Mergent's Handbook of Common Stocks

SPRING 2003

JONATHAN WORRALL, *Chief Executive Officer/Publisher*

SUZANNE WITTEBORT, *Asst. Vice President*
THOMAS WECERA, *Associate Publisher*
BRAD A. ARMBRUSTER, *Editor*

STACY M. CLEELAND, *Editor*

Associate Editors

REGGIE D. CAIN   KEVIN D. HECKERT

Senior Business Analysts

RICHARD K. DEE, JR.   CHRISTALYN Y. DANIEL
MELISSA A. FRANCIS   ANDREW J. KALINSKI

Business Analysts

AVA O. ALEXANDER   ANTHONY E. HARP
TROY GAUNT   TALVI S. YOUNG

MERGENT™

INTRODUCTION

The Handbook of Common Stocks provides quick and easy access to basic financial and business information on more than 900 stocks with high investor interest. The Tab Section provides one-line information on New York Stock Exchange companies for which there is no full page coverage.

The price charts, statistics, and analyses are presented in a format that provides the investor with the necessary perspective for acting on investment advice or suggestions. It also affords investors the opportunity to make investment decisions on their own.

Statistics and analyses are revised quarterly. Every effort is made to secure the most current operating results and dividend information available. In the case of year-end results, preliminary results are shown and analyzed as they are received. Full statistical presentations of annual report information are shown in the following edition. The schedule below describes the publication dates and company reporting periods usually covered in each edition.

The Winter Edition (published in January) covers quarterly reports and preliminary annual reports through September 30.

The Spring Edition (published in April) covers quarterly reports and preliminary annual reports through December 31.

The Summer Edition (published in July) covers quarterly reports and preliminary annual reports through March 31.

The Fall Edition (published in October) covers quarterly reports and preliminary annual reports through June 30.

Note: For various reasons, some companies may not report in time to meet our publication deadlines. Company reports received close to press time are shown in the Addenda. The remainder of late reports are published and analyzed in the next edition of the Handbook.

The special section on these blue pages contains a number of features, including a guide on how to use this book, an index of companies by their major line of business, outstanding stock price movements by company, plus long-term charts on popular stock market averages. The Addenda provide the latest developments available just prior to publication but after the company reports have been completed.

TABLE OF CONTENTS

3a

HOW TO USE THIS BOOK

The presentation of historical data and analytical comments provide the answers to five basic questions.

1. What does the company do?
   (See B,G.)
2. How has it done in the past?
   (See C, E, F, J.)
3. How is it doing now?
   (See E, F, H.)
4. How will it fare in the future?
   (See I.)

A. CAPSULE STOCK INFORMATION

shows where the stock is traded and its symbol, a recent price and price/earnings ratio, plus the yield afforded by the indicated dividend based on a recent price. The indicated dividend is the current annualized dividend based on the most recent regular cash payment. Also shown are the company's market capitalization based on its recent price, and the 52-week range of its stock. Some companies are designated as Dividend Achievers. Dividend Achievers have, by Mergent's criteria, increased their cash dividend payments for at least ten consecutive years, adjusting for splits. The number of years of consecutive increases is given for each Dividend Achiever. The year-end stock price is shown in the Spring edition.

B. MERGENT'S COMMENT

is a concise statement describing the company's earnings trend, merger activity, industry developments or other important factors that have affected the company in the recent quarter, plus our evaluation of the grade (quality) of its common stock.

The grade is based on an analysis of each company's financial strength, including earnings and revenue growth trends and record of dividend payments. Other considerations include conservativeness of capitalization, asset levels, liquidity ratios, and industry position. Evaluation is represented by the following grades:

(1) High Grade
(2) Investment Grade
(3) Upper Medium Grade
(4) Medium Grade
(5) Lower Medium Grade
(6) Speculative Grade

These classifications are a measure of suitability to an individual investor and should not be construed as earnings predictions or advice to buy, sell or hold a stock.

C. LONG-TERM PRICE CHART

illustrates the pattern of monthly stock price movements, fully adjusted for stock dividends and splits. The chart points out the degree of volatility in the price movement of the company's stock and what its long-term trend has been. It indicates areas of price support and resistance, plus other technical points to be considered by the investor. The bars at the base of the long-term price chart indicate the monthly trading volume. Monthly trading volume offers the individual an opportunity to recognize at what periods stock accumulation occurs and what percent of a company's outstanding shares are traded.

Beneath the chart are the 7 Year Price Score and the 12 Month Price Score. These price scores are measured against the New York Stock Exchange Composite Index. A score of 100 indicates that the stock did as well as the the Composite Index during the time period; less than 100 means that the stock did not do as well, and more than 100 means that the stock did better. For example, a score of 85 would indicate a performance 15% worse than the index, and 115 would indicate a 15% better showing.

D. INTERIM EARNINGS

(usually quarterly), are shown for the three previous years and the current year to date.

These figures reveal seasonal patterns and permit comparisons with preceding quarters as well as comparable quarters in prior years. See Earnings Per Share below.

ILLUSTRATIVE, INC.

EXCHANGE	**A** SYM.	REC. PRICE	P/E RATIO	YIELD	MARKET CAP.	RANGE (52-WK.)
NYSE	ILS	89 (2/28/03)	20.7	1.1%	$4.40 bill.	88.50 - 60.00

B UPPER MEDIUM GRADE. THE COMPANY IS ENJOYING STRONG DEMAND FOR ITS NEW PRODUCT LINE.

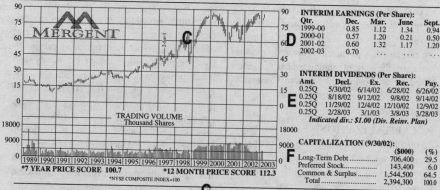

*7 YEAR PRICE SCORE 100.7   *12 MONTH PRICE SCORE 112.3
*NYSE COMPOSITE INDEX=100

D INTERIM EARNINGS (Per Share):

Qtr.	Dec.	Mar.	June	Sept.
1999-00	0.85	1.12	1.34	0.94
2000-01	0.57	1.20	0.21	0.50
2001-02	0.60	1.32	1.17	1.20
2002-03	0.70	...	...	...

E INTERIM DIVIDENDS (Per Share):

Amt.	Decl.	Ex.	Rec.	Pay.
0.25Q	5/30/02	6/14/02	6/28/02	6/26/02
0.25Q	8/18/02	9/12/02	9/8/02	9/14/02
0.25Q	11/29/02	12/4/02	12/10/02	12/9/02
0.25Q	2/28/03	3/1/03	3/8/03	3/28/03

Indicated div.: $1.00 (Div. Reinv. Plan)

F CAPITALIZATION (9/30/02):

	($000)	(%)
Long-Term Debt	706,400	29.5
Preferred Stock	143,400	6.0
Common & Surplus	1,544,500	64.5
Total	2,394,300	100.0

G BUSINESS:

Illustrative, Inc. is engaged in four business segments. The Automotive segment is engaged in the design and manufacture of complete hardware systems, manufacturers of cars, vans and farm machinery. The Controls segment is a worldwide supplier of control systems, services and products providing temperature and ventilation control, security and fire safety for non-residential buildings. The Security segment is a producer of security systems, including alarms and sensor grids. The Gasket segment supplies specialty gaskets. The Company operates facilities in over 43 countries.

H RECENT DEVELOPMENTS:

For the quarter ended 12/31/02, net income rose to $60.4 million compared with $53.4 million in the corresponding prior-year quarter. Net sales were $3.45 billion, up from $3.02 billion in the prior year. Sales in the hardware unit climbed 13.0% to $1.82 billion due to higher levels of system sales in North America, Europe and South America. Sales in the security unit grew 8.0% to $1.22 billion due to growth in the systems facilities management business.

I PROSPECTS:

The Company completed the acquisition of Rialto Gasket Manufacturing for a total of $320.0 million in stock and cash. Rialto's operations will complement the Company's in the Western states. The Security unit has begun marketing Safe At Home, a comprehensive home security system with the Company's patented SensOrSite silent alarm. Initial market reception has surpassed the Company's expectations and strengthens its position in the home security industry. ILS continues to emphasize new product development and is looking for other acquisition targets to expand its product offerings.

J ANNUAL FINANCIAL DATA:

FISCAL YEAR	TOT. REVS. ($mill.)	NET INC. ($mill.)	TOT. ASSETS ($mill.)	OPER. PROFIT %	NET PROFIT %	RET. ON EQUITY %	RET. ON ASSETS %	CURR. RATIO	EARN. PER SH. $	CASH FL. PER SH. $	TANG. BK. VAL. $	DIV. PER SH. $	PRICE RANGE	AVG. P/E RATIO	AVG. YIELD %
9/30/02	11,145.4	③ 220.6	6,048.6	4.7	2.0	13.1	3.6	0.9	③ 4.20	6.67	9.98	0.86	78.00 — 68.25	17.4	2.0
9/30/01	9,210.0	② 222.7	4,991.2	5.2	2.4	14.8	4.5	1.1	② 2.55	9.23	0.82	84.45 — 60.38		14.5	2.2
9/30/00	8,330.3	195.8	4,320.9	5.4	2.4	14.6	4.5	1.1	2.27	6.69	7.04	0.78	83.63 — 58.25	12.7	2.7
9/30/99	6,870.5	165.2	3,806.9	5.3	2.4	13.7	4.3	1.2	1.90	5.05	6.64	0.72	67.88 — 39.88	14.0	2.7
9/30/98	6,181.7	① 137.9	3,230.8	4.8	2.2	12.8	4.3	1.2	① 0.09	4.50	7.60	0.68	49.88 — 37.55	300.0	2.1
9/30/97	5,156.5	123.0	3,179.5	5.1	2.4	10.3	3.9	1.2	1.43	4.09	8.72	0.64	44.60 — 30.50	14.1	3.2
9/30/96	4,559.0	95.1	2,841.0	5.0	2.1	8.9	3.3	1.2	1.10	3.58	8.17	0.62	34.06 — 27.44	13.4	4.2
9/30/95	4,504.0	92.4	2,798.8	5.1	2.1	8.9	3.3	1.2	1.07	3.37	7.68	0.60	30.45 — 26.96	11.6	4.9
9/30/94	3,683.6	97.5	2,415.0	5.6	2.6	10.0	4.0	1.3	1.28	3.21	7.46	0.58	30.13 — 25.75	14.6	3.1
9/30/93	3,099.6	103.5	2,013.3	6.8	3.3	12.1	5.1	1.4	1.42	2.99	9.12	0.55	23.38 — 17.96	11.2	3.5

Statistics are as originally reported. Adj. for 100% stk. div., 3/97. ① Bef. $122.0 mill. ($2.99/sh) acct. chg. ② Bef. $12.0 mill. chg. fr. disc. ops. ③ Bef. $67.9 mill. disc. ops.

OFFICERS:
J. P. Dickens, Chmn. & C.E.O.
C. B. Alexander, V.P. & C.F.O.
D. S. George, Treas.
L. B. Timkin, V.P., Sec. & General Counsel

INVESTOR CONTACT: B. G. Primrose, V.P., (312) 555-2646

PRINCIPAL OFFICE: 1185 Elmwood Road, Chicago, IL 60611

TELEPHONE NUMBER: (312) 555-1200
FAX: (312) 555-5767
WEB: www.illustrative.com

NO. OF EMPLOYEES: 35,200

K SHAREHOLDERS: 47,000

ANNUAL MEETING: In April

INCORPORATED: IL, Aug., 1922

INSTITUTIONAL HOLDINGS:
No. of Institutions: 432
Shares Held: 85,777,000
% Held: 62.6

INDUSTRY: General industrial machinery (SIC: 3569)

TRANSFER AGENT(S): Firstar Trust Company, Milwaukee, WI

E. DIVIDEND INFORMATION includes such details as the most recent quarterly payments, declarations, ex. dates, and dates of record and payment. Stock dividends, stock splits and special cash payments are also shown. Usually the last five cash payments are presented. The current Indicated Dividend is shown, the current annualized cash payment based on the most recent payment. Companies with Dividend Reinvestment Plans are indicated here.

F. CAPITALIZATION shows the breakdown of the company's capital account—long-term debt, preferred stock, deferred taxes, minority interest, capitalized leases, common equity and surplus.

This breakdown helps investors determine the degree of conservatism or financial leverage in a company's balance sheet and its ability to take on additional long-term debt.

Our example, *Illustrative, Inc.,* has a debt to capitalization ratio of 29.5%. Debt in a range of 5% to 10% would be modest while 50% would be high for most industrial companies.

G. COMPANY BACKGROUND is a summary of what a company does in terms of the products or services it sells, its markets, and the position the company occupies in its industry. Complete breakdowns of sales and earnings contributions are often provided, if available.

H. RECENT DEVELOPMENTS keep you up to date on what is happening now. Focus is on the current position of an individual company. In addition to analysis of recently released sales and earnings figures, items covered include where applicable (and if available) new product introductions, expanded operations, acquisitions, labor developments, equity or debt financing, the rate of incoming orders and the level of backlog.

I. PROSPECTS tell you what is anticipated for the company in the immediate future, as well as the outlook for the next few years, based on analysis by Financial Information Services.

J. TEN-YEAR COMPARATIVE STATISTICS AND RATIOS (fully adjusted for stock dividends and splits) provide the necessary historical perspective to make intelligent investment decisions. For industrial companies, operating performance is shown in terms of revenues, net income, operating profitability, net profitability, return on equity and return on assets. The per-share data show the pattern of earnings, cash flow, book value and dividends and common stock prices, plus important ratios such as yield (dividend in relation to price) and P/E (price in relation to earnings). Key balance sheet items such as total assets and current ratio are also included. For non-industrial companies (utilities, banks, real estate investment trusts, etc.), special ratios and relevant statistics are provided (see *Other Definitions* on the following pages).

Fiscal Years are the annual financial reporting periods as determined by each company. Prices and dividends are for calendar years, regardless of the fiscal period.

The *Total Revenues* figure is the total of gross revenues, gross sales, or equivalent items of income from operations. Consolidated statements are used.

Net Income is the amount remaining from total revenues after provisions for all operating and non-operating costs and expenses including interest and taxes have been deducted. Essentially, it is net profit as publicly reported. Generally, extraordinary gains and losses and discontinued operations are excluded and footnoted. Non-extraordinary charges such as restructuring or asset-impairment charges are generally included in net income figures, as is income from minority interests in other companies. Net income is generally shown before preferred dividends have been deducted.

Total Assets represent the sum of the company's tangible and intangible property, as stated on its annual audited balance sheet.

Operating Profit Margin is the percentage of total revenues remaining after all costs and expenses other than those of a non-operating nature such as interest (except for finance companies), minority provisions and income taxes. Extraordinary items are excluded. Trends in the operating profit margin indicate to the investor the company's degree of control over operating expenses. Our example, *Illustrative, Inc.*, has in recent years held its operating margin fairly steady.

Net Profit % is the precentage of total revenues remaining after the deduction of all non-extraordinary costs, including interest and taxes.

Return on Equity % is the ratio of net income to stockholders' equity, expressed as a percentage.

Return on Assets % represents the ratio of net income to total assets and is a measure of how effectively assets are being used to produce profit.

Current Ratio is the ratio of current assets to current liabilities (liabilities due within one year). It is a prime measure of liquidity.

The Earnings Per Share figure essentially is what has been reported by the company, except for adjustments for certain items as footnoted. Earnings per share, and all per share figures, are adjusted for subsequent stock dividends and splits. Earnings per share reported after 12/15/97 are presented on a diluted basis, as described by Financial Accounting Standards Board Statement 128. Prior to that date, earnings per share are presented on a primary basis.

Cash Flow Per Share is computed by dividing the total of net income and non-cash depreciation and amortization charges, less preferred dividends, by average shares outstanding.

Tangible Book Value Per Share is calculated as stockholders equity (the value of common shares, paid-in capital and retained earnings) minus preferred stock and intangibles such as goodwill, patents and excess acquisition costs, divided by year-end shares outstanding. It demonstrates the underlying cash value of each common share if the company were to be liquidated as of that date.

Dividends Per Share is the total of cash payments made per share to shareholders in the calendar year.

Price Ranges are shown for calendar years, regardless of the fiscal reporting period. Where actual stock sales did not take place, a range of lowest bid and highest asked prices is shown.

The Average Price Earnings Ratio is calculated by dividing the mean of the high and low for the year by per share earnings. The higher the number, the greater the valuation. Growth stocks tend to command higher P/Es than cyclical stocks.

Average Yield % is the ratio of dividends to average prices.

EDITOR'S NOTE: In order to preserve the historical relationships between prices, earnings and dividends, figures are not restated to reflect subsequent events. Figures are presented in U.S. dollars unless otherwise indicated.

K. ADDITIONAL INFORMATION on each stock includes the officers of the company, investor relations contact, address, telephone and fax numbers, website, number of employees, number of stockholders, annual meeting date, date and place of incorporation, institutional holdings and transfer agents.

Institutional Holdings indicates the number of investment companies, insurance companies, mutual funds, bank trust and college endowment funds holding the stock and the total number of shares held as last reported. Coverage is as follows:

Investment Companies, Insurance Companies and Mutual Funds – total coverage in the U.S. and Canada; foreign funds limited to those which hold U.S. and/or Canadian stocks.

Banks – national banks reporting under rule 13(F) to the Securities & Exchange Commission. Also included are investment advisors, pension funds, foundations, plus other money managers with equity holdings of $100 million or more who also report under rule 13(F).

Colleges – limited only by a college's willingness to disclose its portfolio publicly.

OTHER DEFINITIONS

FACTORS PERTAINING ESPECIALLY TO UTILITIES

Net Income/Net Property % is the ratio of net income to net plant (including construction work in progress). This figure indicates the realized rate of return on book value of properties.

Net Income/Total Capitalization % is the ratio between net income and capitalization, which includes all long-term debt obligations and shareholders' equity.

Accumulated Depreciation/Gross Property % reflects the percentage of properties that have been depreciated. A lower percentage indicates a higher book value of properties.

Dividend Payout % is the proportion of earnings available for common stock that is paid to common shareholders in the form of cash dividends. It is significant because its complement indicates what percentage of earnings is being reinvested in the business for internal growth.

FACTORS PERTAINING ESPECIALLY TO BANKS

Net Interest Income is interest income less interest expenses. It represents the amount income generated by a bank's primary interest-related business. This figure is presented before any credit loss provisions.

Non-interest Income is any income that is not interest-related. Such income could include, among other things, credit card income, mortgage income, advisory and other bank fees and gains on securities sales.

Total Deposits are total time and demand deposits entrusted to a bank. This figure is also presented in the Capitalization section. (See item F in this section.)

Total Loans are all promissory notes held, including agricultural, commercial, personal, real estate and other loans outstanding, after deducting unearned discount and allowance for possible loan losses.

Equity/Assets % represents the amount of assets that are retained in the Company, or the amount of assets that are not obligated to outside parties.

FACTORS PERTAINING ESPECIALLY TO INSURANCE COMPANIES

Premium Income is the amount of insurance premiums received. This is the primary revenue source for insurance companies.

Net Investment Income is the amount received from investments during a reporting period.

Total Investments represents the invested assets of an insurance company. Certain invested assets may include, among other things, fixed maturities (such as bonds), common equity securities, mortgage loans and short-term investments.

Return on Revenues % (similar to Net Profit %) is the percentage of total revenues remaining after the deduction of all non-extraordinary costs, including interest and taxes.

FACTORS PERTAINING ESPECIALLY TO REAL ESTATE INVESTMENT TRUSTS

Total Income (similar to Total Revenues) is all income from operations. Total Income could include, among other things, rental income, mortgage income and certain interest income.

Net Income + Depreciation/Assets % represents the ratio of net income and non-cash depreciation to total assets. This measures how effectively assets are being used to produce cash profits.

Dividend Payout % is the proportion of earnings paid to shareholders in the form of cash dividends.

HOW TO USE THIS BOOK (Continued)

ABBREVIATIONS
AND
SYMBOLS

* .... Dividend Reinvestment Plan Offered	OTC .... Over-The-Counter Market
ASE .... American Stock Exchange	p .... Preliminary
CBOE .....Chicago Board Options Exchange	P.F. .... Pro Forma
d ....Deficit	PHL .... Philadelphia Stock Exchange
E.. Extra	PSE................... Pacific Stock Exchange
M ....Monthly	Q..Quarterly
MSE................ Montreal Stock Exchange	r.. Revised
N.A. .... Not Available	S .... Semi-annual
N.M.......................... Not Meaningful	Sp............................. Special Dividend
np.. No Par	TSE................. Toronto Stock Exchange
NYSE .... New York Stock Exchange	Y............................Year-end Dividend

For the three-month period beginning December 1, 2002 and ending February 28, 2003, the Dow Jones Industrial Average dropped 11.3%, while the broader New York Stock Exchange Composite Index fell 9.9%. The Dow and NYSE began the period at 8,896.09 and 5,236.85, respectively. The Dow reached its period high on December 2, closing the day at 8,862.57, as investors reacted to stronger-than-expected consumer spending during the first week of the holiday selling season. Meanwhile, the NYSE would wait until January 6 to close at its period high of 5,255.39, fueled by speculation that President Bush's economic-stimulus plan will eliminate taxes investors pay on corporate dividends. Following the strongest three-day start to any year in the Dow Jones Industrial Average's history, the market began to buckle under the weight of continuing worries about a war with Iraq and heightened concerns about another terrorist attack in the U.S. The NYSE slumped to its period low of 4,649.71 on February 12, while the Dow would hit its period low of 7,749.87 the following day. The Dow and the NYSE indices closed the period at 7,891.08 and 4,716.07, respectively.—Richard K. Dee, Jr.

Over the last twelve months, the best performing stock was *Boston Scientific Corporation*, which is benefiting from the introduction of its drug-eluting stent technology and strong worldwide demand for its coronary stent.

The second-best price performer was *Storage Technology Corporation*. Earnings growth is being fueled by market share gains in tape, disk, networking and storage services, along with improved operating margins.

Mylan Laboratories Inc., was the third-best price performer. Results are benefiting from the launch of AMNESTEEM™, which is used to treat severe recalcitrant nodular acne.

Strong demand for the Company's late-stage product development services are positively affecting earnings at *Covance Inc.*, the fourth-best price performer.

Consolidated Graphics, Inc. was the fifth-best price performer, with results benefiting from market share gains and improved performance of recently acquired companies.

The sixth-best performing stock was *Wallace Computer Services, Inc.* On 1/17/03, the Company entered into a definitive agreement to be acquired by Moore Corporation Limited for about $1.30 billion.

US Airways Group, Inc. was the worst performing stock over the last twelve months. Results were negatively affected by weak passenger demand and rising fuel prices.

The second-worst price performer was *UAL Corporation*, which filed for Chapter 11 bankruptcy on 12/9/02 due to unfavorable conditions in the airline industry.

The third-worst performing stock was *OM Group, Inc.* Results were hampered by weak market conditions, particularly for precious metal refining, and non-recurring charges related to restructuring and the disposal of non-core assets.

Aquila, Inc. was the fourth-worst price performer. Earnings were negatively affected by a decline in power prices and an oversupply of generating capacity.

AmeriCredit Corp. was the fifth-worst price performer. Results were hurt by increased net charge-offs and higher delinquency rates, coupled with weakness in recovery values on repossessed vehicles.

The sixth-worst price performer was *Metris Companies, Inc.* Results were hurt by a higher charge-off rate due to higher bankruptcies and the weak economic environment.

SHORT-TERM PRICE SCORES: COMPANY RANKINGS

25 HIGHEST	SHORT-TERM PRICE SCORE♦	LONG-TERM PRICE SCORE♦	PRICE RANGE (52 Wks.)	RECENT PRICE
Boston Scientific Corporation	142.2	126.8	49.94 - 21.42	44.17
Storage Technology Corporation	139.5	92.0	25.82 - 9.66	23.13
Mylan Laboratories Inc.	132.9	136.4	28.66 - 16.73	28.55
Covance Inc.	132.1	...	27.41 - 12.11	23.55
Consolidated Graphics, Inc.	131.7	73.6	25.20 - 14.35	24.15
Wallace Computer Services, Inc.	131.3	92.5	26.89 - 15.80	25.49
Brown Shoe Company, Inc.	129.5	139.0	29.39 - 13.80	27.14
UGI Corporation	126.6	145.1	28.37 - 17.11	27.60
Halliburton Company	126.6	...	21.65 - 8.97	20.26
BMC Software, Inc.	125.6	55.8	19.84 - 10.85	19.40
Doral Financial Corporation	125.4	215.7	32.61 - 21.01	32.41
Citizens Communications Co.	125.2	84.4	11.55 - 2.51	9.81
Alpharma Inc.	124.9	57.3	22.30 - 6.50	16.75
Coach, Inc.	124.7	...	35.80 - 17.19	35.73
Forest Laboratories, Inc.	124.7	227.6	56.36 - 32.13	53.97
Rockwell Automation	124.1	48.8	23.87 - 14.71	23.01
International Game Technology	123.7	204.9	80.70 - 47.75	78.58
Varian Medical Systems, Inc.	123.6	170.0	52.95 - 31.60	50.55
Sealed Air Corporation	123.0	77.0	48.39 - 12.70	36.27
Watson Pharmaceuticals, Inc.	123.0	75.8	33.25 - 17.95	30.93
Fox Entertainment Group, Inc.	122.5	...	29.40 - 16.13	26.73
Energen Corporation	121.4	138.4	32.06 - 21.65	32.06
Harman International Industries, Inc.	121.3	187.6	65.30 - 38.18	63.53
Xerox Corporation	121.0	30.0	11.15 - 4.20	9.00
Handleman Company	120.9	121.2	15.25 - 7.50	14.10

25 LOWEST				
US Airways Group, Inc.	10.2	7.5	7.60 - 0.10	0.16
UAL Corporation	19.1	...	17.90 - 0.64	1.08
OM Group, Inc.	22.5	103.7	73.70 - 4.00	8.46
Aquila, Inc.	25.4	40.9	25.83 - 1.41	1.44
AmeriCredit Corp.	26.8	107.1	46.93 - 1.92	1.99
Metris Companies, Inc.	27.0	...	27.05 - 1.25	1.50
Dynegy Inc.	28.6	33.0	32.19 - 0.49	1.95
AMR Corporation	34.9	29.9	29.20 - 2.25	2.34
Fleming Companies, Inc.	35.7	81.6	26.10 - 1.85	2.07
Mirant Corp.	39.8	...	15.05 - 1.06	1.35
Goodyear Tire & Rubber Company	41.3	37.8	28.85 - 3.35	4.00
Allegheny Energy, Inc.	41.9	69.7	43.86 - 2.95	5.99
Northwestern Corporation	42.5	64.6	23.64 - 2.50	2.64
El Paso Corporation	43.3	55.3	46.89 - 3.33	4.86
PolyOne Corporation	44.9	...	13.40 - 3.03	3.83
Great Atlantic & Pacific Tea Co., Inc.	45.6	63.7	28.44 - 4.55	4.67
Circuit City Stores, Inc.	47.8	66.3	24.59 - 4.11	4.42
Williams Companies, Inc.	48.0	29.3	24.50 - 0.78	3.81
Tower Automotive, Inc.	48.2	58.2	15.40 - 2.66	3.35
Allegheny Technologies Inc.	48.9	34.4	19.10 - 2.75	2.99
Micron Technology, Inc.	49.1	71.2	39.50 - 6.60	7.99
Cypress Semiconductor Corp.	51.4	71.4	25.48 - 3.60	6.41
HEALTHSOUTH Corporation	51.7	57.3	15.90 - 2.79	3.58
Tenet Healthcare Corporation	52.6	168.2	52.50 - 13.70	18.17
Quanta Services, Inc.	52.7	...	18.90 - 1.75	3.30

♦For definition see page 4a.

Over the years, newspapers, once the principal source for news, have met stiff competition from radio, television, and most recently the Internet. As competition grew, the newspaper industry faced dropping advertising and circulation revenues, while newsprint costs climbed. To remain profitable, many successful newspaper companies have expanded into a range of media. Then came the terrorist attacks of September 11, 2001. Americans were galvanized and driven to seek timely information. This need to know has not abated, and has translated into revenue growth for many information companies. Over the last year, virtually all major newspaper companies have outperformed the NYSE Composite.

Knight Ridder publishes 32 daily newspapers in 28 U.S. markets with a readership of 8.5 million daily and 12.1 million on Sunday. For the year ended 12/29/02, income soared 52.4% to $281.7 million, though total revenues were down 2.0% to $2.84 billion. Operating income increased 31.1% to $605.4 million due to a decrease in newsprint and ink costs and efforts to trim labor and other expenses. Knight Ridder Digital revenue rose 31.6% for the year and the unit reached break-even in the fourth quarter. Its Real Cities Network continues to grow, with a total of 56 affiliates. Near-term results are expected to benefit from the growth trend in retail, auto, real estate and general advertising and from increases in daily and Sunday subscriptions.

New York Times Company has diversified interests in newspapers and broadcasting that include 20 regional newspapers, eight network-affiliated television stations, two New York City radio stations and more than 40 Web sites. Net income for the twelve months ended 12/29/02 jumped 48.2% to $299.7 million, while revenues bumped up 2.1% to $3.08 billion, reflecting growth across all business segments.

In its newspaper business, the company has added 162,000 new home delivery customers over the past two years and recently became the sole owner of the International Herald Tribune after buying out its partner, The Washington Post Co. In less traditional media, the company enjoyed 13 million visitors to its nytimes.com website in January and, in a joint venture with Discovery Communications, has launched a digital cable channel, the Discovery Times Channel.

Tribune Company owns and operates 24 major-market television stations, 12 daily newspapers, two 24-hour cable news channels, news and information Web sites in 18 of the nation's 30 markets, and the Chicago Cubs. Income for the year ended 12/29/02 surged to $608.6 million from $111.1 million, reflecting the strength of the Company's mass media franchises in the populous Chicago area. Operating revenue grew 2.5% to $5.38 billion from $5.25 billion the year before. As the year ended the company was enjoying strong growth in advertising revenues, particularly from national and retail accounts. On 12/20/02 the company agreed to acquire television stations in St. Louis and Portland, Oregon. In 2002 revenues from TRB's interactive segment rose 29% to $77.0 million, and the segment's operating profit was $8.7 million, in contrast to a $20.0 million loss in 2001.

With the war in Iraq, interest in current events is at fever pitch. However, once the war is resolved, challenging conditions could lie ahead for the industry if the economy remains weak. But once an economic recovery is in full swing, the companies that are the most flexible, adaptable, and canniest at cutting costs should continue to flourish. –

Ava O. Alexander

NEWSPAPERS

COMPARATIVE STATISTICS

COMPANY	FISCAL DATE	EXCH	SYMBOL	PRICE RANGE (12 MOS.) HIGH	LOW	RECENT PRICE	EARNINGS PER SHARE LATEST: 12 MOS.	1998	1997	1996	IND. CASH DIV.	BOOK VALUE PER SH.	STKHLDR'S EQUITY ($ MILL.)	LONG-TERM DEBT)
Dow Jones & Co., Inc	12/31/02	NYS	DJ	60.20	29.50	35.88	2.41	2.41	1.15	d1.35	1.000	0.37	30.57	75.25
Gannett Co., Inc.	12/30/01	NYS	GCI	79.90	62.76	72.17	4.35	...	3.14	3.65	0.960	†21.58	†5735.92	†44.88
Hollinger International, Inc.	12/31/01	NYS	HLR	13.75	8.16	8.52	d2.88	...	d3.42	1.16	0.200	†3.39	†325.77	†71.31
Journal Register Co.	12/30/01	NYS	JRC	22.20	14.75	15.17	1.16	...	1.85	3.74	nil	†0.87	†d36.20	†100.05

COMPANY	FISCAL DATE	EXCH	SYMBOL	PRICE RANGE (12 MOS.) HIGH	LOW	RECENT PRICE	EARNINGS PER SHARE LATEST: 12 MOS.	1998	1997	1996	IND. CASH DIV.	BOOK VALUE PER SH.	STKHLDR'S EQUITY ($ MILL.)	LONG-TERM DEBT (%)
Knight-Ridder, Inc.	12/29/02	NYS	KRI	70.20	51.35	63.81	3.39	3.39	2.33	4.02	1.080	17.91	1461.48	46.40
Lee Enterprises, Inc.	9/30/02	NYS	LEE	40.09	28.90	32.05	1.94	1.84	1.36	1.59	0.680	16.73	741.26	29.31
McClatchy Co. (The)	12/30/01	NYS	MNI	65.55	50.40	54.22	2.87	...	1.28	1.97	0.440	†21.89	†998.16	†37.34
Media General, Inc.	12/30/01	NYS	MEG	69.49	46.55	50.10	d3.18	...	0.79	2.66	0.760	†50.65	†1163.67	†33.93
New York Times Co.	12/29/02	NYS	NYT	53.00	38.60	46.46	1.98	1.98	1.29	2.37	0.540	8.34	1269.31	35.17
Pulitzer, Inc.	12/30/01	NYS	PTZ	55.80	40.12	42.64	1.63	...	0.58	1.60	0.720	†37.59	†797.24	†27.74
Scripps (E.W.) Co. (New) (OH)	12/31/01	NYS	SSP	87.50	65.13	80.10	...	...	1.75	2.09	0.600	†17.07	†1351.90	†6.84
Tribune Co.	12/30/01	NYS	TRB	49.49	35.66	44.85	1.38	...	0.28	1.06	0.440	†18.96	†651.17	†32.10
Washington Post Co.	12/31/01	NYS	WPO	764.00	516.00	713.50	14.37	...	24.10	14.34	5.800	†177.30	†1683.48	†31.67

† Indicates prior year's data

FINANCIAL DATA – LATEST ANNUAL RANKINGS

REVENUES ($000,000)

RANK COMPANY	2002 AMT		RANK COMPANY	2002 AMT
1 Gannett Co., Inc.	†6344.24		6 Dow Jones & Co., Inc	†559.17
2 Tribune Co.	†5253.37		7 Scripps (E.W.) Co. (New) (OH)	†437.13
3 New York Times Co.	3079.01		8 Hollinger International, Inc.	†146.32
4 Knight-Ridder, Inc.	2841.59		9 McClatchy Co. (The)	†080.05
5 Washington Post Co.	†2416.67			

			RANK COMPANY	2002 AMT
			10 Media General, Inc.	†807.18
			11 Lee Enterprises, Inc.	525.90
			12 Pulitzer, Inc.	†413.51
			13 Journal Register Co.	†394.40

NET INCOME ($000,000)

RANK COMPANY	2002 AMT		RANK COMPANY	2002 AMT
1 Gannett Co., Inc.	†831.20		6 Scripps (E.W.) Co. (New) (OH)	†137.96
2 New York Times Co.	299.75		7 Tribune Co.	†111.14
3 Knight-Ridder, Inc.	281.73		8 Lee Enterprises, Inc.	81.03
4 Washington Post Co.	229.64		9 Journal Register Co.	†78.13
5 Dow Jones & Co., Inc	201.51			

			RANK COMPANY	2002 AMT
			10 McClatchy Co. (The)	†58.00
			11 Media General, Inc.	†17.92
			12 Pulitzer, Inc.	†12.29
			13 Hollinger International, Inc.	†d337.51

NEWSPAPERS

OPERATING PROFIT MARGIN (%)

RANK	COMPANY	2002 AMT
1	Gannett Co., Inc.	†25.06
2	Lee Enterprises, Inc.	23.17
3	Journal Register Co.	†22.45
4	Knight-Ridder, Inc.	21.30
5	Scripps (E.W.) Co. (New) (OH)	†19.10
6	New York Times Co.	17.70
7	McClatchy Co. (The)	†16.10
8	Tribune Co.	†12.38
9	Pulitzer, Inc.	†10.49
10	Washington Post Co.	†9.10
11	Media General, Inc.	†9.01
12	Dow Jones & Co., Inc.	4.82
13	Hollinger International, Inc.	†d3.52

RETURN ON CAPITAL (%)

RANK	COMPANY	2002 AMT
1	Dow Jones & Co., Inc	48.17
2	Journal Register Co.	†15.87
3	New York Times Co.	14.47
4	Scripps (E.W.) Co. (New) (OH)	†8.58
5	Knight-Ridder, Inc.	8.29
6	Washington Post Co.	†7.87
7	Gannett Co., Inc.	†7.09
8	Lee Enterprises, Inc.	5.98
9	McClatchy Co. (The)	†3.40
10	Pulitzer, Inc.	†1.01
11	Tribune Co.	†0.94
12	Media General, Inc.	†0.78
13	Hollinger International, Inc.	…

NET INCOME TO REVENUES (%)

RANK	COMPANY	2002 AMT
1	Journal Register Co.	†19.81
2	Lee Enterprises, Inc.	15.41
3	Gannett Co., Inc.	†13.10
4	Dow Jones & Co., Inc	12.92
5	Knight-Ridder, Inc.	9.91
6	New York Times Co.	9.74
7	Scripps (E.W.) Co. (New) (OH)	†9.60
8	Washington Post Co.	†9.50
9	McClatchy Co. (The)	†5.37
10	Pulitzer, Inc.	†2.97
11	Media General, Inc.	†2.22
12	Tribune Co.	†2.12
13	Hollinger International, Inc.	†29.44

CURRENT RATIO

RANK	COMPANY	2002 AMT
1	Pulitzer, Inc.	†5.29
2	Media General, Inc.	†1.62
3	Hollinger International, Inc.	†1.35
4	Knight-Ridder, Inc.	1.16
5	Gannett Co., Inc.	†1.04
6	Lee Enterprises, Inc.	0.96
7	Washington Post Co.	†0.91
8	Tribune Co.	†0.89
9	McClatchy Co. (The)	†0.81
10	New York Times Co.	0.77
11	Journal Register Co.	†0.71
12	Scripps (E.W.) Co. (New) (OH)	†0.50
13	Dow Jones & Co., Inc	0.40

WORKING CAPITAL ($000,000)

RANK	COMPANY	2002 AMT
1	Pulitzer, Inc.	†221.00
2	Hollinger International, Inc.	†195.71
3	Knight-Ridder, Inc.	72.44
4	Media General, Inc.	†62.54
5	Gannett Co., Inc.	†50.46
6	Lee Enterprises, Inc.	d4.72
7	Journal Register Co.	†d26.56
8	Washington Post Co.	†d37.23
9	McClatchy Co. (The)	†d59.34
10	Tribune Co.	†d169.20
11	New York Times Co.	d172.68
12	Dow Jones & Co., Inc	d371.88
13	Scripps (E.W.) Co. (New) (OH)	†d454.85

NEWSPAPERS

CASH AND SECURITIES ($000,000)

RANK	COMPANY	2002 AMT	RANK	COMPANY	2002 AMT
1	Hollinger International, Inc.	†479.51	6	Dow Jones & Co., Inc	39.35
2	Pulitzer, Inc.	†193.74	7	Knight-Ridder, Inc.	39.33
3	Gannett Co., Inc.	†140.63	8	New York Times Co.	36.96
4	Tribune Co.	†65.84	9	McClatchy Co. (The)	†18.88
5	Washington Post Co.	†47.85	10	Scripps (E.W.) Co. (New) (OH)	†17.42
			11	Lee Enterprises, Inc.	14.38
			12	Media General, Inc.	†9.14
			13	Journal Register Co.	†0.11

PE RATIO

RANK	COMPANY	2002 AMT	RANK	COMPANY	2002 AMT
1	Journal Register Co.	†13.08	6	McClatchy Co. (The)	†18.89
2	Dow Jones & Co., Inc	14.89	7	New York Times Co.	23.46
3	Lee Enterprises, Inc.	16.52	8	Pulitzer, Inc.	†26.16
4	Gannett Co., Inc.	†16.59	9	Tribune Co.	†32.50
5	Knight-Ridder, Inc.	18.82	10	Washington Post Co.	†49.65
			11	Hollinger International, Inc.	...
			12	Media General, Inc.	...
			13	Scripps (E.W.) Co. (New) (OH)	...

YIELD (%)

RANK	COMPANY	2002 AMT	RANK	COMPANY	2002 AMT
1	Dow Jones & Co., Inc	2.79	6	Media General, Inc.	1.52
2	Hollinger International, Inc.	2.35	7	Gannett Co., Inc.	1.33
3	Lee Enterprises, Inc.	2.12	8	New York Times Co.	1.16
4	Knight-Ridder, Inc.	1.69	9	Tribune Co.	0.98
5	Pulitzer, Inc.	1.69	10	Washington Post Co.	0.81
			11	McClatchy Co. (The)	0.81
			12	Scripps (E.W.) Co. (New) (OH)	0.75
			13	Journal Register Co.	...

PRICE SCORE - 12 MONTH

RANK	COMPANY	2002 AMT	RANK	COMPANY	2002 AMT
1	Washington Post Co.	120.29	6	Gannett Co., Inc.	107.76
2	Tribune Co.	116.01	7	Lee Enterprises, Inc.	105.58
3	Scripps (E.W.) Co. (New) (OH)	114.01	8	McClatchy Co. (The)	103.52
4	Knight-Ridder, Inc.	113.72	9	Pulitzer, Inc.	103.46
5	New York Times Co.	108.93	10	Media General, Inc.	103.44
			11	Dow Jones & Co., Inc	97.98
			12	Hollinger International, Inc.	97.28
			13	Journal Register Co.	95.35

PRICE SCORE - 7 YR

RANK	COMPANY	2002 AMT	RANK	COMPANY	2002 AMT
1	McClatchy Co. (The)	169.04	6	Media General, Inc.	133.25
2	Scripps (E.W.) Co. (New) (OH)	152.06	7	Gannett Co., Inc.	129.63
3	New York Times Co.	143.45	8	Lee Enterprises, Inc.	128.10
4	Washington Post Co.	136.30	9	Knight-Ridder, Inc.	127.44
5	Tribune Co.	135.44	10	Dow Jones & Co., Inc	95.27
			11	Hollinger International, Inc.	89.60
			12	Journal Register Co.	...
			13	Pulitzer, Inc.	...

ADVERTISING
* Interpublic Group of Companies, Inc.
Omnicom Group, Inc.
Valassis Communications, Inc.

AGRICULTURAL EQUIPMENT
* Deere & Company
AGCO Corporation

AIRCRAFT & AEROSPACE
* AAR Corporation
Boeing Company
* GenCorp Inc.
United Technologies Corporation

AIRLINES
Alaska Air Group
America West Holdings Corporation
AMR Corporation
Continental Airlines, Inc.
* Delta Air Lines, Inc.
Southwest Airlines Co.
UAL Corp.
US Airways Group, Inc.

AMUSEMENTS
Hasbro, Inc.
* Mattel, Inc.
Russ Berrie and Company, Inc.

APPAREL
Burlington Coat Factory Warehouse Corp.
Jones Apparel Group, Inc.
Kellwood Company
* Liz Claiborne, Inc.
Phillips-Van Heusen Corporation
Polo Ralph Lauren Corporation
* Russell Corp.
* VF Corporation

AUTOMOBILE PARTS
American Axle & Manufacturing Holdings
Applied Industrial Technologies, Inc.
ArvinMeritor, Inc.
Autoliv, Inc.
* Barnes Group, Inc.
BorgWarner Inc.
* Cummins, Inc.
* Dana Corporation
Delphi Corporation
* Eaton Corporation
* Genuine Parts Company
ITT Industries, Inc.
* Johnson Controls, Inc.
Lear Corp.
* Smith (A.O.) Corporation
* SPX Corporation
Superior Industries International, Inc.
* Timken Company (The)
Tower Automotive, Inc.
* Visteon Corporation
Wabtec Corp.

AUTOMOBILES & TRUCKS
* Ford Motor Company
* General Motors Corporation
* Harley-Davidson, Inc.
Navistar International Corp.

BANKS–MAJOR
Bank of America Corporation
* Bank of New York Company Inc.
* Bank One Corporation
Capital One Financial Corp.
MBNA Corp.
* Morgan (J.P.) Chase & Company, Inc.
* Wachovia Corporation
* Wells Fargo & Company

BANKS–MID/ATLANTIC
* First Virginia Banks, Inc.
* M & T Bank Corporation
* Mellon Financial Corporation
* PNC Financial Services Group, Inc.
* Valley National Bancorp
* Wilmington Trust Corp.

BANKS–MIDWEST
* Comerica, Inc.
* KeyCorp.
* Marshall & Illsley Corporation
* National City Corporation
* North Fork Bancorporation, Inc.
* Old National Bancorp
* TCF Financial Corporation
* U.S. Bancorp

BANKS–NORTHEAST
Charter One Financial, Inc.
Chittenden Corporation
Commerce Bancorp, Inc.
* Community Bank Systems, Inc.
* First Commonwealth Financial Corporation
* FleetBoston Financial Corp.
* Hudson United Bancorp
* Sovereign Bancorp, Inc.
State Street Corp.
Webster Financial Corporation

BANKS–SOUTH
* AmSouth Bancorporation
* BancorpSouth, Inc.
* BB&T Corporation
* First Tennessee National Corp.
* Hibernia Corp.
* National Commerce Financial Corporation
* Regions Financial Corporation
* SunTrust Banks, Inc.
Synovus Financial Corp.
Union Planters Corp.

BANKS–WEST
* Bank of Hawaii Corporation
City National Corporation
* UnionBanCal Corp.

BREWING

* Anheuser-Busch Companies, Inc.
  Coors (Adolph) Co.

BUILDING MATERIALS & EQUIPMENT

* Ameron International Corporation
  Martin Marietta Materials, Inc.
  Masco Corporation

CANDY & GUM

* Hershey Foods Corporation
  Tootsie Roll Industries, Inc.
* Wrigley (Wm.) Jr. Company

CEMENT & GYPSUM

* Lafarge North America Inc.
  Texas Industries, Inc.

CHEMICALS

* Air Products & Chemicals, Inc.
* Albemarle Corporation
* Avery Dennison Corporation
* Cabot Corporation
* Crompton Corporation
  Cytec Industries
* Dow Chemical Company (The)
* Du Pont (E.I.) de Nemours & Co.
  Eastman Chemical Co.
* Engelhard Corporation
* Ferro Corporation
  FMC Corporation
* Fuller (H.B.) Company
  Georgia Gulf Corporation
* Goodrich Corporation
  Great Lakes Chemical Corp.
* Hercules, Incorporated
* Lubrizol Corporation (The)
  Lyondell Chemical Company
  Millennium Chemicals Inc.
  Monsanto Co.
  NL Industries, Inc.
* Olin Corporation
  OM Group, Inc.
* PPG Industries, Inc.
  Praxair, Inc.
* Quaker Chemical Corporation
  Rohm & Haas Company
  Solutia Inc.
  Stepan Company (The)

COMPUTERS–COMPONENTS & PERIPHERAL EQUIPMENT

Agere Systems Inc.
Agilent Technologies, Inc.
Cypress Semiconductor Corp.
EMC Corp.
Fairchild Semiconductor International
Ingram Micro Inc.
International Rectifier Corp.
KEMET Corporation
LSI Logic Corp.
NCR Corporation
Storage Technology Corp.
Symbol Technologies, Inc.

COMPUTERS–MAJOR

Gateway Inc.
* International Business Machines Corporation

COMPUTERS–SERVICES & SOFTWARE

Affiliated Computer Services, Inc.
AOL Time Warner, Inc.
Automatic Data Processing, Inc.
Avaya Inc.
BMC Software, Inc.
Cadence Design Systems, Inc.
Ceridian Corporation
Computer Associates International, Inc.
Computer Sciences Corporation
Convergys Corporation
Electronic Data Systems Corporation
First Data Corp.
Gartner Group
GTECH Holdings Corporation
Networks Associates, Inc.
Perot Systems Corporation
Sungard Data Systems Inc.
Sybase, Inc.
Titan Corporation (The)
Total Systems Services Inc.
Unisys Corp.

CONGLOMERATES

Berkshire Hathaway Inc.
* Honeywell International Inc.
  Loews Corporation
  Sequa Corporation
* Tenneco Automotive, Inc.
* Textron, Inc.
* 3M Company
  Valhi, Inc.
  Viad Corp.
* Vulcan Materials Company

CONTAINERS

* Ball Corporation
  Owens-Illinois, Inc.

COPPER

* Phelps Dodge Corporation

COSMETICS, TOILETRIES & FRAGRANCES

Alberto-Culver Company
* Avon Products, Incorporated
* Dial Corporation (The)
  Estee Lauder Cos., Inc. (The)
* Gillette Company (The)
  International Flavors & Fragrances, Inc.

DEFENSE SYSTEMS & EQUIPMENT

Alliant Techsystems Inc.
Curtiss-Wright Corp.
General Dynamics Corporation
* Harris Corporation
  Lockheed Martin Corporation
  L-3 Communications Holdings, Inc.
  Northrop Grumman Corp.
* Raytheon Company
  United Industrial Corp.

DISTILLING
* Brown-Forman Corp.
  Constellation Brands, Inc.
* Fortune Brands, Inc.

DRUGS
* Abbott Laboratories
* Allergan, Inc.
  Alpharma Inc.
* American Home Products Corp.
* Bristol-Myers Squibb Company
  Forest Laboratories, Inc.
  Genentech, Inc.
  ICN Pharmaceuticals, Inc.
  King Pharmaceuticals, Inc.
* Lilly (Eli) & Company
* Merck & Co., Inc.
  Mylan Laboratories, Inc.
* Pfizer Incorporated
* Pharmacia Corporation
* Schering-Plough Corporation
  Watson Pharmaceuticals, Inc.

ELECTRIC POWER - CENTRAL & SOUTHEASTERN
* Alliant Energy Corporation
* Ameren Corp.
* American Electric Power Co., Inc.
* CINergy Corp.
* CLECO Corp.
* CMS Energy Corporation
* DPL Inc.
* DQE, Inc.
* Duke Energy Corp.
* Entergy Corporation
* FPL Group, Inc.
* NiSource, Inc.
* Progress Energy, Inc.
* SCANA Corporation
* Southern Company (The)
* TECO Energy Inc.
* Vectren Corporation
* Wisconsin Energy Corporation
* WPS Resources Corp.

ELECTRIC POWER - NORTHEASTERN
  AES Corp.
* Allegheny Energy
* CH Energy Group, Inc.
* Consolidated Edison, Inc.
* Constellation Energy Group, Inc.
* Dominion Resources Inc.
  DTE Energy Co.
* Energy East Corp.
  Exelon Corporation
  FirstEnergy Corp.
* Northeast Utilities
  NSTAR
* Pepco Holdings, Inc.
* PPL Corporation
* Public Service Enterprise Group Inc.

ELECTRIC POWER - WESTERN
* ALLETE, Inc.
* Avista Corporation
* Black Hills Corporation
* CenterPoint Energy, Inc.
* Edison International

* Great Plains Energy
* Hawaiian Electric Industries, Inc.
* Idacorp, Inc.
* Northwestern Corp.
* OGE Energy Corp.
* PG&E Corp.
* Pinnacle West Capital Corporation
* Puget Energy, Inc.
* Sierra Pacific Resources
* TXU Corporation
  UniSource Energy
* UtiliCorp United Inc.
  Westar Energy, Inc.
  Xcel Energy Inc.

ELECTRICAL EQUIPMENT
* Acuity Brands, Inc.
  AMETEK, Inc.
  Anixter International Inc.
  Baldor Electric Company
* Emerson Electric Co.
* General Electric Company
  Harman International Industires, Inc.
  Hewlett Packard Company
  Hubbell Inc.
  Lennox International Inc.
* Thomas & Betts Corporation

ELECTRICITY GENERATION (WHOLESALE)
  Calpine Corp.
  Mirant Corp.
  Reliant Resources, Inc.

ELECTRONIC COMPONENTS
  Advanced Micro Devices, Inc.
  Amphenol Corporation
  Analog Devices Inc.
  Arrow Electronics, Inc.
* Avnet, Incorporated
  AVX Corporation
  Energizer Holdings Inc.
  ESCO Technologies Inc.
  Federal Signal Corp.
  Jabil Circuit, Inc.
  Micron Technology Inc.
* Motorola, Inc.
  National Semiconductor Corporation
* Rockwell Automation
  Scientific-Atlanta, Inc.
  Solectron Corp.
  Texas Instruments, Inc.
* Varian Medical Systems, Inc.
  Vishay Intertechnology Inc.

ENGINEERING & CONSTRUCTION
  EMCOR Group, Inc.
  Fluor Corp.
  Jacobs Engineering Group Inc.
  Kaydon Corp.
  Shaw Group, Inc. (The)
  URS Corp.

ENTERTAINMENT
  Fox Entertainment Group, Inc.
  Metro Goldwin Mayer
  Regal Entertainment Group
  Westwood One Inc.

EQUIPMENT & VEHICLE LEASING
* Ryder Systems, Inc.
United Rentals, Inc.

FERTILIZER
IMC Global, Inc.
Scotts Company

FINANCE
Affiliated Managers Group, Inc.
Alleghany Corp.
* Allied Capital Corporation
AMBAC Financial Group, Inc.
* American Express Co.
AmeriCredit Corp.
BlackRock, Inc.
* Citigroup Inc.
Countrywide Financial Corporation
Doral Financial Corporation
Eaton Vance Corp.
* Fannie Mae
Federated Investors Inc.
* Freddie Mac
* Household International Inc.
Investment Technology Group, Inc.
* Irwin Financial Corp.
iStar Financial Inc.
Janus Capital Group, Inc.
Metris Companies, Inc.
Morgan Stanley
Nuveen Investments, Inc.
Principal Financial Group, Inc.
Providian Financial Corp.
Prudential Financial, Inc.
SLM Corporation
Student Loan Corporation (The)
Thornburg Mortgage, Inc.

FLOOR COVERINGS & MAINTENANCE
Mohawk Industries, Inc.

FOOD–GRAIN & AGRICULTURE
Archer Daniels Midland Company
* ConAgra Foods, Inc.
* International Multifoods Corp.

FOOD PROCESSING
* Campbell Soup Company
Dole Food Company Inc.
Flowers Foods, Incorporated
* General Mills, Inc.
* Heinz (H.J.) Company
Hormel Foods Corporation
Interstate Bakeries Corp.
* Kellogg Company
Kraft Foods, Inc.
Krispy Kreme Doughnuts, Inc.
McCormick & Company, Inc.
* Sara Lee Corporation
Sensient Technologies Corp.
* Smucker (J.M.) Co. (The)
Tyson Foods, Inc.

FOOD WHOLESALERS
Dean Foods Company
* Fleming Companies, Inc.
* SUPERVALU
* Sysco Corp.

FOREST PRODUCTS
* Georgia-Pacific Group
* Louisiana-Pacific Corporation
Plum Creek Timber Company
* Potlatch Corporation
* Rayonier Inc.
* Weyerhaeuser Company

FREIGHT TRANSPORTATION
Airborne, Inc.
* CNF Inc.
FedEx Corporation
United Parcel Service, Inc.

FURNITURE & FIXTURES
Ethan Allen Interiors, Inc.
Furniture Brands International
Haverty Furniture Companies, Inc.
HON Industries Inc.
La-Z-Boy Chair Co.
Leggett & Platt, Inc.
Simpson Manufacturing Co., Inc.

GAMING
Aztar Corporation
Harrah's Entertainment, Inc.
International Game Technology
Mandalay Resorts Group
MGM Mirage
Park Place Entertainment Corporation

GROCERY CHAINS
* Albertson's, Inc.
Great Atlantic & Pacific Tea Company, Inc.
* Kroger Company (The)
Ruddick Corp.
Safeway Inc.
* Weis Markets, Inc.
* Winn-Dixie Stores, Inc.

HARDWARE & TOOLS
* Black & Decker Corporation
MSC Industrial Direct Co., Inc.
* Newell Rubbermaid Inc.
Snap-on Inc.
* Stanley Works (The)

HEALTHCARE MANAGEMENT & SERVICES
Anthem, Inc.
Caremark RX, Inc.
Covance Inc.
DaVita Inc.
Health Net, Inc.
* Humana Inc.
Laboratory Corp. of America Holdings
Mid Atlantic Medical Services
* Omnicare, Inc.
Orthodontic Centers of America, Inc.
Oxford Health Plans, Inc.
Trigon Healthcare, Inc.
UnitedHealth Group, Inc.
WellPoint Health Networks, Inc.

HOMEBUILDING
Beazer Homes USA, Inc.
Centex Corporation
Clayton Homes, Inc.
Horton (D.R.), Inc.
KB Home, Inc.

Lennar Corporation
Pulte Homes, Inc.
Ryland Group, Inc. (The)
Toll Brothers, Inc.

HOSPITALS & NURSING HOMES
Beverly Enterprises, Inc.
Community Health Systems, Inc.
HCA, Inc.
Health Management Associates, Inc.
HealthSouth Corporation
Manor Care, Inc.
* Tenet Healthcare Corp.
Universal Health Services, Inc.

HOTELS & MOTELS
Extended Stay America, Inc.
Hilton Hotels Corporation
Host Marriott Corporation
Marriott International, Inc.
Starwood Hotels & Resorts Worldwide, Inc.

HOUSEHOLD APPLIANCES & UTENSILS
* Maytag Corporation
* Oneida Ltd.
Salton, Inc.
* Whirlpool Corporation
York International Corporation

INSURANCE–BROKERAGE
Brown & Brown, Inc.
* Marsh & McLennan Cos. Inc.
MBIA, Inc.

INSURANCE–COMBINED
* Aetna Inc.
Allmerica Financial Corporation
American International Group, Inc.
* Aon Corporation
Berkley (W.R.) Corp.
* CIGNA Corp.
Gallagher (Arthur J.) & Co.
Hartford Financial Services Group (The)
Hilb, Rogal & Hamilton Company
* Jefferson-Pilot Corp.
* Lincoln National Corporation
Markel Corporation
* Old Republic International Corp.
* RLI Corp.
St. Paul Companies, Inc.
Stancorp Financial Group Inc.
21st Century Insurance Group
Unitrin, Inc.
Zenith National Insurance Corp.

INSURANCE–LIFE
* AFLAC Inc.
John Hancock Financial Services, Inc.
MetLife Inc.
MONY Group, Inc. (The)
Nationwide Financial Services, Inc.
Protective Life Corp.
Torchmark Corp.
* UnumProvident Corporation

INSURANCE–MORTGAGE
PMI Group Inc. (The)
Radian Group Inc.

INSURANCE–PROPERTY & CASUALTY
* Allstate Corp. (The)
American Financial Group, Inc.
* Chubb Corporation (The)
CNA Financial Corp.
* Fidelity National Financial, Inc.
First American Corporation (The)
Fremont General Corp.
Leucadia National Corp.
* Mercury General Corporation
MGIC Investment Corp.
Progressive Corporation (The)
Reinsurance Group of America, Inc.
Transatlantic Holdings, Inc.

INSURANCE–TITLE
LandAmerica Financial Group Inc.

MACHINERY & EQUIPMENT
Actuant Corporation
American Standard Companies, Inc.
* Briggs & Stratton Corporation
* Caterpillar Inc.
* Cooper Industries, Ltd.
Crane Co.
Dover Corp.
Graco Inc.
IDEX Corporation
* Ingersoll-Rand Company
Manitowoc Company (The)
* Milacron, Inc.
NACCO Industries Inc.
Parker-Hannifin Corp.
* Pentair, Inc.
* Tennant Company
Thermo Electron Corp.
* Toro Co. (The)

MAINTENANCE & SECURITY SERVICES
ABM Industries Inc.
Pittston Company (The)

MEASURING & CONTROL INSTRUMENTS
Applied Biosystems Group
Esterline Technologies Corporation
Fisher Scientific International, Inc.
Flowserve Corporation
Mettler-Toledo International, Inc.
PerkinElmer, Inc.
Roper Industries, Inc.
Steris Corp.
Tektronix, Inc.
* Teleflex Inc.
Teradyne, Inc.
Waters Corp.

MEDICAL & DENTAL EQUIPMENT & SUPPLIES
AmerisourceBergen Corp.
Apogent Technologies, Inc.
* Bard (C.R.), Inc.
* Baxter International Inc.
Beckman Coulter
* Becton, Dickinson & Company
Boston Scientific Corp.
Cooper Companies, Inc.
Diagnostic Products Corp.

Guidant Corporation
* Johnson & Johnson
Medtronic, Incorporated
St. Jude Medical, Inc.
Stryker Corp.
* West Pharmaceutical Services, Inc.
Zimmer Holdings, Inc.

METAL PRODUCTS
Commercial Metals Co.
* Harsco Corporation
Illinois Tool & Works, Inc.
* Kennametal, Inc.
Precision Castparts Corp.

MINING & PROCESSING
* Alcoa, Inc.
Freeport-McMoRan Copper & Gold Inc.
Massey Energy Company
Minerals Technologies, Inc.
* Newmont Mining Corp.
Peabody Energy Corp.

MOBILE HOMES
Fleetwood Enterprises, Inc.
Monaco Coach Corp.
Thor Industries, Inc.
Winnebago Industries, Inc.

NATURAL GAS
Burlington Resources Inc.
Cabot Oil & Gas Corporation
Dynegy Inc.
El Paso Corp.
Forest Oil Corporation
KeySpan Corp.
Kinder Morgan, Inc.
* MDU Resources Group, Inc.
* National Fuel Gas Company
* ONEOK Inc.
* Peoples Energy Corporation
Plains All American Pipeline, L.P.
Questar Corp.
TEPPCO Partners, L.P.
* UGI Corp.
Western Gas Resources, Inc.
Williams Companies, Inc. (The)

NATURAL GAS-DISTRIBUTORS
AGL Resources
* Atmos Energy Corporation
ENERGEN Corp.
* Equitable Resources, Inc.
* NICOR, Inc.
Northwest Natural Gas Company
* Piedmont Natural Gas Company
* Sempra Energy
* WGL Holdings, Inc.

NEWSPAPERS
* Dow Jones & Company, Inc.
* Gannett Company, Inc.
Hollinger International, Inc.
Knight-Ridder Inc.
Lee Enterprises, Inc.
McClatchy Company (The)
* Media General, Inc.
* New York Times Company
Scripps (E.W.) Company (The)
* Tribune Company
Washington Post Company (The)

OFFICE EQUIPMENT & SUPPLIES
Boise Cascade Corporation
Brady Corporation
* Diebold, Inc.
Lexmark International Group, Inc.
Office Depot, Inc.
OfficeMax, Inc.
* Pitney Bowes, Inc.
Reynolds and Reynolds Company (The)
Steelcase Inc.
Wallace Computer Services, Inc.
* Xerox Corporation

OIL
* Amerada Hess Corp.
Anadarko Petroleum Corp.
* Apache Corp.
* Ashland, Inc.
BP, p.l.c.
* ChevronTexaco Corporation
* ConocoPhillips
EOG Resources, Inc.
* Exxon Mobil Corp.
Frontier Oil Corporation
* Kerr-McGee Corporation
* Marathon Oil Corporation
Murphy Oil Corporation
Newfield Exploration Co.
Noble Energy, Inc.
* Occidental Petroleum Corp.
Ocean Energy Inc.
Pioneer Natural Resources Company
Premcor Inc.
* Sunoco, Inc.
Tesoro Petroleum Corp.
* Unocal Corp.
Valero Energy Corporation

OIL SERVICES & EQUIPMENT
Atwood Oceanics, Inc.
Baker Hughes Inc.
BJ Services Co.
Cooper Cameron Corp.
Diamond Offshore Drilling, Inc.
Ensco International Inc.
Halliburton Company
Hanover Compressor Co.
Helmerich & Payne, Inc.
Maverick Tube Corp.
* McDermott International, Inc.
National-Oilwell Inc.
Noble Corporation
Pride International Inc.
Rowan Cos. Inc.
Schlumberger, Ltd.
Smith International, Inc.
Tidewater Inc.
Transocean Inc.
Varco International Inc.
Weatherford International Ltd.

PAINTS & RELATED PRODUCTS
RPM International Inc.
* Sherwin-Williams Company
Valspar Corporation (The)

PAPER
* Albany International Corp.
* Bemis Company Inc.
* Bowater, Inc.
* Chesapeake Corporation

Glatfelter (P.H.) Co.
* International Paper Co.
* Kimberly-Clark Corp.
* MeadWestvaco Corporation
Packaging Corp. of America
Pactiv Corporation
Sonoco Products Company
* Temple-Inland Inc.

PHOTO & OPTICAL
* Bausch & Lomb, Incorporated
* Eastman Kodak Company
Oakley, Inc.

PLASTICS & PLASTIC PRODUCTS
AptarGroup, Inc.
* Myers Industries Inc.
PolyOne Corporation
Sealed Air Corp.
Tupperware Corp.

POLLUTION CONTROL
Allied Waste Industries, Inc.
* Clarcor Inc.
* Donaldson Company, Inc.
* Pall Corporation
Republic Services, Inc.
Waste Management, Inc.

PRINTING & ENGRAVING
* Banta Corporation
Consolidated Graphics, Inc.
Deluxe Corp.
* Donnelley (R.R.) & Sons Co., Inc.
Harland (John H.) Co. (The)

PUBLISHING
American Greetings Corp.
Harte-Hanks, Inc.
* McGraw-Hill Companies, Inc. (The)
Meredith Corporation
Pulitzer Inc.
Reader's Digest Association, Inc. (The)
Wiley (John) & Sons, Inc.

RAILROAD EQUIPMENT
* GATX Corp.

RAILROADS
Burlington Northern Santa Fe Corp.
* CSX Corporation
Florida East Coast Industries, Inc.
Kansas City Southern Industries, Inc.
* Norfolk Southern Corporation
* Union Pacific Corp.

REAL ESTATE
AMB Property Corp.
Kimco Realty Corp.
* Prologis
* Rouse Company (The)
St. Joe Company

REAL ESTATE INVESTMENT TRUSTS
Apartment Investment and Management Co.
* Archstone-Smith Trust Company
AvalonBay Communities Inc.
* Boston Properties Inc.
CarrAmerica Realty Corp.
* Commercial Net Lease Realty, Inc.

Cousins Properties Incorporated
Crescent Real Estate Equity Co.
* Duke Realty Corporation
Eastgroup Properties, Inc.
* Equity Office Properties Trust
* Equity Residential Properties Trust
* Federal Realty Investment Trust
General Growth Properties, Inc.
* Health Care Property Investors, Inc.
Highwoods Properties, Inc.
* IndyMac Bancorp, Inc.
* Liberty Property Trust
* Mack-Cali Realty Corp.
Public Storage Inc.
Simon Property Group, Inc.
* United Dominion Realty Trust, Inc.
* Universal Health Realty Income Trust
Vornado Realty Trust
* Washington Real Estate Investment Trust
* Weingarten Realty Investors

RECREATION
Bally Total Fitness Holding Corp.
* Brunswick Corporation
Callaway Golf Company
Carnival Corporation
* Cedar Fair, L.P.
Disney (Walt) Company
Polaris Industries Inc.
Six Flags Inc.

RESTAURANTS
Brinker International, Inc.
Darden Restaurants, Inc.
IHOP Corp.
* McDonald's Corporation
Outback Steakhouse, Inc.
Ruby Tuesday, Inc.
* Wendy's International, Inc.
Yum! Brands, Inc.

RETAIL–DEPARTMENT STORES
* Dillard's, Inc.
Federated Department Stores, Inc.
Kohl's Corp.
May Department Stores Co. (The)
* Penney (J.C.) Co., Inc.
Saks Incorporated
* Sears, Roebuck and Co.

RETAIL–DISCOUNT & VARIETY STORES
Big Lots Inc.
Dollar General Corp.
Family Dollar Stores, Inc.
Payless ShoeSource Inc.
7-Eleven, Inc.
Shopko Stores, Inc.
* Target Corporation
Wal-Mart Stores, Inc.

RETAIL–DRUG STORES
CVS Corp.
Longs Drug Stores Corp.
* Rite Aid Corporation
* Walgreen Co.

RETAIL–SPECIALTY STORES
Abercrombie & Fitch Co.
AnnTaylor Stores Corp.
AutoNation, Inc.
AutoZone, Inc.
Barnes & Noble, Inc.
Best Buy Co., Inc.
BJ's Wholesale Club, Inc.
Blockbuster, Inc.
Borders Group, Inc.
Circuit City Stores, Inc.
Claire's Stores, Inc.
Coach, Inc.
* Foot Locker, Inc.
GameStop Corp.
Gap, Inc. (The)
Group 1 Automotive, Inc.
Hancock Fabrics, Inc.
Home Depot, Inc. (The)
Limited Brands
Lithia Motors, Inc.
* Lowe's Companies, Inc.
Men's Wearhouse, Inc. (The)
Michaels Stores, Inc.
Neiman-Marcus Group, Inc. (The)
99 Cents Only Stores
Nordstrom, Inc.
* Pep Boys–Manny, Moe & Jack
Pier 1 Imports, Inc.
* RadioShack Corporation
Sonic Automotive, Inc.
Talbots (The), Inc.
Tiffany & Co.
TJX Companies, Inc. (The)
Toys "R" Us
United Auto Group Inc.
Williams-Sonoma Inc.

SAVINGS & LOANS
Golden West Financial Corp.
GreenPoint Financial Corp.
Washington Mutual, Inc.

SECURITIES BROKERAGE
Bear Stearns Companies Inc. (The)
E*TRADE Group, Inc.
Edwards (A.G.), Inc.
Franklin Resources, Inc.
Goldman Sachs Group, Inc. (The)
LaBranche & Co., Inc.
Legg Mason, Inc.
Lehman Brothers Holdings Inc.
* Merrill Lynch & Co., Inc.
Neuberger Berman Inc.
Raymond James Financial, Inc.
* Schwab (Charles) Corp. (The)
Waddell & Reed Financial, Inc.

SERVICES
Administaff, Inc.
ARAMARK Corporation
BISYS Group, Inc. (The)
Block (H&R), Inc.
Catalina Marketing Corp.
CDI Corp.
Cendant Corp.
ChoicePoint Inc.

Concord EFS, Inc.
DeVry, Inc.
DST Systems Inc.
Dun & Bradstreet Corporation (The)
* Equifax, Inc.
Global Payments Inc.
Hillenbrand Industries, Inc.
* IKON Office Solutions, Inc.
IMS Health, Inc.
Iron Mountain Inc.
Labor Ready, Inc.
Manpower Inc.
Moody's Corporation
MPS Group, Inc.
Quanta Services, Inc.
Quest Diagnostics Inc.
Robert Half International
Sabre Holding Corporation
* ServiceMaster Company (The)
Spherion Corporation
Volt Information Sciences, Inc.

SHOE MANUFACTURING
* Brown Shoe Company, Inc.
Genesco, Inc.
Nike, Inc.
Reebok International Ltd.
Timberland Company (The)

SOAPS & CLEANERS
Church & Dwight Co., Inc.
* Clorox Company (The)
* Colgate-Palmolive Co.
* Ecolab, Inc.
* Procter & Gamble Company (The)

SOFT DRINKS
* Coca-Cola Company (The)
Coca-Cola Enterprises, Inc.
Pepsi Bottling Group, Inc.
PepsiAmericas Inc.
* PepsiCo Inc.

STEEL
AK Steel Holding Corporation
Allegheny Technologies Inc.
* Carpenter Technology Corp.
* Nucor Corporation
* Quanex Corporation
Reliance Steel & Aluminum Co.
* Ryerson Tull, Inc.
United States Steel Corporation
Worthington Industries, Inc.

TELECOMMUNICATIONS
* ALLTEL Corp.
* AT&T Corporation
* BCE Inc.
* BellSouth Corp.
BroadWing, Inc.
CenturyTel, Inc.
* Citizens Communications Company
IDT Corp.
Qwest Communications International, Inc.
* SBC Communications
* Sprint Corporation FON Group
* Verizon Communications

TELECOMMUNICATIONS-EQUIPMENT

* Corning Inc.
  Lucent Technologies

TELEVISION & RADIO BROADCASTING

Belo (A.H.) Corporation
Cablevision Systems Corp.
Clear Channel Communications, Inc.
Cox Communications, Inc.
Cox Radio Inc.
Entercom Communications Corp.
Hearst-Argyle Television, Inc.
Hispanic Broadcasting Corp.
Univision Communications, Inc.
Viacom Inc.

TIRES & RUBBER GOODS

* Bandag Incorporated
* Carlisle Companies Incorporated
  Cooper Tire & Rubber Co.
  Danaher Corporation
* Goodyear Tire & Rubber Co.

TOBACCO

* Altria Group, Inc.
  Dimon Incorporated
  R.J. Reynolds Tobacco Holdings, Inc.
* Standard Commercial Corp.
* Universal Corporation
* UST Inc.

WATER

* American States Water Company
  California Water Service Co.
* Philadelphia Suburban Corporation

WHOLESALERS–DISTRIBUTORS–JOBBERS

Cardinal Health, Inc.
Grainger (W.W.), Inc.
* Handleman Company
  Hughes Supply, Inc.
* McKesson Corporation
  Owens & Minor, Inc.
  Watsco, Inc.

* Designates companies offering dividend reinvestment plans.

DOW JONES INDUSTRIAL AVERAGE
PRICES - EARNINGS - DIVIDENDS

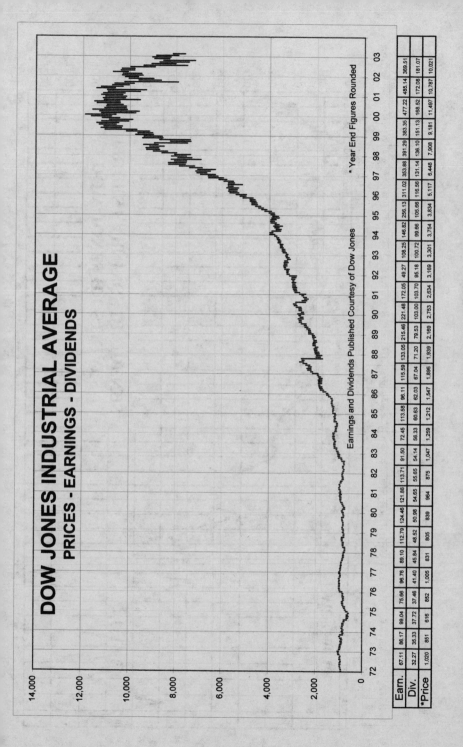

Earnings and Dividends Published Courtesy of Dow Jones

* Year End Figures Rounded

	72	73	74	75	76	77	78	79	80	81	82	83	84	85	86	87	88	89	90	91	92	93	94	95	96	97	98	99	00	01	02	03
Earn.	67.11	86.17	99.04	75.66	96.76	89.10	112.79	124.46	121.86	113.71	91.50	72.45	113.58	96.11	115.59	133.05	215.46	221.48	172.05	49.27	108.25	146.82	256.13	311.02	353.88	391.29	383.35	477.22	485.14	369.51
Div.	32.27	35.33	37.72	37.46	41.40	45.84	48.52	50.98	54.65	55.65	54.14	56.33	60.63	62.03	67.04	71.20	79.53	103.00	103.70	95.18	100.72	99.66	105.66	116.56	131.14	136.10	151.13	168.52	172.08	181.07
*Price	1,020	851	616	852	1,005	831	805	839	964	875	1,047	1,259	1,212	1,547	1,896	1,939	2,169	2,753	2,634	3,169	3,301	3,754	3,834	5,117	6,448	7,908	9,181	11,497	10,787	10,021

25a

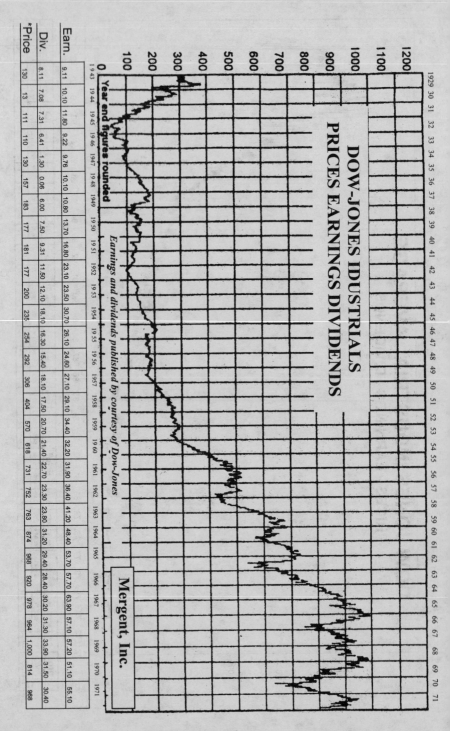

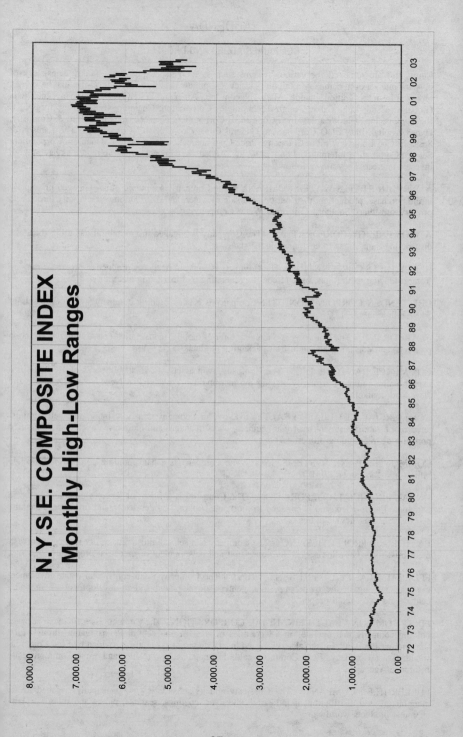

N.Y.S.E. COMPOSITE INDEX
Monthly High-Low Ranges

ADDENDA

COMPANIES ADDED AND DROPPED

Companies are removed for various reasons such as mergers, acquisitions, bankruptcies, lack of investor interest or at company's failure to renew Corporate Visibility. The companies that have been removed from this edition include: Allen Telecom Inc., American Water Works Company, Inc., Asia Global Crossing Ltd., Cable Design Technologies Corporation, Champion Enterprises, Inc., CKE Restaurants, Inc., Clark/Bardes, Inc., Cone Mills Corporation, Conseco, Inc., Crawford & Company, Dynex Capital, Inc., EDO Corporation, General Cable Corp., Kmart Corporation, The Lamson & Sessions Co., Longview Fibre Company, Price Communications Corporation, Quantum Corporation, Service Corporation International and TRW Inc. Added are companies that we regard as having high investor interest. They are as follows:

AMERICAN STATES WATER COMPANY - The Company is a public utility engaged principally in the purchase, production, distribution, and sale of water, and distribution of electricity through its primary subsidiary Southern California Water Company.

ATMOS ENERGY CORPORATION - The Company is engaged in the natural gas utility business distributing natural gas to customers in 12 states.

BLACK HILLS CORPORATION - The Company is engaged in energy production processes ranging from producing natural gas, oil and coal to generating and marketing electricity.

CHITTENDEN CORPORATION - The Company is a bank holding company with total assets of $4.87 billion at 12/31/02.

CLARCOR INC. - The Company is a manufacturer of mobile, industrial and environmental filtration products, and consumer and industrial packaging products.

COMMERCE BANCORP, INC. - The Company, with assets of $16.40 billion as of 12/31/02, is a bank holding company primarily serving the metropolitan Philadelphia, New Jersey, Delaware and New York markets.

COMMERCIAL NET LEASE REALTY, INC. - The Company is a fully integrated, self-administered real estate investment trust that acquires, owns, manages and indirectly develops a diversified portfolio of freestanding properties.

COMMUNITY BANK SYSTEMS, INC. - The Company is a bank holding company with $3.43 billion in assets, as of 12/31/02.

DORAL FINANCIAL CORPORATION - The Company is a financial services company based in San Juan, Puerto Rico, and is engaged in mortgage banking, broker-dealer and investment banking and insurance agency activities.

EASTGROUP PROPERTIES, INC. - The Company is a self-administered, equity real estate investment trust focused on the acquisition, operation and development of industrial properties.

FEDERAL REALTY INVESTMENT TRUST - The Company is an equity real estate investment trust specializing in the ownership, management, development and re-development of shopping centers and street retail properties.

FIRST COMMONWEALTH FINANCIAL CORPORATION - The Company is a financial services holding company that operates in 18 counties in western and central Pennsylvania through First Commonwealth Bank. Financial services and insurance products are also provided by First Commonwealth Trust Company, First Commonwealth Financial Advisors, Inc. and First Commonwealth Insurance Agency.

FULLER (H.B.) COMPANY - The Company and its subsidiaries are principally engaged in the manufacture and distribution of industrial adhesives, coatings, sealants, paints and other specialty chemical products worldwide.

HAVERTY FURNITURE COMPANIES, INC. - The Company is a full-service home furnishings retailer with 111 stores in 14 southern and central states as of 2/14/03.

HILB, ROGAL & HAMILTON COMPANY - The Company places various types of insurance, including property/casualty, marine, aviation and employee benefits, with insurance underwriters on behalf of its clients through a network of wholly-owned subsidiary insurance agencies.

HUDSON UNITED BANCORP - The Company is a bank holding company for Hudson United Bank, a full-service commercial bank that operates over 200 branches throughout New Jersey, Connecticut, lower New York state, and southeastern Pennsylvania.

IRWIN FINANCIAL CORP. - The Company is a diversified financial services company with $4.88 billion in assets at 12/31/02.

NATIONAL COMMERCE FINANCIAL CORPORATION - The Company, with assets of $21.47 billion as of 12/31/02, provides commercial and retail banking services, as well as savings and trust services, through its subsidiaries, National Bank of Commerce, NBC Bank, Federal Savings Bank and Central Carolina Bank.

NUVEEN INVESTMENTS, INC. - The Company is engaged in asset management and related research, as well as the development, marketing and distribution of investment products and services. As of 12/31/02, total assets under management amounted to approximately $79.72 billion.

PHILADELPHIA SUBURBAN CORPORATION - The Company is a holding company for regulated utilities providing water or wastewater services to approximately 2.0 million people in Pennsylvania, Illinois, Ohio, New Jersey, Maine and North Carolina as of 2/5/03.

QUAKER CHEMICAL CORPORATION - The Company develops, produces, and markets a wide range of formulated chemical specialty products for various heavy industrial and manufacturing applications and, in addition, offers and markets chemical management services.

RLI CORP. - The Company is a holding company composed primarily of four main insurance companies.

STEPAN COMPANY - The Company is a producer of specialty and intermediate chemicals that are used in a variety of end products, such as detergents, shampoos, lotions, toothpastes, cosmetics, construction materials and agricultural and industrial products.

TENNANT COMPANY - The Company is a manufacturer of nonresidential floor maintenance and outdoor cleaning equipment, floor coatings and related products.

TEPPCO PARTNERS, L.P. - The Company is a master limited partnership involved in the operation of common carrier pipelines of refined petroleum products, liquefied petroleum gases and crude oil transportation, gathering and marketing.

UNITED DOMINION REALTY TRUST, INC. - The Company is an equity real estate investment trust with activities related to the ownership, development, acquisition, renovation, management, marketing and strategic disposition of multifamily apartment communities.

UNIVERSAL HEALTH REALTY INCOME TRUST - The Company is a real estate investment trust organized in Maryland.

WASHINGTON REAL ESTATE INVESTMENT TRUST - The Company is a self-administered qualified equity real estate investment trust.

WEBSTER FINANCIAL CORPORATION - The Company, with $13.47 billion in assets as of 12/31/02, provides business and consumer banking, mortgage, insurance, trust and investment services through its Webster Bank and Webster Insurance, Inc. subsidiaries.

ADDENDA (Continued)

WEINGARTEN REALTY INVESTORS - The Company is a self-administered and self-managed real estate investment trust that acquires, develops and manages real estate, primarily anchored neighborhood, community shopping centers and industrial properties.

WEST PHARMACEUTICAL SERVICES, INC. - The Company is engaged in drug formulation research and development, clinical research and laboratory services.

RECENT AND PENDING STOCK DIVIDENDS AND SPLITS

Company	Amount	Ex-Div. Date	Date of Record	Payable Date
Alleghany Corporation	2%	3/28/03	4/1/03	4/25/03
Ameron International Corporation	100%	5/28/03	5/1/03	5/27/03
Apache Corporation	5%	3/10/03	3/12/03	4/2/03
Forest Laboratories, Inc.	2-for-1	1/9/03	12/23/02	1/8/03
Mylan Laboratories Inc.	3-for-2	1/28/03	1/17/03	1/27/03
Old National Bancorp	5%	2/27/03	3/3/03	3/17/03
Tootsie Roll Industries, Inc.	3%	2/28/03	3/4/03	4/16/03
Toro Company (The)	100%	4/15/03	4/1/03	4/14/03
UGI Corporation	3-for-2	4/2/03	2/28/03	4/1/03
Weingarten Realty Investors	3-for-2	4/16/03	4/1/03	4/15/03

RECENT DIVIDEND CHANGES

Company	Amount	Payable	Company	Amount	Payable
Increased			**Increased**		
Abbott Laboratories	0.245Q	5/15/03	Diebold, Inc.	0.17Q	3/7/03
Alberto-Culver Company	0.105Q	2/20/03	Dollar General Corporation	0.035Q	4/17/03
Allete, Inc.	0.282Q	3/1/03	Donaldson Company, Inc.	0.09Q	3/14/03
Allied Capital Corp.	0.57Q	3/28/03	Doral Financial Corporation	0.14Q	3/7/03
Allstate Corp. (The)	0.23Q	4/1/03	Eastgroup Properties, Inc.	0.475Q	3/31/03
AMB Property Corporation	0.415Q	4/15/03	Energy East Corporation	0.25Q	2/15/03
Ameron International Corp.	0.40Q	5/20/03	Exelon Corporation	0.46Q	3/10/03
Archstone-Smith Trust Co.	0.427Q	2/28/03	Family Dollar Stores, Inc.	0.075Q	4/15/03
Autoliv, Inc.	0.13Q	3/6/03	Fannie Mae	0.39Q	2/25/03
Avon Products, Inc.	0.21Q	3/3/03	Fidelity National Financial	0.15Q	4/25/03
BellSouth Corporation	0.21Q	5/1/03	FPL Group, Inc.	0.60Q	3/17/03
Bemis Company, Inc.	0.28Q	3/3/03	Freddie Mac	0.26Q	3/31/03
Berkley (W.R.) Corp.	0.10Q	4/1/03	Fremont General Corp.	0.03Q	4/30/03
Black Hills Corp.	0.30Q	3/1/03	Gallagher (Arthur J.) & Co.	0.18Q	4/15/03
Cedar Fair, L.P.	0.44Q	5/15/03	General Dynamics Corp.	0.32Q	5/9/03
CenturyTel, Inc.	0.055Q	3/21/03	Genuine Parts Co.	0.295Q	4/1/03
Chubb Corp. (The)	0.36Q	4/11/03	GreenPoint Financial Corp.	0.3125Q	3/10/03
City National Corp.	0.205Q	2/18/03	Hancock Fabrics, Inc.	0.10Q	4/15/03
Coca-Cola Company (The)	0.22Q	4/1/03	Harte-Hanks Inc.	0.03Q	3/14/03
Colgate-Palmolive Company	0.24Q	5/15/03	Household International Inc.	0.869Q	5/6/03
Comerica, Inc.	0.50Q	4/1/03	Hughes Supply, Inc.	0.10Q	2/14/03
Consolidated Edison, Inc.	0.56Q	3/15/03	Irwin Financial Corp.	0.07Q	3/28/03
Constellation Energy Group	0.26Q	4/1/03	ITT Industries Inc.	0.16Q	4/1/03

ADDENDA (Continued)

Jefferson-Pilot Corp.	0.33Q	6/5/03	**Increased**			
Keycorp	0.305Q	3/14/03	Regions Financial Corp.	0.30Q	4/1/03
Kimberly-Clark Corp.	0.34Q	4/2/03	Rouse Company (The)	0.42Q	3/28/03
Kinder Morgan, Inc.	0.15Q	2/14/03	Russ Berrie & Co., Inc.	0.28Q	3/28/03
Lilly (Eli) & Co.	0.335Q	3/10/03	SCANA Corporation	0.345Q	4/1/03
Limited Brands	0.10Q	3/18/03	Sherwin-Williams Co.	0.155Q	3/10/03
Lockheed Martin Corp.	0.12Q	3/31/03	Student Loan Corp. (The)	0.77Q	3/3/03
May Department Stores Co.	0.24Q	3/15/03	Suntrust Banks, Inc.	0.45Q	3/14/03
MBIA Inc.	0.20Q	4/15/03	Synovus Financial Corp.	0.165Q	4/1/03
MBNA Corporation	0.08Q	4/1/03	TCF Financial Corp.	0.325Q	2/28/03
McClatchy Company (The)	0.11Q	4/1/03	Temple-Inland Inc.	0.34Q	3/14/03
McGraw-Hill Cos., Inc.	0.27Q	3/12/03	U.S. Bancorp	0.205Q	4/15/03
Media General, Inc.	0.19Q	3/15/03	UniSource Energy Corp.	0.15Q	3/7/03
Mercury General Corp.	0.33Q	3/27/03	United Dominion Realty Tr.	0.285Q	4/30/03
Meredith Corp.	0.95Q	3/14/03	United Parcel Service, Inc.	0.21Q	3/11/03
Newmont Mining Corp.	0.04Q	3/19/03	UST, Inc.	0.50Q	3/31/03
NICOR Inc.	0.465Q	5/1/03	Vulcan Materials Co.	0.245Q	3/10/03
North Fork Bancorporation	0.27Q	2/18/03	Wal-Mart Stores, Inc.	0.09Q	4/7/03
Nucor Corporation	0.20Q	5/12/03	Washington Post Co. (The)	1.45Q	2/7/03
Occidental Petroleum Corp.	0.26Q	4/15/03	Wells Fargo & Co.	0.30Q	3/1/03
Parker-Hannifin Corp.	0.19Q	3/7/03	WGL Holdings, Inc.	0.32Q	5/1/03
Pentair, Inc.	0.21Q	5/9/03	Wrigley (Wm.) Jr. Co.	0.22Q	5/1/03
Peoples Energy Corp.	0.53Q	4/15/03			
Piedmont Natural Gas Co.	0.415Q	4/15/03	**Decreased**		
Pier 1 Imports, Inc.	0.06Q	2/19/03	Alliant Energy Corp.	0.25Q	2/15/03
Pitney Bowes Inc.	0.30Q	3/12/03	CenterPoint Energy	0.10Q	3/31/03
PPL Corporation	0.385Q	4/1/03	El Paso Corporation	0.04Q	4/7/03
Praxair, Inc.	0.215Q	3/17/03	Heinz (H.J.) Company	0.27Q	4/10/03
Quanex Corporation	0.17Q	3/31/03	Webstar Energy, Inc.	0.19Q	4/1/03

CHANGES IN COMPANY QUALITY GRADE

COMPANY	Old	New
Albemarle Corporation	Medium	Upper Medium
Alleghany Corporation	Upper Medium	Medium
Allegheny Technologies, Inc.	Lower Medium	Speculative
AmeriCredit Corp.	Medium	Speculative
Ametek, Inc.	Medium	Upper Medium
Ball Corporation	Lower Medium	Medium
Berkley (W.R.) Corp.	Medium	Upper Medium
Circuit City Stores, Inc.	Medium	Lower Medium
Constellation Brands, Inc.	Medium	Upper Medium
Cooper Companies, Inc.	Medium	Upper Medium
Covance Inc.	Medium	Upper Medium
Cypress Semiconductor Corp.	Lower Medium	Speculative
Darden Restaurants, Inc.	Medium	Upper Medium
Diebold, Inc.	Upper Medium	Investment
Duke Energy Corporation	Upper Medium	Medium
Forest Laboratories, Inc.	Upper Medium	Investment
Fox Entertainment Group, Inc.	Medium	Upper Medium
Gap (The), Inc.	Lower Medium	Medium
Goodyear Tire & Rubber Co.	Lower Medium	Speculative

ADDENDA (Continued)

CHANGES IN COMPANY QUALITY GRADE

COMPANY	Old	New
Harman International Industries, Inc.	Medium	Upper Medium
HealthSouth Corporation	Lower Medium	Speculative
Hilb, Roal & Hamilton Company	Medium	Upper Medium
ICN Pharmaceuticals, Inc.	Upper Medium	Medium
International Game Technology	Medium	Upper Medium
McClatchy Company (The)	Medium	Upper Medium
McDonald's Corporation	High	Investment
Micron Technology, Inc.	Lower Medium	Speculative
Mohawk Industries, Inc.	Upper Medium	Investment
MPS Group, Inc.	Lower Medium	Speculative
Mylan Laboratories Inc.	Medium	Upper Medium
National Commercial Financial Corp.	Medium	Upper Medium
Neiman Marcus Group, Inc. (The)	Medium	Upper Medium
NorthWestern Corporation	Lower Medium	Speculative
Oneok Inc.	Investment	Upper Medium
Pactiv Corporation	Medium	Upper Medium
PEPCO Holdings Inc.	Upper Medium	Medium
Pitney Bowes Inc.	Investment	Upper Medium
Scripps (E.W.) Company (The)	Medium	Upper Medium
Sierra Pacific Resources	Lower Medium	Speculative
Spherion Corporation	Lower Medium	Speculative
Tenet Healthcare Corp.	Upper Medium	Medium
Toro Company (The)	Medium	Upper Medium
TXU Corporation	Medium	Lower Medium
Westwood One, Inc.	Medium	Upper Medium
Xcel Energy, Inc.	Medium	Lower Medium

RECENT AND PENDING NAME CHANGES

Old	New
Countrywide Credit Industries, Inc.	Countrywide Financial Corporation
Nuveen (John) Company (The)	Nuveen Investments, Inc.
Philip Morris Companies, Inc.	Altria Group, Inc.
Reliant Energy, Inc.	CenterPoint Energy, Inc.
RPM, Inc.	RPM International Inc.
Stilwell Financial, Inc.	Janus Capital Group, Inc.

LATEST DEVELOPMENTS

OFFICE DEPOT, INC. – On 4/8/03, the Company announced that it has made an offer to acquire the contract sales business of Guilbert S.A. from Pinault-Printemps-Redoute Group for approximately $875.0 million. The transaction, which is subject to European Union approval, is expected to be completed by late spring of 2003.

SEARS, ROEBUCK & CO. – On 3/26/03, the Company announced that it is considering the possible sale of its credit-card business, which had $30.80 billion in receivables as of 12/31/02.

AAR CORPORATION

EXCH.	SYM.	REC. PRICE	P/E RATIO	YLD.	MKT. CAP.	RANGE (52-WK.)	'02 Y/E PR.
NYSE	AIR	4.45 (2/28/03)	...	...	$141.8 mill.	14.00 - 2.92	5.15

LOWER MEDIUM GRADE. SALES ARE BENEFITING FROM STRONG DEMAND FOR THE COMPANY'S SERVICES FROM THE U.S. MILITARY.

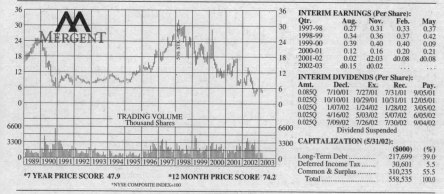

*7 YEAR PRICE SCORE 47.9 ***12 MONTH PRICE SCORE 74.2**
*NYSE COMPOSITE INDEX=100

INTERIM EARNINGS (Per Share):

Qtr.	Aug.	Nov.	Feb.	May
1997-98	0.27	0.31	0.33	0.37
1998-99	0.34	0.36	0.37	0.42
1999-00	0.39	0.40	0.40	0.09
2000-01	0.12	0.16	0.20	0.21
2001-02	0.02	d2.03	d0.08	d0.08
2002-03	d0.15	d0.02	...	...

INTERIM DIVIDENDS (Per Share):

Amt.	Decl.	Ex.	Rec.	Pay.
0.085Q	7/10/01	7/27/01	7/31/01	9/05/01
0.025Q	10/10/01	10/29/01	10/31/01	12/05/01
0.025Q	1/07/02	1/24/02	1/28/02	3/05/02
0.025Q	4/16/02	5/03/02	5/07/02	6/05/02
0.025Q	7/09/02	7/26/02	7/30/02	9/04/02
	Dividend Suspended			

CAPITALIZATION (5/31/02):

	($000)	(%)
Long-Term Debt	217,699	39.0
Deferred Income Tax	30,601	5.5
Common & Surplus	310,235	55.5
Total	558,535	100.0

BUSINESS:

AAR Corporation provides aviation support to the worldwide aerospace/aviation industry and the United States and other governments. The Inventory and Logistic Services segment (40.4% of sales in fiscal 2002) sells new, overhauled and repaired engine and airframe parts and components. The Maintenance, Repair and Overhaul segment (33.9%) includes the repair and overhaul of commercial and military aircraft engine and airframe parts, and parts for industrial gas and steam turbine operators. The Manufacturing segment (15.6%) includes the manufacture and sale of in-plane cargo loading and handling systems, advanced composite materials, containers, pallets and shelters. The Aircraft and Engine Sales and Leasing segment (10.1%) sells and leases used commercial aircraft and new, overhauled and repaired commercial aircraft engines.

RECENT DEVELOPMENTS:

For the quarter ended 11/30/02, net loss totaled $663,000 compared with a net loss of $54.5 million in the prior year. Results for 2001 included asset impairment and other special pre-tax charges of $86.0 million. Total sales grew 5.6% to $153.1 million from $144.9 million a year earlier. Inventory and Logistic Services segment sales climbed 16.7% to $65.2 million, while Manufacturing segment sales rose 15.0% to $29.3 million. Maintenance, Repair and Overhaul segment sales slipped 5.0% to $52.4 million, while Aircraft and Engine Sales and Leasing segment sales fell 26.6% to $6.1 million. Gross profit was $22.9 million, or 15.0% of sales, versus $20.5 million, or 14.2% of sales, in 2001.

PROSPECTS:

Results are benefiting from increased demand for the Company's products and services that support the U.S. Military's tactical deployment activities, which is expected to continue through the remainder of fiscal 2003. Meanwhile, AAR is implementing initiatives expected to generate annual cost savings of $12.0 million in the current fiscal year and going forward. During the second quarter of fiscal 2003, the Company completed the consolidation of its Chicago-based inventory and logistics services warehouses and the sale of the vacated building.

ANNUAL FINANCIAL DATA:

FISCAL YEAR	TOT. REVS. ($mill.)	NET INC. ($mill.)	TOT. ASSETS ($mill.)	OPER. PROFIT %	NET PROFIT %	RET. ON EQUITY %	RET. ON ASSETS %	CURR. RATIO	EARN. PER SH.$	CASH FL. PER SH.$	TANG. BK. VAL.$	DIV. PER SH.$	PRICE RANGE		AVG. P/E RATIO	AVG. YIELD %
5/31/02	638.7	⑤ d58.9	710.2	...	...	...	...	2.9	⑤ d2.08	1.29	8.29	0.28	17.45	6.96	...	2.3
5/31/01	④ 874.3	18.5	701.9	4.6	2.1	5.4	2.6	3.9	0.69	1.38	10.95	0.34	28.50	9.75	27.7	1.8
5/31/00	④ 1,024.3	③ 35.2	741.0	6.9	3.4	10.4	4.7	3.1	③ 1.28	1.98	11.19	0.34	24.00	14.63	15.1	1.8
5/31/99	918.0	41.7	726.6	8.4	4.5	12.8	5.7	2.9	1.49	2.10	10.44	0.34	32.42	17.44	16.7	1.4
5/31/98	782.1	35.7	670.6	8.3	4.6	11.9	5.3	3.1	1.27	1.77	9.90	0.32	27.00	16.17	17.0	1.5
5/31/97	589.3	23.0	529.6	7.3	3.9	8.6	4.3	4.1	0.92	1.41	9.65	0.32	20.83	11.83	17.8	2.0
5/31/96	505.0	16.0	437.8	6.4	3.2	7.8	3.7	4.3	0.67	1.09	8.28	0.32	14.67	8.08	17.1	2.8
5/31/95	451.4	10.5	422.8	5.4	2.3	5.4	2.5	4.4	0.44	0.87	7.85	0.32	11.58	7.92	22.2	3.3
5/31/94	407.8	② 9.5	411.0	5.4	2.3	5.0	2.3	4.5	② 0.40	0.81	7.68	0.32	10.00	7.67	22.1	3.6
5/31/93	382.8	① 0.3	365.2	1.4	0.1	0.1	0.1	3.7	① 0.01	0.47	7.66	0.32	10.58	7.17	677.5	3.6

Statistics are as originally reported. Adj. for 3-for-2 stk. split, 2/98. ① Incl. $7.2 mil after-tax chg. for restruct. ② Bef. $10,000 acctg. cr. ③ Incl. $4.0 mil ($0.11/sh) chg. to incr. bad debt reserves. ④ Incl. pass through sales of $20.6 mil., 5/01; $66.8 mil., 5/00. ⑤ Incl. $86.0 mil pretax impairment and other special chgs.

OFFICERS:
I. A. Eichner, Chmn.
D. P. Storch, Pres., C.E.O., C.O.O.
T. J. Romenesko, V.P., C.F.O.
INVESTOR CONTACT: Ann T. Baldwin, V.P.-Corp. Comm., (630) 227-2082
PRINCIPAL OFFICE: One AAR Place, 1100 North Wood Dale Road, Wood Dale, IL 60191

TELEPHONE NUMBER: (630) 227-2000
FAX: (630) 227-2019
WEB: www.aarcorp.com

NO. OF EMPLOYEES: 2,200 (approx.)

SHAREHOLDERS: 10,000 (approx.)

ANNUAL MEETING: In Oct.

INCORPORATED: DE, 1966

INSTITUTIONAL HOLDINGS:
No. of Institutions: 96
Shares Held: 25,103,968
% Held: 78.8

INDUSTRY: Aircraft engines and engine parts (SIC: 3724)

TRANSFER AGENT(S): First Chicago Trust Company of New York, Jersey City, NJ

ABBOTT LABORATORIES

EXCH.	SYM.	REC. PRICE	P/E RATIO	YLD.	MKT. CAP.	RANGE (52-WK.)	'02 Y/E PR.	DIV. ACH.
NYSE	ABT	35.62 (2/28/03)	20.0	2.8%	$55.68 bill.	57.79 - 29.80	40.00	30 yrs.

HIGH GRADE. THE COMPANY ANNOUNCED THAT IT HAS RECEIVED U.S. FDA APPROVAL EARLIER THAN ANTICIPATED TO MARKET HUMIRA™ FOR THE TREATMENT OF RHEUMATOID ARTHRITIS.

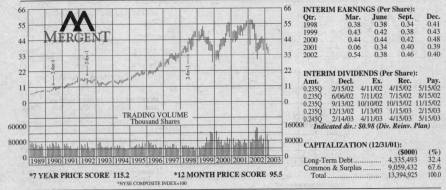

INTERIM EARNINGS (Per Share):

Qtr.	Mar.	June	Sept.	Dec.
1998	0.38	0.38	0.34	0.41
1999	0.43	0.42	0.38	0.43
2000	0.44	0.44	0.42	0.48
2001	0.06	0.34	0.40	0.39
2002	0.54	0.38	0.46	0.40

INTERIM DIVIDENDS (Per Share):

Amt.	Decl.	Ex.	Rec.	Pay.
0.235Q	2/15/02	4/11/02	4/15/02	5/15/02
0.235Q	6/06/02	7/11/02	7/15/02	8/15/02
0.235Q	9/13/02	10/10/02	10/15/02	11/15/02
0.235Q	12/13/02	1/13/03	1/15/03	2/15/03
0.245Q	2/14/03	4/11/03	4/15/03	5/15/03

Indicated div.: $0.98 (Div. Reinv. Plan)

CAPITALIZATION (12/31/01):

	($000)	(%)
Long-Term Debt	4,335,493	32.4
Common & Surplus	9,059,432	67.6
Total	13,394,925	100.0

TRADING VOLUME Thousand Shares

*7 YEAR PRICE SCORE 115.2   ***12 MONTH PRICE SCORE 95.5**

*NYSE COMPOSITE INDEX=100

BUSINESS:

Abbott Laboratories' principal business is the discovery, development, manufacture, and sale of pharmaceuticals, nutritionals, and medical products, including devices and diagnostics. Pharmaceutical products include adult and pediatric pharmaceuticals and vitamins. This segment also includes consumer products, agricultural and chemical products, and bulk pharmaceuticals. Products in the hospital and laboratory segment include diagnostic systems, intravenous and irrigating fluids and related administration equipment, anesthetics, critical care equipment, and other specialty products. Products in the Ross segment include nutritional products such as SIMILAC and ENSURE. ABT also owns 50.0% of the joint venture, TAP Pharmaceutical Products Inc. On 2/8/01, ABT acquired BASF's pharmaceutical business, including the global operations of Knoll, for $6.90 billion in cash.

RECENT DEVELOPMENTS:

For the year ended 12/31/02, net earnings advanced 80.2% to $2.79 billion compared with $1.55 billion the previous year. Results for 2002 and 2001 included pre-tax acquired in-process research and development charges of $107.7 million and $1.33 billion, respectively. Net sales climbed 8.6% to $17.68 billion from $16.29 billion the prior year.

The increase in sales and earnings was due to strong growth in ABT's U.S. pharmaceutical and International sales. U.S. pharmaceutical sales improved 13.5% to $4.27 billion, while U.S. hospital product sales grew 7.2% to $2.98 billion. Total international sales rose 14.0% to $5.0 million.

PROSPECTS:

The Company announced that it has received U.S. FDA approval earlier than anticipated to market HUMIRA™ for the treatment of rheumatoid Arthritis. Going forward, the Company is estimating earnings per share to be in the range of $2.20 to $2.25 for the full-year 2003. Also, the Company expects earnings per share to range from $0.50 to $0.52 for the first quarter of 2003. ABT anticipates that earnings, particularly in the first quarter, to be affected by accelerated spending due to the launch of HUMIRA.

ANNUAL FINANCIAL DATA:

FISCAL YEAR	TOT. REVS. ($mill.)	NET INC. ($mill.)	TOT. ASSETS ($mill.)	OPER. PROFIT %	NET PROFIT %	RET. ON EQUITY %	RET. ON ASSETS %	CURR. RATIO	EARN. PER SH.$	CASH FL. PER SH.$	TANG. BK. VAL.$	DIV. PER SH.$	PRICE RANGE	AVG. P/E RATIO	AVG. YIELD %
p12/31/02	17,684.7	③ 2,793.7							③ 1.78			0.92	58.00 — 29.80	24.7	2.1
12/31/01	16,285.2	③ 1,550.4	23,296.4	11.6	9.5	17.1	6.7	1.1	③ 0.99	1.74	1.14	0.82	57.17 — 42.00	50.1	1.7
12/31/00	13,745.9	② 2,786.0	15,283.3	24.7	20.3	32.5	18.2	1.7	② 1.78	2.31	4.54	0.74	56.25 — 29.38	24.1	1.7
12/31/99	13,177.6	① 2,445.8	14,471.0	23.9	18.6	32.9	16.9	1.4	① 1.57	2.10	3.78	0.66	53.31 — 27.94	25.9	1.6
12/31/98	12,477.8	2,333.2	13,216.2	25.0	18.7	40.8	17.7	1.1	1.51	2.02	2.88	0.58	50.06 — 32.53	27.3	1.4
12/31/97	11,883.5	2,094.5	12,061.1	24.0	17.6	41.9	17.4	1.0	1.34	1.81	2.54	0.53	34.88 — 24.88	22.3	1.8
12/31/96	11,013.5	1,882.0	11,125.6	23.8	17.1	39.0	16.9	1.0	1.21	1.64	2.48	0.47	28.69 — 19.06	19.8	1.9
12/31/95	10,012.2	1,688.7	9,412.6	23.8	16.9	38.4	17.9	1.1	1.06	1.42	2.69	0.41	22.38 — 15.31	17.8	2.2
12/31/94	9,156.0	1,516.7	8,523.7	23.4	16.6	37.5	17.8	1.1	0.94	1.25	2.52	0.37	17.00 — 12.69	15.9	2.5
12/31/93	8,407.8	1,399.1	7,688.6	22.9	16.6	38.1	18.2	1.2	0.85	1.14	2.24	0.33	15.44 — 11.31	15.8	2.5

Statistics are as originally reported. Adjusted for 2-for-1 stock split, 5/98. ① Incl. a nonrecurring pre-tax charge of $168.0 million relating to an FDA consent decree. ② Incl. pre-tax gain of $138.5 mill. on sale of bus. ③ Incl. pre-tax acq. in-process research & dev. chrg. of $107.7 mill., 12/02; $1.33 bill., 12/01.

OFFICERS:
M. D. White, Chmn., C.E.O.
T. C. Freyman, Sr. V.P., C.F.O.
T. C. Kearney, V.P., Treas.

INVESTOR CONTACT: Investor Relations, (847) 937-6400

PRINCIPAL OFFICE: 100 Abbott Park Road, Abbott Park, IL 60064-6400

TELEPHONE NUMBER: (847) 937-6100
FAX: (847) 937-1511
WEB: www.abbott.com

NO. OF EMPLOYEES: 71,426 (avg.)

SHAREHOLDERS: 97,760

ANNUAL MEETING: In Apr.

INCORPORATED: IL, Mar., 1900

INSTITUTIONAL HOLDINGS:
No. of Institutions: 1,047
Shares Held: 903,124,238
% Held: 57.8

INDUSTRY: Pharmaceutical preparations (SIC: 2834)

TRANSFER AGENT(S): EquiServe, Providence, RI

ABERCROMBIE & FITCH CO.

EXCH.	SYM.	REC. PRICE	P/E RATIO	YLD.	MKT. CAP.	RANGE (52-WK.)	'02 Y/E PR.
NYSE	ANF	27.50 (2/28/03)	14.1	...	$2.72 bill.	33.85 - 14.97	20.46

UPPER MEDIUM GRADE. IN FISCAL 2003, THE COMPANY EXPECTS DILUTED EARNINGS OF $0.25 PER SHARE FOR THE FIRST QUARTER AND $0.34 PER SHARE FOR THE SECOND QUARTER.

TRADING VOLUME
Thousand Shares

*7 YEAR PRICE SCORE N/A   ***12 MONTH PRICE SCORE 113.4**

*NYSE COMPOSITE INDEX=100

INTERIM EARNINGS (Per Share):

Qtr.	Apr.	July	Oct.	Jan.
1997-98	0.01	0.02	0.10	0.34
1998-99	0.06	0.10	0.24	0.56
1999-00	0.14	0.17	0.36	0.73
2000-01	0.16	0.21	0.43	0.76
2001-02	0.20	0.24	0.43	0.78
2002-03	0.23	0.31	0.48	0.93

INTERIM DIVIDENDS (Per Share):

Amt.	Decl.	Ex.	Rec.	Pay.
		No dividends paid.		

CAPITALIZATION (2/2/02):

	($000)	(%)
Deferred Income Tax	1,165	0.2
Common & Surplus	595,434	99.8
Total	596,599	100.0

BUSINESS:

Abercrombie & Fitch Co. is a specialty retailer of casual apparel, personal care products and other accessories for men, women and kids. The Company sells merchandise under the ABERCROMBIE & FITCH, HOLLISTER CO. and ABERCROMBIE trade names through its retail stores, catalogues and the Internet. The Company targets its products to men and women approximately 15 to 50 years of age and kids about seven to 14 years of age. As of 2/28/03, the Company operated 598 stores, including 164 Abercrombie locations and 94 Hollister Co. stores.

RECENT DEVELOPMENTS:

For the 52 weeks ended 2/1/03, net income climbed 15.6% to $194.9 million from $168.7 million the year before. Net sales advanced 16.9% to $1.60 billion from $1.36 billion a year earlier. Comparable-store sales declined 5.0% year over year. Gross profit totaled $656.0 million, or 41.1% of net sales, compared with $558.0 million, or 40.9% of net sales, the previous year. Operating income was $312.6 million, up 15.2% versus $271.5 million the year before. For

the 13 weeks ended 2/1/03, net income rose 17.2% to $92.8 million from $79.2 million in 2001. Net sales grew 14.6% to $534.5 million from $466.6 million in the prior year. Comparable-store sales declined 4.0% year over year. Gross profit totaled $243.0 million, or 45.5% of net sales, compared with $208.5 million, or 44.7% of net sales, the previous year. Operating income increased 16.4% to $149.6 million from $128.6 million a year earlier.

PROSPECTS:

Looking ahead, in fiscal 2003, the Company expects diluted earnings of $0.25 per share for the first quarter and $0.34 per share for the second quarter. Additionally, the Company anticipates capital expenditures of approximately

$135.0 million in fiscal 2003. Meanwhile, the Company continues to implement its store expansion program as 125 new stores are scheduled to open in fiscal 2003.

ANNUAL FINANCIAL DATA:

FISCAL YEAR	TOT. REVS. ($mill.)	NET INC. ($mill.)	TOT. ASSETS ($mill.)	OPER. PROFIT %	NET PROFIT %	RET. ON EQUITY %	RET. ON ASSETS %	CURR. RATIO	EARN. PER SH.$	CASH FL. PER SH.$	TANG. BK. VAL.$	PRICE RANGE	AVG. P/E RATIO
p2/01/03	1,595.8	194.9	994.8						1.94			36.65 - 14.97	13.3
2/02/02	1,364.9	168.7	770.5	19.9	12.4	28.3	21.9	2.5	1.65	2.05	6.02	47.50 - 16.21	19.3
2/03/01	1,237.6	158.1	587.5	20.5	12.8	37.4	26.9	2.0	1.55	1.85	4.28	31.31 - 8.00	12.7
1/29/00	1,042.1	149.6	458.2	23.2	14.4	48.1	32.7	2.2	1.39	1.65	3.05	50.75 - 21.00	25.8
1/30/99	815.8	102.1	319.2	20.5	12.5	54.8	32.0	1.8	0.96	1.16	1.81	36.13 - 14.44	26.3
1/31/98	521.6	48.3	183.2	16.1	9.3	82.2	26.4	1.6	0.47	0.63	0.58	18.06 - 6.25	25.9
2/01/97	335.4	24.7	105.8	13.7	7.4	219.6	23.3	1.0	0.27	0.40	0.11	13.50 - 7.88	39.6
3/02/96	235.7	14.3	87.7	10.1	6.1	...	16.3	0.4	0.17	0.27	...	...	...
1/28/95	165.5	8.3	...	8.3	5.0	...	...	...	0.10	0.19	...	...	...

Statistics are as originally reported. Adj. for 2-for-1 stk. split, 6/99.

OFFICERS:
M. S. Jeffries, Chmn., C.E.O.
W. S. McDonald, V.P., C.F.O.
S. R. Johnson, Exec. V.P., C.O.O.

INVESTOR CONTACT: Investor Relations, (614) 283-6751

PRINCIPAL OFFICE: 6301 Fitch Path, New Albany, OH 43054

TELEPHONE NUMBER: (614) 283-6500
FAX: (614) 479-7079
WEB: www.abercrombie.com

NO. OF EMPLOYEES: 3,000 full-time (approx.); 13,700 part-time (approx.)

SHAREHOLDERS: 5,000 (approx.)

ANNUAL MEETING: In May

INCORPORATED: DE, June, 1996

INSTITUTIONAL HOLDINGS:
No. of Institutions: 280
Shares Held: 84,003,758
% Held: 86.4

INDUSTRY: Family clothing stores (SIC: 5651)

TRANSFER AGENT(S): First Chicago Trust Company of New York, Jersey City, NJ

ABM INDUSTRIES INCORPORATED

EXCH.	SYM.	REC. PRICE	P/E RATIO	YLD.	MKT. CAP.	RANGE (52-WK.)	'02 Y/E PR.	DIV. ACH.
NYSE	ABM	15.99 (2/28/03)	18.8	2.4%	$0.78 bill.	19.75 - 12.92	15.50	38 yrs.

UPPER MEDIUM GRADE. NEAR-TERM RESULTS MAY CONTINUE TO BE AFFECTED BY ADVERSE CONDITIONS IN THE COMPANY'S JANITORIAL AND LIGHTING SEGMENTS.

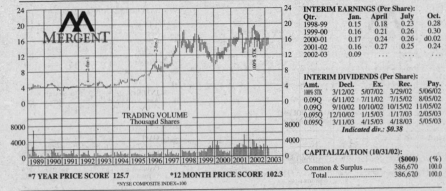

INTERIM EARNINGS (Per Share):

Qtr.	Jan.	April	July	Oct.
1998-99	0.15	0.18	0.23	0.28
1999-00	0.16	0.21	0.26	0.30
2000-01	0.17	0.24	0.26	d0.02
2001-02	0.16	0.27	0.25	0.24
2002-03	0.09	...	...	...

INTERIM DIVIDENDS (Per Share):

Amt.	Decl.	Ex.	Rec.	Pay.
100% STK	3/12/02	5/07/02	3/29/02	5/06/02
0.09Q	6/11/02	7/11/02	7/15/02	8/05/02
0.09Q	9/10/02	10/10/02	10/15/02	11/05/02
0.095Q	12/10/02	1/15/03	1/17/03	2/05/03
0.095Q	3/11/03	4/15/03	4/18/03	5/05/03

Indicated div.: $0.38

TRADING VOLUME
Thousand Shares

*7 YEAR PRICE SCORE 125.7   ***12 MONTH PRICE SCORE 102.3**

NYSE COMPOSITE INDEX=100

CAPITALIZATION (10/31/02):

	($000)	(%)
Common & Surplus	386,670	100.0
Total	386,670	100.0

BUSINESS:

ABM Industries Incorporated is a facility services contractor. The Company provides elevator, engineering, janitorial, lighting, parking, security, mechanical and network services for thousands of commercial, industrial, institutional and retail facilities in hundreds of cities across North America. ABM is comprised of ABM Janitorial, Ampco System Parking, American Commercial Security (ACSS), ABM Engineering, Amtech Elevator, Amtech Lighting, CommAir Mechanical, ABM Lakeside Building Maintenance and ABM Service Network. Contributions to sales for fiscal 2002 were as follows: ABM Janitorial, 58.0%; Ampco System Parking, 16.5%; ABM Engineering, 7.7%; ACSS, 6.5%; Amtech Lighting, 6.0%; and Amtech Elevator, 5.3%.

RECENT DEVELOPMENTS:

For the quarter ended 1/31/03, net income plunged 45.7% to $4.3 million. Earnings were adversely affected by a 28.0% decrease in operating profit for the Company's janitorial segment, substantially the Northeast region, and a 64.4% decline in operating profit for the lighting segment.

Partially offsetting these declines was pre-tax operating profits of $2.6 million generated by ABM Lakeside Building Maintenance, which was acquired in July 2002. Sales and other income rose 10.1% to $580.6 million.

PROSPECTS:

ABM has initiated management changes in its Northeast janitorial region to address a number of problems that affected first quarter results. However, ABM anticipates that this region will continue to perform below earlier expectations for the duration of the fiscal year. Meanwhile, the lighting segment is being adversely affected by higher labor costs, including those related to a number of newer national contracts. Actions have been initiated, although

ABM expects that the second quarter will also be affected. Taking into consideration first quarter results and ABM's recent acquisition of the commercial self-performing janitorial cleaning operations of Horizon National Commercial Services, LLC, ABM now expects earnings for the full-year ending 10/31/02 will be in the range of $0.85 to $0.95 per fully diluted share compared with its previously estimated range of $1.00 to $1.10 per fully diluted share.

ANNUAL FINANCIAL DATA:

FISCAL YEAR	TOT. REVS. ($mill.)	NET INC. ($mill.)	TOT. ASSETS ($mill.)	OPER. PROFIT %	NET PROFIT %	RET. ON EQUITY %	RET. ON ASSETS %	CURR. RATIO	EARN. PER SH.$	CASH FL. PER SH.$	TANG. BK. VAL.$	DIV. PER SH.$	PRICE RANGE	AVG. P/E RATIO	AVG. YIELD %
10/31/02	2,192.0	②③46.7	704.9	3.2	2.1	12.1	6.6	1.9	②③0.92	1.21	4.46	0.36	19.75 - 12.92	17.8	2.2
10/31/01	1,950.0	①32.8	683.1	2.7	1.7	9.1	4.8	2.0	①0.65	1.18	5.08	0.33	19.10 - 12.48	24.3	2.1
10/31/00	1,807.6	44.3	642.0	4.0	2.5	14.0	6.9	2.1	0.93	1.43	4.48	0.31	16.06 - 9.63	13.9	2.4
10/31/99	1,629.7	39.7	563.4	4.1	2.4	14.3	7.0	2.0	0.83	1.27	3.82	0.28	17.25 - 10.00	16.5	2.1
10/31/98	1,501.8	33.9	501.4	3.8	2.3	14.3	6.8	2.1	0.72	1.16	3.12	0.24	18.50 - 12.50	21.5	1.5
10/31/97	1,252.5	27.2	464.3	3.7	2.2	13.8	5.9	1.9	0.67	1.08	2.38	0.20	15.75 - 8.69	18.4	1.6
10/31/96	1,086.9	21.7	379.8	3.5	2.0	13.2	5.7	2.1	0.56	0.92	2.26	0.17	10.09 - 6.75	15.2	2.1
10/31/95	965.4	18.2	335.0	3.3	1.9	12.8	5.4	1.8	0.46	0.78	1.94	0.15	7.13 - 5.25	13.4	2.4
10/31/94	884.6	15.2	299.5	2.8	1.7	12.2	5.1	1.9	0.41	0.69	1.74	0.13	5.97 - 4.31	12.4	2.5
10/31/93	773.3	12.6	268.1	2.6	1.6	11.5	4.7	1.8	0.36	0.57	1.49	0.13	5.44 - 3.66	12.5	2.7

Statistics are as originally reported. Adj. for stk. split: 2-for-1, 8/96 & 5/02. ① Incl. a pre-tax charge of $20.0 million to strengthen the Company's self-insurance. ② Incl. $10.0 mill. gain on insurance claims. ③ Incl. $6.4 mill. after-tax gains rel. to World Trade Center business interruption.

OFFICERS:
M. H. Mandles, Chmn., C.A.O.
H. Slipsager, Pres., C.E.O.
G. B. Sundby, Sr. V.P., C.F.O.
INVESTOR CONTACT: George B. Sundby, Sr. V.P., C.F.O., (415) 733-4000
PRINCIPAL OFFICE: 160 Pacific Avenue, Suite 222, San Francisco, CA 94111

TELEPHONE NUMBER: (415) 733-4000
FAX: (415) 733-7333
WEB: www.abm.com
NO. OF EMPLOYEES: 62,000 (approx.)
SHAREHOLDERS: 4,451 (approx.)
ANNUAL MEETING: In Mar.
INCORPORATED: CA, Apr., 1955; reincorp., DE, May, 1985

INSTITUTIONAL HOLDINGS:
No. of Institutions: 123
Shares Held: 31,007,909
% Held: 62.9
INDUSTRY: Building maintenance services, nec (SIC: 7349)
TRANSFER AGENT(S): Mellon Investor Services LLC, San Francisco, CA

ACTUANT CORPORATION

EXCH.	SYM.	REC. PRICE	P/E RATIO	YLD.	MKT. CAP.	RANGE (52-WK.)	'02 Y/E PR.
NYSE	ATU	37.00 (2/28/03)	17.6	...	$429.0 mill.	49.35 - 30.88	46.45

LOWER MEDIUM GRADE. THE COMPANY IS FORECASTING FISCAL 2003 FULL-YEAR DILUTED EARNINGS PER SHARE, EXCLUDING SPECIAL CHARGES, OF BETWEEN $2.75 AND $3.00 PER SHARE.

MERGENT

TRADING VOLUME
Thousand Shares

*7 YEAR PRICE SCORE N.M.   ***12 MONTH PRICE SCORE 111.5**
*NYSE COMPOSITE INDEX=100

INTERIM EARNINGS (Per Share):

Qtr.	Nov.	Feb.	May	Aug.
1997-98	2.45	2.05	2.75	d3.90
1998-99	2.05	2.40	2.55	2.90
1999-00	1.35	1.45	1.50	d0.85
2000-01	0.50	0.37	0.18	1.86
2001-02	0.54	0.44	0.68	0.69
2002-03	0.15	0.58	...	...

INTERIM DIVIDENDS (Per Share):

Amt.	Decl.	Ex.	Rec.	Pay.
		No dividends paid.		

CAPITALIZATION (8/31/02):

	($000)	(%)
Long-Term Debt	182,783	127.3
Deferred Income Tax	4,409	3.1
Common & Surplus	d43,619	-30.4
Total	143,573	100.0

BUSINESS:

Actuant Corporation (formerly Applied Power Inc.) is a global manufacturer and marketer of a range of industrial products and services, organized into two business segments. Tools & Supplies (56.0% of fiscal 2002 revenues) sells branded, specialized electrical and industrial tools and supplies to hydraulic and electrical wholesale distributors,

to catalog houses and through various retail distribution channels. Engineered Solutions (44.0%) designs, manufacturers and markets customized motion control systems primarily for original equipment manufacturers in diversified niche markets. On 7/31/00, the Company completed the spin-off of its electronics business.

RECENT DEVELOPMENTS:

For the three months ended 2/28/03, net earnings climbed 76.4% to $7.1 million compared with $4.0 million in the corresponding year-earlier period. Net sales rose 31.0% to $142.1 million from $108.4 million the previous year. ATU noted that excluding the results of Heinrich Kopp AG, which was acquired on 9/3/02, and the effect of foreign

currency exchange rate changes on translated results, sales increased approximately 2.0%. Operating profit advanced 6.8% to $16.0 million from $15.0 million the year before. Net financing costs declined to $5.4 million from $9.8 million the year before.

PROSPECTS:

Weakening economic conditions and customer demand in certain of ATU's markets temper the Company's near-term outlook. In response, ATU has indicated that it will initiate plans to reduce costs including headcount reductions and closures. Nevertheless, ATU continues to forecast fiscal

2003 full-year sales in the range of $545.0 million to $575.0 million and diluted earnings per share, excluding special charges, of between $2.75 and $3.00 per share. However, ATU noted that the Company's results will likely be in the lower half of its full-year earnings per share range.

ANNUAL FINANCIAL DATA:

FISCAL YEAR	TOT. REVS. ($mill.)	NET INC. ($mill.)	TOT. ASSETS ($mill.)	OPER. PROFIT %	NET PROFIT %	RET. ON EQUITY %	RET. ON ASSETS %	CURR. RATIO	EARN. PER SH. $	CASH FL. PER SH. $	TANG. BK. VAL. $	PRICE RANGE	AVG. P/E RATIO
8/31/02	463.0	⑨ 25.3	294.6	15.4	5.5	...	8.6	1.2	⑨ 2.39	3.77	...	47.00 - 29.00	15.9
8/31/01	481.9	⑧ 24.4	342.7	14.9	5.1	...	7.1	1.1	⑧ 2.93	5.21	...	34.13 - 12.00	7.9
⑦ 8/31/00	671.6	⑥ 28.0	417.0	12.5	4.2	...	6.7	1.6	⑥ 3.50	6.28	...	218.75 - 10.94	32.8
8/31/99	1,751.0	79.4	1,624.8	10.8	4.5	19.0	4.9	1.3	9.90	19.41	...	194.38 - 106.88	15.2
① 8/31/98	1,230.7	② 26.7	1,174.7	6.2	2.2	7.8	2.3	1.4	② 3.30	9.24	...	200.94 - 101.88	45.9
8/31/97	672.3	42.0	463.6	10.8	6.3	20.6	9.1	1.8	7.30	11.42	11.64	172.50 - 96.25	18.4
8/31/96	571.2	33.7	381.2	10.8	5.9	20.0	8.8	1.9	6.03	9.80	14.05	100.00 - 66.88	13.8
8/31/95	527.1	③ 25.0	332.9	9.9	4.7	19.0	7.5	2.0	③ 4.55	7.90	11.92	87.82 - 56.88	15.9
8/31/94	433.6	④ 16.9	317.4	9.7	3.9	15.7	5.3	1.7	④ 3.18	6.83	7.39	63.44 - 40.63	16.4
8/31/93	360.5	⑤ 8.7	290.7	7.9	1.2	4.9	1.5	1.7	⑤ 1.65	3.84	3.92	46.25 - 36.25	25.0

Statistics are as originally reported. Adj. for 1-for-5 split, 1/01; 100% stk. div., 2/98. ① Refls. 7/98 acq'd of ZERO Corporation. ② Incl. non-recurr. chrg. of $29.6 mill. ③ Bef. extraord. chrg. of $4.9 mill. ④ Bef. disc. ops. loss of $348,000. ⑤ Incl. non-recurr. chrg. $6.7 mill.; bef. disc. ops. loss $5.4 mill. & acctg. chge. chrg. of $4.4 mill. ⑥ Incl. contract termin. recov. of $1.4 mill., corp. reorg. exps. of $12.4 mill. & loss on disp. of prod. lines of $5.4 mill.; bef. extraord. gain of $38.5 mill. & disc. ops. inc. of $585,000. ⑦ Refls. 7/00 spin-off of electronics business. ⑧ Incl. restruct. chrg. of $1.7 mill. & gain of $18.5 mill. on sale of subs. ⑨ Bef. disc. ops. loss of $10.0 mill., extraord. chrg. of $10.6 mill. & acctg. chge. chrg. of $7.2 mill.

OFFICERS:
R. C. Arzbaecher, Chmn., Pres., C.E.O.
A. G. Lampereur, V.P., C.F.O.
T. M. Braatz, Treas.

INVESTOR CONTACT: Andrew Lempereur,
V.P., C.F.O., (414) 352-4160

PRINCIPAL OFFICE: 6100 North Baker Road, Milwaukee, WI 53209

TELEPHONE NUMBER: (414) 352-4160
FAX: (414) 247-5550
WEB: www.actuant.com

NO. OF EMPLOYEES: 2,120 (approx.)

SHAREHOLDERS: 1,657 (approx.)

ANNUAL MEETING: In Jan.

INCORPORATED: WI, 1910

INSTITUTIONAL HOLDINGS:
No. of Institutions: 101
Shares Held: 9,680,140
% Held: 83.4

INDUSTRY: Fluid power cylinders & actuators (SIC: 3593)

TRANSFER AGENT(S): Firstar Trust Company, Milwaukee, WI

ACUITY BRANDS, INC.

EXCH.	SYM.	REC. PRICE	P/E RATIO	YLD.	MKT. CAP.	RANGE (52-WK.)	'02 Y/E PR.
NYSE	AYI	13.30 (2/28/03)	10.8	4.5%	$0.55 bill.	19.40 - 11.00	13.54

MEDIUM GRADE. THE COMPANY EXPECTS IMPROVEMENT IN MANUFACTURING EFFICIENCY AT ITS LIGHTING GROUP.

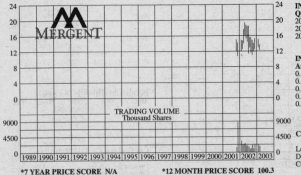

*7 YEAR PRICE SCORE N/A   *12 MONTH PRICE SCORE 100.3
*NYSE COMPOSITE INDEX=100

INTERIM EARNINGS (Per Share):

Qtr.	Nov.	Feb.	May	Aug.
2000-01	----------------	0.99	----------------	
2001-02	0.28	0.26	0.35	0.37
2002-03	0.25	...	...	...

INTERIM DIVIDENDS (Per Share):

Amt.	Decl.	Ex.	Rec.	Pay.
0.15Q	12/20/01	1/15/02	1/17/02	2/01/02
0.15Q	4/03/02	4/11/02	4/15/02	5/01/02
0.15Q	6/26/02	7/15/02	7/17/02	8/01/02
0.15Q	10/02/02	10/10/02	10/15/02	11/01/02
0.15Q	12/19/02	1/13/03	1/15/03	2/03/03

Indicated div.: $0.60 (Div. Reinv. Plan)

CAPITALIZATION (8/31/02):

	($000)	(%)
Long-Term Debt	410,630	49.1
Deferred Income Tax	23,480	2.8
Common & Surplus	401,952	48.1
Total	836,062	100.0

BUSINESS:

Acuity Brands, Inc. was formed from the spin-off of the lighting and chemical operations of National Service Industries, Inc., on 11/30/01. The Acuity Lighting group (74.8% of sales in fiscal 2002) manufactures lighting fixtures for both new construction and renovation and offers indoor and outdoor lighting for commercial and institutional and industrial and residential applications. Lighting brands include LITHONIA®, HOLOPHANE®, HOMEVUE®, LIGHT CONCEPTS®, GOTHAM®, HYDREL®, PEERLESS®, ANTIQUE STREET LAMPS™, and RELOC®. The Acuity Specialty Products group (25.2%) produces specialty chemical products for the institutional and industrial and retail markets, including cleaners, sanitizers, disinfectants, polishes, floor finishes, degreasers, deodorizers, pesticides, insecticides and herbicides. Retail brands include ZEP®, ENFORCER®, and SELIG™.

RECENT DEVELOPMENTS:

For the quarter ended 11/30/02, net income decreased 9.1% to $10.5 million versus $11.5 million in the equivalent 2001 quarter. The decline in net income reflected higher costs for raw materials and increased spending for new product introductions. Total sales increased 4.9% to $505.2 million. Lighting equipment sales advanced 5.1% to $382.7 million due to greater shipments of products to national accounts, utilities, and other key commercial and industrial markets. Specialty products sales rose 4.2% to $122.6 million, primarily due to improved sales to home improvement centers and certain industrial market segments, including food processing and preparation and vehicle wash.

PROSPECTS:

The Company expects manufacturing efficiency at its lighting group to improve due to its supply chain redesign initiative, which is designed to produce inventory optimization, cycle time reductions, strategic sourcing, better utilization of the distribution network and enterprise resource planning platform, and increased Internet capabilities.

Meanwhile, AYI anticipates continued sales growth of its specialty products through home improvement centers and hardware stores. Separately, AYI has reached a licensing agreement with Armor All Products Corporation to sell car wash operators over 100 products under the Armor All® Professional brand name.

ANNUAL FINANCIAL DATA:

FISCAL YEAR	TOT. REVS. ($mill.)	NET INC. ($mill.)	TOT. ASSETS ($mill.)	OPER. PROFIT %	NET PROFIT %	RET. ON EQUITY %	RET. ON ASSETS %	CURR. RATIO	EARN. PER SH.$	CASH FL. PER SH.$	DIV. PER SH.$	PRICE RANGE	AVG. P/E RATIO	AVG. YIELD %
8/31/02	1,972.8	② 52.0	1,358.0	6.1	2.6	12.9	3.8	1.4	② 1.26	2.46	0.60	19.40 - 11.00	13.0	...
8/31/01	1,982.7	① 40.5	1,330.6	7.0	2.0	10.6	3.0	1.3	① 0.99	2.52	...	15.00 - 10.70	...	...
8/31/00	2,023.6	83.7	1,422.9	8.9	4.1	18.9	5.9	1.3	...	...	...	...	...	...
8/31/99	1,701.6	89.1	...	9.0	5.2	...	...	...	...	...	...	...	12.1	3.9

Statistics are as originally reported. ① Incl. restr. chrg. of $4.1 mill. and loss on sale of bus. of $14.6 mill. ② Incl. restr. credit of $853,000.

OFFICERS:
J. S. Balloun, Chmn., Pres., C.E.O.
J. K. Morgan, Sr. Exec. V.P., C.O.O.
V. J. Nagel, Exec. V.P., C.F.O.
INVESTOR CONTACT: Karen Holcom, Investor Relations, (404) 853-1437
PRINCIPAL OFFICE: 1420 Peachtree Street, N.E., Suite 2400, Atlanta, GA 30309

TELEPHONE NUMBER: (404) 853-1400
FAX: (404) 853-1300
WEB: www.acuitybrands.com
NO. OF EMPLOYEES: 11,800 (approx.)
SHAREHOLDERS: 5,346
ANNUAL MEETING: In Dec.
INCORPORATED: DE, June, 2001

INSTITUTIONAL HOLDINGS:
No. of Institutions: 128
Shares Held: 25,920,762
% Held: 62.6
INDUSTRY: Lighting equipment, nec (SIC: 3648)
TRANSFER AGENT(S): Wells Fargo Shareowner Services, St. Paul, MN

ADMINISTAFF, INC.

EXCH.	SYM.	REC. PRICE	P/E RATIO	YLD.	MKT. CAP.	RANGE (52-WK.)	'02 Y/E PR.
NYSE	ASF	7.30 (2/28/03)	...	...	$203.9 mill.	28.40 - 1.99	6.00

LOWER MEDIUM GRADE. THE COMPANY RECENTLY IMPLEMENTED A PLAN DESIGNED TO IMPROVE PROFITABILITY.

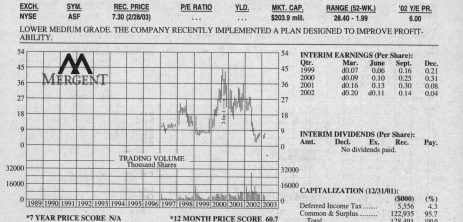

INTERIM EARNINGS (Per Share):

Qtr.	Mar.	June	Sept.	Dec.
1999	d0.07	0.06	0.16	0.21
2000	d0.09	0.10	0.25	0.31
2001	d0.16	0.13	0.30	0.08
2002	d0.20	d0.11	0.14	0.04

INTERIM DIVIDENDS (Per Share):

Amt.	Decl.	Ex.	Rec.	Pay.
		No dividends paid.		

CAPITALIZATION (12/31/01):

	($000)	(%)
Deferred Income Tax	5,556	4.3
Common & Surplus	122,935	95.7
Total	128,491	100.0

TRADING VOLUME Thousand Shares

*7 YEAR PRICE SCORE N/A   *12 MONTH PRICE SCORE 60.7

*NYSE COMPOSITE INDEX=100

BUSINESS:

Administaff, Inc. is a professional employer organization that serves as an off-site, full-service human resources department for small and medium-sized businesses throughout the United States. ASF's Personnel Management System includes employment administration, benefits and payroll administration, health and workers' compensation insurance programs, personal records management, government compliance, employer liability management, owner support, employee recruiting and selection, performance management and training and development services. The Employee Service Center℠, an interactive electronic-service platform, provides clients and worksite employees with information and resources designed to increase the benefit of ASF's core services. As of 2/20/03, ASF operated 38 sales offices in 21 major metropolitan markets.

RECENT DEVELOPMENTS:

For the year ended 12/31/02, the Company reported a net loss of $4.1 million compared with net income of $10.4 million in the previous year. Results for 2002 included a $3.1 million write-off of an investment in eProsper, Inc. Earnings for 2002 were adversely affected by higher benefits and payroll taxes. Revenues advanced 11.1% to $4.86 billion from $4.37 billion a year earlier, primarily due to an 11.3% increase in the number of worksite employees and a 6.1% gross markup per worksite employee per month. Gross profit inched up 0.8% to $166.4 million from $165.0 million the year before. Operating loss amounted to $1.9 million versus operating income of $18.5 million in 2001.

PROSPECTS:

During the fourth quarter of 2002, the Company successfully completed its plan to improve profitability by effectively matching the price and cost of health insurance, and recalibrating its expenses to coincide with its 2003 operating plan. In addition, ASF completed development and implementation of a new pricing and billing system. As new customers are sold and existing clients renew, this new system is expected to eliminate any shortfall in gross markup from changes in worksite employee payroll or benefit elections. In 2003, the Company will focus its efforts on growth.

ANNUAL FINANCIAL DATA:

FISCAL YEAR	TOT. REVS. ($mill.)	NET INC. ($mill.)	TOT. ASSETS ($mill.)	OPER. PROFIT %	NET PROFIT %	RET. ON EQUITY %	RET. ON ASSETS %	CURR. RATIO	EARN. PER SH.$	CASH FL. PER SH.$	TANG. BK. VAL.$	PRICE RANGE	AVG. P/E RATIO
p12/31/02	4,857.7	③ d4.1							③ d0.15			28.40 - 1.99	...
12/31/01	4,373.2	② 10.4	274.0	0.4	0.2	8.4	3.8	1.3	② 0.36	0.95	4.40	36.48 - 15.40	72.0
12/31/00	3,708.5	16.9	242.8	0.6	0.5	16.0	7.0	1.4	0.58	1.00	3.85	44.56 - 10.38	47.4
12/31/99	2,260.7	① 9.4	147.7	0.5	0.4	11.6	6.3	1.6	① 0.34	.61	2.99	17.25 - 5.56	33.5
12/31/98	1,683.1	9.1	142.8	0.7	0.5	10.5	6.4	2.0	0.31	0.46	2.89	26.47 - 10.81	60.1
12/31/97	1,213.6	7.4	109.5	0.8	0.6	11.7	6.8	2.1	0.27	0.36	2.21	13.25 - 6.88	38.0
12/31/96	899.6	2.6	48.4	0.7	0.3	19.6	5.4	1.2	0.12	0.19	0.58	...	...
12/31/95	716.2	1.1	39.5	0.3	0.2	10.4	2.8	1.2	0.05	0.10	0.47	...	...
12/31/94	564.5	3.8	41.1	1.0	0.7	46.7	9.2	1.4	0.19	0.21	0.39	...	...
12/31/93	496.1	1.9		0.6	0.4	...	...	...	0.11	0.13	...	...	...

Statistics are as originally reported. Adj. for 2-for-1 stk. split., 10/00. ① Incl. after-tax non-recurr. chrg. of $920,000. ② Incl. net after-tax non-recurr. chrg. of $7.4 mill. ③ Incl. investment write-off of $3.1 mill.

OFFICERS:
P. J. Sarvadi, Pres., C.E.O.
R. G. Rawson, Exec. V.P., C.F.O., Treas.
J. H. Spurgin II, V.P., Gen. Couns., Sec.
INVESTOR CONTACT: Richard G. Rawson, Exec. V.P., C.F.O., (281) 348-3225
PRINCIPAL OFFICE: 19001 Crescent Springs Drive, Kingwood, TX 77339

TELEPHONE NUMBER: (281) 358-8986
FAX: (281) 348-3977
WEB: www.administaff.com
NO. OF EMPLOYEES: 1,250 (approx.)
SHAREHOLDERS: 156
ANNUAL MEETING: In May
INCORPORATED: TX, 1986; reincorp., DE, 1996

INSTITUTIONAL HOLDINGS:
No. of Institutions: 101
Shares Held: 19,844,874
% Held: 71.2
INDUSTRY: Help supply services (SIC: 7363)
TRANSFER AGENT(S): Computershare Investor Services LLC, Chicago, IL

ADVANCED MICRO DEVICES, INC.

EXCH.	SYM.	REC. PRICE	P/E RATIO	YLD.	MKT. CAP.	RANGE (52-WK.)	'02 Y/E PR.
NYSE	AMD	5.49 (2/28/03)	...	...	$1.83 bill.	17.28 - 3.10	6.46

LOWER MEDIUM GRADE. THE COMPANY EXPECTS TO CONTINUE TO IMPROVE ITS MARKET POSITION IN 2003 WITH THE INTRODUCTION OF NEW PROCESSORS FOR DESKTOPS, SERVERS AND WORKSTATIONS.

*7 YEAR PRICE SCORE 62.7   *12 MONTH PRICE SCORE 71.0

*NYSE COMPOSITE INDEX=100

INTERIM EARNINGS (Per Share):

Qtr.	Mar.	June	Sept.	Dec.
1998	d0.20	d0.23	0.01	0.08
1999	d0.44	0.27	d0.36	0.22
2000	0.58	0.61	1.24	0.53
2001	0.37	0.05	d0.54	d0.05
2002	d0.03	d0.54	d0.74	d2.49

INTERIM DIVIDENDS (Per Share):

Amt.	Decl.	Ex.	Rec.	Pay.
	No dividends paid.			

CAPITALIZATION (12/30/01):

	($000)	(%)
Long-Term Debt	672,945	15.5
Deferred Income Tax	105,305	2.4
Common & Surplus	3,555,055	82.0
Total	4,333,305	100.0

BUSINESS:

Advanced Micro Devices, Inc. designs, manufactures and markets complex integrated circuits. The Company's Core Products segments produces a wide variety of industry-standard digital integrated circuits, which are used in many diverse product applications such as personal computers (PCs), workstations, servers, communications equipment and automotive and consumer electronics. The Company's digital integrated circuits products include personal computer microprocessors (64.7% of net sales in 2002), flash memory products (27.5%) and other integrated circuit products (6.5%). In addition, AMD's Foundry Services segment (1.3%) provides wafer fabrication services.

RECENT DEVELOPMENTS:

For the year ended 12/31/02, the Company reported a net loss of $1.30 billion compared with a net loss of $60.6 million in the previous year. Results for 2002 and 2001 included restructuring and other non-recurring charges of $330.6 million and $89.3 million, and investment impairment charges of $3.6 million and $22.0 million, respectively. Results also included a non-recurring research and development charge of $42.0 million in 2002 and a provision for inventory impairment of $6.9 million in 2001. Net sales dropped 30.7% to $2.70 billion from $3.89 billion a year earlier. Sales of PC processor products fell 27.8% to $1.75 billion, while flash memory products sales decreased 34.6% to $741.0 million. Sales of other integrated circuit products declined 27.3% to $176.0 million.

PROSPECTS:

In 2002, AMD renegotiated its long-term debt associated with its Dresden fabrication facility, and as a result reduced cash requirements for 2003 by $200.0 million. In addition, AMD remains on target to reduce its overall cost structure to below $800.0 million per quarter by the second quarter of 2003. Meanwhile, the Company expects to continue to improve its market position in 2003 with the introduction of new processors for desktops, servers and workstations. Separately, with the transition of all PC processor wafer production to 130-nanometer technology complete, AMD will focus on qualifying 90-nanometer production technology in the coming year.

ANNUAL FINANCIAL DATA:

FISCAL YEAR	TOT. REVS. ($mill.)	NET INC. ($mill.)	TOT. ASSETS ($mill.)	OPER. PROFIT %	NET PROFIT %	RET. ON EQUITY %	RET. ON ASSETS %	CURR. RATIO	EARN. PER SH. $	CASH FL. PER SH. $	TANG. BK. VAL. $	DIV. PER SH. $	PRICE RANGE	AVG. P/E RATIO
p12/31/02	2,697.0	⑥d1,303.0							⑥d3.81				20.60 - 3.10	...
12/30/01	3,891.8	④d60.6	5,647.2	...	...	...	...	1.8	④d0.18	1.69	10.64	...	34.65 - 7.69	...
12/31/00	4,644.2	③1,006.1	5,767.7	19.1	21.7	31.7	17.4	2.2	③2.95	4.53	10.10	...	48.50 - 13.56	10.5
12/26/99	2,857.6	②d88.9	4,377.7	...	...	...	...	1.5	②d0.30	1.45	6.66	...	16.50 - 7.28	...
12/27/98	2,542.1	①d104.0	4,253.0	...	...	...	...	1.9	①d0.36	1.27	6.89	...	16.38 - 6.38	...
12/28/97	2,356.4	d21.1	3,515.3	...	...	...	...	1.6	d0.07	1.33	7.14	...	24.25 - 8.56	...
12/29/96	1,953.0	d68.9	3,145.3	...	...	...	...	1.8	d0.25	0.97	7.35	...	14.19 - 5.13	...
12/31/95	2,429.7	300.5	3,031.3	14.3	12.4	14.3	9.9	1.8	1.43	2.67	10.05	0.01	19.63 - 8.06	9.7
12/25/94	2,134.7	①305.3	2,445.7	24.0	14.3	17.6	12.5	1.7	①1.51	2.62	9.09	...	15.88 - 8.38	8.0
12/26/93	1,648.3	228.8	1,929.2	18.5	13.9	16.9	11.9	2.1	1.15	2.07	7.31	...	16.44 - 8.50	10.8

Statistics are as originally reported. Adj. for 2-for-1 stk. split, 8/21/00. ① Incl. non-recurr. chrg. $11.3 mill., 12/98; $58.0 mill., 12/94. ② Incl. non-recurr. chrg. $38.2 mill. and gain on sale of Vantis of $432.1 mill. ③ Incl. a pre-tax gain on sale of Legerity of $336.9 million. ④ Incl. restr. and oth. non-recurr. chrg. of $89.3 mill. ⑤ Incl. restr. and other non-recurr. chrg. $330.6 mill., invest. impair. chrg. $3.6 mill. and one-time R&D chrg. $42.0 mill.

OFFICERS:
W. J. Sanders III, Chmn.
H. d. Ruiz, Pres., C.E.O.
R. J. Rivet, Sr. V.P., C.F.O.

INVESTOR CONTACT: Mike Haase, Investor Relations, (408) 749-3124

PRINCIPAL OFFICE: One AMD Place, P.O. Box 3453, Sunnyvale, CA 94088

TELEPHONE NUMBER: (408) 732-2400
FAX: (408) 982-6164
WEB: www.amd.com

NO. OF EMPLOYEES: 14,415 (approx.)

SHAREHOLDERS: 7,815

ANNUAL MEETING: In May

INCORPORATED: DE, May, 1969

INSTITUTIONAL HOLDINGS:
No. of Institutions: 269
Shares Held: 186,665,398
% Held: 54.3

INDUSTRY: Semiconductors and related devices (SIC: 3674)

TRANSFER AGENT(S): EquiServe, Providence, RI

AES CORPORATION (THE)

EXCH.	SYM.	REC. PRICE	P/E RATIO	YLD.	MKT. CAP.	RANGE (52-WK.)	'02 Y/E PR.
NYSE	AES	3.32 (2/28/03)	...	...	$1.77 bill.	9.80 - 0.92	3.02

SPECULATIVE GRADE. THE COMPANY ANTICIPATES EARNINGS FROM CONTINUING OPERATIONS IN 2003 TO BE APPROXIMATELY $0.50 PER SHARE.

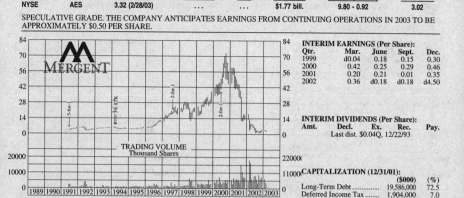

TRADING VOLUME Thousand Shares

*7 YEAR PRICE SCORE 18.9 *12 MONTH PRICE SCORE 85.9

*NYSE COMPOSITE INDEX=100

INTERIM EARNINGS (Per Share):

Qtr.	Mar.	June	Sept.	Dec.
1999	d0.04	0.18	0.15	0.30
2000	0.42	0.25	0.29	0.46
2001	0.20	0.21	0.01	0.35
2002	0.36	d0.18	d0.18	d4.50

INTERIM DIVIDENDS (Per Share):

Amt.	Decl.	Ex.	Rec.	Pay.
Last dist. $0.04Q, 12/22/93				

CAPITALIZATION (12/31/01):

	($000)	(%)
Long-Term Debt	19,586,000	72.5
Deferred Income Tax	1,904,000	7.0
Common & Surplus	5,539,000	20.5
Total	27,029,000	100.0

BUSINESS:

The AES Corporation is a global power company that participates primarily in four lines of business. AES' contract generation business (28.2% of 2002 revenues) is made up of multiple power generation facilities located around the world, including the U.S., Brazil, Chile, Argentina, Ireland, Hungary, the Czech Republic, South Africa, Nigeria, China, Pakistan, India, Georgia, Mexico and Australia. AES' competitive supply business (20.9%) consists of generating facilities and retail supply businesses that sell electricity directly to wholesale and retail customers in competitive markets. AES' large utility business (35.8%) is comprised of four integrated regulated utilities located in North America, the Caribbean and South America. AES' growth distribution business (15.1%) includes distribution facilities that offer significant potential for growth because they are located in developing countries or regions.

RECENT DEVELOPMENTS:

For the year ended 12/31/02, AES reported a loss from continuing operations of $2.59 billion, before an accounting change charge of $346.0 million, versus income from continuing operations of $446.0 million in 2001. Results for 2002 and 2001 included a loss of $2.21 billion and a gain of $18.0 million on the sale of assets and asset impairments, respectively. Results for 2001 also included a non-recurring severance charge of $131.0 million. Sales and services revenue advanced 12.9% to $8.63 billion from $7.65 billion. On a segment basis, contract generation revenue rose 2.5% to $2.48 billion, and large utilities revenue surged 91.9% to $3.15 billion. Competitive supply revenue decreased 6.9% to $1.84 billion, while growth distribution revenue fell 17.8% to $1.33 billion.

PROSPECTS:

The Company completed the sale of AES Mt. Stuart, a 288 megawatt kerosene-powered peaking generation business in Queensland, Australia on 1/22/03. Additionally, on 2/14/03, the Company completed the sale of AES Ecogen Energy, which consists of two gas-fired generation plants in Victoria, Australia. The two transactions were valued at approximately $173.0 million. Separately, AES anticipates earnings from continuing operations in 2003 to be about $0.50 per share.

ANNUAL FINANCIAL DATA:

FISCAL YEAR	TOT. REVS. ($mill.)	NET INC. ($mill.)	TOT. ASSETS ($mill.)	OPER. PROFIT %	NET PROFIT %	NET INC./ NET PROP. %	NET INC./ TOT. CAP. %	RET. ON EQUITY %	ACCUM. DEPR./ GROSS PROP. %	EARN. PER SH. $	TANG. BK. VAL. $	DIV. PER SH. $	DIV. PAYOUT %	PRICE RANGE	AVG. P/E RATIO	AVG. YIELD %
p12/31/02	8,632.0	④ d2,590.0								④ d4.81		...	...	17.92 - 0.92	...	...
③ 12/31/01	9,327.0	② 467.0	36,736.0	22.0	5.0	2.0	1.6	8.4	12.4	② 0.87	4.25	...	...	60.15 - 11.60	41.2	...
12/31/00	6,691.0	① 648.0	31,033.0	24.1	9.7	3.6	2.6	-13.5	6.8	① 1.42	9.77	...	...	72.81 - 34.25	37.7	...
12/31/99	3,253.0	① 245.0	20,880.0	28.4	7.5	1.8	1.4	9.3	5.4	① 0.62	6.24	...	...	38.19 - 16.41	44.0	...
12/31/98	2,398.0	① 307.0	10,781.0	30.6	12.8	5.6	3.6	17.1	8.7	① 0.84	0.84	...	...	29.00 - 11.50	24.2	...
12/31/97	1,411.0	① 188.0	8,909.0	26.1	13.3	4.5	2.5	12.7	8.2	① 0.56	0.55	...	...	24.81 - 11.19	32.4	...
12/31/96	835.0	125.0	3,622.0	33.3	15.0	5.6	3.9	17.3	11.3	0.41	1.99	...	...	12.53 - 5.25	21.9	...
12/31/95	685.0	107.0	2,320.0	36.2	15.6	6.9	5.1	19.5	12.5	0.35	1.57	...	...	6.00 - 4.00	14.2	...
12/31/94	533.0	98.0	1,915.0	43.5	18.4	8.3	5.4	24.4	12.0	0.33	1.21	...	...	5.95 - 3.94	15.2	...
12/31/93	519.0	71.0	1,686.0	37.2	13.7	5.9	4.6	23.0	9.2	0.25	0.97	0.15	59.4	5.66 - 4.21	20.1	3.0

Statistics are as originally reported. Adj. for stk. splits: 2-for-1, 6/00; 8/97; 3% div., 3/94; 3-for-2, 1/94. ① Bef. extraordinary loss of $7.0 mill., 2000; $17.0 mill., 1999; gain of $4.0 mill., 1998; loss of $3.0 mill., 1997. ② Bef. loss from discont. opers. of $194.0 mill.; incl. non-recurring serverance and transaction chrg. of $131.0 mill. ③ Incls. results of IPALCO Enterprises, Inc. acquired on 3/27/01. ④ Bef. an acctg. change chrg. $346.0 mill. and loss fr. disc. oper. $573.0 mill.; incl. loss on asset sale and impair. $2.21 billion.

OFFICERS:
R. W. Sant, Chmn.
R. Darman, Vice-Chmn.
P. T. Hanrahan, Pres., C.E.O.
INVESTOR CONTACT: Kenneth R. Woodcock, (703) 522-1315
PRINCIPAL OFFICE: 1001 North 19th Street, Arlington, VA 22209

TELEPHONE NUMBER: (703) 522-1315
FAX: (703) 528-4510
WEB: www.aesc.com
NO. OF EMPLOYEES: 38,000 (approx.)
SHAREHOLDERS: 9,967 (record)
ANNUAL MEETING: In April
INCORPORATED: DE, Jan., 1981

INSTITUTIONAL HOLDINGS:
No. of Institutions: 310
Shares Held: 366,496,665
% Held: 67.4

INDUSTRY: Electric services (SIC: 4911)

TRANSFER AGENT(S): First Chicago Trust Company, Jersey City, NJ

AETNA, INC.

EXCH.	SYM.	REC. PRICE	P/E RATIO	YLD.	MKT. CAP.	RANGE (52-WK.)	'02 Y/E PR.
NYSE	AET	42.12 (2/28/03)	16.5	0.1%	$6.32 bill.	51.91 - 31.49	41.12

MEDIUM GRADE. GOING FORWARD, THE COMPANY SHOULD BENEFIT FROM THE SUBSTANTIAL IMPROVEMENT IN ITS FINANCIAL PERFORMANCE.

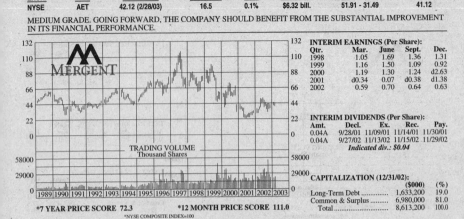

INTERIM EARNINGS (Per Share):

Qtr.	Mar.	June	Sept.	Dec.
1998	1.05	1.69	1.36	1.31
1999	1.16	1.50	1.09	0.92
2000	1.19	1.30	1.24	d2.63
2001	d0.34	0.07	d0.38	d1.38
2002	0.59	0.70	0.64	0.63

INTERIM DIVIDENDS (Per Share):

Amt.	Decl.	Ex.	Rec.	Pay.
0.04A	9/28/01	11/09/01	11/14/01	11/30/01
0.04A	9/27/02	11/13/02	11/15/02	11/29/02

Indicated div.: $0.04

TRADING VOLUME
Thousand Shares

*7 YEAR PRICE SCORE 72.3   ***12 MONTH PRICE SCORE 111.0**

*NYSE COMPOSITE INDEX=100

CAPITALIZATION (12/31/02):

	($000)	(%)
Long-Term Debt	1,633,200	19.0
Common & Surplus	6,980,000	81.0
Total	8,613,200	100.0

BUSINESS:

Aetna, Inc. is a health care benefits company with 13.7 million health members, 11.8 million dental members and 11.7 million group insurance members as of 12/31/02. The Company provides a full spectrum of health and dental products (ranging from managed care to indemnity products), group insurance products (including life, disability and long-term care insurance products) and certain specialty health products. The Company focuses on commercial customers, ranging from small employer groups to large, multi-site national accounts. The Company also has a large case pensions business that manages a variety of retirement products for qualified defined benefit and defined contribution plans of large customers. On 12/13/00, the Company was spun off from the "old" Aetna, with the simultaneous sale of the financial services and international businesses to ING Groep N.V. for $7.70 billion.

RECENT DEVELOPMENTS:

For the year ended 12/31/02, income was $393.2 million, before income from discontinued operations of $50.0 million and an accounting change charge of $2.97 billion, versus a loss of $291.5 million, before income from discontinued operations of $11.4 million and an accounting gain of $500,000, the previous year. Results for 2001 included goodwill amortization of $198.1 million. Total revenue dropped 21.1% to $19.88 billion from $25.19 billion the year before. Revenues from health care premiums fell 24.6% to $15.04 billion.

PROSPECTS:

In 2002, AET's improved financial performance was built on a seven point reduction in the medical cost ratio (MCR), as well as lower administrative costs. This decline in MCR was driven by a reduction of membership with historically higher MCRs, price increases that better aligned AET's prices with competitors' and with its own costs, and more effective contracting, benefit plan designs and medical management programs. The improved financial position should give AET the momentum needed for the next phase of its turnaround plan, which will be built on new customer-focused products and service improvements.

ANNUAL FINANCIAL DATA:

FISCAL YEAR	TOT. REVS. ($mill.)	NET INC. ($mill.)	TOT. ASSETS ($mill.)	OPER. PROFIT %	NET PROFIT %	RET. ON EQUITY %	RET. ON ASSETS %	CURR. RATIO	EARN. PER SH.$	CASH FL. PER SH.$	TANG. BK. VAL.$	DIV. PER SH.$	PRICE RANGE	AVG. P/E RATIO	AVG. YIELD %
12/31/02	19,878.7	③ 393.2	40,047.5	3.3	2.0	5.6	1.0	2.5	③ 2.57	4.54	18.77	0.04	51.91 - 29.90	15.9	0.1
12/31/01	25,190.8	② d291.5	43,255.1	...	...	...	...	2.3	② d2.03	2.14	18.05	0.04	42.69 - 23.01	...	0.1
12/31/00	26,818.9	① d127.4	47,445.7	0.2	...	...	...	2.0	① d0.90	3.26	16.99	...	73.69 - 31.88	...	...
12/31/99	22,109.7	399.4	52,421.9	4.1	1.8	3.7	0.8	2.0	2.54	6.11	14.48	...	99.88 - 46.50	28.8	...
12/31/98	16,589.0	450.4	53,355.2	5.9	2.7	3.9	0.8	2.4	...	...	...	...	89.38 - 60.19	...	...

Statistics are as originally reported. ① Bef. inc. from disc. opers. of $254.5 mill., incl. one-time chrgs. of $452.7 mill. & net realized cap. loss of $40.1 mill. ② Bef. acctg. credit of $500,000 & inc. from disc. opers of $1.4 mill.; incl. net realized cap. gain of $96.1 mill. ③ Bef. inc. fr. disc. opers. of $50.0 mill. & acctg. chrg. $2.97 bill.

OFFICERS:
J. W. Rowe, Chmn., C.E.O.
R. A. Williams, Pres.
A. M. Bennett, Sr. V.P., C.F.O.

INVESTOR CONTACT: Dennis Oakes, Investor Relations, (860) 273-6184

PRINCIPAL OFFICE: 151 Farmington Avenue, Hartford, CT 06156

TELEPHONE NUMBER: (860) 273-0123
FAX: (860) 240-6668
WEB: www.aetna.com

NO. OF EMPLOYEES: 35,700 (approx.)

SHAREHOLDERS: 14,698

ANNUAL MEETING: In March

INCORPORATED: PA, Dec., 1982

INSTITUTIONAL HOLDINGS:
No. of Institutions: 320,
Shares Held: 145,338,395
% Held: 96.5

INDUSTRY: Insurance agents, brokers, & service (SIC: 6411)

TRANSFER AGENT(S): EquiServe Trust Company, N.A., Jersey City, NJ

AFFILIATED COMPUTER SERVICES, INC.

EXCH.	SYM.	REC. PRICE	P/E RATIO	YLD.	MKT. CAP.	RANGE (52-WK.)	'02 Y/E PR.
NYSE	ACS	44.83 (2/28/03)	22.6	...	$5.92 bill.	57.05 - 32.70	52.65

UPPER MEDIUM GRADE. REVENUE FOR THE THIRD QUARTER OF FISCAL 2003 IS EXPECTED TO BE APPROXIMATELY $990.0 MILLION.

TRADING VOLUME
Thousand Shares

1989 1990 1991 1992 1993 1994 1995 1996 1997 1998 1999 2000 2001 2002 2003

*7 YEAR PRICE SCORE 201.6   ***12 MONTH PRICE SCORE 114.7**
*NYSE COMPOSITE INDEX=100

INTERIM EARNINGS (Per Share):

Qtr.	Sept.	Dec.	Mar.	June
1998-99	0.19	0.20	0.22	0.23
1999-00	0.24	0.25	0.27	0.29
2000-01	0.29	0.30	0.32	0.33
2001-02	0.39	0.42	0.46	0.49
2002-03	0.50	0.53	...	...

INTERIM DIVIDENDS (Per Share):

Amt.	Decl.	Ex.	Rec.	Pay.
100% STK	1/22/02	2/25/02	2/15/02	2/22/02

CAPITALIZATION (6/30/02):

	($000)	(%)
Long-Term Debt	708,233	24.4
Deferred Income Tax	95,394	3.3
Common & Surplus	2,095,420	72.3
Total.............................	2,899,047	100.0

BUSINESS:

Affiliated Computer Services, Inc. provides a full range of information technology services to the commercial sector and federal government including business process outsourcing, technology outsourcing and systems integration services primarily in North America, as well as Central America, South America, Europe, Africa and the Middle East. The Company also provides services in loan and mortgage processing, claims processing, accounts payable processing, data capture, storage and retrieval services and trade marketing. Revenues for fiscal 2002 were derived: business process outsourcing, 63.4%; systems integration services, 22.2%; and technology outsourcing, 14.4%.

RECENT DEVELOPMENTS:

For the three months ended 12/31/02, net income advanced 33.2% to $74.0 million compared with $55.6 million in the corresponding quarter of 2001. Revenues were $929.2 million, up 23.8% from $750.4 million in the prior-year period, reflecting internal growth of 17.0% and growth through acquisitions of 7.0%. Operating income increased 28.3% to $125.0 million compared with $97.4 million the year before. New business bookings represented $242.0 million of annualized new revenue compared with $130.0 million in the previous year.

PROSPECTS:

The Company reiterated its revenue projection of approximately $990.0 million for the third quarter of fiscal 2003 and about $1.05 billion for the fourth quarter. Earnings per share for the third quarter and fourth quarter are expected to be $0.56 and $0.59, respectively. Operating margins and pre-tax margins for fiscal 2003 are anticipated to be 13.3% and 12.6%, respectively. Separately, on 1/17/03, the Company announced that it has completed the acquisition of CyberRep, a provider of customer care and customer relationship management applications. The transaction enhances the Company's suite of business process outsourcing applications for commercial clients.

ANNUAL FINANCIAL DATA:

FISCAL YEAR	TOT. REVS. ($mill.)	NET INC. ($mill.)	TOT. ASSETS ($mill.)	OPER. PROFIT %	NET PROFIT %	RET. ON EQUITY %	RET. ON ASSETS %	CURR. RATIO	EARN. PER SH.$	CASH FL. PER SH.$	TANG. BK. VAL.$	PRICE RANGE	AVG. P/E RATIO
6/30/02	3,062.9	② 229.6	3,403.6	13.1	7.5	11.0	6.7	1.8	② 1.76	2.47	0.11	57.05 - 32.70	25.5
6/30/01	2,063.6	134.3	1,891.7	10.8	6.5	15.2	7.1	2.9	1.23	1.96	0.90	53.63 - 26.81	32.7
6/30/00	1,962.5	① 109.3	1,656.4	6.3	5.6	15.4	6.6	2.2	① 1.04	1.74	0.44	31.31 - 15.50	22.6
6/30/99	1,642.2	86.2	1,223.6	9.7	5.3	14.2	7.0	1.9	0.83	1.37	...	26.50 - 15.88	25.5
6/30/98	1,189.1	54.4	949.8	8.3	4.6	10.8	5.7	2.2	0.56	1.01	0.85	22.50 - 11.19	30.3
6/30/97	624.5	38.5	577.4	11.4	6.2	11.0	6.7	1.6	0.53	0.95	0.75	15.13 - 9.75	23.7
6/30/96	396.5	23.8	533.6	10.3	6.0	7.8	4.5	1.4	0.41	0.67	0.86	16.00 - 8.44	29.8
6/30/95	313.2	17.6	225.7	10.1	5.6	16.5	7.8	1.8	0.34	0.57	0.53	9.63 - 4.94	21.2
6/30/94	271.1	23.1	190.1	13.3	8.5	47.9	12.1	2.0	0.26	0.69	...	5.88 - 4.25	19.2
6/30/93	189.1	23.5	187.3	16.7	12.4	42.4	12.6	1.5	0.21	0.66	...	... - ...	...

Statistics are as originally reported. Adj. for 100% stk. div., 2/22/02 and 2-for-1 split, 11/22/96. ① Incl. $72.0 mill. pre-tax non-recur. chgs. & $85.8 mill. pre-tax gain fr. divestitures. ② Incl. $7.4 mill. after-tax non-recur. chg. & $4.3 mill. non-recur. tax benefit.

OFFICERS:
D. Deason, Chmn.
J. A. Rich, C.E.O.
M. A. King, Pres., C.O.O.
W. D. Edwards, Exec. V.P., C.F.O.

INVESTOR CONTACT: Investor Relations, (214) 841-8011

PRINCIPAL OFFICE: 2828 North Haskell Avenue, Dallas, TX 75204

TELEPHONE NUMBER: (214) 841-6111
FAX: (214) 841-8315
WEB: www.acs-inc.com

NO. OF EMPLOYEES: 36,200 (approx.)

SHAREHOLDERS: 1,026

ANNUAL MEETING: In Oct.

INCORPORATED: DE, June, 1988

INSTITUTIONAL HOLDINGS:
No. of Institutions: 355
Shares Held: 121,596,686
% Held: 92.0

INDUSTRY: Data processing and preparation (SIC: 7374)

TRANSFER AGENT(S): FirstCity Transfer Co., Edison, NJ

AFFILIATED MANAGERS GROUP, INC.

EXCH.	SYM.	REC. PRICE	P/E RATIO	YLD.	MKT. CAP.	RANGE (52-WK.)	'02 Y/E PR.
NYSE	AMG	42.41 (2/28/03)	17.2	...	$1.00 bill.	74.50 - 38.75	50.30

UPPER MEDIUM GRADE. THE COMPANY CONTINUES TO DIVERSIFY ITS INVESTMENT STYLES, CLIENT TYPES AND DISTRIBUTION CHANNELS AMONG ITS GROUP OF INVESTMENT MANAGERS.

*7 YEAR PRICE SCORE N/A   *12 MONTH PRICE SCORE 93.3

*NYSE COMPOSITE INDEX=100

TRADING VOLUME
Thousand Shares

INTERIM EARNINGS (Per Share):

Qtr.	Mar.	June	Sept.	Dec.
1998	0.25	0.30	0.30	0.48
1999	0.36	0.41	0.45	1.92
2000	0.60	0.61	0.64	0.65
2001	0.53	0.58	.0.54	0.55
2002	0.63	0.67.	0.57	0.60

INTERIM DIVIDENDS (Per Share):

Amt.	Decl.	Ex.	Rec.	Pay.
		No dividends paid.		

CAPITALIZATION (12/31/01):

	($000)	(%)
Long-Term Debt	200,000	25.6
Deferred Income Tax	38,081	4.9
Common & Surplus	543,340	69.5
Total	781,421	100.0

BUSINESS:

Affiliated Managers Group, Inc. is an asset-management company with equity investments in a diverse group of mid-sized investment management firms. As of 12/31/02, AMG's affiliated investment management firms managed $70.80 billion in assets in three principal distribution channels: High Net Worth, Mutual Fund and Institutional. AMG provides customized investment management services for high net worth individuals through direct relationships, as well as through managed account programs. AMG also provides advisory or sub-advisory services to 27 mutual funds. In addition, AMG offers investment products across 16 different investment styles in the Institutional distribution channel. Net sales for 2001 were derived as follows: high net worth, 32.8%; mutual fund, 27.8%; and institutional, 39.4%.

RECENT DEVELOPMENTS:

For the year ended 12/31/02, net income increased 11.9% to $55.9 million from $50.0 million the year before. Revenue advanced 18.2% to $482.5 million from $408.2 million in the prior year. Operating income grew 26.9% to $195.8 million. Results reflected the strong performance of the Company's value-oriented affiliates such as Tweedy, Browne and Third Avenue, and AMG's growth-oriented affiliates, including Friess and Frontier.

PROSPECTS:

The Company continues to diversify its investment styles, client types and distribution channels among its group of investment managers. For instance, AMG launched its first multi-affiliate product, Multiple Attribute Portfolios, which is a series of diversified portfolios managed by independent specialty managers selected from among AMG's affiliates. Additionally, the Company launched a separate account distribution platform, Portfolio Services Group, which is designed to provide its affiliates with appropriate products to enter the broker-sold channel. The Company also added Third Avenue Management to its group of affiliates, broadening AMG's participation in the mutual fund distribution channel and enhancing its diversity with exposure to real estate and distressed debt investments.

ANNUAL FINANCIAL DATA:

FISCAL YEAR	TOT. REVS. ($000)	NET INC. ($000)	TOT. ASSETS ($000)	OPER. PROFIT %	NET PROFIT %	RET. ON EQUITY %	RET. ON ASSETS %	CURR. RATIO	EARN. PER SH. $	CASH FL. PER SH. $	PRICE RANGE	AVG. P/E RATIO
p12/31/02	482,536	55,942	1,242,994						2.48		74.50 - 38.75	22.8
12/31/01	408,210	49,989	1,160,321	37.8	12.2	9.2	4.3	0.4	2.20	3.89	73.70 - 41.20	26.1
12/31/00	458,708	56,656	793,730	38.0	12.4	11.5	7.1	1.3	2.49	3.85	65.00 - 30.63	19.2
③ 12/31/99	518,726	72,188	909,073	41.0	13.9	15.1	7.9	1.8	3.18	4.33	40.88 - 22.00	9.9
② 12/31/98	238,494	25,551	605,334	38.9	10.7	8.1	4.2	1.5	1.33	2.38	39.50 - 13.38	19.9
12/31/97	95,287	① 1,643	456,990	23.7	1.7	0.6	0.4	2.8	① 0.20	1.24	30.19 - 23.88	135.1
12/31/96	50,384	① d1,389	101,335	14.2	...	...	...	1.0	① d0.36	1.15	...	...
12/31/95	14,182	d2,936	64,699	9.1	...	...	...	4.1	d0.58	0.27	...	...
12/31/94	5,374	d206	...	...	...	...	...	...	d0.05	0.13	...	...

Statistics are as originally reported. ① Bef. extraord. loss of $10.0 mill., 12/97; $983,000, 12/96. ② Reflects affiliate investments in Essex Investment Management Co. in 3/98 and Davis Hamilton Jackson & Associates, L.P. in 12/98. ③ Reflects affiliate investments in Rorer Asset Management, LLC in 1/99 and The Managers Funds LLC in 4/99.

OFFICERS:
W. J. Nutt, Chmn., C.E.O.
S. M. Healey, Pres., C.O.O.
D. W. Crate, Exec. V.P., C.F.O., Treas.

INVESTOR CONTACT: Darrell W. Crate, Exec. V.P., C.F.O. & Treas., (617) 747-3300

PRINCIPAL OFFICE: 600 Hale Street, Prides Crossing, MA 01965

TELEPHONE NUMBER: (617) 747-3300
FAX: (617) 747-3380
WEB: www.amg.com
NO. OF EMPLOYEES: 761 full-time (approx.); 34 part-time (approx.)
SHAREHOLDERS: 46
ANNUAL MEETING: In June
INCORPORATED: DE, 1993

INSTITUTIONAL HOLDINGS:
No. of Institutions: 189
Shares Held: 27,577,934
% Held: 126.8

INDUSTRY: Investment advice (SIC: 6282)

TRANSFER AGENT(S): Mellon Investor Services, New York, NY

AFLAC INCORPORATED

EXCH.	SYM.	REC. PRICE	P/E RATIO	YLD.	MKT. CAP.	RANGE (52-WK.)	'02 Y/E PR.	DIV. ACH.
NYSE	AFL	31.25 (2/28/03)	20.3	0.9%	$16.30 bill.	33.45 - 24.24	30.12	20 yrs.

INVESTMENT GRADE. THE COMPANY IS BENEFITING FROM HIGHER SALES IN THE UNITED STATES AND JAPAN.

*7 YEAR PRICE SCORE 151.3   ***12 MONTH PRICE SCORE 113.5**
NYSE COMPOSITE INDEX=100

INTERIM EARNINGS (Per Share):

Qtr.	Mar.	June	Sept.	Dec.
1997	0.16	0.54	0.17	0.18
1998	0.29	0.19	0.20	0.21
1999	0.36	0.24	0.26	0.19
2000	0.29	0.37	0.30	0.31
2001	0.33	0.28	0.36	0.31
2002	0.34	0.40	0.45	0.35

INTERIM DIVIDENDS (Per Share):

Amt.	Decl.	Ex.	Rec.	Pay.
0.06Q	7/23/02	8/13/02	8/15/02	9/03/02
0.06Q	10/22/02	11/12/02	11/14/02	12/02/02
0.07Q	1/30/03	2/12/03	2/14/03	3/03/03
0.07Q	12/30/99	5/13/03	5/15/03	6/02/03
0.07Q	12/30/99	8/12/03	8/14/03	9/02/03
0.07Q	12/30/99	11/10/03	11/13/03	12/01/03

Indicated div.: $0.28 (Div. Reinv. Plan)

CAPITALIZATION (12/31/01):

	($000)	(%)
Long-Term Debt	1,207,000	13.8
Deferred Income Tax	2,091,000	24.0
Common & Surplus	5,425,000	62.2
Total	8,723,000	100.0

BUSINESS:

AFLAC Incorporated is an international insurance organization whose principal subsidiary is American Family Life Assurance Company of Columbus. In addition to life, and health & accident insurance, AFL has pioneered cancer-expense and intensive-care insurance coverage. AFLAC's subsidiary Communicorp specializes in printing, advertising, audio-visuals, sales incentives, business meetings and mailings. As of 1/30/03, AFL insured more than 40.0 million people worldwide, and offered policies to employees through 248,100 payroll accounts. Also, the Company insures one out of four Japanese households and is the second largest life insurer in Japan in terms of individual policies in force.

RECENT DEVELOPMENTS:

For the year ended 12/31/02, net income climbed 19.5% to $821.0 million from $687.0 million in 2001. Earnings for 2002 included a charge of $26.0 million for the estimated portion of a life insurance industry assessment for Japan's policyholder protection fund. Also, earnings for 2002 and 2001 included realized investment losses of $15.0 million and $34.0 million, and gains of $37.0 million and $1.0 million for changes in the fair value of the interest rate component of the cross-currency swaps related to AFL's senior notes, respectively. Total revenues increased 6.9% to $10.26 billion from $9.60 billion a year earlier due to higher investment activities and solid sales growth in Japan and the U.S.

PROSPECTS:

The Company's outlook remains encouraging, supported by continued strong sales momentum in the U.S. and Japan and favorable investment activities. AFL's objective for both fiscal 2003 and 2004 is to grow operating earnings by at least 15.0% per diluted share, excluding the effect of foreign currency translation. The Company is basing its objectives on the underlying strength of its businesses in Japan and the U.S. as well as the opportunities for further growth that both markets offer.

ANNUAL FINANCIAL DATA:

FISCAL YEAR	PREM. INC. ($mill.)	NET INVST. INC. ($mill.)	TOT. REVS. ($mill.)	NET INC. ($mill.)	TOT. ASSETS ($mill.)	TOT. INVST. ($mill.)	RET. ON REVS. %	RET. ON EQUITY %	RET. ON ASSETS %	EARN. PER SH. $	TANG. BK. VAL. $	AVG. YIELD %	DIV. PER SH. $	PRICE RANGE	AVG. P/E RATIO
p12/31/02			10,257.0	④821.0						④1.55		0.8	0.23	33.45 - 23.10	18.2
12/31/01	8,061.0	1,550.0	9,598.0	687.0	37,860.0	31,941.0	7.2	12.7	1.8	1.28	10.40	0.7	0.19	36.09 - 23.00	23.1
12/31/00	8,239.0	1,550.0	9,720.0	③687.0	37,232.0	31,558.0	7.1	14.6	1.8	③1.26	8.87	0.6	0.17	37.47 - 16.78	21.5
12/31/99	7,264.0	1,369.0	8,640.0	571.0	37,041.0	31,408.0	6.6	14.8	1.5	1.04	7.28	0.6	0.14	28.38 - 19.50	23.1
12/31/98	5,943.0	1,138.0	7,104.0	487.0	31,183.0	26,620.0	6.9	12.9	1.6	0.88	7.09	0.7	0.13	22.66 - 11.34	19.3
12/31/97	5,873.7	1,077.7	7,250.7	②585.0	29,454.0	22,644.2	8.1	17.1	2.0	②1.04	6.44	0.9	0.11	14.47 - 9.38	11.5
12/31/96	5,910.0	1,022.0	7,100.2	②394.4	25,022.8	20,746.5	5.6	18.6	1.6	②0.69	3.57	1.1	0.10	11.00 - 7.06	13.2
12/31/95	6,070.8	1,025.0	7,190.6	349.1	25,338.0	20,040.8	4.9	16.4	1.4	0.58	3.39	1.3	0.08	7.46 - 5.31	11.0
12/31/94	5,180.7	838.8	6,110.8	292.8	20,287.1	15,976.1	4.8	16.7	1.4	0.47	2.75	1.5	0.07	6.02 - 4.21	10.8
12/31/93	4,225.4	689.3	5,000.6	243.9	15,442.7	12,445.7	4.9	17.9	1.6	0.39	2.02	1.3	0.06	5.67 - 4.13	12.6

Statistics are as originally reported. Adj. for stk. splits: 2-for-1, 3/01 & 6/98; 3-for-2, 3/96; 5-for-4, 6/93 ① Bef. acctg. change credit $11.4 mill. ② Incl. non-recurr. credit $267.2 mill., 12/97; $60.3 mill., 12/96 ③ Incl. one-time benefit of $99.0 mill. & realized invest. loss of $69.0 mill. ④ Incls. a one-time net gain of $11.0 mill.

OFFICERS:
D. P. Amos, Chmn. & C.E.O.
K. Cloninger, III, Pres., C.F.O., Treas.

INVESTOR CONTACT: Kenneth S. Janke, Jr., Sr. V.P., Inv. Rel., (800) 235-2667

PRINCIPAL OFFICE: 1932 Wynnton Road, Columbus, GA 31999

TELEPHONE NUMBER: (706) 323-3431
FAX: (706) 596-3488
WEB: www.aflac.com
NO. OF EMPLOYEES: 5,739
SHAREHOLDERS: 70,838 (registered); 182,700 (common approx.)
ANNUAL MEETING: In May
INCORPORATED: GA, 1973

INSTITUTIONAL HOLDINGS:
No. of Institutions: 517
Shares Held: 280,883,715
% Held: 54.4

INDUSTRY: Accident and health insurance (SIC: 6321)

TRANSFER AGENT(S): AFLAC Incorporated, Columbus, GA

AGCO CORPORATION

EXCH.	SYM.	REC. PRICE	P/E RATIO	YLD.	MKT. CAP.	RANGE (52-WK.)	'02 Y/E PR.
NYSE	AG	16.24 (2/28/03)	...	...	$1.22 bill.	26.39 - 14.68	22.10

MEDIUM GRADE. IN 2003, THE COMPANY EXPECTS YEAR-OVER-YEAR NET SALES GROWTH BETWEEN 8.0% AND 10.0%.

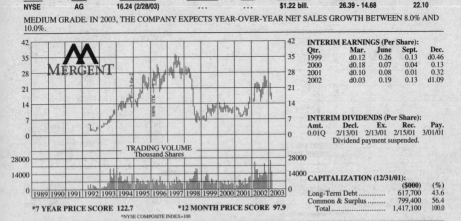

*7 YEAR PRICE SCORE 122.7   *12 MONTH PRICE SCORE 97.9

*NYSE COMPOSITE INDEX=100

INTERIM EARNINGS (Per Share):

Qtr.	Mar.	June	Sept.	Dec.
1999	d0.12	0.26	0.13	d0.46
2000	d0.18	0.07	0.04	0.13
2001	d0.10	0.08	0.01	0.32
2002	d0.03	0.19	0.13	d1.09

INTERIM DIVIDENDS (Per Share):

Amt.	Decl.	Ex.	Rec.	Pay.
0.01Q	2/13/01	2/13/01	2/15/01	3/01/01

Dividend payment suspended.

CAPITALIZATION (12/31/01):

	($000)	(%)
Long-Term Debt	617,700	43.6
Common & Surplus	799,400	56.4
Total	1,417,100	100.0

BUSINESS:

AGCO Corporation manufactures and distributes agricultural equipment and related replacement parts throughout the world. The Company sells a full range of agricultural equipment, including tractors, combines, self-propelled sprayers, hay tools, forage equipment and implements. AG's products are marketed under the following brand names: AGCO®, AGCHEM®, CHALLENGER, FARMHAND®, FENDT™, FIELDSTAR®, GLEANER®, GLENCOE®, HESS TON®, LOR*AL®, MASSEY FERGUSON®, NEW IDEA®, SOILTEQ®, SPRA-COUPE®, SUNFLOWER, TYE®, WHITE PLANTERS and WILLMAR®. In addition, AG provides retail financing in North America, the U.K., France, Germany, Ireland, Spain and Brazil through its joint venture with Cooperative Centrale Raiffeisen-Boerenleenbank B.A. AG acquired Ag-Chem Equipment Co. in April 2001 and Sunflower Manufacturing Co., Inc. in November 2002.

RECENT DEVELOPMENTS:

For the year ended 12/31/02, AG reported a loss of $60.3 million, before an accounting change charge of $24.1 million, versus income of $23.4 million, before an extraordinary loss of $800,000, in the prior year. Results for 2002 and 2001 included restructuring and other one-time expenses of $42.7 million and $13.0 million, and restricted stock compensation expenses of $44.1 million and $7.1 million, respectively. Net sales advanced 15.0% to $2.92 billion from $2.54 billion a year earlier. Gross profit jumped 22.3% to $531.8 million.

PROSPECTS:

For 2003, net sales are expected to increase approximately 8.0% to 10.0%, with growth to be achieved from the Challenger product line introduction, the addition of Sunflower, the impact of new product introductions, and the strengthening of the Euro. Meanwhile, operating margins are expected to improve from cost reduction initiatives, new product offerings, factory rationalizations, and product mix. However, these benefits may be offset by higher pensions costs. Net income before restructuring charges in 2003 is expected to range from $1.60 to $1.75 per share. AG expects restructuring expenses related to the closure of the tractor manufacturing facility in Coventry, England of between $10.0 million and $15.0 million.

ANNUAL FINANCIAL DATA:

FISCAL YEAR	TOT. REVS. ($mill.)	NET INC. ($mill.)	TOT. ASSETS ($mill.)	OPER. PROFIT %	NET PROFIT %	RET. ON EQUITY %	RET. ON ASSETS %	CURR. RATIO	EARN. PER SH.$	CASH FL. PER SH.$	TANG. BK. VAL.$	DIV. PER SH.$	PRICE RANGE	AVG. P/E RATIO	AVG. YIELD %
p12/31/02	2,922.7	⑥d60.3	...	...	...	...	...	...	⑥d0.81	...	...	...	26.39 - 14.60	...	...
12/31/01	2,541.5	⑤23.4	2,173.3	3.8	0.9	2.9	1.1	1.8	⑤0.34	1.43	5.34	0.01	16.95 - 7.90	36.5	0.1
12/31/00	2,336.1	④3.5	2,104.2	2.8	0.1	0.4	0.2	1.9	④0.06	1.23	8.45	0.04	14.50 - 9.44	199.2	0.3
12/31/99	2,413.3	①d11.5	2,273.2	2.4	...	...	...	2.1	①d0.20	1.11	8.67	0.04	14.13 - 6.00	...	0.4
12/31/98	2,941.4	①60.6	2,750.4	5.8	2.1	6.2	2.2	2.4	①0.99	2.29	10.27	0.04	30.94 - 5.25	18.3	0.2
12/31/97	3,224.4	③170.8	2,620.9	9.9	5.3	17.2	6.5	2.1	③2.74	3.91	10.36	0.04	36.31 - 25.00	11.2	0.1
12/31/96	2,317.5	②129.4	2,116.5	9.1	5.6	16.7	6.1	2.0	②2.34	3.31	9.94	0.04	31.63 - 19.25	10.9	0.2
12/31/95	2,125.0	①129.1	2,162.9	12.4	6.1	21.9	6.0	1.5	①2.76	3.53	9.59	0.02	27.31 - 12.38	7.2	0.1
12/31/93	1,359.0	115.5	1,233.5	10.9	8.5	24.2	9.4	1.7	3.07	3.60	16.40	0.01	18.38 - 10.75	4.7	0.1
12/31/93	595.7	34.1	578.3	8.0	5.7	16.1	5.9	3.1	1.11	1.19	10.00	0.01	11.42 - 3.33	6.6	0.2

Statistics are as originally reported. Adj. for stk. splits: 2-for-1, 2/96; 3-for-2, 12/94. ① Incl. non-recurr. chrgs. of $24.5 mill., 1999; $40.0 mill., 1998; $6.0 mill., 1995. ② Bef. extraord. chrg. of $3.5 mill.; incl. non-recurr. chrg. of $15.0 mill. ③ Bef. extraord. loss of $2.1 mill.; incl. non-recurr. chrg. of $18.2 mill. ④ Incl. restr. chrg. of $21.9 mill. ⑤ Bef. extraord. loss of $800,000; incl. restr. chrg. of $13.0 mill. ⑥ Bef. acctg. chng. chrg. of $24.1 mill.; incl. restr. chrg. of $42.7 mill.

OFFICERS:
R. J. Ratliff, Chmn., Pres., C.E.O.
D. R. Millard, Exec. V.P., C.O.O.
A. Beck, Sr. V.P., C.F.O.
INVESTOR CONTACT: Andy Beck, Sr. V.P., C.F.O., (770) 813-6083
PRINCIPAL OFFICE: 4205 River Green Parkway, Duluth, GA 30096

TELEPHONE NUMBER: (770) 813-9200
FAX: (770) 813-6118
WEB: www.agcocorp.com
NO. OF EMPLOYEES: 11,300 (approx.)
SHAREHOLDERS: 768
ANNUAL MEETING: In April
INCORPORATED: DE, April, 1991

INSTITUTIONAL HOLDINGS:
No. of Institutions: 198
Shares Held: 67,070,186
% Held: 89.4
INDUSTRY: Farm machinery and equipment (SIC: 3523)
TRANSFER AGENT(S): SunTrust Bank, Atlanta, GA

AGERE SYSTEMS INC.

EXCH.	SYM.	REC. PRICE	P/E RATIO	YLD.	MKT. CAP.	RANGE (52-WK.)	'02 Y/E PR.
NYSE	AGRA	1.61 (2/28/03)	...	...	$2.63 bill.	4.64 - 0.50	1.44

SPECULATIVE GRADE. THE COMPANY COMPLETED THE SALE OF ITS OPTOELECTRONICS BUSINESS IN JANUARY 2003.

TRADING VOLUME
Thousand Shares

*7 YEAR PRICE SCORE N/A   *12 MONTH PRICE SCORE 84.8

*NYSE COMPOSITE INDEX=100

INTERIM EARNINGS (Per Share):

Qtr.	Dec.	Mar.	June	Sept.
1998-99		----- 0.34 -----		
1999-00		----- d0.07 -----		
2000-01	Nil	d0.15	d0.68	d2.05
2001-02	d0.23	d0.13	d0.20	d0.55
2002-03	d0.09	...	...	...

INTERIM DIVIDENDS (Per Share):

Amt.	Decl.	Ex.	Rec.	Pay.
	No dividends paid.			

CAPITALIZATION (9/30/02):

	($000)	(%)
Long-Term Debt	486,000	39.9
Common & Surplus	732,000	60.1
Total	1,218,000	100.0

BUSINESS:

Agere Systems Inc. provides advanced integrated circuit (IC) products that access, move and store information in a broad range of computing and communications applications. AGRA's Client Systems group (57.8% of 2002 revenues) offers ICs, software and reference designs for a variety of consumer-purchased products such as hard disk drives, personal computers, and cellular telephones.

AGRA's Infrastructure Systems group (42.2%) offers ICs for multi-service networking of high-speed communications systems. Infrastructure products facilitate the transmission and switching of voice, video and data signals within communications networks. AGRA's initial public offering occurred in March 2001. The remaining shares were spun off from Lucent Technologies in June 2002.

RECENT DEVELOPMENTS:

For the first quarter ended 12/31/02, the Company reported a loss from continuing operations of $148.0 million, before an accounting change charge of $5.0 million, compared with a loss of $307.0 million in the corresponding prior-year quarter. Results for 2002 and 2001 included net restructuring and other one-time charges of $25.0 million and $64.0 million, respectively. Earnings excluded income of $7.0 million in 2002 and a loss of $68.0 million in 2001

from discontinued operations. Revenue decreased 2.0% to $436.0 million from $445.0 million a year earlier. Infrastructure Systems group revenue dropped 20.5% to $136.0 million, while Client Systems group revenue climbed 9.5% to $300.0 million. Gross profit jumped 44.9% to $113.0 million, or 25.9% of revenue, from $78.0 million, or 17.5% of revenue, in the previous year. Operating loss narrowed to $114.0 million from $273.0 million the year before.

PROSPECTS:

On 1/2/03, the Company completed its previously announced sale of the majority of its optoelectronics business to TriQuint Semiconductor Inc. for $40.0 million in cash. Separately, on 1/21/03, AGRA completed the exit of its optoelectronic operations with the sale of the optoelec-

tronic components business that provides cable television transmission systems, telecom access and satellite communications to EMCORE Corporation for $25.0 million in cash. Meanwhile, AGRA expects revenues for fiscal 2003 of approximately $1.85 billion.

ANNUAL FINANCIAL DATA:

FISCAL YEAR	TOT. REVS. ($mill.)	NET INC. ($mill.)	TOT. ASSETS ($mill.)	OPER. PROFIT %	NET PROFIT %	RET. ON EQUITY %	RET. ON ASSETS %	CURR. RATIO	EARN. PER SH. $	CASH FL. PER SH. $	TANG. BK. VAL. $	PRICE RANGE
9/30/02	2,177.0	④ d1,811.0	2,864.0	...	...	...	...	1.1	④ d1.11	d0.76	0.38	6.10 - 0.50
9/30/01	4,080.0	③ d4,612.0	6,562.0	...	...	...	...	1.0	③ d3.46	d2.78	1.30	9.50 - 3.10
9/30/00	4,708.0	① d76.0	7,067.0	3.3	...	...	...	1.4	① d0.07	0.57	1.40	...
9/30/99	3,714.0	①② 319.0	3,020.0	12.9	8.6	16.3	10.6	1.3	①② 0.34	0.69	...	...
9/30/98	3,101.0	① 303.0	...	15.1	9.8	...	...	...	① 0.29	0.60	...	...

Statistics are as originally reported. ① Incl. purchase in-process R&D chgs. $446.0 mill., 9/00; $17,000, 9/99; $48.0 mill., 9/98. ② Bef. acctg. change credit of $32.0 mill. ③ Incl. $415.0 mill. amort. of goodwill & intangibles, $2.76 bill. impair. of goodwill, $662.0 mill. restr. chg.; and excl. $4.0 mill. acctg. chg. ④ Incl. impair. chrg. of $220.0 mill., restr. chrg. of $978.0 mill. and gain on asset sale of $294.0 mill.

OFFICERS:
H. Wagner, Chmn.
J. T. Dickson, Pres., C.E.O.
M. T. Greenquist, Exec. V.P., C.F.O.
INVESTOR CONTACT: Vince Keenan, (610) 712-1733
PRINCIPAL OFFICE: 555 Union Blvd., Allentown, PA 18109

TELEPHONE NUMBER: (610) 712-6011
FAX: (610) 712-4106
WEB: www.agere.com
NO. OF EMPLOYEES: 10,700 (approx.)
SHAREHOLDERS: 693,354 (class A); 1,385,080 (class B)
ANNUAL MEETING: In Feb.
INCORPORATED: DE, Aug., 2000

INSTITUTIONAL HOLDINGS:
No. of Institutions: 258
Shares Held: 640,577,019
% Held: 38.8
INDUSTRY: Semiconductors and related devices (SIC: 3674)
TRANSFER AGENT(S): The Bank of New York, New York, NY

AGILENT TECHNOLOGIES, INC.

EXCH.	SYM.	REC. PRICE	P/E RATIO	YLD.	MKT. CAP.	RANGE (52-WK.)	'02 Y/E PR.
NYSE	A	13.20 (2/28/03)	...	...	$6.16 bill.	38.00 - 10.50	17.96

LOWER MEDIUM GRADE. THE COMPANY PLANS TO IMPLEMENT ADDITIONAL RESTRUCTURING INITIATIVES IN AN ATTEMPT TO IMPROVE PROFITABILITY.

TRADING VOLUME
Thousand Shares

*7 YEAR PRICE SCORE N/A   ***12 MONTH PRICE SCORE 84.2**
*NYSE COMPOSITE INDEX=100

INTERIM EARNINGS (Per Share):

Qtr.	Jan.	Apr.	July	Oct.
1997-98	---------------- 0.68 ----------------			
1998-99	0.19	0.41	0.36	0.39
1999-00	0.30	0.36	0.34	0.66
2000-01	0.38	0.18	d0.47	d0.98
2001-02	d0.68	d0.54	0.48	d0.51
2002-03	d0.24	...	...	...

INTERIM DIVIDENDS (Per Share):

Amt.	Decl.	Ex.	Rec.	Pay.
		No dividends paid.		

CAPITALIZATION (10/31/02):

	($000)	(%)
Long-Term Debt	1,150,000	19.9
Common & Surplus	4,627,000	80.1
Total	5,777,000	100.0

BUSINESS:

Agilent Technologies, Inc. provides instruments to markets within the communications, electronics, life sciences and chemical analysis industries in more than 110 countries. The Company was incorporated in May 1999 as a wholly-owned subsidiary of Hewlett-Packard Company and was spun off in November 1999. The Company operates in three business segments: test and measurement; semiconductor products; and life sciences and chemical analysis. The test and measurement unit (55.2% of 2002 revenues)

provides test instruments and monitoring systems for electronic and communication devices. Semiconductor products (25.9%) consist of fiber optic communications devices. Life sciences and chemical analysis (18.9%) provides application-focused solutions that identify, quantify, and analyze the physical and biological properties of substances and products. The Company sold its healthcare applications business to Philips Medical Systems on 8/1/01.

RECENT DEVELOPMENTS:

For the three months ended 1/31/03, the Company reported a loss of $112.0 million, before an accounting change charge of $257.0 million, compared with a loss from continuing operations of $317.0 million in 2001. Net revenue declined 1.0% to $1.41 billion from $1.43 billion in the

prior-year period. Loss from operations narrowed to $256.0 million compared with a loss of $442.0 million the year before. Orders slipped 7.3% to $1.36 billion, primarily due to geopolitical and economic uncertainty.

PROSPECTS:

The Company's outlook for the second quarter of fiscal 2003 calls for a modest improvement in orders and revenues based on a rebound in semiconductor equipment and seasonally higher semiconductor orders. However, the Company is uncertain that business will improve materially in the quarters immediately ahead. As a result, the Com-

pany plans to implement additional restructuring initiatives in an attempt to improve profitability. These actions include the elimination of an additional 4,000 jobs and cutting the Company's cost structure down by an additional $125.0 million per quarter.

ANNUAL FINANCIAL DATA:

FISCAL YEAR	TOT. REVS. ($mill.)	NET INC. ($mill.)	TOT. ASSETS ($mill.)	OPER. PROFIT %	NET PROFIT %	RET. ON EQUITY %	RET. ON ASSETS %	CURR. RATIO	EARN. PER SH.$	CASH FL. PER SH.$	TANG. BK. VAL.$	PRICE RANGE	AVG. P/E RATIO
10/31/02	6,010.0	③ d1,022.0	8,203.0	...	...	...	...	2.2	③ d2.20	d0.62	8.44	38.00 - 10.50	...
10/31/01	8,396.0	② d406.0	7,986.0	...	...	...	...	2.4	② d0.89	0.72	9.95	68.00 - 18.00	...
10/31/00	10,773.0	757.0	8,425.0	9.8	7.0	14.4	9.0	2.1	1.66	2.75	10.37	162.00 - 38.06	60.3
10/31/99	8,331.0	512.0	5,444.0	8.9	6.1	15.1	9.4	2.1	1.35	2.60	8.90	80.00 - 39.81	44.4
10/31/98	7,952.0	① 257.0	4,987.0	5.6	3.2	8.5	5.2	1.9	① 0.68	1.93	7.95	...	...
10/31/97	7,785.0	543.0	5,006.0	11.2	7.0	17.5	10.8	1.9	1.43	2.51	8.18	...	...
10/31/96	7,379.0	542.0	...	11.9	7.3	...	...	...	1.43	2.48	...	...	...

Statistics are as originally reported. ① Incl. $163.0 mill. restr. chg. ② Excl. $652.0 mill. gain fr. disc. ops. & $16.0 mill. after-tax gain fr. acctg. change. ③ Excl. $10.0 mill. loss fr. sale of disc. ops.

OFFICERS:
E. W. Barnholt, Chmn., Pres., C.E.O.
A. T. Dillon, Exec. V.P., C.F.O.
D. C. Nordlund, Sr. V.P., Gen. Couns., Sec.
INVESTOR CONTACT: Hilliard Terry, Investor Relations, (650) 752-5329
PRINCIPAL OFFICE: 395 Page Mill Road, Palo Alto, CA 94306

TELEPHONE NUMBER: (650) 752-5000
FAX: (650) 752-5633
WEB: www.agilent.com
NO. OF EMPLOYEES: 35,000 (approx.)
SHAREHOLDERS: 71,232
ANNUAL MEETING: In Mar.
INCORPORATED: DE, May, 1999

INSTITUTIONAL HOLDINGS:
No. of Institutions: 442
Shares Held: 295,410,365
% Held: 63.3
INDUSTRY: Instruments to measure electricity (SIC: 3825)
TRANSFER AGENT(S): Computershare Investor Services, Chicago, IL

AGL RESOURCES INC.

EXCH.	SYM.	REC. PRICE	P/E RATIO	YLD.	MKT. CAP.	RANGE (52-WK.)	'02 Y/E PR.
NYSE	ATG	22.15 (2/28/03)	12.1	4.9%	$1.22 bill.	25.41 - 17.25	24.30

MEDIUM GRADE. THE COMPANY EXPECTS EARNINGS PER SHARE IN THE RANGE OF $1.85 TO $1.90 FOR FULL-YEAR 2003.

*7 YEAR PRICE SCORE 117.9   *12 MONTH PRICE SCORE 110.0

*NYSE COMPOSITE INDEX=100

INTERIM EARNINGS (Per Share):

Qtr.	Dec.	Mar.	June	Sept.
1998-99	0.28	0.42	0.12	0.48
1999-00	0.30	0.41	0.26	0.32
2000-01	0.41	0.96	0.17	0.09
2001-02	0.45	0.89	0.22	0.17
Qtr.	Mar.	June	Sept.	Dec.
2002	0.89	0.22	0.17	0.55

INTERIM DIVIDENDS (Per Share):

Amt.	Decl.	Ex.	Rec.	Pay.
0.27Q	2/01/02	2/13/02	2/15/02	3/01/02
0.27Q	4/17/02	5/15/02	5/17/02	6/01/02
0.27Q	7/24/02	8/14/02	8/16/02	9/01/02
0.27Q	10/23/02	11/13/02	11/15/02	12/01/02
0.27Q	1/27/03	2/12/03	2/14/03	3/01/03

Indicated div.: $1.08 (Div. Reinv. Plan)

CAPITALIZATION (9/30/01):

	($000)	(%)
Long-Term Debt	845,000	47.7
Deferred Income Tax	255,500	14.4
Common & Surplus	671,400	37.9
Total............................	1,771,900	100.0

BUSINESS:

AGL Resources Inc. (formerly Atlanta Gas Light Company) is an Atlanta-based energy services holding company. At 1/30/03, nearly two million natural gas customers were served in Atlanta through subsidiaries Atlanta Gas Light Company, Virginia Natural Gas and Chattanooga Gas Company. Houston-based subsidiary Sequent Energy Management provides asset optimization services including the wholesale trading, marketing, gathering and transportation of natural gas. As a member of the SouthStar partnership, the Company markets natural gas to consumers in Georgia under the Georgia Natural Gas brand. AGL Networks, the Company's telecommunications subsidiary, owns and operates a fiber optic network in Atlanta and Phoenix. Revenues for 2001 were derived: 99.1% utility and 0.9% non-utility.

RECENT DEVELOPMENTS:

For the year ended 12/31/02, net income advanced 12.8% to $103.0 million compared with $91.3 million the previous year. Results for 2001 included a one-time after-tax gain of $7.1 million on the sale of Utilipro, Inc. Results were driven by improvement in the performance in each of the Company's operating segments. Key performance drivers were lower operating expenses in distribution operations, improved contributions in energy investments from South-Star Energy Services, and better performance in wholesale services. Operating revenues rose 2.6% to $868.9 million from $847.1 million the prior year. Operating margin fell to $600.7 million from $601.5 million a year earlier. Operating income slipped 2.2% to $208.2 million from $212.9 million the year before.

PROSPECTS:

For full-year 2003, the Company expects earnings per share in the range of $1.85 to $1.90. Meanwhile, the distribution operations segment, which benefited from lower payroll and benefits expenses, decreased bad debts expense, as well as increases in operating margin due to increased revenue from Atlanta Gas Light Company's pipeline replacement program, customer growth at Virginia Natural Gas and Chattanooga Gas Company. Meanwhile, the energy investments segment may benefit from lower-of-cost-or-market inventory issues at SouthStar Energy Services.

ANNUAL FINANCIAL DATA:

FISCAL YEAR	TOT. REVS. ($mill.)	NET INC. ($mill.)	TOT. ASSETS ($mill.)	OPER. PROFIT %	NET PROFIT %	NET INC./ NET PROP. %	NET INC./ TOT. CAP. %	RET. ON EQUITY %	ACCUM. DEPR./ GROSS PROP. %	EARN. PER SH. $	TANG. BK. VAL. $	DIV. PER SH. $	DIV. PAYOUT %	PRICE RANGE	AVG. P/E RATIO	AVG. YIELD %
p12/31/02	868.9	103.0								1.82		1.08	59.3	25.00 - 17.25	11.6	5.1
9/30/01	②1,049.3	88.9	3,368.1	19.9	8.5	4.3	5.0	13.2	...	1.62	8.99	1.08	66.7	24.50 - 18.95	13.4	5.0
9/30/00	607.4	71.1	2,019.9	22.7	11.7	4.3	4.9	11.5	33.4	1.29	11.50	1.08	83.7	23.19 - 15.50	15.0	5.6
9/30/99	1,068.6	74.4	1,969.3	14.5	7.0	4.7	5.0	11.2	33.1	1.29	11.44	1.08	83.7	23.38 - 15.56	15.1	5.5
9/30/98	1,338.6	80.6	1,981.8	12.5	6.0	5.3	5.3	12.3	31.5	1.41	11.42	1.08	76.6	23.38 - 17.69	14.6	5.3
9/30/97	1,287.6	29.8	1,925.0	9.7	2.3	2.0	2.0	4.8	31.2	1.37	10.99	1.04	78.8	21.63 - 17.75	14.4	5.5
9/30/96	1,228.6	75.6	1,823.1	13.3	6.2	5.3	5.5	12.9	1.8	1.37	10.56	1.06	77.7	22.00 - 17.13	14.3	5.4
9/30/95	1,068.5	①78.3	1,239.6	8.8	7.3	...	6.7	14.0	...	①0.50	...	...	...	20.00 - 14.88	34.9	...

Statistics are as originally reported. Adjusted for 2-for-1 stock split, 12/95. ① Before $2.9 mill. ($0.08 a sh.) gain from accounting adjustment, but incl. pre-tax restruct. charge of $70.3 mill. ② Reflects the acq. of VNG on 10/1/00.

OFFICERS:
P. G. Rosput, Chmn., Pres., C.E.O.
R. T. O'Brien, Exec. V.P., C.F.O.
T. L. Gleason, Treas.

INVESTOR CONTACT: Steve Cave, Investor Relations, (404) 584-3801

PRINCIPAL OFFICE: 817 West Peachtree Street, N.W., Suite 1000, Atlanta, GA 30308

TELEPHONE NUMBER: (404) 584-9470
FAX: (404) 584-3945
WEB: www.aglresources.com

NO. OF EMPLOYEES: 2,300 (avg.)

SHAREHOLDERS: 621

ANNUAL MEETING: In Feb.

INCORPORATED: GA, Nov., 1995

INSTITUTIONAL HOLDINGS:
No. of Institutions: 191
Shares Held: 29,805,748
% Held: 52.9

INDUSTRY: Natural gas distribution (SIC: 4924)

TRANSFER AGENT(S): EquiServe Trust Company, N.A., Canton, MA

AIR PRODUCTS & CHEMICALS, INC.

EXCH.	SYM.	REC. PRICE	P/E RATIO	YLD.	MKT. CAP.	RANGE (52-WK.)	'02 Y/E PR.	DIV. ACH.
NYSE	APD	38.76 (2/28/03)	16.0	2.2%	$8.81 bill.	53.52 - 36.97	42.75	20 yrs.

UPPER MEDIUM GRADE. THE COMPANY EXPECTS EARNINGS PER SHARE FOR 2003 IN THE RANGE OF $2.40 TO $2.60.

TRADING VOLUME
Thousand Shares

*1989 1990 1991 1992 1993 1994 1995 1996 1997 1998 1999 2000 2001 2002 2003

*7 YEAR PRICE SCORE 126.8   ***12 MONTH PRICE SCORE 98.1**
*NYSE COMPOSITE INDEX=100

INTERIM EARNINGS (Per Share):

Qtr.	Dec.	Mar.	June	Sept.
1997-98	0.72	0.55	0.63	0.59
1998-99	0.59	0.50	0.44	0.57
1999-00	0.23	0.22	d0.89	1.01
2000-01	0.62	0.43	0.60	0.68
2001-02	0.52	0.57	0.63	0.65
2002-03	0.58	...	...	...

INTERIM DIVIDENDS (Per Share):

Amt.	Decl.	Ex.	Rec.	Pay.
0.20Q	3/21/02	3/27/02	4/01/02	5/13/02
0.21Q	5/16/02	6/27/02	7/01/02	8/12/02
0.21Q	9/19/02	9/27/02	10/01/02	11/12/02
0.21Q	11/21/02	12/30/02	1/02/03	2/10/03
0.21Q	3/20/03	3/28/03	4/01/03	5/12/03

Indicated div.: $0.84 (Div. Reinv. Plan)

CAPITALIZATION (9/30/02):

	($000)	(%)
Long-Term Debt	2,041,000	32.8
Deferred Income Tax	725,600	11.7
Common & Surplus	3,460,400	55.6
Total	6,227,000	100.0

BUSINESS:

Air Products & Chemicals, Inc. is an international supplier of industrial and specialty gas products. Principal products of the industrial gases segment (68.0% of 2002 revenues) are oxygen, nitrogen, argon, hydrogen, carbon monoxide, carbon dioxide, synthesis gas and helium. The chemicals segment (26.9%) consists of performance materials, and chemical intermediates. The equipment segment (5.1%) designs and manufactures cryogenic and gas processing equipment for air separation, gas processing, natural gas liquefaction, and hydrogen purification. This segment also designs and builds cryogenic transportation containers for liquid helium and hydrogen.

RECENT DEVELOPMENTS:

For the three months ended 12/31/02, income rose 13.2% to $128.7 million, before an accounting change charge of $2.9 million, compared with net income of $113.7 million in the equivalent period of 2001. Sales amounted to $1.45 billion, up 9.9% from $1.32 billion in the prior-year period. Operating income increased 6.7% to $196.5 million compared with $184.2 million in the previous year. Operating income benefited from the inclusion of acquisitions, higher gas volumes, lower than anticipated fiscal year 2002 incentive compensation costs, and favorable exchange rates, partially offset by increased raw material, energy and pension costs.

PROSPECTS:

The range for U.S. manufacturing growth in fiscal 2003 is anticipated to be 1.0% to 3.0% based on current market conditions. Near-term results may be pressured by increased raw material costs and a slower economic recovery in the first half of the year. Based on these facts, the Company expects earnings per share for fiscal 2003 in the range of $2.40 to $2.60. Separately, on 1/14/02, the Company announced plans to sell its graphic arts business and Langley, South Carolina production facility to UCB Chemicals Corporation for an undisclosed amount. The sale is strategically in line with the Company's plans to focus on core and growth businesses in the Performance Materials division.

ANNUAL FINANCIAL DATA:

FISCAL YEAR	TOT. REVS. ($mill.)	NET INC. ($mill.)	TOT. ASSETS ($mill.)	OPER. PROFIT %	NET PROFIT %	RET. ON EQUITY %	RET. ON ASSETS %	CURR. RATIO	EARN. PER SH. $	CASH FL. PER SH. $	TANG. BK. VAL. $	DIV. PER SH. $	PRICE RANGE	AVG. P/E RATIO	AVG. YIELD %
9/30/02	5,401.2	[8] 525.4	8,495.0	14.3	9.7	15.2	6.2	1.5	[8] 2.36	4.97	13.33	0.82	53.52 - 40.00	19.8	1.8
9/30/01	5,722.7	[7] 431.7	8,084.1	13.0	7.5	13.9	5.3	1.2	[7] 2.33	4.58	13.67	0.78	49.00 - 32.25	17.4	1.9
9/30/00	5,495.5	[6] 124.2	8,270.5	15.1	2.3	4.4	1.5	1.3	[6] 0.57	3.24	9.07	0.74	42.25 - 23.00	57.2	2.3
9/30/99	5,039.8	[5] 450.5	8,235.5	14.4	8.9	15.2	5.5	1.0	[5] 2.09	4.53	11.39	0.70	49.25 - 25.69	17.9	1.9
9/30/98	4,933.8	[2][4] 546.8	7,489.6	17.1	11.1	20.5	7.3	1.3	[2][4] 2.48	4.71	11.08	0.64	45.34 - 29.00	15.0	1.7
9/30/97	4,662.0	429.3	7,244.1	15.6	9.2	16.2	5.9	1.4	1.95	4.04	20.08	0.57	44.81 - 33.19	20.0	1.5
9/30/96	4,033.0	[2] 417.0	6,522.0	14.7	10.3	16.2	6.4	1.1	[2] 1.86	3.71	11.22	0.54	35.31 - 25.19	16.3	1.8
9/30/95	3,891.0	[2] 368.0	5,816.0	15.5	9.5	15.3	6.3	1.0	[2] 1.65	3.35	10.34	0.51	29.81 - 21.94	15.7	2.0
9/30/94	3,483.8	[3] 233.5	5,036.2	14.0	6.7	10.6	4.6	1.1	[3] 1.03	2.58	9.43	0.47	25.19 - 19.38	21.6	2.1
9/30/93	3,355.5	[1] 200.9	4,761.5	11.0	6.0	9.6	4.2	1.4	[1] 0.88	2.40	8.92	0.45	24.25 - 18.75	24.4	2.1

Statistics are as originally reported. Adj. for 2-for-1 split, 6/98. [1] Incl. wkfr. reduc. & ast wt-dwn; $120 mil. [2] Incl. $35.0 mil aft-tx gn, 1998; aft-tx gn $41.0 mil. 1996; $6.6 mil gas plt. sale, 1995. [3] Bef. $14.3 mil. acct. cr. & $74.5 mil. aft-tx chg for spl items. [4] Incl. $58.1 mil. aft-tax gain fr. American Ref-Fuel Co. sale & contract settlements. [5] Incl. $28.3 mil. net chgs. & $23.6 mil. net gain. [6] Incl. $456.5 mil. aft-tax loss fr. currency hedges & $126.8 mil. gain fr. sale of bus. [7] Incl. $67.3 mil. aft-tax chg., $3.7 mil. aft-tax lit. chg., $64.6 mil. aft-tax gain, & excl. $5 mil. aft-tax extraord. loss. [8] Incl. $25.7 mill. aft-tax gain on sale of bus. & $18.9 mill. aft-tax chg. fr. cost-reduc. plan.

OFFICERS:
J. P. Jones III, Chmn., Pres., C.E.O.
J. R. Owings, V.P., C.F.O.
W. D. Brown, V.P., Gen. Couns., Sec.
INVESTOR CONTACT: Alexander W. Massetti, Dir., Inv. Rel., (610) 481-5775
PRINCIPAL OFFICE: 7201 Hamilton Boulevard, Allentown, PA 18195-1501

TELEPHONE NUMBER: (610) 481-4911
FAX: (610) 481-5900
WEB: www.airproducts.com
NO. OF EMPLOYEES: 17,200 (approx.)
SHAREHOLDERS: 11,433
ANNUAL MEETING: In Jan.
INCORPORATED: MI, Oct., 1940; reincorp., DE, June, 1940

INSTITUTIONAL HOLDINGS:
No. of Institutions: 436
Shares Held: 187,851,875
% Held: 86.0

INDUSTRY: Industrial gases (SIC: 2813)

TRANSFER AGENT(S): First Chicago Trust Company of New York, Jersey City, NJ

AIRBORNE, INC.

EXCH.	SYM.	REC. PRICE	P/E RATIO	YLD.	MKT. CAP.	RANGE (52-WK.)	'02 Y/E PR.
NYSE	ABF	14.04 (2/28/03)	45.3	1.1%	$0.68 bill.	23.34 - 10.29	14.83

LOWER MEDIUM GRADE. IN 2003, ABF ANTICIPATES INCREASED OPERATING COSTS DUE TO HIGHER GROUND DELIVERY SERVICE SHIPMENT VOLUMES AND FUEL COSTS.

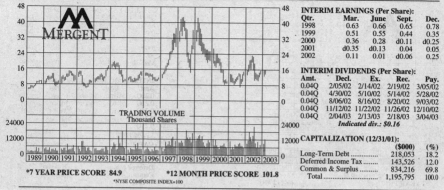

*7 YEAR PRICE SCORE 84.9   ***12 MONTH PRICE SCORE 101.8**

NYSE COMPOSITE INDEX=100

INTERIM EARNINGS (Per Share):

Qtr.	Mar.	June	Sept.	Dec.
1998	0.63	0.66	0.65	0.78
1999	0.51	0.55	0.44	0.35
2000	0.36	0.28	0.11	d0.25
2001	d0.35	d0.13	0.04	0.05
2002	0.11	0.01	d0.06	0.25

INTERIM DIVIDENDS (Per Share):

Amt.	Decl.	Ex.	Rec.	Pay.
0.04Q	2/05/02	2/14/02	2/19/02	3/05/02
0.04Q	4/30/02	5/10/02	5/14/02	5/28/02
0.04Q	8/06/02	8/16/02	8/20/02	9/03/02
0.04Q	11/12/02	11/22/02	11/26/02	12/10/02
0.04Q	2/04/03	2/13/03	2/18/03	3/04/03

Indicated div.: $0.16

CAPITALIZATION (12/31/01):

	($000)	(%)
Long-Term Debt	218,053	18.2
Deferred Income Tax	143,526	12.0
Common & Surplus	834,216	69.8
Total	1,195,795	100.0

BUSINESS:

Airborne, Inc. is the holding company for Airborne Express (formerly Airborne Freight Corporation), Sky Courier (formerly Airborne Forwarding Corp.), and ABX Air, Inc. Airborne Express serves the shipping needs of business customers worldwide. Airborne offers customers time-sensitive delivery of documents, letters, small packages, and freight throughout the U.S. and to more than 200 countries. On 12/21/00, ABF adopted a holding company structure. Net sales for 2002 were derived as follows: domestic, 89.1% and international, 10.9%.

RECENT DEVELOPMENTS:

For the year ended 12/31/02, ABF reported net income of $14.8 million compared with a net loss of $19.5 million the year before. Earnings per share for 2002 and 2001 included after-tax, nonrecurring restructuring and impairment charges of $0.08 and $0.04, respectively. Earnings for 2001 included a pre-tax credit of $13.0 million related to federal legislation compensation. Total revenues increased 3.8% to $3.34 billion from $3.22 billion a year earlier. Domestic revenues grew 39.1% to $2.98 billion, while international revenues rose 1.4% to $365.5 million. Interest expense increased 60.8% to $34.7 million from $21.6 million the year before.

PROSPECTS:

In 2003, the Company anticipates increased operating costs due to higher ground delivery service (GDS) shipment volumes, increased pension and insurance costs, and higher fuel costs. As a result of these increased fuel costs, the Company continues to raise its fuel surcharge to help offset expense levels. Effective 3/3/03, ABF increased its fuel surcharge to 5.1% of revenue on air business and 1.8% on GDS and airborne @home shipments, from previous levels of 4.3% and 1.3%, respectively. Meanwhile, ABF is focused on balancing volume growth with yield improvement in the GDS product. In the first quarter of 2003, ABF expects 200,000 to 210,000 shipments per day, with 3.0% to 5.0% sequential quarterly growth during the year, and 100,000 to 110,000 @home shipments per day, with 2.0% to 4.0% sequential quarterly growth. Separately, ABF expects capital expenditures of up to $150.0 million in 2003.

ANNUAL FINANCIAL DATA:

FISCAL YEAR	TOT. REVS. ($mill.)	NET INC. ($mill.)	TOT. ASSETS ($mill.)	OPER. PROFIT %	NET PROFIT %	RET. ON EQUITY %	RET. ON ASSETS %	CURR. RATIO	EARN. PER SH. $	CASH FL. PER SH. $	TANG. BK. VAL. $	DIV. PER SH. $	PRICE RANGE	AVG. P/E RATIO	AVG. YIELD %
p12/31/02	3,343.7	14.8	1,867.2						0.31			0.16	23.34 - 10.29	54.2	1.0
12/31/01	3,211.1	④d19.5	1,746.8	...	...	...	...	1.0	④d0.40	3.93	17.33	0.16	15.01 - 7.00	...	1.5
12/31/00	3,276.0	③14.3	1,745.9	1.3	0.4	1.7	0.8	1.1	③0.30	4.54	17.96	0.16	26.88 - 8.25	58.5	0.9
12/31/99	3,140.2	②91.2	1,643.3	5.1	2.9	10.6	5.6	1.6	②1.85	5.69	17.63	0.16	42.56 - 19.50	16.8	0.5
12/31/98	3,074.5	137.3	1,501.6	7.6	4.5	17.8	9.1	1.3	2.72	6.04	15.92	0.16	42.88 - 14.25	10.5	0.6
12/31/97	2,912.4	120.1	1,366.0	7.7	4.1	17.9	8.8	1.3	2.44	5.49	13.30	0.15	37.22 - 11.38	10.0	0.6
12/31/96	2,484.3	①27.4	1,307.4	3.2	1.1	6.4	2.1	1.5	①1.28	8.40	20.27	0.15	14.19 - 9.75	9.4	1.3
12/31/95	2,239.4	23.8	1,217.4	3.1	1.1	5.9	2.0	1.4	1.11	7.43	19.27	0.15	14.75 - 9.19	10.8	1.3
12/31/94	1,970.8	38.8	1,078.5	4.5	2.0	10.0	3.6	1.3	1.81	7.89	18.47	0.15	19.94 - 9.00	8.0	1.0
12/31/93	1,720.0	35.3	1,006.9	4.8	2.1	11.1	3.5	1.3	1.66	7.91	16.46	0.15	17.63 - 9.00	8.0	1.1

Statistics are as originally reported. Adj. for 2-for-1 stk. split, 2/98. ① Incl. $3.7 mill. chrg. related to an airplane accident. ② Incl. a gain of $4.6 mill. fr. the sale of securities. ③ Bef. acctg. chrg. of $14.2 mill. ④ Incl. pre-tax credit of $13.0 mill. for federal legislation compensation.

OFFICERS:
C. D. Donaway, Chmn., Pres., C.E.O.
L. H. Michael, Exec. V.P., C.F.O.
D. C. Anderson, V.P., Gen. Coun., Sec.
INVESTOR CONTACT: Lanny H. Michael,
Exec. V.P. & C.F.O., (206) 285-4600
PRINCIPAL OFFICE: 3101 Western Avenue,
P.O. Box 662, Seattle, WA 98111-0662

TELEPHONE NUMBER: (206) 285-4600
FAX: (206) 281-7615
WEB: www.airborne.com
NO. OF EMPLOYEES: 15,300 full-time
(approx.); 7,200 part-time (approx.)
SHAREHOLDERS: 1,206
ANNUAL MEETING: In April
INCORPORATED: DE, May, 1968

INSTITUTIONAL HOLDINGS:
No. of Institutions: 140
Shares Held: 41,520,400
% Held: 85.7

INDUSTRY: Air courier services (SIC: 4513)

TRANSFER AGENT(S): The Bank of New York, New York, NY

AK STEEL HOLDING CORPORATION

EXCH.	SYM.	REC. PRICE	P/E RATIO	YLD.	MKT. CAP.	RANGE (52-WK.)	'02 Y/E PR.
NYSE	AKS	5.49 (2/28/03)	…	…	$0.59 bill.	14.85 - 5.32	8.00

LOWER MEDIUM GRADE. THE COMPANY IS IN THE PROCESS OF ACQUIRING SUBSTANTIALLY ALL OF THE ASSETS OF NATIONAL STEEL CORPORATION.

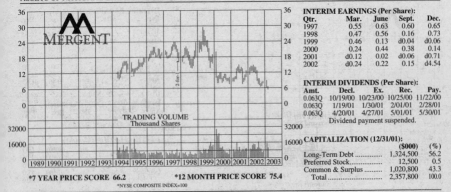

*7 YEAR PRICE SCORE 66.2　　***12 MONTH PRICE SCORE 75.4**

*NYSE COMPOSITE INDEX=100

INTERIM EARNINGS (Per Share):

Qtr.	Mar.	June	Sept.	Dec.
1997	0.55	0.63	0.60	0.65
1998	0.47	0.56	0.16	0.73
1999	0.46	0.13	d0.04	d0.06
2000	0.24	0.44	0.38	0.14
2001	d0.12	0.02	d0.06	d0.71
2002	d0.24	0.22	0.15	d4.54

INTERIM DIVIDENDS (Per Share):

Amt.	Decl.	Ex.	Rec.	Pay.
0.063Q	10/19/00	10/23/00	10/25/01	11/22/00
0.063Q	1/19/01	1/30/01	2/01/01	2/28/01
0.063Q	4/20/01	4/27/01	5/01/01	5/30/01
	Dividend payment suspended.			

CAPITALIZATION (12/31/01):

	($000)	(%)
Long-Term Debt	1,324,500	56.2
Preferred Stock	12,500	0.5
Common & Surplus	1,020,800	43.3
Total	2,357,800	100.0

BUSINESS:

AK Steel Holding Corporation operates through its wholly-owned subsidiary, AK Steel Corporation. AKS is a fully-integrated producer of flat-rolled carbon, stainless and electrical steel products. The Company operates three business segments. AKS' Steel Operations (97.0% of 2002 revenues) consists of seven steelmaking and finishing plants located in Indiana, Kentucky, Ohio and Pennsylvania. The

Snow and Ice Control Products segment (2.7%) manufactures snowplows and salt and sand spreaders for four wheel drive light trucks. Other Operations (0.3%) consist of Greens Port Industrial Park on the Houston, Texas ship channel, which leases land, buildings and rail car storage facilities to third parties and operates a deep water loading dock on the channel.

RECENT DEVELOPMENTS:

For the year ended 12/31/02, loss was $475.6 million compared with a loss from continuing operations of $91.2 million in 2001. Results for 2002 and 2001 included pension and other postretirement expenses of $816.8 million and $192.2 million, respectively. Results for 2002 included a gain of $23.9 million for an insurance settlement, a gain of $24.1 million on the sale of Anthem stock and a charge of

$10.9 million on the impairment of equity investment. Results for 2001 included a gain of $49.9 million on stock received from insurance demutualization. Net sales increased 11.9% to $4.29 billion from $3.83 billion a year earlier. Shipments advanced 3.3% to $5.8 million tons, while AKS' average selling price for steel climbed 7.3% to $703.00 per ton.

PROSPECTS:

On 2/6/03, a federal judge approved a motion making the lead bidder with its offer to acquire substantially all the assets of National Steel Corporation for $1.13 billion. The ruling was made in the U.S. Bankruptcy Court for the Northern District of Illinois in Chicago. AK anticipates the acquisition will give the Company the potential to realize

cost-based synergies in excess of $250.0 million annually. Certain items included in the acquisition will be Nationl Steel's integrated steel plants in Ecorse and River Rouge, Michigan, and Granite City, Illinois, and the Midwest finishing facility in Portage, Indiana.

ANNUAL FINANCIAL DATA:

FISCAL YEAR	TOT. REVS. ($mill.)	NET INC. ($mill.)	TOT. ASSETS ($mill.)	OPER. PROFIT %	NET PROFIT %	RET. ON EQUITY %	RET. ON ASSETS %	CURR. RATIO	EARN. PER SH.$	CASH FL. PER SH.$	TANG. BK. VAL.$	DIV. PER SH.$	PRICE RANGE		AVG. P/E RATIO	AVG. YIELD %
p12/31/02	4,289.0	③ d475.6	5,399.7	…	…	…	…	…	③ d4.67	…	…	…	14.85 -	6.45	…	…
12/31/01	3,994.1	d92.4	5,225.8	…	…	…	…	1.6	d0.87	1.42	7.42	0.13	15.00 -	7.50	…	1.1
12/31/00	4,611.5	132.4	5,239.8	7.3	2.9	10.0	2.5	1.7	1.20	3.03	11.03	0.50	20.13 -	7.50	11.5	3.6
②12/31/99	4,284.8	① 71.3	5,201.5	5.7	1.7	5.6	1.4	1.7	① 0.62	2.90	10.32	0.50	29.63 -	13.75	35.0	2.3
12/31/98	2,393.6	114.5	3,306.3	8.9	4.8	12.3	3.5	1.5	1.92	3.56	15.75	0.50	23.75 -	13.63	9.7	2.7
12/31/97	2,440.5	150.9	3,084.3	11.5	6.2	17.2	4.9	2.2	2.43	3.60	14.46	0.42	24.03 -	16.13	8.3	2.1
12/31/96	2,301.8	145.9	2,650.8	11.5	6.3	18.8	5.5	3.8	2.57	3.97	14.59	0.33	22.06 -	16.50	7.5	1.7
12/31/95	2,257.3	268.6	2,115.5	13.2	11.9	39.8	12.7	2.2	4.82	6.18	13.04	0.07	17.81 -	10.75	3.0	0.5
12/31/94	2,016.6	272.5	1,933.2	9.6	13.5	60.7	14.1	2.0	5.10	6.44	8.61	…	16.63 -	9.63	2.6	…
12/31/93	1,594.5	d25.9	1,560.0	1.3	…	…	…	1.6	d0.96	…	…	…	… -	…	…	…

Statistics are as originally reported. Adj. for 2-for-1 stock split, 11/17/97. ① Incl. an after-tax chrg. of $87.3 mill. fr. spec. chrgs. & other merger-related costs and excl. a gain of $7.5 mil. fr. discont. oper. and an extraord. loss of $13.4 mill. ② Reflects acquisition of Armco Inc. ③ Bef. loss on early retir. of debt of $19.9 mill., loss on sale of Sawhill Tubular of $6.4 mill., loss fr. discont. oper. of $500,000, but incl. unus. exps. of $803.8 mill. & gain on sale of Anthem stock of $24.1 mill.

OFFICERS:
R. M. Wardrop, Jr., Chmn., C.E.O.
J. Hritz, Pres.
J. L. Wainscott, Sr. V.P., C.F.O.
INVESTOR CONTACT: James I. Wainscott, Sr. V.P., C.F.O., Treas., (513) 425-5392
PRINCIPAL OFFICE: 703 Curtis Street, Middletown, OH 45043

TELEPHONE NUMBER: (513) 425-5000
FAX: (513) 425-5220
WEB: www.aksteel.com
NO. OF EMPLOYEES: 11,300 (approx.)
SHAREHOLDERS: 17,396
ANNUAL MEETING: In May
INCORPORATED: DE, Dec., 1993

INSTITUTIONAL HOLDINGS:
No. of Institutions: 165
Shares Held: 79,922,635
% Held: 74.1
INDUSTRY: Blast furnaces and steel mills (SIC: 3312)
TRANSFER AGENT(S): The Fifth Third Bank, Cincinnati, OH

ALASKA AIR GROUP, INC.

EXCH.	SYM.	REC. PRICE	P/E RATIO	YLD.	MKT. CAP.	RANGE (52-WK.)	'02 Y/E PR.
NYSE	ALK	18.15 (2/28/03)	...	...	$481.5 mill.	33.90 - 13.66	21.65

LOWER MEDIUM GRADE. THE COMPANY'S OPERATING PERFORMANCE IS BEING HAMPERED BY LOWER TICKET PRICES AND WEAK PASSENGER DEMAND.

TRADING VOLUME
Thousand Shares

*7 YEAR PRICE SCORE 80.2   *12 MONTH PRICE SCORE 91.5

*NYSE COMPOSITE INDEX=100

INTERIM EARNINGS (Per Share):

Qtr.	Mar.	June	Sept.	Dec.
1995	d1.22	0.52	2.01	d0.06
1996	d0.52	1.24	2.25	d0.38
1997	d0.39	1.41	2.85	0.73
1998	0.56	1.41	1.72	1.02
1999	0.76	1.59	2.07	0.64
2000	d0.28	0.33	0.60	d1.09
2001	d1.25	0.18	0.95	d1.37
2002	d1.30	d0.17	0.40	d1.62

INTERIM DIVIDENDS (Per Share):

Amt.	Decl.	Ex.	Rec.	Pay.
		No dividends paid.		

CAPITALIZATION (12/31/01):

	($000)	(%)
Long-Term Debt	863,300	47.4
Deferred Income Tax	138,400	7.6
Common & Surplus	820,300	45.0
Total	1,822,000	100.0

BUSINESS:

Alaska Air Group, Inc. is the holding company for Alaska Airlines, Inc. and Horizon Air Industries, Inc. As of 12/31/02, Alaska Airlines (82% of 2002 revenues), operates a fleet of 102 aircraft and provides scheduled air transportation to Alaska, Washington, Oregon, California, Arizona, Nevada, Vancouver, Canada and Mexico. The carrier also provides air service between Anchorage and Chicago and between Seattle and Washington D.C. Horizon Air (18%), which was acquired in 1986, provides air service to destinations in Washington, Oregon, California, Idaho, Arizona, Montana and Canada through its fleet of 63 aircraft.

RECENT DEVELOPMENTS:

For the year ended 12/31/02, the Company reported a loss of $67.2 million, before a $51.4 million accounting change charge, compared with a net loss of $43.4 million in the previous year. Results included after-tax gains of $500,000 and $51.3 million in 2002 and 2001, respectively, stemming from the Air Transportation Safety and System Stabilization Act. Results for 2001 also included a $6.4 million after-tax charge for the impairment of Horizon's F-28 fleet. Total operating revenues grew 3.3% to $2.22 billion from $2.15 billion a year earlier. Alaska Airlines' total operating revenues rose 4.0% to $1.83 billion from $1.76 billion the prior year. Horizon Air's total operating revenues increased 1.7% to $415.2 million from $408.4 million. The passenger load factor, or percentage of seats filled, for Alaska Airlines slipped to 68.1% versus 68.4% the year before. Horizon Air's passenger load factor was 62.4% versus 62.8% a year earlier. Comparisons were made with restated prior-year results.

PROSPECTS:

Results are being negatively affected by higher expenses and lower average airfares reflecting continued weak passenger demand due to sluggish U.S. economic conditions. Going forward, the Company is focusing on implementing cost-reduction initiatives and strengthening its network through the redeployment of a portion of its fleet into strategic new markets.

ANNUAL FINANCIAL DATA:

FISCAL YEAR	TOT. REVS. ($mill.)	NET INC. ($mill.)	TOT. ASSETS ($mill.)	OPER. PROFIT %	NET PROFIT %	RET. ON EQUITY %	RET. ON ASSETS %	CURR. RATIO	EARN. PER SH.$	CASH FL. PER SH.$	TANG. BK. VAL.$	PRICE RANGE	AVG. P/E RATIO
p12/31/02	2,224.1	⑤ d67.2							⑤ d4.47			33.90 - 13.66	...
12/31/01	2,140.9	④ d39.5	2,933.8	...	...	...	...	1.2	④ d1.49	6.25	28.98	35.25 - 17.40	...
12/31/00	2,177.2	② d13.4	2,630.0	...	...	...	...	1.1	② d0.51	5.95	30.57	36.88 - 19.50	...
12/31/99	2,082.0	① 134.2	2,180.1	9.6	6.4	14.4	6.2	0.9	① 5.06	10.15	35.85	54.69 - 33.19	8.7
12/31/98	1,897.7	③ 124.4	1,731.8	11.1	6.6	15.8	7.2	1.0	③ 4.81	9.13	27.91	62.56 - 26.00	9.2
12/31/97	1,739.4	72.4	1,533.1	8.0	4.2	15.2	4.7	0.9	3.53	7.75	22.74	40.13 - 20.75	8.6
12/31/96	1,592.2	① 38.0	1,311.4	5.6	2.4	13.9	2.9	0.6	① 2.65	9.84	14.57	30.75 - 15.88	8.8
12/31/95	1,417.5	17.7	1,313.4	5.4	1.2	8.3	1.3	0.8	1.28	8.17	10.98	21.38 - 13.50	13.6
12/31/94	1,315.6	22.5	1,315.8	5.7	1.7	11.8	1.7	0.6	1.68	7.47	9.37	18.88 - 13.13	9.5
12/31/93	1,128.3	d30.9	1,135.0	...	...	...	...	0.8	d2.51	4.28	7.43	18.13 - 12.25	...

Statistics are as originally reported. ① Incl. $2.2 mil ($0.08/sh) after-tax gain fr. sale of Equant N.V., 1999; $3.6 mil gain fr. sale of assets, 1996. ② Bef. $56.9 mil ($2.15/sh) acctg. change chg. & incl. $14.8 mil after-tax chg. related to ALK's frequent-flyer prog. ③ Incl. $10.1 mil ($0.38/sh) after-tax chg. fr. legal settlement. ④ Incl. one-time chrg. of $10.2 mil. and a $4.7 mil. loss on sale of assets. ⑤ Bef. $51.4 mil ($1.94/sh) acctg. change chg. & incl. $500,000 after-tax gain fr. U.S. govt. comp.

OFFICERS:
J. F. Kelly, Chmn., Pres., C.E.O.
B. D. Tilden, Exec. V.P., C.F.O.
K. Loveless, V.P., Gen. Counsel, Sec.

INVESTOR CONTACT: Lou Cancelmi, (206) 433-3170

PRINCIPAL OFFICE: 19300 Pacific Highway South, Seattle, WA 98188

TELEPHONE NUMBER: (206) 431-7040
FAX: (206) 433-3379
WEB: www.alaskaair.com

NO. OF EMPLOYEES: 13,541 (avg.)

SHAREHOLDERS: 4,230

ANNUAL MEETING: In May

INCORPORATED: DE, May, 1985

INSTITUTIONAL HOLDINGS:
No. of Institutions: 117
Shares Held: 20,974,419
% Held: 79.0

INDUSTRY: Air transportation, scheduled (SIC: 4512)

TRANSFER AGENT(S): Fleet National Bank, Providence, RI

ALBANY INTERNATIONAL CORP.

EXCH.	SYM.	REC. PRICE	P/E RATIO	YLD.	MKT. CAP.	RANGE (52-WK.)	'02 Y/E PR.
NYSE	AIN	22.14 (2/28/03)	13.3	1.0%	$0.69 bill.	30.65 - 16.90	20.66

MEDIUM GRADE. THE COMPANY PLANS TO REDUCE COSTS BY AN ADDITIONAL $30.0 MILLION BY JUNE 2004.

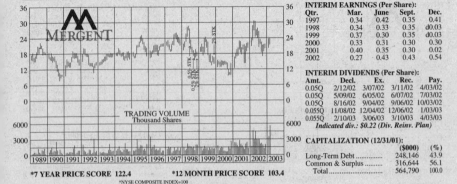

*7 YEAR PRICE SCORE 122.4   ***12 MONTH PRICE SCORE 103.4**
*NYSE COMPOSITE INDEX=100

INTERIM EARNINGS (Per Share):

Qtr.	Mar.	June	Sept.	Dec.
1997	0.34	0.42	0.35	0.41
1998	0.34	0.33	0.35	d0.03
1999	0.37	0.30	0.35	d0.03
2000	0.33	0.31	0.30	0.30
2001	0.40	0.35	0.30	0.02
2002	0.27	0.43	0.43	0.54

INTERIM DIVIDENDS (Per Share):

Amt.	Decl.	Ex.	Rec.	Pay.
0.05Q	2/12/02	3/07/02	3/11/02	4/03/02
0.05Q	5/09/02	6/05/02	6/07/02	7/03/02
0.05Q	8/16/02	9/04/02	9/06/02	10/03/02
0.055Q	11/08/02	12/04/02	12/06/02	1/03/03
0.055Q	2/10/03	3/06/03	3/10/03	4/03/03

Indicated div.: $0.22 (Div. Reinv. Plan)

CAPITALIZATION (12/31/01):

	($000)	(%)
Long-Term Debt	248,146	43.9
Common & Surplus	316,644	56.1
Total	564,790	100.0

BUSINESS:

Albany International Corp. designs, manufactures and markets paper machine clothing (PMC) and produces high-performance industrial doors. AIN is the world's largest maker of PMC, the fabric upon which wood pulp is formed, pressed and dried in the production of paper and paperboard. These custom-designed engineered fabrics are essential to the papermaking process and are manufactured from monofilament and synthetic fiber material. High-performance industrial doors are highly flexible, resistant to damage and need little maintenance. As of 1/28/02, AIN's principal manufacturing facilities are wholly-owned and located in Australia, Brazil, Canada, China, Finland, France, Germany, Great Britain, Italy, Korea, Mexico, the Netherlands, South Africa, Sweden, and the U.S.

RECENT DEVELOPMENTS:

For the year ended 12/31/02, income increased 64.3% to $54.8 million from income of $33.3 million in 2001. Results for 2002 and 2001 excluded an accounting change charge of $5.8 million and $1.1 million, respectively. Results for 2001 included restructuring and other charges of $21.9 million. Net sales slid 2.5% to $816.0 million from $836.7 million a year earlier due to the weakness of the paper and paperboard markets. Operating income grew 21.4% to $102.1 million from $84.1 million in 2001.

PROSPECTS:

The Company has reduced costs by $75.0 million since 1999 through cost reduction initiatives. AIN plans to reduce costs an additional $30.0 million by June 2004. This global initiative will focus on the continued rationalization of assets, the reorganization of its research and development activities, and reductions in selling, technical, and administrative costs. Moreover, during the fourth quarter, the Company announced that it will close a plant in Finland and a plant in Germany. Also, the Company plans to construct a new engineered facility in France, as well as increase capacity at its Helsinki dryer manufacturing facility by installing new equipment. The investments are expected to use about $55.0 million in capital expenditures in 2003.

ANNUAL FINANCIAL DATA:

FISCAL YEAR	TOT. REVS. ($mill.)	NET INC. ($mill.)	TOT. ASSETS ($mill.)	OPER. PROFIT %	NET PROFIT %	RET. ON EQUITY %	RET. ON ASSETS %	CURR. RATIO	EARN. PER SH. $	CASH FL. PER SH. $	TANG. BK. VAL. $	DIV. PER SH. $	PRICE RANGE	AVG. P/E RATIO	AVG. YIELD %
p12/31/02	816.0	④ 54.8							④ 1.68			0.20	30.65 - 16.90	14.1	0.8
12/31/01	836.7	④ 33.3	931.9	10.1	4.0	10.5	3.6	2.0	④ 1.06	2.90	5.62	...	23.00 - 12.38	16.7	...
12/31/00	852.9	③ 38.1	1,112.3	12.2	4.5	11.7	3.4	2.2	③ 1.24	5.30	...	...	15.50 - 9.63	10.1	...
12/31/99	1,556.7	808.6	1,206.8	54.9	51.9	248.5	67.0	2.9	0.99	28.36	4.18	...	24.51 - 13.48	19.2	...
12/31/98	722.7	① 31.8	866.4	9.8	4.4	10.1	3.7	1.9	① 1.01	2.57	8.46	0.20	28.73 - 15.44	21.9	0.9
12/31/97	710.1	49.1	796.9	14.0	6.9	14.3	6.2	2.2	1.50	2.87	9.51	0.39	26.11 - 18.79	15.0	1.8
12/31/96	692.8	② 65.7	824.7	13.8	9.5	20.0	8.0	2.2	② 1.52	...	8.87	0.38	22.01 - 16.30	12.6	2.0
12/31/95	652.6	63.2	796.5	13.6	9.7	20.9	7.9	2.9	1.36	3.35	8.50	0.36	25.22 - 16.30	15.3	1.7
12/31/94	567.6	41.1	721.4	11.1	7.2	15.1	5.7	2.8	0.76	2.53	7.92	0.33	20.22 - 15.35	23.4	1.9
12/31/93	546.1	① 32.0	655.4	7.5	5.9	13.1	4.9	2.7	① 0.55	2.64	6.97	0.33	18.32 - 13.56	28.9	2.1

Statistics are as originally reported. Class A & B common shares. Adj. for stk. split: 0.5%, 7/98 and 10/98; 2.0%, 1/99 and 1/00. ① Incl. a net restruct. chrg. of $21.9 mill., 2001; $20.2 mill., 1998; $419,000, 1993. ② Bef. extraord. loss of $1.3 mill. ($0.04 a sh.). ③ Incl. chrg. of $4.2 mill. for equip. relocation. ④ Bef. an acctg. change chrg. of 2002, $5.8 mill.; 2001, $1.1 mill.

OFFICERS:
F. R. Schmeler, Chmn., C.E.O.
M. C. Nahl, Sr. V.P., C.F.O.
D. C. Michaels, V.P., Treasury, Tax
J. C. Treanor, Treas.
INVESTOR CONTACT: Charles B. Buchanan, V.P., Sec., (518) 445-2284
PRINCIPAL OFFICE: 1373 Broadway, Albany, NY 12204

TELEPHONE NUMBER: (518) 445-2200
FAX: (518) 445-2265
WEB: www.albint.com
NO. OF EMPLOYEES: 6,769 (avg.)
SHAREHOLDERS: 4,600 (approx.)
ANNUAL MEETING: In May
INCORPORATED: NY, 1895; reincorp. in DE, Aug., 1983

INSTITUTIONAL HOLDINGS:
No. of Institutions: 133
Shares Held: 22,487,074
% Held: 69.5
INDUSTRY: Broadwoven fabric mills, man-made (SIC: 2221)
TRANSFER AGENT(S): Computershare Investor Services LLC, Chicago, IL

ALBEMARLE CORPORATION

EXCH.	SYM.	REC. PRICE	P/E RATIO	YLD.	MKT. CAP.	RANGE (52-WK.)	'02 Y/E PR.
NYSE	ALB	24.49 (2/28/03)	14.1	2.3%	$1.02 bill.	33.00 - 23.60	28.45

UPPER MEDIUM GRADE. THE COMPANY EXPECTS VOLUME TRENDS FOR MANY OF ITS BUSINESSES TO REMAIN STABLE IN 2003.

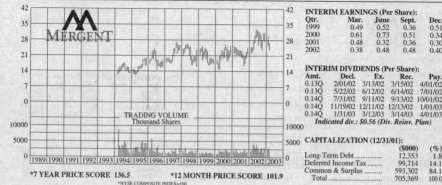

INTERIM EARNINGS (Per Share):

Qtr.	Mar.	June	Sept.	Dec.
1999	0.49	0.52	0.36	0.51
2000	0.61	0.73	0.51	0.34
2001	0.48	0.32	0.36	0.30
2002	0.38	0.48	0.48	0.40

INTERIM DIVIDENDS (Per Share):

Amt.	Decl.	Ex.	Rec.	Pay.
0.13Q	2/01/02	3/13/02	3/15/02	4/01/02
0.13Q	5/22/02	6/12/02	6/14/02	7/01/02
0.14Q	7/31/02	9/11/02	9/13/02	10/01/02
0.14Q	11/19/02	12/11/02	12/13/02	1/01/03
0.14Q	1/31/03	3/12/03	3/14/03	4/01/03

Indicated div.: $0.56 (Div. Reinv. Plan)

CAPITALIZATION (12/31/01):

	($000)	(%)
Long-Term Debt	12,353	1.8
Deferred Income Tax	99,714	14.1
Common & Surplus	593,302	84.1
Total	705,369	100.0

*7 YEAR PRICE SCORE 136.5   *12 MONTH PRICE SCORE 101.9
*NYSE COMPOSITE INDEX=100

BUSINESS:

Albemarle Corporation is a producer of polymer and fine chemicals. A majority of the products are additives to or intermediates for plastics, polymers, and elastomers, cleaning products, agrichemical compounds, pharmaceuticals, photographic chemicals, drilling compounds, ceramics, refractories, paper processing, paints and coatings, and biocides. The Company also performs custom research and development manufacturing campaigns for third parties at its cyclic guanosine monophosphate (cGMP) pilot plant in Dayton, Ohio. The Company produces the majority of its products in the U.S., but also has production facilities in France, Germany and the U.K. Products in the polymer chemicals segment consist of a broad range of chemicals including flame retardants, catalysts and polymer additives, while products in the fine chemicals segment includes pharmaceuticals, agrichemical intermediates and ultraviolet light-curing and performance chemicals.

RECENT DEVELOPMENTS:

For the year ended 12/31/02, net income climbed 9.6% to $74.7 million compared with $68.2 million in 2001. Earnings benefited from the favorable effect of lower raw material and manufacturing costs, higher volume in the performance chemicals business, the integration of the Martinswerk GmbH acquisition, and a favorable income tax settlement. Results for 2002 and 2001 included special charges of $1.6 million and $2.1 million, respectively, related to workforce reductions. Net sales were $980.2 million, up 6.9% from $916.9 million the previous year.

PROSPECTS:

The Company is cautious about its outlook for the year due to uncertainties about the global economy. Nevertheless, ALB expects volume trends for many of its businesses to remain stable in 2003. Moreover, the Company expects its strong cash flow position to continue, which should give it the ability to pursue future acquisitions and lower debt. Separately, on 1/21/03, the Company acquired the fuel and lubricant antioxidants business of Ethyl Corporation for an undisclosed amount. The transaction should strengthen ALB's position in the specialty antioxidants global market.

ANNUAL FINANCIAL DATA:

FISCAL YEAR	TOT. REVS. ($mill.)	NET INC. ($mill.)	TOT. ASSETS ($mill.)	OPER. PROFIT %	NET PROFIT %	RET. ON EQUITY %	RET. ON ASSETS %	CURR. RATIO	EARN. PER SH.$	CASH FL.PER SH.$	TANG. BK. VAL.$	DIV. PER SH.$	PRICE RANGE	AVG. P/E RATIO	AVG. YIELD %
p12/31/02	980.2	④74.7							④1.73			0.54	33.00 — 21.90	15.9	1.9
12/31/01	916.9	①68.2	1,129.5	10.7	7.4	11.5	6.0	1.3	①1.47	3.13	12.34	0.52	25.38 — 16.50	14.2	2.5
12/31/00	917.5	①101.8	981.8	16.4	11.1	18.2	10.4	2.2	②2.18	3.77	11.71	0.43	26.13 — 14.56	9.3	2.1
12/31/99	845.9	②88.8	954.1	13.5	10.5	18.1	9.3	2.5	②1.87	3.46	10.23	0.40	25.31 — 16.63	11.2	1.9
12/31/98	820.9	84.7	937.8	15.3	10.3	18.8	9.0	2.9	1.63	3.06	9.16	0.36	26.19 — 16.00	12.9	1.7
12/31/97	829.9	80.0	888.2	14.5	9.6	15.5	9.0	2.6	1.44	2.68	9.27	0.30	27.25 — 17.38	15.5	1.3
12/31/96	854.5	③156.1	846.3	10.9	18.3	30.9	18.4	1.8	③2.65	3.86	8.76	0.23	24.13 — 14.38	7.3	1.2
12/31/95	1,244.2	③78.2	1,204.5	9.4	6.3	12.6	6.5	2.2	③1.18	2.60	8.98	0.20	20.00 — 12.25	13.7	1.3
12/31/94	1,080.9	51.3	1,139.2	8.7	4.7	9.4	4.5	2.2	0.68	2.27	7.78	0.15	17.63 — 12.50	22.1	1.0
12/31/93	903.4	21.8	1,085.0	5.4	2.4	3.1	2.0	2.2	0.39	1.86	...	...	... — ...	...	...

Statistics are as originally reported. ① Incl. special charge of $2.1 mill., 12/01; gain of $8.1 mill., 12/00. ② Incl. $10.7 mill. special chg. & $22.1 mill. gain fr. sale of investment. ③ Incl. gain fr. sale of businesses of $158.2 mill., 12/96; $23.4 mill., 12/95. ④ Incl. $1.6 mill. special workforce reduction chg.

OFFICERS:
W. M. Gottwald, Chmn.
F. D. Gottwald Jr., Vice-Chmn.
M. C. Rohr, Pres., C.E.O.
INVESTOR CONTACT: Michael J. Zobrist, V.P., Investor Relations, (225) 388-8180
PRINCIPAL OFFICE: 330 South Fourth Street, P.O. Box 1335, Richmond, VA 23210

TELEPHONE NUMBER: (804) 788-6000
FAX: (804) 788-5688
WEB: www.albemarle.com
NO. OF EMPLOYEES: 3,000 (approx.)
SHAREHOLDERS: 5,775 (record)
ANNUAL MEETING: In Mar.
INCORPORATED: VA, Nov., 1993

INSTITUTIONAL HOLDINGS:
No. of Institutions: 162
Shares Held: 20,341,548
% Held: 48.8
INDUSTRY: Plastics materials and resins (SIC: 2821)
TRANSFER AGENT(S): National City Bank, Cleveland, OH

ALBERTO-CULVER COMPANY

EXCH.	SYM.	REC. PRICE	P/E RATIO	YLD.	MKT. CAP.	RANGE (52-WK.)	'02 Y/E PR.	DIV. ACH.
NYSE	ACV	49.71 (2/28/03)	20.5	0.8%	$2.89 bill.	57.91 - 41.55	50.40	18 yrs.

INVESTMENT GRADE. GOING FORWARD, THE COMPANY EXPECTS THE RETAIL ENVIRONMENT TO REMAIN CHALLENGING IN 2003.

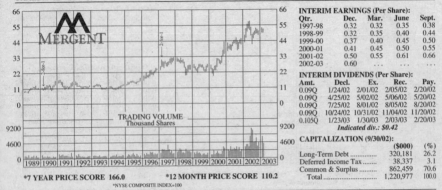

*7 YEAR PRICE SCORE 166.0   ***12 MONTH PRICE SCORE 110.2**
*NYSE COMPOSITE INDEX=100

INTERIM EARNINGS (Per Share):

Qtr.	Dec.	Mar.	June	Sept.
1997-98	0.32	0.32	0.35	0.38
1998-99	0.32	0.35	0.40	0.44
1999-00	0.37	0.40	0.45	0.50
2000-01	0.41	0.45	0.50	0.55
2001-02	0.50	0.55	0.61	0.66
2002-03	0.60	...	...	...

INTERIM DIVIDENDS (Per Share):

Amt.	Decl.	Ex.	Rec.	Pay.
0.09Q	1/24/02	2/01/02	2/05/02	2/20/02
0.09Q	4/25/02	5/02/02	5/06/02	5/20/02
0.09Q	7/25/02	8/01/02	8/05/02	8/20/02
0.09Q	10/24/02	10/31/02	11/04/02	11/20/02
0.105Q	1/23/03	1/30/03	2/03/03	2/20/03

Indicated div.: $0.42

CAPITALIZATION (9/30/02):

	($000)	(%)
Long-Term Debt	320,181	26.2
Deferred Income Tax	38,337	3.1
Common & Surplus	862,459	70.6
Total	1,220,977	100.0

BUSINESS:

Alberto-Culver Company is engaged in developing, manufacturing, distributing and marketing branded consumer products worldwide. Alberto-Culver North America includes ACV's consumer products in the U.S. and Canada, while Alberto-Culver International sells consumer products in more than 120 other countries. ACV's third segment, Specialty Distribution - Sally, consists of Sally Beauty Company, a specialty distributor of professional beauty supplies with 2,743 stores as of 12/31/02, in the U.S., Germany, the United Kingdom, Canada, Japan and Mexico, and its Beauty Systems Group, which sells professional beauty products through over 1,003 professional distributor sales consultants. Brands sold by ACV include ALBERTO VO5, ST. IVES SWISS FORMULA and TRESEMME hair and skin beauty care products.

RECENT DEVELOPMENTS:

For the first quarter ended 12/31/02, net earnings grew 22.9% to $36.0 million from $29.3 million in the equivalent prior-year quarter. The increase in earnings was attributed to strong performances by its Sally Beauty Company and its consumer products unit. Net sales increased 13.4% to $696.8 million from $614.3 million the previous year. Gross profit improved 13.4% to $344.5 million versus $303.7 million a year earlier. Operating income was $61.9 million, up 22.7% from $50.4 million the year before.

PROSPECTS:

The Company's consumer packaged goods business continues to benefit from increased marketing investments behind its established core brands and strong trade and vendor partnerships. Meanwhile, ACV's Sally Beauty and Beauty Systems Group continue to show strong growth both organically and as a result of acquisitions. Going forward, while the Company expects to report improved results in fiscal 2003, the global retail environment is expected to remain challenging due to major competitive product introductions and soft consumer spending in the hair and skin care categories.

ANNUAL FINANCIAL DATA:

FISCAL YEAR	TOT. REVS. ($mill.)	NET INC. ($mill.)	TOT. ASSETS ($mill.)	OPER. PROFIT %	NET PROFIT %	RET. ON EQUITY %	RET. ON ASSETS %	CURR. RATIO	EARN. PER SH.$	CASH FL. PER SH.$	TANG. BK. VAL.$	DIV. PER SH.$	PRICE RANGE	AVG. P/E RATIO	AVG. YIELD %
9/30/02	2,651.0	137.7	1,729.5	8.8	5.2	16.0	8.0	2.1	2.32	3.12	7.55	0.36	57.91 — 41.55	21.4	0.7
9/30/01	2,494.2	110.4	1,516.5	7.6	4.4	15.0	7.3	2.2	1.91	2.80	6.90	0.33	46.26 — 36.88	21.8	0.8
9/30/00	2,247.2	☐ 103.2	1,389.8	7.7	4.6	16.2	7.4	2.2	☐ 1.83	2.71	5.16	0.30	43.50 — 19.38	17.2	1.0
9/30/99	1,975.9	86.3	1,184.5	7.4	4.4	15.2	7.3	1.9	1.51	2.25	5.81	0.26	27.88 — 21.56	16.4	1.1
9/30/98	1,834.7	83.1	1,068.2	7.7	4.5	15.6	7.8	1.9	1.37	1.94	5.75	0.22	32.44 — 19.75	19.0	0.9
9/30/97	1,775.3	☐ 85.4	1,000.1	8.1	4.8	17.2	8.5	1.9	☐ 1.49	2.17	5.57	0.20	32.56 — 23.56	18.8	0.7
9/30/96	1,590.4	☐ 62.7	909.3	7.0	3.9	14.8	6.9	1.8	☐ 1.11	1.70	4.33	0.18	25.00 — 16.25	18.6	0.9
9/30/95	1,358.2	52.7	815.1	6.7	3.9	14.2	6.5	2.3	0.95	1.39	5.08	0.16	18.25 — 12.94	16.5	1.0
9/30/94	1,216.1	44.1	610.2	6.3	3.6	13.5	7.2	1.9	0.79	1.16	4.93	0.14	13.69 — 9.69	14.9	1.2
9/30/93	1,148.0	41.3	593.0	6.3	3.6	13.8	7.0	2.0	0.72	1.06	4.36	0.13	14.13 — 10.06	16.8	1.1

Statistics are as originally reported. Adj. for stk. splits: 2-for-1, 2/97. ☐ Incl. non-recurr. gain 2000, $6.0 mill.; credit 1997, $15.6 mill., 1996, $9.8 mill.

OFFICERS:
L. H. Lavin, Chmn.
B. E. Lavin, Vice-Chmn., Treas., Sec.
H. B. Bernick, Pres., C.E.O.

INVESTOR CONTACT: Wesley C. Davidson, V.P., Invest. Rel., (708) 450-3145

PRINCIPAL OFFICE: 2525 Armitage Avenue, Melrose Park, IL 60160

TELEPHONE NUMBER: (708) 450-3000
FAX: (708) 450-3419
WEB: www.alberto.com

NO. OF EMPLOYEES: 16,900 (approx.)
SHAREHOLDERS: 877 (CL. A); 865 (CL. B)
ANNUAL MEETING: In Jan.
INCORPORATED: DE, Jan., 1961

INSTITUTIONAL HOLDINGS:
No. of Institutions: 225
Shares Held: 22,757,929
% Held: 38.9

INDUSTRY: Toilet preparations (SIC: 2844)

TRANSFER AGENT(S): EquiServe L.P., Providence, RI

ALBERTSON'S, INC.

EXCH.	SYM.	REC. PRICE	P/E RATIO	YLD.	MKT. CAP.	RANGE (52-WK.)	'02 Y/E PR.
NYSE	ABS	18.83 (2/28/03)	8.6	4.0%	$7.66 bill.	35.49 - 18.28	22.26

INVESTMENT GRADE. THE COMPANY ANTICIPATES EARNINGS OF $2.08 TO $2.13 PER SHARE FOR FISCAL 2003.

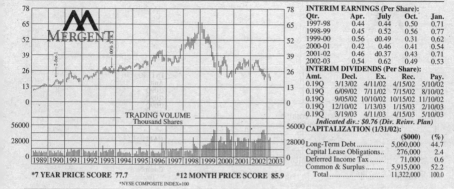

*7 YEAR PRICE SCORE 77.7   *12 MONTH PRICE SCORE 85.9

*NYSE COMPOSITE INDEX=100

INTERIM EARNINGS (Per Share):

Qtr.	Apr.	July	Oct.	Jan.
1997-98	0.44	0.44	0.50	0.71
1998-99	0.45	0.52	0.56	0.77
1999-00	0.56	d0.49	0.31	0.62
2000-01	0.42	0.46	0.41	0.54
2001-02	0.46	d0.37	0.43	0.71
2002-03	0.54	0.62	0.49	0.53

INTERIM DIVIDENDS (Per Share):

Amt.	Decl.	Ex.	Rec.	Pay.
0.19Q	3/13/02	4/11/02	4/15/02	5/10/02
0.19Q	6/09/02	7/11/02	7/15/02	8/10/02
0.19Q	9/05/02	10/10/02	10/15/02	11/10/02
0.19Q	12/10/02	1/13/03	1/15/03	2/10/03
0.19Q	3/19/03	4/11/03	4/15/03	5/10/03

Indicated div.: $0.76 (Div. Reinv. Plan)

CAPITALIZATION (1/31/02):

	($000)	(%)
Long-Term Debt	5,060,000	44.7
Capital Lease Obligations..	276,000	2.4
Deferred Income Tax	71,000	0.6
Common & Surplus	5,915,000	52.2
Total	11,322,000	100.0

BUSINESS:

Albertson's, Inc. is one of the largest retail food-drug chains in the United States. As of 3/19/03, ABS operated approximately 2,300 stores in 30 states under three different formats: combination food-drug, conventional, and warehouse. Combination food-drug units, ranging between 35,000 sq. ft. and 107,000 sq. ft., consist of grocery, general merchandise, and meat and produce departments, along with pharmacy, lobby/video, floral, and bakery service departments. ABS also operated 174 fuel centers, which are generally located in the parking lot of stores. The Company's stores are operated under the Albertson's, Albertson's-Osco, Albertson's-Sav-on, Jewel-Osco, Acme, Sav-on Drugs, Osco Drug, Max Foods and Super Saver banners. On 6/23/99, ABS acquired American Stores Company.

RECENT DEVELOPMENTS:

For the 52 weeks ended 1/30/03, earnings from continuing operations totaled $865.0 million, before a $94.0 million accounting change charge, versus earnings from continuing operations of $496.0 million in the corresponding period the year before. Results for the recent period included a pre-tax restructuring credit of $37.0 million. Results for the prior-year period included a pre-tax restructuring charge of $468.0 million, partially offset by one-time gains totaling $69.0 million. Sales slipped 2.7% to $35.63 billion from $36.61 billion a year earlier. Comparable-store sales declined 0.4% year over year. Gross profit was $10.38 billion, or 29.2% of sales, compared with $10.43 billion, or 28.5% of sales, the previous year.

PROSPECTS:

The Company is targeting full fiscal-2003 earnings of between $2.08 and $2.13 per share. Bottom-line results should benefit from the Company's aggressive cost-control efforts, which are expected to generate cost savings of $500.0 million by mid-2003 and $750.0 million by the end of 2004. Meanwhile, sales are being hurt by intense competitive pressures and economic weakness. Identical-store sales are expected to be positive by year-end 2003, while total square-footage is expected to increase by 2.0% during 2003, excluding closures and acquisitions.

ANNUAL FINANCIAL DATA:

FISCAL YEAR	TOT. REVS. ($mill.)	NET INC. ($mill.)	TOT. ASSETS ($mill.)	OPER. PROFIT %	NET PROFIT %	RET. ON EQUITY %	RET. ON ASSETS %	CURR. RATIO	EARN. PER SH.$	CASH FL. PER SH.$	TANG. BK. VAL.$	DIV. PER SH.$	PRICE RANGE	AVG. P/E RATIO	AVG. YIELD %
p1/30/03	35,626.0	⑦ 865.0							⑦ 2.17			0.76	35.49 - 18.95	12.5	2.8
1/31/02	37,931.0	⑥ 501.0	15,967.0	3.5	1.3	8.5	3.1	1.3	⑥ 1.23	3.74	10.51	0.76	36.99 - 24.00	24.8	2.5
2/01/01	36,762.0	⑤ 765.0	16,078.0	4.5	2.1	13.4	4.8	1.3	⑤ 1.83	4.22	9.85	0.75	39.25 - 20.06	16.2	2.5
④ 2/03/00	37,478.0	③ 427.0	15,701.0	3.3	1.1	7.5	2.7	1.1	③ 1.00	3.17	9.72	0.71	66.63 - 29.00	47.8	1.5
1/28/99	16,005.1	② 567.2	6,234.0	6.1	3.5	20.2	9.1	1.3	② 2.30	3.82	10.84	0.67	67.13 - 44.00	24.2	1.2
1/29/98	14,689.5	516.8	5,218.6	6.1	3.5	21.4	9.9	1.3	2.08	3.40	9.85	0.63	48.63 - 30.50	19.0	1.6
1/30/97	13,776.7	493.8	4,714.6	6.2	3.6	22.0	10.5	1.4	1.96	3.13	8.96	0.58	43.75 - 31.50	19.2	1.5
2/01/96	12,585.0	465.0	4,135.9	6.4	3.7	23.8	11.2	1.2	1.84	2.83	7.75	0.50	34.63 - 27.25	16.8	1.6
2/02/95	11,894.6	① 417.4	3,621.7	6.2	3.5	24.7	11.5	1.1	① 1.65	2.54	6.65	0.42	30.88 - 25.13	17.0	1.5
2/03/94	11,283.7	339.7	3,294.9	5.7	3.0	24.4	10.3	1.1	1.34	2.11	5.48	0.35	29.69 - 23.38	19.8	1.3

Statistics are as originally reported. ① Bef. $17 mil ($0.07/sh) chg. for acctg. adj. ② Incl. $24.4 mil pre-tax impairment chg. for store closures. ③ Bef. $23.3 mil ($0.05/sh) extraord. chg. & incl. one-time pre-tax chgs. totaling $689.0 mil related to the acq. of American Stores Company and a litigation settlement. ④ Refl. acquis. of American Stores Co. in 6/99. ⑤ Incl. $105.0 mil ($0.25/sh) one-time after-tax chg. ⑥ Incl. $468.0 mil pre-tax restr. chg., $54.0 mil gain fr. sale of 80 Osco drugstores and a $15.0 mil merger-related credit. ⑦ Bef. $286.0 mil ($0.72/sh) loss fr. disc. opers. and $94.0 mil ($0.23/sh) acctg. chg. & incl. $37.0 mil pre-tax restr. credit.

OFFICERS:
L. R. Johnston, Chmn., C.E.O.
P. L. Lynch, Pres., C.O.O.
F. D. Thornton, Exec. V.P., C.F.O.
INVESTOR CONTACT: Renee Bergquist,
(208) 395-6622
PRINCIPAL OFFICE: 250 Parkcenter Blvd.,
P.O. Box 20, Boise, ID 83726

TELEPHONE NUMBER: (208) 395-6200
FAX: (208) 395-6777
WEB: www.albertsons.com
NO. OF EMPLOYEES: 200,000 (approx.)
SHAREHOLDERS: 30,400 (approx.)
ANNUAL MEETING: In June
INCORPORATED: DE, Apr., 1969

INSTITUTIONAL HOLDINGS:
No. of Institutions: 396
Shares Held: 277,908,307
% Held: 73.3

INDUSTRY: Grocery stores (SIC: 5411)

TRANSFER AGENT(S): American Stock
Transfer & Trust Company, New York, NY

ALCOA, INC.

EXCH.	SYM.	REC. PRICE	P/E RATIO	YLD.	MKT. CAP.	RANGE (52-WK.)	'02 Y/E PR.
NYSE	AA	19.38 (3/31/03)	34.0	3.1%	$16.37 bill.	39.09 - 17.62	22.78

MEDIUM GRADE. RESTRUCTURING ACTIONS AND DIVESTITURES IN 2003 ARE EXPECTED TO IMPROVE THE COMPANY'S COST POSITION.

*7 YEAR PRICE SCORE 107.2   ***12 MONTH PRICE SCORE 85.0**
*NYSE COMPOSITE INDEX=100

INTERIM EARNINGS (Per Share):

Qtr.	Mar.	June	Sept.	Dec.
1999	0.30	0.33	0.35	0.45
2000	0.48	0.47	0.42	0.45
2001	0.46	0.35	0.39	d0.17
2002	0.22	0.27	0.23	d0.15

INTERIM DIVIDENDS (Per Share):

Amt.	Decl.	Ex.	Rec.	Pay.
0.15Q	12/11/01	2/06/02	2/08/02	2/25/02
0.15Q	3/15/02	5/01/02	5/03/02	5/25/02
0.15Q	7/12/02	7/31/02	8/02/02	8/25/02
0.15Q	9/13/02	11/06/02	11/08/02	11/25/02
0.15Q	1/10/03	2/05/03	2/07/03	2/25/03

Indicated div.: $0.60 (Div. Reinv. Plan)

CAPITALIZATION (12/31/01):

	($000)	(%)
Long-Term Debt [1]	6,388,000	33.8
Deferred Income Tax	556,000	2.9
Minority Interest	1,313,000	6.9
Preferred Stock	56,000	0.3
Common & Surplus	10,558,000	56.1
Total	18,871,000	100.0

BUSINESS:

Alcoa, Inc. (formerly Aluminum Co. of America) produces primary aluminum, fabricated aluminum and alumina, and is active in all major aspects of the industry. AA serves the aerospace, automotive, packaging, building and construction, commercial transportation and industrial markets, providing customers with design, engineering and production capabilities. In addition, AA markets consumer brands including Reynolds Wrap® products, Alcoa® wheels, and Baco® household wraps. AA's other businesses include vinyl siding, closures, precision castings, and vehicle electrical distribution systems. AA has operations in 38 countries. In 2002, revenues were derived as follows: engineered products, 24.8%; flat-rolled products, 22.9%; primary metals, 15.7%; packaging and consumer, 14.2%; alumina and chemicals, 8.6%; and other, 13.8%. In 2002, AA shipped 5,208,000 metric tons of aluminum products.

RECENT DEVELOPMENTS:

For the year ended 12/31/02, the Company reported income from continuing operations of $498.0 million, before an accounting change gain of $34.0 million, compared with $907.0 million in the previous year. Results for 2002 included after-tax restructuring charges of $118.0 million, a divestiture loss of $143.0 million and a goodwill impairment charge of $20.0 million. Results excluded a charge of $112.0 million in 2002 and a gain of $1.0 million in 2001 from discontinued operations. Sales decreased 9.9% to $20.3 million from $22.5 million a year earlier, reflecting lower realized prices for primary aluminum and alumina, and weaknesses in certain end markets.

PROSPECTS:

In 2003, AA will restructure operations of its businesses serving the aerospace, automotive and industrial gas turbine markets, as well as its U.S. smelting operations. The restructuring will affect about 8,000 employees and includes operations that have experienced negligible growth. AA also announced that it intends to divest certain businesses including specialty chemicals, specialty packaging equipment, architectural products in North America, commodity automotive fasteners, certain South American fabricated operations, and certain foil facilities.

ANNUAL FINANCIAL DATA:

FISCAL YEAR	TOT. REVS. ($mill.)	NET INC. ($mill.)	TOT. ASSETS ($mill.)	OPER. PROFIT %	NET PROFIT %	RET. ON EQUITY %	RET. ON ASSETS %	CURR. RATIO	EARN. PER SH. $	CASH FL. PER SH. $	TANG. BK. VAL. $	DIV. PER SH. $	PRICE RANGE	AVG. P/E RATIO	AVG. YIELD %
p12/31/02	20,263.0	[9] 498.0	30,180.0						[9] 0.58			0.60	39.75 - 17.62	49.5	2.1
12/31/01	22,859.0	[8] 908.0	28,355.0	7.5	4.0	8.6	3.2	1.4	[8] 1.05	2.51	5.69	0.60	45.71 - 27.36	34.8	1.6
12/31/00	23,090.0	[7] 1,489.0	31,691.0	14.0	6.4	13.0	4.7	1.0	[7] 1.81	3.29	6.20	0.50	43.63 - 23.13	18.4	1.5
12/31/99	16,447.0	1,054.0	17,066.0	12.4	6.4	16.7	6.2	1.6	1.41	2.62	6.71	0.40	41.69 - 17.97	21.2	1.3
12/31/98	15,489.4	[6] 853.0	17,462.5	11.6	5.5	14.1	4.9	1.5	[6] 1.21	2.43	6.25	0.34	20.31 - 14.50	14.4	2.0
12/31/97	13,481.7	[5] 805.1	13,070.6	12.2	6.0	18.2	6.2	1.8	[5] 1.16	2.24	5.76	0.24	22.41 - 16.06	16.7	1.3
12/31/96	13,128.4	[4] 514.9	13,449.9	10.8	3.9	11.5	3.8	1.8	[4] 0.74	1.83	6.39	0.33	16.56 - 12.28	19.6	2.3
12/31/95	12,654.9	790.5	13,643.4	12.7	6.2	17.8	5.8	1.8	1.11	2.14	5.37	0.23	15.06 - 9.22	11.0	1.9
12/31/94	10,391.5	[3] 443.1	12,353.2	9.7	4.3	11.1	3.6	1.6	[3] 0.62	1.59	4.96	0.20	11.28 - 8.03	15.6	2.1
12/31/93	9,148.9	[2] 4.8	11,596.9	4.7	0.1	0.1	...	1.8	[2] 0.01	1.02	4.99	0.20	9.80 - 7.38	N.M.	2.3

Statistics are as originally reported. Adj. for 2-for-1 stk. split, 6/00, 2/99 & 2/95. [1] Incl. secur. conv. into com. [2] Bef. spec. environ. restruct. costs of $251.6 mill. [3] Incl. nonrecurr. net gains of $300.2 mill. & nonrecurr. net chg. of $117.9 mill.; bef. $67.9 mill. chg. for early debt retire. [4] Incl. net nonrecurr. chg. of $170.4 mill. [5] Incl. a mark-to-mkt. loss of $12.7 mill. on alum. commodity contracts & a gain on asset sales of $43.9 mill. [6] Incl. a mark-to-mkt. loss of $2.7 mill. on alum. commodity contracts. [7] Bef. acctg. chg. of $5.0 mill. [8] Incl. after-tax spec. net chgs. $355.0 mill. [9] Bef. loss from discont. opers. of $112.0 mill. & acctg. chng. gain of $34.0 mill. incl. restr. & divest. chg. of $261.0 mill. & goodwill impair. of $20.0 mill.

OFFICERS:
A. J. Belda, Chmn., C.E.O.
R. B. Kelson, Exec. V.P., C.F.O.
INVESTOR CONTACT: William F. Oplinger, Investor Relations, (212) 836-2674
PRINCIPAL OFFICE: 201 Isabella Street, Pittsburgh, PA 15212-5858

TELEPHONE NUMBER: (412) 553-4707
FAX: (412) 553-4498
WEB: www.alcoa.com
NO. OF EMPLOYEES: 129,000 (avg.)
SHAREHOLDERS: 266,800 (approx.)
ANNUAL MEETING: In April
INCORPORATED: PA, 1888

INSTITUTIONAL HOLDINGS:
No. of Institutions: 624
Shares Held: 643,242,203
% Held: 76.2
INDUSTRY: Primary aluminum (SIC: 3334)
TRANSFER AGENT(S): EquiServe Trust Company, N.A., Providence, RI

ALLEGHANY CORPORATION

EXCH.	SYM.	REC. PRICE	P/E RATIO	YLD.	MKT. CAP.	RANGE (52-WK.)	'02 Y/E PR.
NYSE	Y	161.18 (Adj.; 2/28/03)	22.4	...	$1.18 bill.	190.20 - 157.84	174.02

MEDIUM GRADE. Y EXPECTS AVERAGE INVENTORY COSTS WILL INCREASE IN 2003 DUE TO HIGHER STEEL PRICES FROM CHINA.

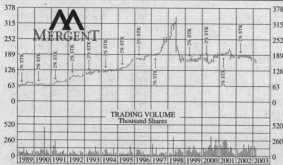

*7 YEAR PRICE SCORE 99.9 ***12 MONTH PRICE SCORE 100.7**

*NYSE COMPOSITE INDEX=100

INTERIM EARNINGS (Per Share):

Qtr.	Mar.	June	Sept.	Dec.
1997	0.88	2.18	2.03	1.95
1998	1.62	2.17	2.51	1.69
1999	1.97	2.65	7.18	0.83
2000	d4.30	14.04	1.14	d6.61
2001	60.31	d1.24	d4.84	d0.19
2002	3.41	1.09	2.92	d0.22

INTERIM DIVIDENDS (Per Share):

Amt.	Decl.	Ex.	Rec.	Pay.
2% STK	3/21/01	3/29/01	4/02/01	4/27/01
2% STK	3/20/02	3/27/02	4/01/02	4/26/02
2% STK	3/19/03	3/28/03	4/01/03	4/25/03

CAPITALIZATION (12/31/01):

	($000)	(%)
Long-Term Debt	181,856	11.6
Common & Surplus	1,390,582	88.4
Total	1,572,438	100.0

BUSINESS:

Alleghany Corporation is engaged in the industrial minerals business through its subsidiaries, World Minerals Inc., Celite Corporation, and Harborlite Corporation. Y conducts a steel fastener importing and distribution business through its subsidiary, Heads & Threads International LLC. The Company is also engaged in property, casualty, fidelity and surety insurance businesses through its subsidiary, Capitol Transamerica Corporation. In addition, through Alleghany Properties, Inc., Y owns and manages properties in Califor-nia. On 11/5/01, Y sold Alleghany Underwriting. On 2/1/01, Y sold Alleghany Asset Management, Inc., its financial services business. On 1/4/02, Y acquired Capitol Transamerica for approximately $182.0 million. As of 3/3/03, the Company owned 4.3% of Burlington Northern Santa Fe Corp. Total revenues for 2002 were derived as follows: mineral and filtration, 43.6%; net insurance premi-ums earned, 21.8%; steel fastener, 19.1%; investment, 6.3%; interest, dividend, and other, 9.2%.

RECENT DEVELOPMENTS:

For the year ended 12/31/02, net income was $54.8 million versus income of $430.6 million, before a loss from discon-tinued operations of $206.3 million, the previous year. Earnings for 2002 included an after-tax investment gain of $23.6 million and a net tax credit of $18.1 million. Earn-ings for 2001 included an after-tax gain from the disposi-tion of Alleghany Asset Management of $474.8 million and an after-tax loss of $50.5 million on the disposition of Alleghany Underwriting. Also, earnings for 2001 included after-tax net investment gains of $7.8 million. Total reve-nues fell 45.8% to $576.9 million, relecting the sale of the asset management business.

PROSPECTS:

Operating earnings from Y's world minerals business is benefiting from businesses acquired in 2001 and 2002, higher profit margins from lower energy costs at U.S. and Latin American plants, and ongoing cost control efforts. Meanwhile, at Heads & Threads, restructuring efforts and lower average inventory costs are offsetting a decline in net sales due to reduced demand in the U.S. economy and reduced sales of certain product lines. However, Y expects average inventory costs will increase in 2003 due to higher steel prices from China.

ANNUAL FINANCIAL DATA:

FISCAL YEAR	TOT. REVS. ($mill.)	NET INC. ($mill.)	TOT. ASSETS ($mill.)	OPER. PROFIT %	NET PROFIT %	RET. ON EQUITY %	RET. ON ASSETS %	CURR. RATIO	⑥ EARN. PER SH. $	CASH FL. PER SH. $	TANG. BK. VAL. $	PRICE RANGE	AVG. P/E RATIO
p12/31/02	576.9	⑥ 54.8							⑤ 7.30			190.20 - 167.16	24.5
12/31/01	925.0	①③ 430.6	1,875.0	59.3	46.5	31.0	23.0	2.6	①③ 57.86	60.52	189.19	215.53 - 173.01	3.4
④ 12/31/00	945.2	①③ 34.0	2,707.6	1.3	3.6	2.9	1.3	...	①③ 4.33	6.76	158.38	195.18 - 151.72	40.0
12/31/99	1,376.2	100.1	4,485.0	14.1	7.3	9.0	2.2	...	12.44	16.51	139.97	190.89 - 160.29	14.1
12/31/98	919.0	63.4	4,282.4	13.4	6.9	5.1	1.5	...	7.94	10.24	159.37	342.83 - 155.79	31.4
② 12/31/97	796.7	① 51.4	3,700.4	12.2	6.5	3.3	1.4	...	① 6.45	9.49	196.97	262.67 - 184.70	34.7
12/31/96	2,062.2	87.0	4,500.6	7.7	4.2	6.1	1.9	...	10.92	17.40	178.00	189.14 - 166.06	16.3
12/31/95	1,784.8	85.3	4,122.5	8.4	4.8	6.5	2.1	...	10.71	16.26	168.57	173.68 - 127.17	14.0
12/31/94	1,827.1	① 68.4	3,587.9	6.7	3.7	6.7	1.9	...	① 8.70	14.41	131.31	130.48 - 116.73	14.2
12/31/93	1,908.5	131.3	6,284.9	9.5	6.9	14.3	2.1	0.9	12.76	22.31	117.80	128.45 - 104.60	9.1

Statistics are as originally reported. Adj. for all 2% stk. divs. through 4/25/03 ① Bef. disc. oper. loss $206.3 mill., 12/01; $34.9 mill.,12/00; $32.7 mill., 12/98; $54.3 mill., 12/97; $69.1 mill., 12/94 ② Reflects the spin-off of Chicago Title and Trust Co. ③ Incl. non-recurr. gain $424.0 mill., 12/01; $136.7 mill., 12/00 ④ Reflects the sale of Underwriters Re Group, Inc. ⑤ Incl. tax gain of $18.1 mill. ⑥ Reflects primary shares.

OFFICERS:
F. Kirby, Chmn.
J. J. Burns Jr., Pres., C.E.O., C.O.O.
D. B. Cuming, Sr. V.P., C.F.O.
INVESTOR CONTACT: R. M. Hart, Inv. Rel.,
(212) 752-1356
PRINCIPAL OFFICE: 375 Park Avenue, New York, NY 10152

TELEPHONE NUMBER: (212) 752-1356
FAX: (212) 759-8149
NO. OF EMPLOYEES: 2,084 (avg.)
SHAREHOLDERS: 1,523 (approx.)
ANNUAL MEETING: In April
INCORPORATED: DE, 1984

INSTITUTIONAL HOLDINGS:
No. of Institutions: 108
Shares Held: 4,591,268 (Adj.)
% Held: 62.2

INDUSTRY: Title insurance (SIC: 6361)

TRANSFER AGENT(S): Computershare Investor Services, Chicago, IL

ALLEGHENY ENERGY, INC.

EXCH.	SYM.	REC. PRICE	P/E RATIO	YLD.	MKT. CAP.	RANGE (52-WK.)	'02 Y/E PR.
NYSE	AYE	5.99 (2/28/03)	...	...	$0.75 bill.	43.86 - 2.95	7.56

LOWER MEDIUM GRADE. THE COMPANY HAS IMPLEMENTED SEVERAL INITIATIVES TO REDUCE ITS COST STRUCTURE, PRESERVE CASH, AND STRENGTHEN ITS BALANCE SHEET.

*7 YEAR PRICE SCORE 69.7   *12 MONTH PRICE SCORE 41.9
*NYSE COMPOSITE INDEX=100

INTERIM EARNINGS (Per Share):

Qtr.	Mar.	June	Sept.	Dec.
1998	0.64	0.44	0.68	0.39
1999	0.80	0.55	0.63	0.66
2000	0.78	0.65	0.69	0.72
2001	0.91	1.01	1.32	0.52
2002	0.81	d0.26	d2.18	...

INTERIM DIVIDENDS (Per Share):

Amt.	Decl.	Ex.	Rec.	Pay.
0.43Q	9/06/01	9/17/01	9/17/01	9/28/01
0.43Q	12/06/01	12/13/01	12/17/01	12/28/01
0.43Q	3/07/02	3/14/02	3/18/02	3/29/02
0.43Q	6/06/02	6/13/02	6/17/02	6/28/02
0.43Q	9/06/02	9/12/02	9/16/02	9/30/02

Dividend payment suspended.

CAPITALIZATION (12/31/01):

	($000)	(%)
Long-Term Debt	3,200,421	46.0
Deferred Income Tax	972,910	14.0
Preferred Stock	74,000	1.1
Common & Surplus	2,709,969	39.0
Total	6,957,300	100.0

BUSINESS:

Allegheny Energy, Inc. (formerly Allegheny Power System, Inc.) is an electric utility holding company, which owns various regulated and non-regulated subsidiaries. The Company conducts its business through its direct and indirect wholly-owned subsidiaries. Monongahela Power Company, The Potomac Edison Company and West Penn Power Company are electric distribution companies. The principal

markets for AYE's electric sales are in the states of Pennsylvania, West Virginia, Maryland, Virginia and Ohio. AYE also has a wholly-owned non-utility subsidiary, Allegheny Ventures, which is involved primarily in energy-related businesses. Revenues for 2001 were derived: unregulated generation, 72.2%; regulated utility, 26.5%; and other unregulated, 1.3%.

RECENT DEVELOPMENTS:

AYE does not expect to file its 2002 Form 10-K in the near term and has delayed its annual meeting to allow enough time to complete its comprehensive review of its financial statements. For the nine months ended 9/30/02, loss was $203.9 million, before an accounting change charge of $130.5 million, compared with income of $384.4 million, before an accounting change charge of $31.1 million, in

2001. Results were hindered by a reduction in the market value of AYE's energy trading portfolio due to changes in valuation model assumptions and market conditions. Total operating revenues slipped 10.3% to $2.32 billion from $2.59 billion in the prior year. Operating loss amounted to $90.2 million compared with operating income of $813.7 million the year before.

PROSPECTS:

AYE implemented several actions to reduce its cost structure, preserve cash, and strengthen its balance sheet. These actions include lowering AYE's reliance on its wholesale energy trading business, reducing pre-tax operating expenses, canceling the development of generating facili-

ties, saving $700.0 million in capital expenditures and reductions in workforce. Separately, on 2/26/03, Allegheny Energy Supply Company, LLC signed a definitive agreement to sell its share of the coal-fired Conemaugh Generating Station for about $51.25 million.

ANNUAL FINANCIAL DATA:

FISCAL YEAR	TOT. REVS. ($mill.)	NET INC. ($mill.)	TOT. ASSETS ($mill.)	OPER. PROFIT %	NET PROFIT %	NET INC./ NET PROP. %	NET INC./ TOT. CAP. %	RET. ON EQUITY %	ACCUM. DEPR./ GROSS PROP. %	EARN. PER SH. $	TANG. BK. VAL. $	DIV. PER SH. $	DIV. PAYOUT %	PRICE RANGE	AVG. P/E RATIO	AVG. YIELD %
12/31/01	⑦ 10,378.9	⑥ 448.9	11,167.6	6.9	4.3	6.6	6.5	16.1	38.2	⑥ 3.73	16.48	1.72	46.1	55.09 — 32.99	11.8	3.9
12/31/00	4,011.9	⑤ 313.7	7,697.0	13.4	7.8	5.7	6.0	17.3	41.7	⑤ 2.84	13.80	1.72	60.6	48.75 — 23.63	12.7	4.8
12/31/99	2,808.4	④ 285.4	6,852.4	16.9	10.2	5.5	5.8	16.1	41.1	④ 2.45	14.97	1.72	70.2	35.19 — 26.19	12.5	5.6
12/31/98	2,576.4	③ 263.0	6,747.8	17.1	10.2	5.0	5.1	11.9	39.3	③ 2.15	16.49	1.72	80.0	34.94 — 26.63	14.3	5.6
12/31/97	2,369.5	281.3	6,654.1	19.1	11.9	5.3	5.1	12.5	37.3	2.30	16.92	1.72	74.8	32.59 — 25.50	12.6	5.9
12/31/96	2,327.6	210.0	6,618.5	16.8	9.0	4.0	3.8	9.7	35.5	② 1.73	16.28	1.69	97.7	31.13 — 28.00	17.1	5.7
12/31/95	2,647.8	② 239.7	6,447.3	15.9	9.1	4.7	4.4	11.3	34.6	② 2.00	16.11	1.65	82.5	29.25 — 21.50	12.7	6.5
12/31/94	2,451.7	① 219.8	6,362.2	15.8	9.0	4.3	4.2	10.7	33.3	① 1.86	14.62	1.64	88.2	26.50 — 19.75	12.4	7.1
12/31/93	2,331.5	215.8	5,949.2	16.1	9.3	4.5	4.4	11.0	33.3	1.88	14.37	1.63	86.7	28.44 — 23.44	13.8	6.3
12/31/92	2,306.7	203.5	5,039.3	15.4	8.8	4.6	4.8	11.1	33.5	1.83	13.72	1.60	87.7	24.38 — 20.75	12.3	7.1

Statistics are as originally reported. Adj. for 2-for-1 split, 11/93. ① Incl. net chg. of $5.3 mill. & bef. the cumulative effect of acctg. chg. ② Incl. after-tax chgs. in connection with restruc. activ. of $62.6 mill. ($0.52/sh), 1996; $14.1 mill. ($0.12/sh), 1995. ③ Excl. $275.4 mill. after-tax extraord. chg. rel. to write-off by West Penn Power in connection with the deregul. in PA. ④ Excl. $27.0 mill. extra chgs., $11.8 mill. merger-related chgs. & a $10.0 mill. chg. for Davis pumped-storage generation project costs. ⑤ Excl. $77.0 mill. extraord. chg. ⑥ Excl. $31.1 mill. acctg. chg. ⑦ Revs. benefited fr. acqs. and addition of generating capacity.

OFFICERS:
A. J. Noia, Chmn., Pres., C.E.O.
B. W. Walenczyk, Sr. V.P., C.F.O.
R. F. Binder, V.P., Treas.
INVESTOR CONTACT: Gregory L. Fries, Investor Relations, (301) 665-2713
PRINCIPAL OFFICE: 10435 Downsville Pike, Hagerstown, MD 21740-1766

TELEPHONE NUMBER: (301) 790-3400
FAX: (301) 665-2746
WEB: www.alleghenyenergy.com
NO. OF EMPLOYEES: 5,600 (avg.)
SHAREHOLDERS: 37,644
ANNUAL MEETING: In May
INCORPORATED: MD, Dec., 1925

INSTITUTIONAL HOLDINGS:
No. of Institutions: 259
Shares Held: 56,090,213
% Held: 44.6

INDUSTRY: Electric services (SIC: 4911)

TRANSFER AGENT(S): Mellon Investor Services, LLC, Ridgefield Park, NJ

ALLEGHENY TECHNOLOGIES INCORPORATED

EXCH.	SYM.	REC. PRICE	P/E RATIO	YLD.	MKT. CAP.	RANGE (52-WK.)	'02 Y/E PR.
NYSE	ATI	2.99 (2/28/03)	...	8.0%	$240.1 mill.	19.10 - 2.75	6.23

SPECULATIVE GRADE. OPERATING RESULTS WERE NEGATIVELY AFFECTED BY CHALLENGING CONDITIOONS IN MOST OF THE COMPANY'S MARKETS.

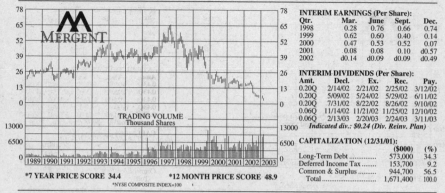

*7 YEAR PRICE SCORE 34.4   ***12 MONTH PRICE SCORE 48.9**

*NYSE COMPOSITE INDEX=100

INTERIM EARNINGS (Per Share):

Qtr.	Mar.	June	Sept.	Dec.
1998	0.28	0.76	0.66	0.74
1999	0.62	0.60	0.40	0.14
2000	0.47	0.53	0.52	0.07
2001	0.08	0.08	0.10	d0.57
2002	d0.14	d0.09	d0.09	d0.49

INTERIM DIVIDENDS (Per Share):

Amt.	Decl.	Ex.	Rec.	Pay.
0.20Q	2/14/02	2/21/02	2/25/02	3/12/02
0.20Q	5/09/02	5/24/02	5/29/02	6/11/02
0.20Q	7/31/02	8/22/02	8/26/02	9/10/02
0.06Q	11/14/02	11/21/02	11/25/02	12/10/02
0.06Q	2/13/03	2/20/03	2/24/03	3/11/03

Indicated div.: $0.24 (Div. Reinv. Plan)

CAPITALIZATION (12/31/01):

	($000)	(%)
Long-Term Debt	573,000	34.3
Deferred Income Tax	153,700	9.2
Common & Surplus	944,700	56.5
Total	1,671,400	100.0

BUSINESS:

Allegheny Technologies Incorporated (formerly Allegheny Teledyne Inc.) is a diversified producer of specialty materials including nickel-based and cobalt-based alloys and superalloys, titanium and titanium alloys, specialty steels, super stainless steel, exotic alloys, which include zirconium, hafium and niobium, tungsten materials, and highly engineered strip and PRECISION ROLLED STRIP® products.

In addition, ATI produces commodity specialty materials, such as stainless steel sheet and plate, silicon and tool steels, and forgings and castings. The Company consists of Flat-Rolled Products (54.9% of 2002 sales), High Performance Metals (33.0%), and Industrial Products (12.1%). On 11/30/99, ATI completed the spin-offs of Teledyne Technologies Incorporated and Water Pik Technologies, Inc.

RECENT DEVELOPMENTS:

For the year ended 12/31/02, the Company reported a net loss of $65.8 million compared with a net loss of $25.2 million in 2001. Results for 2002 and 2001 included restructuring costs of $42.8 million and $74.2 million,

respectively. Sales declined 10.3% to $1.91 billion from $2.13 billion a year earlier, primarily due to challenging conditions in most of the Company's markets. In 2002, ATI generated $111.0 million of free cash flow.

PROSPECTS:

For 2003, the Company will focus on improving profitability in all of its business segments by enhancing its market positions, reducing costs and conserving cash. Meanwhile, a number of contracts awarded during 2002 should improve ATI's position in key markets, beginning in 2003. For instance, in the Flat-Rolled Products segment, the Company was awarded a new long-term agreement (LTA) with a manufacturer of electrical transformers representing

potentially 30,000 new tons annually of silicon electrical steel shipments. In addition, ATI's STAL PRECISION ROLLED STRIP® products operation in Shanghai, China won several new contracts in that rapidly growing market. Finally, in the High Performance Metals segment, ATI finalized a significant LTA and achieved gains with other customers for its premium nickel-based alloys, superalloys and titanium alloys products.

ANNUAL FINANCIAL DATA:

FISCAL YEAR	TOT. REVS. ($mill.)	NET INC. ($mill.)	TOT. ASSETS ($mill.)	OPER. PROFIT %	NET PROFIT %	RET. ON EQUITY %	RET. ON ASSETS %	CURR. RATIO	EARN. PER SH.$	CASH FL. PER SH.$	TANG. BK. VAL.$	DIV. PER SH.$	PRICE RANGE	AVG. P/E RATIO	AVG. YIELD %
p12/31/02	1,907.8	⑥ d65.8							⑥ d0.82			0.66	19.10 - 5.21	...	5.4
12/31/01	2,128.0	⑥ d25.2	2,643.2	...	...	...	...	2.5	⑥ d0.31	0.91	9.42	0.80	21.07 - 12.50	...	4.7
12/31/00	2,460.4	⑤ 132.5	2,776.2	9.3	5.4	12.8	4.8	2.5	⑤ 1.60	2.89	10.51	0.80	26.81 - 12.50	12.3	4.1
12/31/99	2,296.1	③ 111.0	2,750.6	8.0	4.8	9.2	4.0	1.9	③ 1.16	2.15	11.02	1.28	48.38 - 20.25	29.6	3.7
④ 12/31/98	3,923.4	① 241.2	3,175.5	10.2	6.1	18.0	7.6	2.2	① 2.44	3.53	11.12	1.28	59.13 - 28.00	17.9	2.9
12/31/97	3,745.1	② 297.6	2,604.5	11.2	7.9	29.8	11.4	2.2	② 3.34	4.44	9.52	1.28	65.75 - 42.00	16.1	2.4
12/31/96	3,815.6	① 226.5	2,606.4	8.9	5.9	26.0	8.7	2.0	① 2.56	3.79	7.96	0.32	47.50 - 34.75	16.1	0.8
12/31/95	4,048.1	① 276.8	2,628.9	10.0	6.8	35.2	10.7	2.2	① 3.12	4.38	7.16	...	46.00 - 32.75	12.6	...
12/31/94	3,457.3	9.8	...	2.0	0.3	...	...	...	0.12	1.33	...	...	49.75 - 34.00	348.7	...

Statistics are as originally reported. Adj. for stk. split: 1-for-2, 11/99. ① Excl. extraord. chrg. of an undisclosed amount, 1995; $13.5 mill. ($0.08/sh.), 1996. ② Incl. merger and restr. costs of $10.4 mill. ③ Incl. merger and restr. costs of $67.8 mill. ④ Results for 1998 and earlier are for Allegheny Teledyne Inc. prior to the spin-off of Teledyne Technologies Inc. and Water Pik Technologies, Inc. ⑤ Bef. extraord. gain $129.6 mill. and disc. oper. inc. of $59.6 mill.; 1999; incl. non-recurring chrg. of $15.0 mill.; 2000; $7.9 mill., 1999. ⑥ Incl. restruct. chrg. of $42.8 mill., 2002; $74.2 mill., 2001.

OFFICERS:
R. P. Bozzone, Chmn.
J. L. Murdy, Pres., C.E.O.
R. J. Harshman, Sr. V.P., C.F.O.

INVESTOR CONTACT: Dan L. Greenfield, (412) 394-3004

PRINCIPAL OFFICE: 1000 Six PPG Place, Pittsburgh, PA 15222-5479

TELEPHONE NUMBER: (412) 394-2800
FAX: (412) 394-2805
WEB: www.alleghenytechnologies.com
NO. OF EMPLOYEES: 10,000 (approx.)
SHAREHOLDERS: 8,077 (approx.)
ANNUAL MEETING: In May
INCORPORATED: DE, 1996

INSTITUTIONAL HOLDINGS:
No. of Institutions: 180
Shares Held: 42,570,480
% Held: 52.8
INDUSTRY: Semiconductors and related devices (SIC: 3674)
TRANSFER AGENT(S): Mellon Investor Services, Ridgefield Park, NJ

ALLERGAN, INC.

EXCH.	SYM.	REC. PRICE	P/E RATIO	YLD.	MKT. CAP.	RANGE (52-WK.)	'02 Y/E PR.
NYSE	AGN	64.20 (2/28/03)	131.0	0.6%	$8.43 bill.	69.79 - 49.05	57.62

UPPER MEDIUM GRADE. IN 2003, THE COMPANY EXPECTS SALES TO RANGE FROM $1.61 BILLION TO $1.69 BILLION AND DILUTED EARNINGS PER SHARE TO BE IN THE RANGE OF $2.29 TO $2.31.

INTERIM EARNINGS (Per Share):

Qtr.	Mar.	June	Sept.	Dec.
1998	d0.94	0.26	d0.24	0.22
1999	0.26	0.35	0.35	0.44
2000	0.33	0.39	0.41	0.48
2001	0.40	0.16	0.50	0.63
2002	0.33	0.03	d0.28	0.49

INTERIM DIVIDENDS (Per Share):

Amt.	Decl.	Ex.	Rec.	Pay.
0.09Q	1/22/02	2/13/02	2/15/02	3/14/02
0.09Q	4/25/02	5/15/02	5/17/02	6/13/02
0.09Q	7/24/02	8/20/02	8/22/02	9/19/02
0.09Q	10/24/02	11/12/02	11/14/02	12/12/02
0.09Q	1/31/03	2/14/03	2/19/03	3/20/03

Indicated div.: $0.36 (Div. Reinv. Plan)

CAPITALIZATION (12/31/01):

	($000)	(%)
Long-Term Debt	520,600	34.7
Minority Interest	1,200	0.1
Common & Surplus	977,400	65.2
Total	1,499,200	100.0

*7 YEAR PRICE SCORE 135.7   *12 MONTH PRICE SCORE 109.1

*NYSE COMPOSITE INDEX=100

BUSINESS:

Allergan, Inc. is an international provider of specialty therapeutic products principally in the areas of eye and skin care. The specialty pharmaceutical division's eye-care segment develops, manufactures and markets a broad range of prescription ophthalmic products designed to treat diseases and disorders of the eye, including glaucoma, inflammation, infection, allergy and ophthalmic muscle disorders. The skin-care segment markets a line of skin-care products primarily to dermatologists in the United States. The surgical division markets intraocular lenses, surgically related pharmaceuticals, and other ophthalmic surgical products. On 7/1/02, AGN spun-off Advanced Medical Optics, Inc.

RECENT DEVELOPMENTS:

For the year ended 12/31/02, income was $64.0 million, before a gain of $11.2 million from discontinued operations, compared with income of $171.2 million, before an accounting change charge of $1.2 million and gain of $54.9 million from discontinued operations, the previous year. Results for 2002 included a pre-tax legal settlement of $118.7 million, a pre-tax restructuring charge and asset write-off of $62.4 million, a loss of $30.2 million on investments and a $1.7 million unrealized loss on derivative instruments. Results for 2001 included pre-tax net nonrecurring gain of $700,000. Net sales advanced 21.3% to $1.39 billion from $1.14 billion the year before.

PROSPECTS:

In 2003, the Company expects sales to range from $1.61 billion to $1.69 billion and diluted earnings per share to be in the range of $2.29 to $2.31, reflecting revenue growth in the mid-to-high teens and diluted earnings per share growth between 22.0% and 25.0%. Separately, the Company announced that it has completed two Phase III trials of an oral formulation of tazarotene, investigating its use in the treatment of moderate to severe psoriasis. Meanwhile, AGN received FDA approval for RESTASIS™, a therapy for patients with chronic dry eye disease.

ANNUAL FINANCIAL DATA:

FISCAL YEAR	TOT. REVS. ($mill.)	NET INC. ($mill.)	TOT. ASSETS ($mill.)	OPER. PROFIT %	NET PROFIT %	RET. ON EQUITY %	RET. ON ASSETS %	CURR. RATIO	EARN. PER SH. $	CASH FL. PER SH. $	TANG. BK. VAL. $	DIV. PER SH. $	PRICE RANGE	AVG. P/E RATIO	AVG. YIELD %
p12/31/02	1,385.0	⑨ 64.0							⑨ 0.49			0.36	75.10 - 49.05	126.7	0.6
12/31/01	1,745.5	⑦⑧ 226.7	2,046.2	18.4	13.0	23.2	11.1	2.7	⑦⑧ 1.69	2.27	6.48	0.36	99.38 - 59.00	46.9	0.5
12/31/00	1,625.5	⑦ 215.1	1,971.0	18.2	13.2	24.6	10.9	3.1	⑦ 1.61	2.26	5.62	0.32	101.13 - 44.50	45.2	0.4
12/31/99	1,452.4	⑥ 188.2	1,339.1	18.1	13.0	29.7	14.1	1.7	⑥ 1.39	2.00	3.73	0.28	57.81 - 31.69	32.2	0.6
12/31/98	1,296.1	⑤ d90.2	1,334.4	...	...	...	...	1.8	⑤ d0.69	d0.03	3.98	0.26	33.25 - 15.88	...	1.1
12/31/97	1,149.0	④ 128.3	1,398.9	13.0	11.2	15.2	9.2	1.8	④ 0.98	1.58	4.81	0.26	18.59 - 12.94	16.2	1.6
12/31/96	1,156.9	③ 77.1	1,349.8	9.6	6.7	10.3	5.7	1.6	③ 0.59	1.21	3.90	0.24	21.00 - 15.00	30.5	1.4
12/31/95	1,067.2	② 72.5	1,316.3	11.4	6.8	10.8	5.5	1.6	② 0.56	1.09	3.05	0.23	16.88 - 12.88	26.6	1.6
12/31/94	947.2	110.7	1,059.8	16.5	11.7	18.3	10.4	1.5	0.87	1.32	3.98	0.21	15.44 - 10.00	14.7	1.7
12/31/93	858.9	① 104.5	939.8	16.8	12.2	20.3	11.1	1.6	① 0.79	1.14	3.10	0.20	13.19 - 10.38	14.9	1.7

Statistics are as originally reported. Adjusted for a 2-for-1 stock split 12/99. ① Bef. inc. fr. disc. opers of $4.4 mill. ② Incl. an unusual exp. of $50.0 mill. ③ Incl. a restruct. charge of $70.1 mill. & asset write-offs of $7.4 mill. ④ Incl. an inven. adj. chg. of approx. $14.0 mill. & a one-time gain of $9.5 mill. fr. the sale of product rights. ⑤ Incl. a pre-tax chrgs. totaling $315.7 mill. ⑥ Incl. a pre-tax restr. gain of $9.6 mill., a pre-tax asset write-off gain of $1.4 mill., a net gain on invests. of $14.0 mill., & a pre-tax chg. of $6.9 mill. for a contrib. to the AGN Foundation. ⑦ Incl. a pre-tax restr. rever. chrg. $2.0 mill., 2000; $1.7 mill., 2001; net gain/(loss) on invest., $1.0 mill., 2000; ($5.2) mill., 2001. ⑧ Bef. acctg. chrg. of $1.8 mill. & incl. unreal. gain of $5.9 mill. on deriv. instruments. ⑨ Bef. inc. of $11.2 mill. from disc. ops. & incl. net non-recurr. chrgs. of $149.2 mill.

OFFICERS:
D. E. Pyott, Chmn., Pres., C.E.O.
H. W. Boyer Ph.D., Vice-Chmn.
E. K. Brandt, Corp. V.P., C.F.O.
INVESTOR CONTACT: Jim Hindman, Investor Relations, (714) 246-4636
PRINCIPAL OFFICE: 2525 Dupont Drive, P.O. Box 19534, Irvine, CA 92612

TELEPHONE NUMBER: (714) 246-4500
FAX: (714) 246-6987
WEB: www.allergan.com
NO. OF EMPLOYEES: 6,436 (approx.)
SHAREHOLDERS: 7,500 (approx.)
ANNUAL MEETING: In Apr.
INCORPORATED: CA, 1948; reincorp., DE, 1977

INSTITUTIONAL HOLDINGS:
No. of Institutions: 347
Shares Held: 127,415,890
% Held: 98.4
INDUSTRY: Pharmaceutical preparations (SIC: 2834)
TRANSFER AGENT(S): EquiServe Trust Company, N.A., Jersey City, NJ

ALLETE, INC.

EXCH.	SYM.	REC. PRICE	P/E RATIO	YLD.	MKT. CAP.	RANGE (52-WK.)	'02 Y/E PR.
NYSE	ALE	19.38 (2/28/03)	13.4	5.8%	$1.66 bill.	31.10 - 18.50	22.68

UPPER MEDIUM GRADE. ALE IS CONSIDERING A BROADER RANGE OF STRATEGIC OPTIONS WITH RESPECT TO ITS WATER SERVICES BUSINESS.

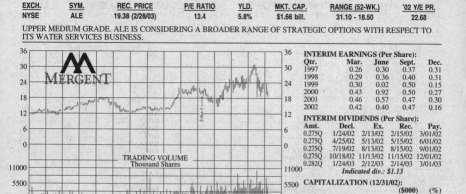

INTERIM EARNINGS (Per Share):

Qtr.	Mar.	June	Sept.	Dec.
1997	0.26	0.30	0.37	0.31
1998	0.29	0.36	0.40	0.31
1999	0.30	0.02	0.50	0.15
2000	0.43	0.92	0.50	0.27
2001	0.46	0.57	0.47	0.30
2002	0.42	0.40	0.47	0.16

INTERIM DIVIDENDS (Per Share):

Amt.	Decl.	Ex.	Rec.	Pay.
0.275Q	1/24/02	2/13/02	2/15/02	3/01/02
0.275Q	4/25/02	5/13/02	5/15/02	6/01/02
0.275Q	7/19/02	8/13/02	8/15/02	9/01/02
0.275Q	10/18/02	11/13/02	11/15/02	12/01/02
0.282Q	1/24/03	2/12/03	2/14/03	3/01/03

Indicated div.: $1.13

TRADING VOLUME
Thousand Shares

*7 YEAR PRICE SCORE 127.8   *12 MONTH PRICE SCORE 91.6

*NYSE COMPOSITE INDEX=100

CAPITALIZATION (12/31/02):

	($000)	(%)
Long-Term Debt	661,300	32.5
Deferred Income Tax	139,800	6.9
Common & Surplus	1,232,400	60.6
Total	2,033,500	100.0

BUSINESS:

ALLETE, Inc. (formerly Minnesota Power, Inc.) operates in three business segments: Electric Services, which include electric and gas services, coal mining and telecommunications; Automotive Services, which include a network of vehicle auctions, a finance company, an auto transport company, a vehicle remarketing company, a company that provides field information services and a company that provides Internet-based parts location and insurance adjustment audit services; and Investments, which includes real estate operations, investments in emerging technologies related to the electric utility industry and a securities portfolio. Revenues for 2002 were derived: 41.8% energy services; 56.0% automotive services; and 2.2% investments.

RECENT DEVELOPMENTS:

For the year ended 12/31/02, ALE reported income of $119.0 million, before income from discontinued operations of $18.2 million, versus income of $130.3 million, before income from discontinued operations of $8.4 million, the previous year. Results for 2002 included a one-time non-cash charge of $5.5 million related to an indefinite delay of a generation project. On a segment basis, income from energy services dropped 19.1% to $41.8 million, primarily due to weak wholesale power prices. Income from automotive services grew 24.2% to $92.9 million. Loss from investments was $15.7 million versus income of $3.8 million the year before.

PROSPECTS:

During 2002, ALE simplified its structure by exiting non-strategic businesses and liquidating its trading securities portfolio. In doing so, ALE strengthened its balance sheet and is focusing on its core businesses, energy and automotive services. Separately, on 3/7/03, ALE announced that a court decision will likely delay the sale of assets of its water services business, Florida Water Services Corporation, to the Florida Water Services Authority. Due to the court's decision, ALE will consider a broader range of strategic options with respect to its water services business, including possible transactions with other buyers. Meanwhile, ALE announced it is undertaking a strategic evaluation of separating its energy and automotive businesses into independent companies.

ANNUAL FINANCIAL DATA:

FISCAL YEAR	TOT. REVS. ($mill.)	NET INC. ($mill.)	TOT. ASSETS ($mill.)	OPER. PROFIT %	NET PROFIT %	RET. ON EQUITY %	RET. ON ASSETS %	CURR. RATIO	EARN. PER SH.$	CASH FL.PER SH.$	TANG. BK. VAL.$	DIV. PER SH.$	PRICE RANGE	AVG. P/E RATIO	AVG. YIELD %
12/31/02	1,506.9	⑤ 119.0	3,147.2	13.1	7.9	9.7	3.8	0.9	⑤ 1.46	2.46	8.09	1.10	31.10 - 18.50	17.0	4.4
12/31/01	1,527.7	② 128.6	3,282.5	13.6	8.4	11.2	3.9	1.3	② 1.68	3.01	7.74	1.07	26.89 - 20.19	14.0	4.5
12/31/00	1,331.9	④ 148.6	2,914.0	14.3	11.2	16.5	5.1	1.0	④ 2.11	3.36	5.73	1.07	25.50 - 14.75	9.5	5.3
12/31/99	1,131.8	③ 68.0	2,312.6	14.7	6.0	8.3	2.9	1.4	③ 0.97	2.09	8.50	1.07	22.09 - 16.00	19.6	5.6
12/31/98	1,039.7	88.5	2,317.1	12.9	8.5	3.7	3.8	1.4	1.35	2.52	30.11	1.02	23.13 - 19.03	15.7	4.8
12/31/97	953.6	77.6	2,188.9	12.1	8.1	3.7	3.5	1.1	1.24	2.39	28.76	1.02	22.00 - 13.50	14.4	5.7
12/31/96	846.9	69.2	2,146.0	9.7	8.2	3.4	3.2	1.0	1.14	2.25	28.13	1.02	18.48 - 13.00	12.2	7.3
12/31/95	672.9	① 61.9	1,947.6	8.7	9.2	3.3	3.2	1.0	① 1.03	2.08	27.38	1.02	14.63 - 12.13	13.0	7.6
12/31/94	637.8	61.3	1,807.8	12.2	9.6	3.4	3.4	1.5	1.03	1.99	28.37	1.01	16.50 - 12.38	14.0	7.0
12/31/93	505.5	① 62.6	1,760.5	15.3	12.4	3.5	3.6	1.9	① 1.10	2.25	28.36	0.99	18.25 - 15.00	15.1	6.0

Statistics are as originally reported. Adj. for stk. splits: 2-for-1, 3/99 ① Bef. extraord. gain $4.8 mill. ② Bef. disc. opers. gain $10.1 mill., 12/01; $2.8 mill., 12/95 ③ Incl. $24.1 mill. non-cash chrg. associated with the final valuation of the acquisition of Capital Re by Ace Limited, which was completed 12/30/99. ④ Incl. income from investment and related disposition of $49.0 mill. ⑤ Bef. inc. fr. disc. opers. of $18.2 mill.; Incl. one-time non-cash chrg. of $5.5 mill.

OFFICERS:
D. G. Gartzke, Chmn., Pres., C.E.O.
J. K. Vizanko, V.P., C.F.O., Treas.
P. R. Halverson, V.P., Sec., Gen. Couns.
INVESTOR CONTACT: Timothy J. Thorp, Dir. Inv. Rel., (218) 723-3953
PRINCIPAL OFFICE: 30 West Superior Street, Duluth, MN 55802-2093

TELEPHONE NUMBER: (218) 279-5000
FAX: (218) 720-2502
WEB: www.mnpower.com
NO. OF EMPLOYEES: 14,000 (approx.)
SHAREHOLDERS: 39,000 (approx.)
ANNUAL MEETING: In May
INCORPORATED: MN, 1906

INSTITUTIONAL HOLDINGS:
No. of Institutions: 190
Shares Held: 32,039,477
% Held: 37.5
INDUSTRY: Electric and other services combined (SIC: 4931)
TRANSFER AGENT(S): Company and Wells Fargo Bank, South St. Paul, MN

ALLIANT ENERGY CORPORATION

EXCH.	SYM.	REC. PRICE	P/E RATIO	YLD.	MKT. CAP.	RANGE (52-WK.)	'02 Y/E PR.
NYSE	LNT	15.76 (2/28/03)	19.0	6.3%	$1.41 bill.	30.85 - 14.28	16.55

LOWER MEDIUM GRADE. THE COMPANY PLANS TO FOCUS ON STRENGTHENING ITS FINANCIAL POSITION.

*7 YEAR PRICE SCORE 79.5   *12 MONTH PRICE SCORE 84.4

*NYSE COMPOSITE INDEX=100

INTERIM EARNINGS (Per Share):

Qtr.	Mar.	June	Sept.	Dec.
1998	0.51	d0.12	0.67	0.38
1999	0.54	0.49	0.91	0.57
2000	0.24	0.54	3.28	0.77
2001	0.28	0.48	0.87	0.66
2002	------------------- 0.84 -------------------			

INTERIM DIVIDENDS (Per Share):

Amt.	Decl.	Ex.	Rec.	Pay.
0.50Q	1/23/02	1/29/02	1/31/02	2/15/02
0.50Q	4/09/02	4/26/02	4/30/02	5/15/02
0.50Q	7/12/02	7/29/02	7/31/02	8/15/02
0.50Q	10/16/02	10/29/02	10/31/02	11/15/02
0.25Q	1/22/03	1/29/03	1/31/03	2/15/03

Indicated div.: $1.00 (Div. Reinv. Plan)

CAPITALIZATION (12/31/01):

	($000)	(%)
Long-Term Debt	2,457,941	47.6
Deferred Income Tax	632,472	12.2
Minority Interest	43,378	0.8
Preferred Stock	113,953	2.2
Common & Surplus	1,918,341	37.1
Total	5,166,085	100.0

BUSINESS:

Alliant Energy Corporation was formed as the result of a three-way merger involving IES Industries Inc., Interstate Power Company and WPL Holdings, Inc. in April 1998. LNT is a diversified holding company for its regulated domestic utilities (82.3% of 2002 revenues), Wisconsin Power and Light Co. (WP&L) and Interstate Power and Light Co. (IP&L), and its non-regulated businesses (17.7%) is

held by Alliant Energy Resources, Inc. LNT's subsidiaries and partners provides electric, natural gas, water, and steam to more than 3.0 million customers worldwide. LNT's non-regulated subsidiaries provide energy products and services to domestic and international markets; provide environmental, engineering and transportation services; and invest in affordable housing and other initiatives.

RECENT DEVELOPMENTS:

For the year ended 12/31/02, the Company reported income from continuing operations of $76.3 million compared with $126.2 million, before an accounting change charge of $12.9 million, in the previous year. The decrease in income was primarily the result of lower earnings from LNT's non-regulated businesses. Results for 2002 included an impairment of available for sale securities of $27.2 million. Earn-

ings for 2002 and 2001 excluded income from discontinued operations of $30.6 million and $59.0 million, respectively. Total revenues slipped 0.6% to $2.61 billion from $2.62 billion a year earlier. Electric utility revenues dipped 0.2% to $1.75 billion, while gas utility revenues dropped 19.2% to $394.0 million. Non-regulated and other revenues advanced 21.6% to $462.3 million.

PROSPECTS:

For 2003, LNT expects earnings in the range of $1.65 to $1.90 per diluted share, before one-time and non-cash charges. The Company expects to pursue the sale of certain non-core businesses in 2003, including its Whiting oil and gas, Australian, affordable housing and several other businesses. As a result of these transactions, LNT expects to

reduce outstanding debt by approximately $800.0 million to $1.00 billion. In addition, LNT has reduced its dividend and expects lower capital spending levels in 2003. Moreover, LNT plans to raise between $200.0 million and $300.0 million of common equity in the coming year.

ANNUAL FINANCIAL DATA:

FISCAL YEAR	TOT. REVS. ($mill.)	NET INC. ($mill.)	TOT. ASSETS ($mill.)	OPER. PROFIT %	NET PROFIT %	NET INC./ NET PROP. %	NET INC./ TOT. CAP. %	RET. ON EQUITY %	ACCUM. DEPR./ GROSS PROP. %	EARN. PER SH.$	TANG. BK. VAL.$	DIV. PER SH.$	DIV. PAYOUT %	PRICE RANGE	AVG. P/E RATIO	AVG. YIELD
p12/31/02	2,608.8	⑥ 76.3								⑥ 0.84		2.00	238.1	31.01 - 14.28	27.0	8.8
12/31/01	2,777.3	⑤ 185.2	6,247.7	13.3	6.7	6.1	3.6	9.1	53.1	⑤ 2.30	21.39	2.00	87.0	33.20 - 27.50	13.2	6.6
12/31/00	2,405.0	④ 382.0	6,733.8	15.8	15.9	10.3	7.6	17.8	51.7	④ 4.82	25.79	2.00	41.5	37.75 - 25.75	6.6	6.3
12/31/99	2,198.0	196.6	6,075.7	17.1	8.9	5.6	4.1	8.7	50.0	③ 2.51	27.29	2.00	79.7	32.38 - 25.19	11.5	6.9
② 12/31/98	2,130.9	96.7	4,959.3	13.3	4.5	2.8	2.4	5.6	48.3	1.26	20.69	2.00	158.7	35.38 - 28.00	25.1	6.3
12/31/97	919.3	61.3	1,861.8	14.0	6.7	4.5	4.4	9.2	46.5	1.99	19.73	2.00	100.5	34.44 - 26.75	15.4	6.5
12/31/96	932.8	① 73.2	1,900.5	15.2	7.8	5.3	5.7	11.0	44.2	① 2.38	19.74	1.97	82.8	32.88 - 27.50	12.7	6.5
12/31/95	807.3	① 71.6	1,872.4	18.1	8.9	5.3	5.4	10.9	42.7	① 2.33	19.41	1.94	83.3	31.75 - 27.25	12.7	6.6
12/31/94	816.2	65.3	1,805.9	15.9	8.0	4.7	4.9	9.9	39.3	2.13	19.43	1.92	90.1	32.88 - 26.38	13.9	6.5
12/31/93	773.1	62.5	1,761.5	16.3	8.1	4.7	4.9	9.7	37.1	2.11	19.15	1.90	90.0	36.75 - 31.25	16.1	5.6

Statistics are as originally reported. Financial data reflects WPL Holdings, Inc. prior to the 1998 merger. ① Bef. disc oper. loss $1.3 mill., 12/96; $13.2 mill., 12/95. ② Reflects the consumation of the merger on 4/21/98. ③ Incl. gains totaling $50.3 mill. ④ Bef. net acctg. credit of $16.7 mill. & incl. non-cash gain of $204.0 mill. ⑤ Bef. acctg. change chrg. of $12.9 mill. ⑥ Bef. disc. opers. of $30.6 mill.; incl. impair. chrg. of $27.2 mill.

OFFICERS:
E. B. Davis Jr., Chmn., Pres., C.E.O.
L. Liu, Vice-Chmn.
T. M. Walker, Exec. V.P., C.F.O.
INVESTOR CONTACT: Eric Mott, Investor Relations, (608) 458-3391
PRINCIPAL OFFICE: 4902 N. Biltmore Lane, Madison, WI 53718-2132

TELEPHONE NUMBER: (608) 458-3311
FAX: (608) 458-4824
WEB: www.alliantenergy.com
NO. OF EMPLOYEES: 8,585 (avg.)
SHAREHOLDERS: 58,288 (approx.)
ANNUAL MEETING: In May
INCORPORATED: WI, April, 1981

INSTITUTIONAL HOLDINGS:
No. of Institutions: 196
Shares Held: 22,862,416
% Held: 24.9
INDUSTRY: Electric and other services combined (SIC: 4931)
TRANSFER AGENT(S): The Company

ALLIANT TECHSYSTEMS INC.

EXCH.	SYM.	REC. PRICE	P/E RATIO	YLD.	MKT. CAP.	RANGE (52-WK.)	'02 Y/E PR.
NYSE	ATK	48.30 (2/28/03)	15.7	...	$1.57 bill.	76.94 - 47.40	62.35

MEDIUM GRADE. THE COMPANY ANTICIPATES REVENUE OF ABOUT $2.14 BILLION AND EARNINGS FROM CONTINUING OPERATIONS OF $3.26 PER SHARE IN FISCAL 2003.

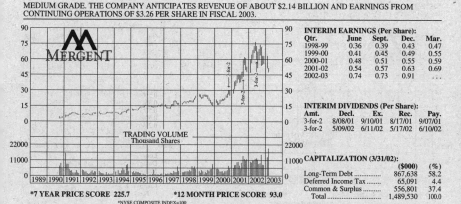

*7 YEAR PRICE SCORE 225.7   ***12 MONTH PRICE SCORE 93.0**
*NYSE COMPOSITE INDEX=100

INTERIM EARNINGS (Per Share):

Qtr.	June	Sept.	Dec.	Mar.
1998-99	0.36	0.39	0.43	0.47
1999-00	0.41	0.45	0.49	0.55
2000-01	0.48	0.51	0.55	0.59
2001-02	0.54	0.57	0.63	0.69
2002-03	0.74	0.73	0.91	...

INTERIM DIVIDENDS (Per Share):

Amt.	Decl.	Ex.	Rec.	Pay.
3-for-2	8/08/01	9/10/01	8/17/01	9/07/01
3-for-2	5/09/02	6/11/02	5/17/02	6/10/02

CAPITALIZATION (3/31/02):

	($000)	(%)
Long-Term Debt	867,638	58.2
Deferred Income Tax	65,091	4.4
Common & Surplus	556,801	37.4
Total	1,489,530	100.0

BUSINESS:

Alliant Techsystems Inc. is an aerospace and defense company operating in two business segments. The Company's Aerospace segment (57.9% of fiscal 2002 revenues) designs, develops and manufactures solid rocket propulsion systems for space, strategic, and tactical applications and composite structures for military and commercial aircraft, space launch vehicles, satellites, spacecraft, and weapons systems. The Defense segment (42.1%) designs, develops and manufactures ammunition, munitions propellants, commercial gunpowder, anti-tank systems, tactical barrier systems, precision-guided munitions, electronic warfare systems, infantry weapon systems, electro-mechanical and electronic fuses and proximity sensors, lithium batteries for military and aerospace applications, reloading equipment and other gun care products and accessories.

RECENT DEVELOPMENTS:

For the three months ended 12/29/02, the Company reported income of $35.9 million, before a $202,000 extraordinary charge and a $63,000 gain from an accounting change, versus income of $22.0 million, before a $383,000 extraordinary charge, in the corresponding prior-year period. Sales climbed 12.0% to $519.8 million from $464.1 million a year earlier, driven by acquisitions completed in 2002 and higher sales of military, small-caliber ammunition. Gross profit was $118.5 million, or 22.8% of sales, versus $97.3 million, or 21.0% of sales, in 2001.

PROSPECTS:

Near-term results are not expected to be hurt by the suspension of space shuttle launches following the loss of the Columbia during re-entry on 2/1/03. However, the long-term impact remains uncertain until the cause of the accident is determined. Production of the reusable solid rocket motors used to launch the space shuttle accounts for 15.0% to 20.0% of ATK's sales. Separately, the Company anticipates revenue of about $2.14 billion in fiscal 2003, and earnings from continuing operations of approximately $3.26 per share. For fiscal 2004, ATK is targeting sales growth in the mid-single digits and earnings from continuing operations of about $3.60 per share.

ANNUAL FINANCIAL DATA:

FISCAL YEAR	TOT. REVS. ($mil.)	NET INC. ($mil.)	TOT. ASSETS ($mil.)	OPER. PROFIT %	NET PROFIT %	RET. ON EQUITY %	RET. ON ASSETS %	CURR. RATIO	EARN. PER SH.$	CASH FL. PER SH.$	TANG. BK. VAL.$	PRICE RANGE	AVG. P/E RATIO
3/31/02	1,801.6	⑤ 86.1	2,211.3	12.4	4.8	15.5	3.9	1.8	⑤ 2.45	4.68	...	62.27 — 26.95	18.2
3/31/01	1,141.9	67.9	879.5	11.9	5.9	34.2	7.7	1.1	2.13	3.54	2.55	30.34 — 15.76	10.8
3/31/00	1,077.5	③ 64.5	906.0	11.2	6.0	56.1	7.1	1.0	③ 1.89	3.28	...	26.08 — 15.11	10.9
3/31/99	1,090.4	④ 67.6	894.3	9.5	6.2	57.0	7.6	1.2	④ 1.64	2.75	...	24.61 — 16.30	12.5
3/31/98	1,075.5	③ 68.0	1,027.4	8.6	6.3	18.8	6.6	1.3	③ 1.51	2.56	5.29	20.45 — 12.00	10.8
3/31/97	1,089.4	36.7	1,009.7	6.5	3.4	16.8	3.6	1.3	③ 0.81	1.98	2.16	17.00 — 12.96	18.5
3/31/96	1,020.6	③ 48.4	1,035.1	9.7	4.7	30.7	4.7	1.1	③ 1.07	2.36	0.74	15.71 — 10.33	12.2
3/31/95	789.1	② d72.6	1,051.8	...	...	...	...	...	② d2.14	d1.40	2.61	12.04 — 6.45	...
3/31/94	775.3	32.5	438.2	5.1	4.2	35.3	7.4	1.1	0.95	1.64	2.21	9.19 — 6.52	8.3
3/31/93	1,005.3	① d45.2	457.2	...	...	...	...	1.5	① d1.39	d0.56	2.00	8.48 — 5.67	...

Statistics are as originally reported. Adj. for stk. splits: 3-for-2, 6/02, 9/01 & 11/00. ① Bef. $37.8 mil loss fr. disc. opers. and $31.2 mil acctg. chrg., incl. $119.9 mil restr. chrg. ② Bef. $1.5 mil acctg. chrg. & incl. $77.6 mil non-recurr. chrgs. ③ Bef. $9.5 mil gain fr. disc. opers., 2000; $225,000 gain fr. disc. opers., 1998; $22.5 mil gain fr. disc. opers., 1997; $623,000 loss fr. disc. opers., 1996. ④ Bef. $16.8 mil extraord. chrg. ⑤ Bef. $4.7 mil loss fr. disc. opers. and $12.1 mil extraord. chrg.

OFFICERS:
P. D. Miller, Chmn., C.E.O.
P. A. Ross, Pres.
N. G. Vlahakis, Sr. V.P., C.O.O.
E. S. Rangen, V.P., C.F.O.
INVESTOR CONTACT: Steve Wold, Director, Investor Relations, (952) 351-3056
PRINCIPAL OFFICE: 5050 Lincoln Drive, Edina, MN 55436-1097

TELEPHONE NUMBER: (952) 351-3000
FAX: (952) 351-3009
WEB: www.atk.com
NO. OF EMPLOYEES: 11,600 (approx.)
SHAREHOLDERS: 9,972
ANNUAL MEETING: In Aug.
INCORPORATED: DE, May, 1990

INSTITUTIONAL HOLDINGS:
No. of Institutions: 265
Shares Held: 30,507,671
% Held: 79.9

INDUSTRY: Small arms (SIC: 3484)

TRANSFER AGENT(S): Mellon Investor Services, Ridgefield Park, NJ

ALLIED CAPITAL CORPORATION

EXCH.	SYM.	REC. PRICE	P/E RATIO	YLD.	MKT. CAP.	RANGE (52-WK.)	'02 Y/E PR.
NYSE	ALD	20.05 (2/28/03)	10.5	11.4%	$2.00 bill.	29.00 - 16.90	21.83

MEDIUM GRADE. DURING THE FOURTH QUARTER OF 2002, THE COMPANY INVESTED A TOTAL OF $78.7 MILLION IN ITS PRIVATE FINANCE PORTFOLIO.

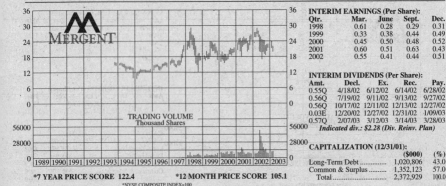

INTERIM EARNINGS (Per Share):

Qtr.	Mar.	June	Sept.	Dec.
1998	0.61	0.28	0.29	0.31
1999	0.33	0.38	0.44	0.49
2000	0.45	0.50	0.48	0.52
2001	0.60	0.51	0.63	0.43
2002	0.55	0.41	0.44	0.51

INTERIM DIVIDENDS (Per Share):

Amt.	Decl.	Ex.	Rec.	Pay.
0.55Q	4/18/02	6/12/02	6/14/02	6/28/02
0.56Q	7/19/02	9/11/02	9/13/02	9/27/02
0.56Q	10/17/02	12/11/02	12/13/02	12/27/02
0.03E	12/20/02	12/27/02	12/31/02	1/09/03
0.57Q	2/07/03	3/12/03	3/14/03	3/28/03

Indicated div.: $2.28 (Div. Reinv. Plan)

TRADING VOLUME
Thousand Shares

CAPITALIZATION (12/31/01):

	($000)	(%)
Long-Term Debt	1,020,806	43.0
Common & Surplus	1,352,123	57.0
Total	2,372,929	100.0

*7 YEAR PRICE SCORE 122.4   *12 MONTH PRICE SCORE 105.1

*NYSE COMPOSITE INDEX=100

BUSINESS:

Allied Capital Corporation is a business development company that provides long-term investment capital to support the expansion of growing companies in a variety of industries and in diverse geographic locations. As of 12/31/02, ALD's investment portfolio totaled $2.49 billion. The Company's investment activity focuses on private finance and commercial real estate finance. Under private finance, ALD provides long-term debt and equity financing to private companies nationwide. ALD's private finance portfo-

lio includes investments in a wide variety of industries, including non-durable consumer products, business services, financial services, light industrial products, retail, education, telecommunications and broadcasting and cable. Under commercial real estate finance, ALD focuses on the investment of non-investment grade commercial mortgage-backed securities. Net sales for 2002 were derived as follows: interest and dividends, 85.2%; fees and other income, 13.9%; and premiums from loan dispositions, 0.9%.

RECENT DEVELOPMENTS:

For the year ended 12/31/02, net income increased 13.7% to $228.3 million compared with $200.7 million the year before. Results for 2002 and 2001 included net realized and unrealized gains of $44.4 million and $21.3 million, respec-

tively. Total interest and related portfolio income advanced 7.2% to $309.9 million from $289.1 million in the prior year. Interest expense grew 8.2% to $70.4 million from $65.1 million the year before.

PROSPECTS:

During January 2003, the Company completed the sale of commercial mortgage-backed securities (CMBS) bonds with a cost basis of $115.7 million, which generated $127.9 million in cash proceeds. The sale resulted in a realized capital gain of $12.2 million. During the fourth quarter of 2002, the Company invested $64.7 million in two new

CMBS transactions. As the Company generally acquires its CMBS investments at significant discounts from the face amounts of the bonds, the unamortized discount on the CMBS portfolio totaled $649.5 million at 12/31/02. Separately, ALD invested a total of $78.7 million in its private finance portfolio during the fourth quarter of 2002.

ANNUAL FINANCIAL DATA:

FISCAL YEAR	TOT. REVS. ($mill.)	NET INC. ($mill.)	TOT. ASSETS ($mill.)	OPER. PROFIT %	NET PROFIT %	RET. ON EQUITY %	RET. ON ASSETS %	CURR. RATIO	EARN. PER SH.$	CASH FL.PER SH.$	TANG. BK. VAL.$	DIV. PER SH.$	PRICE RANGE	AVG. P/E RATIO	AVG. YIELD %
p12/31/02	309.9	②228.3	2,794.3						②2.20			2.20	28.96 - 16.88	10.4	9.6
12/31/01	289.1	②200.7	2,460.7	61.9	69.4	14.8	8.2	...	②2.16	2.02	13.57	2.01	26.50 - 17.96	10.3	9.0
12/31/00	211.6	②④143.1	1,853.8	53.3	67.6	13.9	7.7	...	②④1.94	1.82	12.07	1.82	21.56 - 15.50	9.6	9.8
12/31/99	141.1	②④98.6	1,290.0	50.3	69.8	14.8	7.6	...	②④1.64	1.48	10.12	1.63	24.00 - 16.50	12.3	8.0
12/31/98	106.7	②③78.1	856.1	51.8	73.1	16.1	9.1	14.7	②③1.50	1.40	8.55	1.57	29.25 - 12.00	13.7	7.6
12/31/97	97.4	②61.3	807.8	47.3	62.9	14.6	7.6	2.6	②1.24	1.27	8.07	1.36	22.50 - 13.88	14.7	7.5
12/31/96	10.0	②12.4	68.4	62.3	123.5	29.5	18.1	0.1	②1.32	2.50	9.57	1.30	15.88 - 12.70	10.8	9.1
12/31/95	8.1	②10.5	55.5	67.5	130.3	31.9	18.9	0.2	②1.20	2.33	7.50	1.20	13.25 - 9.50	9.5	10.6
12/31/94	6.1	②9.1	37.6	80.4	150.3	27.8	24.2	0.4	②1.04	2.00	7.50	1.10	15.75 - 9.75	12.3	8.6
12/31/93	4.5	②5.3	35.0	66.1	118.5	16.0	15.1	5.6	②1.03	1.97	7.54	...	16.00 - 14.50	14.8	...

Statistics are as originally reported. ① Incl. pre-tax merger expenses of $5.2 mill. ② Incl. tot. net real. & unreal. gains of $44.4 mill., 2002; $21.3 mill., 2001; $30.4 mill., 2000; $27.5 mill., 1999; $23.6 mill., 1998; $17.9 mill., 1997; $6.3 mill., 1996; $5.3 mill., 1995; $4.5 mill., 1994; $2.7 mill., 1993. ③ Incl. a pre-tax net gain on the securitization of commercial mtge. loans of $14.8 mill. & a special charge of $7.0 mill. ④ Incl. a special charge of $6.2 mill., 2000; $6.8 mill., 1999.

OFFICERS:
W. L. Walton, Chmn., Pres., C.E.O.
P. F. Roll, C.F.O.
S. V. Sparrow, Exec. V.P., Sec.
J. M. Sweeney, C.O.O.
INVESTOR CONTACT: Suzanne V. Sparrow, Dir. of Inv. Rel., (202) 973-6326
PRINCIPAL OFFICE: 1919 Pennsylvania Avenue N.W., Washington, DC 20006

TELEPHONE NUMBER: (202) 331-1112
FAX: (202) 659-2053
WEB: www.alliedcapital.com
NO. OF EMPLOYEES: 97 (avg.)
SHAREHOLDERS: In May
ANNUAL MEETING: In May
INCORPORATED: DE, 1976; reincorp., MD, 1991

INSTITUTIONAL HOLDINGS:
No. of Institutions: 191
Shares Held: 43,460,876
% Held: 42.4
INDUSTRY: Investors, nec (SIC: 6799)
TRANSFER AGENT(S): American Stock Transfer and Trust Company, New York, NY

ALLIED WASTE INDUSTRIES, INC.

EXCH.	SYM.	REC. PRICE	P/E RATIO	YLD.	MKT. CAP.	RANGE (52-WK.)	'02 Y/E PR.
NYSE	AW	8.25 (2/28/03)	11.0	...	$1.62 bill.	14.55 - 5.54	10.00

LOWER MEDIUM GRADE. THE COMPANY EXPECTS FULL-YEAR REVENUES OF APPROXIMATELY $5.50 BILLION FOR 2003.

TRADING VOLUME
Thousand Shares

*7 YEAR PRICE SCORE 73.4   *12 MONTH PRICE SCORE 105.8
*NYSE COMPOSITE INDEX=100

INTERIM EARNINGS (Per Share):

Qtr.	Mar.	June	Sept.	Dec.
1998	0.20	d0.05	0.08	d1.50
1999	0.21	0.29	d1.84	0.08
2000	0.04	0.16	0.02	0.10
2001	d0.05	0.18	Nil	d0.07
2002	0.17	0.18	0.23	0.17

INTERIM DIVIDENDS (Per Share):

Amt.	Decl.	Ex.	Rec.	Pay.
	No dividends paid.			

CAPITALIZATION (12/31/01):

	($000)	(%)
Long-Term Debt	9,861,893	81.9
Deferred Income Tax	418,836	3.5
Preferred Stock	1,169,044	9.7
Common & Surplus	585,779	4.9
Total	12,035,552	100.0

BUSINESS:

Allied Waste Industries, Inc. is a non-hazardous, solid waste management company. The Company operates as a vertically integrated company that provides collection, recycling and disposal services for residential, commercial and industrial customers. As of 12/31/02, the Company operated 340 collection companies, 175 transfer stations, 169 active landfills, and 66 recycling facilities within 39 states. On 12/30/96, AW acquired substantially all of the non-hazardous solid waste management business conducted by Laidlaw Inc. On 8/2/99, the Company acquired Browning-Ferris Industries, Inc.

RECENT DEVELOPMENTS:

For the year ended 12/31/02, income was $225.2 million, before an extraordinary loss of $10.1 million, compared with income of $75.5 million, before an extraordinary loss of $17.0 million, in 2001. Results for 2002 included a $9.3 million gain on the divestiture of assets. Results for 2001 included goodwill amortization of $226.7 million and a $107.0 million loss on the divestiture of assets. Revenues fell 0.9% to $5.52 billion from $5.56 billion a year earlier. Operating income was $1.26 billion versus $1.10 billion the year before. Free cash flow for 2002 was $476.6 million. Debt was reduced to $8.88 billion as of 12/31/02, exceeding the year-end total debt goal of $8.95 billion.

PROSPECTS:

For 2003, the Company expects full-year revenues of approximately $5.50 billion, while earnings before interest, taxes, depreciation and amortization are expected to be about $1.78 billion. This outlook is based on the assumption that economic conditions in 2003 will be similar to those in 2002. Additionally, the Company expects capital expenditures of approximately $520.0 million and free cash flow of $380.0 million in the coming year. Moreover, cash for debt repayment is anticipated to be about $420.0 million in 2003.

ANNUAL FINANCIAL DATA:

FISCAL YEAR	TOT. REVS. ($mill.)	NET INC. ($mill.)	TOT. ASSETS ($mill.)	OPER. PROFIT %	NET PROFIT %	RET. ON EQUITY %	RET. ON ASSETS %	CURR. RATIO	EARN. PER SH. $	CASH FL. PER SH. $	TANG. BK. VAL. $	PRICE RANGE	AVG. P/E RATIO
p12/31/02	5,517.3	⑦225.2							⑦0.76			14.55 - 5.54	13.2
12/31/01	5,565.3	⑥75.5	14,347.1	19.8	1.4	12.9	0.5	0.8	⑥0.01	3.57	...	19.90 - 8.90	N.M.
12/31/00	5,707.5	⑤137.7	14,155.0	21.2	2.4	7.8	1.0	0.8	⑤0.36	3.89	...	14.75 - 5.31	27.9
④12/31/99	3,341.1	③d221.2	14,963.1	5.6	...	...	...	0.9	③d1.33	0.72	...	24.06 - 6.50	...
12/31/98	1,575.6	①②d98.3	3,752.6	1.9	...	...	...	1.1	①②d0.54	0.45	5.04	31.63 - 16.13	...
12/31/97	875.0	①53.6	2,448.7	20.8	6.1	9.0	2.2	0.8	①0.57	1.78	...	24.38 - 7.25	27.7
12/31/96	246.7	①d66.0	2,317.5	...	...	...	...	1.0	①d1.15	d0.61	...	10.38 - 6.44	...
12/31/95	169.9	11.6	458.7	17.9	6.8	8.5	2.5	0.6	0.17	0.89	1.19	10.00 - 3.75	40.4
12/31/94	97.4	①d5.1	315.0	4.6	...	...	...	0.8	①d0.66	0.23	0.62	6.00 - 3.25	...
12/31/93	54.4	1.3	153.2	15.7	2.4	2.0	0.9	1.3	0.04	0.56	2.72	6.88 - 4.00	135.6

Statistics are as originally reported. ① Bef. extraord. chrg. 12/31/98: $124.8 mill.; 12/31/97: $53.2 mill.; 12/31/96: $13.4 mill.; 12/31/94: $3.1 mill. ② Incl. acq.-rel. and unusual chgs. of $247.9 million and asset impairment chg. of $69.7 million. ③ Excl. extraord. loss of $3.2 mill. and acctg. charge of $64.3 mill.; incl. acq. related costs and unusual costs of $588.9 mill. ④ Incl. the Browning-Ferris Industries, Inc. acquisition. ⑤ Incl. acq.-rel. and unusual chgs. of $127.5 mill. & excl. extraord. loss of $13.3 mill. ⑥ Incl. acq.-rel. and unusual chgs. of $27.8 mill., non-cash loss on asset sale of $107.0 mill., excl. extraord. loss of $17.0 mill. ⑦ Incl. a $9.3 million gain on divest. of assets; bef. an extraord. loss of $10.1 mill.

OFFICERS:
T. H. Van Weelden, Chmn., C.E.O.
T. W. Ryan, Exec. V.P., C.F.O.
P. S. Hathaway, Sr. V.P.

INVESTOR CONTACT: Investor Relations,
(480) 627-2700

PRINCIPAL OFFICE: 15880 North Greenway-
Hayden Loop, Suite 100, Scottsdale, AZ
85260

TELEPHONE NUMBER: (480) 627-2700
FAX: (480) 423-9424
WEB: www.alliedwaste.com
NO. OF EMPLOYEES: 29,000 (approx.)
SHAREHOLDERS: 656 (approx.)
ANNUAL MEETING: In May
INCORPORATED: TX, June, 1987; reincorp.,
DE, July, 1989

INSTITUTIONAL HOLDINGS:
No. of Institutions: 213
Shares Held: 158,251,768
% Held: 80.3

INDUSTRY: Refuse systems (SIC: 4953)

TRANSFER AGENT(S): American Stock
Transfer & Trust, New York, NY

ALLMERICA FINANCIAL CORPORATION

EXCH.	SYM.	REC. PRICE	P/E RATIO	YLD.	MKT. CAP.	RANGE (52-WK.)	'02 Y/E PR.
NYSE	AFC	14.15 (2/28/03)	...	...	$0.75 bill.	50.80 - 7.04	10.10

LOWER MEDIUM GRADE. THE COMPANY IS IMPLEMENTING SEVERAL INITIATIVES AIMED AT IMPROVING ITS LIFE INSURANCE CAPITAL POSITION.

*7 YEAR PRICE SCORE 60.2   *12 MONTH PRICE SCORE 54.8

*NYSE COMPOSITE INDEX=100

INTERIM EARNINGS (Per Share):

Qtr.	Mar.	June	Sept.	Dec.
1997	0.32	0.75	1.04	1.58
1998	1.11	1.00	0.13	1.10
1999	2.67	1.21	1.08	1.25
2000	0.56	0.88	1.16	1.11
2001	0.50	0.25	0.59	d1.33
2002	0.97	d1.05	d5.93	0.28

INTERIM DIVIDENDS (Per Share):

Amt.	Decl.	Ex.	Rec.	Pay.
0.25A	10/23/01	11/01/01	11/05/01	11/20/01

Dividend Payment Suspended.

CAPITALIZATION (12/31/01):

	($000)	(%)
Long-Term Debt	199,500	7.7
Common & Surplus	2,391,100	92.3
Total	2,590,600	100.0

BUSINESS:

Allmerica Financial Corporation offers financial products and services in two primary businesses: Asset Accumulation and Risk Management. Asset Accumulation markets insurance and retirement savings products and services to individual and institutional clients through Allmerica Financial Services, and investment management services to institutions, pension funds, and other organizations through Allmerica Asset Management, Inc. Risk Management markets property and casualty insurance products on a regional basis through The Hanover Insurance Company and Citizens Insurance Company of America.

RECENT DEVELOPMENTS:

For the year ended 12/31/02, AFC reported a loss of $302.4 million versus income of $100,000 the previous year. Results for 2002 and 2001 excluded an accounting change charge of $3.7 million and $3.2 million, respectively. Results for 2002 included a charge of $629.4 million to write off deferred acquisition costs, a charge of $106.7 million related to guaranteed minimum death benefit reserves and a related decrease in deferred acquisition cost amortization of $67.6 million. Also, results for 2002 and 2001 included several one-time items that resulted in an after-tax charge of $100.8 million and $85.6 million, respectively. Total revenues rose 3.2% to $3.42 billion from $3.31 billion the year before. Revenues for 2002 and 2001 included net realized investment losses of $162.3 million and $123.9 million, respectively. Premiums revenue grew 2.9% to $2.32 billion.

PROSPECTS:

During the fourth quarter, AFC implemented a series of transactions aimed at improving its life insurance capital position. Among the actions taken, AFC sold through a reinsurance arrangement its interest in a block of fixed universal life policies to John Hancock Life Insurance Company. The transactions resulted in a $90.0 million increase to statutory capital following the retirement of a portion of its long-term funding agreements at less than book value. Other changes included the implementation of a new guaranteed minimum death benefit mortality reinsurance program and the reorganization of the internal ownership structure of AFC's life insurance subsidiaries.

ANNUAL FINANCIAL DATA:

FISCAL YEAR	TOT. REVS. ($mill.)	NET INC. ($mill.)	TOT. ASSETS ($mill.)	OPER. PROFIT %	NET PROFIT %	RET. ON EQUITY %	RET. ON ASSETS %	CURR. RATIO	EARN. PER SH. $	CASH FL. PER SH. $	TANG. BK. VAL. $	DIV. PER SH. $	PRICE RANGE	AVG. P/E RATIO	AVG. YIELD %
p12/31/02	3,419.2	⑤ d302.4							⑤ d5.79			...	50.00 - 7.04	...	...
12/31/01	3,311.8	④ 0.1	30,336.1	...	...	...	...	1.0	④ Nil	0.44	45.20	0.25	71.75 - 36.70	...	0.5
12/31/00	3,087.9	③ 199.9	31,588.0	7.1	6.5	8.3	0.6	1.5	③ 3.70	4.12	45.71	0.25	74.25 - 35.06	14.8	0.5
12/31/99	3,145.2	345.1	30,769.6	14.9	11.0	15.4	1.1	2.5	6.21	6.83	41.33	0.25	64.81 - 46.06	8.9	0.5
12/31/98	3,432.5	201.2	27,607.9	8.1	5.9	8.2	0.7	2.2	3.33	3.70	41.96	0.20	75.25 - 38.38	17.1	0.4
12/31/97	3,006.4	192.6	22,549.0	11.3	6.4	8.1	0.9	2.4	3.52	4.09	39.69	0.20	50.50 - 32.63	11.8	0.5
12/31/96	3,274.7	181.9	18,997.7	10.1	5.6	10.5	1.0	2.3	3.63	4.52	34.43	0.20	34.38 - 24.75	8.1	0.7
12/31/95	3,218.2	② 146.0	17,757.7	8.7	4.5	9.3	0.8	2.6	② 2.61	4.12	31.42	...	28.63 - 23.88	10.1	...
12/31/94	2,788.5	① 40.6	10,502.8	0.3	1.5	6.7	0.4	2.1	...	...	...	...	...	...	...
12/31/93	2,617.4	114.8	10,290.5	1.0	4.4	14.4	1.1	2.0	...	...	...	...	...	...	...

Statistics are as originally reported. ① Incl. equity in net inc. of unconsol. affil. of $38.0 mill. ② Incl. equity in net inc. of unconsol. affil. of $93.2 mill. ③ Incl. restruct. costs of $13.5 mill. ④ Bef. acctg. chrg. $3.2 mill.; incl. restruct. costs of $1.8 mill. & other non-recurr. losses of $136.5 mill. ⑤ Bef. acctg. chrg. $3.7 mill.; incl. a charge of $629.4 million to write-off def. acquisition costs, a chrg. of $106.7 million for guar. min. death benefit reserves & other non-recurr. chrgs. of $100.8 mill.

OFFICERS:
M. P. Angelini, Chmn.
E. J. Parry III, V.P., C.F.O.
J. K. Huber, Sr. V.P., Gen. Couns.
INVESTOR CONTACT: Henry P. St. Cyr, V.P., Inv. Rel., (508) 855-2959
PRINCIPAL OFFICE: 440 Lincoln Street, Worcester, MA 01653

TELEPHONE NUMBER: (508) 855-1000
FAX: (508) 853-6332
WEB: www.allmerica.com
NO. OF EMPLOYEES: 5,600 (approx.)
SHAREHOLDERS: 41,023
ANNUAL MEETING: In May
INCORPORATED: DE, 1995

INSTITUTIONAL HOLDINGS:
No. of Institutions: 138
Shares Held: 33,143,354
% Held: 62.7
INDUSTRY: Fire, marine, and casualty insurance (SIC: 6331)
TRANSFER AGENT(S): Equiserve, L.P., Jersey City, NJ

ALLSTATE CORPORATION (THE)

EXCH.	SYM.	REC. PRICE	P/E RATIO	YLD.	MKT. CAP.	RANGE (52-WK.)	'02 Y/E PR.
NYSE	ALL	31.63 (2/28/03)	15.1	2.9%	$22.52 bill.	41.95 - 31.06	36.99

INVESTMENT GRADE. EARNINGS ARE BENEFITING FROM HIGHER PREMIUM RATES, IMPROVED UNDERWRITING PERFORMANCE AND LOWER EXPENSES.

INTERIM EARNINGS (Per Share):

Qtr.	Mar.	June	Sept	Dec.
1998	1.10	1.05	0.86	0.93
1999	1.27	0.95	0.62	0.54
2000	0.73	0.61	0.87	0.74
2001	0.69	0.23	0.32	0.37
2002	0.60	0.48	0.39	0.63

INTERIM DIVIDENDS (Per Share):

Amt.	Decl.	Ex.	Rec.	Pay.
0.21Q	2/05/02	2/26/02	2/28/02	4/01/02
0.21Q	5/16/02	5/29/02	5/31/02	7/01/02
0.21Q	7/09/02	8/28/02	8/30/02	10/01/02
0.21Q	11/12/02	11/26/02	11/29/02	1/02/03
0.23Q	2/04/03	2/26/03	2/28/03	4/01/03

Indicated div.: $0.92 (Div. Reinv. Plan)

CAPITALIZATION (12/31/01):

	($000)	(%)
Long-Term Debt	3,694,000	17.6
Deferred Income Tax	137,000	0.7
Common & Surplus	17,196,000	81.8
Total	21,027,000	100.0

*7 YEAR PRICE SCORE 113.5   ***12 MONTH PRICE SCORE 102.4**

NYSE COMPOSITE INDEX=100

BUSINESS:

The Allstate Corp. is a holding company for Allstate Insurance Company. Its business is conducted principally through Allstate Insurance Company, Allstate Life Insurance Company and their subsidiaries. The Company is engaged, principally in the United States and Canada, in the personal property and casualty insurance business and the life insurance and savings business. The Company provides insurance products to more than 16.0 million households and has approximately 12,500 exclusive agents and financial specialists in the U.S. and Canada. ALL operates in four business segments: personal property and casualty, life and savings, discontinued lines and coverages, and corporate and other business. On 6/30/95, Sears, Roebuck and Company distributed its 80.3% ownership in ALL's common stock to Sears shareholders. In 1999, the Company acquired American Heritage Life Investment Corp. and the personal lines business of CNA Financial Corp.

RECENT DEVELOPMENTS:

For the year ended 12/31/02, income was $1.48 billion, before an accounting change charge of $331.0 million, versus income of $1.21 billion, before an accounting change charge of $9.0 million, the year before. The increase in earnings reflected higher premium rates, improved underwriting performance and lower expenses. Results for 2002 and 2001 included after-tax restructuring charges of $77.0 million and $84.0 million, respectively. Also, results included an after-tax gain of $2.0 million in 2002 and an after-tax loss of $40.0 million in 2001 related to the disposition of operations. Total revenues grew 2.5% to $29.58 billion from $28.87 billion a year earlier.

PROSPECTS:

Going forward, with the favorable impact of price firming in place, ALL's emphasis in 2003 will be on growing units profitability. The Company expects that its improved profit position in standard auto and homeowners combined with more modest rate increases will allow it to pursue a broader marketing approach in most of the U.S. and will result in sequential unit growth in standard auto and homeowners in the second half of 2003. However, due to concerns about sustained profitability in certain large markets, ALL expect a continued decline in non-standard auto units.

ANNUAL FINANCIAL DATA:

FISCAL YEAR	PREM. INC. ($Mill.)	NET INVST. INC. ($Mill.)	TOT. REVS. ($Mill.)	NET INC. ($Mill.)	TOT. ASSETS ($Mill.)	TOT. INVST. ($Mill.)	RET. ON REVS. %	RET. ON EQUITY %	RET. ON ASSETS %	EARN. PER SH. $	TANG. BK. VAL.$	AVG. YIELD %	DIV. PER SH. $	PRICE RANGE	AVG. P/E RATIO
p12/31/02	23,361.0		29,579.0	④ 1,475.0						④ 1.60		2.2	0.82	41.95 - 31.03	22.8
12/31/01	24,427.0	4,796.0	28,865.0	③ 1,212.0	109,175.0	79,876.0	4.2	7.0	1.1	③ 1.60	22.35	1.9	0.74	45.90 - 30.00	23.7
12/31/00	24,076.0	4,633.0	29,134.0	② 2,252.0	104,808.0	74,483.0	7.7	12.9	2.1	② 2.95	22.26	2.1	0.66	44.75 - 17.19	10.5
12/31/99	21,735.0	4,112.0	26,959.0	① 2,759.0	98,119.0	69,645.0	10.2	16.6	2.8	① 3.38	19.51	1.8	0.58	41.00 - 22.88	9.4
12/31/98	20,826.0	3,890.0	25,879.0	3,333.0	87,691.0	66,525.0	12.9	19.3	3.8	3.94	21.08	1.2	0.53	52.38 - 36.06	11.2
12/31/97	20,106.0	3,861.0	24,949.0	3,144.0	80,918.0	62,548.0	12.6	20.1	3.9	3.56	18.36	1.0	0.36	47.19 - 28.13	10.6
12/31/96	19,702.0	3,813.0	24,299.0	2,079.0	74,508.0	58,329.0	8.6	15.5	2.8	2.32	15.22	1.7	0.42	30.44 - 18.69	10.6
12/31/95	18,908.0	3,627.0	22,793.0	1,904.0	70,029.0	56,505.0	8.4	15.0	2.7	2.12	14.15	2.4	0.39	21.19 - 11.75	7.8
12/31/94	17,861.0	3,401.0	21,464.0	483.0	61,370.0	48,179.0	2.3	5.7	0.8	0.54	9.38	2.7	0.36	14.94 - 11.31	24.3
12/31/93	17,402.0	3,324.0	20,946.0	1,299.0	59,361.0	48,793.0	6.2	12.6	2.2	1.50	11.45	1.2	0.18	17.13 - 13.56	10.3

Statistics are as originally reported. Adj. for stk. split: 2-for-1, 7/98 ① Incl. non-recurr. chrg. $116.0 mill. ② Incl. restruc. chrg. $38.0 mill. ③ Incl. acctg. chng. chrg. $9.0 mill.; Incl. restruc. chrg. $84.0 mill. & loss fr. dispos. of opers. of $40.0 mill. ④ Bef. acctg. chrg. of $331.0 mill.; Incl. after-tax restruct. chrg. of $77.0 mill. & after-tax gain of $2.0 mill. fr. disp. of opers.

OFFICERS:
E. M. Liddy, Chmn., Pres., C.E.O.
D. Hale, Sr. V.P., C.F.O.
R. W. Pike, V.P., Sec.
INVESTOR CONTACT: Investor Relations, (800) 416-8803
PRINCIPAL OFFICE: 2775 Sanders Road, Northbrook, IL 60062

TELEPHONE NUMBER: (847) 402-5000
FAX: (847) 402-0169
WEB: www.allstate.com
NO. OF EMPLOYEES: 40,830 (approx.)
SHAREHOLDERS: 179,166
ANNUAL MEETING: In May
INCORPORATED: DE, Nov., 1992

INSTITUTIONAL HOLDINGS:
No. of Institutions: 617
Shares Held: 490,221,730
% Held: 69.7
INDUSTRY: Fire, marine, and casualty insurance (SIC: 6331)
TRANSFER AGENT(S): First Chicago Trust Company of New York, Jersey City, NJ

ALLTEL CORPORATION

EXCH.	SYM.	REC. PRICE	P/E RATIO	YLD.	MKT. CAP.	RANGE (52-WK.)	'02 Y/E PR.	DIV. ACH.
NYSE	AT	43.42 (2/28/03)	14.7	3.2%	$13.51 bill.	58.30 - 35.33	51.00	42 yrs.

UPPER MEDIUM GRADE. THE COMPANY AGREED TO SELL THE FINANCIAL SERVICES DIVISION OF ITS INFORMATION SERVICES SUBSIDIARY TO FIDELITY NATIONAL FINANCIAL INC. FOR $1.05 BILLION.

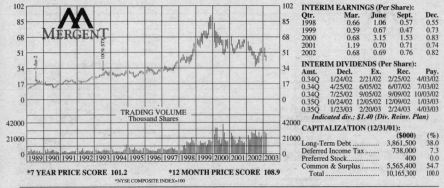

INTERIM EARNINGS (Per Share):

Qtr.	Mar.	June	Sept.	Dec.
1998	0.66	1.06	0.57	0.55
1999	0.59	0.67	0.47	0.73
2000	0.68	3.15	1.53	0.83
2001	1.19	0.70	0.71	0.74
2002	0.68	0.69	0.76	0.82

INTERIM DIVIDENDS (Per Share):

Amt.	Decl.	Ex.	Rec.	Pay.
0.34Q	1/24/02	2/21/02	2/25/02	4/03/02
0.34Q	4/25/02	6/05/02	6/07/02	7/03/02
0.34Q	7/25/02	9/05/02	9/09/02	10/03/02
0.35Q	10/24/02	12/05/02	12/09/02	1/03/03
0.35Q	1/23/03	2/20/03	2/24/03	4/03/03

Indicated div.: $1.40 (Div. Reinv. Plan)

CAPITALIZATION (12/31/01):

	($000)	(%)
Long-Term Debt	3,861,500	38.0
Deferred Income Tax	738,000	7.3
Preferred Stock	400	0.0
Common & Surplus	5,565,400	54.7
Total	10,165,300	100.0

*7 YEAR PRICE SCORE 101.2 ***12 MONTH PRICE SCORE 108.9**
*NYSE COMPOSITE INDEX=100

BUSINESS:

ALLTEL Corporation, with more than 12.0 million communication customers in 26 states as of 1/29/03, provides wireless and wireline local, long-distance, network access and Internet services, wide-area paging service and information processing management services and advanced application software. Telecommunications products are warehoused and sold by the Company's distribution subsidiary. A subsidiary also publishes telephone directories for affiliates and other independent telephone companies. On 7/1/98, AT acquired 360 Communications Company. On 7/2/99, AT acquired Aliant Communications Inc. for $1.80 billion. In August 2002, AT purchased certain local telephone properties from Verizon for $1.90 billion and selected wireless properties from CenturyTel Inc. for $1.57 billion.

RECENT DEVELOPMENTS:

For the twelve months ended 12/31/02, net income was $924.3 million compared with income of $1.05 billion, before an accounting change gain of $19.5 million, the previous year. Results for 2002 and 2001 included integration expenses and other charges of $115.1 million and $92.2 million, and gains on disposal of assets, write-down of investments and other items totaling $985,000 and $357.6 million, respectively. Total revenues and sales rose 6.4% to $7.98 billion. Operating income increased 9.1% to $1.82 billion from $1.66 billion the year before.

PROSPECTS:

On 1/29/03, AT announced that it has agreed to sell the financial services division of its Information Services subsidiary to Fidelity National Financial Inc. for $1.05 billion, payable as $775.0 million in cash and $275.0 million in Fidelity National common stock. The telecom division of ALLTEL Information Services will be retained by AT and will not be part of the transaction. AT noted that assuming the Information Services transaction closes on 3/31/03, the sale will dilute 2003 earnings by about $0.22 per share. AT believes the sale will improve its financial flexibility while allowing the Company to focus on expanding the communications business.

ANNUAL FINANCIAL DATA:

FISCAL YEAR	TOT. REVS. ($mill.)	NET INC. ($mill.)	TOT. ASSETS ($mill.)	OPER. PROFIT %	NET PROFIT %	RET. ON EQUITY %	RET. ON ASSETS %	CURR. RATIO	EARN. PER SH.$	CASH FL. PER SH.$	TANG. BK. VAL.$	DIV. PER SH.$	PRICE RANGE	AVG. P/E RATIO	AVG. YIELD %
p12/31/02	7,983.4	⑧ 924.3							⑧ 2.96			1.36	63.25 - 35.33	16.7	2.8
12/31/01	7,598.9	⑥⑦ 1,047.5	12,609.0	21.9	13.8	18.8	8.3	1.4	⑥⑦ 3.34	7.07	6.87	1.32	68.69 - 49.43	17.7	2.2
12/31/00	7,067.0	⑤⑦ 1,965.4	12,182.0	23.6	27.8	38.6	16.1	1.2	⑤⑦ 6.20	9.31	5.92	1.28	82.94 - 47.75	10.5	2.0
12/31/99	6,302.3	④ 783.6	10,774.2	24.2	12.4	18.6	7.3	1.0	④ 2.47	5.19	7.03	1.22	91.81 - 56.31	30.0	1.6
12/31/98	5,194.0	① 525.5	9,374.2	17.1	10.1	16.1	5.6	0.8	① 1.89	4.44	5.82	1.16	61.38 - 38.25	26.4	2.3
12/31/97	3,263.6	② 507.9	5,633.4	22.9	15.6	23.0	9.0	1.4	② 2.70	5.10	8.67	1.10	41.63 - 29.75	13.2	3.1
12/31/96	3,192.4	② 291.7	5,359.2	18.5	9.1	13.9	5.4	1.2	② 1.53	3.75	8.88	1.04	35.63 - 26.63	20.3	3.3
12/31/95	3,109.7	354.6	5,073.1	22.0	11.4	18.3	7.0	1.3	1.86	4.02	7.64	0.96	31.13 - 23.25	14.6	3.5
12/31/94	2,961.7	③ 271.8	4,713.9	21.4	9.2	16.7	5.8	1.1	③ 1.43	3.34	5.96	0.88	31.38 - 24.00	19.4	3.2
12/31/93	2,342.1	262.0	4,270.5	22.2	11.2	16.9	6.1	0.8	1.39	2.84	5.53	0.80	31.25 - 22.88	19.5	3.0

Statistics are as originally reported. ① Incl. pre-tax net chrg. of 10.8 mill. ② Incl. non-recurr. cr. 12/31/97: $189.7 mill.; chrg. 12/31/96: $74.2 mill. ③ Bef. write-dwn. of $32.0 mill on assets. ④ Incl. chrgs. of $90.5 mill. ⑤ Incl. pre-tax chrgs. of $25.4 mill. & pre-tax gain on disp. of assets & oth. non-recurr. items of $1.93 mill. ⑥ Incl. pre-tax chrgs. of $92.2 mill. & pre-tax gain on disp. of assets & oth. non-recurr. items of $357.6 mill. ⑦ Bef. acctg. chge. cr. 12/31/01: $19.5 mill.; chrg. 12/31/00: $36.6 mill. ⑧ Incl. pre-tax chrgs. of $115.1 mill. & pre-tax gain on disp. of assets & oth. non-recurr. items of $985,000.

OFFICERS:
J. T. Ford, Chmn., C.E.O.
S. T. Ford, Pres., C.O.O.
J. R. Gardner, Sr. V.P., C.F.O.
INVESTOR CONTACT: Rob Clancy, Investor Relations, (501) 905-8991
PRINCIPAL OFFICE: One Allied Drive, Little Rock, AR 72202

TELEPHONE NUMBER: (501) 905-8000
FAX: (501) 905-0962
WEB: www.alltel.com
NO. OF EMPLOYEES: 23,955 (avg.)
SHAREHOLDERS: 256,759 (approx.)
ANNUAL MEETING: In Apr.
INCORPORATED: OH, June, 1960; reincorp., DE, 1990

INSTITUTIONAL HOLDINGS:
No. of Institutions: 535
Shares Held: 193,969,145
% Held: 62.4
INDUSTRY: Telephone communications, exc. radio (SIC: 4813)
TRANSFER AGENT(S): First Union National Bank of North Carolina, Charlotte, NC

ALPHARMA INC.

EXCH.	SYM.	REC. PRICE	P/E RATIO	YLD.	MKT. CAP.	RANGE (52-WK.)	'02 Y/E PR.
NYSE	ALO	16.75 (2/28/03)	...	1.1%	$0.74 bill.	22.30 - 6.50	11.91

LOWER MEDIUM GRADE. THE COMPANY EXPECTS 2003 REVENUES TO GROW 8.0% TO 10.0%.

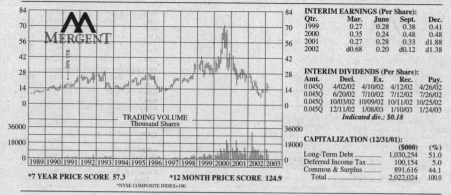

*7 YEAR PRICE SCORE 57.3   *12 MONTH PRICE SCORE 124.9
*NYSE COMPOSITE INDEX=100

INTERIM EARNINGS (Per Share):

Qtr.	Mar.	June	Sept.	Dec.
1999	0.27	0.28	0.38	0.41
2000	0.35	0.24	0.48	0.48
2001	0.27	0.28	0.33	d1.88
2002	d0.68	0.20	d0.12	d1.38

INTERIM DIVIDENDS (Per Share):

Amt.	Decl.	Ex.	Rec.	Pay.
0.045Q	4/02/02	4/10/02	4/12/02	4/26/02
0.045Q	6/20/02	7/10/02	7/12/02	7/26/02
0.045Q	10/03/02	10/09/02	10/11/02	10/25/02
0.045Q	12/11/02	1/08/03	1/10/03	1/24/03

Indicated div.: $0.18

CAPITALIZATION (12/31/01):

	($000)	(%)
Long-Term Debt	1,030,254	51.0
Deferred Income Tax	100,154	5.0
Common & Surplus	891,616	44.1
Total	2,022,024	100.0

BUSINESS:

Alpharma Inc. (formerly A. L. Pharma Inc.) is a multinational pharmaceutical company that develops, manufactures and markets specialty generic and proprietary human pharmaceuticals and animal health products. The Human Pharmaceuticals segment is comprised of the U.S. Pharmaceuticals, International Pharmaceuticals, and Fine Chemicals Divisions. The Animal Health segment is comprised of the Animal Health and Aquatic Animal Health

Divisions. The Human Pharmaceuticals segment accounted for 74.0% of 2002 revenues and the Animal Health segment, 26.0%. ALO conducts business worldwide and has a significant presence in North America, Europe and the Far East. The U.S. generated 35.6% of 2002 Pharmaceutical revenues and the international markets and Active Pharmaceuticals Ingredients accounted for 55.3% and 9.1%, respectively.

RECENT DEVELOPMENTS:

For the year ended 12/31/02, ALO reported a loss of $97.7 million, before an extraordinary loss of $1.1 million, compared with a loss of $35.7 million, before an extraordinary loss of $2.2 million, the previous year. Results for 2002 included a pre-tax asset impairment charge of $159.6 mil-

lion. Total revenues increased 27.0% to $1.24 billion. Human pharmaceuticals revenues advanced 42.7% to $918.3 million, while animal health revenues declined 4.0% to $321.9 million.

PROSPECTS:

ALO expects 2003 revenues to grow 8.0% to 10.0% to between $1.33 billion and $1.35 billion. ALO also estimates diluted earnings to range from $1.15 to $1.25 per share for full-year 2003. ALO expects strong volume growth in its global human pharmaceutical business, reflecting domestic growth of about 10.0% to 13.0% and

international growth of about 8.0% to 11.0%. Revenues in ALO's Active Pharmaceutical Ingredients business are expected to improve significantly, primarily due to price increases on selected products. Revenues for the animal health business are anticipated to be flat in 2003, due to certain products facing continued competitive challenges.

ANNUAL FINANCIAL DATA:

FISCAL YEAR	TOT. REVS. ($mill.)	NET INC. ($mill.)	TOT. ASSETS ($mill.)	OPER. PROFIT %	NET PROFIT %	RET. ON EQUITY %	RET. ON ASSETS %	CURR. RATIO	EARN. PER SH.$	CASH FL.PER SH.$	TANG. BK. VAL.$	DIV. PER SH.$	PRICE RANGE	AVG. P/E RATIO	AVG. YIELD %
p12/31/02	1,238.0	⑥d97.7							⑥d1.96			0.18	28.00 - 6.50		1.0
12/31/01	975.0	⑤d35.7	2,390.0	2.5	...	...	...	1.9	⑤d0.87	1.03	...	0.18	44.25 - 18.00	...	0.6
12/31/00	919.5	④61.1	1,624.5	14.5	6.6	7.1	3.8	3.0	④1.60	2.65	6.15	0.18	71.94 - 29.19	31.6	0.4
12/31/99	742.2	39.6	1,164.5	13.4	5.3	11.2	3.4	2.3	1.34	2.58	...	0.18	43.38 - 24.56	25.3	0.5
12/31/98	604.6	③24.2	908.9	10.8	4.0	9.1	2.7	2.0	③0.92	2.37	...	0.18	36.94 - 18.94	30.4	0.6
12/31/97	500.3	17.4	631.9	9.4	3.5	7.3	2.8	2.0	0.76	2.12	3.50	0.18	23.88 - 11.38	23.2	1.0
12/31/96	486.2	②d11.5	613.4	0.8	...	...	...	1.8	②d0.53	0.92	3.04	0.18	27.38 - 10.63	...	0.9
12/31/95	520.9	18.8	634.9	10.1	3.6	9.2	3.0	1.7	0.86	2.29	3.55	0.18	26.38 - 16.50	24.9	0.8
12/31/94	469.3	①d1.7	592.3	3.4	...	...	...	1.6	①d0.08	1.16	2.43	0.18	20.63 - 12.63	...	1.1
12/31/93	338.2	8.6	423.2	6.2	2.5	4.7	2.0	1.4	0.40	1.23	3.22	0.18	29.38 - 12.75	52.6	0.9

Statistics are as originally reported. ① Bef. an extraord. chrg of $683,000 ($0.03 a sh.) & incl. chrgs. of $17.0 mill. ($0.79 a sh.). ② Incl. after-tax chrgs. of $7.5 mill. rel. to the ration. plans for the Int. Pharm. Div. & the U.S. Pharm. Div. ③ Incl. an after-tax chg. of $3.1 mill. rel. to the acq. of Cox Pharm. ④ Incl. an after-tax chg. of $4.0 mill. rel. to the acq. of Roche MFA bus. ⑤ Incl. an after-tax chg. of $65.5 mill. rel. to the acq. of F. H. Faulding & Co.'s oral solid dose bus.; excl. extraord. loss of $2.2 mill. ⑥ Bef. an extraord. loss of $1.1 mill. & incl. pre-tax asset impair. & other chrgs. of $159.6 mill.

OFFICERS:
E. W. Sissener, Chmn.
I. Wiik, Pres., C.E.O.
M. Farrell, V.P., C.F.O.
INVESTOR CONTACT: Kathleen Makrakis, Investor Relations, (201) 228-5085
PRINCIPAL OFFICE: One Executive Drive, Fort Lee, NJ 07024

TELEPHONE NUMBER: (201) 947-7774
FAX: (201) 947-4879
WEB: www.alpharma.com
NO. OF EMPLOYEES: 4,900 (approx.)
SHAREHOLDERS: 719 (record class A)
ANNUAL MEETING: In May
INCORPORATED: DE, Sept., 1983

ALTRIA GROUP, INC.

EXCH.	SYM.	REC. PRICE	P/E RATIO	YLD.	MKT. CAP.	RANGE (52-WK.)	'02 Y/E PR.	DIV. ACH.
NYSE	MO	37.55 (2/28/03)	7.2	6.8%	$80.83 bill.	57.79 - 35.40	40.53	37 yrs.

INVESTMENT GRADE. THE COMPANY IS PROJECTING FULL-YEAR 2003 DILUTED EARNINGS IN THE RANGE OF $4.60 TO $4.70 PER SHARE.

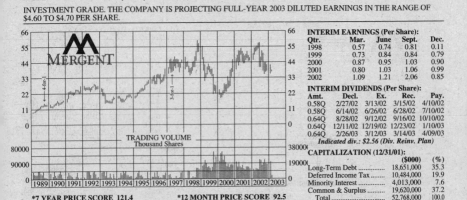

*7 YEAR PRICE SCORE 121.4 ***12 MONTH PRICE SCORE 92.5**
*NYSE COMPOSITE INDEX=100

INTERIM EARNINGS (Per Share):

Qtr.	Mar.	June	Sept.	Dec.
1998	0.57	0.74	0.81	0.11
1999	0.73	0.84	0.84	0.79
2000	0.87	0.95	1.03	0.90
2001	0.80	1.03	1.06	0.99
2002	1.09	1.21	2.06	0.85

INTERIM DIVIDENDS (Per Share):

Amt.	Decl.	Ex.	Rec.	Pay.
0.58Q	2/27/02	3/13/02	3/15/02	4/10/02
0.58Q	6/14/02	6/26/02	6/28/02	7/10/02
0.64Q	8/28/02	9/12/02	9/16/02	10/10/02
0.64Q	12/11/02	12/19/02	12/23/02	1/10/03
0.64Q	2/26/03	3/12/03	3/14/03	4/09/03

Indicated div.: $2.56 (Div. Reinv. Plan)

CAPITALIZATION (12/31/01):

	($000)	(%)
Long-Term Debt	18,651,000	35.3
Deferred Income Tax	10,484,000	19.9
Minority Interest	4,013,000	7.6
Common & Surplus	19,620,000	37.2
Total	52,768,000	100.0

BUSINESS:

Altria Group, Inc. (formerly Philip Morris Companies, Inc.) is one of the world's largest consumer products companies. Tobacco is manufactured and sold through Philip Morris U.S.A., (23.5% of 2002 operating revenues and 29.0% of operating income) and Philip Morris International Inc. (35.7%, 32.8%). Retail packaged foods are processed and marketed through Kraft Foods North America (26.7%, 28.6%) in the U.S. and Canada and Kraft Foods International (10.2%, 7.7%) in Europe and the Asia/Pacific region.

Philip Morris Capital Corporation (0.6%, 0.3%) engages in financing and investment activities. On 7/9/02, MO combined its Miller Brewing Co. (3.3%, 1.6%) with South African Breweries plc, forming SABMiller plc. MO maintains a 36.0% economic interest in SABMiller. On 12/11/00, MO acquired Nabisco Holding Corp. for total consideration of $18.90 billion. As of 1/29/03, MO owned about 84.0% of the outstanding common shares of Kraft Foods Inc.

RECENT DEVELOPMENTS:

For the year ended 12/31/02, net earnings were $11.10 billion versus earnings of $8.57 billion, before an accounting change charge of $6.0 million, the previous year. Results for 2002 and 2001 included non-recurring items resulting in net charges of $544.0 million and $93.0 million, and amortization of intangibles of $7.0 million and

$1.01 billion, respectively. Results for 2002 also included a gain of $2.63 billion related to MO's 7/9/02 merger of Miller Brewing Company into South African Breweries plc. Results for 2001 included a litigation-related charge of $500.0 million. Net revenues slipped to $80.41 billion from $80.88 billion in 2001.

PROSPECTS:

MO's near-term prospects are mixed, reflecting weakness from the Company's domestic tobacco segment due to a poor economic environment, sharp increases in state excise taxes and heightened competition. On the positive side,

MO's international tobacco business is experiencing higher pricing, improved volume/mix and lower costs. Accordingly, MO is projecting full-year 2003 diluted earnings in the range of $4.60 and $4.70 per share.

ANNUAL FINANCIAL DATA:

FISCAL YEAR	TOT. REVS. ($mill.)	NET INC. ($mill.)	TOT. ASSETS ($mill.)	OPER. PROFIT %	NET PROFIT %	RET. ON EQUITY %	RET. ON ASSETS %	CURR. RATIO	EARN. PER SH. $	CASH FL. PER SH. $	DIV. PER SH. $	PRICE RANGE	AVG. P/E RATIO	AVG. YIELD %
p12/31/02	80,408.0	⑥ 11,102.0							⑤ 5.21		2.38	57.79 - 35.40	8.9	5.1
12/31/01	89,924.0	⑤ 8,566.0	84,968.0	17.5	9.5	43.7	10.1	0.8	③ 3.88	4.93	2.17	53.88 - 38.75	11.9	4.7
12/31/00	80,356.0	④ 8,510.0	79,067.0	18.3	10.6	56.7	10.8	0.6	④ 3.75	4.50	1.97	45.94 - 18.69	8.6	6.1
12/31/99	78,596.0	③ 7,675.0	61,381.0	17.2	9.8	50.1	12.5	1.2	③ 3.19	3.90	1.80	55.56 - 21.25	12.0	4.7
12/31/98	74,391.0	② 5,372.0	59,920.0	13.4	7.2	33.2	9.0	1.2	② 2.20	2.89	1.64	59.50 - 34.75	21.4	3.5
12/31/97	72,055.0	① 6,310.0	55,947.0	16.2	8.8	42.3	11.3	1.2	① 2.58	3.25	1.60	48.13 - 36.00	16.3	3.8
12/31/96	69,204.0	6,303.0	54,871.0	17.0	9.1	44.3	11.5	1.0	2.56	3.25	1.40	39.67 - 28.54	13.3	4.1
12/31/95	66,071.0	② 5,478.0	53,811.0	15.9	8.3	39.2	10.2	1.0	② 2.17	2.83	1.16	31.46 - 18.58	11.5	4.6
12/31/94	65,125.0	4,725.0	52,649.0	14.5	7.3	37.0	9.0	1.0	1.82	2.48	0.95	21.50 - 15.75	10.2	5.1
12/31/93	60,901.0	② 3,568.0	51,205.0	12.5	5.9	30.7	7.0	0.9	② 1.35	1.97	0.87	25.88 - 15.00	15.1	4.2

Statistics are as originally reported. Adj. for 3-for-1 stk. split, 4/97. ① Incl. non-recurr. chrg. 12/31/98, $3.38 bill.; 12/31/97, $1.46 bill. ② Bef. acctg. chge. chrg. 12/31/95, $28.0 mill.; 12/31/93, $477.0 mill. ③ Incl. chrgs. of $476.0 mill. for separation programs. ④ Incl. gain of $139.0 mill. on sale of a French confectionery business & $100.0 mill. gain on sale of beer rights. ⑤ Incl. non-recurr. chrg. of $19.0 mill. & loss of $82.0 mill. rel. to sale of factory and integr. costs; bef. acctg. chge. chrg. of $6.0 mill. ⑥ Incl. non-recurr. chrgs. of $624.0 mill., business sales gains of $80.0 mill. & gain of $2.63 bill. on Miller transaction.

OFFICERS:
L. C. Camilleri, Chmn., C.E.O.
D. Devitre, Sr. V.P., C.F.O.

INVESTOR CONTACT: Nicholas M. Rolli, Investor Relations, (917) 663-3460

PRINCIPAL OFFICE: 120 Park Avenue, New York, NY 10017

TELEPHONE NUMBER: (917) 663-5000
FAX: (917) 878-2167
WEB: www.philipmorris.com
NO. OF EMPLOYEES: 175,000 (approx.)
SHAREHOLDERS: 131,700 (approx.)
ANNUAL MEETING: In Apr.
INCORPORATED: VA, Mar., 1985

INSTITUTIONAL HOLDINGS:
No. of Institutions: 909
Shares Held: 1,362,707,519
% Held: 65.9

INDUSTRY: Cigarettes (SIC: 2111)

TRANSFER AGENT(S): First Chicago Trust Company, Jersey City, NJ

AMB PROPERTY CORPORATION

EXCH.	SYM.	REC. PRICE	P/E RATIO	YLD.	MKT. CAP.	RANGE (52-WK.)	'02 Y/E PR.
NYSE	AMB	28.00 (2/28/03)	20.4	5.9%	$2.35 bill.	31.10 - 24.70	27.36

UPPER MEDIUM GRADE. THE COMPANY IS CONTINUING EFFORTS TO DIVEST NON-STRATEGIC ASSETS IN THE U.S.

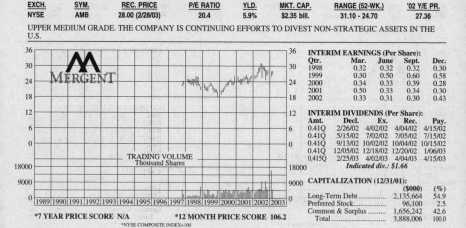

INTEREST EARNINGS (Per Share):

Qtr.	Mar.	June	Sept.	Dec.
1998	0.32	0.32	0.32	0.30
1999	0.30	0.50	0.60	0.58
2000	0.34	0.33	0.39	0.28
2001	0.50	0.33	0.34	0.30
2002	0.33	0.31	0.30	0.43

INTERIM DIVIDENDS (Per Share):

Amt.	Decl.	Ex.	Rec.	Pay.
0.41Q	2/26/02	4/02/02	4/04/02	4/15/02
0.41Q	5/15/02	7/02/02	7/05/02	7/15/02
0.41Q	9/13/02	10/02/02	10/04/02	10/15/02
0.41Q	12/05/02	12/18/02	12/20/02	1/06/03
0.415Q	2/25/03	4/02/03	4/04/03	4/15/03

Indicated div.: $1.66

CAPITALIZATION (12/31/01):

	($000)	(%)
Long-Term Debt	2,135,664	54.9
Preferred Stock	96,100	2.5
Common & Surplus	1,656,242	42.6
Total	3,888,006	100.0

*7 YEAR PRICE SCORE N/A   ***12 MONTH PRICE SCORE 106.2**
*NYSE COMPOSITE INDEX=100

BUSINESS:

AMB Property Corporation is an owner and operator of industrial real estate properties. The Company, through its 94.4%-owned subsidiary, AMB Property, L.P., is engaged in the acquisition, ownership, operation, management, renovation, expansion and development of primarily industrial properties in target markets nationwide. These properties are mainly located in major distribution areas near airports, seaports and ground transportation systems. As of 12/31/02, AMB owned, managed and had renovation and development projects totaling 992 buildings and 94.6 million square feet in 30 metropolitan markets. The Company's portfolio is comprised of High Throughput Distribution® facilities, industrial properties built for speed and benefiting from barriers to entry due to their infill locations.

RECENT DEVELOPMENTS:

For the year ended 12/31/02, net income slipped 9.9% to $124.2 million compared with $138.0 million in 2001. Results for 2002 and 2001 included gains of $8.8 million and $36.4 million, respectively, from developments held for sale and the disposition of real estate. Also, results for 2002 and 2001 included income of $29.9 million and $16.3 million, respectively, from discontinued operations. Additionally, results for 2001 included a loss of $20.8 million on investments. Total revenues climbed 9.4% to $615.8 million from $562.8 million the previous year. Rental revenue increased 11.0% to $588.5 million, while interest and other income dropped 35.9% to $10.5 million.

PROSPECTS:

The Company is continuing to optimize its portfolio through strategic dispositions in the U.S., which include exiting certain non-strategic markets, and pursuing acquisitions in the U.S. and abroad. Although net dispositions of more than $50.0 million in the fourth quarter of 2002 are dilutive in the short-term, the Company expects capital redeployment into investments that are closely aligned with its investment focus will offer stronger long-term returns. Recent transaction activity included entry into Guadalajara, Paris and Singapore and the exit from one-third of the Company's facilities in Dallas, Texas and most facilities in Houston, Texas.

ANNUAL FINANCIAL DATA:

FISCAL YEAR	TOT. INC. ($000)	NET INC. ($000)	TOT. ASSETS ($000)	NET INC. + DEPR./ ASSETS %	RET. ON EQUITY %	RET. ON ASSETS %	EARN. PER SH. $	TANG. BK. VAL. $	DIV. PER SH. $	DIV. PAYOUT %	PRICE RANGE	AVG. P/E RATIO	AVG. YIELD %
p12/31/02	615,843	⑤ 124,237					⑤ 1.37		1.64	119.7	31.10 - 24.70	20.4	5.9
12/31/01	600,845	④ 138,559	4,760,893	5.3	7.9	2.9	④ 1.47	19.76	1.58	107.5	26.69 - 22.75	16.8	6.4
12/31/00	477,707	③ 121,782	4,425,626	4.9	6.9	2.8	③ 1.35	19.87	1.48	109.6	26.06 - 18.81	16.6	6.6
12/31/99	448,183	② 178,593	3,621,550	6.8	9.8	4.9	② 1.97	20.36	1.74	88.4	23.50 - 18.00	10.5	8.4
12/31/98	358,887	112,593	3,562,885	4.8	6.4	3.2	1.27	19.43	1.03	80.9	26.00 - 20.75	18.4	4.4
12/31/97	56,062	18,228	2,506,255	0.9	1.1	0.7	1.38	19.42	0.13	9.7	24.31 - 22.25	16.9	0.6
12/31/96	167,953	① 54,400	1,622,559	5.1	5.3	3.4	...	...	...	...	...	...	...
12/31/95	108,249	32,531	1,117,181	4.5	3.9	2.9	...	...	...	...	...	...	...
12/31/94	51,682	13,194	...	...	...	...	...	...	...	...	...	...	...

Statistics are as originally reported. ① Bef. loss of $1.5 mill. from disc. ops. ② Bef. extraord. chrg. of $2.5 mill.; incls. gain of $53.6 mill. from divest. of real estate. ③ Incls. gain of $7.0 mill. from dispos. of real estate. ④ Incl. $13.2 mill. gain fr. development held for sale & $23.3 mill. gain fr. disp. of real estate and excl. $606,000 extraord. gain. ⑤ Incl. $8.8 mill. gains fr. development held for sale & $29.9 mill. income fr. disc. ops.

OFFICERS:
H. R. Moghadam, Chmn., C.E.O.
W. B. Baird, Pres.
M. A. Coke, Exec. V.P., C.F.O.

INVESTOR CONTACT: Investor Relations, (415) 394-9000

PRINCIPAL OFFICE: Pier 1, Bay 1, San Francisco, CA 94111

TELEPHONE NUMBER: (415) 394-9000
FAX: (415) 394-9001
WEB: www.amb.com

NO. OF EMPLOYEES: 179 (avg.)

SHAREHOLDERS: 382 (approx.)

ANNUAL MEETING: In May

INCORPORATED: MD, 1983

INSTITUTIONAL HOLDINGS:
No. of Institutions: 176
Shares Held: 69,368,262
% Held: 83.9

INDUSTRY: Real estate investment trusts (SIC: 6798)

TRANSFER AGENT(S): Boston EquiServe, Boston, MA

AMBAC FINANCIAL GROUP, INC.

EXCH.	SYM.	REC. PRICE	P/E RATIO	YLD.	MKT. CAP.	RANGE (52-WK.)	'02 Y/E PR.	DIV. ACH.
NYSE	ABK	48.85 (2/28/03)	12.3	0.8%	$5.16 bill.	71.25 - 46.34	56.24	11 yrs.

UPPER MEDIUM GRADE. THE COMPANY IS TARGETING 15.0% GROWTH FOR EARNINGS IN 2003.

*7 YEAR PRICE SCORE 157.7   ***12 MONTH PRICE SCORE 97.7**
*NYSE COMPOSITE INDEX=100

INTERIM EARNINGS (Per Share):

Qtr.	Mar.	June	Sept.	Dec.
1998	0.61	0.57	0.61	0.58
1999	0.69	0.67	0.75	0.79
2000	0.80	0.87	0.85	0.89
2001	0.90	0.99	1.02	1.07
2002	1.07	1.09	1.21	0.59

INTERIM DIVIDENDS (Per Share):

Amt.	Decl.	Ex.	Rec.	Pay.
0.09Q	1/23/02	2/07/02	2/11/02	3/06/02
0.09Q	5/07/02	5/16/02	5/20/02	6/05/02
0.10Q	7/17/02	8/08/02	8/12/02	9/04/02
0.10Q	10/16/02	11/06/02	11/11/02	12/04/02
0.10Q	1/23/03	2/06/03	2/10/03	3/05/03

Indicated div.: $0.40

CAPITALIZATION (12/31/01):

	($000)	(%)
Long-Term Debt	619,315	16.6
Deferred Income Tax	123,077	3.3
Common & Surplus	2,983,688	80.1
Total	3,726,080	100.0

BUSINESS:

AMBAC Financial Group, Inc. is a holding company whose subsidiaries provide financial guarantee products and other financial services to clients in both the public and private sectors. The Company provides financial guarantees for public finance and structured finance obligations through its principal operating subsidiary, Ambac Assurance Corporation. Through its financial services subsidiar-

ies, the Company provides financial and investment products including investment agreements, interest rate and total return swaps, funding conduits, investment advisory and cash management services. These products are sold principally to the Company's financial guarantee clients, which include municipalities and their authorities, school districts, health care organizations and asset-backed issuers.

RECENT DEVELOPMENTS:

For the year ended 12/31/02, net income slipped to $432.6 million from $432.9 million the previous year. Total revenues rose 2.2% to $740.5 million from $724.9 million in the prior year. Revenues for 2002 and 2001 included net security losses of $120.4 million and $5.1 million, respectively. Net premiums written increased 34.5% to $790.5

million from $587.7 million the year before, led by solid growth in all three sectors, including public structured and international finance. Net premiums earned and other credit enhancement fees grew 25.0% to $500.3 million versus $400.4 million a year earlier. Net investment income increased 11.0% to $297.3 million.

PROSPECTS:

Earnings are benefiting from solid business activity across all of the Company's primary markets. In public finance, ABK is benefiting from its continued focus on structured and innovative municipal obligations. Transactions guaranteed during the fourth quarter of 2002 included significant writings in the utility, municipal lease and transportation sectors. Structured finance growth is being driven by

increased activity in the investor-owned utility market, as well as strong demand for both commercial and consumer asset-backed transactions. Meanwhile, healthy premium writings in pooled debt obligations, future flow and other commercial asset-backed financing continue to drive international business. Looking ahead, ABK is targeting 15.0% average growth for earnings in 2003.

ANNUAL FINANCIAL DATA:

FISCAL YEAR	TOT. REVS. ($mill.)	NET INC. ($mill.)	TOT. ASSETS ($mill.)	OPER. PROFIT %	NET PROFIT %	RET. ON EQUITY %	RET. ON ASSETS %	CURR. RATIO	EARN. PER SH.$	CASH FL. PER SH.$	TANG. BK. VAL.$	DIV. PER SH.$	PRICE RANGE	AVG. P/E RATIO	AVG. YIELD %
p12/31/02	740.5	432.6							3.97			0.38	71.25 - 49.86	15.3	0.6
12/31/01	724.9	432.9	12,267.7	84.9	59.7	14.5	3.5	0.2	3.97	3.86	28.26	0.34	64.00 - 42.20	13.4	0.6
12/31/00	621.3	366.2	10,120.3	84.7	58.9	14.1	3.6	0.2	3.41	3.32	24.60	0.31	58.31 - 25.92	12.4	0.7
12/31/99	533.3	307.9	11,345.1	88.8	57.7	15.3	2.7	0.2	2.87	2.86	19.23	0.28	42.00 - 29.79	12.5	0.8
12/31/98	358.3	155.2	11,212.3	85.3	43.3	7.4	1.4	0.2	2.37	1.43	19.98	0.25	43.96 - 27.25	15.0	0.7
12/31/97	282.1	123.3	8,249.7	84.6	43.7	6.6	1.5	0.2	2.09	1.14	17.85	0.23	31.71 - 20.67	12.5	0.9
12/31/96	193.5	181.6	5,876.0	78.8	93.9	11.2	3.1	0.2	2.63	1.74	15.34	0.20	23.17 - 15.17	7.3	1.1
12/31/95	195.7	104.3	5,309.3	80.7	53.3	7.4	2.0	0.5	1.59	1.04	13.35	0.18	15.96 - 12.17	8.8	1.3
12/31/94	149.8	45.3	4,293.3	76.3	30.3	4.4	1.1	0.2	1.34	0.52	9.83	0.17	15.00 - 10.08	9.4	1.3
12/31/93	168.3	76.7	3,807.2	78.5	45.6	7.0	2.0	0.4	1.69	0.79	10.38	0.15	16.58 - 12.67	8.6	1.0

Statistics are as originally reported. Adj. for stk. splits: 50% div., 12/00; 2-for-1, 9/97

OFFICERS:
P. B. Lassiter, Chmn., Pres., C.E.O.
R. Genader, Pres., C.O.O.
T. J. Gandolfo, C.F.O., Contr.
INVESTOR CONTACT: Peter R. Poillon,
Investor Relations, (212) 208-3333
PRINCIPAL OFFICE: One State Street Plaza,
New York, NY 10004

TELEPHONE NUMBER: (212) 668-0340
FAX: (212) 509-9190
WEB: www.ambac.com
NO. OF EMPLOYEES: 370 (avg.)
SHAREHOLDERS: 79
ANNUAL MEETING: In May
INCORPORATED: DE, April, 1991

INSTITUTIONAL HOLDINGS:
No. of Institutions: 375
Shares Held: 103,061,756
% Held: 97.2

INDUSTRY: Surety insurance (SIC: 6351)

TRANSFER AGENT(S): Citibank, N.A., New York, NY

AMERADA HESS CORPORATION

EXCH.	SYM.	REC. PRICE	P/E RATIO	YLD.	MKT. CAP.	RANGE (52-WK.)	'02 Y/E PR.
NYSE	AHC	44.53 (2/28/03)	...	2.7%	$3.95 bill.	84.70 - 42.75	55.05

MEDIUM GRADE. THE RECENT DROP IN PRODUCTION, COUPLED WITH LACKLUSTER REFINING AND MARKET-ING RESULTS, TEMPERS THE COMPANY'S NEAR-TERM OUTLOOK.

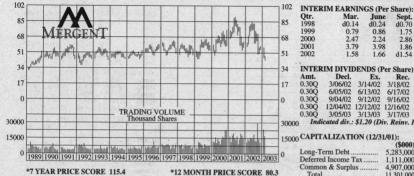

INTERIM EARNINGS (Per Share):

Qtr.	Mar.	June	Sept.	Dec.
1998	d0.14	d0.24	d0.70	d4.70
1999	0.79	0.86	1.75	1.45
2000	2.47	2.24	2.86	3.83
2001	3.79	3.98	1.86	0.61
2002	1.58	1.66	d1.54	d4.20

INTERIM DIVIDENDS (Per Share):

Amt.	Decl.	Ex.	Rec.	Pay.
0.30Q	3/06/02	3/14/02	3/18/02	3/29/02
0.30Q	6/05/02	6/13/02	6/17/02	6/28/02
0.30Q	9/04/02	9/12/02	9/16/02	9/30/02
0.30Q	12/04/02	12/12/02	12/16/02	1/03/03
0.30Q	3/05/03	3/13/03	3/17/03	3/31/03

Indicated div.: $1.20 (Div. Reinv. Plan)

*7 YEAR PRICE SCORE 115.4   ***12 MONTH PRICE SCORE 80.3**

*NYSE COMPOSITE INDEX=100

CAPITALIZATION (12/31/01):

	($000)	(%)
Long-Term Debt	5,283,000	46.7
Deferred Income Tax	1,111,000	9.8
Common & Surplus	4,907,000	43.4
Total	11,301,000	100.0

BUSINESS:

Amerada Hess Corporation and its subsidiaries explore for, produce, purchase, transport and sell crude oil and natural gas. These exploration and production activities take place in the U.S., United Kingdom, Norway, Denmark, Gabon, Indonesia, Thailand, Azerbaijan, Algeria, Colombia, Equatorial Guinea, Malaysia and other countries. AHC also manufactures, purchases, transports, trades and markets refined petroleum and other energy products. As of

12/31/01, AHC owned 50.0% of a refinery joint venture in the U.S. Virgin Islands, and another refining facility, terminals and retail gasoline stations located on the East Coast of the U.S. Retail sales were performed through about 1,158 Hess brand retail outlets. In 2001, revenues were derived as follows: refining, marketing and shipping, 70.5%; exploration and production, 29.5%. On 8/20/01, AHC acquired Triton Energy Limited for approximately $3.20 billion.

RECENT DEVELOPMENTS:

For the year ended 12/31/02, the Company reported a net loss of $218.0 million compared with net income of $914.0 million a year earlier. Results for 2002 included after-tax net special charges of $769.0 million, comprised of an asset impairment charge of $786.0 million, a charge of $43.0 million for an increase in the UK income tax rate, a charge

of $14.0 million related to the reduction in carrying value of intangible assets, a charge of $8.0 million related to severance accrual, and a net gain of $82.0 million from asset sales. Results for 2001 included after-tax non-recurring charges of $31.0 million. Total revenues and other non-operating income decreased 11.2% to $12.09 billion.

PROSPECTS:

Recent production declines, coupled with lackluster refining and marketing results, tempers AHC's near-term outlook. For instance, for the quarter ended 12/31/02, the Company's oil and gas production, on a barrel-of-oil equivalent basis, declined 7.3% to 434,000 barrels per day year-over-year. In addition, AHC recorded an after-tax

impairment charge of $530.0 million in the fourth quarter of 2002 to reduce the carrying value of the Ceiba field in Equatorial Guinea. The non-cash charge principally results from a reduction in probable reserves and higher field development costs associated with extending the field life. There was no revision to Ceiba's proved crude oil reserves.

ANNUAL FINANCIAL DATA:

FISCAL YEAR	TOT. REVS. ($mill.)	NET INC. ($mill.)	TOT. ASSETS ($mill.)	OPER. PROFIT %	NET PROFIT %	RET. ON EQUITY %	RET. ON ASSETS %	CURR. RATIO	EARN. PER SH.$	CASH FL. PER SH.$	TANG. BK. VAL.$	DIV. PER SH.$	PRICE RANGE	AVG. P/E RATIO	AVG. YIELD %
p12/31/02	12,093.0	⑦ d218.0							⑦ d2.48				84.70 — 49.40	...	1.8
12/31/01	13,613.0	⑥ 914.0	15,369.0	10.6	6.7	18.6	5.9	1.1	⑥ 10.25	21.10	44.22	1.05	90.40 — 53.75	7.0	1.5
12/31/00	12,277.0	⑤ 1,023.0	10,274.0	13.6	8.3	26.3	10.0	1.2	⑤ 11.38	19.33	43.76	0.60	76.25 — 47.81	5.5	1.0
12/31/99	7,461.4	④ 437.6	7,727.7	11.1	5.9	14.4	5.7	1.2	④ 4.85	12.03	33.51	0.60	66.31 — 43.75	11.3	1.1
12/31/98	6,621.1	③ d458.9	7,883.0	...	...	...	...	1.1	③ d5.12	2.26	29.26	0.60	61.06 — 46.00	...	1.1
12/31/97	8,340.0	⑦ 7.5	7,934.6	2.5	0.1	0.2	0.1	1.3	⑦ 0.08	7.38	35.16	0.60	64.50 — 47.38	698.3	1.1
12/31/96	8,929.7	① 660.1	7,784.5	11.4	7.4	19.5	8.5	1.4	⑦ 7.09	15.50	36.35	0.60	60.50 — 47.50	7.6	1.1
12/31/95	7,524.8	① d394.4	7,756.4	3.1	...	...	...	1.3	① d4.24	5.36	28.60	0.60	53.63 — 43.25	...	1.2
12/31/94	6,698.8	73.7	8,337.9	3.5	1.1	2.4	0.9	1.4	0.79	10.81	33.33	0.45	52.63 — 43.75	61.0	0.9
12/31/93	5,872.7	② d297.7	8,641.5	...	...	...	...	1.2	② d3.22	5.69	32.71	0.60	56.38 — 42.38	...	1.2

Statistics are as originally reported. ① Incl. nonrecur. net chrg. 12/31/97: $16.8 mil.; net cr. 12/31/96: $424.4 mil.; net chrg. 12/31/95: $381.1 mil. ② Bef. acctg. chge. cr. of $29.5 mil. & incl. nonrecur. chrgs. of $65.0 mil. ③ Incl. loss of $25.7 mil. fr. sale of assets & asset impair. chrg. of $206.5 mil. ④ Incl. cr. of $176.0 mil. fr. asset sales; tax benefit of $54.6 mil. & asset impair. chrg. of $99.5 mil. ⑤ Incl. net aft.-tax gain of $60.0 mil. on acq. termin. & nonrecur. chrg. of $24.0 mil. ⑥ Incl. nonrecur. aft.-tax chrgs. of $31.0 mil. ⑦ Incl. aft.-tax chrgs. of $769.0 mil.

OFFICERS:
J. B. Hess, Chmn., C.E.O.
J. Y. Schreyer, Exec. V.P., C.F.O.
G. A. Jamin, Sr. V.P., Treas.
INVESTOR CONTACT: C. T. Tursi, Investor Relations, (212) 536-8593
PRINCIPAL OFFICE: 1185 Avenue of the Americas, New York, NY 10036

TELEPHONE NUMBER: (212) 997-8500
FAX: (212) 536-8390
WEB: www.hess.com
NO. OF EMPLOYEES: 10,838 (avg.)
SHAREHOLDERS: 6,481
ANNUAL MEETING: In May
INCORPORATED: DE, Feb., 1920

INSTITUTIONAL HOLDINGS:
No. of Institutions: 305
Shares Held: 69,041,162
% Held: 77.4

INDUSTRY: Petroleum refining (SIC: 2911)

TRANSFER AGENT(S): The Bank of New York, New York, NY

AMEREN CORPORATION

EXCH.	SYM.	REC. PRICE	P/E RATIO	YLD.	MKT. CAP.	RANGE (52-WK.)	'02 Y/E PR.
NYSE	AEE	38.99 (2/28/03)	14.7	6.5%	$5.38 bill.	45.19 - 34.72	41.57

MEDIUM GRADE. THE COMPANY RECENTLY COMPLETED THE ACQUISITION OF CILCORP INC.

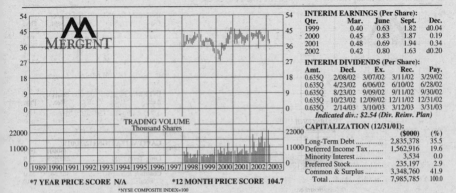

*7 YEAR PRICE SCORE N/A   ***12 MONTH PRICE SCORE 104.7**

*NYSE COMPOSITE INDEX=100

INTERIM EARNINGS (Per Share):

Qtr.	Mar.	June	Sept.	Dec.
1999	0.40	0.63	1.82	d0.04
2000	0.45	0.83	1.87	0.19
2001	0.48	0.69	1.94	0.34
2002	0.42	0.80	1.63	d0.20

INTERIM DIVIDENDS (Per Share):

Amt.	Decl.	Ex.	Rec.	Pay.
0.635Q	2/08/02	3/07/02	3/11/02	3/29/02
0.635Q	4/23/02	6/06/02	6/10/02	6/28/02
0.635Q	8/23/02	9/09/02	9/11/02	9/30/02
0.635Q	10/23/02	12/09/02	12/11/02	12/31/02
0.635Q	2/14/03	3/10/03	3/12/03	3/31/03

Indicated div.: $2.54 (Div. Reinv. Plan)

CAPITALIZATION (12/31/01):

	($000)	(%)
Long-Term Debt	2,835,378	35.5
Deferred Income Tax	1,562,916	19.6
Minority Interest	3,534	0.0
Preferred Stock	235,197	2.9
Common & Surplus	3,348,760	41.9
Total	7,985,785	100.0

BUSINESS:

Ameren Corporation was formed on 12/31/97 upon the merger of Union Electric Company, now known as AmerenUE, and Central Illinois Public Service Company (CIPSCO, Inc.), now known as AmerenCIPS. As of 2/11/03, AEE companies provide energy services to 1.7 million electric and 500,000 natural gas customers throughout its 49,000 square mile territory in Missouri and Illinois. AEE also operates AmerenEnergy Generating Company, a non-regulated electric generating company; AmerenEnergy,

Inc., an energy marketing and trading affiliate; CIPSCO Investment Co., which manages nonutility investments; and Ameren Services, which provides support services to the corporation and its subsidiaries. In 2002, 91.6% of consolidated revenues were derived from the sale of electricity, 8.2% from the sales of natural gas and 0.2% from other sources. On 1/31/03, AEE acquired CILCORP Inc., now known as AmerenCILCO.

RECENT DEVELOPMENTS:

For the year ended 12/31/02, AEE reported net income of $382.0 million versus income of $476.0 million, before an accounting change charge of $7.0 million, in the previous year. Results for 2002 and 2001 included allowances for equity funds of $6.0 million and $13.0 million, respectively. Also, results for 2002 included voluntary retirement

and other restructuring charges of $92.0 million. Total operating revenue slipped 0.4% to $3.84 billion from $3.86 billion a year earlier. Electric revenues increased 0.4% to $3.52 billion, while gas revenues fell 7.9% to $315.0 million. Other revenues dropped 33.3% to $6.0 million. Operating income decreased 6.3% to $623.0 million.

PROSPECTS:

Looking to 2003, AEE expects the challenging operating environment to continue. However, AEE has taken numerous actions to significantly lower costs and benefit future operations, such as recent facility closings and suspensions. Meanwhile, the Company expects to benefit from its recent

acquisition of CILCORP Inc., acquired for approximately $1.40 billion. The acquisition should be accretive to earnings in the first year and provide long-term growth opportunities. Separately, for 2003, AEE expects earnings in the range of $2.80 to $3.05 per share.

ANNUAL FINANCIAL DATA:

FISCAL YEAR	TOT. REVS. ($mill.)	NET INC. ($mill.)	TOT. ASSETS ($mill.)	OPER. PROFIT %	NET PROFIT %	NET INC./ NET PROP. %	NET INC./ TOT. CAP. %	RET. ON EQUITY %	ACCUM. DEPR./ GROSS PROP. %	EARN. PER SH.$	TANG. BK. VAL.$	DIV. PER SH.$	DIV. PAYOUT %	PRICE RANGE	AVG. P/E RATIO	AVG. YIELD %
p12/31/02	3,841.0	⑤ 382.0								⑤ 2.60		2.54	97.7	45.19 - 34.72	15.4	6.4
12/31/01	4,505.9	④ 475.4	10,400.6	14.8	10.6	5.6	6.0	13.3	43.7	④ 3.45	24.26	2.54	73.6	46.00 - 36.53	12.0	6.2
12/31/00	3,855.8	③ 457.1	9,714.4	16.6	11.9	5.9	5.9	13.3	44.6	③ 3.33	23.30	2.54	76.3	46.94 - 27.56	11.2	6.8
12/31/99	3,523.6	385.1	9,177.6	16.0	10.9	5.4	5.3	11.6	45.1	2.81	22.52	2.54	90.4	42.94 - 32.00	13.3	6.8
12/31/98	3,318.2	② 386.5	8,847.4	17.2	11.6	5.6	5.4	11.7	44.7	② 2.82	22.27	2.54	90.1	44.31 - 35.56	14.2	6.4
12/31/97	3,326.5	① 386.5	8,827.5	17.5	11.6	5.5	5.3	11.9	43.1	① 2.82	22.00	...	...	...	...	...
12/31/96	3,328.4	371.7	8,932.6	17.3	11.2	5.3	5.1	11.2	42.0	2.71	21.98	...	...	...	...	...
12/31/95	3,235.9	372.9	...	17.9	11.5	...	...	...	...	2.72	...	...	...	...	...	...

Statistics are as originally reported. Results prior to 1997 are reported on a pro forma basis ① Bef. extraord. chrg. $51.8 mil.; incl. nonrecurr. chrg. $25.0 mill. ② Incl. after-tax nonrecurr. chrg. $31.0 mill. ③ Incl. after-tax nonrecurr. chrg. $15.0 mill. & credit $65.0 mill. assoc. with the alternative rate regulation plan. ④ Bef. an after-tax acctg. change chrg. $6.8 mill. ⑤ Incl. voluntary retirement and oth. restr. chrg. $92.0 mill.

OFFICERS:
C. W. Mueller, Chmn., C.E.O.
G. L. Rainwater, Pres., C.O.O.
S. R. Sullivan, V.P., Gen. Couns., Sec.
INVESTOR CONTACT: Bruce Steinke, (314) 554-2574
PRINCIPAL OFFICE: 1901 Chouteau Avenue, St. Louis, MO 63103

TELEPHONE NUMBER: (314) 621-3222
FAX: (314) 621-2888
WEB: www.ameren.com
NO. OF EMPLOYEES: 7,447
SHAREHOLDERS: 101,455
ANNUAL MEETING: In April
INCORPORATED: MO, Aug., 1995

INSTITUTIONAL HOLDINGS:
No. of Institutions: 304
Shares Held: 74,042,959
% Held: 48.2

INDUSTRY: Electric services (SIC: 4911)

TRANSFER AGENT(S): Ameren Services Company, St. Louis, MO

AMERICA WEST HOLDINGS CORPORATION

EXCH.	SYM.	REC. PRICE	P/E RATIO	YLD.	MKT. CAP.	RANGE (52-WK.)	'02 Y/E PR.
NYSE	AWA	1.85 (2/28/03)	...	...	$92.5 mill.	6.45 - 0.90	1.80

SPECULATIVE GRADE. THE COMPANY IS ELIMINATING ITS HUB OPERATIONS LOCATED IN COLUMBUS, OHIO.

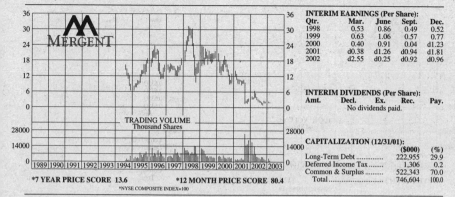

INTERIM EARNINGS (Per Share):

Qtr.	Mar.	June	Sept.	Dec.
1998	0.53	0.86	0.49	0.52
1999	0.63	1.06	0.57	0.77
2000	0.40	0.91	0.04	d1.23
2001	d0.38	d1.26	d0.94	d1.81
2002	d2.55	d0.25	d0.92	d0.96

INTERIM DIVIDENDS (Per Share):

Amt.	Decl.	Ex.	Rec.	Pay.
		No dividends paid.		

TRADING VOLUME
Thousand Shares

CAPITALIZATION (12/31/01):

	($000)	(%)
Long-Term Debt	222,955	29.9
Deferred Income Tax	1,306	0.2
Common & Surplus	522,343	70.0
Total	746,604	100.0

*7 YEAR PRICE SCORE 13.6   ***12 MONTH PRICE SCORE 80.4**

*NYSE COMPOSITE INDEX=100

BUSINESS:

America West Holdings Corporation is an aviation and travel company that operates through two wholly-owned subsidiaries, America West Airlines and The Leisure Company. As of 12/31/02, America West Airlines provided service to 88 destinations in the U.S., Canada and Mexico and operated a fleet of 145 aircraft. America West Airlines' operations are centered around its principal hubs in Phoenix, Arizona and Las Vegas, Nevada. The Leisure Company offers individual and group travel packages directly to consumers, as well as through retail travel agencies in the U.S., Canada and Mexico.

RECENT DEVELOPMENTS:

For the twelve months ended 12/31/02, the Company reported a loss of $157.9 million, before a $272.3 million accounting change charge, compared with a net loss of $147.9 million in the prior year. Results for 2002 included a special pre-tax charge of $58.3 million, partially offset by an $8.5 million pre-tax gain from federal government assistance. Results for 2001 included a pre-tax gain of $108.2 million from federal government assistance, a special pre-tax charge of $38.4 million, and a $19.9 million pre-tax charge for reorganization value amortization. Total operating revenues slipped 0.9% to $2.05 billion from $2.07 billion the previous year. Passenger operating revenues declined 0.6% to $1.93 billion, while cargo operating revenues slid 18.5% to $27.6 million. The passenger load factor, or percentage of seats filled, improved to 73.6% from 71.9% in 2001.

PROSPECTS:

On 2/10/03, the Company announced that it is eliminating its hub operations located in Columbus, Ohio in an effort to boost profitability. As a result, AWA plans to phase 12 regional jets out of its America West Express fleet by mid-June 2003. In addition, New York's LaGuardia Airport will be the only America West destination closed as a result of the elimination of the Columbus hub. However, AWA will continue to serve the New York metropolitan area through both John F. Kennedy and Newark International Airports. Separately, the Company plans to begin service to Memphis in April 2003.

ANNUAL FINANCIAL DATA:

FISCAL YEAR	TOT. REVS. ($mill.)	NET INC. ($mill.)	TOT. ASSETS ($mill.)	OPER. PROFIT %	NET PROFIT %	RET. ON EQUITY %	RET. ON ASSETS %	CURR. RATIO	EARN. PER SH. $	CASH FL. PER SH. $	TANG. BK. VAL. $	PRICE RANGE	AVG. P/E RATIO
p12/31/02	2,047.1	⑥ d157.9							⑥ d4.68			6.45 - 0.90	...
12/31/01	2,065.9	⑤ d147.9	1,570.9	...	...	...	...	0.5	⑤ d4.39	1.43	10.44	14.19 - 1.45	...
12/31/00	2,344.4	7.7	1,568.5	...	0.3	1.2	0.5	0.7	0.22	5.54	20.43	20.94 - 8.94	67.9
12/31/99	2,210.9	① 119.4	1,507.2	9.3	5.4	16.7	7.9	0.7	① 3.03	7.57	14.38	24.13 - 16.00	6.6
12/31/98	2,023.3	① 108.6	1,525.0	10.3	5.4	16.2	7.1	0.6	① 2.40	5.80	14.43	31.31 - 9.56	8.5
12/31/97	1,875.0	75.0	1,546.8	8.6	4.0	11.0	4.8	0.7	1.63	4.41	14.87	18.88 - 12.00	9.5
12/31/96	1,739.5	②④ 9.6	1,597.7	3.9	0.6	1.5	0.6	0.7	②④ 0.21	2.43	13.59	23.75 - 10.88	82.4
12/31/95	1,550.6	②④ 54.8	1,588.7	10.0	3.5	8.4	3.4	0.8	②④ 1.18	2.87	14.36	19.00 - 6.38	10.8
12/31/94	469.8	7.8	1,545.1	8.3	1.7	1.3	0.5	0.9	0.17	0.69	13.55	16.38 - 6.38	66.9
12/31/93	1,325.4	③ 37.2	1,016.7	9.1	2.8	...	3.7	0.6	③ 1.04	4.14	...	...	...

Statistics are as originally reported. ① Incl. Leisure Company expense, 1999, $52.9 mill.; 1998, $39.5 mill. ② Incl. nonrecurr. special chrg., 1996, $65.1 mill.; 1995, $10.5 mill. ③ Incl. reorgan. expenses of $25.0 mill. ④ Bef. extraord. chrg., 1996, $21.1 mill.; 1995, $984,000 ⑤ Incl. $108.2 mill. gain fr. federal grant & $38.4 mill. non-recurr. special chg. ⑥ Bef. $272.3 mill. ($8.07/sh) acctg. chrg., incl. $58.3 mill. non-recurr. special chrg. and $8.5 mill. gain fr. federal grant.

OFFICERS: W. D. Parker, Chmn., Pres., C.E.O. D. Kerr, Sr. V.P., C.F.O. **INVESTOR CONTACT:** Investor Relations, (480) 693-1227 **PRINCIPAL OFFICE:** 111 West Rio Salado Parkway, Tempe, AZ 85281	**TELEPHONE NUMBER:** (480) 693-0800 **FAX:** (480) 693-5546 **WEB:** www.americawest.com **NO. OF EMPLOYEES:** 13,229 **SHAREHOLDERS:** 3 (class A); 4,658 (approx. class B) **ANNUAL MEETING:** In May **INCORPORATED:** DE, Sept., 1981	**INSTITUTIONAL HOLDINGS:** No. of Institutions: 35 Shares Held: 13,225,215 % Held: 39.2 **INDUSTRY:** Air transportation, scheduled (SIC: 4512) **TRANSFER AGENT(S):** Computershare Investor Services, Chicago, IL

AMERICAN AXLE & MANUFACTURING HOLDINGS, INC.

EXCH.	SYM.	REC. PRICE	P/E RATIO	YLD.	MKT. CAP.	RANGE (52-WK.)	'02 Y/E PR.
NYSE	AXL	23.65 (2/28/03)	7.0	...	$1.11 bill.	36.67 - 19.70	23.42

MEDIUM GRADE. THE COMPANY EXPECTS EARNINGS OF APPROXIMATELY $3.65 PER SHARE IN 2003.

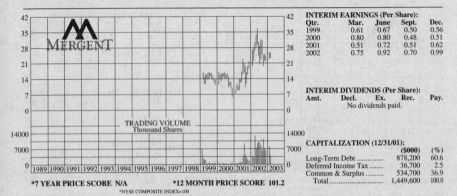

INTERIM EARNINGS (Per Share):

Qtr.	Mar.	June	Sept.	Dec.
1999	0.61	0.67	0.50	0.56
2000	0.80	0.80	0.48	0.51
2001	0.51	0.72	0.51	0.62
2002	0.75	0.92	0.70	0.99

INTERIM DIVIDENDS (Per Share):

Amt.	Decl.	Ex.	Rec.	Pay.
		No dividends paid.		

TRADING VOLUME
Thousand Shares

CAPITALIZATION (12/31/01):

	($000)	(%)
Long-Term Debt	878,200	60.6
Deferred Income Tax	36,700	2.5
Common & Surplus	534,700	36.9
Total	1,449,600	100.0

*7 YEAR PRICE SCORE N/A   ***12 MONTH PRICE SCORE 101.2**
*NYSE COMPOSITE INDEX=100

BUSINESS:

American Axle & Manufacturing Holdings, Inc., formerly the final drive and forge business unit of General Motors (GM), is the parent company of Colfor Manufacturing, Inc., MSP Industries Corporation and Albion Automotive Holdings Limited. The Company, through its subsidiaries, is a Tier 1 automotive supplier that manufactures, engineers and designs, and validates driveline systems, chassis systems and forged products for trucks, buses, sport utility

vehicles and passenger cars. The Company's driveline products include axles, propeller shafts, chassis components, forged products and other products for rear-wheel drive passenger cars. In 2002, sales to General Motors Corp. accounted for approximately 86.0% total sales. As of 1/23/03, AXL operated 14 domestic manufacturing facilities, as well as offices and facilities in Brazil, England, Germany, Japan, Mexico and Scotland.

RECENT DEVELOPMENTS:

For the year ended 12/31/02, net income advanced 53.3% to $176.1 million compared with $114.9 million in the previous year. Results for 2002 included a net gain from an insurance recovery of $10.4 million. Results for 2001 included amortization of intangibles of $4.0 million. Net sales climbed 12.0% to $3.48 billion from $3.11 billion a year earlier. Sales were positively affected by increased

GM light truck production and the successful launches of both the new heavy-duty Dodge Ram program and the HUMMER H2 program. Gross profit rose 20.0% to $491.7 million from $409.7 million in 2001. Operating income jumped 29.0% to $311.2 million from $241.3 million the year before. Net interest expense declined 14.8% to $50.6 million from $59.4 million in the prior year.

PROSPECTS:

The Company is well positioned for further growth in 2003. The Company expects approximately 80.0% of sales to come from new products introduced since mid-1998, products which AXL expects to fit into a growth segment of the market. The Company anticipates 2003 North American

light vehicle production of over 16.0 million units, with vehicles with four-wheel drive or all-wheel drive systems remaining a strong segment of the market. For 2003, AXL has increased its earnings guidance to $3.65 per share from the previous guidance of $3.50 per share.

ANNUAL FINANCIAL DATA:

FISCAL YEAR	TOT. REVS. ($mill.)	NET INC. ($mill.)	TOT. ASSETS ($mill.)	OPER. PROFIT %	NET PROFIT %	RET. ON EQUITY %	RET. ON ASSETS %	CURR. RATIO	EARN. PER SH. $	CASH FL. PER SH. $	TANG. BK. VAL. $	PRICE RANGE	AVG. P/E RATIO
p12/31/02	3,480.2	④ 176.1	2,335.7						④ 3.38			36.67 - 19.55	8.3
12/31/01	3,107.2	① 114.9	2,160.9	7.8	3.7	21.5	5.3	1.0	① 2.36	4.96	8.16	23.10 - 7.56	6.5
12/31/00	3,069.5	129.2	1,902.5	8.5	4.2	34.7	6.8	1.0	2.60	4.77	8.51	17.13 - 5.75	4.4
12/31/99	2,953.1	115.6	1,677.1	8.2	3.9	43.8	6.9	1.1	2.34	4.14	5.69	17.38 - 11.38	6.1
12/31/98	2,040.6	3.5	1,226.2	2.5	0.2	8.7	0.3	0.8	0.08	1.67	1.24	...	...
③ 12/31/97	2,147.5	② 55.3	1,017.7	5.4	2.6	148.4	5.4	0.7	② 0.43	0.83	4.54	...	...
③ 12/31/96	2,022.3	61.7	771.2	4.6	3.1	13.7	8.0	1.4	0.58	1.01	11.88	...	...
③ 12/31/95	1,968.1	70.6	...	5.5	3.6	...	...	...	0.85	1.15	...	...	...

Statistics are as originally reported. ① Financials for American Axle & Manufacturing of Michigan, Inc. ② Incl. pre-tax nonrecurr. chrg. $15.9 mill. ③ Incl. a pre-tax consolidation chrg. of $11.7 mill. ④ Incl. pre-tax net insurance recovery gain of $10.4 mill.

OFFICERS:
R. E. Dauch, Chmn., C.E.O.
J. D. Robinson, Pres., C.O.O.
R. J. Adams, Exec. V.P., C.F.O.
INVESTOR CONTACT: David J. Demos, V.P., Investor Relations, (313) 974-3074
PRINCIPAL OFFICE: 1840 Holbrook Avenue, Detroit, MI 48212-3488

TELEPHONE NUMBER: (313) 974-2000
FAX: (313) 974-3090
WEB: www.aam.com
NO. OF EMPLOYEES: 11,725 (approx.)
SHAREHOLDERS: 482 (approx.)
ANNUAL MEETING: In May
INCORPORATED: DE, 1998

INSTITUTIONAL HOLDINGS:
No. of Institutions: 165
Shares Held: 25,588,819
% Held: 51.5
INDUSTRY: Motor vehicle parts and accessories (SIC: 3714)
TRANSFER AGENT(S): EquiServe Trust Company, N.A., Jersey City, NJ

AMERICAN ELECTRIC POWER COMPANY, INC.

EXCH.	SYM.	REC. PRICE	P/E RATIO	YLD.	MKT. CAP.	RANGE (52-WK.)	'02 Y/E PR.
NYSE	AEP	21.78 (2/28/03)	...	11.0%	$7.02 bill.	48.80 - 15.10	27.33

MEDIUM GRADE. THE COMPANY EXPECTS EARNINGS FOR 2003 IN THE RANGE OF $2.50 TO $2.70 PER SHARE.

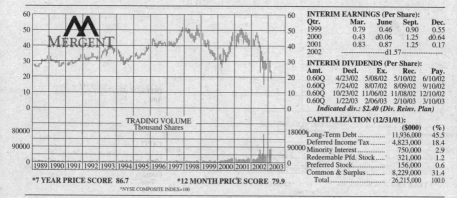

INTERIM EARNINGS (Per Share):

Qtr.	Mar.	June	Sept.	Dec.
1999	0.79	0.46	0.90	0.55
2000	0.43	d0.06	1.25	d0.64
2001	0.83	0.87	1.25	0.17
2002	----------------d1.57----------------			

INTERIM DIVIDENDS (Per Share):

Amt.	Decl.	Ex.	Rec.	Pay.
0.60Q	4/23/02	5/08/02	5/10/02	6/10/02
0.60Q	7/24/02	8/07/02	8/09/02	9/10/02
0.60Q	10/23/02	11/06/02	11/08/02	12/10/02
0.60Q	1/22/03	2/06/03	2/10/03	3/10/03

Indicated div.: $2.40 (Div. Reinv. Plan)

CAPITALIZATION (12/31/01):

	($000)	(%)
Long-Term Debt	11,936,000	45.5
Deferred Income Tax	4,823,000	18.4
Minority Interest	750,000	2.9
Redeemable Pfd. Stock	321,000	1.2
Preferred Stock	156,000	0.6
Common & Surplus	8,229,000	31.4
Total	26,215,000	100.0

TRADING VOLUME
Thousand Shares

*7 YEAR PRICE SCORE 86.7   ***12 MONTH PRICE SCORE 79.9**

*NYSE COMPOSITE INDEX=100

BUSINESS:

American Electric Power Company, Inc. is a holding company that controls one of the largest electric systems in the U.S. As of 3/10/03, AEP owned and operated more than 42,000 megawatts of generating capacity in the U.S. and select international markets. AEP is a wholesale marketer and trader of electricity and natural gas in North America and Europe. In addition to electricity generation, AEP owns and operates natural gas storage and pipeline systems, coal mines, and an inland barge subsidiary in Texas. Also, AEP is a large electric utility with nearly 5.0 million domestic customers as of 3/10/03. On 6/15/00, AEP acquired Central and South West Coporation.

RECENT DEVELOPMENTS:

For the year ended 12/31/02, the Company reported a loss of $519.0 million compared with a income of $971.0 million in the previous year. Results for 2002 included a charge of $1.50 billion for the write-off of assets. Earnings for 2002 were negatively affected by the poor performance of the Company's wholesale investments. Revenues advanced 14.2% to $14.50 billion from $12.70 billion a year earlier. Comparisons were made with restated prior-year results.

PROSPECTS:

The Company expects earnings for 2003 in the range of $2.50 to $2.70 per share. The guidance is based on assumptions that earnings from utility operations will be flat versus 2002 and expected contributions from non-utility investments will continue to erode. Separately, the Company recently sold the assets of its C3 Communications subsidiary to Grande Communications for $7.0 million. In addition, the Company has completed the sale of Mutual Energy Service Company, LLC, the customer-care operation created to manage retail customer accounts in Texas, to Alliance Data Systems in a transaction with a cash value of $30.0 million. The sales are part of an ongoing effort to divest assets that are not a part of AEP's core utility businesses.

ANNUAL FINANCIAL DATA:

FISCAL YEAR	TOT. REVS. (Smill.)	NET INC. (Smill.)	TOT. ASSETS (Smill.)	OPER. PROFIT %	NET PROFIT %	NET INC./ NET PROP. %	NET INC./ TOT. CAP. %	RET. ON EQUITY %	ACCUM. DEPR./ GROSS PROP. %	EARN. PER SH.$	TANG. BK. VAL.$	DIV. PER SH.$	DIV. PAYOUT %	PRICE RANGE	AVG. P/E RATIO	AVG. YIELD %
p12/31/02	14,500.0	d519.0								⑧d1.57		2.40	...	48.80 - 15.10	...	7.5
⑦12/31/01	61,257.0	⑥1,003.0	47,281.0	3.9	1.6	4.1	3.8	12.0	39.7	⑥3.11	20.90	2.40	77.2	51.20 - 39.25	14.5	5.3
⑤12/31/00	13,694.0	④302.0	53,167.0	14.8	2.2	1.3	1.3	3.7	41.2	④0.94	20.72	2.40	255.3	48.94 - 25.94	39.8	6.4
12/31/99	6,916.0	③520.0	21,488.0	18.9	7.5	4.0	3.6	10.1	41.2	③2.69	25.79	2.40	89.2	48.19 - 30.56	14.6	6.1
12/31/98	6,345.9	536.2	19,483.2	15.1	8.4	4.3	3.7	11.0	41.8	2.81	25.24	2.40	85.4	53.31 - 42.06	17.0	5.0
12/31/97	5,879.8	②620.4	16,615.3	16.7	10.6	5.3	4.9	13.1	40.6	②3.28	24.62	2.40	73.2	52.00 - 39.13	13.9	5.3
12/31/96	5,849.2	587.4	15,885.5	17.2	10.0	5.1	4.7	12.7	39.8	3.14	24.15	2.40	76.4	44.75 - 38.63	13.3	5.8
12/31/95	5,670.3	529.9	15,902.3	17.0	9.3	4.7	4.2	11.8	38.4	2.85	23.25	2.40	84.2	40.63 - 31.25	12.6	6.7
12/31/94	5,504.7	500.0	15,712.7	16.9	9.1	4.4	4.1	11.2	37.6	2.71	22.83	2.40	88.6	37.38 - 27.25	11.9	7.4
12/31/93	5,268.8	①353.8	15,341.4	17.6	6.7	3.2	2.9	8.0	37.3	①1.92	22.50	2.40	125.0	40.38 - 32.00	18.8	6.6

Statistics are as originally reported. ① Incl. non-recurr. chrg. $144.5 mill. ② Bef. extraord. chrg. of $109.4 mill. ③ Incl. a chrg of $0.43 per share from restart efforts net of deferrals under Indiana and Michigan settle. agree. ④ Bef. net after-tax extraord. loss of $35.0 mill. ⑤ Incl. opers. of Central & South West Corp., which was acq. on 6/15/00. ⑥ Bef. an after-tax acctg. gain of $18.0 mill. and an after-tax extraord. chrg. of $50.9 mill. ⑦ Revenues going forward reflect settled forward energy transactions from trading operations on a gross basis. ⑧ Incl. asset write-down chrg. $1.50 billion

OFFICERS:
E. L. Draper Jr., Chmn., Pres., C.E.O.
T. V. Shockely III, Vice-Chmn., C.O.O.
S. Tomasky, Exec. V.P., C.F.O.

INVESTOR CONTACT: Bette Jo Rozsa, Investor Relations, (614) 716-2840

PRINCIPAL OFFICE: 1 Riverside Plaza, Columbus, OH 43215

TELEPHONE NUMBER: (614) 223-1000
FAX: (614) 223-1823
WEB: www.aep.com
NO. OF EMPLOYEES: 27,726 (avg.)
SHAREHOLDERS: 150,000 (approx.)
ANNUAL MEETING: In April
INCORPORATED: NY, Dec., 1906; reincorp., NY, Feb., 1925

INSTITUTIONAL HOLDINGS:
No. of Institutions: 408
Shares Held: 197,817,654
% Held: 58.4

INDUSTRY: Electric services (SIC: 4911)

TRANSFER AGENT(S): EquiServe, First Chicago Division, Jersey City, NJ

AMERICAN EXPRESS COMPANY

EXCH.	SYM.	REC. PRICE	P/E RATIO	YLD.	MKT. CAP.	RANGE (52-WK.)	'02 Y/E PR.
NYSE	AXP	33.58 (2/28/03)	19.6	1.0%	$44.69 bill.	44.91 - 26.55	35.35

INVESTMENT GRADE. EARNINGS ARE BENEFITING FROM SOLID GROWTH IN AXP'S CREDIT CARD BUSINESSES, HIGHER REVENUES, LOWER EXPENSES AND STRONG CREDIT QUALITY.

TRADING VOLUME
Thousand Shares

*7 YEAR PRICE SCORE 110.0 ***12 MONTH PRICE SCORE 104.5**
*NYSE COMPOSITE INDEX=100

INTERIM EARNINGS (Per Share):
Qtr.	Mar.	June	Sept.	Dec.
1997	0.31	0.36	0.37	0.35
1998	0.33	0.41	0.42	0.39
1999	0.42	0.47	0.47	0.44
2000	0.48	0.54	0.54	0.50
2001	0.40	0.13	0.22	0.22
2002	0.46	0.51	0.52	0.52

INTERIM DIVIDENDS (Per Share):
Amt.	Decl.	Ex.	Rec.	Pay.
0.08Q	3/22/02	4/03/02	4/05/02	5/10/02
0.08Q	5/22/02	7/02/02	7/05/02	8/09/02
0.08Q	9/23/02	10/02/02	10/04/02	11/08/02
0.08Q	11/18/02	12/31/02	1/03/03	2/10/03
0.08Q	3/24/03	4/03/03	4/04/03	5/09/03

Indicated div.: $0.32 (Div. Reinv. Plan)

CAPITALIZATION (12/31/01):
	($000)	(%)
Long-Term Debt	7,788,000	39.3
Common & Surplus	12,037,000	60.7
Total	19,825,000	100.0

BUSINESS:

American Express Company operates in three primary divisions and is a leader in charge cards, travelers checks, travel products and services, financial planning and international banking. The Travel Related Services division (73.6% of 2002 revenues) provides, among other things, global network services, the American Express® Card and other consumer and corporate lending products, and corporate and consumer travel products and services. The Financial Advisors division (23.3%) provides financial planning and advice, a variety of investment products, personal insurance, and retail brokerage services. The American Express Bank (3.1%) provides financial services for corporations, financial institutions and retail customers, including American Express Travelers Cheques.

RECENT DEVELOPMENTS:

For the year ended 12/31/02, net income jumped to $2.67 billion from $1.31 billion the previous year. Earnings for 2001 included after-tax restructuring charges of $411.0 million, after-tax investment write-down charges of $669.0 million and one-time after-tax costs, including waived fees, of $65.0 million related to the events of 9/11/01. Total revenues increased 5.4% to $23.81 billion. By segment, net income for travel-related services climbed 46.3% to $2.14 billion. Net income from American Express Financial Advisors surged to $632.0 million from $52.0 million in 2001. Net income from American Express Bank was $80.0 million versus a loss of $13.0 million a year earlier.

PROSPECTS:

Results for 2002 reflected several factors, including a solid expansion of AXP's global card businesses, lower expenses due to the success of its ongoing reengineering programs, strong credit quality and the benefits of lower funding costs. Going forward, AXP enters 2003 with strong momentum, but remains cautious due to ongoing uncertainty in the economy and the financial markets. Nonetheless, AXP is encouraged by the early returns of its heavy investment in marketing and product development, particularly in its credit card business as AXP generated strong growth in cardmember spending, higher loan balances and added more than 900,00 new cards in force during the fourth quarter.

ANNUAL FINANCIAL DATA:

FISCAL YEAR	TOT. REVS. ($mil.)	NET INC. ($mil.)	TOT. ASSETS ($mil.)	OPER. PROFIT %	NET PROFIT %	RET. ON EQUITY %	RET. ON ASSETS %	CURR. RATIO	EARN. PER SH. $	CASH FL. PER SH. $	TANG. BK. VAL.$	DIV. PER SH. $	PRICE RANGE		AVG. P/E RATIO	AVG. YIELD %
p12/31/02	23,807.0	2,671.0		13.7	5.8	10.9	0.9	0.6	2.01			0.32	44.91 -	26.55	17.8	0.9
12/31/01	22,582.0	③ 1,311.0	151,100.0						③ 0.98	0.98	9.04	0.32	57.06 -	24.20	41.5	0.8
12/31/00	23,675.0	2,810.0	154,423.0	22.2	11.9	24.0	1.8	0.6	2.07	2.07	8.81	0.32	63.00 -	39.83	24.8	0.6
12/31/99	21,278.0	2,475.0	148,517.0	21.1	11.6	24.5	1.7	0.6	1.81	1.81	7.53	0.30	56.29 -	31.62	24.3	0.7
12/31/98	19,132.0	2,141.0	126,933.0	20.5	11.2	22.1	1.7	0.6	1.54	1.54	7.18	0.30	39.54 -	22.33	20.0	1.0
12/31/97	17,760.0	1,991.0	120,003.0	20.7	11.2	20.8	1.7	0.6	1.38	1.39	6.84	0.30	30.50 -	17.87	17.5	1.2
12/31/96	16,237.0	② 1,901.0	108,512.0	23.3	11.7	22.3	1.8	0.6	② 1.30	1.30	6.01	0.30	20.12 -	12.87	12.7	1.8
12/31/95	15,841.0	1,564.0	107,405.0	21.6	9.9	19.0	1.5	0.6	1.04	1.05	5.53	0.30	15.04 -	9.67	11.9	2.4
12/31/94	14,282.0	① 1,380.0	97,006.0	20.3	9.7	21.5	1.4	0.6	① 0.89	0.90	4.19	0.32	11.04 -	8.42	10.9	3.3
12/31/93	14,173.0	1,605.0	94,132.0	29.0	11.3	18.4	1.7	0.6	1.06	1.07	5.81	0.33	12.21 -	7.46	9.3	3.4

Statistics are as originally reported. Adj. for 3-for-1 stk. splt., 5/00 ① Bef. disc. oper gain $33.0 mill. ② Incl. non-recurr. credit $162.0 mill. ③ Incl. restruct. chrg. $411.0 mill., invest. write-down chrgs. of $669.0 mill. & non-recurr. chrgs. $65.0 mill.

OFFICERS:
K. I. Chenault, Chmn., C.E.O.
J. S. Linen, Vice-Chmn.
G. L. Crittenden, Exec. V.P., C.F.O.
INVESTOR CONTACT: Investor Relations, (212) 640-2000
PRINCIPAL OFFICE: World Financial Center, 200 Vesey Street, New York, NY 10285

TELEPHONE NUMBER: (212) 640-2000
FAX: (212) 619-9230
WEB: www.americanexpress.com
NO. OF EMPLOYEES: 84,417 (avg.)
SHAREHOLDERS: 52,041
ANNUAL MEETING: In April
INCORPORATED: NY, June, 1965

INSTITUTIONAL HOLDINGS:
No. of Institutions: 938
Shares Held: 1,082,044,779
% Held: 82.3
INDUSTRY: Misc. business credit institutions (SIC: 6159)
TRANSFER AGENT(S): Mellon Investor Services, Ridgefield Park, NJ

AMERICAN FINANCIAL GROUP, INC.

EXCH.	SYM.	REC. PRICE	P/E RATIO	YLD.	MKT. CAP.	RANGE (52-WK.)	'02 Y/E PR.
NYSE	AFG	19.83 (2/28/03)	11.0	2.5%	$1.36 bill.	30.30 - 17.90	23.07

LOWER MEDIUM GRADE. GOING FORWARD, AFG WILL CONTINUE TO FOCUS ON DISCIPLINED UNDERWRITING, PROPER RISK SELECTION AND ADEQUATE PRICING.

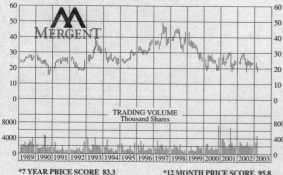

*7 YEAR PRICE SCORE 83.3   *12 MONTH PRICE SCORE 95.8
*NYSE COMPOSITE INDEX=100

INTERIM EARNINGS (Per Share):

Qtr.	Mar.	June	Sept.	Dec.
1997	1.03	1.03	0.57	0.68
1998	1.08	0.65	0.91	d0.63
1999	0.96	0.74	0.48	0.24
2000	0.76	0.28	d0.38	d1.43
2001	0.19	0.09	d0.81	0.46
2002	0.61	0.17	0.39	0.64

INTERIM DIVIDENDS (Per Share):

Amt.	Decl.	Ex.	Rec.	Pay.
0.125Q	1/08/02	1/16/02	1/19/02	1/25/02
0.125Q	4/01/02	4/11/02	4/15/02	4/25/02
0.125Q	7/01/02	7/11/02	7/15/02	7/25/02
0.125Q	10/01/02	10/10/02	10/15/02	10/25/02
0.125Q	1/02/03	1/13/03	1/15/03	1/25/03

Indicated div.: $0.50 (Div. Reinv. Plan)

CAPITALIZATION (12/31/01):

	($000)	(%)
Long-Term Debt	879,712	37.0
Common & Surplus	1,498,379	63.0
Total	2,378,091	100.0

BUSINESS:

American Financial Group, Inc. (formerly American Premier Group, Inc.) is a holding company engaged, through Great American Insurance Group, in the property and casualty insurance business. The Specialty group writes insurance coverage in specialized lines of business or customer groups such as inland and ocean marine, workers' compensation, agriculture, executive and professional liability, and umbrella and excess insurance coverage. The Personal group writes primarily private passenger automobile liability and physical damage insurance. Also, through Great American Financial Resources, Inc., the Company markets and sells retirement annuities products, life and supplemental health insurance products.

RECENT DEVELOPMENTS:

For the year ended 12/31/02, the Company reported income of $125.0 million, before an accounting change charge of $40.4 million, versus a loss of $4.8 million, before an accounting change charge of $10.0 million, the previous year. Earnings for 2002 included an after-tax charge of $19.5 million related to an asbestos litigation settlement and a tax resolution benefit of $31.0 million. Earnings for 2001 included a non-recurring charge of $81.3 million. Also, earnings for 2002 and 2001 included after-tax realized investment losses of $44.7 million and $12.7 million, respectively. Operating revenues declined 3.0% to $3.83 billion.

PROSPECTS:

Going forward, AFG should continue to benefit from current market conditions and expects the ongoing price firming in the commercial casualty markets to continue into 2004. Meanwhile, AFG will continue to focus on disciplined underwriting, proper risk selection and adequate pricing. AFG will continue to target average rate increases of 25.0% or more in 2003. Moreover, the recently completed initial public offering of Infinity Property and Casualty has provided capital that should enable AFG to take advantage of specialty market opportunities. AFG believes that its current mix of specialty businesses positions it for solid growth and improved profitability.

ANNUAL FINANCIAL DATA:

FISCAL YEAR	PREM. INC. ($mill.)	TOT. REVS. ($mill.)	NET INC. ($mill.)	TOT. ASSETS ($mill.)	TOT. INVST. ($mill.)	RET. ON REVS. %	RET. ON EQUITY %	RET. ON ASSETS %	EARN. PER SH. $	TANG. BK. VAL. $	AVG. YIELD %	DIV. PER SH. $	PRICE RANGE	AVG. P/E RATIO
p12/31/02		3,830.2	⑦ 125.0						⑦ 1.81		2.1	0.50	30.30 - 17.90	13.3
12/31/01	2,874.1	3,923.6	⑥ d4.8	17,401.7	11,062.3	...	...	...	⑥ d0.07	5.36	4.1	1.00	30.75 - 18.35	...
12/31/00	2,725.3	3,817.5	⑤ d47.0	16,415.5	10,574.0	...	...	...	⑤ d0.80	6.92	4.2	1.00	29.00 - 18.38	...
12/31/99	2,334.7	3,334.5	④ 147.0	16,054.1	10,431.9	4.4	11.0	0.9	④ 2.44	5.94	2.9	1.00	43.63 - 24.50	14.0
12/31/98	2,869.1	4,050.0	① 125.2	15,845.2	10,946.8	3.1	7.3	0.8	① 2.01	15.93	2.6	1.00	45.75 - 30.50	19.0
12/31/97	2,945.9	4,020.7	① 199.5	15,755.3	11,299.9	5.0	12.0	1.3	① 3.28	13.78	2.5	1.00	49.25 - 32.38	12.4
12/31/96	2,948.1	4,115.4	① 262.0	15,051.1	10,513.0	6.4	16.9	1.7	① 4.31	13.49	2.9	1.00	38.88 - 28.50	7.8
③ 12/31/95	2,648.7	3,629.6	① 190.4	14,953.9	10,097.0	5.2	13.2	1.3	① 3.87	11.74	3.6	1.00	32.13 - 22.88	7.1
12/31/94	1,557.9	1,767.4	② 0.8	4,194.0	2,684.1	...	0.1	...	② 0.02	22.95	3.2	0.99	33.25 - 21.63	N.M.
12/31/93	1,273.6	1,763.3	② 242.7	4,049.6	2,546.4	13.8	14.1	6.0	② 5.03	26.09	2.7	0.84	39.75 - 23.50	6.3

Statistics are as originally reported. ① Bef. extraord. chrg. 1998, $0.7 mill.; 1997, $7.2 mill.; 1996, $28.7 mill.; credit 1995, $0.8 mill. ② Bef. disc. oper. loss 1994, $0.5 mill.; 1993, $10.7 mill. ③ Refl. the merger of American Financial Corp. and American Premier Underwriters, Inc. ④ Incl. a net gain $14.0 mill. & excl. a loss $3.8 mill. for an acctg. change & an extraord. loss $1.7 mill. ⑤ Excl. loss of $9.1 mill. for acctg. chrg. ⑥ Excl. acctg. chrg. $10.0 mill.; Incl. 9/11/01 chrgs. $16.3 mill. & asbestos-related chrgs. of $65.0 mill. ⑦ Bef. acctg. chrg. of $40.4 mill.; incl. after-tax chrg. of $19.5 mill. for asbestos litigation & tax resolution benefit of $31.0 mill.

OFFICERS:
C. H. Lindner, Chmn., C.E.O.
K. E. Lindner, Co-Pres.
S. C. Lindner, Co-Pres.
C. H. Lindner III, Co-Pres.

PRINCIPAL OFFICE: One East Fourth Street, Suite 919, Cincinnati, OH 45202

TELEPHONE NUMBER: (513) 579-2121
FAX: (513) 579-0108
WEB: www.amfnl.com
NO. OF EMPLOYEES: 9,800 (approx.)
SHAREHOLDERS: 13,500 (approx.)
ANNUAL MEETING: In May
INCORPORATED: OH, 1994

AMERICAN GREETINGS CORPORATION

EXCH.	SYM.	REC. PRICE	P/E RATIO	YLD.	MKT. CAP.	RANGE (52-WK.)	'02 Y/E PR.
NYSE	AM	13.12 (2/28/03)	16.8	...	$0.84 bill.	23.80 - 12.41	15.80

MEDIUM GRADE. THE COMPANY CONTINUES TO BENEFIT FROM ITS COST-SAVINGS INITIATIVES.

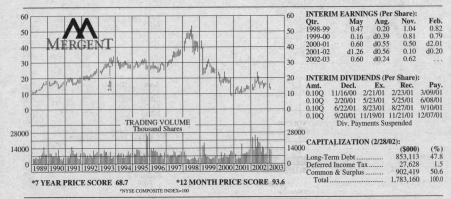

INTERIM EARNINGS (Per Share):

Qtr.	May	Aug.	Nov.	Feb.
1998-99	0.47	0.20	1.04	0.82
1999-00	0.16	d0.39	0.81	0.79
2000-01	0.60	d0.55	0.50	d2.01
2001-02	d1.26	d0.56	0.10	d0.20
2002-03	0.60	d0.24	0.62	...

INTERIM DIVIDENDS (Per Share):

Amt.	Decl.	Ex.	Rec.	Pay.
0.10Q	11/16/00	2/21/01	2/23/01	3/09/01
0.10Q	2/20/01	5/23/01	5/25/01	6/08/01
0.10Q	6/22/01	8/23/01	8/27/01	9/10/01
0.10Q	9/20/01	11/19/01	11/21/01	12/07/01
	Div. Payments Suspended			

*7 YEAR PRICE SCORE 68.7   ***12 MONTH PRICE SCORE 93.6**

*NYSE COMPOSITE INDEX=100

CAPITALIZATION (2/28/02):

	($000)	(%)
Long-Term Debt	853,113	47.8
Deferred Income Tax	27,628	1.5
Common & Surplus	902,419	50.6
Total	1,783,160	100.0

BUSINESS:

American Greetings Corporation designs, manufactures and sells everyday and seasonal greeting cards and other social expression products. More than 15,000 designs of greeting cards as well as gift wrap, paper party goods, candles, balloons, stationery and giftware are manufactured and sold in the U.S. by AM, Plus Mark, Inc., Carlton Cards Retail, Inc. and Quality Greeting Card Distributing Company. AM also manufactures and sells its products in Canada, the U.K, France, Mexico, Australia, New Zealand, and in South Africa. During 1988, AM acquired Camden Graphics Corp. and Hanson White Ltd., both located in the U.K. On 3/2/00, AM acquired Gibson Greetings, Inc. On 9/13/01, AM acquired the BlueMountain.com business, which operates an on-line card and entertainment Internet site.

RECENT DEVELOPMENTS:

For the quarter ended 11/30/02, net income surged to $47.0 million compared with $6.6 million in the corresponding period of the previous year. Earnings reflected AM's cost-savings initiatives. Earnings for 2001 included special after-tax charges of $34.3 million. Net sales rose 2.2% to $588.8 million from $575.9 million a year earlier. Material, labor and other production costs slid 2.3% to $285.3 million. Selling, distribution and marketing expenses decreased 9.6% to $159.7 million, while administrative and general expenses declined 34.0% to $47.0 million.

PROSPECTS:

The Company should continue to benefit from its cost-savings initiatives. Separately, on 12/23/02, the Company announced that it began selling its products at the 1,400 Albertson's Inc. stores that it does not already serve. AM hopes this will offset the losses associated with the termination of grocery store chain Winn-Dixie Stores Inc. as a customer, and the closure of hundreds of stores by another customer, Kmart Corp. Looking ahead, the Company anticipates earnings per share ranging from $1.45 to $1.55 for fiscal 2003, excluding a one-time gain on the sale of an investment.

ANNUAL FINANCIAL DATA:

FISCAL YEAR	TOT. REVS. ($mill.)	NET INC. ($mill.)	TOT. ASSETS ($mill.)	OPER. PROFIT %	NET PROFIT %	RET. ON EQUITY %	RET. ON ASSETS %	CURR. RATIO	EARN. PER SH.$	CASH FL. PER SH.$	TANG. BK. VAL.$	DIV. PER SH.$	PRICE RANGE	AVG. P/E RATIO	AVG. YIELD %
2/28/02	2,355.7	⑤ d122.3	2,615.0	...	...	...	...	1.5	⑤ d1.92	d0.60	11.03	0.40	15.36 — 8.19	...	3.4
2/28/01	2,518.8	② d92.7	2,712.1	6.8	...	...	...	1.1	② d1.46	0.08	12.87	0.82	24.06 — 8.19	...	5.1
2/29/00	2,175.2	④ 90.0	2,518.0	8.2	4.1	7.2	3.6	1.9	④ 1.37	2.35	14.18	0.78	44.31 — 22.00	24.2	2.4
2/28/99	2,205.7	④ 180.2	2,419.3	14.2	8.2	13.4	7.4	2.7	④ 2.53	3.48	15.57	0.74	53.75 — 35.00	17.5	1.7
2/28/97	2,172.3	③ 190.1	2,145.9	14.3	8.6	14.1	8.9	2.0	③ 2.55	3.43	18.90	0.70	38.75 — 27.38	13.0	2.1
2/28/97	2,172.3	167.1	2,135.1	13.1	7.7	12.3	7.8	2.3	2.23	3.10	18.16	0.66	30.50 — 23.50	12.1	2.4
2/29/96	2,012.0	① 115.1	2,005.8	9.9	5.7	9.3	5.7	2.1	① 1.54	2.56	16.53	0.60	33.00 — 25.50	19.0	2.1
2/28/95	1,878.4	148.8	1,761.8	13.0	7.9	12.8	8.4	2.5	2.00	2.92	15.61	0.53	34.00 — 25.88	15.0	1.8
2/28/94	1,780.8	② 130.9	1,565.2	12.7	7.3	12.4	8.4	2.3	② 1.77	2.58	14.21	0.47	34.25 — 22.50	16.0	1.6
2/28/93	1,688.2	112.3	1,548.4	12.3	6.7	14.5	8.5	2.8	1.55	2.22	13.07	0.41	26.19 — 18.56	14.4	1.8

Statistics are as originally reported. Adj. for 2-for-1 stock split, 6/93. ① Incl. $52.1 mill. asset impair. loss. ② Bef. acct. chrgs. of $21.1 mill., 2/01; $17.2 mill., 2/94. ③ Incl. pre-tax gain of $22.1 mill. resulting fr. the divest. of Acme Frame Products and Wilhold, Inc. ④ Incl. pre-tax restruct. chrg. of $38.9 mill., 2/00; $13.9 mill., 2/99. ⑤ Incl. aft.-tax restruct. chrgs. of $35.3 mill. & aft.-tax special chrgs. of $160.6 mill. rel. to various items.

OFFICERS:
M. Weiss, Chmn., C.E.O.
J. C. Spira, Vice-Chmn., Pres., C.O.O.
R. Ryder, Sr. V.P., C.F.O.

INVESTOR CONTACT: Dale A. Cable, V.P. & Treas., (216) 252-7300

PRINCIPAL OFFICE: One American Road, Cleveland, OH 44144

TELEPHONE NUMBER: (216) 252-7300
FAX: (216) 255-6777
WEB: www.americangreetings.com
NO. OF EMPLOYEES: 10,600 full-time (approx.); 27,000 part-time (approx.)
SHAREHOLDERS: 27,000 (approx. class A); 184 (approx. class B)
ANNUAL MEETING: In June
INCORPORATED: OH, Jan., 1944

INSTITUTIONAL HOLDINGS:
No. of Institutions: 215
Shares Held: 85,505,922
% Held: 129.9

INDUSTRY: Greeting cards (SIC: 2771)

TRANSFER AGENT(S): National City Bank, Cleveland, Ohio

AMERICAN INTERNATIONAL GROUP, INC.

EXCH.	SYM.	REC. PRICE	P/E RATIO	YLD.	MKT. CAP.	RANGE (52-WK.)	'02 Y/E PR.	DIV. ACH.
NYSE	AIG	49.29 (2/28/03)	23.5	0.4%	$128.91 bill.	76.75 - 45.90	57.85	17 yrs.

HIGH GRADE. THE COMPANY IS BENEFITING FROM FAVORABLE GENERAL INSURANCE GROWTH TRENDS.

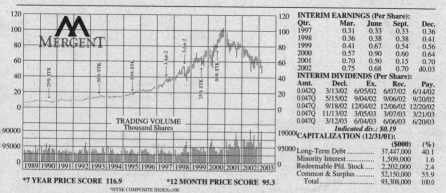

TRADING VOLUME Thousand Shares

*7 YEAR PRICE SCORE 116.9   *12 MONTH PRICE SCORE 95.3

*NYSE COMPOSITE INDEX=100

INTERIM EARNINGS (Per Share):

Qtr.	Mar.	June	Sept.	Dec.
1997	0.31	0.33	0.33	0.36
1998	0.36	0.38	0.38	0.41
1999	0.41	0.67	0.54	0.56
2000	0.57	0.90	0.60	0.64
2001	0.60	0.50	0.15	0.70
2002	0.75	0.68	0.70	d0.03

INTERIM DIVIDENDS (Per Share):

Amt.	Decl.	Ex.	Rec.	Pay.
0.042Q	3/13/02	6/05/02	6/07/02	6/14/02
0.047Q	5/15/02	9/04/02	9/06/02	9/20/02
0.047Q	9/18/02	12/04/02	12/06/02	12/20/02
0.047Q	11/13/02	3/05/03	3/07/03	3/21/03
0.047Q	3/12/03	6/04/03	6/06/03	6/20/03

Indicated div.: $0.19

CAPITALIZATION (12/31/01):

	($000)	(%)
Long-Term Debt	37,447,000	40.1
Minority Interest	1,509,000	1.6
Redeemable Pfd. Stock	2,202,000	2.4
Common & Surplus	52,150,000	55.9
Total	93,308,000	100.0

BUSINESS:

American International Group, Inc. is a holding company that, through its subsidiaries, is engaged in a broad range of insurance and insurance-related activities in the United States and internationally. AIG's primary activities include general and life insurance operations. Other significant activities include financial services, and retirement savings and asset management. AIG's general insurance subsidiaries are multiple line companies writing substantially all lines of property and casualty insurance. On 1/1/99, AIG acquired SunAmerica Inc. for $18.00 billion. On 8/28/01, the Company acquired American General Corporation for approximately $23.00 billion.

RECENT DEVELOPMENTS:

For the year ended 12/31/02, net income was $5.52 billion versus income of $5.50 billion, before an accounting change charge of $136.2 million, the previous year. Results for 2002 included an after-tax charge of $1.79 billion to increase general insurance reserves. Results for 2001 included after-tax acquisition, restructuring and related charges of $1.38 billion and World Trade Center and related losses of $533.0 million. Results for 2002 and 2001 also included after-tax realized capital losses of $1.60 billion and $541.7 million, respectively.

PROSPECTS:

Going forward, AIG should continue to benefit from favorable general insurance growth trends as a result of price increases. The domestic brokerage group expects to benefit from new business opportunities. In the domestic personal lines business, market conditions in the automobile insurance line are showing modest improvement and AIG continues to refine its underwriting capabilities. Foreign general insurance anticipates continued growth due to rate increases and new business. Both AIG's domestic and foreign life insurance operations are performing well. In the U.S., both productivity gains and new marketing initiatives are contributing to growth. For the full-year 2003, net income, excluding realized capital gains and losses, is expected in the range of $9.90 billion to $10.30 billion.

ANNUAL FINANCIAL DATA:

FISCAL YEAR	PREM. INC. ($mill.)	TOT. REVS. ($mill.)	NET INC. ($mill.)	TOT. ASSETS ($mill.)	TOT. INVST. ($mill.)	RET. ON REVS. %	RET. ON EQUITY %	RET. ON ASSETS %	EARN. PER SH.$	TANG. BK. VAL.$	AVG. YIELD %	DIV. PER SH.$	PRICE RANGE	AVG. P/E RATIO
p12/31/02		67,500.0	⑤ 5,518.9						② 2.10		0.3	0.18	80.00 - 47.61	30.4
⑤ 12/31/01	38,608.0	55,459.0	⑤ 5,499.0	492,982.0	297,855.0	9.9	10.5	1.1	② 2.07	19.94	0.2	0.16	98.31 - 66.00	39.7
12/31/00	31,017.0	42,440.0	5,636.0	306,577.0	173,524.0	13.3	14.2	1.8	2.41	16.98	0.2	0.14	103.75 - 52.38	32.4
12/31/99	27,486.0	37,751.0	5,055.0	268,238.0	152,204.0	13.4	15.2	1.9	2.15	14.33	0.2	0.13	75.25 - 51.00	29.3
12/31/98	24,345.0	30,852.0	3,766.0	194,398.0	114,526.0	12.2	13.9	1.9	1.90	13.78	0.3	0.11	54.74 - 34.60	23.5
12/31/97	22,346.7	27,947.4	3,332.3	163,970.7	94,970.6	11.9	13.9	2.0	1.68	12.20	0.3	0.10	40.02 - 25.25	19.4
12/31/96	20,833.1	25,874.3	2,897.3	148,431.0	87,696.9	11.2	13.1	2.0	1.46	11.13	0.4	0.09	27.59 - 20.89	16.6
12/31/95	19,443.9	23,829.9	2,510.4	134,136.4	76,934.5	10.5	12.7	1.9	1.26	9.91	0.4	0.08	22.64 - 15.19	15.1
12/31/94	17,011.2	20,792.8	2,175.5	114,346.1	62,796.8	10.5	13.2	1.9	1.09	8.22	0.5	0.07	15.92 - 12.92	13.3
12/31/93	15,312.7	18,723.0	① 1,918.1	101,014.8	53,970.4	10.2	12.6	1.9	① 0.96	7.57	0.4	0.06	15.84 - 11.60	14.4

Statistics are as originally reported. Adj. for stk. splits: 25% div., 7/30/99; 3-for-2, 7/98, 7/97, 7/95, 5/93 ① Bef. acctg. change credit $20.7 mill. ② Bef. acctg. change $136.2 mill. ③ Incl. after-tax acquisition chrgs. $1.38 bill.; a realized capital loss $541.7 mill. & after-tax loss of $33.0 mill. related to the terrorist attacks on 9/11/01. ④ Refl. acq. of American General Corp. on 8/28/01 ⑤ Incl. after-tax reserve chrg. of $1.79 bill.

OFFICERS:
M. R. Greenberg, Chmn., C.E.O.
M. J. Sullivan, Co-Vice-Chmn., C.O.O.
H. I. Smith, Vice-Chmn., C.F.O.

INVESTOR CONTACT: Investor Relations, (212) 770-7000

PRINCIPAL OFFICE: 70 Pine Street, New York, NY 10270

TELEPHONE NUMBER: (212) 770-7000
FAX: (212) 344-6828
WEB: www.aig.com

NO. OF EMPLOYEES: 81,000 (approx.)

SHAREHOLDERS: 59,000 (approx.)

ANNUAL MEETING: In May

INCORPORATED: DE, June, 1967

INSTITUTIONAL HOLDINGS:
No. of Institutions: 1,252
Shares Held: 1,749,604,490
% Held: 67.1

INDUSTRY: Fire, marine, and casualty insurance (SIC: 6331)

TRANSFER AGENT(S): EquiServe Trust Company, N.A., Jersey City, NJ

AMERICAN STANDARD COMPANIES, INC.

EXCH.	SYM.	REC. PRICE	P/E RATIO	YLD.	MKT. CAP.	RANGE (52-WK.)	'02 Y/E PR.
NYSE	ASD	68.51 (2/28/03)	13.6	...	$4.97 bill.	79.00 - 58.89	71.14

LOWER MEDIUM GRADE. THE COMPANY EXPECTS FIRST QUARTER 2003 DILUTED EARNINGS IN THE RANGE OF $0.85 TO $0.90 PER SHARE.

MERGENT

TRADING VOLUME
Thousand Shares

1989 1990 1991 1992 1993 1994 1995 1996 1997 1998 1999 2000 2001 2002 2003

*7 YEAR PRICE SCORE 156.0   ***12 MONTH PRICE SCORE 106.3**

*NYSE COMPOSITE INDEX=100

INTERIM EARNINGS (Per Share):

Qtr.	Mar.	June	Sept.	Dec.
1997	0.43	0.96	d0.46	0.62
1998	0.50	1.04	0.49	d1.66
1999	0.65	1.23	0.98	0.60
2000	0.82	1.48	1.23	0.82
2001	0.90	1.63	1.23	0.27
2002	0.78	1.71	1.55	1.01

INTERIM DIVIDENDS (Per Share):

Amt.	Decl.	Ex.	Rec.	Pay.
		No dividends paid.		

CAPITALIZATION (12/31/01):

	($000)	(%)
Long-Term Debt	2,142,000	100.2
Deferred Income Tax	85,100	4.0
Common & Surplus	d90,100	-4.2
Total	2,137,000	100.0

BUSINESS:

American Standard Companies, Inc. is a global manufacturer of air conditioning systems and services for commercial, institutional and residential buildings (60.9% of 2002 revenues; 64.6% operating income); plumbing fixtures and fittings for bathrooms and kitchens (25.6%, 18.7%); and vehicle control systems, including electronic braking and air suspension systems, for medium-sized and heavy trucks, buses trailers and utility vehicles (13.5%, 16.7%). ASD's brand names include TRANE and AMERICAN STANDARD for air conditioning systems, AMERICAN STANDARD and IDEAL STANDARD for plumbing products, and WABCO for vehicle control systems. As of 12/31/02, the Company had manufacturing operations in 27 countries. On 2/2/99, ASD acquired Armitage/Dolomite for approximately $427.0 million.

RECENT DEVELOPMENTS:

For the year ended 12/31/02, net income increased 25.8% to $371.0 million compared with $295.0 million in 2001. The improvement in results was primarily attributed to the Company's focus on productivity initiatives, and investments in selling, marketing and product development. Total sales advanced 4.4% to $7.80 billion from $7.47 billion a year earlier. Air Conditioning Systems and Services sales rose 1.1% to $4.74 billion, while Bath & Kitchen sales climbed 10.0% to $1.99 billion. Vehicle Control Systems sales increased 10.1% to $1.06 billion.

PROSPECTS:

Looking ahead, the Company expects year-over-year sales growth in the range of 4.0% to 6.0% for full-year 2003, with diluted earnings per share in the range of $5.40 to $5.80. In addition, the Company expects full-year 2003 free cash flow in the range of $410.0 million and $450.0 million. The Company also expects first quarter 2003 diluted earnings in the range of $0.85 to $0.90 per share. Separately, on 1/31/03, the Company announced that it has acquired Grupo Uralita's sanitary-ware business, known commercially by its name Sangra. This acquisition strengthens ASD's market position in Spain and Europe and provides local manufacturing capability.

ANNUAL FINANCIAL DATA:

FISCAL YEAR	TOT. REVS. ($mill.)	NET INC. ($mill.)	TOT. ASSETS ($mill.)	OPER. PROFIT %	NET PROFIT %	RET. ON ASSETS %	CURR. RATIO	EARN. PER SH. $	CASH FL. PER SH. $	PRICE RANGE	AVG. P/E RATIO
p12/31/02	7,795.0	371.0						5.04		77.50 - 58.20	13.5
12/31/01	7,465.3	295.0	4,831.4	8.6	4.0	6.1	1.1	4.04	7.21	70.90 - 46.75	14.6
12/31/00	7,598.4	⑥315.2	4,744.7	8.6	4.1	6.6	1.1	⑥4.36	7.32	49.75 - 34.31	9.6
12/31/99	7,189.5	⑤261.1	4,686.0	8.9	3.7	5.6	0.8	⑤3.63	6.42	49.44 - 31.13	11.1
12/31/98	6,653.9	①33.6	4,156.2	5.3	0.5	0.8	0.7	①0.46	3.04	49.25 - 21.63	77.0
12/31/97	6,007.5	②119.9	3,764.1	7.1	2.0	3.2	0.8	②1.57	3.73	51.63 - 34.63	27.5
12/31/96	5,804.6	③d46.7	3,519.6	4.4	...	...	1.1	③d0.60	1.27	39.75 - 25.50	...
12/31/95	5,221.5	④141.8	3,430.9	8.4	2.7	4.1	0.9	④1.90	3.82	32.00 - 19.63	13.6
12/31/94	4,457.5	④d77.7	3,156.1	5.5	...	...	1.0	④d1.29	1.28	...	...
12/31/93	3,830.5	④d116.6	2,987.1	5.2	...	...	1.1	④d2.11	0.20	...	...

Statistics are as originally reported. ① Incl. restr. chrg. of $197.0 mill. ② Incl. non-recurr. pre-tax chrg. of $90.0 mill.; bef. extraord. chrg. of $24.0 mill. ③ Incl. non-recurr. chrg. $235.2 mill. ④ Bef. extraord. 12/31/95: $30.0 mill.; chrg. 12/31/94: $8.7 mill.; chrg. 12/31/93: $91.9 mill. ⑤ Incl. restruct. chrgs. of $15.0 mill. ⑥ Incl. restruct. & asset impair. chrg. of $70.0 mill. and $57.0 mill. gain on sale of business.

OFFICERS:
F. M. Poses, Chmn., C.E.O.
G. P. D'Aloia, Sr. V.P., C.F.O.
J. P. McGrath, Sr. V.P., Sec., Gen. Couns.

INVESTOR CONTACT: Investor Relations, (732) 980-6000

PRINCIPAL OFFICE: One Centennial Avenue, P.O. Box 6820, Piscataway, NJ 08855-6820

TELEPHONE NUMBER: (732) 980-6000
FAX: (732) 980-6300
WEB: www.americanstandard.com
NO. OF EMPLOYEES: 60,000 (approx.)
SHAREHOLDERS: 836 (record); 36,000 (approx. beneficial)
ANNUAL MEETING: In May
INCORPORATED: DE, 1988

INSTITUTIONAL HOLDINGS:
No. of Institutions: 259
Shares Held: 54,961,758
% Held: 75.9

INDUSTRY: Refrigeration and heating equipment (SIC: 3585)

TRANSFER AGENT(S): Citibank, NA, New York, NY

AMERICAN STATES WATER COMPANY

EXCH.	SYM.	REC. PRICE	P/E RATIO	YLD.	MKT. CAP.	RANGE (52-WK.)	'02 Y/E PR.	DIV. ACH.
NYSE	AWR	23.48 (2/28/03)	17.7	3.8%	$355.0 mill.	29.01 - 20.25	23.15	49 yrs.

MEDIUM GRADE. THE COMPANY RECENTLY FILED FOR GENERAL RATE INCREASES THAT COULD PROVIDE ADDITIONAL REVENUES IN LATE 2003 AND 2004.

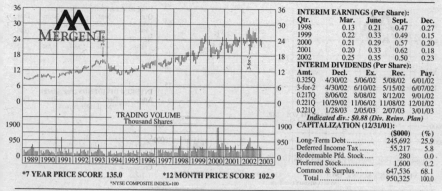

*7 YEAR PRICE SCORE 135.0   ***12 MONTH PRICE SCORE 102.9**
*NYSE COMPOSITE INDEX=100

INTERIM EARNINGS (Per Share):

Qtr.	Mar.	June	Sept.	Dec.
1998	0.13	0.21	0.47	0.27
1999	0.22	0.33	0.49	0.15
2000	0.21	0.29	0.57	0.20
2001	0.20	0.33	0.62	0.18
2002	0.25	0.35	0.50	0.23

INTERIM DIVIDENDS (Per Share):

Amt.	Decl.	Ex.	Rec.	Pay.
0.325Q	4/30/02	5/06/02	5/08/02	6/01/02
3-for-2	4/30/02	6/10/02	5/15/02	6/07/02
0.217Q	8/06/02	8/08/02	8/12/02	9/01/02
0.221Q	10/29/02	11/06/02	11/08/02	12/01/02
0.221Q	1/28/03	2/05/03	2/07/03	3/01/03

Indicated div.: $0.88 (Div. Reinv. Plan)

CAPITALIZATION (12/31/01):

	($000)	(%)
Long-Term Debt	245,692	25.9
Deferred Income Tax	55,217	5.8
Redeemable Pfd. Stock	280	0.0
Preferred Stock	1,600	0.2
Common & Surplus	647,536	68.1
Total	950,325	100.0

BUSINESS:

American States Water Company is a public utility engaged principally in the purchase, production, distribution, and sale of water, and distribution of electricity through its primary subsidiary Southern California Water Company (SCW). SCW is organized into three water service regions and one electric customer service area operating within 75 communities in 10 counties in California and provides water service in 21 customer service areas. As of 2/26/03, SCW served approximately 22,000 electric customers. Through its American States Utility Services (ASUS) sub-

sidiary, the Company contracts to lease, operate and maintain government-owned water and wastewater systems and to provide other services to local governments to assist them in the operation and maintenance of their water and wastewater systems. ASUS has approximately 91,500 accounts under contract. Through its Chaparral City Water Company, the Company serves approximately 12,000 customers in the town of Fountain Hills, Arizona and a portion of the City of Scottsdale, Arizona.

RECENT DEVELOPMENTS:

For the year ended 12/31/02, net income declined 0.5% to $20.3 million compared with $20.4 million in 2001. Operating revenues increased 5.9% to $209.2 million from $197.5 million a year earlier. The improvement in revenues was primarily attributed to contributions from various rate

increases effective during 2001 at Southern California Water Company, a 3.3% increase in water sales, and rate increases at the Bear Valley Electric division of Southern California Water Company. Operating income grew 2.6% to $37.6 million from $36.7 million the year before.

PROSPECTS:

Looking ahead to fiscal 2003, AWR is encouraged by the recent decisions issued by the California Public Utilities Commission (CPUC) that will increase water rates by approximately $6.2 million annually for Southern California Water Company (SCW). Although there was a signifi-

cant delay in the process, this decision by the CPUC effectively addresses the liquidity problems that plagued the Bear Valley electric division of SCW. In addition, AWR has filed general rate increases with the CPUC that could provide additional revenues in late 2003 and 2004.

ANNUAL FINANCIAL DATA:

FISCAL YEAR	TOT. REVS. ($000)	NET INC. ($000)	TOT. ASSETS ($000)	OPER. PROFIT %	NET PROFIT %	RET. ON EQUITY %	RET. ON ASSETS %	CURR. RATIO	EARN. PER SH. $	CASH FL. PER SH. $	TANG. BK. VAL. $	DIV. PER SH. $	PRICE RANGE	AVG. P/E RATIO	AVG. YIELD %
p12/31/02	209,205	20,339	700,666					1.34			0.87	29.01 - 20.25	18.4	3.5
12/31/01	197,514	20,447	683,764	18.6	10.4	3.1	3.0	1.4	1.33	2.51	42.83	0.87	26.40 - 19.00	17.0	3.8
12/31/00	183,960	18,086	616,646	17.6	9.8	3.2	2.9	0.7	1.27	2.36	37.31	0.86	25.29 - 16.67	16.5	4.1
12/31/99	173,421	16,101	533,181	16.4	9.3	3.3	3.0	0.8	1.19	2.26	36.25	0.85	26.50 - 14.79	17.3	4.1
12/31/98	148,060	14,573	484,671	16.9	9.8	3.4	3.0	0.6	1.08	2.04	32.11	0.84	19.50 - 14.08	15.5	5.0
12/31/97	153,755	14,059	457,074	15.3	9.1	3.3	3.1	1.0	1.04	1.89	31.21	0.83	17.08 - 13.50	14.7	5.4
12/31/96	151,529	13,460	430,922	15.5	8.9	3.3	3.1	1.0	1.13	2.01	30.22	0.82	16.08 - 12.50	12.7	5.7
12/31/95	129,813	12,165	406,255	16.5	9.4	3.4	3.0	0.9	1.03	1.79	29.97	0.80	14.00 - 10.50	11.9	6.6
12/31/94	122,675	11,338	383,627	15.4	9.2	3.4	3.0	0.9	0.95	1.68	28.30	0.80	14.67 - 10.17	13.0	6.4
12/31/93	108,506	12,026	358,533	18.5	11.1	3.7	3.4	1.1	1.11	1.82	27.28	0.79	16.25 - 13.08	13.2	5.4

Statistics are as originally reported. Adj. for stk. split: 3-for-2, 6/02.

OFFICERS:
L. E. Ross, Chmn.
F. E. Wicks, Pres., C.E.O.
M. Harris, III, V.P., C.F.O., Treas., Sec.
INVESTOR CONTACT: McClellan Harris, III, (909) 394-3600 ext. 705
PRINCIPAL OFFICE: 630 East Foothill Blvd., San Dimas, CA 91773-9016

TELEPHONE NUMBER: (909) 394-3600
FAX: (909) 394-0711
WEB: www.aswater.com
NO. OF EMPLOYEES: 492 (approx.)
SHAREHOLDERS: 3,404 (approx.)
ANNUAL MEETING: In Apr.
INCORPORATED: CA, Dec., 1929

INSTITUTIONAL HOLDINGS:
No. of Institutions: 101
Shares Held: 5,448,267
% Held: 35.9

INDUSTRY: Water supply (SIC: 4941)

TRANSFER AGENT(S): Mellon Investor Services, L.L.C., Ridgefield Park, NJ

AMERICREDIT CORP.

EXCH.	SYM.	REC. PRICE	P/E RATIO	YLD.	MKT. CAP.	RANGE (52-WK.)	'02 Y/E PR.
NYSE	ACF	1.99 (2/28/03)	0.7	...	$166.0 mill.	46.93 - 1.92	7.74

SPECULATIVE GRADE. THE COMPANY IS PROJECTING THAT CREDIT LOSSES WILL RISE DURING THE FIRST HALF OF 2003.

*7 YEAR PRICE SCORE 107.1 ***12 MONTH PRICE SCORE 26.8**
*NYSE COMPOSITE INDEX=100

INTERIM EARNINGS (Per Share):

Qtr.	Sept.	Dec.	Mar.	June
1998-99	0.23	0.26	0.29	0.33
1999-00	0.35	0.25	0.41	0.46
2000-01	0.51	0.57	0.70	0.81
2001-02	0.88	0.91	1.02	1.06
2002-03	0.81	d0.18	...	...

INTERIM DIVIDENDS (Per Share):

Amt.	Decl.	Ex.	Rec.	Pay.
	No dividends paid.			

CAPITALIZATION (6/30/02):

	($000)	(%)
Long-Term Debt	1,751,974	55.0
Common & Surplus	1,432,316	45.0
Total	3,184,290	100.0

BUSINESS:

AmeriCredit Corp. is engaged in the business of purchasing and servicing automobile sales finance contracts. Through its branch network, ACF purchases auto finance contracts without recourse from franchised and select independent automobile dealerships and, to a lesser extent, makes loans directly to consumers buying late model used and new vehicles. ACF targets consumers who are typically unable to obtain financing from traditional sources. The Company services its automobile lending portfolio at regional centers using automated loan servicing and collection systems. As of 9/30/02, ACF operated 251 auto lending branch offices.

RECENT DEVELOPMENTS:

For the three months ended 12/31/02, ACF posted a net loss of $27.6 million compared with net income of $80.6 million in the same period a year earlier. Total revenues fell 33.3% to $191.2 million from $286.7 million the previous year. AFC noted that this was the first quarter that the Company structured its securitization transactions as secured financing, which did not require the recognition of gain-on-sale revenue. Revenues for 2001 included a gain of $108.7 million on the sale of receivables. Provisions for loan losses climbed to $86.9 million versus $16.7 million the year before.

PROSPECTS:

ACF's near-term outlook is unfavorable, reflecting increasing net charge-offs and higher 60 day plus delinquency rates. For instance, annualized net charge-offs were 5.8% of average managed auto receivables for the quarter ended 12/31/02 versus 5.3% the previous quarter and 4.3% a year earlier. Also, managed auto receivables more than 60 days delinquent were 4.1% of total managed auto receivables as of 12/31/02, compared with 3.8% the year before. These factors, coupled with continued weakness in recovery values on repossessed vehicles and in the overall economy, have led ACF to project that credit losses will rise during the first half of 2003. In response, the Company has reduced both loan origination volume and operating expenses to align loan growth with available liquidity.

ANNUAL FINANCIAL DATA:

FISCAL YEAR	TOT. REVS. ($mill.)	NET INC. ($mill.)	TOT. ASSETS ($mill.)	OPER. PROFIT %	NET PROFIT %	RET. ON EQUITY %	RET. ON ASSETS %	CURR. RATIO	EARN. PER SH. $	CASH FL. PER SH. $	TANG. BK. VAL. $	PRICE RANGE	AVG. P/E RATIO
6/30/02	1,190.2	347.5	4,224.9	47.5	29.2	24.3	8.2	3.7	3.87	4.30	16.69	46.93 - 5.90	6.8
6/30/01	818.2	222.9	3,384.9	44.3	27.2	21.0	6.6	4.0	2.60	2.83	12.71	64.90 - 14.00	15.2
6/30/00	509.7	② 114.5	1,862.3	37.3	22.5	16.6	6.1	2.8	② 1.48	1.72	8.85	31.13 - 10.63	14.1
6/30/99	335.5	74.8	1,063.5	36.3	22.3	18.7	7.0	1.8	1.11	1.30	6.23	18.94 - 9.81	12.9
6/30/98	227.9	60.7	748.6	43.3	26.6	19.8	8.1	2.5	0.93	1.58	4.97	26.94 - 6.63	18.0
6/30/97	137.7	38.7	493.5	45.7	28.1	17.9	7.8	1.8	0.63	1.22	3.15	17.22 - 5.94	18.4
6/30/96	81.0	21.6	330.2	42.3	26.7	13.2	6.5	3.0	0.36	0.49	2.50	10.25 - 5.19	21.7
6/30/95	33.1	28.9	285.7	30.3	87.3	19.6	10.1	61.6	0.48	0.50	2.56	8.13 - 2.63	11.3
6/30/94	15.9	5.1	122.2	31.9	31.9	4.2	4.1	32.4	0.08	0.10	2.08	4.06 - 2.56	41.4
6/30/93	24.5	① d19.4	131.1	...	...	...	...	9.2	① d0.33	0.30	2.11	4.00 - 1.63	...

Statistics are as originally reported. Adj. for 100% stk. div., 10/98. ① Incl. restruct. chrg. of $15.4 mill. ② Incl. chrg. of $10.5 mill. rel. to closure of mtg. ops.

OFFICERS:
C. H. Morris, Jr., Chmn.
M. R. Barrington, Vice-Chmn., Pres., C.E.O.

INVESTOR CONTACT: Susan Sheffield, Investor Relations, (817) 302-7355

PRINCIPAL OFFICE: 801 Cherry Street, Suite 3900, Fort Worth, TX 76102

TELEPHONE NUMBER: (817) 302-7000
FAX: (817) 336-9519
WEB: www.americredit.com
NO. OF EMPLOYEES: 5,258 (avg.)
SHAREHOLDERS: 275 (approx.)
ANNUAL MEETING: In Nov.
INCORPORATED: TX, Aug., 1986; reincorp., TX, May, 1988

INSTITUTIONAL HOLDINGS:
No. of Institutions: 219
Shares Held: 170,244,407
% Held: 111.4

INDUSTRY: Personal credit institutions (SIC: 6141)

TRANSFER AGENT(S): Mellon Investor Services, Ridgefield Park, NJ

AMERISOURCEBERGEN CORPORATION

EXCH.	SYM.	REC. PRICE	P/E RATIO	YLD.	MKT. CAP.	RANGE (52-WK.)	'02 Y/E PR.
NYSE	ABC	55.00 (2/28/03)	16.4	0.2%	$5.86 bill.	82.85 - 50.20	54.31

UPPER MEDIUM GRADE. THE COMPANY SHOULD CONTINUE TO BENEFIT FROM RECENT ACQUISITIONS.

INTERIM EARNINGS (Per Share):

Qtr.	Dec.	Mar.	June	Sept.
1999-00	0.42	0.47	0.48	0.53
2000-01	0.49	0.57	0.57	0.48
2001-02	0.63	0.84	0.82	0.86
2002-03	0.84	...	...	...

INTERIM DIVIDENDS (Per Share):

Amt.	Decl.	Ex.	Rec.	Pay.
0.025Q	4/24/02	5/16/02	5/20/02	6/03/02
0.025Q	7/24/02	8/15/02	8/19/02	9/03/02
0.025Q	10/30/02	11/14/02	11/18/02	12/02/02
0.025Q	1/22/03	2/12/03	2/17/03	3/03/03

Indicated div.: $0.10

CAPITALIZATION (9/30/02):

	($000)	(%)
Long-Term Debt	1,756,494	34.6
Common & Surplus	3,316,338	65.4
Total	5,072,832	100.0

*7 YEAR PRICE SCORE 191.2   ***12 MONTH PRICE SCORE 90.6**

*NYSE COMPOSITE INDEX=100

BUSINESS:

AmerisourceBergen Corporation (formerly AmeriSource Health Corp.) was formed by the merger of AmeriSource Corporation and Bergen Brunswig Corporation on 8/29/01. The Company is a distributor of pharmaceutical products and services to the hospital systems/acute care market, physician's offices, alternate care and mail order facilities, independent community pharmacies, and regional chain pharmacies. The Company also operates in the institutional pharmacy marketplace. In addition, ABC operates in two business segments, pharmaceutical distribution and PharMerica. As of 9/30/02, the Company serves its customers nationwide through 44 distribution facilities.

RECENT DEVELOPMENTS:

For the three months ended 12/31/02, net income jumped 36.6% to $92.7 million compared with $67.9 million in the corresponding quarter of the previous year. Results for 2002 included an after-tax charge of $840,000 for facility consolidations and employee severance, while 2001 results included an after-tax merger charge of $4.5 million. Total revenues increased 12.3% to $12.43 billion from $11.07 billion in the prior-year period. Operating revenue advanced 14.7% to $11.11 billion from $9.69 billion, while revenues from bulk deliveries to customer warehouses declined 4.0% to $1.33 billion from $1.38 billion in the year-earlier quarter.

PROSPECTS:

On 1/17/03, the Company completed the acquisition of US Bioservices Corporation, a privately held company, for approximately $160.0 million, including assumed debt. The transaction also provides for contigent payments of up to about $28.0 million, based on US Bioservices achieving defined earnings targets through the end of the first quarter of calendar year 2004. Separately, on 1/6/03, ABC announced the completion of its purchase of Bridge Medical, Inc., a provider of barcode-enabled point-of-care software, for about $27.0 million and contingent payments of up to $55.0 million based on Bridge Medical achieving significant earnings targets in fiscal 2003 and 2004.

ANNUAL FINANCIAL DATA:

FISCAL YEAR	TOT. REVS. ($mill.)	NET INC. ($mill.)	TOT. ASSETS ($mill.)	OPER. PROFIT %	NET PROFIT %	RET. ON EQUITY %	RET. ON ASSETS %	CURR. RATIO	EARN. PER SH.$	CASH FL. PER SH.$	TANG. BK. VAL.$	DIV. PER SH.$	PRICE RANGE	AVG. P/E RATIO	AVG. YIELD %
9/30/02	45,234.8	⑧ 344.9	11,213.0	1.6	0.8	10.4	3.1	1.4	⑧ 3.16	3.67	10.43	0.10	82.85 - 50.20	21.1	0.2
9/30/01	16,191.4	⑦ 125.1	10,291.2	1.6	0.8	4.4	1.2	1.4	⑦ 2.10	2.39	6.89	0.03	72.00 - 40.13	26.7	...
9/30/00	11,645.0	⑥ 99.0	2,458.6	1.7	0.9	35.1	4.0	1.3	⑥ 1.90	2.24	4.81	...	53.69 - 12.00	17.3	...
9/30/99	9,807.4	⑤ 70.9	2,060.6	1.6	0.7	42.6	3.4	1.4	⑤ 1.38	1.76	2.88	...	41.38 - 11.00	19.0	...
9/30/98	8,668.8	⑤ 50.5	1,552.3	1.4	0.6	67.1	3.3	1.4	⑤ 1.04	1.38	1.55	...	40.38 - 22.23	30.1	...
9/30/97	7,815.9	④ 47.4	1,745.0	1.5	0.6	331.6	2.7	1.4	④ 0.98	1.27	0.26	...	33.16 - 20.63	27.6	...
9/30/96	5,551.7	④ 42.7	1,188.0	1.8	0.8	...	3.6	1.4	④ 0.93	1.18	...	...	24.13 - 13.94	20.6	...
9/30/95	4,668.9	③ 28.2	838.7	2.1	0.6	...	3.4	1.5	③ 0.77	1.05	...	...	17.13 - 9.88	17.5	...
9/30/94	4,301.8	③ d172.4	711.6	...	...	...	...	1.3	③ d5.84	d5.34	...	...	...	...	...
9/30/93	3,719.0	② d7.5	867.9	1.8	...	...	...	1.5	② d0.25	0.26	...	...	...	...	...

Statistics are as originally reported. Adj. for 2-for-1 split 3/99. Results prior to 9/30/01 reflect the operations of AmeriSource Health Corp. ① Incl. non-recurr. chrg. $26.7 mill., 1998 ② Bef. extraord. loss $11.1 mill., but incl. non-recurr chrg. $2.2 mill. ③ Bef. extraord. loss $656,000 and acctg. chrg. $34.6 mill., but incl. non-recurr chrg. $179.8 mill. ④ Bef. extraord. loss $2.0 mill., 1997; $7.2 mill., 1996; $18.0 mill., 1995 ⑤ Bef. extraord. loss $3.4 mill., but incl. non-recurr. chrg. $14.9 mill. ⑥ Incl. one-time credit of $1.1 mill. ⑦ Incl. net chrg. of $10.4 mill. ⑧ Incl. pre-tax merger costs of $24.2 mill.

OFFICERS:
R. E. Martini, Chmn.
R. D. Yost, C.E.O.
K. J. Hilzinger, Pres., C.O.O.
M. D. DiCandilo, Sr. V.P., C.F.O.

INVESTOR CONTACT: Michael N. Kilpatriac, V.P. Inv. Rel., (610) 727-7118

PRINCIPAL OFFICE: 1300 Morris Drive, Suite 100, Chesterbrook, PA 19087

TELEPHONE NUMBER: (610) 727-7000
FAX: (610) 647-0141
WEB: www.amerisourcebergen.net

NO. OF EMPLOYEES: 12,500 full-time (approx.); 1,200 part-time (approx.)

SHAREHOLDERS: 2,431

ANNUAL MEETING: In Feb.
INCORPORATED: DE, 1988

INSTITUTIONAL HOLDINGS:
No. of Institutions: 381
Shares Held: 110,734,291
% Held: 103.5

INDUSTRY: Drugs, proprietaries, and sundries (SIC: 5122)

TRANSFER AGENT(S): Mellon Investor Services, Ridgefield Park, NJ

AMERON INTERNATIONAL CORPORATION

EXCH.	SYM.	REC. PRICE	P/E RATIO	YLD.	MKT. CAP.	RANGE (52-WK.)	'02 Y/E PR.
NYSE	AMN	29.90 (Adj.; 3/31/03)	8.7	2.7%	$236.0 mill.	39.00 - 21.78	27.58

MEDIUM GRADE. NEAR-TERM RESULTS FOR THE WATER TRANSMISSION GROUP SHOULD BENEFIT FROM ITS YEAR-END BACKLOG OF APPROXIMATLEY $151.0 MILLION.

TRADING VOLUME
Thousand Shares

1989 1990 1991 1992 1993 1994 1995 1996 1997 1998 1999 2000 2001 2002 2003

*7 YEAR PRICE SCORE 125.3   ***12 MONTH PRICE SCORE 101.4**

*NYSE COMPOSITE INDEX=100

INTERIM EARNINGS (Per Share):

Qtr.	Feb.	May	Aug.	Nov.
1996-97	0.12	0.65	0.86	0.74
1997-98	d0.12	0.55	0.76	1.36
1998-99	0.13	0.75	0.99	0.81
1999-00	0.12	0.78	1.01	1.30
2000-01	0.21	0.89	1.05	1.31
2001-02	0.22	0.91	1.06	1.27

INTERIM DIVIDENDS (Per Share):

Amt.	Decl.	Ex.	Rec.	Pay.
0.32Q	6/21/02	7/23/02	7/25/02	8/20/02
0.32Q	9/27/02	10/22/02	10/24/02	11/19/02
0.32Q	1/16/03	1/21/03	1/23/03	2/18/03
0.40Q	3/27/03	4/22/03	4/24/03	5/20/03
100% STK	3/27/03	5/28/03	5/01/03	5/27/03

Indicated div.: $0.80 (Adj.; Div. Reinv. Plan)

CAPITALIZATION (11/30/02):

	($000)	(%)
Long-Term Debt	102,823	32.7
Common & Surplus	211,826	67.3
Total	314,649	100.0

BUSINESS:

Ameron International Corporation (formerly Ameron, Inc.) is a multinational manufacturer of highly-engineered products and materials for sale to the chemical, industrial, energy, transportation and infrastructure markets. The Company operates through four business segments: Performance Coatings & Finishes group (33.9% of 2002 sales), the Water Transmission group (26.8%), the Infrastructure Products group (22.9%) and Fiberglass-Composite Pipe group (16.4%). The Company produces water transmission lines; high-performance coatings and finishes for the protection of metals and structures; fiberglass-composite pipe for transporting oil, chemicals and corrosive fluids for the protection of metals and structures; fiberglass-composite pipe for transporting oil, chemicals and corrosive fluids and specialized materials and products used in infrastructure projects. The Company operates businesses in North America, South America, Europe, Australasia and Asia. AMN also participates in several joint venture companies in the U.S., Saudi Arabia, Kuwait, Egypt and Mexico.

RECENT DEVELOPMENTS:

For the year ended 11/30/02, net income rose 1.1% to $28.1 million compared with $27.7 million in 2001. The improvement in earnings was primarily attributed to new products, increased productivity and higher margins. Sales slid 2.2% to $539.5 million. Performance Coatings & Finishes group sales decreased 2.9% to $183.3 million, while Fiberglass-Composite Pipe group sales declined 17.3% to $88.4 million. However, Water Transmission sales group rose 1.3% to $145.0 million. Sales for the Infrastructure Products group grew 8.6% to $123.6 million.

PROSPECTS:

AMN continues to take steps to improve profitability in both the Performance Coatings & Finishes and Fiberglass-Composite Pipe groups. Meanwhile, the Infrastructure Products group is experiencing stronger results, supported by increased construction spending in Hawaii and demand for pole products through the U.S. Near-term results for the Water Transmission group should remain positive, given a year-end backlog of approximately $151.0 million.

ANNUAL FINANCIAL DATA:

FISCAL YEAR	TOT. REVS. ($000)	NET INC. ($000)	TOT. ASSETS ($000)	OPER. PROFIT %	NET PROFIT %	RET. ON EQUITY %	RET. ON ASSETS %	CURR. RATIO	EARN. PER SH. $	CASH FL. PER SH. $	TANG. BK. VAL. $	DIV. PER SH. $	PRICE RANGE	AVG. P/E RATIO	AVG. YIELD %
11/30/02	539,473	28,059	462,942	9.1	5.2	13.2	6.1	2.4	3.49	5.79	25.19	0.64	39.00 - 21.78	8.7	2.1
11/30/01	551,396	27,741	485,080	8.9	5.0	13.6	5.7	2.4	3.45	5.76	24.67	0.64	40.00 - 18.63	8.5	2.3
11/30/00	550,661	25,345	478,449	8.4	4.6	13.9	5.3	2.1	3.21	5.49	21.77	0.64	20.25 - 15.81	5.6	3.5
11/30/99	545,081	22,273	458,967	8.4	4.1	12.5	4.9	2.1	2.77	5.13	20.33	0.64	23.97 - 17.25	7.4	3.1
11/30/98	552,146	③d3,140	500,219	...	...	...	...	2.2	③2.54	1.90	18.51	0.64	31.75 - 16.69	9.5	2.6
11/30/97	533,506	19,372	433,225	6.1	3.6	12.7	4.5	2.8	2.37	4.40	17.69	0.64	35.00 - 23.19	12.3	2.2
11/30/96	496,940	15,410	411,666	5.2	3.1	10.6	3.7	2.2	1.94	4.00	22.23	0.64	26.25 - 17.06	11.2	3.0
11/30/95	481,405	12,452	371,381	4.4	2.6	9.3	3.4	2.2	1.58	3.63	16.93	0.64	19.50 - 14.56	10.8	3.8
11/30/94	417,682	②10,790	350,856	4.1	2.6	8.6	3.1	2.2	②1.38	3.40	15.85	0.64	21.75 - 14.50	13.2	3.5
11/30/93	453,357	①d24,255	339,282	...	...	...	...	1.9	①d3.14	d1.01	15.05	0.64	19.44 - 15.44	...	3.7

Statistics are as originally reported. Adj. for 100% stk. div., 5/03. ① Incl. net restruct. chrg. of $31.5 mill. ② Incl. an after-tax gain from the sale of a subsidiary of $1.8 mill. ($0.46/sh.) ③ Incl. non-recur. gain of $26.9 mill. & asset write-downs and other chrgs. of $21.7 mill.

OFFICERS:
J. S. Marlen, Chmn., Pres., C.E.O.
G. Wagner, Sr. V.P., C.F.O.
J. Solis, Sr. V.P., Gen. Couns., Sec.

INVESTOR CONTACT: Gary Wagner, Sr. V.P., C.F.O., (626)683-4000

PRINCIPAL OFFICE: 245 South Los Robles Avenue, Pasadena, CA 91101-2820

TELEPHONE NUMBER: (626) 683-4000
FAX: (626) 683-4060
WEB: www.ameron.com
NO. OF EMPLOYEES: 2,800 (approx.)
SHAREHOLDERS: 1,172
ANNUAL MEETING: In Mar.
INCORPORATED: DE, Apr., 1929; reincorp., DE, Mar., 1986

INSTITUTIONAL HOLDINGS:
No. of Institutions: 60
Shares Held: 5,105,634 (Adj.)
% Held: 64.7

INDUSTRY: Concrete block and brick (SIC: 3271)

TRANSFER AGENT(S): First Chicago Trust Company of New York, Jersey City, NJ

AMETEK, INC.

EXCH.	SYM.	REC. PRICE	P/E RATIO	YLD.	MKT. CAP.	RANGE (52-WK.)	'02 Y/E PR.
NYSE	AME	32.98 (2/28/03)	13.2	0.7%	$1.08 bill.	40.71 - 26.15	38.49

MEDIUM GRADE. THE COMPANY EXPECTS FULL-YEAR 2003 EARNINGS IN THE RANGE OF $2.65 TO $2.75 PER DILUTED SHARE.

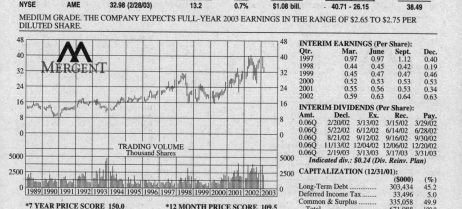

INTERIM EARNINGS (Per Share):

Qtr.	Mar.	June	Sept.	Dec.
1997	0.97	0.97	1.12	0.40
1998	0.44	0.45	0.42	0.19
1999	0.45	0.47	0.47	0.46
2000	0.52	0.53	0.53	0.53
2001	0.55	0.56	0.53	0.34
2002	0.59	0.63	0.64	0.63

INTERIM DIVIDENDS (Per Share):

Amt.	Decl.	Ex.	Rec.	Pay.
0.06Q	2/20/02	3/13/02	3/15/02	3/29/02
0.06Q	5/22/02	6/12/02	6/14/02	6/28/02
0.06Q	8/21/02	9/12/02	9/16/02	9/30/02
0.06Q	11/13/02	12/04/02	12/06/02	12/20/02
0.06Q	2/19/03	3/13/03	3/17/03	3/31/03

Indicated div.: $0.24 (Div. Reinv. Plan)

CAPITALIZATION (12/31/01):

	($000)	(%)
Long-Term Debt	303,434	45.2
Deferred Income Tax	33,496	5.0
Common & Surplus	335,058	49.9
Total	671,988	100.0

*7 YEAR PRICE SCORE 150.0   ***12 MONTH PRICE SCORE 109.5**

*NYSE COMPOSITE INDEX=100

BUSINESS:

Ametek, Inc. manufactures electronic instruments and electric motors through its operations in North America, South America, Europe and Asia. AME markets its products worldwide through its Electronic Instruments Group (EIG) and Electromechanical Group (EMG). EIG (51.8% of 2002 net sales) builds technologically advanced monitoring, testing, and calibration instruments, and display devices for the

aerospace, power generation, process and industrial industries. EMG (48.2%) is a major producer of air-moving electric motors for vacuum cleaners and other floor-care products. This group also produces brushless air-moving motors for aerospace, mass-transit, medical and computer markets, and specialty metals for the electronics, telecommunications, consumer, automotive and other markets.

RECENT DEVELOPMENTS:

For the year ended 12/31/02, net income was $83.7 million compared with $66.1 million a year earlier. Results for 2001 included non-recurring after-tax charges of $15.3 million, partially offset by a tax benefit and related interest income of $10.5 million. Results for 2001 also included after-tax goodwill amortization of $10.2 million. Net sales

rose 2.1% to $1.04 billion from $1.02 billion the previous year. EIG sales increased 8.0% to $539.4 million and operating profits improved 53.4% to $87.5 million, aided by the 2001 acquisitions of Instruments for Research and Applied Science and EDAX. EMG sales fell 3.6% to $501.1 million, while operating profits grew 13.6% to $80.2 million.

PROSPECTS:

On 1/13/03, AME completed the acquisition of Airtechnology Holdings Limited, a supplier of motors, fans and environmental control systems for aerospace and defense markets, from Candover Partners Limited. Airtechnology, located near London, England, has expected sales of about $46.0 million. AME believes the acquisition will greatly expand its presence in high-end technical

motors and strengthen its relationships with large European-based aerospace and defense companies. Separately, AME expects full-year 2003 revenues to be up modestly with earnings in the range of $2.65 to $2.75 per diluted share. This estimate includes the positive effect of AME's acquisition of Airtechnology and approximately $7.0 million of additional pension expense.

ANNUAL FINANCIAL DATA:

FISCAL YEAR	TOT. REVS. ($mill.)	NET INC. ($mill.)	TOT. ASSETS ($mill.)	OPER. PROFIT %	NET PROFIT %	RET. ON EQUITY %	RET. ON ASSETS %	CURR. RATIO	EARN. PER SH. $	CASH FL. PER SH. $	TANG. BK. VAL. $	DIV. PER SH. $	PRICE RANGE	AVG. P/E RATIO	AVG. YIELD %
p12/31/02	1,040.5	83.7							2.49			0.24	40.71 - 26.15	13.4	0.7
12/31/01	1,019.3	⑥66.1	1,029.3	10.7	6.5	19.7	6.4	1.1	①1.98	3.37	...	0.24	34.00 - 21.37	14.0	0.9
12/31/00	1,024.7	68.5	859.0	13.3	6.7	24.4	8.0	1.0	2.11	3.44	...	0.24	26.94 - 15.50	10.1	1.1
12/31/99	924.8	60.8	768.2	12.8	6.6	28.1	7.9	1.0	1.85	3.05	...	0.24	25.75 - 16.50	11.4	1.1
12/31/98	927.5	⑤50.4	699.8	10.4	5.4	29.0	7.2	1.1	②1.50	2.63	0.77	0.24	31.38 - 15.75	15.7	1.0
12/31/97	847.8	②50.3	555.2	10.8	5.9	31.6	9.1	1.4	②1.49	2.45	3.25	0.24	28.00 - 19.88	16.1	1.0
12/31/96	868.7	51.2	537.9	10.9	5.9	39.5	9.5	1.3	1.57	2.64	3.96	0.24	22.25 - 16.00	12.2	1.3
12/31/95	837.5	③43.8	526.7	10.7	5.2	50.3	8.3	1.2	③1.31	2.34	2.65	0.24	19.50 - 15.75	13.5	1.4
12/31/94	808.0	④39.0	502.0	9.8	4.8	53.3	7.8	1.4	④1.05	2.05	2.11	0.24	18.75 - 11.63	14.5	1.6
12/31/93	732.2	⑤d7.3	562.7	...	...	...	...	1.8	⑥d0.17	0.65	3.79	0.57	17.50 - 10.63	...	4.1

Statistics are as originally reported. ① Incl. one-time chrg. of $8.0 mill.; bef. extraord. chrg. of $8.7 mill. ② Bef. inc. of $149,000 fr. disc. ops. ③ Bef. inc. fr. disc. ops. of $11.2 mill. ($0.33/sh.), extraord. chrg. $2.7 mill. & non-recurr. credit of $10.4 mill. ④ Bef. extraord. chrg. of $11.8 mill. & acctg. adj. credit of $3.8 mill. ⑤ Incl. non-recurr. chrg. of $45.1 mill. ⑥ Incl. aft.-tax nonrecurr. chrgs. of $15.3 mill. ($0.46/sh.) and aft.-tax tax benefit & rel. int. inc. of $10.5 mill. ($0.32/sh.)

OFFICERS:
F. S. Hermance, Chmn., C.E.O.
J. J. Molinelli, Exec. V.P., C.F.O.
D. D. Saunders, V.P., Treas.
INVESTOR CONTACT: William J. Burke, (610) 889-5249
PRINCIPAL OFFICE: 37 North Valley Road, Building 4, Paoli, PA 19301-0801

TELEPHONE NUMBER: (610) 647-2121
FAX: (610) 647-0211
WEB: www.ametek.com
NO. OF EMPLOYEES: 8,100 (approx.)
SHAREHOLDERS: 2,590 (approx.)
ANNUAL MEETING: In May
INCORPORATED: DE, Mar., 1930

INSTITUTIONAL HOLDINGS:
No. of Institutions: 169
Shares Held: 23,891,730
% Held: 72.3
INDUSTRY: Motors and generators (SIC: 3621)
TRANSFER AGENT(S): American Stock Transfer & Trust Co., New York, NY

AMPHENOL CORPORATION

EXCH.	SYM.	REC. PRICE	P/E RATIO	YLD.	MKT. CAP.	RANGE (52-WK.)	'02 Y/E PR.
NYSE	APH	40.79 (2/28/03)	21.9	...	$1.73 bill.	49.00 - 27.47	38.00

MEDIUM GRADE. EARNINGS PER SHARE FOR 2003 ARE EXPECTED TO INCREASE BETWEEN 20.0% AND 25.0%.

INTERIM EARNINGS (Per Share):

Qtr.	Mar.	June	Sept.	Dec.
1999	0.23	0.29	0.32	0.37
2000	0.48	0.61	0.67	0.76
2001	0.67	0.53	0.39	0.37
2002	0.40	0.46	0.48	0.52

INTERIM DIVIDENDS (Per Share):

Amt.	Decl.	Ex.	Rec.	Pay.
		No dividends paid.		

CAPITALIZATION (12/31/01):

	($000)	(%)
Long-Term Debt	660,614	86.4
Common & Surplus	103,933	13.6
Total	764,547	100.0

TRADING VOLUME
Thousand Shares

*7 YEAR PRICE SCORE 140.2   ***12 MONTH PRICE SCORE 109.1**

*NYSE COMPOSITE INDEX=100

BUSINESS:

Amphenol Corporation is a producer of electronic and fiber optic connectors, cable and interconnect systems. The Company's products are engineered and manufactured in the Americas, Europe and Asia. The primary end markets for the Company's products are communication systems for the converging technologies of voice, video and data communications, including wired and wireless Internet and broadband networks, and industrial, automotive and aerospace applications. Revenues for 2001 were derived as follows: 82.2% interconnect products; 17.8% cable products.

RECENT DEVELOPMENTS:

For the year ended 12/31/02, net income decreased 4.0% to $80.3 million compared with $83.7 million in the previous year. Results for 2001 included amortization of goodwill of $14.3 million. Net sales declined 3.8% to $1.06 billion from $1.10 billion a year earlier. Operating income fell 11.7% to $173.9 million from $197.0 million the year before. Interest expense dropped 18.1% to $45.9 million.

For the fourth quarter ended 12/31/02, net income jumped 40.2% to $22.5 million from $16.0 million in the corresponding prior-year quarter. Net sales increased 2.6% to $267.0 million from $260.4 million in the year-earlier quarter, due to higher demand from communications and industrial/automotive markets.

PROSPECTS:

The Company's recent sales growth reflects increasing demand from the communications markets for interconnect components and assemblies for mobile handsets and wireless infrastructure, as well as higher demand from the industrial/automotive markets for electronic components used in automobiles. Going forward, the Company expects revenues for 2003 to grow between 4.0% and 7.0%. Earnings per share for 2003 is expected to increase between 20.0% and 25.0%. Separately, the Company has recognized an increase in its long-term pension obligation in 2002 of approximately $66.0 million due to declining equity markets. However, the increase is not likely to require any cash funding in 2003.

ANNUAL FINANCIAL DATA:

FISCAL YEAR	TOT. REVS. ($mill.)	NET INC. ($mill.)	TOT. ASSETS ($mill.)	OPER. PROFIT %	NET PROFIT %	RET. ON EQUITY %	RET. ON ASSETS %	CURR. RATIO	EARN. PER SH. $	CASH FL. PER SH. $	TANG. BK. VAL. $	PRICE RANGE	AVG. P/E RATIO
p12/31/02	1,062.0	80.3	1,078.9						1.85			51.75 - 30.11	22.1
12/31/01	1,103.8	83.7	1,026.7	17.9	7.6	80.5	8.2	1.8	1.95	3.08	...	57.99 - 28.30	22.1
12/31/00	1,359.7	107.9	1,004.3	18.0	7.9	369.1	10.7	1.7	2.52	3.57	...	70.38 - 30.31	20.0
12/31/99	1,010.6	①44.3	836.4	15.9	4.4	...	5.3	2.3	①1.21	2.37	...	35.75 - 14.72	20.9
12/31/98	918.9	36.5	807.4	16.3	4.0	...	4.5	2.3	1.02	2.08	...	32.00 - 13.50	22.3
12/31/97	884.3	②51.3	737.2	17.6	5.8	...	7.0	2.2	②0.92	1.53	...	28.25 - 10.75	21.3
12/31/96	776.2	67.6	710.7	17.8	8.7	18.7	9.5	2.4	0.73	1.04	0.16	13.81 - 9.38	16.0
12/31/95	783.2	62.9	689.9	17.2	8.0	18.3	9.1	2.2	0.67	0.97	0.02	15.19 - 9.38	18.5
12/31/94	692.7	①42.4	...	15.0	6.1	...	...	...	①0.46	0.76	...	12.56 - 7.06	21.6

Statistics are as originally reported. Adj. for 2-for-1 stk. split, 4/00. ① Bef. extraord. chrg. of $8.7 mill., 1999; $4.1 mill., 1994. ② Bef. extraord. chrg. of $24.5 mill. & incl. nonrecurr. chrg. of $2.5 mill.

OFFICERS:
M. H. Loeffler, Chmn., Pres., C.E.O.
E. G. Jepsen, Exec. V.P., C.F.O.
E. C. Wetmore, Sec., Gen. Couns.

INVESTOR CONTACT: Edward G. Jepsen, Exec. V.P., C.F.O., (203) 265-8650

PRINCIPAL OFFICE: 358 Hall Avenue, Wallingford, CT 06492

TELEPHONE NUMBER: (203) 265-8900
FAX: (203) 265-8793
WEB: www.amphenol.com
NO. OF EMPLOYEES: 10,300 (approx.)
SHAREHOLDERS: 98
ANNUAL MEETING: In May
INCORPORATED: DE, Nov., 1991

INSTITUTIONAL HOLDINGS:
No. of Institutions: 118
Shares Held: 21,515,258
% Held: 50.6

INDUSTRY: Electronic connectors (SIC: 3678)

TRANSFER AGENT(S): Boston EquiServe L.P., Canton, MA

AMR CORPORATION

EXCH.	SYM.	REC. PRICE	P/E RATIO	YLD.	MKT. CAP.	RANGE (52-WK.)	'02 Y/E PR.
NYSE	AMR	2.34 (2/28/03)	...	...	$361.5 mill.	29.20 - 2.25	6.60

SPECULATIVE GRADE. THE COMPANY CONTINUES TO TAKE STEPS TO REDUCE OPERATIONAL AND LABOR COSTS.

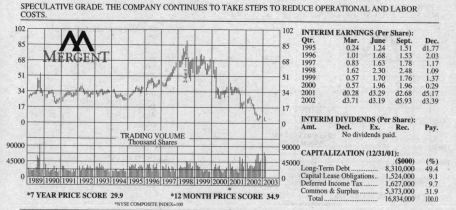

INTERIM EARNINGS (Per Share):

Qtr.	Mar.	June	Sept.	Dec.
1995	0.24	1.24	1.51	d1.77
1996	1.01	1.68	1.53	2.03
1997	0.83	1.63	1.78	1.17
1998	1.62	2.30	2.48	1.09
1999	0.57	1.70	1.76	1.37
2000	0.57	1.96	1.96	0.29
2001	d0.28	d3.29	d2.68	d5.17
2002	d3.71	d3.19	d5.93	d3.39

INTERIM DIVIDENDS (Per Share):

Amt.	Decl.	Ex.	Rec.	Pay.
		No dividends paid.		

CAPITALIZATION (12/31/01):

	($000)	(%)
Long-Term Debt	8,310,000	49.4
Capital Lease Obligations	1,524,000	9.1
Deferred Income Tax	1,627,000	9.7
Common & Surplus	5,373,000	31.9
Total	16,834,000	100.0

*7 YEAR PRICE SCORE 29.9 ***12 MONTH PRICE SCORE 34.9**

*NYSE COMPOSITE INDEX=100

BUSINESS:

AMR Corporation is the parent company of American Airlines, Inc., which provides scheduled jet service to more than 161 destinations throughout North America, the Caribbean, Latin America, Europe and the Pacific as of 12/31/01. AMR also provides regional jet service to smaller markets on American Eagle through its wholly-owned subsidiary, AMR Eagle Holding Corporation. In addition, AMR provides freight and mail services to shippers throughout its system. At 12/31/02, AMR operated a fleet of 1,105 jet aircraft. AMR Investment Services, Inc., a wholly-owned subsidiary, provides investment management activities. On 3/15/00, the Company spun off Sabre, Inc. to AMR shareholders. On 4/9/01, AMR acquired Trans World Airlines, Inc.

RECENT DEVELOPMENTS:

For the year ended 12/31/02, AMR reported a loss of $2.52 billion, before a $988.0 million accounting change charge, versus a net loss of $1.76 billion a year earlier. Results for 2002 and 2001 included net pre-tax special charges of $708.0 million and $610.0 million, respectively. Total operating revenues slipped 8.8% to $17.30 billion from $18.96 billion in 2001. Passenger revenues slid 8.1% to $15.77 billion, while cargo revenues were down 15.3% to $561.0 million. The passenger load factor, or percentage of seats filled, for American Airlines rose to 70.7% versus 69.0% in the prior year. AMR Eagle's passenger load factor improved to 62.7% from 57.6% the year before.

PROSPECTS:

Results are being negatively affected by a combination of factors, including weak economic conditions, higher fuel prices, lingering fears of terrorism and the possibility of war in the Middle East. In an effort to restore profitability, AMR is aggressively implementing initiatives focused on significantly reducing its operational and labor costs. As of year-end 2002, these efforts have resulted in permanent annual savings of about $2.00 billion. Looking ahead, AMR hopes to generate annual cost savings of an additional $2.00 billion.

ANNUAL FINANCIAL DATA:

FISCAL YEAR	TOT. REVS. ($mill.)	NET INC. ($mill.)	TOT. ASSETS ($mill.)	OPER. PROFIT %	NET PROFIT %	RET. ON EQUITY %	RET. ON ASSETS %	CURR. RATIO	EARN. PER SH. $	CASH FL. PER SH. $	TANG. BK. VAL. $	PRICE RANGE	AVG. P/E RATIO
p12/31/02	17,299.0	⑧d2,523.0							⑧d16.22			29.20 - 3.01	...
12/31/01	18,963.0	⑦d1,762.0	32,841.0	...	...	...	...	0.9	⑦d11.43	2.32	17.19	43.94 - 15.10	...
12/31/00	19,703.0	⑥779.0	26,213.0	7.0	4.0	10.9	3.0	0.7	⑥4.81	12.23	39.67	68.75 - 26.00	9.8
12/31/99	17,730.0	⑥656.0	24,374.0	6.5	3.7	9.6	2.7	0.8	⑤4.17	11.13	38.23	75.44 - 52.56	15.3
12/31/98	19,205.0	④1,306.0	22,303.0	12.2	6.8	19.5	5.9	0.9	⑦7.48	14.82	33.90	89.94 - 45.63	9.1
12/31/97	18,570.0	④985.0	20,915.0	10.4	5.3	15.8	4.7	0.9	④5.39	12.25	28.56	66.28 - 39.13	9.8
12/31/96	17,753.0	③1,105.0	20,497.0	10.4	6.2	19.5	5.4	0.8	③6.32	13.42	23.90	48.75 - 34.00	6.5
12/31/95	16,910.0	191.0	19,556.0	6.0	1.1	5.1	1.0	0.7	1.24	9.44	14.89	40.13 - 26.69	26.9
12/31/94	16,137.0	②228.0	19,486.0	6.2	1.4	6.7	1.2	0.6	②1.13	10.48	12.44	36.38 - 24.06	26.7
12/31/93	15,816.0	①d96.0	19,326.0	4.4	...	...	...	0.6	①d1.02	7.06	11.43	36.44 - 27.75	...

Statistics are as originally reported. Adj. for 2-for-1 stk. split, 6/98. ① Bef. $14 mil loss from early retirmnt. of debt & incl. $62 mil in litigation chgs. ② Bef. $29 mil loss from early retirmnt. of debt & incl. $334 mil in restr. chgs. ③ Bef. $89 mil extraord. chg. & incl. $251 mil non-recur. net gain. ④ Incl. $20 mil pre-tax chg. & special items after-tax cr. of $13 mil. ⑤ Bef. $329 mil ($2.09/sh) gain fr. disc. ops., 1999; $8 mil ($0.04/sh) income fr. disc. ops., 1998. ⑥ Bef. $43 mil ($0.27/sh) income fr. disc. ops. and $9 mil ($0.05/sh) extraord. chg. & incl. $36 mil ($0.21/sh) after-tax gain fr. sale of priceline.com warrants. ⑦ Incl. $610.0 mil net special chgs. ⑧ Bef. $988.0 mil ($6.35/sh) acctg. chg. & incl. $708.0 mil net special chgs.

OFFICERS:	TELEPHONE NUMBER: (817) 963-1234	INSTITUTIONAL HOLDINGS:
D. J. Carty, Chmn., C.E.O.	FAX: (817) 967-9641	No. of Institutions: 230
G. J. Arpey, Pres., C.O.O.	WEB: www.amrcorp.com	Shares Held: 119,522,526
J. C. Campbell, Sr. V.P., C.F.O.	NO. OF EMPLOYEES: 105,500 (approx.)	% Held: 76.6
INVESTOR CONTACT: Linda Dill, Dir., Inv. Rel., (817) 967-2970	SHAREHOLDERS: 13,700 (approx.)	INDUSTRY: Air transportation, scheduled (SIC: 4512)
PRINCIPAL OFFICE: 4333 Amon Carter Blvd., Ft. Worth, TX 76155	ANNUAL MEETING: In May	TRANSFER AGENT(S): EquiServe Trust Co., N.A., Jersey City, NJ
	INCORPORATED: DE, Oct., 1982	

AMSOUTH BANCORPORATION

EXCH.	SYM.	REC. PRICE	P/E RATIO	YLD.	MKT. CAP.	RANGE (52-WK.)	'02 Y/E PR.	DIV. ACH.
NYSE	ASO	20.60 (2/28/03)	12.2	4.5%	$7.28 bill.	23.06 - 17.75	19.20	32 yrs.

UPPER MEDIUM GRADE. ON 1/16/03, THE COMPANY INTRODUCED NEW PRODUCTS AND SERVICES TARGETING MID-SIZED AND LARGER BUSINESSES.

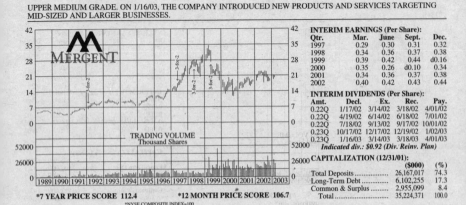

INTERIM EARNINGS (Per Share):

Qtr.	Mar.	June	Sept.	Dec.
1997	0.29	0.30	0.31	0.32
1998	0.34	0.36	0.37	0.38
1999	0.39	0.42	0.44	d0.16
2000	0.35	0.26	d0.10	0.34
2001	0.34	0.36	0.37	0.38
2002	0.40	0.42	0.43	0.44

INTERIM DIVIDENDS (Per Share):

Amt.	Decl.	Ex.	Rec.	Pay.
0.22Q	1/17/02	3/14/02	3/18/02	4/01/02
0.22Q	4/19/02	6/14/02	6/18/02	7/01/02
0.22Q	7/18/02	9/13/02	9/17/02	10/01/02
0.23Q	10/17/02	12/17/02	12/19/02	1/02/03
0.23Q	1/16/03	3/14/03	3/18/03	4/01/03

Indicated div.: $0.92 (Div. Reinv. Plan)

CAPITALIZATION (12/31/01):

	($000)	(%)
Total Deposits	26,167,017	74.3
Long-Term Debt	6,102,255	17.3
Common & Surplus	2,955,099	8.4
Total	35,224,371	100.0

TRADING VOLUME Thousand Shares

*7 YEAR PRICE SCORE 112.4   *12 MONTH PRICE SCORE 106.7

*NYSE COMPOSITE INDEX=100

BUSINESS:

AmSouth Bancorporation is a regional bank holding company headquartered in Birmingham, Alabama. As of 12/31/02, ASO had assets of $40.57 billion and operated 600 branch banking offices and 1,250 ATMs in the following southeastern states: Alabama, Florida, Tennessee, Mississippi, Georgia, and Louisiana. ASO's affiliates, AmSouth N.A., AmSouth Bank of Florida, AmSouth Bank of Tennessee, AmSouth Bank of Georgia and AmSouth

Bank of Alabama, AmSouth Investment Services and AmSouth Leasing Corporation, provide a full line of traditional and nontraditional financial services including consumer and commercial banking, small business banking, mortgage lending, equipment leasing, annuity and mutual fund sales, and trust and investment management services. On 10/1/99, ASO acquired First American Corporation.

RECENT DEVELOPMENTS:

For the year ended 12/31/02, net income climbed 13.6% to $609.1 million from $536.3 million in the previous year. Earnings for 2001 included goodwill amortization of $29.4 million. Net interest income increased 7.8% to $1.50 billion from $1.39 billion a year earlier. Provision for loan losses

grew 14.1% to $213.6 million from $187.1 million the year before. Non-interest revenues decreased 1.2% to $739.4 million from $748.2 million in the previous year. Non-interest expense, excluding amortization, totaled $1.16 billion, essentially unchanged compared with the prior year.

PROSPECTS:

On 1/16/03, the Company introduced its Commercial RelationshiPlus account that features a combination of products and services designed for mid-sized and larger businesses. Commercial RelationshiPlus, which is targeted at companies with at least $5.0 million in annual sales, includes

analyzed checking, a premium money market account, a selection of treasury management services, and a selection of personal banking products for key executives. Meanwhile, near-term results should continue to benefit from growth in consumer loans and deposits.

ANNUAL FINANCIAL DATA:

FISCAL YEAR	NET INT. INC. ($mill.)	NON-INT. INC. ($mill.)	NET INC. ($mill.)	TOT. LOANS ($mill.)	TOT. ASSETS ($mill.)	TOT. DEP. ($mill.)	RET. ON EQUITY %	RET. ON ASSETS %	EQUITY/ ASSETS %	EARN. PER SH.$	TANG. BK. VAL.$	DIV. PER SH.$	PRICE RANGE	AVG. P/E RATIO
p12/31/02	1,503.7		609.1							1.68		0.88	23.06 - 17.75	12.1
12/31/01	1,394.9	748.2	536.3	25,124.5	38,600.4	26,167.0	18.1	1.4	7.7	1.45	8.14	0.84	20.24 - 15.00	12.2
12/31/00	1,379.1	669.5	②329.1	24,616.4	38,936.0	26,623.3	11.7	0.8	7.2	②0.86	7.53	0.80	20.06 - 11.69	18.5
⑤12/31/99	1,507.9	847.6	④340.5	26,436.4	43,406.6	27,912.4	11.5	0.8	6.8	④0.86	7.56	0.67	34.59 - 18.75	31.0
12/31/98	699.0	346.6	③262.7	12,869.9	19,901.7	13,283.8	18.4	1.3	7.4	③1.45	8.05	0.53	30.42 - 20.46	17.6
12/31/97	676.3	266.0	226.2	12,342.8	18,622.3	12,945.2	16.3	1.2	7.4	1.21	7.64	0.50	25.36 - 14.00	16.2
12/31/96	652.4	235.3	②182.7	12,168.6	18,407.3	12,467.6	13.1	1.0	7.6	②0.96	7.38	0.47	15.07 - 10.19	13.2
12/31/95	595.7	231.8	①175.0	11,819.8	17,738.8	13,408.8	12.6	1.0	7.8	①0.89	7.16	0.45	12.26 - 7.63	11.2
12/31/94	567.3	179.0	127.3	11,496.1	16,778.0	13,067.1	9.7	0.8	7.8	0.67	6.69	0.41	10.33 - 7.52	13.4
12/31/93	462.1	194.4	146.2	7,999.9	12,547.9	9,567.9	13.4	1.2	8.7	0.92	6.52	0.34	10.63 - 8.11	10.2

Statistics are as originally reported. Adj. for 3-for-2 splits 5/99, 4/98, 4/97. ① Incl. pre-tax gain on the sale of 3rd party mtg. servicing portfolio to G.E. Capital Services, Inc. & $22.0 mill. in add'l. exps. rel. to the consol. & workforce reduction. ② Incl. SAIF pre-tax chrg. of $24.2 mill. ③ Incl. $28.0 mill. gain fr. sale of assets. ④ Incl. net gain fr. sale of businesses of $8.6 mill. & merger-rel. chrgs. of $301.4 mill. ⑤ Refl. acquis. of First American Corp. in 10/99. ⑥ Incl. pre-tax merger-rel. costs of $110.2 mill. & a gain of $538,000 on the sale of businesses.

OFFICERS:
C. D. Ritter, Chmn., Pres., C.E.O.
S. D. Gibson, Vice-Chmn., C.F.O.
S. A. Yoder, Exec. V.P., Gen. Couns., Sec.

INVESTOR CONTACT: M. List Underwood, Jr., Exec. V.P.-Corp. Fin., (205) 801-0265

PRINCIPAL OFFICE: 1900 Fifth Avenue North, Birmingham, AL 35203

TELEPHONE NUMBER: (205) 320-7151
FAX: (205) 326-4072
WEB: www.amsouth.com

NO. OF EMPLOYEES: 11,900 (approx.)

SHAREHOLDERS: 34,632 (approx.)

ANNUAL MEETING: In Apr.

INCORPORATED: DE, Nov., 1970

INSTITUTIONAL HOLDINGS:
No. of Institutions: 339
Shares Held: 145,090,001
% Held: 40.8

INDUSTRY: State commercial banks (SIC: 6022)

TRANSFER AGENT(S): The Bank of New York, New York, NY

ANADARKO PETROLEUM CORPORATION

EXCH.	SYM.	REC. PRICE	P/E RATIO	YLD.	MKT. CAP.	RANGE (52-WK.)	'02 Y/E PR.
NYSE	APC	46.08 (2/28/03)	14.3	0.9%	$11.47 bill.	58.55 - 36.77	47.90

UPPER MEDIUM GRADE. THE COMPANY ANTICIPATES FULL-YEAR 2003 EARNINGS OF ABOUT $3.90 PER DILUTED SHARE.

TRADING VOLUME
Thousand Shares

MERGENT
100% STK

1989 1990 1991 1992 1993 1994 1995 1996 1997 1998 1999 2000 2001 2002 2003

*7 YEAR PRICE SCORE 123.3   ***12 MONTH PRICE SCORE 104.7**

*NYSE COMPOSITE INDEX=100

INTERIM EARNINGS (Per Share):

Qtr.	Mar.	June	Sept.	Dec.
1998	0.06	0.02	d0.02	d0.47
1999	d0.19	0.06	0.15	0.22
2000	0.37	0.48	1.03	1.75
2001	2.52	1.50	d5.41	0.41
2002	0.34	0.93	0.74	1.21

INTERIM DIVIDENDS (Per Share):

Amt.	Decl.	Ex.	Rec.	Pay.
0.075Q	4/25/02	6/10/02	6/12/02	6/26/02
0.075Q	7/29/02	9/09/02	9/11/02	9/25/02
0.10Q	10/31/02	12/09/02	12/11/02	12/24/02
0.10Q	1/31/03	3/10/03	3/12/03	3/26/03

Indicated div.: $0.40 (Div. Reinv. Plan)

CAPITALIZATION (12/31/01):

	($000)	(%)
Long-Term Debt	4,638,000	32.1
Deferred Income Tax	3,451,000	23.9
Preferred Stock	103,000	0.7
Common & Surplus	6,262,000	43.3
Total	14,454,000	100.0

BUSINESS:

Anadarko Petroleum Corporation is engaged in the exploration, development, production and marketing of natural gas, crude oil, condensate and natural gas liquids (NGLs). APC's major areas of operations are located in the U.S., primarily in Texas, Louisiana, the mid-continent region and the western states, Alaska and in the shallow and deep waters of the Gulf of Mexico, as well as in Canada and Algeria. The Company is also active in Venezuela, Qatar,

Oman, Egypt, Australia, Tunisia, Congo and Gabon. APC owns and operates gas gathering systems in its core producing areas and engages in the hard minerals business through non-operated joint ventures and royalty arrangements. At 12/31/02, proved reserves amounted to: natural gas, 7.18 trillion cubic feet; crude oil, condensate and NGLs, 1.13 billion barrels. On 7/14/00, APC acquired Union Pacific Resources Group Inc.

RECENT DEVELOPMENTS:

For the year ended 12/31/02, net income was $831.0 million versus a loss of $176.0 million, before an accounting change charge of $5.0 million, the previous year. Results for 2002 and 2001 included impairments related to oil and

gas properties of $39.0 million and $2.55 billion, respectively. Results for 2001 also included amortization of goodwill of $73.0 million and a merger expense of $45.0 million. Total revenues decreased 18.2% to $3.86 billion.

PROSPECTS:

APC has set a $2.30 billion capital budget for 2003, a decline of 3.7% from 2002. The Company has allocated $1.48 billion to worldwide development projects in 2003, 34.9% higher than the prior year, primarily for fields in the Gulf of Mexico, Western Canada, East and Central Texas, North Louisiana and Wyoming. Exploration's capital budget for 2003 dropped 56.0% to $381.0 million, while capital for gas gathering and other rose 37.2% to $107.0

million. Full year sales volumes are expected to total 200.0 million barrels of oil equivalent. Separately, APC expects full-year 2003 earnings of about $3.90 per diluted share. For 2003, APC has hedged about 40.0% of its natural gas production through June and 35.0% for July through December 2003. About 35.0% of APC's oil production is hedged through December 2003.

ANNUAL FINANCIAL DATA:

FISCAL YEAR	TOT. REVS. ($mill.)	NET INC. ($mill.)	TOT. ASSETS ($mill.)	OPER. PROFIT %	NET PROFIT %	RET. ON EQUITY %	RET. ON ASSETS %	CURR. RATIO	EARN. PER SH.$	CASH FL. PER SH.$	TANG. BK. VAL.$	DIV. PER SH.$	PRICE RANGE	AVG. P/E RATIO	AVG. YIELD %
p12/31/02	3,860.0	⑦831.0							⑦3.21			0.33	58.55 - 36.77	14.8	0.7
12/31/01	8,369.0	⑧d176.0	16,771.0	...	...	...	...	0.7	⑥d0.73	4.18	19.41	0.23	73.97 - 43.00	...	0.4
⑤12/31/00	5,686.0	④824.0	16,590.0	25.0	14.5	12.1	4.9	1.1	④4.25	7.45	20.80	0.20	75.95 - 27.56	12.2	0.4
12/31/99	701.1	③42.6	4,098.4	25.5	6.1	2.8	1.0	0.9	③0.25	2.01	10.30	0.20	42.75 - 26.25	137.9	0.6
12/31/98	560.3	d42.2	3,633.0	...	...	...	...	0.8	d0.41	1.30	8.65	0.19	44.88 - 24.75	...	0.5
12/31/97	673.2	107.3	2,992.5	30.2	15.9	9.6	3.6	0.9	0.89	2.56	9.17	0.15	38.38 - 25.38	35.8	0.5
12/31/96	569.0	①100.7	2,584.0	34.4	17.7	9.9	3.9	0.9	①0.85	2.28	8.52	0.15	34.44 - 23.38	34.0	0.5
12/31/95	434.0	21.0	2,267.0	14.9	4.8	2.3	0.9	0.9	0.18	1.59	7.58	0.15	27.06 - 17.81	124.6	0.7
12/31/94	482.5	①41.1	2,142.1	18.4	8.5	4.6	1.9	1.1	①0.35	1.83	7.64	0.15	29.25 - 18.50	68.2	0.6
12/31/93	476.3	②40.0	2,022.8	21.9	8.4	4.6	2.0	1.1	②0.35	1.83	7.36	0.15	25.88 - 12.81	55.3	0.8

Statistics are as originally reported. Adj. for 2-for-1 stk. split, 7/98. ① Incl. non-recurr. cr. 12/31/96: $12.3 mill.; chrg. 12/31/94: $6.6 mill. ② Bef. acctg. chge. cr. of $77.4 mill. ③ Incl. non-cash pre-tax chrg. of $24.0 mill. ④ Incl. aft-tax merger-rel. chrgs. of $43.0 mill. & an impair. chrg. of $50.0 mill. rel. to int'l. prop.; bef. acctg. chge. chrg. of $17.0 mill. ⑤ Incl. results for Union Pacific Resources Group Inc. ⑥ Incl. impair. chrg. of $2.55 bill. & merger exp. of $45.0 mill.; bef. acctg. chge. chrg. of $5.0 mill. ⑦ Incl. impair. chrg. of $39.0 mill.

OFFICERS:
R. J. Allison, Jr., Chmn.
J. N. Seitz, Pres., C.E.O.
M. E. Rose, Exec. V.P., C.F.O.
INVESTOR CONTACT: Paul Taylor, V.P., Inv. Rel., (832) 636-3471
PRINCIPAL OFFICE: 1201 Lake Robbins Drive, The Woodlands, TX 77380-1046

TELEPHONE NUMBER: (832) 636-1000
FAX: (874) 874-3385
WEB: www.anadarko.com
NO. OF EMPLOYEES: 3,500 (approx.)
SHAREHOLDERS: 26,000
ANNUAL MEETING: In Apr.
INCORPORATED: DE, 1985

INSTITUTIONAL HOLDINGS:
No. of Institutions: 587
Shares Held: 214,893,613
% Held: 86.4
INDUSTRY: Crude petroleum and natural gas (SIC: 1311)
TRANSFER AGENT(S): Mellon Investor Services LLC, South Hackensack, NJ

ANALOG DEVICES, INC.

EXCH.	SYM.	REC. PRICE	P/E RATIO	YLD.	MKT. CAP.	RANGE (52-WK.)	'02 Y/E PR.
NYSE	ADI	29.16 (2/28/03)	78.8	...	$10.59 bill.	47.95 - 17.88	23.87

MEDIUM GRADE. THE COMPANY EXPECTS SECOND QUARTER EARNINGS OF $0.17 OR $0.18 PER SHARE.

MERGENT

TRADING VOLUME
Thousand Shares

*7 YEAR PRICE SCORE 105.7 *12 MONTH PRICE SCORE 96.3

*NYSE COMPOSITE INDEX=100

INTERIM EARNINGS (Per Share):

Qtr.	Jan.	April	July	Oct.
1998-99	0.09	0.11	0.15	0.20
1999-00	0.25	0.32	0.50	0.52
2000-01	0.50	0.27	0.10	0.06
2001-02	0.06	0.04	0.08	0.09
2002-03	0.16	...	...	...

INTERIM DIVIDENDS (Per Share):

Amt.	Decl.	Ex.	Rec.	Pay.
		No dividends paid.		

CAPITALIZATION (11/2/02):

	($000)	(%)
Long-Term Debt	1,274,487	30.4
Deferred Income Tax	22,612	0.5
Common & Surplus	2,900,016	69.1
Total	4,197,115	100.0

BUSINESS:

Analog Devices, Inc. is a semiconductor company that manufactures high-performance analog, mixed signal and digital signal processing integrated circuits used in signal processing applications. These devices are used by a broad base of markets, including communications, computers and computer peripherals, consumer electronics, industrial, instrumentation, military and space systems and automotive electronics. ADI's products are used in wireless handsets and base stations, cable modems, central-office networking equipment, digital cameras, DVD players, surround sound audio systems, industrial data acquisition systems, automatic process control systems, robotics, environmental control systems, and automatic test equipment. ADI has manufacturing facilities in Massachusetts, California, North Carolina, Ireland, the Philippines, Taiwan and the United Kingdom.

RECENT DEVELOPMENTS:

For the first quarter ended 2/1/03, net income surged to $60.0 million from $24.7 million in the corresponding prior-year quarter. Results for 2003 and 2002 included acquisition related charges of $2.8 million and $20.4 million, respectively. Net sales increased 18.9% to $467.4 million compared with $393.0 million a year earlier, primarily due to strength in the wireless analog and digital signal processing product markets. Gross profit jumped 24.2% to $253.1 million, or 54.2% of net sales, from $203.8 million, or 51.9% of net sales, in the previous year. Operating income amounted to $73.9 million versus $26.6 million the year before.

PROSPECTS:

During the first quarter of fiscal 2003, orders for shipment in the next thirteen weeks grew by approximately 9.0% from the prior quarter. Orders grew sequentially in both the original equipment manufacturer and distributor channels. Consequently, the Company anticipates sequential revenue growth of 3.0% to 5.0% in the second quarter. In addition, ADI expects to hold operating expenses and capital spending relatively flat in the second quarter. As a result, ADI expects second quarter earnings of $0.17 or $0.18 per share. Meanwhile, the Company continues to believe that high-performance analog and digital signal processors should drive long-term growth and profitability.

ANNUAL FINANCIAL DATA:

FISCAL YEAR	TOT. REVS. ($mill.)	NET INC. ($mill.)	TOT. ASSETS ($mill.)	OPER. PROFIT %	NET PROFIT %	RET. ON EQUITY %	RET. ON ASSETS %	CURR. RATIO	EARN. PER SH.$	CASH FL. PER SH.$	TANG. BK. VAL.$	PRICE RANGE	AVG. P/E RATIO
11/02/02	1,707.5	④ 105.3	4,980.2	6.9	6.2	3.6	2.1	7.5	④ 0.28	0.90	7.50	48.84 - 17.88	119.1
11/03/01	2,276.9	③ 356.4	4,884.9	17.9	15.7	12.5	7.3	6.5	③ 0.93	1.48	7.20	64.00 - 29.00	50.0
10/28/00	2,577.5	607.1	4,411.3	29.8	23.6	26.4	13.8	4.9	1.59	2.00	5.90	103.00 - 41.31	45.4
10/30/99	1,450.4	② 196.8	2,218.4	16.7	13.6	12.2	8.9	2.9	② 0.55	0.94	4.53	47.25 - 12.19	54.0
10/31/98	1,230.6	① 119.5	1,861.7	12.8	9.7	10.6	6.4	2.8	① 0.36	0.69	3.47	19.81 - 6.00	36.3
11/01/97	1,243.5	178.2	1,763.9	18.8	14.3	16.4	10.1	3.3	0.52	0.79	3.31	18.34 - 10.31	27.5
11/02/96	1,193.8	171.9	1,515.7	19.0	14.4	19.9	11.3	3.0	0.52	-0.75	2.66	13.32 - 6.38	19.1
10/28/95	941.5	119.3	1,001.6	16.8	12.7	18.2	11.9	2.1	0.38	0.58	2.09	9.88 - 5.00	19.8
10/29/94	773.5	74.5	815.9	13.2	9.6	14.3	9.1	2.5	0.24	0.44	2.50	6.13 - 3.90	20.9
10/30/93	666.3	44.5	678.5	9.4	6.7	10.3	6.6	3.0	0.15	0.34	1.39	4.67 - 2.52	24.6

Statistics are as originally reported. Adj. for stk. splits: 100% div., 3/00; 50% div., 1/95; 3-for-2, 11/95 ① Bef. acctg. change chrg. of $37.1 mill.; incl. pre-tax restr. chrg. of $17.0 mill. and a gain on the sale of a business of $13.1 mill. ② Incl. a pre-tax chrg. of $5.1 mill. for in process R&D ③ Incl. pre-tax chrg. of $9.5 mill. for in-process R&D and a spec. chrg. of $47.0 mill. for cost-reduction activities. ④ Incl. restr. chrg. of $37.4 mill. and impair. chrg. of $11.1 mill.

OFFICERS:
R. Stata, Chmn.
J. G. Fishman, Pres., C.E.O.
J. E. McDonough, V.P., C.F.O.
INVESTOR CONTACT: Maria Tagliaferro, Dir., Corp. Comm., (781) 461-3282
PRINCIPAL OFFICE: One Technology Way, Norwood, MA 02062-9106

TELEPHONE NUMBER: (781) 329-4700
FAX: (791) 326-8703
WEB: www.analog.com
NO. OF EMPLOYEES: 8,600 (approx.)
SHAREHOLDERS: 5,281
ANNUAL MEETING: In March
INCORPORATED: MA, Jan., 1965

INSTITUTIONAL HOLDINGS:
No. of Institutions: 426
Shares Held: 305,529,371
% Held: 83.5
INDUSTRY: Semiconductors and related devices (SIC: 3674)
TRANSFER AGENT(S): EquiServe Trust Company, N.A., Providence, RI

ANHEUSER-BUSCH COMPANIES, INC.

EXCH.	SYM.	REC. PRICE	P/E RATIO	YLD.	MKT. CAP.	RANGE (52-WK.)	'02 Y/E PR.	DIV. ACH.
NYSE	BUD	46.50 (2/28/03)	21.1	1.7%	$40.88 bill.	55.00 - 43.65	48.40	28 yrs.

HIGH GRADE. THE COMPANY IS IMPLEMENTING THE SECOND STAGE OF ITS 2003 PRICING ACTIONS ON APPROXIMATELY 20.0% OF ITS DOMESTIC VOLUME.

*7 YEAR PRICE SCORE 157.7 *12 MONTH PRICE SCORE 103.9

*NYSE COMPOSITE INDEX=100

INTERIM EARNINGS (Per Share):

Qtr.	Mar.	June	Sept.	Dec.
1998	0.27	0.40	0.42	0.18
1999	0.33	0.45	0.49	0.21
2000	0.38	0.52	0.56	0.23
2001	0.43	0.58	0.62	0.26
2002	0.51	0.66	0.71	0.32

INTERIM DIVIDENDS (Per Share):

Amt.	Decl.	Ex.	Rec.	Pay.
0.18Q	1/14/02	2/07/02	2/11/02	3/11/02
0.18Q	4/24/02	5/07/02	5/09/02	6/10/02
0.195Q	7/24/02	8/07/02	8/09/02	9/09/02
0.195Q	10/23/02	11/06/02	11/11/02	12/09/02
0.195Q	1/14/03	2/06/03	2/10/03	3/10/03

Indicated div.: $0.78 (Div. Reinv. Plan)

CAPITALIZATION (12/31/01):

	($000)	(%)
Long-Term Debt	5,983,900	52.8
Deferred Income Tax	1,288,600	11.4
Common & Surplus	4,061,500	35.8
Total	11,334,000	100.0

BUSINESS:

Anheuser-Busch Companies, Inc. is a diversified corporation whose chief subsidiary is Anheuser-Busch, Inc., the world's largest brewer. Beer is sold under brand names including BUDWEISER, MICHELOB, BUSCH, and NATURAL LIGHT. Additionally, theme park operations are conducted through BUD's subsidiary, Busch Entertainment Corporation, which owned nine theme parks as of 12/31/01. BUD also engages in packaging, malt and rice production, international beer, non-beer beverages, real estate development, marketing communications, and transportation services. As of 12/31/01, BUD owned approximately 50.2% of Grupo Modelo, S.A. de C.V., a Mexican brewer.

RECENT DEVELOPMENTS:

For the year ended 12/31/02, net income advanced 13.5% to $1.93 billion compared with $1.70 billion the previous year. Results for 2001 included a pre-tax gain of $17.8 million from the sale of a business. Net sales grew 5.1% to $13.57 billion from $12.91 billion the year before. Domestic beer volume rose 2.1% to 101.8 million barrels, reflecting the continuing favorable introductions of MICHELOB ULTRA and BACARDI SILVER. Meanwhile, International beer volume inched up to 8.0 million barrels, primarily due to volume growth in BUD's three largest markets outside the U.S., which include Canada, China and the U.K.

PROSPECTS:

The Company recently completed the first stage of its pricing actions for 2003 by raising prices during the fourth quarter of 2002 in markets representing almost 45.0% of BUD's domestic volume. The Company is implementing the second stage of its 2003 pricing actions on approximately 20.0% of its domestic volume. Going forward, the combination of higher revenue per barrel, volume growth, and favorable costs should continue to boost operating results. BUD's objective is to grow earnings per share by 12.0% for 2003.

ANNUAL FINANCIAL DATA:

FISCAL YEAR	TOT. REVS. ($mill.)	NET INC. ($mill.)	TOT. ASSETS ($mill.)	OPER. PROFIT %	NET PROFIT %	RET. ON EQUITY %	RET. ON ASSETS %	CURR. RATIO	EARN. PER SH.$	CASH FL. PER SH.$	TANG. BK. VAL.$	DIV. PER SH.$	PRICE RANGE	AVG. P/E RATIO	AVG. YIELD %
p12/31/02	13,566.4	1,933.8	14,119.5						2.20			0.75	55.00 - 43.65	22.4	1.5
12/31/01	12,911.5	5 1,704.5	13,862.0	21.1	13.2	42.0	12.3	0.9	1.89	2.82	4.62	0.69	46.95 - 32.60	21.0	1.7
12/31/00	12,261.8	1,551.6	13,084.5	20.3	12.7	37.6	11.9	0.9	1.69	2.56	4.11	0.63	49.88 - 27.31	22.8	1.6
12/31/99	11,703.7	1,402.2	12,640.4	19.7	12.0	35.8	11.1	0.8	1.47	2.29	4.25	0.58	42.00 - 32.22	25.2	1.6
12/31/98	11,245.8	1,233.3	12,484.3	18.9	11.0	29.3	9.9	0.9	1.27	2.02	4.42	0.54	34.13 - 21.47	22.0	1.9
12/31/97	11,066.2	1 1,179.2	11,727.1	18.6	10.7	29.2	10.1	1.1	1 1.18	1.86	4.15	0.50	24.13 - 19.25	18.4	2.3
12/31/96	10,883.7	4 1,156.1	10,463.6	19.1	10.6	28.7	11.0	1.0	4 1.14	1.73	4.05	0.46	22.50 - 16.19	17.0	2.4
12/31/95	10,340.5	2 886.6	10,590.9	15.8	8.6	20.0	8.4	1.2	2 0.86	1.41	4.36	0.42	17.00 - 12.69	17.3	2.8
12/31/94	12,053.8	1,032.1	11,045.4	15.8	8.6	23.4	9.3	1.1	0.98	1.57	3.82	0.38	13.84 - 11.78	13.1	3.0
12/31/93	11,505.3	3 594.5	10,880.3	10.5	5.2	14.0	5.5	1.0	3 0.54	1.10	3.52	0.34	15.16 - 10.75	23.8	2.6

Statistics are as originally reported. Adj. for 2-for-1 stk. split, 9/00 & 9/96. 1 Bef. acctg. change chrge. of $10.0 mill. 2 Incl. $565.0 mill. restruct. chg. 3 Incl. $160.0 mill. pre-tax write off & excl. disc. oper. loss of $244.3 mill. 4 Incl. $54.7 mill. gain fr. the sale of the St. Louis Cardinals & bef. disc. oper. gain of $33.8 mill. 5 Incl. a pre-tax gain on the sale of SeaWorld Cleveland of $17.8 mill.

OFFICERS:
A. A. Busch III, Chmn.
P. T. Stokes, Pres., C.E.O.
W. R. Baker, V.P., C.F.O.

INVESTOR CONTACT: Carlos Ramierz, Investor Relations, (314) 577-9629

PRINCIPAL OFFICE: One Busch Place, St. Louis, MO 63118

TELEPHONE NUMBER: (314) 577-2000
FAX: (314) 577-2900
WEB: www.anheuser-busch.com

NO. OF EMPLOYEES: 23,432

SHAREHOLDERS: 57,347

ANNUAL MEETING: In Apr.

INCORPORATED: DE, Apr., 1979

INSTITUTIONAL HOLDINGS:
No. of Institutions: 764
Shares Held: 516,104,431
% Held: 60.3

INDUSTRY: Malt beverages (SIC: 2082)

TRANSFER AGENT(S): Mellon Investor Services, LLC, Ridgefield Park, NJ

ANIXTER INTERNATIONAL INC.

EXCH.	SYM.	REC. PRICE	P/E RATIO	YLD.	MKT. CAP.	RANGE (52-WK.)	'02 Y/E PR.
NYSE	AXE	23.45 (2/28/03)	20.8	...	$0.87 bill.	31.29 - 18.80	23.25

LOWER MEDIUM GRADE. THE COMPANY DOES NOT ANTICIPATE A MAJOR IMPROVEMENT IN THE LEVEL OF CORPORATE SPENDING, PARTICULARLY FOR TECHNOLOGY.

TRADING VOLUME
Thousand Shares

*7 YEAR PRICE SCORE 121.0   *12 MONTH PRICE SCORE 101.7
*NYSE COMPOSITE INDEX=100

INTERIM EARNINGS (Per Share):

Qtr.	Mar.	June	Sept.	Dec.
1998	0.35	0.44	0.24	0.07
1999	0.19	0.33	1.06	0.31
2000	0.44	0.62	0.59	0.41
2001	0.53	0.49	d0.32	0.15
2002	0.25	0.33	0.28	0.27

INTERIM DIVIDENDS (Per Share):

Amt.	Decl.	Ex.	Rec.	Pay.
	No dividends paid.			

CAPITALIZATION (12/28/01):

	($000)	(%)
Long-Term Debt	241,100	30.0
Common & Surplus	563,100	70.0
Total	804,200	100.0

BUSINESS:

Anixter International Inc. (formerly Itel Corp.) distributes networking and cable products for network infrastructure requirements through Anixter Inc., a supplier of wiring systems, networking and Internet products for voice, data and video networks and electrical power applications in North America, Europe, Asia and Latin America. AXE stocks and/or sells a full line of these products from a network of 87 locations in the U.S., 16 in Canada, 10 in the United Kingdom, 24 in Europe, 11 in Latin America, 4 in Australia and 9 in Asia as of 12/28/01. AXE sells more than 87,000 products to 85,000 active customers and works with approximately 1,000 active suppliers.

RECENT DEVELOPMENTS:

For the year ended 1/3/03, income was $43.5 million, before an extraordinary loss of $400,000, compared with income of $33.6 million, before an extraordinary loss of $3.3 million, the previous year. Results for 2001 included a pre-tax restructuring charge of $31.7 million. Earnings growth was largely due to the acquisition of Pentacon, Inc. on 9/20/02. Net sales decreased 19.9% to $2.52 billion from $3.14 billion a year earlier. Gross profit declined 17.8% to $605.4 million from $736.9 million the year before. Operating income fell 14.0% to $87.7 million versus $102.0 million the prior year.

PROSPECTS:

The Company does not anticipate a significant improvement in the level of corporate spending, particularly for technology. As a result, it is difficult for AXE to generate significant earnings improvement, as revenue growth will be the key to better leveraging its current operating expense structure. Meanwhile, AXE expects to continue to generate solid free cash flow. In the short-term, AXE will use this cash flow to further reduce debt, and in the long term, use it to support future organic growth or acquisitions. Looking ahead, AXE estimates sales in the first quarter of 2003 to range from $655.0 million to $670.0 million and diluted earnings to range from $0.26 to $0.30 per share.

ANNUAL FINANCIAL DATA:

FISCAL YEAR	TOT. REVS. ($mill.)	NET INC. ($mill.)	TOT. ASSETS ($mill.)	OPER. PROFIT %	NET PROFIT %	RET. ON EQUITY %	RET. ON ASSETS %	CURR. RATIO	EARN. PER SH. $	CASH FL. PER SH. $	TANG. BK. VAL. $	PRICE RANGE	AVG. P/E RATIO
p1/3/03	2,520.1	⑦ 43.5							⑦ 1.14			31.50 - 18.80	22.1
12/28/01	3,144.2	⑥ 33.6	1,198.8	3.2	1.1	6.0	2.8	2.4	⑥ 0.89	1.75	8.98	32.00 - 18.81	28.5
12/29/00	3,514.4	78.7	1,686.0	5.4	2.2	14.2	4.7	2.1	2.03	2.59	8.38	37.38 - 17.56	13.5
12/31/99	2,670.0	⑤ 69.7	1,434.7	4.2	2.6	15.3	4.9	2.3	⑤ 1.83	2.51	6.33	23.75 - 10.63	9.4
1/01/99	2,348.5	④ 44.7	1,335.1	3.7	1.9	10.9	3.3	2.7	④ 0.99	1.58	4.24	22.75 - 11.88	17.5
1/02/98	2,805.2	③ 45.3	1,440.7	4.0	1.6	9.5	3.1	2.3	③ 0.95	1.62	5.79	19.69 - 12.00	16.7
1/03/97	2,475.3	36.1	1,261.0	3.6	1.5	8.3	2.9	2.8	0.73	1.27	5.26	20.00 - 12.63	22.3
12/31/95	2,194.8	39.1	1,184.7	4.5	1.8	8.7	3.3	2.4	0.71	1.10	5.07	22.06 - 16.63	27.2
12/31/94	1,732.6	① 46.2	1,110.9	4.0	2.7	8.5	4.2	2.3	① 1.44	0.97	12.10	18.13 - 11.38	10.2
12/31/93	1,909.2	② 16.1	2,494.4	8.3	0.8	4.0	0.6	1.9	② 0.43	3.15	...	16.81 - 10.13	31.3

Statistics are as originally reported. Adjusted for 2-for-1 stock split, 10/95. ① Bef. inc. fr. dis. opers. of $200.7 mill. ② Bef. loss fr. disc. opers. of $1.3 mill. ③ Incl. nonrecurr. gain of $1.2 mill. in conj. with the merger of AXE's ANTEC affiliate with TSX Corp. ④ Incl. an after-tax gain of $24.3 million assoc./w. the sale of 2.2 million shares of ANTEC common stock & excl. a gain of $20.9 million from disc. opers. ⑤ Incl. a net restr. chg. of $1.8 mill. for staff reduct. & facil. consol. in Latin America, a gain of $24.3 mill. from the rev. of certain tax liabil. assoc./w completing IRS audits for a number of open years, & excl. a net gain of $54.5 mill. for. disc. ⑥ Incl. after-tax chrgs. for restruct. of $19.0 mill.; bef. extraord. loss of $3.3 mill. ⑦ Bef. extraord. loss of $400,000

OFFICERS: S. Zell, Chmn. R. W. Grubbs, Pres., C.E.O. D. J. Letham, Sr. V.P., C.F.O. **INVESTOR CONTACT:** Dennis Letham, Sr. V.P. & C.F.O., (847) 677-2600 **PRINCIPAL OFFICE:** 4711 Golf Road, Skokie, IL 60076	**TELEPHONE NUMBER:** (847) 677-2600 **FAX:** (847) 677-8557 **WEB:** www.anixter.com **NO. OF EMPLOYEES:** 4,900 (approx.) **SHAREHOLDERS:** 3,807 **ANNUAL MEETING:** In May **INCORPORATED:** DE, Dec., 1967	**INSTITUTIONAL HOLDINGS:** No. of Institutions: 137 Shares Held: 24,407,699 % Held: 65.2 **INDUSTRY:** Communications equipment, nec (SIC: 3669) **TRANSFER AGENT(S):** National City Bank, Cleveland, OH

ANNTAYLOR STORES CORPORATION

EXCH.	SYM.	REC. PRICE	P/E RATIO	YLD.	MKT. CAP.	RANGE (52-WK.)	'02 Y/E PR.
NYSE	ANN	19.40 (2/28/03)	11.3	...	$0.85 bill.	33.19 - 17.84	20.42

MEDIUM GRADE. THE COMPANY IS TARGETING FIRST-QUARTER 2003 EARNINGS OF $0.39 TO $0.41 PER SHARE.

7 YEAR PRICE SCORE 137.9 **12 MONTH PRICE SCORE 85.3**
*NYSE COMPOSITE INDEX=100

INTERIM EARNINGS (Per Share):

Qtr.	Apr.	July	Oct.	Jan.
1995-96	0.10	d0.11	0.02	d0.03
1996-97	0.05	0.02	0.09	0.08
1997-98	0.17	0.03	0.05	0.06
1998-99	0.17	0.18	0.33	0.28
1999-00	0.34	0.26	0.43	0.33
2000-01	0.25	0.30	0.52	0.09
2001-02	0.25	0.15	0.27	d0.01
2002-03	0.45	0.39	0.53	0.35

INTERIM DIVIDENDS (Per Share):

Amt.	Decl.	Ex.	Rec.	Pay.
50% STK	4/11/02	5/21/02	5/02/02	5/20/02

CAPITALIZATION (2/2/02):

	($000)	(%)
Long-Term Debt	118,280	16.2
Common & Surplus	612,129	83.8
Total	730,409	100.0

BUSINESS:

AnnTaylor Stores Corporation is a specialty retailer of women's apparel, shoes and accessories sold primarily under the Ann Taylor brand name. Its product line includes career and casual separates, dresses, tops, weekend wear, shoes and accessories. The Company's Ann Taylor stores, which sell better-quality women's fashions, are primarily located in malls and upscale specialty retail centers. ANN also operates Ann Taylor Loft stores, which sell moderately-priced merchandise under the Ann Taylor Loft label. In addition, the Company operates Ann Taylor Factory stores in factory outlet centers. These stores serve primarily as a clearance vehicle for merchandise from Ann Taylor stores. As of 3/11/03, ANN operated 588 stores in 42 states, the District of Columbia and Puerto Rico.

RECENT DEVELOPMENTS:

For the year ended 2/1/03, net income totaled $80.2 million compared with $29.1 million the previous year. Results for fiscal 2001 included amortization of goodwill of $11.0 million. Net sales climbed 6.3% to $1.38 billion from $1.30 billion a year earlier. Comparable-store sales slid 3.9% year over year, reflecting a 5.3% decline at Ann Taylor stores and a 1.0% decline at Ann Taylor Loft stores. Gross profit was $747.5 million, or 54.1% of net sales, versus $647.8 million, or 49.8% of net sales, the prior year. Operating income more than doubled to $135.0 million compared with $60.1 million the year before.

PROSPECTS:

Earnings growth is being fueled by fewer markdowns and increased margins on both full-priced and marked-down merchandise. However, near-term results will likely be hurt by lower levels of customer traffic and reduced sales stemming from unusually harsh winter weather conditions in the eastern U.S. during February and uncertain economic conditions. The Company is targeting earnings per share of between $0.39 and $0.41 for the first quarter of the current fiscal year. Separately, ANN plans to open 75 to 80 new stores in fiscal 2003, including as many as 65 Ann Taylor Loft stores.

ANNUAL FINANCIAL DATA:

FISCAL YEAR	TOT. REVS. ($mill.)	NET INC. ($mill.)	TOT. ASSETS ($mill.)	OPER. PROFIT %	NET PROFIT %	RET. ON EQUITY %	RET. ON ASSETS %	CURR. RATIO	EARN. PER SH.$	CASH FL. PER SH.$	TANG. BK. VAL.$	PRICE RANGE	AVG. P/E RATIO
p2/01/03	1,381.0	80.2							1.72			33.19 - 17.84	14.8
2/02/02	1,299.6	②29.1	883.0	4.6	2.2	4.8	3.3	2.4	②0.67	1.96	7.39	26.19 - 14.07	30.2
2/03/01	1,232.8	②52.4	848.1	8.0	4.2	9.1	6.2	2.2	②1.17	2.13	6.39	29.92 - 10.00	17.0
1/29/00	1,084.5	①65.5	765.1	11.5	6.0	12.7	8.6	2.3	1.39	2.28	4.83	35.38 - 20.79	20.2
1/30/99	911.9	39.3	775.4	10.0	4.3	9.1	5.1	2.3	0.96	1.71	2.90	26.83 - 7.50	17.9
1/31/98	781.0	①12.0	683.7	6.4	1.5	3.1	1.8	2.4	①0.31	1.35	1.39	16.83 - 8.67	40.7
2/01/97	798.1	②8.7	688.1	5.8	1.1	2.3	1.3	2.5	②0.24	1.25	0.75	16.17 - 6.17	46.5
2/03/96	731.1	d0.9	678.7	3.5	...	...	...	1.8	d0.03	0.79	0.35	25.33 - 6.58	...
1/28/95	658.8	①32.6	598.3	11.7	5.0	10.0	5.5	2.6	①0.93	1.55	0.09	29.92 - 13.67	23.4
1/29/94	501.6	①14.3	513.4	9.8	2.9	5.5	2.8	1.8	①0.44	0.99	...	20.00 - 11.67	36.0

Statistics are as originally reported. Adj. for stk. split: 3-for-2, 5/02. ① Bef. $962,000 ($0.02/sh) extraord. loss, 1/00; $173,000 ($0.01/sh), 1/98; $868,000 ($0.03/sh), 1/95; $11.1 mil ($0.34/sh), 1/94. ② Incl. $10.3 mil after-tax chg., 2/02; $10.7 mil one-time pre-tax chg., 2/01; & $4.0 mil ($0.11/sh) after-tax chg. for store closings & employee contract obligs., 2/97.

OFFICERS:
J. P. Spainhour, Chmn., C.E.O.
B. Erdos, Sr. Exec. V.P., C.O.O.
J. M. Smith, Sr. V.P., C.F.O., Treas.

INVESTOR CONTACT: Doreen D. Riely, Dir., Inv. Rel., (212) 541-3484

PRINCIPAL OFFICE: 142 West 57th Street, New York, NY 10019

TELEPHONE NUMBER: (212) 541-3300
FAX: (212) 541-3379
WEB: www.anntaylor.com
NO. OF EMPLOYEES: 4,500 full-time (approx.); 5,000 part-time (approx.)
SHAREHOLDERS: 564
ANNUAL MEETING: In May
INCORPORATED: DE, 1988

INSTITUTIONAL HOLDINGS:
No. of Institutions: 198
Shares Held: 42,729,692
% Held: 95.3

INDUSTRY: Women's clothing stores (SIC: 5621)

TRANSFER AGENT(S): Continental Stock Transfer & Trust Company, New York, NY

ANTHEM, INC.

EXCH.	SYM.	REC. PRICE	P/E RATIO	YLD.	MKT. CAP.	RANGE (52-WK.)	'02 Y/E PR.
NYSE	ATH	59.61 (2/28/03)	13.4	...	$6.16 bill.	75.50 - 53.00	62.90

MEDIUM GRADE. THE COMPANY EXPECTS FULL-YEAR 2003 OPERATING REVENUES OF APPROXIMATELY $17.00 BILLION.

INTERIM EARNINGS (Per Share):

Qtr.	Mar.	June	Sept.	Dec.
2001	---------------- 3.30 ----------------			
2002	0.95	1.01	1.29	1.19

INTERIM DIVIDENDS (Per Share):

Amt.	Decl.	Ex.	Rec.	Pay.
	No dividends paid.			

TRADING VOLUME
Thousand Shares

*7 YEAR PRICE SCORE N/A   *12 MONTH PRICE SCORE 103.0
*NYSE COMPOSITE INDEX=100

CAPITALIZATION (12/31/01):

	($000)	(%)
Long-Term Debt	818,000	28.4
Common & Surplus	2,060,000	71.6
Total	2,878,000	100.0

BUSINESS:

Anthem, Inc. was formed through the conversion of Anthem Insurance from a mutual insurance company, effective 11/2/01. As of 12/31/02, ATH provided health care benefits to almost 11.1 million members, and is the Blue Cross® Blue Shield® licensee for Indiana, Kentucky, Ohio, Connecticut, New Hampshire, Colorado, Nevada, Maine and Virginia, excluding the Northern Virginia suburbs of Washington, D.C. ATH provides a variety of man-

aged care products, including health maintenance organizations, preferred provider organizations, and point of service plans, as well as traditional indemnity products. ATH also offers administrative and managed care services and partially-insured products for employer self-funded plans. Revenues for 2002 were derived 91.9% from fully-insured products, and 8.1% from administrative services and other. On 7/31/02, ATH acquired Trigon Healthcare, Inc.

RECENT DEVELOPMENTS:

For the year ended 12/31/02, net income advanced 60.5% to $549.1 million compared with $342.2 million in the previous year. Results for 2002 and 2001 included after-tax net realized gains on investments of $19.8 million and $39.4 million, and gains on the sale of subsidiary operations of $400,000 and $16.3 million, respectively. Results for 2001 also included demutualization expense of $27.6

million and goodwill amortization of $15.1 million. Total operating revenue increased 28.4% to $12.99 billion from $10.12 billion a year earlier, primarily due to the acquisition of Trigon Healthcare and strong customer growth and retention. Premiums grew 29.2% to $11.94 billion, while administrative fee income rose 17.7% to $962.0 million. Other revenue climbed 50.0% to $87.3 million.

PROSPECTS:

For 2003, ATH expects operating revenues of approximately $17.00 billion. The increase is expected due to a full year of results from Trigon Healthcare as well as continued membership growth and higher premiums. ATH expects enrollment to improve between 4.0% and 6.0% in 2003.

Meanwhile, ATH is continuing with the integration of Trigon as scheduled and expects cost savings of $75.0 million by 2004. ATH expects earnings for 2003 in the range of $4.75 to $4.85 per share. ATH's earnings in the first quarter are expected in the range of $1.00 to $1.05 per share.

ANNUAL FINANCIAL DATA:

FISCAL YEAR	TOT. REVS. ($mill.)	NET INC. ($mill.)	TOT. ASSETS ($mill.)	OPER. PROFIT %	NET PROFIT %	RET. ON EQUITY %	RET. ON ASSETS %	CURR. RATIO	EARN. PER SH. $	CASH FL. PER SH. $	TANG. BK. VAL. $	PRICE RANGE	AVG. P/E RATIO
p12/31/02	12,990.5	③ 549.1		5.0	3.3	16.6	5.5	1.8	③ 4.51			75.50 - 46.40	13.5
12/31/01	10,444.7	② 342.2	6,276.6	5.0	3.3	16.6	5.5	1.8	② 3.30	4.46	15.42	51.90 - 40.35	14.0
12/31/00	8,771.0	226.0	5,708.5	3.8	2.6	11.8	4.0	1.6	...	...	...	...	...
12/31/99	6,270.1	① 50.9	4,816.2	1.0	0.8	3.1	1.1	1.7	...	...	...	...	...
12/31/98	5,682.4	178.4	...	5.1	3.1	...	...	...	...	...	...	...	...

Statistics are as originally reported. Earnings per share amounts for 12/31/01 and prior-year periods are pro forma before the demutualization of the Company on 11/2/01. ① Incls. chrg. of $114.1 mill. fr. endowment of non-profit foundations; bef. loss of $6.0 mill. fr. disc. ops. ② Incls. gain of $25.0 mill. on sale of subsid. ops. & demutualization exp. of $22.6 mill. ③ Incl. aft.-tax net gain on invest. of $19.8 mill. and aft.-tax gain on subsid. sale of $400,000.

OFFICERS:
L. B. Lytle, Chmn.
L. C. Glasscock, Pres., C.E.O.
M. L. Smith, Exec. V.P., C.F.O.
INVESTOR CONTACT: Tami Durle, V.P., Investor Relations, (317) 488-6390
PRINCIPAL OFFICE: 120 Monument Circle, Indianapolis, IN 46204-4903

TELEPHONE NUMBER: (317) 488-6000
FAX: (317) 488-6460
WEB: www.anthem-inc.com
NO. OF EMPLOYEES: 14,800 (approx.)
SHAREHOLDERS: 199,949
ANNUAL MEETING: In May
INCORPORATED: IN, 1944

INSTITUTIONAL HOLDINGS:
No. of Institutions: 374
Shares Held: 103,493,655
% Held: 73.2
INDUSTRY: Hospital and medical service plans (SIC: 6324)
TRANSFER AGENT(S): EquiServe Trust Company, N.A., Providence, RI

AOL TIME WARNER INC.

EXCH.	SYM.	REC. PRICE	P/E RATIO	YLD.	MKT. CAP.	RANGE (52-WK.)	'02 Y/E PR.
NYSE	AOL	11.32 (2/28/03)	...	...	$50.14 bill.	27.95 - 8.70	13.10

LOWER MEDIUM GRADE. REVENUE GROWTH RATE FOR THE FIRST QUARTER OF 2003 IS EXPECTED IN THE LOW-TO-MID-SINGLE DIGIT RANGE.

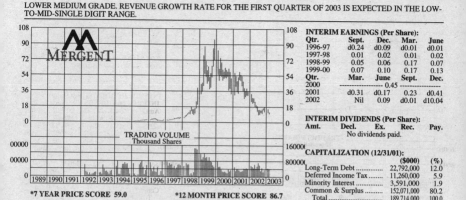

*7 YEAR PRICE SCORE 59.0   ***12 MONTH PRICE SCORE 86.7**

*NYSE COMPOSITE INDEX=100

INTERIM EARNINGS (Per Share):

Qtr.	Sept.	Dec.	Mar.	June
1996-97	d0.24	d0.09	d0.01	d0.01
1997-98	0.01	0.02	0.01	0.02
1998-99	0.05	0.06	0.17	0.07
1999-00	0.07	0.10	0.17	0.13

Qtr.	Mar.	June	Sept.	Dec.
2000			0.45	
2001	d0.31	d0.17	0.23	d0.41
2002	Nil	0.09	d0.01	d10.04

INTERIM DIVIDENDS (Per Share):

Amt.	Decl.	Ex.	Rec.	Pay.
	No dividends paid.			

CAPITALIZATION (12/31/01):

	($000)	(%)
Long-Term Debt	22,792,000	12.0
Deferred Income Tax	11,260,000	5.9
Minority Interest	3,591,000	1.9
Common & Surplus	152,071,000	80.2
Total	189,714,000	100.0

BUSINESS:

AOL Time Warner Inc. (formerly America Online, Inc.) was formed from the acquisition by America Online, Inc. of Time Warner, Inc. in January 2001. AOL classifies its business interests in the following categories: America Online, which consists primarily of interactive services, Web properties, Internet technologies, and electronic commerce services; cable, which consists of interests in cable television systems; filmed entertainment, which consists of interest in filmed entertainment and television production; networks, which consists of interests in cable television and broadcast network programming; music, which consists of interests in recorded music publishing; and publishing, which consists of interests in magazine publishing, book publishing and direct marketing.

RECENT DEVELOPMENTS:

For the year ended 12/31/02, loss was $44.57 billion, before an accounting change charge of $54.24 billion, compared with a loss from continuing operations of $4.90 billion in 2001. Results for 2002 and 2001 included amortization of goodwill and other intangible assets of $732.0 million and $7.19 billion, and merger and restructuring costs of $335.0 million and $250.0 million, respectively.

Results for 2002 also included impairment of goodwill and other intangible assets of $45.54 billion. Results for 2002 and 2001 excluded a net gain of $113.0 million and a net loss of $39.0 million, respectively, from discontinued operations. Revenues rose 10.3% to $41.07 billion from $37.22 billion the year before. Operating loss amounted to $39.88 billion versus operating income of $118.0 million.

PROSPECTS:

The Company expects revenue growth for 2003 in the mid-single digits and earnings before interest, taxes, depreciation and amortization (EBITDA) to be essentially flat year over year. Also, the Company plans to convert 30.0% to 40.0% of EBITDA into free cash flow. Meanwhile, the Company expects revenue growth for the first quarter of 2003 in the low-to-mid-single digit range and EBITDA to be flat to down in the low-single digit range year over year.

ANNUAL FINANCIAL DATA:

FISCAL YEAR	TOT. REVS. ($mill.)	NET INC. ($mill.)	TOT. ASSETS ($mill.)	OPER. PROFIT %	NET PROFIT %	RET. ON EQUITY %	RET. ON ASSETS %	CURR. RATIO	EARN. PER SH. $	CASH FL. PER SH. $	TANG. BK. VAL. $	PRICE RANGE	AVG. P/E RATIO
p12/31/02	41,065.0	⑧ d44,574.0							⑧ d10.01			32.92 — 8.70	...
⑦ 12/31/01	38,234.0	⑥ d4,921.0	208,559.0	1.2	...	...	...	0.8	⑥ d1.11	1.50	...	58.51 — 27.40	...
⑤ 12/31/00	7,703.0	1,152.0	10,827.0	23.6	15.0	17.0	10.6	2.0	0.45	0.59	2.51	83.38 — 32.75	129.0
6/30/00	6,886.0	④ 1,232.0	10,673.0	20.3	17.9	20.0	11.5	1.8	④ 0.48	0.59	2.44	83.38 — 32.75	120.9
6/30/99	4,777.0	③ 762.0	5,348.0	9.6	16.0	25.1	14.2	1.1	③ 0.35	0.39	1.17	95.81 — 32.50	213.8
6/30/98	2,600.0	①② 92.0	2,214.0	3.0	3.5	15.4	4.2	1.0	①② 0.04	0.11	0.12	40.00 — 5.16	512.9
6/30/97	1,685.2	① d499.3	846.7	...	...	...	...	0.6	① d0.33	d0.25	0.04	5.71 — 1.98	...
6/30/96	1,093.9	29.8	958.8	6.0	2.7	5.8	3.1	0.9	0.02	0.11	0.31	4.44 — 1.40	166.6
6/30/95	394.3	d33.6	405.6	...	...	...	...	1.0	d0.06	0.04	0.13	2.89 — 0.77	...
6/30/94	115.7	6.2	155.2	16.7	5.3	17.7	11.3	2.6	0.04	0.03	0.11	0.91 — 0.37	32.0

Statistics are as originally reported. Adj. for 2-for-1 split, 11/94, 4/95, 11/95, 3/98, 11/98, 2/99 & 11/99. ① Incl. $1.0 mill. non-recur. chg., 1998; $482.6 mill., 1997. ② Incl. $132.0 mill. restr., acq. R&D, & settlement chgs. ③ Incl. $567.0 mill. net gain & $120.0 mill. net chgs. ④ Incl. $15.0 mill. merger & restr. chgs. ⑤ Year-end changed from 6/30 to 12/31. ⑥ Incl. $7.23 bill. amort. of goodwill & $250.0 mill. merg. costs. ⑦ Refl. the acq. of Time Warner in Jan. 2001. ⑧ Incl. $335.0 mill. merg. & restr. costs and excl. $54.24 bill. acctg. change chg. & $113.0 mill. gain fr. disc. ops.

OFFICERS:
S. M. Case, Chmn.
R. D. Parsons, C.E.O.
W. H. Pace, Exec. V.P., C.F.O.

INVESTOR CONTACT: John Martin, Inv. Rel., (212) 484-6579

PRINCIPAL OFFICE: 75 Rockefeller Plaza, New York, NY 10019

TELEPHONE NUMBER: (212) 484-8000
FAX: (212) 489-6183
WEB: www.aoltimewarner.com

NO. OF EMPLOYEES: 89,300 (approx.)

SHAREHOLDERS: 66,500 (approx. record); 9 (series LMCN-V com. record)

ANNUAL MEETING: In May

INCORPORATED: DE, May, 1985

INSTITUTIONAL HOLDINGS:
No. of Institutions: 965
Shares Held: 1,630,511,819
% Held: 59.6

INDUSTRY: Information retrieval services (SIC: 7375)

TRANSFER AGENT(S): EquiServe Trust Company, N.A., Boston, MA

AON CORPORATION

EXCH.	SYM.	REC. PRICE	P/E RATIO	YLD.	MKT. CAP.	RANGE (52-WK.)	'02 Y/E PR.
NYSE	AOC	19.45 (2/28/03)	11.9	3.1%	$4.82 bill.	39.63 - 13.30	18.89

UPPER MEDIUM GRADE. THE COMPANY WAS AWARDED AN INSURANCE BROKERAGE LICENSE IN CHINA.

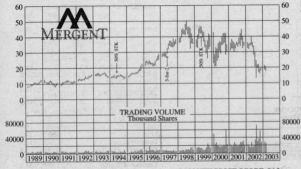

7 YEAR PRICE SCORE 79.9   **12 MONTH PRICE SCORE 86.3**
*NYSE COMPOSITE INDEX=100

INTERIM EARNINGS (Per Share):

Qtr.	Mar.	June	Sept.	Dec.
1997	d0.01	0.32	0.38	0.43
1998	0.53	0.54	0.47	0.53
1999	0.13	0.57	0.52	0.05
2000	0.47	0.49	0.53	0.33
2001	0.07	0.11	0.26	0.30
2002	---------------- 1.64 ----------------			

INTERIM DIVIDENDS (Per Share):

Amt.	Decl.	Ex.	Rec.	Pay.
0.225Q	1/18/02	2/08/02	2/12/02	2/25/02
0.225Q	4/19/02	4/30/02	5/02/02	5/15/02
0.225Q	7/19/02	7/30/02	8/01/02	8/14/02
0.15Q	10/31/02	11/06/02	11/08/02	11/20/02
0.15Q	1/17/03	2/10/03	2/12/03	2/25/03

Indicated div.: $0.60 (Div. Reinv. Plan)

CAPITALIZATION (12/31/01):

	($000)	(%)
Long-Term Debt	1,694,000	32.5
Common & Surplus	3,521,000	67.5
Total	5,215,000	100.0

BUSINESS:

Aon Corporation is a holding company whose subsidiaries operate in three distinct segments: Insurance Brokerage and Other Services, Consulting, and Insurance Underwriting. The Insurance Brokerage and Other Services segment (59.5% of 2002 operating revenues) consists principally of AOC's retail, reinsurance, specialty and wholesale broker-

age operations. The Consulting segment (11.9%) provides a full range of employee benefits, human resources, compensation, and change management services. The Insurance Underwriting segment (28.6%) is comprised of direct sales of life and accident and health, warranty, specialty and other insurance products.

RECENT DEVELOPMENTS:

For the year ended 12/31/02, net income more than tripled to $466.0 million from $147.0 million the year before. Results for 2002 included a charge of $8.0 million for advisory fees related to the previously planned divestiture of the underwriting business. Results for 2002 and 2001 included a gain of $6.0 million and a charge of $218.0 million, respectively, for business transformation initia-

tives. Also, results included an unusual credit of $29.0 million in 2002 and an unusual charge of $158.0 million in 2001 related to the World Trade Center. Total revenue advanced 14.9% to $8.82 billion from $7.68 billion the previous year. Comparisons were made with restated prior-year figures.

PROSPECTS:

On 1/15/03, the Company announced that it was awarded an insurance brokerage license in China. The license will allow AOC to broker insurance through a joint venture with State-owned China National Cereals, Oils & Foodstuffs Import & Export Corp. The joint venture, called Aon-COFCO, will be based in Shanghai and will commence operations by mid-2003. Going forward, U.S. retail and

managing underwriting within the brokerage segment are expected to have significantly better performance in 2003. Meanwhile, consulting revenues are expected to benefit from the large multi-year outsourcing contracts signed in mid-2002. AOC is targeting earnings per share for 2003 in the range of $1.90 to $2.00 per share.

ANNUAL FINANCIAL DATA:

FISCAL YEAR	PREM. INC. ($mill.)	TOT. REVS. ($mill.)	NET INC. ($mill.)	TOT. ASSETS ($mill.)	TOT. INVST. ($mill.)	RET. ON REVS. %	RET. ON EQUITY %	RET. ON ASSETS %	EARN. PER SH. $	TANG. BK. VAL. $	AVG. YIELD %	DIV. PER SH. $	PRICE RANGE	AVG. P/E RATIO
p12/31/02		8,822.0	⑤ 466.0						⑤ 1.64		3.1	0.83	39.63 - 13.30	16.1
12/31/01	2,027.0	7,676.0	④ 203.0	22,386.0	6,146.0	2.6	5.8	0.9	④ 0.73	...	2.4	0.90	44.80 - 29.75	51.1
12/31/00	1,921.0	7,375.0	③ 481.0	22,251.0	6,019.0	6.5	14.2	2.2	③ 1.82	...	2.7	0.87	42.75 - 20.69	17.4
12/31/99	1,854.0	7,070.0	② 352.0	21,132.0	6,184.0	5.0	11.5	1.7	② 1.33	...	2.2	0.81	46.67 - 26.06	27.3
12/31/98	1,706.0	6,493.0	541.0	19,688.0	6,452.0	8.3	17.9	2.7	2.07	...	1.8	0.73	50.38 - 32.17	19.9
12/31/97	1,608.9	5,750.6	298.8	18,691.2	5,922.1	5.2	10.6	1.6	1.12	...	2.1	0.68	38.96 - 26.78	29.3
12/31/96	1,526.7	3,888.2	① 291.8	13,722.7	5,212.8	7.5	10.3	2.1	① 1.10	4.93	2.5	0.63	28.78 - 21.11	22.6
12/31/95	1,426.5	3,465.7	① 304.0	19,735.8	10,639.1	8.8	11.4	1.5	① 1.14	4.38	3.3	0.60	22.61 - 13.95	16.0
12/31/94	1,933.7	4,156.9	360.0	17,921.9	9,782.5	8.7	15.9	2.0	1.40	2.88	3.9	0.56	15.89 - 13.00	10.3
12/31/93	1,823.0	3,844.8	323.8	16,279.1	9,651.7	8.4	14.2	2.0	1.25	3.26	3.4	0.52	17.33 - 13.70	12.4

Statistics are as originally reported. Adj. for stk. splits: 3-for-2, 5/99; 5/97; 5/94 ① Bef. disc. oper. gain 1996, $43.4 mill.; 1995, $99.1 mill. ② Incl. non-recurr. chrg. $313.0 mill. ③ Bef. acctg. change chrg. of $7.0 mill., but incl. special chrgs. of $82.0 mill. ④ Incl. unusual chrgs. $68.0 mill. & special chrgs. of $218.0 mill. ⑤ Incl. unusual gain of $27.0 mill.

OFFICERS:
P. G. Ryan, Chmn., C.E.O.
M. D. O'Halleran, Pres., C.O.O.
H. N. Medvin, Exec. V.P., C.F.O.
INVESTOR CONTACT: Sean P. O'Neill, V.P., Fin. Rel., (312) 381-3983
PRINCIPAL OFFICE: 123 North Wacker Drive, Chicago, IL 60606

TELEPHONE NUMBER: (312) 381-3000
FAX: (312) 381-3080
WEB: www.aon.com
NO. OF EMPLOYEES: 53,000 (approx.)
SHAREHOLDERS: 11,912 (approx.)
ANNUAL MEETING: In April
INCORPORATED: DE, 1979

INSTITUTIONAL HOLDINGS:
No. of Institutions: 299
Shares Held: 236,200,979
% Held: 77.5
INDUSTRY: Accident and health insurance (SIC: 6321)
TRANSFER AGENT(S): EquiServe Trust Company, N.A., Jersey City, NJ

APACHE CORPORATION

EXCH.	SYM.	REC. PRICE	P/E RATIO	YLD.	MKT. CAP.	RANGE (52-WK.)	'02 Y/E PR.
NYSE	APA	62.17 (2/28/03)	17.3	0.6%	$8.95 bill.	64.31 - 42.92	54.28

UPPER MEDIUM GRADE. THE COMPANY ANNOUNCED AGREEMENTS TO ACQUIRE PRODUCING PROPERTIES IN THE NORTH SEA AND THE GULF OF MEXICO FROM BP P.L.C. FOR $1.30 BILLION.

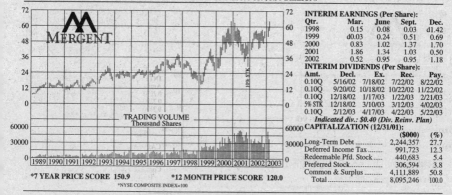

*7 YEAR PRICE SCORE 150.9 ***12 MONTH PRICE SCORE 120.0**

*NYSE COMPOSITE INDEX=100

INTERIM EARNINGS (Per Share):

Qtr.	Mar.	June	Sept.	Dec.
1998	0.15	0.08	0.03	d1.42
1999	d0.03	0.24	0.51	0.69
2000	0.83	1.02	1.37	1.70
2001	1.86	1.34	1.03	0.50
2002	0.52	0.95	0.95	1.18

INTERIM DIVIDENDS (Per Share):

Amt.	Decl.	Ex.	Rec.	Pay.
0.10Q	5/16/02	7/18/02	7/22/02	8/22/02
0.10Q	9/20/02	10/18/02	10/22/02	11/22/02
0.10Q	12/18/02	1/17/03	1/22/03	2/21/03
5% STK	12/18/02	3/10/03	3/12/03	4/02/03
0.10Q	2/12/03	4/17/03	4/22/03	5/22/03

Indicated div.: $0.40 (Div. Reinv. Plan)

CAPITALIZATION (12/31/01):

	($000)	(%)
Long-Term Debt	2,244,357	27.7
Deferred Income Tax	991,723	12.3
Redeemable Pfd. Stock	440,683	5.4
Preferred Stock	306,594	3.8
Common & Surplus	4,111,889	50.8
Total	8,095,246	100.0

BUSINESS:

Apache Corporation is an independent energy company that explores for, develops and produces natural gas, crude oil and natural gas liquids. In North America, APA's exploration and production interests are focused in the Gulf of Mexico, the Gulf Coast, the Permian Basin, the Anadarko Basin and the Western Sedimentary Basin of Canada. APA also has exploration and production interests offshore Western Australia, Egypt and Argentina, and exploration interests in Poland and offshore The People's Republic of China. As of 12/31/02, total proved reserves were: oil, natural gas liquids and condensate 636.8 million barrels; and natural gas 4.05 trillion cubic feet.

RECENT DEVELOPMENTS:

For the year ended 12/31/02, net income was $554.3 million compared with $723.4 million a year earlier. Results for 2002 and 2001 included international impairment charges of $19.6 million and $65.0 million, respectively. Total revenues declined 8.9% to $2.56 billion. Operating income fell 22.4% to $1.03 billion versus $1.33 billion the year before. APA's average natural gas price dropped 22.4% to $2.87 per thousand cubic feet. For full-year 2002, APA produced 341,491 barrels of oil equivalent (boe) per day compared with 344,129 boe per day in 2001.

PROSPECTS:

On 1/13/03, the Company announced agreements to acquire producing properties in the North Sea and the Gulf of Mexico from BP P.L.C. for $1.30 billion. According to APA, the acquisition should add an estimated 29.0% to its 2002 production. The Company also noted that it has a physical sale agreement with BP to take all of APA's North Sea production for two years at a combination of fixed and floating prices. A large portion of the oil and gas production, both in the North Sea and the Gulf of Mexico, has been hedged through 2004. About two-thirds of the reserves and daily oil production APA is acquiring from BP are in the North Sea's Forties oil field. The Gulf of Mexico properties are located offshore Texas and Louisiana. The effective date of the transaction is 1/1/03, with closing on the Gulf portion anticipated on or about 3/31/03 and the North Sea portion projected by 5/31/03. APA intends to finance the acquisition with a combination of internally generated funds, equity and debt.

ANNUAL FINANCIAL DATA:

FISCAL YEAR	TOT. REVS. ($mill.)	NET INC. ($mill.)	TOT. ASSETS ($mill.)	OPER. PROFIT %	NET PROFIT %	RET. ON EQUITY %	RET. ON ASSETS %	CURR. RATIO	EARN. PER SH.$	CASH FL. PER SH.$	TANG. BK. VAL.$	DIV. PER SH.$	PRICE RANGE	AVG. P/E RATIO	AVG. YIELD %
p12/31/02	2,559.9	③ 554.3							③ 3.60			0.38	57.75 - 42.25	13.9	0.7
12/31/01	2,777.1	③ 723.4	8,933.7	47.7	26.0	16.4	8.1	1.3	③ 4.73	9.61	27.25	0.24	63.10 - 33.12	10.2	0.5
12/31/00	2,283.9	② 720.6	7,482.0	57.4	31.6	19.2	9.6	1.1	② 4.96	8.93	24.15	0.24	64.23 - 27.81	9.3	0.5
12/31/99	1,300.5	200.9	5,502.5	22.6	15.4	7.5	3.7	1.0	1.49	4.89	20.27	0.24	43.13 - 15.26	19.6	0.8
12/31/98	875.7	d129.4	3,996.1	...	...	...	...	0.7	d1.16	4.41	15.08	0.24	33.55 - 18.24	...	0.9
12/31/97	1,176.3	154.9	4,138.6	28.1	13.2	9.0	3.7	1.0	1.43	4.73	16.05	0.24	39.02 - 26.08	22.8	0.7
12/31/96	977.2	121.4	3,432.4	26.8	12.4	8.0	3.5	0.9	1.23	4.46	14.60	0.24	32.79 - 21.10	21.9	0.9
12/31/95	750.7	① 20.2	2,681.5	13.8	2.7	1.9	0.8	0.9	① 0.24	3.89	12.22	0.24	26.84 - 19.26	94.9	1.1
12/31/94	545.6	42.8	1,879.0	17.4	7.9	5.2	2.3	0.9	0.61	3.94	11.50	0.24	25.32 - 19.26	36.8	1.1
12/31/93	466.6	37.3	1,592.4	18.2	8.0	4.8	2.3	0.7	0.61	3.52	11.14	0.24	29.00 - 15.26	36.5	1.1

Statistics are as originally reported. Adjusted for 5% stk. div., 4/03; 10% stk. div., 1/02. ① Incl. non-recurr. pre-tax chrg. of $10.0 mill. ② Bef. after-tax acctg. chge. chrg. of $7.5 mill. ($0.06/sh.). ③ Incl. international impairments chrg. of $19.6 mill., 12/31/02; $65.0 mill., 12/31/00.

OFFICERS:
R. Plank, Chmn.
G. S. Farris, Pres., C.E.O., C.O.O.
R. B. Plank, Exec. V.P., C.F.O.
INVESTOR CONTACT: Robert J. Dye, V.P.,
Investor Relations, (713) 296-6662
PRINCIPAL OFFICE: One Post Oak Central,
2000 Post Oak Blvd., Houston, TX 77056

TELEPHONE NUMBER: (713) 296-6000
FAX: (713) 296-6480
WEB: www.apachecorp.com
NO. OF EMPLOYEES: 1,915 (avg.)
SHAREHOLDERS: 9,000 (approx. common);
110,000 (approx. beneficial)
ANNUAL MEETING: In May
INCORPORATED: DE, Dec., 1954

INSTITUTIONAL HOLDINGS:
No. of Institutions: 532
Shares Held: 133,153,530 (Adj.)
% Held: 88.1
INDUSTRY: Crude petroleum and natural gas
(SIC: 1311)
TRANSFER AGENT(S): Wells Fargo Bank
Shareowner Services, South St. Paul, MN

APARTMENT INVESTMENT & MANAGEMENT COMPANY

EXCH.	SYM.	REC. PRICE	P/E RATIO	YLD.	MKT. CAP.	RANGE (52-WK.)	'02 Y/E PR.
NYSE	AIV	36.77 (2/28/03)	39.5	8.9%	$3.45 bill.	51.46 - 33.90	37.48

MEDIUM GRADE. THE COMPANY ESTIMATES FUNDS FROM OPERATIONS TO BE IN THE RANGE OF $4.20 TO $4.42 PER SHARE FOR FISCAL 2003.

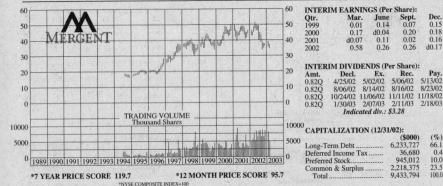

*7 YEAR PRICE SCORE 119.7   ***12 MONTH PRICE SCORE 95.7**
*NYSE COMPOSITE INDEX=100

INTERIM EARNINGS (Per Share):

Qtr.	Mar.	June	Sept.	Dec.
1999	0.01	0.14	0.07	0.15
2000	0.17	d0.04	0.20	0.18
2001	d0.07	0.11	0.02	0.16
2002	0.58	0.26	0.26	d0.17

INTERIM DIVIDENDS (Per Share):

Amt.	Decl.	Ex.	Rec.	Pay.
0.82Q	4/25/02	5/02/02	5/06/02	5/13/02
0.82Q	8/06/02	8/14/02	8/16/02	8/23/02
0.82Q	10/24/02	11/06/02	11/11/02	11/18/02
0.82Q	1/30/03	2/07/03	2/11/03	2/18/03

Indicated div.: $3.28

CAPITALIZATION (12/31/02):

	($000)	(%)
Long-Term Debt	6,233,727	66.1
Deferred Income Tax	36,680	0.4
Preferred Stock	945,012	10.0
Common & Surplus	2,218,375	23.5
Total	9,433,794	100.0

BUSINESS:

Apartment Investment & Management Company is a self-administered and self-managed real estate investment trust engaged in the ownership, acquisition, development, expansion and management of multi-family apartment properties. As of 2/26/03, AIV had 19 regional operating centers, which hold a geographically diversified portfolio of apartment communities. AIV, through its subsidiaries, operates about 1,790 properties, including about 318,000 apartment units, and serves about one million residents each year. AIV's properties are located in 47 states, the District of Columbia and Puerto Rico. On 3/11/02, AIV acquired 17,383 apartment units from Casden Properties for about $1.50 billion. On 8/12/02, AIV acquired 4,323 apartments in the New England area for $500.0 million.

RECENT DEVELOPMENTS:

For the year ended 12/31/02, income was $175.2 million, before a loss of $6.1 million from discontinued operations, compared with income of $103.1 million, before a gain of $4.2 million from discontinued operations, the previous year. Results for 2002 and 2001 included provision for losses on receivables of $9.0 million and $6.6 million, respectively. The 2002 and 2001 results also included a loss of $27.9 million and a gain of $17.4 million, respectively, on the disposition of real estate. Rental and other property revenues advanced 14.8% to $1.41 billion from $1.22 billion, while management fees and other income from affiliates decreased 36.5% to $100.6 million from $158.4 million the year before. Income from investment management business dropped 33.8% to $18.3 million.

PROSPECTS:

The Company continues to be hampered by weakness in the multi-family sector, largely due to the effects of the difficult economic climate. Consequently, the Company is experiencing further declines in occupancy and downward pressure on rent levels in certain markets, particularly in Atlanta, Denver, Charlotte and Phoenix. Meanwhile, the Company will continue to upgrade its portfolio by the sale of lower-rated assets. AIV estimates funds from operations in the range of $4.20 to $4.42 per share for fiscal 2003.

ANNUAL FINANCIAL DATA:

FISCAL YEAR	TOT. INC. ($mill.)	NET INC. ($mill.)	TOT. ASSETS ($mill.)	NET INC. +DEPR./ ASSETS %	RET. ON EQUITY %	RET. ON ASSETS %	EARN. PER SH.$	TANG. BK. VAL.$	DIV. PER SH.$	DIV. PAYOUT %	PRICE RANGE	AVG. P/E RATIO	AVG. YIELD %
12/31/02	1,506.2	④ 175.2	10,316.6	4.5	5.5	1.7	④ 0.94	23.66	3.28	348.9	51.46 - 33.90	45.4	7.7
12/31/01	1,463.6	③ 107.4	8,322.5	5.7	4.0	1.3	③ 0.23	20.01	3.12	N.M.	50.13 - 39.25	194.2	7.0
12/31/00	1,100.7	① 99.2	7,699.9	5.6	4.0	1.3	① 0.52	23.32	2.80	538.4	50.06 - 36.31	83.0	6.5
12/31/99	577.4	① 81.0	5,685.0	3.8	3.6	1.4	① 0.38	24.27	2.50	657.7	44.13 - 34.06	102.9	6.4
12/31/98	401.2	① 64.5	4,268.3	3.7	3.4	1.5	① 0.80	20.26	2.25	281.2	41.00 - 30.00	44.4	6.3
12/31/97	206.9	①② 28.9	2,100.5	3.2	2.8	1.4	①② 1.08	19.34	1.85	171.3	38.00 - 25.50	29.4	5.8
12/31/96	108.9	① 13.0	827.7	4.0	6.0	1.6	① 1.04	14.10	1.70	163.4	28.38 - 18.38	22.5	7.3
12/31/95	83.1	13.4	478.7	6.1	7.9	2.8	0.86	13.59	1.66	193.0	21.25 - 17.13	22.3	8.7
12/31/94	28.1	7.1	416.7	2.9	5.1	1.7	0.42	14.63	0.29	69.0	18.63 - 16.25	41.5	1.7
11/30/93	7.5	0.7	...	3.2	29.1	23.2	...	...	...	...	... ...	...	...

Statistics are as originally reported. ① Incl. diposition of property gain, $17.4 mill., 2001; $26.3 mill., 12/00; loss, $1.8 mill., 12/99; gain, $4.7 mill., 12/98; $2.7 mill., 12/97; $44,000, 12/96 ② Bef. extraord. chrg. $269,000. ③ Incl. pre-tax earnings of $16.7 mill. of unconsolidated real estate partnerships. ④ Bef. disc. opers. loss of $6.1 mill.; incl. pre-tax prov. for losses on rec. of $9.0 mill. & loss of $27.9 mill. on disp. of real estate.

OFFICERS:
T. Considine, Chmn., C.E.O.
P. K. Kompaniez, Vice-Chmn., Pres.
P. J. McAuliffe, Exec. V.P., C.F.O.

INVESTOR CONTACT: Jennifer Martin, V.P., Investor Relations, (303) 691-4440

PRINCIPAL OFFICE: 4582 South Ulster Street Parkway, Suite 1100, Denver, CO 80237

TELEPHONE NUMBER: (303) 757-8101
FAX: (303) 759-3226
WEB: www.aimco.com

NO. OF EMPLOYEES: 7,500 (approx.)

SHAREHOLDERS: 4,451 (class A common)

ANNUAL MEETING: In Apr.

INCORPORATED: MD, Jan., 1994

INSTITUTIONAL HOLDINGS:
No. of Institutions: 195
Shares Held: 77,574,518
% Held: 82.8

INDUSTRY: Real estate investment trusts (SIC: 6798)

TRANSFER AGENT(S): EquiServe, Providence, RI

APOGENT TECHNOLOGIES, INC.

EXCH.	SYM.	REC. PRICE	P/E RATIO	YLD.	MKT. CAP.	RANGE (52-WK.)	'02 Y/E PR.
NYSE	AOT	15.60 (2/28/03)	12.6	...	$1.65 bill.	25.49 - 15.45	20.80

MEDIUM GRADE. THE COMPANY WILL FOCUS ITS EFFORTS ON INITIATED PROGRAMS TO CONSOLIDATE CERTAIN OPERATIONS AND STREAMLINE PRODUCTION AT OTHERS TO ENHANCE RESULTS.

TRADING VOLUME
Thousand Shares

*7 YEAR PRICE SCORE 99.9   *12 MONTH PRICE SCORE 94.4

*NYSE COMPOSITE INDEX=100

INTERIM EARNINGS (Per Share):

Qtr.	Dec.	Mar.	June	Sept.
1998-99	0.22	0.31	0.31	0.34
1999-00	0.20	0.24	0.22	0.16
2000-01	0.21	0.28	0.26	0.27
2001-02	0.28	0.30	0.33	0.34
2002-03	0.27	...	...	...

INTERIM DIVIDENDS (Per Share):

Amt.	Decl.	Ex.	Rec.	Pay.
		No dividends paid.		

CAPITALIZATION (9/30/02):

	($000)	(%)
Long-Term Debt	635,020	36.4
Deferred Income Tax	132,100	7.6
Common & Surplus	975,138	56.0
Total	1,742,258	100.0

BUSINESS:

Apogent Technologies, Inc. (formerly Sybron International Corp.) develops, manufactures value-added products for the labware and life sciences, clinical diagnostics, and laboratory equipment industries. AOT's products include: reusable and disposable plastic products; products for critical packaging applications; microscope slides, cover glass, glass tubes and vials; stains and reagents; diagnostic test kits, cultural media, diagnostic reagents, and other products used in detecting causes of various infections or diseases; heating, stirring and temperature control apparatus; systems for producing ultra pure water; constant temperature equipment; and furnaces, fluorometers, spectrophotometers and strip chart recorders. On 12/11/00, the Company spun off its dental business.

RECENT DEVELOPMENTS:

For the three months ended 12/31/02, income from continuing operations was $28.9 million compared with income of $30.1 million in the corresponding quarter of the previous year. Results for 2002 and 2001 excluded losses of $163,000 and $122,000, respectively, from discontinued operations. Net sales climbed 9.6% to $266.5 million from $243.2 million in the year-earlier period. Clinical diagnostics segment sales rose 7.8% to $126.7 million from $117.5 million, while labware and life sciences segment sales increased 15.8% to $111.3 million from $96.1 million in the prior-year quarter. Sales of the laboratory equipment segment slipped 3.3% to $28.6 million from $29.6 million in 2001. Operating income grew 1.3% to $56.3 million versus $57.1 million the year before.

PROSPECTS:

Due to expected continued softness in instrument sales and lower-than-expected growth in the Clinical Diagnostics area, AOT lowered its guidance for fiscal year 2003 from $1.33 to $1.39 per share excluding restructuring charges. Meanwhile, AOT will focus its efforts on initiated programs to consolidate certain operations and streamline production at others to help enhance operating returns. Separately, on 1/3/03, Barnstead International, a subsidiary of AOT, acquired Tempyros Company Inc., which designs, manufactures and sells high-temperature ovens.

ANNUAL FINANCIAL DATA:

FISCAL YEAR	TOT. REVS. ($mill.)	NET INC. ($mill.)	TOT. ASSETS ($mill.)	OPER. PROFIT %	NET PROFIT %	RET. ON EQUITY %	RET. ON ASSETS %	CURR. RATIO	EARN. PER SH. $	CASH FL. PER SH. $	PRICE RANGE	AVG. P/E RATIO
9/30/02	1,074.6	⑧ 135.2	2,036.1	23.8	12.6	13.9	6.6	2.1	1.24	1.80	26.50 - 16.70	17.4
9/30/01	984.5	④ 109.9	1,835.1	22.8	11.2	13.1	6.0	1.6	④ 1.02	1.74	26.52 - 17.88	21.8
9/30/00	863.6	①⑤ 86.7	1,792.4	22.3	10.0	11.6	4.8	2.1	①⑤ 0.81	1.44	33.06 - 16.38	30.5
9/30/99	1,103.2	③ 125.3	1,842.9	24.0	11.4	20.0	6.8	2.6	③ 1.18	1.80	30.81 - 20.69	21.8
9/30/98	960.7	①②78.0	1,545.1	19.9	8.1	16.6	5.1	2.0	①②0.75	1.30	29.13 - 16.38	30.3
9/30/96	795.1	①57.6	1,221.5	22.6	10.3	22.3	6.7	2.5	0.83	1.32	24.25 - 13.38	22.8
9/30/96	674.5	①57.6	974.6	20.3	8.5	20.3	5.9	2.0	0.60	1.06	16.88 - 10.81	23.1
9/30/95	519.2	51.8	852.1	21.0	10.0	22.8	6.1	1.8	0.55	0.91	12.06 - 8.06	18.3
9/30/94	439.7	43.0	557.7	20.9	9.8	24.3	7.7	1.9	0.46	0.79	9.06 - 6.88	17.2
9/30/93	395.4	①25.8	480.0	20.1	6.5	20.4	5.4	1.8	①0.28	0.59	8.00 - 5.00	23.0

Statistics are as originally reported. Adj. for stk. split: 2-for-1, 12/95; 100%, 2/98. ① Incl. pre-tax restruct. chrg. of $4.0 mill., 1993; $7.5 mill., 1996; $23.3 mill., 1998; $10.3 mill., 2000. ② Incl. pre-tax mgr., transaction & integration exp. of $10.5 mill. ③ Incls. restr. chrg. of $932,000 & mgr., trans. & integrat. chrg. of $2.6 mill.; excl. after-tax chrg. of $17.3 mill. from disc. opers. ④ Excl. income of $11.0 mill. from disc. opers. ⑤ Excl. net loss of $30.6 mill. from disc. oper. and extraord. loss of $700,000. ⑥ Bef. disc. oper. of $14.1 mill. & incl. restr. chrg. of $1.3 mill.

OFFICERS:
K. F. Yontz, Chmn.
F. H. Jellinek Jr., Pres., C.E.O.

INVESTOR CONTACT: Dennis Brown, Investor Relations, (603) 433-6131

PRINCIPAL OFFICE: 30 Penhallow Street, Portsmouth, NH 03801

TELEPHONE NUMBER: (603) 433-6131
FAX: (603) 274-6561
WEB: www.apogent.com
NO. OF EMPLOYEES: 6,900 (approx.)
SHAREHOLDERS: 357 (common record)
ANNUAL MEETING: In Jan.
INCORPORATED: NY, 1965; reincorp., WI, 1987

INSTITUTIONAL HOLDINGS:
No. of Institutions: 191
Shares Held: 101,204,354
% Held: 95.4
INDUSTRY: Dental equipment and supplies (SIC: 3843)
TRANSFER AGENT(S): Fleet National Bank c/o EquiServe, Providence, RI

APPLERA CORP. - APPLIED BIOSYSTEMS GROUP

EXCH.	SYM.	REC. PRICE	P/E RATIO	YLD.	MKT. CAP.	RANGE (52-WK.)	'02 Y/E PR.
NYSE	ABI	18.35 (2/28/03)	25.8	0.9%	$5.21 bill.	24.49 - 13.00	17.54

UPPER MEDIUM GRADE. PERCENTAGE REVENUE GROWTH FOR FISCAL 2003 IS EXPECTED TO BE IN THE HIGH SINGLE DIGITS.

INTERIM EARNINGS (Per Share):

Qtr.	Sept.	Dec.	Mar.	June
1998-99	---------- 0.72 ----------			
1999-00	0.14	0.21	0.26	0.26
2000-01	0.22	0.26	0.26	0.22
2001-02	0.15	0.23	0.23	0.18
2002-03	0.16	0.14	...	...

INTERIM DIVIDENDS (Per Share):

Amt.	Decl.	Ex.	Rec.	Pay.
0.043Q	1/17/02	2/27/02	3/01/02	4/01/02
0.043Q	4/08/02	5/30/02	6/03/02	7/01/02
0.043Q	8/15/02	8/29/02	9/03/02	10/01/02
0.043Q	11/21/02	11/27/02	12/02/02	1/02/03
0.043Q	1/16/03	1/27/03	3/03/03	4/01/03

Indicated div.: $0.17 (Div. Reinv. Plan)

*7 YEAR PRICE SCORE N/A   ***12 MONTH PRICE SCORE 99.6**

*NYSE COMPOSITE INDEX=100

CAPITALIZATION (6/30/02):

	($000)	(%)
Common & Surplus	1,125,231	100.0
Total	1,125,231	100.0

BUSINESS:

Applied Biosystems Group (formerly PE Biosystems Group), a subsidiary of Applera Corporation, develops and markets instrument-based systems, reagents, software, and contract services to the life science industry and research community. Customers use these tools to analyze nucleic acids (DNA and RNA), small molecules, and proteins to make scientific discoveries leading to the development of new pharmaceuticals, and to conduct standardized testing. On 5/5/99, The Perkin-Elmer Corporation changed its name to PE Corporation and created two new classes of common stock, PE Biosystems Group and Celera Genomics Group. On 11/30/00, the name of PE Corporation was changed to Applera Corporation and the name of PE Biosystems Group was changed to the Applied Biosystems Group.

RECENT DEVELOPMENTS:

For the three months ended 12/31/02, net income fell 40.4% to $29.2 million compared with $49.0 million in the same period of 2001. Results for 2002 included a special charge of $24.3 million for asset write-offs, severance costs and office closings, while results for 2001 included an acquired research and development charge of $2.2 million.

Net revenues were $444.7 million, up 8.2% from $411.1 million in the prior-year period, primarily due to the success of ABI's instrument products. Gross margin climbed 2.1% to $218.9 million from $214.4 million the year before. Operating income dropped 48.6% to $33.9 million compared with $65.9 million in the previous year.

PROSPECTS:

The Company is unable to forecast near-term results due to erratic spending patterns in the pharmaceutical and biotechnology segments, delays in the appropriations for the National Institute of Health for the current federal government fiscal year, vague government funding levels in Japan and parts of Europe, and unpredictable trends in the consumption of sequencing reagents. Considering these uncertainties, the Company expects percentage revenue growth for fiscal 2003 to be in the high single digits. Furthermore, the Company remains on track to meet its earnings per share forecast for fiscal 2003 in the range of $0.74 to $0.84, including special charges.

ANNUAL FINANCIAL DATA:

FISCAL YEAR	TOT. REVS. ($mill.)	NET INC. ($mill.)	TOT. ASSETS ($mill.)	OPER. PROFIT %	NET PROFIT %	RET. ON EQUITY %	RET. ON ASSETS %	CURR. RATIO	EARN. PER SH.$	CASH FL. PER SH.$	TANG. BK. VAL.$	DIV. PER SH.$	PRICE RANGE	AVG. P/E RATIO	AVG. YIELD %
6/30/02	1,604.0	⑥ 168.5	1,818.6	...	...	...	...	3.2	⑥ 0.78	0.27	7.84	0.17	39.28 - 13.00	33.5	0.7
6/30/01	1,619.5	⑤ 212.4	2,887.9	...	1.7	1.3	0.9	3.5	⑤ 0.96	0.56	7.86	0.17	94.25 - 18.49	58.7	0.3
6/30/00	1,388.1	④ 186.2	1,698.1	15.4	13.4	19.9	11.0	1.7	④ 0.86	1.11	4.46	0.17	160.00 - 42.81	117.9	0.2
6/30/99	1,221.7	③ 148.4	1,347.6	15.4	12.1	27.8	11.0	1.4	③ 0.72	1.87	5.20	0.17	62.94 - 23.81	60.2	0.4
6/30/98	940.1	② 24.0	1,128.9	5.7	2.6	4.2	2.1	1.8	...	...	...	0.17	...	...	...
6/30/97	767.5	① 132.7	...	13.1	17.3	...	...	...	...	...	...	0.17	...	...	...

Statistics are as originally reported. Adj. for 2-for-1 split, 7/99. Adj. for 100% stk. div., 2/00. ① Excls. income from disc. ops. of $27.9 mill. ② Incl. $28.9 mill. pre-tax acquired research and develop. chg. & $44.0 mill. net restr. chg., bef. income of $40.7 mill. from disc. ops. ③ Incl. $1.5 mill. chg. for merger costs, $6.1 mill. gain, excl. $79.1 mill. gain on disp. of disc. ops. ④ Incl. $42.1 mill. spl. chg. fr. merger costs & $48.6 mill. gain fr. sale of investments. ⑤ Incl. $15.0 mill. gain fr. sale of investments. ⑥ Incl. $2.2 mill. acq. R&D chg. and $8.6 mill. loss fr. investments.

OFFICERS:
T. L. White, Chmn., Pres., C.E.O.
D. L. Winger, Sr. V.P., C.F.O.
W. B. Sawch, Sr. V.P., Gen. Couns.
INVESTOR CONTACT: Peter Dworkin, V.P., Investor Relations, (203) 554-2479
PRINCIPAL OFFICE: 301 Merritt 7, Norwalk, CT 06851-1070

TELEPHONE NUMBER: (203) 840-2000
FAX: (203) 762-6000
WEB: www.appliedbiosystems.com
NO. OF EMPLOYEES: 5,950 (approx.)
SHAREHOLDERS: 6,244 (approx.)
ANNUAL MEETING: In Oct.
INCORPORATED: NY, Dec., 1939; reincorp., DE, 1998

INSTITUTIONAL HOLDINGS:
No. of Institutions: 294
Shares Held: 200,638,617
% Held: 95.9
INDUSTRY: Analytical instruments (SIC: 3826)
TRANSFER AGENT(S): BankBoston, N.A., c/o EquiServe, Boston, MA

APPLIED INDUSTRIAL TECHNOLOGIES, INC.

EXCH.	SYM.	REC. PRICE	P/E RATIO	YLD.	MKT. CAP.	RANGE (52-WK.)	'02 Y/E PR.
NYSE	AIT	16.39 (2/28/03)	21.6	2.9%	$314.7 mill.	21.25 - 14.70	18.90

MEDIUM GRADE. THE COMPANY RECENTLY ACQUIRED CERTAIN ASSETS OF INDUSTRIAL EQUIPMENT CO. LTD. FOR APPROXIMATELY $12.0 MILLION.

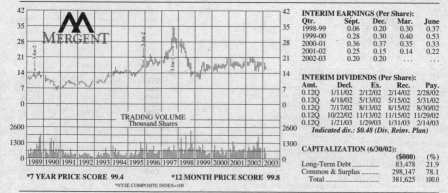

INTERIM EARNINGS (Per Share):

Qtr.	Sept.	Dec.	Mar.	June
1998-99	0.06	0.20	0.30	0.37
1999-00	0.28	0.30	0.40	0.53
2000-01	0.36	0.37	0.35	0.33
2001-02	0.25	0.15	0.14	0.22
2002-03	0.20	0.20	...	...

INTERIM DIVIDENDS (Per Share):

Amt.	Decl.	Ex.	Rec.	Pay.
0.12Q	1/11/02	2/12/02	2/14/02	2/28/02
0.12Q	4/18/02	5/13/02	5/15/02	5/31/02
0.12Q	7/17/02	8/13/02	8/15/02	8/30/02
0.12Q	10/22/02	11/13/02	11/15/02	11/29/02
0.12Q	1/21/03	1/29/03	1/31/03	2/14/03

Indicated div.: $0.48 (Div. Reinv. Plan)

*7 YEAR PRICE SCORE 99.4   ***12 MONTH PRICE SCORE 99.8**

*NYSE COMPOSITE INDEX=100

CAPITALIZATION (6/30/02):

	($000)	(%)
Long-Term Debt	83,478	21.9
Common & Surplus	298,147	78.1
Total	381,625	100.0

BUSINESS:

Applied Industrial Technologies, Inc. distributes industrial, fluid power, fabricated rubber products and engineered systems. In addition, the Company offers rubber and fluid power shop services as well as engineering, design and fabrication services related to electrical, gearing and material handling systems. AIT offers technical application support for its products and provides applications to help customers minimize downtime and reduce procurement and maintenance costs. As of 1/15/03, the Company operated over 450 facilities across North America. AIT's Fluid Power unit operates in various regions of the U.S. under the names Air and Hydraulics Engineering, Air Draulics Engineering, Dees Fluid Power, Elect-Air, Engineered Sales, ESI Power Hydraulics and Kent Fluid Power.

RECENT DEVELOPMENTS:

For the second quarter ended 12/31/02, net income advanced 32.3% to $3.9 million compared with $2.9 million in the equivalent 2001 quarter. Results for 2002 included a gain of $1.2 million on the sale of unneeded real estate. Net sales increased 2.3% to $355.7 million from $347.6 million a year earlier, primarily due to one additional sales day in the quarter and contributions from an acquisition. Gross profit grew 4.8% to $91.2 million from $87.0 million the year before. The increase in gross profit reflected higher discounts and allowances from suppliers. Operating income jumped 21.4% to $7.3 million from $6.0 million in the prior-year period.

PROSPECTS:

The Company recently acquired certain assets of Industrial Equipment Co. Ltd., a western Canadian distributor of bearings, power transmission and fluid power products, for approximately $12.0 million. The acquired operations are being integrated with Applied Industrial Technologies, Ltd., AIT's wholly-owned Canadian subsidiary. The acquisition adds 16 additional service center locations and should strengthen the Company's presence in Alberta and British Columbia. Separately, the Company expects earnings for fiscal 2003 to range from $0.75 to $0.90 per share on sales ranging from $1.45 billion to $1.50 billion.

ANNUAL FINANCIAL DATA:

FISCAL YEAR	TOT. REVS. ($mill.)	NET INC. ($mill.)	TOT. ASSETS ($mill.)	OPER. PROFIT %	NET PROFIT %	RET. ON EQUITY %	RET. ON ASSETS %	CURR. RATIO	EARN. PER SH.$	CASH FL. PER SH.$	TANG. BK. VAL.$	DIV. PER SH.$	PRICE RANGE	AVG. P/E RATIO	AVG. YIELD %
6/30/02	1,446.6	③ 14.8	534.6	2.1	1.0	4.9	2.8	2.9	③ 0.76	1.66	13.11	0.48	21.25 - 14.70	23.6	2.7
6/30/01	1,625.8	28.0	578.9	3.4	1.7	9.0	4.8	3.2	1.41	2.54	12.54	0.48	20.69 - 15.65	12.9	2.6
6/30/00	1,571.7	31.0	594.7	3.7	2.0	10.4	5.2	2.6	1.50	2.61	11.57	0.48	21.00 - 14.31	11.8	2.7
6/30/99	1,527.9	② 19.9	574.3	2.8	1.3	6.8	3.5	2.9	② 0.93	1.98	10.96	0.48	19.06 - 11.13	16.2	3.2
6/30/98	1,491.4	30.1	606.1	3.9	2.0	10.2	5.0	2.1	1.38	2.34	10.92	0.48	29.31 - 12.00	15.0	2.3
6/30/97	1,160.3	① 27.1	394.1	4.4	2.3	13.1	6.9	2.4	① 1.47	2.25	10.88	0.44	34.81 - 18.25	18.0	1.7
6/30/96	1,143.7	23.3	404.1	4.3	2.0	12.3	5.8	2.1	1.27	2.10	9.91	0.39	22.50 - 16.00	15.2	2.0
6/30/95	1,054.8	16.9	359.2	3.5	1.6	10.2	4.7	2.4	0.98	...	9.17	0.33	19.75 - 12.22	16.3	2.1
6/30/94	936.3	12.7	343.5	3.0	1.4	8.4	3.7	2.4	0.75	...	8.86	0.29	16.67 - 12.33	19.4	2.0
6/30/93	831.4	8.9	315.9	2.5	1.1	6.6	2.8	2.4	0.55	...	8.19	0.28	13.83 - 9.11	21.0	2.5

Statistics are as originally reported. Adj. for stk. splits: 3-for-2, 12/95, 9/97 ① Incl. non-recurr. chg. $4.0 mill. ② Incl. pretax restruct. & other spec. chrgs. totaling $5.4 mill. ③ Bef. acctg. chrg. of $12.1 mill.

OFFICERS:
D. L. Pugh, Chmn., C.E.O.
B. L. Purser, Pres., C.O.O.
J. R. Whitten, V.P., C.F.O., Treas.

INVESTOR CONTACT: John R. Whitten, V.P.,
C.F.O., Treas., (216) 426-4000

PRINCIPAL OFFICE: One Applied Plaza,
Cleveland, OH 44115

TELEPHONE NUMBER: (216) 426-4000
FAX: (216) 426-4884
WEB: www.appliedindustrial.com
NO. OF EMPLOYEES: 4,500 (approx.)
SHAREHOLDERS: 6,489 (record)
ANNUAL MEETING: In Oct.
INCORPORATED: DE, Nov., 1928; reincorp.,
OH, Oct., 1988

INSTITUTIONAL HOLDINGS:
No. of Institutions: 91
Shares Held: 12,580,858
% Held: 65.9

INDUSTRY: Industrial supplies (SIC: 5085)

TRANSFER AGENT(S): Computershare Investor Services LLC, Chicago, IL

APTARGROUP INC.

EXCH.	SYM.	REC. PRICE	P/E RATIO	YLD.	MKT. CAP.	RANGE (52-WK.)	'02 Y/E PR.
NYSE	ATR	30.30 (2/28/03)	16.6	0.8%	$1.12 bill.	38.74 - 24.84	31.24

MEDIUM GRADE. THE POSITIVE MOMENTUM IN THE PERSONAL CARE, FRAGRANCE/COSMETIC AND FOOD/BEVERAGE MARKETS THAT ATR EXPERIENCED IN LATE 2002 IS EXPECTED TO CONTINUE INTO 2003.

INTERIM EARNINGS (Per Share):

Qtr.	Mar.	June	Sept.	Dec.
1998	0.36	0.39	0.39	0.51
1999	0.39	0.44	0.35	0.42
2000	0.45	0.49	0.45	0.40
2001	0.50	0.41	0.43	0.27
2002	0.36	0.48	0.49	0.50

INTERIM DIVIDENDS (Per Share):

Amt.	Decl.	Ex.	Rec.	Pay.
0.06Q	1/22/02	2/04/02	2/06/02	2/28/02
0.06Q	4/18/02	4/29/02	5/01/02	5/22/02
0.06Q	7/18/02	7/26/02	7/30/02	8/20/02
0.06Q	10/16/02	10/28/02	10/30/02	11/20/02
0.06Q	1/21/03	2/03/03	2/05/03	2/27/03

Indicated div.: $0.24

CAPITALIZATION (12/31/01):

	($000)	(%)
Long-Term Debt	239,387	32.3
Deferred Income Tax	28,026	3.8
Minority Interest	5,099	0.7
Common & Surplus	469,204	63.3
Total	741,716	100.0

*7 YEAR PRICE SCORE 121.7   ***12 MONTH PRICE SCORE 100.0**

*NYSE COMPOSITE INDEX=100

BUSINESS:

AptarGroup, Inc. is a global supplier of dispensing systems for the fragrance/cosmetic, personal care, pharmaceutical, household and food/beverage markets. The Company operates in the packaging components industry. ATR focuses on providing value-added dispensing systems (pumps, dispensing closures and aerosol valves) to global consumer product marketers. ATR has manufacturing facilities located in North America, Europe, Asia and South America. The SeaquistPerfect segment sells primarily aerosol valves and certain pumps limited to the personal care, household and, to a lesser extent, the food/beverage markets. In fiscal 2002, net sales were derived as follows: Dispensing Systems, 81.8%, and SeaquistPerfect, 18.2%.

RECENT DEVELOPMENTS:

For the year ended 12/31/02, net income increased 13.1% to $66.6 million compared with income of $58.9 million, before an accounting change charge of $64,000, in 2001. Results for 2002 and 2001 included after-tax non-recurring charges of $3.8 million and $6.0 million, respectively.

Results for 2001 also included goodwill amortization of $3.6 million. Net sales rose 3.9% to $926.7 million due to increased sales to the pharmaceutical market, personal care and food/beverage markets, partially offset by decreased sales to the fragrance/cosmetic market.

PROSPECTS:

Looking ahead to 2003, ATR is not certain as to how developments in the Middle East may affect its customers and end consumers. Barring any significant negative outcome from events there, ATR is cautiously optimistic about the year ahead. The positive momentum in the personal care, fragrance/cosmetic and food/beverage markets that ATR experienced in late 2002 is expected to continue into 2003. ATR anticipates sales of its products to the pharmaceutical market in early 2003 will be lower than the level seen in early 2002. However, indications point to sales to this market improving as the year progresses. ATR anticipates first quarter diluted earnings per share to be in the range of $0.48 to $0.53.

ANNUAL FINANCIAL DATA:

FISCAL YEAR	TOT. REVS. ($mill.)	NET INC. ($mill.)	TOT. ASSETS ($mill.)	OPER. PROFIT %	NET PROFIT %	RET. ON EQUITY %	RET. ON ASSETS %	CURR. RATIO	EARN. PER SH. $	CASH FL. PER SH. $	TANG. BK. VAL. $	DIV. PER SH. $	PRICE RANGE	AVG. P/E RATIO	AVG. YIELD %
p12/31/02	926.7	④ 66.6	1,047.7		6.6	12.6	6.4	2.4	④ 1.82	3.63		0.24	38.74 - 24.84	17.5	0.8
12/31/01	892.0	③ 58.9	915.3	11.4	6.6	14.7	6.8	2.0	③ 1.61	3.63	9.37	0.20	37.21 - 26.44	19.8	0.7
12/31/00	883.5	64.7	952.2	12.9	7.3	14.7	6.8	2.0	1.78	3.73	8.55	0.20	30.13 - 19.38	13.9	0.8
12/31/99	834.3	② 58.7	863.3	13.0	7.0	14.0	6.8	2.2	② 1.59	3.45	8.03	0.18	31.50 - 22.50	17.0	0.7
12/31/98	713.5	① 60.8	714.7	13.3	8.5	14.6	8.5	1.9	① 1.65	3.13	10.13	0.16	33.44 - 19.69	16.1	0.6
12/31/97	655.4	46.5	585.4	12.1	7.1	13.6	7.9	2.0	1.28	2.64	8.38	0.15	29.56 - 16.38	18.0	0.7
12/31/96	615.8	37.5	576.1	10.4	6.1	11.2	6.5	2.0	1.05	2.39	8.06	0.14	21.56 - 14.50	17.3	0.8
12/31/95	557.5	35.7	559.2	10.6	6.4	11.4	6.4	1.8	1.00	2.21	7.37	0.13	19.13 - 12.31	15.8	0.8
12/31/94	474.3	27.3	465.4	10.3	5.7	10.1	5.9	1.7	0.83	2.04	6.44	0.12	14.50 - 10.06	14.9	0.9
12/31/93	411.5	21.6	408.0	10.0	5.2	11.3	5.4	1.0	0.67	1.67	4.67	0.05	11.00 - 8.00	14.2	0.5

Statistics are as originally reported. ① Incl. lawsuit settlement gain of $9.9 mill. ② Incl. in-process research & dev. write-off of $3.3 mill. ③ Incl. strategic initiative chrg. of $7.6 mill., but excl. acctg. change chrg. of $64,000. ④ Incl. after-tax charges totaling $3.8 million related to the strategic initative and a patent dispute settlement.

OFFICERS:
K. Harris, Chmn.
P. Pfeiffer, Vice-Chmn.
C. A. Siebel, Pres., C.E.O.
S. J. Hagge, Exec. V.P., C.F.O., Sec.

INVESTOR CONTACT: Stephen J. Hagge, Exec. V.P., C.F.O., Sec., (815) 477-0424

PRINCIPAL OFFICE: 475 West Terra Cotta Avenue, Suite E, Crystal Lake, IL 60014

TELEPHONE NUMBER: (815) 477-0424
FAX: (815) 477-0481
WEB: www.aptargroup.com
NO. OF EMPLOYEES: 6,600 (approx.)
SHAREHOLDERS: 600 (approx.)
ANNUAL MEETING: In May
INCORPORATED: DE, Sept., 1992

INSTITUTIONAL HOLDINGS:
No. of Institutions: 167
Shares Held: 31,652,668
% Held: 88.1

INDUSTRY: Plastics products, nec (SIC: 3089)

TRANSFER AGENT(S): Mellon Investor Services, L.L.C., Ridgefield Park, NJ

AQUILA, INC.

EXCH.	SYM.	REC. PRICE	P/E RATIO	YLD.	MKT. CAP.	RANGE (52-WK.)	'02 Y/E PR.
NYSE	ILA	1.44 (2/28/03)	...	...	$167.0 mill.	25.83 - 1.41	1.77

SPECULATIVE GRADE. LOOKING AHEAD, THE COMPANY WILL FOCUS ON RESTRUCTURING OR TERMINATING ITS LONG-TERM POWER PURCHASE AGREEMENTS.

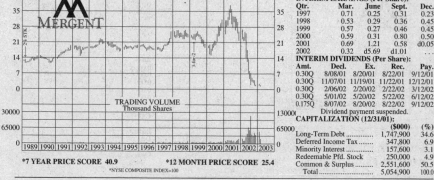

INTERIM EARNINGS (Per Share):

Qtr.	Mar.	June	Sept.	Dec.
1997	0.71	0.25	0.31	0.23
1998	0.53	0.29	0.36	0.45
1999	0.57	0.27	0.46	0.45
2000	0.59	0.31	0.80	0.50
2001	0.69	1.21	0.58	d0.05
2002	0.32	d5.69	d1.01	...

INTERIM DIVIDENDS (Per Share):

Amt.	Decl.	Ex.	Rec.	Pay.
0.30Q	8/08/01	8/20/01	8/22/01	9/12/01
0.30Q	11/07/01	11/19/01	11/22/01	12/12/01
0.30Q	2/06/02	2/20/02	2/22/02	3/12/02
0.30Q	5/01/02	5/20/02	5/22/02	6/12/02
0.175Q	8/07/02	8/20/02	8/22/02	9/12/02

Dividend payment suspended.

CAPITALIZATION (12/31/01):

	($000)	(%)
Long-Term Debt	1,747,900	34.6
Deferred Income Tax	347,800	6.9
Minority Interest	157,600	3.1
Redeemable Pfd. Stock	250,000	4.9
Common & Surplus	2,551,600	50.5
Total	5,054,900	100.0

*7 YEAR PRICE SCORE 40.9   ***12 MONTH PRICE SCORE 25.4**

*NYSE COMPOSITE INDEX=100

BUSINESS:

Aquila, Inc. (formerly UtiliCorp United Inc.) is a multinational energy company operating electricity and natural gas distribution networks. As of 9/30/02, ILA served 431,000 electric distribution customers in Missouri, Kansas, and Colorado; and 874,000 natural gas distribution customers in Missouri, Kansas, Colorado, Nebraska, Iowa, Michigan, and Minnesota. ILA's wholly-owned Canadian operation provided electricity for 377,000 electric distribution customers in Alberta and 140,000 in British Columbia. ILA's U.K. subsidiary provided retail power to 2.3 million customers in and around the city of Birmingham, England. Through its affiliates, the Company distributed energy to 571,000 electric customers and 625,000 natural gas customers in Melbourne, Victoria in Australia. On 12/31/00, ILA completed the acquisitions of GPU International and St. Joseph Light & Power Company.

RECENT DEVELOPMENTS:

For the third quarter ended 9/30/02, the Company reported a loss of $180.6 million, before a loss from discontinued operations of $151.0 million, versus income of $64.8 million, before income from discontinued operations of $4.1 million, in the corresponding prior-year quarter. Results for 2002 included restructuring charges of $116.2 million and impairment charges of $39.0 million. Total sales dropped 28.3% to $576.5 million from $804.0 million a year earlier.

PROSPECTS:

Efforts are ongoing to restructure ILA's long-term power purchase agreements and further reduce debt. While asset sales continue, ILA has sold approximately $1.30 billion of non-strategic assets since October 2002. ILA is working closely with its banking group to renew its short-term credit facility. The Company will be using available nonregulated collateral, as well as pursuing filings with state regulatory commission, to renew the facility before its 4/12/03 expiration date. ILA expects to record significant charges in the fourth quarter of 2002 related to the renegotiation of contracts, the exiting from wholesale commodity positions, severance costs and possible additional asset impairments.

ANNUAL FINANCIAL DATA:

FISCAL YEAR	TOT. REVS. ($mill.)	NET INC. ($mill.)	TOT. ASSETS ($mill.)	OPER. PROFIT %	NET PROFIT %	NET INC./ NET PROP. %	NET INC./ TOT. CAP. %	RET. ON EQUITY %	ACCUM. DEPR./ GROSS PROP. %	EARN. PER SH. $	TANG. BK. VAL.$	DIV. PER SH. $	DIV. PAYOUT %	PRICE RANGE	AVG. P/E RATIO	AVG. YIELD %
p12/31/02										0.78				26.95 - 1.56		5.5
12/31/01	40,376.8	⑨ 279.4	11,948.3	1.0	0.7	8.2	5.5	10.9	41.0	⑨ 2.42	22.01	1.20	49.6	37.85 - 21.85	12.3	4.0
⑩ 12/31/00	28,974.9	⑦ 206.8	14,115.6	1.1	0.7	5.7	3.9	10.9	38.4	⑦ 2.21	17.94	1.20	54.3	31.31 - 15.19	10.5	5.2
12/31/99	18,621.5	160.5	7,538.6	1.8	0.9	4.4	3.5	10.5	29.7	1.75	16.30	1.20	68.6	26.00 - 18.56	12.7	5.4
⑧ 12/31/98	12,563.4	132.2	5,991.2	1.9	1.1	4.0	3.8	9.1	30.4	1.63	15.82	1.20	73.6	26.63 - 22.50	15.1	4.9
12/31/97	8,926.3	⑤ 134.1	5,113.5	2.7	1.5	5.4	4.4	11.5	34.7	⑤ 1.51	14.49	1.17	77.9	26.04 - 16.75	14.2	5.5
12/31/96	4,332.3	①④ 105.8	4,704.9	5.2	2.4	4.4	3.4	8.9	34.2	①④ 1.47	14.49	1.17	80.0	20.17 - 17.17	12.7	6.3
12/31/95	2,798.5	①③ 79.8	3,885.9	8.0	2.9	3.5	2.9	8.2	33.2	①③ 1.15	13.72	1.15	100.0	19.75 - 17.58	16.3	6.1
12/31/94	1,514.6	94.4	3,111.1	15.2	6.2	3.9	4.3	10.1	36.1	1.39	13.55	1.13	81.7	21.25 - 16.75	13.7	6.0
12/31/93	1,571.6	② 86.4	2,850.5	9.7	5.5	3.8	3.9	9.2	35.4	② 1.30	13.51	1.08	83.1	22.67 - 18.08	15.7	5.3

Statistics are as originally reported. Adj. for stk. split: 3-for-2, 3/99 ① Inc. non-recurr. gain $11.8 mill., 12/96; chrgs. $6.8 mill, 12/96; $19.6 mill., 12/95 ② Inc. gain fr. sale of stk. of subsid. $3.0 mill. ③ Incl. non-recurr. chrg. $19.6 mill. ④ Inc. gain $11.8 mill. & net chrg. $6.8 mill. ⑤ Incl. gain $53.0 mill. for merger terminate. fee, a pre-tax chrg. $26.5 mill. for asset impairs., & a pre-tax chrg. $6.5 mill. for add. reserves; & exc. a net extraord. chrg. $7.2 mill. and a net chrg. of $4.8 mill. for acctg. change ⑥ Refl. increased interest in Power New Zealand to 78.6%. ⑦ Incls. impairments & oth. chrgs. of $27.2 mill. ⑧ Refl. acqs. of TrustPower assets in New Zealand & 25% stake in Australian opers. ⑨ Incl. net non-recurr. chrg. of $2.4 mill. ⑩ Refl. the acqs. of St. Joseph Light & Power Company & GPU International.

OFFICERS:
R. C. Green Jr., Chmn., C.E.O.
R. K. Green, Pres., C.O.O.
R. Dobson, C.F.O. (interim)
INVESTOR CONTACT: Neala Clark, Inv. Rel.,
(816) 467-3562
PRINCIPAL OFFICE: 20 West Ninth Street,
Kansas City, MO 64105

TELEPHONE NUMBER: (816) 421-6600
FAX: (816) 467-3435
WEB: www.aquila.com
NO. OF EMPLOYEES: 7,377 (avg.)
SHAREHOLDERS: 40,000 (approx.)
ANNUAL MEETING: In May
INCORPORATED: MO, April, 1950;
reincorp., DE, April, 1987

INSTITUTIONAL HOLDINGS:
No. of Institutions: 190
Shares Held: 75,763,715
% Held: 42.0
INDUSTRY: Electric and other services combined (SIC: 4931)
TRANSFER AGENT(S): UMB Bank, N.A.,
Kansas City, MO

ARAMARK CORPORATION

EXCH.	SYM.	REC. PRICE	P/E RATIO	YLD.	MKT. CAP.	RANGE (52-WK.)	'02 Y/E PR.
NYSE	RMK	21.95 (2/28/03)	16.0	...	$4.10 bill.	28.30 - 18.39	23.50

MEDIUM GRADE. THE COMPANY EXPECTS WEAK EMPLOYMENT LEVELS TO ADVERSELY AFFECT RESULTS IN FISCAL 2003.

7 YEAR PRICE SCORE N/A   **12 MONTH PRICE SCORE 105.2**
*NYSE COMPOSITE INDEX=100

INTERIM EARNINGS (Per Share):

Qtr.	Dec.	Mar.	June	Sept.
2000-01	0.24	0.13	0.27	0.34
2001-02	0.27	0.31	0.35	0.40
2002-03	0.31	...	...	...

INTERIM DIVIDENDS (Per Share):

Amt.	Decl.	Ex.	Rec.	Pay.
		No dividends paid.		

CAPITALIZATION (9/27/02):

	($000)	(%)
Long-Term Debt	1,835,713	68.1
Common & Surplus	858,185	31.9
Total	2,693,898	100.0

BUSINESS:

ARAMARK Corporation is a provider of managed services. The Food & Support Services segments (78.4% of 2002 sales) provides food, refreshment, specialized dietary and support services, including facility maintenance and housekeeping to business, educational, governmental and healthcare institutions and in sports, entertainment, recreational and other facilities in North America, Europe and Asia. The Uniform & Career Apparel segments (16.4%) provides rental, sale, cleaning, maintenance and delivery of personalized uniform and career apparel and other textile items on a contract basis. The Educational Resources segment (5.2%) provides infant, toddler, pre-school and school-age learning programs through community-based child care centers, before and after school programs, employer on-site child care centers and private elementary schools. RMK was privately-held for 17 years prior to its initial public offering on 12/11/01. In 2002, RMK acquired the Fine Host Corp. for about $100.0 million.

RECENT DEVELOPMENTS:

For the quarter ended 12/27/02, net income advanced 21.9% to $62.7 million versus $51.4 million in the equivalent 2001 quarter. Total sales increased 12.9% to $2.39 billion from $2.11 billion a year earlier. On a segment basis, U.S. Food & Support Services sales jumped 18.1% to $1.56 billion, and International Food & Support Services sales climbed 10.4% to $335.7 million. Uniform & Career Apparel rentals rose 1.6% to $254.7 million, while Uniform & Career Apparel sales inched up 0.5% to $129.2 million. Education Resources sales slipped 1.2% to $111.8 million. Operating income improved 15.1% to $135.8 million from $117.9 million in 2001.

PROSPECTS:

Looking forward, RMK expects weak employment levels to continue to negatively affect sales growth, particularly in the uniform businesses. Meanwhile, in December 2002, RMK completed the previously announced acquisition of Fine Host Corporation for about $100.0 million. The acquisition is expected to be cash flow positive and reduce diluted earnings per share for full-year 2003 by $0.01 to $0.02 due to the timing of transition costs and the realization of cost savings. RMK also expects second quarter earnings in the range of $0.21 to $0.22 per diluted share.

ANNUAL FINANCIAL DATA:

FISCAL YEAR	TOT. REVS. ($mill.)	NET INC. ($mill.)	TOT. ASSETS ($mill.)	OPER. PROFIT %	NET PROFIT %	RET. ON EQUITY %	RET. ON ASSETS %	CURR. RATIO	EARN. PER SH. $	CASH FL. PER SH. $	PRICE RANGE	AVG. P/E RATIO
9/27/02	8,769.8	① 269.6	4,259.3	6.4	3.1	31.5	6.3	0.8	① 1.34	2.61	28.30 - 18.39	17.4
9/28/01	7,788.7	176.5	3,216.4	5.6	2.3	71.5	5.5	0.9	0.98	2.30	...	...
9/29/00	7,262.9	168.0	3,199.4	5.8	2.3	150.6	5.2	1.0	0.88	2.04	...	...
10/01/99	6,742.3	150.2	...	5.6	2.2	...	...	...	0.74	1.69	...	...

Statistics are as originally reported. ① Incl. pre-tax net non-recurr. gain of $5.8 mill. and a pre-tax gain of $37.9 mill. on sale of interest in Boston Red Sox Baseball Club and a rel. entity.

OFFICERS:
J. Neubauer, Chmn., C.E.O.
W. Leonard, Pres., C.O.O.
L. F. Sutherland, Exec. V.P., C.F.O.
INVESTOR CONTACT: Gary Sender, Investor Relations, (215) 238-3361
PRINCIPAL OFFICE: ARAMARK Tower, 1101 Market St., Philadelphia, PA 19107

TELEPHONE NUMBER: (215) 238-3000
WEB: www.ARAMARK.com
NO. OF EMPLOYEES: 200,000 (approx.)
SHAREHOLDERS: 570 (approx. class B); 3,600 (approx. class A)
ANNUAL MEETING: In Feb.
INCORPORATED: DE, 1959

INSTITUTIONAL HOLDINGS:
No. of Institutions: 114
Shares Held: 51,671,838
% Held: 27.6

INDUSTRY: Eating places (SIC: 5812)

TRANSFER AGENT(S): Mellon Investor Services, Ridgefield Park, NJ

ARCHER DANIELS MIDLAND COMPANY

EXCH.	SYM.	REC. PRICE	P/E RATIO	YLD.	MKT. CAP.	RANGE (52-WK.)	'02 Y/E PR.	DIV. ACH.
NYSE	ADM	10.90 (2/28/03)	15.1	2.2%	$7.16 bill.	14.85 - 10.00	12.40	28 yrs.

UPPER MEDIUM GRADE. EARNINGS ARE BEING HURT BY SHARPLY HIGHER SOYBEAN PRICES.

*7 YEAR PRICE SCORE 99.4 ***12 MONTH PRICE SCORE 101.4**

*NYSE COMPOSITE INDEX=100

INTERIM EARNINGS (Per Share):

Qtr.	Sept.	Dec.	Mar.	June
1997-98	0.19	0.21	0.10	0.10
1998-99	0.17	0.16	0.02	0.07
1999-00	0.06	0.15	0.15	0.10
2000-01	0.16	0.19	0.14	0.09
2001-02	0.20	0.23	0.18	0.17
2002-03	0.17	0.20	...	...

INTERIM DIVIDENDS (Per Share):

Amt.	Decl.	Ex.	Rec.	Pay.
0.05Q	1/29/02	2/06/02	2/08/02	3/05/02
0.05Q	5/02/02	5/08/02	5/10/02	6/03/02
0.06Q	8/08/02	8/15/02	8/19/02	9/09/02
0.06Q	11/07/02	11/15/02	11/19/02	12/12/02
0.06Q	1/28/03	2/05/03	2/07/03	3/04/03
Indicated div.: $0.24				

CAPITALIZATION (6/30/02):

	($000)	(%)
Long-Term Debt	3,111,294	29.6
Deferred Income Tax	631,923	6.0
Common & Surplus	6,754,821	64.3
Total	10,498,038	100.0

BUSINESS:

Archer Daniels Midland Company is engaged in procuring, transporting, storing, processing and merchandising agricultural commodities and products. The Company processes soybeans, cottonseed, sunflower seeds, canola, peanuts, flaxseed and corn germ into vegetable oils and meals primarily for the food and feed industries. In addition, ADM's corn milling operations produce products for the food and beverage industry, along with ethyl alcohol, or ethanol, which is used as a gasoline additive. The Company also processes wheat, corn and milo into flour. Sales (and operating profit) for fiscal 2002 were derived as follows: oilseeds processing, 38.3% (37.3%); agricultural services, 35.3% (16.3%); corn processing, 8.3% (20.7%); wheat processing, 5.8% (7.6%); and other, 12.3% (18.1%).

RECENT DEVELOPMENTS:

For the three months ended 12/31/02, net earnings declined 12.5% to $131.2 million from $150.0 million in the corresponding prior-year period. Results for 2002 and 2001 included charges of $2.7 million and $20.0 million, respectively, from securities transactions. Net sales and other operating income climbed 42.9% to $7.81 billion from $5.46 billion the year before. Gross profit totaled $490.9 million, or 6.3% of net sales and other operating income, versus $507.3 million, or 9.3% of net sales and other operating income, a year earlier. Operating profit slid 12.9% to $297.4 million from $341.3 million the previous year.

PROSPECTS:

Earnings are being hurt by reduced oilseed processing margins stemming from sharply higher soybean prices. As a result, on 12/16/02, ADM announced plans to close or cut production at six of its U.S. soybean processing plants. However, the Company plans to double the capacity at its biggest soybean plant in Brazil to take advantage of lower land and labor costs, as well as cheap, abundant foreign crops. Meanwhile, results should benefit from ChevronTexaco Corp.'s decision to use ethanol, a fuel additive made from corn, in gasoline it sells in California by May 2003.

ANNUAL FINANCIAL DATA:

FISCAL YEAR	TOT. REVS. ($mill.)	NET INC. ($mill.)	TOT. ASSETS ($mill.)	OPER. PROFIT %	NET PROFIT %	RET. ON EQUITY %	RET. ON ASSETS %	CURR. RATIO	EARN. PER SH. $	CASH FL. PER SH. $	TANG. BK. VAL. $	DIV. PER SH. $	PRICE RANGE	AVG. P/E RATIO	AVG. YIELD %
6/30/02	23,453.6	⑧ 511.1	15,416.3	3.7	2.2	7.6	3.3	1.6	⑧ 0.78	1.71	10.60	0.22	14.85 - 10.00	15.9	1.8
6/30/01	⑦ 20,051.4	⑥ 383.3	14,339.9	3.5	1.9	6.1	2.7	1.6	⑥ 0.58	1.51	9.64	0.19	15.80 - 10.24	22.4	1.5
6/30/00	12,876.8	⑤ 300.9	14,423.1	3.8	2.3	4.9	2.1	1.4	⑤ 0.45	1.42	9.39	0.18	14.47 - 7.80	24.8	1.7
6/30/99	14,283.3	④ 281.3	14,029.9	3.7	2.0	4.5	2.0	1.5	④ 0.41	1.32	9.13	0.17	14.74 - 10.38	30.8	1.4
6/30/98	16,108.6	③ 403.6	13,833.5	4.5	2.5	6.2	2.9	1.5	③ 0.59	1.40	9.47	0.17	19.44 - 12.80	27.3	1.0
6/30/97	13,853.3	③ 377.3	11,354.4	4.5	2.7	6.2	3.3	1.9	③ 0.54	1.24	8.92	0.16	20.26 - 13.32	30.9	0.9
6/30/96	13,314.0	② 695.9	10,449.9	6.9	5.2	11.3	6.7	2.7	② 0.99	1.59	8.82	0.15	18.12 - 12.92	15.4	1.0
6/30/95	12,671.9	795.9	9,756.9	9.6	6.3	13.6	8.2	3.2	1.10	1.66	8.34	0.09	14.93 - 10.66	11.7	0.7
6/30/94	11,374.4	484.1	8,746.9	6.7	4.3	9.6	5.5	3.5	0.66	1.17	6.94	0.05	15.01 - 10.10	19.1	0.4
6/30/93	9,811.4	① 534.5	8,404.1	7.5	5.4	10.9	6.4	4.1	① 0.75	1.16	6.75	0.04	12.46 - 9.46	14.6	0.4

Statistics are as originally reported. Adj. for all stk. divs. & splits through 9/01. ① Bef. $33 mil ($0.07/sh) chg. for acctg. adj. ② Incl. $0.04/sh net chg. ③ Incl. $48 mil ($0.07/sh) chg. for fines & litig. costs & $0.04/sh gain fr secs. transactions, 1998; & $0.18/sh net chg., 1997. ④ Excl. $15.3 mil ($0.02/sh) extraord. chg. & incl. $63.0 mil ($0.10/sh) gain fr. secs. transactions. ⑤ Incl. $72.0 mil ($0.11/sh) chg. for plant closings, $60.0 mil ($0.10/sh) tax credit & $6.0 mil ($0.01/sh) after-tax gain fr. secs. transactions. ⑥ Incl. $0.09/sh gain fr. secs. transactions & $0.03/sh loss fr. invests. ⑦ Reflects the adoption of new accounting standards related to recognizing sales. ⑧ Incl. $38.3 mil (0.03/sh) gain fr. secs. transactions, a $147.0 mil gain fr. a litigation settlement, and a $83.0 mil chg. fr. asset write down.

OFFICERS:
G. A. Andreas, Chmn., C.E.O.
P. B. Mulhollem, Pres., C.O.O.
D. J. Schmalz, Sr. V.P., C.F.O.

INVESTOR CONTACT: Dwight Grimestad, V.P., Inv. Rel., (217) 424-4586

PRINCIPAL OFFICE: 4666 Faries Parkway, Box 1470, Decatur, IL 62525

TELEPHONE NUMBER: (217) 424-5200
FAX: (217) 424-5381
WEB: www.admworld.com
NO. OF EMPLOYEES: 24,746 (avg.)
SHAREHOLDERS: 26,715
ANNUAL MEETING: In Nov.
INCORPORATED: DE, May, 1923

INSTITUTIONAL HOLDINGS:
No. of Institutions: 362
Shares Held: 394,616,217
% Held: 61.0

INDUSTRY: Soybean oil mills (SIC: 2075)

TRANSFER AGENT(S): Hickory Point Bank & Trust, Decatur, IL

ARCHSTONE-SMITH TRUST COMPANY

EXCH.	SYM.	REC. PRICE	P/E RATIO	YLD.	MKT. CAP.	RANGE (52-WK.)	'02 Y/E PR.
NYSE	ASN	22.05 (2/28/03)	14.3	7.8%	$3.85 bill.	29.19 - 20.94	23.54

MEDIUM GRADE. ON 12/19/02, THE COMPANY ANNOUNCED THE SALE OF CONSOLIDATED ENGINEERING SERVICES, INC. FOR APPROXIMATELY $178.0 MILLION.

INTERIM EARNINGS (Per Share):

Qtr.	Mar.	June	Sept.	Dec.
1998	0.42	0.25	0.36	0.43
1999	0.27	0.36	0.46	0.37
2000	0.28	0.57	0.61	0.31
2001	0.52	0.58	0.36	0.37
2002	0.28	0.42	0.28	0.56

INTERIM DIVIDENDS (Per Share):

Amt.	Decl.	Ex.	Rec.	Pay.
0.425Q	12/06/01	2/12/02	2/14/02	2/28/02
0.425Q	5/01/02	5/14/02	5/16/02	5/30/02
0.425Q	8/01/02	8/13/02	8/15/02	8/29/02
0.425Q	11/01/02	11/12/02	11/14/02	11/29/02
0.427Q	12/05/02	2/12/03	2/14/03	2/28/03

Indicated div.: $1.71 (Div. Reinv. Plan)

CAPITALIZATION (12/31/01):

	($000)	(%)
Long-Term Debt	3,853,032	52.9
Common & Surplus	3,427,030	47.1
Total	7,280,062	100.0

*7 YEAR PRICE SCORE 111.9   ***12 MONTH PRICE SCORE 97.8**

*NYSE COMPOSITE INDEX=100

BUSINESS:

Archstone-Smith Trust Company (formerly Archstone Communities Trust) is a major owner, developer, acquirer and operator of apartments in protected locations in major metropolitan areas across the country. The Company has divisional offices in Arlington, Va., Irvine, Calif., and Atlanta. At the end of 2002, 83.2% of the Company's wholly-owned operations portfolio was concentrated in Washington D.C., Boston, Chicago, California, Southeast Florida, Seattle and New York City. As of 12/31/02, the Company's portfolio consisted of 287 garden-style and high-rise properties, representing a total of 99,840 units, including 2,295 units under construction. On 10/31/01, the Company acquired Charles E. Smith Residential Realty, Inc.

RECENT DEVELOPMENTS:

For the year ended 12/31/02, income from continuing operations was $271.5 million, before an extraordinary loss of $30.2 million, compared with income of $249.1 million, before an extraordinary loss of $2.2 million, the previous year. Results for 2002 and 2001 included gains on dispositions of depreciated real estate of $36.0 million and $100.3 million, respectively, and excluded gains of $73.7 million and $11.0 million, respectively, from discontinued operations. Also, results for 2001 included a provision of $14.9 million for possible loss on investments. Total revenues soared 59.3% to $1.08 billion. Comparisons were made with restated prior-year figures.

PROSPECTS:

On 12/19/02, ASN announced the sale of Consolidated Engineering Services, Inc., an unconsolidated entity it acquired in the merger with Charles E. Smith Residential in 2001, to EMCOR Group for about $178.0 million. The sale of CES is an important strategic transaction for ASN as it represents the divestiture of a non-core business unit. Separately, ASN expects to rollout its revenue management system, Lease Rent Optimizer™ (LRO) to the rest of its high rise portfolio by the end of the second quarter of 2003. LRO enables ASN to more precisely forecast market demand and availability to optimize pricing for its apartments, thereby maximizing revenues.

ANNUAL FINANCIAL DATA:

FISCAL YEAR	TOT. INC. ($mill.)	NET INC. ($mill.)	TOT. ASSETS ($mill.)	NET INC. +DEPR./ ASSETS %	RET. ON EQUITY %	RET. ON ASSETS %	EARN. PER SH.$	TANG. BK. VAL.$	DIV. PER SH.$	DIV. PAYOUT %	PRICE RANGE	AVG. P/E RATIO	AVG. YIELD %
p12/31/02	1,082.3	⑤271.5					⑤1.35		1.70	125.9	29.19 - 21.31	18.7	6.7
12/31/01	728.9	②260.2	8,549.9	4.6	7.6	3.0	②1.81	19.64	1.64	90.6	27.85 - 23.00	14.0	6.5
12/31/00	723.2	①②262.3	5,109.5	7.9	11.6	5.1	①②1.78	15.99	1.54	86.5	26.56 - 19.25	12.9	6.7
12/31/99	666.9	①②229.4	5,302.4	6.8	8.9	4.3	①②1.47	16.33	1.48	100.7	23.50 - 18.94	14.4	7.0
12/31/98	513.6	①③199.5	5,059.9	5.8	7.6	3.9	①③1.49	16.44	1.39	93.8	24.50 - 17.88	14.2	6.6
12/31/97	355.7	①④72.9	2,805.7	4.5	4.7	2.6	①④0.65	14.04	1.63	250.0	25.13 - 21.00	35.5	7.0
12/31/96	326.2	①②131.6	2,282.4	7.7	10.4	5.8	①②1.47	13.27	1.24	84.3	23.63 - 19.00	14.5	5.8
12/31/95	264.9	①84.3	1,841.0	6.6	6.6	4.6	①0.93	13.03	1.15	123.6	20.50 - 16.38	19.8	6.2
12/31/94	186.1	46.7	1,295.8	5.5	5.6	3.6	0.66	12.10	1.00	151.5	21.75 - 15.50	28.2	5.4
12/31/93	78.4	①25.5	890.3	4.0	3.4	2.9	①0.66	11.76	0.82	124.2	21.63 - 14.00	27.0	4.6

Statistics are as originally reported. ① Incl. from disposition of investments: gain, 2001, $100.3 mill.; 2000, $93.1 mill.; 1999, $62.1 mill.; 1998, $65.5 mill.; 1997, $48.2 mill.; 1996, $37.5 mill.; 1995, $2.6 mill.; 1993, $2.3 mill. ② Bef. extraord. chrg. 2001, $2.3 mill.; 2000, $911,000; 1999, $1.1 mill.; 1996, $870,000. ③ Bef. extraord. chrg. of $1.5 mill.; Incls. one-time chrg. of $2.2 mill ④ Incls. one-time chrg. of $71.7 mill. ⑤ Bef. extraord. loss of $30.2 mill. & gain of $73.7 mill. from disc. ops. & incl. gain of $36.0 mill. from disp. of depr. real estate.

OFFICERS:
R. S. Sellers, Chmn., C.E.O.
C. E. Mueller, Sr. V.P., C.F.O.
J. L. Freeman, C.O.O.

INVESTOR CONTACT: Jack R. Callinson, Jr., Investor Relations, (800) 982-9293

PRINCIPAL OFFICE: 9200 E. Panorama Circle, Suite 400, Englewood, CO 80112

TELEPHONE NUMBER: (303) 708-5959
FAX: (303) 708-5999
WEB: www.archstonesmith.com

NO. OF EMPLOYEES: 3,450 (approx.)

SHAREHOLDERS: 3,342 (approx.)

ANNUAL MEETING: In May

INCORPORATED: MD, 1982

INSTITUTIONAL HOLDINGS:
No. of Institutions: 235
Shares Held: 144,204,378
% Held: 79.8

INDUSTRY: Real estate investment trusts (SIC: 6798)

TRANSFER AGENT(S): Mellon Investor Services, Ridgefield Park, NJ

ARROW ELECTRONICS, INC.

EXCH.	SYM.	REC. PRICE	P/E RATIO	YLD.	MKT. CAP.	RANGE (52-WK.)	'02 Y/E PR.
NYSE	ARW	14.38 (2/28/03)	102.7	...	$1.44 bill.	30.49 - 8.60	12.79

LOWER MEDIUM GRADE. ON 2/28/02, ARW ANNOUNCED THAT IT HAS COMPLETED ITS ACQUISITION OF PIONEER-STANDARD'S INDUSTRIAL ELECTRONICS DIVISION FOR $230.0 MILLION.

TRADING VOLUME Thousand Shares

*7 YEAR PRICE SCORE 77.1   ***12 MONTH PRICE SCORE 76.7**

*NYSE COMPOSITE INDEX=100

INTERIM EARNINGS (Per Share):

Qtr.	Mar.	June	Sept.	Dec.
1998	0.43	0.37	0.37	0.34
1999	0.30	0.16	0.38	0.46
2000	0.65	0.84	1.02	1.09
2001	0.68	0.07	d1.61	0.07
2002	0.03	0.01	0.01	0.09

INTERIM DIVIDENDS (Per Share):

Amt.	Decl.	Ex.	Rec.	Pay.
No dividends paid.				

CAPITALIZATION (12/31/01):

	($000)	(%)
Long-Term Debt	2,441,983	58.0
Common & Surplus	1,766,461	42.0
Total	4,208,444	100.0

BUSINESS:

Arrow Electronics, Inc. distributes electronic components and computer products. ARW serves more than 175,000 original equipment manufacturers, contract manufacturers and commercial customers in 40 countries. ARW's electronics distribution network encompasses over 200 selling locations supported by 23 primary distribution centers as of 2/20/03. Through its subsidiaries, ARW is the largest electronics distributor in Europe and the Asia/Pacific region. Through its network, Arrow offers a wide range of value-added services designed to help its customers reduce time to market, lower total cost of ownership, and enhance overall competitiveness.

RECENT DEVELOPMENTS:

For the year ended 12/31/02, income from continuing operations was $12.1 million, before an extraordinary loss of $12.9 million and accounting change charge of $603.7 million, compared with a loss from continuing operations of $75.6 million the previous year. Results for 2002 included a pre-tax severance charge of $5.4 million and excluded a loss of $5.9 million from discontinued operations. The

2001 results included pre-tax restructuring costs and other special charges of $77.1 million, a pre-tax integration charge of $9.4 million, a pre-tax loss on investments of $53.0 million, and excluded a gain of $1.8 million from discontinued operations. Sales declined 22.1% to $7.39 billion from $9.49 billion the year before. Operating income climbed 9.7% to $167.5 million.

PROSPECTS:

On 2/28/02, the Company announced that it has completed its previously-announced acquisition of Pioneer-Standard's Industrial Electronics Division (IED). The purchase price for IED, estimated to be approximately $230.0 million, is subject to adjustment based upon an audit of the assets and

liabilities being acquired. Meanwhile, in an attempt to reduce ARW's cost structure by at least $40.0 million per year, the Company recently has taken a series of additional steps to make its organizational structure, systems, and processes in North America more efficient.

ANNUAL FINANCIAL DATA:

FISCAL YEAR	TOT. REVS. ($mill.)	NET INC. ($mill.)	TOT. ASSETS ($mill.)	OPER. PROFIT %	NET PROFIT %	RET. ON EQUITY %	RET. ON ASSETS %	CURR. RATIO	EARN. PER SH. $	CASH FL. PER SH. $	TANG. BK. VAL. $	PRICE RANGE	AVG. P/E RATIO
p12/31/02	7,390.2	[5] 12.1							[5] 0.12			32.97 - 8.60	173.2
12/31/01	10,127.6	[4] d73.8	5,359.0	1.5	...	...	...	3.3	[4] d0.75	0.83	5.43	33.44 - 18.00	...
12/31/00	12,959.3	357.9	7,604.5	6.1	2.8	18.7	4.7	2.2	3.62	4.63	6.88	46.00 - 20.50	9.2
12/31/99	9,312.6	[3] 124.2	4,483.3	3.6	1.3	8.0	2.8	2.4	[3] 1.29	2.11	6.15	26.56 - 13.19	15.4
12/31/98	8,344.7	145.8	3,839.9	4.2	1.7	9.8	3.8	2.5	1.50	2.07	8.01	36.25 - 11.75	16.0
12/31/97	7,763.9	[1] 163.7	3,537.9	4.8	2.1	12.0	4.6	2.2	[1] 1.64	2.11	7.38	36.00 - 25.13	18.6
12/31/96	6,534.6	202.7	2,710.4	6.1	3.1	14.9	7.5	2.5	1.98	2.36	12.08	27.69 - 17.63	11.5
12/31/95	5,919.4	202.5	2,701.0	7.1	3.4	16.9	7.5	2.4	2.11	2.47	8.06	29.88 - 15.56	11.3
12/31/94	4,649.2	[2] 111.9	2,038.8	5.5	2.4	13.4	5.5	2.3	[2] 1.20	1.52	5.45	22.56 - 16.81	16.4
12/31/93	2,535.6	81.6	1,191.3	7.2	3.2	17.8	6.8	2.6	1.31	1.63	4.12	21.56 - 13.25	13.3

Statistics are as originally reported. Adj. for stk. splits: 2-for-1, 10/97 [1] Incl. realignment chrgs. of $59.6 mill [2] Incl. non-recurr. chrg. $45.4 mill. fr. integration of Gasts/FA Distributing Inc. [3] Incl. one-time chrg. of $24.6 mill. for the acq. and integration of the electronics distrib. group of Bell industries and Richey Electronics. [4] Incl. pre-tax restruct. and other rel chrgs. of $77.1 mill. & pre-tax integration chrg. of $9.4 mill. [5] Incl. pre-tax severance chrg. of $5.4 mill. & excl. extraord. loss of $12.9 mill., acctg. chng. chrg. of $603.7 mill. & loss of $5.9 mill. from disc. ops.

OFFICERS:
D. W. Duval, Chmn.
W. E. Mithell, Pres., C.E.O.
P. J. Reilly, V.P., C.F.O.
P. S. Brown, Sr. V.P., Gen. Couns.
INVESTOR CONTACT: Robert E. Klatell, Exec. V.P., (516) 391-1830
PRINCIPAL OFFICE: 25 Hub Drive, Melville, NY 11747

TELEPHONE NUMBER: (516) 391-1300
FAX: (516) 391-1640
WEB: www.arrow.com
NO. OF EMPLOYEES: 12,200
SHAREHOLDERS: 3,000 (Approx.)
ANNUAL MEETING: In May
INCORPORATED: NY, Nov., 1946

INSTITUTIONAL HOLDINGS:
No. of Institutions: 202
Shares Held: 93,198,881
% Held: 93.3
INDUSTRY: Electronic parts and equipment (SIC: 5065)
TRANSFER AGENT(S): Mellon Shareholder Services, Ridgefield Park, NJ

ARVINMERITOR, INC.

EXCH.	SYM.	REC. PRICE	P/E RATIO	YLD.	MKT. CAP.	RANGE (52-WK.)	'02 Y/E PR.
NYSE	ARM	15.28 (2/28/03)	6.1	2.6%	$1.04 bill.	32.50 - 14.39	16.67

MEDIUM GRADE. THE COMPANY ANNOUNCED IT WILL REDUCE ITS WORKFORCE BY 575 EMPLOYEES.

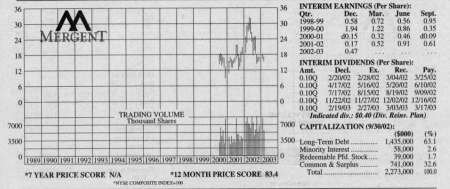

INTERIM EARNINGS (Per Share):

Qtr.	Dec.	Mar.	June	Sept.
1998-99	0.58	0.72	0.56	0.95
1999-00	1.94	1.22	0.86	0.35
2000-01	d0.15	0.32	0.46	d0.09
2001-02	0.17	0.52	0.91	0.61
2002-03	0.47	...	...	...

INTERIM DIVIDENDS (Per Share):

Amt.	Decl.	Ex.	Rec.	Pay.
0.10Q	2/20/02	2/28/02	3/04/02	3/25/02
0.10Q	4/17/02	5/16/02	5/20/02	6/10/02
0.10Q	7/17/02	8/15/02	8/19/02	9/09/02
0.10Q	11/22/02	11/27/02	12/02/02	12/16/02
0.10Q	2/19/03	2/27/03	3/03/03	3/17/03

Indicated div.: $0.40 (Div. Reinv. Plan)

CAPITALIZATION (9/30/02):

	($000)	(%)
Long-Term Debt	1,435,000	63.1
Minority Interest	58,000	2.6
Redeemable Pfd. Stock	39,000	1.7
Common & Surplus	741,000	32.6
Total	2,273,000	100.0

*7 YEAR PRICE SCORE N/A　　***12 MONTH PRICE SCORE 83.4**

*NYSE COMPOSITE INDEX=100

BUSINESS:

ArvinMeritor, Inc., formed through the acquisition of Arvin Industries, Inc. by Meritor Automotive, Inc. on 7/7/00, provides integrated automotive systems, modules and components to light vehicle, commercial truck, trailer and specialty original equipment manufacturers (OEMs) and aftermarket customers. ARM also offers coil coating services for the transportation, appliance, construction and furniture industries. The Light Vehicle Systems segment (52.8% of 2002 sales) supplies aperture, undercarriage, and exhaust systems for passenger cars, light trucks and sport utility vehicles to OEMs. The Commercial Vehicle Systems segment (33.7%) supplies drivetrain systems and components for commercial trucks. The Light Vehicle Aftermarket segment (12.2%) supplies exhaust, ride control and filter products and accessories to the light vehicle aftermarket. Other products represented 2.3% of sales.

RECENT DEVELOPMENTS:

For the first quarter ended 12/31/02, the Company reported net income of $32.0 million compared with income of $11.0 million, before an accounting change charge of $11.0 million, in the corresponding prior-year quarter. Results for 2001 included a restructuring charge of $15.0 million. Total sales increased 9.1% to $1.71 billion from $1.57 billion a year earlier. Light vehicle system sales rose 6.7% to $903.0 million, while commercial vehicle system sales jumped 19.4% to $572.0 million. Light vehicle aftermarket sales declined 1.5% to $197.0 million, while other sales were flat versus the year-earlier period at $37.0 million. Gross profit climbed 13.0% to $174.0 million.

PROSPECTS:

On 1/21/03, the Company announced it would reduce its global light vehicle systems (LVS) workforce by approximately 300 salaried employees. In addition, LVS will close its apertures facility in Gordonsville, Tennessee, affecting a further 275 hourly employees. Separately, ARM expects revenues for fiscal 2003 of $7.80 billion, up from previous guidance of $7.10 billion. The new outlook includes sales related to the recent acquisition of the remaining 51.0% interest in Zeuna Starker GmbH & Co. KG, a German exhaust subsidiary, as well as new business in the commercial vehicle system group. Earnings for 2003 are expected in the range of $2.50 to $2.70 per diluted share.

ANNUAL FINANCIAL DATA:

FISCAL YEAR	TOT. REVS. ($mill.)	NET INC. ($mill.)	TOT. ASSETS ($mill.)	OPER. PROFIT %	NET PROFIT %	RET. ON EQUITY %	RET. ON ASSETS %	CURR. RATIO	EARN. PER SH. $	CASH FL. PER SH. $	TANG. BK. VAL. $	DIV. PER SH. $	PRICE RANGE	AVG. P/E RATIO	AVG. YIELD %
9/30/02	6,882.0	⑤ 149.0	4,651.0	5.0	2.2	20.1	3.2	1.1	⑤ 2.22	5.13	...	0.40	32.50 - 14.39	10.6	1.7
9/30/01	6,805.0	④ 35.0	4,362.0	2.9	0.5	5.4	0.8	1.0	④ 0.53	3.81	...	0.64	21.87 - 11.00	31.0	3.9
9/30/00	5,153.0	③ 218.0	4,720.0	8.3	4.2	27.5	4.6	1.3	③ 4.12	7.18	0.54	0.44	18.63 - 8.88	3.3	3.2
② 9/30/99	4,450.0	① 194.0	2,796.0	8.0	4.4	55.7	6.9	1.2	① 3.75	6.27	...	...	...	...	...
9/30/98	3,836.0	147.0	...	7.8	3.8	...	...	...	2.84	4.51	...	...	...	...	...

Statistics are as originally reported. ① Incl. one-time chrg. 1999, $4.0 mill.; 1997, $29.0 mill.; 1996 $36.0 mill. ② Financials for 1999 and prior are for Meritor Automotive, Inc. ③ Incl. pre-tax restr. chrg. of $26.0 mill., merger exp. of $10.0 mill. and $89.0 mill. gain on the sale of assets. ④ Incl. restr. chrgs. of $84.0 mill. ⑤ Bef. acctg. change chrg. of $42.0 mill.; incl. restr. chrg. of $15.0 mill. and gain on sale of bussiness of $6.0 mill.

OFFICERS:
L. D. Yost, Chmn., C.E.O.
T. E. O'Rourke, Pres., C.O.O.
S. C. Soderstrom, Sr. V.P., C.F.O.
INVESTOR CONTACT: Beth Gurnack, V.P., Investor Relations, (248) 655-2159
PRINCIPAL OFFICE: 2135 West Maple Road, Troy, MI 48084-7186

TELEPHONE NUMBER: (248) 435-1000
FAX: (248) 435-1393
WEB: www.arvinmeritor.com
NO. OF EMPLOYEES: 32,000 (approx.)
SHAREHOLDERS: 34,091 (Record)
ANNUAL MEETING: In Feb.
INCORPORATED: IN, July, 2000

INSTITUTIONAL HOLDINGS:
No. of Institutions: 207
Shares Held: 39,554,608
% Held: 58.2
INDUSTRY: Motor vehicle parts and accessories (SIC: 3714)
TRANSFER AGENT(S): EquiServe, First Chicago Trust Division, Jersey City, NJ

ASHLAND, INC.

EXCH.	SYM.	REC. PRICE	P/E RATIO	YLD.	MKT. CAP.	RANGE (52-WK.)	'02 Y/E PR.
NYSE	ASH	27.81 (2/28/03)	20.8	4.0%	$1.89 bill.	46.47 - 23.60	28.53

MEDIUM GRADE. INCREASED CRUDE OIL PRICES AND HIGHER THAN USUAL PRECIPITATION NEGATIVELY AFFECTED THE OPERATING RESULTS OF THE COMPANY'S MAP AND APAC BUSINESS SEGMENTS.

TRADING VOLUME
Thousand Shares

*7 YEAR PRICE SCORE 86.8   ***12 MONTH PRICE SCORE 90.5**

*NYSE COMPOSITE INDEX=100

INTERIM EARNINGS (Per Share):

Qtr.	Dec.	Mar.	June	Sept.
1997-98	0.68	0.37	1.59	Nil
1998-99	d0.14	1.16	1.35	1.57
1999-00	0.55	0.35	1.83	1.38
2000-01	0.84	0.37	2.79	1.77
2001-02	0.54	d0.31	0.93	0.68
2002-03	0.04	...	...	...

INTERIM DIVIDENDS (Per Share):

Amt.	Decl.	Ex.	Rec.	Pay.
0.275Q	1/30/02	2/21/02	2/25/02	3/15/02
0.275Q	5/16/02	5/28/02	5/30/02	6/15/02
0.275Q	7/17/02	8/22/02	8/26/02	9/15/02
0.275Q	11/07/02	11/21/02	11/25/02	12/15/02
0.275Q	1/29/03	2/20/03	2/24/03	3/15/03

Indicated div.: $1.10 (Div. Reinv. Plan)

CAPITALIZATION (9/30/02):

	($000)	(%)
Long-Term Debt	1,606,000	39.8
Deferred Income Tax	256,000	6.3
Common & Surplus	2,173,000	53.9
Total	4,035,000	100.0

BUSINESS:

Ashland, Inc. is an energy company with operations in five industry segments. APAC (34.8% of 2002 sales and operating revenues) performs asphalt and concrete contract construction work. Ashland Distribution (33.2%) distributes industrial chemicals and solvents, plastics, composite materials and fine ingredients. Ashland Specialty Chemical (16.9%) manufactures composites, adhesives, and casting binder chemicals for use in the transportation and construction industries. Valvoline (15.1%) is a producer and marketer of motor oil and automotive chemicals, including appearance products, antifreeze, filters, rust preventives and coolants. Valvoline is also engaged in the "fast oil change" business through outlets operating under the Valvoline Instant Oil Change® name. Refining and marketing operations are conducted through 38%-owned Marathon Ashland Petroleum LLC (MAP), a joint venture formed on 1/1/98 with Marathon Oil Company. On 2/2/01, ASH sold its remaining ownership interest in Arch Coal.

RECENT DEVELOPMENTS:

For the quarter ended 12/31/02, income from continuing operations was $3.0 million versus $38.0 million the previous year. Earnings for 2002 included an after-tax charge of $95.0 million associated with estimated future asbestos liabilities less probable insurance recoveries. Earnings for 2001 included a non-recurring after-tax charge of $18.0 million. Operating results were hurt by a 67.6% drop in income from MAP due to higher crude oil prices and a heavy turnaround maintenance schedule. Results from APAC fell to break-even levels versus a profit of $36.0 million the prior year, due in part to higher than usual precipitation. Total revenue fell 2.0% to $1.85 billion.

PROSPECTS:

ASH's goals for fiscal 2003 include identifying and divesting assets that cannot achieve desired market strength and returns; reducing debt over time to a target of 35.0% of total capital; reducing general and administrative expenses by $25.0 million a year; improve returns from Ashland Distribution or seek strategic alternatives for the business; and achieving a 10.0% after-tax return from APAC in fiscal 2004.

ANNUAL FINANCIAL DATA:

FISCAL YEAR	TOT. REVS. ($mill.)	NET INC. ($mill.)	TOT. ASSETS ($mill.)	OPER. PROFIT %	NET PROFIT %	RET. ON EQUITY %	RET. ON ASSETS %	CURR. RATIO	EARN. PER SH.$	CASH FL. PER SH.$	TANG. BK. VAL.$	DIV. PER SH.$	PRICE RANGE	AVG. P/E RATIO	AVG. YIELD %
9/30/02	7,792.0	⑤ 129.0	6,725.0	4.3	1.7	5.9	1.9	1.3	⑤ 1.83	4.99	24.29	1.10	46.98 - 23.60	19.3	3.1
9/30/01	8,547.0	④ 406.0	6,945.0	10.0	4.8	18.2	5.8	1.5	④ 5.77	9.37	24.61	1.10	46.54 - 34.39	7.0	2.7
9/30/00	8,436.0	③ 292.0	6,771.0	8.0	3.5	14.9	4.3	1.3	③ 4.10	7.45	20.40	1.10	37.19 - 28.63	8.0	3.3
9/30/99	7,251.0	290.0	6,424.0	8.6	4.0	13.2	4.5	1.5	3.89	6.91	27.50	1.10	50.63 - 30.31	10.4	2.7
9/30/98	② 6,933.0	203.0	6,082.0	6.4	2.9	9.5	3.3	1.3	2.63	4.99	25.39	1.10	57.94 - 42.25	19.0	2.2
9/30/97	14,319.0	① 192.0	7,777.0	3.4	1.3	9.5	2.5	1.3	① 3.80	10.63	25.39	1.10	55.00 - 39.25	12.4	2.3
9/30/96	12,968.0	136.0	7,089.0	2.8	1.0	8.9	1.9	1.2	2.97	7.51	21.89	1.10	48.88 - 34.25	14.0	2.6
9/30/95	12,239.0	24.0	6,992.0	1.6	0.2	1.8	0.3	1.2	0.08	7.94	19.61	1.10	38.38 - 30.38	429.2	3.2
9/30/94	10,382.0	197.0	5,815.0	3.5	1.9	15.1	3.4	1.3	2.94	7.97	20.03	1.02	44.50 - 31.25	12.9	2.7
9/30/93	10,256.3	142.2	5,551.8	2.9	1.4	12.2	2.6	1.2	2.26	7.56	18.28	1.00	35.63 - 24.25	13.2	3.3

Statistics are as originally reported. ① Bef. cr. of $96.0 mill. fr. disc. ops. & extraord. chrg. of $9.0 mill. ② Refl. formation of Marathon Ashland Petroleum LLC (MAP). ASH accounts for its invest. in MAP using the equity method of acctg. ③ Bef. disc. oper. loss of $215.0 mill. ($3.03/sh.), costs of spin-off of disc. oper. of $3.0 mill. ($0.04/sh.) & extraord. loss of $4.0 mill. ($0.05/sh.) ④ Bef. disc. oper. inc. of $19.0 mill. ($0.26/sh.), extraord. loss of $3.0 mill. ($0.04/sh.) & acctg. chge. chrg. of $5.0 mill. ($0.06/sh.) ⑤ Bef. acctg. chrg. of $12.0 mill.

OFFICERS:
J. J. O'Brien, Chmn., C.E.O.
J. M. Quin, Sr. V.P., C.F.O.
D. L. Porter, Treas.

INVESTOR CONTACT: William E. Henderson, III, Dir., Inv. Rel., (859) 815-4454

PRINCIPAL OFFICE: 50 E. RiverCenter Blvd., P.O. Box 391, Covington, KY 41012

TELEPHONE NUMBER: (859) 815-3333
FAX: (859) 815-5188
WEB: www.ashland.com

NO. OF EMPLOYEES: 24,300 (approx.)

SHAREHOLDERS: 17,700 (record)

ANNUAL MEETING: In Jan.

INCORPORATED: KY, Oct., 1936

INSTITUTIONAL HOLDINGS:
No. of Institutions: 229
Shares Held: 44,889,828
% Held: 65.8

INDUSTRY: Petroleum refining (SIC: 2911)

TRANSFER AGENT(S): National City Bank, Cleveland, OH

AT&T CORP.

EXCH.	SYM.	REC. PRICE	P/E RATIO	YLD.	MKT. CAP.	RANGE (52-WK.)	'02 Y/E PR.
NYSE	T	18.54 (2/28/03)	14.7	4.0%	$13.14 bill.	82.40 - 17.06	26.11

LOWER MEDIUM GRADE. THE COMPANY ANTICIPATES TOTAL TELECOM INDUSTRY SPENDING WILL DECREASE IN 2003.

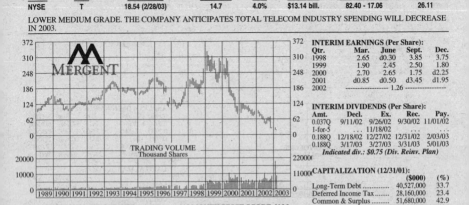

INTERIM EARNINGS (Per Share):

Qtr.	Mar.	June	Sept.	Dec.
1998	2.65	d0.30	3.85	3.75
1999	1.90	2.45	2.50	1.80
2000	2.70	2.65	1.75	d2.25
2001	d0.85	d0.50	d3.45	d1.95
2002	---------------- 1.26 ----------------			

INTERIM DIVIDENDS (Per Share):

Amt.	Decl.	Ex.	Rec.	Pay.
0.037Q	9/11/02	9/26/02	9/30/02	11/01/02
1-for-5	...	11/18/02		
0.188Q	12/18/02	12/27/02	12/31/02	2/03/03
0.188Q	3/17/03	3/27/03	3/31/03	5/01/03

Indicated div.: $0.75 (Div. Reinv. Plan)

CAPITALIZATION (12/31/01):

	($000)	(%)
Long-Term Debt	40,527,000	33.7
Deferred Income Tax	28,160,000	23.4
Common & Surplus	51,680,000	42.9
Total	120,367,000	100.0

TRADING VOLUME
Thousand Shares

1989 1990 1991 1992 1993 1994 1995 1996 1997 1998 1999 2000 2001 2002 2003

*7 YEAR PRICE SCORE N.M.   *12 MONTH PRICE SCORE N.M.
*NYSE COMPOSITE INDEX=100

BUSINESS:

AT&T Corp. provides voice, data and video communications services and products, serving more than 80.0 million customers including consumers, large and small businesses, and government entities (AT&T Business Services). AT&T and its subsidiaries furnish domestic long distance, international long distance, regional, local services and cable television, and provide billing, directory and calling card services to support its communications operations. Also,

AT&T is a supplier of data and Internet services for businesses and is a direct Internet service provider to consumers in the U.S. On 3/9/99, AT&T acquired Tele-Communications, Inc. On 6/15/00, AT&T acquired MediaOne Group in a transaction valued at about $44.00 billion. In July 2001, AT&T completed its spin-off of AT&T Wireless. On 11/18/02, AT&T completed its spin-off of AT&T Broadband.

RECENT DEVELOPMENTS:

For the year ended 12/31/02, AT&T Group, which excludes the results of Liberty Media Group that was tracked as a separate class of stock through the 8/20/01 split-off date, posted income from continuing operations of $963.0 million versus income from continuing operations of $71.0 million in 2001. Results for 2002 and 2001 included net restructuring and other charges of $1.44 billion and $1.04 billion, respectively. Revenues fell 10.4% to $37.83 billion, reflecting continued declines in long distance voice services.

PROSPECTS:

T has stated that it does not yet see a significant turnaround in the overall business services industry, and, as a result, anticipates total telecom industry spending will decrease in 2003. T expects AT&T Business, which posted a 4.1% drop in revenue in 2002, to experience a slower rate of revenue decline for 2003. AT&T Consumer, which posted a revenue decline of 22.3% in 2002, is expected to see a slightly higher revenue decline rate for 2003.

ANNUAL FINANCIAL DATA:

FISCAL YEAR	TOT. REVS. ($mill.)	NET INC. ($mill.)	TOT. ASSETS ($mill.)	OPER. PROFIT %	NET PROFIT %	RET. ON EQUITY %	RET. ON ASSETS %	CURR. RATIO	EARN. PER SH.$	CASH FL. PER SH.$	TANG. BK. VAL.$	DIV. PER SH.$	PRICE RANGE	AVG. P/E RATIO	AVG. YIELD %
p12/31/02	37,827.0	⑨ 963.0			...	...	...		⑧⑨ 1.26			0.75	95.55 - 16.81	44.6	1.3
12/31/01	52,550.0	⑧ d6,842.0	165,282.0	7.1	...	...	...	0.9	⑧⑧ d6.65	...	38.12	0.75	125.75 - 73.75	...	0.8
12/31/00	65,981.0	⑦ 4,669.0	242,223.0	6.5	7.1	4.5	1.9	0.3	⑥⑦ 4.40	21.07	77.25	4.40	304.07 - 82.50	43.9	2.3
12/31/99	62,391.0	③ 3,428.0	169,406.0	17.4	5.5	4.3	2.0	0.5	⑤⑥ 8.70	17.24	98.46	4.40	333.35 - 207.50	31.1	1.6
12/31/98	53,223.0	④ 5,235.0	59,550.0	14.1	9.8	20.5	8.8	0.9	⑨ 9.70	18.27	33.40	4.40	263.35 - 161.26	21.9	2.1
12/31/97	51,319.0	② 4,472.0	58,635.0	13.6	8.7	19.7	7.6	1.0	⑨ 9.13	16.97	29.39	4.40	213.34 - 102.51	17.3	2.8
12/31/96	52,184.0	① 5,608.0	55,552.0	16.9	10.7	27.6	10.1	1.1	② 11.57	17.22	25.11	4.40	229.59 - 110.84	14.7	2.6
12/31/95	79,609.0	③ 139.0	88,884.0	1.5	0.2	0.8	0.2	1.0	③ 0.30	10.44	19.25	4.40	228.34 - 158.76	645.0	2.3
12/31/94	75,094.0	④ 4,710.0	79,262.0	10.7	6.3	26.3	5.9	1.2	③ 10.03	18.65	29.04	4.40	190.43 - 157.51	17.3	2.5
12/31/93	67,156.0	④ 3,974.0	60,766.0	9.3	5.9	28.7	6.5	1.2	④ 9.80	18.72	34.14	4.40	216.68 - 167.09	19.6	2.3

Statistics are as originally reported. Adj. for stk. splits: 1-for-5, 11/18/02; 3-for-2 stk., 4/15/99 ① Incl. non-recur. pre-tax chrg. of $2.51 bil.; bef. disc. ops. gain of $1.29 bill. & extraord. chrg. of $137.0 mil. ② Bef. disc. ops. cr. 12/31/97: $166.0 mil.; cr. 12/31/96: $300.0 mil. ③ Incl. non-recur. chrg. 12/31/95: $7.85 bil.; 12/31/94: $169.0 mil. ④ Bef. acctg. adj. of $7.77 bil.; incl. cr. of $217.0 mil. & restr. chrg. of $498.0 mil. ⑤ Incl. non-recur. chrg. of $1.51 bil. ⑥ Refl. AT&T Common Stock Group, which excl. results of Liberty Media Group. ⑦ Incl. net restr. & oth. chrgs. of $7.03 bil. ⑧ Incl. net restr. & oth. chrgs. of $2.53 bil., net equity losses fr. Liberty Media Group of $2.71 bil. & oth. equity invest. net losses of $4.85 bil.; bef. inc. fr. disc. ops. of $150.0 mil., disc. ops disp. gain of $13.50 bil. & acctg. chg. cr. of $904.0 mil. ⑨ Incl. net restr. & oth. chrgs. of $1.44 bil.; bef. loss fr. disc. ops. of $14.51 bil., disc. ops disp. gain of $1.32 bil. & acctg. chg. chrg. of $856.0 mil.

OFFICERS:
D. W. Dorman, Chmn., C.E.O.
B. J. Bernard, Pres.
T. W. Horton, Sr. Exec. V.P., C.F.O.
INVESTOR CONTACT: Investor Relations, (908) 221-3655
PRINCIPAL OFFICE: 32 Avenue of Americas, New York, NY 10013-2412

TELEPHONE NUMBER: (212) 387-5400
FAX: (908) 221-2528
WEB: www.att.com
NO. OF EMPLOYEES: 117,800 (approx.)
SHAREHOLDERS: 4,500,000 (approx.)
ANNUAL MEETING: In May
INCORPORATED: NY, Mar., 1885

INSTITUTIONAL HOLDINGS:
No. of Institutions: 584
Shares Held: 502,163,295
% Held: 65.2
INDUSTRY: Telephone communications, exc. radio (SIC: 4813)
TRANSFER AGENT(S): BankBoston, NA, Boston, MA

ATMOS ENERGY CORPORATION

EXCH.	SYM.	REC. PRICE	P/E RATIO	YLD.	MKT. CAP.	RANGE (52-WK.)	'02 Y/E PR.	DIV. ACH.
NYSE	ATO	21.28 (2/28/03)	13.7	5.6%	$0.87 bill.	24.55 - 17.56	23.32	15 yrs.

MEDIUM GRADE. THE COMPANY RECENTLY ACQUIRED MISSISSIPPI VALLEY GAS COMPANY.

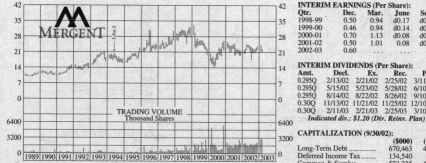

*7 YEAR PRICE SCORE 99.7   ***12 MONTH PRICE SCORE 109.1**

*NYSE COMPOSITE INDEX=100

INTERIM EARNINGS (Per Share):

Qtr.	Dec.	Mar.	June	Sept.
1998-99	0.50	0.94	d0.17	d0.68
1999-00	0.46	0.94	d0.14	d0.11
2000-01	0.70	1.13	d0.08	d0.19
2001-02	0.50	1.01	0.08	d0.14
2002-03	0.60	...	...	...

INTERIM DIVIDENDS (Per Share):

Amt.	Decl.	Ex.	Rec.	Pay.
0.295Q	2/13/02	2/21/02	2/25/02	3/11/02
0.295Q	5/15/02	5/23/02	5/28/02	6/10/02
0.295Q	8/14/02	8/22/02	8/26/02	9/10/02
0.30Q	11/13/02	11/21/02	11/25/02	12/10/02
0.30Q	2/11/03	2/21/03	2/25/03	3/10/03

Indicated div.: $1.20 (Div. Reinv. Plan)

CAPITALIZATION (9/30/02):

	($000)	(%)
Long-Term Debt	670,463	48.6
Deferred Income Tax	134,540	9.8
Common & Surplus	573,235	41.6
Total	1,378,238	100.0

BUSINESS:

Atmos Energy Corporation is primarily engaged in the natural gas utility business (97.4% of revenues in fiscal 2002) as well as certain non-regulated businesses (2.6%). The Company distributes natural gas through sales and transportation arrangements to approximately 1.7 million residential, commercial public authority and industrial customers through its regulated utility operations in twelve states. In addition, ATO transports natural gas for others through its distribution system. ATO's non-regulated businesses provide natural gas storage services and own an interest in storage fields in Kansas, Kentucky and Louisiana. The Company also provides energy management and gas marketing services and electrical power generation as well as markets gas to wholesale customers in Texas and Louisiana. ATO also holds an indirect equity interest in Heritage Propane Partners, L.P.

RECENT DEVELOPMENTS:

For the first quarter ended 12/31/02, net income advanced 25.0% to $25.8 million compared with $20.6 million in the corresponding prior-year quarter. Earnings benefited from more normal weather conditions, which were 16.0% colder than the first quarter of fiscal 2002. Operating revenues jumped 48.0% to $401.5 million from $271.3 million a year earlier. Gross profit increased 21.2% to $132.6 million from $109.4 million the year before. Gas trading margin fell 36.1% to $4.6 million from $7.2 million in 2001. Total throughput amounted to 71.2 billion cubic feet (Bcf) versus 57.0 Bcf in the same period a year ago. Operating income rose 21.1% to $52.6 million versus $43.4 million in the previous year.

PROSPECTS:

On 12/3/02, the Company acquired Mississippi Valley Gas Company, a natural gas utility, for total consideration of approximately $195.0 million, including the assumption of long-term debt. ATO expects the acquired operations to be slightly accretive to fiscal 2003 earnings. Looking ahead, the Company anticipates 2003 earnings to be in the range of $1.52 to $1.58 per diluted share. Earnings for the second quarter of fiscal 2003 are expected to be between $1.00 and $1.10 per diluted share, including a non-cash charge related to a change in accounting principle.

ANNUAL FINANCIAL DATA:

FISCAL YEAR	TOT. REVS. ($000)	NET INC. ($000)	TOT. ASSETS ($000)	OPER. PROFIT %	NET PROFIT %	NET INC./ NET PROP. %	NET INC./ TOT. CAP. %	RET. ON EQUITY %	ACCUM. DEPR./ GROSS PROP. %	EARN. PER SH.$	TANG. BK. VAL.$	DIV. PER SH.$	DIV. PAYOUT %	PRICE RANGE	AVG. P/E RATIO	AVG. YIELD %
9/30/02	950,849	59,656	1,980,221	16.3	6.3	4.6	4.3	10.4	38.9	1.45	9.19	1.19	81.7	24.55 - 17.56	14.5	5.6
9/30/01	1,442,275	56,090	2,036,180	9.0	3.9	4.2	4.0	9.6	36.7	1.47	12.43	1.17	79.2	25.75 - 19.45	15.4	5.2
9/30/00	850,152	35,918	1,348,758	10.0	4.2	3.7	4.0	9.2	37.8	1.14	12.28	1.15	100.4	26.25 - 14.25	17.8	5.7
9/30/99	690,196	17,744	1,230,537	7.9	2.6	1.8	2.0	4.7	37.7	0.58	12.09	1.11	191.3	33.00 - 19.63	45.4	4.2
9/30/98	848,208	55,265	1,141,390	13.3	6.5	6.0	6.5	14.9	36.5	1.84	12.21	1.07	58.1	32.25 - 24.75	15.5	3.8
③9/30/97	906,835	②23,838	1,088,311	7.3	2.6	2.8	3.3	7.3	36.3	②0.81	11.04	1.02	125.9	30.50 - 22.13	32.5	3.9
9/30/96	483,744	23,949	501,861	10.8	5.0	5.8	7.2	13.9	37.9	1.51	10.75	0.97	64.2	31.00 - 20.88	17.2	3.7
9/30/95	435,820	18,873	445,783	9.6	4.3	5.2	5.8	11.9	39.0	1.22	10.20	0.93	76.2	23.00 - 16.13	16.0	4.8
①9/30/94	499,808	14,679	416,678	6.9	2.9	4.5	4.6	9.8	39.8	0.97	9.78	0.89	91.7	20.25 - 15.88	18.6	4.9
9/30/93	388,495	15,712	323,694	9.1	4.0	6.5	6.8	13.3	39.8	0.97	6.93	0.86	89.1	21.17 - 15.17	18.8	4.7

Statistics are as originally reported. Adjusted for 3-for-2 stock split, 5/94. ① Incl. results of Greeley Gas Co. ② Incl. a non-recurr. after-tax chg. of $2.8 mill. related to mgmt. changes & an after-tax charge of $12.6 mill. for merger & integration exps. ③ Incl. results of United Cities Gas Company

OFFICERS:
R. W. Best, Chmn., Pres., C.E.O.
J. P. Reddy, Sr. V.P., C.F.O.
L. P. Gregory, Sr. V.P., Gen. Couns.
INVESTOR CONTACT: Susan Kappes, (972) 855-3729
PRINCIPAL OFFICE: 3 Lincoln Centre, Ste. 1800, 5430 LBJ Freeway, Dallas, TX 75240

TELEPHONE NUMBER: (972) 934-9227
FAX: (972) 855-3040
WEB: www.atmosenergy.com
NO. OF EMPLOYEES: 2,338
SHAREHOLDERS: 28,829 (record)
ANNUAL MEETING: In Feb.
INCORPORATED: TX, Oct., 1983

INSTITUTIONAL HOLDINGS:
No. of Institutions: 125
Shares Held: 17,356,584
% Held: 41.6
INDUSTRY: Natural gas transmission (SIC: 4922)
TRANSFER AGENT(S): EquiServe Trust Company, N.A., Providence, RI

ATWOOD OCEANICS, INC.

EXCH.	SYM.	REC. PRICE	P/E RATIO	YLD.	MKT. CAP.	RANGE (52-WK.)	'02 Y/E PR.
NYSE	ATW	25.24 (3/31/03)	16.7	...	$349.4 mill.	50.32 - 24.39	30.10

UPPER MEDIUM GRADE. DELIVERY OF THE COMPANY'S NEW $125.0 MILLION ULTRA-PREMIUM JACK-UP, THE ATWOOD BEACON, IS EXPECTED AROUND JUNE 2003.

*7 YEAR PRICE SCORE 99.7   *12 MONTH PRICE SCORE 88.9
*NYSE COMPOSITE INDEX=100

INTERIM EARNINGS (Per Share):

Qtr.	Dec.	Mar.	June	Sept.
1996-97	0.29	0.23	0.27	0.37
1997-98	0.63	0.84	0.72	0.65
1998-99	0.49	0.64	0.53	0.35
1999-00	0.36	0.43	0.37	0.49
2000-01	0.58	0.43	0.39	0.56
2001-02	0.59	0.49	0.44	0.51
2002-03	0.07	...	...	...

INTERIM DIVIDENDS (Per Share):

Amt.	Decl.	Ex.	Rec.	Pay.
		No dividends paid.		

CAPITALIZATION (9/30/02):

	($000)	(%)
Long-Term Debt	115,000	28.3
Deferred Income Tax	15,545	3.8
Common & Surplus	276,133	67.9
Total	406,678	100.0

BUSINESS:

Atwood Oceanics, Inc., together with its wholly-owned subsidiaries, is engaged in the international offshore drilling of exploratory and developmental oil and gas wells in offshore areas and related support, management and consulting services. As of 9/30/02, ATW's fleet included seven active, wholly-owned drilling units, which include two semisubmersibles capable of drilling in up to 5,000 feet of water, one semisubmersible capable of drilling in up to 3,500 feet of water, one semisubmersible capable of drilling in up to 2,000 feet of water, one 300 feet cantilever jack-up, one semisubmersible self-erecting tender-assist rig and one submersible unit. In addition to the owned rigs, ATW manages the operations of two operator-owned platform rigs offshore northwest Australia.

RECENT DEVELOPMENTS:

For the quarter ended 12/31/02, net income declined to $950,000 versus $8.2 million in the same period a year earlier. The drop in net income was primarily due to lower contract drilling revenues, coupled with a 19.3% increase in contract drilling expenses. Total revenues fell 19.9% to $29.8 million. Also, in January 2003, ATW announced that its RICHMOND rig has been awarded a contract by Ocean Energy, Inc. to drill three firm wells plus options for four additional wells. This drilling program will start immediately following completion of the rig's current contract, which is estimated to be mid-February 2003. The three firm wells have an estimated duration of 90 to 120 days.

PROSPECTS:

ATW's near-term outlook is tempered by softness in certain semi-submersible markets. Additionally, the Company noted that the ATWOOD HUNTER's current drilling program in Egypt is expected to be completed in early to mid-February 2003. Contract opportunities for ongoing work are being pursued in the Mediterranean area; however, it is possible that the rig could be idle for the balance of the fiscal 2003 second quarter. ATW's longer-term outlook appears brighter. The Company stands to benefit from the construction of its new $125.0 million ultra-premium jack-up, the ATWOOD BEACON, which is moving ahead in Singapore and currently within budget. Delivery of the rig is expected around June 2003. Several work opportunities for the ATWOOD BEACON are currently being pursued.

ANNUAL FINANCIAL DATA:

FISCAL YEAR	TOT. REVS. ($000)	NET INC. ($000)	TOT. ASSETS ($000)	OPER. PROFIT %	NET PROFIT %	RET. ON EQUITY %	RET. ON ASSETS %	CURR. RATIO	EARN. PER SH. $	CASH FL. PER SH. $	TANG. BK. VAL. $	PRICE RANGE	AVG. P/E RATIO
9/30/02	149,157	28,285	444,530	26.9	19.0	10.2	6.4	2.9	2.02	3.76	19.94	50.32 - 24.39	18.5
9/30/01	147,541	27,346	353,878	28.9	18.5	11.0	7.7	2.2	1.96	3.79	17.91	49.90 - 23.76	18.8
9/30/00	134,514	23,148	313,251	27.6	17.2	10.6	7.4	3.7	1.66	3.82	15.79	69.88 - 30.20	30.1
9/30/99	150,009	27,720	293,604	32.2	18.5	14.4	9.4	2.7	2.01	3.78	14.06	38.81 - 16.13	13.7
9/30/98	151,809	39,364	281,737	40.6	25.9	24.0	14.0	1.9	2.84	4.13	12.02	61.38 - 15.06	13.5
9/30/97	89,082	15,619	215,330	27.2	17.5	12.7	7.3	2.4	1.16	1.94	9.06	61.63 - 25.38	37.5
9/30/96	79,455	11,368	159,309	16.4	14.3	10.8	7.1	2.5	0.86	1.63	7.89	32.75 - 12.25	26.3
9/30/95	72,231	7,060	152,853	8.0	9.8	7.4	4.6	1.7	0.54	1.41	7.16	13.50 - 5.19	17.3
9/30/94	68,794	6,209	153,460	9.5	9.0	7.2	4.0	2.9	0.47	1.55	6.53	7.44 - 5.50	13.8
9/30/93	54,245	d1,791	149,853	...	...	...	...	2.2	d0.13	0.85	6.06	6.00 - 4.38	...

Statistics are as originally reported. Adj. for 2-for-1 stk. split, 11/97.

OFFICERS:
J. R. Irwin, Pres., C.E.O.
J. M. Holland, Sr. V.P., Sec.
G. P. Kelley, V.P.
INVESTOR CONTACT: James M. Holland, Sr. V.P., Sec., (281) 749-7804
PRINCIPAL OFFICE: 15835 Park Ten Place Drive, Houston, TX 77084

TELEPHONE NUMBER: (281) 749-7800
FAX: (281) 749-7940
WEB: www.atwd.com
NO. OF EMPLOYEES: 800 (approx.)
SHAREHOLDERS: 750 (approx. beneficial)
ANNUAL MEETING: In Feb.
INCORPORATED: TX, Oct., 1968

INSTITUTIONAL HOLDINGS:
No. of Institutions: 109
Shares Held: 11,225,209
% Held: 81.1
INDUSTRY: Drilling oil and gas wells (SIC: 1381)
TRANSFER AGENT(S): Continental Stock Transfer & Trust Company, New York, NY

AUTOLIV, INC.

EXCH.	SYM.	REC. PRICE	P/E RATIO	YLD.	MKT. CAP.	RANGE (52-WK.)	'02 Y/E PR.
NYSE	ALV	20.70 (2/28/03)	11.3	2.5%	$2.03 bill.	25.90 - 16.75	20.93

MEDIUM GRADE. THE COMPANY HAS DECIDED TO CONSOLIDATE ITS NORTH AMERICAN MANUFACTURING BASE.

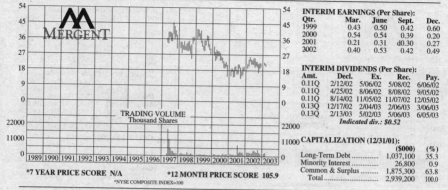

INTERIM EARNINGS (Per Share):

Qtr.	Mar.	June	Sept.	Dec.
1999	0.43	0.50	0.42	0.60
2000	0.54	0.54	0.39	0.20
2001	0.21	0.31	d0.30	0.27
2002	0.40	0.53	0.42	0.49

INTERIM DIVIDENDS (Per Share):

Amt.	Decl.	Ex.	Rec.	Pay.
0.11Q	2/12/02	5/06/02	5/08/02	6/06/02
0.11Q	4/25/02	8/06/02	8/08/02	9/05/02
0.11Q	8/14/02	11/05/02	11/07/02	12/05/02
0.13Q	12/17/02	2/04/03	2/06/03	3/06/03
0.13Q	2/13/03	5/02/03	5/06/03	6/05/03

Indicated div.: $0.52

CAPITALIZATION (12/31/01):

	($000)	(%)
Long-Term Debt	1,037,100	35.3
Minority Interest	26,800	0.9
Common & Surplus	1,875,300	63.8
Total	2,939,200	100.0

*7 YEAR PRICE SCORE N/A ***12 MONTH PRICE SCORE 105.9**
*NYSE COMPOSITE INDEX=100

BUSINESS:

Autoliv, Inc. develops and manufactures automotive safety systems for all major automobile manufacturers in the world through its two principal operating subsidiaries. Autoliv AB, Inc. is a Swedish-based company that develops and manufactures seat belt pretensioners, frontal airbags, side-impact airbags, steering wheels and seat subsystems. Autoliv ASP, Inc. develops and manufactures seat belts, steering wheels, airbag modules, inflators and cushions. ALV's 2002 net sales were derived 71.1% from airbags and associated products and 28.9% from seat belts and associated products. As of 1/8/03, ALV, along with its joint ventures, operated close to 80 facilities in more than 30 countries.

RECENT DEVELOPMENTS:

For the year ended 12/31/02, the Company reported net income of $180.5 million compared with $47.9 million in the previous year. Results for 2002 and 2001 included amortization of intangibles of $19.4 million and $73.3 million, respectively. Results for 2001 also included a pre-tax non-recurring charge of $65.0 million. Net sales increased 11.3% to $4.44 billion from $3.99 billion a year earlier. Airbag product sales advanced 12.2% to $3.16 billion, while seat belt product sales rose 9.3% to $1.28 billion. Gross profit jumped 23.8% to $810.8 million from $654.8 million the year before. Operating income surged 90.4% to $330.8 million from $173.7 million in 2001.

PROSPECTS:

The Company has decided to consolidate its North American manufacturing base by shifting production from operations in Indianapolis, Indiana and Denver, Colorado, which together employ 800 people, to plants in Kentucky, Utah and Mexico. The consolidation is expected to result in savings of $5.0 million in 2003 and over $20.0 million annually starting in 2004. Meanwhile, the Company recently opened a new seat belt plant in Poland, that is expected to add nearly 5.0% to ALV's European seat belt capacity. Looking ahead, the Company expects sales and earnings for the first quarter of 2003 to increase by at least 15.0% year over year.

ANNUAL FINANCIAL DATA:

FISCAL YEAR	TOT. REVS. ($mill.)	NET INC. ($mill.)	TOT. ASSETS ($mill.)	OPER. PROFIT %	NET PROFIT %	RET. ON EQUITY %	RET. ON ASSETS %	CURR. RATIO	EARN. PER SH. $	CASH FL. PER SH. $	TANG. BK. VAL. $	DIV. PER SH. $	PRICE RANGE	AVG. P/E RATIO	AVG. YIELD %
p12/31/02	4,443.4	180.5							1.84			0.44	25.90 - 16.75	11.6	2.1
12/31/01	3,991.0	② 47.9	4,004.3	4.4	1.2	2.6	1.2	1.5	② 0.49	3.59	1.94	0.44	21.63 - 13.25	35.6	2.5
12/31/00	4,116.1	168.7	4,067.8	8.2	4.1	8.8	4.1	1.1	1.67	4.34	1.75	0.44	31.81 - 14.50	13.9	1.9
12/31/99	3,812.2	199.9	3,646.5	9.7	5.2	10.4	5.5	1.1	1.95	4.43	3.28	0.44	41.88 - 27.25	17.7	1.3
12/31/98	3,488.7	188.3	3,668.1	10.1	5.4	10.2	5.1	1.1	1.84	4.07	1.92	0.44	37.25 - 24.44	16.8	1.4
12/31/97	2,739.6	① d579.6	3,430.5	...	...	...	...	1.0	① d6.70	d4.82	0.09	0.22	45.50 - 30.50	...	0.6

Statistics are as originally reported. ① Incl. chrg. of $732.3 mill. fr. write-off of acqd. R&D. ② Incl. an after-tax restr. chrg. of $46.8 mill.

OFFICERS:
S. J. Stewart, Chmn.
L. Westerberg, Pres., C.E.O.
M. Lindquist, V.P., C.F.O.

INVESTOR CONTACT: Patrick Jarboe, Dir., Investor Relations, (248) 475-0407

PRINCIPAL OFFICE: 3350 Airport Road, Ogden, UT 84405

TELEPHONE NUMBER: (801) 625-9200
FAX: (801) 625-4911
WEB: www.autoliv.com

NO. OF EMPLOYEES: 30,100

SHAREHOLDERS: 60,000 (approx.)

ANNUAL MEETING: In April

INCORPORATED: DE, 1996

INSTITUTIONAL HOLDINGS:
No. of Institutions: 127
Shares Held: 29,799,760
% Held: 30.4

INDUSTRY: Motor vehicle parts and accessories (SIC: 3714)

TRANSFER AGENT(S): EquiServe Trust Company, N.A., Jersey City, NJ

AUTOMATIC DATA PROCESSING, INC.

EXCH.	SYM.	REC. PRICE	P/E RATIO	YLD.	MKT. CAP.	RANGE (52-WK.)	'02 Y/E PR.	DIV. ACH.
NYSE	ADP	32.50 (2/28/03)	18.2	1.5%	$20.03 bill.	58.85 - 31.15	39.25	27 yrs.

INVESTMENT GRADE. THE COMPANY AGREED TO ACQUIRE PROBUSINESS SERVICES, INC. FOR APPROXIMATELY $500.0 MILLION IN CASH.

7 YEAR PRICE SCORE 114.4   **12 MONTH PRICE SCORE 89.8**
*NYSE COMPOSITE INDEX=100

INTERIM EARNINGS (Per Share):

Qtr.	Sept.	Dec.	Mar.	June
1997-98	0.18	0.25	0.31	0.26
1998-99	0.20	0.27	0.36	0.30
1999-00	0.23	0.31	0.42	0.35
2000-01	0.27	0.32	0.45	0.40
2001-02	0.31	0.42	0.56	0.46
2002-03	0.34	0.43	...	...

INTERIM DIVIDENDS (Per Share):

Amt.	Decl.	Ex.	Rec.	Pay.
0.115Q	1/16/02	3/13/02	3/15/02	4/01/02
0.115Q	5/14/02	6/12/02	6/14/02	7/01/02
0.115Q	8/12/02	9/11/02	9/13/02	10/01/02
0.12Q	11/12/02	12/11/02	12/13/02	1/01/03
0.12Q	1/28/03	3/12/03	3/14/03	4/01/03

Indicated div.: $0.48 (Div. Reinv. Plan)

CAPITALIZATION (6/30/02):

	($000)	(%)
Long-Term Debt	90,648	1.7
Deferred Income Tax	237,633	4.4
Common & Surplus	5,114,205	94.0
Total	5,442,486	100.0

BUSINESS:

Automatic Data Processing, Inc. is an independent computer services firm with over 500,000 clients. ADP's Employer Services group (62.9% of fiscal 2002 revenues) provides employers with payroll, human resources, tax deposit and reporting services. Brokerage Services (26.5% of revenues) provides securities transaction processing, investor support tools, market data services, and investor communications-related services to the financial community worldwide. ADP Dealer Services (10.6% of revenues) is a major provider of computing, data and professional services to auto and truck dealers in the U.S., Canada, Europe, Asia and Latin America.

RECENT DEVELOPMENTS:

For the three months ended 12/31/02, net earnings slipped 1.1% to $261.7 million compared with $264.6 million in the corresponding quarter of 2001. Total revenues were unchanged at $1.68 billion versus the prior-year period. Revenue in the Employer Services segment climbed 3.7% to $1.06 billion from $1.03 billion, while revenues in the Dealer Services segment grew 12.1% to $195.0 million from $174.0 million. Revenues in the Brokerage Services segment declined 13.7% to $315.0 million from $365.0 million, primarily due to the effect of industry consolidation, lower retail trading activity and reduced discretionary spending in the financial services industry.

PROSPECTS:

On 1/6/03, the Company entered into a definitive agreement to acquire ProBusiness Services, Inc., a provider of comprehensive payroll and human resource processing applications to large employers in the U.S., for approximately $500.0 million in cash. The transaction is a strategic fit for the Company's Employer Services segment and should enhance ADP's position in the domestic and international markets. The acquisition is subject to shareholder and regulatory approvals. Separately, the Company adjusted its guidance for revenue and earnings per share in fiscal 2003 from the mid-single digit to low-single digit range. This guidance was changed due to lower-than-anticipated interest rates and activity in the brokerage services environment.

ANNUAL FINANCIAL DATA:

FISCAL YEAR	TOT. REVS. ($mill.)	NET INC. ($mill.)	TOT. ASSETS ($mill.)	OPER. PROFIT %	NET PROFIT %	RET. ON EQUITY %	RET. ON ASSETS %	CURR. RATIO	EARN. PER SH.$	CASH FL.PER SH.$	TANG. BK. VAL.$	DIV. PER SH.$	PRICE RANGE	AVG. P/E RATIO	AVG. YIELD %
6/30/02	7,004.3	1,100.8	18,276.5	23.9	15.7	21.5	6.0	2.0	1.75	2.19	5.25	0.46	59.53 - 31.15	25.9	1.0
6/30/01	7,017.6	④ 924.7	17,889.1	23.0	13.2	19.7	5.2	2.3	④ 1.44	1.93	4.97	0.41	63.56 - 41.00	36.3	0.8
6/30/00	6,287.5	840.8	16,850.8	21.2	13.4	18.3	5.0	2.4	1.31	1.74	4.71	0.35	69.94 - 40.00	42.0	0.6
6/30/99	5,540.1	③ 696.8	5,824.8	19.9	12.6	17.4	12.0	1.7	③ 1.10	1.52	3.97	0.30	54.81 - 36.25	41.4	0.7
6/30/98	4,798.1	605.3	5,175.4	18.9	12.6	17.8	11.7	1.5	0.99	1.37	2.90	0.27	42.16 - 28.78	35.8	0.7
6/30/97	4,112.2	② 513.5	4,382.8	18.3	12.5	19.3	11.7	1.8	② 0.88	1.27	2.30	0.23	31.34 - 19.75	29.0	0.9
6/30/96	3,566.6	454.7	3,839.9	18.6	12.7	19.6	11.8	1.7	0.79	1.14	1.86	0.20	22.88 - 17.81	25.9	1.0
6/30/95	2,893.7	394.8	3,201.1	19.3	13.6	18.8	12.3	2.2	0.69	0.99	2.41	0.16	20.59 - 14.38	25.2	0.9
6/30/94	2,469.0	① 334.1	2,705.6	18.9	13.5	19.8	12.3	2.1	① 0.59	0.86	1.92	0.14	14.94 - 11.91	22.6	1.0
6/30/93	2,223.4	294.2	2,439.4	18.3	13.2	19.7	12.1	1.9	0.52	0.77	1.63	0.12	14.22 - 11.72	24.9	0.9

Statistics are as originally reported. Adj. for 2-for-1 stk. split, 1/99 & 1/96. ① Excl. acctg. chg. of $4.8 mill. ② Incl. non-recur. chg. of $11.7 mill. ③ Incl. about $37.0 pre-tax gain, $40.0 mill. provision for taxes, & $14.0 mill. net non-recur. adjustment. ④ Incl. $54.0 mill. non-cash, non-recur. write-off of investment.

OFFICERS:
A. F. Weinbach, Chmn., C.E.O.
G. C. Butler, Pres., C.O.O.
K. E. Dykstra, V.P., Fin.

INVESTOR CONTACT: Karen E. Dykstra, V.P., Fin., (973) 974-5000

PRINCIPAL OFFICE: One ADP Boulevard, Roseland, NJ 07068

TELEPHONE NUMBER: (973) 974-5000
FAX: (973) 974-5390
WEB: www.adp.com

NO. OF EMPLOYEES: 40,000 (approx.)

SHAREHOLDERS: 34,536 (approx. record)

ANNUAL MEETING: In Nov.

INCORPORATED: DE, June, 1961

INSTITUTIONAL HOLDINGS:
No. of Institutions: 780
Shares Held: 428,670,686
% Held: 71.6

INDUSTRY: Data processing and preparation (SIC: 7374)

TRANSFER AGENT(S): Mellon Investor Services, Ridgefield Park, NJ

AUTONATION, INC.

EXCH.	SYM.	REC. PRICE	P/E RATIO	YLD.	MKT. CAP.	RANGE (52-WK.)	'02 Y/E PR.
NYSE	AN	13.23 (2/28/03)	11.1	...	$4.26 bill.	18.73 - 9.05	12.56

MEDIUM GRADE. RESULTS ARE BENEFITING FROM THE COMPANY'S ACQUISITION ACTIVITY.

TRADING VOLUME Thousand Shares

*7 YEAR PRICE SCORE 83.5   *12 MONTH PRICE SCORE 104.8
*NYSE COMPOSITE INDEX=100

INTERIM EARNINGS (Per Share):

Qtr.	Mar.	June	Sept.	Dec.
1997	0.08	0.17	0.28	d0.07
1998	0.17	0.27	0.38	0.22
1999	0.11	0.21	0.22	d0.71
2000	0.18	0.27	0.26	0.21
2001	0.17	0.26	0.24	0.06
2002	0.28	0.32	0.33	0.26

INTERIM DIVIDENDS (Per Share):

Amt.	Decl.	Ex.	Rec.	Pay.
		No dividends paid.		

CAPITALIZATION (12/31/01):

	($000)	(%)
Long-Term Debt	647,300	12.1
Deferred Income Tax	853,800	16.0
Common & Surplus	3,827,900	71.8
Total	5,329,000	100.0

BUSINESS:

AutoNation, Inc. (formerly Republic Industries, Inc.) operates more than 370 automotive retail franchises in 17 states, as of 2/6/03, which sell new and used vehicles under a wide range of regional brand names. Approximately 95.0% of the new vehicles sold by AN in 2001 were manufactured by Ford, General Motors, DaimlerChrysler, Toyota, Nissan, Honda and BMW. On 4/28/99, the Company completed the sale of Republic Services, Inc., a provider of non-hazardous solid waste collection and disposal services in the U.S. In December, 1999, AN closed its chain of used-car megastore outlets. On 6/30/00, AN spun off ANC Rental Corporation, comprised of the Alamo Rent-A-Car, National Car Rental and CarTemps USA vehicle rental companies.

RECENT DEVELOPMENTS:

For the year ended 12/31/02, net income totaled $381.6 million, up 55.8% compared with income from continuing operations of $245.0 million a year earlier. Results for 2002 included a nonrecurring after-tax gain of $7.7 million, while results for 2001 included a nonrecurring after-tax charge of $45.8 million. Total revenue slipped 2.6% to $19.48 billion from $19.99 billion the year before. New vehicle revenue slid 2.5% to $11.69 billion, while used vehicle revenue was down 2.5% to $3.79 billion. Parts and service revenue rose 2.0% to $2.45 billion, while finance and insurance revenue grew 4.2% to $510.2 million. Gross profit totaled $2.91 billion, or 14.9% of revenue, versus $2.87 billion, or 14.4% of revenue, the previous year.

PROSPECTS:

The Company expects earnings in the range of $0.28 to $0.30 per share in the first quarter of 2003, along with full-year 2003 earnings of $1.25 to $1.30 per share. Results are benefiting from AN's efforts to reduce expenses and an aggressive acquisition program. In 2002, AN spent approximately $160.0 milion to acquire dealerships with combined annual revenues of about $500.0 million. The Company anticipates similar expansion activity in 2003.

ANNUAL FINANCIAL DATA:

FISCAL YEAR	TOT. REVS. ($mill.)	NET INC. ($mill.)	TOT. ASSETS ($mill.)	OPER. PROFIT %	NET PROFIT %	RET. ON EQUITY %	RET. ON ASSETS %	CURR. RATIO	EARN. PER SH.$	CASH FL. PER SH.$	TANG. BK. VAL.$	PRICE RANGE	AVG. P/E RATIO
p12/31/02	19,478.5	① 381.6							① 1.19			18.73 - 9.05	11.7
12/31/01	19,989.3	⑥ 245.0	8,065.4	2.2	1.2	6.4	3.0	1.2	⑥ 0.73	1.19	2.99	13.07 - 4.94	12.3
12/31/00	20,609.6	① ② 328.1	8,830.0	3.5	1.6	8.5	3.7	1.3	① ② 0.91	1.28	2.65	10.75 - 4.63	8.4
12/31/99	20,111.8	① ② d31.5	9,613.4	...	...	...	...	1.3	① ② d0.07	0.21	4.72	18.38 - 7.50	...
12/31/98	16,118.2	② ③ 334.6	13,925.8	3.3	2.1	6.2	2.4	1.5	② ③ 0.71	2.94	6.44	30.00 - 10.00	28.2
④ 12/31/97	10,305.6	② ⑤ 200.2	10,527.3	1.9	1.9	5.7	1.9	1.6	② ⑤ 0.46	2.79	4.34	44.38 - 19.00	68.9
④ 12/31/96	2,365.5	① ⑤ d27.9	3,776.1	...	...	...	...	1.2	① ⑤ d0.12	2.15	4.05	34.63 - 13.19	...
12/31/95	260.3	② 23.2	542.1	14.1	8.9	5.3	4.3	3.2	② 0.19	0.31	2.21	18.06 - 1.50	52.8
12/31/94	48.8	② 8.5	132.4	19.5	17.4	9.7	6.4	1.4	② 0.16	0.24	1.41	2.06 - 1.25	10.7
12/31/93	102.7	① d18.5	155.5	...	...	...	...	1.1	① d0.33	d0.21	1.00	2.75 - 1.38	...

Statistics are as originally reported. Adj. for 2-for-1 stk. split, 6/96. ① Incl. $7.7 mil after-tax non-recurr. gain, 2002; $3.8 mil pre-tax asset impairment gain, 2000; $390.2 mil one-time pre-tax chg., 1999; $179.1 mil chg., 1997; $38.3 mil chg., 1996; $24.9 mil chg., 1993. ② Bef. $1.8 mil disc. ops. gain, 2000; $314.4 mil ($0.73/sh) gain, 1999; $164.9 mil ($0.35/sh) gain, 1998; $239.5 mil ($0.56/sh) gain, 1997; $293,000 loss, 1995; $2.7 mil ($0.05/sh) gain, 1994. ③ Bef. $31.6 mil ($0.13/sh) extraord. chg. ④ Incl. results of Alamo Rent-A-Car, Inc., acq. on 11/25/96. ⑤ Incl. results of National Car Rental System, Inc., acq. on 2/25/97. ⑥ Bef. $12.7 mil ($0.04/sh) loss fr. disc. opers., incl. $52.3 mil ($0.16/sh) chg. fr. exiting auto loan bus.; $11.8 mil ($0.04/sh) gain fr. sale of dealer & $5.3 mil ($0.02/sh) oth. one-time chg.

OFFICERS:
M. J. Jackson, Chmn., C.E.O.
M. E. Maroone, Pres., C.O.O.

INVESTOR CONTACT: Investor Relations, (954) 769-7339

PRINCIPAL OFFICE: 110 S.E. 6th Street, Ft. Lauderdale, FL 33301

TELEPHONE NUMBER: (954) 769-6000
FAX: (954) 779-3884
WEB: www.autonation.com
NO. OF EMPLOYEES: 30,000 (approx.)
SHAREHOLDERS: 3,400 (approx.)
ANNUAL MEETING: In May
INCORPORATED: OK, Nov., 1980; reincorp., DE, May, 1991

INSTITUTIONAL HOLDINGS:
No. of Institutions: 199
Shares Held: 202,295,785
% Held: 64.7

INDUSTRY: Automotive dealers, nec (SIC: 5599)

TRANSFER AGENT(S): EquiServe, Jersey City, NJ

AUTOZONE, INC.

EXCH.	SYM.	REC. PRICE	P/E RATIO	YLD.	MKT. CAP.	RANGE (52-WK.)	'02 Y/E PR.
NYSE	AZO	65.80 (2/28/03)	15.3	...	$6.53 bill.	89.34 - 58.21	70.65

UPPER MEDIUM GRADE. RESULTS ARE BENEFITING FROM INCREASED SALES TO COMMERCIAL CUSTOMERS.

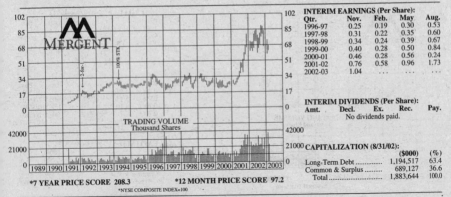

7 YEAR PRICE SCORE 208.3   **12 MONTH PRICE SCORE 97.2**
*NYSE COMPOSITE INDEX=100

INTERIM EARNINGS (Per Share):

Qtr.	Nov.	Feb.	May	Aug.
1996-97	0.25	0.19	0.30	0.53
1997-98	0.31	0.22	0.35	0.60
1998-99	0.34	0.24	0.39	0.67
1999-00	0.40	0.28	0.50	0.84
2000-01	0.46	0.28	0.56	0.24
2001-02	0.76	0.58	0.96	1.73
2002-03	1.04	...	...	...

INTERIM DIVIDENDS (Per Share):

Amt.	Decl.	Ex.	Rec.	Pay.
		No dividends paid.		

CAPITALIZATION (8/31/02):

	($000)	(%)
Long-Term Debt	1,194,517	63.4
Common & Surplus	689,127	36.6
Total	1,883,644	100.0

BUSINESS:

AutoZone, Inc. operates a chain of retail stores that offer a wide assortment of new and remanufactured automotive replacement parts for domestic and foreign cars, vans and light trucks, as well as spark plugs, chemicals, motor oil, maintenance items and various other automotive accessories. AZO sells its products primarily to the do-it-yourself market through its chain of 3,098 AutoZone stores in 44 states and 40 AutoZone stores in Mexico as of 11/23/02. The Company also sells automotive diagnostic and repair software through ALLDATA and www.alldatadiy.com. AZO acquired Chief Auto Parts in June 1998. In December 2001, the Company sold its heavy-duty truck parts subsidiary TruckPro.

RECENT DEVELOPMENTS:

For the 12 weeks ended 11/23/02, net income totaled $104.9 million, up 24.8% compared with $84.1 million in the corresponding period the year before. Net sales climbed 3.6% to $1.22 billion from $1.18 billion the previous year. Comparable-store sales at the Company's U.S. auto parts stores increased 4.5% year over year. Gross profit was $549.4 million, or 45.1% of net sales, versus $516.1 million, or 43.9% of net sales, in the prior year. Operating profit advanced 21.1% to $188.3 million from $155.5 million the previous year. During the first quarter, the Company opened 31 new domestic auto parts stores, replaced one existing location and closed one store. AZO also opened one new auto parts store in Mexico.

PROSPECTS:

Results are being positively affected by higher average customer transaction levels, additional sales from new stores opened, and the Company's efforts to control costs. In addition, AZO is enjoying strong sales to commercial customers, reflecting positive customer response to the Company's service and product offerings. Looking ahead, AZO anticipates opening approximately 150 new auto parts stores in the U.S. during the current fiscal year.

ANNUAL FINANCIAL DATA:

FISCAL YEAR	TOT. REVS. ($mill.)	NET INC. ($mill.)	TOT. ASSETS ($mill.)	OPER. PROFIT %	NET PROFIT %	RET. ON EQUITY %	RET. ON ASSETS %	CURR. RATIO	EARN. PER SH. $	CASH FL. PER SH. $	TANG. BK. VAL. $	PRICE RANGE	AVG. P/E RATIO
8/31/02	5,325.5	428.1	3,477.8	14.5	8.0	62.1	12.3	0.9	4.00	5.10	3.87	89.34 - 59.20	18.6
8/25/01	4,818.2	① 175.5	3,432.5	8.0	3.6	20.3	5.1	1.0	① 1.54	2.70	5.13	80.00 - 24.37	33.9
8/26/00	4,482.7	267.6	3,333.2	11.4	6.0	27.0	8.0	1.1	2.00	2.95	5.49	32.50 - 21.00	13.4
8/28/99	4,116.4	244.8	3,284.8	10.5	5.9	18.5	7.5	1.2	1.63	2.48	6.83	37.31 - 22.56	18.4
8/29/98	3,242.9	227.9	2,748.1	11.8	7.0	17.5	8.3	1.3	1.48	2.11	7.37	38.00 - 20.50	19.8
8/30/97	2,691.4	195.0	1,884.0	11.9	7.2	18.1	10.4	1.3	1.29	1.81	7.00	32.81 - 19.50	20.3
8/31/96	2,242.6	167.2	1,498.4	12.0	7.5	19.3	11.2	1.0	1.13	1.55	5.65	37.63 - 22.13	26.4
8/26/95	1,808.1	138.8	1,111.8	12.6	7.7	20.3	12.5	1.1	0.93	1.25	4.54	30.13 - 22.00	28.0
8/27/94	1,508.0	116.4	882.1	12.6	7.7	22.0	13.2	1.3	0.78	1.00	3.51	30.75 - 21.63	33.6
8/28/93	1,216.8	86.9	697.3	11.6	7.1	21.9	12.5	1.3	0.59	0.74	2.62	29.50 - 16.88	39.3

Statistics are as originally reported. Adj. for 100% stk. div., 4/94. ① Incl. $95.8 mil ($0.84/sh) non-recur. chgs.

OFFICERS:
S. Odland, Chmn., Pres., C.E.O.
M. G. Archbold, Sr. V.P., C.F.O.
H. L. Goldsmith, Sr. V.P., Sec., Gen. Couns.

INVESTOR CONTACT: Ray Pohlman, Investor Relations, (901) 495-7962

PRINCIPAL OFFICE: 123 South Front Street, Memphis, TN 38103

TELEPHONE NUMBER: (901) 495-6500
FAX: (901) 495-8300
WEB: www.autozone.com
NO. OF EMPLOYEES: 27,000 full-time (approx.); 17,179 part-time (approx.)
SHAREHOLDERS: 2,956
ANNUAL MEETING: In Dec.
INCORPORATED: DE, May, 1986; reincorp., NV, Dec., 1991

INSTITUTIONAL HOLDINGS:
No. of Institutions: 352
Shares Held: 92,444,682
% Held: 94.9

INDUSTRY: Auto and home supply stores (SIC: 5531)

TRANSFER AGENT(S): EquiServe, Jersey City, NJ

AVALONBAY COMMUNITIES, INC.

EXCH.	SYM.	REC. PRICE	P/E RATIO	YLD.	MKT. CAP.	RANGE (52-WK.)	'02 Y/E PR.
NYSE	AVB	36.71 (2/28/03)	16.5	7.6%	$2.52 bill.	52.65 - 35.61	39.14

MEDIUM GRADE. THE COMPANY EXPECTS EARNINGS PER SHARE FOR FULL YEAR 2003 IN THE RANGE OF $1.93 TO $2.13.

7 YEAR PRICE SCORE 116.4   *12 MONTH PRICE SCORE 93.7*
NYSE COMPOSITE INDEX=100

INTERIM EARNINGS (Per Share):

Qtr.	Mar.	June	Sept.	Dec.
1998	0.34	0.34	0.37	0.34
1999	0.10	0.80	0.37	0.78
2000	0.55	0.60	0.71	0.99
2001	0.61	0.57	1.14	0.81
2002	0.51	0.46	0.35	0.91

INTERIM DIVIDENDS (Per Share):

Amt.	Decl.	Ex.	Rec.	Pay.
0.70Q	3/04/02	3/27/02	4/01/02	4/15/02
0.70Q	6/17/02	6/26/02	6/28/02	7/15/02
0.70Q	9/16/02	9/27/02	10/01/02	10/15/02
0.70Q	12/16/02	12/27/02	12/31/02	1/15/03
0.70Q	3/13/03	3/28/03	4/01/03	4/15/03

Indicated div.: $2.80

CAPITALIZATION (12/31/01):

	($000)	(%)
Long-Term Debt	1,635,000	41.4
Preferred Stock	96	0.0
Common & Surplus	2,314,459	58.6
Total	3,949,555	100.0

BUSINESS:

AvalonBay Communities, Inc. is a real estate investment trust company focused on developing, redeveloping, acquiring and managing luxury apartment communities in high barrier-to-entry markets of the United States. These markets include Northern California, Southern California and the Northeast, Mid-Atlantic, Midwest and Northwest regions of the country. As of 2/1/03, the Company owned or held interest in 137 apartment communities containing 40,179 apartment homes in eleven states and the District of Columbia, of which twelve communities were under construction and two were under reconstruction. In addition, the Company holds future development rights for 38 communities.

RECENT DEVELOPMENTS:

For the year ended 12/31/02, income was $121.2 million, before a gain of $52.4 million from discontinued operations, compared with income of $245.4 million, before a gain of $3.6 million from discontinued operations, the previous year. Results for 2002 included a pre-tax impairment loss of $6.8 million, while 2001 results included a gain of $62.9 million on sale of communities. Total revenues inched up to $639.0 million from $633.8 million the year before. Rental income rose to $630.5 million from $629.5 million, while revenues from management fees grew 2.3% to $1.4 million from $1.3 million the prior year. Other income more than doubled to $7.1 million from $3.0 million a year earlier.

PROSPECTS:

Going forward, the Company expects earnings per share for full-year 2003 in the range of $1.93 to $2.13. The Company estimates funds from operations per share to range from $3.15 to $3.35. The Company also expects a 50.0% reduction in new development starts in 2003. This will likely result in a significant reduction in development activity for 2003. Moreover, capital used to fund development activity in 2003 is expected to range between $275.0 million and $310.0 million, down from approximately $450.0 million in 2002.

ANNUAL FINANCIAL DATA:

FISCAL YEAR	TOT. INC. ($mill.)	NET INC. ($mill.)	TOT. ASSETS ($mill.)	NET INC. + DEPR./ ASSETS %	RET. ON EQUITY %	RET. ON ASSETS %	EARN. PER SH. $	TANG. BK. VAL. $	DIV. PER SH. $	DIV. PAYOUT %	PRICE RANGE	AVG. P/E RATIO	AVG. YIELD %
p12/31/02	639.0	④ 121.2					④ 1.49		2.74	183.9	52.65 - 36.38	29.7	6.2
12/31/01	641.7	③ 249.0	4,664.3	8.1	10.8	5.3	③ 3.12	33.68	2.48	79.5	51.90 - 42.45	15.1	5.3
12/31/00	573.4	② 210.6	4,397.2	7.6	8.6	4.8	② 2.53	36.35	2.20	87.0	50.63 - 32.63	16.5	5.3
12/31/99	504.5	② 172.3	4,154.7	6.8	7.3	4.1	② 2.00	36.04	2.05	102.5	37.00 - 30.81	17.0	6.0
12/31/98	352.9	94.4	4,030.2	4.3	4.0	2.3	1.37	36.62	1.02	74.4	39.25 - 30.50	25.5	2.9
12/31/97	126.0	② 38.9	1,317.7	5.0	4.9	3.0	② 1.40	30.39	...	...	40.63 - 32.13	26.0	...
12/31/96	82.6	① 20.1	711.9	5.5	4.9	2.8	① 1.05	21.69	...	...	36.00 - 22.63	27.9	...
12/31/95	53.5	11.5	477.2	5.3	4.8	2.4	0.91	20.58	...	...	24.50 - 16.75	22.7	...
12/31/94	32.0	7.5	390.0	4.1	3.8	1.9	0.65	17.04	...	...	22.75 - 17.75	31.1	...
12/31/93	24.8	d0.4	165.4	...	...	...	...	...	...	...	...	...	...

Statistics are as originally reported. ① Bef. extraord. chrg. $511,000 ② Incl. non-recurr. chrg. 1999, $16.8 mill.; 1997, $710,000. ③ Incl. gain on the sale of communities of $62.9 mill., 2001; $40.8 mill, 2000. ④ Bef. inc. of $52.4 mill. & incl. pre-tax impair. loss of $6.8 mill.

OFFICERS:
B. Blair, Chmn., Pres., C.E.O.
T. J. Sargeant, Exec. V.P., C.F.O., Treas.
T. Naughton, C.O.O.

INVESTOR CONTACT: Thomas J. Sargeant, Exec. V.P., C.F.O. & Treas., (703) 317-4635

PRINCIPAL OFFICE: 2900 Eisenhower Avenue, Suite 300, Alexandria, VA 22314

TELEPHONE NUMBER: (703) 329-6300
FAX: (408) 984-7060
WEB: www.avalonbay.com
NO. OF EMPLOYEES: 1,775 (approx.)
SHAREHOLDERS: 795
ANNUAL MEETING: In May
INCORPORATED: CA, 1978; reincorp., MD, July, 1995

INSTITUTIONAL HOLDINGS:
No. of Institutions: 211
Shares Held: 53,207,807
% Held: 77.6

INDUSTRY: Real estate investment trusts (SIC: 6798)

TRANSFER AGENT(S): First Union National Bank, Charlotte, NC

AVAYA INC.

EXCH.	SYM.	REC. PRICE	P/E RATIO	YLD.	MKT. CAP.	RANGE (52-WK.)	'02 Y/E PR.
NYSE	AV	2.19 (2/28/03)	...	...	$627.88 bill.	7.60 - 1.12	2.45

SPECULATIVE GRADE. THE COMPANY HAS BEGUN A CONCENTRATED EFFORT TO BUILD AWARENESS OF THE AVAYA NAME IN KEY MARKETS.

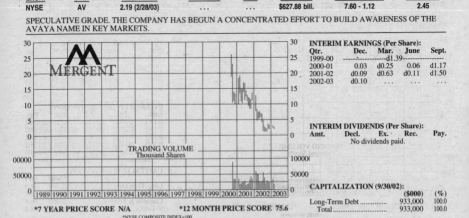

*7 YEAR PRICE SCORE N/A   *12 MONTH PRICE SCORE 75.6
*NYSE COMPOSITE INDEX=100

INTERIM EARNINGS (Per Share):

Qtr.	Dec.	Mar.	June	Sept.
1999-00	------------d1.39---------------			
2000-01	0.03	d0.25	0.06	d1.17
2001-02	d0.09	d0.63	d0.11	d1.50
2002-03	d0.10	...	...	...

INTERIM DIVIDENDS (Per Share):

Amt.	Decl.	Ex.	Rec.	Pay.
No dividends paid.				

CAPITALIZATION (9/30/02):

	($000)	(%)
Long-Term Debt	933,000	100.0
Total	933,000	100.0

BUSINESS:

Avaya Inc. is a provider of communications systems, applications and services for enterprises, including businesses, government agencies and other organizations. AV's converged systems and applications segment, which accounted for 42.0% of 2002 revenues, is focused on large enterprises and includes its converged systems products, unified communications solutions and customer relationship management offerings. The small and medium business solutions segment (4.8%) develops, markets and sells converged and traditional voice communications solutions for small and mid-sized enterprises and includes all Internet Protocol telephony systems and applications, as well as messaging products. The services segment (41.7%) offers a portfolio of services to help customers plan, design, build and manage their communications networks. The connectivity solutions segment (11.5%) includes AV's structured cabling systems and electronic cabinets. AV was spun off from Lucent Technologies Inc. on 9/30/00.

RECENT DEVELOPMENTS:

For the quarter ended 12/31/02, AV posted a net loss of $37.6 million versus a net loss of $19.5 million in the same period a year earlier. Results for 2002 and 2001 included pre-tax restructuring and related charges of $4.2 million and $5.5 million, respectively. Revenue fell 18.3% to $1.07 billion. Products revenue slid 20.2% to $605.2 million, while services revenues dropped 15.8% to $461.6 million. Gross margin decreased 18.1% to $423.2 million. However, gross margin as a percentage of revenue improved slightly to 39.7% versus 39.6% the year before.

PROSPECTS:

The ongoing restraint in spending by AV's customers appears to ensure that the Company will continue to face challenging business conditions over the near term. Nevertheless, AV's results going forward may begin to demonstrate the benefits of continued sequential improvement in gross margin percentage and lower spending for selling, general and administrative expenses as a result of the Company's restructuring initiatives. For instance, selling, general and administrative expenses for the quarter ended 12/31/02 were 17.6% lower than the previous year. Meanwhile, AV has begun a concentrated effort to build awareness of the Avaya name in key markets.

ANNUAL FINANCIAL DATA:

FISCAL YEAR	TOT. REVS. ($mill.)	NET INC. ($mill.)	TOT. ASSETS ($mill.)	OPER. PROFIT %	NET PROFIT %	RET. ON EQUITY %	RET. ON ASSETS %	CURR. RATIO	EARN. PER SH. $	CASH FL. PER SH. $	TANG. BK. VAL. $	PRICE RANGE
9/30/02	4,956.0	③ d666.0	3,897.0	...	...	...	...	1.7	③ d2.44	d1.61	...	12.73 - 1.12
9/30/01	6,793.0	② d352.0	4,648.0	...	...	...	...	1.4	② d1.33	d0.28	0.79	19.24 - 8.50
9/30/00	7,680.0	① d375.0	5,037.0	...	...	...	...	1.3	① d1.39	d0.58	1.99	26.00 - 10.00
9/30/99	8,268.0	186.0	4,239.0	4.5	2.2	10.2	4.4	1.9	1.03	1.46	5.47	...
9/30/98	7,754.0	43.0	4,177.0	4.0	0.6	2.4	1.0	2.0	0.17	0.91	...	...

Statistics are as originally reported. ① Incl. nonrecurr. chrgs. of $757.0 mill. for restruct. & separation fr. Lucent Technologies Inc. ② Incl. business restruct. & rel. chrgs. of $837.0 mill. ③ Incl. business restruct. & rel. chrgs. of $209.0 mill. and goodwill & impairmnt. chrg. of $71.0 mill.

OFFICERS:
D. K. Peterson, Chmn., C.E.O.
G. K. McGuire, Sr., Sr. V.P., C.F.O.
P. F. Craven, Sr. V.P., Sec., Gen. Couns.
INVESTOR CONTACT: Investor Relations, (866) 462-8292
PRINCIPAL OFFICE: 211 Mount Airy Road, Basking Ridge, NJ 07920

TELEPHONE NUMBER: (908) 953-6000
WEB: www.avaya.com
NO. OF EMPLOYEES: 18,800 (approx.)
SHAREHOLDERS: 1,035,892 (approx.)
ANNUAL MEETING: In Feb.
INCORPORATED: DE, Feb., 2000

INSTITUTIONAL HOLDINGS:
No. of Institutions: 295
Shares Held: 208,705,027
% Held: 57.3
INDUSTRY: Telephone and telegraph apparatus (SIC: 3661)
TRANSFER AGENT(S): Bank of New York, New York, NY

AVERY DENNISON CORPORATION

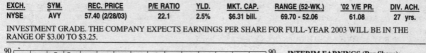

EXCH.	SYM.	REC. PRICE	P/E RATIO	YLD.	MKT. CAP.	RANGE (52-WK.)	'02 Y/E PR.	DIV. ACH.
NYSE	AVY	57.40 (2/28/03)	22.1	2.5%	$6.31 bill.	69.70 - 52.06	61.08	27 yrs.

INVESTMENT GRADE. THE COMPANY EXPECTS EARNINGS PER SHARE FOR FULL-YEAR 2003 WILL BE IN THE RANGE OF $3.00 TO $3.25.

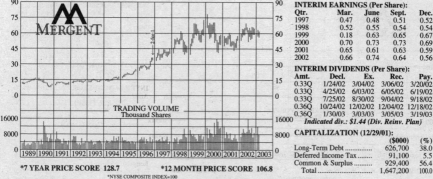

*7 YEAR PRICE SCORE 128.7   ***12 MONTH PRICE SCORE 106.8**

*NYSE COMPOSITE INDEX=100

INTERIM EARNINGS (Per Share):

Qtr.	Mar.	June	Sept.	Dec.
1997	0.47	0.48	0.51	0.52
1998	0.52	0.55	0.54	0.54
1999	0.18	0.63	0.65	0.67
2000	0.70	0.73	0.73	0.69
2001	0.65	0.61	0.63	0.59
2002	0.66	0.74	0.64	0.56

INTERIM DIVIDENDS (Per Share):

Amt.	Decl.	Ex.	Rec.	Pay.
0.33Q	1/24/02	3/04/02	3/06/02	3/20/02
0.33Q	4/25/02	6/03/02	6/05/02	6/19/02
0.33Q	7/25/02	8/30/02	9/04/02	9/18/02
0.36Q	10/24/02	12/02/02	12/04/02	12/18/02
0.36Q	1/30/03	3/03/03	3/05/03	3/19/03

Indicated div.: $1.44 (Div. Reinv. Plan)

CAPITALIZATION (12/29/01):

	($000)	(%)
Long-Term Debt	626,700	38.0
Deferred Income Tax	91,100	5.5
Common & Surplus	929,400	56.4
Total	1,647,200	100.0

BUSINESS:

Avery Dennison Corporation is a worldwide manufacturer of pressure-sensitive adhesives and materials, office products and converted products. A portion of self-adhesive material is converted into labels and other products through embossing, printing, stamping and die-cutting, and some are sold in unconverted form as base materials, tapes and reflective sheeting. AVY also manufactures and sells a variety of office products and other items not involving pressure-sensitive components, such as notebooks, three-ring binders, organization systems, felt-tip markers, glues, fasteners, business forms, tickets, tags, and imprinting equipment. Sales for 2002 were derived: pressure-sensitive adhesives and materials, 58.6%; and consumer and converted products, 41.4%.

RECENT DEVELOPMENTS:

For the twelve months ended 12/28/02, net income climbed 5.7% to $257.2 million compared with income of $243.4 million, before an accounting change charge of $200,000, in 2001. Results for 2002 included asset impairment charges, lease cancellation costs and restructuring charges totaling $32.1 million. Net sales were $4.21 billion, up 10.6% from $3.80 billion in the prior year. Sales for the pressure-sensitive adhesives and materials segment increased 17.3% to $2.57 billion from $2.19 billion, while sales for the consumer and converted products segment grew 1.6% to $1.81 billion from $1.78 billion. Gross profit rose 9.2% to $1.35 billion compared with $1.24 billion in the previous year.

PROSPECTS:

In the near-term, AVY may continue to encounter some weakness in a number of markets due to economic conditions; however, it should benefit from a number of long-term opportunities. Going forward, AVY plans to introduce a variety of innovative products, applications and new or expanded business lines. Meanwhile, earnings per share for the full-year 2003 are expected to be in the range of $3.00 to $3.25 per share, assuming sales growth between 14.0% to 18.0%, augmented by the effects of acquisitions completed in 2002 and currency exchange rates.

ANNUAL FINANCIAL DATA:

FISCAL YEAR	TOT. REVS. ($mill.)	NET INC. ($mill.)	TOT. ASSETS ($mill.)	OPER. PROFIT %	NET PROFIT %	RET. ON EQUITY %	RET. ON ASSETS %	CURR. RATIO	EARN. PER SH.$	CASH FL. PER SH.$	TANG. BK. VAL.$	DIV. PER SH.$	PRICE RANGE	AVG. P/E RATIO	AVG. YIELD %
p12/28/02	4,206.9	④257.2							④2.59			1.35	69.70 - 52.06	23.5	2.2
12/29/01	3,803.3	③243.4	2,819.2	10.8	6.4	26.2	8.6	1.0	③2.47	4.05	4.70	1.23	60.50 - 43.25	21.0	2.4
12/30/00	3,893.5	283.5	2,699.1	12.4	7.3	34.2	10.5	1.2	2.84	4.41	4.35	1.11	78.50 - 41.13	21.1	1.9
1/01/00	3,768.2	②215.4	2,592.5	9.9	5.7	26.6	8.3	1.1	②2.13	3.61	4.18	0.99	73.00 - 39.38	26.4	1.8
1/02/99	3,459.9	223.3	2,142.6	10.7	6.5	26.8	10.4	1.2	2.15	3.37	6.88	0.87	62.06 - 39.44	23.6	1.7
12/27/97	3,345.7	205.3	2,046.5	10.2	6.1	24.5	10.0	1.3	1.93	3.03	6.87	0.72	45.31 - 33.38	20.4	1.8
12/28/96	3,222.5	①175.9	2,036.7	9.6	5.5	21.1	8.6	1.2	①1.68	2.76	6.72	0.62	36.50 - 23.75	17.9	2.1
12/30/95	3,113.9	①143.7	1,963.6	8.6	4.6	17.6	7.3	1.2	①1.35	2.36	6.52	0.56	25.06 - 16.56	15.4	2.7
12/31/94	2,856.7	109.4	1,763.1	7.6	3.8	15.0	6.2	1.2	0.98	1.91	6.84	0.49	18.00 - 13.19	15.9	3.2
1/01/94	2,608.7	83.3	1,639.0	6.7	3.2	11.6	5.1	1.3	0.72	1.54	6.98	0.45	15.75 - 12.56	19.7	3.2

Statistics are as originally reported. Adj. for 2-for-1 split, 12/96. ① Incl. non-recur. chgs. of $2.1 mill., 1996; $1.5 mill., 1995. ② Incl. $65.0 mill. one-time restr. chg. ③ Excl. $200,000 acct. chg. ④ Incl. $32.1 mill. asset impair. chg., lease cancel. costs, & restr. costs.

OFFICERS:
P. M. Neal, Chmn., C.E.O.
D. A. Scarborough, Pres., C.O.O.
D. R. O'Bryant, Sr. V.P., C.F.O

INVESTOR CONTACT: Cynthia S. Guenther,
V.P., Investor Relations, (626) 304-2204

PRINCIPAL OFFICE: 150 North Orange
Grove Boulevard, Pasadena, CA 91103

TELEPHONE NUMBER: (626) 304-2000
FAX: (626) 792-7312
WEB: www.averydennison.com

NO. OF EMPLOYEES: 17,300 (avg.)

SHAREHOLDERS: 12,368

ANNUAL MEETING: In Apr.

INCORPORATED: DE, Sept., 1946

INSTITUTIONAL HOLDINGS:
No. of Institutions: 390
Shares Held: 73,753,138
% Held: 67.2

INDUSTRY: Paper coated and laminated, nec
(SIC: 2672)

TRANSFER AGENT(S): First Chicago Trust
Company of New York, Jersey City, NJ

AVISTA CORPORATION

EXCH.	SYM.	REC. PRICE	P/E RATIO	YLD.	MKT. CAP.	RANGE (52-WK.)	'02 Y/E PR.
NYSE	AVA	10.21 (2/28/03)	15.2	4.7%	$486.3 mill.	16.60 - 8.75	11.56

LOWER MEDIUM GRADE. GOING FORWARD, EARNINGS ARE LIKELY TO BE HAMPERED BY REDUCED WHOLE-SALE ENERGY ACTIVITY AND HIGHER OPERATING EXPENSES.

MERGENT

TRADING VOLUME
Thousand Shares

*7 YEAR PRICE SCORE 69.1   *12 MONTH PRICE SCORE 96.6
*NYSE COMPOSITE INDEX=100

INTERIM EARNINGS (Per Share):

Qtr.	Mar.	June	Sept.	Dec.
1997	0.29	0.28	0.31	0.40
1998	0.57	0.27	0.14	0.30
1999	0.34	0.08	0.52	d0.98
2000	d0.28	d0.47	0.72	1.42
2001	0.61	0.47	0.12	0.19
2002	0.32	0.18	d0.04	0.21

INTERIM DIVIDENDS (Per Share):

Amt.	Decl.	Ex.	Rec.	Pay.
0.12Q	2/11/02	2/20/02	2/22/02	3/15/02
0.12Q	5/13/02	5/21/02	5/23/02	6/14/02
0.12Q	8/12/02	8/20/02	8/22/02	9/13/02
0.12Q	11/11/02	11/20/02	11/22/02	12/13/02
0.12Q	2/10/03	2/19/03	2/21/03	3/14/03

Indicated div.: $0.48 (Div. Reinv. Plan)

CAPITALIZATION (12/31/01):

	($000)	(%)
Long-Term Debt	1,175,715	46.1
Deferred Income Tax	517,428	20.3
Redeemable Pfd. Stock	100,000	3.9
Preferred Stock	35,000	1.4
Common & Surplus	720,063	28.3
Total	2,548,206	100.0

BUSINESS:

Avista Corporation (formerly The Washington Water Power Company), is involved in the generation, transmission and distribution of energy, as well as other energy-related businesses. The Company's operations are organized into four lines of business: Avista Utilities, Energy Trading and Marketing, Information and Technology, and Other. Avista Utilities (91.2% of 2002 operating revenue) represents the regulated utility operations that are responsi-ble for electric generation and transmission, and electric and natural gas distribution services. The Energy Trading and Marketing line of business (5.5%) includes Avista Energy, Inc. and Avista Power, LLC. The Information and Technology line of business (1.8%) includes Avista Advantage and Avista Labs. The Other line of business (1.5%) includes Avista Ventures, Inc., Avista Capital and several other minor subsidiaries.

RECENT DEVELOPMENTS:

For the year ended 12/31/02, income was $34.3 million, before income from discontinued operations of $1.1 million and an accounting change charge of $4.1 million, versus income of $59.6 million, before a loss from discontinued operations of $47.4 million, the previous year. Operating revenues slid 29.7% to $980.4 million from $1.40 billion in 2001. Revenue for the prior-year period was restated to reflect a change in energy trading contracts, which will now be reported on a net basis rather than a gross basis.

PROSPECTS:

Going forward, earnings will likely to be hampered by a continued reduction of activity in wholesale energy markets and increased expenses, such as pension and insurance costs. Moreover, hydro-generation conditions are expected to be below normal in 2003 and may force AVA to purchase higher-priced energy to meet retail demand. During the first quarter of 2003, AVA expects to absorb the entire $9.0 million allowed under the energy recovery mechanism in Washington. For the balance of 2003, 90.0% of any increased power costs will be deferred for future recovery. Despite these challenges, AVA maintains its 2003 target earnings per share range of $0.80 to $1.00.

ANNUAL FINANCIAL DATA:

FISCAL YEAR	TOT. REVS. ($mill.)	NET INC. ($mill.)	TOT. ASSETS ($mill.)	OPER. PROFIT %	NET PROFIT %	NET INC./ NET PROP. %	NET INC./ TOT. CAP. %	RET. ON EQUITY %	ACCUM. DEPR./ GROSS PROP. %	EARN. PER SH. $	TANG. BK. VAL. $	DIV. PER SH. $	DIV. PAYOUT %	PRICE RANGE		AVG. P/E RATIO	AVG. YIELD
p12/31/02	8 980.4	9 34.3								9 0.67		0.48	71.6	16.35 -	8.75	18.7	3.8
12/31/01	6,009.8	7 59.6	4,037.2	2.8	1.0	3.8	2.3	7.9	32.9	7 1.20	15.12	0.48	40.0	23.97 -	10.60	14.4	2.8
12/31/00	7,911.5	6 91.7	12,563.9	2.6	1.2	6.0	4.6	12.1	32.2	6 1.47	15.34	0.48	32.7	68.00 -	14.63	28.1	1.2
12/31/99	7,905.0	5 26.0	3,713.5	0.4	0.3	1.7	1.4	3.8	32.3	5 0.12	11.04	0.48	399.7	19.56 -	14.63	142.3	2.9
12/31/98	4 3,684.0	78.1	3,253.6	4.7	2.1	5.3	3.9	9.9	31.3	1.28	12.06	1.05	82.0	24.88 -	16.13	16.0	5.1
12/31/97	1,302.2	3 114.8	2,411.8	14.5	8.8	8.0	5.7	14.6	30.7	3 1.96	13.38	1.24	63.3	24.81 -	17.38	10.8	5.9
12/31/96	945.0	2 83.5	2,177.3	19.8	8.8	6.0	4.4	10.5	29.8	2 1.35	12.70	1.24	91.8	19.88 -	17.13	13.7	6.7
12/31/95	755.0	87.1	2,098.9	25.1	11.5	6.4	4.6	10.9	28.7	1.41	12.82	1.24	87.9	18.13 -	13.50	11.2	7.8
12/31/94	670.8	77.2	1,994.3	23.2	11.5	5.8	4.2	10.1	27.4	1.28	12.45	1.24	96.9	18.88 -	13.63	12.7	7.6
12/31/93	640.6	1 82.8	1,837.8	25.1	12.9	6.6	4.9	12.1	27.2	1 1.44	12.02	1.24	86.1	21.00 -	17.38	13.3	6.5

Statistics are as originally reported. Adj. for stk. splits: 2-for-1, 11/93. 1 Incl. pre-tax gain $9.9 mill. fr. sale of subsidiary stock. 2 Incl. non-recurr. chrg. $21.4 mill. 3 Incl. non-recurr. after-tax gain of $41.0 mill. 4 Reflects the start-up of National Energy Trading and Marketing operations. 5 Incl. one-time chrg. of $42.9 mill. & a net gain of $57.5 mill. 6 Incl. restruct. chrg. $1.9 mill. and exit costs $4.9 mill. 7 Bef. loss fr. disc. opers. of $47.4 mill. 8 Refl. a change in energy trading contracts, which will now be reported on a net basis rather than a gross basis 9 Bef. inc. fr. disc. opers. of $1.1 mill. & acctg. chrg. $4.1 mill.

OFFICERS:
G. G. Ely, Chmn., Pres., C.E.O.
J. E. Eliassen, Sr. V.P., C.F.O.
R. R. Peterson, V.P., Treas.
INVESTOR CONTACT: Investor Relations, (509) 489-0500
PRINCIPAL OFFICE: 1411 East Mission Ave., Spokane, WA 99202-2600

TELEPHONE NUMBER: (509) 489-0500
FAX: (509) 482-4361
WEB: www.avistacorp.com
NO. OF EMPLOYEES: 2,175 (approx.)
SHAREHOLDERS: 18,120 (approx.)
ANNUAL MEETING: In May
INCORPORATED: WA, March, 1989

INSTITUTIONAL HOLDINGS:
No. of Institutions: 117
Shares Held: 24,277,711
% Held: 50.6
INDUSTRY: Electric and other services combined (SIC: 4931)
TRANSFER AGENT(S): The Bank of New York, New York, NY

AVNET, INC.

EXCH.	SYM.	REC. PRICE	P/E RATIO	YLD.	MKT. CAP.	RANGE (52-WK.)	'02 Y/E PR.
NYSE	AVT	10.30 (2/28/03)	...	...	$1.23 bill.	29.24 - 5.55	10.83

LOWER MEDIUM GRADE. THE COMPANY'S RECENT COST CUTTING ACTIONS ARE EXPECTED TO RESULT IN ANNUALIZED SAVINGS OF $90.0 MILLION.

*7 YEAR PRICE SCORE 70.3   ***12 MONTH PRICE SCORE 70.8**

*NYSE COMPOSITE INDEX=100

INTERIM EARNINGS (Per Share):

Qtr.	Sept.	Dec.	Mar.	June
1998-99	0.21	0.37	0.37	1.51
1999-00	0.32	0.19	0.47	0.74
2000-01	0.81	0.78	0.42	d1.96
2001-02	d0.16	d0.02	d0.01	d0.51
2002-03	Nil	d0.49	...	...

INTERIM DIVIDENDS (Per Share):

Amt.	Decl.	Ex.	Rec.	Pay.
0.075Q	1/30/01	3/14/01	3/16/01	4/02/01
0.075Q	5/25/01	6/13/01	6/15/01	7/02/01
0.075Q	7/27/01	9/17/01	9/14/01	10/01/01
0.075Q	11/30/01	12/12/01	12/14/01	1/02/02
Dividend payment suspended.				

CAPITALIZATION (6/28/02):

	($000)	(%)
Long-Term Debt	1,565,836	46.5
Common & Surplus	1,804,510	53.5
Total	3,370,346	100.0

BUSINESS:

Avnet, Inc, is an industrial distributor of electronic components, enterprise network and computer equipment and embedded subsystems. The Electronics Marketing (EM) group (54.3% of 2002 sales) engages in global marketing, assembly and processing of electronic and electromechanical components and certain computer products. In addition, the EM group offers value-added services such as supply-chain management, connector and cable assembly and semiconductor programming. The Computer Marketing (CM) group (26.9%) distributes computer products to value-added resellers and end users internationally. The Applied Computing (AC) group (18.8%) markets original equipment manufacturer system- and sub-system level components. As of 1/23/03, AVT served customers in 63 countries.

RECENT DEVELOPMENTS:

For the second quarter ended 12/27/02, the Company reported a net loss of $58.7 million compared with a net loss of $2.6 million in the corresponding prior-year quarter. Results for fiscal 2003 included after-tax non-recurring charges of $65.8 million. Total sales slipped 0.6% to $2.35 billion from $2.36 billion a year earlier. CM group sales decreased 3.1% to $682.9 million, while AC group sales fell 4.8% to $459.7 million. EM group sales increased 2.7% to $1.20 billion. Gross profit was down 1.0% to $315.6 million from $318.6 million in 2001. Operating loss amounted to $75.2 million versus operating income of $23.8 million the year before.

PROSPECTS:

AVT believes that the electronics components industry is in a stagnant but stable market, and it remains committed to improving profitability in this environment. Cost cutting actions taken in the second quarter of fiscal 2003 exceeded previous estimates and are expected to result in annualized savings of $90.0 million. Looking ahead, AVT expects revenues for the third quarter of fiscal 2003 should be in the range of $2.25 billion to $2.30 billion, with earnings between $0.07 and $0.09 per share. Full-year earnings are expected to exceed $0.21 per share, before special charges.

ANNUAL FINANCIAL DATA:

FISCAL YEAR	TOT. REVS. ($mill.)	NET INC. ($mill.)	TOT. ASSETS ($mill.)	OPER. PROFIT %	NET PROFIT %	RET. ON EQUITY %	RET. ON ASSETS %	CURR. RATIO	EARN. PER SH.$	CASH FL. PER SH.$	TANG. BK. VAL.$	DIV. PER SH.$	PRICE RANGE	AVG. P/E RATIO	AVG. YIELD %
6/28/02	8,920.2	⑤ d84.4	4,682.0	...	...	...	...	2.5	⑤ d0.71	0.16	8.04	0.07	29.24 - 5.55	...	0.4
6/29/01	12,814.0	④ 0.1	5,864.1	2.0	...	...	...	1.5	④ Nil	1.01	8.23	0.30	28.45 - 17.06	N.M.	1.3
6/30/00	9,172.2	③ 145.1	5,244.4	3.6	1.6	7.6	2.8	2.0	③ 1.75	2.66	11.83	0.30	40.56 - 17.19	16.5	1.0
7/02/99	6,350.0	174.5	2,984.7	2.7	2.7	12.5	5.8	2.9	2.43	3.16	14.38	0.30	30.47 - 17.00	9.8	1.3
6/26/98	5,916.3	② 151.4	2,733.7	4.6	2.6	11.5	5.5	3.4	② 1.90	2.54	11.72	0.30	33.13 - 17.47	13.3	1.2
6/27/97	5,390.6	182.8	2,594.1	6.1	3.4	12.2	7.0	3.3	2.13	2.70	12.47	0.30	37.25 - 27.56	15.2	0.9
6/28/96	5,207.8	188.3	2,521.7	6.7	3.6	12.5	7.5	3.5	2.16	...	11.64	0.30	30.56 - 19.00	11.5	1.2
6/30/95	4,300.0	140.3	2,125.6	6.1	3.3	11.3	6.6	3.3	1.66	2.04	10.05	0.30	27.81 - 17.88	13.8	1.3
7/01/94	3,552.5	① 88.1	1,787.7	4.8	2.5	7.9	4.9	3.4	① 1.08	1.47	13.63	0.30	22.50 - 15.38	17.5	1.6
6/30/93	2,258.3	69.1	1,247.3	5.5	3.1	8.0	5.5	3.9	0.96	1.20	12.18	0.30	21.13 - 14.50	18.6	1.7

Statistics are as originally reported. Adj. for 2-for-1 stk. split, 9/00. ① Incl. non-recurr. chrg. $22.7 mill. fr restruc. ② Incl. non-recurr. gain $33.8 mill. ③ Incl. after-tax spec. chrgs. of $30.4 mill. ④ Bef. inc. of $15.3 mill. from disc. ops.; incl. after-tax spec. chrg. of $236.7 mill. ⑤ Bef. acctg. change chrg. of $580.5 mill.; incl. pretax spec. chrgs. of $79.6 mill.

OFFICERS:
R. Vallee, Chmn., C.E.O.
R. Sadowski, Sr. V.P., C.F.O., Asst. Sec.
D. R. Birk, Sr. V.P., Sec., Gen. Couns.

INVESTOR CONTACT: John J. Hovis, V.P., Investor Relations, (480) 643-7053

PRINCIPAL OFFICE: 2211 South 47th Street, Phoenix, AZ 85034

TELEPHONE NUMBER: (480) 643-2000
FAX: (480) 643-7370
WEB: www.avnet.com

NO. OF EMPLOYEES: 11,000 (approx.)

SHAREHOLDERS: 5,650 (approx. record)

ANNUAL MEETING: In Nov.

INCORPORATED: NY, July, 1955

AVON PRODUCTS, INC.

EXCH.	SYM.	REC. PRICE	P/E RATIO	YLD.	MKT. CAP.	RANGE (52-WK.)	'02 Y/E PR.	DIV. ACH.
NYSE	AVP	52.00 (2/28/03)	23.4	1.6%	$12.23 bill.	57.10 - 43.49	53.87	12 yrs.

UPPER MEDIUM GRADE. THE COMPANY ANNOUNCED PLANS TO REALIGN ITS NORTH AMERICAN MANUFACTURING OPERATIONS.

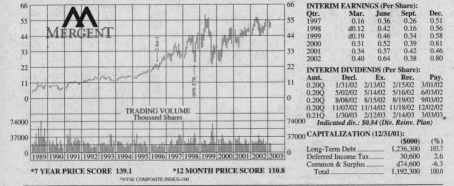

*7 YEAR PRICE SCORE 139.1 ***12 MONTH PRICE SCORE 110.8**
*NYSE COMPOSITE INDEX=100

INTERIM EARNINGS (Per Share):

Qtr.	Mar.	June	Sept.	Dec.
1997	0.16	0.36	0.26	0.51
1998	d0.12	0.42	0.16	0.56
1999	d0.19	0.46	0.34	0.58
2000	0.31	0.52	0.39	0.81
2001	0.34	0.57	0.42	0.46
2002	0.40	0.64	0.38	0.80

INTERIM DIVIDENDS (Per Share):

Amt.	Decl.	Ex.	Rec.	Pay.
0.20Q	1/31/02	2/13/02	2/15/02	3/01/02
0.20Q	5/02/02	5/14/02	5/16/02	6/03/02
0.20Q	8/08/02	8/15/02	8/19/02	9/03/02
0.20Q	11/07/02	11/14/02	11/18/02	12/02/02
0.21Q	1/30/03	2/12/03	2/14/03	3/03/03

Indicated div.: $0.84 (Div. Reinv. Plan)

CAPITALIZATION (12/31/01):

	($000)	(%)
Long-Term Debt	1,236,300	103.7
Deferred Income Tax	30,600	2.6
Common & Surplus	d74,600	-6.3
Total	1,192,300	100.0

BUSINESS:

Avon Products, Inc. is a global manufacturer and marketer of beauty and related products. AVP's products fall into four product categories: Beauty, which consists of cosmetics, fragrance and toiletries; Beauty Plus, which consists of jewelry, watches and apparel and accessories; Beyond Beauty, which consists of home products, gifts and candles; and women's health and wellness, which consists of vitamins and nutrition supplements, exercise and fitness items, and self-care and stress relief products. Avon product lines include such brands as AVON COLOR, ANEW, SKIN-SO-SOFT, ADVANCE TECHNIQUES HAIR CARE, BEСOMING and AVON WELLNESS. As of 12/31/02, the Company had operations in 58 countries and its products were distributed in 85 more for coverage in 143 countries. Sales are made principally by approximately 3.9 million independent Avon representatives. In 2002, net sales by geographic area consisted of: North America, 39.1%; Latin America, 27.6%; Europe, 19.9% and Pacific, 13.4%.

RECENT DEVELOPMENTS:

For the year ended 12/31/02, net income was $534.6 million versus income of $444.9 million, before an accounting change charge of $300,000, in the previous year. Results for 2002 included a net after-tax charge of $25.2 million related to the Company's business transformation initiative. Results for 2001 included a special after-tax charge of $68.3 million and an after-tax settlement gain of $15.7 million. Total revenue increased 3.8% to $6.23 billion from $6.00 billion the prior year. The Company attributed the increase in revenue to record unit growth of 13.0% and a 10.0% increase in active representatives, with all geographic regions contributing to the gains.

PROSPECTS:

On 1/22/03, AVP announced it will realign its North American manufacturing operations as part of its business transformation initiatives. The Company will phase out its Montreal-based manufacturing facility by the first quarter of 2004 and transfer the production to its larger U.S. plants in Springdale, Ohio, and Morton Grove, Illinois. Separately, on 1/31/03, AVP announced that it will end its retail alliance with J.C. Penney and begin to sell its BEСOMING brand through its direct selling channel in the U.S.

ANNUAL FINANCIAL DATA:

FISCAL YEAR	TOT. REVS. ($mill.)	NET INC. ($mill.)	TOT. ASSETS ($mill.)	OPER. PROFIT %	NET PROFIT %	RET. ON EQUITY %	RET. ON ASSETS %	CURR. RATIO	EARN. PER SH. $	CASH FL. PER SH. $	TANG. BK. VAL.$	DIV. PER SH. $	PRICE RANGE	AVG. P/E RATIO	AVG. YIELD %
p12/31/02	6,228.3	⑥ 534.6							⑥ 2.22			0.80	57.10 - 43.49	22.7	1.6
12/31/01	5,994.5	③⑤ 430.3	3,193.1	12.5	7.2	...	13.5	1.3	③⑤ 1.79	2.25	...	0.76	50.12 - 35.55	23.9	1.8
12/31/00	5,714.6	③ 485.1	2,826.4	13.8	8.5	...	17.2	1.1	③ 2.02	2.40	...	0.74	49.75 - 25.25	18.6	2.0
12/31/99	5,289.1	④ 302.4	2,528.6	10.4	5.7	...	12.0	0.8	④ 1.17	1.49	...	0.72	59.13 - 23.31	35.2	1.7
12/31/98	5,212.7	② 270.0	2,433.5	9.1	5.2	94.7	11.1	1.0	② 1.02	1.29	1.09	0.68	46.25 - 25.00	34.9	1.9
12/31/97	5,079.4	338.8	2,272.9	10.6	6.7	118.9	14.9	1.0	1.27	1.54	1.08	0.63	39.00 - 25.31	25.3	2.0
12/31/96	4,814.2	317.9	2,222.4	11.3	6.6	131.5	14.3	1.0	1.19	1.43	0.91	0.58	29.75 - 18.16	20.1	2.4
12/31/95	4,492.1	① 286.1	2,052.8	11.3	6.4	148.5	13.9	1.0	① 1.05	1.26	0.71	0.53	19.59 - 13.50	15.8	3.2
12/31/94	4,266.5	①③ 264.8	1,978.3	11.6	6.2	142.7	13.4	1.0	①③ 0.94	1.14	0.67	0.47	15.91 - 12.09	14.9	3.4
12/31/93	4,007.6	①③ 249.6	1,958.0	11.4	6.2	79.5	12.7	...	①③ 0.87	1.08	1.09	0.42	16.09 - 11.91	16.2	3.0

Statistics are as originally reported. Adj. for stk. splits: 2-for-1, 9/98; 6/96. ① Bef. disc. oper. loss $29.6 mill., 12/95; $25.0 mill., 12/94; $10.0 mill., 12/93 ② Incl. non-recur. chrg. $70.5 mill. ③ Bef. acctg. change chrg., 12/01; $6.7 mill., 12/01; $45.2 mill., 12/94; $107.5 mill., 12/93 ④ Incl. pre-tax special chrg. of $105.2 mill. ⑤ Incl. after-tax cash settlement gain $15.7 mill.; after-tax liab. chrg. $3.4 mill.; asset impair. chrg. $14.5 mill.; after-tax spec. chrg. $68.3 mill. ⑥ Incl. included a net after-tax chrg. of $25.2 mill. for bus. trans.

OFFICERS:
A. Jung., Chmn., C.E.O.
S. J. Kropf, Pres., C.O.O.
R. J. Corti, Exec. V.P., C.F.O.
INVESTOR CONTACT: Ruth M. Scharankov, Investor Relations, (212) 282-5623
PRINCIPAL OFFICE: 1345 Avenue of the Americas, New York, NY 10105-0196

TELEPHONE NUMBER: (212) 282-5000
FAX: (212) 282-6035
WEB: www.avon.com
NO. OF EMPLOYEES: 43,800 (avg.)
SHAREHOLDERS: 21,393
ANNUAL MEETING: In May
INCORPORATED: NY, Jan., 1916

·INSTITUTIONAL HOLDINGS:
No. of Institutions: 434
Shares Held: 197,939,233
% Held: 84.1

INDUSTRY: Toilet preparations (SIC: 2844)

TRANSFER AGENT(S): EquiServe, Jersey City, NJ

AVX CORPORATION

EXCH.	SYM.	REC. PRICE	P/E RATIO	YLD.	MKT. CAP.	RANGE (52-WK.)	'02 Y/E PR.
NYSE	AVX	9.46 (2/28/03)	946.0	1.6%	$1.65 bill.	23.60 - 7.31	9.80

LOWER MEDIUM GRADE. THE COMPANY'S REORGANIZATION OF CERTAIN EUROPEAN MANUFACTURING FACILITIES AND THE TRANSFER OF PRODUCTION TO ITS FACILITY IN CHINA ARE ON SCHEDULE.

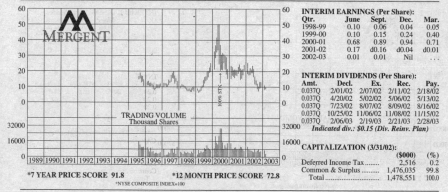

*7 YEAR PRICE SCORE 91.8   ***12 MONTH PRICE SCORE 72.8**

*NYSE COMPOSITE INDEX=100

TRADING VOLUME Thousand Shares

INTERIM EARNINGS (Per Share):

Qtr.	June	Sept.	Dec.	Mar.
1998-99	0.10	0.06	0.04	0.05
1999-00	0.10	0.15	0.24	0.40
2000-01	0.68	0.89	0.94	0.71
2001-02	0.17	d0.16	d0.04	d0.01
2002-03	0.01	0.01	Nil	...

INTERIM DIVIDENDS (Per Share):

Amt.	Decl.	Ex.	Rec.	Pay.
0.037Q	2/01/02	2/07/02	2/11/02	2/18/02
0.037Q	4/20/02	5/02/02	5/06/02	5/13/02
0.037Q	7/23/02	8/07/02	8/09/02	8/16/02
0.037Q	10/25/02	11/06/02	11/08/02	11/15/02
0.037Q	2/06/03	2/19/03	2/21/03	2/28/03
Indicated div.: $0.15 (Div. Reinv. Plan)				

CAPITALIZATION (3/31/02):

	($000)	(%)
Deferred Income Tax	2,516	0.2
Common & Surplus	1,476,035	99.8
Total	1,478,551	100.0

BUSINESS:

AVX Corporation is a manufacturer and supplier of a broad line of passive electronic components and related products. AVX's electronic components include ceramic and tantalum capacitors, film capacitors, ferrites, varistors and non-linear resistors. Capacitors are used in virtually all electronic products and applications to store, filter and regulate electrical energy. The Company also manufactures and sells electronic connectors and distributes and sells certain passive components and connectors. For the year ended 3/31/02, passive components accounted for 91.8% of net sales, while connectors accounted for 8.2% of net sales.

RECENT DEVELOPMENTS:

For the third quarter ended 12/31/02, AVX reported a net loss of $694,000 compared with a net loss of $6.5 million in the corresponding prior-year quarter. Results for 2001 included a restructuring charge of $7.8 million and a charge related to facility consolidation and headcount reductions of $2.7 million. Net sales declined 7.1% to $282.6 million from $304.3 million a year earlier, primarily due to lower selling prices and soft demand across all markets, particularly the telecommunications and information technology hardware industries. Passive component sales decreased 7.4% to $258.0 million, while connector sales were down 4.4% to $24.7 million. Gross profit dropped 36.9% to $13.6 million, or 4.8% of net sales, from $21.5 million, or 7.1% of net sales, in the previous year.

PROSPECTS:

Uncertainty in the global economy may lead to continued soft near-term demand for electronic components. In addition, the Company anticipates a continuing, but more modest decline in average selling prices for certain commodity related products resulting from the imbalance in the electronic component industry's supply capacity and end market demand. Lower selling prices may also continue to depress operating margins and negatively affect the carrying value of inventories and future purchase commitments. Meanwhile, in reaction to the slow-down in near-term demand, AVX has significantly reduced its labor force and operating costs. AVX's previously initiated reorganization of certain European manufacturing facilities and the transfer of production to its facility in China are on schedule.

ANNUAL FINANCIAL DATA:

FISCAL YEAR	TOT. REVS. ($mill.)	NET INC. ($mill.)	TOT. ASSETS ($mill.)	OPER. PROFIT %	NET PROFIT %	RET. ON EQUITY %	RET. ON ASSETS %	CURR. RATIO	EARN. PER SH. $	CASH FL. PER SH. $	TANG. BK. VAL.$	DIV. PER SH. $	PRICE RANGE	AVG. P/E RATIO	AVG. YIELD %
3/31/02	1,250.0	③ d7.2	1,691.6	...	...	...	...	5.9	③ d0.04	0.75	8.06	0.15	24.45 - 14.51	...	0.8
3/31/01	2,608.1	567.5	1,885.4	31.6	21.8	37.7	30.1	3.9	3.22	3.99	8.20	0.14	50.00 - 15.13	10.1	0.4
3/31/00	1,630.3	156.9	1,308.3	13.6	9.6	16.0	12.0	3.0	0.90	1.46	5.21	0.13	25.22 - 6.28	17.5	0.8
3/31/99	1,245.5	41.5	1,058.0	4.3	3.3	5.0	3.9	3.5	0.24	0.78	4.36	0.13	11.69 - 6.75	38.4	1.4
3/31/98	1,267.7	134.7	1,048.7	14.7	10.6	15.8	12.8	4.3	0.76	1.26	4.63	0.12	19.81 - 8.84	18.9	0.8
3/31/97	1,126.2	121.3	949.3	15.3	10.8	16.6	12.8	3.5	0.69	1.16	3.96	0.11	13.75 - 8.00	15.8	1.0
3/31/96	1,207.8	137.7	867.5	16.9	11.4	22.1	15.9	2.8	0.79	1.19	3.34	0.03	19.00 - 10.56	18.7	0.2
3/31/95	988.9	74.9	670.7	11.1	7.6	16.4	11.2	2.3	0.44	0.79	2.43	...	...	...	...
3/31/94	795.5	② 35.2	574.0	7.0	4.4	8.8	6.1	2.4	② 0.21	0.53	2.10	...	...	...	...
3/31/93	718.2	① 28.9	...	6.8	4.0	...	...	...	① 0.17	0.47	...	...	...	...	...

Statistics are as originally reported. Adj. for stk. split., 2-for-1, 6/00. ① Bef. extraord. credit $2.5 mill. ② Bef. acctg. change chrg. $5.0 mill. ③ Incl. restr. chrg. of $24.6 mill., inventory write-downs and facility consolid. chrgs. of $32.5 mill., and a write-down of customer receivs. $3.0 mill.

OFFICERS:
B. P. Rosen, Chmn.
K. Itoh, Vice-Chmn.
J. S. Gilbertson, Pres., C.E.O.
INVESTOR CONTACT: Kurt P. Cummings, V.P., C.F.O., Treas., Sec., (843) 946-0691
PRINCIPAL OFFICE: 801 17th Avenue South, Myrtle Beach, SC 29577

TELEPHONE NUMBER: (843) 448-9411
FAX: (843) 448-6091
WEB: www.avxcorp.com
NO. OF EMPLOYEES: 12,900 (approx.)
SHAREHOLDERS: 525 (approx.)
ANNUAL MEETING: In July
INCORPORATED: DE, 1972

INSTITUTIONAL HOLDINGS:
No. of Institutions: 129
Shares Held: 32,196,104
% Held: 18.5
INDUSTRY: Electronic connectors (SIC 3678)
TRANSFER AGENT(S): The American Stock Transfer & Trust Company, New York, NY

AZTAR CORPORATION

EXCH.	SYM.	REC. PRICE	P/E RATIO	YLD.	MKT. CAP.	RANGE (52-WK.)	'02 Y/E PR.
NYSE	AZR	11.83 (2/28/03)	7.8	...	$433.5 mill.	25.90 - 11.00	14.28

MEDIUM GRADE. THE COMPANY IS ADDING IMPROVEMENTS TO EXISTING SPACE IN THE TROPICANA, INCLUDING A MAJOR RENOVATION OF THE TROPICANA'S BOARDWALK FACADE:

INTERIM EARNINGS (Per Share):

Qtr.	Mar.	June	Sept.	Dec.
1999	0.06	0.13	0.18	0.10
2000	0.25	0.51	0.34	0.12
2001	0.28	0.40	0.46	0.33
2002	0.35	0.42	0.43	0.31

INTERIM DIVIDENDS (Per Share):

Amt.	Decl.	Ex.	Rec.	Pay.
		No dividends paid.		

CAPITALIZATION (1/3/02):

	($000)	(%)
Long-Term Debt	458,659	49.1
Deferred Income Tax	15,846	1.7
Redeemable Pfd. Stock	5,959	0.6
Common & Surplus	453,841	48.6
Total	934,305	100.0

*7 YEAR PRICE SCORE 158.4   *12 MONTH PRICE SCORE 84.8

*NYSE COMPOSITE INDEX=100

BUSINESS:

Aztar Corporation operates in the major domestic gaming markets with casino/hotel facilities in Atlantic City, New Jersey, and in Las Vegas and Laughlin, Nevada. In addition, AZR operates riverboat casinos in Caruthersville, Missouri and Evansville, Indiana. As of 12/31/01, the Tropicana Casino and Resort encompassed about 14 acres and had 220 yards of ocean beach frontage along the Boardwalk in Atlantic City. The Tropicana Resort and Casino is located on a 34-acre site on the southeast corner of the Strip and Tropicana Avenue in Las Vegas. The Ramada Express Hotel and Casino is located on about 31 acres in Laughlin, Nevada. Total sales for 2002 were derived from the following: casino, 79.7%; rooms, 8.8%; food and beverage, 6.7%; and other, 4.8%.

RECENT DEVELOPMENTS:

For the year ended 1/2/03, net income increased 1.5% to $58.9 million from $58.0 million the year before. Total revenues slipped 1.8% to $834.3 million compared with $849.5 million a year earlier. Casino revenues slid 1.9% to $665.0 million from $678.2 million in the prior year.

Rooms revenues declined 2.8% to $73.7 million from $75.8 million in the previous year. Food and beverage revenues decreased 1.2% to $56.2 million, while other revenues improved 2.1% to $39.9 million.

PROSPECTS:

The expansion of the Tropicana Atlantic City, which is scheduled to be completed by 3/1/04, will create the largest hotel, third largest casino and only indoor Las Vegas-style retail/dining/entertainment complex in Atlantic City. The expansion includes 502 additional hotel rooms, 20,000 square feet of meeting space, 2,400 parking spaces, and the "Quarter," the project's centerpiece, a 200,000-square-foot dining, entertainment and retail center. Additionally, the Company is adding improvements to existing space in the Tropicana, including a major renovation of the Tropicana's boardwalk facade and the addition of 280 slot machines and dining and retail facilities in an area named "The Marketplace at the Boardwalk."

ANNUAL FINANCIAL DATA:

FISCAL YEAR	TOT. REVS. ($mill.)	NET INC. ($mill.)	TOT. ASSETS ($mill.)	OPER. PROFIT %	NET PROFIT %	RET. ON EQUITY %	RET. ON ASSETS %	CURR. RATIO	EARN. PER SH.$	CASH FL. PER SH.$	TANG. BK. VAL.$	PRICE RANGE	AVG. P/E RATIO
p1/02/03	834.3	58.9							1.51			25.90 - 11.00	12.2
1/03/02	849.5	58.0	1,061.0	15.5	6.8	12.8	5.5	1.4	1.48	2.85	12.38	18.66 - 8.88	9.3
12/28/00	848.1	③ 53.1	1,011.7	13.6	6.3	12.6	5.3	1.1	③ 1.23	2.54	10.92	16.69 - 8.50	10.2
12/31/99	800.3	① 22.1	1,049.0	11.2	2.8	5.2	2.1	1.3	① 0.46	1.69	9.96	11.13 - 4.19	16.6
12/31/98	806.1	① 11.5	1,077.7	10.1	1.4	2.5	1.1	1.2	① 0.23	1.44	10.02	9.94 - 2.88	27.8
1/01/98	782.4	③ 4.4	1,091.5	8.6	0.6	1.0	0.4	1.0	③ 0.08	1.26	9.82	8.50 - 5.88	89.7
1/02/97	777.5	②③ 20.6	1,119.6	7.6	2.7	4.7	1.8	0.9	②③ 0.47	1.73	9.76	14.13 - 6.50	21.9
12/28/95	572.9	② d5.0	1,013.2	7.5	...	...	...	0.7	② d0.14	0.97	9.40	10.50 - 5.63	...
12/29/94	541.4	① 16.8	915.4	12.8	3.1	4.7	1.8	1.3	① 0.42	1.47	9.65	7.88 - 5.38	15.8
12/30/93	518.8	11.4	877.2	7.2	2.2	3.3	1.3	1.1	0.28	1.20	9.29	10.13 - 6.00	28.8

Statistics are as originally reported. ① Bef. extra. chrg. $15.7 mill., 1999; $1.3 mill., 1998; chrg. $2.7 mill., 1994. ② Incl. pre-opening expen. of $2.9 mill., 1996; & $7.7 mill., 1995. ③ Incl. tax benefits of $7.5 mill., 2000; $2.2 mill., 1997 & $22.6 mill., 1996.

OFFICERS:
P. E. Rubeli, Chmn., C.E.O.
R. M. Haddock, Exec. V.P., C.F.O.
N. W. Armstrong Jr., V.P., Admin., Sec.
N. A. Ciarfalia, Treas.
INVESTOR CONTACT: Joe Cole, V.P., Corp. Commun., (602) 381-4111
PRINCIPAL OFFICE: 2390 East Camelback Road, Suite 400, Phoenix, AZ 85016-3452

TELEPHONE NUMBER: (602) 381-4100
FAX: (602) 381-4107
WEB: www.aztar.com
NO. OF EMPLOYEES: 9,900 (avg.)
SHAREHOLDERS: 7,192
ANNUAL MEETING: In May
INCORPORATED: DE, June, 1989

INSTITUTIONAL HOLDINGS:
No. of Institutions: 136
Shares Held: 31,618,634
% Held: 84.7
INDUSTRY: Amusement and recreation, nec (SIC: 7999)
TRANSFER AGENT(S): Mellon Investor Services, Los Angeles, CA

BAKER HUGHES INC.

EXCH.	SYM.	REC. PRICE	P/E RATIO	YLD.	MKT. CAP.	RANGE (52-WK.)	'02 Y/E PR.
NYSE	BHI	31.02 (2/28/03)	55.4	1.5%	$10.42 bill.	39.95 - 22.60	32.19

MEDIUM GRADE. THE COMPANY EXPECTS FULL-YEAR 2003 INCOME FROM CONTINUING OPERATIONS OF BETWEEN $1.00 AND $1.10 PER DILUTED SHARE.

*7 YEAR PRICE SCORE 103.4   ***12 MONTH PRICE SCORE 106.3**
*NYSE COMPOSITE INDEX=100

INTERIM EARNINGS (Per Share):

Qtr.	Mar.	June	Sept.	Dec.
1998	0.35	0.36	d1.65	0.02
1999	0.14	0.22	0.05	d0.25
2000	0.04	0.19	0.20	d0.12
2001	0.21	0.31	0.41	0.37
2002	0.10	0.21	0.26	d0.01

INTERIM DIVIDENDS (Per Share):

Amt.	Decl.	Ex.	Rec.	Pay.
0.115Q	1/30/02	2/07/02	2/11/02	2/25/02
0.115Q	4/24/02	5/02/02	5/06/02	5/24/02
0.115Q	7/24/02	8/01/02	8/05/02	8/23/02
0.115Q	10/23/02	10/31/02	11/04/02	11/22/02
0.115Q	1/29/03	2/06/03	2/10/03	2/21/03

Indicated div.: $0.46

CAPITALIZATION (12/31/01):

	($000)	(%)
Long-Term Debt	1,682,400	32.2
Deferred Income Tax	210,300	4.0
Common & Surplus	3,327,800	63.7
Total	5,220,500	100.0

BUSINESS:

Baker Hughes Inc. is primarily engaged in the oilfield and process industries. The oilfield services segment supplies wellbore related products, services and systems to the worldwide oil and gas industry. Through its six oilfield service operations, Baker Atlas, Baker Hughes INTEQ, Baker Oil Tools, Baker Petrolite, Centrilift and Hughes Christensen, BHI provides equipment, products and services for drilling, formation evaluation, completion and production of oil and gas wells. The process division provides manufactures, markets and services a broad range of separation and treatment solutions and continuous and batch centrifuges and specialty filters to a wide range of markets. As of 12/31/02, BHI also owned 30.0% of the Western GECO seismic venture, formed through the 11/30/00 combination of the Company's Western Geophysical division and Schlumberger's Geco-Prakla division.

RECENT DEVELOPMENTS:

For the year ended 12/31/02, income from continuing operations was $223.7 million versus income from continuing operations of $418.1 million a year earlier. Results included a 2002 credit of $1.9 million and a 2001 charge of $1.8 million related to restructuring actions. Results for 2001 also included a nonrecurring gain of $2.4 million. Revenues fell 2.3% to $5.02 billion. Separately, in February 2003, BHI's Baker Atlas business unit acquired certain assets and intellectual property of the borehole seismic acquisition business of Compagnie Generale Geophysique and formed a venture for processing and interpreting borehole seismic data. BHI owns 51.0% of the venture.

PROSPECTS:

BHI's near-term results are likely to be affected by the ongoing political and economic situation in Venezuela, which is resulting in a significant reduction in oil production. However, BHI expects overall business activity to improve as 2003 unfolds. Accordingly, BHN is projecting full-year 2003 income from continuing operations of between $1.00 and $1.10 per diluted share. Separately, in December 2002, BHI entered into exclusive negotiations for the sale of its interest in its oil-producing operations in West Africa, and received $10.0 million as a deposit.

ANNUAL FINANCIAL DATA:

FISCAL YEAR	TOT. REVS. ($mill.)	NET INC. ($mill.)	TOT. ASSETS ($mill.)	OPER. PROFIT %	NET PROFIT %	RET. ON EQUITY %	RET. ON ASSETS %	CURR. RATIO	EARN. PER SH.$	CASH FL. PER SH.$	TANG. BK. VAL.$	DIV. PER SH.$	PRICE RANGE	AVG. P/E RATIO	AVG. YIELD %
p12/31/02	5,020.4	⑨ 223.7							⑨ 0.66			0.46	39.95 - 22.60	47.4	1.5
12/31/01	5,382.2	⑧ 438.7	6,676.2	13.6	8.2	13.2	6.6	2.2	⑧ 1.30	2.32	5.69	0.46	45.29 - 25.76	27.3	1.3
12/31/00	5,233.8	⑥ 102.3	6,452.7	7.5	2.0	3.4	1.6	2.5	⑥ 0.31	2.14	4.64	0.46	43.38 - 19.63	101.6	1.5
12/31/99	4,546.7	⑤ 52.3	7,039.8	4.5	1.2	1.7	0.7	2.3	⑤ 0.16	2.52	4.17	0.46	36.25 - 15.00	160.1	1.8
① 12/31/98	6,311.9	② d297.4	7,810.8	...	...	...	...	2.1	② d0.92	1.43	3.98	0.46	44.13 - 15.00	...	1.6
⑦ 12/31/97	1,572.9	111.2	7,230.6	12.9	7.1	3.2	1.5	2.1	0.34	...	6.26	...	49.63 - 32.63	120.9	...
9/30/97	3,685.4	③ 109.1	4,756.3	7.1	3.0	4.2	2.3	2.4	③ 0.71	1.93	9.16	0.46	49.63 - 32.63	57.9	1.1
9/30/96	3,027.7	176.4	3,297.4	10.1	5.8	10.4	5.3	2.7	1.23	2.30	6.45	0.46	38.88 - 22.75	25.0	1.5
9/30/95	2,637.5	③ 120.0	3,166.6	9.7	4.5	7.9	3.8	2.7	⑥ 0.67	1.94	5.21	0.46	24.88 - 16.75	31.1	2.2
9/30/94	2,504.8	④ 131.1	2,999.7	7.4	5.2	8.0	4.4	2.6	④ 0.85	2.14	5.95	0.46	22.13 - 17.00	23.0	2.4

Statistics are as originally reported. ① Refl. acq. of Western Atlas, Inc. ② Incl. chrgs. of $414.1 mill. ③ Bef. acctg. chrg. 9/30/97, $12.1 mill.; chrg. 9/30/95, $14.6 mill. ④ Bef. extraord. loss of $44.3 mill. & net acctg. chge. of $44.2 mill. ⑤ Incl. cr. of $7.2 mill.; bef. loss of $19.0 mill. fr. disc. ops. ⑥ Incl. net unusual chrg. of $69.6 mill. & $14.1 mill. gain on securities. ⑦ 3 mos. only due to fiscal yr.-end chge. ⑧ Incl. unusual chrg. of $1.6 mill.; bef. extraord. loss of $1.5 mill. & acctg. chge. chrg. of $800,000 ⑨ Incl. restruct. cr. of $1.9 mill.; bef. loss of $12.3 mill. fr. disc. ops. & acctg. chge. chrg. of $42.5 mill.

OFFICERS:
M. E. Wiley, Chmn., Pres., C.E.O.
G. S. Finley, Sr. V.P., C.F.O.
D. C. Doty, V.P., Treas.
INVESTOR CONTACT: Gary R. Flaharty, Dir., Investor Relations, (713) 439-8039
PRINCIPAL OFFICE: 3900 Essex Lane, Suite 1200, Houston, TX 77027-5177

TELEPHONE NUMBER: (713) 439-8600
FAX: (713) 739-8699
WEB: www.bakerhughes.com
NO. OF EMPLOYEES: 26,800 (avg.)
SHAREHOLDERS: 75,581 (approx.)
ANNUAL MEETING: In Apr.
INCORPORATED: DE, Apr., 1987

INSTITUTIONAL HOLDINGS:
No. of Institutions: 382
Shares Held: 299,636,127
% Held: 89.3
INDUSTRY: Oil and gas field machinery (SIC: 3533)
TRANSFER AGENT(S): Mellon Investor Services, LLC, Ridgefield Park, NJ

BALDOR ELECTRIC COMPANY

EXCH.	SYM.	REC. PRICE	P/E RATIO	YLD.	MKT. CAP.	RANGE (52-WK.)	'02 Y/E PR.
NYSE	BEZ	22.00 (2/28/03)	31.4	2.4%	$0.75 bill.	25.24 - 17.30	19.75

MEDIUM GRADE. THE COMPANY SHOULD CONTINUE TO BENEFIT FROM CONTINUED INVESTMENTS IN PRODUCTIVITY, EMPLOYEE TRAINING, AND ADDING NEW CUSTOMERS.

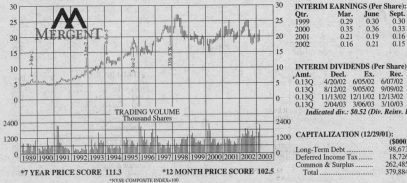

*7 YEAR PRICE SCORE 111.3   ***12 MONTH PRICE SCORE 102.5**

*NYSE COMPOSITE INDEX=100

INTERIM EARNINGS (Per Share):

Qtr.	Mar.	June	Sept.	Dec.
1999	0.29	0.30	0.30	0.30
2000	0.35	0.36	0.33	0.29
2001	0.21	0.19	0.16	0.10
2002	0.16	0.21	0.15	0.18

INTERIM DIVIDENDS (Per Share):

Amt.	Decl.	Ex.	Rec.	Pay.
0.13Q	4/20/02	6/05/02	6/07/02	6/28/02
0.13Q	8/12/02	9/05/02	9/09/02	9/30/02
0.13Q	11/13/02	12/11/02	12/13/02	1/03/03
0.13Q	2/04/03	3/06/03	3/10/03	3/31/03

Indicated div.: $0.52 (Div. Reinv. Plan)

CAPITALIZATION (12/29/01):

	($000)	(%)
Long-Term Debt	98,673	26.0
Deferred Income Tax	18,726	4.9
Common & Surplus	262,485	69.1
Total	379,884	100.0

BUSINESS:

Baldor Electric Company designs, manufactures and markets a line of electric motors, drives, generators and related products. The motor product and controls line BEZ makes range from ⅟₅₀ HP through 1,500 HP A.C. and ⅟₅₀ HP through 800 HP D.C. The adjustable speed controls product line ranges from ⅟₅₀ HP to 700 HP. The Company sells industrial control products, which include servo products, DC controls, and inverter and vector drives. BEZ's motors and drives are designed, manufactured and marketed for general purposes and individual customer requirements and specifications.

RECENT DEVELOPMENTS:

For the fiscal year ended 12/28/02, net income climbed 6.7% to $23.9 million compared with $22.4 million the previous year. Net sales declined 1.4% to $549.5 million from $557.5 million the year before. The growth in earnings was primarily due to an improved operating profit margin resulting from continued investments in productivity. Gross profit decreased 2.1% to $152.7 million from $156.0 million the prior year. Operating income inched up 1.2% to $45.3 million versus $44.7 million a year earlier.

PROSPECTS:

During 2002, BEZ achieved a strengthened balance sheet and permanent cost reductions, and made efforts to improve its competitive position. In the long term, the Company will continue to focus on new product development in motors, drives, and generators. Moverover, the Company should benefit from continued investments in productivity, employee training, and adding new customers. Separately, on 2/13/03, the Company announced that it has reached an agreement to purchase Energy Dynamics, Inc., a designer, assembler, and marketer of industrial generator sets. Terms of the transaction were not disclosed.

ANNUAL FINANCIAL DATA:

FISCAL YEAR	TOT. REVS. ($000)	NET INC. ($000)	TOT. ASSETS ($000)	OPER. PROFIT %	NET PROFIT %	RET. ON EQUITY %	RET. ON ASSETS %	CURR. RATIO	EARN. PER SH. $	CASH FL. PER SH. $	TANG. BK. VAL.$	DIV. PER SH. $	PRICE RANGE	AVG. P/E RATIO	AVG. YIELD %
p12/28/02	549,507	23,895						0.69				0.52	25.24 - 17.30	30.8	2.4
12/29/01	558,298	22,385	457,527	7.3	4.0	8.5	4.9	3.2	0.65	1.25	6.05	0.52	25.15 - 18.00	33.2	2.4
12/30/00	623,080	46,263	464,978	13.4	7.4	17.7	9.9	3.0	1.34	1.91	7.72	0.49	22.50 - 14.88	13.9	2.6
1/01/00	579,262	43,723	423,941	13.8	7.5	16.4	10.3	3.1	1.19	1.79	7.48	0.43	21.69 - 17.00	16.3	2.2
1/02/99	591,425	44,610	411,926	13.8	7.5	16.9	10.8	3.2	1.17	1.71	7.21	0.40	27.19 - 19.06	19.8	1.7
1/03/98	559,783	40,365	355,889	13.3	7.2	16.6	11.3	2.8	1.09	1.61	6.76	0.35	23.82 - 18.19	19.3	1.6
12/28/96	505,372	35,173	325,486	12.8	7.0	17.6	10.8	3.1	0.97	1.45	5.73	0.29	18.76 - 13.88	16.9	1.8
12/30/95	475,699	32,305	313,462	12.6	6.8	15.3	10.3	3.4	0.84	1.24	5.69	0.25	19.88 - 12.94	19.5	1.5
12/31/94	419,820	26,359	283,155	11.7	6.3	14.3	9.3	2.9	0.70	1.04	5.03	0.20	13.75 - 10.63	17.5	1.6
1/01/94	357,993	19,426	237,950	10.2	5.4	12.1	8.2	3.5	0.52	0.85	4.50	0.16	12.35 - 8.07	19.6	1.6

Statistics are as originally reported. Adj. for a 3-for-2 stock split 9/95; 6-for-5, 1/94; 4-for-3, 12/97.

OFFICERS:
R. S. Boreham Jr., Chmn.
R. L. Quails, Vice-Chmn.
J. A. McFarland, Pres., C.E.O.
R. E. Tucker, C.F.O., Treas., Sec.

INVESTOR CONTACT: Lloyd G. Davis, V.P., C.O.O., Sec., (479) 646-4711

PRINCIPAL OFFICE: 5711 R. S. Boreham, Jr. Street, Ft. Smith, AR 72901

TELEPHONE NUMBER: (479) 646-4711
FAX: (479) 648-5752
WEB: www.baldor.com

NO. OF EMPLOYEES: 3,684

SHAREHOLDERS: 4,456

ANNUAL MEETING: In Apr.

INCORPORATED: MO, Mar., 1920

INSTITUTIONAL HOLDINGS:
No. of Institutions: 111
Shares Held: 17,698,513
% Held: 51.9

INDUSTRY: Motors and generators (SIC: 3621)

TRANSFER AGENT(S): Continental Stock Transfer & Trust Company, New York, NY

BALL CORPORATION

EXCH.	SYM.	REC. PRICE	P/E RATIO	YLD.	MKT. CAP.	RANGE (52-WK.)	'02 Y/E PR.
NYSE	BLL	53.28 (2/28/03)	19.2	0.7%	$3.08 bill.	54.49 - 32.82	51.19

MEDIUM GRADE. THE COMPANY ACQUIRED SCHMALBACH-LUBECA AG, THE SECOND LARGEST MANUFAC-
TURER OF BEVERAGE CANS IN EUROPE, FOR ABOUT 900.0 MILLION EUROS IN CASH.

*7 YEAR PRICE SCORE 213.9   ***12 MONTH PRICE SCORE 120.6**
*NYSE COMPOSITE INDEX=100

INTERIM EARNINGS (Per Share):

Qtr.	Mar.	June	Sept.	Dec.
1997	0.11	0.34	0.37	0.12
1998	0.07	0.29	0.38	d0.31
1999	0.24	0.48	0.57	0.30
2000	0.31	d0.28	0.72	0.31
2001	0.31	d2.96	0.61	0.14
2002	0.48	0.87	0.87	0.56

INTERIM DIVIDENDS (Per Share):

Amt.	Decl.	Ex.	Rec.	Pay.
0.09Q	1/23/02	2/27/02	3/01/02	3/15/02
0.09Q	4/24/02	5/30/02	6/03/02	6/17/02
0.09Q	7/24/02	8/29/02	9/03/02	9/16/02
0.09Q	10/23/02	11/27/02	12/02/02	12/16/02
0.09Q	1/22/03	2/27/03	3/03/03	3/17/03

Indicated div.: $0.36 (Div. Reinv. Plan)

CAPITALIZATION (12/31/01):

	($000)	(%)
Long-Term Debt	1,225,100	70.8
Common & Surplus	504,100	29.2
Total	1,729,200	100.0

BUSINESS:

Ball Corporation is a manufacturer of metal and plastic packaging, primarily for beverages and foods, and a supplier of aerospace and other technologies and services to commercial and governmental customers. The packaging segment (87.3% of 2002 sales) includes metal packaging, comprised primarily of two-piece beverage containers and two and three-piece food containers; and PET (polyethylene terephthalate) plastic beverage and food containers. The aerospace and technologies segment (12.7% of 2002 sales) consists of two divisions: the aerospace systems division and the telecommunication products division.

RECENT DEVELOPMENTS:

For the year ended 12/31/02, earnings jumped to $159.3 million, before an extraordinary loss from the early extinguishment of debt of $3.2 million, versus a net loss of $99.2 million in 2001. Results for 2002 and 2001 included business consolidation costs and other charges of $2.3 million and $271.2 million, respectively. Net sales grew 4.7% to $3.86 billion from $3.69 billion. Results benefited from improved profitability levels in the metal beverage container operations, improved pricing, decreased inventories and better asset utilization. The aerospace segment benefited from strong demand for products and services it provides to governmental and commercial customers.

PROSPECTS:

On 12/19/02, the Company completed the acquisition of Schmalbach-Lubeca AG, the second largest manufacturer of beverage cans in Europe, for about 900.0 million euros in cash. The acquired business will operate under the new name of Ball Packaging Europe. The transaction marks the largest acquisition in the Company's history and should be accretive to 2003 results by more than 15.0%. As a result, the Company expects earnings per share in 2003 of more than $3.60. Meanwhile, the seasonality related to the European market and purchase accounting adjustments should make the acquisition accretive to earnings in the first quarter of 2003.

ANNUAL FINANCIAL DATA:

FISCAL YEAR	TOT. REVS. ($mill.)	NET INC. ($mill.)	TOT. ASSETS ($mill.)	OPER. PROFIT %	NET PROFIT %	RET. ON EQUITY %	RET. ON ASSETS %	CURR. RATIO	EARN. PER SH. $	CASH FL. PER SH. $	TANG. BK. VAL.$	DIV. PER SH. $	PRICE RANGE	AVG. P/E RATIO	AVG. YIELD %
p12/31/02	3,858.9	⑧ 159.3							⑧ 2.77			0.36	54.49 - 32.60	15.7	0.8
12/31/01	3,686.1	⑦ d99.2	2,313.6	...	...	...	...	1.4	⑦ d1.85	1.01	...	0.30	36.06 - 19.04	...	1.1
12/31/00	3,664.7	⑥ 68.2	2,649.8	5.7	1.9	10.0	2.6	1.5	⑥ 1.07	3.62	...	0.30	23.97 - 13.00	17.3	1.6
12/31/99	3,584.2	104.2	2,732.1	7.8	2.9	15.1	3.8	1.3	1.58	4.07	...	0.30	29.56 - 17.69	15.0	1.3
12/31/98	2,896.4	⑤ 32.0	2,854.8	3.7	1.1	5.1	1.1	1.3	⑤ 0.46	2.82	...	0.30	24.47 - 14.31	42.6	1.5
12/31/97	2,388.5	④ 58.3	2,090.1	5.8	2.4	9.2	2.8	1.0	④ 0.87	2.68	10.22	0.30	19.50 - 11.88	18.0	1.9
12/31/96	2,184.4	③ 13.1	1,700:8	2.9	0.6	4.1	0.8	1.5	③ 0.17	1.71	8.89	0.30	16.13 - 11.56	81.4	2.2
12/31/95	2,591.7	② d18.6	1,612.5	0.8	...	...	...	1.2	② d0.36	1.53	7.49	0.30	19.38 - 12.88	...	1.9
12/31/94	2,593.4	② 73.0	1,759:8	6.2	2.8	12.1	4.1	1.4	② 1.18	3.32	7.63	0.30	16.06 - 12.19	12.0	2.1
12/31/93	2,440.9	① d32.5	1,795.6	...	...	...	...	1.5	① d0.62	1.40	6.60	0.62	18.63 - 12.56	...	4.0

Statistics are as originally reported. Adj. for 2-for-1 split, 2/02. ① Incl. $58.0 mill. restr. chg.; Bef. $34.7 mill. acct. adj. & $2.1 mill. fr. disc. ops. ② Incl. $1.4 mill. non-recur. net chg., 1994; Incl. net loss on disp. of bus. & $118.2 mill. oth., 1995. ③ Bef. $11.1 mill. income fr. disc. ops. & incl. $21.0 mill. loss on disp. of bus. ④ Incl. $9.0 mill. gain. ⑤ Incl. $73.9 mill. chg. for relocation & $600,000 loss fr. deprec. of Thai currency and excl. $12.1 mill. chg. for debt refinan. & $3.3 mill. for acct. costs. ⑥ Incl. $76.4 mill. chg. fr. bus. consolidation costs and other chgs. ⑦ Incl. $205.2 mill. after-tax benefit fr. bus. consol. costs. ⑧ Incl. $2.3 mill. bus. consol. chg. & excl. $3.2 mill. extraord. loss.

OFFICERS:
R. D. Hoover, Chmn., Pres., C.E.O.
R. J. Seabrook, Sr. V.P., C.F.O.
S. Morrison, V.P., Treas.
INVESTOR CONTACT: Ann T. Scott, Manager, Inv. Rel., (303) 469-3131
PRINCIPAL OFFICE: 10 Longs Peak Drive, P.O. Box 5000, Broomfield, CO 80021-2510

TELEPHONE NUMBER: (303) 469-3131
FAX: (303) 460-2127
WEB: www.ball.com
NO. OF EMPLOYEES: 9,950 (approx.)
SHAREHOLDERS: 5,834
ANNUAL MEETING: In Apr.
INCORPORATED: IN, 1922

INSTITUTIONAL HOLDINGS:
No. of Institutions: 248
Shares Held: 46,975,648
% Held: 82.7

INDUSTRY: Metal cans (SIC: 3411)

TRANSFER AGENT(S): First Chicago Trust Company of New York, Jersey City, NJ

BALLY TOTAL FITNESS HOLDING CORPORATION

EXCH.	SYM.	REC. PRICE	P/E RATIO	YLD.	MKT. CAP.	RANGE (52-WK.)	'02 Y/E PR.
NYSE	BFT	5.70 (2/28/03)	71.3	...	$184.6 mill.	24.10 - 5.25	7.09

LOWER MEDIUM GRADE. THE COMPANY PLANS TO GROW ITS CORE BUSINESS WITH IMPROVED NEW MEMBERSHIP SALES.

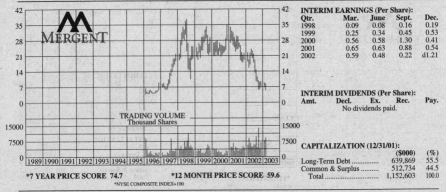

*7 YEAR PRICE SCORE 74.7   *12 MONTH PRICE SCORE 59.6
*NYSE COMPOSITE INDEX=100

INTERIM EARNINGS (Per Share):

Qtr.	Mar.	June	Sept.	Dec.
1998	0.09	0.08	0.16	0.19
1999	0.25	0.34	0.45	0.53
2000	0.56	0.58	1.30	0.41
2001	0.65	0.63	0.88	0.54
2002	0.59	0.48	0.22	d1.21

INTERIM DIVIDENDS (Per Share):

Amt.	Decl.	Ex.	Rec.	Pay.
No dividends paid.				

CAPITALIZATION (12/31/01):

	($000)	(%)
Long-Term Debt	639,869	55.5
Common & Surplus	512,734	44.5
Total	1,152,603	100.0

BUSINESS:

Bally Total Fitness Holding Corporation is a holding company that operates fitness centers. The majority of the Company's fitness centers use the Bally Total Fitness®, Crunch Fitness®, Sports Clubs of Canada®, Gorilla Sports®, Pinnacle Fitness® and Bally Sports Clubs® brands. With more than 150.0 million annual visits to its fitness centers, BFT offers a platform for distribution of a wide range of products and services through membership programs. BFT's fitness centers provide a selection of cardiovascular, conditioning and strength equipment and offer aerobic and other specialty group fitness training programs. In addition, many of BFT's fitness centers include pools, racquet courts and other athletic facilities. As of 2/12/03, BFT had approximately four million members and over 420 facilities located in 29 states, Canada, Asia and the Caribbean. On 12/31/01, BFT acquired Crunch Fitness International, Inc.

RECENT DEVELOPMENTS:

For the year ended 12/31/02, net income plunged 95.6% to $3.5 million compared with $80.7 million in 2001. Results for 2002 and 2001 included special charges of $72.2 million and $6.7 million, respectively. Net revenues increased 13.6% to $968.1 million from $852.0 million the year before, including 9.0% attributable to the Crunch Fitness acquisition completed at the end of 2001. Same club net revenues grew 3.0%, driven by increases in monthly membership dues and products and services, partially offset by a decline in new member initiation fees.

PROSPECTS:

Going forward, BFT may continue to experience softness in membership originations due to the challenging economy and increased competition. BFT is addressing these issues through enhanced marketing and advertising strategies. In addition, BFT plans to lower operating costs, improve margins and reduce overall capital spending. Capital spending for 2003 could be as low as $45.0 million and is not expected to exceed $55.0 million, compared with $93.0 million in 2002. New club spending is not expected to exceed $25.0 million for 2003, and club improvements should be less than or equal to the 2002 level. Moreover, BFT remains fully committed to exiting the financing business.

ANNUAL FINANCIAL DATA:

FISCAL YEAR	TOT. REVS. ($mill.)	NET INC. ($mill.)	TOT. ASSETS ($mill.)	OPER. PROFIT %	NET PROFIT %	RET. ON EQUITY %	RET. ON ASSETS %	CURR. RATIO	EARN. PER SH. $	CASH FL. PER SH. $	TANG. BK. VAL. $	PRICE RANGE	AVG. P/E RATIO
p12/31/02	968.1	③3.5	1,771.9						③0.11			24.10 — 5.70	135.4
12/31/01	852.0	③80.7	1,716.9	6.8	9.5	15.7	4.7	0.8	③2.70	5.28	8.51	33.94 — 17.85	9.6
12/31/00	1,007.1	78.6	1,560.6	12.6	7.8	26.4	5.0	0.7	2.84	5.35	5.94	34.88 — 20.56	9.8
12/31/99	861.1	②42.4	1,348.6	10.8	4.9	20.0	3.1	0.7	②1.56	3.62	3.17	34.38 — 19.13	17.1
12/31/98	742.5	13.3	1,128.8	7.1	1.8	8.2	1.2	0.7	0.51	2.44	2.51	37.56 — 10.50	47.1
12/31/97	661.0	①d23.5	967.6	3.0	...	...	...	0.7	①d2.88	1.55	...	22.00 — 5.63	...
12/31/96	625.6	①d41.2	813.5	0.6	...	...	...	1.0	①d3.38	1.47	8.87	9.06 — 3.75	...
12/31/95	661.7	d25.2	846.3	1.1	...	...	...	1.1	d3.08	3.00	10.99	...	...
12/31/94	661.5	d50.8	973.6	...	...	...	...	1.4	...	0.84	6.30	...	...
12/31/93	694.8	d28.0	928.3	0.1	...	...	...	1.0	...	...	6.94	...	...

Statistics are as originally reported. ① Excl. extraord. loss of $21.4 mill., 1997; gain of $5.7 mill., 1996. ② Excl. acctg. change chrg. of $262,000. ③ Incl. special chrgs. of $72.2 mill., 2002; $6.7 mill., 2001.

OFFICERS:
L. S. Hillman, Chmn.
P. A. Toback, Pres., C.E.O.
J. W. Dwyer, Exec. V.P., C.F.O.
INVESTOR CONTACT: Jon Harris, (773) 864-6850
PRINCIPAL OFFICE: 8700 West Bryn Mawr Avenue, Chicago, IL 60631

TELEPHONE NUMBER: (773) 380-3000
FAX: (773) 693-2982
WEB: www.ballyfitness.com
NO. OF EMPLOYEES: 10,050 full-time (approx.); 11,200 part-time
SHAREHOLDERS: 8,101
ANNUAL MEETING: In June
INCORPORATED: DE, Mar., 1983

INSTITUTIONAL HOLDINGS:
No. of Institutions: 105
Shares Held: 27,663,371
% Held: 83.4
INDUSTRY: Membership sports & recreation clubs (SIC: 7997)
TRANSFER AGENT(S): LaSalle National Bank, N.A., Chicago, IL

BANCORPSOUTH, INC.

EXCH.	SYM.	REC. PRICE	P/E RATIO	YLD.	MKT. CAP.	RANGE (52-WK.)	'02 Y/E PR.	DIV. ACH.
NYSE	BXS	18.65 (2/28/03)	13.3	3.4%	$1.51 bill.	22.21 - 16.61	19.42	16 yrs.

UPPER MEDIUM GRADE. THE COMPANY IS TAKING STEPS EXPECTED TO HELP BOOST NON-INTEREST REVENUE.

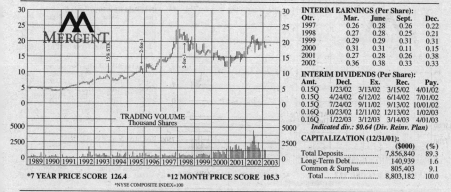

INTERIM EARNINGS (Per Share):

Qtr.	Mar.	June	Sept.	Dec.
1997	0.26	0.28	0.26	0.22
1998	0.27	0.28	0.25	0.21
1999	0.29	0.29	0.31	0.31
2000	0.31	0.31	0.11	0.15
2001	0.27	0.28	0.26	0.38
2002	0.36	0.38	0.33	0.33

INTERIM DIVIDENDS (Per Share):

Amt.	Decl.	Ex.	Rec.	Pay.
0.15Q	1/23/02	3/13/02	3/15/02	4/01/02
0.15Q	4/24/02	6/12/02	6/14/02	7/01/02
0.15Q	7/24/02	9/11/02	9/13/02	10/01/02
0.16Q	10/23/02	12/11/02	12/13/02	1/02/03
0.16Q	1/22/03	3/12/03	3/14/03	4/01/03

Indicated div.: $0.64 (Div. Reinv. Plan)

CAPITALIZATION (12/31/01):

	($000)	(%)
Total Deposits	7,856,840	89.3
Long-Term Debt	140,939	1.6
Common & Surplus	805,403	9.1
Total	8,803,182	100.0

*7 YEAR PRICE SCORE 126.4   ***12 MONTH PRICE SCORE 105.3**

*NYSE COMPOSITE INDEX=100

BUSINESS:

BancorpSouth, Inc. is a bank holding company headquartered in Tupelo, Mississippi with assets of $10.19 billion and total deposits of $8.55 billion as of 12/31/02. BXS operates approximately 250 commercial banking, insurance, trust, broker/dealer and consumer finance locations in Alabama, Arkansas, Louisiana, Mississippi, Tennessee and Texas. BXS and its subsidiaries provide a range of financial services to individuals and small-to-medium size businesses. BXS operates investment services, consumer finance, credit life insurance and insurance agency subsidiaries. BXS trust department offers a variety of services including personal trust and estate services, and certain employee benefit accounts and plans. On 2/28/02, BXS completed its acquisition of Pinnacle Bancshares, Inc.

RECENT DEVELOPMENTS:

For the year ended 12/31/02, net income climbed 13.8% to $112.0 million from $98.5 million in the prior year. Net interest revenue increased 12.8% to $371.5 million from $329.4 million a year earlier. Net interest margin improved to 4.15% compared with 3.94% in 2001. Provision for credit losses jumped 32.1% to $29.4 million from $22.3 million in 2001. Total non-interest revenue slipped 1.3% to $132.2 million, while total non-interest expense rose 5.8% to $312.4 million.

PROSPECTS:

Results may benefit from the Company's efforts to boost non-interest revenue. BXS plans to increase sales of various non-interest bearing products, including a variety of deposit, insurance, cash management and investment brokerage services, to existing retail and small-to-medium size business customers. Meanwhile, results are being positively affected by a reduction in non-performing assets stemming from the Company's focus on improving loan quality despite increasing loan volume. As of 12/31/02, non-performing assets totaled $52.2 million, or 0.82% of net loans, compared with $60.0 million, or 0.99% of net loans, at 12/31/01.

ANNUAL FINANCIAL DATA:

FISCAL YEAR	NET INT. INC. ($mill.)	NON-INT. INC. ($mill.)	NET INC. ($mill.)	TOT. LOANS ($mill.)	TOT. ASSETS ($mill.)	TOT. DEP. ($mill.)	RET. ON EQUITY %	RET. ON ASSETS %	EQUITY/ ASSETS %	EARN. PER SH.$	TANG. BK. VAL.$	DIV. PER SH.$	PRICE RANGE	AVG. P/E RATIO
p12/31/02	371.5		112.0							1.39		0.60	22.21 - 15.90	13.7
12/31/01	334.7	128.6	98.5	6,127.0	9,395.4	7,856.8	12.2	1.0	8.6	1.19	9.92	0.56	17.00 - 12.06	12.2
12/31/00	327.2	85.6	②74.4	6,161.1	9,044.0	7,480.9	9.4	0.8	8.7	②0.88	9.39	0.52	17.25 - 11.88	16.5
12/31/99	217.5	79.3	69.0	4,131.4	5,776.9	4,815.4	13.9	1.2	8.6	1.20	8.68	0.48	19.44 - 15.38	14.5
12/31/98	196.1	53.0	54.5	3,561.4	5,203.7	4,441.9	11.9	1.0	8.8	1.01	8.48	0.44	24.00 - 16.81	20.2
12/31/97	163.0	43.7	45.4	2,852.9	4,180.1	3,540.3	12.6	1.1	8.6	1.02	8.09	0.38	23.78 - 13.25	18.2
12/31/96	151.4	40.7	42.9	2,554.1	3,617.2	3,161.4	13.6	1.2	8.7	1.01	7.50	0.34	14.25 - 10.06	12.0
12/31/95	138.0	31.2	35.5	2,371.7	3,306.2	2,863.6	12.3	1.1	8.7	0.85	6.86	0.30	11.94 - 8.06	11.8
12/31/94	103.9	23.4	25.4	1,795.1	2,518.4	2,171.7	12.4	1.0	8.2	0.80	6.49	0.27	9.06 - 7.25	10.2
12/31/93	96.5	22.6	①23.4	1,558.7	2,306.7	2,031.5	12.4	1.0	8.2	①0.75	5.99	0.23	9.35 - 7.39	11.2

Statistics are as originally reported. Adj. for 2-for-1 split, 5/98; 100% stk. div., 11/95. ① Bef. $3.2 mill. acct. chrg. ② Incl. after-tax merger-related charges of $22.5 mill.

OFFICERS:
A. B. Patterson, Chmn., C.E.O.
J. V. Kelley, Pres., C.O.O.
L. N. Allen, Jr., C.F.O., Treas.

INVESTOR CONTACT: Investor Relations, (662) 680-2000

PRINCIPAL OFFICE: One Mississippi Plaza, 201 South Spring Street, Tupelo, MS 38804

TELEPHONE NUMBER: (662) 680-2000
FAX: (662) 680-2570
WEB: www.bancorpsouth.com

NO. OF EMPLOYEES: 3,920

SHAREHOLDERS: 10,178 (record)

ANNUAL MEETING: In Apr.

INCORPORATED: MS, July, 1982

INSTITUTIONAL HOLDINGS:
No. of Institutions: 103
Shares Held: 12,573,460
% Held: 16.1

INDUSTRY: State commercial banks (SIC: 6022)

TRANSFER AGENT(S): SunTrust Bank, Atlanta, GA

BANDAG, INC.

EXCH.	SYM.	REC. PRICE	P/E RATIO	YLD.	MKT. CAP.	RANGE (52-WK.)	'02 Y/E PR.	DIV. ACH.
NYSE	BDG	30.32 (2/28/03)	11.8	4.2%	$0.63 bill.	42.01 - 26.00	38.68	26 yrs.

MEDIUM GRADE. REVENUES CONTINUE TO BE HAMPERED BY SOFT MARKET CONDITIONS AT THE COMPANY'S TIRE DISTRIBUTION SYSTEMS, INC. SUBSIDIARY.

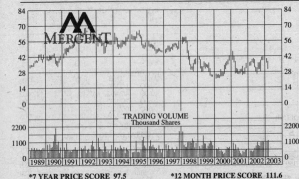

*7 YEAR PRICE SCORE 97.5   ***12 MONTH PRICE SCORE 111.6**

NYSE COMPOSITE INDEX=100

INTERIM EARNINGS (Per Share):

Qtr.	Mar.	June	Sept.	Dec.
1999	0.46	0.73	0.82	0.38
2000	0.48	0.85	0.86	0.71
2001	0.11	0.46	0.71	0.84
2002	0.06	0.57	1.02	0.91

INTERIM DIVIDENDS (Per Share):

Amt.	Decl.	Ex.	Rec.	Pay.
0.315Q	3/12/02	3/20/02	3/22/02	4/19/02
0.315Q	5/14/02	6/17/02	6/19/02	7/19/02
0.315Q	8/27/02	9/17/02	9/19/02	10/18/02
0.32Q	11/12/02	12/17/02	12/19/02	1/17/03
0.32Q	3/11/03	3/19/03	3/21/03	4/17/03

Indicated div.: $1.28 (Div. Reinv. Plan)

CAPITALIZATION (12/31/01):

	($000)	(%)
Long-Term Debt	40,921	7.7
Deferred Income Tax	2,580	0.5
Common & Surplus	488,996	91.8
Total	532,497	100.0

BUSINESS:

Bandag, Inc. is engaged in the manufacture of pre-cured tread rubber, equipment, and supplies primarily for the re-treading of truck and bus tires by a patented cold-bonding reaction process. The Company also does some custom processing of rubber compounds. As of 12/31/02, revenues were generated by more than 1,100 franchised dealers in the U.S. and abroad who are licensed to produce and market cold process retreads utilizing the Bandag process.

BDG's wholly-owned subsidiary, Tire Management Solutions, Inc., provides tire management systems outsourcing for commercial truck fleets. Tire Distribution Systems, Inc., also a wholly-owned subsidiary, sells and services new and retread tires. In 2002, the traditional retread rubber, equipment and supplier for re-treading accounted for 59.5% of net sales and Tire Distribution Systems accounted for 40.5% of net sales.

RECENT DEVELOPMENTS:

For the year ended 12/31/02, the Company reported income of $50.1 million, before an accounting change charge of $47.3 million, compared with net income of $43.8 million in the previous year. Results for 2002 and 2001 included litigation costs of $10.7 million and $18.3 million, respectively. Results for 2001 also included a non-recurring charge of $3.4 million. Total revenue declined 5.7% to

$912.0 million from $966.7 million a year earlier. Net sales decreased 5.1% to $900.5 million, primarily due to lower re-tread volumes and weakness at Tire Distribution Systems, Inc. Interest income fell 30.9% to $5.0 million, while other income dropped 36.2% to $6.4 million. Cost of products sold decreased 8.0% to $563.7 million from $612.6 million the year before.

PROSPECTS:

During 2002, Tire Distribution Systems' (TDS') results were hampered by soft market conditions and the loss of several significant customers. These items are likely to continue to challenge TDS' performance in the coming year. Meanwhile, the restructuring of the Company's Euro-

pean operations is moving forward. Separately, recent strength in BDG's traditional re-tread equipment and supplies business is encouraging, particularly in North America.

ANNUAL FINANCIAL DATA:

FISCAL YEAR	TOT. REVS. ($mill.)	NET INC. ($mill.)	TOT. ASSETS ($mill.)	OPER. PROFIT %	NET PROFIT %	RET. ON EQUITY %	RET. ON ASSETS %	CURR. RATIO	EARN. PER SH.$	CASH FL. PER SH.$	TANG. BK. VAL.$	DIV. PER SH.$	PRICE RANGE	AVG. P/E RATIO	AVG. YIELD %
p12/31/02	912.0	③ 50.1	609.8		5.5	11.8	8.2	2.8	② 2.52			1.26	42.01 - 26.0	13.5	3.7
12/31/01	982.2	② 43.8	718.6	7.5	4.5	9.0	6.1	2.4	② 2.12	4.35	21.22	1.22	46.75 - 25.01	16.9	3.4
12/31/00	1,013.4	60.3	714.5	10.7	6.0	12.7	8.4	3.2	2.90	5.33	20.03	1.18	42.63 - 21.88	11.1	3.7
12/31/99	1,027.9	② 52.3	722.4	9.9	5.1	11.5	7.2	2.8	② 2.40	4.87	18.62	1.14	41.63 - 23.50	13.6	3.5
12/31/98	1,079.5	② 59.3	784.2	10.2	5.5	12.0	7.6	2.5	② 2.63	4.91	19.14	1.10	59.75 - 28.31	16.7	2.5
12/31/97	931.7	① 122.0	899.9	22.1	13.1	26.3	13.6	2.0	① 5.33	6.93	17.00	1.00	55.75 - 45.00	9.5	2.0
12/31/96	769.0	81.6	588.3	17.2	10.6	19.9	13.9	2.5	3.44	4.89	17.85	0.90	55.88 - 44.50	14.6	1.8
12/31/95	755.3	97.0	558.3	20.8	12.8	24.0	17.4	2.7	3.82	5.18	16.60	0.80	65.88 - 49.00	15.0	1.4
12/31/94	665.7	94.0	590.9	22.8	14.1	21.2	15.9	3.0	3.51	4.83	16.95	0.70	63.50 - 49.13	16.0	1.2
12/31/93	601.1	78.7	564.0	21.2	13.1	18.5	14.0	3.1	2.88	4.10	15.70	0.65	60.25 - 44.75	18.2	1.2

Statistics are as originally reported. ① Incl. nonrecurr. gain of $78.6 mill. on sale of secur. ② Incl. nonrecurr. chrg. of $2.0 mill., 2001; $13.5 mill., 1999; $4.2 mill., 1998. ③ Bef. an acctg. chng. chrg. of $47.3 mill.; incl. litigation chrg. of $10.7 mill.

OFFICERS:
M. G. Carver, Chmn., Pres., C.E.O.
W. W. Heidbreder, V.P., C.F.O., Sec.
L. A. Carver, Treas.
INVESTOR CONTACT: Warren W. Heidbreder, V.P., C.F.O., (319) 262-1260
PRINCIPAL OFFICE: 2905 North Highway 61, Muscatine, IA 52761-5886

TELEPHONE NUMBER: (563) 262-1400
FAX: (563) 262-1284
WEB: www.bandag.com
NO. OF EMPLOYEES: 4,014 (approx.)
SHAREHOLDERS: 1,879 (common); 1,070 (class A); 210 (class B)
ANNUAL MEETING: In May
INCORPORATED: IA, Dec., 1957

INSTITUTIONAL HOLDINGS:
No. of Institutions: 104
Shares Held: 4,964,093
% Held: 25.9
INDUSTRY: Tires and inner tubes (SIC: 3011)
TRANSFER AGENT(S): BankBoston, c/o EquiServe, Boston, MA

BANK OF AMERICA CORPORATION

EXCH.	SYM.	REC. PRICE	P/E RATIO	YLD.	MKT. CAP.	RANGE (52-WK.)	'02 Y/E PR.	DIV. ACH.
NYSE	BAC	69.24 (2/28/03)	11.7	3.7%	$103.91 bill.	77.09 - 53.95	69.57	25 yrs.

INVESTMENT GRADE. THE COMPANY ACQUIRED 24.9% OF GRUPO FINANCIERO SANTANDER SERFIN, THE MOST PROFITABLE BANK IN MEXICO.

*7 YEAR PRICE SCORE 123.5   ***12 MONTH PRICE SCORE 111.3**

*NYSE COMPOSITE INDEX=100

INTERIM EARNINGS (Per Share):

Qtr.	Mar.	June	Sept.	Dec.
1998	0.51	1.43	0.21	0.66
1999	1.08	1.07	1.23	1.10
2000	1.33	1.23	1.10	0.85
2001	1.15	1.24	0.51	1.28
2002	1.38	1.40	1.45	1.69

INTERIM DIVIDENDS (Per Share):

Amt.	Decl.	Ex.	Rec.	Pay.
0.60Q	1/23/02	2/27/02	3/01/02	3/22/02
0.60Q	4/24/02	6/05/02	6/07/02	6/28/02
0.60Q	7/24/02	9/04/02	9/06/02	9/27/02
0.64Q	10/23/02	12/04/02	12/06/02	12/27/02
0.64Q	1/22/03	3/05/03	3/07/03	3/28/03

Indicated div.: $2.56 (Div. Reinv. Plan)

CAPITALIZATION (12/31/01):

	($000)	(%)
Total Deposits	373,495,000	77.1
Long-Term Debt	62,496,000	12.9
Preferred Stock	65,000	0.0
Common & Surplus	48,455,000	10.0
Total	484,511,000	100.0

BUSINESS:

Bank of America Corporation (formerly NationsBank Corporation) is a bank holding company with $660.46 billion in total assets as of 12/31/02. The Company was formed on 9/30/98 as a result of BankAmerica's merging into NationsBank. The Company adopted its present name on 4/29/99. As of 12/31/02, BAC provided financial products and services through 4,208 banking centers and 13,013 automatic teller machines, as well as 30 international offices serving clients in 150 countries, and an Internet Web site that provides on-line access for 4.7 million active users, including 1.8 million active bill pay users. BAC maintains full-service operations in 21 states and the District of Columbia.

RECENT DEVELOPMENTS:

For the year ended 12/31/02, net income jumped 36.2% to $9.25 billion compared with $6.79 billion in the previous year. Earnings for 2002 included an income tax settlement benefit of $488.0 million. Earnings for 2001 included after-tax business exit costs of $1.25 billion. Net interest income increased 3.1% to $20.92 billion from $20.29 billion a year earlier, primarily due to growth in consumer loans and deposits, partially offset by the subprime business exited in 2001. Provision for credit losses fell 13.8% to $3.70 billion. Non-interest income decreased 5.4% to $13.57 billion. Non-interest expense declined 11.0% to $18.44 billion. Net charge-offs fell 12.9% to $3.70 billion.

PROSPECTS:

On 3/5/03, BAC announced the completed acquisition of 24.9% of Grupo Financiero Santander Serfin, the most profitable bank in Mexico, from Santander Central Hispano for approximately $1.60 billion in cash. The investment should increase 2003 earnings by approximately $0.04 per share. Separately, the Company acquired Framework, Inc., a privately held technology company. The acquisition is expected to help simplify mortgage transactions for consumers. Meanwhile, the Company announced that it is reorganizing its Global Markets group to improve client service and more effectively link BAC's originate-to-distribute model across its Global Corporate and Investment Bank.

ANNUAL FINANCIAL DATA:

FISCAL YEAR	NET INT. INC. ($mill.)	NON-INT. INC. ($mill.)	NET INC. ($mill.)	TOT. LOANS ($mill.)	TOT. ASSETS ($mill.)	TOT. DEP. ($mill.)	RET. ON EQUITY %	RET. ON ASSETS %	EQUITY/ ASSETS %	EARN. PER SH. $	TANG. BK. VAL. $	DIV. PER SH. $	PRICE RANGE	AVG. P/E RATIO
p12/31/02			9,249.0							5.91		2.44	77.09 - 53.95	11.1
12/31/01	20,290.0	14,348.0	⑥ 6,792.0	329,153.0	621,764.0	373,495.0	14.0	1.1	7.8	⑤ 4.18	20.09	2.28	65.54 - 45.00	13.2
12/31/00	18,442.0	14,514.0	③ 7,517.0	392,193.0	642,191.0	364,244.0	15.8	1.2	7.4	③ 4.52	19.00	2.06	61.00 - 36.31	10.8
12/31/99	18,237.0	14,309.0	③ 7,882.0	370,662.0	632,574.0	347,273.0	17.7	1.2	7.0	③ 4.48	15.66	1.85	76.38 - 47.63	13.8
④ 12/31/98	18,298.0	13,206.0	⑤ 5,165.0	357,328.0	617,679.0	357,260.0	11.2	0.8	7.4	② 2.90	16.68	1.59	88.44 - 44.00	22.8
12/31/97	7,898.0	5,155.0	3,077.0	146,417.0	264,562.0	138,194.0	14.4	1.2	8.1	4.17	14.86	1.37	71.69 - 48.00	14.4
12/31/96	6,329.0	3,713.0	② 2,375.0	125,031.0	185,794.0	106,498.0	17.3	1.3	7.4	② 4.00	18.43	1.20	52.63 - 32.19	10.6
12/31/95	5,447.0	3,107.0	1,995.0	119,020.0	187,298.0	100,691.0	15.6	1.1	6.8	3.56	19.08	1.04	37.38 - 22.31	8.4
12/31/94	5,211.0	2,584.0	1,690.0	105,033.0	169,604.0	100,470.0	15.3	1.0	6.5	3.06	16.64	0.94	28.69 - 21.69	8.2
12/31/93	4,637.0	2,185.0	① 1,301.0	93,262.0	157,686.0	91,113.0	13.0	0.8	6.3	① 2.50	15.51	0.82	29.00 - 22.25	10.2

Statistics are as originally reported. Adj. for 2-for-1 stk. split, 2/97. ① Bef. acctg. cred. of $200.0 mill. ② Incl. aft.-tax merger-rel. chgs. of $77.0 mill. ③ Incl. merg.-rel. & restr. chgs. of $346.0 mill., 2000; $358.0 mill., 1999; $1.80 bill., 1998. ④ Refl. merger of NationsBank Corp. & BankAmerica Corp. on 9/30/98. ⑤ Incl. a loss of $1.30 bill. rel. to the exit of certain consumer finance businesses; restruct. chrgs. of $550.0 mill.; and a loss of $231.0 mill. assoc. with Co.'s credit exposure to Enron.

OFFICERS:
K. D. Lewis, Chmn., Pres., C.E.O.
J. H. Hance Jr., Vice-Chmn., C.F.O.

INVESTOR CONTACT: Kevin Stitt, (704) 386-5667

PRINCIPAL OFFICE: Bank of America Corporate Center, Charlotte, NC 28255

TELEPHONE NUMBER: (704) 386-8486
FAX: (704) 386-6699
WEB: www.bankofamerica.com

NO. OF EMPLOYEES: 133,944

SHAREHOLDERS: 244,000

ANNUAL MEETING: In April

INCORPORATED: NC, July, 1968; reincorp., DE, Sept., 1998

INSTITUTIONAL HOLDINGS:
No. of Institutions: 972
Shares Held: 878,273,920
% Held: 58.7

INDUSTRY: National commercial banks (SIC: 6021)

TRANSFER AGENT(S): Mellon Investor Services LLC, South Hackensack, NJ

BANK OF HAWAII CORPORATION

EXCH.	SYM.	REC. PRICE	P/E RATIO	YLD.	MKT. CAP.	RANGE (52-WK.)	'02 Y/E PR.	DIV. ACH.
NYSE	BOH	31.10 (2/28/03)	18.3	2.4%	$1.96 bill.	31.50 - 22.79	30.39	25 yrs.

MEDIUM GRADE. THE COMPANY EXPECTS CONSTRUCTION AND REAL ESTATE INVESTMENTS TO CONTINUE TO DRIVE THE HAWAIIAN ECONOMY IN 2003.

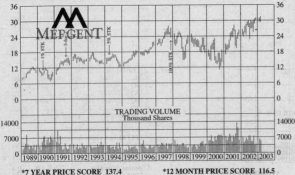

*7 YEAR PRICE SCORE 137.4   ***12 MONTH PRICE SCORE 116.5**
NYSE COMPOSITE INDEX=100

INTERIM EARNINGS (Per Share):

Qtr.	Mar.	June	Sept.	Dec.
1999	0.44	0.47	0.27	0.47
2000	0.50	0.08	0.44	0.41
2001	0.42	0.32	0.37	0.34
2002	0.41	0.42	0.43	0.44

INTERIM DIVIDENDS (Per Share):

Amt.	Decl.	Ex.	Rec.	Pay.
0.18Q	1/28/02	2/22/02	2/26/02	3/14/02
0.18Q	4/22/02	5/22/02	5/24/02	6/14/02
0.18Q	7/22/02	8/21/02	8/23/02	9/16/02
0.19Q	10/23/02	11/20/02	11/22/02	12/13/02
0.19Q	1/27/03	2/20/03	2/24/03	3/14/03

Indicated div.: $0.76 (Div. Reinv. Plan)

CAPITALIZATION (12/31/01):

	($000)	(%)
Total Deposits	6,673,596	79.5
Long-Term Debt	469,735	5.6
Common & Surplus	1,247,012	14.9
Total	8,390,343	100.0

BUSINESS:

Bank of Hawaii Corporation (formerly Pacific Century Financial Corporation), with assets of $9.52 billion as of 12/31/02, is a bank holding company that was initially organized as Hawaii Bancorporation, Inc. In 1979, it changed its name to Bancorp Hawaii, Inc., and in 1997 to Pacific Century Financial Corp. Its present name was adopted 4/29/02. BOH provides a broad range of products and services to businesses, consumers and governments in Hawaii, the West Pacific, and American Samoa. In 2001, BOH sold its credit card portfolio to American Express Centurion Bank and its investment in the Bank of Queensland Ltd. in Australia, and closed branches in Hong Kong, Tokyo, Taipei, Seoul, Singapore, California and Arizona. BOH's principal subsidiary is the Bank of Hawaii.

RECENT DEVELOPMENTS:

For the year ended 12/31/02, net income increased 2.9% to $121.2 million compared with $117.8 million in the previous year. Results for 2002 and 2001 included restructuring charges of $2.4 million and $104.8 million, respectively. Results also included an information technology systems replacement charge of $13.6 million in 2002 and a net gain on the sale of banking operations of $173.4 million in 2001.

Net interest income decreased 19.5% to $370.2 million from $459.7 million a year earlier, primarily due to divestitures and the managed reduction of loans to reduce credit risk. Provision for loan and lease losses amounted to $11.6 million versus $74.3 million in 2001. Total non-interest income dropped 55.4% to $199.9 million, while total non-interest expense fell 37.6% to $370.8 million.

PROSPECTS:

The Company expects construction and real estate investments to continue to drive the Hawaiian economy in 2003. In addition, tourism growth is expected from both domestic and international travelers in 2003. Looking ahead, the Company expects net income of approximately $131.0 million for full-year 2003. Meanwhile, BOH anticipates technology system conversion costs of about $7.7 million in the first quarter of 2003. Separately, BOH has made progress in reducing its credit exposure to air transportation, lodging and telecommunications companies.

ANNUAL FINANCIAL DATA:

FISCAL YEAR	NET INT. INC. ($mill.)	NON-INT. INC. ($mill.)	NET INC. ($mill.)	TOT. LOANS ($mill.)	TOT. ASSETS ($mill.)	TOT. DEP. ($mill.)	RET. ON EQUITY %	RET. ON ASSETS %	EQUITY/ ASSETS %	EARN. PER SH.$	TANG. BK. VAL.$	DIV. PER SH.$	PRICE RANGE	AVG. P/E RATIO
p12/31/02	370.2	199.9	④ 121.2	5,399.1	9,516.4	6,920.2	11.9	1.3	10.7	④ 1.70		0.73	31.05 - 23.79	16.1
12/31/01	459.7	452.6	③ 117.8	6,109.2	10,627.8	6,673.6	9.4	1.1	11.7	③ 1.46	16.16	0.72	28.30 - 16.88	15.5
12/31/00	556.2	263.4	② 113.7	9,668.3	14,013.8	9,080.6	8.7	0.8	9.3	② 1.42	13.93	0.71	23.19 - 11.06	12.1
12/31/99	574.7	265.6	① 133.0	9,717.6	14,440.3	9,394.2	11.0	0.9	8.4	① 1.64	12.57	0.68	24.94 - 17.38	12.9
12/31/98	576.6	211.8	① 107.0	9,854.0	15,016.6	9,576.3	9.0	0.7	7.9	① 1.32	12.07	0.66	25.88 - 14.75	15.4
12/31/97	536.3	187.8	139.5	9,498.4	14,995.5	9,621.3	12.5	0.9	7.5	1.72	11.47	0.63	28.06 - 20.31	14.1
12/31/96	482.3	164.5	133.1	8,699.3	14,009.2	8,684.1	12.5	1.0	7.6	1.63	12.13	0.58	22.00 - 16.56	11.8
12/31/95	428.5	146.4	121.8	8,152.4	13,206.6	7,576.8	11.6	0.9	8.0	1.45	11.69	0.54	18.56 - 12.44	10.7
12/31/94	449.3	128.4	117.7	7,892.0	12,586.4	7,115.1	12.2	0.9	7.7	1.38	10.42	0.52	17.38 - 12.06	10.7
12/31/93	473.4	129.3	132.6	7,258.4	12,462.1	7,005.0	14.1	1.1	7.5	1.55	9.79	0.45	17.96 - 13.33	10.1

Statistics are as originally reported. Adj. for stk. split: 100% div., 12/97; 50% div., 3/94. ① Incl. a restr. chrg. of $22.5 mill., 1999; $19.4 mill., 1998. ② Incl. a pre-tax gain of $11.9 mill. on the settlement of pension obligs. ③ Incl. a pre-tax gain of $173.4 mill. on the sale of banking ops. & venture invest. loss & pre-tax restr. & oth. rel. costs of $104.8 mill. ④ Incl. pre-tax restr. chrg. of $2.4 mill. and info. tech. systems replacement chrg. of $13.6 mill.

OFFICERS:
M. E. O'Neill, Chmn., Pres., C.E.O.
A. R. Landon, Vice-Chmn., C.F.O.
A. T. Kuioka, Vice-Chmn.

INVESTOR CONTACT: Cindy Wyrick, (808) 537-8430

PRINCIPAL OFFICE: 130 Merchant Street, Honolulu, HI 96813

TELEPHONE NUMBER: (808) 538-4727
FAX: (808) 538-4007
WEB: www.boh.com
NO. OF EMPLOYEES: 3,175 (avg.)
SHAREHOLDERS: 10,918
ANNUAL MEETING: In April
INCORPORATED: HI, Aug., 1971; reincorp., DE, April, 1998

INSTITUTIONAL HOLDINGS:
No. of Institutions: 166
Shares Held: 42,938,229
% Held: 66.2

INDUSTRY: State commercial banks (SIC: 6022)

TRANSFER AGENT(S): Continental Stock Transfer & Trust Company, New York, NY

BANK OF NEW YORK COMPANY, INC. (THE)

EXCH.	SYM.	REC. PRICE	P/E RATIO	YLD.	MKT. CAP.	RANGE (52-WK.)	'02 Y/E PR.	DIV. ACH.
NYSE	BK	22.78 (2/28/03)	18.2	3.3%	$16.64 bill.	44.69 - 20.85	23.96	10 yrs.

UPPER MEDIUM GRADE. THE COMPANY AGREED TO ACQUIRE THE PERSHING UNIT OF CREDIT SUISSE FIRST BOSTON FOR $2.00 BILLION.

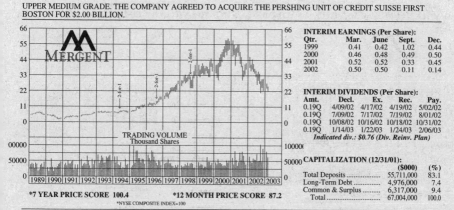

TRADING VOLUME
Thousand Shares

*7 YEAR PRICE SCORE 100.4   ***12 MONTH PRICE SCORE 87.2**
*NYSE COMPOSITE INDEX=100

INTERIM EARNINGS (Per Share):

Qtr.	Mar.	June	Sept.	Dec.
1999	0.41	0.42	1.02	0.44
2000	0.46	0.48	0.49	0.50
2001	0.52	0.52	0.33	0.45
2002	0.50	0.50	0.11	0.14

INTERIM DIVIDENDS (Per Share):

Amt.	Decl.	Ex.	Rec.	Pay.
0.19Q	4/09/02	4/17/02	4/19/02	5/02/02
0.19Q	7/09/02	7/17/02	7/19/02	8/01/02
0.19Q	10/08/02	10/16/02	10/18/02	10/31/02
0.19Q	1/14/03	1/22/03	1/24/03	2/06/03

Indicated div.: $0.76 (Div. Reinv. Plan)

CAPITALIZATION (12/31/01):

	($000)	(%)
Total Deposits	55,711,000	83.1
Long-Term Debt	4,976,000	7.4
Common & Surplus	6,317,000	9.4
Total	67,004,000	100.0

BUSINESS:

The Bank of New York Company, Inc. is a bank holding company with assets of $77.17 billion as of 12/31/02. BK provides a broad range of banking and other financial services to corporations and individuals worldwide through its basic businesses, including securities servicing and global payment services, corporate banking, BNY asset management and private client services, retail banking and global market services. BK's primary subsidiaries are the Bank of New York, BNY Holdings (Delaware) Corporation, and The Bank of New York (Delaware). BK has operating centers in London, Brussels, Dublin, Singapore and Luxembourg and 28 non-U.S. branch and representative offices in 25 countries and provides securities servicing in over 100 markets.

RECENT DEVELOPMENTS:

For the year ended 12/31/02, net income fell 32.8% to $902.0 million compared with $1.34 billion in the previous year. Results for 2002 and 2001 included securities losses of $118.0 million and securities gains of $154.0 million, respectively. Net interest income decreased 1.0% to $1.67 billion from $1.68 billion a year earlier. Provision for credit losses surged 82.7% to $685.0 million from $375.0 million the year before, primarily due weakness in its portfolio of corporate loans and aircraft leases. Total non-interest income declined 12.0% to $3.14 billion, while total non-interest expense slipped 2.4% to $2.75 billion. Comparisons were made with restated prior-year results.

PROSPECTS:

On 1/8/02, the Company announced an agreement to acquire the Pershing unit of Credit Suisse First Boston for $2.00 billion in cash. Pershing is the largest global provider of correspondent clearing services and outsourcing services for brokers, asset managers and other financial intermediaries. The purchase will be financed from the public issuance of approximately $900.0 million of debt and $1.10 billion of equity. The transaction is expected to close by the end of the second quarter of 2003. Excluding one-time integration charges, the deal is expected to be dilutive to earnings by $0.02 to $0.03 per share in 2003 and accretive to earnings by $0.02 to $0.03 per share in 2004.

ANNUAL FINANCIAL DATA:

FISCAL YEAR	NET INT. INC. ($mill.)	NON-INT. INC. ($mill.)	NET INC. ($mill.)	TOT. LOANS ($mill.)	TOT. ASSETS ($mill.)	TOT. DEP. ($mill.)	RET. ON EQUITY %	RET. ON ASSETS %	EQUITY/ ASSETS %	EARN. PER SH. $	TANG. BK. VAL. $	DIV. PER SH. $	PRICE RANGE	AVG. P/E RATIO
p12/31/02	1,665.0	3,143.0	902.0		77,170.0	55,379.0				1.24		0.76	46.50 - 20.85	27.2
12/31/01	1,681.0	3,540.0	⑥ 1,343.0	35,747.0	81,025.0	55,711.0	21.3	1.7	7.8	⑥ 1.81	5.80	0.72	58.13 - 29.75	24.3
12/31/00	1,870.0	3,109.0	1,429.0	36,261.0	77,114.0	56,376.0	23.2	1.9	8.0	1.92	8.30	0.66	59.38 - 29.75	23.2
12/31/99	1,701.0	3,493.0	⑤ 1,739.0	37,547.0	74,756.0	55,751.0	33.8	2.3	6.9	⑤ 2.27	6.95	0.58	45.19 - 31.81	17.0
12/31/98	1,651.0	2,283.0	1,192.0	38,386.0	63,503.0	44,632.0	21.9	1.9	8.6	1.53	7.05	0.54	40.56 - 24.00	21.1
12/31/97	1,855.0	2,137.0	④ 1,104.0	35,127.0	59,961.0	41,357.0	22.1	1.8	8.3	④ 1.36	6.67	0.49	29.28 - 16.38	16.8
12/31/96	1,961.0	2,130.0	1,020.0	37,006.0	55,765.0	39,343.0	19.9	1.8	9.2	1.24	6.50	0.42	18.06 - 10.88	11.7
12/31/95	2,029.0	1,491.0	②③ 914.0	37,687.0	53,720.0	35,918.0	17.5	1.7	9.7	②③ 1.14	6.46	0.34	12.25 - 7.13	8.5
12/31/94	1,717.0	1,289.0	② 749.0	33,083.0	48,879.0	34,091.0	17.4	1.5	8.8	② 0.98	5.58	0.27	8.31 - 6.24	7.4
12/31/93	1,497.0	1,319.0	① 559.0	30,570.0	45,546.0	32,159.0	13.7	1.2	8.9	① 0.72	5.02	0.21	7.81 - 6.33	9.8

Statistics are as originally reported. Adj. for 2-for-1 split, 8/98, 8/96 & 5/94. ① Incl. $30.0 mill. restruct. chg. ② Incl. $58.0 mill. aft.-tax gain on sale ARCS Inc. mtg. svcs. ptf., 1995; $22.0 mill. pre-tax gain on sale of interest in Wing Hang Bank, 1994. ③ Incl. $13.0 mill. chg. fr. settlement of litigation. ④ Incl. a pre-tax gain of $177.0 million fr. sale of BK's cred. card ops. & a $100.0 mill. prov. for cred. losses. ⑤ Incl. a pre-tax gain of $1.02 bill. on the sale of BNY Financial Corp. ⑥ Incl. a pre-tax one-time spec. chrg. of $235.0 mill. & a pre-tax ins. recovery of $175.0 mill.

OFFICERS:
T. A. Renyi, Chmn., C.E.O.
A. R. Griffith, Vice-Chmn.
G. L. Hassell, Pres.
INVESTOR CONTACT: John M. Roy, (212) 635-8005
PRINCIPAL OFFICE: One Wall Street, New York, NY 10286

TELEPHONE NUMBER: (212) 495-1784
FAX: (212) 635-1799
WEB: www.bankofny.com
NO. OF EMPLOYEES: 19,181 (avg.)
SHAREHOLDERS: 28,313
ANNUAL MEETING: In May
INCORPORATED: NY, July, 1968

INSTITUTIONAL HOLDINGS:
No. of Institutions: 652
Shares Held: 459,494,548
% Held: 63.4
INDUSTRY: State commercial banks (SIC: 6022)
TRANSFER AGENT(S): The Bank of New York, New York, NY

BANK ONE CORPORATION

EXCH.	SYM.	REC. PRICE	P/E RATIO	YLD.	MKT. CAP.	RANGE (52-WK.)	'02 Y/E PR.
NYSE	ONE	36.03 (2/28/03)	12.9	2.3%	$41.94 bill.	42.88 - 31.60	36.55

MEDIUM GRADE. THE COMPANY COMPLETED ITS ILLINOIS SYSTEMS CONVERSION, WHICH INVOLVED 2.4 MILLION CONSUMER ACCOUNTS, 52,000 COMMERCIAL ACCOUNTS AND 238 BANKING CENTERS.

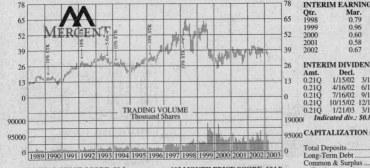

INTERIM EARNINGS (Per Share):

Qtr.	Mar.	June	Sept.	Dec.
1998	0.79	0.68	0.89	0.19
1999	0.96	0.83	0.79	0.36
2000	0.60	d1.11	0.50	d0.44
2001	0.58	0.60	0.64	0.46
2002	0.67	0.71	0.70	0.72

INTERIM DIVIDENDS (Per Share):

Amt.	Decl.	Ex.	Rec.	Pay.
0.21Q	1/15/02	3/13/02	3/15/02	4/01/02
0.21Q	4/16/02	6/12/02	6/14/02	7/01/02
0.21Q	7/16/02	9/11/02	9/13/02	10/01/02
0.21Q	10/15/02	12/11/02	12/13/02	1/01/03
0.21Q	1/21/03	3/12/03	3/14/03	4/01/03

Indicated div.: $0.84 (Div. Reinv. Plan)

CAPITALIZATION (12/31/02):

	($000)	(%)
Total Deposits	170,008,000	73.2
Long-Term Debt	39,919,000	17.2
Common & Surplus	22,440,000	9.7
Total	232,367,000	100.0

*7 YEAR PRICE SCORE 99.3   *12 MONTH PRICE SCORE 104.8

*NYSE COMPOSITE INDEX=100

BUSINESS:

Bank One Corporation (formerly Banc One Corporation), with assets of $277.38 billion as of 12/31/02, is the nation's sixth-largest bank holding company. The Company, formed on 10/1/98, upon the acquisition of First Chicago NBD Corporation by Banc One Corporation, is the third-largest credit card issuer in the U.S. and the largest VISA credit card issuer in the world. ONE offers a variety of financial services to corporate, retail and trust customers. As of 12/31/02, ONE operated 1,795 banking centers and 3,960 ATMs nationwide. ONE also operates affiliates that engage in data processing, venture capital, merchant banking, trust, investment management, brokerage, equipment leasing, consumer finance and insurance.

RECENT DEVELOPMENTS:

For the year ended 12/31/02, the Company reported net income of $3.30 billion compared with income of $2.68 billion, before an accounting charge of $44.0 million, the year before. Earnings included merger and restructuring-related charges of $63.0 million in 2002 and merger and restructuring-related gains of $351.0 million in 2001. Net interest income slipped to $8.60 billion from $8.64 billion a year earlier. Provision for credit losses slid to $2.49 billion from $2.51 billion in the prior year. Non-interest income advanced 14.0% to $8.24 billion. Operating non-interest expense grew to $9.58 billion from $9.55 billion in 2001.

PROSPECTS:

On 11/14/02, the Company announced that it completed its Illinois systems conversion, which involved 2.4 million consumer accounts, 52,000 commercial accounts and 238 banking centers. This conversion, along with three previous major conversions, is the result of a two-year effort under which the Company invested $500.0 million to improve and consolidate its systems. The Company anticipates annual operating savings of $200.0 million as a result of the four conversions. Separately, on 2/6/03, One Equity Partners, Bank One's private equity group, acquired beTRUSTed, PricewaterhouseCoopers' third-party identity management subscription service provider. Looking ahead, ONE expects results in 2003 to be weaker in the beginning of the year and stronger as the year proceeds.

ANNUAL FINANCIAL DATA:

FISCAL YEAR	NET INT. INC. ($mill.)	NON-INT. INC. ($mill.)	NET INC. ($mill.)	TOT. LOANS ($mill.)	TOT. ASSETS ($mill.)	TOT. DEP. ($mill.)	RET. ON EQUITY %	RET. ON ASSETS %	EQUITY/ ASSETS %	EARN. PER SH. $	TANG. BK. VAL. $	DIV. PER SH. $	PRICE RANGE	AVG. P/E RATIO
12/31/02	8,595.0	8,236.0	④ 3,295.0	148,125.0	277,383.0	170,008.0	14.7	1.2	8.1	② 2.80	19.28	0.84	42.88 - 31.60	13.3
12/31/01	8,638.0	7,223.0	④⑤ 2,682.0	156,733.0	268,954.0	167,530.0	13.3	1.0	7.5	④⑤ 2.28	17.11	0.84	41.56 - 27.00	15.0
12/31/00	8,836.0	5,090.0	④ d511.0	174,251.0	269,300.0	167,077.0	. . .	. . .	6.9	④ d0.45	15.56	1.47	39.00 - 23.19	. . .
12/31/99	9,021.0	8,692.0	④ 3,479.0	163,877.0	269,425.0	162,278.0	17.3	1.3	7.5	④ 2.95	17.03	1.64	63.56 - 29.75	15.8
12/31/98	9,347.0	8,071.0	④ 3,108.0	155,398.0	261,496.0	161,542.0	15.1	1.2	7.9	④ 2.61	17.02	1.49	65.63 - 36.06	19.5
12/31/97	5,392.3	3,835.9	④ 1,305.7	82,052.8	115,901.3	77,414.3	12.6	1.1	9.0	④ 1.99	14.74	1.35	54.43 - 35.68	22.6
12/31/96	4,855.5	2,227.5	③ 1,426.5	74,193.9	101,848.1	72,373.1	16.5	1.4	8.5	③ 2.94	16.95	1.21	43.52 - 28.41	12.2
12/31/95	4,129.4	1,870.0	1,277.9	65,328.7	90,454.0	67,320.2	15.6	1.4	9.1	2.65	16.38	1.10	33.16 - 20.77	10.2
12/31/94	4,188.6	1,419.6	② 1,005.1	61,992.9	88,922.6	68,090.1	13.3	1.4	8.5	② 2.00	14.68	1.00	31.41 - 19.94	12.8
12/31/93	4,090.1	1,491.7	① 1,120.6	53,845.6	79,918.6	60,943.2	15.9	1.4	8.8	① 2.42	14.23	0.85	36.97 - 26.67	13.1

Statistics are as originally reported. Adj. for 5-for-4 stock split, 8/93 & 10% stk. div. 2/98, 3/96, 3/94. ① Bef. an acct. cr. $19.4 mill. ② Incl. $40.0 mill. chrg. for acq. of Liberty Bancorp, mtg. loan ctr. consol. & liti. costs. ③ Incl. one-time SAIF chrg. of $34.3 mill. ④ Incl. pre-tax merger-rel. & restr. chrgs.: gain $63.0 mill., 2002; $351.0 mill., 2001; $161.0 mill., 2000; $554.0 mill., 1999; $1.06 bil., 1998; $337.3 mill., 1997. ⑤ Bef. acctg. chrg. of $44.0 mill.

OFFICERS:
J. Dimon, Chmn., C.E.O.
H. G. Miller, C.F.O.

INVESTOR CONTACT: Amy R. Fahey, Investor Relations, (312) 732-5771

PRINCIPAL OFFICE: 1 Bank One Plaza, Chicago, IL 60670

TELEPHONE NUMBER: (312) 732-4000
FAX: (312) 732-1704
WEB: www.bankone.com
NO. OF EMPLOYEES: 73,685
SHAREHOLDERS: 103,589
ANNUAL MEETING: In April
INCORPORATED: DE, April, 1998

INSTITUTIONAL HOLDINGS:
No. of Institutions: 692
Shares Held: 774,214,057
% Held: 66.4
INDUSTRY: National commercial banks
(SIC: 6021)
TRANSFER AGENT(S): First Chicago Trust Company of New York, Jersey City, NJ

BANTA CORPORATION

EXCH.	SYM.	REC. PRICE	P/E RATIO	YLD.	MKT. CAP.	RANGE (52-WK.)	'02 Y/E PR.	DIV. ACH.
NYSE	BN	28.49 (2/28/03)	16.7	2.2%	$0.70 bill.	39.10 - 27.00	31.27	24 yrs.

MEDIUM GRADE. THE COMPANY ANNOUNCED A RESTRUCTURING PLAN THAT IS EXPECTED TO GENERATE ANNUALIZED SAVINGS OF BETWEEN $8.0 MILLION TO $10.0 MILLION.

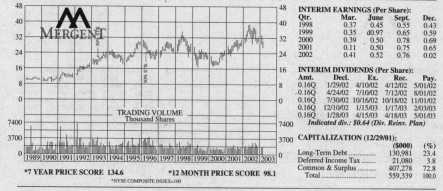

INTERIM EARNINGS (Per Share):

Qtr.	Mar.	June	Sept.	Dec.
1998	0.37	0.45	0.55	0.43
1999	0.35	d0.97	0.65	0.59
2000	0.39	0.50	0.78	0.69
2001	0.11	0.50	0.75	0.65
2002	0.41	0.52	0.76	0.02

INTERIM DIVIDENDS (Per Share):

Amt.	Decl.	Ex.	Rec.	Pay.
0.16Q	1/29/02	4/10/02	4/12/02	5/01/02
0.16Q	4/24/02	7/10/02	7/12/02	8/01/02
0.16Q	7/30/02	10/16/02	10/18/02	11/01/02
0.16Q	12/10/02	1/15/03	1/17/03	2/03/03
0.16Q	1/28/03	4/15/03	4/18/03	5/01/03

Indicated div.: $0.64 (Div. Reinv. Plan)

CAPITALIZATION (12/29/01):

	($000)	(%)
Long-Term Debt	130,981	23.4
Deferred Income Tax	21,080	3.8
Common & Surplus	407,278	72.8
Total	559,339	100.0

TRADING VOLUME
Thousand Shares

*7 YEAR PRICE SCORE 134.6   ***12 MONTH PRICE SCORE 98.1**

NYSE COMPOSITE INDEX=100

BUSINESS:

Banta Corporation provides a broad range of printing and digital imaging services. BN operates in three business segments: print, turnkey services, and healthcare. The print segment provides products and services to publishers of educational and general books and special interest magazines. The print segment also supplies direct marketing materials and consumer and business catalogs. The turnkey services segment provides supply-chain management, product assembly, fulfillment and product localization services to technology companies. The healthcare products are primarily engaged in the production of disposable products used in outpatient clinics, dental offices and hospitals. Sales (and operating income) for 2002 were derived: printing and digital imaging, 71.5% (69.9%); supply-chain management, 21.4% (22.0%); and healthcare, 7.1% (8.1%).

RECENT DEVELOPMENTS:

For the twelve months ended 12/31/02, net income declined 12.4% to $43.8 million compared with $50.0 million in 2001. Results for 2002 included an asset impairment charge of $26.8 million, while results for 2001 included a write-off of $12.5 million for an investment. Net sales were $1.37 billion, down 6.3% from $1.46 billion in the prior year. Results were negatively affected by reductions in advertising and promotional spending, and lower pricing, primarily in the printing and digital imaging segment. Gross profit grew 1.8% to $303.5 million compared with $298.1 million the year before. Earnings from operations decreased 24.7% to $81.6 million.

PROSPECTS:

The Company announced a restructuring plan that involves its consumer catalog business and a realignment of operating activities within its supply-chain management segment. This plan, which will be implemented in 2003, will consolidate operations, leverage existing capacity, improve operating efficiencies and lower costs. As a result, the Company will incur pre-tax charges of $15.0 million to $18.0 million, the majority of which will be expensed in the second and third quarter of 2003. The plan is expected to generate annualized savings of $8.0 million to $10.0 million beginning in 2004, with modest benefit expected in the fourth quarter of 2003.

ANNUAL FINANCIAL DATA:

FISCAL YEAR	TOT. REVS. ($mill.)	NET INC. ($mill.)	TOT. ASSETS ($mill.)	OPER. PROFIT %	NET PROFIT %	RET. ON EQUITY %	RET. ON ASSETS %	CURR. RATIO	EARN. PER SH.$	CASH FL. PER SH.$	TANG. BK. VAL.$	DIV. PER SH.$	PRICE RANGE	AVG. P/E RATIO	AVG. YIELD %
p12/31/02	1,366.5	③ 43.8							③ 1.71			0.64	39.10 - 29.05	19.9	1.9
12/29/01	1,457.9	② 50.0	788.0	7.4	3.4	12.3	6.3	2.0	② 2.01	5.04	13.89	0.61	31.04 - 22.49	13.3	2.3
12/30/00	1,537.7	58.7	854.5	7.5	3.8	15.8	6.9	1.7	2.35	5.38	12.41	0.60	25.70 - 17.19	9.1	2.8
1/01/00	1,278.3	① 16.0	773.3	3.8	1.3	4.5	2.1	1.5	① 0.59	3.10	12.31	0.56	27.38 - 16.75	37.4	2.5
1/02/99	1,335.8	52.9	770.0	7.3	4.0	12.9	6.9	1.8	1.80	4.06	11.83	0.51	35.25 - 21.81	15.8	1.8
1/03/98	1,202.5	① 43.3	781.2	6.6	3.6	10.5	5.5	1.8	① 1.44	3.50	11.80	0.47	29.88 - 21.63	17.9	1.8
12/28/96	1,083.8	50.9	719.2	8.5	4.7	12.1	7.1	2.7	1.63	3.49	12.29	0.44	30.67 - 20.50	15.7	1.7
12/31/95	1,022.7	53.6	678.8	9.6	5.2	13.8	7.9	2.5	1.75	3.42	16.83	0.37	30.08 - 19.00	14.0	1.5
12/31/94	811.3	47.2	577.8	10.3	5.8	14.2	8.2	1.7	1.56	2.92	15.29	0.35	25.67 - 18.00	14.0	1.6
1/01/94	691.2	41.0	457.4	10.5	5.9	14.0	9.0	2.2	1.36	2.47	9.17	0.31	24.67 - 17.78	15.6	1.5

Statistics are as originally reported. Adj. for 50% stk. div., 3/1/96. ① Incl. restr. charges of $55.0 mill., 1/00; $13.5 mill., 1/98. ② Incl. $12.5 mill. write-down of invest. ③ Incl. $26.8 mill. asset impair. chg.

OFFICERS:
D. D. Belcher, Chmn.
S. A. Streeter, Pres., C.E.O.
G. A. Hensler, Interim C.F.O.
INVESTOR CONTACT: Gerald A. Henseler, Exec. V.P., (920) 751-7777
PRINCIPAL OFFICE: 225 Main Street, Menasha, WI 54952

TELEPHONE NUMBER: (920) 751-7777
FAX: (920) 751-7790
WEB: www.banta.com
NO. OF EMPLOYEES: 8,000 (approx.)
SHAREHOLDERS: 1,898 (record)
ANNUAL MEETING: In Apr.
INCORPORATED: WI, 1901

INSTITUTIONAL HOLDINGS:
No. of Institutions: 166
Shares Held: 19,741,597
% Held: 77.9
INDUSTRY: Commercial printing, nec (SIC: 2759)
TRANSFER AGENT(S): Firstar Bank, N.A., Milwaukee, WI

BARD (C.R.), INC.

EXCH.	SYM.	REC. PRICE	P/E RATIO	YLD.	MKT. CAP.	RANGE (52-WK.)	'02 Y/E PR.	DIV. ACH.
NYSE	BCR	59.10 (2/28/03)	20.1	1.5%	$3.10 bill.	59.87 - 45.75	58.00	31 yrs.

INVESTMENT GRADE. ON 1/24/03, THE COMPANY ANNOUNCED THAT IT HAS ACQUIRED THE RIGHT TO PURCHASE THE ASSETS OF GENYX MEDICAL, INC., A PRIVATELY-HELD MEDICAL DEVICE COMPANY.

*7 YEAR PRICE SCORE 134.3   ***12 MONTH PRICE SCORE 112.3**
NYSE COMPOSITE INDEX=100

INTERIM EARNINGS (Per Share):

Qtr.	Mar.	June	Sept.	Dec.
1998	0.44	0.71	0.42	3.03
1999	0.51	0.55	0.58	0.64
2000	0.62	0.65	0.66	0.16
2001	0.65	0.68	0.68	0.74
2002	0.65	0.83	0.57	0.89

INTERIM DIVIDENDS (Per Share):

Amt.	Decl.	Ex.	Rec.	Pay.
0.21Q	12/12/01	1/16/02	1/21/02	2/01/02
0.21Q	4/17/02	4/25/02	4/29/02	5/10/02
0.22Q	7/10/02	7/18/02	7/22/02	8/02/02
0.22Q	10/09/02	10/17/02	10/21/02	11/01/02
0.22Q	12/11/02	1/15/03	1/20/03	1/31/03

Indicated div.: $0.88 (Div. Reinv. Plan)

CAPITALIZATION (12/31/01):

	($000)	(%)
Long-Term Debt	156,400	16.5
Common & Surplus	788,700	83.5
Total	945,100	100.0

BUSINESS:

Bard (C.R.), Inc. is a major multinational developer, manufacturer and marketer of health care products. BCR engages in the design, manufacture, packaging, distribution and sale of medical, surgical, diagnostic and patient-care devices. Bard holds strong positions in the fields of vascular, urology, oncology and surgical specialty products. BCR's products are marketed worldwide to hospitals, individual health care professionals, extended care facilities, alternate site facilities and the home, employing a combination of direct delivery and medical specialty distributors. Hospitals, physicians and nursing homes purchase about 90% of BCR's products as of 12/31/01. The Vascular Group accounted for 20.4% of 2002 sales; Urology, 32.9%; Oncology, 23.5%; Surgery, 18.0%; and other, 5.2%.

RECENT DEVELOPMENTS:

For the twelve months ended 12/31/02, net income climbed 8.2% to $155.0 million compared with $143.2 million the previous year. Results for 2002 included pre-tax non-recurring charges of $34.9 million and a pre-tax tax credit of $3.5 million. Results for 2001 included a pre-tax charge of $13.2 million for goodwill amortization. Net sales rose 7.8% to $1.27 billion from $1.18 billion the year before.

Vascular net sales grew 3.5% to $259.7 million from 250.9 million, while urology net sales advanced 7.6% to $419.7 million from $390.1 million in 2001. Oncology net sales increased 8.9% to $299.0 million from $274.6 million, and surgery net sales improved 11.8% to $229.5 million from $205.2 million the prior year.

PROSPECTS:

On 1/24/03, the Company announced that it has acquired the right to purchase the assets of Genyx Medical, Inc., a privately-held medical device company that develops, manufacturers and markets URYX®, a proprietary injectable bulking agent for the treatment of stress urinary incontinence. Terms of the agreement were not disclosed. Separately, the Company expects revenue growth in the range of 7.0% to 8.0% for 2003 and earnings per share to improve 12.0% over 2002 results, excluding non-recurring items. Meanwhile, BCR plans to increase its research and development funding in 2003 by more than 30.0%.

ANNUAL FINANCIAL DATA:

FISCAL YEAR	TOT. REVS. ($mill.)	NET INC. ($mill.)	TOT. ASSETS ($mill.)	OPER. PROFIT %	NET PROFIT %	RET. ON EQUITY %	RET. ON ASSETS %	CURR. RATIO	EARN. PER SH.$	CASH FL. PER SH.$	TANG. BK. VAL.$	DIV. PER SH.$	PRICE RANGE	AVG. P/E RATIO	AVG. YIELD %
p12/31/02	1,273.8	⑧ 155.0	1,416.7						② 2.94			0.86	63.94 - 44.10	18.4	1.6
12/31/01	1,181.3	143.2	1,231.1	17.3	12.1	18.2	11.6	2.8	2.75	3.78	7.94	0.84	64.95 - 40.86	19.2	1.6
12/31/00	1,098.8	⑦ 106.9	1,089.2	14.0	9.7	17.4	9.8	2.3	⑦ 2.09	3.06	5.06	0.82	54.94 - 35.00	21.5	1.8
12/31/99	1,036.5	⑥ 118.1	1,126.4	16.7	11.4	20.6	10.5	1.5	⑥ 2.28	3.22	4.67	0.78	59.88 - 41.69	22.3	1.5
12/31/98	1,164.7	⑤ 252.3	1,079.8	39.9	21.7	44.5	23.4	1.6	⑤ 4.51	5.56	4.05	0.74	50.25 - 28.50	8.7	1.9
12/31/97	1,213.5	④ 72.3	1,279.3	8.6	6.0	12.6	5.7	1.8	④ 1.26	2.26	2.62	0.70	39.00 - 26.38	25.9	2.1
12/31/96	1,194.4	③ 92.5	1,332.5	8.9	7.7	15.4	6.9	1.7	③ 1.62	2.63	2.71	0.66	37.38 - 25.88	19.5	2.1
12/31/95	1,137.8	① 86.8	1,091.0	10.9	7.6	15.4	8.0	1.8	① 1.53	2.42	4.36	0.62	32.25 - 25.50	18.9	2.1
12/31/94	1,018.2	74.9	958.4	14.8	7.4	17.0	7.8	1.2	1.44	2.20	3.35	0.58	30.50 - 22.25	18.3	2.2
12/31/93	970.8	② 62.1	798.6	13.2	6.4	16.2	7.8	1.6	② 1.19	1.87	4.49	0.54	35.25 - 20.50	23.4	1.9

Statistics are as originally reported. ① Incl. one-time chg. of $17.7 mill. ② Incl. one-time gain of $17.6 mill. & bef. acctg. adj. of $6.1 mill. ③ Incl. net nonrecur. chgs. of $12.9 mill. ④ Incl. pre-tax restruct chg. of $44.1 mill. & a nonrecurr. net gain of $3.9 mill. ⑤ Incl. net gain of $163.8 mill. fr. the sale of cardiology bus. & several nonrecur. chgs. total. $25.9 mill. ⑥ Incl. gain of $9.2 mill. fr. the sale cardiology bus. ⑦ Incl. gain of $15.4 mill. fr. the sale cardiology bus. ⑧ Incl. pre-tax non-recurring chrgs. of $34.9 mill. & pre-tax credit of $3.5 mill.

OFFICERS:
W. H. Longfield, Chmn., C.E.O., Pres.
C. P. Slacik, Sr. V.P., C.F.O.
N. J. Bernstein, V.P., Gen. Couns., Sec.
INVESTOR CONTACT: Todd Schermerhorn, Investor Relations, (908) 277-8139
PRINCIPAL OFFICE: 730 Central Avenue, Murray Hill, NJ 07974

TELEPHONE NUMBER: (908) 277-8000
FAX: (908) 277-8078
WEB: www.crbard.com
NO. OF EMPLOYEES: 7,700 (approx.)
SHAREHOLDERS: 5,859
ANNUAL MEETING: In Apr.
INCORPORATED: NJ, Feb., 1923

INSTITUTIONAL HOLDINGS:
No. of Institutions: 267
Shares Held: 44,040,445
% Held: 85.2
INDUSTRY: Surgical and medical instruments (SIC: 3841)
TRANSFER AGENT(S): EquiServe, Jersey City, NJ

BARNES & NOBLE, INC.

EXCH.	SYM.	REC. PRICE	P/E RATIO	YLD.	MKT. CAP.	RANGE (52-WK.)	'02 Y/E PR.
NYSE	BKS	17.63 (2/28/03)	13.5	...	$1.18 bill.	34.43 - 16.06	18.07

MEDIUM GRADE. THE COMPANY COMPLETED THE ACQUISITION OF STERLING PUBLISHING, A PUBLISHER OF HOW-TO BOOKS, IN A TRANSACTION VALUED AT APPROXIMATELY $115.0 MILLION.

*7 YEAR PRICE SCORE 98.7   *12 MONTH PRICE SCORE 80.9

*NYSE COMPOSITE INDEX=100

INTERIM EARNINGS (Per Share):

Qtr.	Apr.	July	Oct.	Jan.
1998-99	d0.05	d0.08	d0.07	1.47
1999-00	d0.02	0.33	0.05	1.48
2000-01	d0.06	d0.13	d0.08	d0.52
2001-02	d0.18	d0.03	0.10	1.09
2002-03	d0.25	0.02	0.05	1.49

INTERIM DIVIDENDS (Per Share):

Amt.	Decl.	Ex.	Rec.	Pay.
	No dividends paid.			

CAPITALIZATION (2/2/02):

	($000)	(%)
Long-Term Debt	449,000	33.6
Common & Surplus	888,110	66.4
Total	1,337,110	100.0

BUSINESS:

Barnes & Noble, Inc. is a retailer of trade books, mass market paperbacks, children's books, off-price bargain books and magazines. As of 3/20/03, the Company operated 628 bookstores under the Barnes & Noble Booksellers, Bookstop and Bookstar names. In addition, BKS operated 285 mall-based bookstores under the B. Dalton Bookseller, Doubleday Book Shops and Scribner's Bookstore names.

Through its approximate 60.0% interest in GameStop, Inc., BKS operated 1,231 video game and entertainment software stores under the GameStop, Babbage's, Software Etc. and FuncoLand names. As of 3/20/03, BKS owned approximately 37.0% of Barnes & Noble.com. On 10/28/99, BKS acquired Babbage's Etc., a computer software retailer. On 6/19/00, BKS acquired Funco, Inc.

RECENT DEVELOPMENTS:

For the 52 weeks ended 2/1/03, net income advanced 56.2% to $99.9 million from $64.0 million the year before. Earnings for fiscal 2002 and fiscal 2001 included pre-opening expenses of $10.2 million and $8.0 million, and equity in net losses of barnesandnoble.com of $26.8 million and $88.4 million, respectively. Earnings for fiscal 2002 also

included an impairment charge of $25.3 million, while earnings for fiscal 2001 included a legal settlement expense of $4.5 million. Sales climbed 8.2% to $5.27 billion. Comparable-store sales at Barnes & Noble were flat, while comparable-store sales at B. Dalton slipped 6.4% year over year. GameStop's comparable-store sales increased 11.4%.

PROSPECTS:

On 1/22/03, the Company announced that it completed the acquisition of Sterling Publishing, a publisher of how-to books, in a transaction valued at about $115.0 million. Sterling has an active list of more than 4,500 titles, and publishes more than 1,000 new titles annually. Looking ahead, BKS expects earnings per share growth for fiscal

year 2003 of approximately 40.0%, ranging from $1.93 to $2.01 per share. Bookstores are anticipated to earn between $1.62 and $1.65 per share in fiscal 2003. For fiscal year 2003, Barnes & Noble comparable-store sales are expected to range from 0.0% to 1.0%, while B. Dalton comparable-store sales are expected to decline between 6.0% and 7.0%.

ANNUAL FINANCIAL DATA:

FISCAL YEAR	TOT. REVS. ($mill.)	NET INC. ($mill.)	TOT. ASSETS ($mill.)	OPER. PROFIT %	NET PROFIT %	RET. ON EQUITY %	RET. ON ASSETS %	CURR. RATIO	EARN. PER SH.$	CASH FL. PER SH.$	TANG. BK. VAL.$	PRICE RANGE	AVG. P/E RATIO
p2/01/03	5,269.3	③⑤ 99.9	2,995.4						③⑤ 1.39			35.00 - 16.77	18.6
2/02/02	4,870.4	⑥ 64.0	2,623.2	5.0	1.3	7.2	2.4	1.4	⑥ 0.96	2.75	7.96	43.99 - 21.63	34.2
2/03/01	4,375.8	⑤ d52.0	2,557.5	3.1	...	...	...	1.6	⑤ d0.81	1.47	6.43	29.94 - 16.31	...
1/29/00	3,486.0	④ 129.0	2,413.8	6.7	3.7	15.2	5.3	1.4	④ 1.81	3.39	8.37	44.38 - 20.06	17.8
1/30/99	3,005.6	③ 92.4	1,807.6	6.3	3.1	13.6	5.1	1.4	③ 1.29	2.53	8.61	48.00 - 22.19	27.2
1/31/98	2,796.9	② 64.7	1,591.2	5.3	2.3	12.2	4.1	1.4	② 0.93	2.05	6.50	33.94 - 12.88	25.2
2/01/97	2,448.1	51.2	1,446.6	4.9	2.1	11.2	3.5	1.3	0.74	1.63	5.46	18.88 - 11.63	20.6
1/27/96	1,976.9	d53.0	1,315.3	...	...	...	...	1.4	d0.85	d0.04	4.60	21.13 - 13.06	...
1/28/95	1,622.7	25.5	1,026.4	4.2	1.6	7.1	2.5	1.3	0.41	1.03	3.72	15.69 - 10.00	31.7
1/29/94	1,337.4	③ 7.8	895.9	3.2	0.6	2.4	0.9	1.5	①③ 0.15	0.54	3.19	17.00 - 11.31	94.3

Statistics are as originally reported. Adj. for 2-for-1 stk. split, 9/97. ① Pro-forma. ② Bef. $11.5 mil extraord. chg. ③ Incl. $26.8 mil net loss from the Company's equity interest in barnesandnoble.com, 2/03; $4.5 mil, 1/99; bef. $10.6 mil chg. for pfd. stk. redempt. premium, 1/94. ④ Bef. $4.5 mil acctg. chrg. & incl. $25.0 mil non-recur. pre-tax gain fr. formation of barnesandnoble.com. ⑤ Incl. $25.3 mil impairment chrg., 2/03; $92.4 mil, 2/01. ⑥ Incl. $4.5 mil pre-tax chg. fr. legal settlement.

OFFICERS:
L. Riggio, Chmn.
S. Riggio, Vice-Chmn., C.E.O.
L. S. Zilavy, C.F.O.

INVESTOR CONTACT: Larry Zilavy, C.F.O., (212) 633-3336

PRINCIPAL OFFICE: 122 Fifth Avenue, New York, NY 10011

TELEPHONE NUMBER: (212) 633-3300
FAX: (212) 366-5186
WEB: www.barnesandnobleinc.com

NO. OF EMPLOYEES: 37,000 (avg.)

SHAREHOLDERS: 1,986 (approx.)

ANNUAL MEETING: In June

INCORPORATED: DE, Nov., 1986

INSTITUTIONAL HOLDINGS:
No. of Institutions: 186
Shares Held: 41,854,582
% Held: 64.8

INDUSTRY: Book stores (SIC: 5942)

TRANSFER AGENT(S): The Bank of New York, New York, NY

BARNES GROUP INC.

EXCH.	SYM.	REC. PRICE	P/E RATIO	YLD.	MKT. CAP.	RANGE (52-WK.)	'02 Y/E PR.
NYSE	B	19.20 (2/28/03)	13.5	4.2%	$354.5 mill.	26.75 - 17.30	20.35

MEDIUM GRADE. ON 2/6/03, THE COMPANY ACQUIRED KAR PRODUCTS FOR $78.5 MILLION.

*7 YEAR PRICE SCORE 103.3   *12 MONTH PRICE SCORE 98.6
*NYSE COMPOSITE INDEX=100

INTERIM EARNINGS (Per Share):

Qtr.	Mar.	June	Sept.	Dec.
1997	0.49	0.53	0.50	0.47
1998	0.58	0.23	0.52	0.36
1999	0.50	0.41	0.45	0.08
2000	0.50	0.49	0.49	0.41
2001	0.39	0.46	0.39	d0.04
2002	0.36	0.45	0.36	0.25

INTERIM DIVIDENDS (Per Share):

Amt.	Decl.	Ex.	Rec.	Pay.
0.20Q	2/06/02	2/27/02	3/01/02	3/12/02
0.20Q	4/10/02	5/29/02	5/31/02	6/11/02
0.20Q	7/10/02	8/28/02	8/30/02	9/10/02
0.20Q	10/09/02	11/26/02	11/29/02	12/10/02
0.20Q	2/13/03	2/26/03	2/28/03	3/11/03
Indicated div.: $0.80 (Div. Reinv. Plan)				

CAPITALIZATION (12/31/01):

	($000)	(%)
Long-Term Debt	178,365	47.3
Common & Surplus	198,837	52.7
Total	377,202	100.0

BUSINESS:

Barnes Group Inc. is a diversified company that manufactures and provides products and services to industrial markets. Associated Spring (40.7% of 2002 revenues) is a manufacturer of precision springs and custom made metal parts for the automotive, home appliance, farm machinery, heavy construction and electronics industries. Barnes Distribution (36.2%) distributes high-strength fasteners, automotive replacement parts, spray chemicals, adhesives, sealants and welding supplies for maintenance and repair to the industrial aftermarket. Barnes Distribution services customers under the brand names of Bowman Distribution, Curtis Industries, Mechanics Choice, Raymond, Motalink and Autoliaison. The Barnes Aerospace group (23.1%) produces machine components for the primary engine manufacturers serving the commercial aircraft and defense industries.

RECENT DEVELOPMENTS:

For the year ended 12/31/02, net income surged 42.0% to $27.1 million compared with $19.1 million in 2001. Results for 2001 included a charge of $4.8 million related to a Texas plant closure. Net sales rose 2.0% to $784.0 million from $768.8 million a year earlier. Sales growth was primarily attributed to contributions from acquisitions, partially offset by the decline at Barnes Aerospace, which coincides with a decline in the aerospace industry, and the negative effect on Barnes Distribution of adverse market conditions in the manufacturing, industrial and transport services sectors. Operating income increased 11.2% to $44.8 million from $40.3 million the year before.

PROSPECTS:

On 2/6/03, the Company completed the acquisition of Kar Products, a full-service distributor of maintenance, repair and operating supplies to industrial, construction, transportation and other markets, for about $78.5 million. Looking ahead, B expects results at Associated Springs to continue to benefit from recent acquisitions, and growth in sales of products for the transportation sector and sales of nitrogen gas spring products. Meanwhile, Barnes Distribution expects growth initiatives rolled out in 2001 and the integration of Kar Products to have a positive financial effect. Barnes Aerospace is positioned to remain profitable based on its backlog of $152.0 million as of 12/31/02.

ANNUAL FINANCIAL DATA:

FISCAL YEAR	TOT. REVS. ($000)	NET INC. ($000)	TOT. ASSETS ($000)	OPER. PROFIT %	NET PROFIT %	RET. ON EQUITY %	RET. ON ASSETS %	CURR. RATIO	EARN. PER SH. $	CASH FL. PER SH. $	TANG. BK. VAL. $	DIV. PER SH. $	PRICE RANGE	AVG. P/E RATIO	AVG. YIELD %
p12/31/02	784,036	27,151	652,530						1.42			0.80	26.75 - 17.30	15.5	3.6
12/31/01	768,821	② 19,121	636,505	5.2	2.5	9.6	3.0	1.4	② 1.01	2.97	2.11	0.80	24.99 - 17.81	21.2	3.7
12/31/00	740,032	35,665	636,941	8.5	4.8	17.7	5.6	1.9	1.90	3.85	2.45	0.79	22.38 - 12.00	9.0	4.6
12/31/99	622,356	28,612	516,282	7.3	4.6	15.8	5.5	1.9	1.46	3.01	4.88	0.75	30.00 - 15.25	15.5	3.3
12/31/98	651,183	34,494	418,904	8.5	5.3	18.3	8.2	2.1	1.69	3.08	8.59	0.69	34.00 - 21.25	16.3	2.5
12/31/97	642,660	40,423	407,978	10.2	6.3	22.4	9.9	2.3	1.96	3.32	8.04	0.65	30.38 - 19.79	12.8	2.6
12/31/96	594,989	① 32,568	389,956	9.3	5.5	20.7	8.4	2.4	① 1.63	2.97	6.89	0.60	20.67 - 11.67	9.9	3.7
12/31/95	592,509	27,484	361,549	8.2	4.6	21.3	7.6	2.2	1.40	2.76	5.53	0.53	15.25 - 11.96	9.7	3.9
12/31/94	569,197	20,316	351,956	6.4	3.6	19.0	5.8	2.0	1.07	2.31	4.49	0.48	13.29 - 9.83	10.8	4.2
12/31/93	502,292	4,383	333,296	2.5	0.9	4.8	1.3	2.1	0.23	1.47	3.74	0.47	11.00 - 9.96	45.0	4.5

Statistics are as originally reported. Adj. for stk splits: 3-for-1, 4/97. ① Incl. non-recurr. chrg. $1.3 mill. ② Incl. non-recurr. pre-tax chrg. of $4.8 mill.

OFFICERS:
T. O. Barnes, Chmn.
E. M. Carpenter, Pres. & C.E.O.
W. C. Denninger, Sr. V.P., C.F.O.
INVESTOR CONTACT: Phillip J. Penn, Investor Relations, (860) 973-2126
PRINCIPAL OFFICE: 123 Main Street, Bristol, CT 06010-0489

TELEPHONE NUMBER: (860) 583-7070
FAX: (860) 589-3507
WEB: www.barnesgroupinc.com
NO. OF EMPLOYEES: 5,150 (avg.)
SHAREHOLDERS: 18,464,330
ANNUAL MEETING: In Apr.
INCORPORATED: DE, Jan., 1925

INSTITUTIONAL HOLDINGS:
No. of Institutions: 81
Shares Held: 8,591,557
% Held: 45.5
INDUSTRY: Fabricated metal products, nec (SIC: 3499)
TRANSFER AGENT(S): Mellon Shareholder Services, L.L.C., Ridgefield Park, NJ

BAUSCH & LOMB, INC.

EXCH.	SYM.	REC. PRICE	P/E RATIO	YLD.	MKT. CAP.	RANGE (52-WK.)	'02 Y/E PR.
NYSE	BOL	30.80 (2/28/03)	23.2	1.7%	$1.63 bill.	44.80 - 27.16	36.00

MEDIUM GRADE. THE COMPANY EXPECTS REVENUES FOR 2003 TO GROW IN THE MID-SINGLE DIGITS.

TRADING VOLUME
Thousand Shares

1989 1990 1991 1992 1993 1994 1995 1996 1997 1998 1999 2000 2001 2002 2003

*7 YEAR PRICE SCORE 80.6   ***12 MONTH PRICE SCORE 104.4**

*NYSE COMPOSITE INDEX=100

INTERIM EARNINGS (Per Share):

Qtr	Mar.	June	Sept.	Dec.
1998	d0.89	0.98	0.65	d0.77
1999	0.39	0.49	0.71	0.29
2000	0.68	0.64	0.27	0.06
2001	d0.02	0.13	0.43	0.24
2002	0.16	0.40	0.17	0.60

INTERIM DIVIDENDS (Per Share):

Amt.	Decl.	Ex.	Rec.	Pay.
0.26Q	2/26/02	3/06/02	3/08/02	4/01/02
0.13Q	4/25/02	5/30/02	6/03/02	7/01/02
0.13Q	7/23/02	8/29/02	9/03/02	10/01/02
0.13Q	10/28/02	11/27/02	12/02/02	1/02/03
0.13Q	2/25/03	3/05/03	3/07/03	4/01/03

Indicated div.: $0.52 (Div. Reinv. Plan)

CAPITALIZATION (12/29/01):

	($000)	(%)
Long-Term Debt [1]	703,200	32.1
Deferred Income Tax	297,200	13.6
Minority Interest	214,600	9.8
Common & Surplus [3]	975,000	44.5
Total	2,190,000	100.0

BUSINESS:

Bausch & Lomb, Inc. is a developer of healthcare products for the eye. The Company operates five major product categories. The contact lens category (28.8% of 2002 sales) includes traditional, planned replacement disposable, daily disposable, rigid gas permeable, continuous wear and toric lenses. The lens care category (25.7%) includes BOL's multipurpose solutions, enzyme cleaners and saline solutions. The pharmaceutical category (21.8%) includes generic and proprietary prescription pharmaceuticals and vision accessories. The cataract category (16.6%) includes products and equipment for cataract and retinal surgery. The refractive category (7.1%) includes lasers, microkeratomes, and other products and equipment used in refractive surgery. BOL's brands include BAUSCH & LOMB®, SOFLENS™, PUREVISION™, BOSTON®, RENU®, STORZ® and TECHNOLAS™.

RECENT DEVELOPMENTS:

For the year ended 12/28/02, net income was $72.5 million versus income of $42.0 million, before a loss from discontinued operations of $21.1 million and an accounting gain of $300,000, the previous year. Results for 2002 and 2001 included several after-tax non-recurring items that resulted in a net charge of $21.0 million and $7.6 million, respectively. Total net sales grew 9.1% to $1.82 billion from $1.67 billion in 2001. Contact lens sales increased 13.2% to $523.9 million. Lens care sales rose 11.9% to $465.5 million. Pharmaceuticals sales increased 14.9% to $396.1 million. Cataract revenue slipped 0.7% to $301.8 million, while refractive sales declined 6.4% to $129.4 million.

PROSPECTS:

Going forward, BOL expects upper-single-digit sales growth from contact lenses and cataract products, with mid-single-digit growth in pharmaceuticals and low-single-digit growth in the lens care and refractive categories. Meanwhile, the Company expects operating profit margins in excess of 12.0% for the full-year 2003. In addition, BOL expects full-year 2003 earnings per share of about $2.05, with each quarter growing between 15.0% and 20.0%.

ANNUAL FINANCIAL DATA:

FISCAL YEAR	TOT. REVS. ($mill.)	NET INC. ($mill.)	TOT. ASSETS ($mill.)	OPER. PROFIT %	NET PROFIT %	RET. ON EQUITY %	RET. ON ASSETS %	CURR. RATIO	EARN. PER SH.$	CASH FL. PER SH.$	TANG. BK. VAL.$	DIV. PER SH.$	PRICE RANGE	AVG. P/E RATIO	AVG. YIELD %
p12/31/02	1,816.7	[12] 72.5							[1] 1.34			0.78	44.80 - 27.16	26.9	2.2
12/29/01	1,711.9	[11] 42.0	2,993.5	5.1	2.5	4.3	1.4	2.0	[11] 0.78	3.67	2.50	1.04	54.93 - 27.20	52.6	2.5
12/30/00	1,772.4	[10] 82.0	3,085.9	8.0	4.6	7.9	2.7	2.0	[10] 1.49	4.20	4.18	1.04	80.88 - 33.56	38.4	1.8
12/25/99	1,756.1	[9] 102.7	3,273.5	12.2	5.8	8.3	3.1	2.9	[9] 1.79	4.42	11.05	1.04	84.75 - 51.38	38.0	1.5
12/26/98	2,362.8	[8] 25.2	3,491.7	5.2	1.1	3.0	0.7	2.0	[8] 0.45	3.35	1.52	1.04	60.00 - 37.75	108.6	2.1
12/27/97	1,915.7	[7] 49.4	2,772.9	7.7	2.6	6.0	1.8	1.2	[7] 0.89	2.90	7.45	1.04	47.88 - 32.50	45.1	2.6
12/28/96	1,926.8	[5][6] 83.1	2,603.4	9.9	4.3	9.4	3.2	1.0	[5][6] 1.47	3.47	8.86	1.04	44.50 - 32.50	26.2	2.7
12/30/95	1,932.9	[4] 112.0	2,550.1	10.9	5.8	12.1	4.4	1.1	[4] 1.94	3.76	9.62	0.99	44.50 - 30.88	19.4	2.6
12/31/94	1,850.6	13.5	2,457.7	5.1	0.7	1.5	0.5	1.4	0.23	1.89	8.79	0.93	53.88 - 30.63	183.6	2.2
12/25/93	1,872.2	[2] 156.5	2,511.9	13.4	8.4	16.9	6.2	2.0	[2] 2.60	4.01	7.95	0.86	57.50 - 43.00	19.3	1.7

Statistics are as originally reported. [1] Incl. cap. lse. obligs. [2] Incl. $40.0 mill. pre-tax restruct. chg. [3] Incl. Cl. B. common. [4] Incl. restruct. chgs. of $17.4 mill.; gain on sale of Sport Div. of $20.8 mill. and lit. prov. of $14.2 mill. [5] Incl. $15.1 mill. restruct. chg. [6] Incl. a net loss of $26.1 mill. on sale of Oral Care div., an after-tax chg. of $16.1 mill. for lit. exps. & a gain of $27.6 mill. on the sale of Steri-Oss. [7] Incl. net chgs. of $76.2 mill. [8] Incl. a net chg. of $84.2 mill. [9] Incl. a pre-tax gain of $6.7 mill.; after-tax restr. chg. $34.2 mill., excl. net gain fr. disc. opers. $342.1 mill. [10] Incl. pre-tax restruct. chrg. of $33.7 mill. & purch. in proc. res. of $23.8 mill. [11] Incl. pre-tax restruct.chrg. of $21.2 mill. & excl. gain from acctg. chg. of $300,000 and loss from disc. opers. of $21.1 mill. [12] Incl. net chrgs. of $21.0 mill.

OFFICERS:
R. L. Zarrella, Chmn., C.E.O.
S. C. McCluski, Sr. V.P., C.F.O.
A. H. Resnick, V.P., Treas.
INVESTOR CONTACT: Daniel L. Ritz, Dir., Investor Relations, (585) 338-5802
PRINCIPAL OFFICE: One Bausch & Lomb Place, Rochester, NY 14604-2701

TELEPHONE NUMBER: (585) 338-6000
FAX: (585) 338-6007
WEB: www.bausch.com
NO. OF EMPLOYEES: 11,500
SHAREHOLDERS: 6,400 (approx.)
ANNUAL MEETING: In April
INCORPORATED: NY, March, 1908

INSTITUTIONAL HOLDINGS:
No. of Institutions: 211
Shares Held: 56,346,113
% Held: 104.5

INDUSTRY: Ophthalmic goods (SIC: 3851)

TRANSFER AGENT(S): Mellon Investor Services, South Hackensack, NJ

BAXTER INTERNATIONAL INC.

EXCH.	SYM.	REC. PRICE	P/E RATIO	YLD.	MKT. CAP.	RANGE (52-WK.)	'02 Y/E PR.
NYSE	BAX	28.39 (2/28/03)	25.6	2.1%	$17.00 bill.	59.90 - 24.07	28.00

MEDIUM GRADE. THE COMPANY EXPECTS TO ACHIEVE SALES GROWTH IN THE RANGE OF 8.0% TO 12.0% AND DILUTED EARNINGS PER SHARE IN THE RANGE OF $2.10 TO $2.20 IN 2003

INTERIM EARNINGS (Per Share):

Qtr.	Mar.	June	Sept.	Dec.
1998	0.29	0.31	d0.22	0.37
1999	0.31	0.35	0.34	0.39
2000	0.33	0.08	0.39	0.45
2001	0.36	0.42	0.45	d0.13
2002	0.41	0.32	0.51	0.42

INTERIM DIVIDENDS (Per Share):

Amt.	Decl.	Ex.	Rec.	Pay.
2-for-1	2/28/01	5/31/01	5/09/01	5/30/01
0.582A	11/28/01	12/12/01	12/14/01	1/07/02
0.582A	11/18/02	12/11/02	12/13/02	1/06/03

Indicated div.: $0.58 (Div. Reinv. Plan)

CAPITALIZATION (12/31/01):

	($000)	(%)
Long-Term Debt③	2,486,000	38.5
Deferred Income Tax	218,000	3.4
Common & Surplus	3,757,000	58.1
Total	6,461,000	100.0

*7 YEAR PRICE SCORE 119.9   ***12 MONTH PRICE SCORE 78.3**

NYSE COMPOSITE INDEX=100

BUSINESS:

Baxter International Inc. develops, distributes, and manufactures products and technologies related to the blood and circulatory system. Operations are divided into three business segments. The I.V. Systems/Medical Products segment develops technologies and systems to improve intravenous medication delivery and distributes medical products. The BioScience segment develops biopharmaceutical and blood collection and separation products and technologies. The Renal segment develops products and provides services for the treatment of end-stage kidney disease. As of 12/31/02, BAX manufactured products in 29 countries and sold them in over 100 countries. BAX's products are used by hospitals, clinical and medical research laboratories, blood and dialysis centers, rehabilitation centers, nursing homes, doctors' offices and by patients, at home, under physician supervision.

RECENT DEVELOPMENTS:

For the year ended 12/31/02, income was $1.03 billion, before a loss of $255.0 million from discontinued operations, versus income of $675.0 million, before an accounting change charge of $52.0 million and a loss of $11.0 million from discontinued operations, the prior year. Results for 2002 and 2001 included in-process research and development and other special charges of $189.0 million and $280.0 million, respectively. The 2001 results also included pre-tax charges of $189.0 million. Net sales rose 10.3% to $8.11 billion from $7.36 billion in 2001.

PROSPECTS:

Going forward, the Company expects to achieve sales growth in the range of 8.0% to 12.0% and diluted earnings per share in the range of $2.10 to $2.20 in fiscal 2003. BAX also expects to generate cash flow from operations of $1.30 billion to $1.50 billion before capital expenditures for 2003. Meanwhile, BAX should benefit from the launch of several new products, including ADVATE, a factor VIII recombinant therapy. Separately, BAX announced that it completed the acquisition of the majority of ESI Lederle, a division of Wyeth, for approximately $305.0 million.

ANNUAL FINANCIAL DATA:

FISCAL YEAR	TOT. REVS. ($mill.)	NET INC. ($mill.)	TOT. ASSETS ($mill.)	OPER. PROFIT %	NET PROFIT %	RET. ON EQUITY %	RET. ON ASSETS %	CURR. RATIO	EARN. PER SH. $	CASH FL. PER SH. $	TANG. BK. VAL. $	DIV. PER SH. $	PRICE RANGE	AVG. P/E RATIO	AVG. YIELD %
p12/31/02	8,110.0	⑪ 1,033.0							⑪ 1.67			0.58	59.90 - 24.07	25.1	1.4
12/31/01	7,663.0	⑩ 664.0	10,343.0	15.8	8.7	17.7	6.4	1.2	⑩ 1.09	1.81	3.44	0.58	55.90 - 40.06	44.0	1.2
12/31/00	6,896.0	⑨ 738.0	8,733.0	14.7	10.7	27.8	8.5	1.1	⑨ 1.24	1.91	2.42	0.15	45.13 - 25.88	28.7	0.4
12/31/99	6,380.0	⑧ 779.0	9,644.0	18.0	12.2	23.3	8.1	1.4	⑧ 1.35	1.99	4.18	0.58	38.00 - 28.41	24.6	1.8
12/31/98	6,599.0	⑦ 315.0	10,085.0	10.5	4.8	11.1	3.1	1.6	⑦ 0.55	1.28	1.79	0.58	33.00 - 24.25	52.0	2.0
12/31/97	6,138.0	⑥ 300.0	8,707.0	10.6	4.9	11.5	3.4	1.5	⑥ 0.66	0.67	...	0.56	30.13 - 19.94	37.9	2.3
12/31/96	5,438.0	⑤ 575.0	7,596.0	16.8	10.6	23.0	7.6	1.4	⑤ 1.06	1.70	2.06	⑫ 0.58	24.06 - 19.88	20.8	2.7
12/31/95	5,048.0	④ 371.0	9,437.0	14.1	7.3	10.0	3.9	1.4	④ 0.67	1.30	4.79	0.55	22.38 - 13.38	26.7	3.0
12/31/94	9,324.0	596.0	10,002.0	11.0	6.4	16.0	6.0	1.6	1.07	2.00	2.54	0.51	14.44 - 10.81	11.9	4.0
12/31/93	8,879.0	① d268.0	10,545.0	2.7	...	...	...	1.5	① d0.48	0.41	1.25	0.48	16.38 - 10.00	...	3.7

Statistics are as originally reported. Adj. for 2-for-1 stk. split, 5/01. ① Bef. gain of $70.0 mil., & incl. a pre-tax nonrecur. chrg. of $1.03 bil. ② 1 sh. of Allegiance Corp. for each sh. held effect. 10/1/96. ③ Incl. lease obligs. ④ Excl. inc. fr. disc. opers. of $278.0 mil. & pre-tax nonrecur. chgs. of $133.0 mil. ⑤ Excl. inc. fr. disc. opers. of $94.0 mil. ⑥ Incl. pre-tax nonrecur. chrg. of $116.0 mil. & pre-tax spec. chrg. of $309.0 mil. ⑦ Excl. net gain of $64.0 mil. fr. disc. opers., net nonrecur. chrg. of $19.0 mil. & net acctg. chrg. of $27.0 mil. ⑧ Bef. disc. ops. of $2.0 mil. ⑨ Incl. one-time chrg. of $469.0 mill. & excl. acctg. chg. of $52.0 mill. ⑩ Bef. loss of $255.0 mill. from disc. ops. & incl. in proc. R&D & other spec. chrgs. of $189.0 mill.

OFFICERS:
H. M. Jansen Kraemer Jr., Chmn.,C.E.O.
B. P. Anderson, Sr. V.P., C.F.O.
S. J. Meyer, Treas.

INVESTOR CONTACT: Neville J. Jehareijah, V.P., Fin. Rel., (847) 948-4550

PRINCIPAL OFFICE: One Baxter Parkway, Deerfield, IL 60015-4633

TELEPHONE NUMBER: (847) 948-2000
FAX: (847) 948-2964
WEB: www.baxter.com
NO. OF EMPLOYEES: 54,600 (approx.)
SHAREHOLDERS: 62,900
ANNUAL MEETING: In May
INCORPORATED: DE, Oct., 1931

INSTITUTIONAL HOLDINGS:
No. of Institutions: 668
Shares Held: 487,089,671
% Held: 82.1
INDUSTRY: Surgical and medical instruments (SIC: 3841)
TRANSFER AGENT(S): Equiserve, Jersey City, NJ

BB&T CORPORATION

EXCH.	SYM.	REC. PRICE	P/E RATIO	YLD.	MKT. CAP.	RANGE (52-WK.)	'02 Y/E PR.	DIV. ACH.
NYSE	BBT	33.56 (1/31/03)	12.4	3.5%	$15.29 bill.	39.47 - 31.03	36.99	31 yrs.

INVESTMENT GRADE. RESULTS ARE BENEFITING FROM GROWTH IN MORTGAGE BANKING INCOME, INSURANCE COMMISSIONS AND BROKERAGE FEES.

*7 YEAR PRICE SCORE 127.6   ***12 MONTH PRICE SCORE 108.1**

*NYSE COMPOSITE INDEX=100

INTERIM EARNINGS (Per Share):

Qtr.	Mar.	June	Sept.	Dec.
1998	0.39	0.42	0.44	0.46
1999	0.44	0.49	0.44	0.47
2000	0.46	0.48	0.12	0.56
2001	0.53	0.54	0.48	0.61
2002	0.64	0.68	0.68	0.70

INTERIM DIVIDENDS (Per Share):

Amt.	Decl.	Ex.	Rec.	Pay.
0.26Q	12/18/01	1/16/02	1/18/02	2/04/02
0.26Q	2/26/02	4/10/02	4/12/02	5/01/02
0.29Q	6/25/02	7/10/02	7/12/02	8/01/02
0.29Q	8/27/02	10/09/02	10/11/02	11/01/02
0.29Q	12/17/02	1/15/03	1/17/03	2/03/03

Indicated div.: $1.16 (Div. Reinv. Plan)

CAPITALIZATION (12/31/01):

	($000)	(%)
Total Deposits	44,733,275	71.5
Long-Term Debt	11,721,076	18.7
Common & Surplus	6,150,209	9.8
Total	62,604,560	100.0

BUSINESS:

BB&T Corporation, a multi-bank holding company with assets of $80.22 billion as of 12/31/02, owns 1,122 banking offices in the Carolinas, Virginia, West Virginia, Tennessee, Kentucky, Georgia, Maryland, Florida, Alabama, Indiana and Washington, D.C. BBT's largest subsidiary is Branch Banking and Trust Company (BB&T-NC). BB&T-NC's subsidiaries include BB&T Leasing Corp., BB&T Investment Services, and BB&T Insurance Services. BBT's other subsidiaries include Branch Banking and Trust Co. of South Carolina, Branch Banking and Trust Co. of Virginia, and Fidelity Service Corporation. On 3/26/99, BBT acquired Scott & Stringfellow Financial, Inc. On 1/13/00, BBT acquired Premier Bancshares, Inc. On 7/7/00, BBT acquired One Valley Bancorp Inc. On 9/16/02, the Company acquired Regional Financial Corporation.

RECENT DEVELOPMENTS:

For the year ended 12/31/02, BBT reported income of $1.29 billion, before a $9.8 million accounting gain, versus net income of $973.6 million in the prior year. Results for 2002 and 2001 included after-tax merger-related charges of $14.9 million and $126.5 million, respectively. Provision for loan and lease losses increased 17.6% to $263.7 million versus $224.3 million a year earlier. Net interest income grew 12.9% to $2.75 billion. Non-interest income climbed 22.6% to $1.69 billion, while non-interest expense rose 7.0% to $2.39 billion.

PROSPECTS:

Looking ahead, the Company is targeting full-year 2003 earnings of between $2.95 and $3.05 per share. Meanwhile, BBT continues to expand through strategic acquisitions in fast-growing markets. On 11/12/02, the Company opened its first branches in Florida following the integration of Regional Financial Corporation, which was acquired on 9/16/02. Separately, on 12/4/02, BBT announced plans to acquire Southeastern Fidelity Corporation, an insurance premium finance company based in Tallahassee, Florida. Terms of the transaction were not disclosed.

ANNUAL FINANCIAL DATA:

FISCAL YEAR	NET INT. INC. ($mill.)	NON-INT. INC. ($mill.)	NET INC. ($mill.)	TOT. LOANS ($mill.)	TOT. ASSETS ($mill.)	TOT. DEP. ($mill.)	RET. ON EQUITY %	RET. ON ASSETS %	EQUITY/ ASSETS %	EARN. PER SH. $	TANG. BK. VAL. $	DIV. PER SH. $	PRICE RANGE	AVG. P/E RATIO
p12/31/02	2,747.5		⑧1,293.2							② 2.70		1.10	39.47 - 31.03	13.1
12/31/01	2,434.5	1,378.7	⑦ 973.6	48,404.6	70,869.9	44,733.3	15.8	1.4	8.7	②2.12	13.50	0.98	38.84 - 30.24	16.3
12/31/00	2,017.6	777.0	⑥626.4	41,933.8	59,340.2	38,014.5	13.1	1.1	8.1	⑦1.55	11.91	0.86	38.25 - 21.69	19.3
12/31/99	1,581.7	761.4	⑤612.8	30,152.2	43,481.0	27,251.1	19.2	1.4	7.4	⑥1.83	9.66	0.75	40.63 - 27.19	18.5
12/31/98	1,247.4	528.0	⑤501.8	23,375.2	34,427.2	23,046.9	18.2	1.5	8.0	⑤1.71	9.51	0.66	40.75 - 26.25	19.6
12/31/97	1,099.5	474.9	④359.9	20,012.0	29,177.6	20,210.1	16.1	1.2	7.7	④1.30	8.22	0.58	32.50 - 17.50	19.2
12/31/96	828.5	297.4	③283.7	14,524.6	21,246.6	14,953.9	16.4	1.3	8.1	③1.28	7.91	0.50	18.50 - 12.88	12.3
12/31/95	741.5	226.4	②178.1	13,636.2	20,492.9	14,684.1	10.6	0.9	8.2	②0.83	8.08	0.43	14.00 - 9.38	14.1
12/31/94	322.7	83.0	109.6	5,434.9	8,756.1	6,165.1	17.3	1.3	7.2	1.19	7.12	0.37	11.00 - 8.44	8.2
12/31/93	310.5	87.7	①8.2	4,838.3	8,274.5	6,394.9	1.5	0.1	6.8	①0.04	8.81	0.32	11.75 - 9.25	299.1

Statistics are as originally reported. Adj. for 100% stock div., 8/98. ① Bef. acct. chrg. of $27.2 mill. & incl. $49.1 mill. loss on the bulk sale of assets. ② Incl. $108.0 pre-tax merger-rel. chgs., $19.8 mill. in sec. losses, & $12.3 mill. gain on the sale of divest. deposits. ③ Incl. one-time after-tax SAIF chg. of $21.3 mill. ④ Incl. $42.7 mill. in after-tax UCB merger-rel. chgs. ⑤ Incl. after-tax merger costs of $10.9 mill. ⑥ Incl. non-recur. chrg. of $46.2 mill. ⑦ Incl. aft.-tax nonrecur. chrgs. of $126.5 mill., 12/01; $248.6 mill., 12/00. ⑧ Bef. $9.8 mill. acctg. gain & incl. $14.9 mill. after-tax nonrecur. chrg.

OFFICERS:
J. A. Allison IV, Chmn., C.E.O.
K. S. King, Pres.
S. E. Reed, Sr. Exec. V.P., C.F.O.
H. G. Williamson, C.O.O.

INVESTOR CONTACT: Thomas A. Nicholson, Jr., Senior Vice Pres, (336) 733-3058

PRINCIPAL OFFICE: 200 West Second Street, Winston-Salem, NC 27101

TELEPHONE NUMBER: (336) 733-2000
FAX: (336) 671-2399
WEB: www.bbandt.com

NO. OF EMPLOYEES: 20,400 (approx.)

SHAREHOLDERS: 114,461

ANNUAL MEETING: In Apr.

INCORPORATED: NC, 1897; reincorp., NC, 1968

INSTITUTIONAL HOLDINGS:
No. of Institutions: 377
Shares Held: 128,524,726
% Held: 26.8

INDUSTRY: National commercial banks (SIC: 6021)

TRANSFER AGENT(S): Branch Banking & Trust Company, Wilson, NC

BCE INC.

EXCH.	SYM.	REC. PRICE	P/E RATIO	YLD.	MKT. CAP.	RANGE (52-WK.)	'02 Y/E PR.
NYSE	BCE	18.74 (2/28/03)	...	...	...	21.96 - 14.59	18.01

MEDIUM GRADE. THE COMPANY EXPECTS FULL-YEAR 2003 EARNINGS OF BETWEEN C$1.85 AND C$1.95 PER SHARE, BEFORE NON-RECURRING ITEMS.

7 YEAR PRICE SCORE N.M.   **12 MONTH PRICE SCORE 116.2**
NYSE COMPOSITE INDEX=100

INTERIM EARNINGS (Per Share):

Qtr.	Mar.	June	Sept.	Dec.
1998	0.24	0.39	5.70	0.86
1999	d0.18	0.68	0.19	1.02
2000	0.16	0.04	1.10	d0.04
2001	0.83	d0.04	d0.10	d0.40
2002	0.37	0.38	0.42	0.91

INTERIM DIVIDENDS (Per Share):

Amt.	Decl.	Ex.	Rec.	Pay.
0.30Q	11/27/02	12/11/02	12/13/02	1/15/03
0.30Q	2/26/03	3/13/03	3/17/03	4/15/03
0.30Q	3/28/03	6/12/03	6/16/03	7/15/03
0.30Q	8/27/03	9/11/03	9/15/03	10/15/03
0.30Q	11/25/03	12/11/03	12/15/03	1/15/04

Indicated div.: $1.20 (Div. Reinv. Plan)

CAPITALIZATION (12/31/01):

	($000)	(%)
Long-Term Debt	9,350,541	38.6
Deferred Income Tax	581,381	2.4
Minority Interest	3,583,294	14.8
Preferred Stock	817,960	3.4
Common & Surplus	9,872,148	40.8
Total	24,205,324	100.0

BUSINESS:

BCE Inc. is a communications company. Bell Canada (85.8% of 2002 revenue) provides an integrated platform of telecommunications services including voice, data, wireline, wireless and directory communications and satellite entertainment to Canadian customers. Bell Globemedia (6.3%) provides integrated information, communications and entertainment services to Canadian customers. BCE Ventures (5.2%) includes the activities of CGI Group, Telesat Canada and other investments. BCE Emergis (2.7%) provides business to business e-commerce infrastructures. BCE distributed its 35% interest in Nortel Networks to its common shareholders on 5/1/00.

RECENT DEVELOPMENTS:

For the year ended 12/31/02, earnings from continuing operations were C$1.90 billion ($1.21 billion) versus C$3.57 billion ($2.25 billion) the previous year. Results for 2002 and 2001 included restructuring and other charges of C$887.0 million ($565.0 million) and C$980.0 million ($616.6 million), respectively. Results for 2002 also included an impairment charge of C$770.0 million ($490.5 million). Operating revenues rose 2.2% to C$19.77 billion ($12.59 billion) from C$19.34 billion ($12.16 billion) in 2001. Comparisons were made using the following exchange rates: US$1=C$1.57 as of 12/29/02; US$1=C$1.59 as of 12/28/01.

PROSPECTS:

On 12/2/02, BCE announced the completion of its purchase of about 16.0% in Bell Canada from an affiliate of SBC Communications for C$4.99 billion, lifting its ownership of Bell Canada to 100.0%. Also, on 11/29/02, BCE announced the closing of the sale of its Bell Canada directories business for C$3.00 billion in cash to Kohlberg Kravis Roberts & Co and the Teachers' Merchant Bank. Separately, BCE expects full-year 2003 revenues to range from C$19.30 billion to C$20.0 billion and earnings of between C$1.85 and C$1.95 per share, before non-recurring items.

ANNUAL FINANCIAL DATA:

FISCAL YEAR	TOT. REVS. ($mil.)	NET INC. ($mil.)	TOT. ASSETS ($mil.)	OPER. PROFIT %	NET PROFIT %	RET. ON EQUITY %	RET. ON ASSETS %	CURR. RATIO	EARN. PER SH. $	CASH FL. PER SH. $	TANG. BK. VAL. $	DIV. PER SH. $	PRICE RANGE	AVG. P/E RATIO
p12/31/02	12,591.1	⑧ 1,208.9							⑧ 1.36			1.20	23.22 - 14.59	13.9
12/31/01	13,660.6	⑦ 1,522.0	34,187.6	7.9	11.1	14.2	4.5	0.5	⑦ 1.82	8.80	1.13	1.20	29.44 - 20.59	13.7
12/31/00	12,072.3	⑥ 591.1	34,282.7	9.3	4.9	5.1	1.7	0.6	⑥ 0.84	5.49	...	1.28	137.50 - 21.00	94.3
⑤ 12/31/99	9,841.8	④ 3,779.8	25,591.1	7.7	38.4	30.5	14.8	1.0	④ 5.78	11.46	14.86	1.36	98.31 - 37.31	11.7
12/31/98	18,144.3	③ 3,038.8	21,196.4	3.2	16.7	38.5	14.3	0.5	③ 4.67	9.24	11.53	1.36	46.63 - 25.63	7.7
12/31/97	23,117.5	② 984.9	28,067.6	13.5	4.2	17.4	3.5	1.2	② 1.47	d0.38	7.14	1.36	33.88 - 22.00	19.0
12/31/96	20,592.9	842.2	30,165.9	13.1	4.0	10.9	2.8	1.2	2.49	4.80	20.95	1.36	25.38 - 17.19	8.6
12/31/95	18,046.9	573.1	28,361.0	12.4	3.1	7.8	2.0	1.1	1.63	3.07	20.59	1.36	17.50 - 14.50	9.8
12/31/94	15,448.5	839.8	27,155.8	13.0	5.3	11.6	3.1	1.1	2.51	4.80	21.36	1.34	19.38 - 15.81	7.0
12/31/93	14,971.4	③ 120.1	27,725.6	9.3	0.8	1.6	0.4	0.9	③ 0.16	d1.92	19.51	1.32	19.00 - 16.00	110.3

Statistics are as originally reported. All figures are in U.S. dollars unless otherwise noted. Exchange rates are as follows: US$1=C$1.57, 12/29/02; US$1=C$1.59, 12/28/01; US$1=C$1.50, 12/31/00; US$1=C$1.44, 12/31/99; US$1=C$1.51, 12/31/98; C$1.44, 12/31/97; C$1.37, 12/31/96; C$1.36, 12/31/95; C$1.40, 12/31/94; C$1.32, 12/31/93. Adj. for 2-for-1 stk. split, 5/97. ① Incl. cr. of $2.90 bill. ② Bef. extraord. chrg. of $2.05 bill. ③ Bef. loss fr. disc. ops. of $615.6 mill. ④ Incl. cr. of $3.40 bill. ⑤ Excl. Nortel Networks ⑥ Incl. cr. of $3.57 bill. ⑦ Incl. pre-tax & oth. restr. chrgs. of $1.18 bill. and Nortel stk. sale gain of $3.7 bill. ⑧ Incl. restr. & oth. chrgs. of $565.0 mill., impairmnt. chrg. of $490.5 mill.; bef. inc. fr. disc. ops. of $367.5 mill. ⑨ In Canadian $

OFFICERS:
R. J. Currie, Chmn.
M. J. Sabia, Pres., C.E.O.
S. A. Vanaselja, C.F.O.
INVESTOR CONTACT: Isabelle Morin, Inv. Rel., (514) 786-3845
PRINCIPAL OFFICE: 1000 rue de La Gauchetiere Ouest, Suite 4100, Montreal, Quebec, Canada

TELEPHONE NUMBER: (514) 786-3891
FAX: (514) 870-4914
WEB: www.bce.ca
NO. OF EMPLOYEES: 75,000
SHAREHOLDERS: 181,377 (common)
ANNUAL MEETING: In May
INCORPORATED: CAN, Feb., 1970

INSTITUTIONAL HOLDINGS:
No. of Institutions: 135
Shares Held: 296,485,425
% Held: 32.8
INDUSTRY: Telephone communications, exc. radio (SIC: 4813)
TRANSFER AGENT(S): Computershare Trust Company of New York, New York, NY

BEAR STEARNS COMPANIES INC. (THE)

EXCH.	SYM.	REC. PRICE	P/E RATIO	YLD.	MKT. CAP.	RANGE (52-WK.)	'02 Y/E PR.
NYSE	BSC	65.60 (3/31/03)	10.1	1.0%	$6.56 bill.	67.91 - 50.50	59.40

UPPER MEDIUM GRADE. DESPITE THE DOWNTURN IN THE ECONOMY, THE COMPANY CONTINUES TO REPORT RECORD PROFITS AS IT FOCUSES ON AGGRESSIVE EXPENSE MANAGEMENT.

*7 YEAR PRICE SCORE 146.6   *12 MONTH PRICE SCORE 110.8

*NYSE COMPOSITE INDEX=100

INTERIM EARNINGS (Per Share):

Qtr.	Sept.	Dec.	Mar.	June
1999-00	0.95	1.64	...	...
Qtr.	Feb.	May	Aug.	Nov.
2000	1.89	0.77	1.32	1.36
2001	1.10	1.18	0.95	1.08
2002	1.29	2.59	1.23	1.36

INTERIM DIVIDENDS (Per Share):

Amt.	Decl.	Ex.	Rec.	Pay.
0.15Q	3/27/02	4/12/02	4/16/02	4/30/02
0.15Q	6/20/02	7/15/02	7/17/02	7/31/02
0.17Q	9/18/02	10/15/02	10/17/02	10/31/02
0.17Q	1/08/03	1/15/03	1/17/03	1/31/03
0.17Q	3/26/03	4/14/03	4/16/03	4/30/03

Indicated div.: $0.68

CAPITALIZATION (11/30/02):

	($000)	(%)
Long-Term Debt	23,681,399	78.8
Preferred Stock	692,832	2.3
Common & Surplus	5,689,251	18.9
Total	30,063,482	100.0

BUSINESS:

The Bear Stearns Companies Inc. is the parent company of Bear, Stearns and Company Inc., a worldwide investment banking, securities trading and brokerage firm. The firm's business includes corporate finance and mergers and acquisitions, public finance, institutional equities and fixed income sales and trading, private client services and asset management. Through its wholly-owned subsidiary, Bear Stearns Securities Corp., BSC provides professional and correspondent clearing services. The revenue breakdown for the fiscal year ended 11/30/02 was principal transactions, 36.8%; interest & dividends, 32.4%; commissions, 16.1%; investment banking, 12.1%; and other, 2.6%.

RECENT DEVELOPMENTS:

For the year ended 11/30/02, the Company reported net income of $878.3 million compared with income of $625.0 million, before an accounting charge of $6.3 million, the year before. Total revenues fell 20.8% to $6.89 billion from $8.70 billion a year earlier. Revenues, net of interest expense, grew 4.5% to $5.13 billion from $4.91 billion in the prior year. Principal transactions revenues rose 11.2% to $2.54 billion, and investment banking increased 7.9% to $833.5 million. However, interest and dividend revenues dropped 48.6% to $2.23 billion, while commission revenues slipped 0.5% to $1.11 billion. As of 11/30/02, assets under management totaled $24.00 billion, down 8.3% from $24.20 billion the year before.

PROSPECTS:

Despite the downturn in the economy, the Company continues to report record profits as it focuses on aggressive expense management. Moreover, BSC continues to perform well in its fixed income division, principally driven by the mortgage- and asset-backed areas. However, revenues from the private client service area continue to reflect low levels of retail investor activity. Additionally, the asset management business continues to report decreased revenues, primarily due to reduced income from investments and commissions.

ANNUAL FINANCIAL DATA:

FISCAL YEAR	TOT. REVS. ($Mill.)	NET INC. ($Mill.)	TOT. ASSETS ($Mill.)	OPER. PROFIT %	NET PROFIT %	RET. ON EQUITY %	RET. ON ASSETS %	CURR. RATIO	EARN. PER SH.$	CASH FL. PER SH.$	TANG. BK. VAL.$	DIV. PER SH.$	PRICE RANGE	AVG. P/E RATIO	AVG. YIELD %
11/30/02	6,890.8	878.3	184,854.4	19.0	12.7	13.8	0.5	0.8	6.47	6.86	56.88	0.62	67.55 - 50.50	9.1	1.1
11/30/01	8,701.0	④ 625.0	185,530.2	10.7	7.2	11.1	0.3	0.9	④ 4.27	5.48	48.26	0.60	64.45 - 40.65	12.3	1.1
11/30/00	10,276.6	③ 773.2	171,166.5	11.4	7.5	13.7	0.5	0.9	③ 5.35	5.84	44.54	0.55	72.50 - 36.50	10.2	1.0
② 11/26/99	3,470.3	285.8	162,038.0	13.1	8.2	5.8	0.2	0.9	1.78	2.01	34.97	0.56	50.48 - 31.91	23.1	1.4
6/30/99	7,882.0	673.0	153,894.3	13.5	8.5	13.6	0.4	0.8	4.27	4.63	33.07	0.56	50.48 - 31.91	9.7	1.4
6/30/98	7,979.9	① 660.4	154,495.9	13.3	8.3	15.4	0.4	0.8	① 4.17	4.47	28.39	0.54	58.05 - 23.58	9.8	1.3
6/30/97	6,077.3	613.3	121,433.5	16.7	10.1	18.7	0.5	0.6	3.81	4.17	21.90	0.54	44.05 - 23.22	8.8	1.5
6/30/96	4,963.9	490.6	92,085.2	16.8	9.9	17.9	0.5	0.6	2.97	3.27	17.72	0.51	24.51 - 15.73	6.8	2.5
6/30/95	3,753.6	240.6	74,597.2	10.3	6.4	10.2	0.3	0.8	1.40	1.69	13.43	0.48	19.23 - 11.95	11.2	3.1
6/30/94	3,441.1	387.0	67,392.0	18.7	11.2	17.9	0.6	0.9	2.26	2.66	11.94	0.46	18.47 - 11.56	6.6	3.1

Statistics are as originally reported. Adj. for all stk. dividends thru 11/99. ① Includes special charges of $108.0 million related to an increase in litigation reserves. ② For five months due to change in fiscal year-end. ③ Incl. an after-tax charge of $96.0 mill. related to increased legal reserves following a jury verdict. ④ Bef. an after-tax acctg. chrg. of $6.3 mill.

OFFICERS:
J. E. Cayne, Chmn., C.E.O.
A. D. Schwartz, Pres., Co-C.O.O.
W. J. Spector, Pres., Co-C.O.O.
S. L. Molinaro Jr., Exec. V.P., C.F.O.

INVESTOR CONTACT: Elizabeth Ventura, Investor Relations, (212) 272-9251

PRINCIPAL OFFICE: 383 Madison Avenue, New York, NY 10179

TELEPHONE NUMBER: (212) 272-2000
FAX: (212) 272-4785
WEB: www.bearstearns.com

NO. OF EMPLOYEES: 10,506

SHAREHOLDERS: 2,134

ANNUAL MEETING: In Mar.

INCORPORATED: DE, Aug., 1985

INSTITUTIONAL HOLDINGS:
No. of Institutions: 329
Shares Held: 74,550,885
% Held: 77.5

INDUSTRY: Security brokers and dealers (SIC: 6211)

TRANSFER AGENT(S): Mellon Investor Services LLC, Ridgefield, NJ

BEAZER HOMES USA, INC.

EXCH.	SYM.	REC. PRICE	P/E RATIO	YLD.	MKT. CAP.	RANGE (52-WK.)	'02 Y/E PR.
NYSE	BZH	58.36 (2/28/03)	5.3	...	$0.50 bill.	95.05 - 51.40	60.60

UPPER MEDIUM GRADE. THE COMPANY EXPECTS THE STRONG HOMEBUILDING TREND TO CONTINUE IN THE COMING YEARS.

INTERIM EARNINGS (Per Share):

Qtr.	Dec.	Mar.	June	Sept.
1999-00	0.85	1.02	1.26	1.92
2000-01	1.61	1.92	2.07	2.58
2001-02	2.47	2.56	2.59	3.03
2002-03	2.75	...	...	...

INTERIM DIVIDENDS (Per Share):

Amt.	Decl.	Ex.	Rec.	Pay.
		No dividends paid.		

*7 YEAR PRICE SCORE 217.0   ***12 MONTH PRICE SCORE 92.8**
*NYSE COMPOSITE INDEX=100

CAPITALIZATION (9/30/02):

	($000)	(%)
Long-Term Debt	739,100	48.0
Common & Surplus	799,515	52.0
Total	1,538,615	100.0

BUSINESS:

Beazer Homes USA, Inc. is a designer, builder and seller of single-family homes with domestic operations in nineteen states. BZH builds homes that cater primarily to entry-level and first move-up homebuyers. During fiscal year 2002, the average sales price of the Company's homes sold was approximately $190,800. BZH also provides mortgage origination and title services to its homebuyers. The Company's homebuilding and marketing activities are conducted under the name of Beazer Homes in each of its markets except in Colorado (Sanford Homes) and Tennessee (Phillips Builders). In April 2002, BZH acquired Crossmann Communities, Inc.

RECENT DEVELOPMENTS:

For the quarter ended 12/31/02, net income surged 59.5% to $36.9 million compared with $23.2 million in the equivalent 2001 quarter. Revenues jumped 43.0% to $700.2 million from $489.7 million a year earlier. The increase in revenues stemmed from a 47.2% rise in closings to 3,482.

Operating income grew 59.2% to $59.1 million versus $37.1 million the year before. Gross margin increased 130 basis points to 21.2% from 19.9% in 2001, reflecting the strong housing environment and the Company's ability to control costs and build more efficiently.

PROSPECTS:

Going forward, the Company will continue to focus on controlling its building costs through increased use of national purchasing contracts and more efficient product design, which is expected to yield significant benefits in the coming years. In addition, strong population growth fueled by immigration, a limited supply of housing and the consolidation of the housing industry should further strengthen the Company's business. Moreover, fiscal 2003 results should benefit from BZH's solid backlog, which amounted to $1.23 billion at 12/31/02. Meanwhile, BZH expects fiscal 2003 earnings per share to be approximately $12.25, up 14.0% from a year ago. This target is based on 16,500 home closings with an average price in the low $190,000 range.

ANNUAL FINANCIAL DATA:

FISCAL YEAR	TOT. REVS. ($mill.)	NET INC. ($mill.)	TOT. ASSETS ($mill.)	OPER. PROFIT %	NET PROFIT %	RET. ON EQUITY %	RET. ON ASSETS %	CURR. RATIO	EARN. PER SH. $	CASH FL. PER SH. $	TANG. BK. VAL. $	PRICE RANGE	AVG. P/E RATIO
9/30/02	2,641.2	122.6	1,892.8	7.3	4.6	15.3	6.5	14.5	10.74	11.57	42.49	95.05 - 51.40	6.8
9/30/01	1,805.2	① 75.6	995.3	6.8	4.2	21.5	7.6	13.3	① 8.26	9.27	39.09	79.35 - 33.69	6.8
9/30/00	1,527.9	43.6	698.9	4.9	2.9	16.1	6.2	5.9	5.05	5.85	31.03	41.00 - 17.06	5.7
9/30/99	1,394.1	36.9	594.6	4.4	2.6	15.7	6.2	12.2	4.15	4.40	25.25	27.38 - 15.63	5.2
9/30/98	977.4	23.2	525.6	3.8	2.4	11.6	4.4	9.8	2.66	2.57	30.37	27.13 - 16.50	8.2
9/30/97	851.1	② 11.2	399.6	2.1	1.3	6.2	2.8	5.0	② 1.15	1.50	28.63	20.63 - 12.75	14.5
9/30/96	866.6	18.3	356.6	3.5	2.1	10.2	5.1	10.9	2.20	2.44	26.41	21.00 - 13.63	7.9
9/30/95	647.8	11.4	345.2	2.9	1.8	6.9	3.3	8.2	1.23	1.39	24.10	20.63 - 11.50	13.1
9/30/94	536.5	16.5	314.9	5.1	3.1	10.5	5.2	6.1	1.76	1.92	15.54	18.75 - 11.13	8.5
9/30/93	275.1	12.3	245.3	7.3	4.5	12.8	5.0	7.0	...	...	...	...	...

Statistics are as originally reported. ① Excl. an extraord. loss of $733,000. ② Incl. writedown of inventory of $6.3 mill.

OFFICERS:
B. C. Beazer, Chmn.
I. J. McCarthy, Pres., C.E.O.
D. S. Weiss, Exec. V.P., C.F.O.

INVESTOR CONTACT: David S. Weiss, Exec. V.P., C.F.O., (404) 250-3420

PRINCIPAL OFFICE: 5775 Peachtree Dunwoody Road, Suite B-200, Atlanta, GA 30342

TELEPHONE NUMBER: (404) 250-3420
FAX: (404) 250-3428
WEB: www.beazer.com

NO. OF EMPLOYEES: 2,890 (avg.)

SHAREHOLDERS: 77 (approximate record)

ANNUAL MEETING: In Feb.

INCORPORATED: DE, Nov., 1993

INSTITUTIONAL HOLDINGS:
No. of Institutions: 158
Shares Held: 12,676,546
% Held: 98.2

INDUSTRY: Operative builders (SIC: 1531)

TRANSFER AGENT(S): American Stock Transfer & Trust Company, New York, NY

BECKMAN COULTER, INC.

EXCH.	SYM.	REC. PRICE	P/E RATIO	YLD.	MKT. CAP.	RANGE (52-WK.)	'02 Y/E PR.	DIV. ACH.
NYSE	BEC	33.10 (2/28/03)	15.8	1.1%	$2.03 bill.	53.00 - 25.20	29.52	11 yrs.

MEDIUM GRADE. ON 1/20/03, THE COMPANY ANNOUNCED A RESTRUCTURING PLAN RESULTING IN AN AFTER-TAX CHARGE OF APPROXIMATELY $10.0 MILLION TO FIRST QUARTER EARNINGS.

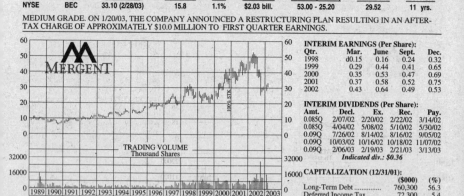

*7 YEAR PRICE SCORE 140.5   *12 MONTH PRICE SCORE 87.0

*NYSE COMPOSITE INDEX=100

INTERIM EARNINGS (Per Share):

Qtr.	Mar.	June	Sept.	Dec.
1998	d0.15	0.16	0.24	0.32
1999	0.29	0.44	0.41	0.65
2000	0.35	0.53	0.47	0.69
2001	0.37	0.58	0.52	0.75
2002	0.43	0.64	0.49	0.53

INTERIM DIVIDENDS (Per Share):

Amt.	Decl.	Ex.	Rec.	Pay.
0.085Q	2/07/02	2/20/02	2/22/02	3/14/02
0.085Q	4/04/02	5/08/02	5/10/02	5/30/02
0.09Q	7/26/02	8/14/02	8/16/02	9/05/02
0.09Q	10/03/02	10/16/02	10/18/02	11/07/02
0.09Q	2/06/03	2/19/03	2/21/03	3/13/03

Indicated div.: $0.36

CAPITALIZATION (12/31/01):

	($000)	(%)
Long-Term Debt	760,300	56.3
Deferred Income Tax	72,300	5.4
Common & Surplus	518,200	38.4
Total	1,350,800	100.0

BUSINESS:

Beckman Coulter, Inc. (formerly Beckman Instruments Inc.) designs, manufactures, sells, and services laboratory systems for biological analysis and investigation into life processes. The Company targets three markets: the life sciences laboratory market, specialty testing and the hospital and clinical diagnostic laboratory market. Customers such as universities, research institutions, pharmaceutical companies, hospitals and clinical laboratories use BEC's products across the entire spectrum of biologically-based endeavors, from basic scientific research to daily analysis of blood samples. Beckman Coulter markets its products in approximately 130 countries. BEC's products are used in all phases of the battle against disease to improve methodologies for biological discovery and diagnosis.

RECENT DEVELOPMENTS:

For the year ended 12/31/02, net earnings declined 4.2% to $135.5 million compared with earnings of $141.5 million, before an accounting change charge of $3.1 million, the prior year. Results for 2002 included pre-tax litigation settlement and related expenses of $39.3 million, while 2001 results included a pre-tax restructuring credit of $500,000.

Sales rose 3.8% to $2.06 billion from $1.98 billion the year before. Clinical Diagnostics sales climbed 6.5% to $1.42 billion, while Life Science Research sales fell 3.1% to $444.9 million. Specialty Testing sales slipped 1.2% to $196.0 million. Operating income decreased 6.7% to $223.5 million versus $239.6 million in 2001.

PROSPECTS:

On 1/20/03, the Company announced a restructuring plan resulting in an after-tax charge of approximately $10.0 million to first quarter earnings. The charge will cover costs associated with the formation of the Biomedical Research division, a refocusing in the Company's international operations and a workforce reduction of approximately 300 positions. The Biomedical Research division is the result of the combination of the Life Science Research and Specialty Testing divisions. Meanwhile, the Company estimates a sales increase of 5.5% to 6.5%, depending on currency, and earnings per share growth of 11.0% to 14.0%, excluding the restructuring charge, in 2003.

ANNUAL FINANCIAL DATA:

FISCAL YEAR	TOT. REVS. ($mill.)	NET INC. ($mill.)	TOT. ASSETS ($mill.)	OPER. PROFIT %	NET PROFIT %	RET. ON EQUITY %	RET. ON ASSETS %	CURR. RATIO	EARN. PER SH.$	CASH FL.PER SH.$	TANG. BK. VAL.$	DIV. PER SH.$	PRICE RANGE	AVG. P/E RATIO	AVG. YIELD %
p12/31/02	2,059.4	⑦ 135.5	2,236.6						⑦ 2.08			0.35	53.00 - 25.20	18.8	0.9
12/31/01	1,984.0	⑥ 141.5	2,178.0	12.1	7.1	27.3	6.5	2.0	⑥ 2.21	4.19	...	0.34	47.60 - 32.80	18.2	0.8
12/31/00	1,886.9	⑤ 125.5	2,018.2	12.3	6.7	36.5	6.2	1.9	⑤ 2.03	4.23	...	0.33	42.44 - 22.78	16.1	1.0
12/31/99	1,808.7	⑤ 106.0	2,110.8	12.0	5.9	46.5	5.0	1.7	⑤ 1.79	4.20	...	0.32	27.88 - 19.75	13.3	1.3
12/31/98	1,718.2	④ 33.5	2,133.3	6.7	1.9	26.4	1.6	1.3	④ 0.57	3.17	...	0.30	32.47 - 20.03	46.0	1.2
12/31/97	1,198.0	③ d264.4	2,331.0	...	...	...	...	1.1	③ d4.79	d2.81	...	0.30	26.16 - 18.69	...	1.3
12/31/96	1,028.0	74.7	960.1	11.9	7.3	18.7	7.8	2.1	1.29	2.81	7.13	0.26	20.56 - 16.00	14.2	1.4
12/31/95	930.1	① 48.9	907.8	8.9	5.3	14.1	5.4	2.1	① 0.85	2.22	5.97	0.22	17.94 - 13.00	18.2	1.4
12/31/94	888.6	①② 47.3	829.1	9.9	5.3	14.9	5.7	1.9	①② 0.84	2.09	5.66	0.20	16.25 - 11.50	16.5	1.4
12/31/93	875.7	①② d33.6	820.0	...	...	...	...	1.7	①② d0.60	0.54	4.95	0.18	14.13 - 9.81	...	1.5

Statistics are as originally reported. Adj. for 2-for-1 stk. split., 12/00. ① Incl. pre-tax restruct. chgs. of $27.7 mill., 1995; $11.3 mill., 1994; & $114.7 mill., 1993; & bef. acctg. adj. of $4.0 mill. ② Bef. acctg. chrg. of $5.1 mill., 1994; & ch. $4.0 mill., 1993. ③ Incl. a $0.05 per sh. dil. for exps. assoc./w the acq. of the Access® immunoassay product line & incl. after-tax chrgs. totaling $318.4 mill. ④ Incl. after-tax chrgs. of $110.9 mill. ⑤ Incl. a pre-tax restruct. gain of $2.4 mill., 2000; $200,000, 1999. ⑥ Bef. acctg. chrg. of $3.1 mill.; incl. restruct. credit of $500,000. ⑦ Incl. pre-tax litig. settlement & other exps. of $39.3 mill.

OFFICERS:
J. P. Wareham, Chmn., Pres., C.E.O.
A. I. Khalifa, V.P., C.F.O.
J. T. Glover, V.P., Treas.
INVESTOR CONTACT: Jeanie Herbert Investor Relations, (714) 773-7620
PRINCIPAL OFFICE: 4300 N. Harbor Boulevard, Fullerton, CA 92834-3100

TELEPHONE NUMBER: (714) 871-4848
FAX: (714) 773-8283
WEB: www.beckmancoulter.com
NO. OF EMPLOYEES: 10,094 (approx.)
SHAREHOLDERS: 6,239 (approx.)
ANNUAL MEETING: In Apr.
INCORPORATED: DE, July, 1988

INSTITUTIONAL HOLDINGS:
No. of Institutions: 242
Shares Held: 51,460,658
% Held: 82.6
INDUSTRY: Analytical instruments (SIC: 3826)
TRANSFER AGENT(S): First Chicago Trust Company of New York, Jersey City, NJ

BECTON, DICKINSON AND COMPANY

EXCH.	SYM.	REC. PRICE	P/E RATIO	YLD.	MKT. CAP.	RANGE (52-WK.)	'02 Y/E PR.	DIV. ACH.
NYSE	BDX	34.40 (2/28/03)	18.6	1.2%	$8.79 bill.	38.60 - 24.70	30.69	30 yrs.

UPPER MEDIUM GRADE. THE COMPANY CONTINUES TO BENEFIT FROM STRONG REVENUE GROWTH PACED BY ITS MEDICAL SYSTEMS AND CLINICAL LABORATORY SOLUTIONS SEGMENTS.

*7 YEAR PRICE SCORE 114.0   ***12 MONTH PRICE SCORE 107.6**
*NYSE COMPOSITE INDEX=100

INTERIM EARNINGS (Per Share):

Qtr.	Dec.	Mar.	June	Sept.
1998-99	0.29	0.34	0.12	0.29
1999-00	0.29	0.45	0.43	0.32
2000-01	0.23	0.44	0.46	0.49
2001-02	0.37	0.48	0.44	0.50
2002-03	0.43	...	...	...

INTERIM DIVIDENDS (Per Share):

Amt.	Decl.	Ex.	Rec.	Pay.
0.098Q	1/22/02	3/06/02	3/08/02	3/29/02
0.098Q	5/21/02	6/05/02	6/07/02	6/28/02
0.098Q	7/23/02	9/05/02	9/09/02	9/30/02
0.10Q	11/26/02	12/10/02	12/12/02	1/02/03
0.10Q	1/28/03	3/06/03	3/10/03	3/31/03

Indicated div.: $0.40 (Div. Reinv. Plan)

CAPITALIZATION (9/30/02):

	($000)	(%)
Long-Term Debt	802,967	23.6
Deferred Income Tax	105,459	3.1
Preferred Stock	37,945	1.1
Common & Surplus	2,450,029	72.1
Total	3,396,400	100.0

BUSINESS:

Becton, Dickinson & Company is principally engaged in the manufacture and sale of a broad line of medical supplies and devices and diagnostic systems used by healthcare professionals, medical research institutions and the general public. BDX's operations consist of three worldwide business segments: Medical Systems, (53.3% of 2002 revenues); Clinical Laboratory Solutions, (30.7%); and Biosciences, (16.0%). Major products in the Medical Systems segment are hypodermic products, specially designed devices for diabetes care, prefillable drug delivery systems, infusion therapy products, elastic support products and thermometers. Major products in the Clinical Laboratory Solutions segment are specimen collection products and services. Major products in the Biosciences segment are clinical and industrial microbiology products, sample collection products, cellular analysis systems, and hematology instruments.

RECENT DEVELOPMENTS:

For the three months ended 12/31/02, net income advanced 14.0% to $113.6 million compared with $99.7 million in the previous year. Revenues improved 11.3% to $1.05 billion from $944.9 million in the year-earlier period. Revenues in the medical systems segment increased 13.6% to $571.6 million from $503.0 million, while revenues in the clinical laboratory solutions segment climbed 12.5% to $331.7 million from $294.7 million the year before. Revenues in the biosciences segment rose to $148.4 million from $147.2 million in the prior-year quarter.

PROSPECTS:

The Company continues to benefit from strong revenue growth paced by its medical systems and clinical laboratory solutions segments. This growth reflects contributions from safety-engineered products, prefillable drug delivery devices and BDX's BD ProbeTec ET™ diagnostic instrument platform. Separately, the Company announced the U.S. availability of the BD Logic ™ Blood Glucose Monitor and the BD Latitude™ Diabetes Management systems. The FDA approved blood glucose monitoring products are designed to help improve diabetes management.

ANNUAL FINANCIAL DATA:

FISCAL YEAR	TOT. REVS. ($mill.)	NET INC. ($mill.)	TOT. ASSETS ($mill.)	OPER. PROFIT %	NET PROFIT %	RET. ON EQUITY %	RET. ON ASSETS %	CURR. RATIO	EARN. PER SH. $	CASH FL. PER SH. $	TANG. BK. VAL. $	DIV. PER SH. $	PRICE RANGE	AVG. P/E RATIO	AVG. YIELD %
9/30/02	4,033.1	⑤ 480.0	5,040.5	16.8	11.9	19.3	9.5	1.5	⑤ 1.79	2.93	4.95	0.39	38.60 - 24.70	17.7	1.2
9/30/01	3,754.3	① 438.4	4,802.3	17.2	11.7	18.8	9.1	1.4	① 1.63	2.76	5.35	0.38	39.25 - 29.96	21.2	1.1
9/30/00	3,618.3	④ 392.9	4,505.1	14.2	10.9	20.1	8.7	1.2	④ 1.49	2.59	3.80	0.37	35.31 - 23.75	19.8	1.3
9/30/99	3,418.4	275.7	4,437.0	13.0	8.1	15.6	6.2	1.3	1.04	2.02	2.74	0.34	44.19 - 22.38	32.0	1.0
9/30/98	3,116.9	②③ 236.6	3,846.0	13.0	7.6	14.7	6.2	1.4	②③ 0.90	1.78	3.30	0.29	49.63 - 24.38	41.1	0.8
9/30/97	2,810.5	300.1	3,080.3	16.0	10.7	21.7	9.7	1.9	1.21	2.08	4.11	0.26	27.81 - 20.94	20.1	1.1
9/30/96	2,769.8	283.4	2,889.8	15.6	10.2	21.4	9.8	1.7	1.10	1.91	4.43	0.23	22.75 - 17.69	18.4	1.1
9/30/95	2,712.5	251.7	2,999.5	14.6	9.3	18.0	8.4	1.8	0.90	1.42	4.46	0.20	19.00 - 12.00	17.3	1.3
9/30/94	2,559.5	227.2	3,159.5	12.7	8.9	15.3	7.2	2.0	0.76	1.47	4.30	0.18	12.47 - 8.50	13.7	1.8
9/30/93	2,465.4	① 212.8	3,087.6	11.0	8.6	14.6	6.9	1.8	0.68	1.31	3.96	0.17	10.19 - 8.16	13.5	1.8

Statistics are as originally reported. Adj. for 2-for-1 stock split, 2/93, 8/96, 8/98. ① Bef. acctg. adj. charge of $141.1 mill., 1993; $36.8 mill., 2001. ② Incl. a one-time chg. of $7.0 mill. for in-prog. res. & dev. rel. to two recent acqs. and incl. a spec. pre-tax chg. of $90.9 mill. ③ Incl. a one-time gain of $7.0 mill. from a fav. tax judge. in Brazil; a pre-tax chg. of $76.0 mill. rel. to exiting of prod. lines & other activities, the impair. of assets, & an enhanced vol. retire. program; a pre-tax chg. of $27.0 mill ④ Incl. a one-time pre-tax spec. chrg. of $57.5 mill. and net gains on invest. of $76.2 mill. ⑤ Incl. a one-time spec. chrg. of $21.5 mill.

OFFICERS:
E. J. Ludwig, Chmn., Pres., C.E.O.
J. R. Considine, Exec. V.P., C.F.O.
B. M. Healy, Exec. V.P., Gen. Couns., Sec.

INVESTOR CONTACT: Dean J. Paranicas, Investors Relations, (201) 847-7102

PRINCIPAL OFFICE: 1 Becton Drive, Franklin Lakes, NJ 07417-1880

TELEPHONE NUMBER: (201) 847-6800
FAX: (201) 847-6475
WEB: www.bd.com
NO. OF EMPLOYEES: 25,249 (avg.)
SHAREHOLDERS: 10,035 (approx. record)
ANNUAL MEETING: In Feb.
INCORPORATED: NJ, Nov., 1906

INSTITUTIONAL HOLDINGS:
No. of Institutions: 411
Shares Held: 213,782,056
% Held: 83.7
INDUSTRY: Surgical and medical instruments (SIC: 3841)
TRANSFER AGENT(S): First Chicago Trust Company of New York, Jersey City, NJ

BELLSOUTH CORPORATION

EXCH.	SYM.	REC. PRICE	P/E RATIO	YLD.	MKT. CAP.	RANGE (52-WK.)	'02 Y/E PR.
NYSE	BLS	21.67 (2/28/03)	14.6	3.9%	$40.67 bill.	39.90 - 18.32	25.87

UPPER MEDIUM GRADE. THE COMPANY ADDED 97,000 NEW DIGITAL SUBSCRIBER LINE HIGH-SPEED INTERNET SERVICE CUSTOMERS IN THE FOURTH QUARTER OF 2002.

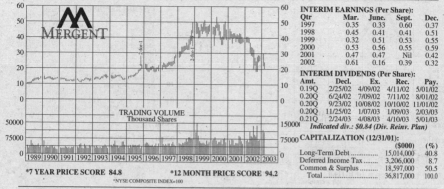

*7 YEAR PRICE SCORE 84.8   ***12 MONTH PRICE SCORE 94.2**

*NYSE COMPOSITE INDEX=100

INTERIM EARNINGS (Per Share):

Qtr	Mar.	June.	Sept.	Dec.
1997	0.35	0.33	0.60	0.37
1998	0.45	0.41	0.41	0.51
1999	0.32	0.51	0.53	0.55
2000	0.53	0.56	0.55	0.59
2001	0.47	0.47	Nil	0.42
2002	0.61	0.16	0.39	0.32

INTERIM DIVIDENDS (Per Share):

Amt.	Decl.	Ex.	Rec.	Pay.
0.19Q	2/25/02	4/09/02	4/11/02	5/01/02
0.20Q	6/24/02	7/09/02	7/11/02	8/01/02
0.20Q	9/23/02	10/08/02	10/10/02	11/01/02
0.20Q	11/25/02	1/07/03	1/09/03	2/01/03
0.21Q	2/24/03	4/08/03	4/10/03	5/01/03

Indicated div.: $0.84 (Div. Reinv. Plan)

CAPITALIZATION (12/31/01):

	($000)	(%)
Long-Term Debt	15,014,000	40.8
Deferred Income Tax	3,206,000	8.7
Common & Surplus	18,597,000	50.5
Total	36,817,000	100.0

BUSINESS:

BellSouth Corporation is one of seven regional holding companies divested by AT&T on 1/1/84. Through its Bell-South Telecommunications Inc. subsidiary, BLS provides wireline communications services, including local exchange, network access and intraLATA long distance services throughout its nine-state territory in Alabama, Florida, Georgia, Kentucky, Louisiana, Mississippi, North Carolina, South Carolina and Tennessee. BLS's international operations consist primarily of wireless service providers operating in 14 countries in Latin America, Asia and Europe. BLS also owns a group of companies that publish, print, sell advertising in and perform related services concerning alphabetical and classified telephone directories in both paper and electronic formats. As of 12/31/02, BLS owned more than 70.0 million access lines. In April 2000, BLS contributed its wireless operations to a joint venture with SBC Communications and formed Cingular Wireless, a provider of wireless voice and data communications services in the U.S. BLS owns 40.0% of Cingular, which has over 21.9 million U.S. wireless subscribers as of 12/31/02.

RECENT DEVELOPMENTS:

For the year ended 12/31/02, BLS reported income of $2.71 billion, before an accounting charge of $1.29 billion, versus net income of $2.57 billion the year before. Results for 2002 and 2001 included provisions for restructuring and asset impairments of $1.00 billion and $358.0 million, respectively. Total operating revenues declined 7.0% to $22.44 billion, reflecting weak demand for communications services in both the U.S. and Latin America.

PROSPECTS:

Operating results continue to be negatively affected by weakness in demand for communications services, retail access line market share losses, and currency devaluations in Argentina and Venezuela. On the positive side, BLS added 97,000 new digital subscriber line high-speed Internet service customers in the fourth quarter of 2002. Also, on 12/19/02, with endorsements in Florida and Tennessee, BLS became the first incumbent local telecommunications company to receive Federal Communications Commission approval to provide long distance service in all of its markets.

ANNUAL FINANCIAL DATA:

FISCAL YEAR	TOT. REVS. ($mill.)	NET INC. ($mill.)	TOT. ASSETS ($mill.)	OPER. PROFIT %	NET PROFIT %	RET. ON EQUITY %	RET. ON ASSETS %	CURR. RATIO	EARN. PER SH. $	CASH FL. PER SH. $	TANG. BK. VAL. $	DIV. PER SH. $	PRICE RANGE	AVG. P/E RATIO	AVG. YIELD %
p12/31/02	22,440.0	⑥⑦ 2,708.0	49,479.0						⑥⑦ 0.76			0.78	40.90 - 18.32	39.0	2.6
12/31/01	⑧ 24,130.0	④ 2,570.0	52,046.0	26.3	10.7	13.8	4.9	0.7	④ 1.36	3.90	7.51	0.76	45.88 - 36.26	30.2	1.9
12/31/00	26,151.0	④ 4,220.0	50,925.0	26.3	16.1	25.0	8.3	0.6	④ 2.23	4.84	6.81	0.76	53.50 - 34.94	19.8	1.7
12/31/99	25,224.0	③ 3,448.0	43,453.0	25.5	13.7	23.3	7.9	0.6	④ 1.80	4.24	5.86	0.76	51.31 - 39.75	25.3	1.7
12/31/98	23,123.0	① 3,527.0	39,410.0	25.5	15.3	21.9	8.9	1.0	1.78	3.97	6.79	0.72	50.00 - 27.06	21.6	1.9
12/31/97	20,561.0	② 3,270.0	36,301.0	26.1	15.9	21.6	9.0	0.9	② 1.65	3.64	6.66	0.72	29.06 - 19.06	14.6	3.0
12/31/96	19,040.0	② 2,863.0	32,568.0	25.1	15.0	21.6	8.8	1.0	1.44	3.31	5.98	0.72	22.94 - 17.63	14.1	3.6
12/31/95	17,886.0	③ 1,564.0	31,880.0	18.4	8.7	13.2	4.9	0.9	③ 0.79	2.53	5.18	0.70	21.94 - 13.41	22.5	3.9
12/31/94	16,844.0	2,160.0	34,400.0	24.1	12.8	15.0	6.3	0.7	1.09	2.73	6.52	0.69	15.88 - 12.63	13.1	4.8
12/31/93	15,880.3	② 1,034.1	32,873.3	14.4	6.5	7.7	3.1	0.7	② 0.52	3.62	6.78	0.69	15.97 - 12.59	27.5	4.8

Statistics are as originally reported. Adj. for 2-for-1 stk. splits, 12/98 & 11/95. ① Incl. asset sale gain of $335.0 mill. ② Incl. pre-tax cr. 12/31/97: $787.0 mill.; aft-tax cr. 12/31/96: $344.0 mill.; pre-tax chrg. $1.20 bill. ③ Bef. extraord. chrg. of $2.72 bill. ④ Bef. extraord. chrg. of $40.7 mill. ⑤ Incl. restruct. & asset impair. chrgs. of $1.00 bill., 2002; $358.0 mill., 2001; $528.0 mill., 2000; $320.0 mill., 1999. ⑥ Refl. the Apr. 2000 formation of Cingular Wireless. ⑦ Bef. acctg. chrg. of $1.29 bill.

OFFICERS:
F. D. Ackerman, Chmn., Pres., C.E.O.
R. M. Dunn, Sr. V.P., Corp. Sec.
R. M. Dykes, C.F.O.
INVESTOR CONTACT: Jeff Battcher, Investor Relations, (404) 249-2793
PRINCIPAL OFFICE: 1155 Peachtree Street N.E., Atlanta, GA 30309-3610

TELEPHONE NUMBER: (404) 249-2000
FAX: (404) 249-2071
WEB: www.bellsouth.com
NO. OF EMPLOYEES: 80,882
SHAREHOLDERS: 811,067
ANNUAL MEETING: In April
INCORPORATED: GA, Dec., 1983

INSTITUTIONAL HOLDINGS:
No. of Institutions: 887
Shares Held: 961,249,449
% Held: 51.4
INDUSTRY: Telephone communications, exc. radio (SIC: 4813)
TRANSFER AGENT(S): Mellon Investor Services, LLC, Ridgefield Park, NJ

BELO CORPORATION

EXCH.	SYM.	REC. PRICE	P/E RATIO	YLD.	MKT. CAP.	RANGE (52-WK.)	'02 Y/E PR.
NYSE	BLC	21.55 (2/28/03)	18.6	...	...	24.52 - 17.75	21.32

MEDIUM GRADE. IT APPEARS THAT THE OPERATING MOMENTUM GAINED IN 2002 HAS CARRIED OVER INTO THE CURRENT YEAR.

*7 YEAR PRICE SCORE 118.9   ***12 MONTH PRICE SCORE 106.2**
*NYSE COMPOSITE INDEX=100

INTERIM EARNINGS (Per Share):

Qtr.	Mar.	June	Sept.	Dec.
1997	0.19	0.21	0.12	0.19
1998	0.11	0.24	0.08	0.10
1999	0.11	0.14	0.15	0.58
2000	0.13	0.27	0.15	0.76
2001	0.01	Nil	Nil	d0.02
2002	0.15	0.36	0.25	0.40

INTERIM DIVIDENDS (Per Share):

Amt.	Decl.	Ex.	Rec.	Pay.
0.075Q	7/29/02	8/14/02	8/16/02	9/16/02
0.075Q	9/27/02	11/13/02	11/15/02	12/06/02
0.075Q	12/06/02	2/12/03	2/14/03	3/07/03
0.075Q	2/07/03	5/14/03	5/16/03	6/06/03
		Indicated div.: $0.30		

CAPITALIZATION (12/31/01):

	($000)	(%)
Long-Term Debt	1,696,900	49.4
Deferred Income Tax	416,500	12.1
Common & Surplus	1,320,745	38.5
Total	3,434,145	100.0

BUSINESS:

Belo Corporation is a media company, with a diversified group of television broadcasting, newspaper publishing, interactive media and cable news operations in several markets and regions, including Texas, the Pacific Northwest, the Southwest, Rhode Island, and the mid-Atlantic region. BLC owns and operates 19 network-affiliated television stations; four daily newspapers, including THE DALLAS MORNING NEWS, THE PROVIDENCE JOURNAL and THE PRESS-ENTERPRISE in Riverside, California; and six local or regional cable news channels. The Company also manages one television station through a local marketing agreement. Six of the Company's stations are in the top 16 U.S. television markets. The Company's television group reaches 13.7% of all U.S. television households. Revenues for 2002 were derived: newspaper publishing, 51.4%; television, 46.1%; interactive media, 1.4%; and other, 1.1%.

RECENT DEVELOPMENTS:

For the year ended 12/31/02, net earnings soared to $131.1 million compared with a net loss of $2.7 million in 2001. Results for 2002 included a gain of $2.4 million on the sale of BLC's interest in the Dallas Mavericks and the American Airlines Center, and a credit of $4.8 million for the favorable settlement of properties sold in December 2000.

Results for 2001 included a charge of $28.8 million for the write-downs of investments. Net operating revenues climbed 4.6% to $1.43 billion from $1.36 billion in the previous year, primarily due to increased revenues from the television and cable news segments.

PROSPECTS:

The Company recently noted that the revenue momentum gained throughout 2002 has carried over into the current year. With continued high ratings and increased revenue share at its television stations, along with the growing circulation of its newspapers, BLC should be well-positioned to capitalize on a continued advertising recovery. On a segment basis, near-term results for the Company's television group should benefit from almost $2.0 million of revenue related to the Super Bowl. In the newspaper group, results should benefit from anticipated increases in all major advertising categories, with the exception of classified employment.

ANNUAL FINANCIAL DATA:

FISCAL YEAR	TOT. REVS. ($mill.)	NET INC. ($mill.)	TOT. ASSETS ($mill.)	OPER. PROFIT %	NET PROFIT %	RET. ON EQUITY %	RET. ON ASSETS %	CURR. RATIO	EARN. PER SH. $	CASH FL. PER SH. $	DIV. PER SH. $	PRICE RANGE	AVG. P/E RATIO	AVG. YIELD %
p12/31/02	1,427.8	④ 131.1							④ 1.15		0.30	24.52 - 17.75	18.4	1.4
12/31/01	1,364.6	d2.7	3,672.2	12.0	...	...	...	1.8	d0.02	1.64	0.30	20.10 - 15.15	...	0.4
12/31/00	1,588.8	③ 150.8	3,893.3	19.1	9.5	11.2	3.9	1.4	③ 1.29	2.87	0.28	20.00 - 12.31	12.5	1.7
12/31/99	1,434.0	③ 178.3	3,976.3	18.4	12.4	12.8	4.5	1.4	③ 1.50	2.91	0.26	24.50 - 16.38	13.6	1.3
12/31/98	1,407.3	64.9	3,539.1	16.6	4.6	5.2	1.8	1.5	0.52	1.80	0.24	28.47 - 13.94	40.8	1.1
12/31/97	1,248.4	83.0	3,623.0	19.3	6.6	6.3	2.3	1.3	0.71	1.86	0.22	27.56 - 16.63	31.1	1.0
12/31/96	824.3	87.5	1,224.1	20.1	10.6	23.6	7.1	1.9	1.06	1.84	0.20	20.88 - 15.50	17.2	1.1
12/31/95	735.3	66.6	1,154.0	18.6	9.1	17.1	5.8	2.0	0.84	1.59	0.16	18.38 - 13.91	19.2	1.0
12/31/94	628.1	68.9	913.8	20.9	11.0	18.0	7.5	1.6	0.85	1.43	0.15	14.31 - 10.78	14.8	1.2
12/31/93	544.8	①② 44.5	796.2	16.4	8.2	12.9	5.6	2.0	①② 0.55	1.02	0.14	13.25 - 9.69	20.8	1.2

Statistics are as originally reported. Adj. for stk. splits: 2-for-1, 6/98 and 5/95. ① Bef. acctg. credit $6.6 mill. ② Incl. non-recurr. chrg. $5.8 mill. ③ Incl. gain on sale of subsidaires & invest., 2000, $104.6 mill.; 1999, $117.8 mill. ④ Incl. $2.4 mill. gain fr. sale of interest & credit of $4.8 mill.

OFFICERS:	TELEPHONE NUMBER: (214) 977-6606	INSTITUTIONAL HOLDINGS:
R. W. Decherd, Chmn., Pres., C.E.O.	FAX: (214) 977-6603	No. of Institutions: 225
D. A. Shive, Exec. V.P., C.F.O.	WEB: www.belo.com	Shares Held: 69,597,171
G. Kerr, Sr. V.P., Gen. Couns., Sec.	NO. OF EMPLOYEES: 7,820 (approx.)	% Held: 61.8
INVESTOR CONTACT: Carey P. Hendrickson, V.P., Investor Relations, (214) 977-6626	SHAREHOLDERS: 9,985 (approx. series A); 540 (approx. series B)	
PRINCIPAL OFFICE: P.O. Box 655237, Dallas, TX 75265	ANNUAL MEETING: In May	INDUSTRY: Newspapers (SIC: 2711)
	INCORPORATED: DE, May, 1987	TRANSFER AGENT(S): BankBoston, NA, Boston, MA

BEMIS COMPANY, INC.

EXCH.	SYM.	REC. PRICE	P/E RATIO	YLD.	MKT. CAP.	RANGE (52-WK.)	'02 Y/E PR.	DIV. ACH.
NYSE	BMS	41.86 (2/28/03)	13.6	2.7%	$2.21 bill.	58.24 - 39.40	49.63	19 yrs.

UPPER MEDIUM GRADE. THE COMPANY ANTICIPATES CLOSING THE SALE OF ITS PRESSURE-SENSITIVE MATERI-
ALS BUSINESS IN THE FIRST HALF OF 2003.

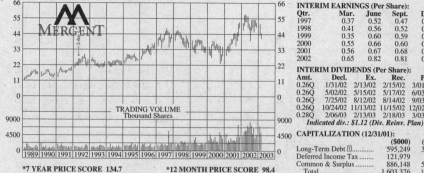

*7 YEAR PRICE SCORE 134.7   ***12 MONTH PRICE SCORE 98.4**

*NYSE COMPOSITE INDEX=100

INTERIM EARNINGS (Per Share):

Qtr.	Mar.	June	Sept.	Dec.
1997	0.37	0.52	0.47	0.64
1998	0.41	0.56	0.52	0.60
1999	0.35	0.60	0.59	0.63
2000	0.55	0.66	0.60	0.63
2001	0.56	0.67	0.68	0.73
2002	0.65	0.82	0.81	0.80

INTERIM DIVIDENDS (Per Share):

Amt.	Decl.	Ex.	Rec.	Pay.
0.26Q	1/31/02	2/13/02	2/15/02	3/01/02
0.26Q	5/02/02	5/15/02	5/17/02	6/03/02
0.26Q	7/25/02	8/12/02	8/14/02	9/03/02
0.26Q	10/24/02	11/13/02	11/15/02	12/02/02
0.28Q	2/06/03	2/13/03	2/18/03	3/03/03

Indicated div.: $1.12 (Div. Reinv. Plan)

CAPITALIZATION (12/31/01):

	($000)	(%)
Long-Term Debt ⬜	ˉ595,249	37.1
Deferred Income Tax	121,979	7.6
Common & Surplus	886,148	55.3
Total	1,603,376	100.0

BUSINESS:

Bemis Company, Inc. is a manufacturer of flexible packaging and pressure-sensitive materials used by food, consumer products, manufacturing, and other companies worldwide. Flexible packaging products include a broad range of consumer and industrial packaging consisting of high-barrier products that include advanced multi-layer coextruded, coated and laminated film structures; polyethylene products; and paper products. Pressure-Sensitive Materials include roll label products, graphics and distribution products, and technical and industrial products. As of 1/23/03, the Company manufactured from 51 facilities in nine countries. In 2002, sales were as follows: flexible packaging, 80.0%, and pressure-sensitive materials, 20.0%.

RECENT DEVELOPMENTS:

For the year ended 12/31/02, net income increased 18.0% to $165.5 million compared with $140.3 million in 2001. Net sales rose 3.3% to $2.37 billion from $2.29 billion a year earlier. Net sales for the flexible packaging business segment grew 4.0% to $1.90 billion due to recent acquisitions. This was partially offset by decreases in both polyethylene and paper product lines due to capacity limitations, weak economic activity and highly competitive pricing in the industrial markets. Net sales for the pressure sensitive materials business segment climbed 1.6% to $499.0 million.

PROSPECTS:

On 12/12/02, the Company announced that the sale of its pressure-sensitive materials business segment to UPM-Kymmene for $420.0 million will be delayed in order to accommodate the ongoing review of information by the U.S. regulatory authorities. BMS anticipates completing the transaction during the first half of 2003. The closing should occur within about 30 days of receiving U.S. regulatory approval. Looking ahead, the Company expects first quarter 2003 earnings per share in the range of $0.70 to $0.73, which includes an estimated $0.06 to $0.08 per share from the pressure sensitive materials business. For the full-year 2003, BMS anticipates earnings per share in the range of $3.15 to $3.25, excluding an expected gain on the sale of the pressure sensitive materials business segment.

ANNUAL FINANCIAL DATA:

FISCAL YEAR	TOT. REVS. ($mill.)	NET INC. ($mill.)	TOT. ASSETS ($mill.)	OPER. PROFIT %	NET PROFIT %	RET. ON EQUITY %	RET. ON ASSETS %	CURR. RATIO	EARN. PER SH. $	CASH FL. PER SH. $	TANG. BK. VAL.$	DIV. PER SH. $	PRICE RANGE	AVG. P/E RATIO	AVG. YIELD %
p12/31/02	2,369.0	165.5	2,256.7						3.08			1.04	58.24 - 39.40	15.9	2.1
12/31/01	2,293.1	140.3	1,923.0	11.3	6.1	15.8	7.3	˙2.5	2.64	4.98	8.78	1.00	52.47 - 28.69	15.4	2.5
12/31/00	2,164.6	130.6	1,888.6	11.3	6.0	16.4	6.9	1.3	2.44	4.46	9.52	0.96	39.31 - 22.94	·12.8	3.1
12/31/99	1,918.0	114.8	1,532.1	11.4	6.0	15.8	7.5	2.3	2.18	4.04	13.91	0.92	40.38 - 30.19	16.2	2.6
12/31/98	1,848.0	111.4	1,453.1	11.3	6.0	16.6	7.7	2.1	2.09	3.76	12.83	0.88	46.94 - 33.50	19.2	2.2
12/31/97	1,877.2	107.6	1,362.6	10.4	5.7	16.8	7.9	2.1	2.00	3.46	12.08	0.80	47.94 - 33.63	20.4	2.0
12/31/96	1,655.4	101.1	1,168.8	10.6	6.1	17.8	8.6	2.2	1.90	3.14	10.83	0.72	37.63 - 25.63	16.6	2.3
12/31/95	1,523.4	85.2	1,030.6	9.7	5.6	16.6	8.3	2.0	1.63	2.74	9.76	0.64	30.00 - 23.00	16.3	2.4
12/31/94	1,390.5	72.8	923.3	9.3	5.2	17.4	7.9	2.0	1.40	2.40	8.16	0.54	25.75 - 20.50	16.5	2.3
12/31/93	1,203.5	②46.1	789.8	8.4	3.8	12.4	5.8	1.8	②0.89	1.80	7.24	0.50	27.38 - 19.88	26.5	2.1

Statistics are as originally reported. ⬜ Incl. capital lease obligations. ② Incl. restruct. chg. of approx. $13 mill. ($0.25/sh.), and bef. acctg. change chrg. $1.7 mill. ($0.03/sh.).

OFFICERS:
J. H. Roe, Chmn.
J. H. Curler, Pres., C.E.O.
B. R. Field, III, Sr. V.P., C.F.O., Treas.
INVESTOR CONTACT: Melanie E.R. Miller, Dir., Investor Relations, (612) 376-3030
PRINCIPAL OFFICE: 222 South 9th Street, Suite 2300, Minneapolis, MN 55402-4099

TELEPHONE NUMBER: (612) 376-3000
FAX: (612) 340-6174
WEB: www.bemis.com
NO. OF EMPLOYEES: 11,012 (avg.)
SHAREHOLDERS: 4,747
ANNUAL MEETING: In May
INCORPORATED: MO, May, 1885

INSTITUTIONAL HOLDINGS:
No. of Institutions: 247
Shares Held: 32,270,614
% Held: 61.0
INDUSTRY: Paper coated & laminated, packaging (SIC: 2671)
TRANSFER AGENT(S): Wells Fargo Bank Minnesota, South St. Paul, MN

BERKLEY (W.R.) CORPORATION

EXCH.	SYM.	REC. PRICE	P/E RATIO	YLD.	MKT. CAP.	RANGE (52-WK.)	'02 Y/E PR.
NYSE	BER	40.60 (2/28/03)	12.4	0.9%	$2.02 bill.	41.40 - 29.90	39.61

UPPER MEDIUM GRADE. BER ANNOUNCED THAT IT INTENDS TO FORM A U.K.-BASED INSURANCE COMPANY.

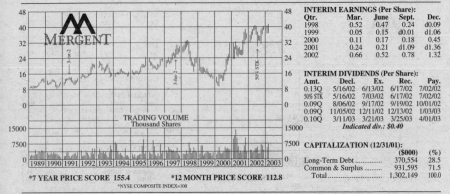

INTERIM EARNINGS (Per Share):

Qtr.	Mar.	June	Sept.	Dec.
1998	0.52	0.47	0.24	d0.09
1999	0.05	0.15	d0.01	d1.06
2000	0.11	0.17	0.18	0.45
2001	0.24	0.21	d1.09	d1.36
2002	0.66	0.52	0.78	1.32

INTERIM DIVIDENDS (Per Share):

Amt.	Decl.	Ex.	Rec.	Pay.
0.13Q	5/16/02	6/13/02	6/17/02	7/02/02
50% STK	5/16/02	7/03/02	6/17/02	7/02/02
0.09Q	8/06/02	9/17/02	9/19/02	10/01/02
0.09Q	11/05/02	12/11/02	12/13/02	1/03/03
0.10Q	3/11/03	3/21/03	3/25/03	4/01/03

Indicated div.: $0.40

CAPITALIZATION (12/31/01):

	($000)	(%)
Long-Term Debt	370,554	28.5
Common & Surplus	931,595	71.5
Total	1,302,149	100.0

*7 YEAR PRICE SCORE 155.4   *12 MONTH PRICE SCORE 112.8

*NYSE COMPOSITE INDEX=100

BUSINESS:

W. R. Berkley Corporation is an insurance holding company that, through its subsidiaries, operates in all segments of the property casualty insurance business. The Company's operating units are grouped in five segments according to market served: Regional Property Casualty Insurance, Reinsurance, Specialty Insurance, Alternative Markets and International. The Company's regional insurance operations are conducted primarily in the New England, Mid-Atlantic, Midwest and Southern sections of the United States. The reinsurance, specialty insurance, and alternative insurance operations are conducted on a nationwide basis. Presently, international operations are conducted primarily in Argentina and the Philippines.

RECENT DEVELOPMENTS:

For the year ended 12/31/02, net income was $175.0 million versus a net loss of $91.5 million in 2001. Total revenues climbed 32.1% to $2.57 billion. Net premiums earned grew 34.0% to $2.25 billion. Net investment income declined 3.7% to $187.9 million. Revenues included realized investment gains of $15.2 million in 2002 versus losses of $12.3 million in 2001. Results reflected strategic decisions made over the past several years to consolidate operations and focus on the most profitable lines of business. This focus also resulted in the early recognition of past reserve deficiencies, and thus, BER was able to benefit from higher prices and improved terms and conditions.

PROSPECTS:

Going forward, BER will continue its cautious reserving practices to guard against the possibility of future adverse reserve development. Meanwhile, BER expects overall industry problems will result in a continuation of the current pricing environment of increasing rates at least through 2003. As a result, the Company expects significantly better results in 2003. Separately, on 3/4/03, BER announced that it intends to form a United Kingdom operation. BER expects this new operation to be based in London and to specialize principally in writing domestic U.K. casualty risks. The U.K. unit is expected to commence operation in the third quarter of 2003, subject to certain approvals, including the approval of the U.K. Financial Services Authority.

ANNUAL FINANCIAL DATA:

FISCAL YEAR	PREM. INC. ($mill.)	TOT. REVS. ($mill.)	NET INC. ($mill.)	TOT. ASSETS ($mill.)	TOT. INVST. ($mill.)	RET. ON REVS. %	RET. ON EQUITY %	RET. ON ASSETS %	EARN. PER SH.$	TANG. BK. VAL.$	AVG. YIELD %	DIV. PER SH.$	PRICE RANGE	AVG. P/E RATIO
p12/31/02	2,252.5	2,566.1	175.0						3.31		1.0	0.35	40.80 - 29.90	10.6
12/31/01	1,680.5	1,941.8	④ d91.5	5,633.5	2,778.8	...	...	...	④ d2.09	17.39	1.1	0.35	38.94 - 23.29	
12/31/00	1,491.0	1,781.3	③ 36.2	5,022.1	2,703.0	2.0	5.3	0.7	③ 0.93	15.83	1.7	0.35	31.75 - 9.33	22.2
12/31/99	1,414.4	1,673.7	② d34.5	4,784.8	2,577.9	...	...	...	② d0.89	13.41	1.8	0.34	24.17 - 13.21	
12/31/98	1,278.4	1,582.5	① 51.2	4,983.4	2,931.9	3.2	5.9	1.0	① 1.17	19.73	1.3	0.31	33.25 - 16.83	21.3
12/31/97	1,111.7	1,400.3	91.2	4,599.3	2,903.4	6.5	9.6	2.0	2.01	19.71	1.1	0.26	30.92 - 19.20	12.4
12/31/96	981.2	1,225.2	76.4	4,073.3	2,611.0	6.2	8.7	1.9	1.71	18.25	1.1	0.23	23.89 - 17.89	12.2
12/31/95	803.3	1,021.9	49.8	3,618.7	2,391.6	4.9	5.4	1.4	1.27	18.95	1.0	0.21	24.67 - 15.33	15.7
12/31/94	655.0	830.8	24.7	3,582.3	1,687.6	3.0	4.1	0.7	0.64	14.36	1.2	0.19	18.67 - 14.45	25.9
12/31/93	420.3	581.8	51.6	2,156.5	1,363.6	8.9	9.8	2.4	1.28	12.31	0.9	0.17	22.45 - 14.22	14.4

Statistics are as originally reported. Adj. for stk. splits: 50.0% div., 7/2/02; 3-for-2, 9/18/97 ① Incl. non-recurr. chrg. $11.5 mill. ② Bef. acctg. change chrg. $3.3 mill. and extraord. gain $735,000 ③ Incl. a restructuring charge of $1.9 mill. ④ Incl. restructuring chrgs. of $3.2 mill.

OFFICERS:
W. R. Berkley, Chmn., Pres., C.E.O.
E. G. Ballard, Sr. V.P., C.F.O., Treas.
I. S. Lederman, Sr. V.P., Gen. Couns., Sec.
INVESTOR CONTACT: Eugene G. Ballard, Sr. V.P., C.F.O., (203) 629-3000
PRINCIPAL OFFICE: 475 Steamboat Rd., Greenwich, CT 06830

TELEPHONE NUMBER: (203) 629-3000
FAX: (203) 629-3492
WEB: www.wrberkley.com
NO. OF EMPLOYEES: 4,244 (avg.)
SHAREHOLDERS: 624 (approx.)
ANNUAL MEETING: In May
INCORPORATED: DE, Jan., 1970

INSTITUTIONAL HOLDINGS:
No. of Institutions: 168
Shares Held: 45,270,780
% Held: 83.3
INDUSTRY: Fire, marine, and casualty insurance (SIC: 6331)
TRANSFER AGENT(S): Mellon Investor Services, Ridgefield Park, NJ

BERKSHIRE HATHAWAY INC.

EXCH.	SYM.	REC. PRICE	P/E RATIO	YLD.	MKT. CAP.	RANGE (52-WK.)	'02 Y/E PR.
NYSE	BRKB	2065.00 (2/28/03)	22.2	...	$433.53 bill.	2620.00 - 1925.00	2423.00

UPPER MEDIUM GRADE. THE COMPANY ENTERED INTO A DEFINITIVE AGREEMENT TO ACQUIRE CLAYTON HOMES, INC.

TRADING VOLUME Thousand Shares

1989 1990 1991 1992 1993 1994 1995 1996 1997 1998 1999 2000 2001 2002 2003

*7 YEAR PRICE SCORE N/A   ***12 MONTH PRICE SCORE 103.9**

*NYSE COMPOSITE INDEX=100

INTERIM EARNINGS (Per Share):

Qtr.	Mar.	June	Sept.	Dec.
1998	19.40	31.57	9.77	14.80
1999	11.87	12.53	9.20	0.57
2000	17.70	14.03	17.43	23.67
2001	13.23	16.87	d14.82	2.10
2002	19.93	22.70	24.80	25.73

INTERIM DIVIDENDS (Per Share):

Amt.	Decl.	Ex.	Rec.	Pay.
	No dividends paid.			

CAPITALIZATION (12/31/01):

	($000)	(%)
Long-Term Debt	3,485,000	5.7
Common & Surplus	57,950,000	94.3
Total	61,435,000	100.0

BUSINESS:

Berkshire Hathaway Inc. is engaged in diverse business activities. As of 12/31/01, BRKB's insurance and reinsurance business activities were conducted through 36 domestic and 16 foreign-based insurance companies including GEICO and General RE. FlightSafety International provides training of aircraft and ship operators. Executive Jet provides fractional ownership programs for general aviation aircraft. Nebraska Furniture Mart, R.C. Willey Home Furnishings, Star Furniture, and Jordans Furniture are retailers of home furnishings. Borsheims, Helzberg Diamond Shops and Ben Bridge Jeweler are retailers of fine jewelry. Scott Fetzer is a diversified manufacturer and distributor of commercial and industrial products. BRK has substantial equity stakes in The Coca-Cola Co., American Express Co., The Gillette Co., and Wells Fargo & Co. On 1/2/01, BRKB acquired Johns Manville Corp. and Benjamin Moore & Co. In 2002, BRKB acquired The Pampered Chef, Ltd., CTB International Corp. and Garan, Inc.

RECENT DEVELOPMENTS:

For the year ended 12/31/02, net income surged to $4.29 billion compared with $795.0 million the year before. Results for 2002 and 2001 included realized investment gains of $637.0 million and $1.36 billion, and gains from equity in net earnings of MidAmerican Energy of $317.0 million and $115.0 million, respectively. Results for 2001 also included goodwill amortization of $572.0 million. Total revenues increased 9.6% to $42.35 billion. Total costs and expenses were $35.17 billion, down 2.8% from $36.20 billion the year before.

PROSPECTS:

On 4/1/03, the Company announced that it has entered into a definitive agreement to acquire Clayton Homes, Inc. Under the transaction, Clayton Homes stockholders will receive cash of $12.50 per share. Clayton Homes is a vertically integrated manufactured housing company with 20 manufacturing plants, 297 Company-owned stores, 610 independent retailers, 85 manufactured housing communities, and financial services operations that provide mortgage services for 165,000 customers and insurance protection for 100,000 families.

ANNUAL FINANCIAL DATA:

FISCAL YEAR	PREM. INC. ($mill.)	NET INVST. INC. ($mill.)	TOT. REVS. ($mill.)	NET INC. ($mill.)	TOT. ASSETS ($mill.)	TOT. INVST. ($mill.)	RET. ON REVS. %	RET. ON EQUITY %	RET. ON ASSETS %	EARN. PER SH. $	TANG. BK. VAL. $	PRICE RANGE	AVG. P/E RATIO
p12/31/02	19,182.0	3,061.0	42,353.0	4,286.0	169,544.0					93.17 [1]		2620.00 - 1925.00	24.4
12/31/01	17,905.0	2,765.0	37,668.0	②795.0	162,752.0	68,984.0	2.1	1.4	0.5	②17.37	225.10	2525.00 - 1977.00	129.6
12/31/00	19,343.0	2,686.0	33,976.0	3,328.0	135,792.0	73,542.0	9.8	5.4	2.5	72.83	925.84	2375.00 - 1351.00	25.6
12/31/99	14,306.0	2,314.0	24,028.0	1,557.0	131,416.0	69,730.0	6.5	2.7	1.2	34.17	865.47	2713.00 - 1700.50	64.6
12/31/98	5,481.0	1,049.0	13,832.0	2,830.0	122,237.0	61,007.0	20.5	4.9	2.3	75.40	202.27	2795.00 - 1529.00	28.7
12/31/97	4,761.0	916.0	10,430.0	1,901.0	56,110.9	46,545.5	18.2	6.0	3.4	51.40	789.89	1624.00 - 1088.00	26.4
12/31/96	4,118.0	778.0	10,500.0	2,489.0	43,409.5	34,197.5	23.7	10.6	5.7	68.83	561.53	1220.00 - 990.00	16.1
12/31/95	957.5	474.8	4,487.7	725.2	29,928.8	23,658.2	16.2	4.2	2.4	20.37	480.66	...	...
12/31/94	923.2	426.1	3,847.5	494.8	21,338.2	18,080.6	12.9	4.2	2.3	14.00	336.02	...	...
12/31/93	656.3	479.8	3,653.5	759.1	19,521.6	14,648.8	20.8	7.3	3.9	21.87	295.09	...	...

Statistics are as originally reported. ① Earnings per share data represent B shares, which have economic rights equal to one-thirtieth of the economic rights of Cl. A common stk. ② Incl. a cost of $2.28 billion rel. to the terrorist attacks that occurred in U.S. on 9/11/01.

OFFICERS:
W. E. Buffett, Chmn., C.E.O.
C. T. Munger, Vice-Chmn.

INVESTOR CONTACT: Marc D. Hamburg, Invsetor Relations, (402) 346-1400

PRINCIPAL OFFICE: 1440 Kiewit Plaza, Omaha, NE 68131

TELEPHONE NUMBER: (402) 346-1400
WEB: www.berkshirehathaway.com

NO. OF EMPLOYEES: 110,000 (approx.)

SHAREHOLDERS: 8,500 (approx. class A); 14,000 (approx. class B)

ANNUAL MEETING: In May

INCORPORATED: DE, Aug., 1973

INSTITUTIONAL HOLDINGS:
No. of Institutions: 557
Shares Held: 77,973,876
% Held: 0.0

INDUSTRY: Fire, marine, and casualty insurance (SIC: 6331)

TRANSFER AGENT(S): Fleet National Bank, N.A. c/o EquiServe, Providence, RI

BEST BUY CO., INC.

EXCH.	SYM.	REC. PRICE	P/E RATIO	YLD.	MKT. CAP.	RANGE (52-WK.)	'02 Y/E PR.
NYSE	BBY	29.07 (2/28/03)	16.6	...	$9.28 bill.	53.75 - 16.99	24.15

INVESTMENT GRADE. IN FISCAL 2004, THE COMPANY IS TARGETING SALES GROWTH OF BETWEEN 10.0% AND 12.0%.

*7 YEAR PRICE SCORE 141.5   ***12 MONTH PRICE SCORE 90.0**

*NYSE COMPOSITE INDEX=100

INTERIM EARNINGS (Per Share):

Qtr.	May	Aug.	Nov.	Feb.
1996-97	0.01	0.02	d0.05	0.03
1997-98	d0.01	0.03	0.10	0.22
1998-99	0.05	0.14	0.17	0.35
1999-00	0.15	0.19	0.25	0.52
2000-01	0.23	0.24	0.18	0.59
2001-02	0.17	0.26	0.25	1.08
2002-03	0.22	0.19	0.26	...

INTERIM DIVIDENDS (Per Share):

Amt.	Decl.	Ex.	Rec.	Pay.
50% STK	4/15/02	5/13/02	4/26/02	5/10/02

CAPITALIZATION (3/2/02):

	($000)	(%)
Long-Term Debt	813,000	24.4
Common & Surplus	2,521,000	75.6
Total	3,334,000	100.0

BUSINESS:

Best Buy Co., Inc. is one of the nation's largest consumer-electronics and major-appliance specialty retailers. The Company sells nationally-recognized, name-brand consumer electronics, personal computers and home-office products, major appliances, entertainment software and photographic equipment through 554 Best Buy stores in the U.S. and Canada as of 1/9/03. In addition, the Company operates 1,326 music and video retail stores through its Musicland Stores Corporation subsidiary under the names Sam Goody, Suncoast, On Cue, Media Play, Magnolia Hi-Fi and Future Shop. For the fiscal year ended 3/2/02, the product sales mix was derived as follows: Consumer Electronics, 33%; Home Office, 31%; Entertainment Software, 22%; Appliances, 6%; and Other, 8%.

RECENT DEVELOPMENTS:

For the quarter ended 11/30/02, net earnings grew 6.3% to $85.0 million from $80.0 million in the prior year. Revenues climbed 15.7% to $5.51 billion from $4.76 billion a year earlier. Sales growth was driven by the addition of 68 new Best Buy stores in the past twelve months, along with the inclusion of a full quarter of sales from about 100 Future Shop stores, which were acquired on 11/4/01. Comparable-store sales slid 0.4% year over year. Gross profit rose 15.5% to $1.19 billion from $1.03 billion the year before. Operating income was up 7.8% to $139.0 million.

PROSPECTS:

The Company is targeting sales growth of between 10.0% and 12.0% in fiscal 2004, which begins on 3/2/03. This growth will primarily be fueled by the opening of 80 to 85 new stores in North America during the year. In fiscal 2004, BBY plans to open between 17 and 19 new stores in Canada, with stores in new markets of Edmonton, Alberta; Winnipeg, Manitoba; and Ottawa, London, and Windsor, Ontario. Separately, on 1/8/03, BBY closed about 110 Musicland locations, including 90 Sam Goody stores and 20 Suncoast stores, due to weak sales of pre-recorded music and sluggish mall traffic levels. In an effort to increase productivity and boost profitability, the Company plans to realign its Musicland business into its domestic Best Buy operations.

ANNUAL FINANCIAL DATA:

FISCAL YEAR	TOT. REVS. ($mill.)	NET INC. ($mill.)	TOT. ASSETS ($mill.)	OPER. PROFIT %	NET PROFIT %	RET. ON EQUITY %	RET. ON ASSETS %	CURR. RATIO	EARN. PER SH.$	CASH FL. PER SH.$	TANG. BK. VAL.$	PRICE RANGE	AVG. P/E RATIO
3/02/02	19,597.0	570.0	7,375.0	4.8	2.9	22.6	7.7	1.2	1.77	2.73	5.48	50.14 - 18.54	19.4
3/03/01	15,326.6	395.8	4,839.6	3.9	2.6	21.7	8.2	1.1	1.24	1.77	4.60	59.25 - 14.00	29.5
2/26/00	12,494.0	347.1	2,995.3	4.3	2.8	31.7	11.6	1.3	1.09	1.43	3.65	53.67 - 20.58	34.2
2/27/99	10,077.9	224.4	2,512.5	3.6	2.2	21.1	8.9	1.5	0.71	0.96	3.48	20.75 - 6.00	18.8
2/28/98	8,358.2	94.5	2,056.3	2.2	1.1	16.9	4.6	1.7	0.35	0.55	2.08	6.83 - 1.31	11.7
3/01/97	7,770.7	②1.7	1,734.3	0.7	...	0.4	0.1	1.7	②0.01	0.26	1.69	4.38 - 1.63	422.6
3/02/96	7,217.4	48.0	1,890.8	1.7	0.7	11.1	2.5	1.6	0.18	0.39	1.68	5.60 - 2.67	22.6
2/25/95	5,079.6	57.7	1,507.1	2.4	1.1	15.3	3.8	2.0	0.22	0.37	1.48	7.54 - 3.17	24.1
2/26/94	3,006.5	①41.7	952.5	2.6	1.4	13.4	4.4	1.9	①0.17	0.26	1.24	5.24 - 1.80	20.9
2/27/93	1,620.0	19.9	439.1	2.2	1.2	10.9	4.5	1.6	0.10	0.17	0.88	2.22 - 0.79	15.8

Statistics are as originally reported. Adj. for 2-for-1 stk. split, 3/99, 5/98, 4/94 & 50% stk. div., 5/02, 9/93. ① Bef. $425,000 ($0.01/sh) acctg. chg. ② Incl. $25 mil pre-tax chg. for write-down of inventory.

OFFICERS:
R. M. Schulze, Chmn.
B. H. Anderson, Vice-Chmn., C.E.O.
A. U. Lenzmeier, Pres., C.O.O.
D. R. Jackson, Exec. V.P., C.F.O., Treas.
INVESTOR CONTACT: Jennifer Driscoll, Investor Relations, (952) 947-2350
PRINCIPAL OFFICE: 7075 Flying Cloud Drive, Eden Prairie, MN 55344

TELEPHONE NUMBER: (952) 947-2000
FAX: (952) 947-2422
WEB: www.bestbuy.com
NO. OF EMPLOYEES: 94,000 (avg.)
SHAREHOLDERS: 2,013 (record)
ANNUAL MEETING: In June
INCORPORATED: MI, 1966

INSTITUTIONAL HOLDINGS:
No. of Institutions: 447
Shares Held: 205,247,388
% Held: 63.8

INDUSTRY: Radio, TV, & electronic stores (SIC: 5731)

TRANSFER AGENT(S): First Chicago Trust Company of New York, Jersey City, NJ

BEVERLY ENTERPRISES, INC.

EXCH.	SYM.	REC. PRICE	P/E RATIO	YLD.	MKT. CAP.	RANGE (52-WK.)	'02 Y/E PR.
NYSE	BEV	1.96 (2/28/03)	...	...	$204.4 mill.	9.18 - 1.60	2.85

SPECULATIVE GRADE. ON 1/24/03, THE COMPANY ANNOUNCED THE SALE OF THE OUTPATIENT REHABILITA-TION CLINIC OPERATIONS OF MATRIX REHABILITATION, INC., TO BENCHMARK MEDICAL HOLDINGS, INC.

INTERIM EARNINGS (Per Share):

Qtr.	Mar.	June	Sept.	Dec.
1998	0.17	0.20	0.21	d0.90
1999	0.06	d1.13	0.08	d0.32
2000	0.06	0.08	d0.22	d0.45
2001	d0.50	0.05	0.11	d2.56
2002	0.19	d0.13	0.15	d0.63

INTERIM DIVIDENDS (Per Share):

Amt.	Decl.	Ex.	Rec.	Pay.
	No dividends paid.			

CAPITALIZATION (12/31/01):

	($000)	(%)
Long-Term Debt ☐	677,442	69.6
Common & Surplus	296,497	30.4
Total	973,939	100.0

*7 YEAR PRICE SCORE 53.9   ***12 MONTH PRICE SCORE 52.7**

*NYSE COMPOSITE INDEX=100

BUSINESS:

Beverly Enterprises, Inc. is a long-term health care company operating nursing facilities, subacute units, institutional pharmacies, retirement living centers, and home health centers. The Company also provides ancillary services, which include occupational, physical, speech, respiratory and IV therapy, as well as sales of pharmaceutical products. The patient population is made up of Medicaid, Medicare and other patients. Changes in the patient mix can significantly affect earnings. BEV also operates retirement living projects and villas, which are affiliated with nearby nursing facilities operated by the Company, as well as durable medical equipment outlets and pharmacies.

RECENT DEVELOPMENTS:

For the year ended 12/31/02, BEV reported a loss of $32.1 million, before an accounting change charge of $77.2 million and loss of $36.8 million from discontinued operations, compared with a loss of $237.4 million, before a loss of $63.9 million from discontinued operations. Results for 2002 and 2001 included charges for asset impairments, workforce reductions and other unusual items of $79.5 million and $197.4 million, and a special credit of $9.4 million and special charge of $77.5 million respectively. The 2002 results also included net non-recurring charges of $28.5 million. Total revenue declined 6.8% to $2.42 billion from $2.60 billion the year before.

PROSPECTS:

On 1/24/03, the Company announced the sale of the outpatient rehabilitation clinic operations of MATRIX Rehabilitation, Inc., to Benchmark Medical Holdings, Inc. The transaction involves 141 MATRIX outpatient therapy clinics in nine states, which generated $74.0 million in revenues during 2002. Meanwhile, BEV will look to retain the financial capability to support continued improvements in its business unit. Also, BEV will implement a plan of divesting the nursing homes that account for more than half of its projected patient care liability costs.

ANNUAL FINANCIAL DATA:

FISCAL YEAR	TOT. REVS. ($mill.)	NET INC. ($mill.)	TOT. ASSETS ($mill.)	OPER. PROFIT %	NET PROFIT %	RET. ON EQUITY %	RET. ON ASSETS %	CURR. RATIO	EARN. PER SH.$	CASH FL. PER SH.$	TANG. BK. VAL.$	PRICE RANGE	AVG. P/E RATIO
p12/31/02	**2,424.7**	☑ **d32.1**							☑ **d0.31**			**9.50 - 1.60**	...
12/31/01	2,712.9	☑ d301.3	1,681.1	...	...	...	...	1.1	☑ d2.90	d1.96	1.45	12.10 - 5.20	...
12/31/00	2,628.3	☑ d54.5	1,876.0	0.1	...	...	...	0.8	☑ d0.53	0.47	3.66	8.25 - 2.50	...
12/31/99	2,551.0	☑ d134.6	1,982.9	...	...	...	...	1.3	☑ d1.31	0.32	4.01	8.19 - 3.50	...
12/31/98	2,822.9	☑ d24.9	2,160.5	0.5	...	...	...	1.9	☑ d0.24	0.69	5.46	16.25 - 5.25	...
12/31/97	3,230.3	☑ 58.6	2,073.5	5.9	1.8	6.8	2.8	1.8	☑ 0.57	1.63	7.21	17.50 - 12.13	26.0
12/31/96	3,281.0	☑ 52.0	2,525.1	6.6	1.6	6.0	2.1	1.8	☑ 0.50	1.61	5.10	13.75 - 9.25	23.0
12/31/95	3,242.8	☑ d8.1	2,428.5	2.4	...	...	...	1.5	☑ d0.16	1.01	4.27	16.13 - 9.00	...
12/31/94	2,983.8	☑ 76.9	2,322.6	6.0	2.6	9.3	3.3	1.6	☑ 0.79	1.86	4.76	16.13 - 11.75	17.6
12/31/93	2,885.9	☑☑ 60.3	1,993.5	5.3	2.1	8.2	3.0	1.4	☑☑ 0.45	1.86	6.00	14.75 - 9.25	26.7

Statistics are as originally reported. ☐ Incl. debs. conv. into com. ☑ Bef. an extraord. chg. of $1.7 mill., 1996; $2.4 mill., 1994; $2.2 mill., 1993; dr$8.8, 1992. ☑ Bef. chg. to retained earns. of $20.0 mill. ☑ Incl. a pre-tax chg. of $68.1 mill. for acctg. changes, 1995; dr$5.5 mill., 1992. ☑ Incl. pre-tax trans. costs of $40.0 mill. ☑ Incl. a pre-tax non-recurring chrgs. of $181.7 mill., 1998; $243.2 mill., 1999; $90.2 mill., 2000. ☑ Incl. net pre-tax chrgs. of $134.6 mill. ☑ Incl. net pre-tax chrgs. of $315.6 mill. ☑ Incl. net pre-tax chrgs. of $98.5 mill. & excl. acctg. chng. chrg. of $77.2 mill. & loss of $36.8 mill. from discs. ops.

OFFICERS:
W. R. Floyd, Chmn., Pres., C.E.O.
J. P. Freimark, Exec. V.P., C.F.O.
S. Hollingsworth Jr., Sr. V.P., Treas.

INVESTOR CONTACT: James M. Griffith, Investor Relations, (479) 201-5514

PRINCIPAL OFFICE: One Thousand Beverly Way, Fort Smith, AR 72919

TELEPHONE NUMBER: (479) 201-2000
FAX: (479) 452-5131
WEB: www.beverlynet.com

NO. OF EMPLOYEES: 57,000 (approx.)

SHAREHOLDERS: 5,049

ANNUAL MEETING: In May

INCORPORATED: DE, Feb., 1987

INSTITUTIONAL HOLDINGS:
No. of Institutions: 105
Shares Held: 70,284,719
% Held: 67.0

INDUSTRY: Skilled nursing care facilities (SIC: 8051)

TRANSFER AGENT(S): The Bank of New York, New York, NY

BIG LOTS, INC.

EXCH.	SYM.	REC. PRICE	P/E RATIO	YLD.	MKT. CAP.	RANGE (52-WK.)	'02 Y/E PR.
NYSE	BLI	11.05 (2/28/03)	16.5	...	$1.26 bill.	19.90 - 9.92	13.23

MEDIUM GRADE. THE COMPANY IS TARGETING FULL-YEAR 2003 EARNINGS OF BETWEEN $0.74 AND $0.78 PER SHARE.

7 YEAR PRICE SCORE 73.6   **12 MONTH PRICE SCORE 90.2**

NYSE COMPOSITE INDEX=100

INTERIM EARNINGS (Per Share):

Qtr.	Apr.	July	Oct.	Jan.
1996-97	0.05	d0.08	d0.03	1.26
1997-98	d0.08	0.01	0.04	0.60
1998-99	0.01	0.06	d0.15	1.06
1999-00	d0.03	d0.04	d0.14	1.06
2000-01	d0.12	0.08	0.06	0.61
2001-02	Nil	d0.09	d0.14	d0.02
2002-03	0.11	0.03	d0.04	0.57

INTERIM DIVIDENDS (Per Share):

Amt.	Decl.	Ex.	Rec.	Pay.
0.01RR	...	8/29/01	8/31/01	9/10/01

CAPITALIZATION (2/2/02):

	($000)	(%)
Long-Term Debt	204,000	16.8
Deferred Income Tax	79,802	6.6
Common & Surplus	927,533	76.6
Total	1,211,335	100.0

BUSINESS:

Big Lots, Inc. (formerly Consolidated Stores Corporation) is a retailer of close-out merchandise. As of 2/26/03, the Company operated 1,380 stores in 45 states under the names Big Lots and Big Lots Furniture. The Company's stores offer substantial savings on a wide variety of name-brand consumer products, including food items, health and beauty aids, electronics, housewares, tools, paint, lawn and garden, hardware, sporting goods and toys. The Company's wholesale operations are conducted through Big Lots Wholesale, Consolidated International and Wisconsin Toy. On 1/16/98, BLI acquired Mac Frugal's Bargains*Close-outs, Inc. On 12/7/00, BLI completed the sale of its K*B Toy division.

RECENT DEVELOPMENTS:

For the 52 weeks ended 2/1/03, the Company reported net income of $76.6 million compared with a loss from continuing operations of $28.7 million in the corresponding period the previous year. Results for the prior year included an after-tax non-recurring charge of $50.4 million. Sales climbed 12.7% to $3.87 billion from $3.43 billion a year earlier. Comparable-store sales, including all stores open two years at the beginning of the fiscal year, were up 7.7% year over year, fueled by a 2.8% increase in customer transactions and a 4.9% increase in the average purchase amount. Gross margin totaled $1.63 billion, or 42.2% of sales, versus $1.34 billion, or 39.1% of sales, the year before. Operating profit was $146.7 million compared with an operating loss of $27.3 million in the prior year.

PROSPECTS:

The Company is targeting full-year 2003 earnings of between $0.74 and $0.78 per share and sales growth in the high single-digit range. Results should benefit from increased advertising and the addition of furniture departments in about 145 new and existing stores. BLI plans to launch its first ever national television advertising campaign in April 2003. Meanwhile, the Company expects to open 60 net new stores, remodel more than 200 stores in eastern U.S. markets, and build a distribution center in Durant, Oklahoma during 2003.

ANNUAL FINANCIAL DATA:

FISCAL YEAR	TOT. REVS. ($mill.)	NET INC. ($mill.)	TOT. ASSETS ($mill.)	OPER. PROFIT %	NET PROFIT %	RET. ON EQUITY %	RET. ON ASSETS %	CURR. RATIO	EARN. PER SH.$	CASH FL. PER SH.$	TANG. BK. VAL.$	PRICE RANGE	AVG. P/E RATIO
p2/01/03	3,868.6	76.6						3.1	0.66			19.90 - 9.75	22.5
2/02/02	3,433.3	⑤d28.7	1,533.2	...	...	...	...	3.1	⑤d0.25	0.35	8.11	15.75 - 7.15	...
2/03/01	3,277.1	④98.3	1,585.4	5.7	3.0	10.6	6.2	3.4	④0.87	1.43	8.28	16.38 - 8.25	14.2
1/29/00	4,700.2	96.1	2,186.8	3.6	2.0	7.4	4.4	2.0	0.85	1.74	11.71	38.13 - 13.69	30.5
1/30/99	4,193.7	③109.4	2,042.5	4.9	2.6	9.3	5.4	2.9	③0.97	1.71	10.79	46.13 - 15.50	31.8
1/31/98	4,055.3	②85.9	1,746.4	5.7	2.1	8.3	4.9	2.1	②0.77	1.47	9.60	50.00 - 24.50	48.4
2/01/97	2,647.5	①113.3	1,330.5	7.4	4.3	16.6	8.5	2.0	①1.35	1.92	8.15	28.32 - 12.40	15.1
2/03/96	1,512.3	64.4	639.8	7.4	4.3	16.5	10.1	2.3	0.85	1.24	5.22	16.40 - 10.08	15.7
1/28/95	1,278.6	55.2	551.6	7.7	4.3	17.5	10.0	2.2	0.74	1.09	4.30	12.96 - 7.36	13.8
1/29/94	1,055.3	43.0	468.2	7.2	4.1	16.6	9.2	2.3	0.58	0.89	3.56	14.24 - 9.04	20.2

Statistics are as originally reported. Adj. for 5-for-4 stk. split, 6/97 & 12/96. ① Bef. $1.9 mil ($0.03/sh) extraord. chg.; bef. $8.6 mil ($0.10/sh) loss fr. discont. opers.; & bef. $18.9 mil ($0.22/sh) loss fr. disp. of opers. ② Incl. pre-tax merger-related chg. of $45.0 mil. ③ Bef. $12.6 mil ($0.11/sh) acctg. chg. ④ Bef. $479.0 mil ($4.26/sh) loss fr. discont. opers. ⑤ Bef. $8.5 mil ($0.07/sh) disc. oper. gain and incl. $50.0 mil ($0.44/sh) non-recurr. chg.

OFFICERS:
M. J. Potter, Chmn., Pres., C.E.O.
A. J. Bell, Vice-Chmn., C.A.O.
J. G. Naylor, Sr. V.P., C.F.O.
J. R. Cooper, V.P., Treas.

INVESTOR CONTACT: Joe R. Cooper, V.P., Treas., (614) 278-6622

PRINCIPAL OFFICE: 300 Phillipi Road, Columbus, OH 43228

TELEPHONE NUMBER: (614) 278-6800
FAX: (614) 278-6666
WEB: www.biglots.com
NO. OF EMPLOYEES: 16,966 full-time; 23,933 part-time
SHAREHOLDERS: 1,382
ANNUAL MEETING: In May
INCORPORATED: DE, 1983

INSTITUTIONAL HOLDINGS:
No. of Institutions: 222
Shares Held: 113,420,871
% Held: 97.7

INDUSTRY: Department stores (SIC: 5311)

TRANSFER AGENT(S): National City Bank, Cleveland, OH

BISYS GROUP, INC. (THE)

EXCH.	SYM.	REC. PRICE	P/E RATIO	YLD.	MKT. CAP.	RANGE (52-WK.)	'02 Y/E PR.
NYSE	BSG	15.64 (2/28/03)	16.5	...	$1.87 bill.	36.20 - 13.02	15.90

MEDIUM GRADE. THE COMPANY CONTINUES TO MAKE STRATEGIC ACQUISITIONS OF DISTRIBUTORS OF LIFE-RELATED INSURANCE PRODUCTS.

*7 YEAR PRICE SCORE 157.1   *12 MONTH PRICE SCORE 70.4

*NYSE COMPOSITE INDEX=100

INTERIM EARNINGS (Per Share):

Qtr.	Sept.	Dec.	Mar.	June
1999-00	0.11	0.14	0.18	0.20
2000-01	0.11	0.16	0.21	0.24
2001-02	0.16	0.22	0.27	0.30
2002-03	0.14	0.24	...	...

INTERIM DIVIDENDS (Per Share):

Amt.	Decl.	Ex.	Rec.	Pay.
100% STK	1/24/02	2/25/02	2/08/02	2/22/02

CAPITALIZATION (6/30/02):

	($000)	(%)
Long-Term Debt	300,000	30.0
Deferred Income Tax	16,670	1.7
Common & Surplus	682,618	68.3
Total	999,288	100.0

BUSINESS:

The BISYS Group, Inc. supplies services to over 20,000 financial institutions and corporate clients. BSG's investment services group (52.0% of 2002 revenue) provides distribution, administration, fund accounting and transfer agency services to over 350 clients representing approximately 1,900 investment funds. It also provides 401(k) plan administration services to financial companies. The insurance and education services group (25.2%) provides outsourcing for the distribution of life insurance, annuities, long-term care and disability products. It also provides training and education programs to enable securities brokers, insurance agents and securities traders to obtain licensure, advanced designations, and continuing education. The information services group (22.8%) provides information processing services to banking institutions through its TOTALPLUS^{SM} services and products.

RECENT DEVELOPMENTS:

For the second quarter ended 12/31/02, net income increased 8.7% to $28.7 million compared with $26.4 million in the equivalent quarter of 2001. Results for 2002 and 2001 included amortization of intangible assets of $4.4 million and $3.1 million, respectively. Total revenues advanced 11.1% to $233.1 million from $209.9 million a year earlier. Investment services revenue jumped 12.7% to $121.9 million, while insurance and education revenue grew 9.6% to $58.8 million. Information services revenue climbed 9.0% to $52.4 million. Operating earnings rose 8.6% to $50.0 million from $46.0 million the year before.

PROSPECTS:

On 12/26/02, the Company announced the acquisition of New York-based Career Brokerage, an insurance brokerage firm specializing in the wholesale distribution of life, annuity, disability and long-term care insurance products. The Company also recently acquired Washington-based Select Insurance Marketing Corporation, an insurance brokerage firm specializing in the wholesale distribution of long-term care insurance. Terms of the transactions were not disclosed. Both transactions support BSG's strategy to continually expand its portfolio of life-related insurance products and enhance its market presence and potential in strategic geographical areas.

ANNUAL FINANCIAL DATA:

FISCAL YEAR	TOT. REVS. ($000)	NET INC. ($000)	TOT. ASSETS ($000)	OPER. PROFIT %	NET PROFIT %	RET. ON EQUITY %	RET. ON ASSETS %	CURR. RATIO	EARN. PER SH. $	CASH FL. PER SH. $	TANG. BK. VAL. $	PRICE RANGE	AVG. P/E RATIO
6/30/02	865,705	③ 115,861	1,246,151	23.1	13.4	17.0	9.3	1.4	③ 0.94	1.26	...	36.20 - 13.02	26.2
6/30/01	701,757	① 85,120	1,003,201	20.9	12.1	16.1	8.5	2.3	① 0.71	1.06	0.01	32.61 - 21.25	38.2
6/30/00	571,401	① 70,204	601,051	20.3	12.3	19.4	11.7	1.5	① 0.62	0.89	1.56	27.88 - 11.81	32.3
6/30/99	472,676	①② 38,116	459,661	15.9	8.1	13.2	8.3	1.1	①② 0.34	0.55	0.86	16.38 - 10.34	39.3
6/30/98	386,344	① 40,024	334,101	16.0	10.4	16.8	12.0	2.4	① 0.37	0.50	1.27	13.06 - 8.13	29.0
6/30/97	318,988	① 40,751	265,085	20.6	12.8	21.2	15.4	2.4	① 0.39	0.50	1.15	10.53 - 6.97	22.5
6/30/96	247,061	① 18,024	214,625	12.1	7.3	12.6	8.4	1.6	① 0.18	0.28	0.63	10.84 - 6.81	49.0
6/30/95	200,527	① d6,484	...	...	...	...	...	...	① d0.07	0.05	...	7.78 - 4.38	...

Statistics are as originally reported. Adj. for stk. split: 2-for-1, 9/21/00 and 2/22/02. ① Incl. bus. divestiture, merger exps. & other chg. $4.2 mill., 6/01; credit $520,000, 6/00; chrg. $400,000, 6/99; $12.0 mill., 6/98; $1.5 mill., 6/97; $22.3 mill., 6/96; $28.3 mill., 6/95 ② Incl. acq. in-process research & develop. exp. $19.0 mill. ③ Incl. restr. chrg. of $6.5 mill.

OFFICERS:
L. J. Mangum, Chmn.
D. R. Sheehan, Pres., C.E.O.
A. C. Corbin, Exec. V.P., C.F.O.
INVESTOR CONTACT: Andy Corbin, Exec. V.P., C.F.O., (212) 907-6079
PRINCIPAL OFFICE: 90 Park Avenue, New York, NY 10016

TELEPHONE NUMBER: (212) 907-6000
FAX: (212) 907-6001
WEB: www.bisys.com
NO. OF EMPLOYEES: 4,800 (approx.)
SHAREHOLDERS: 1,141 (record); 22,500 (approx. benef.)
ANNUAL MEETING: In Nov.
INCORPORATED: DE, Aug., 1989

INSTITUTIONAL HOLDINGS:
No. of Institutions: 239
Shares Held: 104,100,313
% Held: 86.5
INDUSTRY: Data processing and preparation (SIC: 7374)
TRANSFER AGENT(S): Wachovia Bank, N.A., Charlotte, NC

BJ SERVICES COMPANY

EXCH.	SYM.	REC. PRICE	P/E RATIO	YLD.	MKT. CAP.	RANGE (52-WK.)	'02 Y/E PR.
NYSE	BJS	34.37 (2/28/03)	41.4	...	$5.52 bill.	39.49 - 23.00	32.31

UPPER MEDIUM GRADE. THE COMPANY EXPECTS THAT FULL-YEAR FISCAL 2003 EARNINGS WILL BE IN THE RANGE OF $1.05 TO $1.15 PER SHARE.

*7 YEAR PRICE SCORE 162.6   ***12 MONTH PRICE SCORE 109.7**

*NYSE COMPOSITE INDEX=100

INTERIM EARNINGS (Per Share):

Qtr.	Dec.	Mar.	June	Sept.
1996-97	0.16	0.08	0.16	0.23
1997-98	0.29	0.24	0.22	0.01
1998-99	d0.05	d0.08	d0.12	0.03
1999-00	0.13	0.18	0.16	0.25
2000-01	0.38	0.48	0.63	0.61
2001-02	0.42	0.24	0.17	0.21
2002-03	0.21	...	...	...

INTERIM DIVIDENDS (Per Share):

Amt.	Decl.	Ex.	Rec.	Pay.
100% STK	3/22/01	6/01/01	5/17/01	5/31/01

CAPITALIZATION (9/30/02):

	($000)	(%)
Long-Term Debt	489,062	25.5
Deferred Income Tax	9,213	0.5
Common & Surplus	1,418,628	74.0
Total	1,916,903	100.0

BUSINESS:

BJ Services Company is a provider of pressure pumping and other oilfield services for the worldwide petroleum industry. Pressure pumping services consist of cementing and stimulation services used in the completion of new oil and natural gas wells and in remedial work on existing wells, both onshore and offshore. Other oilfield services include completion tools, completion fluids and tubular services provided to the oil and natural gas exploration and production industry, commissioning and inspection services provided to refineries, pipelines and offshore platforms, and specialty chemical services. During the year ended 9/30/02, BJS generated 86.4% of its revenue from pressure pumping services and 13.6% from other oilfield services.

RECENT DEVELOPMENTS:

For the three months ended 12/31/02, net income fell 50.0% to $33.5 million compared with $66.9 million in the corresponding year-earlier period. Revenues declined 7.2% to $473.1 million. U.S./Mexico pressure pumping revenue slid 22.4% to $212.0 million due to a 16.0% decline in drilling activity, a 10.0% drop in workover activity and price deterioration. International pressure pumping revenue fell 4.3% to $178.9 million. However, other oilfield services revenue rose 64.5% to $82.3 million from $50.0 million the year before. BJS attributed the jump in other oilfield services revenue primarily to the addition of completion fluids and completion tools service lines acquired with OSCA, Inc. in May 2002. In addition, revenues and pipeline services, tubular services and production chemicals increased 13.0%, 14.0%, and 3.0%, respectively, versus the prior year.

PROSPECTS:

The Company's results reflect market activity declines and price deterioration in U.S./Mexico pressure pumping services, as evidenced by the drop in operating margins for the quarter ended 12/31/02 to 11.5% from 20.6% the previous year. Although BJS remains optimistic about increased activity in the U.S. gas market based on fundamentals, it is now projecting that activity will continue at the present lackluster levels until late Spring 2003. Consequently, BJS now believes that full-year fiscal 2003 earnings will range between $1.05 and $1.15 per share.

ANNUAL FINANCIAL DATA:

FISCAL YEAR	TOT. REVS. ($mill.)	NET INC. ($mill.)	TOT. ASSETS ($mill.)	OPER. PROFIT %	NET PROFIT %	RET. ON EQUITY %	RET. ON ASSETS %	CURR. RATIO	EARN. PER SH. $	CASH FL. PER SH. $	TANG. BK. VAL. $	PRICE RANGE	AVG. P/E RATIO
9/30/02	1,865.8	166.5	2,442.4	14.1	8.9	11.7	6.8	1.8	1.04	1.69	3.48	39.49 - 23.00	30.0
9/30/01	2,233.5	349.3	1,985.4	24.0	15.6	25.5	17.6	1.9	2.09	2.72	5.57	43.10 - 14.55	13.8
9/30/00	1,555.4	118.0	1,785.2	12.6	7.6	10.1	6.6	1.5	0.70	1.30	4.20	38.38 - 19.06	41.0
9/30/99	1,131.3	d29.7	1,824.8	...	...	...	...	1.0	d0.21	0.50	2.72	21.72 - 6.72	...
9/30/98	1,527.5	117.4	1,743.7	12.9	7.7	13.0	6.7	0.9	0.72	1.29	2.82	21.91 - 5.94	19.3
9/30/97	1,466.6	107.9	1,726.8	12.4	7.4	11.2	6.2	1.2	0.66	1.20	2.90	22.69 - 9.56	24.6
9/30/96	965.3	40.5	1,709.2	7.8	4.2	4.8	2.4	1.4	0.32	0.85	1.80	13.13 - 6.28	30.8
9/30/95	633.7	9.9	989.7	3.2	1.6	2.1	1.0	1.3	0.12	0.61	2.45	7.38 - 3.88	48.9
9/30/94	434.5	10.8	410.1	4.3	2.5	5.7	2.6	1.3	0.17	0.58	2.69	5.63 - 4.06	28.5
9/30/93	394.4	14.6	369.5	5.1	3.7	7.8	3.9	1.6	0.24	0.63	2.67	7.91 - 3.41	24.1

Statistics are as originally reported. Adj. for stk. splits, 3-for-1, 2/98; 2-for-1, 5/01. ☐ Incl. nonrecurr. pre-tax chrgs. of $39.7 mill.

OFFICERS:
J. W. Stewart, Chmn., Pres., C.E.O.
T. M. Whichard, V.P., C.F.O.
J. Smith, Treas.
INVESTOR CONTACT: Robert C. Coons, Corp. Comm. Mgr., (713) 462-4239
PRINCIPAL OFFICE: 5500 Northwest Central Drive, Houston, TX 77092

TELEPHONE NUMBER: (713) 462-4239
FAX: (713) 895-5603
WEB: www.bjservices.com
NO. OF EMPLOYEES: 11,130
SHAREHOLDERS: 3,175 (approx.)
ANNUAL MEETING: In Jan.
INCORPORATED: DE, 1990

INSTITUTIONAL HOLDINGS:
No. of Institutions: 335
Shares Held: 148,486,789
% Held: 94.2
INDUSTRY: Oil and gas field services, nec (SIC: 1389)
TRANSFER AGENT(S): The Bank of New York, New York, NY

BJ'S WHOLESALE CLUB, INC.

EXCH.	SYM.	REC. PRICE	P/E RATIO	YLD.	MKT. CAP.	RANGE (52-WK.)	'02 Y/E PR.
NYSE	BJ	13.98 (2/28/03)	7.5	...	$1.00 bill.	47.20 - 13.36	18.30

UPPER MEDIUM GRADE. THE COMPANY IS TARGETING EARNINGS OF $1.25 TO $1.35 PER SHARE, BEFORE ONE-TIME CHARGES, IN THE CURRENT FISCAL YEAR.

MERGENT

TRADING VOLUME
Thousand Shares

1989 1990 1991 1992 1993 1994 1995 1996 1997 1998 1999 2000 2001 2002 2003

*7 YEAR PRICE SCORE N/A   ***12 MONTH PRICE SCORE 59.5**

*NYSE COMPOSITE INDEX=100

INTERIM EARNINGS (Per Share):

Qtr.	Apr.	July	Oct.	Jan.
1997-98	---------	0.91	---------	
1998-99	0.14	0.24	0.19	0.50
1999-00	0.19	0.34	0.31	0.63
2000-01	0.24	0.42	0.37	0.74
2001-02	0.31	0.49	d0.46	0.77
2002-03	0.32	0.50	0.33	0.71

INTERIM DIVIDENDS (Per Share):

Amt.	Decl.	Ex.	Rec.	Pay.
		No dividends paid.		

CAPITALIZATION (2/2/02):

	($000)	(%)
Capital Lease Obligations..	63,700	8.5
Common & Surplus	686,567	91.5
Total	750,267	100.0

BUSINESS:

BJ's Wholesale Club, Inc. sells brand name food and general merchandise at discounted prices through warehouse clubs in the eastern United States. As of 2/1/03, BJ operated 140 clubs and two distribution centers in 16 states. In addition, the Company has gas stations in operation at 68 of its clubs. BJ sells food items such as frozen foods, fresh meats, dairy products, dry grocery items, fresh produce and flowers, canned goods, and household paper products and cleaning supplies. General merchandise includes office supplies and equipment, consumer electronics, small appliances, auto accessories, tires, jewelry, housewares, health and beauty aids, computer software, books, greeting cards, apparel, tools, toys, and seasonal items. The customers at the Company's warehouse clubs are generally limited to members who pay an annual fee of $40.

RECENT DEVELOPMENTS:

For the year ended 2/1/03, the Company reported income from continuing operations of $145.8 million compared with income from continuing operations of $83.8 million a year earlier. Results included an after-tax gain of $12.0 million and an after-tax charge of $63.0 million in fiscal 2002 and fiscal 2001, respectively, for contingent lease obligations related to House2Home, Inc., which filed for bankruptcy on 11/7/01. Total revenues increased 12.2% to $5.86 billion from $5.22 billion the previous year. Comparable-club sales were up 2.0% year-over-year.

PROSPECTS:

The Company is targeting earnings in the range of $1.25 to $1.35 per share, before one-time charges, in the current fiscal year. Meanwhile, results are being negatively affected by increased competition and weak economic conditions. The Company has lowered prices on dairy products and produce to help spur sales of these items. In an effort to boost sales of computers, electronics and housewares, the Company plans to reduce prices and increase its selection of higher-quality merchandise.

ANNUAL FINANCIAL DATA:

FISCAL YEAR	TOT. REVS. ($mill.)	NET INC. ($mill.)	TOT. ASSETS ($mill.)	OPER. PROFIT %	NET PROFIT %	RET. ON EQUITY %	RET. ON ASSETS %	CURR. RATIO	EARN. PER SH.$	CASH FL. PER SH.$	TANG. BK. VAL.$	PRICE RANGE	AVG. P/E RATIO
p2/01/03	5,859.7	③ 145.8							③ 2.05			48.19 - 14.42	15.3
2/02/02	5,279.7	② 82.3	1,421.9	4.4	1.6	12.0	5.8	1.2	② 1.11	1.95	9.59	57.24 - 36.44	42.2
2/03/01	4,932.1	131.5	1,233.7	4.2	2.7	19.8	10.7	1.3	1.77	2.51	9.18	41.38 - 26.75	19.2
1/29/00	4,206.2	111.1	1,073.4	4.2	2.6	19.2	10.4	1.3	1.47	2.09	7.85	38.75 - 20.25	20.1
1/30/99	3,552.2	① 81.8	907.6	3.8	2.3	16.9	9.0	1.3	① 1.07	1.61	6.57	23.16 - 14.63	17.7
1/31/98	3,226.5	68.3	811.6	3.7	2.1	15.3	8.4	1.4	0.91	1.40	5.95	16.00 - 13.00	16.0
1/25/97	2,922.8	53.6	737.2	3.6	1.8	19.5	7.3	1.2	...	...	4.21	...	...
1/27/96	2,529.6	41.6	676.7	3.3	1.6	18.7	6.1	1.3	...	...	3.39	...	...
1/28/95	2,293.1	30.9	...	2.8	1.3	...	...	...	...	...	...	...	...

Statistics are as originally reported. Adj. for 2-for-1 stk. split, 3/99. ① Bef. $19.3 mil ($0.25/sh) acctg. chg. ② Incl. $63.8 mil after-tax chg. related to losses from House2Home, Inc. leases. ③ Bef. $14.9 mil ($0.21/sh) loss fr. disc. opers. & incl. $12.0 mil after-tax gain related to House2Home leases.

OFFICERS:
H. J. Zarkin, Chmn.
M. T. Wedge, Pres., C.E.O.
F. D. Forward, Exec. V.P., C.F.O.

INVESTOR CONTACT: Cathy Maloney, V.P., Inv. Rel., (508) 651-6650

PRINCIPAL OFFICE: One Mercer Road, Natick, MA 01760

TELEPHONE NUMBER: (508) 651-7400
FAX: (508) 651-6114
WEB: www.bjs.com

NO. OF EMPLOYEES: 15,800 (approx.)

SHAREHOLDERS: 2,300 (approx.)

ANNUAL MEETING: In May

INCORPORATED: DE, July, 1997

INSTITUTIONAL HOLDINGS:
No. of Institutions: 232
Shares Held: 63,658,773
% Held: 91.7

INDUSTRY: Variety stores (SIC: 5331)

TRANSFER AGENT(S): EquiServe Trust Company, N.A., Jersey City, NJ

BLACK & DECKER CORPORATION

EXCH.	SYM.	REC. PRICE	P/E RATIO	YLD.	MKT. CAP.	RANGE (52-WK.)	'02 Y/E PR.
NYSE	BDK	36.70 (2/28/03)	12.9	1.4%	$2.92 bill.	50.50 - 34.24	42.89

MEDIUM GRADE. THE COMPANY IS MAKING EXCELLENT PROGRESS WITH ITS RESTRUCTURING PROGRAM, INITIATED IN EARLY 2002.

*7 YEAR PRICE SCORE 108.9   ***12 MONTH PRICE SCORE 94.6**
*NYSE COMPOSITE INDEX=100

INTERIM EARNINGS (Per Share):

Qtr.	Mar.	June	Sept.	Dec.
1997	0.27	0.47	0.60	1.00
1998	d10.21	0.61	0.72	1.03
1999	0.44	0.80	0.85	1.31
2000	0.69	0.97	1.03	0.64
2001	0.40	0.57	0.57	d0.16
2002	0.41	0.81	0.68	0.94

INTERIM DIVIDENDS (Per Share):

Amt.	Decl.	Ex.	Rec.	Pay.
0.12Q	2/14/02	3/12/02	3/14/02	3/28/02
0.12Q	4/30/02	6/12/02	6/14/02	6/28/02
0.12Q	7/18/02	9/11/02	9/13/02	9/27/02
0.12Q	10/23/02	12/11/02	12/13/02	12/27/02
0.12Q	2/13/03	3/12/03	3/14/03	3/28/03

Indicated div.: $0.48 (Div. Reinv. Plan)

CAPITALIZATION (12/31/01):

	($000)	(%)
Long-Term Debt	1,191,400	54.1
Deferred Income Tax	261,100	11.8
Common & Surplus	751,000	34.1
Total	2,203,500	100.0

BUSINESS:

Black & Decker Corporation is a global marketer and manufacturer of products used in and around the home and for commercial applications. The Power Tools and Accessories (PT&A) segment (71.1% of 2002 sales) manufactures and sells consumer and professional power tools and accessories, electric lawn and garden tools, and electric cleaning and lighting products, and offers product service. It also sells plumbing products to customers outside the U.S. and Canada. The Hardware and Home Improvement segment (17.4%) manufactures and sells security hardware and manufactures plumbing products as well as sells plumbing products to customers in the U.S. and Canada. The Fastening and Assembly Systems segment (11.5%) manufactures and sells fastening and assembly systems.

RECENT DEVELOPMENTS:

For the year ended 12/31/02, net income more than doubled to $229.7 million compared with $108.0 million in 2001. Results for 2002 and 2001 included restructuring and exit costs of $50.7 million and $99.8 million, respectively. Sales rose 3.5% to $4.39 billion from $4.25 billion a year earlier, supported by sales increased across most of the Company's businesses in spite of weak economic conditions. Moreover, sales were particularly stronger in the Company's North American Power Tools and Accessories businesses.

PROSPECTS:

The Company is making excellent progress with its restructuring program, initiated in January 2002. The cost of the program is now expected to be about $170.0 million, and generate $100.0 million in annual savings by 2004. In addition to the net savings of $25.0 million incurred in 2002, the program is expected to generate incremental savings of about $35.0 million in 2003 and $40.0 million in 2004. Further, BDK will implement a plan to revive sales and profitability at Price Pfister®. In fiscal 2003, the Company expects sales growth of a low single-digit rate, and diluted earnings in the range of $3.45 to $3.65 per share.

ANNUAL FINANCIAL DATA:

FISCAL YEAR	TOT. REVS. ($mill.)	NET INC. ($mill.)	TOT. ASSETS ($mill.)	OPER. PROFIT %	NET PROFIT %	RET. ON EQUITY %	RET. ON ASSETS %	CURR. RATIO	EARN. PER SH. $	CASH FL. PER SH. $	TANG. BK. VAL. $	DIV. PER SH. $	PRICE RANGE	AVG. P/E RATIO	AVG. YIELD %
p12/31/02	4,394.0	⑦229.7	...	...	...	...	...	...	⑦2.84	...	...	0.48	50.50 - 35.00	15.1	1.1
12/31/01	4,333.1	⑦108.0	4,014.2	5.7	2.5	14.4	2.7	1.8	⑦1.33	3.30	0.51	0.48	46.95 - 28.26	28.3	1.3
12/31/00	4,560.8	⑦282.0	4,089.7	11.0	6.2	40.7	6.9	1.2	⑦3.34	5.28	...	0.48	52.38 - 27.56	12.0	1.2
12/31/99	4,520.5	⑧300.3	4,012.7	11.9	6.6	37.5	7.5	1.2	⑧3.40	5.21	0.66	0.48	64.63 - 41.00	15.5	0.9
12/31/98	4,559.9	⑤d754.8	3,852.5	...	...	...	...	1.3	⑤d8.22	d6.53	...	0.48	65.50 - 37.94	...	0.9
12/31/97	4,940.5	227.2	5,360.7	9.9	4.6	12.7	4.2	1.5	2.35	4.57	...	0.48	43.44 - 29.63	15.5	1.3
12/31/96	4,914.4	⑥159.2	5,153.5	7.3	3.2	9.8	3.1	1.2	⑥1.64	4.09	...	0.48	44.25 - 29.00	22.3	1.3
②12/31/95	4,766.1	③216.5	5,545.3	8.9	4.5	15.2	3.9	1.2	③2.33	4.81	...	0.40	38.13 - 22.88	13.1	1.3
12/31/94	5,248.3	127.4	5,433.7	7.5	2.4	10.9	2.3	1.0	1.37	3.91	...	0.40	25.75 - 17.00	15.6	1.9
12/31/93	4,882.2	①95.2	5,310.6	6.9	1.9	9.1	1.8	1.2	①1.00	3.40	...	0.40	22.25 - 16.63	19.4	2.1

Statistics are as originally reported. ① Incl. pre-tax gain of $6.3 mill.; bef. acctg. change chrg. $29.2 mill. ② Reflects sale of PRC Inc. ③ Bef. extraord. chrg. of $30.9 mill. and inc. fr. disc. opers. of $38.4 mill. ④ Excl. inc. fr. discont. oper. of $70.4 mill.; incl. non-recurr. chrg. $91.3 mill. ⑤ Incl. gain of $114.5 million before tax; a write-off chrg. of $900.0 mill. for goodwill; and restruct. chrg. of $164.7 mill. ⑥ Incl. nonrecurr. after-tax gain of $13.1 million from the sale of a business. ⑦ Incl. restruct. and exit costs of $50.7 mill., 2002; $99.8 mill., 2001; $39.1 mill., 2000 and a gain on the sale of a business of $20.1 mill., 2000.

OFFICERS:
N. D. Archibald, Chmn., Pres., C.E.O.
M. D. Mangan, Sr. V.P., C.F.O.
M. M. Rothleitner, V.P., Treas.

INVESTOR CONTACT: V. P. Shelley, Mgr.- Investor Relations, (410) 716-3979

PRINCIPAL OFFICE: 701 East Joppa Road, Towson, MD 21286

TELEPHONE NUMBER: (410) 716-3900
FAX: (410) 716-2610
WEB: www.bdk.com

NO. OF EMPLOYEES: 22,700 (approx.)

SHAREHOLDERS: 15,923

ANNUAL MEETING: In Apr.

INCORPORATED: MD, Sept., 1910

INSTITUTIONAL HOLDINGS:
No. of Institutions: 305
Shares Held: 68,442,296
% Held: 85.0

INDUSTRY: Power-driven handtools (SIC: 3546)

TRANSFER AGENT(S): EquiServe, Jersey City, NJ

BLACK HILLS CORPORATION

EXCH.	SYM.	REC. PRICE	P/E RATIO	YLD.	MKT. CAP.	RANGE (52-WK.)	'02 Y/E PR.	DIV. ACH.
NYSE	BKH	23.63 (2/28/03)	10.3	5.1%	$0.64 bill.	36.90 - 18.35	26.52	31 yrs.

LOWER MEDIUM GRADE. THE COMPANY EXPECTS TO DOUBLE ITS OIL AND GAS RESERVES WITH THE ACQUISI-TION OF MALLON RESOURCES.

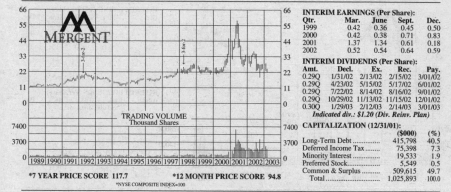

TRADING VOLUME
Thousand Shares

7 YEAR PRICE SCORE 117.7   *12 MONTH PRICE SCORE 94.8*

NYSE COMPOSITE INDEX=100

INTERIM EARNINGS (Per Share):

Qtr.	Mar.	June	Sept.	Dec.
1999	0.42	0.36	0.45	0.50
2000	0.42	0.38	0.71	0.83
2001	1.37	1.34	0.61	0.18
2002	0.52	0.54	0.64	0.59

INTERIM DIVIDENDS (Per Share):

Amt.	Decl.	Ex.	Rec.	Pay.
0.29Q	1/31/02	2/13/02	2/15/02	3/01/02
0.29Q	4/23/02	5/15/02	5/17/02	6/01/02
0.29Q	7/22/02	8/14/02	8/16/02	9/01/02
0.29Q	10/29/02	11/13/02	11/15/02	12/01/02
0.30Q	1/29/03	2/12/03	2/14/03	3/01/03

Indicated div.: $1.20 (Div. Reinv. Plan)

CAPITALIZATION (12/31/01):

	($000)	(%)
Long-Term Debt	415,798	40.5
Deferred Income Tax	75,398	7.3
Minority Interest	19,533	1.9
Preferred Stock	5,549	0.5
Common & Surplus	509,615	49.7
Total	1,025,893	100.0

BUSINESS:

Black Hills Corporation is an energy and communications company with three business groups. Black Hills Energy, Inc. (54.0% of 2002 revenues) is the integrated energy unit that generates electricity, produces natural gas, oil and coal and markets energy. BHE produces coal natural gas and crude oil primarily in the Rocky Mountain region, which it sells nationwide. Black Hills Power, Inc. (38.3%) is an

electric utility serving customers in western South Dakota, northeastern Wyoming and southeastern Montana. Black Hills FiberCom, LLC (7.7%) provides broadband communications to residential and business customers in Rapid City and the northern Black Hills region of South Dakota. Broadband offerings include bundled telephone, high speed Internet and cable entertainment services.

RECENT DEVELOPMENTS:

For the year ended 12/31/02, the Company reported income from continuing operations of $63.2 million, before an accounting change gain of $896,000, compared with $87.6 million in the previous year. Earnings for 2002 included an after-tax gain of $1.9 million related to the collection of receivables reserved in prior periods. Earnings for 2001 included non-recurring items that resulted in a net after-tax gain of $700,000. Earnings excluded a loss of $2.6 million

in 2002 and a gain of $493,000 in 2001 from discontinued operations. Total revenues declined 8.2% to $423.9 million from $461.9 million a year earlier. Revenues from the Integrated Energy group decreased to $229.1 million from $229.3 million in 2001, while Electric Utility group revenues fell 23.6% to $162.2 million. However, Communications group revenues jumped 61.3% to $32.7 million. Coal production increased 15.0% to 4.1 million tons.

PROSPECTS:

During 2002, the Company's natural gas and oil production grew to a record 7.40 billion cubic feet of gas equivalents (BCFE) and gas and oil reserves grew to 57.80 BCFE. Looking ahead, BKH expects to double its reserves with the acquisition of Mallon Resources, a natural gas and oil

company, scheduled to be completed in the first quarter of 2003. Separately, the Company's 90 megawatt coal-fired Wygen power plant in Wyoming is in testing and on schedule to become operational. The Wygen plant will use approximately 500,000 tons of BKH's coal annually.

ANNUAL FINANCIAL DATA:

FISCAL YEAR	TOT. REVS. ($mill.)	NET INC. ($mill.)	TOT. ASSETS ($mill.)	OPER. PROFIT %	NET PROFIT %	NET INC./ NET PROP. %	NET INC./ TOT. CAP. %	RET. ON EQUITY %	ACCUM. DEPR./ GROSS PROP. %	EARN. PER SH. $	TANG. BK. VAL. $	DIV. PER SH. $	DIV. PAYOUT %	PRICE RANGE		AVG. P/E RATIO	AVG. YIELD %
p12/31/02	③ 423.9	② 63.2			14.9					② 2.33		1.16	49.8	36.90 -	18.35	11.9	4.2
12/31/01	1,558.6	88.1	1,658.8	10.9	5.7	16.3	8.6	17.1	44.5	3.42	18.95	1.12	32.7	58.50 -	26.00	12.4	2.7
12/31/00	1,623.8	52.8	1,320.3	7.1	3.3	6.7	7.7	18.7	28.9	2.37	12.14	1.08	45.6	46.06 -	20.44	14.0	3.2
12/31/99	791.9	37.1	674.8	7.8	4.7	8.0	8.5	17.1	37.3	1.73	10.14	1.04	60.1	26.50 -	20.31	13.5	4.4
12/31/98	679.3	① 25.8	559.4	7.2	3.8	6.6	6.1	12.5	37.1	① 1.19	9.52	1.00	84.0	27.94 -	20.69	20.4	4.1
12/31/97	313.7	32.4	508.7	18.8	10.3	8.1	7.7	15.8	33.0	1.49	9.46	0.95	63.5	24.29 -	17.50	14.0	4.5
12/31/96	162.6	30.3	467.4	33.4	18.6	7.6	7.4	15.7	31.1	1.40	8.91	0.92	65.7	19.17 -	15.15	12.3	5.4
12/31/95	149.8	25.6	448.8	28.1	17.1	6.5	6.5	14.0	29.5	1.19	8.43	0.89	75.3	17.42 -	13.17	12.9	5.8
12/31/94	145.4	23.8	436.9	26.7	16.4	6.6	6.9	13.6	30.2	1.11	8.13	0.88	79.5	15.17 -	11.83	12.2	6.5
12/31/93	139.4	22.9	352.9	27.1	16.5	8.2	7.9	13.7	33.9	1.11	7.85	0.85	77.1	18.83 -	14.58	15.1	5.1

Statistics are as originally reported. Adj. for 3-for-2 stk. split, 3/98 ① Inc. non-recurr. chrg. $8.8 mill. ② Bef. acctg. change gain of $896,000 and loss fr. discont. opers. of $2.6 mill. ③ Reflects new reporting requirement to show trading rev. net of exp.

OFFICERS:
D. P. Landguth, Chmn., C.E.O.
E. E. Hoyt, Pres., C.O.O.
M. T. Thies, Sr. V.P., C.F.O.
INVESTOR CONTACT: Dale T. Jahr, Dir., Investor Relations, (605) 721-2326
PRINCIPAL OFFICE: 625 Ninth Street, Rapid City, SD 57701

TELEPHONE NUMBER: (605) 721-1700
FAX: (605) 721-2599
WEB: www.blackhillscorp.com
NO. OF EMPLOYEES: 785
SHAREHOLDERS: 5,509 (record); 16,000 (approx. benef.)
ANNUAL MEETING: In May
INCORPORATED: SD, Aug., 1941

INSTITUTIONAL HOLDINGS:
No. of Institutions: 144
Shares Held: 11,606,514
% Held: 43.1

INDUSTRY: Electric services (SIC: 4911)

TRANSFER AGENT(S): Wells Fargo Shareowner Services, South St. Paul, MN

BLACKROCK, INC.

EXCH.	SYM.	REC. PRICE	P/E RATIO	YLD.	MKT. CAP.	RANGE (52-WK.)	'02 Y/E PR.
NYSE	BLK	41.60 (2/28/03)	20.4	...	$2.68 bill.	47.60 - 33.55	39.40

UPPER MEDIUM GRADE. THE COMPANY EXPECTS DILUTED EARNINGS PER SHARE RANGING FROM $0.52 TO $0.54 FOR THE FIRST QUARTER OF 2003 AND BETWEEN $2.28 AND $2.38 FOR THE FULL YEAR.

INTERIM EARNINGS (Per Share):

Qtr.	Mar.	June	Sept.	Dec.
1999	0.22	0.25	0.30	0.27
2000	0.30	0.32	0.35	0.38
2001	0.39	0.40	0.42	0.44
2002	0.48	0.53	0.51	0.52

INTERIM DIVIDENDS (Per Share):

Amt.	Decl.	Ex.	Rec.	Pay.
		No dividends paid.		

TRADING VOLUME
Thousand Shares

*7 YEAR PRICE SCORE N/A   *12 MONTH PRICE SCORE 106.9
*NYSE COMPOSITE INDEX=100

CAPITALIZATION (12/31/01):

	($000)	(%)
Common & Surplus	486,117	100.0
Total	486,117	100.0

BUSINESS:

BlackRock, Inc. is an investment management firm with assets under management of $272.80 billion as of 12/31/02. BLK manages assets on behalf of institutional and individual investors worldwide through a variety of equity, fixed income, liquidity and alternative investment separate accounts and mutual funds, including BlackRock Funds and BlackRock Provident Institutional Funds. In addition, BLK provides risk management and investment system services to institutional investors under the BlackRock Solu-

tions name. Clients are served from BLK's headquarters in New York City, as well as offices in Wilmington, Delaware; San Francisco, California; Boston, Massachusetts; Edinburgh, Scotland; Tokyo, Japan; and Hong Kong. BlackRock is a member of The PNC Financial Services Group, a diversified financial services organization. As of 6/30/02, BLK was approximately 69.0%-owned by PNC, 15.0%-owned by BlackRock employees, and 16.0%-owned by the public.

RECENT DEVELOPMENTS:

For the year ended 12/31/02, net income increased 24.0% to $133.2 million compared with $107.4 million the year before. Earnings for 2002 and 2001 included amortization of intangible assets of $824,000 and $10.5 million. Total revenue improved 8.2% to $577.0 million from $533.1

million in the prior year. This improvement primarily reflected higher separate account revenue and increased other income, partially offset by a decrease in mutual fund revenue. Operating income grew 26.4% to $215.1 million.

PROSPECTS:

In November 2002, the Company completed the acquisition of Cyllenius Capital Management, an all-cap growth equity hedge fund manager based in Boston. Cyllenius manages over $100.0 million on behalf of institutional and high net worth investors. Separately, net new business continues to

be strong, including $2.10 billion from international clients in 2002. Looking ahead, the Company expects diluted earnings per share ranging from $0.52 to $0.54 for the first quarter of 2003 and between $2.28 and $2.38 for the full year.

ANNUAL FINANCIAL DATA:

FISCAL YEAR	TOT. REVS. ($000)	NET INC. ($000)	TOT. ASSETS ($000)	OPER. PROFIT %	NET PROFIT %	RET. ON EQUITY %	RET. ON ASSETS %	CURR. RATIO	EARN. PER SH. $	CASH FL. PER SH. $	TANG. BK. VAL. $	PRICE RANGE	AVG. P/E RATIO
p12/31/02	576,977	133,249	864,188						2.04			47.60 - 33.55	19.9
12/31/01	533,144	107,434	684,478	31.9	20.2	22.1	15.7	1.5	1.65	2.06	4.72	44.50 - 30.76	22.8
12/31/00	476,872	87,361	537,003	30.0	18.3	23.7	16.3	1.7	1.35	1.66	2.75	48.00 - 15.00	23.3
12/31/99	380,981	59,417	447,582	29.1	15.6	21.2	13.3	1.4	1.04	1.35	1.35	19.38 - 12.50	15.3
12/31/98	339,482	35,615	440,784	23.4	10.5	33.5	8.1	0.7	0.66	0.90	...	...	...
12/31/97	205,473	22,086	335,507	27.2	10.7	49.1	6.6	0.4	0.49	0.76	...	...	...

Statistics are as originally reported.

OFFICERS:
L. D. Fink, Chmn., C.E.O.
R. Schlosstein, Pres.
P. L. Audet, C.F.O.

INVESTOR CONTACT: Paul L. Audet, Investor Relations, (212) 409-3555

PRINCIPAL OFFICE: 40 East 52nd Street, New York, NY 10022

TELEPHONE NUMBER: (212) 754-5300
FAX: (212) 754-3123
WEB: www.blackrock.com
NO. OF EMPLOYEES: 804
SHAREHOLDERS: 313 (class A); 56 (class B)
ANNUAL MEETING: In May
INCORPORATED: DE, 1998

INSTITUTIONAL HOLDINGS:
No. of Institutions: 90
Shares Held: 13,524,969
% Held: 20.9

INDUSTRY: Investment offices, nec (SIC: 6726)

TRANSFER AGENT(S): Mellon Investor Services, L.L.C., Ridgefield Park, NJ

BLOCK (H & R), INC.

EXCH.	SYM.	REC. PRICE	P/E RATIO	YLD.	MKT. CAP.	RANGE (52-WK.)	'02 Y/E PR.
NYSE.	HRB	40.57 (2/28/03)	13.8	1.8%	$7.35 bill.	53.50 - 29.00	40.20

UPPER MEDIUM GRADE. THE COMPANY EXPECTS EARNINGS FOR THE CURRENT FISCAL YEAR TO BE IN THE RANGE OF $3.10 TO $3.25 PER SHARE.

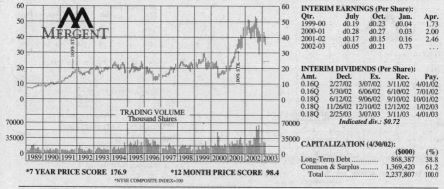

*7 YEAR PRICE SCORE 176.9   *12 MONTH PRICE SCORE 98.4

*NYSE COMPOSITE INDEX=100

INTERIM EARNINGS (Per Share):

Qtr.	July	Oct.	Jan.	Apr.
1999-00	d0.19	d0.23	d0.04	1.73
2000-01	d0.28	d0.27	0.03	2.00
2001-02	d0.17	d0.15	0.16	2.46
2002-03	d0.05	d0.21	0.73	...

INTERIM DIVIDENDS (Per Share):

Amt.	Decl.	Ex.	Rec.	Pay.
0.16Q	2/27/02	3/07/02	3/11/02	4/01/02
0.16Q	5/30/02	6/06/02	6/10/02	7/01/02
0.18Q	6/12/02	9/06/02	9/10/02	10/01/02
0.18Q	11/26/02	12/10/02	12/12/02	1/02/03
0.18Q	2/25/03	3/07/03	3/11/03	4/01/03

Indicated div.: $0.72

CAPITALIZATION (4/30/02):

	($000)	(%)
Long-Term Debt	868,387	38.8
Common & Surplus	1,369,420	61.2
Total	2,237,807	100.0

BUSINESS:

H&R Block, Inc. is a diversified company offering tax services and financial advice, investment and mortgage products and services and business accounting and consulting services. In fiscal 2002, H&R Block Tax Services Inc. (57.7% of 2002 revenues) provided tax return preparation and filing services for about 23.0 million customers through over 10,400 offices worldwide and with software and on-line services. H&R Block Financial Advisors (7.6%) provide consumers with financial planning and investment products. Option One Mortgage Corporation and H&R Block Mortgage Corporation (22.2%) offer a range of home mortgage products and services. RSM McGladrey Inc. and HRB Business Services Inc. offer accounting, tax and consulting services primarily for mid-sized businesses. On 12/1/99, HRB acquired Olde Financial Corp. and Financial Marketing Services, Inc.

RECENT DEVELOPMENTS:

For the third quarter ended 1/31/03, net earnings surged to $132.3 million from $29.6 million in the equivalent prior-year quarter. Total revenues advanced 30.7% to $958.4 million compared with $733.5 million a year earlier. U.S. tax operations revenue increased 8.5% to $403.6 million, while international tax operations revenue climbed 10.1% to $8.8 million. Mortgage operations revenue shot up 120.8% to $397.0 million, primarily due to a $130.9 million gain on the sale of mortgage residual assets. Investment services revenue fell 21.3% to $48.0 million, and business services revenue declined 5.9% to $100.7 million.

PROSPECTS:

HRB's strategy to enhance client service while controlling costs coupled with the strength of its mortgage operations may result in better-than-expected earnings for the current fiscal year. HRB expects earnings to be in the range of $3.10 to $3.25 per share, up 34.2% to 40.7% versus prior-year earnings of $2.31 per share. In addition, revenues are likely to exceed HRB's target growth range of 10.0% to 15.0% for the year. Separately, for the tax filing season through 2/15/03, results were weaker than expected for HRB's retail offices and showed slower growth across all filing channels. However, early results were negatively affected by challenging weather in some parts of the U.S.

ANNUAL FINANCIAL DATA:

FISCAL YEAR	TOT. REVS. ($mill.)	NET INC. ($mill.)	TOT. ASSETS ($mill.)	OPER. PROFIT %	NET PROFIT %	RET. ON EQUITY %	RET. ON ASSETS %	CURR. RATIO	EARN. PER SH.$	CASH FL. PER SH.$	TANG. BK. VAL.$	DIV. PER SH.$	PRICE RANGE	AVG. P/E RATIO	AVG. YIELD %
4/30/02	3,317.7	434.4	4,230.8	21.6	13.1	31.7	10.3	1.2	2.31	3.13	1.45	0.61	46.37 - 18.31	14.0	1.9
4/30/01	3,001.6	③ 276.7	4,121.6	15.5	9.2	23.6	6.7	1.1	③ 1.50	2.61	0.56	0.56	24.75 - 13.47	12.8	2.9
4/30/00	2,451.9	251.9	5,699.4	16.5	10.3	20.7	4.4	1.1	1.28	2.02	0.57	0.51	29.75 - 19.00	19.1	2.1
4/30/99	1,644.7	② 237.8	1,910.2	21.6	14.5	22.4	12.4	2.0	② 1.18	1.55	0.43	0.42	24.53 - 17.66	17.9	2.0
4/30/98	1,306.8	① 174.2	2,904.1	19.6	13.3	13.0	6.0	1.7	① 0.81	1.07	4.83	0.40	22.88 - 14.00	22.8	2.2
4/30/97	1,929.7	47.8	1,906.3	0.9	2.5	4.8	2.5	1.8	0.23	1.58	4.41	0.64	21.06 - 11.81	73.0	3.9
4/30/96	894.4	① 125.1	1,417.6	22.1	14.0	12.0	8.8	3.7	① 0.59	0.74	4.82	0.63	24.44 - 16.69	34.8	3.1
4/30/95	1,360.3	107.3	1,078.0	16.2	7.9	15.6	9.9	1.8	0.51	0.83	2.90	0.58	24.38 - 16.50	40.5	2.8
4/30/94	1,238.7	① 164.0	1,074.7	22.9	13.2	23.2	15.3	2.1	① 0.77	1.04	2.99	0.52	21.38 - 15.94	24.2	2.8
4/30/93	1,525.3	180.7	1,005.8	19.4	11.8	27.8	18.0	1.8	0.84	1.09	2.47	0.46	20.56 - 15.06	21.2	2.6

Statistics are as originally reported. Adj. for 2-for-1 stk. split, 6/01. ① Bef. disc. oper. gain 1998, $218.0 mill.; 1996, $52.1 mill.; 1994, $36.5 mill. ② Bef. disc. oper. loss $22.4 mill. ③ Bef. $4.4 mill. acctg. chg.

OFFICERS:
M. A. Ernst, Chmn., Pres., C.E.O.
F. J. Cotroneo, Sr. V.P., C.F.O.
J. W. Yabuki, Exec. V.P., C.O.O.
INVESTOR CONTACT: Mark Barnett, Dir., Investor Relations, (816) 701-4443
PRINCIPAL OFFICE: 4400 Main Street, Kansas City, MO 64111

TELEPHONE NUMBER: (816) 753-6900
FAX: (816) 932-8390
WEB: www.hrblock.com
NO. OF EMPLOYEES: 10,900 (approx.)
SHAREHOLDERS: 30,946
ANNUAL MEETING: In Sept.
INCORPORATED: MO, 1955

INSTITUTIONAL HOLDINGS:
No. of Institutions: 450
Shares Held: 147,428,439
% Held: 82.5
INDUSTRY: Tax return preparation services (SIC: 7291)
TRANSFER AGENT(S): Mellon Investor Services, Ridgefield Park, NJ

BLOCKBUSTER INC.

EXCH.	SYM.	REC. PRICE	P/E RATIO	YLD.	MKT. CAP.	RANGE (52-WK.)	'02 Y/E PR.
NYSE	BBI	15.30 (2/28/03)	14.6	0.5%	$2.71 bill.	30.25 - 11.80	12.25

MEDIUM GRADE. THE COMPANY ANTICIPATES OPENING 300 TO 400 NEW COMPANY-OPERATED STORES IN 2003.

INTERIM EARNINGS (Per Share):

Qtr.	Mar.	June	Sept.	Dec.
1998	0.11	d2.21	d0.15	d0.09
1999	d0.02	d0.28	d0.12	d0.04
2000	d0.02	d0.16	d0.11	d0.14
2001	0.03	d0.09	d1.28	d0.03
2002	0.37	0.23	0.28	0.17

INTERIM DIVIDENDS (Per Share):

Amt.	Decl.	Ex.	Rec.	Pay.
0.02Q	1/24/02	2/14/02	2/19/02	3/11/02
0.02Q	5/21/02	5/30/02	6/03/02	6/17/02
0.02Q	7/23/02	8/22/02	8/26/02	9/16/02
0.02Q	10/09/02	11/06/02	11/11/02	12/02/02
0.02Q	1/28/03	2/12/03	2/14/03	3/10/03

Indicated div.: $0.08

TRADING VOLUME
Thousand Shares

CAPITALIZATION (12/31/01):

	($000)	(%)
Long-Term Debt	458,400	7.2
Capital Lease Obligations..	88,000	1.4
Deferred Income Tax	111,500	1.7
Common & Surplus	5,748,700	89.7
Total	6,406,600	100.0

*7 YEAR PRICE SCORE N/A   ***12 MONTH PRICE SCORE 68.7**

*NYSE COMPOSITE INDEX=100

BUSINESS:

Blockbuster Inc. is a major renter of home videocassettes, DVDs and video games throughout the Americas, Europe, Asia and Australia. As of 12/31/02, BBI operated 4,518 stores in the United States and 2,389 internationally. In addition, 1,638 locations were operated by franchisees and/or as joint ventures. The Company's stores offer a wide selection of pre-recorded videos and DVDs for rent or purchase, along with video games for use with Sony PlayStation, Nintendo and other video game platforms. BBI also rents video game consoles, as well as VHS and DVD players, in most of its domestic Company-operated stores, and sells other complementary products. As of 2/28/02, Viacom International Inc. owned 81.0% of BBI's Class A common stock and all of its Class B common stock.

RECENT DEVELOPMENTS:

For the twelve months ended 12/31/02, the Company reported income of $189.4 million, before a $1.82 billion accounting change charge, compared with a net loss of $240.3 million a year earlier. Results for 2001 included net after-tax non-recurring charges of $252.0 million, primarily related to inventory reductions. Total revenues climbed 7.9% to $5.57 billion from $5.16 billion the year before.

Rental revenues grew 3.4% to $4.46 billion from $4.31 billion the previous year, while merchandise sales advanced 38.7% to $1.02 billion from $735.2 million in the prior year. Worldwide same-store revenues were up 5.1% year over year. Gross profit was $3.21 billion, or 57.6% of total revenues, versus $2.74 billion, or 53.1% of total revenues, in 2001.

PROSPECTS:

The Company is targeting full-year 2003 earnings per share growth of at least 20.0%, along with a mid-single digit increase in worldwide same-store sales. In addition, BBI expects a mid-single digit increase for gross profit in 2003, fueled by a combination of increased sales and rental margin improvement stemming from growth in higher-margin DVD rentals and lower rental product costs. Meanwhile, in 2003, BBI expects to open between 300 and 400 new Company-operated stores and anticipates capital expenditures in the range of $150.0 million to $175.0 million for the full year.

ANNUAL FINANCIAL DATA:

FISCAL YEAR	TOT. REVS. ($mill.)	NET INC. ($mill.)	TOT. ASSETS ($mill.)	OPER. PROFIT %	NET PROFIT %	CURR. RATIO	EARN. PER SH. $	CASH FL. PER SH. $	TANG. BK. VAL. $	DIV. PER SH. $	PRICE RANGE	AVG. P/E RATIO	AVG. YIELD %
p12/31/02	5,565.9	② 189.4		...	...	0.6	② 1.04			0.08	30.25 - 11.80	20.2	0.4
12/31/01	5,156.7	① d240.3	7,752.4	...	...	0.6	① d1.37	6.03	0.70	0.08	28.66 - 8.19	...	0.4
12/31/00	4,960.1	d75.9	8,548.9	1.5	...	0.7	d0.43	6.39	1.14	0.08	14.88 - 6.88	...	0.7
12/31/99	4,463.5	d69.2	8,540.8	2.7	...	0.6	d0.44	6.39	0.85	0.02	17.13 - 11.38	...	0.1
12/31/98	3,893.4	d336.6	8,274.8	...	...	0.7	d2.34	8.21	...	...		...	...
12/31/97	3,313.6	d318.2	8,731.0	...	...	...	d2.21	6.28	9.90	...		...	...
12/31/96	2,942.1	① 77.8	...	9.1	2.6	...	① 0.54	7.13	...	...		...	...

Statistics are as originally reported. ① Incl. $252.0 mil ($1.42/sh) after-tax chg. primarily related to inventory reductions, 2001; $50.2 mil restr. chg., 1996. ② Bef. $1.82 bil ($10.01/sh) acctg. change chg.

OFFICERS:
J. F. Antioco, Chmn., C.E.O.
N. Travis, Pres., C.O.O.
L. J. Zine, Exec. V.P., C.F.O.
INVESTOR CONTACT: Mary Bell, V.P., Inv. Rel., (214) 854-3863
PRINCIPAL OFFICE: 1201 Elm Street, Dallas, TX 75270

TELEPHONE NUMBER: (214) 854-3000
FAX: (214) 854-4848
WEB: www.blockbuster.com
NO. OF EMPLOYEES: 89,100 (avg.)
SHAREHOLDERS: 277 (class A); 1 (class B)
ANNUAL MEETING: In May
INCORPORATED: DE, Oct., 1989

INSTITUTIONAL HOLDINGS:
No. of Institutions: 130
Shares Held: 35,312,143
% Held: 19.7
INDUSTRY: Video tape rental (SIC: 7841)
TRANSFER AGENT(S): EquiServe, Providence, RI

BMC SOFTWARE, INC.

EXCH.	SYM.	REC. PRICE	P/E RATIO	YLD.	MKT. CAP.	RANGE (52-WK.)	'02 Y/E PR.
NYSE	BMC	19.40 (2/28/03)	194.0	...	$4.68 bill.	19.84 - 10.85	17.11

LOWER MEDIUM GRADE. THE COMPANY EXPECTS EARNINGS PER SHARE FOR FULL-YEAR FISCAL 2003 IN THE RANGE OF $0.46 TO $0.49, EXCLUDING SPECIAL ITEMS.

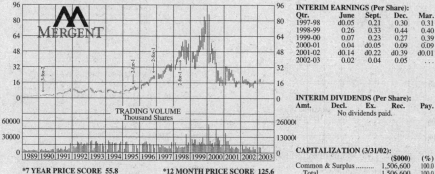

*7 YEAR PRICE SCORE 55.8   *12 MONTH PRICE SCORE 125.6
*NYSE COMPOSITE INDEX=100

INTERIM EARNINGS (Per Share):

Qtr.	June	Sept.	Dec.	Mar.
1997-98	d0.05	0.21	0.30	0.31
1998-99	0.26	0.33	0.44	0.40
1999-00	0.07	0.23	0.27	0.39
2000-01	0.04	d0.05	0.09	0.09
2001-02	d0.14	d0.22	d0.39	d0.01
2002-03	0.02	0.04	0.05	...

INTERIM DIVIDENDS (Per Share):

Amt.	Decl.	Ex.	Rec.	Pay.
		No dividends paid.		

CAPITALIZATION (3/31/02):

	($000)	(%)
Common & Surplus	1,506,600	100.0
Total	1,506,600	100.0

BUSINESS:

BMC Software, Inc. is a worldwide developer and vendor of more than 100 software solutions for automating application and data management across host-based and open systems environments. The Company's products are primarily designed to facilitate database and network management, maintenance and recovery and to increase the speed and efficiency of data-communications. As of 12/31/02, the Company has more than 10,000 customers and 821,000 software licenses worldwide. Revenues for fiscal 2002 were derived: license, 48.5%; maintenance, 44.7%; and professional services, 6.8%.

RECENT DEVELOPMENTS:

For the three months ended 12/31/02, net earnings jumped to $12.1 million compared with a net loss of $94.5 million in the equivalent quarter of 2001. Results for 2002 and 2001 included amortization and impairment of acquired technology, goodwill and intangibles of $17.8 million and $103.9 million, and restructuring and severance costs of $300,000 and $8.2 million, respectively. Results for 2002 also included an acquired research and development charge of $12.0 million, whiles results for 2001 included merger-related costs and compensation charges of $5.8 million. Total revenues climbed 8.9% to $349.6 million from $321.0 million in the prior-year period.

PROSPECTS:

Looking ahead, the Company expects revenues in the fourth quarter of fiscal 2003 in the range of $374.0 million to $387.0 million and expenses, including special items, in the range of $340.0 million to $350.0 million. Earnings per share for full-year fiscal 2003 are expected to range between $0.46 and $0.49, excluding special items. In addition, gross deferred revenue for fiscal 2003 is expected to range from $130.0 million to $145.0 million and net deferred license revenue in the range of $80.0 million to $100.0 million. Separately, during the third quarter of fiscal 2003, the Company completed the acquisition of Remedy, a provider of service management software applications, from Peregrine Systems for $355.0 million in cash.

ANNUAL FINANCIAL DATA:

FISCAL YEAR	TOT. REVS. ($mill.)	NET INC. ($mill.)	TOT. ASSETS ($mill.)	OPER. PROFIT %	NET PROFIT %	RET. ON EQUITY %	RET. ON ASSETS %	CURR. RATIO	EARN. PER SH. $	CASH FL. PER SH. $	TANG. BK. VAL. $	PRICE RANGE	AVG. P/E RATIO
3/31/02	1,288.9	④ d184.1	2,676.2	...	...	...	...	1.5	④ d0.75	0.78	4.82	33.00 - 11.50	...
3/31/01	1,504.0	③ 42.4	3,033.9	...	2.8	2.3	1.4	1.1	③ 0.17	1.42	5.07	86.63 - 13.00	292.8
3/31/00	1,719.2	② 242.5	2,962.1	15.7	14.1	13.6	8.2	1.0	② 0.96	1.89	5.14	84.06 - 30.00	59.4
3/31/99	1,303.9	② 364.2	2,282.7	31.8	27.9	27.3	16.0	1.3	② 1.46	1.77	5.22	60.25 - 29.25	30.6
3/31/98	730.6	① 165.9	1,248.5	31.0	22.7	21.8	13.3	1.1	① 0.77	1.03	3.37	35.63 - 19.81	36.0
3/31/97	563.2	163.9	844.2	38.5	29.1	30.0	19.4	1.2	0.77	0.92	2.53	23.38 - 9.31	21.4
3/31/96	428.9	105.6	608.2	34.4	24.6	27.5	17.4	1.2	0.51	0.57	1.70	12.88 - 6.75	19.4
3/31/95	345.0	77.5	502.6	31.5	22.5	25.3	15.4	1.2	0.38	0.47	1.43	8.88 - 5.03	18.3
3/31/94	288.5	① 56.5	417.5	27.7	19.6	22.6	13.5	1.3	① 0.27	0.34	1.14	10.52 - 4.84	28.4
3/31/93	238.5	65.4	378.7	36.1	27.4	29.3	17.3	1.6	0.31	0.36	0.99	9.88 - 4.66	23.2

Statistics are as originally reported. Adj. for stk. splits: 2-for-1, 5/15/98; 2-for-1, 11/18/96; 2-for-1, 8/14/95. ① Incl. non-recurr. chrg. $150.3 mill., 3/00; $7.3 mill., 3/98; $32.0 mill., 3/94. ② Bef. acctg. change chrg. of $1.5 mill., but incl. non-recurr. chrg. $38.3 mill. ③ Incl. $8.6 mill. merger-related chgs. & $6.1 mill. severance chg. ④ Incl. $52.9 mill. restr. & sev. costs and $12.8 mill. merger-rel. costs & compensation chgs.

OFFICERS:
B. G. Cupp, Chmn.
R. E. Beauchamp, Pres., C.E.O.
J. W. Cox, V.P., C.F.O., C.A.O.

INVESTOR CONTACT: Neil Yekell, Investor Relations, (713) 918-4233

PRINCIPAL OFFICE: 2101 CityWest Boulevard, Houston, TX 77042-2827

TELEPHONE NUMBER: (713) 918-8800
FAX: (713) 918-8000
WEB: www.bmc.com

NO. OF EMPLOYEES: 6,335

SHAREHOLDERS: 1,585

ANNUAL MEETING: In Aug.

INCORPORATED: TX, 1980; reincorp., DE, July, 1988

INSTITUTIONAL HOLDINGS:
No. of Institutions: 303
Shares Held: 190,142,137
% Held: 80.8

INDUSTRY: Prepackaged software (SIC: 7372)

TRANSFER AGENT(S): Fleet National Bank, Boston, MA

BOEING COMPANY (THE)

EXCH.	SYM.	REC. PRICE	P/E RATIO	YLD.	MKT. CAP.	RANGE (52-WK.)	'02 Y/E PR.
NYSE	BA	27.56 (2/28/03)	9.6	2.5%	$23.15 bill.	51.07 - 27.24	32.99

UPPER MEDIUM GRADE. THE COMPANY IS TARGETING REVENUE OF ABOUT $49.00 BILLION IN 2003 AND EARNINGS IN THE RANGE OF $1.90 TO $2.10 PER SHARE.

7 YEAR PRICE SCORE 88.5*   *12 MONTH PRICE SCORE 89.1

*NYSE COMPOSITE INDEX=100

INTERIM EARNINGS (Per Share):

Qtr.	Mar.	June	Sept.	Dec.
1996	0.18	0.68	0.37	0.38
1997	0.55	0.48	d0.72	d0.51
1998	0.05	0.26	0.36	0.48
1999	0.50	0.75	0.52	0.74
2000	0.48	0.71	0.70	0.55
2001	1.45	0.99	0.80	0.12
2002	0.72	0.96	0.46	0.73

INTERIM DIVIDENDS (Per Share):

Amt.	Decl.	Ex.	Rec.	Pay.
0.17Q	12/10/01	2/06/02	2/08/02	3/01/02
0.17Q	4/29/02	5/15/02	5/17/02	6/07/02
0.17Q	6/24/02	8/14/02	8/16/02	9/06/02
0.17Q	10/28/02	11/13/02	11/15/02	12/06/02
0.17Q	12/09/02	2/05/03	2/07/03	3/07/03

Indicated div.: $0.68 (Div. Reinv. Plan)

CAPITALIZATION (12/31/01):

	($000)	(%)
Long-Term Debt	10,866,000	49.7
Deferred Income Tax	177,000	0.8
Common & Surplus	10,825,000	49.5
Total	21,868,000	100.0

BUSINESS:

The Boeing Company is a major commercial aerospace and defense concern, operating in three main business segments. The Commercial Airplanes segment (53.2% of 2002 revenues) principally involves development, production and marketing of commercial aircraft and provides related support services mainly to commercial customers. Operations in the Military Aircraft and Missiles segment (26.2%) involve research, development, production and modification of military aircraft, including fighter, transport and attack aircraft, helicopters and missiles. The Space and Communications segment (20.6%) provides research, development, production, modification for space systems, missile defense systems, satellite launching vehicles, rocket engines, and information and battle management systems. On 8/1/97, BA acquired McDonnell Douglas Corp. On 10/6/00, BA acquired the space and communications operations of Hughes Electronics Corporation.

RECENT DEVELOPMENTS:

For the year ended 12/31/02, earnings totaled $2.32 billion, before a $1.83 billion accounting change charge, compared with earnings of $2.83 billion, before a $1.0 billion accounting change gain, the year before. Earnings included nonrecurring items that resulted in a net after-tax gain of $20.0 million and a net after-tax charge of $181.0 million in 2002 and 2001, respectively. Sales and other operating revenues slid 7.1% to $54.07 billion from $58.20 billion a year earlier. Earnings from operations slipped 0.7% to $3.87 billion from $3.90 billion the prior year.

PROSPECTS:

The Company is targeting full-year 2003 revenue of about $49.00 billion, rising to between $52.00 billion and $54.00 billion in 2004. Meanwhile, BA anticipates earnings per share in the range of $1.90 to $2.10 in 2003 and between $2.10 and $2.30 in 2004. Strong demand in the Company's military aircraft and missiles segment is expected to be offset by continued weakness in the commercial aviation market. BA also expects to deliver approximately 280 airplanes in 2003, and between 275 and 300 in 2004.

ANNUAL FINANCIAL DATA:

FISCAL YEAR	TOT. REVS. ($mill.)	NET INC. ($mill.)	TOT. ASSETS ($mill.)	OPER. PROFIT %	NET PROFIT %	RET. ON EQUITY %	RET. ON ASSETS %	CURR. RATIO	EARN. PER SH. $	CASH FL. PER SH. $	TANG. BK. VAL. $	DIV. PER SH. $	PRICE RANGE	AVG. P/E RATIO	AVG. YIELD
p12/31/02	54,069.0	④ 2,319.0							④ 2.87			0.68	51.07 - 28.53	13.9	1.7
12/31/01	58,198.0	③ 2,826.0	48,343.0	6.7	4.9	26.1	5.8	0.8	③ 3.41	5.52	5.23	0.68	69.85 - 27.60	14.3	1.4
12/31/00	51,321.0	② 2,128.0	42,028.0	6.0	4.1	19.3	5.1	0.9	② 2.44	4.14	6.63	0.56	70.94 - 32.00	21.1	1.1
12/31/99	57,993.0	② 2,309.0	36,147.0	5.5	4.0	20.1	6.4	1.2	② 2.49	4.27	10.15	0.56	48.50 - 32.56	16.3	1.4
12/31/98	56,154.0	② 1,120.0	37,024.0	2.8	2.0	9.1	3.0	1.2	② 1.15	2.81	10.25	0.56	56.25 - 29.00	37.1	1.3
12/31/97	45,800.0	② d178.0	38,024.0	...	...	...	...	1.4	② d0.18	1.32	10.56	0.56	60.50 - 43.00	...	1.1
12/31/96	22,681.0	② 1,095.0	27,254.0	6.0	4.8	10.0	4.0	1.7	② 1.60	3.03	11.75	0.55	53.75 - 37.06	28.5	1.2
12/31/95	19,515.0	① 393.0	22,098.0	1.5	2.0	4.0	1.8	1.8	① 0.58	2.08	14.39	0.50	40.00 - 22.19	54.1	1.6
12/31/94	21,924.0	856.0	21,463.0	5.2	3.9	8.8	4.0	1.5	1.26	2.93	14.22	0.50	25.06 - 21.06	18.4	2.2
12/31/93	25,438.0	1,244.0	20,450.0	6.6	4.9	13.8	6.1	1.4	1.83	3.34	13.21	0.50	22.38 - 16.69	10.7	2.6

Statistics are as originally reported. Adj. for 2-for-1 stk. split, 6/97. ① Incl. $600 mil non-recur. pre-tax chg. for spcl. retirmnt. program. ② Incl. $616 mil ($0.44/sh) pre-tax non-recur. chg., 2000; $87 mil pre-tax gain, 1999; $219 mil non-recur. chg., 1998; $1.90 bil net non-recur. chg., 1997; $6 mil gain, 1996. ③ Bef. $1.0 mil. acctg. cr. and incl. $181.0 mil net after-tax non-recur. chg. ④ Bef. $1.83 bil ($2.26/sh) acctg. chg. & incl. $20.0 mil net after-tax non-recur. gain.

OFFICERS:
P. M. Condit, Chmn., C.E.O.
H. C. Stonecipher, Vice-Chmn.
M. M. Sears, Exec. V.P., C.F.O.

PRINCIPAL OFFICE: 100 North Riverside, Chicago, IL 60606-1596

TELEPHONE NUMBER: (312) 544-2000
FAX: (312) 544-2082
WEB: www.boeing.com
NO. OF EMPLOYEES: 188,000
SHAREHOLDERS: 145,000 (approx.)
ANNUAL MEETING: In Apr.
INCORPORATED: DE, July, 1934

INSTITUTIONAL HOLDINGS:
No. of Institutions: 694
Shares Held: 497,441,004
% Held: 62.2

INDUSTRY: Aircraft (SIC: 3721)

TRANSFER AGENT(S): EquiServe, Providence, RI

BOISE CASCADE CORPORATION

EXCH.	SYM.	REC. PRICE	P/E RATIO	YLD.	MKT. CAP.	RANGE (52-WK.)	'02 Y/E PR.
NYSE	BCC	24.12 (2/28/03)	...	2.5%	$1.40 bill.	38.81 - 19.61	25.22

LOWER MEDIUM GRADE. NEAR-TERM RESULTS ARE EXPECTED TO BE PRESSURED BY THE SLOWDOWN IN THE U.S. ECONOMY AND RISING PENSION COSTS.

INTERIM EARNINGS (Per Share):

Qtr.	Mar.	June	Sept.	Dec.
1998	d0.18	d1.20	0.72	d0.25
1999	0.26	0.92	0.74	1.18
2000	0.60	0.46	1.33	0.34
2001	d0.68	0.28	0.20	d0.78
2002	d0.17	Nil	0.09	0.05

INTERIM DIVIDENDS (Per Share):

Amt.	Decl.	Ex.	Rec.	Pay.
0.15Q	2/08/02	3/27/02	4/01/02	4/15/02
0.15Q	4/18/02	6/27/02	7/01/02	7/15/02
0.15Q	7/25/02	9/27/02	10/01/02	10/15/02
0.15Q	12/13/02	12/27/02	1/01/03	1/15/03
0.15Q	2/14/03	3/28/03	4/01/03	4/15/03

Indicated div.: $0.60 (Div. Reinv. Plan)

TRADING VOLUME
Thousand Shares

*7 YEAR PRICE SCORE 93.0   ***12 MONTH PRICE SCORE 94.8**

*NYSE COMPOSITE INDEX=100

CAPITALIZATION (12/31/01):

	($000)	(%)
Long-Term Debt 🔟............	1,143,755	37.7
Deferred Income Tax	308,305	10.2
Preferred Stock..................	201,626	6.7
Common & Surplus	1,376,727	45.4
Total	3,030,413	100.0

BUSINESS:

Boise Cascade Corporation is an integrated paper and forest products company with domestic and international operations. BCC manufactures and distributes paper, corrugated containers and wood products, distributes office products and building materials, and owns and manages timberlands to support those operations. BCC's segments consist of Office Solutions (44.9% of 2002 total revenues), Building Solutions (31.3%) and Paper Solutions (23.8%). As of 12/31/01, BCC owned or controlled more than 2.0 million acres of timberland in the Pacific Northwest, the upper Midwest, and the South. Other operations consist of information services, leasing, transportation and insurance. In 1995, BCC spun off Boise Cascade Office Products (BCOP). Effective 4/20/00, BCC purchased the minority public shares of BCOP for a total of $216.1 million, and BCOP again became a wholly-owned subsidiary of BCC.

RECENT DEVELOPMENTS:

For the year ended 12/31/02, net income amounted to $11.3 million compared with a net loss of $42.5 million in 2001. Results included a nonrecurring after-tax gain of $4.0 million in 2002 and a nonrecurring after-tax charge of $89.3 million in 2001. Sales slid 0.1% to $7.41 billion from $7.42 billion a year earlier. Sales growth in BCC's building materials distribution business was offset by lower sales in its paper business due to reduced product prices. Operating income grew 45.9% to $118.3 million versus $81.1 million the year before.

PROSPECTS:

The Company expects near-term results to be pressured by the weak domestic economy and rising pension costs. The Company also expects Boise Office Solutions to report positive quarterly same-store sales comparisons relative to 2002, with operating margins in the range of 3.0% to 4.0%. However, Boise Paper Solutions is expected to post a sequential decline due to weak sales volumes, market-related production curtailments, maintenance projects, and higher energy, fiber and other operating costs. Meanwhile, Boise Building Solutions results in the first quarter of 2003 will likely be seasonally slow with sequentially flat results.

ANNUAL FINANCIAL DATA:

FISCAL YEAR	TOT. REVS. ($mill.)	NET INC. ($mill.)	TOT. ASSETS ($mill.)	OPER. PROFIT %	NET PROFIT %	RET. ON EQUITY %	RET. ON ASSETS %	CURR. RATIO	EARN. PER SH. $	CASH FL. PER SH. $	TANG. BK. VAL. $	DIV. PER SH. $	PRICE RANGE	AVG. P/E RATIO	AVG. YIELD %
p12/31/02	7,412.3	🔟 11.3							🔟 d0.03	4.40	16.68	0.60	38.81 - 19.61	...	2.1
12/31/01	7,422.2	d42.5	4,934.0	1.1	...	...	...	1.0	d0.96	4.40	16.68	0.60	38.00 - 26.99	...	1.8
12/31/00	7,806.7	178.6	5,266.9	5.7	2.3	10.2	3.4	1.6	2.73	7.76	19.93	0.60	43.94 - 21.75	12.0	1.8
12/31/99	6,952.7	⑥ 199.8	5,138.4	7.2	2.9	12.4	3.9	1.4	③ 3.06	7.96	15.77	0.60	47.19 - 28.75	12.4	1.6
12/31/98	6,162.1	⑤ d28.4	4,966.7	2.2	...	...	...	1.2	d0.75	4.18	12.17	0.60	40.38 - 22.25	...	1.9
12/31/97	5,493.1	d30.4	4,969.9	1.9	...	...	...	1.5	d1.19	3.73	13.01	0.60	45.56 - 27.75	...	1.6
12/31/96	5,122.7	9.1	4,710.7	3.0	0.2	0.5	0.2	1.5	d0.63	4.42	34.67	0.60	47.25 - 27.38	...	1.6
12/31/95	5,057.7	④ 351.9	4,656.2	13.0	7.0	20.8	7.6	1.7	④ 5.93	11.35	35.48	0.60	47.50 - 26.25	6.2	1.6
12/31/94	4,141.8	③ d62.6	4,294.1	2.2	...	...	...	1.4	③ d3.08	5.03	35.65	0.60	30.50 - 19.00	...	2.4
12/31/93	3,982.4	② d77.1	4,513.0	0.5	...	...	...	1.5	② d3.17	5.32	39.61	0.60	27.50 - 19.50	...	2.6

Statistics are as originally reported. 🔟 Incl. cv. subord. debs. and guarantee of 8.5% ESOP debt. ② Incl. gain of $13.9 mill. from sale of assets. ③ Incl. chrg. of $27 mill. rel. to sale of secur. ④ Incl. gains of $66.2 mill. from the IPO of Boise Cascade Office Products Corp.; $183 mill. fr. the divestment of BCC's int. in Rainy River Forest Products. ⑤ Incl. pre-tax nonrecurr. chrg. of $92.3 mill., but bef. accts. gain of $8.6 mill. ⑥ Incl. nonrecurr. items that reulted in a net gain of a $51.5 mill. ⑦ Incl. after-tax nonrecurr. gain of $4.0 mill.

OFFICERS:	TELEPHONE NUMBER: (208) 384-6161	INSTITUTIONAL HOLDINGS:
G. J. Harad, Chmn., C.E.O.	FAX: (208) 384-7189	No. of Institutions: 206
T. Crumley, Sr. V.P., C.F.O.	WEB: www.bc.com	Shares Held: 50,346,203
I. Littman, V.P., Treas.		% Held: 86.4

OFFICERS:
G. J. Harad, Chmn., C.E.O.
T. Crumley, Sr. V.P., C.F.O.
I. Littman, V.P., Treas.

INVESTOR CONTACT: Investor Relations, (208) 384-6390

PRINCIPAL OFFICE: 1111 West Jefferson Street, P.O. Box 50, Boise, ID 83728-0001

TELEPHONE NUMBER: (208) 384-6161
FAX: (208) 384-7189
WEB: www.bc.com

NO. OF EMPLOYEES: 24,168 (avg.)

SHAREHOLDERS: 14,866 (approx.)

ANNUAL MEETING: In Apr.

INCORPORATED: DE, Apr., 1931

INSTITUTIONAL HOLDINGS:
No. of Institutions: 206
Shares Held: 50,346,203
% Held: 86.4

INDUSTRY: Paper mills (SIC: 2621)

TRANSFER AGENT(S): Boise Cascade Corporation, Boise, Idaho

BORDERS GROUP, INC.

EXCH.	SYM.	REC. PRICE	P/E RATIO	YLD.	MKT. CAP.	RANGE (52-WK.)	'02 Y/E PR.
NYSE	BGP	14.20 (2/28/03)	10.2	...	$1.15 bill.	24.49 - 13.79	16.10

MEDIUM GRADE. THE COMPANY ANTICIPATES FULL FISCAL-2003 EARNINGS OF BETWEEN $1.50 AND $1.60 PER SHARE.

TRADING VOLUME Thousand Shares

*7 YEAR PRICE SCORE 98.6   ***12 MONTH PRICE SCORE 88.5**
*NYSE COMPOSITE INDEX=100

INTERIM EARNINGS (Per Share):

Qtr.	Apr.	July	Oct.	Jan.
1996-97	d0.05	d0.03	d0.04	0.82
1997-98	Nil	0.01	Nil	0.96
1998-99	0.05	0.03	d0.01	1.06
1999-00	d0.05	0.03	d0.02	1.23
2000-01	d0.01	d0.02	d0.06	0.64
2001-02	d0.24	Nil	d0.04	1.32
2002-03	0.05	0.04	d0.02	1.32

INTERIM DIVIDENDS (Per Share):

Amt.	Decl.	Ex.	Rec.	Pay.
No dividends paid.				

CAPITALIZATION (1/27/02):

	($000)	(%)
Capital Lease Obligations..	49,700	5.0
Common & Surplus	949,900	95.0
Total	999,600	100.0

BUSINESS:

Borders Group, Inc. is the second largest operator of book superstores and the largest operator of mall-based bookstores, based on both sales and number of stores. As of 1/26/03, the Company operated 404 superstores under the Borders name in the U.S. and 30 international stores in the United Kingdom, Australia, Puerto Rico, New Zealand and Singapore. The Company also operated 778 mall-based and other bookstores primarily under the Waldenbooks name, and 37 bookstores under the Books etc. name in the United Kingdom. Fiscal 2002 sales were derived as follows: Borders, 66.5%; Waldenbooks, 24.5%; and International, 9.0%.

RECENT DEVELOPMENTS:

For the year ended 1/26/03, net income climbed 27.8% to $111.7 million from $87.4 million in the prior year. Results included non-recurring after-tax charges of $5.3 million and $21.9 million in fiscal 2002 and fiscal 2001, respectively. Total sales grew 2.9% to $3.49 billion from $3.39 billion the year before. Sales for Borders superstores rose 3.8% to $2.32 billion. Comparable-store sales at Borders locations were down 1.2% year over year, while comparable-store sales at Waldenbooks stores slipped 3.2%. Gross margin was $960.9 million, or 27.6% of total sales, versus $938.6 million, or 27.7% of total sales, the previous year. Operating income totaled $193.9 million, up 23.5% compared with $157.0 million a year earlier.

PROSPECTS:

Higher sales of DVDs, gifts and stationery are being partially offset by slightly lower book sales and a decline in music sales. The Company anticipates earnings per share of approximately breakeven for the first quarter of the current fiscal year. Looking ahead, BGP is targeting full fiscal-2003 earnings in the range of $1.50 to $1.60 per share. Sales are expected to benefit from the June 2003 release of the fifth book in the Harry Potter series. Separately, the Company plans to continue expanding its Borders store base in 2003, with 35 to 40 new domestic stores and six to eight new international locations expected to open during the year. Meanwhile, BGP will close between 40 and 50 existing Waldenbooks stores in 2003.

ANNUAL FINANCIAL DATA:

FISCAL YEAR	TOT. REVS. ($mil.)	NET INC. ($mil.)	TOT. ASSETS ($mil.)	OPER. PROFIT %	NET PROFIT %	RET. ON EQUITY %	RET. ON ASSETS %	CURR. RATIO	EARN. PER SH. $	CASH FL. PER SH. $	TANG. BK. VAL. $	PRICE RANGE	AVG. P/E RATIO
p1/26/03	3,486.1	⑤ 111.7							⑤ 1.36			24.49 - 14.68	14.4
1/27/02	3,387.9	④ 87.4	2,179.3	4.6	2.6	9.2	4.0	1.3	④ 1.06	2.22	10.61	24.43 - 11.00	16.7
1/28/01	3,271.2	③ 73.8	2,047.1	4.1	2.3	8.7	3.6	1.2	③ 0.92	2.11	9.70	17.88 - 10.88	15.6
1/23/00	2,999.2	90.3	1,914.8	5.5	3.0	11.3	4.7	1.2	1.13	2.18	8.76	25.75 - 11.75	16.6
1/24/99	2,595.0	92.1	1,766.6	6.4	3.5	12.9	5.2	1.1	1.12	1.92	7.84	41.75 - 17.88	26.6
1/25/98	2,266.0	80.2	1,534.9	6.1	3.5	13.4	5.2	1.2	0.98	1.64	6.48	32.31 - 17.06	25.2
1/26/97	1,958.8	57.9	1,211.0	5.3	3.0	11.3	4.8	1.3	0.70	1.22	6.23	19.63 - 8.19	19.9
1/28/96	1,749.0	② d211.1	1,052.3	...	...	...	...	1.4	② d2.53	d2.03	5.74	10.94 - 6.94	...
1/22/95	1,511.0	② 20.9	1,355.9	2.9	1.4	2.9	1.5	1.5	② 0.24	0.76	8.12	...	...
1/23/94	1,370.6	① d55.6	1,006.3	...	...	...	...	1.2	...	...	...	...	...

Statistics are as originally reported. Adj. for stk. split, 2-for-1, 3/97. ① Bef. $5.6 mil acctg. chg. & incl. $142.8 mil pre-tax restr. chg. ② Incl. $63.1 mil pre-tax non-recur. chg., 1/96; $6.4 mil, 1/95. ③ Bef. $30.2 mil pre-tax $(0.38/sh) loss fr discont. oper. & incl. $36.2 pre-tax chg. fr asset impairments and other writedowns. ④ Incl. $25.4 mil pre-tax chg. fr. asset impair. and oth. writedowns & $2.4 mil chg. fr. a legal settlement. ⑤ Incl. $5.3 mil ($0.07/sh) after-tax non-recur. chg.

OFFICERS:
G. P. Josefowicz, Chmn., Pres., C.E.O.
E. Wilhelm, Sr. V.P., C.F.O.

INVESTOR CONTACT: Ed Wilhelm, (734) 477-4245

PRINCIPAL OFFICE: 100 Phoenix Drive, Ann Arbor, MI 48108

TELEPHONE NUMBER: (734) 477-1100
FAX: (734) 477-4538
WEB: www.borders.com
NO. OF EMPLOYEES: 15,000 full-time (approx.); 17,000 part-time (approx.)
SHAREHOLDERS: 3,845 (record)
ANNUAL MEETING: In May
INCORPORATED: DE, Aug., 1994

INSTITUTIONAL HOLDINGS:
No. of Institutions: 193
Shares Held: 73,975,831
% Held: 93.4

INDUSTRY: Book stores (SIC: 5942)

TRANSFER AGENT(S): EquiServe Trust Company, N.A., Jersey City, NJ

BORGWARNER INC.

EXCH.	SYM.	REC. PRICE	P/E RATIO	YLD.	MKT. CAP.	RANGE (52-WK.)	'02 Y/E PR.
NYSE	BWA	52.22 (2/28/03)	9.4	1.4%	$1.38 bill.	68.95 - 38.38	50.42

UPPER MEDIUM GRADE. THE COMPANY EXPECTS 2003 EARNINGS IN THE RANGE OF $6.20 TO $6.35 PER SHARE.

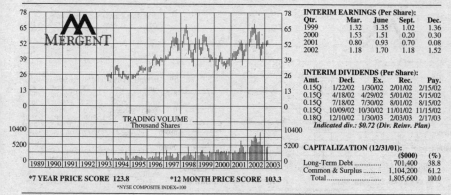

*7 YEAR PRICE SCORE 123.8   ***12 MONTH PRICE SCORE 103.3**
*NYSE COMPOSITE INDEX=100

INTERIM EARNINGS (Per Share):

Qtr.	Mar.	June	Sept.	Dec.
1999	1.32	1.35	1.02	1.36
2000	1.53	1.51	0.20	0.30
2001	0.80	0.93	0.70	0.08
2002	1.18	1.70	1.18	1.52

INTERIM DIVIDENDS (Per Share):

Amt.	Decl.	Ex.	Rec.	Pay.
0.15Q	1/22/02	1/30/02	2/01/02	2/15/02
0.15Q	4/18/02	4/29/02	5/01/02	5/15/02
0.15Q	7/18/02	7/30/02	8/01/02	8/15/02
0.15Q	10/09/02	10/30/02	11/01/02	11/15/02
0.18Q	12/10/02	1/30/03	2/03/03	2/17/03

Indicated div.: $0.72 (Div. Reinv. Plan)

CAPITALIZATION (12/31/01):

	($000)	(%)
Long-Term Debt	701,400	38.8
Common & Surplus	1,104,200	61.2
Total	1,805,600	100.0

BUSINESS:

BorgWarner Inc. (formerly BorgWarner Automotive, Inc.) is a global supplier of highly engineered systems and components, primarily for automotive powertrain applications. These products are manufactured and sold worldwide, primarily to original equipment manufacturers of passenger cars, sport utility vehicles and light trucks, including Ford, DaimlerChrysler, General Motors, Toyota, Honda, Caterpillar, Navistar International, PSA and VW Group. As of 2/4/03, BWA operated 50 manufacturing and technical facilities in 14 countries serving auto makers in North America, Europe, and Asia. BWA's operating segments include Morse TEC (37.5% of 2002 sales), TorqTransfer Systems (22.5%), Transmission Systems (17.7%), Air/Fluid Systems (13.9%) and Cooling Systems (8.4%). BWA acquired Eaton Corp.'s Fluid Power division on 10/1/99.

RECENT DEVELOPMENTS:

For the year ended 12/31/02, BWA reported earnings of $149.9 million, before an accounting change charge of $269.0 million, compared with net earnings of $66.4 million in the previous year. Results for 2001 included goodwill amortization of $42.0 million and restructuring and other non-recurring charges of $28.4 million. Net sales advanced 16.1% to $2.73 billion from $2.35 billion a year earlier. Morse TEC sales grew 20.4% to $1.05 billion, while TorqTransfer Systems sales jumped 26.0% to $630.1 million. Transmission Systems sales rose 15.5% to $495.2 million. Operating income climbed 76.5% to $252.0 million from $142.8 million the year before.

PROSPECTS:

The Company expects 2003 earnings in a range of $6.20 to $6.35 per share. New business and increased penetration of the faster growing parts of the auto market are expected to drive growth in 2003. Strong demand is expected in Europe for AVT's more fuel efficient engine and transmission systems, and in North America for computer-controlled four-wheel and all-wheel drive systems designed to enhance vehicle stability. Despite flat production levels in 2003, Europe remains AVT's fastest growth market due to high fuel costs and stricter emissions regulations. AVT expects to launch several new fuel-efficient products in Europe in 2003.

ANNUAL FINANCIAL DATA:

FISCAL YEAR	TOT. REVS. ($mill.)	NET INC. ($mill.)	TOT. ASSETS ($mill.)	OPER. PROFIT %	NET PROFIT %	RET. ON EQUITY %	RET. ON ASSETS %	CURR. RATIO	EARN. PER SH.$	CASH FL. PER SH.$	TANG. BK. VAL.$	DIV. PER SH.$	PRICE RANGE	AVG. P/E RATIO	AVG. YIELD %
p12/31/02	**2,731.1**	③ 149.9							③ 5.58			0.60	68.95 - 38.38	9.6	1.1
12/31/01	2,351.6	② 66.4	2,770.9	7.2	2.8	6.0	2.4	1.0	② 2.51	8.03	...	0.60	55.19 - 34.20	17.8	1.3
12/31/00	2,645.9	② 94.0	2,765.9	9.6	3.6	8.6	3.4	0.8	② 3.54	9.04	...	0.60	45.00 - 29.75	10.6	1.6
12/31/99	2,458.6	132.3	2,970.7	9.9	5.4	12.5	4.5	0.8	5.07	9.81	...	0.60	60.00 - 36.75	9.5	1.2
12/31/98	1,836.8	94.7	1,846.1	8.7	5.2	12.2	5.1	0.8	4.00	7.87	9.27	0.60	68.38 - 33.06	12.7	1.2
12/31/97	1,767.0	103.2	1,736.3	9.8	5.8	14.9	5.9	0.8	4.31	7.95	6.29	0.60	61.50 - 38.38	11.6	1.2
12/31/96	1,540.1	① 41.8	1,623.6	8.3	2.7	6.6	2.6	0.7	① 1.77	5.37	3.10	0.60	43.00 - 28.38	20.2	1.7
12/31/95	1,329.1	74.2	1,335.2	8.2	5.6	12.4	5.6	0.8	3.15	6.44	12.45	0.60	33.88 - 22.38	8.9	2.1
12/31/94	1,223.4	64.4	1,240.3	9.2	5.3	12.0	5.2	0.8	2.75	5.76	10.24	0.55	34.00 - 21.63	10.1	2.0
12/31/93	985.4	32.8	1,159.4	6.6	3.3	7.1	2.8	1.0	1.41	4.31	6.77	...	28.00 - 20.50	17.2	...

Statistics are as originally reported. ① Incl. non-recurr. chrg. $35.0 mill. for the sale of assets ② Incl. pre-tax nonrecurr. chrgs. of $28.4 mill., 2001; $62.9 mill., 2000. ③ Bef. acctg. change chrg. of $269.0 mill.

OFFICERS:
J. F. Fiedler, Chmn., C.E.O.
T. M. Manganello, Pres., C.O.O.
G. E. Strickler, Exec. V.P., C.F.O.
INVESTOR CONTACT: Mary Brevard, Dir. Investor Relations, (312) 322-8683
PRINCIPAL OFFICE: 200 South Michigan Avenue, Chicago, IL 60604

TELEPHONE NUMBER: (312) 322-8500
FAX: (312) 322-8599
WEB: www.bwauto.com
NO. OF EMPLOYEES: 13,000 (approx.)
SHAREHOLDERS: 3,150 (approx. record)
ANNUAL MEETING: In April
INCORPORATED: DE, 1987

INSTITUTIONAL HOLDINGS:
No. of Institutions: 224
Shares Held: 22,396,999
% Held: 83.3
INDUSTRY: Motor vehicle parts and accessories (SIC: 3714)
TRANSFER AGENT(S): Mellon Investor Services, Ridgefield Park, NJ

BOSTON PROPERTIES, INC.

EXCH.	SYM.	REC. PRICE	P/E RATIO	YLD.	MKT. CAP.	RANGE (52-WK.)	'02 Y/E PR.
NYSE	BXP	37.20 (2/28/03)	8.5	6.6%	$3.38 bill.	41.55 - 32.95	36.86

MEDIUM GRADE. GOING FORWARD, THE COMPANY SHOULD CONTINUE TO BENEFIT FROM THE SALE OF REAL ESTATE.

INTERIM EARNINGS (Per Share):

Qtr.	Mar.	June	Sept.	Dec.
1998	0.36	0.48	0.40	0.37
1999	0.39	0.41	0.40	0.51
2000	0.45	0.50	0.52	0.52
2001	0.51	0.53	0.56	0.61
2002	0.53	0.59	0.62	2.64

INTERIM DIVIDENDS (Per Share):

Amt.	Decl.	Ex.	Rec.	Pay.
0.58Q	3/18/02	3/26/02	3/29/02	4/30/02
0.61Q	5/02/02	6/26/02	6/28/02	7/30/02
0.61Q	9/19/02	9/26/02	9/30/02	10/30/02
0.61Q	12/19/02	12/26/02	12/30/02	1/29/03
0.61Q	3/17/03	3/26/03	3/28/03	4/30/03

Indicated div.: $2.44 (Div. Reinv. Plan)

CAPITALIZATION (12/31/01):

	($000)	(%)
Long-Term Debt	4,314,942	71.1
Common & Surplus	1,754,047	28.9
Total	6,068,989	100.0

*7 YEAR PRICE SCORE N/A   *12 MONTH PRICE SCORE 105.2
*NYSE COMPOSITE INDEX=100

BUSINESS:

Boston Properties, Inc. is a fully integrated, self-administered and self-managed real estate investment trust. The Company develops, redevelops, acquires, manages, operates and owns a diverse portfolio of office, industrial and hotel properties. The Company is one of the largest owners and developers of office properties in the United States, concentrated in four core markets: Boston, Washington DC, Midtown Manhattan and San Francisco. As of 12/31/02, the Company's portfolio consisted of 142 properties comprising more than 42.4 million square feet, including six properties under development totaling 2.8 million square feet. The overall occupancy rate for the properties in service as of 12/31/02 was 93.9%.

RECENT DEVELOPMENTS:

For the year ended 12/31/02, the Company reported income of $419.9 million versus income of $212.0 million in the previous year. Results for 2002 excluded income from discontinued operations of $26.5 million and an extraordinary loss of $2.0 million, while results for 2001 excluded a gain from discontinued operations of $2.8 million and an accounting change charge of $6.8 million. Results for 2002 and 2001 included gains on the sale of real estate of $190.4 million and $9.1 million, and net derivative losses of $11.8 million and $26.5 million, respectively. Total revenue climbed 18.0% to $1.23 billion from $1.02 billion the year before.

PROSPECTS:

On 2/4/03, BXP announced that it has completed the sales of 875 Third Avenue in New York City and The Candler Building in Baltimore, Maryland. These actions are part of an ongoing strategy to finance the acquisition of the property on 399 Park Avenue in midtown Manhattan, which was acquired on 9/25/02 for approximately $1.06 billion. Separately, on 11/22/02, BXP announced that it has completed the sale of One and Two Independence Square in Washington, D.C. for $345.0 million. Going forward, with modest re-leasing exposure of 4.4% of annual base rents maturing in 2003 and 7.5% in 2004, the Company's revenue stream should be somewhat protected as the markets that BXP operates in continue to contend with higher vacancies and slower rent growth.

ANNUAL FINANCIAL DATA:

FISCAL YEAR	TOT. INC. ($mill.)	NET INC. ($mill.)	TOT. ASSETS ($mill.)	NET INC. + DEPR./ ASSETS %	RET. ON EQUITY %	RET. ON ASSETS %	EARN. PER SH.$	TANG. BK. VAL.$	DIV. PER SH.$	DIV. PAYOUT %	PRICE RANGE	AVG. P/E RATIO	AVG. YIELD %
p12/31/02	1,234.8	①②419.9					①②4.40		2.38	54.1	41.55 - 32.95	8.5	6.4
12/31/01	1,033.0	③214.8	7,253.5	5.0	12.2	3.0	③2.26	19.32	2.22	98.2	43.88 - 26.55	15.6	6.3
12/31/00	879.4	①②153.3	6,226.5	4.6	9.3	2.5	①②2.01	19.02	1.96	97.5	44.88 - 29.00	18.4	5.3
12/31/99	786.6	②119.8	5,434.8	4.4	11.3	2.2	②1.71	15.57	1.73	100.9	37.50 - 27.25	18.9	5.3
12/31/98	513.8	①98.6	5,235.1	3.3	10.4	1.9	①1.61	14.93	1.64	101.9	36.06 - 23.44	18.5	5.5
12/31/97	145.6	①27.4	1,672.5	2.9	15.7	1.6	①0.70	4.52	0.44	62.8	35.25 - 26.06	43.8	1.4
12/31/96	269.9	①8.3	896.5	5.0	...	0.9	...	...	...	...	...	...	...
12/31/95	248.7	d4.0	922.8	...	...	...	...	...	...	...	...	...	...
12/31/94	244.1	7.2	...	...	...	...	...	...	...	...	...	...	...

Statistics are as originally reported. ① Excl. an extraord. chrg., $2.0 mill., 12/02; $5.5 mill., 12/98; gain, $7.9 mill., 12/97; chrg., $994,000, 12/96 ② Incl. gain on sale of real estate, $190.4 mill., 12/02; $9.1 mill., 12/01; $234,000, 12/00; $6.5 mill., 12/99 ③ Excl. acctg. chrg. $6.8 mill.

OFFICERS:
M. B. Zuckerman, Chmn.
E. H. Linde, Pres., C.E.O.
D. T. Linde, Sr. V.P., C.F.O., Treas.
INVESTOR CONTACT: Investor Relations, (617) 236-3300
PRINCIPAL OFFICE: 800 Boylston Street, Boston, MA 02199

TELEPHONE NUMBER: (617) 236-3300
FAX: (617) 536-3128
WEB: www.bostonproperties.com
NO. OF EMPLOYEES: 675 (approx.)
SHAREHOLDERS: 633 (approx.)
ANNUAL MEETING: In May
INCORPORATED: DE, March, 1997

INSTITUTIONAL HOLDINGS:
No. of Institutions: 234
Shares Held: 84,569,687
% Held: 88.7
INDUSTRY: Subdividers and developers, nec (SIC: 6552)
TRANSFER AGENT(S): EquiServe, Canton, MA

BOSTON SCIENTIFIC CORPORATION

EXCH.	SYM.	REC. PRICE	P/E RATIO	YLD.	MKT. CAP.	RANGE (52-WK.)	'02 Y/E PR.
NYSE	BSX	44.17 (2/28/03)	49.1	...	$17.90 bill.	49.94 - 21.42	42.52

MEDIUM GRADE. THE COMPANY ANTICIPATES FAVORABLE MARKET OPPORTUNITIES IN 2003 AND 2004 ACROSS ITS BUSINESSES.

*7 YEAR PRICE SCORE 126.8   ***12 MONTH PRICE SCORE 142.2**

*NYSE COMPOSITE INDEX=100

INTERIM EARNINGS (Per Share):

Qtr.	Mar.	June	Sept.	Dec.
1999	0.25	0.27	0.13	0.26
2000	0.26	0.30	0.21	0.15
2001	d0.01	d0.43	0.14	0.16
2002	0.20	0.06	0.39	0.25

INTERIM DIVIDENDS (Per Share):

Amt.	Decl.	Ex.	Rec.	Pay.
		No dividends paid.		

CAPITALIZATION (12/31/01):

	($000)	(%)
Long-Term Debt	973,000	32.1
Deferred Income Tax	43,000	1.4
Common & Surplus	2,015,000	66.5
Total	3,031,000	100.0

BUSINESS:

Boston Scientific Corporation is a developer, manufacturer and marketer of medical devices. The Company sells a broad range of products that are used by physicians to perform less invasive medical specialties, including cardiology, gastroenterology, pulmonary medicine, radiology, urology and vascular surgery. Less invasive procedures provide effective alternatives to traditional surgery by reducing procedural trauma, complexity, cost and recovery time. BSX's products are generally inserted into the human body through natural openings or small incisions in the skin and can be guided to most areas of the anatomy to diagnose and treat a wide range of medical problems.

RECENT DEVELOPMENTS:

For the year ended 12/31/02, net income was $373.0 million compared with a net loss of $54.0 million the previous year. Results for 2002 and 2001 included pre-tax restructuring related charges of $1.44 billion and $1.65 billion, respectively. The 2002 results also included a pre-tax credit of $99.0 million related to litigation settlements. Results for 2002 and 2001 also included pre-tax charges of $85.0 million and $282.0 million, respectively, for purchased research and development. Net sales climbed 9.2% to $2.92 billion from $2.67 billion the year before. Gross profit increased 16.8% to $2.05 billion from $1.75 billion in 2001. Operating income soared to $610.0 million.

PROSPECTS:

The Company anticipates favorable market opportunities in 2003 and 2004 across its businesses, particularly those related to the introduction of its drug-eluting stent technology. The Company expects to launch its TAXUS drug-eluting stent in Europe and a number of other international markets in the first quarter of 2003 and in the U.S. later in the year, subject to regulatory approvals. Sales for 2003 are targeted to be approximately $3.40 billion, reflecting worldwide coronary stent sales of approximately $540.0 million, of which about $180.0 million represent drug-eluting stent sales. Earnings per share for 2003 is expected to be about $1.29, excluding any special charges.

ANNUAL FINANCIAL DATA:

FISCAL YEAR	TOT. REVS. ($mill.)	NET INC. ($mill.)	TOT. ASSETS ($mill.)	OPER. PROFIT %	NET PROFIT %	RET. ON EQUITY %	RET. ON ASSETS %	CURR. RATIO	EARN. PER SH. $	CASH FL. PER SH. $	TANG. BK. VAL. $	PRICE RANGE	AVG. P/E RATIO
p12/31/02	2,919.0	⑨ 373.0							⑨ 0.90			44.30 - 20.48	36.0
12/31/01	2,673.0	⑧ d54.0	3,974.0	3.7	...	...	...	1.3	⑧ d0.13	...	...	27.89 - 13.25	...
12/31/00	2,664.0	⑦ 373.0	3,427.0	21.8	14.0	19.3	10.9	1.2	⑦ 0.91	1.36	3.98	29.19 - 12.19	22.7
12/31/99	2,842.0	⑥ 371.0	3,572.0	24.2	13.1	21.5	10.4	1.0	⑥ 0.92	1.33	3.44	47.06 - 17.56	35.1
12/31/98	2,233.6	⑤ d264.4	3,892.7	...	...	...	...	0.8	⑤ d0.68	d0.35	1.25	40.84 - 20.13	...
12/31/97	1,872.3	④ 160.4	1,967.8	14.4	8.6	16.3	8.2	1.3	④ 0.35	0.62	1.74	39.22 - 20.50	85.3
12/31/96	1,462.0	③ 167.1	1,512.1	21.2	11.4	18.2	11.1	1.6	③ 0.46	0.63	1.70	30.75 - 18.88	53.9
12/31/95	1,129.2	①② 6.4	1,075.3	6.6	0.6	0.9	0.6	2.0	①② 0.02	0.13	1.74	24.69 - 8.31	820.7
12/31/94	448.9	79.7	431.8	29.0	17.8	23.5	18.5	3.6	0.41	0.45	1.57	8.94 - 5.94	18.4
12/31/93	380.1	69.7	323.2	28.6	18.3	28.2	21.6	3.8	0.35	0.38	1.19	11.81 - 4.69	23.6

Statistics are as originally reported. Adj. for 2-for-1 stk. split 11/30/98. ① Incl. after-tax and spec. chgs. of $195.3 mill. ② Incl. acq. ops. of Meadox Medicals, Inc. Heart Technology, Inc., Scimed Life Systems, Inc., and Cardiovascular Imaging Systems, Inc.. ③ Incl. pre-tax nonrecurr. & spec. chrgs. rel. to acqs. of $128.3 mill. ④ Incl. after-tax merger-rel. exps. of $192.0 mill. & excl. a net chg. of $21.1 mill. for acctg. chng. chrg. ⑤ Incl. a spec. prov. for excess inv. of about $62.0 mill., a prov. for legal exps. of $22.0 mill., a spec. credit of $10.0 mill. ⑥ Incl. a net credit of $10.0 mill. ⑦ Incl. pre-tax purch. R&D chrg. of $58.0 mill. & spec. chrg. of $1.25 bill. ⑧ Incl. pre-tax purch. R&D chrg. of $282.0 mill. ⑨ Incl. pre-tax restruct. chrg. of $1.44 bill. & pre-tax credit of $99.0 mill. from litig. settle.

OFFICERS:
P. M. Nicholas, Chmn.
J. R. Tobin, Pres., C.E.O.
L. C. Best, Sr. V.P., C.F.O.
INVESTOR CONTACT: Milan Kofol, Investor Relations, (508) 650-8569
PRINCIPAL OFFICE: One Boston Scientific Place, Natick, MA 01760-1537

TELEPHONE NUMBER: (508) 650-8000
FAX: (508) 647-2200
WEB: www.bsci.com
NO. OF EMPLOYEES: 14,400 (avg.)
SHAREHOLDERS: 10,419 (approx.)
ANNUAL MEETING: In May
INCORPORATED: DE, 1979

INSTITUTIONAL HOLDINGS:
No. of Institutions: 404
Shares Held: 263,633,439
% Held: 64.6
INDUSTRY: Surgical and medical instruments (SIC: 3841)
TRANSFER AGENT(S): Equiserve, L.P., Boston, MA

BOWATER INC.

EXCH.	SYM.	REC. PRICE	P/E RATIO	YLD.	MKT. CAP.	RANGE (52-WK.)	'02 Y/E PR.
NYSE	BOW	37.95 (2/28/03)	...	2.1%	$2.08 bill.	55.80 - 31.00	41.95

MEDIUM GRADE. THE COMPANY HAS IMPLEMENTED A COST REDUCTION PROGRAM THAT IS EXPECTED TO REDUCE ANNUAL COSTS BY $75.0 MILLION.

*7 YEAR PRICE SCORE 98.9   ***12 MONTH PRICE SCORE 100.6**
*NYSE COMPOSITE INDEX=100

INTERIM EARNINGS (Per Share):

Qtr.	Mar.	June	Sept.	Dec.
1998	0.59	0.44	d0.69	0.45
1999	1.89	0.10	d0.98	0.38
2000	0.32	0.63	0.96	1.12
2001	0.72	0.36	d0.04	0.33
2002	0.22	0.95	d0.57	d1.17

INTERIM DIVIDENDS (Per Share):

Amt.	Decl.	Ex.	Rec.	Pay.
0.20Q	1/30/02	3/07/02	3/11/02	4/01/02
0.20Q	5/08/02	6/06/02	6/10/02	7/01/02
0.20Q	7/31/02	9/06/02	9/10/02	10/01/02
0.20Q	11/13/02	12/06/02	12/10/02	1/02/03
0.20Q	1/29/03	3/06/03	3/10/03	4/01/03

Indicated div.: $0.80 (Div. Reinv. Plan)

CAPITALIZATION (12/31/01):

	($000)	(%)
Long-Term Debt	1,828,000	40.3
Deferred Income Tax	601,700	13.3
Minority Interest	85,200	1.9
Common & Surplus	2,024,700	44.6
Total	4,539,600	100.0

BUSINESS:

Bowater Inc. is a global producer of newsprint. In addition, the Company makes coated and uncoated groundwood papers, bleached kraft pulp and lumber products. As of 1/28/03, BOW had 12 pulp and paper mills in the United States, Canada and South Korea and 13 North American sawmills that produce softwood and hardwood lumber. The Company also operates two facilities that convert a groundwood base sheet to coated products. These operations are supported by approximately 1.5 million acres of timberlands owned or leased in the United States and Canada and over 32.0 million acres of timber cutting rights in Canada. BOW completed the sale of its Great Northern Paper, Inc. subsidiary for $250.0 million in the third quarter of 1999. The Company is one of the world's largest consumers of recycled newspapers and magazines.

RECENT DEVELOPMENTS:

For the year ended 12/31/02, BOW incurred a net loss of $142.4 million compared with net income of $70.5 million in 2001. Earnings were adversely affected by lower transaction prices for newsprint, coated and specialty papers, market pulp and lumber, and lower shipments. Results for 2002 and 2001 included gains on the sale of assets of $85.7 million and $163.3 million. Results for 2002 also included impairment of assets of $28.5 million. Sales rose 5.2% to $2.58 billion from $2.45 billion in 2001. Results include Alliance Forest Products, Inc., acquired on 9/24/01.

PROSPECTS:

In October 2002, BOW announced that it will begin a new cost reduction program consisting of workforce reductions, lowering of manufacturing costs and rationalization of production. In 2003, these actions should reduce annual costs by $75.0 million and permanently remove about 100,000 metric tons of annual news capacity. In addition, the planned sale of 240,000 acres of timberland and four sawmills is expected to be completed during the first half of 2003. BOW expects to record a fourth quarter pre-tax charge of about $13.0 million for these reductions.

ANNUAL FINANCIAL DATA:

FISCAL YEAR	TOT. REVS. ($mill.)	NET INC. ($mill.)	TOT. ASSETS ($mill.)	OPER. PROFIT %	NET PROFIT %	RET. ON EQUITY %	RET. ON ASSETS %	CURR. RATIO	EARN. PER SH.$	CASH FL. PER SH.$	TANG. BK. VAL.$	DIV. PER SH.$	PRICE RANGE	AVG. P/E RATIO	AVG. YIELD %
p12/31/02	2,581.1	⑦⑧ d142.4							⑦⑧ d2.50			0.80	38.50 - 31.00	...	2.3
12/31/01	2,449.2	⑦ 73.2	5,765.4	13.0	3.0	3.6	1.3	0.8	⑦ 1.37	7.40	21.60	0.80	58.75 - 40.30	36.2	1.6
12/31/00	2,333.7	⑦ 159.4	5,004.1	15.6	6.8	8.8	3.2	0.6	⑦ 3.02	62.45	18.50	0.80	59.56 - 41.88	16.8	1.6
12/31/99	2,134.7	⑤⑥ 78.7	4,552.2	11.4	3.7	4.4	1.7	1.3	⑤⑥ 1.41	52.14	14.80	0.80	60.56 - 36.94	34.6	1.6
12/31/98	1,995.0	⑤ d18.5	5,091.4	7.1	...	...	...	0.9	⑤ d0.44	52.55	15.98	0.80	60.50 - 31.19	...	1.7
12/31/97	1,484.5	53.7	2,745.8	9.1	3.6	4.7	2.0	3.7	1.25	5.48	27.93	0.80	57.00 - 36.88	37.5	1.7
12/31/96	1,718.3	④ 204.1	2,865.5	17.5	11.9	17.4	7.1	3.0	④ 4.71	8.96	27.93	0.75	41.63 - 31.50	7.8	2.1
12/31/95	2,001.1	③ 258.2	2,908.2	27.4	12.9	23.6	8.9	2.4	③ 5.60	10.16	23.91	0.60	54.38 - 26.38	7.2	1.5
12/31/94	1,359.0	② d4.8	2,851.4	3.1	...	...	...	2.4	② d0.59	4.47	17.43	0.60	29.63 - 20.38	...	2.4
12/31/93	1,353.7	① d64.5	2,726.2	...	...	...	...	1.8	① d1.84	2.71	18.53	0.75	24.63 - 18.00	...	3.5

Statistics are as originally reported. ① Incl. gain of $30.6 mill. ② Incl. gains of $43.1 mill. fr. the sale of timberlands. ③ Incl. gains of $2.2 mill., chrgs. of $30 mill., restruct. chrgs. of $24 mill., bef. $7.1 mill. extraord. chrg. ④ Bef. an extraord. chrg. of $3.9 mill. ($0.09 a sh.); incl. pre-tax of $98.1 mill. ⑤ Incl. a chrg. of $120.0 mill. to reduce the book value of assets at the Millinocket, Maine paper mill, 1998; $92.0 mill., Great Northern Paper, Inc., 1999. ⑥ Incl. a pre-tax gain of $225.4 million. ⑦ Incl. nonrecurr. gain of $85.7 mill., 2002; $167.7 mill., 2001; $7.3 mill., 2000. ⑧ Incl. impairment of assets of $28.5 mill.

OFFICERS: A. M. Nemirow, Chmn., Pres., C.E.O. A. Fuller, Exec. V.P. D. G. Maffuci, Sr. V.P., C.F.O. **INVESTOR CONTACT:** Donald J. D'Antuono, V.P. Corp. Development, (864) 282-9370 **PRINCIPAL OFFICE:** 55 East Camperdown Way, P.O. Box 1028, Greenville, SC 29602-1028	**TELEPHONE NUMBER:** (864) 271-7733 **FAX:** (864) 282-9482 **WEB:** www.bowater.com **NO. OF EMPLOYEES:** 9,400 (avg.) **SHAREHOLDERS:** 5,365 (of record) **ANNUAL MEETING:** In May **INCORPORATED:** DE, 1964	**INSTITUTIONAL HOLDINGS:** No. of Institutions: 191 Shares Held: 54,939,510 % Held: 99.4 **INDUSTRY:** Paper mills (SIC: 2621) **TRANSFER AGENT(S):** The Bank of New York, New York, NY

BP P.L.C.

EXCH.	SYM.	REC. PRICE	P/E RATIO	YLD.	MKT. CAP.	RANGE (52-WK.)	'02 Y/E PR.
NYSE	BP	38.11 (2/28/03)	...	...	...	53.98 - 34.67	40.65

UPPER MEDIUM GRADE. THE COMPANY HAS AGREED IN PRINCIPLE TO ENTER INTO A STRATEGIC PARTNERSHIP IN RUSSIA.

TRADING VOLUME
Thousand Shares

*7 YEAR PRICE SCORE 105.3   ***12 MONTH PRICE SCORE 95.1**
*NYSE COMPOSITE INDEX=100

INTERIM EARNINGS (Per Share):

Qtr.	Mar.	June	Sept.	Dec.
1998	---------- 1.03 ----------			
1999	0.21	0.51	0.58	0.53
2000	0.95	0.83	0.92	0.63
2001	0.88	0.84	0.52	d0.11
2002	0.35	0.54	0.76	0.18

INTERIM DIVIDENDS (Per Share):

Amt.	Decl.	Ex.	Rec.	Pay.
0.345	... 02/20/02	02/22/02	03/18/02	
0.345	... 05/15/02	05/17/02	06/10/02	
0.36	... 08/14/02	08/16/02	09/09/02	
0.36	... 11/13/02	11/15/02	12/09/02	
0.375	... 2/26/03	2/28/03	3/24/03	

CAPITALIZATION (12/31/01):

	($000)	(%)
Capital Lease Obligations..	12,327,000	13.9
Deferred Income Tax	1,655,000	1.9
Minority Interest	627,000	0.7
Common & Surplus	74,367,000	83.6
Total	88,976,000	100.0

BUSINESS:

BP p.l.c. was formed through the 1/4/99 merger of British Petroleum Company, P.L.C. and U.S.-based Amoco Corp., creating one of the largest energy companies in the world in terms of revenues, market value and oil and natural gas reserves. BP's exploration and production activities (12.7% of 2002 revenues) include oil and natural gas exploration and field development and production, together with pipeline transportation and natural gas processing. Gas, power

and renewables activities (18.4%) include marketing and trading of natural gas, liquefied natural gas, natural gas liquids and power. The activities of refining and marketing (62.1%) include oil supply and trading as well as refining and marketing. Chemicals activities (6.5%) include petrochemicals manufacturing and marketing. BP's other businesses includes its corporate activities (0.3%). On 4/18/00, BP acquired Atlantic Richfield Company.

RECENT DEVELOPMENTS:

For the year ended 12/31/02, net income was $6.85 billion versus $6.56 billion a year earlier. Results for 2002 and 2001 included nonrecurring gains of $1.44 billion and $683.0 million, respectively. Revenues rose 2.6% to

$178.72 billion. The increase in revenues reflected refining and marketing and chemicals gains, partially offset by lower revenues from exploration and production as well as gas, power and renewables activities.

PROSPECTS:

On 2/11/03, BP and the Alfa Group and Access-Renova (AAR) said that they have agreed in principle to combine their interests in Russia. For its 50.0% stake in the new company, BP will pay AAR $3.00 billion in cash on completion of the deal and three subsequent annual tranches of $1.25 billion in BP shares. The transaction, which will be

effective from 1/1/03, is scheduled for completion in the summer of 2003. Separately, on 1/13/03, BP announced that it has agreed in principle to sell its 96.14% stake in the North Sea Forties oilfield, together with a package of shallow-water assets in the Gulf of Mexico, to Apache Corp. for $1.30 billion.

ANNUAL FINANCIAL DATA:

FISCAL YEAR	TOT. REVS. ($mill.)	NET INC. ($mill.)	TOT. ASSETS ($mill.)	OPER. PROFIT %	NET PROFIT %	RET. ON EQUITY %	RET. ON ASSETS %	CURR. RATIO	EARN. PER SH. $	DIV. PER SH. $	PRICE RANGE	AVG. P/E RATIO	AVG. YIELD %
p12/31/02	178,721.0	⑤ 6,845.0							⑤ 1.82	1.41	53.98 - 36.25	24.8	3.1
12/31/01	174,218.0	⑨ 8,010.0	141,158.0	8.2	4.6	10.8	5.7	1.0	⑨ 2.13	1.29	55.20 - 42.20	22.9	2.6
⑧ 12/31/00	148,062.0	⑨ 11,870.0	143,938.0	10.4	8.0	16.2	8.2	1.1	⑨ 3.24	1.22	60.63 - 43.13	15.9	2.3
12/31/99	83,566.0	④ 5,008.0	89,561.0	8.8	6.0	11.6	5.6	1.0	④ 1.55	1.52	62.63 - 40.19	66.0	3.0
12/31/98	68,304.0	③ 3,260.0	84,500.0	6.4	4.8	7.8	3.9	0.9	③ 1.03	1.21	48.66 - 36.50	41.3	2.8
② 12/31/97	72,960.6	③ 4,146.6	55,193.9	8.8	5.7	17.5	7.5	1.0	③ 2.20	1.36	46.50 - 32.44	17.9	3.5
12/31/96	75,796.7	③ 4,324.4	55,193.5	8.2	5.7	19.9	7.8	1.0	③ 2.33	0.86	35.94 - 23.63	12.7	2.9
12/31/95	56,072.6	③ 1,742.5	50,242.7	7.9	3.1	9.5	3.5	1.0	③ 0.95	0.64	25.97 - 18.91	23.6	2.8
12/31/94	51,826.5	2,468.0	48,652.7	7.1	4.8	14.3	5.1	1.0	1.37	0.44	21.31 - 14.59	13.1	2.4
12/31/93	51,767.9	③ 910.9	45,942.4	5.8	1.8	6.3	2.0	1.0	③ 0.51	0.41	16.34 - 10.53	26.5	3.1

Statistics are as originally reported. All figs. in U.S. dollars unless noted. Per sh. figs. & ratios are calc. using ADRs. One ADR=six ord. shs. Exch. rates: $1US=£0.62, 12/28/02; £0.69, 12/28/01; £0.67, 12/31/00; £0.62, 12/31/99; £0.61, 12/31/98; £0.71, 12/31/97; £0.59, 12/31/96; £0.64, 12/31/95; £0.64, 12/31/94; £0.68, 12/31/93. Adj. for 2-for-1 stk. split, 10/4/99 & 6/97 ① Incl cr of $623.0 mil ② Prior results refl ops of British Petroleum only ③ Incl chrgs 12/31/97, $57.0 mil; chrgs 12/31/96, $733.0 mil; chrgs 12/31/95, $1.41 bil; chrgs 12/31/93, $343.0 mil ④ Incl aft-tax chrgs of $2.05 bil ⑤ Incl nonrecur gain, 12/31/02: $1.44 bil; 12/31/01: $535.0 mil; 12/31/00: $222.0 mil ⑥ Refl acq of Atlantic Richfield Co.

OFFICERS:
P. D. Sutherland, Chmn.
J. Browne, Group Chief Exec.
B. Grote, C.F.O.
INVESTOR CONTACT: Terry LaMore, Investor Relations, (212) 451-8034 (U.S.)
PRINCIPAL OFFICE: Britannic House, 1 Finsbury Circus, London, United Kingdom

TELEPHONE NUMBER: (212) 421-5010 (U.S.)
FAX: (212) 421-5084 (U.S.)
WEB: www.bp.com
NO. OF EMPLOYEES: 110,150 (avg.)
SHAREHOLDERS: 359,647 ordinary
ANNUAL MEETING: In Apr.
INCORPORATED: U.K., 1909

INSTITUTIONAL HOLDINGS:
No. of Institutions: 873
Shares Held: 510,456,029
% Held: 13.6
INDUSTRY: Crude petroleum and natural gas (SIC: 1311)
DEPOSITARY BANKS(S): JP Morgan Chase Bank, Boston, MA (United States)

BRADY CORPORATION

EXCH.	SYM.	REC. PRICE	P/E RATIO	YLD.	MKT. CAP.	RANGE (52-WK.)	'02 Y/E PR.	DIV. ACH.
NYSE	BRC	26.63 (2/28/03)	24.9	3.0%	$0.61 bill.	40.70 - 25.05	33.35	18 yrs.

UPPER MEDIUM GRADE. THE COMPANY IS TARGETING FISCAL 2003 EARNINGS OF $1.27 TO $1.37 PER SHARE.

*7 YEAR PRICE SCORE 119.5   ***12 MONTH PRICE SCORE 96.3**

*NYSE COMPOSITE INDEX=100

INTERIM EARNINGS (Per Share):

Qtr.	Oct.	Jan.	Apr.	July
1998-99	0.38	0.35	0.57	0.43
1999-00	0.54	0.43	0.51	0.57
2000-01	0.49	0.37	0.44	d0.12
2001-02	0.34	0.26	0.36	0.24
2002-03	0.35	0.12	...	...

INTERIM DIVIDENDS (Per Share):

Amt.	Decl.	Ex.	Rec.	Pay.
0.19Q	2/19/02	4/08/02	4/10/02	4/30/02
0.19Q	5/14/02	7/09/02	7/11/02	7/31/02
0.20Q	9/10/02	10/09/02	10/11/02	10/31/02
0.20Q	11/14/02	1/08/03	1/11/03	1/31/03
0.20Q	2/18/03	4/08/03	4/10/03	4/30/03

Indicated div.: $0.80 (Div. Reinv. Plan)

CAPITALIZATION (7/31/02):

	($000)	(%)
Long-Term Debt	3,751	1.1
Preferred Stock	2,855	0.9
Common & Surplus	321,387	98.0
Total	327,993	100.0

BUSINESS:

Brady Corporation (formerly W.H. Brady Co.) is an international manufacturer and marketer of identification products and specialty coated materials, which are designed to help companies improve safety, security, productivity and performance. BRC's array of labels are used in applications ranging from marking wires and cables in facilities, electrical, telecommunication and transportation equipment to

marking electronic components and printed circuit boards that require identification for purposes such as maintenance, work-in-process or asset tracking. Offerings ranging from signs, pipemakers, lockout/tagout devices, labels and tags to services including consulting, product installation and training enable companies to comply with safety and environmental regulations.

RECENT DEVELOPMENTS:

For the quarter ended 1/31/03, net income totaled $2.8 million, down 54.1% compared with $6.1 million in the corresponding prior-year period. Earnings were hurt by unfavorable sales mix changes and temporary disruptions related to the implementation of a new computer system for BRC's North American direct marketing business. Net sales climbed 7.4% to $129.6 million from $120.6 million a

year earlier. Cost of products sold increased 8.1% to $65.9 million from $61.0 million the year before, while selling, general and administrative expenses rose 18.3% to $54.5 million from $46.1 million the previous year. Operating income fell 51.5% to $4.5 million from $9.4 million in the prior year.

PROSPECTS:

The Company is targeting sales of between $552.0 million and $562.0 million in the current fiscal year, along with earnings of $1.27 to $1.37 per share. On 1/20/03, BRC announced that it has completed its acquisition of Tiscor,

Inc., a developer of software used in safety and security applications for hand-held computing devices. Meanwhile, the Company continues to expand its operations in Asia, with new manufacturing facilities in Malaysia and China.

ANNUAL FINANCIAL DATA:

FISCAL YEAR	TOT. REVS. ($000)	NET INC. ($000)	TOT. ASSETS ($000)	OPER. PROFIT %	NET PROFIT %	RET. ON EQUITY %	RET. ON ASSETS %	CURR. RATIO	EARN. PER SH. $	CASH FL. PER SH. $	TANG. BK. VAL. $	DIV. PER SH. $	PRICE RANGE	AVG. P/E RATIO	AVG. YIELD %
7/31/02	516,962	① 28,253	420,525	8.0	5.5	8.7	6.7	2.8	① 1.20	1.92	9.23	0.77	40.70 - 26.70	28.1	2.3
7/31/01	545,944	① 27,546	392,476	8.2	5.0	9.1	7.0	2.7	① 1.18	2.17	8.89	0.73	39.24 - 25.55	27.5	2.3
7/31/00	541,077	47,201	398,134	12.8	8.7	16.2	11.9	2.3	2.05	2.84	8.25	0.69	34.94 - 24.50	14.5	2.3
7/31/99	470,862	① 39,584	351,120	13.5	8.4	15.2	11.3	2.8	① 1.73	2.41	8.17	0.65	36.31 - 19.50	16.1	2.3
7/31/98	455,150	① 28,036	311,824	10.1	6.2	12.0	9.0	3.1	① 1.23	1.83	7.87	0.61	35.75 - 16.25	21.1	2.3
7/31/97	426,081	31,707	291,662	11.8	7.4	15.4	10.9	3.3	1.44	1.05	7.64	0.54	35.00 - 21.63	19.7	1.9
7/31/96	359,542	28,027	261,835	11.4	7.8	14.8	10.7	3.4	1.27	0.88	6.96	0.43	27.50 - 18.00	17.9	1.9
7/31/95	314,362	27,911	230,005	12.9	8.9	16.3	12.1	4.8	1.28	1.71	7.69	0.30	27.00 - 15.67	16.7	1.4
7/31/94	255,841	18,540	202,509	11.5	7.2	12.8	9.2	4.2	0.85	1.29	6.54	0.24	16.33 - 14.08	17.9	1.6
7/31/93	242,970	① 16,856	179,901	10.4	6.9	13.2	9.4	3.8	① 0.78	1.25	5.79	0.21	14.33 - 11.33	16.5	1.6

Statistics are as originally reported. Adj. for stk. splits: 3-for-1, 12/95. ① Incl. non-recur. pre-tax chrg. in 2002 of $2.7 mill.; 2001, $9.6 mill.; gain of $611,000, 1999; $5.4 mill. chrg., 1998; $1.2 mill. gain, 1993.

OFFICERS:
K. M. Hudson, Chmn.
F. M. Jaehnert, Pres., C.E.O.
D. W. Schroeder, Sr. V.P., C.F.O.
D. Rearic, Sr. V.P., Treas., Asst. Sec.

INVESTOR CONTACT: Barbara Bolens, Dir., Invest. Rel., (414) 438-6940

PRINCIPAL OFFICE: 6555 West Good Hope Road, Milwaukee, WI 53223-0571

TELEPHONE NUMBER: (414) 358-6600
FAX: (414) 438-6910
WEB: www.bradycorp.com

NO. OF EMPLOYEES: 3,200 (approx.)

SHAREHOLDERS: 350 (class A); 3 (class B)

ANNUAL MEETING: In Nov.

INCORPORATED: WI, 1939

INSTITUTIONAL HOLDINGS:
No. of Institutions: 88
Shares Held: 16,070,010
% Held: 69.6

INDUSTRY: Signs and advertising specialities (SIC: 3993)

TRANSFER AGENT(S): Wells Fargo Shareowner Services, St. Paul, MN

BRIGGS & STRATTON CORPORATION

EXCH.	SYM.	REC. PRICE	P/E RATIO	YLD.	MKT. CAP.	RANGE (52-WK.)	'02 Y/E PR.	DIV. ACH.
NYSE	BGG	39.50 (2/28/03)	12.8	3.2%	$0.85 bill.	48.39 - 30.75	42.47	11 yrs.

MEDIUM GRADE. THE COMPANY IS PROJECTING FULL-YEAR FISCAL 2003 NET INCOME OF APPROXIMATELY $72.0 MILLION.

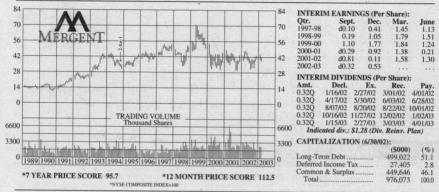

*7 YEAR PRICE SCORE 95.7   *12 MONTH PRICE SCORE 112.5
*NYSE COMPOSITE INDEX=100

INTERIM EARNINGS (Per Share):

Qtr.	Sept.	Dec.	Mar.	June
1997-98	d0.10	0.41	1.45	1.13
1998-99	0.19	1.05	1.79	1.51
1999-00	1.10	1.77	1.84	1.24
2000-01	d0.29	0.92	1.38	0.21
2001-02	d0.81	0.11	1.58	1.30
2002-03	d0.32	0.53	...	...

INTERIM DIVIDENDS (Per Share):

Amt.	Decl.	Ex.	Rec.	Pay.
0.32Q	1/16/02	2/27/02	3/01/02	4/01/02
0.32Q	4/17/02	5/30/02	6/03/02	6/28/02
0.32Q	8/07/02	8/20/02	8/22/02	10/01/02
0.32Q	10/16/02	11/27/02	12/02/02	1/02/03
0.32Q	1/15/03	2/27/03	3/03/03	4/01/03

Indicated div.: $1.28 (Div. Reinv. Plan)

CAPITALIZATION (6/30/02):

	($000)	(%)
Long-Term Debt	499,022	51.1
Deferred Income Tax	27,405	2.8
Common & Surplus	449,646	46.1
Total	976,073	100.0

BUSINESS:

Briggs & Stratton Corporation is a producer of air-cooled gasoline engines for outdoor power equipment. The Company designs, manufactures, markets and services these products for original equipment manufacturers (OEMs) worldwide. These engines are primarily aluminum alloy gasoline engines ranging from 3 through 25 horsepower. BGG's engines are used primarily by the lawn and garden equipment industry. Major lawn and garden equipment applications include walk-behind lawn mowers, riding lawn mowers and garden tillers. Briggs & Stratton engines are marketed under various brand names including CLASSIC™, SPRINT™, QUATTRO™, QUANTUM®, INTEK™, I/C®, INDUSTRIAL PLUS™ and VANGUARD™. BGG also designs, manufactures and markets portable generators, pressure washers and related accessories. On 5/15/01, BGG acquired Generac Portable Products for net cash of $267.0 million. Dividends have been paid since 1929.

RECENT DEVELOPMENTS:

For the quarter ended 12/31/02, net income was $11.7 million compared with $2.4 million in the same period a year earlier. BGG attributed the improved earnings to the absence of an early retirement charge experienced in December 2001, increased utilization of production capacity, greater revenues from export sales due to a strengthening Euro and realization of cost reductions from planned initiatives. Net sales rose 5.7% to $352.6 million. Gross profit improved to $67.1 million, or 19.0% of net sales, versus $54.9 million, or 16.4% of net sales, the year before.

PROSPECTS:

BGG's near-term outlook appears solid. The Company expects that fiscal 2003 annual production volumes for its engine segment will be higher and unit sales volume will be flat compared with the previous year. Meanwhile, the power products segment, which has benefited from increased generator unit sales and production volume due to storm activity, is expected to post higher sales of pressure washer units over the second half of fiscal 2003 due to increased placement at retailers. Accordingly, BGG is projecting full-year fiscal 2003 net income of approximately $72.0 million and net sales approximately 4.0% higher than the prior fiscal year.

ANNUAL FINANCIAL DATA:

FISCAL YEAR	TOT. REVS. ($mill.)	NET INC. ($mill.)	TOT. ASSETS ($mill.)	OPER. PROFIT %	NET PROFIT %	RET. ON EQUITY %	RET. ON ASSETS %	CURR. RATIO	EARN. PER SH. $	CASH FL. PER SH. $	TANG. BK. VAL. $	DIV. PER SH. $	PRICE RANGE	AVG. P/E RATIO	AVG. YIELD %
6/30/02	1,529.4	53.1	1,349.0	7.7	3.5	11.8	3.9	2.5	²2.36	4.87	13.34	1.27	48.39 - 30.75	16.8	3.2
7/01/01	1,312.4	48.0	1,296.2	7.6	-3.7	11.4	3.7	2.5	2.21	4.90	11.53	1.24	48.38 - 29.65	17.7	3.2
7/02/00	1,590.6	②136.5	930.2	12.9	8.6	33.3	14.7	1.5	②5.97	8.22	18.51	1.21	53.88 - 30.38	7.1	2.9
6/27/99	1,501.7	106.1	875.9	12.0	7.1	29.0	12.1	1.6	4.52	6.64	15.45	1.17	71.13 - 46.69	13.0	2.0
6/28/98	1,327.6	70.6	793.4	9.4	5.3	22.3	8.9	1.7	2.85	4.78	12.87	1.13	52.44 - 33.63	15.1	2.6
6/29/97	1,316.4	61.6	842.2	7.9	4.7	17.5	7.3	2.0	2.16	3.68	13.40	1.10	53.63 - 42.63	22.3	2.3
6/30/96	1,287.0	92.4	838.2	11.9	7.2	18.5	11.0	2.4	3.19	4.68	17.17	1.06	46.88 - 36.50	13.1	2.5
7/02/95	1,339.7	104.8	798.5	12.7	7.8	23.8	13.1	2.3	3.62	5.16	15.19	1.01	44.13 - 32.25	10.5	2.6
7/03/94	1,285.5	①102.5	777.4	13.4	8.0	25.4	13.2	2.3	①3.54	5.03	13.96	0.91	45.13 - 30.50	10.7	2.4
6/27/93	1,139.5	70.3	656.1	11.4	6.2	19.5	10.7	2.2	2.43	4.06	12.44	0.86	44.75 - 23.38	14.0	2.5

Statistics are as originally reported. Adj. for 2-for-1 stk. split, 11/94. ① Bef. acctg. chg. of $32.6 mill.; incls. non-recurr. credit of $2.8 mill. ② Incl. non-recurr. gain $16.5 mill.

OFFICERS:
J. S. Shiely, Chmn., Pres., C.E.O.
J. E. Brenn, Sr. V.P., C.F.O.
C. R. Twinem, Treas.
INVESTOR CONTACT: G. R. Thompson, V.P., Corp. Comm., (414) 259-5312
PRINCIPAL OFFICE: 12301 West Wirth Street, Wauwatosa, WI 53222

TELEPHONE NUMBER: (414) 259-5333
FAX: (414) 259-9594
WEB: www.briggsandstratton.com
NO. OF EMPLOYEES: 7,019 (avg.)
SHAREHOLDERS: 4,669 (record)
ANNUAL MEETING: In Oct.
INCORPORATED: DE, June, 1924; reincorp., WI, Oct., 1992

INSTITUTIONAL HOLDINGS:
No. of Institutions: 164
Shares Held: 18,272,230
% Held: 84.4
INDUSTRY: Internal combustion engines, nec (SIC: 3519)
TRANSFER AGENT(S): U.S. Bank, N.A., Milwaukee, WI

BRINKER INTERNATIONAL, INC.

EXCH.	SYM.	REC. PRICE	P/E RATIO	YLD.	MKT. CAP.	RANGE (52-WK.)	'02 Y/E PR.
NYSE	EAT	27.72 (2/28/03)	17.2	...	$2.70 bill.	36.00 - 24.07	32.25

UPPER MEDIUM GRADE. THE COMPANY EXPECTS THIRD QUARTER EARNINGS FOR FISCAL 2003 TO RANGE FROM $0.46 TO $0.47 PER SHARE.

*7 YEAR PRICE SCORE 170.9   ***12 MONTH PRICE SCORE 107.1**

NYSE COMPOSITE INDEX=100

INTERIM EARNINGS (Per Share):

Qtr.	Sept.	Dec.	Mar.	June
1998-99	0.21	0.17	0.21	0.27
1999-00	0.27	0.25	0.29	0.36
2000-01	0.35	0.32	0.34	0.42
2001-02	0.39	0.35	0.34	0.44
2002-03	0.45	0.38	...	...

INTERIM DIVIDENDS (Per Share):

Amt.	Decl.	Ex.	Rec.	Pay.
		No dividends paid.		

CAPITALIZATION (6/26/02):

	($000)	(%)
Long-Term Debt	426,679	30.0
Deferred Income Tax	17,295	1.2
Common & Surplus	977,096	68.8
Total	1,421,070	100.0

BUSINESS:

Brinker International, Inc. (formerly Chili's, Inc.) operates and develops full-service restaurants. As of 12/25/02, the Company owned, operated or franchised 1,343 restaurants under the names CHILI'S GRILL & BAR, ROMANO'S MACARONI GRILL, ON THE BORDER MEXICAN GRILL & CANTINA, COZYMEL'S COASTAL GRILL, MAGGIANO'S LITTLE ITALY, CORNER BAKERY CAFE, BIG BOWL ASIAN KITCHEN, and ROCKFISH SEAFOOD GRILL. CHILI'S operates full-service restaurants, featuring a casual atmosphere and limited menu of broadly appealing food items. ROMANO'S operates upscale and casual full-service Italian-theme restaurants. ON THE BORDER is a full-service, casual, Tex-Mex theme restaurant featuring Southwest specialties. COZYMEL'S restaurants are casual and upscale, authentic Mexican restaurants.

RECENT DEVELOPMENTS:

For the 13 weeks ended 12/25/02, net income advanced 7.5% to $37.2 million from $34.6 million in the corresponding prior-year period. Earnings for 2002 included after-tax charges of $6.4 million associated with store closings and impairment charges. Revenues increased 15.9% to $794.5 million from $685.8 million a year earlier. The increase in revenues was driven by an increase in overall comparable same-store sales for all concepts, which were up 2.1% year over year. Same-store sales were up 4.1% and 1.5% at Chili's and Maggiano's, respectively, but were down 0.6% and 2.4% at Macaroni Grill and On The Border, respectively. Operating income improved 3.9% to $59.0 million. Interest expense declined 13.6% to $2.5 million.

PROSPECTS:

On 12/23/02, EAT signed an agreement with Waterloo Restaurant Ventures, Inc. to become the first domestic franchisee for Romano's Macaroni Grill. Waterloo will develop and operate Romano's Macaroni Grills in the Pacific Northwest, including Oregon and Washington. Separately, EAT expects third quarter earnings for fiscal 2003 to range from $0.46 to $0.47 per share based on expectations of comparable same-store sales growth in the 1.0% to 2.0% range. Fiscal 2003 earnings per share are anticipated to range from $1.88 to $1.92, excluding charges.

ANNUAL FINANCIAL DATA:

FISCAL YEAR	TOT. REVS. ($mill.)	NET INC. ($mill.)	TOT. ASSETS ($mill.)	OPER. PROFIT %	NET PROFIT %	RET. ON EQUITY %	RET. ON ASSETS %	CURR. RATIO	EARN. PER SH. $	CASH FL. PER SH. $	TANG. BK. VAL. $	PRICE RANGE	AVG. P/E RATIO
6/26/02	2,887.1	③ 152.7	1,783.3	8.6	5.3	15.6	8.6	0.5	③ 1.52	2.89	8.04	36.00 - 24.07	19.8
6/27/01	2,473.7	145.1	1,442.3	9.3	5.9	16.1	10.1	0.6	1.42	2.41	7.66	31.30 - 21.30	18.5
6/28/00	2,159.8	117.8	1,162.3	9.1	5.5	15.5	10.1	0.4	1.17	2.08	6.99	28.88 - 13.83	18.3
6/30/99	1,870.6	② 85.2	1,085.6	8.2	4.6	12.9	7.9	0.5	② 0.83	1.64	5.94	20.42 - 13.25	20.2
6/24/98	1,574.4	69.1	989.4	7.5	4.4	11.6	7.0	0.5	0.68	1.54	5.23	19.50 - 10.00	21.7
6/25/97	1,335.3	60.5	996.9	7.3	4.5	11.6	6.1	0.7	0.54	1.24	4.55	11.92 - 7.08	17.6
6/26/96	1,163.0	① 34.4	888.8	7.3	3.0	5.7	3.9	0.7	① 0.29	0.85	4.62	12.67 - 8.50	36.1
6/28/95	1,042.2	72.7	732.8	10.4	7.0	14.6	9.9	1.0	0.65	1.18	4.53	13.92 - 7.92	16.7
6/29/94	878.5	61.6	558.7	10.8	7.0	14.8	11.0	0.5	0.55	1.01	3.84	22.45 - 10.00	29.3
6/30/93	652.9	48.9	435.3	11.1	7.5	14.6	11.2	0.4	0.46	0.80	3.25	20.56 - 12.15	35.7

Statistics are as originally reported. Adj. for stk. splits: 50.0%, 1/01; 3-for-2, 3/94. ① Incl. non-recurr. chrg. $50.0 mill. & credit $9.3 mill. ② Bef. acctg. charge of $6.4 mill. ③ Incl. after-tax non-recurr. chrg. of $13.1 mill.

OFFICERS:
R. A. McDougall, Chmn., C.E.O.
D. H. Brooks, Pres., C.O.O.
C. Sonsteby, Exec. V.P., C.F.O.
INVESTOR CONTACT: Jeremy Wilson, Investor Relations, (972) 770-7228
PRINCIPAL OFFICE: 6820 LBJ Freeway, Dallas, TX 75240

TELEPHONE NUMBER: (972) 980-9917
FAX: (972) 770-9593
WEB: www.brinker.com
NO. OF EMPLOYEES: 90,000 (approx.)
SHAREHOLDERS: 1,126
ANNUAL MEETING: In Nov.
INCORPORATED: DE, Sept., 1983

INSTITUTIONAL HOLDINGS:
No. of Institutions: 287
Shares Held: 88,274,891
% Held: 91.1

INDUSTRY: Eating places (SIC: 5812)

TRANSFER AGENT(S): Mellon Investor Services, LLC, Dallas, TX

BRISTOL-MYERS SQUIBB COMPANY

EXCH.	SYM.	REC. PRICE	P/E RATIO	YLD.	MKT. CAP.	RANGE (52-WK.)	'02 Y/E PR.	DIV. ACH.
NYSE	BMY	23.30 (2/28/03)	24.3	4.8%	$45.10 bill.	51.20 - 19.49	23.15	30 yrs.

MEDIUM GRADE. THE COMPANY EXPECTS DILUTED EARNINGS TO RANGE FROM $1.60 TO $1.65 PER SHARE FOR 2003.

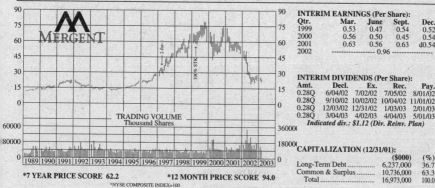

INTERIM EARNINGS (Per Share):

Qtr.	Mar.	June	Sept.	Dec.
1999	0.53	0.47	0.54	0.52
2000	0.56	0.50	0.45	0.54
2001	0.63	0.56	0.63	d0.54
2002	------------------ 0.96 ------------------			

INTERIM DIVIDENDS (Per Share):

Amt.	Decl.	Ex.	Rec.	Pay.
0.28Q	6/04/02	7/02/02	7/05/02	8/01/02
0.28Q	9/10/02	10/02/02	10/04/02	11/01/02
0.28Q	12/03/02	12/31/02	1/03/03	2/01/03
0.28Q	3/04/03	4/02/03	4/04/03	5/01/03

Indicated div.: $1.12 (Div. Reinv. Plan)

TRADING VOLUME
Thousand Shares

CAPITALIZATION (12/31/01):

	($000)	(%)
Long-Term Debt	6,237,000	36.7
Common & Surplus	10,736,000	63.3
Total	16,973,000	100.0

*7 YEAR PRICE SCORE 62.2   ***12 MONTH PRICE SCORE 94.0**

*NYSE COMPOSITE INDEX=100

BUSINESS:

Bristol-Myers Squibb Company, through its divisions and subsidiaries, is a major producer and distributor of medicines. Major products include PRAVACHOL® (12.5% of 2002 sales), a cholesterol-lowering agent; PLAVIX® (10.4%), a platelet aggregation inhibitor; and GLUCOPHAGE® (1.6%), an oral medication for treatment of non-insulin dependent (type 2) diabetes. The Company also produces and distributes infant formulas, ostomy products and wound care products. In August 2001, BMY completed the tax-free spin-off of its Zimmer business. On 11/15/01, the Company sold its Clairol beauty care subsidiary for $4.95 billion.

RECENT DEVELOPMENTS:

For the year ended 12/31/02, income was $1.86 billion, before a gain of $33.0 million from discontinued operations, versus income of $2.15 billion, before a gain of $2.79 billion from discontinued operations, in 2001. Results for 2002 included a pre-tax acquired in-process research and development charge of $169.0 million, a pre-tax provision for restructuring and other items of $649.0 million, a pre-tax gain of $30.0 million from the sale of businesses/products lines, and a pre-tax asset impairment charge of $403.0 million. Results for 2001 included net non-recurring charges of $2.88 billion. Revenues climbed to $18.12 billion from $17.99 billion the year before. Comparisons were made with restated prior-year figures.

PROSPECTS:

The Company's revenues are benefiting from higher worldwide sales of PRAVACHOL® and increased sales of TAXOL in Japan. However, this growth is being partially offset by increased generic competition for domestic products, including GLUCOPHAGE® IR, TAXOL and BUSPAR®. Looking ahead to 2003, BMY expects diluted earnings to range from $1.60 and $1.65 per share, excluding non-recurring items and any in-process research and development that may result from external development activities. This earnings guidance is partly based on revenue growth of BMY's key products, growth in its Oncology Therapeutics Network and the introduction of new products.

ANNUAL FINANCIAL DATA:

FISCAL YEAR	TOT. REVS. ($mill.)	NET INC. ($mill.)	TOT. ASSETS ($mill.)	OPER. PROFIT %	NET PROFIT %	RET. ON EQUITY %	RET. ON ASSETS %	CURR. RATIO	EARN. PER SH. $	CASH FL. PER SH. $	TANG. BK. VAL.$	DIV. PER SH.$	PRICE RANGE	AVG. P/E RATIO	AVG. YIELD %
p12/31/02	18,119.0	⑥ 1,862.0							⑥ 0.96			1.12	51.95 - 19.49	37.2	3.1
12/31/01	19,423.0	⑤ 2,527.0	27,057.0	14.0	13.0	23.5	9.3	1.4	⑤ 1.29	1.68	1.70	1.10	73.50 - 48.50	47.3	1.8
12/31/00	18,216.0	④ 4,096.0	17,578.0	30.1	22.5	44.6	23.3	1.7	④ 2.05	2.42	3.96	0.98	74.88 - 42.44	28.6	1.7
12/31/99	20,222.0	4,167.0	17,114.0	28.9	20.6	48.2	24.3	1.7	2.06	2.39	3.61	0.86	79.25 - 57.25	33.1	1.3
12/31/98	18,284.0	③ 3,141.0	16,272.0	29.1	17.2	41.5	19.3	1.5	③ 1.55	1.85	3.01	0.78	67.63 - 44.16	36.1	1.4
12/31/97	16,701.0	③ 3,205.0	14,977.0	25.2	19.2	44.4	21.4	1.5	③ 1.57	1.86	2.82	0.76	49.09 - 26.63	24.1	2.0
12/31/96	15,065.0	2,850.0	14,685.0	26.2	18.9	43.4	19.4	1.5	1.42	1.68	2.53	0.75	29.09 - 19.50	17.1	3.1
12/31/95	13,767.0	① 1,812.0	13,930.0	24.0	13.2	31.1	13.0	1.5	①⑦ 0.90	1.12	2.28	0.74	21.78 - 14.44	20.2	4.1
12/31/94	11,984.0	1,842.0	12,911.0	26.9	15.4	32.3	14.3	1.6	0.91	1.07	2.35	0.73	15.25 - 12.50	15.3	5.3
12/31/93	11,413.0	1,959.0	12,102.0	25.4	17.2	33.0	16.2	2.1	0.95	1.10	2.81	0.72	16.81 - 12.72	15.5	4.9

Statistics are as originally reported. Adj. for 2-for-1 stk. split, 2/97 & 2/99. ① Incl. spec. after-tax chg. of $590.0 mill. & $98.0 mill. prov. for litig. ② Incl. pre-tax prov. of $225.0 mill. for restr. & $225.0 mill. gain on sale of bus. ③ Incl. spec. chg. of $800.0 mill., pre-tax prov. for restr. of $201.0 mill., & gain of $201.0 mill. on sale of bus. ④ Bef. gain fr. disc. ops. of $615.0 mill.; incl. pre-tax prov. for restr./oth. chrgs. of $386.0 mill. & gain of $160.0 mill. on sale of bus. ⑤ Bef. gain fr. disc. ops. of $2.72 bill.; incl. net pre-tax chrgs. of $3.13 bill. ⑥ Bef. gain fr. disc. ops. of $33.0 mill; & incl. chrg. of $169.0 mill., prov. of $649.0 mill. for restr., gain of $30.0 mill. & asset impair. chrg. of $403.0 mill.

OFFICERS:
P. R. Dolan, Chmn., C.E.O.
R. J. Lane, Sr. V.P., C.F.O.

INVESTOR CONTACT: Timothy Costs, Investor Relations, (212) 546-4103

PRINCIPAL OFFICE: 345 Park Avenue, New York, NY 10154-0037

TELEPHONE NUMBER: (212) 546-4000
FAX: (212) 546-4020
WEB: www.bms.com

NO. OF EMPLOYEES: 46,000 (approx.)
SHAREHOLDERS: 107,626 (approx.)
ANNUAL MEETING: In May
INCORPORATED: DE, Aug., 1933

INSTITUTIONAL HOLDINGS:
No. of Institutions: 1,090
Shares Held: 1,255,926,989
% Held: 64.8
INDUSTRY: Pharmaceutical preparations (SIC: 2834)
TRANSFER AGENT(S): Mellon Investor Services, Ridgefield Park, NJ

BROADWING, INC.

EXCH.	SYM.	REC. PRICE	P/E RATIO	YLD.	MKT. CAP.	RANGE (52-WK.)	'02 Y/E PR.
NYSE	BRW	3.76 (2/28/03)	...	...	$0.82 bill.	8.90 - 1.09	3.52

SPECULATIVE GRADE. THE COMPANY HAS REACHED AN AGREEMENT TO SELL THE ASSETS OF ITS BROADBAND BUSINESS TO PRIVATELY HELD C III COMMUNICATIONS, LLC, FOR $129.0 MILLION IN CASH.

TRADING VOLUME
Thousand Shares

*7 YEAR PRICE SCORE 18.6   ***12 MONTH PRICE SCORE 115.8**
*NYSE COMPOSITE INDEX=100

INTERIM EARNINGS (Per Share):

Qtr.	Mar.	June	Sept.	Dec.
1998	0.16	0.31	0.82	0.16
1999	0.18	0.20	0.22	d0.25
2000	d0.28	d0.15	d0.12	d1.26
2001	d0.17	d0.14	d0.14	d0.91
2002	d0.17	d0.10	0.01	d10.92

INTERIM DIVIDENDS (Per Share):

Amt.	Decl.	Ex.	Rec.	Pay.
		No dividends paid.		

CAPITALIZATION (12/31/01):

	($000)	(%)
Long-Term Debt	2,702,000	61.7
Preferred Stock	129,400	3.0
Common & Surplus	1,549,000	35.4
Total	4,380,400	100.0

BUSINESS:

Broadwing, Inc. (formerly Cincinnati Bell, Inc.) provides diversified communications services through businesses in four segments: The Broadband segment (49.5% of 2002 revenues) provides data, voice and Internet communications services nationwide over approximately 18,700 route miles of fiber-optic transmission facilities, as of 3/27/03. The Local Communications segment (39.4%) provides local telephone service, network access, data transport, high-speed Internet access, and switched long distance. The Wireless segment (12.1%) is comprised of the operations of Cincinnati Bell Wireless LLC, an 80.1%-owned venture with AT&T Wireless Services, as of 12/31/02. The Other segment (3.7%) and Intersegment revenues (-4.7%) accounted for the balance of revenues.

RECENT DEVELOPMENTS:

For the year ended 12/31/02, BRW posted a loss from continuing operations of $2.43 billion versus a loss from continuing operations of $315.8 million in 2001. Results for 2002 and 2001 included restructuring charges of $37.1 million and $93.4 million, and asset impairments and other charges of $2.20 billion and $152.0 million, respectively. Total revenue fell 5.1% to $2.16 billion. On 2/25/03, BRW announced that it reached an agreement to sell the assets of its broadband business, Broadwing Communications Services Inc., for $129.0 million in cash.

PROSPECTS:

On 3/27/03, BRW announced a recapitalization that includes an amendment to its bank credit facility for, among other things, extension of its scheduled maturities. As part of the agreement, BRW obtained a waiver from the holder of its 6.75% convertible debt under which the coupon will rise to 9.0% through the maturity. Furthermore, BRW closed and funded $350.0 million in new financing and will use the proceeds primarily to retire a portion of its bank debt. The notes will pay a 16.0% coupon, of which 12.0% is cash interest and 4.0% is payable in-kind. BRW will also issue to the investor group warrants for 17.5 million shares of its common stock at $3.00 per share.

ANNUAL FINANCIAL DATA:

FISCAL YEAR	TOT. REVS. ($mill.)	NET INC. ($mill.)	TOT. ASSETS ($mill.)	OPER. PROFIT %	NET PROFIT %	RET. ON EQUITY %	RET. ON ASSETS %	CURR. RATIO	EARN. PER SH. $	CASH FL. PER SH. $	TANG. BK. VAL. $	DIV. PER SH. $	PRICE RANGE	AVG. P/E RATIO	AVG. YIELD %
p12/31/02	2,155.9	⑩ d2,431.2							⑩ d11.18				10.62 - 1.09	...	...
12/31/01	2,350.5	⑨ d286.2	6,312.0	...	...	...	...	0.5	⑨ d1.36	1.19	...	...	28.88 - 7.50	...	...
12/31/00	2,050.1	⑧ d376.5	6,477.6	1.9	...	...	...	0.6	⑧ d1.82	0.35	...	...	41.06 - 19.06	...	...
12/31/99	1,131.1	⑦ 38.0	⑦ 6,508.6	12.7	3.4	1.6	0.6	0.7	⑦ 0.24	1.44	...	0.30	37.88 - 16.06	112.3	1.1
12/31/98	885.1	⑥ 81.8	1,041.0	20.3	9.2	57.6	7.9	0.5	⑥ 0.59	1.40	0.28	0.40	38.63 - 20.88	50.4	1.3
12/31/97	1,756.8	⑤ 193.6	1,498.7	17.8	11.0	33.4	12.9	0.8	⑤ 1.41	2.75	2.83	0.40	33.75 - 23.06	20.1	1.4
12/31/96	1,573.7	⑤ 185.0	1,670.9	19.5	11.8	29.2	11.1	0.8	③ 1.35	2.61	3.18	0.40	30.81 - 15.88	17.3	1.7
12/31/95	1,336.1	④ d25.3	1,591.7	3.5	...	...	...	0.8	④ d0.19	1.03	2.29	0.40	17.63 - 8.44	...	3.1
12/31/94	1,228.2	③ 75.5	1,723.4	13.5	6.1	13.7	4.4	1.0	⑥ 0.58	1.75	2.69	0.40	10.06 - 7.69	15.4	4.5
12/31/93	1,089.6	③ d56.8	1,664.1	...	...	...	...	0.9	③ d0.46	0.79	2.49	0.40	12.19 - 8.06	...	4.0

Statistics are as originally reported. Adj. for 2-for-1 stk. split, 5/97. ① Bef. inc. fr. disc. ops. of $69.1 mill. & extraord. chrg. of $1.0 mill. ② Incl. chrgs. of $9.7 mill.; bef. extraord. chrg. of $210.0 mill. ③ Incl. non-recurr. cr. 12/31/96: $17.4 mill.; chrg. 12/31/93: $88.0 mill. ④ Incl. non-recurr. chrg. of $84.1 mill.; bef. extraord. chrg. of $7.0 mill. ⑤ Bef. acctg. chg. of $2.9 mill. ⑥ Bef. extraord. chrg. of $6.6 mill. ⑦ Refl. acquis. of IXC Communications, Inc. ⑧ Incl. non-recurr. cr. of $800,000; net loss on invest. of $356.3 mill.; bef. disc. ops. of $200,000 and oth. chrgs. of $800,000. ⑨ Incl. restruct. & oth. chrgs. of $241.9 mill. and gain on invest. of $11.8 mill. ⑩ Incl. restruct. chrg. of $37.1 mill. and asset impair. & oth. chrgs. of $2.20 bill.; bef. inc fr. disc. ops. of $217.6 mill. & acctg. chge. chrg. of $2.01 bill.

OFFICERS:
D. J. Meyer, Chmn.
K. W. Mooney, C.E.O.
T. L. Shilling, C.F.O.

INVESTOR CONTACT: Mike Hemsath, (513) 397-7788

PRINCIPAL OFFICE: 2301 East Fourth Street, Cincinnati, OH 45202

TELEPHONE NUMBER: (513) 397-9900
FAX: (513) 397-1081
NO. OF EMPLOYEES: 5,400 (approx.)
SHAREHOLDERS: 105,500 (approx. record)
ANNUAL MEETING: In Mar.
INCORPORATED: OH, July, 1873

INSTITUTIONAL HOLDINGS:
No. of Institutions: 179
Shares Held: 145,209,507
% Held: 66.3
INDUSTRY: Telephone communications, exc. radio (SIC: 4813)
TRANSFER AGENT(S): Fifth Third Bank, Cincinnati, OH

BROWN & BROWN, INC.

EXCH.	SYM.	REC. PRICE	P/E RATIO	YLD.	MKT. CAP.	RANGE (52-WK.)	'02 Y/E PR.
NYSE	BRO	28.82 (2/28/03)	23.6	0.8%	$1.82 bill.	37.00 - 24.00	32.32

UPPER MEDIUM GRADE. GOING FORWARD, THE COMPANY EXPECTS TO BENEFIT FROM CONTINUED INTERNAL GROWTH AND ACQUISITIONS.

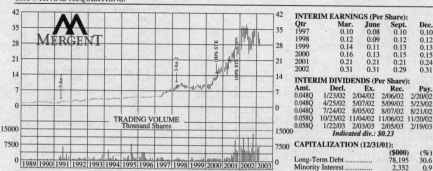

*7 YEAR PRICE SCORE 231.4   ***12 MONTH PRICE SCORE 104.5**
*NYSE COMPOSITE INDEX=100

INTERIM EARNINGS (Per Share):

Qtr	Mar.	June	Sept.	Dec.
1997	0.10	0.08	0.10	0.10
1998	0.12	0.09	0.12	0.12
1999	0.14	0.11	0.13	0.13
2000	0.16	0.13	0.15	0.15
2001	0.21	0.21	0.21	0.24
2002	0.31	0.31	0.29	0.31

INTERIM DIVIDENDS (Per Share):

Amt.	Decl.	Ex.	Rec.	Pay.
0.048Q	1/23/02	2/04/02	2/06/02	2/20/02
0.048Q	4/25/02	5/07/02	5/09/02	5/23/02
0.048Q	7/24/02	8/05/02	8/07/02	8/21/02
0.058Q	10/23/02	11/04/02	11/06/02	11/20/02
0.058Q	1/22/03	2/03/03	2/05/03	2/19/03

Indicated div.: $0.23

CAPITALIZATION (12/31/01):

	($000)	(%)
Long-Term Debt	78,195	30.6
Minority Interest	2,352	0.9
Common & Surplus	175,285	68.5
Total	255,832	100.0

BUSINESS:

Brown & Brown, Inc. (formerly Poe & Brown, Inc.) is a diversified insurance brokerage that sells primarily property and casualty insurance products and services in the U.S. The Company's business is divided into four divisions: the Retail Division, which markets and sells insurance products to commercial, professional and individual clients; the National Programs Division, which develops and adminis-

ters property and casualty insurance and employee benefits coverage; the Service Division, which provides services such as third-party administration for workers' compensation and employee benefit markets; and the Brokerage Division, which markets and sells commercial insurance primarily through independent agents and brokers.

RECENT DEVELOPMENTS:

For the year ended 12/31/02, net income climbed 54.2% to $83.1 million from $53.9 million the previous year. Results for 2002 and 2001 included non-cash stock compensation charges of $3.8 million and $2.0 million, respectively. Total revenues advanced 24.9% to $455.7 million from

$365.0 million the prior year. Revenues were fueled by acquired agencies and new business production. Commissions and fees amounted to $452.3 million, up 25.7% from $359.7 million a year earlier. Employee compensation and benefits expenses increased 19.8% to $224.8 million.

PROSPECTS:

The Company expects results to be enhanced by new merger and acquisition relationships. Furthermore, BRO anticipates the continuation of firm insurance rates and rationed capacity to help it maintain favorable internal growth through 2003 and beyond. Separately, on 1/1/03, BRO acquired MFC&V Insurance Services, a provider of residential and business insurance in California. MFC&V generates annual revenues of about $12.0 million. Also, on

1/1/03, the Company acquired Coleman Company Insurance Services, L.P., a retail commercial property and casualty insurance agency serving the San Antonio, Texas region. On 2/15/03, BRO acquired J.C. Whilt & Company, Insurance Services, Inc., a multi-line commercial insurance agency, which provides property and casualty, employee benefits and personal insurance services in Central California.

ANNUAL FINANCIAL DATA:

FISCAL YEAR	TOT. REVS. ($000)	NET INC. ($000)	TOT. ASSETS ($000)	OPER. PROFIT %	NET PROFIT %	RET. ON EQUITY %	RET. ON ASSETS %	CURR. RATIO	EARN. PER SH. $	CASH FL. PER SH. $	TANG. BK. VAL. $	DIV. PER SH. $	PRICE RANGE	AVG. P/E RATIO	AVG. YIELD %
p12/31/02	455,742	① 83,122						① 1.22				0.20	37.00 — 24.00	25.0	0.7
12/31/01	365,029	① 53,913	488,837	26.9	14.8	30.8	11.0	0.8	① 0.85	1.21	...	0.16	31.50 — 14.38	27.0	0.7
12/31/00	209,706	33,186	276,719	26.0	15.8	27.2	12.0	1.0	0.58	0.81	0.35	0.14	17.94 — 7.81	22.2	1.0
12/31/99	176,413	27,172	235,163	25.4	15.4	26.4	11.6	0.9	0.50	0.71	0.20	0.12	10.16 — 7.33	17.7	1.3
12/31/98	153,791	23,053	230,513	24.7	15.0	27.4	10.0	1.0	0.43	0.60	0.09	0.10	10.63 — 7.20	20.7	1.2
12/31/97	129,191	19,387	194,129	29.1	15.0	25.1	10.0	1.1	0.37	0.52	0.53	0.09	7.83 — 4.25	16.3	1.5
12/31/96	118,680	16,498	179,743	27.6	13.9	24.5	9.2	1.1	0.32	0.46	0.33	0.08	4.58 — 3.79	13.2	2.0
12/31/95	106,365	14,799	151,121	26.6	13.9	27.2	9.8	1.1	0.28	0.41	0.34	0.08	4.21 — 3.38	13.4	2.1
12/31/94	99,507	13,285	139,335	26.0	13.4	30.2	9.5	1.1	0.26	0.38	0.22	0.07	3.79 — 2.83	12.7	2.1
12/31/93	95,570	8,003	133,329	19.8	8.4	29.4	6.0	1.0	0.16	0.29	...	0.07	3.54 — 2.67	19.6	2.1

Statistics are as originally reported. Adj. for stk. splits: 100% div., 11/01; 8/00; 3-for-2, 2/98. ① Incl. non-cash stock compen. chrg. $3.8 mill., 12/02; $2.0 mill., 12/01

OFFICERS:
J. H. Brown, Chmn., Pres., C.E.O.
C. T. Walker, V.P., C.F.O., Treas.
L. Gramming, V.P., Sec., Gen. Couns.
INVESTOR CONTACT: Cory T. Walker, V.P., C.F.O., (386) 239-7250
PRINCIPAL OFFICE: 220 South Ridgewood Ave., Daytona Beach, FL 32114

TELEPHONE NUMBER: (386) 252-9601
FAX: (386) 239-5729
WEB: www.bbinsurance.com
NO. OF EMPLOYEES: 3,000 (approx.)
SHAREHOLDERS: 973 (approx.)
ANNUAL MEETING: In April
INCORPORATED: FL, 1959

INSTITUTIONAL HOLDINGS:
No. of Institutions: 184
Shares Held: 39,959,680
% Held: 58.6
INDUSTRY: Insurance agents, brokers, & service (SIC: 6411)
TRANSFER AGENT(S): Wachovia Bank, N.A., Charlotte, NC

BROWN SHOE COMPANY, INC.

EXCH.	SYM.	REC. PRICE	P/E RATIO	YLD.	MKT. CAP.	RANGE (52-WK.)	'02 Y/E PR.
NYSE	BWS	27.14 (2/28/03)	10.8	1.5%	$474.5 mill.	29.39 - 13.80	23.83

MEDIUM GRADE. THE COMPANY EXPECTS EARNINGS FOR FISCAL 2003 TO BE ABOUT $2.75 PER SHARE.

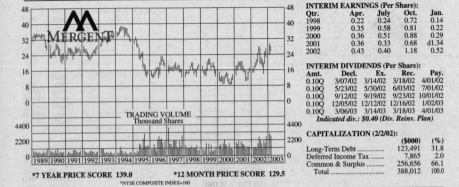

INTERIM EARNINGS (Per Share):

Qtr.	Apr.	July	Oct.	Jan.
1998	0.22	0.24	0.72	0.14
1999	0.35	0.58	0.81	0.22
2000	0.36	0.51	0.88	0.29
2001	0.36	0.33	0.68	d1.34
2002	0.43	0.40	1.18	0.52

INTERIM DIVIDENDS (Per Share):

Amt.	Decl.	Ex.	Rec.	Pay.
0.10Q	3/07/02	3/14/02	3/18/02	4/01/02
0.10Q	5/23/02	5/30/02	6/03/02	7/01/02
0.10Q	9/12/02	9/19/02	9/23/02	10/01/02
0.10Q	12/05/02	12/12/02	12/16/02	1/02/03
0.10Q	3/06/03	3/14/03	3/18/03	4/01/03

Indicated div.: $0.40 (Div. Reinv. Plan)

CAPITALIZATION (2/2/02):

	($000)	(%)
Long-Term Debt	123,491	31.8
Deferred Income Tax	7,865	2.0
Common & Surplus	256,656	66.1
Total	388,012	100.0

*7 YEAR PRICE SCORE 139.0   *12 MONTH PRICE SCORE 129.5

*NYSE COMPOSITE INDEX=100

BUSINESS:

Brown Shoe Company, Inc. (formerly Brown Group, Inc.) is a $1.84 billion dollar footwear company with worldwide operations. The Company's retail footwear segment manufactures, supplies and sells women's and children's footwear and operates shoe stores and leased retail shoe departments in department stores. This segment includes the operations of Famous Footwear, which as of 12/30/02 had 918 stores, and Naturalizer, which had 389 stores, in the U.S. & Canada. The Company's wholesale brands are sold in department stores, multi-line shoe stores and branded specialty stores through its Brown Branded, Brown Pagoda and Canada Wholesale divisions. These brands include: NATURALIZER, LIFESTRIDE, CONNIE and BUSTER BROWN. The division also licenses brands including DR. SCHOLL'S BARBIE, CARLOS and other kids' character footwear. The Brown Pagoda Division markets branded and private label footwear to mass-merchandise, mid-tier and department stores throughout the U.S.

RECENT DEVELOPMENTS:

For the year ended 2/1/03, net income was $45.2 million versus a net loss of $4.0 million the prior year. Results for 2003 included an after-tax non-recurring gain of $1.2 million, while results for 2002 included an after-tax non-recurring charge of $32.2 million. Net sales grew 4.9% to $1.84 billion from $1.76 billion a year earlier. Total Famous Footwear sales rose 2.9% to $1.08 billion, mainly due to higher sales from new stores and increased square footage, partially offset by a 1.3% decline in same-store sales. Wholesale sales climbed 12.5% to $566.4 million.

PROSPECTS:

BWS' prospects are encouraging due to success with its aggressive merchandising strategy and inventory management initiatives. These initiatives lead to a year-over-year gain in operating earnings of 81.6%. In addition, despite a tough consumer environment, BWS' wholesale businesses continue to perform well, due to improved product design processes, which have allowed the Company to increase its market share. Furthermore, BWS completed the elimination of its underperforming Naturalizer retail stores in the U.S. and expects operating improvement throughout the year. Separately, BWS anticipates earnings of about $2.75 a share for the full year.

ANNUAL FINANCIAL DATA:

FISCAL YEAR	TOT. REVS. ($mill.)	NET INC. ($mill.)	TOT. ASSETS ($mill.)	OPER. PROFIT %	NET PROFIT %	RET. ON EQUITY %	RET. ON ASSETS %	CURR. RATIO	EARN. PER SH.$	CASH FL. PER SH.$	TANG. BK. VAL.$	DIV. PER SH.$	PRICE RANGE	AVG. P/E RATIO	AVG. YIELD
p2/01/03	1,841.4	② 45.2							② 2.52			0.40	28.10 - 13.80	8.3	1.9
2/02/02	1,755.8	④ 0.9	700.9	0.9	0.1	0.4	0.1	1.7	④ 0.05	1.58	14.68	0.40	20.50 - 10.25	307.5	2.6
2/03/01	1,684.9	36.4	740.1	4.2	2.2	13.5	4.9	1.9	2.04	3.38	15.46	0.40	15.19 - 8.44	5.8	3.4
1/29/00	1,592.5	35.5	650.3	4.2	2.2	14.2	5.5	2.2	1.96	3.37	13.69	0.40	21.75 - 12.69	8.8	2.3
1/30/99	1,538.5	23.7	655.2	4.0	1.5	10.9	3.6	2.0	1.32	2.82	11.95	0.40	20.00 - 12.44	12.3	2.5
1/31/98	1,567.2	d20.9	695.0	1.2	...	...	...	1.9	d1.19	0.32	11.04	1.00	20.13 - 12.44	...	6.1
2/01/97	1,525.1	20.3	722.4	3.0	1.3	8.6	2.8	2.1	1.15	2.61	13.19	1.00	23.38 - 11.88	15.3	5.7
2/03/96	1,455.9	①② 0.7	661.1	0.9	...	0.3	0.1	1.7	①② 0.04	1.40	12.92	1.45	33.38 - 12.50	572.0	6.3
1/28/95	1,461.6	① 33.6	636.5	4.3	2.3	13.4	5.3	2.2	① 1.91	3.16	13.90	1.60	38.88 - 30.63	18.2	4.6
1/29/94	1,597.8	①③ d6.7	771.7	1.7	...	...	...	1.6	①③ d0.39	0.93	13.27	1.60	35.88 - 28.38	...	5.0

Statistics are as originally reported. ① Bef. disc. oper. gain $2.6 mill., 2/96; $5.8 mill., 1/95; loss $22.7 mill., 1/94. ② Bef. non-recurr. chrg. $1.7 mill., 2/03; $3.6 mill. 2/96 ③ Bef. acctg. change chrg. $2.2 mill. ④ Bef. extraord. chrg. $4.9 mill; Incl. after-tax restruct. chrgs. $27.3 mill.

OFFICERS:
R. A. Fromm, Chmn., Pres., C.E.O.
A. M. Rosen, C.F.O., Treas.
R. D. Pickle, V.P., Gen. Couns., Sec.
INVESTOR CONTACT: Investor Relations, (314) 854-4000
PRINCIPAL OFFICE: 8300 Maryland Ave., St. Louis, MO 63105-3693

TELEPHONE NUMBER: (314) 854-4000
FAX: (314) 854-4274
WEB: www.brownshoe.com
NO. OF EMPLOYEES: 11,500 (approx.)
SHAREHOLDERS: 5,500 (approx.)
ANNUAL MEETING: In May
INCORPORATED: NY, Jan., 1913

INSTITUTIONAL HOLDINGS:
No. of Institutions: 110
Shares Held: 12,392,965
% Held: 70.2
INDUSTRY: Women's footwear, except athletic (SIC: 3144)
TRANSFER AGENT(S): First Chicago Trust Company of New York, Jersery City, NJ

BROWN-FORMAN CORPORATION

EXCH.	SYM.	REC. PRICE	P/E RATIO	YLD.	MKT. CAP.	RANGE (52-WK.)	'02 Y/E PR.	DIV. ACH.
NYSE	BFB	69.55 (2/28/03)	20.0	2.2%	$4.75 bill.	80.54 - 58.69	65.36	18 yrs.

UPPER MEDIUM GRADE. FISCAL 2004 EARNINGS SHOULD BENEFIT FROM COST SAVINGS RESULTING FROM BUSINESS-IMPROVEMENT INITIATIVES MADE IN 2002 AND 2003.

*7 YEAR PRICE SCORE 127.6   ***12 MONTH PRICE SCORE 104.4**

*NYSE COMPOSITE INDEX=100

INTERIM EARNINGS (Per Share):

Qtr.	July	Oct.	Jan.	Apr.
1999-00	0.56	1.06	0.80	0.76
2000-01	0.62	1.17	0.80	0.79
2001-02	0.57	1.17	0.84	0.75
2002-03	0.53	1.18	1.02	...

INTERIM DIVIDENDS (Per Share):

Amt.	Decl.	Ex.	Rec.	Pay.
0.35Q	1/24/02	3/01/02	3/05/02	4/01/02
0.35Q	5/23/02	6/04/02	6/06/02	7/01/02
0.35Q	7/25/02	8/30/02	9/04/02	10/01/02
0.375Q	11/21/02	12/04/02	12/06/02	1/01/03
0.375Q	1/23/03	2/28/03	3/04/03	4/01/03

Indicated div.: $1.50 (Div. Reinv. Plan)

CAPITALIZATION (4/30/02):

	($000)	(%)
Long-Term Debt	40,000	2.8
Deferred Income Tax	58,000	4.1
Common & Surplus	1,311,000	93.0
Total	1,409,000	100.0

BUSINESS:

Brown-Forman Corporation, with assets as of 1/31/03 of $2.14 billion, operates in two business segments: wines and spirits and consumer durables. The wines and spirits segment includes the production, importing and marketing of wines and distilled spirits under brand names of JACK DANIEL'S, SOUTHERN COMFORT, FINLANDIA Vodka, CANADIAN MIST, KORBEL CALIFORNIA champagnes, and FETZER and BOLLA wines. The consumer durables segment includes tableware and flatware sold under the LENOX, GORHAM and DANSK brand names, as well as HARTMANN luggage. In fiscal 2002, sales (operating income) were as follows: 73.4% (95.2%), wine and spirits; 26.6% (4.8%) consumer durables.

RECENT DEVELOPMENTS:

For the quarter ended 1/31/03, net income advanced 22.2% to $70.0 million from $57.3 million in the corresponding prior-year period, reflecting solid demand for JACK DANIEL'S and SOUTHERN COMFORT, increased profitability in the U.K. from a new distribution arrangement, and benefits from a weaker U.S. dollar. Net sales increased 10.5% to $635.6 million from $575.1 million the year before. Sales for the wine and spirits segment improved 18.1% to $472.8 million, while sales for the consumer durables segment slipped 6.9% to $162.8 million from $174.9 million.

PROSPECTS:

On 2/11/03, the Company completed its acquisition of an additional 55.0% interest in Tuaca liquer, increasing its ownership to 100%. In addition, on 12/31/02, BFB acquired an additional 35.0% interest in Finlandia Vodka Worldwide, BFB's joint venture with Altia Corporation. The transaction increases BFB's ownership to 80.0%. Meanwhile, earnings per share growth for fiscal 2003 is expected to range from 6.0% to 10.0%. Fiscal 2004 earnings should benefit from cost savings resulting from business-improvement initiatives made in fiscal 2002 and 2003, as well as from a full year of higher margins resulting from the new distribution arrangement for BFB's spirits brands in the U.K.

ANNUAL FINANCIAL DATA:

FISCAL YEAR	TOT. REVS. ($mill.)	NET INC. ($mill.)	TOT. ASSETS ($mill.)	OPER. PROFIT %	NET PROFIT %	RET. ON EQUITY %	RET. ON ASSETS %	INC. TAX CURR. RATIO	EARN. PER SH. $	CASH FL. PER SH. $	TANG. BK. VAL.$	DIV. PER SH. $	PRICE RANGE	AVG. P/E RATIO	AVG. YIELD %
4/30/02	2,208.0	228.0	2,016.0	16.0	10.3	17.4	11.3	2.1	3.33	4.13	15.58	1.32	72.00 - 57.65	19.5	2.0
4/30/01	2,180.0	233.0	1,939.0	17.2	10.7	19.6	12.0	1.8	3.40	4.33	13.50	1.24	69.25 - 41.88	16.3	2.2
4/30/00	2,134.0	218.0	1,802.0	16.3	10.2	20.8	12.1	2.0	3.18	4.08	11.36	1.18	77.25 - 54.94	20.8	1.8
4/30/99	2,030.0	202.0	1,735.0	15.9	10.0	22.0	11.6	1.9	2.93	3.74	9.53	1.12	76.88 - 51.75	21.9	1.7
4/30/98	1,924.0	185.0	1,494.0	16.0	9.6	22.6	12.4	2.3	2.67	3.42	8.04	1.08	55.38 - 42.00	18.2	2.2
4/30/97	1,841.0	169.0	1,428.0	15.6	9.2	23.2	11.8	2.0	2.45	3.17	6.73	1.04	47.50 - 35.25	16.9	2.5
4/30/96	1,807.0	160.0	1,381.0	15.2	8.9	25.2	11.6	2.5	2.31	2.99	5.26	0.99	40.75 - 29.38	15.2	2.8
4/30/95	1,679.6	148.6	1,285.6	15.9	8.8	27.2	11.6	2.4	2.15	2.78	3.94	0.95	32.50 - 26.13	13.6	3.2
4/30/94	1,628.5	① 161.1	1,233.8	14.8	9.9	34.7	13.1	2.3	① 2.04	2.63	2.50	0.91	29.58 - 24.33	13.2	3.4
4/30/93	1,691.7	156.2	1,311.0	15.1	9.2	19.1	11.9	3.4	1.88	2.42	6.37	0.81	30.00 - 24.00	14.4	3.0

Statistics are as originally reported. Adj. for 200% stk. div. 5/94. ① Bef. acct. chge. of $32.5 mill. & gain fr. sale of bus. of $30.1 mill.

OFFICERS:
O. Brown II, Chmn., C.E.O.
W. M. Street, Pres.
P. A. Wood, Exec. V.P., C.F.O.

INVESTOR CONTACT: Phil Lynch, V.P. & Dir. of Corp. Comm., (502) 774-7928

PRINCIPAL OFFICE: 850 Dixie Highway, Louisville, KY 40210

TELEPHONE NUMBER: (502) 585-1100
FAX: (502) 774-7876
WEB: www.brown-forman.com
NO. OF EMPLOYEES: 5,400 full-time (approx.); 1,600 part-time (approx.)
SHAREHOLDERS: 3,734 (cl A); 4,453 (cl B)
ANNUAL MEETING: In July
INCORPORATED: KY, 1901; reincorp., DE, 1933

INSTITUTIONAL HOLDINGS:
No. of Institutions: 187
Shares Held: 28,764,727
% Held: 42.0

INDUSTRY: Wines, brandy, and brandy spirits (SIC: 2084)

TRANSFER AGENT(S): National City Bank, Cleveland, OH

BRUNSWICK CORPORATION

EXCH.	SYM.	REC. PRICE	P/E RATIO	YLD.	MKT. CAP.	RANGE (52-WK.)	'02 Y/E PR.
NYSE	BC	18.90 (2/28/03)	16.6	2.6%	$1.70 bill.	30.01 - 18.23	19.86

MEDIUM GRADE. THE COMPANY EXPECTS FIRST QUARTER 2003 EARNINGS IN THE RANGE OF $0.20 TO $0.22 PER SHARE.

*7 YEAR PRICE SCORE 105.3   *12 MONTH PRICE SCORE 92.2
*NYSE COMPOSITE INDEX=100

INTERIM EARNINGS (Per Share):

Qtr.	Mar.	June	Sept.	Dec.
1998	0.59	0.83	0.04	0.34
1999	0.62	0.89	0.19	d1.30
2000	0.69	0.97	0.20	0.48
2001	0.45	0.47	0.07	d0.03
2002	0.15	0.51	0.26	0.22

INTERIM DIVIDENDS (Per Share):

Amt.	Decl.	Ex.	Rec.	Pay.
0.125Q	2/06/01	2/22/01	2/26/01	3/15/01
0.125Q	5/01/01	5/23/01	5/25/01	6/15/01
0.125Q	7/31/01	8/22/01	8/24/01	9/14/01
0.125Q	10/22/01	11/21/01	11/26/01	12/14/01
0.50A	10/23/02	11/21/02	11/25/02	12/13/02

Indicated div.: $0.50 (Div. Reinv. Plan)

CAPITALIZATION (12/31/01):

	($000)	(%)
Long-Term Debt	600,200	31.7
Deferred Income Tax	185,200	9.8
Common & Surplus	1,110,900	58.6
Total	1,896,300	100.0

BUSINESS:

Brunswick Corporation is a global manufacturer and marketer of consumer brands including MERCURY and MARINER outboard engines; MERCURY MERCRUISER sterndrives and inboard engines; SEA RAY, BAYLINER, MAXUM, HATTERAS, SEALINE and MERIDIAN pleasure boats; BAJA high-performance boats; BOSTON WHALER and TROPHY offshore fishing boats; PRINCECRAFT fishing, deck and pontoon boats; LIFE FITNESS, HAMMER STRENGTH and PARABODY fitness equipment; BRUNSWICK bowling centers, equipment and consumer products; and BRUNSWICK billiards tables.

RECENT DEVELOPMENTS:

For the year ended 12/31/02, income increased 22.2% to $103.5 million, before an accounting change charge of $25.1 million, compared with income of $84.7 million, before an accounting change charge of $2.9 million, in 2001. Net sales advanced 10.1% to $3.71 billion from $3.37 billion a year earlier. The improvement in sales was primarily attributed to higher marine engine sales and double-digit growth in fitness equipment as well as incremental sales from boat companies acquired in 2001. Operating income climbed 2.9% to $196.6 million, supported by higher sales volumes at MERCURY and LIFE FITNESS, cost reductions and contribution from acquisitions.

PROSPECTS:

For 2003, BC will continue to focus on reducing costs to improve its competitive position, introducing new products, enhancing its marketing and brand building efforts and improving its distribution channels. The Company will introduce 50 new products in 2003 in LIFE FITNESS in order to extend its sales momentum. Also, the Company's bowling capital equipment and products business is expected to break-even in the coming year due to reduced costs and improved products and supply chain management. BC expects first quarter 2003 earnings in the range of $0.20 to $0.22 per share, and full-year 2003 earnings of $1.40 to $1.60 per share. Meanwhile, on 12/16/02, BC announced that it has acquired North Star Technologies, Inc., a supplier of marine navigation electronics.

ANNUAL FINANCIAL DATA:

FISCAL YEAR	TOT. REVS. ($mill.)	NET INC. ($mill.)	TOT. ASSETS ($mill.)	OPER. PROFIT %	NET PROFIT %	RET. ON EQUITY %	RET. ON ASSETS %	CURR. RATIO	EARN. PER SH. $	CASH FL. PER SH. $	TANG. BK. VAL. $	DIV. PER SH. $	PRICE RANGE	AVG. P/E RATIO	AVG. YIELD %
p12/31/02	3,711.9	⑧ 103.5							⑧ 1.14			0.50	30.01 - 18.30	21.2	2.1
12/31/01	3,370.8	⑧ 84.7	3,157.5	5.7	2.5	7.6	2.7	1.6	⑧ 0.96	2.78	5.78	0.50	25.01 - 14.03	20.3	2.6
12/31/00	3,811.9	③⑦ 202.2	3,396.5	10.4	5.3	18.9	6.0	1.5	③⑦ 2.28	3.96	6.40	0.50	22.13 - 14.75	8.1	2.7
12/31/99	4,283.8	⑥ 37.9	3,354.8	2.6	0.9	2.9	1.1	1.5	⑥ 0.41	2.20	6.99	0.50	30.00 - 18.06	58.6	2.1
12/31/98	3,945.2	⑤ 178.6	3,351.5	8.6	4.5	13.6	5.3	1.4	⑤ 1.80	3.42	5.35	0.50	35.69 - 12.00	13.2	2.1
12/31/97	3,657.4	④ 151.2	3,241.4	7.4	4.1	11.5	4.7	1.4	④ 1.51	3.07	4.75	0.50	37.00 - 23.13	19.9	1.7
12/31/96	3,160.3	185.8	2,802.4	9.6	5.9	15.5	6.6	1.5	1.88	3.19	7.18	0.50	25.88 - 17.25	11.5	2.3
12/31/95	3,041.4	①③ 134.2	2,360.5	7.2	4.4	12.9	5.7	1.9	①③ 1.39	2.65	6.58	0.50	24.00 - 16.25	14.5	2.5
12/31/94	2,700.1	129.0	2,122.3	7.8	4.8	14.2	6.1	1.7	1.35	2.60	5.41	0.44	25.38 - 17.00	15.7	2.1
12/31/93	2,206.8	② 54.5	1,983.7	4.5	2.5	6.8	2.7	1.6	② 0.57	1.81	4.29	0.44	18.50 - 12.50	27.2	1.7

Statistics are as originally reported. ① Incl. a nonrecur. chrg. of $24.4 mill. ② Bef. loss of $12.2 mill. fr. discont. oper., an extraord. chrg. of $4.6 mill., and an acctg. adj. chrg. of $14.6 mill. ③ Bef. discont. oper. loss of $2.9 mill., 2001; $298.0 mill., 2000; $7.0 mill. ($0.07/sh.), 1995. ④ Incl. strategic chrg. of $63.0 mill. & bef. acctg. adj. chrg. of $700,000. ⑤ Incl. strategic chrg. of $60.0 mill.; Bef. after-tax gain of $7.7 mill. fr. discont. oper. ⑥ Incl. a litigation charge of $116.0 mill. and strategic chrg. of $151.0 mill. ⑦ Incl. nonrecurr. after-tax chrg. $40.0 mill. ⑧ Bef. acctg. chg. chrg. of $25.1 mill.

OFFICERS:
G. W. Buckley, Chmn., C.E.O.
P. B. Hamilton, Vice-Chmn.
V. J. Reich, Sr. V.P., C.F.O.

INVESTOR CONTACT: Investor Relations, (847) 735-4294

PRINCIPAL OFFICE: One North Field Court, Lake Forest, IL 60045-4811

TELEPHONE NUMBER: (847) 735-4700
FAX: (847) 735-4765
WEB: www.brunswick.com

NO. OF EMPLOYEES: 20,700 (approx.)

SHAREHOLDERS: 13,200 (approx.)

ANNUAL MEETING: In May

INCORPORATED: DE, Dec., 1907

INSTITUTIONAL HOLDINGS:
No. of Institutions: 226
Shares Held: 74,686,507
% Held: 82.8

INDUSTRY: Boat building and repairing (SIC: 3732)

TRANSFER AGENT(S): Brunswick Shareholder Services, Lake Forest, IL

BURLINGTON COAT FACTORY WAREHOUSE CORP.

EXCH.	SYM.	REC. PRICE	P/E RATIO	YLD.	MKT. CAP.	RANGE (52-WK.)	'02 Y/E PR.
NYSE	BCF	15.70 (2/28/03)	9.8	0.1%	$0.70 bill.	23.50 - 15.47	17.95

MEDIUM GRADE. RESULTS ARE BENEFITING FROM THE COMPANY'S STORE EXPANSION PROGRAM.

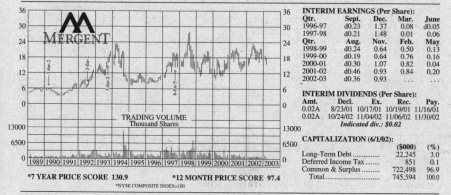

*7 YEAR PRICE SCORE 130.9   ***12 MONTH PRICE SCORE 97.4**

*NYSE COMPOSITE INDEX=100

INTERIM EARNINGS (Per Share):

Qtr.	Sept.	Dec.	Mar.	June
1996-97	d0.23	1.37	0.08	d0.05
1997-98	d0.21	1.48	0.01	0.06
Qtr.	Aug.	Nov.	Feb.	May
1998-99	d0.24	0.64	0.50	0.13
1999-00	d0.19	0.64	0.76	0.16
2000-01	d0.30	1.07	0.82	0.04
2001-02	d0.46	0.93	0.84	0.20
2002-03	d0.36	0.93	...	...

INTERIM DIVIDENDS (Per Share):

Amt.	Decl.	Ex.	Rec.	Pay.
0.02A	8/23/01	10/17/01	10/19/01	11/16/01
0.02A	10/24/02	11/04/02	11/06/02	11/30/02

Indicated div.: $0.02

CAPITALIZATION (6/1/02):

	($000)	(%)
Long-Term Debt	22,245	3.0
Deferred Income Tax	851	0.1
Common & Surplus	722,498	96.9
Total	745,594	100.0

BUSINESS:

Burlington Coat Factory Warehouse Corp. operated 333 stores in 42 states as of 1/10/03, which sell off-price apparel, shoes and accessories for men, women and children. Most of the Company's stores also sell home furnishings, linens and children's furniture. BCF operates stores under the names Burlington Coat Factory Warehouse, Cohoes Fashions, Decelle, Luxury Linens, Totally 4 Kids, and Baby Depot. The Company's stores range in size from approximately 16,000 square feet to about 163,000 square feet, with an average area of approximately 75,700 square feet. In fiscal 2002, net revenues were derived: 76.8% apparel and 23.2% home products.

RECENT DEVELOPMENTS:

For the three months ended 11/30/02, the Company reported net income of $41.6 million compared with $41.3 million in the corresponding period a year earlier. Net sales climbed 5.2% to $782.8 million from $744.2 million the year before. Meanwhile, other income advanced 37.3% to $8.6 million from $6.3 million the prior year. Comparable store sales were down 1.3% year over year. Cost of sales totaled $476.3 million, or 60.8% of net sales, versus $449.9 million, or 60.4% of net sales, the previous year. Selling and administrative expenses rose 4.3% to $228.9 million from $219.4 million in 2001.

PROSPECTS:

Results are being positively affected by the Company's efforts to expand its store base. During the first half of the current fiscal year, BCF opened twelve new Burlington Coat Factory stores and four stand-alone MJM Designer Shoe stores. In addition, the Company relocated two existing stores and expanded or remodeled twelve stores. The Company anticipates opening an additional six Burlington Coat Factory stores and two MJM Designer Shoe stores during the remainder of the current fiscal year.

ANNUAL FINANCIAL DATA:

FISCAL YEAR	NET REVS. ($mill.)	NET INC. ($mill.)	TOT. ASSETS ($mill.)	OPER. PROFIT %	NET PROFIT %	RET. ON EQUITY %	RET. ON ASSETS %	CURR. RATIO	EARN. PER SH.$	CASH FL. PER SH.$	TANG. BK. VAL.$	DIV. PER SH.$	PRICE RANGE	AVG. P/E RATIO	AVG. YIELD %
6/01/02	2,604.6	66.9	1,273.8	4.1	2.6	9.3	5.2	1.5	1.51	2.85	16.24	0.02	21.98 - 12.81	11.5	0.1
6/02/01	2,428.9	③ 71.8	1,060.8	4.8	3.0	11.0	6.8	1.8	③ 1.62	2.73	14.76	0.02	19.25 - 9.69	8.9	0.1
6/03/00	2,226.2	62.5	1,046.0	4.7	2.8	10.7	6.0	1.6	1.37	2.26	13.16	0.02	20.75 - 10.75	11.5	0.1
5/29/99	2,005.7	47.8	941.6	4.1	2.4	8.7	5.1	2.0	1.02	1.76	11.81	0.02	28.06 - 12.75	20.0	0.1
② 5/30/98	1,813.9	63.6	909.8	6.2	3.5	12.3	7.0	2.2	1.34	1.96	10.89	0.02	20.00 - 10.21	11.3	0.1
6/28/97	1,776.8	56.5	775.1	5.8	3.2	12.3	7.3	2.3	1.18	1.81	9.30	0.02	20.00 - 10.21	12.9	0.1
6/29/96	1,610.9	29.0	704.7	3.8	1.8	7.0	4.1	2.4	0.59	1.21	8.38	...	11.15 - 7.81	16.0	...
7/01/95	1,597.0	14.9	735.3	2.4	0.9	3.9	2.0	2.0	0.31	0.84	7.88	...	11.98 - 7.08	30.9	...
7/02/94	1,480.7	45.4	725.4	5.6	3.1	12.3	6.3	2.1	0.93	1.37	7.57	...	23.65 - 8.54	17.2	...
7/03/93	1,216.8	① 42.3	585.5	6.3	3.5	13.1	7.2	2.7	① 0.88	1.22	6.63	...	20.42 - 10.97	17.9	...

Statistics are as originally reported. Adj. for stk. splits: 6-for-5, 10/97 & 3-for-2, 10/93. ① Bef. acctg. change chrg. $601.0 mill. ② Results for 11 months only to reflect change in fiscal year to the Saturday nearest the last day in May. Fourth quarter results are for two months due to year-end change. ③ Bef. $823,000 ($0.02/sh) extraord. chg.

OFFICERS:
M. G. Milstein, Chmn., Pres., C.E.O.
M. A. Nesci, Exec. V.P., C.O.O.
P. C. Tang, Exec. V.P., Gen. Couns., Asst. Sec.

INVESTOR CONTACT: Robert L. LaPenta, Jr., (609) 387-7800 ext. 1216

PRINCIPAL OFFICE: 1830 Route 130 North, Burlington, NJ 08016

TELEPHONE NUMBER: (609) 387-7800
FAX: (609) 387-7071
WEB: www.coat.com

NO. OF EMPLOYEES: 26,000 (approx.)

SHAREHOLDERS: 258

ANNUAL MEETING: In Oct.

INCORPORATED: DE, Apr., 1983

INSTITUTIONAL HOLDINGS:
No. of Institutions: 106
Shares Held: 14,982,870
% Held: 33.7

INDUSTRY: Family clothing stores (SIC: 5651)

TRANSFER AGENT(S): American Stock Transfer & Trust Company, New York, NY

BURLINGTON NORTHERN SANTA FE CORPORATION

EXCH.	SYM.	REC. PRICE	P/E RATIO	YLD.	MKT. CAP.	RANGE (52-WK.)	'02 Y/E PR.
NYSE	BNI	24.90 (3/31/03)	12.4	1.9%	$9.36 bill.	30.93 - 23.18	26.01

MEDIUM GRADE. THE COMPANY HAS EXPANDED ITS GUARANTEED ON-TIME CARLOAD RAIL SERVICE.

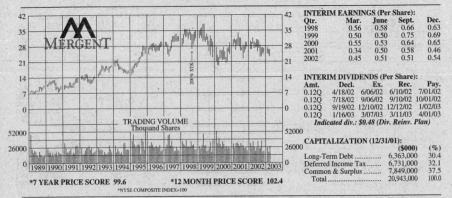

INTERIM EARNINGS (Per Share):

Qtr.	Mar.	June	Sept.	Dec.
1998	0.56	0.58	0.66	0.63
1999	0.50	0.50	0.75	0.69
2000	0.55	0.53	0.64	0.65
2001	0.34	0.50	0.58	0.46
2002	0.45	0.51	0.51	0.54

INTERIM DIVIDENDS (Per Share):

Amt.	Decl.	Ex.	Rec.	Pay.
0.12Q	4/18/02	6/06/02	6/10/02	7/01/02
0.12Q	7/18/02	9/06/02	9/10/02	10/01/02
0.12Q	9/19/02	12/10/02	12/12/02	1/02/03
0.12Q	1/16/03	3/07/03	3/11/03	4/01/03
Indicated div.: $0.48 (Div. Reinv. Plan)				

TRADING VOLUME
Thousand Shares

*7 YEAR PRICE SCORE 99.6   *12 MONTH PRICE SCORE 102.4

*NYSE COMPOSITE INDEX=100

CAPITALIZATION (12/31/01):

	($000)	(%)
Long-Term Debt	6,363,000	30.4
Deferred Income Tax	6,731,000	32.1
Common & Surplus	7,849,000	37.5
Total	20,943,000	100.0

BUSINESS:

Burlington Northern Santa Fe Corporation, created through the merger of Burlington Northern, Inc. and Santa Fe Pacific Corp. on 9/22/95, owns one of the largest railroad networks in the U.S., with approximately 33,000 route miles stretching across 28 states and two Canadian provinces, as of 1/21/03, to provide single-line service to shippers. BNI's principal subsidiary, The Burlington Northern and Santa Fe Railway Company (BNSF), transports a range of products and commodities, including consumer products (37.8% of total 2002 revenues), industrial products (23.0%), coal (23.3%) and agricultural commodities (15.9%).

RECENT DEVELOPMENTS:

For the twelve months ended 12/31/02, net income increased 4.0% to $760.0 million compared with $731.0 million a year earlier. Total operating revenues declined 2.5% to $8.98 billion from $9.21 billion the previous year. Freight revenues slipped 2.4% to $8.87 billion, reflecting revenue declines across each of the Company's major product sectors. BNI's railway operating ratio, which measures the percentage of railway operating revenues consumed by railway operating expenses, edged down to 81.3% from 80.7% the year before. Operating income was $1.66 billion, 5.4% lower than the prior year.

PROSPECTS:

As part of BNI's ongoing efforts to focus on customer service and generate new business opportunities, BNSF has expanded its guaranteed on-time carload rail service to seven lanes, including three additional lanes from the Pacific Northwest to Arizona and northern/southern California, and two from northern/southern California to the Midwest. The guarantee allows shippers to purchase, for a premium, a guarantee for on-time carload rail service in any of these lanes.

ANNUAL FINANCIAL DATA:

FISCAL YEAR	TOT. REVS. ($mill.)	NET INC. ($mill.)	TOT. ASSETS ($mill.)	OPER. PROFIT %	NET PROFIT %	RET. ON EQUITY %	RET. ON ASSETS %	CURR. RATIO	EARN. PER SH.$	CASH FL. PER SH.$	TANG. BK. VAL.$	DIV. PER SH.$	PRICE RANGE	AVG. P/E RATIO	AVG. YIELD %
p12/31/02	8,979.0	760.0							2.00			0.48	31.75 - 23.18	13.7	1.7
12/31/01	9,208.0	⑥737.0	24,721.0	19.1	8.0	9.4	3.0	0.3	⑥1.89	4.21	20.35	0.49	34.00 - 22.40	14.9	1.7
12/31/00	9,205.0	⑤980.0	24,375.0	22.9	10.6	13.1	4.0	0.4	⑤2.36	4.52	19.10	0.48	29.56 - 19.06	10.3	2.0
12/31/99	9,100.0	1,137.0	23,700.0	24.2	12.5	13.9	4.8	0.5	2.44	4.36	17.98	0.48	37.94 - 22.88	12.5	1.6
12/31/98	8,941.0	1,155.0	22,690.0	24.1	12.9	14.9	5.1	0.5	2.43	4.17	16.52	0.42	35.71 - 26.88	12.9	1.3
12/31/97	8,413.0	①885.0	21,336.0	21.0	10.5	13.0	4.1	0.6	①1.88	3.52	14.53	0.40	33.65 - 23.42	15.2	1.4
12/31/96	8,187.0	889.0	19,846.0	21.4	10.9	14.9	4.5	0.6	1.90	3.52	12.95	0.40	30.04 - 24.50	14.4	1.5
12/31/95	6,183.0	②198.0	18,269.0	8.5	3.2	3.9	1.1	0.5	②0.55	2.24	11.22	0.40	28.25 - 15.17	39.2	1.8
③12/31/94	4,995.0	④426.0	7,772.0	17.1	8.5	19.0	5.5	0.7	④1.49	2.91	7.10	0.40	22.21 - 15.50	12.6	2.1
12/31/93	4,699.0	296.0	8,282.0	14.1	6.3	15.4	3.6	0.3	1.02	2.41	5.94	0.40	19.63 - 14.00	16.5	2.4

Statistics are as originally reported. Adj. for 3-for-1 stk. split, 9/98. ① Incl. non-recurr. chrg. of $57.0 mill. ② Bef. extraord. chrg. of $6.0 mill.; acctg. adj. chrg. of $100.0 mill.; & incls. pre-tax chrg. of $735.0 mill. ③ Figures for '94 & earlier are for Burlington Northern Inc. ④ Bef. acctg. adj. chrg. of $10.0 mill. ⑤ Incl. pre-tax merger-related chrg. of $20.0 mill. & gain of $29.0 mill. fr. disp. of prop. ⑥ Bef. extraord. chrg. of $6.0 mill.

OFFICERS:
M. K. Rose, Chmn., Pres., C.E.O.
T. N. Hund, Exec. V.P., C.F.O., Treas.
C. R. Ice, V.P., C.O.O.

INVESTOR CONTACT: Marsha K. Morgan, V.P., Inv. Rel., Corp. Sec., (817) 352-6452

PRINCIPAL OFFICE: 2650 Lou Menk Drive, Fort Worth, TX 76131-2830

TELEPHONE NUMBER: (817) 333-2000
FAX: (817) 333-2377
WEB: www.bnsf.com

NO. OF EMPLOYEES: 39,000 (approx.)

SHAREHOLDERS: 41,000 (approx.)

ANNUAL MEETING: In Apr.

INCORPORATED: DE, Mar., 1981

INSTITUTIONAL HOLDINGS:
No. of Institutions: 419
Shares Held: 283,467,326
% Held: 75.1

INDUSTRY: Railroads, line-haul operating (SIC: 4011)

TRANSFER AGENT(S): EquiServe, Jersey City, NJ

BURLINGTON RESOURCES INC.

EXCH.	SYM.	REC. PRICE	P/E RATIO	YLD.	MKT. CAP.	RANGE (52-WK.)	'02 Y/E PR.
NYSE	BR	46.35 (2/28/03)	20.6	1.2%	$9.31 bill.	47.75 - 32.00	42.65

MEDIUM GRADE. THE COMPANY HAS HEDGED ITS 2003 NORTH AMERICAN NATURAL GAS PRODUCTION.

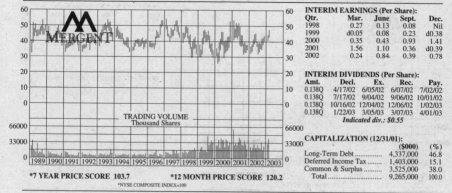

INTERIM EARNINGS (Per Share):

Qtr.	Mar.	June	Sept.	Dec.
1998	0.27	0.13	0.08	Nil
1999	d0.05	0.08	0.23	d0.38
2000	0.35	0.43	0.93	1.41
2001	1.56	1.10	0.36	d0.39
2002	0.24	0.84	0.39	0.78

INTERIM DIVIDENDS (Per Share):

Amt.	Decl.	Ex.	Rec.	Pay.
0.138Q	4/17/02	6/05/02	6/07/02	7/02/02
0.138Q	7/17/02	9/04/02	9/06/02	10/01/02
0.138Q	10/16/02	12/04/02	12/06/02	1/02/03
0.138Q	1/22/03	3/05/03	3/07/03	4/01/03

Indicated div.: $0.55

CAPITALIZATION (12/31/01):

	($000)	(%)
Long-Term Debt	4,337,000	46.8
Deferred Income Tax	1,403,000	15.1
Common & Surplus	3,525,000	38.0
Total	9,265,000	100.0

*7 YEAR PRICE SCORE 103.7   ***12 MONTH PRICE SCORE 120.2**

*NYSE COMPOSITE INDEX=100

BUSINESS:

Burlington Resources Inc. is engaged in the exploration for and the development, production and marketing of crude oil, natural gas liquids and natural gas. Its principal subsidiaries include: Burlington Resources Oil & Gas LP (formerly known as Burlington Resources Oil & Gas Company), The Louisiana Land and Exploration Company, Burlington Resources Canada Energy Ltd. (formerly known as Poco Petroleums Ltd.), Canadian Hunter Explo-

ration Ltd., and their affiliated companies, BR is one of North America's largest producers of natural gas with an asset base dominated by North American natural gas properties. BR also has operations in the Northwest European Shelf, North Africa, Latin America, the Far East and West Africa. At 12/31/02, total proved reserves were 8.20 trillion cubic feet of gas equivalents. BR acquired Canadian Hunter Exploration Ltd. on 12/5/01 for about $2.10 billion.

RECENT DEVELOPMENTS:

For the year ended 12/31/02, net income was $454.0 million versus income of $558.0 million, before an accounting change credit of $3.0 million, a year earlier. Results for 2002 and 2001 included gains of $68.0 million and $8.0 million, respectively, on the disposal of assets. Results for 2001 also included an impairment of oil and gas properties

charge of $184.0 million. Revenues fell 13.6% to $2.92 billion. Total production for 2002 rose 7.8% to 2,571 million cubic feet of natural gas equivalent per day. Average price realizations for natural gas slid 21.0% to $3.13 per thousand cubic feet (Mcf). However, oil price realizations increased 2.8% to $24.11 per barrel.

PROSPECTS:

BR anticipates that production volume growth during 2003 will be at the low end of the Company's long-term 3.0% to 8.0% average annual growth target. Separately, BR stated that as of 1/29/03 it has hedged its 2003 North American natural gas production using costless price collars. For the first quarter ended 3/31/03, 490 million cubic feet of natu-

ral gas per day (MMcfd) is hedged at a floor of $3.38 per Mcf and ceiling of $5.18 per Mcf. For the second and third quarters of 2003, 540 MMcfd is hedged at a floor of $3.43 per Mcf and ceiling of $5.26 per Mcf. For the fourth quarter ended 12/31/03, 510 MMcfd is hedged at a floor of $3.41 per Mcf and a ceiling of $5.22 per Mcf.

ANNUAL FINANCIAL DATA:

FISCAL YEAR	TOT. REVS. ($mill.)	NET INC. ($mill.)	TOT. ASSETS ($mill.)	OPER. PROFIT %	NET PROFIT %	RET. ON EQUITY %	RET. ON ASSETS %	CURR. RATIO	EARN. PER SH. $	CASH FL. PER SH. $	TANG. BK. VAL. $	DIV. PER SH. $	PRICE RANGE	AVG. P/E RATIO	AVG. YIELD %
p12/31/02	2,919.0	[7] 454.0							[7] 2.25			0.55	45.34 - 32.00	17.2	1.4
12/31/01	3,326.0	[6] 558.0	10,582.0	32.6	16.8	15.8	5.3	1.0	[6] 2.69	6.19	13.66	0.55	53.63 - 31.69	15.9	1.3
12/31/00	3,147.0	675.0	7,506.0	37.8	21.4	18.0	9.0	1.3	3.12	6.38	17.40	0.55	52.88 - 25.75	12.6	1.4
12/31/99	2,065.0	[2] 1.0	7,191.0	11.4	...	...	...	1.0	[2] 0.01	2.91	15.03	0.55	47.63 - 29.50	N.M.	1.4
12/31/98	1,637.0	86.0	5,917.0	13.3	5.3	2.8	1.5	0.9	0.48	3.50	19.86	0.55	49.63 - 29.44	82.3	1.4
[1] 12/31/97	2,000.0	[2] 319.0	5,821.0	25.2	16.0	10.6	5.5	1.3	[2] 1.79	4.84	17.07	0.55	54.50 - 39.75	26.3	1.2
12/31/96	1,293.0	255.0	4,316.0	32.3	19.7	10.9	5.9	1.2	2.02	4.77	18.68	0.55	53.50 - 35.13	21.9	1.2
12/31/95	872.5	[2] d279.6	4,141.8	...	...	...	...	0.8	[2] d2.20	0.73	17.54	0.55	42.25 - 33.63	...	1.4
[3] 12/31/94	1,054.8	154.2	4,808.6	16.6	14.6	6.0	3.2	1.0	1.20	3.81	20.30	0.55	49.63 - 33.13	34.5	1.3
12/31/93	1,043.2	[4][5] 255.2	4,447.7	24.5	24.5	9.8	5.7	0.9	[4][5] 1.95	4.13	20.11	0.54	53.88 - 36.50	23.2	1.2

Statistics are as originally reported. [1] Refl. acq. of Louisiana Land & Exploration Co. [2] Incl. non-recurr. chrgs. 12/31/99: $262.0 mill.; 12/31/01: $40.0 mill.; chrg. 12/31/95: $304.0 mill. [3] Revs. in '94 incl. net amts. fr. sale of NGLs. [4] Incl. non-recurr. gain of ($0.50/sh.) & ($0.09/sh.) gain on exchg. of BR debt into stk. of Anadarko Petroleum stk. [5] Bef. disc. ops. cr. of $200,000. [6] Incl. impair. of oil & gas prop. chrg. of $184.0 mill.; bef. acctg. cr. of $3.0 mill. [7] Incl. gain of $68.0 mill. on disp. of assets.

OFFICERS:
B. S. Shackouls, Chmn., Pres., C.E.O.
S. J. Shapiro, Exec. V.P., C.F.O.
P. W. Cook, V.P., Contr.
INVESTOR CONTACT: John Carrara, Inv. Rel., (713) 624-9548
PRINCIPAL OFFICE: 5051 Westheimer, Suite 1400, Houston, TX 77056

TELEPHONE NUMBER: (713) 624-9500
FAX: (713) 624-9645
WEB: www.br-inc.com
NO. OF EMPLOYEES: 2,167
SHAREHOLDERS: 17,531
ANNUAL MEETING: In Apr.
INCORPORATED: DE, 1988

INSTITUTIONAL HOLDINGS:
No. of Institutions: 451
Shares Held: 167,681,345
% Held: 83.3
INDUSTRY: Natural gas transmission (SIC: 4922)
TRANSFER AGENT(S): Fleet National Bank, Providence, RI

CABLEVISION SYSTEMS CORPORATION

EXCH.	SYM.	REC. PRICE	P/E RATIO	YLD.	MKT. CAP.	RANGE (52-WK.)	'02 Y/E PR.
NYSE	CVC	17.79 (2/28/03)	...	...	$4.80 bil.	39.36 - 4.67	16.74

SPECULATIVE GRADE. THE COMPANY SOLD THE WIZ CONSUMER ELECTRONICS CHAIN.

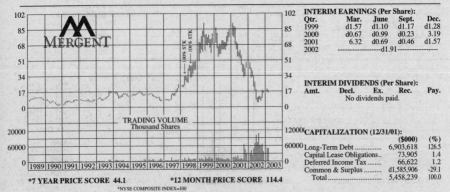

INTERIM EARNINGS (Per Share):

Qtr.	Mar.	June	Sept.	Dec.
1999	d1.57	d1.10	d1.17	d1.28
2000	d0.67	d0.99	d0.23	3.19
2001	6.32	d0.69	d0.46	1.57
2002	----------------d1.91----------------			

INTERIM DIVIDENDS (Per Share):

Amt.	Decl.	Ex.	Rec.	Pay.
	No dividends paid.			

CAPITALIZATION (12/31/01):

	($000)	(%)
Long-Term Debt	6,903,618	126.5
Capital Lease Obligations..	73,905	1.4
Deferred Income Tax	66,622	1.2
Common & Surplus	d1,585,906	-29.1
Total	5,458,239	100.0

*7 YEAR PRICE SCORE 44.1   *12 MONTH PRICE SCORE 114.4

*NYSE COMPOSITE INDEX=100

BUSINESS:

Cablevision Systems Corporation, a telecommunications and entertainment company, consists of the Cablevision NY Group (83.7% of net sales as of 12/31/02) and the Rainbow Media Group (16.3%). As of 2/11/03, CVC's cable television operations served 3.0 million households located in the New York metropolitan area. CVC offers integrated business communications services, Internet service, and digital television service. RMG operates programming businesses including American Movie Classics,

Bravo, The Independent Film Channel and other national and regional services. In addition, RMG is a 50.0% partner in Fox Sports Net. Cablevision also owns a controlling interest and operates Madison Square Garden and its sports teams, including the Knicks and Rangers, Radio City Music Hall, and Clearview Cinemas in the New York metropolitan area. On 3/7/03, CVC sold THE WIZ consumer electronics chain.

RECENT DEVELOPMENTS:

For the year ended 12/31/02, CVC reported a loss from continuing operations of $560.8 million versus income of $1.08 billion the year before. Results included a net loss of $64.0 million in 2002 and a net gain of $2.39 billion in

2001 related to one-time items. Results excluded a gain of $651.0 million in 2002 and a loss of $74.8 million in 2001 from discontinued operations. Net revenues grew 3.2% to $4.00 billion from $3.88 billion the year before.

PROSPECTS:

On 3/7/03, the Company announced that it sold THE WIZ consumer electronics chain to GBO Electronic Acquisition LLC in a stock transaction. Separately, on 12/19/02, CVC's partner, Northcoast Communications, announced an agreement to sell its spectrum license covering 50 U.S. markets to Verizon Wireless. CVC plans to use its share of the

proceeds, about $635.0 million, to pay down debt. The transaction is expected to close in the second quarter of 2003. Looking ahead, revenue growth for the telecommunications segment is expected to range from 12.0% to 14.0%, while revenue growth for the Company is anticipated between 10.0% and 12.0% in 2003.

ANNUAL FINANCIAL DATA:

FISCAL YEAR	TOT. REVS. ($mill.)	NET INC. ($mill.)	TOT. ASSETS ($mill.)	OPER. PROFIT %	NET PROFIT %	RET. ON ASSETS %	CURR. RATIO	EARN. PER SH.$	CASH FL. PER SH.$	PRICE RANGE	AVG. P/E RATIO
p12/31/02	4,003.4	④ d560.8						④ d1.91	9.83	48.25 — 4.67	...
12/31/01	4,404.5	③ 1,007.7	10,216.8	...	22.9	9.9	0.6	③ 3.71	9.83	91.50 — 32.50	16.7
12/31/00	4,411.0	① 229.3	8,273.3	...	5.2	2.8	0.2	1.29	7.23	86.88 — 55.00	55.0
12/31/99	3,943.0	d800.6	7,130.3	...	...	...	0.1	d5.12	0.66	91.88 — 49.88	...
12/31/98	3,265.1	① d448.5	7,061.1	...	...	...	0.2	① d3.16	2.07	50.25 — 21.78	...
12/31/97	1,949.4	① 136.7	5,625.1	4.2	7.0	2.4	0.1	① d0.12	4.97	24.56 — 6.78	...
12/31/96	1,315.1	d332.1	3,034.7	5.7	...	...	0.1	d4.63	d0.59	15.09 — 6.25	...
12/31/95	1,078.1	① d317.5	2,502.3	7.4	...	...	0.1	① d3.54	0.02	17.44 — 12.19	...
12/31/94	837.2	② d315.2	...	7.5	...	...	...	② d3.43	d0.33	16.97 — 9.75	...

Statistics are as originally reported. In Mar. 2001, Co. created a tracking stk. for its Rainbow Media Group. Cablevision owns 77.5% of Rainbow Media, with NBC owning the remaining 22.5%, as of 4/1/02. Fin.'l data reflects the combined opers., while per share figures reflect the Cablevision NY Group only beg. in 2001. Adj. for 100% stk. div., 8/98 & 3/98. ① Incl. gain on sales of programs int. & cable assets, 2000, $1.21 bill.; 1998, $170.9 mill.; 1997, $372.1 mill.; 1995, $36.0 mill. ② Incl. restruct. exps. of $4.3 mill. ③ Incl. a pre-tax net gain of $2.39 bill. rel. to var. items, primarily sale of cable assets. ④ Incl. a net loss of $64.0 mill. rel. to var. items; bef. gain of $651.0 mill. fr. disc. ops.

OFFICERS: C. F. Dolan, Chmn. J. L. Dolan, Pres., C.E.O. **INVESTOR CONTACT:** Frank J. Golden, Sr., V.P., Inv. Rel., (516) 803-2270 **PRINCIPAL OFFICE:** 1111 Stewart Avenue, Bethpage, NY 11714-3581	**TELEPHONE NUMBER:** (516) 803-2300 **FAX:** (516) 803-2273 **WEB:** www.cablevision.com **NO. OF EMPLOYEES:** 19,904 **SHAREHOLDERS:** 1,018 (Cablevision NY Group class A) **ANNUAL MEETING:** In June **INCORPORATED:** DE, Mar., 1998	**INSTITUTIONAL HOLDINGS:** No. of Institutions: 225 Shares Held: 196,589,255 % Held: 65.1 **INDUSTRY:** Cable and other pay TV services (SIC: 4841) **TRANSFER AGENT(S):** Mellon Investor Services, Ridgefield Park, NJ

CABOT CORPORATION

EXCH.	SYM.	REC. PRICE	P/E RATIO	YLD.	MKT. CAP.	RANGE (52-WK.)	'02 Y/E PR.
NYSE	CBT	21.90 (2/28/03)	14.6	2.4%	$1.35 bill.	37.22 - 19.45	26.54

UPPER MEDIUM GRADE. THE COMPANY IS CAUTIOUS ABOUT ITS NEAR-TERM OUTLOOK.

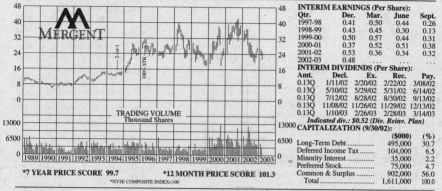

INTERIM EARNINGS (Per Share):

Qtr.	Dec.	Mar.	June	Sept.
1997-98	0.41	0.50	0.44	0.26
1998-99	0.43	0.45	0.30	0.13
1999-00	0.50	0.57	0.44	0.31
2000-01	0.37	0.52	0.51	0.38
2001-02	0.53	0.36	0.34	0.32
2002-03	0.48	...	...	...

INTERIM DIVIDENDS (Per Share):

Amt.	Decl.	Ex.	Rec.	Pay.
0.13Q	1/11/02	2/20/02	2/22/02	3/08/02
0.13Q	5/10/02	5/29/02	5/31/02	6/14/02
0.13Q	7/12/02	8/28/02	8/30/02	9/13/02
0.13Q	11/08/02	11/26/02	11/29/02	12/13/02
0.13Q	1/10/03	2/26/03	2/28/03	3/14/03

Indicated div.: $0.52 (Div. Reinv. Plan)

CAPITALIZATION (9/30/02):

	($000)	(%)
Long-Term Debt	495,000	30.7
Deferred Income Tax	104,000	6.5
Minority Interest	35,000	2.2
Preferred Stock	75,000	4.7
Common & Surplus	902,000	56.0
Total	1,611,000	100.0

*7 YEAR PRICE SCORE 99.7   ***12 MONTH PRICE SCORE 101.3**

*NYSE COMPOSITE INDEX=100

BUSINESS:

Cabot Corporation is a global company with businesses in specialty chemicals, performance materials, and specialty fluids. CBT and its affiliates operate manufacturing facilities in the U.S. and more than 20 other countries. The Company manufactures, markets and distributes fine powders through four specialty chemical businesses: carbon black; fumed metal oxides; inkjet colorants; and aerogels. In September 2000, CBT spun off Cabot Microelectronics Corporation. In February 2002, the Company purchased the remaining 50.0% of the shares it did not own in Showa Cabot Supermetals KK in Japan. Revenues for fiscal 2002 were derived: chemicals businesses, 78.7%; performance materials, 19.5%; and specialty fluids, 1.8%.

RECENT DEVELOPMENTS:

For the three months ended 12/31/02, net income declined 13.2% to $33.0 million compared with $38.0 million in the corresponding quarter of 2001. Net sales and other operating revenues were $408.0 million, up 8.2% from $377.0 million in the prior-year period. The improvement in sales was attributable to higher sales volumes of both carbon black and fumed metal oxides and higher average selling prices for CBT's performance materials segment, partially offset by lower volumes within the specialty fluids division. Gross profit was unchanged at $117.0 million versus the previous year. Income from operations slipped 6.9% to $54.0 million compared with $58.0 million the year before.

PROSPECTS:

The Company is cautious about its near-term outlook in light of uncertain economic and political conditions and the rapid rise in oil and natural gas prices. Although CBT's businesses continue to perform reasonable well and the Company has succeeded in providing greater stability to its tantalum business, it is unclear as to when a significant and sustainable recovery in volumes and margins can be expected. Meanwhile, the Company remains optimistic about the long-term prospects of its developing businesses, inkjet colorants, aerogels and specialty fluids, as all three businesses are progressing well.

ANNUAL FINANCIAL DATA:

FISCAL YEAR	TOT. REVS. ($mill.)	NET INC. ($mill.)	TOT. ASSETS ($mill.)	OPER. PROFIT %	NET PROFIT %	RET. ON EQUITY %	RET. ON ASSETS %	CURR. RATIO	EARN. PER SH.$	CASH FL. PER SH.$	TANG. BK. VAL.$	DIV. PER SH.$	PRICE RANGE	AVG. P/E RATIO	AVG. YIELD %
9/30/02	1,557.0	[7] 105.0	2,067.0	9.5	6.7	10.7	5.1	3.4	[7] 1.48	2.97	12.81	0.52	37.22 - 19.45	19.1	1.8
9/30/01	1,698.0	[6] 121.0	1,919.0	12.1	7.1	12.7	6.3	3.3	[6] 1.62	3.15	13.63	0.50	42.24 - 24.44	20.6	1.5
9/30/00	1,523.0	[5] 108.0	2,134.0	13.1	7.1	10.3	5.1	2.4	[5] 1.46	3.21	14.05	0.44	38.44 - 18.19	19.4	1.6
9/30/99	1,699.0	[4] 97.0	1,842.0	12.1	5.7	13.7	5.3	1.5	[4] 1.31	3.00	9.10	0.44	29.81 - 17.94	18.2	1.8
9/30/98	1,652.8	[3] 121.6	1,805.2	13.3	7.4	17.2	6.7	1.2	[3] 1.61	3.13	9.01	0.43	39.94 - 21.75	19.2	1.4
9/30/97	1,636.7	92.7	1,823.6	11.8	5.7	12.7	5.1	1.1	1.27	2.82	8.83	0.40	29.25 - 21.50	20.0	1.6
9/30/96	1,865.2	[2] 194.1	1,857.6	14.4	10.4	26.1	10.4	1.3	[2] 2.60	3.93	8.76	0.37	31.63 - 22.75	10.5	1.4
9/30/95	1,840.9	171.9	1,654.3	15.6	9.3	25.1	10.4	1.7	2.17	3.39	7.97	0.41	29.38 - 14.00	10.0	1.9
9/30/94	1,686.6	[2] 78.7	1,616.8	10.8	4.7	14.0	4.9	1.3	[2] 0.98	2.12	3.08	0.27	14.63 - 12.19	13.7	2.0
9/30/93	1,618.5	[1] 37.4	1,489.5	6.7	2.3	8.5	2.5	1.5	[1] 0.45	1.59	4.29	0.26	14.63 - 9.28	26.6	2.2

Statistics are as originally reported. Adj. for 2-for-1 split, 3/96 & 7/94. [1] Bef. $26.1 mill. loss fr. acct. adj. [2] Incl. $69.7 mill. net pre-tax gain, 1996; $32.6 mill., 1995; $6.2 mill., 1994. [3] Incl. $60.0 mill. asset impairment chg., $25.0 mill. pre-tax chg. & $90.3 mill. pre-tax gain. [4] Incl. $110.9 mill. pre-tax chgs. & $9.9 mill. pre-tax gain fr. sale of securities. [5] Incl. $10.0 mill. chg. fr. cost reduction efforts & excl. $36.0 mill. net inc. fr. disc. ops. & $309.0 mill. gain fr. sale of bus. [6] Incl. $21.0 mill. special chgs. & excl. $3.0 mill. gain fr. sale of bus. [7] Incl. $17.0 mill. special chgs. & excl. $1.0 mill. gain fr. disc. ops.

OFFICERS:
K. F. Burnes, Chmn., Pres., C.E.O.
J. A. Shaw, Exec. V.P., C.F.O.
H. Kim, V.P., Gen Couns.

INVESTOR CONTACT: James P. Kelly, Investor Relations, (617) 345-0100

PRINCIPAL OFFICE: Two Seaport Lane, Suite 1300, Boston, MA 02210-2019

TELEPHONE NUMBER: (617) 345-0100
FAX: (617) 342-6103
WEB: www.cabot-corp.com
NO. OF EMPLOYEES: 4,500 (approx.)
SHAREHOLDERS: 1,600 (approx. record)
ANNUAL MEETING: In Mar.
INCORPORATED: DE, 1960

CABOT OIL & GAS CORPORATION

EXCH.	SYM.	REC. PRICE	P/E RATIO	YLD.	MKT. CAP.	RANGE (52-WK.)	'02 Y/E PR.
NYSE	COG	24.07 (2/28/03)	48.1	0.7%	$0.77 bill.	26.55 - 17.75	24.78

MEDIUM GRADE. THE RECENT STRENGTHENING OF NATURAL GAS PRICES ENHANCES THE COMPANY'S NEAR-TERM OUTLOOK.

*7 YEAR PRICE SCORE 119.6   ***12 MONTH PRICE SCORE 113.9**

*NYSE COMPOSITE INDEX=100

INTERIM EARNINGS (Per Share):

Qtr.	Mar.	June	Sept.	Dec.
1998	0.12	0.09	d0.10	d0.03
1999	d0.13	Nil	0.15	0.19
2000	0.18	0.05	0.21	0.58
2001	1.32	0.45	0.32	d0.49
2002	d0.03	0.07	0.19	0.27

INTERIM DIVIDENDS (Per Share):

Amt.	Decl.	Ex.	Rec.	Pay.
0.04Q	1/28/02	2/06/02	2/08/02	2/22/02
0.04Q	5/03/02	5/15/02	5/17/02	5/24/02
0.04Q	8/01/02	8/08/02	8/12/02	8/26/02
0.04Q	10/25/02	11/06/02	11/08/02	11/22/02
0.04Q	1/24/03	2/05/03	2/07/03	2/21/03

Indicated div.: $0.16

CAPITALIZATION (12/31/01):

	($000)	(%)
Long-Term Debt	393,000	41.8
Deferred Income Tax	200,859	21.4
Common & Surplus	346,552	36.9
Total	940,411	100.0

BUSINESS:

Cabot Oil & Gas Corporation is an independent oil and gas company engaged in the exploration, development, acquisition and exploitation of oil and gas properties located in three principal areas of the United States: the Gulf Coast, including onshore Texas and Louisiana; the West, with the Rocky Mountains and Mid-Continent; and the East. COG also transports, stores, gathers and purchases natural gas for resale. Cabot Oil & Gas was organized in 1989 as the successor to the oil and gas business of Cabot Corporation, founded in 1891. As of 12/31/02, COG's proved reserves totaled 1.17 trillion cubic feet equivalent. On 8/16/01, COG acquired Cody Company for $231.2 million.

RECENT DEVELOPMENTS:

For the year ended 12/31/02, net income was $16.1 million compared with $47.1 million a year earlier. Results for 2002 and 2001 included pre-tax gains of $244,000 and $26,000, respectively, on the sale of assets, and impairment of long-lived asset charges of $2.7 million and $6.9 million, respectively. Net operating revenues slid 20.9% to $353.8 million from $447.0 million in 2001. COG attributed the lower results primarily to decreased realized commodity prices. For instance, the Company's average realized natural gas price fell 30.7% to $3.02 per thousand cubic feet (Mcf) compared with $4.36 per Mcf the year before. Oil prices declined 4.5% to $23.79 per barrel. However, year-over year production rose 12.3% to 91.1 billion cubic feet equivalent, aided by a full year of production from the Cody acquisition versus a five-month contribution in 2001, and organic drilling results.

PROSPECTS:

COG's near-term outlook appears to be improving, reflecting in part the recent strengthening of natural gas and oil prices. Additionally, the Company has indicated that it intends to move forward with its $150.0 million production program that includes testing 30 exploration prospects during 2003, which is triple the amount spent by COG on its 2002 program. COG believes that spending at these levels, coupled with its hedging program and current solid commodity prices, should provide the Company with additional flexibility over the course of 2003 to pursue further debt reduction and/or increase drilling exposure.

ANNUAL FINANCIAL DATA:

FISCAL YEAR	TOT. REVS. ($000)	NET INC. ($000)	TOT. ASSETS ($000)	OPER. PROFIT %	NET PROFIT %	RET. ON EQUITY %	RET. ON ASSETS %	CURR. RATIO	EARN. PER SH. $	CASH FL. PER SH. $	TANG. BK. VAL.$	DIV. PER SH. $	PRICE RANGE	AVG. P/E RATIO	AVG. YIELD %
p12/31/02	353,756	③ 16,103							③ 0.51			0.16	26.55 - 17.75	43.4	0.7
12/31/01	447,042	② 47,084	1,069,031	21.3	10.5	13.6	4.4	0.8	② 1.53	4.22	10.86	0.16	34.35 - 16.25	16.5	0.6
12/31/00	368,651	① 25,472	735,634	17.6	6.9	10.5	3.5	0.9	① 1.06	2.99	8.31	0.16	32.00 - 14.06	21.7	0.7
12/31/99	181,873	8,519	659,480	21.7	4.7	4.6	1.3	0.7	0.21	2.36	7.52	0.16	20.00 - 10.75	73.2	1.0
12/31/98	159,606	5,304	704,160	17.2	3.3	2.9	0.8	0.7	0.08	1.72	7.31	0.16	24.00 - 12.63	228.6	0.9
12/31/97	185,127	28,334	541,805	34.5	15.3	15.4	5.2	0.8	0.97	2.67	7.46	0.16	25.19 - 15.38	20.9	0.8
12/31/96	163,061	20,824	561,341	19.4	12.8	13.0	3.7	1.1	0.67	2.54	7.03	0.16	18.50 - 13.13	23.6	1.0
12/31/95	213,923	d86,618	528,155	...	...	...	...	0.9	d4.05	d1.97	6.48	0.16	17.00 - 12.38	...	1.1
12/31/94	237,067	d995	688,352	6.3	...	...	...	1.0	d0.25	2.07	10.67	0.16	23.75 - 13.38	...	0.9
12/31/93	164,295	3,520	445,001	12.2	2.1	2.3	0.8	1.2	0.10	1.64	7.46	0.16	27.00 - 15.38	211.7	1.1

Statistics are as originally reported. ① Incl. bad debt exp. of $2.1 mill., loss on sale of assets of $39,000 & impairment of long-lived assets chrg. of $9.1 mill. ② Incl. bad debt exp. of $2.3 mill., gain on sale of assets of $26,000 & impairment of long-lived assets chrg. of $6.9 mill. ③ Incl. gain on sale of assets of $244,000 & impairment of long-lived assets chrg. of $2.7 mill.

OFFICERS:
D. O. Dinges, Chmn., C.E.O., Pres.
S. C. Schroeder, V.P., C.F.O.
L. A. Machesney, V.P., Corp. Sec.
INVESTOR CONTACT: Scott C. Schroeder, V.P., C.F.O., (281) 589-4993
PRINCIPAL OFFICE: 1200 Enclave Parkway, Houston, TX 77077

TELEPHONE NUMBER: (281) 589-4600
FAX: (281) 589-4653
WEB: www.cabotog.com
NO. OF EMPLOYEES: 366 (avg.)
SHAREHOLDERS: 849
ANNUAL MEETING: In May
INCORPORATED: DE, Dec., 1989

INSTITUTIONAL HOLDINGS:
No. of Institutions: 135
Shares Held: 28,900,507
% Held: 90.9
INDUSTRY: Crude petroleum and natural gas (SIC: 1311)
TRANSFER AGENT(S): Bank Boston N.A., Boston, MA

CADENCE DESIGN SYSTEMS, INC.

EXCH.	SYM.	REC. PRICE	P/E RATIO	YLD.	MKT. CAP.	RANGE (52-WK.)	'02 Y/E PR.
NYSE	CDN	10.59 (2/28/03)	40.7	...	$2.86 bill.	24.19 - 8.65	11.79

LOWER MEDIUM GRADE. THE COMPANY EXPECTS FIRST QUARTER 2003 REVENUES TO RANGE FROM $245.0 MILLION TO $255.0 MILLION.

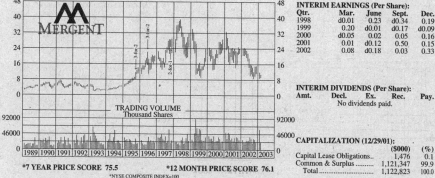

*7 YEAR PRICE SCORE 75.5   ***12 MONTH PRICE SCORE 76.1**

*NYSE COMPOSITE INDEX=100

INTERIM EARNINGS (Per Share):

Qtr.	Mar.	June	Sept.	Dec.
1998	d0.01	0.23	d0.34	0.19
1999	0.20	d0.01	d0.17	d0.09
2000	d0.05	0.02	0.05	0.16
2001	0.01	0.12	0.50	0.15
2002	0.08	d0.18	0.03	0.33

INTERIM DIVIDENDS (Per Share):

Amt.	Decl.	Ex.	Rec.	Pay.
	No dividends paid.			

CAPITALIZATION (12/29/01):

	($000)	(%)
Capital Lease Obligations..	1,476	0.1
Common & Surplus	1,121,347	99.9
Total	1,122,823	100.0

BUSINESS:

Cadence Design Systems, Inc. provides software and other technology and offers design and methodology services for the product development requirements of the world's electronics companies. The Company licenses its electronic design automation software technology and provides a range of professional services to companies ranging from consulting services to helping customers optimize their product development processes. CDN is a supplier of end-to-end products and services that are used by companies to design and develop complex chips and electronic systems including semiconductors, computer systems and peripherals, telecommunications and networking equipment, mobile and wireless devices, automotive electronics, and consumer products. Revenues for 2002 were derived: product, 62.8%; services, 11.6%; and maintenance, 25.6%.

RECENT DEVELOPMENTS:

For the year ended 12/28/02, net income fell 49.1% to $71.9 million versus $141.3 million in 2001. Results for 2002 and 2001 included amortization of acquired intangibles of $82.5 million and $92.3 million, and amortization of deferred stock compensation of $37.5 million and $17.9 million, respectively. Results for 2002 and 2001 also included special charges of $216.0 million and $168.1 million, and restructuring and asset impairments of $133.6 million and $64.4 million, respectively. Total revenues slipped 9.6% to $1.29 billion from $1.43 billion in 2001.

PROSPECTS:

The Company remains cautious about its near-term outlook due to ongoing difficult market conditions in the semiconductor industry. As a result, the Company expects product bookings in the first quarter of 2003 to be down sequentially. Moreover, total revenue for the first quarter is expected to range from $245.0 million to $255.0 million, with subscription revenue comprising approximately 80.0% to 90.0% of software product bookings. Separately, on 1/15/03, the Company acquired Celestry Design Technologies, Inc., a supplier of silicon modeling tools and expanded full-chip circuit simulation technology, for an undisclosed amount.

ANNUAL FINANCIAL DATA:

FISCAL YEAR	TOT. REVS. ($Mill.)	NET INC. ($Mill.)	TOT. ASSETS ($Mill.)	OPER. PROFIT %	NET PROFIT %	RET. ON EQUITY %	RET. ON ASSETS %	CURR. RATIO	EARN. PER SH.$	CASH FL. PER SH.$	TANG. BK. VAL.$	PRICE RANGE	AVG. P/E RATIO
p12/28/02	1,293.1	⑥ 71.9							⑥ 0.27			24.39 — 8.65	61.2
12/29/01	1,430.4	⑤ 141.3	1,730.0	16.8	9.9	12.6	8.2	1.3	⑤ 0.55	1.44	2.78	32.69 — 14.10	42.5
12/30/00	1,279.6	②④ 50.0	1,477.3	5.0	3.9	5.5	3.4	1.1	②④ 0.19	0.98	2.35	28.94 — 13.00	110.3
1/01/00	1,093.3	② d14.1	1,459.7	...	...	...	...	1.1	② d0.06	0.62	2.36	34.13 — 9.19	...
1/02/99	1,216.1	② 32.0	1,406.0	8.6	2.6	3.7	2.2	1.8	② 0.14	0.58	2.84	39.00 — 19.13	207.4
1/03/98	926.4	②③ 180.4	1,023.9	25.1	19.5	24.3	17.4	2.3	②③ 0.77	1.08	3.34	29.13 — 13.06	25.7
12/28/96	741.5	② 29.0	717.0	12.3	3.9	6.7	4.0	2.1	② 0.16	0.44	2.31	22.19 — 10.69	102.7
12/31/95	548.4	97.3	374.0	21.5	17.7	73.6	26.1	1.0	0.52	0.77	0.62	14.13 — 4.28	17.6
12/31/94	429.1	② 36.6	361.0	10.3	7.4	18.3	8.9	1.2	② 0.19	0.39	0.79	4.83 — 2.28	19.0
12/31/93	368.6	① d0.6	339.3	...	...	...	...	1.9	① d0.77	0.22	0.89	5.42 — 1.83	...

Statistics are as originally reported. Adj. for 3-for-2 stk. split, 5/31/96; 2-for-1 stk. split, 11/17/97. ① Incl. $13.5 mill. restr. chg. and excl. $6.0 mill. loss on disp. of disc. ops. & $12.2 mill. loss fr. disc. ops. ② Incl. unusual chg. of $14.7 mill., 1994; $100.5 mill., 1996; $44.1 mill., 1997; $263.6 mill., 1998; $59.3 mill., 1999; and $6.8 mill., 2000. ③ Excl. $12.3 mill. acctg. change chg. ④ Incl. $11.4 mill. amort. of def. stk chg. ⑤ Incl. $92.3 mill. amort. of acq. intang., $17.9 mill. amort. of def. stk comp., $168.1 mill. unusual credit, $83.3 mill. restr. chg. & $25.8 mill. goodwill write-off. ⑥ Incl. one-time chgs. of $349.6 mill.

OFFICERS:
D. L. Lucas, Chmn.
H. R. Bingham, Pres, C.E.O.
W. Porter, Sr. V.P., C.F.O.

INVESTOR CONTACT: Investor Relations, (408) 236-5972

PRINCIPAL OFFICE: 2655 Seely Avenue, Building 5, San Jose, CA 95134

TELEPHONE NUMBER: (408) 943-1234
FAX: (408) 943-0513
WEB: www.cadence.com
NO. OF EMPLOYEES: 5,600 (approx.)
SHAREHOLDERS: 1,444 (approx. of record); 32,161 (approx. beneficial)
ANNUAL MEETING: In May
INCORPORATED: DE, May, 1988

INSTITUTIONAL HOLDINGS:
No. of Institutions: 247
Shares Held: 216,331,688
% Held: 80.5
INDUSTRY: Prepackaged software (SIC: 7372)
TRANSFER AGENT(S): Mellon Investor Services, South Hackensack, NJ

CALIFORNIA WATER SERVICE GROUP

EXCH.	SYM.	REC. PRICE	P/E RATIO	YLD.	MKT. CAP.	RANGE (52-WK.)	'02 Y/E PR.	DIV. ACH.
NYSE	CWT	25.41 (2/28/03)	20.5	4.4%	$385.8 mill.	26.89 - 20.45	23.65	35 yrs.

MEDIUM GRADE. THE COMPANY EXPECTS A FINAL DECISION ON ITS GENERAL RATE APPLICATIONS IN THE FIRST OR SECOND QUARTERS OF 2003.

*7 YEAR PRICE SCORE 107.4   ***12 MONTH PRICE SCORE 109.8**

*NYSE COMPOSITE INDEX=100

INTERIM EARNINGS (Per Share):

Qtr.	Mar.	June	Sept.	Dec.
1998	0.12	0.28	0.72	0.33
1999	0.20	0.44	0.62	0.30
2000	0.09	0.38	0.60	0.23
2001	0.01	0.37	0.39	0.20
2002	0.12	0.43	0.50	0.19

INTERIM DIVIDENDS (Per Share):

Amt.	Decl.	Ex.	Rec.	Pay.
0.28Q	1/30/02	2/06/02	2/08/02	2/22/02
0.28Q	4/24/02	5/02/02	5/06/02	5/20/02
0.28Q	7/24/02	8/01/02	8/05/02	8/19/02
0.28Q	10/23/02	10/31/02	11/04/02	11/18/02
0.281Q	1/29/03	2/05/03	2/07/03	2/21/03

Indicated div.: $1.13 (Div. Reinv. Plan)

CAPITALIZATION (12/31/01):

	($000)	(%)
Long-Term Debt	202,600	47.0
Deferred Income Tax	28,816	6.7
Preferred Stock	3,475	0.8
Common & Surplus	196,619	45.6
Total	431,510	100.0

BUSINESS:

California Water Service Group is a public utility water company that provides regulated and non-regulated water utility services to more than 2.0 million customers in 98 communities in California, Washington and New Mexico as of 1/29/03. CWT is the parent company of California Water Service Company, Washington Water Service Company, New Mexico Water Service Company and CWS Util-ity Services. The sole business of the Company consists of the production, purchase, storage, purification, distribution and sale of water for domestic, industrial, public, and irrigation uses, and for fire protection. Annual water production totaled nearly 127 billion gallons for 2001, with 51.6% from wells and surface supplies and 48.4% from purchased water.

RECENT DEVELOPMENTS:

For the year ended 12/31/02, net income increased 27.5% to $19.1 million compared with $15.0 million in 2001. Results for 2002 and 2001 included a gain on the sale of non-utility property of $3.0 million and $3.9 million, respectively. Operating revenue rose 6.6% to $263.2 million from $246.8 million the year before. The improvement in revenues was primarily attributed to favorable weather and, to a lesser extent, sales to new customers and rate increases. Total operating expenses advanced 5.0% to $232.9 million due to increases in both purchased water and purchased power costs. Net operating income jumped 20.5% to $30.3 million from $25.2 million a year earlier.

PROSPECTS:

The Company is awaiting a decision on general rate applications for 14 of its 25 California districts plus the General Office operation, filed in mid-2001. The California Public Utilities Commission has issued a draft decision on the applications, and is expected to issue a final decision in the first or second quarter of 2003. If the draft decision is adopted without modification, it would increase annual revenue by $12.8 million. In addition, the Company has applied to recover increases in purchased water and electricity costs incurred prior to 11/29/01, and not yet billed to customers. CWT anticipates decisions on those requests, which total $4.6 million, late in the first quarter 2003.

ANNUAL FINANCIAL DATA:

FISCAL YEAR	TOT. REVS. ($000)	NET INC. ($000)	TOT. ASSETS ($000)	OPER. PROFIT %	NET PROFIT %	NET INC./ NET PROP. %	NET INC./ TOT. CAP. %	RET. ON EQUITY %	ACCUM. DEPR./ GROSS PROP. %	EARN. PER SH. $	TANG. BK. VAL. $	DIV. PER SH. $	DIV. PAYOUT %	PRICE RANGE		AVG. P/E RATIO	AVG. YIELD %
p12/31/02	263,151	☐ 19,073								☐ 1.25		1.12	89.6	26.89	- 20.45	18.9	4.7
12/31/01	246,820	14,965	710,214	10.2	6.1	2.4	3.5	7.5	31.4	0.97	12.95	1.11	114.9	28.60	- 22.88	26.5	4.3
12/31/00	244,806	19,963	666,605	13.6	8.2	3.4	4.8	9.9	31.6	1.31	13.13	1.10	84.0	31.38	- 21.50	20.2	4.2
12/31/99	206,440	19,919	587,618	14.8	9.6	3.9	5.6	11.0	30.1	1.53	13.70	1.08	70.9	32.00	- 22.56	17.8	4.0
12/31/98	186,273	18,395	548,499	16.1	9.9	3.8	5.5	10.7	29.7	1.45	13.38	1.07	73.8	33.75	- 20.75	18.8	3.9
12/31/97	195,324	23,305	531,297	17.6	11.9	5.1	7.0	13.9	28.9	1.83	13.00	1.05	57.6	29.38	- 18.63	13.1	4.4
12/31/96	182,764	19,067	512,390	16.6	10.4	4.3	5.9	12.1	28.3	1.51	12.22	1.04	69.1	21.88	- 16.25	12.7	5.5
12/31/95	165,086	14,698	484,883	15.4	8.9	3.5	4.7	9.8	27.8	1.17	11.72	1.02	87.5	17.63	- 14.81	13.9	6.3
12/31/94	157,271	14,408	464,228	16.2	9.2	3.5	5.0	9.7	27.1	1.22	11.56	0.99	81.1	20.50	- 14.69	14.4	5.6
12/31/93	151,716	15,501	446,619	18.4	10.2	4.0	5.8	12.2	26.5	1.35	10.90	0.96	71.1	20.63	- 16.13	13.6	5.2

Statistics are as originally reported. Adj. for stk. split: 2-for-1, 1/98   ☐ Incl. gain of $3.0 mill. on sale of non-utility property.

OFFICERS:
R. W. Foy, Chmn.
P. C. Nelson, Pres., C.E.O.
G. F. Feeney, V.P., C.F.O., Treas.

INVESTOR CONTACT: Gerald F. Feeney,
(408) 367-8216

PRINCIPAL OFFICE: 1720 North First Street,
San Jose, CA 95112

TELEPHONE NUMBER: (408) 367-8200
FAX: (408) 437-9185
WEB: www.calwater.com

NO. OF EMPLOYEES: 783 (avg.)

SHAREHOLDERS: 11,000 (approx.)

ANNUAL MEETING: In Apr.

INCORPORATED: CA, Dec., 1926

INSTITUTIONAL HOLDINGS:
No. of Institutions: 63
Shares Held: 2,659,830
% Held: 17.5

INDUSTRY: Water supply (SIC: 4941)

TRANSFER AGENT(S): Fleet National Bank
c/o EquiServe, L.P., Providence, RI

CALLAWAY GOLF COMPANY

EXCH.	SYM.	REC. PRICE	P/E RATIO	YLD.	MKT. CAP.	RANGE (52-WK.)	'02 Y/E PR.
NYSE	ELY	11.48 (2/28/03)	10.3	2.4%	$0.87 bill.	20.68 - 9.42	13.25

UPPER MEDIUM GRADE. THE COMPANY EXPECTS NET SALES FOR THE FIRST QUARTER OF 2003 TO BE UP 5.0% TO ABOUT $270.0 MILLION YEAR OVER YEAR.

TRADING VOLUME
Thousand Shares

1989 1990 1991 1992 1993 1994 1995 1996 1997 1998 1999 2000 2001 2002 2003

7 YEAR PRICE SCORE 76.2   **12 MONTH PRICE SCORE 90.9**
*NYSE COMPOSITE INDEX=100

INTERIM EARNINGS (Per Share):

Qtr.	Mar.	June	Sept.	Dec.
1997	0.34	0.66	0.52	0.34
1998	0.16	0.30	0.08	d0.93
1999	0.18	0.35	0.25	Nil
2000	0.22	0.62	0.28	0.04
2001	0.49	0.36	0.09	d0.14
2002	0.45	0.55	0.19	d0.08

INTERIM DIVIDENDS (Per Share):

Amt.	Decl.	Ex.	Rec.	Pay.
0.07Q	2/06/02	2/15/02	2/20/02	3/13/02
0.07Q	5/06/02	5/16/02	5/20/02	6/10/02
0.07Q	8/20/02	8/29/02	9/03/02	9/24/02
0.07Q	11/06/02	11/18/02	11/20/02	12/11/02
0.07Q	2/27/03	3/11/03	3/13/03	4/03/03

Indicated div.: $0.28

CAPITALIZATION (12/31/01):

	($000)	(%)
Long-Term Debt	3,160	0.6
Common & Surplus	514,349	99.4
Total	517,509	100.0

BUSINESS:

Callaway Golf Company manufactures golf equipment. ELY's golf clubs are sold at premium prices to average and skilled golfers on the basis of performance, ease of use and appearance. Primary products include BIG BERTHA® metal woods and irons, including GREAT BIG BERTHA™ II titanium drivers and fairway woods, BIG BERTHA C4™ compression cured carbon composite drivers, BIG BERTHA ERC™ II forged titanium drivers, BIG BERTHA ERC™ forged titanium fairway woods, BIG BERTHA HAWK EYE® VFT® and BIG BERTHA HAWK EYE® VFT® PRO SERIES titanium drivers and fairway woods, BIG BERTHA STEEL HEAD™ III stainless steel drivers and fairway woods, HAWK EYE VFT TUNGSTEN INJECTED™ titanium irons, BIG BERTHA stainless steel irons, STEELHEAD X-16™ and STEELHEAD X-16™ PRO SERIES stainless steel irons, STEELHEAD X-14® and STEELHEAD X-14 PRO SERIES stainless steel irons and Callaway Golf forged wedges. ELY also makes and sells ODYSSEY® putters, including WHITE HOT®, TRIHOT™, DFX™ and DUAL FORCE® putters. Callaway Golf Ball Company, a subsidiary, makes and sells the Callaway Golf® HX™ BLUE and HX RED balls, CTU 30™ BLUE and CTU 30 RED balls, HX 2-Piece BLUE and HX 2-Piece RED balls, CB1™ BLUE and CB1 RED balls, and the WARBIRD™.

RECENT DEVELOPMENTS:

For the year ended 12/31/02, net income increased 19.0% to $69.4 million compared with $58.4 million in 2001. Results for 2002 included a $10.5 million after-tax non-cash gain associated with an adjustment to ELY's warranty reserves. Results for 2001 included a $14.2 million after-tax non-cash charge associated with ELY's long-term energy supply agreement. Net sales decreased 3.0% to $792.1 million due to a decline in sales of woods products.

PROSPECTS:

Looking ahead, the Company expects net sales for the first quarter of 2003 to be up 5.0% to about $270.0 million year over year. However, full-year 2003 net sales are expected to be flat year over year. The Company is targeting earnings per share growth in the low double digits based on ELY's long-term strategic plan and assuming some improvement in the global economy.

ANNUAL FINANCIAL DATA:

FISCAL YEAR	TOT. REVS. ($mill.)	NET INC. ($mill.)	TOT. ASSETS ($mill.)	OPER. PROFIT %	NET PROFIT %	RET. ON EQUITY %	RET. ON ASSETS %	CURR. RATIO	EARN. PER SH. $	CASH FL. PER SH. $	TANG. BK. VAL. $	DIV. PER SH. $	PRICE RANGE	AVG. P/E RATIO	AVG. YIELD %
p12/31/02	792.1	⑦ 69.4	679.8						⑦ 1.03			0.28	20.68 — 9.42	14.6	1.9
12/31/01	816.2	⑥ 58.4	647.6	13.8	7.2	11.3	9.0	3.5	⑥ 0.82	1.34	5.05	0.28	27.18 — 11.83	23.8	1.4
12/31/00	837.6	⑤ 82.0	630.9	14.6	9.8	16.0	13.0	3.1	⑤ 1.14	1.71	5.38	0.28	20.63 — 10.94	13.8	1.8
12/31/99	714.5	④ 55.3	616.8	11.2	7.7	11.1	9.0	2.9	④ 0.78	1.35	4.98	0.28	18.19 — 9.31	17.6	2.0
12/31/98	697.6	③ d26.6	655.8	...	...	...	...	1.8	③ d0.38	0.13	4.33	0.28	33.94 — 9.38	...	1.3
12/31/97	842.9	② 132.7	561.7	24.8	15.7	27.6	23.6	3.9	② 1.85	2.12	4.97	0.14	38.50 — 25.88	17.4	0.5
12/31/96	678.5	122.3	428.4	28.0	18.0	33.8	28.5	5.1	1.73	1.91	4.97	0.24	36.63 — 18.50	15.9	0.9
12/31/95	553.3	97.7	290.0	27.9	17.7	43.5	33.7	3.3	1.40	1.55	3.17	0.20	22.63 — 11.25	12.1	1.2
12/31/94	448.7	78.0	243.6	28.2	17.4	41.9	32.0	3.3	1.07	1.15	2.74	0.10	21.69 — 12.06	15.8	0.6
12/31/93	254.6	① 41.2	144.5	26.9	16.2	35.3	28.5	4.0	① 0.60	0.64	3.45	0.03	16.31 — 4.30	17.3	0.2

Statistics are as originally reported. Adj. for stk. split: 2-for-1, 3/95, 3/94 & 3/93. ① Bef. gain fr. acctg. adj. chrg. of $1.7 mill. ② Incl. nonrecur. chrg. of $12 mill. ③ Incl. restruct. chrg. of $54.2 mill. and reserves for excess inventory chrg. of $30.0 mill. ④ Incl. restruct. chrg. of $5.9 mill. ⑤ Incl. one-time tax benefit of $0.05 per share assoc. with consol. of ELY's club and ball operations. ⑥ Incl. an after-tax, non-cash charge of $14.2 mill. rel. to long-term energy supply contract. ⑦ Incl. an after-tax, non-cash gain of $10.5 mill. assoc. w/ adj. to warranty reser.

OFFICERS:
R. A. Drapeau, Chmn., Pres., C.E.O.
B. J. Holiday, Exec. V.P., C.F.O.

INVESTOR CONTACT: Barb West, (760) 804-4132

PRINCIPAL OFFICE: 2180 Rutherford Road, Carlsbad, CA 92008-8815

TELEPHONE NUMBER: (760) 931-1771
FAX: (760) 931-8013
WEB: www.callawaygolf.com
NO. OF EMPLOYEES: 2,500 (approx.)
SHAREHOLDERS: 9,000 (approx.)
ANNUAL MEETING: In May
INCORPORATED: CA, Sept., 1982; reincorp., DE, July, 1999

INSTITUTIONAL HOLDINGS:
No. of Institutions: 181
Shares Held: 61,912,636
% Held: 81.5

INDUSTRY: Sporting and athletic goods, nec (SIC: 3949)

REGISTRAR(S): Mellon Investor Services, Ridgefield, NJ

CALPINE CORPORATION

EXCH.	SYM.	REC. PRICE	P/E RATIO	YLD.	MKT. CAP.	RANGE (52-WK.)	'02 Y/E PR.
NYSE	CPN	2.79 (2/28/03)	27.9	...	$0.86 bill.	14.99 - 1.55	3.26

SPECULATIVE GRADE. EARNINGS FOR 2003 ARE EXPECTED TO RANGE FROM $0.40 TO $0.50 PER SHARE.

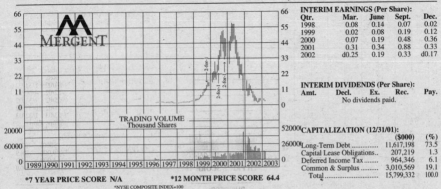

*7 YEAR PRICE SCORE N/A   *12 MONTH PRICE SCORE 64.4

*NYSE COMPOSITE INDEX=100

INTERIM EARNINGS (Per Share):

Qtr.	Mar.	June	Sept.	Dec.
1998	0.08	0.14	0.07	0.02
1999	0.02	0.08	0.19	0.12
2000	0.07	0.19	0.48	0.36
2001	0.31	0.34	0.88	0.33
2002	d0.25	0.19	0.33	d0.17

INTERIM DIVIDENDS (Per Share):

Amt.	Decl.	Ex.	Rec.	Pay.
		No dividends paid.		

CAPITALIZATION (12/31/01):

	($000)	(%)
Long-Term Debt	11,617,198	73.5
Capital Lease Obligations..	207,219	1.3
Deferred Income Tax	964,346	6.1
Common & Surplus	3,010,569	19.1
Total	15,799,332	100.0

BUSINESS:

Calpine Corporation is an independent power company engaged in the development, acquisition, ownership and operation of power generation facilities, and the sale of electricity predominantly in the U.S., but also in Canada and the U.K. As of 2/13/03, CPN owned interests in 76 power plants, which have an aggregate capacity of more than 19,000 megawatts. In addition, CPN is the world's largest producer of renewable geothermal energy, and owns approximately 1.30 trillion cubic feet equivalent of proved natural gas reserves in Canada and the U.S. Revenues for 2002 were derived: electric generation, 86.0%; oil and gas production, 13.3%; trading, 0.3%; unconsolidated investments in power projects, 0.2%; and other, 0.2%.

RECENT DEVELOPMENTS:

For the year ended 12/31/02, income from continuing operations dropped 88.5% to $69.5 million versus income of $605.1 million, before an accounting change charge of $1.0 million, in 2001. Earnings reflected a significant decrease in electricity prices versus the same period of 2001, primarily due an increase in supply. Results for 2002 included an equipment cancellation and asset impairment charge of $404.7 million, while results for 2001 included a merger expense of $41.6 million. Results for 2002 and 2001 excluded net gains of $72.1 million and $42.0 million, respectively, from discontinued operations. Total revenue climbed 10.5% to $7.48 billion from $6.77 billion in 2001.

PROSPECTS:

CPN expects earnings for 2003 to range from $0.40 to $0.50 per share and earnings before interest, taxes, depreciation and amortization between $1.40 billion and $1.50 billion. This guidance is based on average on-peak market spark spreads, which show the daily margin between the cost of input spot fuels and price fetched by output electricity, in the range of $8.00 to $10.00 per megawatt-hour and cost-reduction efforts. Separately, CPN restructured its agreements with major gas and steam turbine manufacturers. The new agreements give CPN the option to cancel its existing orders for 87 gas turbines and 44 steam turbines.

ANNUAL FINANCIAL DATA:

FISCAL YEAR	TOT. REVS. ($mill.)	NET INC. ($mill.)	TOT. ASSETS ($mill.)	OPER. PROFIT %	NET PROFIT %	NET INC./ NET PROP. %	NET INC./ TOT. CAP. %	RET. ON EQUITY %	ACCUM. DEPR./ GROSS PROP. %	EARN. PER SH. $	TANG. BK. VAL. $	PRICE RANGE	AVG. P/E RATIO
p12/31/02	7,482.8	⑥ 69.5								⑥ 0.19		17.28 - 1.55	49.6
⑤ 12/31/01	7,590.0	④ 641.1	21,309.3	14.4	8.4	4.2	4.1	21.3	-5.8	④ 1.85	9.80	58.04 - 10.00	18.4
12/31/00	2,282.8	③ 324.7	9,933.1	26.4	14.2	4.4	4.4	14.5	4.2	③ 1.11	7.88	52.97 - 16.09	31.1
12/31/99	847.7	③ 96.2	3,991.6	26.7	11.4	3.4	3.0	10.0	7.3	③ 0.43	3.82	16.38 - 3.16	22.5
12/31/98	555.9	③ 46.3	1,728.9	26.4	8.3	4.2	3.1	16.1	15.7	③ 0.27	1.78	3.45 - 1.59	9.2
12/31/97	276.3	34.7	1,381.0	35.2	12.6	4.8	3.1	14.5	17.1	0.21	1.50	2.87 - 1.55	10.7
12/31/96	214.6	18.7	1,030.2	31.1	8.7	2.9	2.2	9.2	13.4	0.16	1.28	2.50 - 2.00	14.1
12/31/95	132.1	7.4	554.5	32.3	5.6	1.6	1.7	29.2	11.9	0.07	0.29	...	...
12/31/94	94.8	② 6.0	421.4	33.5	6.4	1.8	1.6	32.3	9.2	② 0.07	1.80	...	...
12/31/93	69.9	① 4.2	301.3	30.1	6.0	1.7	1.5	31.0	4.8	① 0.24	0.84	...	...

Statistics are as originally reported. Adj. for 5.194-for-1 split, 9/96. Adj. for 2-for-1 split, 10/99, 6/00 & 11/00. ① Excl. $413,000 cumulative effect of acctg. change. ② Incl. $1.0 mill. provision for write-off of project costs. ③ Excl. net extraord. chgs. of $641,000, 1998; $793,000, 1999; $796,000, 2000. ④ Incl. $41.6 mill. merger exp. & excl. $6.0 mill. extraord. gain and $1.0 mill. acctg. credit. ⑤ Reflects CPN's program to expand in key North American mkts. & Calpine Energy Services' risk mgmt. program. ⑥ Incl. $404.7 mill. equip. cancel. & asset impair. chg. and excl. $72.1 mill. gain fr. disc. ops.

OFFICERS:
P. Cartwright, Chmn., Pres., C.E.O.
A. B. Curtis, Vice-Chmn., Exec. V.P., Sec.
R. D. Kelly, Exec. V.P., C.F.O.
INVESTOR CONTACT: Richard D. Barraza, Sr. V.P., Inv. Rel., (408) 995-5115 ext. 1125
PRINCIPAL OFFICE: 50 West San Fernando Street, San Jose, CA 95113-2429

TELEPHONE NUMBER: (408) 995-5115
FAX: (408) 995-0505
WEB: www.calpine.com
NO. OF EMPLOYEES: 3,719
SHAREHOLDERS: 1,347 (approx., record)
ANNUAL MEETING: In May
INCORPORATED: CA, June, 1984; reincorp., DE, Sept., 1996

INSTITUTIONAL HOLDINGS:
No. of Institutions: 341
Shares Held: 226,028,502
% Held: 59.8

INDUSTRY: Electric services (SIC: 4911)

TRANSFER AGENT(S): First Chicago Trust Company of New York, Jersey City, NJ

CAMPBELL SOUP COMPANY

EXCH.	SYM.	REC. PRICE	P/E RATIO	YLD.	MKT. CAP.	RANGE (52-WK.)	'02 Y/E PR.
NYSE	CPB	20.74 (2/28/03)	14.9	3.0%	$8.50 bill.	28.40 - 19.65	23.47

LOWER MEDIUM GRADE. RESULTS ARE BENEFITING FROM INCREASED SOUP SHIPMENTS IN THE U.S.

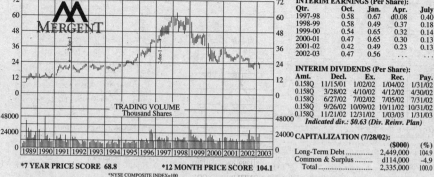

*7 YEAR PRICE SCORE 68.8   ***12 MONTH PRICE SCORE 104.1**

*NYSE COMPOSITE INDEX=100

INTERIM EARNINGS (Per Share):

Qtr.	Oct.	Jan.	Apr.	July
1997-98	0.58	0.67	d0.08	0.40
1998-99	0.58	0.49	0.37	0.18
1999-00	0.54	0.65	0.32	0.14
2000-01	0.47	0.65	0.30	0.13
2001-02	0.42	0.49	0.23	0.13
2002-03	0.47	0.56	...	...

INTERIM DIVIDENDS (Per Share):

Amt.	Decl.	Ex.	Rec.	Pay.
0.158Q	11/15/01	1/02/02	1/04/02	1/31/02
0.158Q	3/28/02	4/10/02	4/12/02	4/30/02
0.158Q	6/27/02	7/02/02	7/05/02	7/31/02
0.158Q	9/26/02	10/09/02	10/11/02	10/31/02
0.158Q	11/21/02	12/31/02	1/03/03	1/31/03

Indicated div.: $0.63 (Div. Reinv. Plan)

CAPITALIZATION (7/28/02):

	($000)	(%)
Long-Term Debt	2,449,000	104.9
Common & Surplus	d114,000	-4.9
Total	2,335,000	100.0

BUSINESS:

Campbell Soup Company is a major manufacturer and marketer of prepared convenience foods. Well-known brand names include CAMPBELL's, SWANSON, PEPPERIDGE FARM, V-8, PACE, PREGO, and GODIVA chocolates. Products sold by CPB under these brand names include: canned foods such as ready-to-serve soups, juices, gravies, pasta, meat and vegetables; frozen foods such as dinners, breakfasts and entrees; other items including salsa, pickles and relishes, various condiments, chocolate, salads and confectionery items. For fiscal year 2002, sales were derived: North America Soup and Away From Home, 41.1%; Biscuits and Confectionery, 24.6%; North America Sauces and Beverages, 19.3%; and International Soup and Sauces, 15.0%.

RECENT DEVELOPMENTS:

For the three months ended 1/26/03, net earnings increased 13.8% to $231.0 million from $203.0 million in the corresponding quarter of the prior year. Results for 2002 included a $1.0 million restructuring charge. Net sales grew 6.0% to $1.92 billion from $1.81 billion the previous year. North America Soup and Away From Home segment sales rose 1.5% to $824.0 million from $812.0 million the year before, while North America Sauces and Beverages segment sales slipped to $318.0 million from $319.0 million a year earlier. Biscuits and Confectionery segment sales climbed 13.6% to $486.0 million, while International Soup and Sauces segment sales advanced 15.5% to $290.0 million. Earnings before taxes were up 10.4% to $339.0 million.

PROSPECTS:

Results are benefiting from increased soup shipments in the U.S. Improved sales of the Company's condensed vegetable soups are being fueled by a new marketing program that began during the second quarter. Meanwhile, CPB is enjoying strong sales of its CHUNKY and SELECT ready-to-serve soups, as well as its SOUP AT HAND sippable soups. Separately, the Company is targeting third-quarter earnings in the range of $0.25 to $0.27 per share, along with full fiscal-2003 earnings, before accounting changes, of approximately $1.47 per share.

ANNUAL FINANCIAL DATA:

FISCAL YEAR	TOT. REVS. ($mill.)	NET INC. ($mill.)	TOT. ASSETS ($mill.)	OPER. PROFIT %	NET PROFIT %	RET. ON EQUITY %	RET. ON ASSETS %	CURR. RATIO	EARN. PER SH.$	CASH FL. PER SH.$	TANG. BK. VAL.$	DIV. PER SH.$	PRICE RANGE	AVG. P/E RATIO	AVG. YIELD %
7/28/02	6,133.0	③ 525.0	5,721.0	16.0	8.6	...	9.2	0.4	③ 1.28	2.05	...	0.63	30.00 - 19.65	19.4	2.5
7/29/01	6,664.0	③ 649.0	5,927.0	17.9	9.7	...	10.9	0.4	③ 1.55	2.19	...	0.83	35.44 - 25.52	19.7	2.7
7/30/00	6,267.0	714.0	5,196.0	20.2	11.4	521.2	13.7	0.4	1.65	2.23	...	0.90	39.63 - 23.75	19.2	2.8
8/01/99	6,424.0	③ 724.0	5,522.0	19.8	11.3	308.1	13.1	0.4	③ 1.63	2.20	...	0.90	55.75 - 37.44	28.6	1.9
8/02/98	6,696.0	④ 689.0	5,633.0	18.6	10.3	78.8	12.2	0.5	④ 1.50	2.07	...	0.84	62.88 - 46.69	36.5	1.5
8/03/97	7,964.0	③ 713.0	6,459.0	15.9	9.0	50.2	11.0	0.5	③ 1.51	2.21	...	0.77	59.44 - 39.38	32.7	1.6
7/28/96	7,678.0	② 802.0	6,632.0	17.2	10.4	29.2	12.1	0.7	② 1.61	2.27	1.64	0.69	42.13 - 28.00	21.8	2.0
7/30/95	7,278.0	698.0	6,315.0	15.8	9.6	28.3	11.1	0.7	1.40	1.99	1.20	0.62	30.63 - 20.50	18.3	2.4
7/31/94	6,690.0	630.0	4,992.0	15.4	9.4	31.7	12.6	1.0	1.26	1.76	2.78	0.56	23.00 - 17.13	16.0	2.8
8/01/93	6,586.2	① 257.2	4,897.5	9.0	3.9	15.1	5.3	0.9	① 0.51	0.99	2.36	0.48	23.00 - 17.63	39.5	2.4

Statistics are as originally reported. Adj. for 2-for-1 stk. split, 3/97. ① Bef. $249 mil chg. for acctg. adj. & incl. $300 mil ($1.19/sh) restr. chg. ② Incl. $0.05/sh non-recur. gain, 1996. ③ Incl. $1.0 mil pre-tax restr. chg., 2002; $10.0 mil, 2001; $36.0 mil, 1999; & $160.1 mil ($0.34/sh) after-tax restr. chg., 1997. ④ Incl. $262 mil pre-tax restr. chg.; bef. $11 mil acctg. chg.; & bef. $54 mil loss from discont. opers.

OFFICERS:
G. M. Sherman, Chmn.
D. R. Conant, Pres., C.E.O.
R. A. Schiffner, Sr. V.P., C.F.O.

INVESTOR CONTACT: Leonard F. Griehs, V.P., Investor Relations, (856) 342-6428

PRINCIPAL OFFICE: Campbell Place, Camden, NJ 08103-1799

TELEPHONE NUMBER: (856) 342-4800
FAX: (856) 342-3878
WEB: www.campbellsoup.com

NO. OF EMPLOYEES: 25,000 (approx.)

SHAREHOLDERS: 34,531

ANNUAL MEETING: In Nov.

INCORPORATED: NJ, Nov., 1922

INSTITUTIONAL HOLDINGS:
No. of Institutions: 299
Shares Held: 125,143,120
% Held: 30.5

INDUSTRY: Canned specialties (SIC: 2032)

TRANSFER AGENT(S): Equiserve, Jersey City, NJ

CAPITAL ONE FINANCIAL CORP.

EXCH.	SYM.	REC. PRICE	P/E RATIO	YLD.	MKT. CAP.	RANGE (52-WK.)	'02 Y/E PR.
NYSE	COF	30.97 (2/28/03)	7.9	0.3%	$7.01 bill.	66.50 - 24.05	29.72

UPPER MEDIUM GRADE. THE COMPANY IS TARGETING EARNINGS PER SHARE FOR 2003 AT ABOUT $4.55.

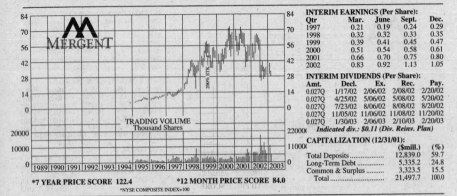

*7 YEAR PRICE SCORE 122.4   ***12 MONTH PRICE SCORE 84.0**

*NYSE COMPOSITE INDEX=100

INTERIM EARNINGS (Per Share):

Qtr	Mar.	June	Sept.	Dec.
1997	0.21	0.19	0.24	0.29
1998	0.32	0.32	0.33	0.35
1999	0.39	0.41	0.45	0.47
2000	0.51	0.54	0.58	0.61
2001	0.66	0.70	0.75	0.80
2002	0.83	0.92	1.13	1.05

INTERIM DIVIDENDS (Per Share):

Amt.	Decl.	Ex.	Rec.	Pay.
0.027Q	1/17/02	2/06/02	2/08/02	2/20/02
0.027Q	4/25/02	5/06/02	5/08/02	5/20/02
0.027Q	7/23/02	8/06/02	8/08/02	8/20/02
0.027Q	11/05/02	11/06/02	11/08/02	11/20/02
0.027Q	1/30/03	2/06/03	2/10/03	2/20/03

Indicated div.: $0.11 (Div. Reinv. Plan)

CAPITALIZATION (12/31/01):

	($mill.)	(%)
Total Deposits	12,839.0	59.7
Long-Term Debt	5,335.2	24.8
Common & Surplus	3,323.5	15.5
Total	21,497.7	100.0

BUSINESS:

Capital One Financial Corp. is a holding company whose subsidiaries provide a variety of financial products and services to consumers. The Company's subsidiary Capital One Bank offers credit card products. Capital One, F.S.B. provides certain consumer lending and deposit services. Capital One Services, Inc., provides various operating and administrative services. Prior to November 22, 1994, the Company operated as the credit card division of Signet

Bank. The Company is among the largest providers of MasterCard and Visa credit cards in the world. Also, the Company provides financial services on the Internet, with on-line accounts, real-time account numbering and on-line retail deposits. The Company's subsidiaries collectively had 47.4 million customers and $59.75 billion in managed customer loans as of 12/31/02.

RECENT DEVELOPMENTS:

For the year ended 12/31/02, net income climbed 40.1% to $899.6 million from $642.0 million the previous year. Earnings benefited from higher service charges, increased account volume and higher average earning assets. Total interest income increased 43.1% to $4.18 billion. Net interest income jumped 55.4% to $2.72 billion from $1.75 bil-

lion in 2001. Provision for loan losses soared 91.8% to $2.15 billion versus $1.12 billion a year earlier. Total non-interest income grew 22.5% to $5.47 billion from $4.46 billion the prior year. Total non-interest expenses amounted to $4.59 billion, up 13.0% from $4.06 billion the year before.

PROSPECTS:

Looking ahead, net interest margin is expected to fluctuate somewhat due to the scheduled repricings of certain introductory rate credit card products and a gradual shift toward superprime assets, but is expected to stabilize at about 9.0% to 10.0% in 2003. Non-interest income is expected to remain stable in 2003, consistent with a gradual shift

towards higher credit quality assets. Meanwhile, COF expects its managed charge-off rate to increase to the mid-to-high 6.0% range during the first half of 2003 and decline to the low-to-mid 6.0% range in the second half due to the continued maturation of its subprime assets. COF is targeting earnings per share for 2003 at about $4.55.

ANNUAL FINANCIAL DATA:

FISCAL YEAR	NET INT. INC. ($mill.)	NON-INT. INC. ($mill.)	NET INC. ($mill.)	TOT. LOANS ($mill.)	TOT. ASSETS ($mill.)	TOT. DEP. ($mill.)	RET. ON EQUITY %	RET. ON ASSETS %	EQUITY/ ASSETS %	EARN. PER SH.$	TANG. BK. VAL.$	DIV. PER SH.$	PRICE RANGE	AVG. P/E RATIO
p12/31/02	2,719.1	5,466.8	899.6							3.93		0.11	66.50 - 24.05	11.5
12/31/01	1,663.4	4,419.9	642.0	20,921.0	28,184.0	12,839.0	19.3	2.3	11.8	2.91	15.33	0.11	72.58 - 36.40	18.7
12/31/00	1,588.9	3,034.4	469.6	15,112.7	18,889.3	8,379.0	23.9	2.5	10.4	2.24	9.94	0.11	73.25 - 32.06	23.5
12/31/99	1,052.6	2,372.4	363.1	9,913.5	13,336.4	3,783.8	24.0	2.7	11.4	1.72	7.69	0.11	60.24 - 35.81	27.9
12/31/98	687.3	1,488.3	275.2	6,157.1	9,419.4	2,000.0	21.7	2.9	13.5	1.32	6.45	0.11	43.31 - 16.85	22.8
12/31/97	383.1	1,069.1	189.4	4,861.7	7,078.3	1,313.7	21.2	2.7	12.6	0.93	4.55	0.11	17.96 - 10.17	15.1
12/31/96	365.5	763.4	155.3	4,343.9	6,467.4	943.0	21.0	2.4	11.4	0.77	3.72	0.11	12.29 - 7.25	12.7
12/31/95	208.0	553.0	126.5	2,921.7	4,759.3	696.0	21.1	2.7	11.4	0.63	3.02	0.08	9.87 - 5.12	11.8
12/31/94	165.0	396.9	95.3	2,228.5	3,092.0	452.2	20.1	3.1	15.3	0.48	2.39	...	5.54 - 4.62	10.6
12/31/93	191.9	194.8	110.5	1,862.7	1,991.2	...	65.4	5.5	8.5	0.56	0.85	...	...	...

Statistics are as originally reported. Adj. for stk. split: 3-for-1, 6/99.

OFFICERS:
R. D. Fairbank, Chmn., C.E.O.
N. W. Morris, Pres., C.O.O.
D. Lawson, Interim C.F.O.
INVESTOR CONTACT: Paul Paquin, V.P.,
Investor Relations, (703) 205-1039
PRINCIPAL OFFICE: 2980 Fairview Park Dr.,
Suite 1300, Falls Church, VA 22042-4525

TELEPHONE NUMBER: (703) 205-1000
FAX: (703) 205-1755
WEB: www.capitalone.com
NO. OF EMPLOYEES: 21,648
SHAREHOLDERS: 10,065
ANNUAL MEETING: In April
INCORPORATED: DE, July, 1994

INSTITUTIONAL HOLDINGS:
No. of Institutions: 419
Shares Held: 194,442,385
% Held: 87.6
INDUSTRY: Personal credit institutions (SIC: 6141)
TRANSFER AGENT(S): First Chicago Trust Company of New York, Jersey City, NJ

CARDINAL HEALTH, INC.

EXCH.	SYM.	REC. PRICE	P/E RATIO	YLD.	MKT. CAP.	RANGE (52-WK.)	'02 Y/E PR.
NYSE	CAH	57.29 (2/28/03)	20.8	0.2%	$25.71 bill.	73.70 - 46.60	59.19

UPPER MEDIUM GRADE. ON 1/1/03, THE COMPANY COMPLETED ITS ACQUISITION OF SYNCOR INTERNATIONAL CORPORATION.

7 YEAR PRICE SCORE 148.3   **12 MONTH PRICE SCORE 100.3**
*NYSE COMPOSITE INDEX=100

INTERIM EARNINGS (Per Share):

Qtr.	Sept.	Dec.	Mar.	June
1997-98	0.22	0.27	0.22	0.26
1998-99	0.29	0.33	0.19	0.35
1999-00	0.29	0.41	0.45	0.46
2000-01	0.41	0.49	0.42	0.55
2001-02	0.53	0.62	0.66	0.64
2002-03	0.64	0.82	...	...

INTERIM DIVIDENDS (Per Share):

Amt.	Decl.	Ex.	Rec.	Pay.
0.025Q	2/08/02	3/27/02	4/01/02	4/15/02
0.025Q	5/08/02	6/27/02	7/01/02	7/15/02
0.025Q	8/07/02	9/27/02	10/01/02	10/15/02
0.025Q	11/06/02	12/27/02	1/01/03	1/15/03
0.025Q	2/05/03	3/28/03	4/01/03	4/15/03

Indicated div.: $0.10

CAPITALIZATION (6/30/02):

	($000)	(%)
Long-Term Debt	2,207,000	25.7
Common & Surplus	6,393,000	74.3
Total	8,600,000	100.0

BUSINESS:

Cardinal Health, Inc. (formerly Cardinal Distribution, Inc.) is a holding company whose subsidiaries provide products and services for healthcare providers and manufacturers including pharmaceutical packing and distribution, drug delivery systems development, automated dispensing systems manufacturing, hospital pharmacy management, retail pharmacy franchising, and healthcare information systems

development. On 8/7/98, CAH acquired R.P. Scherer, a manufacturer of drug delivery systems. On 2/3/99, CAH completed the acquisition of Allegiance Corp., a distributor and manufacturer of medical and laboratory products. On 8/16/00, the Company acquired Bergen Brunswig Medical Corp. On 2/14/01, CAH acquired Bindley Western Industries, Inc., a wholesale distributor of pharmaceuticals.

RECENT DEVELOPMENTS:

For the three months ended 12/31/02, net earnings advanced 29.7% to $367.5 million from $283.3 million in the corresponding quarter a year earlier. Results for 2002 included an after-tax special gain of $22.1 million, while results for 2001 included an after-tax special charge of $10.3 million. Operating revenue increased 13.2% to

$12.71 billion from $11.22 billion the previous year. Gross margin was $1.08 billion, or 8.5% of operating revenue, compared with $1.00 billion, or 8.9% of operating revenue, the year before. Operating earnings climbed 25.8% to $590.9 million from $469.7 million the prior year.

PROSPECTS:

On 1/1/03, the Company completed its acquisition of Syncor International Corporation, a major provider of nuclear pharmacy services, for approximately $781.0 million of CAH common stock and the assumption of about $120.0 million of debt. Looking ahead, results should benefit from an expanded distribution agreement with Express

Scripts, Inc. Beginning in February 2003, Express Scripts will outsource to the Company an additional $1.80 billion per year of branded pharmaceuticals previously purchased direct and self distributed. Separately, CAH is targeting earnings per share growth in the range of 20.0% to 22.0% for fiscal 2003.

ANNUAL FINANCIAL DATA:

FISCAL YEAR	TOT. REVS. ($mill.)	NET INC. ($mill.)	TOT. ASSETS ($mill.)	OPER. PROFIT %	NET PROFIT %	RET. ON EQUITY %	RET. ON ASSETS %	CURR. RATIO	EARN. PER SH. $	CASH FL. PER SH. $	TANG. BK. VAL. $	DIV. PER SH. $	PRICE RANGE	AVG. P/E RATIO	AVG. YIELD %
6/30/02	51,135.7	③ 1,126.3	16,438.0	3.6	2.2	17.6	6.9	1.7	③ 2.45	0.53	10.92	0.10	73.70 - 46.60	24.6	0.2
6/30/01	47,947.6	① 857.4	14,642.4	3.1	1.8	15.8	5.9	1.6	① 1.88	2.50	9.50	0.09	77.32 - 56.67	35.6	0.1
6/30/00	29,870.6	① 679.7	10,264.9	4.0	2.3	17.1	6.6	1.6	① 1.59	2.17	7.28	0.07	69.96 - 24.67	29.7	0.2
6/30/99	25,033.6	① 456.3	8,289.0	3.5	1.8	13.2	5.5	1.7	① 1.09	1.65	6.14	0.07	55.50 - 24.67	36.7	0.2
6/30/98	15,918.1	① 247.1	3,961.1	2.6	1.6	15.2	6.2	1.8	① 0.99	1.24	4.99	0.05	50.92 - 30.97	41.5	0.1
6/30/97	10,968.0	① 181.1	3,108.5	3.0	1.7	13.6	5.8	1.8	① 0.74	0.95	4.93	0.04	35.00 - 22.89	39.2	0.2
6/30/96	8,862.4	① 111.9	2,681.1	2.4	1.3	12.0	4.2	1.6	① 0.51	0.66	3.94	0.04	26.00 - 15.54	40.5	0.2
6/30/95	7,806.1	85.0	1,841.8	2.1	1.1	15.5	4.6	1.6	0.60	0.15	3.87	0.04	17.22 - 12.30	24.8	0.2
② 6/30/94	5,790.4	① 35.1	1,395.6	1.5	0.6	9.5	2.5	1.6	① 0.26	0.13	2.89	0.03	14.30 - 9.84	47.3	0.3
3/31/93	1,966.5	33.6	656.5	3.2	1.7	13.2	5.1	2.7	0.42	0.51	3.17	...	8.06 - 5.63	16.3	...

Statistics are as originally reported. Adj. for 3-for-2 stk. split, 4/01, 10/98 & 12/96; & 5-for-4 stk. split, 6/94. ① Incl. $85.3 mil ($0.19/sh) net merger costs, 6/01; $49.8 mil ($0.11/sh), 6/00; $117.6 mil ($0.28/sh), 6/99; $41 mil, 6/98; $40.2 mil, 6/97; $47.8 mil, 6/96; & $28.2 mil, 6/94. ② Changed fiscal year end to 6/30 from 3/31. ③ Bef. $70.1 mil ($0.15/sh) acctg. chg. and incl. $87.1 mil ($0.19/sh) net after-tax special chrgs.

OFFICERS:
R. D. Walter, Chmn., C.E.O.
R. J. Miller, Exec. V.P., C.F.O.
A. J. Rucci, Exec. V.P., Chief Admin. Off.

INVESTOR CONTACT: Debra Dendahl Haley, Dir., Inv. Rel., (614) 757-7481

PRINCIPAL OFFICE: 7000 Cardinal Place, Dublin, OH 43017

TELEPHONE NUMBER: (614) 757-5000
FAX: (614) 717-6000
WEB: www.cardinal.com
NO. OF EMPLOYEES: 50,000 (approx.)
SHAREHOLDERS: 21,000 (approx.)
ANNUAL MEETING: In Nov.
INCORPORATED: OH, July, 1982

INSTITUTIONAL HOLDINGS:
No. of Institutions: 731
Shares Held: 355,709,089
% Held: 80.4

INDUSTRY: Drugs, proprietaries, and sundries (SIC: 5122)

TRANSFER AGENT(S): EquiServe, Providence, RI

CAREMARK RX, INC.

EXCH.	SYM.	REC. PRICE	P/E RATIO	YLD.	MKT. CAP.	RANGE (52-WK.)	'02 Y/E PR.
NYSE	CMX	17.46 (2/28/03)	5.5	...	$3.95 bill.	21.95 - 12.24	16.25

LOWER MEDIUM GRADE. THE COMPANY ANTICIPATES REVENUE GROWTH OF 25.0% TO 30.0% FOR THE FULL-YEAR 2003.

TRADING VOLUME
Thousand Shares

*7 YEAR PRICE SCORE 130.0   *12 MONTH PRICE SCORE 111.4
*NYSE COMPOSITE INDEX=100

INTERIM EARNINGS (Per Share):

Qtr.	Mar.	June	Sept.	Dec.
1998	0.24	d0.12	0.04	0.06
1999	0.06	0.06	0.07	0.10
2000	0.09	0.09	0.11	0.14
2001	0.15	0.16	0.19	0.23
2002	0.24	0.27	0.31	2.34

INTERIM DIVIDENDS (Per Share):

Amt.	Decl.	Ex.	Rec.	Pay.
		No dividends paid.		

CAPITALIZATION (12/31/01):

	($000)	(%)
Long-Term Debt	695,625	...
Common & Surplus	d772,467	...
Total	d-76,842	100.0

BUSINESS:

Caremark Rx, Inc. (formerly MedPartners, Inc.) is a major pharmaceutical services company, providing comprehensive drug benefit services to over 1,200 health plan sponsors and holding contracts to serve participants throughout the U.S. Caremark's clients include corporate health plans, managed care organizations, insurance companies, unions, government agencies, and other funded benefit plans. As of 2/11/03, the Company operated a national retail pharmacy network with over 55,000 participating pharmacies, four state-of-the-art mail service pharmacies, the industry's only FDA-regulated repackaging plant and 21 specialty distribution mail service pharmacies for delivery of advanced medications to individuals with chronic or genetic diseases and disorders. The Company acquired Caremark International Inc. on 9/5/96.

RECENT DEVELOPMENTS:

For the year ended 12/31/02, income was $818.9 million, before a loss of $37.5 million from discontinued operations, compared with net income of $177.3 million the prior year. Results for 2002 included a $520.0 million benefit from the recognition of a deferred tax asset. The increase in earnings was largely due to new business wins and growth in mail-order product lines. Net revenues advanced 21.2% to $6.81 billion. During 2002, mail pharmacy prescriptions climbed 11.0% to 20.2 million. For the year, mail-order prescriptions represented 45.0% of all prescriptions processed on a retail-adjusted basis. Retail claims for the period jumped 11.8% to 71.3 million.

PROSPECTS:

Going forward, the Company's new business wins and mail order product lines should continue to drive revenue growth, margin improvement and cash flow. Results should also benefit from CMX's ability to drive higher generic dispensing rates. As a result of CMX's strong financial performance, revenues for the full-year 2003 are expected to increase by 25.0% to 30.0% over the prior year. Diluted earnings per share from continuing operations for 2003 are expected in the range of $1.02 to $1.04, using an expected tax rate of 40.0%.

ANNUAL FINANCIAL DATA:

FISCAL YEAR	TOT. REVS. ($mill.)	NET INC. ($mill.)	TOT. ASSETS ($mill.)	OPER. PROFIT %	NET PROFIT %	RET. ON ASSETS %	CURR. RATIO	EARN. PER SH. $	CASH FL. PER SH. $	TANG. BK. VAL. $	PRICE RANGE	AVG. P/E RATIO
p12/31/02	6,805.3	7 818.9						7 3.15			21.95 - 12.24	5.4
12/31/01	5,614.0	190.5	873.7	3.7	3.4	21.8	1.0	0.73	0.83	...	18.50 - 10.75	20.0
12/31/00	4,430.1	6 104.7	685.5	2.6	2.4	15.3	0.7	6 0.43	0.61	...	13.94 - 3.75	20.6
12/31/99	3,307.8	5 59.1	770.8	1.9	1.8	7.7	0.9	6 0.29	0.42	...	9.00 - 2.88	20.5
12/31/98	2,634.0	5 30.8	1,862.1	1.9	1.2	1.7	1.1	5 0.16	0.29	...	22.38 - 1.63	75.0
12/31/97	6,331.2	4 d693.7	2,890.5	...	...	...	1.1	4 d3.73	d3.09	...	32.00 - 17.88	...
3 12/31/96	4,813.5	1 d89.8	2,266.0	...	...	...	1.2	1 d0.58	d0.05	0.49	36.00 - 16.38	...
12/31/95	725.7	d9.6	355.0	...	...	...	1.2	d0.30	0.24	1.09	34.50 - 14.75	...
12/31/94	75.2	d1.6	56.3	...	...	...	2.0	d0.14	d0.03	...	...	...
12/31/93	1.2	2 d1.3	13.9	...	...	...	12.9	2 d0.11	d0.11	...	...	...

Statistics are as originally reported. ① Incl. pre-tax merger exps. of $308.7 mill. and excl. loss fr. disc. opers. of $68.7 mill. ② Bef. gain from acctg. chng. of $298,000. ③ Refl. the acq. of Caremark International, Inc. ④ Incl. a pre-tax merger exp. of $59.4 mill., a pre-tax chg. of $664.7 mill. for restruct. & impair. chgs., a net loss of $96.0 mill. fr. disc. opers. and a net chg. of $30.9 mill. for the cum. effect of a chng. in acctg. prin. ⑤ Incl. a pre-tax restruct. chrg. of $9.5 mill.; excl. a loss of $1.28 bill. from disc. oper. & a loss of $6.3 mill. fr. acctg chng. ⑥ Bef. loss from disc. oper. of $268.0 mill., 2000; $199.3 mill., 1999. ⑦ Bef. loss from disc. oper. of $37.5 mill, incl. def. tax ben. of $520.0 mill.

OFFICERS:
E. M. Crawford, Chmn., C.E.O.
A. Frazier Jr., Pres., C.O.O.
H. A. McLure, Exec. V.P., C.F.O.
INVESTOR CONTACT: Peter J. Clemens IV, Sr. V.P., (205) 733-8996
PRINCIPAL OFFICE: 3000 Galleria Tower, Suite 1000, Birmingham, AL 35244

TELEPHONE NUMBER: (205) 733-8996
FAX: (205) 733-9780
WEB: www.caremark.com
NO. OF EMPLOYEES: 4,037 (avg.)
SHAREHOLDERS: 23,292
ANNUAL MEETING: In May
INCORPORATED: DE, Jan., 1993

INSTITUTIONAL HOLDINGS:
No. of Institutions: 321
Shares Held: 217,719,548
% Held: 85.1
INDUSTRY: Health and allied services, nec (SIC: 8099)
TRANSFER AGENT(S): First Chicago Trust Company of New York, Jersey City, NJ

CARLISLE COMPANIES INCORPORATED

EXCH.	SYM.	REC. PRICE	P/E RATIO	YLD.	MKT. CAP.	RANGE (52-WK.)	'02 Y/E PR.	DIV. ACH.
NYSE	CSL	42.61 (2/28/03)	18.1	2.0%	$1.29 bill.	47.23 - 32.36	41.38	26 yrs.

MEDIUM GRADE. THE COMPANY EXPECTS EARNINGS IN THE RANGE OF $2.60 TO $2.80 PER SHARE FOR 2003.

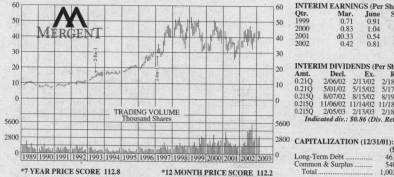

INTERIM EARNINGS (Per Share):

Qtr.	Mar.	June	Sept.	Dec.
1999	0.71	0.91	0.81	0.70
2000	0.83	1.04	0.92	0.35
2001	d0.33	0.54	0.36	0.25
2002	0.42	0.81	0.65	0.48

INTERIM DIVIDENDS (Per Share):

Amt.	Decl.	Ex.	Rec.	Pay.
0.21Q	2/06/02	2/13/02	2/18/02	3/01/02
0.21Q	5/01/02	5/15/02	5/17/02	6/01/02
0.215Q	8/07/02	8/15/02	8/19/02	9/01/02
0.215Q	11/06/02	11/14/02	11/18/02	12/01/02
0.215Q	2/05/03	2/13/03	2/18/03	3/01/03

Indicated div.: $0.86 (Div. Reinv. Plan)

*7 YEAR PRICE SCORE 112.8   ***12 MONTH PRICE SCORE 112.2**

*NYSE COMPOSITE INDEX=100

CAPITALIZATION (12/31/01):

	($000)	(%)
Long-Term Debt	461,744	46.1
Common & Surplus	540,284	53.9
Total	1,002,028	100.0

BUSINESS:

Carlisle Companies Incorporated produces and sells a diverse line of products in six industry segments. The Industrial Components segment (31.5% of 2002 revenue) manufactures and distributes tire and wheel assemblies and high-performance wire/cable and cable assemblies. The Construction Materials segment (24.8%) manufactures membranes and accessories for rubber and plastic roofing systems for non-residential flat roofs. The General Industry segment (20.3%) consists of several businesses with prod-

ucts, including stainless steel in-plant processing equipment, food service products and cheese making systems. The Automotive Components segment (12.0%) manufactures highly engineered plastic and rubber components for the automotive industry. The Transportation Products segment (6.1%) produces specialty and high-payload trailers and dump bodies. The Specialty Products segment (5.3%) manufactures heavy-duty friction and braking systems for trucks and off-highway equipment.

RECENT DEVELOPMENTS:

For the year ended 12/31/02, CSL reported income of $72.4 million, before an accounting change charge of $43.8 million, versus net income of $24.8 million the previous year. Results included an after-tax restructuring charge of $21.5 million in 2001. Net sales increased 6.6% to $1.97 billion from $1.85 billion a year earlier. Industrial components sales jumped 30.5% to $621.6 million, primarily due to the

acquisition of Dayco Industrial Power Transmission. Construction materials sales rose 5.0% to $488.0 million, while automotive components sales decreased 6.4% to $235.8 million. Specialty products sales fell 9.1% to $105.3 million, while general industry sales declined 4.6% to $401.0 million.

PROSPECTS:

The Company has aggressively pursued cost reductions, manufacturing efficiencies, and the introduction of new products into many of the markets it serves. Accordingly, these actions are expected to support sales and earnings

growth going forward. For 2003, CSL expects earnings in the range of $2.60 to $2.80 per share. Separately, based on its balance sheet debt, CSL's debt-to-total capitalization ratio improved to 35.0% in 2002 from 46.0% in 2001.

ANNUAL FINANCIAL DATA:

FISCAL YEAR	TOT. REVS. ($mill.)	NET INC. ($mill.)	TOT. ASSETS ($mill.)	OPER. PROFIT %	NET PROFIT %	RET. ON EQUITY %	RET. ON ASSETS %	CURR. RATIO	EARN. PER SH. $	CASH FL. PER SH. $	TANG. BK. VAL.$	DIV. PER SH. $	PRICE RANGE	AVG. P/E RATIO	AVG. YIELD %
p12/31/02	1,971.3	③ 72.4	1,315.9		3.7	13.1	5.5		③ 2.37			0.85	47.23 - 32.36	16.8	2.1
12/31/01	1,849.5	② 24.8	1,398.0	3.5	1.3	4.6	1.8	2.0	② 0.82	2.92	6.72	0.82	44.00 - 25.50	42.4	2.4
12/31/00	1,771.1	96.2	1,305.7	9.9	5.4	17.6	7.4	1.4	3.14	5.09	9.79	0.76	51.00 - 30.94	13.0	1.9
12/31/99	1,611.3	① 95.8	1,080.7	10.4	5.9	20.0	8.9	2.3	① 3.13	4.67	10.63	0.68	52.94 - 30.63	13.3	1.6
12/31/98	1,517.5	84.9	1,022.9	10.0	5.6	20.9	8.3	1.9	2.77	4.24	8.85	0.60	53.06 - 32.56	15.5	1.4
12/31/97	1,260.6	70.7	861.2	10.1	5.6	20.3	8.2	1.8	2.28	3.53	7.48	0.53	47.75 - 27.00	16.4	1.4
12/31/96	1,017.5	55.7	866.8	9.5	5.5	18.1	6.4	2.0	1.80	2.76	6.55	0.47	30.50 - 17.50	13.7	1.9
12/31/95	822.5	44.1	542.4	9.3	5.4	16.1	8.1	2.2	1.41	2.15	7.71	0.42	21.81 - 17.25	13.9	2.2
12/31/94	692.7	35.6	485.3	8.9	5.1	14.4	7.3	2.5	1.15	1.86	7.44	0.38	18.06 - 15.13	14.4	2.3
12/31/93	611.3	28.4	420.4	8.0	4.6	12.9	6.8	2.6	0.92	1.59	6.71	0.35	17.25 - 11.53	15.7	2.4

Statistics are as originally reported. Adj. for stk. split: 2-for-1, 1/97 ① Incl. non-recurr. gain of $685,000. ② Incl. after-tax restructuring chrg. of $21.5 mill. ③ Bef. acctg. change chrg. of $43.8 mill.

OFFICERS:
S. P. Munn, Chmn.
R. D. McKinnish, Pres., C.E.O.
K. F. Vincent, V.P., C.F.O.
INVESTOR CONTACT: Kirk F. Vincent, V.P., C.F.O., (704) 501-1100
PRINCIPAL OFFICE: 13925 Ballantyne Corporate Place, Ste. 400, Charlotte, NC 28277

TELEPHONE NUMBER: (704) 501-1100
FAX: (704) 501-1190
WEB: www.carlisle.com
NO. OF EMPLOYEES: 11,710 (approx.)
SHAREHOLDERS: 2,257 (record)
ANNUAL MEETING: In April
INCORPORATED: DE, Sept., 1917; reincorp., DE, May, 1986

INSTITUTIONAL HOLDINGS:
No. of Institutions: 168
Shares Held: 18,014,670
% Held: 58.9
INDUSTRY: Tires and inner tubes (SIC: 3011)
TRANSFER AGENT(S): Computershare Investor Services, Chicago, IL

CARNIVAL CORPORATION

EXCH.	SYM.	REC. PRICE	P/E RATIO	YLD.	MKT. CAP.	RANGE (52-WK.)	'02 Y/E PR.
NYSE	CCL	22.97 (2/28/03)	13.3	1.8%	...	34.64 - 21.85	24.95

UPPER MEDIUM GRADE. THE COMPANY'S PROPOSED DUAL-LISTED COMPANY STRUCTURE WITH P&O PRINCESS IS EXPECTED TO CLOSE IN THE SECOND QUARTER OF 2003.

MERGENT

TRADING VOLUME
Thousand Shares

1989 1990 1991 1992 1993 1994 1995 1996 1997 1998 1999 2000 2001 2002 2003

*7 YEAR PRICE SCORE 102.3   *12 MONTH PRICE SCORE 96.4
*NYSE COMPOSITE INDEX=100

INTERIM EARNINGS (Per Share):

Qtr.	Feb.	May	Aug.	Nov.
1998-99	0.26	0.33	0.67	0.40
1999-00	0.28	0.34	0.67	0.33
2000-01	0.22	0.32	0.84	0.20
2001-02	0.22	0.33	0.85	0.33
2002-03	0.22	...	...	...

INTERIM DIVIDENDS (Per Share):

Amt.	Decl.	Ex.	Rec.	Pay.
0.105Q	1/23/02	2/26/02	2/28/02	3/14/02
0.105Q	4/22/02	5/29/02	5/31/02	6/14/02
0.105Q	7/18/02	8/28/02	8/30/02	9/13/02
0.105Q	11/20/02	11/26/02	11/30/02	12/16/02
0.105Q	1/13/03	2/26/03	2/28/03	3/14/03

Indicated div.: $0.42 (Div. Reinv. Plan)

CAPITALIZATION (11/30/02):

	($000)	(%)
Long-Term Debt [1]	3,011,969	28.9
Common & Surplus	7,417,903	71.1
Total	10,429,872	100.0

BUSINESS:

Carnival Corporation (formerly Carnival Cruise Lines, Inc.) is a major multiple-night cruise company. The Company offers a broad range of major cruise brands serving the contemporary cruise market through Carnival Cruise Lines, the premium cruise market through Holland America Line and the luxury cruise market through Cunard Line, Seabourn Cruise Line, Windstar Cruises and Holland America Tours. CCL also owns Costa Crociere S.p.A., an Italian cruise and integrated leisure travel group of companies. Costa targets the contemporary cruise market. CCL's various brands operate 45 ships in the Bahamas, the Caribbean, Alaska, Europe, Mexico, South America, and other destinations.

RECENT DEVELOPMENTS:

For the quarter ended 2/28/03, net income declined 2.1% to $126.9 million compared with $129.6 million in the equivalent 2002 quarter. Results for 2002 included income from net insurance proceeds of $19.0 million. Revenues grew 13.7% to $1.03 billion from $906.5 million a year earlier. Revenues benefited from an increase in CCL's passenger capacity, partially offset by a decline in the number of guests purchasing air transportation from the Company. Operating income decreased 9.3% to $132.3 million from $145.8 million the year before.

PROSPECTS:

Near-term prospects remain uncertain as CCL continues to face challenging market conditions, which have been magnified by continued economic weakness and concerns over the war with Iraq. These factors are expected to continue to impact bookings over the balance of the year. As of 3/21/03, booking volumes for the second half of 2003 remained slightly ahead of prior-year levels, but do not commensurate with the higher capacity expected for the second half of the year. Pricing remains slightly below the previous year. Separately, CCL's proposed dual-listed company structure with P&O Princess is awaiting approval by both CCL and P&O Princess shareholders and is expected to close in the second quarter of 2003. Meanwhile, CCL expects to ramp-up 13 new ships for delivery by mid-2006.

ANNUAL FINANCIAL DATA:

FISCAL YEAR	TOT. REVS. ($mill.)	NET INC. ($mill.)	TOT. ASSETS ($mill.)	OPER. PROFIT %	NET PROFIT %	RET. ON EQUITY %	RET. ON ASSETS %	CURR. RATIO	EARN. PER SH.$	CASH FL. PER SH.$	TANG. BK. VAL.$	DIV. PER SH.$	PRICE RANGE	AVG. P/E RATIO	AVG. YIELD %
11/30/02	4,368.3	[3] 1,015.9	12,334.8	23.9	23.3	13.7	8.2	0.7	[3] 1.73	2.38	11.48	0.42	34.64 - 22.07	16.4	1.5
11/30/01	4,535.8	[2] 926.2	11,563.6	19.7	20.4	14.1	8.0	1.3	[2] 1.58	2.21	10.13	0.42	34.94 - 16.95	16.4	1.6
11/30/00	3,778.4	965.5	9,831.3	26.0	25.6	16.4	9.8	0.3	1.60	2.08	8.37	0.42	51.25 - 18.31	21.7	1.3
11/30/99	3,573.2	1,027.2	8,286.4	28.5	28.7	17.3	12.4	0.6	1.66	2.06	8.86	0.38	53.50 - 38.13	27.6	0.8
11/30/98	3,086.0	835.9	7,179.3	29.1	27.1	19.5	11.6	0.3	1.40	1.73	6.46	0.32	48.50 - 19.00	24.1	0.9
11/30/97	2,500.6	666.1	5,426.8	28.6	26.6	18.5	12.3	0.4	1.20	1.40	5.71	0.24	27.63 - 15.69	18.0	1.1
11/30/96	2,258.5	566.3	5,101.9	26.5	25.1	18.7	11.1	0.4	0.98	1.23	4.77	0.19	16.56 - 11.63	14.4	1.3
11/30/95	1,998.2	451.1	4,105.5	24.5	22.6	19.2	11.0	0.4	0.80	...	3.72	0.14	13.56 - 10.00	14.8	1.3
11/30/94	1,806.0	381.8	3,669.8	24.6	21.1	19.8	10.4	0.4	0.68	...	3.00	0.14	13.06 - 9.56	16.8	1.3
11/30/93	1,556.9	318.2	3,218.9	22.3	20.4	19.6	9.9	0.5	0.57	...	2.46	0.14	12.50 - 7.56	17.8	1.4

Statistics are as originally reported. All figures are in U.S. dollars unless otherwise noted. Adj. for stock splits; 2-for-1, 6/12/98 and 12/14/94. [1] Incl. zero coupon convert. deb. [2] Incl. nonrecurr. chrg. of $140.4 mill. [3] Incl. nonrecurr. chrg. of $20.0 mill.

OFFICERS:
M. Arison, Chmn., C.E.O.
H. S. Frank, Vice-Chmn., C.O.O.
G. R. Cahill, Sr. V.P. C.F.O.
L. Zemnick, V.P., Treas.

INVESTOR CONTACT: Investor Relations, (305) 599-2600

PRINCIPAL OFFICE: Carnival Place, 3655 N.W. 87th Avenue, Miami, FL 33178-2428

TELEPHONE NUMBER: (305) 599-2600
FAX: (305) 471-4700
WEB: www.carnivalcorp.com
NO. OF EMPLOYEES: 35,100 full-time (approx.); 2,100 part-time (approx.)
SHAREHOLDERS: 4,556 (approx. record)
ANNUAL MEETING: In Apr.
INCORPORATED: PAN, Nov., 1974

INSTITUTIONAL HOLDINGS:
No. of Institutions: 446
Shares Held: 336,840,260
% Held: 57.4

INDUSTRY: Water passenger transportation, nec (SIC: 4489)

TRANSFER AGENT(S): First Union National Bank, Charlotte, NC

CARPENTER TECHNOLOGY CORPORATION

EXCH.	SYM.	REC. PRICE	P/E RATIO	YLD.	MKT. CAP.	RANGE (52-WK.)	'02 Y/E PR.
NYSE	CRS	11.64 (2/28/03)	...	2.8%	$260.1 mill.	30.55 - 10.25	12.45

LOWER MEDIUM GRADE. THE COMPANY EXPECTS TO BE PROFITABLE IN THE SECOND HALF OF ITS FISCAL YEAR.

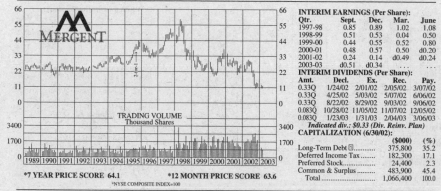

TRADING VOLUME
Thousand Shares

*7 YEAR PRICE SCORE 64.1   ***12 MONTH PRICE SCORE 63.6**

*NYSE COMPOSITE INDEX=100

INTERIM EARNINGS (Per Share):

Qtr.	Sept.	Dec.	Mar.	June
1997-98	0.85	0.89	1.02	1.08
1998-99	0.51	0.53	0.04	0.50
1999-00	0.44	0.55	0.52	0.80
2000-01	0.48	0.57	0.50	0.20
2001-02	0.24	0.14	d0.49	d0.24
2003-03	d0.51	d0.34	...	...

INTERIM DIVIDENDS (Per Share):

Amt.	Decl.	Ex.	Rec.	Pay.
0.33Q	1/24/02	2/01/02	2/05/02	3/07/02
0.33Q	4/25/02	5/03/02	5/07/02	6/06/02
0.33Q	8/22/02	8/29/02	9/03/02	9/06/02
0.083Q	10/28/02	11/05/02	11/07/02	12/05/02
0.083Q	1/23/03	1/31/03	2/04/03	3/06/03

Indicated div.: $0.33 (Div. Reinv. Plan)

CAPITALIZATION (6/30/02):

	($000)	(%)
Long-Term Debt [1]	375,800	35.2
Deferred Income Tax	182,300	17.1
Preferred Stock.................	24,400	2.3
Common & Surplus	483,900	45.4
Total	1,066,400	100.0

BUSINESS:

Carpenter Technology Corporation is an international manufacturer of high performance alloys, specialty metals, and advanced materials for use in the aerospace, automotive, electronic, medical and consumer products industries. The Company operates in two business segments: Specialty Metals (86.9% of 2002 sales) and Engineered Products (13.1%). The Company primarily processes basic raw materials such as chromium, nickel, titanium, iron scrap and other metal alloying elements through various melting, hot forming and cold working facilities to produce finished products in the form of billet, bar, rod, wire, narrow strip, special shapes and hollow forms in many sizes and finishes, and produces certain metal powders and fabricated metal products. In addition, ceramic and metal injection molded products are produced from various raw materials using molding, heating and other processes.

RECENT DEVELOPMENTS:

For the quarter ended 12/31/02, CRS incurred a net loss of $7.1 million compared with net income of $3.5 million in the equivalent 2001 quarter. Results for 2002 included an after-tax special charge of $7.7 million related primarily to severance and pension related costs of an early retirement program for certain production and maintenance employees. Net sales declined 15.3% to $210.2 million, reflecting reduced demand for certain high temperature alloys, titanium alloys and ceramic products due to lower build rates of commercial aircraft and industrial gas turbines. Free cash flow rose 62.6% to $17.4 million, while net debt decreased 24.4% to $401.1 million.

PROSPECTS:

Based on current market conditions, the Company expects to be profitable in the second half of its fiscal year ending 6/30/03, driven primarily by the cost reduction initiatives it has undertaken. Workforce reductions, combined with other cost savings initiatives, should result in annual savings of $40.0 million to $45.0 million. In addition, CRS expects to generate free cash flow in excess of $40.0 million for the current fiscal year. Meanwhile, the Company plans to further improve its operating efficiencies through process improvements, which are expected to enhance CRS' profitability as the U.S. manufacturing sector recovers.

ANNUAL FINANCIAL DATA:

FISCAL YEAR	TOT. REVS. ($mill.)	NET INC. ($mill.)	TOT. ASSETS ($mill.)	OPER. PROFIT %	NET PROFIT %	RET. ON EQUITY %	RET. ON ASSETS %	CURR. RATIO	EARN. PER SH. $	CASH FL. PER SH. $	TANG. BK. VAL. $	DIV. PER SH. $	PRICE RANGE	AVG. P/E RATIO	AVG. YIELD %
6/30/02	977.1	② d46.0	1,479.5	2.1	...	...	...	1.8	② d0.35	2.68	18.40	1.07	30.55 - 10.25	...	5.3
6/30/01	1,324.1	③ 35.2	1,691.5	10.0	2.7	5.4	2.1	1.3	② 1.50	4.70	20.83	1.32	34.81 - 19.80	18.2	4.8
6/30/00	1,095.8	53.3	1,745.9	9.1	4.9	8.2	3.1	1.2	2.31	5.33	20.73	1.32	38.25 - 18.75	12.3	4.6
6/30/99	1,036.7	④ 37.1	1,607.8	9.6	5.9	2.3	1.4	1.8	④ 1.58	4.45	19.47	1.32	37.13 - 22.19	18.8	4.5
6/30/98	1,176.7	84.0	1,698.9	14.3	7.1	12.7	4.9	1.8	3.84	6.55	20.26	1.32	58.94 - 30.00	11.6	3.0
6/30/97	939.0	60.0	1,223.0	12.2	6.4	13.4	4.9	1.6	3.30	5.70	16.24	1.32	52.44 - 34.75	13.2	3.0
6/30/96	865.3	60.1	912.0	13.4	7.0	16.6	6.6	1.9	3.51	5.72	15.75	1.32	42.00 - 31.25	10.4	3.6
6/30/95	757.5	47.5	831.8	11.9	6.3	18.0	5.7	1.8	2.81	4.90	13.47	1.26	44.00 - 26.63	12.6	3.6
6/30/94	628.8	③ 38.3	729.9	12.5	6.1	16.0	5.2	1.7	③ 2.28	4.17	12.99	1.20	33.19 - 26.56	13.1	4.0
6/30/93	576.2	② 26.5	699.6	10.1	4.6	12.1	3.8	3.0	② 1.56	3.34	11.85	1.20	29.13 - 23.69	17.0	4.5

Statistics are as originally reported. Adj. for stk. split: 2-for-1, 9/95. ⬜ Incl. cap. lease oblig. ② Bef. acctg. chrg. of $112.3 million, 2002; $74.7 mill. (d$4.66/sh.), 1993. ③ Bef. extraord. chrg. of $2.0 mill. ($0.12/sh.). ④ Incl. special chrgs. of $14.2 mill. ⑤ Incl. special charge of $36.0 mill. and excl. acctg. change chrg. of $14.1 mill.

OFFICERS:
D. M. Draeger, Chmn., C.E.O.
R. J. Torcolini, Pres., C.O.O.
T. E. Geremski, Sr. V.P., C.F.O.
INVESTOR CONTACT: Jaime Vasquez, V.P., Treas., (610) 208-2165
PRINCIPAL OFFICE: 1047 North Park Road, Wyomissing, PA 19610-1339

TELEPHONE NUMBER: (610) 208-2000
FAX: (610) 208-2361
WEB: www.cartech.com
NO. OF EMPLOYEES: 5,163 (avg.)
SHAREHOLDERS: 5,211
ANNUAL MEETING: In Oct.
INCORPORATED: DE, 1968

INSTITUTIONAL HOLDINGS:
No. of Institutions: 108
Shares Held: 12,247,195
% Held: 54.8
INDUSTRY: Blast furnaces and steel mills (SIC: 3312)
TRANSFER AGENT(S): First Chicago Trust Company of New York, Jersey City, NJ

CARRAMERICA REALTY CORPORATION

EXCH.	SYM.	REC. PRICE	P/E RATIO	YLD.	MKT. CAP.	RANGE (52-WK.)	'02 Y/E PR.
NYSE	CRE	24.41 (2/28/03)	23.5	8.2%	$1.27 bill.	33.30 - 21.94	25.05

MEDIUM GRADE. GOING FORWARD, RESULTS MAY BE NEGATIVELY AFFECTED BY REDUCED DEMAND FOR OFFICE SPACE AND HIGHER VACANCY RATES FOR OFFICE PROPERTIES.

INTERIM EARNINGS (Per Share):

Qtr.	Mar.	June	Sept.	Dec.
1999	0.30	0.19	0.18	0.23
2000	0.36	0.31	0.60	0.25
2001	0.32	0.38	0.32	d0.38
2002	0.14	0.18	0.39	0.34

INTERIM DIVIDENDS (Per Share):

Amt.	Decl.	Ex.	Rec.	Pay.
0.50Q	5/02/02	5/15/02	5/17/02	5/31/02
0.50Q	8/01/02	8/14/02	8/16/02	8/30/02
0.50Q	11/07/02	11/14/02	11/18/02	12/02/02
0.50Q	2/07/03	2/13/03	2/18/03	2/28/03

Indicated div.: $2.00

TRADING VOLUME Thousand Shares

*7 YEAR PRICE SCORE 107.8   ***12 MONTH PRICE SCORE 97.6**
*NYSE COMPOSITE INDEX=100

CAPITALIZATION (12/31/02):

	($000)	(%)
Long-Term Debt	1,603,949	61.6
Preferred Stock	254,518	9.8
Common & Surplus	743,273	28.6
Total	2,601,740	100.0

BUSINESS:

CarrAmerica Realty Corporation is a fully integrated, self-administered and self-managed publicly-traded real estate investment trust that focuses primarily on the acquisition, development, ownership and operation of office properties in growth markets across the United States. As of 2/07/03, CRE and its affiliates owned, directly or through joint ventures, interests in a portfolio of 296 operating office properties and have four office buildings under development in four key growth markets. CRE's markets include Atlanta, Austin, Chicago, Dallas, Denver, Los Angeles/Orange County, Portland, Salt Lake City, San Diego, San Francisco Bay Area, Seattle and metropolitan Washington, D.C.

RECENT DEVELOPMENTS:

For the year ended 12/31/02, income was $86.1 million, before a gain of $23.3 million from discontinued operations, compared with income of $71.9 million, before a gain of $7.2 million from discontinued operations, the previous year. Results for 2002 included a net non-recurring gain of $4.0 million, while 2001 results included a net non-recurring loss of $39.3 million. Operating revenue inched up to $527.7 million from $525.8 million the year before. Rental revenue grew 1.7% to $503.2 million, while real estate service revenue decreased 20.9% to $24.5 million.

PROSPECTS:

As a result of the ongoing weak economic climate, the real estate markets have been materially affected. The sustained lack of job growth has reduced demand for office space and overall vacancy rates for office properties have increased in most of CRE's markets. In reviewing various outlooks for the economy, CRE believes that the vacancy rates will not improve in any material fashion until at least 2004. During 2002, CRE's markets weakened significantly and its operations in those markets were adversely affected. The occupancy in CRE's portfolio of stabilized operating properties decreased to 92.3% at 12/31/02. Market rental rates have declined in most markets from peak levels and CRE anticipates there will be additional declines in some markets in 2003.

ANNUAL FINANCIAL DATA:

FISCAL YEAR	TOT. INC. ($mill.)	NET INC. ($mill.)	TOT. ASSETS ($mill.)	NET INC. + DEPR./ ASSETS %	RET. ON EQUITY %	RET. ON ASSETS %	EARN. PER SH. $	TANG. BK. VAL. $	DIV. PER SH. $	DIV. PAYOUT %	PRICE RANGE	AVG. P/E RATIO	AVG. YIELD %
12/31/02	527.7	⑧86.1	2,815.7	7.6	8.6	3.1	①1.04	14.34	2.00	192.3	33.30 - 21.94	26.6	7.2
12/31/01	538.6	⑦79.1	2,775.6	7.4	6.7	2.8	⑦0.71	22.66	1.85	260.5	33.29 - 27.00	42.5	6.1
12/31/00	558.0	⑥147.2	3,072.8	9.0	8.9	4.8	⑥1.65	25.33	1.85	112.1	31.50 - 19.69	15.5	7.2
12/31/99	515.9	①96.3	3,479.1	6.2	5.7	2.8	①0.90	25.24	1.85	205.5	26.75 - 17.75	24.7	8.3
12/31/98	602.6	①126.5	3,793.5	6.3	7.0	3.3	③1.32	22.20	1.85	140.1	31.69 - 19.00	19.2	7.3
12/31/97	359.4	②78.7	2,744.1	5.7	5.1	2.9	②1.23	25.27	1.75	142.3	33.44 - 26.25	24.3	5.9
12/31/96	166.7	②④24.8	1,536.6	4.1	3.1	1.6	②④0.90	17.98	1.75	194.4	29.50 - 21.88	28.5	6.8
12/31/95	100.9	④12.1	458.9	6.7	12.6	2.6	④0.90	7.13	1.76	195.5	24.63 - 16.75	23.0	8.5
12/31/94	99.2	12.1	407.9	6.5	11.4	3.0	1.06	8.00	1.74	163.9	24.50 - 17.38	19.8	8.3
⑤12/31/93	75.2	②4.1	279.9	4.8	6.8	1.5	②0.41	6.11	1.06	258.0	27.50 - 20.00	57.9	4.5

Statistics are as originally reported. ① Bef. loss from discont. oper. of $7.9 mill. and extraord. gain on sale of assets of $54.8 mill.; incl. $4.5 mill. loss on treas. stock. ② Bef. extraord. loss, 1997, $608,000; 1996, $484,000; 1993, $5.6 mill. ③ Incl. $13.7 mill. gain on treas. stock. ④ Incl. loss on write off of investments, 1996, $2.3 mill.; 1995, $1.9 mill. ⑤ From 2/15/93 (commencement of operations) ⑥ Bef. inc. from disc. oper. of $32.3 mill. and extraord. gain on sale of assets of $36.4 mill. ⑦ Incl. impairment loss of $42.2 mill. on invest. ⑧ Incl. net non-recurring gain of $4.0 mill. & excl. a gain of $23.2 mill. from disc. ops.

OFFICERS:
T. A. Carr, Chmn., C.E.O.
P. L. Hawkins, Pres., C.O.O.
S. E. Riffee, C.F.O., Treas., Contr.
L. A. Madrid, Sec., Gen. Couns.
INVESTOR CONTACT: Stephen Walsh, Investor Relations, (202) 729-1764
PRINCIPAL OFFICE: 1850 K Street N.W., Washington, DC 20006

TELEPHONE NUMBER: (202) 729-1700
FAX: (202) 729-1150
WEB: www.carramerica.com
NO. OF EMPLOYEES: 780 (approx.)
SHAREHOLDERS: 314 (record)
ANNUAL MEETING: In May
INCORPORATED: MD, July, 1992

INSTITUTIONAL HOLDINGS:
No. of Institutions: 161
Shares Held: 46,928,912
% Held: 88.3

INDUSTRY: Real estate investment trusts (SIC: 6798)

TRANSFER AGENT(S): BankBoston, NA, Boston, MA

CATALINA MARKETING CORPORATION

EXCH.	SYM.	REC. PRICE	P/E RATIO	YLD.	MKT. CAP.	RANGE (52-WK.)	'02 Y/E PR.
NYSE	POS	18.10 (2/28/03)	16.6	...	$1.00 bill.	37.80 - 16.95	18.50

UPPER MEDIUM GRADE. FOR FISCAL 2003, POS EXPECTS REVENUE GROWTH OF 7.0% TO 9.0%, WITH EARNINGS PER SHARE RANGING FROM $1.09 TO $1.11, AFTER THE EFFECT OF A ONE-TIME CHARGE.

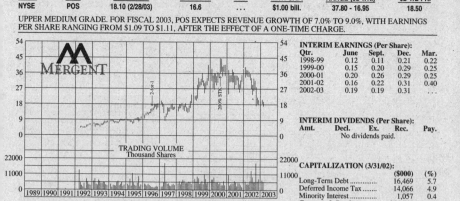

TRADING VOLUME
Thousand Shares

*7 YEAR PRICE SCORE 112.3   *12 MONTH PRICE SCORE 76.5

*NYSE COMPOSITE INDEX=100

INTERIM EARNINGS (Per Share):

Qtr.	June	Sept.	Dec.	Mar.
1998-99	0.12	0.11	0.21	0.22
1999-00	0.15	0.20	0.29	0.25
2000-01	0.20	0.26	0.29	0.25
2001-02	0.16	0.22	0.31	0.40
2002-03	0.19	0.19	0.31	...

INTERIM DIVIDENDS (Per Share):

Amt.	Decl.	Ex.	Rec.	Pay.
		No dividends paid.		

CAPITALIZATION (3/31/02):

	($000)	(%)
Long-Term Debt	16,469	5.7
Deferred Income Tax	14,066	4.9
Minority Interest	1,057	0.4
Common & Surplus	254,868	89.0
Total	286,460	100.0

BUSINESS:

Catalina Marketing Corporation provides a wide range of strategic targeted marketing services for consumer goods companies, pharmaceutical manufacturers and their respective retailers. Through its operating groups, POS is able to reach consumers internationally and domestically in-store, using incentives, loyalty programs, sampling and advertising messages; and at-home, through direct mailings and on-line. POS is composed of three business groups: Catalina

Marketing Services Worldwide, Health Services Marketing and Emerging Businesses. The products and services offered by POS originate from the Catalina Marketing Network®, the Company's proprietary, electronic marketing system. As of 12/31/02, POS' installed store base was 17,333 retail stores and 17,686 pharmacies in the U.S., and 4,069 retail stores throughout the U.K., France, Italy and Japan.

RECENT DEVELOPMENTS:

For the quarter ended 12/31/02, net income decreased 2.9% to $16.9 million versus $17.4 million in the corresponding prior-year period. Results reflected reduced spending by manufacturer clients in the Company's domestic business. Revenue advanced 3.8% to $119.1 million from $114.7

million a year earlier. As of 12/31/02, POS calculated its weekly U.S. shopper reach at 212.0 million compared with 209.0 million, and its weekly international shopper reach at 47.0 million versus 37.0 million the year before.

PROSPECTS:

The Company's international business units continue to perform well. Recently, Catalina Marketing Japan, an international division of POS, announced the expansion of its in-store network with 174 Ito Yokado stores and 200 Maruetsu stores. Ito Yokado amd Maruetso are both premier Japanese supermarket retailers. Looking ahead, earn-

ings per share are anticipated to range from $0.41 to $0.43 during the fourth quarter of fiscal 2003. For the full fiscal year, POS expects revenue growth of 7.0% to 9.0%, with earnings per share ranging from $1.09 to $1.11, after the effect of a one-time charge.

ANNUAL FINANCIAL DATA:

FISCAL YEAR	TOT. REVS. ($000)	NET INC. ($000)	TOT. ASSETS ($000)	OPER. PROFIT %	NET PROFIT %	RET. ON EQUITY %	RET. ON ASSETS %	CURR. RATIO	EARN. PER SH. $	CASH FL. PER SH. $	TANG. BK. VAL. $	PRICE RANGE	AVG. P/E RATIO
3/31/02	446,668	61,880	403,802	22.4	13.9	24.3	15.3	1.1	1.08	1.82	1.84	40.06 - 24.00	28.8
3/31/01	417,881	58,135	388,048	22.5	13.9	27.5	15.0	0.9	1.00	1.75	1.37	44.63 - 26.50	35.6
3/31/00	350,922	51,348	303,752	24.3	14.6	36.4	16.9	0.8	0.89	1.49	1.29	40.83 - 20.19	34.4
3/31/99	264,783	37,608	221,047	25.6	14.2	31.1	17.0	1.1	0.66	1.14	1.55	23.50 - 13.12	27.7
3/31/98	217,150	32,871	157,066	24.4	15.1	36.5	20.9	1.0	0.58	1.00	1.29	20.00 - 8.37	24.6
3/31/97	172,143	27,241	154,696	25.2	15.8	28.1	17.6	1.2	0.44	0.74	1.33	18.50 - 9.73	31.9
3/31/96	134,155	22,028	114,187	25.9	16.4	30.9	19.3	1.6	0.37	0.61	1.22	10.81 - 6.67	23.7
3/31/95	113,254	17,229	96,556	24.9	15.2	31.0	17.8	1.4	0.29	0.54	0.94	9.37 - 6.87	28.5
3/31/94	91,448	12,670	85,476	20.3	13.9	28.2	14.8	1.3	0.21	0.40	0.76	8.37 - 4.75	31.7
3/31/93	71,947	8,229	52,065	17.1	11.4	28.0	15.8	1.0	0.14	0.29	0.51	6.54 - 4.04	39.2

Statistics are as originally reported. Adj. for stk. split: 200% stk. div., 8/00; 2-for-1, 6/96.

OFFICERS:
D. D. Granger, Chmn., Pres., C.E.O.
C. W. Wolf, Sr. V.P., C.F.O., Treas.

INVESTOR CONTACT: Investor Relations, (727) 579-5000

PRINCIPAL OFFICE: 200 Carillon Parkway, St. Petersburg, FL 33716-2325

TELEPHONE NUMBER: (727) 579-5000
FAX: (727) 570-8507
WEB: www.catalinamarketing.com
NO. OF EMPLOYEES: 1,295 full-time (approx.); 302 part-time (approx.)
SHAREHOLDERS: 918 (approx.)
ANNUAL MEETING: In July
INCORPORATED: CA, 1983; reincorp., DE, Mar., 1992

INSTITUTIONAL HOLDINGS:
No. of Institutions: 176
Shares Held: 47,101,814
% Held: 86.5

INDUSTRY: Advertising agencies (SIC: 7311)

TRANSFER AGENT(S): Mellon Investor Services, LLC, South Hackensack, NJ

CATERPILLAR INC.

EXCH.	SYM.	REC. PRICE	P/E RATIO	YLD.	MKT. CAP.	RANGE (52-WK.)	'02 Y/E PR.
NYSE	CAT	47.00 (2/28/03)	20.4	3.0%	$16.14 bill.	59.99 - 33.75	45.72

MEDIUM GRADE. THE COMPANY EXPECTS SALES AND REVENUES FOR FULL-YEAR 2003 TO BE UNCHANGED VERSUS THE PRIOR YEAR AND PROFITS TO DECLINE ABOUT 5.0%.

TRADING VOLUME Thousand Shares

*7 YEAR PRICE SCORE 108.0   *12 MONTH PRICE SCORE 104.3

*NYSE COMPOSITE INDEX=100

INTERIM EARNINGS (Per Share):

Qtr.	Mar.	June	Sept.	Dec.
1998	1.15	1.20	0.92	0.83
1999	0.57	0.78	0.61	0.67
2000	0.73	0.90	0.62	0.76
2001	0.47	0.78	0.59	0.48
2002	0.23	0.58	0.61	0.88

INTERIM DIVIDENDS (Per Share):

Amt.	Decl.	Ex.	Rec.	Pay.
0.35Q	12/12/01	1/17/02	1/22/02	2/20/02
0.35Q	4/10/02	4/18/02	4/22/02	5/20/02
0.35Q	6/12/02	7/18/02	7/22/02	8/20/02
0.35Q	10/09/02	10/17/02	10/21/02	11/20/02
0.35Q	12/11/02	1/16/03	1/21/03	2/20/03

Indicated div.: $1.40 (Div. Reinv. Plan)

CAPITALIZATION (12/31/01):

	($000)	(%)
Long-Term Debt	11,291,000	66.8
Common & Surplus	5,611,000	33.2
Total	16,902,000	100.0

BUSINESS:

Caterpillar Inc. operates in three principal lines of business. The machinery division designs, manufactures and markets construction, mining, agricultural and forestry machinery. Products include track and wheel tractors and loaders, pipelayers, backhoe loaders, mining shovels, log loaders, off-highway trucks, paving products, skid steer loaders, and related parts. The engines division designs, manufactures and markets engines for Caterpillar machinery; on-highway trucks and locomotives; marine, petroleum, construction, industrial, agricultural, and other applications; electric power generation systems; and related parts. Engines range from 5 to over 22,000 horsepower, and turbines range from 1,600 to 19,500 horsepower. The financial products division, provides financing to customers and dealers for the purchase and lease of Caterpillar and noncompetitive related equipment, as well as some financing for Caterpillar sales to dealers. The financial products division also provides various forms of insurance to customers and dealers.

RECENT DEVELOPMENTS:

For the year ended 12/31/02, net income slipped to $798.0 million versus $805.0 million the previous year. Total sales and revenues fell 1.5% to $20.15 billion. Operating profit was $1.32 billion, up slightly from $1.31 billion in 2001.

Separately, on 2/10/03, CAT and BHP Billiton announced a five-year global alliance during which it will supply an estimated $1.50 billion in equipment and support to BHP Billiton's diversified global resources operations.

PROSPECTS:

CAT expects sales and revenues for full-year 2003 to be unchanged versus the prior year, due to continuing uncertainty in the political environment and prolonged weakness in capital spending. Profits are expected to decline about 5.0% compared with 2002. Separately, on 2/6/03, CAT announced its intention to acquire all outstanding shares in the Company's Indian diesel engine joint venture, Hindu-

stan Powerplus Limited. The acquisition will include outstanding public shares, as well as those held by its joint venture partner, the C.K. Birla Group. Also, on 12/19/02, the Company announced the sale of its rubber-belted track component business to Camoplast, of Quebec, Canada, who will supply these components to CAT for use in its Mobiltrac™ systems.

ANNUAL FINANCIAL DATA:

FISCAL YEAR	TOT. REVS. ($mill.)	NET INC. ($mill.)	TOT. ASSETS ($mill.)	OPER. PROFIT %	NET PROFIT %	RET. ON EQUITY %	RET. ON ASSETS %	CURR. RATIO	EARN. PER SH. $	CASH FL. PER SH. $	TANG. BK. VAL. $	DIV. PER SH. $	PRICE RANGE	AVG. P/E RATIO	AVG. YIELD %
p12/31/02	20,152.0	798.0							2.30			1.40	59.99 - 33.75	20.4	3.0
12/31/01	20,450.0	②805.0	30,657.0	9.6	3.9	14.3	2.6	1.3	②2.32	5.69	11.47	1.38	56.83 - 39.75	20.8	2.9
12/31/00	20,175.0	1,053.0	28,464.0	12.0	5.2	18.8	3.7	1.5	3.02	5.95	11.92	1.33	55.13 - 29.56	14.0	3.1
12/31/99	19,702.0	946.0	26,635.0	10.4	4.8	17.3	3.6	1.4	2.63	5.26	11.09	1.25	66.44 - 42.00	20.6	2.3
12/31/98	20,977.0	1,513.0	25,128.0	13.1	7.2	29.5	6.0	1.5	4.11	6.46	10.89	1.10	60.75 - 39.06	12.1	2.2
12/31/97	18,949.0	1,665.0	20,756.0	14.7	8.8	35.6	8.0	1.5	4.37	6.31	12.10	0.90	61.63 - 36.25	11.2	1.8
12/31/96	16,522.0	1,361.0	18,728.0	13.8	8.2	33.1	7.3	1.3	3.54	5.33	10.22	0.75	40.50 - 27.00	9.5	2.2
12/31/95	16,072.0	1,136.0	16,830.0	12.3	7.1	33.5	6.7	1.3	2.86	4.59	8.29	0.60	37.63 - 24.13	10.8	1.9
12/31/94	14,328.0	955.0	16,250.0	11.5	6.7	32.8	5.9	1.3	2.35	4.03	6.68	0.23	30.38 - 22.19	11.2	0.9
12/31/93	11,615.0	①681.0	14,807.0	6.9	5.9	31.0	4.6	1.3	①1.68	3.34	4.52	0.15	23.28 - 13.47	10.9	0.8

Statistics are as originally reported. Adj. for 2-for-1 stk. splits, 9/97 & 7/94. ① Incl. non-recurr. credit of $336.0 mill.; bef. extraord. chrg. of $29.0 mill. ② Incl. non-recurr. chrg. of $153.0 mill.

OFFICERS:
G. A. Barton, Chmn., C.E.O.
R. R. Atterbury III, V.P., Couns., Sec.
F. L. McPheeters, V.P., C.F.O.
INVESTOR CONTACT: James W. Anderson, Dir., Investor Relations, (309) 675-4549
PRINCIPAL OFFICE: 100 NE Adams Street, Peoria, IL 61629-7310

TELEPHONE NUMBER: (309) 675-1000
FAX: (309) 675-4332
WEB: www.cat.com
NO. OF EMPLOYEES: 68,990
SHAREHOLDERS: 36,339
ANNUAL MEETING: In Apr.
INCORPORATED: CA, Apr., 1925; reincorp., DE, May, 1986

INSTITUTIONAL HOLDINGS:
No. of Institutions: 529
Shares Held: 230,145,238
% Held: 66.9
INDUSTRY: Construction machinery (SIC: 3531)
TRANSFER AGENT(S): Mellon Investor Services, South Hackensack, NJ

CDI CORP.

EXCH.	SYM.	REC. PRICE	P/E RATIO	YLD.	MKT. CAP.	RANGE (52-WK.)	'02 Y/E PR.
NYSE	CDI	22.75 (2/28/03)	113.8	...	$435.2 mill.	32.55 - 20.98	26.98

MEDIUM GRADE. GOING FORWARD, THE COMPANY IS WELL-POSITIONED FOR PROFITABLE GROWTH.

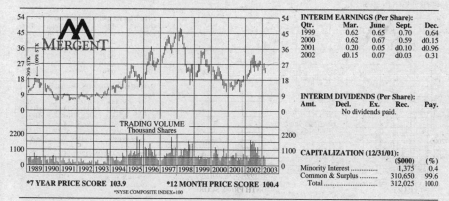

*7 YEAR PRICE SCORE 103.9   ***12 MONTH PRICE SCORE 100.4**

*NYSE COMPOSITE INDEX=100

INTERIM EARNINGS (Per Share):

Qtr.	Mar.	June	Sept.	Dec.
1999	0.62	0.65	0.70	0.64
2000	0.62	0.67	0.59	d0.15
2001	0.20	0.05	d0.10	d0.96
2002	d0.15	0.07	d0.03	0.31

INTERIM DIVIDENDS (Per Share):

Amt.	Decl.	Ex.	Rec.	Pay.
		No dividends paid.		

CAPITALIZATION (12/31/01):

	($000)	(%)
Minority Interest	1,375	0.4
Common & Surplus	310,650	99.6
Total	312,025	100.0

BUSINESS:

CDI Corp. is a provider of specialized staffing, professional services and project outsourcing services. The Professional Services segment, which contributed 53.3% to 2002 revenues, combines the former CDI Information Technology Services staffing business and the staffing elements of CDI Technical Services. It also includes UK-based AndersElite, specializing in professional staffing services. The Project Management segment, 26.6%, is comprised of CDI's engineering, information technology and telecommunications project management businesses. Temporary Staffing, 12.8%, is comprised of Todays Staffing and focuses on temporary clerical, administrative and legal professional staffing in select markets. Permanent Placement, 7.3%, consists of Management Recruiters International and focuses on mid-level and senior-level recruitment and placement. As of 1/14/03, CDI and its franchisees operated more than 1,400 offices in 27 countries.

RECENT DEVELOPMENTS:

For the year ended 12/31/02, CDI reported income from continuing operations of $4.1 million, before an accounting change charge of $14.0 million, versus a loss of $16.7 million in 2001. Results for 2002 and 2001 included after-tax restructuring charges of $13.3 million and $19.2 million, respectively. Revenues decreased 19.8% to $1.17 billion from $1.46 billion a year earlier. On a segment basis, Professional Services revenue dropped 23.1% to $622.9 million, while Project Management revenues declined 11.6% to $311.3 million. Todays Staffing revenue fell 22.9% to $149.4 million, and Management Recruiters revenues were down 16.7% to $85.9 million.

PROSPECTS:

In the fourth quarter of 2002, the Company signed contracts valued at up to $98.0 million in annualized revenue. About two-thirds of this new business represents longer cycle engineering assignments that should help to offset the effect of cutbacks in other accounts. Meanwhile, CDI does not anticipate any improvement or deterioration in the near-term business environment. However, regardless of the economy, CDI should be well positioned for profitable growth, reflecting the exit of low-margin accounts, a lower break-even point and its focus on higher value business.

ANNUAL FINANCIAL DATA:

FISCAL YEAR	TOT. REVS. ($mill.)	NET INC. ($mill.)	TOT. ASSETS ($mill.)	OPER. PROFIT %	NET PROFIT %	RET. ON EQUITY %	RET. ON ASSETS %	CURR. RATIO	EARN. PER SH.$	CASH FL. PER SH.$	TANG. BK. VAL.$	PRICE RANGE	AVG. P/E RATIO
p12/31/02	1,169.5	③ 4.1							③ 0.21			32.55 - 18.58	121.7
12/31/01	1,488.1	② d15.6	472.6	...	...	...	...	2.1	② d0.82	0.66	11.63	20.50 - 11.05	...
12/31/00	1,717.2	② 33.0	572.0	3.5	1.9	10.1	5.8	2.2	② 1.73	2.97	12.35	25.88 - 11.00	10.7
12/31/99	1,601.9	① 49.7	531.7	5.4	3.1	16.9	9.3	2.4	① 2.60	3.56	10.72	36.00 - 19.50	10.7
12/31/98	1,540.5	① 44.2	435.8	4.9	2.9	18.3	10.2	2.3	① 2.25	2.98	10.10	47.94 - 15.00	14.0
12/31/97	1,496.8	① 46.9	348.8	5.3	3.1	21.7	13.5	2.4	① 2.36	2.96	10.02	45.19 - 27.75	15.5
12/31/96	1,374.9	① 42.5	340.2	5.4	3.1	24.0	12.5	2.7	① 2.14	2.70	8.14	37.25 - 18.00	12.9
12/31/95	1,270.5	① 30.7	328.8	4.4	2.4	21.1	9.3	2.5	① 1.55	2.17	7.33	26.63 - 13.50	12.9
12/31/94	1,097.6	22.4	297.7	3.7	2.0	16.1	7.5	2.3	1.13	1.85	5.93	19.88 - 10.25	13.3
12/31/93	921.3	7.8	266.7	1.8	0.8	6.7	2.9	2.3	0.40	1.17	4.70	13.13 - 6.88	25.0

Statistics are as originally reported. Statistics are as originally reported. ① Bef. disc. oper., inc 1999, $2.8 mill.; 1998, $1.3 mill., loss 1997, $9.3 mill.; 1996, $11.1 mill.; 1995, $25.5 mill. ② Incl. pre-tax non-recurr. chrgs. of $22.4 mill., 2001; $11.7 mill., 2000. ③ Bef. acctg. change chrg. of $14.0 mill. and a gain fr. disc. opers. of $527,000; incl. after-tax restr. chrg. of $13.3 mill.

OFFICERS:
W. R. Garrison, Chmn.
R. H. Ballou, Pres., C.E.O.
J. G. Stuart, C.F.O.
INVESTOR CONTACT: Jay Stuart, C.F.O., (215) 636-1141
PRINCIPAL OFFICE: 1717 Arch Street, 35th Floor, Philadelphia, PA 19103-2768

TELEPHONE NUMBER: (215) 569-2200
FAX: (215) 569-1750
WEB: www.cdicorp.com
NO. OF EMPLOYEES: 23,570 (approx.)
SHAREHOLDERS: 505 (record); 4,400 (approx.); (beneficial)
ANNUAL MEETING: In May
INCORPORATED: PA, Sept., 1950

INSTITUTIONAL HOLDINGS:
No. of Institutions: 104
Shares Held: 9,246,835
% Held: 47.9
INDUSTRY: Help supply services (SIC: 7363)
TRANSFER AGENT(S): Mellon Investor Services LLC, Ridgefield Park, NJ

CEDAR FAIR, L.P.

EXCH.	SYM.	REC. PRICE	P/E RATIO	YLD.	MKT. CAP.	RANGE (52-WK.)	'02 Y/E PR.	DIV. ACH.
NYSE	FUN	23.90 (2/28/03)	15.7	7.4%	$1.21 bill.	24.50 - 19.59	23.60	15 yrs.

MEDIUM GRADE. THE COMPANY PLANS TO INVEST $48.0 MILLION IN CAPITAL IMPROVEMENTS AT ITS ELEVEN PROPERTIES IN 2003.

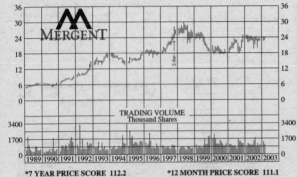

TRADING VOLUME
Thousand Shares

*7 YEAR PRICE SCORE 112.2   *12 MONTH PRICE SCORE 111.1

*NYSE COMPOSITE INDEX=100

INTERIM EARNINGS (Per Share):

Qtr.	Mar.	June	Sept.	Dec.
1997	d0.37	0.31	1.81	d0.28
1998	d0.44	0.37	1.79	d0.14
1999	d0.41	0.37	1.83	d0.15
2000	d0.51	0.36	1.83	d0.17
2001	d0.60	0.13	2.10	d0.50
2002	d0.63	0.40	2.01	d0.26

INTERIM DIVIDENDS (Per Share):

Amt.	Decl.	Ex.	Rec.	Pay.
0.41Q	3/11/02	4/01/02	4/03/02	5/15/02
0.41Q	6/17/02	7/01/02	7/03/02	8/15/02
0.42Q	9/26/02	10/01/02	10/03/02	11/15/02
0.42Q	12/19/02	1/02/03	1/06/03	2/14/03
0.44Q	3/10/03	4/01/03	4/03/03	5/15/03

Indicated div.: $1.76 (Div. Reinv. Plan)

CAPITALIZATION (12/31/01):

	($000)	(%)
Long-Term Debt	373,000	54.8
Common & Surplus	308,250	45.2
Total	681,250	100.0

BUSINESS:

Cedar Fair, L.P. is a limited partnership managed by Cedar Fair Management Company. The partnership owns and operates six amusement parks: Cedar Point, located on Lake Erie in Sandusky, OH; Knott's Berry Farm, located in Buena Park, CA; Dorney Park & Wildwater Kingdom, near Allentown, PA; Valleyfair, located near Minneapolis, MN; Worlds of Fun, located in Kansas City, MO; and Michigan's Adventure, located near Muskegon, MI. The partner-

ship's five water parks are located near San Diego and Palm Springs, CA, and adjacent to Cedar Point, Knott's Berry Farm and Worlds of Fun. All principal rides and attractions are owned and operated by the partnership. FUN owns and operates four hotel facilities. FUN also operates Knott's Camp Snoopy at the Mall of America in Bloomington, MN under a management contract.

RECENT DEVELOPMENTS:

For the year ended 12/31/02, net income rose 23.4% to $71.4 million compared with $57.9 million in 2001. Results for 2002 and 2001 included a non-cash unit option expense of $4.0 million and $11.7 million, respectively. Results for 2002 also included a provision for loss on retirement of

assets of $3.2 million. Net revenues rose 5.4% to $502.9 million, on a 4.0% increase in combined attendance, a 9.0% jump in out-of-park revenues, including resort hotels, and a slight improvement in combined in-park guest per capita spending.

PROSPECTS:

In 2003 the Company plans to invest $48.0 million in capital improvements at its eleven properties. The major projects include the introduction of Cedar Point's 420-foot-tall Top Thrill Dragster, which will be the world's tallest and fastest roller coaster, and the addition of a double-impulse roller coaster, called Steel Venom, at Valleyfair.

Meanwhile, FUN expects internal growth of 3.0% to 5.0% in net revenues, driven primarily by increases in attendance at both Cedar Point and Valleyfair, and improvements in guest per capita spending across all eleven properties. In addition, the Company plans to continue disciplined expense control during the year.

ANNUAL FINANCIAL DATA:

FISCAL YEAR	TOT. REVS. ($000)	NET INC. ($000)	TOT. ASSETS ($000)	OPER. PROFIT %	NET PROFIT %	RET. ON EQUITY %	RET. ON ASSETS %	CURR. RATIO	EARN. PER SH. $	CASH FL. PER SH. $	TANG. BK. VAL.$	DIV. PER SH. $	PRICE RANGE	AVG. P/E RATIO	AVG. YIELD %
p12/31/02	502,851	②③71,417							②③1.39			1.65	24.80 - 19.59	16.0	7.4
12/31/01	477,256	②57,894	810,231	20.7	12.1	18.8	7.1	0.3	②1.13	1.96	5.88	1.58	25.00 - 17.80	18.9	7.4
12/31/00	472,920	①77,806	764,143	24.4	16.5	23.5	10.2	0.2	①1.50	2.27	6.31	1.50	20.88 - 17.44	12.8	7.8
12/31/99	438,001	85,774	708,961	26.6	19.6	24.5	12.1	0.3	1.63	2.31	6.56	1.39	26.00 - 18.44	13.6	6.2
12/31/98	419,500	83,441	631,325	26.8	19.9	24.4	13.2	0.3	1.58	2.20	6.38	1.38	30.13 - 21.75	16.4	5.0
12/31/97	264,137	68,458	599,619	28.9	25.9	24.0	11.4	0.4	1.47	1.95	5.24	1.26	28.25 - 17.69	15.6	5.5
12/31/96	250,523	74,179	304,104	32.4	29.6	43.6	24.4	0.3	1.59	2.02	3.47	1.18	19.50 - 16.13	11.2	6.6
12/31/95	218,197	66,136	274,717	33.5	30.3	43.7	24.1	0.3	1.45	1.83	3.06	1.13	18.56 - 14.06	11.2	6.9
12/31/94	198,358	62,825	223,982	34.3	31.7	54.6	28.0	0.2	1.40	1.75	2.33	1.03	18.31 - 13.38	11.4	6.5
12/31/93	178,943	61,879	218,359	32.1	34.6	61.9	28.3	0.2	1.38	1.72	1.98	0.94	18.31 - 13.50	11.6	5.9

Statistics are as originally reported. Adj. for stk. split: 2-for-1, 11/7/97. ① Incl. nonrecurr. chrg. of $7.8 mill. to terminate general partner fees.
② Incl. non-cash unit option exp. of $4.0 mill., 2002; $11.7 mill., 2001. ③ Incl. prov. for loss on retirement of assets of $3.2 mill.

OFFICERS:
R. L. Kinzel, Pres., C.E.O.
B. A. Jackson, Corp. V.P., C.F.O.
T. W. Salamone, Treas.

INVESTOR CONTACT: Brian C. Witherow, Corporate Director - Investor Relations, (419) 627-2233

PRINCIPAL OFFICE: One Cedar Point Drive, Sandusky, OH 44870-5259

TELEPHONE NUMBER: (419) 626-0830
FAX: (419) 627-2234
WEB: www.cedarfair.com
NO. OF EMPLOYEES: 1,400 (approx.)
SHAREHOLDERS: 10,000 (approx.)
ANNUAL MEETING: N/A
INCORPORATED: MN, 1983; reincorp., DE, 1987

INSTITUTIONAL HOLDINGS:
No. of Institutions: 111
Shares Held: 9,996,300
% Held: 19.8

INDUSTRY: Amusement parks (SIC: 7996)

TRANSFER AGENT(S): American Stock Transfer & Trust Company, New York, NY

CENDANT CORPORATION

EXCH.	SYM.	REC. PRICE	P/E RATIO	YLD.	MKT. CAP.	RANGE (52-WK.)	'02 Y/E PR.
NYSE	CD	12.31 (2/28/03)	11.5	...	$12.70 bill.	20.15 - 8.90	10.48

MEDIUM GRADE. THE COMPANY EXPECTS EARNINGS OF APPROXIMATELY $1.46 PER SHARE IN 2003.

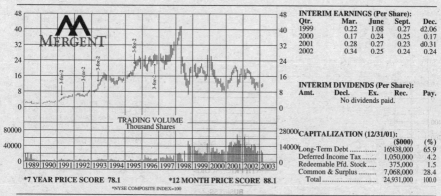

*7 YEAR PRICE SCORE 78.1   *12 MONTH PRICE SCORE 88.1
*NYSE COMPOSITE INDEX=100

INTERIM EARNINGS (Per Share):

Qtr.	Mar.	June	Sept.	Dec.
1999	0.22	1.08	0.27	d2.06
2000	0.17	0.24	0.25	0.17
2001	0.28	0.27	0.23	d0.31
2002	0.34	0.25	0.24	0.24

INTERIM DIVIDENDS (Per Share):

Amt.	Decl.	Ex.	Rec.	Pay.
		No dividends paid.		

CAPITALIZATION (12/31/01):

	($000)	(%)
Long-Term Debt	16,438,000	65.9
Deferred Income Tax	1,050,000	4.2
Redeemable Pfd. Stock	375,000	1.5
Common & Surplus	7,068,000	28.4
Total	24,931,000	100.0

BUSINESS:

Cendant Corporation was formed through the merger of CUC International and HFS Inc. in 1997. The Real Estate Services segment (33.3% of 2002 revenue) assists in employee relocation, provides home buyers with mortgages and franchises real estate brokerage businesses. The Vehicle Services segment (29.7%) rents vehicles and provides fleet management and fuel card services. The Hospitality segment (15.5%) franchises hotel and car rental businesses and facilitates vacation timeshare sales and exchanges. The Travel Distribution segment (12.1%) provides global distribution and computer reservation services to airlines, hotels, car rental companies and other travel suppliers. The Financial Services segment (9.4%) provides enhancement packages to financial institutions, insurance-based products to consumers, loyalty programs to businesses, tax preparation services and membership programs offering discounts to consumers. CD acquired NRT Incorporated on 4/17/02 and Budget Group, Inc. on 11/22/02.

RECENT DEVELOPMENTS:

For the year ended 12/31/02, CD reported income of $1.08 billion, before an extraordinary loss of $30.0 million, versus income of $342.0 million, before an accounting change charge of $38.0 million in 2001. Results for 2002 included acquisition and integration costs of $285.0 million, a litigation charge of $103.0 million, and a restructuring credit of $14.0 million. Results for 2001 included after-tax net one-time charges of $524.0 million. Net revenues advanced 63.6% to $14.09 billion from $8.61 billion a year earlier, primarily due to several acquisitions, including NRT Incorporated, Equivest Finance, Inc. and Budget Group, Inc.

PROSPECTS:

On 2/4/03, the Company announced the acquisition of FFD Development Company, LLC for $27.0 million in cash and the assumption of about $58.0 million in debt. FFD is the primary developer of timeshare inventory for CD's subsidiary, Fairfield Resorts, Inc. Separately, CD expects total revenues for 2003 to range between $17.68 billion and $18.35 billion. The Company also expects earnings of approximately $1.46 per share for 2003.

ANNUAL FINANCIAL DATA:

FISCAL YEAR	TOT. REVS. ($mill.)	NET INC. ($mill.)	TOT. ASSETS ($mill.)	OPER. PROFIT %	NET PROFIT %	RET. ON EQUITY %	RET. ON ASSETS %	CURR. RATIO	EARN. PER SH. $	CASH FL. PER SH. $	TANG. BK. VAL. $	PRICE RANGE	AVG. P/E RATIO
p12/31/02	14,088.0	⑦ 1,081.0							⑦ 1.04			20.15 - 8.90	14.0
12/31/01	8,950.4	⑥ 423.0	33,452.0	8.7	4.7	6.0	1.3	0.8	⑥ 0.45	2.83	...	21.53 - 9.63	34.6
12/31/00	3,930.0	⑤ 576.0	14,516.0	24.9	14.7	20.8	4.0	1.2	⑤ 0.78	1.39	...	26.31 - 8.13	22.1
12/31/99	5,402.0	④ d229.0	15,149.0	...	...	...	...	0.8	④ d0.30	1.12	...	26.94 - 13.63	...
12/31/98	5,283.8	③ 159.9	20,216.5	6.0	3.0	3.3	0.8	1.4	③ 0.18	1.98	...	41.69 - 6.50	133.8
① 12/31/97	5,314.7	② 55.4	14,851.2	5.5	1.0	1.2	0.4	1.5	② 0.06	2.41	0.89	33.81 - 19.25	441.5
1/31/97	2,347.7	164.1	2,473.4	11.8	7.0	13.1	6.6	3.0	0.41	2.14	2.02	27.42 - 18.33	56.5
1/31/96	1,415.0	172.1	1,141.3	19.4	12.2	23.7	15.1	5.1	0.37	1.43	1.05	26.17 - 14.50	54.5
1/31/95	1,044.7	118.2	764.9	18.3	11.3	26.9	15.5	4.6	0.30	1.25	0.63	15.95 - 11.11	45.5
1/31/94	879.3	88.6	612.8	16.3	10.1	31.1	14.5	3.1	0.23	1.11	0.28	17.67 - 7.37	54.9

Statistics are as originally reported. Adj. for stk. splits through 10/96 ① Results prior to 12/97 were for CUC Intl. ② Incl. one-time chg. $1.15 bill. ③ Bef. disc. oper. inc. $379.7 mill., incl. one-time chg. $838.3 mill. ④ Bef. disc. oper. gain $174.1 mill.; incl. one-time chgs. $3.03 bill. ⑤ Bef. acctg. chg. $56.0 mill., net gain fr. disc. opers. $84.0 mill. & extr. loss $2.0 mill.; incl. net pre-tax one-time chg. $99.0 mill. ⑥ Bef. acctg. chg. $423.0 mill.; incl. after-tax net one-time chgs. $524.0 mill. ⑦ Bef. extr. loss $30.0 mill. and net loss fr. disc. oper. $205.0 mill.; incl. acquis. chg. $285.0 mill., litig chg. $103.0 mill. and a restr. credit $14.0 mill.

OFFICERS:
H. R. Silverman, Chmn., Pres., C.E.O.
J. E. Buckman, Vice-Chmn., Gen. Couns.
S. P. Holmes, Vice-Chmn.
INVESTOR CONTACT: Sam Levenson, Investor Relations, (212) 413-1834
PRINCIPAL OFFICE: 9 West 57th Street, New York, NY 10019

TELEPHONE NUMBER: (212) 413-1800
FAX: (212) 413-1924
WEB: www.cendant.com
NO. OF EMPLOYEES: 85,000 (approx.)
SHAREHOLDERS: 10,093 (approx., record)
ANNUAL MEETING: In May
INCORPORATED: DE, 1973; reincorp., DE, 1974

INSTITUTIONAL HOLDINGS:
No. of Institutions: 526
Shares Held: 812,678,370
% Held: 78.4
INDUSTRY: Miscellaneous personal services, nec (SIC: 7299)
TRANSFER AGENT(S): Mellon Investor Services, South Hackensack, NJ

CENTERPOINT ENERGY, INC.

EXCH.	SYM.	REC. PRICE	P/E RATIO	YLD.	MKT. CAP.	RANGE (52-WK.)	'02 Y/E PR.
NYSE	CNP	4.65 (2/28/03)	2.3	8.6%	$4,650	26.30 - 4.24	8.50

LOWER MEDIUM GRADE. THE COMPANY EXPECTS 2003 EARNINGS PER SHARE IN THE RANGE OF $0.85 TO $1.00.

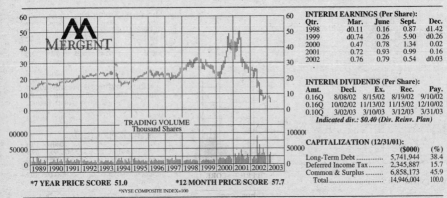

INTERIM EARNINGS (Per Share):

Qtr.	Mar.	June	Sept.	Dec.
1998	d0.11	0.16	0.87	d1.42
1999	d0.74	0.26	5.90	d0.26
2000	0.47	0.78	1.34	0.02
2001	0.72	0.93	0.99	0.16
2002	0.76	0.79	0.54	d0.03

INTERIM DIVIDENDS (Per Share):

Amt.	Decl.	Ex.	Rec.	Pay.
0.16Q	8/08/02	8/15/02	8/19/02	9/10/02
0.16Q	10/02/02	11/13/02	11/15/02	12/10/02
0.10Q	3/02/03	3/10/03	3/12/03	3/31/03
Indicated div.: $0.40 (Div. Reinv. Plan)				

CAPITALIZATION (12/31/01):

	($000)	(%)
Long-Term Debt	5,741,944	38.4
Deferred Income Tax	2,345,887	15.7
Common & Surplus	6,858,173	45.9
Total..............................	14,946,004	100.0

*7 YEAR PRICE SCORE 51.0　　***12 MONTH PRICE SCORE 57.7**

*NYSE COMPOSITE INDEX=100

BUSINESS:

CenterPoint Energy, Inc.(formerly Reliant Energy, Incorporated) is a public utility holding company, created on 8/31/01 as part of a corporate restructuring of Reliant Energy. The Company's wholly-owned operating subsidiaries own and operate electric generation plants, electric transmission and distribution facilities, natural gas distribution facilities and natural gas pipelines. As of 2/28/03, the Company served nearly five million customers primarily in Arkansas, Louisiana, Minnesota, Mississippi, Missouri, Oklahoma, and Texas. On 9/30/02, the Company completed the spin-off of its 83.0%-owned energy services subsidiary, Reliant Resources, Inc. to its shareholders.

RECENT DEVELOPMENTS:

For the year ended 12/31/02, income was $386.3 million versus income of $446.9 million the year before. Results for 2002 and 2001 excluded income from discontinued operations of $82.2 million and $475.1 million, respectively. Also, results for 2002 excluded a loss on the disposal of discontinued operations of $4.37 billion and an extraordinary loss of $17.2 million, while results for 2001 excluded an accounting gain of $58.6 million. Results for 2002 and 2001 included losses on its AOL Time Warner investment of $499.7 million and $70.2 million, and gains on indexed debt securities of $480.0 million and $58.0 million, respectively. Results for 2001 also included net impairment charges of $79.4 million. Total revenues dropped 25.7% to $7.92 billion from $10.66 billion.

PROSPECTS:

On 2/19/03, CNP announced the sale of its Argentina-based cogeneration facility for $23.1 million. This action is in line with CNP's strategy to focus on its core energy delivery business in the U.S. Separately, on 2/28/03, CNP announced it was able to amend its $3.85 billion credit facility. The amendment extends the term to June 2005, eliminates $1.20 billion in mandatory payments required in 2003 and should provide financial stability during CNP's transition period, by which time CNP expects to recover its investment in its generating assets and return to a more typical debt level. Looking ahead, CNP expects 2003 diluted earnings per share in the range of $0.85 to $1.00.

ANNUAL FINANCIAL DATA:

FISCAL YEAR	TOT. REVS. ($mill.)	NET INC. ($mill.)	TOT. ASSETS ($mill.)	OPER. PROFIT %	NET PROFIT %	NET INC./ NET PROP. %	NET INC./ TOT. CAP. %	RET. ON EQUITY %	ACCUM. DEPR./ GROSS PROP. %	EARN. PER SH. $	TANG. BK. VAL. $	DIV. PER SH. $	DIV. PAYOUT %	PRICE RANGE		AVG. P/E RATIO	AVG. YIELD %
⑧ p12/31/02	7,922.5	⑨ 386.3								⑨ 1.29		1.07	82.9	27.10 -	4.24	12.1	6.8
12/31/01	46,225.8	918.9	30,680.5	4.3	2.0	5.8	5.5	3.9	. . .	3.14	13.05	1.50	47.8	50.45 -	23.27	11.7	4.1
12/31/00	29,339.4	⑦ 771.1	32,076.7	6.4	2.6	5.1	5.6	14.1	. . .	⑦ 2.68	8.10	1.50	56.0	49.00 -	19.75	12.8	4.4
12/31/99	15,302.8	⑥ 1,768.2	26,220.9	8.1	11.6	13.3	13.2	33.3	34.1	⑥ 5.82	7.70	1.50	25.8	32.50 -	22.75	4.7	5.4
⑤ 12/31/98	11,488.5	④ d82.7	19,138.5	12.8	. . .	. . .	. . .	. . .	32.3	④ d0.50	7.47	1.50	. . .	33.38 -	25.00	. . .	5.1
12/31/97	6,873.4	③ 421.1	18,414.6	15.5	6.1	3.7	3.2	8.6	29.7	③ 1.66	9.69	1.50	90.4	26.75 -	18.88	13.7	6.6
12/31/96	4,095.3	② 404.9	12,287.9	24.2	9.9	4.6	4.3	10.2	32.7	② 1.66	15.52	0.94	56.5	25.63 -	20.50	13.9	4.1
12/31/95	3,730.2	② 397.4	11,819.6	24.3	10.7	4.5	3.8	8.9	30.6	② 1.60	15.70	1.50	93.7	24.50 -	17.69	13.2	7.1
12/31/94	3,746.1	① 424.0	11,453.2	26.6	11.3	4.7	4.3	11.4	28.0	1.73	12.83	1.50	87.0	23.88 -	15.00	11.3	7.7
12/31/93	4,323.9	416.0	12,230.2	23.6	9.6	4.5	3.9	11.5	26.7	1.60	8.76	1.50	93.7	24.88 -	21.25	14.4	6.5

Statistics are as originally reported. Adj. for 2-for-1 split, 12/95. ① Incl. non-recurr. after-tax chrg. $46.1 mill. ② Bef. acctg. chrg. $8.2 mill. and disc. opers. gain of $691.6 mill. ③ Incl. non-recurr. chrg. 1997, $42.3 mill.; 1996, $66.9 mill. ④ Incl. unrealized acctg. loss of $1.18 bill. Refl. first full year of results since the acq. of Reliant Energy Resources Corp. on 8/6/97. ⑤ Incl. one-time unrealized gain of $2.45 bill. on Time Warner investments, but bef. extraord. loss of $183.3 mill. ⑥ Bef. disc. opers. chrg., $331.1 and extraord. gain, $7.4 mill.; incl. one-time unrealized loss of $205.0 mill. fr. Time Warner invest. ⑦ Refl. spin-off of Reliant Resources, Inc to shareholders. ⑧ Bef. disc. opers. $82.2 mill., loss fr. disposal of disc. opers fr. $4.37 bill. & extraord. loss of $17.2 mill.; Incl. one-time loss of $499.7 mill. fr. Time Warner invest.

OFFICERS:	TELEPHONE NUMBER: (713) 207-1111	INSTITUTIONAL HOLDINGS:
M. Carroll, Chmn.	FAX: (713) 207-3169	No. of Institutions: 225
D. M. McClanahan, Pres., C.E.O.	WEB: centerpointenergy.com	Shares Held: 136,484,284
G. L. Whitlock, Exec. V.P., C.F.O.	NO. OF EMPLOYEES: 11,000 (approx.)	% Held: 44.8
	SHAREHOLDERS: N/A	
PRINCIPAL OFFICE: 1111 Louisiana, Houston, TX 77002	ANNUAL MEETING: In June	INDUSTRY: Electric services (SIC: 4911)
	INCORPORATED: TX, Aug., 2002	TRANSFER AGENT(S): The Company

CENTEX CORPORATION

EXCH.	SYM.	REC. PRICE	P/E RATIO	YLD.	MKT. CAP.	RANGE (52-WK.)	'02 Y/E PR.
NYSE	CTX	55.28 (2/28/03)	7.3	0.3%	$3.38 bill.	63.09 - 38.31	50.20

UPPER MEDIUM GRADE. THE COMPANY EXPECTS HOME SALES TO REMAIN ROBUST IN FISCAL 2003.

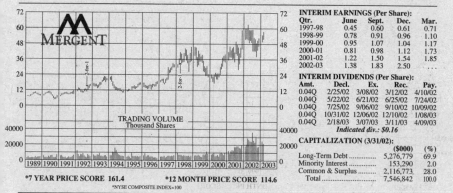

*7 YEAR PRICE SCORE 161.4   ***12 MONTH PRICE SCORE 114.6**

*NYSE COMPOSITE INDEX=100

INTERIM EARNINGS (Per Share):

Qtr.	June	Sept.	Dec.	Mar.
1997-98	0.45	0.60	0.61	0.71
1998-99	0.78	0.91	0.96	1.10
1999-00	0.95	1.07	1.04	1.17
2000-01	0.81	0.98	1.12	1.73
2001-02	1.22	1.50	1.54	1.85
2002-03	1.38	1.83	2.50	...

INTERIM DIVIDENDS (Per Share):

Amt.	Decl.	Ex.	Rec.	Pay.
0.04Q	2/25/02	3/08/02	3/12/02	4/10/02
0.04Q	5/22/02	6/21/02	6/25/02	7/24/02
0.04Q	7/25/02	9/06/02	9/10/02	10/09/02
0.04Q	10/31/02	12/06/02	12/10/02	1/08/03
0.04Q	2/18/03	3/07/03	3/11/03	4/09/03

Indicated div.: $0.16

CAPITALIZATION (3/31/02):

	($000)	(%)
Long-Term Debt	5,276,779	69.9
Minority Interest	153,290	2.0
Common & Surplus	2,116,773	28.0
Total	7,546,842	100.0

BUSINESS:

Centex Corporation has operations in home building, contracting and construction services, construction products, and investment real estate. The Financial Services segment consists of CTX's mortgage banking operations. As of 12/31/02, CTX owned approximately 65.1% of publicly-held Centex Construction Products, Inc., which manufactures cement, concrete and aggregate, and gypsum wallboard. Centex Development Co., L.P. con-

ducts CTX's real estate development activities. In 2002, revenues (and operating income) were derived as follows: Home Building, which includes conventional and manufactured housing, 66.2% (65.7%); Contracting and Construction Services, 17.2% (4.5%); Financial Services, 9.3% (14.3%); Construction Products, 6.3% (9.5%); and Investment Real Estate, 1.0% (6.0%).

RECENT DEVELOPMENTS:

For the quarter ended 12/31/02, net income increased 62.1% to $155.9 million compared with $96.1 million in the equivalent 2001 quarter. Earnings reflected a 16.9% increase in the number of closings to 6,509, and a 3.5% improvement in average unit sales price to $219,909. Revenues grew 21.7% to $2.30 billion from $1.89 billion in the

prior-year period. Home Building revenues jumped 21.3% to $1.47 billion, while revenues from Construction Services increased 27.9% to $411.1 million. Financial Services' revenues rose 22.0% to $223.1 million, while revenues from Construction Products climbed 5.6% to $119.1 million.

PROSPECTS:

The Company expects home sales orders to remain vigorous due to historically low mortgage rates. In addition, CTX's home building margins are expected to continue to increase as a result of higher unit volume and lower brick-and-mortar costs. On 1/7/03, the Company closed on the acquisition of substantially all of the St. Louis and Indian-

apolis home building operations of The Jones Company. The transaction includes about 5,000 owned or controlled lots. For the twelve months ended 3/31/02, The Jones Company delivered 733 homes at an average sales price of $260,000.

ANNUAL FINANCIAL DATA:

FISCAL YEAR	TOT. REVS. ($mill.)	NET INC. ($mill.)	TOT. ASSETS ($mill.)	OPER. PROFIT %	NET PROFIT %	RET. ON EQUITY %	RET. ON ASSETS %	CURR. RATIO	EARN. PER SH.$	CASH FL.PER SH.$	TANG. BK. VAL.$	DIV. PER SH.$	PRICE RANGE	AVG. P/E RATIO	AVG. YIELD %
3/31/02	7,748.4	382.2	8,985.5	8.0	4.9	18.1	4.3	4.9	6.11	7.56	28.89	0.16	58.80 - 28.03	7.1	0.4
3/31/01	6,710.7	282.0	6,649.0	7.0	4.2	16.5	4.2	2.3	4.65	5.32	23.20	0.16	40.00 - 17.50	6.2	0.6
3/31/00	5,956.4	257.1	4,038.7	8.1	4.3	18.1	6.4	1.5	4.22	5.02	19.66	0.16	45.75 - 22.38	8.1	0.5
3/31/99	5,154.8	232.0	4,334.7	8.3	4.5	19.4	5.4	0.8	3.75	4.33	16.43	0.15	45.75 - 26.38	9.6	0.4
3/31/98	3,975.5	144.8	3,416.2	6.9	3.6	14.6	4.2	0.8	2.36	2.78	14.40	0.11	33.00 - 16.75	10.5	0.4
3/31/97	3,785.0	106.6	2,678.8	5.2	2.8	12.8	4.0	1.0	1.81	2.04	12.62	0.10	18.88 - 12.63	8.7	0.6
3/31/96	3,103.0	53.4	2,337.0	2.0	1.7	7.4	2.3	1.2	0.92	1.13	12.71	0.10	18.00 - 10.94	15.8	0.7
3/31/95	3,277.5	92.2	2,049.7	2.1	2.8	13.8	4.5	1.3	1.52	1.63	11.90	0.10	22.88 - 10.06	10.8	0.6
3/31/94	3,214.5	①85.2	2,580.4	4.2	2.6	12.7	3.3	0.9	①1.30	1.60	10.56	0.10	22.63 - 13.38	13.8	0.6
3/31/93	2,502.7	61.0	2,272.1	3.7	2.4	10.6	2.7	0.9	0.96	1.21	9.29	0.10	16.44 - 9.94	13.8	0.8

Statistics are as originally reported. Adj. for stk. split: 2-for-1, 2/98. ① Incl. a net gain of $37.5 mill. on the sale of interest in Centex Construction Products, Inc.

OFFICERS:
L. E. Hirsch, Chmn., C.E.O.
T. R. Eller, Pres., C.O.O.
L. E. Echols, Exec. V.P., C.F.O.
INVESTOR CONTACT: Investor Relations, (214) 981-6770
PRINCIPAL OFFICE: 2728 N. Harwood, Dallas, TX 75201-1516

TELEPHONE NUMBER: (214) 981-5000
FAX: (214) 981-6859
WEB: www.centex.com
NO. OF EMPLOYEES: 16,249 (avg.)
SHAREHOLDERS: 3,344 (approx.)
ANNUAL MEETING: In July
INCORPORATED: NV, Nov., 1968

INSTITUTIONAL HOLDINGS:
No. of Institutions: 314
Shares Held: 56,883,426
% Held: 92.3

INDUSTRY: Operative builders (SIC: 1531)

TRANSFER AGENT(S): Mellon Investor Services LLC, Ridgefield Park, NJ

CENTURYTEL, INC.

EXCH.	SYM.	REC. PRICE	P/E RATIO	YLD.	MKT. CAP.	RANGE (52-WK.)	'02 Y/E PR.	DIV. ACH.
NYSE	CTL	27.40 (2/28/03)	20.6	0.8%	$3.87 bill.	35.50 - 21.13	29.38	29 yrs.

UPPER MEDIUM GRADE. THE COMPANY EXPECTS FULL-YEAR 2003 DILUTED EARNINGS TO RANGE BETWEEN $2.05 AND $2.15 PER SHARE.

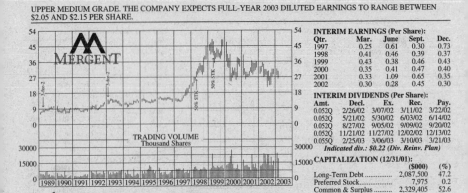

*7 YEAR PRICE SCORE 107.6   ***12 MONTH PRICE SCORE 110.3**

*NYSE COMPOSITE INDEX=100

INTERIM EARNINGS (Per Share):

Qtr.	Mar.	June	Sept.	Dec.
1997	0.25	0.61	0.30	0.73
1998	0.41	0.46	0.39	0.37
1999	0.43	0.38	0.46	0.43
2000	0.35	0.41	0.47	0.40
2001	0.33	1.09	0.65	0.35
2002	0.30	0.28	0.45	0.30

INTERIM DIVIDENDS (Per Share):

Amt.	Decl.	Ex.	Rec.	Pay.
0.052Q	2/26/02	3/07/02	3/11/02	3/22/02
0.052Q	5/21/02	5/30/02	6/03/02	6/14/02
0.052Q	8/27/02	9/05/02	9/09/02	9/20/02
0.052Q	11/21/02	11/27/02	12/02/02	12/13/02
0.055Q	2/25/03	3/06/03	3/10/03	3/21/03

Indicated div.: $0.22 (Div. Reinv. Plan)

CAPITALIZATION (12/31/01):

	($000)	(%)
Long-Term Debt	2,087,500	47.2
Preferred Stock................	7,975	0.2
Common & Surplus	2,329,405	52.6
Total	4,424,880	100.0

BUSINESS:

CenturyTel, Inc. (formerly Century Telephone Enterprises, Inc.) is a regional diversified telecommunications company that is primarily engaged in providing local exchange telephone services. CTL also provides long distance, Internet access, competitive local exchange carrier, broadband data, security monitoring, and other communications and business information services in certain local and regional markets. As of 12/31/02, CTL's telephone subsidiaries provided service to more than 3.0 million customers in 22 states, with the largest customer bases located in Wisconsin, Arkansas, Washington, Missouri, Michigan, Louisiana and Colorado. On 7/31/00 and 9/29/00, CTL acquired over 490,000 telephone access lines from Verizon Communications, Inc. in four separate transactions for about $1.50 billion in cash. On 8/1/02, CTL sold its wireless business to ALLTEL for $1.57 billion. On 7/1/02 and 8/31/02, CTL acquired about 654,000 telephone access lines in two separate transactions from Verizon for about $2.16 billion.

RECENT DEVELOPMENTS:

For the year ended 12/31/02, income from continuing operations was $189.9 million compared with income from continuing operations of $144.1 million a year earlier. Results for 2002 and 2001 included pre-tax non-recurring gains of $3.7 million and $33.0 million, respectively. Total revenues climbed 17.4% to $1.97 billion from $1.68 billion the previous year, due in part to the July and August 2002 acquisitions from Verizon Communications, Inc. that added 654,000 telephone access lines. Telephone revenues grew 15.1% to $1.73 billion and operating income improved 28.3% to $543.1 million. Other operations revenues, which include long distance, Internet and competitive long distance service, climbed 31.2% to $238.4 million, while operating profit jumped 97.2% to $43.6 million.

PROSPECTS:

The Company expects full-year 2003 diluted earnings to range between $2.05 and $2.15 per share. CTL noted that these figures give effect to a full year's operations of the Company's Verizon properties that were acquired in 2002, anticipated increases in pension expense and pre- and post-retirement medical costs, and anticipated amortization expense and operating costs as the Company converts to a new billing and customer care system.

ANNUAL FINANCIAL DATA:

FISCAL YEAR	TOT. REVS. ($mill.)	NET INC. ($mill.)	TOT. ASSETS ($mill.)	OPER. PROFIT %	NET PROFIT %	RET. ON EQUITY %	RET. ON ASSETS %	CURR. RATIO	EARN. PER SH.$	CASH FL. PER SH.$	TANG. BK. VAL.$	DIV. PER SH.$	PRICE RANGE	AVG. P/E RATIO	AVG. YIELD %
p12/31/02	1,972.0	⑤ 189.9							⑤ 1.33			0.21	35.50 - 21.13	21.3	0.7
12/31/01	2,117.5	④ 343.0	6,318.7	26.3	16.2	14.7	5.4	0.2	④ 2.41	5.63	...	0.20	39.88 - 25.45	13.6	0.6
12/31/00	1,845.9	③ 231.5	6,393.3	28.5	12.5	11.4	3.6	0.5	③ 1.63	4.37	...	0.19	47.31 - 24.44	22.0	0.5
12/31/99	1,676.7	③ 239.8	4,705.4	30.3	14.3	13.0	5.1	0.9	③ 1.70	4.16	1.39	0.18	49.00 - 35.19	24.8	0.4
12/31/98	1,577.1	① 228.8	4,935.5	30.4	14.5	14.9	4.6	0.7	① 1.64	3.98	...	0.17	45.17 - 21.56	20.3	0.5
12/31/97	901.5	② 256.0	4,709.2	29.7	28.4	19.7	5.4	0.9	② 1.87	3.02	...	0.16	22.42 - 12.67	9.4	0.9
12/31/96	749.7	② 129.1	2,028.5	29.8	17.2	12.6	6.4	0.8	② 0.96	1.94	3.61	0.16	15.78 - 12.67	14.9	1.1
12/31/95	644.8	114.8	1,862.4	31.5	17.8	12.9	6.2	0.7	0.88	1.75	2.95	0.15	14.72 - 12.00	15.3	1.1
12/31/94	540.2	100.2	1,643.3	31.4	18.6	15.4	6.1	0.3	0.84	1.63	1.71	0.14	14.33 - 9.72	14.4	1.2
12/31/93	433.2	69.0	1,319.4	28.8	15.9	13.4	5.2	0.4	0.60	1.35	2.03	0.14	14.83 - 10.33	21.0	1.1

Statistics are as originally reported. Adj. for 50% stk. div., 3/99 & 3/98. ① Incl. non-recurr. pre-tax credit of $49.9 mill. ② Incl. pre-tax credit 12/31/97: $169.9 mill.; credit 12/31/96, $815,000. ③ Incl. pre-tax gain on sales of assets of $20.6 mill., 2000; $62.8 mill., 1999. ④ Incl. pre-tax non-recurr. gain of $200.0 mill. ⑤ Incl. pre-tax non-recurr. gain of $3.7 mill.; bef. inc. fr. disc. ops. of $611.7 mill.

OFFICERS:
G. F. Post III, Chmn., C.E.O.
K. A. Puckett, Pres., C.O.O.
R. S. Ewing, Jr., Exec. V.P., C.F.O.
INVESTOR CONTACT: Tony Davis, Inv. Rel., (318) 388-9525
PRINCIPAL OFFICE: 100 CenturyTel Drive, Monroe, LA 71203

TELEPHONE NUMBER: (318) 388-9000
FAX: (318) 789-8656
WEB: www.centurytel.com
NO. OF EMPLOYEES: 6,900 (approx.)
SHAREHOLDERS: 5,300 (approx.)
ANNUAL MEETING: In May
INCORPORATED: LA, Apr., 1968

INSTITUTIONAL HOLDINGS:
No. of Institutions: 315
Shares Held: 113,254,099
% Held: 79.4
INDUSTRY: Telephone communications, exc. radio (SIC: 4813)
TRANSFER AGENT(S): Computershare Investor Services, LLC, Chicago, IL

CERIDIAN CORPORATION

EXCH.	SYM.	REC. PRICE	P/E RATIO	YLD.	MKT. CAP.	RANGE (52-WK.)	'02 Y/E PR.
NYSE	CEN	13.80 (2/28/03)	22.3	...	$2.02 bill.	23.05 - 11.40	14.42

MEDIUM GRADE. EARNINGS FOR 2003 ARE EXPECTED TO RANGE BETWEEN $0.83 AND $0.90 PER SHARE.

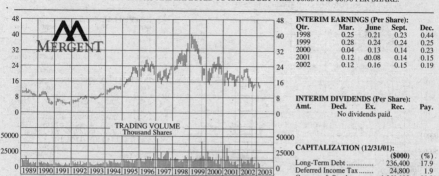

INTERIM EARNINGS (Per Share):

Qtr.	Mar.	June	Sept.	Dec.
1998	0.25	0.21	0.23	0.44
1999	0.28	0.24	0.24	0.25
2000	0.04	0.13	0.14	0.23
2001	0.12	d0.08	0.14	0.15
2002	0.12	0.16	0.15	0.19

INTERIM DIVIDENDS (Per Share):

Amt.	Decl.	Ex.	Rec.	Pay.
		No dividends paid.		

CAPITALIZATION (12/31/01):

	($000)	(%)
Long-Term Debt	236,400	17.9
Deferred Income Tax	24,800	1.9
Common & Surplus	1,061,100	80.2
Total	1,322,300	100.0

*7 YEAR PRICE SCORE 78.7   ***12 MONTH PRICE SCORE 91.4**

*NYSE COMPOSITE INDEX=100

BUSINESS:

Ceridian Corporation was formed as a result of the 3/30/01 spin-off of the human resources division, human resource services, and Comdata subsidiaries of Ceridian Corporation (old). The spun-off entities retained the Ceridian Corporation name. The business comprising the Company's human resource services business offers a broad range of services and software designed to help employees more effectively manage their work forces and information that is integral to human resource processes. The Company's Comdata subsidiary provides transaction processing and regulatory compliance services to the transportation and other industries. Revenues in 2002 were derived: human resource services, 73.6%; and Comdata, 26.4%.

RECENT DEVELOPMENTS:

For the year ended 12/31/02, net earnings soared 89.3% to $93.7 million compared with income from continuing operations of $49.5 million in 2001. Results benefited from strong revenue growth from the Human Resource Services segment as total Human Resource Services orders were up 15.0% over the prior year, despite the cancellation of a large total outsourcing order in the fourth quarter. Results for 2001 excluded a gain of $5.2 million from discontinued operations. Revenues were $1.19 billion, up 0.2% from $1.19 billion the previous year. Human Resource Services revenue grew 0.5% to $878.1 million from $873.8 million. However, revenue from Comdata Corporation slipped 0.4% to $314.6 million from $316.0 million a year earlier.

PROSPECTS:

The Company expects earnings for 2003 to range between $0.83 and $0.90 per share. Operating results for the year will be hampered by incremental expenses of about $15.0 million related to the Company's pension plan. Additionally, decreases in interest rates and employment levels may negatively affect revenue and earnings in 2003, mostly in the first half of the year. As a result, earnings per share for the first quarter of 2003 are expected to range between $0.17 and $0.19 and revenue is expected to range between $309.0 million and $318.0 million.

ANNUAL FINANCIAL DATA:

FISCAL YEAR	TOT. REVS. ($mill.)	NET INC. ($mill.)	TOT. ASSETS ($mill.)	OPER. PROFIT %	NET PROFIT %	RET. ON EQUITY %	RET. ON ASSETS %	CURR. RATIO	EARN. PER SH.$	CASH FL. PER SH.$	PRICE RANGE	AVG. P/E RATIO
p12/31/02	1,192.7	93.7							0.62		23.05 - 11.40	27.8
12/31/01	1,182.3	③ 49.5	4,037.0	8.2	4.2	4.7	1.2	1.5	③ 0.33	1.04	21.85 - 13.65	53.8
12/31/00	1,175.7	② 79.5	2,088.0	13.9	6.8	8.5	3.8	1.5	② 0.54	1.14	29.19 - 14.75	40.7
12/31/99	1,127.0	104.4	1,988.5	16.5	9.3	12.9	5.3	1.4	0.71	1.19	40.50 - 16.63	40.2
12/31/98	967.6	① 125.3	...	16.8	12.9	...	...	...	① 0.85	1.16	36.00 - 21.75	34.0

Statistics are as originally reported. Adj. for 2-for-1 split, 2/99. ① Incl. $24.3 mill. gain fr. sale of bus. & land and excl. $25.4 mill. gain fr. disc. ops. ② Excl. $20.7 mill. from disc. ops. ③ Excl. $5.2 mill. inc. fr. disc. ops.

OFFICERS:
R. L. Turner, Chmn., Pres., C.E.O.
J. R. Eickhoff, Exec. V.P., C.F.O.
G. M. Nelson, Exec. V.P., Sec., Gen. Couns.

INVESTOR CONTACT: Craig Manson, V.P. of Inv. Rel., (952) 853-6022

PRINCIPAL OFFICE: 311 East Old Shakopee Road, Minneapolis, MN 55425

TELEPHONE NUMBER: (952) 853-8100
FAX: (952) 853-3932
WEB: www.ceridian.com

NO. OF EMPLOYEES: 8,727 full-time (approx.); 688 part-time (approx.)

SHAREHOLDERS: 11,400 (approx.)

ANNUAL MEETING: In May
INCORPORATED: DE, Mar., 2001

INSTITUTIONAL HOLDINGS:
No. of Institutions: 181
Shares Held: 138,846,878
% Held: 93.5

INDUSTRY: Management consulting services (SIC: 8742)

TRANSFER AGENT(S): The Bank of New York, New York, NY

CH ENERGY GROUP, INC.

EXCH.	SYM.	REC. PRICE	P/E RATIO	YLD.	MKT. CAP.	RANGE (52-WK.)	'02 Y/E PR.
NYSE	CHG	41.18 (2/28/03)	16.3	5.2%	$0.67 bill.	52.39 - 39.90	46.63

MEDIUM GRADE. DESPITE CONTINUED VOLATILITY IN THE INVESTMENT MARKETS, THE COMPANY PROJECTS EARNINGS PER SHARE FOR 2003 OF BETWEEN $2.55 TO $2.75.

*7 YEAR PRICE SCORE 126.8   ***12 MONTH PRICE SCORE 100.3**
*NYSE COMPOSITE INDEX=100

INTERIM EARNINGS (Per Share):

Qtr.	Mar.	June	Sept.	Dec.
1997	1.18	0.55	0.72	0.52
1998	1.06	0.54	0.77	0.52
1999	1.09	0.51	0.77	0.51
2000	1.07	0.47	0.87	0.68
2001	1.12	0.20	0.58	1.21
2002	1.19	0.31	0.37	0.66

INTERIM DIVIDENDS (Per Share):

Amt.	Decl.	Ex.	Rec.	Pay.
0.54Q	3/22/02	4/08/02	4/10/02	5/01/02
0.54Q	6/28/02	7/08/02	7/10/02	8/01/02
0.54Q	9/27/02	10/08/02	10/10/02	11/01/02
0.54Q	12/20/02	1/08/03	1/10/03	2/03/03
0.54Q	3/14/03	4/08/03	4/10/03	5/02/03

Indicated div.: $2.16 (Div. Reinv. Plan)

CAPITALIZATION (12/31/01):

	($000)	(%)
Long-Term Debt	216,124	27.4
Deferred Income Tax	21,360	2.7
Preferred Stock	56,030	7.1
Common & Surplus	496,309	62.8
Total	789,823	100.0

BUSINESS:

CH Energy Group, Inc. (formerly Central Hudson Gas & Electric Corp.) became the holding company of Central Hudson Gas & Electric Corporation and Central Hudson Energy Services, Inc. on 12/15/99. CHG generates, purchases, and distributes electricity, and purchases and distributes gas to communities along the Hudson River. Central Gas & Electric is a regulated electric and natural gas utility serving approximately 345,000 customers as of 1/31/03 in portions of eight counties in New York's Mid-Hudson Valley region. Central Hudson Energy Services, Inc. serves more than 80,000 customers in 11 Northeastern and Mid-Atlantic states with electricity, heating oil, motor fuels, natural gas, propane and value-added energy services.

RECENT DEVELOPMENTS:

For the twelve months ended 12/31/02, income from continuing operations declined 28.6% to $38.6 million compared with net income of $54.1 million in 2001. Earnings were restricted by increased operating expenses related to storm repair and service restoration efforts, as well as the negative effect on energy deliveries due to a warmer winter and hotter summer. Results for 2002 excluded a net gain of $4.8 million from discontinued operations. Total operating revenues slipped 4.5% to $695.5 million from $727.9 million in the prior year. Operating income declined to $41.4 million from $47.7 million in 2001.

PROSPECTS:

Looking ahead, the Company projects earnings per share for 2003 of between $2.55 and $2.75, despite continued volatility in the investment markets. In addition, the Company expects earnings per share for Central Hudson Gas & Electric Corporation, CHG's regulated subsidiary, of between $2.15 and $2.30, and earnings per share from Central Hudson Enterprises Corporation, CHG's competitive fuel delivery subsidiary of between $0.30 and $0.50. Separately, on 2/19/03, Central Hudson Enterprises Corporation acquired Cook's Fuel and Energy Services and MIFCO, which supply product and services including, heating oil and motor fuels in Maryland and Virginia, respectively.

ANNUAL FINANCIAL DATA:

FISCAL YEAR	TOT. REVS. ($mill.)	NET INC. ($mill.)	TOT. ASSETS ($mill.)	OPER. PROFIT %	NET PROFIT %	NET INCJ NET PROP. %	NET INCJ TOT. CAP. %	RET. ON EQUITY %	ACCUM. DEPRJ GROSS PROP. %	EARN. PER SH.$	TANG. BK. VAL.$	DIV. PER SH.$	DIV. PAYOUT %	PRICE RANGE	AVG. P/E RATIO	AVG. YIELD %
p12/31/02	695.5	③ 38.6								③ 2.53		2.16	85.4	52.39 - 39.90	18.2	4.7
12/31/01	728.4	② 50.8	1,188.6	6.5	7.0	9.0	6.4	9.2	38.7	② 3.11	25.47	2.16	69.5	45.88 - 38.30	13.5	5.1
12/31/00	749.9	51.6	1,531.0	10.5	6.8	5.5	4.8	9.5	43.2	3.05	25.20	2.16	70.8	46.31 - 26.13	11.7	10.8
12/31/99	521.9	① 48.6	1,335.9	13.5	9.3	5.3	4.5	9.0	42.4	① 2.88	28.73	2.16	75.0	45.00 - 30.56	14.6	6.0
12/31/98	503.5	52.5	1,316.0	14.2	10.4	5.7	4.8	9.9	40.5	2.90	28.00	2.15	74.1	47.06 - 38.88	13.1	5.7
12/31/97	520.3	51.9	1,252.1	13.5	10.0	5.6	4.7	9.7	38.9	2.97	27.60	2.13	71.7	43.56 - 29.75	14.8	5.0
12/31/96	514.0	51.4	1,249.1	14.8	10.0	5.5	4.7	9.7	37.0	2.99	26.87	2.11	70.6	31.50 - 28.75	12.3	5.8
12/31/95	512.2	52.7	1,250.1	13.8	10.3	5.6	4.8	10.3	35.6	2.74	25.96	2.09	76.3	31.88 - 25.38	10.1	7.0
12/31/94	515.7	45.8	1,309.4	14.2	8.9	4.9	4.0	8.8	34.3	2.68	25.34	2.07	77.2	30.38 - 22.88	10.4	7.3
12/31/93	517.4	50.4	1,328.2	14.4	9.7	5.5	4.5	10.1	32.9	2.68	24.65	2.03	75.7	35.75 - 28.38	9.9	7.8

Statistics are as originally reported. ① Incl. $432,000 non-recur. chg. fr. favorable ins. settlement & $455,000 non-recur. chg. ② Incl. $429,000 chg. for allow. for equity funds used during constr. ③ Excl. $4.8 mill. gain fr. disc. ops.

OFFICERS:
P. J. Ganci, Chmn., C.E.O.
S. V. Lant, C.F.O., C.O.O.
C. M. Capone, Treas.
INVESTOR CONTACT: Denise D. VanBuren, Inv. Rel., (845) 471-8323
PRINCIPAL OFFICE: 284 South Avenue, Poughkeepsie, NY 12601-4879

TELEPHONE NUMBER: (845) 452-2000
FAX: (845) 486-5782
WEB: www.chenergygroup.com
NO. OF EMPLOYEES: 902
SHAREHOLDERS: 18,577
ANNUAL MEETING: In Apr.
INCORPORATED: NY, Dec., 1926

INSTITUTIONAL HOLDINGS:
No. of Institutions: 125
Shares Held: 6,995,515
% Held: 43.2
INDUSTRY: Electric and other services combined (SIC: 4931)
TRANSFER AGENT(S): First Chicago Trust Company of New York, New York, NY

CHARTER ONE FINANCIAL, INC.

EXCH.	SYM.	REC. PRICE	P/E RATIO	YLD.	MKT. CAP.	RANGE (52-WK.)	'02 Y/E PR.	DIV. ACH.
NYSE	CF	28.91 (2/28/03)	11.9	3.0%	$6.50 bill.	34.77 - 23.89	28.73	14 yrs.

UPPER MEDIUM GRADE. EARNINGS PER SHARE ARE EXPECTED TO RANGE FROM $2.66 TO $2.72 IN 2003.

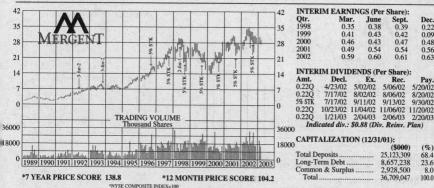

INTERIM EARNINGS (Per Share):

Qtr.	Mar.	June	Sept.	Dec.
1998	0.35	0.38	0.39	0.22
1999	0.41	0.43	0.42	0.09
2000	0.46	0.43	0.47	0.48
2001	0.49	0.54	0.54	0.56
2002	0.59	0.60	0.61	0.63

INTERIM DIVIDENDS (Per Share):

Amt.	Decl.	Ex.	Rec.	Pay.
0.22Q	4/23/02	5/02/02	5/06/02	5/20/02
0.22Q	7/17/02	8/02/02	8/06/02	8/20/02
5% STK	7/17/02	9/11/02	9/13/02	9/30/02
0.22Q	10/23/02	11/04/02	11/06/02	11/20/02
0.22Q	1/21/03	2/04/03	2/06/03	2/20/03

Indicated div.: $0.88 (Div. Reinv. Plan)

CAPITALIZATION (12/31/01):

	($000)	(%)
Total Deposits	25,123,309	68.4
Long-Term Debt	8,657,238	23.6
Common & Surplus	2,928,500	8.0
Total	36,709,047	100.0

*7 YEAR PRICE SCORE 138.8   ***12 MONTH PRICE SCORE 104.2**

*NYSE COMPOSITE INDEX=100

BUSINESS:

Charter One Financial, Inc. is a bank holding company whose principal line of business is consumer banking, which includes retail banking, mortgage banking and other related financial services. As of 12/31/02, CF, with $41.90 billion in total assets, had 461 branch locations in Ohio, Michigan, Illinois, New York, Massachusetts and Vermont, and operated 913 automated teller machines at various banking offices. As of 12/31/02, Charter One Mortgage Corp., CF's mortgage banking subsidiary, operated 26 loan production offices nationwide. On 10/1/99, CF acquired St. Paul Bancorp, Inc. On 11/5/99, CF acquired fourteen Vermont National Bank offices from Chittenden Corporation. On 7/2/01, CF acquired Alliance Bancorp.

RECENT DEVELOPMENTS:

For the year ended 12/31/02, net income increased 15.4% to $577.7 million from $500.7 million the year before. Earnings for 2002 and 2001 included pre-tax non-recurring net gains of $205.0 million and $114.3 million, respectively. Net interest income improved 18.1% to $1.17 billion from $990.4 million the year before. Provision for loan and lease losses increased 90.5% to $192.0 million from $100.8 million in 2001. Total other income rose 15.6% to $547.5 million, while total administrative expenses increased 7.8% to $679.0 million.

PROSPECTS:

On 1/16/03, the Company announced that it has signed a definitive agreement to acquire Cook County, Illinois-based Advance Bancorp in a stock-for-stock transaction valued at $72.0 million. Advance has approximately $632.0 million in assets, $491.0 million in deposits, and operates 14 branch offices. Going forward, earnings per share are expected to range from $2.66 to $2.72 in 2003, reflecting the Company's balance sheet strength and flexibility combined with the operating momentum of CF's retail banking operation. During the fourth quarter, the Company opened 138,000 new checking accounts, increasing the average banking center to 1,300 accounts in 2002, up from 1,000 in 2001. During 2002, the number of active accounts grew by 5.0% to 1.3 million.

ANNUAL FINANCIAL DATA:

FISCAL YEAR	NET INT. INC. ($mill.)	NON-INT. INC. ($mill.)	NET INC. ($mill.)	TOT. LOANS ($mill.)	TOT. ASSETS ($mill.)	TOT. DEP. ($mill.)	RET. ON EQUITY %	RET. ON ASSETS %	EQUITY/ ASSETS %	EARN. PER SH.$	TANG. BK. VAL.$	DIV. PER SH.$	PRICE RANGE	AVG. P/E RATIO
p12/31/02	1,169.8	547.5	④ 577.7							② 2.45		0.83	34.77 - 23.89	12.0
12/31/01	990.4	473.6	④ 500.7	25,842.1	38,174.5	25,123.3	17.1	1.3	7.7	④ 2.11	10.94	0.72	31.41 - 22.29	12.8
12/31/00	903.0	392.9	③ 434.0	24,297.4	32,971.4	19,605.7	17.7	1.3	7.4	1.81	9.95	0.61	28.57 - 13.83	11.7
12/31/99	934.1	230.6	① ② 335.5	22,545.8	31,819.1	19,074.0	14.0	1.1	7.5	① ② 1.32	9.12	0.52	27.75 - 15.87	16.5
12/31/98	729.1	211.6	① ② 277.0	17,688.0	24,467.3	15,165.1	14.8	1.1	7.7	① ② 1.33	8.54	0.43	30.13 - 15.23	17.0
12/31/97	527.0	110.8	① ② 151.1	12,360.1	19,760.3	10,219.2	11.0	0.8	7.0	② 0.91	7.76	0.37	26.33 - 16.11	23.2
12/31/96	383.4	57.1	127.7	8,295.0	13,904.6	7,841.2	13.8	0.9	6.7	1.05	7.29	0.32	17.53 - 10.54	13.4
12/31/95	317.8	d47.8	① 34.0	6,842.9	13,578.9	7,012.5	4.0	0.3	6.2	① 0.28	6.91	0.27	12.45 - 7.04	35.1
12/31/94	178.1	28.1	② 67.6	3,635.6	6,130.2	4,368.2	18.3	1.1	6.0	② 1.09	. . .	0.21	8.96 - 6.62	7.2
12/31/93	170.3	26.2	61.4	3,297.0	5,215.4	4,179.4	16.6	1.2	7.1	1.00	6.12	0.15	9.33 - 6.34	7.9

Statistics are as originally reported. Adj. for stk. splits: 5% stk. div., 9/02; 9/01, 9/00, 9/99; 9/98; 2-for-1, 5/98; 5% stk. div., 10/97; 5% stk. div., 9/96; 3-for-2, 11/93. ① Incl. non-recurr. chrg. $37.5 mill., 1995; $60.6 mill., 1997; $55.7 mill., 1998; $63.5 mill., 1999. ② Bef. extraord. credit $7.0 mill., 1994; chrg. $2.7 mill., 1997; chrg. $61.7 mill., 1998; chrg. $1.6 mill., 1999. ③ Incl. pre-tax merger expenses of $29.5 mill. & non-recurr. net gains of $9.3 mill. ④ Incl. pre-tax nonrecurr. net gains of $205.0 mill., 2002; $114.3 mill., 2001.

OFFICERS:
C. J. Koch, Chmn., Pres., C.E.O.
H. G. Chorbajian, Vice-Chmn.
J. L. Schostak, Vice-Chmn.
R. W. Neu, Exec. V.P., C.F.O.

INVESTOR CONTACT: Ellen L. Batkie, Senior V.P., (800) 262-6301

PRINCIPAL OFFICE: 1215 Superior Avenue, Cleveland, OH 44114

TELEPHONE NUMBER: (216) 566-5300
FAX: (216) 566-1465
WEB: www.charterone.com

NO. OF EMPLOYEES: 6,997

SHAREHOLDERS: 20,000 (approx.)

ANNUAL MEETING: In April

INCORPORATED: DE, 1987

INDUSTRY: Federal savings institutions (SIC: 6035)

TRANSFER AGENT(S): EquiServe, Providence, RI

CHESAPEAKE CORPORATION

EXCH.	SYM.	REC. PRICE	P/E RATIO	YLD.	MKT. CAP.	RANGE (52-WK.)	'02 Y/E PR.
NYSE	CSK	15.19 (2/28/03)	11.3	5.8%	$230.9 mill.	29.30 - 12.62	17.85

MEDIUM GRADE. THE COMPANY EXPECTS FULL-YEAR 2003 EARNINGS PER SHARE TO BE IN THE RANGE OF $1.15 TO $1.45.

*7 YEAR PRICE SCORE 78.1 ***12 MONTH PRICE SCORE 83.6**
*NYSE COMPOSITE INDEX=100

TRADING VOLUME
Thousand Shares

INTERIM EARNINGS (Per Share):

Qtr.	Mar.	June	Sept.	Dec.
1997	d0.15	1.57	0.41	0.34
1998	0.37	0.49	0.60	0.10
1999	0.39	0.39	3.16	9.50
2000	0.14	0.11	d0.11	0.15
2001	0.02	0.17	0.13	0.37
2002	d0.02	0.02	0.60	0.75

INTERIM DIVIDENDS (Per Share):

Amt.	Decl.	Ex.	Rec.	Pay.
0.22Q	2/20/02	4/10/02	4/12/02	5/15/02
0.22Q	4/24/02	7/10/02	7/12/02	8/15/02
0.22Q	10/08/02	10/23/02	10/25/02	11/15/02
0.22Q	12/09/02	1/08/03	1/10/03	2/14/03
0.22Q	2/19/03	4/09/03	4/11/03	5/15/03

Indicated div.: $0.88 (Div. Reinv. Plan)

CAPITALIZATION (12/30/01):

	($000)	(%)
Long-Term Debt	488,300	51.2
Deferred Income Tax	34,300	3.6
Common & Surplus	431,000	45.2
Total	953,600	100.0

BUSINESS:

Chesapeake Corporation is a supplier of value-added specialty paperboard and plastic packaging, including folding cartons, leaflets and labels, as well as plastic containers, bottles, preforms and closures. CSK's primary end-use markets are pharmaceuticals and healthcare, premium branded products, multimedia and technology, agrochemicals, beverages and food and household. Chesapeake also has a land development business segment that holds approximately 20,000 acres of real estate in Virginia. This land is slated to be sold over the next few years. As of 1/28/03, the Company had 50 locations in Europe, North America, Africa and Asia. Contributions to revenues in 2002 were paperboard packaging, 82.5%; plastic packaging, 12.6% and land development, 4.9%.

RECENT DEVELOPMENTS:

For the year ended 12/29/02, income surged 95.2% to $20.5 million compared with income of $10.5 million in 2001. Results for 2002 and 2001 included after-tax restructuring charges of $1.8 million and $9.3 million, respectively. Results for 2001 included goodwill amortization of $14.4 million. Net sales increased 4.0% to $822.2 million. The improvement in sales reflected strengthening of major European currencies relative to the U.S. dollar, increased land sales and higher sales volumes in the premium branded market sector and the African plastics beverage market sector.

PROSPECTS:

Looking ahead, the Company expects full-year 2003 earnings per share in the range of $1.15 to $1.45. Meanwhile, CSK substantially completed the consolidation of two Scottish facilities, broke ground on two plants in Germany, and opened new facilities in China and Mauritius during 2002. As a result, the Company expects to realize improved operational efficiencies due to the plant consolidations and other process improvements that it has completed. In addition, on 2/10/03, the Company announced that it completed a plant expansion in Oss, Netherlands, which nearly doubles the size of the plant and increases production capacity by 35.0%.

ANNUAL FINANCIAL DATA:

FISCAL YEAR	TOT. REVS. ($mill.)	NET INC. ($mill.)	TOT. ASSETS ($mill.)	OPER. PROFIT %	NET PROFIT %	RET. ON EQUITY %	RET. ON ASSETS %	CURR. RATIO	EARN. PER SH. $	CASH FL. PER SH. $	TANG. BK. VAL. $	DIV. PER SH. $	PRICE RANGE	AVG. P/E RATIO	AVG. YIELD %
p12/29/02	822.2	② 20.5							⑦ 1.35			0.88	30.80 - 12.62	16.1	4.0
12/30/01	790.5	⑥ 10.5	1,247.4	4.6	1.3	2.4	0.8	1.2	⑦ 0.69	5.39	…	0.88	29.91 - 19.63	35.9	3.6
12/31/00	654.7	⑤ 11.2	1,540.9	10.0	1.7	53.3	0.7	1.1	⑤ 0.70	5.30	23.10	0.88	35.75 - 16.75	37.5	3.4
12/31/99	1,162.0	⑤ 250.8	1,373.2	3.4	21.6	45.5	18.3	1.9	⑥ 12.29	16.27	14.59	0.88	38.63 - 25.75	2.6	2.7
12/31/98	950.4	④ 34.0	979.4	7.0	3.6	7.7	3.5	2.0	④ 1.57	4.46	18.27	0.80	41.75 - 31.75	23.4	2.2
12/31/97	1,021.0	② 50.9	913.0	1.9	5.0	12.1	5.6	2.3	② 2.18	5.42	19.81	0.80	36.75 - 27.13	14.6	2.5
12/31/96	1,158.6	30.1	1,290.2	6.4	2.6	6.4	2.3	2.0	1.27	5.09	20.05	0.80	31.75 - 23.13	21.6	2.9
12/31/95	1,233.7	② 93.4	1,146.3	13.1	7.6	19.9	8.1	2.0	② 3.88	7.04	19.68	0.76	39.00 - 27.50	8.6	2.3
12/31/94	990.5	② 37.6	1,013.1	8.2	3.8	9.6	3.7	2.1	② 1.58	4.66	16.53	0.72	35.88 - 22.25	18.4	2.5
12/31/93	885.0	② 10.4	919.3	5.0	1.2	2.8	1.1	1.9	① 0.44	3.53	15.66	0.72	25.75 - 17.13	48.7	3.4

Statistics are as originally reported. ① Incl. net gain of $3.6 mil. fr. disposal of assets. ② Incl. chrg. of $6.2 mill., 1995; $700,000, 1994. ③ Incl. $49.1 mill. gain & $10.8 mill. restruct. chrg.; excl. $2.3 mill. extraord. loss. ④ Bef. acctg. gain of $13.3 mill., but incl. non-recurr. chrgs. of $8.8 mill. ⑤ Incl. after-tax nonrecurr. gain of $242.0 mill. on sale of tissue, building products and timberlands bus. ⑥ Incl. after-tax nonrecurr. chrg. of $4.7 mill., but excl. an after-tax extraord. loss of $1.5 mill. and an after-tax loss of $33.8 million from disc. opers. ⑦ Bef. discont. oper. gain of $1.4 mill., 2002; $112.4 mill., 2001; but incl. restruct. chrg. of $2.6 mill., 2002; $14.6 mill., 2001.

OFFICERS:
T. H. Johnson, Chmn., Pres., C.E.O.
K. Gilchrist, Exec. V.P., C.O.O.
A. J. Kohut, Exec. V.P., C.F.O.
INVESTOR CONTACT: Joel Mostrom, Inv. Rel., (804) 697-1147
PRINCIPAL OFFICE: 1021 East Cary Street, James Center II, Richmond, VA 23219

TELEPHONE NUMBER: (804) 697-1000
FAX: (804) 697-1199
WEB: www.cskcorp.com
NO. OF EMPLOYEES: 5,900 (avg.)
SHAREHOLDERS: 5,036
ANNUAL MEETING: In Apr.
INCORPORATED: VA, Oct., 1918

INSTITUTIONAL HOLDINGS:
No. of Institutions: 99
Shares Held: 9,668,417
% Held: 63.8

INDUSTRY: Paper mills (SIC: 2621)

TRANSFER AGENT(S): Computershare Investor Services LLC, Chicago, IL

CHEVRONTEXACO CORP.

EXCH.	SYM.	REC. PRICE	P/E RATIO	YLD.	MKT. CAP.	RANGE (52-WK.)	'02 Y/E PR.	DIV. ACH.
NYSE	CVX	64.17 (2/28/03)	60.0	4.4%	$68.48 bill.	91.60 - 61.31	66.48	15 yrs.

INVESTMENT GRADE. THE COMPANY ANNOUNCED AN $8.50 BILLION CAPITAL AND EXPLORATORY SPENDING PROGRAM FOR 2003.

MERGENT

*7 YEAR PRICE SCORE 101.0   *12 MONTH PRICE SCORE 93.8

*NYSE COMPOSITE INDEX=100

TRADING VOLUME
Thousand Shares

INTERIM EARNINGS (Per Share):

Qtr.	Mar.	June	Sept.	Dec.
1998	0.76	0.88	0.70	0.66
1999	0.50	0.53	0.88	1.23
2000	1.59	1.71	2.35	2.32
2001	2.29	1.99	1.66	d2.24
2002	0.68	0.39	d0.85	0.85

INTERIM DIVIDENDS (Per Share):

Amt.	Decl.	Ex.	Rec.	Pay.
0.70Q	4/24/02	5/15/02	5/17/02	6/10/02
0.70Q	7/31/02	8/15/02	8/19/02	9/10/02
0.70Q	10/30/02	11/14/02	11/18/02	12/10/02
0.70Q	1/29/03	2/12/03	2/14/03	3/10/03

Indicated div.: $2.80 (Div. Reinv. Plan)

CAPITALIZATION (12/31/01):

	($000)	(%)
Long-Term Debt	8,704,000	17.6
Capital Lease Obligations..	285,000	0.6
Deferred Income Tax	6,132,000	12.4
Minority Interest	283,000	0.6
Common & Surplus	33,958,000	68.8
Total	49,362,000	100.0

BUSINESS:

ChevronTexaco Corp. (formerly Chevron Corp.) is a global energy company engaged in the exploration and production, refining, marketing and transportation of crude oil, natural gas and natural gas liquids. CVX is also engaged in chemicals manufacturing and sales, and holds investments in power generation and gasification businesses. Formed as a result of the acquisition by Chevron Corporation of Texaco Inc. on 10/9/01, CVX operates in the U.S. and about 180 other countries. As of 12/31/02, oil and gas reserves totaled about 11.80 billion barrels of oil and gas equivalent. In addition, CVX operated 22 refineries and more than 21,000 branded service stations worldwide.

RECENT DEVELOPMENTS:

For the year ended 12/31/02, net income was $1.13 billion compared with income of $3.93 billion, before an extraordinary loss of $643.0 million, the previous year. Results for 2002 and 2001 included special charges of $2.95 billion and $1.74 billion, and merger-related charges of $386.0 million and $1.78 billion, respectively. Total revenue and other income decreased 6.8% to $99.05 billion from $106.25 billion the year before. Overall results were negatively affected by lower average prices for natural gas and refined products, lower refined products sales and lower oil-equivalent production.

PROSPECTS:

On 1/29/03, CVX announced an $8.50 billion capital and exploratory spending program for 2003 including $1.60 billion in affiliates' expenditures. Approximately 75.0% of total capital spending, or $6.40 billion, will be invested in worldwide exploration and production. About $1.30 billion, or 15.0% of total spending, will be invested in global downstream. Refining and marketing investments will total about $400.0 million in the U.S., and $700.0 million internationally. Transportation investments, including pipelines to support expanded upstream production, will total about $200.0 million. Investments in power and related businesses will total about $300.0 million, about 50.0% less than what was invested in 2002. Investments in chemicals will total about $300.0 million.

ANNUAL FINANCIAL DATA:

FISCAL YEAR	TOT. REVS. ($mill.)	NET INC. ($mill.)	TOT. ASSETS ($mill.)	OPER. PROFIT %	NET PROFIT %	RET. ON EQUITY %	RET. ON ASSETS %	CURR. RATIO	EARN. PER SH.$	CASH FL. PER SH.$	TANG. BK. VAL.$	DIV. PER SH.$	PRICE RANGE	AVG. P/E RATIO	AVG. YIELD %
p12/31/02	99,049.0	ⓐ 1,132.0							⑥ 1.07			2.80	91.60 - 65.41	73.4	3.6
④ 12/31/01	106,245.0	⑤ 3,931.0	77,572.0	8.7	3.7	11.6	5.1	0.9	⑤ 3.70	10.34	31.82	2.65	98.49 - 78.44	23.9	3.0
12/31/00	52,129.0	⑤ 5,185.0	41,264.0	18.7	10.1	26.0	12.6	1.1	⑤ 7.97	12.34	31.08	2.60	94.88 - 69.94	10.3	3.2
12/31/99	36,586.0	② 2,070.0	40,668.0	11.3	5.7	11.7	5.1	0.9	② 3.14	7.48	27.04	2.48	104.44 - 73.13	28.3	2.8
12/31/98	30,557.0	1,339.0	36,540.0	7.3	4.4	7.9	3.7	0.9	2.04	5.57	25.81	2.44	90.19 - 67.75	38.7	3.1
12/31/97	41,950.0	3,256.0	35,473.0	13.9	7.8	18.6	9.2	1.0	4.95	8.44	26.64	2.28	89.19 - 61.75	15.2	3.0
12/31/96	43,893.0	2,607.0	34,854.0	11.6	5.9	16.7	7.5	0.9	① 3.99	7.39	23.82	2.08	68.38 - 51.00	15.0	3.5
12/31/95	37,082.0	① 930.0	34,330.0	5.9	2.5	6.5	2.7	0.8	① 1.43	6.61	22.02	1.93	53.63 - 43.38	33.9	4.0
12/31/94	35,854.0	1,693.0	34,407.0	8.8	4.7	11.6	4.9	0.8	2.60	6.33	22.39	1.85	47.31 - 39.88	16.8	4.2
12/31/93	37,082.0	① 1,265.0	34,736.0	7.4	3.4	9.0	3.6	0.8	① 1.95	5.72	21.47	1.75	49.38 - 33.69	21.4	4.2

Statistics are as originally reported. Adj. for 2-for-1 stk. split 5/94. The financial data for 12/31/00 and prior years reflects the former operations of Chevron Corporation only. ① Incl. nonrecur. chrg. 12/31/96: $44.0 mill.; chrgs. totaling 12/31/95: $1.03 bill.; chrg. 12/31/93: $552.0 mill. ② Incl. spec. chrgs. of $216.0 mill. ③ Incl. spec. chrgs. of $252.0 mill. ④ Refl. acq. of Texaco Inc. ⑤ Incl. spec. chrgs. of $1.74 bill. & merger-rel. chrgs. of $1.78 bill.; bef. extraord. loss of $643.0 mill. ⑥ Incl. spec. chrgs. of $2.95 bill. & merger-rel. chrgs. of $386.0 mill.

OFFICERS:
D. J. O'Reilly, Chmn., C.E.O.
P. J. Robertson, Vice-Chmn., V.P.
J. Watson, V.P., C.F.O.

INVESTOR CONTACT: Pierre Breber, Mgr., Inv. Rel., (925) 842-3523

PRINCIPAL OFFICE: 6001 Bollinger Canyon Rd., San Ramon, CA 94583

TELEPHONE NUMBER: (925) 842-1000
WEB: www.chevrontexaco.com

NO. OF EMPLOYEES: 55,763 (avg.)

SHAREHOLDERS: 250,000 (approx.)

ANNUAL MEETING: In May

INCORPORATED: DE, Jan., 1926

INSTITUTIONAL HOLDINGS:
No. of Institutions: 1,076
Shares Held: 619,463,231
% Held: 58.0

INDUSTRY: Petroleum refining (SIC: 2911)

TRANSFER AGENT(S): Mellon Investor Services, Ridgefield Park, NJ

CHITTENDEN CORPORATION

EXCH.	SYM.	REC. PRICE	P/E RATIO	YLD.	MKT. CAP.	RANGE (52-WK.)	'02 Y/E PR.	DIV. ACH.
NYSE	CHZ	26.14 (3/31/03)	13.3	3.1%	$0.93 bill.	34.18 - 23.18	25.48	10 yrs.

MEDIUM GRADE. THE COMPANY SIGNED A DEFINITIVE AGREEMENT TO ACQUIRE GRANITE STATE BANC-SHARES, INC.

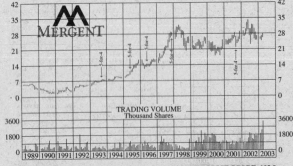

*7 YEAR PRICE SCORE 127.0   *12 MONTH PRICE SCORE 102.9
*NYSE COMPOSITE INDEX=100

INTERIM EARNINGS (Per Share):

Qtr.	Mar.	June	Sept.	Dec.
1998	0.40	0.42	0.42	0.43
1999	0.34	d1.26	0.44	0.39
2000	0.41	0.42	0.44	0.45
2001	0.44	0.44	0.46	0.46
2002	0.46	0.47	0.48	0.55

INTERIM DIVIDENDS (Per Share):

Amt.	Decl.	Ex.	Rec.	Pay.
0.19Q	1/16/02	1/30/02	2/01/02	2/15/02
0.20Q	4/17/02	5/01/02	5/03/02	5/17/02
0.20Q	7/17/02	7/31/02	8/02/02	8/16/02
0.20Q	10/16/02	10/30/02	11/01/02	11/15/02
0.20Q	1/15/03	1/29/03	1/31/03	2/14/03
Indicated div.: $0.80				

CAPITALIZATION (12/31/01):

	($000)	(%)
Long-Term Debt	44,409	10.7
Common & Surplus	370,654	89.3
Total	415,063	100.0

BUSINESS:

Chittenden Corporation is a bank holding company with total assets of $4.87 billion at December 31, 2002. The Company's subsidiary banks are Chittenden Bank, The Bank of Western Massachusetts, Flagship Bank and Trust Company, Maine Bank & Trust Company and Ocean National Bank. Chittenden Bank also operates under the name Mortgage Service Center, and it owns Chittenden Insurance Group and Chittenden Securities, Inc. The Company offers a broad range of financial products and services, including deposit accounts and services; consumer, commercial, and public sector loans; insurance; brokerage; and investment and trust services to individuals, businesses, and the public sector.

RECENT DEVELOPMENTS:

For the year ended 12/31/02, net income grew 8.8% to $63.6 million compared with $58.5 million in 2001. Net interest income rose 13.1% to $192.6 million versus $170.3 million in 2001. Provision for loan losses increased 3.6% to $8.3 million from $8.0 million the year before. Total noninterest income advanced 2.1% to $65.1 million. Total noninterest expense grew 11.6% to $151.5 million. Total loans rose 4.8% to $2.97 billion versus $2.84 billion in 2001 due to the acquisition of Ocean National Bank, completed 2/28/02. Total deposits increased 12.4% to $4.13 billion from $3.67 billion the year before.

PROSPECTS:

The Company continues to grow through acquisitions. On 11/7/02, the Company announced that it signed a definitive merger agreement whereby CHZ will acquire Granite State Bancshares, Inc. and its subsidiary, Granite Bank, in a transaction valued at about $247.0 million. The transaction is subject to the approval of Granite State shareholders and various bank regulatory agencies. The transaction is expected to close in the second quarter of 2003. Under the terms of the agreement, Granite State shareholders can elect to receive $46.00 per share in cash or 1.64 shares of CHZ common stock for each share of Granite stock they own, plus cash in lieu of any fractional share interest or 50.0% of the consideration in CHZ common stock and 50.0% in cash.

ANNUAL FINANCIAL DATA:

FISCAL YEAR	NET INVST. INC. ($mill.)	TOT. REVS. ($mill.)	NET INC. ($mill.)	TOT. ASSETS ($mill.)	TOT. INVST. ($mill.)	RET. ON REVS. %	RET. ON EQUITY %	RET. ON ASSETS %	EARN. PER SH. $	TANG. BK. VAL. $	AVG. YIELD %	DIV. PER SH. $	PRICE RANGE	AVG. P/E RATIO
p12/31/02	259.0		63.6						1.96		2.7	0.79	34.18 – 23.18	14.6
12/31/01	266.5	330.2	58.5	4,153.7	3,630.8	17.7	15.8	1.4	1.80	9.44	3.0	0.77	28.99 – 21.75	14.1
12/31/00	288.1	342.9	① 58.7	3,769.9	3,362.7	17.1	17.2	1.6	① 1.72	9.13	3.5	0.75	25.25 – 18.05	12.6
12/31/99	288.2	352.4	① d2.5	3,827.3	3,430.5	...	...	...	① d0.07	9.69	2.9	0.69	26.90 – 20.80	...
12/31/98	151.5	183.9	30.7	2,122.0	1,829.0	16.7	17.5	1.4	1.67	9.18	2.4	0.62	32.00 – 20.35	15.7
12/31/97	150.2	178.4	29.4	1,977.2	1,712.6	16.5	18.1	1.5	1.55	8.23	4.7	④ 1.03	28.80 – 14.80	14.0
12/31/96	142.6	167.5	26.7	1,988.7	1,631.7	16.0	15.3	1.3	1.37	8.56	3.2	0.46	16.80 – 12.29	10.6
12/31/95	115.2	145.2	② 20.9	1,521.1	1,280.7	14.4	15.3	1.4	② 1.30	7.74	2.3	0.28	16.38 – 8.40	9.6
12/31/94	84.9	108.5	② 15.5	1,213.9	1,073.9	14.3	15.8	1.3	② 1.01	6.81	2.4	0.19	9.01 – 6.96	7.9
12/31/93	79.8	104.1	②③ 11.6	1,231.0	1,016.3	11.1	11.9	0.9	②③ 0.77	6.44	1.3	0.08	7.78 – 4.83	8.2

Statistics are as originally reported. ① Incl. special chrgs. of $833,000, 2000; $58.5 mill., 1999. ② Incl. losses on & writedowns of other real estate owned 1995, income $236,000; 1994, income $67,000; 1993, loss $1.5.mill. ③ Excl. acct. change chrg. of $575,000. ④ Incl. special div. of $0.75 payable on 11/14/97.

OFFICERS:
P. A. Perrault, Chmn., Pres., C.E.O.
K. W. Walters, Exec. V.P., C.F.O., Treas.
F. S. Prentice, Sr. V.P., Gen. Couns., Sec.
INVESTOR CONTACT: F. Sheldon Prentice, Sec., (802) 660-1412
PRINCIPAL OFFICE: Two Burlington Square, P.O. Box 820, Burlington, VT 05401

TELEPHONE NUMBER: (802) 658-4000
FAX: (802) 660-1591
WEB: www.chittenden.com
NO. OF EMPLOYEES: 1,842 (avg.)
SHAREHOLDERS: 4,796
ANNUAL MEETING: In Apr.
INCORPORATED: VT, 1971

INSTITUTIONAL HOLDINGS:
No. of Institutions: 116
Shares Held: 17,063,245
% Held: 53.4
INDUSTRY: State commercial banks (SIC: 6022)
TRANSFER AGENT(S): BankBoston, N.A., Boston, MA

CHOICEPOINT, INC.

EXCH.	SYM.	REC. PRICE	P/E RATIO	YLD.	MKT. CAP.	RANGE (52-WK.)	'02 Y/E PR.
NYSE	CPS	33.75 (2/28/03)	26.4	. . .	$2.82 bill.	48.15 - 29.75	39.49

UPPER MEDIUM GRADE. THE COMPANY EXPECTS NEW BUSINESS INITIATIVES TO DRIVE LONG-TERM REVENUE GROWTH.

*7 YEAR PRICE SCORE N/A   ***12 MONTH PRICE SCORE 99.1**

*NYSE COMPOSITE INDEX=100

INTERIM EARNINGS (Per Share):

Qtr.	Mar.	June	Sept.	Dec.
1998	0.13	0.14	0.14	0.19
1999	0.15	0.16	0.17	0.18
2000	0.18	d0.08	0.21	0.23
2001	0.08	0.23	Nil	0.26
2002	0.31	0.27	0.35	0.35

INTERIM DIVIDENDS (Per Share):

Amt.	Decl.	Ex.	Rec.	Pay.
3-for-2	1/31/01	3/08/01	2/16/01	3/07/01
33% STK	4/25/02	6/07/02	5/16/02	6/06/02

CAPITALIZATION (12/31/01):

	($000)	(%)
Long-Term Debt	2,390	0.5
Common & Surplus	484,821	99.5
Total	487,211	100.0

BUSINESS:

Choicepoint, Inc. is a provider of risk management and fraud prevention information and technology. CPS was spun off from Equifax Inc. to its shareholders on 8/8/97. CPS operates in three primary service groups: Insurance services (44.2% of revenues in 2001), Business & Government services (41.0%), and Marketing services (14.1%). Insurance services include underwriting and claims information, such as motor vehicle reports, CPS' Comprehensive Loss Underwriting Exchange database services, vehi-

cle registration services, credit reports, modeling services, ChoicePointLink™, and driver's license information. Business and Government services include risk management and fraud prevention services and related technology and shareholder locator services to corporations, asset-based lenders, legal and professional service providers, individuals and local, state and federal government agencies. Marketing services include customer relationship management, direct marketing support and telephone services.

RECENT DEVELOPMENTS:

For the year ended 12/31/02, CPS reported income of $114.2 million, before an accounting change charge of $24.4 million, versus net income of $50.3 million in 2001. Results for 2002 and 2001 included merger-related costs of $7.4 million and $18.0 million, respectively. Results for 2001 also included a loss on the sale of a business of $10.9

million. Total revenue advanced 14.1% to $791.6 million from $694.0 million a year earlier. Insurance services revenue climbed 18.3% to $332.5 million, while business and government services revenue rose 15.5% to $308.8 million. Marketing services revenue jumped 38.4% to $105.8 million, while royalty revenue fell 14.0% to $5.9 million.

PROSPECTS:

CPS believes that its internal growth rate for its base businesses in 2003 will be in the range of 10.0% to 11.0% with successes in new business initiatives driving the growth rate into the 12.0% to 15.0% range over the long term. Additionally, CPS continues to pursue acquisitions, which

should enhance revenue growth. CPS recently acquired National Data Retrieval, Inc., a provider of public records information for bankruptcies, civil judgements and tax liens. CPS also acquired The List Source, Inc., a direct marketing company.

ANNUAL FINANCIAL DATA:

FISCAL YEAR	TOT. REVS. ($000)	NET INC. ($000)	TOT. ASSETS ($000)	OPER. PROFIT %	NET PROFIT %	RET. ON EQUITY %	RET. ON ASSETS %	CURR. RATIO	EARN. PER SH. $	CASH FL. PER SH. $	TANG. BK. VAL. $	PRICE RANGE	AVG. P/E RATIO
p12/31/02	791,562	④ 114,243							④ 1.28			48.15 - 29.75	30.4
12/31/01	655,967	③ 50,334	832,392	18.2	7.7	10.4	6.0	0.7	③ 0.58	1.26	0.41	38.99 - 22.16	52.9
12/31/00	593,533	① 43,822	704,439	15.2	7.4	10.9	6.2	1.7	① 0.52	1.16	0.38	33.50 - 16.25	48.1
12/31/99	430,143	①② 39,389	532,872	18.2	9.2	19.4	7.4	1.8	①② 0.65	1.28	. . .	20.97 - 11.34	24.8
12/31/98	406,475	①② 35,419	534,199	15.1	8.7	22.2	6.6	1.1	①② 0.59	1.11	. . .	16.13 - 9.34	21.6
12/31/97	417,321	①② 28,944	359,971	11.0	6.9	22.7	8.0	1.9	①② 0.48	0.95	. . .	12.03 - 7.69	20.5
12/31/96	366,481	23,280	301,824	13.0	6.4	11.9	7.7	2.0	. . .	. . .	. . .	. . . - . . .	. . .
12/31/95	328,990	① 14,865	200,779	9.7	4.5	14.2	7.4	1.9	. . .	. . .	. . .	. . . - . . .	. . .

Statistics are as originally reported. Adj. for stk. splits: 2-for-1, 11/99; 3-for-2, 3/01; 4-for-3; 6/02. ① Incl. non-recurr. chrgs., $28.9 mill., 2000; $1.6 mill., 1999; $3.8 mill., 1998; $6.2 mill., 1997; $9.2 mill., 1995. ② Incl. net gain on sale of bus. $2.5 mill., 1999; $8.8 mill., 1998; $14.0 mill., 1997. ③ Incl. merger and oth. non-recurr. chrgs. of $18.0 mill. and a loss on the sale of a bus. of $10.9 mill. ④ Bef. acctg. change chrg. of $24.4 mill.; incl. merger-related costs of $7.4 mill.

OFFICERS:
D. V. Smith, Chmn., C.E.O.
D. C. Curling, Pres., C.O.O.
S. W. Surbaugh, C.F.O.
INVESTOR CONTACT: John Mongelli, V.P., Investor Relations, (770) 752-6171
PRINCIPAL OFFICE: 1000 Alderman Drive, Alpharetta, GA 30005

TELEPHONE NUMBER: (770) 752-6000
FAX: (770) 752-6250
WEB: www.choicepoint.net
NO. OF EMPLOYEES: 5,000 (approx.)
SHAREHOLDERS: 4,290 (approx.)
ANNUAL MEETING: In April
INCORPORATED: GA, 1997

INSTITUTIONAL HOLDINGS:
No. of Institutions: 274
Shares Held: 63,191,945
% Held: 73.6
INDUSTRY: Credit reporting services (SIC: 7323)
TRANSFER AGENT(S): SunTrust Bank, Atlanta, GA

CHUBB CORPORATION (THE)

EXCH.	SYM.	REC. PRICE	P/E RATIO	YLD.	MKT. CAP.	RANGE (52-WK.)	'02 Y/E PR.	DIV. ACH.
NYSE	CB	47.82 (2/28/03)	38.0	3.0%	$8.19 bill.	78.64 - 45.57	52.20	38 yrs.

INVESTMENT GRADE. THE COMPANY'S OUTLOOK FOR CONTINUED REVENUE AND EARNINGS GROWTH IS ENCOURAGING.

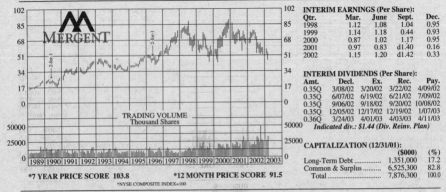

INTERIM EARNINGS (Per Share):

Qtr.	Mar.	June	Sept.	Dec.
1998	1.12	1.08	1.04	0.95
1999	1.14	1.18	0.44	0.93
2000	0.87	1.02	1.17	0.95
2001	0.97	0.83	d1.40	0.16
2002	1.15	1.20	d1.42	0.33

INTERIM DIVIDENDS (Per Share):

Amt.	Decl.	Ex.	Rec.	Pay.
0.35Q	3/08/02	3/20/02	3/22/02	4/09/02
0.35Q	6/07/02	6/19/02	6/21/02	7/09/02
0.35Q	9/06/02	9/18/02	9/20/02	10/08/02
0.35Q	12/05/02	12/17/02	12/19/02	1/07/03
0.36Q	3/24/03	4/01/03	4/03/03	4/11/03

Indicated div.: $1.44 (Div. Reinv. Plan)

CAPITALIZATION (12/31/01):

	($000)	(%)
Long-Term Debt	1,351,000	17.2
Common & Surplus	6,525,300	82.8
Total	7,876,300	100.0

*7 YEAR PRICE SCORE 103.8   ***12 MONTH PRICE SCORE 91.5**

*NYSE COMPOSITE INDEX=100

BUSINESS:

The Chubb Corporation is a holding company with subsidiaries principally engaged in the property and casualty insurance business. The property and casualty insurance subsidiaries provide insurance coverages principally in North America, Europe, Latin America, Asia and Australia. CB also has investments in high quality bonds, U.S. Treasury, government agency, mortgage-backed securities and corporate issues as well as equity securities. CB has a real estate group that is composed of Bellemead Development Corporation and its subsidiaries. The group's activities involve commercial development primarily in New Jersey and residential development activities primarily in central Florida. In 2002, the combined loss and expense ratio after policyholder's dividends was 106.7%.

RECENT DEVELOPMENTS:

For the year ended 12/31/02, net income nearly doubled to $222.9 million from $111.5 million in the prior year. Results for 2002 included a $741.1 million pre-tax charge in net loss reserves for asbestos claims, a $40.0 million tax valuation allowance relating to CB's European losses and an $88.0 million pre-tax benefit resulting from the settlement in the Mahonia/Enron surety bond lawsuit. Results for 2001 included pre-tax costs of $645.0 million related to the events of 9/11/01 and a pre-tax charge of $220.0 million relating to CB's Enron surety exposure. Net premiums written climbed 30.0% to $9.05 billion, while premiums earned advanced 21.5% to $8.09 billion.

PROSPECTS:

CB's outlook for continued revenue and earnings growth is encouraging, based on favorable market conditions for Chubb Commercial Insurance, continuing rate increases and an expected leveling off of claim activity for Chubb Specialty Insurance. Also, CB anticipates a gradually improving homeowners outlook for Chubb Personal Insurance, and improved cash generations that will result in higher investment income. For fiscal 2003, CB expects net premiums written to grow 20.0% to 25.0%, with full-year operating earnings ranging from $4.60 to $5.00 per share. Moreover, CB expects a combined ratio of between 96.0% and 99.0% for 2003. Separately, CB announced that it is reviewing strategic alternatives with respect to Chubb Financial Solutions, its non-insurance operations.

ANNUAL FINANCIAL DATA:

FISCAL YEAR	PREM. INC. ($mill.)	TOT. REVS. ($mill.)	NET INC. ($mill.)	TOT. ASSETS ($mill.)	TOT. INVST. ($mill.)	RET. ON REVS. %	RET. ON EQUITY %	RET. ON ASSETS %	EARN. PER SH. $	TANG. BK. VAL. $	AVG. YIELD %	DIV. PER SH. $	PRICE RANGE	AVG. P/E RATIO
p12/31/02	8,085.3		④ 222.9						④ 1.29		2.1	1.39	78.20 — 51.91	50.4
12/31/01	6,656.4	7,754.0	③ 111.5	29,449.0	19,234.2	1.4	1.7	0.4	③ 0.63	35.62	1.9	1.35	86.63 — 55.54	112.8
12/31/00	6,145.9	7,251.5	714.6	25,026.7	18,128.8	9.9	10.2	2.9	4.01	37.13	2.0	1.31	90.25 — 43.25	16.6
12/31/99	5,652.0	6,729.6	621.1	23,537.0	17,188.3	9.2	9.9	2.6	3.66	32.85	2.1	1.27	76.38 — 44.00	16.4
12/31/98	5,303.8	6,349.8	707.0	20,746.0	15,501.3	11.1	12.5	3.4	4.19	34.78	1.7	1.22	88.81 — 55.38	17.2
12/31/97	5,157.4	6,664.0	769.5	19,615.6	14,839.6	11.5	13.6	3.9	4.39	32.11	1.8	1.14	78.50 — 51.13	14.8
12/31/96	4,569.3	5,680.5	② 486.2	19,938.9	13,685.0	8.6	8.9	2.4	② 2.75	31.24	2.2	1.05	56.25 — 40.88	17.7
12/31/95	4,770.1	4,630.1	696.6	22,996.5	15,630.0	11.4	13.2	3.0	3.93	30.14	2.2	0.96	50.31 — 38.06	11.3
12/31/94	4,612.6	5,709.5	528.5	20,723.1	14,118.7	9.3	12.4	2.6	2.98	24.46	2.4	0.91	41.56 — 34.31	12.8
12/31/93	4,306.1	5,499.7	① 344.2	19,436.9	13,551.1	6.3	8.2	1.8	① 1.96	23.92	2.0	0.84	48.19 — 38.00	22.0

Statistics are as originally reported. Adj. for stk. split: 2-for-1, 5/96 ① Bef. acctg. change chrg. $20.0 mill. ② Bef. disc. oper. gain $26.5 mill. ③ Incl. after-tax chrg. of $143.0 mill. fr. 9/11/01 attacks & after-tax chrgs. of $143.0 mill. from Enron. ④ Incl. a pre-tax charg. of $700.0 mill. for asbestos claims, a pre-tax tax valuation allowance of $40.0 mill., & a pre-tax settlement gain of $88.0 mill.

OFFICERS:
J. Cohen, Chmn.
J. D. Finnegan, Pres., C.E.O.
W. M. Hicks, Sr. V.P., C.F.O.
INVESTOR CONTACT: Mary Jane Murphy, Asst. Sec., (908) 903-3579
PRINCIPAL OFFICE: 15 Mountain View Rd., P.O. Box 1615, Warren, NJ 07061-1615

TELEPHONE NUMBER: (908) 903-2000
FAX: (908) 903-2101
WEB: www.chubb.com
NO. OF EMPLOYEES: 12,600 (approx.)
SHAREHOLDERS: 6,300 (approx.)
ANNUAL MEETING: In April
INCORPORATED: NJ, June, 1967

INSTITUTIONAL HOLDINGS:
No. of Institutions: 464
Shares Held: 140,196,672
% Held: 82.0
INDUSTRY: Fire, marine, and casualty insurance (SIC: 6331)
TRANSFER AGENT(S): EquiServe Trust Company, N.A., Jersey City, NJ

CHURCH & DWIGHT COMPANY, INC.

EXCH.	SYM.	REC. PRICE	P/E RATIO	YLD.	MKT. CAP.	RANGE (52-WK.)	'02 Y/E PR.
NYSE	CHD	29.80 (2/28/03)	18.6	1.0%	$1.17 bill.	36.50 - 26.43	30.43

UPPER MEDIUM GRADE. THE COMPANY EXPECTS EARNINGS FOR 2003 TO RANGE BETWEEN $1.77 TO $1.81 PER SHARE.

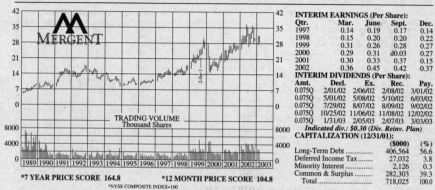

*7 YEAR PRICE SCORE 164.8   *12 MONTH PRICE SCORE 104.8
*NYSE COMPOSITE INDEX=100

INTERIM EARNINGS (Per Share):

Qtr.	Mar.	June	Sept.	Dec.
1997	0.14	0.19	0.17	0.14
1998	0.15	0.20	0.20	0.22
1999	0.31	0.26	0.28	0.27
2000	0.29	0.31	d0.03	0.27
2001	0.30	0.33	0.37	0.15
2002	0.36	0.45	0.42	0.37

INTERIM DIVIDENDS (Per Share):

Amt.	Decl.	Ex.	Rec.	Pay.
0.075Q	2/01/02	2/06/02	2/08/02	3/01/02
0.075Q	5/01/02	5/08/02	5/10/02	6/03/02
0.075Q	7/29/02	8/07/02	8/09/02	9/02/02
0.075Q	10/25/02	11/06/02	11/08/02	12/02/02
0.075Q	1/31/03	2/05/03	2/07/03	3/03/03

Indicated div.: $0.30 (Div. Reinv. Plan)

CAPITALIZATION (12/31/01):

	($000)	(%)
Long-Term Debt	406,564	56.6
Deferred Income Tax	27,032	3.8
Minority Interest	2,126	0.3
Common & Surplus	282,303	39.3
Total	718,025	100.0

BUSINESS:

Church & Dwight Company, Inc. is the world's leading producer of sodium bicarbonate, popularly known as baking soda. The Company sells its products, primarily under the ARM & HAMMER trademark, to consumers through supermarkets, drug stores and mass merchandisers and to industrial customers and distributors. CHD operates two business divisions. Consumer Products (82.5% of 2002 sales) produces ARM & HAMMER products such as baking

soda, carpet and room deodorizers, dental care products and laundry products. Specialty Products (17.5%) produces sodium bicarbonate and related products for the food, pharmaceuticals, animal feed and industrial markets. On 5/21/01, the Company acquired USA Detergents, Inc. On 9/28/01, the Company acquired the consumer products business of Carter-Wallace for approximately $739.0 million.

RECENT DEVELOPMENTS:

For the year ended 12/31/02, net income climbed 41.9% to $66.7 million from $47.0 million the prior year. Results for 2001 included a benefit of $660,000 for impairment and other one-time items. Net sales increased 9.1% to $1.05 billion from $959.1 million the previous year, due in part to

contributions from acquisitions in 2001. Consumer product sales grew 9.8% to $864.1 million, while specialty product sales rose 5.9% to $183.0 million. Operating income amounted to $104.5 million, up 11.8% from $93.5 million the year before.

PROSPECTS:

The Company intends to strengthen its product lineup with the launch of several new product initiatives during the year. As a result of the timing of these new product introductions, CHD expects moderate earnings growth for the first half of the 2003. However, the Company expects improved margins, combined with significantly higher marketing and new product spending, should enable it to

achieve solid operating performance for the year, with earnings ranging from $1.77 to $1.81 per share for 2003. CHD also maintains its objectives for average annual growth for 2003 to 2005, with organic sales growth in excess of 5.0% a year; gross margin improvement of 100 to 150 basis points a year; and earnings per share growth of 12.5% to 15.0% per year.

ANNUAL FINANCIAL DATA:

FISCAL YEAR	TOT. REVS. ($000)	NET INC. ($000)	TOT. ASSETS ($000)	OPER. PROFIT %	NET PROFIT %	RET. ON EQUITY %	RET. ON ASSETS %	CURR. RATIO	EARN. PER SH. $	CASH FL. PER SH. $	TANG. BK. VAL. $	DIV. PER SH. $	PRICE RANGE	AVG. P/E RATIO	AVG. YIELD %
p12/31/02	1,047,149	66,690							1.60			0.30	36.50 - 25.54	19.4	1.0
12/31/01	1,080,864	④46,984	949,085	8.7	4.3	16.6	5.0	1.5	④1.15	1.83	0.46	0.29	28.44 - 19.56	20.9	1.2
12/31/00	795,725	33,559	455,632	6.6	4.2	14.3	7.4	1.1	0.84	3.93	0.28	0.28	27.75 - 14.69	25.3	1.3
12/31/99	730,036	③45,357	476,306	9.3	6.2	20.0	9.5	1.3	③1.11	1.57	3.59	0.26	30.19 - 16.50	21.0	1.1
12/31/98	684,393	30,289	391,438	6.2	4.4	15.5	7.7	1.3	0.76	1.17	4.39	0.24	18.00 - 13.28	20.7	1.5
12/31/97	574,906	24,506	351,014	5.3	4.3	13.7	7.0	1.2	0.62	0.97	4.61	0.23	16.38 - 10.81	22.1	1.7
12/31/96	527,771	21,228	307,971	5.2	4.0	12.8	6.9	1.4	0.55	0.89	4.25	0.22	11.63 - 8.75	18.7	2.2
12/31/95	485,759	②10,152	293,180	1.7	2.1	6.6	3.5	1.2	②0.26	0.60	3.84	0.22	12.44 - 8.50	40.2	2.1
12/31/94	491,048	①⑤6,117	295,587	0.3	1.2	4.0	2.1	1.2	①⑤0.16	0.45	3.94	0.22	14.63 - 8.31	73.9	1.9
12/31/93	507,651	②29,486	281,741	7.0	5.8	17.4	10.5	1.8	①②0.73	0.99	4.22	0.21	16.44 - 11.44	19.1	1.5

Statistics are as originally reported. Adj. for 2-for-1 split, 9/99 ① Incl. non-recurr. chrg. 1995, $4.0 mill.; 1994, $6.5 mill.; gain 1993, $1.2 mill. ② Bef. acctg. change chrg. $6.2 mill. ③ Incl. pre-tax impairment chrg. of $6.2 mill. ④ Incl. non-recurr. chrg. $1.4 mill. & inventory chrgs. of $13.7 mill.

OFFICERS:
R. A. Davies III, Chmn., C.E.O.
S. P. Cugine, Pres., C.O.O. (acting)
Z. Eiref, V.P., C.F.O.

INVESTOR CONTACT: Zvi Eiref, V.P., C.F.O., (609) 279-7666

PRINCIPAL OFFICE: 469 North Harrison Street, Princeton, NJ 08543-5297

TELEPHONE NUMBER: (609) 683-5900
FAX: (609) 497-7269
WEB: www.churchdwight.com
NO. OF EMPLOYEES: 2,099
SHAREHOLDERS: 10,000 (approx.)
ANNUAL MEETING: In May
INCORPORATED: DE, 1925

INSTITUTIONAL HOLDINGS:
No. of Institutions: 167
Shares Held: 25,774,582
% Held: 64.6
INDUSTRY: Alkalies and chlorine (SIC: 2812)
TRANSFER AGENT(S): Mellon Investor Services, Ridgefield Park, NJ

CIGNA CORPORATION

EXCH.	SYM.	REC. PRICE	P/E RATIO	YLD.	MKT. CAP.	RANGE (52-WK.)	'02 Y/E PR.
NYSE	CI	42.97 (2/28/03)	...	3.1%	$5.99 bill.	111.00 - 34.70	41.12

UPPER MEDIUM GRADE. THE COMPANY EXPECTS THE REORGANIZATION OF ITS HEALTH CARE BUSINESS TO YIELD AFTER-TAX COST SAVINGS OF APPROXIMATELY $100.0 MILLION IN 2003.

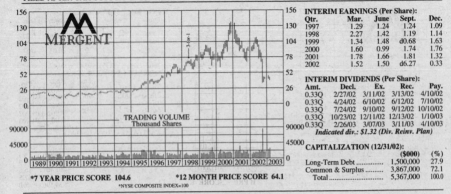

INTERIM EARNINGS (Per Share):

Qtr.	Mar.	June	Sept.	Dec.
1997	1.29	1.24	1.24	1.09
1998	2.27	1.42	1.19	1.14
1999	1.34	1.48	d0.68	1.63
2000	1.60	0.99	1.74	1.76
2001	1.78	1.66	1.81	1.32
2002	1.52	1.50	d6.27	0.33

INTERIM DIVIDENDS (Per Share):

Amt.	Decl.	Ex.	Rec.	Pay.
0.33Q	2/27/02	3/11/02	3/13/02	4/10/02
0.33Q	4/24/02	6/10/02	6/12/02	7/10/02
0.33Q	7/24/02	9/10/02	9/12/02	10/10/02
0.33Q	10/23/02	12/11/02	12/13/02	1/10/03
0.33Q	2/26/03	3/07/03	3/11/03	4/10/03

Indicated div.: $1.32 (Div. Reinv. Plan)

TRADING VOLUME
Thousand Shares

*7 YEAR PRICE SCORE 104.6   *12 MONTH PRICE SCORE 64.1
*NYSE COMPOSITE INDEX=100

CAPITALIZATION (12/31/02):

	($000)	(%)
Long-Term Debt	1,500,000	27.9
Common & Surplus	3,867,000	72.1
Total	5,367,000	100.0

BUSINESS:

CIGNA Corporation is a provider of health care products and services, group life, accident and disability insurance, retirement products and services and investment management. The Employee Health Care, Life and Disability Benefits segment offers a wide range of traditional indemnity products and services and is a provider of managed care and cost containment products and services to 13.1 million members as of 12/31/02. The Employee Retirement Benefits and Investment Services segment provides investment products and professional services, and had $53.80 billion in assets under management as of 12/31/02. CI's International Life, Health and Employee Benefits segment provides individual and group life, accident and health, health care and employee benefits outside the U.S. Other operations include a reinsurance business. On 11/98, CI sold its individual life insurance and annuity business. On 7/2/99, CI sold its property and casualty businesses.

RECENT DEVELOPMENTS:

For the year ended 12/31/02, CI reported a loss of $397.0 million, before a loss from discontinued operations of $1.0 million, versus income of $971.0 million, before income from discontinued operations of $18.0 million, the previous year. Results for 2002 included an after-tax charge of $720.0 million for variable annuity death benefit expenses, an after-tax charge of $317.0 million for Unicover reinsurance matters, and an after-tax restructuring charge of $95.0 million. Also, results included several one-time items that resulted in a net charge of $45.0 million in 2002 and a net gain of $17.0 million in 2001. Total revenues grew 4.0% to $19.35 billion from $18.61 billion the prior year.

PROSPECTS:

CI is in the process of taking a number of steps to improve the operational and financial performance of its health care business. The initiatives undertaken include a realignment and consolidation of the sales organization, centralization of medical management resources and streamlining of non-service support functions. As part of this effort, CI expects to eliminate about 3,900 positions in 2003. These actions are expected to yield after-tax cost savings of approximately $100.0 million in 2003.

ANNUAL FINANCIAL DATA:

FISCAL YEAR	PREM. INC. ($mill.)	TOT. REVS. ($mill.)	NET INC. ($mill.)	TOT. ASSETS ($mill.)	TOT. INVST. ($mill.)	RET. ON REVS. %	RET. ON EQUITY %	RET. ON ASSETS %	EARN. PER SH.$	TANG. BK. VAL.$	AVG. YIELD %	DIV. PER SH.$	PRICE RANGE	AVG. P/E RATIO
12/31/02	15,737.0	19,348.0	④ d397.0	88,950.00	40,362.0	...	...	...	④ d2.83	16.12	1.8	1.31	111.00 - 34.70	...
12/31/01	15,367.0	19,115.0	③ 989.0	91,589.0	38,261.0	5.2	19.6	1.1	③ 6.59	22.94	1.2	1.27	134.95 - 69.86	15.5
12/31/00	16,328.0	19,994.0	987.0	95,088.0	39,808.0	4.9	18.2	1.0	6.08	23.26	1.2	1.23	136.75 - 60.75	16.2
12/31/99	15,079.0	18,781.0	① ② 699.0	95,333.0	38,295.0	3.7	11.4	0.7	① ② 3.54	24.71	1.5	1.19	98.63 - 63.44	22.9
12/31/98	16,413.0	21,437.0	1,292.0	114,612.0	50,707.0	6.0	15.6	1.1	6.05	28.12	1.6	1.14	82.38 - 56.00	11.4
12/31/97	14,935.0	20,038.0	1,086.0	108,199.0	56,578.0	5.4	13.7	1.0	4.88	24.95	2.0	1.10	66.92 - 44.71	11.4
12/31/96	13,916.0	18,950.0	1,056.0	98,932.0	56,534.0	5.6	14.7	1.1	4.62	27.66	2.6	1.05	47.79 - 33.58	8.8
12/31/95	13,914.0	18,955.0	211.0	95,903.0	57,710.0	1.1	2.9	0.2	0.95	27.96	3.4	1.01	38.33 - 20.75	31.0
12/31/94	13,912.0	18,392.0	554.0	86,102.0	50,919.0	3.0	9.5	0.6	2.55	21.51	4.6	1.01	24.67 - 19.00	8.6
12/31/93	13,712.0	18,402.0	234.0	84,975.0	50,728.0	1.3	3.6	0.3	1.08	24.60	4.9	1.01	22.79 - 18.83	19.2

Statistics are as originally reported. Adj. for stk. split: 3-for-1, 5/98 ① Bef. acctg. change chrg. $91.0 mill. ② Bef. disc. oper. gain $1.17 bill. ③ Incl. an after-tax gain fr. sale of reinsurance of $69.0 mill., after-tax gain fr. sale of Japanese Life Insurance of $35.0 mill. & after-tax cost fr. 9/11/01 of $25.0 mill. & after-tax restr. chrgs. of $62.0 mill. ④ Bef. loss fr. disc. opers. of $1.0 mill.; Incl. after-tax chrg. of $720.0 mill. for reinsur., after-tax chrg. of $317.0 mill. for Unicover, after-tax restruct. chrg. of $95.0 mill & other one-time chrgs. of $45.0 mill.

OFFICERS:
H. E. Hanway, Chmn., C.E.O.
J. G. Stewart, Exec. V.P., C.F.O.
T. J. Wagner, Exec. V.P., Gen. Couns.
INVESTOR CONTACT: Shareholder Services, (215) 761-3516
PRINCIPAL OFFICE: One Liberty Place, 1650 Market Street, Philadelphia, PA 19192-1550

TELEPHONE NUMBER: (215) 761-1000
FAX: (215) 761-5515
WEB: www.cigna.com
NO. OF EMPLOYEES: 41,200 (approx.)
SHAREHOLDERS: 11,532
ANNUAL MEETING: In March
INCORPORATED: DE, Nov., 1981

INSTITUTIONAL HOLDINGS:
No. of Institutions: 374
Shares Held: 119,794,283
% Held: 85.9
INDUSTRY: Fire, marine, and casualty insurance (SIC: 6331)
TRANSFER AGENT(S): EquiServe Trust Company, N.A., Jersey City, NJ

CINERGY CORPORATION

EXCH.	SYM.	REC. PRICE	P/E RATIO	YLD.	MKT. CAP.	RANGE (52-WK.)	'02 Y/E PR.
NYSE	CIN	32.23 (2/28/03)	13.8	5.7%	$5.14 bill.	37.19 - 25.40	33.72

MEDIUM GRADE. THE COMPANY'S SUBSIDIARY, PSI ENERGY, RECENTLY FILED A PETITION WITH THE INDIANA UTILITY REGULATORY COMMISSION FOR A RATE INCREASE OF $225.0 MILLION.

TRADING VOLUME Thousand Shares

*7 YEAR PRICE SCORE 110.9   ***12 MONTH PRICE SCORE 106.7**

*NYSE COMPOSITE INDEX=100

INTERIM EARNINGS (Per Share):

Qtr.	Mar.	June	Sept.	Dec.
1999	0.80	0.37	0.76	0.60
2000	0.87	0.47	0.58	0.58
2001	0.75	0.51	0.80	0.69
2002	0.58	0.26	0.77	0.73

INTERIM DIVIDENDS (Per Share):

Amt.	Decl.	Ex.	Rec.	Pay.
0.45Q	1/25/02	1/31/02	2/04/02	2/15/02
0.45Q	5/02/02	5/06/02	5/08/02	5/15/02
0.45Q	7/24/02	8/01/02	8/05/02	8/15/02
0.45Q	9/30/02	10/10/02	10/15/02	11/15/02
0.46Q	1/14/03	1/22/03	1/24/03	2/15/03

Indicated div.: $1.84 (Div. Reinv. Plan)

CAPITALIZATION (12/31/01):

	($000)	(%)
Long-Term Debt	3,596,730	45.9
Deferred Income Tax	1,301,407	16.6
Common & Surplus	2,941,459	37.5
Total	7,839,596	100.0

BUSINESS:

Cinergy Corporation is the parent company of the Cincinnati Gas and Electric Company (CG&E) and PSI Energy, Inc. CIN provides electricity, natural gas, and other energy services through two core business units: Regulated Businesses (74.8% of net income in 2002), with 6,000 MW of generation; and Energy Merchant (35.0%), with 7,000 megawatts (MW) of generation; as well as its Power Technology and Infrastructure Services segment (-9.8%). Energy Merchant manages wholesale generation, energy marketing and trading of energy commodities and operates and maintains the regulated and non-regulated generating plants. Regulated Businesses consists of a regulated, integrated utility, and regulated electric and gas transmission and distribution systems. As of 1/31/03, CIN's regulated operations served about 1.5 million electric customers and about 500,000 gas customers in Indiana, Ohio and Kentucky.

RECENT DEVELOPMENTS:

For the year ended 12/31/02, CIN reported income from continuing operations of $396.9 million, before an accounting change charge of $10.9 million, versus $458.8 million in 2001. Results for 2002 included charges of $0.55 per share for early debt retirement and severance. Earnings for 2002 and 2001 excluded losses from discontinued operations of $25.4 million and $16.5 million, respectively. Total revenues decreased 8.0% to $11.96 billion from $13.00 billion a year earlier. Electric revenues fell 16.3% to $6.91 billion, while gas revenues increased 5.4% to $4.92 billion. Other revenues jumped 67.2% to $130.8 million. Comparisons were made with restated prior-year results.

PROSPECTS:

PSI Energy recently filed a petition with the Indiana Utility Regulatory Commission for a rate increase of $225.0 million. If approved, the average customer electric bill would increase between 16.0% and 19.0%. The proposed increase would provide for major construction projects related to environmental compliance, growing power demands of customers and transmission and distribution system improvements to maintain reliable service. If approved, the increase is expected to be effective in early 2004. Separately, CIN expects earnings for full-year 2003 to range from $2.55 to $2.70 per share.

ANNUAL FINANCIAL DATA:

FISCAL YEAR	TOT. REVS. ($mill.)	NET INC. ($mill.)	TOT. ASSETS ($mill.)	OPER. PROFIT %	NET PROFIT %	NET INC./ NET PROP. %	NET INC./ TOT. CAP. %	RET. ON EQUITY %	ACCUM. DEPR./ GROSS PROP. %	EARN. PER SH.$	TANG. BK. VAL. $	DIV. PER SH.$	DIV. PAYOUT %	PRICE RANGE	AVG. P/E RATIO	AVG. YIELD %
p12/31/02	11,960.1	⑥ 396.9								⑥ 2.34		1.80	76.9	37.19 - 25.40	13.4	5.8
12/31/01	⑤ 12,922.5	442.3	12,299.8	7.3	3.4	5.4	5.6	15.0	56.6	2.75	17.98	1.80	65.5	35.60 - 28.00	11.6	5.7
12/31/00	8,422.0	④ 399.5	12,329.7	10.2	4.7	6.0	5.8	14.3	40.7	④ 2.50	17.54	1.80	72.0	35.25 - 20.00	11.0	6.5
12/31/99	5,937.9	③ 403.6	9,616.9	11.7	6.8	6.3	5.8	15.2	39.9	③ 2.53	16.70	1.80	71.1	34.88 - 23.44	11.5	6.2
12/31/98	5,876.3	261.0	10,298.8	9.6	4.4	4.1	4.1	10.3	38.9	1.65	16.02	1.80	109.1	39.88 - 30.81	21.4	5.1
12/31/97	4,352.8	② 422.6	8,858.2	12.4	9.7	6.7	6.9	16.6	37.6	② 1.59	16.10	1.80	113.2	39.13 - 32.00	22.4	5.1
12/31/96	3,242.7	① 366.0	8,848.5	17.2	11.3	5.8	5.7	14.2	36.3	① 2.12	16.39	1.74	82.1	34.25 - 27.50	14.6	5.6
12/31/95	3,023.4	368.0	8,220.1	19.4	12.2	5.9	5.6	14.4	35.0	2.22	16.17	1.72	77.5	31.13 - 23.38	12.3	6.3
12/31/94	2,924.2	211.5	8,149.8	15.1	7.2	3.4	3.2	8.8	33.8	1.30	15.56	0.10	7.9	24.00 - 20.75	17.2	0.5
12/31/93	2,840.1	① 50.3	7,803.9	17.0	1.8	0.8	0.8	2.3	32.7	① 0.43	15.17	...	...	... - ...	...	...

Statistics are as originally reported. ① Incl. non-recurr. chrg. 1993, $233.0 mill.; 1996, $0.24/sh. ② Bef. extraord. chrg. $109.4 mill. ③ Incl. pre-tax $99.3 gain on sale of assets. ④ Incl. one-time chrg. of $0.11 per share. ⑤ Reflects increased volume and realized prices on wholesale gas & energy marketing and trading activities. ⑥ Bef. loss fr. disc. opers. of $25.4 mill. and acctg. change chrg. of $10.9 mill.

OFFICERS:
J. E. Rogers, Chmn., Pres., C.E.O.
R. F. Duncan, Exec. V.P., C.F.O.
INVESTOR CONTACT: Steve Schrader, (513) 287-1083
PRINCIPAL OFFICE: 139 East Fourth Street, Cincinnati, OH 45202

TELEPHONE NUMBER: (513) 421-9500
FAX: (513) 651-9196
WEB: www.cinergy.com
NO. OF EMPLOYEES: 8,769 (avg.)
SHAREHOLDERS: 58,601
ANNUAL MEETING: In May
INCORPORATED: DE, Oct., 1994

INSTITUTIONAL HOLDINGS:
No. of Institutions: 314
Shares Held: 101,745,229
% Held: 60.4
INDUSTRY: Electric and other services combined (SIC: 4931)
TRANSFER AGENT(S): The Company

CIRCUIT CITY STORES, INC.

EXCH.	SYM.	REC. PRICE	P/E RATIO	YLD.	MKT. CAP.	RANGE (52-WK.)	'02 Y/E PR.
NYSE	CC	4.42 (2/28/03)	5.9	1.6%	$0.92 bill.	24.59 - 4.11	7.42

LOWER MEDIUM GRADE. RESULTS ARE BEING HURT BY WEAKER SALES OF DIGITAL SATELLITE SYSTEMS AND WIRELESS COMMUNICATION PRODUCTS.

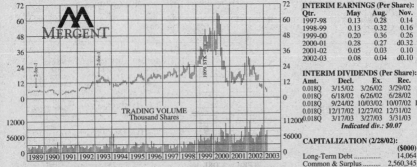
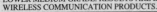

*7 YEAR PRICE SCORE 66.3   ***12 MONTH PRICE SCORE 47.8**

*NYSE COMPOSITE INDEX=100

INTERIM EARNINGS (Per Share):

Qtr.	May	Aug.	Nov.	Feb.
1997-98	0.13	0.28	0.14	0.58
1998-99	0.13	0.32	0.16	0.86
1999-00	0.20	0.36	0.26	0.79
2000-01	0.28	0.27	d0.32	0.49
2001-02	0.05	0.03	0.10	0.73
2002-03	0.08	0.04	d0.10	...

INTERIM DIVIDENDS (Per Share):

Amt.	Decl.	Ex.	Rec.	Pay.
0.018Q	3/15/02	3/26/02	3/29/02	4/15/02
0.018Q	6/18/02	6/26/02	6/28/02	7/15/02
0.018Q	9/24/02	10/03/02	10/07/02	10/15/02
0.018Q	12/17/02	12/27/02	12/31/02	1/15/03
0.018Q	3/17/03	3/27/03	3/31/03	4/15/03

Indicated div.: $0.07

CAPITALIZATION (2/28/02):

	($000)	(%)
Long-Term Debt	14,064	0.5
Common & Surplus	2,560,345	99.5
Total	2,574,409	100.0

BUSINESS:

Circuit City Stores, Inc. (formerly Circuit City Group) is a specialty retailer of brand-name electronics including VCRs, cameras, stereo systems, compact disc players, telephones, personal computers and entertainment software. As of 1/7/03, the Company operated 611 Circuit City Super-stores and 17 mall-based Circuit City Express Stores throughout the U.S. The Company exited the major appliance category in November 2000. On 10/1/02, CC spun off of its 64.1% interest in the CarMax Group, a retailer of new and used cars.

RECENT DEVELOPMENTS:

For the three months ended 11/30/02, the Company reported a loss from continuing operations of $21.3 million compared with income from continuing operations of $9.2 million in the corresponding prior-year period. Results included one-time remodeling and relocation charges of $11.4 million and $2.2 million in 2002 and 2001, respectively. Net sales and operating revenues increased 7.0% to $2.42 billion from $2.26 billion a year earlier. Comparable-store sales were up 6.0% year over year. Gross profit was $548.1 million, or 22.6% of net sales, versus $551.2 million, or 24.4% of net sales, the previous year.

PROSPECTS:

Earnings are being negatively affected by weaker sales of high-margin digital satellite systems and wireless communication products, partially offset by higher sales of entertainment software such as DVD movies and video games. Results are also being hurt by increased price competition across a wide range of products and aggressive price markdowns throughout the holiday selling season. The Company is taking steps to reduce costs in an effort to boost profitability. Meanwhile, customers are responding favorably to the newly remodeled video departments, in 301 of CC's stores as of 11/30/02, that feature an expanded selection of digital and big-screen televisions.

ANNUAL FINANCIAL DATA:

FISCAL YEAR	TOT. REVS. ($mill.)	NET INC. ($mill.)	TOT. ASSETS ($mill.)	OPER. PROFIT %	NET PROFIT %	RET. ON EQUITY %	RET. ON ASSETS %	CURR. RATIO	EARN. PER SH.$	CASH FL. PER SH.$	TANG. BK. VAL.$	DIV. PER SH.$	PRICE RANGE	AVG. P/E RATIO	AVG. YIELD %
2/28/02	9,589.8	② 190.8	4,133.2	2.2	2.0	7.5	4.6	2.2	② 0.92	1.57	12.26	0.07	26.65 - 9.55	19.7	0.4
2/28/01	10,458.0	② 149.2	3,452.6	1.8	1.4	6.6	4.3	2.4	② 0.73	1.34	10.90	0.07	65.19 - 8.69	50.6	0.2
2/29/00	10,599.4	① 327.6	3,537.4	5.1	3.1	15.9	9.3	2.1	① 1.60	2.25	10.08	0.07	53.88 - 23.69	24.2	0.2
2/28/99	9,338.1	148.4	3,134.8	3.1	1.6	8.1	4.7	2.3	1.48	2.78	18.05	0.07	27.25 - 14.41	14.1	0.4
2/28/98	7,996.6	112.1	3,061.6	3.1	1.4	6.8	3.7	2.3	1.13	2.26	16.60	0.07	22.75 - 14.31	16.4	0.4
2/28/97	7,153.6	136.7	3,008.3	3.6	1.9	9.0	4.5	2.2	1.40	2.40	15.55	0.07	19.38 - 12.50	11.4	0.4
2/29/96	6,753.3	179.4	...	4.7	2.7	...	...	...	1.86	2.68	...	0.06	19.00 - 10.50	7.9	0.4

Statistics are as originally reported. Adj. for 2-for-1 stk. split, 7/99. ① Bef. loss from disc. Digital Video Express ops. $130.2 mil ($0.64/sh). ② Incl. $10.0 mil one-time pre-tax chg. to exit the appliance business, 2002; $30.0 mil. chg., 2001.

OFFICERS:
W. A. McCollough, Chmn., Pres., C.E.O.
J. W. Froman, Exec. V.P., C.O.O.
M. T. Chalifoux, Exec. V.P., C.F.O., Sec.

INVESTOR CONTACT: Ann M. Collier, V.P.-Fin. & Pub. Rel., (804) 527-4058

PRINCIPAL OFFICE: 9950 Mayland Drive, Richmond, VA 23233

TELEPHONE NUMBER: (804) 527-4000
FAX: (804) 527-4164
WEB: www.circuitcity.com

NO. OF EMPLOYEES: 41,679 (avg.)

SHAREHOLDERS: 8,195

ANNUAL MEETING: In June

INCORPORATED: VA, Sept., 1949

INSTITUTIONAL HOLDINGS:
No. of Institutions: 277
Shares Held: 172,189,968
% Held: 82.0

INDUSTRY: Radio, TV, & electronic stores (SIC: 5731)

TRANSFER AGENT(S): Wells Fargo Shareowner Services, South St. Paul, MN

CITIGROUP INC.

EXCH.	SYM.	REC. PRICE	P/E RATIO	YLD.	MKT. CAP.	RANGE (52-WK.)	'02 Y/E PR.	DIV. ACH.
NYSE	C	33.34 (2/28/03)	11.5	2.4%	$170.66 bill.	50.49 - 24.48	35.19	16 yrs.

INVESTMENT GRADE. THE COMPANY CONTINUES TO GROW ITS GLOBAL PRESENCE IN RUSSIA AND CHINA.

*7 YEAR PRICE SCORE 119.1　　***12 MONTH PRICE SCORE 101.7**
NYSE COMPOSITE INDEX=100

INTERIM EARNINGS (Per Share):

Qtr.	Mar.	June	Sept.	Dec.
1998	0.46	0.47	0.11	0.14
1999	0.52	0.53	0.53	0.56
2000	0.78	0.65	0.67	0.55
2001	0.70	0.71	0.61	0.74
2002	0.93	0.78	0.72	0.47

INTERIM DIVIDENDS (Per Share):

Amt.	Decl.	Ex.	Rec.	Pay.
0.16Q	1/15/02	1/31/02	2/04/02	2/22/02
0.18Q	4/16/02	5/02/02	5/06/02	5/24/02
0.18Q	7/16/02	8/01/02	8/05/02	8/23/02
0.18Q	10/15/02	10/31/02	11/04/02	11/22/02
0.20Q	1/21/03	1/30/03	2/03/03	2/28/03

Indicated div.: $0.80 (Div. Reinv. Plan)

CAPITALIZATION (12/31/01):

	($mill.)	(%)
Long-Term Debt	121,631.0	57.9
Redeemable Pfd. Stock	7,125.0	3.4
Preferred Stock	1,525.0	0.7
Common & Surplus	79,722.0	38.0
Total	210,003.0	100.0

BUSINESS:

Citigroup Inc., (formerly Travelers Group Inc.) was formed on 10/8/98 by the merger of Travelers and Citicorp. The Company consists of businesses that produce a broad range of financial services -- consumer banking and credit, corporate and investment banking, insurance, securities brokerage, and asset management -- and use diverse channels to make them available to consumers, governments and institutions around the world. Major brand names include Citibank, CitiFinancial, Primerica, Salomon Smith Barney, Banamex, and Travelers Life and Annuity. On 1/18/00, the Company acquired Shroders PLC. On 11/30/00, the Company acquired Associates First Capital Corporation. On 8/6/01, the Company acquired Grupo Financiero Banamex-Accival for approximately $12.48 billion.

RECENT DEVELOPMENTS:

For the year ended 12/31/02, income rose 1.7% to $13.45 billion versus income of $13.23 billion in 2001. Results for 2002 and 2001 excluded accounting change charges of $47.0 million and $158.0 million. Results for 2002 included a loss of $215.0 million from C's realized insurance investment portfolio and an after-tax charge of $10.0 million for restructuring items. Results for 2001 included an after-tax restructuring-related loss of $282.0 million and a gain of $94.0 million from its realized insurance investment portfolio. Revenues grew 7.0% to $75.76 billion.

PROSPECTS:

During the fourth quarter ended 12/31/02, the Company completed the acquisition of Golden State Bancorp, which added 352 branches and $25.00 billion in deposits to C's retail banking franchise, primarily in California and Nevada, as well as giving C a strong base in the growing Hispanic banking market. Separately, during the fourth quarter ended 12/31/02, the Company launched retail banking operations in Russia and announced an equity investment in and joint venture with the Shanghai Pudong Development Bank to market credit cards to consumers in China.

ANNUAL FINANCIAL DATA:

FISCAL YEAR	PREM. INC ($bill.)	NET INVST. INC. ($bill.)	TOT. REVS. ($bill.)	NET INC. ($bill.)	TOT. ASSETS ($bill.)	RET. ON REVS. %	RET. ON EQUITY %	RET. ON ASSETS %	EARN. PER SH. $	TANG. BK. VAL. $	AVG. YIELD %	DIV. PER SH. $	PRICE RANGE	AVG. P/E RATIO
p12/31/02	13.65		75.76	①②④ 13.45					①②④ 2.94			0.70	52.20 - 24.48	13.0
12/31/01	13.46	66.57	112.02	②④⑦ 14.28	1,051.45	12.8	12.8	1.3	②④⑦ 2.75	15.57	1.3	0.60	57.38 - 34.51	16.7
12/31/00	12.43	64.94	111.83	⑦ 13.52	902.21	12.1	20.4	1.5	⑦ 2.62	12.84	1.1	0.52	59.13 - 35.34	18.0
12/31/99	10.44	44.90	82.01	②④⑨ 9.99	716.94	12.2	20.1	1.4	②④ 2.15	10.64	1.2	0.41	43.69 - 24.50	15.9
⑥ 12/31/98	9.85	46.24	76.43	④ 5.81	668.64	7.6	13.6	0.9	④ 1.22	8.94	1.1	0.28	36.75 - 14.25	21.0
③ 12/31/97	9.00	17.62	37.61	3.10	386.56	8.3	14.9	0.8	1.27	6.99	0.9	0.20	28.69 - 14.58	17.0
12/31/96	7.63	6.71	21.35	② 2.30	151.07	10.8	17.6	1.5	② 1.15	4.95	1.2	0.15	15.83 - 9.42	11.0
12/31/95	5.00	5.47	16.58	①④ 1.63	114.48	9.8	13.9	1.4	①④ 0.81	4.74	1.7	0.13	10.65 - 5.40	9.9
⑤ 12/31/94	7.59	4.67	18.47	④ 1.33	115.30	7.2	15.3	1.2	④ 0.64	3.04	1.6	0.10	7.19 - 5.06	9.5
12/31/93	1.48	1.67	6.63	② 0.95	101.36	14.3	10.2	0.9	② 0.65	3.24	1.3	0.08	8.25 - 4.01	9.5

Statistics are as originally reported. Adj. for stk. splits: 33.3% stk. div., 8/25/00; 3-for-2, 5/99; 11/97; 4-for-3, 8/00, 11/96 & 8/93; 3-for-2, 5/96 & 2/93. ① Bef. disc. oper. gain 2002, $1.88 bill.; 1996, $31.0 mill.; 1995, $206.0 mill. ② Bef. acctg. change chrgs. 2002, $47.0 mill.; 2001, $158.0 mill.; 1999, $127.0 mill.; 1993, $35.0 mill. ③ Results reflect the acquisition of Salomon Inc. in 11/97. ④ Incl. non-recurr. chrg. 2002, $225.0 mill.; 2001, $621.0 mill.; credit 1999, $47.0 mill.; 1998, $795.0 mill.; chrg. 1997, $255.4 mill.; credit 1996, $397.0 mill.; 1995, $117.0 mill.; 1994, $87.8 mill. ⑤ Results reflect merger of Primerica & Old Travelers in 12/93. ⑥ Results prior to fourth quarter of 1998 are for Travelers Group. ⑦ Incl. restruct. & merger related items 2001, $285.0 mill.; 2000, $621.0 mill.

OFFICERS:
S. I. Weill, Chmn., C.E.O.
W. R. Rhodes, Sr. Vice-Chmn.
M. T. Masin, Vice-Chmn, C.O.O.
R. B. Willumstad, Pres.

INVESTOR CONTACT: Sheri Ptashek, Investor Relations, (212) 559-2718

PRINCIPAL OFFICE: 399 Park Avenue, New York, NY 10043

TELEPHONE NUMBER: (212) 559-1000
FAX: (212) 816-8913
WEB: www.citigroup.com

NO. OF EMPLOYEES: 250,000 (approx.)

SHAREHOLDERS: 221,400 (approx. record)

ANNUAL MEETING: In Apr.

INCORPORATED: DE, Dec., 1993

INSTITUTIONAL HOLDINGS:
No. of Institutions: 1,271
Shares Held: -1,153,615,992
% Held: 62.1

INDUSTRY: National commercial banks (SIC: 6021)

TRANSFER AGENT(S): Citibank Shareholder Services, Jersey City, NJ

CITIZENS COMMUNICATIONS CO.

EXCH.	SYM.	REC. PRICE	P/E RATIO	YLD.	MKT. CAP.	RANGE (52-WK.)	'02 Y/E PR.
NYSE	CZN	9.81 (2/28/03)	...	...	$2.76 bill.	11.55 - 2.51	10.55

LOWER MEDIUM GRADE. THE COMPANY ENTERED INTO A DEFINITIVE AGREEMENT TO SELL ITS HAWAIIAN GAS DIVISION TO K-1 USA VENTURES, INC. FOR $115.0 MILLION IN CASH.

TRADING VOLUME
Thousand Shares

*7 YEAR PRICE SCORE 84.4 ***12 MONTH PRICE SCORE 125.2**
*NYSE COMPOSITE INDEX=100

INTERIM EARNINGS (Per Share):

Qtr.	Mar.	June	Sept.	Dec.
1997	0.13	d0.50	0.09	0.32
1998	0.12	0.06	0.06	0.01
1999	0.21	0.03	0.05	0.26
2000	0.03	0.01	0.01	d0.15
2001	0.07	d0.05	0.15	d0.39
2002	d0.16	0.15	d2.49	d0.09

INTERIM DIVIDENDS (Per Share):

Amt.	Decl.	Ex.	Rec.	Pay.
		No dividends paid.		

CAPITALIZATION (12/31/01):

	($000)	(%)
Long-Term Debt	5,534,906	68.2
Deferred Income Tax	429,544	5.3
Redeemable Pfd. Stock	201,250	2.5
Common & Surplus	1,946,142	24.0
Total	8,111,842	100.0

BUSINESS:

Citizens Communications Co. (formerly Citizens Utilities Co.) is a telecommunications company providing wireline communications services primarily to rural areas, small and medium sized cities and towns throughout the U.S. as an incumbent local exchange carrier. As of 11/1/02, CZN served about 2.5 million access lines in 24 states. In addition, CZN provides competitive local exchange carrier services to business customers and to other communications carriers in the western U.S. through Electric Lightwave

Inc., its wholly-owned subsidiary. CZN also provides public utility services including natural gas transmission and distribution, electric transmission and distribution services to primarily rural and suburban customers in Vermont, Hawaii and Arizona. On 6/29/01, CZN acquired Global Crossing's local exchange telephone business (Frontier Telephone) for $3.50 billion. On 1/15/02, CZN sold its water and wastewater treatment operations to American Water Works for $979.0 million.

RECENT DEVELOPMENTS:

For the year ended 12/31/02, CZN posted a loss from continuing operations of $904.1 million versus a loss from continuing operations of $160.6 million a year earlier. Results for 2002 and 2001 included restructuring and other

expenses of $37.2 million and $19.3 million, and asset sale gains of $9.8 million and $139.3 million, respectively. Results for 2002 also included an impairment charge of $1.07 billion. Revenues rose 8.6% to $2.67 billion.

PROSPECTS:

On 12/19/02, CZN announced that it has entered into a definitive agreement to sell its Hawaiian gas division to K-1 USA Ventures, Inc. for $115.0 million in cash. The transaction is expected to close during the fourth quarter of 2003. Meanwhile, CZN has stated that it remains focused on improving its balance sheet through the generation of

free cash flow. In addition, the sale of the Company's Arizona Electric and Gas divisions for $230.0 million in cash and the aforementioned sale of The Gas Company of Hawaii division for $115.0 million in cash are expected to close during the second half of 2003. The net proceeds from these sales will be used to further reduce debt.

ANNUAL FINANCIAL DATA:

FISCAL YEAR	TOT. REVS. ($mill.)	NET INC. ($mill.)	TOT. ASSETS ($mill.)	OPER. PROFIT %	NET PROFIT %	RET. ON EQUITY %	RET. ON ASSETS %	CURR. RATIO	EARN. PER SH.$	CASH FL. PER SH.$	TANG. BK. VAL.$	PRICE RANGE	AVG. P/E RATIO
p12/31/02	2,669.3	⑥ d904.1							⑥ d2.43			11.52 — 2.51	...
12/31/01	2,457.0	⑤ d63.9	10,553.6	9.5	...	...	...	1.6	⑤ d0.28	2.03	...	15.88 — 8.20	...
12/31/00	1,802.4	④ d40.1	6,955.0	6.8	...	...	...	2.3	④ d0.11	1.15	4.09	19.00 — 12.50	...
12/31/99	1,087.4	③ 117.1	5,771.7	0.7	10.8	6.1	2.0	0.7	③ 0.45	1.89	7.30	14.31 — 7.25	24.0
12/31/98	1,542.4	① 59.4	5,292.9	11.6	3.9	3.3	1.1	0.8	① 0.23	1.22	6.90	11.20 — 6.89	39.3
12/31/97	1,393.6	② 10.1	4,872.9	1.1	0.7	0.6	0.2	0.9	② 0.04	0.94	6.58	11.72 — 7.62	241.2
12/31/96	1,306.5	184.5	4,523.1	22.6	14.1	11.0	4.1	0.9	0.71	1.62	6.64	11.24 — 9.46	14.6
12/31/95	1,069.0	159.5	3,918.2	23.8	14.9	10.2	4.1	0.5	0.64	1.34	6.42	11.99 — 9.13	16.5
12/31/94	916.0	144.0	3,576.6	24.9	15.7	12.4	4.0	0.4	0.63	1.26	5.43	14.43 — 10.44	19.7
12/31/93	619.4	125.6	2,627.1	26.0	20.3	12.9	4.8	0.4	0.55	0.92	4.80	15.73 — 10.53	23.8

Statistics are as originally reported. Adj. for all stk. splits & divs. thru 12/98. ① Bef. acctg. chg. chrg. of $2.3 mill. ② Incl. non-recurr. chrg. of $78.7 mill. ③ Bef. disc. ops. gain of $27.4 mill. ④ Incl. acq. assimil. exp. of $39.9 mill.; bef. inc. fr. disc. ops of $11.7 mill. ($0.04/sh.) ⑤ Incl. acq. assimil. exp. of $21.4 mill., restruct. chrg. of $19.3 mill., write-down of receiv. of $21.2 mill. & gain on sale of assets of $139.3 mill.; bef. inc. fr. disc. ops. of $17.9 mill. & extraord. exp. of $43.6 mill. ⑥ Incl. restruct. & oth. exp. of $37.2 mill., loss on impairmnt. of $1.07 bill. and gain on sale of assets of $9.8 mill.; bef. net gain on disp. of water seg. of $181.4 mill. & acctg. chg. gain of $39.8 mill.

OFFICERS:
L. Tow, Chmn., C.E.O.
S. N. Schneider, Vice-Chmn., Pres., C.O.O.
J. Elliott, V.P., C.F.O.
INVESTOR CONTACT: Brigid M. Smith, Asst. V.P., Corp. Comm., (203) 614-5042
PRINCIPAL OFFICE: 3 High Ridge Park, Stamford, CT 06905

TELEPHONE NUMBER: (203) 614-5600
FAX: (203) 614-4602
WEB: www.czn.net
NO. OF EMPLOYEES: 10,121 (approx.)
SHAREHOLDERS: 34,264 (approx.)
ANNUAL MEETING: In May
INCORPORATED: DE, Nov., 1935

INSTITUTIONAL HOLDINGS:
No. of Institutions: 253
Shares Held: 217,972,341
% Held: 77.2
INDUSTRY: Telephone communications, exc. radio (SIC: 4813)
TRANSFER AGENT(S): Illinois Stock Transfer Company, Chicago, IL

CITY NATIONAL CORPORATION

EXCH.	SYM.	REC. PRICE	P/E RATIO	YLD.	MKT. CAP.	RANGE (52-WK.)	'02 Y/E PR.
NYSE	CYN	46.56 (2/28/03)	13.1	1.8%	$2.24 bill.	56.42 - 40.10	43.99

UPPER MEDIUM GRADE. THE COMPANY ENTERED INTO A DEFINITIVE AGREEMENT TO ACQUIRE CONVERGENT CAPITAL MANGEMENT LLC, AND SUBSTANTIALLY ALL OF ITS ASSET MANAGEMENT HOLDINGS.

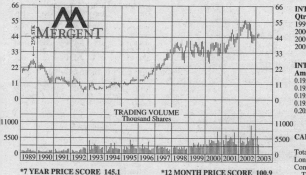

INTERIM EARNINGS (Per Share):

Qtr.	Mar.	June	Sept.	Dec.
1999	0.55	0.55	0.60	0.60
2000	0.66	0.68	0.70	0.68
2001	0.69	0.74	0.75	0.78
2002	0.87	0.88	0.94	0.87

INTERIM DIVIDENDS (Per Share):

Amt.	Decl.	Ex.	Rec.	Pay.
0.195Q	1/24/02	2/04/02*	2/06/02	2/19/02
0.195Q	4/25/02	5/06/02	5/08/02	5/20/02
0.195Q	7/24/02	8/05/02	8/07/02	8/19/02
0.195Q	10/23/02	11/04/02	11/06/02	11/18/02
0.205Q	1/22/03	2/03/03	2/05/03	2/18/03

Indicated div.: $0.82

TRADING VOLUME
Thousand Shares

*7 YEAR PRICE SCORE 145.1   ***12 MONTH PRICE SCORE 100.9**
*NYSE COMPOSITE INDEX=100

CAPITALIZATION (12/31/01):

	($000)	(%)
Total Deposits	8,131,202	85.7
Long-Term Debt	466,174	4.9
Common & Surplus	890,577	9.4
Total	9,487,953	100.0

BUSINESS:

City National Corporation, with assets of $11.87 billion as of 12/31/02, conducts its business through City National Bank. The bank operates in Alameda, Contra Costa, Los Angeles, Orange, San Diego, Riverside, Ventura, San Bernardino, San Mateo, Santa Clara and San Francisco counties, as well as a loan production office in Sacramento. CYN is engaged in one operating segment: providing private and business banking, including investment and trust services. The Bank offers a broad range of loans, deposit,

cash management, international banking, and other products and services. Through City National Investments, a division of CYN, and Reed, Conner & Buckwell, Inc., acquired on 1/4/01, the bank offers personal and employee benefit trust services, manages investments for clients and engages in securities sales and tradings. The Bank also manages and offers mutual funds under the name of CNI Charter Funds. On 2/28/02, CYN acquired Civic Bancorp.

RECENT DEVELOPMENTS:

For the year ended 12/31/02, net income rose 15.1% to $183.1 million from $146.2 million the year before, reflecting strong growth in deposits. Earnings for 2002 included income tax benefits of $4.6 million, while earnings for

2001 included amortization of goodwill of $12.9 million. Net interest income grew 19.0% to $515.3 million. Provision for credit losses increased 91.4% to $67.0 million. Non-interest income improved 10.5% to $146.3 million.

PROSPECTS:

On 1/31/03, the Company entered into a definitive agreement to acquire Convergent Capital Mangement LLC and substantially all of its asset management holdings in a transaction valued at $56.5 million. The acquisition, which is expected to close in the second quarter of 2003, will nearly double CYN's assets under management to $13.90 billion. Separately, for 2003, diluted earnings per share

growth is anticipated to range from about 8.0% to 10.0%; average loan growth is expected to be between 6.0% and 8.0%; and average deposit growth is anticipated to range from 5.0% to 7.0%. Moreover, provision for credit losses for 2003 is expected to range from $60.0 million to $75.0 million, and non-interest income growth is anticipated to be between 6.0% and 8.0%.

ANNUAL FINANCIAL DATA:

FISCAL YEAR	NET INT. INC. ($mill.)	NON-INT. INC. ($mill.)	NET INC. ($mill.)	TOT. LOANS ($mill.)	TOT. ASSETS ($mill.)	TOT. DEP. ($mill.)	RET. ON EQUITY %	RET. ON ASSETS %	EQUITY/ ASSETS %	EARN. PER SH. $	TANG. BK. VAL. $	DIV. PER SH. $	PRICE RANGE	AVG. P/E RATIO
p12/31/02	515.3	146.3	⑤183.1		11,871.4					⑤3.56		0.78	56.42 — 40.10	13.6
12/31/01	434.2	132.4	146.2	7,159.2	10,176.3	8,131.2	16.4	1.4	8.8	2.96	14.81	0.74	49.75 — 32.97	14.0
12/31/00	406.5	109.5	131.7	6,527.1	9,096.7	7,408.7	17.7	1.4	8.2	2.72	11.50	0.70	40.81 — 25.50	12.2
12/31/99	322.0	87.2	②108.1	5,490.7	7,213.6	5,669.4	18.9	1.5	7.9	②2.30	9.78	0.66	41.56 — 29.63	15.5
12/31/98	293.7	67.7	②96.2	4,530.4	6,427.8	4,887.4	17.1	1.5	8.7	②2.00	10.61	0.56	41.63 — 25.75	16.8
12/31/97	253.7	53.4	②80.1	3,825.2	5,252.0	4,228.3	15.8	1.5	9.7	②1.68	9.83	0.44	35.38 — 20.38	16.6
12/31/96	199.7	44.0	②66.6	2,845.6	4,216.5	3,386.5	16.6	1.6	9.5	②1.52	8.90	0.36	22.25 — 12.63	11.5
12/31/95	162.3	34.6	④48.8	2,355.0	4,157.6	3,248.0	13.3	1.2	8.8	④1.08	8.12	0.26	15.38 — 9.75	11.6
12/31/94	143.4	32.8	②37.2	1,653.8	3,012.8	2,417.8	11.2	1.2	11.0	②0.81	7.32	0.05	12.13 — 7.13	11.9
12/31/93	127.8	45.8	①②③d14.0	1,634.4	3,100.6	2,526.8	…	…	9.6	①②③d0.35	6.62	…	11.63 — 6.38	…

Statistics are as originally reported. ① Bef. a gain from disc. opers. of $7.1 mill., 1993; $804,000, 1992. ② Incl. a gain on the sale of assets of $2.1 mill., 1999; $1.8 mill., 1998; $1.6 mill., 1997; $1.1 mill., 1996; $1.5 mill., 1994; $1.9 mill., 1993. ③ Incl. a gain of the sale of loans of $4.5 mill. ④ Incl. a loss of $83,000 on the sale of assets. ⑤ Incl. inc. tax benef. of about $4.6 mill.

OFFICERS:
B. Goldsmith, Chmn.
R. Goldsmith, Vice-Chmn., C.E.O.
INVESTOR CONTACT: Frank P. Pekny, Exec. V.P., C.F.O. & Treas., (310) 888-6700
PRINCIPAL OFFICE: City National Center, 400 North Roxbury Drive, Beverly Hills, CA 90210

TELEPHONE NUMBER: (310) 888-6000
FAX: (310) 858-3334
WEB: www.cnb.com
NO. OF EMPLOYEES: 2,084
SHAREHOLDERS: 1,959 (approx.)
ANNUAL MEETING: In April
INCORPORATED: DE, Oct., 1968

INSTITUTIONAL HOLDINGS:
No. of Institutions: 215
Shares Held: 31,759,577
% Held: 63.6
INDUSTRY: National commercial banks (SIC: 6021)
TRANSFER AGENT(S): City National Bank, Beverly Hills, CA

CLAIRE'S STORES, INC.

EXCH.	SYM.	REC. PRICE	P/E RATIO	YLD.	MKT. CAP.	RANGE (52-WK.)	'02 Y/E PR.
NYSE	CLE	22.82 (2/28/03)	14.3	0.7%	$1.11 bill.	26.97 - 16.25	22.07

UPPER MEDIUM GRADE. THE COMPANY IS TARGETING FULL-YEAR SALES OF ABOUT $1.04 BILLION AND EARNINGS OF $1.76 PER SHARE.

TRADING VOLUME
Thousand Shares

*7 YEAR PRICE SCORE 116.3   ***12 MONTH PRICE SCORE 116.1**
*NYSE COMPOSITE INDEX=100.

INTERIM EARNINGS (Per Share):

Qtr.	Apr.	July	Oct.	Jan.
1997-98	0.17	0.22	0.22	0.60
1998-99	0.20	0.25	0.21	0.66
1999-00	0.27	0.40	0.25	0.80
2000-01	0.08	0.34	0.28	0.61
2001-02	0.16	d0.12	0.15	0.61
2002-03	0.17	0.31	0.25	0.87

INTERIM DIVIDENDS (Per Share):

Amt.	Decl.	Ex.	Rec.	Pay.
0.04Q	2/04/02	3/04/02	3/06/02	3/20/02
0.04Q	5/23/02	6/04/02	6/06/02	6/20/02
0.04Q	8/22/02	9/04/02	9/06/02	9/20/02
0.04Q	11/21/02	12/04/02	12/06/02	12/20/02
0.04Q	2/27/03	3/06/03	3/10/03	3/21/03
			Indicated div.: $0.16	

CAPITALIZATION (2/2/02):

	($000)	(%)
Long-Term Debt	110,104	21.4
Common & Surplus	404,188	78.6
Total	514,292	100.0

BUSINESS:

Claire's Stores, Inc. is a mall-based retailer of fashion accessories, including costume jewelry, hair ornaments and earrings, and apparel for pre-teens and teenagers. At 2/1/03, the Company operated 2,912 stores in all 50 U.S. states, Canada, the Caribbean, Puerto Rico, the United Kingdom, Switzerland, Austria, Germany, France, Ireland and Japan. CLE's stores operate primarily under the trade names CLAIRE'S BOUTIQUES, CLAIRE'S ACCESSORIES, AFTER THOUGHTS, THE ICING, ICING BY CLAIRE'S and BIJOUX ONE. On 12/1/99, CLE acquired 768 Afterthoughts stores. In January 1999, the Company discontinued Just Nikki, Inc. In May 2002, CLE sold its 154-store MR. RAGS men's apparel chain.

RECENT DEVELOPMENTS:

For the twelve months ended 2/1/03, income from continuing operations totaled $78.0 million, up 89.6% compared with income from continuing operations of $41.1 million in the corresponding prior-year period. Net sales climbed 9.0% to $1.00 billion from $918.7 million the previous year. Same-store sales increased 5.0% year over year. Gross profit was $514.7 million, or 51.4% of net sales, versus $445.0 million, or 48.4% of net sales, a year earlier.

PROSPECTS:

The Company anticipates first-quarter sales of about $225.0 million and earnings of $0.19 per share. Looking ahead, CLE is targeting full-year sales of approximately $1.04 billion, same-store sales growth of 3.0% to 4.0%, and earnings per share of $1.76. During the current fiscal year, the Company plans to open 150 new stores, primarily in Europe, and close 89 existing locations. Meanwhile, results are being positively affected by the Company's efforts to manage inventory levels, improve margins and control expenses, partially offset by weak mall traffic and increased shipping costs. However, mall traffic is expected to remain weak during the current fiscal year due to uncertain economic conditions and the possible outbreak of a war with Iraq.

ANNUAL FINANCIAL DATA:

FISCAL YEAR	TOT. REVS. ($mil.)	NET INC. ($mil.)	TOT. ASSETS ($mil.)	OPER. PROFIT %	NET PROFIT %	RET. ON EQUITY %	RET. ON ASSETS %	CURR. RATIO	EARN. PER SH. $	CASH FL. PER SH. $	TANG. BK. VAL. $	DIV. PER SH. $	PRICE RANGE	AVG. P/E RATIO	AVG. YIELD %
p2/01/03	1,001.5	☐ 78.0							☐ 1.59			0.16	26.97 - 14.70	13.1	0.8
2/02/02	918.7	☐ 41.1	611.6	7.7	4.5	10.2	6.7	2.6	☐ 0.84	1.72	4.34	0.16	22.70 - 11.50	20.4	0.9
2/03/01	1,060.4	65.0	668.5	10.4	6.1	16.3	9.7	2.6	1.30	2.18	4.27	0.16	24.94 - 15.63	15.6	0.8
1/29/00	846.9	☐ 87.9	702.1	16.5	10.4	22.1	12.5	3.0	☐ 1.71	2.27	3.65	0.16	36.88 - 14.75	15.1	0.6
1/30/99	661.9	☐ 71.7	394.3	17.0	10.8	22.8	18.2	3.5	☐ 1.40	1.83	6.01	0.15	24.13 - 14.31	13.7	0.8
1/31/98	500.2	58.2	306.3	17.2	11.6	23.1	19.0	4.3	1.19	1.54	5.20	0.12	24.00 - 12.13	15.2	0.7
2/01/97	440.2	45.1	242.9	15.7	10.3	23.2	18.6	3.5	0.95	1.28	4.31	0.09	26.63 - 7.56	18.0	0.5
2/03/96	344.9	30.9	187.8	13.8	9.0	20.2	16.4	3.4	0.66	0.98	3.23	0.05	10.22 - 5.00	11.5	0.7
1/28/95	301.4	23.9	158.6	12.5	7.9	19.5	15.0	2.6	0.51	0.81	2.61	0.05	10.28 - 4.22	14.2	0.7
1/29/94	281.7	23.6	135.2	13.4	8.4	23.7	17.5	2.6	0.51	0.79	2.14	0.04	8.67 - 5.33	13.7	0.6

Statistics are as originally reported. Adj. for 3-for-2 stk. split, 9/96 & 2/96. ☐ Bef. $235,000 loss from disc. ops., 2003; $21.5 mil ($0.44/sh), 2002; $9.4 mil ($0.18/sh) loss, 1999. ☐ Incl. $5.5 mil ($0.11/sh) non-recur. after-tax restr. chg.

OFFICERS:
R. Schaefer, Chmn., Pres., C.E.O.
M. Schaefer, Vice-Chmn.
E. B. Schaefer, Vice-Chmn.
I. D. Kaplan, Sr. V.P., C.F.O.

INVESTOR CONTACT: Sonia Rohan, Dir.,
Inv. Rel., (212) 594-3127

PRINCIPAL OFFICE: 3 S.W. 129th Avenue,
Pembroke Pines, FL 33027

TELEPHONE NUMBER: (954) 433-3900
FAX: (954) 433-3999
WEB: www.clairestores.com
NO. OF EMPLOYEES: 16,300 (approx.)
SHAREHOLDERS: 1,488 (approx. common);
505 (approx. Class A)
ANNUAL MEETING: In June
INCORPORATED: DE, Oct., 1961; reincorp.,
FL, June, 2000

INSTITUTIONAL HOLDINGS:
No. of Institutions: 189
Shares Held: 35,075,647
% Held: 71.7

INDUSTRY: Women's accessory & specialty
stores (SIC: 5632)

TRANSFER AGENT(S): First Union National
Bank, Charlotte, NC

CLARCOR INC.

EXCH.	SYM.	REC. PRICE	P/E RATIO	YLD.	MKT. CAP.	RANGE (52-WK.)	'02 Y/E PR.	DIV. ACH.
NYSE	CLC	33.44 (2/28/03)	18.2	1.4%	$0.83 bill.	36.30 - 25.03	32.27	22 yrs.

UPPER MEDIUM GRADE. THE COMPANY EXPECTS EARNINGS TO BE IN THE RANGE OF $1.92 TO $2.02 PER SHARE IN 2003.

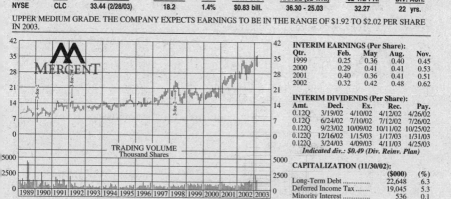

INTERIM EARNINGS (Per Share):

Qtr.	Feb.	May	Aug.	Nov.
1999	0.25	0.36	0.40	0.45
2000	0.29	0.41	0.41	0.53
2001	0.40	0.36	0.41	0.51
2002	0.32	0.42	0.48	0.62

INTERIM DIVIDENDS (Per Share):

Amt.	Decl.	Ex.	Rec.	Pay.
0.12Q	3/19/02	4/10/02	4/12/02	4/26/02
0.12Q	6/24/02	7/10/02	7/12/02	7/26/02
0.12Q	9/23/02	10/09/02	10/11/02	10/25/02
0.12Q	12/16/02	1/15/03	1/17/03	1/31/03
0.12Q	3/24/03	4/11/03	4/15/03	4/25/03

Indicated div.: $0.49 (Div. Reinv. Plan)

CAPITALIZATION (11/30/02):

	($000)	(%)
Long-Term Debt	22,648	6.3
Deferred Income Tax	19,045	5.3
Minority Interest	536	0.1
Common & Surplus	315,461	88.2
Total	357,690	100.0

*7 YEAR PRICE SCORE 159.3   ***12 MONTH PRICE SCORE 117.8**

*NYSE COMPOSITE INDEX=100

BUSINESS:

CLARCOR, Inc. manufactures mobile, industrial and environmental filtration products and consumer and industrial packaging products for domestic and international markets. The Industrial/Environmental Filtration segment (53.6% of fiscal 2002 net sales) includes products used primarily for commercial, residential and industrial applications. The segment markets commercial and industrial air filters and systems, electrostatic contamination control equipment and electrostatic high precision spraying equipment. The Engine/Mobile Filtration segment (36.8%) markets a full line of oil, air, fuel, coolant and hydraulic fluid filters. The Packaging segment (9.6%) includes a variety of custom styled containers and packaging items used primarily by the food, confectionery, spice, drug, toiletries and chemical specialties industries. In June 2001, CLC acquired Total Filtration Systems, Inc. for $33.3 million.

RECENT DEVELOPMENTS:

For the year ended 11/30/02, net earnings advanced 11.2% to $46.6 million compared with $41.9 million in the previous year. Net sales increased 7.3% to $715.6 million from $667.0 million a year earlier. Engine/Mobile Filtration segment sales rose 5.0% to $263.5 million, while Industrial/Environmental Filtration segment sales climbed 10.7% to $383.6 million. Packaging segment sales decreased 1.7% to $68.4 million. Gross profit grew 6.0% to $207.3 million from $195.5 million in 2001. Operating income improved 2.6% to $77.8 million from $75.8 million the year before. Other expense amounted to $6.4 million versus $10.1 million in the prior year.

PROSPECTS:

For fiscal 2003, the Company expects continued sales growth of heavy-duty, environmental and industrial filters. Conversely, CLC's sales to the dust collection and air quality systems market should remain subdued in the coming year. Nevertheless, CLC plans to introduce several new products for this market. Separately, the Company expects earnings in the range of $1.92 to $2.02 per share in 2003. Moreover, excess free cash generated in 2003 will be used to further reduce CLC's bank debt. Elsewhere, with its China operations growing at a double-digit pace, CLC has plans to expand production and to manufacture new types of products in China over the next several years.

ANNUAL FINANCIAL DATA:

FISCAL YEAR	TOT. REVS. ($000)	NET INC. ($000)	TOT. ASSETS ($000)	OPER. PROFIT %	NET PROFIT %	RET. ON EQUITY %	RET. ON ASSETS %	CURR. RATIO	EARN. PER SH.$	CASH FL. PER SH.$	TANG. BK. VAL.$	DIV. PER SH.$	PRICE RANGE	AVG. P/E RATIO	AVG. YIELD %
11/30/02	715,563	46,601	546,119	10.9	6.5	14.8	8.5	1.5	1.85	2.64	7.74	0.48	34.00 - 25.03	16.0	1.6
11/30/01	666,964	41,893	530,617	11.4	6.3	15.3	7.9	2.6	1.68	2.56	6.40	0.47	28.88 - 19.00	14.2	2.0
11/30/00	652,148	40,237	501,930	11.7	6.2	16.6	8.0	2.4	1.64	2.50	5.75	0.46	21.50 - 16.06	11.5	2.5
11/27/99	477,869	35,412	472,991	11.7	7.4	16.8	7.5	2.3	1.46	2.09	4.98	0.45	21.38 - 14.25	12.2	2.5
11/28/98	426,773	32,079	305,766	12.1	7.5	17.2	10.5	2.7	1.30	1.80	6.90	0.44	24.67 - 14.25	15.0	2.3
11/29/97	394,264	☐26,918	282,519	11.3	6.8	15.7	9.5	3.0	☐1.11	1.60	6.41	0.43	20.83 - 13.33	15.3	2.5
11/30/96	333,388	24,978	243,964	12.2	7.5	17.1	10.2	2.8	1.12	1.56	5.87	0.43	16.75 - 12.42	13.0	2.9
11/30/95	290,194	21,954	223,262	12.2	7.6	16.8	9.8	2.8	0.99	1.36	5.23	0.42	18.00 - 12.42	15.4	2.8
11/30/94	270,123	20,625	188,448	12.0	7.6	17.6	10.9	2.5	0.93	1.26	4.62	0.41	14.92 - 10.58	13.8	3.3
11/30/93	225,319	17,251	169,896	12.9	7.7	16.5	10.2	2.6	0.77	1.06	4.00	0.41	14.08 - 10.67	16.0	3.3

Statistics are as originally reported. Adj. for stk. split: 3-for-2, 4/98 ☐ Incl. non-recurr. credit of $1.7 mill. & non-recurr. chrg. of $3.0 mill.

OFFICERS:
N. E. Johnson, Chmn., Pres., C.E.O.
B. A. Klein, V.P., C.F.O.
D. J. Boyd, V.P., Sec., Gen. Couns.
INVESTOR CONTACT: Bruce A. Klein, V.P., C.F.O., (815) 962-8867
PRINCIPAL OFFICE: 2323 Sixth Street, P.O. Box 7007, Rockford, IL 61125

TELEPHONE NUMBER: (815) 962-8867
FAX: (815) 962-0417
WEB: www.clarcor.com
NO. OF EMPLOYEES: 4,545 (approx.)
SHAREHOLDERS: 1,500 (record)
ANNUAL MEETING: In March
INCORPORATED: IL, 1904; reincorp., DE, 1969

INSTITUTIONAL HOLDINGS:
No. of Institutions: 148
Shares Held: 18,897,222
% Held: 75.9
INDUSTRY: Motor vehicle parts and accessories (SIC: 3714)
TRANSFER AGENT(S): EquiServe, First Chicago Trust Division, Jersey City, NJ

CLAYTON HOMES, INC.

EXCH.	SYM.	REC. PRICE	P/E RATIO	YLD.	MKT. CAP.	RANGE (52-WK.)	'02 Y/E PR.
NYSE	CMH	11.04 (3/31/03)	12.3	0.6%	$1.52 bill.	19.60 - 9.23	12.18

UPPER MEDIUM GRADE. ON 4/2/03, THE COMPANY ANNOUNCED THAT IT WILL BE ACQUIRED BY BERKSHIRE HATHAWAY INC. FOR APPROXIMATELY $1.70 BILLION.

TRADING VOLUME
Thousand Shares

*7 YEAR PRICE SCORE 113.4   ***12 MONTH PRICE SCORE 93.0**
*NYSE COMPOSITE INDEX=100

INTERIM EARNINGS (Per Share):

Qtr.	Sept.	Dec.	Mar.	June
1996-97	0.18	0.18	0.18	0.27
1997-98	0.20	0.21	0.21	0.30
1998-99	0.22	0.24	0.24	0.36
1999-00	0.25	0.25	0.26	0.27
2000-01	0.21	0.20	0.17	0.19
2001-02	0.19	0.24	0.21	0.25
2002-03	0.22	0.22	...	...

INTERIM DIVIDENDS (Per Share):

Amt.	Decl.	Ex.	Rec.	Pay.
0.016Q	1/25/01	3/26/01	3/28/01	4/18/01
0.016Q	4/25/01	6/25/01	6/27/01	7/18/01
0.064A	10/30/01	12/31/01	1/03/02	1/24/02
0.064A	10/30/02	1/07/03	1/09/03	1/30/03

Indicated div.: $0.06 (Div. Reinv. Plan)

CAPITALIZATION (6/30/02):

	($000)	(%)
Long-Term Debt[1]	92,912	6.9
Common & Surplus	1,261,957	93.1
Total	1,354,869	100.0

BUSINESS:

Clayton Homes, Inc. builds, sells, finances and insures manufactured homes, and owns and operates 85 residential manufactured housing communities in 12 states. The Manufacturing group is a producer of homes with 20 plants supplying 622 independent retail centers. The Retail group sells, installs and services factory built homes. As of 12/31/02, Company-owned retail centers numbered 290.

The Financial Services group provides financing and insurance for homebuyers of Company-owned and selected independent retail sales centers through Vanderbilt Mortgage and Finance, a wholly-owned subsidiary. In addition, the Company's financial services operations provide mortgage services for 165,000 customers and insurance protection for 100,000 families.

RECENT DEVELOPMENTS:

For the quarter ended 12/31/02, net income declined 9.3% to $30.6 million compared with $33.7 million in the equivalent 2001 quarter. Results for 2001 included a nonrecurring $0.02 per share servicing gain from a $900.0 million portfolio acquisition. Operating revenue climbed 1.1% to $300.0 million from $296.8 million a year earlier. CMH's retail same-store sales increased 10.0% for the

quarter, and total sales climbed 3.5% to $214.9 million. Financial services revenues declined 5.5% to $66.7 million and rental and other income slipped 0.7% to $18.3 million. Net manufacturing unit sales fell 22.6% to 1,635, and total retail unit sales slid 1.3% to 3,712. However, total community unit sales grew 15.5% to 283.

PROSPECTS:

On 4/2/03, the Company announced that it will be acquired by Berkshire Hathaway Inc. for approximately $1.70 billion. Under the terms of the agreement, CMH's stockholders will receive $12.50 per share, with approximately 136 million shares outstanding. The acquisition is subject to the

approval of the Company's stockholders. In the near-term, CMH expects the operating environment to be challenging for manufacturing due to continued independent store closings and the cannibalization of new home production by the sale of foreclosures.

ANNUAL FINANCIAL DATA:

FISCAL YEAR	TOT. REVS. ($mill.)	NET INC. ($mill.)	TOT. ASSETS ($mill.)	OPER. PROFIT %	NET PROFIT %	RET. ON EQUITY %	RET. ON ASSETS %	CURR. RATIO	EARN. PER SH. $	CASH FL. PER SH. $	TANG. BK. VAL. $	DIV. PER SH. $	PRICE RANGE	AVG. P/E RATIO	AVG. YIELD %
6/30/02	1,198.8	124.1	1,828.4	16.8	10.4	9.8	6.8	9.0	0.89	1.13	9.14	0.064	19.60 — 9.23	16.2	0.4
6/30/01	1,151.0	106.7	1,654.2	14.8	9.3	9.3	6.4	9.1	0.77	1.02	8.32	0.05	17.62 — 10.00	-17.9	0.3
6/30/00	1,293.3	144.0	1,506.4	17.6	11.1	13.9	9.6	7.7	1.03	1.20	7.54	0.06	13.06 — 7.69	10.1	0.6
6/30/99	1,344.3	155.0	1,417.2	18.7	11.5	16.4	10.9	6.9	1.06	1.18	6.66	0.06	15.44 — 8.25	11.2	0.5
6/30/98	1,127.8	137.7	1,457.8	19.2	12.2	15.6	9.4	7.3	0.92	1.02	5.93	0.06	18.10 — 10.65	15.6	0.4
6/30/97	1,021.7	119.5	1,045.8	18.4	11.7	15.8	11.4	6.9	0.80	0.89	5.09	0.06	15.60 — 10.10	16.1	0.5
6/30/96	928.7	106.8	886.4	18.1	11.5	16.4	12.0	6.3	0.71	0.79	4.38	0.05	14.48 — 9.92	17.1	0.4
6/30/95	758.1	[3]87.0	761.2	17.4	11.5	16.0	11.4	7.5	[2]0.58	0.64	3.69	0.04	14.98 — 7.17	19.0	0.4
6/30/94	628.2	[2]69.6	770.5	17.3	11.1	15.1	9.9	8.4	[2]0.48	0.53	3.93	...	10.96 — 6.30	18.0	...
6/30/93	476.2	53.8	587.0	17.5	11.3	15.4	9.2	11.6	0.48	0.47	3.19	...	10.08 — 6.76	17.5	...

Statistics are as originally reported. Adj. for stk. split: 25% stk. divs., 12/93, 12/94, 12/95, 12/96 & 12/98. [1] Incl. debentures conv. into common stock. [2] Bef. an acctg. cr. of $3.0 mill. ($0.02/sh.). [3] Incl. a $4.8 mill. pretax gain from the sale of CMH's interest in two communities.

OFFICERS:
J. L. Clayton, Chmn.
K. T. Clayton, Pres., C.E.O.
J. J. Kalec, Sr. V.P., C.F.O.
G. A. Hamilton, V.P., Controller
INVESTOR CONTACT: Investor Relations, (865) 380-3206
PRINCIPAL OFFICE: Box 15169, Knoxville, TN 37901

TELEPHONE NUMBER: (865) 380-3000
FAX: (865) 380-3750
WEB: www.clayton.net
NO. OF EMPLOYEES: 6,554 (avg.)
SHAREHOLDERS: 9,185 (record); 44,000 (approx. beneficial)
ANNUAL MEETING: In Oct.
INCORPORATED: TN, May, 1968

INSTITUTIONAL HOLDINGS:
No. of Institutions: 173
Shares Held: 87,575,164
% Held: 64.4

INDUSTRY: Mobile homes (SIC: 2451)

TRANSFER AGENT(S): American Stock Transfer & Trust Company, New York, NY

CLEAR CHANNEL COMMUNICATIONS, INC.

EXCH.	SYM.	REC. PRICE	P/E RATIO	YLD.	MKT. CAP.	RANGE (52-WK.)	'02 Y/E PR.
NYSE	CCU	36.51 (2/28/03)	30.9	...	$22.38 bill.	54.90 - 20.00	37.29

LOWER MEDIUM GRADE. NEAR-TERM GROWTH MAY BE HAMPERED BY ONGOING ECONOMIC AND GEOPOLITICAL UNCERTAINTY.

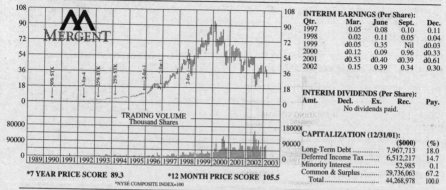

INTERIM EARNINGS (Per Share):

Qtr.	Mar.	June	Sept.	Dec.
1997	0.05	0.08	0.10	0.11
1998	0.02	0.11	0.05	0.04
1999	d0.05	0.35	Nil	d0.03
2000	0.12	0.09	0.96	d0.33
2001	d0.53	d0.40	d0.39	d0.61
2002	0.15	0.39	0.34	0.30

INTERIM DIVIDENDS (Per Share):

Amt.	Decl.	Ex.	Rec.	Pay.
	No dividends paid.			

CAPITALIZATION (12/31/01):

	($000)	(%)
Long-Term Debt	7,967,713	18.0
Deferred Income Tax	6,512,217	14.7
Minority Interest	52,985	0.1
Common & Surplus	29,736,063	67.2
Total	44,268,978	100.0

*7 YEAR PRICE SCORE 89.3   *12 MONTH PRICE SCORE 105.5

*NYSE COMPOSITE INDEX=100

BUSINESS:

Clear Channel Communications, Inc. is a diversified media company with radio and television stations, outdoor advertising displays, and live entertainment venues in 64 countries around the world. As of 12/31/01, Clear Channel Radio operated approximately 1,225 radio stations in the United States and has equity interests in approximately 240 radio stations internationally. Also, Clear Channel Outdoor operated approximately 776,000 outdoor advertising displays as of 12/31/01, including billboards, street furniture and transit panels across the world. Clear Channel Entertainment is one of the world's largest diversified promoters, producers and presenters of live entertainment events and is a fully integrated sports marketing and management company. Clear Channel also operates 37 television stations in the United States and owns the largest media representation firm, Katz Media Group. On 6/14/02, the Company acquired The Ackerley Group in a transaction valued at about $848.5 million.

RECENT DEVELOPMENTS:

For the year ended 12/31/02, net income was $724.8 million compared with a net loss of $1.14 billion the previous year. Results for 2002 included a net pre-tax gain of $49.1 million related to the sale of a television license, extinguishment of long-term debt, a sale of marketable securities, a sale of other assets and a litigation settlement. Results for 2001 included a net pre-tax charge of $205.0 million related to non-cash compensation, a sale of assets and a sale of marketable securities. Revenue increased 5.7% to $8.42 billion from $7.97 billion a year earlier. Radio revenues grew 7.6% to $3.72 billion, while outdoor revenues increased 6.4% to $1.86 billion.

PROSPECTS:

Earnings are benefiting from an improved advertising climate. This improvement is especially evident in the Company's core radio division, which saw a 9.9% revenue gain during the fourth quarter of 2002. Meanwhile, stronger percentage gains are also being experienced in the Company's live-entertainment and outdoor-advertising divisions, up 28.0% and 17.3%, respectively, from the prioryear levels. Going forward, CCU remains cautious about its near-term outlook as uncertain geopolitical and economic events may soften advertising volume.

ANNUAL FINANCIAL DATA:

FISCAL YEAR	TOT. REVS. ($mill.)	NET INC. ($mill.)	TOT. ASSETS ($mill.)	OPER. PROFIT %	NET PROFIT %	RET. ON EQUITY %	RET. ON ASSETS %	CURR. RATIO	EARN. PER SH.$	CASH FL. PER SH.$	TANG. BK. VAL.$	PRICE RANGE	AVG. P/E RATIO
p12/31/02	8,421.1	⑤ 724.8							⑤ 1.18			54.90 - 20.00	31.7
12/31/01	7,970.0	④ d1,144.0	47,603.1	...	...	...	...	0.7	④ d1.93	2.45	...	68.08 - 35.20	...
③ 12/31/00	5,345.3	② 248.8	50,056.5	5.7	4.7	0.8	0.5	1.1	② 0.57	3.83	...	95.50 - 43.88	122.2
12/31/99	2,678.2	① 85.7	16,821.5	9.5	3.2	0.8	0.5	1.3	① 0.26	2.54	...	91.50 - 52.00	275.9
12/31/98	1,350.9	54.0	7,539.9	17.8	4.0	1.2	0.7	1.6	0.22	1.51	0.35	62.31 - 31.00	212.0
12/31/97	697.1	63.6	3,455.6	24.0	9.1	3.6	1.8	2.3	0.34	1.06	...	39.94 - 16.81	84.7
12/31/96	351.7	37.7	1,324.7	28.2	10.7	7.3	2.8	2.6	0.25	0.66	...	22.63 - 10.19	65.6
12/31/95	243.8	32.0	563.0	29.3	13.1	19.6	5.7	2.0	0.23	0.55	...	11.06 - 6.27	38.0
12/31/94	173.1	22.0	411.6	24.8	12.7	16.9	5.3	1.9	0.16	0.41	...	6.50 - 3.93	33.0
12/31/93	118.2	9.1	227.6	18.0	7.7	9.3	4.0	1.5	0.07	0.26	...	4.61 - 1.62	42.6

Statistics are as originally reported. Adj. for stk. splits: 2-for-1, 7/98, 12/96 & 12/95; 25% div., 2/94 & 2/93. ① Incl. gain on sale of stations of $138.7 mill. & excl. extraord. loss of $13.2 mill. ② Incl. non-cash compen. exp. of $16.0 mill. & gain on sale of assets of $783.4 mill. ③ Reflect the acqs. of SFX Entertainment, Inc. and AMFM Inc. on 8/1/00 and 9/30/00, respectively ④ Incl. non-cash chrg. $17.1 mill., gain on marketable securities of $28.8 mill. & a loss on the sale of assets of $213.7 mill. ⑤ Incl. net non-recurr. gains of $49.1 mill.

OFFICERS:
L. L. Mays, Chmn., C.E.O.
M. P. Mays, Pres., C.O.O.
R. T. Mays, Exec. V.P., C.F.O.
INVESTOR CONTACT: Randy Palmer, Investor Relations, (210) 832-3315
PRINCIPAL OFFICE: 200 East Basse Road, San Antonio, TX 78209-8328

TELEPHONE NUMBER: (210) 822-2828
FAX: (210) 822-2299
WEB: www.clearchannel.com
NO. OF EMPLOYEES: 36,200 (approx.)
SHAREHOLDERS: 3,388 (approx.)
ANNUAL MEETING: In April
INCORPORATED: TX, April, 1974

INSTITUTIONAL HOLDINGS:
No. of Institutions: 556
Shares Held: 480,213,707
% Held: 78.4
INDUSTRY: Television broadcasting stations (SIC: 4833)
TRANSFER AGENT(S): Bank of New York, New York, NY

CLECO CORPORATION

EXCH.	SYM.	REC. PRICE	P/E RATIO	YLD.	MKT. CAP.	RANGE (52-WK.)	'02 Y/E PR.	DIV. ACH.
NYSE	CNL	11.69 (2/28/03)	8.1	7.7%	$0.55 bill.	24.90 - 9.74	14.00	21 yrs.

MEDIUM GRADE. FULL-YEAR 2003 EARNINGS ARE EXPECTED IN THE RANGE OF $1.65 TO $1.75 PER SHARE.

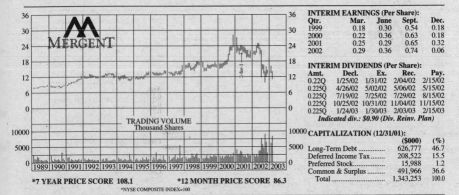

*7 YEAR PRICE SCORE 108.1   ***12 MONTH PRICE SCORE 86.3**
NYSE COMPOSITE INDEX=100

INTERIM EARNINGS (Per Share):

Qtr.	Mar.	June	Sept.	Dec.
1999	0.18	0.30	0.54	0.18
2000	0.22	0.36	0.63	0.18
2001	0.25	0.29	0.65	0.32
2002	0.29	0.36	0.74	0.06

INTERIM DIVIDENDS (Per Share):

Amt.	Decl.	Ex.	Rec.	Pay.
0.22Q	1/25/02	1/31/02	2/04/02	2/15/02
0.225Q	4/26/02	5/02/02	5/06/02	5/15/02
0.225Q	7/19/02	7/25/02	7/29/02	8/15/02
0.225Q	10/25/02	10/31/02	11/04/02	11/15/02
0.225Q	1/24/03	1/30/03	2/03/03	2/15/03

Indicated div.: $0.90 (Div. Reinv. Plan)

CAPITALIZATION (12/31/01):

	($000)	(%)
Long-Term Debt	626,777	46.7
Deferred Income Tax	208,522	15.5
Preferred Stock	15,988	1.2
Common & Surplus	491,966	36.6
Total	1,343,253	100.0

BUSINESS:

Cleco Corporation, under an energy services holding structure, is the parent company of Cleco Power LLC and Cleco Midstream Resources LLC. Cleco Power LLC (78.4% of 2002 revenues) is a regulated electric utility company that provides electricity to approximately 250,000 customers in Louisiana. Cleco Midstream Resources LLC (21.6%) is a non-regulated regional energy services group that develops

and operates electric power generation facilities, invests in and develops natural gas pipelines and other gas-related assets, and provides energy services to organizations that operate electric utility systems. The other segment consists of a shared services subsidiary, an investment subsidiary and a retail subsidiary.

RECENT DEVELOPMENTS:

For the year ended 12/31/02, the Company reported net income of $71.9 million compared with income from continuing operations of $72.3 million in the previous year. Results for 2002 included a restructuring charge of $10.2 million and an asset impairment charge of $3.6 million. Total operating revenue decreased 3.7% to $721.2 million from $748.8 million a year earlier. Electric operations revenue declined 4.1% to $568.1 million, while net energy trading revenues fell 76.2% to $1.7 million. Energy operations revenue dropped 49.0% to $30.1 million. However, tolling operations revenue jumped 49.1% to $90.3 million. Operating income increased 0.2% to $160.6 million from $160.2 million the year before.

PROSPECTS:

Going forward, the Company's primary goals include extracting value from existing wholesale generating assets and reducing risks and reinforcing its balance sheet. Meanwhile, Cleco Power is expected to contribute $1.00 to $1.10 per share to earnings in the coming year, assuming normal weather. In 2003, CNL expects to report increases in power capacity costs, insurance premiums, pension and 401(k) costs, interest expense, depreciation expense and property taxes. For full-year 2003, the Company anticipates total earnings in the range of $1.65 to $1.75 per share.

ANNUAL FINANCIAL DATA:

FISCAL YEAR	TOT. REVS. ($mill.)	NET INC. ($mill.)	TOT. ASSETS ($mill.)	OPER. PROFIT %	NET PROFIT %	NET INC./ NET PROP. %	NET INC./ TOT. CAP. %	RET. ON EQUITY %	ACCUM. DEPR./ GROSS PROP. %	EARN. PER SH.$	TANG. BK. VAL.$	DIV. PER SH.$	DIV. PAYOUT %	PRICE RANGE		AVG. P/E RATIO	AVG. YIELD %
p12/31/02	721.2	③ 71.9	2,344.6		10.0			12.4		③ 1.47	10.94	0.90	61.2	24.90	9.74	11.8	5.2
12/31/01	1,058.6	② 72.3	1,768.1	14.1	6.8	5.9	5.4	14.2	34.9	② 1.51	10.94	0.87	57.6	27.25	19.25	15.4	3.7
12/31/00	820.0	① 69.3	1,845.7	18.0	8.5	5.6	4.8	14.4	32.9	① 1.46	10.33	0.84	58.1	28.25	15.06	14.9	3.9
12/31/99	768.2	56.8	1,704.7	14.6	7.4	4.7	3.9	12.5	31.4	1.19	9.77	0.83	34.8	17.75	14.13	13.4	5.2
12/31/98	515.2	53.8	1,429.0	15.6	10.4	4.9	4.7	12.3	33.6	1.12	9.45	0.81	36.0	18.06	14.31	14.5	5.0
12/31/97	456.2	52.5	1,361.0	17.3	11.5	5.1	4.6	12.5	33.6	1.09	9.10	0.79	36.0	16.56	12.38	13.3	5.5
12/31/96	435.4	52.1	1,321.8	18.0	12.0	5.5	4.8	12.9	33.3	1.12	8.76	0.77	34.3	14.63	12.56	12.2	5.7
12/31/95	394.4	48.7	1,266.0	18.9	12.3	5.2	4.4	12.6	32.2	1.04	8.41	0.75	35.8	14.06	11.00	12.0	6.0
12/31/94	379.6	45.0	1,178.2	18.6	11.9	4.9	4.8	12.2	31.0	0.96	7.61	0.73	37.8	12.81	10.44	12.1	6.3
12/31/93	382.4	41.8	1,161.6	16.9	10.9	4.7	4.4	11.7	29.8	0.89	7.88	0.71	39.6	13.56	11.50	14.1	5.7

Statistics are as originally reported. Adj. for 2-for-1 stock split 5/21/01. ① Bef. extraord. gain of $2.5 mill. & disc. opers. loss $6.9 mill. ② Bef. a loss from discont. opers. of $2.0 mill. ③ Incl. restr. chrg. of $10.2 mill. and asset impair. chrg. of $3.6 mill.

OFFICERS:
D. M. Eppler, Pres., C.E.O.
D. Samil, Sr. V.P., C.F.O.
K. F. Nolen, Treas.

INVESTOR CONTACT: Rodney J. Hamilton, Dir., Inv. Rel., (318) 484-7593

PRINCIPAL OFFICE: 2030 Donahue Ferry Road, Pineville, LA 71360-5226

TELEPHONE NUMBER: (318) 484-7400
FAX: (318) 484-7465
WEB: www.cleco.com

NO. OF EMPLOYEES: 1,392

SHAREHOLDERS: 8,990

ANNUAL MEETING: In April

INCORPORATED: LA, Dec., 1932

INSTITUTIONAL HOLDINGS:
No. of Institutions: 152
Shares Held: 24,975,533
% Held: 53.1

INDUSTRY: Electric services (SIC: 4911)

TRANSFER AGENT(S): EquiServe Trust Company, N.A., Jersey City, NJ

CLOROX COMPANY (THE)

EXCH.	SYM.	REC. PRICE	P/E RATIO	YLD.	MKT. CAP.	RANGE (52-WK.)	'02 Y/E PR.	DIV. ACH.
NYSE	CLX	42.31 (2/28/03)	21.9	1.9%	$9.44 bill.	47.95 - 31.92	41.25	26 yrs.

INVESTMENT GRADE. CLX RAISED ITS EARNINGS PER SHARE GUIDANCE TO A RANGE OF $2.21 TO $2.27.

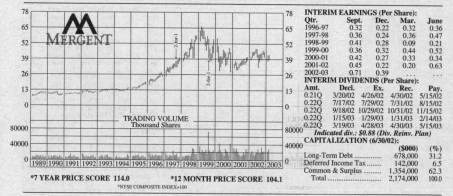

*7 YEAR PRICE SCORE 114.0   ***12 MONTH PRICE SCORE 104.1**
*NYSE COMPOSITE INDEX=100

INTERIM EARNINGS (Per Share):

Qtr.	Sept.	Dec.	Mar.	June
1996-97	0.32	0.22	0.32	0.36
1997-98	0.36	0.24	0.36	0.47
1998-99	0.41	0.28	0.09	0.21
1999-00	0.36	0.32	0.44	0.52
2000-01	0.42	0.27	0.33	0.34
2001-02	0.45	0.22	0.20	0.63
2002-03	0.71	0.39	...	...

INTERIM DIVIDENDS (Per Share):

Amt.	Decl.	Ex.	Rec.	Pay.
0.21Q	3/20/02	4/26/02	4/30/02	5/15/02
0.22Q	7/17/02	7/29/02	7/31/02	8/15/02
0.22Q	9/18/02	10/29/02	10/31/02	11/15/02
0.22Q	1/15/03	1/29/03	1/31/03	2/14/03
0.22Q	3/19/03	4/28/03	4/30/03	5/15/03

Indicated div.: $0.88 (Div. Reinv. Plan)

CAPITALIZATION (6/30/02):

	($000)	(%)
Long-Term Debt	678,000	31.2
Deferred Income Tax	142,000	6.5
Common & Surplus	1,354,000	62.3
Total	2,174,000	100.0

BUSINESS:

The Clorox Company is a manufacturer and marketer of household products, both domestic and international, and products for institutional markets. CLX operates in four business segments. The U.S. Home Care and Cleaning segment (54.1% of fiscal 2002 sales) includes products such as SOFT SCRUB, CLOROX, TUFFY FORMULA 409, LIQUID PLUMR, PINE - SOL, TILEX, and SOS. The U.S. Specialty Products segment (32.1%) includes brand names such as ARMOR ALL, STP and KINGSFORD CHARCOAL. Products in

the U.S. Food, Food Preparation and Storage segment include HIDDEN VALLEY and K C MASTERPIECE dressings and sauces, BRITA, GLAD, and GLADWARE businesses and SCOOP AWAY, and FRESH STEP cat litters. The international segment (13.8%), which includes CLX's overseas operations, exports and Puerto Rico, primarily focuses on the laundry, household cleaning and insecticide categories. On 1/29/99, the Company acquired First Brands Corp. for $2.00 billion.

RECENT DEVELOPMENTS:

For the quarter ended 12/31/02, income jumped to $87.0 million, before income from discontinued operations of $2.0 million, from income of $42.0 million, before income from discontinued operations of $9.0 million, in the equivalent prior-year quarter. Earnings for 2002 and 2001 included restructuring and asset impairment charges of

$30.0 million and $66.0 million, respectively. Net sales increased 4.4% to $926.0 million from $887.0 million the previous year. North American household products sales grew 7.7% to $545.0 million, while household product sales in Latin America slid 15.9% to $116.0 million. Sales of specialty products rose 9.1% to $265.0 million.

PROSPECTS:

For the third quarter of fiscal 2003, CLX expects volume to be equal to or slightly below the year-ago levels, with sales lagging volume because of promotional expenses associated with new product introductions. For the fourth quarter, CLX anticipates low- to mid-single digit volume and sales

growth driven by new product introductions. For the full-year, CLX continues to expect low-single-digit volume and sales growth, and has increased its expectations for earnings per diluted share to a range of $2.21 to $2.27.

ANNUAL FINANCIAL DATA:

FISCAL YEAR	TOT. REVS. ($mill.)	NET INC. ($mill.)	TOT. ASSETS ($mill.)	OPER. PROFIT %	NET PROFIT %	RET. ON EQUITY %	RET. ON ASSETS %	CURR. RATIO	EARN. PER SH.$	CASH FL. PER SH.$	TANG. BK. VAL.$	DIV. PER SH.$	PRICE RANGE	AVG. P/E RATIO	AVG. YIELD %
6/30/02	4,061.0	④ 322.0	3,630.0	12.6	7.9	23.8	8.9	0.8	④ 1.37	2.18	0.24	0.86	47.95 - 31.92	29.1	2.2
6/30/01	3,903.0	④ 325.0	3,995.0	15.7	8.3	17.1	8.1	1.0	④ 1.36	2.30	1.38	0.84	40.85 - 29.95	26.0	2.4
6/30/00	4,083.0	④ 394.0	4,353.0	18.2	9.6	22.0	9.1	0.9	④ 1.64	2.48	1.10	0.82	56.38 - 28.38	25.8	1.9
③ 6/30/99	4,003.0	④ 246.0	4,132.0	13.8	6.1	15.7	6.0	0.8	④ 1.03	1.87	0.31	0.76	66.47 - 37.50	50.5	1.5
6/30/98	2,741.3	298.0	3,030.0	19.6	10.9	27.5	9.8	0.7	1.41	2.06	...	0.68	58.75 - 37.19	34.0	1.4
6/30/97	2,532.7	249.4	2,778.0	18.4	9.8	24.1	9.0	0.8	1.21	1.82	...	0.61	40.19 - 24.31	26.8	1.9
6/30/96	2,217.8	222.1	2,178.9	18.7	10.0	23.8	10.2	0.9	1.07	1.63	1.11	0.56	27.56 - 17.50	21.1	2.5
6/30/95	1,984.2	200.8	1,906.7	18.1	10.1	21.3	10.5	1.3	0.95	1.43	1.68	0.51	19.81 - 13.81	17.8	3.0
6/30/94	1,836.9	180.0	1,697.6	17.7	9.8	19.8	10.6	1.3	① 0.84	1.27	1.82	0.47	14.88 - 11.75	15.9	3.5
6/30/93	1,634.2	① ① 167.9	1,649.2	18.1	10.3	19.1	10.2	1.4	① 0.77	1.15	1.89	0.44	13.84 - 11.00	16.2	3.6

Statistics are as originally reported. Adj. for stk. splits: 2-for-1, 8/99 and 9/97. ① Bef. disc. oper. gain $32.1 mill., 6/94; loss $867,000, 6/93. ② Bef. acctg. change chrg. $2.0 mill., 6/01 ③ Incl. results of First Brands Corp. ④ Incl. one-time chrgs. $241.0 mill., 6/02; $98.0 mill., 6/01; $21.0 mill., 6/00; $180.0 mill., 6/99.

OFFICERS:
G. C. Sullivan, Chmn., C.E.O.
G. E. Johnston, Pres., C.O.O.
K. M. Rose, V.P., C.F.O.
INVESTOR CONTACT: Doug Hughes, Investor Relations, (510) 271-2270
PRINCIPAL OFFICE: 1221 Broadway, Oakland, CA 94612-1888

TELEPHONE NUMBER: (510) 271-7000
FAX: (510) 832-1463
WEB: www.clorox.com
NO. OF EMPLOYEES: 11,000 (approx.)
SHAREHOLDERS: 15,365 (approx.)
ANNUAL MEETING: In Nov.
INCORPORATED: DE, 1986

INSTITUTIONAL HOLDINGS:
No. of Institutions: 423
Shares Held: 110,175,619
% Held: 50.1
INDUSTRY: Polishes and sanitation goods (SIC: 2842)
TRANSFER AGENT(S): EquiServe Trust Company, N.A., Providence, RI

CMS ENERGY CORPORATION

EXCH.	SYM.	REC. PRICE	P/E RATIO	YLD.	MKT. CAP.	RANGE (52-WK.)	'02 Y/E PR.
NYSE	CMS	4.50 (2/28/03)	1.3	...	$0.60 bill.	23.63 - 4.05	9.44

SPECULATIVE GRADE. THE COMPANY ANTICIPATES 2003 EARNINGS WILL RANGE FROM BREAK-EVEN TO $0.10 PER SHARE.

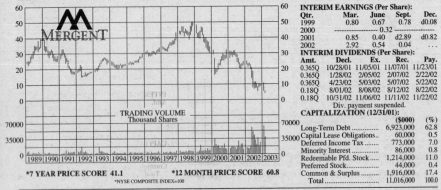

INTERIM EARNINGS (Per Share):

Qtr.	Mar.	June	Sept.	Dec.
1999	0.80	0.67	0.78	d0.08
2000	-------------	0.32	-------------	
2001	0.85	0.40	d2.89	d0.82
2002	2.92	0.54	0.04	...

INTERIM DIVIDENDS (Per Share):

Amt.	Decl.	Ex.	Rec.	Pay.
0.365Q	10/28/01	11/05/01	11/07/01	11/23/01
0.365Q	1/28/02	2/05/02	2/07/02	2/22/02
0.365Q	4/23/02	5/03/02	5/07/02	5/22/02
0.18Q	8/01/02	8/08/02	8/12/02	8/22/02
0.18Q	10/31/02	11/06/02	11/11/02	11/22/02

Div. payment suspended.

CAPITALIZATION (12/31/01):

	($000)	(%)
Long-Term Debt	6,923,000	62.8
Capital Lease Obligations..	60,000	0.5
Deferred Income Tax	773,000	7.0
Minority Interest	86,000	0.8
Redeemable Pfd. Stock ...	1,214,000	11.0
Preferred Stock	44,000	0.4
Common & Surplus	1,916,000	17.4
Total	11,016,000	100.0

*7 YEAR PRICE SCORE 41.1   ***12 MONTH PRICE SCORE 60.8**

*NYSE COMPOSITE INDEX=100

BUSINESS:

CMS Energy Corporation is a holding company for Consumers Energy Company and CMS Enterprises Company. Consumers Energy Company provides natural gas and electricity to residents of the lower Michigan peninsula. Consumers Energy Company currently has 1.7 million electric customers and 1.6 million gas customers. CMS Enterprises

Company offers several domestic and international energy businesses through its subsidiaries including: natural gas transmission, storage and processing; independent power generation; oil and gas exploration and production; international energy distribution; and energy marketing, services and trading.

RECENT DEVELOPMENTS:

For the third quarter ended 9/30/02, CMS reported income from continuing operations of $6.0 million compared with a loss from continuing operations of $363.0 million a year earlier. Results excluded income of $17.0 million in 2002 and a loss of $206.0 million in 2001 from discontinued operations. Results for 2002 included a net gain on asset sales of $12.0 million. Total operating revenues were

unchanged at $1.33 billion. Electric utility revenues increased 5.1% to $776.0 million, while marketing, services and trading revenues climbed 12.8% to $159.0 million. Gas utility revenues declined 10.1% to $134.0 million, while natural gas transmission revenues fell 17.1% to $170.0 million. Independent power production revenues slipped 4.1% to $93.0 million.

PROSPECTS:

The Company recently announced an agreement to sell CMS Marketing, Services and Trading's wholesale electric book and related supply portfolio to Constellation Power Sources, Inc. In addition, the Company's pipeline subsidiary agreed to sell its one-third equity interest in Centennial Pipeline LLC to Centennial's two other partners for $40.0 million. Separately CMS expects to report a loss in the

range of $4.25 to $4.75 for 2002. Looking ahead, CMS anticipates 2003 earnings will range from break-even to $0.10 per share. Going forward, CMS expects to sell other non-core assets such as its Guardian pipeline, CMS Field Services and international distribution companies and selected power plants. CMS expects to reduce capital spending by $350.0 million in 2003.

ANNUAL FINANCIAL DATA:

FISCAL YEAR	TOT. REVS. ($Mill.)	NET INC. ($Mill.)	TOT. ASSETS ($Mill.)	OPER. PROFIT %	NET PROFIT %	NET INC./ NET PROP. %	NET INC./ TOT. CAP. %	RET. ON EQUITY %	ACCUM. DEPR./ GROSS PROP. %	EARN. PER SH. $	TANG. BK. VAL.$	DIV. PER SH. $	DIV. PAYOUT %	PRICE RANGE	AVG. P/E RATIO	AVG. YIELD %
12/31/01	9,597.0	⑥ d331.0	17,128.0	3.1	...	...	...	...	45.0	⑥ d2.76	8.31	1.46	...	31.80 — 19.49	...	5.7
12/31/00	8,998.0	⑤ 41.0	15,851.0	8.1	0.5	0.5	0.4	1.7	44.4	⑤ 0.32	12.13	1.46	456.1	32.25 — 16.06	75.5	6.0
12/31/99	6,103.0	④ 277.0	15,462.0	14.9	4.5	3.4	2.4	11.1	43.1	④ 2.42	13.49	1.39	57.4	48.44 — 30.31	16.3	3.5
12/31/98	5,141.0	③ 242.0	11,168.0	15.1	4.7	4.0	3.0	10.5	46.3	③ 2.62	17.79	1.26	48.1	50.13 — 38.75	17.0	2.8
12/31/97	4,787.0	268.0	9,793.0	15.6	5.6	4.9	4.0	12.1	49.2	2.61	19.59	1.14	43.7	43.38 — 31.13	14.3	3.1
12/31/96	4,333.0	240.0	8,615.0	15.9	5.5	4.5	4.1	11.7	48.0	2.45	16.52	1.02	41.6	33.75 — 27.81	12.6	3.3
12/31/95	3,890.0	② 204.0	8,143.0	15.5	5.2	4.0	3.7	11.2	47.7	② 2.27	14.84	0.90	39.6	30.00 — 22.63	11.6	3.4
12/31/94	3,619.0	179.0	7,384.0	13.9	4.9	3.7	3.7	12.2	47.1	2.09	12.72	0.78	37.3	25.00 — 19.63	10.7	3.5
12/31/93	3,482.0	150.0	6,964.0	12.6	4.3	3.3	3.6	13.3	46.7	1.90	11.36	0.60	31.6	27.50 — 18.13	12.0	2.6
12/31/92	3,073.0	① d297.0	6,848.0	7.7	...	...	...	...	46.6	① d3.72	9.09	0.48	...	22.75 — 14.88	...	2.6

Statistics are as originally reported. ① Incl. non-recurr. chrg. $282.0 mill. ② Incl. non-recurr. credit $15.0 mill. ③ Bef. acctg. chrg. credit $43.0 mill. ④ Incl. special net chrg. of $49.0 mill. and a one-time chrg. of $84.0 mill. ⑤ Bef. acctg. chrg. $5.0 mill. & incl. net loss of $268.0 mill. fr. sale of an investment. ⑥ Bef. discont. opers. of $185.0 mill., extraord. chrg. of $18.0 mill. & acctg. change chrg. of $11.0 mill.; incl. net non-recurr. chrgs. of $516.0 mill.

OFFICERS:
K. Whipple, Chmn., C.E.O.
S. K. Smith Jr., Vice-Chmn., Gen. Couns.
D. W. Joos, Pres., C.O.O.
INVESTOR CONTACT: Investor Relations, (517) 788-2590
PRINCIPAL OFFICE: 330 Town Center Drive, Suite 1100, Dearborn, MI 48126

TELEPHONE NUMBER: (313) 436-9200
FAX: (313) 436-9225
WEB: www.cmsenergy.com
NO. OF EMPLOYEES: 11,343 full-time; 83 part-time
SHAREHOLDERS: 65,739
ANNUAL MEETING: In May
INCORPORATED: MI, 1987

INSTITUTIONAL HOLDINGS:
No. of Institutions: 233
Shares Held: 95,482,323
% Held: 66.3
INDUSTRY: Electric and other services combined (SIC: 4931)
TRANSFER AGENT(S): Investor Services Department, Jackson, MI

CNA FINANCIAL CORPORATION

EXCH.	SYM.	REC. PRICE	P/E RATIO	YLD.	MKT. CAP.	RANGE (52-WK.)	'02 Y/E PR.
NYSE	CNA	22.99 (2/28/03)	20.7	...	$5.14 bill.	30.99 - 21.45	25.60

MEDIUM GRADE. THE COMPANY IS ENCOURAGED BY THE PERFORMANCE OF ITS KEY BUSINESSES.

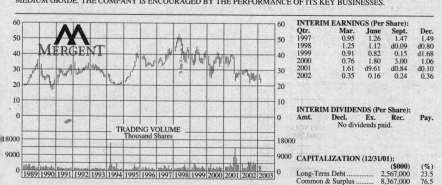

*7 YEAR PRICE SCORE 77.5   ***12 MONTH PRICE SCORE 100.6**
*NYSE COMPOSITE INDEX=100

INTERIM EARNINGS (Per Share):

Qtr.	Mar.	June	Sept.	Dec.
1997	0.95	1.26	1.47	1.49
1998	1.25	1.12	d0.09	d0.80
1999	0.91	0.82	0.15	d1.68
2000	0.76	1.80	3.00	1.06
2001	1.61	d9.61	d0.84	d0.10
2002	0.35	0.16	0.24	0.36

INTERIM DIVIDENDS (Per Share):

Amt.	Decl.	Ex.	Rec.	Pay.
	No dividends paid.			

CAPITALIZATION (12/31/01):

	($000)	(%)
Long-Term Debt	2,567,000	23.5
Common & Surplus	8,367,000	76.5
Total	10,934,000	100.0

BUSINESS:

CNA Financial Corporation's principal business is as a multiple-line insurer, underwriting property, casualty, life, accident and health coverage and pension products and annuities. Property and casualty insurance operations are conducted by Continental Casualty Co. and its affiliates, and life insurance operations are conducted primarily by Continental Assurance Co. The Company also provides services that include risk management, information services, health care management and claims administration. The Company acquired The Continental Corporation on 5/10/95. Loews Corporation owns 89.0% of CNA Financial Corp.'s outstanding common stock as of 12/31/01.

RECENT DEVELOPMENTS:

For the year ended 12/31/02, income was $279.0 million versus a loss of $1.59 billion the year before. Results for 2002 excluded a loss from discontinued operations of $35.0 million and an accounting change charge of $57.0 million, while results for 2001 excluded a gain from discontinued operations of $11.0 million and an accounting change charge of $61.0 million. Results for 2002 and 2001 included a pre-tax benefit of $37.0 million and a charge of $251.0 million, respectively, for restructuring and other related items. Also, results for 2001 included after-tax reserve charges of $2.01 billion and an after-tax charge of $304.0 million related to the World Trade Center event. Total revenues declined 5.8% to $12.34 billion. Comparisons were made with restated prior-year figures.

PROSPECTS:

The Company is encouraged by the underlying performance of its key businesses. The strong rate achievement and growth in new business experienced during the first three quarters of 2002 continued through the fourth quarter. These factors led to an approximate 11.0 point improvement in the full-year gross accident year loss ratio for the primary property and casualty businesses. Separately, CNA announced that it is restating its financial statements for 2000, 2001 and the first three quarters of 2002 to reflect an adjustment in how the Company accounts for its investment in life-settlement contracts. The change reduced net income by $9.0 million for the full-year 2002, and shareholder equity by $254.0 million.

ANNUAL FINANCIAL DATA:

FISCAL YEAR	PREM. INC. ($mill.)	TOT. REVS. ($mill.)	NET INC. ($mill.)	TOT. ASSETS ($mill.)	TOT. INVST. ($mill.)	RET. ON REVS. %	RET. ON EQUITY %	RET. ON ASSETS %	EARN. PER SH.$	TANG. BK. VAL.$	PRICE RANGE	AVG. P/E RATIO
p12/31/02		12,336.0	④ 279.0						④ 1.25		30.99 - 21.45	21.0
12/31/01	9,365.0	13,203.0	③ d1,583.0	65,968.0	35,475.0	...	...	...	③ d8.16	36.23	40.24 - 23.00	...
12/31/00	11,474.0	15,614.0	1,214.0	62,068.0	34,801.0	7.8	12.6	2.0	6.61	50.91	41.94 - 24.56	5.0
12/31/99	13,282.0	16,403.0	② 47.0	61,219.0	35,250.0	0.3	0.5	0.1	② 0.19	45.88	45.31 - 33.00	206.0
12/31/98	13,375.0	17,074.0	① 282.0	62,359.0	36,849.0	1.7	3.1	0.5	① 1.49	45.89	53.31 - 34.50	29.5
12/31/97	13,362.0	17,072.0	966.0	61,269.0	35,900.0	5.7	11.6	1.6	5.17	40.66	44.08 - 32.13	7.4
12/31/96	13,479.0	16,987.8	964.8	60,455.7	35,135.2	5.7	13.7	1.6	5.17	35.02	39.17 - 31.92	6.9
12/31/95	11,735.1	14,699.7	757.0	59,901.8	35,597.7	5.1	11.2	1.3	4.05	33.06	41.08 - 21.58	7.7
12/31/94	9,474.4	10,999.5	36.5	44,320.4	26,815.4	0.3	0.8	0.1	0.17	23.62	27.42 - 20.00	139.4
12/31/93	8,688.8	11,010.8	267.5	41,912.3	25,246.1	2.4	5.0	0.6	1.42	28.22	33.67 - 24.75	20.6

Statistics are as originally reported. Adj. for stk. split: 3-for-1, 6/98 ① Incl. restruct. chrg. $246.0 mill. ② Incl. restruct. chrg. $54.0 mill.; bef. acctg. change chrg. $177.0 mill. ③ Bef. acctg. change $61.0 mill.; incl. non-recurr. chrgs. $3.74 bill. ④ Bef. acctg. change chrg. $57.0 mill. & loss.fr. disc. opers. of $35.0 mill.; Incl. pre-tax restruct. benefit of $37.0 mill.

OFFICERS:
B. L. Hengesbaugh, Chmn.
S. W. Lilienthal, C.E.O.
R. V. Deutsch, Sr. V.P., C.F.O.
INVESTOR CONTACT: Donald P. Lofe, Jr., V.P., (312) 822-3993
PRINCIPAL OFFICE: CNA Plaza, Chicago, IL 60685

TELEPHONE NUMBER: (312) 822-5000
FAX: (312) 822-6419
WEB: www.cna.com
NO. OF EMPLOYEES: 17,274 (approx.)
SHAREHOLDERS: 2,473
ANNUAL MEETING: In May
INCORPORATED: DE, Sept., 1967

INSTITUTIONAL HOLDINGS:
No. of Institutions: 117
Shares Held: 219,925,844
% Held: 98.4
INDUSTRY: Fire, marine, and casualty insurance (SIC: 6331)
TRANSFER AGENT(S): EquiServe Trust Company, N.A. Canton, MA

CNF INC.

EXCH.	SYM.	REC. PRICE	P/E RATIO	YLD.	MKT. CAP.	RANGE (52-WK.)	'02 Y/E PR.
NYSE	CNF	28.77 (2/28/03)	14.7	...	$1.41 bill.	38.28 - 27.36	33.24

MEDIUM GRADE. IN 2003, THE COMPANY EXPECTS EARNINGS PER SHARE RANGING FROM $0.24 TO $0.30 FOR THE FIRST QUARTER AND TOTALING $2.24 FOR THE FULL YEAR.

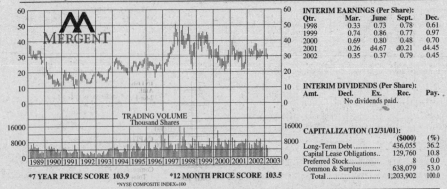

INTERIM EARNINGS (Per Share):

Qtr.	Mar.	June	Sept.	Dec.
1998	0.33	0.73	0.78	0.61
1999	0.74	0.86	0.77	0.97
2000	0.69	0.80	0.48	0.70
2001	0.26	d4.67	d0.21	d4.45
2002	0.35	0.37	0.79	0.45

INTERIM DIVIDENDS (Per Share):

Amt.	Decl.	Ex.	Rec.	Pay.
		No dividends paid.		

CAPITALIZATION (12/31/01):

	($000)	(%)
Long-Term Debt	436,055	36.2
Capital Lease Obligations..	129,760	10.8
Preferred Stock..................	8	0.0
Common & Surplus	638,079	53.0
Total	1,203,902	100.0

TRADING VOLUME
Thousand Shares

*7 YEAR PRICE SCORE 103.9   ***12 MONTH PRICE SCORE 103.5**

NYSE COMPOSITE INDEX=100

BUSINESS:

CNF Inc. (formerly CNF Transportation, Inc.) is a provider of regional less-than-truckload (LTL) trucking, heavy air freight, contract logistics, and trailer manufacturing. CNF operates in two primary segments: Con-Way Transportation Services, which provides regional LTL trucking services in all 50 states, and Menlo Worldwide group, which provides customers globally with a full range of logistics services through Menlo Worldwide Logistics, Emery Forwarding, Vector SCM, and Menlo Worldwide Technologies. CNF also provides other transportation services, including truckload services, ocean forwarding and customs brokerage.

RECENT DEVELOPMENTS:

For the year ended 12/31/02, CNF reported income from continuing operations of $114.2 million compared with a loss from continuing operations of $433.6 million the year before. Results excluded a loss of $12.4 million in 2002 and a gain of $39.0 million in 2001 from discontinued operations. Results for 2001 included restructuring charges of $652.2 million. Total revenues slipped 2.1% to $4.76 billion from $4.86 billion the year before. Con-Way Transportation Services revenue grew 5.2% to $2.01 billion. Emery Forwarding revenue decreased 13.0% to $1.78 billion, while revenue for Menlo Worldwide Logistics rose 7.9% to $969.1 million. Revenue for CNF's other operations dropped 61.8% to $2.8 million.

PROSPECTS:

On 2/13/03, Emery Forwarding opened a new logistics facility in Fotan, Hong Kong, providing full transportation, logistics and warehousing capabilities, as part of the strategic expansion of its operations and services. Additionally, Emery plans to change its name to Menlo Worldwide Forwarding. The name change, which should be completed by 1/1/04, is intended to make it easier for customers to identify and use the full range of supply chain services that Menlo Worldwide supplies. Separately, in 2003, the Company expects earnings per share ranging from $0.24 to $0.30 for the first quarter and totaling $2.24 for the full year.

ANNUAL FINANCIAL DATA:

FISCAL YEAR	TOT. REVS. ($mill.)	NET INC. ($mill.)	TOT. ASSETS ($mill.)	OPER. PROFIT %	NET PROFIT %	RET. ON EQUITY %	RET. ON ASSETS %	CURR. RATIO	EARN. PER SH. $	CASH FL. PER SH. $	TANG. BK. VAL. $	DIV. PER SH. $	PRICE RANGE	AVG. P/E RATIO	AVG. YIELD %
p12/31/02	4,762.1	③ 114.2	2,739.8			...			③ 1.96			0.40	38.28 - 27.36	16.7	1.2
12/31/01	4,862.7	⑥ d433.6	2,990.0	...	...	...	...	1.5	⑥ d9.06	d4.90	6.50	0.40	39.88 - 21.05	...	1.3
12/31/00	5,572.4	③⑤ 151.3	3,244.9	5.2	2.7	14.2	4.7	1.3	③⑤ 2.65	6.10	16.59	0.40	36.88 - 20.19	10.8	1.4
12/31/99	5,592.8	④ 190.5	3,049.0	6.4	3.4	19.7	6.2	1.1	④ 3.35	6.87	14.49	0.40	45.88 - 28.38	11.1	1.1
12/31/97	4,941.5	139.0	2,682.6	5.9	2.8	17.9	5.2	1.2	2.45	5.48	10.61	0.40	49.94 - 21.56	14.6	1.1
12/31/96	4,266.8	120.9	2,421.5	6.2	2.8	18.4	5.0	1.3	2.19	4.59	8.03	0.40	50.88 - 20.25	16.2	1.1
② 12/31/96	3,662.2	③ 80.2	2,081.9	5.2	2.2	11.1	3.9	1.0	③ 1.59	3.71	9.87	0.40	29.38 - 16.25	14.3	1.8
12/31/95	5,281.1	57.4	2,750.1	2.7	1.1	6.0	2.1	1.2	1.10	4.39	14.67	0.41	28.75 - 20.25	22.3	1.7
12/31/94	4,680.5	⑥ 60.3	2,472.7	3.0	1.3	6.6	2.4	1.2	⑥ 1.11	5.02	16.30	...	29.25 - 17.88	21.2	...
12/31/93	4,191.8	50.6	2,306.7	2.9	1.2	5.7	2.2	1.1	0.87	4.92	14.53	...	24.00 - 13.63	21.6	...

Statistics are as originally reported. ① Bef. extra. chg. of $5.5 mill. ② Refl. spin-off of Consolidated Freightways Corp. ③ Bef. loss from disc. ops. of $12.4 mill., 2002; $13.5 mill., 2000; $52.6 mill., 1996. ④ Incl. various pre-tax net gains of $26.6 mill. ⑤ Incl. various after-tax losses of $10.1 mill. ⑥ Bef. a gain of $39.0 mill. fr. discont. opers. & incl. pre-tax restruct. & related chrgs. of $652.2 mill.

OFFICERS:
D. E. Moffitt, Chmn.
G. L. Quesnel, Pres., C.E.O.
C. Ratnathicam, Sr. V.P., C.F.O.

INVESTOR CONTACT: Patrick Fossenier, Investor Relations, (650) 494-2900

PRINCIPAL OFFICE: 3240 Hillview Avenue, Palo Alto, CA 94304

TELEPHONE NUMBER: (650) 494-2900
FAX: (650) 813-0160
WEB: www.cnf.com
NO. OF EMPLOYEES: 26,100 (approx.)
SHAREHOLDERS: 8,561
ANNUAL MEETING: In April
INCORPORATED: WA, Aug., 1929; reincorp., DE, 1958

INSTITUTIONAL HOLDINGS:
No. of Institutions: 184
Shares Held: 43,141,656
% Held: 87.6

INDUSTRY: Trucking, except local (SIC: 4213)

TRANSFER AGENT(S): First Chicago Trust Company of New York, Jersey City, NJ

COACH, INC.

EXCH.	SYM.	REC. PRICE	P/E RATIO	YLD.	MKT. CAP.	RANGE (52-WK.)	'02 Y/E PR.
NYSE	COH	35.73 (2/28/03)	28.8	...	$3.20 bill.	35.80 - 17.19	32.92

INVESTMENT GRADE. THE COMPANY'S OUTLOOK REMAINS BRIGHT.

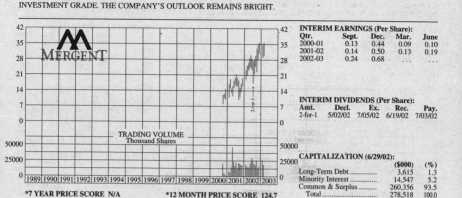

*7 YEAR PRICE SCORE N/A   *12 MONTH PRICE SCORE 124.7
*NYSE COMPOSITE INDEX=100

INTERIM EARNINGS (Per Share):

Qtr.	Sept.	Dec.	Mar.	June
2000-01	0.13	0.44	0.09	0.10
2001-02	0.14	0.50	0.13	0.19
2002-03	0.24	0.68	...	...

INTERIM DIVIDENDS (Per Share):

Amt.	Decl.	Ex.	Rec.	Pay.
2-for-1	5/02/02	7/05/02	6/19/02	7/03/02

CAPITALIZATION (6/29/02):

	($000)	(%)
Long-Term Debt	3,615	1.3
Minority Interest	14,547	5.2
Common & Surplus	260,356	93.5
Total	278,518	100.0

BUSINESS:

Coach, Inc. is a designer, producer and marketer of accessories and gifts for women and men. The Company's product offerings include handbags, women's and men's accessories, business cases, weekend and travel accessories, leather outerwear, gloves, scarves and personal planning products. Together with its licensing partners, the Company also offers watches, footwear and home and office furniture with the Coach brand name. The Company's products are sold worldwide through the Coach stores, selected department stores and specialty stores, through the Coach catalogue and its Web site. As of 12/28/02, the Company operated 150 retail stores and 76 factory stores. In 2001, the Company was spun off from Sara Lee Corp.

RECENT DEVELOPMENTS:

For the 13 weeks ended 12/28/02, net income grew 41.4% to $62.4 million compared with $44.2 million in the equivalent 2001 quarter. Net sales advanced 30.9% to $308.5 million from $235.8 million a year earlier. Gross profit climbed 34.2% to $216.8 million from $161.6 million in 2001. Gross profit as a percentage of sales expanded to 70.3% from 68.6%, driven by improved sourcing cost initiatives, product mix and channel mix. Operating income surged 46.7% to $102.6 million from $69.9 million the year before.

PROSPECTS:

Looking ahead, the Company expects third quarter earnings of at least $0.29 per diluted share, supported by continued strong sales trends in all channels and further expansion of its operating margins. Moreover, COH expects full-year 2003 sales of at least $900.0 million and earnings per share of at least $1.40. Separately, the Company plans to add seven more retail stores in the U.S. during the spring, bringing the total to 20 new retail stores in fiscal 2003. Also, COH plans to add at least six new locations in Japan during the second half, including its second flagship store in the Shibuya area of Tokyo, further leveraging its opportunity in that under-penetrated market. In March 2003, the Company is set to introduce two new groups, SOHO twill and HAMPTON WEEKEND, which are expected to increase COH's appeal in the casual, weekend market.

ANNUAL FINANCIAL DATA:

FISCAL YEAR	TOT. REVS. ($mill.)	NET INC. ($mill.)	TOT. ASSETS ($mill.)	OPER. PROFIT %	NET PROFIT %	RET. ON EQUITY %	RET. ON ASSETS %	CURR. RATIO	EARN. PER SH. $	CASH FL. PER SH. $	TANG. BK. VAL. $	PRICE RANGE	AVG. P/E RATIO
6/29/02	719.4	Ⓘ 85.8	440.6	18.6	11.9	33.0	19.5	1.8	Ⓘ 0.94	1.22	2.66	35.70 - 17.19	28.1
6/30/01	616.1	Ⓘ 64.0	258.7	16.5	10.4	43.2	24.7	1.5	Ⓘ 0.76	1.05	1.70	21.38 - 10.00	20.6
7/01/00	548.9	38.6	296.7	10.2	7.0	18.1	13.0	1.7	0.55	0.87	3.04	14.69 - 8.00	20.6
7/03/99	507.8	Ⓘ 16.7	282.1	3.8	3.3	8.2	5.9	1.7	Ⓘ 0.24	0.56	...	...	...
7/27/98	522.2	20.7	...	4.8	4.0	...	...	...	...	...	...	...	...

Statistics are as originally reported. Adj. for stk. split: 2-for-1, 7/02. Ⓘ Incl. reorg. costs, $3.4 mill., 6/02; $4.6 mill., 6/01; $7.1 mill., 7/99.

OFFICERS:
L. Frankfort, Chmn., C.E.O.
K. Monda, Pres., C.O.O.
M. Devine, III, Sr. V.P., C.F.O.
INVESTOR CONTACT: Andrea Shaw Resnick, Inv. Rel., (212) 629-2618
PRINCIPAL OFFICE: 516 West 34th Street, New York, NY 10001

TELEPHONE NUMBER: (212) 594-1850
FAX: (212) 594-1682
WEB: www.coach.com
NO. OF EMPLOYEES: 2,900 (approx.)
SHAREHOLDERS: 20,000
ANNUAL MEETING: In Nov.
INCORPORATED: MD, June, 2000

INSTITUTIONAL HOLDINGS:
No. of Institutions: 283
Shares Held: 81,161,229
% Held: 91.5
INDUSTRY: Personal leather goods, nec (SIC: 3172)
TRANSFER AGENT(S): Mellon Investor Services, New York, NY

COCA-COLA COMPANY (THE)

EXCH.	SYM.	REC. PRICE	P/E RATIO	YLD.	MKT. CAP.	RANGE (52-WK.)	'02 Y/E PR.	DIV. ACH.
NYSE	KO	40.22 (2/28/03)	23.8	2.2%	$100.00 bill.	57.91 - 38.85	43.84	40 yrs.

HIGH GRADE. THE COMPANY EXPECTS PRE-TAX BENEFITS OF AT LEAST $100.0 MILLION ON AN ANNUALIZED BASIS BEGINNING IN 2004 AS A RESULT OF RECENTLY IMPLEMENTED STREAMLINING INITIATIVES.

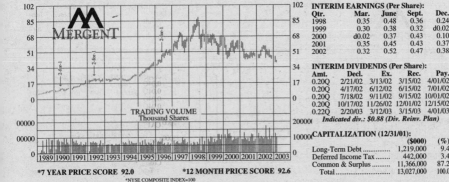

*7 YEAR PRICE SCORE 92.0   ***12 MONTH PRICE SCORE 92.6**

*NYSE COMPOSITE INDEX=100

INTERIM EARNINGS (Per Share):

Qtr.	Mar.	June	Sept.	Dec.
1998	0.35	0.48	0.36	0.24
1999	0.30	0.38	0.32	d0.02
2000	d0.02	0.37	0.43	0.10
2001	0.35	0.45	0.43	0.37
2002	0.32	0.52	0.47	0.38

INTERIM DIVIDENDS (Per Share):

Amt.	Decl.	Ex.	Rec.	Pay.
0.20Q	2/21/02	3/13/02	3/15/02	4/01/02
0.20Q	4/17/02	6/12/02	6/15/02	7/01/02
0.20Q	7/18/02	9/11/02	9/15/02	10/01/02
0.20Q	10/17/02	11/26/02	12/01/02	12/15/02
0.22Q	2/20/03	3/12/03	3/15/03	4/01/03

Indicated div.: $0.88 (Div. Reinv. Plan)

CAPITALIZATION (12/31/01):

	($000)	(%)
Long-Term Debt	1,219,000	9.4
Deferred Income Tax	442,000	3.4
Common & Surplus	11,366,000	87.2
Total	13,027,000	100.0

BUSINESS:

The Coca-Cola Company is engaged in the manufacturing, distributing and marketing of soft drink concentrates and syrups. Principal beverage products include: COCA-COLA, COCA-COLA CLASSIC, DIET COKE, CHERRY COKE, FANTA, SPRITE, MR. PIBB, MELLO YELLOW, BARQ'S ROOT BEER, POWERADE, FRUITOPIA, DASANI plus other assorted diet and caffeine-free versions. The Minute Maid Company produces, juice and juice-drink products. Brands include MIN-UTE MAID, FIVE ALIVE, BACARDI brand tropical fruit mixers and HI-C. Coca-Cola Nestle Refreshments, KO's joint venture with Nestle S.A., markets ready-to-drink teas and coffees in certain countries. In 2002, sales were derived: North America, 32.4%; Europe, Eurasia & Middle East, 27.2%; Asia, 26.1%; Latin America, 10.8%; and Africa, 3.5%. As of 12/31/01, KO held an approximate 38.0% interest in Coca-Cola Enterprises, Inc.

RECENT DEVELOPMENTS:

For the year ended 12/31/02, income of $3.98 billion was essentially unchanged versus the previous year. Results for 2002 included a non-recurring charge of $157.0 million, primarily related to investments in Latin America. Results for 2002 and 2001 excluded accounting change charges of $926.0 million and $10.0 million, respectively. Net operating revenues climbed 11.5% to $19.56 billion, reflecting a 5.0% increase in the pricing of concentrate, the consolidation of the bottling operations in Germany, and the inclusion of EVIAN and the DANONE water brands. Worldwide unit case volume rose 5.0%, comprised of 6.0% volume growth in North America and 5.0% internationally.

PROSPECTS:

During the first quarter of 2003, KO initiated steps to streamline its operations, primarily in North America and Germany. In North America, KO is integrating the operations of its three separate North American business units that will result 1,000 job losses. In Germany, Coca-Cola Erfrischungsgetraenke AG has taken steps to improve its efficiency in sales and distribution, including the closure of three bottling plants in 2003, that is expected to affect about 900 employees in Germany. As a result of these initiatives, KO expects pre-tax benefits of at least $50.0 million in 2003 and $100.0 million on an annualized basis beginning in 2004.

ANNUAL FINANCIAL DATA:

FISCAL YEAR	TOT. REVS. ($mill.)	NET INC. ($mill.)	TOT. ASSETS ($mill.)	OPER. PROFIT %	NET PROFIT %	RET. ON EQUITY %	RET. ON ASSETS %	CURR. RATIO	EARN. PER SH.$	CASH FL. PER SH.$	TANG. BK. VAL.$	DIV. PER SH.$	PRICE RANGE	AVG. P/E RATIO	AVG. YIELD %
p12/31/02	19,564.0	⑥ 3,976.0							⑥ 1.23			0.80	57.91 - 42.90	41.0	1.6
12/31/01	20,092.0	⑤ 3,979.0	22,417.0	26.6	19.8	35.0	17.7	0.9	⑤ 1.60	1.92	3.53	0.72	62.19 - 42.37	32.7	1.4
12/31/00	20,458.0	④ 2,177.0	20,834.0	18.0	10.6	23.4	10.4	0.7	④ 0.88	1.19	2.98	0.68	66.88 - 42.88	62.4	1.2
12/31/99	19,805.0	③ 2,431.0	21,623.0	20.1	12.3	25.6	11.2	0.7	③ 0.98	1.30	3.06	0.64	70.88 - 47.31	60.3	1.1
12/31/98	18,813.0	3,533.0	19,145.0	26.4	18.8	42.0	18.5	0.7	1.42	1.67	3.19	0.60	88.94 - 53.63	50.2	0.8
12/31/97	18,868.0	① 4,129.0	16,940.0	26.5	21.9	56.5	24.4	0.8	① 1.64	1.89	2.66	0.56	72.63 - 50.00	37.4	0.9
12/31/96	18,546.0	3,492.0	16,161.0	21.1	18.8	56.7	21.6	0.8	1.40	1.59	2.18	0.50	54.25 - 36.06	32.3	1.1
12/31/95	18,018.0	2,986.0	15,041.0	22.3	16.6	55.4	19.9	0.7	1.18	1.36	1.78	0.44	40.19 - 24.38	27.4	1.4
12/31/94	16,172.0	2,554.0	13,873.0	22.9	15.8	48.8	18.4	0.8	0.99	1.15	1.79	0.39	26.75 - 19.44	23.3	1.7
12/31/93	13,957.0	② 2,188.0	12,021.0	22.2	15.7	47.7	18.2	0.9	② 0.84	0.98	1.55	0.34	22.56 - 18.75	24.6	1.6

Statistics are as originally reported. Adj. for 2-for-1 stk. split, 5/96. ① Incl. non-recurr. net gain of $290.0 mill. ② Bef. acctg. chge. chrg. of $12.0 mill. ③ Incl. non-recurr. chrg. of $813.0 mill. ④ Incl. non-recurr. chrgs. of $1.04 bill. & asset writedown of $405.0 mill. ⑤ Incl. non-recurr. gain of $91.0 mill.; bef. acctg. chge. chrg. of $10.0 mill. ⑥ Incl. non-recurr. chrg. of $157.0 mill.; bef. acctg. chge. chrg. of $926.0 mill.

OFFICERS:
D. N. Daft, Chmn., C.E.O.
B. G. Dyson, Vice-Chmn.
S. J. Heyer, Pres., C.O.O.
INVESTOR CONTACT: Institutional Investor Inquires, (404) 676-5766
PRINCIPAL OFFICE: One Coca-Cola Plaza, Atlanta, GA 30313

TELEPHONE NUMBER: (404) 676-2121
FAX: (404) 676-6792
WEB: www.coca-cola.com
NO. OF EMPLOYEES: 38,000 (approx.)
SHAREHOLDERS: 371,794 (record)
ANNUAL MEETING: In Apr.
INCORPORATED: DE, Sept., 1919

INSTITUTIONAL HOLDINGS:
No. of Institutions: 1,024
Shares Held: 1,403,611,769
% Held: 56.6
INDUSTRY: Bottled and canned soft drinks (SIC: 2086)
TRANSFER AGENT(S): EquiServe, Jersey City, NJ

COCA-COLA ENTERPRISES INC.

EXCH.	SYM.	REC. PRICE	P/E RATIO	YLD.	MKT. CAP.	RANGE (52-WK.)	'02 Y/E PR.
NYSE	CCE	20.18 (2/28/03)	18.7	0.8%	$8.98 bill.	24.50 - 16.74	21.72

MEDIUM GRADE. THE COMPANY EXPECTS FULL-YEAR 2003 EARNINGS BETWEEN $1.15 AND $1.22 PER SHARE.

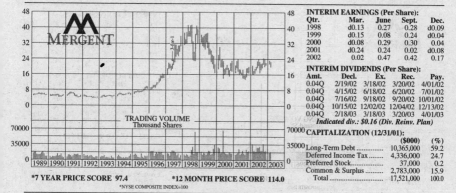

INTERIM EARNINGS (Per Share):

Qtr.	Mar.	June	Sept.	Dec.
1998	d0.13	0.27	0.28	d0.09
1999	d0.15	0.08	0.24	d0.04
2000	d0.08	0.29	0.30	0.04
2001	d0.24	0.24	0.02	d0.08
2002	0.02	0.47	0.42	0.17

INTERIM DIVIDENDS (Per Share):

Amt.	Decl.	Ex.	Rec.	Pay.
0.04Q	2/19/02	3/18/02	3/20/02	4/01/02
0.04Q	4/15/02	6/18/02	6/20/02	7/01/02
0.04Q	7/16/02	9/18/02	9/20/02	10/01/02
0.04Q	10/15/02	12/02/02	12/04/02	12/13/02
0.04Q	2/18/03	3/18/03	3/20/03	4/01/03

Indicated div.: $0.16 (Div. Reinv. Plan)

CAPITALIZATION (12/31/01):

	($000)	(%)
Long-Term Debt	10,365,000	59.2
Deferred Income Tax	4,336,000	24.7
Preferred Stock	37,000	0.2
Common & Surplus	2,783,000	15.9
Total	17,521,000	100.0

TRADING VOLUME Thousand Shares

*7 YEAR PRICE SCORE 97.4   ***12 MONTH PRICE SCORE 114.0**

*NYSE COMPOSITE INDEX=100

BUSINESS:

Coca-Cola Enterprises Inc. markets, produces, and distributes products of The Coca-Cola Company. CCE also distributes A&W, CANADA DRY, DR PEPPER, APPLETISER, BUXTON, NESTEA and numerous other beverage brands in North America and Europe. CCE is in the nonalcoholic beverage business, which extends its product line beyond traditional carbonated soft drink categories to beverages such as still and sparkling waters, juices, isotonics, coffee-based drinks, and teas. As of 12/31/01, CCE's bottling territories in North America were located in 46 states of the U.S., the District of Columbia and all ten provinces of Canada. CCE also has bottling territories in Europe, including Belgium, continental France, Great Britain, Luxembourg, Monaco, and the Netherlands. As of 2/20/02, The Coca-Cola Company owned about 38.0% of CCE's outstanding common shares. On 7/10/01, CCE acquired Hondo Incorporated and Herbco Enterprises, Inc. in a transaction valued at about $1.40 billion.

RECENT DEVELOPMENTS:

For the year ended 12/31/02, net income was $494.0 million versus a loss of $19.0 million, before an accounting change charge of $302.0 million, the previous year. Results for 2002 and 2001 included nonrecurring income tax benefits of $20.0 million and $56.0 million, respectively. Net operating revenues rose 8.2% to $16.89 billion. Physical case bottle and can volume, which includes the number of units that were actually produced, regardless of package configuration, increased 4.0% on a comparable basis. North American volume grew 3.5% and volume in Europe advanced 4.5%. Operating income jumped to $1.36 billion from $601.0 million the year before, due to volume growth, gross margin expansion and controlled growth in operating expense.

PROSPECTS:

CCE's outlook appears positive, reflecting anticipated 2003 volume growth of 3.0% in North America and growth ranging ranging from 4.0% to 6.0% in Europe. Furthermore, the Company expects to benefit from enhanced marketing programs from The Coca-Cola Company, a new media campaign, and additional brand initiatives. Accordingly, CCE is projecting full-year 2003 diluted earnings between $1.15 and $1.22 per share.

ANNUAL FINANCIAL DATA:

FISCAL YEAR	TOT. REVS. ($Mill.)	NET INC. ($Mill.)	TOT. ASSETS ($Mill.)	OPER. PROFIT %	NET PROFIT %	RET. ON EQUITY %	RET. ON ASSETS %	CURR. RATIO	EARN. PER SH. $	CASH FL. PER SH. $	TANG. BK. VAL. $	DIV. PER SH. $	PRICE RANGE	AVG. P/E RATIO	AVG. YIELD %
p12/31/02	16,889.0	⑦494.0							⑦1.07			0.16	24.50 - 15.94	18.9	0.8
12/31/01	15,700.0	⑥d19.0	23,719.0	3.8	...	...	...	0.6	⑥d0.75	3.08	6.25	0.16	23.90 - 13.46	...	0.9
12/31/00	14,750.0	⑤236.0	22,162.0	7.6	1.6	8.3	1.1	0.9	⑤0.54	3.48	6.67	0.16	30.25 - 14.00	41.0	0.7
12/31/99	14,406.0	④59.0	22,730.0	5.8	0.4	2.0	0.3	0.7	④0.13	3.22	6.83	0.16	37.50 - 16.81	208.7	0.6
12/31/98	13,414.0	③113.0	21,132.0	6.5	0.8	4.6	0.5	0.7	③0.35	3.03	5.95	0.14	41.56 - 22.88	92.0	0.5
②12/31/97	11,278.0	③113.0	17,487.0	6.4	1.0	6.2	0.6	0.6	③0.43	2.67	4.69	0.08	35.81 - 15.71	59.9	0.3
12/31/96	7,921.0	③114.0	11,234.0	6.9	1.4	7.6	1.0	0.8	③0.28	1.97	3.65	0.03	16.38 - 8.00	43.5	0.3
12/31/95	6,773.0	82.0	9,064.0	6.9	1.2	6.0	0.9	1.1	0.21	1.58	3.45	0.02	9.96 - 5.92	37.8	0.2
12/31/94	6,011.0	69.0	8,738.0	7.3	1.1	5.3	0.8	0.7	0.17	1.35	3.28	0.02	6.50 - 4.67	32.3	0.3
12/31/93	5,465.0	①d15.0	8,682.0	7.0	...	...	...	0.7	①d0.04	1.04	3.17	0.02	5.29 - 3.92	...	0.4

Statistics are as originally reported. Adj. for 3-for-1 stk. split, 5/97. ① Bef. income tax rate chge. benefit 12/31/98: $29.0 mill.; benefit 12/31/97, $58.0 mill. ② Incl. results from acqs. of Coke Canada & Coke New York. ③ Incl. non-recurr. credit 12/31/96: $10.0 mill.; 12/31/93: $40.0 mill. ④ Incl. non-recurr. chrg. of $103.0 mill. ⑤ Incl. non-recurr. chrg. of $12.0 mill. & insur. proceeds of $20.0 mill. ⑥ Incl. restruct. & non-recurr. chrgs. of $78.0 mill.; bef. acctg. chge. chrge. of $302.0 mill. ⑦ Incl. non-recurr. tax benefit of $20.0 mill.

OFFICERS:
L. F. Kline, Chmn., C.E.O.
J. R. Alm, Pres., C.O.O.
V. R. Palmer, Sr. V.P., Treas.
INVESTOR CONTACT: Scott Anthony, Investor Relations, (770) 989-3105
PRINCIPAL OFFICE: 2500 Windy Ridge Parkway, Suite 700, Atlanta, GA 30339

TELEPHONE NUMBER: (770) 989-3000
FAX: (770) 989-3788
WEB: www.cokecce.com
NO. OF EMPLOYEES: 72,000 (approx.)
SHAREHOLDERS: 16,012
ANNUAL MEETING: In Apr.
INCORPORATED: DE, 1944

INSTITUTIONAL HOLDINGS:
No. of Institutions: 261
Shares Held: 156,621,216
% Held: 34.9
INDUSTRY: Bottled and canned soft drinks (SIC: 2086)
TRANSFER AGENT(S): American Stock Transfer & Trust Company, New York, NY

COLGATE-PALMOLIVE COMPANY

EXCH.	SYM.	REC. PRICE	P/E RATIO	YLD.	MKT. CAP.	RANGE (52-WK.)	'02 Y/E PR.	DIV. ACH.
NYSE	CL	50.31 (2/28/03)	22.9	1.9%	$27.71 bill.	58.86 – 44.05	52.43	40 yrs.

INVESTMENT GRADE. NEW PRODUCT INTRODUCTIONS AND INCREASED MARKET SHARE ARE HELPING DRIVE EARNINGS GROWTH.

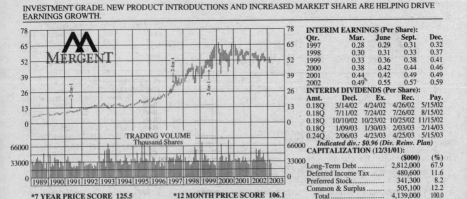

*7 YEAR PRICE SCORE 125.5   ***12 MONTH PRICE SCORE 106.1**
*NYSE COMPOSITE INDEX=100

INTERIM EARNINGS (Per Share):

Qtr.	Mar.	June	Sept.	Dec.
1997	0.28	0.29	0.31	0.32
1998	0.30	0.31	0.33	0.37
1999	0.33	0.36	0.38	0.41
2000	0.38	0.42	0.44	0.46
2001	0.44	0.42	0.49	0.49
2002	0.49	0.55	0.57	0.59

INTERIM DIVIDENDS (Per Share):

Amt.	Decl.	Ex.	Rec.	Pay.
0.18Q	3/14/02	4/24/02	4/26/02	5/15/02
0.18Q	7/11/02	7/24/02	7/26/02	8/15/02
0.18Q	10/10/02	10/23/02	10/25/02	11/15/02
0.18Q	1/09/03	1/30/03	2/03/03	2/14/03
0.24Q	2/06/03	4/23/03	4/25/03	5/15/03

Indicated div.: $0.96 (Div. Reinv. Plan)

CAPITALIZATION (12/31/01):

	($000)	(%)
Long-Term Debt	2,812,000	67.9
Deferred Income Tax	480,600	11.6
Preferred Stock	341,300	8.2
Common & Surplus	505,100	12.2
Total	4,139,000	100.0

BUSINESS:

Colgate-Palmolive Company is a consumer products company that markets its products in over 200 countries. The Company operates five segments. Oral, Personal, Fabric and Household Surface Care accounted for 86.0% of 2002 revenues and consists of tooth pastes, toothbrushes, soaps, shampoos, baby products, deodorants, detergents, cleaners, shave products and other similar items under brand names including COLGATE, PALMOLIVE, MENNEN, SOFTSOAP, IRISH SPRING, PROTEX, SORRISO, KOLYNOS, AJAX, AXION, SOUPLINE, SUAVITEL and FAB. Pet Nutrition, 14.0%, consists of pet food products manufactured and marketed by Hill's Pet Nutrition. Hill's markets pet foods primarily under SCIENCE DIET, which is sold by authorized pet supply retailers, breeders and veterinarians for every day nutritional needs, and PRESCRIPTION DIET for dogs and cats with disease conditions.

RECENT DEVELOPMENTS:

For the year ended 12/31/02, net income increased 12.4% to $1.29 billion from $1.15 billion the previous year. Net sales increased 2.3% to $9.29 billion from $9.08 billion in the prior year. On a segment basis, North American unit volume grew 6.0%, sales grew 3.0% and operating profit grew 12.0%. In Latin America, unit volume increased 2.5%, while sales and operating profit declined 5.5% and 2.0%, respectively. European unit volume grew 5.0%, sales increased 8.0%, and operating profit increased 19.0%. In the Asia/Africa region, unit volume increased 4.5%, sales grew 4.0% and operating profit increased 19.0% year over year. Lastly, unit volume for Hill's Pet Nutrition increased 5.5%, sales grew 7.0% and operating profit grew 13.0% versus 2001.

PROSPECTS:

Earnings growth is being supported by new product introductions and increased global market share in key categories, including toothpaste, liquid hand soap, body wash, fabric softeners and pet-nutrition products. Moreover, the Company is enjoying higher margins and increased marketing spending, which should provide an excellent foundation for growth in the coming year. Looking ahead, CL expects its accelerated new product activity and full pipeline of new products in each core category to propel growth throughout 2003 and into 2004.

ANNUAL FINANCIAL DATA:

FISCAL YEAR	TOT. REVS. ($mill.)	NET INC. ($mill.)	TOT. ASSETS ($mill.)	OPER. PROFIT %	NET PROFIT %	RET. ON EQUITY %	RET. ON ASSETS %	CURR. RATIO	EARN. PER SH.$	CASH FL. PER SH.$	DIV. PER SH.$	PRICE RANGE	AVG. P/E RATIO	AVG. YIELD %
p12/31/02	9,294.3	1,288.3							2.19		0.72	58.86 – 44.05	23.5	1.4
12/31/01	9,427.8	① 1,146.6	6,984.8	20.5	12.2	135.5	16.4	1.0	① 1.89	2.44	0.68	64.75 – 48.50	30.0	1.2
12/31/00	9,357.9	1,063.8	7,252.3	19.2	11.4	72.5	14.7	1.0	1.70	2.23	0.63	66.75 – 40.50	31.5	1.2
12/31/99	9,118.2	937.3	7,423.1	18.0	10.3	51.1	12.6	1.0	1.47	2.00	0.59	65.00 – 36.56	34.5	1.2
12/31/98	8,971.6	848.6	7,685.2	16.5	9.5	40.7	11.0	1.1	1.31	1.82	0.55	49.44 – 32.53	31.4	1.3
12/31/97	9,056.7	740.4	7,538.7	15.0	8.2	34.0	9.8	1.1	1.14	1.63	0.53	39.34 – 22.50	27.2	1.7
12/31/96	8,749.0	635.0	7,901.5	14.2	7.3	31.2	8.0	1.2	1.05	1.62	0.47	24.13 – 17.22	19.7	2.3
12/31/95	8,358.2	① 172.0	7,642.3	8.0	2.1	10.2	2.3	1.3	① 0.26	0.81	0.44	19.34 – 14.50	65.1	2.6
12/31/94	7,587.9	① 580.2	6,142.4	13.8	7.6	31.8	9.4	1.4	① 0.96	1.39	0.39	16.34 – 12.38	15.0	2.7
12/31/93	7,141.3	② 548.1	5,761.2	13.4	7.7	29.2	9.5	1.5	② 0.85	1.22	0.34	16.81 – 11.69	16.9	2.4

Statistics are as originally reported. Adj. for stk. splits: 2-for-1, 6/99 & 5/97 ① Incl. non-recurr. chrgs. $15.0 mill., 12/01; $369.2 mill., 12/95; $5.2 mill., 12/94 ② Bef. acctg. change chrg. $358.2 mill.

OFFICERS:
R. Mark, Chmn., C.E.O.
W. S. Shanahan, Pres., C.O.O.
S. C. Patrick, C.F.O.
INVESTOR CONTACT: Bina Thompson, Inv. Rel., (212) 310-3072
PRINCIPAL OFFICE: 300 Park Ave., New York, NY 10022-7499

TELEPHONE NUMBER: (212) 310-2000
FAX: (212) 310-3284
WEB: www.colgate.com
NO. OF EMPLOYEES: 38,500 (avg.)
SHAREHOLDERS: 40,900
ANNUAL MEETING: In May
INCORPORATED: DE, July, 1923

INSTITUTIONAL HOLDINGS:
No. of Institutions: 759
Shares Held: 372,701,175
% Held: 69.2

INDUSTRY: Toilet preparations (SIC: 2844)

TRANSFER AGENT(S): First Chicago Trust Company of New York, Jersey City, NJ

COMERICA, INC.

EXCH.	SYM.	REC. PRICE	P/E RATIO	YLD.	MKT. CAP.	RANGE (52-WK.)	'02 Y/E PR.	DIV. ACH.
NYSE	CMA	40.98 (2/28/03)	11.5	4.9%	$7.26 bill.	66.09 - 35.20	43.24	19 yrs.

INVESTMENT GRADE. FOR 2003, EARNINGS PER SHARE ARE EXPECTED TO RANGE FROM $4.20 TO $4.40.

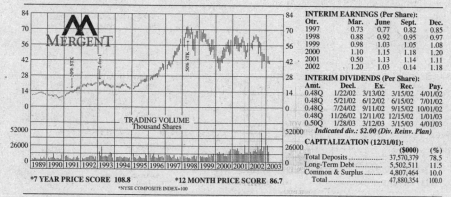

INTERIM EARNINGS (Per Share):

Qtr.	Mar.	June	Sept.	Dec.
1997	0.73	0.77	0.82	0.85
1998	0.88	0.92	0.95	0.97
1999	0.98	1.03	1.05	1.08
2000	1.10	1.15	1.18	1.20
2001	0.50	1.13	1.14	1.11
2002	1.20	1.03	0.14	1.18

INTERIM DIVIDENDS (Per Share):

Amt.	Decl.	Ex.	Rec.	Pay.
0.48Q	1/22/02	3/13/02	3/15/02	4/01/02
0.48Q	5/21/02	6/12/02	6/15/02	7/01/02
0.48Q	7/24/02	9/11/02	9/15/02	10/01/02
0.48Q	11/26/02	12/11/02	12/15/02	1/01/03
0.50Q	1/28/03	3/12/03	3/15/03	4/01/03

Indicated div.: $2.00 (Div. Reinv. Plan)

CAPITALIZATION (12/31/01):

	($000)	(%)
Total Deposits	37,570,379	78.5
Long-Term Debt	5,502,511	11.5
Common & Surplus	4,807,464	10.0
Total	47,880,354	100.0

*7 YEAR PRICE SCORE 108.8   ***12 MONTH PRICE SCORE 86.7**

*NYSE COMPOSITE INDEX=100

BUSINESS:

Comerica, Inc. is a bank holding company headquartered in Detroit, Michigan. The Company, as of 12/31/02, had assets of $53.30 billion and total deposits of $41.78 billion. CMA operates banking subsidiaries in Michigan, Texas and California, banking operations in Florida, and businesses in several other states. CMA is a diversified financial services provider, offering a broad range of financial products and services for businesses and individuals. CMA has an investment services affiliate, Munder Capital Management, and operates banking subsidiaries in Canada and Mexico. On 1/30/01, CMA acquired Imperial Bancorp in a transaction valued at $1.30 billion.

RECENT DEVELOPMENTS:

For the year ended 12/31/02, net income decreased 15.4% to $601.0 million versus $710.0 million the year before. Earnings for 2002 and 2001 included net gains on sales of businesses of $12.0 million and $31.0 million, respectively. Earnings for 2002 included goodwill impairment losses of $86.0 million. Earnings for 2001 included a pre-tax restructuring charge of $152.0 million. Net interest income grew 1.4% to $2.13 billion from $2.10 billion the year before.

Net interest margin fell to 4.55% from 4.61% in 2001, primarily due to a competitive deposit rate environment as a result of decreasing interest rates. Provision for loan losses jumped to $635.0 million from $241.0 million a year earlier, as a result of the continued weak market environment. Total non-interest income increased 7.5% to $900.0 million, while total non-interest expense declined 4.5% to $1.52 billion.

PROSPECTS:

Operating results are being adversely affected by difficult market conditions resulting from prolonged weakness in the U.S. economy. However, the Company's commercial lending business continues to perform well, generating modest growth despite the slow business environment.

Going forward, the Company will continue to take actions necessary to address credit quality and to invest in company-wide technology. CMA expects full-year earnings for 2003 to range from $4.20 to $4.40 per share, provided there is an improvement in the business climate of its markets.

ANNUAL FINANCIAL DATA:

FISCAL YEAR	NET INT. INC. ($mill.)	NON-INT. INC. ($mill.)	NET INC. ($mill.)	TOT. LOANS ($mill.)	TOT. ASSETS ($mill.)	TOT. DEP. ($mill.)	RET. ON EQUITY %	RET. ON ASSETS %	EQUITY/ ASSETS %	EARN. PER SH.$	TANG. BK. VAL.$	DIV. PER SH.$	PRICE RANGE	AVG. P/E RATIO
p12/31/02	2,132.0	900.0	④ 601.0							④ 3.40		1.88	66.09 — 35.20	14.9
12/31/01	2,103.3	803.3	②③ 709.6	41,196.3	50,732.0	37,570.4	14.8	1.4	9.5	②③ 3.88	27.15	1.72	65.15 — 44.02	14.1
12/31/00	1,658.9	825.9	② 749.3	36,060.3	41,985.2	27,168.0	18.7	1.8	9.5	② 4.63	23.94	1.56	61.13 — 32.94	10.2
12/31/99	1,547.1	716.9	672.6	32,693.3	38,653.3	23,291.4	19.4	1.7	9.0	4.14	20.60	1.40	70.00 — 44.00	13.8
12/31/98	1,461.3	603.1	① 607.1	30,604.9	36,600.8	24,313.1	19.9	1.7	8.3	① 3.72	17.94	1.25	73.00 — 46.50	16.1
12/31/97	1,442.8	528.0	530.5	28,895.0	36,292.4	22,586.3	19.2	1.5	7.6	3.19	16.02	1.12	61.88 — 34.17	15.1
12/31/96	1,412.3	507.0	① 417.2	26,206.7	34,206.1	22,367.2	15.9	1.2	7.6	① 2.37	14.21	0.99	39.58 — 24.17	13.5
12/31/95	1,299.9	498.7	413.4	24,442.3	35,469.9	23,167.2	15.9	1.2	7.4	2.36	15.17	0.89	28.50 — 16.08	9.4
12/31/94	1,230.1	450.2	387.2	22,209.2	33,429.9	22,432.3	16.2	1.2	7.2	2.19	13.64	0.80	20.83 — 16.08	8.4
12/31/93	1,133.5	449.7	① 340.6	19,099.9	30,294.9	20,949.9	15.6	1.1	7.2	① 1.90	12.66	0.70	23.50 — 16.75	10.6

Statistics are as originally reported. Adj. for 50% stk. div., 4/98; 2-for-1 split, 1/93. ① Incl. merger-related or restructuring charges: $6.8 mill., 1998; $90.0 mill., 1996; $22.0 mill., 1993. ② Incl. a pre-tax net gain on the sales of businesses of $31.2 mill., 2001; $47.6 mill., 2000. ③ Incl. pre-tax restr. chrg. of $151.7 mill. ④ Incl. pre-tax net gain on the sales of businesses of $12.0 mill. & goodwill impairment losses of $86.0 mill.

OFFICERS:
R. W. Babb Jr., Chmn., Pres., C.E.O.
J. D. Lewis, Vice-Chmn.
E. S. Acton, Exec. V.P., C.F.O.
INVESTOR CONTACT: Judith S. Love, Investor Relations, (313) 222-2840
PRINCIPAL OFFICE: Comerica Tower at Detroit Center, 500 Woodward Avenue, MC 3391, Detroit, MI 48226-3509

TELEPHONE NUMBER: (313) 222-9743
FAX: (313) 222-6091
WEB: www.comerica.com
NO. OF EMPLOYEES: 10,307 full-time; 1,485 part-time
SHAREHOLDERS: 16,915 (approx.)
ANNUAL MEETING: In May
INCORPORATED: DE, 1973

INSTITUTIONAL HOLDINGS:
No. of Institutions: 384
Shares Held: 101,949,515
% Held: 58.4

INDUSTRY: National commercial banks (SIC: 6021)

TRANSFER AGENT(S): Wells Fargo Shareowner Services, South St. Paul, MN

COMMERCE BANCORP, INC.

EXCH.	SYM.	REC. PRICE	P/E RATIO	YLD.	MKT. CAP.	RANGE (52-WK.)	'02 Y/E PR.	DIV. ACH.
NYSE	CBH	41.32 (2/28/03)	20.3	1.7%	$2.72 bill.	50.49 - 36.10	43.19	11 yrs.

UPPER MEDIUM GRADE. THE COMPANY EXPECTS REVENUE AND NET INCOME GROWTH OF 25.0%, AND EARNINGS PER SHARE GROWTH OF 20.0% IN 2003.

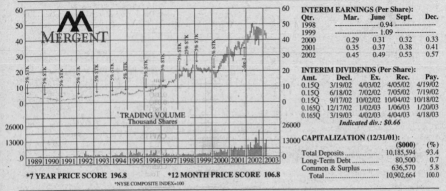

*7 YEAR PRICE SCORE 196.8   ***12 MONTH PRICE SCORE 106.8**
*NYSE COMPOSITE INDEX=100

INTERIM EARNINGS (Per Share):

Qtr.	Mar.	June	Sept.	Dec.
1998	------------------ 0.94 ------------------			
1999	------------------ 1.09 ------------------			
2000	0.29	0.31	0.32	0.33
2001	0.35	0.37	0.38	0.41
2002	0.45	0.49	0.53	0.57

INTERIM DIVIDENDS (Per Share):

Amt.	Decl.	Ex.	Rec.	Pay.
0.15Q	3/19/02	4/03/02	4/05/02	4/19/02
0.15Q	6/18/02	7/02/02	7/05/02	7/19/02
0.15Q	9/17/02	10/02/02	10/04/02	10/18/02
0.165Q	12/17/02	1/02/03	1/06/03	1/20/03
0.165Q	3/19/03	4/02/03	4/04/03	4/18/03

Indicated div.: $0.66

CAPITALIZATION (12/31/01):

	($000)	(%)
Total Deposits	10,185,594	93.4
Long-Term Debt	80,500	0.7
Common & Surplus	636,570	5.8
Total	10,902,664	100.0

BUSINESS:

Commerce Bancorp, Inc. with assets of $16.40 billion as of 12/31/02, is a bank holding company primarily serving the Metropolitan Philadelphia, New Jersey, Delaware and New York markets. The Company operates five bank subsidiaries including, Commerce Bank, N.A., Commerce Bank/Pennsylvania, N.A., Commerce Bank/Shore, N.A., Commerce Bank/Delaware, N.A. and Commerce Bank/North. As of 12/31/02, these banks provided a full range of retail and commercial banking services for consumers and small and mid-sized companies through 224 retail branch offices. In addition, CBH operates non-banking subsidiaries Commerce Capital Markets, Inc., which is engaged in various securities, investment banking and brokerage activities, and Commerce National Insurance Services, Inc., which operates an insurance brokerage agency concentrating on commercial property, casualty and surety as well as personal lines of insurance.

RECENT DEVELOPMENTS:

For the year ended 12/31/02, net income increased 40.6% to $144.8 million compared with $103.0 million in the previous year. Net interest income advanced 42.7% to $572.8 million from $401.3 million the year before. Net interest margin was 4.69% versus 4.76% in 2001, primarily reflecting lower reinvestment rates. Provision for loan losses grew 25.6% to $33.2 million from $26.4 million a year earlier. Total non-interest income improved 30.8% to $257.5 million, primarily as a result of increased deposit charges and service fees. Total non-interest expense grew 37.9% to $579.2 million.

PROSPECTS:

The Company expects revenue and net income growth of 25.0%, and earnings per share growth of 20.0% in 2003. Meanwhile, the Company had over 140 new offices in development as of 1/13/03 with plans to open approximately 13 branch offices in metropolitan Philadelphia and 32 branch offices in metropolitan New York in the current year. CBH's recent entry into markets in Manhattan and Long Island has been met with tremendous customer acceptance as total customers in these markets exceed 57,000 and 18,000, respectively.

ANNUAL FINANCIAL DATA:

FISCAL YEAR	NET INT. INC. ($mill.)	NON-INT. INC. ($mill.)	NET INC. ($mill.)	TOT. LOANS ($mill.)	TOT. ASSETS ($mill.)	TOT. DEP. ($mill.)	RET. ON EQUITY %	RET. ON ASSETS %	EQUITY/ ASSETS %	EARN. PER SH.$	TANG. BK. VAL.$	DIV. PER SH.$	PRICE RANGE	AVG. P/E RATIO
p12/31/02	572.8		144.8							2.04		0.60	50.49 - 36.10	21.2
12/31/01	401.3	196.8	103.0	4,583.4	11,363.7	10,185.6	16.2	0.9	5.6	1.51	9.67	0.55	39.60 - 26.00	21.7
12/31/00	296.9	150.8	80.0	3,687.3	8,296.5	7,387.6	16.3	1.0	5.9	1.25	7.75	0.48	35.41 - 15.44	20.4
12/31/99	244.4	114.6	66.0	2,961.1	6,635.8	5,608.9	18.5	1.0	5.4	1.09	5.98	0.41	23.81 - 18.45	19.5
12/31/98	173.7	88.9	49.3	1,931.4	4,894.1	4,435.1	16.4	1.0	6.1	0.94	5.97	0.44	24.04 - 15.05	20.7
12/31/97	147.1	57.4	40.3	1,411.3	3,939.0	3,369.4	16.1	1.0	6.4	0.81	5.28	0.28	17.95 - 9.03	16.8
12/31/96	108.5	30.0	26.6	1,096.2	2,862.0	2,573.4	14.7	0.9	6.3	0.76	4.93	0.23	10.94 - 6.62	11.6
12/31/95	95.3	21.5	23.5	907.5	2,415.9	2,225.1	14.5	1.0	6.7	0.70	4.99	0.20	8.03 - 4.86	9.2
12/31/94	90.5	17.5	20.4	802.0	2,291.3	1,834.6	18.2	0.9	4.9	0.78	4.09	0.18	7.09 - 4.41	7.4
12/31/93	69.7	17.3	14.6	701.4	2,032.6	1,744.9	14.7	0.7	4.9	0.64	4.30	0.14	5.12 - 3.86	7.5

Statistics are as originally reported. Adjusted for stk. splits and stk. divs. thru 12/01.

OFFICERS:
V. W. Hill II, Chmn., Pres., C.E.O.
D. J. Pauls, Sr. V.P., C.F.O.
P. M. Musumeci Jr., Exec. V.P., Treas.
INVESTOR CONTACT: C. Edward Jordan, Jr., Exec. Vice-Pres., (856) 751-9000
PRINCIPAL OFFICE: Commerce Atrium, 1701 Route 70 East, Cherry Hill, NJ 08034

TELEPHONE NUMBER: (856) 751-9000
FAX: (856) 751-9260
WEB: www.commerceonline.com
NO. OF EMPLOYEES: 5,300 (approx.)
SHAREHOLDERS: 24,000 (approx. record)
ANNUAL MEETING: In May
INCORPORATED: NJ, Dec., 1982

INSTITUTIONAL HOLDINGS:
No. of Institutions: 245
Shares Held: 40,944,170
% Held: 60.7
INDUSTRY: National commercial banks (SIC: 6021)
TRANSFER AGENT(S): Mellon Investor Services, LLC, Ridgefield Park, NJ

COMMERCIAL METALS COMPANY

EXCH.	SYM.	REC. PRICE	P/E RATIO	YLD.	MKT. CAP.	RANGE (52-WK.)	'02 Y/E PR.
NYSE	CMC	14.07 (2/28/03)	13.4	2.3%	$401.3 mill.	24.87 - 13.75	16.24

UPPER MEDIUM GRADE. THE COMPANY HAS IMPLEMENTED A PRICE INCREASE FOR ITS STEEL MILL PRODUCTS IN ORDER TO RESTORE MARGINS FOR ITS STEEL MINIMILLS.

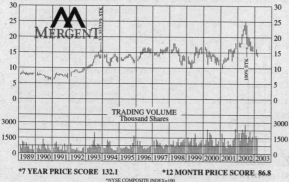

*7 YEAR PRICE SCORE 132.1   *12 MONTH PRICE SCORE 86.8
*NYSE COMPOSITE INDEX=100

INTERIM EARNINGS (Per Share):

Qtr.	Nov.	Feb.	May	Aug.
1997-98	0.27	0.28	0.38	0.50
1998-99	0.38	0.29	0.38	0.58
1999-00	0.35	0.35	0.46	0.47
2000-01	d0.09	0.07	0.41	0.54
2001-02	0.33	0.24	0.56	0.31
2002-03	0.08	0.10	...	...

INTERIM DIVIDENDS (Per Share):

Amt.	Decl.	Ex.	Rec.	Pay.
100% STK	5/20/02	7/01/02	6/07/02	6/28/02
0.08Q	6/18/02	7/02/02	7/05/02	7/19/02
0.08Q	9/23/02	10/02/02	10/04/02	10/18/02
0.08Q	12/18/02	12/30/02	1/02/03	1/23/03
0.08Q	3/17/03	4/02/03	4/04/03	4/18/03

Indicated div.: $0.32

CAPITALIZATION (8/31/02):

	($000)	(%)
Long-Term Debt	255,969	32.4
Deferred Income Tax	32,813	4.2
Common & Surplus	501,306	63.4
Total	790,088	100.0

BUSINESS:

Commercial Metals Company's businesses are organized into three segments and operated through a network of over 130 locations as of 3/18/03. The Manufacturing segment consists of the CMC Steel Group and the Howell Metal Company, a manufacturer of copper tubing. The Recycling segment is engaged in processing secondary (scrap) metals for recycling into new metal products through 44 recycling plants. The segment also operates through The Commercial Metals Railroad Salvage Company, a railroad salvage company. The Marketing and Trading segment is involved in buying and selling primary and secondary metals and other commodities and products through a global network of trading offices.

RECENT DEVELOPMENTS:

For the quarter ended 2/28/03, net income dropped 55.4% to $2.9 million compared with $6.6 million in the equivalent 2001 quarter. The decline in earnings was primarily attributed to the weak domestic commercial construction market and the sluggish industrial side of the economy, partially offset by better demand for the Recycling segment products and the benefits of the relatively strong markets outside the U.S. Net sales grew 15.1% to $660.8 million from $574.3 million a year earlier. For the quarter, shipments rose 7.2% to 537,000 tons. The average annual mill selling price grew 1.9% to $271.00 per ton, and the average selling price for finished goods increased 2.6% to $277.00 per ton.

PROSPECTS:

The Company expects markets to perform better in the second half of 2003, resulting in improvements in production, shipments and prices. Also, during its second quarter, the Company implemented two steel mill product price increases on most of its products totaling $35.00 per ton, which partly become effective in the fiscal third quarter and become fully effective during the fourth quarter, which should help restore margins for its steel minimills. Separately, on 1/9/03, the Company announced that it acquired substantially all of the operating assets of D&G Enterprises, Inc., a rebar fabrication company.

ANNUAL FINANCIAL DATA:

FISCAL YEAR	TOT. REVS. ($mill.)	NET INC. ($mill.)	TOT. ASSETS ($mill.)	OPER. PROFIT %	NET PROFIT %	RET. ON EQUITY %	RET. ON ASSETS %	CURR. RATIO	EARN. PER SH.$	CASH FL. PER SH.$	TANG. BK. VAL.$	DIV. PER SH.$	PRICE RANGE	AVG. P/E RATIO	AVG. YIELD %
8/31/02	2,446.8	③ 40.5	1,230.1	3.9	1.7	8.1	3.3	1.9	③ 1.43	3.61	17.58	0.29	24.87 - 15.50	14.1	1.4
8/31/01	2,441.2	① 24.3	1,084.8	3.2	1.0	5.6	2.2	1.8	① 0.93	3.48	16.65	0.26	18.30 - 9.88	15.2	1.8
8/31/00	2,661.4	② 46.3	1,172.9	4.5	1.7	11.0	3.9	1.6	② 1.63	3.96	15.97	0.26	16.97 - 11.00	8.6	1.9
8/31/99	2,251.4	① 47.1	1,079.0	4.9	2.1	11.3	4.4	1.8	① 1.61	3.39	14.52	0.26	17.09 - 9.84	8.4	1.9
8/31/98	2,367.6	42.7	1,002.6	4.5	1.8	11.2	4.3	1.6	1.41	2.98	13.09	0.26	18.00 - 10.78	10.2	1.8
8/31/97	2,258.4	38.6	839.1	4.0	1.7	10.9	4.6	2.1	1.27	2.74	12.02	0.26	16.94 - 13.56	12.1	1.7
8/31/96	2,322.4	46.0	766.8	4.4	2.0	13.7	6.0	2.0	1.51	2.86	11.10	0.24	16.75 - 12.19	9.6	1.7
8/31/95	2,116.8	③ 38.2	748.1	4.0	1.8	12.6	3.9	2.0	① 1.26	2.52	9.86	0.24	14.50 - 11.50	10.3	1.8
8/31/94	1,666.2	26.2	604.9	3.5	1.6	10.8	2.9	1.6	0.88	1.60	8.50	0.24	14.56 - 10.50	14.3	1.7
8/31/93	1,568.5	21.7	542.0	3.3	1.4	9.2	2.1	1.9	0.73	1.31	7.98	0.20	15.00 - 9.71	16.9	1.6

Statistics are as originally reported. Adj. for stk. splits: 4-for-3, 12/93; 2-for-1, 6/02. ① Incl. a litigation chrg. of $8.3 mill., 2001; $3.3 mill., 1999; $6.7 mill., 1995. ② Incl. nonrecurr. chrg. of $1.2 mill. ③ Incl. after-tax write-downs of $3.0 mill.

OFFICERS:
S. A. Rabin, Chmn., Pres., C.E.O.
W. B. Larson, V.P., C.F.O.
D. M. Sudbury, V.P., Gen. Couns., Sec.
INVESTOR CONTACT: Debbie L. Okie, Dir., Public Relations, (214)689-4354
PRINCIPAL OFFICE: 7800 Stemmons Freeway, Dallas, TX 75247

TELEPHONE NUMBER: (214) 689-4300
FAX: (214) 689-5886
WEB: www.commercialmetals.com
NO. OF EMPLOYEES: 7,728 (approx.)
SHAREHOLDERS: 2,242 (approx.)
ANNUAL MEETING: In Jan.
INCORPORATED: DE, 1946

INSTITUTIONAL HOLDINGS:
No. of Institutions: 107
Shares Held: 16,057,318
% Held: 56.5
INDUSTRY: Metals service centers and offices (SIC: 5051)
TRANSFER AGENT(S): Mellon Investor Services, LLC, Ridgefield Park, NJ

COMMERCIAL NET LEASE REALTY, INC.

EXCH.	SYM.	REC. PRICE	P/E RATIO	YLD.	MKT. CAP.	RANGE (52-WK.)	'02 Y/E PR.	DIV. ACH.
NYSE	NNN	14.85 (2/28/03)	14.0	8.6%	$0.60 bill.	16.40 - 12.60	15.33	13 yrs.

MEDIUM GRADE. THE COMPANY WILL LOOK TO CAPITALIZE ON ITS IMPROVED OCCUPANCY RATES AND THE PROFITABILITY OF COMMERCIAL NET LEASE REALTY SERVICES, INC.

TRADING VOLUME
Thousand Shares

*7 YEAR PRICE SCORE 118.4   *12 MONTH PRICE SCORE 108.2
*NYSE COMPOSITE INDEX=100

INTERIM EARNINGS (Per Share):

Qtr.	Mar.	June	Sept.	Dec.
1998	0.15	0.32	0.34	0.29
1999	0.32	0.23	0.29	0.31
2000	0.28	0.28	0.28	0.41
2001	0.38	0.34	0.24	d0.01
2002	0.29	0.27	0.23	0.27

INTERIM DIVIDENDS (Per Share):

Amt.	Decl.	Ex.	Rec.	Pay.
0.315Q	1/15/02	1/29/02	1/31/02	2/15/02
0.315Q	4/15/02	4/26/02	4/30/02	5/15/02
0.32Q	7/15/02	7/29/02	7/31/02	8/15/02
0.32Q	10/15/02	10/29/02	10/31/02	11/15/02
0.32Q	1/16/03	1/29/03	1/31/03	2/14/03

Indicated div.: $1.28 (Div. Reinv. Plan)

CAPITALIZATION (12/31/01):

	($000)	(%)
Long-Term Debt	435,333	43.5
Preferred Stock	50,000	5.0
Common & Surplus	514,640	51.5
Total	999,973	100.0

BUSINESS:

Commercial Net Lease Realty, Inc. is a fully integrated, self-administered real estate investment trust that acquires, owns, manages and indirectly develops a diversified portfolio of freestanding properties. The Company invests in single-tenant, freestanding retail properties that are located in intensive commercial corridors with purchase prices up to $8.0 million. As of 2/3/03, the Company owned 345 properties in 39 states that are generally leased to major retail businesses under long-term commercial net leases. These businesses include Barnes & Noble, Best Buy, Eckerd and OfficeMax. On 12/1/01, NNN acquired Captec Net Lease Realty, Inc.

RECENT DEVELOPMENTS:

For the year ended 12/31/02, income from continuing operations was $46.1 million compared with income of $27.0 million the previous year. Results for 2002 included a provision for loss on the impairment of real estate of $1.9 million, while 2001 results included pre-tax expenses of $12.6 million incurred in acquiring advisor. Total revenues advanced 20.5% to $93.8 million from $77.9 million in 2001. Rental and earned income jumped 26.9% to $85.3 million from $67.2 million, while interest and other income decreased 20.2% to $8.5 million from $10.7 million the year before.

PROSPECTS:

Going forward, NNN will look to capitalize on priorities from the prior year, which included improving its occupancy rates and the profitability of Commercial Net Lease Realty Services, Inc., an unconsolidated subsidiary that operates in built-to-suit development. Also, operating results should benefit from contributions from newer investments as NNN and its affiliated subsidiaries invested about $45.8 million in 35 properties and construction in progress during 2002. Conversely, NNN sold 19 properties in the previous year generating about $29.9 million in net proceeds. As of 12/31/02, four tenants in NNN's property portfolio each accounted for more than 5.0% of annualized base rent (Eckerd 13.0%, Best Buy 6.7%, OfficeMax 6.2%, Barnes & Noble 5.5%).

ANNUAL FINANCIAL DATA:

FISCAL YEAR	TOT. INC. ($000)	NET INC. ($000)	TOT. ASSETS ($000)	NET INC. +DEPR./ ASSETS %	RET. ON EQUITY %	RET. ON ASSETS %	EARN. PER SH.$	TANG. BK. VAL.$	DIV. PER SH.$	DIV. PAYOUT %	PRICE RANGE	AVG. P/E RATIO	AVG. YIELD %
p12/31/02	93,827	③ 46,060	954,108				③ 1.04		1.27	122.1	16.40 - 12.60	13.9	8.8
12/31/01	80,526	① 28,963	1,006,628	3.8	5.1	2.9	① 0.91	12.68	1.26	138.4	14.25 - 10.13	13.4	10.3
12/31/00	80,891	①② 38,618	761,611	6.3	9.8	5.1	①② 1.27	12.93	1.25	98.0	11.50 - 9.50	8.3	11.9
12/31/99	76,543	① 35,311	749,789	5.9	9.0	4.7	① 1.16	12.94	1.24	106.9	13.94 - 9.44	10.1	10.6
12/31/98	64,773	① 32,441	685,595	5.7	8.5	4.7	① 1.10	13.00	1.23	111.8	18.31 - 12.50	14.0	8.0
12/31/97	50,135	① 30,385	537,014	6.6	8.4	5.7	① 1.25	12.96	1.20	96.0	18.13 - 13.88	12.8	7.5
12/31/96	33,369	① 19,839	370,953	6.3	7.9	5.3	① 1.18	15.04	1.18	100.0	16.38 - 12.75	12.3	8.1
12/31/95	20,580	12,707	219,257	6.7	9.4	5.8	1.09	11.65	1.16	106.4	13.75 - 11.75	11.7	9.1
12/31/94	12,289	8,915	152,211	6.7	6.5	5.9	1.04	11.72	1.14	109.6	14.50 - 11.88	12.7	8.6
12/31/93	5,069	① 3,522	91,620	4.5	3.9	3.8	① 0.95	11.89	1.10	115.8	15.00 - 11.75	14.1	8.2

Statistics are as originally reported. ① Incl. gain on sale of investment $4.6 mill., 2001; $4.1 mill., 2000; $6.7 mill., 1999; $1.4 mill., 1998; $651,000, 1997; $73,000, 1996; $374,000, 1993. ② Excl. acctg. chg. of $367,000. ③ Excl. disc. oper. of $2.0 mill. & incl. pre-tax prov. of $1.9 mill. for loss on the impair. of real estate.

OFFICERS:
J. M. Seneff Jr., Chmn., C.E.O.
R. A. Bourne, Vice-Chmn.
G. M. Ralston, Pres., C.O.O.

INVESTOR CONTACT: Kevin B. Habicht,
Investor Relations, (407) 265-7348

PRINCIPAL OFFICE: 450 South Orange Avenue, Orlando, FL 32801

TELEPHONE NUMBER: (407) 265-7348
FAX: (407) 423-2894
WEB: www.cnlreit.com
NO. OF EMPLOYEES: 35
SHAREHOLDERS: 1,303 (common); 43 (preferred)
ANNUAL MEETING: In May
INCORPORATED: DE, June, 1984; reincorp., MD, June, 1994

INSTITUTIONAL HOLDINGS:
No. of Institutions: 95
Shares Held: 11,723,321
% Held: 29.0

INDUSTRY: Real estate investment trusts (SIC: 6798)

TRANSFER AGENT(S): First Union National Bank, Charlotte, NC

COMMUNITY BANK SYSTEM, INC.

EXCH.	SYM.	REC. PRICE	P/E RATIO	YLD.	MKT. CAP.	RANGE (52-WK.)	'02 Y/E PR.	DIV. ACH.
NYSE	CBU	32.69 (2/28/03)	11.8	3.5%	$421.8 mill.	34.23 - 26.50	31.35	11 yrs.

MEDIUM GRADE. THE COMPANY EXPECTS FULL-YEAR 2003 EARNINGS OF APPROXIMATELY $2.95 PER SHARE.

MERGENT

TRADING VOLUME
Thousand Shares

*7 YEAR PRICE SCORE 126.2   *12 MONTH PRICE SCORE 113.5

*NYSE COMPOSITE INDEX=100

INTERIM EARNINGS (Per Share):

Qtr.	Mar.	June	Sept.	Dec.
1998	0.48	0.50	0.56	0.51
1999	0.50	0.55	0.68	0.69
2000	0.70	0.72	0.72	0.70
2001	0.50	0.18	0.55	0.39
2002	0.57	0.62	0.84	0.73

INTERIM DIVIDENDS (Per Share):

Amt.	Decl.	Ex.	Rec.	Pay.
0.27Q	2/21/02	3/13/02	3/15/02	4/10/02
0.27Q	5/16/02	6/12/02	6/14/02	7/10/02
0.29Q	8/22/02	9/12/02	9/16/02	10/10/02
0.29Q	11/21/02	12/12/02	12/16/02	1/10/03
0.29Q	2/20/03	3/12/03	3/14/03	4/10/03

Indicated div.: $1.16 (Div. Reinv. Plan)

CAPITALIZATION (12/31/01):

	($000)	(%)
Total Deposits	2,545,970	80.7
Long-Term Debt	263,100	8.3
Redeemable Pfd. Stock	77,819	2.5
Common & Surplus	267,980	8.5
Total	3,154,869	100.0

BUSINESS:

Community Bank System, Inc. is a bank holding company with $3.43 billion in assets, as of 12/31/02. As of 12/31/02, CBU's wholly-owned community banking subsidiary, Community Bank, N.A., operated 116 customer facilities and 85 automated teller machines located from Northern New York to the Southern Tier, west to Lake Erie, and in Northeastern Pennsylvania. Other subsidiaries include Elias Asset Management, Inc., an investment management firm;

Benefit Plans Administrative Services, Inc., a pension administration and consulting firm serving sponsors of defined benefit and defined contribution plans; and Community Investment Services, Inc., a broker-dealer delivering financial products, including mutual funds, annuities, individual stocks and bonds, and long-term health care and other selected insurance products.

RECENT DEVELOPMENTS:

For the year ended 12/31/02, net income was $38.5 million compared with $19.1 million the previous year. Earnings for 2002 and 2001 included pre-tax acquisition and unusual expenses of $700,000 and $8.2 million, respectively. Net interest income climbed 32.3% to $127.9 million, driven in

part by the improved contribution of the Company's three 2001 acquisitions. Loan loss provision was $12.2 million versus $7.1 million the year before. Total noninterest income rose 23.5% to $32.6 million, while noninterest expense increased 7.7% to $95.8 million.

PROSPECTS:

Looking ahead, CBU expects portfolio loan growth for 2003 in the low single digits. The Company noted that this reflects a resumption of commercial loan growth and higher installment loan growth, both in the mid-single digits. Its residential mortgage portfolio is likely to grow only marginally as a result of an overall market slowdown. CBU

anticipates that total noninterest income growth will be in the high single digits for 2003. Growth of recurring banking noninterest expenses is expected to be in the 7.0% to 8.0% range. Accordingly, CBE believes that the full-year 2003 estimate of $2.95 per share is consistent with its current expectations.

ANNUAL FINANCIAL DATA:

FISCAL YEAR	NET INT. INC. ($mill.)	NON-INT. INC. ($mill.)	NET INT. INC. ($mill.)	TOT. LOANS ($mill.)	TOT. ASSETS ($mill.)	TOT. DEP. ($mill.)	RET. ON EQUITY %	RET. ON ASSETS %	EQUITY/ ASSETS %	EARN. PER SH.$	TANG. BK. VAL.$	DIV. PER SH.$	PRICE RANGE	AVG. P/E RATIO	AVG. YIELD %
p12/31/02	127.9		③ 38.5							③ 2.93		1.10	34.21 - 25.91	10.3	3.7
12/31/01	96.7	29.1	② 20.7	1,733.1	3,210.8	2,546.0	7.7	0.6	8.3	② 1.62	9.74	1.08	29.85 - 24.75	16.9	4.0
12/31/00	71.2	21.0	20.3	1,093.8	2,022.6	1,457.7	14.6	1.0	6.9	2.85	12.64	1.02	26.25 - 20.00	8.1	4.4
12/31/99	67.9	15.5	17.6	1,006.1	1,840.7	1,360.3	16.3	1.0	5.9	2.42	8.09	0.94	33.63 - 22.63	11.6	3.3
12/31/98	64.4	17.0	① 15.5	916.0	1,680.7	1,378.1	12.9	0.9	7.1	① 2.05	9.01	0.83	38.25 - 24.81	15.4	2.6
12/31/97	62.9	11.8	15.6	845.0	1,633.7	1,345.7	13.2	1.0	7.2	2.02	7.82	0.74	34.00 - 19.25	13.2	2.8
12/31/96	55.3	8.9	14.1	658.4	1,343.9	1,027.2	12.9	1.1	8.1	1.84	9.85	0.68	20.13 - 15.13	9.6	3.8
12/31/95	47.1	6.6	11.5	573.6	1,152.0	1,016.9	11.5	1.0	8.7	1.71	8.37	0.60	18.38 - 12.13	8.9	3.9
12/31/94	39.4	5.1	10.1	510.7	915.6	679.6	15.3	1.1	7.2	1.80	10.79	0.56	15.88 - 12.88	8.0	3.9
12/31/93	37.8	3.9	9.6	443.6	713.1	588.3	15.4	1.3	8.7	1.72	11.20	0.51	15.38 - 11.50	7.8	3.8

Statistics are as originally reported. Adj. for 2-for-1 stk. split, 3/97. ① Bef. acctg. chg. credit of $193,860. ② Incl. acquisition & unusual exp. of $8.2 mill.; bef. extraord. loss of $1.6 mill. ③ Incl. acquisition & unusual exp. of $700,000.

OFFICERS:
J. A. Gabriel, Chmn.
S. A. Belden, Pres., C.E.O.
D. G. Wallace, Exec. V.P., C.F.O.

INVESTOR CONTACT: David G. Wallace, Exec. V.P., C.F.O., (315) 445-2282

PRINCIPAL OFFICE: 5790 Widewaters Parkway, DeWitt, NY 13214-1883

TELEPHONE NUMBER: (315) 445-2282
FAX: (315) 445-2997
WEB: www.communitybankna.com

NO. OF EMPLOYEES: 1,115

SHAREHOLDERS: 9,000 (approx. record)

ANNUAL MEETING: In May

INCORPORATED: DE, Apr., 1983

INSTITUTIONAL HOLDINGS:
No. of Institutions: 82
Shares Held: 4,388,989
% Held: 33.8

INDUSTRY: National commercial banks (SIC: 6021)

TRANSFER AGENT(S): Mellon Investor Services, L.L.C., Ridgefield Park, NJ

COMMUNITY HEALTH SYSTEMS, INC.

EXCH.	SYM.	REC. PRICE	P/E RATIO	YLD.	MKT. CAP.	RANGE (52-WK.)	'02 Y/E PR.
NYSE	CYH	18.75 (2/28/03)	18.0	...	$1.85 bill.	30.55 - 15.84	20.59

MEDIUM GRADE. ON 1/3/03, THE COMPANY ANNOUNCED THE ACQUISITION OF SEVEN WEST TENNESSEE HOSPITALS FROM METHODIST HEALTHCARE OF MEMPHIS, TENNESSEE.

TRADING VOLUME
Thousand Shares

*7 YEAR PRICE SCORE N/A   *12 MONTH PRICE SCORE 84.2

*NYSE COMPOSITE INDEX=100

INTERIM EARNINGS (Per Share):

Qtr.	Mar.	June	Sept.	Dec.
1999	0.04	d0.03	d0.08	d0.23
2000	0.02	Nil	0.02	0.09
2001	0.12	0.11	0.11	0.18
2002	0.27	0.24	0.25	0.28

INTERIM DIVIDENDS (Per Share):

Amt.	Decl.	Ex.	Rec.	Pay.
		No dividends paid.		

CAPITALIZATION (12/31/01):

	($000)	(%)
Long-Term Debt	980,083	45.8
Deferred Income Tax	44,675	2.1
Common & Surplus	1,115,665	52.1
Total	2,140,423	100.0

BUSINESS:

Community Health Systems, Inc. is a non-urban provider of general hospital healthcare services in the United States. The Company's hospitals typically have 50 to 200 beds and are located in non-urban markets with populations of 20,000 to 80,000 people and economically diverse employment bases. The Company's facilities, together with its medical staffs, provide a range of inpatient and outpatient general hospital services and a variety of specialty services. As of 12/31/02, the Company owned, leased or operated 63 hospitals, geographically diversified across 22 states, with an aggregate of 6,310 licensed beds.

RECENT DEVELOPMENTS:

For the year ended 12/31/02, income was $105.3 million, before an extraordinary loss of $5.3 million, compared with income of $48.6 million, before an extraordinary loss of $3.8 million, the previous year. Results for 2001 included amortization of goodwill of $28.8 million. Net operating revenues advanced 29.9% to $2.20 billion from $1.69 billion the year before, reflecting 4.4% growth in total admissions to 176,959, and a 5.1% increase in adjusted admissions on a same-store basis to 327,201. Total expenses jumped 30.2% to $1.96 billion from $1.50 billion a year earlier. Operating income improved 27.8% to $241.5 million versus $189.0 million the prior year.

PROSPECTS:

On 1/3/03, the Company announced the closing of the acquisition of seven West Tennessee hospitals from Methodist Healthcare of Memphis, Tennessee. The acquisition includes Methodist hospitals in Brownsville, Dyersburg, Jackson, Lexington, Martin, McKenzie and Selmer, as well as Methodist's wholly owned outpatient care and ancillary services located in these areas. Separately, on 1/14/03, the Company announced the execution of a definitive agreement to acquire the 408-bed Southside Regional Medical Center in Petersburg, Virginia, including several satellite clinics and two paramedical educational programs. The transaction, structured as a lease of real estate and purchase of other assets is subject to regulatory approvals.

ANNUAL FINANCIAL DATA:

FISCAL YEAR	TOT. REVS. ($mill.)	NET INC. ($mill.)	TOT. ASSETS ($mill.)	OPER. PROFIT %	NET PROFIT %	RET. ON EQUITY %	RET. ON ASSETS %	CURR. RATIO	EARN. PER SH. $	CASH FL. PER SH. $	TANG. BK. VAL. $	PRICE RANGE	AVG. P/E RATIO
p12/31/02	2,200.4	① 105.3	...	...	...	...	...	...	① 1.05	...	...	30.55 - 18.50	23.4
12/31/01	1,693.6	① 48.6	2,460.7	11.2	2.9	4.4	2.0	1.7	① 0.54	1.86	1.17	35.45 - 21.25	52.5
12/31/00	1,337.5	9.6	2,213.8	11.6	0.7	1.3	0.4	1.7	0.14	1.55	...	37.20 - 15.63	188.5
12/31/99	1,080.0	d16.8	1,895.1	9.7	...	...	...	1.3	d0.31	1.19	...	...	...
12/31/98	854.6	d182.9	1,747.0	...	...	...	...	1.0	d3.37	d1.96	...	...	...
12/31/97	742.4	d32.2	...	7.2	...	...	...	...	d0.60	0.69	...	...	...

Statistics are as originally reported. ① Bef. extraord loss of $3.8 mill., 2001; $5.3 mill., 2002.

OFFICERS:
W. T. Smith, Chmn., Pres., C.E.O.
W. L. Cash, Exec. V.P., C.F.O.

INVESTOR CONTACT: W. Larry Cash, Exec. V.P., C.F.O., (615) 373-9600

PRINCIPAL OFFICE: 155 Franklin Road, Suite 400, Brentwood, TN 37027

TELEPHONE NUMBER: (615) 373-9600
FAX: (615) 373-1068
WEB: www.chs.net
NO. OF EMPLOYEES: 13,200 full-time (approx.); 7,300 part-time (approx.)
SHAREHOLDERS: 61 (approx.); 6,350 (approx. beneficial)
ANNUAL MEETING: In May
INCORPORATED: DE, 1996

INSTITUTIONAL HOLDINGS:
No. of Institutions: 129
Shares Held: 55,014,921
% Held: 55.7

INDUSTRY: General medical & surgical hospitals (SIC: 8062)

TRANSFER AGENT(S): Mellon Investor Services, Dallas, TX

COMPUTER ASSOCIATES INTERNATIONAL, INC.

EXCH.	SYM.	REC. PRICE	P/E RATIO	YLD.	MKT. CAP.	RANGE (52-WK.)	'02 Y/E PR.
NYSE	CA	13.35 (2/28/03)	...	0.6%	$7.71 bill.	22.09 - 7.47	13.50

LOWER MEDIUM GRADE. THE COMPANY EXPECTS REVENUE FOR THE FOURTH QUARTER OF FISCAL 2003 TO BE IN THE RANGE OF $785.0 MILLION TO $800.0 MILLION.

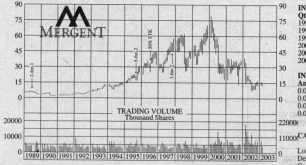

*7 YEAR PRICE SCORE 41.7   *12 MONTH PRICE SCORE 104.0

*NYSE COMPOSITE INDEX=100

INTERIM EARNINGS (Per Share):

Qtr.	June	Sept.	Dec.	Mar.
1997-98	0.28	0.48	0.60	0.75
1998-99	0.34	0.52	0.64	0.83
1999-00	d0.80	0.60	0.72	0.98
2000-01	0.04	0.54	d0.59	d0.71
2001-02	d0.59	d0.50	d0.40	d0.41
2002-03	d0.11	d0.09	d0.08	...

INTERIM DIVIDENDS (Per Share):

Amt.	Decl.	Ex.	Rec.	Pay.
0.04S	5/22/01	6/20/01	6/22/01	7/05/01
0.04S	12/11/01	12/19/01	12/21/01	1/09/02
0.04S	5/14/02	6/18/02	6/20/02	7/08/02
0.04S	12/13/02	12/19/02	12/23/02	1/08/03

Indicated div.: $0.08 (Div. Reinv. Plan)

CAPITALIZATION (3/31/02):

	($000)	(%)
Long-Term Debt	3,334,000	36.2
Deferred Income Tax	1,267,000	13.7
Common & Surplus	4,617,000	50.1
Total	9,218,000	100.0

BUSINESS:

Computer Associates International, Inc. is a business software company that delivers the end-to-end infrastructure to enable e-business through technology, education and services. CA provides software applications for all types of businesses throughout the world. The Company has a portfolio of more than 800 products, including enterprise management, database and application development, as well as

products that provide the infrastructure for e-business and e-commerce over the Internet. Many of CA's products provide tools to measure and improve computer hardware and software performance and programmer productivity. Revenues for fiscal 2002 were derived: maintenance, 32.3%; subscription, 27.9%; financing fees, 15.0%; software fees and other, 14.6%; and professional services, 10.2%.

RECENT DEVELOPMENTS:

For the quarter ended 12/31/02, CA reported a net loss of $44.0 million versus a net loss of $231.0 million in the same period of 2001. Results for 2002 and 2001 included amortization of capitalized software costs of $116.0 million and $122.0 million, and depreciation/amortization of goodwill and other intangibles of $35.0 million and $153.0

million, respectively. Total revenue climbed 4.1% to $778.0 million from $747.0 million the year before. CA also reported new deferred subscription revenue of $538.0 million with an average contract duration of about 2.8 years. As of 12/31/02, aggregate deferred subscription revenue totaled approximately $3.50 billion.

PROSPECTS:

The Company expects to continue to implement growth strategies despite challenging technology spending conditions. Near-term results may continue to benefit from a rise in the number of large multi-million dollar licenses, increases in the number of license transactions and the

performance of CA's European business. As a result, the Company expects revenue for the fourth quarter of fiscal 2003 in the range of $785.0 million to $800.0 million and earnings per share in the range of $0.05 to $0.06.

ANNUAL FINANCIAL DATA:

FISCAL YEAR	TOT. REVS. ($mill.)	NET INC. ($mill.)	TOT. ASSETS ($mill.)	OPER. PROFIT %	NET PROFIT %	RET. ON EQUITY %	RET. ON ASSETS %	CURR. RATIO	EARN. PER SH. $	CASH FL. PER SH. $	TANG. BK. VAL. $	DIV. PER SH. $	PRICE RANGE	AVG. P/E RATIO	AVG. YIELD %
3/31/02	2,964.0	⑦ d1,102.0	12,226.0	...	...	...	...	1.3	⑦ d1.91	d0.01	...	0.08	39.03 - 12.92	...	0.3
⑥ 3/31/01	4,198.0	⑤ d591.0	14,143.0	...	...	...	...	1.2	⑤ d1.02	0.89	...	0.08	79.44 - 18.13	...	0.2
3/31/00	6,103.0	④ 696.0	18,053.0	31.6	11.4	9.2	3.9	1.3	④ 1.25	2.32	...	0.08	70.63 - 32.13	41.1	0.2
3/31/99	5,253.0	③ 626.0	8,430.0	21.6	11.9	20.3	7.4	1.4	③ 1.11	1.69	2.32	0.08	61.94 - 26.00	39.6	0.2
3/31/98	4,719.0	② 1,169.0	6,914.0	42.7	24.8	43.5	16.9	1.2	② 2.06	2.68	2.38	0.07	57.50 - 24.83	20.0	0.2
3/31/97	4,040.0	366.0	6,138.0	25.6	9.1	23.5	6.0	1.0	0.65	1.39	...	0.06	45.25 - 22.56	52.4	0.2
3/31/96	3,504.6	① d56.4	4,933.2	...	...	...	...	1.0	① d0.11	0.64	0.09	0.06	31.33 - 13.89	...	0.3
3/31/95	2,623.0	① 431.9	3,154.8	26.9	16.5	29.5	13.7	1.4	① 0.76	1.22	1.45	0.05	15.07 - 8.11	15.3	0.4
3/31/94	2,148.5	① 401.3	2,524.0	29.3	18.7	31.5	15.9	1.8	① 1.04	1.58	2.11	0.04	13.11 - 5.96	13.7	0.4
3/31/93	1,841.0	245.5	2,365.9	21.1	13.3	22.9	10.4	1.6	0.28	0.52	0.50	0.03	6.15 - 3.22	11.0	0.6

Statistics are as originally reported. Adj. for 3-for-2 split, 8/95, 7/96 & 11/97. ① Incl. after-tax write-off for purch. R&D of: $154.6 mill. rel. to acq. of The ASK Group, Inc., 1994; $808.0 mill. rel. to acq. of Legent Corp., 1995; $598.0 mill. rel. to acq. of Cheyenne Software, Inc., 1996. ② Excl. $33.8 mill. pre-tax chg. rel. to CSC tender offer. ③ Incl. $1.07 bill. chg. rel. to the vesting of stock ownership. ④ Incl. $796.0 mill. in-process R&D chg. & $50.0 mill. non-cash asset write-down chg. ⑤ Incl. $184.0 mill. gain fr. special items & $31.0 mill. write-off fr. bankrpt filing of Inacom Corp. ⑥ ꟿ fiscal 2001, CA began accounting for contract revs. over life of the contract & licenses, resulting in lower rev. figures. ⑦ Incl. $59.0 mill. loss fr. special items.

OFFICERS:
S. Kumar, Chmn., Pres., C.E.O.
I. Zar, Exec. V.P., C.F.O.
S. M. Woghin, Sr. V.P., Gen. Couns.
INVESTOR CONTACT: Investor Relations, (631) 342-5601
PRINCIPAL OFFICE: One Computer Associates Plaza, Islandia, NY 11749

TELEPHONE NUMBER: (631) 342-6000
FAX: (631) 342-5329
WEB: www.ca.com
NO. OF EMPLOYEES: 16,600 (approx.)
SHAREHOLDERS: 9,000 (approx.)
ANNUAL MEETING: In Aug.
INCORPORATED: DE, June, 1974

INSTITUTIONAL HOLDINGS:
No. of Institutions: 361
Shares Held: 362,332,309
% Held: 63.2
INDUSTRY: Prepackaged software (SIC: 7372).
TRANSFER AGENT(S): Mellon Investor Services, Ridgefield Park, NJ

COMPUTER SCIENCES CORPORATION

EXCH.	SYM.	REC. PRICE	P/E RATIO	YLD.	MKT. CAP.	RANGE (52-WK.)	'02 Y/E PR.
NYSE	CSC	31.26 (2/28/03)	12.9	...	$5.35 bill.	53.47 - 24.30	34.45

MEDIUM GRADE. THE COMPANY SHOULD STRENGTHEN ITS POSITION IN THE U.S. FEDERAL MARKETPLACE WITH THE ACQUISITION OF DYNCORP.

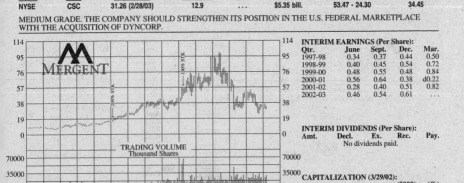

*7 YEAR PRICE SCORE 78.2　　***12 MONTH PRICE SCORE 92.7**
NYSE COMPOSITE INDEX=100

INTERIM EARNINGS (Per Share):

Qtr.	June	Sept.	Dec.	Mar.
1997-98	0.34	0.37	0.44	0.50
1998-99	0.40	0.45	0.54	0.72
1999-00	0.48	0.55	0.48	0.84
2000-01	0.56	0.64	0.38	d0.22
2001-02	0.28	0.40	0.51	0.82
2002-03	0.46	0.54	0.61	...

INTERIM DIVIDENDS (Per Share):

Amt.	Decl.	Ex.	Rec.	Pay.
		No dividends paid.		

CAPITALIZATION (3/29/02):

	($000)	(%)
Long-Term Debt	1,873,100	34.1
Common & Surplus	3,623,600	65.9
Total	5,496,700	100.0

BUSINESS:

Computer Sciences Corporation offers an array of professional services to industry and government and specializes in the application of advanced and complex information technology to achieve its customers' strategic objectives. CSC's services include: outsourcing, which includes operating all or a portion of a customer's technology infrastructure, including systems analysis, applications development, network operations and data center management; systems integration, which includes designing, developing, implementing and integrating complete information systems; and information technology and management consulting and other professional services. Revenues for the year ended 3/29/02 were derived as follows: U.S. Commercial, 37.7%; Europe, 25.8%; other international, 11.1%; Department of Defense, 15.7%; and civil agencies, 9.7%.

RECENT DEVELOPMENTS:

For the third quarter ended 12/27/02, net income jumped 21.4% to $105.7 million compared with $87.1 million in the equivalent quarter of 2001. Earnings were enhanced by strong performances from the Company's North American consulting and systems integration and federal sectors, along with efforts to improve operating efficiencies. Revenues slipped 3.5% to $2.79 billion from $2.89 billion in the prior-year period, reflecting softness in worldwide demand for commercial information technology services in the financial services vertical market and shorter-term project-oriented services. During the quarter, the Company announced new business awards totaling approximately $400.0 million.

PROSPECTS:

On 12/13/02, the Company announced that it has agreed to acquire DynCorp, an employee-owned information technology and outsourcing firm that focuses on large defense, security and civil markets, for approximately $950.0 million, including the assumption of DynCorp's debt. The acquisition is expected to be accretive to earnings in 2004, excluding the effect of a special charge related to the transaction. In addition, the acquisition, which is subject to shareholder approval, should strengthen the Company's position in the U.S. federal marketplace.

ANNUAL FINANCIAL DATA:

FISCAL YEAR	TOT. REVS. ($Mill.)	NET INC. ($Mill.)	TOT. ASSETS ($Mill.)	OPER. PROFIT %	NET PROFIT %	RET. ON EQUITY %	RET. ON ASSETS %	CURR. RATIO	EARN. PER SH. $	CASH FL. PER SH. $	TANG. BK. VAL. $	PRICE RANGE	AVG. P/E RATIO
3/29/02	11,426.0	344.1	8,610.5	5.6	3.0	9.5	4.0	1.2	2.01	7.02	9.39	66.71 - 28.99	23.8
3/30/01	10,524.0	④ 233.2	8,174.8	6.2	2.2	7.3	2.9	0.9	④ 1.37	5.17	7.48	99.88 - 58.25	57.7
3/31/00	9,370.7	④ 402.9	5,874.1	7.4	4.3	13.2	6.9	1.4	④ 2.37	5.59	11.18	94.63 - 52.38	31.0
4/02/99	7,660.0	341.2	5,007.7	7.1	4.5	14.2	6.8	1.3	2.11	4.85	9.92	74.88 - 39.97	27.2
4/03/98	6,600.8	③ 260.4	4,046.8	7.0	3.9	13.0	6.4	1.6	③ 1.64	4.08	8.52	43.88 - 28.94	22.2
3/28/97	5,616.0	② 192.4	3,580.9	6.8	3.4	11.5	5.4	1.5	② 1.23	6.72	12.73	43.25 - 32.06	30.6
3/29/96	4,242.4	141.7	2,595.8	6.2	3.3	10.9	5.5	1.5	1.24	6.88	14.08	37.63 - 23.25	24.5
3/31/95	3,372.5	110.7	2,333.7	6.0	3.3	9.6	4.7	1.4	1.05	5.35	11.70	26.31 - 15.81	20.2
4/01/94	2,582.7	90.9	1,806.4	6.2	3.5	11.3	5.0	1.3	0.89	4.31	8.22	16.71 - 11.67	16.0
4/02/93	2,479.8	① 78.1	1,453.6	5.8	3.2	11.2	5.4	1.7	① 0.78	3.91	7.08	14.00 - 9.50	15.2

Statistics are as originally reported. Adj. for 3-for-1 split, 1/94; 100% stk. split, 3/98. Fiscal yr. ends 3/31 of the following yr. ① Excl. $4.9 mill. ($0.05/sh.) acct. chg. ② Incl. $35.3 mill. ($0.23/sh.) non-recur. chg., 1996; cr$1.7 mill., 1997. ③ Incl. $13.9 mill. after-tax spl. chg. rel. to an unsolicited take-over attempt. ④ Incl. after-tax spl. chgs. of $29.8 mill., 2000; $156.0 mill., 2001.

OFFICERS:
V. B. Honeycutt, Chmn., C.E.O.
E. P. Boykin, Pres., C.O.O.
L. J. Level, V.P., C.F.O.
INVESTOR CONTACT: Lisa Runge, Manager, Investor Relations, (310) 615-1680
PRINCIPAL OFFICE: 2100 East Grand Avenue, El Segundo, CA 90245

TELEPHONE NUMBER: (310) 615-0311
FAX: (310) 640-2648
WEB: www.csc.com
NO. OF EMPLOYEES: 67,000 (approx.)
SHAREHOLDERS: 10,182
ANNUAL MEETING: In Aug.
INCORPORATED: NV, Apr., 1959

INSTITUTIONAL HOLDINGS:
No. of Institutions: 390
Shares Held: 144,054,557
% Held: 83.9
INDUSTRY: Computer integrated systems design (SIC: 7373)
TRANSFER AGENT(S): Mellon Investor Services, Ridgefield Park, NJ

CONAGRA FOODS, INC.

EXCH.	SYM.	REC. PRICE	P/E RATIO	YLD.	MKT. CAP.	RANGE (52-WK.)	'02 Y/E PR.	DIV. ACH.
NYSE	CAG	23.07 (2/28/03)	15.1	4.3%	$12.39 bill.	27.65 - 20.90	25.01	25 yrs.

UPPER MEDIUM GRADE. THE COMPANY IS TARGETING EARNINGS OF ABOUT $1.60 PER SHARE IN THE CURRENT FISCAL YEAR.

TRADING VOLUME
Thousand Shares

*7 YEAR PRICE SCORE 104.3   *12 MONTH PRICE SCORE 108.3
*NYSE COMPOSITE INDEX=100

INTERIM EARNINGS (Per Share):

Qtr.	Aug.	Nov.	Feb.	May
1997-98	0.48	0.46	0.30	0.36
1998-99	0.23	0.46	0.36	d0.30
1999-00	0.21	0.39	0.30	d0.04
2000-01	0.30	0.58	0.19	0.23
2001-02	0.36	0.44	0.31	0.36
2002-03	0.42	0.44	...	...

INTERIM DIVIDENDS (Per Share):

Amt.	Decl.	Ex.	Rec.	Pay.
0.235Q	12/06/01	1/30/02	2/01/02	3/01/02
0.235Q	4/08/02	5/01/02	5/03/02	6/01/02
0.235Q	7/12/02	7/31/02	8/02/02	9/01/02
0.247Q	9/26/02	10/30/02	11/01/02	12/01/02
0.247Q	12/05/02	1/29/03	1/31/03	3/01/03

Indicated div.: $0.99 (Div. Reinv. Plan)

CAPITALIZATION (5/26/02):

	($000)	(%)
Long-Term Debt	5,743,700	57.1
Common & Surplus	4,308,200	42.9
Total	10,051,900	100.0

BUSINESS:

ConAgra Foods, Inc. (formerly ConAgra, Inc.) operates in four industry segments: Packaged Foods (44.8% of sales and 78.2% of operating profit in fiscal 2002) includes branded shelf-stable, frozen and refrigerated products for retail and foodservice markets. Meat Processing (36.3%, 13.1%) includes the Company's fresh beef, pork and poultry operations. Agricultural Products (12.9%, 0.9%) includes CAG's crop inputs distribution business and its agricultural merchandising operations. Food Ingredients (6.0%, 7.8%) includes spices, grain milling and ingredients for food products. The Company's major brands include: HEALTHY CHOICE, BANQUET, CHEF BOYARDEE, WESSON, HUNT'S, ORVILLE REDENBACHER'S, SLIM JIM, PETER PAN, PARKAY, VAN CAMP'S, PAM, SWISS MISS, LOUIS KEMP, REDDI-WIP, ACT II, LA CHOY, BUTTERBALL, ARMOUR and BUMBLE BEE.

RECENT DEVELOPMENTS:

For the 13 weeks ended 11/24/02, net income totaled $235.8 million up 1.8% compared with $231.6 million in the corresponding prior-year period. Net sales slid 19.0% to $5.96 billion from $7.36 billion the year prior, primarily reflecting the 9/19/02 divestiture of the Company's fresh beef and pork processing business, partially offset by higher sales in the Agricultural Products and Food Ingredients segments. Operating profit slipped 0.2% to $552.1 million from $553.0 million in the previous year.

PROSPECTS:

The Company is targeting earnings of approximately $1.60 per share in the current fiscal year. Results are expected to benefit from CAG's efforts to control costs and increase advertising in the Packaged Foods segment, along with lower administrative and operating costs in the Agricultural Products segment. Separately, operating profit in the Food Ingredients segment is being negatively affected by increased costs and lower margins for certain seasonings and flavorings products, partially offset by improved prices and profitability from the Company's flour milling operations.

ANNUAL FINANCIAL DATA:

FISCAL YEAR	TOT. REVS. ($mill.)	NET INC. ($mill.)	TOT. ASSETS ($mill.)	OPER. PROFIT %	NET PROFIT %	RET. ON EQUITY %	RET. ON ASSETS %	CURR. RATIO	EARN. PER SH.$	CASH FL. PER SH.$	TANG. BK. VAL.$	DIV. PER SH.$	PRICE RANGE	AVG. P/E RATIO	AVG. YIELD %
5/26/02	27,629.6	☐ 785.0	15,496.2	6.0	2.8	18.2	5.1	1.5	☐ 1.47	2.67	...	0.91	26.00 - 17.50	14.8	4.2
5/27/01	27,194.2	☐ 682.5	16,480.8	5.6	2.5	17.1	4.1	1.1	☐ 1.33	2.48	...	0.84	26.19 - 15.06	15.5	4.1
5/28/00	25,385.8	☒ 413.0	12,295.8	5.1	1.6	13.9	3.4	1.1	☐ 0.86	1.98	1.22	0.74	34.38 - 20.63	32.0	2.7
5/30/99	24,594.3	☒ 358.4	12,146.1	5.9	1.5	12.3	3.0	1.1	☒ 0.75	1.80	1.02	0.65	33.63 - 22.56	37.5	2.3
5/31/98	23,840.5	☐ 628.0	11,702.8	5.5	2.6	22.6	5.4	1.1	☐ 1.36	2.33	0.85	0.56	38.75 - 24.50	23.3	1.8
5/25/97	24,002.1	615.0	11,277.1	5.4	2.6	24.9	5.5	1.0	1.34	2.24	0.08	0.49	27.38 - 18.81	17.2	2.1
5/26/96	24,821.6	☒ 188.9	11,196.6	4.9	0.8	8.4	1.7	1.1	☒ 0.40	1.28	...	0.43	20.88 - 14.88	45.2	2.4
5/28/95	24,108.9	495.6	10,801.0	4.6	2.1	19.9	4.6	1.3	1.03	1.85	0.15	0.37	16.56 - 12.75	14.2	2.6
5/29/94	23,512.2	437.1	10,721.8	4.1	1.9	19.6	4.1	1.1	0.91	1.71	...	0.32	16.81 - 11.38	15.6	2.3
5/30/93	21,519.1	☒ 391.5	9,988.7	4.0	1.8	19.1	3.9	1.1	☒ 0.79	1.54	...	0.28	17.88 - 12.25	19.1	1.9

Statistics are as originally reported. Adj. for 2-for-1 stk. split, 10/97. ☐ Bef. $2.0 mil acctg. chg., 2002; $43.9 mil ($0.09/sh), 2001; $14.8 mil ($0.03/sh), 1998; & $121.2 mil, 1993. ☒ Incl. $621.4 mil pre-tax, non-recur. chg., 2000; $337.9 mil ($0.71/sh) after-tax, non-recur chg., 1999; & $356.3 mil ($0.78/sh) after-tax, non-recur. chg., 1996.

OFFICERS:
B. C. Rohde, Chmn., Pres., C.E.O.
J. P. O'Donnell, Exec. V.P., C.F.O., Sec.
K. W. Gerhardt, Sr. V.P., Chief Info. Off.

INVESTOR CONTACT: Shareholder Services, (800) 214-0349

PRINCIPAL OFFICE: One ConAgra Drive, Omaha, NE 68102-5001

TELEPHONE NUMBER: (402) 595-4000
FAX: (402) 595-4707
WEB: www.conagra.com
NO. OF EMPLOYEES: 89,000 (approx.)
SHAREHOLDERS: 34,000 (record); 190,000 (approx. beneficial)
ANNUAL MEETING: In Sept.
INCORPORATED: NE, Sept., 1919; reincorp., DE, Dec., 1975

INSTITUTIONAL HOLDINGS:
No. of Institutions: 485
Shares Held: 329,230,240
% Held: 61.3

INDUSTRY: Meat packing plants (SIC: 2011)

TRANSFER AGENT(S): Wells Fargo Shareowner Services, St. Paul, MN

CONCORD EFS, INC.

EXCH.	SYM.	REC. PRICE	P/E RATIO	YLD.	MKT. CAP.	RANGE (52-WK.)	'02 Y/E PR.
NYSE	CE	11.10 (2/28/03)	19.1	...	$5.64 bill.	35.06 - 9.60	15.74

UPPER MEDIUM GRADE. IN 2003, DILUTED EARNINGS PER SHARE ARE EXPECTED TO RANGE FROM $0.75 TO $0.79.

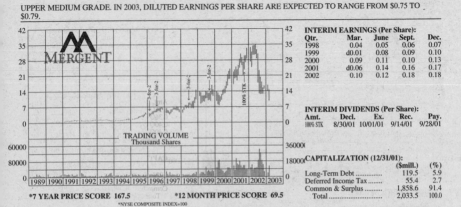

INTERIM EARNINGS (Per Share):

Qtr.	Mar.	June	Sept.	Dec.
1998	0.04	0.05	0.06	0.07
1999	d0.01	0.08	0.09	0.10
2000	0.09	0.11	0.10	0.13
2001	d0.06	0.14	0.16	0.17
2002	0.10	0.12	0.18	0.18

INTERIM DIVIDENDS (Per Share):

Amt.	Decl.	Ex.	Rec.	Pay.
100% STK	8/30/01	10/01/01	9/14/01	9/28/01

CAPITALIZATION (12/31/01):

	($mill.)	(%)
Long-Term Debt	119.5	5.9
Deferred Income Tax	55.4	2.7
Common & Surplus	1,858.6	91.4
Total	2,033.5	100.0

TRADING VOLUME Thousand Shares

*7 YEAR PRICE SCORE 167.5   *12 MONTH PRICE SCORE 69.5

*NYSE COMPOSITE INDEX=100

BUSINESS:

Concord EFS, Inc. is a vertically-integrated electronic transaction processor, providing transaction authorization, data capture, settlement and funds transfer services to financial institutions, supermarkets, petroleum retailers, convenience stores, restaurants and other independent retailers. CEFT's primary activities consist of Network Services, which provide ATM processing, debit card processing, deposit risk management, and coast-to-coast debit network access principally for financial institutions, and Payment Services, which provide payment processing for supermarkets, major retailers, petroleum dealers, convenience stores, restaurants, trucking companies, and independent retailers.

RECENT DEVELOPMENTS:

For the year ended 12/31/02, net income increased 39.0% to $300.8 million from $216.4 million the year before. Results for 2002 and 2001 included acquisition and restructuring and write-off charges of $77.9 million and $125.4 million, respectively. Results for 2002 also included pre-tax litigation settlement charges of $8.8 million. Revenues advanced 27.7% to $2.17 billion from $1.70 billion the year before, reflecting strong transaction growth. Operating income increased 37.7% to $390.0 million compared with $283.1 million a year earlier.

PROSPECTS:

On 1/9/03, the Company announced that it signed a non-binding letter of intent to acquire the Credit Union 24® Network-owned ATM and point-of-sale network based in Tallahassee, Florida. The Credit Union 24® Network connects over 400 credit unions via 7,200 ATMs and 7.0 million cardholders in 35 states. Looking ahead, diluted earnings per share are expected to range from $0.75 to $0.79 in 2003, based on an ongoing low interest-rate environment, continued uncertainty about the economy, and increasing competition. The Company will continue to focus on cross-selling services and improving its cost structure.

ANNUAL FINANCIAL DATA:

FISCAL YEAR	TOT. REVS. ($mill.)	NET INC. ($mill.)	TOT. ASSETS ($mill.)	OPER. PROFIT %	NET PROFIT %	RET. ON EQUITY %	RET. ON ASSETS %	CURR. RATIO	EARN. PER SH.$	CASH FL. PER SH.$	TANG. BK. VAL.$	PRICE RANGE	AVG. P/E RATIO
p12/31/02	2,174.4	⧉ 300.8							⧉ 0.57			35.06 - 12.60	41.8
12/31/01	1,707.0	⧉ 216.4	2,729.4	16.8	12.7	11.6	7.9	3.1	0.42	0.60	3.18	33.36 - 17.00	59.9
12/31/00	1,229.4	⧉ 187.5	1,553.6	20.9	15.2	19.4	12.1	2.5	0.42	0.59	1.92	24.06 - 7.66	37.8
12/31/99	830.1	⧉ 101.7	1,096.9	18.2	12.2	14.5	9.3	2.7	⧉ 0.25	0.40	1.44	16.75 - 8.46	51.4
12/31/98	375.7	63.8	519.6	22.3	17.0	18.4	12.3	4.7	0.21	0.27	1.18	14.63 - 4.44	45.4
12/31/97	240.0	42.7	360.7	23.2	17.8	15.8	11.9	4.5	0.15	0.19	0.97	7.25 - 3.61	35.9
12/31/96	166.7	26.8	292.8	22.4	16.1	12.5	9.1	2.7	0.10	0.13	0.79	7.00 - 2.79	48.9
12/31/95	127.8	18.3	156.9	20.6	14.3	20.5	11.7	2.1	0.07	0.10	0.35	4.44 - 1.45	42.0
12/31/94	96.2	12.7	99.5	18.8	13.2	20.5	12.8	2.2	0.05	0.08	0.25	1.68 - 0.87	24.9
12/31/93	75.4	9.9	71.0	19.1	13.1	19.6	13.9	2.8	0.04	0.06	0.21	1.48 - 0.78	28.2

Statistics are as originally reported. Adj. for stk. splits: 100% div., 9/28/01; 3-for-2, 9/22/99; 3-for-2, 6/8/98; 3-for-2, 6/28/96; 3-for-2, 1/18/96. ⧉ Incl. non-recurr. chrgs. $86.2 mill., 2002; $125.4 mill., 12/01; $11.7 mill., 12/00; $36.2 mill., 12/99.

OFFICERS:
D. M. Palmer, Chmn., C.E.O.
E. A. Labry III, Pres.
E. T. Haslam, Sr. V.P., C.F.O., Treas.

INVESTOR CONTACT: Ed Winnick, Investor Relations, (302) 791-8484

PRINCIPAL OFFICE: 2525 Horizon Lake Drive, Suite 120, Memphis, TN 38133

TELEPHONE NUMBER: (901) 371-8000
FAX: (901) 371-8050
WEB: www.concordefs.com

NO. OF EMPLOYEES: 2,628 (avg.)

SHAREHOLDERS: 74,000 (approx.)

ANNUAL MEETING: In May

INCORPORATED: MA, Jan., 1970; reincorp., DE, 1990

INSTITUTIONAL HOLDINGS:
No. of Institutions: 492
Shares Held: 417,353,877
% Held: 82.0

INDUSTRY: Data processing and preparation (SIC: 7374)

TRANSFER AGENT(S): State Street Bank and Trust Company, Providence, RI

CONOCOPHILLIPS

EXCH.	SYM.	REC. PRICE	P/E RATIO	YLD.	MKT. CAP.	RANGE (52-WK.)	'02 Y/E PR.
NYSE	COP	50.70 (2/28/03)	35.7	3.2%	$20.77 bill.	64.10 – 44.03	48.39

UPPER MEDIUM GRADE. THE COMPANY ANNOUNCED THAT IT WILL DISPOSE OF A SUBSTANTIAL PORTION OF ITS COMPANY-OWNED RETAIL SITES AND EXIT CERTAIN GEOGRAPHIC MARKETS.

*7 YEAR PRICE SCORE 113.5   ***12 MONTH PRICE SCORE 101.1**

*NYSE COMPOSITE INDEX=100

INTERIM EARNINGS (Per Share):

Qtr.	Mar.	June	Sept.	Dec.
1998	0.92	0.58	0.18	d0.83
1999	0.28	0.27	0.87	0.98
2000	0.98	1.73	1.66	2.88
2001	1.90	2.40	1.34	0.42
2002	d0.27	0.95	d0.11	0.85

INTERIM DIVIDENDS (Per Share):

Amt.	Decl.	Ex.	Rec.	Pay.
0.36Q	4/08/02	4/26/02	4/30/02	5/31/02
0.36Q	7/29/02	8/07/02	8/09/02	9/03/02
0.40Q	10/22/02	10/31/02	11/04/02	12/02/02
0.40Q	2/10/03	2/18/03	2/20/03	3/03/03

Indicated div.: $1.60 (Div. Reinv. Plan)

CAPITALIZATION (12/31/01):

	($000)	(%)
Long-Term Debt	8,645,000	32.0
Deferred Income Tax	4,015,000	14.9
Common & Surplus	14,340,000	53.1
Total	27,000,000	100.0

BUSINESS:

ConocoPhillips (formerly Phillips Petroleum Company) is an integrated global petroleum company formed by the August 2002 acquisition of Conoco Inc. by Phillips Petroleum Company. COP's exploration and production segment explores for and produces crude oil, natural gas and natural gas liquids on a worldwide basis. The gas gathering, processing and marketing segment includes COP's 30.3% equity interest in Duke Energy Field Services, LLC. The refining, marketing and transportation segment refines,

markets and transports crude oil and petroleum products, primarily in the U.S. The chemicals segment manufactures and markets petrochemicals and plastics on a worldwide basis, primarily through its 50.0% equity investment in Chevron Phillips Chemical Company LLC. The Company acquired Atlantic Richfield Company's Alaskan businesses on 8/1/00 for about $6.90 billion. On 9/14/02, the Company acquired Tosco Corporation in a $7.00 billion stock transaction.

RECENT DEVELOPMENTS:

For the year ended 12/31/02, income from continuing operations was $732.0 million versus income from continuing operations of $1.61 billion a year earlier. Earnings for 2002 and 2001 included after-tax special charges of $1.79 billion and $16.0 million, respectively. Total revenues were $57.22 billion versus $24.77 billion the previous year.

Results for the twelve months ended 12/31/02 included eight months of activity for Phillips and four months of activity for ConocoPhillips, which was formed by the 8/30/02 acquisition of Conoco Inc. by Phillips Petroleum Company. The prior-year period reflects only Phillips results.

PROSPECTS:

COP's outlook is clouded by the recent political and economic events in Venezuela that have resulted in the Company's total Venezuela crude oil production of 75,000 to 80,000 barrels per day to remain shut in, reducing refinery

run rates. Meanwhile, COP has announced that as part of the Company's rationalization plan for its marketing assets it will dispose of a substantial portion of its Company-owned retail sites and exit certain geographic markets.

ANNUAL FINANCIAL DATA:

FISCAL YEAR	TOT. REVS. ($mill.)	NET INC. ($mill.)	TOT. ASSETS ($mill.)	OPER. PROFIT %	NET PROFIT %	RET. ON EQUITY %	RET. ON ASSETS %	CURR. RATIO	EARN. PER SH.$	CASH FL.PER SH.$	TANG. BK. VAL.$	DIV. PER SH.$	PRICE RANGE	AVG. P/E RATIO	AVG. YIELD %
p12/31/02	57,224.0	⑨ 732.0							⑨ 1.51			1.48	64.10 – 44.03	35.8	2.7
⑧ 12/31/01	26,868.0	⑦ 1,643.0	35,217.0	12.6	6.1	11.5	4.7	1.0	⑦ 5.57	10.28	26.23	1.40	68.00 – 50.00	10.6	2.4
12/31/00	21,227.0	⑥ 1,862.0	20,509.0	20.5	8.8	29.5	9.1	0.7	⑥ 7.26	11.86	22.26	1.36	70.00 – 35.94	7.3	2.6
12/31/99	13,852.0	⑤ 609.0	15,201.0	11.7	4.4	13.4	4.0	1.1	⑤ 2.39	5.94	16.13	1.36	57.25 – 37.69	19.9	2.9
12/31/98	11,845.0	④ 237.0	14,216.0	5.3	2.0	5.6	1.7	1.1	④ 0.91	5.92	16.35	1.36	53.25 – 40.19	51.3	2.9
12/31/97	15,424.0	③ 959.0	13,860.0	13.6	6.2	19.9	6.9	1.1	③ 3.61	6.88	18.30	1.34	52.25 – 37.38	12.4	3.0
12/31/96	15,807.0	② 1,303.0	13,548.0	11.8	8.2	30.7	9.6	1.1	② 4.96	8.53	16.16	1.25	45.88 – 31.13	7.8	3.2
12/31/95	13,521.0	469.0	11,978.0	10.1	3.5	14.7	3.9	0.9	1.79	5.11	12.17	1.20	37.13 – 29.88	18.7	3.6
12/31/94	12,367.0	484.0	11,436.0	9.0	3.9	16.4	4.2	1.0	1.85	4.88	11.27	1.12	37.25 – 25.50	17.0	3.6
12/31/93	12,545.0	① 245.0	10,868.0	6.8	2.0	9.1	2.3	1.0	① 0.94	4.16	10.30	1.12	37.38 – 24.50	32.9	3.6

Statistics are as originally reported. Results for 12/31/01 & earlier are for Phillips Petroleum Company prior to acq. of Conoco Inc. on 8/30/02. ① Incl. non-recurr. cr. 12/31/97, $412.0 mill.; chrgs. 12/31/96, $412.0 mill.; chrg. 12/31/95, $49.0 mill. ② Bef. acctg. adj. chrg. of $44.0 mill. ③ Bef. extraord. chrg. of $2.0 mill. ④ Incl. non-recurr. net chrgs. of $138.0 mill. ⑤ Incl. one-time gain of $61.0 mill. ⑥ Incl. special chrg. of $54.0 mill. ⑦ Bef. extraord. chrg. of $10.0 mill. & acctg. chg. credit of $28.0 mill. ⑧ Refl. acq. of Tosco Corporation. ⑨ Incl. after-tax special chrgs. of $1.79 bill.; bef. loss fr. disc. ops. of $993.0 mill. & extraord. chrg. of $16.0 mill.

OFFICERS:
A. W. Dunham, Chmn.
J. J. Mulva, Pres., C.E.O.
J. A. Carrig, Exec. V.P., C.F.O.

INVESTOR CONTACT: Clayton Reasor, Investor Relations, (212) 207-1996

PRINCIPAL OFFICE: 600 North Dairy Ashford Road, Houston, TX 77079

TELEPHONE NUMBER: (281) 293-1000
WEB: www.conocophillips.com

NO. OF EMPLOYEES: 57,000 (approx.)

SHAREHOLDERS: 54,195

ANNUAL MEETING: In May

INCORPORATED: DE, June, 1917

INSTITUTIONAL HOLDINGS:
No. of Institutions: 701
Shares Held: 507,152,781
% Held: 74.9

INDUSTRY: Petroleum refining (SIC: 2911)

TRANSFER AGENT(S): Mellon Investor Services, L.L.C., Ridgefield, NJ

CONSOLIDATED EDISON, INC.

EXCH.	SYM.	REC. PRICE	P/E RATIO	YLD.	MKT. CAP.	RANGE (52-WK.)	'02 Y/E PR.	DIV. ACH.
NYSE	ED	39.00 (2/28/03)	12.5	5.7%	$8.27 bill.	46.02 - 32.65	42.82	28 yrs.

UPPER MEDIUM GRADE. THE COMPANY EXPECTS EARNINGS PER SHARE FOR 2003 IN THE RANGE OF $2.90 TO $3.05.

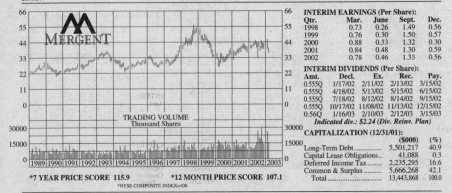

TRADING VOLUME
Thousand Shares

*7 YEAR PRICE SCORE 115.9   *12 MONTH PRICE SCORE 107.1
*NYSE COMPOSITE INDEX=100

INTERIM EARNINGS (Per Share):

Qtr.	Mar.	June	Sept.	Dec.
1998	0.73	0.26	1.49	0.56
1999	0.76	0.30	1.50	0.57
2000	0.88	0.33	1.32	0.30
2001	0.84	0.48	1.30	0.59
2002	0.78	0.46	1.33	0.56

INTERIM DIVIDENDS (Per Share):

Amt.	Decl.	Ex.	Rec.	Pay.
0.555Q	1/17/02	2/11/02	2/13/02	3/15/02
0.555Q	4/18/02	5/13/02	5/15/02	6/15/02
0.555Q	7/18/02	8/12/02	8/14/02	9/15/02
0.555Q	10/17/02	11/08/02	11/13/02	12/15/02
0.56Q	1/16/03	2/10/03	2/12/03	3/15/03

Indicated div.: $2.24 (Div. Reinv. Plan)

CAPITALIZATION (12/31/01):

	($000)	(%)
Long-Term Debt	5,501,217	40.9
Capital Lease Obligations..	41,088	0.3
Deferred Income Tax	2,235,295	16.6
Common & Surplus	5,666,268	42.1
Total	13,443,868	100.0

BUSINESS:

Consolidated Edison, Inc. (formerly Consolidated Edison Company of New York) provides a range of energy-related products and services through six subsidiaries. Consolidated Edison Company of New York is a regulated utility providing electric, gas and steam service to New York City and Westchester County, New York. Orange and Rockland Utilities, Inc. is a regulated utility serving customers in southeastern New York state and adjacent sections of New Jersey and northeastern Pennsylvania. Con Edison Solutions is a retail energy services company and Con Edison Energy is a wholesale energy supply company. Con Edison Development is an infrastructure development company and Con Edison Communications is a telecommunications infrastructure company. Sales for 2002 were derived: electric, 73.7%; gas, 14.2%; steam, 4.8%; and non-utility, 7.3%.

RECENT DEVELOPMENTS:

For the twelve months ended 12/31/02, income slipped 2.1% to $668.1 million, before an accounting change charge of $22.1 million, compared with net income of $682.2 million in 2001. Earnings reflected the negative effect of milder winter weather conditions in the first quarter of 2002 and the soft economy, partially offset by hot summer weather and productivity improvements. Total operating revenues declined 9.7% to $8.48 billion from $9.39 billion in the prior year. Electric operating revenues slipped 9.2% to $6.25 billion, while gas operating revenue decreased 17.9% to $1.20 billion. Steam operating revenues fell 19.8% to $404.0 million. However, non-utility revenues grew 17.3% to $622.9 million. Operating income declined 6.0% to $1.06 billion.

PROSPECTS:

Despite the effect of the relatively weak economy, ED's financial condition remains strong with a solid balance sheet and good liquidity. Looking ahead, the Company expects earnings for 2003 in the range of $2.90 to $3.05 per share. This estimate reflects ED's expectations for the timing of the economic recovery from the current downturn. In addition, the forecast reflects an anticipated decline of $54.0 million in after-tax net credits for pensions and other post-retirement benefits in 2003. Meanwhile, capital expenditures for 2003 should be about $1.31 billion.

ANNUAL FINANCIAL DATA:

FISCAL YEAR	TOT. REVS. ($mill.)	NET INC. ($mill.)	TOT. ASSETS ($mill.)	OPER. PROFIT %	NET PROFIT %	NET INC./ NET PROP. %	NET INC./ TOT. CAP. %	RET. ON EQUITY %	ACCUM. DEPR./ GROSS PROP. %	EARN. PER SH. $	TANG. BK. VAL.$	DIV. PER SH. $	DIV. PAYOUT %	PRICE RANGE	AVG. P/E RATIO	AVG. YIELD %
p12/31/02	8,481.9	② 668.1								② 3.13		2.22	70.9	45.40 - 32.65	12.5	5.7
12/31/01	9,634.0	695.8	16,996.1	11.7	7.2	5.7	5.1	11.8	26.8	3.21	24.21	2.20	68.5	43.37 - 31.44	11.7	5.9
12/31/00	9,431.4	① 596.4	16,767.2	10.8	6.3	5.0	4.4	10.5	30.8	① 2.74	26.39	2.18	79.6	39.50 - 26.19	12.0	6.6
12/31/99	7,491.3	714.2	15,531.5	13.6	9.5	6.3	5.7	12.7	29.6	3.13	25.90	2.14	68.4	53.44 - 33.56	13.9	4.9
12/31/98	7,093.0	729.7	14,381.4	14.9	10.3	6.4	5.7	11.7	29.5	3.04	25.88	2.12	69.7	56.13 - 39.06	15.7	4.5
12/31/97	7,121.3	712.8	14,722.5	14.7	10.0	6.3	5.6	11.6	28.2	2.95	25.18	2.10	71.2	41.50 - 27.00	11.6	6.1
12/31/96	6,959.7	694.1	14,057.2	14.6	10.0	6.3	5.5	11.6	28.1	2.93	24.37	2.08	71.0	34.75 - 25.88	10.3	6.9
12/31/95	6,536.9	723.9	13,949.9	15.9	11.1	6.7	5.8	11.9	27.3	2.93	23.51	2.04	69.6	32.25 - 25.50	9.9	7.1
12/31/94	6,444.5	734.3	13,728.4	16.3	11.5	7.0	6.0	12.5	26.8	2.98	22.62	2.00	67.1	32.38 - 23.00	9.3	7.2
12/31/93	6,265.4	658.5	13,483.5	15.2	10.5	6.5	5.6	11.7	26.3	2.66	21.63	1.94	72.9	37.75 - 30.25	12.8	5.7

Statistics are as originally reported. ① Incl. approx. $84.9 mill. chg. fr. replacement power costs. ② Excl. $22.1 mill. acctg. change chg.

OFFICERS:
E. R. McGrath, Chmn., Pres., C.E.O.
J. S. Freilich, Exec. V.P., C.F.O.
C. E. McTiernan, Jr., Gen. Couns.
INVESTOR CONTACT: Jan C. Childress, Dir. of Inv. Rel., (212) 460-6611
PRINCIPAL OFFICE: 4 Irving Place, New York, NY 10003

TELEPHONE NUMBER: (212) 460-4600
FAX: (212) 475-0734
WEB: www.conedison.com
NO. OF EMPLOYEES: 13,953 (avg.)
SHAREHOLDERS: 103,380 (record)
ANNUAL MEETING: In May
INCORPORATED: NY, Nov., 1884

INSTITUTIONAL HOLDINGS:
No. of Institutions: 357
Shares Held: 83,140,427
% Held: 38.9
INDUSTRY: Electric and other services combined (SIC: 4931)
TRANSFER AGENT(S): The Bank of New York, NY

CONSOLIDATED GRAPHICS, INC.

EXCH.	SYM.	REC. PRICE	P/E RATIO	YLD.	MKT. CAP.	RANGE (52-WK.)	'02 Y/E PR.
NYSE	CGX	24.15 (2/28/03)	16.4	...	$318.9 mill.	25.20 - 14.35	22.25

MEDIUM GRADE. THE COMPANY'S TOP LINE IS BENEFITING FROM EXISTING AND NEWLY-ACQUIRED COMPANIES.

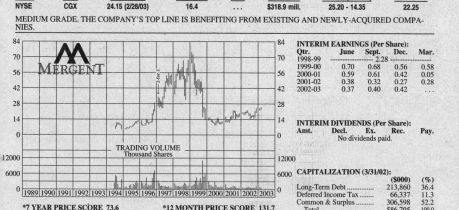

INTERIM EARNINGS (Per Share):

Qtr.	June	Sept.	Dec.	Mar.
1998-99	------------- 2.28 -------------			
1999-00	0.70	0.68	0.56	0.58
2000-01	0.59	0.61	0.42	0.05
2001-02	0.38	0.32	0.27	0.28
2002-03	0.37	0.40	0.42	...

INTERIM DIVIDENDS (Per Share):

Amt.	Decl.	Ex.	Rec.	Pay.
	No dividends paid.			

*7 YEAR PRICE SCORE 73.6   ***12 MONTH PRICE SCORE 131.7**

*NYSE COMPOSITE INDEX=100

CAPITALIZATION (3/31/02):

	($000)	(%)
Long-Term Debt	213,860	36.4
Deferred Income Tax	66,337	11.3
Common & Surplus	306,598	52.2
Total	586,795	100.0

BUSINESS:

Consolidated Graphics, Inc. is a provider of general commercial printing services with printing operations in 25 states as of 1/22/03. The majority of the Company's sales are derived from traditional printing services, including electronic prepress, printing, finishing, storage and delivery of high-quality, custom-designed products. These products include multicolor product and capability brochures, shareholder communications, catalogs, training manuals, point-of-purchase marketing materials, trading cards and direct mail pieces. The Company has a diverse customer base, including both national and local corporations, mutual fund companies, advertising agencies, graphic design firms, catalog retailers and direct mail distributors. The Company also offers an extensive and growing range of digital and Internet-based services marketed through CGXmedia.

RECENT DEVELOPMENTS:

For the three months ended 12/31/02, net income soared 60.8% to $5.7 million compared with $3.6 million in the corresponding period a year earlier. Sales were $186.3 million, up 21.2% from $153.8 million in the prior-year period. The increase in sales was driven by existing and newly-acquired companies and reflected CGX's efforts to grow market share. Gross profit grew 13.9% to $44.9 million. Operating margin was 6.3%. CGX noted that year-over-year comparisons benefited from the particularly weak 2001 December quarter, which was negatively affected by the events of September 11th.

PROSPECTS:

Although the Company reported improved results for the third quarter of fiscal 2003, volatile economic conditions continue to negatively affect the commercial printing industry. As a result, operating margins are expected to remain at depressed levels. Looking ahead to the fourth quarter of fiscal 2003, the Company expects operating margins and earnings per share to be in line with the third quarter. Going forward, the Company will continue to evaluate a number of acquisition opportunities.

ANNUAL FINANCIAL DATA:

FISCAL YEAR	TOT. REVS. ($000)	NET INC. ($000)	TOT. ASSETS ($000)	OPER. PROFIT %	NET PROFIT %	RET. ON EQUITY %	RET. ON ASSETS %	CURR. RATIO	EARN. PER SH.$	CASH FL. PER SH.$	TANG. BK. VAL.$	PRICE RANGE	AVG. P/E RATIO
3/31/02	643,948	16,680	676,733	6.7	2.6	5.4	2.5	1.9	1.25	4.33	8.12	22.10 - 11.20	13.3
3/31/01	683,396	② 22,111	674,667	8.5	3.2	7.7	3.3	1.9	② 1.68	4.62	6.49	15.75 - 8.50	7.2
3/31/00	624,895	38,479	677,277	12.4	6.2	14.1	5.7	1.6	2.51	4.65	5.39	74.50 - 13.31	17.5
3/31/99	435,961	32,275	489,654	13.9	7.4	15.0	6.6	1.6	2.28	3.72	6.33	67.63 - 31.50	21.7
3/31/98	231,282	18,390	237,645	14.4	8.0	17.5	7.7	1.6	1.40	2.17	5.95	56.19 - 23.88	28.6
3/31/97	144,082	10,100	135,720	12.7	7.0	15.2	7.4	2.1	0.83	1.31	4.85	29.00 - 8.13	22.4
3/31/96	85,133	① 3,985	87,809	8.2	4.7	8.0	4.5	2.5	① 0.36	0.70	3.78	13.06 - 4.75	24.7
3/31/95	57,166	4,482	60,288	12.8	7.8	11.7	7.4	2.3	0.46	0.88	3.49	11.25 - 4.88	17.5
3/31/94	48,643	3,511	36,809	13.0	7.2	39.1	9.5	1.9	0.53	...	1.60	...	...
3/31/93	28,851	2,102	34,674	14.0	7.3	34.9	6.1	1.5	0.37	...	...	...	...

Statistics are as originally reported. Adj. for 2-for-1 stock split, 1/10/97. ① Incl. restr. chg. of $1.5 mill. ② Incl. $6.5 mill. special chg.

OFFICERS:
J. R. Davis, Chmn., C.E.O.
G. C. Colville, Exec. V.P., C.F.O.

INVESTOR CONTACT: G. Christopher Colville, Exec. V.P., C.F.O., (713) 787-0977

PRINCIPAL OFFICE: 5858 Westheimer Road, Suite 200, Houston, TX 77057

TELEPHONE NUMBER: (713) 787-0977
FAX: (713) 787-5013
WEB: www.consolidatedgraphics.com
NO. OF EMPLOYEES: 4,600
SHAREHOLDERS: 148 (record); 5,000 (beneficial).
ANNUAL MEETING: In July
INCORPORATED: TX, 1985

INSTITUTIONAL HOLDINGS:
No. of Institutions: 89
Shares Held: 7,584,756
% Held: 57.0

INDUSTRY: Commercial printing, nec (SIC: 2759)

TRANSFER AGENT(S): American Stock Transfer & Trust Company, New York, NY

CONSTELLATION BRANDS, INC.

EXCH.	SYM.	REC. PRICE	P/E RATIO	YLD.	MKT. CAP.	RANGE (52-WK.)	'02 Y/E PR.
NYSE	STZ	22.70 (3/31/03)	11.7	...	$2.01 bill.	32.00 - 21.90	23.71

UPPER MEDIUM GRADE. THE COMPANY REACHED AN AGREEMENT TO ACQUIRE BRL HARDY LIMITED, AN AUSTRALIAN WINE PRODUCER, FOR ABOUT $1.40 BILLION.

TRADING VOLUME
Thousand Shares

*7 YEAR PRICE SCORE 186.6   *12 MONTH PRICE SCORE 100.4
*NYSE COMPOSITE INDEX=100

INTERIM EARNINGS (Per Share):

Qtr.	May	Aug.	Nov.	Feb.
1998-99	0.18	0.21	0.27	0.09
1999-00	0.15	0.29	0.40	0.21
2000-01	0.24	0.35	0.47	0.25
2001-02	0.28	0.41	0.56	0.32
2002-03	0.40	0.53	0.69	...

INTERIM DIVIDENDS (Per Share):

Amt.	Decl.	Ex.	Rec.	Pay.
100% STK	4/12/01	5/15/01	4/30/01	5/14/01
2-for-1	4/10/02	5/14/02	4/30/02	5/13/02

CAPITALIZATION (2/28/02):

	($000)	(%)
Long-Term Debt	1,293,183	53.6
Deferred Income Tax	163,146	6.8
Common & Surplus	955,736	39.6
Total	2,412,065	100.0

BUSINESS:

Constellation Brands, Inc. (formerly Canandaigua Brands, Inc.) is a producer, marketer and distributor of premier branded beverage alcohol products in the U.S. and the U.K. STZ's business is broken into five segments: Popular and Premium Wine; Imported Beer and Spirits; U.K. Brands and Wholesale (branded wine, cider and bottled water, and wholesale wine, cider, distilled spirits, beer and soft drinks); Fine Wine; and Corporate Operations and Other. STZ's key products include CORONA EXTRA, PACIFICO, ST. PAULI GIRL, BLACK VELVET, FLEISCHMANN'S, SIMI, ESTANCIA, RAVENSWOOD, ALICE WHITE, TALUS, VENDANGE, ALMADEN, ARBOR MIST, STOWELLS OF CHELSEA, BLACKTHORN, BLACKSTONE, and BANROCK STATION.

RECENT DEVELOPMENTS:

For the quarter ended 11/30/02, net income increased 29.6% to $64.3 million from $49.6 million in the corresponding prior-year period. Earnings for 2002 and 2001 included gains of $4.2 million and $1.2 million, respectively, from equity in earning of joint venture. Net sales rose 5.2% to $738.4 million from $701.9 million the year before. Net sales of imported beer and spirits improved 10.1% to $276.1 million, primarily due to volume gains, price increases on STZ's Mexican beer portfolio, and an increase in bulk whiskey sales. Net sales of the U.K. brands and wholesale segment grew 7.4% to $211.4 million, while fine wine segment net sales inched up 3.4% to $42.4 million. However, net sales of the popular and premium wine segment slipped 2.6% to $213.3 million.

PROSPECTS:

On 1/16/03, the Company announced that it has reached an agreement to acquire BRL Hardy Limited, an Australian wine producer, for about $1.40 billion. The acquisition, which is expected to close in early April 2003, should increase STZ's overall sales to $3.20 billion annually, with wine sales of $1.70 billion. Going forward, diluted earnings per share are expected to range from $0.40 to $0.42 for the fourth quarter of fiscal 2003 and be between $2.03 and $2.05 for the full year. In 2004, diluted earnings per share are expected to range from $2.29 to $2.35, excluding the impact of the acquisition of BRL Hardy.

ANNUAL FINANCIAL DATA:

FISCAL YEAR	TOT. REVS. ($mill.)	NET INC. ($mill.)	TOT. ASSETS ($mill.)	OPER. PROFIT %	NET PROFIT %	RET. ON EQUITY %	RET. ON ASSETS %	CURR. RATIO	EARN. PER SH. $	CASH FL. PER SH. $	TANG. BK. VAL. $	PRICE RANGE	AVG. P/E RATIO
2/28/02	2,820.5	⑤ 138.0	3,069.4	12.1	4.9	14.4	4.5	2.1	⑤ 1.57	2.55	10.80	23.25 - 13.25	11.6
2/28/01	2,396.7	97.3	2,512.2	11.3	4.1	15.8	3.9	2.8	1.30	2.25	8.24	14.75 - 10.09	9.6
2/29/00	2,340.5	④ 77.4	2,348.8	10.0	3.3	14.9	3.3	2.3	④ 1.05	1.93	7.16	15.38 - 10.72	12.5
2/28/99	1,497.3	③ 61.9	1,793.8	9.7	4.1	14.2	3.5	2.1	③ 0.83	1.34	6.06	14.94 - 8.81	14.2
2/28/98	1,212.8	50.1	1,073.2	9.7	4.1	12.1	4.7	2.0	0.66	1.09	5.54	14.41 - 5.47	15.2
2/28/97	1,135.0	27.7	1,020.9	7.2	2.4	7.6	2.7	2.0	0.35	0.76	4.83	9.88 - 3.94	19.6
2/29/96	535.0	② 3.3	1,054.6	4.5	0.6	0.9	0.3	1.7	② 0.04	0.22	4.54	... - ...	...
8/31/95	906.5	② 41.0	785.9	10.1	4.5	11.7	5.2	2.3	② 0.54	0.81	4.49	13.25 - 7.44	19.3
8/31/94	629.6	② 11.7	826.6	5.9	1.9	5.7	1.4	1.9	② 0.19	0.40	3.19	9.63 - 5.06	39.7
8/31/93	306.3	15.6	355.2	10.2	5.1	12.4	4.4	2.5	0.33	0.51	2.48	8.00 - 3.38	11.5

Statistics are as originally reported. Adj. for stk. splits: 2-for-1, 5/02 & 5/01. ① For 6 mos. ended 2/29/96 due to fiscal yr-end change. ② Incl. non-recurr. chrg. of $2.4 mill., 2/96; $2.2 mill., 8/95; $24.0 mill., 8/94. ③ Bef. extraord. loss of $11.4 mill.; incl. nonrecurr. chrg. of $2.6 mill. ④ Incl. pre-tax nonrecurr. chrgs. of approx. $6.0 mill. ⑤ Bef. extraord. loss of $1.6 mill.

OFFICERS:
Richard Sands, Chmn., C.E.O.
Robert Sands, Pres., C.O.O.
T. S. Summer, Exec. V.P., C.F.O.
INVESTOR CONTACT: Lynn Fetterman, Sr. V.P., (716) 394-7900
PRINCIPAL OFFICE: 300 Willowbrook Office Park, Fairport, NY 14450

TELEPHONE NUMBER: (585) 218-3600
FAX: (585) 394-4839
WEB: www.cbrands.com
NO. OF EMPLOYEES: 5,080 (approx.)
SHAREHOLDERS: 954 (Class A common); 249 (Class B common)
ANNUAL MEETING: In July
INCORPORATED: DE, Dec., 1972

INSTITUTIONAL HOLDINGS:
No. of Institutions: 275
Shares Held: 60,238,676
% Held: 66.7
INDUSTRY: Wines, brandy, and brandy spirits (SIC: 2084)
TRANSFER AGENT(S): Mellon Investor Services, Ridgefield Park, NJ

CONSTELLATION ENERGY GROUP, INC.

EXCH.	SYM.	REC. PRICE	P/E RATIO	YLD.	MKT. CAP.	RANGE (52-WK.)	'02 Y/E PR.
NYSE	CEG	26.22 (2/28/03)	8.2	4.0%	$4.29 bill.	32.38 - 19.30	27.82

UPPER MEDIUM GRADE. THE ACQUISITION OF CMS MARKETING, SERVICES & TRADING CO. SHOULD COMPLEMENT THE COMPANY'S EXISTING SUPPLY BUSINESS.

TRADING VOLUME
Thousand Shares

1989 1990 1991 1992 1993 1994 1995 1996 1997 1998 1999 2000 2001 2002 2003

*7 YEAR PRICE SCORE 93.6   *12 MONTH PRICE SCORE 107.6

*NYSE COMPOSITE INDEX=100

INTERIM EARNINGS (Per Share):

Qtr.	Mar.	June	Sept.	Dec.
1998	0.50	0.39	1.08	0.09
1999	0.55	0.45	0.91	0.26
2000	0.48	0.26	0.98	0.57
2001	0.74	0.46	1.00	d1.59
2002	1.40	0.50	0.92	0.39

INTERIM DIVIDENDS (Per Share):

Amt.	Decl.	Ex.	Rec.	Pay.
0.24Q	1/30/02	3/07/02	3/11/02	4/01/02
0.24Q	5/24/02	6/06/02	6/10/02	7/01/02
0.24Q	7/19/02	9/06/02	9/10/02	10/01/02
0.24Q	10/18/02	12/06/02	12/10/02	1/02/03
0.26Q	1/24/03	3/06/03	3/10/03	4/01/03

Indicated div.: $1.04 (Div. Reinv. Plan)

CAPITALIZATION (12/31/01):

	($000)	(%)
Long-Term Debt	2,712,500	34.0
Deferred Income Tax	1,431,000	17.9
Common & Surplus	3,843,600	48.1
Total	7,987,100	100.0

BUSINESS:

Constellation Energy Group, Inc. (formerly Baltimore Gas & Electric Co.) is the holding company for Baltimore Gas and Electric Company (BGE) and Constellation Enterprises, Inc. As of 1/31/03, BGE provided service to more than 1.1 million electric customers and about 600,000 natural gas customers in Central Maryland. Constellation Enterprises is a holding company for several diversified businesses engaged in energy services. Constellation Nuclear is a wholly-owned subsidiary of CEG. The energy services, which includes wholesale generation and power marketing and retail energy businesses are Constellation Power Source, Inc.; Constellation Power, Inc. and Constellation Energy Source, Inc. Revenues in 2002 were derived: nonregulated, 46.1%; electric, 41.8%; and gas, 12.1%.

RECENT DEVELOPMENTS:

For the year ended 12/31/02, net income amounted to $525.6 million compared with income of $82.4 million, before an accounting change gain of $8.5 million, in 2001. Results for 2002 and 2001 included workforce reduction costs of $62.8 million and $105.7 million, impairment losses and other costs of $25.2 million and $158.8 million, and net gains on sales of investments and other assets of $261.3 million and $6.2 million, respectively. Results for 2001 also included a contract termination fee of $224.8 million. Revenues rose 21.2% to $4.70 billion from $3.88 billion in the prior year. Results benefited from the Company's decision to sell non-core assets and lower debt.

PROSPECTS:

On 2/19/03, the Company announced that it has agreed to acquire substantially all of the customer load-serving contracts and supply portfolio of CMS Marketing, Services & Trading Co. for an undisclosed amount. The acquisition complements CEG's existing supply business to large commercial and industrial customers. Separately, on 1/22/03, the Company announced that it has purchased the electricity division of Dynergy Canada Inc. for an undisclosed amount. The newly-purchased division expands the Company's reach in North American markets.

ANNUAL FINANCIAL DATA:

FISCAL YEAR	TOT. REVS. ($mill.)	NET INC. ($mill.)	TOT. ASSETS ($mill.)	OPER. PROFIT %	NET PROFIT %	NET INC./ NET PROP. %	NET INC./ TOT. CAP. %	RET. ON EQUITY %	ACCUM. DEPR./ GROSS PROP. %	EARN. PER SH.$	TANG. BK. VAL.$	DIV. PER SH.$	DIV. PAYOUT %	PRICE RANGE	AVG. P/E RATIO	AVG. YIELD %
p12/31/02	4,703.0	⑧ 525.6								⑧ 3.20		0.84	26.3	32.38 - 19.30	8.1	3.3
12/31/01	3,928.3	⑦ 82.4	14,077.6	9.1	2.1	1.1	1.0	2.1	35.1	⑦ 0.52	23.48	0.78	150.0	50.14 - 20.90	68.3	2.2
12/31/00	3,878.5	⑥ 345.3	12,384.6	21.7	8.9	5.2	4.4	10.3	36.4	⑥ 2.30	20.95	1.68	73.0	52.06 - 27.06	17.2	4.2
12/31/99	3,786.2	④⑤ 326.4	9,683.8	20.1	8.6	5.9	4.6	10.3	38.6	④⑤ 2.18	20.05	1.68	77.1	31.50 - 24.69	12.9	6.0
12/31/98	3,358.1	④ 327.7	9,195.0	22.1	9.8	5.8	4.3	10.3	35.3	④ 2.06	19.98	1.68	81.5	35.25 - 29.25	15.7	5.2
12/31/97	3,307.6	②④ 282.8	8,773.4	21.9	8.6	5.0	3.8	9.2	33.5	②④ 1.72	19.40	1.62	70.9	34.31 - 24.75	17.2	5.5
12/31/96	3,153.2	② 310.8	8,551.0	21.2	9.9	5.6	4.3	10.1	31.9	② 1.85	19.35	1.58	85.4	29.50 - 25.00	12.0	5.8
12/31/95	2,934.8	② 338.0	8,316.7	23.7	11.5	6.1	4.7	11.0	31.1	② 2.02	19.07	1.54	76.2	29.00 - 22.00	12.6	6.0
12/31/94	2,783.0	② 323.6	8,143.5	22.8	11.6	6.0	4.7	11.1	29.9	② 1.93	18.42	1.50	77.7	25.50 - 20.50	11.9	6.5
12/31/93	2,668.7	① 309.9	7,987.0	23.3	11.6	6.0	4.4	11.0	29.4	① 1.85	17.94	1.46	78.9	27.50 - 22.38	13.5	5.9

Statistics are as originally reported. ① Incl. $11.00 mill. net rel. to empl. sev. programs. ② Incl. $37.5 mill. net write-offs, 1997; $9.7 mill., 1995; $11.0 mill., 1994. ③ Incl. $62.0 mill. one-time disallow. for replacement energy during nuclear plt. outages in 1989-91. ④ Incl. $45.4 mill. in spl. chgs. and write-down of invtmts., 1999; $23.7 mill., 1998; $46.0 mill., 1997. ⑤ Excl. $66.3 mill. extraord. chg. ⑥ Incl. aft-tax chg. of $150.0 mill. for CEG's trans. to deregul. of its electric bus. & a $4.2 mill. net chg. for empl. who participated in volun. spl early retiremnt prog. ⑦ Incl. $105.7 mill. workforce costs & $426.9 mill. impair. losses; bef. acctg. change benefit of $8.5 mill. ⑧ Incl. $62.8 mill. workforce costs, $25.2 mill. impair. losses & $261.3 mill. net gain fr. sale of invest.

OFFICERS:
M. A. Shattuck III, Chmn., Pres., C.E.O.
E. F. Smith, Sr. V.P., C.F.O.
K. Chagnon, V.P., Gen. Couns., Corp. Sec.
INVESTOR CONTACT: Investor Relations, (410) 783-3670
PRINCIPAL OFFICE: 250 W. Pratt Street, Baltimore, MD 21201

TELEPHONE NUMBER: (410) 234-5000
FAX: (410) 234-5367
WEB: www.constellationenergy.com
NO. OF EMPLOYEES: 9,200 (approx.)
SHAREHOLDERS: 53,435
ANNUAL MEETING: In Apr.
INCORPORATED: MD, June, 1906

INSTITUTIONAL HOLDINGS:
No. of Institutions: 281
Shares Held: 111,575,708
% Held: 67.7
INDUSTRY: Electric and other services combined (SIC: 4931)
TRANSFER AGENT(S): The Company

CONTINENTAL AIRLINES, INC.

EXCH.	SYM.	REC. PRICE	P/E RATIO	YLD.	MKT. CAP.	RANGE (52-WK.)	'02 Y/E PR.
NYSE	CAL	5.10 (2/28/03)	. . .	. . .	$322.2 mill.	35.25 - 3.59	7.25

SPECULATIVE GRADE. THE COMPANY EXPECTS TO REPORT A SIGNIFICANT LOSS IN 2003.

INTERIM EARNINGS (Per Share):

Qtr.	Mar.	June	Sept.	Dec.
1996	1.60	3.05	0.42	0.82
1997	1.28	2.22	1.97	1.26
1998	1.06	2.11	0.97	0.91
1999	1.19	1.80	1.53	2.42
2000	0.21	2.46	2.24	0.70
2001	0.16	0.74	0.05	d2.58
2002	d2.61	d2.18	d0.58	d1.67

INTERIM DIVIDENDS (Per Share):

Amt.	Decl.	Ex.	Rec.	Pay.
		No dividends paid.		

CAPITALIZATION (12/31/01):

	($000)	(%)
Long-Term Debt	4,198,000	66.5
Deferred Income Tax	710,000	11.2
Redeemable Pfd. Stock	243,000	3.8
Common & Surplus	1,161,000	18.4
Total	6,312,000	100.0

TRADING VOLUME
Thousand Shares

*7 YEAR PRICE SCORE 41.3   ***12 MONTH PRICE SCORE 52.9**

*NYSE COMPOSITE INDEX=100

BUSINESS:

Continental Airlines, Inc. is a major U.S. air carrier engaged in the business of transporting passengers, cargo and mail. CAL, together with its subsidiaries Continental Express, Inc. and Continental Micronesia, Inc., flies to 131 domestic and 93 international destinations and offers additional connecting service through alliances with domestic and foreign carriers. CAL provides service to Europe, Mexico, Central America and South America, and through its Guam hub, provides service in the western Pacific, including Japan. Major hubs include New York, Houston, Cleveland and Guam. Through its alliance with Northwest Airlines, Inc., CAL's domestic route system connects with Northwest's hubs in Minneapolis, Detroit and Memphis. At 12/31/02, CAL operated 366 aircraft.

RECENT DEVELOPMENTS:

For the year ended 12/31/02, net loss totaled $451.0 million compared with a net loss of $95.0 million in the previous year. Results for 2002 included non-recurring pre-tax charges totaling $254.0 million, primarily related to fleet disposition, impairment and other special charges. Results for 2001 included a pre-tax charge related to fleet disposition, impairment and other special charges of $124.0 million and a $417.0 million pre-tax gain from the Stabilization Act grant. Total operating revenue slid 6.3% to $8.40 billion from $8.97 billion a year earlier. Operating loss was $312.0 million versus operating income of $144.0 million the year before. The passenger load factor, or percentage of seats filled, improved to 73.3% from 71.8% the prior year.

PROSPECTS:

The combination of weak passenger traffic levels, widespread industry fare discounting, and higher fuel costs are expected to hurt operating performance during 2003, resulting in a significant loss for the year. The Company ended 2002 with about $1.34 billion of cash and short-term investments, however, CAL is using approximately $1.5 million per day for required debt payments and capital expenditures. The Company projects that it will not be able to support its current size and cost structure beyond 2003 if economic conditions do not improve.

ANNUAL FINANCIAL DATA:

FISCAL YEAR	TOT. REVS. ($mill.)	NET INC. ($mill.)	TOT. ASSETS ($mill.)	OPER. PROFIT %	NET PROFIT %	RET. ON EQUITY %	RET. ON ASSETS %	CURR. RATIO	EARN. PER SH.$	CASH FL.PER SH.$	TANG. BK. VAL.$	PRICE RANGE	AVG. P/E RATIO
p12/31/02	8,402.0	⑪ d451.0							⑪ d7.02			35.25 - 3.59	. . .
12/31/01	8,969.0	⑤ d95.0	9,791.0	1.6	. . .	. . .	0.7	⑤ d1.72	6.88	2.03	57.88 - 12.35	. . .
12/31/00	9,899.0	④ 348.0	9,201.0	6.9	3.5	30.0	3.8	0.8	④ 5.54	11.94	1.35	54.81 - 29.00	7.6
12/31/99	8,639.0	①③ 488.0	8,223.0	6.9	5.6	30.6	5.9	0.9	①③ 6.64	11.47	7.06	48.00 - 30.00	5.9
12/31/98	7,951.0	①② 387.0	7,086.0	8.8	4.9	32.4	5.5	1.0	①② 5.06	8.48	0.19	65.13 - 28.88	9.3
12/31/97	7,213.0	② 389.0	5,830.0	9.9	5.4	42.5	6.7	0.8	② 5.03	7.91	. . .	50.19 - 27.00	7.7
12/31/96	6,360.0	①② 325.0	5,206.0	8.3	5.1	55.9	6.2	0.8	①② 4.97	8.83	. . .	31.44 - 19.44	5.1
12/31/95	5,825.0	② 224.0	4,821.0	6.6	3.8	73.4	4.6	0.7	② 3.60	7.31	. . .	23.75 - 3.25	3.7
12/31/94	5,670.0	d613.0	4,601.0	. . .	. . .	. . .	. . .	0.4	d11.88	d6.94	. . .	13.63 - 3.75	. . .
12/31/93	3,906.0	d38.0	5,106.0	2.4	. . .	. . .	. . .	0.7	. . .	. . .	. . .	15.31 - 6.50	. . .

Statistics are as originally reported. Adj. for 2-for-1 stk. split, 7/96. ① Incl. $254 mil pre-tax chg., 2002; $132 mil after-tax gain, 1999; $77 mil after-tax fleet disposition chrg.; 1998; $59.5 mil chrg., 1996; & $108 mil pre-tax gain, 1995. ② Bef. $4 mil ($0.07/sh) after-tax extraord. chrg., 2000; $4 mil ($0.04/sh) after-tax extraord. chrg., 1998; $4 mil ($0.04/sh) after-tax extraord. loss, 1997; $6 mil ($0.12/sh) after-tax extraord. loss, 1996. ③ Bef. $33 mil ($0.44/sh) acctg. change chrg. ④ Bef. $6.0 mil ($0.09/sh) extraord. chg. & incl. $6 mil after-tax gain fr sale of invest. in America West. ⑤ Incl. $263.0 mil after-tax gain fr. U.S. government financial aid program and $92.0 mil. after-tax special chgs.

OFFICERS:
G. M. Bethune, Chmn., C.E.O.
L. W. Kellner, Pres.
J. J. Misner, Sr. V.P., C.F.O.
INVESTOR CONTACT: Diane Schad, Staff V.P.-Fin., (713) 324-5242
PRINCIPAL OFFICE: 1600 Smith Street, Dept. HQSEO, Houston, TX 77002

TELEPHONE NUMBER: (713) 324-2950
FAX: (713) 520-6329
WEB: www.flycontinental.com
NO. OF EMPLOYEES: 48,000 (approx.)
SHAREHOLDERS: 13,499 approx.
ANNUAL MEETING: In Apr.
INCORPORATED: DE, 1985

INSTITUTIONAL HOLDINGS:
No. of Institutions: 125
Shares Held: 52,800,098
% Held: 80.3
INDUSTRY: Air transportation, scheduled (SIC: 4512)
TRANSFER AGENT(S): Computershare Investor Services, Chicago, IL

CONVERGYS CORPORATION

EXCH.	SYM.	REC. PRICE	P/E RATIO	YLD.	MKT. CAP.	RANGE (52-WK.)	'02 Y/E PR.
NYSE	CVG	12.30 (2/28/03)	14.3	...	$2.13 bill.	32.85 - 11.30	15.15

MEDIUM GRADE. THE COMPANY EXPECTS LOWER NEAR-TERM REVENUES FOR BOTH ITS INFORMATION MANAGEMENT AND CUSTOMER MANAGEMENT GROUPS.

*7 YEAR PRICE SCORE N/A　　　　***12 MONTH PRICE SCORE 74.9**

*NYSE COMPOSITE INDEX=100

INTERIM EARNINGS (Per Share):

Qtr.	Mar.	June	Sept.	Dec.
1998	d0.02	0.17	0.18	0.22
1999	0.21	0.21	0.26	0.21
2000	0.28	0.29	0.32	0.34
2001	0.34	0.16	0.02	0.33
2002	0.35	0.35	0.34	d0.18

INTERIM DIVIDENDS (Per Share):

Amt.	Decl.	Ex.	Rec.	Pay.
		No dividends paid.		

CAPITALIZATION (12/31/01):

	($000)	(%)
Long-Term Debt	3,600	0.3
Common & Surplus	1,226,600	99.7
Total	1,230,200	100.0

BUSINESS:

Convergys Corporation is a provider of outsourced, integrated billing and customer care software and services. CVG serves clients in the telecommunications, cable, broadband, satellite broadcasting, Internet services, technology, and financial services industries and other industries in more than 40 countries. CVG operates in two segments: the Information Management Group, which provides outsourced billing and information services and software, and the Customer Management Group, which provides outsourced marketing and customer support services and outsourced employee care services. CVG was spun off from Cincinnati Bell Inc. (now Broadwing, Inc.) on 12/31/98. Revenues for 2002 were derived from the Information Management Group, 39.2%, and the Customer Management Group, 60.8%.

RECENT DEVELOPMENTS:

For the twelve months ended 12/31/02, net income climbed 5.1% to $145.9 million compared with $138.8 million in 2001. Results for 2002 and 2001 included restructuring and impairment charges of $107.7 million and $58.0 million, respectively. Results for 2001 also included an acquisition and integration charge of $31.8 million. Total revenues slipped 1.5% to $2.29 billion from $2.32 billion in the prior year. Revenues for the Information Management Group declined 4.1% to $899.2 million, while revenues for the Customer Management Group grew 0.2% to $1.40 billion. Operating income decreased 8.4% to $253.3 million compared with $276.6 million the year before.

PROSPECTS:

In the near term, the Company expects revenue for the Information Management Group to be adversely affected by further reductions in professional and consulting revenue. Additionally, near-term revenue for the Customer Management Group is expected to be lower. However, the Company expects margin pressures associated with the lower revenues and increases in pension, healthcare and other costs to be partially offset by benefits from restructuring. Separately, on 2/3/03, the Company acquired Cygent, Inc., a software company specializing in Web-based customer, order, and service management platforms for the communications industry, for less than $5.0 million in cash.

ANNUAL FINANCIAL DATA:

FISCAL YEAR	TOT. REVS. ($mill.)	NET INC. ($mill.)	TOT. ASSETS ($mill.)	OPER. PROFIT %	NET PROFIT %	RET. ON EQUITY %	RET. ON ASSETS %	CURR. RATIO	EARN. PER SH.$	CASH FL. PER SH.$	TANG. BK. VAL.$	PRICE RANGE	AVG. P/E RATIO
p12/31/02	**2,286.2**	④ **145.9**							④ **0.88**			37.98 - 12.50	28.7
12/31/01	2,320.6	③ 138.8	1,742.9	11.9	6.0	11.3	8.0	1.1	③ 0.80	1.81	3.03	50.25 - 24.46	46.7
12/31/00	2,162.5	② 194.7	1,779.5	15.2	9.0	17.5	10.9	1.3	② 1.23	2.25	2.41	55.44 - 26.63	33.4
12/31/99	1,762.9	① 137.0	1,579.5	13.3	7.8	14.8	8.7	0.8	① 0.89	1.73	1.13	31.75 - 14.50	26.0
12/31/98	1,447.2	81.0	1,450.9	9.7	5.6	11.1	5.6	0.5	0.57	1.28	0.29	23.75 - 9.63	29.3
12/31/97	987.5	86.6	654.4	11.6	8.8	20.1	13.2	1.2	0.63	1.08	1.85	...	...
12/31/96	842.4	78.0	619.2	14.2	9.3	21.4	12.6	1.0	0.57	0.95	1.22	...	...
12/31/95	644.7	d3.5	...	4.8	...	...	...	...	d0.03	0.31	...	...	...

Statistics are as originally reported. ① Incl. $6.9 mill. special chgs. ② Incl. $300,000 chg. fr. year 2000 programming. ③ Incl. $58.0 mill. restr. & impair. chg. and $31.8 mill. acq. & integration chg. ④ Incl. $107.7 mill. restr. & impair. chg.

OFFICERS:
J. F. Orr, Chmn., Pres., C.E.O.
S. G. Rolls, C.F.O.
W. H. Hawkins II, Gen. Couns., Sec.
INVESTOR CONTACT: Ron Harris, Director, Investor Relations, (888) 284-9900
PRINCIPAL OFFICE: 201 East Fourth Street, Cincinnati, OH 45202

TELEPHONE NUMBER: (513) 723-7000
FAX: (513) 421-8624
WEB: www.convergys.com
NO. OF EMPLOYEES: 46,000 (approx.)
SHAREHOLDERS: 19,564 (record)
ANNUAL MEETING: In Apr.
INCORPORATED: OH, May, 1998

INSTITUTIONAL HOLDINGS:
No. of Institutions: 289
Shares Held: 102,812,447
% Held: 59.3
INDUSTRY: Computer integrated systems design (SIC: 7373)
TRANSFER AGENT(S): The Fifth Third Bank, Corporate Trust Services, Cincinnati, OH

COOPER CAMERON CORPORATION

EXCH.	SYM.	REC. PRICE	P/E RATIO	YLD.	MKT. CAP.	RANGE (52-WK.)	'02 Y/E PR.
NYSE	CAM	52.00 (2/28/03)	48.1	...	$2.81 bill.	59.60 - 35.94	49.82

MEDIUM GRADE. THE COMPANY EXPECTS FULL-YEAR 2003 EARNINGS TO RANGE BETWEEN $1.80 AND $2.00 PER SHARE.

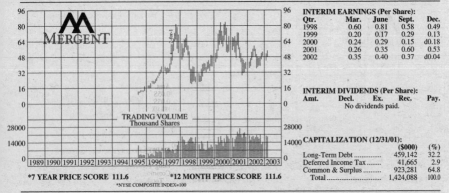

*7 YEAR PRICE SCORE 111.6   *12 MONTH PRICE SCORE 111.6
*NYSE COMPOSITE INDEX=100

INTERIM EARNINGS (Per Share):

Qtr.	Mar.	June	Sept.	Dec.
1998	0.60	0.81	0.58	0.49
1999	0.20	0.17	0.29	0.13
2000	0.24	0.29	0.15	d0.18
2001	0.26	0.35	0.60	0.53
2002	0.35	0.40	0.37	d0.04

INTERIM DIVIDENDS (Per Share):

Amt.	Decl.	Ex.	Rec.	Pay.
		No dividends paid.		

CAPITALIZATION (12/31/01):

	($000)	(%)
Long-Term Debt	459,142	32.2
Deferred Income Tax	41,665	2.9
Common & Surplus	923,281	64.8
Total	1,424,088	100.0

BUSINESS:

Cooper Cameron Corporation is an international manufacturer of oil and gas pressure control equipment. Cameron (59.7% of 2002 revenues) is an international manufacturer of oil and gas pressure control equipment, including wellheads, chokes, blowout preventers and assembled systems for oil and gas drilling, production and transmission used in onshore, offshore and subsea applications. Cooper Cameron Valves (17.8%) provides a full range of ball valves,

gate valves, butterfly valves and accessories. Cooper Compression (22.5%) provides centrifugal air compressors and aftermarket productions to manufacturing companies and chemical process industries worldwide. In addition, this segment provides power and compression for the oil and gas production, gas transmission, process and independent power industries.

RECENT DEVELOPMENTS:

For the twelve months ended 12/31/02, net income was $60.5 million compared with $98.3 million a year earlier. Results for 2002 and 2001 included non-recurring charges of $33.3 million and $20.2 million, respectively. Total rev-

enues slipped 1.6% to $1.54 billion from $1.56 billion the previous year, due in part to weakness in North American exploration and production activity, which contributed to reduced margins.

PROSPECTS:

CAM expects full-year 2003 earnings to approximate $1.80 to $2.00 per share, primarily due to growth in revenues related to the Company's subsea business from its Cameron business segment. For instance, as of 12/31/02, CAM's total backlog was $828.0 million, an increase of 19.1% from the prior year. However, the majority of the increase is reflected in Cameron's new equipment subsea backlog, which increased by more than $150.0 million during 2002.

Separately, capital expenditures during 2003 are expected to be approximately $65.0 million to $70.0 million versus $82.0 million in 2002. On 12/30/02, CAM announced the acquisition of Nutron Industries, a privately-held valve manufacturer located in Edmonton, Canada, for approximately $50.0 million in cash. For the twelve months ended 9/30/02, Nutron generated revenues of about $36.0 million.

ANNUAL FINANCIAL DATA:

FISCAL YEAR	TOT. REVS. ($mill.)	NET INC. ($mill.)	TOT. ASSETS ($mill.)	OPER. PROFIT %	NET PROFIT %	RET. ON EQUITY %	RET. ON ASSETS %	CURR. RATIO	EARN. PER SH. $	CASH FL. PER SH. $	TANG. BK. VAL. $	PRICE RANGE	AVG. P/E RATIO
p12/31/02	1,538.1	① 60.5							① 1.10			59.60 - 35.94	43.4
12/31/01	1,563.7	① 98.3	1,875.1	10.8	6.3	10.7	5.2	2.6	① 1.75	3.12	11.66	73.00 - 28.85	29.1
② 12/31/00	1,386.7	① 27.7	1,493.9	10.0	2.0	3.3	1.9	2.0	① 0.50	1.87	10.75	83.88 - 42.38	126.2
12/31/99	1,464.8	① 43.0	1,470.7	7.5	2.9	6.0	2.9	1.7	① 0.78	2.31	8.57	50.00 - 22.25	46.3
12/31/98	1,882.1	① 136.2	1,823.6	13.3	7.2	17.4	7.5	1.8	① 2.48	3.80	9.22	71.00 - 20.13	18.4
12/31/97	1,806.1	140.6	1,643.2	12.6	7.8	21.9	8.6	1.8	2.53	3.71	7.61	81.75 - 30.25	22.1
12/31/96	1,388.2	① 64.2	1,468.9	8.7	4.6	12.4	4.4	1.8	① 2.41	2.50	5.01	38.25 - 15.94	11.2
12/31/95	1,144.0	d500.1	1,135.4	0.8	...	...	...	1.7	① d19.87	d8.55	3.78	17.75 - 9.25	...
12/31/94	1,110.1	d3.7	1,710.4	2.1	...	...	...	2.3	...	1.33	...	...	...
12/31/93	1,340.8	51.2	1,713.7	7.8	3.8	6.1	3.0	2.1	...	...	...	...	...

Statistics are as originally reported. Adj. for 2-for-1 stk. split, 6/97. ① Incls. net nonrecurr. chrg. of $33.3 mill., 2002; $20.2 mill., 2001; $77.4 mill., 2000; $10.6 mill., 1999; $22.0 mill., 1998; $7.3 mill., 1996; $41.5 mill., 1995. ② Beginning with 12/31/00 results, shipping & handling costs are class. as cost of rev. rather than part of revs.

OFFICERS:
S. R. Erikson, Chmn., Pres., C.E.O.
F. Myers, Sr. V.P., C.F.O.
W. C. Lemmer, V.P., Sec., Gen. Couns.
INVESTOR CONTACT: R. S. Amann, Investor Relations, (713) 513-3344
PRINCIPAL OFFICE: 1333 West Loop South, Suite 1700, Houston, TX 77027

TELEPHONE NUMBER: (713) 513-3300
FAX: (713) 513-3320
WEB: www.coopercameron.com
NO. OF EMPLOYEES: 8,000 (approx.)
SHAREHOLDERS: 1,693 (approx. record)
ANNUAL MEETING: In May
INCORPORATED: DE, Nov., 1994

INSTITUTIONAL HOLDINGS:
No. of Institutions: 201
Shares Held: 50,260,137
% Held: 92.5
INDUSTRY: Oil and gas field machinery (SIC: 3533)
TRANSFER AGENT(S): First Chicago Trust Company of New York, Jersey City, NJ

COOPER COMPANIES, INC.

EXCH.	SYM.	REC. PRICE	P/E RATIO	YLD.	MKT. CAP.	RANGE (52-WK.)	'02 Y/E PR.
NYSE	COO	29.05 (2/28/03)	17.0	0.2%	$0.90 bill.	31.47 - 19.18	25.02

UPPER MEDIUM GRADE. IN FISCAL 2003, THE COMPANY EXPECTS EARNINGS PER SHARE WILL RANGE FROM $1.98 TO $2.03, UP 26.0% TO 29.0%.

TRADING VOLUME
Thousand Shares

| 1989 | 1990 | 1991 | 1992 | 1993 | 1994 | 1995 | 1996 | 1997 | 1998 | 1999 | 2000 | 2001 | 2002 | 2003 |

*7 YEAR PRICE SCORE 164.2   ***12 MONTH PRICE SCORE 114.3**

*NYSE COMPOSITE INDEX=100

INTERIM EARNINGS (Per Share):

Qtr.	Jan.	Apr.	July	Oct.
1999-00	0.17	0.24	0.30	0.32
2000-01	0.22	0.29	0.34	0.38
2001-02	0.31	0.32	0.43	0.52
2002-03	0.44	...	...	...

INTERIM DIVIDENDS (Per Share):

Amt.	Decl.	Ex.	Rec.	Pay.
0.05S	12/05/01	12/12/01	12/14/01	1/04/02
0.05S	5/16/02	6/11/02	6/13/02	7/03/02
100% STK	11/05/02	11/25/02	11/14/02	11/22/02
0.03S	12/05/02	12/12/02	12/16/02	1/06/03

Indicated div.: $0.06

CAPITALIZATION (10/31/02):

	($000)	(%)
Long-Term Debt	127,318	29.0
Common & Surplus	311,442	71.0
Total	438,760	100.0

BUSINESS:

The Cooper Companies, Inc. develop, manufacture and market specialty healthcare products. COO operates in two businesses. CooperVision (CVI) markets a range of contact lenses for the vision care market. CVI manufacturers its products in the U.S., Canada, Australia, England and Spain.

CooperSurgical (CSI) markets diagnostic products, surgical instruments and accessories for the synecological market, in the U.S., Canada, Sweden and Germany. Revenues (and operating income) for 2002: CVI, 77.4% (81.1%) and CSI, 22.6% (18.9%).

RECENT DEVELOPMENTS:

For the quarter ended 1/31/03, net income jumped 47.3% to $13.9 million compared with $9.4 million in the previous year. Net sales increased 61.8% to $94.0 million from $51.8 million in the prior-year period. CooperVision revenues advanced 72.9% to $72.8 million from $42.1 million in the year-earlier quarter, reflecting higher sales of soft contact lens products to commercial customers and growth

in all disposable and planned replacement products. CooperSurgical revenues climbed 32.5% to $21.2 million from $16.0 million the year before, due to the addition of three new product lines through acquisition during fiscal 2002. Gross profit soared 58.4% to $59.4 million from $37.5 million in 2001. Operating income improved 51.2% to $19.8 million versus $13.1 million in the previous year.

PROSPECTS:

CooperSurgical should continue benefit from its efforts to consolidate in-office women's healthcare operations as a result of completing three acquisitions during fiscal 2002. Meanwhile, COO's CooperVision unit expects to achieve about $300.0 million in worldwide soft contact lens reve-

nues, growing at about one and a half to two times faster than the worldwide soft lens market. Moreover, COO expects revenue of $380.0 million to $400.0 million, up 21.0% to 27.0%, and earnings per share ranging from $1.98 to $2.03, up 26.0% to 29.0%, in fiscal 2003.

ANNUAL FINANCIAL DATA:

FISCAL YEAR	TOT. REVS. ($000)	NET INC. ($000)	TOT. ASSETS ($000)	OPER. PROFIT %	NET PROFIT %	RET. ON EQUITY %	RET. ON ASSETS %	CURR. RATIO	EARN. PER SH. $	CASH FL. PER SH. $	TANG. BK. VAL. $	DIV. PER SH. $	PRICE RANGE	AVG. P/E RATIO	AVG. YIELD %
10/31/02	315,306	48,875	571,115	21.2	15.5	15.7	8.6	1.6	1.57	1.93	1.87	0.05	31.47 - 19.18	16.1	0.2
10/31/01	234,572	37,136	396,849	23.3	15.8	14.5	9.4	2.3	1.22	1.58	3.64	0.04	27.86 - 17.45	18.6	0.2
10/31/00	197,317	⑧ 29,400	322,565	23.8	14.9	14.8	9.1	1.7	⑥ 1.02	1.31	3.03	0.04	20.75 - 12.50	16.4	0.2
10/31/99	165,328	⑤ 22,001	285,873	23.5	13.3	13.4	7.7	2.4	⑤ 0.77	1.00	2.97	0.02	15.94 - 5.88	14.2	0.2
10/31/98	147,192	④ 57,810	296,041	20.2	39.3	39.8	19.5	2.5	④ 1.90	2.17	2.11	...	25.84 - 7.00	8.7	...
10/31/97	141,473	48,390	175,298	18.2	34.2	43.4	27.6	2.0	1.85	2.01	2.53	...	21.00 - 7.94	7.8	...
10/31/96	109,131	16,603	102,909	15.4	15.2	108.3	16.1	1.3	0.71	0.85	...	...	8.69 - 3.19	8.4	...
10/31/95	97,090	③ 115	91,992	8.2	0.1	...	0.1	1.0	③ 0.01	0.15	...	...	5.63 - 2.63	817.5	...
10/31/94	95,645	d4,697	95,058	0.4	...	...	...	1.0	d0.23	d0.03	...	...	5.26 - 0.66	...	...
② 10/31/93	92,652	① d34,072	109,524	...	...	...	...	1.0	① d1.71	d1.47	...	...	1.88 - 0.42	...	...

Statistics are as originally reported. Adj. for 2-for-1, 11/02; 1-for-3 rev. split, 9/95. ① Bef. disc. opers. chg. of $13.7 mill. & an extraord. gain of $924,000. ② Results reflect sale of Cooper Technicon Inc. in 6/89. ③ Incl. $1.5 mill. for restruct & $3.4 mill. for settle. of dispute. ④ Excl. $22.3 mill. loss on sale of ops. & $18.0 mill. loss fr. disc. ops. ⑤ Excl. a gain of $3.1mill. from disc. ops. ⑥ Bef. after-tax acctg. chrg. of $432,000.

OFFICERS:
A. T. Bender, Chmn.., C.E.O.
R. S. Weiss, Exec. V.P., C.F.O., Treas.
C. R. Kaufman, V.P., Sec., C.A.O.

INVESTOR CONTACT: B. Norris Battin, V.P., Investor Relations, (888) 822-2600

PRINCIPAL OFFICE: 6140 Stoneridge Mall Road, Suite 590, Pleasanton, CA 94588

TELEPHONE NUMBER: (925) 460-3600
FAX: (949) 597-0662
WEB: www.coopercos.com

NO. OF EMPLOYEES: 3,500 (approx.)

SHAREHOLDERS: 865

ANNUAL MEETING: In Mar.

INCORPORATED: DE, Mar., 1980

INSTITUTIONAL HOLDINGS:
No. of Institutions: 176
Shares Held: 34,925,970
% Held: 114.0

INDUSTRY: Ophthalmic goods (SIC: 3851)

TRANSFER AGENT(S): American Stock Transfer & Trust Company, New York, NY

COOPER INDUSTRIES, LTD.

EXCH.	SYM.	REC. PRICE	P/E RATIO	YLD.	MKT. CAP.	RANGE (52-WK.)	'02 Y/E PR.
NYSE	CBE	37.85 (2/28/03)	16.6	3.7%	$3.53 bill.	47.01 - 27.14	36.45

UPPER MEDIUM GRADE. THE COMPANY EXPECTS MODEST GROWTH IN REVENUES IN 2003 THROUGH NEW PRODUCT INTRODUCTIONS AND MARKET PENETRATION.

TRADING VOLUME
Thousand Shares

*7 YEAR PRICE SCORE N/A   *12 MONTH PRICE SCORE N/A
*NYSE COMPOSITE INDEX=100

INTERIM EARNINGS (Per Share):

Qtr.	Mar.	June	Sept.	Dec.
1998	0.76	0.88	0.59	1.27
1999	0.80	0.92	0.89	0.89
2000	0.89	0.99	0.97	0.95
2001	0.60	0.72	0.78	0.66
2002	0.52	0.78	0.68	0.30

INTERIM DIVIDENDS (Per Share):

Amt.	Decl.	Ex.	Rec.	Pay.
0.35Q	2/13/02	2/27/02	3/01/02	4/01/02
0.35Q	4/30/02	5/13/02	5/15/02	7/01/02
0.35Q	8/06/02	9/11/02	9/13/02	10/01/02
0.35Q	11/05/02	11/27/02	12/02/02	1/02/03
0.35Q	2/13/03	2/26/03	3/03/03	4/01/03

Indicated div.: $1.40 (Div. Reinv. Plan)

CAPITALIZATION (12/31/01):

	($000)	(%)
Long-Term Debt	1,107,000	35.4
Common & Surplus	2,023,200	64.6
Total	3,130,200	100.0

BUSINESS:

Cooper Industries, Ltd. operates in two business segments: The Electrical Products segment (84.0% of 2002 revenues) manufactures, markets and sells electrical and circuit protection products, including fittings, support systems, enclosures, wiring devices, plugs, receptacles, lighting fixtures, fuses, emergency lighting, fire detection systems and security products for use in residential, commercial and industrial construction, maintenance and repair applications. This segment also manufactures, markets and sells products for use by utilities and in industry for electrical power transmission and distribution. The Tools & Hardware segment (16.0%) manufactures, markets and sells hand tools for industrial, construction and consumer markets; automated assembly systems for industrial markets; and electric and pneumatic industrial power tools for general industry, primarily automotive and aerospace manufacturers. On 10/9/98, CBE sold its former Automotive Products division to Federal-Mogul Corporation for $1.90 billion.

RECENT DEVELOPMENTS:

For the year ended 12/31/02, net income was $213.7 million compared with income of $261.3 million, before a loss of $30.0 million from discontinued operations, the previous year. Results for 2002 and 2001 included pre-tax non-recurring charges of $39.1 million and $74.1 million, respectively. Revenues declined 5.9% to $3.96 billion from $4.21 billion the year before. Electrical Products segment revenues fell 4.6% to $3.32 billion from $3.49 billion, while Tools and Hardware segment revenues decreased 12.2% to $635.6 million from $724.0 million a year earlier.

PROSPECTS:

Looking ahead, the Company expects modest growth in revenues for both the Electrical Products and Tools & Hardware segments in 2003 through new product introductions and market penetration. However, CBE does not anticipate any meaningful improvement in business conditions for the better part of 2003. Nevertheless, CBE expects that the strategic improvement programs and commercial initiatives that it is implementing will generate growth and earnings even if markets remain flat. As a result, the Company anticipates diluted earnings per share will range from $2.85 to $3.05 for full-year 2003.

ANNUAL FINANCIAL DATA:

FISCAL YEAR	TOT. REVS. ($mill.)	NET INC. ($mill.)	TOT. ASSETS ($mill.)	OPER. PROFIT %	NET PROFIT %	RET. ON EQUITY %	RET. ON ASSETS %	CURR. RATIO	EARN. PER SH. $	CASH FL. PER SH. $	TANG. BK. VAL.$	DIV. PER SH. $	PRICE RANGE	AVG. P/E RATIO	AVG. YIELD
p12/31/02	3,960.5	⑧ 213.7							⑦ 2.28			1.40	47.01 - 27.14	16.3	3.8
12/31/01	4,209.5	⑥ 261.3	4,611.4	9.5	6.2	12.9	5.7	1.5	⑥ 2.75	4.72	0.69	1.40	60.45 - 31.61	16.7	3.0
12/31/00	4,459.9	357.4	4,789.3	14.6	8.0	18.8	7.5	1.5	3.80	5.65	...	1.38	47.00 - 29.38	10.0	3.6
12/31/99	3,868.9	331.9	4,143.4	14.8	8.6	19.0	8.0	1.4	3.50	5.05	0.04	1.32	56.75 - 39.63	13.8	2.7
⑤ 12/31/98	3,651.2	① 335.9	3,779.1	17.1	9.2	21.5	8.9	1.5	① 2.93	4.13	0.04	1.32	70.38 - 36.88	18.3	2.5
12/31/97	5,288.8	② 394.6	6,052.5	13.6	7.5	15.3	6.5	1.5	② 3.26	5.23	1.55	1.32	58.63 - 40.00	15.1	2.7
12/31/96	5,283.7	315.4	5,950.4	10.4	6.0	16.7	5.3	1.5	2.93	5.11	...	1.32	44.63 - 34.13	13.4	3.4
12/31/95	4,885.9	③ 280.6	6,063.9	12.9	5.7	16.3	4.6	1.5	③ 2.51	4.48	...	1.32	40.50 - 32.88	14.6	3.6
④ 12/31/94	4,588.0	③ 292.8	6,400.7	12.6	6.4	10.7	4.6	1.6	③ 2.10	4.31	4.76	1.32	52.25 - 31.63	20.0	3.1
12/31/93	6,273.8	367.1	7,147.8	11.5	5.9	12.3	5.1	1.5	2.75	5.87	3.17	1.30	54.75 - 45.63	18.2	2.6

Statistics are as originally reported. ① Incls. one-time pre-tax credit of $81.6 mill.; bef. income fr. disc. ops. of $87.1 mill. ② Incls. non-recurr. pre-tax gain of $9.1 mill. ③ Bef. loss fr. disc. ops. 12/31/95: $186.6 mill. ($1.67/sh.); loss 12/31/94: $313.4 mill. ($2.75/sh.). ④ Refls. discontinuance of several business units. ⑤ Refls. sale of Automotive division. ⑥ Excl. loss fr. disc. ops. of $30.0 mill. & incl. pre-tax non-recurr chrg. of $74.1 mill. ⑦ Incl. pre-tax non-recurr. chrg. of $39.1 mill.

OFFICERS:
H. J. Riley Jr., Chmn., Pres., C.E.O.
T. A. Klebe, Sr. V.P., C.F.O.
A. J. Hill, V.P., Treas.

INVESTOR CONTACT: Richard J. Bajenski,
V.P. Investor Relations, (713) 209-8610

PRINCIPAL OFFICE: 600 Travis, Suite 5800, Houston, TX 77002

TELEPHONE NUMBER: (713) 209-8400
FAX: (713) 209-8996
WEB: www.cooperindustries.com
NO. OF EMPLOYEES: 28,462 (approx.)
SHAREHOLDERS: 26,509
ANNUAL MEETING: In Apr.
INCORPORATED: OH, Jan., 1919; Reincorp., Bermuda, 2002

INSTITUTIONAL HOLDINGS:
No. of Institutions: N/A
Shares Held: N/A
% Held: N/A
INDUSTRY: Commercial lighting fixtures (SIC: 3646)
TRANSFER AGENT(S): EquiServe Trust Company, N.A., Jersey City, NJ

COOPER TIRE & RUBBER COMPANY

EXCH.	SYM.	REC. PRICE	P/E RATIO	YLD.	MKT. CAP.	RANGE (52-WK.)	'02 Y/E PR.
NYSE	CTB	14.01 (2/28/03)	9.3	3.0%	$1.02 bill.	26.10 - 12.25	15.34

MEDIUM GRADE. IN THE NEAR TERM, THE COMPANY EXPECTS SOFT TIRE DEMAND AND HIGHER RAW MATERIAL COSTS.

*7 YEAR PRICE SCORE 103.4   *12 MONTH PRICE SCORE 87.7

*NYSE COMPOSITE INDEX=100

INTERIM EARNINGS (Per Share):

Qtr.	Mar.	June	Sept.	Dec.
1999	0.41	0.50	0.46	0.42
2000	0.41	0.48	0.32	0.09
2001	0.05	0.25	d0.27	0.22
2002	0.36	0.52	0.31	0.32

INTERIM DIVIDENDS (Per Share):

Amt.	Decl.	Ex.	Rec.	Pay.
0.105Q	2/07/02	2/28/02	3/04/02	3/28/02
0.105Q	5/07/02	5/30/02	6/03/02	6/28/02
0.105Q	7/18/02	9/03/02	9/05/02	9/27/02
0.105Q	11/18/02	11/27/02	12/02/02	12/30/02
0.105Q	2/06/03	2/27/03	3/03/03	3/28/03

Indicated div.: $0.42 (Div. Reinv. Plan)

CAPITALIZATION (12/31/01):

	($000)	(%)
Long-Term Debt	882,134	48.7
Deferred Income Tax	20,012	1.1
Common & Surplus	910,240	50.2
Total	1,812,386	100.0

BUSINESS:

Cooper Tire & Rubber Company specializes in manufacturing and marketing primarily rubber-based products for the transportation industry. CTB has two reportable operating segments. The Tire segment (52.7% of revenues and 53.9% of income in 2002) produces automobile, truck and motorcycle tires and inner tubes primarily for sale in the replacement market to independent dealers, wholesale distributors, and large retail chains. The Automotive segment (47.3%,

46.1%) produces body sealing systems, active and passive vibration control systems, and fluid handling systems primarily for the global automotive original equipment manufacturing and replacement markets. At 2/6/03, CTB operated 52 manufacturing facilities in 13 countries. On 1/28/00, CTB acquired Seibe Automotive, the automotive fluid handling division of Invensys plc. On 10/27/99, CTB acquired The Standard Products Company.

RECENT DEVELOPMENTS:

For the year ended 12/31/02, CTB reported net income of $111.8 million versus $18.2 million in the previous year. Results for 2002 and 2001 included restructuring charges of $4.6 million and $8.6 million, respectively. Results for 2001 also included class action litigation costs of $72.2 million and goodwill amortization of $15.7 million. Net sales increased 5.6% to $3.33 billion from $3.15 billion a

year earlier. Tire segment sales rose 3.8% to $1.77 billion, primarily due to higher demand from regional retailers. Automotive segment sales advanced 7.3% to $1.59 billion due to new business launches and increased content per vehicle, as well as higher North American vehicle production. Gross profit advanced 14.0% to $490.2 million from $430.0 million the year before.

PROSPECTS:

The Company anticipates weaker tire demand for the first half of 2003 along with higher raw material costs. However, in the second half of 2003, the Company believes economic conditions will improve and tire demand should return to near normal conditions. Recently implemented tire

price increases should help to offset higher raw material costs, while new products and growing demand for replacement tires as well as new automotive business launches should lead to improved capacity utilization and operating efficiency.

ANNUAL FINANCIAL DATA:

FISCAL YEAR	TOT. REVS. ($mill.)	NET INC. ($mill.)	TOT. ASSETS ($mill.)	OPER. PROFIT %	NET PROFIT %	RET. ON EQUITY %	RET. ON ASSETS %	CURR. RATIO	EARN. PER SH.$	CASH FL. PER SH.$	TANG. BK. VAL.$	DIV. PER SH.$	PRICE RANGE	AVG. P/E RATIO	AVG. YIELD %
p12/31/02	3,330.0	③ 111.8							③ 1.51			0.42	26.10 - 12.25	12.7	2.2
12/31/01	3,154.7	② 18.2	2,764.3	3.4	0.6	1.9	0.7	1.5	② 0.25	. . .	6.64	0.42	17.43 - 10.55	55.9	3.0
12/31/00	3,472.4	① 96.7	2,922.0	7.3	2.8	10.2	3.3	1.7	① 1.31	3.88	7.07	0.42	16.00 - 9.19	9.6	3.3
12/31/99	2,196.3	135.5	2,757.6	10.9	6.2	13.9	4.9	2.4	1.79	3.44	7.15	0.42	25.00 - 13.25	10.7	2.2
12/31/98	1,879.8	127.0	1,541.3	11.4	6.8	14.6	8.2	3.0	1.64	2.97	11.45	0.39	26.25 - 15.44	12.7	1.9
12/31/97	1,814.4	122.4	1,496.0	11.6	6.7	14.7	8.2	2.8	1.55	2.75	10.58	0.35	28.44 - 18.00	15.0	1.5
12/31/96	1,620.2	107.9	1,273.0	10.7	6.7	13.7	8.5	2.4	1.30	2.22	9.67	0.31	27.38 - 17.88	17.4	1.4
12/31/95	1,497.5	112.8	1,143.7	12.1	7.5	15.1	9.9	2.7	1.35	2.11	8.95	0.27	29.63 - 22.25	19.2	1.0
12/31/94	1,405.5	128.5	1,039.7	15.0	9.1	19.4	12.4	3.0	1.54	2.20	7.92	0.23	29.50 - 21.63	16.6	0.9
12/31/93	1,194.2	102.2	889.6	14.0	8.6	18.6	11.5	2.6	1.22	1.78	6.58	0.20	39.63 - 20.00	24.4	0.7

Statistics are as originally reported. ① Incl. pre-tax non-recurr. chrg. of $38.7 mill. ② Incl. pre-tax litigation chrg. of $72.2 mill. and a pre-tax restr. chrg. of $8.6 mill. ③ Incl. restr. chrg. of $4.6 mill.

OFFICERS:
T. A. Dattilo, Chmn., Pres., C.E.O.
P. G. Weaver, V.P., C.F.O.
R. D. Teeple, V.P., Gen. Couns., Sec.
INVESTOR CONTACT: Roger S. Hendriksen, Investor Relations Dir., (419) 427-4768
PRINCIPAL OFFICE: 701 Lima Avenue, Findlay, OH 45840

TELEPHONE NUMBER: (419) 423-1321
FAX: (419) 424-4108
WEB: www.coopertire.com
NO. OF EMPLOYEES: 23,268 (avg.)
SHAREHOLDERS: 4,146
ANNUAL MEETING: In May
INCORPORATED: DE, March, 1930

INSTITUTIONAL HOLDINGS:
No. of Institutions: 223
Shares Held: 50,732,776
% Held: 69.0
INDUSTRY: Tires and inner tubes (SIC: 3011)
TRANSFER AGENT(S): Fifth Third Bank, Cincinnati, OH

COORS (ADOLPH) COMPANY

EXCH.	SYM.	REC. PRICE	P/E RATIO	YLD.	MKT. CAP.	RANGE (52-WK.)	'02 Y/E PR.
NYSE	RKY	48.10 (2/28/03)	10.9	1.7%	$1.73 bill.	70.15 - 47.03	61.25

INVESTMENT GRADE. THE COMPANY CONTINUES TO PERFORM WELL, PRIMARILY DRIVEN BY THE ADDITION OF RESULTS FROM UNITED KINGDOM-BASED COORS BREWERS LTD.

MERGENT

TRADING VOLUME
Thousand Shares

*7 YEAR PRICE SCORE 142.1   ***12 MONTH PRICE SCORE 101.9**
*NYSE COMPOSITE INDEX=100

INTERIM EARNINGS (Per Share):

Qtr.	Mar.	June	Sept.	Dec.
1998	0.26	1.06	0.24	0.25
1999	0.32	1.23	0.58	0.33
2000	0.40	1.29	0.92	0.32
2001	0.49	1.33	1.05	0.44
2002	0.75	1.84	1.28	0.55

INTERIM DIVIDENDS (Per Share):

Amt.	Decl.	Ex.	Rec.	Pay.
0.205Q	2/15/02	2/26/02	2/28/02	3/15/02
0.205Q	5/16/02	5/29/02	5/31/02	6/17/02
0.205Q	8/15/02	8/28/02	8/31/02	9/16/02
0.205Q	11/14/02	11/26/02	11/30/02	12/16/02
0.205Q	2/14/03	2/26/03	2/28/03	3/17/03

Indicated div.: $0.82

CAPITALIZATION (12/30/01):

	($000)	(%)
Long-Term Debt	20,000	1.9
Deferred Income Tax	61,635	6.0
Common & Surplus	951,312	92.1
Total	1,032,947	100.0

BUSINESS:

Adolph Coors Company, through its principal operating subsidiary Coors Brewing Company (CBC), produces, markets and sells malt-based beverages. The Company's portfolio of products includes COORS LIGHT®, ORIGINAL COORS®, COORS DRY® and COORS NON-ALCOHOLIC®. CBC produces and markets COORS EXTRA GOLD® and ZIMA®, a malt-based, above-premium beverage. CBC also offers specialty, above-premium beers, including WINTERFEST® and BLUEMOON™ ales. In addition, CBC sells licensed products, including GEORGE KILLIAN'S® products, and popular-priced products, including KEY STONE® products. RKY also owns London-based Coors Brewing International, Ltd. and Coors Canada, Inc. On 2/4/02, RKY acquired the Carling business portion of Bass Brewers in a transaction valued at $1.70 billion, and renamed it Coors Brewers Ltd. For the year ended 12/29/02, net sales were derived as The Americas, 63.5% and Europe, 36.5%.

RECENT DEVELOPMENTS:

For the 52 weeks ended 12/29/02, net income increased 31.5% to $161.7 million versus $123.0 million the year before. Earnings for 2002 and 2001 included special pretax charges of $6.3 million and $23.2 million, respectively. Earnings for 2001 also included gains of $27.7 million on the sale of distributorships. Net sales grew 55.4% to $3.78 billion from $2.43 billion a year earlier. Net sales for the Americas segment slid 0.9% to $2.40 billion, while net sales for the Europe segment amounted to $1.38 billion.

PROSPECTS:

The Company continues to perform well, primarily driven by the addition of results from the United Kingdom-based Coors Brewers Limited, which was acquired on 2/2/02. The Company continues to make significant investments to build its brands and improve operations. RKY's goal is to build on its success in the United Kingdom, grow its United States volume, further reduce its costs, and maximize cash generation to reduce debt. Meanwhile, sales volume in the Company's Europe segment increased at a low-single-digit percent rate, while Volume for Carling, a beer brand in the United Kingdom, grew at mid-single-digit percentage rates for 2002.

ANNUAL FINANCIAL DATA:

FISCAL YEAR	TOT. REVS. ($mill.)	NET INC. ($mill.)	TOT. ASSETS ($mill.)	OPER. PROFIT %	NET PROFIT %	RET. ON EQUITY %	RET. ON ASSETS %	CURR. RATIO	EARN. PER SH.$	CASH FL. PER SH.$	TANG. BK. VAL.$	DIV. PER SH.$	PRICE RANGE	AVG. P/E RATIO	AVG. YIELD %
p12/31/02	3,776.3	③ 161.7							③ 4.42			0.82	70.15 - 50.50	13.6	1.4
12/30/01	2,429.5	② 123.0	1,739.7	6.2	5.1	12.9	7.1	1.2	② 3.31	6.56	24.94	0.80	81.19 - 42.65	18.7	1.3
12/31/00	2,414.4	① 109.6	1,629.3	6.2	4.5	11.8	6.7	1.3	① 2.93	6.38	24.32	0.72	82.31 - 37.38	20.4	1.2
12/26/99	2,056.6	① 92.3	1,546.4	6.9	4.5	11.0	6.0	1.6	① 2.46	5.77	22.06	0.65	65.81 - 45.25	22.6	1.2
12/27/98	1,899.5	① 67.8	1,460.6	5.5	3.6	8.7	4.6	1.4	① 1.81	4.89	20.51	0.60	56.75 - 29.25	23.8	1.4
12/28/97	1,822.2	② 82.3	1,412.1	8.1	4.5	11.2	5.8	1.4	② 2.16	5.24	19.36	0.55	41.25 - 17.50	13.6	1.9
12/29/96	1,732.2	43.4	1,362.5	4.7	2.5	6.1	3.2	1.4	1.14	4.33	18.30	0.50	24.25 - 16.75	18.0	2.4
12/31/95	1,675.4	43.2	1,386.9	4.8	2.6	6.2	3.1	1.1	1.13	4.35	17.59	0.50	23.25 - 15.13	17.0	2.6
12/25/94	1,662.7	58.1	1,371.6	6.5	3.5	8.6	4.2	0.9	1.52	4.67	13.77	0.50	20.88 - 14.75	11.7	2.8
12/26/93	1,581.8	d41.9	1,350.9	...	...	...	...	1.0	d1.10	2.03	16.21	0.50	22.63 - 15.00	...	2.7

Statistics are as originally reported. ① Incl. non-recurr. chrg. $15.2 mill., 2000; $5.7 mill., 1999; chrge. $19.4 mill. 1998; credit $31.5 mill., 1997. ② Incl. a pre-tax gain of $27.7 mill. on the sale of distributorships & a pre-tax special chrg. of $23.2 mill. primarily rel. to restructuring several areas of the Co. ③ Incl. special pre-tax charges of $6.3 million.

OFFICERS:
W. K. Coors, Chmn.
P. Coors, Pres., C.E.O.
T. V. Wolf, V.P., C.F.O.
INVESTOR CONTACT: Dave Dunnewald,
Investor Relations, (303) 279-6565
PRINCIPAL OFFICE: 311 Tenth Street,
Golden, CO 80401

TELEPHONE NUMBER: (303) 279-6565
FAX: (303) 425-7967
WEB: www.coorsinvestor.com
NO. OF EMPLOYEES: 5,500 (approx.)
SHAREHOLDERS: 2,916 (approx. cl. B com.)
ANNUAL MEETING: In May
INCORPORATED: CO, 1913

INSTITUTIONAL HOLDINGS:
No. of Institutions: 243
Shares Held: 22,191,234
% Held: 61.1

INDUSTRY: Malt beverages (SIC: 2082)

TRANSFER AGENT(S): BankBoston, N.A.,
Canton, MA

CORNING INCORPORATED

EXCH.	SYM.	REC. PRICE	P/E RATIO	YLD.	MKT. CAP.	RANGE (52-WK.)	'02 Y/E PR.
NYSE	GLW	4.92 (2/28/03)	...	...	$4.53 bill.	8.90 - 1.10	3.31

SPECULATIVE GRADE. THE COMPANY EXPECTS TO RETURN TO PROFITABILITY BY THE THIRD QUARTER OF 2003.

*7 YEAR PRICE SCORE 19.2 ***12 MONTH PRICE SCORE 118.6**

NYSE COMPOSITE INDEX=100

INTERIM EARNINGS (Per Share):

Qtr.	Mar.	June	Sept.	Dec.
1998	0.09	0.08	0.15	0.15
1999	0.12	0.16	0.18	0.18
2000	0.09	0.17	0.28	d0.08
2001	0.14	d5.13	d0.24	d0.69
2002	d0.10	d0.39	d0.25	d0.96

INTERIM DIVIDENDS (Per Share):

Amt.	Decl.	Ex.	Rec.	Pay.
0.06Q	2/07/01	3/01/01	3/05/01	3/30/01
0.06Q	4/27/01	5/31/01	6/04/01	6/29/01
	Dividend payment suspended.			

CAPITALIZATION (12/31/01):

	($000)	(%)
Long-Term Debt	4,461,000	44.6
Minority Interest	119,000	1.2
Redeemable Pfd. Stock	7,000	0.1
Common & Surplus	5,414,000	54.1
Total	10,001,000	100.0

BUSINESS:

Corning Incorporated is a global, technology-based corporation. The Telecommunications segment (51.9% of 2002 revenues) produces optical fiber and cable, optical hardware and equipment, photonic modules and components and optical networking devices for the worldwide telecommunications industry. The Technologies segment (48.1%) manufactures specialized products with unique properties for customer applications utilizing glass, glass ceramic and polymer technologies. The Technologies segment also manufactures glass panels and funnels for televisions and CRTs, liquid crystal display glass for flat panel displays and projection video lens assemblies. On 4/1/98, GLW sold its consumer housewares business to an affiliate of Borden, Inc.

RECENT DEVELOPMENTS:

For the year ended 12/31/02, GLW posted a loss from continuing operations of $1.78 billion versus a loss from continuing operations of $5.53 billion the previous year. Results for 2002 and 2001 included restructuring, impairment and other charges of $2.08 billion and $5.72 billion, respectively. Results for 2002 also included a gain of $176.0 million from the repurchase of debt, while results for 2001 included amortization of goodwill of $363.0 million. Net sales fell 47.7% to $3.16 billion, reflecting poor demand from GLW's Telecommunications businesses.

PROSPECTS:

GLW has indicated that it expects to be profitable in the third quarter of 2003 despite weakness from its Telecommunications segment. Key elements of GLW's 2003 plan to restore profitability include stable sales volume in optical fiber and cable, significant cost reduction benefits from its 2002 restructuring actions primarily in its Telecommunications segment, continued growth in the Corning Technologies segment, and reduced corporate operating expenses. GLW noted that it expects to experience annual revenue growth of at least 20.0% to 40.0% over the next several years from its liquid crystal displays business. Separately, GLW stated that it is actively considering all options for its photonics business, including partnerships, further product reductions or exiting the photonics market entirely.

ANNUAL FINANCIAL DATA:

FISCAL YEAR	TOT. REVS. ($mill.)	NET INC. ($mill.)	TOT. ASSETS ($mill.)	OPER. PROFIT %	NET PROFIT %	RET. ON EQUITY %	RET. ON ASSETS %	CURR. RATIO	EARN. PER SH.$	CASH FL. PER SH.$	TANG. BK. VAL.$	DIV. PER SH.$	PRICE RANGE		AVG. P/E RATIO	AVG. YIELD %
p12/31/02	3,164.0	⑨d1,780.0		...	...	...	...	2.1	⑨d1.85	d4.74	3.39	...	11.15	- 1.10	...	...
12/31/01	6,272.0	⑧d5,498.0	12,793.0	...	...	...	...	2.1	⑧d5.89	d4.74	3.39	0.12	72.19	- 6.92	...	0.3
12/31/00	⑦7,273.1	⑥409.5	17,525.7	11.6	5.6	3.9	2.3	2.4	⑥0.46	1.34	3.56	0.24	113.28	- 34.33	160.4	0.3
12/31/99	4,368.1	⑤476.9	6,012.2	17.0	10.9	21.4	7.9	1.2	⑤0.64	1.15	2.59	0.24	43.02	- 14.92	45.0	0.8
12/31/98	3,572.1	④327.5	4,981.9	15.5	9.2	21.8	6.6	1.2	④0.46	0.85	1.72	0.24	15.23	- 7.62	24.7	2.1
12/31/97	4,129.1	439.8	4,811.4	19.4	10.7	35.3	9.1	1.4	0.62	1.03	1.27	0.24	21.71	- 11.25	26.7	1.5
12/31/96	3,684.5	③342.9	4,321.3	16.1	9.3	35.7	7.9	1.8	③0.50	0.93	0.92	0.24	15.42	- 9.29	24.7	1.9
12/31/95	5,346.1	②d50.8	5,987.1	11.6	...	...	...	1.6	②d0.08	0.48	1.00	0.24	12.46	- 8.04	...	2.3
1/01/95	4,799.2	②281.3	6,022.7	12.7	5.9	12.4	4.7	1.6	②0.44	0.98	1.25	0.23	11.69	- 9.21	23.7	2.2
1/02/94	4,038.9	①d15.2	5,231.7	7.1	...	...	...	1.4	①d0.03	0.46	1.12	0.23	13.00	- 8.00	...	2.2

Statistics are as originally reported. Adj. for 3-for-1 stk. split, 10/00. ① Incl. chg. of $323.6 mil ② Incl. $40.5 mil aft.-tax chrg. & $365.5 mil equity loss for Dow Corning invt., 12/31/95; $82.3 mil chrg., 1/01/95 ③ Bef. loss fr. disc. ops. of $167.3 mil ④ Bef. loss fr. disc. ops. of $66.5 mil; incl. aft.-tax chrg. of $26.3 mil ⑤ Bef. loss fr. disc. ops. of $4.8 mil; incl. aft.-tax gain of $8.1 mil ⑥ Bef. loss fr. disc. ops. of $12.5 mil; incl. chrgs. of $707.6 mil ⑦ Refl. strong sales growth fr. GLW's telecom. segment. ⑧ Incl. impair. & restr. chrgs. of $5.73 bil ⑨ Bef. inc. fr. disc. ops. of $478.0 mil; incl. impair. & restr. chrgs. of $2.08 bil

OFFICERS:
J. R. Houghton, Chmn., C.E.O.
J. B. Flaws, Vice-Chmn., C.F.O.
W. P. Weeks, Pres., C.O.O.
INVESTOR CONTACT: Kenneth C. Sofio, (607) 974-7705
PRINCIPAL OFFICE: One Riverfront Plaza, Corning, NY 14831-0001

TELEPHONE NUMBER: (607) 974-9000
FAX: (607) 974-8688
WEB: www.corning.com
NO. OF EMPLOYEES: 31,700 (avg.)
SHAREHOLDERS: 26,030
ANNUAL MEETING: In Apr.
INCORPORATED: NY, Dec., 1936

INSTITUTIONAL HOLDINGS:
No. of Institutions: 502
Shares Held: 651,208,261
% Held: 56.7

INDUSTRY: Glass containers (SIC: 3221)

TRANSFER AGENT(S): Computershare Investor Services LLC, Chicago, IL

COUNTRYWIDE FINANCIAL CORPORATION

EXCH.	SYM.	REC. PRICE	P/E RATIO	YLD.	MKT. CAP.	RANGE (52-WK.)	'02 Y/E PR.
NYSE	CFC	53.39 (2/28/03)	8.2	0.9%	$6.55 bill.	55.82 - 39.50	51.65

UPPER MEDIUM GRADE. THE COMPANY EXPECTS ITS CORE MORTGAGE BANKING BUSINESS AND ITS DIVERSIFICATION INITIATIVES WILL PROVIDE A SOLID FOUNDATION FOR FUTURE GROWTH.

*7 YEAR PRICE SCORE 135.6   ***12 MONTH PRICE SCORE 119.9**

*NYSE COMPOSITE INDEX=100

INTERIM EARNINGS (Per Share):

Qtr.	May	Aug.	Nov.	Feb.
1998-99	0.78	0.81	0.84	0.86
1999-00	0.88	0.91	0.87	0.87
2000-01	0.72	0.77	0.80	0.85
2001-02		3.89		

Qtr.	Mar.	June	Sept.	Dec.
2002	1.32	1.48	1.74	1.94

INTERIM DIVIDENDS (Per Share):

Amt.	Decl.	Ex.	Rec.	Pay.
0.10Q	4/23/02	5/10/02	5/14/02	5/31/02
0.03E	4/23/02	5/10/02	5/14/02	5/31/02
0.11Q	7/24/02	8/12/02	8/14/02	8/30/02
0.12Q	10/24/02	11/07/02	11/12/02	11/29/02
0.12Q	1/24/03	2/07/03	2/11/03	2/28/03

Indicated div.: $0.48

CAPITALIZATION (12/31/01):

	($000)	(%)
Long-Term Debt	16,549,999	73.7
Deferred Income Tax	1,815,254	8.1
Common & Surplus	4,087,642	18.2
Total	22,452,895	100.0

BUSINESS:

Countrywide Financial Corporation (formerly Countrywide Credit Industries, Inc.) is a provider of mortgage banking and diversified financial services in domestic and international markets. Principal subsidiaries include Countrywide Home Loans, Inc, which originates, purchases, securitizes, sells and services prime-quality loans; Full Spectrum Lending, Inc., a sub-prime residential lender; LandSafe, Inc., a provider of loan closing services; Countrywide Insurance Services, Inc., a national insurance agency offering home-

related insurance products; Balboa Life & Casualty Group, whose companies are providers of property, liability and life insurance; Balboa Reinsurance, a captive mortgage reinsurance company; Countrywide Capital Markets, a mortgage-related investment banker; and Treasury Bank, National Association, a bank offering customers CDs, money market accounts, and home loan products. In addition, as of 11/12/02, CFC owned 70.0% of Global Home Loans, Ltd., a European mortgage banking joint venture.

RECENT DEVELOPMENTS:

For the year ended 12/31/02, net earnings climbed 56.6% to $841.8 million from $537.5 million in the 12 months ended 12/31/01. Total revenues increased 58.0% to $4.52 billion from $2.86 billion in comparable 2001 period. Revenues for 2002 and 2001 included $3.42 billion and $2.35 billion,

respectively, for impairment of retained interests. Gains on the sale of loans and securities soared 99.5% to $3.56 billion. Net interest income leapt 184.2% to $792.2 million. Results for the prior year included only ten months of performance.

PROSPECTS:

CFC anticipates its core mortgage banking business and its diversification initiatives will provide a solid foundation for future growth. With respect to CFC's core mortgage banking, the market environment remains strong and competitive industry trends remain favorable. The servicing portfolio is positioned to generate significant earnings when

interest rates ultimately rise. In addition, the business model has been expanded by synergistic businesses that are designed to maximize and diversify earnings. These businesses include capital markets, banking, insurance and global, which provided about 28.0% of consolidated earnings in the most recent quarter.

ANNUAL FINANCIAL DATA:

FISCAL YEAR	TOT. REVS. ($mill.)	NET INC. ($mill.)	TOT. ASSETS ($mill.)	OPER. PROFIT %	NET PROFIT %	RET. ON EQUITY %	RET. ON ASSETS %	CURR. RATIO	EARN. PER SH. $	CASH FL. PER SH. $	TANG. BK. VAL.$	DIV. PER SH. $	PRICE RANGE	AVG. P/E RATIO	AVG. YIELD %
p12/31/02	4,519.5	841.8							6.49		...	0.46	55.00 - 37.60	7.1	1.0
③ 12/31/01	2,635.7	486.0	37,216.8	29.9	18.4	11.9	1.3	0.8	3.89	21.31	...	0.40	52.00 - 37.39	11.5	0.9
2/28/01	2,056.3	374.2	22,955.5	28.5	18.2	10.5	1.6	1.2	3.14	15.62	...	0.40	50.50 - 22.31	11.6	1.1
2/29/00	2,018.7	② 410.2	15,822.3	31.3	20.3	14.2	2.6	1.5	② 3.52	5.63	...	0.38	51.44 - 24.63	10.8	1.0
2/28/99	1,979.0	385.4	15,648.3	31.9	19.5	15.3	2.5	...	3.29	12.37	...	0.32	56.25 - 28.63	12.9	0.8
2/28/98	1,509.0	① 345.0	12,219.2	37.5	22.9	16.5	2.8	...	① 3.09	8.53	...	0.32	43.25 - 24.38	10.9	0.9
2/28/97	1,112.5	257.4	8,089.3	37.9	23.1	16.0	3.2	1.8	2.44	3.78	...	0.32	30.25 - 19.75	10.2	1.3
2/29/96	860.7	195.7	8,657.7	37.9	22.7	14.8	2.3	1.3	1.95	5.68	...	0.32	26.75 - 12.50	10.1	1.6
2/28/95	602.7	88.4	5,579.7	24.4	14.7	9.4	1.6	3.1	0.96	2.28	...	0.31	19.08 - 12.38	16.4	2.0
2/28/94	755.6	179.5	5,585.5	39.6	23.8	20.4	3.2	1.2	1.97	4.83	0.48	0.32	23.33 - 15.24	9.8	1.4

Statistics are as originally reported. Adj. for stk. split: 3-for-2, 5/94 ① Incl. non-recurr. credit $57.4 mill. ② Incl. non-recurr. gain $25.0 mill. ③ For 10 mos. due to fiscal year-end change

OFFICERS:
A. R. Mozilo, Chmn., Pres., C.E.O.
T. K. McLaughlin, C.F.O.
S. L. Kurland, C.O.O.
INVESTOR CONTACT: Lisa Riordan, Sr. V.P., Investor Relations, (818) 225-3550
PRINCIPAL OFFICE: 4500 Park Granada, Calabasas, CA 91302

TELEPHONE NUMBER: (818) 225-3000
FAX: (818) 304-5979
WEB: www.countrywide.com
NO. OF EMPLOYEES: 25,000 (avg.)
SHAREHOLDERS: 2,167
ANNUAL MEETING: In July
INCORPORATED: NY, March, 1969

INSTITUTIONAL HOLDINGS:
No. of Institutions: 369
Shares Held: 121,865,286
% Held: 96.4
INDUSTRY: Mortgage bankers and correspondents (SIC: 6162)
TRANSFER AGENT(S): Bank of New York, New York, NY

COUSINS PROPERTIES INCORPORATED

EXCH.	SYM.	REC. PRICE	P/E RATIO	YLD.	MKT. CAP.	RANGE (52-WK.)	'02 Y/E PR.	DIV. ACH.
NYSE	CUZ	24.68 (2/28/03)	24.7	6.0%	$1.22 bill.	27.32 - 20.05	24.70	11 yrs.

MEDIUM GRADE. THE COMPANY EXPECTS DEMAND FOR OFFICE SPACE TO REMAIN WEAK IN MOST OF ITS MARKETS IN 2003.

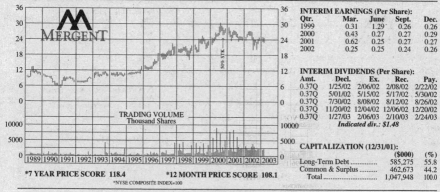

INTERIM EARNINGS (Per Share):

Qtr.	Mar.	June	Sept.	Dec.
1999	0.31	1.29	0.26	0.26
2000	0.43	0.27	0.27	0.29
2001	0.62	0.25	0.27	0.27
2002	0.25	0.25	0.24	0.26

INTERIM DIVIDENDS (Per Share):

Amt.	Decl.	Ex.	Rec.	Pay.
0.37Q	1/25/02	2/06/02	2/08/02	2/22/02
0.37Q	5/01/02	5/15/02	5/17/02	5/30/02
0.37Q	7/30/02	8/08/02	8/12/02	8/26/02
0.37Q	11/20/02	12/04/02	12/06/02	12/20/02
0.37Q	1/27/03	2/06/03	2/10/03	2/24/03

Indicated div.: $1.48

CAPITALIZATION (12/31/01):

	($000)	(%)
Long-Term Debt	585,275	55.8
Common & Surplus	462,673	44.2
Total	1,047,948	100.0

*7 YEAR PRICE SCORE 118.4   *12 MONTH PRICE SCORE 108.1

NYSE COMPOSITE INDEX=100

BUSINESS:

Cousins Properties Incorporated is a fully-integrated, self-administered equity real estate investment trust. The Company has three reportable segments. The Office division develops, leases and manages office buildings. The Retail division develops, leases and manages retail centers. The Land division owns various tracts of land being held for future development. Also, the Land division develops single-family residential communities which are parceled into lots and sold to home builders. As of 2/11/03, the Company's portfolio consisted of interests in 13.3 million square feet of office space, 3.3 million square feet of retail space and 900,000 square feet of medical office space, and more than 300 acres of strategically located land for future commercial development. CUZ also provides leasing and management services to third-party investors.

RECENT DEVELOPMENTS:

For the year ended 12/31/02, income from continuing operations declined 29.2% to $50.0 million, before an extraordinary loss of $3.5 million, compared with $70.6 million in the previous year. Results for 2002 and 2001 included gains on the sale of investment property of $6.3 million and $23.5 million, respectively. Earnings excluded gains from discontinued operations of $1.4 million and $221,000 in 2002 and 2001, respectively. Total revenues increased 12.9% to $199.8 million from $177.0 million a year earlier. Rental property revenues climbed 16.1% to $168.0 million, primarily due to properties becoming operational that had previously been under development. Funds from operations rose 9.6% to $114.4 million, or $2.29 per share, from $104.4 million, or $2.08 per share, in 2001.

PROSPECTS:

Although the office markets remain soft, CUZ is equipped to deal with leasing issues and maintain its portfolios at respectable leased levels. CUZ's operating office portfolio ended the year 94.0% leased, and its operating retail portfolio ended the year at 96.0% leased. Looking ahead, CUZ expects weak office demand as vacancy rates continue to rise in most of its major markets. In addition, tenant credit issues also continue to be of concern.

ANNUAL FINANCIAL DATA:

FISCAL YEAR	TOT. INC. ($mill.)	NET INC. ($mill.)	TOT. ASSETS ($mill.)	NET INC. + DEPR./ ASSETS %	RET. ON EQUITY %	RET. ON ASSETS %	EARN. PER SH. $	TANG. BK. VAL. $	DIV. PER SH. $	DIV. PAYOUT %	PRICE RANGE	AVG. P/E RATIO	AVG. YIELD %
p12/31/02	199.8	④ 50.0					④ 1.00		1.48	148.0	27.31 - 20.05	23.7	6.3
12/31/01	177.7	③ 70.8	1,212.0	9.5	15.3	5.8	③ 1.41	9.36	1.39	98.6	28.75 - 23.30	18.5	5.3
12/31/00	144.6	② 62.6	1,115.8	8.5	13.8	5.6	② 1.26	9.24	1.24	98.4	30.42 - 21.92	20.8	4.7
12/31/99	97.8	① 104.1	932.9	13.0	23.8	11.2	① 2.12	9.07	1.12	52.8	25.50 - 19.04	10.5	5.0
12/31/98	98.3	① 45.3	752.9	8.0	11.9	6.0	① 0.94	7.94	0.99	105.7	21.71 - 16.13	20.1	5.3
12/31/97	86.0	① 37.3	617.7	8.3	10.1	6.0	① 0.84	7.85	0.86	102.4	22.50 - 16.17	23.0	4.4
12/31/96	58.5	① 41.0	556.6	8.7	13.7	7.4	① 0.96	6.90	0.75	77.8	18.75 - 12.25	16.1	4.8
12/31/95	41.0	26.3	418.0	7.4	9.5	6.3	0.63	6.56	0.66	105.2	13.67 - 10.38	19.2	5.5
12/31/94	31.1	26.9	330.8	9.3	9.9	8.1	0.65	6.53	0.60	92.9	11.32 - 9.51	16.1	5.8
12/31/93	19.0	12.0	319.7	4.7	4.4	3.7	0.35	6.48	0.49	137.8	11.56 - 8.96	29.0	4.7

Statistics are as originally reported. Adj. for 3-for-2 stk. split, 10/00. ① Incl. gains on sales of prop. of $6.4 mill., 1994; $1.9 mill.; 1995; $12.8 mill., 1996; $6.0 mill., 1997; $3.9 mill., 1998; $58.8 mill., 1999. ② Bef. acctg. chng. chrg. of $566,000; incl. gain of $11.9 mill. on sale of prop. ③ Incl. gain of $23.5 mill. on the sale of invest. prop. ④ Bef. extraord loss of $3.5 mill. and gain fr. disc. opers. of $1.4 mill.; incl. gain on sale of invest. prop. of $6.3 mill.

OFFICERS:
T. G. Cousins, Chmn., C.E.O.
T. D. Bell Jr., Vice-Chmn., Pres., C.E.O.
T. G. Charlesworth, Exec. V.P., C.F.O.

INVESTOR CONTACT: Tom Charlesworth, (770) 857-2376

PRINCIPAL OFFICE: 2500 Windy Ridge Pkwy., Atlanta, GA 30339-5683

TELEPHONE NUMBER: (770) 955-2200
FAX: (770) 857-2360
WEB: www.cousinsproperties.com
NO. OF EMPLOYEES: 431 (avg.)
SHAREHOLDERS: 1,114
ANNUAL MEETING: In May
INCORPORATED: GA, Nov., 1961; reincorp., GA, June, 1972

INSTITUTIONAL HOLDINGS:
No. of Institutions: 124
Shares Held: 19,156,522
% Held: 39.4

INDUSTRY: Real estate investment trusts (SIC: 6798)

TRANSFER AGENT(S): First Union National Bank, Charlotte, NC

COVANCE INC.

EXCH.	SYM.	REC. PRICE	P/E RATIO	YLD.	MKT. CAP.	RANGE (52-WK.)	'02 Y/E PR.
NYSE	CVD	23.55 (2/28/03)	22.9	...	$1.41 bill.	27.41 - 12.11	24.59

UPPER MEDIUM GRADE. THE COMPANY SHOULD CONTINUE TO BENEFIT FROM STRONG DEMAND FOR LATE-STAGE AND EARLY DEVELOPMENT SERVICES.

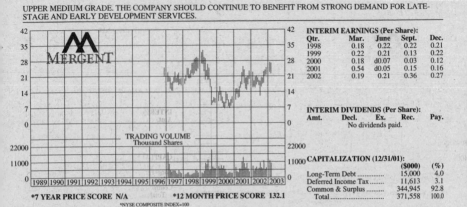

7 YEAR PRICE SCORE N/A　　**12 MONTH PRICE SCORE 132.1**

NYSE COMPOSITE INDEX=100

INTERIM EARNINGS (Per Share):

Qtr.	Mar.	June	Sept.	Dec.
1998	0.18	0.22	0.22	0.21
1999	0.22	0.21	0.13	0.22
2000	0.18	d0.07	0.03	0.12
2001	0.54	d0.05	0.15	0.16
2002	0.19	0.21	0.36	0.27

INTERIM DIVIDENDS (Per Share):

Amt.	Decl.	Ex.	Rec.	Pay.
		No dividends paid.		

CAPITALIZATION (12/31/01):

	($000)	(%)
Long-Term Debt	15,000	4.0
Deferred Income Tax	11,613	3.1
Common & Surplus	344,945	92.8
Total	371,558	100.0

BUSINESS:

Covance Inc. is a contract research organization providing a wide range of product development services on a worldwide basis primarily to the pharmaceutical, biotechnology and medical device industries. CVD also provides laboratory testing services to the chemical, agrochemical and food industries. The Company's services are divided into two reportable segments: early development services, which include preclinical and Phase I clinical service capabilities; and late-stage development services, which include central laboratory, clinical development, commercialization and other clinical support services. In February 2001, CVD sold its pharmaceutical packaging business, which offered full-service contract drug packaging services for clinical trials, for $137.5 million. In June 2001, CVD sold its biomanufacturing unit, Covance Biotechnology Services Inc., which manufactured recombinant proteins for biotechnology and pharmaceutical clients, for $190.0 million.

RECENT DEVELOPMENTS:

For the year ended 12/31/02, net income jumped 33.2% to $63.8 million compared with $47.9 million the previous year. Results for 2001 included pre-tax special charges of $8.2 million and a net gain of $30.8 million on the sale of businesses. Total revenues rose 3.2% to $924.7 million from $896.0 million the year before. Net revenues grew 3.2% to $883.1 million from $855.9 million, while reimbursable out-of-pockets revenues climbed 3.6% to $41.6 million from $40.2 million the prior year. Income from operations leapt 73.2% to $94.7 million versus $54.7 million a year earlier. As of 12/31/02, the Company's backlog was $1.12 billion versus $1.01 billion at 12/31/01.

PROSPECTS:

The Company should continue to benefit from strong demand for late-stage and early development services. Meanwhile, CVD raised its full-year 2003 diluted earnings per share guidance to approximately $1.20, in light of continually improving operating performance. Furthermore, the Company expects solid double-digit revenue growth and operating margin increases over 2002 levels of 10.7%.

ANNUAL FINANCIAL DATA:

FISCAL YEAR	TOT. REVS. ($mill.)	NET INC. ($mill.)	TOT. ASSETS ($mill.)	OPER. PROFIT %	NET PROFIT %	RET. ON EQUITY %	RET. ON ASSETS %	CURR. RATIO	EARN. PER SH.$	CASH FL.PER SH.$	TANG. BK. VAL.$	PRICE RANGE	AVG. P/E RATIO
p12/31/02	924.7	63.8							1.03			25.00 - 12.11	18.0
12/31/01	855.9	①③47.9	612.0	6.4	5.6	13.9	7.8	1.4	①③0.79	1.58	4.86	25.50 - 10.38	22.7
12/31/00	868.1	①15.2	771.1	5.1	1.8	5.7	2.0	0.8	①0.27	1.21	3.19	16.50 - 6.50	42.6
12/31/99	829.0	①45.8	700.3	10.4	5.5	17.4	6.5	1.5	①0.78	1.60	3.12	32.88 - 8.13	26.3
12/31/98	731.6	48.6	593.4	12.6	6.6	21.6	8.2	1.4	0.83	1.47	2.62	29.69 - 17.69	28.5
12/31/97	590.7	39.8	484.0	13.1	6.7	25.3	8.2	1.3	0.69	1.23	1.84	23.19 - 14.50	27.3
12/31/96	494.8	②12.7	451.0	7.7	2.6	11.5	2.8	1.4	②0.22	0.66	1.01	25.00 - 20.88	104.2
12/31/95	409.2	①24.2	322.5	11.6	5.9	29.4	7.5	1.1	...	...	...	...	...
12/31/94	319.5	19.6	272.0	12.1	6.1	30.7	7.2	1.1	...	...	...	...	...
12/31/93	289.7	16.8	...	11.6	5.8	...	...	...	...	...	...	...	...

Statistics are as originally reported. ① Incl. spec chrg. of $4.6 mill., 1995; $7.7 mill., 1999, $12.5 mill., 2000; $8.2 mill., 2001. ② Incl. spin-off rel. chrg. of $27.4 mill. ③ Incl. net gain of $30.4 mill. on sale of bus.

OFFICERS:
C. A. Kuebler, Chmn., C.E.O.
J. L. Herring, Pres., C.O.O.

INVESTOR CONTACT: Parag P. Bhansali, Investor Relations, (609) 452-4953

PRINCIPAL OFFICE: 210 Carnegie Center, Princeton, NJ 08540

TELEPHONE NUMBER: (609) 452-4440
FAX: (609) 452-9375
WEB: www.covance.com

NO. OF EMPLOYEES: 6,900 (approx.)

SHAREHOLDERS: 6,290

ANNUAL MEETING: In May

INCORPORATED: DE, 1996

INSTITUTIONAL HOLDINGS:
No. of Institutions: 220
Shares Held: 49,527,358
% Held: 82.8

INDUSTRY: Commercial physical research (SIC: 8731)

TRANSFER AGENT(S): Computershare Investor Services, Chicago, IL

COX COMMUNICATIONS, INC.

EXCH.	SYM.	REC. PRICE	P/E RATIO	YLD.	MKT. CAP.	RANGE (52-WK.)	'02 Y/E PR.
NYSE	COX	29.65 (2/28/03)	...	...	$17.78 bill.	40.05 - 18.95	28.40

LOWER MEDIUM GRADE. FOR 2003, THE COMPANY EXPECTS REVENUE GROWTH IN THE RANGE OF 14.0% TO 15.0%.

INTERIM EARNINGS (Per Share):

Qtr.	Mar.	June	Sept.	Dec.
1997	d0.07	0.12	d0.15	d0.15
1998	d0.19	d0.02	1.95	0.56
1999	0.45	0.90	0.02	0.18
2000	1.74	0.15	1.37	d0.12
2001	1.12	0.05	0.24	d0.18
2002	0.22	d0.86	d0.12	0.28

INTERIM DIVIDENDS (Per Share):

Amt.	Decl.	Ex.	Rec.	Pay.
		No dividends paid.		

CAPITALIZATION (12/31/01):

	($000)	(%)
Long-Term Debt	8,417,675	46.5
Preferred Stock.................	4,836	0.0
Common & Surplus	9,670,955	53.4
Total	18,093,466	100.0

*7 YEAR PRICE SCORE 105.5   ***12 MONTH PRICE SCORE 106.0**

*NYSE COMPOSITE INDEX=100

BUSINESS:

Cox Communications, Inc. is a multi-service broadband communications company serving approximately 6.3 million customers nationwide as of 2/12/03. The Company is the nation's fourth-largest cable television provider, and offers both traditional analog video programming under the Cox Cable brand as well as advanced digital video programming under the Cox Digital Cable brand. In addition, COX provides an array of other communications and entertainment services, including local and long distance telephone under the Cox Digital Telephone brand; high-speed Internet access with 1.4 million customers as of 2/12/03 under the brands Cox High Speed Internet and Cox Express; and commercial voice and data services via its affiliate Cox Business Services, LLC. The Company is also an investor in programming networks including The Discovery Channel.

RECENT DEVELOPMENTS:

For the year ended 12/31/02, the Company posted a net loss of $274.0 million versus income of $37.9 million, before an accounting gain of $717.1 million, the previous year. Earnings included a gain of $1.13 billion in 2002 and a loss of $212.0 million in 2001 on derivative instruments, and a loss of $1.35 billion in 2002 and a gain of $1.11 billion in 2001 on investments. Results also included a loss on the sale of Cable Systems of $3.9 million in 2002 and a one-time charge of $148.0 million related to the transition of high-speed Internet customers from Excite@Home in 2001. Total revenues grew 18.5% to $5.04 billion from $4.25 billion the year before.

PROSPECTS:

The Company's outlook remains encouraging, supported by strong gains in digital telephone and broadband Internet subscribers. Full-year 2002 broadband customer levels rose 59.0% to 1.4 million, while 58.0% more customers picked up digital telephone service, bringing the total to more than 718,400 customers. For 2003, COX expects revenue to increase between 14.0% and 15.0% over 2002 levels, with operating cash flow to increase in the range of 14.0% and 15.0%, and capital expenditures of about $1.60 billion. Basic video customers are expected to increase 1.0% over 2002 and new-service revenue generating unit net additions are expected to be between 1.0 to 1.1 million.

ANNUAL FINANCIAL DATA:

FISCAL YEAR	TOT. REVS. ($mill.)	NET INC. ($mill.)	TOT. ASSETS ($mill.)	OPER. PROFIT %	NET PROFIT %	RET. ON EQUITY %	RET. ON ASSETS %	CURR. RATIO	EARN. PER SH.$	CASH FL.PER SH.$	TANG. BK. VAL.$	PRICE RANGE	AVG. P/E RATIO
p12/31/02	5,038.6	d274.0		...	...	...	...	...	d0.45	...	...	42.09 - 18.95	...
12/31/01	4,067.0	② 37.9	25,061.4	...	0.9	0.4	0.2	0.1	② 0.06	2.59	...	50.25 - 36.40	720.9
12/31/00	3,506.9	1,925.3	24,720.8	4.0	54.9	20.9	7.8	0.1	3.16	5.20	...	58.38 - 31.69	14.3
12/31/99	2,318.1	727.2	26,614.5	4.7	31.4	6.3	2.7	...	1.51	2.47	2.25	52.00 - 32.00	27.8
12/31/98	1,716.8	① 1,270.7	12,878.1	11.7	74.0	23.6	9.9	0.1	① 2.30	3.13	2.55	35.38 - 17.19	11.4
12/31/97	1,610.4	① d136.5	6,556.6	12.7	...	...	...	0.4	① d0.25	0.50	...	19.97 - 9.00	...
12/31/96	1,460.3	① d51.6	5,784.6	15.2	...	...	...	0.3	① d0.09	0.52	...	12.06 - 8.31	...
12/31/95	1,286.2	103.8	5,555.3	17.6	8.1	4.5	1.9	0.3	...	...	...	10.75 - 7.00	...
12/31/94	736.3	26.6	1,874.7	19.0	3.6	3.2	1.4	0.2	...	...	...	...	...
12/31/93	708.0	77.1	1,527.4	25.4	10.9	10.8	5.0	0.3	...	...	...	...	...

Statistics are as originally reported. Adj. for stk. split: 2-for-1, 12/99 ① Incl. gain on issuance of stk. by affiliated companies: 1998, $165.3 mill.; 1997, $90;8 mill., 1996, $50.1 mill. ② Excl. acctg. change chrg. $717.1 mill.

OFFICERS:
J. C. Kennedy, Chmn.
J. O. Robbins, Pres., C.E.O.
J. W. Hayes, Exec. V.P., C.F.O.
INVESTOR CONTACT: Lacey Lewis, Investor Relations, (404) 269-7608
PRINCIPAL OFFICE: 1400 Lake Hearn Drive N.E., Atlanta, GA 30319

TELEPHONE NUMBER: (404) 843-5000
FAX: (404) 843-5030
WEB: www.cox.com
NO. OF EMPLOYEES: 20,700 (approx.)
SHAREHOLDERS: 5,924 (class A); 2 (class C); 3 (pref.)
ANNUAL MEETING: In May
INCORPORATED: DE, May, 1994

INSTITUTIONAL HOLDINGS:
No. of Institutions: 319
Shares Held: 209,997,310
% Held: 33.9
INDUSTRY: Cable and other pay TV services (SIC: 4841)
TRANSFER AGENT(S): Wachovia Bank, N.A., Charlotte, NC

COX RADIO, INC.

EXCH.	SYM.	REC. PRICE	P/E RATIO	YLD.	MKT. CAP.	RANGE (52-WK.)	'02 Y/E PR.
NYSE	CXR	21.40 (2/28/03)	36.3	...	$2.14 bill.	31.73 - 18.60	22.81

MEDIUM GRADE. THE COMPANY IS BENEFITING FROM ITS LONG-TERM FOCUS ON BUILDING STRONG LOCAL BRANDS.

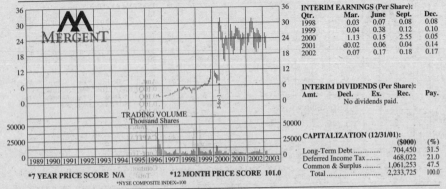

INTERIM EARNINGS (Per Share):

Qtr.	Mar.	June	Sept.	Dec.
1998	0.03	0.07	0.08	0.08
1999	0.04	0.38	0.12	0.10
2000	1.13	0.15	2.55	0.05
2001	d0.02	0.06	0.04	0.14
2002	0.07	0.17	0.18	0.17

INTERIM DIVIDENDS (Per Share):

Amt.	Decl.	Ex.	Rec.	Pay.
	No dividends paid.			

CAPITALIZATION (12/31/01):

	($000)	(%)
Long-Term Debt	704,450	31.5
Deferred Income Tax	468,022	21.0
Common & Surplus	1,061,253	47.5
Total	2,233,725	100.0

*7 YEAR PRICE SCORE N/A   *12 MONTH PRICE SCORE 101.0
*NYSE COMPOSITE INDEX=100

TRADING VOLUME
Thousand Shares

BUSINESS:

Cox Radio, Inc. is the third-largest radio broadcasting company in the U.S., based on net revenues. As of 2/20/03, CXR owned, operated, or provided sales and marketing services for 79 stations (68 FM and 11 AM) clustered in 18 markets, including major markets such as Atlanta, Houston, Miami, Tampa, Orlando and San Antonio. CXR is an indirect majority-owned subsidiary of Cox Enterprises, Inc. Cox Enterprises indirectly owned approximately 62.0% of the Company's common stock and had approximately 94.0% of the voting power in CXR as of 11/8/02.

RECENT DEVELOPMENTS:

For the year ended 12/31/02, income was $59.9 million, before an accounting change charge of $13.9 million, versus income of $21.5 million, before an accounting change charge of $787,000, the year before. Results for 2002 and 2001 included gains on the sale of radio stations of $304,000 and $2.4 million, and losses on the sale of assets of $617,000 and $337,000, respectively. Also, results for 2001 included a one-time tax benefit of $10.9 million

related to a revision of CXR's state income tax rate. Total net revenues increased 6.4% to $420.6 million from $395.3 million the previous year, reflecting strong growth from a majority of CXR's markets, including double-digit revenue growth in Houston, Miami, Jacksonville, Tampa, Long Island, Richmond, Honolulu and Louisville. Local net revenues grew 5.6% to $308.9 million, while national net revenues improved 10.7% to $89.9 million.

PROSPECTS:

The improved financial performance was primarily the result of the Company's long-term focus on building strong local brands. Looking ahead, CXR continues to remain cautious in its outlook as advertisers may hold back on spending amid the uncertain economic and geo-political climate. Nevertheless, CXR maintains a strong internal cash flow and solid competitive positions within its mar-

kets. For the first quarter of 2003, CXR expects to report net revenue growth of about 6.0% and diluted earnings per share of approximately $0.08. This guidance includes the effect of the WFOX-FM reformat in Atlanta, and additional marketing and promotion costs associated with competitive situations in Atlanta, Miami and Birmingham.

ANNUAL FINANCIAL DATA:

FISCAL YEAR	TOT. REVS. ($mill.)	NET INC. ($mill.)	TOT. ASSETS ($mill.)	OPER. PROFIT %	NET PROFIT %	RET. ON EQUITY %	RET. ON ASSETS %	CURR. RATIO	EARN. PER SH.$	CASH FL. PER SH.$	TANG. BK. VAL.$	PRICE RANGE	AVG. P/E RATIO
p12/31/02	420.6	③ 59.9							③ 0.60			30.45 - 18.60	40.9
12/31/01	395.3	② 21.5	2,286.7	17.2	5.4	2.0	0.9	2.0	② 0.22	0.91	...	29.38 - 17.69	106.9
12/31/00	369.4	① 305.9	2,317.8	153.2	82.8	29.6	13.2	2.6	① 3.26	3.71	...	32.00 - 6.72	5.9
12/31/99	300.5	55.3	986.6	39.2	18.4	14.6	5.6	2.2	0.64	0.97	...	11.89 - 4.15	12.6
12/31/98	261.2	23.0	753.1	23.9	8.8	7.4	3.1	2.3	0.27	0.54	...	5.71 - 2.92	16.1
12/31/97	199.6	49.7	654.6	22.8	24.9	17.3	7.6	2.2	0.58	d0.36	...	4.83 - 1.89	5.8
12/31/96	132.9	14.9	261.7	20.8	11.2	4.6	5.7	2.9	0.23	0.29	1.15	2.74 - 1.72	9.7
12/31/95	123.6	8.2	191.8	16.6	6.6	17.3	4.3	2.7	0.02	0.19	...	...	...
12/31/94	111.5	11.2	180.0	22.9	10.0	27.7	6.2	2.7	...	...	...	...	...
12/31/93	95.0	4.4	...	17.1	4.6	...	...	...	...	...	...	...	...

Statistics are as originally reported. Adj. for 3-for-1 stk. spl., 5/00 ① Incl. net after-tax gain $244.6 mill. ② Bef. acctg. chng. chrg. $787,000; incl. net non-recurr. gain of $2.1 mill. ③ Bef. acctg. chng. chrg. $13.9 mill.; Incl. net non-recurr. loss of $313,000

OFFICERS:
D. E. Easterly, Chmn.
R. F. Neil, Pres., C.E.O.
N. O. Johnston, V.P., C.F.O.
INVESTOR CONTACT: Charles Odom, (404) 843-5000
PRINCIPAL OFFICE: 1400 Lake Hearn Drive, Atlanta, GA 30319

TELEPHONE NUMBER: (404) 843-5000
FAX: (404) 843-5890
WEB: www.coxradio.com
NO. OF EMPLOYEES: 2,336
SHAREHOLDERS: N/A
ANNUAL MEETING: In May
INCORPORATED: DE, 1996

INSTITUTIONAL HOLDINGS:
No. of Institutions: 142
Shares Held: 40,842,878
% Held: 40.7
INDUSTRY: Radio broadcasting stations (SIC: 4832)
TRANSFER AGENT(S): Wachovia Bank, N.A., Charlotte, NC

CRANE CO.

EXCH.	SYM.	REC. PRICE	P/E RATIO	YLD.	MKT. CAP.	RANGE (52-WK.)	'02 Y/E PR.
NYSE	CR	17.28 (2/28/03)	64.0	2.3%	$1.03 bill.	28.99 - 15.19	19.93

MEDIUM GRADE. THE COMPANY ACQUIRED GENERAL TECHNOLOGY CORPORATION FOR $25.0 MILLION IN CASH AND ASSUMED DEBT.

*7 YEAR PRICE SCORE 95.1   *12 MONTH PRICE SCORE 85.1
*NYSE COMPOSITE INDEX=100

INTERIM EARNINGS (Per Share):

Qtr.	Mar.	June	Sept.	Dec.
1997	0.33	0.42	0.45	0.43
1998	0.43	0.53	0.53	0.51
1999	0.49	0.57	0.27	0.22
2000	0.45	0.78	0.35	0.44
2001	0.33	0.54	0.30	0.30
2002	0.35	0.44	0.34	d0.86

INTERIM DIVIDENDS (Per Share):

Amt.	Decl.	Ex.	Rec.	Pay.
0.10Q	1/28/02	2/27/02	3/01/02	3/12/02
0.10Q	5/20/02	5/30/02	6/03/02	6/12/02
0.10Q	8/19/02	8/29/02	9/03/02	9/12/02
0.10Q	10/28/02	11/29/02	12/03/02	12/12/02
0.10Q	1/27/03	2/27/03	3/03/03	3/12/03

Indicated div.: $0.40 (Div. Reinv. Plan)

CAPITALIZATION (12/31/01):

	($000)	(%)
Long-Term Debt	302,368	31.0
Deferred Income Tax	20,888	2.1
Common & Surplus	651,295	66.8
Total	974,551	100.0

BUSINESS:

Crane Co. is a diversified manufacturer of engineered industrial products. Products include vending machines, airplane braking devices, pumps, valves and other industrial goods. Industries served range from aerospace manufacturing, power generation and hydrocarbon processing to commercial and residential building, plumbing, and food and beverage production. The Company has five reporting segments: Fluid Handling, which accounted for 44.5% of 2002 sales, Aerospace 21.5%, Engineered Materials 19.0%, Merchandising Systems 10.7%, and Controls 4.3%.

RECENT DEVELOPMENTS:

For the year ended 12/31/02, income was $16.6 million, before an accounting change charge of $28.1 million, versus net income of $88.6 million a year earlier. Results for 2002 and 2001 included pre-tax asbestos charges of $115.3 million and $2.2 million, respectively. CR noted that the asbestos charge for 2002 reflects the recent significant increase in the rate of new claims filed and the estimated settlement and defense costs of pending and future asbestos claims through 2007, net of estimated insurance recoveries. CR believes that the level of uncertainty is too great to provide for reasonable estimation beyond 2007. Results for 2001 also included a special stock-based retirement charge of $6.1 million and goodwill amortization of $18.1 million. Total net sales fell 4.5% to $1.52 billion, reflecting lower sales results across CR's five reporting segments with the exception of Fluid Handling.

PROSPECTS:

CR's near-term prospects look to be challenging. On the plus side, the Company expects the recreational vehicle market to remain strong and the truck trailer transportation market to improve in 2003. Also, CR sees a 20.0% improvement in Fluid Handling operating profit in 2003. However, weakness from CR's Aerospace and Merchandise Systems segments temper the Company's overall outlook. Separately, on 11/25/02, CR announced the purchase of General Technology Corporation for $25.0 million in cash and assumed debt. General Technology, which posted 2001 sales of about $22.0 million, provides high-reliability customized contract manufacturing services and products focused on military and defense applications.

ANNUAL FINANCIAL DATA:

FISCAL YEAR	TOT. REVS. ($mill.)	NET INC. ($mill.)	TOT. ASSETS ($mill.)	OPER. PROFIT %	NET PROFIT %	RET. ON EQUITY %	RET. ON ASSETS %	CURR. RATIO	EARN. PER SH.$	CASH FL. PER SH.$	TANG. BK. VAL.$	DIV. PER SH.$	PRICE RANGE	AVG. P/E RATIO	AVG. YIELD %
p12/31/02	1,516.3	④ 16.6							④ 0.28			0.40	28.99 - 17.72	83.4	1.7
12/31/01	1,587.2	① 88.6	1,292.1	10.8	5.6	13.6	6.9	2.1	① 1.47	2.70	3.87	0.40	32.25 - 19.95	17.8	1.5
12/31/00	1,491.2	③ 123.7	1,143.9	12.3	8.3	20.4	10.8	2.2	③ 2.03	2.92	4.11	0.40	29.50 - 18.63	11.9	1.7
12/31/99	1,553.7	② 100.9	1,175.4	10.9	6.5	17.8	8.6	2.2	② 1.50	2.40	3.10	0.40	32.75 - 16.06	16.3	1.6
12/31/98	2,268.5	138.4	1,454.7	10.5	6.1	21.5	9.5	2.0	2.00	2.88	3.33	0.37	37.58 - 21.75	14.8	1.2
12/31/97	2,036.8	112.8	1,185.9	9.7	5.5	21.2	9.5	2.1	1.63	2.42	3.81	0.33	31.50 - 18.33	15.3	1.3
12/31/96	1,847.7	⑤ 92.1	1,088.9	9.0	5.0	19.9	8.5	2.1	⑤ 1.34	2.05	2.95	0.33	21.00 - 16.00	13.8	1.8
12/31/95	1,782.3	76.3	998.4	8.0	4.3	20.4	7.6	2.1	1.11	1.82	2.14	0.33	17.56 - 11.50	13.1	2.3
12/31/94	1,653.5	55.9	1,008.0	6.6	3.4	17.1	5.5	2.0	0.83	1.48	1.38	0.33	13.11 - 10.72	14.4	2.8
12/31/93	1,310.2	48.9	744.2	6.6	3.7	16.8	6.6	1.4	0.73	1.15	2.55	0.33	13.72 - 10.06	16.4	2.8

Statistics are as originally reported. Adj. for all stk. splits & divs. thru 50%, 9/98. ① Incl. non-recurr. chrg. 12/31/01: $6.1 mill.; chrg. 12/31/96: $2.3 mill. ② Bef. inc. of $13.7 mill. fr. disc. ops. & incl. pre-tax spec. chgs. of $35.0 mill. ③ Incl. gain fr. sale of investments of $28.9 mill. ($0.26/sh.) ④ Incl. pre-tax asbestos chrg. of $115.3 mill.; bef. acctg. change chrg. of $28.1 mill.

OFFICERS:
R. S. Evans, Chmn.
E. C. Fast, Pres., C.E.O.
A. I. duPont, V.P., Sec., Gen. Couns.
INVESTOR CONTACT: Shareholder Relations, (888) 272-6327
PRINCIPAL OFFICE: 100 First Stamford Place, Stamford, CT 06092

TELEPHONE NUMBER: (203) 363-7300
FAX: (203) 363-7295
WEB: www.craneco.com
NO. OF EMPLOYEES: 9,600 (approx.)
SHAREHOLDERS: 4,525 (approx. record)
ANNUAL MEETING: In Apr.
INCORPORATED: DE, May, 1985

INSTITUTIONAL HOLDINGS:
No. of Institutions: 189
Shares Held: 34,332,233
% Held: 57.7
INDUSTRY: Fluid power valves & hose fittings (SIC: 3492)
TRANSFER AGENT(S): Equiserve/First Chicago Trust Division, Jersey City, NJ

CRESCENT REAL ESTATE EQUITIES COMPANY

EXCH.	SYM.	REC. PRICE	P/E RATIO	YLD.	MKT. CAP.	RANGE (52-WK.)	'02 Y/E PR.
NYSE	CEI	14.75 (2/28/03)	22.0	10.2%	$1.54 bill.	20.15 - 13.18	16.64

MEDIUM GRADE. THE COMPANY SHOULD CONTINUE TO BENEFIT FROM THE SALE OF HOTEL/RESORT AND RESIDENTIAL DEVELOPMENT PROPERTIES.

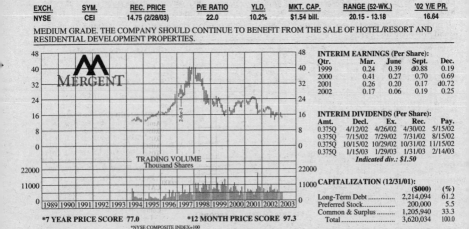

*7 YEAR PRICE SCORE 77.0 ***12 MONTH PRICE SCORE 97.3**
*NYSE COMPOSITE INDEX=100

INTERIM EARNINGS (Per Share):

Qtr.	Mar.	June	Sept.	Dec.
1999	0.24	0.39	d0.88	0.19
2000	0.41	0.27	0.70	0.69
2001	0.26	0.20	0.17	d0.72
2002	0.17	0.06	0.19	0.25

INTERIM DIVIDENDS (Per Share):

Amt.	Decl.	Ex.	Rec.	Pay.
0.375Q	4/12/02	4/26/02	4/30/02	5/15/02
0.375Q	7/15/02	7/29/02	7/31/02	8/15/02
0.375Q	10/15/02	10/29/02	10/31/02	11/15/02
0.375Q	1/15/03	1/29/03	1/31/03	2/14/03

Indicated div.: $1.50

CAPITALIZATION (12/31/01):

	($000)	(%)
Long-Term Debt	2,214,094	61.2
Preferred Stock	200,000	5.5
Common & Surplus	1,205,940	33.3
Total	3,620,034	100.0

BUSINESS:

Crescent Real Estate Equities Company operates as a real estate investment trust and provides management, leasing and development services. CEI operates in five investment segments: Office, Resorts and Hotels, Residential Development, Temperature-controlled Logistics, and Behavioral Healthcare. As of 12/31/02, the office segment consisted of 73 office properties, with 29.5 million square feet of rentable space in major metropolitan markets across theSouthwest. The resort and hotel segment is comprised of three luxury resorts and spas and two Canyon Ranch destination fitness resorts and spas. The residential development segment consisted of five residential corporations that own 19 properties through joint venture or partnership agreements. The temperature-controlled logistics segment consisted of 89 facilities, while the behavioral healthcare segment consisted of 21 properties, all of which are up for sale. CEI's other investments include four full-service hotels.

RECENT DEVELOPMENTS:

For the year ended 12/31/02, income was $88.4 million, before an accounting change charge of $9.2 million and income of $8.5 million from discontinued operations, versus income of $3.3 million, before an extraordinary loss of $10.8 million and income of $2.8 million from discontinued operations. Results for 2002 and 2001 included net pre-tax impairment and other charges of $12.2 million and $118.1 million, respectively, and pre-tax gains of $39.0 million and $4.4 million, respectively, from property sales. Total revenues advanced 48.9% to $1.02 billion from $682.5 million the year before, due to higher sales of resort/hotel and residential development property.

PROSPECTS:

On 1/2/03, the Company announced that it agreed to sell the City of Houston land in front of Houston's downtown George R. Brown Convention Center as part of a litigation settlement related to the intended use of the Compaq Center, located in CEI's Greenway Plaza. CEI received approximately $33.0 million in proceeds from the sale. Separately, CEI announced that it has acquired a 30.0% interest in 5 Post Oak Park, a 28-story, 567,000 square-foot class A office building in the Galleria submarket of Houston, for $65.0 million.

ANNUAL FINANCIAL DATA:

FISCAL YEAR	TOT. INC. ($mill.)	NET INC. ($mill.)	TOT. ASSETS ($mill.)	NET INC. +DEPR./ ASSETS %	RET. ON EQUITY %	RET. ON ASSETS %	EARN. PER SH.$	TANG. BK. VAL.$	DIV. PER SH.$	DIV. PAYOUT %	PRICE RANGE	AVG. P/E RATIO	AVG. YIELD %
p12/31/02	1,016.4	⑤ 88.4					⑤ 0.64		1.50	234.4	20.15 - 13.18	26.0	9.0
12/31/01	696.1	④ 6.1	4,142.1	3.4	0.4	0.2	④ d0.07	11.53	2.02	...	25.24 - 16.30	...	9.7
12/31/00	718.4	①② 252.1	4,531.8	8.5	14.6	5.6	①②③ 2.05	12.57	2.20	107.3	23.44 - 15.75	9.6	11.2
12/31/99	746.3	② 11.0	4,950.6	3.1	0.5	0.2	② d0.06	15.28	2.20	...	25.50 - 15.13	...	10.8
12/31/98	698.3	165.6	5,043.4	5.8	6.8	3.3	1.21	17.84	1.69	139.7	40.38 - 21.06	25.4	5.5
12/31/97	447.4	117.3	4,180.0	4.7	5.3	2.8	1.20	18.62	1.29	107.9	40.75 - 25.13	27.4	3.9
12/31/96	208.9	① 38.4	1,730.9	4.7	4.4	2.2	① 0.72	11.97	1.13	156.9	26.63 - 16.06	29.6	5.3
12/31/95	130.0	27.4	964.2	6.0	6.7	2.8	0.66	12.67	1.02	156.5	17.94 - 12.50	23.2	6.7
⑤ 12/31/94	50.3	①② 9.2	538.4	4.5	3.9	1.7	①② 0.28	7.33	0.40	141.0	15.00 - 12.25	48.6	2.9
12/31/93	55.6	①② d53.0	290.9	...	...	...	...	...	...	...	...	...	...

Statistics are as originally reported. ① Bef. extraord. chrg., 2000, $3.9 mill.; 1996, $1.3 mill.; 1994, $949,000; credit, 1993, $58.4 mill. ② Incl. non-recurr. gain, 2000, $119.6 mill.; chrgs., 1999, $193.8 mill.; 1994, $1.9 mill.; 1993, $37.6 mill. ③ For the period from 5/5/94 ④ Bef. extraord. loss of $10.8 mill., incl. impair. & other chrgs. of $118.1 mill. & gain of $4.4 mill. on the sale of prop. ⑤ Incl. pre-tax impair. chrg. of $12.2 mill. & pre-tax gain of $39.0 mill. from prop. sales; excl. acctg. chng. chrg. of $9.2 mill. & income of $8.5 mill. from disc. ops.

OFFICERS:
R. E. Rainwater, Chmn.
J. C. Goff, Vice-Chmn.C.E.O.
D. Alberts, Pres., C.O.O.
INVESTOR CONTACT: Jane E. Mody, Investor Relations, (817) 321-1086
PRINCIPAL OFFICE: 777 Main Street, Suite 2100, Fort Worth, TX 76102

TELEPHONE NUMBER: (817) 321-2100
FAX: (817) 321-2000
WEB: www.cei-crescent.com
NO. OF EMPLOYEES: 794
SHAREHOLDERS: 1,040 (approx., record)
ANNUAL MEETING: In June
INCORPORATED: MD, Feb., 1994

INSTITUTIONAL HOLDINGS:
No. of Institutions: 168
Shares Held: 59,086,858
% Held: 58.5
INDUSTRY: Real estate investment trusts (SIC: 6798)
TRANSFER AGENT(S): Boston Equiserve L.P., Boston, MA

CROMPTON CORPORATION

EXCH.	SYM.	REC. PRICE	P/E RATIO	YLD.	MKT. CAP.	RANGE (52-WK.)	'02 Y/E PR.
NYSE	CK	4.69 (2/28/03)	36.1	4.3%	$0.53 bill.	13.00 - 4.69	5.95

LOWER MEDIUM GRADE. THE COMPANY ANTICIPATES EARNINGS PER SHARE FOR 2003 TO BE IN THE RANGE OF $0.45 TO $0.55, EXCLUDING SPECIAL ITEMS.

*7 YEAR PRICE SCORE N/A   ***12 MONTH PRICE SCORE 67.3**
*NYSE COMPOSITE INDEX=100

INTERIM EARNINGS (Per Share):

Qtr.	Mar.	June	Sept.	Dec.
1998	0.42	0.52	0.40	1.11
1999	0.86	0.57	d2.21	d0.77
2000	0.26	0.36	0.19	d0.03
2001	0.14	0.12	d0.60	d0.76
2002	0.06	d0.06	0.11	0.02

INTERIM DIVIDENDS (Per Share):

Amt.	Decl.	Ex.	Rec.	Pay.
0.05Q	1/22/02	1/30/02	2/01/02	2/22/02
0.05Q	4/30/02	5/01/02	5/03/02	5/24/02
0.05Q	7/23/02	7/31/02	8/02/02	8/23/02
0.05Q	10/23/02	10/30/02	11/01/02	11/22/02
0.05Q	1/21/03	2/05/03	2/07/03	2/28/03

Indicated div.: $0.20

CAPITALIZATION (12/31/01):

	($000)	(%)
Long-Term Debt	1,392,833	71.8
Common & Surplus	547,541	28.2
Total	1,940,374	100.0

BUSINESS:

Crompton Corporation (formerly CK Witco Corporation) was formed on 9/1/99 through the merger of Crompton & Knowles Corporation and Witco Corporation. The Company is a manufacturer and marketer of specialty chemicals and polymers. The Company operates in two businesses: polymer products and specialty products. These products include polymers, polymer additives, rubber chemicals, urethane chemicals, polymer processing equipment, organosilicones, crop protection chemicals, industrial surfactants, petroleum additives, refined products, industrial colors and glycerine/fatty acids. The Company does business in more than 120 countries. Major subsidiaries include: Witco; Uniroyal Chemical; OSI Specialties; and Davis-Standard Corporation. Revenues for 2002 were derived: polymer products, 60.4%; and specialty products, 39.6%.

RECENT DEVELOPMENTS:

For the year ended 12/31/02, earnings were $15.5 million, before an accounting change charge of $299.0 million, versus a net loss of $123.9 million in 2001. Results for 2002 and 2001 included charges of $23.3 million and $106.5 million, respectively, from facility closures, severance and related costs. Results for 2002 also included antitrust investigation costs of $6.3 million, while results for 2001 included impairment of long-lived assets of $80.4 million. Net sales declined 6.3% to $2.55 billion from $2.72 billion in the prior year, primarily due to lower selling prices.

PROSPECTS:

Improved unit volume and favorable currency translation are helping to offset lower selling prices. Near-term results should continue to benefit from the Company's divestiture of the industrial specialties business in 2002 and debt reduction efforts. CK's primary goal for 2003 will be to continue to focus on debt reduction initiatives in an attempt to offset sluggish economic conditions. The Company estimates earnings per share for 2003 to be in the range of $0.45 to $0.55, excluding special items.

ANNUAL FINANCIAL DATA:

FISCAL YEAR	TOT. REVS. ($mill.)	NET INC. ($mill.)	TOT. ASSETS ($mill.)	OPER. PROFIT %	NET PROFIT %	RET. ON EQUITY %	RET. ON ASSETS %	CURR. RATIO	EARN. PER SH.$	CASH FL. PER SH.$	DIV. PER SH.$	PRICE RANGE	AVG. P/E RATIO	AVG. YIELD %
p12/31/02	2,546.9	⑧ 15.5							⑧ 0.13		0.20	13.00 - 5.44	70.9	2.2
12/31/01	2,718.8	⑦ d123.9	3,232.2	...	...	...	...	1.2	⑦ d1.10	0.55	0.20	12.19 - 6.20	...	2.2
12/31/00	3,038.4	⑥ 89.3	3,528.3	8.8	2.9	11.8	2.5	1.5	⑥ 0.78	2.36	0.20	14.19 - 6.94	13.5	1.9
12/31/99	2,092.4	⑤ d159.4	3,726.6	0.1	...	...	...	1.1	⑤ d1.91	d0.51	0.05	17.50 - 7.25	...	0.4
12/31/98	1,796.1	④ 183.2	1,408.9	12.2	10.2	274.7	13.0	1.5	④ 2.42	3.48	...	...	...	...
12/31/97	1,851.2	③ 92.1	1,548.8	12.1	5.0	...	5.9	2.0	③ 1.22	2.28	...	...	...	...
① 12/31/96	1,804.0	② d22.1	1,657.2	5.7	...	...	...	...	② d0.31	0.84	...	...	...	...

Statistics are as originally reported. Results for 1998 and earlier are for Crompton & Knowles Corp. ① Incl. results of Uniroyal Chem. Corp., acq. in 8/96. ② Excl. $441,000 extraord. chg. and incl. $85.0 merg. chgs. & $30.0 mill. spl. environ. provision. ③ Excl. $5.2 mill. extraord. loss. ④ Excl. $21.5 mill. extraord. loss and incl. $5.0 mill. net chg. for acct. chg. & $92.1 mill. net gain fr. sale of int. in bus. ⑤ Bef. $15.7 mill. extraord. loss and incl. $26.8 mill. gain fr. sale of bus., $195.0 mill. acq. in-process R&D chg., $20.6 mill. merg. chg., & $65.5 mill. loss fr. sale of bus. ⑥ Incl. $15.0 mill. chg. fr. facility shutdown costs. ⑦ Incl. $75.0 mill. chg. fr. facility closings, $50.8 mill. impair. of assets & $14.1 mill. loss fr. sale of bus. ⑧ Incl. $23.3 mill. fr. facility closings, $6.3 mill. antitrust invest. costs & excl. $299.0 mill. acctg. chg.

OFFICERS:
V. A. Calarco, Chmn., Pres., C.E.O.
P. Barna, Sr. V.P., C.F.O.
J. R. Jespen, V.P., Treas.
INVESTOR CONTACT: William A. Kuser, Investor Relations, (203) 552-2213
PRINCIPAL OFFICE: One American Lane, Greenwich, CT 06831-2559

TELEPHONE NUMBER: (203) 552-2000
FAX: (203) 353-5424
WEB: www.cromptoncorp.com
NO. OF EMPLOYEES: 7,340 (approx.)
SHAREHOLDERS: 6,040
ANNUAL MEETING: In Apr.
INCORPORATED: DE, Sept., 1999

INSTITUTIONAL HOLDINGS:
No. of Institutions: 165
Shares Held: 92,577,718
% Held: 81.4
INDUSTRY: Industrial organic chemicals, nec (SIC: 2869)
TRANSFER AGENT(S): Mellon Investor Services, Ridgefield Park, NJ

CSX CORPORATION

EXCH.	SYM.	REC. PRICE	P/E RATIO	YLD.	MKT. CAP.	RANGE (52-WK.)	'02 Y/E PR.
NYSE	CSX	26.86 (2/28/03)	12.3	1.5%	$5.74 bill.	41.40 - 25.09	28.31

MEDIUM GRADE. THE COMPANY REACHED AN AGREEMENT TO SELL ITS DOMESTIC CONTAINER SHIPPING UNIT, CSX LINES, LLC FOR APPROXIMATELY $300.0 MILLION IN CASH AND SECURITIES.

TRADING VOLUME
Thousand Shares

*7 YEAR PRICE SCORE 85.2   ***12 MONTH PRICE SCORE 94.7**

*NYSE COMPOSITE INDEX=100

INTERIM EARNINGS (Per Share):

Qtr.	Mar.	June	Sept.	Dec.
1998	0.41	0.68	0.88	0.51
1999	0.36	0.53	d0.54	d0.12
2000	0.12	0.23	0.28	0.26
2001	0.10	0.51	0.47	0.31
2002	0.32	0.63	0.60	0.64

INTERIM DIVIDENDS (Per Share):

Amt.	Decl.	Ex.	Rec.	Pay.
0.10Q	4/23/02	5/22/02	5/24/02	6/14/02
0.10Q	7/10/02	8/21/02	8/23/02	9/13/02
0.10Q	10/10/02	11/20/02	11/22/02	12/13/02
0.10Q	2/12/03	2/25/03	2/25/03	3/14/03

Indicated div.: $0.40 (Div. Reinv. Plan)

CAPITALIZATION (12/28/01):

	($000)	(%)
Long-Term Debt	5,839,000	37.5
Deferred Income Tax	3,621,000	23.2
Common & Surplus	6,120,000	39.3
Total	15,580,000	100.0

BUSINESS:

CSX Corporation is a freight transportation company with principal business units providing rail, intermodal, domestic container-shipping, and international terminal operations. The rail system, CSX Transportation Inc., operated over a more than 23,000 route-mile network in 23 states, the District of Columbia and two Canadian provinces, as of 12/31/02. CSX Intermodal Inc. operates a network of dedicated intermodal facilities across North America. CSX Lines provides domestic ocean liner service and operated 17 U.S.-flagged vessels and 22,000 containers serving the trade between ports on the U.S. mainland and Alaska, Guam, Hawaii and Puerto Rico, as of 12/31/02. CSX World Terminals operates terminal facilities at locations in Hong Kong, China, Australia, Europe, Russia and Latin America. As of 12/31/02, CSX and Norfolk Southern, through a jointly-owned acquisition entity, held economic interests in Conrail 42.0% and 58.0%, respectively.

RECENT DEVELOPMENTS:

For the year ended 12/27/02, earnings were $467.0 million, before an accounting change charge of $43.0 million, versus net earnings of $293.0 million a year earlier. Results for 2001 included a non-recurring litigation provision of $60.0 million. Operating revenues were $8.15 billion versus $8.11 billion the previous year, reflecting the weak economy. Rail and intermodal revenues slipped to $7.18 billion from $7.19 billion the year before. Operating income rose 17.8% to $1.13 billion from $957.0 million in 2001. Interest expense decreased 14.1% to $445.0 million.

PROSPECTS:

CSX's near-term outlook appears favorable, reflecting the Company's expectations of continued productivity gains and cost-reduction efforts. CSX noted that it expects to post revenue gains in 2003 in spite of a flat economy, due to the Company's pricing programs and modal conversion initiatives. Separately, on 12/17/02, CSX announced that it has reached an agreement to sell its domestic container shipping unit, CSX Lines, LLC, to a venture formed with The Carlyle Group for approximately $300.0 million in cash and securities. Closing of this transaction, which furthers CSX's strategy of becoming a more rail-based organization, is expected to take place by 3/31/03.

ANNUAL FINANCIAL DATA:

FISCAL YEAR	TOT. REVS. ($mill.)	NET INC. ($mill.)	TOT. ASSETS ($mill.)	OPER. PROFIT %	NET PROFIT %	RET. ON EQUITY %	RET. ON ASSETS %	CURR. RATIO	EARN. PER SH.$	CASH FL. PER SH.$	TANG. BK. VAL.$	DIV. PER SH.$	PRICE RANGE	AVG. P/E RATIO	AVG. YIELD %
p12/27/02	8,152.0	⑤467.0							⑤2.19			0.40	41.40 - 25.09	15.2	1.2
12/28/01	8,110.0	④293.0	20,801.0	11.8	3.6	4.8	1.4	0.6	④1.38	4.31	28.64	0.80	41.30 - 24.81	24.0	2.4
12/29/00	8,191.0	③186.0	20,491.0	9.8	2.3	3.1	0.9	0.4	③0.88	3.72	28.28	1.20	33.44 - 19.50	30.1	4.5
12/31/99	10,811.0	②51.0	20,720.0	5.6	0.5	0.9	0.2	0.7	②0.24	3.16	26.35	1.20	53.94 - 28.81	172.3	2.9
12/25/98	9,898.0	537.0	20,427.0	11.7	5.4	9.1	2.6	0.8	2.51	5.45	27.08	1.20	60.75 - 36.50	19.4	2.5
12/26/97	10,621.0	①799.0	19,957.0	14.9	7.5	13.9	4.0	0.8	①3.72	6.74	26.41	1.08	62.44 - 41.25	13.9	2.1
12/27/96	10,536.0	855.0	16,965.0	14.4	8.1	17.1	5.0	0.8	4.00	6.89	23.02	1.04	53.13 - 42.13	11.9	2.2
12/29/95	10,504.0	①618.0	14,282.0	11.2	5.9	14.6	4.3	0.6	①2.94	5.80	20.20	0.92	46.13 - 34.69	13.7	2.3
12/30/94	9,608.0	652.0	13,724.0	12.8	6.8	17.5	4.8	0.7	3.12	5.88	17.85	0.88	46.19 - 31.56	12.5	2.3
12/31/93	8,940.0	①359.0	15,385.0	10.2	4.0	11.3	2.3	0.4	①1.73	4.48	15.29	0.79	44.06 - 33.19	22.3	2.0

Statistics are as originally reported. Adj. for 2-for-1 stk. split, 12/95. ① Incl. non-recurr. chrgs. 12/31/97: $97.0 mill.; net chrg. 12/31/95: $206.0 mill.; chrg. 12/31/93: $61.0 mill. ② Incl. non-recurr. after-tax chrgs. of $34.0; non-recurr. after-tax gain of $17.0 mill.; non-recurr. chrg. of $271.0 mill.; Bef. acctg. chge. chrg. of $49.0 mill. ③ Bef. inc. fr. disc. opers. of $379.0 mill. ④ Incl. after-tax chrg. of $37.0 mill. for proposed litigation settlement. ⑤ Bef. acctg. chge. chrg. of $43.0 mill.

OFFICERS:
M. J. Ward, Chmn., Pres., C.E.O.
P. R. Goodwin, Vice-Chmn., C.F.O.
D. A. Boor, V.P., Treas.
INVESTOR CONTACT: Karen L. Kennedy, Admin., Shareholder Serv., (804) 782-1465
PRINCIPAL OFFICE: 901 East Cary Street, Richmond, VA 23219-4031

TELEPHONE NUMBER: (804) 782-1400
FAX: (804) 782-1409
WEB: www.csx.com
NO. OF EMPLOYEES: 38,916 (approx.)
SHAREHOLDERS: 62,048
ANNUAL MEETING: In Apr.
INCORPORATED: VA, 1980

INSTITUTIONAL HOLDINGS:
No. of Institutions: 358
Shares Held: 144,745,165
% Held: 67.9
INDUSTRY: Railroads, line-haul operating (SIC: 4011)
TRANSFER AGENT(S): Computershare Investor Services LLC, Chicago IL

CUMMINS INC.

EXCH.	SYM.	REC. PRICE	P/E RATIO	YLD.	MKT. CAP.	RANGE (52-WK.)	'02 Y/E PR.
NYSE	CUM	23.97 (2/28/03)	14.1	5.0%	$0.99 bill.	50.29 - 19.60	28.13

MEDIUM GRADE. THE COMPANY EXPECTS EARNINGS TO RANGE FROM $1.80 TO $2.00 PER SHARE IN 2003.

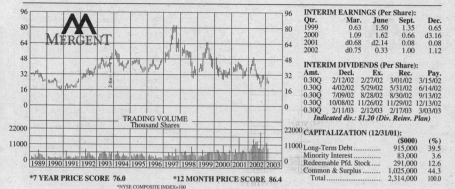

*7 YEAR PRICE SCORE 76.0   *12 MONTH PRICE SCORE 86.4

*NYSE COMPOSITE INDEX=100

INTERIM EARNINGS (Per Share):

Qtr.	Mar.	June	Sept.	Dec.
1999	0.63	1.50	1.35	0.65
2000	1.09	1.62	0.66	d3.16
2001	d0.68	d2.14	0.08	0.08
2002	d0.75	0.33	1.00	1.12

INTERIM DIVIDENDS (Per Share):

Amt.	Decl.	Ex.	Rec.	Pay.
0.30Q	2/12/02	2/27/02	3/01/02	3/15/02
0.30Q	4/02/02	5/29/02	5/31/02	6/14/02
0.30Q	7/09/02	8/28/02	8/30/02	9/13/02
0.30Q	10/08/02	11/26/02	11/29/02	12/13/02
0.30Q	2/11/03	2/12/03	2/17/03	3/03/03

Indicated div.: $1.20 (Div. Reinv. Plan)

CAPITALIZATION (12/31/01):

	($000)	(%)
Long-Term Debt	915,000	39.5
Minority Interest	83,000	3.6
Redeemable Pfd. Stock	291,000	12.6
Common & Surplus	1,025,000	44.3
Total	2,314,000	100.0

BUSINESS:

Cummins Inc. (formerly Cummins Engine Company Inc.) is a worldwide designer and manufacturer of electrical power generation systems, engines and related products including fuel systems, controls, air handling, filtration, and emission products. The Engine Group (55.5% of 2002 sales) offers diesel engines for heavy-duty trucks, medium-duty trucks, and bus and light commercial vehicles. The

Power Generation Group (19.8%) offers diesel, natural gas, and gasoline-fueled power generation sets. The Filtration Group and Other segment (15.4%) offers technical solutions including engine filters, hydraulic fluids and air. The International Distributor Group (9.3%) consists of 17 wholly-owned and three joint venture retail distributors that sell the Company's products.

RECENT DEVELOPMENTS:

For the year ended 12/31/02, the Company reported earnings of $70.0 million, before an accounting change gain of $3.0 million, compared with a net loss of $102.0 million a year earlier. Results for 2002 and 2001 included a credit of $14.0 million and a charge of $125.0 million for restructuring, asset impairment and other non-recurring charges. Results for 2002 also included a loss of $8.0 million on the early extinguishment of debt. Net sales increased 3.0% to

$5.85 billion from $5.68 billion a year earlier. Engine segment sales climbed 10.1% to $3.44 billion, while Filtration and other segment sales grew 7.0% to $951.0 million. International Distributor segment sales improved 2.1% to $574.0 million, while Power Generation segment sales fell 13.8% to $1.23 billion. Gross profit inched up 0.8% to $1.03 billion from $1.02 billion the year before.

PROSPECTS:

Due to the continuing weakness of power generation markets, the Company is setting its earnings guidance for 2003 at $1.80 to $2.00 per share. Meanwhile, CUM still expects year-over-year revenue growth of 5.0% to 10.0% in 2003, assuming modest economic recovery in the second half of

the year. Free cash flow for the coming year is expected to range from $70.0 million to $80.0 million, after capital expenditures of approximately $130.0 million. Separately, CUM expects to provide additional funding to its pension plans of about $30.0 million in 2003.

ANNUAL FINANCIAL DATA:

FISCAL YEAR	TOT. REVS. ($mill.)	NET INC. ($mill.)	TOT. ASSETS ($mill.)	OPER. PROFIT %	NET PROFIT %	RET. ON EQUITY %	RET. ON ASSETS %	CURR. RATIO	EARN. PER SH.$	CASH FL. PER SH.$	TANG. BK. VAL.$	DIV. PER SH.$	PRICE RANGE	AVG. P/E RATIO	AVG. YIELD %
p12/31/02	5,853.0	② 70.0							② 1.82			1.20	50.29 - 19.60	19.2	3.4
12/31/01	5,681.0	① d91.0	4,335.0	...	...	...	...	1.7	① d2.66	3.66	16.47	1.20	45.50 - 28.00		3.3
12/31/00	6,597.0	① 8.0	4,500.0	1.2	0.1	0.6	0.2	1.5	① 0.20	6.49	23.72	1.20	50.00 - 27.06	192.6	3.1
12/31/99	6,639.0	① 160.0	4,697.0	5.0	2.4	11.2	3.4	1.7	① 4.13	10.18	25.66	1.13	65.69 - 34.56	12.1	2.2
12/31/98	6,266.0	① d21.0	4,542.0	2.8	...	...	...	1.8	① d0.55	4.62	21.14	1.10	62.75 - 28.31		2.4
12/31/97	5,625.0	212.0	3,765.0	4.9	3.8	14.9	5.6	1.6	5.48	9.56	33.49	1.07	83.00 - 44.25	11.6	1.7
12/31/96	5,257.0	160.0	3,369.0	4.0	3.0	12.2	4.7	1.5	4.01	7.76	33.30	1.00	47.75 - 34.50	10.3	2.4
12/31/95	5,245.0	① 224.0	3,056.0	3.8	4.3	18.9	7.3	1.3	① 5.52	9.02	29.43	1.00	48.63 - 34.00	7.5	2.4
12/31/94	4,737.2	252.9	2,706.3	6.5	5.3	23.6	9.3	1.5	6.11	9.19	25.78	0.63	57.63 - 35.88	7.7	1.3
12/31/93	4,247.9	182.6	2,390.6	5.8	4.3	22.2	7.6	1.5	4.95	8.49	18.41	0.20	54.38 - 37.38	9.3	0.4

Statistics are as originally reported. ① Incl. non-recurr. chrgs. $125.0 mill., 2001; $160.0 mill., 2000; $60.0 mill., 1999; $161.0 mill., 1998; and $77.0 mill., 1995. ② Bef. acctg. change gain of $3.0 mill.; incl. non-recurring credit of $14.0 mill. and loss of $8.0 mill. on early debt extinguish.

OFFICERS:
T. M. Solso, Chmn., C.E.O.
J. S. Blackwell, C.F.O.

INVESTOR CONTACT: Jason Rawlings, (812) 377-7719

PRINCIPAL OFFICE: 500 Jackson Street, Box 3005, Columbus, IN 47202-3005

TELEPHONE NUMBER: (812) 377-5000
FAX: (812) 377-4937
WEB: www.cummins.com
NO. OF EMPLOYEES: 24,900
SHAREHOLDERS: 4,600 (approx.)
ANNUAL MEETING: In April
INCORPORATED: IN, Feb., 1919

INSTITUTIONAL HOLDINGS:
No. of Institutions: 201
Shares Held: 27,883,599
% Held: 67.2
INDUSTRY: Internal combustion engines, nec (SIC: 3519)
TRANSFER AGENT(S): EquiServe Trust Company, N.A., Jersey City, NJ

CURTISS-WRIGHT CORPORATION

EXCH.	SYM.	REC. PRICE	P/E RATIO	YLD.	MKT. CAP.	RANGE (52-WK.)	'02 Y/E PR.
NYSE	CW	54.60 (2/28/03)	12.6	1.1%	$0.55 bill.	80.20 - 52.08	63.82

UPPER MEDIUM GRADE. THE COMPANY CONTINUES TO EXPAND THROUGH STRATEGIC ACQUISITIONS.

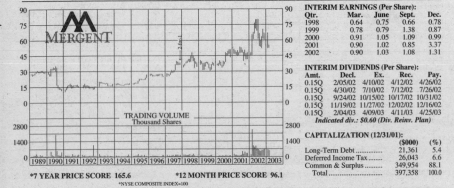

*7 YEAR PRICE SCORE 165.6   ***12 MONTH PRICE SCORE 96.1**
*NYSE COMPOSITE INDEX=100

INTERIM EARNINGS (Per Share):

Qtr.	Mar.	June	Sept.	Dec.
1998	0.64	0.75	0.66	0.78
1999	0.78	0.79	1.38	0.87
2000	0.91	1.05	1.09	0.99
2001	0.90	1.02	0.85	3.37
2002	0.90	1.03	1.08	1.31

INTERIM DIVIDENDS (Per Share):

Amt.	Decl.	Ex.	Rec.	Pay.
0.15Q	2/05/02	4/10/02	4/12/02	4/26/02
0.15Q	4/30/02	7/10/02	7/12/02	7/26/02
0.15Q	9/24/02	10/15/02	10/17/02	10/31/02
0.15Q	11/19/02	11/27/02	12/02/02	12/16/02
0.15Q	2/04/03	4/09/03	4/11/03	4/25/03

Indicated div.: $0.60 (Div. Reinv. Plan)

CAPITALIZATION (12/31/01):

	($000)	(%)
Long-Term Debt	21,361	5.4
Deferred Income Tax	26,043	6.6
Common & Surplus	349,954	88.1
Total	397,358	100.0

BUSINESS:

Curtiss-Wright Corporation designs, develops and manufactures flight control actuation systems and components for the aerospace industry and provides metal-treating services such as shot peening and heat treating. In addition, the Company designs, manufactures, refurbishes and tests highly engineered valves of various types and sizes. As of 12/31/02, CW reported its operations in three segments: Motion Control (45.5% of sales), Metal Treatment (20.9% of sales), and Flow Control (33.6% of sales).

RECENT DEVELOPMENTS:

For the year ended 12/31/02, net income increased 28.2% to $45.1 million versus $62.9 million the year before. Earnings for 2002 and 2001 included gains on the sale of real property of $681,000 and $38.9 million, respectively. Net sales grew 49.6% to $513.3 million from $343.2 million in the prior year, primarily due to recent acquisitions and increases in some of CW's base businesses, particularly in aerospace defense. Sales for the Motion Control segment leapt 70.3% to $233.4 and sales for the Flow Control segment jumped 75.5% to $172.5 million. However, sales for the Metal Treatment segment slipped to $107.4 million from $107.8 million a year earlier. Operating income advanced 31.1% to $61.8 million. Backlog increased 97.5% to $478.5 million at 12/31/02 from $242.3 million at 12/31/01.

PROSPECTS:

The Company continues to expand through strategic acquisitions. For instance, on 3/3/03, CW announced that it has acquired Collins Technologies for $12.0 million. Collins is a designer and manufacturer of aerospace electronic interface devices. In December 2002, CW acquired the assets of TAPCO International, Inc. for $10.5 million in cash and assumption of certain operating liabilities. TAPCO designs, engineers and manufactures valves, as well as provides inspection and installation for harsh environment flow control systems. Separately, on 1/2/03, CW was awarded a $10.0 million contract for various spare parts in support of the U.S. Army's Bradley Fighting Vehicle program.

ANNUAL FINANCIAL DATA:

FISCAL YEAR	TOT. REVS. ($000)	NET INC. ($000)	TOT. ASSETS ($000)	OPER. PROFIT %	NET PROFIT %	RET. ON EQUITY %	RET. ON ASSETS %	CURR. RATIO	EARN. PER SH.$	CASH FL. PER SH.$	TANG. BK. VAL.$	DIV. PER SH.$	PRICE RANGE	AVG. P/E RATIO	AVG. YIELD %
p12/31/02	513,278	⑥ 45,136	812,924						⑥ 4.33			0.60	80.20 - 45.10	14.5	1.0
12/31/01	343,167	⑥ 62,880	500,428	13.7	18.3	18.0	12.6	3.0	⑥ 6.14	7.58	25.71	0.54	53.70 - 39.82	7.6	1.2
12/31/00	329,575	④ 41,074	409,416	15.8	12.5	14.2	10.0	3.9	④ 4.03	5.44	24.23	0.52	51.13 - 33.44	10.5	1.2
12/31/99	293,263	④ 39,045	387,126	17.4	13.3	15.1	10.1	3.2	④ 3.82	5.08	20.72	0.52	40.63 - 30.38	9.3	1.5
12/31/98	249,413	③ 29,053	352,740	14.6	11.6	12.7	8.2	2.9	③ 2.82	3.76	19.51	0.52	48.38 - 33.06	14.4	1.3
12/31/97	219,395	② 27,885	284,708	15.2	12.7	13.6	9.8	4.4	② 2.71	3.59	19.76	0.51	39.88 - 24.75	11.9	1.6
12/31/96	170,536	16,109	267,164	11.2	9.4	8.8	6.0	3.7	1.59	2.47	18.04	0.50	27.63 - 24.81	16.5	1.9
12/31/95	167,551	18,169	246,201	16.7	10.8	10.6	7.4	4.6	1.80	2.73	16.95	0.50	26.88 - 17.56	12.4	2.3
12/31/94	166,189	① 19,547	238,694	17.5	11.8	12.3	8.2	4.0	① 1.93	3.01	15.69	0.50	18.63 - 16.31	9.1	2.9
12/31/93	170,264	① d2,952	236,947	1.1	...	...	...	3.1	① d0.29	0.84	15.23	0.50	20.13 - 15.56	...	2.8

Statistics are as originally reported. Adj. for 2-for-1 stock split, 12/97. ① Bef acct. chrg. of $2.7 mill., 1993; $244,000, 1994. ② Incl. gain of $2.0 mill. fr. the sale of excess real estate. ③ Incl. aft.-tax chgs. of $1.3 mill. fr. consol. chgs. & insur. claim proceeds. ④ Incl. an after-tax gain of $7.4 mill. rel. to an insur. claim settlement & a chrg. of $2.3 mill. rel. to consol. of facilities. ⑤ Incl. net after-tax gains of $3.2 mill. ⑥ Incl. a pre-tax gain on the sale of real property of $681,000, 2002; $38.9 mill., 2001.

OFFICERS:
M. R. Benante, Chmn., C.E.O.
G. Nachman, Exec. V.P.
G. J. Benschip, Treas.

INVESTOR CONTACT: Gary Benschip, Treasurer, (973) 597-4700

PRINCIPAL OFFICE: 4 Becker Farm Rd., Roseland, NJ 07068

TELEPHONE NUMBER: (973) 597-4700
FAX: (973) 597-4799
WEB: www.curtisswright.com
NO. OF EMPLOYEES: 4,200
SHAREHOLDERS: 3,395 approx. com.; 6,503 approx. cl. B com.
ANNUAL MEETING: In April
INCORPORATED: DE, Aug., 1929

INSTITUTIONAL HOLDINGS:
No. of Institutions: 115
Shares Held: 4,891,461
% Held: 47.7

INDUSTRY: Metal heat treating (SIC: 3398)

TRANSFER AGENT(S): American Stock Transfer & Trust Company, New York, NY

CVS CORPORATION

EXCH.	SYM.	REC. PRICE	P/E RATIO	YLD.	MKT. CAP.	RANGE (52-WK.)	'02 Y/E PR.
NYSE	CVS	24.90 (2/28/03)	14.2	0.9%	$9.73 bill.	35.70 - 21.84	24.97

UPPER MEDIUM GRADE. THE COMPANY IS TARGETING EARNINGS OF $1.92 TO $2.00 PER SHARE FOR 2003.

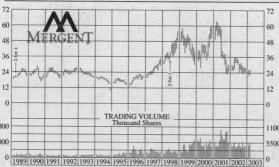

TRADING VOLUME
Thousand Shares

|1989|1990|1991|1992|1993|1994|1995|1996|1997|1998|1999|2000|2001|2002|2003|

*7 YEAR PRICE SCORE 85.4   ***12 MONTH PRICE SCORE 93.5**

*NYSE COMPOSITE INDEX=100

INTERIM EARNINGS (Per Share):

Qtr.	Mar.	June	Sept.	Dec.
1997	0.26	d0.69	0.21	0.31
1998	0.34	0.03	0.25	0.36
1999	0.40	0.40	0.30	0.46
2000	0.47	0.46	0.39	0.51
2001	0.54	0.48	0.30	d0.34
2002	0.43	0.43	0.40	0.49

INTERIM DIVIDENDS (Per Share):

Amt.	Decl.	Ex.	Rec.	Pay.
0.058Q	3/06/02	4/19/02	4/23/02	5/03/02
0.058Q	7/10/02	7/18/02	7/22/02	8/02/02
0.058Q	9/11/02	10/17/02	10/21/02	11/01/02
0.058Q	1/08/03	1/21/03	1/23/03	2/04/03
0.058Q	3/05/03	4/17/03	4/22/03	5/02/03

Indicated div.: $0.23 (Div. Reinv. Plan)

CAPITALIZATION (12/29/01):

	($000)	(%)
Long-Term Debt	810,400	15.0
Deferred Income Tax	35,300	0.7
Preferred Stock	261,200	4.8
Common & Surplus	4,305,700	79.5
Total	5,412,600	100.0

BUSINESS:

CVS Corporation (formerly Melville Corporation) operates a chain of 4,087 drug stores in 32 states and the District of Columbia as of 1/25/03. In addition to prescription drugs and services, the Company's stores offer a broad selection of general merchandise, including over-the-counter drugs, greeting cards, film and photo-finishing services, beauty and cosmetics, seasonal merchandise and convenience foods. In May 1997, CVS acquired Revco D.S., Inc. and in March 1998, CVS acquired Arbor Drugs Inc.

RECENT DEVELOPMENTS:

For the 52 weeks ended 12/28/02, net earnings advanced 73.4% to $716.6 million from $413.2 million in the corresponding prior-year period. Results for 2002 included a $2.0 million after-tax charge from a litigation settlement, while results for 2001 included net non-recurring charges of $228.4 million. Net sales climbed 8.7% to $24.18 billion from $22.24 billion a year earlier. Same-store sales were up 8.4%, driven by an 11.7% gain in pharmacy same-store sales. Gross profit totaled $6.07 billion, or 25.1% of net sales, compared with $5.69 billion, or 25.6% of net sales, the year before. Operating profit increased 56.5% to $1.21 billion from $770.6 million in 2001. During 2002, CVS opened 174 new stores, closed 278 stores, and relocated 92 existing stores.

PROSPECTS:

The Company anticipates revenue growth of between 8.0% and 11.0% in 2003, with sales at stores open at least a year expected to increase by approximately 7.0%. In addition, CVS is targeting full-year 2003 earnings of $1.92 to $2.00 per share. Meanwhile, earnings are benefiting from increased sales of generic drugs and the Company's focus on controlling costs. CVS is lowering its promotional spending and taking aggressive steps to reduce losses from theft to help boost profitability.

ANNUAL FINANCIAL DATA:

FISCAL YEAR	TOT. REVS. ($mill.)	NET INC. ($mill.)	TOT. ASSETS ($mill.)	OPER. PROFIT %	NET PROFIT %	RET. ON EQUITY %	RET. ON ASSETS %	CURR. RATIO	EARN. PER SH. $	CASH FL. PER SH. $	TANG. BK. VAL. $	DIV. PER SH. $	PRICE RANGE	AVG. P/E RATIO	AVG. YIELD %
p12/28/02	24,181.5	⑧ 716.6							⑤ 1.75			0.23	35.70 - 23.03	16.8	0.8
12/29/01	22,241.4	⑧ 413.2	8,628.2	3.5	1.9	9.0	4.8	1.8	⑤ 1.00	1.76	8.90	0.23	63.75 - 22.89	43.3	0.5
12/30/00	20,087.5	⑥ 746.0	7,949.5	6.6	3.7	17.3	9.4	1.7	⑤ 1.83	2.52	8.20	0.23	60.44 - 27.75	24.1	0.5
1/01/00	18,098.3	635.1	7,275.4	6.3	3.5	17.3	8.7	1.6	1.55	2.20	6.88	0.23	58.38 - 30.00	28.5	0.5
12/31/98	15,273.6	⑤ 396.4	6,736.2	5.1	2.6	12.7	5.9	1.4	⑤ 0.98	1.56	5.40	0.22	56.00 - 30.44	44.1	0.5
④ 12/31/97	12,738.2	③ 37.3	5,636.9	1.6	0.3	1.6	0.7	1.3	③ 0.07	0.72	3.96	0.22	35.00 - 19.50	388.7	0.8
⑥ 12/31/96	5,528.1	② 239.6	2,831.8	5.4	4.3	19.2	8.5	1.7	② 1.06	1.70	3.87	0.22	23.00 - 13.63	17.3	1.2
⑦ 12/31/95	9,689.1	① d615.7	3,961.6	...	...	...	...	1.4	① d3.01	d1.84	4.84	0.76	19.94 - 14.31	...	4.4
12/31/94	11,285.6	307.5	4,735.5	5.4	2.7	12.9	6.5	1.6	1.38	2.44	7.54	0.76	20.81 - 14.75	12.9	4.3
12/31/93	10,435.4	331.8	4,272.4	6.0	3.2	14.8	7.8	1.8	1.50	2.49	6.91	0.76	27.38 - 19.44	15.6	3.2

Statistics are as originally reported. Adj. for 2-for-1 stk. split, 6/98. ① Incl. $799 mil restr. chg. & bef. $547,000 gain fr disc. ops. & $42 mil acctg. cr. ② Bef. $164.2 mil ($0.78/sh) loss fr disc. ops., incl. $121.4 mil ($0.34/sh) gain fr sale of secs., & incl. $148 mil ($0.70/sh) restr. chg. ③ Incl. $442.7 mil merger & restr. chg., bef. $17.1 mil ($0.05/sh) extraord. chg., & bef. $17.5 mil gain fr disc. ops. ④ Refls incl. of acqd. Revco ops. ⑤ Incl. $2.0 mil after-tax non-recur. chg., 2002; $11.5 mil ($0.03/sh) after-tax non-recur. gain, 2000; $158.3 mil pre-tax non-recur. chg., 1998. ⑥ Refls. sale of Kay-Bee Center, Inc. ⑦ Refls. sale of Marshalls div. ⑧ Incl. $230.5 mil ($0.56/sh) after-tax restr. and asset impair. chg. & $50.3 mil. gain fr. lawsuit settle.

OFFICERS:
T. M. Ryan, Chmn., Pres., C.E.O.
D. B. Rickard, Exec. V.P., C.F.O.

INVESTOR CONTACT: Nancy R. Christal, V.P., Inv. Rel., (914) 722-4704

PRINCIPAL OFFICE: One CVS Drive, Woonsocket, RI 02895

TELEPHONE NUMBER: (401) 765-1500
FAX: (401) 762-2137
WEB: www.cvs.com
NO. OF EMPLOYEES: 107,000 (approx.)
SHAREHOLDERS: 11,000 (approx.)
ANNUAL MEETING: In Apr.
INCORPORATED: NY, May, 1914; reincorp., DE, Nov., 1996

INSTITUTIONAL HOLDINGS:
No. of Institutions: 539
Shares Held: 326,754,438
% Held: 83.2

INDUSTRY: Drug stores and proprietary stores (SIC: 5912)

TRANSFER AGENT(S): The Bank of New York, New York, NY

CYPRESS SEMICONDUCTOR CORPORATION

EXCH.	SYM.	REC. PRICE	P/E RATIO	YLD.	MKT. CAP.	RANGE (52-WK.)	'02 Y/E PR.
NYSE	CY	6.41 (2/28/03)	...	...	$0.78 bill.	25.48 - 3.60	5.72

SPECULATIVE GRADE. THE COMPANY ANTICIPATES TAKING ADDITIONAL ACTIONS TO REDUCE COSTS IN THE FIRST QUARTER OF 2003.

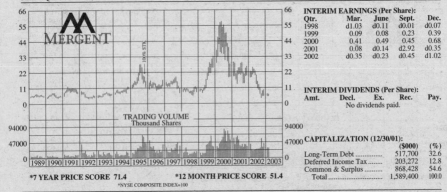

INTERIM EARNINGS (Per Share):

Qtr.	Mar.	June	Sept.	Dec.
1998	d1.03	d0.11	d0.01	d0.07
1999	0.09	0.08	0.23	0.39
2000	0.41	0.49	0.45	0.68
2001	0.08	d0.14	d2.92	d0.35
2002	d0.35	d0.23	d0.45	d1.02

INTERIM DIVIDENDS (Per Share):

Amt.	Decl.	Ex.	Rec.	Pay.
		No dividends paid.		

CAPITALIZATION (12/30/01):

	($000)	(%)
Long-Term Debt	517,700	32.6
Deferred Income Tax	203,272	12.8
Common & Surplus	868,428	54.6
Total	1,589,400	100.0

*7 YEAR PRICE SCORE 71.4   ***12 MONTH PRICE SCORE 51.4**

*NYSE COMPOSITE INDEX=100

BUSINESS:

Cypress Semiconductor Corporation is a global supplier of high-performance digital and mixed-signal integrated circuits to a broad range of markets, including data communications, telecommunications, computation, consumer products and industrial control. CY's operating segments include non-memory products and memory products. The Company's portfolio of non-memory products consists of programmable logic products and programming software,

programmable-skew clocking, data communications products, computer products, microcontrollers and non-volatile memory products. The Company's memory products line primarily consists of static random access memory products. CY's market segments include: wide area networks/storage area networks, wireless terminals/wireless infrastructure and computation and other.

RECENT DEVELOPMENTS:

For the year ended 12/29/02, the Company reported a net loss of $249.1 million compared with a net loss of $407.4 million the previous year. Results for 2002 and 2001 included restructuring charges of $38.3 million and $132.1 million, acquisition charges of $44.1 million and $94.7 million, and other non-recurring charges of $40.8 million and $66.6 million, respectively. Revenues decreased 5.4%

to $774.7 million from $819.2 million a year earlier. However, gross profit jumped 24.1% to $331.4 million, or 42.8% of revenues, from $266.9 million, or 32.6% of revenues, the year before. Operating loss narrowed to $231.3 million from $459.6 million a year earlier. Net interest and other expense amounted to $14.9 million versus net interest and other income of $22.4 million in 2001.

PROSPECTS:

The Company's restructuring actions taken in the fourth quarter of 2002 included a reduction in force of approximately 360 employees and further reduction of wafer fabrication capacity due to continuing softness in demand. However, these restructuring actions are no longer suffi-

cient given the Company's current level of sales and near-term outlook. As a result, CY has identified incremental actions to be taken in the first quarter of 2003 to lower its breakeven sales further and keep its objective of returning to profitability. Near-term sales are expected to be flat.

ANNUAL FINANCIAL DATA:

FISCAL YEAR	TOT. REVS. ($mil.)	NET INC. ($mil.)	TOT. ASSETS ($mil.)	OPER. PROFIT %	NET PROFIT %	RET. ON EQUITY %	RET. ON ASSETS %	CURR. RATIO	EARN. PER SH.$	CASH FL. PER SH.$	TANG. BK. VAL.$	PRICE RANGE	AVG. P/E RATIO
p12/31/02	774.7	⑤ d249.1		...	...	...	...		⑤ d2.02			25.48 - 3.60	...
12/30/01	819.2	④ d411.8	1,886.4	...	...	...	...	2.5	④ d3.32	d1.31	7.15	29.25 - 13.72	...
12/31/00	1,287.8	①③ 277.3	2,361.8	25.5	21.5	20.9	11.7	4.3	①③ 2.03	2.97	10.57	58.00 - 18.25	18.8
1/02/00	705.5	①③ 91.1	1,117.2	7.5	12.9	13.0	8.2	2.8	①③ 0.81	1.79	6.32	33.50 - 7.38	25.2
1/03/99	486.8	② d110.8	756.3	...	...	...	...	2.8	② d1.24	0.03	5.76	12.00 - 5.50	...
12/29/97	544.4	18.4	956.3	3.4	3.4	2.9	1.9	4.3	0.21	1.41	7.10	18.94 - 7.38	62.6
12/30/96	528.4	① 53.0	794.0	15.4	10.0	10.4	6.7	1.8	① 0.63	1.83	6.30	16.63 - 9.13	20.4
1/01/96	596.1	② 102.5	750.7	26.7	17.2	21.7	13.7	2.2	② 1.15	1.90	5.79	27.75 - 10.75	16.7
1/02/95	406.4	50.5	555.7	19.1	12.4	14.3	9.1	3.5	0.61	1.18	4.54	12.06 - 6.56	15.3
1/03/94	304.5	①③ 8.0	340.6	3.5	2.6	3.0	2.4	3.0	①③ 0.11	0.65	3.75	8.38 - 4.31	57.6

Statistics are as originally reported. Adj. for 2-for-1 stk. split, 11/95. ① Incl. special credit of $485,000, 2000; $3.8 mill., 1999; $7.0 mill., 1996; $408,000, 1993. ② Incl. restr. & oth. non-recurr. chrgs. of $58.9 mill., 1998; $17.8 mill., 1995. ③ Incl. acq.-related nonrecurr. chrg. of $56.2 mill., 2000; $37.9 mill., 1999; $18.3 mill., 1993. ④ Bef. an after-tax extraord. gain of $4.3 mill.; incl. restr. chrg. of $132.1 mill. and acquis. chrg. of $161.3 mill. ⑤ Incl. restr. chrg. of $38.3 mill., acquis. chrg. of $44.1 mill., and oth. non-recurr. chrg. of $40.8 mill.

OFFICERS:
E. A. Benhamou, Chmn.
T. J. Rodgers, Pres., C.E.O.
E. T. Hernandez, V.P., C.F.O.
INVESTOR CONTACT: Manny Hernandez, (408) 943-2754
PRINCIPAL OFFICE: 3901 North First Street, San Jose, CA 95134-1599

TELEPHONE NUMBER: (408) 943-2600
FAX: (408) 943-6841
WEB: www.cypress.com
NO. OF EMPLOYEES: 4,160
SHAREHOLDERS: 74,000 (approx.)
ANNUAL MEETING: In May
INCORPORATED: CA, Dec., 1982; reincorp., DE, Feb., 1987

INSTITUTIONAL HOLDINGS:
No. of Institutions: 211
Shares Held: 81,314,213
% Held: 65.7
INDUSTRY: Semiconductors and related devices (SIC: 3674)
TRANSFER AGENT(S): EquiServe, L.P., Canton, MA

CYTEC INDUSTRIES, INC.

EXCH.	SYM.	REC. PRICE	P/E RATIO	YLD.	MKT. CAP.	RANGE (52-WK.)	'02 Y/E PR.
NYSE	CYT	28.95 (2/28/03)	14.8	...	$1.12 bill.	34.00 - 19.20	27.28

MEDIUM GRADE. THE COMPANY EXPECTS EARNINGS PER SHARE FOR THE FIRST QUARTER OF 2003 IN THE RANGE OF $0.47 TO $0.52.

*7 YEAR PRICE SCORE 91.7   ***12 MONTH PRICE SCORE 113.6**

*NYSE COMPOSITE INDEX=100

INTERIM EARNINGS (Per Share):

Qtr.	Mar.	June	Sept.	Dec.
1997	0.56	0.59	0.60	0.65
1998	0.66	0.73	0.59	0.71
1999	0.63	0.63	0.79	0.68
2000	0.74	0.95	0.65	1.82
2001	0.41	0.50	0.51	0.17
2002	0.17	0.52	0.78	0.49

INTERIM DIVIDENDS (Per Share):

Amt.	Decl.	Ex.	Rec.	Pay.
	No dividends paid.			

CAPITALIZATION (12/31/01):

	($000)	(%)
Long-Term Debt	314,700	33.1
Preferred Stock	100	0.0
Common & Surplus	636,800	66.9
Total	951,600	100.0

BUSINESS:

Cytec Industries, Inc. develops manufactures and markets water and industrial process chemicals, specialty material, building block chemicals and performance products. Performance products (33.6% of 2002 revenues) include specialty resins, polymer additives, surfactants, specialty monomers and urethane systems. The specialty materials product category (29.4%) includes aerospace adhesives and advanced composites; acrylic plastics and methyl methcrylate; refinery and styrene catalysts and other specialty materials. The water and industrial process chemicals product category (24.6%) principally includes water treating, paper mining and phosphine chemicals. Building block chemicals (12.4%) include acrylonitrile, acrylamide, melamine methanol, and other building block chemicals. CYT has manufacturing facilities in nine countries and sell its products worldwide.

RECENT DEVELOPMENTS:

For the year ended 12/31/02, net earnings rose 19.8% to $79.3 million versus earnings of $66.2 million, before an extraordinary gain of $4.9 million, in 2001. Results for 2002 and 2001 included amortization of acquisition intangibles of $3.1 million and $12.8 million, respectively. Earnings also included non-recurring items that resulted in net after-tax charges of $3.2 million and $6.5 million in 2002 and 2001, respectively. Net sales were $1.35 billion, down 2.9% from $1.39 billion in the prior year. Earnings from operations climbed 4.2% to $117.4 million versus $112.7 million the year before.

PROSPECTS:

The Company is cautious about its near-term earnings due to continued economic uncertainty and increased raw material, employee benefits and insurance costs. As a result, the Company expects earnings per share for the first quarter of 2003 in the range of $0.47 to $0.52. CYT forecasts a stable market for the Water and Industrial Products segment and expects to report modest sales increases of about 3.0% in 2003 due to new product introductions and geographical expansion. Sales for the Performance Products segment is anticipated to increase about 4.0% in 2003.

ANNUAL FINANCIAL DATA:

FISCAL YEAR	TOT. REVS. ($mill.)	NET INC. ($mill.)	TOT. ASSETS ($mill.)	OPER. PROFIT %	NET PROFIT %	RET. ON EQUITY %	RET. ON ASSETS %	CURR. RATIO	EARN. PER SH.$	CASH FL. PER SH.$	TANG. BK. VAL.$	PRICE RANGE	AVG. P/E RATIO
p12/31/02	1,346.2	⑥ 79.3							⑥ 1.96			34.00 - 19.20	13.6
12/31/01	1,387.1	⑤ 66.2	1,650.4	8.1	4.8	10.4	4.0	1.8	⑤ 1.59	3.76	6.58	39.50 - 19.00	18.4
12/31/00	1,492.5	④ 177.6	1,719.4	11.8	11.9	28.8	10.3	1.6	④ 4.15	6.41	5.77	41.31 - 22.38	7.7
12/31/99	1,412.5	③ 121.3	1,759.9	13.1	8.6	24.0	6.9	1.3	③ 2.73	4.86	2.66	31.94 - 19.50	9.4
12/31/98	1,444.5	② 124.7	1,730.6	12.8	8.6	28.9	7.2	1.2	② 2.68	4.56	1.88	58.56 - 14.88	13.7
12/31/97	1,290.6	① 113.6	1,614.1	9.2	8.8	29.3	7.0	1.2	① 2.39	4.05	2.03	50.94 - 33.88	17.7
12/31/96	1,259.6	100.1	1,261.1	10.8	7.9	31.8	7.9	1.3	2.01	3.79	6.53	40.88 - 20.38	15.2
12/31/95	1,260.1	282.2	1,293.8	9.7	22.4	82.3	21.8	1.3	1.80	6.54	6.49	21.42 - 10.58	8.9
12/31/94	1,101.3	56.1	1,199.4	6.2	5.1	67.3	4.7	1.4	1.05	3.60	1.64	13.96 - 4.21	8.6
12/31/93	1,008.1	d285.7	1,082.1	...	...	...	...	1.2	...	...	...	5.04 - 3.96	...

Statistics are as originally reported. Adj. for 3-for-1 stk. split, 7/96. ① Incl. $71.0 mill. pre-tax restr. & oth. chgs., $24.4 mill. gain for reversal of tax valu. allowance, & $13.6 mill. gain rel. to the divest. of the acrylic fibers product line. ② Incl. $2.8 mill. after-tax gain fr. sale of business. ③ Incl. $8.0 mill. income exp., $2.5 mill. external chg. & $600,000 restr. chgs. ④ Incl. $8.7 mill. net gain fr. insurance settlement, $57.8 mill. net gain fr. sale of bus., and $10.6 mill. net expense fr. restr. & other chgs. ⑤ Bef. extraord. gain of $4.9 mill. ⑥ Incl. $3.2 mill. net after-tax chgs.

OFFICERS:
D. Lilley, Chmn., Pres., C.E.O.
J. P. Cronin, Exec. V.P., C.F.O.
R. Smith, V.P., Gen. Couns., Sec.
INVESTOR CONTACT: D. M. Drillock, V.P., Contr., Inv. Rel., (973) 357-3249
PRINCIPAL OFFICE: Five Garret Mountain Plaza, West Paterson, NJ 07424

TELEPHONE NUMBER: (973) 357-3100
FAX: (973) 357-3061
WEB: www.cytec.com
NO. OF EMPLOYEES: 4,450 (approx.)
SHAREHOLDERS: 13,800 (approx., record)
ANNUAL MEETING: In Mar.
INCORPORATED: DE, Dec., 1993

INSTITUTIONAL HOLDINGS:
No. of Institutions: 177
Shares Held: 30,346,870
% Held: 77.4
INDUSTRY: Chemical preparations, nec (SIC: 2899)
TRANSFER AGENT(S): Mellon Investor Services, Ridgefield Park, NJ

DANA CORPORATION

EXCH.	SYM.	REC. PRICE	P/E RATIO	YLD.	MKT. CAP.	RANGE (52-WK.)	'02 Y/E PR.
NYSE	DCN	8.56 (2/28/03)	21.4	0.5%	$1.27 bill.	23.22 - 8.41	11.76

MEDIUM GRADE. THE COMPANY AGREED TO SELL CERTAIN ENGINE MANAGEMENT OPERATIONS TO STANDARD MOTOR PRODUCTS FOR ABOUT $120.0 MILLION.

TRADING VOLUME
Thousand Shares

*7 YEAR PRICE SCORE 52.5   ***12 MONTH PRICE SCORE 73.9**
NYSE COMPOSITE INDEX=100

INTERIM EARNINGS (Per Share):

Qtr.	Mar.	June	Sept.	Dec.
1999	0.84	1.14	0.97	Nil
2000	1.54	0.95	0.19	d0.57
2001	d0.18	0.10	0.08	d2.01
2002	d0.06	0.35	0.02	0.09

INTERIM DIVIDENDS (Per Share):

Amt.	Decl.	Ex.	Rec.	Pay.
0.01Q	2/12/02	2/27/02	3/01/02	3/15/02
0.01Q	4/16/02	5/29/02	5/31/02	6/14/02
0.01Q	7/16/02	8/28/02	8/30/02	9/13/02
0.01Q	10/22/02	11/26/02	11/29/02	12/13/02
0.01Q	2/12/03	2/26/03	2/28/03	3/14/03

Indicated div.: $0.04 (Div. Reinv. Plan)

CAPITALIZATION (12/31/01):

	($000)	(%)
Long-Term Debt	3,008,000	59.2
Minority Interest	112,000	2.2
Common & Surplus	1,958,000	38.6
Total	5,078,000	100.0

BUSINESS:

Dana Corporation manufactures and markets vehicle components and provides services for original equipment markets and distribution markets. DCN produces axles driveshafts, structural products, transfer cases, brakes, integrated modules and systems, internal engine hard parts, chassis products, filtration products for a variety of applications, sealing products, sensors, drivetrain components, trailer products, power-shift transmissions, and electronic controls. DCN manufactures products for light, medium and heavy-duty vehicles as well as leisure and outdoor power equipment and construction, agriculture and mining equipment. The Company is organized into the Automotive Systems group (37.1% of 2002 net sales), Automotive Aftermarket group (22.9%), Engine and Fluid Management group (20.5%), Heavy Vehicle Technologies and Systems group (18.9%) and other (0.6%). DCN's subsidiary, Dana Credit Corporation provides lease financing services in selected markets.

RECENT DEVELOPMENTS:

For the year ended 12/31/02, the Company reported income from continuing operations of $58.0 million, before an accounting change charge of $220.0 million, compared with a loss from continuing operations of $216.0 million in 2001. Results for 2002 and 2001 included restructuring charges of $194.0 million and $317.0 million, respectively.

Earnings for 2002 and 2001 exluded losses from discontinued operations of $20.0 million and $82.0 million, respectively. Total revenues inched up 0.1% to $9.69 billion from $9.68 billion a year earlier. Net sales increased slightly to $9.50 billion from $9.49 billion the year before.

PROSPECTS:

On 2/10/03, DCN announced a definitive agreement to sell a significant portion of the engine management operations of its Automotive Aftermarket group to Standard Motor Products for approximately $120.0 million, subject to postclosing adjustments. The sale involves nine U.S. operations with approximately 1,900 employees. Meanwhile, DCN anticipates sales of about $9.50 billion in 2003, reflecting current economic conditions and slightly lower North American light-vehicle production. Net income for 2003 is expected to range from $185.0 million to $205.0 million.

ANNUAL FINANCIAL DATA:

FISCAL YEAR	TOT. REVS. ($mill.)	NET INC. ($mill.)	TOT. ASSETS ($mill.)	OPER. PROFIT %	NET PROFIT %	RET. ON EQUITY %	RET. ON ASSETS %	CURR. RATIO	EARN. PER SH.$	CASH FL. PER SH.$	TANG. BK. VAL.$	DIV. PER SH.$	PRICE RANGE	AVG. P/E RATIO	AVG. YIELD %
p12/31/02	9,694.0	③ 58.0							③ 0.39			0.04	23.22 - 9.28	41.7	2.5
12/31/01	10,469.0	① d298.0	10,207.0	...	...	...	...	1.1	① d2.01	1.68	13.18	0.94	26.90 - 10.25	...	5.1
12/31/00	12,691.0	① 334.0	11,236.0	6.2	2.6	12.7	3.0	1.0	① 2.18	5.60	17.76	1.24	33.25 - 12.81	10.6	5.4
12/31/99	13,353.0	① 513.0	11,123.0	7.6	3.8	17.3	4.6	1.2	① 3.08	6.20	18.12	1.24	54.06 - 26.00	13.0	3.1
12/31/98	12,838.7	① 534.1	10,137.5	9.0	4.2	18.2	5.3	1.1	① 3.20	6.12	17.74	1.14	61.50 - 31.31	14.5	2.5
12/31/97	12,402.4	① 320.1	9,511.1	6.9	2.6	12.3	3.4	1.1	① 1.94	4.68	15.89	1.04	54.38 - 30.63	21.9	2.4
12/31/96	7,890.7	306.0	6,160.0	8.2	3.9	21.4	5.0	1.2	3.01	5.74	13.87	0.98	35.50 - 27.25	10.4	3.1
12/31/95	7,794.5	288.1	5,694.1	8.5	3.7	24.7	5.1	1.5	2.84	5.27	11.47	0.90	32.63 - 21.38	9.5	3.3
12/31/94	6,740.5	228.2	5,110.8	7.5	3.4	24.3	4.5	1.1	2.31	4.45	9.51	0.83	30.69 - 19.63	10.9	3.3
12/31/93	5,563.3	② 128.5	4,631.9	6.6	2.3	16.0	2.8	1.1	② 1.39	3.50	16.29	0.80	30.13 - 22.00	18.7	3.1

Statistics are as originally reported. Adj. for stk. splits: 2-for-1, 6/15/94 ① Includes non-recurr. chrgs. $390.0 mill., 12/01; $173.0 mill., 12/00; $181.0 mill., 12/99; $167.3 mill., 12/98; $327.6 mill., 12/97. ② Bef. acctg. change chrg. $48.9 mill. ③ Bef. acctg. change chrg. $220.0 mill. and loss from disc. oper. $20.0 mill.; incl. restr. chrg. $194.0 mill.

OFFICERS:
J. M. Magliochetti, Chmn., Pres., C.E.O., C.O.O.
R. C. Richter, V.P., C.F.O.
INVESTOR CONTACT: Investor Relations, (419) 535-4635
PRINCIPAL OFFICE: 4500 Dorr Street, Toledo, OH 43615

TELEPHONE NUMBER: (419) 535-4500
FAX: (419) 535-4643
WEB: www.dana.com
NO. OF EMPLOYEES: 60,000 (approx.)
SHAREHOLDERS: 37,000 (approx.)
ANNUAL MEETING: In April
INCORPORATED: NJ, 1905; reincorp., VA, Oct., 1916

INSTITUTIONAL HOLDINGS:
No. of Institutions: 257
Shares Held: 101,660,651
% Held: 68.4
INDUSTRY: Motor vehicle parts and accessories (SIC: 3714)
TRANSFER AGENT(S): Mellon InvestorServices, Ridgefield Park, NJ

DANAHER CORPORATION

EXCH.	SYM.	REC. PRICE	P/E RATIO	YLD.	MKT. CAP.	RANGE (52-WK.)	'02 Y/E PR.
NYSE	DHR	65.02 (2/28/03)	23.3	0.2%	$9.32 bill.	75.46 - 52.60	65.70

INVESTMENT GRADE. THE COMPANY EXPECTS EARNINGS PER SHARE TO BE IN THE RANGE OF $3.13 TO $3.28 FOR THE FULL YEAR 2003.

*7 YEAR PRICE SCORE 148.4   ***12 MONTH PRICE SCORE 109.3**

*NYSE COMPOSITE INDEX=100

INTERIM EARNINGS (Per Share):

Qtr.	Mar.	June	Sept.	Dec.
1999	0.39	0.45	0.42	0.51
2000	0.49	0.56	0.58	0.60
2001	0.56	0.63	0.59	0.23
2002	0.55	0.66	0.74	0.84

INTERIM DIVIDENDS (Per Share):

Amt.	Decl.	Ex.	Rec.	Pay.
0.02Q	3/21/02	3/26/02	3/29/02	4/30/02
0.02Q	6/20/02	6/26/02	6/28/02	7/31/02
0.025Q	9/17/02	9/25/02	9/27/02	10/31/02
0.025Q	12/17/02	12/24/02	12/27/02	1/31/03
0.025Q	3/20/03	3/26/03	3/28/03	4/30/03

Indicated div.: $0.10

CAPITALIZATION (12/31/01):

	($000)	(%)
Long-Term Debt	1,119,333	33.4
Common & Surplus	2,228,586	66.6
Total	3,347,919	100.0

BUSINESS:

Danaher Corporation is a manufacturer of industrial and consumer products, with emphasis on proprietary technology, and operates through two business segments. The Process/Environmental Controls segment produces and sells compact, professional electronic test tools, underground storage tank leak detection systems and motion, position, speed, temperature, level and position instruments and sensing devices, power switches and controls, liquid flow, and quality measuring devices. The Tools and Components segment produces and distributes general purpose mechanics' hand tools and automotive specialty tools. Other products include tool boxes and storage devices, diesel engine retarders, and wheel service equipment.

RECENT DEVELOPMENTS:

For the year ended 12/31/02, income was $434.1 million, before an accounting charge of $173.8 million and reduction of income of $30.0 million related to previously discontinued operations, compared with net income of $297.7 million the previous year. Results for 2002 and 2001 included an after-tax restructuring credit and charge of $4.1 million and $43.5 million, respectively. Results for 2002 also included an after-tax gain of $3.9 million from the sale of real estate. Net sales increased 21.0% to $4.58 billion from $3.78 billion the year before. Operating income jumped 39.7% to $701.1 million versus $502.0 million in 2001.

PROSPECTS:

The Company expects earnings per share to be in the range of $3.13 to $3.28 for the full year 2003 and from $0.61 to $0.66 for the first quarter of 2003. Separately, DHR completed the acquisition of Willett International Ltd. for approximately $110.0 million and $27.0 million in assumed debt. Willett is a manfacturer and marketer of product identification equipment and consumables. Meanwhile, on 3/10/03, DHR announced that it completed the acquisition of the assets of Gasboy International, Inc., a manufacturer and marketer of commercial electronic and mechanical petroleum dispensing systems, fleet management systems and transfer pumps, for about $38.3 million.

ANNUAL FINANCIAL DATA:

FISCAL YEAR	TOT. REVS. ($mill.)	NET INC. ($mill.)	TOT. ASSETS ($mill.)	OPER. PROFIT %	NET PROFIT %	RET. ON EQUITY %	RET. ON ASSETS %	CURR. RATIO	EARN. PER SH.$	CASH FL.PER SH.$	TANG. BK. VAL.$	DIV. PER SH.$	PRICE RANGE	AVG. P/E RATIO	AVG. YIELD %
p12/31/02	4,577.2	⑥ 434.1							⑥ 2.79			0.09	75.46 - 52.60	22.9	0.1
12/31/01	3,782.4	⑤ 297.7	4,820.5	13.3	7.9	13.4	6.2	1.8	⑤ 2.01	3.14	...	0.08	68.69 - 43.90	28.0	0.1
12/31/00	3,777.8	324.2	4,031.7	14.6	8.6	16.7	8.0	1.4	2.23	3.26	0.55	0.07	69.81 - 36.44	23.8	0.1
12/31/99	3,197.2	④ 261.6	3,047.1	14.3	8.2	15.3	8.6	1.7	④ 1.79	2.66	2.92	0.06	69.00 - 42.75	31.2	0.1
12/31/98	2,910.0	182.9	2,738.7	12.6	6.3	13.5	6.7	1.3	1.32	2.10	0.50	0.05	55.25 - 28.00	31.5	0.1
12/31/97	2,051.0	③ 154.8	1,879.7	13.0	7.5	16.9	8.2	1.2	③ 1.29	1.92	0.60	0.05	32.00 - 19.50	20.0	0.2
12/31/96	1,811.9	② 128.0	1,765.1	12.5	7.1	16.0	7.2	1.2	② 1.07	1.64	0.06	0.04	23.31 - 14.63	17.8	0.2
12/31/95	1,486.8	② 105.8	1,486.0	12.1	7.1	18.0	7.1	1.2	② 0.89	1.37	...	0.04	17.19 - 12.13	16.6	0.3
12/31/94	1,288.7	81.7	1,134.9	11.3	6.3	17.1	7.2	1.0	0.70	1.08	0.31	0.03	13.28 - 9.00	15.9	0.3
12/31/93	1,075.5	① 53.7	872.5	9.4	5.0	14.8	6.2	1.2	① 0.47	0.82	0.23	0.02	9.81 - 6.03	17.0	...

Statistics are as originally reported. Adj. for stk. splits: 2-for-1; 1/95, 5/98 ① Bef. acctg. change chrg. $36.0 mill. ② Bef disc. opers. gain $2.6 mill., 1995 & $79.8 mill, 1996 ③ Incl. non-recurr. credit $6.0 mill. from sale of investment. ④ Incls. one-time after-tax chrg. of $11.8 mill. for acqs. ⑤ Incl. pre-tax restruct. chrg. of $69.7 mill. ⑥ Incl. after-tax restruct. credit of $4.1 mill. & after-tax gain of $3.9 mill. on sale of real estate & excl. reduct. of tax res. of $30.0 mill. & acctg. chng. chrg. of $173.8 mill.

OFFICERS:
S. M. Rales, Chmn.
L. Culp Jr., Pres., C.E.O.
P. W. Allender, Exec. V.P., C.F.O., Sec.
INVESTOR CONTACT: Patrick Allender, Exec. V.P., C.F.O. & Sec., (202) 828-0850
PRINCIPAL OFFICE: 2099 Pennsylvania Ave. NW, 12th Floor, Washington, DC 20006-1813

TELEPHONE NUMBER: (202) 828-0850
FAX: (202) 828-0860
WEB: www.danaher.com

NO. OF EMPLOYEES: 23,000 (approx.)

SHAREHOLDERS: 3,000 (approx.)

ANNUAL MEETING: In May

INCORPORATED: DE, 1987

DARDEN RESTAURANTS, INC.

EXCH.	SYM.	REC. PRICE	P/E RATIO	YLD.	MKT. CAP.	RANGE (52-WK.)	'02 Y/E PR.
NYSE	DRI	17.81 (2/28/03)	13.1	0.4%	$3.07 bill.	29.77 - 16.50	20.45

UPPER MEDIUM GRADE. THE COMPANY CONTINUES TO EXPAND THROUGH THE OPENING OF NEW RESTAURANTS.

7 YEAR PRICE SCORE 183.6   **12 MONTH PRICE SCORE 97.9**
*NYSE COMPOSITE INDEX=100

INTERIM EARNINGS (Per Share):

Qtr.	Aug.	Nov.	Feb.	May
1998-99	0.16	0.07	0.18	0.25
1999-00	0.23	0.12	0.24	0.31
2000-01	0.31	0.16	0.27	0.33
2001-02	0.34	0.20	0.36	0.40
2002-03	0.40	0.21	0.35	...

INTERIM DIVIDENDS (Per Share):

Amt.	Decl.	Ex.	Rec.	Pay.
0.04S	9/20/01	10/05/01	10/10/01	11/01/01
0.04S	3/21/02	4/08/02	4/10/02	5/01/02
50% STK	3/21/02	5/02/02	4/10/02	5/01/02
0.04S	9/18/02	10/08/02	10/10/02	11/01/02
0.04S	3/20/03	4/08/03	4/10/03	5/01/03

Indicated div.: $0.08 (Div. Reinv. Plan)

CAPITALIZATION (5/26/02):

	($000)	(%)
Long-Term Debt	662,506	34.7
Deferred Income Tax	117,709	6.2
Common & Surplus	1,128,877	59.1
Total	1,909,092	100.0

BUSINESS:

Darden Restaurants, Inc. and its subsidiaries, as of 2/23/03, operated a total of 1,254 restaurant locations in the U.S., including 672 RED LOBSTER locations, 516 OLIVE GARDEN locations, 32 BAHAMA BREEZE locations and 34 SMOKEY BONES BBQ SPORTS BAR restaurants. In addition, the Company operated 37 restaurants in Canada, including 31 RED LOBSTER units and six OLIVE GARDEN units. All of the restaurants in North America are Company-operated.

RED LOBSTER is a full-service, seafood-specialty restaurant offering a menu featuring fresh fish, shrimp, crab, lobster, scallops, and other seafood in a casual atmosphere. THE OLIVE GARDEN is a full-service Italian restaurant featuring recipes from both northern and southern Italy. BAHAMA BREEZE has a Caribbean theme. SMOKEY BONES BBQ SPORTS BAR restaurant combines barbecue with sports entertainment in a mountain lodge setting.

RECENT DEVELOPMENTS:

For the quarter ended 2/23/03, net earnings decreased 6.7% to $61.8 million versus $66.2 million in the corresponding period of the prior year. Results for the current quarter were negatively affected by unanticipated worker's compensation and insurance costs, higher-than-expected utility expense, increased marketing expense, and severe winter weather. Sales advanced 5.1% to $1.18 billion from $1.12 billion a year earlier. OLIVE GARDEN sales grew 5.7% to $505.4 million, while RED LOBSTER sales climbed 2.3% to $620.6 million. Same-store sales at RED LOBSTER and OLIVE GARDEN increased 1.2% and 0.3%, respectively.

PROSPECTS:

The Company continues to expand through the opening of new restaurants. During fiscal 2002, the Company opened three BAHAMA BREEZE restaurants, and is scheduled to open two more restaurants located in Cleveland and Seattle during the fiscal fourth quarter. Additionally, the Company opened 17 SMOKEY BONES restaurants during fiscal 2002, and plans to open at least 20 restaurants in fiscal 2003. Meanwhile, subsequent to its fiscal third quarter, the Company opened SEASONS 52^{SM}, a new test restaurant in Orlando. SEASONS 52^{SM} is described as a casually sophisticated fresh grill and wine bar with seasonally inspired menus.

ANNUAL FINANCIAL DATA:

FISCAL YEAR	TOT. REVS. ($mill.)	NET INC. ($mill.)	TOT. ASSETS ($mill.)	OPER. PROFIT %	NET PROFIT %	RET. ON EQUITY %	RET. ON ASSETS %	CURR. RATIO	EARN. PER SH.$	CASH FL. PER SH.$	TANG. BK. VAL.$	DIV. PER SH.$	PRICE RANGE	AVG. P/E RATIO	AVG. YIELD %
5/26/02	4,368.7	⑤ 237.8	2,529.7	9.2	5.4	21.1	9.4	0.7	⑤ 1.30	2.24	6.56	0.05	24.98 - 12.67	14.5	0.3
5/27/01	4,021.2	197.0	2,218.5	8.3	4.9	19.0	8.9	0.6	1.06	1.89	5.88	0.05	18.00 - 8.29	12.4	0.4
5/28/00	3,701.3	④ 176.7	1,971.4	8.0	4.8	18.4	9.0	0.5	④ 0.89	1.58	5.24	0.05	15.58 - 10.42	14.6	0.4
5/30/99	3,458.1	③ 140.5	1,905.7	6.8	4.1	14.6	7.4	0.6	③ 0.66	1.28	4.86	0.05	12.63 - 7.83	15.5	0.5
5/31/98	3,287.0	101.7	1,984.7	5.3	3.1	10.0	5.1	0.7	0.45	1.02	4.82	0.05	8.33 - 4.50	14.4	0.8
5/25/97	3,171.8	① d91.0	1,963.7	...	...	...	...	0.7	① d0.39	0.21	4.94	0.05	9.33 - 5.00	...	0.4
5/26/96	3,191.8	① 74.4	2,088.5	4.2	2.3	6.1	3.6	0.6	① 0.31	0.89	5.17	0.03	8.08 - 6.08	22.6	0.4
5/28/95	3,163.3	② 52.4	2,113.4	2.8	1.7	4.5	2.5	0.6	② 0.22	0.79	4.95	...	...	...	...
5/29/94	2,963.0	② 123.1	1,879.7	7.2	4.2	8.6	6.5	0.7	② 0.51	1.04	...	...	...	...	...
5/28/93	2,737.0	① 91.6	1,632.0	6.5	3.3	7.4	5.6	0.7	① 0.37	0.85	...	...	...	...	...

Statistics are as originally reported. Adj. for 50.0% stk. div., 5/02 ① Incl. non-recurr. chrg. 5/25/97, $229.9 mill.; 5/26/96, $75.0 mill.; 5/28/95, $99.3 mill.; 5/28/93, $30.6 mill. ② Bef. acctg. change credit $3.7 mill. ③ Incls. restr. chrg. of $8.5 mill. ④ Incl. pre-tax restr. & asset impair. credit of $5.9 mill. ⑤ Incl. a credit from restr. of $2.6 mill.

OFFICERS:
J. R. Lee, Chmn., C.E.O.
R. E. Rivera, Pres., C.O.O.
L. J. Dimopoulos, C.F.O.

INVESTOR CONTACT: Matthre Stroud, (407) 245-5192

PRINCIPAL OFFICE: 5900 Lake Ellenor Drive, Orlando, FL 32809

TELEPHONE NUMBER: (407) 245-4000
FAX: (407) 245-4989
WEB: www.darden.com
NO. OF EMPLOYEES: 133,200 (approx.)
SHAREHOLDERS: 38,027 (approx.)
ANNUAL MEETING: In Sept.
INCORPORATED: FL, Mar., 1995

INSTITUTIONAL HOLDINGS:
No. of Institutions: 339
Shares Held: 124,877,057
% Held: 73.1

INDUSTRY: Eating places (SIC: 5812)

TRANSFER AGENT(S): First Union National Bank, Charlotte, NC

DAVITA INC.

EXCH.	SYM.	REC. PRICE	P/E RATIO	YLD.	MKT. CAP.	RANGE (52-WK.)	'02 Y/E PR.
NYSE	DVA	20.75 (2/28/03)	8.8	…	$1.75 bill.	26.21 - 19.00	24.67

MEDIUM GRADE. DURING THE FOURTH QUARTER, THE COMPANY ANNOUNCED THAT IT ACQUIRED FOUR CENTERS AND OPENED EIGHT DE NOVO CENTERS.

INTERIM EARNINGS (Per Share):

Qtr.	Mar.	June	Sept.	Dec.
1998	d0.61	0.20	0.33	0.16
1999	0.28	d0.27	0.03	d1.86
2000	0.05	d0.19	0.16	0.18
2001	0.35	0.32	0.47	0.36
2002	0.40	0.43	0.72	0.81

INTERIM DIVIDENDS (Per Share):

Amt.	Decl.	Ex.	Rec.	Pay.
		No dividends paid.		

CAPITALIZATION (12/31/01):

	($000)	(%)
Long-Term Debt	811,190	59.7
Deferred Income Tax	23,441	1.7
Minority Interest	20,722	1.5
Common & Surplus	503,637	37.1
Total	1,358,990	100.0

*7 YEAR PRICE SCORE N/A   *12 MONTH PRICE SCORE 107.1

*NYSE COMPOSITE INDEX=100

BUSINESS:

DaVita Inc. (formerly Total Renal Care Holding, Inc.) is a provider of dialysis services in the United States for patients suffering from chronic kidney failure, also known as end stage renal disease, or ESRD. As of 12/31/02, the Company treated 45,000 patients through a network of 515 owned and managed dialysis facilities located in 33 states and the District of Columbia. In addition, the Company provided acute dialysis services in 270 hospitals.

RECENT DEVELOPMENTS:

For the year ended 12/31/02, net income was $186.7 million, before an extraordinary loss of $29.4 million, compared with net income of $136.3 million, before an extraordinary gain of $977,000, the previous year. Results for 2002 included a pre-tax charge of $380,000 for impairments and valuation adjustments. Net operating revenues increased 12.4% to $1.85 billion from $1.65 billion the year before. Total operating expenses climbed 9.8% to $1.46 billion from $1.33 billion a year earlier. Operating income advanced 23.1% to $391.3 million versus $318.0 million the prior year.

PROSPECTS:

The Company recently acquired four centers and opened eight de novo centers. The Company also closed one center that did not have enough private patients to cover the Medicare reimbursement deficit. As a result, DVA added approximately 3,400 patients in 30 centers under management. Meanwhile, the Company continues to be well-positioned to benefit from increases in its revenue per treatment, which excludes lab management fees and other revenue. Going forward, the Company expects normal operating earnings before depreciation and amortization, debt expenses and taxes, to be in the range of $380.0 million to $400.0 million.

ANNUAL FINANCIAL DATA:

FISCAL YEAR	TOT. REVS. ($mill.)	NET INC. ($mill.)	TOT. ASSETS ($mill.)	OPER. PROFIT %	NET PROFIT %	RET. ON EQUITY %	RET. ON ASSETS %	CURR. RATIO	EARN. PER SH.$	CASH FL. PER SH.$	TANG. BK. VAL.$	PRICE RANGE	AVG. P/E RATIO
p12/31/02	1,854.6	④ 186.7							④ 2.28			26.21 - 19.00	9.9
12/31/01	1,650.8	③ 136.3	1,662.7	19.3	8.3	27.1	8.2	1.6	③ 1.51	2.33	…	24.50 - 14.00	12.7
12/31/00	1,486.3	②③ 17.0	1,596.6	11.8	1.1	4.9	1.1	1.6	②③ 0.20	1.55	…	17.81 - 9.25	67.6
12/31/99	1,445.4	② d147.3	2,056.7	…	…	…	…	0.4	② d1.81	d0.43	…	…	…
12/31/98	1,204.9	① 15.3	1,915.6	11.8	1.3	3.2	0.8	3.2	① 0.19	1.31	…	…	…
12/31/97	438.2	37.0	695.3	18.2	8.4	13.5	5.3	4.7	0.82	1.41	…	…	…
12/31/96	272.9	23.7	374.1	17.9	8.7	10.3	6.3	4.1	0.55	0.91	1.14	…	…
12/31/95	89.7	6.5	164.0	20.6	7.2	7.8	3.9	3.6	0.22	0.37	0.62	…	…
5/31/95	99.0	4.9	77.6	17.3	4.9	…	6.3	2.0	0.20	0.31	…	…	…
5/31/94	80.5	5.7	43.6	13.5	7.1	16.5	13.1	3.9	…	…	…	…	…
5/31/93	71.6	d2.5	…	15.9	…	…	…	…	…	…	…	…	…

Statistics are as originally reported. Adj. for stk. splits: 1,000-for-1, 1994; 2-for-3, 1997. ① Incl. per-tax merger-related costs of $78.2 mill. ② Incl. pre-tax impairment and valuation adjust. of $139.8 mill., 1999; $4.6 mill., 2000. ③ Bef. extraord. loss of $3.5 mill., 2000; gain of $977,000, 2001. ④ Bef. extraord. loss of $29.4 mill. & incl. pre-tax chrg. of $380,000 for impair. & val. adjust.

OFFICERS:
K. J. Thiry, Chmn., C.E.O.
R. K. Whitney, C.F.O.
S. Udicious, V.P., Sec. Gen. Couns.

INVESTOR CONTACT: LeAnne Zumwalt, V.P. Inv. Rel., (310) 750-2072

PRINCIPAL OFFICE: 21250 Hawthorne Blvd., Suite 800, Torrance, CA 90503-5517

TELEPHONE NUMBER: (310) 792-2600
FAX: (310) 792-8928
WEB: www.davita.com

NO. OF EMPLOYEES: 13,000

SHAREHOLDERS: 2,604

ANNUAL MEETING: In June

INCORPORATED: DE, Apr., 1994

INSTITUTIONAL HOLDINGS:
No. of Institutions: 155
Shares Held: 59,192,821
% Held: 97.8

INDUSTRY: Kidney dialysis centers (SIC: 8092)

TRANSFER AGENT(S): The Bank of New York, New York, NY

DEAN FOODS COMPANY

EXCH.	SYM.	REC. PRICE	P/E RATIO	YLD.	MKT. CAP.	RANGE (52-WK.)	'02 Y/E PR.
NYSE	DF	42.17 (2/28/03)	15.9	...	$3.71 bill.	42.78 - 27.07	37.10

UPPER MEDIUM GRADE. ON 1/8/03, THE COMPANY SOLD ITS DAIRY OPERATIONS IN PUERTO RICO FOR APPROXIMATELY $122.0 MILLION IN CASH.

7 YEAR PRICE SCORE N/A **12 MONTH PRICE SCORE 116.6**
*NYSE COMPOSITE INDEX=100

INTERIM EARNINGS (Per Share):

Qtr.	Mar.	June	Sept.	Dec.
1997	0.35	0.28	0.31	d0.30
1998	0.23	0.41	0.38	0.38
1999	0.30	0.44	0.42	0.39
2000	0.35	0.52	0.51	0.55
2001	0.41	0.56	0.48	0.43
2002	0.56	0.72	0.68	0.70

INTERIM DIVIDENDS (Per Share):

Amt.	Decl.	Ex.	Rec.	Pay.
2-for-1	2/21/02	4/24/02	4/08/02	4/24/02

CAPITALIZATION (12/31/01):

	($000)	(%)
Long-Term Debt	2,971,525	55.9
Deferred Income Tax	281,229	5.3
Redeemable Pfd. Stock	584,605	11.0
Common & Surplus	1,475,880	27.8
Total	5,313,239	100.0

BUSINESS:

Dean Foods Company (formerly Suiza Foods Corporation) is a major processor and distributor of food and beverage products. DF produces a full line of Company-branded and private-label dairy products including milk and milk-based beverages, ice cream, coffee creamers, half-and-half, whipping cream, whipped toppings, sour cream, cottage cheese, yogurt, dips, dressings and soy milk. The Company is also a supplier of pickles and other specialty food products, juice, juice drinks and water. On 12/21/01, the Company acquired Dean Foods Company.

RECENT DEVELOPMENTS:

For the year ended 12/31/02, income from continuing operations totaled $267.8 million, before an $85.0 million accounting charge, versus income from continuing operations of $112.0 million, before a $4.3 million extraordinary charge and a $1.4 million acounting charge, in the prior year. Results included non-recurring pre-tax charges of $19.1 million and $14.0 million in 2002 and 2001, respectively. Net sales advanced 50.5% to $8.99 billion from $5.97 billion the year before. Sales growth was attributed primarily to the addition of the legacy Dean dairies. Gross profit totaled $2.35 billion, or 26.1% of net sales, versus $1.40 billion, or 23.4% of net sales, the previous year. Operating income jumped 72.1% to $662.6 million from $385.1 million a year earlier.

PROSPECTS:

On 1/8/03, DF announced that it has completed the sale of its dairy operations in Puerto Rico to Grupo Gloria, a Peruvian conglomerate, for approximately $122.0 million in cash. The sale is expected to be slightly dilutive to earnings in 2003. The Company is targeting first-quarter 2003 earnings in the range of $0.62 to $0.64, and full-year earnings of between $3.11 and $3.16 per share, before one-time charges. Results should benefit from continued growth of DF's strategic branded products, including INTERNATIONAL DELIGHT coffee creamers, SILK soy milk and HERSHEY'S flavored milks. DF plans to spend about $190.0 million for marketing and promotional activities to help support and grow these products, up from approximately $130.0 million spent in 2002.

ANNUAL FINANCIAL DATA:

FISCAL YEAR	TOT. REVS. ($mill.)	NET INC. ($mill.)	TOT. ASSETS ($mill.)	OPER. PROFIT %	NET PROFIT %	RET. ON EQUITY %	RET. ON ASSETS %	CURR. RATIO	EARN. PER SH.$	CASH FL.PER SH.$	TANG. BK. VAL.$	PRICE RANGE	AVG. P/E RATIO
p12/31/02	8,991.5	⑤ 267.8							⑤ 2.66			40.55 - 27.07	12.7
12/31/01	6,230.1	④ 115.6	6,731.9	6.3	1.9	7.8	1.7	1.3	④ 1.86	3.67	16.80	36.24 - 21.00	15.4
12/31/00	5,756.3	①② 113.8	3,780.5	6.4	2.0	19.0	3.0	1.2	①② 1.84	3.53	10.97	26.22 - 18.00	12.0
12/31/99	4,482.0	①② 108.8	2,658.9	6.2	2.4	18.6	4.1	1.3	①② 1.56	2.63	9.97	25.13 - 14.81	12.8
12/31/98	3,320.9	①③ 103.1	3,013.8	7.3	3.1	15.7	3.4	1.5	①③ 1.45	2.32	9.76	33.50 - 12.84	16.0
12/31/97	1,794.9	①②③ 39.3	1,403.5	5.3	2.2	10.9	2.8	1.7	①②③ 0.63	1.34	5.84	30.88 - 9.63	32.4
12/31/96	520.9	①② 29.1	384.1	6.9	5.6	31.1	7.6	1.4	①② 1.41	2.24	4.35	10.38 - 7.00	6.2
12/31/95	430.5	①② 18.9	232.5	9.5	4.4	199.8	8.1	1.0	①② d0.13	2.69	0.75	...	...
12/31/94	341.1	①② 7.6	239.0	8.0	2.2	76.5	3.2	1.0	①② 0.35	1.68	...	...	...
12/31/93	51.7	1.4	...	16.8	2.7	...	...	...	0.29	1.18	...	...	...

Statistics are as originally reported. Adj. for 2-for-1 stk. split, 4/02. ① Bef. $5.0 mil ($0.07/sh) extraord. gain, 2000; $904,000 gain, 1999; $31.7 mil ($0.38/sh) gain, 1998; $11.3 mil chg., 1997; $2.2 mil chg., 1996; $8.5 mil chg., 1995; & $197,000 chg., 1994. ② Incl. $3.4 mil non-recur. pre-tax chg., 2000; $17.5 mil, 1999; $37.0 mil, 1997; $571,000, 1996; $12.0 mil, 1995; & $1.7 mil 1994. ③ Bef. $3.2 mil discont. oper chg., 1998; & $717,000 gain, 1997. ④ Bef. $4.3 mil ($0.08/sh) extraord. chg. and $1.4 mil ($0.02/sh) acctg. chg. & incl. $14.0 mil non-recur. pre-tax chg. ⑤ Bef. $7.4 mil ($0.07/sh) loss fr. discont. opers., $85.0 mil ($0.78/sh) acctg. change chg., & incl. $19.1 mil non-recur. pre-tax chg.

OFFICERS:
G. L. Engles, Chmn., C.E.O.
B. A. Fromberg, Exec. V.P., C.F.O.

INVESTOR CONTACT: Cory M. Olson, Sr. V.P. & Treas., (214) 303-3645

PRINCIPAL OFFICE: 2515 McKinney Avenue, Suite 1200, Dallas, TX 75201

TELEPHONE NUMBER: (214) 303-3400
FAX: (214) 303-2850
WEB: www.deanfoods.com
NO. OF EMPLOYEES: 31,503 (avg.)
SHAREHOLDERS: 6,100 (approx.)
ANNUAL MEETING: In May
INCORPORATED: DE, Sept., 1994

INSTITUTIONAL HOLDINGS:
No. of Institutions: 290
Shares Held: 79,357,064
% Held: 87.0
INDUSTRY: Ice cream and frozen desserts (SIC: 2024)
TRANSFER AGENT(S): Computershare Investor Services, Dallas, TX

DEERE & COMPANY

EXCH.	SYM.	REC. PRICE	P/E RATIO	YLD.	MKT. CAP.	RANGE (52-WK.)	'02 Y/E PR.
NYSE	DE	41.38 (2/28/03)	23.5	2.1%	$9.89 bill.	51.60 - 37.50	45.85

LOWER MEDIUM GRADE. THE COMPANY IS TARGETING FULL-YEAR 2003 NET INCOME IN THE RANGE OF $500.0 MILLION TO $600.0 MILLION.

*7 YEAR PRICE SCORE 111.9   ***12 MONTH PRICE SCORE 103.8**

*NYSE COMPOSITE INDEX=100

INTERIM EARNINGS (Per Share):

Qtr.	Jan.	Apr.	July	Oct.
1996-97	0.69	1.25	1.00	0.84
1997-98	0.81	1.45	1.19	0.71
1998-99	0.21	0.65	0.29	d0.13
1999-00	0.16	0.87	0.72	0.30
2000-01	0.24	0.54	0.30	d1.36
2001-02	d0.16	0.59	0.61	0.28
2002-03	0.28	...	...	...

INTERIM DIVIDENDS (Per Share):

Amt.	Decl.	Ex.	Rec.	Pay.
0.22Q	2/27/02	3/26/02	3/31/02	5/01/02
0.22Q	5/29/02	6/26/02	6/30/02	8/01/02
0.22Q	8/28/02	9/26/02	9/30/02	11/01/02
0.22Q	12/04/02	12/27/02	12/31/02	2/01/03
0.22Q	2/26/03	3/27/03	3/31/03	5/01/03

Indicated div.: $0.88 (Div. Reinv. Plan)

CAPITALIZATION (10/31/02):

	($000)	(%)
Long-Term Debt	8,950,400	73.7
Deferred Income Tax	24,500	0.2
Common & Surplus	3,163,200	26.1
Total	12,138,100	100.0

BUSINESS:

Deere & Company manufactures and distributes agricultural equipment, lawn and grounds care products, and industrial equipment for construction, forestry, and public works. The Company also provides credit and health care products. The farm equipment segment produces a full range of equipment including: tractors; tillage, soil preparation, planting and harvesting machinery; and crop-handling equipment. The industrial equipment segment produces crawler dozers and loaders; four-wheel-drive loaders; elevating scrapers; motor graders; excavators; log skidders; and tree harvesting equipment. The lawn and garden operation manufactures and distributes mowers, golf course equipment and other outdoor power products.

RECENT DEVELOPMENTS:

For the three months ended 1/31/03, net income totaled $68.0 million compared with a net loss of $38.0 million in the corresponding period a year earlier. Results for 2002 included pre-tax restructuring charges of $17.0 million. Net sales and revenues climbed 10.8% to $2.79 billion from $2.52 billion the previous year. Agricultural equipment net sales rose 7.7% to $1.27 billion from $1.18 billion the year before. Commercial and consumer equipment net sales advanced 34.9% to $483.0 million, while construction and forestry net sales grew 32.3% to $512.0 million. Operating profit was $156.0 million versus an operating loss of $11.0 million in the prior year.

PROSPECTS:

The Company anticipates full-year 2003 equipment sales growth of 7.0% to 9.0%, along with net income in the range of $500.0 million to $600.0 million, reflecting the Company's aggressive efforts to control costs. Worldwide sales of agricultural equipment are expected to increase by 7.0% to 9.0% in 2003, driven by further expansion in Western Europe. Meanwhile, DE projects shipments of commercial and consumer equipment will climb 13.0% to 15.0% in 2003, while sales of construction and forestry equipment are expected to grow slightly in 2003 due to the full-year inclusion of Hitachi sales.

ANNUAL FINANCIAL DATA:

FISCAL YEAR	TOT. REVS. ($mill.)	NET INC. ($mill.)	TOT. ASSETS ($mill.)	OPER. PROFIT %	NET PROFIT %	RET. ON EQUITY %	RET. ON ASSETS %	CURR. RATIO	EARN. PER SH.$	CASH FL. PER SH.$	TANG. BK. VAL.$	DIV. PER SH.$	PRICE RANGE	AVG. P/E RATIO	AVG. YIELD %
10/31/02	13,947.0	① 319.2	23,768.0	8.9	2.3	10.1	1.3	2.4	① 1.33	4.34	9.49	0.88	51.60 - 37.50	33.2	2.0
10/31/01	13,292.9	① d64.0	22,663.1	5.6	...	...	...	1.9	① d0.27	2.76	13.14	0.88	46.13 - 33.50	...	2.2
10/31/00	13,136.8	485.5	20,469.4	11.1	3.7	11.3	2.4	1.8	2.06	4.80	15.56	0.88	49.63 - 30.31	19.4	2.2
10/31/99	11,750.9	239.2	17,577.6	7.8	2.0	5.8	1.4	2.0	1.02	3.21	16.25	0.88	45.94 - 30.19	37.3	2.3
10/31/98	13,821.5	1,021.4	18,001.5	15.0	7.4	25.0	5.7	1.8	4.16	5.86	16.63	0.88	64.13 - 28.38	11.1	1.9
10/31/97	12,791.4	960.1	16,320.0	15.1	7.5	23.2	5.9	1.9	3.78	5.22	15.94	0.80	60.50 - 39.88	13.3	1.6
10/31/96	11,229.4	- 817.3	14,653.1	15.0	7.3	23.0	5.6	2.0	3.14	4.33	12.72	0.80	47.13 - 33.00	12.8	2.0
10/31/95	10,290.5	706.1	13,848.0	14.4	6.9	22.9	5.1	2.0	2.71	3.80	10.61	0.75	36.00 - 21.67	10.6	2.6
10/31/94	9,029.8	603.6	12,781.1	13.6	6.7	23.6	4.7	2.0	2.34	3.32	8.80	0.68	30.29 - 20.42	10.8	2.7
10/31/93	7,753.5	② 184.4	11,466.5	8.3	2.4	8.8	1.6	2.4	② 0.80	1.72	7.71	0.67	26.13 - 14.13	25.2	3.3

Statistics are as originally reported. Adj. for 3-for-1 stk. split, 11/95. ① Incl. $45.0 mil ($0.18/sh) after-tax special chg., 2002; $216.6 mil ($0.91/sh) net restr. chg., 2001. ② Incl. $107.2 mil non-recur. restr. chg. & bef. $1.11 bill. acctg. change chg.

OFFICERS:
R. W. Lane, Chmn., Pres., C.E.O.
N. J. Jones, Sr. V.P., C.F.O.
J. R. Jenkins, Sr. V.P., Gen. Couns.

INVESTOR CONTACT: Marie Ziegler, Director, Investor Relations, (309) 765-4491

PRINCIPAL OFFICE: One John Deere Place, Moline, IL 61265

TELEPHONE NUMBER: (309) 765-8000
FAX: (309) 765-9929
WEB: www.deere.com

NO. OF EMPLOYEES: 43,000 (approx.)

SHAREHOLDERS: 31,238 (record)

ANNUAL MEETING: In Feb.

INCORPORATED: DE, Apr., 1958

INSTITUTIONAL HOLDINGS:
No. of Institutions: 409
Shares Held: 187,204,011
% Held: 78.2

INDUSTRY: Farm machinery and equipment (SIC: 3523)

TRANSFER AGENT(S): The Bank of New York, New York, NY

DELPHI CORPORATION

EXCH.	SYM.	REC. PRICE	P/E RATIO	YLD.	MKT. CAP.	RANGE (52-WK.)	'02 Y/E PR.
NYSE	DPH	7.73 (2/28/03)	12.7	3.6%	$4.31 bill.	17.40 - 6.60	8.05

LOWER MEDIUM GRADE. IN 2003, THE COMPANY EXPECTS TO BENEFIT FROM STABLE PRODUCTION IN MAJOR AUTOMOTIVE MARKETS, STEADY GROWTH OF ITS NON-GM BUSINESS AND COST-SAVINGS INITIATIVES.

*7 YEAR PRICE SCORE N/A   ***12 MONTH PRICE SCORE 83.6**

*NYSE COMPOSITE INDEX=100

INTERIM EARNINGS (Per Share):

Qtr.	Mar.	June	Sept.	Dec.
1999	0.55	0.70	0.24	0.48
2000	0.51	0.75	0.26	0.36
2001	d0.77	0.29	0.05	d0.23
2002	d0.09	0.39	0.10	0.21

INTERIM DIVIDENDS (Per Share):

Amt.	Decl.	Ex.	Rec.	Pay.
0.07Q	3/13/02	3/21/02	3/25/02	4/22/02
0.07Q	6/27/02	7/3/02	7/8/02	8/5/02
0.07Q	9/4/02	9/12/02	9/16/02	10/15/02
0.07Q	12/4/02	12/12/02	12/16/02	1/15/02
0.07Q	3/26/03	4/3/03	4/7/03	5/5/03

Indicated div.: $0.28 (Div. Reinv. Plan)

CAPITALIZATION (12/31/01):

	($000)	(%)
Long-Term Debt	2,083,000	47.4
Common & Surplus	2,312,000	52.6
Total	4,395,000	100.0

BUSINESS:

Delphi Corporation (formerly Delphi Automotive Systems Corporation) is a supplier of components, integrated systems and modules to the automotive industry. The Company provides its products directly to automotive manufacturers and to the worldwide aftermarket for replacement parts, and to other industrial customers. The Company operates its business along two major product sectors: Electrical, Electronics, Safety and Interior, and Dynamics, Propulsion and Thermal. As of 2/10/03, DPH operated 179 wholly-owned manufacturing facilities, 42 joint ventures, 53 customer centers and sales offices and 32 technical centers in 41 countries. On 2/10/99, General Motors made an initial public offering of 100.0 million shares of DPH's $0.01 par value common stock. In May 1999, GM spun-off 80.1% of DPH common stock to GM $1 2/3 par value common stockholders to complete DPH's divestiture.

RECENT DEVELOPMENTS:

For the year ended 12/31/02, the Company reported net income of $343.0 million compared with a net loss of $370.0 million. Results for 2002 included net after-tax restructuring and product line charges of $174.0 million. Results for 2001 included after-tax restructuring and impairment charges of $590.0 million and after-tax goodwill amortization of $28.0 million. Total net sales increased 5.1% to $27.43 billion from $26.09 billion a year earlier. Net sales to GM and affiliates rose 1.4% to $17.86 billion, while net sales to other customers advanced 13.0% to $9.57 billion. Operating income amounted to $690.0 million versus an operating loss of $284.0 million the year before.

PROSPECTS:

Going forward, the Company should benefit from stable production in major automotive markets, steady growth of its non-GM business and savings related to ongoing restructuring and cost containment. The ramp-up of several new products, including passive occupant detection, mobile multimedia, diesel engine management systems and connection systems should continue to result in strong overall gains in sales to major auto makers, commercial vehicle manufacturers and the independent aftermarket. Meanwhile, DPH expects first quarter revenues to range between $6.90 billion and $7.00 billion, and net income of $120.0 million to $130.0 million.

ANNUAL FINANCIAL DATA:

FISCAL YEAR	TOT. REVS. ($mill.)	NET INC. ($mill.)	TOT. ASSETS ($mill.)	OPER. PROFIT %	NET PROFIT %	RET. ON EQUITY %	RET. ON ASSETS %	CURR. RATIO	EARN. PER SH.$	CASH FL.PER SH.$	TANG. BK. VAL.$	DIV. PER SH.$	PRICE RANGE	AVG. P/E RATIO	AVG. YIELD %
p12/31/02	27,427.0	③ 343.0	...	...	...	...	...	...	③ 0.61	...	...	0.28	17.40 - 6.60	19.7	2.3
12/31/01	26,088.0	② d370.0	18,602.0	...	...	...	...	1.3	② d0.66	1.39	4.13	0.28	17.50 - 9.50	...	2.1
12/31/00	29,139.0	① 1,062.0	18,521.0	5.8	3.6	28.2	5.7	1.4	① 1.88	3.55	6.73	0.28	21.13 - 10.50	8.4	1.8
12/31/99	29,192.0	1,083.0	18,350.0	5.8	3.7	33.8	5.9	1.6	1.95	3.50	5.69	0.14	22.25 - 14.00	9.3	0.8
12/31/98	28,479.0	d93.0	15,506.0	...	...	...	...	1.6	d0.20	2.17	0.02	...	...	...	...
12/31/97	31,447.0	215.0	15,026.0	1.1	0.7	...	1.4	1.6	0.46	4.70	...	...	...	...	...
12/31/96	31,032.0	853.0	15,390.0	4.1	2.7	92.5	5.5	1.7	1.83	3.65	1.98	...	...	...	...
12/31/95	31,661.0	1,307.0	...	6.8	4.1	...	...	...	2.81	4.47	...	...	...	...	...
12/31/94	31,044.0	1,233.0	14,494.0	6.7	4.0	N.M.	8.5	...	2.10	...	...	...	...	...	...

Statistics are as originally reported. ① Incl. non-recurr. after-tax chrg. $32.0 mill. ② Incl. after-tax restr. chrg. of $404.0 mill. and after-tax impairment chrg. of $186.0 mill. ③ Incl. after-tax restr. and prod. line chrg. of $174.0 mill.

OFFICERS:
J. T. Battenberg III, Chmn., Pres., C.E.O.
A. S. Dawes, Vice-Chmn., C.F.O.
J. G. Blahnik, V.P., Treas.
INVESTOR CONTACT: Paula M. Angelo, (248) 813-2626
PRINCIPAL OFFICE: 5725 Delphi Drive, Troy, MI 48098

TELEPHONE NUMBER: (248) 813-2000
FAX: (248) 813-2670
WEB: www.delphiauto.com
NO. OF EMPLOYEES: 192,000 (approx.)
SHAREHOLDERS: 407,797 (record)
ANNUAL MEETING: In May
INCORPORATED: DE, 1998

INSTITUTIONAL HOLDINGS: .
No. of Institutions: 384
Shares Held: 412,012,039
% Held: 73.8
INDUSTRY: Motor vehicle parts and accessories (SIC: 3714)
TRANSFER AGENT(S): The Bank of New York, New York, NY

DELTA AIR LINES, INC.

EXCH.	SYM.	REC. PRICE	P/E RATIO	YLD.	MKT. CAP.	RANGE (52-WK.)	'02 Y/E PR.
NYSE	DAL	8.40 (2/28/03)	...	1.2%	$1.04 bill.	38.69 - 6.10	12.10

SPECULATIVE GRADE. ON 4/15/03, THE COMPANY WILL BEGIN SERVICE BETWEEN THE NORTHEAST AND FLORIDA ON ITS NEW LOW-COST AIRLINE CALLED SONG.

INTERIM EARNINGS (Per Share):

Qtr.	Sept.	Dec.	Mar.	June
1998-99	2.08	1.29	1.42	2.40
1999-00	2.38	2.50	1.67	3.51

Qtr.	Mar.	June	Sept.	Dec.
2000	...	...	1.77	0.12
2001	d1.11	d0.76	d2.13	d5.98
2002	d3.25	d1.54	d2.67	d2.98

INTERIM DIVIDENDS (Per Share):

Amt.	Decl.	Ex.	Rec.	Pay.
0.025Q	1/24/02	2/04/02	2/06/02	3/01/02
0.025Q	4/26/02	5/06/02	5/08/02	6/01/02
0.025Q	7/25/02	8/05/02	8/07/02	9/01/02
0.025Q	10/24/02	11/04/02	11/06/02	12/01/02
0.025Q	1/23/03	2/03/03	2/05/03	3/01/03

Indicated div.: $0.10 (Div. Reinv. Plan)

CAPITALIZATION (12/31/01):

	($000)	(%)
Long-Term Debt	8,279,000	65.8
Capital Lease Obligations	68,000	0.5
Deferred Income Tax	465,000	3.7
Common & Surplus	3,769,000	30.0
Total	12,581,000	100.0

*7 YEAR PRICE SCORE 43.7   ***12 MONTH PRICE SCORE 62.4**

*NYSE COMPOSITE INDEX=100

BUSINESS:

Delta Air Lines, Inc. is a major air carrier providing scheduled passenger and cargo service through a network of routes throughout the U.S. and abroad. Delta, Delta Express, Delta Shuttle, the Delta Connection carriers and Delta's Worldwide Partners operate 5,826 flights each day to 437 cities in 78 countries. As of 12/31/02, the Company operated a fleet of 831 aircraft. On 5/11/99, the Company acquired ASA Holdings, Inc., the parent of Atlantic Southeast Airlines. DAL acquired various assets of Pan Am Corp. in 1991.

RECENT DEVELOPMENTS:

For the twelve months ended 12/31/02, net loss totaled $1.27 billion compared with a net loss of $1.22 billion in the corresponding period a year earlier. Results for 2002 and 2001 included net after-tax charges of $314.0 million and $189.0 million, respectively, primarily related to asset impairments and workforce reductions. Total operating revenues slipped 4.1% to $13.31 billion from $13.88 billion the previous year. Operating loss totaled $1.31 billion versus an operating loss of $1.60 billion the year before. The passenger load factor, or percentage of seats filled, improved to 72.0% from 68.8% in the prior year.

PROSPECTS:

On 1/29/03, the Company introduced Song, a wholly-owned subsidiary that will provide low-fare air service initially between the Northeast and Florida. Song, which will begin passenger service on 4/15/03, is expected to provide 144 daily flights utilizing a fleet of 36 Boeing 757 aircraft by October 2003. Meanwhile, DAL is taking aggressive steps to reduce costs and capacity in an effort to restore profitability. In 2003, unit costs are expected to rise 4.0% to 5.0% due to increased pension costs and sharply higher fuel prices. The Company anticipates reduced demand for air travel through at least mid-2004, as well as net losses in both the first quarter of 2003 and the full year.

ANNUAL FINANCIAL DATA:

FISCAL YEAR	TOT. REVS. ($mill.)	NET INC. ($mill.)	TOT. ASSETS ($mill.)	OPER. PROFIT %	NET PROFIT %	RET. ON EQUITY %	RET. ON ASSETS %	CURR. RATIO	EARN. PER SH.$	CASH FL. PER SH.$	TANG. BK. VAL.$	DIV. PER SH.$	PRICE RANGE	AVG. P/E RATIO	AVG. YIELD %
p12/31/02	13,305.0	⑧ d1,272.0		...	...	...	...		⑧ d10.44			0.10	38.69 - 6.10	...	0.4
12/31/01	13,879.0	⑦ d1,216.0	23,605.0	...	...	...	...	0.6	⑦ d9.99	0.43	12.84	0.10	52.94 - 20.00	...	0.3
⑥ 12/31/00	16,741.0	⑤ 928.0	21,931.0	9.8	5.5	16.6	4.2	0.6	⑤ 7.05	16.05	23.30	0.10	58.31 - 39.63	6.9	0.2
6/30/00	15,888.0	④ 1,369.0	20,566.0	8.1	8.6	26.9	6.7	0.6	④ 9.90	18.15	19.04	0.10	58.31 - 39.63	4.9	0.2
6/30/99	14,711.0	1,101.0	16,544.0	12.7	7.5	23.7	6.7	0.5	7.20	13.47	23.64	0.10	72.00 - 45.69	8.2	0.2
6/30/98	14,138.0	1,001.0	14,603.0	12.0	7.1	23.8	6.9	0.7	6.34	11.77	18.94	0.10	71.81 - 40.88	8.9	0.2
6/30/97	13,590.0	③ 854.0	12,741.0	11.3	6.3	27.0	6.7	0.7	③ 5.65	10.39	15.55	0.10	60.31 - 34.63	8.4	0.2
6/30/96	12,455.0	② 156.0	12,226.0	3.7	1.3	5.8	1.3	0.9	② 0.71	6.79	13.19	0.10	43.50 - 33.38	54.1	0.3
6/30/95	12,194.0	② 294.0	12,143.0	5.4	2.4	15.1	2.4.	0.9	② 2.04	7.55	9.91	0.10	46.03 - 25.13	16.2	0.3
6/30/94	12,359.0	① d409.0	11,896.0	...	...	...	...	0.9	① d5.16	0.96	5.79	0.10	28.94 - 19.75	...	0.4

Statistics are as originally reported. Adj. for 2-for-1 stk. split, 11/98. ① Incl. $829 mil restr. chrg., 1996; $526 mil. 1994. ② Bef. $114 mil acctg. cr. ③ Incl. $20.3 mil pre-tax chg. for lawsuit & $52 mil pre-tax chg. for restr. ④ Bef. $66.0 mil acctg. chg.; incl. pre-tax gain of $1.20 bil fr sale of invest & non-recur. chg. of $555.0 mil fr disposal of surplus parts and asset write downs. ⑤ Bef. $100.0 mil acctg. chg. & incl. $108.0 mil pre-tax chg. for asset write downs and other special chgs. & incl. $301.0 mil pre-tax gain fr sale of invest. ⑥ Results for 12 months to refl change in fiscal year end. ⑦ Incl. $1.12 bil. pre-tax chg. fr. asset write-downs and oth. spec. chgs.; $634.0 mil. pre-tax gain fr. airline stabilization act & $127.0 mil gain fr. sale of invest. ⑧ Incl. $314.0 mil ($2.55/sh) after-tax chg. for asset impairments and other special chgs.

OFFICERS:
L. F. Mullin, Chmn., C.E.O.
F. W. Reid, Pres., C.O.O.
M. M. Burns, Exec. V.P., C.F.O.

INVESTOR CONTACT: Investor Relations, (404) 715-2170

PRINCIPAL OFFICE: Hartsfield Atlanta International Airport, P.O. Box 20706, Atlanta, GA 30320

TELEPHONE NUMBER: (404) 715-2600
FAX: (404) 715-5042
WEB: www.delta-air.com

NO. OF EMPLOYEES: 75,100

SHAREHOLDERS: 21,953

ANNUAL MEETING: In Apr.

INCORPORATED: DE, Mar., 1967

INSTITUTIONAL HOLDINGS:
No. of Institutions: 235
Shares Held: 83,591,357
% Held: 67.8

INDUSTRY: Air transportation, scheduled (SIC: 4512)

TRANSFER AGENT(S): EquiServe Trust Company, N.A., Jersey City, NJ

DELUXE CORPORATION

EXCH.	SYM.	REC. PRICE	P/E RATIO	YLD.	MKT. CAP.	RANGE (52-WK.)	'02 Y/E PR.
NYSE	DLX	40.30 (2/28/03)	12.0	3.7%	$2.58 bill.	50.13 - 33.02	42.10

UPPER MEDIUM GRADE. THE COMPANY EXPECTS 2003 DILUTED EARNINGS PER SHARE OF AT LEAST $3.40.

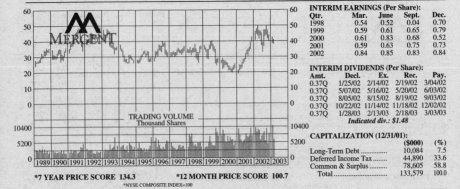

*7 YEAR PRICE SCORE 134.3   ***12 MONTH PRICE SCORE 100.7**

*NYSE COMPOSITE INDEX=100

INTERIM EARNINGS (Per Share):

Qtr.	Mar.	June	Sept.	Dec.
1998	0.54	0.52	0.04	0.70
1999	0.59	0.61	0.65	0.79
2000	0.61	0.83	0.68	0.52
2001	0.59	0.63	0.75	0.73
2002	0.84	0.85	0.83	0.84

INTERIM DIVIDENDS (Per Share):

Amt.	Decl.	Ex.	Rec.	Pay.
0.37Q	1/25/02	2/14/02	2/19/02	3/04/02
0.37Q	5/07/02	5/16/02	5/20/02	6/03/02
0.37Q	8/05/02	8/15/02	8/19/02	9/03/02
0.37Q	10/22/02	11/14/02	11/18/02	12/02/02
0.37Q	1/28/03	2/13/03	2/18/03	3/03/03

Indicated div.: $1.48

CAPITALIZATION (12/31/01):

	($000)	(%)
Long-Term Debt	10,084	7.5
Deferred Income Tax	44,890	33.6
Common & Surplus	78,605	58.8
Total	133,579	100.0

BUSINESS:

Deluxe Corporation provides personal and business checks, business forms, labels, self-inking stamps, fraud prevention services and customer retention programs to banks, credit unions, financial services companies, consumers and small businesses. The Company reaches clients and customers through a number of distribution channels: the Internet, direct mail, the telephone and a nationwide sales force. DLX operates in three business segments: Financial Services (58.7% of 2002 revenues); Direct Checks (24.2%); and Business Services (17.1%).

RECENT DEVELOPMENTS:

For the year ended 12/31/02, net income rose 15.3% to $214.3 million compared with $185.9 million in 2001. Results for 2002 included asset impairment and disposition losses of $300,000 versus $2.1 million the year before. Results for 2001 also included goodwill amortization expense of $6.2 million. Revenues climbed 0.4% to $1.28 billion, due to a 4.4% increase in revenue per unit and a unit decline of 3.7% due primarily to fewer conversion programs and the soft economy. Revenue for financial services decreased 1.9%, while revenue for direct checks and business services increased 1.7% and 7.2%, respectively. Gross margin improved to 66.1% from 64.5% in the previous year, reflecting an increase in revenue per unit, productivity improvements and cost-reduction efforts.

PROSPECTS:

The Company expects results for 2003 to be slightly better than 2002, despite sluggish economic conditions, a decrease in check volume due to the increased use of electronic payments and competitive pricing. However, the Company plans to grow revenue and operating income in 2003 over the prior year. Going forward, the Company will continue to invest in growth opportunities, while pursuing cost-reduction initiatives. Capital spending is expected to be approximately $45.0 million in 2003. Meanwhile, earnings per share for 2003 are expected to be at least $3.40.

ANNUAL FINANCIAL DATA:

FISCAL YEAR	TOT. REVS. ($mill.)	NET INC. ($mill.)	TOT. ASSETS ($mill.)	OPER. PROFIT %	NET PROFIT %	RET. ON EQUITY %	RET. ON ASSETS %	CURR. RATIO	EARN. PER SH. $	CASH FL. PER SH. $	TANG. BK. VAL.$	DIV. PER SH. $	PRICE RANGE	AVG. P/E RATIO	AVG. YIELD %
p12/31/02	1,284.0	⑧ 214.3							⑧ 3.36		...	1.48	50.13 - 33.02	12.4	3.6
12/31/01	1,278.4	⑦ 185.9	537.7	23.6	14.5	236.5	34.6	0.2	⑦ 2.69	3.76	...	1.48	42.65 - 18.85	11.4	4.8
12/31/00	1,262.7	⑥ 169.5	649.5	22.0	13.4	64.5	26.1	0.7	⑥ 2.34	3.29	0.55	1.48	29.00 - 19.63	10.4	6.1
12/31/99	1,650.5	203.0	992.6	18.3	12.3	48.7	20.5	1.0	2.64	3.73	2.89	1.48	40.50 - 24.44	12.3	4.6
12/31/98	1,931.8	⑤ 145.4	1,203.0	12.8	7.5	23.9	12.1	1.4	⑤ 1.80	2.86	5.15	1.48	38.19 - 26.06	17.8	4.5
12/31/97	1,919.4	④ 44.7	1,148.4	8.1	2.3	7.3	3.9	1.3	④ 0.55	1.73	5.44	1.48	37.00 - 29.75	60.7	4.4
12/31/96	1,895.7	③ 65.5	1,176.4	4.6	3.5	9.2	5.6	1.3	③ 0.80	2.09	6.00	1.48	39.75 - 27.00	41.7	4.4
12/31/95	1,858.0	② 94.4	1,295.1	9.9	5.1	12.1	7.3	1.0	② 1.15	2.40	4.96	1.48	34.00 - 25.75	26.0	5.0
12/31/94	1,747.9	① 140.9	1,256.3	13.9	8.1	17.3	11.2	1.4	① 1.71	2.75	5.90	1.46	38.00 - 25.63	18.6	4.6
12/31/93	1,581.8	① 141.9	1,252.0	14.7	9.0	17.7	11.3	1.8	① 1.71	2.58	6.15	1.42	47.88 - 31.75	23.3	3.6

Statistics are as originally reported. ① Incl. $10.0 mill. pre-tax credit, 1994; $49.0 mill. pre-tax chg., 1993. ② Bef. $7.4 mill. loss fr. disc. oper.; incl. $62.5 mill. pre-tax non-recur. chg. ③ Incl. $142.3 mill. net pre-tax chg. for goodwill impair., restr., gains & losses on sales of bus., & oth. costs. ④ Incl. $180.0 mill. net pre-tax chg. rel. to write-dwn of impaired assets, write-offs of some bus. units, legal proceedings, addl. facility closings, elim. of some job func., & oth. bal. sheet adj. ⑤ Incl. $70.2 mill. pre-tax chg. ⑥ Excl. $7.5 mill. net income fr. disc. ops. ⑦ Incl. $2.1 mill. loss fr. asset dispos. ⑧ Incl. $300,000 pre-tax asset impair. & disp. losses.

OFFICERS:
L. J. Mosner, Chmn., C.E.O.
R. E. Eilers, Pres., C.O.O.
D. J. Treff, Sr. V.P., C.F.O.

INVESTOR CONTACT: Stu Alexander, V.P., Inv. Rel., (651) 483-7358

PRINCIPAL OFFICE: 3680 Victoria Street North, Shoreview, MN 55126-2966

TELEPHONE NUMBER: (651) 483-7111
FAX: (651) 483-7337
WEB: www.deluxe.com

NO. OF EMPLOYEES: 6,840 (approx.)

SHAREHOLDERS: 11,462

ANNUAL MEETING: In May

INCORPORATED: MN, Mar., 1920

INSTITUTIONAL HOLDINGS:
No. of Institutions: 261
Shares Held: 48,266,111
% Held: 78.2

INDUSTRY: Blankbooks and looseleaf binders (SIC: 2782)

TRANSFER AGENT(S): Wells Fargo Shareowner Services, St. Paul, MN

DEVRY INC.

EXCH.	SYM.	REC. PRICE	P/E RATIO	YLD.	MKT. CAP.	RANGE (52-WK.)	'02 Y/E PR.
NYSE	DV	17.08 (2/28/03)	17.4	...	$1.19 bill.	34.76 - 12.10	16.61

MEDIUM GRADE. GOING FORWARD, THE COMPANY WILL CONTINUE TO OPEN ADDITIONAL ADULT LEARNING CENTERS AND ADD NEW DEGREE PROGRAMS.

TRADING VOLUME
Thousand Shares

*7 YEAR PRICE SCORE 99.8   ***12 MONTH PRICE SCORE 86.3**

*NYSE COMPOSITE INDEX=100

INTERIM EARNINGS (Per Share):

Qtr.	Sept.	Dec.	Mar.	June
1998-99	0.11	0.15	0.15	0.14
1999-00	0.14	0.18	0.19	0.17
2000-01	0.17	0.22	0.23	0.20
2001-02	0.20	0.26	0.26	0.23
2002-03	0.16	0.33	...	...

INTERIM DIVIDENDS (Per Share):

Amt.	Decl.	Ex.	Rec.	Pay.
		No dividends paid.		

CAPITALIZATION (6/30/02):

	($000)	(%)
Common & Surplus	353,546	100.0
Total	353,546	100.0

BUSINESS:

DeVry Inc. is a holding company for DeVry University and Becker Conviser Professional Review. Devry University offers undergraduate degrees in business, technology and management. The university's Keller Graduate School of Management offers graduate degree programs. As of 10/07/02, DeVry University provided its degree programs through 26 undergraduate campuses and 37 adult learning centers, in the U.S. and Canada, as well as through DeVry University Online, serving a total enrollment of over 56,000 full- and part-time students. Summer 2002 undergraduate enrollment was 43,567, while enrollment at Keller Graduate School for the 2002 September term was 10,713. Becker Conviser Professional Review is an international training firm that offers preparatory coursework for the Certified Public Accountant, Certified Management Accountant and Chartered Financial Analyst exams.

RECENT DEVELOPMENTS:

For the second quarter ended 12/31/02, net income grew 24.6% to $23.0 million versus $18.4 million in the corresponding prior-year quarter. Earnings for 2002 included income tax benefits of $8.1 million. Total revenues increased 3.5% to $172.5 million from $166.7 million a year earlier. Tuition revenues climbed 3.5% to $159.2 million, while other educational revenues improved 3.6% to $13.3 million. Total costs and expenses rose 9.2% to $148.8 million, or 86.2% of revenues, from $136.3 million, or 81.8% of revenues, in the previous year. Income before income taxes was $23.8 million versus $30.4 million a year earlier.

PROSPECTS:

During the second quarter, the Company continued its geographic expansion with the opening of new DeVry University Centers in Plano, Texas, and Valley Forge, Pennsylvania. In addition, seven existing Keller Graduate School of Management centers were converted to the DeVry University Center format, bringing the total number of university centers to 18 as of 12/31/02. Meanwhile, DeVry University received approval from The Higher Learning Commission of the North Central Association to offer on-line its remaining undergraduate degree programs. Going forward, the Company will continue to open additional adult learning centers and add new degree programs.

ANNUAL FINANCIAL DATA:

FISCAL YEAR	TOT. REVS. ($000)	NET INC. ($000)	TOT. ASSETS ($000)	OPER. PROFIT %	NET PROFIT %	RET. ON EQUITY %	RET. ON ASSETS %	CURR. RATIO	EARN. PER SH.$	CASH FL. PER SH.$	TANG. BK. VAL.$	PRICE RANGE	AVG. P/E RATIO
6/30/02	648,134	67,055	467,628	17.2	10.3	19.0	14.3	1.1	0.95	1.42	3.94	34.76 - 12.10	24.7
6/30/01	568,177	57,776	391,675	17.0	10.2	20.3	14.8	0.9	0.82	1.27	2.95	40.25 - 22.75	38.4
6/30/00	506,824	47,781	327,079	15.7	9.4	21.2	14.6	0.9	0.68	1.04	2.17	41.50 - 16.06	42.3
6/30/99	420,635	38,830	260,691	15.1	9.2	22.1	14.9	1.1	0.55	0.80	1.98	31.88 - 15.63	43.2
6/30/98	353,471	30,724	223,892	14.5	8.7	22.5	13.7	1.1	0.44	0.64	1.42	30.63 - 14.00	50.7
6/30/97	308,319	24,186	206,703	13.9	7.8	23.2	11.7	1.2	0.36	0.52	0.97	16.34 - 9.50	36.4
6/30/96	260,007	19,245	178,089	13.0	7.4	34.1	10.8	1.2	0.29	0.40	0.28	12.69 - 6.44	33.5
6/30/95	228,593	14,896	126,671	12.6	6.5	40.2	11.8	1.2	0.22	0.32	0.53	7.03 - 3.81	24.3
6/30/94	211,437	12,225	106,798	12.1	5.8	55.1	11.4	1.2	0.18	0.29	0.30	4.19 - 2.94	19.5
6/30/93	191,915	9,431	99,210	11.7	4.9	97.6	9.5	0.8	0.14	0.24	0.11	3.74 - 2.44	21.9

Statistics are as originally reported. Adj. for stk. split 100%, 6/98; 2-for-1, 12/96; 2-for-1, 6/95.

OFFICERS:
D. J. Keller, Chmn., Co-C.E.O.
R. L. Taylor, Pres., Co-C.E.O., C.O.O.
N. M. Levine, Sr. V.P., C.F.O.
INVESTOR CONTACT: Joan Bates, Investor Relations, (630) 574-1949
PRINCIPAL OFFICE: One Tower Lane, Suite 1000, Oakbrook Terrace, IL 60181

TELEPHONE NUMBER: (630) 571-7700
FAX: (630) 571-0317
WEB: www.devry.com
NO. OF EMPLOYEES: 4,300 (avg.)
SHAREHOLDERS: 749
ANNUAL MEETING: In Nov.
INCORPORATED: IL, 1973; reincorp., DE, Aug., 1987

INSTITUTIONAL HOLDINGS:
No. of Institutions: 178
Shares Held: 50,339,214
% Held: 72.0
INDUSTRY: Schools & educational services, nec (SIC: 8299)
TRANSFER AGENT(S): Computershare Investor Services, LLC, Chicago, IL

DIAGNOSTIC PRODUCTS CORPORATION

EXCH.	SYM.	REC. PRICE	P/E RATIO	YLD.	MKT. CAP.	RANGE (52-WK.)	'02 Y/E PR.
NYSE	DP	33.91 (2/28/03)	21.1	0.7%	$0.96 bill.	52.99 - 30.00	38.62

UPPER MEDIUM GRADE. RESULTS ARE BEING DRIVEN BY INCREASED SALES OF IMMULITE PRODUCTS.

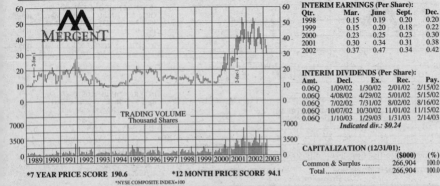

*7 YEAR PRICE SCORE 190.6   ***12 MONTH PRICE SCORE 94.1**

*NYSE COMPOSITE INDEX=100

INTERIM EARNINGS (Per Share):

Qtr.	Mar.	June	Sept.	Dec.
1998	0.15	0.19	0.20	0.20
1999	0.15	0.20	0.18	0.22
2000	0.23	0.25	0.23	0.30
2001	0.30	0.34	0.31	0.38
2002	0.37	0.47	0.34	0.42

INTERIM DIVIDENDS (Per Share):

Amt.	Decl.	Ex.	Rec.	Pay.
0.06Q	1/09/02	1/30/02	2/01/02	2/15/02
0.06Q	4/08/02	4/29/02	5/01/02	5/15/02
0.06Q	7/02/02	7/31/02	8/02/02	8/16/02
0.06Q	10/07/02	10/30/02	11/01/02	11/15/02
0.06Q	1/10/03	1/29/03	1/31/03	2/14/03

Indicated div.: $0.24

CAPITALIZATION (12/31/01):

	($000)	(%)
Common & Surplus	266,904	100.0
Total	266,904	100.0

BUSINESS:

Diagnostic Products Corporation develops, manufactures and markets medical immunodiagnostic test kits and related instrumentation. DP's products are used by hospitals, clinical, veterinary, and forensic laboratories and doctors' offices to obtain identification and measurement of hormones, drugs, viruses, bacteria, and other substances present in body fluids and tissues in small concentrations. The Company's instrument systems include IMMULITE, a family of chemiluminescent immunoassay analyzers, ALASTAT for non-invasive allergy testing, and the MARK 55 HSS for automated immunohistochemical staining. The principal clinical applications of the Company's more than 400 assays relate to diagnosis of conditions including anemia, cancer, diabetes, infectious diseases, reproductive disorders, substance abuse, thyroid disorders and veterinary applications. DP's products are sold in over 100 countries.

RECENT DEVELOPMENTS:

For the year ended 12/31/02, net income advanced 21.2% to $47.3 million compared with $39.0 million the previous year. Total sales increased 14.5% to $324.1 million from $283.1 million the prior year. Sales to non-affiliated customers improved 14.5% to $293.3 million from $256.1 million, while sales to unconsolidated affiliates climbed 14.0% to $30.8 million from $27.0 million the year before. IMMULITE product line sales grew 20.1% to $276.8 million. The Company shipped 1,083 IMMULITE instruments during the year. Gross profit rose 14.7% to $186.3 million. Operating income jumped 19.7% to $69.2 million versus $57.8 million in 2001.

PROSPECTS:

Going forward, the Company should continue to benefit from increased sales of IMMULITE products, which constituted approximately 85.0% of total sales for full-year 2002. However, the Company may continue to experience a decline in sales of its mature radioimmunoassays product line. Separately, on 1/22/03, the Company and Compugen Ltd. announced that Compugen granted to DP a license to develop and commercialize diagnostic assays based on two novel prostate-specific proteins for the screening, detection and monitoring of prostate and other cancers.

ANNUAL FINANCIAL DATA:

FISCAL YEAR	TOT. REVS. ($000)	NET INC. ($000)	TOT. ASSETS ($000)	OPER. PROFIT %	NET PROFIT %	RET. ON EQUITY %	RET. ON ASSETS %	CURR. RATIO	EARN. PER SH.$	CASH FL.PER SH.$	TANG. BK. VAL.$	DIV. PER SH.$	PRICE RANGE	AVG. P/E RATIO	AVG. YIELD %
p12/31/02	324,087	47,313							1.60			0.24	52.99 - 30.45	26.1	0.6
12/31/01	283,430	39,029	325,767	20.4	13.8	14.6	12.0	2.9	1.32	2.13	8.95	0.24	53.25 - 22.00	28.5	0.6
12/31/00	247,867	28,250	280,484	16.9	11.4	12.7	10.1	3.0	1.01	1.61	7.70	0.24	30.38 - 10.84	20.4	1.2
12/31/99	216,193	20,488	250,494	13.1	9.5	9.9	8.2	3.0	0.75	1.28	7.06	0.24	17.66 - 10.94	19.2	1.7
12/31/98	196,643	20,213	246,224	13.5	10.3	10.1	8.2	2.8	0.73	1.37	6.81	0.24	16.44 - 10.19	18.2	1.8
12/31/97	186,264	18,248	222,180	12.7	9.8	9.8	8.2	3.3	0.66	1.13	6.28	0.24	16.75 - 12.75	22.3	1.6
12/31/96	176,832	22,947	207,002	16.2	13.0	12.6	11.1	4.3	0.83	1.23	6.16	0.24	21.44 - 12.50	20.6	1.4
12/31/95	159,649	24,169	189,462	18.4	15.1	14.8	12.8	3.7	0.88	1.16	5.44	0.23	22.44 - 12.13	19.7	1.3
12/31/94	126,453	16,700	152,735	16.2	13.2	12.4	10.9	4.4	0.62	0.84	4.68	0.20	13.31 - 8.88	17.9	1.8
12/31/93	106,791	14,166	137,149	16.9	13.3	11.5	10.3	5.0	0.52	0.61	4.15	0.20	15.38 - 8.56	23.0	1.7

Statistics are as originally reported. Adj. for 2-for-1 stk. split., 6/01.

OFFICERS:
M. Ziering, Chmn., Pres., C.E.O.
S. A. Aroesty, C.O.O.
J. L. Brill, C.F.O.

INVESTOR CONTACT: James L. Brill, C.F.O., (310) 546-8200

PRINCIPAL OFFICE: 5700 West 96th Street, Los Angeles, CA 90045

TELEPHONE NUMBER: (310) 645-8200
FAX: (310) 645-9999
WEB: www.dpcweb.com

NO. OF EMPLOYEES: 1,955 (avg.)

SHAREHOLDERS: 258

ANNUAL MEETING: In May

INCORPORATED: CA, 1971

INSTITUTIONAL HOLDINGS:
No. of Institutions: 139
Shares Held: 16,580,339
% Held: 58.1

INDUSTRY: Diagnostic substances (SIC: 2835)

TRANSFER AGENT(S): Mellon Investor Services, Los Angeles, CA

DIAL CORPORATION (THE)

EXCH.	SYM.	REC. PRICE	P/E RATIO	YLD.	MKT. CAP.	RANGE (52-WK.)	'02 Y/E PR.
NYSE	DL	18.19 (2/28/03)	14.6	0.9%	$1.73 bill.	22.45 - 15.82	20.37

MEDIUM GRADE. THE COMPANY REACHED AN AGREEMENT TO SELL ITS ARGENTINA BUSINESS.

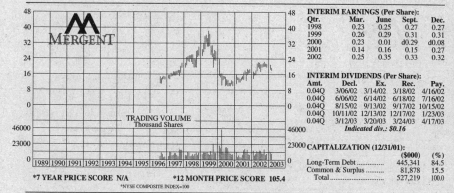

INTERIM EARNINGS (Per Share):

Qtr.	Mar.	June	Sept.	Dec.
1998	0.23	0.25	0.27	0.27
1999	0.26	0.29	0.31	0.31
2000	0.23	0.01	d0.29	d0.08
2001	0.14	0.16	0.15	0.27
2002	0.25	0.35	0.33	0.32

INTERIM DIVIDENDS (Per Share):

Amt.	Decl.	Ex.	Rec.	Pay.
0.04Q	3/06/02	3/14/02	3/18/02	4/16/02
0.04Q	6/06/02	6/14/02	6/18/02	7/16/02
0.04Q	8/15/02	9/13/02	9/17/02	10/15/02
0.04Q	10/11/02	12/13/02	12/17/02	1/23/03
0.04Q	3/12/03	3/20/03	3/24/03	4/17/03

Indicated div.: $0.16

CAPITALIZATION (12/31/01):

	($000)	(%)
Long-Term Debt	445,341	84.5
Common & Surplus	81,878	15.5
Total	527,219	100.0

*7 YEAR PRICE SCORE N/A   ***12 MONTH PRICE SCORE 105.4**
*NYSE COMPOSITE INDEX=100

BUSINESS:

The Dial Corporation was created on 8/15/96 by the spin-off of the consumers products group from the former Dial Corp. DL is a worldwide manufacturer and marketer of consumer products whose business is organized into three segments: domestic branded, international, and commercial markets and other. The domestic branded has leading brands in each of its four core product segments: personal care products include DIAL, BRECK and TONE; laundry products include PUREX, BORATEEM and STA-FLO; air

fresheners includes a wide variety of air freshener forms and fragrances marketed under the RENUZIT brand; and food products include ARMOUR and ARMOUR STAR canned meat products. DL's commercial markets and other business segment includes a broad range of branded products through various channels, including amenity products for hotels and soap and cleaning products for healthcare and janitorial customers.

RECENT DEVELOPMENTS:

For the year ended 12/31/02, the Company reported income of $115.2 million, before a loss from discontinued operations of $55.0 million and an accounting change charge of $43.3 million, versus income of $74.3 million, before a loss from discontinued operations of $206.6 million, in the pre-

vious year. Results for 2002 and 2001 included a gain of $1.7 million and a charge of $8.7 million, respectively, for asset write downs and other special items. Net sales increased 7.8% to $1.28 billion from $1.19 billion in the year-earlier period.

PROSPECTS:

On 12/23/02, DL announced that it has agreed to sell its Argentina business to an entity designated by Southern Cross Group, a private equity investor in Argentina. The transaction, which is subject to negotiated closing conditions and receipt of governmental approvals, should close in the first half of 2003. Going forward, DL will continue

its focus on brand building through internal innovation and continued product updates of its core businesses. DL noted that it will consider acquisitions, debt repayment, stock repurchases and raising its dividend as its cash position grows. Meanwhile, sales for 2003 are expected to rise 3.0% to 4.0%.

ANNUAL FINANCIAL DATA:

FISCAL YEAR	TOT. REVS. ($mill.)	NET INC. ($mill.)	TOT. ASSETS ($mill.)	OPER. PROFIT %	NET PROFIT %	RET. ON EQUITY %	RET. ON ASSETS %	CURR. RATIO	EARN. PER SH. $	CASH FL. PER SH. $	DIV. PER SH. $	PRICE RANGE	AVG. P/E RATIO	AVG. YIELD %
p12/31/02	1,282.2	⑤115.2	...	...	...	...	...	...	⑤1.22	...	0.16	22.45 - 13.80	14.9	0.9
12/31/01	1,663.3	④69.8	1,024.1	9.5	4.2	85.3	6.8	1.2	④0.76	1.31	0.16	18.78 - 11.19	19.7	1.1
12/31/00	1,638.5	③d11.0	1,382.0	3.6	...	...	...	1.0	③d0.12	0.47	0.32	24.06 - 9.88	...	1.9
12/31/99	1,721.6	116.8	1,269.7	12.5	6.8	28.4	9.2	1.0	1.17	1.60	0.32	38.38 - 19.50	24.7	1.1
12/31/98	1,524.5	102.6	1,175.4	12.1	6.7	26.3	8.7	1.0	1.02	1.38	0.32	30.25 - 19.38	24.3	1.3
1/03/98	1,362.6	83.7	883.9	11.9	6.1	26.2	9.5	1.0	0.89	1.23	0.32	21.81 - 13.38	19.8	1.8
12/28/96	1,406.4	②29.9	866.1	5.0	2.1	21.3	3.5	1.2	②0.33	0.67	0.08	15.00 - 11.13	39.6	0.6
①12/31/95	1,365.3	②d27.5	798.4	...	...	...	...	1.2	...	...	...	...	...	...
①12/31/94	1,511.4	91.1	887.4	10.6	6.0	16.4	10.3	1.2	...	...	...	...	...	...
①12/31/93	1,420.2	84.2	...	9.8	5.9	...	...	...	...	...	...	...	...	...

Statistics are as originally reported. ① Pro forma ② Incl. non-recurr. chrg. 1996, $32.1 mill.; 1995, $135.6 mill. ③ Incl. asset write-down & disc. product inventories chrg. of $49.2 mill., a restruct. chrg. and other assets write-downs of $18.2 mill.; and a pre-tax gain of $9.2 mill. ④ Excl. disc. oper. loss of $202.1 mill.; Incl. asset write-down & disc product inventories chrg. $10.4 mill., restruct. & other assets writedowns of $330,000 ⑤ Excl. loss from disc. opers. of $55.0 mill. & an acctg. chrg. $43.3 million; incl. asset writedown & other spec. chrgs. $1.7 million.

OFFICERS:
H. M. Baum, Chmn., Pres., C.E.O.
C. A. Conrad, Exec. V.P., C.F.O.
C. J. Littlefield, Sr. V.P., Gen. Couns., Sec.
INVESTOR CONTACT: Investor Relations Dept., (480) 754-2386
PRINCIPAL OFFICE: 15501 North Dial Blvd., Scottsdale, AZ 85260-1619

TELEPHONE NUMBER: (480) 754-3425
FAX: (480) 754-1098
WEB: www.dialcorp.com
NO. OF EMPLOYEES: 3,139 (approx.)
SHAREHOLDERS: 30,462
ANNUAL MEETING: In June
INCORPORATED: DE, 1996

INSTITUTIONAL HOLDINGS:
No. of Institutions: 244
Shares Held: 68,643,326
% Held: 72.2
INDUSTRY: Soap and other detergents (SIC: 2841)
TRANSFER AGENT(S): Wells Fargo Shareowner Services, South St. Paul, MN

DIAMOND OFFSHORE DRILLING, INC.

EXCH.	SYM.	REC. PRICE	P/E RATIO	YLD.	MKT. CAP.	RANGE (52-WK.)	'02 Y/E PR.
NYSE	DO	21.95 (2/28/03)	46.7	2.3%	$2.90 bill.	34.99 - 17.30	21.85

MEDIUM GRADE. THE COMPANY COMPLETED ITS PURCHASE OF THE SEMISUBMERSIBLE DRILLING RIG WEST VANGUARD FOR $68.5 MILLION.

TRADING VOLUME
Thousand Shares

*7 YEAR PRICE SCORE 78.5   ***12 MONTH PRICE SCORE 92.9**

*NYSE COMPOSITE INDEX=100

INTERIM EARNINGS (Per Share):

Qtr.	Mar.	June	Sept.	Dec.
1998	0.56	0.76	0.75	0.58
1999	0.37	0.37	0.27	0.10
2000	0.21	0.03	0.08	0.20
2001	0.27	0.37	0.38	0.29
2002	0.17	0.09	0.16	0.05

INTERIM DIVIDENDS (Per Share):

Amt.	Decl.	Ex.	Rec.	Pay.
0.125Q	1/18/02	1/30/02	2/01/02	3/01/02
0.125Q	4/16/02	4/29/02	5/01/02	6/03/02
0.125Q	7/15/02	7/30/02	8/01/02	9/03/02
0.125Q	10/16/02	10/30/02	11/01/02	12/02/02
0.125Q	1/24/03	1/30/03	2/03/03	3/03/03

Indicated div.: $0.50

CAPITALIZATION (12/31/01):

	($000)	(%)
Long-Term Debt	920,636	29.2
Deferred Income Tax	376,095	11.9
Common & Surplus	1,853,146	58.8
Total	3,149,877	100.0

BUSINESS:

Diamond Offshore Drilling, Inc. is engaged principally in the operations of contract drilling of offshore oil and gas wells. Contract drilling services are conducted through DO's fleet of 46 offshore rigs. As of 12/31/02, the fleet consisted of 31 semisubmersibles, 14 jack-ups and one drillship. Principal markets for DO's operations are the Gulf of Mexico, the U.K. sector of the North Sea, South America, Africa, Australia and Southeast Asia. The Company also provides a portfolio of drilling services, including project management, extended well tests, and drilling and completion operations through its wholly-owned subsidiary, Diamond Offshore Team Solutions, Inc. As of 12/31/01, Loews Corporation owned 53.1% of the outstanding common stock of DO.

RECENT DEVELOPMENTS:

For the twelve months ended 12/31/02, net income was $62.5 million compared with $173.8 million the previous year. Results for 2002 and 2001 included gains on the sale of marketable securities of $36.5 million and $27.1 million, respectively. Revenues fell 18.6% to $752.6 million, reflecting lower utilization and dayrates from across the Company's drilling fleet, which it classifies as high specification floaters, other semisubmersibles and jack-ups. Operating income decreased 76.9% to $51.9 million versus $225.1 million the year before.

PROSPECTS:

DO's near-term outlook remains challenging. On the positive side, utilization rates appeared to have stabilized. For instance, for the quarter ended 12/31/02, DO's high specification floaters and jack-up rig utilization rates improved to 84.0% and 68.0%, respectively versus 80.0% and 65.0% the previous quarter. Other semi-submersibles rig utilization rates were flat at 61.0%. However, dayrates, with the exception of jack-ups, have lagged, which could restrain top line growth over the immediate term. Separately, on 12/17/02, DO announced that its subsidiary, Diamond Offshore Drilling Limited, completed its purchase of the semisubmersible drilling rig WEST VANGUARD. The rig, purchased for $68.5 million, has been renamed OCEAN VANGUARD.

ANNUAL FINANCIAL DATA:

FISCAL YEAR	TOT. REVS. ($mill.)	NET INC. ($mill.)	TOT. ASSETS ($mill.)	OPER. PROFIT %	NET PROFIT %	RET. ON EQUITY %	RET. ON ASSETS %	CURR. RATIO	EARN. PER SH.$	CASH FL. PER SH.$	TANG. BK. VAL.$	DIV. PER SH.$	PRICE RANGE	AVG. P/E RATIO	AVG. YIELD %
p12/31/02	752.6	62.5							0.47			0.50	34.99 — 17.30	55.6	1.9
12/31/01	885.3	③ 181.5	3,502.5	25.4	20.5	9.8	5.2	4.3	③ 1.31	2.46	13.74	0.50	45.65 — 22.83	26.1	1.5
12/31/00	659.4	② 72.3	3,079.5	8.6	11.0	4.1	2.3	8.9	② 0.53	1.56	12.86	0.50	47.94 — 26.50	70.2	1.3
12/31/99	821.0	① 156.1	2,681.0	27.3	19.0	8.5	5.8	6.4	① 1.11	2.06	13.02	0.50	41.00 — 20.25	27.6	1.6
12/31/98	1,208.8	383.7	2,609.7	47.1	31.7	21.9	14.7	5.9	2.66	3.48	11.81	0.50	54.63 — 20.06	14.0	1.3
12/31/97	956.1	278.6	2,298.6	43.9	29.1	18.1	12.1	5.5	1.93	2.63	10.17	0.14	67.50 — 27.69	24.7	0.3
12/31/96	611.4	146.4	1,574.5	34.9	23.9	12.3	9.3	1.9	1.18	1.78	7.79	...	32.50 — 16.63	20.9	...
12/31/95	336.6	d7.0	618.1	3.5	...	...	...	2.2	d0.10	...	4.93	...	17.25 — 11.69	...	...
12/31/94	307.9	d34.8	587.2	...	...	...	...	2.3	...	...	...	...	...	...	...
12/31/93	288.1	d16.6	592.2	1.5	...	...	...	2.3	...	...	...	...	...	...	...

Statistics are as originally reported. Adj. for 2-for-1 stk. split, 8/97. ① Incls. after-tax chrg. of $6.9 mill. related to a non-cash impairment of investment securities. ② Incls. gain of $14.3 mill. on the sale of assets. ③ Incls. gain of $327,000 on the sale of assets; bef. extraord. chrg. of $7.7 mill.

OFFICERS:
J. S. Tisch, Chmn., C.E.O.
L. R. Dickerson, Pres., C.O.O.
G. T. Krenek, V.P., C.F.O.

INVESTOR CONTACT: Caren W. Steffes, (281) 492-5393

PRINCIPAL OFFICE: 15415 Katy Freeway, Houston, TX 77094

TELEPHONE NUMBER: (281) 492-5300
FAX: (281) 492-5316
WEB: www.diamondoffshore.com

NO. OF EMPLOYEES: 4,100 (approx.)

SHAREHOLDERS: 387 (approx.)

ANNUAL MEETING: In May

INCORPORATED: DE, Apr., 1989

INSTITUTIONAL HOLDINGS:
No. of Institutions: 168
Shares Held: 125,120,963
% Held: 96.0

INDUSTRY: Drilling oil and gas wells (SIC: 1381)

TRANSFER AGENT(S): Mellon Investor Services LLC, Ridgefield Park, NJ

DIEBOLD, INC.

EXCH.	SYM.	REC. PRICE	P/E RATIO	YLD.	MKT. CAP.	RANGE (52-WK.)	'02 Y/E PR.	DIV. ACH.
NYSE	DBD	36.36 (2/28/03)	19.9	1.9%	$2.59 bill.	42.99 - 30.30	41.22	49 yrs.

INVESTMENT GRADE. THE COMPANY ACQUIRED DATA INFORMATION MANAGEMENT SYSTEMS, A PROVIDER OF VOTER REGISTRATION SYSTEMS IN THE U.S.

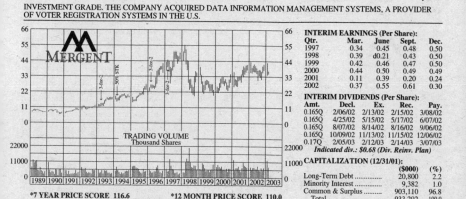

*7 YEAR PRICE SCORE 116.6   ***12 MONTH PRICE SCORE 110.0**

NYSE COMPOSITE INDEX=100

INTERIM EARNINGS (Per Share):

Qtr.	Mar.	June	Sept.	Dec.
1997	0.34	0.45	0.48	0.50
1998	0.39	d0.21	0.43	0.50
1999	0.42	0.46	0.47	0.50
2000	0.44	0.50	0.49	0.49
2001	0.11	0.39	0.20	0.24
2002	0.37	0.55	0.61	0.30

INTERIM DIVIDENDS (Per Share):

Amt.	Decl.	Ex.	Rec.	Pay.
0.165Q	2/06/02	2/13/02	2/15/02	3/08/02
0.165Q	4/25/02	5/15/02	5/17/02	6/07/02
0.165Q	8/07/02	8/14/02	8/16/02	9/06/02
0.165Q	10/09/02	11/13/02	11/15/02	12/06/02
0.17Q	2/05/03	2/12/03	2/14/03	3/07/03

Indicated div.: $0.68 (Div. Reinv. Plan)

CAPITALIZATION (12/31/01):

	($000)	(%)
Long-Term Debt	20,800	2.2
Minority Interest	9,382	1.0
Common & Surplus	903,110	96.8
Total	933,292	100.0

BUSINESS:

Diebold, Inc. provides card-based transaction systems, security products, and customer service solutions to the financial, education, and healthcare industries. The Company develops, manufactures, sells and services the following products: automated teller machines, electronic and physical security systems, bank facility equipment, electronic voting systems, software and integrated systems for global financial and commercial markets. The products segment accounted for 51.2% of revenues, while the services segment accounted for 48.8% for the year ended 12/31/02.

RECENT DEVELOPMENTS:

For the year ended 12/31/02, income totaled $132.3 million, before a $33.1 million accounting change charge, compared with net income of $66.9 million in the prior year. Results for 2001 included one-time pre-tax realignment charges of $42.3 million and other pre-tax special charges totaling $31.4 million. Total net sales rose 10.2% to $1.94 billion from $1.76 billion a year earlier. Product net sales climbed 7.7% to $993.0 million, while service net sales advanced 13.0% to $947.1 million. Gross profit was $594.6 million, or 30.6% of net sales, versus $530.8 million, or 30.2% of net sales, the previous year. Operating profit increased 73.6% to $241.2 million from $138.9 million in 2001.

PROSPECTS:

On 1/23/03, the Company announced that it has acquired Data Information Management Systems, a provider of voter registration systems supporting information for more than 14.0 million voters in the U.S., including more than 55.0% of the registered voters in California. Meanwhile, the Company is targeting full-year 2003 revenue growth of between 5.0% and 10.0%, fueled by strong revenue growth of DBD's voting systems and security products and services. In addition, the Company anticipates 2003 earnings in the range of $2.32 to $2.45 per share.

ANNUAL FINANCIAL DATA:

FISCAL YEAR	TOT. REVS. ($mill.)	NET INC. ($mill.)	TOT. ASSETS ($mill.)	OPER. PROFIT %	NET PROFIT %	RET. ON EQUITY %	RET. ON ASSETS %	CURR. RATIO	EARN. PER SH.$	CASH FL. PER SH.$	TANG. BK. VAL.$	DIV. PER SH.$	PRICE RANGE	AVG. P/E RATIO	AVG. YIELD %
p12/31/02	1,940.2	② 132.3							② 1.83			0.66	43.55 - 30.30	20.2	1.8
12/31/01	1,760.3	① 66.9	1,651.9	7.9	3.8	7.4	4.0	1.4	① 0.93	1.57	8.79	0.64	41.50 - 25.75	36.2	1.9
12/31/00	1,743.6	136.9	1,585.4	13.1	7.9	14.6	8.6	1.4	1.92	2.42	8.94	0.62	34.75 - 21.50	14.6	2.2
12/31/99	1,259.2	① 128.9	1,298.8	14.8	10.2	15.3	9.9	1.7	① 1.85	2.35	9.63	0.60	39.88 - 19.69	16.1	2.0
12/31/98	1,185.7	① 76.1	1,004.2	9.0	6.4	10.9	7.6	2.3	① 1.10	1.47	9.87	0.56	55.31 - 19.13	33.8	1.5
12/31/97	1,226.9	122.5	991.1	15.0	10.0	18.3	12.4	2.3	1.76	2.03	9.69	0.50	50.63 - 28.00	22.3	1.3
12/31/96	1,030.2	97.4	859.1	13.6	9.5	16.9	11.3	2.1	1.42	1.72	8.36	0.45	42.33 - 22.45	22.8	1.4
12/31/95	863.4	76.2	745.2	12.4	8.8	15.1	10.2	2.0	1.11	1.32	7.37	0.43	27.61 - 14.67	19.0	2.0
12/31/94	760.2	63.5	666.2	11.9	8.4	13.8	9.5	2.1	0.93	1.12	6.70	0.39	20.78 - 15.07	19.2	2.2
12/31/93	623.3	48.4	609.0	11.1	7.8	11.3	7.9	2.3	0.71	0.89	6.27	0.36	18.26 - 11.58	21.0	2.4

Statistics are as originally reported. Adj. for 3-for-2 stk. split, 2/97, 2/96 & 3/94. ① Incl. $73.7 mil pre-tax chrg. for realignment and other special charges, 2001; $1.2 mil one-time pre-tax chg., 1999; $41.9 mil ($0.60/sh) after-tax chrg. for realignment program, 1998. ② Bef. $33.1 mil ($0.46/sh) acctg. change chrg.

OFFICERS:
W. W. O'Dell, Chmn., Pres., C.E.O.
W. B. Vance, C.O.O.
G. T. Geswein, Sr. V.P., C.F.O.
R. J. Warren, V.P., Treas.

INVESTOR CONTACT: Sandy K. Upperman, Mgr., Inv. Rel., (800) 766-5859

PRINCIPAL OFFICE: 5995 Mayfair Road, P.O. Box 3077, North Canton, OH 44720-8077

TELEPHONE NUMBER: (330) 490-4000
FAX: (330) 588-3794
WEB: www.diebold.com

NO. OF EMPLOYEES: 13,000 (approx.)

SHAREHOLDERS: 82,001 (approx.)

ANNUAL MEETING: In Apr.

INCORPORATED: OH, Aug., 1876

INSTITUTIONAL HOLDINGS:
No. of Institutions: 283
Shares Held: 50,963,682
% Held: 70.7

INDUSTRY: Calculating and accounting equipment (SIC: 3578)

TRANSFER AGENT(S): The Bank of New York, New York, NY

DILLARD'S, INC.

EXCH.	SYM.	REC. PRICE	P/E RATIO	YLD.	MKT. CAP.	RANGE (52-WK.)	'02 Y/E PR.
NYSE	DDS	13.95 (2/28/03)	8.7	1.1%	$1.17 bill.	31.20 - 13.46	15.86

MEDIUM GRADE. EARNINGS ARE BEING HURT BY INCREASED MERCHANDISE MARKDOWNS.

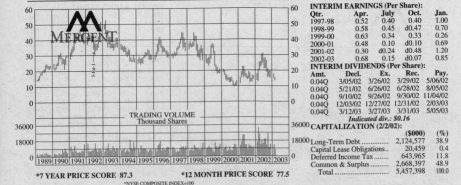

INTERIM EARNINGS (Per Share):

Qtr.	Apr.	July	Oct.	Jan.
1997-98	0.52	0.40	0.40	1.00
1998-99	0.58	0.45	d0.47	0.70
1999-00	0.63	0.34	0.33	0.26
2000-01	0.48	0.10	d0.10	0.69
2001-02	0.30	d0.24	d0.48	1.20
2002-03	0.68	0.15	d0.07	0.85

INTERIM DIVIDENDS (Per Share):

Amt.	Decl.	Ex.	Rec.	Pay.
0.04Q	3/05/02	3/26/02	3/29/02	5/06/02
0.04Q	5/21/02	6/26/02	6/28/02	8/05/02
0.04Q	9/10/02	9/26/02	9/30/02	11/04/02
0.04Q	12/03/02	12/27/02	12/31/02	2/03/03
0.04Q	3/12/03	3/27/03	3/31/03	5/05/03

Indicated div.: $0.16

CAPITALIZATION (2/2/02):

	($000)	(%)
Long-Term Debt	2,124,577	38.9
Capital Lease Obligations..	20,459	0.4
Deferred Income Tax	643,965	11.8
Common & Surplus	2,668,397	48.9
Total	5,457,398	100.0

*7 YEAR PRICE SCORE 87.3   ***12 MONTH PRICE SCORE 77.5**

*NYSE COMPOSITE INDEX=100

BUSINESS:

Dillard's, Inc. (formerly Dillard Department Stores, Inc.) operates a chain of retail department stores located primarily in the Southwest, Southeast and Midwest. As of 2/1/03, the Company operated 333 stores in 29 states. DDS offers merchandise aimed at middle to upper-middle income consumers, with an emphasis on brand names, fashion-oriented apparel, cosmetics, accessories, and home furnishings.

DDS acquired Mercantile Stores Co., Inc. in 1998, the Higbee Company in 1992 and J.B. Ivey & Co. in 1990. The 2003 sales breakdown was: Women's & Juniors' Clothing, 31.0%; Shoes, Accessories & Lingerie, 20.8%; Men's Clothing & Accessories, 18.4%; Cosmetics, 13.9%; Home, 8.9%; and Children's Clothing, 7.0%.

RECENT DEVELOPMENTS:

For the 52 weeks ended 2/1/03, the Company reported income of $136.3 million, before a $530.3 million accounting change charge and a $4.4 million extraordinary charge, compared with income of $65.8 million, before a $6.0 million extraordinary gain, in the corresponding prior-year period. Results for fiscal 2002 and fiscal 2001 included pre-

tax asset impairment and store closing charges of $52.2 million and $3.7 million, respectively. Total revenues were $8.23 billion, down 2.0% versus $8.40 billion a year earlier. Comparable-store sales slipped 3.0% year over year. Cost of sales declined 4.6% to $5.25 billion from $5.51 billion the previous year.

PROSPECTS:

Results are being negatively affected by the Company's aggressive markdown activity in response to increased competitive pressures and sluggish consumer spending. Meanwhile, DDS is focused on expanding its selection of private-brand apparel in an effort to boost profitability.

Separately, the Company anticipates capital expenditures of about $250.0 million and rental expense of approximately $65.0 million in the current fiscal year. DDS plans to open five new stores, including one replacement store, in 2003.

ANNUAL FINANCIAL DATA:

FISCAL YEAR	TOT. REVS. ($mill.)	NET INC. ($mill.)	TOT. ASSETS ($mill.)	OPER. PROFIT %	NET PROFIT %	RET. ON EQUITY %	RET. ON ASSETS %	CURR. RATIO	EARN. PER SH.$	CASH FL. PER SH.$	TANG. BK. VAL.$	DIV. PER SH.$	PRICE RANGE	AVG. P/E RATIO	AVG. YIELD %
p2/01/03	8,233.9	⑤ 136.3							⑤ 1.60			0.16	31.20 - 12.94	13.8	0.7
2/02/02	8,388.3	④ 65.8	7,074.6	4.5	0.8	2.5	0.9	3.0	④ 0.78	4.52	25.02	0.16	22.50 - 11.44	21.8	0.9
2/03/01	8,817.8	③ 96.8	7,199.3	5.6	1.1	3.7	1.3	3.2	③ 1.06	4.42	24.05	0.16	20.81 - 9.44	14.3	1.1
1/29/00	8,921.2	② 163.7	7,918.2	7.5	1.8	5.8	2.1	4.2	② 1.55	4.35	22.50	0.16	37.44 - 17.75	17.8	0.6
1/30/99	8,011.7	② 135.3	8,177.6	6.0	1.7	4.8	1.7	3.1	② 1.26	3.52	20.41	0.16	44.50 - 26.50	28.2	0.5
1/31/98	6,816.9	258.3	5,591.8	8.7	3.8	9.2	4.6	2.7	2.31	4.10	25.70	0.16	44.75 - 28.00	15.7	0.4
2/01/97	6,412.1	238.6	5,059.7	8.7	3.7	8.8	4.7	3.1	2.09	3.81	23.91	0.13	41.75 - 27.13	16.5	0.4
2/03/96	6,097.1	① 167.2	4,778.5	9.4	2.7	6.7	3.5	3.1	① 1.48	3.19	21.91	0.12	33.88 - 24.00	19.6	0.4
1/28/95	5,728.6	251.8	4,577.8	10.4	4.4	10.8	5.5	3.3	2.23	3.93	20.55	0.09	37.63 - 25.50	14.2	0.3
1/29/94	5,312.4	241.1	4,430.3	11.2	4.5	11.6	5.4	3.1	2.14	3.67	18.42	0.08	52.88 - 33.13	20.1	0.2

Statistics are as originally reported. ① Incl. $55.5 mil ($0.55/sh) after-tax chg. for impairment of assets, 2000; $78.5 mil ($0.69/sh) chg., 1996. ② Incl. $140.2 mil ($1.30/sh) after-tax chg. related to Mercantile Stores purchase. ③ Bef. $27.3 mil ($0.30/sh) extraord. gain. from early debt repayment, $130.0 mil ($1.42/sh) acctg. chg. & incl. $51.4 mil pre-tax asset impairment and store closing charge. ④ Bef. $6.0 mil ($0.07/sh) extraord. gain from early debt repayment & incl. $3.8 mil pre-tax asset impairment and store closing charge. ⑤ Bef. $530.3 mil ($6.22/sh) acctg. chg. & $4.4 mil ($0.05/sh) extraord. chg. & incl. $52.2 mil pre-tax asset impairment and store closing charge.

OFFICERS:
W. Dillard, II, Chmn., C.E.O.
A. Dillard, Pres.
J. I. Freeman, Sr. V.P., C.F.O.

INVESTOR CONTACT: Julie J. Bull, Dir. of Investor Relations, (501) 376-5965

PRINCIPAL OFFICE: 1600 Cantrell Road, Little Rock, AR 72201

TELEPHONE NUMBER: (501) 376-5200
FAX: (501) 376-5917
WEB: www.dillards.com
NO. OF EMPLOYEES: 57,257
SHAREHOLDERS: 4,968 (class A common); 8 (class B common)
ANNUAL MEETING: In May
INCORPORATED: DE, 1964

INSTITUTIONAL HOLDINGS:
No. of Institutions: 210
Shares Held: 68,853,160
% Held: 81.3

INDUSTRY: Department stores (SIC: 5311)

TRANSFER AGENT(S): Registrar and Transfer Company, Cranford, NJ

DIMON INCORPORATED

EXCH.	SYM.	REC. PRICE	P/E RATIO	YLD.	MKT. CAP.	RANGE (52-WK.)	'02 Y/E PR.
NYSE	DMN	6.12 (2/28/03)	9.7	4.9%	$273.2 mill.	7.95 - 5.35	6.00

LOWER MEDIUM GRADE. THE COMPANY SEES WORLDWIDE TRADING CONDITIONS FOR LEAF TOBACCO AS FAVORABLE.

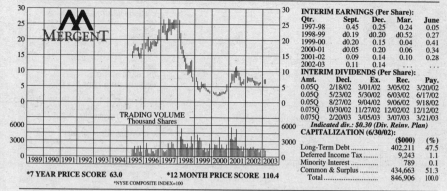

*7 YEAR PRICE SCORE 63.0   ***12 MONTH PRICE SCORE 110.4**

*NYSE COMPOSITE INDEX=100

INTERIM EARNINGS (Per Share):

Qtr.	Sept.	Dec.	Mar.	June
1997-98	0.45	0.25	0.24	0.05
1998-99	d0.19	d0.20	d0.52	0.27
1999-00	d0.20	0.15	0.04	0.41
2000-01	d0.05	0.20	0.06	0.34
2001-02	0.09	0.14	0.10	0.28
2002-03	0.11	0.14	...	...

INTERIM DIVIDENDS (Per Share):

Amt.	Decl.	Ex.	Rec.	Pay.
0.05Q	2/18/02	3/01/02	3/05/02	3/20/02
0.05Q	5/23/02	5/30/02	6/03/02	6/17/02
0.05Q	8/27/02	9/04/02	9/06/02	9/18/02
0.075Q	10/30/02	11/27/02	12/02/02	12/12/02
0.075Q	2/20/03	3/05/03	3/07/03	3/21/03

Indicated div.: $0.30 (Div. Reinv. Plan)

CAPITALIZATION (6/30/02):

	($000)	(%)
Long-Term Debt	402,211	47.5
Deferred Income Tax	9,243	1.1
Minority Interest	789	0.1
Common & Surplus	434,663	51.3
Total	846,906	100.0

BUSINESS:

DIMON Incorporated is the successor to Dibrell Brothers, Inc. and Monk-Austin Inc., which merged on 4/1/95. DMN is engaged in selecting, purchasing, processing, storing, packing and shipping leaf tobacco. As of 6/30/02, the Company sold its tobacco to manufacturers of cigarettes and other consumer tobacco products in about 90 countries around the world. DMN also provides agronomy

expertise and financing for growing leaf tobacco in certain developing markets. As of 6/30/02, DMN owned tobacco processing facilities in Virginia and North Carolina, as well as ownership or interests in processing facilities in Brazil, Malawi, Zimbabwe, Tanzania, Germany, Greece, Italy, Turkey, and Thailand.

RECENT DEVELOPMENTS:

For the second quarter ended 12/31/02, net income was $6.3 million versus $6.2 million in the same period a year earlier. Results for 2002 and 2001 included pre-tax recoveries related to derivative financial instruments of $202,000 and $382,000, respectively. Results for 2001 also included after-tax goodwill amortization of $1.7 million. Sales and

other operating revenues fell 18.8% to $305.7 million. DMN attributed the lower revenues primarily to delayed shipments from Zimbabwe, which are expected to be realized during the quarter ended 3/31/03. Gross profit as a percentage of sales and other operating revenues improved to 14.4% from 12.6% the year before.

PROSPECTS:

DMN's near-term outlook appears good. The Company indicated that worldwide trading conditions for leaf tobacco continue to be favorable, and uncommitted inventories remain at an optimal level. Accordingly, DMN confirmed its earnings guidance of between $1.00 and $1.05 per basis share for fiscal 2003, excluding any effects from market valuation adjustments for derivatives. DMN cautioned that

the operating environment in Zimbabwe, which accounted for 13.0% of the dollar value of tobacco purchased during fiscal 2002, continues to be a concern as the economic and political situation further deteriorates. However, to date, these operations have not seen any material disruption. DMN expects the remainder of the current year Zimbabwe crop to be largely shipped during the quarter ended 3/31/03.

ANNUAL FINANCIAL DATA:

FISCAL YEAR	TOT. REVS. ($mill.)	NET INC. ($mill.)	TOT. ASSETS ($mill.)	OPER. PROFIT %	NET PROFIT %	RET. ON EQUITY %	RET. ON ASSETS %	CURR. RATIO	EARN. PER SH.$	CASH FL. PER SH.$	TANG. BK. VAL.$	DIV. PER SH.$	PRICE RANGE	AVG. P/E RATIO	AVG. YIELD %
6/30/02	1,259.7	④ 27.5	1,277.1	7.6	2.2	6.3	2.2	2.2	④ 0.61	1.54	6.21	0.23	8.29 - 5.35	11.2	3.3
6/30/01	1,401.0	③ 25.0	1,182.1	6.6	1.8	6.1	2.1	1.3	③ 0.56	1.56	5.49	0.20	11.61 - 4.75	14.6	2.4
6/30/00	1,473.6	② 18.0	1,266.7	5.5	1.2	4.5	1.4	2.4	② 0.40	1.39	5.06	0.20	5.81 - 1.94	9.7	5.2
6/30/99	1,815.2	① d28.4	1,471.3	1.6	...	...	...	1.9	① d0.63	0.38	4.53	0.24	7.94 - 2.81	...	4.5
6/30/98	2,171.8	41.8	1,797.5	6.4	1.9	9.9	2.3	2.4	0.94	1.91	4.77	0.60	26.31 - 6.56	17.5	3.7
6/30/97	2,513.2	77.2	1,987.6	7.0	3.1	18.9	3.9	2.0	1.79	2.65	4.46	0.62	26.75 - 19.75	13.0	2.7
6/30/96	2,167.5	39.9	1,020.0	5.3	1.8	12.6	3.9	2.7	1.00	1.86	6.03	0.56	23.25 - 16.00	19.6	2.8
6/30/95	1,927.7	d30.2	1,082.1	0.6	...	...	...	1.6	d0.79	0.04	4.52	0.41	18.75 - 13.75	...	2.5
6/30/94	528.3	2.6	414.4	2.9	0.5	1.6	0.6	1.5	0.14	0.46	8.76	...	...	...	...
6/30/93	611.4	28.7	365.8	6.4	4.7	17.4	7.8	1.9	1.68	1.96	9.11	...	...	...	...

Statistics are as originally reported. ① Incl. non-recurr. pre-tax chrg. of $23.1 mill.; bef. gain of $23.8 mill. from disc. ops. ② Incl. restruct. recov. credit of $605,000 & chrg. of $2.0 mill. rel. to deriv. fin. instruments. ③ Incl. restruct. recov. credit of $1.4 mill., litig. recov. of $3.9 mill. & chrg. of $4.7 mill. rel. to deriv. fin. instrmnts.; bef. net acctg. chge. chrg. of $103,000. ④ Incl. chrg. of $10.2 mill. rel. to deriv. fin. instrmnts.

OFFICERS:
J. L. Lanier, Jr., Chmn.
B. J. Harker, Pres., C.E.O.
J. A. Cooley, Sr. V.P., C.F.O.
INVESTOR CONTACT: Ritchie L. Bond, Sr.
V.P. & Treas., (434) 791-6952
PRINCIPAL OFFICE: 512 Bridge Street, Danville, VA 24541

TELEPHONE NUMBER: (434) 792-7511
FAX: (434) 791-0377
WEB: www.dimon.com
NO. OF EMPLOYEES: 3,900 (approx.)
SHAREHOLDERS: 950 (approx. record);
5,075 (approx. beneficial)
ANNUAL MEETING: In Oct.
INCORPORATED: NC, June, 1990

INSTITUTIONAL HOLDINGS:
No. of Institutions: 97
Shares Held: 25,928,379
% Held: 58.0
INDUSTRY: Farm-product raw materials, nec
(SIC: 5159)
TRANSFER AGENT(S): First Union National
Bank, Charlotte, NC

DISNEY (WALT) COMPANY (THE)

EXCH.	SYM.	REC. PRICE	P/E RATIO	YLD.	MKT. CAP.	RANGE (52-WK.)	'02 Y/E PR.
NYSE	DIS	17.06 (2/28/03)	31.0	1.2%	$34.44 bill.	25.17 - 13.48	16.31

UPPER MEDIUM GRADE. IN FISCAL 2003, THE COMPANY EXPECTS EARNINGS PER SHARE TO INCREASE IN THE RANGE OF 25.0% TO 35.0% YEAR OVER YEAR.

TRADING VOLUME
Thousand Shares

*7 YEAR PRICE SCORE 72.7   *12 MONTH PRICE SCORE 98.9
*NYSE COMPOSITE INDEX=100

INTERIM EARNINGS (Per Share):

Qtr.	Dec.	Mar.	June	Sept.
1997-98	0.37	0.55	0.20	0.14
1998-99	0.30	0.11	0.18	0.03
1999-00	0.25	0.08	0.21	0.11
2000-01	0.16	d0.26	0.19	0.03
2001-02	0.21	0.13	0.18	0.11
2002-03	0.13	...	...	...

INTERIM DIVIDENDS (Per Share):

Amt.	Decl.	Ex.	Rec.	Pay.
0.21A	11/27/01	12/05/01	12/07/01	12/21/01
0.21A	12/03/02	12/11/02	12/13/02	1/09/03

Indicated div.: $0.21

CAPITALIZATION (9/30/02):

	($000)	(%)
Long-Term Debt 8	12,467,000	32.0
Deferred Income Tax	2,597,000	6.7
Minority Interest	434,000	1.1
Common & Surplus	23,445,000	60.2
Total	38,943,000	100.0

BUSINESS:

The Walt Disney Company is a diversified international entertainment company. Media Networks, which accounted for 38.4% of revenues in 2002, includes broadcasting and cable networks. Studio Entertainment, 26.5%, includes theatrical films and home video. Parks and Resorts, 25.5%, includes Walt Disney World Resort, Disney Regional Entertainment, and Anaheim Sports, Inc. Consumer Products, 9.6%, includes character merchandise and publica-tions licensing, The Disney Stores, and books and magazines. On 2/29/96, DIS acquired Capital Cities/ABC, Inc. for $18.90 billion. On 3/20/01, DIS converted each share of its outstanding Internet Group stock to 0.19353 of a share of DIS common. On 10/24/01, DIS acquired Fox Family Worldwide for $5.20 billion. As of 12/31/02, the Company had a 39.0% interest in Euro Disney S.C.A., which operates the Disneyland Resort Paris.

RECENT DEVELOPMENTS:

For the quarter ended 12/31/02, net income decreased 41.5% to $256.0 million compared with $438.0 million in the equivalent 2001 quarter. Results for 2002 included an after-tax charge of $83.0 million for the write-off of an investment in aircraft leveraged leases with United Airlines. Results for 2001 included a gain of $216.0 million resulting from the sale of shares of Knight-Ridder, Inc. held by the Company. Revenues rose 6.4% to $7.47 billion from $7.02 billion a year earlier. Operating income in the Media Networks segment declined 7.0% to 225.0 million, while operating income in the Studio Entertainment segment fell 7.4% to $138.0 million.

PROSPECTS:

Looking ahead, DIS expects earnings per share in fiscal 2003 of 25.0% to 35.0%, with similar growth fiscal in 2004. This projection assumes a steady improvement in the economic climate. Separately, during the quarter, DIS invested $193.0 million in parks, resorts and other properties. Meanwhile, DIS announced the reorganization of the feature animation group in an effort to increase production of cartoon series for its cable and broadcast networks.

ANNUAL FINANCIAL DATA:

FISCAL YEAR	TOT. REVS. ($mill.)	NET INC. ($mill.)	TOT. ASSETS ($mill.)	OPER. PROFIT %	NET PROFIT %	RET. ON EQUITY %	RET. ON ASSETS %	CURR. RATIO	EARN. PER SH.$	CASH FL. PER SH.$	TANG. BK. VAL.$	DIV. PER SH.$	PRICE RANGE	AVG. P/E RATIO	AVG. YIELD %
9/30/02	25,329.0	3 1,236.0	50,045.0	9.5	4.9	5.3	2.5	1.0	2 0.60	1.11	1.78	...	25.17 - 13.48	32.2	...
9/30/01	25,269.0	7 120.0	43,699.0	5.5	0.5	0.5	0.3	1.1	2 0.11	0.87	4.03	0.21	34.80 - 10.50	205.7	0.9
9/30/00	25,402.0	6 920.0	45,027.0	11.2	3.6	3.8	2.0	1.2	6 0.57	2.60	3.78	0.21	43.88 - 26.00	61.3	0.6
9/30/99	23,402.0	5 1,300.0	43,679.0	13.2	5.6	6.2	3.0	1.3	5 0.62	2.44	2.55	0.21	38.69 - 23.38	50.0	0.7
9/30/98	22,976.0	4 1,850.0	41,378.0	17.5	8.1	9.5	4.5	1.2	4 0.89	2.70	1.34	0.20	42.79 - 22.50	36.7	0.6
9/30/97	22,473.0	3 1,966.0	37,776.0	19.2	8.7	11.4	5.2	1.4	3 0.95	3.36	0.63	0.17	33.42 - 22.13	29.1	0.6
9/30/96	18,739.0	2 1,214.0	37,306.0	16.2	6.5	7.5	3.3	1.2	2 0.65	2.78	...	0.14	25.75 - 17.75	33.3	0.6
9/30/95	12,112.1	1,380.1	14,605.8	18.7	11.4	20.8	9.4	1.9	0.87	2.03	4.23	0.12	21.42 - 15.00	21.0	0.6
9/30/94	10,055.1	1,110.4	12,826.3	19.5	11.0	20.2	8.7	1.5	0.68	1.61	3.50	0.10	16.21 - 12.58	21.2	0.7
9/30/93	8,529.2	671.3	11,751.1	20.2	7.9	13.3	5.7	1.3	0.41	1.04	3.13	0.08	15.96 - 12.00	34.1	0.6

Statistics are as originally reported. Adj. for stk. splits: 4-for-1, 5/92; 200%, 7/98. Results from 1996 & forward incl. Capital Cities/ABC, Inc., acq. on 2/29/96 for $18.90 bill. 1 Bef. acctg. chrg. of $371.5 mill. 2 Incl. acctg. chrg. of $300.0 mill. & acq. costs of $225 mill. 3 Incl. 2002, $250.0 mill.; 1997, $135 mill. gain. 4 Incl. $24.0 mill. gain. Incl. chrg. of $64.0 mill. 5 Incl. restruct. chrg. of $132.0 mill. & gain on sale of Starwave of $345.0 mill. 6 Incl. retained interest in the Internet Group loss of $741.0 mill., gain of $243.0 mill. for sale of Fairchild Publications and gain of $93.0 mill. for the disposition of Eurosport. 7 Incl. gain of $22.0 mill., restruct. & impairment chrg. of $1.45 bill. Bef. acctg. chrg. of $278.0 mill. 8 Total debt; DIS does not distinguish between cur. & noncur. assets and liab.

OFFICERS:
M. D. Eisner, Chmn., C.E.O.
R. E. Disney, Vice-Chmn.
R. A. Iger, Pres., C.O.O.

INVESTOR CONTACT: Investor Relations, (818) 560-5300

PRINCIPAL OFFICE: 500 South Buena Vista Street, Burbank, CA 91521

TELEPHONE NUMBER: (818) 560-1000
FAX: (818) 569-1930
WEB: www.disney.com
NO. OF EMPLOYEES: 112,000 (approx.)
SHAREHOLDERS: 995,000 (approx.)
ANNUAL MEETING: In Mar.
INCORPORATED: CA, Sept., 1938; reincorp., DE, Feb., 1987

INSTITUTIONAL HOLDINGS:
No. of Institutions: 904
Shares Held: 1,223,616,451
% Held: 59.9

INDUSTRY: Amusement parks (SIC: 7996)

TRANSFER AGENT(S): The Walt Disney Company, Glendale, CA

DOLE FOOD COMPANY, INC.

EXCH.	SYM.	REC. PRICE	P/E RATIO	YLD.	MKT. CAP.	RANGE (52-WK.)	'02 Y/E PR.
NYSE	DOL	32.80 (2/28/03)	11.9	1.8%	$1.83 bill.	33.99 - 24.14	32.58

LOWER MEDIUM GRADE. DAVID H. MURDOCK ENTERED INTO AN AGREEMENT TO ACQUIRE ABOUT 76.0% OF DOL'S COMMON STOCK FOR $33.50 PER SHARE.

*7 YEAR PRICE SCORE 105.3   *12 MONTH PRICE SCORE 117.8
*NYSE COMPOSITE INDEX=100

INTERIM EARNINGS (Per Share):

Qtr.	Mar.	June	Sept.	Dec.
1997	0.70	1.17	0.40	0.38
1998	0.37	1.35	0.26	d1.82
1999	0.65	0.83	d0.14	d0.51
2000	0.65	0.81	d0.13	d0.12
2001	0.62	0.66	d1.68	0.07
2002	0.99	1.18	0.26	0.32

INTERIM DIVIDENDS (Per Share):

Amt.	Decl.	Ex.	Rec.	Pay.
0.15Q	2/06/02	2/21/02	2/25/02	3/21/02
0.15Q	3/21/02	5/14/02	5/16/02	6/13/02
0.15Q	7/22/02	8/27/02	8/29/02	9/19/02
0.15Q	10/10/02	11/05/02	11/07/02	12/05/02
0.15Q	2/06/03	2/20/03	2/24/03	3/18/03

Indicated div.: $0.60

CAPITALIZATION (12/29/01):

	($000)	(%)
Long-Term Debt	816,124	51.5
Minority Interest	32,018	2.0
Common & Surplus	736,030	46.5
Total	1,584,172	100.0

BUSINESS:

Dole Food Company, Inc. produces and markets fresh fruits, vegetables, flowers and packaged foods worldwide. Operations are in North America, Europe, Latin America, and Asia. DOL's principal products are produced both directly on Company-owned or leased land and through associated producer and independent grower arrangements. DOL's products are primarily packaged and processed by Dole and sold to retail and institutional customers and other food product companies. In 1995, the Company sold its juice and beverage business, excluding the canned pineapple juice business, to The Seagram Co. Ltd. and completed the distribution of its real estate and resorts business, Castle & Cooke, to DOL's shareholders. On 11/29/01, DOL sold its Honduran beverage operations.

RECENT DEVELOPMENTS:

For the year ended 12/28/02, the Company reported income from continuing operations of $156.2 million compared with a loss from continuing operations of $37.1 million in the corresponding period the previous year. Results for 2001 included a $132.7 million pre-tax charge primarily related to business reconfiguration programs and an $8.2 million pre-tax gain on an investment. Net revenue rose 1.8% to $4.39 billion from $4.31 billion a year earlier. Gross profit was $704.3 million, or 16.0% of revenue, versus $433.0 million, or 10.0% of revenue, the year before. Operating income was $283.4 million compared with $49.8 million in 2001.

PROSPECTS:

On 12/19/02, the Company and David H. Murdock, Chairman and Chief Executive Officer of DOL, signed a definitive agreement under which Mr. Murdock will acquire approximately 76.0% of the Company's common stock that he and his family do not already own for $33.50 in cash. The transaction, which has been approved by the board of directors, is expected to be completed in March 2003, subject to shareholder approval. Separately, the Company is targeting full-year 2003 income from continuing operations of between $2.83 and $2.93 per share.

ANNUAL FINANCIAL DATA:

FISCAL YEAR	TOT. REVS. ($mill.)	NET INC. ($mill.)	TOT. ASSETS ($mill.)	OPER. PROFIT %	NET PROFIT %	RET. ON EQUITY %	RET. ON ASSETS %	CURR. RATIO	EARN. PER SH.$	CASH FL.PER SH.$	TANG. BK. VAL.$	DIV. PER SH.$	PRICE RANGE	AVG. P/E RATIO	AVG. YIELD
p12/28/02	4,392.1	⑥ 156.2							⑥ 2.76			0.60	33.99 - 24.14	10.5	2.1
12/29/01	4,449.3	② d37.1	2,746.7	1.1	...	...	...	1.6	② d0.66	1.44	8.59	0.40	27.65 - 14.60	...	1.9
12/30/00	4,763.1	⑤ 67.7	2,844.7	3.9	1.4	12.2	2.4	1.5	⑤ 1.21	3.65	4.95	0.40	21.50 - 11.75	13.7	2.4
1/01/00	5,060.6	④ 48.5	3,034.5	2.8	1.0	9.1	1.6	1.5	④ 0.85	3.17	4.20	0.40	34.13 - 13.75	28.2	1.7
1/02/99	4,424.2	④ 12.1	2,915.1	1.9	0.3	1.9	0.4	1.5	④ 0.20	2.22	5.80	0.40	57.31 - 28.06	213.3	0.9
1/03/98	4,336.1	160.2	2,463.9	5.6	3.7	24.0	6.5	1.6	2.65	4.51	11.10	0.40	50.06 - 33.75	15.8	1.0
12/28/96	3,840.3	③ 89.0	2,486.8	4.3	2.3	16.2	3.6	1.7	③ 1.47	3.31	9.18	0.40	43.75 - 30.88	25.4	1.1
12/31/95	3,803.8	①② 119.8	2,442.2	5.1	3.2	23.6	4.9	1.7	①② 2.00	3.90	8.49	0.40	38.63 - 23.00	15.4	1.3
12/31/94	3,841.6	67.9	3,848.7	4.5	1.8	6.3	1.8	1.9	1.14	3.61	18.17	0.40	35.50 - 22.50	25.4	1.4
.1/01/94	3,430.5	① 77.9	3,387.9	4.1	2.3	7.4	2.3	1.7	① 1.30	3.53	17.70	0.40	37.88 - 25.88	24.5	1.3

Statistics are as originally reported. ① Incl. $61.7 mil gain from sale of bus., 1995; $42.5 mil pre-tax, non-recur. chg., $30.9 mil gain on sale of stk., & $9.4 mil gain on sale of bus., 1993. ② Bef. $18.9 mil ($0.34/sh) inc. fr. discont. opers. & $168.6 mil ($2.99/sh) gain fr. disp. of discont. opers, & incl. $132.7 mil pre-tax restr. chg., 2001; $96.5 mil gain fr. discont. opers., 1995. ③ Incl. $50 mil pre-tax restr. chg. ④ Incl. $20.6 mil pre-tax, non-recur. chg., 1999; & $120.0 mil chg., 1998. ⑤ Incl. $42.5 mil net insur. proceeds fr. Hurricane Mitch, $8.6 mil pre-tax gain fr. sale of Cal. and Ariz. citrus assets, & $45.8 mil pre-tax business downsizing chg. ⑥ Bef. $119.9 mil ($2.12/sh) acctg. change chg.

OFFICERS:
D. H. Murdock, Chmn., C.E.O.
L. A. Kern, Pres., C.O.O.
R. J. Dahl, V.P., C.F.O.

INVESTOR CONTACT: Lawrence A. Kern, Pres., C.O.O., (818) 879-6808

PRINCIPAL OFFICE: One Dole Drive, Westlake Village, CA 91362

TELEPHONE NUMBER: (818) 879-6600
FAX: (818) 879-6615
WEB: www.dole.com
NO. OF EMPLOYEES: 59,000 (approx.)
SHAREHOLDERS: 9,266 (approx. record)
ANNUAL MEETING: In June
INCORPORATED: HI, 1894; reincorp., DE, July, 2001

DOLLAR GENERAL CORPORATION

EXCH.	SYM.	REC. PRICE	P/E RATIO	YLD.	MKT. CAP.	RANGE (52-WK.)	'02 Y/E PR.
NYSE	DG	10.39 (2/28/03)	13.2	1.3%	$3.46 bill.	19.95 - 9.50	11.95

UPPER MEDIUM GRADE. THE COMPANY ANTICIPATES EARNINGS GROWTH OF BETWEEN 11.0% AND 15.0%, BEFORE ONE-TIME ITEMS, IN THE CURRENT FISCAL YEAR.

MERGENT

10% STK
5-for-4 5-for-4 5-for-4 5-for-4 5-for-4 5-for-4 5-for-4

TRADING VOLUME
Thousand Shares

|1989|1990|1991|1992|1993|1994|1995|1996|1997|1998|1999|2000|2001|2002|2003|

*7 YEAR PRICE SCORE 97.0   ***12 MONTH PRICE SCORE 82.9**

*NYSE COMPOSITE INDEX=100

INTERIM EARNINGS (Per Share):

Qtr.	Apr.	July	Oct.	Jan.
1997-98	0.06	0.08	0.10	0.19
1998-99	0.09	0.10	0.12	0.23
1999-00	0.11	0.12	0.15	0.27
2000-01	0.14	0.12	0.15	0.21
2001-02	0.11	0.08	0.14	0.29
2002-03	0.14	0.13	0.20	0.32

INTERIM DIVIDENDS (Per Share):

Amt.	Decl.	Ex.	Rec.	Pay.
0.032Q	3/18/02	3/27/02	4/01/02	4/15/02
0.032Q	6/03/02	6/13/02	6/17/02	7/01/02
0.032Q	8/13/02	8/22/02	8/26/02	9/09/02
0.032Q	11/11/02	12/30/02	1/02/03	1/16/03
0.035Q	3/13/03	4/01/03	4/03/03	4/17/03

Indicated div.: $0.14 (Div. Reinv. Plan)

CAPITALIZATION (2/1/02):

	($000)	(%)
Long-Term Debt	339,470	23.9
Deferred Income Tax	37,646	2.7
Common & Surplus	1,041,718	73.4
Total	1,418,834	100.0

BUSINESS:

Dollar General Corporation sells general merchandise at everyday low prices through a chain of 6,113 stores in 27 states as of 1/31/03. The Company also operates distribution centers in Florida, Kentucky, Mississippi, Missouri, Ohio, Oklahoma and Virginia. The Company offers hard goods, including health and beauty aids, cleaning supplies, housewares, stationery, and seasonal goods. DG also markets soft goods, including apparel for the whole family, shoes, and domestics. In addition to its regular hard good and soft goods inventory, the Company also sells manufacturers' overruns, closeouts, and "irregulars" at a discount from regular prices. DG emphasizes even-dollar pricing of its merchandise, most of which is priced at $1 or in increments of $1.

RECENT DEVELOPMENTS:

For the year ended 1/31/03, net income advanced 27.7% to $264.9 million from $207.5 million in the prior year. Results for fiscal 2002 included a restatement-related gain of $23.1 million, while results for fiscal 2001 included a restatement-related charge of $28.4 million. Results for fiscal 2002 also included a $29.5 million gain from a litigation settlement. Net sales rose 14.6% to $6.10 billion from $5.32 billion in the previous year, helped by the addition of 573 net new stores. Same-store sales increased 5.7% year over year. Gross profit was $1.72 billion, or 28.3% of sales, versus $1.51 billion, or 28.4% of sales, the year before. Operating income climbed 22.4% to $457.3 million from $373.6 million a year earlier.

PROSPECTS:

The Company is targeting earnings growth of between 11.0% and 15.0%, before one-time items, in the current fiscal year. In addition, DG is projecting revenue growth in the range of 13.0% to 15.0% for the year, while same-store sales are expected to increase by 4.0% to 6.0%. During the current fiscal year, the Company plans to open approximately 650 new stores, close between 50 and 70 stores, and remodel or relocate approximately 145 existing locations. DG anticipates capital expenditures for the year of about $165.0 million.

ANNUAL FINANCIAL DATA:

FISCAL YEAR	TOT. REVS. ($mill.)	NET INC. ($mill.)	TOT. ASSETS ($mill.)	OPER. PROFIT %	NET PROFIT %	RET. ON EQUITY %	RET. ON ASSETS %	CURR. RATIO	EARN. PER SH. $	CASH FL. PER SH. $	TANG. BK. VAL. $	DIV. PER SH. $	PRICE RANGE	AVG. P/E RATIO	AVG. YIELD %
p1/31/03	6,100.4	② 264.9							② 0.79			0.13	19.95 - 11.70	20.0	0.8
2/01/02	5,322.9	207.5	2,552.4	7.0	3.9	19.9	8.1	1.4	0.62	0.99	3.13	0.13	24.05 - 10.50	27.9	0.7
2/02/01	4,550.6	① 70.6	2,282.5	3.4	1.6	8.2	3.1	2.1	① 0.21	0.55	2.60	0.12	23.19 - 13.44	87.2	0.7
1/28/00	3,888.0	219.4	1,450.9	9.0	5.6	23.7	15.1	2.3	0.65	0.84	2.80	0.10	26.10 - 15.08	31.8	0.5
1/29/99	3,221.0	182.0	1,211.8	9.0	5.7	25.1	15.0	1.9	0.54	0.70	2.61	0.08	24.19 - 11.26	32.6	0.5
1/30/98	2,627.3	144.6	914.8	9.0	5.5	24.8	15.8	2.2	0.43	0.52	1.70	0.07	16.38 - 7.80	28.2	0.6
1/31/97	2,134.4	115.1	718.1	8.9	5.4	23.7	16.0	2.2	0.34	0.43	1.78	0.05	9.14 - 4.04	19.3	0.8
1/31/96	1,764.2	87.8	680.0	8.4	5.0	20.9	12.9	2.0	0.26	0.34	1.52	0.04	7.13 - 4.09	21.4	0.7
1/31/95	1,448.6	73.6	540.9	8.4	5.1	22.7	13.6	2.0	0.22	0.28	0.96	0.03	5.12 - 3.29	18.8	0.8
1/31/94	1,133.0	48.6	397.2	7.1	4.3	20.2	12.2	2.1	0.15	0.19	0.74	0.02	4.66 - 2.26	22.9	0.7

Statistics are as originally reported. Adj. for all stk. splits & divs. through 5/00. ① Incl. $162.0 mil. pre-tax litigation chrg. ② Incl. $29.5 mil. pre-tax litigation gain and a net pre-tax restatement-related gain of $23.1 mil.

OFFICERS:
C. Turner, Jr., Chmn.
D. S. Shaffer, Pres., C.O.O., acting C.E.O.
J. J. Hagan, Exec. V.P., C.F.O.

INVESTOR CONTACT: Kiley Fleming, Dir., Inv. Rel., (615) 855-5525

PRINCIPAL OFFICE: 100 Mission Ridge, Goodlettsville, TN 37072

TELEPHONE NUMBER: (615) 855-4000
FAX: (615) 855-5527
WEB: www.dollargeneral.com
NO. OF EMPLOYEES: 48,000 (approx.)
SHAREHOLDERS: 16,039 (approx.)
ANNUAL MEETING: In June
INCORPORATED: KY, 1955; reincorp., TN, June, 1998

INSTITUTIONAL HOLDINGS:
No. of Institutions: 294
Shares Held: 210,267,382
% Held: 63.1

INDUSTRY: Variety stores (SIC: 5331)

TRANSFER AGENT(S): Registrar and Transfer Company, Cranford, NJ

DOMINION RESOURCES, INC.

EXCH.	SYM.	REC. PRICE	P/E RATIO	YLD.	MKT. CAP.	RANGE (52-WK.)	'02 Y/E PR.
NYSE	D	53.90 (2/28/03)	11.2	4.8%	$14.27 bill.	67.06 - 35.40	54.90

UPPER MEDIUM GRADE. IN RESPONSE TO DIFFICULT ENERGY AND FINANCIAL MARKET CONDITIONS, THE COMPANY HAS REDUCED ITS FUTURE CAPITAL SPENDING PLANS.

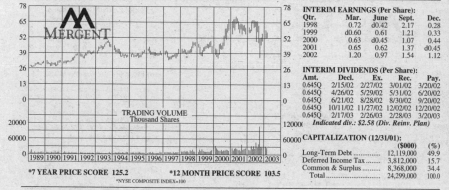

*7 YEAR PRICE SCORE 125.2   *12 MONTH PRICE SCORE 103.5
*NYSE COMPOSITE INDEX=100

INTERIM EARNINGS (Per Share):

Qtr.	Mar.	June	Sept.	Dec.
1998	0.72	d0.42	2.17	0.28
1999	d0.60	0.61	1.21	0.33
2000	0.63	d0.45	1.07	0.44
2001	0.65	0.62	1.37	d0.45
2002	1.20	0.97	1.54	1.12

INTERIM DIVIDENDS (Per Share):

Amt.	Decl.	Ex.	Rec.	Pay.
0.645Q	2/15/02	2/27/02	3/01/02	3/20/02
0.645Q	4/26/02	5/29/02	5/31/02	6/20/02
0.645Q	6/21/02	8/28/02	8/30/02	9/20/02
0.645Q	10/11/02	11/27/02	12/02/02	12/20/02
0.645Q	2/17/03	2/26/03	2/28/03	3/20/03

Indicated div.: $2.58 (Div. Reinv. Plan)

CAPITALIZATION (12/31/01):

	($000)	(%)
Long-Term Debt	12,119,000	49.9
Deferred Income Tax	3,812,000	15.7
Common & Surplus	8,368,000	34.4
Total	24,299,000	100.0

BUSINESS:

Dominion Resources, Inc. is active in regulated and unregulated electric, natural gas and oil development services. The Company operates through three business lines: Dominion Energy, Dominion Delivery and Dominion Exploration and Production. As of 1/23/03, Dominion Energy managed 24,000 megawatts of generation, 7,700 miles of gas transmission pipeline, and over a 960.00 billion cubic feet of storage capacity. It also manages D's generation growth strategy, energy trading, marketing and risk management activities. Dominion Delivery manages

the local electric and gas distribution systems serving 3.9 million customers, about 6,000 miles of electric transmission lines and customer service operations. Dominion Exploration and Production manages the onshore and offshore gas and oil exploration, development and production activities, including the properties acquired from the acquisition of Louis Dreyfus. Dominion Exploration and production has about 6.1 trillion cubic feet equivalent of proved natural gas reserves and an annual production capacity exceeding 450.00 billion cubic feet.

RECENT DEVELOPMENTS:

For the twelve months ended 12/31/02, net income more than doubled to $1.36 billion compared with $544.0 million in 2001. Earnings benefited from the acquisitions of State Line power station and the Cove Point LNG facility, and the successful integration of Louis Dreyfus Natural Gas,

acquired in November 2001. Results for 2002 and 2001 included after-tax special charges of $3.0 million and $509.0 million, respectively. Total operating revenues and income slipped 3.2% to $10.22 billion from $10.56 billion in the prior year.

PROSPECTS:

The Company has significantly reduced its future capital spending plans in response to difficult energy and financial market conditions. The Company has reduced its planned net capital investments to about $2.50 billion in 2003 and

to about $2.20 billion in 2004. As a result, the Company expects to be between $100.0 million and $300.0 million free cash flow negative in 2003 and between $300.0 million and $500.0 million free cash flow positive in 2004.

ANNUAL FINANCIAL DATA:

FISCAL YEAR	TOT. REVS. ($mill.)	NET INC. ($mill.)	TOT. ASSETS ($mill.)	OPER. PROFIT %	NET PROFIT %	NET INC./ NET PROP. %	NET INC./ TOT. CAP. %	RET. ON EQUITY %	ACCUM. DEPR./ GROSS PROP. %	EARN. PER SH.$	TANG. BK. VAL.$	DIV. PER SH.$	DIV. PAYOUT %	PRICE RANGE	AVG. P/E RATIO	AVG. YIELD %
p12/31/02	10,218.0	⑦ 1,362.0								⑧ 4.82	2.58	53.5	67.06 - 35.40	10.6	5.0
12/31/01	10,558.0	⑦ 544.0	34,369.0	16.9	5.2	2.9	2.2	6.5	43.6	⑦ 1.76	15.71	2.58	120.0	69.99 - 55.13	29.1	4.1
12/31/00	9,260.0	⑥ 415.0	29,348.0	16.5	4.5	2.8	2.0	5.9	47.0	⑥ 1.76	18.73	2.58	146.6	67.94 - 34.81	29.2	5.0
12/31/99	5,520.0	⑤ 551.0	17,747.0	23.8	10.0	5.1	4.0	11.6	42.3	⑤ 2.81	24.80	2.58	91.8	48.38 - 36.56	15.3	6.0
12/31/98	6,086.2	④ 535.6	17,517.0	17.9	8.8	5.0	4.1	10.1	41.3	④ 2.75	26.56	2.58	93.8	48.94 - 37.81	15.8	5.9
12/31/97	7,677.6	③ 399.2	20,192.7	19.2	5.2	3.2	2.6	7.9	35.8	③ 2.15	16.55	2.58	120.0	42.88 - 33.25	17.7	6.8
12/31/96	4,842.3	② 472.1	14,905.6	22.8	9.7	4.5	4.0	9.6	37.5	② 2.65	27.17	2.58	97.4	44.38 - 36.88	15.3	6.4
12/31/95	4,651.7	② 425.0	13,903.3	22.1	9.1	4.1	3.8	9.0	35.4	② 2.45	26.88	2.58	105.3	41.63 - 34.88	15.6	6.7
12/31/94	4,491.1	① 478.2	13,562.2	23.1	10.6	4.7	4.3	10.4	33.5	① 2.81	26.60	2.55	90.7	45.38 - 34.88	14.3	6.4
12/31/93	4,433.9	516.6	13,349.5	25.4	11.7	5.1	4.7	11.6	32.0	3.12	26.38	2.48	79.5	49.50 - 38.25	14.1	5.7

Statistics are as originally reported. ① Incl. $42.0 mill. chg. for employee-reduction program. ② Incl. approx. $92.0 mill. ($0.33/sh.) restr. & oth. chgs., 1996; $80.0 mill. ($0.46/sh.), 1995. ③ Incl. $157.0 mill. one-time, pre-tax windfall profits tax. ④ Incl. $201.0 mill. after-tax non-recur. chg. fr. VA Power settlement & $200.7 mill. after-tax gain fr. sale of East Midlands. ⑤ Bef. $255.0 mill. extraord. chg. ⑥ Incl. $198.0 mill. net restr. chg., $186.0 mill. net chg. for write-down of assets, $13.0 mill. net gain & excl. $21.0 mill. credit fr. acctg. change. ⑦ Incl. $3.0 mill. after-tax special chgs., 2002; $509.0 mill., 2001.

OFFICERS:
T. E. Capps, Chmn., Pres., C.E.O.
T. N. Chewning, Exec. V.P., C.F.O.
G. S. Hetzer, Sr. V.P., Treas.

INVESTOR CONTACT: Thomas P. Wohlfarth,
Investor Relations, (804) 819-2150
PRINCIPAL OFFICE: 120 Tredegar Street,
Richmond, VA 23219

TELEPHONE NUMBER: (804) 819-2000
FAX: (804) 775-5819
WEB: www.dom.com
NO. OF EMPLOYEES: 17,100 (approx.)
SHAREHOLDERS: 184,000
ANNUAL MEETING: In Apr.
INCORPORATED: VA, Feb., 1983

DONALDSON COMPANY, INC.

EXCH.	SYM.	REC. PRICE	P/E RATIO	YLD.	MKT. CAP.	RANGE (52-WK.)	'02 Y/E PR.
NYSE	DCI	34.85 (2/28/03)	17.7	1.0%	$1.53 bill.	44.99 - 29.91	36.00

UPPER MEDIUM GRADE. THE COMPANY EXPECTS STEADY TRUCK SALES RESULTS FOR THE REMAINDER OF 2003.

*7 YEAR PRICE SCORE 156.5   *12 MONTH PRICE SCORE 101.6
*NYSE COMPOSITE INDEX=100

INTERIM EARNINGS (Per Share):

Qtr.	Oct.	Jan.	Apr.	July
1997-98	0.28	0.25	0.32	0.30
1998-99	0.28	0.27	0.37	0.39
1999-00	0.36	0.37	0.38	0.40
2000-01	0.37	0.40	0.39	0.50
2001-02	0.43	0.45	0.47	0.55
2002-03	0.50	0.45	...	...

INTERIM DIVIDENDS (Per Share):

Amt.	Decl.	Ex.	Rec.	Pay.
0.08Q	1/18/02	2/20/02	2/22/02	3/14/02
0.08Q	5/17/02	5/22/02	5/24/02	6/13/02
0.085Q	7/26/02	8/21/02	8/23/02	9/12/02
0.085Q	11/15/02	11/27/02	12/02/02	12/13/02
0.09Q	1/17/03	2/26/03	2/28/03	3/14/03

Indicated div.: $0.36 (Div. Reinv. Plan)

CAPITALIZATION (7/31/02):

	($000)	(%)
Long-Term Debt	105,019	21.0
Deferred Income Tax	13,376	2.7
Common & Surplus	382,621	76.4
Total	501,016	100.0

BUSINESS:

Donaldson Company, Inc. is a worldwide manufacturer of filtration systems and replacement parts. The Company's product mix includes air and liquid filters and exhaust and emission control products for mobile equipment; in-plant air cleaning systems; compressed air purfication systems; air intake systems for industrial gas turbines; and special-ized filters for such diverse applications as computer disk drives, aircraft passenger cabins and semiconductor processing. Products are manufactured at more than three dozen Donaldson plants around the world and through four joint ventures. In fiscal 2002, sales were derived as follows: Engine Products, 54.3%; and Industrial Products, 45.7%.

RECENT DEVELOPMENTS:

For the quarter ended 1/31/03, net income declined 3.6% to $20.0 million compared with $20.8 million in the equivalent 2002 quarter. Net sales climbed 7.6% to $284.4 million from $264.3 million a year earlier. The improve-ment in sales was primarily attributed to contributions from a recent acquisition, partially offset by weak North Ameri-can sales in gas turbine products. Gross profit advanced 11.7% to $90.8 million from $81.3 million the year before. Operating income slid 0.4% to $28.2 million from $28.3 million in 2002.

PROSPECTS:

Looking ahead, the Engine Products segment's North American heavy-duty truck product group is expected to see an improvement in build rates this Spring based on growing orders, which should last for several quarters. DCI's North American light-duty vehicle product group's new PowerCore® systems programs have ramped up quickly and should lift truck results for the remainder of 2003. Worldwide sales of off-road products are expected to remain steady as slight improvement in the agriculture mar-ket is tempered by a weaker global construction outlook. Meanwhile, the Industrial Product segment will likely ben-efit from the expected stable near-term industrial air filtra-tion markets. However, DCI expects declining gas turbine sales. Separately, DCI is focused on continually improving operating efficiency through product cost reductions, man-ufacturing infrastructure improvements, discretionary expense controls, and completing the integration of ultrafil-ter international AG, acquired 7/12/02.

ANNUAL FINANCIAL DATA:

FISCAL YEAR	TOT. REVS. ($mill.)	NET INC. ($mill.)	TOT. ASSETS ($mill.)	OPER. PROFIT %	NET PROFIT %	RET. ON EQUITY %	RET. ON ASSETS %	CURR. RATIO	EARN. PER SH. $	CASH FL. PER SH. $	TANG. BK. VAL. $	DIV. PER SH. $	PRICE RANGE	AVG. P/E RATIO	AVG. YIELD %
7/31/02	1,126.0	86.9	850.1	11.0	7.7	22.7	10.2	1.7	1.90	2.60	6.35	0.33	44.99 - 29.91	19.7	0.9
7/31/01	1,137.0	75.5	706.8	9.9	6.6	23.7	10.7	1.9	1.66	2.50	5.80	0.30	40.35 - 24.45	19.5	0.9
7/31/00	1,092.3	70.2	669.7	9.7	6.4	25.1	10.5	1.6	1.51	2.24	4.84	0.28	28.88 - 18.81	15.8	1.2
7/31/99	944.1	62.4	528.4	9.4	6.6	23.8	11.8	2.1	1.31	1.89	5.69	0.25	25.94 - 17.06	16.4	1.2
7/31/98	940.4	57.1	499.3	9.2	6.1	22.3	11.4	1.7	1.14	1.64	5.28	0.21	26.75 - 13.50	17.7	1.0
7/31/97	833.3	50.6	454.4	9.9	6.1	20.8	11.1	1.5	0.99	1.41	4.93	0.18	27.69 - 15.31	21.7	0.9
7/31/96	758.6	43.4	402.9	10.0	5.7	19.0	10.8	1.8	0.84	1.26	4.52	0.17	17.00 - 12.00	17.3	1.1
7/31/95	704.0	38.5	381.0	9.3	5.5	17.4	10.1	2.0	0.73	1.11	4.22	0.14	14.00 - 11.25	17.4	1.1
7/31/94	593.5	①31.9	337.4	8.8	5.4	16.8	9.5	1.9	①0.59	0.89	3.58	0.14	13.13 - 10.00	19.8	1.2
7/31/93	533.3	28.2	300.2	8.5	5.3	16.2	9.4	2.1	0.51	0.77	3.19	0.11	11.06 - 8.31	19.2	1.1

Statistics are as originally reported. Adj. for stk. splits: 2-for-1, 4/94 & 1/98. ① Bef. a cr. of $2.2 mill. from acctg. changes.

OFFICERS:
W. G. Van Dyke, Chmn., Pres., C.E.O.
W. M. Cook, Sr. V.P., C.F.O.
N. C. Linnell, V.P., Gen. Couns., Sec.
INVESTOR CONTACT: Rich Sheffer, Investor Relations, (952) 887-3753
PRINCIPAL OFFICE: 1400 West 94th Street, Minneapolis, MN 55431

TELEPHONE NUMBER: (952) 887-3131
FAX: (952) 887-3155
WEB: www.donaldson.com
NO. OF EMPLOYEES: 8,500 (approx.)
SHAREHOLDERS: 1,871 (approx.)
ANNUAL MEETING: In Nov.
INCORPORATED: DE, Dec., 1936

INSTITUTIONAL HOLDINGS:
No. of Institutions: 195
Shares Held: 26,468,847
% Held: 60.8

INDUSTRY: Blowers and fans (SIC: 3564)

TRANSFER AGENT(S): Wells Fargo Share-holder Services, N.A., South St.Paul, MN

DONNELLEY (R.R.) & SONS CO.

EXCH.	SYM.	REC. PRICE	P/E RATIO	YLD.	MKT. CAP.	RANGE (52-WK.)	'02 Y/E PR.	DIV. ACH.
NYSE	DNY	18.26 (2/28/03)	13.6	5.5%	$2.07 bill.	32.10 - 17.65	21.77	33 yrs.

UPPER MEDIUM GRADE. THE COMPANY EXPECTS EARNINGS PER SHARE FOR 2003 IN THE RANGE OF $1.25 TO $1.40, INCLUDING A RESTRUCTURING CHARGE OF $0.06 PER SHARE.

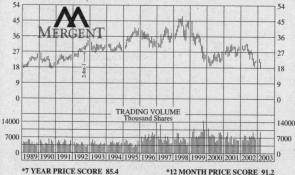

INTERIM EARNINGS (Per Share):

Qtr.	Mar.	June	Sept.	Dec.
1997	0.24	0.31	0.56	0.31
1998	0.30	0.61	0.71	0.67
1999	0.33	0.40	0.67	1.01
2000	0.38	0.46	0.75	0.58
2001	0.12	0.05	0.36	d0.33
2002	0.20	0.30	0.42	0.42

INTERIM DIVIDENDS (Per Share):

Amt.	Decl.	Ex.	Rec.	Pay.
0.24Q	1/24/02	2/04/02	2/06/02	3/01/02
0.24Q	3/28/02	5/08/02	5/10/02	6/01/02
0.25Q	7/25/02	8/08/02	8/12/02	8/31/02
0.25Q	9/26/02	11/06/02	11/08/02	11/30/02
0.25Q	1/23/03	2/03/03	2/05/03	3/01/03

Indicated div.: $1.00 (Div. Reinv. Plan)

CAPITALIZATION (12/31/01):

	($000)	(%)
Long-Term Debt	881,318	44.5
Deferred Income Tax	212,099	10.7
Common & Surplus	888,407	44.8
Total	1,981,824	100.0

*7 YEAR PRICE SCORE 85.4   ***12 MONTH PRICE SCORE 91.2**

*NYSE COMPOSITE INDEX=100

BUSINESS:

Donnelley (R.R.) & Sons Co. provides comprehensive, integrated communications applications that produce, manage and deliver its customers' content, regardless of the communication medium. The Company's services include content creation, digital content management, production and distribution. The Company operates primarily in two business segments, commercial print and logistic services. DNY serves the following end-markets: long-run magazines, catalogs and inserts; telecommunications; book publishing services; and financial services. The Company also operates through specialized publishing services, RRD Direct, Premedia Technologies, and R.R. Donnelley Logistics. DNY operates facilities in North and South America, Europe and the Asia/Pacific Basin. Sales for 2002 industry segment data were derived: print solutions, 65.0%; logistics services, 16.5%; and other, 18.5%.

RECENT DEVELOPMENTS:

For the twelve months ended 12/31/02, net income soared to $142.2 million compared with $25.0 million in 2001. Results benefited from the Company's efforts to reduce its fixed costs and improve productivity. Results for 2002 and 2001 included after-tax restructuring and impairment charges of $54.0 million and $137.0 million, and non-recurring charges of $5.4 million and $23.9 million, respectively. Results for 2002 also included an after-tax gain of $30.0 million from the reversal of excess tax reserves. Net sales were $4.75 billion, down 10.2% from $5.30 billion in the prior year. Gross profit declined 4.7% to $867.6 million from $910.5 million in the previous year. Earnings from operations jumped 66.3% to $244.9 million compared with $147.3 million the year before.

PROSPECTS:

Looking ahead, the Company expects earnings per share in 2003 in the range of $1.25 to $1.40, including a restructuring charge of $0.06 per share. Results in 2003 are expected to continue to benefit from productivity improvements and restructuring efforts. These factors are anticipated to offset challenging pricing conditions in the Company's magazine, catalog and retail markets. Meanwhile, capital spending for 2003 is expected to be lower than $250.0 million, which is comparable to 2002 levels. In addition, cash flow in 2003 is anticipated to be sufficient to fund future investments.

ANNUAL FINANCIAL DATA:

FISCAL YEAR	TOT. REVS. ($mill.)	NET INC. ($mill.)	TOT. ASSETS ($mill.)	OPER. PROFIT %	NET PROFIT %	RET. ON EQUITY %	RET. ON ASSETS %	CURR. RATIO	EARN. PER SH. $	CASH FL. PER SH. $	TANG. BK. VAL. $	DIV. PER SH. $	PRICE RANGE	AVG. P/E RATIO	AVG. YIELD %
p12/31/02	4,754.9	⑦ 142.2							⑦ 1.24			0.98	32.10 - 18.50	20.4	3.9
12/31/01	5,297.8	⑦ 25.0	3,400.0	2.8	0.5	2.8	0.7	1.0	⑦ 0.21	3.41	3.15	0.94	31.90 - 24.30	133.7	3.3
12/31/00	5,764.3	⑥ 266.9	3,914.2	8.7	4.6	21.7	6.8	1.0	⑥ 2.17	5.34	5.06	0.90	27.50 - 19.00	10.7	3.9
12/31/99	5,183.4	⑤ 311.5	3,853.5	10.2	6.0	27.4	8.1	1.0	⑤ 2.40	5.29	6.01	0.86	44.75 - 21.50	13.8	2.6
12/31/98	5,018.4	④ 294.6	3,787.8	8.1	5.9	22.6	7.8	1.3	④ 2.08	4.67	6.85	0.82	48.00 - 33.75	19.7	2.0
12/31/97	4,850.0	③ 206.5	4,134.2	7.6	4.3	13.0	5.0	1.4	③ 1.40	3.91	8.31	0.78	41.75 - 29.50	25.4	2.2
12/31/96	6,599.0	② d253.1	4,849.0	...	...	...	...	1.5	② d1.04	0.90	7.49	0.74	39.88 - 29.38	...	2.1
12/31/95	6,511.8	189.0	5,384.8	8.6	2.9	8.7	3.5	1.7	1.95	6.42	7.46	0.68	41.25 - 28.88	18.0	1.9
12/31/94	4,888.8	215.1	4,452.1	9.4	4.4	10.9	4.8	1.7	1.75	5.47	7.13	0.60	32.50 - 26.88	17.0	2.0
12/31/93	4,387.8	① 178.9	3,654.0	7.4	4.1	9.7	4.9	1.6	① 1.16	2.93	8.76	0.54	32.75 - 26.13	25.4	1.8

Statistics are as originally reported. ① Bef. $127.7 mill. acct. adj. & $60.8 mill. aft-tax restr. chg. ② Incl. $560.6 mill. pre-tax restr. chg. & $80.0 mill. gains from IPO's. ③ Bef. loss fr. disc. ops. of $76.9 mill. ($0.51/sh) & incl. $70.7 mill. pre-tax restr. chg. ④ Incl. $168.9 mill. gain fr. sale of subsidiaries & $80.1 mill. loss fr. businesses held for sale. ⑤ Incl. $42.8 mill. gain fr. sale of bus. & excl. $3.2 mill. loss fr. disc. ops. ⑥ Excl. $13.0 mill. pre-tax gain fr. sale of shares. ⑦ Incl. $88.9 mill. restr. & impair. chgs., 2002; $195.5 mill., 2001.

OFFICERS:
W. L. Davis, Chmn., Pres., C.E.O.
G. A. Stoklosa, Exec. V.P., C.F.O.
M. M. Fohrman, Sr. V.P., Sec., Gen. Couns.
INVESTOR CONTACT: Christopher Curtis, Director, Investor Relations, (312) 326-8313
PRINCIPAL OFFICE: 77 West Wacker Drive, Chicago, IL 60601

TELEPHONE NUMBER: (312) 326-8000
FAX: (312) 326-8543
WEB: www.rrdonnelley.com
NO. OF EMPLOYEES: 31,000 (approx.)
SHAREHOLDERS: 8,786
ANNUAL MEETING: In Mar.
INCORPORATED: DE, May, 1956

INSTITUTIONAL HOLDINGS:
No. of Institutions: 290
Shares Held: 85,306,619
% Held: 75.3
INDUSTRY: Commercial printing, lithographic (SIC: 2752)
TRANSFER AGENT(S): EquiServe Trust Company, N.A., Jersey City, NJ

DORAL FINANCIAL CORPORATION

EXCH.	SYM.	REC. PRICE	P/E RATIO	YLD.	MKT. CAP.	RANGE (52-WK.)	'02 Y/E PR.	DIV. ACH.
NYSE	DRL	32.41 (2/28/03)	11.4	1.7%	$2.32 bill.	32.61 - 21.01	28.60	13 yrs.

MEDIUM GRADE. THE COMPANY IS BENEFITING FROM HIGH DEMAND FOR NEW HOUSING IN PUERTO RICO.

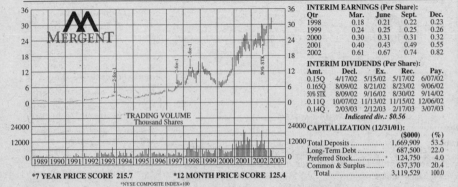

*7 YEAR PRICE SCORE 215.7 ***12 MONTH PRICE SCORE 125.4**

*NYSE COMPOSITE INDEX=100

INTERIM EARNINGS (Per Share):

Qtr	Mar.	June	Sept.	Dec.
1998	0.18	0.21	0.22	0.23
1999	0.24	0.25	0.25	0.26
2000	0.30	0.31	0.31	0.32
2001	0.40	0.43	0.49	0.55
2002	0.61	0.67	0.74	0.82

INTERIM DIVIDENDS (Per Share):

Amt.	Decl.	Ex.	Rec.	Pay.
0.15Q	4/17/02	5/15/02	5/17/02	6/07/02
0.165Q	8/09/02	8/21/02	8/23/02	9/06/02
50% STK	8/09/02	9/16/02	8/30/02	9/14/02
0.11Q	10/07/02	11/13/02	11/15/02	12/06/02
0.14Q	2/03/03	2/12/03	2/17/03	3/07/03

Indicated div.: $0.56

CAPITALIZATION (12/31/01):

	($000)	(%)
Total Deposits	1,669,909	53.5
Long-Term Debt	687,500	22.0
Preferred Stock	124,750	4.0
Common & Surplus	637,370	20.4
Total	3,119,529	100.0

BUSINESS:

Doral Financial Corporation (formerly First Financial Caribbean Corporation) is a financial services company engaged in mortgage banking, banking (including thrift operations), broker-dealer and investment banking and insurance agency activities. The Company conducts its mortgage banking activities in Puerto Rico primarily through its HF Mortgage Bankers division, and through its subsidiaries, Doral Mortgage Corporation, Centro Hipotecario de Puerto Rico, Inc. and Sana Investment Mortgage Bankers, Inc. In the U.S., DRL conducts its mortgage banking activities through Doral Mortgage Corporation and through its indirect subsidiary, Doral Money, Inc. The Company's broker-dealer and insurance agency activities are conducted through Doral Securities and Doral Agency, respectively. As of 12/31/02, DRL had consolidated assets of $8.42 billion and deposits of $2.22 billion.

RECENT DEVELOPMENTS:

On 1/8/03, the Company began trading on the NYSE under the new ticker symbol ''DRL''. For the year ended 12/31/02, net income amounted to $221.0 million versus income of $137.9 million, before an accounting change gain of $5.9 million, the previous year. Net interest income leapt 80.5% to $152.4 million. DRL attributed the jump in net interest income to the positive effects of reductions in interest rates and the increase in its interest earning assets. Provision for loan losses rose 67.1% to $7.4 million. Total non-interest income grew 33.6% to $255.4 million, reflecting higher net gains on mortgage loan sales and fees and, to a lesser extent, increased gains on the sale of investment securities. Total non-interest expense climbed 23.5% to $139.4 million. The volume of mortgage loan production for the year ended 12/31/02 grew 23.8% to $5.20 billion.

PROSPECTS:

DRL's near-term outlook appears positive, reflecting strong demand for new housing in Puerto Rico. DRL noted that while it is experiencing higher refinancing activity as a result of reduced rates, the increase was substantially lower than in the mainland United States. For instance, 57.0% of the Company's internal loan originations consisted of refinanced loans, which, according to DRL, is consistent with its historical experience for the last 30 years.

ANNUAL FINANCIAL DATA:

FISCAL YEAR	NET INT. INC. ($000)	NON-INT. INC. ($000)	NET INC. ($000)	TOT. LOANS ($000)	TOT. ASSETS ($000)	TOT. DEP. ($000)	RET. ON EQUITY %	RET. ON ASSETS %	EQUITY/ ASSETS %	EARN. PER SH.$	TANG. BK. VAL.$	DIV. PER SH.$	PRICE RANGE		AVG. P/E RATIO	AVG. YIELD %
p12/31/02			220,968							2.84		0.42	30.26	20.18	8.9	1.7
12/31/01	84,427	191,132	①137,922	669,899	6,694,283	1,669,909	18.1	2.1	11.4	①1.88	8.89	0.32	26.93	13.88	10.9	1.6
12/31/00	42,304	164,585	84,656	440,639	5,463,386	1,303,525	16.7	1.5	9.3	1.23	5.84	0.25	17.33	5.75	9.4	2.2
12/31/99	49,884	126,911	67,926	277,550	4,537,343	1,010,424	17.6	1.5	8.5	1.00	6.16	0.20	15.38	7.00	11.2	1.8
12/31/98	33,265	88,340	52,832	216,866	2,918,113	533,113	19.6	1.8	9.2	0.84	4.35	0.15	15.83	6.83	13.5	1.4
12/31/97	28,693	45,286	②32,548	134,618	1,857,789	300,494	17.4	1.8	10.1	②0.57	3.27	0.13	8.67	4.04	11.2	2.0
12/31/96	66,987	40,846	27,041	130,046	1,101,955	158,902	18.0	2.5	13.7	0.50	2.63	0.11	4.79	2.96	7.8	2.8
12/31/95	61,907	29,930	19,560	51,980	916,118	95,740	15.2	2.1	14.1	0.44	2.30	0.10	3.33	1.75	5.7	3.8
12/31/94	46,508	25,535	16,216	35,250	768,019	66,471	17.9	2.1	11.8	0.38	1.94	0.09	3.17	1.75	6.4	3.7
12/31/93	23,775	46,454	21,320	...	486,431	26,451	27.7	4.4	15.8	0.53	1.73	0.05	3.04	1.65	4.5	2.1

Statistics are as originally reported. Adj. for stk. splits: 50% div., 9/02; 2-for-1, 5/98, 8/97. ① Excl. acctg. change credit $5.9 mill. ② Excl. extraord. chrg. $12.3 mill.

OFFICERS:
S. Levis, Chmn., C.E.O.
Z. Lewis, Pres., C.O.O.
INVESTOR CONTACT: Richard F. Bonini, Sr. V.P., C.F.O., Treas., (212) 329-3729
PRINCIPAL OFFICE: 1451 Franklin D. Roosevelt Ave., San Juan, Puerto Rico 00920

TELEPHONE NUMBER: (787) 474-6700
FAX: (787) 749-8267
WEB: www.doralfinancial.com
NO. OF EMPLOYEES: 1,930 (avg.)
SHAREHOLDERS: 582 Approx.
ANNUAL MEETING: In Mar.
INCORPORATED: PRI, Dec., 1972

INSTITUTIONAL HOLDINGS:
No. of Institutions: 168
Shares Held: 41,771,742
% Held: 58.1
INDUSTRY: Mortgage bankers and correspondents (SIC: 6162)
TRANSFER AGENT(S): Mellon Investor Services, LLC, Ridgefield Park, NJ

DOVER CORPORATION

EXCH.	SYM.	REC. PRICE	P/E RATIO	YLD.	MKT. CAP.	RANGE (52-WK.)	'02 Y/E PR.	DIV. ACH.
NYSE	DOV	25.52 (2/28/03)	25.5	2.1%	$5.17 bill.	43.55 - 23.54	29.16	47 yrs.

UPPER MEDIUM GRADE. THE COMPANY IS HOPEFUL THAT ITS CIRCUIT BOARD ASSEMBLY AND TEST AND SPECIALTY ELECTRONIC COMPONENTS UNITS WILL RETURN TO PROFITABILITY IN 2003.

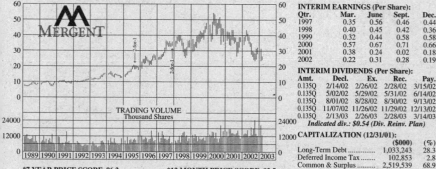

INTERIM EARNINGS (Per Share):

Qtr.	Mar.	June	Sept.	Dec.
1997	0.35	0.56	0.46	0.44
1998	0.40	0.45	0.42	0.36
1999	0.32	0.44	0.58	0.58
2000	0.57	0.67	0.71	0.66
2001	0.38	0.24	0.02	0.18
2002	0.22	0.31	0.28	0.19

INTERIM DIVIDENDS (Per Share):

Amt.	Decl.	Ex.	Rec.	Pay.
0.135Q	2/14/02	2/26/02	2/28/02	3/15/02
0.135Q	5/02/02	5/29/02	5/31/02	6/14/02
0.135Q	8/01/02	8/28/02	8/30/02	9/13/02
0.135Q	11/07/02	11/26/02	11/29/02	12/13/02
0.135Q	2/13/03	2/26/03	2/28/03	3/14/03

Indicated div.: $0.54 (Div. Reinv. Plan)

CAPITALIZATION (12/31/01):

	($000)	(%)
Long-Term Debt	1,033,243	28.3
Deferred Income Tax	102,853	2.8
Common & Surplus	2,519,539	68.9
Total	3,655,635	100.0

*7 YEAR PRICE SCORE 96.2   ***12 MONTH PRICE SCORE 92.5**

*NYSE COMPOSITE INDEX=100

BUSINESS:

Dover Corporation is a diversified industrial manufacturing corporation encompassing over 50 operating companies. Dover Diversified (28.5% of 2002 revenues), builds packaging and printing machinery, heat transfer equipment, food refrigeration and display cases, specialized bearings, construction and agricultural cabs, as well as products for use in the defense, aerospace and automotive industries. Dover Industries (26.8%) makes products for use in the waste handling, bulk transport, automotive service, commercial food service and packaging, welding, cash dispenser and construction industries. Dover Technologies (24.7%) builds automated assembly and testing equipment and specialized electronic components for the electronics industry, and industrial printers for coding and marking. Dover Resources Inc. (20.0%), manufactures products primarily for the automotive, fluid handling, petroleum, winch and chemical equipment industries. On 1/5/99, DOV sold Dover Elevator for $1.16 billion.

RECENT DEVELOPMENTS:

For the year ended 12/31/02, earnings from continuing operations were $211.1 million compared with earnings of $181.8 million a year earlier. Results for 2001 included after-tax goodwill amortization of $42.2 million. Sales declined 4.2% to $4.18 billion from $4.37 billion the previous year. Operating profit increased 2.1% to $365.4 million, reflecting improvement across the Company's industry segments with the exception of Dover Technologies, which posted an operating loss of $30.3 million versus operating profit of $5.6 million in 2001.

PROSPECTS:

The Company's near-term outlook remains lackluster, reflecting its expectations of little or no economic growth for 2003. Consequently, DOV will attempt to improve earnings by developing new products, expanding market share and presence and continuing to look for earnings growth opportunities, both internal and external. Meanwhile, recent efforts to restructure DOV's circuit board assembly and test and specialty electronic components companies are expected to lead to modest profitability for these businesses in 2003, assuming no further adverse market conditions.

ANNUAL FINANCIAL DATA:

FISCAL YEAR	TOT. REVS. ($mill.)	NET INC. ($mill.)	TOT. ASSETS ($mill.)	OPER. PROFIT %	NET PROFIT %	RET. ON EQUITY %	RET. ON ASSETS %	CURR. RATIO	EARN. PER SH. $	CASH FL. PER SH. $	TANG. BK. VAL. $	DIV. PER SH. $	PRICE RANGE	AVG. P/E RATIO	AVG. YIELD %
p12/31/02	4,183.7	⑧ 211.1							⑥ 1.04			0.54	43.55 - 23.54	32.3	1.6
12/31/01	4,459.7	⑧ 166.8	4,602.2	6.7	3.7	6.6	3.6	2.0	⑤ 0.82	1.90	1.97	0.52	43.55 - 26.40	42.6	1.5
12/31/00	5,400.7	④ 533.2	4,892.1	15.6	9.9	21.8	10.9	1.2	④ 2.61	3.60	1.79	0.48	54.38 - 34.13	17.0	1.1
12/31/99	4,446.4	③ 405.1	4,131.9	14.3	9.1	19.9	9.8	1.2	③ 1.92	2.79	1.07	0.44	47.94 - 29.31	20.1	1.1
12/31/98	3,977.7	① 326.4	3,627.3	13.4	8.2	17.1	9.0	1.3	① 1.45	2.00	2.11	0.40	39.94 - 25.50	22.6	1.2
12/31/97	4,547.7	② 405.4	3,277.5	13.5	8.9	23.8	12.4	1.3	② 1.79	2.54	2.66	0.36	36.69 - 24.13	17.0	1.2
12/31/96	4,076.3	② 390.2	2,993.4	13.2	9.6	26.2	13.0	1.3	② 1.73	2.27	2.29	0.32	27.56 - 18.31	13.3	1.4
12/31/95	3,745.9	② 278.3	2,666.7	11.7	7.4	22.7	10.4	1.3	② 1.23	1.70	1.79	0.28	20.84 - 12.91	13.8	1.7
12/31/94	3,085.3	202.4	2,070.6	10.5	6.6	20.3	9.8	1.5	0.89	1.30	1.86	0.24	16.72 - 12.44	16.5	1.7
12/31/93	2,483.9	158.3	1,773.7	10.2	6.4	18.2	8.9	1.5	0.70	1.03	1.42	0.23	15.47 - 11.25	19.2	1.7

Statistics are as originally reported. Adj. for 2-for-1 stk. split, 12/97; 100% stk. div., 9/95. ① Bef. inc. fr. disc. ops. of $52.4 mill. ② Incl. pretax cr. 12/31/97: $32.2 mill.; cr. 12/31/96: $75.1 mill.; chrg. 12/31/95: $31.9 mill. ③ Incl. non-recurr. gain of $10.3 mill.; bef. gain fr. disc. ops. of $523.9 mill. ④ Incl. non-recurr. gain of $10.5 mill.; bef. loss fr. disc. ops. of $13.6 mill. ⑤ Bef. inc. fr. disc. ops. of $81.7 mill. ⑥ Bef. loss fr. disc. ops. of $39.4 mill. & acctg. chg. chrg. of $293.0 mill.

OFFICERS:
T. L. Reece, Chmn., Pres., C.E.O.
R. G. Kuhbach, V.P., C.F.O.
J. W. Schmidt, V.P., Sec., Gen. Couns.
INVESTOR CONTACT: John F. McNiff, V.P., (212) 922-1640
PRINCIPAL OFFICE: 280 Park Avenue, New York, NY 10017-1292

TELEPHONE NUMBER: (212) 922-1640
FAX: (212) 922-1656
WEB: www.dovercorporation.com
NO. OF EMPLOYEES: 26,600 (approx.)
SHAREHOLDERS: 16,000 (approx.)
ANNUAL MEETING: In Apr.
INCORPORATED: DE, 1947

INSTITUTIONAL HOLDINGS:
No. of Institutions: 368
Shares Held: 158,619,724
% Held: 78.4
INDUSTRY: Construction machinery (SIC: 3531)
TRANSFER AGENT(S): Mellon Investor Services, Ridgefield Park, NJ

DOW CHEMICAL COMPANY

EXCH.	SYM.	REC. PRICE	P/E RATIO	YLD.	MKT. CAP.	RANGE (52-WK.)	'02 Y/E PR.
NYSE	DOW	27.30 (2/28/03)	...	4.9%	$24.70 bill.	34.73 - 24.10	29.70

MEDIUM GRADE. THE COMPANY PLANS TO IMPLEMENT SEVERAL INITIATIVES IN ORDER TO OFFSET THE EFFECTS OF HIGHER FEEDSTOCK AND ENERGY COSTS.

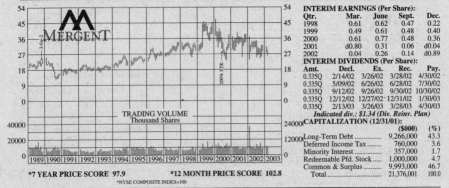

INTERIM EARNINGS (Per Share):

Qtr.	Mar.	June	Sept.	Dec.
1998	0.61	0.62	0.47	0.22
1999	0.49	0.61	0.48	0.40
2000	0.61	0.77	0.48	0.36
2001	d0.80	0.31	0.06	d0.04
2002	0.04	0.26	0.14	d0.89

INTERIM DIVIDENDS (Per Share):

Amt.	Decl.	Ex.	Rec.	Pay.
0.335Q	2/14/02	3/26/02	3/28/02	4/30/02
0.335Q	5/09/02	6/26/02	6/28/02	7/30/02
0.335Q	9/12/02	9/26/02	9/30/02	10/30/02
0.335Q	12/12/02	12/27/02	12/31/02	1/30/03
0.335Q	2/13/03	3/26/03	3/28/03	4/30/03

Indicated div.: $1.34 (Div. Reinv. Plan)

CAPITALIZATION (12/31/01):

	($000)	(%)
Long-Term Debt	9,266,000	43.3
Deferred Income Tax	760,000	3.6
Minority Interest	357,000	1.7
Redeemable Pfd. Stock	1,000,000	4.7
Common & Surplus	9,993,000	46.7
Total	21,376,001	100.0

TRADING VOLUME Thousand Shares

*7 YEAR PRICE SCORE 97.9   ***12 MONTH PRICE SCORE 102.8**

NYSE COMPOSITE INDEX=100

BUSINESS:

Dow Chemical Company is a diversified, worldwide manufacturer and supplier of more than 3,200 product families, which are grouped into the following industry segments: performance plastics, 25.8% of 2002 net sales; plastics, 23.6%; performance chemicals, 18.7%; chemicals, 12.3%; agricultural sciences, 9.9%; hydrocarbons and energy,

8.9%; and unallocated and other businesses, 0.8%. DOW serves customers in more than 170 countries. Geographic sales in 2002 were derived: U.S., 40.4%; Europe, 33.6%; and other countries, 26.0%. On 2/6/01, the Company acquired Union Carbide Corporation.

RECENT DEVELOPMENTS:

For the twelve months ended 12/31/02, loss narrowed to $405.0 million, before an accounting change gain of $67.0 million, versus a loss of $417.0 million, before an accounting change gain of $32.0 million, in 2001. Results for 2002 and 2001 included amortization of intangibles of $65.0 million and $178.0 million, and merger-related expenses

and restructuring costs of $280.0 million and $1.49 billion, respectively. Results also included an asbestos-related charge of $828.0 million for 2002, and a purchased in-process research and development charge of $69.0 million for 2001. Net sales were $27.43 billion, down 1.3% from $27.81 billion in the prior year.

PROSPECTS:

The Company expects the first quarter of 2003 to be particularly challenging due to increased feedstock and energy costs. As a result, the Company has taken steps to reach its key goals in 2003 in an attempt to improve earnings and restore its financial strength. These steps include price

increases, decreased capital spending by $400.0 million, as well as the elimination of up to 4,000 jobs due to the high cost of crude oil and natural gas, along with weak U.S. industrial demand.

ANNUAL FINANCIAL DATA:

FISCAL YEAR	TOT. REVS. ($mill.)	NET INC. ($mill.)	TOT. ASSETS ($mill.)	OPER. PROFIT %	NET PROFIT %	RET. ON EQUITY %	RET. ON ASSETS %	CURR. RATIO	EARN. PER SH. $	CASH FL. PER SH. $	TANG. BK. VAL.$	DIV. PER SH. $	PRICE RANGE	AVG. P/E RATIO	AVG. YIELD %
p12/31/02	27,434.0	⑨ d405.0							⑨ d0.44			1.34	37.00 - 23.66	...	4.4
12/31/01	27,805.0	⑧ d417.0	35,515.0	...	...	...	...	1.3	⑧ d0.46	1.55	7.58	1.25	39.67 - 25.06	...	3.9
12/31/00	23,008.0	⑦ 1,513.0	27,645.0	9.6	6.6	16.5	5.5	1.2	⑦ 2.22	4.14	10.77	1.16	47.16 - 23.00	15.8	3.3
12/31/99	19,989.0	⑥ 1,326.0	25,499.0	11.1	6.6	15.9	5.2	1.4	⑥ 1.98	3.90	9.69	1.16	46.00 - 28.50	18.8	3.1
12/31/98	18,441.0	⑤ 1,304.0	23,830.0	7.5	7.1	16.1	5.5	1.2	⑤ 1.92	3.83	9.80	1.16	33.81 - 24.89	15.3	4.0
12/31/97	20,018.0	④ 1,802.0	24,040.0	13.6	9.0	21.2	7.5	1.2	④ 2.57	4.39	9.94	1.08	34.00 - 25.46	11.6	3.6
12/31/96	20,053.0	① 1,900.0	24,673.0	15.4	9.5	21.9	7.7	1.6	① 2.57	4.33	10.76	1.00	30.83 - 22.75	10.4	3.7
12/31/95	20,200.0	②③ 1,884.0	23,582.0	19.3	9.3	23.4	8.0	1.9	②③ 2.34	4.13	9.45	0.93	26.00 - 20.46	9.9	4.0
12/31/94	16,742.0	765.0	26,490.0	10.9	4.6	8.6	2.9	1.3	0.92	2.50	5.42	0.87	26.41 - 18.83	24.5	3.8
12/31/93	15,052.0	① 566.0	25,505.0	7.1	3.8	6.5	2.2	1.4	① 0.69	2.33	5.12	0.87	20.66 - 16.33	26.8	4.7

Statistics are as originally reported. Adj. for 200% stk. div., 6/00. ① Incl. $120.0 mil. gain on sale of int., 1996; $592.0 mil. gain on sale & $180.0 mill. restr. chg., 1993. ② Bef. $187.0 mil. aft-tax gain on inc. & sale of pharm. unit. ③ Incl. $330.0 mil. chg. rel. to invest. in Dow Corning Corp. ④ Incl. $186.0 mil. gain on sale of bus. ⑤ Incl. $1.00 bil. gains fr. sale of bus., $338.0 mil. chg. fr. purch. in-process R&D rel. to acqs., cr$1.0 mil., $458.0 mil. chg. for sever. costs & asset write-dwns, & restr. costs. ⑥ Incl. $6.0 mil. purch. in-process R&D chgs. & $94.0 mil. fr. sever. exps. ⑦ Incl. $98.0 mil. pre-tax gain fr. sale of bus. & $6.0 mil. purch. in-process R&D chgs. ⑧ Incl. $178.0 mil. amort. of intang., $69.0 mil. in-process R&D chg., $1.49 bil. merg. costs and excl. $32.0 mil. acctg. credit. ⑨ Incl. $65.0 mil. amort. of intang., $280.0 mil. merg-rel. chg., $828.0 mil. asbestos chg. and excl. $67.0 mil. acctg. chg. gain.

OFFICERS:
W. S. Stavropoulos, Chmn., Pres., C.E.O.
A. J. Carbone, Vice-Chmn.
J. P. Reinhard, Exec. V.P., C.F.O.
INVESTOR CONTACT: Teri S. LeBea, Coporate Director, Inv. Rel., (989) 636-8193
PRINCIPAL OFFICE: 2030 Dow Center, Midland, MI 48674

TELEPHONE NUMBER: (989) 636-1000
FAX: (989) 636-3518
WEB: www.dow.com
NO. OF EMPLOYEES: 52,689 (avg.)
SHAREHOLDERS: 124,094; 365,000 (shareholder held in nominee names)
ANNUAL MEETING: In May
INCORPORATED: DE, June, 1947

INSTITUTIONAL HOLDINGS:
No. of Institutions: 636
Shares Held: 617,306,419
% Held: 67.8
INDUSTRY: Plastics materials and resins (SIC: 2821)
TRANSFER AGENT(S): EquiServe, L.P., Boston, MA

DOW JONES & COMPANY, INC.

EXCH.	SYM.	REC. PRICE	P/E RATIO	YLD.	MKT. CAP.	RANGE (52-WK.)	'02 Y/E PR.
NYSE	DJ	35.88 (2/28/03)	15.1	2.8%	$3.04 bill.	60.20 - 29.50	43.23

UPPER MEDIUM GRADE. EARNINGS PER SHARE IN THE FIRST QUARTER OF 2003 ARE EXPECTED IN THE MID TO UPPER SINGLE-DIGIT RANGE, BEFORE SPECIAL ITEMS.

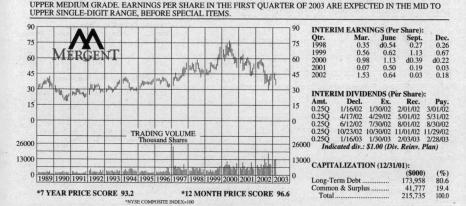

*7 YEAR PRICE SCORE 93.2   ***12 MONTH PRICE SCORE 96.6**

*NYSE COMPOSITE INDEX=100

INTERIM EARNINGS (Per Share):

Qtr.	Mar.	June	Sept.	Dec.
1998	0.35	d0.54	0.27	0.26
1999	0.56	0.62	1.13	0.67
2000	0.98	1.13	d0.39	d0.22
2001	0.07	0.50	0.19	0.03
2002	1.53	0.64	0.03	0.18

INTERIM DIVIDENDS (Per Share):

Amt.	Decl.	Ex.	Rec.	Pay.
0.25Q	1/16/02	1/30/02	2/01/02	3/01/02
0.25Q	4/17/02	4/29/02	5/01/02	5/31/02
0.25Q	6/12/02	7/30/02	8/01/02	8/30/02
0.25Q	10/23/02	10/30/02	11/01/02	11/29/02
0.25Q	1/16/03	1/30/03	2/03/03	2/28/03

Indicated div.: $1.00 (Div. Reinv. Plan)

CAPITALIZATION (12/31/01):

	($000)	(%)
Long-Term Debt	173,958	80.6
Common & Surplus	41,777	19.4
Total	215,735	100.0

BUSINESS:

Dow Jones & Company, Inc. is a global provider of business and financial news and information. The print publishing segment (60.9% of 2002 revenues and d33.1% of operating income) contains the operations of THE WALL STREET JOURNAL, as well as its international editions in Europe and Asia; BARRONS; SMART MONEY magazines; Dow Jones interactive publishing; THE FAR EASTERN ECONOMIC REVIEW; and DJ's television operations. The electronic publishing segment (19.8%, 72.4%) includes the operations of Dow Jones newswires, Consumer Electronic Publishing and Dow Jones Indexes/Ventures. Community newspapers (19.3%, 60.7%) published by Ottaway Newspapers, Inc., a wholly-owned subsidiary, include 16 general interest dailies. DJ is also the co-owner with Reuters Group of Factiva, with Hearst of SmartMoney and with NBC of the CNBC television operations in Asia and Europe.

RECENT DEVELOPMENTS:

For the twelve months ended 12/31/02, net income more than doubled to $201.5 million compared with $98.2 million in 2001. Results for 2002 and 2001 included restructuring charges and other special items of $23.8 million and $73.2 million, respectively. Results for 2002 also included a gain of $197.9 million on the sale of five Ottaway Community Newspaper properties. Total revenues were $1.56 billion, down 12.1% from $1.77 billion in the prior year, reflecting a difficult global advertising environment. Print publishing revenue declined 14.3% to $948.9 million from $1.11 billion, while electronic publishing revenue slipped 2.7% to $309.5 million from $318.0 million.

PROSPECTS:

Looking ahead to the first quarter of 2003, DJ expects lineage trends, which is a section of the newspaper that is sold for advertising, at THE WALL STREET JOURNAL to be down between 10.0% and 12.0% compared with the first quarter of 2002. In addition, DJ expects earnings per share in the first quarter in the mid to upper single-digit range, before special items. Meanwhile, the Company will not issue full-year guidance due to the uncertainty of lineage trends at THE WALL STREET JOURNAL in 2003 and no signs of significant business-to-business recovery.

ANNUAL FINANCIAL DATA:

FISCAL YEAR	TOT. REVS. ($mill.)	NET INC. ($mill.)	TOT. ASSETS ($mill.)	OPER. PROFIT %	NET PROFIT %	RET. ON EQUITY %	RET. ON ASSETS %	CURR. RATIO	EARN. PER SH.$	CASH FL. PER SH.$	TANG. BK. VAL.$	DIV. PER SH.$	PRICE RANGE	AVG. P/E RATIO	AVG. YIELD %
p12/31/02	1,559.2	⑧201.5							⑧2.40			1.00	60.20 - 29.50	18.7	2.2
12/31/01	1,773.1	⑦98.2	1,298.3	6.2	5.5	235.1	7.6	0.4	⑦1.14	2.36	...	1.00	64.30 - 43.05	47.1	1.9
12/31/00	2,202.6	⑥d119.0	1,362.1	22.6	...	...	...	0.6	⑥d1.35	d0.13	0.98	1.00	77.31 - 51.38	...	1.6
12/31/99	2,001.8	⑤272.4	1,530.6	19.5	13.6	49.2	17.8	0.8	⑤2.99	4.13	5.24	0.96	71.38 - 43.63	19.2	1.7
12/31/98	2,158.1	④8.8	1,491.3	10.1	0.4	1.7	0.6	0.7	④0.09	1.57	4.60	0.96	59.00 - 41.56	31.4	1.9
12/31/97	2,572.5	③d802.1	1,919.7	...	...	...	...	0.8	③d8.36	d5.74	4.07	0.96	55.88 - 33.38	...	2.2
12/31/96	2,481.6	①190.0	2,923.6	13.6	7.7	11.6	6.5	0.7	①1.96	4.22	3.64	0.96	41.88 - 31.88	18.8	2.6
12/31/95	2,283.8	189.6	2,748.2	13.3	8.3	11.8	6.9	0.6	1.96	4.08	3.01	0.92	40.13 - 30.63	18.0	2.6
12/31/94	2,091.0	②181.2	2,579.3	17.1	8.7	12.2	7.0	0.6	②1.82	3.90	1.83	0.84	41.88 - 28.13	19.2	2.4
12/31/93	1,931.8	147.5	2,354.4	16.4	7.6	9.9	6.3	0.6	1.48	3.37	1.45	0.80	39.00 - 26.75	22.2	2.4

Statistics are as originally reported. ① Incl. $8.8 mill. net gain, 1996; $5.3 mill., 1995. ② Bef. $3.0 mill. acct. adj. chg. ③ Incl. $1.0 bill. pretax restr. chg. & $52.6 mill. pre-tax gain on disp. of bus. & invest. ④ Incl. $24.2 mill. gain on disp. of bus. & invest. & $76.1 mill. restr. chgs. ⑤ Incl. $67.9 mill. after-tax gain fr. sale of portion of interest in bus. & $1.6 mill. net restr. chg. ⑥ Incl. $24.1 mill. gain fr. dispost. of bus. & invest. and $178.5 mill. chg. fr. write-down of invest. ⑦ Incl. $73.2 mill. restr. chg. & $8.8 mill. write-down of invest. ⑧ Incl. $23.8 mill. restr. & spl. chgs. and $197.9 mill. gain fr. sale of bus.

OFFICERS:
P. R. Kann, Chmn., C.E.O.
C. W. Vieth, C.F.O.
P. G. Skinner, Exec. V.P., Gen. Couns., Sec.
INVESTOR CONTACT: Valerie L. Gerard, Director-Investor Relations, (609) 520-5660
PRINCIPAL OFFICE: 200 Liberty Street, New York, NY 10281

TELEPHONE NUMBER: (212) 416-2000
FAX: (212) 416-2829
WEB: www.dowjones.com
NO. OF EMPLOYEES: 8,077
SHAREHOLDERS: 10,838 (approx. common); 3,934 (approx. class B common)
ANNUAL MEETING: In Apr.
INCORPORATED: DE, Nov., 1949

INSTITUTIONAL HOLDINGS:
No. of Institutions: 225
Shares Held: 56,461,567
% Held: 68.5

INDUSTRY: Newspapers (SIC: 2711)

TRANSFER AGENT(S): Mellon Investor Services, L.L.C., South Hackensack, NJ

DPL INC.

EXCH.	SYM.	REC. PRICE	P/E RATIO	YLD.	MKT. CAP.	RANGE (52-WK.)	'02 Y/E PR.
NYSE	DPL	12.10 (2/28/03)	16.8	7.8%	$1.53 bill.	27.25 - 11.75	15.34

MEDIUM GRADE. EARNINGS FOR 2003 MAY BE AFFECTED BY SOFT MARKET CONDITIONS FOR WHOLESALE ENERGY, INCREASED CORPORATE COSTS AND DOWNTIME DUE TO PLANNED POWER PLANT MAINTENANCE.

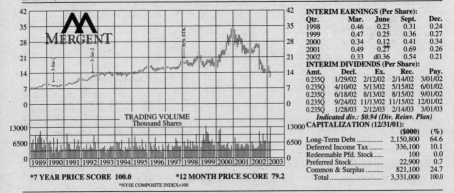

TRADING VOLUME Thousand Shares

*7 YEAR PRICE SCORE 100.0   *12 MONTH PRICE SCORE 79.2
*NYSE COMPOSITE INDEX=100

INTERIM EARNINGS (Per Share):

Qtr.	Mar.	June	Sept.	Dec.
1998	0.46	0.23	0.31	0.24
1999	0.47	0.25	0.36	0.27
2000	0.34	0.12	0.41	0.34
2001	0.49	0.27	0.49	0.26
2002	0.33	d0.36	0.54	0.21

INTERIM DIVIDENDS (Per Share):

Amt.	Decl.	Ex.	Rec.	Pay.
0.235Q	1/29/02	2/12/02	2/14/02	3/01/02
0.235Q	4/10/02	5/13/02	5/15/02	6/01/02
0.235Q	6/18/02	8/13/02	8/15/02	9/01/02
0.235Q	9/24/02	11/13/02	11/15/02	12/01/02
0.235Q	1/28/03	2/12/03	2/14/03	3/01/03

Indicated div.: $0.94 (Div. Reinv. Plan)

CAPITALIZATION (12/31/01):

	($000)	(%)
Long-Term Debt	2,150,800	64.6
Deferred Income Tax	336,100	10.1
Redeemable Pfd. Stock	100	0.0
Preferred Stock	22,900	0.7
Common & Surplus	821,100	24.7
Total	3,331,000	100.0

BUSINESS:

DPL Inc. is a holding company for Dayton Power and Light Company (DP&L) and DPL Energy. DP&L sells electricity to residential, commercial and governmental customers in West Central Ohio. Electricity is generated at eight power plants in 24 counties and distributed to 500,000 retail customers. DPL Energy operates over 4,600 mega-watts of generation capacity and markets wholesale energy throughout the eastern half of the United States. Principal industries served by the Company include food processing, automotive, paper, technology, and defense. In 2002, revenues were derived: Electric, 98.9% and Other, 1.1%. In October 2000, DPL sold its natural gas business.

RECENT DEVELOPMENTS:

For the year ended 12/31/02, net income was $87.3 million compared with income of $196.9 million, before an accounting change charge of $1.0 million, the previous year. The decrease in earnings was primarily due to lower wholesale revenues and the write-down of certain assets in DPL's financial portfolio. Total revenues slipped 1.3% to $1.19 billion from $1.20 billion the year before. Electric revenues declined 1.1% to $1.17 billion, while other revenues, net of fuel costs, decreased 17.3% to $12.9 million. Operating income fell 6.6% to $426.7 million. DPL recorded an investment loss of $105.7 million in 2002 versus investment income of $25.2 million in 2001. Comparisons were made with restated prior-year figures.

PROSPECTS:

Going forward, the Company expects to continue to generate strong operational results and achieve low production costs; however, DPL anticipates a continuing soft market for wholesale energy and capacity which may affect 2003 results. DPL noted that earnings for 2003 may also be affected by increased corporate costs and the timing of planned power plant maintenance. Additionally, DPL expects to experience pressure on sales from continued weakness in the economy. Accordingly, the Company anticipates full-year 2003 basic earnings per share from the utility operations in the range of $1.10 to $1.15, excluding results from DPL's financial asset portfolio.

ANNUAL FINANCIAL DATA:

FISCAL YEAR	TOT. REVS. ($mill.)	NET INC. ($mill.)	TOT. ASSETS ($mill.)	OPER. PROFIT %	NET PROFIT %	NET INC./ NET PROP. %	NET INC./ TOT. CAP. %	RET. ON EQUITY %	ACCUM. DEPR./ GROSS PROP. %	EARN. PER SH. $	TANG. BK. VAL. $	DIV. PER SH. $	DIV. PAYOUT %	PRICE RANGE	AVG. P/E RATIO	AVG. YIELD %
p12/31/02	1,186.4	87.3								0.72		0.94	130.6	27.25 - 13.60	28.4	4.6
12/31/01	1,199.6	② 215.5	4,253.5	38.1	18.0	8.7	6.5	25.5	40.6	② 1.70	6.49	0.94	55.3	33.31 - 22.05	16.3	3.4
12/31/00	1,436.9	① 284.9	4,436.0	30.9	19.8	12.6	9.2	31.1	41.2	② 2.14	6.98	0.94	43.9	33.81 - 16.38	11.7	3.7
12/31/99	1,338.9	204.2	4,340.4	30.1	15.3	9.0	6.2	13.8	41.9	1.35	9.20	0.94	69.6	22.00 - 16.31	14.2	4.9
12/31/98	1,379.6	189.1	3,855.9	29.2	13.7	8.4	6.4	13.4	40.2	1.24	8.58	0.94	75.8	21.75 - 16.63	15.5	4.9
12/31/97	1,355.8	181.4	3,585.2	27.6	13.4	8.0	6.6	13.9	38.1	1.20	8.03	0.91	75.5	19.13 - 15.25	14.3	5.3
12/31/96	1,282.1	172.9	3,418.7	28.6	13.5	7.6	6.3	14.1	36.1	1.15	7.55	0.87	75.6	17.42 - 14.42	13.9	5.4
12/31/95	1,284.8	164.7	3,322.8	28.2	12.8	7.2	5.9	13.9	34.4	1.09	7.28	0.83	76.0	17.08 - 13.33	14.0	5.4
12/31/94	1,218.0	154.9	3,232.7	29.1	12.7	6.7	5.6	13.5	32.3	1.03	7.03	0.79	76.6	14.42 - 12.25	13.0	5.9
12/31/93	1,178.0	139.0	3,305.0	27.4	11.8	6.0	5.0	12.5	30.2	0.95	6.62	0.75	78.8	14.58 - 12.33	14.2	5.5

Statistics are as originally reported. Adj. for stk. div. 50% 1/98 ① Bef. an extraord. chrg. of $41.4 mill.; incl. pre-tax gain of $116.9 mill. on gas purch. for resale. ② Bef. an acctg. chrg. of $1.0 mill.

OFFICERS:
P. H. Forster, Chmn.
S. F. Koziar Jr., Pres., C.E.O.
E. McCarthy, Group V.P., C.F.O.

INVESTOR CONTACT: Elizabeth M. McCarthy, Investor Relations, (937) 259-7210

PRINCIPAL OFFICE: 1065 Woodman Drive, Dayton, OH 45432

TELEPHONE NUMBER: (937) 224-6000
FAX: (937) 224-6500
WEB: www.dplinc.com
NO. OF EMPLOYEES: 1,231 full-time; 247 part-time
SHAREHOLDERS: 31,856
ANNUAL MEETING: In Apr.
INCORPORATED: OH, 1985

INSTITUTIONAL HOLDINGS:
No. of Institutions: 206
Shares Held: 43,564,308
% Held: 34.4

INDUSTRY: Electric and other services combined (SIC: 4931)

TRANSFER AGENT(S): EquiServe, Boston, MA

DQE, INC.

EXCH.	SYM.	REC. PRICE	P/E RATIO	YLD.	MKT. CAP.	RANGE (52-WK.)	'02 Y/E PR.
NYSE	DQE	13.50 (2/28/03)	...	7.4%	$0.75 bill.	22.25 - 10.90	15.24

LOWER MEDIUM GRADE. THE COMPANY SHOULD CONTINUE TO BENEFIT FROM THE SUCCESS OF ITS CORE UTILITY BUSINESS.

7 YEAR PRICE SCORE 56.0   **12 MONTH PRICE SCORE 100.8**
*NYSE COMPOSITE INDEX=100

INTERIM EARNINGS (Per Share):

Qtr.	Mar.	June	Sept.	Dec.
1998	0.58	0.51	0.78	0.62
1999	0.61	0.53	0.63	0.84
2000	0.62	0.23	1.02	0.44
2001	0.22	d2.17	0.40	d1.19
2002	0.29	d1.69	0.36	d0.64

INTERIM DIVIDENDS (Per Share):

Amt.	Decl.	Ex.	Rec.	Pay.
0.42Q	2/28/02	3/07/02	3/11/02	4/01/02
0.42Q	5/28/02	6/06/02	6/10/02	7/01/02
0.25Q	7/25/02	9/06/02	9/10/02	10/01/02
0.25Q	11/22/02	12/09/02	12/11/02	1/01/03
0.25Q	2/27/03	3/06/03	3/10/03	4/01/03

Indicated div.: $1.00 (Div. Reinv. Plan)

CAPITALIZATION (12/31/01):

	($000)	(%)
Long-Term Debt	1,198,759	51.7
Deferred Income Tax	611,429	26.4
Common & Surplus	508,461	21.9
Total	2,318,649	100.0

BUSINESS:

DQE, Inc. is a multi-utility delivery and services company providing electricity, water and communications to more than one million customers throughout the U.S. DQE's expanded business lines include propane distribution, communication systems, and financing and insurance services for DQE and various affiliates. DQE's subsidiaries are

Duquesne Power, Inc., Duquesne Light Company, AquaSource, Inc., DQE Capital Corp., DQE Energy Services, Inc., DQE Energy Partners, Inc., DQE Enterprises, Inc., DQE Financial Corp., DQE Communications, Inc., ProAm, Inc. and Cherrington Insurance Ltd.

RECENT DEVELOPMENTS:

For the year ended 12/31/02, net income was $26.7 million, before a loss of $127.6 million from discontinued operations, compared with a loss of $44.5 million, before an accounting change charge of $113.7 million and a loss of $108.9 million from discontinued operations, the previous year. Results for 2002 and 2001 included after-tax non-recurring charges of $52.2 million and $100.3 million,

respectively. Total operating revenues declined 10.2% to $1.02 billion from $1.14 billion the year before. Electricity sales decreased 10.2% to $928.0 million from $1.03 billion, while other revenues fell 10.7% to $91.4 million from $102.4 million a year earlier. Operating income soared to $92.2 million from $3.1 million in 2001.

PROSPECTS:

The Company continues to expect earnings to range from $95.0 to $100.0 million, comprised of $84.0 million to $88.0 million from continuing operations and $11.0 million to $12.0 million from AquaSource, or $1.27 to $1.34 per share. Meanwhile, the Company should continue to benefit

from the success of its core utility business and a more stable stream of earnings and cash flow. Separately, on 12/16/02, the Company announced the sale of its ProAm subsidiary to Ferreligas Partners, L.P., a retail marketer of propane, for approximately $42.0 million.

ANNUAL FINANCIAL DATA:

FISCAL YEAR	TOT. REVS. ($mill.)	NET INC. ($mill.)	TOT. ASSETS ($mill.)	OPER. PROFIT %	NET PROFIT %	NET INC./ NET PROP. %	NET INC./ TOT. CAP. %	RET. ON EQUITY %	ACCUM. DEPR./ GROSS PROP. %	EARN. PER SH. $	TANG. BK. VAL. $	DIV. PER SH. $	DIV. PAYOUT %	PRICE RANGE	AVG. P/E RATIO	AVG. YIELD %
p12/31/02	1,019.4	④ 26.7								④ d3.28		1.34		22.25 - 10.90	...	8.1
12/31/01	1,296.1	③ d153.4	3,225.9	...	...	...	...	31.0		③ d2.75	9.09	1.68	...	33.70 - 16.55	...	6.7
12/31/00	1,327.6	② 138.1	3,866.0	7.9	10.4	8.1	4.3	13.4	29.2	② 2.39	14.02	1.60	66.9	53.00 - 30.75	17.5	3.8
12/31/99	1,341.2	201.4	5,609.0	23.8	15.0	11.0	4.7	12.3	58.2	2.62	18.78	1.52	58.0	44.25 - 33.63	14.9	3.9
12/31/98	1,269.6	① 196.7	5,247.6	21.4	15.5	11.5	5.0	11.2	64.8	① 2.48	19.18	1.44	58.1	44.13 - 31.56	15.3	3.8
12/31/97	1,230.2	199.1	4,694.4	22.8	16.2	7.5	5.2	11.4	42.4	2.54	19.30	1.36	53.5	34.63 - 26.50	12.0	4.4
12/31/96	1,225.2	179.1	4,639.0	24.6	14.6	6.4	4.6	11.0	41.1	2.32	18.01	1.28	55.2	31.50 - 25.75	12.3	4.5
12/31/95	1,220.2	170.6	4,458.8	26.4	14.0	5.6	4.7	12.0	35.5	2.20	17.13	1.19	53.9	30.75 - 15.83	10.6	5.1
12/31/94	1,223.9	156.8	4,427.0	25.9	12.8	5.0	4.1	11.2	33.3	1.98	16.27	1.12	56.6	23.00 - 18.42	10.5	5.4
12/31/93	1,195.6	141.4	4,574.0	21.2	11.8	4.5	3.5	10.5	31.5	1.78	15.48	1.07	59.9	24.67 - 20.92	12.8	4.7

Statistics are as originally reported. Adj. for stk. splits: 3-for-2, 5/95 ① Bef. extraordinary item of $82.5 mill. ② Excl. acct. chng. credit of $15.9 mill. ③ Incl. one-time chrgs. of $216.8 mill. ④ Incl. after-tax non-recurr. chrg. of $52.2 mill.

OFFICERS:
R. P. Bozzone, Chmn.
D. E. Boyce, Vice-Chmn.
M. K. O'Brien, Pres., C.E.O., C.O.O.
F. C. Cordisco, V.P., Treas.

INVESTOR CONTACT: Investor Relations, (412) 393-1238

PRINCIPAL OFFICE: 411 Seventh Avenue, Pittsburgh, PA 15219

TELEPHONE NUMBER: (412) 393-6000
FAX: (412) 393-6065
WEB: www.dqe.com

NO. OF EMPLOYEES: 2,538

SHAREHOLDERS: 56,000 (approx.)

ANNUAL MEETING: In Jun.

INCORPORATED: PA, 1989

INSTITUTIONAL HOLDINGS:
No. of Institutions: 158
Shares Held: 32,222,963
% Held: 43.4

INDUSTRY: Electric services (SIC: 4911)

TRANSFER AGENT(S): BankBoston, N.A., Boston, MA

DST SYSTEMS, INC.

EXCH.	SYM.	REC. PRICE	P/E RATIO	YLD.	MKT. CAP.	RANGE (52-WK.)	'02 Y/E PR.
NYSE	DST	28.02 (2/28/03)	16.3	...	$3.37 bill.	51.15 - 24.14	35.55

UPPER MEDIUM GRADE. THE COMPANY EXPECTS FULL-YEAR 2003 EARNINGS IN THE RANGE OF $1.89 TO $1.94 PER SHARE.

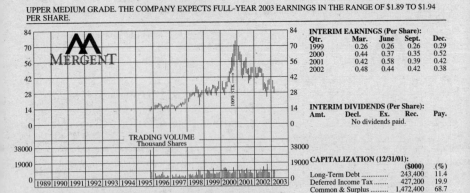

INTERIM EARNINGS (Per Share):

Qtr.	Mar.	June	Sept.	Dec.
1999	0.26	0.26	0.26	0.29
2000	0.44	0.37	0.35	0.52
2001	0.42	0.58	0.39	0.42
2002	0.48	0.44	0.42	0.38

INTERIM DIVIDENDS (Per Share):

Amt.	Decl.	Ex.	Rec.	Pay.
	No dividends paid.			

CAPITALIZATION (12/31/01):

	($000)	(%)
Long-Term Debt	243,400	11.4
Deferred Income Tax	427,200	19.9
Common & Surplus	1,472,400	68.7
Total	2,143,000	100.0

*7 YEAR PRICE SCORE 124.8   ***12 MONTH PRICE SCORE 93.4**

*NYSE COMPOSITE INDEX=100

BUSINESS:

DST Systems, Inc. provides information technology products and services to businesses. The Financial Services segment (43.1% of 2002 revenues) provides information processing and computer software services and products primarily to mutual funds, investment managers, insurance companies, banks, brokers and financial planners. The Output Solutions segment (45.4%) provides complete bill and statement processing services, including electronic presen-

tation. The Customer Management segment (9.4%) provides customer management and open billing services to the video/broadband, direct broadcast satellite, telephony, Internet and utility markets worldwide. Investments and other segment contributed 2.1% to 2002 revenues. On 7/31/01, DST acquired EquiServe, Inc. At 12/31/02, EquiServe serviced 24.7 million shareowner accounts.

RECENT DEVELOPMENTS:

For the year ended 12/31/02, net income decreased 8.4% to $209.0 million versus $228.2 million in 2001. Results for 2002 and 2001 included net gains on securities of $2.3 million and $8.8 million, and lease abandonment charges of $1.2 million and $2.6 million, respectively. Also, results for 2002 also included a consolidation charge of $7.9 million,

while results for 2001 included a gain on the sale of DST's portfolio accounting systems business of $20.0 million and an impairment charge of $12.7 million. Total revenues were flat versus the prior year at $2.38 billion. Financial services revenue increased 6.4% to $1.11 billion, while output solutions revenue slipped 3.3% to $1.17 billion.

PROSPECTS:

The output solutions segment is continuing with its facility consolidations and closings to improve its operational efficiency. Meanwhile, the customer management segment recently signed long-term extensions to its agreements with Comcast and DirectTV to continue subscriber processing

and billing services. Separately, the Company expects full-year earnings in the range of $1.89 to $1.94 per share, excluding non-recurring items. For the first quarter of 2003, earnings are expected to range from $0.43 to $0.45 per share.

ANNUAL FINANCIAL DATA:

FISCAL YEAR	TOT. REVS. ($mill.)	NET INC. ($mill.)	TOT. ASSETS ($mill.)	OPER. PROFIT %	NET PROFIT %	RET. ON EQUITY %	RET. ON ASSETS %	CURR. RATIO	EARN. PER SH.$	CASH FL.PER SH.$	TANG. BK. VAL.$	PRICE RANGE	AVG. P/E RATIO
p12/31/02	2,383.8	⑤ 209.0							⑤ 1.72			51.15 - 24.14	21.9
12/31/01	1,660.0	④ 228.2	2,704.0	17.7	13.7	15.5	8.4	1.3	④ 1.81	3.08	10.58	69.94 - 36.25	29.3
12/31/00	1,362.1	③ 215.8	2,552.4	19.4	15.8	13.8	8.5	1.7	③ 1.67	2.66	12.55	74.94 - 25.81	30.2
12/31/99	1,203.3	138.1	2,326.3	16.6	11.5	9.4	5.9	1.6	1.07	2.01	11.46	38.19 - 25.47	29.9
12/31/98	1,096.1	② 71.6	1,897.0	10.9	6.5	6.1	3.8	1.4	② 0.56	1.40	9.27	35.28 - 17.00	47.1
12/31/97	650.7	① 59.0	1,355.4	14.2	9.1	7.1	4.4	1.6	① 0.59	1.40	8.52	22.72 - 12.13	29.5
12/31/96	580.8	① 167.2	1,121.6	9.8	28.8	24.1	14.9	1.6	① 1.68	2.46	7.01	19.00 - 12.31	9.3
12/31/95	484.1	① 27.6	749.5	8.4	5.7	5.9	3.7	1.4	① 0.39	0.98	4.66	15.88 - 11.81	35.9
12/31/94	401.7	33.4	510.4	8.7	8.3	18.5	6.5	1.1	0.43	0.94	2.96	... - ...	...
12/31/93	341.2	22.8	401.7	8.7	6.7	14.5	5.7	1.4	...	...	2.57	... - ...	...

Statistics are as originally reported. Adj. for stk. split, 2-for-1, 10/00. ① Incl. a pre-tax gain of $1.5 mill. fr. the sale of Continuum, 1997; $223.4 mill., 1996; $44.9 mill., 1995. ② Incl. merger-related exp. of $33.1 mill. ③ Incl. after-tax nonrecurr. gains $19.7 mill. ④ Incl. after-tax gain of $20.0 mill. on the sale of a business, a $13.5 mill. state sales tax refund, an after-tax secur. gain of $8.8 mill., an impairment chrg. of $12.7 mill. and a lease abandonement chrg. of $2.6 mill. ⑤ Incl. gain on secur. of $2.3 mill., lease abandon. chrg. of $1.2 mill. and consol. chrg. of $7.9 mill.

OFFICERS:
T. A. McDonnell, Pres., C.E.O.
C. W. Schellhorn, Vice-Chmn.
K. V. Hager, V.P., C.F.O., Treas.
INVESTOR CONTACT: Kenneth V. Hager, C.F.O., (816) 435-8603
PRINCIPAL OFFICE: 333 West 11th Street, Kansas City, MO 64105

TELEPHONE NUMBER: (816) 435-1000
FAX: (816) 435-8630
WEB: www.dstsystems.com
NO. OF EMPLOYEES: 11,200 (approx.)
SHAREHOLDERS: 30,300 (approx. benef.)
ANNUAL MEETING: In May
INCORPORATED: Aug., 1968; reincorp., DE, Aug., 1995

INSTITUTIONAL HOLDINGS:
No. of Institutions: 208
Shares Held: 53,255,847
% Held: 44.5
INDUSTRY: Information retrieval services (SIC: 7375)
TRANSFER AGENT(S): EquiServe Trust Company, N.A., Providence, RI

DTE ENERGY CO.

EXCH.	SYM.	REC. PRICE	P/E RATIO	YLD.	MKT. CAP.	RANGE (52-WK.)	'02 Y/E PR.
NYSE	DTE	41.44 (2/28/03)	10.8	5.0%	$5.91 bill.	49.50 - 33.05	46.40

MEDIUM GRADE. ON 2/28/02, THE COMPANY ANNOUNCED THAT IT HAS COMPLETED THE SALE OF ITS SUBSIDIARY, INTERNATIONAL TRANSMISSION CO. FOR APPROXIMATELY $610.0 MILLION IN CASH.

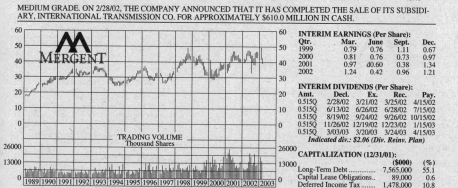

*7 YEAR PRICE SCORE 121.5   *12 MONTH PRICE SCORE 107.9
*NYSE COMPOSITE INDEX=100

INTERIM EARNINGS (Per Share):
Qtr.	Mar.	June	Sept.	Dec.
1999	0.79	0.76	1.11	0.67
2000	0.81	0.76	0.73	0.97
2001	0.97	d0.60	0.38	1.34
2002	1.24	0.42	0.96	1.21

INTERIM DIVIDENDS (Per Share):
Amt.	Decl.	Ex.	Rec.	Pay.
0.515Q	2/28/02	3/21/02	3/25/02	4/15/02
0.515Q	6/13/02	6/26/02	6/28/02	7/15/02
0.515Q	8/19/02	9/24/02	9/26/02	10/15/02
0.515Q	11/26/02	12/19/02	12/23/02	1/15/03
0.515Q	3/03/03	3/20/03	3/24/03	4/15/03

Indicated div.: $2.06 (Div. Reinv. Plan)

CAPITALIZATION (12/31/01):
	($000)	(%)
Long-Term Debt	7,565,000	55.1
Capital Lease Obligations..	89,000	0.6
Deferred Income Tax	1,478,000	10.8
Common & Surplus	4,589,000	33.4
Total	13,721,000	100.0

BUSINESS:

DTE Energy Co. is a holding company whose principal subsidiary is Detroit Edison Co. Detroit Edison supplied energy to 2.1 million customers in Southeastern Michigan as of 12/31/02. The Company added a second subsidiary in 2001, MichCon. MichCon served 1.2 million customers across Michigan as of 12/31/02. Eight wholly-owned subsidiaries, along with various affiliates of DTE, are engaged in non-regulated businesses, including energy-related services and products. Such services and products include the operations of a pulverized coal facility and a coke oven battery, coal sales and brokering, energy technologies, real estate development, power marketing, specialty engineering services and retail marketing of energy products. On 5/31/01, DTE acquired MCN Energy Group for about $3.90 billion.

RECENT DEVELOPMENTS:

For the year ended 12/31/02, net income rocketed 92.1% to $632.0 million compared with income of $329.0 million, before an accounting change credit of $3.0 million, the previous year. Results for 2001 included pre-tax merger and restructuring charges of $268.0 million. The improvement in earnings was largely due to increased contributions from both regulated and non-regulated businesses. Operating revenues increased 16.5% to $6.75 billion from $5.79 billion the year before. Operating income advanced 58.8% to $1.11 billion versus $696.0 million a year earlier.

PROSPECTS:

On 2/28/02, the Company announced that it has completed the sale of its subsidiary, International Transmission Co., to an investor group including Kohlberg Kravis Roberts & Co. and Trimaran Capital Partners L.L.C. for approximately $610.0 million in cash. Meanwhile, the Company expects continued earnings growth in fiscal 2003, but believes that slow economic recovery, slow growth in electric markets, and costs pressures from pension and health care expenses may hamper year-over-year comparisons. Nevertheless, the Company estimates earnings per share to range from $3.90 to $4.10 for 2003.

ANNUAL FINANCIAL DATA:

FISCAL YEAR	TOT. REVS. ($mill.)	NET INC. ($mill.)	TOT. ASSETS ($mill.)	OPER. PROFIT %	NET PROFIT %	NET INC./ NET PROP. %	NET INC./ TOT. CAP. %	RET. ON EQUITY %	ACCUM. DEPR./ GROSS PROP. %	EARN. PER SH. $	TANG. BK. VAL. $	DIV. PER SH. $	DIV. PAYOUT %	PRICE RANGE	AVG. P/E RATIO	AVG. YIELD %
p12/31/02	6,749.0	632.0								3.83		2.06	53.3	47.70 - 33.05	10.5	5.1
12/31/01	7,849.0	④ 329.0	19,228.0	8.9	4.2	3.4	2.4	7.2	44.1	④ 2.14	18.13	2.06	96.3	47.13 - 34.65	18.8	5.0
12/31/00	5,597.0	③ 468.0	12,662.0	14.8	8.4	6.3	4.7	11.7	43.9	③ 3.27	28.15	2.06	63.0	41.31 - 28.44	10.7	5.9
12/31/99	4,728.0	483.0	12,316.0	19.1	10.2	6.8	4.9	12.4	43.9	3.33	26.95	2.06	61.9	44.69 - 31.06	11.4	5.4
12/31/98	4,221.0	443.0	12,088.0	22.2	10.5	6.4	4.5	12.0	43.0	3.05	25.50	2.06	67.5	49.25 - 33.44	13.6	5.0
12/31/97	3,764.0	417.0	11,223.0	26.6	11.1	4.7	4.2	11.3	41.9	2.88	24.55	2.06	71.5	34.13 - 26.13	10.5	6.8
12/31/96	3,645.4	② 309.3	11,014.9	16.8	8.5	3.5	3.2	9.0	37.8	② 2.13	23.73	2.06	96.7	37.25 - 27.63	15.2	6.4
12/31/95	3,635.5	① 405.9	11,130.6	20.3	11.2	4.6	4.2	11.8	35.8	① 2.80	23.68	2.06	73.6	34.88 - 25.75	10.8	6.8
12/31/94	3,519.3	390.3	10,993.0	20.4	11.1	4.4	4.0	11.7	33.7	2.67	22.96	2.06	77.2	30.25 - 24.25	10.2	7.6
12/31/93	3,555.2	491.1	...	23.7	13.8	...	...	...	...	3.34	...	2.04	61.1	37.13 - 29.88	10.0	6.1

Statistics are as originally reported. ① Incl. an after-tax write-off of $32.0 mill. ② Incl. non-recurr. after-tax charge of $97.0 mill. ③ Incl. after-tax merger and restruct. chrgs. of $175.0 mill., 2001; $16.0 mill., 2000. ④ Incl. merger & restr. chrg. of $268.0 mill.; bef. acctg. chrg. of $3.0 mill.

OFFICERS:
A. F. Earley Jr., Chmn., Pres., C.E.O., C.O.O.
D. E. Meador, Sr. V.P., Treas., C.F.O.
S. M. Beale, V.P., Sec.
INVESTOR CONTACT: Investor Relations, (313) 235-4000
PRINCIPAL OFFICE: 2000 2nd Avenue, Room 2412, Detroit, MI 48226-1279

TELEPHONE NUMBER: (313) 235-4000
FAX: (313) 235-8030
WEB: www.dteenergy.com
NO. OF EMPLOYEES: 11,030
SHAREHOLDERS: 114,556 (record).
ANNUAL MEETING: In Apr.
INCORPORATED: MI, 1995

INSTITUTIONAL HOLDINGS:
No. of Institutions: 317
Shares Held: 95,748,051
% Held: 57.2

INDUSTRY: Electric services (SIC: 4911)

TRANSFER AGENT(S): The Detroit Edison Company, Detroit, MI

E.I. DU PONT DE NEMOURS AND COMPANY

EXCH.	SYM.	REC. PRICE	P/E RATIO	YLD.	MKT. CAP.	RANGE (52-WK.)	'02 Y/E PR.
NYSE	DD	36.67 (2/28/03)	19.9	3.8%	$36.74 bill.	49.80 - 35.02	42.40

UPPER MEDIUM GRADE. GOING FORWARD, THE COMPANY SHOULD BENEFIT FROM MODEST GROWTH IN MANY OF ITS MARKETS.

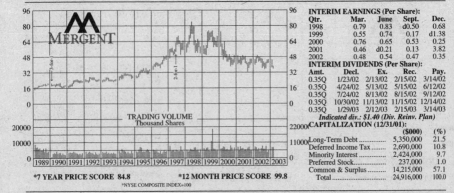

*7 YEAR PRICE SCORE 84.8   ***12 MONTH PRICE SCORE 99.8**
*NYSE COMPOSITE INDEX=100

INTERIM EARNINGS (Per Share):

Qtr.	Mar.	June	Sept.	Dec.
1998	0.79	0.83	d0.50	0.68
1999	0.55	0.74	0.17	d1.38
2000	0.76	0.65	0.53	0.25
2001	0.46	d0.21	0.13	3.82
2002	0.48	0.54	0.47	0.35

INTERIM DIVIDENDS (Per Share):

Amt.	Decl.	Ex.	Rec.	Pay.
0.35Q	1/23/02	2/13/02	2/15/02	3/14/02
0.35Q	4/24/02	5/13/02	5/15/02	6/12/02
0.35Q	7/24/02	8/13/02	8/15/02	9/12/02
0.35Q	10/30/02	11/13/02	11/15/02	12/14/02
0.35Q	1/29/03	2/12/03	2/15/03	3/14/03

Indicated div.: $1.40 (Div. Reinv. Plan)

CAPITALIZATION (12/31/01):

	($000)	(%)
Long-Term Debt	5,350,000	21.5
Deferred Income Tax	2,690,000	10.8
Minority Interest	2,424,000	9.7
Preferred Stock	237,000	1.0
Common & Surplus	14,215,000	57.1
Total	24,916,000	100.0

BUSINESS:

E.I. du Pont de Nemours and Company provides science and technology products for a range of industries including high-performance materials, synthetic fibers, electronics, specialty chemicals, agriculture and biotechnology. DD has a portfolio of trademarks and brands, including such consumer brands as LYCRA®, TEFLON®, STAINMASTER®, KEVLAR®, PIONEER®, TYVEK®, DACRON®, CORDURA®, CORIAN®, COOLMAX® and TACTEL®. Revenues in 2002 were derived: textiles & interiors, 23.5%; coatings & color technologies, 18.8%; performance materials, 18.2%; agricultural & nutrition. 16.9%; safety & protection, 13.0%; electronic & communication technologies, 9.5%; and other, 0.1%. On 10/1/01, DD sold DuPont Pharmaceuticals to Bristol-Myers Squibb.

RECENT DEVELOPMENTS:

For the year ended 12/31/02, income dropped 57.5% to $1.84 billion, before an accounting change charge of $2.94 billion, versus income of $4.33 billion, before an accounting change charge of $11.0 million, in 2001. Results for 2002 and 2001 included amortization of goodwill and other intangible assets of $218.0 million and $434.0 million, employee separation costs and the write-down of assets of $290.0 million and $1.08 billion, and gains on the sale of DuPont Pharmaceuticals of $25.0 million and $6.14 billion, respectively. Revenues slipped 3.3% to $24.52 billion.

PROSPECTS:

Going forward, the Company should benefit from modest growth in many of its markets. However, there are two factors that are expected to influence results for 2003. The combined impact of pension and other postretirement expenses is expected to negatively affect earnings per share for 2003 by $0.34 to $0.39 versus the prior year. Also, the Company expects its full-year base income tax rate to be 30.0% versus the 31.4% average actual base rate for the period 1999-2001. Based on current market conditions, the Company expects earnings per share for the first quarter of 2003 to be similar to prior-year results, before special items.

ANNUAL FINANCIAL DATA:

FISCAL YEAR	TOT. REVS. ($mill.)	NET INC. ($mill.)	TOT. ASSETS ($mill.)	OPER. PROFIT %	NET PROFIT %	RET. ON EQUITY %	RET. ON ASSETS %	CURR. RATIO	EARN. PER SH.$	CASH FL. PER SH.$	TANG. BK. VAL.$	DIV. PER SH.$	PRICE RANGE	AVG. P/E RATIO	AVG. YIELD
p12/31/02	24,522.0	⑦1,841.0							⑦1.84			1.40	49.80 - 35.02	23.0	3.3
12/31/01	25,370.0	⑥4,328.0	40,319.0	29.3	17.1	29.9	10.7	1.8	⑥4.15	5.84	7.30	1.40	49.88 - 32.64	9.9	3.4
12/31/00	29,202.0	⑤2,314.0	39,426.0	14.6	7.9	17.4	5.9	1.3	⑤2.19	3.97	4.50	1.40	74.00 - 38.19	25.6	2.5
12/31/99	27,892.0	④219.0	40,777.0	8.0	0.8	1.7	0.5	1.1	④0.19	1.74	12.09	1.40	75.19 - 50.06	329.4	2.2
⑧12/31/98	25,748.0	③②1,648.0	38,536.0	12.2	6.4	11.8	4.3	0.8	③②1.43	2.71	12.18	1.40	84.44 - 51.69	47.6	2.1
12/31/97	46,653.0	③3,087.0	42,942.0	11.4	6.6	27.4	7.2	0.8	③2.08	4.76	9.76	1.23	69.75 - 46.38	27.9	2.1
12/31/96	45,150.0	4,305.0	37,987.0	14.8	9.5	40.2	11.3	1.0	3.24	6.17	12.12	1.11	49.69 - 34.81	13.1	2.6
12/31/95	43,262.0	③3,838.0	37,312.0	14.2	8.9	45.5	10.3	0.9	③2.81	5.61	9.46	1.01	36.50 - 26.31	11.2	3.2
12/31/94	40,259.0	③3,088.0	36,892.0	12.3	7.7	24.1	8.4	1.5	③2.00	4.46	9.07	0.91	31.19 - 24.13	13.8	3.3
12/31/93	37,841.0	③⑤566.0	37,053.0	4.1	1.5	5.2	1.5	1.2	③⑤0.42	2.51	8.11	0.88	26.94 - 22.25	59.2	3.6

Statistics are as originally reported. Adj. for 2-for-1 split, 6/97. ① Incl. non-recur. chgs. $2.07 bill., 1998; $1.99 bill., 1997; $96.0 mill., 1995; cr$142.0 mill., 1994; $1.62 bill., 1993. ② Bef. disc. oper. inc. $3.03 bill. & extraord. chg. $201.0 mill. ③ Bef. extraord. chg. $11.0 mill. ④ Incl. $2.25 bill. in-process R&D chg., $524.0 mill. employee sep. costs & excl. $7.47 bill. net gain fr. disc. ops. ⑤ Incl. $101.0 mill. sep. chg., $29.0 mill. gain. fr. issuance of stock & $11.0 mill. purch. in-process R&D chg. ⑥ Incl. $1.08 bill. employee sep. chg., $6.14 bill. gain & excl. $11.0 mill. acctg. chg. ⑦ Incl. $290.0 mill. empl. sep. costs & write-down of assets & $25.0 mill. gain on sale of bus. & excl. $2.94 bill. acctg. chg. ⑧ Revs. reflect the divest. of the petroleum bus.

OFFICERS:
C. O. Holliday Jr., Chmn., C.E.O.
G. M. Pfeiffer, Sr. V.P., C.F.O.
S. J. Mobley, Sr. V.P., C.A.O., Gen. Couns.

INVESTOR CONTACT: Stockholder Relations, (302) 774-4994

PRINCIPAL OFFICE: 1007 Market Street, Wilmington, DE 19898

TELEPHONE NUMBER: (302) 774-1000
FAX: (302) 774-0748
WEB: www.dupont.com
NO. OF EMPLOYEES: 79,000 (avg.)
SHAREHOLDERS: 126,718
ANNUAL MEETING: In Apr.
INCORPORATED: DE, Sept., 1915

INSTITUTIONAL HOLDINGS:
No. of Institutions: 849
Shares Held: 616,343,017
% Held: 62.0
INDUSTRY: Plastics materials and resins (SIC: 2821)
TRANSFER AGENT(S): First Chicago Trust Company of New York, Jersey City, NJ

DUKE ENERGY CORPORATION

EXCH.	SYM.	REC. PRICE	P/E RATIO	YLD.	MKT. CAP.	RANGE (52-WK.)	'02 Y/E PR.
NYSE	DUK	13.51 (2/28/03)	10.8	8.1%	$12.09 bill.	39.60 - 13.00	19.54

MEDIUM GRADE. THE COMPANY ANNOUNCED THAT IT PLANS TO CUT ITS CAPITAL SPENDING BY APPROXI-MATELY $200.0 MILLION IN 2003 TO FREE UP CASH TO PAY OFF MORE OF ITS DEBT.

*7 YEAR PRICE SCORE 92.5   ***12 MONTH PRICE SCORE 73.2**

*NYSE COMPOSITE INDEX=100

INTERIM EARNINGS (Per Share):

Qtr.	Mar.	June	Sept.	Dec.
1998	0.45	0.38	0.59	0.30
1999	0.42	0.39	0.60	d0.27
2000	0.53	0.44	1.04	0.38
2001	0.73	0.53	1.01	0.28
2002	0.48	0.56	0.27	d0.06

INTERIM DIVIDENDS (Per Share):

Amt.	Decl.	Ex.	Rec.	Pay.
0.275Q	4/25/02	5/15/02	5/17/02	6/17/02
0.275Q	6/27/02	8/14/02	8/16/02	9/16/02
0.275Q	10/29/02	11/13/02	11/15/02	12/16/02
0.275Q	1/03/03	2/12/03	2/14/03	3/17/03

Indicated div.: $1.10 (Div. Reinv. Plan)

CAPITALIZATION (12/31/01):

	($000)	(%)
Long-Term Debt	12,321,000	38.7
Deferred Income Tax	4,307,000	13.5
Minority Interest	2,246,000	7.1
Redeemable Pfd. Stock ...	234,000	0.7
Common & Surplus	12,689,000	39.9
Total	31,797,000	100.0

BUSINESS:

Duke Energy Corporation (formerly Duke Power Company) is a diversified multinational energy-services corporation that conducts business through four subsidiaries. The Franchised Electric Group generates, transmits, distributes and sells electricity in central and western North Carolina and western South Carolina. The Natural Gas Transmission Group provides transportation and storage of natural gas for customers throughout the East Coast and Southern U.S. and in Canada. The Field Services Group gathers, compresses, treats, processes, transports, trades and markets, and stores natural gas; and produces, transports, trades and markets, and stores natural gas liquids. Duke Energy North America develops, operates and manages merchant power generation facilities and engages in commodity sales and services related to natural gas and electric power. PanEnergy Corporation was acquired on 5/28/97.

RECENT DEVELOPMENTS:

For the year ended 12/31/02, net income was $1.03 billion compared with income of $1.99 billion, before an accounting change charge of $96.0 million, the previous year. Total operating revenues decreased 18.0% to $15.19 billion from $18.53 billion the year before. Revenues from the generation, transmission and distribution of electricity slipped 2.0% to $7.08 billion, while revenues from sales of natural gas and petroleum products dropped 34.3% to $4.06 billion. However, revenues from the transportation and storage of natural gas advanced 56.9% to $1.56 billion.

PROSPECTS:

The Company announced that it plans to cut its capital spending by approximately $200.0 million in 2003 to free up cash to pay off more of its debt. Originally, the Company had planned to spend about $3.20 billion on capital expenditures. On 3/7/03, DUK announced that it plans to sell the assets of a unit that financed merchant power operations. The finance business at Duke Energy's Duke Capital Partners subsidiary had about $350.0 million in assets that will be sold over the next two years. Separately, on 2/7/03, DUK announced that it has completed the sale of the Empire State Pipeline to National Fuel Gas Co. for approximately $240.0 million, including $58.0 million in debt. Looking to the long term, DUK should be well positioned for growth, due to its focus on operational efficiency, cash generation, and capital management.

ANNUAL FINANCIAL DATA:

FISCAL YEAR	TOT. REVS. ($mill.)	NET INC. ($mill.)	TOT. ASSETS ($mill.)	OPER. PROFIT %	NET PROFIT %	NET INC./ NET PROP. %	NET INC./ TOT. CAP. %	RET. ON EQUITY %	ACCUM. DEPR./ GROSS PROP. %	EARN. PER SH.$	TANG. BK. VAL.$	DIV. PER SH.$	DIV. PAYOUT %	PRICE RANGE	AVG. P/E RATIO	AVG. YIELD %
p12/31/02	15,186.0	1,034.0								1.22		1.10	90.2	40.00 - 16.42	23.1	3.9
7 12/31/01	59,503.0	6 1,994.0	48,375.0	6.9	3.4	7.0	6.3	15.7	28.0	6 2.56	14.10	1.10	43.0	47.74 - 32.22	15.6	2.8
12/31/00	49,318.0	1,776.0	58,176.0	7.7	3.6	7.3	6.4	17.7	29.3	2.38	11.49	1.10	46.2	45.22 - 22.88	14.3	3.2
12/31/99	21,742.0	4 847.0	33,409.0	8.3	3.9	4.0	3.8	9.4	31.0	4 1.13	11.14	1.10	97.8	32.66 - 23.38	24.9	3.9
5 12/31/98	17,610.0	3 1,260.0	26,806.0	13.8	7.2	7.5	6.7	15.5	37.8	3 1.71	10.54	1.10	64.3	35.50 - 26.56	18.1	3.5
5 12/31/97	16,308.9	2 974.4	24,028.8	12.1	6.0	6.2	5.3	12.9	38.2	2 1.25	9.78	1.08	86.4	28.28 - 20.94	19.7	4.4
12/31/96	4,758.0	730.0	13,469.7	28.6	15.3	7.4	6.4	14.9	37.2	1.69	12.13	1.04	61.7	26.50 - 21.69	14.3	4.3
12/31/95	4,676.7	1 714.5	13,358.5	28.8	15.3	7.4	6.2	14.9	36.5	1 1.63	11.51	1.00	61.5	23.94 - 18.69	13.1	4.7
12/31/94	4,488.9	638.9	12,862.2	26.3	14.2	6.7	5.7	14.1	35.3	1.44	11.06	0.96	66.7	21.50 - 16.44	13.2	5.1
12/31/93	4,281.9	626.4	12,193.1	19.0	14.6	6.8	5.9	14.4	34.4	1.40	7.23	0.92	65.7	22.44 - 17.69	14.3	4.6

Statistics are as originally reported. Adj. for 2-for-1, 1/01 ① Incl. non-recurr. gain $42.0 mill. ($0.12/sh) ② Incl. non-recurr. chrg. $46.8 mill. ③ Bef. extraord. chrg. $8.0 mill. ④ Excl. net extraord. gain of $660.0 mill. ⑤ Results reflect the acquisition of PanEnergy Corporation. ⑥ Bef. acctg. chg. of $96.0 mill. ⑦ Energy trading rev. reported on a gross basis for 2001 and prior years.

OFFICERS:
R. B. Priory, Chmn., Pres., C.E.O.
R. Brace, Exec. V.P., C.F.O.
INVESTOR CONTACT: Terry Franscisco, Investor Services, (704) 373-6680
PRINCIPAL OFFICE: 526 South Church Street, Charlotte, NC 28202-1904

TELEPHONE NUMBER: (704) 594-6200
FAX: (704) 382-0230
WEB: www.duke-energy.com
NO. OF EMPLOYEES: 24,000 (approx.)
SHAREHOLDERS: 149,051 (approx.)
ANNUAL MEETING: In Apr.
INCORPORATED: NC, June, 1964

INSTITUTIONAL HOLDINGS:
No. of Institutions: 672
Shares Held: 569,810,863
% Held: 63.9

INDUSTRY: Electric services (SIC: 4911)

TRANSFER AGENT(S): The Company

DUKE REALTY CORPORATION

EXCH.	SYM.	REC. PRICE	P/E RATIO	YLD.	MKT. CAP.	RANGE (52-WK.)	'02 Y/E PR.
NYSE	DRE	25.95 (2/28/03)	22.2	...	$3.41 bill.	28.95 - 21.40	25.45

MEDIUM GRADE. THE COMPANY ANTICIPATES EARNINGS GROWTH MAY RESUME BEGINNING IN LATE 2003 AND INTO 2004.

*7 YEAR PRICE SCORE 123.4   ***12 MONTH PRICE SCORE 109.0**
NYSE COMPOSITE INDEX=100

INTERIM EARNINGS (Per Share):

Qtr.	Mar.	June	Sept.	Dec.
1999	0.32	0.33	0.35	0.32
2000	0.39	0.36	0.35	0.57
2001	0.45	0.38	0.58	0.34
2002	0.33	0.34	0.29	0.21

INTERIM DIVIDENDS (Per Share):

Amt.	Decl.	Ex.	Rec.	Pay.
0.43Q	4/25/01	5/11/01	5/15/01	5/31/01

CAPITALIZATION (12/31/01):

	($000)	(%)
Long-Term Debt	1,814,856	39.5
Preferred Stock	608,664	13.2
Common & Surplus	2,176,345	47.3
Total	4,599,865	100.0

BUSINESS:

Duke Realty Corporation (formerly Duke-Weeks Realty Corp.) is a self-administered and self-managed real estate investment trust company that focuses on major cities in the Midwest and the Southeast. As of 12/31/02, the Company owned or held an interest in approximately 108.0 million square feet of office, industrial and retail assets. The Company also owns or controls over 3,800 acres of

land that can support approximately 59.0 million square feet of future development. Through its service operations, the Company also provides, on a fee basis, leasing, property and asset management, development, construction, build-to-suit, and other tenant-related services. In July 1999, Duke Realty Corporation merged with Weeks Corporation.

RECENT DEVELOPMENTS:

For the year ended 12/31/02, net income dropped 29.9% to $161.3 million compared with $230.0 million the year before. Revenues slipped 1.9% to $780.1 million from $795.2 million the year before. Earnings from rental operations decreased 13.8% to $219.1 million from $254.1 million, while earnings from services operations declined

13.8% to $30.3 million from $35.1 million the year before. As of 12/31/02, the Company's total portfolio consisted of 927 properties totaling more than 108.0 million square feet that were 86.8 percent leased, including projects under development.

PROSPECTS:

During 2002, the Company renewed 72.0% of leases up for renewel with an average increase in net effective rents of 3.3%. Meanwhile, DRE believes the declining fundamentals it has experienced in the past two years have bottomed out. As a result, DRE anticipates earnings growth may

resume beginning in late 2003 and into 2004. Separately, on 2/3/03, DRE sold The Office Centre at Southpoint and 4.76 acres of developable land in Jacksonville, Florida, and its ownership interest in Beacon Station Business Park to Flagler Development Company.

ANNUAL FINANCIAL DATA:

FISCAL YEAR	TOT. INC. ($mill.)	NET INC. ($mill.)	TOT. ASSETS ($mill.)	NET INC. + DEPR./ ASSETS %	RET. ON EQUITY %	RET. ON ASSETS %	EARN. PER SH. $	TANG. BK. VAL. $	DIV. PER SH. $	DIV. PAYOUT %	PRICE RANGE	AVG. P/E RATIO	AVG. YIELD %
p12/31/02	780.1	161.3					1.19		1.81	152.1	28.95 - 21.40	21.2	7.2
12/31/01	803.8	282.4	5,330.0	8.3	10.1	5.3	1.75	16.56	1.76	100.6	26.17 - 21.60	13.6	7.4
12/31/00	794.6	261.9	5,460.0	7.7	9.7	4.8	1.66	16.45	1.64	98.8	25.75 - 17.75	13.1	7.5
12/31/99	589.6	182.2	5,486.2	5.3	6.8	3.3	1.32	16.36	1.46	110.6	24.25 - 16.63	15.5	7.1
12/31/98	373.3	110.7	2,853.7	6.3	7.1	3.9	1.12	14.20	1.28	114.3	25.00 - 19.50	19.9	5.8
12/31/97	252.1	78.5	2,176.2	5.7	6.4	3.6	0.98	13.36	1.10	112.7	25.00 - 17.13	21.5	5.2
12/31/96	182.1	53.4	1,361.1	6.3	7.1	3.9	0.91	11.58	1.00	110.5	19.31 - 14.19	18.5	6.0
12/31/95	131.4	35.0	1,045.6	5.7	6.5	3.3	0.77	11.07	0.96	124.7	15.88 - 12.50	18.4	6.8
12/31/94	107.8	26.2	774.9	5.7	5.9	3.4	0.77	10.92	0.92	120.2	14.13 - 10.13	15.8	7.6
12/31/93	39.2	5.0	632.9	2.0	1.4	0.8	0.46	10.81	...	...	13.13 - 1.88	16.3	...

Statistics are as originally reported. Adj. for 100% stk. divs., 8/97

OFFICERS:
T. L. Hefner, Chmn., Pres., C.E.O.
D. E. Zink Jr., Exec. V.P., C.F.O.
G. Burk, Co-C.O.O.
D. Oklak, Co-C.O.O.

INVESTOR CONTACT: Thomas K. Peek, Investor Relations, (317) 808-6168

PRINCIPAL OFFICE: 600 East 96th Street, Suite 100, Indianapolis, IN 46240

TELEPHONE NUMBER: (317) 808-6000
FAX: (317) 808-6770
WEB: www.dukerealty.com

NO. OF EMPLOYEES: 1,050 (avg.)

SHAREHOLDERS: 10,865

ANNUAL MEETING: In Apr.

INCORPORATED: DE, Nov., 1985; reincorp., IN, May, 1992

INSTITUTIONAL HOLDINGS:
No. of Institutions: 273
Shares Held: 70,898,900
% Held: 52.6

INDUSTRY: Real estate investment trusts (SIC: 6798)

TRANSFER AGENT(S): American Stock Transfer & Trust Company, New York, NY

DUN & BRADSTREET CORPORATION (THE)

EXCH.	SYM.	REC. PRICE	P/E RATIO	YLD.	MKT. CAP.	RANGE (52-WK.)	'02 Y/E PR.
NYSE	DNB	35.90 (2/28/03)	19.3	...	$2.76 bill.	43.40 - 28.26	34.49

MEDIUM GRADE. ON 3/3/03, THE COMPANY COMPLETED THE ACQUISITION OF HOOVER'S INC.

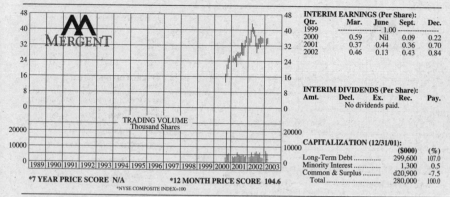

*7 YEAR PRICE SCORE N/A   *12 MONTH PRICE SCORE 104.6
*NYSE COMPOSITE INDEX=100

INTERIM EARNINGS (Per Share):

Qtr.	Mar.	June	Sept.	Dec.
1999	---------------- 1.00 ----------------			
2000	0.59	Nil	0.09	0.22
2001	0.37	0.44	0.36	0.70
2002	0.46	0.13	0.43	0.84

INTERIM DIVIDENDS (Per Share):

Amt.	Decl.	Ex.	Rec.	Pay.
	No dividends paid.			

CAPITALIZATION (12/31/01):

	($000)	(%)
Long-Term Debt	299,600	107.0
Minority Interest	1,300	0.5
Common & Surplus	d20,900	-7.5
Total	280,000	100.0

BUSINESS:

The Dun & Bradstreet Corporation collects and organizes business information. DNB operates a comprehensive database containing information on more than 75.0 million public and private business entities located in 214 countries. The database is the information source for DNB's product and service offerings. DNB's Risk Management Solutions (69.1% of 2002 revenues) are designed for credit and transaction risk management, while Sales & Marketing Solutions (28.0%) are used for the purpose of finding and retaining profitable customers. Supply Management Solutions (2.9%) are designed to help manage customer and vendor relationships more efficiently. On 7/1/98, R. H. Donnelley was spun off as a tax-free dividend to shareholders. On 9/30/00, DNB separated into two independent, publicly traded companies, The Dun & Bradstreet Corporation and Moody's Corporation.

RECENT DEVELOPMENTS:

For the year ended 12/31/02, net income decreased 4.3% to $143.4 million compared with $149.9 million in 2001. Results for 2002 and 2001 included net after-tax restructuring charges of $21.6 million and $24.1 million, respectively. Also, results for 2001 included after-tax asset write-offs and impairments of $16.4 million, credit for excess accrued reorganization costs of $5.6 million and gains on the sale of assets of $45.3 million. Total revenue declined 2.2% to $1.28 billion from $1.30 billion a year earlier. Revenues for 2001 included revenue from Receivables Management Services and other divested businesses of $79.2 million. Notably, Risk Management Solutions revenue rose 1.9% to $880.8 million, while Sales & Marketing Solutions revenue climbed 7.8% to $357.3 million.

PROSPECTS:

On 3/3/03, DNB acquired Hoover's Inc., a provider of industry and market information on public and private companies, for a total of $119.0 million, or $81.0 million net of cash acquired. Separately, DNB recently announced a series of financial flexibility initiatives designed to deliver $50.0 million in savings in 2003 and $75.0 million annually thereafter. Actions include the elimination of about 550 employees by July 2003 and selling non-core businesses and assets. Earnings for 2003 are expected to range from $2.25 to $2.29 per share, including one-time items.

ANNUAL FINANCIAL DATA:

FISCAL YEAR	TOT. REVS. ($mill.)	NET INC. ($mill.)	TOT. ASSETS ($mill.)	OPER. PROFIT %	NET PROFIT %	RET. ON ASSETS %	CURR. RATIO	EARN. PER SH.$	CASH FL. PER SH.$	PRICE RANGE	AVG. P/E RATIO
p12/31/02	1,275.6	③143.4						③1.87		43.40 - 28.26	19.2
12/31/01	1,308.8	②153.2	1,431.2	17.4	11.7	10.7	0.9	②1.88	3.04	36.90 - 20.99	15.4
12/31/00	1,417.6	①73.6	1,423.6	12.2	5.2	5.2	0.7	①0.90	2.25	27.00 - 13.00	22.2
12/31/99	1,407.7	①81.3	1,574.8	11.4	5.8	5.2	0.6	①1.00	2.55	...	...
12/31/98	1,420.5	86.2	1,574.7	13.2	6.1	5.5	0.6	1.00	2.47	...	...
12/31/97	1,353.6	93.2	...	15.3	6.9	...	...	1.08	2.42	...	...

Statistics are as originally reported. ① Excl. inc. fr. discont. opers. of $174.7 mill., 1999; $133.0 mill., 2000 ② Incl. net after-tax gain of $10.4 mill. ③ Incl. after-tax restr. chrg. $21.6 mill.

OFFICERS:
A. Z. Loren, Chmn., C.E.O.
S. W. Alesio, Pres., C.O.O.
S. Mathew, Sr. V.P., C.F.O.
INVESTOR CONTACT: Sandy Parker, V.P.,
Inv. Rel., Treas., (973) 921-5693
PRINCIPAL OFFICE: 103 John F. Kennedy Parkway, Short Hills, NJ 07078

TELEPHONE NUMBER: (973) 921-5500
FAX: (866) 560-7035
WEB: www.dnb.com
NO. OF EMPLOYEES: 7,800 (approx.)
SHAREHOLDERS: 5,136
ANNUAL MEETING: In April
INCORPORATED: DE, April, 2000

INSTITUTIONAL HOLDINGS:
No. of Institutions: 270
Shares Held: 63,955,594
% Held: 86.0
INDUSTRY: Business services, nec (SIC: 7389)
TRANSFER AGENT(S): EquiServe, First Chicago Trust Division, Jersey City, NJ

DYNEGY INC.

EXCH.	SYM.	REC. PRICE	P/E RATIO	YLD.	MKT. CAP.	RANGE (52-WK.)	'02 Y/E PR.
NYSE	DYN	1.95 (2/28/03)	…	…	$0.69 bill.	32.19 - 0.49	1.18

SPECULATIVE GRADE. THE COMPANY WILL CONTINUE TO RESTRUCTURE AROUND ITS CORE ENERGY BUSINESSES.

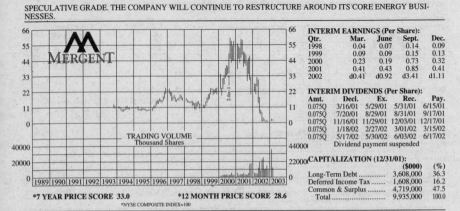

*7 YEAR PRICE SCORE 33.0   ***12 MONTH PRICE SCORE 28.6**

*NYSE COMPOSITE INDEX=100

INTERIM EARNINGS (Per Share):

Qtr.	Mar.	June	Sept.	Dec.
1998	0.04	0.07	0.14	0.09
1999	0.09	0.09	0.15	0.13
2000	0.23	0.10	0.73	0.32
2001	0.41	0.43	0.85	0.41
2002	d0.41	d0.92	d3.41	d1.11

INTERIM DIVIDENDS (Per Share):

Amt.	Decl.	Ex.	Rec.	Pay.
0.075Q	3/16/01	5/29/01	5/31/01	6/15/01
0.075Q	7/20/01	8/29/01	8/31/01	9/17/01
0.075Q	11/16/01	11/29/01	12/03/01	12/17/01
0.075Q	1/18/02	2/27/02	3/01/02	3/15/02
0.075Q	5/17/02	5/30/02	6/03/02	6/17/02
	Dividend payment suspended			

CAPITALIZATION (12/31/01):

	($000)	(%)
Long-Term Debt	3,608,000	36.3
Deferred Income Tax	1,608,000	16.2
Common & Surplus	4,719,000	47.5
Total	9,935,000	100.0

BUSINESS:

Dynegy Inc. (formerly NGC Corporation) is a provider of energy products and services in North America, the United Kingdom and in continental Europe. The Company's businesses include power generation and wholesale and direct commercial and industrial marketing of power, natural gas, coal and other similar products. The Company is also engaged in the transportation, gathering and processing of natural gas liquids and the transmission and distribution of electricity and natural gas to retail consumers. Moreover, DYN maintains a fiber optic and metropolitan network in key cities in the U.S. and Europe. On 2/1/00, the Company completed its acquisition of Illinova Corporation.

RECENT DEVELOPMENTS:

For the year ended 12/31/02, DYN reported a loss of $2.03 billion, before an accounting change charge of $234.0 million and loss of $543.0 million from discontinued operations, compared with income of $472.0 million, before a loss of $42.0 million from discontinued operations, the previous year. Results for 2002 included non-recurring after-tax charges of $1.76 billion. The decrease in earnings was due to the loss on the sale of Northern Natural Gas in the third quarter of 2002. Operating revenues dropped 46.4% to $4.95 billion from $9.24 billion the year before. Operating loss was $2.02 billion versus operating income of $835.0 million a year earlier.

PROSPECTS:

On 2/18/03, the Company announced that it is selling its liquefied natural gas project in Hackberry, Louisiana, to a unit of Sempra Energy for an initial payment of $20.0 million with additional contingent payments based on project development milestones and performance. Separately, on 1/23/03, DYN announced the sale of its European communications business to an affiliate of Klesch & Company, a private equity firm specializing in European restructurings. These actions reflect the Company's commitment to restructure around its core energy businesses.

ANNUAL FINANCIAL DATA:

FISCAL YEAR	TOT. REVS. ($mill.)	NET INC. ($mill.)	TOT. ASSETS ($mill.)	OPER. PROFIT %	NET PROFIT %	RET. ON EQUITY %	RET. ON ASSETS %	CURR. RATIO	EARN. PER SH.$	CASH FL. PER SH.$	TANG. BK. VAL.$	DIV. PER SH.$	PRICE RANGE	AVG. P/E RATIO	AVG. YIELD
p12/31/02	4,950.0	⑧d2,025.0							⑧d6.44				32.19 - 0.49		
12/31/01	42,242.0	⑦646.0	24,874.0	2.3	1.5	13.7	2.6	1.1	⑦1.90	3.24	9.16	0.30	59.00 - 20.00	20.8	0.8
12/31/00	29,445.0	⑥501.0	21,406.0	2.5	1.7	13.9	2.3	1.1	⑥1.48	2.72	6.30	0.25	59.88 - 19.25	26.7	0.6
12/31/99	15,430.0	151.8	6,525.2	1.4	1.0	11.6	2.3	1.1	0.46	0.78	3.95	…	24.75 - 10.13	38.3	…
12/31/98	14,258.0	108.4	5,264.2	0.8	0.8	9.6	2.1	1.0	0.33	0.63	3.46	…	17.50 - 9.38	40.7	…
⚊12/31/97	13,378.4	②d87.7	4,516.9	…	…	…	…	1.2	②d0.34	0.85	3.12	…	24.13 - 14.75	…	…
12/31/96	7,260.2	②113.3	4,186.8	2.7	1.6	10.1	2.7	1.3	②0.42	0.67	3.47	…	24.75 - 8.63	40.2	…
③12/31/95	3,665.9	④92.7	1,875.3	2.2	2.5	16.8	4.9	1.1	④0.50	0.59	2.50	…	11.75 - 8.38	50.3	…
12/31/94	584.0	②2.8	756.6	6.8	0.5	1.2	0.4	1.2	②0.05	0.69	4.14	…	12.25 - 8.00	202.1	…
⑤12/31/93	591.1	13.9	745.4	9.6	2.4	6.0	1.9	1.2	0.27	0.96	4.11	…	13.13 - 10.13	43.9	…

Statistics are as originally reported. Adj. for 2-for-1 split, 8/22/00. ⚊ Refls. the acq. of Destec Energy. ② Incls. non-recurr. chrgs. totaling 12/31/97: $289.8 mill.; 12/31/96: $2.5 mill.; pre-tax gain 12/31/94: $2.7 mill. ③ Refls. acq. of Natural Gas Clearinghouse. ④ Incls. net deferred tax benefit of $45.7 mill. & non-recurr. chrg. of $1.1 mill. ⑤ Initial public offering 11/93. ⑥ Excls. non-recurr. pre-tax gain of $83.3 mill. ⑦ Bef. acctg. chg. of $2.0 mill.; incl. pre-tax, one-time chrgs. of $103.0 mill. ⑧ Bef. acctg. chng. chrg. of $234.0 mill. & loss of $543.0 mill. from disc. ops., incl. non-recurr. after-tax chrgs. of $1.76 bill.

OFFICERS:
D. L. Dienstbier, Chmn.
B. A. Williamson, Pres., C.E.O.
N. J. Caruso, Exec. V.P., C.F.O.

INVESTOR CONTACT: Arthur Shannon, Investors Relations, (713) 507-6466

PRINCIPAL OFFICE: 1000 Louisiana, Suite 5800, Houston, TX 77002

TELEPHONE NUMBER: (713) 507-6400
FAX: (713) 507-6888
WEB: www.dynegy.com

NO. OF EMPLOYEES: 6,139 (avg.)

SHAREHOLDERS: 23,408

ANNUAL MEETING: In May

INCORPORATED: DE, 1993; reincorp., IL, 2000

INSTITUTIONAL HOLDINGS:
No. of Institutions: 217
Shares Held: 81,968,234
% Held: 22.1

INDUSTRY: Crude petroleum and natural gas (SIC: 1311)

TRANSFER AGENT(S): Mellon Investor Services, Ridgefield Park, NJ

E*TRADE GROUP, INC.

EXCH.	SYM.	REC. PRICE	P/E RATIO	YLD.	MKT. CAP.	RANGE (52-WK.)	'02 Y/E PR.
NYSE	ET	4.20 (2/28/03)	15.0	...	$1.46 bill.	10.45 - 2.81	4.86

SPECULATIVE GRADE. E*TRADE ACCESS INC. ACQUIRED A PORTFOLIO OF MORE THAN 4,000 ATMS FROM XTRACASH ATM, INC.

MERGENT

TRADING VOLUME
Thousand Shares

| 1989 | 1990 | 1991 | 1992 | 1993 | 1994 | 1995 | 1996 | 1997 | 1998 | 1999 | 2000 | 2001 | 2002 | 2003 |

*7 YEAR PRICE SCORE N/A   ***12 MONTH PRICE SCORE 89.2**

NYSE COMPOSITE INDEX=100

INTERIM EARNINGS (Per Share):

Qtr.	Dec.	Mar.	June	Sept.
1999-00	d0.02	d0.08	0.02	0.15
2000-01	Nil	...	...	...

Qtr.	Mar.	June	Sept.	Dec.
2001	d0.02	d0.04	d0.77	0.02
2002	0.05	0.09	0.06	0.08

INTERIM DIVIDENDS (Per Share):

Amt.	Decl.	Ex.	Rec.	Pay.
		No dividends paid.		

CAPITALIZATION (12/31/01):

	($000)	(%)
Long-Term Debt	4,930,690	75.8
Common & Surplus	1,570,914	24.2
Total	6,501,604	100.0

BUSINESS:

E*Trade Group, Inc. is a global provider of on-line personal financial services, including value-added investing, banking, research tools, customer service and a proprietary Stateless Architecture® infrastructure. ET offers automated order placement and execution, financial products and services that can be personalized, including portfolio tracking, charting and quote applications, and "real-time" market commentary and analysis. ET's products also include mutual funds, proprietary mutual funds, and bond trading. On 1/12/00, ET acquired Telebanc Financial Corp., a pure-play Internet bank, for about $1.20 billion. On 5/8/00, ET acquired Card Capture Services, Inc., now E*TRADE Access, Inc., an independent network of centrally-managed ATMs in the U.S. and Canada. On 2/1/01, ET acquired LoansDirect, an on-line mortgage originator. On 8/6/01, ET acquired Web Street, Inc., an on-line brokerage firm.

RECENT DEVELOPMENTS:

For the year ended 12/31/02, ET reported income of $107.3 million, before an accounting change charge of $293.7 million, compared with a net loss of $241.5 million the year before. Earnings for 2002 and 2001 included nonrecurring items that resulted in net pre-tax charges of $29.9 million and $277.5 million, respectively. Results also included amortization of goodwill and other intangibles of $28.3 million in 2002 and $43.1 million in 2001. Total revenues grew 4.0% to $1.33 billion. Revenues for 2002 and 2001 included gains on the sale of originated loans of $128.5 million and $95.5 million, and net gains on loans held for sale of $84.0 million and $75.8 million, respectively.

PROSPECTS:

On 2/4/03, E*TRADE Access, Inc. acquired a portfolio of more than 4,000 ATMs from XtraCash ATM, Inc. As a result, ET's ATM network now totals more than 15,000, making it the second largest ATM network in the U.S. Separately, on 12/24/02, E*TRADE Bank acquired Ganis Credit Corp. for $101.0 million. The acquisition expands ET's consumer finance business by adding recreational vehicle, marine and motorsport loans to its existing suite of consumer lending products, which already include mortgages, auto loans and home equity loans.

ANNUAL FINANCIAL DATA:

FISCAL YEAR	TOT. REVS. ($mill.)	NET INC. ($mill.)	TOT. ASSETS ($mill.)	OPER. PROFIT %	NET PROFIT %	RET. ON EQUITY %	RET. ON ASSETS %	CURR. RATIO	EARN. PER SH. $	CASH FL. PER SH. $	TANG. BK. VAL. $	PRICE RANGE	AVG. P/E RATIO
p12/31/02	1,325.9	⑤ 107.3	...	...	...	...	...	...	⑤ d0.52	...	...	12.64 - 2.81	...
④ 12/31/01	2,062.1	③ d270.8	18,172.4	...	...	...	...	0.7	③ d0.81	d0.25	2.55	15.38 - 4.07	...
9/30/00	1,368.3	② 19.2	17,317.4	...	1.0	1.0	0.1	1.4	② 0.06	0.37	4.51	34.25 - 6.66	340.3
9/30/99	621.4	① d54.4	3,927.0	...	...	...	...	1.1	① d0.23	d0.09	3.81	72.25 - 12.74	...
9/30/98	245.3	d0.7	1,968.9	...	...	...	...	1.5	...	0.07	3.14	16.25 - 2.50	...
9/30/97	142.7	13.9	989.9	16.3	9.7	4.9	1.4	1.4	0.10	0.13	1.82	11.94 - 2.75	73.4
9/30/96	51.6	d0.8	294.9	...	...	...	...	1.2	d0.01	...	0.59	3.47 - 2.06	...
9/30/95	23.3	2.6	14.2	18.5	11.1	23.2	18.2	4.0	0.03	0.03	0.19	...	...
9/30/94	10.9	0.8	2.2	2.2	7.2	...	36.3	0.8	0.01	0.01	...	...	...

Statistics are as originally reported. Total revenues include interest income, net of interest expense; adj. for stk. splits: 2-for-1, 5/21/99; 1/29/99. ① Incl. non-recurr. credit $34.6 mill. ② Incl. a pre-tax gain on the sale of investments of $211.1 mill. and pre-tax acq.-rel. exps. of $36.4 mill. ③ Bef. extraord. gain of $29.3 mill.; incl. facility restruct. & oth. nonrecurr. chrgs. of $233.0 mill. and a net loss of $95.7 mill. rel. to various items. ④ Co. changed its fiscal year-end to 12/31 from 9/30. ⑤ Bef. acctg. chrg. of $293.7 mill.; incl. net pre-tax chrgs. of $29.9 million related to various items.

OFFICERS:
M. H. Caplan, Pres., C.E.O.
L. C. Purkis, C.F.O., Chief Admin. Officer

INVESTOR CONTACT: Erica Gessert, Sr. Mgr., Inv. Rel., (650) 331-5397

PRINCIPAL OFFICE: 4500 Bohannon Drive, Menlo Park, CA 94025

TELEPHONE NUMBER: (650) 331-6000
FAX: (650) 842-2552
WEB: www.etrade.com
NO. OF EMPLOYEES: 3,495 (avg.)
SHAREHOLDERS: 2,507
ANNUAL MEETING: In May
INCORPORATED: CA, 1982; reincorp., DE, July, 1996

INSTITUTIONAL HOLDINGS:
No. of Institutions: 200
Shares Held: 193,225,615
% Held: 53.5
INDUSTRY: National commercial banks (SIC: 6021)
TRANSFER AGENT(S): American Stock Transfer & Trust Company, New York, NY

EASTGROUP PROPERTIES, INC.

EXCH.	SYM.	REC. PRICE	P/E RATIO	YLD.	MKT. CAP.	RANGE (52-WK.)	'02 Y/E PR.	DIV. ACH.
NYSE	EGP	25.49 (2/28/03)	30.7	7.5%	$405.6 mill.	26.50 - 22.10	25.50	10 yrs.

UPPER MEDIUM GRADE. THE COMPANY ESTIMATES FUNDS FROM OPERATIONS PER SHARE BEFORE GAINS ON SECURITIES IN THE RANGE OF $2.42 TO $2.54 FOR THE FULL-YEAR 2003.

INTERIM EARNINGS (Per Share):

Qtr.	Mar.	June	Sept.	Dec.
1998	0.30	0.33	0.56	0.47
1999	0.33	0.29	1.11	0.24
2000	0.28	0.29	0.29	0.76
2001	0.27	0.53	0.38	0.32
2002	0.22	0.27	0.16	0.18

INTERIM DIVIDENDS (Per Share):

Amt.	Decl.	Ex.	Rec.	Pay.
0.47Q	3/07/02	3/18/02	3/20/02	3/29/02
0.47Q	5/29/02	6/17/02	6/19/02	6/28/02
0.47Q	9/05/02	9/16/02	9/18/02	9/27/02
0.47Q	12/06/02	12/13/02	12/17/02	12/27/02
0.475Q	3/06/03	3/17/03	3/19/03	3/31/03

Indicated div.: $1.90

CAPITALIZATION (12/31/01):

	($000)	(%)
Long-Term Debt	205,014	35.6
Preferred Stock	108,535	18.9
Common & Surplus	262,175	45.5
Total	575,724	100.0

*7 YEAR PRICE SCORE 129.9   ***12 MONTH PRICE SCORE 109.7**

*NYSE COMPOSITE INDEX=100

BUSINESS:

Eastgroup Properties, Inc. is a self-administered, equity real estate investment trust focused on the acquisition, operation and development of industrial properties in major sunbelt markets throughout the United States. The Company's strategy for growth is based on its property portfolio orientation toward premier distribution facilities located near major transportation centers. The Company's portfolio included 18.5 million square feet with an additional 561,000 square feet of properties under development as of 12/31/02.

RECENT DEVELOPMENTS:

For the year ended 12/31/02, income from continuing operations decreased 30.6% to $23.7 million from $34.2 million the previous year, primarily due to lower average occupancy. Results for 2002 and 2001 included pre-tax gains on the sale of real estate investments of $93,000 and $4.3 million, respectively. Results for 2002 and 2001 excluded a loss of $79,000 and a gain of $17,000, respectively, from discontinued operations. Revenues increased slightly to $105.8 million from $105.1 million the year before. Funds from operations declined 5.6% to $49.9 million from $52.9 million in the prior year.

PROSPECTS:

The Company is estimating funds from operations per share before gains on securities ranging from $2.42 to $2.54 for the full-year 2003. The projection assumes occupancy of 89.0% to 91.5%, exisiting and proposed development contributing $0.13 per share before interest expense, same-store net operating income change of -0.5% to 3.0% and no lease termination fees. Going forward, the Company will continue to focus on improving occupancy, and anticipates the change in same property net operating income to turn positive in the third quarter of 2003.

ANNUAL FINANCIAL DATA:

FISCAL YEAR	TOT. INC. ($mill.)	NET INC. ($mill.)	TOT. ASSETS ($mill.)	NET INC. +DEPR./ ASSETS %	RET. ON EQUITY %	RET. ON ASSETS %	EARN. PER SH. $	TANG. BK. VAL. $	DIV. PER SH. $	DIV. PAYOUT %	PRICE RANGE	AVG. P/E RATIO	AVG. YIELD %
p12/31/02	105.8	② 23.7	702.3				② 0.84		1.88	223.8	26.50 - 22.09	28.9	7.7
12/31/01	105.3	34.2	683.8	9.0	9.2	5.0	1.51	16.48	1.80	119.2	24.25 - 20.00	14.7	8.1
12/31/00	98.1	36.5	666.2	9.0	9.7	5.5	1.68	16.84	1.58	94.0	24.00 - 17.50	12.4	7.6
12/31/99	86.2	① 38.8	632.2	9.3	10.5	6.1	① 1.99	16.76	1.48	74.4	21.88 - 15.38	9.4	7.9
12/31/98	76.7	29.3	567.5	8.1	9.3	5.2	1.66	16.25	1.40	84.3	22.13 - 16.31	11.6	7.3
12/31/97	53.6	20.8	413.1	7.5	8.1	5.0	1.56	15.88	1.34	85.7	22.94 - 17.38	12.9	6.6
12/31/96	39.8	12.5	281.5	7.2	8.6	4.4	0.96	9.18	1.28	133.3	18.33 - 13.83	16.8	8.0
12/31/95	30.3	7.7	158.0	8.4	9.3	4.9	1.21	13.06	1.23	101.1	14.92 - 11.50	10.9	9.3
12/31/94	24.9	7.2	154.9	7.4	8.7	4.6	1.16	12.98	1.16	100.0	14.08 - 11.00	10.8	9.2
12/31/93	16.1	6.4	107.5	8.6	13.1	6.0	1.74	13.22	1.03	59.4	16.17 - 11.00	7.8	7.6

Statistics are as originally reported. Adj, for 3-for-2 stk. spl., 4/97. ① Bef. acctg. chrg. of $418,000. ② Bef. loss from disc. opers. of $79,000.

OFFICERS:
L. R. Speed, Chmn.
D. H. Hoster II, Pres., C.E.O.
N. K. McKey, Exec. V.P., C.F.O., Sec.

INVESTOR CONTACT: Investor Relations, (601) 354-3555

PRINCIPAL OFFICE: 300 One Jackson Place, 188 East Capitol Street, Jackson, MS 39201

TELEPHONE NUMBER: (601) 354-3555
FAX: (601) 352-1441
WEB: www.eastgroup.net

NO. OF EMPLOYEES: 49 full-time; 2 part-time

SHAREHOLDERS: 1,300 (approx.)

ANNUAL MEETING: In June

INCORPORATED: MD, July, 1969

INSTITUTIONAL HOLDINGS:
No. of Institutions: 91
Shares Held: 6,665,889
% Held: 41.4

INDUSTRY: Real estate investment trusts
(SIC: 6798)

TRANSFER AGENT(S): First Chicago Trust Company of New York, Jersey City, NJ

EASTMAN CHEMICAL COMPANY

EXCH.	SYM.	REC. PRICE	P/E RATIO	YLD.	MKT. CAP.	RANGE (52-WK.)	'02 Y/E PR.
NYSE	EMN	32.19 (2/28/03)	31.3	5.5%	$2.48 bill.	49.55 - 31.06	36.77

LOWER MEDIUM GRADE. THE COMPANY'S RESULTS MAY CONTINUE TO BE ADVERSELY AFFECTED BY HIGHER RAW MATERIAL COSTS.

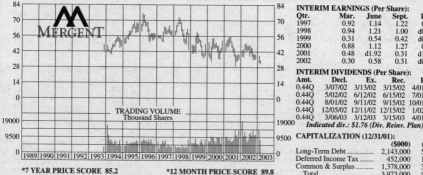

INTERIM EARNINGS (Per Share):

Qtr.	Mar.	June	Sept.	Dec.
1997	0.92	1.14	1.22	0.35
1998	0.94	1.21	1.00	d0.02
1999	0.31	0.54	0.42	d0.67
2000	0.88	1.12	1.27	0.68
2001	0.48	d1.92	0.31	d1.20
2002	0.30	0.58	0.31	d0.16

INTERIM DIVIDENDS (Per Share):

Amt.	Decl.	Ex.	Rec.	Pay.
0.44Q	3/07/02	3/13/02	3/15/02	4/01/02
0.44Q	5/02/02	6/12/02	6/15/02	7/01/02
0.44Q	8/01/02	9/11/02	9/15/02	10/01/02
0.44Q	12/05/02	12/11/02	12/15/02	1/02/03
0.44Q	3/06/03	3/12/03	3/15/03	4/01/03

Indicated div.: $1.76 (Div. Reinv. Plan)

CAPITALIZATION (12/31/01):

	($000)	(%)
Long-Term Debt	2,143,000	53.9
Deferred Income Tax	452,000	11.4
Common & Surplus	1,378,000	34.7
Total	3,973,000	100.0

*7 YEAR PRICE SCORE 85.2   ***12 MONTH PRICE SCORE 89.8**

*NYSE COMPOSITE INDEX=100

BUSINESS:

Eastman Chemical Company manufactures and sells a broad range of plastics, chemicals and fibers. The Company is the largest producer of polyethlene terephthalate (PET) for packaged goods based on market share. The Company has 41 manufacturing sites in 17 countries that supply major chemicals, fibers and plastic products to customers around the world. The Company operates in five segments. The Eastman division, previously called the chemicals group, contains the coatings, adhesives, specialty polymers, and inks segment; the performance chemicals and intermediates segment; and the specialty plastics segment. The Voridian division, previously called the polymers group, contains the polymers segment and the fibers segment. Sales (and operating income) for 2002 were derived: chemicals, 62.0% (17.6%); and polymers, 38.0% (82.4%).

RECENT DEVELOPMENTS:

For the twelve months ended 12/31/02, net income jumped to $79.0 million, before an accounting change charge of $18.0 million, versus a net loss of $175.0 million in 2001. Results for 2002 and 2001 included asset impairment and restructuring charges of $5.0 million and $396.0 million, respectively. Results for 2001 also included a non-recurring charge of $50.0 million. Sales slipped 1.3% to $5.32 billion versus $5.39 billion the previous year, primarily due to declines in selling prices, particularly in the polymers and the performance chemicals and intermediates segments. Operating earnings climbed to $208.0 million versus an operating loss of $120.0 million the year before.

PROSPECTS:

Looking ahead to the first quarter of 2003, the Company expects to continue to see increased raw material costs and challenging global economic conditions. As a result, the Company is implementing initiatives to raise selling prices as well as cost-reduction actions. Based on the Company's current business outlook and global and economic uncertainties, EMN expects earnings in the first quarter of 2003 to be similar to the first quarter of 2002.

ANNUAL FINANCIAL DATA:

FISCAL YEAR	TOT. REVS. ($mill.)	NET INC. ($mill.)	TOT. ASSETS ($mill.)	OPER. PROFIT %	NET PROFIT %	RET. ON EQUITY %	RET. ON ASSETS %	CURR. RATIO	EARN. PER SH. $	CASH FL. PER SH. $	TANG. BK. VAL. $	DIV. PER SH. $	PRICE RANGE	AVG. P/E RATIO	AVG. YIELD %
p12/31/02	5,320.0	⑥ 79.0							⑥ 1.02			1.76	49.55 - 34.53	41.2	4.2
12/31/01	5,384.0	⑤ d179.0	6,086.0	....	...	...	...	1.5	⑤ d2.33	3.33	9.92	1.76	55.65 - 29.03	...	4.2
12/31/00	5,292.0	④ 303.0	6,550.0	10.6	5.7	16.7	4.6	1.2	④ 3.94	9.36	15.64	1.76	54.75 - 33.63	11.2	4.0
12/31/99	4,590.0	③ 48.0	6,303.0	4.4	1.0	2.7	0.8	0.9	③ 0.61	5.50	16.81	1.76	60.31 - 36.00	78.9	3.7
12/31/98	4,481.0	② 249.0	5,876.0	9.7	5.6	12.9	4.2	1.4	② 3.13	7.55	24.42	1.76	72.94 - 43.50	18.6	3.0
12/31/97	4,678.0	① 286.0	5,778.0	10.8	6.1	16.3	4.9	1.6	① 3.63	7.78	22.47	1.76	65.38 - 50.75	16.0	3.0
12/31/96	4,782.0	380.0	5,266.0	13.9	7.9	23.2	7.2	1.7	4.80	...	21.01	1.70	76.25 - 50.75	13.2	2.7
12/31/95	5,040.0	559.0	4,854.0	19.1	11.1	36.6	11.5	1.7	6.78	...	18.41	1.62	69.50 - 48.50	8.7	2.7
12/31/94	4,329.0	336.0	4,375.0	14.7	7.8	25.9	7.7	1.5	4.05	...	15.60	1.20	56.00 - 39.50	11.8	2.5
12/31/93	3,903.0	267.0	4,341.0	11.6	6.8	25.2	6.2	2.4	2.46	...	12.78	...	48.13 - 42.88	18.5	...

Statistics are as originally reported. ① Incl. $62.0 mill. pre-tax chg. for early retirements. ② Incl. $40.0 mill. non-recur. pre-tax chgs. & $15.0 mill. gain fr. tax settlement. ③ Incl. $123.0 mill. pre-tax non-recur. chg. and $29.0 mill. pre-tax gain & excl. $15.0 mill. fr. disc. ops. ④ Incl. $9.0 mill. write-off of in-process R&D and $38.0 mill. gain fr. sale of equity investment. ⑤ Incl. $396.0 mill. asset impair. & restr. chg. and $50.0 mill. other non-recur. items. ⑥ Incl. $5.0 mill. asset impair. & restr. chg. and excl. $18.0 mill. acctg. chg.

OFFICERS:
J. B. Ferguson, Chmn., C.E.O.
J. P. Rogers, Sr. V.P., C.F.O.
T. K. Lee, Sr. V.P., Sec., Gen. Couns.

INVESTOR CONTACT: Gregory A. Riddle, Inv. Rel. Mgr., (423) 229-8692

PRINCIPAL OFFICE: 100 N. Eastman Road, Kingsport, TN 37660

TELEPHONE NUMBER: (423) 229-2000
FAX: (423) 224-0208
WEB: www.eastman.com

NO. OF EMPLOYEES: 15,800 (approx.)

SHAREHOLDERS: 41,917 (record)

ANNUAL MEETING: In May

INCORPORATED: DE, July, 1993

INSTITUTIONAL HOLDINGS:
No. of Institutions: 267
Shares Held: 65,317,078
% Held: 84.6

INDUSTRY: Plastics materials and resins (SIC: 2821)

TRANSFER AGENT(S): First Chicago Trust Company of New York, Jersey City, NJ

EASTMAN KODAK COMPANY

EXCH.	SYM.	REC. PRICE	P/E RATIO	YLD.	MKT. CAP.	RANGE (52-WK.)	'02 Y/E PR.
NYSE	EK	29.60 (2/28/03)	11.0	6.1%	$8.61 bill.	41.08 - 25.59	35.04

MEDIUM GRADE. EARNINGS FOR 2003 ARE EXPECTED TO RANGE BETWEEN $2.35 TO $2.95 PER SHARE.

TRADING VOLUME
Thousand Shares

*7 YEAR PRICE SCORE 56.9   ***12 MONTH PRICE SCORE 110.7**
*NYSE COMPOSITE INDEX=100

INTERIM EARNINGS (Per Share):

Qtr.	Mar.	June	Sept.	Dec.
1998	0.69	1.51	1.21	0.83
1999	0.59	1.52	0.73	1.50
2000	0.93	1.62	1.36	0.66
2001	0.52	0.12	0.33	d0.71
2002	0.13	0.97	1.15	0.45

INTERIM DIVIDENDS (Per Share):

Amt.	Decl.	Ex.	Rec.	Pay.
0.44Q	4/25/01	5/30/01	6/01/01	7/02/01
0.44Q	7/25/01	8/30/01	9/04/01	10/01/01
0.45Q	10/12/01	11/29/01	12/03/01	12/20/01
0.90S	4/11/02	5/30/02	6/03/02	7/16/02
0.90S	10/10/02	10/30/02	11/01/02	12/13/02

Indicated div.: $1.80 (Div. Reinv. Plan)

CAPITALIZATION (12/31/01):

	($000)	(%)
Long-Term Debt ②	1,666,000	36.5
Common & Surplus	2,894,000	63.5
Total	4,560,000	100.0

BUSINESS:

Eastman Kodak Company is engaged primarily in developing, manufacturing and marketing consumer, professional, health and other imaging products. The consumer imaging segment supplies films, photographic papers, processing services, photofinishing equipment, photographic chemicals, cameras and projectors for traditional consumer amateur photography. The professional segment offers films, photographic papers, digital cameras, printers and scanners, chemicals, and services targeted to professional customers. Products in the health imaging segment are used to capture, store, process, print and display images and information for customers in the health care industry. Products in the other imaging segment include motion picture films, audiovisual equipment, certain digital cameras and printers, copiers, microfilm products, applications software, printers, scanners and other business equipment.

RECENT DEVELOPMENTS:

For the year ended 12/31/02, income was $793.0 million, before a loss from discontinued operations of $23.0 million, versus income of $81.0 million, before a loss from discontinued operations of $5.0 million, the year before. Results for 2002 and 2001 included pre-tax restructuring charges of $98.0 million and $659.0 million, respectively. Net sales declined 3.0% to $12.84 billion from $13.23 billion in the prior year. Photography sales fell 4.3% to $9.00 billion. Health imaging sales grew 3.7% to $565.0 million, while commercial imaging sales climbed 3.2% to $354.0 million.

PROSPECTS:

As part of the EK's focused cost-reduction effort, the Company expects to reduce employment by a range of 2,300 to 2,900 in 2003. The Company expects these actions will generate annual savings of $65.0 million to $85.0 million, with $35.0 million to $50.0 million being realized in 2003.

Going forward, EK anticipates revenue in 2003 to increase slightly over 2002 levels and earnings per share to range between $2.35 to $2.95, reflecting sustained weak economic pressure, rising geopolitical concerns and increased consumer use of digital photography.

ANNUAL FINANCIAL DATA:

FISCAL YEAR	TOT. REVS. ($mill.)	NET INC. ($mill.)	TOT. ASSETS ($mill.)	OPER. PROFIT %	NET PROFIT %	RET. ON EQUITY %	RET. ON ASSETS %	CURR. RATIO	EARN. PER SH.$	CASH FL. PER SH.$	TANG. BK. VAL.$	DIV. PER SH.$	PRICE RANGE	AVG. P/E RATIO	AVG. YIELD %
p12/31/02	12,835.0	⑩ 793.0							⑩ 2.72			1.80	38.30 — 25.58	11.7	5.6
12/31/01	13,234.0	⑨ 76.0	13,362.0	2.6	0.6	2.6	0.6	0.9	⑨ 0.26	3.42	6.69	2.21	49.95 — 24.40	142.9	5.9
12/31/00	13,994.0	⑧ 1,407.0	14,212.0	15.8	10.1	41.0	9.9	0.9	⑧ 4.59	7.49	8.54	1.76	67.50 — 35.31	11.2	3.4
12/31/99	14,089.0	⑦ 1,392.0	14,370.0	14.1	9.9	35.6	9.7	0.9	⑦ 4.33	7.19	9.44	1.76	80.38 — 56.63	15.8	2.6
12/31/98	13,406.0	⑥ 1,390.0	14,733.0	14.1	10.4	34.9	9.4	0.9	⑥ 4.24	6.84	8.54	1.76	88.94 — 57.94	17.3	2.4
12/31/97	14,538.0	⑤ 5.0	13,145.0	…	…	0.2	…	1.1	⑤ 0.01	2.51	8.09	1.72	94.75 — 53.31	N.M.	2.3
12/31/96	15,968.0	④ 1,011.0	14,438.0	8.5	6.3	21.4	7.0	1.3	④ 3.00	5.68	12.51	1.60	85.00 — 65.13	25.0	2.1
12/31/95	14,980.0	1,252.0	14,477.0	11.4	8.4	24.4	8.6	1.6	3.67	6.34	13.25	1.60	70.38 — 47.13	16.0	2.7
12/31/94	13,557.0	③ 554.0	14,968.0	7.5	4.1	13.8	3.7	1.3	③ 1.65	4.34	10.00	1.70	56.38 — 40.69	29.4	3.5
12/31/93	16,364.0	① 475.0	20,325.0	7.4	2.9	14.2	2.3	1.6	① 1.44	4.84	…	2.00	65.00 — 40.25	36.5	3.8

Statistics are as originally reported. ① Bef. acctg. adj. ch. of $2.17 bill., inc. fr. dis. ops. of $192.0 mill. & extra. chg. of $14.0 mill. ② Incl. conv. subord. debt. ③ Bef. extra. ch. of $266.0 mill. & dis. ops. of $269.0 mill. ④ Excl. inc. fr. dis. ops. of $277.0 mill. & incl. after-tax restruct. chg. of $256.0 mill. ⑤ Incl. pre-tax chg. of $186.0 mill. assoc./w the acq. of Wang Laboratories, Inc., a pre-tax prov. of $46.0 mill. for litigation, & an after-tax chg. of $1.29 billion for restruct. costs & asset impair. ⑥ Incl. pre-tax gain per sh., a pre-tax gain of $66.0 mill. & a pre-tax chg. of $42.0 mill. ⑦ Incl. pre-tax chg. of $350.0 mill. for restr. costs, asset impair., and other chrgs. ⑧ Incl. pre-tax nonrecurr. gain. of $44.0 mill. ⑨ Incl. after-tax restr. and other chgs. of $594.0 mill. ⑩ Excl. loss fr. dis. ops. of $23.0 mill.; Incl. pre-tax restruct. chrg. of $98.0 mill.

OFFICERS:
D. A. Carp, Chmn., Pres., C.E.O.
R. H. Brust, Exec. V.P., C.F.O.
G. P. Van Graafeiland, Sr. V.P., Couns.
INVESTOR CONTACT: Gerard Meuchner, Investor Relations, (716) 724-4513
PRINCIPAL OFFICE: 343 State Street, Rochester, NY 14650

TELEPHONE NUMBER: (716) 724-4000
FAX: (716) 724-0663
WEB: www.kodak.com
NO. OF EMPLOYEES: 75,100 (avg.)
SHAREHOLDERS: 91,893
ANNUAL MEETING: In Jan.
INCORPORATED: NJ, Oct., 1901

INSTITUTIONAL HOLDINGS:
No. of Institutions: 446
Shares Held: 246,308,018
% Held: 84.4
INDUSTRY: Photographic equipment and supplies (SIC: 3861)
REGISTRAR(S): BankBoston, N.A., Boston, MA

EATON CORPORATION

EXCH.	SYM.	REC. PRICE	P/E RATIO	YLD.	MKT. CAP.	RANGE (52-WK.)	'02 Y/E PR.
NYSE	ETN	70.95 (2/28/03)	18.0	2.5%	$4.93 bill.	88.68 - 59.10	78.11

UPPER MEDIUM GRADE. ETN EXPECTS ONLY MARGINAL GROWTH IN THE FIRST HALF OF 2003, WITH STRONG GROWTH LIKELY IN THE SECOND HALF.

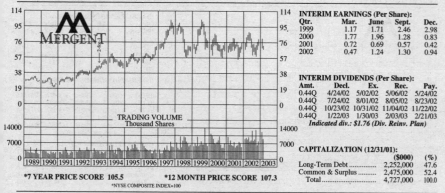

*7 YEAR PRICE SCORE 105.5   *12 MONTH PRICE SCORE 107.3
*NYSE COMPOSITE INDEX=100

INTERIM EARNINGS (Per Share):

Qtr.	Mar.	June	Sept.	Dec.
1999	1.17	1.71	2.46	2.98
2000	1.77	1.96	1.28	0.83
2001	0.72	0.69	0.57	0.42
2002	0.47	1.24	1.30	0.94

INTERIM DIVIDENDS (Per Share):

Amt.	Decl.	Ex.	Rec.	Pay.
0.44Q	4/24/02	5/02/02	5/06/02	5/24/02
0.44Q	7/24/02	8/01/02	8/05/02	8/23/02
0.44Q	10/23/02	10/31/02	11/04/02	11/22/02
0.44Q	1/22/03	1/30/03	2/03/03	2/21/03

Indicated div.: $1.76 (Div. Reinv. Plan)

CAPITALIZATION (12/31/01):

	($000)	(%)
Long-Term Debt	2,252,000	47.6
Common & Surplus	2,475,000	52.4
Total	4,727,000	100.0

BUSINESS:

Eaton Corporation is a global industrial manufacturer of fluid power systems, electrical power quality, distribution and control, automotive engine air management and fuel economy, and intelligent truck systems for fuel economy and safety. Revenues for 2002 were comprised of the following: Fluid Power, 34.1%; Industrial and Commercial Controls, 27.6%; Automotive, 22.1%; and Truck, 16.2%. As of 1/31/03, the Company sold products in more than 50 countries. On 4/9/99, Eaton acquired Aeroquip-Vickers, Inc., for $1.70 billion.

RECENT DEVELOPMENTS:

For the year ended 12/31/02, net income advanced 66.3% to $281.0 million compared with $169.0 million the previous year. Results for 2002 and 2001 included after-tax gains of $13.0 million and $22.0 million, respectively, from the sales of businesses. Results for 2002 and 2001 also included after-tax unusual charges of $47.0 million and $86.0 million, respectively. Total net sales slipped 1.2% to $7.21 billion from $7.30 billion the year before. Fluid Power segment net sales fell 2.0% to $2.46 billion and Industrial & Commercial Controls segment net sales declined 9.4% to $1.99 billion. Automotive segment net sales climbed 7.7% to $1.59 billion.

PROSPECTS:

After a survey of its end markets, ETN expects only marginal growth in the first half of 2003, with stronger growth likely in the second half. For the year as a whole, ETN is anticipating growth in its end markets of approximately 1.0% to 2.0%. As in 2002, ETN expects to outgrow its end markets by approximately 2.0% to 3.0%. ETN will also record additional growth during 2003 from the recently completed acquisitions of Boston Weatherhead, the aerospace circuit breaker business of Mechanical Products, and the power systems business of Commonwealth Sprague Capacitor, as well as from the acquisition of the electrical division of Delta plc. For full-year 2003, ETN projects operating earnings per share to be between $5.00 and $5.25.

ANNUAL FINANCIAL DATA:

FISCAL YEAR	TOT. REVS. ($mill.)	NET INC. ($mill.)	TOT. ASSETS ($mill.)	OPER. PROFIT %	NET PROFIT %	RET. ON EQUITY %	RET. ON ASSETS %	CURR. RATIO	EARN. PER SH.$	CASH FL. PER SH.$	TANG. BK. VAL.$	DIV. PER SH.$	PRICE RANGE	AVG. P/E RATIO	AVG. YIELD %
p12/31/02	7,209.0	⑥281.0							⑥3.92			1.76	88.68 - 59.10	18.8	2.4
12/31/01	7,299.0	⑤169.0	7,646.0	4.8	2.3	6.8	2.2	1.4	⑤2.39	8.77	0.58	1.76	81.43 - 55.12	28.6	2.6
12/31/00	8,309.0	④363.0	8,180.0	7.8	4.4	15.1	4.4	1.2	④5.00	11.36	...	1.76	86.56 - 57.50	14.4	2.4
12/31/99	8,402.0	③617.0	8,437.0	8.7	7.3	23.5	7.3	1.1	③8.36	14.36	1.27	1.76	103.50 - 62.00	9.9	2.1
12/31/98	6,625.0	349.0	5,665.0	7.3	5.3	17.0	6.2	1.3	4.80	9.35	14.33	1.76	99.63 - 57.50	16.4	2.2
12/31/97	7,563.0	②464.0	5,465.0	8.1	6.1	22.4	8.5	1.5	②5.93	10.33	14.73	1.72	103.38 - 67.25	14.4	2.0
12/31/96	6,961.0	349.0	5,307.0	7.7	5.0	16.2	6.6	1.6	4.50	8.69	15.48	1.60	70.88 - 50.38	13.5	2.6
12/31/95	6,822.0	399.0	5,053.0	9.4	5.8	20.2	7.9	1.7	5.13	8.74	13.92	1.50	62.50 - 45.25	10.5	2.8
12/31/94	6,052.0	333.0	4,682.0	9.3	5.5	19.8	7.1	1.7	4.40	0.77	10.64	1.20	62.13 - 43.88	12.0	2.3
12/31/93	4,401.0	①180.0	3,268.0	7.2	4.1	16.3	5.5	1.9	①2.57	5.37	11.83	1.15	55.38 - 38.25	18.2	2.5

Statistics are as originally reported. Adj. for 2-for-1 stk. split, 6/93 ① Inc. non-recurr. chrg. $55.0 mill. & bef. extraord. chrg. $7.0 mill. ② Bef. extraord. loss $54.0 mill., but incl. $91.0 mill. gain on sale of business ③ Incl. $340.0 mill. gain from sale of businesses. ④ Bef. inc. of $90.0 mill. from disc. ops. ⑤ Incl. pre-tax gain of $61.0 mill. on sales of businesses. ⑥ Incl. after-tax gain of $13.0 mill. on sale of bus. & unusual chrg. of $47.0 million.

OFFICERS:
A. M. Cutler, Chmn., Pres., C.E.O.
R. E. Pearson, V.P., C.F.O.
R. E. Parmenter, V.P., Treas.

INVESTOR CONTACT: William C. Hartman, Investor Relations, (216) 523-4501

PRINCIPAL OFFICE: Eaton Center, 1111 Superior Avenue, Cleveland, OH 44114-2584

TELEPHONE NUMBER: (216) 523-5000
FAX: (216) 479-7092
WEB: www.eaton.com

NO. OF EMPLOYEES: 51,000

SHAREHOLDERS: 11,193 (record)

ANNUAL MEETING: In Apr.

INCORPORATED: OH, Aug., 1916

INSTITUTIONAL HOLDINGS:
No. of Institutions: 324
Shares Held: 63,092,942
% Held: 89.5

INDUSTRY: Electrical equipment & supplies, nec (SIC: 3699)

TRANSFER AGENT(S): First Chicago Trust Company of New York, Jersey City, NJ

EATON VANCE CORPORATION

EXCH.	SYM.	REC. PRICE	P/E RATIO	YLD.	MKT. CAP.	RANGE (52-WK.)	'02 Y/E PR.	DIV. ACH.
NYSE	EV	25.54 (2/28/03)	15.9	1.3%	$1.77 bill.	41.00 - 22.46	28.25	21 yrs.

INVESTMENT GRADE. THE COMPANY IS STRENGTHENING ITS POSITION IN MANAGED ACCOUNTS FOR BROKER/DEALER CLIENTS.

*7 YEAR PRICE SCORE 178.7   ***12 MONTH PRICE SCORE 97.9**
*NYSE COMPOSITE INDEX=100

INTERIM EARNINGS (Per Share):

Qtr.	Jan.	Apr.	July	Oct.
1997-98	0.14	0.15	0.18	d0.08
1998-99	d0.14	0.14	0.35	0.35
1999-00	0.39	0.40	0.38	0.42
2000-01	0.44	0.29	0.44	0.44
2001-02	0.46	0.46	0.44	0.34
2002-03	0.37	...	...	...

INTERIM DIVIDENDS (Per Share):

Amt.	Decl.	Ex.	Rec.	Pay.
0.072Q	1/16/02	1/29/02	1/31/02	2/11/02
0.072Q	4/17/02	4/26/02	4/30/02	5/13/02
0.072Q	7/10/02	7/29/02	7/31/02	8/12/02
0.08Q	10/16/02	10/29/02	10/31/02	11/11/02
0.08Q	1/15/03	1/29/03	1/31/03	2/10/03

Indicated div.: $0.32

CAPITALIZATION (10/31/02):

	($000)	(%)
Long-Term Debt	124,118	22.7
Deferred Income Tax	50,531	9.2
Common & Surplus	372,302	68.1
Total	546,951	100.0

BUSINESS:

Eaton Vance Corporation creates, markets and manages mutual funds and provides management and counseling services to institutions and individuals. The Company conducts its investment management and counseling business through two wholly-owned subsidiaries, Eaton Vance Management and Boston Management and Research. As of 10/31/02, the Company provided investment advisory or administration services to 180 funds, 1,370 separately managed individual and institutional accounts, and participated in 40 managed account broker/dealer programs. EV's funds consist of money markets, equities, bank loans, and taxable and non-taxable fixed income. As of 1/31/03, assets under management totaled $55.75 billion.

RECENT DEVELOPMENTS:

For the quarter ended 1/31/03, net income declined 21.9% to $25.9 million compared with $33.2 million in the equivalent 2002 quarter. Earnings for 2003 and 2002 included a gain of $1.9 million and $1.4 million, respectively, on the sale of investments. Total revenues decreased 7.9% to $124.9 million from $135.7 million a year earlier, reflecting lower average assets under management. Total expenses of $86.5 million were essentially unchanged versus the prior year. Operating income fell 22.5% to $38.4 million from $49.5 million in 2002.

PROSPECTS:

Looking ahead, the Company should continue to benefit from the acquisitions of 70.0% of Atlanta Capital Management Company, LLC and 80.0% of Fox Asset Management, acquired in late 2001. The two acquisitions have helped broaden and strengthen EV's array of mutual funds, as well as increase its presence in managed accounts for broker/dealers. For instance, EV participated in approximately 40 broker/dealer managed account programs as of 10/31/02 versus only one program 15 months prior. Also, the Company should continue to benefit from increasing interest in tax-managed equity funds, assisted by investors' growing awareness of the benefits of tax efficiency.

ANNUAL FINANCIAL DATA:

FISCAL YEAR	TOT. REVS. ($000)	NET INC. ($000)	TOT. ASSETS ($000)	OPER. PROFIT %	NET PROFIT %	RET. ON EQUITY %	RET. ON ASSETS %	CURR. RATIO	EARN. PER SH. $	CASH FL. PER SH. $	TANG. BK. VAL. $	DIV. PER SH. $	PRICE RANGE	AVG. P/E RATIO	AVG. YIELD %
10/31/02	522,985	⑤ 121,057	616,619	35.2	23.1	32.5	19.6	3.1	⑤ 1.70	2.94	3.83	0.30	41.00 — 22.46	18.7	0.9
10/31/01	486,372	⑤⑥ 116,020	675,301	39.2	23.9	38.5	17.2	2.8	⑤⑥ 1.60	2.67	2.81	0.25	39.22 — 26.50	20.5	0.8
10/31/00	429,566	⑥ 116,051	432,989	42.5	27.0	45.5	26.8	1.9	⑥ 1.58	2.74	3.65	0.20	32.94 — 18.13	16.2	0.8
10/31/99	348,950	③ 52,405	358,229	22.3	15.0	27.0	14.6	1.9	③⑤ 0.71	1.58	2.73	0.16	20.00 — 9.34	20.8	1.1
10/31/98	249,987	④ 30,523	380,260	19.5	12.2	14.4	8.0	2.7	④ 0.41	1.29	2.94	0.13	12.55 — 8.72	26.2	1.2
10/31/97	200,910	40,234	387,375	31.8	20.0	17.8	10.4	4.1	0.52	1.26	3.03	0.10	9.50 — 5.22	14.2	1.4
10/31/96	181,361	① 35,834	360,262	32.5	19.8	17.0	9.9	5.4	① 0.47	1.19	2.77	0.09	6.22 — 3.25	10.1	1.9
10/31/95	167,922	② 26,968	357,586	28.1	16.1	13.9	7.5	4.0	② 0.36	1.07	2.59	0.08	4.91 — 3.41	11.4	2.0
10/31/94	171,216	②③ 25,810	455,506	28.0	15.1	15.6	5.7	0.3	②③ 0.34	1.07	2.25	0.07	4.69 — 3.06	11.4	1.9
10/31/93	152,276	② 25,517	425,547	29.0	16.8	17.6	6.0	0.3	② 0.36	0.97	1.96	0.06	5.16 — 3.63	12.2	1.4

Statistics are as originally reported. Adj. for 2-for-1 stk. split: 11/00, 8/98 & 5/97. ① Bef. extraord. credit $1.6 mill. ② Bef. disc. oper. gain 10/31/95: $3.4 mill.; 10/31/94: $2.7 mill.; 10/31/93: $1.8 mill. ③ Bef. acct. chrg. of $36.6 mill., 10/31/99; $1.3 mill., 10/31/94. ④ Incl. an impairment loss on real estate of $2.6 mill. & a gain of $2.1 mill. from the sale of an investment. ⑤ Incl. a gain on the sale of investments of $1.3 mill., 10/31/02; loss of $2.6 mill., 10/31/01; gain of $226,000, 10/31/00; gain of $7.3 mill., 10/31/99. ⑥ Incl. an impairment loss on investments of $15.1 mill.

OFFICERS:
J. B. Hawkes, Chmn., Pres., C.E.O.
W. M. Steul, V.P., C.F.O., Treas.
A. R. Dynner, V.P., Sec.

INVESTOR CONTACT: William M. Steul, C.F.O., (617) 482-8260

PRINCIPAL OFFICE: 255 State Street, Boston, MA 02109

TELEPHONE NUMBER: (617) 482-8260
FAX: (617) 482-2396
WEB: www.eatonvance.com
NO. OF EMPLOYEES: 575
SHAREHOLDERS: 1,100 (approx.)
ANNUAL MEETING: In May
INCORPORATED: MD, May, 1959; reincorp., MD, Feb., 1981

INSTITUTIONAL HOLDINGS:
No. of Institutions: 183
Shares Held: 34,841,430
% Held: 50.3

INDUSTRY: Investment advice (SIC: 6282)

TRANSFER AGENT(S): EquiServe Trust Company, N.A., Providence, RI

ECOLAB, INC.

EXCH.	SYM.	REC. PRICE	P/E RATIO	YLD.	MKT. CAP.	RANGE (52-WK.)	'02 Y/E PR.	DIV. ACH.
NYSE	ECL	49.05 (2/28/03)	30.3	1.2%	$6.27 bill.	51.80 - 36.53	49.50	10 yrs.

UPPER MEDIUM GRADE. RESULTS ARE BENEFITING FROM INCREASED SALES AND LOWER COSTS.

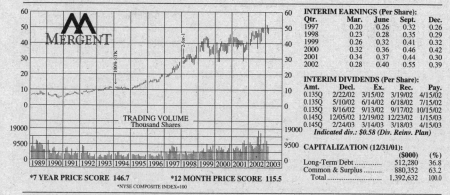

INTERIM EARNINGS (Per Share):

Qtr.	Mar.	June	Sept.	Dec.
1997	0.20	0.26	0.32	0.26
1998	0.23	0.28	0.35	0.29
1999	0.26	0.32	0.41	0.32
2000	0.32	0.36	0.46	0.42
2001	0.34	0.37	0.44	0.30
2002	0.28	0.40	0.55	0.39

INTERIM DIVIDENDS (Per Share):

Amt.	Decl.	Ex.	Rec.	Pay.
0.135Q	2/22/02	3/15/02	3/19/02	4/15/02
0.135Q	5/10/02	6/14/02	6/18/02	7/15/02
0.135Q	8/16/02	9/13/02	9/17/02	10/15/02
0.145Q	12/05/02	12/19/02	12/23/02	1/15/03
0.145Q	2/24/03	3/14/03	3/18/03	4/15/03

Indicated div.: $0.58 (Div. Reinv. Plan)

CAPITALIZATION (12/31/01):

	($000)	(%)
Long-Term Debt	512,280	36.8
Common & Surplus	880,352	63.2
Total	1,392,632	100.0

*7 YEAR PRICE SCORE 146.7   ***12 MONTH PRICE SCORE 115.5**

*NYSE COMPOSITE INDEX=100

BUSINESS:

Ecolab, Inc. develops and markets cleaning, sanitizing, pest elimination, maintenance and repair products and services. The Cleaning and Sanitizing segment (48.2% of revenue in 2002) consists of seven business units and offers cleaners, sanitizers, detergents, lubricants, chemical cleaning, animal health, water treatment, infection control and janitorial products to customers in the U.S. Other U.S. Services (9.2%) consists of two business units focused on the elimination and prevention of pests, and the manufacturing of dishwashing and customized machines for the foodservice industry. The International segment (42.6%) serves customers in Europe, Asia Pacific, Canada, Latin America, the Middle East and Africa. Customers include hotels and restaurants, foodservice, healthcare and educational facilities, commercial laundries, light industry, and food processors. On 11/30/01, the Company acquired the remaining 50.0% of its Henkel-Ecolab joint venture for approximately $430.0 million.

RECENT DEVELOPMENTS:

For the year ended 12/31/02, income was $211.9 million, before income from discontinued operations of $1.9 million and an accounting change charge of $4.0 million, versus net income of $188.2 million the year before. Results for 2002 and 2001 included net special charges of $37.0 million and $824,000, respectively. Net sales climbed 46.7% to $3.40 billion. Sales from the U.S. cleaning and sanitizing segment improved 4.3% to $1.62 billion, while operating income jumped 50.7% to $271.8 million. Sales from other U.S. services grew 12.9% to $308.3 million and operating income rose 12.7% to $33.1 million. Sales from the international segment soared to $1.43 billion from $472.1 million while operating income jumped to $131.4 million from $44.2 million in 2001.

PROSPECTS:

Going forward, results should continue to benefit from growth in key customer segments, focused sales efforts, favorable performances from all geographic regions and additional cost savings. As a result, sales for the first quarter of 2003 are expected to increase between 9.0% to 10.0% year over year, and diluted earnings per share are expected to be in the $0.40 to $0.42 range. For the full-year 2003, ECL anticipates diluted earnings per share of about $2.05.

ANNUAL FINANCIAL DATA:

FISCAL YEAR	TOT. REVS. ($mill.)	NET INC. ($mill.)	TOT. ASSETS ($mill.)	OPER. PROFIT %	NET PROFIT %	RET. ON EQUITY %	RET. ON ASSETS %	CURR. RATIO	EARN. PER SH.$	CASH FL PER SH.$	TANG. BK. VAL.$	DIV. PER SH.$	PRICE RANGE	AVG. P/E RATIO	AVG. YIELD %
p12/31/02	3,403.6	⑤ 211.9							⑤ 1.62			0.54	50.40 - 36.53	26.8	1.2
12/31/01	2,354.7	④ 188.2	2,525.0	13.5	8.0	21.4	7.5	1.1	④ 1.45	2.70	0.82	0.52	44.19 - 28.50	25.1	1.4
12/31/00	2,264.3	③ 208.6	1,714.0	15.2	9.2	27.5	12.2	1.1	③ 1.58	2.71	5.95	0.48	45.69 - 28.00	23.3	1.3
12/31/99	2,080.0	175.8	1,585.9	13.9	8.5	23.1	11.1	1.2	1.31	2.31	5.89	0.42	44.44 - 31.69	29.1	1.1
12/31/98	1,888.2	② 154.5	1,471.0	13.9	8.2	22.4	10.5	1.3	② 1.15	2.06	5.33	0.38	38.00 - 26.13	27.9	1.2
12/31/97	1,640.4	134.0	1,416.3	13.3	8.2	24.3	9.5	1.3	1.00	1.75	4.27	0.32	27.81 - 18.13	23.0	1.4
12/31/96	1,490.0	113.2	1,208.4	12.4	7.6	21.8	9.4	1.3	1.75	3.14	8.02	0.28	19.75 - 14.56	9.8	1.6
12/31/95	1,340.9	99.2	1,060.9	12.1	7.4	21.7	9.3	1.2	1.50	2.65	7.06	0.25	15.88 - 10.00	8.6	1.6
12/31/94	1,207.6	84.6	1,020.4	11.3	7.0	18.3	8.3	1.6	1.25	2.24	6.82	0.22	11.75 - 9.63	8.5	2.1
12/31/93	1,041.5	① 75.9	867.2	11.7	7.3	20.0	8.8	1.5	① 1.20	2.15	6.00	0.19	11.91 - 9.06	8.7	1.5

Statistics are as originally reported. Adj. for stk. splits: 2-for-1, 1/98, 1/94 ① Excl. acctg. change credit of $4.7 mill. & extraord. chrg. $4.0 mill. ② Excl. disc. opers. gain of $38.0 mill. ③ Bef. acctg. chrg., $2.4 mill.; incl. gain on sale of business of $25.9 mill. & restruct. chrg. of $5.2 mill. ④ Incl. net non-recurr. chrg. of $824,000 ⑤ Excl. disc. opers. gain of $1.9 mill. & acctg. chrg. $4.0 mill.; Incl. net spec. chrgs. $37.0 mill.

EDISON INTERNATIONAL

EXCH.	SYM.	REC. PRICE	P/E RATIO	YLD.	MKT. CAP.	RANGE (52-WK.)	'02 Y/E PR.
NYSE	EIX	12.36 (2/28/03)	3.5	...	$4.03 bill.	19.60 - 7.80	11.85

LOWER MEDIUM GRADE. THE COMPANY IS MAKING PROGRESS TOWARDS IMPROVING ITS FINANCIAL HEALTH AND CREDIT-WORTHINESS.

***7 YEAR PRICE SCORE 70.5**   ***12 MONTH PRICE SCORE 97.7**

*NYSE COMPOSITE INDEX=100

INTERIM EARNINGS (Per Share):

Qtr.	Mar.	June	Sept.	Dec.
1997	0.35	0.34	0.70	0.37
1998	0.38	0.40	0.60	0.46
1999	0.40	0.37	0.73	0.28
2000	0.32	0.41	1.10	d7.83
2001	d1.93	0.18	2.46	6.66
2002	0.26	2.01	1.07	0.17

INTERIM DIVIDENDS (Per Share):

Amt.	Decl.	Ex.	Rec.	Pay.
Last Dist. $0.28Q, 10/31/00				

CAPITALIZATION (12/31/01):

	($000)	(%)
Long-Term Debt	12,674,000	52.8
Deferred Income Tax	6,367,000	26.5
Minority Interest	345,000	1.4
Redeemable Pfd. Stock	1,204,000	5.0
Preferred Stock	129,000	0.5
Common & Surplus	3,272,000	13.6
Total	23,991,000	100.0

BUSINESS:

Edison International (formerly SCEcorp), through its subsidiary Southern California Edison, provides electric service to a 50,000-square-mile area of Central and Southern California, which includes some 800 cities and communities, with a population of more than 11.0 million people. The Company's nonutility businesses are Edison Mission Energy, which is engaged in developing, acquiring, owning or leasing, and operating electric power generation facilities worldwide; Edison Capital, a provider of capital and financial services for energy and infrastructure projects; and Edison Enterprises, which provides integrated energy services, utility outsourcing, and consumer products and services.

RECENT DEVELOPMENTS:

For the year ended 12/31/02, income was $1.14 billion, before a loss from discontinued operations of $58.0 million, compared with income of $2.40 billion, before a loss from discontinued operations of $1.37 billion, the year before. Earnings included a gain of $1.50 billion in 2002 and a loss of $3.21 billion in 2001 for net provisions for regulatory adjustment clauses, respectively. Results also included gains of $5.0 million in 2002 and $6.0 million in 2001 on sale of utility plant. Total operating revenue grew 4.5% to $11.76 billion from $11.26 billion a year earlier. Operating income fell to $2.66 billion from $5.46 billion a year earlier.

PROSPECTS:

The Company is making progress towards recovering from the California power crisis. Core earnings for Southern California Edison (SCE) grew by $340.0 million from 2001 levels due to higher revenue from rate increases, lower interest expenses and improved income from Units 2 & 3 from the San Onofre Nuclear Generating Station. Meanwhile, as of 12/31/02, $574.0 million of SCE's $3.60 billion in uncollected procurement costs remained to be recovered. The Company noted that a full recovery of the balance may occur as early as mid year, allowing rates to drop shortly thereafter. Going forward, EIL will focus on restoring its financial health and improving its credit-worthiness. EIX noted that it was committed to renewing a dividend payment to shareholders by the end of 2003.

ANNUAL FINANCIAL DATA:

FISCAL YEAR	TOT. REVS. ($mill.)	NET INC. ($mill.)	TOT. ASSETS ($mill.)	OPER. PROFIT %	NET PROFIT %	NET INC./ NET PROP. %	NET INC./ TOT. CAP. %	RET. ON EQUITY %	ACCUM. DEPR./ GROSS PROP. %	EARN. PER SH.$	TANG. BK. VAL.$	DIV. PER SH.$	DIV. PAYOUT %	PRICE RANGE	AVG. P/E RATIO	AVG. YIELD %
p12/31/02	11,764.0	③ 1,135.0								③ 3.46		...	...	19.60 - 7.80	4.0	...
12/31/01	11,436.0	② 2,402.0	36,774.0	47.7	21.0	30.0	10.0	70.6	49.9	② 7.36	8.10	...	...	16.12 - 6.25	1.5	...
12/31/00	11,717.0	d1,943.0	35,100.0	...	...	...	...	...	50.0	d5.84	7.43	1.11	...	30.00 - 14.13	...	5.0
12/31/99	9,670.0	623.0	36,229.0	18.0	6.4	8.5	2.4	11.7	50.6	1.79	14.94	1.07	59.8	29.63 - 21.63	14.3	4.2
12/31/98	10,208.0	668.0	24,698.0	12.2	6.5	9.2	3.7	12.8	48.7	1.84	14.55	1.03	56.0	31.00 - 25.13	15.3	3.7
12/31/97	9,235.0	① 700.0	25,101.0	22.0	7.6	6.4	3.7	12.3	49.1	① 1.73	14.71	1.00	57.8	27.81 - 19.38	13.6	4.2
12/31/96	8,545.0	① 717.0	24,559.0	23.9	8.4	6.1	3.7	10.7	44.6	① 1.64	15.12	1.00	61.0	20.38 - 15.00	10.8	5.7
12/31/95	8,405.0	739.0	23,946.0	22.7	8.8	6.1	3.8	11.1	41.4	1.66	14.34	1.00	60.2	18.00 - 14.38	9.8	6.2
12/31/94	8,345.0	681.0	22,390.0	21.3	8.2	5.5	3.8	10.5	38.3	1.52	13.72	1.21	79.6	20.50 - 12.38	10.8	7.4
12/31/93	7,821.0	639.0	21,379.0	21.5	8.2	5.2	3.7	10.1	36.7	1.43	13.31	1.41	98.6	25.75 - 19.88	16.0	6.2

Statistics are as originally reported. Adj. for stk. splits: 2-for-1, 6/93 ① Incl. non-recurr. chrg. 1996, $0.06/sh.; 1997, $0.04/sh. for workforce reductions. ② Bef. loss from disc. opers. of $1.37 bill.; Incl. asset impair. chrgs. $1.27 bill. & a procurement and generation-related adjustment gain of $1.98 bill. ③ Bef. loss of disc. opers. of $58.0 mill.; Incl. a gain of $1.50 bill. for net provisions for reg. adj. clauses & gain of $5.0 mill for sale of util. plant.

OFFICERS:
J. E. Bryson, Chmn., Pres., C.E.O.
T. F. Craver Jr., Exec. V.P., C.F.O., Treas.
K. S. Stewart, Asst. Gen. Couns., Asst. Sec.
INVESTOR CONTACT: Jo Ann Goddard,
V.P., Inv. Rel. (626) 302-2515
PRINCIPAL OFFICE: 2244 Walnut Grove
Avenue Rosemead, CA 91770

TELEPHONE NUMBER: (626) 302-2222
FAX: (626) 302-9935
WEB: www.edison.com
NO. OF EMPLOYEES: 14,964
SHAREHOLDERS: 72,774
ANNUAL MEETING: In May
INCORPORATED: CA, April, 1987

INSTITUTIONAL HOLDINGS:
No. of Institutions: 290
Shares Held: 224,387,851
% Held: 68.9

INDUSTRY: Electric services (SIC: 4911)

TRANSFER AGENT(S): Wells Fargo Shareowner Services, South St. Paul, MN

EDWARDS (A.G.), INC.

EXCH.	SYM.	REC. PRICE	P/E RATIO	YLD.	MKT. CAP.	RANGE (52-WK.)	'02 Y/E PR.
NYSE	AGE	26.67 (2/28/03)	36.0	2.4%	$2.15 bill.	46.15 - 25.50	32.96

MEDIUM GRADE. THE COMPANY IS EXPANDING ITS HEADQUARTERS WITH AN ADDITIONAL OFFICE BUILDING AND LEARNING CENTER.

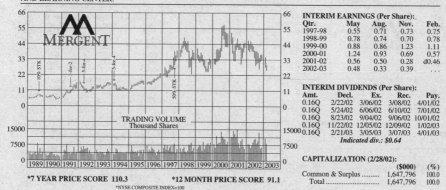

INTERIM EARNINGS (Per Share):

Qtr.	May	Aug.	Nov.	Feb.
1997-98	0.55	0.71	0.73	0.75
1998-99	0.78	0.74	0.70	0.78
1999-00	0.88	0.86	1.23	1.11
2000-01	1.24	0.93	0.69	0.57
2001-02	0.56	0.50	0.28	d0.46
2002-03	0.48	0.33	0.39	...

INTERIM DIVIDENDS (Per Share):

Amt.	Decl.	Ex.	Rec.	Pay.
0.16Q	2/22/02	3/06/02	3/08/02	4/01/02
0.16Q	5/24/02	6/06/02	6/10/02	7/01/02
0.16Q	8/23/02	9/04/02	9/06/02	10/01/02
0.16Q	11/22/02	12/05/02	12/09/02	1/02/03
0.16Q	2/21/03	3/05/03	3/07/03	4/01/03

Indicated div.: $0.64

*7 YEAR PRICE SCORE 110.3   ***12 MONTH PRICE SCORE 91.1**

*NYSE COMPOSITE INDEX=100

CAPITALIZATION (2/28/02):

	($000)	(%)
Common & Surplus	1,647,796	100.0
Total	1,647,796	100.0

BUSINESS:

A.G. Edwards, Inc. is a holding company whose subsidiaries provide securities and commodities brokerage, investment banking, trust, asset management, and insurance services. As of 12/19/02, AGE's principal subsidiary, A.G. Edwards & Sons, Inc., operated 709 brokerage offices in 49 states, the District of Columbia and London, England. A.G. Edwards & Sons provides a full range of financial products and services to individual and institutional investors and offers investment banking services to corporate, governmental and municipal clients.

RECENT DEVELOPMENTS:

For the quarter ended 11/30/02, net earnings increased 43.8% to $32.0 million from $22.2 million in the corresponding prior-year period. Results for 2002 included a tax benefit of $8.9 million, while results for 2001 included a charge of $20.0 million resulting from a reserve established in connection with a partially secured margin loan. Total revenues fell 8.2% to $513.5 million from $559.7 million the previous year. Commissions declined 7.7% to $204.7 million from $221.7 million a year earlier. Asset management and service fees decreased 10.7% to $146.4 million, primarily due to lower distribution fees received from certain money funds that reached expense caps due to current money fund yields. Investment banking revenue slipped 3.2% to $65.6 million. Interest revenue dropped 27.4% to $26.0 million, while revenues from principal transactions slid 2.6% to $69.4 million. Interest expense was $539,000 compared with $3.8 million the year before.

PROSPECTS:

Revenues continue to be negatively affected by the ongoing hesitancy of individual investors to reinvest in the equity markets and the adverse effects of current interest rates on certain revenue streams. Separately, the Company is expanding its headquarters with an additional office building and learning center. The cost of construction is estimated to be $185.0 million. The completion date is expected to be in the first quarter of fiscal 2004.

ANNUAL FINANCIAL DATA:

FISCAL YEAR	TOT. REVS. ($mill.)	NET INC. ($mill.)	TOT. ASSETS ($mill.)	OPER. PROFIT %	NET PROFIT %	RET. ON EQUITY %	RET. ON ASSETS %	CURR. RATIO	EARN. PER SH.$	CASH FL. PER SH.$	TANG. BK. VAL.$	DIV. PER SH.$	PRICE RANGE	AVG. P/E RATIO	AVG. YIELD %
2/28/02	2,363.8	②71.5	4,187.2	5.0	3.0	4.3	1.7	1.4	②0.88	2.67	20.42	0.64	52.19 - 29.76	46.6	1.6
2/28/01	2,839.1	287.5	4,860.0	19.5	10.1	17.7	5.9	1.3	3.43	5.01	20.29	0.63	57.94 - 29.56	12.8	1.4
2/29/00	2,819.0	①382.9	5,347.6	22.9	13.6	22.3	7.2	1.4	①4.08	5.12	19.69	0.59	41.00 - 24.25	8.0	1.8
2/28/99	2,240.8	292.1	3,803.1	21.3	13.0	17.9	7.7	1.6	3.00	3.78	17.16	0.54	48.81 - 22.63	11.9	1.5
2/28/98	2,004.1	269.3	4,193.3	21.9	13.4	18.4	6.4	1.4	2.75	3.39	15.54	0.48	39.50 - 20.50	10.9	1.6
2/28/97	1,696.5	219.1	4,244.3	21.0	12.9	17.4	5.2	1.3	2.24	2.88	13.12	0.43	23.33 - 15.00	8.6	2.2
2/29/96	1,454.5	170.6	3,102.1	19.2	11.7	15.7	5.5	1.4	1.77	2.31	11.33	0.37	18.00 - 11.67	8.4	2.5
2/28/95	1,178.3	124.1	2,224.3	17.5	10.5	13.5	5.6	1.5	1.33	1.84	9.84	0.37	16.25 - 11.00	10.2	2.7
2/28/94	1,278.6	154.9	2,236.6	19.1	12.1	19.6	6.9	1.4	1.71	2.24	8.72	0.31	16.93 - 12.00	8.4	2.1
2/28/93	1,074.4	119.4	2,111.2	17.9	11.1	19.4	5.7	1.3	1.38	1.71	7.11	0.27	17.17 - 9.20	9.6	2.0

Statistics are as originally reported. Adj. for all stock dividends and splits through 10/97. ① Includes a gain of $75.2 million from an investment in a privately-held investment management company. ② Incl. pre-tax restruct. chrgs. of $82.5 mill.

OFFICERS:
R. L. Bagby, Chmn., C.E.O.
B. F. Edwards IV, Vice-Chmn., Pres.
R. J. Kessler, Vice-Chmn.
D. L. Kelly, C.F.O., Treas., Sec.

INVESTOR CONTACT: Investor Relations, (314) 955-5913

PRINCIPAL OFFICE: One North Jefferson Avenue, St. Louis, MO 63103

TELEPHONE NUMBER: (314) 955-3000
FAX: (314) 955-5913
WEB: www.agedwards.com

NO. OF EMPLOYEES: 16,791

SHAREHOLDERS: 25,400 (approx.).

ANNUAL MEETING: In June

INCORPORATED: DE, 1983

INSTITUTIONAL HOLDINGS:
No. of Institutions: 224
Shares Held: 40,562,114
% Held: 51.5

INDUSTRY: Security brokers and dealers (SIC: 6211)

TRANSFER AGENT(S): The Bank of New York, New York, NY

EL PASO CORPORATION

EXCH.	SYM.	REC. PRICE	P/E RATIO	YLD.	MKT. CAP.	RANGE (52-WK.)	'02 Y/E PR.	DIV. ACH.
NYSE	EP	4.86 (2/28/03)	...	3.3%	$2.58 bill.	46.89 - 3.33	6.96	10 yrs.

LOWER MEDIUM GRADE. THE COMPANY HAS SIGNED AGREEMENTS FOR OR COMPLETED MORE THAN 50.0% OF THE $3.40 BILLION OF NON-CORE ASSET SALES IT EXPECTS IN 2003.

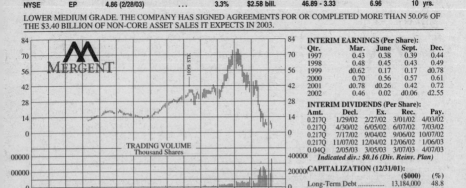

*7 YEAR PRICE SCORE 55.3   ***12 MONTH PRICE SCORE 43.3**
*NYSE COMPOSITE INDEX=100

INTERIM EARNINGS (Per Share):

Qtr.	Mar.	June	Sept.	Dec.
1997	0.43	0.38	0.39	0.44
1998	0.48	0.45	0.43	0.49
1999	d0.62	0.17	0.17	d0.78
2000	0.70	0.56	0.57	0.61
2001	d0.78	d0.26	0.42	0.72
2002	0.46	0.02	d0.06	d2.55

INTERIM DIVIDENDS (Per Share):

Amt.	Decl.	Ex.	Rec.	Pay.
0.217Q	1/29/02	2/27/02	3/01/02	4/03/02
0.217Q	4/30/02	6/05/02	6/07/02	7/03/02
0.217Q	7/17/02	9/04/02	9/06/02	10/07/02
0.217Q	11/07/02	12/04/02	12/06/02	1/06/03
0.04Q	2/05/03	3/05/03	3/07/03	4/07/03

Indicated div.: $0.16 (Div. Reinv. Plan)

CAPITALIZATION (12/31/01):

	($000)	(%)
Long-Term Debt	13,184,000	48.8
Deferred Income Tax	4,459,000	16.5
Common & Surplus	9,356,000	34.7
Total	26,999,000	100.0

BUSINESS:

El Paso Corporation (formerly El Paso Energy Corp.) has operations in natural gas transportation, gathering, processing and storage; natural gas and oil exploration, development and production; energy and energy-related commodities and product marketing; power generation; energy infrastructure facility development and operation; petroleum refining; and chemicals production. On 1/29/01, EPG acquired The Coastal Corporation for $24.00 billion.

RECENT DEVELOPMENTS:

For the twelve months ended 12/31/02, EP reported a loss from continuing operations of $1.29 billion compared with income from continuing operations of $72.0 million a year earlier. Results for 2002 and 2001 included restructuring and merger-related charges of $81.0 million and $1.52 billion, losses on long-lived assets of $282.0 million and $183.0 million, and ceiling test charges of $269.0 million and $135.0 million, respectively. Results for 2002 also included a charge of $899.0 million related to the Company's Western Energy Settlement. Operating revenues declined 10.7% to $12.19 billion from $13.65 billion the previous year.

PROSPECTS:

On 3/13/03, EP announced that it has completed the sale of its Mid-Continent natural gas and oil reserves to Chesapeake Energy Corporation and closed on a $1.20 billion two-year secured loan. Proceeds from the secured loan were used to retire the approximately $825.0 million net balance of the Company's Trinity River financing. As of 3/27/03, EP has completed or signed additional asset sales that have resulted in transactions totaling over $1.70 billion since 1/1/03. This total represents more than 50.0% of EP's asset sales goal of $3.40 billion for 2003. The asset sales and financing activities support EP's previously announced 2003 five-point business plan, which includes exiting non-core businesses and strengthening and simplifying its balance sheet while maximizing liquidity.

ANNUAL FINANCIAL DATA:

FISCAL YEAR	TOT. REVS. ($mill.)	NET INC. ($mill.)	TOT. ASSETS ($mill.)	OPER. PROFIT %	NET PROFIT %	NET INC./ NET PROP. %	NET INC./ TOT. CAP. %	RET. ON EQUITY %	ACCUM. DEPR./ GROSS PROP. %	EARN. PER SH. $	TANG. BK. VAL. $	DIV. PER SH. $	DIV. PAYOUT %	PRICE RANGE		AVG. P/E RATIO	AVG. YIELD %
p12/31/02	⑩ 12,194.0	⑨ 1,289.0								⑨ d2.30		0.87	...	46.89 —	4.39	...	3.4
12/31/01	⑧ 57,475.0	⑦ 67.0	48,171.0	1.4	0.1	0.3	0.2	0.7	36.9	⑦ 0.13	17.63	0.84	648.3	75.30 —	36.00	427.7	1.5
12/31/00	⑥ 21,950.0	⑤ 582.0	27,445.0	6.1	2.7	5.0	4.0	16.3	40.0	⑤ 2.44	15.20	0.82	33.5	74.25 —	30.31	21.4	1.6
12/31/99	④ 10,581.0	④ d242.0	16,657.0	...	...	...	...	...	42.7	④ d1.06	10.47	0.79	...	43.44 —	30.69	...	2.1
12/31/98	5,782.0	225.0	10,069.0	8.8	3.9	3.1	3.3	10.7	17.4	1.85	13.09	0.76	40.9	38.94 —	24.69	17.2	2.4
12/31/97	5,638.0	186.0	9,532.0	9.2	3.3	2.6	3.1	9.5	16.4	1.59	16.32	0.72	45.4	33.38 —	24.44	18.2	2.5
12/31/96	① 3,010.0	② 38.0	8,712.0	5.6	1.3	0.6	0.7	2.3	...	② 0.53	14.82	0.69	129.5	26.63 —	14.31	38.6	3.4
12/31/95	1,038.0	85.4	2,534.6	20.5	8.2	4.3	4.7	12.0	...	1.24	4.85	0.65	104.6	16.25 —	12.38	23.2	4.5
12/31/94	869.9	② 89.6	2,331.8	25.6	10.3	4.8	5.0	12.6	...	② 1.23	9.92	0.59	48.3	20.94 —	14.81	14.6	3.3
12/31/93	908.9	91.7	2,269.7	25.2	10.1	5.2	5.1	13.0	...	1.23	9.60	0.54	43.7	20.19 —	15.13	14.4	3.0

Statistics are as originally reported. Adj. for 100% stk. div., 4/98 ① Refl. acq. of Tenneco ② Incl. non-recurr. chrgs. 12/31/96, $64.6 mill.; chrg. 12/31/94, $12.0 mill. ③ Incl. one-time chrgs. of $909.0 mill.; bef. acctg. change chrg. of $13.0 mill. ④ Refl. acq. of Sonat Inc. in 10/99. ⑤ Incl. merger rel. costs & asset impair. chrgs. of $91.0 mill.; bef. extraord. gain of $70.0 mill. ⑥ Refl. growth of energy commodities revs. ⑦ Incl. merger-rel. costs & asset impair. chrgs. of $1.84 bill. and ceiling test chrg. of $135.0 mill.; bef. extraord. gain of $26.0 mill. ⑧ Refl. acq. of The Coastal Corporation on 1/29/01. ⑨ Incl. restruct. & merger-rel. chrgs. of $81.0 mill., ceiling test chrg. of $269.0 mill. and Western Energy settlmnt. chrg. of $899.0 mill.; bef. loss fr. disc. ops. of $124.0 mill. & acctg. chge. chrg. of $54.0 mill. ⑩ Refl. adopt. of Emerging Issues Task Force Issue No. 02-3, which requires EP to report all physical sales of energy commodities in its energy trading activs. on a net basis.

OFFICERS:
R. L. Kuehn, Jr., Chmn., C.E.O.
H. B. Austin, Pres., C.O.O.
P. Heeg, Exec. V.P., Gen. Couns.

INVESTOR CONTACT: Bruce Connery, V.P. Investor Relations, (713) 420-5855

PRINCIPAL OFFICE: El Paso Building, 1001 Louisiana Street, Houston, TX 77002

TELEPHONE NUMBER: (713) 420-2600
FAX: (713) 420-4417
WEB: www.elpaso.com
NO. OF EMPLOYEES: 14,180 (approx.)
SHAREHOLDERS: 55,069 (approx.)
ANNUAL MEETING: In May
INCORPORATED: DE, 1928

INSTITUTIONAL HOLDINGS:
No. of Institutions: 463
Shares Held: 471,015,379
% Held: 78.6

INDUSTRY: Natural gas transmission (SIC: 4922)

TRANSFER AGENT(S): Fleet National Bank c/o EquiServe, Providence, RI

ELECTRONIC DATA SYSTEMS CORPORATION

EXCH.	SYM.	REC. PRICE	P/E RATIO	YLD.	MKT. CAP.	RANGE (52-WK.)	'02 Y/E PR.
NYSE	EDS	15.57 (2/28/03)	7.6	3.9%	$7.43 bill.	65.91 - 10.09	18.43

UPPER MEDIUM GRADE. THE COMPANY EXPECTS FULL-YEAR 2003 EARNINGS PER SHARE OF $1.80 TO $2.00, EXCLUDING DISCONTINUED OPERATIONS.

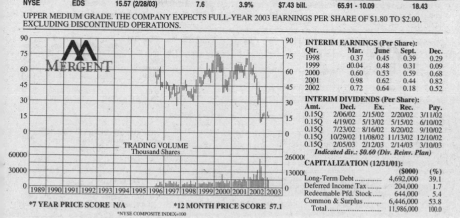

INTERIM EARNINGS (Per Share):

Qtr.	Mar.	June	Sept.	Dec.
1998	0.37	0.45	0.39	0.29
1999	d0.04	0.48	0.31	0.09
2000	0.60	0.53	0.59	0.68
2001	0.98	0.62	0.44	0.82
2002	0.72	0.64	0.18	0.52

INTERIM DIVIDENDS (Per Share):

Amt.	Decl.	Ex.	Rec.	Pay.
0.15Q	2/06/02	2/15/02	2/20/02	3/11/02
0.15Q	4/19/02	5/13/02	5/15/02	6/10/02
0.15Q	7/23/02	8/16/02	8/20/02	9/10/02
0.15Q	10/29/02	11/08/02	11/13/02	12/10/02
0.15Q	2/05/03	2/12/03	2/14/03	3/10/03

Indicated div.: $0.60 (Div. Reinv. Plan)

CAPITALIZATION (12/31/01):

	($000)	(%)
Long-Term Debt	4,692,000	39.1
Deferred Income Tax	204,000	1.7
Redeemable Pfd. Stock	644,000	5.4
Common & Surplus	6,446,000	53.8
Total	11,986,000	100.0

*7 YEAR PRICE SCORE N/A   ***12 MONTH PRICE SCORE 57.1**

NYSE COMPOSITE INDEX=100

BUSINESS:

Electronic Data System Corporation is a global provider of information technology using advanced computer and communications technologies to meet the business needs of its clients. EDS operates in four business lines: A.T. Kearney, E.solutions, Business Process Management, and Information Solutions. A.T. Kearney provides business consulting and executive searches. E.solutions is the global solutions

consulting line of business. Business Process Management is the customer services and claims processing unit. Information Solutions is the centralized outsourcing business that manages customer mainframe data. Revenues for 2002 were derived: Operating Solutions, 66.8%; Solutions Consulting, 27.1%; PLM Solutions, 4.1%; and other, 2.0%.

RECENT DEVELOPMENTS:

For the year ended 12/31/02, income from continuing operations declined 25.6% to $1.01 billion from $1.35 billion, before an accounting change charge of $24.0 million, in 2001. Results for 2002 and 2001 included restructuring and other charges of $3.0 million and $15.0 million, respectively. Results for 2001 also included a research and devel-

opment charge of $144.0 million and a reclassification of investment gain from equity of $315.0 million. In addition, results for 2002 and 2001 excluded income of $109.0 million and $33.0 million, respectively, from discontinued operations. Revenues climbed 1.7% to $21.50 billion from $21.14 billion in 2001.

PROSPECTS:

The Company is maintaining a cautious outlook as market conditions in the information technology services sector remain challenging with companies continuing to limit their discretionary spending. Based on this continued weakness, the Company expects full-year 2003 earnings per

share of $1.80 to $2.00, excluding the effect of discontinued operations. Moreover, base revenues for full-year 2003 are expected to increase in the low-to-mid-single digit percentage range, while revenues from business with General Motors is expected to decline.

ANNUAL FINANCIAL DATA:

FISCAL YEAR	TOT. REVS. ($mill.)	NET INC. ($mill.)	TOT. ASSETS ($mill.)	OPER. PROFIT %	NET PROFIT %	RET. ON EQUITY %	RET. ON ASSETS %	CURR. RATIO	EARN. PER SH.$	CASH FL. PER SH.$	TANG. BK. VAL.$	DIV. PER SH.$	PRICE RANGE	AVG. P/E RATIO	AVG. YIELD %
p12/31/02	21,502.0	⑧ 1,007.0							⑧ 2.06			0.60	68.55 - 10.09	19.1	1.5
12/31/01	21,543.0	⑦ 1,387.0	16,353.0	9.7	6.4	21.5	8.5	1.7	⑦ 2.86	5.93	3.06	0.60	72.45 - 50.90	21.6	1.0
12/31/00	19,226.8	⑥ 1,143.3	12,700.3	9.5	5.9	22.2	9.0	1.4	⑥ 2.40	5.40	4.53	0.60	76.69 - 38.38	24.0	1.0
12/31/99	18,534.2	⑤ 420.9	12,522.3	2.6	2.3	9.3	3.4	1.2	⑤ 0.85	3.73	3.93	0.60	70.00 - 44.13	67.1	1.1
12/31/98	16,891.0	④ 743.4	11,526.1	6.3	4.4	12.6	6.4	1.5	④ 1.50	4.31	9.02	0.60	51.31 - 30.44	27.2	1.5
12/31/97	15,235.6	③ 730.6	11,174.1	8.0	4.8	13.8	6.5	1.6	③ 1.48	3.93	7.65	0.60	49.63 - 25.50	25.4	1.6
12/31/96	14,441.3	① 431.5	11,192.9	5.5	3.0	9.0	3.9	1.6	① 0.89	...	6.93	② 0.60	63.38 - 40.75	58.5	0.6
12/31/95	12,422.1	938.9	10,832.4	12.3	7.6	17.7	8.7	1.3	1.96	4.23	7.13	0.52	...	...	...
12/31/94	9,960.1	740.7	8,786.5	12.5	7.4	17.5	8.4	1.2	1.71	...	6.15	0.48	...	...	...
12/31/93	8,507.3	669.5	...	13.1	7.9	...	...	...	1.51	...	...	0.40	...	...	...

Statistics are as originally reported. ① Incl. $850.0 mill. one-time chg. & $45.5 mill. one-time split-off costs. ② Incl. $0.30 per sh. payable as General Motors class E common stock. ③ Incl. $329.6 mill. pre-tax restr. chg. & asset write-downs. ④ Incl. $70.3 mill. in-process R&D and asset write-downs chg., $49.4 mill. chg. for exec. retirements, cr$22.2 mill. restr. chgs. & $49.6 mill. gain fr. sale of stock. ⑤ Incl. $199.5 mill. pre-tax gain & $1.04 bill. pre-tax restr. & other chgs. ⑥ Incl. $24.2 mill. chg. fr. in-process R&D and $21.7 mill. restr. & other chgs. ⑦ Incl. $144.0 mill. in-process R&D, $15.0 mill. restr. credit, $315.0 mill. gain fr. reclass. of invest., and excl. $24.0 mill. acctg. chg. ⑧ Incl. $3.0 mill. restr. chg. & excl. $109.0 mill. gain fr. disc. ops.

OFFICERS:
R. H. Brown, Chmn., C.E.O.
R. H. Swan, Exec. V.P., C.F.O.

INVESTOR CONTACT: Jeff Baum, Investor Relations, (972) 797-9495

PRINCIPAL OFFICE: 5400 Legacy Drive, Plano, TX 75024

TELEPHONE NUMBER: (972) 604-6000
FAX: (972) 605-6796
WEB: www.eds.com
NO. OF EMPLOYEES: 143,000 (approx.)
SHAREHOLDERS: 143,910 (approx.)
ANNUAL MEETING: In Apr.
INCORPORATED: TX, 1962; reincorp., DE, 1994

INSTITUTIONAL HOLDINGS:
No. of Institutions: 533
Shares Held: 402,275,177
% Held: 84.4
INDUSTRY: Data processing and preparation (SIC: 7374)
TRANSFER AGENT(S): The Bank of New York, New York, NY

EMC CORPORATION

EXCH.	SYM.	REC. PRICE	P/E RATIO	YLD.	MKT. CAP.	RANGE (52-WK.)	'02 Y/E PR.
NYSE	EMC	7.39 (2/28/03)	...	...	$16.41 bill.	12.75 - 3.67	6.14

SPECULATIVE GRADE. REVENUE IN THE FIRST QUARTER OF 2003 IS EXPECTED BETWEEN $1.35 BILLION AND $1.40 BILLION.

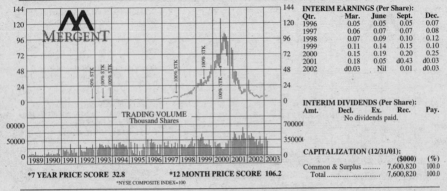

*7 YEAR PRICE SCORE 32.8   ***12 MONTH PRICE SCORE 106.2**
NYSE COMPOSITE INDEX=100

INTERIM EARNINGS (Per Share):

Qtr.	Mar.	June	Sept.	Dec.
1996	0.05	0.05	0.05	0.07
1997	0.06	0.07	0.07	0.08
1998	0.07	0.09	0.10	0.12
1999	0.11	0.14	0.15	0.10
2000	0.15	0.19	0.20	0.25
2001	0.18	0.05	d0.43	d0.03
2002	d0.03	Nil	0.01	d0.03

INTERIM DIVIDENDS (Per Share):

Amt.	Decl.	Ex.	Rec.	Pay.
		No dividends paid.		

CAPITALIZATION (12/31/01):

	($000)	(%)
Common & Surplus	7,600,820	100.0
Total	7,600,820	100.0

BUSINESS:

EMC Corporation designs, manufactures and markets a wide range of storage platforms and software offerings, as well as related services that enable its customers to store, manage, protect and share electronic information. These integrated applications enable organizations to create an enterprise information infrastructure or an E-Infostructure. The Company's products are sold to customers who use a range of computing platforms for key applications, including transaction processing, enterprise resource planning, customer relationship management, data warehousing, electronic commerce and Web hosting. The Company operates in two segments: information storage systems and software, and other businesses. The Company's information storage systems include its SYMMETRIX systems, CLARiiON systems, CELERRA systems, and CONNECTRIX systems.

RECENT DEVELOPMENTS:

For the twelve months ended 12/31/02, the Company reported a net loss of $118.7 million compared with a net loss of $507.7 million in 2001. Results for 2002 and 2001 included restructuring and other special charges of $150.4 million and $398.5 million, respectively. Total revenues declined 23.3% to $5.44 billion from $7.09 billion in the prior year. Operating loss narrowed to $493.8 million from $697.8 million in the previous year. Overall results reflected double-digit sequential revenue growth across the Company's major businesses, as well as increased market share, particularly in mid-tier storage and storage software.

PROSPECTS:

The Company expects revenue in the first quarter of 2003 between $1.35 billion and $1.40 billion and earnings per diluted share of about $0.01, excluding restructuring charges. In addition, EMC expects its overall cost structure to improve, and result in a break-even level of under $1.30 billion by the end of the second quarter of 2003. The Company also expects continued improvement in gross margins and operating margins, even though quarterly margins may vary during the year based on volume. Meanwhile, research and development expenditures for 2003 is expected to be slightly lower than the $781.0 million, which was invested in 2002.

ANNUAL FINANCIAL DATA:

FISCAL YEAR	TOT. REVS. ($mill.)	NET INC. ($mill.)	TOT. ASSETS ($mill.)	OPER. PROFIT %	NET PROFIT %	RET. ON EQUITY %	RET. ON ASSETS %	CURR. RATIO	EARN. PER SH.$	CASH FL. PER SH.$	TANG. BK. VAL.$	PRICE RANGE	AVG. P/E RATIO
p12/31/02	5,438.4	⑥d118.7							⑥ d0.05			17.97 - 3.67	...
12/31/01	7,090.6	⑤d507.7	9,889.6	...	...	...	...	2.3	⑤ d0.23	0.08	3.42	82.00 - 10.01	...
12/31/00	8,872.8	1,782.1	10,628.3	25.4	20.1	21.8	16.8	2.9	0.79	1.04	3.72	127.00 - 47.50	110.4
④12/31/99	6,715.6	③1,010.6	7,173.3	18.5	15.0	20.4	14.1	3.1	③0.46	0.66	2.38	55.50 - 21.00	83.1
12/31/98	3,973.7	793.4	4,569.7	24.7	20.0	23.9	17.4	4.8	0.37	0.46	1.65	21.66 - 6.00	36.9
12/31/97	2,937.9	538.5	3,490.1	22.5	18.3	22.7	15.4	5.2	0.26	0.32	1.20	8.14 - 3.97	23.3
12/31/96	2,273.7	386.2	2,293.5	21.8	17.0	23.6	16.8	4.2	0.20	0.24	0.84	4.55 - 1.89	16.4
①12/30/95	1,921.3	②326.8	1,745.7	22.7	17.0	28.7	18.7	3.7	②0.17	0.19	0.61	3.42 - 1.63	14.8
12/31/94	1,377.5	250.7	1,317.5	25.4	18.2	34.4	19.0	3.0	0.15	0.16	0.46	3.00 - 1.56	15.4
1/01/94	782.6	127.1	829.6	23.1	16.2	30.3	15.3	4.9	0.04	0.09	0.28	2.44 - 0.64	34.9

Statistics are as originally reported. Adj. for 2-for-1 split, 6/93, 12/93, 11/97, 5/99 & 6/00. ① Incl. results of McDATA Corp., acq. on 12/7/95 on a pooling-of-interests basis. ② Excl. $38.6 mill. ($0.15/sh.) one-time after-tax chg. ③ Incl. $208.2 mill. restr. chg. ④ Refl. acq. of Data General Corp. on 10/12/99. ⑤ Incl. $398.5 mill. restr. & special chgs. ⑥ Incl. $150.4 mill. restr. and other spl. chgs.

OFFICERS:
M. C. Ruettgers, Exec. Chmn.
J. M. Tucci, Pres., C.E.O.
W. J. Teuber Jr., Exec. V.P., C.F.O.
INVESTOR CONTACT: Marc Frederickson, Investor Relations, (508) 293-7137
PRINCIPAL OFFICE: 35 Parkwood Drive, Hopkinton, MA 01748

TELEPHONE NUMBER: (508) 435-1000
FAX: (508) 435-5222
WEB: www.emc.com
NO. OF EMPLOYEES: 20,100 (approx.)
SHAREHOLDERS: 16,678
ANNUAL MEETING: In May
INCORPORATED: MA, 1979

INSTITUTIONAL HOLDINGS:
No. of Institutions: 817
Shares Held: 1,288,982,815
% Held: 58.6
INDUSTRY: Computer storage devices (SIC: 3572)
TRANSFER AGENT(S): Boston EquiServe, Boston, MA

EMCOR GROUP, INC.

EXCH.	SYM.	REC. PRICE	P/E RATIO	YLD.	MKT. CAP.	RANGE (52-WK.)	'02 Y/E PR.
NYSE	EME	48.30 (2/28/03)	11.9	...	$0.72 bill.	64.35 - 44.71	53.01

UPPER MEDIUM GRADE. THE COMPANY'S RECENT ACQUISITION OF CONSOLIDATED ENGINEERING SERVICE, INC. IS EXPECTED TO STRENGTHEN ITS FACILITIES SERVICES OFFERINGS.

*7 YEAR PRICE SCORE 207.0   ***12 MONTH PRICE SCORE 99.3**

NYSE COMPOSITE INDEX=100

INTERIM EARNINGS (Per Share):

Qtr.	Mar.	June	Sept.	Dec.
1996	d0.37	0.93	0.19	0.20
1997	0.03	0.20	0.34	0.33
1998	0.08	0.34	0.55	0.69
1999	0.20	0.45	0.66	0.88
2000	0.40	0.68	0.83	1.04
2001	0.44	0.81	1.00	1.14
2002	0.47	0.96	1.26	1.38

INTERIM DIVIDENDS (Per Share):

Amt.	Decl.	Ex.	Rec.	Pay.
	No dividends paid.			

CAPITALIZATION (12/31/01):

	($000)	(%)
Long-Term Debt	848	0.2
Common & Surplus	421,933	99.8
Total	422,781	100.0

BUSINESS:

EMCOR Group, Inc. is a mechanical and electrical construction and facilities services company. As of 12/31/02, EME provided services to a broad range of commercial, industrial, utility and institutional customers through approximately 70 principal operating subsidiaries, joint ventures and a majority-owned interest in a limited liability company. The Company specializes in the design, integration, installation, start-up, operation and maintenance of systems for generation and distribution of electrical power; lighting systems; low-voltage systems, such as fire alarm, security, communications and process control systems; voice and data communications systems; heating, ventilation, air conditioning, refrigeration and clean-room process ventilation systems; and plumbing, process and high-purity piping systems.

RECENT DEVELOPMENTS:

For the year ended 12/31/02, net income increased 25.8% to $62.9 million compared with $50.0 million in 2001. Revenues advanced 16.0% to $3.97 billion from $3.42 billion a year earlier. Results for 2001 included goodwill amortization of $5.5 million. The improvement in results was due to EME's 3/1/02 acquisitions of 19 Midwestern companies from Comfort Systems USA and internal revenue growth of 1.3%. Operating income rose 29.0% to $114.4 million, or 2.9% of revenues, from $88.7 million, or 2.6% of revenues the prior year.

PROSPECTS:

On 12/19/02, the Company announced that it has acquired Consolidated Engineering Services, Inc. (CES), a subsidiary of Archstone-Smith Engineering Services, Inc. Under the terms of the agreement, EME paid Archstone-Smith about $178.0 million in cash. The CES acquisition is expected to be immediately accretive to the Company's earnings and strengthens its facilities services offerings. In 2003, EME expects full-year revenues in the range of $4.40 billion to $4.60 billion, and diluted earnings per share in the range of $4.25 to $4.60. The Company expects its recent acquisition of CES to contribute between $400.0 million and $450.0 million to 2003 revenues and to provide earnings of between $0.20 and $0.35 per diluted share.

ANNUAL FINANCIAL DATA:

FISCAL YEAR	TOT. REVS. ($mill.)	NET INC. ($mill.)	TOT. ASSETS ($mill.)	OPER. PROFIT %	NET PROFIT %	RET. ON EQUITY %	RET. ON ASSETS %	CURR. RATIO	EARN. PER SH. $	CASH FL. PER SH. $	TANG. BK. VAL. $	PRICE RANGE	AVG. P/E RATIO
p12/31/02	3,968.1	62.9							4.07			64.35 - 44.71	13.4
12/31/01	3,419.9	50.0	1,349.7	2.6	1.5	11.9	3.7	1.4	3.40	4.48	24.70	49.14 - 24.44	10.8
12/31/00	3,460.2	40.1	1,261.9	2.3	1.2	17.2	3.2	1.3	2.95	3.76	15.84	28.13 - 16.81	7.6
12/31/99	2,894.0	27.8	1,056.5	2.0	1.0	16.3	2.6	1.3	2.21	2.90	11.00	26.00 - 16.06	9.5
12/31/98	2,210.4	① 17.1	801.0	1.7	0.8	14.3	2.1	1.4	① 1.46	2.03	13.50	23.13 - 12.50	12.2
12/31/97	1,950.9	① 8.6	660.7	1.4	0.4	9.0	1.3	1.4	① 0.84	1.65	9.94	22.25 - 12.75	20.8
12/31/96	1,669.3	9.4	614.7	1.0	0.6	11.3	1.5	1.4	0.95	1.74	8.82	17.38 - 9.38	14.1
12/31/95	1,588.7	③ d10.9	710.9	0.4	...	...	...	1.2	③ d1.13	d0.20	7.49	9.75 - 7.25	...
12/31/94	1,764.0	④ d118.9	707.5	...	...	...	...	1.2	④ d12.62	d10.95	8.61	...	...
12/31/93	2,194.7	② d114.0	806.4	...	...	...	...	0.6	② d2.84	d1.93		...	...

Statistics are as originally reported. ① Bef. extraord. chrg. 12/31/98: $4.8 mill. ($0.35/sh.); chrg. 12/31/97: $1.0 mill. ($0.10/sh.) ② Bef. disc. oper. loss $9.1 mill. ($0.22/sh.). ③ Incl. loss of $926,000 from sale of bus. ④ Incls. net loss of $3.3 mill. & reorg. chrgs. of $91.3 mill.; Bef. inc. of $10.2 mill. from disc. ops. & acctg. chrg. of $2.1 mill.

OFFICERS:
F. T. MacInnis, Chmn., C.E.O.
J. M. Levy, Pres., C.O.O.
L. E. Chesser, Exec. V.P., C.F.O.
INVESTOR CONTACT: R. Kevin Matz, (203) 849-7938
PRINCIPAL OFFICE: 101 Merritt Seven Corporate Park, Norwalk, CT 06851-1060

TELEPHONE NUMBER: (203) 849-7800
FAX: (203) 849-7900
WEB: www.emcorgroup.com
NO. OF EMPLOYEES: 20,000 (approx.)
SHAREHOLDERS: 138 (of record); 3,800 (approx. beneficial)
ANNUAL MEETING: In July
INCORPORATED: DE, 1987

INSTITUTIONAL HOLDINGS:
No. of Institutions: 165
Shares Held: 15,289,210
% Held: 102.6

INDUSTRY: Electrical work (SIC: 1731)

TRANSFER AGENT(S): Bank of New York, New York, NY

EMERSON ELECTRIC CO.

EXCH.	SYM.	REC. PRICE	P/E RATIO	YLD.	MKT. CAP.	RANGE (52-WK.)	'02 Y/E PR.	DIV. ACH.
NYSE	EMR	47.07 (2/28/03)	19.4	3.3%	$19.80 bill.	66.09 - 41.74	50.85	46 yrs.

INVESTMENT GRADE. EARNINGS FOR FISCAL 2003 ARE EXPECTED TO RANGE FROM $2.60 TO $2.75 PER SHARE.

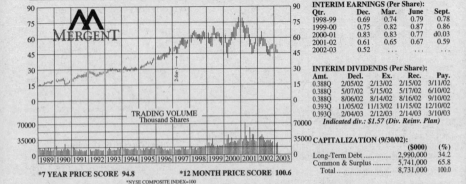

*7 YEAR PRICE SCORE 94.8   ***12 MONTH PRICE SCORE 100.6**
*NYSE COMPOSITE INDEX=100

INTERIM EARNINGS (Per Share):

Qtr.	Dec.	Mar.	June	Sept.
1998-99	0.69	0.74	0.79	0.78
1999-00	0.75	0.82	0.87	0.86
2000-01	0.83	0.83	0.77	d0.03
2001-02	0.61	0.65	0.67	0.59
2002-03	0.52	...	...	...

INTERIM DIVIDENDS (Per Share):

Amt.	Decl.	Ex.	Rec.	Pay.
0.388Q	2/05/02	2/13/02	2/15/02	3/11/02
0.388Q	5/07/02	5/15/02	5/17/02	6/10/02
0.388Q	8/06/02	8/14/02	8/16/02	9/10/02
0.393Q	11/05/02	11/13/02	11/15/02	12/10/02
0.393Q	2/04/03	2/12/03	2/14/03	3/10/03

Indicated div.: $1.57 (Div. Reinv. Plan)

CAPITALIZATION (9/30/02):

	($000)	(%)
Long-Term Debt	2,990,000	34.2
Common & Surplus	5,741,000	65.8
Total	8,731,000	100.0

BUSINESS:

Emerson Electric Co. is a global manufacturer of electrical, electromechanical and electronic products and systems sold through independent distributors and to original equipment manufacturers. The appliance and tools segment (24.2% of 2002 sales) provides motors, controls and other components for appliances, refrigeration and comfort control applications as well as disposers, tools and storage products. The process control segment (23.9%) provides measurement and fluid flow instrumentation, valves and control systems as well as services for process and industrial applications. The industrial automation segment (17.6%) provides industrial motors, drives, controls and equipment. The electronics and telecommunications segment (17.4%) provides power supplies and power distribution, protection and conversion equipment, and fiber optic conduits. The heating, ventilating and air conditioning (HVAC) segment (16.9%) provides components and systems for refrigeration and comfort control markets.

RECENT DEVELOPMENTS:

For the quarter ended 12/31/02, EMR reported net earnings of $217.0 million versus earnings of $255.0 million, before an accounting change charge of $938.0 million, in the equivalent 2001 quarter. Results for 2002 and 2001 included gains from divestitures of $15.0 million and $85.0 million, and rationalization charges of $29.0 million and $53.0 million, respectively. Net sales decreased 1.6% to $3.24 billion from $3.30 billion a year earlier. On a segment basis, process control sales declined 3.0% to $772.0 million, industrial automation sales decreased 5.0% to $623.0 million, and electronics and telecommunications sales fell 10.4% to $569.0 million. Heating, ventilating and air conditioning sales grew 11.5% to $512.0 million, while appliance and tools sales rose 2.5% to $852.0 million.

PROSPECTS:

Capital spending and business investment across many of the industries served by the Company continue to be restrained by heightened political uncertainty and the sluggish economic climate. Nevertheless, the Company expects to achieve improved earnings and margins in 2003 by driving companywide cost initiatives and delivering restructuring benefits. Earnings for fiscal 2003 are expected to range from $2.60 to $2.75 per share.

ANNUAL FINANCIAL DATA:

FISCAL YEAR	TOT. REVS. ($mill.)	NET INC. ($mill.)	TOT. ASSETS ($mill.)	OPER. PROFIT %	NET PROFIT %	RET. ON EQUITY %	RET. ON ASSETS %	CURR. RATIO	EARN. PER SH.$	CASH FL. PER SH.$	TANG. BK. VAL.$	DIV. PER SH.$	PRICE RANGE	AVG. P/E RATIO	AVG. YIELD %
9/30/02	13,824.0	③ 1,060.0	14,545.0	13.0	7.7	18.5	7.3	1.1	③ 2.52	3.80	1.98	1.56	66.09 - 41.74	21.4	2.9
9/30/01	15,479.6	② 1,031.8	15,046.4	12.2	6.7	16.9	6.9	1.0	② 2.40	4.05	2.22	1.54	79.25 - 44.04	25.7	2.5
9/30/00	15,544.8	1,422.4	15,164.3	15.9	9.2	22.2	9.4	1.1	3.30	4.87	2.53	1.46	79.75 - 40.50	18.2	2.4
9/30/99	14,269.5	1,313.6	13,623.5	15.5	9.2	21.3	9.6	1.1	3.00	4.45	4.43	1.33	71.44 - 51.44	20.5	2.2
9/30/98	13,447.2	1,228.6	12,659.8	15.4	9.1	21.2	9.7	•1.2	2.77	•4.03	4.79	1.21	67.44 - 54.50	22.0	2.0
9/30/97	12,298.6	1,121.9	11,463.3	15.5	9.1	20.7	9.8	1.2	2.52	3.67	5.23	1.10	60.38 - 45.00	20.9	2.1
9/30/96	11,149.9	1,018.5	10,481.0	15.6	9.1	19.0	9.7	1.4	2.27	3.31	5.75	1.00	51.75 - 38.75	19.9	2.2
9/30/95	10,012.9	929.0	9,399.0	15.3	9.3	19.1	9.9	1.2	2.03	2.99	5.55	0.92	40.88 - 30.75	17.6	2.6
9/30/94	8,607.2	① 904.4	8,215.0	15.4	10.5	20.8	11.0	1.3	① 1.76	2.83	5.54	0.80	32.94 - 28.06	17.3	2.6
9/30/93	8,173.8	708.1	7,814.5	15.1	8.7	18.1	9.7	1.1	1.58	2.33	4.63	0.73	31.19 - 26.38	18.3	2.6

Statistics are as originally reported. Adjusted for 2-for-1 stock split 11/96. ① Bef. charge for cum. eff. of change in acctg. principle of $115.9 mill. ② Incl. pre-tax rationalization chrg. of $377.0 mill. ③ Bef. acctg. change chrg. of $938.0 mill.; incl. divestiture gain of $231.0 mill. and rational. chrg. of $207.0 mill.

OFFICERS:
C. F. Knight, Chmn.
D. N. Farr, C.E.O.
J. G. Berges, Pres.
INVESTOR CONTACT: Mark Polzin, (314) 982-1700
PRINCIPAL OFFICE: 8000 W. Florissant Ave., P.O. Box 4100, St. Louis, MO 63136

TELEPHONE NUMBER: (314) 553-2000
FAX: (314) 553-3527
WEB: www.gotoemerson.com
NO. OF EMPLOYEES: 111,500 (approx.)
SHAREHOLDERS: 32,700 (approx.)
ANNUAL MEETING: In Feb.
INCORPORATED: MO, Sept., 1890

INSTITUTIONAL HOLDINGS:
No. of Institutions: 789
Shares Held: 287,889,002
% Held: 68.4
INDUSTRY: Process control instruments (SIC: 3823)
TRANSFER AGENT(S): Mellon Investor Services, LLC, South Hackensack, NJ

ENERGEN CORPORATION

EXCH.	SYM.	REC. PRICE	P/E RATIO	YLD.	MKT. CAP.	RANGE (52-WK.)	'02 Y/E PR.	DIV. ACH.
NYSE	EGN	32.06 (3/31/03)	14.8	2.2%	$0.99 bill.	32.06 - 21.65	29.10	20 yrs.

UPPER MEDIUM GRADE. THE COMPANY RAISED ITS EARNINGS GUIDANCE FOR 2003 TO A RANGE OF $2.40 TO $2.50 PER DILUTED SHARE.

TRADING VOLUME
Thousand Shares

*7 YEAR PRICE SCORE 138.4   *12 MONTH PRICE SCORE 121.4

*NYSE COMPOSITE INDEX=100

INTERIM EARNINGS (Per Share):

Qtr.	Dec.	Mar.	June	Sept.
1999-00	0.30	1.36	0.15	d0.06
2000-01	0.44	1.52	0.33	d0.10
Qtr.	Mar.	June	Sept.	Dec.
2001	...	...	...	0.12
2002	1.24	0.37	0.01	0.54

INTERIM DIVIDENDS (Per Share):

Amt.	Decl.	Ex.	Rec.	Pay.
0.175Q	1/30/02	2/13/02	2/15/02	3/01/02
0.175Q	5/01/02	5/13/02	5/15/02	6/03/02
0.18Q	7/31/02	8/13/02	8/15/02	9/03/02
0.18Q	10/30/02	11/13/02	11/15/02	12/02/02
0.18Q	1/29/03	2/12/03	2/14/03	3/03/03

Indicated div.: $0.72 (Div. Reinv. Plan)

CAPITALIZATION (12/31/01):

	($000)	(%)
Long-Term Debt	544,133	53.4
Common & Surplus	474,205	46.6
Total	1,018,338	100.0

BUSINESS:

Energen Corporation is a diversified energy holding company engaged in the business of natural gas distribution and oil and gas exploration and production. EGN provides natural gas to residential, commercial and industrial customers located in Alabama. Alagasco, EGN's principal subsidiary, is the largest natural gas distribution utility in the State of Alabama. EGN's utility operations are subject to regulation by the Alabama Public Service Commission. The oil and gas exploration and production arm of EGN is Energen Resources, which conducts its activities in the Gulf of Mexico. In fiscal 2002, revenues were derived: 62.7% natural gas distribution and 37.3% oil and gas production activities.

RECENT DEVELOPMENTS:

For the year ended 12/31/02, income was $70.6 million, before an accounting change charge of $2.2 million, compared with income from continuing operations of $56.6 million the previous year. Results for 2002 and 2001 excluded gains of $273,000 and $1.3 million, respectively, from discontinued operations. Total operating revenues declined 9.7% to $677.2 million from $749.6 million the year before. Revenues from oil and gas operations increased 15.9% to $252.7 million from $218.1 million, while natural gas distribution revenues dropped 20.1% to $424.4 million from $531.4 million the prior year. Operating income jumped 29.4% to $136.1 million. The average sales price of natural gas rose to $3.16 per thousand cubic feet from $3.15 per thousand cubic feet, while the average sales price of oil slipped to $24.03 per barrel from $24.23 per barrel in 2001.

PROSPECTS:

As a result of the Company's significant hedge position and strong commodity prices, the Company raised its earnings guidance for 2003 to a range of $2.40 to $2.50 per diluted share from its previous range of $2.25 to $2.40 per diluted share. Going forward, the Company will continue to monitor the commodity price environment and remains prepared to enter into additional oil and gas hedge contracts. Production for 2003 is estimated to reach 85.00 billion cubic feet equivalent, including approximately 2.00 billion cubic feet equivalent from potential property acquisitions.

ANNUAL FINANCIAL DATA:

FISCAL YEAR	TOT. REVS. ($000)	NET INC. ($000)	TOT. ASSETS ($000)	OPER. PROFIT %	NET PROFIT %	NET INC./ NET PROP. %	NET INC./ TOT. CAP. %	RET. ON EQUITY %	ACCUM. DEPR./ GROSS PROP. %	EARN. PER SH.$	TANG. BK. VAL.$	DIV. PER SH.$	DIV. PAYOUT %	PRICE RANGE	AVG. P/E RATIO	AVG. YIELD %
p12/31/02	677,175	[4] 70,586								[4] 2.09		0.71	34.0	29.99 — 21.65	12.4	2.7
[3] 12/31/01	147,328	[2] 3,658	1,240,356	7.5	2.5	0.4	0.4	0.8	38.0	[2] 0.12	15.18	...	...	...	...	...
9/30/01	784,973	67,896	1,223,879	15.8	8.6	6.8	6.6	14.1	37.2	2.18	15.61	0.69	31.6	40.25 — 21.50	14.2	2.2
9/30/00	555,595	[1] 53,018	1,203,041	17.2	9.5	5.8	7.0	13.2	36.5	[1] 1.75	13.21	0.67	38.3	33.56 — 14.69	13.8	2.8
9/30/99	497,517	41,410	1,184,895	15.6	8.3	4.8	5.6	11.5	34.9	1.38	12.09	0.65	47.1	21.25 — 13.13	12.5	3.8
9/30/98	502,627	36,249	993,455	12.2	7.2	4.8	5.2	11.0	34.5	1.23	11.23	0.63	51.2	22.50 — 15.13	15.3	3.3
9/30/97	448,230	28,997	799,797	11.6	6.5	4.3	5.0	9.6	36.2	1.16	13.49	0.61	52.8	20.63 — 14.50	15.2	3.5
9/30/96	399,442	21,541	570,971	9.7	5.4	4.8	5.6	11.4	42.7	0.98	8.44	0.59	60.5	15.63 — 10.88	13.6	4.5
9/30/95	321,204	19,308	459,084	10.1	6.0	5.9	6.3	11.1	48.1	0.89	7.96	0.57	64.4	12.56 — 10.06	12.8	5.0
9/30/94	377,073	23,751	411,314	9.5	6.3	8.3	8.3	14.2	49.3	1.10	7.65	0.55	50.2	11.94 — 9.63	9.8	5.1

Statistics are as originally reported. Adjusted for 2-for-1 stock split, 3/98. [1] Incl. an after-tax gain of $1.9 mill. on the sale of offshore properties. [2] Excl. one-time, non-cash exp. of $5.5 mill. assoc. w/the oil and gas unit's open hedge contracts w/Enron Corporation. [3] Reflects change in fiscal year-end date. [4] Excl. income of $273,000 from disc. oper.

OFFICERS:
W. M. Warren Jr., Chmn., Pres., C.E.O.
G. C. Ketcham, Exec. V.P., C.F.O., Treas.
J. D. Woodruff, Jr., Gen. Couns., Sec.

INVESTOR CONTACT: Julie S. Ryland, Asst.
V.P., Inv. Rel., (800) 654-3206

PRINCIPAL OFFICE: 605 Richard Arrington
Jr. Boulevard North, Birmingham, AL
35203-2707

TELEPHONE NUMBER: (205) 326-2700
FAX: (205) 326-2704
WEB: www.energen.com

NO. OF EMPLOYEES: 1,485

SHAREHOLDERS: 8,400 (approx.)

ANNUAL MEETING: In Jan.

INCORPORATED: AL, Jan., 1978

INSTITUTIONAL HOLDINGS:
No. of Institutions: 168
Shares Held: 20,064,771
% Held: 57.9

INDUSTRY: Natural gas distribution (SIC: 4924)

TRANSFER AGENT(S): EquiServe Trust
Company, Jersey City, NJ

ENERGIZER HOLDINGS, INC.

EXCH.	SYM.	REC. PRICE	P/E RATIO	YLD.	MKT. CAP.	RANGE (52-WK.)	'02 Y/E PR.
NYSE	ENR	26.55 (2/28/03)	12.1	...	$2.35 bill.	31.92 - 20.99	27.90

MEDIUM GRADE. THE COMPANY AGREED TO PURCHASE THE SCHICK-WILKINSON SWORD BUSINESS FROM PFIZER INC. FOR $930.0 MILLION.

TRADING VOLUME
Thousand Shares

1989 1990 1991 1992 1993 1994 1995 1996 1997 1998 1999 2000 2001 2002 2003

*7 YEAR PRICE SCORE N/A   *12 MONTH PRICE SCORE 103.9
*NYSE COMPOSITE INDEX=100

INTERIM EARNINGS (Per Share):

Qtr.	Dec.	Mar.	June	Sept.
1999-00	1.07	0.18	0.24	0.38
2000-01	0.57	0.06	0.17	d1.25
2001-02	0.76	0.21	0.43	0.61
2002-03	0.95	...	...	...

INTERIM DIVIDENDS (Per Share):

Amt.	Decl.	Ex.	Rec.	Pay.
		No dividends paid.		

CAPITALIZATION (9/30/02):

	($000)	(%)
Long-Term Debt	160,000	18.5
Common & Surplus	704,800	81.5
Total	864,800	100.0

BUSINESS:

Energizer Holdings, Inc. was formed on 4/1/00, when the Company was spun-off from Ralston Purina Company. ENR manufactures batteries, flashlights and portable lighting devices. ENR offers a full line of products in five categories: alkaline batteries (68.3% of 2002 sales), carbon zinc batteries (14.0%), lighting products (6.3%), miniature batteries (4.0%) and other products (7.4%). ENR's line of alkaline and carbon zinc batteries is sold under the brand names of ENERGIZER and EVEREADY in more than 140 countries. In addition, ENR produces lithium batteries in various sizes. Miniature batteries are offered in silver oxide, zinc-air and manganese dioxide systems. Although the Company sold its rechargeable battery manufacturing and assembly business in November 1999, ENR continues to market a line of rechargeable batteries for retail sale to consumers.

RECENT DEVELOPMENTS:

For the first quarter ended 12/31/02, net earnings advanced 22.7% to $86.4 million compared with $70.4 million in the corresponding prior-year quarter. Results for 2002 included after-tax intellectual property rights income of $3.7 million. Results for 2001 included after-tax restructuring provisions and related costs of $2.9 million. Net sales increased slightly to $572.4 million from $567.7 million a year earlier. Lighting products sales grew 10.2% to $35.5 million, and miniature battery sales rose 12.7% to $18.7 million. Alkaline battery sales decreased 2.4% to $410.4 million, while sales of carbon-zinc batteries slipped 0.5% to $66.3 million. Sales of other products jumped 30.9% to $41.5 million. Operating income climbed 3.4% to $133.1 million from $128.7 million a year earlier.

PROSPECTS:

On 1/21/03, the Company announced a definitive agreement to purchase the Schick-Wilkinson Sword business from Pfizer Inc. for $930.0 million. Schick-Wilkinson Sword is a manufacturer and marketer of men's and women's wet shave products with operations in over 80 countries. Products include Xtreme 3, Protector, Slim Twin and Silk Effects. The Company expects the acquisition to close in the Spring of 2003, pending customary approvals. ENR anticipates the acquisition will be accretive to fiscal 2004 earnings.

ANNUAL FINANCIAL DATA:

FISCAL YEAR	TOT. REVS. ($mill.)	NET INC. ($mill.)	TOT. ASSETS ($mill.)	OPER. PROFIT %	NET PROFIT %	RET. ON EQUITY %	RET. ON ASSETS %	CURR. RATIO	EARN. PER SH. $	CASH FL. PER SH. $	TANG. BK. VAL. $	PRICE RANGE	AVG. P/E RATIO
9/30/02	1,739.7	⑤ 186.4	1,588.1	17.2	10.7	26.4	11.7	1.7	⑤ 2.01	2.59	7.97	31.92 - 18.50	12.5
9/30/01	1,694.2	④ d39.0	1,497.6	3.8	...	...	...	1.6	④ d0.42	0.43	6.63	27.55 - 15.00	...
9/30/00	1,914.3	②③ 180.2	1,793.5	16.0	9.4	24.4	10.0	1.8	②③ 1.87	2.72	7.73	24.94 - 14.81	10.6
9/30/99	1,872.3	①② 163.0	1,833.7	13.7	8.7	12.4	8.9	2.0	...	...	...	...	...
9/30/98	1,921.8	①② 208.2	2,077.6	14.2	10.8	13.6	10.0	1.9	...	...	...	...	...
9/30/97	2,005.8	①② 159.3	...	10.9	7.9	...	...	...	...	...	...	...	...

Statistics are as originally reported. ① Incl. provision for restruct. of $7.8 mill., 1999; $21.0 mill., 1998; $78.5 mill., 1997. ② Incl. net gain fr. disc. opers. of $1.2 mill., 2000; loss $79.8 mill., 1999; loss $43.5 mill., 1998; gain $500,000, 1997. ③ Incl. net nonrecurr. gain of $10.2 mill. ④ Incl. net nonrecurr. chrg. of $126.1 mill. ⑤ Incl. restr. chrg. of $29.8 mill., goodwill impair. chrg. of $119.0 mill. and intellect. prop. rights income of $20.0 mill.

OFFICERS:
W. P. Stiritz, Chmn.
J. P. Mulcahy, C.E.O.
P. C. Mannix, Pres.
INVESTOR CONTACT: Jacqueline E. Buritz, V.P., Investor Relations, (314) 985-2169
PRINCIPAL OFFICE: 533 Maryville University Drive, St. Louis, MO 63141

TELEPHONE NUMBER: (314) 985-2000
FAX: (314) 985-2200
WEB: www.energizer.com
NO. OF EMPLOYEES: 9,963 (avg.)
SHAREHOLDERS: 16,750
ANNUAL MEETING: In Jan.
INCORPORATED: MO, Sept., 1999

INSTITUTIONAL HOLDINGS:
No. of Institutions: 225
Shares Held: 61,942,926
% Held: 70.0
INDUSTRY: Primary batteries, dry and wet (SIC: 3692)
TRANSFER AGENT(S): Continental Stock Transfer & Trust Company, New York, NY

ENERGY EAST CORPORATION

EXCH.	SYM.	REC. PRICE	P/E RATIO	YLD.	MKT. CAP.	RANGE (52-WK.)	'02 Y/E PR.
NYSE	EAS	18.82 (2/28/03)	12.7	5.3%	$2.20 bill.	23.71 - 15.75	22.09

MEDIUM GRADE. THE COMPANY PLANS TO DECREASE ITS WORKFORCE BY APPROXIMATELY 650 EMPLOYEES, OR 8.0%, BY 4/30/03.

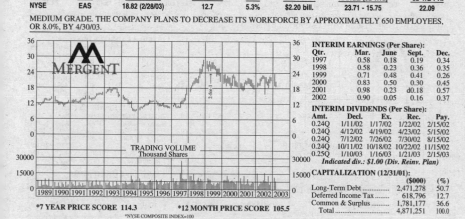

INTERIM EARNINGS (Per Share):

Qtr.	Mar.	June	Sept.	Dec.
1997	0.58	0.18	0.19	0.34
1998	0.58	0.23	0.36	0.35
1999	0.71	0.48	0.41	0.26
2000	0.83	0.50	0.30	0.45
2001	0.98	0.23	d0.18	0.57
2002	0.90	0.05	0.16	0.37

INTERIM DIVIDENDS (Per Share):

Amt.	Decl.	Ex.	Rec.	Pay.
0.24Q	1/11/02	1/17/02	1/22/02	2/15/02
0.24Q	4/12/02	4/19/02	4/23/02	5/15/02
0.24Q	7/12/02	7/26/02	7/30/02	8/15/02
0.24Q	10/11/02	10/18/02	10/22/02	11/15/02
0.25Q	1/10/03	1/16/03	1/21/03	2/15/03

Indicated div.: $1.00 (Div. Reinv. Plan)

TRADING VOLUME
Thousand Shares

*7 YEAR PRICE SCORE 114.3   *12 MONTH PRICE SCORE 105.5

*NYSE COMPOSITE INDEX=100

CAPITALIZATION (12/31/01):

	($000)	(%)
Long-Term Debt	2,471,278	50.7
Deferred Income Tax	618,796	12.7
Common & Surplus	1,781,177	36.6
Total	4,871,251	100.0

BUSINESS:

Energy East Corporation (formerly New York State Electric & Gas Corporation) is a holding company that provides electricity and gas service in New York, Massachusetts, Maine, New Hampshire, Vermont, and New Jersey. As of 1/31/03, EAS served 1.8 million electric customers, 900,000 natural gas customers and 300,000 other retail energy customers in New York and New England. Revenues in 2002 were divided: 64.0% electric, 25.8% gas and

10.2% other. Retail electric revenues in 2001 were derived: residential, 37.0%; commercial, 28.0%; industrial, 28.1%; and other, 6.9%. The electricity generated is fueled by 72%, coal; 24%, nuclear; and 4%, hydro. The Company merged with Connecticut Energy Corporation on 2/18/00, and then merged with CMP Group, Inc., CTG Resources, and Berkshire Energy Resources on 9/1/00. EAS acquired with RGS Energy Group, Inc. on 6/28/02.

RECENT DEVELOPMENTS:

For the year ended 12/31/02, net income climbed 0.5% to $188.6 million versus $187.6 million in 2001. Results for 2002 included a restructuring charge of $40.6 million, while results for 2001 included a gain on the sale of generation assets of $84.1 million and a deferral of asset sale gain of $71.8 million. Operating revenues increased 6.6% to $4.01 billion from $3.76 billion in the prior year. Operating

income decreased 7.0% to $592.2 million versus $636.9 million the year before. The decrease in earnings was primarily due to an electric rate reduction of $205.0 million, which became effective 3/1/02. Other items that reduced earnings included higher operating costs, merger integration costs, fewer wholesale sales at lower market prices and a loss on the early retirement of debt.

PROSPECTS:

The Company has implemented several restructuring initiatives related to voluntary early retirement and involuntary severance programs. These programs, which are the result of a detailed integration effort the Company undertook in 2002, are expected to result in a decrease in the overall

workforce by approximately 650 employees, or 8.0%, by 4/30/03. This number includes nearly 500 employees who accepted the voluntary early retirement program in December 2002.

ANNUAL FINANCIAL DATA:

FISCAL YEAR	TOT. REVS. ($mill.)	NET INC. ($mill.)	TOT. ASSETS ($mill.)	OPER. PROFIT %	NET PROFIT %	NET INC./ NET PROP. %	NET INC./ TOT. CAP. %	RET. ON EQUITY %	ACCUM. DEPR./ GROSS PROP. %	EARN. PER SH.$	TANG. BK. VAL.$	DIV. PER SH.$	DIV. PAYOUT %	PRICE RANGE	AVG. P/E RATIO	AVG. YIELD
p12/31/02	4,008.9	⑦ 188.6								⑦ 1.44		0.96	66.7	23.13 - 15.75	13.5	4.9
12/31/01	3,759.8	⑥ 187.6	7,269.2	16.9	5.0	5.2	3.9	10.5	38.5	⑥ 1.61	7.57	0.92	57.1	22.14 - 16.96	12.1	4.7
12/31/00	2,959.5	⑤ 236.7	7,003.6	17.4	8.0	6.5	5.0	13.8	46.0	⑤ 2.06	6.49	0.88	42.7	23.63 - 17.94	10.1	4.2
12/31/99	2,278.6	④ 236.3	3,769.4	24.0	10.4	11.0	8.1	16.8	48.7	④ 1.88	13.02	0.84	44.7	28.63 - 20.56	13.1	3.4
12/31/98	2,499.4	194.2	4,883.3	19.0	7.8	5.0	4.7	11.3	36.4	1.29	13.73	0.70	25.7	29.00 - 16.53	15.1	3.4
12/31/97	2,130.0	③ 184.6	5,028.7	20.8	8.7	4.7	4.2	10.2	34.8	③ 1.29	13.73	0.70	54.5	17.88 - 10.31	11.0	5.0
12/31/96	2,059.4	② 178.2	5,059.7	22.2	8.7	4.5	4.1	10.1	32.7	② 1.19	12.70	0.70	59.1	13.19 - 10.19	9.6	6.0
12/31/95	2,009.5	196.7	5,114.3	16.8	9.8	5.0	4.5	11.3	31.1	1.25	12.19	0.70	56.2	13.38 - 9.50	9.2	6.1
12/31/94	1,898.9	187.6	5,222.9	17.0	9.9	4.7	4.7	11.3	29.2	1.19	11.64	1.00	84.4	15.25 - 8.88	10.2	8.3
12/31/93	1,800.1	① 166.0	5,276.0	16.7	9.2	4.2	4.2	10.3	28.2	① 1.04	11.44	1.09	104.8	18.25 - 14.38	15.7	6.7

Statistics are as originally reported. Adj. for 2-for-1 stock split, 4/99. ① Incl. $26.0 mill. chg. rel. to restr. ② Incl. $0.14/sh. chg. to write down an investment in EnerSoft Corp. ③ Incl. $0.24/sh. chg. for fees rel. to an unsolicited tender offer. ④ Excl. $17.6 mill. extraordinary chg. fr. early exting. of debt & incl. $0.12 per share non-recur. gain. ⑤ Excl. $1.6 mill. extraord. chg. ⑥ Bef. extr. loss; incls. one-time items. ⑦ Incl. $40.6 mill. restr. chg.

OFFICERS:
W. W. von Schack, Chmn., Pres., C.E.O.
K. M. Jasinski, Exec. V.P., C.F.O.
R. D. Kump, V.P., Treas., Secy.
INVESTOR CONTACT: Fausto Gentile, Investor Relations, (607) 347-2561
PRINCIPAL OFFICE: P.O. Box 12904, Albany, NY 12212

TELEPHONE NUMBER: (518) 434-3049
FAX: (607) 762-4345
WEB: www.energyeast.com
NO. OF EMPLOYEES: 5,816
SHAREHOLDERS: 34,354
ANNUAL MEETING: In Apr.
INCORPORATED: NY, Oct., 1852

INSTITUTIONAL HOLDINGS:
No. of Institutions: 221
Shares Held: 67,392,715
% Held: 46.6
INDUSTRY: Electric and other services combined (SIC: 4931)
TRANSFER AGENT(S): Mellon Investor Services, South Hackensack, NJ

ENGELHARD CORP.

EXCH.	SYM.	REC. PRICE	P/E RATIO	YLD.	MKT. CAP.	RANGE (52-WK.)	'02 Y/E PR.
NYSE	EC	20.75 (2/28/03)	15.7	1.9%	$2.68 bill.	33.00 - 19.10	22.35

UPPER MEDIUM GRADE. EARNINGS PER SHARE FOR THE FIRST QUARTER OF 2003 ARE EXPECTED TO BE DOWN ABOUT $0.10 TO $0.12 FROM THE COMPARABLE PERIOD OF 2002.

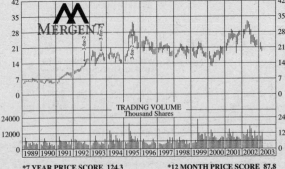

*7 YEAR PRICE SCORE 124.3   ***12 MONTH PRICE SCORE 87.8**
*NYSE COMPOSITE INDEX=100

INTERIM EARNINGS (Per Share):

Qtr.	Mar.	June	Sept.	Dec.
1997	0.26	0.31	0.27	d0.50
1998	0.30	0.35	0.31	0.33
1999	0.28	0.41	0.40	0.39
2000	0.45	0.47	0.40	d0.01
2001	0.37	0.45	0.43	0.46
2002	0.40	0.46	0.02	0.44

INTERIM DIVIDENDS (Per Share):

Amt.	Decl.	Ex.	Rec.	Pay.
0.10Q	3/07/02	3/13/02	3/15/02	3/29/02
0.10Q	5/02/02	6/12/02	6/14/02	6/28/02
0.10Q	8/08/02	9/12/02	9/16/02	9/30/02
0.10Q	10/03/02	12/12/02	12/16/02	12/31/02
0.10Q	2/06/03	3/12/03	3/14/03	3/31/03

Indicated div.: $0.40 (Div. Reinv. Plan)

CAPITALIZATION (12/31/01):

	($000)	(%)
Long-Term Debt	237,853	19.2
Common & Surplus	1,003,506	80.8
Total	1,241,359	100.0

BUSINESS:

Engelhard Corp. develops, manufactures and markets technology-based performance products and engineered materials for a range of industrial customers. EC operates in four business units: Environmental Technologies, Process Technologies, Appearance and Performance Technologies, and Materials Services. The Environmental Technologies unit consists of automotive emission systems and performance systems. The Process Technologies unit is the chemical catalysts and petroleum catalysts business. The Appearance and Performance Technologies unit provides pigments and performance additives. The Materials Services provides certain precious metals, base metals and related products and services. Revenues for 2002 were derived: Environmental Technologies, 18.1%; Process Technologies, 14.4%; Appearance and Performance Technologies, 17.3%; Materials Services, 48.9%; and other, 1.3%.

RECENT DEVELOPMENTS:

For the year ended 12/31/02, net earnings declined 24.0% to $171.4 million versus $225.6 million in 2001. Results for 2002 included a non-cash charge of $57.7 million for an equity investment impairment related to the write-down of the Company's investment in Engelhard-CLAL, a 50.0% owned joint venture, and a loss on investments of $6.7 million. Net sales were $3.75 billion, down 26.4% from $5.10 billion in the prior year, primarily due to reduced prices and volumes for precious metals. Gross profit slipped 1.4% to $653.8 million from $663.2 million the year before. Operating earnings slipped 2.7% to $311.5 million versus $320.1 million a year earlier.

PROSPECTS:

In the near term, earnings could be negatively affected by the absence of stronger results from the gas turbine market and weaker comparisons from the Materials Services segment. Also, charges related to productivity programs and certain resource reductions may hamper first quarter results by about $0.05 per share, which could bring the outlook for earnings per share to about $0.10 to $0.12 below comparisons from 2002. Going forward, the Company expects full-year 2003 results to benefit from new product introductions, price-mix enhancements and the implementation of productivity improvements in early 2003.

ANNUAL FINANCIAL DATA:

FISCAL YEAR	TOT. REVS. ($mill.)	NET INC. ($mill.)	TOT. ASSETS ($mill.)	OPER. PROFIT %	NET PROFIT %	RET. ON EQUITY %	RET. ON ASSETS %	CURR. RATIO	EARN. PER SH.$	CASH FL PER SH.$	TANG. BK. VAL.$	DIV. PER SH.$	PRICE RANGE	AVG. P/E RATIO	AVG. YIELD %
p12/31/02	3,753.6	⑥ 171.4							⑥ 1.31			0.40	33.00 - 21.18	20.7	1.5
12/31/01	5,096.9	⑤ 225.6	2,995.5	6.3	4.4	22.5	7.5	1.0	⑤ 1.71	2.53	5.44	0.40	29.20 - 18.20	13.9	1.7
12/31/00	5,542.6	④ 168.3	3,166.8	4.8	3.0	19.2	5.3	1.0	④ 1.31	2.23	4.51	0.40	21.50 - 12.56	13.0	2.3
12/31/99	4,404.9	③ 197.5	2,904.0	7.2	4.5	25.8	6.8	1.0	③ 1.47	2.30	3.49	0.40	23.69 - 16.25	13.6	2.0
12/31/98	4,174.6	187.1	2,866.3	7.4	4.5	20.8	6.5	1.1	1.29	1.98	4.02	0.40	22.81 - 15.75	14.9	2.1
12/31/97	3,630.7	② 47.8	2,586.3	5.1	1.3	6.1	1.8	1.0	② 0.33	0.93	3.95	0.38	23.75 - 17.06	61.8	1.9
12/31/96	3,184.4	150.4	2,494.9	8.1	4.7	18.1	6.0	1.1	1.05	1.57	5.79	0.36	26.13 - 17.88	21.0	1.6
12/31/95	2,840.1	137.5	1,943.3	7.6	4.8	18.6	7.1	1.1	0.96	1.41	5.13	0.35	32.50 - 14.92	24.7	1.5
12/31/94	2,385.8	118.0	1,440.8	7.5	4.9	19.2	8.2	1.1	0.82	1.30	4.31	0.31	21.00 - 13.92	21.3	1.8
12/31/93	2,150.9	① 16.7	1,279.1	. . .	0.8	3.1	1.3	1.1	① 0.11	0.58	3.69	0.28	19.95 - 12.89	149.1	1.7

Statistics are as originally reported. Adj. for 3-for-2 split, 6/95 & 9/93. ① Bef. $16.0 mill. acct. adj. ② Incl. $96.4 mill. ($0.67/sh.) after-tax chg. & $305,000 pre-tax gain fr. sale of investment. ③ Incl. $8.6 mill. gain fr. sale of investments & land. ④ Incl. gain of $18.8 mill. fr. disposal of investments & land and $82.5 mill. special chg. ⑤ Incl. $7.1 mill. special chg. ⑥ Incl. $57.7 mill. eq. invest. impair. & $6.7 mill. loss on invest.

OFFICERS:
B. W. Perry, Chmn., C.E.O.
M. A. Sperduto, V.P., C.F.O.
A. A. Dornbusch II, V.P., Sec., Gen. Couns.
INVESTOR CONTACT: Peter Martin, Investor Relations, (732) 205-6106
PRINCIPAL OFFICE: 101 Wood Avenue, Iselin, NJ 08830

TELEPHONE NUMBER: (732) 205-5000
FAX: (732) 632-9253
WEB: www.engelhard.com
NO. OF EMPLOYEES: 5,870 (approx.)
SHAREHOLDERS: 5,498 (record)
ANNUAL MEETING: In May
INCORPORATED: DE, Nov., 1938

INSTITUTIONAL HOLDINGS:
No. of Institutions: 262
Shares Held: 112,632,527
% Held: 88.1
INDUSTRY: Industrial inorganic chemicals, nec (SIC: 2819)
TRANSFER AGENT(S): Mellon Investor Services, Ridgefield Park, NJ

ENSCO INTERNATIONAL INC.

EXCH.	SYM.	REC. PRICE	P/E RATIO	YLD.	MKT. CAP.	RANGE (52-WK.)	'02 Y/E PR.
NYSE	ESV	27.98 (2/28/03)	65.1	0.4%	$4.17 bill.	35.50 - 21.19	29.45

MEDIUM GRADE. THE COMPANY'S OUTLOOK IS TEMPERED BY LACKLUSTER CONDITIONS IN ITS GULF OF MEXICO MARKET, POSSIBLE SOFTNESS IN THE NORTH SEA, AND SCHEDULED SHIPYARD DOWNTIME.

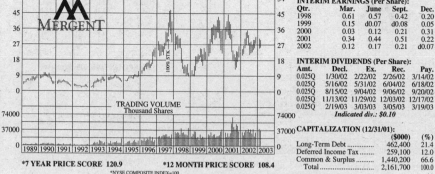

*7 YEAR PRICE SCORE 120.9   ***12 MONTH PRICE SCORE 108.4**

*NYSE COMPOSITE INDEX=100

INTERIM EARNINGS (Per Share):

Qtr.	Mar.	June	Sept.	Dec.
1998	0.61	0.57	0.42	0.20
1999	0.15	d0.07	d0.08	0.05
2000	0.03	0.12	0.21	0.31
2001	0.34	0.44	0.51	0.22
2002	0.12	0.17	0.21	d0.07

INTERIM DIVIDENDS (Per Share):

Amt.	Decl.	Ex.	Rec.	Pay.
0.025Q	1/30/02	2/22/02	2/26/02	3/14/02
0.025Q	5/16/02	5/31/02	6/04/02	6/18/02
0.025Q	8/15/02	9/04/02	9/06/02	9/20/02
0.025Q	11/13/02	11/29/02	12/03/02	12/17/02
0.025Q	2/19/03	3/03/03	3/05/03	3/19/03

Indicated div.: $0.10

CAPITALIZATION (12/31/01):

	($000)	(%)
Long-Term Debt	462,400	21.4
Deferred Income Tax	259,100	12.0
Common & Surplus	1,440,200	66.6
Total	2,161,700	100.0

BUSINESS:

ENSCO International Inc. is an international offshore contract drilling company that also provides marine transportation services in the Gulf of Mexico. As of 12/31/02, ESV's fleet consisted of 56 offshore drilling rigs. ESV conducts its marine transportation operations through a wholly-owned subsidiary, ENSCO Marine Company. As of 12/31/02, ESV owned a marine transportation fleet of 27 vessels. In August 2002, ESV completed its acquisition of Chiles Offshore Inc.

RECENT DEVELOPMENTS:

For the twelve months ended 12/31/02, net income was $59.3 million compared with $207.3 million a year earlier. Results for 2002 included impairment of assets charges of $59.9 million and $9.2 million, respectively. Results for 2002 also included a $5.8 million gain in connection with an insurance claim relating to the ENSCO 51 jackup rig that sustained extensive damage from a natural gas fire in March 2001 and has recently returned to service after extensive shipyard work. Operating revenue decreased 14.6% to $698.1 million from $817.4 million the previous year. Utilization for the Company's jackup fleet increased to 86.0% for the quarter ended 12/31/02 compared with 77.0% in the same quarter the year before. Excluding rigs in the shipyard for regulatory inspection and enhancement, jackup utilization was 93.0% versus 78.0% a year earlier.

PROSPECTS:

Continued lackluster conditions in ESV's Gulf of Mexico market, coupled with possible near-term softness in the North Sea and scheduled shipyard downtime, limit the Company's immediate prospects. The Company noted that the timing of an expected recovery of drilling activity in Venezuela, which has been severely affected by a nation-wide strike and economic unrest, is uncertain under the current circumstances.

ANNUAL FINANCIAL DATA:

FISCAL YEAR	TOT. REVS. ($mill.)	NET INC. ($mill.)	TOT. ASSETS ($mill.)	OPER. PROFIT %	NET PROFIT %	RET. ON EQUITY %	RET. ON ASSETS %	CURR. RATIO	EARN. PER SH. $	CASH FL. PER SH. $	TANG. BK. VAL. $	DIV. PER SH. $	PRICE RANGE	AVG. P/E RATIO	AVG. YIELD %
p12/31/02	698.1	⑥ 59.3							⑥ 0.42			0.10	35.50 - 20.87	67.1	0.4
12/31/01	817.4	⑤ 207.3	2,323.8	38.8	25.4	14.4	8.9	3.1	⑤ 1.50	2.48	10.70	0.10	44.49 - 12.81	19.1	0.3
12/31/00	533.8	85.4	2,108.0	24.6	16.0	6.4	4.1	2.5	0.61	1.37	9.59	0.10	43.13 - 20.25	51.9	0.3
12/31/99	363.7	6.7	1,978.0	1.0	1.8	0.5	0.3	2.0	0.05	0.83	9.05	0.10	25.00 - 8.75	336.8	0.6
12/31/98	813.2	253.9	1,992.8	47.4	31.2	20.4	12.7	3.0	1.81	2.47	9.08	0.10	33.56 - 8.69	11.7	0.5
12/31/97	815.1	② 234.9	1,772.0	47.8	28.8	21.8	13.3	3.4	② 1.64	2.44	7.57	0.05	47.00 - 20.25	20.5	0.1
12/31/96	468.8	95.4	1,315.4	31.7	20.3	11.3	7.3	2.0	0.72	1.37	5.97	...	25.06 - 10.00	24.3	...
12/31/95	279.1	① 41.8	821.5	19.8	15.0	7.9	5.1	1.9	① 0.35	0.86	4.38	...	11.50 - 5.63	24.8	...
12/31/94	262.0	④ 37.2	775.4	19.6	14.2	7.4	4.8	2.4	④ 0.31	0.80	3.92	...	9.63 - 5.38	24.6	...
12/31/93	246.2	① ③ 16.7	691.4	14.7	6.8	4.2	2.4	2.9	① ③ 0.16	0.56	3.27	...	8.13 - 1.75	31.8	...

Statistics are as originally reported. Adj. for 2-for-1 stk. split, 9/97. ① Bef. disc. ops. credit, 1995, $6.3 mill.; 1993, $2.3 mill. ② Bef. $1.0 mill. extraord. chrg. ③ Bef. $2.5 mill. acctg. change chrg. ④ Incl. gain of $670,000 on sale of subsidiary stk. ⑤ Incl. after-tax non-recurr. gain of $12.7 mill. ⑥ Incl. impairment chrg. of $59.9 mill.

OFFICERS:
C. F. Thorne, Chmn., C.E.O.
R. A. LeBlanc, Treas.
C. A. Moomjian, Jr., V.P., Gen. Couns., Sec.

INVESTOR CONTACT: Investor Relations,
(214) 922-1500

PRINCIPAL OFFICE: 2700 Fountain Place, 1445 Ross Avenue, Dallas, TX 75202-2792

TELEPHONE NUMBER: (214) 922-1500
FAX: (214) 855-0300
WEB: www.enscous.com

NO. OF EMPLOYEES: 3,500 (approx.)

SHAREHOLDERS: 1,600 (approx.)

ANNUAL MEETING: In May

INCORPORATED: TX, Apr., 1975; reincorp., DE, Sept., 1987

INSTITUTIONAL HOLDINGS:
No. of Institutions: 296
Shares Held: 124,104,327
% Held: 83.3

INDUSTRY: Drilling oil and gas wells (SIC: 1381)

TRANSFER AGENT(S): American Stock Transfer & Trust Company, New York, NY

ENTERCOM COMMUNICATIONS CORP.

EXCH.	SYM.	REC. PRICE	P/E RATIO	YLD.	MKT. CAP.	RANGE (52-WK.)	'02 Y/E PR.
NYSE	ETM	46.24 (2/28/03)	41.3	...	$2.31 bill.	59.45 - 35.80	46.92

MEDIUM GRADE. THE COMPANY ENTERS 2003 WITH A POSITIVE LONG-TERM OUTLOOK FOR GROWTH.

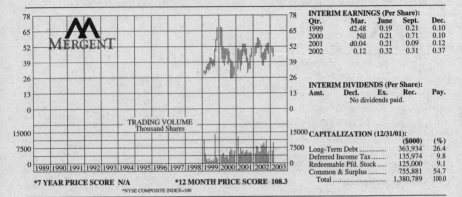

*7 YEAR PRICE SCORE N/A   *12 MONTH PRICE SCORE 108.3

*NYSE COMPOSITE INDEX=100

INTERIM EARNINGS (Per Share):

Qtr.	Mar.	June	Sept.	Dec.
1999	d2.48	0.19	0.21	0.10
2000	Nil	0.21	0.71	0.10
2001	d0.04	0.21	0.09	0.12
2002	0.12	0.32	0.31	0.37

INTERIM DIVIDENDS (Per Share):

Amt.	Decl.	Ex.	Rec.	Pay.
	No dividends paid.			

CAPITALIZATION (12/31/01):

	($000)	(%)
Long-Term Debt	363,934	26.4
Deferred Income Tax	135,974	9.8
Redeemable Pfd. Stock	125,000	9.1
Common & Surplus	755,881	54.7
Total	1,380,789	100.0

BUSINESS:

Entercom Communications Corp. is a radio broadcasting company, the fifth largest in the United States in terms of revenues. As of 2/12/03, the Company operated a nationwide portfolio of 100 radio stations in 19 markets, including 11 of the country's top 50 radio revenue markets. Moreover, ETM's station groups rank among the top three in revenue market share in 18 of the 19 markets in which the Company operates. ETM's markets include Boston, Seattle, Denver, Portland, Sacramento, Kansas City, Milwaukee, Norfolk, New Orleans, Greensboro, Buffalo, Memphis, Rochester, Greenville/Spartanburg, Wilkes-Barre/Scranton, Wichita, Madison, Gainesville/Ocala and Longview/Kelso, WA.

RECENT DEVELOPMENTS:

For the year ended 12/31/02, income was $55.8 million, before an accounting change charge of $138.9 million, versus income of $17.8 million, before an accounting change charge of $566,000, the previous year. Results for 2002 included a time brokerage agreement fee of $7.4 million, a non-cash compensation charge of $1.2 million, and a net gain on the sale of assets of $1.2 million, while results for 2001 included a non-cash compensation charge of $536,000, a net loss on the sale of assets of $16,000 and a loss on investments of $2.0 million. Also, results for 2002 and 2001 included net losses on the sale of derivative instruments of $2.3 million and $912,000, respectively. Net revenues grew 17.5% to $391.3 million.

PROSPECTS:

ETM enters 2003 with a positive long-term outlook for growth, supported by continued acquisition efforts. During 2002, ETM enhanced its competitive position by adding new stations in Denver and Greensboro. In addition, ETM strengthened its balance sheet by increasing its free cash flow to $105.0 million, a gain of over 40.0% from $75.0 million in 2001. Looking ahead, although recent geopolitical events raise concerns, operating fundamentals should continue to improve as ETM capitalizes on improving industry conditions and focuses on gaining market share.

ANNUAL FINANCIAL DATA:

FISCAL YEAR	TOT. REVS. ($000)	NET INC. ($000)	TOT. ASSETS ($000)	OPER. PROFIT %	NET PROFIT %	RET. ON EQUITY %	RET. ON ASSETS %	CURR. RATIO	EARN. PER SH. $	CASH FL. PER SH. $	PRICE RANGE	AVG. P/E RATIO
p12/31/02	391,289	⑦ 55,824	1,438,740	21.9	5.4	2.4	1.2	1.6	⑦ 1.12		59.45 - 36.04	42.6
12/31/01	332,897	⑥ 17,834							⑥ 0.39	1.40	54.40 - 30.00	108.2
12/31/00	352,025	47,254	1,473,928	37.2	13.4	6.4	3.2	3.3	1.04	1.99	68.69 - 25.31	45.2
12/31/99	215,001	②③ d59,958	1,396,048	23.6	...	...	...	2.6	②③ d1.58	d1.00	67.75 - 28.31	...
①12/31/98	47,363	43,455	681,034	168.0	91.7	19.3	6.4	5.0	0.64	1.98	...	...
9/30/98	132,998	②④ 9,439	522,945	18.4	7.1	5.2	1.8	3.1	②④ 0.12	1.01	...	...
9/30/97	93,862	④⑤ 176,770	364,743	23.6	188.3	98.7	48.5	3.5	④⑤ 4.59	8.57	...	...
9/30/96	48,675	② 6,779	...	24.8	13.9	...	...	...	② 0.20	0.45	...	...

Statistics are as originally reported. ① Fiscal year changed from 9/30 to 12/31. ② Bef. extraord. chrg. 12/31/99, $918,000; 9/30/98, $2.4 mill.; 9/30/96, $539,000. ③ Incl. $2.0 mill. gain on sale of assets and non-recurr. chrg. $1.8 mill. ④ Incl. chrg. for adj. to reflect indexing of notes $8.8 mill., 9/98; $29.1 mill., 9/97 ⑤ Incl. gain on sale of assets $197.1 mill. ⑥ Bef. acctg. chrg. $566,000; Incl. loss fr. sale of assets of $16,000 & invest. loss $2.9 mill. ⑦ Bef. acctg. chrg. $138.9 mill.; Incl. gain fr. sale of assets of $1.2 mill., time brokerage agreement chrg. of $7.4 mill., non-cash chrg. of $1.2 mill. & net loss on invest. of $2.3 mill.

OFFICERS:
J. M. Field, Chmn.
D. J. Field, Pres., C.E.O.
S. F. Fisher, Exec. V.P., C.F.O.
INVESTOR CONTACT: Steve Fisher, Exec. V.P., C.F.O., (610) 660-5647
PRINCIPAL OFFICE: 401 City Avenue, Suite 409, Bala Cynwyd, PA 19004

TELEPHONE NUMBER: (610) 660-5510
FAX: (610) 660-5620
WEB: www.entercom.com
NO. OF EMPLOYEES: 1,641 full-time; 658 part-time
SHAREHOLDERS: 75 (class A); 3 (class B)
ANNUAL MEETING: In May
INCORPORATED: PA, 1968

INSTITUTIONAL HOLDINGS:
No. of Institutions: 184
Shares Held: 38,149,367
% Held: 76.6
INDUSTRY: Radio broadcasting stations (SIC: 4832)
TRANSFER AGENT(S): Wachovia Bank, N.A., Charlotte, NC

ENTERGY CORPORATION

EXCH.	SYM.	REC. PRICE	P/E RATIO	YLD.	MKT. CAP.	RANGE (52-WK.)	'02 Y/E PR.
NYSE	ETR	45.55 (2/28/03)	17.3	3.1%	$10.05 bill.	48.38 - 32.12	45.59

MEDIUM GRADE. THE COMPANY REMAINS COMMITTED TO GROWING ITS NUCLEAR BUSINESS AND REINFORCING ITS ENERGY TRADING CAPABILITY.

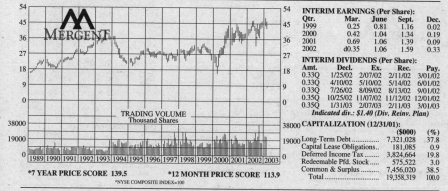

INTERIM EARNINGS (Per Share):

Qtr.	Mar.	June	Sept.	Dec.
1999	0.25	0.81	1.16	0.02
2000	0.42	1.04	1.34	0.19
2001	0.69	1.06	1.39	0.09
2002	d0.35	1.06	1.59	0.33

INTERIM DIVIDENDS (Per Share):

Amt.	Decl.	Ex.	Rec.	Pay.
0.33Q	1/25/02	2/07/02	2/11/02	3/01/02
0.33Q	4/10/02	5/10/02	5/14/02	6/01/02
0.33Q	7/26/02	8/09/02	8/13/02	9/01/02
0.35Q	10/25/02	11/07/02	11/12/02	12/01/02
0.35Q	1/31/03	2/07/03	2/11/03	3/01/03

Indicated div.: $1.40 (Div. Reinv. Plan)

CAPITALIZATION (12/31/01):

	($000)	(%)
Long-Term Debt	7,321,028	37.8
Capital Lease Obligations..	181,085	0.9
Deferred Income Tax	3,824,664	19.8
Redeemable Pfd. Stock	575,522	3.0
Common & Surplus	7,456,020	38.5
Total	19,358,319	100.0

*7 YEAR PRICE SCORE 139.5   ***12 MONTH PRICE SCORE 113.9**

NYSE COMPOSITE INDEX=100

BUSINESS:

Entergy Corporation is a public utility holding company engaged principally in the businesses of power production, distribution operations, and related diversified services. Through Entergy-Koch, L.P., it is a provider of wholesale energy marketing and trading services. The Company has five wholly-owned domestic retail electric utility subsidiaries: Entergy Arkansas, Entergy Gulf States, Entergy Louisiana, Entergy Mississippi, and Entergy New Orleans. As of

2/4/03, these utility companies provided retail electric service to approximately 2.6 million customers primarily in portions of the states of Arkansas, Louisiana, Mississippi, and Texas. During 2002, the domestic utility companies' combined retail electric sales as a percentage of total electric sales were: residential, 36.7%; industrial, 27.9%; commercial, 25.2%; wholesale, 7.5%; and governmental, 2.7%.

RECENT DEVELOPMENTS:

For the year ended 12/31/02, net income was $623.1 million compared with income of $727.5 million, before an accounting change charge of $23.5 million, the previous year. Results for 2002 and 2001 included net gains of $6.6 million and $5.2 million, respectively. Results for 2002 included a pre-tax provision of $428.5 million for turbine

commitments, asset impairments, and restructuring. Total operating revenues decreased 13.7% to $8.31 billion from $9.62 billion the year before. Domestic electric revenues fell 8.3% to $6.65 billion, while natural gas revenues dropped 32.6% to $125.4 million. Competitive businesses revenue declined 30.0% to $1.53 billion.

PROSPECTS:

In 2003, the Company remains committed to growing its nuclear business and reinforcing its energy trading capability. ETR's utility operations should continue to benefit from higher sales volumes, provided further strengthening in the U.S. economy. Meanwhile, ETR should focus on

strengthening operating performance within its competitive non-regulated business, which has been adversely affected by the closing of ETR's wholesale power development operations. ETR expects operational earnings per share to range from $3.75 to $3.95 for full-year 2003.

ANNUAL FINANCIAL DATA:

FISCAL YEAR	TOT. REVS. ($mill.)	NET INC. ($mill.)	TOT. ASSETS ($mill.)	OPER. PROFIT %	NET PROFIT %	NET INC./ NET PROP. %	NET INC./ TOT. CAP. %	RET. ON EQUITY %	ACCUM. DEPR./ GROSS PROP. %	EARN. PER SH. $	TANG. BK. VAL. $	DIV. PER SH. $	DIV. PAYOUT %	PRICE RANGE		AVG. P/E RATIO	AVG. YIELD
p12/31/02	8,305.0	⑥ 623.1								⑥ 2.64		1.34	50.8	46.85	— 32.12	15.0	3.4
12/31/01	9,620.9	⑤ 727.0	25,910.3	16.4	7.6	4.1	3.8	9.8		⑤ 3.13	33.78	1.27	40.7	44.67	— 32.56	12.3	3.3
12/31/00	10,016.1	⑤ 710.9	22,374.6	15.4	7.1	4.2	4.6	17.1	40.3	⑤ 2.97	17.36	1.22	40.9	43.88	— 15.94	10.1	4.1
12/31/99	8,773.2	⑤ 595.0	20,198.6	14.3	6.8	3.8	3.9	12.3	40.8	⑤ 2.25	18.13	1.20	53.3	33.50	— 23.69	12.7	4.2
12/31/98	11,494.8	.785.6	22,848.0	13.2	6.8	5.1	4.3	10.3	39.7	3.00	28.82	1.50	50.0	32.44	— 23.25	9.3	5.4
12/31/97	9,561.7	④ 300.9	27,000.7	19.4	3.1	1.7	1.4	4.2	34.6	④ 1.03	27.23	1.80	174.7	30.00	— 22.38	25.4	6.9
12/31/96	7,163.5	④ 420.0	22,966.3	23.4	5.9	2.6	2.2	5.8	35.4	④ 1.83	28.51	1.80	98.4	30.38	— 24.88	15.1	6.5
12/31/95	6,274.4	④ 484.6	22,265.9	19.4	7.7	3.1	2.7	6.8	34.3	④ 2.13	28.41	1.80	84.5	29.25	— 20.00	11.6	7.3
12/31/94	5,963.3	② 341.8	22,613.5	17.9	5.7	2.1	1.8	4.8	32.4	② 1.49	27.61	1.80	120.8	37.38	— 21.25	19.7	6.1
12/31/93	4,485.3	①③ 458.1	22,876.7	22.1	10.2	2.9	2.4	6.3	30.9	①③ 2.62	28.27	1.65	63.0	39.88	— 32.50	13.8	4.6

Statistics are as originally reported. ① Bef. disc. opers. ② Incl. non-recurr. chrg. $154.3 mill. ($0.67/sh) ③ Bef. acctg. change credit: 1993, $93.8 mill. ($0.54/sh); 1995, $35.4 mill. ④ Incl. non-recurr. chrg. 1995, $15.2 mill. ($0.07/sh);1996, $174.0 mill.;1997 $293.7 mill. ⑤ Incl. net gain of $71.9 mill. from the sale of assets, 1999; net gain of $2.3 mill., 2000; net gain of $5.2 mill., 2001. ⑥ Incl. prov. of $428.5 mill for turbine commit., asset impair., & restruct. chrgs. & net gain of $6.6 mill. on sales of assets.

OFFICERS:
R. V. Luft, Chmn.
J. W. Leonard, C.E.O.
D. C. Hintz, Pres.
C. J. Wilder, Exec. V.P., C.F.O.

INVESTOR CONTACT: Nancy Morovich, Investor Relations, (504) 576-4947

PRINCIPAL OFFICE: 639 Loyola Avenue, New Orleans, LA 70113

TELEPHONE NUMBER: (504) 576-4000
FAX: (504) 576-4428
WEB: www.entergy.com

NO. OF EMPLOYEES: 15,000 (approx.)

SHAREHOLDERS: 60,327

ANNUAL MEETING: In May

INCORPORATED: FL, May, 1949; reincorp., DE,

INSTITUTIONAL HOLDINGS:
No. of Institutions: 356
Shares Held: 172,660,644
% Held: 77.8

INDUSTRY: Electric services (SIC: 4911)

TRANSFER AGENT(S): Mellon Investor Services, Ridgefield Park, NJ

EOG RESOURCES, INC.

EXCH.	SYM.	REC. PRICE	P/E RATIO	YLD.	MKT. CAP.	RANGE (52-WK.)	'02 Y/E PR.
NYSE	EOG	41.30 (2/28/03)	63.5	0.4%	…	44.15 - 30.02	39.92

MEDIUM GRADE. THE COMPANY HAS ELECTED TO SECURE PRICE PROTECTION FOR SLIGHTLY OVER 20.0% OF ITS 2003 NORTH AMERICAN NATURAL GAS PRODUCTION THROUGH COLLARS AND FINANCIAL PRICE SWAPS.

*7 YEAR PRICE SCORE 145.8   ***12 MONTH PRICE SCORE 113.5**
*NYSE COMPOSITE INDEX=100

INTERIM EARNINGS (Per Share):

Qtr.	Mar.	June	Sept.	Dec.
1998	0.17	0.09	0.04	0.06
1999	0.03	0.13	3.68	0.25
2000	0.33	0.63	0.95	1.33
2001	1.79	1.13	0.59	d0.24
2002	d0.23	0.30	0.22	0.36

INTERIM DIVIDENDS (Per Share):

Amt.	Decl.	Ex.	Rec.	Pay.
0.04Q	2/12/02	4/12/02	4/16/02	4/30/02
0.04Q	5/07/02	7/15/02	7/17/02	7/31/02
0.04Q	9/10/02	10/15/02	10/17/02	10/31/02
0.04Q	12/10/02	1/15/03	1/17/03	1/31/03
0.04Q	2/20/03	4/14/03	4/16/03	4/30/03

Indicated div.: $0.16

CAPITALIZATION (12/31/01):

	($000)	(%)
Long-Term Debt	855,969	28.1
Deferred Income Tax	551,020	18.1
Preferred Stock	147,582	4.8
Common & Surplus	1,495,104	49.0
Total	3,049,675	100.0

BUSINESS:

EOG Resources, Inc. (formerly Enron Oil & Gas Company) is engaged in the exploration for, and the development, production and marketing of, natural gas and crude oil primarily in major producing basins in the United States, as well as in Canada and Trinidad and, to a lesser extent, selected other international areas. As of 12/31/01 the Company's estimated net proved natural gas reserves were 3,796.50 billion cubic feet and estimated net proved crude oil, condensate and natural gas liquids reserves were 72.1 million barrels.

RECENT DEVELOPMENTS:

For the twelve months ended 12/31/02, net income was $87.2 million compared with $398.6 million a year earlier. Results for 2001 included charges of $19.2 million associated with the Enron bankruptcy. Total net operating revenues decreased 33.8% to $1.10 billion from $1.65 billion the previous year, primarily due to a 31.8% drop in average natural gas prices to $2.60 per thousand cubic feet. In addition, revenues included a loss of $48.5 million for 2002 and a gain of $97.8 million for 2001 on mark-to-market commodity derivative contracts. Revenues for 2002 and 2001 also included gains of $1.1 million and $934,000, respectively, on net sales of reserves and related assets and other items.

PROSPECTS:

EOG appears well positioned to benefit from potentially higher natural gas commodity prices that could be sustained for several years. The Company indicated that during 2002, total aggregate U.S. natural gas production decreased by an estimated 5.0% resulting in a tightening supply-demand situation. No significant easing of this supply-constrained environment is anticipated in either 2003 or 2004. Meanwhile, EOG expects its 2003 North American natural gas production to increase, while Trinidad is expected to post strong growth. Separately, the Company noted that it has elected to secure price protection for slightly over 20.0% of its 2003 North American natural gas production through collars and financial price swaps.

ANNUAL FINANCIAL DATA:

FISCAL YEAR	TOT. REVS. ($mill.)	NET INC. ($mill.)	TOT. ASSETS ($mill.)	OPER. PROFIT %	NET PROFIT %	RET. ON EQUITY %	RET. ON ASSETS %	CURR. RATIO	EARN. PER SH.$	CASH FL. PER SH.$	TANG. BK. VAL.$	DIV. PER SH.$	PRICE RANGE	AVG. P/E RATIO	AVG. YIELD %
p12/31/02	1,095.0	87.2							0.65			0.16	44.15 - 30.02	57.1	0.4
12/31/01	1,654.9	② 398.6	3,414.0	40.8	24.1	24.3	11.7	0.9	② 3.30	6.64	12.95	0.15	55.50 - 25.80	12.3	0.4
12/31/00	1,489.9	396.9	3,000.8	46.8	26.6	28.7	13.2	1.1	3.24	6.35	10.55	0.13	56.69 - 13.69	10.9	0.4
12/31/99	801.4	① 569.1	2,610.8	2.3	71.0	50.4	21.8	0.9	① 3.99	7.22	8.25	0.12	25.38 - 14.38	5.0	0.6
12/31/98	769.2	56.2	3,018.1	14.8	7.3	4.4	1.9	0.9	0.36	2.11	8.33	0.12	24.50 - 11.75	50.3	0.7
12/31/97	783.5	122.0	2,723.4	24.6	15.6	9.5	4.5	1.0	0.77	2.26	8.26	0.12	27.00 - 17.50	28.9	0.5
12/31/96	730.6	140.0	2,458.4	28.6	19.2	11.1	5.7	1.0	0.88	2.18	7.92	0.12	30.63 - 22.38	30.1	0.5
12/31/95	648.7	142.1	2,147.3	30.1	21.9	12.2	6.6	1.3	0.89	1.97	7.28	0.12	25.38 - 17.13	23.9	0.6
12/31/94	625.8	148.0	1,861.9	25.5	23.6	14.2	7.9	1.0	0.93	2.44	6.52	0.12	24.63 - 17.38	22.6	0.6
12/31/93	581.0	138.0	1,811.2	19.9	23.8	14.8	7.6	1.1	0.86	2.42	5.84	0.12	27.00 - 13.38	23.5	0.6

Statistics are as originally reported. Adj. for 2-for-1 stk. split, 6/94. ① Incls. gain on share exchange of $575.2 mill. ② Incls. non-recurr. chrgs. of $19.2 mill.

OFFICERS:
M. G. Papa, Chmn., C.E.O.
E. P. Segner III, Pres.
D. R. Looney, V.P., Treas.

INVESTOR CONTACT: Investor Relations, (713) 651-7000

PRINCIPAL OFFICE: 333 Clay Street, Suite 4200, Houston, TX 77002-7361

TELEPHONE NUMBER: (713) 651-7000
FAX: (713) 651-6992
WEB: www.eogresources.com
NO. OF EMPLOYEES: 960 (approx.)
SHAREHOLDERS: 370 (approx. record); 57,700 (approx. benef.)
ANNUAL MEETING: In May
INCORPORATED: DE, June, 1985

INSTITUTIONAL HOLDINGS:
No. of Institutions: 297
Shares Held: 117,286,495
% Held: 101.5

INDUSTRY: Crude petroleum and natural gas (SIC: 1311)

TRANSFER AGENT(S): EquiServe Trust Company, N.A., Jersey City, NJ

EQUIFAX INC.

EXCH.	SYM.	REC. PRICE	P/E RATIO	YLD.	MKT. CAP.	RANGE (52-WK.)	'02 Y/E PR.
NYSE	EFX	19.18 (2/28/03)	13.9	0.4%	$2.61 bill.	31.10 - 17.99	23.14

MEDIUM GRADE. THE COMPANY EXPECTS EARNINGS IN 2003 TO BE BETWEEN $1.46 AND $1.52 PER SHARE.

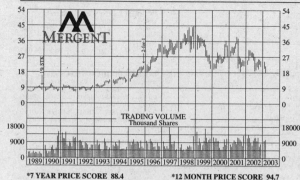

*7 YEAR PRICE SCORE 88.4   ***12 MONTH PRICE SCORE 94.7**

*NYSE COMPOSITE INDEX=100

INTERIM EARNINGS (Per Share):

Qtr.	Mar.	June	Sept.	Dec.
1999	0.31	0.37	0.42	0.45
2000	0.31	0.39	0.47	0.50
2001	0.25	0.28	0.26	0.07
2002	0.30	0.34	0.36	0.38

INTERIM DIVIDENDS (Per Share):

Amt.	Decl.	Ex.	Rec.	Pay.
0.02Q	2/06/02	2/20/02	2/23/02	3/15/02
0.02Q	5/01/02	5/22/02	5/24/02	6/14/02
0.02Q	8/07/02	8/21/02	8/23/02	9/13/02
0.02Q	11/06/02	11/20/02	11/22/02	12/13/02
0.02Q	1/29/03	2/19/03	2/21/03	3/14/03

Indicated div.: $0.08 (Div. Reinv. Plan)

CAPITALIZATION (12/31/01):

	($000)	(%)
Long-Term Debt	693,600	67.6
Deferred Income Tax	88,600	8.6
Common & Surplus	243,500	23.7
Total	1,025,700	100.0

BUSINESS:

Equifax Inc. enables and secures global commerce through its information management, consumer credit, marketing services, business information, authentication and e-commerce businesses. The Company serves many industries including the financial services, retail, telecommunications/utilities, information technology, brokerage, insurance and business lending industries and government. EFX also enables consumers to manage and protect their financial health with services offered at www.equifax.com. As of 1/23/03, the Company had businesses located in 12 countries. In August 1997, the Company completed the spin-off of its Insurance Services Group. In July 2001, EFX completed the spin-off of its Payment Services division, Certegy.

RECENT DEVELOPMENTS:

For the year ended 12/31/02, the Company reported income from continuing operations of $191.3 million compared with $117.3 million in the previous year. Results for 2001 included a pre-tax restructuring charge of $60.4 million. Earnings excluded a loss of $13.3 million in 2002 and income of $5.2 million in 2001 from discontinued operations. Total revenues decreased 2.6% to $1.11 billion from $1.14 billion a year earlier. North American revenue advanced 5.8% to $902.2 million. European revenue fell 10.6% to $126.1 million, and Latin American revenue dropped 28.2% to $76.6 million. Operating income jumped 38.4% to $351.3 million from $253.8 million a year earlier.

PROSPECTS:

Earnings for 2003 should benefit from the recent acquisition of consumer credit files and certain customer contracts from CBC Companies, Inc., as well as the previously reported acquisition of Naviant, Inc., a provider of e-marketing services. The Company expects earnings per share growth of 6.0% to 9.0% in 2003, or earnings between $1.46 and $1.52 per share. Revenue growth for the coming year is expected to range from 4.0% to 7.0%. Separately, on 1/22/03, the Company announced an agreement to offer its Equifax Decision Power® to Pershing LLC's broker-dealer customers, providing access to tools that help meet the requirements of the USA PATRIOT Act.

ANNUAL FINANCIAL DATA:

FISCAL YEAR	TOT. REVS. (Smill.)	NET INC. (Smill.)	TOT. ASSETS (Smill.)	OPER. PROFIT %	NET PROFIT %	RET. ON EQUITY %	RET. ON ASSETS %	CURR. RATIO	EARN. PER SH.$	CASH FL.PER SH.$	TANG. BK. VAL.$	DIV. PER SH.$	PRICE RANGE	AVG. P/E RATIO	AVG. YIELD %
p12/31/02	1,109.3	⑤191.3							⑤1.38			0.08	31.30 - 18.95	18.2	0.3
12/31/01	1,139.0	④117.3	1,422.6	22.3	10.3	48.2	8.2	1.3	④0.84	1.61	...	0.23	38.76 - 18.60	34.1	0.8
12/31/00	1,965.9	228.0	2,069.6	23.2	11.6	59.4	11.0	1.4	1.68	2.77	...	0.37	36.50 - 19.88	16.8	1.3
12/31/99	1,772.7	215.9	1,839.8	23.4	12.2	100.1	11.7	1.2	1.55	2.44	...	0.36	39.88 - 20.13	19.4	1.2
12/31/98	1,621.0	193.4	1,828.8	22.6	11.9	52.8	10.6	1.2	1.34	2.06	...	0.35	45.00 - 29.75	27.9	0.9
12/31/97	1,366.1	②③185.5	1,177.1	21.9	13.6	53.1	15.8	1.2	②③1.26	1.78	...	0.34	37.19 - 26.50	25.3	1.1
12/31/96	1,811.2	177.6	1,301.9	16.8	9.8	41.8	13.6	0.9	1.22	1.81	0.19	0.33	34.50 - 17.75	21.4	1.3
12/31/95	1,623.0	①147.7	1,053.7	16.2	9.1	41.8	14.0	1.5	①0.98	1.48	...	0.32	21.75 - 12.63	17.5	1.8
12/31/94	1,422.0	120.3	1,021.2	15.1	8.5	33.3	11.8	1.3	0.81	1.26	...	0.30	15.25 - 10.94	16.2	2.3
12/31/93	1,217.2	①63.5	731.2	9.8	5.2	25.0	8.7	2.0	①0.43	0.79	0.36	0.28	13.69 - 8.69	26.3	2.5

Statistics are as originally reported. Adj. for stk. splits: 2-for-1, 11/95 ① Incl. non-recurr. credit 1995, $98,000; chrg. 1993, $48.4 mill. ② Bef. disc. oper. gain $1.4 mill. ③ Bef. acctg. change chrg. $3.2 mill. ④ Bef. disc. oper. gain of $5.2 mill.; incl. after-tax restr. chrg. of $35.3 mill. ⑤ Bef. disc. oper. loss of $13.3 mill.

OFFICERS:
T. F. Chapman, Chmn., C.E.O.
M. E. Miller, Pres., C.O.O.
D. T. Heroman, V.P., C.F.O.

INVESTOR CONTACT: Jeff Dodge, Investor Relations, (404) 885-8804

PRINCIPAL OFFICE: 1550 Peachtree Street, N.W., Atlanta, GA 30309

TELEPHONE NUMBER: (404) 885-8000
FAX: (404) 885-8682
WEB: www.equifax.com

NO. OF EMPLOYEES: 5,200 (approx.)

SHAREHOLDERS: 10,268 (approx.)

ANNUAL MEETING: In May

INCORPORATED: GA, Dec., 1913

INSTITUTIONAL HOLDINGS:
No. of Institutions: 309
Shares Held: 95,051,053
% Held: 70.1

INDUSTRY: Credit reporting services (SIC: 7323)

TRANSFER AGENT(S): SunTrust Bank, Atlanta, GA

EQUITABLE RESOURCES, INC.

EXCH.	SYM.	REC. PRICE	P/E RATIO	YLD.	MKT. CAP.	RANGE (52-WK.)	'02 Y/E PR.
NYSE	EQT	36.30 (2/28/03)	17.8	1.9%	$2.26 bill.	37.84 - 28.67	35.04

UPPER MEDIUM GRADE. THE COMPANY EXPECTS EARNINGS PER SHARE TO RANGE FROM $2.70 TO $2.80 FOR 2003.

INTERIM EARNINGS (Per Share):

Qtr.	Mar.	June	Sept.	Dec.
1999	0.42	0.11	0.09	0.40
2000	0.59	0.25	0.29	0.48
2001	1.08	0.47	0.38	0.37
2002	0.80	0.45	0.42	0.67

INTERIM DIVIDENDS (Per Share):

Amt.	Decl.	Ex.	Rec.	Pay.
0.17Q	4/18/02	5/08/02	5/10/02	6/01/02
0.17Q	7/18/02	8/14/02	8/16/02	9/01/02
0.17Q	10/17/02	11/13/02	11/15/02	12/01/02
0.17Q	1/17/03	2/05/03	2/07/03	3/01/03

Indicated div.: $0.68 (Div. Reinv. Plan)

CAPITALIZATION (12/31/02):

	($000)	(%)
Long-Term Debt	447,000	28.4
Deferred Income Tax	350,690	22.2
Common & Surplus	778,639	49.4
Total	1,576,329	100.0

*7 YEAR PRICE SCORE 166.7   ***12 MONTH PRICE SCORE 113.0**

*NYSE COMPOSITE INDEX=100

BUSINESS:

Equitable Resources, Inc. is an integrated energy company operating through three business segments: Equitable Supply, Equitable Utilities and NORESCO. The production segment's operations include exploration and production activities in the East (Appalachian) and Gulf regions, as well as Appalachian area natural gas gathering and liquids processing. The utilities segment's activities are comprised of EQT's natural gas supply, natural gas transmission and distribution operations and energy-management services for customers throughout the U.S. EQT also has energy-service management projects in selected international markets. In December 1998, EQT sold its Gulf area midstream operations. On 2/15/00, EQT purchased the Appalachian oil and gas properties of Statoil Energy, Inc.

RECENT DEVELOPMENTS:

For the year ended 12/31/02, income was $150.6 million, before an accounting change charge of $5.5 million and income of $9.0 million from discontinued operations, compared with net income of $151.8 million, the previous year. Results for 2002 included a pre-tax impairment of long-lived assets charge of $5.3 million. Operating revenues declined 3.6% to $1.07 billion from $1.11 billion the year before. Net operating revenue decreased to $562.7 million to $567.6 million the prior year. Operating income climbed 9.1% to $277.6 million.

PROSPECTS:

The Company's utility segment is being favorably affected by increased revenues resulting from colder weather and higher commercial and industrial net revenue. In addition, the Company's supply segment continues to be hampered by lower realized natural gas prices and a reduction in volume from the sale in December 2001 of EQT's oil dominated fields. Meanwhile, results for the Company's NORESCO segment may weaken due to a lower construction backlog and higher expenses. Going forward, the Company expects earnings per share to range from $2.70 to $2.80 for 2003. Also, EQT anticipates $228.0 million of capital expenditures for 2003.

ANNUAL FINANCIAL DATA:

FISCAL YEAR	TOT. REVS. ($mill.)	NET INC. ($mill.)	TOT. ASSETS ($mill.)	OPER. PROFIT %	NET PROFIT %	RET. ON EQUITY %	RET. ON ASSETS %	CURR. RATIO	EARN. PER SH.$	CASH FL. PER SH.$	TANG. BK. VAL.$	DIV. PER SH.$	PRICE RANGE	AVG. P/E RATIO	AVG. YIELD
12/31/02	1,069.1	⑥ 150.6	2,436.9	26.0	14.1	19.3	6.2	0.8	⑥ 2.36	3.49	11.66	0.67	37.55 - 28.67	14.0	2.0
12/31/01	1,764.5	151.8	2,518.7	14.4	8.6	17.9	6.0	1.0	2.30	3.43	12.35	0.63	40.49 - 26.00	14.5	1.9
12/31/00	1,652.2	⑤ 106.2	2,455.9	13.0	6.4	15.3	4.3	0.7	⑤ 1.60	3.09	9.73	0.59	33.38 - 16.13	15.5	2.4
12/31/99	1,062.7	69.1	1,789.6	13.4	6.5	10.8	3.9	0.8	1.01	2.81	8.84	0.59	19.50 - 11.63	15.5	3.8
12/31/98	882.6	④ d27.1	1,854.2	...	...	...	...	1.0	④ d0.36	0.85	8.93	0.59	17.63 - 10.28	...	4.2
12/31/97	2,151.0	③ 78.1	2,411.0	5.2	3.6	9.5	3.2	0.9	③ 1.08	2.40	10.25	0.59	17.31 - 13.69	14.4	3.8
12/31/96	1,861.8	② 59.4	2,096.3	6.9	3.2	8.0	2.8	0.9	② 0.85	2.01	10.38	0.59	15.75 - 12.63	16.8	4.2
12/31/95	1,426.0	1.5	1,961.8	1.5	0.1	0.2	0.1	1.0	0.02	1.53	10.21	0.59	15.69 - 12.94	712.1	4.1
12/31/94	1,397.3	60.7	2,019.1	7.9	4.3	3.2	3.0	0.6	0.88	2.23	27.48	0.57	19.38 - 12.75	18.3	3.6
12/31/93	1,094.8	73.5	1,946.9	11.9	6.7	4.0	3.8	0.6	1.14	2.32	26.62	0.55	22.13 - 16.50	17.0	2.8

Statistics are as originally reported. Adj. for 2-for-1 stock split, 6/01 & 3-for-2 stock split, 1/93. ① Incl. nonrecurr. revs. of $45.0 mill. & incl. non-recurr. chgs. of $121.1 mill. ② Incl. a net non-recurr. gain of $3.8 mill. ③ Incl. a net gain of $28.3 mill. ④ Incl. a pre-tax chg. of $81.8 mill. for restr., impairs. & oth. nonrecurr. chgs. & a loss of $1.6 mill. on the sale of assets; excl. a net losses of $17.1 mill. ⑤ Excl. an after-tax chrg. of $12.3 mill. for costs rel. to the Kentucky West labor settlement & an after-tax gain of $4.3 mill. for the sale of Westport Resource's stk. ⑥ Bef. acctg. chng. chrg. of $5.5 mill. & inc. of $9.0 mill. & incl. pre-tax chrg. of $5.3 mill.

OFFICERS: M. S. Gerber, Chmn., Pres., C.E.O. D. L. Porges, Exec. V.P., C.F.O. P. P. Conti, V.P., Treas. **INVESTOR CONTACT:** Patrick Kane, Investor Relations, (412) 553-5869 **PRINCIPAL OFFICE:** One Oxford Centre, 301 Grant Street, Suite 3300, Pittsburgh, PA 15219	**TELEPHONE NUMBER:** (412) 553-5700 **FAX:** (412) 553-5732 **WEB:** www.eqt.com **NO. OF EMPLOYEES:** 1,500 (approx.) **SHAREHOLDERS:** 4,647 (approx.) **ANNUAL MEETING:** In May **INCORPORATED:** PA, Mar., 1925	**INSTITUTIONAL HOLDINGS:** No. of Institutions: 222 Shares Held: 42,528,312 % Held: 68.0 **INDUSTRY:** Gas transmission and distribution (SIC: 4923) **TRANSFER AGENT(S):** Mellon Investor Services, Pittsburgh, PA

EQUITY OFFICE PROPERTIES TRUST

EXCH.	SYM.	REC. PRICE	P/E RATIO	YLD.	MKT. CAP.	RANGE (52-WK.)	'02 Y/E PR.
NYSE	EOP	24.53 (2/28/03)	14.4	8.2%	$10.17 bill.	31.36 - 22.78	24.98

MEDIUM GRADE. THE COMPANY EXPECTS A SLOW RECOVERY IN 2003.

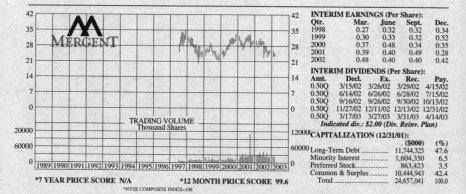

TRADING VOLUME
Thousand Shares

| 1989 | 1990 | 1991 | 1992 | 1993 | 1994 | 1995 | 1996 | 1997 | 1998 | 1999 | 2000 | 2001 | 2002 | 2003 |

*7 YEAR PRICE SCORE N/A   ***12 MONTH PRICE SCORE 99.6**

NYSE COMPOSITE INDEX=100

INTERIM EARNINGS (Per Share):

Qtr.	Mar.	June	Sept.	Dec.
1998	0.27	0.32	0.32	0.34
1999	0.30	0.33	0.32	0.52
2000	0.37	0.48	0.34	0.35
2001	0.39	0.40	0.49	0.28
2002	0.48	0.40	0.40	0.42

INTERIM DIVIDENDS (Per Share):

Amt.	Decl.	Ex.	Rec.	Pay.
0.50Q	3/15/02	3/26/02	3/29/02	4/15/02
0.50Q	6/14/02	6/26/02	6/28/02	7/15/02
0.50Q	9/16/02	9/26/02	9/30/02	10/15/02
0.50Q	11/27/02	12/11/02	12/13/02	12/31/02
0.50Q	3/17/03	3/27/03	3/31/03	4/14/03

Indicated div.: $2.00 (Div. Reinv. Plan)

CAPITALIZATION (12/31/01):

	($000)	(%)
Long-Term Debt	11,744,325	47.6
Minority Interest	1,604,350	6.5
Preferred Stock	863,423	3.5
Common & Surplus	10,444,943	42.4
Total	24,657,041	100.0

BUSINESS:

Equity Office Properties Trust is a fully integrated real estate investment trust company and is the nation's largest publicly-held owner and manager of office properties, in terms of its property portfolio as of 2/11/03. EOP is engaged in acquiring, owning, managing and leasing office properties and parking facilities. As of 2/11/03, the Company owned or had an interest in 731 buildings comprising 125.6 million square feet in 20 states and the District of Columbia. In addition, EOP has an ownership presence in 32 Metropolitan Statistical Areas and in 137 submarkets. In June 2000, the Company acquired Cornerstone Properties Inc. On 7/2/01, EOP acquired Spieker Properties, Inc.

RECENT DEVELOPMENTS:

For the year ended 12/31/02, income was $732.0 million, before income from discontinued operations of $38.2 million, versus income of $598.3 million, before income from discontinued operations of $22.1 million, an extraordinary loss of $1.0 million and an accounting change charge of $1.1 million, in the previous year. Results for 2001 included pre-tax impairment charges of $135.2 million and a gain on the sale of real estate of $81.7 million. Total revenues increased 13.8% to $3.51 billion from $3.08 billion the prior year. Revenues reflected an increase in rental rates and tenant reimbursements. For full-year 2002, office occupancy declined to 88.6% from 91.8% at 12/31/01. Industrial occupancy declined 3.5 percentage points to 89.3% at year-end versus 92.8% at 12/31/01.

PROSPECTS:

Looking ahead, the Company predicts a slow recovery in 2003, but remains optimistic that office job growth will continue to accelerate throughout the year, leading to a modest firming of rents and occupancies, particularly during the second half of 2003. Meanwhile, the Company remains well-positioned for future growth as EOP closed over $500.0 million in asset sales during the year, providing added liquidity. The Company expects diluted funds from operations for full-year 2003 in the range of $2.80 to $3.00 per share, assuming office job growth of about 1.0% and lease termination fees ranging from $25.0 to $30.0 million.

ANNUAL FINANCIAL DATA:

FISCAL YEAR	TOT. INC. ($mill.)	NET INC. ($mill.)	TOT. ASSETS ($mill.)	NET INC. +DEPR./ ASSETS %	RET. ON EQUITY %	RET. ON ASSETS %	EARN. PER SH. $	TANG. BK. VAL. $	DIV. PER SH. $	DIV. PAYOUT %	PRICE RANGE	AVG. P/E RATIO	AVG. YIELD %
p12/31/02	3,506.1	③ 732.0					③ 1.70		2.00	117.6	31.36 - 22.78	15.9	7.4
12/31/01	3,130.1	② 629.7	25,808.4	4.7	5.6	2.4	② 1.55	25.20	1.90	122.6	33.19 - 26.20	19.2	6.4
12/31/00	2,264.2	① 472.7	18,794.3	4.8	5.9	2.5	① 1.52	24.28	1.74	114.5	33.50 - 22.88	18.5	6.2
12/31/99	1,942.2	① 441.9	14,046.1	5.7	6.5	3.1	① 1.48	24.69	1.58	106.7	29.38 - 20.81	17.0	6.3
12/31/98	1,679.7	① 356.5	14,261.3	4.6	5.1	2.5	① 1.24	24.76	1.38	111.3	32.00 - 20.19	21.0	5.3
12/31/97	413.0	① 88.1	11,751.7	1.3	1.4	0.7	① 0.43	24.87	0.56	130.2	34.69 - 25.25	69.7	1.9
12/31/96	508.1	73.4	3,912.6	4.2	4.3	1.9	...	...	...	...	...	...	...
12/31/95	371.5	① 3.2	2,650.9	2.8	0.3	0.1	...	...	...	...	...	...	...
12/31/94	240.9	① 14.9	...	...	...	...	...	...	...	...	...	...	...

Statistics are as originally reported. ① Bef. extraord. chrg. 2000, $1.8 mill.; 1999, $10.5 mill.; 1998, $7.5 mill.; 1997, $16.4 mill.; 1994, $1.7 mill.; credit, 1995, $31.3 mill. ② Bef. extraord. chrg. of $10.4 mill. & acctg. chng. chrg. of $1.1 mill.; incl. pre-tax impair. chrgs. of $135.2 mill. & gain of $81.7 mill. on sale of real estate. ③ Bef. income fr. disc. opers. of $38.2 mill.

OFFICERS:
S. Zell, Chmn., Pres., C.E.O.
M. C. Williams, Exec. V.P., C.F.O.
M. O. Fear, Sr. V.P., Treas.
S. M. Stevens, Exec. V.P., Sec.

INVESTOR CONTACT: Diane M. Morefield, Sr. V.P., Inv. Rel., (312) 466-3286

PRINCIPAL OFFICE: Two North Riverside Plaza, Suite 2100, Chicago, IL 60606

TELEPHONE NUMBER: (312) 466-3300
FAX: (312) 466-0332
WEB: www.equityoffice.com

NO. OF EMPLOYEES: 2,700 (approx.)

SHAREHOLDERS: 1,817 (approx.)

ANNUAL MEETING: In May

INCORPORATED: MD, Oct., 1996

INSTITUTIONAL HOLDINGS:
No. of Institutions: 421
Shares Held: 319,351,671
% Held: 77.6

INDUSTRY: Real estate investment trusts (SIC: 6798)

TRANSFER AGENT(S): EquiServe Trust Company, Providence, RI

EQUITY RESIDENTIAL PROPERTIES TRUST

EXCH.	SYM.	REC. PRICE	P/E RATIO	YLD.	MKT. CAP.	RANGE (52-WK.)	'02 Y/E PR.
NYSE	EQR	24.28 (2/28/03)	20.6	7.1%	$6.44 bill.	30.96 - 21.55	24.58

MEDIUM GRADE. THE COMPANY EXPECTS FUNDS FROM OPERATIONS FOR 2003 TO BE AT THE LOWER END OF A RANGE OF $2.25 TO $2.40 PER SHARE.

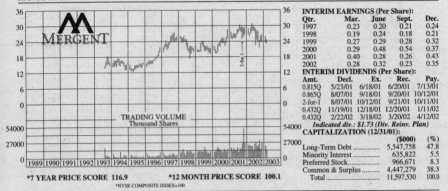

*7 YEAR PRICE SCORE 116.9   ***12 MONTH PRICE SCORE 100.1**
*NYSE COMPOSITE INDEX=100

INTERIM EARNINGS (Per Share):

Qtr.	Mar.	June	Sept.	Dec.
1997	0.23	0.20	0.21	0.24
1998	0.19	0.24	0.18	0.21
1999	0.27	0.29	0.28	0.32
2000	0.29	0.48	0.54	0.37
2001	0.40	0.28	0.26	0.43
2002	0.28	0.32	0.23	0.35

INTERIM DIVIDENDS (Per Share):

Amt.	Decl.	Ex.	Rec.	Pay.
0.815Q	5/23/01	6/18/01	6/20/01	7/13/01
0.865Q	8/07/01	9/18/01	9/20/01	10/12/01
2-for-1	8/07/01	10/12/01	9/21/01	10/11/01
0.432Q	11/19/01	12/18/01	12/20/01	1/11/02
0.432Q	2/22/02	3/18/02	3/20/02	4/12/02

Indicated div.: $1.73 (Div. Reinv. Plan)

CAPITALIZATION (12/31/01):

	($000)	(%)
Long-Term Debt	5,547,758	47.8
Minority Interest	635,822	5.5
Preferred Stock	966,671	8.3
Common & Surplus	4,447,279	38.3
Total	11,597,530	100.0

BUSINESS:

Equity Residential Properties Trust is a self-administered and self-managed equity real estate investment trust. The Company, through its subsidiaries, is engaged in the acquisition, disposition, ownership, management and operation of multifamily properties. As of 2/5/03, the Company owned or had interests in a portfolio of 1,039 multifamily properties containing 223,591 apartment units in 36 states. On 10/31/00, the Company acquired Grove Property Trust, a Maryland real estate investment trust company, for approximately $174.7 million in cash and the issuance of approximately 344,142 operating partnership units.

RECENT DEVELOPMENTS:

For the year ended 12/31/02, income was $301.5 million, before income from discontinued operations of $16.3 million and an extraordinary loss of $792,000, versus income of $362.2 million, before a loss from discontinued operations of $36.7 million, an extraordinary gain of $444,000 and an accounting change charge of $1.3 million, the year before. Results for 2002 and 2001 excluded gains from the sale of discontinued operations of $104.3 million and $148.9 million. Results for 2002 and 2001 included a gain of $5.1 million and $387,000, respectively, from sales of unconsolidated entities, as well as charges of $1.2 million and $11.8 million, respectively, for impairment of technology investments. Also, 2002 results included a charge of $17.1 million for impairment on EQR's corporate housing business. Total revenues declined 2.2% to $1.99 billion.

PROSPECTS:

Earnings continue to be hampered by overall weakness in the economy and the strength of the housing market. Looking ahead, while supply and demand fundamentals and same-store revenue growth are likely to continue to be challenging in the near-term, a stabilization of the housing market combined with a resolution to geopolitical issues and predicted job growth in the second half of 2003 should have a positive impact on the Company in the long-term. EQR is anticipating funds from operations for 2003 to be at the lower end of a range of $2.25 to $2.40 per share.

ANNUAL FINANCIAL DATA:

FISCAL YEAR	TOT. INC. ($mill.)	NET INC. ($mill.)	TOT. ASSETS ($mill.)	NET INC. + DEPR./ ASSETS %	RET. ON EQUITY %	RET. ON ASSETS %	EARN. PER SH.$	TANG. BK. VAL.$	DIV. PER SH.$	DIV. PAYOUT %	PRICE RANGE	AVG. P/E RATIO	AVG. YIELD %
p12/31/02	1,994.1	⑤ 301.5					⑤ 1.18		1.73	146.6	30.96 - 21.55	22.3	6.6
12/31/01	2,170.6	④ 474.4	12,235.6	7.7	8.8	3.9	④ 1.36	16.59	1.25	91.7	30.45 - 24.80	20.3	4.5
12/31/00	2,030.3	③ 555.0	12,264.0	8.3	9.9	4.5	③ 1.67	16.47	1.57	94.3	28.63 - 19.34	14.4	6.6
12/31/99	1,753.1	①③ 300.8	11,715.7	6.1	5.5	2.6	①③ 1.15	16.46	1.47	128.4	24.19 - 19.06	18.9	6.8
12/31/98	1,337.4	② 236.5	10,700.3	5.1	4.4	2.2	② 0.82	16.58	1.36	166.9	26.28 - 17.34	26.8	6.2
12/31/97	747.3	① 162.8	7,094.6	4.5	4.4	2.3	① 0.88	14.86	1.58	180.1	27.50 - 19.88	26.9	6.7
12/31/96	478.4	①② 82.7	2,986.1	6.0	5.7	2.8	①②⑤ 0.85	...	1.18	138.8	21.75 - 14.13	21.1	6.6
12/31/95	388.9	①③ 44.1	2,141.3	5.6	5.0	2.1	①③ 0.84	8.66	1.05	125.6	15.94 - 12.44	16.9	7.4
12/31/94	231.0	34.4	1,847.7	4.0	5.6	1.9	0.67	8.98	0.98	145.9	17.56 - 12.88	22.7	6.4
12/31/93	112.1	4.3	535.9	4.3	2.9	0.8	0.21	5.02	0.10	50.0	18.38 - 13.69	76.3	0.7

Statistics are as originally reported. Adj. for 2-for-1 stk. spl., 10/01 ① Bef. gain on dispos. of properties, 1999, $93.5 mill.; 1998, $21.7 mill.; 1997, $13.8 mill.; 1996, $22.4 mill.; 1995, $21.6 mill. ② Bef. $3.5 mill. write-off of unamort. costs of refin. ③ Bef. gain on early exting. of debt., 2000, $5.6 mill.; 1999, $451,000; 1995, $2.0 mill. ④ Bef. extraord. gain of $444,000 & acctg. chrg. of $1.3 mill.; incl. pre-tax impair. chrgs. of $71.8 mill. & net gain of $149.3 mill. on sales of real estate. ⑤ Bef. inc. fr. disc. opers. of $16.3 mill. & extraord. loss of $792,000; incl. pre-tax impair. chrgs. of $18.3 mill. & net gain on sale of opers. of $104.3 mill.

OFFICERS:
S. Zell, Chmn.
B. W. Duncan, Pres., C.E.O.
D. J. Neithercut, Exec. V.P., C.F.O.
INVESTOR CONTACT: Cynthia H. McHugh, V.P. Inv. Rel., (312) 466-3779
PRINCIPAL OFFICE: Two North Riverside Plaza, Chicago, IL 60606

TELEPHONE NUMBER: (312) 474-1300
FAX: (312) 454-8703
WEB: www.eqr.com
NO. OF EMPLOYEES: 6,400 (approx.)
SHAREHOLDERS: 63,900 (approx. benef.)
ANNUAL MEETING: In Sept.
INCORPORATED: MD, March, 1993

INSTITUTIONAL HOLDINGS:
No. of Institutions: 355
Shares Held: 230,568,588
% Held: 85.1
INDUSTRY: Real estate investment trusts (SIC: 6798)
TRANSFER AGENT(S): Boston EquiServe, Boston, MA

ESCO TECHNOLOGIES INC.

EXCH.	SYM.	REC. PRICE	P/E RATIO	YLD.	MKT. CAP.	RANGE (52-WK.)	'02 Y/E PR.
NYSE	ESE	33.95 (2/28/03)	18.8	...	$425.5 mill.	41.15 - 25.80	37.00

UPPER MEDIUM GRADE. THE COMPANY INCREASED ITS YEAR-OVER-YEAR REVENUE GROWTH EXPECTATION FROM GREATER THAN 10.0% TO GREATER THAN 15.0%.

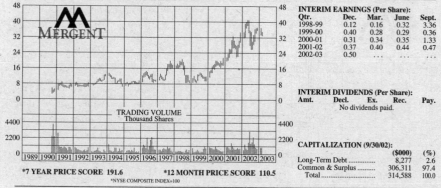

*7 YEAR PRICE SCORE 191.6   *12 MONTH PRICE SCORE 110.5
*NYSE COMPOSITE INDEX=100

INTERIM EARNINGS (Per Share):

Qtr.	Dec.	Mar.	June	Sept.
1998-99	0.12	0.16	0.32	3.36
1999-00	0.40	0.28	0.29	0.36
2000-01	0.31	0.34	0.35	1.33
2001-02	0.37	0.40	0.44	0.47
2002-03	0.50	...	...	...

INTERIM DIVIDENDS (Per Share):

Amt.	Decl.	Ex.	Rec.	Pay.
	No dividends paid.			

CAPITALIZATION (9/30/02):

	($000)	(%)
Long-Term Debt	8,277	2.6
Common & Surplus	306,311	97.4
Total	314,588	100.0

BUSINESS:

ESCO Technologies Inc. (formerly Esco Electronics Corporation) is a supplier of engineered filtration products to the process, healthcare and transportation markets worldwide. ESE's filtration products include depth filters, membrane-based microfiltration products and precision screen filters. Major applications include semiconductor production processes, blood collection, water purification, food and beverage processing, oil production and removal of contaminants in fuel lube and hydraulic systems. Esco's filtration business contributed approximately 52.4% to total sales as of 9/30/02. Remaining sales are derived primarily from RF shielding and test products and special purpose communication systems. In addition, Esco provides a communication system called TWACS® to the electric utility industry. The TWACS® system is currently used primarily for automatic meter reading.

RECENT DEVELOPMENTS:

For the three months ended 12/31/02, net income jumped 37.3% to $6.6 million from $4.8 million in the previous year. Results for 2002 included an after-tax charge of $400,000 related to the management transition agreement. Net sales advanced 32.6% to $111.8 million. Filtration segment sales increased 13.1% to $50.2 million, due to higher shipments of automotive and aerospace products. Communications segment sales more than doubled to $39.5 million, reflecting higher shipments of Automatic Meter Reading products. Test segment sales climbed 10.1% to $19.6 million, largely due to higher sales of large of electromagnetic compatibility test chambers.

PROSPECTS:

The Company has increased its year-over-year revenue growth expectation from greater than 10.0% to greater than 15.0%, absent any additional fiscal 2003 acquisitions or divestitures. ESE expects revenue growth of greater than 30.0% in the Communications segment. In the Test segment, ESE anticipates revenue growth of at least 15.0%. Filtration segment revenue growth is expected to be in the low to mid-single-digit range. In addition, the Company estimates earnings per share for the full-year 2003 to be in the range of $1.95 to $2.05, including a charge of $0.06 to $0.08 in the first half of the year related to the management transition agreement.

ANNUAL FINANCIAL DATA:

FISCAL YEAR	TOT. REVS. ($000)	NET INC. ($000)	TOT. ASSETS ($000)	OPER. PROFIT %	NET PROFIT %	RET. ON EQUITY %	RET. ON ASSETS %	CURR. RATIO	EARN. PER SH. $	CASH FL. PER SH. $	TANG. BK. VAL. $	PRICE RANGE	AVG. P/E RATIO
9/30/02	367,525	③ 21,781	407,688	10.0	5.9	7.1	5.3	2.6	③ 1.67	2.62	16.20	41.15 - 25.80	20.0
9/30/01	344,904	② 30,107	375,577	10.7	8.7	10.5	8.0	2.4	② 2.35	3.53	14.90	34.70 - 19.75	11.6
9/30/00	300,157	16,819	331,133	10.0	5.6	6.5	5.1	1.9	1.33	2.45	13.73	21.50 - 11.50	12.4
9/30/99	416,102	① 50,455	378,385	4.8	12.1	20.3	13.3	2.2	① 4.00	5.35	12.50	13.94 - 8.56	2.8
9/30/98	365,083	11,296	409,302	7.4	3.1	5.0	2.8	1.6	0.90	2.29	12.22	20.75 - 8.50	16.2
9/30/97	378,524	11,797	378,187	7.3	3.1	5.8	3.1	1.7	0.96	2.14	12.72	19.94 - 9.63	15.4
9/30/96	438,543	26,136	307,832	...	6.0	13.7	8.5	2.1	2.26	3.42	14.41	14.63 - 8.63	5.1
9/30/95	441,023	d30,260	378,001	...	...	...	...	1.5	d2.76	d1.48	14.70	9.75 - 6.63	...
9/30/94	473,855	8,308	347,486	5.1	1.8	4.4	2.4	1.8	0.72	1.90	15.27	13.38 - 6.50	13.8
9/30/93	459,725	5,189	335,251	4.3	1.1	3.0	1.5	1.7	0.47	2.29	14.43	12.88 - 8.00	21.1

Statistics are as originally reported. ① Incl. pre-tax gain of $59.9 mill. from sale of SEI subsidiary and nonrecurring charges of $9.1 mill.; Excl. acctg. charge of $25.0 mill. ② Incl. gain of $12.7 mill. from elimination of def. tax. val. allow. ③ Incl. after-tax chrg. of $400,000 from management transition agreement.

OFFICERS:
D. J. Moore, Chmn.
V. L. Richey Jr., C.E.O.
G. E. Muenster, V.P., C.F.O.
INVESTOR CONTACT: Patricia Moore, Investor Relations, (314) 213-2090
PRINCIPAL OFFICE: 8888 Ladue Road, Suite 200, St. Louis, MO 63124-2090

TELEPHONE NUMBER: (314) 213-7200
FAX: (314) 213-7250
WEB: www.escostl.com
NO. OF EMPLOYEES: 2,500 (approx.)
SHAREHOLDERS: 4,100 (approx. record)
ANNUAL MEETING: In Feb.
INCORPORATED: MO, Aug., 1990

INSTITUTIONAL HOLDINGS:
No. of Institutions: 125
Shares Held: 10,882,282
% Held: 86.4
INDUSTRY: Search and navigation equipment (SIC: 3812)
TRANSFER AGENT(S): Mellon Investor Services, Ridgefield Park, NJ

ESTEE LAUDER COMPANIES, INC. (THE)

EXCH.	SYM.	REC. PRICE	P/E RATIO	YLD.	MKT. CAP.	RANGE (52-WK.)	'02 Y/E PR.
NYSE	EL	28.05 (2/28/03)	36.0	0.7%	$6.66 bill.	38.80 - 25.20	26.40

MEDIUM GRADE. THE COMPANY EXPECTS EARNINGS PER SHARE FOR THE SECOND HALF OF FISCAL 2003 TO BE BETWEEN $0.55 AND $0.60.

*7 YEAR PRICE SCORE 97.0   ***12 MONTH PRICE SCORE 101.2**
*NYSE COMPOSITE INDEX=100

INTERIM EARNINGS (Per Share):

Qtr.	Sept.	Dec.	Mar.	June
1996-97	0.18	0.23	0.10	0.09
1997-98	0.24	0.30	0.17	0.16
1998-99	0.28	0.38	0.20	0.18
1999-00	0.32	0.45	0.22	0.21
2000-01	0.37	0.50	0.24	0.06
2001-02	0.30	0.35	0.19	d0.13
2002-03	0.28	0.44	...	...

INTERIM DIVIDENDS (Per Share):

Amt.	Decl.	Ex.	Rec.	Pay.
0.05Q	8/23/01	9/17/01	9/14/01	10/02/01
0.05Q	10/31/01	12/12/01	12/14/01	1/03/02
0.05Q	2/26/02	3/13/02	3/15/02	4/02/02
0.05Q	5/14/02	6/12/02	6/14/02	7/02/02
0.20A	10/30/02	12/10/02	12/12/02	1/03/03

Indicated div.: $0.20

CAPITALIZATION (6/30/02):

	($000)	(%)
Long-Term Debt	403,900	21.6
Common & Surplus	1,461,900	78.4
Total	1,865,800	100.0

BUSINESS:

The Estee Lauder Companies, Inc. manufactures and markets prestige skin care, makeup, fragrance and hair care products. The Company's products are sold in over 130 countries and territories under the following brand names: ESTEE LAUDER, CLINIQUE, ARAMIS, PRESCRIPTIVES, ORIGINS, M.A.C., BOBBI BROWN, LA MER, jane, AVEDA, STILA, Jo MALONE and BUMBLE AND bUMBLE. The Company also owns licensees for fragrances and cosmetics sold under the TOMMY HILFIGER, DONNA KARAN and KATE SPADE brands. Each brand is distinctly positioned within the cosmetics market. Contributions to sales for 2002 were as follows: skin care, 35.9%; makeup, 37.7%; fragrance, 21.4%; hair care, 4.5%; other, 0.5%.

RECENT DEVELOPMENTS:

For the third quarter ended 12/31/02, net income increased 21.6% to $109.6 million from $90.1 million in the corresponding 2001 quarter. Net sales climbed 8.9% to $1.41 billion from $954.9 million the previous year, reflecting growth in all product categories and geographic regions due to new and recent product launches, as well as solid sales from EL's core products. Skin care sales increased 7.8% to $479.3 million from $444.8 million in 2001. Makeup sales advanced 11.4% to $476.8 million, fueled by double-digit growth from the Company's makeup artist brands, M-A-C, BOBBI BROWN and STILA. Fragrance sales rose 6.6% to $386.3 million, while hair care sales improved 3.1% to $60.2 million. Operating income was $170.0 million, up 18.5% from $143.5 million a year earlier.

PROSPECTS:

The Company expects its rate of growth to slow down in the the second half of fiscal 2003 as economic and political disruptions may translate into a softer retail market. Net sales are expected to grow between 5.0% and 6.0% on a constant currency basis versus the prior-year period. Sales gains are expected to be lead by the hair care and skin care categories, followed by makeup and fragrance. Meanwhile, the positive effect of changes in exchange rates in Europe and Asia may increase sales growth by about 2.5% to 3.5%. As a result, EL expects to achieve earnings per diluted share of between $0.55 and $0.60 for the second half of fiscal 2003.

ANNUAL FINANCIAL DATA:

FISCAL YEAR	TOT. REVS. ($mill.)	NET INC. ($mill.)	TOT. ASSETS ($mill.)	OPER. PROFIT %	NET PROFIT %	RET. ON EQUITY %	RET. ON ASSETS %	CURR. RATIO	EARN. PER SH.$	CASH FL. PER SH.$	TANG. BK. VAL.$	DIV. PER SH.$	PRICE RANGE	AVG. P/E RATIO	AVG. YIELD %
6/30/02	4,743.7	①② 212.5	3,416.5	7.2	4.5	14.5	6.2	2.0	①② 0.78	1.46	3.23	0.15	38.80 - 25.20	41.0	0.5
6/30/01	4,608.1	①② 307.4	3,218.8	10.8	6.7	22.7	9.6	2.0	①② 1.17	1.85	2.64	0.20	44.35 - 29.25	31.5	0.5
6/30/00	4,633.8	① 314.1	3,043.3	11.8	7.2	27.1	10.3	1.8	① 1.20	1.80	1.77	0.20	55.88 - 33.75	37.3	0.4
6/30/99	3,961.5	272.9	2,746.7	11.5	6.9	29.5	9.9	1.8	1.03	1.52	1.33	0.18	56.50 - 37.25	45.5	0.4
6/30/98	3,618.0	236.8	2,512.8	11.3	6.5	34.0	9.4	1.7	0.90	1.30	0.56	0.17	43.25 - 23.34	37.2	0.5
6/30/97	3,381.6	197.6	1,873.1	10.6	5.8	36.1	10.5	1.7	0.73	1.05	1.63	0.17	28.19 - 19.50	32.7	0.7
6/30/96	3,194.5	160.4	1,821.6	9.7	5.0	40.7	8.8	1.5	0.59	0.69	1.06	0.09	26.75 - 16.06	36.6	0.4
6/30/95	2,899.1	121.2	1,721.7	8.0	4.2	36.2	7.0	1.6	0.45	0.60	1.25	...	18.38 - 15.88	38.0	...
6/30/94	2,576.4	93.0	1,453.2	6.8	3.6	16.1	6.4	1.7	...	...	...	...	...	...	...
6/30/93	2,447.7	① 76.4	...	6.1	3.1	...	...	...	...	...	...	...	...	...	...

Statistics are as originally reported. Adj. for stock split, 2-for-1, 6/99 ① Bef. acctg. change chrg. $20.6 mill., 6/02; $2.2 mill., 6/01; $2.2 mill., 6/00; $13.5 mill., 6/93. ② Incl. after-tax non-recurr. chrgs. $76.9 mill., 6/02; $63.0 mill., 6/01

OFFICERS:
L. A. Lauder, Chmn.
F. H. Langhammer, Pres., C.E.O.
R. J. Bigler, Sr. V.P., C.F.O.
INVESTOR CONTACT: Dennis D'Andrea, V.P., Inv, Rel., (212) 572-4384
PRINCIPAL OFFICE: 767 Fifth Avenue, New York, NY 10153

TELEPHONE NUMBER: (212) 572-4200
FAX: (212) 572-3941
WEB: www.elcompanies.com
NO. OF EMPLOYEES: 19,900 (approx.)
SHAREHOLDERS: 4,087 (approx. Class A); 15 (Class B)
ANNUAL MEETING: In Nov.
INCORPORATED: DE, 1946

INSTITUTIONAL HOLDINGS:
No. of Institutions: 247
Shares Held: 92,496,675
% Held: 39.7

INDUSTRY: Toilet preparations (SIC: 2844)

TRANSFER AGENT(S): Mellon Investor Services, South Hackensack, NJ

ESTERLINE TECHNOLOGIES CORPORATION

EXCH.	SYM.	REC. PRICE	P/E RATIO	YLD.	MKT. CAP.	RANGE (52-WK.)	'02 Y/E PR.
NYSE	ESL	17.18 (2/28/03)	13.5	...	$357.1 mill.	24.00 - 15.40	17.67

MEDIUM GRADE. EARNINGS PER SHARE ARE ANTICIPATED TO RANGE FROM $1.50 TO $1.60 IN FISCAL 2003.

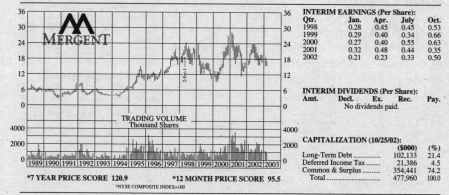

7 YEAR PRICE SCORE 120.9   **12 MONTH PRICE SCORE 95.5**
*NYSE COMPOSITE INDEX=100

INTERIM EARNINGS (Per Share):

Qtr.	Jan.	Apr.	July	Oct.
1998	0.28	0.45	0.45	0.53
1999	0.29	0.40	0.34	0.66
2000	0.27	0.40	0.55	0.63
2001	0.32	0.48	0.44	0.35
2002	0.21	0.23	0.33	0.50

INTERIM DIVIDENDS (Per Share):

Amt.	Decl.	Ex.	Rec.	Pay.
		No dividends paid.		

CAPITALIZATION (10/25/02):

	($000)	(%)
Long-Term Debt	102,133	21.4
Deferred Income Tax	21,386	4.5
Common & Surplus	354,441	74.2
Total	477,960	100.0

BUSINESS:

Esterline Technologies Corporation is a manufacturing company with operations primarily serving the aerospace and defense markets. The Avionics and Controls segment (39.6% of sales as of 10/25/02) focuses on technology interface systems for commercial and military aircraft and similar devices for land- and sea-based military vehicles, secure specialized medical equipment, communications systems and applications. The Sensors & Systems segment (24.2%) includes operations that produce high-precision temperature and pressure sensors, fluid and motion control components and other related systems principally for aerospace and defense customers. The Advanced Materials segment (36.2%) focuses on process related technologies including high-performance elastomer products used in a wide range of commercial aerospace and military applications, and combustible ordinance and electronic warfare countermeasure devices. On 7/31/02, the Company announced plans to sell its Automation business segment, which should be completed in July 2003.

RECENT DEVELOPMENTS:

For the quarter ended 1/3/03, ESL reported net income of $5.8 million compared with income from continuing operations of $6.6 million in the corresponding prior-year period. Results for 2001 excluded a loss from discontinued operations of $2.3 million, and an accounting charge of $7.6 million. Net sales increased 30.5% to $126.3 million. On a segmented basis, Advanced Materials jumped 44.6% to $51.6 million due to two acquisitions completed in the latter half of fiscal 2002. Avionics & Controls sales grew 23.9% to $48.3 million, primarily reflecting strong sales to military original equipment manufacturers. Sensors & Systems rose 19.6% to $26.2 million.

PROSPECTS:

On 1/6/03, the Company acquired the assets of BVR Aero Precision, a maker of precision gear assemblies and electronic data concentrators based in Rockford, Illinois. Separately, ESL acquired a small British trackball manufactuer, which will enable the Company to better serve overseas customers as well as open new European market opportunities. Looking ahead, earnings per share are anticipated to range from $1.50 to $1.60 in fiscal 2003.

ANNUAL FINANCIAL DATA:

FISCAL YEAR	TOT. REVS. ($mill.)	NET INC. ($mill.)	TOT. ASSETS ($mill.)	OPER. PROFIT %	NET PROFIT %	RET. ON EQUITY %	RET. ON ASSETS %	CURR. RATIO	EARN. PER SH. $	CASH FL. PER SH. $	TANG. BK. VAL. $	PRICE RANGE	AVG. P/E RATIO
10/25/02	434.8	⑤31.3	571.0	10.8	7.2	8.8	5.5	2.3	⑤1.49	2.19	6.49	24.00 - 15.55	13.3
10/26/01	491.2	④32.9	559.8	10.0	6.7	9.4	5.9	3.3	④1.64	1.64	10.37	28.38 - 11.25	12.1
10/27/00	491.0	②32.6	474.3	10.9	6.6	13.1	6.9	2.1	②1.85	3.08	6.41	26.88 - 9.25	9.8
10/31/99	461.0	②29.9	453.1	9.6	6.5	13.3	6.6	2.4	②1.69	2.87	6.88	24.13 - 10.25	10.2
10/31/98	453.9	30.1	387.2	10.8	6.6	15.3	7.8	1.6	1.70	2.73	5.60	24.50 - 15.50	11.8
10/31/97	391.0	25.3	289.8	10.0	6.5	14.6	8.7	1.9	1.44	2.50	7.86	21.75 - 11.94	11.7
10/31/96	352.8	21.4	276.6	9.8	6.1	14.7	7.7	1.7	1.31	2.37	5.95	14.00 - 9.38	9.0
10/31/95	351.9	17.4	225.7	8.8	4.9	20.6	7.7	1.3	1.27	2.47	3.77	15.19 - 6.25	8.5
10/31/94	294.0	7.6	216.0	5.0	2.6	11.1	3.5	1.1	0.58	1.82	1.81	7.38 - 3.19	9.2
10/31/93	285.2	①d25.6	205.7	...	...	...	...	1.1	①d1.95	d0.48	1.19	6.50 - 3.63	...

Statistics are as originally reported. Adj. for 2-for-1 split, 4/98. ① Incl. $40.6 mill. restr. chg. ② Incl. $8.0 mill. loss fr. sale of bus. ③ Incl. $2.6 mill. gain fr. sale of bus. ④ Bef. acctg. chrg. of $403,000; incl. unrealized loss of $786,000 on derivative financial instruments & a nonrecurr. gain of $4.6 mill. fr. an insurance settlement. ⑤ Bef. a loss of $25.0 mill. fr. disc. opers. & an acctg. chrg. of $7.6 mill.

OFFICERS: R. W. Cremin, Chmn., Pres., C.E.O. R. D. George, V.P., C.F.O., Treas., Sec. **INVESTOR CONTACT:** Brian D. Keogh, Investor Relations, (425) 453-9400 **PRINCIPAL OFFICE:** 10800 NE 8th Street, Bellevue, WA 98004	**TELEPHONE NUMBER:** (425) 453-9400 **FAX:** (425) 453-2916 **WEB:** www.esterline.com **NO. OF EMPLOYEES:** 4,200 (approx.) **SHAREHOLDERS:** 625 **ANNUAL MEETING:** In Mar. **INCORPORATED:** DE, Aug., 1967	**INSTITUTIONAL HOLDINGS:** No. of Institutions: 114 Shares Held: 17,095,735 % Held: 82.3 **INDUSTRY:** Special industry machinery, nec (SIC: 3559) **TRANSFER AGENT(S):** Mellon Investor Services, Ridgefield Park, NJ

ETHAN ALLEN INTERIORS, INC.

EXCH.	SYM.	REC. PRICE	P/E RATIO	YLD.	MKT. CAP.	RANGE (52-WK.)	'02 Y/E PR.
NYSE	ETH	29.07 (2/28/03)	13.0	0.8%	$1.15 bill.	42.20 - 27.15	34.37

UPPER MEDIUM GRADE. THE COMPANY HAS EXPANDED ITS OVERSEAS PRESENCE WITH THE OPENING OF ITS FIRST RETAIL STORE IN CHINA.

*7 YEAR PRICE SCORE 135.4   ***12 MONTH PRICE SCORE 99.5**

*NYSE COMPOSITE INDEX=100

INTERIM EARNINGS (Per Share):

Qtr.	Sept.	Dec.	Mar.	June
1998-99	0.38	0.50	0.50	0.54
1999-00	0.45	0.59	0.57	0.59
2000-01	0.52	0.58	0.50	0.39
2001-02	0.42	0.53	0.58	0.54
2002-04	0.52	0.60	...	...

INTERIM DIVIDENDS (Per Share):

Amt.	Decl.	Ex.	Rec.	Pay.
0.04Q	1/23/02	4/08/02	4/10/02	4/25/02
0.06Q	4/25/02	7/08/02	7/10/02	7/25/02
0.06Q	8/01/02	10/08/02	10/10/02	10/25/02
0.06Q	11/21/02	1/08/03	1/10/03	1/27/03
0.06Q	1/28/03	4/08/03	4/10/03	4/25/03

Indicated div.: $0.24

CAPITALIZATION (6/30/02):

	($000)	(%)
Long-Term Debt	9,214	1.7
Deferred Income Tax	37,158	6.7
Common & Surplus	511,189	91.7
Total	557,561	100.0

BUSINESS:

Ethan Allen Interiors, Inc., is a manufacturer and retailer of home furnishings, furniture products and home accessories. The Company manufactures and distributes three principal products lines: case goods, which consist primarily of bedroom and dining room furniture, wall units and tables; upholstered products, consisting of sofas, loveseats, chairs, and recliners; and home accessories and other, which include carpeting and area rugs, lighting, clocks, wall decor, bedding ensembles, draperies, decorative accessories and indoor/outdoor furnishings. As of 1/16/03, the Company operated a network of 314 retail stores in the U.S. and abroad, and had 17 manufacturing facilities, which included three sawmills located in the U.S.

RECENT DEVELOPMENTS:

For the quarter ended 12/31/02, net income increased 8.9% to $23.1 million compared with $21.2 million in the equivalent 2001 quarter. Net sales rose 3.1% to $229.7 million from $222.9 million a year earlier. The improvement in sales was primarily attributed to the continued growth of the Company's retail segment, which experienced a 19.2% increase to $139.3 million in net delivered sales, partially offset by a 4.0% decrease in comparable-store sales year over year. Gross profit grew 12.0% to $115.8 million versus $103.4 million the year before. Operating income jumped 12.0% to $37.2 million from $33.2 million in 2001.

PROSPECTS:

Looking ahead, ETH expects full-year 2003 earnings per share to grow between 12.0% and 15.0%, assuming no further deterioration in the economy or consumer confidence. However, the Company has lowered its sales outlook from its previously stated range of 8.0% to 10.0% due to the challenges presented by the current difficult economic environment. Separately, on 12/27/02, the Company announced that it has opened its first Ethan Allen store in China. The new store is part of an agreement with Markor Furniture International Ltd. to develop a chain of Ethan Allen retail stores in China. Located in the city of Tianjin, it is the 23rd ETH store outside the United States and is the first of three stores slated to open in China.

ANNUAL FINANCIAL DATA:

FISCAL YEAR	TOT. REVS. ($mill.)	NET INC. ($mill.)	TOT. ASSETS ($mill.)	OPER. PROFIT %	NET PROFIT %	RET. ON EQUITY %	RET. ON ASSETS %	CURR. RATIO	EARN. PER SH. $	CASH FL. PER SH. $	TANG. BK. VAL. $	DIV. PER SH. $	PRICE RANGE	AVG. P/E RATIO	AVG. YIELD %
6/30/02	892.3	②82.3	688.8	14.6	9.2	16.1	11.9	2.5	②2.06	2.54	11.48	0.20	43.45 - 27.15	17.1	0.6
6/30/01	904.1	79.7	619.1	13.9	8.8	12.9	2.7	2.7	1.98	2.48	10.45	0.16	42.30 - 26.51	17.4	0.5
6/30/00	856.2	90.6	543.6	17.1	10.6	23.2	16.7	2.2	2.20	2.61	8.52	0.16	33.75 - 20.50	12.3	0.6
6/30/99	762.2	81.3	480.6	17.4	10.7	23.2	16.9	2.4	1.92	2.31	7.31	0.13	37.75 - 24.67	16.3	0.4
6/30/98	679.3	71.9	433.1	17.6	10.6	22.9	16.6	2.6	1.63	1.99	6.23	0.09	44.42 - 15.75	18.5	0.3
6/30/97	571.8	48.7	427.8	15.0	8.5	18.4	11.4	3.1	1.11	1.49	4.94	0.07	28.58 - 12.33	18.4	0.3
6/30/96	509.8	28.1	396.0	10.9	5.5	12.8	7.1	2.8	0.65	1.04	3.87	0.03	13.00 - 6.54	15.1	0.3
6/30/95	476.1	①22.7	408.3	9.7	4.8	11.8	-5.6	3.3	①0.51	0.93	3.18	...	8.33 - 5.75	13.8	...
6/30/94	437.3	22.6	413.3	11.5	5.2	13.2	5.5	2.6	0.51	...	2.65	...	10.67 - 6.50	16.8	...
6/30/93	384.2	d2.3	396.2	9.2	...	...	...	2.6	0.37	...	1.47	...	10.50 - 5.42	21.3	...

Statistics are as originally reported. ① Incl. restruct. chrgs. of $1.6 mill. ② Incl. restruct. & impair. chrg. of $5.1 mill.

OFFICERS:
M. F. Kathwari, Chmn., Pres., C.E.O.
E. D. Teplitz, V.P., C.F.O.
G. Burdo, V.P., Treas.
INVESTOR CONTACT: Peg Lupton, (203) 743-8234
PRINCIPAL OFFICE: Ethan Allen Drive, P.O. Box 1966, Danbury, CT 06811

TELEPHONE NUMBER: (203) 743-8000
FAX: (203) 743-8298
WEB: www.ethanallen.com
NO. OF EMPLOYEES: 7,600 (approx.)
SHAREHOLDERS: 429 (approx.)
ANNUAL MEETING: In Nov.
INCORPORATED: DE, May, 1989

INSTITUTIONAL HOLDINGS:
No. of Institutions: 188
Shares Held: 32,792,041
% Held: 86.8
INDUSTRY: Wood household furniture (SIC: 2511)
TRANSFER AGENT(S): Computershare Investor Services, LLC, Chicago, IL

EXELON CORPORATION

EXCH.	SYM.	REC. PRICE	P/E RATIO	YLD.	MKT. CAP.	RANGE (52-WK.)	'02 Y/E PR.
NYSE	EXC	49.15 (2/28/03)	9.5	3.7%	$15.78 bill.	56.99 - 37.85	52.77

MEDIUM GRADE. FOR THE FULL-YEAR 2003, THE COMPANY EXPECTS EARNINGS PER SHARE IN THE RANGE OF $4.80 TO $5.00.

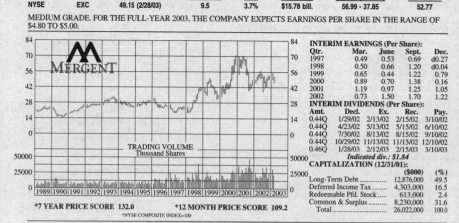

INTERIM EARNINGS (Per Share):

Qtr.	Mar.	June	Sept.	Dec.
1997	0.49	0.53	0.69	d0.27
1998	0.50	0.66	1.20	d0.04
1999	0.65	0.44	1.22	0.79
2000	0.89	0.70	1.38	0.16
2001	1.19	0.97	1.25	1.05
2002	0.73	0.97	1.70	1.22

INTERIM DIVIDENDS (Per Share):

Amt.	Decl.	Ex.	Rec.	Pay.
0.44Q	1/29/02	2/13/02	2/15/02	3/10/02
0.44Q	4/23/02	5/13/02	5/15/02	6/10/02
0.44Q	7/30/02	8/13/02	8/15/02	9/10/02
0.44Q	10/29/02	11/13/02	11/15/02	12/10/02
0.46Q	1/28/03	2/12/03	2/15/03	3/10/03

Indicated div.: $1.84

CAPITALIZATION (12/31/01):

	($000)	(%)
Long-Term Debt	12,876,000	49.5
Deferred Income Tax	4,303,000	16.5
Redeemable Pfd. Stock	613,000	2.4
Common & Surplus	8,230,000	31.6
Total	26,022,000	100.0

*7 YEAR PRICE SCORE 132.0   ***12 MONTH PRICE SCORE 109.2**

*NYSE COMPOSITE INDEX=100

BUSINESS:

Exelon Corporation (formerly PECO Energy Company) was formed from the acquisition by PECO Energy Company of Unicom Corporation on 10/20/00. Exelon is the holding company for ComEd, PECO Energy Company, Genco and other subsidiaries. As of 2/7/03, the Company distributed electricity to approximately five million customers in Illinois and Pennsylvania and gas to 444,000 customers in the Philadelphia area. EXC is the nation's largest operator of commercial nuclear power plants and the third largest in the world. The Company also has holdings in the competitive businesses of energy, infrastructure services and energy services. Revenues for 2002 were derived as follows: energy delivery, 54.0%; generation, 35.5%; and enterprises, 10.5%.

RECENT DEVELOPMENTS:

For the year ended 12/31/02, income rose 17.9% to $1.67 billion, before an accounting change charge of $230.0 million, compared with income of $1.42 billion, before an accounting change gain of $12.0 million, in 2001. Earnings benefited from higher sales, including increased weather-related kilowatt-hour deliveries, lower interest expense, higher interest income and the cessation of goodwill amortization. Results were partially offset by lower energy margins due to decreased wholesale power prices. Total operating revenues climbed 0.2% to $14.96 billion from $14.92 billion in the prior year. Operating income slipped 1.9% to $3.30 billion compared with $3.36 billion the year before.

PROSPECTS:

The Company's energy delivery segment should continue to benefit from increased sales to residential customers; however, the generation segment may continue to be negatively affected by higher average supply costs and increased operating and maintenance expenses. Moreover, the enterprises segment should benefit from increased revenues and margins in infrastructure services, mark-to-market adjustments and cost-savings efforts. Based on the current outlook, the Company anticipates earnings per share in the range of $4.80 to $5.00 for the full-year 2003.

ANNUAL FINANCIAL DATA:

FISCAL YEAR	TOT. REVS. ($mill.)	NET INC. ($mill.)	TOT. ASSETS ($mill.)	OPER. PROFIT %	NET PROFIT %	NET INC./ NET PROP. %	NET INC./ TOT. CAP. %	RET. ON EQUITY %	ACCUM. DEPR./ GROSS PROP. %	EARN. PER SH. $	TANG. BK. VAL. $	DIV. PER SH. $	DIV. PAYOUT %	PRICE RANGE	AVG. P/E RATIO	AVG. YIELD %
p12/31/02	14,955.0	⑦ 1,670.0								⑦ 5.15		1.76	34.2	56.99 - 37.85	9.2	3.7
⑥ 12/31/01	15,140.0	⑦ 1,416.0	34,821.0	22:2	9.4	10.3	5.4	17.2	44.5	⑦ 4.39	9.02	1.82	41.5	70.26 - 38.75	12.4	3.3
⑥ 12/31/00	7,499.0	⑤ 566.0	34,597.0	20.4	7.5	4.4	2.2	7.8	42.7	⑤ 2.77	11.90	0.91	32.8	71.00 - 33.00	18.8	1.7
12/31/99	5,436.8	④ 619.0	13,119.5	19.3	11.4	12.3	5.9	32.4	56.7	④ 3.08	9.12	1.00	32.5	50.50 - 30.75	13.2	2.5
12/31/98	5,210.5	③ 532.4	12,048.4	24.6	10.2	11.2	5.9	16.7	39.3	③ 2.32	13.61	1.00	43.1	42.19 - 18.88	13.2	3.3
12/31/97	4,617.9	② 336.6	12,356.6	21.8	7.3	7.2	3.5	11.8	38.2	② 1.44	12.25	1.80	125.0	26.38 - 18.75	15.7	8.0
12/31/96	4,283.7	517.2	15,260.6	21.1	12.1	4.7	4.0	10.7	32.3	2.24	20.88	1.75	78.3	32.50 - 23.00	12.4	6.3
12/31/95	4,186.2	609.7	14,960.6	24.0	14.6	5.6	4.8	12.9	30.4	2.64	20.40	1.65	62.5	30.25 - 24.25	10.3	6.1
12/31/94	4,040.6	① 426.7	15,092.8	20.5	10.6	3.9	3.3	9.3	28.5	① 1.76	19.41	1.54	87.8	30.00 - 23.63	15.2	5.8
12/31/93	3,988.1	590.6	15,032.3	26.0	14.8	5.4	4.4	12.6	27.2	2.45	19.25	1.43	58.4	33.50 - 25.50	12.0	4.8

Statistics are as originally reported. ① Incl. $253.9 mill. pre-tax chg. for workforce reduct. ② Incl. $214.0 mill. pre-tax non-recur. chg. & bef. $1.83 bill. extraord. chg. ③ Incl. $74.0 mill. spl. chg. rel. to sever. costs & excl. $19.0 mill. extraord. item. ④ Excl. $25.4 mill. net extraord. chg. for the early retire. of debt. ⑤ Incl. $276.0 mill. merger chg. and excl. $4.0 mill. net extraord. chg. & $24.0 mill. net cumul. acctg. credit ⑥ Results reflect the combined operations of PECO Energy Company & Unicom Corp. from 10/20/00. ⑦ Excl. net acctg. chrg. of $230.0 mill., 2002; credit of $12.0 mill., 2001.

OFFICERS:
J. W. Rowe, Chmn., C.E.O.
R. S. Shapard, Exec. V.P., C.F.O.
R. E. Mehrberg, Sr. V.P., Gen. Couns.

INVESTOR CONTACT: Linda Byus, V.P., Investor Relations, (312) 394-4321

PRINCIPAL OFFICE: 10 South Dearborn Street, 37th Floor, P.O. Box 805379, Chicago, IL 60680-5379

TELEPHONE NUMBER: (312) 394-7398
WEB: www.exeloncorp.com

NO. OF EMPLOYEES: 29,200 (approx.)

SHAREHOLDERS: 202,312 (approx.)

ANNUAL MEETING: In Apr.

INCORPORATED: PA, Oct., 1929

INSTITUTIONAL HOLDINGS:
No. of Institutions: 427
Shares Held: 220,719,312
% Held: 68.3

INDUSTRY: Electric and other services combined (SIC: 4931)

TRANSFER AGENT(S): First Chicago Trust Company of New York, Jersey City, NJ

EXTENDED STAY AMERICA, INC.

EXCH.	SYM.	REC. PRICE	P/E RATIO	YLD.	MKT. CAP.	RANGE (52-WK.)	'02 Y/E PR.
NYSE	ESA	10.80 (2/28/03)	18.0	...	$1.01 bill.	18.20 - 10.39	14.75

MEDIUM GRADE. THE COMPANY HAS DEFERRED THE COMMENCEMENT OF NEW CONSTRUCTION PROJECTS UNTIL CONDITIONS IN THE HOTEL INDUSTRY IMPROVE.

INTERIM EARNINGS (Per Share):

Qtr	Mar.	June	Sept.	Dec.
1998	0.05	0.10	0.06	0.08
1999	0.07	0.15	0.17	0.10
2000	0.12	0.22	0.23	0.15
2001	0.17	0.21	0.20	0.08
2002	0.12	0.18	0.22	0.08

INTERIM DIVIDENDS (Per Share):

Amt.	Decl.	Ex.	Rec.	Pay.
		No dividends paid.		

*7 YEAR PRICE SCORE 115.7 ***12 MONTH PRICE SCORE 92.3**

*NYSE COMPOSITE INDEX=100

CAPITALIZATION (12/31/01):

	($000)	(%)
Long-Term Debt	1,132,250	49.9
Deferred Income Tax	126,752	5.6
Common & Surplus	1,007,783	44.5
Total	2,266,785	100.0

BUSINESS:

Extended Stay America, Inc. develops, owns, and operates lodging facilities under three brands: StudioPLUS Deluxe Studios®, EXTENDED STAYAMERICA Efficiency Studios®, and Crossland Economy Studios®. Each brand is designed to appeal to different price points generally below $500.00 per week, and all three brands offer the same core components, a living/sleeping area, a fully-equipped kitchen or kitchenette and a bathroom. StudioPLUS serves the mid-price category and feature larger guest rooms, an exercise area, and a swimming pool. EXTENDED STAYAMERICA is designed to compete in the economy category, while Crossland Economy Studios® are targeted for the budget category. As of 2/3/03, ESA owned and operated 457 extended-stay lodging hotels in 42 states.

RECENT DEVELOPMENTS:

For the year ended 12/31/02, the Company reported net income of $57.1 million compared with income of $64.0 million, before an extraordinary charge of $5.9 million and an accounting change charge of $669,000, in the previous year. Results for 2001 included a headquarters relocation cost of $9.0 million. Revenue increased 1.2% to $547.9 million from $541.5 million a year earlier. Property operating expenses climbed 9.7% to $252.4 million, or 46.1% of revenue, from $230.2 million, or 42.5% of revenue in the previous year. For the fourth quarter, revenue per available room at comparable hotels declined 2.7% versus the year-earlier quarter.

PROSPECTS:

Due to continued weakness in the U.S. economy, declines in occupancy and the increasing likelihood of further reductions in travel as a result of geo-political events, the Company plans to defer the commencement of new construction projects. However, as of 12/31/02, ESA had 20 EXTENDED STAYAMERICA Efficiency Studios under construction. These hotels are scheduled to open throughout 2003 and the first quarter of 2004. Separately, for 2003, ESA anticipates revenue per available room at comparable hotels will decline between 2.0% and 4.0%. The Company expects earnings to range from $0.04 to $0.06 per share for the first quarter and $0.46 to $0.54 per share for full-year 2003.

ANNUAL FINANCIAL DATA:

FISCAL YEAR	TOT. REVS. ($mill.)	NET INC. ($mill.)	TOT. ASSETS ($mill.)	OPER. PROFIT %	NET PROFIT %	RET. ON EQUITY %	RET. ON ASSETS %	CURR. RATIO	EARN. PER SH.$	CASH FL. PER SH.$	TANG. BK. VAL.$	PRICE RANGE	AVG. P/E RATIO
p12/31/02	547.9	57.1							0.59	1.45	10.55	18.20 - 10.90	24.7
12/31/01	541.5	②64.0	2,371.9	33.7	11.8	6.4	2.7	0.7	②0.66	1.46	10.11	19.35 - 11.45	23.3
12/31/00	518.0	70.0	2,121.6	37.2	13.5	7.1	3.3	0.8	0.72	1.16	10.11	16.31 - 6.00	-15.5
12/31/99	417.7	①48.0	1,927.2	32.6	11.5	5.2	2.5	0.7	①0.50	1.16	9.37	12.69 - 6.94	19.6
12/31/98	283.1	①28.0	1,694.6	23.8	9.9	3.2	1.7	0.3	①0.29	0.73	8.83	15.25 - 6.00	36.6
12/31/97	130.8	①2.6	1,070.9	...	2.0	0.3	0.2	0.2	①0.03	0.25	8.64	20.75 - 10.63	521.2
12/31/96	15.7	3.4	522.6	...	21.8	0.7	0.7	7.9	0.06	0.10	7.12	23.00 - 10.00	274.5
12/31/95	0.9	d1.3	149.6	...	...	...	...	51.9	d0.05	d0.05	3.21	14.00 - 10.13	...

Statistics are as originally reported. Adj. for 2-for-1 stk. split, 7/96 ① Incls. one-time chrgs. of $1.1 mill., 1999; $12.0 mill., 1998; $19.9 mill., 1997 ② Bef. an after-tax extraord. chrg. of $5.9 mill. and an after-tax acctg. change chrg. of $669,000; incl. a pre-tax relocation chrg. of $9.0 mill.

OFFICERS:
H. W. Huizenga, Chmn.
G. D. Johnson Jr., C.E.O.
R. A. Brannon, Pres., C.O.O.
INVESTOR CONTACT: Gregory R. Moxley, V.P., C.F.O., (864) 573-1635
PRINCIPAL OFFICE: 101 North Pine Street, Spartanburg, SC 29302

TELEPHONE NUMBER: (864) 573-1600
FAX: (864) 573-1695
WEB: www.exstay.com
NO. OF EMPLOYEES: 2,525 full-time (approx.); 4,200 part-time (approx.)
SHAREHOLDERS: 301 (approx. record)
ANNUAL MEETING: In May
INCORPORATED: DE, Jan., 1995

INSTITUTIONAL HOLDINGS:
No. of Institutions: 123
Shares Held: 68,167,333
% Held: 72.7

INDUSTRY: Hotels and motels (SIC: 7011)

TRANSFER AGENT(S): Computershare Investor Services, Chicago, IL

EXXON MOBIL CORPORATION

EXCH.	SYM.	REC. PRICE	P/E RATIO	YLD.	MKT. CAP.	RANGE (52-WK.)	'02 Y/E PR.	DIV. ACH.
NYSE	XOM	34.02 (2/28/03)	21.0	2.7%	$227.93 bill.	44.58 - 29.75	34.94	20 yrs.

HIGH GRADE. THE COMPANY'S BOTTOM LINE HAS BEEN HURT BY DOWNSTREAM MARKET WEAKNESS.

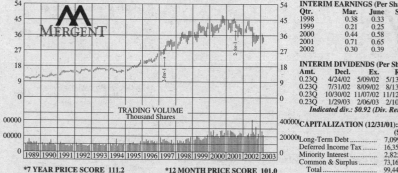

*7 YEAR PRICE SCORE 111.2　　　***12 MONTH PRICE SCORE 101.0**

*NYSE COMPOSITE INDEX=100

INTERIM EARNINGS (Per Share):

Qtr.	Mar.	June	Sept.	Dec.
1998	0.38	0.33	0.29	0.31
1999	0.21	0.25	0.31	0.33
2000	0.44	0.58	0.59	0.71
2001	0.71	0.65	0.46	0.39
2002	0.30	0.39	0.39	0.54

INTERIM DIVIDENDS (Per Share):

Amt.	Decl.	Ex.	Rec.	Pay.
0.23Q	4/24/02	5/09/02	5/13/02	6/10/02
0.23Q	7/31/02	8/09/02	8/13/02	9/10/02
0.23Q	10/30/02	11/07/02	11/12/02	12/10/02
0.23Q	1/29/03	2/06/03	2/10/03	3/10/03

Indicated div.: $0.92 (Div. Reinv. Plan)

CAPITALIZATION (12/31/01):

	($000)	(%)
Long-Term Debt	7,099,000	7.1
Deferred Income Tax	16,359,000	16.5
Minority Interest	2,825,000	2.8
Common & Surplus	73,161,000	73.6
Total	99,444,000	100.0

BUSINESS:

Exxon Mobil Corporation's principal business is energy, involving exploration for, and production of, crude oil and natural gas, manufacturing of petroleum products and transportation and sale of crude oil, natural gas and petroleum products. Exxon Mobil is a major manufacturer and marketer of basic petrochemicals, including olefins, aromatics, polyethylene and polypropylene plastics and a wide variety of specialty products. Exxon Mobil is engaged in exploration for, and mining and sale of coal, copper and other minerals. Exxon Mobil also has interests in electric power generation facilities. As of 12/31/01, XOM owned 69.6% of Imperial Oil Limited. In 2001, worldwide proved reserves were: crude oil and natural gas liquids, 11,491 million barrels; and natural gas, 55,946 billion cubic feet. On 11/30/99, Exxon Corp. acquired Mobil Corporation in a transaction valued at $81.00 billion.

RECENT DEVELOPMENTS:

For the twelve months ended 12/31/02, income from continuing operations was $11.01 billion versus income from continuing operations of $15.00 billion a year earlier. Results for 2002 and 2001 included merger charges of $275.0 million and $525.0 million, respectively. Results for 2001 also included a regulatory divestiture charge of $40.0 million. Total revenues fell 3.9% to $204.51 billion from $212.79 billion the previous year. Upstream earnings decreased 10.6% to $9.60 billion. Downstream earnings slid 69.2% to $1.30 billion, reflecting lower natural gas realizations and poor market conditions. Chemicals earnings decreased 5.9% to $830.0 million.

PROSPECTS:

XOM has indicated that plans for long-term capacity increases remain on track as reflected by the Company's higher capital spending. For instance, capital and exploration expenditures for the three and twelve months ended 12/31/02 increased 4.2% and 13.4% to $4.03 billion and $13.96 billion, respectively, compared with $3.86 billion and $12.31 billion the year before. XOM's outlook is further strengthened by its ability to successfully achieve cost savings across the Company's business lines.

ANNUAL FINANCIAL DATA:

FISCAL YEAR	TOT. REVS. ($mill.)	NET INC. ($mill.)	TOT. ASSETS ($mill.)	OPER. PROFIT %	NET PROFIT %	RET. ON EQUITY %	RET. ON ASSETS %	CURR. RATIO	EARN. PER SH. $	CASH FL. PER SH. $	TANG. BK. VAL. $	DIV. PER SH. $	PRICE RANGE	AVG. P/E RATIO	AVG. YIELD
p12/31/02	204,506.0	⑦ 11,011.0							⑦ 1.61			0.92	44.58 - 29.75	23.1	2.5
12/31/01	213,488.0	⑥ 15,105.0	143,174.0	11.7	7.1	20.6	10.6	1.2	⑥ 2.18	3.32	10.74	0.91	45.84 - 35.01	18.5	2.3
⑤ 12/31/00	232,748.0	④ 15,990.0	149,000.0	12.1	6.9	22.6	10.7	1.1	④ 2.28	3.43	10.21	0.88	47.72 - 34.94	18.2	2.1
12/31/99	185,527.0	③ 7,910.0	144,521.0	6.5	4.3	12.5	5.5	0.8	③ 1.13	2.35	9.12	0.83	43.63 - 32.16	33.7	2.2
12/31/98	117,772.0	① 6,440.0	92,630.0	7.9	5.5	14.7	7.0	0.9	① 1.31	2.43	8.99	0.82	38.66 - 28.31	25.7	2.4
12/31/97	137,242.0	② 8,460.0	96,064.0	9.9	6.2	19.4	8.8	1.1	② 1.69	2.78	8.85	0.81	33.63 - 24.13	17.1	2.8
12/31/96	134,249.0	② 7,510.0	95,527.0	9.5	5.6	17.2	7.9	1.0	② 1.51	2.58	8.70	0.78	25.31 - 19.41	14.9	3.5
12/31/95	123,920.0	6,470.0	91,296.0	9.1	5.2	16.0	7.1	0.9	1.30	2.39	8.05	0.75	21.50 - 15.03	14.1	4.1
12/31/94	113,904.0	5,100.0	87,862.0	7.7	4.5	13.6	5.8	0.8	1.02	2.04	7.42	0.73	16.84 - 14.03	15.2	4.7
12/31/93	111,211.0	5,280.0	84,145.0	8.1	4.7	15.2	6.3	0.8	1.05	2.05	6.87	0.72	17.25 - 14.44	15.0	4.5

Statistics are as originally reported. Adj. for stk. splits: 2-for-1, 4/97 & 7/01. ① Bef. acctg. chrg. of $70.0 mill. ② Incl. non-recurr. credit 12/31/97: $305.0 mill.; credit 12/31/96: $90.0 mill. ③ Incl. non-recurr. chrg. of $625.0 mill. ④ Incl. merger rel. exp. of $1.41 bill.; bef. extraord. gain fr. required asset divest. of $1.73 bill. ($0.50/sh.) ⑤ Incl. results of Mobil Corporation. ⑥ Incl. merger rel. exp. of $748.0 mill.; bef. extraord. gain of $215.0 mill. ⑦ Incl. merger rel. exp. of $275.0 mill.; bef. disc. ops. of $449.0 mill.

OFFICERS:
L. R. Raymond, Chmn., C.E.O.
H. J. Longwell, Exec. V.P.
E. G. Galante, Exec. V.P.

INVESTOR CONTACT: Media Relations,
(972) 444-1109

PRINCIPAL OFFICE: 5959 Las Colinas Blvd.,
Irving, TX 75039-2298

TELEPHONE NUMBER: (972) 444-1000
FAX: (972) 444-1348
WEB: www.exxonmobil.com

NO. OF EMPLOYEES: 97,900 (approx.)

SHAREHOLDERS: 697,972

ANNUAL MEETING: In May

INCORPORATED: NJ, Aug., 1882

INSTITUTIONAL HOLDINGS:
No. of Institutions: 1,282
Shares Held: 3,336,600,000
% Held: 49.8

INDUSTRY: Petroleum refining (SIC: 2911)

TRANSFER AGENT(S): ExxonMobil Shareholder Services c/o EquiServe Trust Company, NA, Boston, MA

FAIRCHILD SEMICONDUCTOR INTERNATIONAL, INC.

EXCH.	SYM.	REC. PRICE	P/E RATIO	YLD.	MKT. CAP.	RANGE (52-WK.)	'02 Y/E PR.
NYSE	FCS	12.16 (2/28/03)	...	...	$1.22 bill.	32.03 - 6.85	10.71

LOWER MEDIUM GRADE. A PRODUCTION RAMP AT FCS' NEW FACILITY IN CHINA SHOULD IMPROVE TECHNOLOGY, LOWER COSTS AND BOLSTER EFFICIENCY.

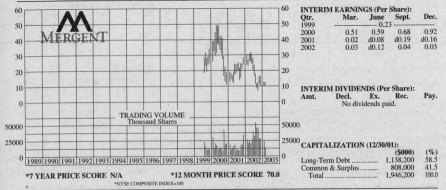

*7 YEAR PRICE SCORE N/A   ***12 MONTH PRICE SCORE 70.0**

NYSE COMPOSITE INDEX=100

INTERIM EARNINGS (Per Share):

Qtr.	Mar.	June	Sept.	Dec.
1999	-------------	0.23	-------------	
2000	0.51	0.59	0.68	0.92
2001	0.02	d0.08	d0.19	d0.16
2002	0.03	d0.12	0.04	0.03

INTERIM DIVIDENDS (Per Share):

Amt.	Decl.	Ex.	Rec.	Pay.
		No dividends paid.		

CAPITALIZATION (12/30/01):

	($000)	(%)
Long-Term Debt	1,138,200	58.5
Common & Surplus	808,000	41.5
Total	1,946,200	100.0

BUSINESS:

Fairchild Semiconductor International, Inc. is a global supplier of high-performance semiconductors used in the communications, computing, consumer, industrial, and automotive end markets. The discrete products group includes individual diodes or transistors that perform basic signal amplification and switching functions in electronic circuits. The analog and mixed signal products group consists of high-performance analog and mixed signal integrated circuits. The interface and logic products group consists of high-performance interface and logic devices utilizing three wafer fabrication processes. Other products include non-volatile memory and optoelectronic products. FCS also provides contract manufacturing services.

RECENT DEVELOPMENTS:

For the year ended 12/29/02, the Company reported a net loss of $2.5 million compared with a net loss of $41.7 million in the previous year. Results for 2002 and 2001 included amortization of acquisition-related intangibles of $37.8 million and $53.1 million, and restructuring and impairment charges of $12.2 million and $21.4 million, respectively. Results for 2002 and 2001 also included purchased in-process research and development charges of $1.7 million and $13.8 million, respectively. Total revenues were flat versus the prior year at $1.41 billion. Net sales increased 1.9% to $1.36 billion, while contract manufacturing revenue fell 31.1% to $47.4 million. Meanwhile, operating income more than doubled to $71.2 million from $28.5 million a year earlier.

PROSPECTS:

During the first quarter of 2003, the Company plans to initiate a project that should double its advanced submicron PowerTrench® process production capability in its 8-inch wafer fabrication facility in Mountaintop, Pennsylvania. This technology expansion should allow FCS to service a more profitable segment of the power MOSFET market from a more efficient facility and allow for the closure of its older 6-inch Mountaintop facility. In addition, FCS is planning a production ramp in its new Suzhou, China assembly and test facility. These actions are expected to bolster efficiency, lower costs, and improve technical capabilities across FCS' manufacturing base.

ANNUAL FINANCIAL DATA:

FISCAL YEAR	TOT. REVS. ($mill.)	NET INC. ($mill.)	TOT. ASSETS ($mill.)	OPER. PROFIT %	NET PROFIT %	RET. ON EQUITY %	RET. ON ASSETS %	CURR. RATIO	EARN. PER SH.$	CASH FL. PER SH.$	TANG. BK. VAL.$	PRICE RANGE	AVG. P/E RATIO
p12/29/02	1,411.9	⑤d2.5		2.0	...	...	...	4.4	⑤d0.02			32.03 - 6.85	...
12/30/01	1,407.7	④d41.7	2,149.2		...	...	...	3.0	④d0.42	1.38	3.28	28.20 - 11.86	...
12/31/00	1,783.2	②273.1	1,837.5	18.4	15.3	32.6	14.9	2.2	②2.69	4.18	5.43	49.50 - 11.19	11.3
③12/26/99	786.2	21.3	1,137.6	10.5	2.7	10.0	1.9	2.2	0.23	1.24	...	34.13 - 18.50	114.4
5/30/99	735.1	②d114.1	1,095.7	...	...	...	...	2.0	②d1.97	d0.17	...	...	...
5/31/98	789.2	①22.1	635.7	11.1	2.8	...	3.5	1.5	①0.20	1.64	...	...	...
5/25/97	692.0	15.5	555.0	4.6	2.2	...	2.8	...	...	...	...	...	...

Statistics are as originally reported. ① Bef. acctg. chrg. $1.5 mill.; incl. nonrecurr. chrg. $15.5 mill. ② Incl. nonrecurr. chrg. $3.4 mill., 2000; $55.3 mill., 5/99. ③ Results for 7 months only to reflect change in fiscal year. ④ Incls. a restr. and impair. chrg. $21.4 mill. and purch. in-process R&D $13.8 mill. ⑤ Incl. restr. chrg. $12.2 mill. and purch. in-process R&D chrg. $1.7 mill.

OFFICERS:
K. P. Pond, Chmn., Pres., C.E.O.
J. R. Martin, Exec. V.P., C.F.O.

INVESTOR CONTACT: Pete Groth, Investor Relations, (207) 775-8660

PRINCIPAL OFFICE: 82 Running Hill Road, South Portland, ME 04106

TELEPHONE NUMBER: (207) 775-8100
FAX: (207) 761-6139
WEB: www.fairchildsemi.com
NO. OF EMPLOYEES: 9,798 (avg.)
SHAREHOLDERS: 348 (approx. class A)
ANNUAL MEETING: In May
INCORPORATED: ME, March, 1997

INSTITUTIONAL HOLDINGS:
No. of Institutions: 200
Shares Held: 95,816,521
% Held: 81.9
INDUSTRY: Semiconductors and related devices (SIC: 3674)
TRANSFER AGENT(S): EquiServe Trust Company, Providence, RI

FAMILY DOLLAR STORES, INC.

EXCH.	SYM.	REC. PRICE	P/E RATIO	YLD.	MKT. CAP.	RANGE (52-WK.)	'02 Y/E PR.	DIV. ACH.
NYSE	FDO	28.22 (2/28/03)	21.9	1.1%	$4.89 bill.	37.25 - 23.75	31.21	26 yrs.

INVESTMENT GRADE. THE COMPANY CONTINUES TO AGGRESSIVELY EXPAND ITS STORE BASE.

*7 YEAR PRICE SCORE 170.5   ***12 MONTH PRICE SCORE 106.0**

*NYSE COMPOSITE INDEX=100

INTERIM EARNINGS (Per Share):

Qtr.	Nov.	Feb.	May	Aug.
1996-97	0.11	0.12	0.14	0.09
1997-98	0.14	0.16	0.18	0.12
1998-99	0.17	0.24	0.24	0.16
1999-00	0.21	0.32	0.29	0.18
2000-01	0.24	0.35	0.31	0.20
2001-02	0.29	0.37	0.35	0.24
2002-03	0.33	...	...	...

INTERIM DIVIDENDS (Per Share):

Amt.	Decl.	Ex.	Rec.	Pay.
0.065Q	1/17/02	3/13/02	3/15/02	4/15/02
0.065Q	5/16/02	6/12/02	6/14/02	7/15/02
0.065Q	8/20/02	9/12/02	9/16/02	10/15/02
0.065Q	11/07/02	12/12/02	12/16/02	1/15/03
0.075Q	1/16/03	3/12/03	3/14/03	4/15/03

Indicated div.: $0.30

CAPITALIZATION (8/31/02):

	($000)	(%)
Deferred Income Tax	68,891	5.6
Common & Surplus	1,154,948	94.4
Total	1,223,839	100.0

BUSINESS:

Family Dollar Stores, Inc. operated 4,690 discount stores as of 1/4/03. The stores are located in a contiguous 41-state area ranging as far northwest as South Dakota, northeast to Maine, southeast to Florida and southwest to Arizona. The stores' relatively small size, generally 7,500 to 9,500 square feet, gives FDO flexibility to open them in various markets from small rural towns to large urban centers. The stores are located in strip shopping centers or as freestanding buildings convenient to FDO's low- and middle-income customer base. The merchandise, which is generally priced under $10.00, is sold in a no-frills, low overhead, self-service environment.

RECENT DEVELOPMENTS:

For the three months ended 11/30/02, net income climbed 14.5% to $57.5 million from $50.2 million in the corresponding prior-year period. Net sales totaled $1.11 billion, up 13.5% compared with $977.1 million the previous year. Results for fiscal 2002 benefited from a 3.0% increase in existing-store sales and sales from new stores opened as part of the Company's store expansion program. During the quarter, the Company opened 91 stores, closed 29 stores, expanded or relocated 30 stores and remodeled 20 stores. Gross margin advanced 13.9% to $380.8 million from $334.4 million the year before. In the first quarter, FDO's customer count, as measured by the number of register transactions in existing stores, rose about 0.2%, while the average transaction grew approximately 2.6% to $8.70.

PROSPECTS:

The Company is targeting full fiscal-year 2003 earnings per share growth of 14.0% to 16.0%. Meanwhile, FDO is projecting existing-store sales growth of between 3.0% and 5.0% during the second half of fiscal 2003. Separately, the Company is continuing to aggressively expand its store base. During the current fiscal year, FDO plans to open approximately 575 new stores, close about 50 existing stores, expand or relocate 150 stores, remodel 50 stores, and open a seventh distribution center.

ANNUAL FINANCIAL DATA:

FISCAL YEAR	TOT. REVS. (Smill.)	NET INC. (Smill.)	TOT. ASSETS (Smill.)	OPER. PROFIT %	NET PROFIT %	RET. ON EQUITY %	RET. ON ASSETS %	CURR. RATIO	EARN. PER SH.$	CASH FL. PER SH.$	TANG. BK. VAL.$	DIV. PER SH.$	PRICE RANGE	AVG. P/E RATIO	AVG. YIELD %
8/31/02	4,162.7	216.9	1,754.6	8.2	5.2	18.8	12.4	2.0	1.25	1.69	6.66	0.26	37.25 - 23.75	24.4	0.8
9/01/01	3,665.4	189.5	1,399.7	8.1	5.2	19.8	13.5	2.1	1.10	1.49	5.57	0.23	31.35 - 18.38	22.6	0.9
8/26/00	3,132.6	172.0	1,243.7	8.6	5.5	21.6	13.8	1.8	1.00	1.31	4.66	0.21	24.50 - 14.25	19.4	1.1
8/28/99	2,751.2	140.1	1,095.3	8.1	5.1	20.3	12.8	1.9	0.81	1.07	4.00	0.20	26.75 - 14.00	25.2	1.0
8/29/98	2,361.9	103.3	942.2	7.0	4.4	17.9	11.0	1.9	0.60	0.80	3.36	0.17	22.44 - 11.50	28.3	1.0
8/31/97	1,995.0	74.7	780.3	6.1	3.7	14.9	9.6	2.1	0.44	0.61	2.75	0.16	15.06 - 6.25	24.5	1.5
8/31/96	1,714.6	60.6	696.8	5.8	3.5	13.6	8.7	2.2	0.35	0.50	2.61	0.14	7.44 - 3.67	15.2	2.7
8/31/95	1,546.9	58.1	636.2	6.1	3.8	14.3	9.1	2.3	0.34	0.47	2.40	0.13	6.58 - 3.63	14.9	2.5
8/31/94	1,428.4	☐ 62.0	592.8	7.0	4.3	16.7	10.5	2.1	☐ 0.37	0.48	2.06	0.11	6.13 - 3.33	12.9	2.3
8/31/93	1,297.4	64.4	537.4	7.9	5.0	19.9	12.0	2.0	0.38	0.48	1.91	0.10	7.88 - 5.04	16.9	1.5

Statistics are as originally reported. Adj. for 2-for-1 stk. split, 4/98 & 3-for-2 stk. split, 7/97. ☐ Bef. $1.1 mil ($0.01/sh) cr. for acctg. adj.

OFFICERS:
L. Levine, Chmn.
R. J. Kelly, Vice-Chmn., C.F.O.
H. R. Levine, Pres., C.E.O.
R. D. Alexander, Exec. V.P., C.O.O.

INVESTOR CONTACT: George R. Mahoney, Jr., (704) 814-3252

PRINCIPAL OFFICE: 10401 Old Monroe Road, P.O. Box 1017, Charlotte, NC 28101

TELEPHONE NUMBER: (704) 847-6961
FAX: (704) 847-5534
WEB: www.familydollar.com

NO. OF EMPLOYEES: 22,800 full-time (approx.); 16,600 part-time (approx.)

SHAREHOLDERS: 1,875 (approx.)

ANNUAL MEETING: In Nov.

INCORPORATED: DE, Nov., 1969

INSTITUTIONAL HOLDINGS:
No. of Institutions: 291
Shares Held: 141,565,091
% Held: 81.8

INDUSTRY: Variety stores (SIC: 5331)

TRANSFER AGENT(S): Mellon Investors Services, Ridgefield Park, NJ

FANNIE MAE

EXCH.	SYM.	REC. PRICE	P/E RATIO	YLD.	MKT. CAP.	RANGE (52-WK.)	'02 Y/E PR.	DIV. ACH.
NYSE	FNM	64.10 (2/28/03)	13.7	2.4%	$63.91 bill.	84.10 - 58.85	64.33	17 yrs.

HIGH GRADE. THE COMPANY EXPECTS GROWTH IN OPERATING EARNINGS PER SHARE IN THE RANGE OF 12.0% TO 13.0% FOR 2003.

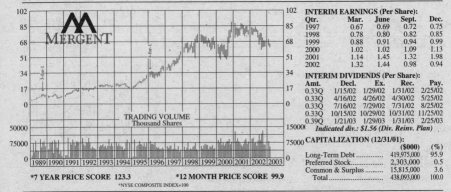

INTERIM EARNINGS (Per Share):

Qtr.	Mar.	June	Sept.	Dec.
1997	0.67	0.69	0.72	0.75
1998	0.78	0.80	0.82	0.85
1999	0.88	0.91	0.94	0.99
2000	1.02	1.02	1.09	1.13
2001	1.14	1.45	1.32	1.98
2002	1.32	1.44	0.98	0.94

INTERIM DIVIDENDS (Per Share):

Amt.	Decl.	Ex.	Rec.	Pay.
0.33Q	1/15/02	1/29/02	1/31/02	2/25/02
0.33Q	4/16/02	4/26/02	4/30/02	5/25/02
0.33Q	7/16/02	7/29/02	7/31/02	8/25/02
0.33Q	10/15/02	10/29/02	10/31/02	11/25/02
0.39Q	1/21/03	1/29/03	1/31/03	2/25/03

Indicated div.: $1.56 (Div. Reinv. Plan)

CAPITALIZATION (12/31/01):

	($000)	(%)
Long-Term Debt	419,975,000	95.9
Preferred Stock	2,303,000	0.5
Common & Surplus	15,815,000	3.6
Total	438,093,000	100.0

*7 YEAR PRICE SCORE 123.3   ***12 MONTH PRICE SCORE 99.9**

*NYSE COMPOSITE INDEX=100

BUSINESS:

Fannie Mae (formerly Federal National Mortgage Association) is the largest investor in home mortgage loans in the U.S. The Company was established in 1938 as a U.S. government agency to provide supplemental liquidity to the mortgage market and was transformed into a stockholder-owned and privately-managed company by legislation enacted in 1968. FNM provides funds to the mortgage market by purchasing mortgage loans from lenders, thereby replenishing their funds for additional lending. FNM also issues mortgage-backed securities (MBS), primarily in exchange for pools of mortgage loans from lenders, which also increases the liquidity of residential mortgage loans. FNM receives guaranty fees for its guaranty of timely payment of principal of and interest on MBS certificates.

RECENT DEVELOPMENTS:

For the year ended 12/31/02, net income was $4.62 billion versus income of $5.73 billion, before an accounting gain of $167.9 million, in the previous year. Earnings were hampered by a sharp decline in the value of the derivatives FNM uses to hedge its exposure to interest rate risk. Results for 2002 and 2001 included purchased options expenses of $4.54 billion and $37.4 million, respectively.

Results for 2001 included a special contribution charge of $300.0 million. Net interest income climbed 30.6% to $10.57 billion from $8.09 billion in 2001. Guaranty fee income increased 22.5% to $1.82 billion, while fee and other income surged 53.8% to $232.2 million. Comparisons were made with restated prior-year figures.

PROSPECTS:

For 2003, FNM expects operating earnings per share in the range of 12.0% to 13.0%. The growth in operating earnings may be hampered by a decline in the net interest margin and reduced amounts of losses on the repurchase of debt. Meanwhile, FNM anticipates continued healthy growth in the overall mortgage market, and noted that if purchases of fixed-rate mortgages by banks and fixed-income investors eased from 2002 levels, FNM's 2003 portfolio growth will likely be in the mid-teens. Moreover, 2003 credit losses will probably be higher than in 2003.

ANNUAL FINANCIAL DATA:

FISCAL YEAR	NET INT. INC. ($mill.)	NON-INT. INC. ($mill.)	NET INC. ($mill.)	TOT. LOANS ($mill.)	TOT. ASSETS ($mill.)	RET. ON EQUITY %	RET. ON ASSETS %	EQUITY/ ASSETS %	EARN. SH. $	TANG. BK. VAL. $	DIV. PER SH. $	PRICE RANGE	AVG. P/E RATIO
p12/31/02	10,566.1		4,618.8						4.53		1.32	84.10 - 58.85	15.8
12/31/01	8,090.0	1,633.0	①②6,067.0	707,476.0	799,791.0	33.5	0.8	2.3	①②5.89	15.86	1.20	87.94 - 72.08	13.6
12/31/00	5,674.0	1,307.0	①4,416.0	610,122.0	675,072.0	21.2	0.7	3.1	①4.26	18.58	1.12	89.38 - 47.88	16.1
12/31/99	4,894.0	1,473.0	①3,921.0	523,941.0	575,167.0	22.2	0.7	3.1	①3.73	16.02	1.08	75.88 - 58.56	18.0
12/31/98	4,110.0	1,504.0	①3,444.0	414,515.0	485,014.0	22.3	0.7	3.2	①3.26	13.95	0.96	76.19 - 49.56	19.3
12/31/97	3,949.0	1,399.0	①3,068.0	316,678.0	391,673.0	22.2	0.8	3.5	①2.84	12.34	0.84	57.31 - 36.13	16.4
12/31/96	3,592.0	1,282.0	①2,754.0	286,259.0	351,041.0	21.6	0.8	3.6	①2.50	11.10	0.76	41.63 - 27.50	13.8
12/31/95	3,047.0	1,179.0	①2,155.0	252,588.0	316,550.0	19.7	0.5	3.5	①1.96	10.04	0.68	31.50 - 17.19	12.4
12/31/94	2,823.0	1,226.0	2,141.0	220,525.0	272,508.0	22.4	0.8	3.5	1.95	8.75	0.60	22.59 - 17.03	10.2
12/31/93	2,533.0	1,220.0	2,042.0	189,892.0	216,979.0	25.4	0.9	3.7	1.86	7.40	0.46	21.53 - 18.22	10.7

Statistics are as originally reported. Adj. for stk. split: 4-for-1, 1/96. ① Bef. extraord. chrg. $340.5 mill.; 12/01; gain $31.5 mill. 12/00; chrg., $9.2 mill.,12/99; $10.7 mill., 12/98; $12.8 mill.,12/97; $29.0 mill., 12/96; $11.4 mill., 12/95; $9.0 mill., 12/94; $169.3 mill., 12/93. ② Bef. acctg. gain of $167.9 mill.

OFFICERS:
F. D. Raines, Chmn., C.E.O.
D. H. Mudd, Vice-Chmn., C.O.O.
J. T. Howard, Exec. V.P., C.F.O.
L. K. Knight, Sr. V.P., Treas.
INVESTOR CONTACT: Janis Smith, Inv. Rel.
(202) 752-6673
PRINCIPAL OFFICE: 3900 Wisconsin Ave.,
N.W., Washington, DC 20016-2892

TELEPHONE NUMBER: (202) 752-7000
FAX: (202) 752-4934
WEB: www.fanniemae.com
NO. OF EMPLOYEES: 4,500 (approx.)
SHAREHOLDERS: 26,000 (approx.)
ANNUAL MEETING: In May
INCORPORATED: 1938

INSTITUTIONAL HOLDINGS:
No. of Institutions: 1,020
Shares Held: 811,217,054
% Held: 82.0

INDUSTRY: Federal & fed.-sponsored credit
(SIC: 6111)

TRANSFER AGENT(S): First Chicago Trust
Company of New York, Jersey City, NJ

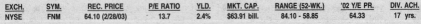

FEDERAL REALTY INVESTMENT TRUST

EXCH.	SYM.	REC. PRICE	P/E RATIO	YLD.	MKT. CAP.	RANGE (52-WK.)	'02 Y/E PR.	DIV. ACH.
NYSE	FRT	29.31 (2/28/03)	47.3	6.6%	$1.17 bill.	29.60 - 21.83	28.12	35 yrs.

MEDIUM GRADE. THE COMPANY IS BENEFITING FROM STRONG DEMAND FOR ITS RETAIL PROPERTIES.

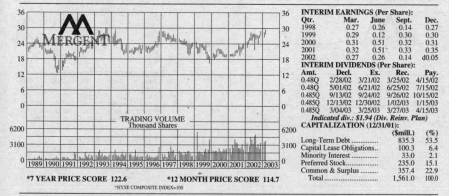

TRADING VOLUME Thousand Shares

*7 YEAR PRICE SCORE 122.6   *12 MONTH PRICE SCORE 114.7

*NYSE COMPOSITE INDEX=100

INTERIM EARNINGS (Per Share):

Qtr.	Mar.	June	Sept.	Dec.
1998	0.27	0.26	0.14	0.27
1999	0.29	0.12	0.30	0.30
2000	0.31	0.51	0.32	0.31
2001	0.32	0.51ˇ	0.33	0.35
2002	0.27	0.26	0.14	d0.05

INTERIM DIVIDENDS (Per Share):

Amt.	Decl.	Ex.	Rec.	Pay.
0.48Q	2/28/02	3/21/02	3/25/02	4/15/02
0.48Q	5/01/02	6/21/02	6/25/02	7/15/02
0.485Q	9/13/02	9/24/02	9/26/02	10/15/02
0.485Q	12/13/02	12/30/02	1/02/03	1/15/03
0.485Q	3/04/03	3/25/03	3/27/03	4/15/03

Indicated div.: $1.94 (Div. Reinv. Plan)

CAPITALIZATION (12/31/01):

	($mill.)	(%)
Long-Term Debt	835.3	53.5
Capital Lease Obligations	100.3	6.4
Minority Interest	33.0	2.1
Preferred Stock	235.0	15.1
Common & Surplus	357.4	22.9
Total	1,561.0	100.0

BUSINESS:

Federal Realty Investment Trust is an equity real estate investment trust specializing in the ownership, management, development and redevelopment of shopping centers and street retail properties. As of 2/13/03, the Company's portfolio contained over 15.0 million square feet located in major metropolitan markets across the United States. The operating portfolio is currently 95.0% occupied by over 2,000 national, regional and local retailers, with no single tenant accounting for more than 2.5% of rental revenue.

RECENT DEVELOPMENTS:

For the year ended 12/31/02, income from continuing operations was $44.6 million compared with income of $56.1 million the year before. Results for 2002 included restructuring charges of $22.3 million. Also, results for 2002 and 2001 excluded income from discontinued operations of $1.3 million and $3.5 million, and a gain on the sale of real estate net loss on abandoned developments held for sale of $9.5 million and $9.2 million, respectively. Total revenues increased 8.0% to $318.8 million from $295.1 million the previous year, primarily due to higher rental and other property income. Revenues from rental income improved 8.6% to $298.1 million from $274.6 million a year earlier. Funds from operations was $90.5 million versus $110.4 million the year before.

PROSPECTS:

Despite the difficult economic climate, demand for the Company's retail space remains strong. For instance, FRT signed leases for more than 310,000 square feet of retail space during the fourth quarter. Also, rent increases on comparable space leased during 2002 averaged 13.0% on a cash basis. Moreover, overall occupancy, excluding the Company's Santana Row investment, remained strong at 95.5% at year-end versus 95.6% on 12/31/01. Separately, FRT announced that it expects limited impact from Kmart Corporation's plan to close three of the five Kmart stores at its properties. FMT noted that new tenants at these sites should improve traffic, sales and rents for those properties.

ANNUAL FINANCIAL DATA:

FISCAL YEAR	TOT. INC. ($mill.)	NET INC. ($mill.)	TOT. ASSETS ($mill.)	NET INC. + DEPR./ ASSETS %	RET. ON EQUITY %	RET. ON ASSETS %	EARN. PER SH.$	TANG. BK. VAL.$	DIV. PER SH.$	DIV. PAYOUT %	PRICE RANGE	AVG. P/E RATIO	AVG. YIELD %
p12/31/02	318.8	① 44.6	1,999.4				① 0.60		1.93	321.7	28.92 - 21.83	42.3	7.6
12/31/01	300.5	68.8	1,838.0	7.0	11.6	3.7	1.52	8.92	1.89	124.3	23.96 - 18.97	14.1	8.8
12/31/00	279.3	60.5	1,621.1	7.0	12.9	3.7	1.35	9.31	1.82	134.8	22.31 - 17.75	14.8	9.1
12/31/99	264.7	48.4	1,534.0	6.4	9.7	3.2	1.02	10.00	1.77	173.5	24.88 - 16.38	20.2	6.4
12/31/98	238.5	45.0	1,484.3	6.1	8.5	3.0	0.94	10.73	1.73	184.0	25.94 - 19.38	24.1	7.6
12/31/97	204.3	46.5	1,316.6	6.7	8.4	3.5	1.14	11.59	1.69	148.2	28.75 - 24.50	23.4	6.3
12/31/96	179.1	28.7	1,035.3	6.5	7.4	2.8	0.86	10.84	1.65	191.8	28.75 - 20.25	28.5	6.7
12/31/95	154.4	23.1	886.2	6.5	7.1	2.6	0.72	10.18	1.59	221.5	23.63 - 19.75	30.1	7.4
12/31/94	137.8	20.5	753.7	6.7	5.9	2.7	0.67	10.92	1.57	234.3	29.50 - 19.63	36.7	6.4
12/31/93	115.3	16.1	690.9	6.0	5.7	2.3	0.60	10.14	1.55	258.3	30.25 - 23.88	45.1	5.7

Statistics are as originally reported. ① Excl. inc. fr. disc. opers. of $1.3 mill. & a gain fr. sales of real estate of $9.5 mill.; Incl. restruct. chrgs. of $22.3 mill.

OFFICERS:
D. C. Wood, Pres., C.E.O.
L. E. Finger, Sr. V.P., C.F.O., Treas.
D. Becker, V.P., Gen. Consl.

INVESTOR CONTACT: Andrew Blocher, V.P., Investor Relations, (301) 998-8166

PRINCIPAL OFFICE: 1626 East Jefferson Street, Rockville, MD 20852-4041

TELEPHONE NUMBER: (301) 998-8100
FAX: (301) 998-3700
WEB: www.federalrealty.com

NO. OF EMPLOYEES: 243

SHAREHOLDERS: 5,932

ANNUAL MEETING: In May

INCORPORATED: DC, 1962; reincorp., MD, June, 1999

INSTITUTIONAL HOLDINGS:
No. of Institutions: 140
Shares Held: 26,659,101
% Held: 61.5

INDUSTRY: Real estate investment trusts (SIC: 6798)

TRANSFER AGENT(S): American Stock Transfer & Trust Company, New York, NY

FEDERAL SIGNAL CORP.

EXCH.	SYM.	REC. PRICE	P/E RATIO	YLD.	MKT. CAP.	RANGE (52-WK.)	'02 Y/E PR.	DIV. ACH.
NYSE	FSS	14.20 (3/31/03)	13.9	5.6%	$0.6 mill.	25.98 - 13.60	19.42	15 yrs.

INVESTMENT GRADE. THE INCREASE IN EARNINGS WAS MAINLY ATTRIBUTABLE TO STRONGER RESULTS FOR THE COMPANY'S SAFETY AND ENVIRONMENTAL PRODUCTS GROUPS.

TRADING VOLUME
Thousand Shares

*7 YEAR PRICE SCORE 95.4   ***12 MONTH PRICE SCORE 81.8**

*NYSE COMPOSITE INDEX=100

INTERIM EARNINGS (Per Share):

Qtr.	Mar.	June	Sept.	Dec.
1999	0.29	0.30	0.30	0.37
2000	0.30	0.36	0.32	0.29
2001	0.26	0.37	0.20	0.21
2002	0.22	0.24	0.28	0.28

INTERIM DIVIDENDS (Per Share):

Amt.	Decl.	Ex.	Rec.	Pay.
0.20Q	4/18/02	6/11/02	6/13/02	7/02/02
0.20Q	7/18/02	9/10/02	9/12/02	10/01/02
0.20Q	10/17/02	12/11/02	12/13/02	1/03/03
0.20Q	2/06/03	3/11/03	3/13/03	4/01/03

Indicated div.: $0.80 (Div. Reinv. Plan)

CAPITALIZATION (12/31/01):

	($000)	(%)
Long-Term Debt	446,595	53.5
Deferred Income Tax	29,280	3.5
Common & Surplus	359,436	43.0
Total	835,311	100.0

BUSINESS:

Federal Signal Corp. is a manufacturer and worldwide supplier of public safety, signaling and communications equipment, fire trucks, emergency and street sweeping vehicles, parking control equipment, custom on-premise signage, carbide cutting tools, precision punches and related die components. The Environmental Products Group manufactures street sweeping, industrial vacuuming and municipal catch basin/sewer cleaning vehicles, hydroexcavation equipment, glycol recovery vehicles and high-pressure water blasting equipment. The Fire Rescue Group makes commercial fire apparatus and rescue vehicles. The Safety Products Group provides warning, signal and communication products. Standard and special die components and precision parts are manufactured by the Tool Group. Revenues for 2002 were derived: fire rescue; 31.6%, environmental products, 28.0%; safety products, 25.6%; and tool group, 14.8%.

RECENT DEVELOPMENTS:

For the year ended 12/31/02, income was $46.2 million, before an accounting change charge of $8.0 million, compared with income from continuing operations of $46.6 million the prior year. Results for 2001 included an after-tax goodwill expense of $5.5 million and excluded a gain tax-goodwill expense of $5.5 million and excluded a gain of $983,000 from discontinued operations. Revenues declined 1.4% to $1.06 billion. Environmental product sales increased 5.6% to $296.4 million, and safety products sales advanced 5.4% to $270.3 million, Fire rescue sales fell 10.5% to $334.2 million.

PROSPECTS:

Going forward, the Safety Products Group should continue to benefit from strong European police and global warning systems sales. The Environmental Products Group is expected to benefit from the addition of refuse truck body sales. However, operating earnings for this segment may be hampered by lower capital spending and weak municipal demand for street sweepers. Fire Rescue Group's results remain disappointing, although FSS' U.S. operations are focused on making significant improvements. The Tool Group is expected to benefit from aggressive cost containment efforts.

ANNUAL FINANCIAL DATA:

FISCAL YEAR	TOT. REVS. ($mill.)	NET INC. ($mill.)	TOT. ASSETS ($mill.)	OPER. PROFIT %	NET PROFIT %	RET. ON EQUITY %	RET. ON ASSETS %	CURR. RATIO	EARN. PER SH.$	CASH FL. PER SH.$	TANG. BK. VAL.$	DIV. PER SH.$	PRICE RANGE	AVG. P/E RATIO	AVG. YIELD %
p12/31/02	1,057.2	⑤ 46.2	1,168.4						⑤ 1.01			0.80	27.07 - 16.00	21.3	3.7
12/31/01	1,072.2	④ 46.6	1,014.7	8.6	4.3	13.0	4.6	1.9	④ 1.03	1.69	1.74	0.78	24.63 - 17.00	20.2	3.7
12/31/00	1,106.1	③ 57.7	991.1	10.5	5.2	16.1	5.8	1.2	③ 1.27	1.90	1.82	0.76	24.13 - 14.75	15.3	3.9
12/31/99	1,061.9	57.5	961.0	10.0	5.4	18.5	6.0	1.3	1.25	1.84	1.67	0.73	28.13 - 15.06	17.3	3.4
12/31/98	1,002.8	59.4	836.0	10.1	5.9	18.5	7.1	1.4	1.30	1.81	1.98	0.70	27.50 - 20.00	18.3	2.9
12/31/97	924.9	59.0	727.9	10.8	6.4	19.7	8.1	1.2	1.29	1.73	2.45	0.65	27.50 - 19.88	18.4	2.7
12/31/96	896.4	② 62.0	703.9	11.5	6.9	22.7	8.8	0.7	② 1.35	1.75	2.36	0.56	28.25 - 20.88	18.2	2.3
12/31/95	816.1	① 51.6	620.0	11.8	6.3	20.8	8.3	0.7	① 1.13	1.47	2.24	0.48	25.88 - 19.63	20.1	2.1
12/31/94	677.6	46.8	521.6	11.6	6.9	21.2	9.0	0.8	1.02	1.33	2.31	0.41	21.38 - 16.94	18.8	2.1
12/31/93	566.2	39.8	405.7	11.5	7.0	20.0	9.8	0.9	0.86	1.06	2.92	0.35	21.01 - 15.66	21.3	1.9

Statistics are as originally reported. Adj for 3-for-2 split, 4/92; 4-for-3 split, 3/94. ① Incl. $4.2 mill. ($0.09/sh) chg. for litigation. ② Incl. $2.8 mill. after-tax gain on sale of assets. ③ Bef. inc. from disc. opers. of $726,000 and accts. change chrg. of $844,000 & incl. pre-tax restruct. chrg. of $3.7 mill. ④ Bef. income from disc. oper. of $983,000 & incl. pre-tax restruct. chrg. of $2.3 mill. ⑤ Bef. acctg. chng. chrg. of $8.0 mill.

OFFICERS:
J. J. Ross, Chmn., C.E.O.
S. K. Kushner, V.P., C.F.O.

INVESTOR CONTACT: Stephanie K. Kushner, V.P., C.F.O., (630) 954-2020

PRINCIPAL OFFICE: 1415 West 22nd Street, Oak Brook, IL 60523-2004

TELEPHONE NUMBER: (630) 954-2000
FAX: (630) 954-2030
WEB: www.federalsignal.com
NO. OF EMPLOYEES: 6,631 (avg.)
SHAREHOLDERS: 3,872
ANNUAL MEETING: In Apr.
INCORPORATED: IL, Mar., 1901; reincorp., DE, Mar., 1969

INSTITUTIONAL HOLDINGS:
No. of Institutions: 159
Shares Held: 30,066,244
% Held: 63.0
INDUSTRY: Motor vehicles and car bodies (SIC: 3711)
TRANSFER AGENT(S): EquiServe Trust Company, Jersey City, NJ

FEDERATED DEPARTMENT STORES, INC.

EXCH.	SYM.	REC. PRICE	P/E RATIO	YLD.	MKT. CAP.	RANGE (52-WK.)	'02 Y/E PR.
NYSE	FD	25.50 (2/28/03)	7.8	...	$5.12 bill.	44.26 - 23.51	28.76

MEDIUM GRADE. THE COMPANY IS TARGETING EARNINGS OF BETWEEN $3.05 AND $3.25 PER SHARE IN ITS NEXT FISCAL YEAR.

MERGENT

TRADING VOLUME
Thousand Shares

7 YEAR PRICE SCORE 93.4   *12 MONTH PRICE SCORE 85.2*

*NYSE COMPOSITE INDEX=100

INTERIM EARNINGS (Per Share):

Qtr.	Apr.	July	Oct.	Jan.
1996-97	d0.18	d0.13	0.20	1.39
1997-98	0.12	0.31	0.48	1.66
1998-99	0.27	0.47	0.50	1.88
1999-00	0.40	0.61	0.56	2.04
2000-01	0.41	0.30	d3.32	1.65
2001-02	0.29	0.55	0.07	1.55
2002-03	0.43	0.66	0.38	1.78

INTERIM DIVIDENDS (Per Share):

Amt.	Decl.	Ex.	Rec.	Pay.
		No dividends paid.		

CAPITALIZATION (2/2/02):

	($000)	(%)
Long-Term Debt	3,859,000	35.8
Deferred Income Tax	1,345,000	12.5
Common & Surplus	5,564,000	51.7
Total	10,768,000	100.0

BUSINESS:

Federated Department Stores, Inc., as of 2/25/03, operated more than 450 full-line department stores in 34 states, Puerto Rico and Guam under the names of Macy's, Bloomingdale's, The Bon Marche, Burdines, Goldsmith's, Lazarus and Rich's-Macy's. FD's stores sell men's, women's and children's apparel and accessories, cosmetics, home furnishings, and other consumer goods, and are diversified by size of store, merchandising character, and character of community served. FD also operates direct-to-customer catalog and e-commerce subsidiaries under the names of Bloomingdale's By Mail and macys.com. FD sold its specialty store chain on 8/1/98.

RECENT DEVELOPMENTS:

For the 52 weeks ended 2/1/03, income from continuing operations totaled $638.0 million versus income from continuing operations of $518.0 million in the corresponding prior-year period. Results for 2002 included a pre-tax charge of $68.0 million related to store consolidations and closings. Results for 2001 included pre-tax non-recurring charges of $244.0 million. Net sales were $15.44 billion, down 1.4% compared with $15.65 billion the previous year. Same-store sales slid 3.0% year-over-year. Operating income advanced 21.6% to $1.34 billion from $1.10 billion a year earlier.

PROSPECTS:

Results are benefiting from the Company's aggressive efforts to reduce inventory levels, partially offset by sluggish sales. Looking ahead, FD anticipates earnings of between $3.05 and $3.25 per share in its next fiscal year, including expected store-closing costs of about $45.0 million. Meanwhile, same-store sales are expected to be flat to down 1.5% year over year. During fiscal 2003, the Company plans to open twelve new stores, including five Bloomingdale's department stores, three Macy's stores, two The Bon March locations, as well as two Rich's-Macy's furniture galleries that will open in former Macy's locations.

ANNUAL FINANCIAL DATA:

FISCAL YEAR	TOT. REVS. ($mill.)	NET INC. ($mill.)	TOT. ASSETS ($mill.)	OPER. PROFIT %	NET PROFIT %	RET. ON EQUITY %	RET. ON ASSETS %	CURR. RATIO	EARN. PER SH.$	CASH FL. PER SH.$	TANG. BK. VAL.$	PRICE RANGE	AVG. P/E RATIO
p2/01/03	15,435.0	⑤ 638.0							⑤ 3.21			44.26 - 23.59	10.6
2/02/02	15,651.0	① 518.0	15,044.0	7.1	3.3	9.3	3.4	2.0	① 2.59	6.08	24.31	49.90 - 26.05	14.7
2/03/01	18,407.0	③ d184.0	17,012.0	3.0	...	...	...	1.8	③ d0.90	2.71	24.93	53.88 - 21.00	...
1/29/00	17,716.0	795.0	17,692.0	9.6	4.5	12.1	4.5	1.9	3.62	7.01	19.89	57.06 - 36.44	12.9
1/30/99	15,833.0	② 685.0	13,464.0	9.2	4.3	12.0	5.1	1.9	② 3.06	5.83	24.35	56.19 - 32.81	14.5
1/31/98	15,668.0	② 575.0	13,738.0	8.6	3.7	10.9	4.2	2.0	② 2.58	5.22	21.75	48.88 - 30.00	15.3
2/01/97	15,229.0	③ 265.9	14,266.1	5.9	1.7	5.7	1.9	1.8	③ 1.28	3.98	19.00	37.00 - 25.00	24.2
④2/03/96	15,048.5	③ 74.6	14,295.1	4.4	0.5	1.7	0.5	2.1	③ 0.39	3.10	18.26	30.00 - 17.88	61.4
1/28/95	8,315.9	187.6	12,379.7	6.6	2.3	5.2	1.5	1.9	1.41	3.87	14.42	25.25 - 18.00	15.3
1/29/94	7,229.4	② 196.8	7,419.4	7.4	2.7	8.6	2.7	2.5	② 1.56	3.59	15.36	25.00 - 17.38	13.6

Statistics are as originally reported. ① Bef. $784.0 mil ($3.92/sh) loss fr. discont. opers and $10.0 mil ($0.05/sh) extraord. chg. & incl. $162.0 mil asset impair. and restr. chg. and $53.0 mil inv. val. chg. ② Bef. $23 mil ($0.10/sh) extraord. loss, 1/99; $38.7 mil ($0.18/sh) extraord. loss, 1/98; $4.5 mil ($0.03/sh), 1/94. ③ Incl. $962.0 mil pre-tax chg. for Fingerhut restructuring and asset impairment, 2/01; $308.6 mil chg. for bus. integration & consol., 2/97; $293.9 mil non-recur. chg., 2/96. ④ Results include opers. of acqd. Broadway stores. ⑤ Bef. $180 mil ($0.91/sh) gain fr. discont. opers & incl. $68.0 mil ($0.20/sh) chg. fr. store consol. and closings.

OFFICERS:
J. M. Zimmerman, Chmn.
T. J. Lundgren, Pres., C.E.O.
K. M. Hoguet, Sr. V.P., C.F.O.

INVESTOR CONTACT: Susan Robinson, Investor Relations, (513) 579-7780

PRINCIPAL OFFICE: 151 West 34th Street, New York, NY 10001

TELEPHONE NUMBER: (212) 494-1602
FAX: (212) 494-1838
WEB: www.federated-fds.com

NO. OF EMPLOYEES: 115,000 (approx.)

SHAREHOLDERS: 11,400 (approx.)

ANNUAL MEETING: In May

INCORPORATED: DE, Nov., 1929

INSTITUTIONAL HOLDINGS:
No. of Institutions: 352
Shares Held: 176,277,876
% Held: 92.7

INDUSTRY: Department stores (SIC: 5311)

TRANSFER AGENT(S): The Bank of New York, New York, NY

FEDERATED INVESTORS, INC.

EXCH.	SYM.	REC. PRICE	P/E RATIO	YLD.	MKT. CAP.	RANGE (52-WK.)	'02 Y/E PR.
NYSE	FII	25.32 (2/28/03)	14.6	0.9%	$2.92 bill.	36.18 - 23.43	25.37

INVESTMENT GRADE. THE COMPANY EXPECTS EARNINGS PER SHARE OF APPROXIMATELY $1.90 IN 2003.

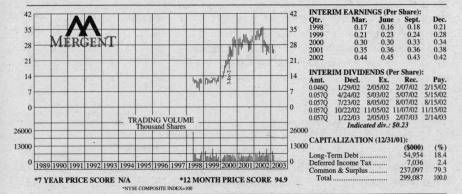

INTERIM EARNINGS (Per Share):

	Mar.	June	Sept.	Dec.
1998	0.17	0.16	0.18	0.21
1999	0.21	0.23	0.24	0.28
2000	0.30	0.30	0.33	0.34
2001	0.35	0.36	0.36	0.38
2002	0.44	0.45	0.43	0.42

INTERIM DIVIDENDS (Per Share):

Amt.	Decl.	Ex.	Rec.	Pay.
0.046Q	1/29/02	2/05/02	2/07/02	2/15/02
0.057Q	4/24/02	5/03/02	5/07/02	5/15/02
0.057Q	7/23/02	8/05/02	8/07/02	8/15/02
0.057Q	10/22/02	11/05/02	11/07/02	11/15/02
0.057Q	1/22/03	2/05/03	2/07/03	2/14/03

Indicated div.: $0.23

CAPITALIZATION (12/31/01):

	($000)	(%)
Long-Term Debt	54,954	18.4
Deferred Income Tax	7,036	2.4
Common & Surplus	237,097	79.3
Total	299,087	100.0

*7 YEAR PRICE SCORE N/A   ***12 MONTH PRICE SCORE 94.9**

*NYSE COMPOSITE INDEX=100

BUSINESS:

Federated Investors, Inc. and its consolidated subsidiaries are a major provider of investment management and related financial services. The Company sponsors, markets and provides investment advisory, distribution and administrative services primarily to mutual funds. As of 12/31/02, the Company had approximately $195.35 billion in assets under management in over 135 mutual funds and various separate accounts. These funds are offered through banks, broker/dealers and other financial intermediaries who use them to meet the needs of their customers, which include retail investors, corporations, and retirement plans. The Company also provides mutual fund administrative services to its managed funds and to funds sponsored by third parties, where FII also acts as fund distributor.

RECENT DEVELOPMENTS:

For the year ended 12/31/02, the Company reported net income of $203.8 million compared with income of $172.7 million, before an extraordinary loss of $4.3 million, the year before. Total revenue declined 1.2% to $711.1 million from $719.8 million a year earlier. Net investment advisory fees climbed 7.2% to $453.6 million, while net administrative service fees increased 8.2% to $141.1 million. Net other service fees dropped 31.0% to $111.2 million, and revenue from commission income grew 6.8% to $3.3 million. Comparisons are made with restated 2001 figures.

PROSPECTS:

Looking ahead, the Company expects revenue growth of 6.0%, earnings per share growth between 7.0% to 10.0%, and earnings per share of approximately $1.90 in 2003. Although earnings continue to benefit from FII's heavy focus on money-market funds, weaker stock prices have sharply reduced the amount of equity fund assets the Company manages. However, FII maintains its long-term growth rate target of 15.0% to 20.0% a year, which it has consistently met for the past five years. Separately, the Company aims to raise $1.00 billion in new money in the separately managed account area in 2003, an increase from $40.0 million FII attracted in its initial phase of business in 2002. Meanwhile, FII is entering the 529 college savings plan business.

ANNUAL FINANCIAL DATA:

FISCAL YEAR	TOT. REVS. ($000)	NET INC. ($000)	TOT. ASSETS ($000)	OPER. PROFIT %	NET PROFIT %	RET. ON EQUITY %	RET. ON ASSETS %	CURR. RATIO	EARN. PER SH. $	CASH FL. PER SH. $	TANG. BK. VAL. $	DIV. PER SH. $	PRICE RANGE	AVG. P/E RATIO	AVG. YIELD %
p12/31/02	711,069	203,760	529,872	43.3	24.1	72.8	40.0	1.0	1.74	2.02	0.79	0.22	36.18 - 23.43	17.1	0.7
12/31/01	715,777	① 172,716	431,553	43.3	24.1	72.8	40.0	1.0	① 1.44	2.02	0.79	0.17	32.80 - 23.31	19.5	0.6
12/31/00	680,768	155,360	704,750	42.1	22.8	105.1	22.0	2.5	1.27	1.88	0.86	0.14	31.69 - 12.46	17.4	0.6
12/31/99	601,098	② 124,020	673,193	39.4	20.6	104.4	18.4	2.5	② 0.96	1.48	0.70	0.11	14.13 - 10.04	12.6	0.9
12/31/98	522,127	92,369	580,020	34.9	17.7	100.7	15.9	2.8	0.71	1.18	0.44	0.05	13.46 - 7.33	14.6	0.5
12/31/97	403,719	① 51,026	337,156	27.2	12.6	...	15.1	1.2	① 0.41	0.75	...	...	...	...	...
12/31/96	321,793	① 13,605	247,377	16.0	4.2	...	5.5	0.8	① 0.09	0.35	...	...	...	...	...
12/31/95	279,831	28,531	...	22.5	10.2	...	...	...	0.17	0.36	...	...	...	...	...

Statistics are as originally reported. Adj. for 3-for-2 stk. split, 7/00 ① Bef. extraordinary loss $4.3 mill., 2001; $449,000, 1997; $986,000, 1996. ② Excl. after-tax gain $2.0 mill. from the sale of non-earnings assets.

OFFICERS:
J. F. Donahue, Chmn.
J. C. Donahue, Pres., C.E.O.
T. R. Donahue, V.P., C.F.O., Treas.
J. W. McGonigle, Exec. V.P., Sec.

INVESTOR CONTACT: Investor Relations, (412) 288-1054

PRINCIPAL OFFICE: Federated Investors Tower, Pittsburgh, PA 15222-3779

TELEPHONE NUMBER: (412) 288-1900
FAX: (412) 288-2919
WEB: www.federatedinvestors.com

NO. OF EMPLOYEES: 1,829 (avg.)

SHAREHOLDERS: 11,606 (approx.)

ANNUAL MEETING: In April

INCORPORATED: PA, 1955

INSTITUTIONAL HOLDINGS:
No. of Institutions: 188
Shares Held: 47,787,975
% Held: 42.0

INDUSTRY: Investment advice (SIC: 6282)

TRANSFER AGENT(S): EquiServe Trust Company, N.A., Providence, RI

FEDEX CORPORATION

EXCH.	SYM.	REC. PRICE	P/E RATIO	YLD.	MKT. CAP.	RANGE (52-WK.)	'02 Y/E PR.
NYSE	FDX	51.40 (2/28/03)	20.6	0.4%	$15.35 bill.	61.35 - 42.75	54.22

UPPER MEDIUM GRADE. FOR THE FULL-YEAR FISCAL 2003, THE COMPANY ANTICIPATES DILUTED EARNINGS PER SHARE TO TOTAL $2.77.

TRADING VOLUME
Thousand Shares

*7 YEAR PRICE SCORE 145.4   ***12 MONTH PRICE SCORE 110.5**
*NYSE COMPOSITE INDEX=100

INTERIM EARNINGS (Per Share):

Qtr.	Aug.	Nov.	Feb.	May
1998-99	0.50	0.61	0.26	0.73
1999-00	0.52	0.57	0.39	0.85
2000-01	0.58	0.67	0.37	0.38
2001-02	0.41	0.81	0.39	0.78
2002-03	0.52	0.81	. . .	. . .

INTERIM DIVIDENDS (Per Share):

Amt.	Decl.	Ex.	Rec.	Pay.
0.05Q	5/31/02	6/13/02	6/17/02	7/08/02
0.05Q	8/16/02	9/05/02	9/09/02	10/01/02
0.05Q	12/02/02	12/10/02	12/12/02	1/02/03
0.05Q	2/14/03	3/06/03	3/10/03	4/01/03

Indicated div.: $0.20

CAPITALIZATION (5/31/02):

	($000)	(%)
Long-Term Debt	1,800,000	20.1
Deferred Income Tax	599,000	6.7
Common & Surplus	6,545,000	73.2
Total	8,944,000	100.0

BUSINESS:

FedEx Corporation (formerly FDX Corporation) is a holding company that provides comprehensive transportation, logistics and supply chain management solutions. The Company's principal operating subsidiaries are FedEx Express, an express transportation company; FedEx Ground (formerly RPS, Inc.), a provider of small-package ground delivery service; FedEx Custom Critical, an interna-

tional provider of expedited time-critical shipments; FedEx Trade Networks Inc., a provider of customs brokerage, consulting, information technology and trade facilitation solutions; and FedEx Freight, a provider of regional less-than-truckload freight services. Net sales for fiscal 2002 were derived as follows: FedEx Express, 74.4%; FedEx Ground, 13.2%; FedEx Freight, 9.5%; and other, 2.9%.

RECENT DEVELOPMENTS:

For the quarter ended 11/30/02, net income remained the same at $245.0 million compared with the year before. Total revenue improved 10.4% to $5.67 billion from $5.14 billion the year before. Revenue for FedEx Express grew 7.4% to $4.10 billion, while revenue for FedEx Ground

rose 27.5% to $863.0 million. Revenue for FedEx Freight improved 12.2% to $547.0 million. Total average daily package volume at FedEx Express and FedEx Ground grew a combined 13.0%. FedEx Ground volume advanced 25.0%, while FedEx Express package volume rose 5.0%.

PROSPECTS:

FedEx Ground and FedEx Freight are reporting healthy increases in revenue and profit, while FedEx Express continues to achieve solid growth in its international operations and strong results from its U.S. Postal Service transportation agreement. Separately, nearly 31,000 shippers use FedEx Home Delivery, which is more than double the number the year before. The number of shippers is

expected to continue to grow as the service is able to provide evening, weekend, and day-and time-specific delivery options to nearly 100% of U.S. residences. In fiscal 2003, the Company anticipates diluted earnings per share to range from $0.45 to $0.55 in the third quarter, and total $2.77 for the full year. Capital expenditures are expected to be $1.70 billion in fiscal 2003.

ANNUAL FINANCIAL DATA:

FISCAL YEAR	TOT. REVS. ($mill.)	NET INC. ($mill.)	TOT. ASSETS ($mill.)	OPER. PROFIT %	NET PROFIT %	RET. ON EQUITY %	RET. ON ASSETS %	CURR. RATIO	EARN. PER SH.$	CASH FL. PER SH. $	TANG. BK. VAL.$	PRICE RANGE	AVG. P/E RATIO
5/31/02	20,607.0	③ 725.0	13,812.0	6.4	3.5	11.1	5.2	1.2	③ 2.39	6.89	18.38	53.48 - 33.15	18.1
5/31/01	19,629.0	584.4	13,340.0	5.5	3.0	9.9	4.4	1.1	1.99	6.34	16.20	49.85 - 30.56	20.2
5/31/00	18,256.9	688.3	11,527.1	6.7	3.8	14.4	6.0	1.1	2.32	6.22	14.35	61.88 - 34.88	20.9
5/31/99	16,773.5	631.3	10,648.2	6.9	3.8	13.5	5.9	1.1	2.10	5.54	14.50	46.56 - 21.81	16.3
5/31/98	15,872.8	① 498.2	9,686.1	6.4	3.1	12.6	5.1	1.0	① 1.67	4.90	12.23	42.25 - 21.00	18.9
5/31/97	14,237.9	196.1	9,044.3	3.6	1.4	5.6	2.2	1.0	0.67	3.86	10.60	22.50 - 16.72	29.3
5/31/96	12,721.8	② 400.2	. . .	6.1	3.1	. . .	. . .	. . .	② 1.38	4.35	. . .	21.50 - 14.63	13.1

Statistics are as originally reported. Years prior to and including fiscal 1998 are pro forma; adj. for 2-for-1 split, 5/99. ① Incl. merger expenses of $88.0 mill. & bef. disc. oper. gain of $4.9 mill. ② Bef. disc. oper. loss of $119.6 mill. ③ Incl. credit of $119.0 mill. rel. to airline stabilization compensation; bef. an acctg. chrg. of $15.0 mill.

OFFICERS:
F. W. Smith, Chmn., Pres., C.E.O.
A. B. Graf Jr., Exec. V.P., C.F.O.

INVESTOR CONTACT: Jim Clippard, (901) 818-7468

PRINCIPAL OFFICE: 942 South Shady Grove Road, Memphis, TN 38120

TELEPHONE NUMBER: (901) 818-7500
FAX: (901) 346-1013
WEB: www.fedex.com

NO. OF EMPLOYEES: 214,000 (avg.)

SHAREHOLDERS: 18,075

ANNUAL MEETING: In Sept.

INCORPORATED: DE, Oct., 1997

INSTITUTIONAL HOLDINGS:
No. of Institutions: 461
Shares Held: 201,805,782
% Held: 67.7

INDUSTRY: Air transportation, scheduled (SIC: 4512)

TRANSFER AGENT(S): First Chicago Trust Company of New York, Jersey City, NJ

FERRO CORP.

EXCH.	SYM.	REC. PRICE	P/E RATIO	YLD.	MKT. CAP.	RANGE (52-WK.)	'02 Y/E PR.
NYSE	FOE	21.26 (2/28/03)	23.1	2.7%	$0.73 bill.	30.55 - 20.55	24.43

MEDIUM GRADE. THE COMPANY EXPECTS TO BE WELL-POSITIONED TO TAKE ADVANTAGE OF GROWTH OPPORTUNITIES ONCE ECONOMIC CONDITIONS IMPROVE.

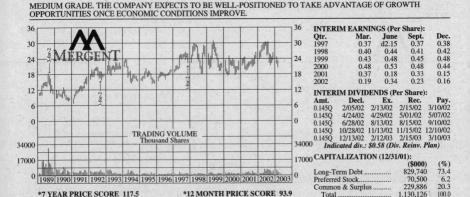

INTERIM EARNINGS (Per Share):

Qtr.	Mar.	June	Sept.	Dec.
1997	0.37	d2.15	0.37	0.38
1998	0.40	0.44	0.41	0.42
1999	0.43	0.48	0.45	0.48
2000	0.48	0.53	0.48	0.44
2001	0.37	0.18	0.33	0.15
2002	0.19	0.34	0.23	0.16

INTERIM DIVIDENDS (Per Share):

Amt.	Decl.	Ex.	Rec.	Pay.
0.145Q	2/05/02	2/13/02	2/15/02	3/10/02
0.145Q	4/24/02	4/29/02	5/01/02	5/07/02
0.145Q	6/28/02	8/13/02	8/15/02	9/10/02
0.145Q	10/28/02	11/13/02	11/15/02	12/10/02
0.145Q	12/13/02	2/12/03	2/15/03	3/10/03

Indicated div.: $0.58 (Div. Reinv. Plan)

CAPITALIZATION (12/31/01):

	($000)	(%)
Long-Term Debt	829,740	73.4
Preferred Stock	70,500	6.2
Common & Surplus	229,886	20.3
Total	1,130,126	100.0

*7 YEAR PRICE SCORE 117.5   ***12 MONTH PRICE SCORE 93.9**

*NYSE COMPOSITE INDEX=100

BUSINESS:

Ferro Corp. is a worldwide producer of specialty materials through organic and inorganic chemistry. FOE operates in two segments: Coatings and Performance Chemicals. Coatings products include ceramics and color, industrial coatings and electronic materials. Performance Chemicals consists of polymer additives, performance and fine chemicals, plastic compounds and plastic colorants. FOE's products are used primarily in the markets of building and renovation, major appliances, automotive, household furnishings, transportation, industrial products, telecommunications, and pharmaceuticals. As of 2/6/03, FOE operated globally through manufacturing facilities in 20 countries and sold products in more than 100 countries. In 2002, sales and operating income were derived: coatings, (64.5%, 73.5%); and performance chemicals, (35.5%, 26.5%). On 9/9/01, FOE completed the acquisition of certain businesses of dmc2, including electronic materials, performance pigments, glass systems and Cerdec ceramics.

RECENT DEVELOPMENTS:

For the twelve months ended 12/31/02, income from continuing operations rose 12.4% to $33.7 million compared with $30.0 million in 2001. Results for 2002 included a pre-tax charge of $9.8 million related to integration and overall consolidation costs. Results for 2001 included non-recurring items that resulted in a net pre-tax charge of $9.3 million. Results for 2002 and 2001 excluded gains of $40.0 million and $9.2 million, respectively, from discontinued operations. Total net sales were $1.53 billion, up 22.6% from $1.25 billion in the prior year, primarily due to increased volumes related to the dmc2 acquisition in September 2001.

PROSPECTS:

The Company expects to be well-positioned for 2003 due to efforts to divest non-strategic businesses, improve its cost structure and reduce debt by about $377.0 million in 2002. The Company also expects to benefit from the full-year effect of the integration of the dmc2 businesses. Meanwhile, FOE is benefiting from an increase in orders in certain markets; however, the rate of sustainability is still uncertain.

ANNUAL FINANCIAL DATA:

FISCAL YEAR	TOT. REVS. ($mill.)	NET INC. ($mill.)	TOT. ASSETS ($mill.)	OPER. PROFIT %	NET PROFIT %	RET. ON EQUITY %	RET. ON ASSETS %	CURR. RATIO	EARN. PER SH. $	CASH FL. PER SH. $	TANG. BK. VAL. $	DIV. PER SH. $	PRICE RANGE	AVG. P/E RATIO	AVG. YIELD %
p12/31/02	1,528.5	④ 33.7							④ 0.81			0.58	30.55 - 21.37	32.0	2.2
12/31/01	1,501.1	③ 39.2	1,732.6	5.6	2.6	13.0	2.3	1.5	③ 1.04	2.80	1.72	0.58	26.50 - 19.41	22.1	2.5
12/31/00	1,447.3	73.1	1,127.0	9.6	5.1	23.7	6.5	1.2	1.92	3.19	1.24	0.58	25.13 - 17.31	11.1	2.7
12/31/99	1,355.3	73.0	971.8	10.1	5.4	24.6	7.5	1.5	1.85	3.03	3.78	0.55	30.94 - 19.19	13.5	2.2
12/31/98	1,361.8	69.3	849.2	9.5	5.1	24.5	8.2	1.6	1.67	2.68	4.59	0.54	30.13 - 18.00	14.4	2.1
12/31/97	1,381.3	② d37.3	785.7	...	...	...	...	1.5	② d1.08	0.10	3.97	0.43	26.67 - 18.67	...	1.9
12/31/96	1,355.7	54.6	870.5	7.8	4.0	14.2	6.3	1.7	1.28	2.52	5.73	0.39	20.08 - 15.25	13.8	2.2
12/31/95	1,323.0	49.3	875.9	7.3	3.7	12.9	5.6	1.7	1.09	2.20	5.36	0.36	20.42 - 14.25	15.9	2.1
12/31/94	1,194.2	47.4	801.4	7.2	4.0	16.0	5.9	1.8	1.01	2.01	5.88	0.36	23.92 - 14.42	18.9	1.9
12/31/93	1,065.7	① 57.5	767.9	8.9	5.4	16.0	7.5	2.1	① 1.22	2.09	5.11	0.34	23.17 - 17.42	16.6	1.7

Statistics are as originally reported. Adj. for 3-for-2 splits, 12/97. ① Bef. $23.6 mill. acct. adj. ② Excl. $152.8 mill. pre-tax restr. chg. ③ Incl. $19.8 mill. gain fr. foreign currency contracts. ④ Incl. $9.8 mill. pre-tax chg. & excl. $40.0 mill. gain fr. disc. ops.

OFFICERS:
H. R. Ortino, Chmn., Pres., C.E.O.
J. W. Heitman, V.P., Fin., Acting C.F.O.
J. C. Bays, V.P., Gen. Couns.

INVESTOR CONTACT: Aidan Gormley, Dir., Investor Relations, (216) 875-7155

PRINCIPAL OFFICE: 1000 Lakeside Ave., Cleveland, OH 44114

TELEPHONE NUMBER: (216) 641-8580
FAX: (216) 696-6930
WEB: www.ferro.com

NO. OF EMPLOYEES: 9,348

SHAREHOLDERS: 2,037 (record)

ANNUAL MEETING: In Apr.

INCORPORATED: OH, Oct., 1919

INSTITUTIONAL HOLDINGS:
No. of Institutions: 142
Shares Held: 34,073,739
% Held: 84.3

INDUSTRY: Paints and allied products (SIC: 2851)

TRANSFER AGENT(S): National City Bank, Cleveland, OH

FIDELITY NATIONAL FINANCIAL, INC.

EXCH.	SYM.	REC. PRICE	P/E RATIO	YLD.	MKT. CAP.	RANGE (52-WK.)	'02 Y/E PR.	DIV. ACH.
NYSE	FNF	32.83 (2/28/03)	6.1	1.8%	$3.09 bill.	34.70 - 23.35	32.83	15 yrs.

INVESTMENT GRADE. THE COMPANY HAS ENTERED INTO A DEFINITIVE AGREEMENT TO ACQUIRE THE FINANCIAL SERVICES DIVISION OF ALLTEL INFORMATION SERVICES FOR $1.05 BILLION IN CASH AND STOCK.

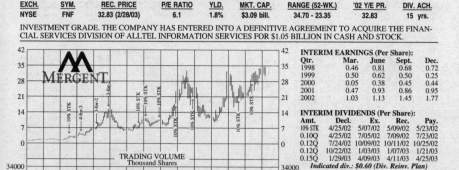

INTERIM EARNINGS (Per Share):

Qtr.	Mar.	June	Sept.	Dec.
1998	0.46	0.81	0.68	0.72
1999	0.50	0.62	0.50	0.25
2000	0.05	0.38	0.45	0.44
2001	0.47	0.93	0.86	0.95
2002	1.03	1.13	1.45	1.77

INTERIM DIVIDENDS (Per Share):

Amt.	Decl.	Ex.	Rec.	Pay.
10% STK	4/25/02	5/07/02	5/09/02	5/23/02
0.10Q	4/25/02	7/05/02	7/09/02	7/23/02
0.12Q	7/24/02	10/09/02	10/11/02	10/25/02
0.12Q	10/22/02	1/03/03	1/07/03	1/21/03
0.15Q	1/29/03	4/09/03	4/11/03	4/25/03

Indicated div.: $0.60 (Div. Reinv. Plan)

CAPITALIZATION (12/31/01):

	($000)	(%)
Long-Term Debt	565,690	25.5
Deferred Income Tax	14,074	0.6
Common & Surplus	1,638,870	73.9
Total	2,218,634	100.0

*7 YEAR PRICE SCORE 168.4   ***12 MONTH PRICE SCORE 120.9**

*NYSE COMPOSITE INDEX=100

BUSINESS:

Fidelity National Financial, Inc., through its principal subsidiaries, is a major title insurance and diversified real estate-related services business. FNF's title insurance underwriters are Fidelity National Title, Chicago Title, Ticor Title, Security Union Title and Alamo Title. As of 12/31/02, FNF provided title insurance in 49 states, the District of Columbia, Guam, Mexico, Puerto Rico, the U.S. Virgin Islands and Canada. FNF also performs other real estate-related services such as escrow, default management and exchange intermediary services, and homeowners and home warranty insurance. FNF also provides real estate and technology services through its majority-owned, publicly traded subsidiary, Fidelity National Information Solutions. On 3/20/00, FNF acquired Chicago Title Corporation.

RECENT DEVELOPMENTS:

For the year ended 12/31/02, net income was $531.7 million versus income of $311.2 million, before an accounting change charge of $5.7 million, the previous year. Results for 2001 included amortization of cost in excess of net assets acquired of $54.2 million. Total revenues rose 31.2% to $5.08 billion. Separately, on 1/29/03, FNF announced that it has entered into a definitive agreement to acquire the financial services division of ALLTEL Information Services, a wholly-owned subsidiary of ALLTEL Corporation for $775.0 million in cash and $275.0 million in FNF stock issued to ALLTEL. The transaction is expected to close by 3/31/03.

PROSPECTS:

On 1/10/03, FNF announced the signing of a definitive agreement under which the Company will acquire all of the outstanding common stock of ANFI, Inc. that it does not currently own. FNF currently owns, directly or indirectly, about 33.0% of the outstanding stock of ANFI, a provider of title insurance and other real estate related services. Under the terms, each share of ANFI common stock will be exchanged for 0.4540 shares of FNF common stock. The transaction is expected to close by 6/30/03. Also in January 2003, FNF closed on its acquisition of certain assets of Bankers Insurance Group, and announced it has entered into a definitive agreement to acquire Lender's Service, Inc., a provider of appraisal, title and closing services to residential mortgage originators.

ANNUAL FINANCIAL DATA:

FISCAL YEAR	PREM. INC. ($mill.)	TOT. REVS. ($mill.)	NET INC. ($mill.)	TOT. ASSETS ($mill.)	TOT. INVST. ($mill.)	RET. ON REVS. %	RET. ON EQUITY %	RET. ON ASSETS %	EARN. PER SH. $	TANG. BK. VAL. $	AVG. YIELD %	DIV. PER SH. $	PRICE RANGE	AVG. P/E RATIO
12/31/02	3,547.7	5,082.6	531.7						5.38		1.4	0.40	33.98 — 21.55	5.2
12/31/01	2,694.5	3,874.1	④311.2	4,416.0	1,803.8	8.0	19.0	7.0	④3.22	17.39	1.4	0.34	31.51 — 16.28	7.4
12/31/00	1,946.2	2,742.0	108.3	3,834.0	1,685.3	4.0	9.8	2.8	1.47	14.48	1.6	0.33	32.54 — 9.61	14.3
12/31/99	939.5	1,352.2	70.9	1,029.2	506.9	5.2	16.4	6.9	1.88	13.15	1.3	0.23	25.41 — 11.11	9.7
12/31/98	910.3	1,288.5	③105.7	969.5	510.5	8.2	26.6	10.9	③2.67	11.35	0.8	0.21	32.78 — 17.23	9.4
12/31/97	533.2	746.7	②41.5	600.6	326.3	5.6	21.1	6.9	②1.56	8.19	1.2	0.19	23.62 — 7.86	10.1
12/31/96	476.0	636.9	24.3	509.3	227.7	3.8	22.1	4.8	1.17	5.41	1.9	0.17	11.18 — 7.45	8.0
12/31/95	285.6	409.8	①7.6	405.1	180.1	1.9	9.8	1.9	①0.36	3.94	1.8	0.15	10.73 — 5.57	22.5
12/31/94	369.3	492.8	①9.7	418.1	217.6	2.0	13.2	2.3	①0.37	4.61	1.4	0.14	15.17 — 5.50	28.0
12/31/93	429.8	575.4	36.3	396.3	236.5	6.3	31.6	9.2	1.34	4.24	1.1	0.12	15.38 — 6.27	8.1

Statistics are as originally reported. Adjusted for 10.0% stk. div., 5/02, 8/01, 12/98, 12/97, 12/96, 1/96, 9/95. ① Excl. extraord. gain of $813,000, 12/95; $2.4 mill., 12/94 ② Excl. net extraord. loss of $1.7 mill. ③ Incl. $7.3 mil in pre-tax merger-related expenses. ④ Excl. acctg. chrg. $5.7 mill.; Incl. after-tax non-recurr. chrgs. $10.0 mill.

OFFICERS:
W. P. Foley II, Chmn., C.E.O.
R. R. Quirk, Pres.
A. L. Stinson, Exec. V.P., C.F.O.
INVESTOR CONTACT: Dan Murphy, Dir., Inv. Rel., (949) 622-4333
PRINCIPAL OFFICE: 17911 Von Karman Avenue, Suite 300, Irvine, CA 92614

TELEPHONE NUMBER: (949) 622-4333
FAX: (949) 622-4153
WEB: www.fnf.com
NO. OF EMPLOYEES: 17,600 (approx.)
SHAREHOLDERS: 1,797 (approx. record)
ANNUAL MEETING: In June
INCORPORATED: DE, Nov., 1984

INSTITUTIONAL HOLDINGS:
No. of Institutions: 272
Shares Held: 66,119,020
% Held: 69.2

INDUSTRY: Title insurance (SIC: 6361)

REGISTRAR(S): Continental Stock Transfer & Trust Co., New York, NY

FIRST AMERICAN CORPORATION (THE)

EXCH.	SYM.	REC. PRICE	P/E RATIO	YLD.	MKT. CAP.	RANGE (52-WK.)	'02 Y/E PR.
NYSE	FAF	23.10 (2/28/03)	7.9	1.7%	$1.59 bill.	23.62 - 16.14	22.20

MEDIUM GRADE. ORDER COUNTS IN FAF'S REAL ESTATE-RELATED BUSINESSES ARE EXPECTED TO REMAIN AT ELEVATED LEVELS DURING THE FIRST HALF OF 2003.

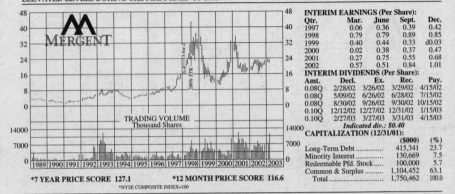

*7 YEAR PRICE SCORE 127.1   ***12 MONTH PRICE SCORE 116.6**
*NYSE COMPOSITE INDEX=100

INTERIM EARNINGS (Per Share):

Qtr.	Mar.	June	Sept.	Dec.
1997	0.06	0.36	0.39	0.42
1998	0.79	0.79	0.89	0.85
1999	0.40	0.44	0.33	d0.03
2000	0.02	0.38	0.37	0.47
2001	0.27	0.75	0.55	0.68
2002	0.57	0.51	0.84	1.01

INTERIM DIVIDENDS (Per Share):

Amt.	Decl.	Ex.	Rec.	Pay.
0.08Q	2/28/02	3/26/02	3/29/02	4/15/02
0.08Q	5/09/02	6/26/02	6/28/02	7/15/02
0.08Q	8/30/02	9/26/02	9/30/02	10/15/02
0.10Q	12/12/02	12/27/02	12/31/02	1/15/03
0.10Q	2/27/03	3/27/03	3/31/03	4/15/03

Indicated div.: $0.40

CAPITALIZATION (12/31/01):

	($000)	(%)
Long-Term Debt	415,341	23.7
Minority Interest	130,669	7.5
Redeemable Pfd. Stock	100,000	5.7
Common & Surplus	1,104,452	63.1
Total	1,750,462	100.0

BUSINESS:

The First American Corporation (formerly First American Financial Corp.) is a provider of insurance business information and related services. The Company operates within seven primary business segments: Title Insurance and Services (73.2% of 2002 revenues), Specialty Insurance (3.0%), Trust and Other Services (1.2%), Mortgage Information (10.3%), Property Information (5.6%), Credit Information (4.6%) and Screening Information (2.1%). As of 2/12/03, the Company had approximately 1,300 offices throughout the United States and abroad.

RECENT DEVELOPMENTS:

For the year ended 12/31/02, net income climbed 40.1% to $234.4 million from $167.3 million the previous year. Results benefited from a healthy housing market and strong demand for the Company's services. Total revenues increased 25.4% to $4.70 billion from $3.75 billion in the prior year. Revenues included a net realized investment loss of $18.9 million in 2002 and a net realized investment gain of $6.6 million in 2001. Operating revenues advanced 26.5% to $4.63 billion from $3.66 billion a year earlier. Investment and other income grew 10.8% to $89.8 million versus $81.1 million the year before.

PROSPECTS:

Order counts in the Company's real estate-related businesses remain at elevated levels, which should bode well for the company's results during the first half of 2003. Meanwhile, FAF's focus will continue to be on steady margin improvement through technology initiatives, back-office consolidation and solid expense controls. In addition, the Company's acquisition of US Search, which is expected to close in the second quarter 2003, is expected to provide significant growth opportunities in the rapidly expanding screening services industry. Separately, on 2/27/03, FAF's subsidiary, First American Title Insurance Company, announced that it will launch a new operating divvision designed to increase market share and improve profitability.

ANNUAL FINANCIAL DATA:

FISCAL YEAR	TOT. REVS. ($mill.)	NET INC. ($mill.)	TOT. ASSETS ($mill.)	OPER. PROFIT %	NET PROFIT %	RET. ON EQUITY %	RET. ON ASSETS %	CURR. RATIO	EARN. PER SH. $	CASH FL. PER SH. $	TANG. BK. VAL. $	DIV. PER SH. $	PRICE RANGE	AVG. P/E RATIO	AVG. YIELD %
p12/31/02	4,704.2	234.4							2.92			0.31	23.20 - 16.14	6.7	1.6
12/31/01	3,750.7	167.3	2,837.3	9.6	4.5	15.1	5.9	2.0	2.27	3.63	9.78	0.26	35.49 - 16.30	11.4	1.0
12/31/00	2,934.3	82.2	2,199.7	6.1	2.8	9.4	3.7	1.6	1.24	2.55	8.20	0.24	32.88 - 10.25	17.4	1.0
12/31/99	2,988.2	☐88.6	2,116.4	6.3	3.0	10.9	4.2	1.6	☐1.34	2.50	8.17	0.24	35.19 - 11.50	17.4	1.0
12/31/98	2,877.3	☐198.7	1,784.8	13.2	6.9	27.1	11.1	1.7	☐3.32	4.32	9.28	0.20	43.00 - 15.94	8.9	0.7
12/31/97	1,887.5	64.7	1,168.1	6.4	3.4	15.7	5.5	1.4	1.21	1.93	5.35	0.16	16.22 - 6.97	9.6	1.4
12/31/96	1,597.6	53.6	979.8	6.0	3.4	15.2	5.5	1.5	1.04	1.47	5.10	0.15	9.14 - 5.50	7.0	2.0
12/31/95	1,250.2	7.6	873.8	1.8	0.6	2.5	0.9	1.9	0.15	0.50	4.50	0.13	6.11 - 3.67	32.8	2.7
12/31/94	1,376.4	18.9	828.6	3.0	1.4	6.5	2.3	2.3	0.37	0.75	4.50	0.13	8.33 - 3.56	16.1	2.2
12/31/93	1,398.4	62.1	786.4	8.1	4.4	21.9	7.9	2.0	1.22	1.54	4.49	0.11	8.72 - 5.00	5.6	1.5

Statistics are as originally reported. Adj. for stk. splits: 200% div., 7/98; 3-for-2, 1/98 ☐ Excl. investment gain of $32.4 mill. ☐ Bef. acctg. chrg. $55.6 mill.

OFFICERS:
D. P. Kennedy, Chmn.
P. S. Kennedy, Pres.
T. A. Klemens, Exec. V.P., C.F.O.

INVESTOR CONTACT: Denise M. Warren, Dir., Investor Relations, (800) 854-3643

PRINCIPAL OFFICE: 1 First American Way, Santa Ana, CA 92707-5913

TELEPHONE NUMBER: (714) 800-3000
FAX: (714) 541-6372
WEB: www.firstam.com

NO. OF EMPLOYEES: 25,000 (approx.)

SHAREHOLDERS: 3,681 (approx.)

ANNUAL MEETING: In May

INCORPORATED: CA, 1894

INSTITUTIONAL HOLDINGS:
No. of Institutions: 183
Shares Held: 41,865,031
% Held: 58.0

INDUSTRY: Title insurance (SIC: 6361)

TRANSFER AGENT(S): First American Trust, FSB, Santa Ana, CA

FIRST COMMONWEALTH FINANCIAL CORPORATION

EXCH.	SYM.	REC. PRICE	P/E RATIO	YLD.	MKT. CAP.	RANGE (52-WK.)	'02 Y/E PR.	DIV. ACH.
NYSE	FCF	11.75 (2/28/03)	14.0	5.3%	$0.69 bill.	14.23 - 10.55	11.50	15 yrs.

MEDIUM GRADE. THE COMPANY CHANGED THE NAME OF ALL 90 OF ITS RETAIL COMMUNITY BANKING OFFICES TO FIRST COMMONWEALTH.

TRADING VOLUME
Thousand Shares

1989 1990 1991 1992 1993 1994 1995 1996 1997 1998 1999 2000 2001 2002 2003

*7 YEAR PRICE SCORE 115.9   ***12 MONTH PRICE SCORE 106.2**
*NYSE COMPOSITE INDEX=100

INTERIM EARNINGS (Per Share):

Qtr.	Mar.	June	Sept.	Dec.
1997	0.18	0.17	0.20	0.16
1998	0.16	0.17	0.19	0.03
1999	0.20	0.24	0.22	0.21
2000	0.20	0.23	0.20	0.19
2001	0.21	0.21	0.22	0.23
2002	0.22	0.19	0.21	0.22

INTERIM DIVIDENDS (Per Share):

Amt.	Decl.	Ex.	Rec.	Pay.
0.15Q	3/12/02	3/26/02	3/29/02	4/15/02
0.15Q	6/11/02	6/26/02	6/28/02	7/15/02
0.15Q	9/17/02	9/26/02	9/30/02	10/15/02
0.155Q	12/19/02	12/27/02	12/31/02	1/15/03
0.155Q	3/18/03	3/27/03	3/31/03	4/15/03

Indicated div.: $0.62 (Div. Reinv. Plan)

CAPITALIZATION (12/31/01):

	($000)	(%)
Total Deposits	3,093,150	74.9
Long-Term Debt	629,220	15.2
Redeemable Pfd. Stock	35,000	0.8
Common & Surplus	370,066	9.0
Total	4,127,436	100.0

BUSINESS:

First Commonwealth Financial Corporation is a financial services holding company with $4.54 billion in assets, as of 12/31/02. The Company operates in 18 counties in western and central Pennsylvania through First Commonwealth Bank, a Pennsylvania chartered bank. Financial services and insurance products are also provided by First Commonwealth Trust Company, First Commonwealth Financial Advisors, Inc. and First Commonwealth Insurance Agency. The Company also operates First Commonwealth Systems Corporation, a data processing subsidiary, First Commonwealth Professional Resources, Inc., a support services subsidiary, and jointly owns Commonwealth Trust Credit Life Insurance Company, a credit life reinsurance company.

RECENT DEVELOPMENTS:

For the year ended 12/31/02, net income declined 13.3% to $43.5 million compared with $50.2 million in 2001. Results for 2001 and 2000 included securities gains of $642,000 and $3.3 million, and intangible amortization of $203,000 and $490,000, respectively. Results for 2002 also included a $6.1 million restructuring charge and an $8.0 million litigation settlement, while results for 2001 included goodwill amortization of $920,000. Net interest income advanced 7.9% to $152.9 million from $141.7 million the previous year. Provision for credit losses grew 6.3% to $12.2 million versus $11.5 million the year before. Total interest income slipped 10.8% to $275.6 million from $308.9 million, while total interest expense decreased 26.6% to $122.7 million from $167.2 million the prior year.

PROSPECTS:

On 10/14/02, the Company changed the name of all 90 of its retail community banking offices to First Commonwealth. Previously, the Company operated the community offices as separate divisions with different names. The name change and new logo is part of a marketing strategy to better promote the full range of financial products offered by the Company. The name change should enable the Company to realize system-wide process efficiencies and many market synergies across the 18 counties in central and western Pennsylvania that it operates in.

ANNUAL FINANCIAL DATA:

FISCAL YEAR	NET INT. INC. ($mill.)	NON-INT. INC. ($mill.)	NET INC. ($mill.)	TOT. LOANS ($mill.)	TOT. ASSETS ($mill.)	TOT. DEP. ($mill.)	RET. ON EQUITY %	RET. ON ASSETS %	EQUITY/ ASSETS %	EARN. PER SH. $	TANG. BK. VAL. $	DIV. PER SH. $	PRICE RANGE	AVG. P/E RATIO
p12/31/02	152.9	32.4	① 43.5	2,569.2	4,583.5	3,093.2				① 0.74		0.60	14.23 - 10.55	16.7
12/31/01	141.7	32.4	50.2	2,569.2	4,583.5	3,093.2	13.6	1.1	8.1	0.86	6.33	0.58	15.10 - 9.44	14.3
12/31/00	137.3	33.4	47.2	2,492.9	4,372.3	3,064.1	14.1	1.1	7.6	0.82	5.74	0.56	12.13 - 8.63	12.7
12/31/99	144.9	25.9	53.0	2,503.7	4,340.8	2,948.8	18.5	1.2	6.6	0.88	4.93	0.49	14.88 - 10.06	14.2
12/31/98	135.1	26.3	34.0	2,382.2	4,096.8	2,931.1	9.6	0.8	8.7	0.55	5.74	0.44	17.41 - 11.25	26.0
12/31/97	97.1	19.8	30.5	1,937.7	2,929.3	2,242.5	11.2	1.0	9.3	0.70	6.17	0.40	16.81 - 8.56	18.3
12/31/96	94.0	13.7	27.6	1,778.1	2,584.6	2,104.8	10.6	1.1	10.1	0.63	5.89	0.36	9.88 - 8.38	14.5
12/31/95	93.3	10.4	25.5	1,531.2	2,364.3	1,962.8	10.1	1.1	10.7	0.58	5.64	0.32	8.94 - 6.56	13.4
12/31/94	90.5	16.2	28.7	1,422.3	2,334.9	1,881.1	12.8	1.2	9.6	0.64	5.02	0.28	10.13 - 6.75	13.2
12/31/93	73.7	12.1	22.7	1,037.7	1,955.3	1,575.6	12.2	1.2	9.5	0.61	5.00	0.25	8.81 - 6.19	12.3

Statistics are as originally reported. Adj. for 100% stk. div., 10/99; 2/94. ① Incl. $6.1 mill. restr. chg. & $8.0 mill. litigation settlement.

OFFICERS:
E. J. Trimarchi, Chmn.
D. S. Dahlman, Vice-Chmn.
J. E. O'Dell, Pres., C.E.O.

INVESTOR CONTACT: Shareholder Relations, (800) 331-4107

PRINCIPAL OFFICE: 22 North Sixth Street, Indiana, PA 15701

TELEPHONE NUMBER: (724) 349-7220
WEB: www.fcfbank.com

NO. OF EMPLOYEES: 1,465

SHAREHOLDERS: 13,000 (approx.)

ANNUAL MEETING: In Apr.

INCORPORATED: PA, Nov., 1983

INSTITUTIONAL HOLDINGS:
No. of Institutions: 71
Shares Held: 9,560,923
% Held: 16.2

INDUSTRY: National commercial banks (SIC: 6021)

TRANSFER AGENT(S): The Bank of New York, New York, NY

FIRST DATA CORPORATION

EXCH.	SYM.	REC. PRICE	P/E RATIO	YLD.	MKT. CAP.	RANGE (52-WK.)	'02 Y/E PR.
NYSE	FDC	34.65 (2/28/03)	21.1	0.2%	$26.37 bill.	45.08 - 23.75	35.41

UPPER MEDIUM GRADE. THE COMPANY AGREED TO ACQUIRE TELECASH KOMMUNIKATIONS-SERVICE GMBH FOR AN UNDISCLOSED AMOUNT.

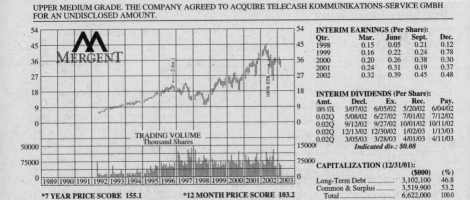

INTERIM EARNINGS (Per Share):

Qtr.	Mar.	June	Sept.	Dec.
1998	0.15	0.05	0.21	0.12
1999	0.16	0.22	0.24	0.78
2000	0.20	0.26	0.38	0.30
2001	0.24	0.31	0.19	0.37
2002	0.32	0.39	0.45	0.48

INTERIM DIVIDENDS (Per Share):

Amt.	Decl.	Ex.	Rec.	Pay.
100% STK	3/07/02	6/05/02	5/20/02	6/04/02
0.02Q	5/08/02	6/27/02	7/01/02	7/12/02
0.02Q	9/12/02	9/27/02	10/01/02	10/11/02
0.02Q	12/13/02	12/30/02	1/02/03	1/13/03
0.02Q	3/05/03	3/28/03	4/01/03	4/11/03

Indicated div.: $0.08

CAPITALIZATION (12/31/01):

	($000)	(%)
Long-Term Debt	3,102,100	46.8
Common & Surplus	3,519,900	53.2
Total	6,622,000	100.0

*7 YEAR PRICE SCORE 155.1   ***12 MONTH PRICE SCORE 103.2**

*NYSE COMPOSITE INDEX=100

BUSINESS:

First Data Corporation operates in four business segments: payment services, merchant services, card issuing services and emerging payments. Payment services is a provider of non-bank domestic and international money transfer and payment services to consumers and commercial entities. Merchant services provides merchants with credit and debit card transaction processing services, including authorization, transaction capture, settlement, Internet-based transaction processing, check verification and guarantee services.

Card issuing services provide a line of processing and related services to financial institutions issuing credit and debit cards and to issuers of oil and private label credit cards. The emerging payments segment consists of eONE Global, a provider of emerging technologies that support Internet and wireless payment products. Revenues for 2002 were derived: payment services, 39.3%; merchant services, 34.0%; card issuing services, 23.8%; emerging payments, 1.8%; and other, 1.1%.

RECENT DEVELOPMENTS:

For the year ended 12/31/02, net income jumped 43.0% to $1.25 billion compared with income of $874.6 million, before an accounting change charge of $2.7 million, in 2001. Results for 2002 and 2001 included net restructuring charges of $5.1 million and $20.8 million, impairment charges of $11.3 million and $14.7 million, an investment

gain of $700,000 and an investment loss of $184.2 million, and net divestiture charges of $4.2 million and $28.2 million, respectively. Results for 2002 also included a litigation and regulatory settlement charge of $38.0 million. Total revenues were $7.64 billion, up 14.8% from $6.65 billion in the prior year.

PROSPECTS:

On 2/24/03, the Company signed an agreement to acquire TeleCash Kommunikations-Service GmbH, an electronic payment network operator that allows merchants to accept debit, credit and charge payments through a network of

166,000 point of sale terminals, from T-Systems International GmbH. The acquisition strengthens the Company's commitment to meet the payment processing needs of banks and merchants in Europe.

ANNUAL FINANCIAL DATA:

FISCAL YEAR	TOT. REVS. ($mill.)	NET INC. ($mill.)	TOT. ASSETS ($mill.)	OPER. PROFIT %	NET PROFIT %	RET. ON EQUITY %	RET. ON ASSETS %	CURR. RATIO	EARN. PER SH.$	CASH FL. PER SH.$	TANG. BK. VAL.$	DIV. PER SH.$	PRICE RANGE	AVG. P/E RATIO	AVG. YIELD %
p12/31/02	7,636.2	⑨ 1,250.7		20.6	13.6	24.8	4.0	...	⑨ 1.62			0.08	45.08 — 23.75	21.2	0.2
12/31/01	6,450.8	⑧ 874.6	21,912.2	24.7	16.3	24.9	5.4	...	⑦ 1.10	1.90	...	0.04	40.10 — 24.32	29.5	0.1
12/31/00	5,705.2	⑦ 929.6	17,295.1	24.7	16.3	24.9	5.4	...	⑦ 1.13	1.83	0.19	0.04	28.84 — 18.50	21.0	0.2
12/31/99	5,539.8	⑥ 1,199.7	17,004.8	34.8	21.7	30.7	7.1	...	⑥ 1.38	2.09	0.51	0.04	25.75 — 15.66	15.0	0.2
12/31/98	5,117.6	⑤ 465.7	16,587.0	15.9	9.1	12.4	2.8	...	⑤ 0.52	1.18	...	0.04	18.03 — 9.84	26.8	0.3
12/31/97	5,234.5	④ 356.7	15,315.2	15.7	6.8	9.8	2.3	...	④ 0.40	0.95	...	0.04	23.06 — 12.50	45.0	0.2
12/31/96	4,938.1	③ 636.5	14,340.1	23.1	12.9	17.2	4.4	...	③ 0.71	1.18	...	0.03	22.00 — 15.19	27.1	0.2
②12/31/95	4,186.2	① d84.2	12,217.8	6.5	...	...	...	...	① d0.10	...	...	0.03	17.81 — 11.50	...	0.2
12/31/94	1,652.2	208.1	5,419.4	24.1	12.6	20.5	3.8	1.0	0.47	0.84	...	0.03	12.66 — 10.13	24.4	0.3
12/31/93	1,490.3	173.0	4,148.1	22.3	11.6	18.1	4.2	1.2	0.39	0.66	...	0.03	10.56 — 7.81	23.6	0.3

Statistics are as originally reported. Adj. for 2-for-1 split, 11/96 & 6/02. ① Incl. $539.9 mill. net after-tax merg., integra. & impair. chg. ② Incl. First Financial Mgmt. Corp., acq. on 10/27/95 as a pooling-of-interests. ③ Incl. $8.3 mill. net non-recur. gain. ④ Incl. $334.0 mill. restr. chgs. ⑤ Incl. $231.5 mill. after-tax non-recur. chgs. ⑥ Incl. $429.8 mill. in net after-tax gains. ⑦ Incl. $201.6 mill. gain fr. sale of bus., $96.7 mill. restr. chg. & $33.6 mill. chg. for write-down of invest. ⑧ Incl. $184.8 mill. net non-recur. chg. & excl. $2.7 mill. acctg. chg. ⑨ Incl. $5.1 mill. net restr. chg., $11.3 impair., $38.0 mill. lit. & settlmnt., $700,000 invest. gain and $4.2 mill. net divest.

OFFICERS:
C. T. Fote, Chmn., Pres., C.E.O.
K. S. Patmore, Exec. V.P., C.F.O.
M. T. Whealy, Exec. V.P., Gen. Couns.
INVESTOR CONTACT: David Banks, Investor Relations, (303) 967-6756
PRINCIPAL OFFICE: 6200 South Quebec Street, Greenwood Village, CO 80111

TELEPHONE NUMBER: (303) 967-8000
FAX: (303) 967-6262
WEB: www.firstdatacorp.com
NO. OF EMPLOYEES: 29,000 (approx.)
SHAREHOLDERS: 2,966
ANNUAL MEETING: In May
INCORPORATED: DE, Feb., 1992

INSTITUTIONAL HOLDINGS:
No. of Institutions: 735
Shares Held: 718,190,974
% Held: 95.5
INDUSTRY: Data processing and preparation (SIC: 7374)
TRANSFER AGENT(S): Wells Fargo Shareowner Services, South St. Paul, MN

FIRST TENNESSEE NATIONAL CORPORATION

EXCH.	SYM.	REC. PRICE	P/E RATIO	YLD.	MKT. CAP.	RANGE (52-WK.)	'02 Y/E PR.
NYSE	FTN	38.19 (2/28/03)	13.2	3.1%	$4.81 bill.	41.00 - 29.76	35.94

UPPER MEDIUM GRADE. EARNINGS CONTINUE TO BENEFIT FROM THE STRONG PERFORMANCE OF FIRST HORIZON, WHICH PRODUCED RECORD ORIGINATIONS OF $32.90 BILLION IN 2002.

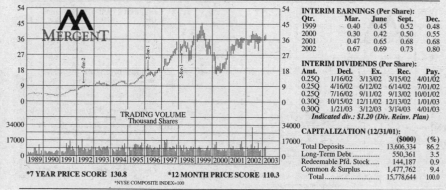

INTERIM EARNINGS (Per Share):

Qtr.	Mar.	June	Sept.	Dec.
1999	0.40	0.45	0.52	0.48
2000	0.30	0.42	0.50	0.55
2001	0.47	0.65	0.68	0.68
2002	0.67	0.69	0.73	0.80

INTERIM DIVIDENDS (Per Share):

Amt.	Decl.	Ex.	Rec.	Pay.
0.25Q	1/16/02	3/13/02	3/15/02	4/01/02
0.25Q	4/16/02	6/12/02	6/14/02	7/01/02
0.25Q	7/16/02	9/11/02	9/13/02	10/01/02
0.30Q	10/15/02	12/11/02	12/13/02	1/01/03
0.30Q	1/21/03	3/12/03	3/14/03	4/01/03

Indicated div.: $1.20 (Div. Reinv. Plan)

CAPITALIZATION (12/31/01):

	($000)	(%)
Total Deposits	13,606,334	86.2
Long-Term Debt	550,361	3.5
Redeemable Pfd. Stock	144,187	0.9
Common & Surplus	1,477,762	9.4
Total	15,778,644	100.0

TRADING VOLUME
Thousand Shares

*7 YEAR PRICE SCORE 130.8   ***12 MONTH PRICE SCORE 110.3**

*NYSE COMPOSITE INDEX=100

BUSINESS:

First Tennessee National Corporation, the parent company of First Tennessee Bank N.A., held assets of $23.82 billion as of 12/31/02 and is a nationwide, diversified financial services institution. FTN is one of the 50 largest bank holding companies in the U.S. in asset size and market capitalization. Banking and other financial services are provided through the regional banking group and three national lines of business: First Horizon, which includes home loans, equity lending and money centers; FTN Financial, which includes capital markets, equity research, investment banking, strategic alliances and correspondent services; and Transaction Processing, which includes credit card merchant processing and nationwide payment processing.

RECENT DEVELOPMENTS:

For the year ended 12/31/02, FTN reported net income of $376.5 million versus income of $326.4 million, before an accounting charge of $8.2 million, the year before. Results for 2002 and 2001 included gains from divestitures of $4.6 million and $80.4 million, securities losses of $9.2 million and $4.3 million, and amortization of intangible assets of $6.2 million and $10.8 million, respectively. Net interest income grew 9.7% to $752.5 million from $686.3 million a year earlier. Provision for loan losses 1.1% to $92.2 million. Total non-interest income improved 22.3% to $1.54 billion, while total non-interest expense increased 20.5% to $1.64 billion.

PROSPECTS:

Earnings continue to benefit from the strong performance of First Horizon, which produced record originations of $32.90 billion in 2002, driven by the ongoing low interest rate environment. Going forward, revenues could be dependent on the expansion of FTN's customer base, the volume of investment banking transactions and the introduction of new products, as well as the strength of loan growth in the U.S. economy and volatility in the interest rate environment and the equity markets. Separately, on 1/9/03, First Horizon Merchant Service, Inc. acquired substantially all of the assets of Merchant Card Management Systems, a provider of card-based processing services to the U.S. ski industry.

ANNUAL FINANCIAL DATA:

FISCAL YEAR	NET INT. INC. ($mill.)	NON-INT. INC. ($mill.)	NET INC. ($mill.)	TOT. LOANS ($mill.)	TOT. ASSETS ($mill.)	TOT. DEP. ($mill.)	RET. ON EQUITY %	RET. ON ASSETS %	EQUITY/ ASSETS %	EARN. PER SH. $	TANG. BK. VAL. $	DIV. PER SH. $	PRICE RANGE	AVG. P/E RATIO
p12/31/02	752.5	1,541.1	② 376.5		23,823.1					② 2.89	4.99	1.05	41.00 - 29.76	12.2
12/31/01	686.3	1,259.6	① 329.6	10,283.1	20,616.8	13,606.3	22.3	1.6	7.2	① 2.51	0.88	0.88	37.49 - 27.13	12.9
12/31/00	598.4	1,063.4	232.6	10,239.5	18,555.1	12,188.7	16.8	1.3	7.5	1.77	4.03	0.88	29.31 - 15.94	12.8
12/31/99	589.5	1,123.1	247.5	9,362.2	18,373.4	11,358.7	19.9	1.3	6.8	1.85	2.17	0.76	45.38 - 27.38	19.7
12/31/98	540.5	985.5	226.4	8,557.1	18,734.0	11,723.0	20.6	1.2	5.9	1.72	2.34	0.66	38.38 - 23.38	17.9
12/31/97	483.1	668.1	197.5	8,311.4	14,387.9	9,671.8	20.7	1.4	6.6	1.50	3.38	0.60	34.81 - 18.38	17.7
12/31/96	451.2	571.1	179.9	7,728.2	13,058.9	9,033.1	18.8	1.4	7.3	1.34	4.26	0.53	19.44 - 14.25	12.6
12/31/95	390.7	496.6	164.9	8,122.5	12,076.9	8,582.2	18.9	1.4	7.2	1.21	4.43	0.47	15.44 - 9.81	10.4
12/31/94	380.6	389.2	146.3	6,347.5	10,522.4	7,688.4	19.5	1.4	7.1	1.14	1.83	0.42	11.94 - 9.25	9.3
12/31/93	346.6	270.5	120.7	5,279.1	9,608.8	7,146.8	17.8	1.3	7.1	1.07	1.87	0.36	11.81 - 8.94	9.7

Statistics are as originally reported. Adj. for stk. splits: 2-for-1, 2/20/98; 2-for-1, 2/16/96. ① Incl. debt restructurings of $3.2 mill. & an acctg. change chrg. of $8.2 mill. ② Incl. a gain from divestitures of $4.6 mill.

OFFICERS:
R. Horn, Chmn.
K. Glass, Pres., C.E.O.
J. K. Glass, C.O.O.
E. L. Thomas Jr., Exec. V.P., C.F.O.
INVESTOR CONTACT: Marty Mosby, Investor Relations, (901) 523-5620
PRINCIPAL OFFICE: 165 Madison Avenue, Memphis, TN 38103

TELEPHONE NUMBER: (901) 523-4444
FAX: (901) 523-4336
WEB: www.firsttennessee.com
NO. OF EMPLOYEES: 9,861
SHAREHOLDERS: 9,338 (record)
ANNUAL MEETING: In April
INCORPORATED: TN, 1968

INSTITUTIONAL HOLDINGS:
No. of Institutions: 291
Shares Held: 66,866,420
% Held: 53.3
INDUSTRY: National commercial banks (SIC: 6021)
TRANSFER AGENT(S): Wells Fargo Bank Minnesota, South St. Paul, MN

FIRST VIRGINIA BANKS, INC.

EXCH.	SYM.	REC. PRICE	P/E RATIO	YLD.	MKT. CAP.	RANGE (52-WK.)	'02 Y/E PR.	DIV. ACH.
NYSE	FVB	40.90 (2/28/03)	15.9	2.7%	$2.93 bill.	44.61 - 30.93	37.23	25 yrs.

UPPER MEDIUM GRADE. BB&T CORPORATION PLANS TO ACQUIRE THE COMPANY THROUGH A STOCK SWAP VALUED AT $3.38 BILLION.

TRADING VOLUME
Thousand Shares

*7 YEAR PRICE SCORE 134.1   *12 MONTH PRICE SCORE 119.3
*NYSE COMPOSITE INDEX=100

INTERIM EARNINGS (Per Share):

Qtr.	Mar.	June	Sept.	Dec.
1997	0.41	0.42	0.45	0.37
1998	0.41	0.41	0.45	0.45
1999	0.59	0.45	0.50	0.47
2000	0.47	0.49	0.51	0.55
2001	0.58	0.54	0.64	0.56
2002	0.59	0.65	0.66	0.67

INTERIM DIVIDENDS (Per Share):

Amt.	Decl.	Ex.	Rec.	Pay.
0.41Q	5/29/02	6/26/02	6/28/02	7/15/02
50% STK	5/29/02	8/19/02	7/31/02	8/16/02
0.273Q	8/28/02	9/26/02	9/30/02	10/25/02
0.28Q	11/20/02	12/27/02	12/31/02	1/13/03
0.28Q	2/26/03	3/27/03	3/31/03	4/25/03

Indicated div.: $1.12 (Div. Reinv. Plan)

CAPITALIZATION (12/31/01):

	($000)	(%)
Total Deposits	8,649,636	88.1
Long-Term Debt	19,526	0.2
Preferred Stock	421	0.0
Common & Surplus	1,152,065	11.7
Total	9,821,648	100.0

BUSINESS:

First Virginia Banks, Inc. with assets of $11.23 billion as of 12/31/02, provides retail, commercial, international, and mortgage banking; insurance; trust and asset management services; and personal investment services through its subsidiaries. There are eight banks in the First Virginia group with 298 offices in Virginia, 55 offices in Maryland and 11 offices in East Tennessee. In addition, FVB operates a full-service insurance agency, First Virginia Insurance Services, Inc. On 7/2/01, FVB acquired James River Bankshares, Inc.

RECENT DEVELOPMENTS:

For the year ended 12/31/02, net income increased 11.8% to $183.9 million from $164.5 million in 2001. Results for 2002 and 2001 included amortization of intangibles of $8.8 million and $14.8 million, and securities gains of $516,000 and $4.5 million, respectively. Results for 2001 also included non-recurring income of $21.5 million. Net interest income improved 10.7% to $487.8 million from $440.6 million in the previous year. Provision for loan losses jumped 47.4% to $10.0 million from $6.8 million a year earlier. Total non-interest income was down 8.5% to $137.2 million from $150.0 million the year before. Total non-interest expense climbed 1.4% to $337.4 million from $332.7 million in the prior year.

PROSPECTS:

Growth in real estate loans is helping offset declines in consumer installment and business loans. On 1/21/03, BB&T Corporation announced plans to acquire the Company in a $3.38 billion stock swap. The acquisition will increase BB&T's assets to more than $91.00 billion and will create the 11th largest financial institution in the U.S. The transaction is subject to regulatory and shareholder approval and is expected to be completed in the third quarter of 2003. If approved, the exchange ratio will be fixed at 1.26 BB&T shares for each FVB share held.

ANNUAL FINANCIAL DATA:

FISCAL YEAR	NET INT. INC. ($mill.)	NON-INT. INC. ($mill.)	NET INC. ($mill.)	TOT. LOANS ($mill.)	TOT. ASSETS ($mill.)	TOT. DEP. ($mill.)	RET. ON EQUITY %	RET. ON ASSETS %	EQUITY/ ASSETS %	EARN. PER SH.$	TANG. BK. VAL.$	DIV. PER SH.$	PRICE RANGE	AVG. P/E RATIO
p12/31/02	487.8	137.2	④ 183.9	6,510.6	10,623.0	8,649.6	14.9	1.6	11.0	④ 2.55	13.27	1.08	39.98 - 30.93	13.9
12/31/01	440.6	150.0	164.5	6,366.5	9,516.5	7,825.8	14.3	1.5	10.8	2.32	12.05	1.03	34.77 - 25.69	13.0
12/31/00	424.5	118.0	142.0	6,366.5	9,516.5	7,825.8	14.3	1.5	10.4	2.01	12.05	0.97	32.63 - 19.33	12.9
12/31/99	433.7	136.6	③ 150.9	6,385.4	9,451.8	7,863.9	14.6	1.6	10.9	③ 2.00	11.66	0.88	35.09 - 27.00	15.5
12/31/98	429.3	116.8	130.2	6,093.2	9,564.7	8,055.1	13.1	1.4	10.4	1.69	10.71	0.77	39.63 - 26.46	19.6
12/31/97	408.2	103.6	② 124.8	5,938.0	9,011.6	7,619.8	12.3	1.4	11.2	② 1.63	10.75	0.68	35.59 - 20.56	17.2
12/31/96	374.9	98.5	① 116.3	5,364.8	8,236.1	7,042.7	13.4	1.4	10.6	① 1.56	10.65	0.63	21.78 - 17.00	12.5
12/31/95	358.1	89.9	111.6	5,038.1	8,221.5	7,056.1	12.8	1.4	10.6	1.46	10.13	0.60	19.56 - 14.22	11.6
12/31/94	342.0	84.7	113.2	5,352.5	7,865.4	6,815.8	14.0	1.4	10.3	-1.56	9.41	0.56	17.95 - 14.06	10.3
12/31/93	339.8	82.5	116.0	4,345.8	7,036.9	6,136.4	16.8	1.6	9.8	1.59	9.24	0.48	18.22 - 14.11	10.2

Statistics are as originally reported. Adj. for 3-for-2 splits, 8/02 & 9/97. ① Incl. one-time pre-tax SAIF chg. of $1.1 mill. ② Incl. $2.1 mill. gain fr. the sale of seven offices. ③ Incl. a pre-tax gain of $17.9 mill. fr. the sale of the Co.'s credit card portfolio. ④ Incl. $516,000 gain fr. securities.

OFFICERS:
B. J. Fitzpatrick, Chmn., Pres., C.E.O.
R. F. Bowman, Exec. V.P., C.F.O., Treas.
B. J. Chapman, V.P., Sec.
T. P. Jennings, Sr. V.P., Gen. Couns.

INVESTOR CONTACT: Barbara J. Chapman, V.P., Sec., (800) 995-9416

PRINCIPAL OFFICE: 6400 Arlington Boulevard, Falls Church, VA 22042-2336

TELEPHONE NUMBER: (703) 241-4000
FAX: (703) 241-3360
WEB: www.firstvirginia.com

NO. OF EMPLOYEES: 4,913 full-time; 481 part-time

SHAREHOLDERS: 19,886 (record); 547 (preferred)

ANNUAL MEETING: In May
INCORPORATED: VA, Oct., 1949

INSTITUTIONAL HOLDINGS:
No. of Institutions: 197
Shares Held: 21,433,163
% Held: 29.9

INDUSTRY: State commercial banks (SIC: 6022)

TRANSFER AGENT(S): Registrar and Transfer Company, Cranford, NJ

FIRSTENERGY CORPORATION

EXCH.	SYM.	REC. PRICE	P/E RATIO	YLD.	MKT. CAP.	RANGE (52-WK.)	'02 Y/E PR.
NYSE	FE	29.50 (2/28/03)	12.7	5.1%	$8.78 bill.	39.12 - 24.85	32.97

MEDIUM GRADE. THE COMPANY ESTIMATES EARNINGS PER SHARE IN THE RANGE OF $3.35 TO $3.55 FOR FULL-YEAR 2003, EXCLUDING INCREMENTAL EXPENSES ASSOCIATED WITH THE DAVIS-BESSE RESTART EFFORT.

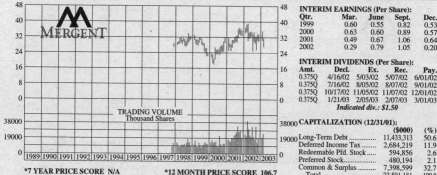

INTERIM EARNINGS (Per Share):

Qtr.	Mar.	June	Sept.	Dec.
1999	0.60	0.55	0.82	0.53
2000	0.63	0.60	0.89	0.57
2001	0.49	0.67	1.06	0.64
2002	0.29	0.79	1.05	0.20

INTERIM DIVIDENDS (Per Share):

Amt.	Decl.	Ex.	Rec.	Pay.
0.375Q	4/16/02	5/03/02	5/07/02	6/01/02
0.375Q	7/16/02	8/05/02	8/07/02	9/01/02
0.375Q	10/17/02	11/05/02	11/07/02	12/01/02
0.375Q	1/21/03	2/05/03	2/07/03	3/01/03

Indicated div.: $1.50

CAPITALIZATION (12/31/01):

	($000)	(%)
Long-Term Debt	11,433,313	50.6
Deferred Income Tax	2,684,219	11.9
Redeemable Pfd. Stock	594,856	2.6
Preferred Stock	480,194	2.1
Common & Surplus	7,398,599	32.7
Total	22,591,181	100.0

*7 YEAR PRICE SCORE N/A   ***12 MONTH PRICE SCORE 106.7**

*NYSE COMPOSITE INDEX=100

BUSINESS:

FirstEnergy Corporation was formed upon the merger of Ohio Edison and Centerior Energy on 11/8/97. FE has seven electric utility operating companies: Ohio Edison, Pennsylvania Power, The Cleveland Electric Illuminating Company, Metropolitan Edison, Pennsylvania Electric, Toledo Edison and Jersey Central Power & Light. As of 1/30/02, these companies comprised the nation's fourth-largest investor-owned electric system, based on serving 4.3 million customers in a 36,100 square mile service area from the Ohio-Indiana border to the New Jersey shore. FE's subsidiaries and affiliates provide a wide range of energy and energy-related products and services, including the generation and sale of electricity; exploration and production of oil and natural gas; transmission and marketing of natural gas; mechanical and electricity contracting and construction; energy management; and telecommunications. On 11/7/01, FE acquired GPU, Inc.

RECENT DEVELOPMENTS:

For the year ended 12/31/02, income was $686.4 million, before an accounting change charge of $57.1 million, compared with income of $654.9 million, before an accounting change charge of $8.5 million, the previous year. The improvement in earnings reflected the November 2001 acquisition of GPU, Inc., lower purchased gas expenses and increased electric sales. Total revenues advanced 51.9% to $12.15 billion from $8.00 billion a year earlier. Electric sales jumped 58.4% to $9.70 billion from $6.12 billion the year before.

PROSPECTS:

Going forward, the Company estimates earnings per share in the range of $3.35 to $3.55 for full-year 2003, excluding incremental expenses associated with the Davis-Besse Nuclear Power Station restart effort and any accounting change charges. Meanwhile, the Company is benefiting from increased residential electric distribution deliveries primarily due to colder weather. The Company will remain focused on reducing its debt in 2003, and will help support this effort through its free cash flow, which is projected to exceed $700.0 million in 2003.

ANNUAL FINANCIAL DATA:

FISCAL YEAR	TOT. REVS. ($mill.)	NET INC. ($mill.)	TOT. ASSETS ($mill.)	OPER. PROFIT %	NET PROFIT %	NET INC./ NET PROP. %	NET INC./ TOT. CAP. %	RET. ON EQUITY %	ACCUM. DEPR./ GROSS PROP. %	EARN. PER SH. $	TANG. BK. VAL. $	DIV. PER SH. $	DIV. PAYOUT %	PRICE RANGE	AVG. P/E RATIO	AVG. YIELD %
p12/31/02	12,152.0	⑤ 686.4								⑤ 2.33		1.50	64.4	39.12 — 24.85	13.7	4.7
④ 12/31/01	7,999.4	③ 654.9	37,351.5	21.1	8.2	5.3	2.9	8.3	39.6	② 2.84	6.04	1.50	52.8	36.98 — 25.10	10.9	4.8
12/31/00	7,029.0	599.0	17,941.3	21.4	8.5	7.9	4.5	11.3	41.0	2.69	11.42	1.50	55.8	32.13 — 18.00	9.3	6.0
12/31/99	6,319.6	568.3	18,224.0	24.3	9.0	6.2	4.1	10.9	39.4	2.50	10.47	1.50	60.0	33.19 — 22.13	11.1	5.4
12/31/98	5,861.3	② 441.4	18,063.5	23.3	7.5	4.8	3.1	8.6	39.4	① 1.95	9.62	1.50	76.9	34.06 — 27.06	15.7	4.9
12/31/97	2,821.4	① 305.8	18,080.8	19.7	10.8	3.2	2.1	6.3	37.1	① 1.94	8.91	...	...	28.81 — 26.88	14.4	...
12/31/96	2,469.8	302.7	9,054.5	21.5	12.3	5.5	4.1	11.1	36.9	2.10	16.41	...	...	...	...	...
12/31/95	2,465.8	294.7	...	23.0	12.0	...	...	...	...	2.05	...	...	...	...	...	...

Statistics are as originally reported. ① Incl. non-recurr. chrg. $34.0 mill. ($0.17/sh) ② Bef. extraordinary loss of $30.5 mill. ③ Bef. acctg. chng. chrg. of $8.5 mill. ④ Reflects the acquisition of GPU, Inc. on 11/7/01. ⑤ Bef. acctg. chng. chrg. of $57.1 mill.

OFFICERS:
H. P. Burg, Chmn., C.E.O.
A. J. Alexander, Pres., C.O.O.
R. H. Marsh, Sr. V.P., C.F.O.
INVESTOR CONTACT: Kurt E. Turosky, Manager, Dir., Investor Relations, (330) 384-5500
PRINCIPAL OFFICE: 76 South Main Street, Akron, OH 44308-1890

TELEPHONE NUMBER: (800) 633-4766
FAX: (330) 384-3772
WEB: www.firstenergycorp.com
NO. OF EMPLOYEES: 18,700 (avg.)
SHAREHOLDERS: 173,121
ANNUAL MEETING: In May
INCORPORATED: OH, Nov., 1997

INSTITUTIONAL HOLDINGS:
No. of Institutions: 332
Shares Held: 211,272,558
% Held: 71.0

INDUSTRY: Electric services (SIC: 4911)

TRANSFER AGENT(S): The Company

FISHER SCIENTIFIC INTERNATIONAL INC.

EXCH.	SYM.	REC. PRICE	P/E RATIO	YLD.	MKT. CAP.	RANGE (52-WK.)	'02 Y/E PR.
NYSE	FSH	28.73 (2/28/03)	17.2	...	$1.56 bill.	33.43 - 22.85	30.08

LOWER MEDIUM GRADE. FOR 2003, THE COMPANY EXPECTS EARNINGS PER SHARE IN THE RANGE OF $2.20 TO $2.30, EXCLUDING NON-RECURRING CHARGES.

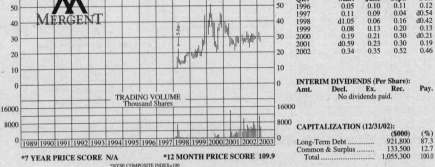

INTERIM EARNINGS (Per Share):

Qtr.	Mar.	June	Sept.	Dec.
1996	0.05	0.10	0.11	0.12
1997	0.11	0.09	0.04	d0.54
1998	d1.05	0.06	0.16	d0.42
1999	0.08	0.13	0.20	0.13
2000	0.19	0.21	0.30	d0.21
2001	d0.59	0.23	0.30	0.19
2002	0.34	0.35	0.52	0.46

INTERIM DIVIDENDS (Per Share):

Amt.	Decl.	Ex.	Rec.	Pay.
	No dividends paid.			

CAPITALIZATION (12/31/02):

	($000)	(%)
Long-Term Debt	921,800	87.3
Common & Surplus	133,500	12.7
Total	1,055,300	100.0

*7 YEAR PRICE SCORE N/A ***12 MONTH PRICE SCORE 109.9**

*NYSE COMPOSITE INDEX=100

BUSINESS:

Fisher Scientific International Inc. is engaged in the supply, marketing, service and manufacture of scientific, clinical, educational, occupational health and safety products. As of 2/3/03, FSH provided more than 600,000 scientific products and services to research, healthcare, industrial, educational and governmental markets in 145 countries. FSH serves scientists engaged in biomedical, biotechnology, pharmaceutical, chemical and other fields of R&D, and is a supplier to clinical laboratories, hospitals, healthcare alliances, physicians' offices, environmental testing centers, remediation companies, quality-control laboratories and many other customers. On 1/21/98, FSH acquired FSI Merger Corporation and recapitalized. FSH completed the spin-off of its ProcureNet, Inc. subsidiary on 4/15/99.

RECENT DEVELOPMENTS:

For the twelve months ended 12/31/02, income soared to $96.7 million, before an accounting change charge of $46.1 million, compared with net income of $16.4 million in 2001. Results reflected strong performances across all of the Company's business segments. Results for 2002 and 2001 included restructuring and other credits of $2.2 million and charges of $59.7 million, respectively. Sales were $3.24 billion, up 12.4% from $2.88 billion in the prior year. Revenue from domestic distribution grew 13.8% to $2.78 billion from $2.44 billion, while revenue from international distribution climbed 5.4% to $448.4 million from $425.4 million the year before. Revenue from laboratory workstations rose 8.6% to $193.9 million from $178.6 million a year earlier.

PROSPECTS:

The Company expects revenue growth for 2003, excluding foreign-exchange effects, of about 5.0% to 6.0%. Operating margins are anticipated in the 7.7% to 7.9% range. FSH expects earnings per share for 2003, excluding non-recurring charges, to range from $2.20 to $2.30, which is up from its previous guidance of $2.10 to $2.15. Operating cash flow is expected to be in the $180.0 million to $190.0 million range. Capital expenditures are estimated to be about $60.0 million due to ongoing facility consolidation and increased investment in chemical manufacturing and pharmaceutical services.

ANNUAL FINANCIAL DATA:

FISCAL YEAR	TOT. REVS. ($mill.)	NET INC. ($mill.)	TOT. ASSETS ($mill.)	OPER. PROFIT %	NET PROFIT %	RET. ON EQUITY %	RET. ON ASSETS %	CURR. RATIO	EARN. PER SH. $	CASH FL. PER SH. $	TANG. BK. VAL. $	PRICE RANGE	AVG. P/E RATIO
12/31/02	3,238.4	⑦96.7	1,871.4	7.6	3.0	72.4	5.2	1.3	⑥1.67	2.96	...	33.43 - 22.85	16.9
12/31/01	2,880.0	⑥16.4	1,839.2	4.6	0.6	70.4	0.9	1.2	⑥0.31	1.86	...	40.00 - 21.00	98.4
12/31/00	2,622.3	⑤22.7	1,385.7	6.0	0.9	...	1.6	1.3	⑤0.51	1.94	...	51.00 - 19.88	69.5
12/31/99	2,469.7	④23.4	1,402.6	5.9	0.9	...	1.7	1.2	④0.55	2.00	...	44.00 - 16.13	54.6
12/31/98	2,252.3	③d49.5	1,357.6	1.0	...	...	...	1.2	③d1.24	0.09	...	22.50 - 9.56	...
12/31/97	2,175.3	②d30.5	1,176.5	1.0	...	...	...	1.7	②d0.30	0.16	0.94	...	...
12/31/96	2,144.4	①36.8	1,262.7	4.4	1.7	9.5	2.9	1.7	①0.39	0.78	0.93	...	...
12/31/95	1,435.8	①3.2	1,270.5	1.3	0.2	1.4	0.3	1.7	①0.04	0.39	...	...	...
12/31/94	1,126.7	35.7	722.5	5.7	3.2	16.3	4.9	1.8	0.44	...	0.87	...	...
12/31/93	978.4	32.6	673.8	6.2	3.3	18.0	4.8	1.9	0.40	...	0.83	...	...

Statistics are as originally reported. Adj. for 5-for-1 split, 4/98. ① Incl. $11.0 mill. non-recur. chgs., 1996; $31.5 mill., 1995. ② Incl. $76.5 mill. one-time noncash chgs. ③ Incl. $71.0 mill. trans-related costs, $23.6 mill. restr. & other chgs. & $15.1 mill. loss fr. disp. ops. ④ Incl. $11.3 mill. loss fr. disposal of ops. & $1.5 mill. non-recur. credits. ⑤ Incl. $8.4 mill. non-recur. expense. ⑥ Incl. $59.7 mill. restr. chg. ⑦ Bef. $46.1 mill. acctg. chrg.; incl. $2.2 mill. restr. credit.

OFFICERS:
P. M. Montrone, Chmn., C.E.O.
P. M. Meister, Vice-Chmn.
D. T. Della Penta, Pres., C.O.O.
INVESTOR CONTACT: Carolyn Miller, Investor Relations, (603) 929-2381
PRINCIPAL OFFICE: One Liberty Lane, Hampton, NH 03842

TELEPHONE NUMBER: (603) 926-5911
FAX: (603) 929-2449
WEB: www.fisherscientific.com
NO. OF EMPLOYEES: 9,100 (approx.)
SHAREHOLDERS: 137 (approx. record)
ANNUAL MEETING: In May
INCORPORATED: DE, Sept., 1991

INSTITUTIONAL HOLDINGS:
No. of Institutions: 169
Shares Held: 49,654,680
% Held: 90.9
INDUSTRY: Professional equipment, nec (SIC: 5049)
TRANSFER AGENT(S): Mellon Investor Services, Ridgefield Park, NJ

FLEETBOSTON FINANCIAL CORPORATION

EXCH.	SYM.	REC. PRICE	P/E RATIO	YLD.	MKT. CAP.	RANGE (52-WK.)	'02 Y/E PR.
NYSE	FBF	24.56 (2/28/03)	17.1	5.7%	$25.64 bill.	37.56 - 17.65	24.30

UPPER MEDIUM GRADE. THE COMPANY ANTICIPATES ELIMINATING 1,900 EMPLOYEES, OR 3.8% OF ITS WORKFORCE, DURING THE FIRST QUARTER OF 2003.

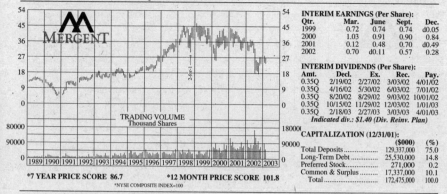

INTERIM EARNINGS (Per Share):

Qtr.	Mar.	June	Sept.	Dec.
1999	0.72	0.74	0.74	d0.05
2000	1.03	0.91	0.90	0.84
2001	0.12	0.48	0.70	d0.49
2002	0.70	d0.11	0.57	0.28

INTERIM DIVIDENDS (Per Share):

Amt.	Decl.	Ex.	Rec.	Pay.
0.35Q	2/19/02	2/27/02	3/03/02	4/01/02
0.35Q	4/16/02	5/30/02	6/03/02	7/01/02
0.35Q	8/20/02	8/29/02	9/03/02	10/01/02
0.35Q	10/15/02	11/29/02	12/03/02	1/01/03
0.35Q	2/18/03	2/27/03	3/03/03	4/01/03

Indicated div.: $1.40 (Div. Reinv. Plan)

CAPITALIZATION (12/31/01):

	($000)	(%)
Total Deposits	129,337,000	75.0
Long-Term Debt	25,530,000	14.8
Preferred Stock	271,000	0.2
Common & Surplus	17,337,000	10.1
Total	172,475,000	100.0

TRADING VOLUME
Thousand Shares

*7 YEAR PRICE SCORE 86.7   *12 MONTH PRICE SCORE 101.8

NYSE COMPOSITE INDEX=100

BUSINESS:

FleetBoston Financial Corporation (formerly Fleet Financial Group, Inc.), with assets of $190.45 billion as of 12/31/02, is a diversified financial services firm with offices nationwide. FBF's products and services include: consumer banking, government banking, mortgage banking and commercial real estate lending, corporate finance, credit cards, insurance services, cash management, asset-based lending, equipment leasing, and investment management services. FBF operates one of the nation's largest discount brokerage firms through its subsidiary, Quick and Reilly, Inc. On 10/1/99, FBF acquired BankBoston Corporation.

RECENT DEVELOPMENTS:

For the year ended 12/31/02, income from continuing operations amounted to $1.52 billion versus $968.0 million in 2001. Results for 2002 and 2001 included merger and restructuring costs and a loss on the sale of a business of $101.0 million and $1.14 billion, respectively. Results for 2002 and 2001 also included amortization of intangibles of $93.0 million and $381.0 million, respectively. Earnings excluded losses from discontinued operations of $336.0 million in 2002 and $37.0 million in 2001. Net interest income declined 11.7% to $6.48 billion from $7.34 billion a year earlier. FBF's provision for credit losses climbed 18.8% to $2.76 billion. Non-interest income rose 10.6% to $5.04 billion. Non-performing assets increased 87.1% to $3.46 billion from $1.85 billion the prior year.

PROSPECTS:

During 2002, the Company exited the investment banking business and significantly reduced its domestic wholesale and Latin American exposures. However, as a result of continuing economic weakness, the Company anticipates eliminating 1,900 employees, or 3.8% of its workforce through the first quarter of 2003. The job cuts are part of FBF's efforts to reduce its expenses. Looking ahead, the Company expects strong consumer loan growth to continue, while commercial loan demand is expected to be fairly modest. For 2003, FBF is comfortable with the earnings estimate of $2.50 per share.

ANNUAL FINANCIAL DATA:

FISCAL YEAR	NET INT. INC. ($mill.)	NON-INT. INC. ($mill.)	NET INC. ($mill.)	TOT. LOANS ($mill.)	TOT. ASSETS ($mill.)	TOT. DEP. ($mill.)	RET. ON EQUITY %	RET. ON ASSETS %	EQUITY/ ASSETS %	EARN. PER SH. $	TANG. BK. VAL. $	DIV. PER SH. $	PRICE RANGE	AVG. P/E RATIO
p12/31/02	6,483.0	5,036.0	⑦1,524.0	190,453.0	125,814.0	9.1	0.8	8.8	⑦1.44		1.40	37.56 — 17.65	19.2
12/31/01	7,397.0	5,340.0	⑥931.0	128,180.0	203,638.0	129,337.0	5.3	0.5	8.6	⑥0.83	11.75	1.32	44.19 — 31.27	45.5
12/31/00	6,521.0	9,024.0	④3,420.0	109,372.0	179,519.0	101,290.0	21.1	1.9	9.0	④3.68	9.85	1.20	43.75 — 25.13	9.4
⑤12/31/99	6,742.0	6,974.0	③2,038.0	119,700.0	190,692.0	114,896.0	13.3	1.1	8.0	③2.10	7.78	1.08	46.81 — 33.25	19.1
12/31/98	3,869.0	3,237.0	1,532.0	69,396.0	104,382.0	69,678.0	16.3	1.5	9.0	2.52	7.36	0.98	45.38 — 30.00	15.0
12/31/97	3,627.0	2,247.0	②1,303.0	61,179.0	85,535.0	63,735.0	16.2	1.5	9.4	②2.37	6.54	0.90	37.59 — 24.38	13.1
12/31/96	3,403.0	2,201.0	1,139.0	58,844.0	85,518.0	67,071.0	15.4	1.3	8.7	1.98	6.10	0.86	21.63 — 18.81	11.9
12/31/95	3,020.0	1,675.0	①610.0	51,525.0	84,432.0	57,122.0	9.6	0.7	7.5	①0.79	6.79	0.80	21.63 — 14.94	23.3
12/31/94	1,982.0	1,173.0	613.0	27,541.0	48,757.0	34,806.0	18.1	1.2	6.8	1.88	6.80	0.65	20.69 — 14.94	9.5
12/31/93	2,051.0	1,465.0	488.0	26,310.0	47,923.0	31,085.0	13.4	1.0	7.4	1.51	8.12	0.47	18.94 — 14.13	11.0

Statistics are as originally reported. Adj. for 2-for-1 stk. split, 10/98. ① Incl. aft.-tax merger chg. & loss on assets held for disposition of $429.0 mill. ② Incl. pre-tax gain of $175.0 mill fr. the sale of bus. & pre-tax restr. chg. of $155.0 mill. ③ Incl. aft.-tax merger & rel. chgs. of $760.0 mill. ④ Incl. aft.-tax BankBoston Corp. integration chgs. of $137.0 mill. & aft.-tax divest. gain of $420.0 mill. ⑤ Incl. the acq. of BankBoston Corp. on 10/1/99. ⑥ Incl. pre-tax merger chg. & loss on Fleet Mtge. of $1.07 bill. & pre-tax gains of $430.0 mill. on branch divests. ⑦ Incl. merger & restr. chg. & loss on bus. divest. of $101.0 mill.

OFFICERS:
C. K. Gifford, Chmn., C.E.O.
E. M. McQuade, Pres., C.O.O.
P. J. Manning, Vice-Chmn.
INVESTOR CONTACT: John A. Kahwaty, (617) 434-3650
PRINCIPAL OFFICE: 100 Federal Street, Boston, MA 02110-2010

TELEPHONE NUMBER: (617) 434-2200
FAX: (617) 346-4000
WEB: www.fleet.com
NO. OF EMPLOYEES: 56,000 (approx.)
SHAREHOLDERS: 85,312
ANNUAL MEETING: In April
INCORPORATED: RI, May, 1970

INSTITUTIONAL HOLDINGS:
No. of Institutions: 681
Shares Held: 668,626,810
% Held: 63.7
INDUSTRY: National commercial banks (SIC: 6021)
TRANSFER AGENT(S): EquiServe Trust Company, N.A., Providence, RI

FLEETWOOD ENTERPRISES, INC.

EXCH.	SYM.	REC. PRICE	P/E RATIO	YLD.	MKT. CAP.	RANGE (52-WK.)	'02 Y/E PR.
NYSE	FLE	4.05 (2/28/03)	...	...	$142.9 mill.	11.90 - 2.37	7.85

SPECULATIVE GRADE. IN THE NEAR-TERM, THE COMPANY EXPECTS CONTINUED LOSSES IN ITS MANUFACTURED HOUSING SEGMENT.

TRADING VOLUME
Thousand Shares

*7 YEAR PRICE SCORE 35.8   ***12 MONTH PRICE SCORE 82.9**

*NYSE COMPOSITE INDEX=100

INTERIM EARNINGS (Per Share):

Qtr.	July	Oct.	Jan.	Apr.
1997-98	0.84	0.77	0.57	0.81
1998-99	0.86	0.84	0.59	0.66
1999-00	0.72	0.84	0.48	0.37
2000-01	d0.61	d0.10	d6.26	d1.36
2001-02	d0.34	d0.38	0.31	d1.15
2002-03	d0.04	0.13	d0.51	...

INTERIM DIVIDENDS (Per Share):

Amt.	Decl.	Ex.	Rec.	Pay.
0.04Q	3/13/01	4/04/01	4/06/01	5/09/01
0.04Q	6/12/01	7/03/01	7/06/01	8/08/01
0.04Q	9/11/01	10/03/01	10/05/01	11/14/01
Dividend payment suspended.				

CAPITALIZATION (4/28/03):

	($000)	(%)
Long-Term Debt	8,741	4.8
Common & Surplus	174,743	95.2
Total	183,484	100.0

BUSINESS:

Fleetwood Enterprises, Inc. is a producer of recreational vehicles and manufactured homes. FLE's motor homes, travel trailers, folding trailers and slide-in truck campers are used for leisure-time activities, including vacation, sightseeing and fishing trips. As of 3/17/03, FLE operated 23 facilities nationwide, selling homes through around 1,200 retail home centers. In addition, FLE operates five supply companies, which provide components for the manufactured housing and recreational vehicle operations, while also generating outside sales. Products are marketed through independent dealers. For the fiscal year ended 4/28/02, sales were derived: RVs, 53.2%; manufactured housing, 45.3%; and supply operations, 1.5%.

RECENT DEVELOPMENTS:

For the third quarter ended 1/26/03, net loss was $18.4 million compared with a net loss of $17.3 million in the equivalent 2002 quarter. Sales declined 5.6% to $493.2 million from $522.4 million a year earlier due to a 26.2% decline in the Company's manufactured housing segment. Revenues in FLE's recreational vehicle group were up 11.5% for the same period, with the majority of the increase coming from motor home sales.

PROSPECTS:

The lack of retail financing for manufactured housing remains a problem for FLE. As a result, the Company is addressing the problem internally with the buildup of its own HomeOne Credit finance subsidiary as it awaits industry-wide relief from the current lending conditions. Meanwhile, the recreational vehicle group should continue to perform relatively well despite the recent erosion in consumer confidence and dealer reluctance to take on new inventory. For the fourth quarter 2003, FLE anticipates that losses in the housing group, which will include charges related to plant closings, will offset the operating profits of the recreational vehicle segment, and that the Company as a whole will not be profitable.

ANNUAL FINANCIAL DATA:

FISCAL YEAR	TOT. REVS. ($mill.)	NET INC. ($mill.)	TOT. ASSETS ($mill.)	OPER. PROFIT %	NET PROFIT %	RET. ON EQUITY %	RET. ON ASSETS %	CURR. RATIO	EARN. PER SH.$	CASH FL. PER SH.$	TANG. BK. VAL.$	DIV. PER SH.$	PRICE RANGE	AVG. P/E RATIO	AVG. YIELD %
4/28/02	2,280.4	[7] d81.3	984.9	...	...	...	...	1.6	[7] d1.53	d1.41	4.77	0.16	17.25 — 8.10	...	1.3
4/29/01	2,531.5	[6] d272.8	1,142.5	...	...	...	...	1.2	[6] d8.33	d7.21	6.09	0.76	21.00 — 8.69	...	5.1
4/30/00	3,713.0	[5] 83.5	1,536.7	4.4	2.2	14.3	5.4	1.6	[5] 2.41	3.03	10.08	0.74	39.81 — 18.00	12.0	2.6
4/25/99	3,490.2	107.1	1,531.2	5.5	3.1	18.3	7.0	1.6	2.94	3.46	9.63	0.70	48.00 — 25.00	12.4	1.9
4/26/98	3,050.6	[4] 108.5	1,129.5	5.6	3.6	28.9	9.6	2.1	[4] 3.01	3.69	11.96	0.66	42.81 — 24.38	11.2	2.0
4/27/97	2,874.4	[3] 90.1	871.5	4.9	3.1	20.3	10.3	1.9	[3] 2.30	3.00	12.40	0.62	37.25 — 23.13	13.1	2.1
4/28/96	2,809.3	[2] 69.9	1,108.9	4.7	2.5	10.8	6.3	3.5	[2] 1.50	2.09	14.22	0.58	26.38 — 17.75	14.7	2.6
4/30/95	2,855.7	84.6	1,345.1	4.8	3.0	13.9	6.3	1.7	1.82	2.34	13.20	0.53	27.25 — 17.88	12.4	2.3
4/24/94	2,369.4	[1] 81.6	1,224.1	4.4	2.8	12.3	5.5	1.7	[1] 1.43	1.90	11.88	0.49	26.88 — 16.50	15.2	2.3
4/25/93	1,941.9	56.6	1,061.9	4.3	2.9	11.3	5.3	1.8	1.23	1.61	11.01	0.45	24.56 — 12.69	15.1	2.4

Statistics are as originally reported. Adj. for stk. split: 2-for-1, 3/93. [1] Bef. acctg. chrg. of $1.5 mill. [2] Bef. discont. oper. gain $9.7 mill. and incl. non-recurring chrg. of $16.4 mill. [3] Bef. discont. oper. gain of $34.8 mill. [4] Incl. non-recurr. pre-tax gain $16.2 mill. [5] Incl. non-recurr. pre-tax chrg. of $4.0 mill. [6] Incl. non-recurr. pre-tax chrg. of $200.7 mill.; bef. acctg. chrg. of $11.2 mill. [7] Incl. non-recurr. pre-tax chrg. of $19.9 mill.; bef. acctg. chrg. of $80.6 mill.

OFFICERS:
T. B. Pitcher, Interim Chmn.
E. Caudill, Pres., C.E.O.
C. A. Wilkinson, Exec. V.P., C.O.O.
B. R. Plowman, Exec. V.P., C.F.O.

INVESTOR CONTACT: Kathy A. Munson, Dir., Investor Relations, (909) 351-3650

PRINCIPAL OFFICE: 3125 Myers Street, Riverside, CA 92503-5527

TELEPHONE NUMBER: (909) 351-3500
FAX: (909) 351-3690
WEB: www.fleetwood.com

NO. OF EMPLOYEES: 13,600 (approx.)

SHAREHOLDERS: 1,200 (approx. record)

ANNUAL MEETING: In Sept.

INCORPORATED: CA, 1957; reincorp. DE, Sept., 1977

INSTITUTIONAL HOLDINGS:
No. of Institutions: 115
Shares Held: 44,815,784
% Held: 124.7

INDUSTRY: Motor homes (SIC: 3716)

TRANSFER AGENT(S): BankBoston, N.A., Boston, MA

FLEMING COMPANIES, INC.

EXCH.	SYM.	REC. PRICE	P/E RATIO	YLD.	MKT. CAP.	RANGE (52-WK.)	'02 Y/E PR.
NYSE	FLM	2.07 (2/28/03)	2.6	3.9%	$92.0 mill.	26.10 - 1.85	6.57

SPECULATIVE GRADE. ON 4/1/03, THE COMPANY FILED FOR CHAPTER 11 BANKRUPTCY.

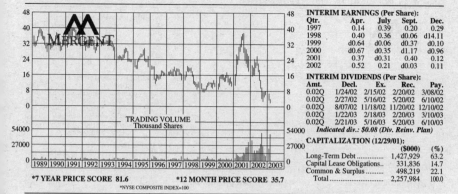

INTERIM EARNINGS (Per Share):

Qtr.	Apr.	July	Sept.	Dec.
1997	0.14	0.39	0.20	0.29
1998	0.40	0.36	d0.06	d14.11
1999	d0.64	d0.06	d0.37	d0.10
2000	d0.67	d0.35	d1.17	d0.96
2001	0.37	0.31	0.40	0.12
2002	0.52	0.21	d0.03	0.11

INTERIM DIVIDENDS (Per Share):

Amt.	Decl.	Ex.	Rec.	Pay.
0.02Q	1/24/02	2/15/02	2/20/02	3/08/02
0.02Q	2/27/02	5/16/02	5/20/02	6/10/02
0.02Q	8/07/02	11/18/02	11/20/02	12/10/02
0.02Q	1/22/03	2/18/03	2/20/03	3/10/03
0.02Q	2/21/03	5/16/03	5/20/03	6/10/03

Indicated div.: $0.08 (Div. Reinv. Plan)

CAPITALIZATION (12/29/01):

	($000)	(%)
Long-Term Debt	1,427,929	63.2
Capital Lease Obligations..	331,836	14.7
Common & Surplus	498,219	22.1
Total	2,257,984	100.0

*7 YEAR PRICE SCORE 81.6   ***12 MONTH PRICE SCORE 35.7**

*NYSE COMPOSITE INDEX=100

TRADING VOLUME
Thousand Shares

BUSINESS:

Fleming Companies, Inc. distributes food and non-food products to approximately 50,000 retail locations including supermarkets, convenience stores, supercenters, discount stores, concessions, limited assortment, drug, specialty, casinos, gift shops and military exchanges. In 2002, the Company discontinued its retail operations, which included 110 price-impact supermarkets, primarily under the Food4Less and Rainbow Foods banners, and 17 limited-assortment retail stores under the yes!Less banner. During 2001, FLM's product mix as a percentage of product sales was comprised as follows: groceries, 61.0%; perishables, 33.0%; and general merchandise, 6.0%. Kmart Corporation accounted for approximately 20.0% of the Company's total net sales in 2002.

RECENT DEVELOPMENTS:

For the 52 weeks ended 12/28/02, income from continuing operations was $40.2 million, before a $7.9 million charge from early retirement of debt, versus income from continuing operations of $9.0 million, before a $3.5 million charge from the early retirement of debt, a year earlier. Results included one-time pre-tax impairment/restructuring charges of $27.4 million and $13.9 million in 2002 and 2001, respectively. Results for 2001 also included a $48.6 million pre-tax litigation charge. Net sales climbed 17.2% to $15.50 billion from $13.23 billion the previous year.

PROSPECTS:

On 4/1/03, the Company filed for reorganization under Chapter 11 of the U.S. Bankruptcy Code. On 3/8/03, FLM terminated shipments to Kmart Corporation as part of an agreement reached between the two companies in early February 2003. On 2/25/03, FLM launched a series of cost-control initiatives that should help offset costs associated with the termination of the Kmart supply agreement. The Company expects to generate annual cost savings of about $60.0 million by the fourth quarter of 2003 through facility closures and an anticipated workforce reduction of approximately 1,800 positions. In addition, FLM expects to reduce its debt by more than $200.0 million in 2003 through the use of the proceeds from the sale of its discontinued retail operations and a reduction of capital expenditures.

ANNUAL FINANCIAL DATA:

FISCAL YEAR	TOT. REVS. ($mill.)	NET INC. ($mill.)	TOT. ASSETS ($mill.)	OPER. PROFIT %	NET PROFIT %	RET. ON EQUITY %	RET. ON ASSETS %	CURR. RATIO	EARN. PER SH.$	CASH FL. PER SH.$	TANG. BK. VAL.$	DIV. PER SH.$	PRICE RANGE	AVG. P/E RATIO	AVG. YIELD %
p12/28/02	15,502.9	⑥ 40.2							⑥ 0.80			0.08	26.10 - 2.60	17.9	0.6
12/29/01	15,627.7	⑤ 26.8	3,654.7	1.5	0.2	5.4	0.7	1.4	⑤ 0.60	4.45	...	0.08	37.89 - 10.75	40.5	0.3
12/30/00	14,443.8	④ d122.1	3,402.8	1.1	...	...	...	1.3	④ d3.15	1.34	...	0.08	17.63 - 8.69	...	0.6
12/25/99	14,645.6	④ d44.7	3,573.2	1.2	...	...	...	1.3	④ d1.17	3.07	...	0.08	13.44 - 7.19	...	0.8
12/26/98	15,069.3	③④ d510.6	3,490.8	1.3	...	...	...	1.2	③④ d13.48	d8.58	...	0.08	20.75 - 8.63	...	0.5
12/27/97	15,372.7	①③ 38.7	3,924.0	1.5	0.3	3.6	1.0	1.3	①③ 1.02	5.81	3.31	0.08	20.38 - 13.38	16.5	0.5
12/28/96	16,486.7	② 26.7	4,055.2	1.3	0.2	2.5	0.7	1.2	② 0.71	5.67	2.10	0.36	20.88 - 11.50	22.8	2.2
12/31/95	17,501.6	42.0	4,296.7	1.3	0.2	3.9	1.0	1.3	1.12	5.93	1.65	1.20	29.88 - 19.13	21.9	4.9
12/31/94	15,753.5	56.2	4,608.3	1.2	0.4	5.2	1.2	1.4	1.51	5.42	2.42	1.20	30.00 - 22.63	17.4	4.6
12/25/93	13,092.1	① 37.5	3,102.6	1.6	0.3	3.5	1.2	1.5	① 1.02	3.77	15.93	1.20	34.38 - 23.75	28.5	4.1

Statistics are as originally reported. ① Bef. $13.3 mil ($0.35/sh) extraord. chg. for early retirement of debt. ② Incl. $107.8 mil pre-tax chg. & bef. $2.3 mil ($0.06/sh) extraord. chg. ③ Incl. $7.8 mil chg. for litigation, 1998; $21 mil chg., 1997; & $20 mil chg., 1996. ④ Incl. pre-tax restruc. chg. of $212.8 mil, 2000; $103.0 mil, 1999; & $652.7 mil, 1998. ⑤ Bef. $3.5 mil ($0.08/sh) extraord. chg. and incl. $25.0 mil net chgs. fr. asset impairment, litigation settlements and restructuring. ⑥ Bef. $116.1 mil ($2.31/sh) loss fr. disc. opers. and $7.9 mil ($0.16/sh) extraord. chg. & incl. $27.4 mil pre-tax restr. chg.

OFFICERS:
A. R. Dykes, Chmn.
P. S. Willmott, Pres., & C.E.O.
N. J. Rider, Exec. V.P., C.F.O.
INVESTOR CONTACT: Mark Shapiro, Investor Relations, (972) 906-8110
PRINCIPAL OFFICE: 1945 Lakepointe Drive, Box 299013, Lewisville, TX 75029

TELEPHONE NUMBER: (972) 906-8000
FAX: (972) 841-8149
WEB: www.fleming.com
NO. OF EMPLOYEES: 23,000 (approx.)
SHAREHOLDERS: 14,000
ANNUAL MEETING: In May
INCORPORATED: KS, Dec., 1915; reincorp., OK, Apr., 1981

INSTITUTIONAL HOLDINGS:
No. of Institutions: 161
Shares Held: 57,063,085
% Held: 94.7
INDUSTRY: Groceries, general line (SIC: 5141)
TRANSFER AGENT(S): EquiServe, Jersey City, NJ

FLORIDA EAST COAST INDUSTRIES, INC.

EXCH.	SYM.	REC. PRICE	P/E RATIO	YLD.	MKT. CAP.	RANGE (52-WK.)	'02 Y/E PR.
NYSE	FLA	23.44 (2/28/03)	...	0.4%	$0.86 bill.	30.00 - 20.94	23.20

MEDIUM GRADE. THE COMPANY COMPLETED THE SALE OF ITS WHOLLY OWNED TELECOMMUNICATIONS SUBSIDIARY, EPIK COMMUNICATIONS INCORPORATED.

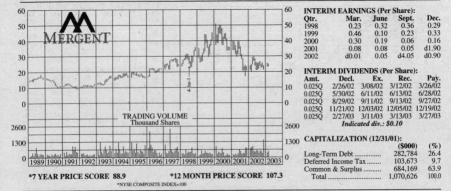

*7 YEAR PRICE SCORE 88.9   *12 MONTH PRICE SCORE 107.3
*NYSE COMPOSITE INDEX=100

INTERIM EARNINGS (Per Share):

Qtr.	Mar.	June	Sept.	Dec.
1998	0.23	0.32	0.36	0.29
1999	0.46	0.10	0.23	0.33
2000	0.30	0.19	0.06	0.16
2001	0.08	0.08	0.05	d1.90
2002	d0.01	0.05	d4.05	d0.90

INTERIM DIVIDENDS (Per Share):

Amt.	Decl.	Ex.	Rec.	Pay.
0.025Q	2/26/02	3/08/02	3/12/02	3/26/02
0.025Q	5/30/02	6/11/02	6/13/02	6/28/02
0.025Q	8/29/02	9/11/02	9/13/02	9/27/02
0.025Q	11/21/02	12/03/02	12/05/02	12/19/02
0.025Q	2/27/03	3/11/03	3/13/03	3/27/03

Indicated div.: $0.10

CAPITALIZATION (12/31/01):

	($000)	(%)
Long-Term Debt	282,784	26.4
Deferred Income Tax	103,673	9.7
Common & Surplus	684,169	63.9
Total	1,070,626	100.0

BUSINESS:

Florida East Coast Industries, Inc. conducts operations through two wholly-owned subsidiaries. Flagler Development Company owns, develops, leases and manages about 6.9 million square feet of office, service and warehouse space, including a number of industrial and commercial parks in Jacksonville, Orlando and Miami, and owns approximately 1,030 acres of entitled land and 5,500 acres of additional Florida property, as of 2/11/03. Florida East Coast Railway Company (FECR) is a regional freight railroad that operates 351 miles of mainline track from Jacksonville to Miami and provides intermodal drayage services at terminals located in Atlanta, Jacksonville and Miami.

RECENT DEVELOPMENTS:

For the year ended 12/31/02, income from continuing operations was $50.0 million versus income from continuing operations of $38.6 million a year earlier. Operating revenues rose 21.9% to $301.5 million. Separately, on 12/4/02, FLA announced that it has completed the sale of its wholly owned telecommunications subsidiary, EPIK Communications to Odyssey Telecorp, Inc. for a cash payment of $500,000, a potential earnout payment of up to $30.0 million based on EPIK's future performance, and a warrant to acquire 15.0% of the outstanding stock of Odyssey.

PROSPECTS:

On 12/6/02, FLA announced that its wholly-owned subsidiary FECR has completed the sale of its former Buena Vista rail yard located in Miami to Biscayne Development Partners LLC for $34.5 million. The sale is part of FLA's ongoing program to exploit the Company's non-core assets. As part of this program, FLA's subsidiaries have additional properties under contract totaling about $54.0 million and other properties currently listed for sale at asking prices totaling approximately $70.0 million, of which about half is expected to be placed under contract and close in 2003. Separately, on 2/3/03, FLA announced that its Flagler Development subsidiary has closed a transaction with Duke Realty Corporation. Flagler acquired The Office Centre at Southpoint and 4.76 acres of developable land in Jacksonville, Florida, and also has acquired the 50.0% partnership interest not already owned by Flagler in three buildings at Flagler's Beacon Station Business Park in South Florida. The transaction is valued at $23.3 million.

ANNUAL FINANCIAL DATA:

FISCAL YEAR	TOT. REVS. ($mill.)	NET INC. ($mill.)	TOT. ASSETS ($mill.)	OPER. PROFIT %	NET PROFIT %	RET. ON EQUITY %	RET. ON ASSETS %	CURR. RATIO	EARN. PER SH. $	CASH FL. PER SH. $	TANG. BK. VAL. $	DIV. PER SH. $	PRICE RANGE	AVG. P/E RATIO	AVG. YIELD %
p12/31/02	301.5	③ 50.0							③ 1.37			0.10	30.00 - 20.10	18.3	0.4
12/31/01	298.8	② d61.4	1,200.7	...	...	...	...	1.0	② d1.69	d0.22	18.73	0.10	40.07 - 17.00	...	0.4
12/31/00	276.3	25.8	1,111.5	12.7	9.3	3.4	2.3	0.8	0.70	1.84	20.50	0.10	51.00 - 33.75	60.5	0.2
12/31/99	324.3	40.8	910.9	18.9	12.6	5.6	4.5	2.4	1.12	1.98	19.90	0.10	45.38 - 25.88	31.8	0.3
12/31/98	247.8	43.6	867.8	23.3	17.6	6.4	5.0	2.8	1.20	2.00	18.91	0.10	36.00 - 23.00	24.6	0.3
12/31/97	250.5	40.1	825.5	20.9	16.0	6.2	4.9	2.4	1.11	1.77	17.88	0.10	29.00 - 21.50	22.8	0.4
12/31/96	208.0	30.4	789.7	18.1	14.6	5.0	3.9	2.0	0.84	1.49	16.81	0.10	22.53 - 16.84	23.4	0.5
12/31/95	201.1	26.6	756.2	17.2	13.2	4.6	3.5	2.2	0.74	1.35	16.07	0.10	20.19 - 16.03	24.5	0.6
12/31/94	199.5	34.6	722.5	23.3	17.3	6.3	4.8	2.2	0.96	1.57	15.34	0.10	19.41 - 14.41	17.6	0.6
12/31/93	181.1	① 20.8	688.4	18.3	11.5	4.0	3.0	2.2	① 0.58	1.14	14.53	0.10	17.56 - 11.50	25.1	0.7

Statistics are as originally reported. Adj. for 4-for-1 stk. split, 6/98. ① Bef. acctg. adj. chge. of $1.5 mill. ($0.17/sh.) ② Incl. pre-tax restruct. & asset impairment chrgs. of $110.2 mill. ($1.85/sh.) ③ Bef. loss of $157.8 mill. fr. disc. ops.

OFFICERS:
R. W. Anestis, Chmn., Pres., C.E.O.
R. G. Smith, Exec. V.P., C.F.O.
H. J. Eddins, Exec. V.P., Sec., Gen. Couns.
INVESTOR CONTACT: Bradley D. Lehan, (904) 819-2128
PRINCIPAL OFFICE: One Malaga Street, St. Augustine, FL 32084

TELEPHONE NUMBER: (904) 829-3421
FAX: (904) 396-4042
WEB: www.feci.com
NO. OF EMPLOYEES: 1,144 (avg.)
SHAREHOLDERS: 573 (class A); 1,123 (class B)
ANNUAL MEETING: In May
INCORPORATED: FL, Dec., 1983

INSTITUTIONAL HOLDINGS:
No. of Institutions: 74
Shares Held: 11,577,641
% Held: 31.6
INDUSTRY: Railroads, line-haul operating (SIC: 4011)
TRANSFER AGENT(S): First Union National Bank, Charlotte, NC

FLOWERS FOODS, INC.

EXCH.	SYM.	REC. PRICE	P/E RATIO	YLD.	MKT. CAP.	RANGE (52-WK.)	'02 Y/E PR.
NYSE	FLO	24.80 (2/28/03)	124.0	0.8%	$0.74 bill.	26.93 - 16.23	19.51

MEDIUM GRADE. ON 1/30/03, THE COMPANY AGREED TO SELL ITS MRS. SMITH'S BAKERIES' FROZEN DESSERT BUSINESS TO THE SCHWAN FOOD COMPANY FOR ABOUT $240.0 MILLION.

*7 YEAR PRICE SCORE N/A   ***12 MONTH PRICE SCORE 107.2**
*NYSE COMPOSITE INDEX=100

INTERIM EARNINGS (Per Share):

Qtr.	Apr.	July	Oct.	Dec.
2000		d1.41		
2001		d0.61		
2002	0.06	0.20	0.27	d0.33

INTERIM DIVIDENDS (Per Share):

Amt.	Decl.	Ex.	Rec.	Pay.
50% STK	11/16/01	1/03/02	12/14/01	1/02/02
0.05Q	11/15/02	11/26/02	11/29/02	12/13/02
0.05Q	2/21/03	3/05/03	3/07/03	3/21/03

Indicated div.: $0.20

CAPITALIZATION (12/29/01):

	($000)	(%)
Long-Term Debt	242,057	28.0
Common & Surplus	621,637	72.0
Total	863,694	100.0

BUSINESS:

Flowers Foods, Inc. was formed as a result of a spin-off from Flowers Industries, Inc. on 3/26/01. The Company produces and markets fresh baked breads, rolls and snack foods and frozen baked breads, desserts and snack foods. Products are distributed primarily in the Southeast, Central and Western U.S., and are sold chiefly to restaurants, fast-food chains, wholesalers, institutions, supermarkets and vending companies. Major brands include MRS SMITH'S, NATURE'S OWN, MRS. FRESHLEY'S and COBBLESTONE MILL. FLO acquired Mrs. Smith's Pies in May 1996, Allied Bakery Products in September 1997, and President Baking Company, Inc. and Keebler Foods Co. in September 1998. On 3/26/01, Flowers Industries sold its controlling interest in Keebler Foods Co. and merged into Kellogg Company. The Flowers Bakeries and Mrs. Smith's businesses were combined to form Flowers Foods, Inc.

RECENT DEVELOPMENTS:

For the 52 weeks ended 12/28/02, the Company reported income of $6.1 million, before a $23.1 million accounting change charge, compared with a loss of $18.2 million, before a $4.0 million extraordinary gain, in the corresponding period a year earlier. Results for 2002 and 2001 included pre-tax non-recurring charges of $27.6 million and $36.4 million, respectively. Sales rose 1.5% to $1.65 billion from $1.63 billion the previous year. Flowers Bakeries' sales grew 1.0% to $1.07 billion from $1.06 billion the year before, while Mrs. Smith's Bakeries sales increased 3.8% to $435.2 million from $419.5 million in 2001. The Company's snack group sales slipped 0.9% to $150.3 million.

PROSPECTS:

On 1/30/03, the Company announced that it has entered into an agreement to sell its Mrs. Smith's Bakeries' frozen dessert business, which has annual sales of about $350.0 million, to The Schwan Food Company for approximately $240.0 million. The transaction is expected to be completed during the first quarter of 2003. Meanwhile, the Company will keep the frozen bread and roll operations of the Mrs. Smith's business, which is expected to generate sales of about $125.0 million in 2003, primarily to foodservice and in-store bakery customers.

ANNUAL FINANCIAL DATA:

FISCAL YEAR	TOT. REVS. ($mil.)	NET INC. ($mil.)	TOT. ASSETS ($mil.)	OPER. PROFIT %	CURR. RATIO	EARN. PER SH.$	CASH FL. PER SH.$	TANG. BK. VAL.$	DIV. PER SH.$	PRICE RANGE	AVG. P/E RATIO	AVG. YIELD %
p12/28/02	1,652.2	④ 6.1				④ 0.20	1.86	16.64	...	28.96 - 10.70	...	...
12/29/01	1,629.0	③ d18.2	1,099.7	0.4	1.4	③ d0.61	0.82	12.65	...	...	...	...
12/30/00	1,620.0	② d42.3	1,562.6	0.6	1.5	② d1.41	0.64	13.76	...	...	...	...
1/01/00	1,568.2	① d34.7	1,567.0	...	1.9	① d1.15	1.80		...	...	...	...
1/02/99	1,538.9	d1.2	...	2.8	...	d0.04			0.05	26.66 - 16.76	108.6	0.2

Statistics are as originally reported. Adj. for 3-for-2 stk. split, 1/02. ① Incl. $60.4 mil pre-tax, non-recur. chg. ② Bef. $47.3 mil ($1.57/sh) inc. fr. disc. ops., incl. $17.7 mil pre-tax non-recur. chg. & $17.2 mil pre-tax gain fr insur. proceeds. ③ Bef. $4.0 mil ($0.13/sh) extraord. gain, incl. $43.9 mil pre-tax non-recur. chg. & $7.5 mil pre-tax gain fr insur. proceeds. ④ Bef. $23.1 mil ($0.76/sh) acctg. chg., incl. $26.5 mil asset impair chg. and $1.1 mil severance and oth. chg.

OFFICERS:
A. R. McMullian, Chmn., C.E.O.
G. E. Deese, Pres., C.O.O.
J. M. Woodward, Sr. V.P., C.F.O.

INVESTOR CONTACT: Lisa Hay, Investor Relations, (229) 227-2216

PRINCIPAL OFFICE: 1919 Flowers Circle, Thomasville, GA 31757

TELEPHONE NUMBER: (229) 226-9110
FAX: (229) 226-9231
WEB: www.flowersfoods.com

NO. OF EMPLOYEES: 8,000 (approx.)

SHAREHOLDERS: 5,389 (approx.)

ANNUAL MEETING: In May

INCORPORATED: GA, Oct., 2000

INSTITUTIONAL HOLDINGS:
No. of Institutions: 96
Shares Held: 16,087,778
% Held: 53.7

INDUSTRY: Frozen bakery products, except bread (SIC: 2053)

TRANSFER AGENT(S): Wachovia Bank, N.A., Charlotte, NC

FLOWSERVE CORPORATION

EXCH.	SYM.	REC. PRICE	P/E RATIO	YLD.	MKT. CAP.	RANGE (52-WK.)	'02 Y/E PR.
NYSE	FLS	11.96 (2/28/03)	11.7	...	$0.54 bill.	35.09 - 7.58	14.79

LOWER MEDIUM GRADE. THE COMPANY ANTICIPATES TOUGH YEAR-OVER-YEAR COMPARISONS FOR THE FIRST HALF OF 2003.

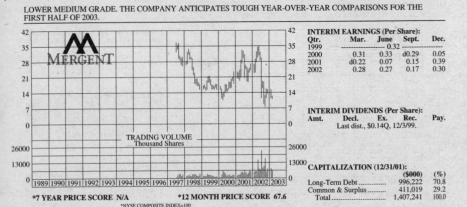

INTERIM EARNINGS (Per Share):

Qtr.	Mar.	June	Sept.	Dec.
1999	---------------- 0.32 ----------------			
2000	0.31	0.33	d0.29	0.05
2001	d0.22	0.07	0.15	0.39
2002	0.28	0.27	0.17	0.30

INTERIM DIVIDENDS (Per Share):

Amt.	Decl.	Ex.	Rec.	Pay.
	Last dist., $0.14Q, 12/3/99.			

CAPITALIZATION (12/31/01):

	($000)	(%)
Long-Term Debt	996,222	70.8
Common & Surplus	411,019	29.2
Total	1,407,241	100.0

*7 YEAR PRICE SCORE N/A   ***12 MONTH PRICE SCORE 67.6**

*NYSE COMPOSITE INDEX=100

BUSINESS:

Flowserve Corporation is a manufacturer and aftermarket service provider of comprehensive flow control systems. FLS develops and manufactures precision-engineered flow control equipment for critical service applications. The flow control system components include pumps, valves and mechanical seals. The Company's products and services are used in several industries, including petroleum, chemical, power generation and water treatment. FLS operates mainly through the three following segments: Pump Division, Flow Solutions Division and Flow Control Division. The Pump Division (53.4% of 2002 revenues) supplies engineered pumps. The Flow Control Division (32.0%) supplies valves and related products. The Flow Solutions Division (14.6%) provides mechanical seals and aftermarket services.

RECENT DEVELOPMENTS:

For the year ended 12/31/02, earnings were $60.4 million, before an extraordinary charge of $7.4 million, compared with earnings of $16.4 million, before an extraordinary charge of $17.9 million, in 2001. Results for 2002 and 2001 included integration expenses of $16.2 million and $63.0 million, respectively. Results for 2002 included a restructuring charge of $4.3 million versus a restructuring credit of $1.2 million in 2001. Sales increased 17.4% to $2.25 billion from $1.92 billion in the prior year, reflecting strong activity in the seals business.

PROSPECTS:

The Company is cautious about its near-term outlook due to weakness in some of its key end-markets. Moreover, the Company does not expect a turnaround or any significant improvement in its end-markets in the first half of 2003. As a result, FLS will continue to focus on cash flow generation and debt repayment. Furthermore, year-over-year comparisons for the first half of 2003 will be tough. Accordingly, earnings per share for the first quarter of 2003 are expected to be in the range of $0.20 to $0.28, excluding special items. However, full-year 2003 earnings per share, excluding special items, are expected to be comparable to 2002.

ANNUAL FINANCIAL DATA:

FISCAL YEAR	TOT. REVS. ($mill.)	NET INC. ($mill.)	TOT. ASSETS ($mill.)	OPER. PROFIT %	NET PROFIT %	RET. ON EQUITY %	RET. ON ASSETS %	CURR. RATIO	EARN. PER SH.$	CASH FL. PER SH.$	TANG. BK. VAL.$	DIV. PER SH.$	PRICE RANGE	AVG. P/E RATIO	AVG. YIELD
p12/31/02	2,251.3	⑨ 60.4							⑧ 1.02			...	35.09 - 7.58	20.9	...
12/31/01	1,917.5	⑧ 16.4	2,051.6	7.4	0.9	4.1	0.8	2.2	⑧ 0.42	2.50	...	...	33.30 - 18.70	61.9	...
12/31/00	1,538.3	⑦ 15.3	2,110.1	6.0	1.0	5.2	0.7	2.1	⑦ 0.40	1.91	...	...	23.50 - 10.56	42.6	3.1
12/31/99	1,061.3	⑥ 12.2	838.2	3.0	1.1	4.0	1.5	2.3	⑥ 0.32	1.37	5.66	0.56	21.56 - 15.00	57.1	2.3
12/31/98	1,083.1	⑤ 47.7	870.2	7.9	4.4	13.8	5.5	2.2	⑤ 1.20	2.18	6.73	0.56	33.75 - 15.38	20.5	1.8
12/31/97	1,152.2	④ 51.6	880.0	7.3	4.5	13.0	5.9	2.2	④ 1.26	2.21	7.77	0.56	36.69 - 26.00	24.9	...
12/31/96	605.5	③ 43.3	425.5	10.6	7.1	21.6	10.2	2.6	③ 1.77	2.59	8.51	0.52	...	...	...
12/31/95	532.7	② 30.7	395.4	9.4	5.8	15.7	7.8	2.5	② 1.24	2.01	8.02	0.46	...	...	...
12/31/94	345.4	17.2	274.1	7.8	5.0	12.3	6.3	2.8	0.90	1.63	7.34	0.42	...	...	...
12/31/93	313.9	① 15.9	247.9	8.2	5.1	12.4	6.4	3.1	① 0.87	1.45	6.73	0.40	...	...	...

Statistics are as originally reported. ① Excl. $385,000 acctg. chg. ② Incl. $5.0 mill. integr. exp. ③ Incl. $5.8 mill. restr. & merg. trans. exp. ④ Incl. $44.5 mill. restr. exp., $7.0 mill. integr. exp. & $11.4 mill. gain fr. sale of sub. ⑤ Incl. $38.3 mill. integr. exp. & excl. $1.2 mill. acctg. chg. ⑥ Incl. $15.9 mill. restr. exp. & $14.2 mill. integr. exp. ⑦ Incl. $19.4 mill. restr. exp., $35.2 mill. integr. exp. & excl. $2.1 mill. extraord. loss. ⑧ Incl. $1.2 mill. restr. gain, $63.0 mill. integr. exp. & excl. extraord. loss of $17.9 mill. ⑨ Incl. $16.2 mill. integr. exp., $4.3 mill. restr. exp., & excl. $7.4 mill. extraord. chrg.

OFFICERS:
C. S. Greer, Chmn., Pres., C.E.O.
R. J. Hornbaker, V.P., C.F.O.
D. F. Chevenson, V.P., Treas.
INVESTOR CONTACT: Mike Conley, Dir., Investor Relations, (972) 443-6557
PRINCIPAL OFFICE: 222 W. Las Colinas Blvd., Suite 1500, Irving, TX 75039

TELEPHONE NUMBER: (972) 443-6500
FAX: (972) 443-6800
WEB: www.flowserve.com
NO. OF EMPLOYEES: 11,000 (approx.)
SHAREHOLDERS: 1,800 (approximately); 12,100 approximate beneficial
ANNUAL MEETING: In Apr.
INCORPORATED: NY, May, 1912

INSTITUTIONAL HOLDINGS:
No. of Institutions: 163
Shares Held: 48,350,894
% Held: 87.6
INDUSTRY: Pumps and pumping equipment (SIC: 3561)
TRANSFER AGENT(S): National City Bank, Cleveland, OH

FLUOR CORPORATION

EXCH.	SYM.	REC. PRICE	P/E RATIO	YLD.	MKT. CAP.	RANGE (52-WK.)	'02 Y/E PR.
NYSE	FLR	28.23 (2/28/03)	13.3	2.3%	$2.26 bill.	44.95 - 20.06	28.00

MEDIUM GRADE. THE COMPANY'S NEAR-TERM AND LONG-TERM PROSPECTS APPEAR BRIGHT.

*7 YEAR PRICE SCORE N/A ***12 MONTH PRICE SCORE 98.7**

*NYSE COMPOSITE INDEX=100

INTERIM EARNINGS (Per Share):

Qtr.	Jan.	April	July	Oct.
1998-99	0.40	d1.19	0.44	0.70
1999-00	0.49	0.48	0.12	0.22
Qtr.	Mar.	June	Sept.	Dec.
2000	. . .	. . .	. . .	d0.05
2001	0.15	0.43	0.56	0.39
2002	0.45	0.54	0.58	0.56

INTERIM DIVIDENDS (Per Share):

Amt.	Decl.	Ex.	Rec.	Pay.
0.16Q	2/06/02	3/07/02	3/11/02	4/01/02
0.16Q	5/08/02	6/06/02	6/10/02	7/01/02
0.16Q	8/06/02	9/06/02	9/10/02	10/01/02
0.16Q	11/06/02	12/06/02	12/10/02	1/02/03
0.16Q	2/05/03	3/07/03	3/11/03	4/01/03

Indicated div.: $0.64

CAPITALIZATION (12/31/01):

	($000)	(%)
Long-Term Debt	17,594	2.2
Common & Surplus	789,266	97.8
Total	806,860	100.0

BUSINESS:

Fluor Corporation is a holding company that provides services on a global basis in the fields of engineering, procurement, construction, operations, maintenance and project management. These services are grouped into five business segments: Energy & Chemicals, Industrial & Infrastructure, Power, Global Services and Government Services. On 11/30/00, the old Fluor Corporation completed a reverse spin-off transaction wherein two publicly-traded companies were created: Massey Energy Company and a "new" Fluor Corporation.

RECENT DEVELOPMENTS:

For the year ended 12/31/02, income from continuing operations increased 33.0% to $170.0 million compared with income from continuing operations of $127.8 million in 2001. Results for 2002 and 2001 excluded losses from discontinued operations of $6.4 million and $108.4 million, respectively. Revenues advanced 11.0% to $9.96 billion from $8.97 billion a year earlier. Results benefited from lower expenses, new project activity and the completion of a record number of projects.

PROSPECTS:

Now that funding issues have been resolved, the Company expects to move forward with the Tengizchevroil (TCO) project, an oil producing partnership in Kazakhstan, that had been suspended in November 2002. Meanwhile, the Company is focusing on near-term opportunities in the areas of federal services, life sciences, and transportation. Moreover, longer-term business prospects look promising as FLR's clients continue to indicate their long-term commitment to invest in an assortment of major upstream oil and gas projects. As of 12/31/02, new awards and backlog amounted to $8.60 billion and $9.70 billion, respectively. FLR expects full-year 2003 earnings in the range of $2.13 to $2.35 per share. Separately, in January 2003, the Company agreed to acquire DEL-JEN, INC., a provider of outsourced services to the U.S. Government. This acquisition should help FLR to achieve its strategic objective to broaden its participation in the large, relatively stable government services market.

ANNUAL FINANCIAL DATA:

FISCAL YEAR	TOT. REVS. ($mill.)	NET INC. ($mill.)	TOT. ASSETS ($mill.)	OPER. PROFIT %	NET PROFIT %	RET. ON EQUITY %	RET. ON ASSETS %	CURR. RATIO	EARN. PER SH.$	CASH FL.PER SH.$	TANG. BK. VAL.$	DIV. PER SH.$	PRICE RANGE	AVG. P/E RATIO	AVG. YIELD %
p12/31/02	9,959.0	⑥ 170.0							⑥ 2.13			0.64	44.95 - 20.06	15.3	2.0
⑤ 12/31/01	8,972.2	⑥ 127.8	3,091.2	2.1	1.4	16.2	4.1	1.0	⑥ 1.61	3.09	9.57	0.48	63.20 - 31.20	29.3	1.0
① 10/31/00	9,970.2	④ 99.8	3,652.7	1.6	1.0	6.2	2.7	0.9	④ 1.31	5.47	19.96	. . .	33.31 - 21.00	20.7	. . .
① 10/31/99	11,334.4	③ 26.7	4,886.1	0.7	0.2	1.7	0.5	0.9	③ 0.35	4.54	19.27	. . .	. . .	. . .	. . .
① 10/31/98	12,377.5	② 135.9	. . .	1.7	1.1	. . .	. . .	. . .	② 1.72	5.37	. . .	. . .	. . .	. . .	. . .

Statistics are as originally reported. ① Pro forma ② Bef. discont. oper. of $99.4 mill. ③ Bef. discont. oper. of $77.5 mill., but incl. a spec. prov. loss of $117.2 mill. to implement a strategic reorg. ④ Bef. inc. from discont. oper. of $49.1 mill., bef. net loss on disposal of $25.0 mill., but incl. a reverse spec. prov. credit of $17.9 mill. ⑤ For fourteen months due to fiscal year end change to 12/31. ⑥ Bef. discont. oper. loss of $6.4 mill, 2002; $108.4 mill., 2001.

OFFICERS:
A. L. Boeckmann, Chmn., C.E.O.
D. M. Steuert, Sr. V.P., C.F.O.
L. N. Fisher, Sr. V.P., Sec.

INVESTOR CONTACT: Lila Churney, Inv. Rel., (949) 349-3909

PRINCIPAL OFFICE: One Enterprise Drive, Aliso Viejo, CA 92656

TELEPHONE NUMBER: (949) 349-2000
FAX: (949) 349-7220
WEB: www.fluor.com

NO. OF EMPLOYEES: 51,313 (avg.)

SHAREHOLDERS: 11,725 (record)

ANNUAL MEETING: In May

INCORPORATED: DE, Sept., 2000

INSTITUTIONAL HOLDINGS:
No. of Institutions: 230
Shares Held: 62,724,343
% Held: 78.1

INDUSTRY: Engineering services (SIC: 8711)

TRANSFER AGENT(S): Mellon Investor Services LLC, Los Angeles, CA

FMC CORPORATION

EXCH.	SYM.	REC. PRICE	P/E RATIO	YLD.	MKT. CAP.	RANGE (52-WK.)	'02 Y/E PR.
NYSE	FMC	15.53 (2/28/03)	7.8	...	$486.2 mill.	42.30 - 15.53	27.32

LOWER MEDIUM GRADE. THE COMPANY EXPECTS BUSINESS CONDITIONS IN 2003 TO CONTINUE TO BE CHALLENGING.

*7 YEAR PRICE SCORE 51.5   *12 MONTH PRICE SCORE 73.5

*NYSE COMPOSITE INDEX=100

INTERIM EARNINGS (Per Share):

Qtr.	Mar.	June	Sept.	Dec.
1997	'1.05	1.90	1.43	d4.50
1998	0.75	1.89	1.60	1.06
1999	0.92	2.10	1.98	1.69
2000	1.05	1.20	1.79	1.57
2001	d0.68	d9.62	0.66	d1.14
2002	0.28	0.57	0.79	0.35

INTERIM DIVIDENDS (Per Share):

Amt.	Decl.	Ex.	Rec.	Pay.
		No dividends paid.		

CAPITALIZATION (12/31/01):

	($000)	(%)
Long-Term Debt	651,800	71.2
Minority Interest	44,800	4.9
Common & Surplus	218,800	23.9
Total	915,400	100.0

BUSINESS:

FMC Corporation is a diversified chemical company that serves agricultural, industrial and consumer markets globally. The Company is divided into three operating segments: Agricultural Products, Specialty Chemicals and Industrial Chemicals. On 12/31/01, the Company completed the separation of FMC Technologies, Inc. through the distribution of all of its remaining shares of FMC Technologies common stock. The distribution completed the separation of the Company into two independent public companies. Revenues for 2002 were derived: Industrial Chemicals, 40.6%; Agricultural Products, 33.1%; and Specialty Chemicals, 26.3%.

RECENT DEVELOPMENTS:

For the twelve months ended 12/31/02, income from continuing operations amounted to $69.1 million compared with a loss from continuing operations of $306.3 million, before an accounting change charge of $900,000, in 2001. Results for 2002 and 2001 included restructuring and other charges of $30.1 million and $280.4 million, respectively. Results for 2001 also included an asset impairment charge of $323.1 million. Results for 2002 and 2001 excluded losses of $3.3 million and $30.5 million, respectively, from discontinued operations. Revenue was $1.85 billion, down 4.6% from $1.94 billion in the prior year, reflecting lower herbicide sales in the Agricultural Products segment and reduced soda ash volumes, lower oxygen prices, as well as decreased prices and volumes at Foret.

PROSPECTS:

The Company expects challenging business conditions to continue in 2003, particularly in the Industrial Chemicals segment. However, the Company is confident that year-over-year operating profit will be achieved in the Agricultural Products and Specialty Chemicals segments. Global selling prices of phosphorus chemicals continue to be pressured. This will likely lead to further deterioration of performance in FMC's phosphorus businesses. Nevertheless, the Company expects earnings per share for full-year 2003 in the range of $1.75 to $2.00.

ANNUAL FINANCIAL DATA:

FISCAL YEAR	TOT. REVS. ($mill.)	NET INC. ($mill.)	TOT. ASSETS ($mill.)	OPER. PROFIT %	NET PROFIT %	RET. ON EQUITY %	RET. ON ASSETS %	CURR. RATIO	EARN. PER SH.$	CASH FL. PER SH.$	TANG. BK. VAL.$	PRICE RANGE	AVG. P/E RATIO
p12/31/02	1,852.9	9 69.1							9 2.01			42.30 - 22.90	16.2
8 12/31/01	1,943.0	7 d306.3	2,477.2	...	...	...	...	0.8	7 d9.85	d5.63	3.27	84.00 - 45.65	...
12/31/00	3,925.5	6 177.3	3,745.9	8.4	4.5	22.2	4.7	0.9	6 5.62	11.60	9.98	77.19 - 46.06	11.0
12/31/99	4,110.6	5 216.0	3,995.8	8.8	5.3	29.0	5.4	0.9	6.67	12.56	7.84	75.25 - 39.25	8.6
12/31/98	4,378.4	4 185.3	4,166.4	8.3	4.2	25.4	4.4	1.2	4 5.30	11.22	10.10	82.19 - 48.25	12.3
12/31/97	4,312.6	3 d24.5	4,113.1	6.5	...	...	...	1.2	3 d0.67	5.81	9.74	91.44 - 59.38	...
12/31/96	5,080.6	2 218.1	4,989.8	6.3	4.3	25.5	4.4	1.1	5.73	12.41	9.60	78.00 - 60.88	12.1
12/31/95	4,566.6	1 215.6	4,301.1	6.2	4.7	33.0	5.0	1.0	5.72	12.31	8.38	80.00 - 57.13	12.0
12/31/94	4,051.3	173.4	3,351.5	6.2	4.3	41.6	5.2	1.1	4.66	10.82	8.01	65.13 - 45.50	11.9
12/31/93	3,789.0	1 41.0	2,813.1	1.1	1.1	18.9	1.5	1.0	1 1.11	7.04	3.46	54.00 - 41.50	43.0

Statistics are as originally reported. ① Incl. $99.7 mill. gain & $134.5 mill. restr. chgs., 1995; bef. $4.7 mill. extraord. chg. (but incl. $172.3 mill. restr. chg.), 1993. ② Bef. $7.4 mill. loss fr. disc. ops. ③ Incl. $224.0 mill. pre-tax chg. fr asset impair.: $40.9 mill. pre-tax restr. chgs.; excl. $4.5 mill. net acct. chgs.; and $191.4 mill. gain fr. disc. ops. ④ Excl. d$36.1 mill. net effect of acct. chg. ⑤ Excl. $3.4 mill. net gain fr. disc. ops. and incl. $55.5 mill. gain fr. sale of bus., $29.1 mill. asset impair. chg., & $14.7 mill. restr. chgs. ⑥ Incl. $56.6 mill. asset impair. & restr. chgs. and excl. $66.7 mill. loss fr. disc. ops. ⑦ Incl. $323.1 mill. asset impair. & $280.4 mill. restr. chg. and excl. $30.5 mill. loss fr. disc. ops. & $900,000 acctg. chg. ⑧ Refl. spin-off of FMC Technologies, Inc. ⑨ Incl. $30.1 mill. restr. chg. & excl. $3.3 mill. gain fr. disc. ops.

OFFICERS:	TELEPHONE NUMBER: (215) 299-6000	INSTITUTIONAL HOLDINGS:
W. G. Walter, Chmn., Pres., C.E.O.	FAX: (215) 299-6618	No. of Institutions: 168
W. K. Foster, Sr. V.P., C.F.O.	WEB: www.fmc.com	Shares Held: 27,562,934
A. E. Utecht, V.P., Gen. Couns., Sec.	NO. OF EMPLOYEES: 6,000 (approx.)	% Held: 78.6
INVESTOR CONTACT: Elisabeth Azzarello, Director, Investor Relations, (312) 861-6921	SHAREHOLDERS: 8,022 (registered)	INDUSTRY: Industrial machinery and equipment (SIC: 5084)
PRINCIPAL OFFICE: 1735 Market Street, Philadelphia, PA 19103	ANNUAL MEETING: In Apr.	TRANSFER AGENT(S): Computershare Investor Services, Chicago, IL
	INCORPORATED: DE, Aug., 1928	

FOOT LOCKER, INC.

EXCH.	SYM.	REC. PRICE	P/E RATIO	YLD.	MKT. CAP.	RANGE (52-WK.)	'02 Y/E PR.
NYSE	FL	10.20 (2/28/03)	9.3	1.2%	$1.43 bill.	17.95 - 8.20	10.50

LOWER MEDIUM GRADE. EARNINGS ARE BENEFITING FROM INCREASED SALES OF PRIVATE-LABEL APPAREL AND THE COMPANY'S EXPANSION ACTIVITY IN EUROPE.

TRADING VOLUME Thousand Shares

*7 YEAR PRICE SCORE 86.1   ***12 MONTH PRICE SCORE 90.6**
*NYSE COMPOSITE INDEX=100

INTERIM EARNINGS (Per Share):

Qtr.	Apr.	July	Oct.	Jan.
1996-97	d0.17	0.17	0.52	0.74
1997-98	0.01	0.19	0.41	0.85
1998-99	d0.04	d0.09	d0.29	0.21
1999-00	d0.08	0.30	0.05	0.44
2000-01	0.11	0.07	0.18	0.31
2001-02	0.24	0.03	0.23	0.28
2002-03	0.26	0.22	0.29	0.33

INTERIM DIVIDENDS (Per Share):

Amt.	Decl.	Ex.	Rec.	Pay.
0.03Q	11/20/02	1/15/03	1/17/03	1/31/03
0.03Q	2/19/03	4/15/03	4/17/03	5/02/03

Indicated div.: $0.12

CAPITALIZATION (2/2/02):

	($000)	(%)
Long-Term Debt	365,000	26.9
Common & Surplus	992,000	73.1
Total	1,357,000	100.0

BUSINESS:

Foot Locker, Inc. (formerly Venator Group, Inc.) is primarily a mall-based retailer of athletic apparel and footwear. As of 2/1/03, the Company operated 3,625 stores in 14 countries in North America, Europe and Australia, under the names Foot Locker, Lady Foot Locker, Kids Foot Locker and Champs Sports, as well as Footlocker.com/Eastbay, the Company's Internet and catalog operations. In 1998, FL sold its 357-store German General Merchandise business, its six-store nursery chain, and divested its Specialty Footwear segment, comprised of 467 Kinney shoe stores and 103 Footquarters stores. In 1999, the Company sold its 768-store Afterthoughts fashion accessory chain. In 2001, FL divested its Northern Group chain of apparel stores.

RECENT DEVELOPMENTS:

For the year ended 2/1/03, income from continuing operations totaled $162.0 million compared with income from continuing operations of $111.0 million in the prior year. Results included a pre-tax restructuring credit of $2.0 million in fiscal 2002 and a pre-tax restructuring charge of $34.0 million in fiscal 2001. Sales were $4.51 billion, up 3.0% versus $4.38 billion the previous year. Comparable-store sales inched up 0.1% year over year. Income before taxes climbed 40.6% to $246.0 million from $175.0 million a year earlier. On 3/31/03, the Company's common stock began trading on the NYSE under the ticker symbol FL.

PROSPECTS:

Earnings growth is being fueled by significant growth of the Company's European operations and improved profitability from Champs Sports stores. In addition, results are benefiting from continued growth of the Company's catalog and Internet direct-to-customer businesses, an expanded selection of private-label apparel, and the implementation of cost-control initiatives. Meanwhile, challenging retail market conditions are expected to persist over the near term due to economic uncertainties stemming from a possible war with Iraq.

ANNUAL FINANCIAL DATA:

FISCAL YEAR	TOT. REVS. ($mill.)	NET INC. ($mill.)	TOT. ASSETS ($mill.)	OPER. PROFIT %	NET PROFIT %	RET. ON EQUITY %	RET. ON ASSETS %	CURR. RATIO	EARN. PER SH. $	CASH FL. PER SH. $	TANG. BK. VAL.$	DIV. PER SH. $	PRICE RANGE	AVG. P/E RATIO	AVG. YIELD %
p2/01/03	4,509.0	⑩ 162.0							⑩ 1.10			...	17.95 - 8.20	11.9	...
2/02/02	4,379.0	⑨ 111.0	2,290.0	4.5	2.5	11.2	4.8	2.1	⑨ 0.77	1.80	5.91	...	19.10 - 9.75	18.7	...
2/03/01	4,356.0	⑧ 107.0	2,232.0	4.2	2.5	10.6	4.8	1.6	⑧ 0.77	1.85	6.28	...	16.50 - 5.00	14.0	...
1/29/00	4,647.0	⑦ 17.0	2,515.0	...	0.4	1.5	0.7	1.4	⑦ 0.13	1.43	7.18	...	12.00 - 3.19	58.4	...
1/30/99	4,555.0	⑥ 3.0	2,876.0	...	0.1	0.3	0.1	1.3	⑥ 0.02	1.14	6.39	...	27.25 - 5.81	822.5	...
1/31/98	6,624.0	⑤ 213.0	3,182.0	5.3	3.2	16.8	6.7	1.9	⑤ 1.57	2.81	9.41	...	28.75 - 18.25	15.0	...
1/25/97	8,092.0	④ 169.0	3,476.0	3.9	2.1	12.7	4.9	2.1	④ 1.26	2.66	9.96	...	25.25 - 9.38	13.7	...
1/27/96	8,224.0	③ d164.0	3,506.0	1.0	...	...	...	1.9	③ d1.23	0.56	9.24	0.15	19.38 - 12.25	...	0.9
1/28/95	8,238.0	② 47.0	4,173.0	1.8	0.6	3.5	1.1	1.2	② 0.36	2.12	10.29	0.88	26.25 - 12.88	54.3	4.5
1/29/94	9,626.0	① 63.0	4,593.0	...	0.7	4.7	1.4	1.2	① d3.76	2.42	10.21	1.15	32.75 - 20.50	...	4.3

Statistics are as originally reported. ① Incl. $391 mil ($2.97/sh) after-tax restr. chg. & $104 mil ($0.79/sh) chg. for sale of opers. ② Incl. $30 mil prov for disp. of opers. & incl. $41 mil gain fr sale of secs. ③ Incl. $165 mil chg. for writedown of assets & $5 mil chg. for sale of opers. ④ Incl. $10 mil net loss fr disposal of opers. & sale of real est. ⑤ Incl. $9 mil net gain & bef. $223 mil ($1.64/sh) net loss from discont. opers. ⑥ Bef. discont. opers. loss $139.0 mil ($1.02/sh) ⑦ Incl. $144 mil pre-tax restr. chg. & bef. $23 mil ($0.16/sh) inc. fr. disc. opers. & $8 mil ($0.06/sh) acctg. gain. ⑧ Bef. $346 mil ($2.49/sh) loss fr. disc. opers., $1 mil ($0.01/sh) acctg. chrg. & incl. $1 mil restr. chg. ⑨ Bef. $19 mil ($0.13/sh) loss fr. disc. opers. & incl. $34 mil pre-tax restr. chg. ⑩ Bef. $18 mil ($0.11/sh) loss fr. disc. opers. & incl. $2 mil pre-tax restr. gain.

OFFICERS:
J. C. Bacot, Chmn.
M. D. Serra, Pres., C.E.O.
B. L. Hartman, Exec. V.P., C.F.O.
INVESTOR CONTACT: Juris Pagrabs, Dir., Investor Relations, (212) 553-2600
PRINCIPAL OFFICE: 112 West 34th Street, New York, NY 10120

TELEPHONE NUMBER: (212) 720-3700
FAX: (212) 553-7026
WEB: www.footlocker-inc.com
NO. OF EMPLOYEES: 40,104 (approx.)
SHAREHOLDERS: 31,085
ANNUAL MEETING: In June
INCORPORATED: NY, Dec., 1911; reincorp., NY, 1989

INSTITUTIONAL HOLDINGS:
No. of Institutions: 200
Shares Held: 129,184,342
% Held: 91.6

INDUSTRY: Shoe stores (SIC: 5661)

TRANSFER AGENT(S): The Bank of New York, New York, NY

FORD MOTOR COMPANY

EXCH.	SYM.	REC. PRICE	P/E RATIO	YLD.	MKT. CAP.	RANGE (52-WK.)	'02 Y/E PR.
NYSE	F	8.32 (2/28/03)	55.5	4.8%	$15.87 bill.	18.23 - 6.90	9.30

LOWER MEDIUM GRADE. THE COMPANY EXPECTS FULL-YEAR 2003 EARNINGS OF APPROXIMATELY $0.70 PER DILUTED SHARE.

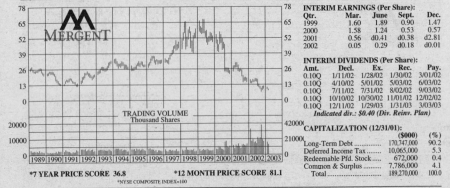

INTERIM EARNINGS (Per Share):

Qtr.	Mar.	June	Sept.	Dec.
1999	1.60	1.89	0.90	1.47
2000	1.58	1.24	0.53	0.57
2001	0.56	d0.41	d0.38	d2.81
2002	0.05	0.29	d0.18	d0.01

INTERIM DIVIDENDS (Per Share):

Amt.	Decl.	Ex.	Rec.	Pay.
0.10Q	1/11/02	1/28/02	1/30/02	3/01/02
0.10Q	4/10/02	5/01/02	5/03/02	6/03/02
0.10Q	7/11/02	7/31/02	8/02/02	9/03/02
0.10Q	10/10/02	10/30/02	11/01/02	12/02/02
0.10Q	12/11/02	1/29/03	1/31/03	3/03/03

Indicated div.: $0.40 (Div. Reinv. Plan)

CAPITALIZATION (12/31/01):

	($000)	(%)
Long-Term Debt	170,747,000	90.2
Deferred Income Tax	10,065,000	5.3
Redeemable Pfd. Stock	672,000	0.4
Common & Surplus	7,786,000	4.1
Total	189,270,000	100.0

*7 YEAR PRICE SCORE 36.8   ***12 MONTH PRICE SCORE 81.1**

*NYSE COMPOSITE INDEX=100

BUSINESS:

Ford Motor Company is the world's second largest automaker. Its automotive brands included Ford, Mercury, Lincoln, Volvo, Jaguar, Land Rover, Aston Martin and TH!NK. In addition, Ford owns 33.4% of Mazda Motor Corp. Ford operates through two segments. The Automotive segment (82.7% of 2002 revenues) engages in the design, manufacture, sale and service of cars, trucks, automotive components and systems. The Financial Services segment (17.3%), operates through Ford Motor Credit Company and The Hertz Corporation, and engages in vehicle-related financing, leasing and insurance and rental of vehicles and equipment. Ford acquired Land Rover on 6/30/00. On 1/28/00, Ford spun off Visteon Corp. On 3/9/01, Ford acquired The Hertz Corp.

RECENT DEVELOPMENTS:

For the year ended 12/31/02, the Company reported income from continuing operations of $284.0 million, before an accounting change charge of $1.00 billion, compared with a loss of $5.35 billion in the previous year. Results for 2002 and 2001 excluded losses from discontinued operations of $262.0 million and $104.0 million, respectively. Total sales and revenues increased 1.1% to $162.59 billion from $160.75 billion a year earlier. Automotive sales advanced 2.8% to $134.43 billion, while financial services revenues fell 5.9% to $28.16 billion. Cost of automotive sales decreased 2.6% to $125.14 billion, or 93.1% of sales, from $128.42 billion, or 98.2% of sales, the year before.

PROSPECTS:

The Company continues to make progress towards its revitalization plan goals. During 2002, the Company exceeded nearly all of its commitments and remains on track to reach its target of an annual pre-tax operating profit of $7.00 billion by the middle of this decade. In 2003, Ford will focus on improving total cost and will accelerate the implementation of key elements of its revitalization plan. Separately, while the outlook for the U.S. economy continues to be uncertain, Ford expects 2003 to be another good year for car and truck sales. The Company expects full-year 2003 earnings of approximately $0.70 per diluted share.

ANNUAL FINANCIAL DATA:

FISCAL YEAR	TOT. REVS. ($mill.)	NET INC. ($mill.)	TOT. ASSETS ($mill.)	OPER. PROFIT %	NET PROFIT %	RET. ON EQUITY %	RET. ON ASSETS %	CURR. RATIO	EARN. PER SH.$	CASH FL. PER SH.$	TANG. BK. VAL.$	DIV. PER SH.$	PRICE RANGE	AVG. P/E RATIO	AVG. YIELD %
p12/31/02	162,586.0	⑥ 284.0		7.9	...	...	0.7	⑥ 0.15			0.40	18.23 - 6.90	83.8	3.2
12/31/01	162,412.0	⑤ d5,453.0	276,543.0		...	...		⑤ d3.02	2.06	4.08	1.05	31.42 - 14.70		4.6
12/31/00	170,064.0	④ 5,410.0	284,421.0	14.5	3.2	29.1	1.9	0.8	④ 3.59	14.19	9.75	1.80	57.25 - 21.69	11.0	4.6
12/31/99	162,558.0	7,237.0	276,229.0	15.2	4.5	26.3	2.6	1.0	3.58	18.18	22.53	1.88	67.88 - 46.25	9.7	3.3
12/31/98	144,416.0	③ 22,071.0	237,545.0	16.2	15.3	94.3	9.3	1.0	③ 17.76	29.34	19.17	1.72	65.94 - 38.81	2.9	3.3
12/31/97	153,627.0	② 6,920.0	279,097.0	19.5	4.5	22.5	2.5	1.0	② 5.62	16.71	25.55	1.65	50.25 - 30.00	7.1	4.1
12/31/96	146,991.0	① 4,446.0	262,867.0	16.7	3.0	16.6	1.7	0.9	① 3.72	14.56	22.51	1.47	37.25 - 27.25	8.7	4.6
12/31/95	137,137.0	4,139.0	243,283.0	17.1	3.0	17.7	1.7	0.9	3.58	14.53	20.14	1.23	32.88 - 24.63	8.0	4.3
12/31/94	128,439.0	5,308.0	219,354.0	17.3	4.1	24.9	2.4	1.0	4.97	14.21	20.80	0.91	35.06 - 25.63	6.1	3.0
12/31/93	108,521.0	2,529.0	198,938.0	14.1	2.3	16.2	1.3	0.7	2.27	9.85	15.61	0.80	33.06 - 21.50	12.0	2.9

Statistics are as originally reported. Adj. for stk. splits: 2-for-1, 7/94. ① Incl. non-recurr credit $512.0 mill. & chrg. $669.0 mill. ② Incl. non-recurr. credit $269.0 mill. from the IPO of Hertz Corp. & fr sale of Ford's heavy truck bus. ③ Incl. non-recurring gain $15.96 billion from spin-off of Associates First Capital. ④ Bef. net loss from disc. ops. of $1.94 bill. ⑤ Incl. restr. and other non-recurr. chrg. of $4.67 billion. ⑥ Bef. an acctg. change chrg. of $1.00 billion and a loss from disc. opers. of $262.0 mill.

OFFICERS: W. C. Ford Jr., Chmn., C.E.O. A. Gilmour, Vice-Chmn., C.F.O. N. V. Scheele, Pres., C.O.O. **INVESTOR CONTACT:** Investor Relations, (313) 845-8540 **PRINCIPAL OFFICE:** One American Road, Dearborn, MI 48126	**TELEPHONE NUMBER:** (313) 322-3000 **FAX:** (313) 845-7512 **WEB:** www.ford.com **NO. OF EMPLOYEES:** 335,000 (approx.) **SHAREHOLDERS:** 184,938 (approx.) **ANNUAL MEETING:** In May **INCORPORATED:** DE, July, 1919	**INSTITUTIONAL HOLDINGS:** No. of Institutions: 560 Shares Held: 643,341,916 % Held: 35.1 **INDUSTRY:** Motor vehicles and car bodies (SIC: 3711) **TRANSFER AGENT(S):** EquiServe, First Chicago Trust Division, Jersey City, NJ

FOREST LABORATORIES, INC.

EXCH.	SYM.	REC. PRICE	P/E RATIO	YLD.	MKT. CAP.	RANGE (52-WK.)	'02 Y/E PR.
NYSE	FRX	53.97 (3/31/03)	43.9	...	$19.35 bill.	56.36 - 32.13	49.11

INVESTMENT GRADE. GOING FORWARD, RESULTS SHOULD CONTINUE TO BENEFIT FROM GROWTH IN THE COMPANY'S ANTIDEPRESSANT FRANCHISE.

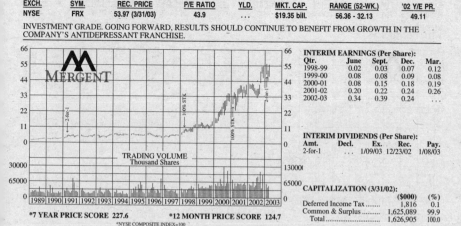

INTERIM EARNINGS (Per Share):

Qtr.	June	Sept.	Dec.	Mar.
1998-99	0.02	0.03	0.07	0.12
1999-00	0.08	0.08	0.09	0.08
2000-01	0.08	0.15	0.18	0.19
2001-02	0.20	0.22	0.24	0.26
2002-03	0.34	0.39	0.24	...

INTERIM DIVIDENDS (Per Share):

Amt.	Decl.	Ex.	Rec.	Pay.
2-for-1	...	1/09/03	12/23/02	1/08/03

*7 YEAR PRICE SCORE 227.6   ***12 MONTH PRICE SCORE 124.7**

*NYSE COMPOSITE INDEX=100

CAPITALIZATION (3/31/02):

	($000)	(%)
Deferred Income Tax	1,816	0.1
Common & Surplus	1,625,089	99.9
Total	1,626,905	100.0

BUSINESS:

Forest Laboratories, Inc. develops, manufactures and markets branded and generic forms of ethical drug products, which require a physician's prescription, as well as non-prescription pharmaceuticals sold over-the-counter, which are used for the treatment of a wide range of illnesses. FRX products include, CELEXA™, for the treatment of depression; TIAZAC®, for the treatment of angina and hypertension; BENICAR™, for the treatment of hypertension and AEROBID®, for the treatment of asthma. FRX's products are marketed principally in the United States, western and eastern Europe, and in Puerto Rico and other Caribbean Islands. Marketing is conducted by FRX and through independent distributors and under exclusive marketing contracts with major pharmaceutical companies. In fiscal 2002, sales outside the U.S. contributed 2.7% to net sales.

RECENT DEVELOPMENTS:

For the three months ended 12/31/02, net income nearly doubled to $174.6 million compared with $87.4 million in the corresponding quarter of the previous year. Net revenues soared 44.2% to $593.9 million from $411.9 million in the year-earlier period. Net sales advanced 45.6% to $586.8 million from $403.1 million, while other income decreased 19.7% to $7.1 million from $8.8 million in the prior-year quarter. Sales of CELEXA™, a selective serotonin reuptake inhibitor, improved 32.3% to $371.2 million from $280.5 million the year before. Sales of LEXAPRO™, FRX's recently introduced selective serotonin reuptake inhibitor, were $81.0 million.

PROSPECTS:

The Company expects the U.S. Food and Drug Administration to approve its antidepressant, LEXAPRO, for the additional indication of general anxiety disorder in early 2004. LEXAPRO is a next-generation version of FRX's CELEXA, which will lose patent exclusivity in January 2004. In anticipation, the Company has stopped promoting CELEXA, and is working to switch patients over to LEXAPRO. Separately, the Company announced that its new drug application for memantin, for the treatment of Alzheimer's disease, was accepted for filing by the U.S. FDA. FRX should receive an initial action letter from the FDA by the end of 2003.

ANNUAL FINANCIAL DATA:

FISCAL YEAR	TOT. REVS. ($mill.)	NET INC. ($mill.)	TOT. ASSETS. ($mill.)	OPER. PROFIT %	NET PROFIT %	RET. ON EQUITY %	RET. ON ASSETS %	CURR. RATIO	EARN. PER SH. $	CASH FL. PER SH. $	TANG. BK. VAL. $	PRICE RANGE	AVG. P/E RATIO
3/31/02	1,601.8	338.0	1,951.9	29.4	21.1	20.8	17.3	3.7	0.91	1.06	3.75	41.60 - 23.25	35.6
3/31/01	1,205.2	215.1	1,446.9	24.8	17.8	17.6	14.9	4.0	0.59	0.71	2.64	35.33 - 14.34	42.1
3/31/00	899.3	② 112.7	1,097.6	17.5	12.5	12.7	10.3	3.1	② 0.32	0.44	1.79	15.44 - 10.31	40.2
3/31/99	624.0	77.2	875.1	17.8	12.4	10.4	8.8	3.9	0.23	0.29	1.60	13.31 - 6.08	43.1
3/31/98	474.7	① 36.7	744.3	11.5	7.7	6.0	4.9	2.9	① 0.11	0.17	1.24	6.04 - 3.95	45.4
3/31/97	309.1	① d23.5	700.3	...	...	...	...	4.9	① d0.07	d0.01	1.22	6.97 - 3.53	...
3/31/96	459.9	104.2	899.4	35.3	22.7	12.9	11.6	5.3	0.28	0.32	1.58	6.53 - 5.05	20.8
3/31/95	404.8	100.1	757.2	38.6	24.7	14.3	13.2	6.1	0.27	0.31	1.43	6.56 - 5.00	21.5
3/31/94	361.3	80.2	619.2	34.7	22.2	14.0	13.0	6.7	0.22	0.25	1.21	5.98 - 3.44	21.5
3/31/93	296.4	64.3	520.5	34.6	21.7	13.3	12.4	7.6	0.18	0.21	0.99	5.61 - 3.75	26.3

Statistics are as originally reported. Adj. for stk. split: 2-for-1, 3/25/98, 1/11/01 & 1/08/03 ① Incl. non-recurr. chrg. 3/31/98: $32.3 mill.; credit 3/31/97: $19.1 mill. ② Incl. one-time chrg. of $14.0 mill. rel. to the term. of the Warner-Lambert co-prom. agree.

OFFICERS:
H. Solomon, Chmn., C.EO.
K. E. Goodman, Pres., C.O.O.
J. E. Eggers, V.P., C.F.O.
INVESTOR CONTACT: Investor Relations, (212) 421-7850
PRINCIPAL OFFICE: 909 Third Avenue, New York, NY 10022-4731

TELEPHONE NUMBER: (212) 421-7850
FAX: (212) 750-9152
WEB: www.forestlaboratories.com
NO. OF EMPLOYEES: 3,731
SHAREHOLDERS: 1,875 (record)
ANNUAL MEETING: In Aug.
INCORPORATED: DE, Apr., 1956

INSTITUTIONAL HOLDINGS:
No. of Institutions: 459
Shares Held: 376,761,770
% Held: 208.2
INDUSTRY: Pharmaceutical preparations (SIC: 2834)
TRANSFER AGENT(S): Mellon Investor Services, Ridgefield Park, NJ

FOREST OIL CORPORATION

EXCH.	SYM.	REC. PRICE	P/E RATIO	YLD.	MKT. CAP.	RANGE (52-WK.)	'02 Y/E PR.
NYSE	FST	22.75 (2/28/03)	44.6	...	$1.06 bill.	32.44 - 20.69	27.65

MEDIUM GRADE. THE COMPANY IS PROJECTING HIGHER FULL-YEAR 2003 DAILY PRODUCTION COMPARED WITH THE PRIOR YEAR.

*7 YEAR PRICE SCORE N/A *12 MONTH PRICE SCORE 101.0
*NYSE COMPOSITE INDEX=100

INTERIM EARNINGS (Per Share):

Qtr.	Mar.	June	Sept.	Dec.
1999	0.02	0.18	0.22	0.36
2000	0.48	0.38	0.70	1.16
2001	1.60	1.04	0.05	d0.56
2002	d0.03	0.25	0.10	0.19

INTERIM DIVIDENDS (Per Share):

Amt.	Decl.	Ex.	Rec.	Pay.
		No dividends paid.		

CAPITALIZATION (12/31/01):

	($000)	(%)
Long-Term Debt	594,178	38.7
Deferred Income Tax	16,426	1.1
Common & Surplus	923,943	60.2
Total	1,534,547	100.0

BUSINESS:

Forest Oil Corporation is an independent oil and gas company engaged in the exploration, development, acquisition, production and marketing of natural gas and liquids. FST's principal reserves and producing properties are all located in North America. In the U.S., FST operates in the following areas: offshore Gulf of Mexico, onshore Gulf Coast, the Western U.S. and Alaska. In Canada, FST's oil and gas operations are conducted by its wholly-owned subsidiary,

Canadian Forest Oil Ltd. The Company also has interests in other countries, principally South Africa, Gabon, Italy, Germany, Albania and Romania. In addition, FST conducts marketing and trading activities in Canada through Producers Marketing Ltd., a subsidiary of Canadian Forest. As of 12/31/02, FST's estimated proved reserves were 1,560 billion cubic feet equivalent of which about 52.0% was natural gas. On 12/7/00, FST acquired Forcenergy Inc.

RECENT DEVELOPMENTS:

For the year ended 12/31/02, earnings were $24.5 million versus $109.4 million a year earlier. Earnings included realized and unrealized losses on derivative instruments of $1.3 million and $788,000, respectively for 2002 and realized and unrealized gains of $11.6 million and $376,000 for 2001. Earnings for 2001 also included merger and seismic

licensing expenses of $9.8 million and impairment charges totaling $21.3 million. Earnings for 2002 and 2001 excluded extraordinary losses of $3.2 million and $5.6 million, respectively. Total revenue fell 33.8% to $475.7 million. FST attributed the lower results to decreased production volumes and lower average oil and gas sales prices.

PROSPECTS:

For 2003, FST expects that it will incur between $300.0 million and $350.0 million of capital expenditures, versus $354.2 million incurred in 2002 for acquisition, exploration and development activities. Also, FST is projecting full-

year 2003 daily production of between 420.0 million cubic feet equivalent per day (MMCFE) and 470.0 MMCFE, up from 394.4 MMCFE in 2002. FST expects production to be higher at year-end than the beginning of the year.

ANNUAL FINANCIAL DATA:

FISCAL YEAR	TOT. REVS. ($mill.)	NET INC. ($mill.)	TOT. ASSETS ($mill.)	OPER. PROFIT %	NET PROFIT %	RET. ON EQUITY %	RET. ON ASSETS %	CURR. RATIO	EARN. PER SH.$	CASH FL. PER SH.$	TANG. BK. VAL.$	PRICE RANGE	AVG. P/E RATIO
p12/31/02	⑨475.7	④24.5							④0.51			32.44 - 20.69	52.1
12/31/01	1,018.4	⑧109.4	1,796.4	24.0	10.7	11.8	6.1	0.8	⑧2.22	6.84	19.48	37.85 - 22.75	13.6
12/31/00	913.1	⑦130.6	1,752.4	22.2	14.3	15.2	7.5	1.0	⑦2.64	7.18	17.41	37.50 - 28.94	12.6
12/31/99	357.3	⑥19.6	800.1	12.5	5.5	6.2	2.5	0.8	⑥0.82	4.55	11.04	...	
12/31/98	321.8	⑤d197.8	759.7	...	...	...	...	1.0	⑤d9.66	d4.73	7.15	...	
12/31/97	339.6	④3.1	647.8	9.0	0.9	1.2	0.5	1.3	④0.16	4.80	12.97	...	
12/31/96	317.5	③1.1	563.5	9.4	0.4	0.5	0.2	0.8	③d0.08	4.66	12.91	...	
12/31/95	82.5	d18.0	321.0	8.9	...	...	...	0.7	d5.48	6.37	4.15	...	
12/31/94	115.9	②d67.9	324.8	14.6	...	...	...	0.5	②d54.80	d1.62	...	...	
12/31/93	105.1	①d9.4	426.8	12.4	...	...	...	0.7	①d11.10	22.27	25.90	...	

Statistics are as originally reported. Adj. for 1-for-2 reverse stock split, 12/00. ① Bef. net acctg. chng. chrg. of $1.1 mill. & extraord. loss of $10.5 mill. ② Incl. impairment chrg. of $58.0 mill.; bef. acctg. chng. chrg. of $14.0 mill. ③ Bef. extraord. gain of $2.2 mill. ④ Bef. extraord. loss of $3.2 mill., 12/31/02; $12.4 mill., 12/31/97. ⑤ Incl. impairment chrg. of $199.5 mill.; bef. extraord. gain of $6.2 mill. ⑥ Bef. extraord. loss of $598,000. ⑦ Incl. impairment chrg. of $5.9 mill. and merger & seismic licens. exp. of $31.6 mill. ⑧ Incl. impairment chrgs. of $21.3 mill. and merger & seismic licens. exp. of $9.8 mill.; bef. extraord. loss of $5.6 mill. ⑨ Refl. adoption of Emerging Issues Task Force issue No. 02-03, which incls. the netting of marketing & processing revenue and related expenses.

OFFICERS:
R. S. Boswell, Chmn., C.E.O.
H. C. Clark, Pres., C.O.O.
D. H. Keyte, Exec. V.P., C.F.O.
INVESTOR CONTACT: David H. Keyte, Exec. V.P., C.F.O., (303) 812-1663
PRINCIPAL OFFICE: 1600 Broadway, Suite 2200, Denver, CO 80202

TELEPHONE NUMBER: (303) 812-1400
FAX: (303) 592-2602
WEB: www.forestoil.com
NO. OF EMPLOYEES: 493 (avg.)
SHAREHOLDERS: 1,825 (record)
ANNUAL MEETING: In May
INCORPORATED: NY, 1916; reincorp., NY, 1924

INSTITUTIONAL HOLDINGS:
No. of Institutions: 155
Shares Held: 27,487,293
% Held: 58.5
INDUSTRY: Crude petroleum and natural gas (SIC: 1311)
TRANSFER AGENT(S): Mellon Investor Services, Dallas, TX

FORTUNE BRANDS, INC.

EXCH.	SYM.	REC. PRICE	P/E RATIO	YLD.	MKT. CAP.	RANGE (52-WK.)	'02 Y/E PR.
NYSE	FO	43.84 (2/28/03)	12.9	2.5%	$6.49 bill.	57.86 - 41.65	46.51

UPPER MEDIUM GRADE. THE COMPANY ANTICIPATES DOUBLE-DIGIT EARNINGS PER SHARE GROWTH IN THE FIRST QUARTER OF 2003.

*7 YEAR PRICE SCORE 133.9   ***12 MONTH PRICE SCORE 97.1**
*NYSE COMPOSITE INDEX=100

INTERIM EARNINGS (Per Share):

Qtr.	Mar.	June	Sept.	Dec.
1998	0.30	0.50	0.32	0.55
1999	0.32	d7.04	0.28	0.61
2000	0.42	0.61	0.46	d2.41
2001	0.39	0.66	0.60	0.84
2002	0.55	1.27	0.73	0.86

INTERIM DIVIDENDS (Per Share):

Amt.	Decl.	Ex.	Rec.	Pay.
0.25Q	1/29/02	2/11/02	2/13/02	3/01/02
0.25Q	4/30/02	5/13/02	5/15/02	6/03/02
0.25Q	7/30/02	8/12/02	8/14/02	9/03/02
0.27Q	9/24/02	11/04/02	11/06/02	12/02/02
0.27Q	1/30/03	2/10/03	2/12/03	3/03/03

Indicated div.: $1.08 (Div. Reinv. Plan)

CAPITALIZATION (12/31/01):

	($000)	(%)
Long-Term Debt	950,300	31.1
Preferred Stock	8,600	0.3
Common & Surplus	2,094,100	68.6
Total	3,053,000	100.0

BUSINESS:

Fortune Brands, Inc. (formerly American Brands, Inc.) is an international consumer products holding company. FO has premier brands and leading market positions in home and office products. Home and office brands include MOEN faucets, MASTER locks, ARISTOKRAFT, SCHROCK and OMEGA cabinets and WATERLOO tool storage sold by units of Masterbrand Industries, and DAY TIMER, KENSINGTON, WILSON JONES and SWINGLINE sold by units of ACCO World Corp. Acushnet Company's golf brands include TITLEIST, COBRA and FOOTJOY. Spirit and wine brands sold by units of Jim Beam Brands Worldwide, Inc. include JIM BEAM and KNOB CREEK bourbons, DeKUYPER cordials, THE DALMORE single malt scotch, VOX vodka and GEYSER PEAK and CANYON ROAD wines. Net sales for 2002 were derived as follows: home products, 44.6%; office products, 19.5%; spirits and wine, 18.2%; and golf products, 17.7%.

RECENT DEVELOPMENTS:

For the year ended 12/31/02, net income advanced 36.2% to $525.6 million from $386.0 million the year before. Results for 2002 and 2001 included restructuring and special charges of $55.8 million and $98.1 million, respectively. Also, results for 2001 included a write-down of indentifiable intangibles/goodwill of $73.3 million. Net sales increased 2.1% to $5.68 billion from $5.56 billion the year before. On a segment basis, home product sales grew 22.4% to $2.53 billion, while golf products sales rose 6.5% to $1.01 billion. Spirits and wine sales fell 24.5% to $1.03 billion, and office products sales slid 6.0% to $1.11 billion.

PROSPECTS:

The Company anticipates double-digit earnings per share growth in the first quarter of 2003, partially benefiting from the final incremental quarter of the acquisition of the OMEGA cabinets. Moreover, the Company expects to benefit from strategic initiatives, including brand investments and new product development, particularly with its home and golf brands. During the first quarter of 2003, Fortune Brands, Inc. introduced two golf ball models, two driver models and an iron line. On 3/4/03, Jim Beam Brands Co. announced that it will launch Beam and Cola, a new ready-to-drink beverage consisting of Jim Beam® bourbon and cola.

ANNUAL FINANCIAL DATA:

FISCAL YEAR	TOT. REVS. ($mill.)	NET INC. ($mill.)	TOT. ASSETS ($mill.)	OPER. PROFIT %	NET PROFIT %	RET. ON EQUITY %	RET. ON ASSETS %	CURR. RATIO	EARN. PER SH. $	CASH FL. PER SH. $	TANG. BK. VAL. $	DIV. PER SH. $	PRICE RANGE	AVG. P/E RATIO	AVG. YIELD %
p12/31/02	5,677.7	⑦ 525.6							③ 3.41			1.02	57.86 — 36.85	13.9	2.2
12/31/01	5,678.7	⑤⑥ 386.0	5,300.9	9.4	6.8	18.4	7.3	1.6	2.49	3.89	2.06	0.97	40.54 — 28.38	13.8	2.8
12/31/00	5,844.5	①⑤ d137.7	5,764.1	3.1	...	...	...	1.1	①⑤ d0.88	0.63	0.89	0.93	33.25 — 19.19	...	3.5
12/31/99	5,524.7	①⑤ d890.6	6,417.1	...	...	...	...	1.2	①⑤ d5.35	d3.96	0.59	0.89	45.88 — 29.38	...	2.4
12/31/98	5,240.9	② 293.6	7,359.7	11.8	5.6	7.2	4.0	1.2	② 1.67	1.64	1.91	0.85	42.25 — 25.25	20.2	2.5
12/31/97	4,844.5	⑧ 41.5	6,942.5	5.6	0.9	1.0	0.6	1.2	⑧ 0.23	1.64	2.91	1.41	56.00 — 30.38	187.7	3.3
12/31/96	11,579.3	①② 496.8	9,504.2	8.6	4.3	13.5	5.2	1.0	①② 2.86	4.45	...	2.00	50.13 — 39.88	15.7	4.5
12/31/95	11,367.1	①② 543.1	8,021.2	9.6	4.8	14.0	6.8	1.3	①② 2.90	4.28	3.13	2.00	47.25 — 36.63	14.5	4.8
12/31/94	13,146.5	①④ 885.1	9,794.4	10.0	6.7	19.1	9.0	1.5	①④ 4.38	5.95	5.33	1.99	38.38 — 29.38	7.7	5.9
12/31/93	13,701.4	③ 668.2	16,339.0	10.2	4.9	15.6	4.1	0.7	③ 3.30	4.84	2.64	1.97	40.63 — 28.50	10.5	5.7

Statistics are as originally reported. ① Incl. pre-tax restruct. & oth. non-recurr. chrg.: $45.4 mill., 2001; $73.0 mill., 2000; $196.0 mill., 1999; $59.9 mill., 1996; cr$20.0 mill., 1995; cr$332.9 mill., 1994 ② Bef. extraord. chrg.: $30.5 mill., 1998; $10.3 mill., 1998; $2.7 mill., 1995. ③ Bef. acctg. change chrg. $198.4 mill. ④ Bef. disc. oper. loss $151.0 mill. ⑤ Incl. a write-off of goodwill of $73.3 mill., 2001; $502.6 mill., 2000; $1.13 bill., 1999. ⑥ Incl. pre-tax restruct. & oth. non-recurr. chrg. of $209.1 mill.; bef. extraord. chrg. of $8.1 mill. & disc. opers. gain of $65.1 mill. ⑦ Incl. restr. & special chrgs. of $55.8 mill.

OFFICERS:
N. H. Wesley, Chmn., C.E.O.
C. P. Omtvedt, Sr. V.P., C.F.O.
INVESTOR CONTACT: Anthony J. Diaz, Investor Relations, (847) 484-4410
PRINCIPAL OFFICE: 300 Tower Parkway, Lincolnshire, IL 60069-3640

TELEPHONE NUMBER: (847) 484-4400
FAX: (847) 478-0073
WEB: www.fortunebrands.com
NO. OF EMPLOYEES: 24,998 (approx.)
SHAREHOLDERS: 30,275
ANNUAL MEETING: In April
INCORPORATED: DE, Oct., 1985

INSTITUTIONAL HOLDINGS:
No. of Institutions: 452
Shares Held: 107,343,424
% Held: 71.9
INDUSTRY: Hardware, nec (SIC: 3429)
TRANSFER AGENT(S): Bank of New York, New York, NY

FOX ENTERTAINMENT GROUP, INC.

EXCH.	SYM.	REC. PRICE	P/E RATIO	YLD.	MKT. CAP.	RANGE (52-WK.)	'02 Y/E PR.
NYSE	FOX	26.73 (2/28/03)	35.6	...	$22.72 bill.	29.40 - 16.13	25.93

UPPER MEDIUM GRADE. THE COMPANY IS BENEFITING FROM STRONGER RESULTS FROM ITS FILMED ENTERTAINMENT AND TELEVISION STATION OPERATIONS.

INTERIM EARNINGS (Per Share):

Qtr.	Sept.	Dec.	Mar.	June
1998-99	0.10	0.17	0.01	0.05
1999-00	0.06	0.13	0.03	d0.02
2000-01	0.05	0.01	d0.01	0.24
2001-02	0.01	0.54	0.13	0.05
2002-03	0.25	0.32	...	...

INTERIM DIVIDENDS (Per Share):

Amt.	Decl.	Ex.	Rec.	Pay.
		No dividends paid.		

TRADING VOLUME
Thousand Shares

CAPITALIZATION (6/30/02):

	($000)	(%)
Long-Term Debt	942,000	6.3
Deferred Income Tax	1,912,000	12.8
Common & Surplus	12,095,000	80.9
Total	14,949,000	100.0

*7 YEAR PRICE SCORE N/A   *12 MONTH PRICE SCORE 122.5

*NYSE COMPOSITE INDEX=100

BUSINESS:

Fox Entertainment Group, Inc. is principally engaged in the development, production and worldwide distribution of feature films and television programs, television broadcasting and cable network programming. The Company's studios, production facilities and film and television library provide content and the Company's broadcasting and cable networks provide extensive distribution platforms for the Company's programs. FOX primarily operates in four business segments: Filmed Entertainment (38.1% of revenues in 2002); Television Stations (21.3%), which included 35 owned and operated stations as of 12/31/02; Television Broadcast Network (18.6%); and Cable Network Programming (22.0%). As of 12/31/02, the News Corporation Limited owned an 80.6% equity interest in the Company.

RECENT DEVELOPMENTS:

For the quarter ended 12/31/02, net income declined 37.8% to $283.0 million from $455.0 million in the equivalent 2001 quarter. Results for 2001 included a provision of $909.0 million for sports contracts and a gain of $1.59 billion related to the sale of FOX's investments in Fox Family Worldwide and Outdoor Life. Net revenues grew 14.9% to $3.15 billion. By segment, net revenues for Filmed Entertainment climbed 19.8% to $1.34 billion. Net revenue for the Television Broadcast Network rose 3.7% to $749.0 million, while net revenue for the Television Stations segment improved 12.7% to $593.0 million. Net revenue for Cable Network Programming climbed 25.0% to $470.0 million. Operating income was $500.0 million versus an operating loss of $695.0 million the year before.

PROSPECTS:

The Company's outlook is encouraging, supported by solid revenue growth from FOX's film business, which is thriving from a string of successful theatrical releases and from strong growth in the home entertainment market. Moreover, the Company continues to enjoy accelerated levels of revenue and income growth at both its cable and television station operations due to strong ratings and advertising growth at Fox News Channel and FX, as well as higher affiliate rates at the Regional Sports Network Programming.

ANNUAL FINANCIAL DATA:

FISCAL YEAR	TOT. REVS. ($mill.)	NET INC. ($mill.)	TOT. ASSETS ($mill.)	OPER. PROFIT %	NET PROFIT %	RET. ON EQUITY %	RET. ON ASSETS %	CURR. RATIO	EARN. PER SH.$	CASH FL. PER SH.$	TANG. BK. VAL.$	PRICE RANGE	AVG. P/E RATIO
6/30/02	9,725.0	② 607.0	22,876.0	...	6.2	5.0	2.7	1.2	② 0.72	1.34	...	29.65 - 16.94	83.2
6/30/01	8,504.0	① 206.0	17,856.0	7.7	2.4	2.6	1.2	1.5	① 0.28	0.94	0.44	34.75 - 15.44	125.4
6/30/00	8,589.0	145.0	17,930.0	7.6	1.7	1.8	0.8	1.2	0.20	0.81	0.57	...	...
6/30/99	8,057.0	205.0	13,163.0	8.9	2.5	3.1	1.6	1.2	0.33	0.83	1.26	30.00 - 19.50	75.0
6/30/98	7,023.0	176.0	12,630.0	9.4	2.5	4.5	1.4	1.2	0.32	0.76	...	25.75 - 19.38	70.5
6/30/97	5,847.0	30.0	11,697.0	5.5	0.5	0.8	0.3	1.2	0.05	0.38	...	...	...
6/30/96	4,548.0	411.0	...	10.6	9.0	...	...	...	0.75	0.93	...	...	...

Statistics are as originally reported. ① Bef. acctg. change chrg. of $494.0 mill., incl. rest. chrg. of $89.0 mill. ② Bef. acctg. change chrg. of $26.0 mill.; incl. one-time gains of $1.54 bill.

OFFICERS:
K. R. Murdoch, Chmn., C.E.O.
P. Chernin, Pres., C.O.O.
D. F. DeVoe, Sr. Exec. V.P., C.F.O.

INVESTOR CONTACT: Reed Nolte, V.P., Inv. Relations, (212) 852-7092

PRINCIPAL OFFICE: 1211 Avenue of the Americas, New York, NY 10036

TELEPHONE NUMBER: (212) 852-7111
FAX: (212) 852-7145
WEB: www.fox.com

NO. OF EMPLOYEES: 12,800 (approx.)

SHAREHOLDERS: 877 (approx. class A)

ANNUAL MEETING: In Nov.

INCORPORATED: DE, 1985

INSTITUTIONAL HOLDINGS:
No. of Institutions: 253
Shares Held: 159,751,135
% Held: 18.8

INDUSTRY: Motion picture & video production (SIC: 7812)

TRANSFER AGENT(S): The Bank of New York, New York, NY

FPL GROUP, INC.

EXCH.	SYM.	REC. PRICE	P/E RATIO	YLD.	MKT. CAP.	RANGE (52-WK.)	'02 Y/E PR.
NYSE	FPL	56.01 (2/28/03)	13.9	4.3%	$9.86 bill.	64.99 - 45.00	60.13

UPPER MEDIUM GRADE. THE COMPANY EXPECTS EARNINGS FOR 2003 IN THE RANGE OF $4.80 TO $5.00 PER SHARE.

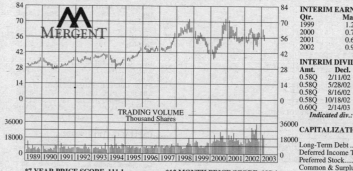

INTERIM EARNINGS (Per Share):

Qtr.	Mar.	June	Sept.	Dec.
1999	1.22	0.45	1.70	0.71
2000	0.71	1.20	1.84	0.38
2001	0.65	1.30	1.98	0.68
2002	0.98	1.46	0.85	0.73

INTERIM DIVIDENDS (Per Share):

Amt.	Decl.	Ex.	Rec.	Pay.
0.58Q	2/11/02	2/20/02	2/22/02	3/15/02
0.58Q	5/28/02	6/05/02	6/07/02	6/17/02
0.58Q	8/16/02	8/28/02	8/30/02	9/16/02
0.58Q	10/18/02	11/26/02	11/29/02	12/16/02
0.60Q	2/14/03	2/26/03	2/28/03	3/17/03

Indicated div.: $2.40 (Div. Reinv. Plan)

CAPITALIZATION (12/31/01):

	($000)	(%)
Long-Term Debt	4,858,000	38.9
Deferred Income Tax	1,390,000	11.1
Preferred Stock	226,000	1.8
Common & Surplus	6,015,000	48.2
Total	12,489,000	100.0

*7 YEAR PRICE SCORE 111.1   *12 MONTH PRICE SCORE 109.4

*NYSE COMPOSITE INDEX=100

BUSINESS:

FPL Group, Inc. is a holding company whose principal operating subsidiary, Florida Power & Light Company, is engaged in the generation, transmission, distribution and sale of electric energy. FPL supplies service throughout most of the east and lower west coasts of Florida. As of 1/24/02, Florida Power & Light Company served more than 4.0 million customer accounts. On 2/15/98, FPL formed FPL Energy, LLC, its unregulated independent power pro-

duction unit, which produces electricity primarily from clean and renewable fuels. FPL Energy's project portfolio included over 80 natural gas, hydro, wind, solar, geothermal, biomass generating and nuclear facilities with nearly 7,300 megawatts of capacity in operation as of 1/30/03. FPL FiberNet LLC provides wholesale fiber-optic service to telephone and cable companies, Internet service providers and other Communications businesses within Florida.

RECENT DEVELOPMENTS:

For the year ended 12/31/02, the Company reported income of $695.0 million, before an accounting change charge of $222.0 million, compared with net income of $781.0 million in the previous year. Results for 2002 included an after-tax restructuring and impairment charge of $167.0 million and a nonrecurring gain of $31.0 million mainly

from settlement of IRS litigation. Results for 2001 included a net nonrecurring charge of $11.0 million. Operating revenues slipped 0.6% to $8.28 billion from $8.33 billion a year earlier. Operating income decreased 12.0% to $1.23 billion from $1.40 billion the year before.

PROSPECTS:

The Company expects earnings growth in the range of 4.0% to 5.0%, or ranging between $725.0 million and $735.0 million at its Florida Power & Light Company utility subsidiary. In 2003, FPL Energy will continue to focus on being a low-cost, reliable supplier, expanding its wind portfolio, and successfully completing projects currently under construction. FPL Energy expects to add between

700 and 1,200 megawatts of additional wind-powered generation in 2003. In addition, gas-fired projects currently under construction should add nearly 2,900 megawatts in mid- to late-2003 and nearly 750 megawatts in 2004. Overall, the Company expects earnings for 2003 in the range of $4.80 to $5.00 per share.

ANNUAL FINANCIAL DATA:

FISCAL YEAR	TOT. REVS. ($mill.)	NET INC. ($mill.)	TOT. ASSETS ($mill.)	OPER. PROFIT %	NET PROFIT %	NET INC./ NET PROP. %	NET INC./ TOT. CAP. %	RET. ON EQUITY %	ACCUM. DEPR./ GROSS PROP. %	EARN. PER SH. $	TANG. BK. VAL.$	DIV. PER SH. $	DIV. PAYOUT %	PRICE RANGE	AVG. P/E RATIO	AVG. YIELD %
p12/31/02	8,280.0	⑤ 695.0								⑤ 4.01		2.32	57.9	64.99 - 45.00	13.7	4.2
12/31/01	8,475.0	④ 781.0	17,463.0	16.5	9.2	6.7	6.3	12.5	50.1	④ 4.62	34.18	2.24	48.5	71.63 - 51.21	13.3	3.6
12/31/00	7,082.0	③ 704.0	15,300.0	17.5	9.9	7.1	6.2	12.1	52.7	③ 4.14	31.82	2.16	52.2	73.00 - 36.38	13.2	3.9
12/31/99	6,438.0	② 697.0	13,441.0	14.3	10.8	7.5	6.8	12.5	52.6	② 4.07	30.07	2.08	51.1	61.94 - 41.13	12.7	4.0
12/31/98	6,661.0	664.0	12,029.0	18.8	10.0	7.8	7.3	12.4	52.3	3.85	28.37	2.00	51.9	72.56 - 56.06	16.7	3.1
12/31/97	6,369.0	618.0	12,449.0	19.3	9.7	6.6	6.4	12.2	47.5	3.57	26.66	1.92	53.8	60.00 - 42.63	14.4	3.7
12/31/96	6,036.8	579.5	12,219.3	19.4	9.6	6.2	6.0	11.9	45.4	3.33	25.12	1.84	55.3	48.13 - 41.50	13.5	4.1
12/31/95	5,592.5	553.3	12,459.2	21.4	9.9	5.6	5.6	11.8	41.6	3.16	23.78	1.76	55.7	46.50 - 34.00	12.7	4.4
12/31/94	5,422.7	518.7	12,617.6	21.2	9.6	5.1	5.0	11.2	38.3	2.91	22.50	1.88	64.6	39.13 - 26.88	11.3	5.7
12/31/93	5,316.3	① 428.7	13,720.3	18.3	8.1	4.2	3.9	8.3	35.8	① 2.30	24.95	2.47	107.4	41.00 - 35.50	16.6	6.5

Statistics are as originally reported. ① Bef. disc. opers. loss $135.6 mill. & Incl. non-recurr. chrg. $56.1 mill. ② Incl. one-time net gains of $162.0 mill. & incl. one-time net charges totaling $146.0 mill. ③ Incl. nonrecurr. chrg. of $67.0 mill. ④ Bef. acctg. change gain of $8.0 mill.; incl. merger-related chrg. of $19.0 mill. ⑤ Bef. acctg. change chrg. $222.0 mill.; incl. aft.-tax restr. & impair. chrg. $167.0 mill.

OFFICERS:
L. Hay III, Chmn., Pres., C.E.O.
M. Dewhurst, V.P., C.F.O.
INVESTOR CONTACT: Investor Relations, (561) 694-4697
PRINCIPAL OFFICE: 700 Universe Blvd., Juno Beach, FL 33408

TELEPHONE NUMBER: (561) 694-4000
FAX: (561) 694-4999
WEB: www.fplgroup.com
NO. OF EMPLOYEES: 10,992 (avg.)
SHAREHOLDERS: 39,319 (approx.)
ANNUAL MEETING: In May
INCORPORATED: FL, Sept., 1984

INSTITUTIONAL HOLDINGS:
No. of Institutions: 491
Shares Held: 128,926,368
% Held: 70.6
INDUSTRY: Electric services (SIC: 4911)
REGISTRAR(S): EquiServe Trust Company, N.A, Providence, RI

FRANKLIN RESOURCES, INC.

EXCH.	SYM.	REC. PRICE	P/E RATIO	YLD.	MKT. CAP.	RANGE (52-WK.)	'02 Y/E PR.	DIV. ACH.
NYSE	BEN	32.67 (2/28/03)	20.0	0.9%	$8.52 bill.	44.48 - 27.90	34.08	13 yrs.

UPPER MEDIUM GRADE. THE COMPANY RECENTLY LAUNCHED EQUITY PRODUCTS IN KOREA, TAIWAN, JAPAN AND AUSTRALIA AND FIXED-INCOME PRODUCTS IN KOREA AND INDIA.

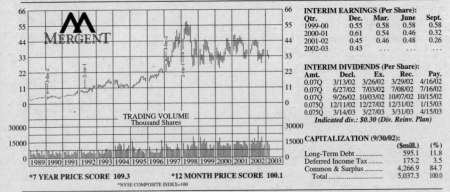

*7 YEAR PRICE SCORE 109.3   *12 MONTH PRICE SCORE 100.1
*NYSE COMPOSITE INDEX=100

INTERIM EARNINGS (Per Share):

Qtr.	Dec.	Mar.	June	Sept.
1999-00	0.55	0.58	0.58	0.58
2000-01	0.61	0.54	0.46	0.32
2001-02	0.45	0.46	0.48	0.26
2002-03	0.43	...	...	...

INTERIM DIVIDENDS (Per Share):

Amt.	Decl.	Ex.	Rec.	Pay.
0.07Q	3/13/02	3/26/02	3/29/02	4/16/02
0.07Q	6/27/02	7/03/02	7/08/02	7/16/02
0.07Q	9/26/02	10/03/02	10/07/02	10/15/02
0.075Q	12/11/02	12/27/02	12/31/02	1/15/03
0.075Q	3/14/03	3/27/03	3/31/03	4/15/03

Indicated div.: $0.30 (Div. Reinv. Plan)

CAPITALIZATION (9/30/02):

	($mill.)	(%)
Long-Term Debt	595.1	11.8
Deferred Income Tax	175.2	3.5
Common & Surplus	4,266.9	84.7
Total	5,037.3	100.0

BUSINESS:

Franklin Resources, Inc., operating as Franklin Templeton Investments, is engaged in providing investment management, marketing, distribution, transfer agency and other administrative services to the open-end investment companies of the Franklin Templeton Group and to U.S. and international managed and institutional accounts. The Company also provides investment management and related services to a number of closed-end investment companies. In addition, the Company provides investment management, marketing and distribution services to certain sponsored investment companies organized in the Grand Duchy of Luxembourg. Moreover, the Company provides advisory services, variable annuity products, and sponsors and manages public and private real estate programs. As of 12/31/02, BEN's subsidiaries had $257.74 billion in assets under management. On 4/10/01, BEN acquired Fiduciary Trust Company International for approximately $775.0 million.

RECENT DEVELOPMENTS:

For the quarter ended 12/31/02, net income decreased 7.4% to $109.8 million compared with $118.5 million the year before. Total operating revenues slipped 2.1% to $605.5 billion. Investment management fees slid 1.5% to $351.4 million, while underwriting and distribution fees declined 3.2% to $185.9 million. However, shareholder servicing fees rose 1.5% to $48.1 million. Operating income decreased 2.4% to $139.5 million.

PROSPECTS:

The Company continues to strengthen its presence overseas. For instance, during the first quarter of fiscal 2003, BEN created a fund management joint venture in China with Sealand Securities Co. Ltd. Also, BEN launched equity products in Korea, Taiwan, Japan and Australia and fixed-income products in Korea and India. Separately, the Company was awarded a $600.0 million international equity assignment from Employees Retirement System of Texas. As of 12/31/02, the Company's total assets under management were comprised of 48.5% equity assets, 34.3% fixed-income assets, 14.9% hybrid assets, and 2.3% money.

ANNUAL FINANCIAL DATA:

FISCAL YEAR	TOT. REVS. ($mill.)	NET INC. ($mill.)	TOT. ASSETS ($mill.)	OPER. PROFIT %	NET PROFIT %	RET. ON EQUITY %	RET. ON ASSETS %	CURR. RATIO	EARN. PER SH.$	CASH FL. PER SH.$	TANG. BK. VAL.$	DIV. PER SH.$	PRICE RANGE	AVG. P/E RATIO	AVG. YIELD %
9/30/02	2,518.5	③ 432.7	6,422.7	23.2	17.2	10.1	6.7	2.5	③ 1.65	2.35	8.69	0.28	44.48 - 27.90	21.9	0.8
9/30/01	2,354.8	① 484.7	6,265.7	21.7	20.6	12.2	7.7	2.1	① 1.91	2.79	7.63	0.26	48.30 - 30.85	20.7	0.7
9/30/00	2,340.1	562.1	4,042.4	31.9	24.0	19.0	13.9	2.0	2.28	3.09	7.37	0.24	45.63 - 24.63	15.4	0.7
9/30/99	2,262.5	② 426.7	3,666.8	27.3	18.9	16.1	11.6	2.1	② 1.69	2.48	5.79	0.22	45.00 - 27.00	21.3	0.6
9/30/98	2,577.3	500.5	3,480.0	28.4	19.4	21.9	14.4	1.6	1.98	2.74	4.08	0.20	57.88 - 25.75	21.1	0.5
9/30/97	2,163.3	434.1	3,095.2	31.3	20.1	23.4	14.0	1.7	1.72	2.20	2.50	0.17	51.91 - 22.08	21.6	0.5
9/30/96	1,522.6	314.7	2,374.2	27.4	20.7	22.5	13.3	2.3	1.26	1.42	3.15	0.15	24.92 - 15.46	16.0	0.7
9/30/95	845.8	268.9	2,244.7	43.5	31.8	23.2	12.0	1.6	1.08	1.27	2.06	0.13	19.33 - 11.00	14.0	0.9
9/30/94	826.9	251.3	1,738.0	44.7	30.4	27.0	14.5	2.2	1.00	1.17	1.03	0.11	17.00 - 11.21	14.1	0.8
9/30/93	640.7	175.5	1,598.2	44.5	27.4	23.8	11.0	1.7	0.71	0.82	0.16	0.09	17.29 - 10.67	19.8	0.7

Statistics are as originally reported. Adj. for stk. splits: 3-for-2, 12/96; 2-for-1, 12/97. ① Incl. restr. chrg. $58.5 mill. ② Incl. one-time chrg. of $7.6 mill. ③ Incl. a chrg. of $60.1 mill. rel. to an unreal. loss in BEN's corp. investments.

OFFICERS:
C. B. Johnson, Chmn., C.E.O.
H. E. Burns, Vice-Chmn.
R. H. Johnson Jr., Vice-Chmn.
M.L. Flanagan, Pres., C.F.O.
INVESTOR CONTACT: Alan Weinfeld, Investor Relations, (650) 525-8900
PRINCIPAL OFFICE: One Franklin Parkway, San Mateo, CA 94403

TELEPHONE NUMBER: (650) 312-2000
FAX: (650) 312-3655
WEB: www.frk.com
NO. OF EMPLOYEES: 6,670
SHAREHOLDERS: 5,100 (approx.)
ANNUAL MEETING: In Jan.
INCORPORATED: DE, Nov., 1969

INSTITUTIONAL HOLDINGS:
No. of Institutions: 311
Shares Held: 107,926,049
% Held: 41.9

INDUSTRY: Investment advice (SIC: 6282)

TRANSFER AGENT(S): Bank of New York, New York, NY

FREDDIE MAC

EXCH.	SYM.	REC. PRICE	P/E RATIO	YLD.	MKT. CAP.	RANGE (52-WK.)	'02 Y/E PR.	DIV. ACH.
NYSE	FRE	54.65 (2/28/03)	7.0	1.9%	$38.00 bill.	68.50 - 52.60	59.05	12 yrs.

INVESTMENT GRADE. THE COMPANY ANNOUNCED THAT ITS FINANCIAL STATEMENTS FROM 2002, 2001 AND POSSIBLY 2000 WOULD BE RESTATED.

*7 YEAR PRICE SCORE 132.3   ***12 MONTH PRICE SCORE 103.3**

*NYSE COMPOSITE INDEX=100

INTERIM EARNINGS (Per Share):

Qtr.	Mar.	June	Sept.	Dec.
1997	0.44	0.46	0.49	0.51
1998	0.54	0.56	0.58	0.62
1999	0.68	0.74	0.74	0.78
2000	0.81	0.83	0.86	0.89
2001	1.12	1.29	1.49	2.06
2002	2.07	1.50	1.90	2.38

INTERIM DIVIDENDS (Per Share):

Amt.	Decl.	Ex.	Rec.	Pay.
0.22Q	3/01/02	3/07/02	3/11/02	3/29/02
0.22Q	6/07/02	6/13/02	6/17/02	6/28/02
0.22Q	9/06/02	9/12/02	9/16/02	9/30/02
0.22Q	12/06/02	12/12/02	12/16/02	12/31/02
0.26Q	3/07/03	3/13/03	3/17/03	3/31/03

Indicated div.: $1.04 (Div. Reinv. Plan)

CAPITALIZATION (12/31/01):

	($000)	(%)
Long-Term Debt	314,733,000	95.3
Preferred Stock	4,596,000	1.4
Common & Surplus	10,777,000	3.3
Total	330,106,000	100.0

BUSINESS:

Freddie Mac (formerly The Federal Home Loan Mortgage Corporation) is a federally chartered and stockholder-owned corporation. FRE purchases conventional residential mortgages from mortgage lending institutions and finances most of its purchases with sales of guaranteed mortgage securities called Mortgage Participation Certificates for which FRE ultimately assumes the risk of borrower default.

FRE also maintains an investment portfolio that consists principally of federal funds sold, reverse repurchase agreements and tax-advantaged and other short-term investments. FRE's financial performance is driven primarily by the growth of its total servicing portfolio, the mix of sold versus retained portfolios, the spreads earned on the sold and retained portfolios and mortgage default costs.

RECENT DEVELOPMENTS:

For the year ended 12/31/02, net income amounted to $5.76 billion compared with income of $4.14 billion, before an accounting change charge of $5.0 million, the previous year. Earnings were driven by a record volume of home loan issuance as homeowners took advantage of low interest rates to refinance existing mortgages. Results for 2002 included a special contributions charge of $225.0 million.

Total revenues increased 34.5% to $9.43 billion from $7.01 billion the prior year. Revenues for 2002 and 2001 included a gain on investment activity of $94.0 million and $115.0 million, respectively. Net interest income climbed 23.7% to $6.78 billion from $5.48 billion a year earlier. Management and guarantee income grew 16.6% to $1.91 billion.

PROSPECTS:

On 1/27/03, the Company announced that its financial statements from 2002, 2001 and possibly 2000 will be restated. The restatement, which is anticipated to materially increase the reported levels of earnings, will affect the Company's treatment of gains it makes on the derivatives options used to hedge its exposure to interest-rate risk.

Although the expected adjustments will not affect FRE's fair market value disclosures or market risk disclosures, the adjustments are expected to increase its cumulative capital surplus under regulatory capital requirements and may result in more volatility in reported quarterly earnings for those periods.

ANNUAL FINANCIAL DATA:

FISCAL YEAR	NET INT. INC. ($mill.)	NON-INT. INC. ($mill.)	NET INC. ($mill.)	TOT. LOANS ($mill.)	TOT. ASSETS ($mill.)	RET. ON EQUITY %	RET. ON ASSETS %	EQUITY/ ASSETS %	EARN. PER SH.$	TANG. BK. VAL.$	DIV. PER SH.$	PRICE RANGE	AVG. P/E RATIO
p12/31/02	6,777.0	1,911.0	④ 5,764.0						④ 7.95		0.88	69.50 - 52.60	7.7
12/31/01	5,480.0	1,639.0	②③ 4,373.0	494,585.0	617,340.0	28.4	0.7	2.5	②③ 5.96	15.50	0.80	71.25 - 58.75	10.9
12/31/00	2,838.0	1,489.0	③ 2,539.0	385,451.0	459,297.0	17.1	0.6	3.2	③ 3.39	16.81	0.68	70.13 - 36.88	15.8
12/31/99	2,540.0	1,405.0	② 2,218.0	322,914.0	386,684.0	19.2	0.6	3.0	② 2.96	11.98	0.60	65.25 - 45.38	18.7
12/31/98	1,927.0	1,307.0	1,700.0	255,670.0	321,421.0	15.7	0.5	3.4	2.31	11.55	0.48	66.38 - 38.69	22.7
12/31/97	1,631.0	1,298.0	1,395.0	164,543.0	194,597.0	18.5	0.7	3.9	1.88	8.74	0.40	44.56 - 26.69	18.9
12/31/96	1,542.0	1,249.0	① 1,258.0	137,826.0	173,866.0	18.7	0.7	3.9	① 1.67	9.62	0.35	29.00 - 19.06	14.4
12/31/95	1,396.0	1,087.0	1,091.0	107,706.0	137,181.0	18.6	0.8	4.3	1.42	8.14	0.30	20.91 - 12.47	11.7
12/31/94	1,112.0	1,108.0	① 1,027.0	72,585.0	106,199.0	19.9	1.0	4.9	① 1.27	7.08	0.26	15.72 - 11.75	10.8
12/31/93	852.0	1,033.0	①② 786.0	55,938.0	83,880.0	17.7	0.9	5.3	①② 1.02	6.08	0.22	14.19 - 11.31	12.5

Statistics are as originally reported. Adj. for stk. splits: 4-for-1, 1/97. ① Bef. extraord. chrg. $15.0 mill., 12/96; $44.0 mill., 12/94; $20.0 mill., 12/93 ② Bef. acctg. change credit $5.0 mill., 12/01; $20.0 mill., 12/93 ③ Bef. extraord. gain $231.0 mill., 12/01; $8.0 mill., 12/00; $5.0 mill., 12/99 ④ Incl. special contributions chrg. $225.0 mill.

OFFICERS:
L. C. Brendsel, Chmn., C.E.O.
D. W. Glenn, Vice-Chmn., Pres.
V. A. Clarke, Exec. V.P., C.F.O.
INVESTOR CONTACT: Shareholder Relations, (800) 373-3343
PRINCIPAL OFFICE: 8200 Jones Branch Drive, McLean, VA 22102-3110

TELEPHONE NUMBER: (703) 903-2000
FAX: (703) 903-2759
WEB: www.freddiemac.com
NO. OF EMPLOYEES: 3,500 (approx.)
SHAREHOLDERS: 5,627 (approx.)
ANNUAL MEETING: In May
INCORPORATED: July, 1970

INSTITUTIONAL HOLDINGS:
No. of Institutions: 760
Shares Held: 602,187,528
% Held: 86.9
INDUSTRY: Federal & fed.-sponsored credit (SIC: 6111)
TRANSFER AGENT(S): EquiServe Trust Company, N.A., Jersey City, NJ

FREEPORT-MCMORAN COPPER & GOLD INC.

EXCH.	SYM.	REC. PRICE	P/E RATIO	YLD.	MKT. CAP.	RANGE (52-WK.)	'02 Y/E PR.
NYSE	FCX	17.02 (2/28/03)	20.5	2.1%	$2.45 bill.	20.83 - 9.95	16.78

LOWER MEDIUM GRADE. FCX EXPECTS TO USE EXCESS CASH FLOW OF ABOUT $350.0 MILLION IN 2003 TO REDUCE NET DEBT AND MANDATORILY REDEEMABLE PREFERRED STOCK.

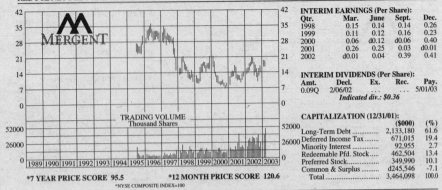

*7 YEAR PRICE SCORE 95.5   ***12 MONTH PRICE SCORE 120.6**
*NYSE COMPOSITE INDEX=100

INTERIM EARNINGS (Per Share):

Qtr.	Mar.	June	Sept.	Dec.
1998	0.15	0.14	0.14	0.26
1999	0.11	0.12	0.16	0.23
2000	0.06	d0.12	d0.06	0.40
2001	0.26	0.25	0.03	d0.01
2002	d0.01	0.04	0.39	0.41

INTERIM DIVIDENDS (Per Share):

Amt.	Decl.	Ex.	Rec.	Pay.
0.09Q	2/06/02			5/01/03

Indicated div.: $0.36

CAPITALIZATION (12/31/01):

	($000)	(%)
Long-Term Debt	2,133,180	61.6
Deferred Income Tax	671,015	19.4
Minority Interest	92,955	2.7
Redeemable Pfd. Stock	462,504	13.4
Preferred Stock	349,990	10.1
Common & Surplus	d245,546	-7.1
Total	3,464,098	100.0

BUSINESS:

Freeport-McMoRan Copper & Gold Inc. is engaged in exploring for and recovering copper, gold, and silver. FCX has two operating segments: Mining & Exploration and Smelting & Refining. The Mining & Exploration segment includes the Company's 90.6% ownership interest in PT Freeport Indonesia's copper and gold mining operations in Indonesia and FCX's Indonesian exploration activities. The Smelting & Refining segment includes Atlantic Copper's operations in Spain and PT Freeport Indonesia's equity investment in PT Smelting in Gresik, Indonesia. As of 12/31/02, proven reserves included approximately 53.30 billion pounds of copper and 62.6 million ounces of gold.

RECENT DEVELOPMENTS:

For the year ended 12/31/02, FCX reported income of $167.7 million, before an accounting change charge of $3.0 million, versus net income of $113.0 million in the previous year. Earnings for 2002 reflected FCX's increased ownership interest in its PT Freeport Indonesia mining subsidiary. Revenues increased 3.9% to $1.91 billion from $1.84 billion a year earlier. Sales volume included 1.52 billion pounds of copper at an average price of $0.71 per pound, 2.3 million ounces of gold at an average price of $311.97 per ounce and 4.1 million ounces of silver at an average price of $4.66 per ounce. Total cost of sales decreased 2.3% to $1.20 billion from $1.23 billion the year before. Operating income advanced 17.9% to $640.1 million from $542.9 million in 2001.

PROSPECTS:

Assuming recent gold prices of $350 per ounce and sales of 2.6 million ounces, the Company expects 2003 unit net production costs of a net credit of $0.07 per pound of copper. Moreover, PT Freeport Indonesia anticipates sales for 2003 to approximate 1.40 billion pounds of copper and 2.6 million ounces of gold, with expected first quarter sales of about 370.0 million pounds of copper and 580,000 ounces of gold. FCX estimates capital expenditures for 2003 will total approximately 160.0 million, including $40.0 million to complete the expansion of the Deep Ore Zone underground mine and complete the Grasberg mine overburden system. FCX expects to use excess cash flow in 2003 to reduce net debt and mandatorily redeemable preferred stock by about $350.0 million.

ANNUAL FINANCIAL DATA:

FISCAL YEAR	TOT. REVS. ($mill.)	NET INC. ($mill.)	TOT. ASSETS ($mill.)	OPER. PROFIT %	NET PROFIT %	RET. ON EQUITY %	RET. ON ASSETS %	CURR. RATIO	EARN. PER SH. $	CASH FL. PER SH. $	TANG. BK. VAL. $	DIV. PER SH. $	PRICE RANGE		AVG. P/E RATIO	AVG. YIELD
p12/31/02	1,910.5	⑥ 167.7							⑥ 0.89		...	...	20.83	9.95	17.3	...
12/31/01	1,838.9	113.0	4,211.9	29.5	6.1	108.2	2.7	0.9	0.53	2.49	...	...	17.15	8.31	24.0	...
12/31/00	1,868.6	⑤ 77.0	3,950.7	25.6	4.1	203.0	1.9	0.9	⑤ 0.26	2.09	...	...	21.44	6.75	54.2	...
12/31/99	1,887.3	④ 136.5	4,082.9	30.9	7.2	...	3.3	1.1	④ 0.61	2.39	...	...	21.38	9.13	25.0	...
12/31/98	1,757.1	153.8	4,192.6	32.7	8.8	148.8	3.7	1.1	0.67	2.26	...	0.20	21.44	9.81	23.3	1.3
12/31/97	2,000.9	③ 245.1	4,152.2	33.2	12.2	87.9	5.9	1.0	③ 1.06	2.14	...	0.90	34.88	14.94	23.5	3.6
12/31/96	1,905.0	226.2	3,865.5	33.5	11.9	33.5	5.9	1.1	0.89	1.79	1.61	0.90	36.13	27.38	35.7	2.8
12/31/95	1,834.3	253.6	3,581.7	32.5	13.8	28.8	7.1	1.2	0.98	1.58	2.59	0.68	30.75	22.63	27.2	2.5
12/31/94	1,212.3	② 130.2	3,040.2	23.1	10.7	13.1	4.3	1.4	② 0.38	0.75	2.04	0.60	...	...	...	...
12/31/93	925.9	① 60.7	2,116.7	16.7	6.6	6.4	2.9	1.5	① 0.16	0.50	1.87	...	...	...	...	...

Statistics are as originally reported. ① Bef. acctg. change chrg. of $9.9 mill.; incl. restr. chrg. of $20.8 mill. ② Incl. a $32.6 mill. gain on insurance settlement. ③ Incl. a net gain of $12.3 mill. for the reversal of stock appreciation rights costs. ④ Incl. a $1.2 mill. nonrecur. chg. for a vol. severance/early retire. program, a $500,000 chg. for costs of stock appreciation rights rel. to the incr. in FCX's stock price during the second quarter of 1999. ⑤ Incl. net pre-tax net chrgs. of $8.0 mill. ⑥ Bef. acctg. change chrg. of $3.0 mill.

OFFICERS:
J. R. Moffett, Chmn., C.E.O.
B. M. Rankin Jr., Vice-Chmn.
R. C. Adkerson, Pres., C.F.O.
INVESTOR CONTACT: David P. Joint, (504) 582-4203
PRINCIPAL OFFICE: 1615 Poydras Street, New Orleans, LA 70112

TELEPHONE NUMBER: (504) 582-4000
FAX: (504) 582-3265
WEB: www.fcx.com
NO. OF EMPLOYEES: 10,049 (avg.)
SHAREHOLDERS: 9,681 (class B common)
ANNUAL MEETING: In May
INCORPORATED: DE, Nov., 1987

INSTITUTIONAL HOLDINGS:
No. of Institutions: 265
Shares Held: 126,036,382
% Held: 87.0

INDUSTRY: Copper ores (SIC: 1021)

TRANSFER AGENT(S): Mellon Investor Services, LLC, Ridgefield Park, NJ

FREMONT GENERAL CORPORATION

EXCH.	SYM.	REC. PRICE	P/E RATIO	YLD.	MKT. CAP.	RANGE (52-WK.)	'02 Y/E PR.
NYSE	FMT	6.07 (2/28/03)	4.3	2.0%	$429.7 mill.	7.20 - 2.98	4.49

LOWER MEDIUM GRADE. FMT IS BENEFITING FROM AN INCREASED LEVEL OF INTEREST-BEARING ASSETS.

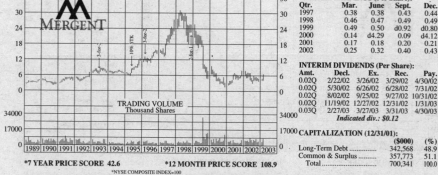

INTERIM EARNINGS (Per Share):

Qtr.	Mar.	June	Sept.	Dec.
1997	0.38	0.38	0.43	0.44
1998	0.46	0.47	0.49	0.49
1999	0.49	0.50	d0.92	d0.80
2000	0.14	d4.29	0.09	d4.12
2001	0.17	0.18	0.20	0.21
2002	0.25	0.32	0.40	0.43

INTERIM DIVIDENDS (Per Share):

Amt.	Decl.	Ex.	Rec.	Pay.
0.02Q	2/22/02	3/26/02	3/29/02	4/30/02
0.02Q	5/30/02	6/26/02	6/28/02	7/31/02
0.02Q	8/02/02	9/25/02	9/27/02	10/31/02
0.02Q	11/19/02	12/27/02	12/31/02	1/31/03
0.03Q	2/27/03	3/27/03	3/31/03	4/30/03

Indicated div.: $0.12

CAPITALIZATION (12/31/01):

	($000)	(%)
Long-Term Debt	342,568	48.9
Common & Surplus	357,773	51.1
Total	700,341	100.0

*7 YEAR PRICE SCORE 42.6   ***12 MONTH PRICE SCORE 108.9**

*NYSE COMPOSITE INDEX=100

BUSINESS:

Fremont General Corporation is a financial services holding company engaged primarily in commercial and residential real estate lending through its industrial bank subsidiary, Fremont Investment & Loan. Commercial and residential real estate lending represented approximately 99.2% of loan interest revenues in 2002. Interest in syndicated commercial loans account for substantially all of the remaining loan interest revenues. In December 1999, FMT sold its commercial finance subsidiary that provided commercial working capital lines of credit. In July 2002, the Company sold its workers' compensation insurance operation.

RECENT DEVELOPMENTS:

For the year ended 12/31/02, net income was $102.2 million, before a loss from discontinued operations of $77.8 million and an extraordinary gain of $1.9 million, versus income of $53.3 million, before income from discontinued operations of $2.3 million and an extraordinary gain of $5.0 million, the previous year. Results for 2002 and 2001 included gains from the sale of real estate loans of $143.0 million and $46.2 million, respectively. Total interest income rose 3.9% to $436.9 million. Net interest income climbed 37.1% to $278.4 million from $203.1 million a year earlier. Provision for loan losses jumped 84.8% to $108.1 million from $53.4 million in 2001. Non-interest income rose 2.7% to $16.8 million, while non-interest expense increased 29.7% to $95.7 million.

PROSPECTS:

The Company is benefiting from an increased level of interest-bearing assets, primarily residential real estate loans. FMT's loans receivable, before allowance for loan losses, amounted to $4.14 billion at 12/31/02 compared with $3.86 billion at 12/31/01. Separately, FMT is taking steps to improve its financial position. FMT has extinguished about 38.0% of its original $425.0 million in outstanding debt. In addition, during the first quarter of 2003, FMT sold all of its residual interests in its three securitizations of residential real estate loans for $40.2 million in cash. As of 2/27/03, the Company had approximately $85.0 million in cash and short-term investments.

ANNUAL FINANCIAL DATA:

FISCAL YEAR	PREM. INC. ($mill.)	NET INVST. INC. ($mill.)	TOT. REVS. ($mill.)	NET INC. ($mill.)	TOT. ASSETS ($mill.)	TOT. INVST. ($mill.)	RET. ON REVS. %	RET. ON EQUITY %	RET. ON ASSETS %	EARN. PER SH.$	TANG. BK. VAL.$	AVG. YIELD %	DIV. PER SH.$	PRICE RANGE		AVG. P/E RATIO
p12/31/02			596.7	⑧102.2						⑧1.40		1.9	⑦0.10	7.79	2.98	3.9
⑥12/31/01	...	422.9	422.9	⑤53.3	8,009.0	383.7	12.6	14.9	0.7	⑤0.76	5.05	2.0	⑦0.10	7.90	2.25	6.7
12/31/00	1,016.1	540.2	1,577.2	④d483.7	8,164.1	2,031.0	...	...	...	④d8.23	3.16	5.0	0.28	9.63	1.50	...
12/31/99	831.0	536.0	1,397.6	②③10.6	8,015.2	2,268.8	0.8	1.4	0.1	②③d0.64	7.16	2.1	0.32	25.69	4.69	...
12/31/98	552.1	427.6	1,037.6	①155.1	7,369.6	2,386.8	14.9	16.3	2.1	①1.90	11.24	1.2	0.30	31.06	18.00	12.9
12/31/97	601.2	344.1	974.3	132.9	6,090.6	2,442.8	13.6	16.0	2.2	1.62	9.89	1.5	0.30	27.50	13.19	12.6
12/31/96	486.9	287.3	795.8	115.1	4,307.5	1,484.3	14.5	20.6	2.7	1.63	8.75	2.2	0.29	15.75	10.75	8.1
12/31/95	606.9	282.5	923.8	97.2	4,477.4	1,937.9	10.5	19.5	2.2	1.31	8.42	2.7	0.25	12.42	5.72	6.9
12/31/94	433.6	190.2	653.1	79.8	3,067.4	888.9	12.2	22.7	2.6	1.08	10.47	3.1	0.22	7.88	6.52	6.7
12/31/93	455.8	164.4	651.4	42.7	2,601.2	1,055.3	6.6	11.6	1.6	0.93	...	2.8	0.21	8.71	6.36	8.1

Statistics are as originally reported. Adj. for stk. splits: 2-for-1, 12/98; 3-for-2 spl., 2/96 & 6/93; 10% div., 6/95. ① Bef. acctg. change credit $43.5 mill. ② Bef. disc. ops. loss. $25.0 mill. ③ Incl. pre-tax chrg. $75.0 mill. & gain of $10.3 mill. ④ Bef. extraord. gain of $12.4 mill. for debt extinguishment, but incl. a write-down of intangibles and restruct. chrg. of $267.8 mill. ⑤ Bef. gain fr. disc. opers. of $2.3 mill. & extraord. gain of $5.0 mill. ⑥ Absence of premiums revenue reflect the discontinuation of FMT's property and casualty insurance business ⑦ Incl. a special div. $0.02 per share, 12/02; $0.02 per share, 12/01. ⑧ Bef. loss fr. disc. opers. of $77.8 mill. & extraord. gain of $1.9 mill.

OFFICERS:
J. A. Mcintyre, Chmn., C.E.O.
L. J. Rampino, Pres., C.O.O.
W. R. Bailey, Exec. V.P., C.F.O., Treas.
INVESTOR CONTACT: Investor Relations, (310) 315-5500
PRINCIPAL OFFICE: 2020 Santa Monica Blvd., Suite 600, Santa Monica, CA 90404

TELEPHONE NUMBER: (310) 315-5500
FAX: (310) 315-5599
NO. OF EMPLOYEES: 1,600 (avg.)
SHAREHOLDERS: 2,028 (record)
ANNUAL MEETING: In May
INCORPORATED: NV, 1972

INSTITUTIONAL HOLDINGS:
No. of Institutions: 98
Shares Held: 33,673,177
% Held: 44.8
INDUSTRY: State commercial banks (SIC: 6022)
TRANSFER AGENT(S): Mellon Investor Services, South Hackensack, NJ

FRONTIER OIL CORPORATION

EXCH.	SYM.	REC. PRICE	P/E RATIO	YLD.	MKT. CAP.	RANGE (52-WK.)	'02 Y/E PR.
NYSE	FTO	16.35 (2/28/03)	545.0	1.2%	$422.1 mill.	22.75 - 10.68	17.22

LOWER MEDIUM GRADE. THE COMPANY IS OPTIMISTIC ABOUT PRODUCT PRICES FOR 2003 DUE TO LOWER DOMESTIC INVENTORIES AND A HEAVY TURNAROUND SCHEDULE.

TRADING VOLUME
Thousand Shares

*7 YEAR PRICE SCORE 200.0   *12 MONTH PRICE SCORE 107.7
*NYSE COMPOSITE INDEX=100

INTERIM EARNINGS (Per Share):

Qtr.	Mar.	June	Sept.	Dec.
1998	d0.03	0.33	0.33	0.04
1999	d0.18	0.14	0.30	d0.90
2000	d0.22	1.13	0.36	0.05
2001	0.17	2.86	1.27	d0.41
2002	0.01	d0.12	0.03	0.11

INTERIM DIVIDENDS (Per Share):

Amt.	Decl.	Ex.	Rec.	Pay.
0.05Q	3/18/02	3/26/02	3/28/02	4/15/02
0.05Q	6/17/02	6/26/02	6/28/02	7/15/02
0.05Q	9/09/02	9/25/02	9/27/02	10/14/02
0.05Q	12/13/02	12/24/02	12/27/02	1/13/03
0.05Q	3/14/03	3/26/03	3/28/03	4/14/03

Indicated div.: $0.20

CAPITALIZATION (12/31/01):

	($000)	(%)
Long-Term Debt	208,880	53.1
Deferred Income Tax	15,080	3.8
Common & Surplus	169,204	43.0
Total	393,164	100.0

BUSINESS:

Frontier Oil Corporation is an independent energy company engaged in crude oil refining and the wholesale marketing of refined petroleum products. FTO operates refineries in Cheyenne, WY and in El Dorado, KS with a total crude oil capacity of over 156,000 barrels per day, as of 2/11/03. FTO focuses its marketing efforts in the Rocky Mountain region, which includes the states of CO, WY, MT and UT, and the Plains States, which includes KS, NE, IA, MO, ND and SD. As of 12/31/01, FTO's refinery product mix included gasoline (52.6%), diesel and jet fuel (32.4%), asphalt (4.3%), chemicals (0.9%) and other refined petroleum products (9.8%). On 11/16/99, FTO acquired the refinery located in El Dorado, KS from Equilon Enterprises LLC for about $170.0 million.

RECENT DEVELOPMENTS:

For the twelve months ended 12/31/02, net income was $1.0 million compared with $107.7 million a year earlier. Results for 2002 included an impairment charge of $363,000 related to a loss on assets to be sold. FTO's lower earnings were attributable to significantly lower refined product margins. Revenues fell 4.0% to $1.81 billion from $1.89 billion the previous year. Operating income of $27.9 million was 83.0% less than the year before.

PROSPECTS:

FTO's near-term prospects are mixed. The Company is optimistic about product prices for 2003, citing lower domestic inventories and a heavy turnaround schedule. However, the ongoing Venezuelan oil industry strike and political unrest in that country, coupled with the threat of war in Iraq clouds FTO's outlook. On the positive side, FTO's crude oil supply agreement with Baytex Energy commenced on 1/1/03, which should provide the Company with some stability in the crude oil environment. The agreement provides for the purchase by FTO of 9,000 barrels per day (bpd) of a Lloydminster crude oil blend, a heavy Canadian crude, rising to 20,000 bpd by October of 2003. FTO intends to process the contract crude oil primarily at its Cheyenne, Wyoming refinery and expects the agreement will result in lower volatility in the refinery's light/heavy crude oil spread, or the discount at which heavy, higher sulfur content crude oil sells compared with the sales price of light, lower sulfur content crude oil.

ANNUAL FINANCIAL DATA:

FISCAL YEAR	TOT. REVS. ($000)	NET INC. ($000)	TOT. ASSETS ($000)	OPER. PROFIT %	NET PROFIT %	RET. ON EQUITY %	RET. ON ASSETS %	CURR. RATIO	EARN. PER SH.$	CASH FL.PER SH.$	TANG. BK. VAL.$	DIV. PER SH.$	PRICE RANGE	AVG. P/E RATIO	AVG. YIELD %
p12/31/02	1,813,750	1,028							④ 0.04			0.20	22.75 - 10.68	417.9	0.2
12/31/01	1,888,401	④ 107,653	581,746	8.7	5.7	63.6	18.5	1.7	4.00	4.93	6.55	0.10	20.25 - 6.38	3.3	0.8
12/31/00	③ 2,045,157	37,206	588,213	3.5	1.8	45.7	6.3	1.2	1.34	2.17	3.06	...	9.13 - 5.13	5.3	...
12/31/99	503,600	d17,061	521,493	...	...	...	...	1.1	d0.62	d0.15	1.86	...	8.25 - 4.56	...	...
12/31/98	299,368	① 18,818	182,026	8.6	6.3	26.7	10.3	1.9	① 0.65	1.03	2.53	...	9.31 - 4.00	10.2	...
12/31/97	376,418	② 7,812	177,915	5.8	2.1	14.0	4.4	1.4	② 0.28	0.75	1.99	...	8.50 - 3.13	20.8	...
12/31/96	403,952	d6,892	239,865	2.6	...	...	...	0.9	d0.25	0.38	0.93	...	4.13 - 2.63	...	...
12/31/95	362,745	d19,125	238,382	0.3	...	...	...	1.0	d0.70	0.08	1.19	...	5.00 - 2.63	...	...
12/31/94	353,715	d12,607	277,536	2.1	...	...	...	1.0	d0.46	0.52	1.81	...	5.88 - 3.88	...	...
12/31/93	366,556	2,504	296,811	6.1	0.7	3.8	0.8	1.0	0.10	1.05	2.44	...	5.88 - 3.50	46.8	...

Statistics are as originally reported. ① Bef. extraord. chrg. of $3.0 mill. ② Bef. disc. oper. gain of $15.2 mill.; bef. extraord. chrg. of $3.9 mill. ③ Incl. results of the El Dorado refinery. ④ Incl. impairment chrg. of $363,000.

OFFICERS:
J. R. Gibbs, Chmn., Pres., C.E.O.
J. H. Edwards, Exec. V.P., C.F.O.
J. C. Bechtol, V.P., Gen. Couns., Sec.
INVESTOR CONTACT: Doug Aron, Sr. Fin. Analyst, (713) 688-9600, ext. 145
PRINCIPAL OFFICE: 10000 Memorial Drive, Suite 600, Houston, TX 77024-3411

TELEPHONE NUMBER: (713) 688-9600
FAX: (713) 688-0610
WEB: www.frontieroil.com
NO. OF EMPLOYEES: 726 (approx.)
SHAREHOLDERS: 1,420
ANNUAL MEETING: In Apr.
INCORPORATED: WY, Dec., 1976

INSTITUTIONAL HOLDINGS:
No. of Institutions: 103
Shares Held: 19,093,627
% Held: 73.1

INDUSTRY: Petroleum refining (SIC: 2911)

TRANSFER AGENT(S): Computershare Investor Services, Chicago, IL

FULLER (H.B.) COMPANY

EXCH.	SYM.	REC. PRICE	P/E RATIO	YLD.	MKT. CAP.	RANGE (52-WK.)	'02 Y/E PR.	DIV. ACH.
NYSE	FUL	22.05 (2/28/03)	22.5	2.0%	$0.63 bill.	33.32 - 21.50	25.88	35 yrs.

UPPER MEDIUM GRADE. THE COMPANY SHOULD BENEFIT FROM AN IMPROVED COST STRUCTURE DUE TO ITS RESTRUCTURING, WHICH IS NEAR COMPLETION.

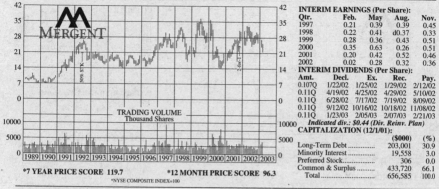

INTERIM EARNINGS (Per Share):

Qtr.	Feb.	May	Aug.	Nov.
1997	0.21	0.39	0.39	0.45
1998	0.22	0.41	d0.37	0.33
1999	0.28	0.36	0.43	0.51
2000	0.35	0.63	0.26	0.51
2001	0.20	0.42	0.52	0.46
2002	0.02	0.28	0.32	0.36

INTERIM DIVIDENDS (Per Share):

Amt.	Decl.	Ex.	Rec.	Pay.
0.107Q	1/22/02	1/25/02	1/29/02	2/12/02
0.11Q	4/19/02	4/25/02	4/29/02	5/10/02
0.11Q	6/28/02	7/17/02	7/19/02	8/09/02
0.11Q	9/12/02	10/16/02	10/18/02	11/08/02
0.11Q	1/23/03	2/05/03	2/07/03	2/21/03

Indicated div.: $0.44 (Div. Reinv. Plan)

CAPITALIZATION (12/1/01):

	($000)	(%)
Long-Term Debt	203,001	30.9
Minority Interest	19,558	3.0
Preferred Stock	306	0.0
Common & Surplus	433,720	66.1
Total	656,585	100.0

*7 YEAR PRICE SCORE 119.7   ***12 MONTH PRICE SCORE 96.3**

*NYSE COMPOSITE INDEX=100

BUSINESS:

H.B. Fuller and Company and its subsidiaries are principally engaged in the manufacture and distribution of industrial adhesives, coatings, sealants, paints and other specialty chemical products worldwide. These products, in thousands of formulations, are sold to customers in a wide range of industries. Also, the Company is a producer and supplier of specialty chemical products for a variety of applications such as ceramic tile installation, HVAC insulation, powder coatings applied to metal surfaces such as office furniture, appliances and lawn and garden equipment, specialty hot melt adhesives for packaging applications, and liquid paint sold through retail outlets.

RECENT DEVELOPMENTS:

On 12/2/02, the Company began trading on the New York Stock Exchange under the ticker symbol "FUL." For the 52 weeks ended 11/30/02, net income decreased 37.3% to $28.2 million compared with $44.9 million the year before. Earnings for 2002 and 2001 included after-tax charges of $19.1 million and $1.5 million, respectively, for asset impairments, severance and other costs related to the Company's restructuring initiative. Net sales slid 1.4% to $1.26 billion from $1.27 billion a year earlier, reflecting lower sales volumes and pricing, partially offset by positive currency effects. Gross profit slipped 2.2% to $338.0 million from $345.6 million, while gross profit as a percentage of sales declined to 26.9% from 27.1% the year before. Selling, administrative and other expenses increased 9.4% to $281.6 million. Interest expense decreased 18.7% to $17.3 million.

PROSPECTS:

The Company should benefit from an improved cost structure due to its restructuring, which is near completion. Separately, on 3/15/03, the Company's adhesives business segment implemented a price increase of 6.5% for water based adhesives, 4.5% for hot melt adhesives and specific individual increases for various other products. These price increases should help FUL safeguard against the run-up in raw material prices and increased transportation costs, which have resulted in part from the uncertainty surrounding the political situation in the Middle East.

ANNUAL FINANCIAL DATA:

FISCAL YEAR	TOT. REVS. ($mill.)	NET INC. ($mill.)	TOT. ASSETS ($mill.)	OPER. PROFIT %	NET PROFIT %	RET. ON EQUITY %	RET. ON ASSETS %	CURR. RATIO	EARN. PER SH.$	CASH FL. PER SH.$	TANG. BK. VAL.$	DIV. PER SH.$	PRICE RANGE	AVG. P/E RATIO	AVG. YIELD %
p12/31/02	1,256.2	③ 28.2							③ 0.98			0.44	33.32 - 24.15	29.3	1.5
12/01/01	1,274.1	① 44.9	966.2	6.9	3.5	10.4	4.7	2.0	① 1.59	3.51	12.37	0.43	31.19 - 17.25	15.2	1.8
12/02/00	1,352.6	49.2	1,010.4	7.6	3.6	12.1	4.9	1.9	1.74	3.59	11.07	0.42	35.88 - 14.06	14.3	1.7
11/27/99	1,364.5	② 44.1	1,025.6	7.6	3.2	11.7	4.3	1.7	② 1.58	3.39	9.88	0.41	36.44 - 19.06	17.6	1.5
11/28/98	1,347.2	② 16.0	1,046.2	4.5	1.2	4.7	1.5	1.6	② 0.58	2.37	8.51	0.39	32.50 - 17.00	43.0	1.6
11/29/97	1,306.8	① 40.3	917.6	6.7	3.1	11.9	4.4	1.7	① 1.43	3.09	10.51	0.36	30.13 - 22.50	18.4	1.4
11/30/96	1,275.7	45.4	869.3	6.3	3.6	13.6	5.2	1.6	1.61	3.27	10.06	0.33	24.81 - 14.75	12.3	1.7
11/30/95	1,243.8	① 31.2	828.9	5.6	2.5	10.4	3.8	1.6	① 1.11	2.57	8.71	0.31	19.88 - 14.88	15.7	1.8
11/30/94	1,097.4	30.9	742.6	6.0	2.8	11.2	4.2	1.6	1.10	2.29	7.75	0.29	21.13 - 13.88	15.9	1.6
11/30/93	975.3	①② 21.7	564.5	5.5	2.2	8.7	3.8	1.7	①② 0.78	1.83	8.22	0.27	21.38 - 15.63	23.9	1.5

Statistics are as originally reported. Adj. for 2-for-1 stk. split, 11/16/01. ① Bef. acctg. chrg.: 12/1/01, $501,000; 11/29/97, $3.4 mill.; 11/30/95, $2.5 mill. ② Incl. non-recurr. chrg. 11/27/99: $17.2 mill.; 11/28/98: $26.7 mill. ③ Incl. after-tax restructuring costs of $19.1 mill.

OFFICERS:
A. P. Stroucken, Chmn., Pres., C.E.O.
R. A. Tucker, Sr. V.P., C.F.O., Treas.
W. L. Gacki, V.P., Treas.
INVESTOR CONTACT: Scott Dvorak, Director of Investor Relations, (651) 236-5150
PRINCIPAL OFFICE: 1200 Willow Lake Boulevard, Vadnais Heights, MN 55110-5101

TELEPHONE NUMBER: (651) 236-5900
FAX: (651) 236-5161
WEB: www.hbfuller.com
NO. OF EMPLOYEES: 4,900 (approx.)
SHAREHOLDERS: 3,606
ANNUAL MEETING: In April
INCORPORATED: MN, Dec., 1915

INSTITUTIONAL HOLDINGS:
No. of Institutions: 137
Shares Held: 17,540,469
% Held: 61.9
INDUSTRY: Adhesives and sealants (SIC: 2891)
TRANSFER AGENT(S): Wells Fargo Shareowner Services, Minnesota, MN

FURNITURE BRANDS INTERNATIONAL INC.

EXCH.	SYM.	REC. PRICE	P/E RATIO	YLD.	MKT. CAP.	RANGE (52-WK.)	'02 Y/E PR.
NYSE	FBN	18.21 (2/28/03)	8.6	...	$0.99 bill.	42.74 - 18.12	23.85

MEDIUM GRADE. FOR FULL-YEAR 2003, THE COMPANY EXPECTS EARNINGS PER SHARE OF BETWEEN $2.40 AND $2.50.

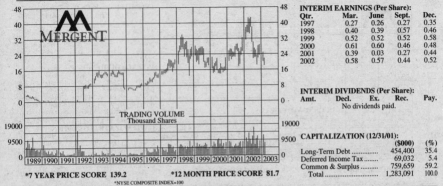

7 YEAR PRICE SCORE 139.2   **12 MONTH PRICE SCORE 81.7**
*NYSE COMPOSITE INDEX=100

INTERIM EARNINGS (Per Share):

Qtr.	Mar.	June	Sept.	Dec.
1997	0.27	0.26	0.27	0.35
1998	0.40	0.39	0.57	0.46
1999	0.52	0.52	0.52	0.58
2000	0.61	0.60	0.46	0.48
2001	0.39	0.03	0.27	0.44
2002	0.58	0.57	0.44	0.52

INTERIM DIVIDENDS (Per Share):

Amt.	Decl.	Ex.	Rec.	Pay.
		No dividends paid.		

CAPITALIZATION (12/31/01):

	($000)	(%)
Long-Term Debt	454,400	35.4
Deferred Income Tax	69,032	5.4
Common & Surplus	759,659	59.2
Total	1,283,091	100.0

BUSINESS:

Furniture Brands International Inc. is a manufacturer of residential furniture in the U.S. FBN markets its products across a broad spectrum of price categories and distributes them through an extensive system of independently owned national, regional and local retailers. FBN markets its products through its six operating subsidiaries: Broyhill Furniture Industries, Inc.; Lane Furniture Industries, Inc.; Thomasville Furniture Industries, Inc.; Henredon Furniture Industries; Drexel Heritage Furnishings; and Maitland-Smith. FBN manufactures and distributes case goods, consisting of bedroom, dining room and living room furniture; stationary upholstery products, consisting of sofas, loveseats, sectionals and chairs; occasional furniture, consisting of wood tables, accent pieces, home entertainment centers and home office furniture; recliners, motion furniture and sleep sofas; and accessories. On 12/28/01, FBN acquired the assets of Henredon Furniture Industries, Drexel Heritage Furnishings and Maitland-Smith.

RECENT DEVELOPMENTS:

For the year ended 12/31/02, net income surged 104.8% to $118.8 million compared with $58.0 million in 2001. Results for 2001 included an asset impairment charge of $18.0 million. Net sales increased 26.8% to $2.40 billion from $1.89 billion a year earlier. The improvement in sales was primarily attributed to strong demand for middle-price point products of Broyhill and Lane, partially offset by soft demand for upper-end price-point products. Operating income soared 104.3% to $202.4 million from $99.1 million in 2001.

PROSPECTS:

In the near-term, FBN expects current business conditions to persist based on incoming order trends. Consequently, first quarter 2003 sales are projected to be flat quarter over quarter, with earnings per share in the range of $0.55 to $0.60. For full-year 2003, FBN expects earnings per share of between $2.40 and $2.50. FBN also expects operating profit margin improvement to continue in 2003, as its implements its cost-reduction program at each operating company. Also, FBN will focus on expanding its market share by leveraging its strategic initiatives in sourcing and distribution.

ANNUAL FINANCIAL DATA:

FISCAL YEAR	TOT. REVS. ($mill.)	NET INC. ($mill.)	TOT. ASSETS ($mill.)	OPER. PROFIT %	NET PROFIT %	RET. ON EQUITY %	RET. ON ASSETS %	CURR. RATIO	EARN. PER SH. $	CASH FL. PER SH. $	TANG. BK. VAL. $	PRICE RANGE	AVG. P/E RATIO
p12/31/02	2,397.7	118.8	1,567.4						2.11			42.74 - 18.40	14.5
12/31/01	1,891.3	④ 58.0	1,503.5	5.2	3.1	7.6	3.9	4.4	④ 1.13	2.22	7.18	32.50 - 17.65	22.2
12/31/00	2,116.2	② 108.4	1,304.8	9.1	5.1	18.6	8.3	4.8	② 2.15	3.30	5.92	22.44 - 13.94	8.5
12/31/99	2,088.1	111.9	1,288.8	10.1	5.4	23.6	8.7	4.4	2.14	3.22	3.46	28.44 - 17.00	10.6
12/31/98	1,960.3	97.9	1,303.2	9.4	5.0	23.7	7.5	4.1	1.82	2.85	1.86	34.13 - 12.94	12.9
12/31/97	1,808.3	67.1	1,257.2	8.1	3.7	20.7	5.3	4.5	1.15	2.10	...	21.50 - 13.63	15.3
12/31/96	1,696.8	② 54.2	1,269.2	7.7	3.2	12.9	4.3	4.2	② 0.88	1.75	1.23	15.00 - 8.25	13.2
12/31/95	1,073.9	②③ 34.2	1,291.7	7.4	3.2	11.4	2.6	4.4	②③ 0.67	1.39	...	9.25 - 5.50	11.0
12/31/94	1,072.7	① 27.9	891.9	7.9	2.6	10.1	3.1	4.1	① 0.54	1.24	...	15.75 - 6.13	20.3
12/31/93	1,656.8	45.4	1,205.7	8.0	2.7	13.4	3.8	4.2	0.88	1.59	1.76	15.75 - 9.38	14.3

Statistics are as originally reported. ① Bef. disc. oper. credit of $10.3 mill. ② Bef. extraord. loss, 2000, $2.5 mill.; 1996, $7.4 mill.; 1995, $5.8 mill. ③ Gain on insurance settlement of $7.9 mill. ④ Incl. asset impairment chrg. of $18.0 mill.

OFFICERS:
W. G. Holliman, Chmn., Pres., C.E.O.
D. P. Howard, V.P., C.F.O., Treas.
L. Chipperfield, Sr. V.P., C.A.O.
INVESTOR CONTACT: Lynn Chipperfield, (314) 863-1100
PRINCIPAL OFFICE: 101 South Hanley Road, St. Louis, MO 63105-3493

TELEPHONE NUMBER: (314) 863-1100
FAX: (314) 863-5306
WEB: www.furniturebrands.com
NO. OF EMPLOYEES: 23,850 (approx.)
SHAREHOLDERS: 2,150 (approx.)
ANNUAL MEETING: In Apr.
INCORPORATED: DE, Mar., 1921

INSTITUTIONAL HOLDINGS:
No. of Institutions: 186
Shares Held: 47,746,891
% Held: 84.8
INDUSTRY: Household furniture, nec (SIC: 2519)
TRANSFER AGENT(S): The Bank of New York, New York, NY

GALLAGHER (ARTHUR J.) & COMPANY

EXCH.	SYM.	REC. PRICE	P/E RATIO	YLD.	MKT. CAP.	RANGE (52-WK.)	'02 Y/E PR.	DIV. ACH.
NYSE	AJG	24.47 (2/28/03)	17.4	2.9%	$2.08 bill.	37.20 - 21.70	29.38	18 yrs.

INVESTMENT GRADE. GOING FORWARD, EARNINGS SHOULD BENEFIT FROM CONTINUED NEW BUSINESS DEVELOPMENT AND ACCOUNT RETENTION FOR EXISTING BUSINESS.

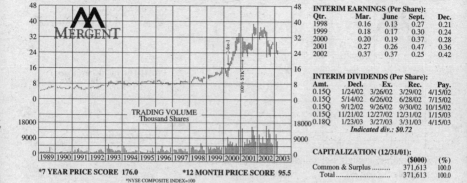

*7 YEAR PRICE SCORE 176.0   ***12 MONTH PRICE SCORE 95.5**

*NYSE COMPOSITE INDEX=100

INTERIM EARNINGS (Per Share):

Qtr.	Mar.	June	Sept.	Dec.
1998	0.16	0.13	0.27	0.21
1999	0.18	0.17	0.30	0.24
2000	0.20	0.19	0.37	0.28
2001	0.27	0.26	0.47	0.36
2002	0.37	0.37	0.25	0.42

INTERIM DIVIDENDS (Per Share):

Amt.	Decl.	Ex.	Rec.	Pay.
0.15Q	1/24/02	3/26/02	3/29/02	4/15/02
0.15Q	5/14/02	6/26/02	6/28/02	7/15/02
0.15Q	9/12/02	9/26/02	9/30/02	10/15/02
0.15Q	11/21/02	12/27/02	12/31/02	1/15/03
0.18Q	1/23/03	3/27/03	3/31/03	4/15/03

Indicated div.: $0.72

CAPITALIZATION (12/31/01):

	($000)	(%)
Common & Surplus	371,613	100.0
Total	371,613	100.0

BUSINESS:

Arthur J. Gallagher & Company is engaged in providing insurance brokerage, risk management, employee benefit and other related services to clients in the United States and abroad. The Company's principal activity is the negotiation and placement of insurance for its clients. In addition, AJG specializes in furnishing risk management services that include assisting clients in analyzing risks and determining whether proper protection is best obtained through the purchase of insurance or through retention of those risks and the adoption of corporate risk management policies and cost-effective loss control and prevention programs. Risk management also includes claims management, loss control consulting and property appraisals. As of 1/29/03, the Company had offices in seven countries and served clients in more than 100 countries around the world through a network of correspondent brokers and consultants.

RECENT DEVELOPMENTS:

For the year ended 12/31/02, net income grew 3.6% to $129.7 million from $125.3 million in the previous year. Results for 2002 included an investment loss, net of related incentive compensation, other and income tax expense, of $10.4 million versus a gain of $9.8 million in 2001. Total operating revenues climbed 24.0% to $1.12 billion from $903.9 million a year earlier. The increase in revenues was the result of strong new business development, account retention, property/casualty rate increases and acquisitions. Revenues from commissions increased 23.1% to $663.5 million from $539.0 million in 2001. Revenues from fees rose 19.7% to $388.9 million. Comparisons were made with restated prior-year figures.

PROSPECTS:

Going forward, AJG's earnings should benefit from continued new business development and account retention for existing business. The company expects premium rates in the property/casualty market to remain solid throughout 2003, which should continue to have a positive impact on its revenues. Separately, AJG noted that it expects salaries and employee benefits costs to be higher than normal throughout most of 2003 due to the annualized impact of the new employees hired in 2002 and increases in pension and medical insurance costs.

ANNUAL FINANCIAL DATA:

FISCAL YEAR	TOT. REVS. ($mill.)	NET INC. ($mill.)	TOT. ASSETS ($mill.)	TOT. INVST. ($mill.)	RET. ON REVS. %	RET. ON EQUITY %	RET. ON ASSETS %	EARN. PER SH.$	TANG. BK. VAL.$	AVG. YIELD %	DIV. PER SH.$	PRICE RANGE	AVG. P/E RATIO
p12/31/02	1,120.8	⊡ 129.7						⊡ 1.41		2.0	0.58	37.24 - 22.10	21.0
12/31/01	910.0	125.3	1,471.8	70.9	13.8	33.7	8.5	1.39	3.60	1.7	0.51	38.82 - 21.88	21.8
12/31/00	740.6	87.8	1,062.3	83.3	11.9	27.9	8.3	1.05	3.75	1.9	0.45	34.25 - 11.53	21.8
12/31/99	605.8	67.8	884.1	84.1	11.2	27.9	7.7	0.88	3.14	2.9	0.39	16.56 - 10.56	15.4
12/31/98	540.7	56.5	746.0	77.5	10.5	27.9	7.6	0.78	2.69	3.4	0.34	11.69 - 8.39	13.0
12/31/97	488.0	53.3	641.8	101.9	10.9	32.5	8.3	0.78	2.31	3.6	0.30	9.56 - 7.44	10.9
12/31/96	456.7	45.8	590.4	90.3	10.0	34.0	7.8	0.66	1.89	3.3	0.28	9.88 - 7.28	13.0
12/31/95	412.0	41.5	495.8	87.8	10.1	35.1	8.4	0.64	1.79	2.8	0.24	9.50 - 7.53	13.4
12/31/94	356.4	34.5	451.1	80.5	9.7	35.7	7.7	0.54	1.50	2.6	0.21	9.09 - 7.03	14.8
12/31/93	317.7	32.3	466.1	113.6	10.2	26.0	6.9	0.51	1.92	2.2	0.17	9.34 - 6.38	15.6

Statistics are as originally reported. Adjusted for 2-for-1 stock split: 1/01 & 3/00. ⊡ Incl. after-tax invest. chrg. $10.4 mill.

OFFICERS:
R. E. Gallagher, Chmn.
J. P. Gallagher, Jr., Pres., C.E.O.

INVESTOR CONTACT: Marsha J. Akin, Investor Relations, (630) 773-3800

PRINCIPAL OFFICE: Two Pierce Place, Itasca, IL 60143-3141

TELEPHONE NUMBER: (630) 773-3800
FAX: (630) 285-4000
WEB: www.ajg.com

NO. OF EMPLOYEES: 6,500 (approx.)

SHAREHOLDERS: 700 (approx.)

ANNUAL MEETING: In May

INSTITUTIONAL HOLDINGS:
No. of Institutions: 238
Shares Held: 59,446,649
% Held: 67.6
INDUSTRY: Insurance agents, brokers, & service (SIC: 6411)
TRANSFER AGENT(S): Computershare Investor Services, Chicago, IL

GAMESTOP CORP.

EXCH.	SYM.	REC. PRICE	P/E RATIO	YLD.	MKT. CAP.	RANGE (52-WK.)	'02 Y/E PR.
NYSE	GME	10.50 (2/28/03)	12.2	...	$378.1 mill.	24.30 - 7.50	9.80

MEDIUM GRADE. THE COMPANY EXPECTS TO ACCELERATE ITS STORE OPENINGS TO BETWEEN 235 AND 265 NEW STORES IN 2003.

*7 YEAR PRICE SCORE N/A   ***12 MONTH PRICE SCORE 59.5**
*NYSE COMPOSITE INDEX=100

INTERIM EARNINGS (Per Share):

Qtr.	Apr.	July	Oct.	Jan.
2002-03	0.08	0.10	0.16	0.52

INTERIM DIVIDENDS (Per Share):

Amt.	Decl.	Ex.	Rec.	Pay.
		No dividends paid.		

CAPITALIZATION (2/2/02):

	($000)	(%)
Long-Term Debt	399,623	100.2
Deferred Income Tax	3,065	0.8
Common & Surplus	d3,985	-1.0
Total	398,703	100.0

BUSINESS:

GameStop Corp., formerly a wholly-owned subsidiary of Barnes & Noble, Inc., went public with an initial offering of its common stock on 2/12/02. With more than 30.0 million customers, GME is the largest video game and entertainment software specialty retailer in the nation, based on revenues and number of stores. As of 3/19/03, GME operated 1,231 retail stores in 49 states, and Puerto Rico, under the GAMESTOP®, BABBAGES®, SOFTWARE ETC™ and FUNCOLAND® brands. GME sells new

software, hardware and game accessories for the personal computer and next-generation video game systems from Sony, Nintendo, and Microsoft, and also resells used video games. In addition, GME sells computer and video game magazines and strategy guides, action figures and other related merchandise. GME also owns a commerce-enabled Web property, GameStop.com and Game Informer magazine. As of 3/19/03, Barnes & Noble, Inc., owned approximately 60.0% interest in GME.

RECENT DEVELOPMENTS:

For the 52 weeks ended 2/1/03, net income surged to $52.4 million compared with $7.0 million in the corresponding 53-week period a year earlier. Results for 2002 included goodwill amortization of $11.1 million. Sales increased 20.7% to $1.35 billion from $1.12 billion a year earlier.

Comparable-store sales improved 11.0% year over year. Expenses were reduced by 80 basis points due to economies of scale as well as distribution and systems enhancements that increased operating efficiencies. Operating income soared 155.4% to $87.1 million.

PROSPECTS:

The Company expects to accelerate its store openings to between 235 and 265 new stores in 2003 due to the solid results in 2002 and the availability of suitable real estate. GME also expects total revenues for the fiscal year ending 1/31/04 to increase between 14.0% to 16.0% year over

year, with corresponding comparable-store sales growth in the range of 4.0% to 6.0%. Earnings per share in fiscal 2003 are expected to range from $1.02 to $1.06 per share, which represents earnings per share growth of 17.0% to 22.0% from a year earlier.

ANNUAL FINANCIAL DATA:

FISCAL YEAR	TOT. REVS. ($mill.)	NET INC. ($mill.)	TOT. ASSETS ($mill.)	OPER. PROFIT %	NET PROFIT %	RET. ON ASSETS %	CURR. RATIO	EARN. PER SH. $	CASH FL. PER SH. $
p2/1/03	1,352.8	52.4	803.9					0.87	
2/02/02	1,121.1	7.0	606.8	3.0	0.6	1.1	1.2	0.18	0.95

Statistics are as originally reported.

OFFICERS:
R. R. Fontaine, Chmn., C.E.O.
D. A. DeMatteo, Pres., C.O.O.
D. W. Carlson, Exec. V.P., C.F.O., Asst. Sec.

INVESTOR CONTACT: David W. Carlson, (817) 424-2130

PRINCIPAL OFFICE: 2250 William D. Tate Avenue, Grapevine, TX 76051

TELEPHONE NUMBER: (817) 424-2000
FAX: (817) 424-2820
WEB: www.gamestop.com

NO. OF EMPLOYEES: 2,700 (approx.)

SHAREHOLDERS: 3,849 (approx.)

ANNUAL MEETING: N/A

INCORPORATED: DE, Aug., 2001

INSTITUTIONAL HOLDINGS:
No. of Institutions: 100
Shares Held: 19,977,979
% Held: 35.0

INDUSTRY: Computer and software stores (SIC: 5734)

TRANSFER AGENT(S): Fleet National Bank, Providence, RI

GANNETT CO., INC.

EXCH.	SYM.	REC. PRICE	P/E RATIO	YLD.	MKT. CAP.	RANGE (52-WK.)	'02 Y/E PR.	DIV. ACH.
NYSE	GCI	72.17 (2/28/03)	16.7	1.3%	$19.34 bill.	79.90 - 62.76	71.80	31 yrs.

INVESTMENT GRADE. THE COMPANY FACES DIFFICULT COMPARISONS FOR 2003 COMPARED WITH 2002, WHICH BENEFITED FROM INCREASED ADVERTISING.

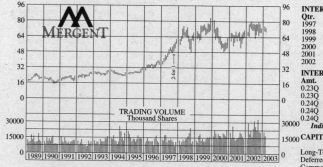

*7 YEAR PRICE SCORE 129.6   *12 MONTH PRICE SCORE 107.8
*NYSE COMPOSITE INDEX=100

INTERIM EARNINGS (Per Share):

Qtr.	Mar.	June	Sept.	Dec.
1997	0.48	0.69	0.27	0.80
1998	1.20	0.78	0.62	0.92
1999	0.64	0.98	0.74	1.01
2000	0.74	1.00	0.79	1.12
2001	0.66	0.88	0.66	0.93
2002	0.91	1.13	0.99	1.29

INTERIM DIVIDENDS (Per Share):

Amt.	Decl.	Ex.	Rec.	Pay.
0.23Q	2/19/02	3/06/02	3/08/02	4/01/02
0.23Q	5/07/02	6/05/02	6/07/02	7/01/02
0.24Q	8/07/02	9/11/02	9/13/02	10/01/02
0.24Q	10/22/02	12/10/02	12/12/02	1/02/03
0.24Q	2/25/03	3/05/03	3/07/03	4/01/03

Indicated div.: $0.96 (Div. Reinv. Plan)

CAPITALIZATION (12/30/01):

	($000)	(%)
Long-Term Debt	5,080,025	44.9
Deferred Income Tax	503,397	4.4
Common & Surplus	5,735,922	50.7
Total	11,319,344	100.0

BUSINESS:

Gannett Co., Inc. is a diversified news and information company that publishes newspapers and operates broadcasting stations. GCI is also engaged in marketing, commercial printing, a newswire service, data services, and news programming. GCI has operations in 43 states, the District of Columbia, Guam, the United Kingdom, Belgium, Germany, Italy and Hong Kong. GCI is the largest U.S. newspaper group in terms of circulation, with 94 daily newspapers, including USA TODAY, more than 400 non-daily publications and USA WEEKEND, a weekly newspaper magazine. In the U.K., GCI subsidiary Newsquest plc publishes nearly 300 titles, including 15 daily newspapers. GCI owns and operates 22 television stations in major markets. Results for 2002 were derived: newspaper publishing, 88.0%; and television, 12.0%.

RECENT DEVELOPMENTS:

For the year ended 12/29/02, net income jumped 39.6% to $1.16 billion compared with $831.2 million in 2001. Results for 2002 and 2001 included amortization of intangible assets of $7.3 million and $241.3 million, respectively. Total operating revenues were $6.42 billion, up 1.9% from $6.30 billion in the previous year. Operating income increased 21.2% to $1.93 billion compared with $1.59 billion the year before. Results reflected very strong television results and improved newspaper performance. The television segment achieved strong year-over-year gains due to political advertising spending and a favorable advertising environment. The newspaper segment benefited from a decline in newsprint costs.

PROSPECTS:

Looking ahead to 2003, the Company faces difficult comparisons with its 2002 performance because it benefited from political advertising on television as well as from television broadcasts of the Winter Olympics. Newsprint could also be of concern. However, the Company is comfortable with first quarter earnings per share estimates of $0.94 to $0.96 but warned global strife could hinder the slow recovery in the advertising sector.

ANNUAL FINANCIAL DATA:

FISCAL YEAR	TOT. REVS. ($mill.)	NET INC. ($mill.)	TOT. ASSETS ($mill.)	OPER. PROFIT %	NET PROFIT %	RET. ON EQUITY %	RET. ON ASSETS %	CURR. RATIO	EARN. PER SH. $	CASH FL. PER SH. $	TANG. BK. VAL. $	DIV. PER SH. $	PRICE RANGE	AVG. P/E RATIO	AVG. YIELD %
p12/29/02	6,422.2	1,160.1							4.31			0.93	79.90 - 62.76	16.5	1.3
12/30/01	6,344.2	831.2	13,096.1	25.1	13.1	14.5	6.3	1.0	3.12	4.78	...	0.89	71.14 - 53.00	19.9	1.4
12/31/00	6,222.3	④971.9	12,980.4	29.2	15.6	19.0	7.5	1.1	④3.63	5.03	...	0.85	81.56 - 48.38	17.9	1.3
12/26/99	5,260.2	③919.4	9,006.4	29.7	17.5	19.9	10.2	1.2	③3.26	4.26	...	0.81	83.63 - 60.63	22.1	1.1
12/27/98	5,121.3	②999.9	6,979.5	28.2	19.5	25.1	14.3	1.2	②3.50	4.59	0.66	0.80	75.13 - 47.63	17.5	1.3
12/28/97	4,729.5	712.7	6,890.4	27.8	15.1	20.5	10.3	1.2	2.50	3.55	...	0.73	61.69 - 35.69	19.5	1.5
12/31/96	4,421.1	①624.0	6,349.6	24.1	14.1	21.3	9.8	1.1	①2.22	3.23	...	0.70	39.38 - 29.50	15.5	2.0
12/31/95	4,006.7	477.3	6,503.8	21.3	11.9	22.2	7.3	1.1	1.71	2.45	...	0.69	32.44 - 24.75	16.8	2.4
12/25/94	3,824.5	465.4	3,707.1	21.3	12.2	25.5	12.6	1.2	1.62	2.34	1.25	0.67	29.50 - 23.06	16.3	2.5
12/26/93	3,641.6	397.8	3,823.8	19.6	10.9	20.8	10.4	1.1	1.36	2.07	1.38	0.65	39.13 - 23.38	19.3	2.5

Statistics are as originally reported. Adj. for 2-for-1 spl., 10/97. ① Excl. $294.6 mill. after-tx gain & $24.5 mill. inc. fr. disc. ops; incl. $93.0 mill. after-tx gain. ② Incl. $184.0 mill. after-tax gain fr. disp. of five radio stations & alarm security bus. ③ Incl. $33.0 mill. net gain fr. exchange of TV stations & excl. $38.5 mill. gain fr. disc. ops. ④ Excl. $2.4 mill. net inc. fr. disc. ops. & $744.7 mill. net gain fr. sale of bus.

OFFICERS:
D. H. McCorkindale, Chmn., Pres., C.E.O.
G. Mortore, Sr. V.P., C.F.O.

INVESTOR CONTACT: Gracia Martore, Sr. V.P., C.F.O., (703) 854-6918

PRINCIPAL OFFICE: 7950 Jones Branch Drive, McLean, VA 22107

TELEPHONE NUMBER: (703) 854-6000
FAX: (703) 364-0855
WEB: www.gannett.com
NO. OF EMPLOYEES: 51,500 (approx.)
SHAREHOLDERS: 13,700 (approx.)
ANNUAL MEETING: In May
INCORPORATED: NY, Dec., 1923; reincorp., DE, May, 1972

INSTITUTIONAL HOLDINGS:
No. of Institutions: 654
Shares Held: 217,417,928
% Held: 81.3

INDUSTRY: Newspapers (SIC: 2711)

TRANSFER AGENT(S): Wells Fargo Bank Minnesota, N.A., St. Paul, MN

GAP, INC. (THE)

EXCH.	SYM.	REC. PRICE	P/E RATIO	YLD.	MKT. CAP.	RANGE (52-WK.)	'02 Y/E PR.
NYSE	GPS	13.04 (2/28/03)	25.1	0.7%	$11.29 bill.	23.54 - 8.35	15.52

MEDIUM GRADE. THE COMPANY IS TAKING STEPS TO BOOST SALES AND EARNINGS GROWTH.

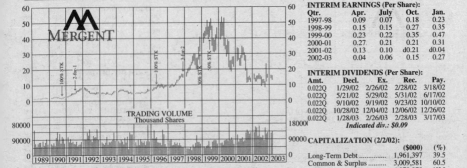

INTERIM EARNINGS (Per Share):

Qtr.	Apr.	July	Oct.	Jan.
1997-98	0.09	0.07	0.18	0.23
1998-99	0.15	0.15	0.27	0.35
1999-00	0.23	0.22	0.35	0.47
2000-01	0.27	0.21	0.21	0.31
2001-02	0.13	0.10	d0.21	d0.04
2002-03	0.04	0.06	0.15	0.27

INTERIM DIVIDENDS (Per Share):

Amt.	Decl.	Ex.	Rec.	Pay.
0.022Q	1/29/02	2/26/02	2/28/02	3/18/02
0.022Q	5/21/02	5/29/02	5/31/02	6/17/02
0.022Q	9/10/02	9/19/02	9/23/02	10/10/02
0.022Q	10/28/02	12/04/02	12/06/02	12/26/02
0.022Q	1/28/03	2/26/03	2/28/03	3/17/03

Indicated div.: $0.09

CAPITALIZATION (2/2/02):

	($000)	(%)
Long-Term Debt	1,961,397	39.5
Common & Surplus	3,009,581	60.5
Total	4,970,978	100.0

*7 YEAR PRICE SCORE 63.6   ***12 MONTH PRICE SCORE 114.0**
NYSE COMPOSITE INDEX=100

BUSINESS:

The Gap, Inc. is a specialty retailer that operates stores selling casual and activewear apparel for men, women, and children under five brand names: GAP, GAPKIDS and BABY GAP, which offer gender-specific contemporary clothing; BANANA REPUBLIC, which offers upscale clothing, jewelry, and small leather products; and OLD NAVY CLOTHING CO., which offers value-priced merchandise in a warehouse for-

mat. As of 2/1/03, the Company operated 3,592 stores in the U.S.: 2,309 Gap stores, 842 Old Navy stores, and 441 Banana Republic stores. All stores are leased and no stores are franchised or operated by others. In addition to the U.S., the Company operated 660 stores located in Canada, the United Kingdom, Japan, France, and Germany.

RECENT DEVELOPMENTS:

For the 52 weeks ended 2/1/03, net earnings totaled $477.5 million compared with a net loss of $7.8 million in the corresponding prior-year period. Net sales climbed 4.4% to $14.45 billion from $13.85 billion the previous year. Old Navy sales advanced 13.7% to $5.80 billion from $5.10

billion the year before, while sales at Banana Republic were essentially flat at $1.90 billion. Sales at international Gap stores rose 6.3% to $1.70 billion, while sales at Gap stores in the U.S. slipped 1.9% to $5.10 billion. Comparable-store sales were down 3.0% year-over-year.

PROSPECTS:

Near-term earnings are expected to be negatively affected by increased merchandise markdowns, harsh weather conditions on the East Coast in February, and weak consumer spending due to uncertain economic conditions. Meanwhile, the Company plans to increase marketing spending during the first half of fiscal 2003 to help boost sales. A

Gap television ad campaign is planned for the first quarter, along with increased distribution of Old Navy promotional circulars. Separately, in an effort to boost operating profitability, the Company anticipates closing more stores than it opens in fiscal 2003. GPS expects net square footage will decline by about 2.0% in the current fiscal year.

ANNUAL FINANCIAL DATA:

FISCAL YEAR	TOT. REVS. ($mill.)	NET INC. ($mill.)	TOT. ASSETS ($mill.)	OPER. PROFIT %	NET PROFIT %	RET. ON EQUITY %	RET. ON ASSETS %	CURR. RATIO	EARN. PER SH. $	CASH FL. PER SH. $	TANG. BK. VAL. $	DIV. PER SH. $	PRICE RANGE	AVG. P/E RATIO	AVG. YIELD %
p2/01/03	14,454.7	477.5							0.54			0.09	23.54 - 8.35	29.5	0.6
2/02/02	13,847.9	① d7.8	7,591.3	2.4	...	...	...	1.5	① d0.01	0.93	3.48	0.09	34.98 - 11.12	...	0.4
2/03/01	13,673.5	877.5	7,012.9	10.6	6.4	30.0	12.5	0.9	1.00	1.67	3.43	0.09	53.75 - 18.50	36.1	0.2
1/29/00	11,635.4	1,127.1	5,188.8	15.6	9.7	50.5	21.7	1.3	1.26	1.75	2.63	0.09	52.69 - 30.81	33.1	0.2
1/30/99	9,054.5	824.5	3,963.9	14.7	9.1	52.4	20.8	1.2	0.91	1.27	1.83	0.09	40.92 - 15.31	30.8	0.3
1/31/98	6,507.8	533.9	3,337.5	13.1	8.2	33.7	16.0	1.8	0.58	0.87	1.79	0.09	17.15 - 8.26	21.9	0.7
2/01/97	5,284.4	452.9	2,626.9	13.8	8.6	27.4	17.2	1.7	0.47	0.69	1.79	0.09	10.82 - 6.22	18.1	1.0
2/03/96	4,395.3	354.0	2,343.1	13.0	8.1	21.6	15.1	2.3	0.37	0.57	1.69	0.07	7.56 - 4.41	16.2	1.2
1/28/95	3,722.9	320.2	2,003.5	13.9	8.6	23.3	16.0	2.1	0.33	0.50	1.41	0.07	7.32 - 4.28	17.8	1.2
1/29/94	3,295.7	258.4	1,763.1	12.9	7.8	22.9	14.7	2.1	0.26	0.41	1.15	0.06	6.30 - 3.78	19.1	1.1

Statistics are as originally reported. Adj. for 3-for-2 stk. split, 6/99, 11/98 & 12/97; 2-for-1 stk. split, 4/96. ① Incl. $131.0 mill. tax chg. & $73.0 mill. after-tax chg. from cancelled orders, workforce reductions, sublease losses and distribution center closures.

OFFICERS:
D. G. Fisher, Chmn.
P. S. Pressler, Pres., & C.E.O.
B. Pollitt, Exec. V.P., C.F.O.
J. B. Wilson, Exec. V.P., C.O.O.

INVESTOR CONTACT: Evan Price, Investor Relations, (650) 874-2021

PRINCIPAL OFFICE: One Harrison Street, San Francisco, CA 94105

TELEPHONE NUMBER: (650) 952-4400
FAX: (650) 952-4407
WEB: www.gap.com

NO. OF EMPLOYEES: 165,000 (approx.)

SHAREHOLDERS: 10,505

ANNUAL MEETING: In May

INCORPORATED: CA, July, 1969; reincorp., DE, May, 1988

INSTITUTIONAL HOLDINGS:
No. of Institutions: 417
Shares Held: 539,829,199
% Held: 61.1

INDUSTRY: Family clothing stores (SIC: 5651)

TRANSFER AGENT(S): Computershare Investor Services, Chicago, IL

GARTNER GROUP, INC.

EXCH.	SYM.	REC. PRICE	P/E RATIO	YLD.	MKT. CAP.	RANGE (52-WK.)	'02 Y/E PR.
NYSE	IT	7.32 (2/28/03)	91.5	...	$0.60 bill.	13.70 - 4.90	9.20

LOWER MEDIUM GRADE. THE COMPANY EXPECTS TOTAL REVENUE FOR FISCAL 2003 TO RANGE BETWEEN $850.0 MILLION AND $890.0 MILLION.

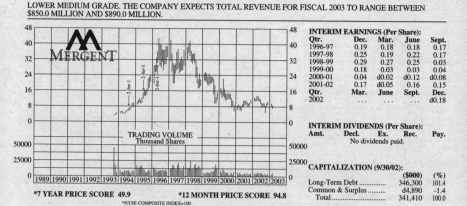

INTERIM EARNINGS (Per Share):

Qtr.	Dec.	Mar.	June	Sept.
1996-97	0.19	0.18	0.18	0.17
1997-98	0.25	0.19	0.22	0.17
1998-99	0.29	0.27	0.25	0.03
1999-00	0.18	0.03	0.03	0.04
2000-01	0.04	d0.02	d0.12	d0.08
2001-02	0.17	d0.05	0.16	0.15

Qtr.	Mar.	June	Sept.	Dec.
2002	...	...	...	d0.18

INTERIM DIVIDENDS (Per Share):

Amt.	Decl.	Ex.	Rec.	Pay.
	No dividends paid.			

CAPITALIZATION (9/30/02):

	($000)	(%)
Long-Term Debt	346,300	101.4
Common & Surplus	d4,890	-1.4
Total	341,410	100.0

*7 YEAR PRICE SCORE 49.9   ***12 MONTH PRICE SCORE 94.8**

*NYSE COMPOSITE INDEX=100

BUSINESS:

Gartner Group, Inc. is an independent provider of research and analysis on the computer hardware, software, communications and related information technology industries. IT's core business is researching and analyzing significant information technology industry trends and developments, packaging its analysis into annually renewable subscription-based products and distributing the products through print and electronic media. IT is organized into three businesses. The Research segment (55.6% of 2002 revenues) offers products that highlight industry developments, review products and technologies, provide market research, and analyze industry trends. The Consulting segment (30.7%) consists of consulting and measurement services that provide assessments of cost performance, efficiency and quality. The Events segment (13.7%) consists of vendor and user focused expositions and conferences.

RECENT DEVELOPMENTS:

The Company changed its year-end to 12/31 from 9/30. For the three months ended 12/31/02, net loss was $14.4 million compared with net income of $19.0 million in the corresponding quarter of 2001, primarily due to difficult business conditions. Results for 2002 and 2001 included amortization of intangibles of $482,000 and $502,000, net gains on the sale of investments of $78,000 and $792,000, and a net loss of $1.7 million and a net gain of $79,000 from minority-owned investments, respectively. Results for 2002 also included a non-recurring charge of $32.2 million. Total revenues slipped 7.9% to $229.8 million from $249.4 million in the previous year.

PROSPECTS:

The Company expects total revenue for fiscal 2003 to range between $850.0 million and $890.0 million and normalized earnings per share in the range of $0.45 to $0.50, excluding other charges, net gain/loss on sale of investments, net gain/loss from minority-owned investments and net gain/loss from sale of a business. Research revenue is expected to range between $453.0 million and $478.0 million, with consulting revenue between $275.0 million and $285.0 million. Events revenue is anticipated to range from $104.0 million to $108.0 million.

ANNUAL FINANCIAL DATA:

FISCAL YEAR	TOT. REVS. ($000)	NET INC. ($000)	TOT. ASSETS ($000)	OPER. PROFIT %	NET PROFIT %	RET. ON EQUITY %	RET. ON ASSETS %	CURR. RATIO	EARN. PER SH.$	CASH FL. PER SH.$	TANG. BK. VAL.$	DIV. PER SH.$	PRICE RANGE		AVG. P/E RATIO	AVG. YIELD %
9/30/02	907,174	⑥ 48,578	824,850	10.6	5.4	...	5.9	1.0	⑥ 0.47	0.71	...	...	13.70	4.90	19.8	...
9/30/01	952,042	⑤ d220	839,002	4.5	...	...	...	0.9	⑤ Nil	0.62	...	...	11.70	5.80	...	...
9/30/00	858,671	④ 27,275	1,002,965	5.6	3.2	36.5	2.7	0.9	④ 0.30	0.93	...	...	22.25	5.65	46.5	...
9/30/99	734,234	③ 88,271	803,444	17.8	12.0	118.5	11.0	0.9	③ 0.84	1.14	...	1.19	25.75	9.56	21.0	6.8
9/30/98	641,957	② 88,347	832,871	22.4	13.8	21.3	10.6	1.2	② 0.84	1.09	2.28	...	41.75	17.31	35.2	...
9/30/97	511,239	73,130	645,312	22.8	14.3	27.1	11.3	1.1	0.71	0.89	1.42	...	42.25	19.75	43.7	...
9/30/96	394,672	16,438	444,108	12.5	4.2	10.9	3.7	1.1	0.17	0.30	0.61	...	43.13	19.75	184.8	...
9/30/95	229,152	25,539	300,598	18.9	11.1	29.9	8.5	1.0	0.28	0.37	0.32	...	24.13	8.88	58.9	...
9/30/94	169,002	14,975	232,557	16.2	8.9	30.5	6.4	1.0	0.17	0.24	...	...	9.88	4.00	42.0	...
9/30/93	122,544	① 6,766	133,685	11.9	5.5	52.6	5.1	0.7	① 0.07	0.16	...	...	4.66	3.09	57.8	...

Statistics are as originally reported. Adj. for 2-for-1 split, 8/94, 6/95 & 3/96. ① Bef. $765,000 ($0.01/sh.) extraord. chg. ② Incl. $9.1 mill. pre-tax non-recur. chgs. & $2.0 mill. loss on sale of GartnerLearning. ③ Incl. $30.1 mill. non-recur. chg. ④ Incl. $29.6 mill. net gain fr. sale of investments & excl. $1.7 mill. net extraord. loss fr. exting. of debt. ⑤ Incl. $12.4 mill. amort. of intang., $46.6 mill. other chgs., & $640,000 loss fr. sale of invest., and excl. $26.1 mill. loss fr. disc. ops. & $39.9 mill. loss fr. disp. of disc. ops. ⑥ Incl. $1.9 mill. amort. of intang., $17.2 mill. other chgs., $787,000 gain fr. sale of invest. & $2.4 mill. loss fr. minor-owned invest.

OFFICERS:
M. D. Fleisher, Chmn., C.E.O., Pres.
M. E. O'Connell, Exec. V.P., C.F.O.
L. Schwartz, Sr. V.P., Gen. Couns.
INVESTOR CONTACT: Heather McConnell, Investor Relations, (203) 316-6768
PRINCIPAL OFFICE: P.O. Box 10212, 56 Top Gallant Road, Stamford, CT 06904

TELEPHONE NUMBER: (203) 316-1111
FAX: (203) 316-1100
WEB: www.gartner.com
NO. OF EMPLOYEES: 4,039 (avg.)
SHAREHOLDERS: 111 (approx. class A); 3729 (approx. class B)
ANNUAL MEETING: In Feb.
INCORPORATED: DE, 1990

INSTITUTIONAL HOLDINGS:
No. of Institutions: 105
Shares Held: 41,855,218
% Held: 50.6
INDUSTRY: Management services (SIC: 8741)
TRANSFER AGENT(S): Mellon Investor Services, L.L.C., Ridgefield Park, NJ

GATEWAY INC.

EXCH.	SYM.	REC. PRICE	P/E RATIO	YLD.	MKT. CAP.	RANGE (52-WK.)	'02 Y/E PR.
NYSE	GTW	2.18 (2/28/03)	...	...	$0.71 bill.	6.65 - 2.02	3.14

SPECULATIVE GRADE. ON 4/1/03, THE COMPANY ANNOUNCED IT WILL BE RESTATING REVENUES FOR 2000 AND 2001.

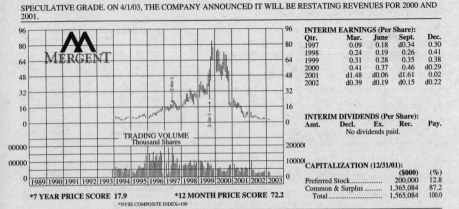

INTERIM EARNINGS (Per Share):

Qtr.	Mar.	June	Sept.	Dec.
1997	0.09	0.18	d0.34	0.30
1998	0.24	0.19	0.26	0.41
1999	0.31	0.28	0.35	0.38
2000	0.41	0.37	0.46	d0.29
2001	d1.48	d0.06	d1.61	0.02
2002	d0.39	0.19	0.15	d0.22

INTERIM DIVIDENDS (Per Share):

Amt.	Decl.	Ex.	Rec.	Pay.
		No dividends paid.		

CAPITALIZATION (12/31/01):

	($000)	(%)
Preferred Stock	200,000	12.8
Common & Surplus	1,365,084	87.2
Total	1,565,084	100.0

*7 YEAR PRICE SCORE 17.9 ***12 MONTH PRICE SCORE 72.2**

*NYSE COMPOSITE INDEX=100

BUSINESS:

Gateway Inc. (formerly Gateway 2000, Inc.) is a direct marketer of personal computers and related products and services. Gateway develops, manufactures, markets, and supports a broad line of desktop and portable PCs, digital media (convergence) PCs, servers, workstations and PC-related products used by individuals, families, businesses, government agencies and educational institutions. Gateway markets its products directly to PC customers through television advertisements, newspapers, magazines, radio, the Internet, the Company's Internet Web site, local promotions, trade shows and its 274 Gateway Country® stores. Gateway began offering nationwide Internet provider service directly to its customers in November 1997.

RECENT DEVELOPMENTS:

For the year ended 12/31/02, the Company reported a net loss of $297.7 million compared with a loss of $1.01 billion, before an extraordinary gain of $4.3 million and an accounting change charge of $23.9 million, in 2001. Net sales were $4.17 billion, down 31.4% from $6.08 billion in the prior year. Total unit sales for the year were 2.7 million, down 24.0% over the year before, which included GTW's international operations in 2001. On a comparable U.S. only basis, unit sales declined 15.0%. Gross profit declined 32.4% to $566.2 million from $838.2 million the year before. Operating loss amounted to $511.2 million compared with an operating loss of $1.18 billion a year earlier.

PROSPECTS:

On 4/1/03, GTW announced it will be restating revenues for 2000 and 2001, reducing them by $340.0 million for 2000 and by $130.0 million for 2001. The revision concerns payments for AOL Internet Service that were bundled into sales of the Company's computers. The revised figures will account for these amounts on a net basis rather than a gross basis. The restatement will reduce sales for 2000 and 2001 by 3.5% and 2.5%, respectively.

ANNUAL FINANCIAL DATA:

FISCAL YEAR	TOT. REVS. ($mill.)	NET INC. ($mill.)	TOT. ASSETS ($mill.)	OPER. PROFIT %	NET PROFIT %	RET. ON EQUITY %	RET. ON ASSETS %	CURR. RATIO	EARN. PER SH. $	CASH FL. PER SH. $	TANG. BK. VAL. $	PRICE RANGE	AVG. P/E RATIO
p12/31/02	4,171.3	d297.7	2,986.9	...	...	...	...	1.9	d0.95	d2.52	4.10	10.60 - 2.61	...
12/31/01	6,079.5	③ d1,014.4	3,385.3	...	...	...	...	1.9	③ d3.14	4.24	...	24.21 - 4.24	...
12/31/00	9,600.6	② 253.3	4,152.5	5.3	2.6	10.6	6.1	1.4	② d0.03	1.34	6.85	75.13 - 16.43	...
12/31/99	8,645.6	427.9	3,954.7	6.9	4.9	21.2	10.8	1.5	1.32	1.73	6.15	84.00 - 23.72	40.8
12/31/98	7,467.9	346.4	2,890.4	6.6	4.6	25.8	12.0	1.6	1.09	1.42	4.08	34.38 - 15.50	22.9
12/31/97	6,293.7	① 109.8	2,039.3	2.8	1.7	11.8	5.4	1.5	① 0.35	0.63	2.62	23.13 - 11.78	49.9
12/31/96	5,035.2	250.7	1,673.4	7.1	5.0	30.7	15.0	1.6	0.80	0.99	2.41	16.56 - 4.50	13.1
12/31/95	3,676.3	173.0	1,124.0	6.8	4.7	31.1	15.4	1.6	0.55	0.67	1.67	9.38 - 4.00	12.2
12/31/94	2,701.2	96.0	770.6	5.2	3.6	25.5	12.5	1.9	0.31	0.36	1.20	6.19 - 2.31	13.9
12/31/93	1,731.7	151.2	564.3	8.6	8.7	53.9	26.8	2.0	0.35	0.56	0.96	...	7.6

Statistics are as originally reported. Adj. for 2-for-1 split, 9/99 & 6/97. ① Incl. $95.0 mill. after-tax non-recur. chg. ② Incl. $187.0 mill. pretax chg. fr. the write-down of investments. ③ Excl. $4.3 mill. net extraord. gain & $23.9 mill. net acctg. chg.

OFFICERS:
T. W. Waitt, Chmn., C.E.O.
R. Sherwood III, Exec. V.P., C.F.O.
M. J. Chaudhri, Sr. V.P., Gen. Couns.

INVESTOR CONTACT: Marlys Johnson, Manager of Investor Relations, (800) 846-4503

PRINCIPAL OFFICE: 14303 Gateway Place, Poway, CA 92064

TELEPHONE NUMBER: (858) 848-3401
FAX: (858) 799-3459
WEB: www.gateway.com

NO. OF EMPLOYEES: 14,000 (approx.)

SHAREHOLDERS: 4,681

ANNUAL MEETING: In May

INCORPORATED: IA, 1986; reincorp., DE, Dec., 1991

INSTITUTIONAL HOLDINGS:
No. of Institutions: 217
Shares Held: 146,733,020
% Held: 45.3

INDUSTRY: Electronic computers (SIC: 3571)

TRANSFER AGENT(S): UMB Bank, NA, Kansas City, MO

GATX CORPORATION

EXCH.	SYM.	REC. PRICE	P/E RATIO	YLD.	MKT. CAP.	RANGE (52-WK.)	'02 Y/E PR.	DIV. ACH.
NYSE	GMT	15.44 (2/28/03)	25.7	8.3%	$0.75 bill.	35.91 - 15.43	22.82	17 yrs.

UPPER MEDIUM GRADE. THE COMPANY INTENDS TO SELL ITS GATX VENTURES BUSINESS UNIT.

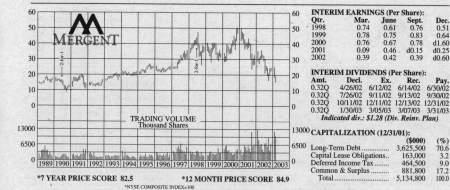

TRADING VOLUME
Thousand Shares

*7 YEAR PRICE SCORE 82.5   ***12 MONTH PRICE SCORE 84.9**

NYSE COMPOSITE INDEX=100

INTERIM EARNINGS (Per Share):

Qtr.	Mar.	June	Sept.	Dec.
1998	0.74	0.61	0.76	0.51
1999	0.78	0.75	0.83	0.64
2000	0.76	0.67	0.78	d1.60
2001	0.09	0.46	d0.15	d0.25
2002	0.39	0.42	0.39	d0.60

INTERIM DIVIDENDS (Per Share):

Amt.	Decl.	Ex.	Rec.	Pay.
0.32Q	4/26/02	6/12/02	6/14/02	6/30/02
0.32Q	7/26/02	9/11/02	9/13/02	9/30/02
0.32Q	10/11/02	12/11/02	12/13/02	12/31/01
0.32Q	1/30/03	3/05/03	3/07/03	3/31/03

Indicated div.: $1.28 (Div. Reinv. Plan)

CAPITALIZATION (12/31/01):

	($000)	(%)
Long-Term Debt	3,625,500	70.6
Capital Lease Obligations..	163,000	3.2
Deferred Income Tax	464,500	9.0
Common & Surplus	881,800	17.2
Total	5,134,800	100.0

BUSINESS:

GATX Corporation operates in two industry segments. The Financial Services segment provides financing for equipment and other capital assets on a worldwide basis and consists of four business units: Air, Technology, Venture Finance and Specialty Finance. The GATX Rail segment is principally engaged in leasing rail equipment, including tank cars, freight cars and locomotives. As of 12/31/02, GMT owned or had an interest in about 107,000 railcars in North America. In March 2001, GMT purchased Dyrekcja

Eksploatacji Cystern, Poland's national tank car fleet. As of 12/31/02, GATX Rail also owned KVG Kesselwagen Vermietgesellschaft mbH, a German and Austrian-based tank car and specialty railcar leasing company, and a 37.5% interest in Switzerland-based AAE Cargo. During 2001 GMT completed the sale of most of its Integrated Solution Group, which included GATX Terminals and GATX Logistics, Inc.

RECENT DEVELOPMENTS:

For the year ended 12/31/02, income from continuing operations was $29.0 million versus income from continuing operations of $7.5 million a year earlier. Earnings for 2002 and 2001 included asset impairment charges of $40.5 million and $85.2 million, and workforce reduction charges of

$16.9 million and $13.4 million, respectively. Results for 2002 also included a gain on the extinguishment of debt of $18.0 million. Results for 2001 included a nonrecurring gain of $13.1 million. Revenues fell 13.9% to $1.28 billion from $1.49 billion the previous year.

PROSPECTS:

On 12/17/02, GMT announced that it intends to sell GATX Ventures, its business unit that specializes in providing secured financing to early stage companies. In addition, GMT announced that it will further curtail new investment in its specialty finance unit. GMT expects to use the cash generated from the exit of its venture business and the

return of capital from the specialty unit for reinvestment in its core rail, air, and technology leasing businesses, and for general corporate purposes. Separately, on 12/18/02, GMT announced that it has acquired the remaining interest in the companies comprising KVG Kesselwagen, a European railcar lessor.

ANNUAL FINANCIAL DATA:

FISCAL YEAR	TOT. REVS. ($mill.)	NET INC. ($mill.)	TOT. ASSETS ($mill.)	OPER. PROFIT %	NET PROFIT %	RET. ON EQUITY %	RET. ON ASSETS %	CURR. RATIO	EARN. PER SH.$	CASH FL.PER SH.$	TANG. BK. VAL.$	DIV. PER SH.$	PRICE RANGE	AVG. P/E RATIO	AVG. YIELD %
p12/31/02	1,281.7	④ 29.0			0.5	0.9	0.1	2.8	④ 0.59			1.28	35.91 - 16.30	44.2	4.9
12/31/01	1,488.6	③ 7.5	6,109.7	16.3	0.5	0.9	0.1	2.8	③ 0.15	8.61	18.09	1.24	49.94 - 23.65	245.1	3.4
12/31/00	1,311.8	② 30.8	6,263.7	28.8	2.3	3.9	0.5	1.7	② 0.63	7.50	16.25	1.20	50.50 - 28.38	62.6	3.0
12/31/99	1,773.0	151.3	5,866.8	22.6	8.5	18.1	2.6	1.4	3.01	9.14	17.20	1.10	40.88 - 28.06	11.5	3.2
12/31/98	1,701.9	131.9	4,939.3	22.5	7.5	18.0	2.7	1.5	2.62	7.92	14.87	1.00	47.56 - 26.25	14.1	2.7
12/31/97	1,414.4	① d50.9	4,947.8	7.9	...	...	...	1.5	① d1.27	4.32	13.39	0.92	36.00 - 23.75	...	3.1
12/31/96	1,246.4	102.7	4,750.2	23.4	7.3	13.3	2.2	1.7	2.19	7.13	16.73	0.86	25.63 - 21.50	10.8	3.6
12/31/95	1,155.0	100.8	4,042.9	23.0	8.1	14.0	2.5	1.6	2.15	6.37	15.60	0.80	27.13 - 20.19	11.0	3.4
12/31/94	1,086.9	91.5	3,650.7	23.0	7.9	13.8	2.5	1.4	1.94	6.04	14.52	0.76	22.31 - 19.13	10.7	3.7
12/31/93	1,019.1	① 72.7	3,392.1	23.6	6.7	12.3	2.1	1.7	① 1.50	5.61	14.89	0.70	21.13 - 15.69	12.3	3.8

Statistics are as originally reported. Adj. for 2-for-1 stk. split, 6/98. ① Incl. non-recurr. chrg. 12/31/97: $163.0 mill.; chrg. 12/31/93: $8.5 mill. ② Incl. litig. chrg. of $160.5 mill.; bef. inc. fr. disc. ops. of $35.8 mill. ③ Incl. workforce chrgs. of $13.4 mill., asset impair. chrgs. of $85.2 mill. & nonrecurr. gain of $13.1 mill.; bef. disc. ops. inc. of $165.4 mill. ④ Incl. workforce chrgs. of $16.9 mill. & asset impair. chrgs. of $40.5 mill.; bef. disc. ops. inc. of $6.2 mill. & acctg. chge. chrg. of $34.9 mill.

OFFICERS:
R. H. Zech, Chmn., Pres., C.E.O.
B. A. Kenney, Sr. V.P., C.F.O.
R. J. Cinancio, V.P., Sec., Gen. Couns.
INVESTOR CONTACT: Irma Dominguez, Inv. Rel. Coord., (312) 621-8799
PRINCIPAL OFFICE: 500 West Monroe Street, Chicago, IL 60661-3676

TELEPHONE NUMBER: (312) 621-6200
FAX: (312) 621-6665
WEB: www.gatx.com
NO. OF EMPLOYEES: 1,900 (approx.)
SHAREHOLDERS: 3,618
ANNUAL MEETING: In Apr.
INCORPORATED: NY, July, 1916

INSTITUTIONAL HOLDINGS:
No. of Institutions: 190
Shares Held: 45,339,901
% Held: 92.6
INDUSTRY: Rental of railroad cars (SIC: 4741)
TRANSFER AGENT(S): Mellon Investor Services, Ridgefield Park, NJ

GENCORP INC.

EXCH.	SYM.	REC. PRICE	P/E RATIO	YLD.	MKT. CAP.	RANGE (52-WK.)	'02 Y/E PR.
NYSE	GY	6.80 (2/28/03)	10.0	1.8%	$292.2 mill.	16.25 - 6.38	7.92

LOWER MEDIUM GRADE. THE COMPANY IS TARGETING FISCAL 2003 EARNINGS OF $0.41 TO $0.46 PER SHARE.

MERGENT

TRADING VOLUME
Thousand Shares

1989 1990 1991 1992 1993 1994 1995 1996 1997 1998 1999 2000 2001 2002 2003

*7 YEAR PRICE SCORE 70.8   *12 MONTH PRICE SCORE 77.1
*NYSE COMPOSITE INDEX=100

INTERIM EARNINGS (Per Share):

Qtr.	Feb.	May	Aug.	Nov.
1996	d0.35	0.42	0.47	0.69
1997	0.32	2.45	0.50	0.52
1998	0.31	0.51	0.41	0.77
1999	0.41	0.77	0.48	0.26
2000	0.25	0.45	0.46	0.16
2001	0.33	0.12	0.07	2.47
2002	0.07	0.14	0.19	0.28

INTERIM DIVIDENDS (Per Share):

Amt.	Decl.	Ex.	Rec.	Pay.
0.03Q	1/30/02	2/07/02	2/11/02	2/28/02
0.03Q	3/27/02	4/29/02	5/01/02	5/31/02
0.03Q	7/12/02	7/30/02	8/01/02	8/30/02
0.03Q	9/05/02	10/30/02	11/01/02	11/29/02
0.03Q	2/05/03	2/13/03	2/18/03	2/28/03

Indicated div.: $0.12 (Div. Reinv. Plan)

CAPITALIZATION (11/30/02):

	($000)	(%)
Long-Term Debt	365,000	50.3
Common & Surplus	360,000	49.7
Total	725,000	100.0

BUSINESS:

GenCorp Inc. operates in three segments: GDX Automotive (71.0% of fiscal 2002 sales), Aerospace and Defense (24.4%) and Fine Chemicals (4.6%). GDX Automotive develops and manufactures highly-engineered extruded and molded rubber sealing systems for vehicle bodies and windows for original equipment manufacturers. Aerojet-General Corporation manufactures space electronics and smart munitions, as well as solid and liquid rocket propulsion systems and related defense products and services. Aerojet Fine Chemicals supplies special intermediates and active pharmaceutical ingredients primarily to commercial customers. On 10/1/99, GY spun off its polymer products and building products businesses under the name OMNOVA Solutions Inc. On 12/29/00, GY acquired the Draftex International Car Body Seals division of The Laird Group.

RECENT DEVELOPMENTS:

For the year ended 11/30/02, net income totaled $30.0 million compared with $128.0 million the year before. Results for fiscal 2002 included $17.0 million of restructuring and other non-recurring charges. Results for fiscal 2001 included a $111.0 million gain, primarily related to the October 2001 sale of the Aerojet Electronic and Information Systems (EIS) business. Net sales slid 23.6% to $1.14 billion from $1.49 billion a year earlier. GDX Automotive segment net sales were $806.0 million versus $808.0 million the previous year. Net sales for the Aerospace and Defense segment fell 56.7% to $277.0 million, due to the sale of EIS, while Fine Chemicals segment net sales advanced 36.8% to $52.0 million, driven by new products launched in 2001.

PROSPECTS:

The Company is targeting earnings in the range of $0.41 to $0.46 per share in fiscal 2003. Meanwhile, sales in GY's GDX Automotive segment are expected to be between $700.0 million and $730.0 million in fiscal 2003, due to anticipated price reductions and the discontinuation of certain unprofitable products. Aerospace and Defense segment sales in fiscal 2003 are projected to be $265.0 million to $275.0 million, while Fine Chemical segment sales are expected to be in the range of $52.0 million to $57.0 million in fiscal 2003.

ANNUAL FINANCIAL DATA:

FISCAL YEAR	TOT. REVS. ($mill.)	NET INC. ($mill.)	TOT. ASSETS ($mill.)	OPER. PROFIT %	NET PROFIT %	RET. ON EQUITY %	RET. ON ASSETS %	CURR. RATIO	EARN. PER SH.$	CASH FL. PER SH.$	TANG. BK. VAL.$	DIV. PER SH.$	PRICE RANGE	AVG. P/E RATIO	AVG. YIELD %
11/30/02	1,135.0	② 30.0	1,636.0	6.8	2.6	8.3	1.8	1.0	② 0.69	1.98	5.45	0.12	16.25 — 6.38	16.4	1.1
11/30/01	1,486.0	④ 128.0	1,450.0	3.2	8.6	41.3	8.8	0.9	④ 3.00	4.81	5.75	0.12	14.55 — 9.13	3.9	1.0
11/30/00	1,047.0	③ 55.0	1,324.0	9.7	5.3	28.2	4.2	1.1	③ 1.31	2.50	4.64	0.12	10.81 — 6.63	6.7	1.4
11/30/99	1,071.0	①② 46.0	1,230.0	5.9	4.3	57.5	3.7	1.0	①② 1.09	2.19	1.91	0.48	26.50 — 7.63	15.7	2.8
11/30/98	1,737.0	② 84.0	1,743.0	8.5	4.8	24.4	4.8	1.2	② 1.99	3.31	8.29	0.60	31.19 — 16.44	12.0	2.5
11/30/97	1,568.0	137.0	1,432.0	7.8	8.7	48.8	9.6	1.2	3.63	5.21	6.80	0.60	31.00 — 17.63	6.7	2.5
11/30/96	1,515.0	② 42.0	1,330.0	7.5	2.8	75.0	3.2	1.2	② 1.25	3.18	1.67	0.60	19.13 — 11.50	12.2	3.9
11/30/95	1,772.0	② 38.0	1,458.0	5.5	2.1	108.6	2.6	1.2	② 1.17	3.47	1.05	0.60	14.13 — 10.00	10.3	5.0
11/30/94	1,740.0	③ d13.0	1,455.0	5.6	...	...	...	1.1	③ d0.41	2.01	...	0.60	16.38 — 9.88	...	4.6
11/30/93	1,905.0	43.0	1,164.0	4.8	2.3	18.3	3.7	1.3	1.35	4.07	7.41	0.60	17.38 — 11.25	10.6	4.2

Statistics are as originally reported. ① Bef. $26.4 mil ($0.63/sh) gain fr. discont. opers. ② Incl. $17.0 non-recurr. chg., 2002; $11.8 mil gain, 1999; $5.0 mil gain, 1998; $42.0 mil chg., 1996; $5.0 mil chg., 1995. ③ Bef. $74.0 mil ($1.76/sh) acctg. change chg., 2000; $212.7 mil ($6.69/sh), 1994 & incl. $5.0 mil non-recur. gain, 2000; $82.8 mil chg., 1994. ④ Incl. $151.0 mil gain fr. sale of business & $40.0 mil restr. chg.

OFFICERS:
R. A. Wolfe, Chmn.
T. L. Hall, Pres, C.E.O.
Y. R. Seyal, Sr. V.P., C.F.O.
G. K. Scott, Sr. V.P., Gen. Couns., Sec.

PRINCIPAL OFFICE: Highway 50 and Aerojet Road, Rancho Cordova, CA 95670

TELEPHONE NUMBER: (916) 355-4000
FAX: (916) 351-8668
WEB: www.gencorp.com
NO. OF EMPLOYEES: 10,112
SHAREHOLDERS: 11,148
ANNUAL MEETING: In Mar.
INCORPORATED: OH, Sept., 1915

INSTITUTIONAL HOLDINGS:
No. of Institutions: 125
Shares Held: 34,311,277
% Held: 79.4
INDUSTRY: Space propulsion units and parts (SIC: 3764)
TRANSFER AGENT(S): The Bank of New York, New York, NY

GENENTECH, INC.

EXCH.	SYM.	REC. PRICE	P/E RATIO	YLD.	MKT. CAP.	RANGE (52-WK.)	'02 Y/E PR.
NYSE	DNA	35.36 (2/28/03)	294.7	...	$18.13 bill.	54.81 - 25.10	33.16

MEDIUM GRADE. THE COMPANY REPORTED THAT ITS RESEARCH AND DEVELOPMENT PROGRAMS IN THE AREAS OF ONCOLOGY, IMMUNOLOGY AND VASCULAR BIOLOGY SHOULD DRIVE RESULTS.

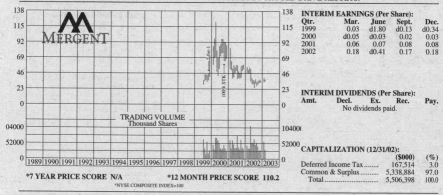

INTERIM EARNINGS (Per Share):

Qtr.	Mar.	June	Sept.	Dec.
1999	0.03	d1.80	d0.13	d0.34
2000	d0.05	d0.03	0.02	0.03
2001	0.06	0.07	0.08	0.08
2002	0.18	d0.41	0.17	0.18

INTERIM DIVIDENDS (Per Share):

Amt.	Decl.	Ex.	Rec.	Pay.
		No dividends paid.		

TRADING VOLUME
Thousand Shares

*7 YEAR PRICE SCORE N/A   *12 MONTH PRICE SCORE 110.2

*NYSE COMPOSITE INDEX=100

CAPITALIZATION (12/31/02):

	($000)	(%)
Deferred Income Tax	167,514	3.0
Common & Surplus	5,338,884	97.0
Total	5,506,398	100.0

BUSINESS:

Genentech, Inc. is a biotechnology company that uses human genetic information to discover, develop, manufacture and market human pharmaceuticals. DNA manufactures and markets ten protein-based pharmaceuticals including PROTROPIN®, used for growth hormone deficiency (GHD) in children; HERCEPTIN®, for the treatment of one type of metastic breast cancer; ACTIVASE®, which dissolves blood clots that cause strokes and heart attacks;

RITUXAN®, a single-agent therapy for the treatment of a certain type of non-Hodgkins lymphoma; PULMOZYME®, used for treatment of cystic fibrosis; NUTROPIN® and NUTROPIN AQ®, used for GHD in children and adults. NUTROPIN DEPOT™, for treatment of GHD in children. As of 12/31/02, Roche Holdings, Inc. owned about 59.8% of DNA, following a recapitalization in July 1999.

RECENT DEVELOPMENTS:

For the year ended 12/31/02, net income was $63.8 million compared with income of $155.9 million, before an accounting change charge of $5.6 million the previous year. Results for 2002 and 2001 included pre-tax recurring charges of $155.7 million and $321.8 million, respectively, related to redemption. Results for 2002 also included a pre-

tax special litigation charge of $543.9 million. Total revenues increased 22.9% to $2.72 billion from $2.21 billion the year before. The increase in revenues was primarily attributable to solid demand for the Company's biooncology products, RITUXAN® and HERCEPTIN®.

PROSPECTS:

Looking ahead, the Company expects to deliver strong and consistent growth between the years 2003 and 2005. The Company reported that its research and development programs in the areas of oncology, immunology and vascular biology should drive results. Meanwhile, for 2003, the Company anticipates FDA licensing decisions on Xolair for

allergic asthma and Raptiva for psoriasis, and data from two Phase III oncology clinical trials. DNA expects future sales growth would be dependent on increasing market penetration for labeled indications and developing new markets for its existing products.

ANNUAL FINANCIAL DATA:

FISCAL YEAR	TOT. REVS. ($mill.)	NET INC. ($mill.)	TOT. ASSETS ($mill.)	OPER. PROFIT %	NET PROFIT %	RET. ON EQUITY %	RET. ON ASSETS %	CURR. RATIO	EARN. PER SH.$	CASH FL. PER SH.$	TANG. BK. VAL.$	PRICE RANGE	AVG. P/E RATIO
12/31/02	2,719.2	[5] 63.8	6,777.3	1.1	2.3	1.2	0.9	3.2	[5] 0.12	0.65	6.00	55.15 - 25.10	334.1
12/31/01	2,212.3	[4] 155.9	7,134.8	13.1	7.0	2.6	2.2	3.4	[4] 0.29	1.09	6.63	84.00 - 37.99	210.3
12/31/00	1,736.4	[3] d16.4	6,711.8	22.1	...	...	...	4.0	[3] d0.03	0.86	5.59	122.50 - 42.25	...
12/31/99	1,421.4	[2] d1,144.5	6,554.4	21.1	...	...	...	-2.7	[2] d2.23	d1.68	4.26	71.50 - 29.13	...
12/31/98	1,150.9	181.9	2,855.4	22.3	15.8	7.8	6.4	4.3	0.35	0.50	4.61	...	...
12/31/97	1,016.7	129.0	2,507.6	17.1	12.7	6.4	5.1	4.1	0.26	0.38	4.09	...	...
12/31/96	968.7	118.3	2,226.4	15.8	12.2	6.6	5.3	3.8	0.24	0.36	3.71	...	...
12/31/95	917.8	[1] 146.4	2,011.0	22.4	16.0	9.1	7.3	4.5	[1] 0.30	0.42	3.36	...	...
12/31/94	795.4	124.4	1,745.1	17.2	15.6	9.2	7.1	4.5	0.26	0.37	2.88	...	...
12/31/93	649.7	58.9	1,468.8	10.1	9.1	5.3	4.0	4.6	0.13	0.22	2.43	...	...

Statistics are as originally reported. Adj. for 2-for-1 split, 10/00 & 11/99. [1] Incl. a spec. nonrecurr. pre-tax chrg. of $25.0 mill. [2] Incl. a spec. pre-tax chrg. of $1.44 bill. & pre-tax recurr. chrgs. of $198.4 mill. [3] Bef. acctg. chg. chrg. of $57.8 mill.; incl. recurr. chrg. of $375.3 mill. [4] Bef. acctg. chg. chrg. of $5.6 mill.; incl. recurr. chrg. of $321.8 mill. [5] Incl. pre-tax recurr. chrgs. of $155.7 mill. & spec. litig. chrgs. of $543.9 mill.

OFFICERS:
A. D. Levinson, Chmn., Pres., C.E.O.
L. J. Lavigne Jr., Exec. V.P., C.F.O.
T. T. Thomas II, Treas.
INVESTOR CONTACT: Kathee Littrell, Investor Relations, (650) 225-1034
PRINCIPAL OFFICE: 1 DNA Way, South San Francisco, CA 94080-4990

TELEPHONE NUMBER: (650) 225-1000
FAX: (650) 225-6000
WEB: www.gene.com
NO. OF EMPLOYEES: 5,252 (avg.)
SHAREHOLDERS: 2,036 (approx.)
ANNUAL MEETING: In Apr.
INCORPORATED: CA, Apr., 1976; reincorp., DE, Jan., 1987

INSTITUTIONAL HOLDINGS:
No. of Institutions: 347
Shares Held: 169,427,568
% Held: 32.9
INDUSTRY: Pharmaceutical preparations (SIC: 2834)
TRANSFER AGENT(S): EquiServe, LP, Providence, RI

GENERAL DYNAMICS CORPORATION

EXCH.	SYM.	REC. PRICE	P/E RATIO	YLD.	MKT. CAP.	RANGE (52-WK.)	'02 Y/E PR.	DIV. ACH.
NYSE	GD	59.26 (2/28/03)	11.7	2.2%	$11.90 bill.	111.18 - 58.40	79.37	11 yrs.

HIGH GRADE. THE COMPANY ENTERED INTO A DEFINITIVE AGREEMENT TO ACQUIRE GENERAL MOTORS DEFENSE IN A CASH TRANSACTION VALUED AT $1.10 BILLION.

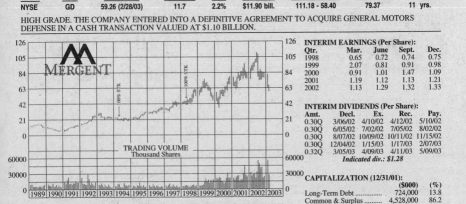

7 YEAR PRICE SCORE 154.5 **12 MONTH PRICE SCORE 87.0**
*NYSE COMPOSITE INDEX=100

INTERIM EARNINGS (Per Share):

Qtr.	Mar.	June	Sept.	Dec.
1998	0.65	0.72	0.74	0.75
1999	2.07	0.81	0.91	0.98
2000	0.91	1.01	1.47	1.09
2001	1.19	1.12	1.13	1.21
2002	1.13	1.29	1.32	1.33

INTERIM DIVIDENDS (Per Share):

Amt.	Decl.	Ex.	Rec.	Pay.
0.30Q	3/06/02	4/10/02	4/12/02	5/10/02
0.30Q	6/05/02	7/02/02	7/05/02	8/02/02
0.30Q	8/07/02	10/09/02	10/11/02	11/15/02
0.30Q	12/04/02	1/15/03	1/17/03	2/07/03
0.32Q	3/05/03	4/09/03	4/11/03	5/09/03

Indicated div.: $1.28

CAPITALIZATION (12/31/01):

	($000)	(%)
Long-Term Debt	724,000	13.8
Common & Surplus	4,528,000	86.2
Total	5,252,000	100.0

BUSINESS:

General Dynamics Corporation is a major defense contractor operating in four business segments. Information Systems and Technology (26.6% of net sales for 2002) provides defense and commercial customers with infrastructure and systems integration skills required to process, communicate and manage information. Marine Systems (26.4%) provides the U.S. Navy with combat vessels, including nuclear submarines, surface combatants and auxiliary ships. Aerospace (23.8%) designs, develops, manu-

factures, markets, and provides maintenance and support services for technologically advanced business jet aircraft. Combat Systems (21.1%) provides systems integration, design, development, production and support for armored vehicles, armaments, munitions and components. Other (2.1%) businesses consist of a coal mining operation, an aggregates operation and a leasing operation for liquefied natural gas tankers. On 1/26/01, GD acquired Primex Technologies, Inc.

RECENT DEVELOPMENTS:

For the year ended 12/31/02, the Company reported income from continuing operations of $1.05 billion versus net income of $943.0 million the year before. Results for 2001 included a tax settlement gain of $28.0 million. Earnings for 2002 excluded a net loss of $134.0 million from discontinued operations. Net sales rose 14.7% to $13.83 billion.

Information Systems and Technology segment sales improved 36.8% to $3.68 million, while Combat Systems segment sales advanced 32.3% to $2.92 billion. Marine Systems segment sales inched up 1.1% to $3.65 billion. Aerospace segment sales grew slightly to $3.29 billion from $3.27 billion in 2001.

PROSPECTS:

On 12/19/02, the Company entered into a definitive agreement to acquire General Motors Defense in a cash transaction valued at $1.10 billion. GM Defense, with revenues of about $950.0 million, and a backlog of more than $1.50

billion as of 12/31/02, produces wheeled armored vehicles and turrets. The acquisition, which is expected to be completed by the end of the first quarter of 2003, should be immediately accretive to earnings.

ANNUAL FINANCIAL DATA:

FISCAL YEAR	TOT. REVS. ($mill.)	NET INC. ($mill.)	TOT. ASSETS ($mill.)	OPER. PROFIT %	NET PROFIT %	RET. ON EQUITY %	RET. ON ASSETS %	CURR. RATIO	EARN. PER SH.$	CASH FL. PER SH.$	TANG. BK. VAL.$	DIV. PER SH.$	PRICE RANGE	AVG. P/E RATIO	AVG. YIELD %
p12/31/02	13,829.0	⑤ 1,051.0							⑤ 5.18			1.18	111.18 - 73.25	17.8	1.3
12/31/01	12,163.0	④ 943.0	11,069.0	12.2	7.8	20.8	8.5	1.1	④ 4.65	5.98	3.84	1.10	96.00 - 60.50	16.8	1.4
12/31/00	10,356.0	④ 901.0	7,987.0	12.8	8.7	23.6	11.3	1.2	④ 4.48	5.60	6.43	1.02	79.00 - 36.25	12.9	1.8
12/31/99	8,959.0	880.0	7,774.0	13.4	9.8	27.8	11.3	1.0	4.36	5.35	3.27	0.94	75.44 - 46.19	13.9	1.5
12/31/98	4,970.0	364.0	4,572.0	10.9	7.3	16.4	8.0	1.3	2.86	3.86	5.46	0.86	62.00 - 40.25	17.9	1.7
12/31/97	4,062.0	316.0	4,091.0	11.0	7.8	16.5	7.7	1.3	2.50	3.20	5.64	0.82	45.75 - 31.56	15.5	2.1
12/31/96	3,581.0	270.0	3,299.0	9.9	7.5	15.8	8.2	2.2	2.14	2.67	13.60	0.80	37.75 - 28.50	15.5	2.4
12/31/95	3,067.0	③ 247.0	3,164.0	10.3	8.1	15.8	7.8	2.3	③ 1.96	2.26	12.44	0.74	31.50 - 21.19	13.4	2.8
12/31/94	3,058.0	② 223.0	2,673.0	10.5	7.3	16.9	8.3	2.9	② 1.76	2.08	10.44	0.68	23.81 - 19.00	12.2	3.2
12/31/93	3,187.0	① 270.0	2,635.0	9.7	8.5	22.9	10.2	2.1	① 2.17	2.59	9.34	12.95	30.00 - 20.09	11.5	51.7

Statistics are as originally reported. Adj. for 100% stk. div., 4/98 & 4/94. ① Bef. loss of $30.0 mill. & gain on disp. of $645.0 mill. ② Bef. inc. fr. disc. ops. of $15.0 mill. & incl. nonrecur. gain of $62.0 mill. ③ Bef. gain on disp. of $74.0 mill. ④ Incl. research & dev. tax credit of $28.0 mill., 2001; $90.0 mill., 2000. ⑤ Bef. a net loss of $134.0 mill. fr. disc. opers.

OFFICERS:
N. D. Chabraja, Chmn., C.E.O.
M. J. Mancuso, Sr. V.P., C.F.O.
D. H. Fogg, V.P., Treas.

INVESTOR CONTACT: R. Lewis, Inv. Rel., (703) 876-3195

PRINCIPAL OFFICE: 3190 Fairview Park Drive, Falls Church, VA 22042-4523

TELEPHONE NUMBER: (703) 876-3000
FAX: (703) 876-3125
WEB: www.generaldynamics.com

NO. OF EMPLOYEES: 54,000 (approx.)

SHAREHOLDERS: 17,900 (approx.)

ANNUAL MEETING: In May

INCORPORATED: DE, Feb., 1952

INSTITUTIONAL HOLDINGS:
No. of Institutions: 571
Shares Held: 136,774,151
% Held: 68.1

INDUSTRY: Guided missiles and space vehicles (SIC: 3761)

TRANSFER AGENT(S): First Chicago Trust Company of New York, Jersey City, NJ

GENERAL ELECTRIC COMPANY

EXCH.	SYM.	REC. PRICE	P/E RATIO	YLD.	MKT. CAP.	RANGE (52-WK.)	'02 Y/E PR.	DIV. ACH.
NYSE	GE	24.05 (2/28/03)	15.9	3.2%	$238.72 bill.	41.84 - 21.30	24.35	27 yrs.

HIGH GRADE. GE IS TARGETING 2003 EARNINGS PER SHARE IN THE $1.55 TO $1.70 RANGE, UP 3.0% TO 13.0% OVER 2002.

TRADING VOLUME
Thousand Shares

*7 YEAR PRICE SCORE 93.1   ***12 MONTH PRICE SCORE 90.2**

*NYSE COMPOSITE INDEX=100

INTERIM EARNINGS (Per Share):

Qtr.	Mar.	June	Sept.	Dec.
1998	0.19	0.25	0.23	0.27
1999	0.22	0.29	0.27	0.31
2000	0.26	0.34	0.32	0.36
2001	0.30	0.39	0.33	0.39
2002	0.35	0.44	0.41	0.31

INTERIM DIVIDENDS (Per Share):

Amt.	Decl.	Ex.	Rec.	Pay.
0.18Q	2/15/02	2/27/02	3/01/02	4/25/02
0.18Q	6/14/02	6/26/02	6/28/02	7/25/02
0.18Q	9/13/02	9/25/02	9/27/02	10/25/02
0.19Q	12/13/02	12/27/02	12/31/02	1/27/03
0.19Q	2/14/03	2/26/03	2/28/03	4/25/03

Indicated div.: $0.76 (Div. Reinv. Plan)

CAPITALIZATION (12/31/01):

	($000)	(%)
Long-Term Debt	79,806,000	55.5
Deferred Income Tax	9,130,000	6.4
Common & Surplus	54,824,000	38.1
Total	143,760,000	100.0

BUSINESS:

General Electric Company's businesses and their contributions to 2002 revenues are as follows: Financial Services (43.2%) are provided by GE Commercial Finance, GE Insurance, GE Consumer Finance and GE Equipment Management. The Materials, Power Systems, and Technical Products and Services (29.6%) sectors are providers of medical systems, power generation, motors and transporta-

tion systems. The Industrial Products and Systems segment (7.3%) includes transportation systems, industrial systems, and GE Supply. Aircraft Engines (8.3%) develops and manufactures engines for commercial aircraft. Consumer Products segment (6.3%) includes appliances and lighting. Broadcasting (5.3%) operations are conducted through NBC.

RECENT DEVELOPMENTS:

For the year ended 12/31/02, income was $15.13 billion, before an accounting change charge of $1.02 billion, compared with earnings of $14.13 billion, before an accounting change charge of $444.0 million, the prior year. Total revenues rose 4.6% to $131.70 billion from $125.91 billion a

year earlier. Sales of goods and services climbed 6.8% to $76.23 billion from $71.40 billion, while revenues for GE Capital Services inched up to $54.45 billion from $54.28 billion the year before.

PROSPECTS:

GE is targeting 2003 earnings per share in the $1.55 to $1.70 range, up 3.0% to 13.0% over 2002. Performance gains will be broad-based, with 11 of GE's 13 businesses in line to deliver double-digit operating profit growth. GE's businesses supporting the airline industry should see positive earnings growth in 2003. Power Systems earnings from

gas turbine will decline as anticipated after several years of solid growth; however, the rest of power systems, particularly its services, oil and gas, and wind businesses, should deliver strong performances and provide a solid platform for future earnings growth.

ANNUAL FINANCIAL DATA:

FISCAL YEAR	TOT. REVS. ($mill.)	NET INC. ($mill.)	TOT. ASSETS ($mill.)	OPER. PROFIT %	NET PROFIT %	RET. ON EQUITY %	RET. ON ASSETS %	CURR. RATIO	EARN. PER SH.$	CASH FL.PER SH.$	TANG. BK. VAL.$	DIV. PER SH.$	PRICE RANGE	AVG. P/E RATIO	AVG. YIELD %
p12/31/02	131,698.0	④ 15,133.0							④ 1.51			0.72	41.84 - 21.40	20.9	2.3
12/31/01	125,913.0	④ 14,476.0	489,808.0	49.0	11.5	26.4	3.0	0.6	④ 1.41	2.15	2.33	0.64	53.55 - 28.50	29.1	1.6
12/31/00	129,853.0	13,162.0	432,070.0	49.0	10.1	26.1	3.0	0.7	1.27	2.08	2.32	0.55	60.50 - 41.64	40.2	1.1
12/31/99	111,630.0	11,082.0	399,986.0	49.0	9.9	26.0	2.8	0.7	1.07	1.78	1.68	0.47	53.16 - 31.35	39.4	1.1
12/31/98	100,469.0	9,561.0	351,660.0	48.4	9.5	24.6	2.7	0.7	0.93	1.54	1.55	0.40	34.64 - 23.00	30.9	1.4
12/31/97	90,840.0	③ 8,443.0	300,330.0	46.8	9.3	24.5	2.8	0.8	③ 0.82	1.37	1.56	0.35	25.52 - 15.98	25.3	1.7
12/31/96	79,179.0	7,549.0	269,395.0	50.1	9.5	24.3	2.8	0.8	0.73	1.14	1.53	0.31	17.69 - 11.58	20.0	2.1
12/31/95	70,028.0	6,777.0	225,079.0	48.2	9.7	22.9	3.0	0.7	0.65	1.03	1.63	0.27	12.19 - 8.31	15.8	2.7
12/31/94	60,109.0	② 6,085.0	192,637.0	37.3	10.1	23.1	3.2	0.6	② 0.58	0.91	1.47	0.24	9.15 - 7.50	14.4	2.9
12/31/93	60,562.0	① 4,575.0	187,715.0	47.0	7.6	17.7	2.4	1.2	① 0.43	0.76	1.51	0.21	8.92 - 6.74	18.1	2.7

Statistics are as originally reported. Adj. for 3-for-1 stock split, 2/00; 2-for-1, 5/97 & 5/94. ① Excl. an acctg. change of $862.0 mill. ② Bef. disc. opers. of d$1.19 bill. ③ Incl. an after-tax gain of $1.50 bill. from the exchange of Lockheed Martin pfd. stk. & after-tax charges of $1.50 bill. for restruct. & oth. spec. matters. ④ Bef. acctg. chrg. chrg. of $444.0 mill., 2001; $1.02 bill., 2002.

OFFICERS:
J. R. Immelt, Chmn., C.E.O.
D. D. Dammerman, Vice-Chmn.
G. L. Rogers, Vice-Chmn.
R. C. Wright, Vice-Chmn.

INVESTOR CONTACT: Pauline Telep, Shareholder Relations, (203) 373-2816

PRINCIPAL OFFICE: 3135 Easton Turnpike, Fairfield, CT 06828-0001

TELEPHONE NUMBER: (203) 373-2211
FAX: (203) 373-3131
WEB: www.ge.com

NO. OF EMPLOYEES: 310,000 (avg.)

SHAREHOLDERS: 634,000 (approx.)

ANNUAL MEETING: In Apr.

INCORPORATED: NY, Apr., 1892

INSTITUTIONAL HOLDINGS:
No. of Institutions: 1,333
Shares Held: 739,041,984
% Held: 50.6

INDUSTRY: Electric lamps (SIC: 3641)

TRANSFER AGENT(S): GE Share Owner Services, c/o The Bank of New York, New York, NY

GENERAL GROWTH PROPERTIES, INC.

EXCH.	SYM.	REC. PRICE	P/E RATIO	YLD.	MKT. CAP.	RANGE (52-WK.)	'02 Y/E PR.
NYSE	GGP	52.27 (2/28/03)	17.8	5.3%	$3.24 bill.	52.89 - 41.35	52.00

UPPER MEDIUM GRADE. GGP IS FORECASTING FUNDS FROM OPERATIONS FOR 2003 IN THE RANGE OF $6.08 TO $6.25 PER DILUTED SHARE.

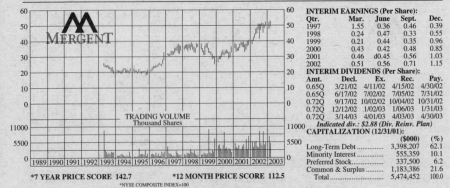

INTERIM EARNINGS (Per Share):

Qtr.	Mar.	June	Sept.	Dec.
1997	1.55	0.36	0.46	0.39
1998	0.24	0.47	0.33	0.55
1999	0.21	0.44	0.35	0.96
2000	0.43	0.42	0.48	0.85
2001	0.46	d0.45	0.56	1.03
2002	0.51	0.56	0.71	1.15

INTERIM DIVIDENDS (Per Share):

Amt.	Decl.	Ex.	Rec.	Pay.
0.65Q	3/21/02	4/11/02	4/15/02	4/30/02
0.65Q	6/17/02	7/02/02	7/05/02	7/31/02
0.72Q	9/17/02	10/02/02	10/04/02	10/31/02
0.72Q	12/12/02	1/02/03	1/06/03	1/31/03
0.72Q	3/14/03	4/01/03	4/03/03	4/30/03

Indicated div.: $2.88 (Div. Reinv. Plan)

CAPITALIZATION (12/31/01):

	($000)	(%)
Long-Term Debt	3,398,207	62.1
Minority Interest	555,359	10.1
Preferred Stock	337,500	6.2
Common & Surplus	1,183,386	21.6
Total	5,474,452	100.0

*7 YEAR PRICE SCORE 142.7   ***12 MONTH PRICE SCORE 112.5**

*NYSE COMPOSITE INDEX=100

BUSINESS:

General Growth Properties, Inc. is a self-administered regional mall real estate investment trust. As of 2/7/03, the Company owned or had an ownership interest in 169 operating regional mall shopping centers in 41 states. GGP's regional mall shopping centers have approximately 146.0 million square feet of gross retail space and include over 16,000 retailers and anchor department stores, as well as theaters, sit-down restaurants, ice skating rinks and other forms of family entertainment.

RECENT DEVELOPMENTS:

For the year ended 12/31/02, income was $186.1 million, before an extraordinary loss of $1.3 million, compared with income of $85.2 million, before an extraordinary loss of $14.0 million and an accounting change charge of $3.3 million, the previous year. Results for 2001 included net-work discontinuance costs of $66.0 million. Total revenues increased 21.3% to $974.6 million from $803.7 million the prior year. Funds from operations advanced 32.8% to $365.1 million, or $5.58 per diluted share, from $275.0 million, or $4.96 per diluted share, a year earlier.

PROSPECTS:

AIG is benefiting from a favorable rent environment and stable occupancy trends. Average rent per square foot for new/renewal leases signed during 2002 was $36.00 versus $33.29 in 2001. Average rent on expiring leases in 2002 was $29.90 per square foot, up 9.1% from the prior year. Mall shop occupancy and annualized sales per square foot remained constant at 91.0% and $355.00, respectively, as of 12/31/02, compared with 12/31/01. Looking ahead, GGP is forecasting funds from operations for 2003 in the range of $6.08 to $6.25 per diluted share. Separately, on 1/23/03, GGP announced plans to transform the vacant 220,000 square-foot JCPenney building at its Ala Moana Center in Honolulu, Hawaii into spaces for 30 or more retailers, including specialty stores, fashion boutiques, restaurants and one-of-a-kind retailers. On 2/4/03, GGP announced that it had been awarded the management, leasing and marketing contract for the Dallas Galleria, an up-scale shopping mall in Dallas, Texas.

ANNUAL FINANCIAL DATA:

FISCAL YEAR	TOT. INC. ($mill.)	NET INC. ($mill.)	TOT. ASSETS ($mill.)	NET INC. + DEPR./ ASSETS %	RET. ON EQUITY %	RET. ON ASSETS %	EARN. PER SH.$	TANG. BK. VAL.$	DIV. PER SH.$	DIV. PAYOUT %	PRICE RANGE	AVG. P/E RATIO	AVG. YIELD %
p12/31/02	974.6	① 186.1		4.5	7.2	1.9	① 2.97		2.67	89.9	52.29 — 38.00	15.2	5.9
12/31/01	803.7	② 109.7	5,646.8	5.0	10.8	2.6	② 1.61	19.11	2.24	139.1	40.50 — 32.80	22.8	6.1
12/31/00	698.8	137.9	5,284.1	5.0	10.8	2.6	2.18	17.95	2.04	93.6	36.50 — 26.38	14.4	6.5
12/31/99	612.3	① 114.9	4,954.9	4.6	9.1	2.3	① 1.96	17.95	1.94	99.0	38.63 — 25.00	16.2	6.1
12/31/98	426.6	① 71.2	4,027.5	3.6	7.7	1.8	① 1.59	15.02	1.86	117.0	39.25 — 32.50	22.6	5.2
12/31/97	291.1	① 90.7	2,097.7	6.6	18.2	4.3	① 2.76	16.19	1.78	64.5	38.38 — 30.25	12.4	5.2
12/31/96	217.4	① 62.0	1,757.7	5.8	18.8	3.5	① 2.20	10.73	1.72	78.2	32.88 — 20.63	12.2	6.4
12/31/95	167.4	43.1	1,456.0	5.1	18.8	3.0	1.69	8.41	1.64	97.0	22.63 — 18.13	12.1	8.0
12/31/94	152.6	14.9	906.5	4.7	9.6	1.6	0.65	6.78	1.54	236.9	22.63 — 19.25	32.2	7.4
12/31/93	142.2	14.4	789.5	5.0	8.3	1.8	0.63	7.60	0.68	107.9	26.00 — 19.25	35.9	3.0

Statistics are as originally reported. ① Bef. extraord. loss $1.3 mill. 12/02; $13.8 mill., 12/99; $4.7 mill., 12/98; $1.2 mill., 12/97; $2.3 mill., 12/96. ② Bef. extraord. loss $14.0 mill. & acctg. chrg. $3.3 mill.; incl. $66.0 mill. chrg. for network discontinuance.

OFFICERS:
M. Bucksbaum, Chmn.
R. Michaels, Pres.
J. Bucksbaum, C.E.O.
B. Freibaum, Exec. V.P., C.F.O.
INVESTOR CONTACT: Investor Relations, (312) 960-5000
PRINCIPAL OFFICE: 110 North Wacker Drive, Chicago, IL 60606

TELEPHONE NUMBER: (312) 960-5000
FAX: (312) 960-5475
WEB: www.generalgrowth.com
NO. OF EMPLOYEES: 3,429
SHAREHOLDERS: 1,484 (approx.)
ANNUAL MEETING: In May
INCORPORATED: DE, 1986

INSTITUTIONAL HOLDINGS:
No. of Institutions: 233
Shares Held: 56,209,882
% Held: 90.1
INDUSTRY: Real estate investment trusts (SIC: 6798)
TRANSFER AGENT(S): Mellon Investor Services, South Hackensack, NJ

GENERAL MILLS, INC.

EXCH.	SYM.	REC. PRICE	P/E RATIO	YLD.	MKT. CAP.	RANGE (52-WK.)	'02 Y/E PR.
NYSE	GIS	42.87 (2/28/03)	27.3	2.6%	$15.73 bill.	50.40 - 37.38	46.95

UPPER MEDIUM GRADE. THE COMPANY IS TARGETING EARNINGS PER SHARE OF BETWEEN $2.60 AND $2.62 FOR FISCAL 2003.

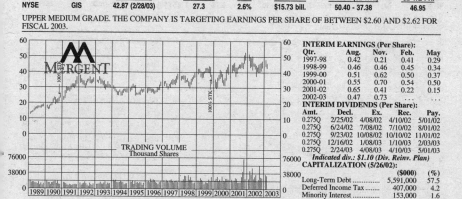

TRADING VOLUME
Thousand Shares

*7 YEAR PRICE SCORE 123.7   ***12 MONTH PRICE SCORE 111.9**
*NYSE COMPOSITE INDEX=100

INTERIM EARNINGS (Per Share):

Qtr.	Aug.	Nov.	Feb.	May
1997-98	0.42	0.21	0.41	0.29
1998-99	0.46	0.46	0.45	0.34
1999-00	0.51	0.62	0.50	0.37
2000-01	0.55	0.70	0.54	0.50
2001-02	0.65	0.41	0.22	0.15
2002-03	0.47	0.73	...	...

INTERIM DIVIDENDS (Per Share):

Amt.	Decl.	Ex.	Rec.	Pay.
0.275Q	2/25/02	4/08/02	4/10/02	5/01/02
0.275Q	6/24/02	7/08/02	7/10/02	8/01/02
0.275Q	9/23/02	10/08/02	10/10/02	11/01/02
0.275Q	12/16/02	1/08/03	1/10/03	2/03/03
0.275Q	2/24/03	4/08/03	4/10/03	5/01/03

Indicated div.: $1.10 (Div. Reinv. Plan)

CAPITALIZATION (5/26/02):

	($000)	(%)
Long-Term Debt	5,591,000	57.5
Deferred Income Tax	407,000	4.2
Minority Interest	153,000	1.6
Common & Surplus	3,576,000	36.8
Total	9,727,000	100.0

BUSINESS:

General Mills, Inc. is a major producer of packaged consumer foods including cereals, snack products, dessert mixes, dinner and side dishes, flour, baking mix, and yogurt. Products include CHEERIOS, WHEATIES, TOTAL, and BIG G cereals, and products under the brand names BETTY CROCKER, GOLD MEDAL, BISQUICK, YOPLAIT, CHEX and COLOMBO. GIS is party to two joint ventures (% equity interest in): Cereal Partners Worldwide (50.0%) and Snack Ventures Europe (40.5%). On 5/28/95, GIS completed the spin-off of its restaurant operations, Darden Restaurants, Inc. The Company also sold its Gorton's frozen and canned seafood products business on 5/18/95. On 10/31/01, the Company acquired The Pillsbury Company.

RECENT DEVELOPMENTS:

For the 13 weeks ended 11/24/02, net earnings totaled $276.0 million compared with $131.0 million in the corresponding period the year before. Results for 2002 included a one-time after-tax charge of $14.0 million related to the 10/31/01 acquisition of Pillsbury's domestic operations, partially offset by a pre-tax gain of $3.0 million stemming from additional insurance proceeds. Meanwhile, results for 2001 included a one-time after-tax charge of $68.0 million. Net sales advanced 60.3% to $2.95 billion from $1.84 billion a year earlier, primarily due to the Pillsbury acquisition. Operating profit was $541.0 million versus $278.0 million the previous year.

PROSPECTS:

Results are benefiting from unit volume growth in the U.S. for the Company's established cereal brands, including HONEY NUT CHEERIOS, LUCKY CHARMS and CINNAMON TOAST CRUNCH. GIS is also enjoying strong unit volume growth for its YOPLAIT yogurt products, as well as GREEN GIANT vegetables, BETTY CROCKER dinner mixes and PROGRESSO soups. Separately, the Company anticipates cost synergies from the integration of Pillsbury will increase from an expected $350.0 million in fiscal 2003 to $475.0 million in fiscal 2004. Going forward, the Company is targeting fiscal 2003 earnings of between $2.60 and $2.62 per share.

ANNUAL FINANCIAL DATA:

FISCAL YEAR	TOT. REVS. ($mill.)	NET INC. ($mill.)	TOT. ASSETS ($mill.)	OPER. PROFIT %	NET PROFIT %	RET. ON EQUITY %	RET. ON ASSETS %	CURR. RATIO	EARN. PER SH. $	CASH FL PER SH. $	TANG. BK. VAL.$	DIV. PER SH. $	PRICE RANGE	AVG. P/E RATIO	AVG. YIELD %
5/26/02	7,949.0	⑤ 461.0	16,540.0	16.0	5.8	12.9	2.8	0.6	⑤ 1.35	2.21	...	1.10	52.86 — 37.26	33.4	2.4
5/27/01	7,077.7	② 665.1	5,091.2	16.5	9.4	N.M.	13.1	0.6	② 2.28	3.04	...	1.10	45.31 — 29.38	16.4	2.9
5/28/00	6,700.2	614.4	4,573.7	16.4	9.2	...	13.4	0.5	2.00	2.68	...	1.10	43.94 — 32.50	19.1	2.9
5/30/99	6,246.1	④ 534.5	4,140.7	16.3	8.6	325.5	12.9	0.6	④ 1.70	2.32	0.54	1.06	39.84 — 29.59	20.4	3.1
5/31/98	6,033.0	421.8	3,861.4	15.8	7.0	221.8	10.9	0.7	1.30	1.90	0.61	1.04	39.13 — 28.88	26.2	3.1
5/25/97	5,609.3	② 445.4	3,902.4	15.3	7.9	90.1	11.4	0.8	② 1.41	1.99	...	0.98	33.75 — 26.00	21.2	3.3
5/26/96	5,416.0	② 476.4	3,294.7	15.9	8.8	154.8	14.5	0.8	② 1.50	2.09	0.62	0.94	32.31 — 24.88	19.1	3.3
③ 5/28/95	5,026.7	259.7	3,358.2	13.7	5.2	184.2	7.7	0.7	② 0.82	1.43	0.07	0.94	31.13 — 24.69	34.0	3.4
5/29/94	8,516.9	① 469.7	5,198.3	11.7	5.5	40.8	9.0	0.6	① 1.48	2.43	3.04	0.89	37.06 — 28.44	22.2	2.7
5/30/93	8,134.6	② 506.1	4,650.8	12.1	6.2	41.5	10.9	0.7	② 1.55	2.39	3.29	0.79	37.94 — 29.38	21.7	2.3

Statistics are as originally reported. Adj. for 100% stk. div., 11/99. ① Bef. $200,000 acctg. change. ② Incl. $21.9 mil ($0.08/sh) after-tax gain, 2001; $400,000 pre-tax gain & $100.1 mil ($0.32/sh) after-tax restr. chg.; 1997; $29.2 mil ($0.09/sh) after-tax chg., 1996; $111.6 mil ($0.36/sh) restr. chg. & $107.7 mil ($0.35/sh) after-tax inc. fr. discont. opers., 1995; $57.3 mil ($0.18/sh) restr. chg., 1993. ③ Refl. spin-offs of rest. & seafood bus. ④ Incl. $32.3 mil ($0.11/sh) after-tax restr. chg. ⑤ Bef. $3.0 mil acctg. chrg. & incl. $120.0 mil ($0.35/sh) after-tax chg.

OFFICERS:
S. W. Sanger, Chmn., C.E.O.
S. R. Demeritt, Vice-Chmn.
J. A. Lawrence, Exec. V.P., C.F.O.

INVESTOR CONTACT: Kris Wenker, V.P., Inv. Rel., (763) 764-2607

PRINCIPAL OFFICE: One General Mills Boulevard, Minneapolis, MN 55426

TELEPHONE NUMBER: (763) 764-7600
FAX: (763) 764-7384
WEB: www.generalmills.com
NO. OF EMPLOYEES: 29,859
SHAREHOLDERS: 38,047
ANNUAL MEETING: In Sept.
INCORPORATED: DE, June, 1928

INSTITUTIONAL HOLDINGS:
No. of Institutions: 521
Shares Held: 199,535,357
% Held: 54.2

INDUSTRY: Cereal breakfast foods (SIC: 2043)

TRANSFER AGENT(S): Wells Fargo Shareowner Services, St. Paul, MN

GENERAL MOTORS CORPORATION

EXCH.	SYM.	REC. PRICE	P/E RATIO	YLD.	MKT. CAP.	RANGE (52-WK.)	'02 Y/E PR.
NYSE	GM	33.77 (2/28/03)	10.3	5.9%	$48.51 bill.	68.17 - 30.80	36.86

MEDIUM GRADE. FOR 2003, THE COMPANY EXPECTS EARNINGS OF APPROXIMATELY $5.00 PER SHARE, EXCLUDING HUGHES AND SPECIAL ITEMS.

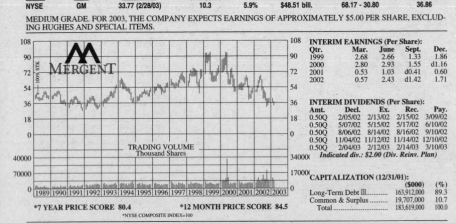

INTERIM EARNINGS (Per Share):

Qtr.	Mar.	June	Sept.	Dec.
1999	2.68	2.66	1.33	1.86
2000	2.80	2.93	1.55	d1.16
2001	0.53	1.03	d0.41	0.60
2002	0.57	2.43	d1.42	1.71

INTERIM DIVIDENDS (Per Share):

Amt.	Decl.	Ex.	Rec.	Pay.
0.50Q	2/05/02	2/13/02	2/15/02	3/09/02
0.50Q	5/07/02	5/15/02	5/17/02	6/10/02
0.50Q	8/06/02	8/14/02	8/16/02	9/10/02
0.50Q	11/04/02	11/12/02	11/14/02	12/10/02
0.50Q	2/04/03	2/12/03	2/14/03	3/10/03

Indicated div.: $2.00 (Div. Reinv. Plan)

CAPITALIZATION (12/31/01):

	($000)	(%)
Long-Term Debt ③	163,912,000	89.3
Common & Surplus	19,707,000	10.7
Total	183,619,000	100.0

*7 YEAR PRICE SCORE 80.4   ***12 MONTH PRICE SCORE 84.5**

*NYSE COMPOSITE INDEX=100

BUSINESS:

General Motors Corporation is the world's largest auto maker. The Automotive segment (79.2% of 2002 revenues) operates through Chevrolet, Pontiac, GMC, Oldsmobile, Buick, Cadillac, Saturn, Hummer, Opel, Vauxhall, Holden, Isuzu and Saab. General Motors Acceptance Corporation (GMAC) operates in the financial and insurance segment (14.5%), which includes vehicle leasing, insurance and financing. Hughes Electronics Corp. (5.1%) is a telecommunications company. Other products (1.2%) include Allison Transmission, which produces medium and heavy duty automatic transmissions for commercial-duty trucks and buses; and GM Locomotive Group, which produces diesel-electric locomotives, diesel engines and components. GM spun-off Delphi Automotive Systems in May 1999.

RECENT DEVELOPMENTS:

For the year ended 12/31/02, net income surged to $1.74 billion from $601.0 million in 2001. Results for 2002 included an after-tax gain of $372.0 million from the Hughes-EchoStar merger termination payment, an after-tax write-down charge of GM's investment in Fiat Auto of $1.37 billion, and a net after-tax charge of $722.0 million from various items. Results for 2001 included a net after-tax one-time charge of $874.0 million. Total net sales and revenues increased 5.4% to $186.76 billion. Net sales and revenues from automotive, communications services and other operations advanced 5.4% to $159.74 billion, while revenues from financing and insurance operations rose 4.9% to $27.03 billion. Total cost and expenses climbed 5.1% to $184.68 billion.

PROSPECTS:

For 2003, GM expects earnings of approximately $5.00 per share, excluding Hughes and special items. In addition, GM anticipates generating $10.00 billion in cash and improving market share in all of its automotive geographic regions. The Company's increasingly competitive products and cost structure should position GM for long-term improvement of its financial performance. GM North America is expected to earn between $1.70 and $1.90 billion, and GM Europe is expected to report improved results in the range of a loss of $200.0 million to break-even.

ANNUAL FINANCIAL DATA:

FISCAL YEAR	TOT. REVS. ($mill.)	NET INC. ($mill.)	TOT. ASSETS ($mill.)	OPER. PROFIT %	NET PROFIT %	RET. ON EQUITY %	RET. ON ASSETS %	CURR. RATIO	EARN. PER SH. $	CASH FL. PER SH. $	TANG. BK. VAL. $	DIV. PER SH. $	PRICE RANGE	AVG. P/E RATIO	AVG. YIELD %
p12/31/02	186,763.0	⑩ 1,736.0							⑩ 3.35			2.00	68.17 – 30.80	14.8	4.0
12/31/01	177,260.0	⑨ 601.0	323,969.0	5.7	0.3	3.0	0.2	0.9	⑨ 1.77	24.12	10.71	2.00	67.80 – 39.17	30.2	3.7
12/31/00	184,632.0	⑧ 4,452.0	303,100.0	9.1	2.4	14.8	1.5	0.8	⑧ 6.68	30.04	41.14	2.00	94.63 – 48.44	10.7	2.6
12/31/99	176,558.0	⑦ 5,576.0	274,730.0	10.5	3.2	27.0	2.0	0.9	⑦ 8.53	27.20	19.56	2.00	94.88 – 59.75	9.1	2.6
12/31/98	161,315.0	⑥ 2,956.0	257,389.0	8.6	1.8	19.7	1.1	1.0	⑥ 4.18	22.39	7.27	2.00	76.69 – 47.06	14.8	3.2
12/31/97	178,174.0	⑤ 6,698.0	228,888.0	8.6	3.8	38.3	2.9	4.1	⑤ 8.62	31.93	8.70	2.00	72.44 – 52.25	7.2	3.2
12/31/96	164,013.0	④ 4,953.0	222,142.0	8.8	3.0	21.2	2.2	4.1	④ 6.06	26.01	8.25	1.60	59.38 – 45.75	8.7	3.0
12/31/95	168,828.6	② 6,932.5	217,123.4	9.9	4.1	29.7	3.2	4.5	② 7.28	24.90	8.85	1.10	53.13 – 37.25	6.2	2.4
12/31/94	154,951.2	② 5,658.7	198,598.7	9.8	3.7	42.6	2.8	4.0	② 6.20	21.13	1.20	0.80	65.38 – 36.13	8.2	1.6
12/31/93	138,219.5	① 2,465.8	188,202.0	7.1	1.8	40.8	1.3	3.8	② 2.13	16.39	...	0.80	57.13 – 32.00	20.9	1.8

Statistics are as originally reported. ① Incl one-time chrg. $478.0 mill. ② Bef. acctg. change chrg. $758.0 mill., 1994; $51.8 mill., 1995. ③ Incl. long-term debt from GMAC. ④ Bef. disc. opers. gain $10.0 mill.; incl. one-time chrg. $938.0 mill. ⑤ Incl. non-recurr. credit $30.0 mill. ⑥ Bef. disc. opers. chrg. $500.0 mill. ⑦ Bef. disc. opers. gain $426.0 mill.; incl. one-time gain $597.0 mill. ⑧ Incl. spec. chrgs. totaling $520.0 mill. ⑨ Incl. acctg. credit of $12.0 mill. & after-tax net spec. chrgs. of $886.0 mill. ⑩ Incl. aft.-tax gain $372.0 mill. fr. Hughes EchoStar termination payment, an aft.-tax write-down of invest. in Fiat Auto $1.37 billion & oth. net after-tax one-time chrg. of $722.0 mill.

OFFICERS:
J. F. Smith Jr., Chmn.
J. M. Devine, Vice-Chmn., C.F.O.
G. R. Wagoner Jr., Pres., C.E.O.
INVESTOR CONTACT: Mark Tanner, (313) 665-3146
PRINCIPAL OFFICE: 300 Renaissance Center, Detroit, MI 48265-3000

TELEPHONE NUMBER: (313) 556-5000
FAX: (313) 556-5108
WEB: www.gm.com
NO. OF EMPLOYEES: 350,000 (avg.)
SHAREHOLDERS: 429,767 ($1 2/3 par common); 177,355 (class H common)
ANNUAL MEETING: In June
INCORPORATED: DE, Oct., 1916

INSTITUTIONAL HOLDINGS:
No. of Institutions: 585
Shares Held: 415,076,122
% Held: 74.1
INDUSTRY: Motor vehicles and car bodies (SIC: 3711)
TRANSFER AGENT(S): EquiServe, Providence, RI

GENESCO, INC.

EXCH.	SYM.	REC. PRICE	P/E RATIO	YLD.	MKT. CAP.	RANGE (52-WK.)	'02 Y/E PR.
NYSE	GCO	13.65 (2/28/03)	9.3	...	$298.1 mill.	28.30 - 10.65	18.63

MEDIUM GRADE. THE COMPANY IS FOCUSING ON BOOSTING PROFITABILITY AT ITS JOHNSTON & MURPHY OPERATIONS.

7 YEAR PRICE SCORE 137.4   **12 MONTH PRICE SCORE 90.9**

*NYSE COMPOSITE INDEX=100

INTERIM EARNINGS (Per Share):

Qtr.	Apr.	July	Oct.	Jan.
1996	0.04	0.08	0.23	0.31
1997	0.08	0.15	0.35	d0.28
1998	0.14	0.25	0.25	1.30
1999	0.16	0.17	0.26	0.45
2000	0.25	0.24	0.36	0.49
2001	0.34	0.26	0.33	0.61
2002	0.33	0.17	0.41	0.56

INTERIM DIVIDENDS (Per Share):

Amt.	Decl.	Ex.	Rec.	Pay.
		No dividends paid.		

CAPITALIZATION (2/2/02):

	($000)	(%)
Long-Term Debt	103,245	39.0
Preferred Stock	7,634	2.9
Common & Surplus	153,553	58.1
Total	264,432	100.0

BUSINESS:

Genesco, Inc. is a retailer and wholesaler of branded footwear. As of 2/1/03, GCO's products were sold at wholesale to more than 2,100 retailers, including the Company's own network of 991 footwear retail stores in the U.S., operated principally under the names Journeys, Journeys Kidz, Johnston & Murphy, Jarman and Underground Station. GCO also sells footwear at wholesale under its JOHNSTON & MURPHY brand and under the licensed DOCKERS brand. The Company disposed of its Western Boot operations in July 1998. On 6/19/00, the Company disposed of its Volunteer Leather Company.

RECENT DEVELOPMENTS:

For the year ended 2/1/03, earnings from continuing operations totaled $36.4 million, down 4.9% compared with earnings from continuing operations of $38.3 million in the previous year. Results included pre-tax restructuring and other charges of $2.5 million and $5.1 million in fiscal 2003 and fiscal 2002, respectively. Net sales climbed 11.0% to $828.3 million from $746.2 million the year before. Sales from Journeys stores rose 14.3% to $436.5 million from $381.7 million in the prior year, while sales at Jarman and Underground Station stores advanced 23.0% to $147.9 million from $120.2 million a year earlier. Licensed brands sales, primarily comprised of DOCKERS footwear, grew 2.4% to $78.5 million, while Johnston & Murphy sales slipped 1.3% to $165.3 million. Comparable-store sales increased 3.0% year over year.

PROSPECTS:

The Company is implementing initiatives expected to help boost profitability at its Johnston & Murphy operations, which are being hurt by increased markdowns on high-end men's footwear. GCO is taking steps to close unprofitable stores and focus its Johnston & Murphy product line on the dress-casual and dress segments of the footwear market. However, unfavorable foreign currency exchange rates, primarily between the U.S. dollar and the euro, will likely hurt Johnston & Murphy's results in 2003, due to a large number of Italian-made shoes in its product line. GCO is exploring alternative product sources to help reduce its exposure to currency rate fluctuations.

ANNUAL FINANCIAL DATA:

FISCAL YEAR	TOT. REVS. ($000)	NET INC. ($000)	TOT. ASSETS ($000)	OPER. PROFIT %	NET PROFIT %	RET. ON EQUITY %	RET. ON ASSETS %	CURR. RATIO	EARN. PER SH. $	CASH FL. PER SH. $	TANG. BK. VAL. $	PRICE RANGE	AVG. P/E RATIO
p2/01/03	828,307	⑦ 36,445							⑦ 1.47			28.30 - 10.65	13.2
2/02/02	746,821	⑥ 38,323	363,554	8.5	5.1	23.8	10.5	3.1	⑦ 1.54	2.00	7.03	35.00 - 15.65	16.4
2/03/01	680,166	⑥ 32,831	352,163	8.8	4.8	23.8	9.3	2.5	⑤ 1.35	1.70	6.02	24.94 - 8.25	12.3
1/29/00	573,720	⑤ 25,922	301,165	8.4	4.5	23.9	8.6	2.8	⑤ 1.05	1.30	4.73	14.63 - 5.38	9.5
1/30/99	549,748	54,923	307,198	7.0	10.0	47.1	17.9	3.1	1.89	2.11	4.56	18.88 - 3.94	6.0
1/31/98	536,107	①②8,820	246,817	3.4	1.6	12.3	3.6	2.6	①②0.31	0.66	2.48	15.44 - 8.50	38.6
1/31/97	461,348	①②10,554	217,654	5.6	2.3	17.4	4.8	3.0	①②0.42	0.75	2.09	11.13 - 3.38	17.3
1/31/96	434,575	d4,281	198,706	0.7	...	...	...	3.2	d0.19	0.13	1.07	4.88 - 2.00	...
1/31/95	462,901	③④d18,514	243,878	...	...	...	...	2.2	③④d0.77	d0.38	0.88	5.63 - 1.63	...
1/31/94	572,860	②③d51,779	309,386	...	...	...	...	3.3	②③d2.16	...	2.97	11.50 - 4.75	...

Statistics are as originally reported. ① Bef. extraord. chrg. $3.7 mill., 1998; $0.2 mill., 1997. ② Incl. non-recurr. chrg. $2.4 mill., 1998; $17.7 mill., 1997; $1.7 mill., 1996; $15.1 mill., 1995; $22.1 mill., 1994. ③ Bef. acctg. change chrg. $2.3 mill. ④ Bef. disc. oper. loss $62.7 mill. ⑤ Incl. non-recurr. chrg. $794,000 and a gain of $79,000. ⑥ Excl. provision for disc. oper. of $3.0 mill., but incl. non-recurr. chrg. of $4.4 mill. ⑦ Bef. $165,000 loss fr. disc. opers., 2003; $1.3 mill., 2002 & incl. $2.5 mill. pre-tax restr. chg., 2003; $5.1 mill., 2002.

OFFICERS:
B. T. Harris, Chmn.
H. N. Pennington, Pres., C.E.O.
J. S. Gulmi, Sr. V.P., C.F.O.
INVESTOR CONTACT: James S. Gulmi, Sr.
V.P. & C.F.O., (615) 367-8325
PRINCIPAL OFFICE: Genesco Park, 1415
Murfreesboro Road, Nashville, TN 37217

TELEPHONE NUMBER: (615) 367-7000
FAX: (615) 367-8278
WEB: www.genesco.com
NO. OF EMPLOYEES: 5,325 (approx.)
SHAREHOLDERS: 5,900 (approx.)
ANNUAL MEETING: In June
INCORPORATED: TN, July, 1925

INSTITUTIONAL HOLDINGS:
No. of Institutions: 117
Shares Held: 21,364,729
% Held: 98.5

INDUSTRY: Shoe stores (SIC: 5661)

REGISTRAR(S): EquiServe Trust Company,
N.A., Jersey City, NJ

GENUINE PARTS COMPANY

EXCH.	SYM.	REC. PRICE	P/E RATIO	YLD.	MKT. CAP.	RANGE (52-WK.)	'02 Y/E PR.	DIV. ACH.
NYSE	GPC	28.80 (2/28/03)	13.6	4.1%	$5.02 bill.	38.80 - 27.10	30.80	46 yrs.

UPPER MEDIUM GRADE. THE COMPANY EXPECTS TO ACHIEVE ADDITIONAL MARKET SHARE GAINS IN 2003.

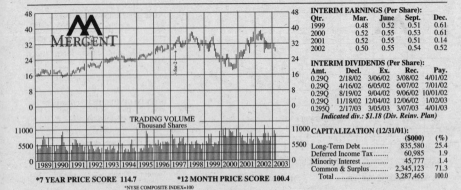

*7 YEAR PRICE SCORE 114.7   ***12 MONTH PRICE SCORE 100.4**

*NYSE COMPOSITE INDEX=100

INTERIM EARNINGS (Per Share):

Qtr.	Mar.	June	Sept.	Dec.
1999	0.48	0.52	0.51	0.61
2000	0.52	0.55	0.53	0.61
2001	0.52	0.55	0.51	0.14
2002	0.50	0.55	0.54	0.52

INTERIM DIVIDENDS (Per Share):

Amt.	Decl.	Ex.	Rec.	Pay.
0.29Q	2/18/02	3/06/02	3/08/02	4/01/02
0.29Q	4/16/02	6/05/02	6/07/02	7/01/02
0.29Q	8/19/02	9/04/02	9/06/02	10/01/02
0.29Q	11/18/02	12/04/02	12/06/02	1/02/03
0.295Q	2/17/03	3/05/03	3/07/03	4/01/03

Indicated div.: $1.18 (Div. Reinv. Plan)

CAPITALIZATION (12/31/01):

	($000)	(%)
Long-Term Debt	835,823	25.4
Deferred Income Tax	60,985	1.9
Minority Interest	45,777	1.4
Common & Surplus	2,345,123	71.3
Total	3,287,465	100.0

BUSINESS:

Genuine Parts Company is a service organization engaged in the distribution of automotive replacement parts, industrial replacement parts, office products and electrical and electronic materials throughout North America. GPC's largest division is its Automotive Parts Group (52.3% sales in 2002), which distributes automotive replacement parts and accessory items to NAPA auto parts stores. The Industrial Parts Group (27.1%) distributes replacement parts, equipment and related supplies. The Office Products Group (16.8%) distributes products including information processing, supplies, furniture and machines. The Electrical and Electronic Materials Group (3.8%) distributes materials for the manufacture and repair of electrical and electronic apparatus. In January 2000, GPC purchased a 15.0% ownership interest in Mitchell Repair Information Company, LLC.

RECENT DEVELOPMENTS:

For the year ended 12/31/02, the Company reported income of $367.5 million, before an accounting change charge of $395.1 million, compared with net income of $297.1 million in the previous year. Results for 2001 included a facility consolidation and impairment charge of $73.9 million. Net sales increased slightly to $8.26 billion from $8.22 billion a year earlier. Automotive sales grew 1.9% to $4.34 billion, while industrial sales inched up 0.5% to $2.25 billion. Sales of office products advanced 1.2% to $1.40 billion, while sales of electrical/electronic materials fell 18.6% to $315.8 million. Gross profit improved 1.3% to $2.55 billion from $2.52 billion the year before.

PROSPECTS:

Looking ahead to 2003, the Company anticipates continued growth in both sales and earnings. Meanwhile, GPC is optimistic that it can achieve additional market share gains. GPC expects most of its gains in 2003 will come from organic growth and increased unit volume. For the coming year, the Company does not anticipate any material acquisitions for its businesses and expects only modest price increases.

ANNUAL FINANCIAL DATA:

FISCAL YEAR	TOT. REVS. ($mill.)	NET INC. ($mill.)	TOT. ASSETS ($mill.)	OPER. PROFIT %	NET PROFIT %	RET. ON EQUITY %	RET. ON ASSETS %	CURR. RATIO	EARN. PER SH. $	CASH FL. PER SH. $	TANG. BK. VAL. $	DIV. PER SH. $	PRICE RANGE	AVG. P/E RATIO	AVG. YIELD %
p12/31/02	8,258.9	③ 367.5	4,019.8						③ 2.11			1.16	38.80 - 27.10	15.6	3.5
12/31/01	8,220.7	② 297.1	4,206.6	6.0	3.6	12.7	7.1	3.4	② 1.71	2.21	10.97	1.13	37.94 - 23.91	18.1	3.7
12/31/00	8,369.9	385.3	4,142.1	7.7	4.6	17.0	9.3	3.1	2.20	2.72	10.50	1.08	26.69 - 18.25	10.2	4.8
12/31/99	7,981.7	377.6	3,929.7	7.9	4.7	17.3	9.6	3.2	2.11	2.61	9.80	1.03	35.75 - 22.25	13.7	3.4
12/31/98	6,614.0	355.8	3,600.4	8.9	5.4	17.3	9.9	3.3	1.98	2.36	9.52	0.99	38.25 - 28.25	16.8	3.0
12/31/97	6,005.2	342.4	2,754.4	9.4	5.7	18.4	12.4	3.8	1.90	2.23	10.39	0.94	35.88 - 28.67	17.0	2.9
12/31/96	5,720.5	330.1	2,521.6	9.5	5.8	19.1	13.1	3.4	1.82	2.10	9.62	0.88	31.67 - 26.67	16.0	3.0
12/31/95	5,261.9	309.2	2,274.1	9.7	5.9	18.7	13.6	3.7	1.68	1.92	9.03	0.82	28.00 - 23.67	15.4	3.2
12/31/94	4,858.4	288.5	2,029.5	9.9	5.9	18.9	14.2	3.8	1.55	1.75	8.30	0.75	26.25 - 22.42	15.7	3.1
12/31/93	4,384.3	① 258.9	1,870.8	9.7	5.9	17.9	13.8	4.3	① 1.39	1.57	7.75	0.70	26.00 - 21.92	17.3	2.9

Statistics are as originally reported. Adj. for stk. splits: 3-for-2, 4/97 ① Bef. acctg change chrg. $1.1 mill. ② Incl. after-tax non-recurr. chrg. $64.4 mill. ③ Bef. acctg. change chrg. $395.1 mill.

OFFICERS:
L. L. Prince, Chmn., C.E.O.
T. C. Gallagher, Pres., C.O.O.
J. W. Nix, Exec. V.P., C.F.O.

INVESTOR CONTACT: Jerry Nix, Exec. V.P., C.F.O., (770) 612-2048

PRINCIPAL OFFICE: 2999 Circle 75 Parkway, Atlanta, GA 30339

TELEPHONE NUMBER: (770) 953-1700
FAX: (770) 956-2211
WEB: www.genpt.com

NO. OF EMPLOYEES: 31,000 (approx.)

SHAREHOLDERS: 7,930

ANNUAL MEETING: In April

INCORPORATED: GA, May, 1928

INDUSTRY: Motor vehicle supplies and new parts (SIC: 5013)

TRANSFER AGENT(S): Sun Trust Bank, Atlanta, GA

GEORGIA GULF CORPORATION

EXCH.	SYM.	REC. PRICE	P/E RATIO	YLD.	MKT. CAP.	RANGE (52-WK.)	'02 Y/E PR.
NYSE	GGC	19.04 (2/28/03)	19.6	1.7%	$0.61 bill.	27.20 - 18.24	23.14

LOWER MEDIUM GRADE. THE COMPANY ANTICIPATES 2003 WILL BE A STRONG YEAR FOR ITS VINYL RESINS AND COMPOUNDS BUSINESSES.

TRADING VOLUME
Thousand Shares

1989 1990 1991 1992 1993 1994 1995 1996 1997 1998 1999 2000 2001 2002 2003

*7 YEAR PRICE SCORE 106.1   ***12 MONTH PRICE SCORE 103.5**
*NYSE COMPOSITE INDEX=100

INTERIM EARNINGS (Per Share):

Qtr.	Mar.	June	Sept.	Dec.
1997	0.35	0.60	0.82	0.63
1998	0.52	0.52	0.33	0.41
1999	0.08	0.13	0.44	0.66
2000	1.00	1.04	0.24	d0.24
2001	d0.21	d0.09	0.08	d0.16
2002	0.02	0.12	0.53	0.30

INTERIM DIVIDENDS (Per Share):

Amt.	Decl.	Ex.	Rec.	Pay.
0.08Q	3/05/02	3/15/02	3/19/02	4/09/02
0.08Q	5/21/02	6/14/02	6/18/02	7/10/02
0.08Q	9/10/02	9/18/02	9/20/02	10/11/02
0.08Q	12/11/02	12/18/02	12/20/02	1/10/03
0.08Q	3/04/03	3/17/03	3/19/03	4/10/03

Indicated div.: $0.32

CAPITALIZATION (12/31/01):

	($000)	(%)
Long-Term Debt	585,415	72.9
Deferred Income Tax	120,868	15.1
Common & Surplus	96,634	12.0
Total	802,917	100.0

BUSINESS:

Georgia Gulf Corporation is a manufacturer and marketer of chemical and plastic products. The Company's products are manufactured through two integrated lines categorized into chlorovinyls and aromatic chemicals. Chlorovinyls products include chlorine, caustic soda, vinyl chloride monomer, vinyl resins and compounds; aromatic chemical products include cumene, phenol and acetone. Sales (and operating income) in 2002 were derived: chlorovinyls, 82.1% (103.0%); and aromatics, 17.9% (d3.0%).

RECENT DEVELOPMENTS:

For the twelve months ended 12/31/02, net income amounted to $31.2 million compared with a net loss of $12.0 million in 2001. Results for 2001 included an asset write-off charge of $5.4 million. Earnings benefited from increased vinyl resins sales volumes and decreased natural gas and raw material costs, partially offset by reduced sales prices for most products, particularly caustic soda, and an oversupply of aromatics. Net sales climbed 2.1% to $1.23 billion from $1.21 billion in the prior year. Sales from the chlorovinyls segment grew 2.8% to $1.01 billion from $983.4 million, while sales from the aromatics segment slipped 1.3% to $219.7 million from $222.5 million. Operating income more than tripled to $98.3 million compared with $30.4 million the year before.

PROSPECTS:

Based on the assumption of a strengthening economy, the Company anticipates 2003 to be a strong year for its vinyl resins and compounds businesses and that caustic prices will continue to trend up. However, the current higher cost of natural gas, particularly in the first quarter of 2003, and a challenging environment for the aromatics business may mitigate the aforementioned positive factors.

ANNUAL FINANCIAL DATA:

FISCAL YEAR	TOT. REVS. ($mill.)	NET INC. ($mill.)	TOT. ASSETS ($mill.)	OPER. PROFIT %	NET PROFIT %	RET. ON EQUITY %	RET. ON ASSETS %	CURR. RATIO	EARN. PER SH.$	CASH FL. PER SH.$	TANG. BK. VAL.$	DIV. PER SH.$	PRICE RANGE	AVG. P/E RATIO	AVG. YIELD %
p12/31/02	1,230.2	31.2							0.97			0.32	27.20 - 17.20	22.9	1.4
12/31/01	1,205.9	⑤d12.0	942.8	2.5	...	...	...	1.6	⑤d0.38	1.91	0.59	0.30	19.95 - 13.51	...	1.8
12/31/00	1,581.7	64.2	1,041.1	10.6	4.1	54.1	6.2	1.5	2.03	4.36	1.21	0.32	30.94 - 10.19	10.1	1.6
12/31/99	857.8	④43.2	1,098.0	12.0	5.0	75.4	3.9	1.5	④1.38	2.98	...	0.32	31.13 - 10.00	14.9	1.6
12/31/98	875.0	③56.3	669.8	14.9	6.4	194.9	8.4	1.7	③1.77	3.21	...	0.32	36.75 - 14.50	14.5	1.2
12/31/97	965.7	②81.2	612.7	15.2	8.4	228.1	13.3	1.5	②2.39	3.51	1.11	0.32	33.50 - 23.00	11.8	1.1
12/31/96	896.2	71.6	588.0	15.2	8.0	385.7	12.2	1.4	1.97	3.06	0.54	0.32	39.50 - 25.75	16.6	1.0
12/31/95	1,081.6	186.5	507.3	30.3	17.2	368.4	36.8	1.6	4.73	5.54	1.36	0.24	40.75 - 26.63	7.1	0.7
12/31/94	955.3	122.2	508.4	24.1	12.8	392.3	24.0	2.0	2.88	3.53	0.74	...	43.25 - 21.63	11.3	...
12/31/93	768.9	①42.2	405.3	14.4	5.5	...	10.4	1.6	①1.01	1.66	...	...	23.75 - 16.50	19.9	...

Statistics are as originally reported. ① Bef. $13.3 mill. ($0.32/sh.) extraord. chg. & cr$13.0 mill. ($0.32/sh.) acct. adj. ② Incl. $8.6 mill. pre-tax gain fr. sale of certain oil & gas props. ③ Incl. $6.0 mill. one-time after-tax chg. for loss on int. rate hedge agreements. ④ Excl. $10.2 mill. loss fr. disc. ops. & disposal of bus. ⑤ Incl. $5.4 mill. asset write-off & other chgs.

OFFICERS:
E. A. Schmitt, Chmn., Pres., C.E.O.
R. B. Marchese, V.P., C.F.O.
J. I. Beerman, V.P., Sec., Gen. Couns.

INVESTOR CONTACT: Dick Marchese, V.P., C.F.O., (770) 395-4531

PRINCIPAL OFFICE: 400 Perimeter Center Terrace, Suite 595, Atlanta, GA 30346

TELEPHONE NUMBER: (770) 395-4500
FAX: (770) 395-4529
WEB: www.ggc.com

NO. OF EMPLOYEES: 1,232

SHAREHOLDERS: 1,160

ANNUAL MEETING: In May

INCORPORATED: DE, Dec., 1984

INSTITUTIONAL HOLDINGS:
No. of Institutions: 135
Shares Held: 23,204,587
% Held: 72.2

INDUSTRY: Industrial inorganic chemicals, nec (SIC: 2819)

TRANSFER AGENT(S): EquiServe, Boston, MA

GEORGIA-PACIFIC GROUP

EXCH.	SYM.	REC. PRICE	P/E RATIO	YLD.	MKT. CAP.	RANGE (52-WK.)	'02 Y/E PR.
NYSE	GP	15.01 (2/28/03)	...	3.3	$3.45 bill.	31.60 - 9.81	16.16

LOWER MEDIUM GRADE. THE COMPANY PLANS TO REDUCE ADMINISTRATIVE OVERHEAD COSTS BY ABOUT $135.0 MILLION BELOW 2002 LEVELS.

*7 YEAR PRICE SCORE 67.1   ***12 MONTH PRICE SCORE 83.4**

*NYSE COMPOSITE INDEX=100

INTERIM EARNINGS (Per Share):

Qtr.	Mar.	June	Sept.	Dec.
1998	0.09	0.17	0.22	0.15
1999	0.57	1.20	1.31	1.00
2000	1.11	1.20	0.76	d0.98
2001	d0.60	0.13	d0.80	0.15
2002	0.26	0.38	0.27	d0.94

INTERIM DIVIDENDS (Per Share):

Amt.	Decl.	Ex.	Rec.	Pay.
0.125Q	2/01/02	2/08/02	2/12/02	2/22/02
0.125Q	5/07/02	5/15/02	5/17/02	5/28/02
0.125Q	8/01/02	8/08/02	8/12/02	8/21/02
0.125Q	11/04/02	11/07/02	11/12/02	11/22/02
0.125Q	1/31/03	2/06/03	2/10/03	2/20/03

Indicated div.: $0.50 (Div. Reinv. Plan)

CAPITALIZATION (12/29/01):

	($000)	(%)
Long-Term Debt	10,221,000	60.2
Deferred Income Tax	1,846,000	10.9
Common & Surplus	4,905,000	28.9
Total	16,972,000	100.0

BUSINESS:

Georgia-Pacific Group (formerly Georgia-Pacific Corporation) is a global manufacturer and distributor of tissue, packaging, paper, building products, pulp and related chemicals. GP's consumer tissue brands include QUILTED NORTHERN, ANGEL SOFT, BRAWNY, SPARKLE, SOFT 'N GENTLE, MARDI GRAS, SO-DRI, GREEN FOREST and VANITY FAIR, as well as the DIXIE brand of disposable cups, plates and cutlery. GP's building products distribution seg-

ment is a wholesale supplier of building products to lumber and building materials dealers and large do-it-yourself wholesale retailers. As of 12/31/02, net sales were derived: 20.9%, North American consumer products; 19.6%, building products manufacturing; 18.2%, paper distribution; 14.6%, building products distribution; 10.5%, packaging; 9.8%, bleached pulp and paper; and 6.4%, international consumer products.

RECENT DEVELOPMENTS:

For the year ended 12/31/02, GP incurred a loss of $190.0 million, before an accounting change charge of $545.0 million, compared with a loss of $476.0 million, before income from discontinued operations of $70.0 million, an extraordinary loss of $12.0 million and an accounting

change credit of $11.0 million, in 2001 due difficult business conditions. Results for 2002 and 2001 included nonrecurring charges of $911.0 million and $585.0 million, respectively. Total net sales declined 7.0% to $23.27 billion from $25.02 billion a year earlier.

PROSPECTS:

GP plans to reduce administrative overhead costs by about $135.0 million below 2002 levels due to continuing difficult market conditions and anticipated higher pension costs in 2003. GP will focus on inventory management and manufacturing to demand to maximize cash flow. Separately,

GP plans to proceed with the the separation of its consumer products and packaging business from its building products business depending on financial and capital market conditions, operating results of its two main businesses, and the market's perception of its asbestos liabilities.

ANNUAL FINANCIAL DATA:

FISCAL YEAR	TOT. REVS. ($mill.)	NET INC. ($mill.)	TOT. ASSETS ($mill.)	OPER. PROFIT %	NET PROFIT %	RET. ON EQUITY %	RET. ON ASSETS %	CURR. RATIO	EARN. PER SH. $	CASH FL. PER SH. $	TANG. BK. VAL. $	DIV. PER SH. $	PRICE RANGE	AVG. P/E RATIO	AVG. YIELD %
p12/31/02	23,271.0	⑧ d190.0							⑧ d0.80				31.60 — 9.81	...	2.4
12/29/01	25,016.0	⑥ d476.0	26,364.0	4.8	...	...	...	0.9	⑥ d2.10	3.82	...	0.50	37.65 — 25.39	...	1.6
12/30/00	22,218.0	⑤ 505.0	30,882.0	6.5	2.3	8.8	1.6	1.0	⑤ 3.94	6.24	...	0.50	51.94 — 19.31	9.0	1.4
1/01/00	17,977.0	⑦ 1,116.0	16,897.0	12.9	6.2	28.8	6.6	1.1	⑦ 8.80	8.21	6.84	0.50	54.13 — 29.34	4.7	1.2
12/31/98	13,336.0	⑤ 289.0	12,700.0	7.0	2.2	9.3	2.3	1.0	⑤ 1.59	3.58	8.36	0.50	40.50 — 18.69	18.6	1.7
12/31/97	13,094.0	④ 129.0	12,950.0	4.4	1.0	3.7	1.0	1.0	④ 0.70	3.14	10.17	1.00	54.28 — 29.50	60.3	2.4
12/31/96	13,024.0	⑦ 161.0	12,818.0	5.6	1.2	4.5	1.3	1.1	⑦ 0.89	6.39	10.24	1.00	40.50 — 31.50	40.4	2.8
12/31/95	14,292.0	① 1,018.0	12,335.0	14.6	7.1	28.9	8.3	1.5	① 5.65	10.24	9.92	0.95	47.88 — 32.88	7.2	2.4
12/31/94	12,738.0	③ 326.0	10,728.0	7.6	2.6	12.4	3.0	0.8	③ 1.83	6.41	4.71	0.80	39.50 — 28.38	18.5	2.4
12/31/93	12,330.0	② d18.0	10,545.0	4.6	...	...	...	0.8	② d0.10	4.61	3.17	0.80	37.50 — 27.50	...	2.5

Statistics are as originally reported. Adj. for stk. split: 100%, 6/99. Full-year results reflect the combined opers. of Georgia-Pacific Group and The Timber Co., while qtrly. EPS are for Georgia-Pacific Group only. ① Incl. nonrecurr. chrg. of $114 mill., 1996; $70 mill., 1995. ② Incl. $7 mill. chrg. & bef. extraord. chrg. of $16 mill. ③ Incl. nonrecurr. gain of $33 mill. Bef. chrg. of $30 mill. ④ Bef. acctg. chrg. of $60 mill.; & incl. restr. chrg. of $80 mill. ⑤ Bef. extraord. chrg. of $13.0 mill. ⑥ Incl. one-time unusual chrgs. of $204.0 mill. and a gain of $88.0 mill. on the disposal of assets, net. ⑦ Incl. nonrecurr. gain of $406.0 mill. ⑧ Bef. acctg. change chrg. of $545.0 mill., 2002; $11.0 mill., 2001 & extraord. loss of $12.0 mill., 2001; incl. nonrecurr. chrg. of $911.0 mill., 2002; $355.0 mill., 2001.

OFFICERS:
A. D. Correll, Chmn., C.E.O.
L. M. Thomas, Pres.
D. W. Huff, Exec. V.P., C.F.O.

INVESTOR CONTACT: Investor Relations, (404) 652-5555

PRINCIPAL OFFICE: 133 Peachtree Street, N.E., Atlanta, GA 30303

TELEPHONE NUMBER: (404) 652-4000
FAX: (404) 230-1674
WEB: www.gp.com
NO. OF EMPLOYEES: 75,000 (approx.)
SHAREHOLDERS: 36,462 (Georgia-Pacific Group)
ANNUAL MEETING: In May
INCORPORATED: GA, Sept., 1927

INSTITUTIONAL HOLDINGS:
No. of Institutions: 314
Shares Held: 188,623,816
% Held: 75.4

INDUSTRY: Wood products, nec (SIC: 2499)

TRANSFER AGENT(S): First Chicago Trust Company of New York, Jersey City, NJ

GILLETTE COMPANY (THE)

EXCH.	SYM.	REC. PRICE	P/E RATIO	YLD.	MKT. CAP.	RANGE (52-WK.)	'02 Y/E PR.
NYSE	G	30.19 (2/28/03)	26.5	2.2%	$31.52 bill.	37.30 - 27.57	30.36

UPPER MEDIUM GRADE. THE COMPANY CONTINUES TO MAKE PROGRESS IN STRENGTHENING ITS BRANDS.

*7 YEAR PRICE SCORE 87.8   ***12 MONTH PRICE SCORE 102.6**

*NYSE COMPOSITE INDEX=100

INTERIM EARNINGS (Per Share):

Qtr.	Mar.	June	Sept.	Dec.
1997	0.26	0.29	0.32	0.41
1998	0.23	0.33	Nil	0.39
1999	0.24	0.26	0.32	0.32
2000	0.24	0.28	0.33	d0.08
2001	0.17	0.22	0.28	0.19
2002	0.21	0.28	0.33	0.32

INTERIM DIVIDENDS (Per Share):

Amt.	Decl.	Ex.	Rec.	Pay.
0.163Q	12/13/01	1/30/02	2/01/02	3/05/02
0.163Q	4/24/02	4/29/02	5/01/02	6/05/02
0.163Q	6/28/02	7/30/02	8/01/02	9/05/02
0.163Q	10/24/02	10/30/02	11/01/02	12/05/02
0.163Q	12/12/02	1/29/03	2/01/03	3/05/03

Indicated div.: $0.65 (Div. Reinv. Plan)

CAPITALIZATION (12/31/01):

	($000)	(%)
Long-Term Debt	1,654,000	38.5
Deferred Income Tax	459,000	10.7
Minority Interest	42,000	1.0
Common & Surplus	2,137,000	49.8
Total	4,292,000	100.0

BUSINESS:

The Gillette Company manufactures and sells a wide variety of consumer products throughout the world. The Company's five primary businesses are: Blades and Razors (40.6% of 2002 sales), which include male shaving systems sold under the MACH3, SENSOREXCEL, SENSOR, ATRA, TRAC II, CUSTOM PLUS and GOOD NEWS brands, and female shaving franchises sold under the GILLETTE FOR WOMEN VENUS, SENSOR EXCEL FOR WOMEN, SENSOR FOR WOMEN, and AGILITY brands; Duracell (22.4%), which include the DURACELL ULTRA and COPPERTOP alkaline batteries and DURACELL primary lithium, zinc air and rechargeable nickel-metal hydride batteries; Oral Care (14.8%), which offers manual and power toothbrushes sold under the BRAUN and ORAL-B brands; Braun (12.5%), which sells electric shavers under the BRAUN brand and hair epilators under the SILK EPIL brand; Personal Care (9.7%), which offers shave preparations, after-shave products and deodorants and antiperspirants under the GILLETTE, SATIN CARE, RIGHT GUARD, SOFT & DRI and DRY IDEA brands.

RECENT DEVELOPMENTS:

For the year ended 12/31/02, income was $1.21 billion, before income from discontinued operations of $7.0 million, versus net income of $910.0 million the previous year. Results for 2002 included an after-tax benefit of $21.0 million from the sale of Vaniga and an after-tax benefit of $6.0 million for the recovery of restructuring reserves.

Results for 2001 included an after-tax restructuring charge of $135.0 million. Net sales improved 4.6% to $8.45 billion from $8.08 billion a year earlier. The improvement was supported by notably higher sales from all of the Company's operating segments, with the exception of its Duracell division.

PROSPECTS:

The Company continues to make good progress in strengthening its brands. Moreover, G's efforts to remove costs and strengthen its capabilities company-wide should continue to enhance its ability to fund increased brand-building investments and heighten the quality of its operating performance. The Company remains on target in meeting its objective of removing more than $300.0 million in overhead expenses by 2006.

ANNUAL FINANCIAL DATA:

FISCAL YEAR	TOT. REVS. ($mill.)	NET INC. ($mill.)	TOT. ASSETS ($mill.)	OPER. PROFIT %	NET PROFIT %	RET. ON EQUITY %	RET. ON ASSETS %	CURR. RATIO	EARN. PER SH.$	CASH FL. PER SH.$	TANG. BK. VAL.$	DIV. PER SH.$	PRICE RANGE	AVG. P/E RATIO	AVG. YIELD %
p12/31/02	8,453.0	④ 1,209							④ 1.14			0.65	37.30 - 27.57	28.5	2.0
12/31/01	8,961.0	② 910.0	9,969.0	16.7	10.2	42.6	9.1	0.9	② 0.86	1.34	0.74	0.65	36.38 - 24.50	35.4	2.1
12/31/00	9,295.0	②③ 821.0	10,402.0	16.3	8.8	42.7	7.9	0.9	②③ 0.77	1.28	0.33	0.64	43.00 - 27.13	45.5	1.8
12/31/99	9,897.0	1,260.0	11,786.0	21.3	12.7	41.2	10.7	1.2	1.14	1.58	0.58	0.57	64.38 - 33.06	42.7	1.2
12/31/98	10,056.0	② 1,081.0	11,902.0	17.8	10.7	23.8	9.1	1.6	② 0.95	1.35	1.81	0.49	62.66 - 35.31	51.6	1.0
12/31/97	10,062.0	1,427.0	10,864.0	23.1	14.2	29.5	13.1	1.8	1.25	1.61	2.07	0.41	53.19 - 36.00	35.8	0.9
12/31/96	9,697.7	② 948.7	10,435.3	16.9	9.8	21.1	9.1	1.6	② 0.86	1.20	1.56	0.34	38.88 - 24.13	36.8	1.1
12/31/95	6,794.7	823.5	6,340.3	20.2	12.1	32.8	13.0	1.5	0.93	1.20	1.34	0.29	27.69 - 17.69	24.5	1.3
12/31/94	6,070.2	698.3	5,494.0	20.2	11.5	34.6	12.7	1.5	0.79	1.03	1.16	0.24	19.13 - 14.44	21.4	1.4
12/31/93	5,410.8	①② 426.9	5,102.3	15.2	7.9	28.9	8.4	1.4	①②④ 0.48	0.73	0.52	0.20	15.94 - 11.84	28.9	1.5

Statistics are as originally reported. Adj. for stk. splits: 2-for-1, 6/98 & 6/95. ① Bef. acctg. change chrg. $138.6 mill. ② Incl. non-recurr. chrgs. $172.0 mill., 12/01; $572.0 mill., 12/00; $535.0 mill., 12/98; $413.0 mill., 12/96; $164.1 mill., 12/93 ③ Bef. loss from disc. opers. $429.0 mill. ④ Bef. inc. fr. disc. opers. of $7.0 mill.; Incl. after-tax net benefit $27.0 mill.

OFFICERS:
J. Kilts, Chmn., C.E.O.
E. F. DeGraan, Pres., C.O.O.
C. W. Cramb Jr., Sr. V.P., C.F.O.
INVESTOR CONTACT: Christopher M. Jakubik, (617) 421-7968
PRINCIPAL OFFICE: Prudential Tower Building, Boston, MA 02199

TELEPHONE NUMBER: (617) 421-7000
FAX: (617) 421-7123
WEB: www.gillette.com
NO. OF EMPLOYEES: 31,500 (approx.)
SHAREHOLDERS: 46,787
ANNUAL MEETING: In May
INCORPORATED: DE, Sept., 1917

INSTITUTIONAL HOLDINGS:
No. of Institutions: 740
Shares Held: 745,698,828
% Held: 70.7
INDUSTRY: Hand and edge tools, nec (SIC: 3423)
TRANSFER AGENT(S): Boston EquiServe, Boston, MA

GLATFELTER (P.H.) COMPANY

EXCH.	SYM.	REC. PRICE	P/E RATIO	YLD.	MKT. CAP.	RANGE (52-WK.)	'02 Y/E PR.
NYSE	GLT	9.95 (2/28/03)	11.6	7.0	$425.4 mill.	19.35 - 9.85	13.16

MEDIUM GRADE. THE COMPANY EXPECTS PRESSURE ON PRODUCT DEMAND AND PRICING TO CONTINUE IN THE NEAR-TERM.

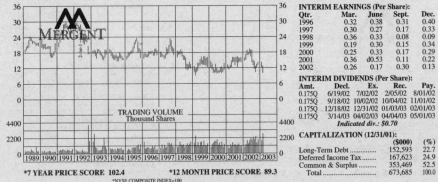

INTERIM EARNINGS (Per Share):

Qtr.	Mar.	June	Sept.	Dec.
1996	0.32	0.38	0.31	0.40
1997	0.30	0.27	0.17	0.33
1998	0.36	0.33	0.08	0.09
1999	0.19	0.30	0.15	0.34
2000	0.25	0.33	0.17	0.29
2001	0.36	d0.53	0.11	0.22
2002	0.26	0.17	0.30	0.13

INTERIM DIVIDENDS (Per Share):

Amt.	Decl.	Ex.	Rec.	Pay.
0.175Q	6/19/02	7/02/02	2/05/02	8/01/02
0.175Q	9/18/02	10/02/02	10/04/02	11/01/02
0.175Q	12/18/02	12/31/02	01/03/03	02/01/03
0.175Q	3/14/03	04/02/03	04/04/03	05/01/03

Indicated div.: $0.70

CAPITALIZATION (12/31/01):

	($000)	(%)
Long-Term Debt	152,593	22.7
Deferred Income Tax	167,623	24.9
Common & Surplus	353,469	52.5
Total	673,685	100.0

*7 YEAR PRICE SCORE 102.4   ***12 MONTH PRICE SCORE 89.3**

*NYSE COMPOSITE INDEX=100

BUSINESS:

P.H. Glatfelter Company is a global manufacturer of specialty papers and engineered products. GLT's specialized printing paper products are directed at the uncoated free-sheet portion of the industry, and are principally used for the printing of case bound and quality paperback books, commercial and financial printing and envelope converting. GLT's engineered papers are used in a variety of products, including tea bags, cigarette papers, cigarette tipping and

plug wrap papers, metalized beverage labels, decorative laminates, food product casings, highway signs and striping, billboard graphics, decorative shopping bags, playing cards, postage stamps, filters, labels and surgical gowns. These papers are generally sold directly to the converter of the paper. GLT's operations include facilities in Spring Grove, Pennsylvania and Neenah, Wisconsin as well as Germany, France and the Philippines.

RECENT DEVELOPMENTS:

For the year ended 12/31/02, net income amounted to $37.6 million compared with $7.0 million in 2001. Earnings for 2002 and 2001 included nonrecurring items that resulted in charges of $1.9 million and $39.7 million, respectively. Net sales declined 14.4% to $543.8 million from $635.7 million

a year earlier. Approximately $90.8 million of the sales in 2001 were attributable to the Ecusta division, which was sold during 2001. Gross margin declined to $117.0 million from $132.1 million the year before.

PROSPECTS:

Looking ahead, results are likely to continue to be adversely affected by weak domestic and global economic conditions, which pressured product demand and pricing, particularly in the printing and converting portion of the

Company's business during 2002. The Company plans to improve its financial performance and enhance efficiency and workforce reductions.

ANNUAL FINANCIAL DATA:

FISCAL YEAR	TOT. REVS. ($000)	NET INC. ($000)	TOT. ASSETS ($000)	OPER. PROFIT %	NET PROFIT %	RET. ON EQUITY %	RET. ON ASSETS %	CURR. RATIO	EARN. PER SH.$	CASH FL. PER SH.$	TANG. BK. VAL.$	DIV. PER SH.$	PRICE RANGE	AVG. P/E RATIO	AVG. YIELD
p12/31/02	543,823	④ 37,595							④ 0.86			0.70	19.35 - 10.22	17.2	4.7
12/31/01	652,539	⑥ 6,958	960,724	13.5	1.1	2.0	0.7	1.1	④ 0.16	1.21	8.27	0.70	16.37 - 11.30	86.4	5.1
12/31/00	739,812	②③ 44,000	1,013,191	11.9	5.9	11.8	4.3	2.4	②③ 1.04	2.12	8.79	0.70	14.63 - 9.81	11.7	5.7
12/31/99	695,806	② 41,425	1,003,780	12.0	6.0	11.6	4.1	2.0	② 0.98	2.10	8.48	0.70	16.50 - 9.06	13.0	5.5
12/31/98	717,705	② 36,133	990,738	12.6	5.0	10.5	3.6	1.9	②③ 0.86	1.99	8.17	0.70	19.13 - 11.19	17.6	4.6
12/31/97	587,212	② 45,284	937,583	15.7	7.7	13.3	4.8	1.3	② 1.07	1.91	8.08	0.70	23.38 - 15.38	18.1	3.6
12/31/96	577,194	② 60,399	715,310	18.6	10.5	18.2	8.4	2.2	② 1.41	2.16	7.78	0.70	19.63 - 15.63	12.5	4.0
12/31/95	636,392	② 65,828	673,107	18.5	10.3	20.9	9.8	1.9	② 1.49	2.23	7.26	0.70	23.63 - 15.38	13.1	3.6
12/31/94	487,503	②③ d118,251	650,810	4.6	...	...	...	1.3	②③ d2.67	d1.71	6.68	0.70	19.38 - 14.63	...	4.1
12/31/93	482,005	① 20,409	842,087	10.7	4.2	4.6	2.4	2.2	① 0.46	1.32	10.03	0.70	19.50 - 15.13	37.6	4.0

Statistics are as originally reported. ① Bef. cum effect acctg. chrg. of $4.2 mill. ② Incl. gain from property dispositions, etc., net of $2.0 mill., 2000; $4.1 mill., 1999; $1.0 mill., 1998; $3.2 mill., 1997; $977,000, 1996; $1.9 mill., 1995; $2.6 mill., 1994. ③ Incl. unusual items of $3.3 mill., 2000; $9.8 mill., 1998; $208.9 mill., 1994. ④ Incl. nonrecurr. charge of $1.9 mill., 2002; $60.9 mill., 2001.

OFFICERS:
G. H. Glatfelter, II, Chmn., C.E.O.
R. P. Newcomer, II, Pres., C.O.O., interim C.F.O.
J. R. Anke, Treas.

INVESTOR CONTACT: Pat Sweeney, Investor Relations, (717) 225-2700

PRINCIPAL OFFICE: 96 South George Street, Suite 500, York, PA 17401

TELEPHONE NUMBER: (717) 225-4711
FAX: (717) 225-6834
WEB: www.glatfelter.com

NO. OF EMPLOYEES: 2,400 (approx.)

SHAREHOLDERS: 2,584

ANNUAL MEETING: In Mar.

INCORPORATED: PA, Dec., 1905

INSTITUTIONAL HOLDINGS:
No. of Institutions: 118
Shares Held: 31,762,040
% Held: 72.8

INDUSTRY: Paper mills (SIC: 2621)

TRANSFER AGENT(S): American Stock Transfer & Trust Company, New York, NY

GLOBAL PAYMENTS INC.

EXCH.	SYM.	REC. PRICE	P/E RATIO	YLD.	MKT. CAP.	RANGE (52-WK.)	'02 Y/E PR.
NYSE	GPN	27.94 (2/28/03)	24.3	0.6%	$1.02 bill.	39.70 - 21.00	32.01

MEDIUM GRADE. THE RECENT IMPROVEMENT IN OPERATING MARGINS BODES WELL FOR THE COMPANY'S NEAR-TERM OUTLOOK.

TRADING VOLUME
Thousand Shares

*7 YEAR PRICE SCORE N/A   *12 MONTH PRICE SCORE 105.0

*NYSE COMPOSITE INDEX=100

INTERIM EARNINGS (Per Share):

Qtr.	Aug.	Nov.	Feb.	May
2000-01	...	...	...	0.02
2001-02	0.34	0.31	0.27	0.13
2002-03	0.39	0.36	...	...

INTERIM DIVIDENDS (Per Share):

Amt.	Decl.	Ex.	Rec.	Pay.
0.04Q	2/01/02	2/12/02	2/14/02	2/28/02
0.04Q	5/03/02	5/15/02	5/17/02	5/31/02
0.04Q	8/02/02	8/14/02	8/16/02	8/30/02
0.04Q	11/01/02	11/13/02	11/15/02	11/29/02
0.04Q	2/03/03	2/12/03	2/14/03	2/28/03

Indicated div.: $0.16

CAPITALIZATION (5/31/02):

	($000)	(%)
Capital Lease Obligations..	4,711	1.6
Deferred Income Tax	1,788	0.6
Common & Surplus	296,288	97.9
Total	302,787	100.0

BUSINESS:

Global Payments Inc. is an integrated provider of high volume electronic transaction processing and end-to-end information services and systems to merchants, independent sales organizations, multinational corporations, financial institutions, and government agencies located throughout the United States, Canada, the United Kingdom and Europe. GPN's merchant service offerings include credit and debt cards, business-to-business purchasing cards, gift cards, electronic benefits transfer cards, check guarantee, check verification and recovery, terminal management services and funds transfer. GPN was formed on 9/1/00 through the stock transfer of the companies that comprised National Data Corporation's (NDC) eCommerce business. On 1/31/01, NDC spun off to its stockholders all of the shares of common stock of GPN.

RECENT DEVELOPMENTS:

For the three months ended 11/30/02, net income rose 16.7% to $13.6 million compared with $11.6 million in the corresponding year-earlier period. Revenues advanced 12.0% to $129.5 million from $115.6 million the previous year. GPN attributed the higher revenues in part to increased levels of sales productivity in the Company's independent sales organizations and direct sales channels. Operating income climbed 14.3% to $23.8 million, or 18.3% of revenues, versus $20.8 million, or 18.0% of revenues, the year before.

PROSPECTS:

Healthy new merchant additions, coupled with ongoing margin improvement through the successful implementation of the National Bank of Canada back-end processing platform and the implementation of other cost control initiatives, solidify GPN's near-term outlook. Accordingly, GPN believes that it remains on track to achieve its fiscal 2003 full-year guidance of $495.0 million to $514.0 million in revenue and $1.35 to $1.41 in diluted earnings per share. Separately, on 12/5/02, GPN announced that Chittenden Corporation, a bank holding company with assets of $5.00 billion, has renewed its agreement for a line of payment services including front and back-end processing, authorization, capture and settlement.

ANNUAL FINANCIAL DATA:

FISCAL YEAR	TOT. REVS. ($mill.)	NET INC. ($mill.)	TOT. ASSETS ($mill.)	OPER. PROFIT %	NET PROFIT %	RET. ON EQUITY %	RET. ON ASSETS %	CURR. RATIO	EARN. PER SH.$	CASH FL. PER SH.$	TANG. BK. VAL.$	DIV. PER SH.$	PRICE RANGE	AVG. P/E RATIO	AVG. YIELD %
5/31/02	462.8	② 39.8	431.4	15.4	8.6	13.4	9.2	0.8	② 1.05	1.83	0.09	0.12	37.30 - 14.94	24.9	0.5
5/31/01	353.2	① 23.7	458.6	15.0	6.7	8.7	5.2	1.0	① 0.82	1.57	...	...	...	...	...
5/31/00	340.0	33.0	287.9	18.6	9.7	27.6	11.5	0.6	1.24	2.00	...	...	...	...	...
5/31/99	330.1	41.3	289.7	23.2	12.5	38.7	14.3	0.5	1.53	2.27	...	...	...	...	...
5/31/98	291.5	31.1	...	19.9	10.7	...	...	...	1.21	1.92	...	...	...	...	...

Statistics are as originally reported. ① Incl. restruct. & other chrgs. of $4.9 mill. ② Incl. restruct. & other chrgs. of $11.0 mill.; bef. acctg. chng. chrg. of $16.0 mill.

OFFICERS:
R. A. Yellowless, Chmn.
P. R. Garcia, Pres., C.E.O.
J. G. Kelly, C.F.O.
INVESTOR CONTACT: Jane M. Forbes, V.P., Planning & Inv. Rel., (404) 728-2719
PRINCIPAL OFFICE: Four Corporate Square, Atlanta, GA 30329-2009

TELEPHONE NUMBER: (404) 728-2719
FAX: (404) 728-3216
WEB: www.globalpaymentsinc.com
NO. OF EMPLOYEES: 1,800 (approx.)
SHAREHOLDERS: 2,981 (record)
ANNUAL MEETING: In Oct.
INCORPORATED: GA, Sept., 2000; reincorp., GA, Sept. 2000

INSTITUTIONAL HOLDINGS:
No. of Institutions: 138
Shares Held: 22,616,661
% Held: 61.3
INDUSTRY: Telegraph & other communications (SIC: 4822)
TRANSFER AGENT(S): SunTrust Bank, Atlanta, GA

GOLDEN WEST FINANCIAL CORPORATION

EXCH.	SYM.	REC. PRICE	P/E RATIO	YLD.	MKT. CAP.	RANGE (52-WK.)	'02 Y/E PR.	DIV. ACH.
NYSE	GDW	72.40 (2/28/03)	11.8	0.5%	$11.26 bill.	76.40 - 56.20	71.81	19 yrs.

HIGH GRADE. THE COMPANY'S EARNINGS EXPOSURE TO SWINGS IN INTEREST RATES SHOULD BE REDUCED BY ITS INCREASED PERCENTAGE OF VARIABLE RATE LOANS.

7 YEAR PRICE SCORE 176.7   **12 MONTH PRICE SCORE 119.4**
NYSE COMPOSITE INDEX=100

INTERIM EARNINGS (Per Share):

Qtr.	Mar.	June	Sept.	Dec.
1998	0.64	0.68	0.62	0.66
1999	0.70	0.72	0.72	0.73
2000	0.78	0.84	0.86	0.93
2001	1.10	1.30	1.28	1.44
2002	1.51	1.44	1.56	1.60

INTERIM DIVIDENDS (Per Share):

Amt.	Decl.	Ex.	Rec.	Pay.
0.072Q	1/24/02	2/13/02	2/15/02	3/11/02
0.072Q	4/30/02	5/13/02	5/15/02	6/10/02
0.072Q	7/25/02	8/13/02	8/15/02	9/10/02
0.085Q	10/25/02	11/13/02	11/15/02	12/10/02
0.085Q	1/31/03	2/12/03	2/15/03	3/10/03

Indicated div.: $0.34

CAPITALIZATION (12/31/01):

	($000)	(%)
Total Deposits	34,472,585	59.9
Long-Term Debt	18,835,235	32.7
Common & Surplus	4,284,190	7.4
Total	57,592,010	100.0

BUSINESS:

Golden West Financial Corporation, with assets of $68.41 billion as of 12/31/02, is the holding company of World Savings Bank, FSB, a federally chartered savings and lending institution. As of 12/31/02, GDW operated 469 savings and lending offices in 38 states under the World name. Also, the Company has two other subsidiaries, Atlas Advisers, Inc., and Atlas Securities, Inc., which provide services to Atlas Assets, Inc., a registered open-end management investment company sponsored by GDW. Atlas Advisers, Inc., is a registered investment adviser and the investment manager of Atlas Assets, Inc.'s portfolios. Atlas Securities, Inc., is a registered broker-dealer and the sole distributor of Atlas Fund shares.

RECENT DEVELOPMENTS:

For the year ended 12/31/02, net income was $958.3 million versus income of $818.8 million, before an accounting change charge of $6.0 million, the year before. Results for 2002 and 2001 included a pre-tax gain of $7.6 million and a pre-tax loss of $9.7 million, respectively, from changes in the fair value of derivatives. Also, results for 2002 and 2001 included gains on the sale of securities, mortgage-backed securities and loans of $45.1 million and $42.5 million, respectively. Net interest income advanced 18.3% to $1.93 billion. Provision for loan losses declined 4.9% to $21.2 million. Total non-interest income rose 4.3% to $247.0 million.

PROSPECTS:

The Company continues to grow its mortgage portfolio, with 92.0% of new loans comprised of adjustable rate mortgages in 2002. This is important, since these variable rate loans should help limit the exposure of the Company's earnings to swings in interest rates. Moreover, earnings should continue to benefit from a higher average primary spread, which is the difference between what the Company charges on loans and what it pays for savings and borrowings. During 2002, GDW's primary spread averaged 2.99% versus 2.70% in 2001. Separately, as of 12/31/02, the Company's ratio of non-performing assets to total assets decreased to 0.62% compared with 0.67% a year earlier.

ANNUAL FINANCIAL DATA:

FISCAL YEAR	NET INT. INC. ($mill.)	NON-INT. INC. ($mill.)	NET INC. ($mill.)	TOT. LOANS ($mill.)	TOT. ASSETS ($mill.)	TOT. DEP. ($mill.)	RET. ON EQUITY %	RET. ON ASSETS %	EQUITY/ ASSETS %	EARN. PER SH. $	TANG. BK. VAL. $	DIV. PER SH. $	PRICE RANGE	AVG. P/E RATIO
p12/31/02	1,930.3	247.0	④ 958.3		68,405.8		19.1	1.4		④ 6.12	27.55	0.30	73.75 — 56.20	10.6
12/31/01	1,631.3	236.7	③ 818.8	41,139.6	58,586.3	34,472.6	19.1	1.4	7.3	③ 5.11	25.90	0.26	70.90 — 45.02	11.3
12/31/00	1,151.2	160.8	545.8	33,860.3	55,704.0	30,047.9	14.8	1.0	6.6	3.41	23.28	0.22	70.50 — 26.88	14.3
12/31/99	1,003.5	143.3	480.0	28,090.1	42,142.2	27,714.9	15.0	1.1	7.6	2.87	19.80	0.19	38.41 — 28.91	11.7
12/31/98	967.3	137.6	② 447.1	25,991.6	38,468.7	26,219.1	14.3	1.2	8.1	② 2.58	18.32	0.17	38.16 — 23.27	11.9
12/31/97	890.5	81.3	354.1	33,553.5	39,590.3	24,109.7	13.1	0.9	6.8	2.04	15.76	0.15	32.33 — 19.62	12.7
12/31/96	831.0	74.9	① 369.9	30,397.2	37,730.6	22,099.9	15.7	1.0	6.2	① 2.11	13.66	0.13	22.91 — 16.33	9.3
12/31/95	722.8	42.5	234.5	28,435.1	35,118.2	20,847.9	10.3	0.7	6.5	1.33	12.12	0.12	19.16 — 11.58	11.5
12/31/94	721.4	37.5	230.4	27,330.5	31,683.7	19,219.4	11.5	0.7	6.3	1.24	10.60	0.10	15.33 — 11.42	10.8
12/31/93	732.8	62.0	273.9	24,171.7	28,829.3	17,422.5	13.3	0.9	7.2	1.43	10.06	0.09	16.79 — 12.37	10.2

Statistics are as originally reported. Adj. for stk. split: 3-for-1, 12/10/99. ① Bef. acct. chrg. of $205.2 mill. & incl. one-time SAIF chg. of $133.0 mill. & a tax benefit of $139.5 mill. ② Bef. extraord. loss of $12.5 mill. ③ Bef. acctg. chrg. of $6.0 mill. ④ Incl. a pre-tax gain fr. changes in the fair value of derivatives of $7.6 mill.

OFFICERS:
H. M. Sandler, Co-Chmn., Co-C.E.O.
M. O. Sandler, Co-Chmn., Co-C.E.O.
R. W. Kettell, Pres., C.F.O., Treas.
M. Roster, Exec. V.P., Sec., Gen. Couns.
INVESTOR CONTACT: William C. Nunan, Sr. Vice-Pres., (510) 446-3614
PRINCIPAL OFFICE: 1901 Harrison Street, Oakland, CA 94612

TELEPHONE NUMBER: (510) 446-3420
FAX: (510) 446-3072
WEB: www.gdw.com
NO. OF EMPLOYEES: 6,113 full-time; 1,025 part-time
SHAREHOLDERS: 1,241
ANNUAL MEETING: In May
INCORPORATED: DE, May, 1959

INSTITUTIONAL HOLDINGS:
No. of Institutions: 338
Shares Held: 104,547,881
% Held: 68.1

INDUSTRY: Federal savings institutions (SIC: 6035)

TRANSFER AGENT(S): Mellon Investor Services, LLC, San Francisco, CA

GOLDMAN SACHS GROUP, INC. (THE)

EXCH.	SYM.	REC. PRICE	P/E RATIO	YLD.	MKT. CAP.	RANGE (52-WK.)	'02 Y/E PR.
NYSE	GS	69.45 (2/28/03)	17.3	0.7%	$32.85 bill.	92.25 - 58.57	68.10

UPPER MEDIUM GRADE. THE COMPANY AND STARWOOD CAPITAL GROUP ACQUIRED NATIONAL GOLF PROPERTIES, INC. AND AMERICAN GOLF CORPORATION.

TRADING VOLUME
Thousand Shares

1989 1990 1991 1992 1993 1994 1995 1996 1997 1998 1999 2000 2001 2002 2003

*7 YEAR PRICE SCORE N/A   ***12 MONTH PRICE SCORE 101.6**

*NYSE COMPOSITE INDEX=100

INTERIM EARNINGS (Per Share):

Qtr.	Feb.	May	Aug.	Nov.
1999	Nil	0.71	1.32	1.48
2000	1.76	1.48	1.62	1.16
2001	1.40	1.06	0.87	0.93
2002	0.98	1.06	1.00	0.98

INTERIM DIVIDENDS (Per Share):

Amt.	Decl.	Ex.	Rec.	Pay.
0.12Q	3/19/02	4/26/02	4/30/02	5/30/02
0.12Q	6/20/02	7/26/02	7/30/02	8/29/02
0.12Q	9/24/02	10/24/02	10/28/02	11/25/02
0.12Q	12/19/02	1/24/03	1/28/03	2/27/03
0.12Q	3/20/03	4/25/03	4/29/03	5/29/03

Indicated div.: $0.48

CAPITALIZATION (11/29/02):

	($000)	(%)
Long-Term Debt	38,711,000	67.1
Common & Surplus	19,003,000	32.9
Total	57,714,000	100.0

BUSINESS:

The Goldman Sachs Group, Inc. is a global investment banking and securities firm that provides a wide range of services worldwide to a substantial and diversified client base that includes corporations, financial institutions, governments and high-net-worth individuals. The Company's activities are divided into two business segments comprised of Global Capital Markets (52.4% of net sales as of 11/29/02), which includes investment banking and trading and principal investments, and Asset Management and Securities Services (47.6%). In November 2000, the Company completed the acquisition of Spear, Leeds & Kellogg L.P., a New York Stock Exchange specialist firm.

RECENT DEVELOPMENTS:

For the year ended 11/29/02, net income decreased 8.5% to $2.11 billion from $2.31 billion the year before. Earnings for 2002 and 2001 included pre-tax expenses of $293.0 million and $464.0 million, respectively, related to the amortization of employee initial public offering and acquisition awards. Total revenues declined 26.6% to $22.85 billion, reflecting continued weakness in capital spending, lower investor confidence, and significant declines in global equity prices and corporate activity. Interest income dropped 32.2% to $11.27 billion, while revenues from asset management and securities services grew 7.9% to $4.95 billion. Revenues from trading and principal investments fell 35.0% to $4.06 billion, and revenues from investment banking declined 30.1% to $2.57 million.

PROSPECTS:

On 2/6/03, an investor group comprised of GS Capital Partners 2000, Goldman Sachs Whitehall Street Real Estate Fund 2001 and Starwood Capital Group, announced the acquisition of National Golf Properties, Inc. and American Golf Corporation in a transaction valued at about $1.00 billion, including the assumption of debt. National Golf's portfolio consists of 118 golf courses at 105 facilities in 22 states, as well as seven golf courses in the U.K. American Golf is a premier operator of golf facilities worldwide. Going forward, general business activity is likely to remain subdued due to weakness in the capital markets combined with industry-wide declines in the volume of equity underwritings, initial public offerings, and mergers and acquisitions.

ANNUAL FINANCIAL DATA:

FISCAL YEAR	TOT. REVS. ($mill.)	NET INC. ($mill.)	TOT. ASSETS ($mill.)	OPER. PROFIT %	NET PROFIT %	RET. ON EQUITY %	RET. ON ASSETS %	CURR. RATIO	EARN. PER SH. $	CASH FL. PER SH. $	TANG. BK. VAL. $	DIV. PER SH. $	PRICE RANGE	AVG. P/E RATIO	AVG. YIELD %
11/29/02	22,854.0	2,114.0	355,574.0	14.2	9.3	11.1	0.6	0.7	4.03	5.44	40.18	0.48	97.25 - 58.57	19.3	0.6
11/30/01	31,138.0	③ 2,310.0	312,218.0	11.9	7.4	12.7	0.7	0.7	③ 4.26	5.87	38.28	0.48	120.00 - 63.27	21.5	0.5
11/24/00	33,000.0	②③ 3,067.0	289,760.0	15.2	9.3	18.6	1.1	0.8	②③ 6.00	6.95	34.19	0.48	133.63 - 65.50	16.6	0.5
11/26/99	25,363.0	①③ 2,708.0	250,491.0	7.9	10.7	26.7	1.1	0.7	①③ 5.57	6.27	22.98	0.24	94.81 - 55.19	13.5	0.3
11/27/98	22,478.0	2,428.0	217,380.0	13.0	10.8	38.0	1.1	0.8	...	...	12.57	...	...	...	...
11/28/97	20,433.0	2,746.0	178,401.0	14.8	13.4	42.0	1.5	0.7	...	...	...	...	...	...	...
11/29/96	17,289.0	2,399.0	...	15.1	13.9	...	...	...	...	...	...	...	...	...	...

Statistics are as originally reported. ① Incl. a non-recurr. exp. of $2.26 billion related to the Co.'s conversion to a public corporation. ② Incl. exps. of $290.0 mill. rel. to nonrecurr. employee initial public offering & acq. awards. ③ Incl. pre-tax exps. rel. to the amort. of employee initial public offering & acq. awards of $293.0 mill., 2002; $464.0 mill., 2001; $428.0 mill., 2000; $268.0 mill., 1999.

OFFICERS:
H. M. Paulson Jr., Chmn., C.E.O.
L. C. Blankfein, Vice-Chmn.
R. S. Kaplan, Vice-Chmn.
INVESTOR CONTACT: John Andrews, Investor Relations, (212) 357-2674
PRINCIPAL OFFICE: 85 Broad Street, New York, NY 10004

TELEPHONE NUMBER: (212) 902-1000
FAX: (212) 902-3000
WEB: www.gs.com
NO. OF EMPLOYEES: 19,739 (avg.)
SHAREHOLDERS: 5,530
ANNUAL MEETING: In Apr.
INCORPORATED: DE, 1989

INSTITUTIONAL HOLDINGS:
No. of Institutions: 526
Shares Held: 299,519,735
% Held: 62.7
INDUSTRY: Security brokers and dealers (SIC: 6211)
TRANSFER AGENT(S): Mellon Investor Services, Ridgefield, NJ

GOODRICH CORPORATION

EXCH.	SYM.	REC. PRICE	P/E RATIO	YLD.	MKT. CAP.	RANGE (52-WK.)	'02 Y/E PR.
NYSE	GR	15.37 (2/28/03)	9.7	5.2	$1.80 bill.	34.45 - 14.17	18.32

MEDIUM GRADE. THE COMPANY AGREED TO SELL ITS AVIONICS BUSINESS TO L-3 COMMUNICATIONS FOR $188.0 MILLION.

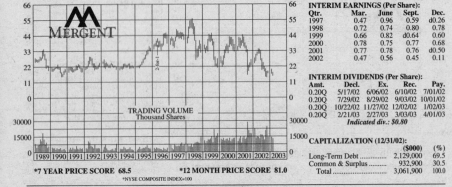

*7 YEAR PRICE SCORE 68.5   ***12 MONTH PRICE SCORE 81.0**

*NYSE COMPOSITE INDEX=100

INTERIM EARNINGS (Per Share):

Qtr.	Mar.	June	Sept.	Dec.
1997	0.47	0.96	0.59	d0.26
1998	0.72	0.74	0.80	0.78
1999	0.66	0.82	d0.64	0.60
2000	0.78	0.75	0.77	0.68
2001	0.77	0.78	0.76	d0.50
2002	0.47	0.56	0.45	0.11

INTERIM DIVIDENDS (Per Share):

Amt.	Decl.	Ex.	Rec.	Pay.
0.20Q	5/17/02	6/06/02	6/10/02	7/01/02
0.20Q	7/29/02	8/29/02	9/03/02	10/01/02
0.20Q	10/22/02	11/27/02	12/02/02	1/02/03
0.20Q	2/21/03	2/27/03	3/03/03	4/01/03

Indicated div.: $0.80

CAPITALIZATION (12/31/02):

	($000)	(%)
Long-Term Debt	2,129,000	69.5
Common & Surplus	932,900	30.5
Total	3,061,900	100.0

BUSINESS:

Goodrich Corporation (formerly The B.F. Goodrich Company) provides aircraft systems and services and manufactures a range of specialty chemicals. The Aerospace segment includes landing systems, sensors and integrated systems, safety systems, and maintenance, repair and overhauls business groups. The Engineered Industrial Products segment manufactures industrial seals, gaskets, packing products, self-lubricating bearings, diesel, gas and dual-fuel engines, air compressors, spray nozzles and vacuum pumps. Revenues for 2002 were derived: aerostructures and aviation technical services, 30.1%; landing systems, 26.5%; engine and safety systems, 16.3%; electronic systems, 20.3%; and aeronautical systems, 6.8%. GR completed the sale of its Performance Materials segment on 2/28/01.

RECENT DEVELOPMENTS:

For the year ended 12/31/02, income from continuing operations declined 6.2% to $165.9 million, before an accounting change charge of $36.1 million, compared with $176.9 million in 2001. Results for 2002 included an after-tax special charge of $78.0 million for certain acquisition-related and consolidation costs, gains or losses from the sale of businesses, asset impairment charges and other restructuring costs. Results for 2002 and 2001 excluded a loss of $11.9 million and a gain of $112.3 million, respectively, from discontinued operations. Sales were $3.91 billion, down 6.6% from $4.18 billion in the prior year. Operating income decreased 5.4% to $420.6 million.

PROSPECTS:

On 1/29/03, the Company entered into a definitive agreement to sell its avionics business to L-3 Communications for $188.0 million. The sale is expected to be completed late in the first quarter or early in the second quarter of 2003. The after-tax proceeds from the sale are expected to be about $134.0 million, and the avionics segment will be reported as a discontinued operation in the first quarter of 2003. Separately, effective 1/1/03, GR reorganized into three business segments: airframe systems, engine systems, and electronic systems. Financial data will be reported for these segments beginning with the first quarter of 2003.

ANNUAL FINANCIAL DATA:

FISCAL YEAR	TOT. REVS. ($mill.)	NET INC. ($mill.)	TOT. ASSETS ($mill.)	OPER. PROFIT %	NET PROFIT %	RET. ON EQUITY %	RET. ON ASSETS %	CURR. RATIO	EARN. PER SH.$	CASH FL.PER SH.$	TANG. BK. VAL.$	DIV. PER SH.$	PRICE RANGE	AVG. P/E RATIO	AVG. YIELD %
12/31/02	3,910.2	⑧ 165.9	5,989.6	9.2	4.2	17.8	2.8	1.3	⑧ 1.57	3.31	...	0.95	34.45 - 14.17	15.5	3.9
12/31/01	4,184.5	⑦ 176.9	4,638.1	9.2	4.2	13.0	3.8	1.7	⑦ 1.65	3.28	4.67	0.82	44.50 - 15.91	18.3	2.7
12/31/00	4,363.8	⑤⑥ 286.3	5,717.5	13.6	6.6	23.3	5.0	1.4	⑤⑥ 2.68	4.39	3.48	1.10	43.13 - 21.56	12.1	3.4
12/31/99	5,537.5	⑥ 169.6	5,455.6	8.5	3.1	13.1	3.1	1.4	⑥ 1.53	3.62	1.41	1.10	45.69 - 21.00	21.8	3.3
12/31/98	3,950.8	⑤ 228.1	4,192.6	12.1	5.8	14.3	5.4	1.6	⑤ 3.04	5.25	9.63	1.10	56.00 - 26.50	13.6	2.7
12/31/97	3,373.0	①④ 113.2	3,493.9	7.4	3.4	8.0	3.2	1.5	①④ 1.53	3.38	11.35	1.10	48.25 - 35.13	27.2	2.6
12/31/96	2,238.8	①④ 106.2	2,663.1	10.7	4.7	10.1	4.0	1.4	①④ 1.97	4.56	8.52	1.10	45.88 - 33.38	20.1	2.8
12/31/95	2,408.6	④ 118.0	2,489.6	10.0	4.9	13.4	4.5	1.6	④ 2.15	4.32	5.74	1.10	36.31 - 20.81	13.3	3.9
12/31/94	2,199.2	③ 65.7	2,468.9	8.2	3.0	7.1	2.7	1.4	③ 1.12	3.30	...	0.82	24.19 - 19.50	19.5	3.8
12/31/93	1,818.3	② 15.3	2,905.8	4.5	0.8	1.7	0.5	1.7	② 0.14	2.26	3.57	1.10	27.13 - 19.75	167.3	4.7

Statistics are as originally reported. Adj. for 2-for-1 split, 4/96. ① Excl. cr$84.3 mill. disc. ops., 1997; cr$45.5 mill. & $19.3 mill. net extra. loss, 1996; $39.6 mill., 2000. ② Bef. $113.0 mill. gain fr. disc. ops. ③ Bef. $10.0 mill. non-recur. tax benefit rel. to divest. ④ Incl. $24.4 mill. net gain, 1997; $2.1 mill., 1996; $12.8 mill., 1995. ⑤ Incl. $6.5 mill. net restr. chg. & excl. $81.6 mill. after-tax loss fr. disc. ops. ⑥ Excl. $29.5 mill. net merg. & consol. chgs., 2000; $192.1 mill., 1999 & $1.7 mill. after-tax impair. chg., 2000. ⑦ Incl. $129.4 mill. merg. & consol. chgs. and excl. $112.3 mill. gain fr. disc. ops. ⑧ Incl. $78.0 mill. after-tax spl. chg. and excl. $11.9 mill. loss fr. disc. ops. & $36.1 mill. acctg. chg.

OFFICERS:
D. L. Burner, Chmn.
M. O. Larsen, Pres., C.E.O.
U. Schmidt, Exec. V.P., C.F.O.
INVESTOR CONTACT: Paul S. Gifford, V.P. of Investor Relations, (704) 423-5517
PRINCIPAL OFFICE: 4 Coliseum Centre, 2730 W. Tyvola Road, Charlotte, NC 28217

TELEPHONE NUMBER: (704) 423-7000
FAX: (704) 423-7075
WEB: www.bfgoodrich.com
NO. OF EMPLOYEES: 19,200 (approx.)
SHAREHOLDERS: 11,073
ANNUAL MEETING: In Apr.
INCORPORATED: OH, May, 1880; reincorp., NY, May, 1912

GOODYEAR TIRE & RUBBER COMPANY

EXCH.	SYM.	REC. PRICE	P/E RATIO	YLD.	MKT. CAP.	RANGE (52-WK.)	'02 Y/E PR.
NYSE	GT	4.00 (2/28/03)	...	...	$0.65 bill.	28.85 - 3.35	6.81

SPECULATIVE GRADE. THE COMPANY IS EXPLORING THE POSSIBLE SALE OF ITS CHEMICAL BUSINESS.

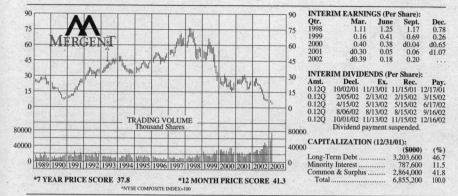

INTERIM EARNINGS (Per Share):

Qtr.	Mar.	June	Sept.	Dec.
1998	1.11	1.25	1.17	0.78
1999	0.16	0.41	0.69	0.26
2000	0.40	0.38	d0.04	d0.65
2001	d0.30	0.05	0.06	d1.07
2002	d0.39	0.18	0.20	...

INTERIM DIVIDENDS (Per Share):

Amt.	Decl.	Ex.	Rec.	Pay.
0.12Q	10/02/01	11/13/01	11/15/01	12/17/01
0.12Q	2/05/02	2/13/02	2/15/02	3/15/02
0.12Q	4/15/02	5/13/02	5/15/02	6/17/02
0.12Q	8/06/02	8/13/02	8/15/02	9/16/02
0.12Q	10/01/02	11/13/02	11/15/02	12/16/02
Dividend payment suspended.				

TRADING VOLUME
Thousand Shares

*7 YEAR PRICE SCORE 37.8   *12 MONTH PRICE SCORE 41.3
*NYSE COMPOSITE INDEX=100

CAPITALIZATION (12/31/01):

	($000)	(%)
Long-Term Debt	3,203,600	46.7
Minority Interest	787,600	11.5
Common & Surplus	2,864,000	41.8
Total	6,855,200	100.0

BUSINESS:

Goodyear Tire & Rubber Company's principal business is the development, manufacture, distribution and sale of tires throughout the world. In addition, GT produces and sells a broad spectrum of rubber, chemical and plastic products for the transportation industry and various industrial and consumer markets. GT also provides automotive repair and other services. As of 3/20/03, GT operated more than 90 facilities in 28 countries. In 2001, revenues were derived: Tire Products, 85.2%; Engineered Products, 7.7% and Chemical Products, 7.1%. On 6/14/99, GT formed a strategic global alliance with Sumitomo Rubber Industries Ltd. for tire manufacturing and sales.

RECENT DEVELOPMENTS:

For the third quarter ended 9/30/02, the Company reported net income of $33.7 million compared with $9.3 million in the corresponding prior-year quarter. Results for 2002 included an after-tax gain from the sale of assets of $8.2 million and an after-tax rationalization charge of $8.9 million. Net sales decreased 4.0% to $3.53 billion from $3.68 billion a year earlier. Sales from tire operations declined 3.8% to $3.15 billion, primarily due to lower tire volume in the North American replacement market. Chemical products sales fell 9.0% to $237.5 million, primarily due to the sale of the specialty chemical business. Engineered products sales increased 2.7% to $274.5 million due to strong for military and custom products. Costs of goods sold were down 4.7% to $2.85 billion from $2.99 billion in 2001.

PROSPECTS:

The Company will release its 2002 financial statements following the completion of the restructuring, refinancing and extension of its loan agreement, which are under discussion with GT's bank lenders. Separately, the Company announced that it will record a fourth quarter non-cash charge of $1.10 billion to establish a valuation allowance against its net U.S. deferred tax assets. In addition to this charge, the Company's shareholders' equity at 12/31/02 will also be reduced by $1.30 billion to reflect an increase in unfunded pension benefit obligations. Meanwhile, on 3/19/02, GT announced that is exploring the possible sale of its chemical business.

ANNUAL FINANCIAL DATA:

FISCAL YEAR	TOT. REVS. ($mill.)	NET INC. ($mill.)	TOT. ASSETS ($mill.)	OPER. PROFIT %	NET PROFIT %	RET. ON EQUITY %	RET. ON ASSETS %	CURR. RATIO	EARN. PER SH.$	CASH FL. PER SH.$	TANG. BK. VAL.$	DIV. PER SH.$	PRICE RANGE	AVG. P/E RATIO	AVG. YIELD %
12/31/01	14,147.2	⑤ d203.6	13,512.9	0.5	...	...	...	1.6	⑤ d1.27	2.71	14.06	1.02	32.10 — 17.37	...	4.1
12/31/00	14,417.1	① 40.3	13,568.0	2.9	0.3	1.2	0.3	1.3	① 0.25	4.22	18.49	1.20	31.63 — 15.60	94.4	5.1
12/31/99	12,880.6	① 241.1	13,102.6	2.6	1.9	6.7	1.8	1.3	① 1.52	5.18	19.83	1.20	66.75 — 25.50	30.3	2.6
12/31/98	12,626.3	①④ 717.0	10,589.3	9.7	5.7	19.1	6.8	1.4	①④ 4.53	7.61	24.02	1.20	76.75 — 45.88	13.5	2.0
12/31/97	13,155.1	① 558.7	9,917.4	7.3	4.2	16.5	5.6	1.3	① 3.53	6.51	21.63	1.14	71.25 — 49.25	17.1	1.9
12/31/96	13,112.8	① 101.7	9,671.8	2.5	0.8	3.1	1.1	1.5	① 0.66	3.63	21.01	1.03	53.00 — 41.50	71.6	2.2
12/31/95	13,165.9	611.0	9,789.6	8.6	4.6	18.6	6.2	1.4	4.02	6.88	21.38	0.95	45.38 — 33.00	9.7	2.4
12/31/94	12,288.2	567.0	9,123.3	8.6	4.6	20.2	6.2	1.3	3.75	6.46	18.51	0.75	49.25 — 31.63	10.8	1.9
12/31/93	11,643.4	③ 488.7	8,436.1	8.7	4.2	21.2	5.8	1.3	③ 3.33	5.99	15.29	0.57	47.25 — 32.56	12.0	1.4
12/31/92	11,784.9	② 367.3	8,563.7	6.9	3.1	19.0	4.3	1.3	② 2.57	5.69	13.36	0.28	38.06 — 26.00	12.5	0.9

Statistics are as originally reported. Adj. for stk. split: 2-for-1, 5/93 ① Incl. non-recurr. chrg. $158.2 mill., 2000; $240.1 mill., 1999; $26.8 mill., 1998; $176.5 mill.; 1997; $572.2 mill., 1996. ② Bef. acctg. change chrg. $1.03 bill. ③ Bef. extraord. chrg. $14.6 mill. fr early exting. debt & bef. acctg. change chrg. $86.3 mill ④ Bef. disc. opers. loss of $34.7 mill. ⑤ Incl. net after-tax non-recurr. chrg. of $170.1 mill.

OFFICERS:
S. G. Gibara, Chmn.
R. J. Keegan, Pres., C.E.O.
R. W. Tieken, Exec. V.P., C.F.O.

INVESTOR CONTACT: Barb Gould, Investor Relations, (330) 796-8576

PRINCIPAL OFFICE: 1144 East Market Street, Akron, OH 44316-0001

TELEPHONE NUMBER: (330) 796-2121
FAX: (330) 796-2222
WEB: www.goodyear.com
NO. OF EMPLOYEES: 92,000 (approx.)
SHAREHOLDERS: 29,836 (record); 30,940 (approx. beneficial)
ANNUAL MEETING: In April
INCORPORATED: OH, Aug., 1898

INSTITUTIONAL HOLDINGS:
No. of Institutions: 238
Shares Held: 99,648,885
% Held: 56.8

INDUSTRY: Tires and inner tubes (SIC: 3011)

TRANSFER AGENT(S): EquiServe Trust Company, N.A., Providence, RI

GRACO INC.

EXCH.	SYM.	REC. PRICE	P/E RATIO	YLD.	MKT. CAP.	RANGE (52-WK.)	'02 Y/E PR.
NYSE	GGG	26.80 (2/28/03)	17.2	1.2%	$1.25 bill.	30.57 - 22.13	28.65

MEDIUM GRADE. THE COMPANY IS CAUTIOUSLY OPTIMISTIC ABOUT PROSPECTS FOR SALES AND EARNINGS GROWTH IN 2003.

*7 YEAR PRICE SCORE 183.0 ***12 MONTH PRICE SCORE 107.4**
*NYSE COMPOSITE INDEX=100

INTERIM EARNINGS (Per Share):

Qtr.	Mar.	June	Sept.	Dec.
1997	0.10	0.18	0.22	0.26
1998	0.15	0.21	0.23	0.31
1999	0.24	0.38	0.32	0.32
2000	0.32	0.39	0.39	0.41
2001	0.28	0.39	0.35	0.32
2002	0.33	0.44	0.42	0.37

INTERIM DIVIDENDS (Per Share):

Amt.	Decl.	Ex.	Rec.	Pay.
3-for-2	5/07/02	6/07/02	5/21/02	6/06/02
0.073Q	6/13/02	7/18/02	7/22/02	8/07/02
0.073Q	9/27/02	10/17/02	10/21/02	11/06/02
0.083Q	12/06/02	1/15/03	1/20/03	2/05/03
0.083Q	2/21/03	4/16/03	4/21/03	5/07/03

Indicated div.: $0.33

CAPITALIZATION (12/28/01):

	($000)	(%)
Deferred Income Tax	1,761	1.0
Common & Surplus	173,740	99.0
Total	175,501	100.0

BUSINESS:

Graco Inc. supplies equipment for the management of fluids in both industrial and commercial settings. GGG designs, manufactures and markets systems and equipment to move, measure, control, dispense and apply fluid materials. GGG manufactures a wide array of specialized pumps, applicators, regulators, valves, meters, atomizing devices, replacement parts, and accessories. These products are used in the movement, measurement, control, dispensing and application of many fluids and semi-solids. The Company offers an extensive line of portable equipment that is used in construction and maintenance businesses for the application of paint and other materials. Revenues for 2002 were derived: contractor, 48.9%; industrial/automotive, 41.9%; and lubrication, 9.2%.

RECENT DEVELOPMENTS:

For the twelve months ended 12/27/02, net earnings rose 15.9% to $75.6 million compared with $65.3 million in 2001. The improvement in earnings was primarily due to the introduction of new products and a strong housing market. Net sales were $487.0 million, up 3.0% from $472.8 million in the prior year. Net sales in the industrial/automotive segment grew 2.4% to $204.2 million from $199.5 million, while net sales in the contractor segment climbed 5.7% to $238.0 million from $225.1 million. Meanwhile, sales in the lubrication segment declined 7.0% to $44.8 million from $48.2 million in the previous year. Gross profit climbed 6.6% to $250.2 million from $234.8 million a year earlier due to price increases, exchange rates, and product and manufacturing cost improvements. Operating earnings increased 12.6% to $112.8 million compared with $100.2 million the year before.

PROSPECTS:

Going forward, the Company will continue to make significant investments in its growth strategies, which include introducing new products, expanding distribution, entering new markets and other initiatives that support long-term growth. The Company is cautiously optimistic about prospects for sales and earnings growth since 2003 is projected to be another year of slow growth for many industrialized countries. However, new product introductions should help GGG maintain its position in product technology and favorable exchange rates should assist revenue growth.

ANNUAL FINANCIAL DATA:

FISCAL YEAR	TOT. REVS. ($mill.)	NET INC. ($mill.)	TOT. ASSETS ($mill.)	OPER. PROFIT %	NET PROFIT %	RET. ON EQUITY %	RET. ON ASSETS %	CURR. RATIO	EARN. PER SH.$	CASH FL. PER SH.$	TANG. BK. VAL.$	DIV. PER SH.$	PRICE RANGE	AVG. P/E RATIO	AVG. YIELD %
p12/27/02	487.0	75.6							1.57			0.37	30.57 - 22.13	16.8	1.4
12/28/01	472.8	65.3	276.1	21.2	13.8	37.6	23.6	2.1	1.38	1.77	3.42	0.27	26.56 - 15.50	15.2	1.3
12/29/00	494.4	70.1	238.0	22.5	14.2	63.2	29.5	1.8	1.51	1.85	3.65	0.25	19.00 - 12.64	10.5	1.6
12/31/99	442.5	59.3	236.0	21.1	13.4	94.3	25.1	1.8	1.26	1.58	1.37	0.20	16.09 - 8.83	9.9	1.6
12/25/98	432.2	②47.3	233.7	17.8	10.9	507.5	20.2	1.6	②0.89	1.15	0.21	0.20	16.22 - 8.83	14.0	1.6
12/26/97	413.9	44.7	264.5	15.8	10.8	28.4	16.9	2.3	0.76	0.99	2.74	0.17	11.76 - 6.96	12.3	1.8
12/27/96	391.8	36.2	247.8	13.5	9.2	28.7	14.6	1.8	0.61	0.83	2.19	0.14	7.70 - 5.26	10.6	2.2
12/29/95	386.3	27.7	217.8	11.7	7.2	26.8	12.7	1.8	0.47	0.66	1.78	0.13	7.56 - 3.90	12.2	2.2
12/30/94	360.0	15.3	228.4	7.3	4.3	18.7	6.7	1.6	0.17	0.29	1.40	①0.64	4.86 - 3.31	23.5	15.8
12/31/93	322.6	9.5	216.4	5.2	2.9	12.7	4.4	1.5	0.11	0.22	1.26	0.10	4.79 - 3.05	36.2	2.6

Statistics are as originally reported. Adj for 3-for-2 split, 6/02, 2/01, 2/98, 2/96, & 2/94. ① Incl. $1.20/sh. special div. ② Incl. $1.7 mill. restr. & non-recur. chgs.

OFFICERS:
L. R. Mitau, Chmn.
D. A. Roberts, Pres., C.E.O.
M. W. Sheahan, V.P., Treas.
INVESTOR CONTACT: Investor Relations, (612) 623-6659
PRINCIPAL OFFICE: 88 - 11th Avenue Northeast, Minneapolis, MN 55413

TELEPHONE NUMBER: (612) 623-6000
FAX: (612) 623-6777
WEB: www.graco.com
NO. OF EMPLOYEES: 1,850 (approx.)
SHAREHOLDERS: 2,600 (record); 5,600 (beneficial)
ANNUAL MEETING: In May
INCORPORATED: MN, 1926

INSTITUTIONAL HOLDINGS:
No. of Institutions: 145
Shares Held: 38,509,034
% Held: 80.9
INDUSTRY: Pumps and pumping equipment (SIC: 3561)
TRANSFER AGENT(S): Wells Fargo Shareowner Services, South St. Paul, MN

GRAINGER (W.W.), INC.

EXCH.	SYM.	REC. PRICE	P/E RATIO	YLD.	MKT. CAP.	RANGE (52-WK.)	'02 Y/E PR.	DIV. ACH.
NYSE	GWW	46.03 (2/28/03)	18.4	1.6%	$4.30 bill.	59.29 - 39.20	51.55	31 yrs.

INVESTMENT GRADE. THE COMPANY IS TARGETING 2003 EARNINGS OF $2.50 TO $2.80 PER SHARE, DRIVEN BY INCREASED SALES AND IMPROVED MARGINS.

MERGENT

TRADING VOLUME
Thousand Shares

1989 1990 1991 1992 1993 1994 1995 1996 1997 1998 1999 2000 2001 2002 2003

*7 YEAR PRICE SCORE 122.2   ***12 MONTH PRICE SCORE 104.8**
*NYSE COMPOSITE INDEX=100

INTERIM EARNINGS (Per Share):

Qtr.	Mar.	June	Sept.	Dec.
1996	0.49	0.48	0.51	0.54
1997	0.52	0.57	0.56	0.63
1998	0.58	0.60	0.57	0.69
1999	0.60	0.53	0.49	0.30
2000	0.44	0.59	0.51	0.51
2001	0.45	0.15	0.59	0.65
2002	0.61	0.57	0.64	0.68

INTERIM DIVIDENDS (Per Share):

Amt.	Decl.	Ex.	Rec.	Pay.
0.175Q	1/30/02	2/07/02	2/11/02	3/01/02
0.18Q	4/24/02	5/02/02	5/06/02	6/01/02
0.18Q	7/31/02	8/08/02	8/12/02	9/01/02
0.18Q	10/30/02	11/06/02	11/11/02	12/01/02
0.18Q	1/29/03	2/06/03	2/10/03	3/01/03

Indicated div.: $0.72

CAPITALIZATION (12/31/01):

	($000)	(%)
Long-Term Debt	118,219	6.9
Deferred Income Tax	1,239	0.1
Minority Interest	139	0.0
Common & Surplus	1,603,189	93.1
Total	1,722,786	100.0

BUSINESS:

W.W. Grainger, Inc. is a nationwide distributor of equipment, components, and supplies to the commercial, industrial, contractor and institutional markets. Products include motors, fans, blowers, pumps, compressors, air and power tools, heating and air conditioning equipment, as well as other items offered in its Grainger Industrial Supply Catalog and through its Grainger.com Web site. The Company serves its customers through its network of approximately 600 branches in the United States, Canada and Mexico. The Company also operates 16 distribution facilities throughout the U.S.

RECENT DEVELOPMENTS:

For the year ended 12/31/02, earnings totaled $235.5 million, before a $23.9 million accounting change charge, versus net earnings of $174.5 million the year before. Results included a non-recurring net pre-tax gain of $9.2 million in 2002 and a non-recurring net pre-tax charge of $59.1 million in 2001. Net sales totaled $4.64 billion, down 2.3% compared with $4.75 billion a year earlier. Gross profit was $1.60 billion, or 34.4% of net sales, versus $1.59 billion, or 33.4% of net sales, in the prior year. Operating earnings climbed 16.1% to $393.2 million from $338.6 million the previous year.

PROSPECTS:

The Company is targeting full-year 2003 sales growth of between 4.0% and 9.0%, and earnings per share of $2.50 to $2.80, driven by increased sales and improved margins. Meanwhile, GWW is implementing initiatives focused on reconfiguring its logistics network in an effort to expand capacity, improve productivity and locate more inventory closer to its customers. These initiatives are expected to generate operating earnings of about $10.0 million in 2004, and up to $20.0 million annually going forward.

ANNUAL FINANCIAL DATA:

FISCAL YEAR	TOT. REVS. ($mill.)	NET INC. ($mill.)	TOT. ASSETS ($mill.)	OPER. PROFIT %	NET PROFIT %	RET. ON EQUITY %	RET. ON ASSETS %	CURR. RATIO	EARN. PER SH.$	CASH FL. PER SH.$	TANG. BK. VAL.$	DIV. PER SH.$	PRICE RANGE	AVG. P/E RATIO	AVG. YIELD %
p12/31/02	4,643.9	④ 235.5							④ 2.50			0.72	59.40 – 39.20	19.7	1.5
12/31/01	4,754.3	③ 174.5	2,331.2	7.1	3.7	10.9	7.5	2.5	③ 1.84	2.93	15.09	0.70	48.99 – 29.51	21.3	1.8
12/31/00	4,977.0	② 192.9	2,459.6	6.7	3.9	12.5	7.8	2.0	② 2.05	3.18	14.08	0.67	56.88 – 24.31	19.8	1.7
12/31/99	4,533.9	180.7	2,564.8	7.0	4.0	12.2	7.0	1.7	1.92	2.96	13.47	0.63	58.13 – 36.88	24.7	1.3
12/31/98	4,341.3	238.5	2,103.9	9.4	5.5	18.7	11.3	1.8	2.44	3.24	11.39	0.58	54.72 – 36.44	18.7	1.3
12/31/97	4,136.6	231.8	1,997.8	9.5	5.6	17.9	11.6	2.2	2.27	3.05	11.13	0.53	49.88 – 35.25	18.7	1.2
12/31/96	3,537.2	208.5	2,119.0	9.8	5.9	14.3	9.8	2.1	2.02	2.74	11.65	0.49	40.75 – 31.31	17.8	1.4
12/31/95	3,276.9	186.7	1,669.2	9.7	5.7	15.8	11.2	2.4	1.82	2.51	10.87	0.45	33.81 – 27.75	16.9	1.4
12/31/94	3,023.1	② 127.9	1,534.8	7.7	4.2	12.4	8.3	2.1	② 1.25	1.88	9.33	0.39	34.56 – 25.75	24.1	1.3
12/31/93	2,628.4	① 149.3	1,376.7	9.6	5.7	15.8	10.8	2.2	① 1.44	1.98	9.29	0.35	33.38 – 25.81	20.5	1.2

Statistics are as originally reported. Adj. for 2-for-1 stk. split, 6/98. ① Bef. $820,000 chg. for acctg. adj. ② Incl. $29.8 mil ($0.19/sh) one-time gain from the sale of an investment security, 2000; $49.8 mil ($0.97/sh) non-recur. chg., 1994. ③ Incl. $39.1 mil restr. chg., a $20.1 mil loss fr. liquidation of equity in unconsol. subsid. and a $138,000 gain on invest. sale. ④ Bef. $23.9 mil ($0.26/sh) acctg. chrg., $1.9 mil restr. cr. & $7.3 mil gain on invest, sale.

OFFICERS:
R. L. Keyser, Chmn., C.E.O.
W. M. Clark, Pres., C.O.O.
P. O. Loux, Sr. V.P., C.F.O.

INVESTOR CONTACT: Robb Kristopher, Mgr., Inv. Rel., (847) 535-0879

PRINCIPAL OFFICE: 100 Grainger Parkway, Lake Forest, IL 60045-5201

TELEPHONE NUMBER: (847) 535-1000
FAX: (847) 535-0878
WEB: www.grainger.com

NO. OF EMPLOYEES: 13,342 full-time; 2,043 part-time

SHAREHOLDERS: 1,700 (approx.)

ANNUAL MEETING: In Apr.

INCORPORATED: IL, Dec., 1928

INSTITUTIONAL HOLDINGS:
No. of Institutions: 324
Shares Held: 57,115,599
% Held: 62.5

INDUSTRY: Electrical apparatus and equipment (SIC: 5063)

TRANSFER AGENT(S): BankBoston, N.A., Boston, MA

GREAT ATLANTIC & PACIFIC TEA COMPANY, INC. (THE)

EXCH.	SYM.	REC. PRICE	P/E RATIO	YLD.	MKT. CAP.	RANGE (52-WK.)	'02 Y/E PR.
NYSE	GAP	4.67 (2/28/03)	...	...	$179.2 mill.	28.44 - 4.55	8.06

SPECULATIVE GRADE. RESULTS ARE BEING HURT BY UNFAVORABLE ECONOMIC CONDITIONS AND INCREASED COMPETITION.

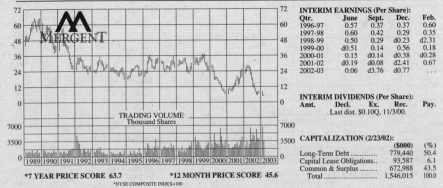

*7 YEAR PRICE SCORE 63.7   ***12 MONTH PRICE SCORE 45.6**

*NYSE COMPOSITE INDEX=100

INTERIM EARNINGS (Per Share):

Qtr.	June	Sept.	Dec.	Feb.
1996-97	0.57	0.37	0.37	0.60
1997-98	0.60	0.42	0.29	0.35
1998-99	0.50	0.29	d0.23	d2.31
1999-00	d0.51	0.14	0.56	0.18
2000-01	0.15	d0.14	d0.38	d0.28
2001-02	d0.19	0.08	d2.41	0.67
2002-03	0.06	d3.76	d0.77	

INTERIM DIVIDENDS (Per Share):

Amt.	Decl.	Ex.	Rec.	Pay.
		Last dist. $0.10Q, 11/3/00.		

CAPITALIZATION (2/23/02):

	($000)	(%)
Long-Term Debt	779,440	50.4
Capital Lease Obligations	93,587	6.1
Common & Surplus	672,988	43.5
Total	1,546,015	100.0

BUSINESS:

The Great Atlantic & Pacific Tea Company, Inc. operates 692 stores, as of 1/10/03, located in 15 states, the District of Columbia and Ontario, Canada. Store names include A&P, Waldbaum's, The Food Emporium, Super Foodmart, Super Fresh, Farmer Jack, Kohl's, Sav-A-Center, Dominion, The Barn Markets, Food Basics and Ultra Food & Drug. The stores deal in groceries, meats, fresh produce, health and beauty aids. Some have specialty food departments, including gourmet products, international cuisine and delicatessens. Through Compass Foods, GAP manufactures and distributes a line of whole-bean coffees under the Eight O'Clock, Bokar and Royale labels. As of 6/15/02, the Tengelmann Group of Germany owned approximately 56.6% of GAP's stock.

RECENT DEVELOPMENTS:

For the 12 weeks ended 11/30/02, net loss totaled $29.7 million compared with a net loss of $89.6 million in the corresponding period a year earlier. Results for 2002 and 2001 included after-tax charges of $11.1 million and $95.5 million, respectively, from asset dispositions. Sales slipped 2.3% to $2.47 billion from $2.53 billion the previous year. Comparable-store sales were up 0.1% year over year. Gross margin was $692.1 million, or 28.1% of sales, versus $726.9 million, or 28.8% of sales, the year before. Comparisons were made with restated prior-year results.

PROSPECTS:

Results are being negatively affected by cautious consumer spending due to ongoing economic uncertainties, along with increased promotional activity and aggressive pricing by competitors. Meanwhile, the Company is accelerating its efforts to reduce costs to help boost profitability going forward. Separately, GAP anticipates opening seven new supermarkets, enlarging or remodeling 15 to 20 supermarkets, and closing approximately five stores during the fourth quarter of fiscal 2003.

ANNUAL FINANCIAL DATA:

FISCAL YEAR	TOT. REVS. ($mill.)	NET INC. ($mill.)	TOT. ASSETS ($mill.)	OPER. PROFIT %	NET PROFIT %	RET. ON EQUITY %	RET. ON ASSETS %	CURR. RATIO	EARN. PER SH.$	CASH FL. PER SH.$	TANG. BK. VAL.$	DIV. PER SH.$	PRICE RANGE	AVG. P/E RATIO	AVG. YIELD %
2/23/02	10,973.3	⑤ d64.7	3,194.3	...	...	...	...	1.0	⑤ d1.69	6.52	17.54	...	25.92 — 6.38	...	...
2/24/01	10,622.9	④ d25.1	3,309.8	0.5	...	...	...	1.1	④ d0.65	6.02	20.79	0.40	29.06 — 6.00	...	2.3
2/26/00	10,151.3	④ 14.2	3,335.5	1.0	0.1	1.7	0.4	1.1	④ 0.37	6.43	22.06	0.40	37.69 — 24.50	84.0	1.3
2/27/99	10,179.4	④ d67.2	3,141.7	...	...	...	...	1.1	④ d1.75	4.35	21.87	0.40	34.38 — 21.88	...	1.4
2/28/98	10,262.2	③ 63.6	2,995.3	1.5	0.6	6.9	2.1	1.3	③ 1.66	7.80	24.22	0.35	36.00 — 23.13	17.8	1.3
2/22/97	10,089.0	73.0	3,002.7	1.7	0.7	8.2	2.4	1.2	1.91	7.94	23.27	0.20	36.75 — 19.50	14.7	0.7
2/24/96	10,101.4	57.2	2,860.8	1.5	0.6	7.0	2.0	1.2	1.50	7.40	21.53	0.20	29.00 — 17.63	15.5	0.9
2/25/95	10,332.0	② d166.6	2,894.8	...	...	...	...	1.1	② d4.36	1.80	20.28	0.80	27.38 — 17.38	...	3.6
2/26/94	10,384.1	4.0	3,098.7	0.7	...	0.4	0.1	1.1	0.10	6.28	26.02	0.80	35.00 — 22.50	287.2	2.8
2/27/93	10,499.5	① d98.5	3,090.9	0.4	...	...	...	1.0	① d2.58	d2.58	27.06	0.80	35.25 — 21.38	...	2.8

Statistics are as originally reported. ① Incl. $89.2 mil ($2.34/sh) net chg. for invt. loss; $42.6 mil ($1.11/sh) chg. for realignment; & bef. $91 mil ($2.38/sh) chg. for acctg. change. ② Bef. $5 mil ($0.13/sh) chg. for acctg. change. ③ Bef. a $544,000 ($0.01/sh) extraord. loss. ④ Incl. $44.1 mil ($1.15/sh) non-recur. after-tax chg., 2001; $59.9 mil ($1.56/sh) 2000; & $118.5 mil ($3.09/sh) 1999. ⑤ Bef. $7.2 mil ($0.19/sh) extraord. chg., incl. $56.7 mil after-tax restr. chg.; $112.3 mil after-tax asset disp. chg.; $35.2 million after-tax gain fr. the demutualization of The Prudential Insurance Co.

OFFICERS:
C. W. Haub, Chmn., C.E.O.
E. Culligan, Pres., C.O.O.
M. P. Goldstein, Sr. V.P., C.F.O.

INVESTOR CONTACT: Rick DeSanta, V.P., Corp. Affairs, (201) 571-4495

PRINCIPAL OFFICE: 2 Paragon Drive, Montvale, NJ 07645

TELEPHONE NUMBER: (201) 573-9700
FAX: (201) 930-8008
WEB: www.aptea.com

NO. OF EMPLOYEES: 30,730 full-time (approx.); 52,270 part-time (approx.)

SHAREHOLDERS: 6,281

ANNUAL MEETING: In July

INCORPORATED: MD, May, 1925

INSTITUTIONAL HOLDINGS:
No. of Institutions: 107
Shares Held: 14,435,111
% Held: 37.5

INDUSTRY: Grocery stores (SIC: 5411)

TRANSFER AGENT(S): American Stock Transfer and Trust Company, New York, NY

GREAT LAKES CHEMICAL CORP.

EXCH.	SYM.	REC. PRICE	P/E RATIO	YLD.	MKT. CAP.	RANGE (52-WK.)	'02 Y/E PR.
NYSE	GLK	21.09 (2/28/03)	22.9	1.7%	$1.06 bill.	29.31 - 20.10	23.88

LOWER MEDIUM GRADE. THE COMPANY STRENGTHENED ITS POSITION IN THE CONSUMER PRODUCTS MARKET WITH THE ACQUISITION OF LIME-O-SOL.

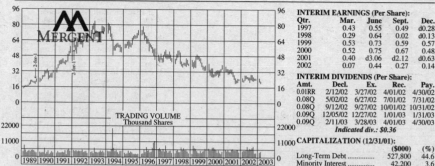

INTERIM EARNINGS (Per Share):

Qtr.	Mar.	June	Sept.	Dec.
1997	0.43	0.55	0.49	d0.28
1998	0.29	0.64	0.02	d0.13
1999	0.53	0.73	0.59	0.57
2000	0.52	0.75	0.67	0.48
2001	0.40	d3.06	d2.12	d0.63
2002	0.07	0.44	0.27	0.14

INTERIM DIVIDENDS (Per Share):

Amt.	Decl.	Ex.	Rec.	Pay.
0.01RR	2/12/02	3/27/02	4/01/02	4/30/02
0.08Q	5/02/02	6/27/02	7/01/02	7/31/02
0.08Q	9/12/02	9/27/02	10/01/02	10/31/02
0.09Q	12/05/02	12/27/02	1/01/03	1/31/03
0.09Q	2/11/03	3/28/03	4/01/03	4/30/03

Indicated div.: $0.36

CAPITALIZATION (12/31/01):

	($000)	(%)
Long-Term Debt	527,800	44.6
Minority Interest	42,200	3.6
Common & Surplus	613,500	51.8
Total	1,183,500	100.0

*7 YEAR PRICE SCORE 67.2   ***12 MONTH PRICE SCORE 97.3**

*NYSE COMPOSITE INDEX=100

BUSINESS:

Great Lakes Chemical Corp. is a producer of specialty chemicals including flame retardants, polymer stabilizers, fire extinguishants, water treatments, and a growing line of performance chemicals for the life sciences industry. Primary manufacturing operations are located in the U.S. and Europe. GLK's products are sold globally. The principal markets include: computer and business equipment, consumer electronics, data processing, construction materials, telecommunications, pharmaceutical and pool and spa dealers and distributors. Revenues for 2002 were derived: polymer additives, 44.1%; water treatment, 38.7%; performance chemicals, 16.6%; and corporate and other, 0.6%.

RECENT DEVELOPMENTS:

For the twelve months ended 12/31/02, income from continuing operations jumped to $48.0 million compared with a loss from continuing operations of $181.2 million in 2001. Operating efficiencies, new product growth and increased free cash flow enhanced results. Results for 2002 and 2001 included net repositioning charges of $5.1 million and $148.6 million, respectively. Results for 2002 and 2001 excluded a net gain of $77.6 million and a net loss of $108.3 million, respectively, from discontinued operations. Net sales were $1.40 billion, up 3.6% from $1.35 billion in the prior year. Operating income amounted to $112.0 million compared with an operating loss of $141.4 million the year before.

PROSPECTS:

On 2/28/03, the Company announced that its BioLab Inc. subsidiary, a provider of recreational and industrial water treatment products, acquired the Lime-O-Sol Company for an undisclosed amount. The acquisition included Lime-O-Sol's brand of specialty household cleaning products marketed under the trade name The Works®. The transaction is strategically in line with the Company's plans to expand its presence in the consumer products market. Separately, on 12/3/02, the Company acquired the non-staining phenolic antioxidants business from Flexsys America for an undisclosed amount. The acquisition enhances GLK's polymer stabilizers business and expands its customer base for the Lowinox® line of non-staining and non-discoloring antioxidants.

ANNUAL FINANCIAL DATA:

FISCAL YEAR	TOT. REVS. ($mill.)	NET INC. ($mill.)	TOT. ASSETS ($mill.)	OPER. PROFIT %	NET PROFIT %	RET. ON EQUITY %	RET. ON ASSETS %	CURR. RATIO	EARN. PER SH. $	CASH FL. PER SH. $	TANG. BK. VAL. $	DIV. PER SH. $	PRICE RANGE	AVG. P/E RATIO	AVG. YIELD %
p12/31/02	1,401.5	8 48.0	...	...	...	...	...	...	9 0.95			0.33	29.31 - 21.24	26.6	1.3
12/31/01	1,594.7	7 d289.5	1,687.6	...	...	...	...	1.5	7 d5.76	d3.75	9.44	0.32	37.63 - 20.00	...	1.1
12/31/00	1,670.5	6 127.0	2,134.4	8.4	7.6	13.4	6.0	2.6	6 2.42	4.33	13.38	0.32	40.50 - 26.50	13.8	1.0
12/31/99	1,453.3	5 139.6	2,261.0	11.2	14.0	6.2	3.8	2.41	5 2.41	3.95	13.74	0.32	50.00 - 33.19	17.3	0.8
12/31/98	1,394.3	4 56.4	2,004.6	5.3	4.0	5.3	2.8	2.9	4 0.95	2.36	16.07	0.48	54.19 - 36.69	47.8	1.1
3 12/31/97	1,311.2	2 71.8	2,270.4	10.8	5.5	5.5	3.2	2.2	2 1.19	2.41	20.23	0.62	54.88 - 41.50	40.5	1.3
12/31/96	2,211.7	250.3	2,661.3	20.1	11.3	16.8	9.4	2.7	3.94	5.90	17.07	0.54	78.63 - 44.25	15.6	0.9
12/31/95	2,361.1	295.6	2,533.7	21.1	12.5	20.9	11.7	2.3	4.52	6.21	15.47	0.42	74.63 - 55.75	14.4	0.7
12/31/94	2,110.7	1 278.7	2,111.5	21.2	11.1	21.3	10.9	2.3	1 4.00	4.77	13.37	0.38	82.00 - 48.75	16.3	0.6
12/31/93	1,827.8	272.8	1,900.9	23.7	15.2	21.7	14.4	2.3	3.82	5.09	12.84	0.34	84.00 - 64.50	19.4	0.5

Statistics are as originally reported. 1 Incl. $0.15 per sh. one-time chg. to acct. adj. 2 Incl. $49.8 mill. pre-tax spl. chg. & $137.0 mill. est. loss of divest. 3 Refl. divest. of petro. add., furfural & deriv., Chemol, Four Seasons & Aquaterra businesses. 4 Incl. $129.0 mill. pre-tax restr. chgs. 5 Incl. $18.2 mill. spl. chg. 6 Incl. $63.4 mill. spl. chg., $60.4 mill. non-tax gain & $4.0 mill. gain. 7 Incl. $267.1 mill. spl. chg. & $9.4 mill. gain fr. sale of stock. 8 Incl. $5.1 mill. spl. chg. & excl. $77.6 mill. net gain fr. disc. ops.

OFFICERS:
M. P. Bulriss, Chmn., Pres., C.E.O.
J. J. Gallagher III, Sr. V.P., C.F.O.
J. M. Lipshaw, Sr. V.P., Gen. Couns., Sec.
INVESTOR CONTACT: Jeffrey Potrzebowski, Dir., Investor Relations, (317) 715-3000
PRINCIPAL OFFICE: 500 East 96th Street, Suite 500, Indianapolis, IN 46240

TELEPHONE NUMBER: (317) 715-3000
FAX: (317) 715-3050
WEB: www.greatlakes.com
NO. OF EMPLOYEES: 5,600 (avg.)
SHAREHOLDERS: 2,278 (approx.)
ANNUAL MEETING: In May
INCORPORATED: MI, 1933; reincorp., DE, Sept., 1933

INSTITUTIONAL HOLDINGS:
No. of Institutions: 190
Shares Held: 46,868,920
% Held: 93.4
INDUSTRY: Chemical preparations, nec (SIC: 2899)
TRANSFER AGENT(S): Computershare Investor Services, Chicago, IL

GREAT PLAINS ENERGY INCORPORATED

EXCH.	SYM.	REC. PRICE	P/E RATIO	YLD.	MKT. CAP.	RANGE (52-WK.)	'02 Y/E PR.
NYSE	GXP	22.67 (2/28/03)	11.1	7.3%	$1.57 bill.	26.98 - 15.69	22.88

UPPER MEDIUM GRADE. FOR 2003, THE COMPANY EXPECTS EARNINGS IN THE RANGE OF $1.90 TO $2.00 PER SHARE.

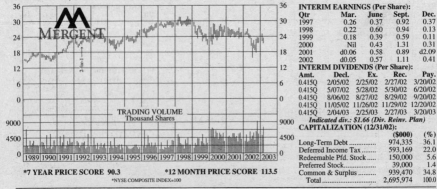

INTERIM EARNINGS (Per Share):

Qtr	Mar.	June	Sept.	Dec.
1997	0.26	0.37	0.92	0.37
1998	0.22	0.60	0.94	0.13
1999	0.18	0.39	0.59	0.11
2000	Nil	0.43	1.31	0.31
2001	d0.06	0.58	0.89	d2.09
2002	d0.05	0.57	1.11	0.41

INTERIM DIVIDENDS (Per Share):

Amt.	Decl.	Ex.	Rec.	Pay.
0.415Q	2/05/02	2/25/02	2/27/02	3/20/02
0.415Q	5/07/02	5/28/02	5/30/02	6/20/02
0.415Q	8/06/02	8/27/02	8/29/02	9/20/02
0.415Q	11/05/02	11/26/02	11/29/02	12/20/02
0.415Q	2/04/03	2/25/03	2/27/03	3/20/03

Indicated div.: $1.66 (Div. Reinv. Plan)

CAPITALIZATION (12/31/02):

	($000)	(%)
Long-Term Debt	974,335	36.1
Deferred Income Tax	593,169	22.0
Redeemable Pfd. Stock	150,000	5.6
Preferred Stock	39,000	1.4
Common & Surplus	939,470	34.8
Total	2,695,974	100.0

*7 YEAR PRICE SCORE 90.3   ***12 MONTH PRICE SCORE 113.5**

*NYSE COMPOSITE INDEX=100

BUSINESS:

Great Plains Energy Incorporated was formed upon the conversion of Kansas City Power & Light Company to a holding company structure on 10/1/01. The Company's three wholly-owned subsidiaries are Kansas City Power & Light Company (KCP&L), a regulated provider of electricity in the Midwest; Strategic Energy LLC, an energy man-agement company providing load aggregation and power supply coordination; and KLT Gas Inc., a subsidiary specializing in coal bed methane exploration and development. Operating revenues for 2001 were derived from the following: KCP&L electric sales, 54.2%; Strategic Energy electric, 42.3%; other, 3.5%.

RECENT DEVELOPMENTS:

For the year ended 12/31/02, the Company's reported income of $129.2 million, before an accounting change charge of $3.0 million, versus a loss of $40.0 million, before an extraordinary gain of $15.9 million, the previous year. Total operating revenues climbed 27.4% to $1.86 billion from $1.46 billion the prior year. Electric revenues from KCP&L rose 4.4% to $1.01 billion from $967.5 million in 2001. Electric revenues from Strategic Energy soared 99.1% to $788.3 million from $396.0 million a year earlier. Other revenue climbed 35.3% to $63.7 million. Operating income was $291.7 million compared with $57.2 million the year before.

PROSPECTS:

The Company's prospects are bright, reflecting strong wholesale sales and cost-reduction programs at KCP&L and continued growth at Strategic Energy. At KCP&L, continued load growth and a 40.0% increase in wholesale MWh sales combined with other net positive impacts of the return to service of Hawthorn No. 5 in mid-2001 are more than offsetting lower sales to industrial customers as a result of a softer economy. Meanwhile, continued growth in retail electric sales resulting from increases in customer accounts and MWh's served are fueling growth at Strategic Energy. For 2003, the Company expects earnings in the range of $1.90 to $2.00 per share.

ANNUAL FINANCIAL DATA:

FISCAL YEAR	TOT. REVS. ($mill.)	NET INC. ($mill.)	TOT. ASSETS ($mill.)	OPER. PROFIT %	NET PROFIT %	NET INC./ NET PROP. %	NET INC./ TOT. CAP. %	RET. ON EQUITY %	ACCUM. DEPR./ GROSS PROP. %	EARN. PER SH. $	TANG. BK. VAL.$	DIV. PER SH.$	DIV. PAYOUT %	PRICE RANGE	AVG. P/E RATIO	AVG. YIELD %
12/31/02	1,861.9	⑤ 129.2	3,506.7	15.7	6.9	5.0	4.8	13.2	42.0	⑤ 2.04	13.58	1.66	81.4	26.98 - 15.69	10.5	7.8
12/31/01	1,461.9	④ d40.0	3,464.4	3.9	...	...	...	...	40.6	④ d0.68	12.59	1.66	...	27.56 - 23.19	...	6.5
12/31/00	1,115.9	③ 128.6	3,293.9	26.2	11.5	5.1	4.7	13.4	39.4	③ 2.05	14.88	1.66	81.0	29.00 - 20.88	12.2	6.7
12/31/99	897.4	② 81.9	2,990.1	16.0	9.1	3.6	3.5	9.1	39.7	② 1.26	13.97	1.66	131.7	29.63 - 20.81	20.0	6.6
12/31/98	938.9	120.7	3,012.4	19.6	12.9	5.2	4.8	12.3	37.9	1.89	14.41	1.64	86.8	31.81 - 28.00	15.8	5.5
12/31/97	895.9	① 76.6	3,058.0	18.2	8.5	3.3	2.8	7.9	36.1	① 1.18	14.19	1.62	137.3	29.94 - 27.38	24.3	5.7
12/31/96	903.9	108.2	2,914.5	19.7	12.0	4.6	4.2	10.8	34.6	1.69	14.71	1.59	94.1	29.38 - 23.63	15.7	6.0
12/31/95	886.0	122.6	2,882.5	18.9	13.8	5.2	5.0	12.4	32.9	1.92	14.51	1.54	80.2	26.63 - 21.50	12.5	6.4
12/31/94	868.3	104.8	2,770.4	17.2	12.1	4.5	4.4	10.9	31.9	1.64	14.13	1.50	91.5	23.88 - 18.63	13.0	7.1
12/31/93	857.5	105.8	2,755.1	18.2	12.3	4.6	4.6	11.1	30.5	1.66	13.99	1.46	87.9	26.25 - 21.75	14.5	6.1

Statistics are as originally reported. ① Incl. non-recurr. chrg. $60.0 mill. ② Incl. net gain of $1.7 mill. and net loss of $15.0 mill. ③ Excl. acctg. credit $30.1 mill. ④ Excl. extraord. gain $15.9 mill.; incl after-tax asset write-off of $140.0 mill. ⑤ Bef. acctg. chrg. of $3.0 mill.

OFFICERS:
B. J. Beaudoin, Chmn., Pres., C.E.O.
J. S. Latz, Exec. V.P., Corp. Sec.
A. F. Bielsker, Sr. V.P., C.F.O., Treas.

INVESTOR CONTACT: Greg Drown, Investor Relations, (816) 556-2312

PRINCIPAL OFFICE: 1201 Walnut Ave., Kansas City, MO 64106-2124

TELEPHONE NUMBER: (816) 556-2200
FAX: (816) 556-2924
WEB: www.greatplainsenergy.com

NO. OF EMPLOYEES: 2,258 (avg.)

SHAREHOLDERS: 18,393

ANNUAL MEETING: In May

INCORPORATED: MO, July, 1922

INSTITUTIONAL HOLDINGS:
No. of Institutions: 182
Shares Held: 21,434,712
% Held: 31.4

INDUSTRY: Power transmission equipment, nec (SIC: 3568)

TRANSFER AGENT(S): United Missouri Bank of Kansas City, N.A., Kansas City, MO

GREENPOINT FINANCIAL CORPORATION

EXCH.	SYM.	REC. PRICE	P/E RATIO	YLD.	MKT. CAP.	RANGE (52-WK.)	'02 Y/E PR.
NYSE	GPT	42.48 (2/28/03)	7.7	2.9%	$4.24 bill.	51.86 - 36.69	45.18

UPPER MEDIUM GRADE. THE COMPANY EXPECTS TO CONTINUE TO BENEFIT FROM THE OPENING OF NEW BRANCHES AND ITS SMALL BUSINESS BANKING PROGRAM.

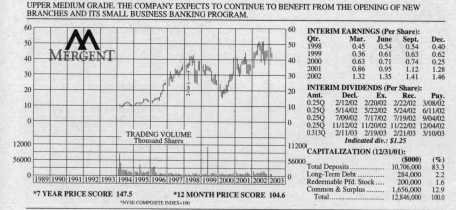

*7 YEAR PRICE SCORE 147.5   ***12 MONTH PRICE SCORE 104.6**

*NYSE COMPOSITE INDEX=100

INTERIM EARNINGS (Per Share):

Qtr.	Mar.	June	Sept.	Dec.
1998	0.45	0.54	0.54	0.40
1999	0.36	0.61	0.63	0.62
2000	0.63	0.71	0.74	0.25
2001	0.86	0.95	1.12	1.28
2002	1.32	1.35	1.41	1.46

INTERIM DIVIDENDS (Per Share):

Amt.	Decl.	Ex.	Rec.	Pay.
0.25Q	2/12/02	2/20/02	2/22/02	3/08/02
0.25Q	5/14/02	5/22/02	5/24/02	6/11/02
0.25Q	7/09/02	7/17/02	7/19/02	9/04/02
0.25Q	11/12/02	11/20/02	11/22/02	12/04/02
0.313Q	2/11/03	2/19/03	2/21/03	3/10/03

Indicated div.: $1.25

CAPITALIZATION (12/31/01):

	($000)	(%)
Total Deposits	10,706,000	83.3
Long-Term Debt	284,000	2.2
Redeemable Pfd. Stock	200,000	1.6
Common & Surplus	1,656,000	12.9
Total	12,846,000	100.0

BUSINESS:

GreenPoint Financial Corporation is a bank holding company that conducts its business through two principal businesses. GreenPoint Mortgage Funding originates adjustable and fixed-rate mortgage loans through a network of brokers, attorneys, bankers, and real estate professionals across the United States. GreenPoint Mortgage also originates commercial real estate loans in the New York metropolitan area. As of 1/21/03, GreenPoint Bank, a chartered savings bank, was the second largest thrift depository in the Greater New York area with $12.00 billion in deposits in 81 branches serving more than 400,000 households. In 1999, the Company acquired Headlands Mortgage Company. In March 2002, GPT completed its exit of the manufactured housing lending business.

RECENT DEVELOPMENTS:

For the year ended 12/31/02, GPT reported income from continuing operations of $498.2 million versus income of $409.5 million the year before. Results for 2002 and 2001 included net pre-tax gains from sales of mortgage loans of $375.3 million and $396.0 million, net gains on securities of $15.2 million and $17.7 million, and losses from a change in the valuation of retained interests of $8.7 million and $400,000, respectively. Results for 2001 also included goodwill amortization of $45.2 million. Results excluded a net gain of $4.8 million in 2002 and a net loss of $704.2 million from discontinued operations. Net interest income grew 21.0% to $753.2 million. Non-interest income fell slightly to $461.7 million from $464.7 million, while non-interest expense declined 1.2% to $426.4 million.

PROSPECTS:

The Company's results continue to reflect growth in both its retail banking and mortgage banking businesses. The Company expects to continue to benefit from the opening of new branches and its small business banking program, which is exceeding GPT's expectations. Additionally, the Company's mortgage production continues to be driven by low interest rates, while its held-for-investment mortgage portfolio remains strong. Meanwhile, GPT opened 133,000 new checking accounts in 2002 compared with 63,000 in 2001.

ANNUAL FINANCIAL DATA:

FISCAL YEAR	NET INT. INC. ($mill.)	NON-INT. INC. ($mill.)	NET INC. ($mill.)	TOT. LOANS ($mill.)	TOT. ASSETS ($mill.)	TOT. DEP. ($mill.)	RET. ON EQUITY %	RET. ON ASSETS %	EQUITY/ ASSETS %	EARN. PER SH. $	TANG. BK. VAL. $	DIV. PER SH. $	PRICE RANGE	AVG. P/E RATIO
p12/31/02	753.2	461.7	⑥ 498.2		21,814.0					⑥ 5.53		1.00	51.86 — 34.76	7.8
12/31/01	622.0	465.0	⑤ 409.0	10,019.0	20,186.0	10,706.0	24.7	2.0	8.2	⑤ 4.50	…	1.00	44.74 — 29.00	8.2
12/31/00	573.4	324.8	④ 213.1	8,696.4	15,764.8	11,176.3	10.4	1.4	13.0	④ 2.34	13.18	1.00	41.31 — 15.00	12.0
12/31/99	539.9	391.7	④ 215.5	9,308.2	15,401.1	11,560.1	10.8	1.4	12.9	④ 2.23	10.03	0.88	37.13 — 23.31	13.6
12/31/98	483.7	75.1	③ 149.5	9,400.3	13,970.3	11,173.1	8.3	1.1	12.9	③ 1.92	8.26	0.64	42.88 — 24.00	17.4
12/31/97	475.0	56.2	④ 147.6	8,935.8	13,083.5	10,973.0	11.6	1.4	9.7	④ 1.86	9.20	0.50	36.75 — 22.75	16.0
12/31/96	446.5	56.9	④ 132.5	7,447.5	13,325.6	11,452.3	9.1	1.0	11.0	④ 1.51	8.85	0.40	25.13 — 11.75	12.2
12/31/95	350.7	35.8	④ 107.5	6,022.4	14,670.5	12,898.3	6.9	0.7	10.6	④ 1.15	8.44	0.40	14.88 — 10.19	10.9
12/31/94	337.5	27.1	112.9	5,758.4	6,955.0	5,223.5	7.4	1.6	21.9	1.11	13.85	0.30	12.63 — 8.75	9.7
①② 12/31/93	158.4	16.2	56.2	5,583.0	7,377.1	5,650.4	7.2	0.8	10.7	…	…	…	… — …	…

Statistics are as originally reported. Adj. for 2-for-1 stk. split, 3/98. ① Fiscal year end changed to 12/31 from 6/30. ② Fin'ls. are for GreenPoint Savings Bank. ③ Incl. non-recurr. exps. $8.3 mill. ④ Incl. restruct. chrg. $4.9 mill., 2000; chrg. $6.0 mill., 1999; chrg. $2.5 mill., 1997; cr$1.6 mill., 1996; chrg. $8.0 mill., 1995. ⑤ Incl. net pre-tax gain of $395.6 mill. & excl. loss of $704.3 mill. fr. disc. ops. ⑥ Bef. a net gain of $4.8 mill. fr. disc. ops.; incl. a net gain on sales of mtge. loans of $375.3 mill. & a loss of $8.7 mill. fr. chng. in valuation of retained ints.

OFFICERS:
T. S. Johnson, Chmn., C.E.O.
P. T. Paul, Vice-Chmn.
B. B. Bhatt, Pres., C.O.O.
J. R. Leeds, Exec. V.P., C.F.O.

INVESTOR CONTACT: Maritza Vicole, Investor Relations, (212) 834-1202

PRINCIPAL OFFICE: 90 Park Avenue, New York, NY 10016

TELEPHONE NUMBER: (212) 834-1000
FAX: (212) 834-1400
WEB: www.greenpoint.com

NO. OF EMPLOYEES: 4,498 full-time; 257 part-time

SHAREHOLDERS: 3,756 (approx.)

ANNUAL MEETING: In May

INCORPORATED: DE, Aug., 1993

INSTITUTIONAL HOLDINGS:
No. of Institutions: 257
Shares Held: 61,613,564
% Held: 63.1

INDUSTRY: Savings institutions, except federal (SIC: 6036)

TRANSFER AGENT(S): Mellon Investor Services, L.L.C., South Hackensack, NJ

GROUP 1 AUTOMOTIVE, INC.

EXCH.	SYM.	REC. PRICE	P/E RATIO	YLD.	MKT. CAP.	RANGE (52-WK.)	'02 Y/E PR.
NYSE	GPI	23.29 (2/28/03)	8.3	...	$0.53 bill.	50.80 - 18.00	23.88

UPPER MEDIUM GRADE. THE COMPANY IS TARGETING FULL-YEAR 2003 EARNINGS IN THE RANGE OF $3.10 TO $3.30 PER SHARE.

INTERIM EARNINGS (Per Share):

Qtr.	Mar.	June	Sept.	Dec.
1998	0.20	0.31	0.35	0.29
1999	0.31	0.42	0.48	0.35
2000	0.40	0.54	0.54	0.41
2001	0.47	0.68	0.75	0.68
2002	0.64	0.78	0.84	0.53

INTERIM DIVIDENDS (Per Share):

Amt.	Decl.	Ex.	Rec.	Pay.
	No dividends paid.			

TRADING VOLUME
Thousand Shares

CAPITALIZATION (12/31/01):

	($000)	(%)
Long-Term Debt :	95,499	19.2
Deferred Income Tax	9,982	2.0
Common & Surplus	392,243	78.8
Total	497,724	100.0

*7 YEAR PRICE SCORE N/A   ***12 MONTH PRICE SCORE 89.7**

*NYSE COMPOSITE INDEX=100

BUSINESS:

Group 1 Automotive, Inc. operates in the automotive retailing industry. As of 2/19/03, the Company owned 73 dealerships, comprised of 114 franchises and 25 collision service centers, located in California, Colorado, Florida, Georgia, Louisiana, Massachusetts, New Mexico, Oklahoma and Texas. The Company, through its dealerships and Internet sites, sells new and used cars and light trucks, provides maintenance and repair services, sells replacement parts and arranges related financing, vehicle service and insurance contracts.

RECENT DEVELOPMENTS:

For the twelve months ended 12/31/02, net income advanced 21.0% to $67.1 million from $55.4 million in the corresponding period a year earlier. Total revenues climbed 5.5% to $4.21 billion from $4.00 billion the previous year. New vehicle retail sales increased 6.5% to $2.53 billion from $2.37 billion in 2001. Used vehicle retail sales slipped 2.9% to $921.4 million, while used vehicle wholesale sales grew 16.8% to $222.5 million. Parts and service revenues rose 11.7% to $402.2 million, while net finance and insurance revenues were up 14.8% to $141.5 million. Gross profit was $652.3 million, or 15.5% of total revenues, versus $607.3 million, or 15.2% of total revenues, the year before. Income from operations totaled $137.6 million, up 4.8% from $131.3 million in the prior year.

PROSPECTS:

Earnings are being negatively affected by weaker sales of both new and used cars. Looking ahead, the Company anticipates full-year 2003 earnings in the range of $3.10 to $3.30 per share. Earnings growth is expected to be fueled by increased parts and service revenue and GPI's aggressive cost-control efforts. Meanwhile, the Company plans to acquire new dealerships with total annual revenues of approximately $800.0 million in 2003. In January 2003, GPI completed the acquisition of Bob Howard Ford-Lincoln-Mercury, and the divestiture of the Bob Howard Mercedes-Benz dealership in Oklahoma City, Oklahoma. These transactions are expected to add net revenues of $84.0 million in 2003.

ANNUAL FINANCIAL DATA:

FISCAL YEAR	TOT. REVS. ($mill.)	NET INC. ($mill.)	TOT. ASSETS ($mill.)	OPER. PROFIT %	NET PROFIT %	RET. ON EQUITY %	RET. ON ASSETS %	CURR. RATIO	EARN. PER SH. $	CASH FL. PER SH. $	TANG. BK. VAL. $	PRICE RANGE	AVG. P/E RATIO
p12/31/02	4,214.4	67.1							2.80			50.80 - 18.00	12.3
12/31/01	3,996.4	55.4	1,054.4	3.3	1.4	14.1	5.3	1.3	2.59	3.40	4.84	34.99 - 8.13	8.3
12/31/00	3,586.1	40.8	1,099.6	3.3	1.1	16.5	3.7	1.1	1.88	2.62	...	16.88 - 8.06	6.6
12/31/99	2,508.3	33.5	842.9	3.4	1.3	14.4	4.0	1.2	1.55	2.05	...	30.00 - 12.75	13.8
12/31/98	1,630.1	20.7	477.7	3.2	1.3	15.2	4.3	1.2	1.16	1.52	0.69	26.00 - 8.63	14.9
12/31/97	404.0	13.8	213.1	2.5	3.4	15.4	6.5	1.5	0.76	0.98	4.25	13.94 - 7.75	14.3

Statistics are as originally reported.

OFFICERS:
B. B. Hollingsworth, Jr., Chmn., Pres., C.E.O.
S. L. Thompson, Exec. V.P., C.F.O., Treas.
J. T. Turner, Exec. V.P.
INVESTOR CONTACT: Scott L. Thompson, Exec. V.P., C.F.O., Treas., (713) 647-5700
PRINCIPAL OFFICE: 950 Echo Lane, Suite 100, Houston, TX 77024

TELEPHONE NUMBER: (713) 647-5700
FAX: (713) 647-5858
WEB: www.group1auto.com
NO. OF EMPLOYEES: 6,000 (approx.)
SHAREHOLDERS: 138
ANNUAL MEETING: In May
INCORPORATED: DE, Dec., 1995

INSTITUTIONAL HOLDINGS:
No. of Institutions: 116
Shares Held: 15,042,586
% Held: 66.9
INDUSTRY: New and used car dealers (SIC: 5511)
TRANSFER AGENT(S): Mellon Investor Services, Dallas, TX

GTECH HOLDINGS CORP.

EXCH.	SYM.	REC. PRICE	P/E RATIO	YLD.	MKT. CAP.	RANGE (52-WK.)	'02 Y/E PR.
NYSE	GTK	29.10 (2/28/03)	14.3	...	$1.67 bill.	30.49 - 17.62	27.86

UPPER MEDIUM GRADE. THE COMPANY ENTERED INTO AN AGREEMENT TO ACQUIRE A 62.8% EQUITY STAKE IN POLCARD S.A. IN A TRANSACTION VALUED AT APPROXIMATELY $62.0 MILLION.

*7 YEAR PRICE SCORE 164.3   *12 MONTH PRICE SCORE 119.1
*NYSE COMPOSITE INDEX=100

INTERIM EARNINGS (Per Share):

Qtr.	May	Aug.	Nov.	Feb.
1998-99	0.23	0.27	0.32	0.28
1999-00	0.25	0.29	0.33	0.44
2000-01	0.29	d0.31	0.27	0.38
2001-02	0.31	0.28	0.37	0.31
2002-03	0.49	0.66	0.57	...

INTERIM DIVIDENDS (Per Share):

Amt.	Decl.	Ex.	Rec.	Pay.
2-for-1	5/06/02	5/24/02	5/16/02	5/23/02

CAPITALIZATION (2/23/02):

	($000)	(%)
Long-Term Debt	329,715	61.5
Deferred Income Tax	3,695	0.7
Common & Surplus	202,955	37.8
Total	536,365	100.0

BUSINESS:

Gtech Holdings Corp., a global information technology company providing software, network and professional services that power transaction processing solutions, is the operator of highly-secure on-line lottery transaction processing systems. As of 2/23/02, GTECH, the wholly-owned subsidiary of the Company, operated on-line lottery systems for, or supplied equipment and services to, 24 of the 39 on-line lottery authorities in the U.S. and 58 of the 105 international on-line lottery authorities. GTK offers its customers a range of lottery technology services, including the design, assembly, installation, operation, maintenance and marketing of on-line lottery systems and instant ticket support systems. GTK's lottery systems consist of numerous lottery terminals located in retail outlets, central computer systems, systems software and game software, and communications equipment that connects the terminals and the central computer systems.

RECENT DEVELOPMENTS:

For the quarter ended 11/23/02, net income advanced 51.8% to $32.8 million compared with $21.6 million in the corresponding prior-year period. Results for 2001 included goodwill amortization of $1.5 million. Total revenues decreased 2.7% to $256.5 million. Services revenues grew 5.8% to $207.8 million as a result of stronger same-sale store sales combined with several new international contracts and higher service revenues from Colombia, partially offset by the weakening of the Brazilian real against the U.S. dollar. Product sales declined 27.5% to $48.7 million, as prior-year product sales included one-time sales of terminals and software to GTK's customer in the U.K.

PROSPECTS:

On 2/28/03, the Company announced that it has acquired a 62.8% equity stake in PolCard S.A., a debit and credit card merchant transaction acquirer and processor company in Poland. The transaction is valued at about $62.0 million. GTK expects PolCard to generate aggregate revenues in the range of $40.0 million to $50.0 million in fiscal 2004. Looking ahead, the Company anticipates same-store sales growth of between 5.0% and 6.0%, diluted earnings per share ranging from $2.50 to $2.60, and product sales between $90.0 million and $100.0 million for fiscal 2004.

ANNUAL FINANCIAL DATA:

FISCAL YEAR	TOT. REVS. ($mill.)	NET INC. ($mill.)	TOT. ASSETS ($mill.)	OPER. PROFIT %	NET PROFIT %	RET. ON EQUITY %	RET. ON ASSETS %	CURR. RATIO	EARN. PER SH. $	CASH FL. PER SH. $	TANG. BK. VAL. $	PRICE RANGE	AVG. P/E RATIO
2/23/02	1,009.7	④⑤75.8	853.8	13.3	7.5	37.3	8.9	1.0	④⑤1.26	4.05	1.50	23.75 - 9.84	13.4
2/24/01	936.5	43.1	938.2	8.7	4.6	13.7	4.6	1.2	0.63	3.14	2.80	11.75 - 7.69	15.5
2/26/00	1,010.8	③93.6	891.0	17.8	9.3	31.6	10.5	1.1	③1.29	3.85	2.38	14.09 - 9.69	9.2
2/27/99	972.9	④89.1	874.2	14.6	9.2	31.4	10.2	1.0	④1.08	3.50	1.91	20.34 - 10.78	14.4
2/28/98	990.6	④27.2	1,023.8	4.5	2.7	7.9	2.7	1.1	④0.32	2.75	2.75	18.69 - 14.19	51.4
2/22/97	904.3	77.8	956.5	14.1	8.6	21.7	8.1	1.2	0.91	2.91	2.89	16.75 - 12.13	16.0
2/24/96	744.1	66.6	859.4	15.9	9.0	22.5	7.8	1.1	0.77	2.30	2.11	15.38 - 9.06	15.9
2/25/95	695.1	②④52.3	779.3	15.0	7.5	22.5	6.7	1.0	②④0.60	1.92	1.67	19.44 - 7.56	22.5
2/26/94	632.8	56.2	680.9	16.4	8.9	24.2	8.2	1.2	0.65	1.77	1.63	22.94 - 13.38	28.1
2/27/93	501.4	①37.8	516.9	16.4	7.5	22.5	7.3	1.5	①0.46	1.29	0.87	22.50 - 8.69	33.9

Statistics are as originally reported. Adj. for 2-for-1 stk. split, 5/02. ① Bef. extraord. loss of $18.5 mill. ② Bef. a loss of $50.0 mill. fr. disc. opers. & an extraord. loss of $1.4 mill. ③ Incl. a special gain of $1.1 mill. ④ Incl. special chrgs. of $42.3 mill., 2/02; $15.0 mill., 2/99; $99.4 mill., 2/98; $11.1 mill., 2/95. ⑤ Bef. extraord. loss of $7.8 mill.

OFFICERS:
W. B. Turner, Chmn., Pres., C.E.O.
D. J. Calabro, Exec. V.P., C.O.O.
J. B. Patel, Sr. V.P., C.F.O.
INVESTOR CONTACT: Investor Relations, (401) 392-6980
PRINCIPAL OFFICE: 55 Technology Way, West Greenwich, RI 02817

TELEPHONE NUMBER: (401) 392-1000
FAX: (401) 392-1234
WEB: www.gtech.com
NO. OF EMPLOYEES: 4,400
SHAREHOLDERS: 790 (approx.)
ANNUAL MEETING: In May
INCORPORATED: DE, 1989

INSTITUTIONAL HOLDINGS:
No. of Institutions: 194
Shares Held: 53,938,329
% Held: 94.5
INDUSTRY: Computer related services, nec (SIC: 7379)
TRANSFER AGENT(S): The Bank of New York, New York, NY

GUIDANT CORPORATION

EXCH.	SYM.	REC. PRICE	P/E RATIO	YLD.	MKT. CAP.	RANGE (52-WK.)	'02 Y/E PR.
NYSE	GDT	35.76 (2/28/03)	17.9	0.9%	$10.96 bill.	43.50 - 24.75	30.85

UPPER MEDIUM GRADE. IN 2003, THE COMPANY DOES NOT EXPECTS SALES TO BE SUBSTANTIALLY ABOVE 2002 LEVELS, AND ESTIMATES ADJUSTED EARNINGS TO RANGE FROM $1.85 TO $2.00 PER SHARE.

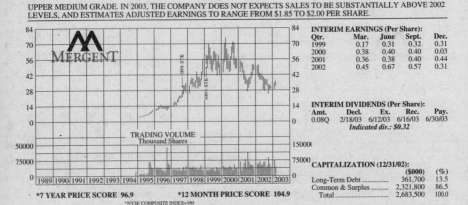

*7 YEAR PRICE SCORE 96.9　　　***12 MONTH PRICE SCORE 104.9**
*NYSE COMPOSITE INDEX=100

INTERIM EARNINGS (Per Share):

Qtr.	Mar.	June	Sept.	Dec.
1999	0.17	0.31	0.32	0.31
2000	0.38	0.40	0.40	0.03
2001	0.36	0.38	0.40	0.44
2002	0.45	0.67	0.57	0.31

INTERIM DIVIDENDS (Per Share):

Amt.	Decl.	Ex.	Rec.	Pay.
0.08Q	2/18/03	6/12/03	6/16/03	6/30/03

Indicated div.: $0.32

CAPITALIZATION (12/31/02):

	($000)	(%)
Long-Term Debt	361,700	13.5
Common & Surplus	2,321,800	86.5
Total	2,683,500	100.0

BUSINESS:

Guidant Corporation is a multinational company that designs, develops, manufactures and markets implantable cardioverter defibrillator systems used to detect and treat abnormally fast heart rhythms (tachycardia), implantable pacemaker systems used to manage slow or irregular heart rhythms (bradycardia), implantable cardiac resynchronization therapy cardioverter defibrillator and pacemaker systems used to treat heart failure and provide backup therapy for tachycardia and bradycardia, coronary and noncoronary stent systems, angioplasty dialation catheters, intravascular radiotherapy systems and related accessories for the treatment of artery and biliary structure disease, and products for emerging therapies including beating heart surgery, endoscopic vessel havesting and less-invasive endovascular procedures for the treatment of abdominal aortic aneurysms. GDT has principal operations in the U.S., Europe and Japan. The Company markets its products in nearly 100 countries through a direct sales force in the U.S. and a combination of direct sales representatives and independent distributors in international markets.

RECENT DEVELOPMENTS:

For the year ended 12/31/02, net income increased 26.4% to $611.8 million compared with $484.0 million the previous year. Earnings for 2002 and 2001 included non-recurring items that resulted in net charges of $26.4 million and $25.0 million, respectively. Net sales advanced 19.6% to $3.24 billion from $2.71 billion the year before. The increase in revenues reflected strong worldwide sales of implantable defibrillator systems and pacemaker products as well as vascular intervention products. Gross profit jumped 19.4% to $2.44 billion.

PROSPECTS:

In 2003, GDT does not expects sales to be substantially above 2002 levels, and estimates adjusted earnings to range from $1.85 to $2.00 per share. Separately, on 3/11/03, GDT signed a definitive agreement to acquire X Technologies, Inc., which manufactures the FX MINIRAIL™, a coronary device for the treatment of de novo lesions and in-stent restenosis. Meanwhile, GDT announced U.S. availability of the INSIGNIA® Entra line of pacemakers.

ANNUAL FINANCIAL DATA:

FISCAL YEAR	TOT. REVS. ($mill.)	NET INC. ($mill.)	TOT. ASSETS ($mill.)	OPER. PROFIT %	NET PROFIT %	RET. ON EQUITY %	RET. ON ASSETS %	CURR. RATIO	EARN. PER SH. $	CASH FL. PER SH. $	TANG. BK. VAL. $	DIV. PER SH. $	PRICE RANGE	AVG. P/E RATIO	AVG. YIELD %
12/31/02	3,239.6	⑨ 611.8	3,716.1	30.2	18.9	26.4	16.5	2.7	⑨ 2.00	2.42	5.58	...	51.00 - 24.75	18.9	...
12/31/01	2,707.6	⑧ 484.0	2,916.8	24.6	17.9	31.3	16.6	1.9	⑧ 1.58	1.71	...	...	55.13 - 26.90	26.0	...
12/31/00	2,548.7	⑦ 374.3	2,521.4	30.8	14.7	31.6	14.8	1.6	⑦ 1.21	1.64	1.75	...	75.38 - 44.00	49.3	...
12/31/99	2,352.3	⑥ 344.5	2,250.7	26.2	14.6	39.7	15.3	1.2	⑧ 1.11	1.49	0.65	...	69.88 - 41.00	49.9	...
12/31/98	1,897.0	⑤ d2.2	1,569.5	27.5	...	...	...	1.3	⑤ d0.01	0.24	1.02	0.03	56.50 - 25.50	...	0.1
12/31/97	1,328.2	④ 150.0	1,225.0	21.0	11.3	25.8	12.2	1.2	④ 0.50	0.72	1.30	0.03	34.75 - 13.41	48.1	0.1
12/31/96	1,048.5	① 65.8	1,003.9	24.4	6.3	14.7	6.6	1.4	① 0.23	0.46	0.84	0.03	15.34 - 9.88	55.3	0.2
12/31/95	931.3	101.1	1,057.4	23.8	10.9	26.3	9.6	1.4	0.35	0.59	1.60	0.01	10.66 - 3.88	20.6	0.2
12/31/94	862.4	92.1	1,103.6	22.2	10.7	34.8	8.3	1.3	...	...	...	...	...	...	...
12/31/93	794.7	② ③ 52.4	1,288.6	11.7	6.6	5.0	4.1	1.7	...	...	...	...	...	...	...

Statistics are as originally reported. Adj. for a 2-for-1 stock split 1/27/99 & 9/16/97. ① Incl. nonrecur. pre-tax chg. of $66.9 mill. ② Excl. exp. assoc. with change in actg. prin. of $1.8 mill. ③ Incl. restruct. & spec. pre-tax chgs. of $81.5 mill. ④ Bef. acctg. chrg. $4.7 mill., incl. non-recurr. chrg. $22.6 mill. ⑤ Incl. a pre-tax chrg. of $309.2 mill. for litigat. settle. & the acqs. of InControl, Inc. and NeoCardia LLC. ⑥ Bef. acctg. chg. of $3.3 mill. but incl. pre-tax nonrecurr. chg. totaling $41.9 mill. from acquisitions. ⑦ Incl. nonrecur. chrg. of $114.1 mill. ⑧ Incl. pre-tax spec. chrg. of $25.0 mill. & pre-tax litig. chrg. of $10.0 mill. ⑨ Incl. pre-tax non-recurr. chgrs. of $26.4 mill.

OFFICERS:
J. M. Cornelius, Chmn.
R. W. Dollens, Pres., C.E.O.
K. E. Brauer, V.P., C.F.O.
INVESTOR CONTACT: Andy Reith, Investor Relations, (317) 971-2061
PRINCIPAL OFFICE: 111 Monument Circle, 29th Floor, Indianapolis, IN 46204-5129

TELEPHONE NUMBER: (317) 971-2000
FAX: (317) 971-2040
WEB: www.guidant.com
NO. OF EMPLOYEES: 14,100
SHAREHOLDERS: 5,790
ANNUAL MEETING: In May
INCORPORATED: IN, Sept., 1994

INSTITUTIONAL HOLDINGS:
No. of Institutions: 492
Shares Held: 267,241,342
% Held: 87.4
INDUSTRY: Surgical and medical instruments (SIC: 3841)
TRANSFER AGENT(S): First Chicago Trust Company of New York, Jersey City, NJ

HALLIBURTON COMPANY

EXCH.	SYM.	REC. PRICE	P/E RATIO	YLD.	MKT. CAP.	RANGE (52-WK.)	'02 Y/E PR.
NYSE	HAL	20.26 (2/28/03)	...	2.5%	$8.79 bill.	21.65 - 8.97	18.71

MEDIUM GRADE. THE COMPANY REACHED AN AGREEMENT IN PRINCIPLE THAT, IF COMPLETED, WOULD RESULT IN A GLOBAL SETTLEMENT OF ALL ASBESTOS AND OTHER PERSONAL INJURY CLAIMS.

TRADING VOLUME
Thousand Shares

1989 1990 1991 1992 1993 1994 1995 1996 1997 1998 1999 2000 2001 2002 2003

*7 YEAR PRICE SCORE 51.1 ***12 MONTH PRICE SCORE 126.6**

*NYSE COMPOSITE INDEX=100

INTERIM EARNINGS (Per Share):

Qtr.	Mar.	June	Sept.	Dec.
1998	0.44	0.51	d1.20	0.15
1999	0.18	0.19	0.13	0.17
2000	0.06	0.12	0.29	d0.05
2001	0.20	0.33	0.42	0.33
2002	0.12	d0.83	0.22	d0.30

INTERIM DIVIDENDS (Per Share):

Amt.	Decl.	Ex.	Rec.	Pay.
0.125Q	2/13/02	2/26/02	2/28/02	3/21/02
0.125Q	5/15/02	6/04/02	6/06/02	6/27/02
0.125Q	8/23/02	9/03/02	9/05/02	9/26/02
0.125Q	11/14/02	11/25/02	11/27/02	12/18/02
0.125Q	2/12/03	3/04/03	3/06/03	3/27/03

Indicated div.: $0.50

CAPITALIZATION (12/31/01):

	($000)	(%)
Long-Term Debt	1,403,000	22.6
Minority Interest	41,000	0.7
Common & Surplus	4,752,000	76.7
Total	6,196,000	100.0

BUSINESS:

Halliburton Company provides a variety of services, products, maintenance, engineering and construction to energy, industrial and governmental customers. The Energy Services Group segment (54.4% of 2002 revenues) consists of Halliburton Energy Services, Landmark Graphics and operations through various product lines in surface/subsea and major projects. This segment provides a range of services and products, as well as integrated solutions to customers for the exploration, development and production of oil and gas. The Engineering and Construction Group segment (45.6%), operating as Halliburton KBR, provides a range of services to energy and industrial customers and governmental entities worldwide. On 4/10/01, HAL completed the sale of Dresser Equipment Group to an investor group in a transaction valued at $1.55 billion, with HAL retaining a 5.1% ownership interest.

RECENT DEVELOPMENTS:

For the year ended 12/31/02, HAL posted a loss from continuing operations of $343.0 million versus income from continuing operations of $551.0 million the previous year. Results for 2002 and 2001 included asbestos charges of $564.0 million and $11.0 million, respectively. Results for 2002 also included restructuring charges of $107.0 million, while results for 2001 included goodwill amortization of $42.0 million. Total revenues slid 3.6% to $12.57 billion. Operating loss was $118.0 million versus income of $1.08 billion in 2001, due in part to lower rig activity.

PROSPECTS:

On 12/18/02, HAL announced it has reached an agreement in principle that, if completed, would result in a global settlement of all asbestos and other personal injury claims. The agreement covers all pending and future personal injury asbestos and other claims against DII Industries, LLC, the Engineering and Construction Group segment and their subsidiaries, as well as Harbison-Walker claims. Separately, 1/17/03, HAL announced that it has reached an agreement to sell its mono pumping business to National Oilwell, Inc. for total consideration of about $87.0 million. The sale of the mono pumping business is part of HAL's plan to divest the Company's non-strategic assets.

ANNUAL FINANCIAL DATA:

FISCAL YEAR	TOT. REVS. ($mill.)	NET INC. ($mill.)	TOT. ASSETS ($mill.)	OPER. PROFIT %	NET PROFIT %	RET. ON EQUITY %	RET. ON ASSETS %	CURR. RATIO	EARN. PER SH. $	CASH FL. PER SH. $	TANG. BK. VAL.$	DIV. PER SH. $	PRICE RANGE	AVG. P/E RATIO	AVG. YIELD %
p12/31/02	12,572.0	⑧ d343.0							⑧ d0.79			0.50	23.00 — 8.60	...	3.2
12/31/01	13,046.0	⑥ 551.0	10,966.0	8.3	4.2	11.6	5.0	1.9	⑥ 1.28	2.52	9.29	0.50	49.25 — 10.94	23.5	1.7
12/31/00	11,944.0	⑤ 188.0	10,103.0	3.9	1.6	4.8	1.9	1.5	⑤ 0.42	1.55	7.80	0.50	55.19 — 32.25	104.1	1.1
12/31/99	14,898.0	④ 298.0	10,728.0	4.4	2.0	7.0	2.8	1.6	④ 0.67	2.02	7.96	0.50	51.75 — 28.13	59.6	1.3
12/31/98	⑦ 17,353.1	① d14.7	11,112.0	2.3	...	...	...	1.5	① d0.03	1.30	7.48	0.50	57.25 — 25.00	...	1.2
12/31/97	8,818.6	② 454.0	5,603.0	9.1	5.2	17.6	8.1	1.7	② 1.75	2.94	8.62	0.50	63.25 — 29.69	26.6	1.1
12/31/96	7,385.1	② 300.4	4,436.6	5.7	4.1	13.9	6.8	1.6	② 1.19	2.25	7.68	0.50	31.81 — 22.38	22.8	1.8
12/31/95	5,698.7	② 233.8	3,646.6	6.7	4.1	13.4	6.4	1.8	② 1.02	2.15	6.74	0.50	25.44 — 16.44	20.5	2.4
12/31/94	5,740.5	177.8	5,268.3	4.1	3.1	9.2	3.4	2.6	0.78	1.92	7.58	0.50	18.63 — 13.94	20.9	3.1
12/31/93	6,350.8	② d161.0	5,403.1	...	...	...	...	2.1	② d0.71	1.38	7.31	0.50	22.00 — 12.88	...	2.9

Statistics are as originally reported. Adj. for 2-for-1 stk. split, 6/97 ① Incl. chrgs. of $980.1 mill. ② Incl. nonrecur. chrg. 12/31/97, $8.6 mill.; chrg. 12/31/96, $85.8 mill.; chrg. 12/31/93, $193.6 mill. ③ Bef. disc. ops. loss of $65.5 mill. ④ Incl. nonrecur. gain of $47.0 mill.; bef. acctg. chrg. of $19.0 mill. & extraordr. cr. of $159.0 mill. ⑤ Incl. chrg. of $193.0 mill.; bef. disc. ops. inc. of $98.0 mill. & disc. ops. disp. gain of $215.0 mill. ⑥ Bef. disc. ops. loss of $42.0 mill., disc. ops. disp. gain of $299.0 mill. & acctg. chge. cr. of $1.0 mill. ⑦ Refl. 9/29/98 acq. of Dresser Industries, Inc. ⑧ Incl. restruct. chrg. of $107.0 mill. & asbestos chrg. of $564.0 mill.; bef. disc. ops. loss of $641.0 mill.

OFFICERS:
D. J. Lesar, Chmn., Pres., C.E.O.
D. L. Foshee, C.O.O.
C. C. Gaut, Exec. V.P., C.F.O.
INVESTOR CONTACT: Guy T. Marcus, V.P., Investor Relations, (214) 978-2691
PRINCIPAL OFFICE: 4100 Clinton Drive, Houston, TX 77020

TELEPHONE NUMBER: (713) 676-3011
FAX: (214) 978-2611
WEB: www.halliburton.com
NO. OF EMPLOYEES: 85,000 (approx.)
SHAREHOLDERS: 25,100 (approx.)
ANNUAL MEETING: In May
INCORPORATED: DE, July, 1924

HANCOCK FABRICS, INC.

EXCH.	SYM.	REC. PRICE	P/E RATIO	YLD.	MKT. CAP.	RANGE (52-WK.)	'02 Y/E PR.
NYSE	HKF	14.28 (2/28/03)	13.5	2.8%	$260.4 mill.	20.40 - 13.64	15.25

MEDIUM GRADE. THE COMPANY CONTINUES TO INTRODUCE NEW HOME-DECORATING DEPARTMENTS THROUGHOUT ITS STORE BASE.

*7 YEAR PRICE SCORE 176.1   ***12 MONTH PRICE SCORE 107.5**

*NYSE COMPOSITE INDEX=100

INTERIM EARNINGS (Per Share):

Qtr.	Apr.	July	Oct.	Jan.
1996-97	0.08	0.06	0.18	0.26
1997-98	0.11	0.08	0.23	0.30
1998-99	0.10	0.02	0.18	d0.14
1999-00	0.06	d0.04	0.14	0.22
2000-01	0.12	0.03	0.19	0.31
2001-02	0.15	0.03	0.22	0.44
2002-03	0.20	0.08	0.31	0.47

INTERIM DIVIDENDS (Per Share):

Amt.	Decl.	Ex.	Rec.	Pay.
0.08Q	3/01/02	3/27/02	4/01/02	4/15/02
0.08Q	6/13/02	6/27/02	7/01/02	7/15/02
0.08Q	9/06/02	9/27/02	10/01/02	10/15/02
0.08Q	12/05/02	12/27/02	1/01/03	1/15/03
0.10Q	2/28/03	3/28/03	4/01/03	4/15/03

Indicated div.: $0.40

CAPITALIZATION (2/3/02):

	($000)	(%)
Common & Surplus	100,603	100.0
Total	100,603	100.0

BUSINESS:

Hancock Fabrics, Inc. is a retail and wholesale merchant of fabrics, crafts and related home sewing and decorating accessories. As of 2/25/03, the Company operated 430 stores in 42 states under the names Hancock Fabrics, Minnesota Fabrics, Fabric Market, Fabric Warehouse and Northwest Fabrics & Crafts, and supplied more than 100 independent wholesale customers. Products include fashion piece goods, patterns, notions, crafts, home decoration items and bridal items. The Company also offers a broad selection of drapery and upholstery fabrics. As a wholesaler of fabrics, HKF also sells to independent retail fabric stores through its wholesale distribution facility. On 11/1/97, the Company acquired 48 Northwest Fabrics & Crafts stores from Silas Creek Retail, L.P.

RECENT DEVELOPMENTS:

For the 52 weeks ended 2/2/03, net earnings totaled $19.9 million, up 35.9% compared with $14.7 million in the corresponding 53-week period the year before. Sales climbed 6.4% to $438.3 million from $411.9 million a year earlier. Comparable-store sales increased 8.3% year over year. Gross profit was $223.9 million, or 51.1% of sales, versus $210.5 million, or 51.1% of sales, the previous year. Selling, general and administrative expenses rose 3.4% to $186.9 million from $180.7 million in the prior year. Earnings before income taxes advanced 35.9% to $31.3 million from $23.0 million in 2001.

PROSPECTS:

The Company continues to expand its store-within-a-store concept for home decorating, which was in operation in 285 stores as of 2/25/03. Between 60 and 70 existing stores will be outfitted with the home decorating concept in 2003, as well as in the 35 to 40 new stores that are scheduled to open during the year. Meanwhile, results should benefit from an expanded selection of quilting and special occasion products, as well as the addition of premium products such as yarn, small furniture and iron beds. Separately, in 2003, the Company plans to expand its 473,000 square-foot distribution facility located in Tupelo, Mississippi by about 40.0% and build a new corporate headquarters facility nearby. Both facilities are expected to be completed in early 2004.

ANNUAL FINANCIAL DATA:

FISCAL YEAR	TOT. REVS. ($000)	NET INC. ($000)	TOT. ASSETS ($000)	OPER. PROFIT %	NET PROFIT %	RET. ON EQUITY %	RET. ON ASSETS %	CURR. RATIO	EARN. PER SH. $	CASH FL. PER SH. $	TANG. BK. VAL.$	DIV. PER SH. $	PRICE RANGE	AVG. P/E RATIO	AVG. YIELD %
p2/02/03	438,287	19,928						1.06				0.28	20.40 - 12.70	15.6	1.7
2/03/02	411,857	14,659	195,549	5.9	3.6	14.6	7.5	2.2	0.85	1.30	5.52	0.14	13.75 - 3.50	10.1	1.7
1/28/01	385,245	10,867	192,729	5.0	2.8	13.2	5.6	2.2	0.65	1.09	4.78	0.10	5.69 - 2.44	6.2	2.5
1/30/00	381,572	6,816	195,562	3.4	1.8	8.9	3.5	2.6	0.38	0.72	4.12	0.40	8.94 - 2.88	15.5	6.8
1/31/99	392,303	①3,556	192,404	1.7	0.9	4.6	1.8	2.8	①0.18	0.45	4.15	0.40	17.13 - 7.50	68.4	3.2
2/01/98	381,910	15,324	195,558	6.5	4.0	14.4	7.8	2.9	0.72	0.93	5.05	0.34	15.00 - 10.13	17.4	2.7
2/02/97	378,218	12,481	187,843	5.6	3.3	11.9	6.6	2.8	0.59	0.88	4.94	0.32	11.75 - 8.00	16.7	3.2
1/28/96	364,192	8,951	201,835	4.6	2.5	8.9	4.4	3.4	0.42	0.68	4.67	0.32	11.75 - 7.75	23.2	3.3
1/29/95	366,816	10,139	208,622	5.2	2.8	10.4	4.9	3.2	0.48	0.73	4.54	0.32	10.00 - 6.50	17.2	3.9
1/30/94	367,745	5,438	208,548	2.9	1.5	5.8	2.6	3.4	0.26	0.50	4.37	0.32	14.50 - 8.00	43.3	2.8

Statistics are as originally reported. ① Incl. $6.3 mil ($0.34/sh) after-tax non-recur. chg.

OFFICERS:
L. G. Kirk, Chmn., C.E.O.
J. W. Busby, Jr., Pres., C.O.O.
B. D. Smith, Sr. V.P., C.F.O., Treas.
INVESTOR CONTACT: Ellen J. Kennedy, Investor Relations, (662) 842-2834 ext.109
PRINCIPAL OFFICE: 3406 W. Main St., Tupelo, MS 38801

TELEPHONE NUMBER: (662) 842-2834
FAX: (662) 842-2834
WEB: www.hancockfabrics.com
NO. OF EMPLOYEES: 6,500 (avg.)
SHAREHOLDERS: 5,526 (record)
ANNUAL MEETING: In June
INCORPORATED: DE, 1987

INSTITUTIONAL HOLDINGS:
No. of Institutions: 90
Shares Held: 12,625,636
% Held: 66.7
INDUSTRY: Sewing, needlework, and piece goods (SIC: 5949).
TRANSFER AGENT(S): Continental Stock Transfer & Trust Co., New York, NY

HANDLEMAN COMPANY

EXCH.	SYM.	REC. PRICE	P/E RATIO	YLD.	MKT. CAP.	RANGE (52-WK.)	'02 Y/E PR.
NYSE	HDL	14.10 (2/28/03)	12.2	...	$374.2 mill.	15.25 - 7.50	11.50

MEDIUM GRADE. THE COMPANY ENTERED INTO A NON-BINDING LETTER OF INTENT TO SELL MADACY ENTERTAINMENT.

*7 YEAR PRICE SCORE 121.2   *12 MONTH PRICE SCORE 120.9
*NYSE COMPOSITE INDEX=100

INTERIM EARNINGS (Per Share):

Qtr.	July	Oct.	Jan.	Apr.
1996-97	d0.24	0.20	0.19	0.01
1997-98	d0.19	0.25	0.21	d0.26
1998-99	d1.86	0.19	0.18	0.39
1999-00	0.02	0.45	0.50	0.35
2000-01	0.06	0.51	0.60	0.37
2001-02	0.08	0.58	0.27	0.45
2002-03	0.10	0.61	Nil	...

INTERIM DIVIDENDS (Per Share):

Amt.	Decl.	Ex.	Rec.	Pay.
Last dist. $0.05Q, 1/10/96				

CAPITALIZATION (4/27/02):

	($000)	(%)
Long-Term Debt	53,749	15.7
Common & Surplus	289,618	84.3
Total	343,367	100.0

BUSINESS:

Handleman Company operates in two business segments: Handleman Entertainment Resources (H.E.R.) and North Coast Entertainment (NCE). H.E.R. (89.5% of fiscal 2002 revenue) is a category manager and distributor of prerecorded music to mass merchants in the U.S., Canada, United Kingdom, Mexico, Brazil and Argentina. H.E.R. provides various merchandising services to retail accounts such as direct-to-store shipments, marketing and instore merchandising. NCE (10.5%) is comprised of two companies. Anchor Bay Entertainment is a major independent home video label. Madacy Entertainment, a major independent record label, markets music and video products. In July, 1998, HDL sold its software publishing subsidiary, Sofsource, Inc., and its book distribution business.

RECENT DEVELOPMENTS:

For the three months ended 1/31/03, the Company reported net income of $24,000 compared with $7.2 million in the corresponding prior-year period. Results included pre-tax charges of $33.1 million and $5.7 million in 2003 and 2002, respectively, for impairment of subsidiary assets. Revenues climbed 12.2% to $437.6 million from $389.9 million the year before. Handleman Entertainment Resources' sales advanced 12.9% to $412.7 million from $365.4 million in the previous year, reflecting increased sales in the U.S., Canada and the United Kingdom. Meanwhile, North Coast Entertainment's sales slipped 3.4% to $28.7 million from $29.7 million a year earlier. Gross profit as a percentage of revenues improved to 20.5% from 19.4% the prior year.

PROSPECTS:

On 2/25/03, the Company announced that it has entered into a non-binding letter of intent to sell Madacy Entertainment. Terms of the transaction, which is expected to be completed within 30 days, were not disclosed, however, the Company expects the sale will generate approximately $41.0 million in cash, including a tax benefit. Meanwhile, HDL is taking steps expected to significantly reduce operating losses from its Handleman Online e-commerce unit. The Company plans to partner with third parties to provide Internet technology services, such as web site hosting, maintenance and support, which will no longer be developed or supported by Handleman Online.

ANNUAL FINANCIAL DATA:

FISCAL YEAR	TOT. REVS. ($mill.)	NET INC. ($mill.)	TOT. ASSETS ($mill.)	OPER. PROFIT %	NET PROFIT %	RET. ON EQUITY %	RET. ON ASSETS %	CURR. RATIO	EARN. PER SH. $	CASH FL. PER SH. $	TANG. BK. VAL. $	DIV. PER SH. $	PRICE RANGE		AVG. P/E RATIO	AVG. YIELD %
4/27/02	1,337.5	37.1	605.5	3.7	2.8	12.8	6.1	1.8	1.39	2.27	10.94	...	17.89 -	7.25	9.0	...
4/28/01	1,193.0	42.0	590.7	6.0	3.5	16.6	7.1	1.6	1.53	2.29	9.54	...	13.50 -	6.44	6.5	...
4/29/00	1,137.6	38.6	519.7	6.1	3.4	17.3	7.4	1.5	1.30	1.98	7.52	...	17.00 -	9.38	10.1	...
5/01/99	1,058.6	☐d35.1	487.9	...	...	...	...	1.7	☐d11.1	d0.46	7.27	...	15.00 -	5.81	...	...
5/02/98	1,104.5	☐ 0.3	613.1	1.1	...	0.1	0.1	2.1	☐0.01	1.01	8.56	...	9.63 -	5.13	730.2	...
5/03/97	1,181.0	5.4	667.9	2.0	0.5	1.9	0.8	2.1	0.16	1.22	8.50	0.05	9.00 -	4.00	40.6	0.8
4/27/96	1,132.6	☐ d22.5	693.9	...	...	...	...	1.9	☐d0.67	0.44	8.35	0.44	11.88 -	5.63	...	5.0
4/29/95	1,226.1	☐ 28.0	754.1	4.3	2.3	9.0	3.7	1.9	☐0.84	1.78	9.29	0.44	14.00 -	10.00	14.3	3.7
4/30/94	1,066.6	27.7	641.0	4.9	2.6	9.2	4.3	1.8	0.83	1.78	8.96	0.43	16.00 -	9.88	15.6	3.3
5/01/93	1,121.7	43.7	655.9	6.9	3.9	15.2	6.7	1.9	1.32	2.23	8.69	0.40	15.88 -	10.63	10.0	3.0

Statistics are as originally reported. ☐ Incl. $127.4 mil pre-tax non-recur. chg. & $31.0 mil one-time pre-tax gain on sale of subsidiary, 1999; $11.2 mil after-tax restr. chg., 1998; $16 mil pre-tax chg., 1996; & $7.5 mil restr. chg., 1995.

OFFICERS:
S. Strome, Chmn., C.E.O.
P. J. Cline, Pres., C.O.O.
T. C. Braun, Jr., Sr. V.P., C.F.O.
INVESTOR CONTACT: Tim C. Oviatt, V.P. & Treas., (248) 362-4400
PRINCIPAL OFFICE: 500 Kirts Boulevard, Troy, MI 48084-4142

TELEPHONE NUMBER: (248) 362-4400
FAX: (248) 362-3615
WEB: www.handleman.com
NO. OF EMPLOYEES: 2,600 (avg.)
SHAREHOLDERS: 2,887 (record)
ANNUAL MEETING: In Sept.
INCORPORATED: MI, July, 1979

INSTITUTIONAL HOLDINGS:
No. of Institutions: 94
Shares Held: 21,281,482
% Held: 82.4

INDUSTRY: Durable goods, nec (SIC: 5099)

TRANSFER AGENT(S): Fifth Third Bank, Cincinnati, OH

HANOVER COMPRESSOR CO.

EXCH.	SYM.	REC. PRICE	P/E RATIO	YLD.	MKT. CAP.	RANGE (52-WK.)	'02 Y/E PR.
NYSE	HC	8.09 (2/28/03)	...	...	$0.64 bill.	20.33 - 6.20	9.18

LOWER MEDIUM GRADE. THE COMPANY HAS IDENTIFIED SEVERAL AREAS WHERE IT COULD IMPROVE ITS ONGOING OPERATING PERFORMANCE.

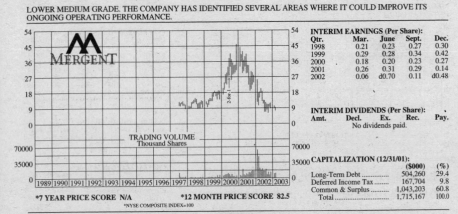

*7 YEAR PRICE SCORE N/A   ***12 MONTH PRICE SCORE 82.5**

*NYSE COMPOSITE INDEX=100

INTERIM EARNINGS (Per Share):

Qtr.	Mar.	June	Sept.	Dec.
1998	0.21	0.23	0.27	0.30
1999	0.29	0.28	0.34	0.42
2000	0.18	0.20	0.23	0.27
2001	0.26	0.31	0.29	0.14
2002	0.06	d0.70	0.11	d0.48

INTERIM DIVIDENDS (Per Share):

Amt.	Decl.	Ex.	Rec.	Pay.
		No dividends paid.		

CAPITALIZATION (12/31/01):

	($000)	(%)
Long-Term Debt	504,260	29.4
Deferred Income Tax	167,704	9.8
Common & Surplus	1,043,203	60.8
Total	1,715,167	100.0

BUSINESS:

Hanover Compressor Co. is engaged in full-service natural gas compression and provides service financing, fabrication and equipment for contract natural gas handling applications. HC provides this equipment on a rental, contract compression, maintenance and acquisition leaseback basis to natural gas production, processing and transportation companies. HC's customers include independent and major producers and distributors. In conjunction with its mainte-nance business, HC has developed a parts and service business to provide services to customers that own their own compression equipment, but want to outsource their operations. HC's compression services are complemented by its compressor and oil and gas production equipment fabrication operations and gas processing and treating, gas measurement and power generation services.

RECENT DEVELOPMENTS:

For the year ended 12/31/02, loss from continuing operations amounted to $74.8 million compared with income from continuing operations of $69.6 million in 2001. Results were negatively affected by increased interest and leasing expenses as well as higher selling, general and administrative expenses. Results for 2002 and 2001 included a loss of $3.2 million and a gain of $7.6 million from a change in the fair value of derivative financial instruments. Results for 2002 also included a goodwill impairment of $52.1 million. Results for 2002 and 2001 excluded a loss of $41.2 million and a gain of $3.0 million, respectively, from discontinued operations. Total revenues slipped 1.2% to $1.03 billion from $1.04 billion the previous year.

PROSPECTS:

During the fourth quarter of 2002, the Company completed a comprehensive review of its operations and lines of business and identified several areas where it could improve its ongoing operating performance by exiting non-core businesses and streamlining its fabrication operations through the consolidation of facilities. As a result of this process, HC will reduce its staffing levels by approximately 500 employees. HC expects pre-tax savings in employee salaries and benefits of approximately $12.0 million in 2003 and annualized pre-tax savings of about $20.0 million.

ANNUAL FINANCIAL DATA:

FISCAL YEAR	TOT. REVS. ($mill.)	NET INC. ($mill.)	TOT. ASSETS ($mill.)	OPER. PROFIT %	NET PROFIT %	RET. ON EQUITY %	RET. ON ASSETS %	CURR. RATIO	EARN. PER SH. $	CASH FL. PER SH. $	TANG. BK. VAL. $	PRICE RANGE	AVG. P/E RATIO
p12/31/02	1,028.8	③ d74.8		13.1	6.8	7.0	3.2	1.8	③ d0.94	2.02	10.07	25.52 - 6.20	...
12/31/01	1,078.2	② 72.8	2,273.0	16.9	9.7	9.2	4.6	2.6	② 0.95	1.58	7.49	44.38 - 19.00	33.4
12/31/00	603.8	58.7	1,289.5	22.8	12.8	11.0	5.3	2.3	0.88	2.58	12.84	46.06 - 16.91	35.8
12/31/99	317.0	① 40.4	756.5	21.8	10.8	9.6	4.9	3.2	① 1.32	2.27	11.08	19.19 - 9.63	10.9
12/31/98	282.0	① 30.4	614.6	20.2	9.1	6.3	3.6	2.6	① 1.01	1.73	10.16	14.81 - 8.66	11.6
12/31/97	198.8	18.1	506.5	17.5	7.6	5.9	3.0	2.7	0.66	1.09	7.72	13.00 - 8.56	16.3
12/31/96	136.0	10.4	341.4	14.2	5.9	4.0	2.2	2.1	0.15	1.16	6.87	...	...
12/31/95	96.0	5.6	252.3	16.1	7.8				0.30	0.89		...	...
12/31/94	56.1	4.4	...						0.30			...	...

Statistics are as originally reported. Adj. for 2-for-1 stk. spl., 6/00. ① Incl. gain on sale of prop., plt. & equip., 1999, $5.9 mill.; 1998, $2.6 mill. ② Excl. $164,000 acct. change chg. ③ Incl. $3.2 mill. loss fr. chg. in fair value of deriv., $52.1 mill. goodwill amort., & excl. $41.2 mill. gain fr. disc. ops.

OFFICERS:
V. E. Grijalva, Chmn.
C. C. Deaton, Pres., C.E.O.
J. E. Jackson, Sr. V.P., C.F.O.
INVESTOR CONTACT: Lee Beckelman, Investor Relations, (281) 447-8787
PRINCIPAL OFFICE: 12001 North Houston Rosslyn, Houston, TX 77086

TELEPHONE NUMBER: (281) 447-8787
FAX: (281) 441-0821
WEB: www.hanover.com
NO. OF EMPLOYEES: 4,800 (approx.)
SHAREHOLDERS: 632 (approx. record)
ANNUAL MEETING: In May
INCORPORATED: DE, Oct., 1990

INSTITUTIONAL HOLDINGS:
No. of Institutions: 165
Shares Held: 49,654,698
% Held: 61.7
INDUSTRY: Equipment rental & leasing, nec (SIC: 7359)
TRANSFER AGENT(S): Mellon Investor Services, Dallas, TX

HARLAND (JOHN H.) COMPANY

EXCH.	SYM.	REC. PRICE	P/E RATIO	YLD.	MKT. CAP.	RANGE (52-WK.)	'02 Y/E PR.
NYSE	JH	22.98 (2/28/03)	13.2	1.3%	$0.66 bill.	34.81 - 18.20	22.13

MEDIUM GRADE. EARNINGS PER SHARE FOR THE FULL-YEAR 2003 ARE EXPECTED TO BE IN THE RANGE OF $1.98 TO $2.03.

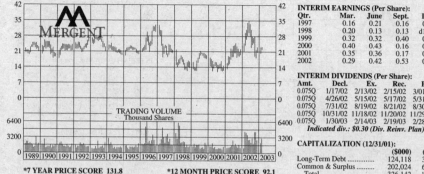

INTERIM EARNINGS (Per Share):

Qtr.	Mar.	June	Sept.	Dec.
1997	0.16	0.21	0.16	0.03
1998	0.20	0.13	0.13	d1.12
1999	0.32	0.32	0.40	0.34
2000	0.40	0.43	0.16	0.01
2001	0.35	0.36	0.17	0.42
2002	0.29	0.42	0.53	0.50

INTERIM DIVIDENDS (Per Share):

Amt.	Decl.	Ex.	Rec.	Pay.
0.075Q	1/17/02	2/13/02	2/15/02	3/01/02
0.075Q	4/26/02	5/15/02	5/17/02	5/31/02
0.075Q	7/31/02	8/19/02	8/21/02	8/30/02
0.075Q	10/31/02	11/18/02	11/20/02	11/29/02
0.075Q	1/30/03	2/14/03	2/19/03	2/28/03

Indicated div.: $0.30 (Div. Reinv. Plan)

CAPITALIZATION (12/31/01):

	($000)	(%)
Long-Term Debt	124,118	38.1
Common & Surplus	202,024	61.9
Total	326,142	100.0

*7 YEAR PRICE SCORE 131.8   *12 MONTH PRICE SCORE 92.1
*NYSE COMPOSITE INDEX=100

BUSINESS:

John H. Harland Company, a provider of software and printed products to the financial markets, operates in three segments. The Printed Products segment includes personal and business checks, computer checks and internal bank forms, which are sold primarily to financial institutions. The Software and Services segment includes Harland Financial Solutions and Harland Analytical Services, and provides lending and mortgage origination and closing applications, database marketing software, host processing applications and business intelligence applications. The Scantron segment provides educational technology products and services primarily to the commercial, financial institution and education markets. Revenues (and operating income) for 2002 were derived: printed products, 68.1% (67.3%); software and services, 17.9% (10.4%); and Scantron, 14.0% (22.3%).

RECENT DEVELOPMENTS:

For the twelve months ended 12/31/02, net income jumped 34.5% to $52.4 million compared with $39.0 million in 2001. Results for 2002 and 2001 included amortization of intangibles of $2.6 million and $14.0 million, and losses from investment write-downs of $303,000 and $7.8 million, respectively. Results for 2002 also included an acquired in-process research and development charge of $3.0 million and a loss on the sale of investments of $1.8 million. Sales were $767.8 million, up 3.3% from $743.2 million in the prior year.

PROSPECTS:

Going forward, JH's printed products segment will focus squarely on profitable revenue growth. The software and services segment should continue to benefit from recent acquisitions and the introduction of new products. The scantron segment should continue to deliver consistent results in a soft environment for expenditures in the K-12 education market. Separately, JH expects earnings per share for the full-year 2003 in the range of $1.98 to $2.03. Although the fourth quarter of 2002 was strong, there are a number of factors that are hampering the Company's outlook for 2003, including the loss of a large customer and weak economic conditions.

ANNUAL FINANCIAL DATA:

FISCAL YEAR	TOT. REVS. ($mill.)	NET INC. ($mill.)	TOT. ASSETS ($mill.)	OPER. PROFIT %	NET PROFIT %	RET. ON EQUITY %	RET. ON ASSETS %	CURR. RATIO	EARN. PER SH.$	CASH FL. PER SH.$	TANG. BK. VAL.$	DIV. PER SH.$	PRICE RANGE	AVG. P/E RATIO	AVG. YIELD
p12/31/02	767.8	⑦ 52.4							⑦ 1.73			0.30	34.81 - 18.20	15.3	1.1
12/31/01	743.2	⑥ 39.0	467.0	11.9	5.2	19.3	8.3	1.1	⑥ 1.31	3.34	2.33	0.30	24.90 - 13.19	14.5	1.6
12/31/00	720.7	⑤ 28.7	522.9	8.4	4.0	16.7	5.5	1.2	⑤ 1.00	2.68	1.00	0.30	18.31 - 11.88	15.1	2.0
12/31/99	702.5	④ 42.7	391.4	10.4	6.1	25.3	10.9	1.6	④ 1.37	2.66	3.76	0.30	21.25 - 12.38	12.3	1.8
12/31/98	566.7	③ d20.6	391.8	...	...	...	...	1.5	③ d0.66	0.70	3.03	0.30	21.88 - 12.25	...	1.8
12/31/97	562.7	② 17.3	426.2	6.2	3.1	9.0	4.1	1.4	② 0.56	1.80	2.49	0.30	32.88 - 18.38	45.8	1.2
12/31/96	609.4	① d13.9	454.7	...	...	...	...	1.0	① d0.45	0.93	1.78	1.02	33.00 - 20.75	...	3.8
12/31/95	561.6	46.8	474.7	14.9	8.3	21.0	9.9	1.2	1.51	3.11	2.91	1.02	23.63 - 19.13	14.2	4.8
12/31/94	521.3	51.2	414.4	17.7	9.8	25.2	12.4	1.5	1.68	3.04	3.34	0.98	24.75 - 19.38	13.1	4.4
12/31/93	519.5	52.5	356.5	16.8	10.1	28.6	14.7	1.3	1.62	2.70	4.3	0.94	28.13 - 20.88	15.1	3.8

Statistics are as originally reported. ① Incl. $63.5 mill. after-tax restr. chgs. for in-process R&D. ② Incl. $0.15/sh. for restr. & costs assoc. with develop. of printing equip. tech. & incl. $0.05/sh. gain fr. sale of bldgs. ③ Incl. $51.1 mill. loss fr. restr. chgs., $12.8 mill. loss fr. development chgs., & $10.9 mill. gain fr. sale of assets. ④ Incl. $0.03 per sh. tax benefit. ⑤ Incl. $8.2 mill. one-time in-process R&D chg. & $14.5 mill. restr. chg. ⑥ Incl. $14.5 mill. restr. chg., $14.0 mill. amort. of intang. & $7.8 mill. invest. of write-down. ⑦ Incl. $3.0 mill. acq. in-process R&D chg., $303,000 loss on invest. write-down & $1.8 mill. loss on sale of invest.

OFFICERS:
T. C. Tuff, Chmn., C.E.O.
C. B. Carden, V.P., C.F.O.
J. Stakel, V.P., Treas.
INVESTOR CONTACT: Victoria P. Weyand, Investor Relations, (770) 593-5128
PRINCIPAL OFFICE: 2939 Miller Rd., Decatur, GA 30035

TELEPHONE NUMBER: (770) 981-9460
FAX: (770) 593-5367
WEB: www.harland.net
NO. OF EMPLOYEES: 4,999 (approx.)
SHAREHOLDERS: 4,576
ANNUAL MEETING: In Apr.
INCORPORATED: GA, June, 1923

INSTITUTIONAL HOLDINGS:
No. of Institutions: 136
Shares Held: 20,387,069
% Held: 69.3
INDUSTRY: Blankbooks and looseleaf binders (SIC: 2782)
TRANSFER AGENT(S): First Chicago Trust Company of New York, Jersey City, NJ

HARLEY-DAVIDSON, INC.

EXCH.	SYM.	REC. PRICE	P/E RATIO	YLD.	MKT. CAP.	RANGE (52-WK.)	'02 Y/E PR.
NYSE	HDI	39.59 (2/28/03)	20.9	0.4%	$11.99 bill.	56.50 - 38.62	46.20

INVESTMENT GRADE. THE COMPANY EXPECTS TO PRODUCE 289,000 HARELY-DAVIDSON MOTORCYCLES IN 2003.

*7 YEAR PRICE SCORE 172.6   ***12 MONTH PRICE SCORE 95.3**
*NYSE COMPOSITE INDEX=100

INTERIM EARNINGS (Per Share):

Qtr.	Mar.	June	Sept.	Dec.
1999	0.19	0.22	0.21	0.24
2000	0.26	0.29	0.27	0.31
2001	0.30	0.38	0.36	0.39
2002	0.39	0.47	0.54	0.49

INTERIM DIVIDENDS (Per Share):

Amt.	Decl.	Ex.	Rec.	Pay.
0.03Q	2/13/02	3/08/02	3/12/02	3/22/02
0.035Q	5/04/02	6/07/02	6/11/02	6/21/02
0.035Q	8/15/02	9/16/02	9/18/02	9/30/02
0.035Q	12/11/02	12/18/02	12/20/02	12/31/02
0.035Q	2/12/03	3/10/03	3/12/03	3/24/03

Indicated div.: $0.14 (Div. Reinv. Plan)

CAPITALIZATION (12/31/01):

	($000)	(%)
Long-Term Debt	380,000	17.6
Deferred Income Tax	17,816	0.8
Common & Surplus	1,756,283	81.5
Total	2,154,099	100.0

BUSINESS:

Harley-Davidson, Inc. operates in two business segments. HDI's Motorcycles and Related Products segment (95.1% of revenue and 88.4% of income in 2002) consists primarily of the Company's wholly-owned subsidiaries, H-D Michigan, Inc., Harley-Davidson Motor Company and Buell Motorcycle Company. The Motorcycles segment designs, manufactures and sells primarily heavyweight touring, custom and sport motorcycles and a broad range of related products, which include motorcycle parts and accessories and general merchandise. The Financial Services segment (4.9%, 11.6%), which is comprised of Harley-Davidson Financial Services, Inc., provides financing and insurance for HDI's dealers and customers.

RECENT DEVELOPMENTS:

For the year ended 12/31/02, net income advanced 32.5% to $580.2 million versus $437.7 million in the previous year. Earnings for 2002 benefited from commemorative sales of parts and accessories and general merchandise related to HDI's 100th anniversary. Net revenues increased 20.1% to $4.09 billion from $3.41 billion a year earlier. Harley-Davidson® motorcycle sales climbed 18.3% to $3.16 billion, while parts and accessories revenues rose 23.5% to $626.2 million. General merchandise sales jumped 41.2% to $231.5 million. Buell® motorcycle sales grew 8.6% to $66.9 million. Operating income increased 33.2% to $882.7 million from $662.5 million the year before. Harley-Davidson motorcycle shipments were up 12.5% to 263,653 units from 234,461 units in 2001.

PROSPECTS:

The Company's 2003 production goal for Harley-Davidson motorcycles is 289,000 units. In addition, excitement surrounding the Company 100th Anniversary should continue to positively affect near-term results, particularly for sales of parts and accessories and general merchandise. The 100th Anniversary celebration will culminate in four days of festivities in the Milwaukee, Wisconsin area in August 2003. Separately, the Company expects full-year 2003 operating income from Harley-Davidson Financial Services, Inc. to grow approximately 20.0% over 2002 performance.

ANNUAL FINANCIAL DATA:

FISCAL YEAR	TOT. REVS. ($mill.)	NET INC. ($mill.)	TOT. ASSETS ($mill.)	OPER. PROFIT %	NET PROFIT %	RET. ON EQUITY %	RET. ON ASSETS %	CURR. RATIO	EARN. PER SH.$	CASH FL. PER SH.$	TANG. BK. VAL.$	DIV. PER SH.$	PRICE RANGE	AVG. P/E RATIO	AVG. YIELD %
p12/31/02	4,302.5	580.2							1.90			0.14	57.25 - 42.60	26.3	0.3
⑥ 12/31/01	3,545.0	437.7	3,118.5	18.7	12.3	24.9	14.0	2.3	1.43	1.93	5.64	0.12	55.99 - 32.00	30.8	0.3
⑤ 12/31/00	2,943.5	④ 347.7	2,436.4	17.5	11.8	24.7	14.3	2.6	④ 1.13	1.56	4.47	0.10	50.63 - 29.53	35.5	0.2
12/31/99	2,480.6	267.2	2,112.1	16.8	10.8	23.0	12.7	1.8	0.87	1.23	3.65	0.09	32.03 - 21.38	30.9	0.3
12/31/98	2,084.2	③ 213.5	1,920.2	16.0	10.2	20.7	11.1	1.8	③ 0.69	0.97	3.20	0.08	23.75 - 12.47	26.2	0.4
12/31/97	1,774.9	174.1	1,598.9	15.2	9.8	21.1	10.9	1.9	0.57	0.79	2.59	0.07	15.63 - 8.34	21.2	0.6
12/31/96	1,539.0	② 143.4	1,320.0	14.8	9.3	21.6	10.9	1.6	② 0.48	0.66	2.05	0.06	12.38 - 6.59	20.0	0.6
12/31/95	1,354.1	② 111.1	1,000.7	13.4	8.2	22.5	11.1	1.4	② 0.37	0.51	1.51	0.05	7.53 - 5.50	17.6	0.7
12/31/94	1,541.8	104.3	778.3	10.4	6.8	24.0	13.4	1.3	0.34	0.46	1.42	0.04	7.47 - 5.41	18.8	0.5
12/31/93	1,217.4	① 18.4	583.3	5.7	1.5	5.7	3.2	1.7	① 0.06	0.17	1.07	0.02	5.94 - 3.94	80.8	0.3

Statistics are as originally reported. Adj. for stk. splits: 2-for-1, 4/00, 9/97, 9/94. ① Incl. non-recurr. chrg. $57.0 mill. fr. write-down of assets & bef. acctg. change chrg. $30.3 mill. ($0.20/sh) ② Bef. disc. opers. gain $1.4 mill., 1995; $22.6 mill., 1996. ③ Bef. extraord. loss $3.2 mill. ④ Incl. pre-tax non-recurr. gain $18.9 mill. fr. sale of Visa card bus. ⑤ 12/00 and prior-year revenues included operating income from the financial services segment. ⑥ Revenues reflect net sales plus financing and insurance revenues.

OFFICERS:
J. L. Bleustein, Chmn., C.E.O.
J. A. McCaslin, Pres., C.O.O.
J. L. Ziemer, V.P., C.F.O.
INVESTOR CONTACT: Investor Relations, (414) 343-4782
PRINCIPAL OFFICE: 3700 West Juneau Avenue, Milwaukee, WI 53208

TELEPHONE NUMBER: (414) 342-4680
FAX: (414) 343-4621
WEB: www.harley-davidson.com
NO. OF EMPLOYEES: 8,650 (avg.)
SHAREHOLDERS: 76,935
ANNUAL MEETING: In May
INCORPORATED: DE, April, 1981; reincorp., WI, June, 1991

INSTITUTIONAL HOLDINGS:
No. of Institutions: 530
Shares Held: 230,258,002
% Held: 76.1
INDUSTRY: Motorcycles, bicycles, and parts (SIC: 3751)
TRANSFER AGENT(S): ComputerShare Investor Services, Chicago, IL

HARMAN INTERNATIONAL INDUSTRIES, INC.

EXCH.	SYM.	REC. PRICE	P/E RATIO	YLD.	MKT. CAP.	RANGE (52-WK.)	'02 Y/E PR.
NYSE	HAR	63.53 (2/28/03)	27.7	0.2%	$2.07 bill.	65.30 - 38.18	59.50

UPPER MEDIUM GRADE. THE COMPANY SHOULD CONTINUE TO EXPERIENCE GROWTH IN DEMAND IN EUROPE FROM MERCEDES-BENZ, BMW, PORSCHE AND AUDI FOR HARMANBECKER'S NEW INFOTAINMENT SYSTEMS.

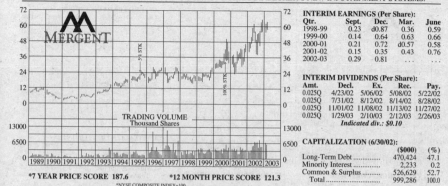

*7 YEAR PRICE SCORE 187.6   ***12 MONTH PRICE SCORE 121.3**

*NYSE COMPOSITE INDEX=100

INTERIM EARNINGS (Per Share):

Qtr.	Sept.	Dec.	Mar.	June
1998-99	0.23	d0.87	0.36	0.59
1999-00	0.14	0.64	0.63	0.66
2000-01	0.21	0.72	d0.57	0.58
2001-02	0.15	0.35	0.43	0.76
2002-03	0.29	0.81	...	...

INTERIM DIVIDENDS (Per Share):

Amt.	Decl.	Ex.	Rec.	Pay.
0.025Q	4/23/02	5/06/02	5/08/02	5/22/02
0.025Q	7/31/02	8/12/02	8/14/02	8/28/02
0.025Q	11/01/02	11/08/02	11/13/02	11/27/02
0.025Q	1/29/03	2/10/03	2/12/03	2/26/03

Indicated div.: $0.10

CAPITALIZATION (6/30/02):

	($000)	(%)
Long-Term Debt	470,424	47.1
Minority Interest	2,233	0.2
Common & Surplus	526,629	52.7
Total	999,286	100.0

BUSINESS:

Harman International Industries, Inc. designs, manufactures and markets high-quality, high-fidelity audio products, including professional and consumer loudspeakers and electronics. HAR's products are sold to worldwide consumer and professional audio markets. The Company is organized in two operating groups: Consumer Systems and Professional. Harman's brand names include JBL, HARMAN KARDON, INFINITY, AKG, CROWN, STUDER, SOUNDCRAFT, SPIRIT, DOD, DIGITECH, LEXICON, DBX, BECKER, MARK LEVINSON, PROCEED, and REVEL.

RECENT DEVELOPMENTS:

For the three months ended 12/31/02, net income more than doubled to $27.6 million compared with $11.7 million in the equivalent period of the previous year. Net sales increased 19.8% to $560.0 million from $467.4 million in the year-earlier period. Net sales for the Consumer Systems Group improved 23.3% to $447.9 million from $363.4 million in 2002, due to increased sales in Europe. Net sales for the Professional Group climbed 7.7% to $112.1 million from $104.1 million the previous year, reflecting strong sales growth at CROWN and AKG. Gross profit advanced 29.0% to $164.3 million from $127.4 million in the prior-year quarter. Operating income leapt 92.1% to $43.3 million versus $22.5 million the year before.

PROSPECTS:

The Company should continue to experience growth in demand in Europe from Mercedes-Benz, BMW, Porsche and Audi for HARMANBECKER's new infotainment systems. The Company should also continue to receive strong demand from Toyota for JBL's branded music systems. Meanwhile, the Company's professional group business is benefiting from strong contributions from CROWN and AKG. For its 2003 fiscal year, HAR expects earnings to be approximately $3.00 per share.

ANNUAL FINANCIAL DATA:

FISCAL YEAR	TOT. REVS. ($mill.)	NET INC. ($mill.)	TOT. ASSETS ($mill.)	OPER. PROFIT %	NET PROFIT %	RET. ON EQUITY %	RET. ON ASSETS %	CURR. RATIO	EARN. PER SH.$	CASH FL. PER SH.$	TANG. BK. VAL.$	DIV. PER SH.$	PRICE RANGE	AVG. P/E RATIO	AVG. YIELD %
6/30/02	1,826.2	57.5	1,480.3	5.7	3.1	10.9	3.9	2.0	1.70	4.00	10.07	0.10	65.30 - 38.18	30.4	0.2
6/30/01	1,716.5	⑤ 32.4	1,162.4	4.1	1.9	7.7	2.8	2.0	⑤ 0.96	2.95	8.66	0.10	46.62 - 23.28	36.4	0.3
6/30/00	1,677.9	72.8	1,137.5	7.3	4.3	15.0	6.4	1.9	2.06	3.89	9.39	0.10	50.35 - 27.50	18.9	0.3
6/30/99	1,500.1	④ 11.7	1,065.8	2.6	0.8	2.5	1.1	2.3	④ 0.33	2.17	9.22	0.10	28.06 - 17.13	69.5	0.4
6/30/98	1,513.3	③ 53.8	1,130.7	6.6	3.6	10.5	4.8	2.1	③ 1.43	3.08	9.40	0.10	23.41 - 15.75	13.7	0.5
6/30/97	1,474.1	54.8	1,014.3	6.9	3.7	11.7	5.4	2.7	1.48	2.91	9.68	0.10	28.53 - 16.19	15.1	0.4
6/30/96	1,361.6	52.0	996.2	7.7	3.8	11.9	5.2	2.4	1.58	3.13	8.23	0.10	28.25 - 16.00	14.0	0.5
6/30/95	1,170.2	41.4	886.9	7.5	3.5	14.3	4.7	1.9	1.30	2.69	5.14	0.09	24.88 - 17.00	16.1	0.4
6/30/94	862.1	① ② 26.4	680.7	7.7	3.1	11.4	3.9	1.8	① ② 0.94	2.09	6.25	0.04	19.00 - 12.25	16.6	0.2
6/30/93	664.9	11.2	431.7	6.2	1.7	10.1	2.6	2.0	0.50	1.51	14.63 - 7.25	22.1	...	

Statistics are as originally reported. Adjusted for a 5% stock dividend, 8/95; 2-for-1, 9/00. ① Bef. extraord. charge of $748,000 ($0.03 per sh.). ② Bef. extraord. charge of $274,000 ($0.01 per sh.). ③ Excl. an after-tax extraord. charge of $3.6 million for the early retirement of debt. ④ Incl. nonrecurring after-tax charges totaling $66.4 million. ⑤ Incl. after-tax non-recurr. chrg. of $25.8 mill.

OFFICERS:
S. Harman, Exec. Chmn.
B. A. Girod, Vice-Chmn., C.E.O.
G. P. Stapleton, Pres., C.O.O.
F. Meredith, Exec. V.P., C.F.O.

INVESTOR CONTACT: Frank Meredith, Exec. V.P., C.F.O., (818) 893-8411

PRINCIPAL OFFICE: 1101 Pennsylvania Avenue, NW, Suite 1010, Washington, DC 20004

TELEPHONE NUMBER: (202) 393-1101
FAX: (202) 393-3064
WEB: www.harman.com

NO. OF EMPLOYEES: 10,389

SHAREHOLDERS: 184 (approx., record)

ANNUAL MEETING: In Nov.

INCORPORATED: DE, 1980

INSTITUTIONAL HOLDINGS:
No. of Institutions: 204
Shares Held: 32,356,961
% Held: 100.3

INDUSTRY: Household audio and video equipment (SIC: 3651)

TRANSFER AGENT(S): Mellon Investor Services, Los Angeles, CA

HARRAH'S ENTERTAINMENT, INC.

EXCH.	SYM.	REC. PRICE	P/E RATIO	YLD.	MKT. CAP.	RANGE (52-WK.)	'02 Y/E PR.
NYSE	HET	32.84 (2/28/03)	11.4	...	$3.69 bill.	51.35 - 30.30	39.60

MEDIUM GRADE. HET'S SHOWBOAT IS SCHEDULED TO EXPAND ITS CASINO IN MID-2003, RENOVATE ITS BOARDWALK ENTRANCE IN FALL 2003, AND OPEN ITS NEW 544-ROOM HOTEL EXPANSION IN SPRING OF 2004.

TRADING VOLUME
Thousand Shares

*7 YEAR PRICE SCORE 169.0   *12 MONTH PRICE SCORE 89.4

*NYSE COMPOSITE INDEX=100

INTERIM EARNINGS (Per Share):

Qtr.	Mar.	June	Sept.	Dec.
1999	0.30	0.37	0.58	0.45
2000	0.25	0.40	0.61	d1.41
2001	0.38	0.40	0.54	0.49
2002	0.75	0.75	0.89	0.48

INTERIM DIVIDENDS (Per Share):

Amt.	Decl.	Ex.	Rec.	Pay.
	No dividends paid.			

CAPITALIZATION (12/31/01):

	($000)	(%)
Long-Term Debt	3,719,443	69.5
Deferred Income Tax	261,119	4.9
Common & Surplus	1,374,113	25.7
Total	5,354,675	100.0

BUSINESS:

Harrah's Entertainment, Inc. (formerly The Promus Companies Inc.), as of 2/5/03, operated 26 casinos nationwide under the HARRAH'S, SHOWBOAT, RIO, and PLAYERS brand names. HET's U.S. markets include Atlantic City, Las Vegas, Reno, Shreveport, North Kansas City, Laughlin and others. HET competes in all four segments of the casino industry: traditional land-based casinos, riverboat and dockside casinos, limited stakes casinos and casinos for Indian communities. HET operates casinos in more markets than any other casino company in the U.S. On 1/1/99 and 3/22/00, HET acquired Rio Hotel & Casino, Inc. and Players International, Inc., respectively. On 7/31/01, HET acquired Harveys Casino Resorts. Net sales for 2001 were derived as follows: casino, 75.7%; food and beverage, 12.4%; rooms, 7.1%; management fees, 1.5%; and other, 3.3%.

RECENT DEVELOPMENTS:

For the year ended 12/31/02, the Company reported income from continuing operations of $324.6 million compared with income of $208.4 million, before an extraordinary gain of $23,000, the year before. Results for 2002 and 2001 included pre-tax project opening costs and other nonrecurring items of $6.8 million and $35.8 million, and amortization of intangible assets of $4.5 million and $25.0 million, respectively. Earnings for 2001 also included reserves of $2.3 million for HET's New Orleans casino. Total revenues grew 12.1% to $4.14 billion.

PROSPECTS:

Harrah's Atlantic City continues to benefit from the 452-room hotel addition and 450 new slot machines that opened in May 2002 and an additional 500 slots added in late December 2002. Additionally, HET's SHOWBOAT is scheduled to expand its casino in mid-2003, renovate its boardwalk entrance in the Fall of 2003, and open its new 544-room hotel expansion in the Spring of 2004. Separately, the Company anticipates the opening of the first phase of a revitalized Louisiana Downs racetrack with 900 slot machines in the Summer of 2003. Meanwhile, on 12/10/02, HET acquired the remaining 37.0% of JCC Holding Company that it did not already own.

ANNUAL FINANCIAL DATA:

FISCAL YEAR	TOT. REVS. ($mill.)	NET INC. ($mill.)	TOT. ASSETS ($mill.)	OPER. PROFIT %	NET PROFIT %	RET. ON EQUITY %	RET. ON ASSETS %	CURR. RATIO	EARN. PER SH.$	CASH FL. PER SH.$	TANG. BK. VAL.$	PRICE RANGE	AVG. P/E RATIO
p12/31/02	4,136.4	⑨ 324.6							⑨ 2.86			51.35 - 34.95	15.1
12/31/01	3,709.0	①⑥ 209.0	6,128.6	15.7	5.6	15.2	3.4	1.1	①⑥ 1.81	4.68	3.80	38.29 - 22.00	16.7
12/31/00	3,471.2	①⑥ d11.3	5,166.1	8.1	...	...	...	0.7	①⑥ d0.09	2.31	5.04	30.06 - 17.00	...
12/31/99	3,024.4	⑦ 219.5	4,766.8	15.9	7.3	14.8	4.6	1.3	⑦ 1.71	3.40	7.89	30.75 - 14.19	13.1
12/31/98	2,004.0	①⑤ 121.7	3,286.3	14.4	6.1	14.3	3.7	1.2	①⑤ 1.19	2.77	4.58	26.38 - 11.06	15.7
12/31/97	1,619.2	①⑤ 107.5	2,005.5	13.2	6.6	14.6	5.4	1.0	①⑤ 1.06	2.27	6.85	23.06 - 15.50	18.2
12/31/96	1,588.1	③⑥ 98.9	1,974.1	15.0	6.2	13.7	5.0	1.0	③⑥ 0.95	1.94	6.99	38.88 - 16.38	29.1
12/31/95	1,550.1	④ 78.8	1,636.7	14.8	5.1	13.5	4.8	0.9	③④ 0.76	1.69	5.70	45.88 - 22.13	44.7
12/31/94	1,339.4	② 50.0	1,738.0	20.1	3.7	8.0	2.9	0.6	② 0.49	1.33	6.09	55.25 - 25.88	82.8
12/31/93	1,251.9	② 91.8	1,793.1	24.3	7.3	17.1	5.1	0.6	② 0.89	1.92	5.24	55.00 - 17.46	40.7

Statistics are as originally reported. Adj. for stk. split: 3-for-2, 10/93 & 2-for-1, 2/93. ① Bef. extraord. loss of $23,000, 2001; $716,000, 2000; $19.7 mill., 1998; $8.1 mill., 1997. ② Bef. disc. ops. gain of $36.3 mill. & acct. chg. of $7.9 mill. ③ Incl. pre-tax write-down & reorg. chgs. of $66.8 mill., 1996; $93.3 mill., 1995. ④ Bef. disc. oper. gain of $36,000; incl. various costs of $450,000. ⑤ Incl. one-time net cost of $1.0 mill. ⑥ Incl. various costs of $43.1 mill., 2001; $297.9 mill., 2000; $21.6 mill., 1998; $5.9 mill., 1996. ⑦ Bef. extraord. loss of $11.0 mill.; incl. a one-time net gain of $37.9 mill. ⑧ Bef. extraord. gain $5.4 mill. ⑨ Incl. loss from disc. ops. of $1.6 mill.; incl. one-time chrg. of $6.8 mill.

OFFICERS:
P. G. Satre, Chmn.
G. W. Loveman, Pres., C.E.O.

INVESTOR CONTACT: Charles Atwood, Sr. V.P. & C.F.O., (702) 407-6406

PRINCIPAL OFFICE: One Harrah's Court, Las Vegas, NV 89119

TELEPHONE NUMBER: (702) 407-6000
WEB: www.harrahs.com

NO. OF EMPLOYEES: 42,000 (approx.)

SHAREHOLDERS: 9,986 (approx.)

ANNUAL MEETING: In May

INCORPORATED: DE, Nov., 1989

INSTITUTIONAL HOLDINGS:
No. of Institutions: 301
Shares Held: 101,181,903
% Held: 90.5

INDUSTRY: Amusement and recreation, nec (SIC: 7999)

TRANSFER AGENT(S): The Bank of New York, New York, NY

HARRIS CORPORATION

EXCH.	SYM.	REC. PRICE	P/E RATIO	YLD.	MKT. CAP.	RANGE (52-WK.)	'02 Y/E PR.
NYSE	HRS	29.96 (2/28/03)	23.2	1.1%	$1.99 bill.	38.70 - 24.09	26.30

UPPER MEDIUM GRADE. EARNINGS PER SHARE FOR FISCAL 2003 ARE EXPECTED TO RANGE FROM $1.30 TO $1.40, EXCLUDING THE IMPACT OF EXPENSES RELATED TO THE MICROWAVE DIVISION'S COST-REDUCTION ACTIONS.

INTERIM EARNINGS (Per Share):

Qtr.	Sept.	Dec.	Mar.	June
1998-99	0.36	0.66	0.52	0.04
1999-00	0.12	0.18	d0.21	0.24
2000-01	d0.51	0.30	0.17	0.44
2001-02	0.26	0.25	0.34	0.40
2002-03	0.30	0.25	. . .	. . .

INTERIM DIVIDENDS (Per Share):

Amt.	Decl.	Ex.	Rec.	Pay.
0.05Q	2/22/02	3/04/02	3/06/02	3/19/02
0.05Q	4/26/02	5/29/02	5/31/02	6/14/02
0.08Q	8/26/02	9/04/02	9/06/02	9/20/02
0.08Q	10/25/02	11/20/02	11/22/02	12/06/02
0.08Q	2/28/03	3/07/03	3/11/03	3/19/03

Indicated div.: $0.32 (Div. Reinv. Plan)

*7 YEAR PRICE SCORE 97.8   *12 MONTH PRICE SCORE 100.0

*NYSE COMPOSITE INDEX=100

CAPITALIZATION (6/28/02):

	($000)	(%)
Long-Term Debt	283,000	19.8
Common & Surplus	1,149,900	80.2
Total	1,432,900	100.0

BUSINESS:

Harris Corporation is an international communications equipment company focused on providing products, systems, and services. The Company provides a wide range of products and services for commercial and government communications markets such as wireless, broadcast, government, and network support. As of 2/5/03, the Company had sales and service facilities in more than 90 countries. On 8/16/99, the Company sold its semiconductor business. On 11/5/99, the Company completed the spin-off of its subsidiary, Lanier Worldwide, to its shareholders. On 8/31/00, the Company acquired Wavtrace, Inc.

RECENT DEVELOPMENTS:

For the quarter ended 12/27/02, net income slipped to $16.3 million from $16.4 million in the corresponding prior-year period. Revenue from product sales and services increased 16.0% to $523.9 million from $451.5 million the year before, primarily due to strong performances from the Company's government businesses. Government communications systems revenue rose 23.7% to $272.7 million, reflecting a major contract win rate and increased government spending. Broadcast communications revenue advanced 18.6% to $94.2 million, driven by new international contract wins. The contract wins included a $64.0 million order for the radio broadcast infrastructure of S.N. Radiocomunicatii S.A., Romania's state-owned broadcast organization.

PROSPECTS:

Earnings per share for fiscal 2003 are expected to range from $1.30 to $1.40, excluding the impact of expenses associated with the Microwave division's cost-reduction actions. Separately, on 2/12/03, HRS announced that it was awarded an imagery contract from the National Imagery and Mapping Agency. Under the terms of the potential 10-year, $750.0 million contract, HRS will supply geospatial and imagery delivered products for the Global Geospatial Intelligence program.

ANNUAL FINANCIAL DATA:

FISCAL YEAR	TOT. REVS. ($mill.)	NET INC. ($mill.)	TOT. ASSETS ($mill.)	OPER. PROFIT %	NET PROFIT %	RET. ON EQUITY %	RET. ON ASSETS %	CURR. RATIO	EARN. PER SH.$	CASH FL. PER SH.$	TANG. BK. VAL.$	DIV. PER SH.$	PRICE RANGE	AVG. P/E RATIO	AVG. YIELD %
6/28/02	1,875.8	82.6	1,858.5	7.4	4.4	7.2	4.4	2.7	1.25	2.08	14.09	0.26	38.70 - 24.09	25.1	0.8
6/29/01	1,955.1	⑤21.4	1,959.9	4.8	1.1	1.9	1.1	2.7	⑤0.32	1.51	13.67	0.20	37.00 - 20.80	90.3	0.7
6/30/00	1,807.4	④25.0	2,326.9	2.0	1.4	1.8	1.1	2.9	④0.34	1.28	17.52	0.20	39.38 - 20.75	88.4	0.7
⑥7/02/99	1,743.5	③49.9	2,958.6	4.3	2.9	3.1	1.7	1.3	③0.63	1.42	19.04	0.77	40.63 - 18.25	46.7	2.6
7/03/98	3,939.1	②133.0	3,784.0	6.9	3.4	8.3	3.5	1.7	②1.66	4.29	17.43	0.92	55.31 - 27.56	25.0	2.2
6/27/97	3,834.6	147.6	3,637.9	8.1	3.8	9.4	4.1	1.6	2.66	4.20	16.96	0.82	50.00 - 33.69	15.7	2.0
6/30/96	3,659.3	115.9	3,206.7	7.5	3.2	8.4	3.6	1.6	2.29	3.68	14.92	0.72	35.69 - 24.44	13.1	2.4
6/30/95	3,480.9	154.5	2,836.0	8.7	4.4	12.4	5.4	1.7	1.98	4.08	13.92	0.65	30.69 - 20.25	12.9	2.6
6/30/94	3,369.4	①121.9	2,677.1	7.5	3.6	10.3	4.6	2.1	①1.54	3.47	13.00	0.59	26.13 - 18.88	14.7	2.6
6/30/93	3,133.3	111.1	2,542.0	7.3	3.5	9.7	4.4	2.2	1.41	3.41	12.35	0.54	23.69 - 16.81	14.4	2.7

Statistics are as originally reported. Adj. for 2-for-1 stk. split, 9/97. ① Bef. acct. chrge. of $10.1 mill. ② Incl. an $86.4 mill. aft.-tax restr. chrg. & $8.0 mill. aft.-tax prov. for costs assoc. with an intnl. contract. ③ Incl. special chrg. of $20.6 mill. for litig. costs & restruct. exps. of $5.1 mill.; excl. gain of $12.4 mill. fr. disc. opers. & extra. loss of $9.2 mill. ④ Bef. disc. opers. loss of $7.0 mill.; incl. non-recurr. chrgs. of $51.7 mill. ⑤ Incl. pre-tax loss from purchased in-process research and development of $73.5 million. ⑥ Reflects the spin-off of HRS' subsidiary, Lanier Worldwide, to its shareholders.

OFFICERS:
P. W. Farmer, Chmn.
H. L. Lance, Pres., C.E.O.
B. R. Roub, Sr. V.P., C.F.O.

INVESTOR CONTACT: Pamela Padgett, V.P.-Inv. Rel., (321) 727-9383

PRINCIPAL OFFICE: 1025 West NASA Boulevard, Melbourne, FL 32919

TELEPHONE NUMBER: (321) 727-9100
FAX: (321) 724-3973
WEB: www.harris.com

NO. OF EMPLOYEES: 9,700 (approx.)

SHAREHOLDERS: 8,755 (approx.)

ANNUAL MEETING: In Oct.

INCORPORATED: DE, Dec., 1926

INSTITUTIONAL HOLDINGS:
No. of Institutions: 256
Shares Held: 55,066,971
% Held: 82.9

INDUSTRY: Radio & TV communications equipment (SIC: 3663)

TRANSFER AGENT(S): ChaseMellon Shareholder Services, LLC, Ridgefield Park, NJ

HARSCO CORPORATION

EXCH.	SYM.	REC. PRICE	P/E RATIO	YLD.	MKT. CAP.	RANGE (52-WK.)	'02 Y/E PR.
NYSE	HSC	30.17 (2/28/03)	14.0	3.5%	$1.21 bill.	44.48 - 24.20	31.89

MEDIUM GRADE. THE COMPANY EXPECTS TO SHOW GRADUALLY IMPROVING YEAR-OVER-YEAR RESULTS.

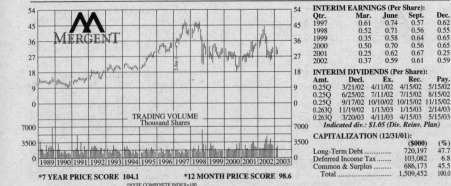

*7 YEAR PRICE SCORE 104.1   ***12 MONTH PRICE SCORE 98.6**

*NYSE COMPOSITE INDEX=100

INTERIM EARNINGS (Per Share):

Qtr.	Mar.	June	Sept.	Dec.
1997	0.61	0.74	0.57	0.62
1998	0.52	0.71	0.56	0.55
1999	0.35	0.58	0.64	0.65
2000	0.50	0.70	0.56	0.65
2001	0.25	0.62	0.67	0.25
2002	0.37	0.59	0.61	0.59

INTERIM DIVIDENDS (Per Share):

Amt.	Decl.	Ex.	Rec.	Pay.
0.25Q	3/21/02	4/11/02	4/15/02	5/15/02
0.25Q	6/25/02	7/11/02	7/15/02	8/15/02
0.25Q	9/17/02	10/10/02	10/15/02	11/15/02
0.263Q	11/19/02	1/13/03	1/15/03	2/14/03
0.263Q	3/20/03	4/11/03	4/15/03	5/15/03

Indicated div.: $1.05 (Div. Reinv. Plan)

CAPITALIZATION (12/31/01):

	($000)	(%)
Long-Term Debt	720,197	47.7
Deferred Income Tax	103,082	6.8
Common & Surplus	686,173	45.5
Total	1,509,452	100.0

BUSINESS:

Harsco Corporation is a global, diversified industrial services and engineered products company. The principal lines of business are: industrial mill services that are provided to steel producers in 40 countries; scaffolding services; railway maintenance of way equipment and services; gas control and containment products; and several other lines of business, including industrial grating and bridge decking,

industrial pipe fittings, process equipment, slag abrasives and roofing granules. HSC's operations fall into four operating groups: Mill Services (35.3% of 2002 sales); Access Services (29.7%); Gas and Fluid Control (17.7%); and Other Infrastructure Products and Services (17.3%). In 1997, HSC sold its 40.0% interest in United Defense, L.P., completing its exit from the Defense business.

RECENT DEVELOPMENTS:

For the year ended 12/31/02, income increased 18.4% to $88.4 million, before income from discontinued operations of $1.7 million, compared with income of $74.6 million, before a loss from discontinued operations of $2.9 million,

in 2001. Results for 2002 and 2001 included net nonrecurring after-tax charges of $300,000 and $23.2 million, respectively. Total revenues slid 2.4% to $1.98 billion. Free cash flow rose 98.9% to $162.9 million.

PROSPECTS:

The Company expects first quarter 2003 earnings per share to be down from the prior-year period due to continuing difficult economic conditions in its Access Services segment and manufacturing businesses, and the inclusion of increased pension expense. Going forward, HSC expects to show gradually improving year over year performance as

the benefits of its cost reduction and organic growth initiatives are realized. Earnings from continuing operations, excluding any net special items but including an increase in pension expense, will be in the range of $0.20 to $0.24 per share for the first quarter of 2003 and between $2.25 and $2.36 per share for the full-year 2003.

ANNUAL FINANCIAL DATA:

FISCAL YEAR	TOT. REVS. ($mill.)	NET INC. ($mill.)	TOT. ASSETS ($mill.)	OPER. PROFIT %	NET PROFIT %	RET. ON EQUITY %	RET. ON ASSETS %	CURR. RATIO	EARN. PER SH.$	CASH FL. PER SH.$	TANG. BK. VAL.$	DIV. PER SH.$	PRICE RANGE	AVG. P/E RATIO	AVG. YIELD %
p12/31/02	1,976.7	⑦88.4	1,999.3						⑦2.17			1.00	44.48 - 24.20	15.8	2.9
12/31/01	2,108.5	⑥71.7	2,090.8	7.8	3.4	10.5	3.4	1.5	⑥1.79	6.20	8.32	0.96	36.00 - 23.60	16.6	3.2
12/31/00	2,004.7	96.8	2,180.9	9.7	4.8	14.4	4.4	1.4	2.42	6.39	7.66	0.94	31.63 - 17.69	10.2	3.8
12/31/99	1,720.8	90.7	1,659.8	9.9	5.3	14.0	5.5	1.4	2.21	5.52	9.77	0.90	34.38 - 23.06	13.0	3.1
12/31/98	1,735.4	⑤107.5	1,623.6	11.1	6.2	15.7	6.6	1.2	⑤2.34	5.20	9.74	0.88	47.25 - 22.31	14.9	2.5
12/31/97	1,629.1	④100.4	1,477.2	11.0	6.2	12.8	6.8	1.9	④2.04	4.41	12.71	0.80	47.88 - 33.25	19.9	2.0
12/31/96	1,608.5	①119.0	1,324.4	13.4	7.4	17.5	9.0	1.7	①2.39	4.58	9.80	0.76	35.06 - 29.00	13.4	2.4
12/31/95	1,554.0	①97.4	1,310.7	11.9	6.3	15.6	7.4	1.4	①1.93	4.01	8.39	0.74	30.25 - 19.81	13.0	3.0
12/31/94	1,465.8	②86.6	1,314.6	12.0	5.9	14.9	6.6	1.9	②1.72	3.71	7.30	0.70	23.19 - 19.19	12.3	3.3
12/31/93	1,422.3	②80.8	1,427.6	8.9	5.7	15.4	5.7	1.4	②1.62	3.11	6.05	0.70	22.50 - 17.50	12.4	3.5

Statistics are as originally reported. Adj. for stk. split: 2-for-1, 2/97. ① Incl. a pretax chrg. of $22.8 mill., 1995; and $3.3 mill., 1996. ② Bef. a $6.8 mill. acctg. cr. & incl. a net gain of $10.7 mill. fr. sale of portion of an equity int. ③ Incl. results of MultiServ International, acq. on 8/31/93, and a net gain of $6.0 mill.; Bef. a $0.14 adj. per sh. gain fr. a settlement claim. ④ Bef. discont. oper. of $11.7 mill. ⑤ Incl. non-recur. chrg. of about $29.0 mill. ⑥ Incl. after-tax nonrecurr. chrg. of $23.2 mill. ⑦ Excl. inc. fr. dis. ops. of $1.7 mill., but incl. net nonrecurr. after-tax chrg. of $300,000.

OFFICERS:
D. C. Hathaway, Chmn., Pres., C.E.O.
S. D. Fazzolari, Sr. V.P., C.F.O., Treas.

INVESTOR CONTACT: Eugene M. Truett, Dir., Investor Relations, (717) 975-5677

PRINCIPAL OFFICE: P.O. Box 8888, Camp Hill, PA 17001-8888

TELEPHONE NUMBER: (717) 763-7064
FAX: (717) 763-6424
WEB: www.harsco.com

NO. OF EMPLOYEES: 17,500 (approx.)

SHAREHOLDERS: 18,000 (approx.)

ANNUAL MEETING: In Apr.

INCORPORATED: DE, Feb., 1956

INSTITUTIONAL HOLDINGS:
No. of Institutions: 166
Shares Held: 20,096,732
% Held: 49.6

INDUSTRY: Miscellaneous metal work (SIC: 3449)

TRANSFER AGENT(S): Mellon Investor Services, L.L.C., South Hackensack, NJ

HARTE-HANKS, INC.

EXCH.	SYM.	REC. PRICE	P/E RATIO	YLD.	MKT. CAP.	RANGE (52-WK.)	'02 Y/E PR.
NYSE	HHS	18.31 (2/28/03)	18.9	0.7%	$1.71 bill.	22.68 - 16.05	18.67

UPPER MEDIUM GRADE. ALTHOUGH HHS EXPECTS EARNINGS PER SHARE IN 2003 TO BE HIGHER COMPARED WITH 2002, RESULTS MAY CONTINUE TO BE NEGATIVELY AFFECTED BY THE DIFFICULT ECONOMIC CLIMATE.

*7 YEAR PRICE SCORE 138.4   *12 MONTH PRICE SCORE 100.0
*NYSE COMPOSITE INDEX=100

INTERIM EARNINGS (Per Share):

Qtr.	Mar.	June	Sept.	Dec.
1998	0.19	0.15	0.15	0.12
1999	0.19	0.17	0.17	0.14
2000	0.17	0.20	0.20	0.21
2001	0.19	0.21	0.21	0.21
2002	0.21	0.25	0.24	0.26

INTERIM DIVIDENDS (Per Share):

Amt.	Decl.	Ex.	Rec.	Pay.
50% STK	5/07/02	5/31/02	5/20/02	5/30/02
0.025Q	5/07/02	6/06/02	6/10/02	6/15/02
0.025Q	8/20/02	8/28/02	8/31/02	9/13/02
0.025Q	11/14/02	11/26/02	11/29/02	12/13/02
0.03Q	1/29/03	2/26/03	3/01/03	3/14/03

Indicated div.: $0.12

CAPITALIZATION (12/31/01):

	($000)	(%)
Long-Term Debt	48,312	8.0
Common & Surplus	552,366	92.0
Total	600,678	100.0

BUSINESS:

Harte-Hanks, Inc. is a direct and interactive services company that provides end-to-end customer relationship management and related services for a host of consumer and business-to-business marketers. The Company has operations in two principal businesses: direct marketing and shoppers. The Company's direct and interactive marketing business operates both nationally and internationally, while its shopper business operates in selected local and regional markets in California and Florida. Direct marketing, which represented 63.1% of the Company's revenue as of 12/31/02, offers a complete range of specialized, coordinated and integrated direct and interactive marketing services from a single source.

RECENT DEVELOPMENTS:

For the year ended 12/31/02, net income slipped 1.0% to $90.7 million compared with $91.7 million the year before. Earnings for 2001 excluded goodwill amortization of $12.0 million after-tax. Operating revenues slid to $908.8 million from $917.9 million in the prior year. Direct marketing operating revenues declined 4.7% to $573.8 million from $601.9 million a year earlier. Shoppers operating revenues increased 6.0% to $335.0 million, reflecting solid growth in in-book advertising, particularly real estate advertising. Operating income decreased 3.6% to $150.3 million.

PROSPECTS:

Although the Company expects its earnings per share in 2003 to be higher compared with 2002, results may continue to be negatively affected by the difficult economic climate. While many of the Company's clients are facing weak demand in their markets, HHS will continue to maintain tight expense controls in an effort to support long-term growth. Meanwhile, during the fourth quarter of 2002, the Company entered into several new agreements to provide marketing programs. For instance, HHS entered into an agreement with a biotechnology company to provide support for their initiatives for a new asthma drug. HHS also signed an agreement with a financial services institution to provide direct marketing services for all lines of the company's business.

ANNUAL FINANCIAL DATA:

FISCAL YEAR	TOT. REVS. ($mill.)	NET INC. ($mill.)	TOT. ASSETS ($mill.)	OPER. PROFIT %	NET PROFIT %	RET. ON EQUITY %	RET. ON ASSETS %	CURR. RATIO	EARN. PER SH.$	CASH FL. PER SH.$	TANG. BK. VAL.$	DIV. PER SH.$	PRICE RANGE	AVG. P/E RATIO	AVG. YIELD %
p12/31/02	908.8	90.7	736.7						0.96			0.10	22.68 - 16.05	20.2	0.5
12/31/01	917.9	79.7	771.0	15.2	8.7	14.4	10.3	1.7	0.82	1.33	1.22	0.08	19.28 - 13.63	20.1	0.5
12/31/00	960.8	81.9	807.1	14.4	8.5	14.9	10.1	1.4	0.79	1.21	1.15	0.07	18.96 - 13.08	20.4	0.4
12/31/99	829.8	72.9	769.4	14.2	8.8	12.6	9.5	1.4	0.67	1.00	1.64	0.05	19.50 - 12.71	23.9	0.3
12/31/98	748.5	⑤68.4	715.2	13.6	9.1	11.8	9.6	2.8	⑤0.60	0.86	2.68	0.04	19.00 - 11.56	25.5	0.3
12/31/97	638.3	④44.3	954.9	12.1	6.9	7.8	4.6	1.7	④0.38	0.58	2.88	0.03	12.90 - 8.46	28.1	0.2
12/31/96	665.9	③40.6	592.3	13.2	6.1	16.1	6.9	1.6	③0.35	0.62	...	0.02	9.50 - 6.54	22.9	0.3
12/31/95	532.9	②34.0	477.7	13.9	6.4	20.6	7.1	1.6	②0.37	0.67	...	0.02	7.53 - 4.14	15.6	0.4
12/31/94	513.6	23.8	496.9	12.5	4.6	22.1	4.8	1.5	0.28	0.58	...	...	4.81 - 3.92	15.8	...
12/31/93	463.5	①d45.5	478.9	...	...	...	...	1.6	①d0.78	d0.33	...	...	4.33 - 3.36	...	...

Statistics are as originally reported. Adj. for stk. splits: 3-for-2, 5/02 & 12/95; 2-for-1, 3/98. ① Incl. goodwill writedown chrg. $55.5 mill. & bef. extraord. loss of $7.4 mill. ② Incl. gain on sale of bus. $13.7 mill. ③ Incl. merger costs $12.1 mill. ④ Bef. inc. from disc. opers. $292.4 mill. & extraord. loss $875,000. ⑤ Incl. pension curtailment gain $2.2 mill.

OFFICERS:
L. D. Franklin, Chmn.
H. H. Harte, Vice-Chmn.
R. M. Hochhauser, Pres., C.E.O.
J. D. Kerrest, Sr. V.P., Fin., C.F.O.

INVESTOR CONTACT: Jaques D. Kerrest, Sr. V.P. & C.F.O., (210) 829-9140

PRINCIPAL OFFICE: 200 Concord Plaza Drive, San Antonio, TX 78216

TELEPHONE NUMBER: (210) 829-9000
FAX: (210) 829-9403
WEB: www.harte-hanks.com
NO. OF EMPLOYEES: 6,894 full-time; 625 part-time
SHAREHOLDERS: 2,700 (approx.)
ANNUAL MEETING: In May
INCORPORATED: DE, Oct., 1970

INSTITUTIONAL HOLDINGS:
No. of Institutions: 180
Shares Held: 44,818,454
% Held: 49.2

INDUSTRY: Miscellaneous publishing (SIC: 2741)

TRANSFER AGENT(S): State Street Bank and Trust Company, Boston, MA

HARTFORD FINANCIAL SERVICES GROUP, INC.

EXCH.	SYM.	REC. PRICE	P/E RATIO	YLD.	MKT. CAP.	RANGE (52-WK.)	'02 Y/E PR.
NYSE	HIG	36.13 (2/28/03)	9.1	3.0%	$9.22 bill.	70.24 - 35.45	45.43

UPPER MEDIUM GRADE. THE COMPANY IS UNDERGOING A COMPREHENSIVE STUDY OF ITS CURRENT ASBES-
TOS LIABILITIES.

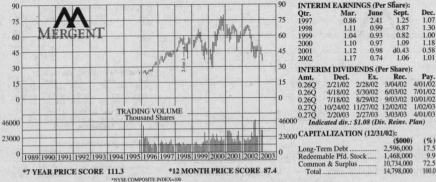

*7 YEAR PRICE SCORE 111.3   ***12 MONTH PRICE SCORE 87.4**
*NYSE COMPOSITE INDEX=100

INTERIM EARNINGS (Per Share):

Qtr.	Mar.	June	Sept.	Dec.
1997	0.86	2.41	1.25	1.07
1998	1.11	0.99	0.87	1.30
1999	1.04	0.93	0.82	1.00
2000	1.10	0.97	1.09	1.18
2001	1.12	d0.43	0.58	
2002	1.17	0.74	1.06	1.01

INTERIM DIVIDENDS (Per Share):

Amt.	Decl.	Ex.	Rec.	Pay.
0.26Q	2/21/02	2/28/02	3/04/02	4/01/02
0.26Q	4/18/02	5/30/02	6/03/02	7/01/02
0.26Q	7/18/02	8/29/02	9/03/02	10/01/02
0.27Q	10/24/02	11/27/02	12/02/02	1/02/03
0.27Q	2/20/03	2/27/03	3/03/03	4/01/03

Indicated div.: $1.08 (Div. Reinv. Plan)

CAPITALIZATION (12/31/02):

	($000)	(%)
Long-Term Debt	2,596,000	17.5
Redeemable Pfd. Stock	1,468,000	9.9
Common & Surplus	10,734,000	72.5
Total	14,798,000	100.0

BUSINESS:

Hartford Financial Services Group, Inc. (formerly ITT Hartford Group, Inc.) is organized into two major operations: Life and Property & Casualty. Life is organized into four reportable operating segments: Investment Products, Individual Life, Group Benefits and Corporate Owned Life Insurance. Life also includes an Other category, which consists of its international operations. HIG's Property & Cas-

ualty operation is organized into six reportable operating segments: the North American underwriting segments of Business Insurance, Affinity Personal Lines, Personal Insurance, Specialty Commercial and Reinsurance; and the International and Other Operations segment. On 12/20/95, the Company was spun off from ITT Corp.

RECENT DEVELOPMENTS:

For the year ended 12/31/02, net income was $1.00 billion compared with income of $541.0 million, before an accounting change charge of $34.0 million, the previous year. Results for 2002 included an after-tax litigation charge of $11.0 million, an after-tax benefit of $8.0 million related to the events of 9/11/01, and a tax benefit of $76.0

million. Results for 2001 included after-tax losses of $440.0 million related to the events of 9/11/01 and a $130.0 million tax benefit. Also, results for 2002 and 2001 included after-tax goodwill amortization of $14.0 million and $52.0 million, respectively. Total revenues rose 5.0% to $15.91 billion.

PROSPECTS:

The Company's outlook is mixed. The pricing environment in the property-casualty market continued to improve in 2002, and it is anticipated that favorable rates and terms will continue in 2003. However, the individual annuity segment continues to be affected by lower equity markets in terms of reduced assets under management. Furthermore, based on changes in interest rates in late 2002, pension

expenses are expected to rise. Accordingly, the Company lowered its expected operating income per share expectations for 2003 to a range of $4.50 to $4.75 per share. Separately, the Company announcement that they are commencing a comprehensive study of its current asbestos liabilities. HIG expects the review to be completed prior to the end of the second quarter of 2003.

ANNUAL FINANCIAL DATA:

FISCAL YEAR	PREM. INC. ($mill.)	NET INVST. INC. ($mill.)	TOT. REVS. ($mill.)	NET INC. ($mill.)	TOT. ASSETS ($mill.)	TOT. INVST. ($mill.)	RET. ON REVS. %	RET. ON EQUITY %	RET. ON ASSETS %	EARN. PER SH. $	TANG. BK. VAL. $	AVG. YIELD %	DIV. PER SH. $	PRICE RANGE	AVG. P/E RATIO
12/31/02	12,878.0	2,953.0	15,907.0	④ 1,000.0	182,043.0	54,530.0	6.3	9.3	0.5	④ 3.97	35.31	1.9	1.04	70.24 - 37.25	13.5
12/31/01	12,042.0	2,850.0	15,147.0	③ 549.0	181,238.0	46,689.0	3.6	6.1	0.3	③ 2.27	29.81	1.7	1.00	71.15 - 45.50	25.7
12/31/00	11,434.0	2,674.0	14,703.0	974.0	171,532.0	40,669.0	6.6	13.0	0.6	4.34	32.98	1.8	0.96	80.00 - 29.38	12.6
12/31/99	10,867.0	2,627.0	13,528.0	862.0	167,051.0	39,141.0	6.4	15.8	0.5	3.79	25.16	1.7	0.90	66.44 - 36.50	13.6
12/31/98	11,616.0	3,102.0	15,022.0	1,015.0	150,632.0	43,696.0	6.8	15.8	0.7	4.30	28.25	1.7	0.83	60.00 - 37.63	11.4
12/31/97	10,323.0	2,655.0	13,305.0	① 1,332.0	131,743.0	41,122.0	10.0	21.9	1.0	① 5.58	25.78	2.0	0.80	46.34 - 32.44	7.1
12/31/96	10,076.0	2,523.0	12,473.0	d99.0	108,840.0	37,639.0	...	...	...	d0.42	19.15	2.1	0.60	34.94 - 22.25	...
12/31/95	9,628.0	2,420.0	12,150.0	562.0	93,855.0	36,675.0	4.6	12.0	0.6	2.39	20.09	...	...	25.06 - 23.69	10.2
12/31/94	8,728.0	2,138.0	10,957.0	② 579.0	72,338.0	30,641.0	5.3	19.7	0.8	...	...	...	...	... - ...	...
12/31/93	8,033.0	1,883.0	10,066.0	503.0	61,270.0	28,578.0	5.0	13.6	0.8	...	...	...	...	... - ...	...

Statistics are as originally reported. Adj. for stk. split: 2-for-1, 7/98 ① Incl. non-recurr. credit $0.4 mill. ② Bef. acctg. change credit $12.0 mill. ③ Bef. extraord. loss $8.0 mill. & acctg chrg. $34.0 mill.; incl. restruct. chrgs. $11.0 mill. & net realized capital losses after-tax $164.0 mill. ④ Incl. after-tax litigation chrg. of $11.0 mill., after-tax 9/11/01 benefit of $8.0 mill. & tax benefit of $76.0 mill.

OFFICERS: R. Ayer, Chmn., Pres., C.E.O. L. A. Smith, Vice-Chmn. D. M. Johnson, Exec. V.P., C.F.O. **INVESTOR CONTACT:** Hans Miller, Investor Rel., (860) 547-2751 **PRINCIPAL OFFICE:** Hartford Plaza, Hartford, CT 06115-1900	**TELEPHONE NUMBER:** (860) 547-5000 **FAX:** (860) 720-6097 **WEB:** www.thehartford.com **NO. OF EMPLOYEES:** 29,000 (approx.) **SHAREHOLDERS:** 115,000 (approx.) **ANNUAL MEETING:** In April **INCORPORATED:** DE, Dec., 1985	**INSTITUTIONAL HOLDINGS:** No. of Institutions: 435 Shares Held: 217,836,694 % Held: 85.4 **INDUSTRY:** Fire, marine, and casualty insurance (SIC: 6331) **TRANSFER AGENT(S):** The Bank of New York, New York, NY

HASBRO, INC.

EXCH.	SYM.	REC. PRICE	P/E RATIO	YLD.	MKT. CAP.	RANGE (52-WK.)	'02 Y/E PR.
NYSE	HAS	12.11 (2/28/03)	28.2	1.0%	$2.09 bill.	16.98 - 9.87	11.55

MEDIUM GRADE. GOING FORWARD, THE COMPANY EXPECTS TO GROW REVENUE BETWEEN 3.0% AND 5.0% PER ANNUM AND GENERATE OPERATING MARGINS OF 10.0% OR BETTER IN FISCAL 2003.

*7 YEAR PRICE SCORE 75.4   ***12 MONTH PRICE SCORE 97.6**
*NYSE COMPOSITE INDEX=100

INTERIM EARNINGS (Per Share):

Qtr.	Mar.	June	Sept.	Dec.
1998	0.04	0.03	0.30	0.65
1999	0.07	0.16	0.43	0.29
2000	0.08	0.04	0.08	d1.05
2001	d0.14	d0.11	0.29	0.30
2002	d0.10	d0.15	0.32	0.36

INTERIM DIVIDENDS (Per Share):

Amt.	Decl.	Ex.	Rec.	Pay.
0.03Q	2/06/02	4/29/02	5/01/02	5/15/02
0.03Q	5/15/02	7/30/02	8/01/02	8/15/02
0.03Q	7/19/02	10/30/02	11/01/02	11/15/02
0.03Q	12/10/02	1/29/03	1/31/03	2/14/03
0.03Q	2/12/03	4/29/03	5/01/03	5/15/03

Indicated div.: $0.12 (Div. Reinv. Plan)

CAPITALIZATION (12/30/01):

	($000)	(%)
Long-Term Debt	1,165,649	46.3
Common & Surplus	1,352,864	53.7
Total	2,518,513	100.0

BUSINESS:

Hasbro, Inc. is a major worldwide toy manufacturer, offering a diverse line of toys, board and card games, dolls, preschool toys, boys' and girls' action toys as well as infant care products. In 1984, the Company acquired Milton Bradley Co. and in 1991, Tonka Corp., which also included Parker Bros. and Kenner. The Company's product lines include PLAYSKOOL®, KENNER®, TONKA®, ODDZON®, SUPER SOAKER®, MILTON BRADLEY®, PARKER BROTH-ERS®, TIGER™, WIZARDS OF THE COAST® and GALOOB®. Toys and games include MR. POTATO HEAD™, FURBY™, G.I. JOE®, TRANSFORMERS®, TONKA® Trucks, EASY-BAKE® Oven, PLAY-DOH®, STAR WARS™, BATMAN™, NERF®, NERDS®, THE GAME OF LIFE®, SCRABBLE®, MONOPOLY® KOOSH® and MICRO MACHINES®. In January 2001, HAS sold the Hasbro Interactive business to Infogrames Entertainment, SA.

RECENT DEVELOPMENTS:

For the year ended 12/29/02, income was $75.1 million, before an accounting change charge of $245.7 million, compared with income of $60.8 million, before an accounting change charge of $1.1 million, the year before. Earnings included nonrecurring items that resulted in a net after-tax gain of $31.7 million and a net after-tax charge of $11.3 million in 2002 and 2001, respectively. Net revenue slipped 1.4% to $2.82 billion from $2.86 billion the year before. The decline in revenues reflected a decrease in demand for licensed trading card games and electronic games, partially offset by strong results in HAS' core product lines including G.I. JOE, TRANSFORMERS, PLAY-DOH, and PLAYSKOOL. Operating income rose 3.8% to $219.3 million versus $211.3 million a year earlier.

PROSPECTS:

Going forward, HAS expects to grow revenue between 3.0% and 5.0% per annum and generate operating margins of 10.0% or better in fiscal 2003. Furthermore, HAS will look to focus on managing its balance sheet in an effort to reduce inventory levels and increase cash. Meanwhile, HAS continues to focus its emphasis on its core brands including G.I. JOE, TRANSFORMERS, PLAY-DOH, LITE BRITE and MAGIC THE GATHERING trading card games.

ANNUAL FINANCIAL DATA:

FISCAL YEAR	TOT. REVS. ($mill.)	NET INC. ($mill.)	TOT. ASSETS ($mill.)	OPER. PROFIT %	NET PROFIT %	RET. ON EQUITY %	RET. ON ASSETS %	CURR. RATIO	EARN. PER SH. $	CASH FL. PER SH. $	TANG. BK. VAL. $	DIV. PER SH. $	PRICE RANGE	AVG. P/E RATIO	AVG. YIELD %
12/29/02	2,816.2	② 75.1	3,369.0	...	...	...	...	1.8	② 0.43	1.66	...	0.12	17.30 - 9.87	31.6	0.9
12/30/01	2,856.3	④ 60.8	3,369.0	7.4	2.1	4.5	1.8	1.8	④ 0.35	1.66	...	0.12	18.44 - 10.31	41.1	0.8
12/31/00	3,787.2	①③ d144.6	3,828.5	...	...	...	...	1.3	③ d0.82	0.68	...	0.24	18.94 - 8.38	...	1.8
12/26/99	4,232.3	① 189.0	4,463.3	7.7	4.5	10.1	4.2	1.0	① 0.93	2.38	0.64	0.23	37.00 - 16.88	29.0	0.9
12/27/98	3,304.5	① 206.4	3,793.8	9.8	6.2	10.6	5.4	1.3	① 1.00	1.83	1.92	0.21	27.29 - 18.67	23.0	0.9
12/28/97	3,188.6	① 135.0	2,899.7	7.4	4.2	7.3	4.7	1.6	① 0.68	1.46	4.36	0.20	24.33 - 15.25	29.1	1.0
12/31/96	3,002.4	199.9	2,701.5	11.1	6.7	12.1	7.4	1.2	1.01	1.71	4.28	0.17	19.67 - 12.83	16.0	1.0
12/31/95	2,858.2	① 155.6	2,616.4	9.6	5.4	10.2	5.9	1.1	① 0.78	1.44	3.61	0.14	15.67 - 12.61	18.1	1.0
12/31/94	2,670.3	①② 179.3	2,378.4	11.1	6.7	12.9	7.5	1.1	①② 0.89	1.50	3.15	0.12	16.28 - 12.39	16.0	0.8
12/26/93	2,747.2	① 200.0	2,293.0	12.8	7.3	15.7	8.7	1.1	① 0.99	1.48	3.11	0.12	17.83 - 12.55	15.4	0.7

Statistics are as originally reported. Adj. for stk. splits: 3-for-2, 3/1/99; 3-for-2, 3/97 ① Incl. non-recurr. chrg. 12/31/00: $64.0 mill.; 12/26/99: $64.2 mill.; 12/27/98: $20.0 mill.; 12/28/97: $125.0 mill.; 12/31/95: $31.1 mill.; 12/31/94: $12.5 mill.; 12/26/93: $15.5 mill. ② Bef. acctg. change chrg. of $4.3 mill. ($0.03/sh.), 1994; $245.7 mill., 2002. ③ Incl. pre-tax chrg. of $44.0 mill. for loss on sale of bus. units. ④ Bef. acctg. change chrg. of $1.1 mill.; incl. pre-tax restruct. chrg. of $1.8 mill.

OFFICERS:
A. G. Hassenfeld, Chmn., C.E.O.
H. P. Gordon, Vice-Chmn.
A. J. Verrecchia, Pres., C.O.O.
D. D. Hargreaves, Exec. V.P., C.F.O.

INVESTOR CONTACT: Karen A. Warren, Investor Relations, (401) 727-5401

PRINCIPAL OFFICE: 1027 Newport Avenue, Pawtucket, RI 02862

TELEPHONE NUMBER: (401) 431-8697
FAX: (401) 727-5544
WEB: www.hasbro.com

NO. OF EMPLOYEES: 8,000 (approx.)

SHAREHOLDERS: 9,100 (approx. record)

ANNUAL MEETING: In May

INCORPORATED: RI, Jan., 1926

INSTITUTIONAL HOLDINGS:
No. of Institutions: 245
Shares Held: 145,899,615
% Held: 84.3

INDUSTRY: Games, toys, and children's vehicles (SIC: 3944)

TRANSFER AGENT(S): Fleet National Bank, Providence, RI

HAVERTY FURNITURE COMPANIES, INC.

EXCH.	SYM.	REC. PRICE	P/E RATIO	YLD.	MKT. CAP.	RANGE (52-WK.)	'02 Y/E PR.	DIV. ACH.
NYSE	HVT	10.85 (2/28/03)	9.9	2.1%	$231.1 mill.	21.45 - 9.40	13.90	32 yrs.

MEDIUM GRADE. THE COMPANY IS CAUTIOUS REGARDING ITS NEAR-TERM OUTLOOK.

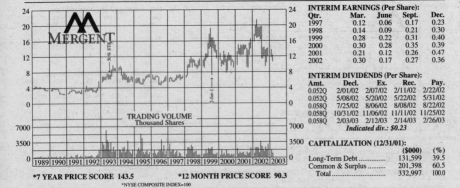

INTERIM EARNINGS (Per Share):

Qtr.	Mar.	June	Sept.	Dec.
1997	0.12	0.06	0.17	0.23
1998	0.14	0.09	0.21	0.30
1999	0.28	0.22	0.31	0.40
2000	0.30	0.28	0.35	0.39
2001	0.21	0.26	0.26	0.47
2002	0.30	0.17	0.27	0.36

INTERIM DIVIDENDS (Per Share):

Amt.	Decl.	Ex.	Rec.	Pay.
0.052Q	2/01/02	2/07/02	2/11/02	2/22/02
0.052Q	5/08/02	5/20/02	5/22/02	5/31/02
0.058Q	7/25/02	8/06/02	8/08/02	8/22/02
0.058Q	10/31/02	11/06/02	11/11/02	11/25/02
0.058Q	2/03/03	2/12/03	2/14/03	2/26/03

Indicated div.: $0.23

CAPITALIZATION (12/31/01):

	($000)	(%)
Long-Term Debt	131,599	39.5
Common & Surplus	201,398	60.5
Total	332,997	100.0

*7 YEAR PRICE SCORE 143.5   ***12 MONTH PRICE SCORE 90.3**

*NYSE COMPOSITE INDEX=100

BUSINESS:

Haverty Furniture Companies, Inc. is a full-service home furnishings retailer with 111 stores in 14 southern and central states as of 2/14/03. The Company's stores, primarily targeted at middle and upper-middle income families, offer a wide selection of well-known brand names of furniture, such as BROYHILL, THOMASVILLE, LANE/ACTION, LA-Z-BOY, BERNHARDT, and CLAYTON MARCUS. The Company has regional warehouses located in Charlotte, North Carolina, Jackson, Mississippi and Ocala, Florida serving all of the Company's local markets except for Dallas, Texas, and Atlanta, Georgia, which each have a metropolitan area warehouse.

RECENT DEVELOPMENTS:

For the year ended 12/31/02, net income increased 7.1% to $24.3 million compared with $22.7 million in 2001. Net sales advanced 3.8% to $704.0 million from $678.1 million a year earlier, with comparable-store sales up 0.7% for the year 2002. Gross profit as a percentage of net sales was 48.2% compared with 47.7% in 2001. The improvement in margins was primarily attributed to an increase in the mix of products imported from Asia and the strong performance of Havertys brand products. Selling, general and administrative expenses increased 7.0% to $304.0 million. However, interest expense fell 38.0% to $6.6 million and provision for doubtful accounts decreased 21.7% to $3.2 million.

PROSPECTS:

In the near-term, the Company expects concerns over the economy, the equity markets and hostilities in the Middle East to cause many customers to postpone some big-ticket purchases, such as furniture. In the meantime, HVT plans to continue to provide a consistent message of the breadth of its merchandise in advertising rather than marketing a variety of discount and promotional opportunities. Nevertheless, the Company is confident that its strong positioning in key markets across the Sunbelt, where growth is expected to outpace most areas of the U.S., will result in continued growth going forward.

ANNUAL FINANCIAL DATA:

FISCAL YEAR	TOT. REVS. ($000)	NET INC. ($000)	TOT. ASSETS ($000)	OPER. PROFIT %	NET PROFIT %	RET. ON EQUITY %	RET. ON ASSETS %	CURR. RATIO	EARN. PER SH. $	CASH FL. PER SH. $	TANG. BK. VAL.$	DIV. PER SH. $	PRICE RANGE	AVG. P/E RATIO	AVG. YIELD %
p12/31/02	703,959	24,315							1.10			0.22	21.45 - 9.40	14.0	1.4
12/31/01	689,178	22,710	460,905	7.4	3.3	11.3	4.9	2.5	1.06	1.81	9.45	0.21	16.55 - 9.10	12.1	1.6
12/31/00	693,575	① 27,851	448,163	8.5	4.0	15.5	6.2	3.1	① 1.31	2.06	8.64	0.20	13.44 - 7.75	8.1	1.9
12/31/99	633,721	27,400	404,648	9.2	4.3	16.2	6.8	2.8	1.19	1.84	7.81	0.19	19.33 - 7.19	11.1	2.1
12/31/97	557,258	16,835	392,901	8.4	3.0	10.7	4.3	3.9	0.72	1.36	7.08	0.17	12.00 - 6.50	12.8	1.8
12/31/97	506,118	13,387	406,514	8.4	2.6	8.4	3.3	2.2	0.57	1.16	6.79	0.16	7.38 - 5.44	11.2	2.5
12/31/96	470,250	12,247	399,875	8.0	2.6	8.1	3.1	2.3	0.53	1.06	6.42	0.15	7.31 - 4.63	11.4	2.6
12/31/95	407,846	12,183	371,778	7.7	3.0	8.6	3.3	2.6	0.53	0.99	6.06	0.15	7.50 - 4.81	11.7	2.4
12/31/94	381,796	12,538	315,103	8.5	3.3	9.6	4.0	2.5	0.55	0.93	5.70	0.14	9.63 - 5.38	13.6	1.8
12/31/93	333,359	9,716	264,353	7.9	2.9	8.1	3.7	4.1	0.46	0.77	5.29	0.13	9.81 - 5.42	16.7	1.7

Statistics are as originally reported. Adj. for stk. split: 2-for-1, 8/25/99. ① Bef. $3.4 mil. ($0.16/sh) acctg. change chrg.

OFFICERS:
C. H. Ridley, Chmn.
C. H. Smith, Pres., C.E.O.
D. L. Fink, Exec. V.P., C.F.O.
J. H. Parker, V.P., Treas., Sec.

INVESTOR CONTACT: Dennis L. Fink, Exec. V.P., C.F.O., (404) 443-2900

PRINCIPAL OFFICE: 780 Johnson Ferry Road, Suite 800, Atlanta, GA 30342

TELEPHONE NUMBER: (404) 443-2900
FAX: (404) 443-4180
WEB: www.havertys.com

NO. OF EMPLOYEES: 3,720 (approx.)

SHAREHOLDERS: 3,400 (approx., common); 200 (class A)

ANNUAL MEETING: In May

INCORPORATED: MD, Sept., 1929

INSTITUTIONAL HOLDINGS:
No. of Institutions: 89
Shares Held: 12,136,129
% Held: 55.8

INDUSTRY: Furniture stores (SIC: 5712)

TRANSFER AGENT(S): SunTrust Bank, Atlanta, GA

HAWAIIAN ELECTRIC INDUSTRIES, INC.

EXCH.	SYM.	REC. PRICE	P/E RATIO	YLD.	MKT. CAP.	RANGE (52-WK.)	'02 Y/E PR.
NYSE	HE	39.80 (2/28/03)	12.4	6.2%	$1.42 bill.	48.65 - 34.55	43.98

LOWER MEDIUM GRADE. THE COMPANY IS BENEFITING FROM HIGHER EARNINGS FROM ITS BANKING AND UTILITY OPERATIONS.

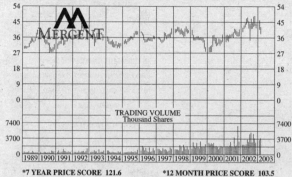

TRADING VOLUME
Thousand Shares

*7 YEAR PRICE SCORE 121.6   ***12 MONTH PRICE SCORE 103.5**
*NYSE COMPOSITE INDEX=100

INTERIM EARNINGS (Per Share):

Qtr.	Mar.	June	Sept.	Dec.
1997	0.64	0.63	0.77	0.71
1998	0.69	0.70	0.86	0.66
1999	0.64	0.71	0.67	0.86
2000	0.90	0.59	0.67	d0.74
2001	0.83	0.76	0.84	0.73
2002	0.75	0.85	0.89	0.72

INTERIM DIVIDENDS (Per Share):

Amt.	Decl.	Ex.	Rec.	Pay.
0.62Q	1/23/02	2/11/02	2/13/02	3/11/02
0.62Q	4/23/02	5/08/02	5/10/02	6/10/02
0.62Q	7/23/02	8/08/02	8/12/02	9/10/02
0.62Q	10/22/02	11/07/02	11/12/02	12/10/02
0.62Q	1/21/03	2/10/03	2/12/03	3/10/03

Indicated div.: $2.48 (Div. Reinv. Plan)

CAPITALIZATION (12/31/01):

	($000)	(%)
Long-Term Debt	2,178,521	66.1
Deferred Income Tax	185,436	5.6
Common & Surplus	929,665	28.2
Total	3,293,622	100.0

BUSINESS:

Hawaiian Electric Industries, Inc., is a holding company whose core businesses are electric utilities and a savings bank. As of 12/31/02, the Company and its subsidiaries, Maui Electric Company, Limited and Hawaii Electric Light Company, Inc., provided electricity to 95.0% of the 1.2 million residents of the State of Hawaii1. The principal communities served include Honolulu, Wailuku and Kahului, and Hilo and Kona. The service areas also include numerous suburban communities, resorts, U.S. Armed Forces installations and agricultural operations. The Company's banking subsidiary, American Savings Bank, is the third largest financial institution in the State of Hawaii. As of 12/31/02, American Savings Bank had 71 retail branches with total assets of $6.30 billion and deposits of $3.80 billion. On 9/30/01, the Company discontinued its international power operations.

RECENT DEVELOPMENTS:

For the year ended 12/31/02, net income amounted to $118.2 million compared with income of $107.7 million, before a loss from discontinued operations of $24.0 million, the previous year. The increase in income was primarily attributed to higher earnings from the Company's utility and banking operatings, partially offset by holding company net losses. Revenues declined 4.3% to $1.65 billion from $1.73 billion in 2001. On a segment basis, electric utility revenues decreased 2.5% to $1.26 billion, while operating income rose to $195.0 million from $193.9 million a year earlier. Bank revenues dropped 10.2% to $399.3 million, while operating income climbed 13.1% to $92.9 million.

PROSPECTS:

The Company's regulated utility business is benefiting from increased usage and growth in the number of residential customers, which led kilowatt-hour sales to grow by 1.9% in 2002, despite cooler weather. Improved operating efficiency and lower interest expense are also having a favorable impact on 2002 utility earnings. Meanwhile, HE's bank subsidiary is experiencing some compression in its interest rate spread as the low interest rate environment is spurring high levels of mortgage refinancing at lowered asset yields while deposits remain at already low levels.

ANNUAL FINANCIAL DATA:

FISCAL YEAR	TOT. REVS. ($Mill.)	NET INC. ($Mill.)	TOT. ASSETS ($Mill.)	OPER. PROFIT %	NET PROFIT %	NET INC./ NET PROP. %	NET INC./ TOT. CAP. %	RET. ON EQUITY %	ACCUM. DEPR./ GROSS PROP. %	EARN. PER SH. $	TANG. BK. VAL. $	DIV. PER SH. $	DIV. PAYOUT %	PRICE RANGE		AVG. P/E RATIO	AVG. YIELD %
p12/31/02	1,653.7	118.2								3.24		2.48	76.5	48.65 - 34.55		12.8	6.0
12/31/01	1,727.3	② 107.7	8,517.9	14.8	6.2	5.2	3.3	11.6	39.2	② 3.18	23.25	2.48	78.0	41.25 - 33.56		11.8	6.6
12/31/00	1,719.0	45.7	8,469.3	9.0	2.7	2.2	1.4	5.5	37.0	1.40	22.43	2.48	177.1	37.94 - 27.69		23.4	7.6
12/31/99	1,523.3	② 92.9	8,291.0	15.4	6.1	4.5	2.9	11.0	35.3	② 2.88	23.00	2.48	86.1	40.50 - 28.06		11.9	7.2
12/31/98	1,485.2	② 94.6	8,199.3	15.1	6.4	4.5	3.5	11.4	33.7	② 2.95	22.17	2.48	84.1	42.56 - 36.38		13.4	6.3
12/31/97	1,464.0	① 86.4	7,953.9	14.1	5.9	4.3	3.4	10.6	32.6	① 2.75	21.70	2.44	88.7	41.31 - 32.88		13.5	6.6
12/31/96	1,410.6	① 78.7	5,935.8	13.3	5.6	4.1	3.2	10.2	31.4	① 2.60	23.85	2.41	92.7	39.50 - 33.25		14.0	6.6
12/31/95	1,295.9	77.5	5,603.7	14.5	6.0	4.3	3.6	10.6	31.1	2.66	23.12	2.37	89.1	39.75 - 32.13		13.5	6.6
12/31/94	1,188.5	73.0	5,174.5	14.7	6.1	4.4	3.3	10.7	30.8	2.60	22.22	2.33	89.6	36.50 - 29.88		13.8	7.0
12/31/93	1,142.2	② 61.7	4,521.6	13.8	5.4	4.0	3.4	9.6	30.5	2.38	21.44	2.29	96.2	38.88 - 31.00		14.7	6.6

Statistics are as originally reported. ① Incl. non-recurr chrg. $2.4 mill., 12/97; $13.8 mill., 12/96; $3.0 mill., 12/93 ② Before loss fr. disc. opers. $24.0 mill., 12/01; gain $4.0 mill., 12/99; loss $8.7 mill., 12/98

OFFICERS:
R. F. Clarke, Chmn., Pres., C.E.O.
R. F. Mougeot, V.P., C.F.O.
E. H. Kawamoto, Treas.
INVESTOR CONTACT: Suzy P. Hollinger, Mgr. Inv. Rel., (808) 543-7385
PRINCIPAL OFFICE: 900 Richards St., Honolulu, HI 96808-0730

TELEPHONE NUMBER: (808) 543-5662
FAX: (808) 543-7966
WEB: www.hei.com
NO. OF EMPLOYEES: 3,189
SHAREHOLDERS: 16,203
ANNUAL MEETING: In April
INCORPORATED: HI, July, 1981

INSTITUTIONAL HOLDINGS:
No. of Institutions: 190
Shares Held: 10,999,258
% Held: 30.0

INDUSTRY: Electric services (SIC: 4911)

TRANSFER AGENT(S): Continental Stock Transfer & Trust Company, New York, NY

HCA INC.

EXCH.	SYM.	REC. PRICE	P/E RATIO	YLD.	MKT. CAP.	RANGE (52-WK.)	'02 Y/E PR.
NYSE	HCA	41.24 (2/28/03)	26.1	0.2	$21.00 bill.	52.05 - 36.21	41.50

MEDIUM GRADE. THE COMPANY SHOULD CONTINUE TO BENEFIT FROM STRONG REVENUE GROWTH.

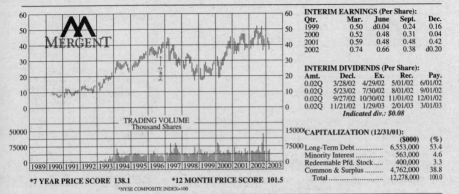

*7 YEAR PRICE SCORE 138.1   ***12 MONTH PRICE SCORE 101.5**
NYSE COMPOSITE INDEX=100

INTERIM EARNINGS (Per Share):

Qtr.	Mar.	June	Sept.	Dec.
1999	0.50	d0.04	0.24	0.16
2000	0.52	0.48	0.31	0.04
2001	0.59	0.48	0.48	0.42
2002	0.74	0.66	0.38	d0.20

INTERIM DIVIDENDS (Per Share):

Amt.	Decl.	Ex.	Rec.	Pay.
0.02Q	3/28/02	4/29/02	5/01/02	6/01/02
0.02Q	5/23/02	7/30/02	8/01/02	9/01/02
0.02Q	9/27/02	10/30/02	11/01/02	12/01/02
0.02Q	11/21/02	1/29/03	2/01/03	3/01/03

Indicated div.: $0.08

CAPITALIZATION (12/31/01):

	($000)	(%)
Long-Term Debt	6,553,000	53.4
Minority Interest	563,000	4.6
Redeemable Pfd. Stock	400,000	3.3
Common & Surplus	4,762,000	38.8
Total	12,278,000	100.0

BUSINESS:

HCA Inc. (formerly HCA-The Healthcare Company) is a holding company whose subsidiaries own and operate hospitals and related health care entities. At 12/31/02, these affiliates owned and operated 179 hospitals and 78 ambulatory surgery centers. Affiliates of HCA are also partners in several 50/50 joint ventures that own and operate six hospitals and four ambulatory surgery centers. The Company's facilities are located in 22 U.S. states, London, England and Geneva, Switzerland. HCA integrates fragmented providers and services (such as hospitals, physicians, outpatient centers, psychiatric facilities and home-health agencies) to create local healthcare networks. HCA typically develops networks by entering a market through the acquisition of a hospital with more than 150 beds. Additional healthcare facilities are then acquired to develop a comprehensive healthcare network in a local market.

RECENT DEVELOPMENTS:

For the year ended 12/31/02, net income decreased 6.0% to $833.0 million compared with $886.0 million the previous year. Results included charges of $603.0 million and $262.0 million in 2002 and 2001, respectively, for settlement with the Federal government. Earnings also included nonrecurring items that resulted in a net charge of $241.0 million in 2002 and a net gain of $84.0 million in 2001. Revenues climbed 9.9% to $19.73 billion from $17.95 billion the year before. Admissions declined 1.2% to 1.6 million patients.

PROSPECTS:

The Company's results reflect continued strength in same-facility admissions, same-facility equivalent admissions and same-facility net revenues, which increased 2.5%, 2.6%, and 11.7%, respectively, in 2002. Separately, HCA plans to change its charitable care policies to provide financial relief to more of its charity patients and needs based discounts to uninsured patients who receive non-elective care at its hospitals. The new policies are subject to approval by the Center for Medicare and Medicaid Services of the Department of Health and Human Services.

ANNUAL FINANCIAL DATA:

FISCAL YEAR	TOT. REVS. ($mill.)	NET INC. ($mill.)	TOT. ASSETS ($mill.)	OPER. PROFIT %	NET PROFIT %	RET. ON EQUITY %	RET. ON ASSETS %	CURR. RATIO	EARN. PER SH. $	CASH FL. PER SH. $	TANG. BK. VAL. $	DIV. PER SH. $	PRICE RANGE	AVG. P/E RATIO	AVG. YIELD %
p12/31/02	19,729.0	⑩ 833.0							⑩ 1.59			0.08	52.05 — 36.21	27.8	0.2
12/31/01	17,953.0	⑨ 903.0	17,730.0	12.0	5.0	19.0	5.1	1.3	⑨ 1.68	3.63	5.32	0.08	47.28 — 33.93	24.2	0.2
12/31/00	16,670.0	⑧ 219.0	17,568.0	12.1	1.3	5.0	1.2	1.1	⑧ 0.39	2.21	4.14	0.08	45.25 — 18.75	82.0	0.3
12/31/99	16,657.0	⑦ 657.0	16,885.0	10.2	3.9	11.7	3.9	1.1	⑦ 1.11	2.96	5.84	0.08	29.44 — 17.25	21.0	0.3
12/31/98	18,681.0	⑥ 532.0	19,429.0	8.1	2.8	7.0	2.7	1.1	⑥ 0.82	2.75	7.27	0.08	34.63 — 17.00	31.5	0.3
12/31/97	18,819.0	⑤ 182.0	22,002.0	8.2	1.0	2.5	0.8	1.6	⑤ 0.27	2.14	5.82	0.08	44.88 — 25.75	130.7	0.3
12/31/96	18,786.0	1,505.0	21,116.0	15.4	8.0	17.5	7.1	1.5	2.22	3.92	7.49	0.08	41.88 — 31.67	16.6	0.2
12/31/95	17,695.0	②③ 1,064.0	19,892.0	14.9	6.0	14.9	5.3	1.5	②③ 1.58	3.04	5.43	0.08	36.00 — 23.58	18.9	0.3
12/31/94	11,132.0	②③ 745.0	12,339.0	14.4	6.7	14.8	6.0	1.4	②③ 1.42	2.63	5.07	0.08	30.17 — 22.17	18.4	0.3
④ 12/31/93	10,252.0	①② 575.0	10,216.0	13.5	5.6	16.6	5.6	1.5	①② 1.13	2.31	4.43	0.02	22.58 — 10.83	14.7	0.1

Statistics are as originally reported. Adj. for 3-for-2 stock split 10/96. ① Bef. loss fr. disc. opers. of $108.0 mill. ② Bef. an extra. chg. of $103.0 mill., 1995; $115.0 mill., 1994; $84.0 mill., 1993. ③ Incl. mgr.-rel. costs $235.0 mill., 1995; $102.0 mill., 1994. ④ Incr. in revs. was due to mgrs. & acqs. ⑤ Incl. chrgs. of $383.0 mill; bef. dis. opers. of $431.0 mill. & net acctg. chg. $56.0 mill. ⑥ Incl. net chrg. of $58.0 mill.; bef. loss $153.0 mill. fr. disc. opers. ⑦ Incl. net chrg. total. $110.0 mill. ⑧ Incl. net chrgs. $985.0 mill. ⑨ Incl. net gain. of $47.0 mill. ⑩ Incl. pretax chrg. of $603.0 mill. for settlement with the Federal govt. & net non-recurr. chrg. of $241.0 mill.

OFFICERS:
J. O. Bovender Jr., Chmn., C.E.O.
R. M. Bracken, Pres., C.O.O.
D. G. Anderson, Sr. V.P.

INVESTOR CONTACT: W. Mark Kimbrough, V.P. Inv. Rel., (615) 344-1199

PRINCIPAL OFFICE: One Park Plaza, Nashville, TN 37203

TELEPHONE NUMBER: (615) 344-9551
FAX: (615) 320-2266
WEB: www.columbia-hca.com
NO. OF EMPLOYEES: 178,000 (approx.)
SHAREHOLDERS: 15,700 (approx.); 1 (nonvoting)
ANNUAL MEETING: In May
INCORPORATED: NV, Jan., 1990; reincorp., DE, Sept. 1993

INSTITUTIONAL HOLDINGS:
No. of Institutions: 492
Shares Held: 488,997,665
% Held: 95.3

INDUSTRY: General medical & surgical hospitals (SIC: 8062)

TRANSFER AGENT(S): National City Bank, Cleveland, OH

HEALTH CARE PROPERTY INVESTORS, INC.

EXCH.	SYM.	REC. PRICE	P/E RATIO	YLD.	MKT. CAP.	RANGE (52-WK.)	'02 Y/E PR.	DIV. ACH.
NYSE	HCP	35.35 (2/28/03)	18.6	9.4%	$2.10 bill.	45.08 - 34.45	38.30	17 yrs.

UPPER MEDIUM GRADE. THE HIGH LEVEL OF NEW INVESTMENT CONSUMMATED IN 2002 IS EXPECTED TO POSITIVELY AFFECT FUNDS FROM OPERATIONS IN 2003.

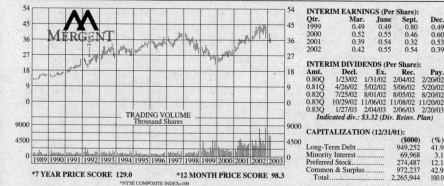

*7 YEAR PRICE SCORE 129.0   ***12 MONTH PRICE SCORE 98.3**
*NYSE COMPOSITE INDEX=100

INTERIM EARNINGS (Per Share):

Qtr.	Mar.	June	Sept.	Dec.
1999	0.49	0.49	0.80	0.49
2000	0.52	0.55	0.46	0.60
2001	0.39	0.54	0.32	0.53
2002	0.42	0.55	0.54	0.39

INTERIM DIVIDENDS (Per Share):

Amt.	Decl.	Ex.	Rec.	Pay.
0.80Q	1/23/02	1/31/02	2/04/02	2/20/02
0.81Q	4/26/02	5/02/02	5/06/02	5/20/02
0.82Q	7/25/02	8/01/02	8/05/02	8/20/02
0.83Q	10/29/02	11/06/02	11/08/02	11/20/02
0.83Q	1/27/03	2/04/03	2/06/03	2/20/03

Indicated div.: $3.32 (Div. Reinv. Plan)

CAPITALIZATION (12/31/01):

	($000)	(%)
Long-Term Debt	949,252	41.9
Minority Interest	69,968	3.1
Preferred Stock	274,487	12.1
Common & Surplus	972,237	42.9
Total	2,265,944	100.0

BUSINESS:

Health Care Property Investors, Inc. is a real estate investment trust that invests in healthcare-related facilities throughout the United States, including long-term care facilities, congregate care and assisted living facilities, acute care and rehabilitation hospitals, medical office buildings and physician group practice clinics. The Company's investment portfolio as of 1/21/03 included 463 facilities in 43 states. The Company's investments include 184 long-

term care facilities, 101 assisted living centers, 90 medical office buildings, 35 physician group practice clinics, 22 acute care hospitals, 14 retirement living communities, nine freestanding rehabilitation facilities and eight health care laboratory and biotech research facilities. On 11/4/99, HCP acquired American Health Properties, Inc., in a stock-for-stock transaction, and its 72 healthcare properties in 22 states.

RECENT DEVELOPMENTS:

For the year ended 12/31/02, income from continuing operations amounted to $137.2 million versus $123.7 million in 2001. Results for 2002 and 2001 included impairment losses on real estate of $9.2 million and $7.4 million, respectively. Earnings excluded a gain of $202,000 in 2002 and a loss of $2.5 million in 2001 from discontinued opera-

tions. Total revenues increased 9.6% to $359.6 million from $328.1 million a year earlier. Rental income from triple net leases improved 7.6% to $240.5 million, while rental income from managed properties advanced 10.3% to $91.2 million. Diluted funds from operations improved 11.9% to $204.6 million.

PROSPECTS:

The Company projects diluted funds from operations for 2003 to range between $3.51 and $3.59 per share. The high level of new investment consummated in 2002 is expected to positively affect funds from operations in 2003. However, internal growth in the Company's portfolio is expected to be flat-to-slightly negative in 2003, primarily

due to rent reductions in the long-term care sector as lower Medicare and Medicaid reimbursement rates will intensify pressure on already low margins achieved by long-term care operators. Meanwhile, HCP anticipates historically low interest rate levels will increase over time resulting in a higher overall cost of capital.

ANNUAL FINANCIAL DATA:

FISCAL YEAR	TOT. INC. ($mill.)	NET INC. ($mill.)	TOT. ASSETS ($mill.)	NET INC. + DEPR./ ASSETS %	RET. ON EQUITY %	RET. ON ASSETS %	EARN. PER SH. $	TANG. BK. VAL. $	DIV. PER SH. $	DIV. PAYOUT %	PRICE RANGE	AVG. P/E RATIO	AVG. YIELD %
p12/31/02	359.6	③ 137.2	2,748.5				③ 1.93		3.26	168.9	45.08 - 35.80	21.0	8.1
12/31/01	332.5	① 121.2	2,431.2	8.4	9.7	5.0	① 1.78	17.24	3.10	174.1	39.03 - 29.25	19.2	9.1
12/31/00	329.8	② 133.5	2,398.7	8.6	11.7	5.6	② 2.13	17.10	2.94	138.0	30.44 - 23.06	12.6	11.0
12/31/99	224.8	① 96.2	2,469.4	5.8	8.0	3.9	① 2.25	17.99	2.78	123.6	33.13 - 21.69	12.2	10.1
12/31/98	161.5	① 87.2	1,356.6	8.8	14.6	6.4	① 2.54	13.15	2.62	103.1	40.00 - 28.25	13.4	7.7
12/31/97	128.5	① 64.8	941.0	9.6	14.6	6.9	① 2.19	12.72	2.46	112.3	40.38 - 31.88	16.5	6.8
12/31/96	120.4	60,641	753.7	11.1	18.0	8.0	2.12	11.74	2.30	108.5	37.75 - 30.50	16.1	6.7
12/31/95	105.7	① 80.3	667.8	14.9	23.6	12.0	① 2.83	11.88	2.14	75.6	35.25 - 28.00	11.2	6.8
12/31/94	99.0	50.0	573.8	11.8	18.6	8.7	1.87	10.08	1.98	105.9	32.63 - 26.25	15.7	6.7
12/31/93	92.5	44.0	549.6	11.3	16.3	8.0	1.66	10.13	1.84	111.1	33.63 - 24.00	17.4	6.4

Statistics are as originally reported. ① Incl non-recurr. credit: 12/31/01, $1.2 mill.; 12/31/99, $10.3 mill.; 12/31/98, $14.1 mill.; 12/31/97, $2.0 mill.; 12/31/95, $23.6 mill. ② Incls. net non-recurr. credit of $9.8 mill.; bef. extraord. gain of $274,000. ③ Bef. income fr. discont. opers. of $1.3 mill. & loss on real estate dispos. of $1.1 mill.; incl. impair. loss on real estate of $9.2 mill.

OFFICERS:
K. B. Roath, Chmn., C.E.O.
J. F. Flaherty, III, Pres., C.O.O.
J. G. Reynolds, Exec. V.P., C.F.O.
INVESTOR CONTACT: James G. Reynolds, Exec. V.P., C.F.O., (949) 221-0600
PRINCIPAL OFFICE: 4675 MacArthur Court, Suite 900, Newport Beach, CA 92660

TELEPHONE NUMBER: (949) 221-0600
FAX: (949) 221-0607
WEB: www.hcpi.com
NO. OF EMPLOYEES: 37
SHAREHOLDERS: 4,800 (approx. record); 70,000 (approx. benef.)
ANNUAL MEETING: In May
INCORPORATED: MD, March, 1985

HEALTH MANAGEMENT ASSOCIATES, INC.

EXCH.	SYM.	REC. PRICE	P/E RATIO	YLD.	MKT. CAP.	RANGE (52-WK.)	'02 Y/E PR.
NYSE	HMA	17.92 (2/28/03)	17.7	0.4%	$4.28 bill.	22.99 - 15.89	17.90

UPPER MEDIUM GRADE. THE COMPANY CONTINUES TO ADD HOSPITALS TO ITS PORTFOLIO THROUGH ITS DISCIPLINED ACQUISITION APPROACH.

*7 YEAR PRICE SCORE 128.4   ***12 MONTH PRICE SCORE 99.0**
*NYSE COMPOSITE INDEX=100

INTERIM EARNINGS (Per Share):

Qtr.	Dec.	Mar.	June	Sept.
1997-98	0.10	0.16	0.15	0.13
1998-99	0.12	0.19	0.15	0.13
1999-00	0.14	0.21	0.18	0.16
2000-01	0.16	0.19	0.21	0.20
2001-02	0.20	0.27	0.26	0.24
2002-03	0.24	...	...	...

INTERIM DIVIDENDS (Per Share):

Amt.	Decl.	Ex.	Rec.	Pay.
0.02Q	10/29/02	11/06/02	11/08/02	12/02/02
0.02Q	1/28/03	2/05/03	2/07/03	3/03/03

Indicated div.: $0.08

CAPITALIZATION (9/30/02):

	($000)	(%)
Long-Term Debt	650,159	31.7
Deferred Income Tax	17,861	0.9
Minority Interest	33,009	1.6
Common & Surplus	1,346,752	65.8
Total	2,047,781	100.0

BUSINESS:

Health Management Associates, Inc. provides health care services, primarily in the Southeast and Southwest, to patients in owned and leased hospitals and also provides management services under contracts to other hospital facilities. As of 1/30/03, the Company, upon completing the previously announced transaction to acquire the 40-bed

Expansion of Heart of Florida Regional Medical Center operates 44 hospitals in 14 states with a total of 6,027 licensed beds. Approximately 59.0% of gross patient service revenues for the year ended 9/30/02 were related to services rendered to patients covered by Medicare and Medicaid programs.

RECENT DEVELOPMENTS:

For the three months ended 12/31/02, net income increased 18.2% to $59.7 million compared with $50.5 million in the equivalent quarter of the previous year. Net patient service revenue advanced 22.9% to $609.4 million from $495.8 million in the year-earlier period. Same-store hospital occupancy grew to 46.8% from 44.3%, while same-store admis-

sions climbed 6.2% to 50,581 from 47,631 in the prior-year quarter. Total hospital occupancy rose to 48.1% from 45.5%, while total hospital surgeries improved 11.7% to 51,331 from 45,967 the year before. Total costs and expenses jumped 23.7% to $510.7 million from $412.7 million in 2001.

PROSPECTS:

The Company continues to add hospitals to its portfolio through its disciplined acquisition approach. For instance, On 1/30/03, the Company announced that it completed a 40-bed addition to the existing 75-bed acute-care hospital at Heart of Florida Regional Medical Center in Greater Haines City, Florida. Separately, on 1/22/03, the Company

announced that it has executed a purchase agreement to acquire 60 acres of land in southeast Collier County, Florida upon which the Company expects to construct the proposed 100-bed Collier Regional Medical Center. Separately, the Company increased it minimum earnings per share objective to 17.0% for fiscal year 2003.

ANNUAL FINANCIAL DATA:

FISCAL YEAR	TOT. REVS. ($mill.)	NET INC. ($mill.)	TOT. ASSETS ($mill.)	OPER. PROFIT %	NET PROFIT %	RET. ON EQUITY %	RET. ON ASSETS %	CURR. RATIO	EARN. PER SH.$	CASH FL. PER SH.$	TANG. BK. VAL.$	DIV. PER SH.$	PRICE RANGE	AVG. P/E RATIO	AVG. YIELD %
9/30/02	2,262.6	246.4	2,364.3	18.0	10.9	18.3	10.4	2.5	0.97	1.31	4.24	0.02	22.99 - 16.24	20.2	0.1
9/30/01	1,879.8	② 195.0	1,941.6	18.1	10.4	15.6	10.0	3.0	② 0.76	1.08	4.08	...	22.22 - 13.42	23.4	...
9/30/00	1,577.8	167.7	1,772.1	19.1	10.6	16.3	9.5	2.9	0.68	0.98	3.27	...	22.75 - 9.63	23.8	...
9/30/99	1,355.7	149.8	1,517.3	18.8	11.1	16.8	9.9	2.4	0.59	0.83	2.89	...	21.63 - 7.00	24.3	...
9/30/98	1,138.8	136.8	1,112.1	20.2	12.0	18.1	12.3	2.6	0.54	0.73	2.82	...	25.75 - 14.92	37.6	...
9/30/97	895.5	108.3	727.6	20.3	12.1	14.9	12.3	2.8	0.43	0.58	2.30	...	17.67 - 9.50	31.4	...
9/30/96	714.3	84.1	591.7	19.7	11.8	20.1	14.2	2.5	0.34	0.45	1.76	...	11.11 - 7.45	27.3	...
9/30/95	531.1	63.3	467.0	20.3	11.9	19.9	13.6	3.4	0.26	0.34	1.36	...	8.00 - 4.64	24.1	...
9/30/94	438.4	① 49.1	398.8	19.6	11.2	19.4	12.3	4.5	① 0.21	0.27	1.10	...	5.27 - 3.56	21.5	...
9/30/93	346.8	32.2	325.8	17.7	9.3	16.7	9.9	2.7	0.14	0.20	0.85	...	3.85 - 1.38	18.2	...

Statistics are as originally reported. Adjusted for 3-for-2 stock splits, 6/98, 10/97, 6/96, 10/95, 6/94 & 11/93. ① Excl. acctg. charge of $2.6 mill. (d$0.03 a sh.). ② Incl. pre-tax, non-cash chrg. of $17.0 mill. for retirement ben. & write down of assets held for sale.

OFFICERS:
W. J. Schoen, Chmn.
J. V. Vumbacco, Pres., C.E.O.
R. E. Farnham, Sr. V.P., C.F.O.

INVESTOR CONTACT: John C. Merriwether,
Dir. Inv. Rel., (239) 598-3131

PRINCIPAL OFFICE: 5811 Pelican Bay
Boulevard, Naples, FL 34108-2710

TELEPHONE NUMBER: (239) 598-3131
FAX: (239) 597-5794
WEB: www.hma-corp.com

NO. OF EMPLOYEES: 23,000 (approx.)

SHAREHOLDERS: 1,500 (approx. record)

ANNUAL MEETING: In Feb.

INCORPORATED: DE, 1979

INSTITUTIONAL HOLDINGS:
No. of Institutions: 337
Shares Held: 228,768,165
% Held: 95.9

INDUSTRY: General medical & surgical hospitals (SIC: 8062)

TRANSFER AGENT(S): First Union National Bank, Charlotte, NC

HEALTH NET, INC.

EXCH.	SYM.	REC. PRICE	P/E RATIO	YLD.	MKT. CAP.	RANGE (52-WK.)	'02 Y/E PR.
NYSE	HNT	25.11 (2/28/03)	13.3	...	$3.11 bill.	30.15 - 20.35	26.40

MEDIUM GRADE. THE COMPANY ANTICIPATES FULL-YEAR 2003 EARNINGS PER SHARE IN THE RANGE OF $2.48 TO $2.52.

*7 YEAR PRICE SCORE 124.2   ***12 MONTH PRICE SCORE 109.9**
*NYSE COMPOSITE INDEX=100

INTERIM EARNINGS (Per Share):

Qtr.	Mar.	June	Sept.	Dec.
1998	0.22	0.01	d0.73	d0.85
1999	0.18	0.23	0.29	0.31
2000	0.28	0.32	0.36	0.37
2001	0.34	d0.12	0.02	0.45
2002	0.47	0.51	0.55	0.36

INTERIM DIVIDENDS (Per Share):

Amt.	Decl.	Ex.	Rec.	Pay.
		No dividends paid.		

CAPITALIZATION (12/31/01):

	($000)	(%)
Long-Term Debt	593,860	33.8
Common & Surplus	1,165,512	66.2
Total	1,759,372	100.0

BUSINESS:

Health Net, Inc. (formerly Foundation Health Systems, Inc.) was formed upon the merger of Foundation Health Corporation and Health Systems International Inc. on 4/1/97. HNT is a managed care organization that administers the delivery of managed healthcare services. HNT's HMO, insured PPO and government contracts subsidiaries provide health benefits to approximately 5.3 million individuals in 15 states through group, individual, Medicare risk, Medicaid and TRICARE programs. HNT's subsidiaries also offer managed health care products related to behavioral health, dental, vision and prescription drugs, and offer managed health care product coordination for multiregion employers and administrative services for medical groups and self-funded benefits programs.

RECENT DEVELOPMENTS:

For the year ended 12/31/02, income was $237.6 million, before an accounting change charge of $8.9 million, compared with net income of $86.5 million the previous year. Results for 2002 and 2001 included pre-tax asset impairment and restructuring charges of $60.3 million and $79.7 million, respectively. The 2002 and 2001 results also included pre-tax losses of $5.0 million and $76.1 million, respectively, on the sale of businesses and assets. Total revenues grew 1.4% to $10.20 billion. Revenues from health plan services inched up to $8.58 billion, while government contracts revenues climbed 11.9% to $1.50 billion.

PROSPECTS:

In the near term, HNT anticipates that its performance will continue to improve. Accordingly, HNT expects earnings for the first quarter of 2003 to be $0.54 per share. Moreover, HNT estimates full-year 2003 earnings to range from $2.48 to $2.52 per share. On a segment basis, health plan services should continue to benefit from higher commercial Medicare and Medicaid premium yields across all of its health plans. The government contracts segment results should continue to reflect an increase in the number of enrollees in its TRICARE contracts.

ANNUAL FINANCIAL DATA:

FISCAL YEAR	TOT. REVS. ($mill.)	NET INC. ($mill.)	TOT. ASSETS ($mill.)	OPER. PROFIT %	NET PROFIT %	RET. ON EQUITY %	RET. ON ASSETS %	CURR. RATIO	EARN. PER SH. $	CASH FL. PER SH. $	TANG. BK. VAL. $	PRICE RANGE	AVG. P/E RATIO
p12/31/02	10,201.5	⑦ 237.6							⑦ 1.89			30.15 - 20.35	13.5
12/31/01	10,064.5	⑦ 86.5	3,559.6	1.4	0.9	7.4	2.4	1.3	⑦ 0.69	1.48	2.94	26.19 - 16.00	30.6
12/31/00	9,076.6	⑥ 163.6	3,670.1	2.9	1.8	15.4	4.5	1.3	⑥ 1.33	2.18	1.61	26.94 - 7.63	13.0
12/31/99	8,706.2	⑤⑥ 147.8	3,696.5	2.8	1.7	16.6	4.0	1.4	⑤⑥ 1.21	2.12	...	20.06 - 6.25	10.9
12/31/98	8,896.1	③④ d165.2	3,929.5	...	...	...	...	1.2	③④ d1.35	d0.30	...	32.63 - 5.88	...
12/31/97	7,235.0	① d67.8	4,076.4	...	...	...	...	1.4	① d0.55	0.25	...	33.94 - 22.06	...
② 12/31/96	3,204.2	73.6	1,211.9	3.5	2.3	20.2	6.1	1.6	1.52	2.61	1.24	37.13 - 19.38	18.6
12/31/95	2,732.1	89.6	1,213.7	5.2	3.3	31.4	7.4	1.3	1.83	2.82	...	34.25 - 24.88	16.2
12/31/94	2,306.2	88.1	894.4	6.3	3.8	39.4	9.8	1.3	1.77	2.57	1.74	36.75 - 20.00	16.0
12/31/93	1,957.3	23.8	834.6	2.7	1.2	15.4	2.9	1.3	0.48	1.17	...	...	...

Statistics are as originally reported. ① Incl. after-tax restruct. & other one-time chgs. of $338.4 mill. & excl. loss fr. disc. opers. ② Statistics for years prior to 1997 are for Health Systems International Inc. ③ Incl. a pre-tax restruct. chg. of $21.1 mill. & excl. an after-tax chg. of $5.4 mill. for the cum. eff. of a change in accg. princ. ④ Incl. a pre-tax gain of $53.6 mill. on the sale of pharmacy ben. mgmt. opers. ⑤ Bef. acctg. change chrg. $5.4 mill., but incl. restr. & other chrgs. of $11.7 mill. ⑥ Incl. a pre-tax loss on the sale of bus. of $409,000, 2000; gain of $58.3 mill., 1999. ⑦ Incl. pre-tax chrg. of $79.7 mill., 2001; $60.3 mill., 2002 & pre-tax loss of $76.1 mill., 2001; $5.0 mill., 2002 on sale of bus. and buildings.

OFFICERS:
J. M. Gellert, Pres., C.E.O.
S. P. Erwin, Exec. V.P., C.F.O.

INVESTOR CONTACT: David W. Olson, Sr. V.P., Inv. Rel., (818) 676-6978

PRINCIPAL OFFICE: 21650 Oxnard Street, Woodland Hills, CA 91367

TELEPHONE NUMBER: (818) 676-6000
FAX: (818) 676-8591
WEB: www.health.net
NO. OF EMPLOYEES: 9,800 (approx.)
SHAREHOLDERS: 1,600 (class A common, approx.)
ANNUAL MEETING: In May
INCORPORATED: DE, June, 1990

INSTITUTIONAL HOLDINGS:
No. of Institutions: 216
Shares Held: 111,747,240
% Held: 90.3

INDUSTRY: Health and allied services, nec (SIC: 8099)

TRANSFER AGENT(S): Computershare Investor Services, Chicago, IL

HEALTHSOUTH CORPORATION

EXCH.	SYM.	REC. PRICE	P/E RATIO	YLD.	MKT. CAP.	RANGE (52-WK.)	'02 Y/E PR.
NYSE	HLSH	3.58 (2/28/03)	...	...	$1.40 bill.	15.90 - 2.79	4.20

SPECULATIVE GRADE. THE COMPANY REMOVED RICHARD SCRUSHY AS CHAIRMAN AND CHIEF EXECUTIVE.

*7 YEAR PRICE SCORE 57.3   ***12 MONTH PRICE SCORE 51.7**
*NYSE COMPOSITE INDEX=100

INTERIM EARNINGS (Per Share):

Qtr.	Mar.	June	Sept.	Dec.
1998	0.27	0.28	0.24	d0.46
1999	0.26	0.27	d0.01	d0.37
2000	0.17	0.17	0.18	0.19
2001	0.19	d0.05	0.20	0.17
2002	0.27	0.14	0.13	d1.03

INTERIM DIVIDENDS (Per Share):

Amt.	Decl.	Ex.	Rec.	Pay.
	No dividends paid.			

CAPITALIZATION (12/31/01):

	($000)	(%)
Long-Term Debt [1]	3,005,035	41.6
Deferred Income Tax	259,535	3.6
Minority Interest	154,541	2.1
Common & Surplus	3,796,924	52.6
Total	7,216,035	100.0

BUSINESS:

HEALTHSOUTH Corporation (formerly HEALTH-SOUTH Rehabilitation Corporation) is the largest provider of outpatient surgery, diagnostic imaging and rehabilitation healthcare services. HRC's rehabilitation services provide inpatient services and management of rehabilitation services to acute care hospitals or organized physician groups.

HRC operates more than 1,700 inpatient and outpatient locations in 50 states, the United Kingdom, Puerto Rico, Australia, Saudi Arabia and Canada as of 3/3/03. The consumer base includes major insurance companies, self-insured employers, physicians, patients and communities at large.

RECENT DEVELOPMENTS:

For the year ended 12/31/02, the Company reported a loss of $186.9 million, before an accounting change charge of $83.2 million, compared with net income of $202.4 million the previous year. Results for 2002 and 2001 included restructuring and other charges of $521.7 million and

$176.3 million, respectively. Results also included a loss of $19.6 million and a gain of $6.5 million on the early extinguishment of debt in 2002 and 2001, respectively. Revenues slipped 1.6% to $4.31 billion. Operating income decreased 18.0% to $267.3 million.

PROSPECTS:

On 3/31/03, the Company removed Richard Scrushy as chairman and chief executive. The government has filed a civil suit alleging that the Company, Scrushy, and other former officers overstated earnings by at least $1.40 billion since 1999 to make it appear HRC was meeting Wall Street expectations. A criminal investigation is also underway. HRC informed the Securities and Exchange Commission it would be unable to file its annual financial statement for

2002 by the 3/31 deadline and is moving to replace its independent auditors. Separately, HRC announced that it is initiating a plan to close, consolidate or sell a number of locations, primarily outpatient rehabilitation facilities, that are duplicative, no longer strategic or are consistent underperformers. On 4/3/03, it announced 165 layoffs at its corporate headquarters.

ANNUAL FINANCIAL DATA:

FISCAL YEAR	TOT. REVS. ($mill.)	NET INC. ($mill.)	TOT. ASSETS ($mill.)	OPER. PROFIT %	NET PROFIT %	RET. ON EQUITY %	RET. ON ASSETS %	CURR. RATIO	EARN. PER SH.$	CASH FL.PER SH.$	TANG. BK. VAL.$	PRICE RANGE	AVG. P/E RATIO
p12/31/02	4,310.8	[9] d186.9							[9] d0.47			15.90 - 2.79	...
12/31/01	4,380.5	[8] 202.4	7,579.2	14.7	4.6	5.3	2.7	4.8	[8] 0.51	1.45	2.74	18.49 - 11.25	29.2
12/31/00	4,195.1	[7] 278.5	7,380.4	18.4	6.6	7.9	3.8	3.7	[7] 0.71	1.64	1.76	17.50 - 4.75	15.7
12/31/99	4,072.1	[7] 76.5	6,832.3	12.7	1.9	2.4	1.1	3.0	[7] 0.18	1.09	0.98	17.75 - 4.56	61.9
12/31/98	4,006.1	[6] 109.0	6,773.0	23.6	2.7	1.4	0.7	3.4	[6] 0.11	0.90	1.10	30.81 - 7.69	174.8
12/31/97	3,017.3	[5] 330.6	5,401.1	24.0	11.0	10.5	6.1	2.1	[5] 0.91	1.59	2.31	28.94 - 17.75	25.6
12/31/96	2,436.5	[4] 220.8	3,372.0	22.2	9.1	14.6	6.5	2.8	[4] 0.68	1.26	1.53	19.88 - 13.50	24.5
12/31/95	1,556.7	[3] 78.9	2,460.1	17.6	5.1	8.5	3.2	2.4	[3] 0.42	1.06	0.99	16.19 - 8.19	29.0
12/31/94	1,127.4	[2] 53.2	1,552.3	14.0	4.7	12.5	3.4	2.2	[2] 0.35	0.85	0.74	9.84 - 5.84	22.4
12/31/93	482.3	[2] 6.7	1,024.3	14.6	1.4	2.3	0.7	1.3	[2] 0.06	0.36	1.03	6.59 - 3.03	87.4

Statistics are as originally reported. Adj. for 2-for-1 stk. split, 3/97 & 4/95. [1] Incl. cap. lease obligs. [2] Incl. nonrecurr. pre-tax chgs. of $11.8 mill., 1994; $49.7 mill., 1993. [3] Incl. after-tax non-recurr. chgs. of $28.1 mill. [4] Incl. after-tax nonrecurr. chgs. of $28.4 mill. [5] Inc. nonrecurr. after-tax merger exps. of $11.5 mill. [6] Incl. net nonrecurr. chg. of $427.0 mill. assoc. with the disc. of substant. all of HRC's home health opers. & other bus. [7] Incl. unusual non-recurr. chrgs. of $352.0 mill., 2000; $275.5 mill., 1999. [8] Incl. impair. of unamort. loan fee costs of $6.5 mill. & gain of $174.1 mill. on sale of assets. [9] Bef. acctg. chng. chrg. of $83.2 mill., incl. net chrgs. of $541.3 mill.

OFFICERS:
Joel C. Gordon, Acting Chmn.
Robert P. May, Acting C.E.O.,
M. E. McVay, Exec. V.P., Treas.
INVESTOR CONTACT: Jason Brown, Investor Relations, (205) 967-7116
PRINCIPAL OFFICE: One Healthsouth Parkway, Birmingham, AL 35243

TELEPHONE NUMBER: (205) 967-7116
FAX: (205) 969-4740
WEB: www.healthsouth.com
NO. OF EMPLOYEES: 33,783 full-time; 17,754 part-time
SHAREHOLDERS: 6,684 (approx. record)
ANNUAL MEETING: In May
INCORPORATED: DE, Feb., 1984

INSTITUTIONAL HOLDINGS:
No. of Institutions: 287
Shares Held: 272,969,947
% Held: 68.9
INDUSTRY: Specialty outpatient clinics, nec (SIC: 8093)
TRANSFER AGENT(S): Mellon Investor Services, Ridgefield Park, NJ

HEARST-ARGYLE TELEVISION, INC.

EXCH.	SYM.	REC. PRICE	P/E RATIO	YLD.	MKT. CAP.	RANGE (52-WK.)	'02 Y/E PR.
NYSE	HTV	22.22 (2/28/03)	19.5	…	$2.04 bill.	28.48 - 19.29	24.11

MEDIUM GRADE. THE COMPANY IS BENEFITING FROM SOLID REVENUE GROWTH FROM SEVERAL CORE ADVERTISING CATEGORIES.

INTERIM EARNINGS (Per Share):

Qtr.	Mar.	June	Sept.	Dec.
1998	0.10	0.39	0.20	0.40
1999	0.04	0.15	0.03	0.17
2000	0.05	0.17	0.10	0.12
2001	0.22	0.10	d0.08	0.08
2002	0.15	0.33	0.27	0.39

INTERIM DIVIDENDS (Per Share):

Amt.	Decl.	Ex.	Rec.	Pay.
		No dividends paid.		

CAPITALIZATION (12/31/01):

	($000)	(%)
Long-Term Debt	1,160,205	33.9
Deferred Income Tax	792,327	23.2
Preferred Stock	2	0.0
Common & Surplus	1,466,612	42.9
Total	3,419,146	100.0

*7 YEAR PRICE SCORE N/A   *12 MONTH PRICE SCORE 106.1

*NYSE COMPOSITE INDEX=100

BUSINESS:

Hearst-Argyle Television, Inc. owned 24 television stations and managed an additional three television stations and two radio stations, as of 2/7/03, in geographically diverse U.S. markets. The Company's television stations reach about 17.7% of U.S. TV households, making it one of the two largest U.S. television station groups not primarily aligned with a single network, as well as one of the seven largest television groups overall as measured by audience deliv-

ered. The Company, through a joint venture with NBC Enterprises, is also involved in television production and syndication, and in the convergence of broadcast television and the Internet through its partnership with Internet Broadcasting Systems. On 1/5/99, HTV acquired Kelly Broadcasting Co. for approximately $520.4 million. On 3/18/99, HTV acquired Pulitzer Broadcasting Company for approximately $1.70 billion.

RECENT DEVELOPMENTS:

For the year ended 12/31/02, net income soared to $108.0 million from $31.1 million the previous year. Results for 2001 included a net gain of $72.6 million from the sale of assets and a charge of $23.8 million for the write-down of investments. Total revenues increased 12.4% to $721.3 million from $641.9 million the previous year. Revenues were

fueled by robust political advertising, as well as strong year-over-year gains from other core advertising categories such as automotive, movies, financial services, beverages, retail and furniture/housewares. Operating income was $265.6 million versus $115.4 million the year before.

PROSPECTS:

Looking ahead, although the Company is currently experiencing strength in a number of revenue categories, HTV's near-term outlook is uncertain. Advertisers worldwide are being cautious with their near-term expenditures, primarily due to concerns about the strength of the national economy and uncertainty regarding world events. Moreover, HTV

will not have Olympics revenue to offset any short-term declines in this period. Therefore, HTV is anticipating its net revenues for the first quarter of 2003 to range from flat to up 2.0%, operating cash flow to have a percentage decline in the mid-single digits, and earnings per share to be in the range of $0.11 to $0.13.

ANNUAL FINANCIAL DATA:

FISCAL YEAR	TOT. REVS. ($mill.)	NET INC. ($mill.)	TOT. ASSETS ($mill.)	OPER. PROFIT %	NET PROFIT %	RET. ON EQUITY %	RET. ON ASSETS %	CURR. RATIO	EARN. PER SH. $	CASH FL. PER SH. $	PRICE RANGE	AVG. P/E RATIO
p12/31/02	721.3	108.0			4.8	2.1	0.8	1.6	1.15		28.48 - 18.80	20.6
12/31/01	641.9	③ 30.6	3,779.7	18.0	4.8	2.1	0.8	1.6	③ 0.32	2.38	24.75 - 16.59	64.6
12/31/00	747.3	② 42.5	3,818.0	27.5	5.7	2.9	1.1	1.9	② 0.44	2.48	29.25 - 17.06	52.6
12/31/99	661.4	① 35.4	3,913.2	26.6	5.4	2.5	0.9	1.9	① 0.41	2.47	35.25 - 19.94	67.3
12/31/98	407.3	① 59.7	1,421.1	34.9	14.7	18.4	4.2	5.8	① 1.08	2.60	41.25 - 24.00	30.2
12/31/97	146.4	① 23.9	1,044.1	38.3	16.3	7.3	2.3	3.2⁻	① 0.48	1.04	32.63 - 26.25	61.3
12/31/96	73.3	① d14.6	328.6	2.7	…	…	…	1.5	① d1.37	1.26	…	…
12/31/95	46.9	d8.0	291.1	8.7	…	…	…	1.5	d1.25	1.43	…	…

Statistics are as originally reported. ① Bef. extraord. loss of $7.8 mill., 12/99; $16.2 mill., 12/98; $10.8 mill., 12/97; 1997; $3.1 mill., 12/96. ② Bef. extraord. gain of $2.5 mill.; Incls. non-recurr. chrg. of $15.4 mill. & $5.0 mill. write-down of carrying value of invest. ③ Bef. extraord. gain of $526,000; incl. net gain of $48.8 mill. from sale of assets & write-down on invest.

OFFICERS:
V. F. Ganz, Chmn.
D. J. Barrett, Pres., C.E.O.
H. T. Hawks, Exec. V.P., C.F.O.
INVESTOR CONTACT: Thomas W. Campo, Investor Relations, (212) 887-6827
PRINCIPAL OFFICE: 888 Seventh Ave., Suite 700, New York, NY 10106

TELEPHONE NUMBER: (212) 887-6800
FAX: (212) 887-6875
WEB: www.hearstargyle.com
NO. OF EMPLOYEES: 3,181
SHAREHOLDERS: 726 (Class A)
ANNUAL MEETING: In May
INCORPORATED: DE, 1994

INSTITUTIONAL HOLDINGS:
No. of Institutions: 1
Shares Held: 19,085,287
% Held: 20.7
INDUSTRY: Television broadcasting stations (SIC: 4833)
TRANSFER AGENT(S): ComputerShare Investor Services, Chicago, IL

HEINZ (H.J.) COMPANY

EXCH.	SYM.	REC. PRICE	P/E RATIO	YLD.	MKT. CAP.	RANGE (52-WK.)	'02 Y/E PR.	DIV. ACH.
NYSE	HNZ	30.70 (2/28/03)	13.3	3.5%	$10.77 bill.	43.48 - 29.60	32.87	39 yrs.

INVESTMENT GRADE. THE COMPANY SPUN OFF OF ITS TUNA, PET FOOD, PRIVATE-LABEL SOUP AND BABY FOOD BUSINESSES TO DEL MONTE FOODS COMPANY.

INTERIM EARNINGS (Per Share):

Qtr.	July	Oct.	Jan.	Apr.
1997-98	0.65	0.51	0.50	0.49
1998-99	0.58	0.63	0.33	d0.25
1999-00	0.57	1.14	0.47	0.27
2000-01	0.57	0.54	0.77	d0.49
2001-02	0.57	0.59	0.57	0.63
2002-03	0.50	0.60	. . .	. . .

INTERIM DIVIDENDS (Per Share):

Amt.	Decl.	Ex.	Rec.	Pay.
0.405Q	3/13/02	3/21/02	3/25/02	4/10/02
0.405Q	6/12/02	6/20/02	6/24/02	7/10/02
0.405Q	9/12/02	9/19/02	9/23/02	10/10/02
0.405Q	12/11/02	12/19/02	12/23/02	1/10/03
0.27Q	3/12/03	3/20/03	3/24/03	4/10/03

Indicated div.: $1.08 (Div. Reinv. Plan)

CAPITALIZATION (5/1/02):

	($000)	(%)
Long-Term Debt	4,642,968	64.5
Deferred Income Tax	394,935	5.5
Minority Interest	440,648	6.1
Preferred Stock	110	0.0
Common & Surplus	1,718,506	23.9
Total	7,197,167	100.0

*7 YEAR PRICE SCORE 90.8   ***12 MONTH PRICE SCORE 96.0**

NYSE COMPOSITE INDEX=100

BUSINESS:

H.J. Heinz Company manufactures and markets an extensive line of processed food products throughout the world, including ketchup and other sauces/condiments, frozen dinners, pet food, baby food, frozen potato products and canned soups, vegetables and fruits. Major U.S. brands include HEINZ, ORE-IDA, BOSTON MARKET and SMART ONES. Overseas, well-known brands include PLASMON, PUDLISZKI, ORLANDO, WATTIE'S, OLIVINE, FARLEY'S,

ABC, and JURAN. Fiscal 2002 sales were derived: Ketchup, Condiments & Sauces, 28.3%; Frozen Foods, 21.2%; Convenience Meals, 12.6%; Seafood, 11.0%; Pet Products, 10.4%; Infant/Nutritional Foods, 9.5%; and Other, 7.0%. On 12/20/02, the Company completed the spin-off of its tuna, pet food, private-label soup and baby food businesses to Del Monte Foods Company.

RECENT DEVELOPMENTS:

For the three months ended 10/31/02, net income rose 1.8% to $212.1 million from $208.2 million in the corresponding quarter the year before. Results for 2002 included a non-recurring after-tax charge of $6.1 million. Sales climbed 6.4% to $2.57 billion from $2.41 billion a year earlier. Sales reflected elevated pricing in highly inflationary countries in developing markets and Europe, favorable exchange rates, and strong performance of recent acquisitions in HNZ's key businesses. Gross profit totaled $904.4 million, or 35.2% of sales, compared with $862.6 million, or 35.7% of sales, the previous year.

PROSPECTS:

On 12/20/02, the Company announced that it has completed the spin off of its tuna, pet food, private-label soup and baby food businesses to Del Monte Foods Company. The Company will operate two business segments, away-from-home, which will focus on HNZ's restaurant and on-the-go eating businesses, and consumer products, which will focus on retail sales of ketchup, condiments and sauces, frozen meals and snacks. Separately, HNZ is targeting full fiscal-2003 earnings of between $2.00 and $2.05 per share.

ANNUAL FINANCIAL DATA:

FISCAL YEAR	TOT. REVS. ($mill.)	NET INC. ($mill.)	TOT. ASSETS ($mill.)	OPER. PROFIT %	NET PROFIT %	RET. ON EQUITY %	RET. ON ASSETS %	CURR. RATIO	EARN. PER SH.$	CASH FL. PER SH.$	TANG. BK. VAL.$	DIV. PER SH.$	PRICE RANGE	AVG. P/E RATIO	AVG. YIELD %
5/01/02	9,431.0	① 833.9	10,278.4	16.9	8.8	48.5	8.1	1.3	① 2.36	3.22	. . .	1.58	47.94 — 36.90	18.0	3.7
5/02/01	9,430.4	③ 494.9	9,035.2	10.4	5.2	36.0	5.5	0.9	③ 1.41	2.28	. . .	1.50	48.00 — 30.81	27.9	3.8
5/03/00	9,407.9	① 890.6	8,850.7	18.4	9.5	55.8	10.1	1.5	① 2.47	3.32	. . .	1.40	58.81 — 39.50	19.9	2.8
4/28/99	9,299.6	① 474.3	8,053.6	11.9	5.1	26.3	5.9	1.0	① 1.29	2.11	. . .	1.29	61.75 — 48.50	42.7	2.3
4/29/98	9,209.3	① 801.6	8,023.4	16.5	8.7	36.2	10.0	1.2	① 2.15	2.99	. . .	1.19	56.69 — 35.25	21.4	2.6
4/30/97	9,357.0	① 301.9	8,437.8	8.1	3.2	12.4	3.6	1.0	① 0.80	1.72	0.03	1.08	38.38 — 29.75	42.6	3.2
5/01/96	9,112.3	659.3	8,623.7	14.1	-7.2	24.4	7.6	1.1	1.74	2.66	0.87	0.98	34.88 — 24.25	17.0	3.3
5/03/95	8,086.8	591.0	8,247.2	14.3	7.3	23.9	7.2	1.1	1.59	2.43	0.34	0.90	26.00 — 20.50	14.6	3.9
4/27/94	7,046.7	② 602.9	6,381.1	15.2	8.6	25.8	9.4	1.4	① 1.57	2.24	2.67	0.82	30.17 — 22.75	16.9	3.1
4/28/93	7,103.4	② 529.9	6,821.3	12.1	7.5	22.8	7.8	0.9	② 1.36	1.96	2.49	0.74	30.33 — 23.42	19.8	2.8

Statistics are as originally reported. Adj. for 3-for-2 stk. split, 9/95. ① Incl. $8.9 mil ($0.03/sh) net chg., 2002; $34.7 mil ($0.10/sh) net chg., 2000; $408.2 mil ($1.11/sh) net chg., 1999; $12.5 mil net gain, 1998; $664.4 mil net chg., 1997; & $127.0 mil gain, 1994. ② Bef. $133.6 mil chg. for acctg. adj. & incl. $117.0 mil non-recur restr. chg. ③ Bef. $16.9 mil ($0.05/sh) acctg. chg. & incl. $494.6 mil ($1.41/sh) net special chg. and $93.2 mil ($0.27/sh) tax gain.

OFFICERS:
W. R. Johnson, Chmn., Pres., C.E.O.
A. Winkleback, Exec. V.P., C.F.O.
L. F. Stein, Sr. V.P., Gen. Couns.

INVESTOR CONTACT: Jack Runkel, V.P., Investor Relations, (412) 456-6034

PRINCIPAL OFFICE: 600 Grant Street, Pittsburgh, PA 15219

TELEPHONE NUMBER: (412) 456-5700
FAX: (412) 456-6128
WEB: www.heinz.com

NO. OF EMPLOYEES: 46,500 (approx.)

SHAREHOLDERS: 54,100 (approx. record)

ANNUAL MEETING: In Sept.

INCORPORATED: PA, July, 1900

INSTITUTIONAL HOLDINGS:
No. of Institutions: 528
Shares Held: 220,334,807
% Held: 62.7

INDUSTRY: Food preparations, nec (SIC 2099)

TRANSFER AGENT(S): Mellon Investor Services, Ridgefield Park, NJ

HELMERICH & PAYNE, INC.

EXCH.	SYM.	REC. PRICE	P/E RATIO	YLD.	MKT. CAP.	RANGE (52-WK.)	'02 Y/E PR.
NYSE	HP	27.50 (2/28/03)	38.2	1.2%	$1.38 bill.	43.24 - 22.60	27.91

MEDIUM GRADE. THE COMPANY IS EXPERIENCING LOWER RIG ACTIVITY FROM BOTH ITS DOMESTIC AND INTERNATIONAL OPERATIONS.

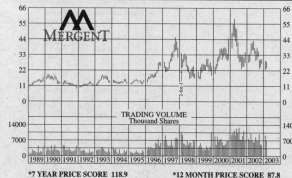

*7 YEAR PRICE SCORE 118.9   ***12 MONTH PRICE SCORE 87.8**

*NYSE COMPOSITE INDEX=100

INTERIM EARNINGS (Per Share):

Qtr.	Dec.	Mar.	June	Sept.
1997-98	0.57	0.38	0.67	0.38
1998-99	0.26	0.15	0.24	0.21
1999-00	0.41	0.39	0.37	0.48
2000-01	0.67	0.82	0.79	0.56
2001-02	0.36	0.16	0.45	0.10
2002-03	0.01	...	...	...

INTERIM DIVIDENDS (Per Share):

	Decl.	Ex.	Rec.	Pay.
0.075Q	3/06/02	5/13/02	5/15/02	6/03/02
0.08Q	6/05/02	8/13/02	8/15/02	9/03/02
0.08Q	9/04/02	11/13/02	11/15/02	12/02/02
0.08Q	12/04/02	2/12/03	2/14/03	3/03/03
0.08Q	3/05/03	5/13/03	5/15/03	6/02/03

Indicated div.: $0.32

CAPITALIZATION (9/30/02):

	($000)	(%)
Long-Term Debt	100,000	8.9
Deferred Income Tax	131,401	11.7
Common & Surplus	895,170	79.5
Total	1,126,571	100.0

BUSINESS:

Helmerich & Payne, Inc. is primarily a contract driller of oil and gas wells for others. As of 2/13/03, HP owned 75 U.S. land rigs, 12 U.S. platform rigs located in the Gulf of Mexico, and 33 rigs located in South America. The Company is also engaged in the ownership, development, and operation of commercial real estate. Revenues (and operating income) for fiscal 2002 were derived as follows: contract drilling, 92.8% (94.2%); real estate, 1.7% (5.8%); and other, 5.5% (Nil). On 9/30/02, HP completed the spin-off of its oil and gas division to HP shareholders.

RECENT DEVELOPMENTS:

For HP's first fiscal quarter ended 12/31/02, net income was $607,000 compared with income from continuing operations of $18.1 million in the same period a year earlier. Total revenues declined 20.5% to $107.3 million from $135.0 million the previous year. Total contract drilling division operating profit dropped 74.7% to $8.0 million, reflecting lower activity and profit margins from both the Company's domestic and international operations. Real estate division operating profit was $1.2 million, 16.5% lower than the year before.

PROSPECTS:

On 2/13/03, the Company announced that it has been informed by one of its major customers that, due to new budget constraints, twelve HP domestic land rigs will be released after the completion of their current contracts. The HP rigs contracted by the customer consist of six FlexRig3s, three FlexRig2s, and three conventional land rigs. It is estimated that all of these rigs will be released by the end of April 2003. HP noted that since release notification, it has obtained verbal contract commitments from other operators for work to begin immediately following the release of three of the FlexRig3s. HP further stated that given the recent increased level of bid activity and the schedule of rig release dates, it anticipates that the remaining FlexRigs and conventional rigs should have jobs by the completion of their current commitments.

ANNUAL FINANCIAL DATA:

FISCAL YEAR	TOT. REVS. ($mill.)	NET INC. ($mill.)	TOT. ASSETS ($mill.)	OPER. PROFIT %	NET PROFIT %	RET. ON EQUITY %	RET. ON ASSETS %	CURR. RATIO	EARN. PER SH.$	CASH FL PER SH.$	TANG. BK. VAL.$	DIV. PER SH.$	PRICE RANGE	AVG. P/E RATIO	AVG. YIELD %
9/30/02	510.9	①53.7	1,227.3	18.0	10.5	6.0	4.4	2.5	①1.07	2.31	17.90	0.31	43.24 - 23.45	31.2	0.9
9/30/01	826.9	144.3	1,364.5	28.4	17.4	14.1	10.6	2.5	2.84	4.59	20.59	0.30	58.73 - 23.40	14.5	0.7
9/30/00	631.1	82.3	1,259.5	22.2	13.0	8.6	6.5	3.4	1.64	3.89	19.12	0.29	44.81 - 19.75	19.7	0.9
9/30/99	564.3	42.8	1,109.7	12.7	7.6	5.0	3.9	2.2	0.86	3.08	17.09	0.28	30.38 - 16.00	27.0	1.2
9/30/98	636.6	101.2	1,090.4	24.1	15.9	12.8	9.3	1.5	2.00	3.77	16.06	0.28	34.13 - 16.13	12.6	1.1
9/30/97	517.9	84.2	1,033.6	25.4	16.3	10.8	8.1	1.7	1.69	3.15	15.60	0.26	45.56 - 20.75	19.6	0.8
9/30/96	393.3	①45.4	821.9	17.9	11.6	7.0	5.5	1.8	①0.92	2.16	12.98	0.26	27.88 - 13.44	22.5	1.2
9/30/95	325.8	9.8	710.2	4.3	3.0	1.7	1.4	1.7	0.20	1.80	11.36	0.25	15.63 - 12.13	69.3	1.8
9/30/94	329.0	②21.0	624.8	9.3	6.4	4.0	3.4	2.6	②0.43	1.49	10.61	0.24	15.69 - 12.38	32.6	1.7
9/30/93	315.1	③24.6	610.9	13.7	7.8	4.8	4.0	3.2	③0.51	1.54	10.33	0.24	18.75 - 11.13	29.6	1.6

Statistics are as originally reported. Adj. for 2-for-1 stk. split, 12/97. ① Bef. disc. oper. inc. of $9.8 mill., 9/30/02; $27.1 mill., 9/30/96. ② Bef. acctg. change credit of $4.0 mill. ③ Incl. non-recurr. credit of $1.3 mill.

OFFICERS:
W. H. Helmerich III, Chmn.
H. C. Helmerich, Pres., C.E.O.
D. E. Fears, V.P., C.F.O.

INVESTOR CONTACT: D. E. Fears, V.P., C.F.O., (918) 742-5531

PRINCIPAL OFFICE: Utica at Twenty-First Street, Tulsa, OK 74114

TELEPHONE NUMBER: (918) 742-5531
FAX: (918) 742-0237
WEB: www.hpinc.com

NO. OF EMPLOYEES: 3,662 full-time; 13 part-time

SHAREHOLDERS: 1,001 (record)

ANNUAL MEETING: In Mar.

INCORPORATED: DE, Feb., 1940

INSTITUTIONAL HOLDINGS:
No. of Institutions: 223
Shares Held: 39,146,690
% Held: 78.3

INDUSTRY: Drilling oil and gas wells (SIC: 1381)

TRANSFER AGENT(S): UMB Bank, Kansas City, MO

HERCULES INC.

EXCH.	SYM.	REC. PRICE	P/E RATIO	YLD.	MKT. CAP.	RANGE (52-WK.)	'02 Y/E PR.
NYSE	HPC	8.03 (2/28/03)	...	...	$0.87 bill.	13.70 - 7.92	8.80

SPECULATIVE GRADE. EARNINGS IN 2003 ARE EXPECTED TO BENEFIT FROM THE COST SAVINGS IMPLEMENTED IN 2002 AND IMPROVED SALES VOLUMES.

TRADING VOLUME
Thousand Shares

*7 YEAR PRICE SCORE 37.9   ***12 MONTH PRICE SCORE 88.7**

*NYSE COMPOSITE INDEX=100

INTERIM EARNINGS (Per Share):

Qtr.	Mar.	June	Sept.	Dec.
1997	1.05	0.75	0.82	0.61
1998	0.70	0.77	0.74	d1.64
1999	0.37	0.56	0.54	0.16
2000	0.34	0.15	0.70	d0.28
2001	d0.09	0.21	d0.66	0.06
2002	d0.03	d0.19	d0.32	0.09

INTERIM DIVIDENDS (Per Share):

Amt.	Decl.	Ex.	Rec.	Pay.
0.08Q	8/25/00	9/01/00	9/06/00	9/29/00

Dividend payment suspended.

CAPITALIZATION (12/31/01):

	($000)	(%)
Long-Term Debt	1,959,000	65.2
Deferred Income Tax	334,000	11.1
Common & Surplus	712,000	23.7
Total	3,005,000	100.0

BUSINESS:

Hercules Inc. is a diversified worldwide producer of chemicals. HPC operates in two industry segments: Performance Products, which includes the Pulp and Paper and Aqualon businesses; and Engineered Materials and Additives, which includes the FiberVisions and Pinova businesses. The pulp and paper business supplies functional, process and water treatment chemical programs for the pulp and paper industry. The Aqualon business manages the properties of water-based systems. The FiberVisions business supplies fine-denier staple fibers for the disposable hygiene product industry. The Pinova business is a producer of pale wood rosin derivatives. On 4/29/02, HPC sold its BetzDearborn water treatment business for $1.80 billion in cash. Sales (and operating income) for 2002 were derived: Performance Products, 81.2% (93.3%); and Engineered Materials and Additives, 18.8% (6.7%).

RECENT DEVELOPMENTS:

For the twelve months ended 12/31/02, loss from continuing operations amounted to $49.0 million, before an accounting change charge of $368.0 million, compared with a loss from continuing operations of $106.0 million in 2001. Results for 2002 and 2001 included goodwill and intangible asset amortization of $9.0 million and $24.0 million, respectively. Results for 2002 and 2001 excluded a net loss of $199.0 million and a net gain of $48.0 million, respectively, from discontinued operations. Net sales slipped 4.0% to $1.71 billion.

PROSPECTS:

Looking ahead, the Company anticipates further growth in earnings before interest, taxes, depreciation and amortization in 2003 even though there is little indication that aggregate market conditions will improve. The challenges in 2003 include higher post-retirement and insurance costs and uncertain market conditions. Driving the improvement in earnings in 2003 will be the fully annualized cost savings implemented in 2002 and further reductions in fixed and variable costs, as well as improved sales volumes.

ANNUAL FINANCIAL DATA:

FISCAL YEAR	TOT. REVS. ($mill.)	NET INC. ($mill.)	TOT. ASSETS ($mill.)	OPER. PROFIT %	NET PROFIT %	RET. ON EQUITY %	RET. ON ASSETS %	CURR. RATIO	EARN. PER SH. $	CASH FL. PER SH. $	TANG. BK. VAL.$	DIV. PER SH. $	PRICE RANGE	AVG. P/E RATIO	AVG. YIELD %
p12/31/02	1,705.0	⑥ d49.0	...	...	...	...	...	...	⑥ d0.45	...	...	...	13.70 - 8.45	...	...
12/31/01	2,620.0	d58.0	5,049.0	11.0	...	...	...	0.9	d0.54	1.42	...	...	20.00 - 6.50	...	...
12/31/00	3,152.0	⑤ 98.0	5,309.0	14.1	3.1	12.0	1.8	1.1	⑤ 0.91	3.20	...	0.62	28.00 - 11.38	21.6	3.1
12/31/99	3,248.0	④ 168.0	5,896.0	14.8	8.3	31.3	4.6	0.9	④ 1.62	5.00	...	1.08	40.69 - 22.38	19.5	3.4
12/31/98	2,145.0	③ 9.0	5,833.0	9.0	0.4	1.6	0.2	0.9	③ 0.10	1.20	...	1.08	51.38 - 24.63	380.0	2.8
12/31/97	1,866.0	② 324.0	2,411.0	12.2	17.4	47.0	13.4	0.9	② 3.18	3.88	7.18	1.00	54.50 - 37.75	14.5	2.2
12/31/96	2,060.0	325.0	2,386.0	21.4	15.8	36.6	13.6	1.1	3.04	4.25	8.75	0.92	66.25 - 42.75	17.9	1.7
12/31/95	2,427.2	332.8	2,493.5	15.0	13.7	30.8	13.3	1.3	2.93	4.09	9.97	0.84	62.25 - 38.25	17.1	1.7
12/31/94	2,821.0	274.2	2,941.3	14.8	9.7	21.2	9.3	1.5	2.29	3.51	11.10	0.75	40.50 - 32.13	15.9	2.1
12/31/93	2,773.4	① 208.4	3,162.0	11.1	7.5	15.2	6.6	1.4	① 1.62	2.93	11.17	0.75	38.29 - 21.08	18.3	2.5

Statistics are as originally reported. Adj. for 3-for-1 split, 1/95. ① Bef. dr$238.2 mill. acct. adj. & $3.6 mill. chg. for debt retire. ② Bef. $5.0 mill. acct. chg. & incl. $0.14/sh. chg. for acq. activity. ③ Incl. $197.0 mill. after-tax non-recur. chg. rel. to acq. of BetzDearborn, $40.0 mill. after-tax non-recur. chg. for legal settlement, & $59.0 mill. chg. for oth. exps. ④ Incl. $35.0 mill. non-recur. chg., $16.0 mill. gain fr. sale of subsidiary & $43.0 mill. in restr. and other chgs. ⑤ Incl. $25.0 mill. chg. rel. to sale of bus., $168.0 mill. gain, $66.0 mill. asset write-down chg. & $28.0 mill. restr. chg. ⑥ Excl. $199.0 mill. loss fr. disc. ops. & $368.0 mill. acctg. chrg.

OFFICERS:
W. H. Joyce, Chmn., C.E.O.
S. C. Shears, V.P., Treas.
I. J. Floyd, Sec., Gen. Couns.

INVESTOR CONTACT: Allen A. Spizzo, Investor Relations, (302) 594-6491

PRINCIPAL OFFICE: 1313 North Market St., Hercules Plaza, Wilmington, DE 19894

TELEPHONE NUMBER: (302) 594-5000
FAX: (302) 594-5400
WEB: www.herc.com

NO. OF EMPLOYEES: 5,280 (approx.)

SHAREHOLDERS: 18,113 (approx. record)

ANNUAL MEETING: In June

INCORPORATED: DE, Oct., 1912

INSTITUTIONAL HOLDINGS:
No. of Institutions: 189
Shares Held: 84,154,492
% Held: 77.1

INDUSTRY: Industrial organic chemicals, nec (SIC: 2869)

TRANSFER AGENT(S): Mellon Investor Services, Ridgefield Park, NJ

HERSHEY FOODS CORPORATION

EXCH.	SYM.	REC. PRICE	P/E RATIO	YLD.	MKT. CAP.	RANGE (52-WK.)	'02 Y/E PR.	DIV. ACH.
NYSE	HSY	64.61 (2/28/03)	22.0	2.0%	$10.73 bill.	79.49 - 56.45	67.44	28 yrs.

INVESTMENT GRADE. SALES SHOULD BENEFIT FROM NEW PRODUCT INTRODUCTIONS IN 2003.

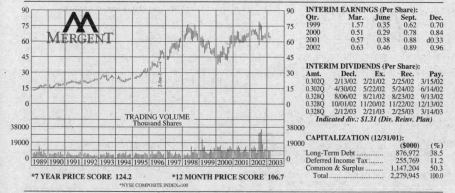

INTERIM EARNINGS (Per Share):

Qtr.	Mar.	June	Sept.	Dec.
1999	1.57	0.35	0.62	0.70
2000	0.51	0.29	0.78	0.84
2001	0.57	0.38	0.88	d0.33
2002	0.63	0.46	0.89	0.96

INTERIM DIVIDENDS (Per Share):

Amt.	Decl.	Ex.	Rec.	Pay.
0.302Q	2/13/02	2/21/02	2/25/02	3/15/02
0.302Q	4/30/02	5/22/02	5/24/02	6/14/02
0.328Q	8/06/02	8/21/02	8/23/02	9/13/02
0.328Q	10/01/02	11/20/02	11/22/02	12/13/02
0.328Q	2/12/03	2/21/03	2/25/03	3/14/03

Indicated div.: $1.31 (Div. Reinv. Plan)

CAPITALIZATION (12/31/01):

	($000)	(%)
Long-Term Debt	876,972	38.5
Deferred Income Tax	255,769	11.2
Common & Surplus	1,147,204	50.3
Total	2,279,945	100.0

TRADING VOLUME
Thousand Shares

2-for-1

*7 YEAR PRICE SCORE 124.2   *12 MONTH PRICE SCORE 106.7
*NYSE COMPOSITE INDEX=100

BUSINESS:

Hershey Foods Corporation and its subsidiaries are engaged in the manufacture, distribution and sale of consumer food products including: chocolate and non-chocolate confectionery products sold in the form of bar goods, bagged items and boxed items; and grocery products sold in the form of baking ingredients, chocolate drink mixes, peanut butter, dessert toppings and beverages. HSY's products are marketed in over 90 countries worldwide under more than 50 brands. Principal brands include: HERSHEY's,

REESE's, MR. GOODBAR, JOLLY RANCHER, KIT KAT, MILK DUDS, WHOPPERS, YORK, TWIZZLERS, and SUPER BUBBLE. In January 1999, HSY sold a 94.0% majority interest in its former U.S. pasta business to New World, LLC. On 12/15/00, HSY acquired Nabisco, Inc.'s mints and gum businesses for $135.0 million. Acquired brands include ICE BREAKERS, BREATH SAVERS COOL BLASTS and BREATH SAVERS mints, and ICE BREAKERS, CARE*FREE, STICK*FREE, BUBBLE YUM, and FRUIT STRIPE gums.

RECENT DEVELOPMENTS:

For the year ended 12/31/02, net income surged 94.8% to $403.6 million from $207.2 million in the previous year. Results for 2002 included pre-tax realignment charges of $34.0 million and expenses of $17.2 million related to the exploration of the possible sale of the Company. Results for 2001 included a pre-tax charge of $278.4 million related to

the realignment initiatives, the gain on the sale of Luden's business and the amortization of goodwill. Net sales slipped 0.4% to $4.12 billion from $4.14 billion a year earlier. Gross profit improved 6.2% to $1.56 billion, or 37.8% of net sales, from $1.47 billion, or 35.5% of net sales, the year before.

PROSPECTS:

The Company's sales mix continues benefit from its focus on higher margin products, packtypes, and channels of trade. Looking ahead, sales are expected to benefit from new product introductions in 2003, including a sugar-free

Reese's chocolate and several new items under the Reese's brand, as well as a recent price increase on selected chocolate bars. Also, earnings for 2003 should benefit from HSY's recent focus on convenience and club stores.

ANNUAL FINANCIAL DATA:

FISCAL YEAR	TOT. REVS. ($mill.)	NET INC. ($mill.)	TOT. ASSETS ($mill.)	OPER. PROFIT %	NET PROFIT %	RET. ON EQUITY %	RET. ON ASSETS %	CURR. RATIO	EARN. PER SH. $	CASH FL. PER SH. $	TANG. BK. VAL. $	DIV. PER SH. $	PRICE RANGE	AVG. P/E RATIO	AVG. YIELD %
p12/31/02	4,120.3	⑤ 403.6	3,480.6		9.8	29.4	11.6		⑤ 2.93			1.26	79.49 - 56.45	23.2	1.9
12/31/01	4,557.2	④ 207.2	3,247.4	8.6	4.5	18.1	6.4	1.9	④ 1.50	2.89	4.32	1.17	70.15 - 55.13	41.8	1.9
12/31/00	4,221.0	334.5	3,447.8	14.8	7.9	28.5	9.7	1.7	2.42	3.69	5.14	1.08	66.44 - 37.75	21.5	2.1
12/31/99	3,970.9	③ 460.3	3,346.7	14.1	11.6	41.9	13.8	1.8	③ 3.26	4.41	4.68	1.00	64.88 - 45.75	17.0	1.8
12/31/98	4,435.6	340.9	3,404.1	14.5	7.7	32.7	10.0	1.4	2.34	3.43	3.58	0.92	76.38 - 59.69	29.1	1.4
12/31/97	4,302.2	336.3	3,291.2	14.6	7.8	39.4	10.2	1.3	2.23	3.24	2.11	0.84	63.88 - 42.13	23.8	1.6
12/31/96	3,989.3	273.2	3,184.8	14.1	6.8	23.5	8.6	1.2	1.77	2.64	3.89	0.76	51.75 - 31.94	23.6	1.8
12/31/95	3,690.7	281.9	2,830.6	13.8	7.6	26.0	10.0	1.1	1.70	2.50	4.23	0.69	33.94 - 24.00	17.0	2.4
12/31/94	3,606.3	② 184.2	2,891.0	10.2	5.1	12.8	6.4	1.2	② 1.06	1.80	5.69	0.63	26.75 - 20.56	22.3	2.6
12/31/93	3,488.2	① 297.2	2,855.1	15.4	8.5	21.0	10.4	1.1	① 1.66	2.29	5.36	0.57	27.94 - 21.75	15.0	2.3

Statistics are as originally reported. Adj. for 2-for-1 stk. split, 9/96. ① Bef. acctg. change chrg. $103.9 mill.; incl. credit of $40.6 mill. ② Incl. non-recurr. chrg. of $80.2 mill. ③ Incl. non-recurr. credit of $165.0 mill. ④ Incl. pre-tax chrg. of $228.3 mill. for business realign. & asset impairmnts. and pre-tax gain of $19.2 mill. on sale of Luden's business. ⑤ Incl. pre-tax realign. chrg. of $34.0 mill. and bus. sale exploration chrg. of $17.2 mill.

OFFICERS:
R. H. Lenny, Chmn., Pres., C.E.O.
F. Cerminara, Sr. V.P., C.F.O.

INVESTOR CONTACT: James A. Edris, (717) 534-7556

PRINCIPAL OFFICE: 100 Crystal A Drive, Hershey, PA 17033

TELEPHONE NUMBER: (717) 534-6799
FAX: (717) 534-7873
WEB: www.hersheys.com
NO. OF EMPLOYEES: 14,400 full-time (approx.); 1,600 part-time (approx.)
SHAREHOLDERS: 40,311 (class B)
ANNUAL MEETING: In April
INCORPORATED: DE, Oct., 1927

INSTITUTIONAL HOLDINGS:
No. of Institutions: 414
Shares Held: 55,829,840
% Held: 41.0

INDUSTRY: Chocolate and cocoa products (SIC: 2066)

TRANSFER AGENT(S): Mellon Investor Services, Ridgefield Park, NJ

HEWLETT-PACKARD COMPANY

EXCH.	SYM.	REC. PRICE	P/E RATIO	YLD.	MKT. CAP.	RANGE (52-WK.)	'02 Y/E PR.
NYSE	HPQ	15.85 (2/28/03)	...	2.0%	$48.24 bill.	21.35 - 10.75	17.36

LOWER MEDIUM GRADE. THE COMPANY'S REVENUES IN THE U.S. AND JAPAN REMAIN SOFT, WHILE REVENUES IN EUROPE AND THE ASIA-PACIFIC REGION CONTINUE TO GROW.

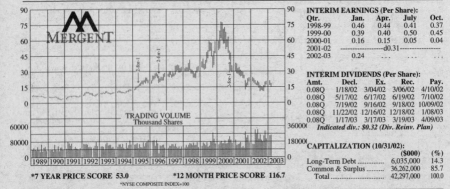

INTERIM EARNINGS (Per Share):

Qtr.	Jan.	Apr.	July	Oct.
1998-99	0.46	0.44	0.41	0.37
1999-00	0.39	0.40	0.50	0.45
2000-01	0.16	0.15	0.05	0.04
2001-02	--------------------d0.31-------------------
2002-03	0.24	...	...	...

INTERIM DIVIDENDS (Per Share):

Amt.	Decl.	Ex.	Rec.	Pay.
0.08Q	1/18/02	3/04/02	3/06/02	4/10/02
0.08Q	5/17/02	6/17/02	6/19/02	7/10/02
0.08Q	7/19/02	9/16/02	9/18/02	10/09/02
0.08Q	11/22/02	12/16/02	12/18/02	1/08/03
0.08Q	1/17/03	3/17/03	3/19/03	4/09/03

Indicated div.: $0.32 (Div. Reinv. Plan)

CAPITALIZATION (10/31/02):

	($000)	(%)
Long-Term Debt	6,035,000	14.3
Common & Surplus	36,262,000	85.7
Total	42,297,000	100.0

*7 YEAR PRICE SCORE 53.0   ***12 MONTH PRICE SCORE 116.7**

*NYSE COMPOSITE INDEX=100

BUSINESS:

Hewlett-Packard Company is a provider of computing and imaging solutions and services for the business and home. On 5/3/02, the Company acquired Compaq Computer Corporation. As a result of the combination of the two companies, operations have been combined into five major operating groups. The Enterprise Systems Group (22.5% of net revenue for 2002) provides servers, storage, networking technology and management software for businesses, telecommunications companies and financial institutions.

HP Services (16.9%) provides information technology consulting and services. The Imaging and Printing Group (27.8%) consists of printers, digital imaging solutions and digital publishing systems. The Personal Systems Group (30.0%) includes personal computers, notebooks, handheld devices, personal storage, emerging internet-access devices and mobility technologies. The Financial Services Group (2.8%) offers leasing and financial asset management services.

RECENT DEVELOPMENTS:

For the three months ended 1/31/03, net earnings advanced 49.0% to $721.0 million compared with $484.0 million in the corresponding quarter of the previous year. Results for 2002 and 2001 included pre-tax acquisition-related charges of $86.0 million and $38.0 million, respectively. Results for

2002 and 2001 included amortization of goodwill and purchased intangible assets of $138.0 million and $50.0 million, respectively. Net revenue increased 57.0% to $17.88 billion. Results are not directly comparable as the prior-year period excluded Compaq.

PROSPECTS:

HPQ's revenues are reflecting ongoing weakness in commercial information technology spending in the U.S. and Japan, while Europe and Asia-Pacific are posting solid revenue growth quarter over quarter. Meanwhile, HPQ is seeing some improvement in its cost structure as a result of

sequential market share gains in each of its businesses leading to stronger gross margins. Going forward, HPQ will look to stay focused on accelerating market share gains and investing in growth. HPQ expects its second quarter 2003 earnings per share to be in the range of $0.27.

ANNUAL FINANCIAL DATA:

FISCAL YEAR	TOT. REVS. ($mill.)	NET INC. ($mill.)	TOT. ASSETS ($mill.)	OPER. PROFIT %	NET PROFIT %	RET. ON EQUITY %	RET. ON ASSETS %	CURR. RATIO	EARN. PER SH.$	CASH FL. PER SH.$	TANG. BK. VAL.$	DIV. PER SH.$	PRICE RANGE	AVG. P/E RATIO	AVG. YIELD %
10/31/02	56,588.0	④ d923.0	70,710.0	...	...	...	...	1.5	④ d0.37	0.48	5.36	0.32	24.12 - 10.75	...	1.8
10/31/01	45,226.0	③ 624.0	32,584.0	3.2	1.4	4.5	1.9	1.5	③ 0.32	1.01	7.20	0.32	37.95 - 12.50	78.8	1.3
10/31/00	48,782.0	② 3,561.0	34,009.0	8.0	7.3	25.1	10.5	1.5	② 1.73	2.37	7.30	0.32	77.75 - 29.13	30.9	0.6
10/31/99	42,370.0	② 3,104.0	35,297.0	8.7	7.3	17.0	8.8	1.5	② 1.49	2.10	9.11	0.32	59.22 - 31.69	30.6	0.7
10/31/98	47,061.0	① 2,945.0	33,673.0	8.2	6.3	17.4	8.7	1.6	① 1.39	2.25	8.33	0.30	41.19 - 23.53	23.4	0.9
10/31/97	42,895.0	3,119.0	31,749.0	10.1	7.3	19.3	9.8	1.9	1.48	2.21	7.76	0.26	36.47 - 24.06	20.5	0.9
10/31/96	38,420.0	2,586.0	27,699.0	9.7	6.7	19.2	9.3	1.7	1.23	1.85	6.63	0.22	28.84 - 18.41	19.2	0.9
10/31/95	31,519.0	2,433.0	24,427.0	11.3	7.7	20.6	10.0	1.5	1.16	1.70	5.80	0.17	24.16 - 12.25	15.7	1.0
10/31/94	24,991.0	1,627.0	19,567.0	10.2	6.5	16.4	8.3	1.5	0.77	1.27	4.87	0.14	12.81 - 8.98	14.2	1.3
10/31/93	20,317.0	1,177.0	16,736.0	9.2	5.8	13.8	7.0	1.5	0.58	1.00	4.22	0.11	11.16 - 9.65	18.5	1.2

Statistics are as originally reported. Adj. for a 2-for-1 stock split 10/27/00, 4/13/95 & 7/15/96. ① Incl. spec. pre-tax chrgs. of approx. $170.0 mill. for volun.-sever. programs & fixed asset write downs. ② Bef. inc. frm. disc. opers. of $136.0 mill., 2000; $387.0 mill., 1999. ③ Bef. extra. gain of $56.0 mill. & acctg. chrg. of $272.0 mill., incl. a loss on divest. of $53.0 mill. & restruct. chrg. of $384.0 mill. ④ Bef. extraord. gain of $20.0 mill., incl. net chrgs. of $3.35 bill., net inv. loss of $100.0 mill. & litig. settle. of $14.0 mill.

OFFICERS:
C. S. Fiorina, Chmn., C.E.O.
R. P. Wayman, Exec. V.P., C.F.O.

INVESTOR CONTACT: Investor Relations,
(800) 825-5497

PRINCIPAL OFFICE: 3000 Hanover Street,
Palo Alto, CA 94304

TELEPHONE NUMBER: (650) 857-1501
FAX: (650) 857-5518
WEB: www.hp.com
NO. OF EMPLOYEES: 141,000 (approx.)
SHAREHOLDERS: 160,800 (approx.)
ANNUAL MEETING: In Feb.
INCORPORATED: CA, Aug., 1947; reincorp., DE, May, 1998

INSTITUTIONAL HOLDINGS:
No. of Institutions: 937
Shares Held: 1,912,436,467
% Held: 62.7

INDUSTRY: Electronic computers (SIC: 3571)

TRANSFER AGENT(S): Computershare Investor Services, Chicago, IL

HIBERNIA CORPORATION

EXCH.	SYM.	REC. PRICE	P/E RATIO	YLD.	MKT. CAP.	RANGE (52-WK.)	'02 Y/E PR.
NYSE	HIB	18.12 (2/28/03)	11.5	3.3%	$2.88 bill.	21.71 - 16.25	19.26

UPPER MEDIUM GRADE. BY THE END OF 2006, THE COMPANY PLANS TO OPEN UP TO 50 SALES OFFICES IN CERTAIN MAJOR TEXAS CITIES.

TRADING VOLUME
Thousand Shares

1989 1990 1991 1992 1993 1994 1995 1996 1997 1998 1999 2000 2001 2002 2003

*7 YEAR PRICE SCORE 132.6   ***12 MONTH PRICE SCORE 104.7**
*NYSE COMPOSITE INDEX=100

INTERIM EARNINGS (Per Share):

Qtr.	Mar.	June	Sept.	Dec.
1997	0.23	0.24	0.25	0.28
1998	0.25	0.27	0.29	0.30
1999	0.18	0.29	0.30	0.30
2000	0.31	0.31	0.33	0.10
2001	0.31	0.34	0.35	0.35
2002	0.37	0.39	0.40	0.41

INTERIM DIVIDENDS (Per Share):

Amt.	Decl.	Ex.	Rec.	Pay.
0.14Q	1/29/02	2/06/02	2/08/02	2/20/02
0.14Q	4/17/02	4/25/02	4/29/02	5/20/02
0.14Q	7/24/02	8/01/02	8/05/02	8/20/02
0.15Q	10/23/02	10/31/02	11/04/02	11/20/02
0.15Q	1/28/03	2/05/03	2/07/03	2/20/03

Indicated div.: $0.60

CAPITALIZATION (12/31/01):

	($000)	(%)
Total Deposits	12,953,112	83.3
Long-Term Debt	1,042,983	6.7
Common & Surplus	1,559,779	10.0
Total	15,555,874	100.0

BUSINESS:

Hibernia Corporation is a bank holding company headquartered in Louisiana. As of 12/31/02, the Company had assets of $17.39 billion and 261 locations in 34 Louisiana parishes, 17 Texas counties and two Mississippi counties. The Company conducts its business through its sole depository institution subsidiary, Hibernia National Bank. In addition, the Company also owns Hibernia Capital Corporation (HCC). HCC is licensed as a small business investment company, which provides private equity investments to small businesses.

RECENT DEVELOPMENTS:

For the year ended 12/31/02, net income increased 14.2% to $249.9 million from $218.8 million the year before. Earnings for 2002 and 2001 included pre-tax gains on the sale of mortgage loans of $28.0 million and $21.1 million, net amortization of goodwill and other intangibles of $57.9 million and $46.6 million, non-cash provisions for the temporary impairment of mortgage servicing rights of $23.2 million and $12.3 million, and net securities losses of $13.4 million and $8.9 million, respectively. Net interest income improved 6.0% to $704.2 million from $664.7 million a year earlier. Provision for loan losses decreased 17.1% to $80.6 million. Non-interest income increased 10.1% to $352.9 million, while non-interest expense rose 7.8% to $593.7 million. Net interest margin improved to 4.62% from 4.39%.

PROSPECTS:

During the quarter, the Company opened a commercial financial center in Addison, Texas as part of its Texas expansion program. Additionally, HIB identified Dallas sites for future new sales offices. By the end of 2006, the Company plans to open up to 50 sales offices in certain major Texas cities, beginning with the Dallas/Fort Worth metroplex. Separately, HIB's Completely Free Checking program, which was introduced in March 2002, continues to perform well, contributing to a 15.0% increase in noninterest-bearing deposits compared with the prior year.

ANNUAL FINANCIAL DATA:

FISCAL YEAR	NET INT. INC. ($mill.)	NON-INT. INC. ($mill.)	NET INC. ($mill.)	TOT. LOANS ($mill.)	TOT. ASSETS ($mill.)	TOT. DEP. ($mill.)	RET. ON EQUITY %	RET. ON ASSETS %	EQUITY/ ASSETS %	EARN. PER SH. $	TANG. BK. VAL.$	DIV. PER SH.$	PRICE RANGE	AVG. P/E RATIO
p12/31/02	704.2	352.9	④⑤ 249.9		17,392.7					④⑤ 1.56		0.57	21.71 - 16.25	12.2
12/31/01	664.7	318.1	④ 218.8	11,241.0	16,618.2	12,953.1	14.0	1.3	9.4	④ 1.35	9.81	0.53	19.35 - 11.75	11.5
12/31/00	610.6	248.7	170.6	12,124.7	16,698.0	12,692.7	11.5	1.0	8.9	1.04	8.83	0.49	13.94 - 8.75	10.9
12/31/99	584.8	214.7	175.1	10,856.7	15,314.2	11,855.9	12.7	1.1	9.0	1.06	7.96	0.43	17.50 - 10.25	13.1
12/31/98	530.5	184.9	178.6	10,006.2	14,011.5	10,603.0	13.6	1.3	9.4	1.10	7.79	0.38	22.00 - 12.25	15.6
12/31/97	427.8	145.4	137.4	7,580.3	11,023.0	8,633.3	13.1	1.2	9.5	0.98	7.15	0.33	19.63 - 12.38	16.3
12/31/96	366.2	110.4	① 110.0	6,043.0	9,306.8	7,821.8	11.7	1.2	10.1	① 0.85	6.50	0.29	13.63 - 9.50	13.6
12/31/95	299.8	97.5	①② 123.9	4,469.4	7,196.2	6,085.1	17.3	1.7	10.0	①② 1.05	6.01	0.25	11.00 - 6.88	8.5
12/31/94	260.1	81.8	84.7	3,375.7	6,335.8	5,506.8	15.2	1.3	8.8	0.52	3.41	0.19	9.13 - 7.25	15.7
12/31/93	195.7	67.2	③ 48.0	2,328.1	4,795.6	4,086.0	11.2	1.0	8.9	③ 0.58	5.12	0.03	9.13 - 5.88	12.9

Statistics are as originally reported. ① Incl. gain on sale of business lines, 1996, $517,000; 1995, $3.4 mill. ② Incl. gain on divestiture of banking offices $2.4 mill. ③ Incl. gain on settlement of acquired loans $1.3 mill. ④ Incl. pre-tax gains on the sales of mtge. loans of $28.0 mill., 2002; $21.1 mill., 2001. ⑤ Incl. non-cash provs. for the temp. impair. of mtge. svcing. rts. of $23.2 mill.

OFFICERS:
E. R. Campbell, Vice-Chmn.
J. H. Boydstun, Pres., C.E.O.
M. M. Gassan, Sr. Exec. V.P., C.F.O.

INVESTOR CONTACT: Trisha Voltz, V.P., Mgr., Investor Relations, (504) 533-2180

PRINCIPAL OFFICE: 313 Carondelet Street, New Orleans, LA 70130

TELEPHONE NUMBER: (504) 533 5332
FAX: (504) 586 2199
WEB: www.hibernia.com

NO. OF EMPLOYEES: 5,398

SHAREHOLDERS: 16,004

ANNUAL MEETING: In April

INCORPORATED: LA, Oct., 1972

INSTITUTIONAL HOLDINGS:
No. of Institutions: 229
Shares Held: 80,735,214
% Held: 51.3

INDUSTRY: National commercial banks (SIC: 6021)

TRANSFER AGENT(S): Mellon Investor Services, Ridgefield Park, NJ

HIGHWOODS PROPERTIES, INC.

EXCH.	SYM.	REC. PRICE	P/E RATIO	YLD.	MKT. CAP.	RANGE (52-WK.)	'02 Y/E PR.
NYSE	HIW	21.01 (2/28/03)	23.6	11.1%	$1.11 bill.	29.45 - 18.97	22.10

MEDIUM GRADE. THE COMPANY IS FOCUSED ON PRESERVING AND INCREASING ITS OCCUPANCY.

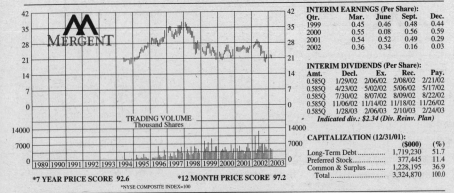

*7 YEAR PRICE SCORE 92.6   ***12 MONTH PRICE SCORE 97.2**

*NYSE COMPOSITE INDEX=100

INTERIM EARNINGS (Per Share):

Qtr.	Mar.	June	Sept.	Dec.
1999	0.45	0.46	0.48	0.44
2000	0.55	0.08	0.56	0.59
2001	0.54	0.52	0.49	0.29
2002	0.36	0.34	0.16	0.03

INTERIM DIVIDENDS (Per Share):

Amt.	Decl.	Ex.	Rec.	Pay.
0.585Q	1/29/02	2/06/02	2/08/02	2/21/02
0.585Q	4/23/02	5/02/02	5/06/02	5/17/02
0.585Q	7/30/02	8/07/02	8/09/02	8/22/02
0.585Q	11/06/02	11/14/02	11/18/02	11/26/02
0.585Q	1/28/03	2/06/03	2/10/03	2/24/03

Indicated div.: $2.34 (Div. Reinv. Plan)

CAPITALIZATION (12/31/01):

	($000)	(%)
Long-Term Debt	1,719,230	51.7
Preferred Stock	377,445	11.4
Common & Surplus	1,228,195	36.9
Total	3,324,870	100.0

BUSINESS:

Highwoods Properties, Inc. is a fully integrated, self-administered real estate investment trust that provides leasing, management, development, construction and other customer-related services for its properties and for third parties. As of 12/31/02, HIW owned or had an interest in 571 in-service office, industrial and retail properties encompassing approximately 44.9 million square feet. HIW also owned approximately 1,300 acres of development land. The Company's properties and development land are located in Florida, Georgia, Iowa, Kansas, Missouri, North Carolina, South Carolina, Tennessee and Virginia.

RECENT DEVELOPMENTS:

For the year ended 12/31/02, income declined 39.0% to $70.7 million, before a gain of $29.3 million from discontinued operations and an extraordinary loss of $378,000, compared with income of $115.8 million, before a gain of $16.1 million from discontinued operations and an extraordinary loss of $714,000, in 2001. Results for 2002 and 2001 included gains on the disposition of assets of $12.2 million and $16.2 million, respectively. Results for 2002 also included a litigation reserve of $2.7 million. Rental revenue declined 3.2% to $454.2 million. Funds from operations fell 15.2% to $201.8 million due to higher bad debt expenses, lower lease termination fee incomes, lower capitalized interest on development projects and the dilution of asset sales.

PROSPECTS:

The Company is focused on preserving and increasing its occupancy through leasing efforts and customer service. HIW's development pipeline of four projects totaling 331,000 square feet is 52.0% pre-leased. Projects in the pipeline have an anticipated total investment of $34.5 million, with $28.1 million funded as of 12/31/02. Full-year 2003 funds from operations are estimated to be between $3.00 and $3.25 per share. The estimates for the year ended 12/31/03 assume an average occupancy of 82.0% to 84.0% on the portfolio, including the vacancies created by WorldCom and US Airways that account for 2.5% of HIW's in-service portfolio.

ANNUAL FINANCIAL DATA:

FISCAL YEAR	TOT. REVS. ($mill.)	NET INC. ($mill.)	TOT. ASSETS ($mill.)	OPER. PROFIT %	NET PROFIT %	RET. ON EQUITY %	RET. ON ASSETS %	CURR. RATIO	EARN. PER SH.$	CASH FL. PER SH.$	TANG. BK. VAL.$	DIV. PER SH.$	PRICE RANGE	AVG. P/E RATIO	AVG. YIELD %
p12/31/02	⑦ 70.7	3,395.4							⑦ 0.75			2.34	29.45 - 18.97	32.3	9.7
12/31/01	540.6	⑥ 131.9	3,648.3	45.0	24.4	8.2	3.6	...	⑥ 1.84	4.11	23.22	2.31	26.78 - 23.35	13.6	9.2
12/31/00	566.4	⑤ 138.2	3,701.6	46.8	24.4	7.7	3.7	...	⑤ 1.78	3.84	23.98	2.25	27.19 - 20.13	13.3	9.5
12/31/99	584.9	④ 145.4	4,016.2	47.2	24.9	7.7	3.6	...	④ 1.83	3.71	24.54	2.19	28.00 - 20.25	13.2	9.1
12/31/98	514.2	③ 126.0	4,314.3	48.1	24.5	6.6	2.9	...	③ 1.74	3.45	25.03	2.10	37.44 - 22.75	17.3	7.0
12/31/97	274.5	③ 77.5	2,722.3	51.0	28.2	5.5	2.8	...	③ 1.65	2.91	23.57	1.98	37.63 - 29.88	20.5	5.9
12/31/96	137.9	③ 41.5	1,443.4	54.3	30.1	5.4	2.9	...	③ 1.59	2.51	21.62	1.86	33.88 - 26.50	19.0	6.2
12/31/95	73.5	③ 24.0	621.1	58.0	32.6	6.8	3.9	...	③ 1.55	2.37	18.23	1.75	28.50 - 19.88	15.6	7.2
② 12/31/94	19.4	③ 6.9	224.8	56.1	35.4	5.1	3.1	1.4	③ 0.77	1.15	15.16	0.50	21.63 - 18.50	26.1	2.5
① 12/31/93	13.5	d13.8	58.7	...	...	...	...	...	...	...	...	...	...	...	...

Statistics are as originally reported. ① Financials are for Highwoods Group (predecessor company) ② From 6/14/94 (commencement of operations) ③ Bef. extraord. loss of $387,000, 12/98; $5.8 mill., 12/97; $2.1 mill., 12/96; $875,000, 12/95, $1.3 mill., 12/94 ④ Bef. extraord. loss of $7.3 mill., incl. gain on dispos. of assets of $8.7 mill. and exp. of $1.5 mill. rel. to unsuccessful ters. ⑤ Bef. extraord. loss of $4.7 mill., incl. gain on dispos. of assets of $4.7 mill. ⑥ Bef. extraord. loss of $714,000, incl. gain on dispos. of assets of $16.2 mill. ⑦ Bef. inc. of $29.3 mill. from discont. oper., & extraord. loss of $378,000, but incl. lit. reserve of $2.7 mill., gain on dispos. of assets of $12.2 mill.

OFFICERS:
O. T. Sloan, Jr., Chmn.
J. L. Turner, Vice-Chmn.
R. P. Gibson, Pres., C.E.O.
INVESTOR CONTACT: Investor Relations,
(919) 872-4924
PRINCIPAL OFFICE: 3100 Smoketree Court,
Suite 600, Raleigh, NC 27604

TELEPHONE NUMBER: (919) 872-4924
FAX: (919) 873-0088
WEB: www.highwoods.com
NO. OF EMPLOYEES: 540 (avg.)
SHAREHOLDERS: 1,474 (record)
ANNUAL MEETING: In May
INCORPORATED: MD, 1994

INSTITUTIONAL HOLDINGS:
No. of Institutions: 165
Shares Held: 27,232,531
% Held: 51.0
INDUSTRY: Real estate investment trusts
(SIC: 6798)
TRANSFER AGENT(S): First Union National
Bank, Charlotte, NC

HILB, ROGAL & HAMILTON COMPANY

EXCH.	SYM.	REC. PRICE	P/E RATIO	YLD.	MKT. CAP.	RANGE (52-WK.)	'02 Y/E PR.	DIV. ACH.
NYSE	HRH	31.24 (3/31/03)	16.5	1.2%	$0.88 bill.	46.15 - 28.41	40.90	16 yrs.

UPPER MEDIUM GRADE. THE COMPANY FORMED HRH AFFINITY MARKETING GROUP.

*7 YEAR PRICE SCORE 241.3   ***12 MONTH PRICE SCORE 91.6**

*NYSE COMPOSITE INDEX=100

INTERIM EARNINGS (Per Share):

Qtr.	Mar.	June	Sept.	Dec.
1998	0.23	0.18	0.13	0.06
1999	0.30	0.12	0.21	0.12
2000	0.24	0.18	0.22	0.15
2001	0.27	0.27	0.32	0.12
2002	0.48	0.40	0.53	0.48

INTERIM DIVIDENDS (Per Share):

Amt.	Decl.	Ex.	Rec.	Pay.
0.087Q	2/12/02	3/13/02	3/15/02	3/29/02
0.09Q	5/07/02	6/12/02	6/14/02	6/28/02
0.09Q	8/19/02	9/12/02	9/16/02	9/30/02
0.09Q	11/25/02	12/12/02	12/16/02	12/31/02
0.09Q	2/11/03	3/12/03	3/14/03	3/31/03

Indicated div.: $0.36

CAPITALIZATION (12/31/01):

	($000)	(%)
Long-Term Debt	114,443	44.5
Common & Surplus	142,801	55.5
Total	257,245	100.0

BUSINESS:

Hilb, Rogal & Hamilton Company places various types of insurance, including property/casualty, marine, aviation and employee benefits, with insurance underwriters on behalf of its clients through the network of its wholly-owned subsidiary insurance agencies. The agencies operate in over 100 offices in the U.S., and the client base consists mainly of middle market commercial and industrial accounts. HRH also advises clients on risk management and employee benefits and provides claims administration and loss control consulting services to clients. On 7/1/02, the Company acquired Hobbs Group, LLC, an independent insurance broker that serves top-tier middle-market and risk management clients.

RECENT DEVELOPMENTS:

For the year ended 12/31/02, income leapt 89.1% to $61.2 million, before an accounting change benefit of $3.9 million, compared with net income of $32.3 million in 2001. Earnings benefited from the acquisition of Hobbs Group, LLC on 7/1/02 and new business. Results for 2002 and 2001 included amortization of intangibles of $5.3 million and $13.9 million, and non-operating gains of $212,000 and $2.7 million, respectively. Total revenues were $452.7 million, up 37.1% from $330.3 million the previous year. Operating margins improved to 26.3% from 23.5% in 2001, primarily due improved operating efficiencies.

PROSPECTS:

On 1/17/03, the Company announced the formation of HRH Affinity Marketing Group, a purchasing alliance that provides health insurance and other products and services to members of trade and professional associations and other multiple-employer purchasing groups. The new group will operate from HRH's current Pittsburgh, Pennsylvania office. Separately, on 1/1/03, the Company completed the acquisition of the Freberg group of companies, which has seven offices in Colorado, Wyoming and Texas, for a combination of stock and cash.

ANNUAL FINANCIAL DATA:

FISCAL YEAR	TOT. REVS. ($000)	NET INC. ($000)	TOT. ASSETS ($000)	OPER. PROFIT %	NET PROFIT %	RET. ON EQUITY %	RET. ON ASSETS %	CURR. RATIO	EARN. PER SH.$	CASH FL. PER SH.$	TANG. BK. VAL.$	DIV. PER SH.$	PRICE RANGE	AVG. P/E RATIO	AVG. YIELD %
p12/31/02	452,726	③ 61,175							③ 1.89			0.36	46.15 - 26.65	19.3	1.0
12/31/01	330,267	32,349	499,301	19.9	9.8	22.7	6.5	0.9	1.07	1.91	...	0.35	31.38 - 16.88	22.5	1.4
12/31/00	262,119	② 22,127	353,371	18.3	8.4	25.1	6.3	0.9	② 0.78	1.33	...	0.34	21.06 - 12.81	21.7	2.0
12/31/99	227,226	① 19,486	317,981	18.2	8.6	27.4	6.1	0.9	① 0.72	1.24	...	0.33	14.56 - 7.78	15.5	2.9
12/31/98	175,364	14,945	188,066	15.8	8.5	32.7	7.9	0.9	0.59	1.04	...	0.32	9.94 - 7.69	14.9	3.6
12/31/97	173,709	12,790	181,607	13.7	7.4	24.9	7.0	0.9	0.49	0.93	...	0.31	9.81 - 6.25	16.6	3.9
12/31/96	158,243	11,406	181,475	12.8	7.2	20.6	6.3	0.9	0.43	0.82	...	0.30	7.00 - 5.69	14.9	4.8
12/31/95	148,147	11,829	163,249	13.6	8.0	20.9	7.2	0.9	0.41	0.75	...	0.29	7.19 - 5.25	15.2	4.6
12/31/94	140,810	11,392	158,895	14.3	8.1	17.1	7.2	1.0	0.39	0.70	0.60	0.25	6.69 - 5.50	15.8	4.1
12/31/93	134,954	8,422	155,676	11.1	6.2	13.1	5.4	1.0	0.31	0.64	0.59	0.23	8.44 - 5.69	23.1	3.2

Statistics are as originally reported. Adj. for 100% stk. div., 12/01. ① Incl. $1.9 mill. integration chg. & $4.9 mill. non-recur. gain. ② Excl. $325,000 cumulative effect of an acctg. chg. ③ Excl. $3.9 mill. cumulative effect of an acctg. gain.

OFFICERS:
A. L. Rogal, Chmn., C.E.O.
M. L. Vaughan III, Pres., C.O.O.
C. Jones, Sr. V.P., C.F.O., Treas.

INVESTOR CONTACT: Carolyn Jones, Sr.
V.P., C.F.O., Treas., (804) 747-6500

PRINCIPAL OFFICE: 4951 Lake Brook Drive,
Suite 500, Glen Allen, VA 23060

TELEPHONE NUMBER: (804) 747-6500
FAX: (804) 747-6046
WEB: www.hrh.com

NO. OF EMPLOYEES: 2,600 (approx.)

SHAREHOLDERS: 594

ANNUAL MEETING: In May

INCORPORATED: VA, 1982

INSTITUTIONAL HOLDINGS:
No. of Institutions: 173
Shares Held: 23,756,199
% Held: 80.7

INDUSTRY: Insurance agents, brokers, & service (SIC: 6411)

TRANSFER AGENT(S): Mellon Investor Services, LLC, Ridgefield Park, NJ

HILLENBRAND INDUSTRIES, INC.

EXCH.	SYM.	REC. PRICE	P/E RATIO	YLD.	MKT. CAP.	RANGE (52-WK.)	'02 Y/E PR.	DIV. ACH.
NYSE	HB	49.95 (2/28/03)	...	2.0%	$3.08 bill.	66.48 - 46.55	48.31	32 yrs.

UPPER MEDIUM GRADE. FOR FISCAL 2003, THE COMPANY EXPECTS RESULTS TO BENEFIT FROM NEW PRODUCT INTRODUCTIONS AND POSSIBLE ACQUISITIONS IN THE HEALTH CARE INDUSTRY.

*7 YEAR PRICE SCORE 126.3   *12 MONTH PRICE SCORE 100.9
*NYSE COMPOSITE INDEX=100

INTERIM EARNINGS (Per Share):

Qtr.	Feb.	May	Aug.	Nov.
1999-00	0.58	0.56	0.54	0.76
2000-01	0.40	0.65	0.65	1.01
Qtr.	Dec.	Mar.	June	Sept.
2001-02	1.00	0.85	0.52	d1.69
2002-03	0.12	...	...	...

INTERIM DIVIDENDS (Per Share):

Amt.	Decl.	Ex.	Rec.	Pay.
0.077E	1/15/02	2/27/02	3/01/02	3/29/02
0.23Q	5/16/02	5/29/02	5/31/02	6/28/02
0.23Q	9/05/02	9/12/02	9/16/02	9/30/02
0.25Q	12/05/02	12/13/02	12/17/02	12/31/02
0.25Q	2/13/03	2/27/03	3/03/03	3/31/03

Indicated div.: $1.00 (Div. Reinv. Plan)

CAPITALIZATION (9/30/02):

	($000)	(%)
Long-Term Debt	322,000	24.2
Deferred Income Tax	10,000	0.8
Common & Surplus	999,000	75.1
Total	1,331,000	100.0

BUSINESS:

Hillenbrand Industries, Inc. is organized into two business groups. The Health Care Group (54.5% of fiscal 2002 revenues) consists of Hill-Rom, Inc., a manufacturer of equipment for the health care market and provider of wound care and pulmonary/trauma management services. Hill-Rom produces adjustable hospital beds, infant incubators, radiant warmers, hospital procedural stretchers, hospital patient room furniture, medical gas and vacuum systems and architectural systems designed to meet the needs of medical-surgical critical care, long-term care, home-care and prenatal providers. The Funeral Services Group consists of Batesville Casket Company, Inc. (29.0%), a manufacturer of caskets and other products for the funeral industry, and Forethought Financial Services, Inc. (16.5%), a provider of funeral planning financial products.

RECENT DEVELOPMENTS:

For the first quarter ended 12/31/02, net income dropped 87.3% to $8.0 million compared with $63.0 million in the corresponding prior-year quarter. Results for 2002 included an impairment charge of $68.0 million and realized capital gains of $12.0 million. Results for 2001 included net capital losses of $26.0 million and an unusual charge of $11.0 million. Total revenues were down 13.3% to $471.0 million from $543.0 million a year earlier. Health care sales fell 18.8% to $194.0 million, while health care therapy rentals decreased 6.9% to $81.0 million. Funeral Services sales slipped 3.8% to $152.0 million, and insurance revenues declined 25.4% to $44.0 million. Gross profit fell 26.3% to $168.0 million, or 35.7% of revenues, from $228.0 million, or 42.0% of revenues, in the previous year.

PROSPECTS:

On 1/2/03, the U.S. District Court for the Western District of Texas reviewed and approved a litigation settlement agreement between HB and Kinetic Concepts, Inc. and dismissed all pending antitrust litigation between the two companies. Going forward, HB anticipates improved operating performance due to new product innovations and possible acquisitions, particularly in the health care industry. For fiscal 2003, the Company expects net revenues to range between $2.27 billion and $2.30 billion, and earnings of $3.78 to $3.84 per diluted share, before special items.

ANNUAL FINANCIAL DATA:

FISCAL YEAR	TOT. REVS. ($mill.)	NET INC. ($mill.)	TOT. ASSETS ($mill.)	OPER. PROFIT %	NET PROFIT %	RET. ON EQUITY %	RET. ON ASSETS %	CURR. RATIO	EARN. PER SH. $	CASH FL. PER SH. $	TANG. BK. VAL.$	DIV. PER SH. $	PRICE RANGE	AVG. P/E RATIO	AVG. YIELD %
⑥ 9/30/02	1,757.0	⑦ d10.0	5,442.0	...	...	...	...	1.7	⑦ d0.16	0.97	12.72	⑧ 1.02	66.48 - 46.55	...	1.8
12/01/01	2,107.0	⑥ 170.0	5,049.0	11.2	8.1	16.6	3.4	2.7	⑤ 2.71	4.30	13.24	0.84	58.51 - 41.56	18.5	1.7
12/02/00	2,096.0	④ 154.0	4,597.0	11.6	7.3	18.5	3.4	2.6	④ 2.44	3.86	10.42	0.80	56.38 - 28.75	17.4	1.9
11/27/99	2,047.0	③ 124.0	4,433.0	10.3	6.1	14.8	2.8	2.1	③ 1.87	3.35	10.17	0.78	56.81 - 26.13	22.2	1.9
11/28/98	2,001.0	② 184.0	4,280.0	11.4	9.2	19.3	4.3	2.3	② 2.73	4.93	11.29	0.72	64.69 - 44.38	20.0	1.3
11/29/97	1,776.0	157.0	3,828.0	14.9	8.8	17.7	4.1	2.3	2.28	3.76	11.09	0.66	50.88 - 35.50	18.9	1.5
11/30/96	1,684.0	140.0	3,396.0	14.0	8.3	17.8	4.1	2.3	2.02	3.44	9.28	0.62	40.25 - 31.88	17.9	1.7
12/02/95	1,624.9	89.9	3,070.3	11.0	5.5	12.0	2.9	2.1	1.27	3.07	8.30	0.60	34.13 - 27.00	24.1	2.0
12/03/94	1,577.0	89.5	2,693.8	10.1	5.7	12.9	3.3	2.3	1.26	2.62	7.12	0.57	43.63 - 26.63	27.9	1.6
11/27/93	1,447.9	① 132.5	2,270.7	16.2	9.2	20.7	5.8	2.0	① 1.86	3.43	7.04	0.45	48.63 - 36.50	22.9	1.1

Statistics are as originally reported. ① Bef. disc. oper. gain $13.3 mill. ② Incl. non-recurr. chrg. $66.0 mill. ③ Incl. unusual chrg. $38.0 mill. ④ Incl. non-recurr. chrgs. of $3.0 mill. ⑤ Incl. non-recurr. chrgs. of $32.0 mill. ⑥ For ten months ⑦ Incl. after-tax litigation chrg. of $158.0 mill. and oth. non-recurr. chrg. of $4.0 mill. ⑧ Incl. spec. div. of $0.08 per sh.

OFFICERS:
R. J. Hillenbrand, Chmn.
F. W. Rockwood, Pres., & C.E.O.
S. K. Sorensen, V.P., C.F.O.
INVESTOR CONTACT: Mark R. Lanning, V.P., Treas., (812) 934-7256
PRINCIPAL OFFICE: 700 State Route 46 East, Batesville, IN 47006-8835

TELEPHONE NUMBER: (812) 934-7000
FAX: (812) 934-7364
WEB: www.hillenbrand.com
NO. OF EMPLOYEES: 10,300 (approx.)
SHAREHOLDERS: 17,600 (approx.)
ANNUAL MEETING: In Feb.
INCORPORATED: IN, Aug., 1969

HILTON HOTELS CORPORATION

EXCH.	SYM.	REC. PRICE	P/E RATIO	YLD.	MKT. CAP.	RANGE (52-WK.)	'02 Y/E PR.
NYSE	HLT	10.99 (2/28/03)	20.7	0.7%	$4.06 bill.	17.09 - 9.56	12.71

MEDIUM GRADE. THE COMPANY ANTICIPATES SOFT ECONOMIC CONDITIONS MAY AFFECT THE RECOVERY OF INDEPENDENT BUSINESS TRAVEL.

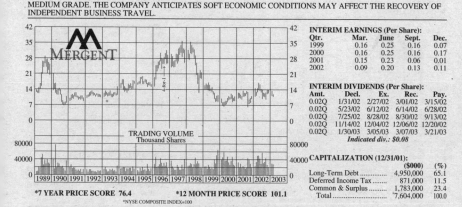

*7 YEAR PRICE SCORE 76.4   *12 MONTH PRICE SCORE 101.1

*NYSE COMPOSITE INDEX=100

INTERIM EARNINGS (Per Share):

Qtr.	Mar.	June	Sept.	Dec.
1999	0.16	0.25	0.16	0.07
2000	0.16	0.25	0.16	0.17
2001	0.15	0.23	0.06	0.01
2002	0.09	0.20	0.13	0.11

INTERIM DIVIDENDS (Per Share):

Amt.	Decl.	Ex.	Rec.	Pay.
0.02Q	1/31/02	2/27/02	3/01/02	3/15/02
0.02Q	5/23/02	6/12/02	6/14/02	6/28/02
0.02Q	7/25/02	8/28/02	8/30/02	9/13/02
0.02Q	11/14/02	12/04/02	12/06/02	12/20/02
0.02Q	1/30/03	3/05/03	3/07/03	3/21/03

Indicated div.: $0.08

CAPITALIZATION (12/31/01):

	($000)	(%)
Long-Term Debt	4,950,000	65.1
Deferred Income Tax	871,000	11.5
Common & Surplus	1,783,000	23.4
Total	7,604,000	100.0

BUSINESS:

Hilton Hotels Corporation is engaged in the ownership, management and development of hotels, resorts and vacation properties and the franchising of lodging properties. The Company's hotel brands include HILTON, EMBASSY SUITES, HILTON GARDEN INN, DOUBLETREE, HAMPTON, HOMEWOOD SUITES by HILTON, CONRAD and HARRISON Conference Centers. In addition, HLT operates Hilton Grand Vacations Company®, a timeshare program. On 11/30/99, HLT acquired Promus Hotel Corp. For 2002 HLT derived 72.5% of revenues from owned hotels, 3.8% from leased hotels, 11.4% from management and franchise fees and 12.3% from other fees and operations. As of 12/31/02, HLT owned, partially owned, leased, franchised or managed 2,084 properties.

RECENT DEVELOPMENTS:

For the year ended 12/31/02, net income advanced 19.8% to $198.0 million versus $166.0 million in 2001. Results for 2002 and 2001 included losses on the disposition of assets of $14.0 million and $44.0 million, respectively. Results for 2002 also included impairment and related costs of $21.0 million. Total revenues decreased 3.7% to $3.85 billion. from $3.99 billion a year earlier. Revenues from owned hotels declined 1.0% to $2.10 billion, while revenues from leased hotels dropped 33.9% to $111.0 million. Revenues and fee income from managed and franchised properties slipped 0.3% to $1.28 billion, while other fees and income fell 15.1% to $355.0 million.

PROSPECTS:

During 2002, the Company added 143 hotels and 18,034 rooms to its system. For 2003, HLT anticipates adding between 100 to 115 hotels and 12,000 to 15,000 rooms. Meanwhile, HLT expects continuing challenges for the lodging industry during 2003. HLT expects soft economic conditions may impact the recovery of independent business travel, which could continue to pressure room rates. For 2003, HLT expects revenue per available room to be approximately flat versus the 2002 rate of $87.43. Separately, for 2003, the Company anticipates revenues of approximately $4.00 billion and earnings in the mid- to high-$0.40 per share range.

ANNUAL FINANCIAL DATA:

FISCAL YEAR	TOT. REVS. ($mill.)	NET INC. ($mill.)	TOT. ASSETS ($mill.)	OPER. PROFIT %	NET PROFIT %	RET. ON EQUITY %	RET. ON ASSETS %	CURR. RATIO	EARN. PER SH. $	CASH FL.PER SH. $	TAN@ BK. VAL. $	DIV. PER SH. $	PRICE RANGE	AVG. P/E RATIO	AVG. YIELD %
p12/31/02	3,847.0	⑧198.0							⑧0.53			0.08	17.09 - 9.56	25.1	0.6
12/31/01	3,050.0	⑦166.0	8,785.0	20.7	5.4	9.3	1.9	1.1	⑦0.45	1.95	1.38	0.08	13.57 - 6.15	21.9	0.8
12/31/00	3,451.0	⑥272.0	9,140.0	24.1	7.9	16.6	3.0	1.3	⑥0.73	1.69	0.91	0.08	12.13 - 6.38	12.7	0.9
12/31/99	2,150.0	⑤176.0	9,253.0	23.0	8.2	12.4	1.9	1.2	⑤0.66	1.75	0.38	0.08	17.13 - 8.38	19.3	0.6
④12/31/98	1,769.0	③188.0	3,944.0	26.2	10.6	100.5	4.8	0.9	③0.71	1.13	0.72	0.32	35.50 - 12.50	33.8	1.3
12/31/97	5,316.0	250.0	7,826.0	11.2	4.7	7.4	3.2	1.1	0.94	1.97	8.25	0.32	35.81 - 24.00	31.8	1.1
12/31/96	3,940.0	②156.0	7,577.0	8.4	4.0	4.9	2.1	1.2	②0.79	1.70	7.63	0.30	31.75 - 15.28	29.8	1.3
12/31/95	1,589.8	172.8	3,060.3	22.2	10.9	13.8	5.6	1.3	0.89	1.62	6.50	0.30	19.94 - 15.09	19.7	1.7
12/31/94	1,456.1	121.7	2,925.9	19.0	8.4	10.8	4.2	2.1	0.63	1.32	5.88	0.30	18.50 - 12.44	24.6	1.9
12/31/93	1,358.0	①102.7	2,674.8	17.7	7.6	9.7	3.8	2.6	①0.54	1.15	5.55	0.30	15.25 - 10.38	23.9	2.3

Statistics are as originally reported. Adj. for stk. split: 4-for-1, 9/96. ① Bef. acctg. change credit $3.4 mill. ② Bef. extraord. chrg. $74.0 mill. ③ Inc. a charge of $0.04 per share for the spin-off of HLT's gaming opers. & excl. a gain of $109. mill. from disc. opers. ④ Reflects the spin-off of the gaming opers. ⑤ Incl. an after-tax chg. of $2.0 mill. for the cum. effect of a chg. in acctg. & pre-tax chrg. of $2.0 mill. assoc. with the pre-opening of the Company's new hotel at Boston's Logan Airport. ⑥ Incl. pre-tax gain of $32.0 mill. & nonrecurr. cr. of $8.0 mill. ⑦ Incl. pre-tax loss $44.0 mill. on the disposition of assets. ⑧ Incl. loss on asset disp. of $14.0 mill. & impair. and oth. chrg. $21.0 mill.

OFFICERS:
B. Hilton, Chmn.
S. F. Bollenbach, Pres., C.E.O.
M. J. Hart, Exec. V.P. & C.F.O.
INVESTOR CONTACT: Marc Grossman, (310) 205-4030
PRINCIPAL OFFICE: 9336 Civic Center Dr., Beverly Hills, CA 90210

TELEPHONE NUMBER: (310) 278-4321
FAX: (310) 205-7824
WEB: www.hilton.com
NO. OF EMPLOYEES: 74,000 (avg.)
SHAREHOLDERS: 19,000 (approx.)
ANNUAL MEETING: In May
INCORPORATED: DE, May, 1946

INSTITUTIONAL HOLDINGS:
No. of Institutions: 265
Shares Held: 273,306,690
% Held: 72.6

INDUSTRY: Hotels and motels (SIC: 7011)

TRANSFER AGENT(S): The Bank of New York, New York, NY

HISPANIC BROADCASTING CORP.

EXCH.	SYM.	REC. PRICE	P/E RATIO	YLD.	MKT. CAP.	RANGE (52-WK.)	'02 Y/E PR.
NYSE	HSP	21.04 (2/28/03)	61.9	...	$2.28 bill.	32.00 - 13.80	20.55

MEDIUM GRADE. HSP'S SHAREHOLDERS HAVE APPROVED THE SALE OF THE COMPANY TO UNIVISION COMMUNICATIONS, INC.

*7 YEAR PRICE SCORE N/A   *12 MONTH PRICE SCORE 100.6

*NYSE COMPOSITE INDEX=100

INTERIM EARNINGS (Per Share):

Qtr.	Mar.	June	Sept.	Dec.
1998	0.05	0.08	0.07	0.08
1999	0.04	0.10	0.10	0.11
2000	0.05	0.11	0.12	0.10
2001	0.03	0.09	0.08	0.08
2002	0.06	0.09	0.11	...

INTERIM DIVIDENDS (Per Share):

Amt.	Decl.	Ex.	Rec.	Pay.
		No dividends paid.		

CAPITALIZATION (12/31/01):

	($000)	(%)
Long-Term Debt	1,418	0.1
Deferred Income Tax	119,486	9.8
Common & Surplus	1,096,816	90.1
Total	1,217,720	100.0

BUSINESS:

Hispanic Broadcasting Corp. is the largest Spanish-language radio broadcasting company in the United States. As of 11/1/02, the Company owned and operated 55 radio stations in 14 of the top 20 Hispanic markets. The Company's stations are located in Los Angeles, New York, Miami, San Francisco/San Jose, Chicago, Houston, San Antonio, Fresno, Las Vegas, Dallas/Fort Worth, McAllen/Brownsville/Harlingen, San Diego, Phoenix and El Paso. In addition, the Company also operates the HBC Radio Network, which is one of the largest Spanish-language radio broadcast networks in the United States. On 6/12/02, the Company announced a definitive agreement to be acquired by Univision Communications Inc.

RECENT DEVELOPMENTS:

For the quarter ended 9/30/02, net income climbed 41.6% to $12.0 million from $8.5 million in the corresponding prior-year quarter. Earnings benefited from a more favorable operating environment in the Company's key markets. Results for 2002 included merger expenses of $572,000. Net revenues grew 6.8% to $70.2 million from $65.8 million in the previous year. Same-station net revenues increased 5.8%. Operating expenses rose 2.9% to $43.0 million. Operating income amounted to $20.4 million, up 60.2% from $12.7 million the year before.

PROSPECTS:

On 2/28/03, the Company announced that its stockholders have approved the sale of Hispanic Broadcasting Corp. to Univision Communications Inc. The transaction remains subject to approval by the Federal Communications Commission. Separately, on 3/3/03, HSP announced that it has entered into a definitive agreement to acquire the assets of KNGT(FM), which serves the Sacramento, California metro area, for $24.0 million in cash. On 3/17/03, the Company agreed to acquire the assets of KTND(FM), which serves Georgetown, Austin and surrounding communities in Texas, for about $16.0 million.

ANNUAL FINANCIAL DATA:

FISCAL YEAR	TOT. REVS. ($mill.)	NET INC. ($mill.)	TOT. ASSETS ($mill.)	OPER. PROFIT %	NET PROFIT %	RET. ON EQUITY %	RET. ON ASSETS %	CURR. RATIO	EARN. PER SH.$	CASH FL. PER SH.$	TANG. BK. VAL.$	PRICE RANGE	AVG. P/E RATIO
12/31/01	240.8	31.0	1,241.7	18.5	12.9	2.8	2.5	4.6	0.28	0.61	0.68	38.88 - 13.58	93.6
12/31/00	237.6	41.5	1,204.6	25.2	17.5	3.9	3.4	8.2	0.38	0.69	1.18	67.50 - 18.69	113.4
12/31/99	197.9	34.2	1,157.1	28.4	17.3	3.3	3.0	10.1	0.33	0.61	1.64	49.81 - 30.06	121.0
12/31/98	164.1	26.9	746.7	25.4	16.4	4.3	3.6	1.6	0.27	0.49	...	...	...
12/31/97	136.6	18.8	512.2	25.6	13.7	4.8	3.7	1.4	0.23	0.40	...	...	...
1 12/31/96	18.3	2.1	163.7	27.2	11.3	14.6	1.3	1.6	0.05	0.08	...	...	...
9/30/96	71.7	2 3 d36.6	165.8	17.6	...	...	...	1.4	2 3 d0.89	d0.76	...	...	...
9/30/95	68.2	3.7	151.6	17.5	5.4	8.5	2.4	2.4	0.09	0.17	...	...	...
9/30/94	27.7	2 0.5	113.4	23.2	1.7	1.0	0.4	3.0	2 0.01	0.11	...	...	...
9/30/93	21.3	2.7	25.8	23.9	12.8	...	10.6	1.1	0.14	0.24	...	...	...

Statistics are as originally reported. Adj. for 2-for-1 stk. spl., 6/00 ☐ Fiscal year end changed from 9/30 to 12/31 ☒ Incl. loss on retirement of debt, 9/96, $7.5 mill.; 9/94, $1.7 mill. ☒ Incl. restruct. chrg. $29.0 mill. & excl. loss from discont. opers., $20.0 mill.

HOLLINGER INTERNATIONAL, INC.

EXCH.	SYM.	REC. PRICE	P/E RATIO	YLD.	MKT. CAP.	RANGE (52-WK.)	'02 Y/E PR.
NYSE	HLR	8.52 (2/28/03)	...	2.3%	$0.82 bill.	13.75 - 8.16	10.16

LOWER MEDIUM GRADE. THE COMPANY EXPECTS EARNINGS BEFORE INTEREST, TAXES, DEPRECIATION AND AMORTIZATION FOR FULL-YEAR 2002 TO BE IN THE RANGE OF $110.0 MILLION TO $120.0 MILLION.

TRADING VOLUME
Thousand Shares

*7 YEAR PRICE SCORE 89.6   *12 MONTH PRICE SCORE 97.3
*NYSE COMPOSITE INDEX=100

INTERIM EARNINGS (Per Share):

Qtr.	Mar.	June	Sept.	Dec.
1999	1.20	0.81	d0.02	0.04
2000	0.25	0.02	d0.06	0.80
2001	d0.01	d0.17	d1.37	d1.91
2002	d0.65	d0.03	d0.33	...

INTERIM DIVIDENDS (Per Share):

Amt.	Decl.	Ex.	Rec.	Pay.
0.11Q	2/27/02	3/27/02	4/01/02	4/15/02
0.11Q	5/23/02	6/27/02	7/01/02	7/15/02
0.05Q	9/11/02	9/27/02	10/01/02	10/15/02
0.05Q	12/06/02	12/27/02	1/01/03	1/15/03
0.05Q	2/27/03	3/28/03	4/01/03	4/15/03

Indicated div.: $0.20

CAPITALIZATION (12/31/01):

	($000)	(%)
Long-Term Debt	809,652	62.4
Deferred Income Tax	163,050	12.6
Common & Surplus	325,775	25.1
Total	1,298,477	100.0

BUSINESS:

Hollinger International, Inc. owns and operates English-language newspapers and magazines in the United States, the United Kingdom, Canada and Israel. HLR's assets include THE DAILY TELEGRAPH and its related publications in the United Kingdom, THE CHICAGO SUN-TIMES, THE JERUSALEM POST and more than 100 titles in the greater Chicago metropolitan area. As of 11/1/02, HLR also owned a 15.6% equity interest in CanWest Global Communica-tions Corp., an international media company, with substantial interests in conventional television, specialty cable channels, radio networks and newspapers. In addition, HLR holds a number of minority investments in various Internet and media-related public and private companies. On 9/1/01, HLR sold its 50.0% interest in The National Post Company.

RECENT DEVELOPMENTS:

For the three months ended 9/30/02, the Company reported a net loss of $31.5 million compared with a net loss of $139.6 million in the same period of 2001. Earnings for 2002 and 2001 included several non-recurring items that resulted in net, after-tax charges of $29.9 million and $127.0 million, respectively. Operating revenues slipped 7.2% to $244.4 million from $263.5 million in the prior-year period. The reduction in revenues primarily resulted from sales of Canadian properties. Advertising operating revenues fell 5.5% to $170.1 million. Operating income amounted to $9.0 million compared with an operating loss of $19.5 million in the previous year.

PROSPECTS:

The Company confirmed its guidance for full-year 2002 of earnings before interest, taxes, depreciation and amortiza-tion (EBITDA) in the range of $110.0 million to $120.0 million. Moreover, HLR expects EBITDA to be in the lower end of the range. In October 2002, HLR announced a comprehensive financing initiative with the purpose of extending debt maturities and securing better borrowing terms. In light of new guidelines and review comments from the SEC, the Company is reevaluating whether certain intangible assets were appropriately reclassified to good-will. As a result, full-year 2002 results have been delayed.

ANNUAL FINANCIAL DATA:

FISCAL YEAR	TOT. REVS. ($mill.)	NET INC. ($mill.)	TOT. ASSETS ($mill.)	OPER. PROFIT %	NET PROFIT %	RET. ON EQUITY %	RET. ON ASSETS %	CURR. RATIO	EARN. PER SH. $	CASH FL. PER SH. $	DIV. PER SH. $	PRICE RANGE	AVG. P/E RATIO	AVG. YIELD %
12/31/01	1,146.3	③ d337.5	1,981.8	...	...	...	...	1.3	③ d3.42	d2.54	0.55	16.49 - 9.08	...	4.3
12/31/00	2,096.0	② 123.4	2,751.0	10.6	5.9	14.4	4.5	0.7	② 1.11	2.29	0.55	17.06 - 9.69	12.0	4.1
12/31/99	2,147.4	② 250.5	3,503.0	9.9	11.7	27.8	7.2	0.8	② 2.13	3.32	0.55	16.81 - 9.75	6.2	4.1
12/31/98	2,197.8	② 202.0	3,251.7	12.8	9.2	24.7	6.2	0.8	② 1.47	2.61	0.40	18.63 - 11.19	10.1	2.9
12/31/97	2,211.5	104.5	3,023.9	13.0	4.7	15.2	3.5	1.1	0.87	1.93	0.40	14.44 - 8.88	13.4	3.4
12/31/96	1,862.7	② 33.8	3,189.1	6.9	1.8	4.5	1.1	0.6	② 0.40	1.75	0.33	13.88 - 9.13	28.7	2.8
12/31/95	965.0	6.2	1,570.1	5.8	0.6	2.1	0.4	0.6	0.11	1.00	0.10	13.00 - 9.25	101.0	0.9
12/31/94	422.6	① 12.9	636.1	9.4	3.0	6.6	2.0	1.0	① 0.63	2.39	0.03	15.00 - 10.00	19.8	0.2
12/31/93	185.0	d1.5	349.6	9.8	...	...	...	0.5	d0.10	d0.10	...	...	...	...
12/31/92	173.2	d7.5	335.0	6.8	...	...	...	0.6	d0.50	1.22	...	...	...	...

Statistics are as originally reported. ① Incl. gain on sale of net assets of cable oper., $300,000 ② Bef. extraord. loss, 2000, $6.3 mill.; 1999, $5.2 mill.; 1998, $5.1 mill.; 1996, $2.2 mill.; ③ Incl. $1.4 mill. stock-based compensation chg.

OFFICERS:
C. M. Black, Chmn., C.E.O.
D. W. Colson, Vice-Chmn.
F. D. Radler, Pres., C.O.O.
INVESTOR CONTACT: Paul B. Healy, V.P., Investor Relations, (212) 586-5666
PRINCIPAL OFFICE: 401 North Wabash Ave-nue, Suite 740, Chicago, IL 60611

TELEPHONE NUMBER: (312) 321-2299
FAX: (312) 321-0629
WEB: www.hollinger.com
NO. OF EMPLOYEES: 5,740 (approx.)
SHAREHOLDERS: 250 (approx. record); 4,000 (approx. beneficial)
ANNUAL MEETING: In May
INCORPORATED: DE, Dec., 1990

INSTITUTIONAL HOLDINGS:
No. of Institutions: 98
Shares Held: 59,319,252
% Held: 55.6

INDUSTRY: Newspapers (SIC: 2711)

TRANSFER AGENT(S): First Chicago Trust Company of New York, Jersey City, NJ

HOME DEPOT (THE), INC.

EXCH.	SYM.	REC. PRICE	P/E RATIO	YLD.	MKT. CAP.	RANGE (52-WK.)	'02 Y/E PR.	DIV. ACH.
NYSE	HD	23.45 (2/28/03)	15.0	1.0%	$55.01 bill.	50.50 - 20.10	24.02	15 yrs.

INVESTMENT GRADE. THE COMPANY ANTICIPATES EARNINGS GROWTH OF 9.0% TO 14.0% DURING THE CURRENT FISCAL YEAR.

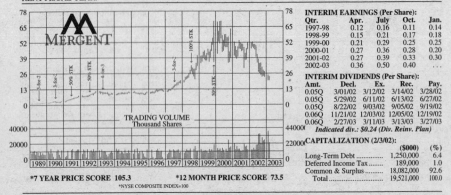

INTERIM EARNINGS (Per Share):

Qtr.	Apr.	July	Oct.	Jan.
1997-98	0.12	0.16	0.11	0.14
1998-99	0.15	0.21	0.17	0.18
1999-00	0.21	0.29	0.25	0.25
2000-01	0.27	0.36	0.28	0.20
2001-02	0.27	0.39	0.33	0.30
2002-03	0.36	0.50	0.40	...

INTERIM DIVIDENDS (Per Share):

Amt.	Decl.	Ex.	Rec.	Pay.
0.05Q	3/01/02	3/12/02	3/14/02	3/28/02
0.05Q	5/29/02	6/11/02	6/13/02	6/27/02
0.05Q	8/22/02	9/03/02	9/05/02	9/19/02
0.06Q	11/21/02	12/03/02	12/05/02	12/19/02
0.06Q	2/27/03	3/11/03	3/13/03	3/27/03

Indicated div.: $0.24 (Div. Reinv. Plan)

CAPITALIZATION (2/3/02):

	($000)	(%)
Long-Term Debt	1,250,000	6.4
Deferred Income Tax	189,000	1.0
Common & Surplus	18,082,000	92.6
Total	19,521,000	100.0

*7 YEAR PRICE SCORE 105.3   ***12 MONTH PRICE SCORE 73.5**

*NYSE COMPOSITE INDEX=100

BUSINESS:

The Home Depot, Inc. operated 1,502 retail warehouse stores as of 12/31/02 in the United States, Canada, Mexico and Puerto Rico that offer a wide assortment of building materials and home improvement products. The average Home Depot store has about 109,000 square feet of interior floor space and is stocked with approximately 40,000 to 50,000 separate items. Most stores have about 22,000 square feet of additional outdoor selling area for landscaping supplies. The Company also operates 52 EXPO Design Center stores that sell products and services primarily for home decorating and remodeling projects, five Home Depot Supply stores, three Home Depot Landscape Supply stores and one Home Depot Floor Store outlet.

RECENT DEVELOPMENTS:

For the three months ended 11/3/02, net earnings climbed 20.8% to $940.0 million from $778.0 million in the corresponding prior-year period. Net sales increased 8.9% to $14.48 billion from $13.29 billion a year earlier. Comparable-store sales were down 2.0% year-over-year. Gross profit totaled $4.58 billion, or 31.6% of net sales, versus $4.01 billion, or 30.2% of net sales, the year before. Operating income advanced 19.0% to $1.50 billion from $1.26 billion the previous year. During the quarter, the Company opened 34 new stores, including two stores in Mexico.

PROSPECTS:

The Company anticipates sales growth of between 9.0% and 12.0% and earnings growth of 9.0% to 14.0% during the current fiscal year. Meanwhile, HD expects to open approximately 200 new stores in 2003. Separately, the Company plans to open five new Home Depot Landscape Supply stores, which stock a wide supply of products for both professional landscapers and do-it-yourself gardeners, in Texas during the spring of 2003. HD opened its first three Home Depot Landscape Supply stores in Atlanta, Georgia in the summer of 2002.

ANNUAL FINANCIAL DATA:

FISCAL YEAR	TOT. REVS. ($mill.)	NET INC. ($mill.)	TOT. ASSETS ($mill.)	OPER. PROFIT %	NET PROFIT %	RET. ON EQUITY %	RET. ON ASSETS %	CURR. RATIO	EARN. PER SH.$	CASH FL. PER SH.$	TANG. BK. VAL.$	DIV. PER SH.$	PRICE RANGE	AVG. P/E RATIO	AVG. YIELD %
2/03/02	53,553.0	3,044.0	26,394.0	9.2	5.7	16.8	11.5	1.6	1.62	7.53	0.17	53.73 – 30.30	32.6	0.4
1/28/01	45,738.0	2,581.0	21,385.0	9.2	5.6	17.2	12.1	1.8	1.10	1.35	6.32	0.16	70.00 – 34.69	47.6	0.3
1/30/00	38,434.0	2,320.0	17,081.0	9.9	6.0	18.8	13.6	1.7	1.00	1.19	5.22	0.11	69.75 – 34.59	52.2	0.2
1/31/99	30,219.0	1,614.0	13,465.0	8.8	5.3	18.5	12.0	1.7	0.71	0.86	3.83	0.08	41.34 – 18.44	42.1	0.3
2/01/98	24,156.0	①1,160.0	11,229.0	7.9	4.8	16.3	10.3	1.8	①0.52	0.63	3.17	0.06	20.17 – 10.61	29.8	0.4
2/02/97	19,535.5	937.7	9,341.7	7.9	4.8	15.7	10.0	2.0	0.43	0.53	2.71	0.05	13.22 – 9.22	26.0	0.5
1/28/96	15,470.4	731.5	7,354.0	7.6	4.7	14.7	9.9	1.9	0.34	0.42	2.28	0.04	11.11 – 8.14	28.1	0.4
1/29/95	12,476.7	604.5	5,778.0	7.9	4.8	17.6	10.5	1.8	0.29	0.34	1.64	0.03	10.72 – 8.11	32.1	0.3
1/30/94	9,238.8	457.4	4,700.9	7.6	5.0	16.3	9.7	2.0	0.23	0.27	1.38	0.03	11.32 – 7.78	42.4	0.3
1/31/93	7,148.4	362.9	3,931.8	7.7	5.1	15.7	9.2	2.1	0.18	0.22	1.14	0.02	11.44 – 6.61	49.6	0.2

Statistics are as originally reported. Adj. for 3-for-2 stk. split, 12/99; 100% stk. div., 7/98; 3-for-2 stk. split, 7/97 & 4-for-3 stk. split, 4/93. ① Incl. $104 mil pre-tax, non-recur. chg.

OFFICERS:
R. L. Nardelli, Chmn. Pres., C.E.O.
C. B. Tome, Exec. V.P., C.F.O.
F. Fernandez, Exec. V.P., Sec., Gen. Couns.

INVESTOR CONTACT: Investor Relations, (770) 384-2666

PRINCIPAL OFFICE: 2455 Paces Ferry Road N.W., Atlanta, GA 30339-4024

TELEPHONE NUMBER: (770) 433-8211
FAX: (770) 431-2707
WEB: www.homedepot.com

NO. OF EMPLOYEES: 256,000 (approx.)

SHAREHOLDERS: 206,988

ANNUAL MEETING: In May

INCORPORATED: DE, June, 1978

INSTITUTIONAL HOLDINGS:
No. of Institutions: 1,093
Shares Held: 1,432,258,534
% Held: 61.6

INDUSTRY: Lumber and other building materials (SIC: 5211)

TRANSFER AGENT(S): EquiServe Trust Company, N.A., Providence, RI

HON INDUSTRIES INCORPORATED

EXCH.	SYM.	REC. PRICE	P/E RATIO	YLD.	MKT. CAP.	RANGE (52-WK.)	'02 Y/E PR.	DIV. ACH.
NYSE	HNI	26.81 (2/28/03)	17.3	1.9%	$1.57 bill.	30.85 - 22.88	28.28	14 yrs.

MEDIUM GRADE. RESULTS ARE BENEFITING FROM OPERATIONAL IMPROVEMENTS, NEW PRODUCT INTRODUC-
TIONS, AND RESTRUCTURING INITIATIVES.

*7 YEAR PRICE SCORE 119.8   *12 MONTH PRICE SCORE 107.2

*NYSE COMPOSITE INDEX=100

INTERIM EARNINGS (Per Share):

Qtr.	Mar.	June	Sept.	Dec.
1997	0.28	0.32	0.43	0.42
1998	0.36	0.38	0.50	0.48
1999	0.19	0.37	0.47	0.41
2000	0.41	0.39	0.57	0.40
2001	0.31	0.07	0.48	0.40
2002	0.27	0.34	0.46	0.48

INTERIM DIVIDENDS (Per Share):

Amt.	Decl.	Ex.	Rec.	Pay.
0.125Q	2/13/02	2/20/02	2/22/02	3/01/02
0.125Q	5/07/02	5/15/02	5/17/02	5/31/02
0.125Q	8/05/02	8/13/02	8/15/02	8/30/02
0.125Q	11/07/02	11/13/02	11/15/02	11/27/02
0.13Q	2/12/03	2/19/03	2/21/03	2/28/03

Indicated div.: $0.52

CAPITALIZATION (12/29/01):

	($000)	(%)
Long-Term Debt	97,876	13.4
Capital Lease Obligations	1,260	0.2
Deferred Income Tax	39,632	5.4
Common & Surplus	592,680	81.0
Total	731,448	100.0

BUSINESS:

Hon Industries Incorporated manufactures and markets office furniture and gas- and wood-burning fireplaces. Office products (75.6% of 2002 net sales) include filing cabinets, seating, including task chairs, executive desk chairs and side chairs, desks, tables, bookcases and credenzas. The office products are sold through mass merchandisers, warehouse clubs, a national system of dealers, retail superstores, end-user customers, and federal and state gov-

ernments. The Hearth Technologies (24.4%) products are comprised of wood-burning, pellet-burning, and gas-burning factory-built fireplaces, fireplace inserts, gas logs, and stoves. The hearth products are sold through wholesalers, a national system of dealers, large regional contractors and Company-owned retail outlets. HNI has locations in the United States, Canada and Mexico.

RECENT DEVELOPMENTS:

For the year ended 12/28/02, net income increased 22.8% to $91.4 million compared with $74.4 million in 2001. Results for 2002 and 2001 included restructuring charges of $3.0 million and $24.0 million, respectively. Net sales slid 5.6% to $1.69 billion. Gross profit declined 1.9% to $599.9

million versus $611.3 million in 2001. However, gross profit as a percentage of sales improved to 35.4% versus 34.1% in 2001 due to operational improvements, new product introductions, and restructuring initiatives.

PROSPECTS:

Looking ahead to 2003, the Company expects the unstable political and economic environment to continue to affect market conditions during the first half of the year. The two primary channels for hearth product sales are the home construction and the remodel/retail channels. Early indications are that the housing market should remain healthy while the retail side, which is closely dependent on con-

sumer confidence, will likely by hampered by market instability. Nevertheless, the Company remains optimistic about growth opportunities from its new products and brand extensions into new markets. These markets include outdoor living products such as outdoor cooking systems and healthy home products such as heat recovery system and a central vacuum system.

ANNUAL FINANCIAL DATA:

FISCAL YEAR	TOT. REVS. ($mill.)	NET INC. ($mill.)	TOT. ASSETS ($mill.)	OPER. PROFIT %	NET PROFIT %	RET. ON EQUITY %	RET. ON ASSETS %	CURR. RATIO	EARN. PER SH. $	CASH FL. PER SH. $	TANG. BK. VAL. $	DIV. PER SH. $	PRICE RANGE	AVG. P/E RATIO	AVG. YIELD %
p12/28/02	1,692.6	☐ 91.4							☐ 1.55			0.50	30.85 - 22.88	17.3	1.9
12/29/01	1,792.4	☐ 74.4	961.9	6.9	4.2	12.6	7.7	1.4	☐ 1.26	2.64	6.45	0.48	28.85 - 19.96	19.4	2.0
12/30/00	2,046.3	106.2	1,022.5	8.7	5.2	18.5	10.4	1.2	1.77	3.08	5.97	0.44	27.88 - 15.56	12.3	2.0
01/01/00	1,789.3	☐ 87.4	906.7	8.2	4.9	17.4	9.6	1.4	☐ 1.44	2.51	6.45	0.38	29.88 - 18.75	16.9	1.6
1/02/99	1,696.4	106.3	864.5	10.6	6.3	23.0	12.3	1.3	1.72	2.58	5.77	0.32	37.19 - 20.00	16.6	1.1
1/03/98	1,362.7	87.0	754.7	10.7	6.4	22.8	11.5	1.5	1.45	2.05	4.59	0.28	32.13 - 16.00	16.6	1.2
12/28/96	998.1	☐ 61.7	513.5	10.0	6.2	24.4	12.0	1.3	☐ 1.13	1.44	3.39	0.25	21.38 - 9.25	13.5	1.6
12/31/95	893.1	41.1	409.5	7.5	4.6	19.0	10.0	1.5	0.67	1.02	3.54	0.24	15.63 - 11.50	20.2	1.8
12/31/94	846.0	54.4	372.6	10.3	6.4	27.9	14.6	1.7	0.87	1.18	3.17	0.22	17.00 - 12.00	16.7	1.5
1/01/94	780.3	44.6	352.4	9.2	5.7	24.9	12.7	1.7	0.70	0.95	2.59	0.20	14.63 - 10.75	18.3	1.6

Statistics are as originally reported. Adj. for stk. split: 2-for-1, 3/27/98. ☐ Incl. non-recurr. chrg. $3.0 mill., 2002; $24.0 mill., 2001; net chrg. $12.5 mill., 1999; credit $3.2 mill., 1996.

OFFICERS:
J. D. Michaels, Chmn., Pres., C.E.O.
J. K. Dittmer, V.P., C.F.O.
J. I. Johnson, V.P., Sec., Gen. Couns.
INVESTOR CONTACT: Jerald K. Dittmer, V.P. & C.F.O., (563) 264-7400
PRINCIPAL OFFICE: 414 East Third Street, P.O. Box 1109, Muscatine, IA 52761-0071

TELEPHONE NUMBER: (563) 264-7400
FAX: (563) 264-7217
WEB: www.honi.com
NO. OF EMPLOYEES: 8,800 full-time (approx.); 200 part-time (approx.)
SHAREHOLDERS: 6,694
ANNUAL MEETING: In May
INCORPORATED: IA, Jan., 1944

INSTITUTIONAL HOLDINGS:
No. of Institutions: 139
Shares Held: 25,500,462
% Held: 43.3
INDUSTRY: Office furniture, except wood (SIC: 2522)
TRANSFER AGENT(S): Computershare Investor Services, LLC, Chicago, IL

HONEYWELL INTERNATIONAL INC.

EXCH.	SYM.	REC. PRICE	P/E RATIO	YLD.	MKT. CAP.	RANGE (52-WK.)	'02 Y/E PR.
NYSE	HON	22.89 (2/28/03)	...	3.3%	$18.65 bill.	40.95 - 18.77	24.00

UPPER MEDIUM GRADE. THE COMPANY IS TARGETING EARNINGS OF $1.60 TO $1.70 PER SHARE FOR 2003.

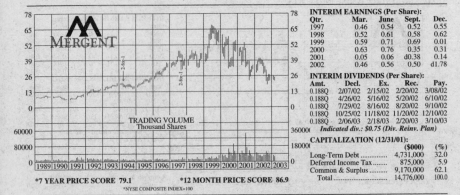

INTERIM EARNINGS (Per Share):

Qtr.	Mar.	June	Sept.	Dec.
1997	0.46	0.54	0.52	0.55
1998	0.52	0.61	0.58	0.62
1999	0.59	0.71	0.69	0.01
2000	0.63	0.76	0.35	0.31
2001	0.05	0.06	d0.38	0.14
2002	0.46	0.56	0.50	d1.78

INTERIM DIVIDENDS (Per Share):

Amt.	Decl.	Ex.	Rec.	Pay.
0.188Q	2/07/02	2/15/02	2/20/02	3/08/02
0.188Q	4/26/02	5/16/02	5/20/02	6/10/02
0.188Q	7/29/02	8/16/02	8/20/02	9/10/02
0.188Q	10/25/02	11/18/02	11/20/02	12/10/02
0.188Q	2/06/03	2/18/03	2/20/03	3/10/03

Indicated div.: $0.75 (Div. Reinv. Plan)

CAPITALIZATION (12/31/01):

	($000)	(%)
Long-Term Debt	4,731,000	32.0
Deferred Income Tax	875,000	5.9
Common & Surplus	9,170,000	62.1
Total	14,776,000	100.0

*7 YEAR PRICE SCORE 79.1   ***12 MONTH PRICE SCORE 86.9**
*NYSE COMPOSITE INDEX=100

BUSINESS:

Honeywell International Inc. (formerly AlliedSignal Inc.) is a diversified technology and manufacturing company, serving customers worldwide with aerospace products and services, control technologies for buildings, homes and industry, automotive products, power generation systems, specialty chemicals, fibers, plastics and electronic and advanced materials. In 2002, revenues (and operating income) were derived: Aerospace, 39.9% (51.0%); Automation & Control Solutions, 31.4% (33.4%); Specialty Materials, 14.4% (2.2%); and Transportation & Power Systems, 14.3% (13.4%). On 12/1/99, HON acquired Honeywell Inc. On 2/4/00, HON acquired Pittway Corp.

RECENT DEVELOPMENTS:

For the year ended 12/31/02, net loss was $220.0 million compared with a net loss of $99.0 million in the corresponding period a year earlier. Results for 2002 and 2001 included net after-tax repositioning, asset impairment, and other charges totaling $2.06 billion and $1.77 billion, respectively. Net sales slipped 5.8% to $22.27 billion from $23.65 billion the year before, reflecting weakness in the commercial aviation industry and the divestiture of the Company's commercial vehicle braking systems business. Loss before taxes was $945.0 million versus a loss before taxes of $422.0 million in 2001.

PROSPECTS:

The Company is targeting full-year 2003 revenues of about $22.20 billion and earnings of between $1.60 and $1.70 per share. Meanwhile, on 1/30/03, the Company announced that it has entered into a letter of intent to sell its Bendix friction materials business, which has annual sales of about $700.0 million, to Federal-Mogul Corporation in exchange for Bankruptcy Court protection against all current and future asbestos liabilities related to Bendix. Completion of the transaction is subject to Bankruptcy Court and government approvals.

ANNUAL FINANCIAL DATA:

FISCAL YEAR	TOT. REVS. ($mill.)	NET INC. ($mill.)	TOT. ASSETS ($mill.)	OPER. PROFIT %	NET PROFIT %	RET. ON EQUITY %	RET. ON ASSETS %	CURR. RATIO	EARN. PER SH. $	CASH FL. PER SH. $	TANG. BK. VAL. $	DIV. PER SH. $	PRICE RANGE	AVG. P/E RATIO	AVG. YIELD %
p12/31/02	22,274.0	④ d220.0							④ d0.27			0.75	40.95 - 18.77	...	2.5
12/31/01	23,652.0	④ d99.0	24,226.0	0.7	...	...	...	1.6	④ d0.12	1.02	3.45	0.75	53.90 - 22.15	...	2.0
12/31/00	25,023.0	③ 1,659.0	25,175.0	11.2	6.6	17.1	6.6	1.5	③ 2.05	3.28	4.72	0.75	60.50 - 32.13	22.6	1.6
12/31/99	23,735.0	② 1,541.0	23,527.0	8.5	6.5	17.9	6.5	1.3	② 1.90	2.99	4.95	0.68	68.63 - 37.81	28.0	1.3
12/31/98	15,128.0	1,331.0	15,560.0	13.0	8.8	25.1	8.6	1.1	2.32	3.38	4.11	0.60	47.56 - 32.63	17.3	1.5
12/31/97	14,472.0	② 1,170.0	13,707.0	11.3	8.1	26.7	8.5	1.3	② 2.02	3.07	3.51	0.52	47.13 - 31.63	19.5	1.3
12/31/96	13,971.0	② 1,020.0	12,829.0	10.8	7.3	105.6	8.0	1.6	② 1.81	2.87	4.88	0.45	37.19 - 23.56	16.8	1.5
12/31/95	14,346.0	875.0	12,465.0	8.8	6.1	68.5	7.0	1.3	1.55	2.63	3.57	0.39	24.94 - 16.69	13.5	1.9
12/31/94	12,817.0	759.0	11,321.0	9.0	5.9	55.4	6.7	1.4	1.34	2.23	3.00	0.34	20.34 - 15.19	13.3	1.9
12/31/93	11,827.0	① 656.0	10,829.0	8.1	5.5	27.4	6.1	1.3	① 1.16	2.13	2.89	0.29	20.03 - 14.38	14.9	1.7

Statistics are as originally reported. Adj. for 2-for-1 stk. split, 9/97 & 3/94. ① Bef. $245 mil ($1.73/sh) acctg. chg. & incl. $16 mil non-recur. chg. ② Incl. $624 mil ($0.77/sh) net chg., 1999; $163 mil ($0.29/sh) net gain from sale of bus., 1997; $368 mil ($1.30/sh), 1996; & $159 mil ($0.28/sh) chg. for envir. costs, 1997; $359 mil ($1.27/sh), 1996. ③ Incl. $71.0 mil ($0.09/sh) after-tax gain fr. prod. line sale & $705.0 mil ($0.87/sh) after-tax repositioning and impairment chgs. ④ Incl. $2.06 bil ($2.51/sh) after-tax repositioning and other chgs., 2002; $1.77 bil ($2.18/sh), 2001.

OFFICERS:
D. M. Cote, Chmn., Pres., C.E.O.
R. F. Williams, Sr. V.P., C.F.O.

INVESTOR CONTACT: Tom Crane, Investor Relations, (973) 455-4732

PRINCIPAL OFFICE: 101 Columbia Road, P.O. Box 4000, Morristown, NJ 07962-2497

TELEPHONE NUMBER: (973) 455-2000
FAX: (973) 455-4807
WEB: www.honeywell.com

NO. OF EMPLOYEES: 108,000 (approx.)

SHAREHOLDERS: 90,386

ANNUAL MEETING: In Apr.

INCORPORATED: NY, Dec., 1920; reincorp., DE, 1985

INDUSTRY: Motor vehicle parts and accessories (SIC: 3714)

TRANSFER AGENT(S): The Bank of New York, New York, NY

HORMEL FOODS CORPORATION

EXCH.	SYM.	REC. PRICE	P/E RATIO	YLD.	MKT. CAP.	RANGE (52-WK.)	'02 Y/E PR.	DIV. ACH.
NYSE	HRL	21.01 (2/28/03)	15.8	2.0%	$2.91 bill.	28.20 - 20.02	23.33	35 yrs.

UPPER MEDIUM GRADE. THE COMPANY ACQUIRED THE DIXIE CRYSTAL BRANDS UNIT OF IMPERIAL SUGAR CO.

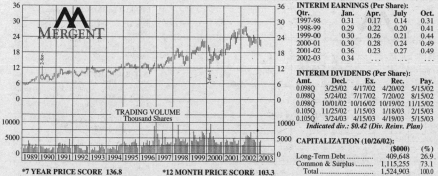

INTERIM EARNINGS (Per Share):

Qtr.	Jan.	Apr.	July	Oct.
1997-98	0.31	0.17	0.14	0.31
1998-99	0.29	0.22	0.20	0.41
1999-00	0.30	0.26	0.21	0.44
2000-01	0.30	0.28	0.24	0.49
2001-02	0.36	0.23	0.27	0.49
2002-03	0.34	...	...	...

INTERIM DIVIDENDS (Per Share):

Amt.	Decl.	Ex.	Rec.	Pay.
0.098Q	3/25/02	4/17/02	4/20/02	5/15/02
0.098Q	5/24/02	7/17/02	7/20/02	8/15/02
0.098Q	10/01/02	10/16/02	10/19/02	11/15/02
0.105Q	11/25/02	1/15/03	1/18/03	2/15/03
0.105Q	3/24/03	4/15/03	4/19/03	5/15/03

Indicated div.: $0.42 (Div. Reinv. Plan)

CAPITALIZATION (10/26/02):

	($000)	(%)
Long-Term Debt	409,648	26.9
Common & Surplus	1,115,255	73.1
Total	1,524,903	100.0

*7 YEAR PRICE SCORE 136.8   ***12 MONTH PRICE SCORE 103.3**

*NYSE COMPOSITE INDEX=100

BUSINESS:

Hormel Foods Corporation (formerly Geo. A. Hormel & Co.) and its subsidiaries produce and market a variety of processed, packaged food products. The Company's main products include: meat and meat products, including hams, sausages, wieners, sliced bacon, luncheon meats, stews, chilies, hash and meat spreads. The products are sold fresh, frozen, cured, smoked, cooked or canned. The majority of its products are sold under the HORMEL name. Other trade names include: SPAM, LIGHT & LEAN, FARM FRESH, DINTY MOORE, BLACK LABEL, TOPSHELF, MARY KITCHEN, KID'S KITCHEN and OLD SMOKEHOUSE. Through its wholly-owned subsidiary, Jennie-O Foods, Inc., the Company is a producer and marketer of whole and processed turkey products.

RECENT DEVELOPMENTS:

For the 13 weeks ended 1/25/03, net earnings slipped 6.8% to $46.9 million from $50.4 million in the corresponding prior-year period. Net sales totaled $1.02 billion, up 3.6% compared with $983.0 million the previous year. Gross profit was $252.2 million, or 24.8% of net sales, versus $246.3 million, or 25.1% of net sales, the year before. Operating income declined 10.2% to $77.1 million from $85.8 million a year earlier. Earnings before taxes slid 9.3% to $71.9 million from $79.3 million in the prior year.

PROSPECTS:

On 12/30/02, the Company announced that it has acquired the Diamond Crystal Brands unit of Imperial Sugar Co. for $115.0 million in stock. Diamond Crystal Brands, which has annual revenues of about $160.0 million, packages and sells various sugar, sugar substitute, salt and pepper products, drink mixes and dessert mixes to retail and foodser-vice customers. The acquisition is expected to be immediately accretive to earnings and will further expand HRL's foodservice product line. Separately, the Company is targeting earnings per share of between $0.22 and $0.28 for the second quarter of the current fiscal year.

ANNUAL FINANCIAL DATA:

FISCAL YEAR	TOT. REVS. ($mill.)	NET INC. ($mill.)	TOT. ASSETS ($mill.)	OPER. PROFIT %	NET PROFIT %	RET. ON EQUITY %	RET. ON ASSETS %	CURR. RATIO	EARN. PER SH. $	CASH FL. PER SH. $	TANG. BK. VAL. $	DIV. PER SH. $	PRICE RANGE	AVG. P/E RATIO	AVG. YIELD %
10/26/02	3,910.3	189.3	2,220.2	8.1	4.8	17.0	8.5	2.3	1.35	1.94	5.41	0.39	28.20 - 20.02	17.9	1.6
10/27/01	4,124.1	182.4	2,162.7	7.3	4.4	18.3	8.4	2.1	1.30	1.95	4.45	0.37	27.35 - 17.00	17.1	1.7
10/28/00	3,675.1	170.2	1,641.9	7.1	4.6	19.5	10.4	2.1	1.20	1.67	5.64	0.35	20.97 - 13.63	14.4	2.0
10/30/99	3,357.8	②163.4	1,685.6	7.2	4.9	19.4	9.7	2.1	②1.11	1.55	5.20	0.33	23.09 - 15.50	17.4	1.7
10/31/98	3,261.0	②139.3	1,555.9	6.5	4.3	17.1	9.0	2.7	②0.93	1.33	4.82	0.32	19.69 - 12.84	17.6	2.0
10/25/97	3,256.6	109.5	1,528.5	5.3	3.4	13.6	7.2	2.6	0.72	1.06	4.55	0.31	16.38 - 11.75	19.7	2.2
10/26/96	3,098.7	②79.4	1,436.1	3.6	2.6	10.1	5.5	2.7	②0.52	0.80	4.27	0.30	14.00 - 9.69	22.8	2.5
10/28/95	3,046.2	120.4	1,223.9	6.0	4.0	16.5	9.8	3.0	0.79	1.03	4.24	0.29	14.00 - 11.44	16.2	2.3
10/29/94	3,064.8	118.0	1,196.7	6.1	3.8	17.8	9.9	2.7	0.77	...	3.79	0.25	13.38 - 9.38	14.8	2.2
10/30/93	2,854.0	①100.8	1,093.6	5.4	3.5	17.7	9.2	2.7	①0.66	...	3.25	0.22	12.75 - 10.13	17.5	1.9

Statistics are as originally reported. Adj. for 2-for-1 stk. split, 2/15/00. ① Bef. $127.5 ($0.83/sh) mil chg. for acctg. adj. ② Incl. $3.8 mil ($0.03/sh) gain, 1999; $17.4 mil ($0.12/sh) after-tax gain, 1998; $5.4 mil ($0.04/sh) non-recur. chg., 1996.

OFFICERS:
J. W. Johnson, Chmn., Pres., C.E.O.
M. J. McCoy, Exec. V.P., C.F.O.
G. J. Ray, Exec. V.P.

INVESTOR CONTACT: Fred Halvin, Investor Relations, (507) 437-5007

PRINCIPAL OFFICE: 1 Hormel Place, Austin, MN 55912-3680

TELEPHONE NUMBER: (507) 437-5611
FAX: (507) 437-5489
WEB: www.hormel.com

NO. OF EMPLOYEES: 15,500 (approx.)

SHAREHOLDERS: 11,600 (approx.)

ANNUAL MEETING: In Jan.

INCORPORATED: DE, Sept., 1928

INSTITUTIONAL HOLDINGS:
No. of Institutions: 174
Shares Held: 33,615,934
% Held: 24.2

INDUSTRY: Meat packing plants (SIC: 2011)

TRANSFER AGENT(S): Wells Fargo Share-owner Services, South St. Paul, MN

HORTON (D.R.) INC.

EXCH.	SYM.	REC. PRICE	P/E RATIO	YLD.	MKT. CAP.	RANGE (52-WK.)	'02 Y/E PR.
NYSE	DHI	18.31 (2/28/03)	6.1	1.5%	$2.68 bill.	29.17 - 16.03	17.35

UPPER MEDIUM GRADE. THE COMPANY EXPECTS FISCAL YEAR 2003 EARNINGS PER SHARE IN THE RANGE OF $3.50 TO $3.55.

*7 YEAR PRICE SCORE 197.5   ***12 MONTH PRICE SCORE 95.3**

*NYSE COMPOSITE INDEX=100

INTERIM EARNINGS (Per Share):

Qtr.	Dec.	Mar.	June	Sept.
1998-99	0.43	0.37	0.29	0.29
1999-00	0.37	0.35	0.43	0.54
2000-01	0.42	0.45	0.59	0.74
2001-02	0.63	0.64	0.67	0.92
2002-03	0.75	...	...	...

INTERIM DIVIDENDS (Per Share):

Amt.	Decl.	Ex.	Rec.	Pay.
50% STK	3/04/02	4/10/02	3/26/02	4/09/02
0.06Q	4/30/02	5/10/02	5/14/02	5/21/02
0.06Q	7/24/02	8/07/02	8/09/02	8/23/02
0.06Q	10/22/02	10/31/02	11/04/02	11/15/02
0.07Q	1/21/03	1/30/03	2/03/03	2/14/03

Indicated div.: $0.28

CAPITALIZATION (9/30/02):

	($000)	(%)
Long-Term Debt	2,486,976	52.3
Common & Surplus	2,269,863	47.7
Total	4,756,839	100.0

BUSINESS:

D.R. Horton, Inc., a national homebuilder, builds high-quality, single-family homes designed principally for the entry-level and move-up markets. As of 1/16/03, the Company built and sold homes under the D.R. Horton, Arappco, Cambridge, Continental, Dietz-Crane, Dobson, Emerald, Melody, Milburn, Schuler, SGS Communities, Stafford, Torrey, Trimark and Western Pacific names in 20 states and 44 markets, with a geographic presence in the Mid-west, Mid-Atlantic, Southeast, Southwest, and Western regions of the United States. The Company also provides mortgage financing and title services for homebuyers through its wholly-owned subsidiaries CH Mortgage, DRH Title Company, Principal Title, Travis Title Company, Metro Title Company, Century Title Company and Custom Title Company.

RECENT DEVELOPMENTS:

For the quarter ended 12/31/02, net income surged 52.3% to $111.8 million compared with $73.4 million in the corresponding quarter of the previous year. Homebuilding revenues leapt 50.4% to $1.71 billion from $1.14 billion a year earlier, while financial services revenues surged 53.4% to $38.2 million. Operating income from homebuilding advanced 49.8% to $158.8 million, while operating income from financial services rose 74.8% to $20.1 million. During the quarter, the number of homes closed increased 32.0% to 7,514 homes from 5,691 homes in 2001. Net sales orders rose 66.3% to $1.70 billion, or 7,252 homes, from $1.02 billion, or 5,144 homes, in the equivalent 2001 quarter.

PROSPECTS:

The Company expects diluted earnings per share for the second quarter of fiscal 2003 to range from $0.73 to $0.76. Additionally, DHI expects diluted earnings per share for fiscal 2003 in the range of $3.50 to $3.55, representing a 22.0% to 24.0% increase versus earnings per share of $2.87 reported in fiscal 2002. Revenues for fiscal 2003 are expected to be around $8.00 billion, based on about 35,000 homes expected to close during the year. As of 12/31/02, the Company's backlog of homes under contract was 12,435 homes, or $2.86 billion, versus 8,716 homes, or $1.83 billion a year earlier.

ANNUAL FINANCIAL DATA:

FISCAL YEAR	TOT. REVS. ($mill.)	NET INC. ($mill.)	TOT. ASSETS ($mill.)	OPER. PROFIT %	NET PROFIT %	RET. ON EQUITY %	RET. ON ASSETS %	CURR. RATIO	EARN. PER SH.$	CASH FL. PER SH.$	TANG. BK. VAL.$	DIV. PER SH.$	PRICE RANGE	AVG. P/E RATIO	AVG. YIELD %
③ 9/30/02	6,738.8	404.7	6,017.5	9.5	6.0	17.8	6.7	3.6	2.87	3.14	11.54	0.22	29.17 - 16.03	7.9	1.0
9/30/01	4,455.5	② 254.9	3,652.2	10.1	5.7	20.4	7.0	4.5	② 2.21	2.52	9.66	0.13	22.33 - 11.67	7.7	0.8
9/30/00	3,653.7	191.7	2,694.6	8.7	5.2	19.8	7.1	4.8	1.69	1.90	7.60	0.09	15.62 - 5.99	6.4	0.8
9/30/99	3,156.2	159.8	2,361.8	8.7	5.1	20.0	6.8	4.2	1.38	1.56	6.01	0.07	12.67 - 5.51	6.6	0.7
9/30/98	2,176.9	① 93.4	1,667.8	8.3	4.3	17.0	5.6	5.0	① 0.86	0.92	4.86	0.05	13.74 - 5.85	11.4	0.5
9/30/97	837.3	36.2	719.8	7.5	4.3	13.8	5.0	1.4	0.56	0.62	3.46	0.04	11.57 - 4.96	14.8	0.5
9/30/96	547.3	27.4	402.9	8.1	5.0	15.4	6.8	1.7	0.48	0.53	2.95	...	6.57 - 4.13	11.2	...
9/30/95	437.4	20.5	318.8	7.6	4.7	19.4	6.4	1.4	0.41	0.45	2.23	...	6.06 - 2.93	11.0	...
9/30/94	393.3	17.7	230.9	7.2	4.5	20.9	7.6	1.5	0.41	0.44	1.97	...	6.23 - 2.97	11.1	...
9/30/93	190.1	8.9	158.7	7.2	4.7	13.4	5.6	1.6	0.21	0.22	1.58	...	5.68 - 2.85	20.5	...

Statistics are as originally reported. Adj. for all stk. splits through 4/02. ① Incl. non-recur merger chrg. of $11.9 mill. ② Bef. acctg. change credit of $2.1 mill. ③ Reflects the acq. of Schuler Homes, Inc.

OFFICERS:
D. R. Horton, Chmn.
D. J. Tomnitz, Vice-Chmn., C.E.O., Pres.
S. R. Fuller, Exec. V.P., C.F.O., Treas.
INVESTOR CONTACT: Stacey Dwyer, Investor Relations, (817) 856-8200
PRINCIPAL OFFICE: 1901 Ascension Blvd., Suite 100, Arlington, TX 76006

TELEPHONE NUMBER: (817) 856-8200
FAX: (817) 856-8429
WEB: www.drhorton.com
NO. OF EMPLOYEES: 5,701 (avg.)
SHAREHOLDERS: 473 (approx.)
ANNUAL MEETING: In Jan.
INCORPORATED: DE, July, 1991

INSTITUTIONAL HOLDINGS:
No. of Institutions: 243
Shares Held: 117,084,364
% Held: 79.9

INDUSTRY: Operative builders (SIC: 1531)

TRANSFER AGENT(S): American Stock Transfer & Trust Co., New York, NY

HOST MARRIOTT CORPORATION

EXCH.	SYM.	REC. PRICE	P/E RATIO	YLD.	MKT. CAP.	RANGE (52-WK.)	'02 Y/E PR.
NYSE	HMT	6.92 (2/28/03)	...	...	$1.82 bill.	12.25 - 6.67	8.85

LOWER MEDIUM GRADE. THE SHORT-TERM OUTLOOK IS EXPECTED TO BE HAMPERED BY THE DIFFICULT BUSINESS ENVIRONMENT.

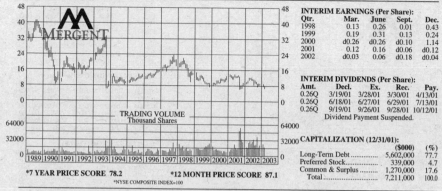

7 YEAR PRICE SCORE 78.2   **12 MONTH PRICE SCORE 87.1**
*NYSE COMPOSITE INDEX=100

INTERIM EARNINGS (Per Share):

Qtr.	Mar.	June	Sept.	Dec.
1998	0.13	0.26	0.01	0.43
1999	0.19	0.31	0.13	0.24
2000	d0.26	d0.26	0.10	1.14
2001	0.12	0.16	d0.06	d0.12
2002	d0.03	0.06	d0.18	d0.04

INTERIM DIVIDENDS (Per Share):

Amt.	Decl.	Ex.	Rec.	Pay.
0.26Q	3/19/01	3/28/01	3/30/01	4/13/01
0.26Q	6/18/01	6/27/01	6/29/01	7/13/01
0.26Q	9/19/01	9/26/01	9/28/01	10/12/01
	Dividend Payment Suspended.			

CAPITALIZATION (12/31/01):

	($000)	(%)
Long-Term Debt	5,602,000	77.7
Preferred Stock	339,000	4.7
Common & Surplus	1,270,000	17.6
Total	7,211,000	100.0

BUSINESS:

Host Marriott Corporation is a lodging real estate company operating through an umbrella partnership structure. As of 2/26/03, the Company owned or held controlling interests in 122 upscale and luxury full-service hotel properties operated primarily under the MARRIOTT, RITZ-CARLTON, HYATT, FOUR SEASONS, SWISSOTEL, and HILTON brand names. In addition, the Company operates as a self-managed and self-administered real estate investment trust and its operations are conducted solely through its subsidiaries. The Company is the sole general partner of the Operating Partnership. HMT spun off its senior living businesses and Crestline Capital Corporation in December 1998.

RECENT DEVELOPMENTS:

For the year ended 12/31/02, HMT reported a loss of $29.0 million, before income from discontinued operations of $7.0 million and an extraordinary gain of $6.0 million, versus income of $56.0 million, before a loss from discontinued operations of $3.0 million and an extraordinary loss of $2.0 million, the year before. Revenue dropped 2.3% to $3.68 billion from $3.77 billion a year earlier. Total hotel sales declined 1.4% to $3.58 billion from $3.63 billion in 2001. Comparable revenues per available room dropped 5.1%, reflecting a 5.9% decline in average room rate, partially offset by a slight increase of about 1.0% in occupancy rates.

PROSPECTS:

The combined influence of a weak economy and the war in the Middle East are expected to dampen business and leisure travel plans throughout the hotel industry in the near-term. Consequently, HMT will continue to maintain high cash reserves, which combined with limited debt maturities, should strengthen its financial flexibility. Moreover, HMT expects to continue to sell assets during 2003, the proceeds of which will be used to reduce debt or reinvest in HMT's portfolio. Once market conditions improve, HMT expects that its properties will be able to reverse recent declines in average occupancy rates, allowing the Company to increase revenues and operating efficiencies.

ANNUAL FINANCIAL DATA:

FISCAL YEAR	TOT. INC. ($mill.)	NET INC. ($mill.)	TOT. ASSETS ($mill.)	NET INC. +DEPR./ ASSETS %	RET. ON EQUITY %	RET. ON ASSETS %	EARN. PER SH. $	TANG. BK. VAL.$	DIV. PER SH.$	DIV. PAYOUT %	PRICE RANGE	AVG. P/E RATIO	AVG. YIELD %
p12/31/02	3,680.0	①② d29.0					①② d0.19			...	12.25 — 7.50	...	...
⑧ 12/31/01	3,754.0	⑦ 53.0	8,338.0	5.2	3.3	0.6	⑦ 0.09	4.83	1.04	N.M.	13.95 — 6.22	111.9	10.3
12/31/00	1,473.0	⑥ 159.0	8,396.0	5.8	11.2	1.9	⑥ 0.64	5.54	0.86	134.4	12.94 — 8.00	16.4	8.2
12/31/99	1,376.0	⑤ 196.0	8,202.0	5.9	13.0	2.4	⑤ 0.87	5.80	0.63	72.4	14.81 — 7.38	12.8	5.7
12/31/98	3,513.0	⑤ 194.0	8,268.0	2.3	14.8	2.3	⑤ 0.84	5.13	...	...	22.13 — 9.88	19.0	...
1/02/98	1,147.0	⑤ 47.0	6,526.0	0.7	3.9	0.7	⑤ 0.23	5.89	...	...	23.75 — 15.25	84.7	...
1/03/97	732.0	d13.0	5,152.0	...	...	...	d0.07	7.04	...	...	16.25 — 11.25	...	...
④ 12/29/95	484.0	①② d62.0	3,557.0	...	...	...	①② d0.39	4.22	...	...	13.88 — 9.13	...	...
12/30/94	1,501.0	①② d19.0	3,822.0	...	...	...	①② d0.13	4.53	...	...	13.75 — 8.25	...	...
12/31/93	1,791.0	①②③ 57.0	3,893.0	1.5	11.3	1.5	①②③ 0.40	3.58	...	...	33.38 — 6.25	49.5	...

Statistics are as originally reported. ① Bef. extraord. credit 2002, $6.0 mill.; 1999, $15.0 mill.; 1997, $3.0 mill.; chrg. 1995, $20.0 mill.; 1994, $6.0 mill.; 1993, $5.0 mill. ② Bef. disc. oper. gain 2002, $7.0 mill.; loss 1995, $61.0 mill.; 1994, $6.0 mill.; 1993, $4.0 mill. ③ Bef. acctg. change chrg. $2.0 mill. ④ Results exclude the opers. of Host Marriott Services which was spun-off through a special dividend distribution. ⑤ Incl. a pre-tax chrg. of $64.0 mill. & a pre-tax benefit of $106.0 mill.; bef. a gain of $1.0 mill. in f. disc. opers. & extraord. chrg. of $148.0 mill. ⑥ Bef. extraord. loss of $3.0 mill., incl. non-recurr. chrg. of $207.0 mill. ⑦ Bef. extraord. loss $2.0 mill.; incl. net property gain $6.0 mill. ⑧ Revenues represented the gross hotel sales rather than rental income from third party lessees that were previously reported.

OFFICERS:
R. E. Marriott, Chmn.
C. J. Nassetta, Pres., C.E.O.
W. E. Walter, C.O.O., C.F.O.

INVESTOR CONTACT: Investor Relations, (301) 380-9000

PRINCIPAL OFFICE: 10400 Fernwood Road, Bethesda, MD 20817

TELEPHONE NUMBER: (301) 380-9000
FAX: (301) 380-6338
WEB: www.hostmarriott.com
NO. OF EMPLOYEES: 199 (avg.)
SHAREHOLDERS: 107,000 (approx.)
ANNUAL MEETING: In May
INCORPORATED: DE, July, 1929

INSTITUTIONAL HOLDINGS:
No. of Institutions: 205
Shares Held: 211,357,836
% Held: 79.5

INDUSTRY: Real estate investment trusts (SIC: 6798)

TRANSFER AGENT(S): EquiServe Trust Company, N.A., Jersey City, NJ

HOUSEHOLD INTERNATIONAL INC.

EXCH.	SYM.	REC. PRICE	P/E RATIO	YLD.	MKT. CAP.	RANGE (52-WK.)	'02 Y/E PR.	DIV. ACH.
NYSE	HI	27.93 (2/28/03)	8.5	12.5%	$12.77 bill.	63.25 - 20.00	27.81	50 yrs.

INVESTMENT GRADE. THE ACQUISITION OF THE COMPANY BY HSBC HOLDINGS PLC WAS COMPLETED ON 3/28/03.

INTERIM EARNINGS (Per Share):

Qtr.	Mar.	June	Sept.	Dec.
1997	0.43	0.49	0.57	0.66
1998	0.51	d1.03	0.63	0.71
1999	0.65	0.67	0.83	0.92
2000	0.78	0.80	0.94	1.03
2001	0.91	0.93	1.07	1.17
2002	1.09	1.07	0.45	0.66

INTERIM DIVIDENDS (Per Share):

Amt.	Decl.	Ex.	Rec.	Pay.
0.22Q	3/13/02	3/26/02	3/28/02	4/15/02
0.25Q	5/15/02	6/26/02	6/28/02	7/15/02
0.25Q	9/10/02	9/26/02	9/30/02	10/15/02
0.25Q	11/12/02	12/27/02	12/31/02	1/15/03
0.869Q	2/12/03	...	3/28/03	5/06/03

Indicated div.: $3.48 (Div. Reinv. Plan)

CAPITALIZATION (12/31/01):

	($000)	(%)
Long-Term Debt	56,823,600	87.4
Common & Surplus	8,202,800	12.6
Total	65,026,400	100.0

*7 YEAR PRICE SCORE 98.7   ***12 MONTH PRICE SCORE 76.8**

*NYSE COMPOSITE INDEX=100

BUSINESS:

Household International Inc. provides middle-market consumers with real estate secured loans, auto finance loans, MasterCard® and Visa® credit cards, private label credit cards and personal non-credit card loans. The Company also offers tax refund anticipation loans in the U.S. and credit and specialty insurance products in the U.S, U.K. and Canada. The Company's operations are divided into three reportable segments: Consumer, Credit Card Services and International. HI's Consumer segment consists of its consumer lending, mortgage services, retail services and auto finance businesses. The Company's Credit Card Services segment includes its domestic MasterCard and Visa credit card businesses. The Company's International segment includes its foreign operations in the U.K. and Canada. As of 12/31/02, HI's managed portfolio consisted of the following: real estate secured, 43.0%; auto finance, 6.9%; MasterCard/Visa, 17.6%; private label, 13.9%; personal non-credit card, 18.2%; and commercial and other, 0.4%.

RECENT DEVELOPMENTS:

For the year ended 12/31/02, net income declined 15.7% to $1.56 billion from $1.85 billion in the previous year. Results for 2002 included an after-tax loss of $240.0 million related to the sale of the assets and deposits of its thrift, Household Bank FSB. Results for 2002 also included an after-tax charge of $333.2 million related to a nationwide settlement with state attorneys general and other regulators. Total revenues increased 6.5% to $14.67 billion. Net interest income grew 15.0% to $6.65 billion.

PROSPECTS:

On 3/28/03, the Company was acquired by Europe's largest bank, HSBC Holdings plc, for $14.24 billion. Going forward, earning may continue to be negatively affected by a rise in bad loans caused by rising unemployment and more bankruptcies. The percentage of the Company's loans that have been written off rose to 4.39% in the fourth quarter of 2002, up from 3.90% in 2001. The percentage of loans more than 60 days late on repayments was 5.24% at the end of the fourth quarter, up from 4.46% in the prior-year quarter.

ANNUAL FINANCIAL DATA:

FISCAL YEAR	TOT. REVS. ($mill.)	NET INC. ($mill.)	TOT. ASSETS ($mill.)	OPER. PROFIT %	NET PROFIT %	RET. ON EQUITY %	RET. ON ASSETS %	CURR. RATIO	EARN. PER SH. $	CASH FL. PER SH. $	TANG. BK. VAL. $	DIV. PER SH. $	PRICE RANGE	AVG. P/E RATIO	AVG. YIELD %
p12/31/02	14,671.6	② 1,557.8							② 3.22			0.94	63.25 - 20.00	12.9	2.3
12/31/01	13,915.7	1,923.5	89,416.0	21.1	13.8	23.4	2.2	4.3	4.08	4.73	14.54	0.82	69.98 - 48.00	14.5	1.4
12/31/00	11,960.9	1,700.7	76,706.3	21.8	14.2	21.0	2.2	3.5	3.55	4.19	13.26	0.72	57.44 - 29.50	12.2	1.7
12/31/99	9,491.1	1,486.4	60,749.4	23.4	15.6	22.5	2.4	3.3	① 3.07	3.67	10.39	0.66	52.31 - 32.19	13.8	1.6
12/31/98	8,897.0	524.1	52,892.7	10.7	5.9	8.2	1.0	3.7	1.03	1.65	9.36	0.59	53.69 - 23.00	37.2	1.5
12/31/97	5,503.1	686.6	30,302.6	18.7	12.5	14.7	2.3	3.1	2.17	2.99	8.59	0.53	43.33 - 26.21	16.0	1.5
12/31/96	5,058.8	538.6	29,594.5	16.3	10.6	17.1	1.8	2.8	1.77	2.58	6.77	0.47	32.71 - 17.33	14.2	1.9
12/31/95	5,144.4	453.2	29,218.8	14.7	8.8	15.6	1.6	1.9	1.44	2.32	7.25	0.43	22.79 - 11.96	12.1	2.5
12/31/94	4,603.3	367.6	34,338.4	11.5	8.0	14.6	1.1	1.7	1.17	2.00	5.35	0.41	13.25 - 9.50	9.7	3.6
12/31/93	4,454.5	298.7	32,961.5	10.1	6.7	12.5	0.9	1.5	0.97	1.81	5.66	0.39	13.48 - 8.98	11.6	3.5

Statistics are as originally reported. Adj. for stk. splits: 3-for-1, 6/98; 2-for-1, 10/93. ① Incl. chrg. of $1.00 bill. for merger costs & gain of $189.4 mill. for sale of Beneficial Canada. ② Incl. after-tax loss. of $240.0 mill. for disp. of thrift assets & dep. & an after-tax settlement chrg. of $333.2 mill.

OFFICERS:
W. F. Aldinger, Chmn., C.E.O.
L. N. Bangs, Vice-Chmn.
D. A. Schoenholz, C.F.O.

INVESTOR CONTACT: Celeste Murphy, Dir. Inv. Rel., (847) 564-7568

PRINCIPAL OFFICE: 2700 Sanders Road, Prospect Heights, IL 60070

TELEPHONE NUMBER: (847) 564-5000
FAX: (847) 205-7490
WEB: www.household.com

NO. OF EMPLOYEES: 32,000 (approx.)

SHAREHOLDERS: 19,089

ANNUAL MEETING: In May

INCORPORATED: DE, Feb., 1981

INSTITUTIONAL HOLDINGS:
No. of Institutions: 500
Shares Held: 386,115,574
% Held: 84.9

INDUSTRY: Personal credit institutions (SIC: 6141)

TRANSFER AGENT(S): Computershare Investor Services, Chicago, IL

HUBBELL, INC.

EXCH.	SYM.	REC. PRICE	P/E RATIO	YLD.	MKT. CAP.	RANGE (52-WK.)	'02 Y/E PR.
NYSE	HUBB	30.76 (2/28/03)	17.0	4.3%	$1.81 bill.	37.30 - 25.73	35.14

MEDIUM GRADE. THE COMPANY EXPECTS EARNINGS FOR 2003 TO RANGE FROM $1.95 TO $2.15 PER SHARE.

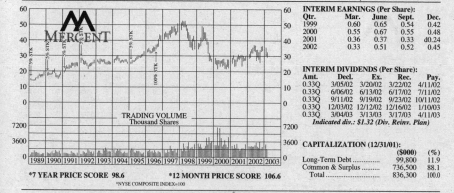

INTERIM EARNINGS (Per Share):

Qtr.	Mar.	June	Sept.	Dec.
1999	0.60	0.65	0.54	0.42
2000	0.55	0.67	0.55	0.48
2001	0.36	0.37	0.33	d0.24
2002	0.33	0.51	0.52	0.45

INTERIM DIVIDENDS (Per Share):

Amt.	Decl.	Ex.	Rec.	Pay.
0.33Q	3/05/02	3/20/02	3/22/02	4/11/02
0.33Q	6/06/02	6/13/02	6/17/02	7/11/02
0.33Q	9/11/02	9/19/02	9/23/02	10/11/02
0.33Q	12/03/02	12/12/02	12/16/02	1/10/03
0.33Q	3/04/03	3/13/03	3/17/03	4/11/03

Indicated div.: $1.32 (Div. Reinv. Plan)

*7 YEAR PRICE SCORE 98.6   ***12 MONTH PRICE SCORE 106.6**
*NYSE COMPOSITE INDEX=100

CAPITALIZATION (12/31/01):

	($000)	(%)
Long-Term Debt	99,800	11.9
Common & Surplus	736,500	88.1
Total	836,300	100.0

BUSINESS:

Hubbell, Inc. specializes in the engineering, manufacture, and sale of electrical and electronic products for the commercial, industrial, utility, and telecommunications markets. These products may be classified into three segments: Electrical (72.0% of 2002 sales), Power (20.5%) and Industrial Technology (7.5%). HUBB operates manufacturing facilities in North America, Switzerland, Puerto Rico, Italy, Mexico, and the U.K. and maintains sales offices in Hong Kong, the People's Republic of China, South Korea, Singapore, and the Middle East. Hubbell participates in joint ventures with partners in Taiwan. On 4/26/02, HUB acquired LCA Group, Inc. for $250.0 million.

RECENT DEVELOPMENTS:

For the year ended 12/31/02, HUBB reported income of $108.6 million, before an accounting change charge of $25.4 million, versus net income of $48.3 million in 2001. Results for 2002 and 2001 included pre-tax restructuring, rationalization and other non-recurring charges of $13.7 million and $53.4 million, and gains on the sale of business of $3.0 million and $4.7 million, respectively. Net sales advanced 21.0% to $1.59 billion. Electrical segment sales jumped 36.4% to $1.14 billion, primarily due to the acquisition of LCA Group, Inc. Power segment sales decreased 2.7% to $325.8 million, while Industrial Technology segment sales fell 14.3% to $119.5 million.

PROSPECTS:

For 2003, the Company expects only modest improvement in industrial markets and continuing weakness in non-residential construction markets. Utility customers are likely to invest in infrastructure only when absolutely necessary. Separately, HUBB expects its rationalization program for its recently expanded lighting business will reduce costs and position the Company for market share growth going forward. HUBB also plans to double the rate of productivity activities in 18 of its largest facilities in 2003. In addition, HUBB is increasing its investment in new product development and expects substantial productivity gains as well as improved working capital efficiency and cash generation. Meanwhile, earnings for 2003 are expect to range from $1.95 to $2.15 per share.

ANNUAL FINANCIAL DATA:

FISCAL YEAR	TOT. REVS. ($mill.)	NET INC. ($mill.)	TOT. ASSETS ($mill.)	OPER. PROFIT %	NET PROFIT %	RET. ON EQUITY %	RET. ON ASSETS %	CURR. RATIO	EARN. PER SH.$	CASH FL. PER SH.$	TANG. BK. VAL.$	DIV. PER SH.$	PRICE RANGE	AVG. P/E RATIO	AVG. YIELD %
p12/31/02	1,587.8	⑤ 108.6							⑤ 1.81			1.32	37.30 - 25.73	17.4	4.2
12/31/01	1,312.2	④ 48.3	1,205.4	4.3	3.7	6.6	4.0	1.8	④ 0.82	1.72	7.98	1.32	30.98 - 23.30	33.1	4.9
12/31/00	1,424.1	③ 138.2	1,454.5	13.0	9.7	18.0	9.5	1.3	③ 2.25	3.15	8.64	1.30	28.81 - 21.63	11.2	5.2
12/31/99	1,451.8	② 145.8	1,399.2	13.4	10.0	17.0	10.4	1.6	② 2.21	3.01	9.56	1.26	49.19 - 26.25	17.1	3.3
12/31/98	1,424.6	169.4	1,390.4	15.9	11.9	20.2	12.2	1.6	2.50	3.21	9.27	1.20	52.75 - 33.88	17.3	2.8
12/31/97	1,378.8	① 130.3	1,284.8	12.4	9.5	15.7	10.1	2.3	① 1.89	2.52	9.54	1.10	50.94 - 40.75	24.3	2.4
12/31/96	1,297.4	141.5	1,186.4	15.2	10.9	19.0	11.9	2.3	2.10	2.74	8.79	0.99	43.88 - 31.75	18.0	2.6
12/31/95	1,143.1	121.9	1,057.2	14.4	10.7	18.0	11.5	2.6	1.83	2.37	8.04	0.89	33.06 - 24.82	15.9	3.1
12/31/94	1,013.7	106.5	1,041.6	13.9	10.5	17.5	10.2	1.3	1.60	2.11	7.09	0.80	29.94 - 25.00	17.2	2.9
12/31/93	832.4	66.3	874.3	8.4	8.0	17.0	7.6	1.6	1.00	1.45	7.48	0.77	28.04 - 24.17	26.1	3.0

Statistics are as originally reported. Adj. for stk. splits, 2-for-1, 8/96; 5%, 2/95 ① Incl. after-tax chrg. $32.2 mill. for consolidation & reorganization. ② Incl. a one-time gain $8.8 mill. fr. the sale of The Kerite Company. ③ Incl. after-tax spec. and nonrecurr. chrgs. $23.7 mill. & a one-time gain $36.2 mill. fr. the sale of WavePacer DSL assets. ④ Incl. a chrg. $40.0 mill. and a $4.7 mill. gain on the sale of business. ⑤ Bef. acctg. chng. chrg. $25.4 mill.; incl. pre-tax restr., rational. & oth. one-time chrg. $13.7 mill. and gain on sale of business $30. mill.

OFFICERS:
G. J. Ratcliffe, Chmn.
T. H. Powers, Pres., C.E.O.
W. T. Tolley, Sr. V.P., C.F.O.

INVESTOR CONTACT: Thomas R. Conlin, (203) 799-4100

PRINCIPAL OFFICE: 584 Derby-Milford Road, Orange, CT 06477-4024

TELEPHONE NUMBER: (203) 799-4100
FAX: (203) 799-4223
WEB: www.hubbell.com

NO. OF EMPLOYEES: 8,771 (approx.)

SHAREHOLDERS: 916 (Class A); 4,174 (Class B)

ANNUAL MEETING: In May
INCORPORATED: CT, May, 1905

INSTITUTIONAL HOLDINGS:
No. of Institutions: 214
Shares Held: 36,077,093
% Held: 61.0

INDUSTRY: Commercial lighting fixtures (SIC: 3646)

TRANSFER AGENT(S): Mellon Investor Services LLC, Ridgefield Park, NJ

HUDSON UNITED BANCORP

EXCH.	SYM.	REC. PRICE	P/E RATIO	YLD.	MKT. CAP.	RANGE (52-WK.)	'02 Y/E PR.	DIV. ACH.
NYSE	HU	31.54 (2/28/03)	11.6	3.6%	$1.44 bill.	33.00 - 22.90	31.10	12 yrs.

MEDIUM GRADE. THE COMPANY ANTICIPATES FULL-YEAR 2003 EARNINGS OF APPROXIMATELY $2.60 PER DILUTED SHARE.

INTERIM EARNINGS (Per Share):

Qtr.	Mar.	June	Sept.	Dec.
1998	0.31	0.10	d0.44	0.51
1999	0.48	0.49	0.50	d0.31
2000	0.53	d0.22	0.45	0.17
2001	0.46	0.49	0.51	0.54
2002	0.93	0.56	0.60	0.63

INTERIM DIVIDENDS (Per Share):

Amt.	Decl.	Ex.	Rec.	Pay.
0.26Q	1/24/02	2/13/02	2/15/02	3/01/02
0.28Q	4/18/02	5/15/02	5/17/02	6/01/02
0.28Q	7/18/02	8/21/02	8/23/02	9/03/02
0.28Q	10/23/02	11/13/02	11/15/02	12/02/02
0.28Q	1/30/03	2/19/03	2/21/03	3/03/03

Indicated div.: $1.12 (Div. Reinv. Plan)

CAPITALIZATION (12/31/01):

	($000)	(%)
Total Deposits	5,983,545	90.4
Long-Term Debt	123,000	1.9
Redeemable Pfd. Stock	125,300	1.9
Common & Surplus	383,904	5.8
Total	6,615,749	100.0

TRADING VOLUME
Thousand Shares

```
42                                                              42
35                                                              35
28                                                              28
21                                                              21
14                                                              14
7                                                               7
0                                                               0
12000                                                           12000
6000                                                            6000
0                                                               0
   1989 1990 1991 1992 1993 1994 1995 1996 1997 1998 1999 2000 2001 2002 2003
```

*7 YEAR PRICE SCORE 125.8   *12 MONTH PRICE SCORE 115.5

*NYSE COMPOSITE INDEX=100

BUSINESS:

Hudson United Bancorp (formerly HUBCO, Inc.) is a bank holding company for Hudson United Bank, a full-service commercial bank that operates over 200 branches throughout New Jersey, Connecticut, lower New York state, and southeastern Pennsylvania. The Company directly owns Hudson United Bank and four additional subsidiaries, which are HUBCO Capital Trust I, HUBCO Capital Trust II, JBI Capital Trust I and Jefferson Delaware Inc. The Company is also the indirect owner, through Hudson United Bank, of nine subsidiaries. At 12/31/02, HU, through its subsidiaries, had total deposits of $6.20 billion and total assets of $7.65 billion.

RECENT DEVELOPMENTS:

For the year ended 12/31/02, net income was $123.2 million compared with $94.5 million the previous year. Results for 2002 and 2001 included gains of $197,000 and $10.2 million, respectively, on assets held for sale. Results for 2002 also included a non-recurring gain of $77.0 million received from Dime Bancorp Inc. related to the uncompleted merger of HU and Dime. This gain was partially offset by expenses of $8.3 million related to the Dime termination payment and an impairment charge of $2.8 million on mortgage-related servicing assets. Net interest income grew 5.4% to $300.8 million. Provision for loan losses rose 50.3% to $51.3 million. Total non-interest income, which included the aforementioned non-recurring items, rose 69.2% to $185.1 million.

PROSPECTS:

HU's near-term outlook appears positive. The Company's non-interest income is benefiting from higher credit card fees, commercial lending fees and increased income from separate account bank owned insurance. Also, HU's non-interest expense should continue to reflect efficiencies realized from the acquisition of Connecticut Bank of Commerce, which took place in June 2002. Looking forward, HU anticipates full-year 2003 earnings of about $2.60 per diluted share.

ANNUAL FINANCIAL DATA:

FISCAL YEAR	NET INT. INC. ($mill.)	NON-INT. INC. ($mill.)	NET INC. ($mill.)	TOT. LOANS ($mill.)	TOT. ASSETS ($mill.)	TOT. DEP. ($mill.)	RET. ON EQUITY %	RET. ON ASSETS %	EQUITY/ ASSETS %	EARN. PER SH.$	TANG. BK. VAL.$	DIV. PER SH.$	PRICE RANGE	AVG. P/E RATIO	AVG. YIELD %
p12/31/02	300.8	185.1	②③ 123.2							③③ 2.72		1.10	33.00 - 22.90	10.3	3.9
12/31/01	285.4	109.4	② 94.5	4,444.6	6,999.5	5,983.5	24.6	1.3	5.5	2.00	6.50	1.01	29.50 - 19.50	12.2	4.1
12/31/00	319.7	31.1	① 49.8	5,277.5	6,817.2	5,813.3	13.5	0.7	5.4	① 0.92	5.58	0.93	25.63 - 16.36	22.8	4.4
12/31/99	343.1	88.7	① 69.3	5,670.5	9,686.3	6,455.3	13.4	0.7	5.4	① 1.18	7.07	0.88	32.11 - 22.67	23.2	3.2
12/31/98	254.2	33.3	① 23.2	3,386.8	6,778.7	5,051.4	5.1	0.3	6.7	① 0.49	8.25	0.78	33.63 - 18.65	52.9	3.0
12/31/97	140.2	41.1	① 49.3	1,773.8	3,046.5	2,314.4	26.5	1.6	6.1	① 1.80	6.32	0.65	32.56 - 18.10	14.1	2.5
12/31/96	131.4	30.3	① 21.5	1,884.4	3,115.7	2,592.1	10.4	0.7	6.6	① 0.77	6.51	0.57	21.21 - 14.74	23.2	3.2
12/31/95	81.1	17.8	23.7	854.0	1,613.2	1,425.0	18.2	1.5	8.1	1.51	7.77	0.48	17.87 - 11.85	9.8	3.3
12/31/94	58.0	10.0	16.9	733.4	1,377.1	1,199.7	17.1	1.2	7.2	1.41	6.91	0.33	12.79 - 10.10	8.1	2.9
12/31/93	47.0	8.6	14.2	534.8	1,041.8	935.7	18.0	1.4	7.6	1.14	6.51	0.25	13.60 - 8.63	9.7	2.2

Statistics are as originally reported. Adj. for all stk. splits thru 12/00. ① Incl. merger-rel. & restruct. costs of $15.0 mill., 2000; $32.0 mill., 1999; $66.4 mill., 1998; $270,000, 1997; $22.0 mill., 1996. ② Incl. trading asset gains of $197,000, 2002; $10.2 mill., 2001. ③ Incl. Dime Bancorp., Inc. merger termination payment of $77.0 mill., non-recurr. chrg. of $8.3 mill. & impairment chrgs. of $2.8 mill.

OFFICERS:
K. T. Neilson, Chmn., Pres., C.E.O.
W. A. Houlihan, Exec. V.P., C.F.O.
D. L. Van Borkulo-Nuzzo, Exec. V.P., Corp. Sec.

INVESTOR CONTACT: William A. Houlihan, Exec. V.P., C.F.O., (201) 236-2803

PRINCIPAL OFFICE: 1000 Macarthur Boulevard, Mahwah, NJ 07430

TELEPHONE NUMBER: (201) 236-2600
FAX: (201) 236-2649
WEB: www.hudsonunitedbank.com

NO. OF EMPLOYEES: 1,777

SHAREHOLDERS: 7,670 (approx.)

ANNUAL MEETING: In Apr.

INCORPORATED: NJ, June, 1982

INSTITUTIONAL HOLDINGS:
No. of Institutions: 165
Shares Held: 20,828,735
% Held: 46.3

INDUSTRY: State commercial banks (SIC: 6022)

TRANSFER AGENT(S): American Stock Transfer Company, New York, NY

HUGHES SUPPLY, INC.

EXCH.	SYM.	REC. PRICE	P/E RATIO	YLD.	MKT. CAP.	RANGE (52-WK.)	'02 Y/E PR.
NYSE	HUG	23.20 (2/28/03)	9.5	1.7%	$0.55 bill.	46.96 - 22.31	27.32

MEDIUM GRADE. EARNINGS ARE BENEFITING FROM THE COMPANY'S EFFORTS TO REDUCE COSTS.

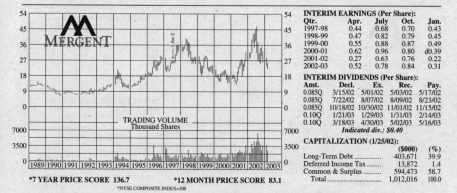

*7 YEAR PRICE SCORE 136.7   ***12 MONTH PRICE SCORE 83.1**

*NYSE COMPOSITE INDEX=100

INTERIM EARNINGS (Per Share):

Qtr.	Apr.	July	Oct.	Jan.
1997-98	0.44	0.68	0.70	0.43
1998-99	0.47	0.82	0.79	0.45
1999-00	0.55	0.88	0.87	0.49
2000-01	0.62	0.96	0.80	d0.39
2001-02	0.27	0.63	0.76	0.22
2002-03	0.52	0.78	0.84	0.31

INTERIM DIVIDENDS (Per Share):

Amt.	Decl.	Ex.	Rec.	Pay.
0.085Q	3/15/02	5/01/02	5/03/02	5/17/02
0.085Q	7/22/02	8/07/02	8/09/02	8/23/02
0.085Q	10/18/02	10/30/02	11/01/02	11/15/02
0.10Q	1/21/03	1/29/03	1/31/03	2/14/03
0.10Q	3/18/03	4/30/03	5/02/03	5/16/03

Indicated div.: $0.40

CAPITALIZATION (1/25/02):

	($000)	(%)
Long-Term Debt	403,671	39.9
Deferred Income Tax	13,872	1.4
Common & Surplus	594,473	58.7
Total	1,012,016	100.0

BUSINESS:

Hughes Supply, Inc. is engaged in wholesale distribution of a broad range of materials, equipment and supplies primarily to the construction industry. HUG distributes over 240,000 products from more than 450 locations in 34 states and Mexico. These products are used by its customers in new construction for commercial, residential, infrastructure and industrial applications and for replacement and renova-

tion projects. Major product lines distributed by HUG include electrical, plumbing, water and sewer, air conditioning and heating, industrial pipe, valves and fittings, building materials, electric utilities, and water systems. On 8/9/02, the Company acquired Utiliserve Holdings, Inc., a wholesale distributor of electrical transmission and distribution products and services.

RECENT DEVELOPMENTS:

For the year ended 1/31/03, net income advanced 31.8% to $58.1 million from $44.1 million in the previous year. Sales rose 0.9% to $3.07 billion from $3.04 billion a year earlier. Sales for the recent year included $95.3 million from the acquisition of Utiliserve Holdings, Inc., which was completed in August 2002. Results for the prior-year period included a pre-tax charge of $734,000 for impairment of

long-lived assets. Gross profit was $710.3 million, or 23.2% of sales, compared with $697.7 million, or 23.0% of sales, the year before. Operating income increased 18.9% to $119.1 million from $100.1 million in the prior year. Income before income taxes grew 31.5% to $98.2 million from $74.7 million the previous year.

PROSPECTS:

Earnings growth is being driven by the implementation of cost-control initiatives. Going forward, the Company will continue its efforts to reduce costs and boost sales despite unfavorable commercial construction market conditions. Meanwhile, on 3/3/03, the Company announced that it has

formed a new department that will focus on the identification, evaluation, pricing, closing and integration of strategic acquisitions, as well as the negotiation, establishment and implementation of strategic alliances.

ANNUAL FINANCIAL DATA:

FISCAL YEAR	TOT. REVS. ($mill.)	NET INC. ($mill.)	TOT. ASSETS ($mill.)	OPER. PROFIT %	NET PROFIT %	RET. ON EQUITY %	RET. ON ASSETS %	CURR. RATIO	EARN. PER SH.$	CASH FL. PER SH.$	TANG. BK. VAL.$	DIV. PER SH.$	PRICE RANGE	AVG. P/E RATIO	AVG. YIELD %
p1/31/03	3,066.3	58.1							2.45			0.34	46.96 - 25.31	14.7	0.9
1/25/02	3,037.7	☑44.1	1,293.3	3.3	1.5	7.4	3.4	3.1	☑1.88	3.21	13.92	0.34	31.95 - 13.22	12.0	1.5
1/26/01	3,310.2	☑46.5	1,400.3	3.2	1.4	8.2	3.3	3.3	☑1.97	3.34	13.55	0.34	21.94 - 13.90	9.1	1.9
1/28/00	2,994.9	65.9	1,369.0	4.4	2.2	12.6	4.8	3.2	2.80	4.06	11.84	0.34	30.00 - 17.88	8.5	1.4
1/29/99	2,536.3	61.4	1,123.5	4.6	2.4	12.7	5.5	3.5	2.55	3.51	12.50	0.33	39.81 - 25.13	12.7	1.0
1/30/98	1,878.7	44.8	942.0	4.5	2.4	10.8	4.8	3.5	2.30	3.24	11.61	0.29	36.13 - 20.33	12.3	1.0
1/31/97	1,516.1	32.5	649.5	3.9	2.1	11.7	5.0	3.3	2.05	2.99	10.95	0.25	29.75 - 17.75	11.6	1.0
1/26/96	1,082.2	16.1	379.1	2.8	1.5	10.4	4.2	2.5	1.56	2.59	15.12	0.18	19.42 - 11.83	10.0	1.2
1/27/95	802.4	10.3	328.9	2.4	1.3	7.9	3.1	2.7	1.19	2.21	14.50	0.14	21.50 - 10.58	13.4	0.9
1/28/94	660.9	6.3	263.4	1.9	1.0	6.7	2.4	3.0	0.90	1.97	13.52	0.09	13.08 - 8.83	12.2	0.9

Statistics are as originally reported. Adj. for 3-for-2 stk. split, 7/97. ☑ Incl. $15.6 mil pre-tax non-recur. chg. for impairment of long-lived assets & $11.0 mil pre-tax gain from the sale of the Company's pool business. ☑ Incl. $734,000 pre-tax non-recur. chg. for impairment of long-lived assets.

OFFICERS:
D. H. Hughes, Chmn.
T. I. Morgan, Pres., C.E.O.
D. Bearman, Exec. V.P., C.F.O.

INVESTOR CONTACT: J. Stephen Zepf, Sr. V.P., (407) 841-4755

PRINCIPAL OFFICE: 20 North Orange Ave., Suite 200, Orlando, FL 32801

TELEPHONE NUMBER: (407) 841-4755
FAX: (407) 649-1670
WEB: www.hughessupply.com

NO. OF EMPLOYEES: 7,156 (avg.)

SHAREHOLDERS: 915 (approx.)

ANNUAL MEETING: In May

INCORPORATED: FL, 1947

INSTITUTIONAL HOLDINGS:
No. of Institutions: 133
Shares Held: 19,826,306
% Held: 83.4

INDUSTRY: Electrical apparatus and equipment (SIC: 5063)

TRANSFER AGENT(S): American Stock Transfer & Trust Company, New York, NY

HUMANA INC.

EXCH.	SYM.	REC. PRICE	P/E RATIO	YLD.	MKT. CAP.	RANGE (52-WK.)	'02 Y/E PR.
NYSE	HUM	9.80 (2/28/03)	11.5	. . .	$1.65 bill.	17.45 - 8.68	10.00

MEDIUM GRADE. THE COMPANY ESTIMATES DILUTED EARNINGS PER SHARE WILL RANGE FROM $1.23 TO $1.28 FOR 2003.

*7 YEAR PRICE SCORE 84.9   ***12 MONTH PRICE SCORE 83.1**

*NYSE COMPOSITE INDEX=100

INTERIM EARNINGS (Per Share):

Qtr.	Mar.	June	Sept.	Dec.
1998	0.30	0.31	d0.18	0.34
1999	d0.10	0.17	0.13	d2.48
2000	0.13	0.11	0.14	0.16
2001	0.16	0.15	0.18	0.21
2002	0.28	0.27	0.31	d0.01

INTERIM DIVIDENDS (Per Share):

Amt.	Decl.	Ex.	Rec.	Pay.
	No dividends paid.			

CAPITALIZATION (12/31/01):

	($000)	(%)
Long-Term Debt	315,489	17.3
Common & Surplus	1,507,949	82.7
Total	1,823,438	100.0

BUSINESS:

Humana Inc. operates through two business segments: Commercial and Government. The Commercial segment (52.7% of 2002 revenues) includes three lines of business: fully insured medical, administrative services only and specialty. The Government segment (47.3%) includes three lines of business, Medicare+Choice, Medicaid and military or TRICARE business. At 12/31/02, HUM had approximately 6.6 million medical members located primarily in 18 states and Puerto Rico.

RECENT DEVELOPMENTS:

For the year ended 12/31/02, net income advanced 21.8% to $142.8 million compared with $117.2 million the previous year. Results for 2002 included a pre-tax restructuring charge of $35.9 million. Total revenues increased 10.7% to $11.28 billion from $10.19 billion the year before. Total premiums advanced 10.0% to $10.93 billion from $9.94 billion, while revenues from administrative services fees leapt 78.3% to $244.4 million from $137.1 million in 2001. Investment income decreased 30.0% to $78.8 million from $112.7 million, while other income jumped 22.7% to $7.6 million from $6.2 million the prior year. Income from operations climbed 9.0% to $227.2 million versus $208.4 million a year earlier. Total medical membership rose 3.3% to 6.6 million from 6.4 million in 2001.

PROSPECTS:

Going forward, the Company estimates diluted earnings per share to be in the range of $1.23 to $1.28 for 2003. In addition, the Company anticipates organic growth for commercial medical membership to range from 4.0% to 5.0% for 2003. Meanwhile, the Company is benefiting from the continued success of its strategy to provide services for employers. Based on its inititiaries in place and targeted opportunities, the Company believes it can further improve its commercial business in 2003, while maintaining strong results in its government segment.

ANNUAL FINANCIAL DATA:

FISCAL YEAR	TOT. REVS. ($mill.)	NET INC. ($mill.)	TOT. ASSETS ($mill.)	OPER. PROFIT %	NET PROFIT %	RET. ON EQUITY %	RET. ON ASSETS %	CURR. RATIO	EARN. PER SH.$	CASH FL. PER SH.$	TANG. BK. VAL.$	DIV. PER SH.$	PRICE RANGE	AVG. P/E RATIO	AVG. YIELD %
p12/31/02	11,280.8	⑤ 142.8		2.0	1.1	7.8	2.7	1.1	⑤ 0.85	1.72	4.33	...	17.45 - 9.78	16.0	...
12/31/01	10,194.9	117.2	4,403.6	2.0	1.1	7.8	2.7	1.1	0.70	1.72	4.33	...	15.63 - 8.38	17.1	...
12/31/00	10,514.0	90.0	4,167.0	1.4	0.9	6.6	2.2	0.9	0.54	1.42	3.37	...	15.81 - 4.75	19.0	...
12/31/99	10,113.0	④ d382.0	4,900.0	...	...	...	...	1.0	④ d2.28	d1.54	2.76	...	20.75 - 5.88	...	...
12/31/98	9,781.0	④ 129.0	5,496.0	2.6	1.3	7.6	2.3	1.2	④ 0.77	1.53	3.01	...	32.13 - 12.25	28.8	...
12/31/97	8,036.0	173.0	5,418.0	3.6	2.2	11.5	3.2	1.2	1.05	1.69	1.69	...	25.31 - 17.38	20.3	...
12/31/96	6,899.0	④ 123.0	3,153.0	2.0	1.8	9.5	3.9	1.3	④ 0.07	1.36	4.93	...	28.88 - 15.00	312.9	...
② 12/31/95	4,702.0	190.0	2,878.0	6.4	4.0	14.8	6.6	1.3	1.17	1.60	4.64	...	28.00 - 17.00	19.2	...
12/31/94	3,654.0	③ 176.0	1,957.0	6.3	4.8	16.6	9.0	1.3	③ 1.10	1.40	5.61	...	25.38 - 15.68	18.7	...
① 12/31/93	3,195.0	89.0	1,731.0	4.7	2.8	10.0	5.1	1.3	0.56	0.86	5.55	0.23	21.38 - 6.13	24.5	1.6

Statistics are as originally reported. ① Refl. 3/1/93 spin-off of acute-care bus. ② Incl. opers. of EMPHESYS Financial Group, Inc. ③ Incl. unusual chrg. of $18.0 mill. ④ Incl. asset write-downs & other chrgs. of $460.0 mill., 12/99; $34.0 mill., 12/98; $96.0 mill., 12/96. ⑤ Incl. pre-tax restuct. chrg. of $35.9 mill.

OFFICERS:
D. A. Jones, Chmn.
D. A. Jones Jr., Vice-Chmn.
M. B. McCallister, Pres., C.E.O.
J. H. Bloem, Sr. V.P., C.F.O.

INVESTOR CONTACT: Regina C. Nethery, Investor Relations, (502) 580-3644

PRINCIPAL OFFICE: 500 West Main Street, Louisville, KY 40202

TELEPHONE NUMBER: (502) 580-1000
FAX: (502) 580-1441
WEB: www.humana.com

NO. OF EMPLOYEES: 14,500 (approx.)

SHAREHOLDERS: 7,200 (approx. record)

ANNUAL MEETING: In May

INCORPORATED: DE, July, 1964

INSTITUTIONAL HOLDINGS:
No. of Institutions: 272
Shares Held: 111,108,030
% Held: 67.2

INDUSTRY: Hospital and medical service plans (SIC: 6324)

TRANSFER AGENT(S): National City Bank, Cleveland, OH

ICN PHARMACEUTICALS, INC.

EXCH.	SYM.	REC. PRICE	P/E RATIO	YLD.	MKT. CAP.	RANGE (52-WK.)	'02 Y/E PR.
NYSE	ICN	9.62 (2/28/03)	41.8	3.2%	$0.79 bill.	33.40 - 6.51	10.91

MEDIUM GRADE. THE COMPANY SHOULD BE WELL-POSITIONED FOR GROWTH IN 2003 DUE TO A REDUCTION IN WHOLESALE INVENTORY LEVELS AND THE SETTING OF NEW STRATEGIC DIRECTIONS.

*7 YEAR PRICE SCORE 72.1   ***12 MONTH PRICE SCORE 72.1**
*NYSE COMPOSITE INDEX=100

INTERIM EARNINGS (Per Share):

Qtr.	Mar.	June	Sept.	Dec.
1999	0.28	0.32	0.39	0.47
2000	0.34	0.38	0.45	0.09
2001	0.26	0.26	0.11	0.40
2002	0.36	0.65	d0.62	d0.16

INTERIM DIVIDENDS (Per Share):

Amt.	Decl.	Ex.	Rec.	Pay.
0.077Q	7/01/02	7/08/02	7/10/02	7/24/02
0.077Q	10/02/02	10/09/02	10/14/02	10/23/02
0.077Q	12/20/02	1/06/03	1/08/03	1/22/03
0.077Q	3/04/03	4/07/03	4/09/03	4/23/03
		Indicated div.: $0.31		

CAPITALIZATION (12/31/01):

	($000)	(%)
Long-Term Debt	734,933	47.3
Minority Interest	7,858	0.5
Common & Surplus	810,717	52.2
Total	1,553,508	100.0

BUSINESS:

ICN Pharmaceuticals, Inc. is a global, research-based pharmaceutical company that develops, manufactures, distributes and sells pharmaceutical, research and diagnostic products. The Company distributes and sells a broad range of prescription and over-the-counter pharmaceutical and nutritional products under the ICN brand name. These pharmaceutical products treat viral and bacterial infections, diseases of the skin, neuromuscular disorders, cancer, cardiovascular disease, diabetes and psychiatric disorders. As of 11/7/02, ICN owned approximately 80.0% interest in Ribapharm, Inc., a biopharmaceutical company.

RECENT DEVELOPMENTS:

For the year ended 12/31/02, income was $84.2 million, before an accounting change charge of $21.8 million and loss of $197.3 million from discontinued operations, compared with income of $76.6 million, before a loss of $12.4 million from discontinued operations, the previous year. Results for 2002 included pre-tax non-recurring and unusual charges of $241.5 million and $4.0 million, respectively. The 2002 results also included a loss of $25.7 million on the extinguishment of debt. Total revenues advanced 18.7% to $737.1 million from $620.8 million the year before. Product sales slipped 3.5% to $466.8 million from $483.8 million, while revenues from royalties leapt 97.3% to $270.3 million from $137.0 million a year earlier.

PROSPECTS:

The Company should be well-positioned for growth in 2003 due to a reduction in wholesale inventory levels and setting new strategic directions. ICN expects revenues in the range of $770.0 million to $780.0 million with earnings from continuing operations, before non-recurring and unusual items, ranging from $1.20 to $1.25 per share for full-year 2003. Meanwhile, the Company remains on track with its inventory reduction plan, which is expected to be completed by the end of the second quarter of 2003. ICN had over ten months of inventory at wholesalers in early 2002 and is working that down to one to three months.

ANNUAL FINANCIAL DATA:

FISCAL YEAR	TOT. REVS. ($mill.)	NET INC. ($mill.)	TOT. ASSETS ($mill.)	OPER. PROFIT %	NET PROFIT %	RET. ON EQUITY %	RET. ON ASSETS %	CURR. RATIO	EARN. PER SH. $	CASH FL. PER SH. $	TANG. BK. VAL. $	DIV. PER SH. $	PRICE RANGE	AVG. P/E RATIO	AVG. YIELD %
p12/31/02	737.1	② 84.2							② 1.00			0.31	33.88 - 6.51	20.2	1.5
12/31/01	858.1	① 85.2	1,754.4	22.1	9.9	10.5	4.9	4.8	① 1.02	1.88	4.46	0.30	34.73 - 20.69	27.2	1.1
12/31/00	800.3	① 93.4	1,477.1	23.0	11.7	12.3	6.3	3.6	① 1.14	1.92	3.99	0.29	41.75 - 18.44	26.4	1.0
12/31/99	747.4	118.6	1,472.3	26.6	15.9	17.4	8.1	4.0	1.45	2.24	2.88	0.27	36.38 - 16.56	18.3	1.0
12/31/98	838.1	d352.1	1,356.4	...	...	...	...	2.2	d4.78	d4.09	1.60	0.23	52.25 - 13.81	...	0.7
12/31/97	752.2	113.9	1,491.7	16.7	15.1	14.3	7.6	3.9	1.69	2.05	7.98	0.21	37.33 - 13.00	14.9	0.8
12/31/96	614.1	86.9	778.7	18.6	14.2	27.6	11.2	3.2	1.51	1.97	5.62	0.15	18.67 - 11.33	9.9	1.0
12/31/95	507.9	67.3	518.3	18.3	13.3	41.5	13.0	3.1	1.47	1.77	3.43	0.18	16.06 - 7.97	8.2	1.5
12/31/94	366.9	d183.6	441.5	15.6	...	...	...	2.3	d4.52	d4.29	1.39	0.08	14.99 - 9.55	...	0.7
12/31/93	62.6	d11.9	207.9	...	...	...	...	1.7	d0.33	d0.13	...	...	... - ...	...	...

Statistics are as originally reported. Adj. for all stock splits through 3/98. ① Bef. extraord. loss of $3.2 mill., 2000; $21.1 mill., 2001. ② Bef. loss of $197.3 mill. from disc. ops. & acctg. chng. chrg. of $21.8 mill. & incl. non-recurr. chrgs. of $241.5 mill. and loss of $25.7 mill. on early exting. of debt.

OFFICERS:
R. W. O'Leary, Chmn., C.E.O.
T. C. Tyson, Pres., C.O.O.
B. G. Bailey, C.F.O.

INVESTOR CONTACT: Mariann Obanesian, Inv. Rel., (714) 545-0100 ext.3230

PRINCIPAL OFFICE: 3300 Hyland Avenue, Costa Mesa, CA 92626

TELEPHONE NUMBER: (714) 545-0100
FAX: (714) 641-7215
WEB: www.icnpharm.com
NO. OF EMPLOYEES: 11,970 (avg.)
SHAREHOLDERS: 6,865
ANNUAL MEETING: In May
INCORPORATED: CA, Dec., 1960; reincorp., DE, Oct., 1986

INSTITUTIONAL HOLDINGS:
No. of Institutions: 170
Shares Held: 64,368,857
% Held: 76.9

INDUSTRY: Pharmaceutical preparations (SIC: 2834)

TRANSFER AGENT(S): American Stock Transfer & Trust Company, New York, NY

IDACORP, INC.

EXCH.	SYM.	REC. PRICE	P/E RATIO	YLD.	MKT. CAP.	RANGE (52-WK.)	'02 Y/E PR.
NYSE	IDA	21.74 (2/28/03)	13.3	8.6%	$0.82 bill.	40.99 - 20.60	24.83

MEDIUM GRADE. EARNINGS FOR 2003 ARE EXPECTED TO RANGE BETWEEN $1.50 AND $1.70 PER SHARE.

*7 YEAR PRICE SCORE 90.0   ***12 MONTH PRICE SCORE 89.0**
*NYSE COMPOSITE INDEX=100

INTERIM EARNINGS (Per Share):

Qtr.	Mar.	June	Sept.	Dec.
1998	0.75	0.54	0.59	0.49
1999	0.78	0.56	0.59	0.49
2000	1.12	0.86	1.11	0.63
2001	0.93	0.96	0.91	0.55
2002	0.66	0.08	0.98	d0.08

INTERIM DIVIDENDS (Per Share):

Amt.	Decl.	Ex.	Rec.	Pay.
0.465Q	3/21/02	5/02/02	5/06/02	5/30/02
0.465Q	7/18/02	8/01/02	8/05/02	8/30/02
0.465Q	9/19/02	11/01/02	11/05/02	11/29/02
0.465Q	1/16/03	2/03/03	2/05/03	2/28/03
0.465Q	3/20/03	5/01/03	5/05/03	5/30/03

Indicated div.: $1.86 (Div. Reinv. Plan)

CAPITALIZATION (12/31/01):

	($000)	(%)
Long-Term Debt	843,000	36.6
Deferred Income Tax	590,000	25.6
Common & Surplus	871,000	37.8
Total	2,304,000	100.0

BUSINESS:

IDACORP, Inc. (formerly Idaho Power Corp.) is a holding company formed in 1998 as the parent of Idaho Power Company, a regulated electric utility, Ida-West Energy Company, an independent power project management and development company, IDACORP Energy Solutions, Inc, a marketer of energy and energy-related products and services, IdaTech, a developer of integrated fuel cell systems, IDACOMM, a provider of telecommunications services, and IDACORP Financial Services, which makes investments primarily in affordable housing projects. As of 12/31/02, Idaho Power Co. provided electric energy to 412,308 customers in over a 20,000-square-mile area of southern Idaho and eastern Oregon. IDA is a combination hydro-thermal utility with 17 hydroelectric plants and part owner in three coal-fired generating plants. In 1997, IDA expanded operations into wholesale marketing of natural gas through trading operations in Boise, Idaho and Houston, Texas.

RECENT DEVELOPMENTS:

For the year ended 12/31/02, net income dropped 50.7% to $61.7 million from $125.2 million the prior year. The decrease in earnings was attributed to the wind down of the Company's energy trading and marketing business, drought-related pressures on the utility's operation and the write-off of disallowed program costs, partially offset by a change in tax method accounting, which resulted in a one-time benefit of $34.7 million. Results for 2002 included a pre-tax non-recurring charge of $8.9 million and a charge of $12.0 million related to disallowed irrigation revenues. Total operating revenues slid 27.2% to $928.8 million versus $1.28 billion the year before.

PROSPECTS:

Going forward, IDA will focus on improving its regulated utility's operations and further strengthening of its balance sheet, liquidity, and credit rating. IDA expects these initiatives will enable it to rebuild earnings growth in 2004 and beyond. IDA expects earnings for 2003 in the range of $1.50 and $1.70 per share. Separately, IDA announced that the wind-down of IDACORP Energy remains on schedule. IDA noted that working capital and liquidity requirements, average value-at-risk, and staffing levels are significantly lower since the wind down strategy was announced.

ANNUAL FINANCIAL DATA:

FISCAL YEAR	TOT. REVS. ($mill.)	NET INC. ($mill.)	TOT. ASSETS ($mill.)	OPER. PROFIT %	NET PROFIT %	NET INC./ NET PROP. %	NET INC./ TOT. CAP. %	RET. ON EQUITY %	ACCUM. DEPR./ GROSS PROP. %	EARN. PER SH. $	TANG. BK. VAL. $	DIV. PER SH. $	DIV. PAYOUT %	PRICE RANGE			AVG. P/E RATIO	AVG. YIELD %
p12/31/02	③ 928.8	④ 61.7								④ 1.63		1.86	114.1	40.99	-	20.87	19.0	6.0
12/31/01	② 5,648.0	125.0	3,642.0	4.3	2.2	6.6	5.4	14.4	39.5	3.35	23.19	1.86	55.5	49.38	-	33.55	12.4	4.5
12/31/00	1,019.4	① 139.9	4,639.3	25.7	13.7	7.7	6.2	15.1	38.9	③ 3.72	21.85	1.86	50.0	53.00	-	25.94	10.6	4.7
12/31/99	658.3	91.3	2,637.0	26.2	13.9	5.2	4.3	10.6	38.1	2.43	20.02	1.86	76.5	36.50	-	26.00	12.9	6.0
12/31/98	1,122.0	89.2	2,451.6	17.0	7.9	5.2	4.0	10.7	37.1	2.37	19.42	1.86	78.5	38.06	-	29.88	14.3	5.5
12/31/97	748.5	92.3	2,405.4	24.7	12.3	5.4	4.7	11.3	35.4	2.32	18.93	1.86	80.2	37.75	-	28.50	14.3	5.6
12/31/96	578.4	90.6	2,295.3	32.4	15.7	5.3	4.6	11.3	34.4	2.21	18.47	1.86	84.2	34.25	-	27.25	13.9	6.0
12/31/95	545.6	86.9	2,241.8	32.3	15.9	5.2	4.6	10.7	33.2	2.10	18.15	1.86	88.6	30.00	-	23.38	12.7	7.0
12/31/94	543.7	74.9	2,191.8	27.5	13.8	4.5	4.0	9.3	31.9	1.80	17.91	1.86	103.3	30.63	-	21.75	14.5	7.1
12/31/93	540.4	84.5	2,097.4	30.0	15.6	5.2	4.6	10.6	31.1	2.14	17.86	1.86	86.9	33.00	-	27.25	14.1	6.2

Statistics are as originally reported. ① Incl. gain of $14.0 mill. from sale of assets. ② Revenues reflect gross amounts rather than net amounts used in prior-year periods. ③ Revenues reflect net amounts rather than gross amounts used in 2001 due to a change in acctg. requirements. ④ Incl. after-tax chrg. of $12.0 mill. for disallow of irrigation revs. & pre-tax non-recurr. chrgs. of $8.9 mill.

OFFICERS:
J. H. Miller, Chmn.
J. B. Packwood, Pres., C.E.O.
D. T. Anderson, V.P., C.F.O., Treas.
INVESTOR CONTACT: Lawrence F. Spencer, Dir. Inv. Rel., (208) 388-2664
PRINCIPAL OFFICE: 1221 West Idaho Street, Boise, ID 83702-5627

TELEPHONE NUMBER: (208) 388-2200
FAX: (208) 388-6916
WEB: www.idacorpinc.com
NO. OF EMPLOYEES: 1,999
SHAREHOLDERS: 20,910
ANNUAL MEETING: In May
INCORPORATED: ME, May, 1915; reincorp., ID, 1915

INSTITUTIONAL HOLDINGS:
No. of Institutions: 149
Shares Held: 11,582,947
% Held: 30.6

INDUSTRY: Electric services (SIC: 4911)

TRANSFER AGENT(S): IDACORP, Inc., Boise, Idaho

IDEX CORPORATION

EXCH.	SYM.	REC. PRICE	P/E RATIO	YLD.	MKT. CAP.	RANGE (52-WK.)	'02 Y/E PR.
NYSE	IEX	27.72 (2/28/03)	16.6	2.0%	$0.85 bill.	39.66 - 25.70	32.70

MEDIUM GRADE. THE COMPANY HAS INDICATED THAT IT WILL CONTINUE TO PURSUE ACQUISITIONS TO SPUR LONGER-TERM GROWTH.

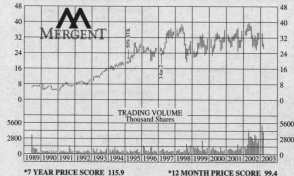

*7 YEAR PRICE SCORE 115.9   *12 MONTH PRICE SCORE 99.4
*NYSE COMPOSITE INDEX=100

INTERIM EARNINGS (Per Share):

Qtr.	Mar.	June	Sept.	Dec.
1998	0.46	0.50	0.47	0.39
1999	0.40	0.47	0.48	0.46
2000	0.52	0.57	0.54	0.44
2001	0.23	0.42	0.26	0.14
2002	0.37	0.48	0.45	0.37

INTERIM DIVIDENDS (Per Share):

Amt.	Decl.	Ex.	Rec.	Pay.
0.14Q	3/26/02	4/11/02	4/15/02	4/30/02
0.14Q	6/25/02	7/11/02	7/15/02	7/31/02
0.14Q	9/24/02	10/10/02	10/15/02	10/31/02
0.14Q	12/17/02	1/13/03	1/15/03	1/31/03
0.14Q	3/25/03	4/11/03	4/15/03	4/30/03

Indicated div.: $0.56

CAPITALIZATION (12/31/01):

	($000)	(%)
Long-Term Debt	291,820	42.1
Common & Surplus	401,112	57.9
Total	692,932	100.0

BUSINESS:

IDEX Corporation manufactures an array of proprietary, engineered industrial products sold to customers in a variety of industries around the world. IDEX's business segments include: The Pump Products Group, (58.6% of 2002 sales) designs, produces, and distributes a variety of industrial pumps, compressors, flow meters and related controls for the movement of liquids, air and gases. The Dispensing Equipment Group, (18.6%) produces engineered equipment for dispensing, metering and mixing colorants, paints, inks and dyes; refinishing equipment; and centralized lubrication systems. The Other Engineered Products Group, (22.8%) manufactures engineered banding and clamping devices, fire fighting pumps, rescue tools, and other components and systems for the fire and rescue industry.

RECENT DEVELOPMENTS:

For the year ended 12/31/02, net income was $54.1 million compared with $32.7 million a year earlier. Results included a credit of $203,000 for 2002 and a charge of $11.2 million for 2001 related to restructuring activity. Results for 2001 also included goodwill amortization of $14.2 million. Net sales rose 2.1% to $742.0 million from $726.9 million the previous year. IEX noted that acquisitions accounted for 3.0% of the sales improvement, and foreign currency translation added another 1.0%, which was partially offset by a 2.0% drop in the Company's base business. Domestic sales climbed 3.0% and international sales, net of foreign currency translation, fell 2.0%. For the twelve months ended 12/31/02, international sales were 41.0% of total sales versus 42.0% the year before.

PROSPECTS:

IEX's near-term prospects appear unfavorable, reflecting the absence of any order growth over the previous four quarters. IEX attributes the lack of order growth to weakness in the U.S. and other worldwide markets the Company serves. On the positive side, recent corporate initiatives, including global sourcing, e-business and utilization of cash flow to reduce debt and interest expense, should allow IEX to capitalize on the eventual economic recovery. IEX noted that it continues to roll out its IDEXconnect.com initiative to its pump distribution customers, with 75 distributors on-line and more scheduled for 2003. In addition, IEX will continue to pursue acquisitions to spur longer-term growth.

ANNUAL FINANCIAL DATA:

FISCAL YEAR	TOT. REVS. ($000)	NET INC. ($000)	TOT. ASSETS ($000)	OPER. PROFIT %	NET PROFIT %	RET. ON EQUITY %	RET. ON ASSETS %	CURR. RATIO	EARN. PER SH.$	CASH FL PER SH.$	DIV. PER SH.$	PRICE RANGE	AVG. P/E RATIO	AVG. YIELD %
p12/31/02	742,014	④ 54,112							④ 1.67		0.56	39.66 - 25.70	19.6	1.7
12/31/01	726,947	③ 32,710	838,804	10.1	4.5	8.2	3.9	2.5	③ 1.05	2.48	0.56	37.20 - 24.90	29.6	1.8
12/31/00	704,276	63,445	758,854	16.5	9.0	16.9	8.4	1.3	2.07	3.27	0.56	36.00 - 22.75	14.2	1.9
12/31/99	655,041	54,428	738,567	16.0	8.3	16.5	7.4	2.3	1.81	2.97	0.56	34.13 - 21.63	15.4	2.0
12/31/98	640,131	① 54,396	695,811	17.1	8.5	19.0	7.8	2.4	① 1.81	2.93	0.54	38.75 - 19.50	16.1	1.9
12/31/97	552,163	② 53,475	599,193	18.8	9.7	22.4	8.9	2.5	② 1.78	2.61	0.48	36.69 - 23.25	16.8	1.6
12/31/96	562,551	50,198	583,773	17.5	8.9	25.7	8.6	2.2	1.69	2.47	0.43	27.67 - 19.83	14.1	1.8
12/31/95	487,336	45,325	466,122	17.7	9.3	30.0	9.7	2.2	1.53	2.11	0.37	29.50 - 18.45	15.6	1.6
12/31/94	399,502	33,610	371,096	16.4	8.4	28.9	9.1	2.2	1.15	1.63	...	19.50 - 15.06	15.1	...
12/31/93	308,638	25,326	258,967	15.6	8.2	30.3	9.8	2.7	0.87	1.28	...	16.00 - 9.67	14.7	...

Statistics are as originally reported. Adj. for 3-for-2 stk. splits, 1/97 & 1/95. ① Bef. inc. fr. disc. ops. of $10.2 mill. & extraord. chrg. of $2.5 mill. ② Bef. inc. fr. disc. ops. of $5.2 mill. ($0.17/sh.) ③ Incl. restruct. chrg. of $11.2 mill. ④ Incl. restruct. credit of $203,000.

OFFICERS:
D. K. Williams, Chmn., Pres., C.E.O.
W. P. Sayatovic, Sr. V.P., C.F.O.
D. C. Lennox, V.P., Treas.

INVESTOR CONTACT: Wayne P. Sayatovic, Sr. V.P. (847) 498-7070

PRINCIPAL OFFICE: 630 Dundee Road, Northbrook, IL 60062

TELEPHONE NUMBER: (847) 498-7070
FAX: (847) 498-3940
WEB: www.idexcorp.com
NO. OF EMPLOYEES: 3,900 (approx.)
SHAREHOLDERS: 5,500 (approx.)
ANNUAL MEETING: In Mar.
INCORPORATED: DE, Sept., 1987

INSTITUTIONAL HOLDINGS:
No. of Institutions: 126
Shares Held: 27,609,320
% Held: 85.1

INDUSTRY: Pumps and pumping equipment (SIC: 3561)

TRANSFER AGENT(S): National City Bank Shareholder Services, Cleveland, OH

IDT CORPORATION

EXCH.	SYM.	REC. PRICE	P/E RATIO	YLD.	MKT. CAP.	RANGE (52-WK.)	'02 Y/E PR.
NYSE	IDTC	15.55 (2/28/03)	...	...	$1.23 bill.	23.32 - 15.05	17.29

LOWER MEDIUM GRADE. THE COMPANY HAS BEEN SELECTED AS THE EXCLUSIVE PREPAID CALLING CARD PROVIDER TO WALGREEN CO.

*7 YEAR PRICE SCORE 158.9   *12 MONTH PRICE SCORE 100.4

*NYSE COMPOSITE INDEX=100

INTERIM EARNINGS (Per Share):

Qtr.	Oct.	Jan.	Apr.	July
1997-98	------------------d0.10------------------			
1998-99	0.07	0.03	0.03	d0.48
1999-00	0.49	1.35	1.66	d0.41
2000-01	11.27	d1.77	d0.73	d2.44
2001-02	d0.16	d0.23	d0.64	d0.99
2002-03	d0.05	d0.16	...	...

INTERIM DIVIDENDS (Per Share):

Amt.	Decl.	Ex.	Rec.	Pay.
	No dividends paid.			

CAPITALIZATION (7/31/02):

	($000)	(%)
Capital Lease Obligations..	45,398	3.9
Deferred Income Tax	241,973	20.9
Common & Surplus	869,530	75.2
Total	1,156,901	100.0

BUSINESS:

IDT Corporation is a facilities-based, multinational carrier that provides a range of telecommunications services to retail and wholesale customers worldwide. IDT's operations are conducted through two main subsidiaries: IDT's telecommunications services, conducted by IDT Telecom, Inc., consists of retail services, including prepaid and rechargeable calling cards and international and domestic long distance services, as well as wholesale carrier services.

New venture related activities of IDT are conducted through IDT Media, Inc. In August 2000, IDT completed the sale of 14.9 million shares of Net2Phone to AT&T for about $1.10 billion in cash. On 10/23/01, IDT entered into an agreement to lead a consortium that would concentrate ownership of Net2Phone, Inc. On 12/19/01, IDT acquired certain of the U.S. voice and data assets of Winstar Communications, Inc.

RECENT DEVELOPMENTS:

For the quarter ended 1/31/03, IDT posted a net loss of $12.5 million versus a net loss of $17.2 million in the corresponding year-earlier period. Results for 2003 included a charge of $395,000 related to the settlement of litigation and restructuring, severance and impairment charges of $653,000. Revenues increased 20.5% to $450.8

million, fueled by gains from the Company's calling card, long distance and wholesale telecom operations. Excluding its Winstar division, acquired on 12/19/01, and Net2Phone, which was not consolidated during fiscal 2002, IDT's revenue would have increased 15.2%.

PROSPECTS:

IDT's near-term results should benefit from further expansion of its European calling card operations and continued aggressive growth of its early-stage South America calling card business. Looking ahead, IDT's recent decision to significantly increase its marketing and advertising expenditures in its consumer long distance business, in an attempt

to accelerate the growth of its customer base, should enhance long-term results. Separately, on 12/10/02, IDT announced that it has been selected as the exclusive prepaid calling card provider to Walgreen Co. IDT expects that this product will generate about $45.0 million in revenues over the next 12 months.

ANNUAL FINANCIAL DATA:

FISCAL YEAR	TOT. REVS. ($mill.)	NET INC. ($mill.)	TOT. ASSETS ($mill.)	OPER. PROFIT %	NET PROFIT %	RET. ON EQUITY %	RET. ON ASSETS %	CURR. RATIO	EARN. PER SH.$	CASH FL. PER SH.$	TANG. BK. VAL.$	PRICE RANGE	AVG. P/E RATIO
7/31/02	1,531.6	④ d156.4	1,607.9	...	...	...	...	3.1	④ d2.08	...	10.80	23.32 - 15.05	...
7/31/01	1,231.0	③ 532.4	1,881.3	...	43.2	49.5	28.3	3.8	③ 7.12	7.93	12.21	20.85 - 8.63	2.1
7/31/00	1,093.9	① 233.8	1,219.1	...	21.4	49.9	19.2	2.2	① 3.11	4.32	4.10	22.50 - 9.66	2.6
7/31/99	732.2	① 6.2	515.3	0.3	0.8	2.4	1.2	2.6	① d0.30	0.33	2.55	17.50 - 4.75	...
7/31/98	335.4	② d6.3	417.2	...	...	...	...	3.7	② d0.10	0.09	2.48	20.13 - 5.94	...
7/31/97	135.2	d3.8	58.5	...	...	...	...	1.2	d0.09	0.02	0.55	12.63 - 2.00	...
7/31/96	57.7	① d15.4	43.8	...	...	...	...	1.8	① d0.42	d0.39	0.64	8.75 - 3.38	...
7/31/95	11.7	d2.1	4.2	...	...	...	...	0.7	d0.06	d0.06	0.03	...	...
7/31/94	3.2	d0.3	2.8	...	...	...	...	2.8	d0.01	d0.01	0.07	...	...
7/31/93	1.7	0.3	...	18.2	18.1	...	...	...	0.01	0.01	...	...	...

Statistics are as originally reported. On 5/31/01, IDT issued a stk. div. of one sh. of Class B com. stk. for every share of com. stk. ① Excl. extraord. loss on retire. of debt of $3.0 mill.; 2000; $3.3 mill., 1999; $234,000, 1996. ② Incl. non-recurr. chrgs. of $25.0 mill. rel. to acquired R&D; bef. extraord. loss on retire. of debt of $132,000. ③ Incl. impair. chrg. of $199.4 mill. & gain of $1.04 bill. on sales of subsid. stk. ④ Incl. impair. chrg. of $114.3 mill.; bef. acctg. change chrg. of $147.0 mill.

OFFICERS:
H. S. Jonas, Chmn.
J. A. Courter, Vice-Chmn., C.E.O.
I. A. Greenstein, Pres.
INVESTOR CONTACT: Mary Jennings, Mgr., Inv. Rel., (973) 438-3124
PRINCIPAL OFFICE: 520 Broad Street, Newark, NJ 07102

TELEPHONE NUMBER: (973) 438-1000
FAX: (973) 438-1609
WEB: www.idt.net
NO. OF EMPLOYEES: 2,533 (avg.)
SHAREHOLDERS: 348 (approx.)
ANNUAL MEETING: In Dec.
INCORPORATED: NY, Aug., 1990; reincorp., DE, Dec., 1995

INSTITUTIONAL HOLDINGS:
No. of Institutions: 98
Shares Held: 14,156,028
% Held: 15.9
INDUSTRY: Computer integrated systems design (SIC: 7373)
TRANSFER AGENT(S): American Stock Transfer & Trust Company, New York, NY

IHOP CORP.

EXCH.	SYM.	REC. PRICE	P/E RATIO	YLD.	MKT. CAP.	RANGE (52-WK.)	'02 Y/E PR.
NYSE	IHP	22.55 (2/28/03)	11.7	...	$467.0 mill.	36.46 - 20.98	24.00

MEDIUM GRADE. IHP ANTICIPATES DILUTED EARNINGS PER SHARE RANGING FROM $1.55 TO $1.70 AND SYSTEM-WIDE SALES BETWEEN $1.55 BILLION AND $1.60 BILLION IN 2003.

*7 YEAR PRICE SCORE 144.1   ***12 MONTH PRICE SCORE 90.7**

*NYSE COMPOSITE INDEX=100

INTERIM EARNINGS (Per Share):

Qtr.	Mar.	June	Sept.	Dec.
1998	0.24	0.32	0.36	0.39
1999	0.33	0.39	0.42	0.44
2000	0.36	0.41	0.50	0.48
2001	0.37	0.49	0.53	0.55
2002	0.46	0.44	0.46	0.56

INTERIM DIVIDENDS (Per Share):

Amt.	Decl.	Ex.	Rec.	Pay.
		No dividends paid.		

CAPITALIZATION (12/31/01):

	($000)	(%)
Long-Term Debt	50,209	8.4
Capital Lease Obligations..	175,177	29.3
Deferred Income Tax	59,084	9.9
Common & Surplus	312,430	52.3
Total	596,900	100.0

BUSINESS:

IHOP Corp. and its subsidiaries develop, franchise and operate International House of Pancakes family restaurants. IHOP restaurants offer a diverse menu for breakfast, lunch and dinner, including more than 16 types of pancakes, as well as omelets, burgers, chicken and steaks. Franchisees and area licensees are third-party operators who operate more than 90.0% of IHOP restaurants and actively participate in day-to-day operations. As of 12/31/02, there were 1,070 IHOP restaurants in the chain located in 45 states and Canada, of which 866 were operated by franchisees, 125 by an area licensee and 79 by the Company. In 2002, IHP had system-wide restaurant sales of $1.48 billion.

RECENT DEVELOPMENTS:

For the year ended 12/31/02, net income improved 1.4% to $40.8 million compared with $40.3 million the year before. System-wide sales increased 9.9% to $1.48 billion from $1.35 billion in 2001. Total revenues advanced 12.8% to $365.9 million from $324.4 million a year earlier. Revenues from franchise operations rose 14.3% to $238.4 million, while sales of franchises and equipment advanced 12.8% to $53.0 million. Revenues for the Company's operations were up 8.2% to $74.4 million. System-wide comparable store sales increased 0.7% year over year. Total costs and expenses climbed 11.7% to $300.5 million, or 82.1% of revenues, from $260.0 million, or 80.1% of revenues, in the previous year.

PROSPECTS:

In January 2003, the Company announced that it plans to transition from company-financed development of new restaurants to a traditional franchise development model during 2003. As a result, IHP intends to develop 55 to 60 company-financed restaurants and 20 to 25 franchise developed restaurants in 2003. Additionally, the Company anticipates diluted earnings per share ranging from $1.55 to $1.70 and system-wide sales between $1.55 billion and $1.60 billion in 2003. Free cash flow is also expected to improve to between a negative $25.0 million and negative $35.0 million as IHP substantially reduces capital expenditures. This compares with negative free cash flow of $63.5 million in 2002.

ANNUAL FINANCIAL DATA:

FISCAL YEAR	TOT. REVS. ($000)	NET INC. ($000)	TOT. ASSETS ($000)	OPER. PROFIT %	NET PROFIT %	RET. ON EQUITY %	RET. ON ASSETS %	CURR. RATIO	EARN.* PER SH. $	CASH FL. PER SH. $	TANG. BK. VAL. $	PRICE RANGE	AVG. P/E RATIO
p12/31/02	365,874	40,848	819,800						1.92			36.46 - 21.08	15.0
12/31/01	324,436	40,288	641,429	26.3	12.4	12.9	6.3	1.3	1.94	2.65	14.57	31.03 - 18.90	12.9
12/31/00	303,244	35,338	562,212	26.3	11.7	13.6	6.3	1.0	1.74	2.41	12.43	22.63 - 13.63	10.4
12/31/99	273,235	32,125	520,402	26.4	11.8	14.2	6.2	1.0	1.58	2.18	10.68	26.00 - 14.94	13.0
12/31/98	256,208	26,111	445,899	24.1	10.2	13.9	5.9	0.9	1.31	1.87	8.90	23.75 - 14.75	14.7
12/31/97	215,458	20,914	382,593	31.3	9.7	13.4	5.5	1.0	1.08	1.59	7.40	18.69 - 11.81	14.2
12/31/96	190,096	18,604	328,889	30.4	9.8	14.4	5.7	1.2	0.98	1.41	6.15	14.94 - 9.63	12.6
12/31/95	164,323	② 16,154	252,057	30.5	9.8	14.9	6.4	1.0	② 0.85	1.22	5.06	15.25 - 10.25	15.0
12/31/94	149,994	15,115	202,553	29.6	10.1	17.1	7.5	1.2	0.80	1.14	4.06	16.88 - 11.25	17.6
12/31/93	142,545	① 10,733	180,026	26.8	7.5	15.1	6.0	1.2	① 0.58	0.88	3.13	15.63 - 9.19	21.6

Statistics are as originally reported. Adj. for 2-for-1 stk. split, 5/99. ① Incl. non-recurr. chrg. $2.5 mill. ② Incl. one-time chrg. of $800,000.

OFFICERS:
L. A. Kay, Chmn.
J. A. Stewart, Pres., C.E.O.
A. S. Unger, C.F.O.
INVESTOR CONTACT: Alan S. Unger, C.F.O., (919) 240-6055
PRINCIPAL OFFICE: 450 North Brand Boulevard, Glendale, CA 91203-1903

TELEPHONE NUMBER: (818) 240-6055
FAX: (818) 247-0694
WEB: www.ihop.com
NO. OF EMPLOYEES: 3,921 (avg.)
SHAREHOLDERS: 4,554 (approx.)
ANNUAL MEETING: In May
INCORPORATED: DE, 1976

INSTITUTIONAL HOLDINGS:
No. of Institutions: 99
Shares Held: 18,682,183
% Held: 88.9
INDUSTRY: Patent owners and lessors (SIC: 6794)
TRANSFER AGENT(S): Mellon Investor Services, LLC, South Hackensack, NJ

IKON OFFICE SOLUTIONS, INC.

EXCH.	SYM.	REC. PRICE	P/E RATIO	YLD.	MKT. CAP.	RANGE (52-WK.)	'02 Y/E PR.
NYSE	IKN	7.01 (2/28/03)	7.2	2.3%	$1.01 bill.	14.24 - 6.38	7.15

LOWER MEDIUM GRADE. THE COMPANY WILL CONTINUE TO PHASE OUT ITS DISTRIBUTION OF LOW-MARGIN TECHNOLOGY HARDWARE THROUGHOUT FISCAL 2003.

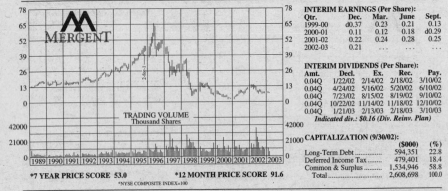

*7 YEAR PRICE SCORE 53.0   ***12 MONTH PRICE SCORE 91.6**

*NYSE COMPOSITE INDEX=100

INTERIM EARNINGS (Per Share):

Qtr.	Dec.	Mar.	June	Sept.
1999-00	d0.37	0.23	0.21	0.13
2000-01	0.11	0.12	0.18	d0.29
2001-02	0.22	0.24	0.28	0.25
2002-03	0.21	...	...	...

INTERIM DIVIDENDS (Per Share):

Amt.	Decl.	Ex.	Rec.	Pay.
0.04Q	1/22/02	2/14/02	2/18/02	3/10/02
0.04Q	4/24/02	5/16/02	5/20/02	6/10/02
0.04Q	7/23/02	8/15/02	8/19/02	9/10/02
0.04Q	10/22/02	11/14/02	11/18/02	12/10/02
0.04Q	1/21/03	2/13/03	2/18/03	3/10/03

Indicated div.: $0.16 (Div. Reinv. Plan)

CAPITALIZATION (9/30/02):

	($000)	(%)
Long-Term Debt	594,351	22.8
Deferred Income Tax	479,401	18.4
Common & Surplus	1,534,946	58.8
Total	2,608,698	100.0

BUSINESS:

IKON Office Solutions, Inc. provides products and services including copiers and printers, color solutions, distributed printing, facilities management, imaging and legal document services, as well as network design and consulting and e-business development. As of 1/23/03, the Company had approximately 600 locations worldwide, including locations in the United States, Canada, Mexico, the United Kingdom, France, Germany, Ireland and Denmark. IKN primarily distributes equipment made by Canon, Ricoh, Hewlett-Packard and Oce. The Company customers include large and small businesses, professional firms and government agencies.

RECENT DEVELOPMENTS:

For the quarter ended 12/31/02, net income decreased 0.3% to $32.5 million compared with $32.6 million in the corresponding prior-year quarter. Total revenues declined 6.1% to $1.14 billion from $1.21 billion a year earlier, primarily due to downsizing and exit strategies employed during the first quarter of the previous year. Net sales dropped 7.4% to $526.8 million, while revenues from services fell 6.0% to $515.3 million. Finance income increased 1.9% to $94.9 million. Gross profit as a percentage of revenues rose to 39.4% from 38.6% the year before.

PROSPECTS:

IKN anticipates continued execution of major initiatives that should provide significant long-term benefits, such as phasing out the distribution of low-margin technology hardware, which is expected to continue throughout fiscal 2003. For 2003, IKN expects to deliver only modest improvements in margins as a result of the uncertain economy and the need to dedicate additional resources to long-term revenue and profit building opportunities, such as the Company's e-IKON implementation. Earnings are expected in the range of $0.94 to $0.98 per diluted share in fiscal 2003. Revenues are expected to decline 2.0% to 4.0% for the year, including a likely decline in technology hardware sales of between $120.0 million and $150.0 million.

ANNUAL FINANCIAL DATA:

FISCAL YEAR	TOT. REVS. ($mill.)	NET INC. ($mill.)	TOT. ASSETS ($mill.)	OPER. PROFIT %	NET PROFIT %	RET. ON EQUITY %	RET. ON ASSETS %	CURR. RATIO	EARN. PER SH.$	CASH FL. PER SH.$	TANG. BK. VAL.$	DIV. PER SH.$	PRICE RANGE	AVG. P/E RATIO	AVG. YIELD %
9/30/02	4,827.5	② 150.3	6,472.6	6.1	3.1	9.8	2.3	1.2	② 0.99	1.81	2.08	0.16	14.25 — 6.38	10.4	1.6
9/30/01	5,273.5	③ 14.0	6,291.0	2.6	0.3	1.0	0.2	1.1	③ 0.10	1.33	0.97	0.16	11.84 — 2.19	70.1	2.3
9/30/00	5,446.9	⑦ 26.0	6,362.6	2.7	0.5	1.8	0.4	1.1	⑦ 0.18	1.49	0.87	0.16	9.38 — 2.00	31.6	2.8
9/30/99	5,522.1	⑥ 33.8	5,801.3	2.7	0.6	2.3	0.6	1.1	⑥ 0.23	1.55	0.50	0.16	16.38 — 5.38	47.3	1.5
9/30/98	5,628.7	⑤ d83.0	5,748.8	...	...	...	...	1.3	⑤ d0.76	0.74	...	0.16	36.25 — 5.00	...	0.8
9/30/97	5,128.4	④ 122.4	5,323.9	5.1	2.4	8.3	2.3	1.5	④ 0.77	1.95	...	0.16	46.63 — 20.63	43.7	0.5
9/30/96	4,099.8	① 164.9	5,239.7	7.6	4.0	7.3	3.1	1.2	① 1.13	2.07	6.67	0.56	66.00 — 37.38	45.7	1.1
9/30/95	3,091.6	① 115.0	3,950.4	6.9	3.7	6.1	2.8	1.1	① 0.86	1.61	5.41	0.53	47.13 — 30.94	45.4	1.4
9/30/94	7,996.1	70.6	3,502.3	4.3	0.9	5.2	2.0	1.6	0.55	1.45	3.85	0.51	32.75 — 24.75	52.3	1.8
9/30/93	6,444.6	① ② 7.6	3,348.9	1.4	0.1	0.7	0.2	1.5	① ② d0.02	0.82	1.36	0.48	27.38 — 17.88	...	2.1

Statistics are as originally reported. Adj. for 2-for-1 stock split, 10/95. ① Bef. inc. from disc. ops. of $7.5 mill., 1993; dr$16.5 mill.; 1995; & dr$45.8 mill. reflect. spin-off of Unisource, 1996. ② Incl. pre-tax chrg. of $175.0 mill. ③ Reflects spin-off of Unisource. ④ Bef. inc. fr. disc. ops. of $20.2 mill. & $12.2 mill. extraord. chrg.; incl. transf. costs of $126.9 mill. ⑤ Bef. inc. fr. disc. ops. of $10.0 mill.; incl. non-recurr. costs of $228.4 mill. ⑥ Incl. cost of $101.1 mill. fr. litigation settlement. ⑦ Bef. extraord. gain of $1.7 mill. & disc. oper. gain of $1.4 mill.; incl. net non-recurr. costs of $84.4 mill. ⑧ Bef. gain of $1.2 mill. fr. disc. ops.; incl. pre-tax net restruct. & asset impairment chrgs. of $60.0 mill. ⑨ Incl. restr. gain of $10.5 mill.

OFFICERS:
M. J. Espe, Chmn., Pres., C.E.O.
W. S. Urkiel, Sr. V.P., C.F.O.
D. H. Liu, Sr. V.P., Gen. Couns., Sec.

INVESTOR CONTACT: Veronica L. Rosa, Investor Relations, (610) 408-7196

PRINCIPAL OFFICE: P.O. Box 834, Valley Forge, PA 19482-0834

TELEPHONE NUMBER: (610) 296-8000
FAX: (610) 644-1574
WEB: www.ikon.com
NO. OF EMPLOYEES: 33,200 (approx.)
SHAREHOLDERS: 12,853 (approx.)
ANNUAL MEETING: In Feb.
INCORPORATED: OH, Nov., 1952

INSTITUTIONAL HOLDINGS:
No. of Institutions: 164
Shares Held: 96,481,767
% Held: 66.7
INDUSTRY: Computers, peripherals & software (SIC: 5045)
TRANSFER AGENT(S): National City Bank, Cleveland, OH

ILLINOIS TOOL WORKS, INCORPORATED

EXCH.	SYM.	REC. PRICE	P/E RATIO	YLD.	MKT. CAP.	RANGE (52-WK.)	'02 Y/E PR.	DIV. ACH.
NYSE	ITW	59.57 (2/28/03)	19.7	1.5%	$18.28 bill.	77.80 - 55.03	64.86	40 yrs.

INVESTMENT GRADE. THE COMPANY EXPECTS FULL-YEAR 2003 EARNINGS PER DILUTED SHARE IN THE RANGE OF $3.02 TO $3.42.

TRADING VOLUME
Thousand Shares

| 1989 | 1990 | 1991 | 1992 | 1993 | 1994 | 1995 | 1996 | 1997 | 1998 | 1999 | 2000 | 2001 | 2002 | 2003 |

*7 YEAR PRICE SCORE 120.9   ***12 MONTH PRICE SCORE 102.3**

NYSE COMPOSITE INDEX=100

INTERIM EARNINGS (Per Share):

Qtr.	Mar.	June	Sept.	Dec.
1997	0.49	0.61	0.59	0.64
1998	0.59	0.70	0.65	0.73
1999	0.65	0.79	0.74	0.59
2000	0.72	0.90	0.87	0.66
2001	0.60	0.76	0.65	0.61
2002	0.63	0.86	0.80	0.74

INTERIM DIVIDENDS (Per Share):

Amt.	Decl.	Ex.	Rec.	Pay.
0.22Q	2/15/02	3/26/02	3/31/02	4/19/02
0.22Q	5/10/02	6/26/02	6/30/02	7/19/02
0.23Q	8/09/02	9/26/02	9/30/02	10/18/02
0.23Q	10/24/02	12/27/02	12/31/02	1/27/03
0.23Q	2/14/03	3/27/03	3/31/03	4/21/03

Indicated div.: $0.92 (Div. Reinv. Plan)

CAPITALIZATION (12/31/01):

	($000)	(%)
Long-Term Debt	1,267,141	17.3
Common & Surplus	6,040,738	82.7
Total	7,307,879	100.0

BUSINESS:

Illinois Tool Works, Incorporated manufactures and markets a variety of products and systems. As of 1/29/03, ITW had more than 600 operations in 44 countries. The Engineered Products-North America segment (30.8% of net sales for 2001) and the Engineered Products-International segment (15.3%) manufacture short lead-time components and fasteners, and specialty products. Specialty Systems-North America segment (35.1%) produces longer lead-time machinery and specialty equipment. The Specialty Systems-International segment (17.3%) manufactures longer lead-time machinery and specialty equipment for industrial spray coating and other applications. The Leasing and Investments segment (1.5%) makes investments in mortgage-related assets, equipment leases and property. ITW acquired Premark International, Inc. in November 1999 for $3.40 billion.

RECENT DEVELOPMENTS:

For the year ended 12/31/02, net income increased 16.1% to $931.8 million, before an accounting change charge of $221.9 million, compared with net income of $802.4 million in 2001. Results for 2002 and 2001 excluded income from discontinued operations of $2.7 million and $3.2 million, respectively. Results for 2002 and 2001 included amortization and impairment of goodwill and other intangibles of $27.9 million and $104.6 million, respectively. Operating revenues rose 1.9% to $9.47 billion versus $9.29 billion in 2001 due to acquisitions. Operating income climbed 15.3% to $1.50 billion from $1.31 billion a year earlier, reflecting higher revenues and reduced costs, primarily in the automotive and general industrial businesses.

PROSPECTS:

Looking ahead, the Company expects full-year 2003 income per diluted share from continuing operations in the range of $3.02 to $3.42. In addition, the Company is now forecasting first quarter 2003 income per diluted share from continuing operations in the range of $0.59 to $0.69. These forecasts are predicated on base business revenue assumptions ranging from a year-over-year decline of 2.0% to a year-over-year increase of 2.0%.

ANNUAL FINANCIAL DATA:

FISCAL YEAR	TOT. REVS. ($mill.)	NET INC. ($mill.)	TOT. ASSETS ($mill.)	OPER. PROFIT %	NET PROFIT %	RET. ON EQUITY %	RET. ON ASSETS %	CURR. RATIO	EARN. PER SH. $	CASH FL. PER SH. $	TANG. BK. VAL. $	DIV. PER SH. $	PRICE RANGE	AVG. P/E RATIO	AVG. YIELD %
p12/31/02	9,467.7	③ 931.8							③ 3.02			0.89	77.80 - 55.03	22.0	1.3
12/31/01	9,292.8	② 802.4	9,822.3	14.1	8.6	13.3	8.2	2.1	② 2.62	3.88	10.82	0.82	71.99 - 49.15	23.1	1.4
12/31/00	9,983.6	958.0	9,603.5	15.7	9.6	17.7	10.0	1.8	3.15	4.50	9.64	0.74	69.00 - 49.50	18.8	1.2
12/31/99	9,333.2	① 841.1	9,060.3	15.1	9.0	17.5	9.3	1.6	① 2.76	3.89	9.27	0.63	82.00 - 58.13	25.4	0.9
12/31/98	5,647.9	672.8	6,118.2	19.1	11.9	20.2	11.0	1.5	2.67	3.50	8.59	0.51	73.19 - 45.19	22.2	0.9
12/31/97	5,220.4	587.0	5,394.8	17.6	11.2	20.9	10.9	1.6	2.33	3.07	8.14	0.43	59.50 - 37.38	20.8	0.9
12/31/96	4,996.7	486.3	4,806.2	16.0	9.7	20.3	10.1	1.4	1.97	2.68	6.80	0.35	43.63 - 25.94	17.7	1.0
12/31/95	4,152.2	387.6	3,613.1	15.1	9.3	20.1	10.7	1.8	1.65	2.29	5.94	0.31	32.75 - 19.88	16.0	1.2
12/31/94	3,461.3	277.8	2,580.5	13.7	8.0	18.0	10.8	2.0	1.23	1.81	5.03	0.27	22.75 - 18.50	16.8	1.3
12/31/93	3,159.2	206.6	2,336.9	11.7	6.5	16.4	8.8	2.0	0.92	1.50	3.95	0.24	20.25 - 16.25	19.9	1.3

Statistics are as originally reported. Adj. for stk. splits: 2-for-1, 6/93 & 5/97. ① Incl. Premark International, Inc. merger-related costs of $81.0 mill. ② Excl. inc. from discont. oper. of $3.2 mill. ③ Excl. acctg. change charge of $221.9 mill., income from discont. oper. of $2.3 mill., but incl. amort. and impairment of goodwill & other intangibles of $27.9 mill.

OFFICERS:
W. J. Farrell, Chmn., C.E.O.
F. S. Ptak, Vice-Chmn.
J. C. Kinney, Sr. V.P., C.F.O.
S. S. Hudnut, Sr. V.P., Gen. Couns., Sec.
INVESTOR CONTACT: Investor Relations, (847) 724-7500
PRINCIPAL OFFICE: 3600 West Lake Avenue, Glenview, IL 60025-5811

TELEPHONE NUMBER: (847) 724-7500
FAX: (847) 657-4261
WEB: www.itw.com
NO. OF EMPLOYEES: 52,000 (approx.)
SHAREHOLDERS: 15,330 (approx.)
ANNUAL MEETING: In May
INCORPORATED: DE, June, 1961

INSTITUTIONAL HOLDINGS:
No. of Institutions: 587
Shares Held: 236,530,442
% Held: 77.2

INDUSTRY: Plastics products, nec (SIC: 3089)

TRANSFER AGENT(S): Computershare Investor Service, L.L.C., Chicago, IL

IMC GLOBAL, INC.

EXCH.	SYM.	REC. PRICE	P/E RATIO	YLD.	MKT. CAP.	RANGE (52-WK.)	'02 Y/E PR.
NYSE	IGL	8.81 (2/28/03)	88.1	0.9%	$1.01 bill.	15.55 - 7.89	10.67

LOWER MEDIUM GRADE. THE COMPANY IS INTRODUCING TWO NEW COST-SAVINGS INITIATIVES DESIGNED TO GENERATE ANNUAL COST SAVINGS OF $80.0 MILLION BY 2005.

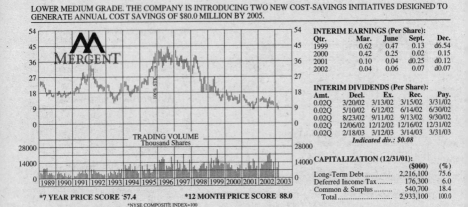

*7 YEAR PRICE SCORE `57.4   ***12 MONTH PRICE SCORE 88.0**
*NYSE COMPOSITE INDEX=100

INTERIM EARNINGS (Per Share):

Qtr.	Mar.	June	Sept.	Dec.
1999	0.62	0.47	0.13	d6.54
2000	0.42	0.25	0.02	0.15
2001	0.10	0.04	d0.25	d0.12
2002	0.04	0.06	0.07	d0.07

INTERIM DIVIDENDS (Per Share):

Amt.	Decl.	Ex.	Rec.	Pay.
0.02Q	3/20/02	3/13/02	3/15/02	3/31/02
0.02Q	5/10/02	6/12/02	6/14/02	6/30/02
0.02Q	8/23/02	9/11/02	9/13/02	9/30/02
0.02Q	12/06/02	12/12/02	12/16/02	12/31/02
0.02Q	2/18/03	3/12/03	3/14/03	3/31/03

Indicated div.: $0.08

CAPITALIZATION (12/31/01):

	($000)	(%)
Long-Term Debt	2,216,100	75.6
Deferred Income Tax	176,300	6.0
Common & Surplus	540,700	18.4
Total	2,933,100	100.0

BUSINESS:

IMC Global, Inc. is a producer and distributor of crop nutrients to the international agricultural community and a manufacturer and distributor of animal feed ingredients to the worldwide industry. IGL mines, processes and distributes potash in the United States and Canada and is the majority joint venture partner in IMC-Agrico Company, a producer, marketer and distributor of phosphate crop nutrients and animal feed ingredients. IGL's current operational structure consists of continuing business units corresponding to its major product lines, IMC Phosfeed (62.4% of 2002 revenues) and IMC Potash (37.6%).

RECENT DEVELOPMENTS:

For the year ended 12/31/02, the Company reported earnings of $11.5 million, before a loss from discontinued operations of $96.4 million, compared with a loss of $27.9 million, before an accounting change charge of $24.5 million, in the previous year. Also, earnings for 2002 and 2001 excluded extraordinary charges of $600,000 and $14.1 million, respectively. Results for 2001 included restructuring and other non-recurring charges of $15.6 million. Net sales increased 5.0% to $2.06 billion from $1.96 billion a year earlier. IMC Phosfeed sales advanced 7.4%, reflecting a 3.1% rise in volume and an increase of 7.0% in average diammonium phosphate prices to $137 per ton. IMC Potash sales slipped 0.7% to $805.9 million, due to lower prices, partially offset by higher potash volumes.

PROSPECTS:

The Company recently announced two new cost-savings initiatives. An organizational restructuring program, scheduled to be implemented before 4/1/03, will focus on reducing overhead levels and costs through rightsizing and efficiency improvements. The second initiative is a multi-year program that is expected to result in increased efficiency, reduced costs and revenue enhancements through core business process redesign and maximization. The programs are targeted to generate total pre-tax annual savings of $80.0 million by 2005.

ANNUAL FINANCIAL DATA:

FISCAL YEAR	TOT. REVS. ($mil.)	NET INC. ($mil.)	TOT. ASSETS ($mil.)	OPER. PROFIT %	NET PROFIT %	RET. ON EQUITY %	RET. ON ASSETS %	CURR. RATIO	EARN. PER SH.$	CASH FL. PER SH.$	TANG. BK. VAL.$	DIV. PER SH.$	PRICE RANGE		AVG. P/E RATIO	AVG. YIELD %
p12/31/02	2,057.4	[11] 11.5							[11] 0.10				0.08	15.55	8.52	120.4	0.7
12/31/01	1,958.7	[10] d27.9	4,248.9	4.9	...	...	...	1.5	[10] d0.24	1.20	4.70	0.08	16.69	8.00	...	0.6
12/31/00	2,095.9	[9] 84.3	4,261.6	11.0	4.0	12.5	2.0	0.9	[9] 0.73	2.23	5.88	0.32	19.38	11.00	20.8	2.1
12/31/99	2,369.3	[8] d611.1	5,195.9	...	...	...	...	1.9	[8] d5.33	d3.31	9.43	0.32	27.13	12.75	...	1.6
12/31/98	2,696.2	[7] 57.1	6,456.9	13.8	2.1	3.1	0.9	1.6	[7] 0.50	2.69	16.27	0.32	39.50	17.81	57.3	1.1
[6] 12/31/97	2,988.6	[5] 87.8	4,673.9	10.1	2.9	4.5	1.9	1.6	[5] 0.93	2.86	16.98	0.32	42.50	29.63	38.8	0.9
6/30/97	2,982.0	[4] 204.5	3,611.6	17.5	6.9	15.3	5.7	2.4	[4] 2.15	4.09	14.32	0.32	42.50	29.63	16.8	0.9
6/30/96	2,981.0	[3] 144.3	3,436.8	16.4	4.8	12.5	4.2	2.5	[3] 1.56	3.38	12.53	0.32	44.50	32.25	24.6	0.8
6/30/95	1,924.0	[2] 127.1	2,693.2	19.8	6.6	16.7	4.7	2.0	[2] 2.15	4.46	12.92	0.28	40.88	20.63	14.3	0.9
6/30/94	1,441.5	[1] d3.6	2,778.3	11.6	...	...	...	2.6	[1] d0.07	2.35	11.12	...	24.63	15.38	...	...

Statistics are as originally reported. Adj. for 100% stk. div., 12/95 [1] Bef. ext. loss $25.2 mill. [2] Bef. ext. loss $6.5 mill. & acctg. chrg. $5.9 mill. [3] Incl. non-recurr. chrg. $43.3 mill. [4] Bef. ext. loss $11.4 mill. [5] Bef. ext. loss $24.9 mill., but incl. non-recurr. chrg. $183.7 mill. [6] For six months due to fiscal year end change [7] Bef. disc. ops. loss $69.1 mill. and ext. gain $3.0 mill.; incl. non-recurr. chrg. $176,100 [8] Bef. disc. ops. loss $155.2 mill., ext. gain $500,000 & acctg. chrg. $7.5 mill. [9] Bef. disc. ops. loss $37.6 mill.; incl. pre-tax restr. credit $1.2 mill. [10] Bef. ext. chrg. $14.1 mill. & acctg. change chrg. $24.5 mill.; incl. pre-tax restr. chrg. $11.0 mill. [11] Bef. disc. fr. disc. ops. $96.4 mill. and ext. chrg. $600,000.

OFFICERS:
D. A. Pertz, Chmn., C.E.O.
J. J. Ferguson, Pres., C.O.O.
J. R. Porter, Exec. V.P., C.F.O.

INVESTOR CONTACT: David A. Prichard, V.P., Investor Relations, (847) 739-1810

PRINCIPAL OFFICE: 100 South Saunders Road, Lake Forest, IL 60045

TELEPHONE NUMBER: (847) 739-1200
FAX: (847) 739-1617
WEB: www.imcglobal.com
NO. OF EMPLOYEES: 5,194 (avg.)
SHAREHOLDERS: 5,495 (record)
ANNUAL MEETING: In May
INCORPORATED: DE, Jan., 1987

INSTITUTIONAL HOLDINGS:
No. of Institutions: 179
Shares Held: 107,101,414
% Held: 93.2

INDUSTRY: Phosphatic fertilizers (SIC: 2874)

TRANSFER AGENT(S): American Stock Transfer & Trust Company, New York, NY

IMS HEALTH, INC.

EXCH.	SYM.	REC. PRICE	P/E RATIO	YLD.	MKT. CAP.	RANGE (52-WK.)	'02 Y/E PR.
NYSE	RX	15.00 (2/28/03)	16.7	0.5%	$4.22 bill.	22.59 - 12.90	16.00

MEDIUM GRADE. ON 2/7/03, THE COMPANY ANNOUNCED THE COMPLETION OF THE EXCHANGE OFFER TO DISTRIBUTE RX'S MAJORITY INTEREST IN COGNIZANT.

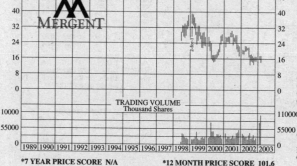

TRADING VOLUME
Thousand Shares

1989 1990 1991 1992 1993 1994 1995 1996 1997 1998 1999 2000 2001 2002 2003

*7 YEAR PRICE SCORE N/A   *12 MONTH PRICE SCORE 101.6
*NYSE COMPOSITE INDEX=100

INTERIM EARNINGS (Per Share):

Qtr.	Mar.	June	Sept.	Dec.
1999	0.18	0.15	0.22	0.28
2000	0.27	0.17	d0.20	0.14
2001	0.22	0.21	0.27	d0.11
2002	0.20	0.21	0.27	0.22

INTERIM DIVIDENDS (Per Share):

Amt.	Decl.	Ex.	Rec.	Pay.
0.02Q	4/16/02	4/26/02	4/30/02	6/07/02
0.02Q	7/08/02	7/19/02	7/23/02	8/30/02
0.02Q	10/15/02	10/25/02	10/29/02	12/06/02
0.02Q	2/11/03	2/21/03	2/25/03	3/31/03

Indicated div.: $0.08

CAPITALIZATION (12/31/01):

	($000)	(%)
Long-Term Debt	150,000	40.7
Common & Surplus	218,366	59.3
Total	368,366	100.0

BUSINESS:

IMS Health, Inc. provides information applications to the pharmaceutical and healthcare industries in more than 100 countries. RX was formed as a result of its spin-off from the Cognizant Corporation on 7/1/98. The Core IMS segment consists of IMS, a provider of information and decision support services including market research, sales management services, sales force automation, and other professional services to pharmaceutical and healthcare industries. In 2/03, RX completed the exchange offer to distribute RX's majority interest in Cognizant Technology Solutions, a provider of software services. On 7/26/99, RX completed the spin-off of the majority of its equity investment in Gartner Group Inc. During 2000, RX discontinued its Transaction Business segment, which consisted of Erisco Managed Care Technologies, Synavant, Inc. and three small non-strategic software businesses.

RECENT DEVELOPMENTS:

For the year ended 12/31/02, net income was $266.1 million compared with income of $138.4 million, before income of $47.0 million from discontinued operations, the previous year. Earnings for 2002 and 2001 included nonrecurring items that resulted in net losses of $7.0 million and $220.1 million, respectively. Total revenues climbed 7.1% to $1.43 billion from $1.33 billion the year before. Total IMS segment revenues rose 3.9% to $1.22 billion, while revenues from Cognizant Technology Solutions increased 31.3% to $208.7 million.

PROSPECTS:

On 2/7/03, the Company and Cognizant Technology Solutions jointly announced the completion of the exchange offer to distribute RX's majority interest in Cognizant. Following the exchange, RX will have reduced its shares outstanding by approximately 13.0%. Meanwhile, the Company should be well-positioned to take advantage of growth opportunities in the coming year, aided by the Company's investments in its core business, entrance into new markets and the launch of new offerings.

ANNUAL FINANCIAL DATA:

FISCAL YEAR	TOT. REVS. ($mill.)	NET INC. ($mill.)	TOT. ASSETS ($mill.)	OPER. PROFIT %	NET PROFIT %	RET. ON EQUITY %	RET. ON ASSETS %	CURR. RATIO	EARN. PER SH.$	CASH FL. PER SH.$	TANG. BK. VAL.$	DIV. PER SH.$	PRICE RANGE	AVG. P/E RATIO	AVG. YIELD %
p12/31/02	**1,428.1**	⑧ **266.1**							⑧ **0.93**			0.08	22.59 - 12.90	19.1	0.5
12/31/01	1,332.9	⑦ 138.4	1,367.6	24.3	10.4	63.4	10.1	1.0	⑦ 0.46	0.69	...	0.08	30.50 - 17.30	51.9	0.3
12/31/00	1,424.4	⑥ 116.1	1,243.0	9.6	8.2	112.2	9.3	0.7	⑥ 0.39	0.69	...	0.08	28.69 - 14.25	55.0	0.4
12/31/99	1,398.0	⑤ 250.4	1,450.8	24.3	17.9	50.7	17.3	0.8	⑤ 0.78	1.10	...	0.08	39.19 - 21.50	38.9	0.3
12/31/98	1,186.5	④ 178.5	1,731.5	11.2	15.0	21.6	10.3	1.2	④ 0.53	0.82	0.92	0.03	38.47 - 25.13	60.0	0.1
12/31/97	1,059.6	③ 234.1	1,502.1	21.5	22.1	29.2	15.6	1.6	③ 0.70	0.96	1.90	...	...	...	...
12/31/96	1,411.2	② 139.8	1,793.4	17.3	9.9	16.0	7.8	1.5	② 0.41	0.73	1.52	...	...	...	...
12/31/95	1,253.7	① 41.3	...	5.4	3.3	...	...	...	① 0.12	0.44	...	...	...	...	...

Statistics are as originally reported. Adj. for stk. split: 2-for-1, 1/99 ① Incls. restr. exps. of $12.8 mill. & gain from dispos. of assets of $15.1 mill., bef. disc. ops. of $47.6 mill. ② Incls. gain of $200,000; bef. income of $55.7 mill. from disc. ops. ③ Incls. gain of $24.1 mill.; bef. income of $78.2 mill. from disc. ops. ④ Incls. gain of $60.9 mill.; bef. income of $42.1 mill. from disc. ops. ⑤ Incls. gain of $25.3 mill. from dispos. of assets; bef. income of $25.7 mill. from disc. ops. ⑥ Incls. one-time chrgs. of $133.8 mill., bef. inc. from disc. ops. of $4.7 mill. ⑦ Incl. net chrgs. of $213.6 mill. in bef. inc. from disc. oper. of $47.0 mill. ⑧ Incl. net losses of $7.0 mill.

OFFICERS:
D. M. Thomas, Chmn., C.E.O.
D. R. Carlucci, Pres., C.O.O.
N. E. Cooper, Sr. V.P., C.F.O.

INVESTOR CONTACT: Darcie Peck, (203) 319-4766

PRINCIPAL OFFICE: 1499 Post Road, Fairfield, CT 06430

TELEPHONE NUMBER: (203) 319-4700
FAX: (203) 222-4201
WEB: www.imshealth.com

NO. OF EMPLOYEES: 5,428 (approx.)

SHAREHOLDERS: 6,056

ANNUAL MEETING: In May

INCORPORATED: DE, Feb., 1998

INSTITUTIONAL HOLDINGS:
No. of Institutions: 393
Shares Held: 270,021,475
% Held: 96.1

INDUSTRY: Data processing and preparation (SIC: 7374)

TRANSFER AGENT(S): American Stock Transfer and Trust Company, New York, NY

INDYMAC BANCORP, INC.

EXCH.	SYM.	REC. PRICE	P/E RATIO	YLD.	MKT. CAP.	RANGE (52-WK.)	'02 Y/E PR.
NYSE	NDE	19.10 (2/28/03)	7.9	...	$1.05 bill.	26.89 - 16.14	18.49

MEDIUM GRADE. THE COMPANY IS ANTICIPATING EARNINGS PER SHARE GROWTH FOR 2003 OF ABOUT 15.0%.

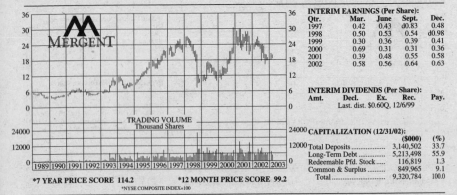

*7 YEAR PRICE SCORE 114.2   *12 MONTH PRICE SCORE 99.2
*NYSE COMPOSITE INDEX=100

INTERIM EARNINGS (Per Share):

Qtr.	Mar.	June	Sept.	Dec.
1997	0.42	0.43	d0.83	0.48
1998	0.50	0.53	0.54	d0.98
1999	0.30	0.36	0.39	0.41
2000	0.69	0.31	0.31	0.36
2001	0.39	0.48	0.55	0.58
2002	0.58	0.56	0.64	0.63

INTERIM DIVIDENDS (Per Share):

Amt.	Decl.	Ex.	Rec.	Pay.
Last. dist. $0.60Q, 12/6/99				

CAPITALIZATION (12/31/02):

	($000)	(%)
Total Deposits	3,140,502	33.7
Long-Term Debt	5,213,498	55.9
Redeemable Pfd. Stock	116,819	1.3
Common & Surplus	849,965	9.1
Total	9,320,784	100.0

BUSINESS:

IndyMac Bancorp, Inc. is the holding company for IndyMac Bank, an Internet-based mortgage banker with proprietary systems to facilitate automated underwriting and risk-based pricing on a nationwide basis. NDE's mortgage banking group offers multi-channel distribution of its mortgage products and services through a nationwide network of mortgage brokers, mortgage bankers and community financial institutions in addition to programs offered directly to consumers and through realtors and home builders. The Company also provides community lending services through its limited Southern California branch system. NDE offers Web-enhanced banking services and provides commercial loans for the purpose of constructing new single-family residences.

RECENT DEVELOPMENTS:

For the year ended 12/31/02, net earnings were $143.4 million compared with income of $126.6 million, before an accounting change charge of $10.2 million, the previous year. Earning for 2002 and 2001 included charges of $11.0 million and $1.4 million, respectively, related to trust preferred securities. Net revenues increased 15.5% to $575.3 million from $498.1 million the prior year. Net interest income rose 3.3% to $209.3 million from $202.6 million in 2001. Provision for loan losses amounted to $16.2 million, down 26.6% from $22.0 million a year earlier. Total non-interest income grew 20.4% to $382.2 million. Total non-interest expenses rose 22.6% to $345.1 million.

PROSPECTS:

The Company is benefiting from low interest rates, which continue to fuel mortgage growth. Mortgage production for 2002 was $20.30 billion, up 23.0% from 2001. Meanwhile, credit risk management efforts continue to improve, despite a challenging environment, as the ratio of non-performing assets to total assets improved to 1.1% from 1.6% a year earlier. Going forward, results should continue to benefit from a strong mortgage pipeline. NDE's pipeline of loans in process as of 12/31/02 was $4.70 billion, up 34.0% over the prior year. The Company is anticipating earnings per share growth for 2003 of about 15.0%.

ANNUAL FINANCIAL DATA:

FISCAL YEAR	NET INT. INC. ($mill.)	NON-INT. INC. ($mill.)	NET INC. ($mill.)	TOT. LOANS ($mill.)	TOT. ASSETS ($mill.)	TOT. DEP. ($mill.)	RET. ON EQUITY %	RET. ON ASSETS %	EQUITY/ ASSETS %	EARN. PER SH.$	TANG. BK. VAL.$	DIV. PER SH.$	PRICE RANGE	AVG. P/E RATIO
12/31/02	209.3	382.2	③143.4	6,189.3	9,574.5	3,140.5	16.9	1.5	8.9	③2.41	14.87	...	26.89 - 16.14	8.9
12/31/01	204.0	317.5	②126.6	5,076.0	7,497.3	3,238.9	15.0	1.7	11.3	②2.00	13.41	...	30.00 - 20.00	12.5
12/31/00	155.0	198.0	①117.9	3,983.1	5,740.2	797.9	16.2	2.1	12.7	①1.69	11.08	...	30.44 - 10.38	12.1
12/31/99	161.0	3.9	115.9	2,802.2	3,726.5	...	14.0	3.1	22.2	1.48	11.02	1.74	17.44 - 9.81	9.2
12/31/98	173.5	d16.3	33.8	3,834.1	4,851.2	...	4.1	0.7	16.9	0.48	10.85	1.89	27.19 - 7.38	36.0
12/31/97	118.5	8.3	①24.3	4,481.6	5,849.1	...	3.5	0.4	12.0	①0.43	11.11	1.71	26.13 - 19.38	52.9
12/31/96	82.9	2.5	69.0	2,643.5	3,370.5	...	14.0	2.0	14.6	1.51	9.82	1.47	21.88 - 14.75	12.1
12/31/95	48.6	1.4	50.0	2,147.6	2,643.6	...	13.8	1.9	13.7	1.25	8.56	1.17	17.25 - 8.50	10.3
12/31/94	25.4	0.9	27.8	1,748.0	1,997.6	...	10.9	1.4	12.8	0.86	7.93	0.72	11.75 - 7.00	10.9
12/31/93	4.1	9.3	7.0	1,275.0	1,440.2	...	2.8	0.5	17.4	0.13	7.83	0.48	11.38 - 5.25	63.9

Statistics are as originally reported. Results through 6/30/99 reflect the operations of IndyMac Mortgage Holdings, Inc. prior to the acquisition of SVG Bancorp, Inc. on 7/3/00. ① Incl. non-recurr. chrg. $4.6 mill., 12/00; $76.0 mill., 12/97 ② Bef. acctg. chrg. $10.2 mill.; incl. $1.4 mill. chrg. fr. trust preferred exp. ③ Incl. $11.0 mill. chrg. fr. trust preferred exp.

OFFICERS:
D. S. Loeb, Chmn.
M. W. Perry, Vice-Chmn., C.E.O.
S. Keys, Exec. V.P., C.F.O.

INVESTOR CONTACT: Pamela Marsh, Inv. Rel., (626) 535-8465

PRINCIPAL OFFICE: 155 North Lake Avenue, Pasadena, CA 91101-7211

TELEPHONE NUMBER: (626) 535-5901
FAX: (626) 535-8203
WEB: www.indymac.com
NO. OF EMPLOYEES: 3,223
SHAREHOLDERS: 1,978
ANNUAL MEETING: In May
INCORPORATED: MD, July, 1985; reincorp., DE, March, 1987

INSTITUTIONAL HOLDINGS:
No. of Institutions: 169
Shares Held: 44,473,390
% Held: 80.5

INDUSTRY: Federal savings institutions (SIC: 6035)

TRANSFER AGENT(S): The Bank of New York, New York, NY

INGERSOLL-RAND COMPANY LIMITED

EXCH.	SYM.	REC. PRICE	P/E RATIO	YLD.	MKT. CAP.	RANGE (52-WK.)	'02 Y/E PR.
NYSE	IR	39.85 (2/28/03)	16.7	1.7%	$6.63 bill.	54.40 - 29.69	43.06

INVESTMENT GRADE. THE COMPANY HAS INDICATED THAT IT IS ON TARGET TO INCREASE ITS SERVICES-RELATED REVENUES TO 25.0% OF TOTAL REVENUES BY THE END OF 2003.

*7 YEAR PRICE SCORE N/A   *12 MONTH PRICE SCORE N/A

*NYSE COMPOSITE INDEX=100

INTERIM EARNINGS (Per Share):

Qtr.	Mar.	June	Sept.	Dec.
1997	0.17	0.69	0.60	0.57
1998	0.60	0.85	0.72	0.91
1999	0.73	0.99	0.80	-0.86
2000	0.80	1.10	0.80	0.66
2001	0.31	0.38	0.20	0.59
2002	0.48	0.63	0.53	0.74

INTERIM DIVIDENDS (Per Share):

Amt.	Decl.	Ex.	Rec.	Pay.
0.17Q	5/02/02	5/16/02	5/20/02	6/03/02
0.17Q	8/07/02	8/15/02	8/19/02	9/03/02
0.17Q	10/28/02	11/14/02	11/18/02	12/02/02
0.17Q	02/06/03	02/13/03	02/18/03	03/03/03

Indicated div.: $0.68 (Div. Reinv. Plan)

CAPITALIZATION (12/31/01):

	($000)	(%)
Long-Term Debt	2,900,700	40.9
Deferred Income Taxes	170,100	2.4
Minority Interest	110,500	1.5
Common & Surplus	3,916,600	55.2
Total	7,097,900	100.0

BUSINESS:

Ingersoll-Rand Company Limited is a provider of security and safety, climate control, industrial productivity and infrastructure products. The infrastructure segment (29.6% of 2002 revenues) supplies products and services for all types of construction projects and industrial and commercial development. The climate control segment 27.6%) offers a range of temperature-control products for protecting food and other perishables. Products include Thermo King transport temperature control units and Hussmann refrigerated display cases. The industrial solutions segment (26.1%) includes a diverse group of businesses offering products and services to enhance industrial efficiency. The security and safety segment (16.7%) markets architectural hardware and access-control products and services for residential, commercial and institutional buildings. On 6/14/00, IR acquired Hussmann International, Inc. for about $1.70 billion. On 8/8/00, IR sold Ingersoll-Dresser Pump Company for $775.0 million.

RECENT DEVELOPMENTS:

For the year ended 12/31/02, earnings from continuing operations were $367.3 million versus earnings from continuing operations of $182.0 million a year earlier. Results for 2002 and 2001 included restructuring charges of $41.9 million and $73.7 million, respectively. Revenues rose 4.0% to $8.95 billion. Excluding acquisitions, revenues increased 3.0%, primarily due to improved sales from the Company's security and safety segment.

PROSPECTS:

On 2/18/03, IR announced that it has completed the sale of its engineered solutions business to The Timken Company for $700.0 million in cash and $140.0 million of Timken common stock. Meanwhile, IR intends to continue aggressively pursuing the development of its recurring revenue stream from installation and maintenance activities, aftermarket parts and service contracts. IR noted that the service-related business offers significantly better profit margins than its other products as well as providing a stable revenue base. IR has indicated that it is on target to increase its services-related revenues to 25.0% of total revenues by the end of 2003. Separately, IR expects full-year 2003 earnings to be between $3.10 and $3.30 per diluted share, excluding the gain on the sale of engineered solutions.

ANNUAL FINANCIAL DATA:

FISCAL YEAR	TOT. REVS. ($mill.)	NET INC. ($mill.)	TOT. ASSETS ($mill.)	OPER. PROFIT %	NET PROFIT %	RET. ON EQUITY %	RET. ON ASSETS %	CURR. RATIO	EARN. PER SH. $	CASH FL. PER SH. $	TANG. BK. VAL. $	DIV. PER SH. $	PRICE RANGE	AVG. P/E RATIO	AVG. YIELD %
p12/31/02	8,951.3	⑥ 367.3							⑥ 2.16			0.68	54.40 - 29.69	19.5	1.6
12/31/01	9,682.0	⑤ 246.2	11,063.7	5.4	2.5	6.3	2.2	1.1	⑤ 1.48	3.69	...	0.68	50.28 - 30.40	27.3	1.7
12/31/00	8,798.2	④ 546.2	10,528.5	12.7	6.2	15.6	5.2	0.8	④ 3.36	5.19	...	0.68	57.75 - 29.50	13.0	1.6
12/31/99	7,666.7	③ 544.9	8,400.2	14.3	7.1	17.7	6.5	1.6	③ 3.29	4.93	...	0.64	73.81 - 44.63	18.0	1.1
12/31/98	8,291.5	509.1	8,309.5	12.6	6.1	18.8	6.1	1.3	3.08	4.78	...	0.60	54.94 - 34.94	14.3	1.4
12/31/97	7,103.3	380.5	8,415.6	10.7	5.4	16.3	4.5	1.1	2.31	3.60	...	0.57	46.25 - 27.83	16.0	1.5
12/31/96	6,702.9	358.0	5,621.6	10.2	5.3	17.1	6.4	2.0	2.22	3.48	5.56	0.52	31.75 - 23.42	12.4	1.9
12/31/95	5,729.0	270.3	5,563.3	8.7	4.7	15.1	4.9	1.8	1.70	2.83	3.29	0.49	28.25 - 18.92	13.9	2.1
12/31/94	4,507.5	211.1	3,596.9	8.4	4.7	13.8	5.9	1.9	1.33	2.17	8.89	0.48	27.75 - 19.67	17.8	2.0
12/31/93	4,021.1	①② 163.5	3,375.3	7.2	4.1	12.1	4.8	1.9	①② 1.04	1.82	7.88	0.47	26.58 - 19.17	22.0	2.0

Statistics are as originally reported. Adj. for 3-for-2 stk. split, 9/97. ① Incl. non-recurr. net chrg. of $5.0 mill. ② Bef. acctg. adj. chrg. of $21.0 mill. ③ Bef. inc. fr. disc. ops. of $46.2 mill. ④ Incl. restruct. chrgs. of $76.2 mill.; bef. inc. fr. disc. ops. of $123.2 mill. ⑤ Incl. restruct. chrgs. of $93.1 mill. ⑥ Incl. restruct. chrgs. of $41.9 mill.; bef. inc. fr. disc. ops. of $93.6 mill. & acctg. chge. chrg. of $634.5 mill.

OFFICERS:
H. L. Henkel, Chmn., Pres., C.E.O.
T. R. McLevish, Sr. V.P., C.F.O.
P. Nachtigal, Sr. V.P., Gen. Couns.
INVESTOR CONTACT: Joseph P. Fimbianti, (201) 573-3113
PRINCIPAL OFFICE: Clarendon House, 2 Church Street, Hamilton, Bermuda 07677

TELEPHONE NUMBER: (441) 295-2838
WEB: www.ingersoll-rand.com
NO. OF EMPLOYEES: 56,000 (approx.)
SHAREHOLDERS: 10,495 (approx.)
ANNUAL MEETING: In May
INCORPORATED: NJ, 1905; reincorp., Bermuda, Dec., 2001

INSTITUTIONAL HOLDINGS:
No. of Institutions: N/A
Shares Held: N/A
% Held: N/A
INDUSTRY: General industrial machinery, nec (SIC: 3569)
TRANSFER AGENT(S): The Bank of New York, New York, NY

INGRAM MICRO INC.

EXCH.	SYM.	REC. PRICE	P/E RATIO	YLD.	MKT. CAP.	RANGE (52-WK.)	'02 Y/E PR.
NYSE	IM	10.36 (2/28/03)	345.3	...	$1.54 bill.	17.10 - 9.30	12.35

LOWER MEDIUM GRADE. SALES FOR THE FIRST QUARTER OF 2003 ARE EXPECTED TO RANGE FROM $5.40 BILLION TO $5.55 BILLION.

INTERIM EARNINGS (Per Share):

Qtr.	Apr.	July	Oct.	Jan.
1998-99	0.38	0.37	0.40	0.49
1999-00	0.26	0.34	0.11	0.51
2000-01	0.65	0.22	0.26	0.39
2001-02	0.18	d0.08	d0.09	0.04
2002-03	0.10	0.06	d0.06	d0.07

INTERIM DIVIDENDS (Per Share):

Amt.	Decl.	Ex.	Rec.	Pay.
		No dividends paid.		

CAPITALIZATION (12/29/01):

	($000)	(%)
Long-Term Debt	205,304	9.9
Common & Surplus	1,867,298	90.1
Total	2,072,602	100.0

*7 YEAR PRICE SCORE N/A   *12 MONTH PRICE SCORE 91.2

*NYSE COMPOSITE INDEX=100

BUSINESS:

Ingram Micro Inc. is a worldwide distributor of information technology products and services. IM markets computer hardware, networking equipment, and software products to nearly 170,000 reseller customers in more than 100 countries. IM also provides logistics and fulfillment services to vendor and reseller customers. IM offers more than 280,000 products, including desktop and notebook personal computers, servers, workstations, mass storage devices, CD-ROM drives, monitors, printers, scanners, and modems. IM also provides a range of outsourcing programs, including tailored financing programs, channel assembly, systems configuration, and marketing programs.

RECENT DEVELOPMENTS:

For the year ended 12/28/02, income fell 39.3% to $5.7 million, before an accounting change charge of $280.9 million, versus income of $9.3 million, before an extraordinary loss of $2.6 million, in 2001. Results for 2002 and 2001 included reorganization charges of $71.1 million and $41.4 million, respectively, primarily related to facility consolidations and workforce reductions. Results for 2002 also included a gain on the sale of securities of $6.5 million, while results for 2001 included special items totaling $22.9 million. Net sales declined 10.8% to $22.46 billion from $25.19 billion in the prior year. Gross profit slipped 7.4% to $1.23 billion from $1.33 billion in the previous year. Income from operations dropped 46.0% to $50.2 million versus $92.9 million the year before.

PROSPECTS:

The Company's improvement in operating performance is being driven by stronger gross margins and tight management of its balance sheet. For instance, IM has eliminated more than $1.00 billion in debt over the last 24 months. Looking ahead, the Company expects sales for the first quarter of 2003 to range from $5.40 billion to $5.55 billion and net income to range from $21.0 million to $24.0 million, or $0.14 to $0.16 per share, before any major-program expenses and other special items. These objectives are based on a flat revenue scenario and are not contingent on a resurgence of demand.

ANNUAL FINANCIAL DATA:

FISCAL YEAR	TOT. REVS. ($mill.)	NET INC. ($mill.)	TOT. ASSETS ($mill.)	OPER. PROFIT %	NET PROFIT %	RET. ON EQUITY %	RET. ON ASSETS %	CURR. RATIO	EARN. PER SH.$	CASH FL. PER SH.$	TANG. BK. VAL.$	PRICE RANGE	AVG. P/E RATIO
p12/28/02	22,459.3	④ 5.7		0.4	...	0.5	0.2	1.4	④ 0.04	0.83	9.12	18.85 - 10.00	360.6
12/29/01	25,186.9	③ 9.3	5,302.0	0.4	...	0.5	0.2	1.4	③ 0.06	2.24	9.87	17.48 - 10.69	234.3
12/30/00	30,715.1	② 223.8	6,609.0	1.2	0.7	11.9	3.4	1.4	② 1.51	2.24	9.87	21.13 - 10.19	10.4
1/01/00	28,068.6	① 179.6	8,271.9	0.7	0.6	9.1	2.2	1.5	① 1.21	1.88	10.46	36.31 - 10.00	19.1
1/02/99	22,034.0	245.2	6,733.4	2.2	1.1	17.5	3.6	1.7	1.64	2.09	8.22	54.63 - 26.63	24.8
1/03/98	16,581.5	193.6	4,932.2	2.3	1.2	18.7	3.9	1.6	1.32	1.65	6.53	34.75 - 19.00	20.4
12/28/96	12,023.5	110.7	3,366.9	2.1	0.9	13.4	3.3	1.4	0.88	1.35	5.96	28.13 - 20.00	27.3
12/30/95	8,616.9	84.3	2,940.9	2.2	1.0	27.1	2.9	1.6	0.69	0.90	2.56	...	...
12/31/94	5,830.2	63.3	1,974.3	2.4	1.1	28.6	3.2	1.5	0.52	0.68	1.71	...	...
1/01/94	4,044.2	50.4	...	2.5	1.2	...	...	...	0.41	0.52	...	...	...

Statistics are as originally reported. ① Excl. $13.0 mill. net tax reorg. costs and $3.8 mill. net extraord. gain. ② Excl. $1.5 mill. net extraord. gain fr. repurchase of debentures. ③ Incl. $64.3 mill. restr. chg. & excl. $2.6 mill. extraord. loss. ④ Incl. $71.1 mill. reorg. costs, $6.5 mill. gain fr. sale of sec. & excl. $280.9 mill. acctg. chg. chrg.

OFFICERS:
K. B. Foster, Chmn., C.E.O.
M. J. Grainger, Pres., C.O.O.
T. A. Madden, Exec. V.P., C.F.O.

INVESTOR CONTACT: Investor Relations,
(714) 382-8282

PRINCIPAL OFFICE: 1600 E. St. Andrew Place, Santa Ana, CA 92799-5125

TELEPHONE NUMBER: (714) 566-1000
FAX: (714) 566-7604
WEB: www.ingrammicro.com
NO. OF EMPLOYEES: 14,500 (approx.)
SHAREHOLDERS: 675 (approx. record);
26,000 (approx. beneficial)
ANNUAL MEETING: In May
INCORPORATED: DE, Apr., 1996

INSTITUTIONAL HOLDINGS:
No. of Institutions: 138
Shares Held: 83,261,875
% Held: 55.3

INDUSTRY: Computers, peripherals & software (SIC: 5045)

TRANSFER AGENT(S): First Chicago Trust Company of New York, Jersey City, NJ

INTERNATIONAL BUSINESS MACHINES CORPORATION

EXCH.	SYM.	REC. PRICE	P/E RATIO	YLD.	MKT. CAP.	RANGE (52-WK.)	'02 Y/E PR.
NYSE	IBM	77.95 (2/28/03)	25.7	0.8%	$134.26 bill.	160.50 - 54.01	77.50

INVESTMENT GRADE. THE COMPANY COMPLETED THE ACQUISITION OF TARIAN SOFTWARE, A PROVIDER OF E-RECORDS MANAGEMENT SOFTWARE, FOR AN UNDISCLOSED AMOUNT.

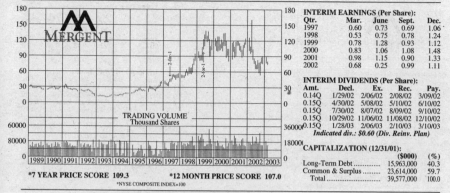

7 YEAR PRICE SCORE 109.3   **12 MONTH PRICE SCORE 107.0**
NYSE COMPOSITE INDEX=100

INTERIM EARNINGS (Per Share):

Qtr.	Mar.	June	Sept.	Dec.
1997	0.60	0.73	0.69	1.06
1998	0.53	0.75	0.78	1.24
1999	0.78	1.28	0.93	1.12
2000	0.83	1.06	1.08	1.48
2001	0.98	1.15	0.90	1.33
2002	0.68	0.25	0.99	1.11

INTERIM DIVIDENDS (Per Share):

Amt.	Decl.	Ex.	Rec.	Pay.
0.14Q	1/29/02	2/06/02	2/08/02	3/09/02
0.15Q	4/30/02	5/08/02	5/10/02	6/10/02
0.15Q	7/30/02	8/07/02	8/09/02	9/10/02
0.15Q	10/29/02	11/06/02	11/08/02	12/10/02
0.15Q	1/28/03	2/06/03	2/10/03	3/10/03

Indicated div.: $0.60 (Div. Reinv. Plan)

CAPITALIZATION (12/31/01):

	($000)	(%)
Long-Term Debt	15,963,000	40.3
Common & Surplus	23,614,000	59.7
Total	39,577,000	100.0

BUSINESS:

International Business Machines Corporation provides information technology services, software, systems, products, financing and technologies. Products and services include servers, personal computer systems, storage and other peripherals, original equipment manufacturers hardware, software, maintenance services, and financing. The personal systems segment produces several major brands, including the Aptiva home personal computers, IntelliStation workstations, IBM xSeries servers, NetVista and ThinkPad mobile systems. The server segment produces the

following major brands: zSeries mainframe servers, e-business infrastructure for mission-critical data and transaction processing, the IBM pSeries servers, and the IBM iSeries mid-range servers. The software segment provides operating systems for IBM's servers and e-business enabling software for IBM and non-IBM platforms. Revenues for 2002 were derived: hardware, 33.8%; services, 44.8%; software, 16.1%; financing, 4.0%; and enterprise investments and other, 1.3%.

RECENT DEVELOPMENTS:

For the year ended 12/31/02, income from continuing operations dropped 34.5% to $5.33 billion versus income of $8.15 billion in 2001. Earnings were hampered by asset write-offs, workforce reductions and a loss related to the discontinued operations of the hard disk drive business. Results for 2002 and 2001 excluded losses of $1.76 billion

and $423.0 million, respectively, from discontinued operations. Total revenues were $81.19 billion, down 2.3% from $83.07 billion in the prior year. Revenues from the Americas were down 3.0% to $36.40 billion, while revenues from Europe/Middle East/Africa climbed 1.0% to $24.30 billion. Asia-Pacific revenues were flat at $17.20 billion.

PROSPECTS:

On 11/15/02, the Company completed the acquisition of Tarian Software, a provider of e-Records management software, for an undisclosed amount. The transaction should enhance the Company's position in the enterprise

content management market and will be integrated into IBM's data management portfolio of products. Separately, on 12/31/02, the Company completed the sale of its hard disk drive business to Hitachi, Ltd.

ANNUAL FINANCIAL DATA:

FISCAL YEAR	TOT. REVS. ($mill.)	NET INC. ($mill.)	TOT. ASSETS ($mill.)	OPER. PROFIT %	NET PROFIT %	RET. ON EQUITY %	RET. ON ASSETS %	CURR. RATIO	EARN. PER SH.$	CASH FL. PER SH.$	TANG. BK. VAL.$	DIV. PER SH.$	PRICE RANGE	AVG. P/E RATIO	AVG. YIELD %
p12/31/02	81,186.0	⑥ 5,334.0							⑥ 3.07			0.60	126.39 - 54.01	29.4	0.7
12/31/01	85,866.0	7,723.0	88,313.0	10.8	9.0	32.7	8.7	1.2	4.35	7.08	13.70	0.55	124.70 - 83.75	24.0	0.5
12/31/00	88,396.0	8,093.0	88,349.0	13.2	9.2	39.2	9.2	1.2	4.44	7.21	11.56	0.51	134.94 - 80.06	24.2	0.5
12/31/99	87,548.0	⑤ 7,712.0	87,495.0	13.6	8.8	37.6	8.8	1.1	⑤ 4.12	7.63	10.99	0.47	139.19 - 80.88	26.7	0.4
12/31/98	81,667.0	6,328.0	86,100.0	11.2	7.7	32.6	7.3	1.2	3.29	5.89	10.04	0.43	94.97 - 47.81	21.7	0.6
12/31/97	78,508.0	6,093.0	81,499.0	11.6	7.8	30.7	7.5	1.2	3.01	5.48	9.68	0.39	56.75 - 31.78	14.7	0.9
12/31/96	75,947.0	⑤ 5,429.0	81,132.0	11.3	7.1	25.1	6.7	1.2	⑤ 2.56	4.93	9.81	0.33	41.50 - 20.78	12.2	1.0
③ 12/31/95	71,940.0	② 4,178.0	80,292.0	10.6	5.8	18.6	5.2	1.3	② 1.81	4.27	9.01	0.25	28.66 - 17.56	12.8	1.1
12/31/94	64,052.0	3,021.0	81,091.0	7.8	4.7	12.9	3.7	1.4	1.26	3.95	8.24	0.25	19.09 - 12.84	12.7	1.6
12/31/93	62,716.0	① d7,987.0	81,113.0	...	...	...	...	1.2	① d3.50	d0.60	6.43	0.40	14.97 - 10.16	...	3.1

Statistics are as originally reported. Adj. for 2-for-1 split, 5/99 & 5/97. ① Incl. $8.95 bill. restr. chg. ② Incl. $488.0 mill. pre-tax chg. & $1.84 bill. chg. rel. to acq. of Lotus Develop. ③ Incl. Lotus Develop., acq. 7/95. ④ Incl. $435.0 mill. one-time chg. ⑤ Incl. $750.0 mill. net gain fr. sale of bus., restr. chgs., & acct. chg. ⑥ Excl. $1.76 bill. loss fr. disc. ops.

OFFICERS:
L. V. Gerstner Jr., Chmn.
J. M. Thompson, Vice-Chmn.
S. J. Palmisano, Pres., C.E.O.
INVESTOR CONTACT: IBM Stockholder Relations, IBM Corporation, (888) 421-8860
PRINCIPAL OFFICE: One New Orchard Road, Armonk, NY 10504

TELEPHONE NUMBER: (914) 499-1900
FAX: (914) 765-4190
WEB: www.ibm.com
NO. OF EMPLOYEES: 335,000 (avg.)
SHAREHOLDERS: 677,418 (common record)
ANNUAL MEETING: In Apr.
INCORPORATED: NY, June, 1911

INSTITUTIONAL HOLDINGS:
No. of Institutions: 1,185
Shares Held: 866,183,702
% Held: 51.3
INDUSTRY: Electronic computers (SIC: 3571)
TRANSFER AGENT(S): First Chicago Trust Company of New York, Jersey City, NJ

INTERNATIONAL FLAVORS & FRAGRANCES, INC.

EXCH.	SYM.	REC. PRICE	P/E RATIO	YLD.	MKT. CAP.	RANGE (52-WK.)	'02 Y/E PR.
NYSE	IFF	31.36 (2/28/03)	17.0	1.9%	$2.97 bill.	37.45 - 26.05	35.10

HIGH GRADE. THE COMPANY SHOULD CONTINUE TO BENEFIT FROM ONGOING COST-SAVING INITIATIVES.

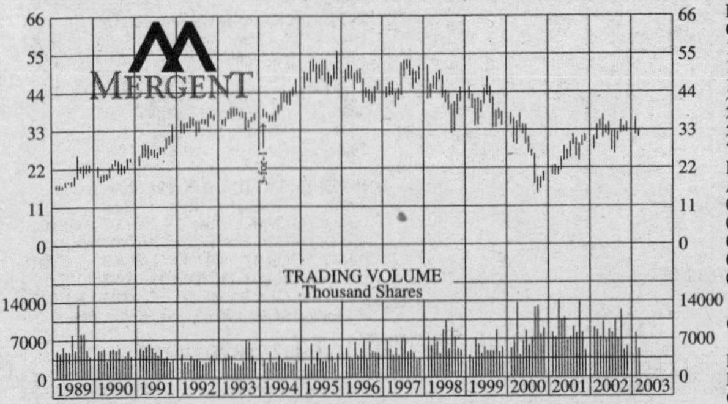

***7 YEAR PRICE SCORE 93.5** ***12 MONTH PRICE SCORE 110.3**

*NYSE COMPOSITE INDEX=100

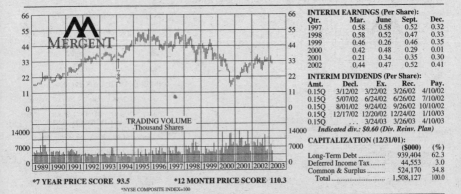

INTERIM EARNINGS (Per Share):

Qtr.	Mar.	June	Sept.	Dec.
1997	0.58	0.58	0.52	0.32
1998	0.58	0.52	0.47	0.33
1999	0.46	0.26	0.46	0.35
2000	0.42	0.48	0.29	0.01
2001	0.21	0.34	0.35	0.30
2002	0.44	0.47	0.52	0.41

INTERIM DIVIDENDS (Per Share):

Amt.	Decl.	Ex.	Rec.	Pay.
0.15Q	3/12/02	3/22/02	3/26/02	4/10/02
0.15Q	5/07/02	6/24/02	6/26/02	7/10/02
0.15Q	8/01/02	9/24/02	9/26/02	10/10/02
0.15Q	12/17/02	12/20/02	12/24/02	1/10/03
0.15Q	...	3/24/03	3/26/03	4/10/03

Indicated div.: $0.60 (Div. Reinv. Plan)

CAPITALIZATION (12/31/01):

	($000)	(%)
Long-Term Debt	939,404	62.3
Deferred Income Tax	44,553	3.0
Common & Surplus	524,170	34.8
Total	1,508,127	100.0

BUSINESS:

International Flavors & Fragrances, Inc. supplies compounds that enhance the aroma or taste of other manufacturers' products. It is one of the largest companies in its field producing and marketing on an international basis. Fragrance products are sold principally to manufacturers of perfumes, cosmetics, toiletries, hair care products, deodorants, soaps, detergents and air care products. Flavor products are sold principally to manufacturers of prepared foods, beverages, dairy foods, pharmaceuticals and confectionery products. As of 1/27/03, the Company had sales, manufacturing and creative facilities in 37 countries worldwide. On 11/3/00, IFF acquired Bush Boak Allen.

RECENT DEVELOPMENTS:

For the year ended 12/31/02, net income climbed 51.7% to $175.9 million from $116.0 million the previous year. Results for 2002 and 2001 included non-recurring charges of $11.7 million and $30.1 million, respectively, related to the Company's reorganization plan. Also, results for 2002 and 2001 included amortization charges of $12.6 million and $46.1 million, respectively. Net sales declined 1.9% to $1.81 billion from $1.84 billion in the year-earlier period, primarily due to weak economies in the Latin American region and the sale of non-core businesses.

PROSPECTS:

The Company remains cautious in regard to its near-term outlook as the strength of the global economy continues to be uncertain. However, the combination of actions IFF has taken to streamline its business, coupled with a renewed focus on research and development initiatives and cost savings realized from reorganization and integration efforts should bode well for future growth. For the full-year 2003, IFF expects sales to increase 7.0% to 8.0%, excluding sales related to non-core businesses disposed of during 2002. Moreover, IFF expects earnings per share for 2003, excluding nonrecurring charges, to increase between 10.0% and 15.0% to a range of $2.12 to $2.20.

ANNUAL FINANCIAL DATA:

FISCAL YEAR	TOT. REVS. ($mill.)	NET INC. ($mill.)	TOT. ASSETS ($mill.)	OPER. PROFIT %	NET PROFIT %	RET. ON EQUITY %	RET. ON ASSETS %	CURR. RATIO	EARN. PER SH. $	CASH FL. PER SH. $	TANG. BK. VAL. $	DIV. PER SH. $	PRICE RANGE	AVG. P/E RATIO	AVG. YIELD %
p12/31/02	**1,809.2**	**1 175.9**							**1 1.84**			**0.60**	**37.45 - 26.05**	**17.3**	**1.9**
12/31/01	1,843.8	1 116.0	2,268.1	18.0	6.3	22.1	5.1	1.6	1 1.20	2.76	...	0.60	31.69 - 19.75	21.4	2.3
12/31/00	1,462.8	1 123.0	2,489.0	17.8	8.4	19.5	4.9	0.9	1 1.22	1.90	...	1.52	37.94 - 14.69	21.6	5.8
12/31/99	1,439.5	1 162.0	1,401.5	19.5	11.3	18.9	11.6	2.3	1 1.53	2.06	8.19	1.52	48.50 - 33.63	26.8	3.7
12/31/98	1,407.3	203.8	1,388.1	21.8	14.5	21.6	14.7	3.1	1.90	2.35	8.91	1.48	51.88 - 32.06	22.1	3.5
12/31/97	1,426.8	218.2	1,422.3	23.3	15.3	21.8	15.3	3.5	1.99	2.45	9.17	1.44	53.44 - 39.88	23.4	3.1
12/31/96	1,436.1	1 189.9	1,506.9	23.7	13.2	17.6	12.6	3.6	1 1.71	2.15	9.79	1.36	51.88 - 40.75	27.1	2.9
12/31/95	1,439.5	248.8	1,534.3	26.7	17.3	22.3	16.2	3.7	2.24	2.60	10.06	1.24	55.88 - 45.13	22.5	2.5
12/31/94	1,315.2	226.0	1,399.7	26.5	17.2	22.4	16.1	3.7	2.03	2.35	9.04	1.08	47.88 - 35.63	20.6	2.6
12/31/93	1,188.6	202.5	1,225.3	25.7	17.0	22.7	16.5	3.9	1.78	2.09	7.96	1.00	39.83 - 33.00	20.5	2.7

Statistics are as originally reported. Adj. for stk. split: 3-for-1, 1/94. 1 Incl. non-recurr. chrgs. $11.7 mill., 12/02; $30.1 mill., 12/01; $41.3 mill., 12/00; $32.9 mill., 12/99; $49.7 mill., 12/96

OFFICERS:
R. A. Goldstein, Chmn., C.E.O.
S. A. Block, Sr. V.P., Gen. Couns., Sec.
D. J. Wetmore, Sr. V.P., C.F.O.

INVESTOR CONTACT: Douglas J. Wetmore, Sr. V.P., C.F.O., (212) 708-7145

PRINCIPAL OFFICE: 521 West 57th Street, New York, NY 10019-2960

TELEPHONE NUMBER: (212) 765-5500
FAX: (212) 708-7132
WEB: www.iff.com

NO. OF EMPLOYEES: 5,929

SHAREHOLDERS: 3,394

ANNUAL MEETING: In May

INCORPORATED: NY, Dec., 1909

INSTITUTIONAL HOLDINGS:
No. of Institutions: 281
Shares Held: 65,406,713
% Held: 69.3

INDUSTRY: Industrial organic chemicals, nec (SIC: 2869)

TRANSFER AGENT(S): Wachovia Bank, N.A., Charlotte, NC

INTERNATIONAL GAME TECHNOLOGY

EXCH.	SYM.	REC. PRICE	P/E RATIO	YLD.	MKT. CAP.	RANGE (52-WK.)	'02 Y/E PR.
NYSE	IGT	78.58 (2/28/03)	22.4	...	$6.82 bill.	80.70 - 47.75	75.92

UPPER MEDIUM GRADE. THE COMPANY ENTERED INTO AN AGREEMENT TO SELL ITS COLORADO CASINO OPERATIONS TO ISLE OF CAPRI BLACK HAWK L.L.C. IN A TRANSACTION VALUED AT $84.0 MILLION.

*7 YEAR PRICE SCORE 204.9   ***12 MONTH PRICE SCORE 123.7**

*NYSE COMPOSITE INDEX=100

INTERIM EARNINGS (Per Share):

Qtr.	Dec.	Mar.	June	Sept.
1997-98	0.26	0.31	0.40	0.37
1998-99	0.32	0.32	0.39	d0.45
1999-00	0.49	0.33	0.51	0.70
2000-01	0.64	0.70	0.73	0.73
2001-02	0.70	0.81	0.90	0.80
2002-03	1.00	...	...	...

INTERIM DIVIDENDS (Per Share):

Amt.	Decl.	Ex.	Rec.	Pay.

Last dist., $0.03Q, 3/1/99.

CAPITALIZATION (9/28/02):

	($000)	(%)
Long-Term Debt	971,375	40.4
Common & Surplus	1,433,144	59.6
Total	2,404,519	100.0

BUSINESS:

International Game Technology manufactures, markets and designs a broad range of gaming machines and proprietary software systems for computerized wide-area gaming machine networks throughout the world. IGT has three major divisions: IGT Gaming, which serves the traditional casino gaming markets primarily within North America; IGT-International, which serves gaming markets internationally; and IGT Lottery, which focuses on the public lottery market. IGT's wide-area progressive games include DOUBLE DIAMOND; MEGABUCKS; PLAYERS EDGEPLUS; RED WHITE AND BLUE; FIVE TIMES PAY; BONUSPOKER; DEUCES WILD; TRIPLE PLAY POKER ELVIS?; and WHEEL OF FORTUNE. In September 1999, IGT acquired Sodak Gaming, Inc. Net sales for 2002 were derived as follows: gaming operations, 47.8%, product sales, 45.8%, and lottery and pari-mutuel systems, 6.4%.

RECENT DEVELOPMENTS:

For the quarter ended 12/28/02, IGT reported income from continuing operations of $87.9 million versus net income of $51.8 million in the corresponding prior-year period. Results for 2002 included costs related to its lottery and pari-mutuel systems of $29.4 million, and excluded a gain of $3.7 million from discontinued operations. Total revenues grew 76.3% to $531.7 million. Product sales grew 20.9% to $241.3 million, while revenues for gaming operations jumped 143.8% to $248.4 million. Lottery and pari-mutuel systems revenue was $42.0 million in 2002.

PROSPECTS:

On 12/26/02, IGT entered into an agreement to sell its Colorado casino operations to Isle of Capri Black Hawk L.L.C. in a transaction valued at $84.0 million. The sale is expected to be completed in the Spring of 2003. Separately, on 2/26/03, IGT sold Anchor Coin to Herbst Gaming, Inc. in a transaction valued at about $61.0 million. Meanwhile, as of 12/28/02, IGT's installed base of recurring revenue games consisted of 32,500 machines, an increase of 600 machines versus the corresponding prior-year period. New game themes expected to be introduced during the remainder of fiscal 2003 include FAMILY FEUD™, HARLEY-DAVIDSON®, S2000®, UNO®, and M*A*S*H™.

ANNUAL FINANCIAL DATA:

FISCAL YEAR	TOT. REVS. ($mill.)	NET INC. ($mill.)	TOT. ASSETS ($mill.)	OPER. PROFIT %	NET PROFIT %	RET. ON EQUITY %	RET. ON ASSETS %	CURR. RATIO	EARN. PER SH.$	CASH FL.PER SH.$	TANG. BK. VAL.$	DIV. PER SH.$	PRICE RANGE	AVG. P/E RATIO	AVG. YIELD %
9/28/02	1,847.6	⑦276.7	3,315.8	28.8	15.0	19.3	8.3	2.3	⑦3.21	4.93	2.18	...	80.10 - 47.75	19.9	...
9/29/01	1,199.2	④⑥213.9	1,923.4	33.0	17.8	72.2	11.1	2.6	④⑥2.80	3.79	1.60	...	71.95 - 35.70	19.2	...
9/30/00	1,004.4	④⑥156.8	1,623.7	26.6	15.6	162.3	9.7	3.1	④⑥2.00	2.73	...	...	49.38 - 17.44	16.7	...
10/02/99	929.7	⑤⑥65.3	1,765.1	12.5	7.0	27.0	3.7	4.6	⑤⑥0.65	1.18	1.03	0.03	24.13 - 14.13	29.4	0.2
9/30/98	824.1	④152.4	1,543.6	26.6	18.5	28.2	9.9	3.3	④1.33	1.69	3.76	0.12	28.69 - 16.13	16.8	0.5
9/30/97	744.0	③137.2	1,215.1	25.7	18.4	26.4	11.3	3.5	③1.13	1.41	4.57	0.12	26.94 - 15.25	18.7	0.6
9/30/96	733.5	②118.0	1,154.2	23.2	16.1	18.9	10.2	4.8	②0.93	1.17	4.96	0.12	23.50 - 10.75	18.4	0.7
9/30/95	620.8	①92.6	971.7	22.4	14.9	16.7	9.5	6.2	①0.71	0.92	4.30	0.12	17.00 - 10.75	19.5	0.9
9/30/94	674.5	140.4	868.0	29.3	20.8	27.0	16.2	7.1	1.07	1.23	3.94	0.12	34.00 - 14.88	22.8	0.5
9/30/93	478.0	105.6	646.6	31.4	22.1	27.9	16.3	5.5	0.85	3.03	0.09	41.38 - 23.75	38.3	0.3

Statistics are as originally reported. Adj. for 2-for-1 stk. split, 3/93. ① Incl one-time chrg. of $14.9 mill. ② Incl. $7.6 mill. gain fr. a lawsuit in Austria, a $3.3 mill. loss on sale of assets & a non-recurring after-tax chrg. of $5.5 mill. ③ Incl. $12.9 mill. gain fr. sale of invts. ④ Incl. pre-tax gain fr. sale of assets of $412,000, 9/01; $3.6 mill., 9/00; $11.1 mill., 9/98. ⑤ Incl. a gain of $4.9 mill. on sale of assets & bef. extraord. loss of $3.3 mill. ⑥ Incl. pre-tax impair. of assets & restruct. gain of $1.1 mill., 9/01; loss of $6,000, 9/00; loss of $98.1 mill., 9/99. ⑦ Bef. a gain of $7.6 mill. fr. disc. opers.; incl. a cost of lottery & pari-mutuel systems of $79.9 mill.

OFFICERS:	TELEPHONE NUMBER: (775) 448-7777	INSTITUTIONAL HOLDINGS:
C. N. Mathewson, Chmn.	FAX: (775) 448-0719	No. of Institutions: 334
G. T. Baker, Pres., C.E.O.	WEB: www.igt.com	Shares Held: 80,269,805
M. T. Mullarkay, Sr. V.P., C.F.O., Treas.	NO. OF EMPLOYEES: 6,200 (approx.)	% Held: 92.3
INVESTOR CONTACT: Investor Relations, (775) 448-0880	SHAREHOLDERS: 2,881 (approx.)	INDUSTRY: Special industry machinery, nec (SIC: 3559)
PRINCIPAL OFFICE: 9295 Prototype Drive, Reno, NV 89521	ANNUAL MEETING: In Mar. INCORPORATED: NV, Dec., 1980	TRANSFER AGENT(S): The Bank of New York, New York, NY

INTERNATIONAL MULTIFOODS CORP.

EXCH.	SYM.	REC. PRICE	P/E RATIO	YLD.	MKT. CAP.	RANGE (52-WK.)	'02 Y/E PR.
NYSE	IMC	19.70 (2/28/03)	14.3	...	$374.2 mill.	28.92 - 16.95	21.19

MEDIUM GRADE. THE COMPANY ANTICIPATES EARNINGS OF $1.70 TO $1.80 PER SHARE FOR FISCAL 2004, ENDING 2/28/04.

MERGENT

3-for-2

TRADING VOLUME
Thousand Shares

1989 1990 1991 1992 1993 1994 1995 1996 1997 1998 1999 2000 2001 2002 2003

*7 YEAR PRICE SCORE 112.9   *12 MONTH PRICE SCORE 104.8
*NYSE COMPOSITE INDEX=100

INTERIM EARNINGS (Per Share):

Qtr.	May	Aug.	Nov.	Feb.
1997-98	0.11	0.25	0.51	0.21
1998-99	d1.30	0.24	0.52	0.37
1999-00	0.24	0.27	0.43	0.37
2000-01	0.25	0.28	0.45	0.14
2001-02	0.11	0.15	d0.01	0.25
2002-03	0.25	0.22	0.66	...

INTERIM DIVIDENDS (Per Share):

Amt.	Decl.	Ex.	Rec.	Pay.
Last dist. $0.20Q, 1/16/01				

CAPITALIZATION (3/2/02):

	($000)	(%)
Long-Term Debt	514,541	62.6
Deferred Income Tax	35,766	4.3
Common & Surplus	272,070	33.1
Total	822,377	100.0

BUSINESS:

International Multifoods Corp. manufactures and markets branded consumer foods and foodservice products in North America. The Company's U.S. Foodservice Products segment (7.6% of fiscal 2002 revenues) produces approximately 1,400 products for retail, wholesale and in-store bakeries and foodservice customers. The Canadian Foods segment (9.9%) consists of IMC's retail and commercial operations in Canada. Through its U.S. Consumer Products (3.9%) segment, IMC markets and distributes products under the following brands, PILLSBURY, MARTHA WHITE, JIM DANDY, GLADIOLA, ROBIN HOOD, LA PINA, RED BAND, SOFTASILK, HUNGRY JACK, IDAHO SPUDS and FARMHOUSE. On 9/9/02, IMC sold its foodservice and vending distribution business (78.6%) for $166.0 million.

RECENT DEVELOPMENTS:

For the quarter ended 11/30/02, earnings from continuing operations totaled $12.8 million compared with a loss from continuing operations of $1.9 million in the corresponding prior-year period. Results included one-time after-tax charges of $3.0 million and $5.8 million in 2002 and 2001, respectively. Net sales more than doubled to $301.2 million from $148.5 million a year earlier, reflecting the November 2001 acquisition of the Pillsbury desserts and specialty products business. Gross profit was $65.2 million, or 21.6% of net sales, versus $25.2 million, or 17.0% of net sales, the previous year. Operating earnings totaled $31.4 million compared with $10.0 million the year before.

PROSPECTS:

The Company is targeting annualized earnings per share growth of between 9.0% and 11.0% over the next three years. For fiscal 2004, ending on 2/28/04, IMC anticipates earnings in the range of $1.70 to $1.80 per share. Separately, on 1/27/03, the Company announced that it has completed the acquisition of a plant in Toledo, Ohio from General Mills, Inc. for $316.0 million. The plant will immediately begin manufacturing PILLSBURY baking mixes and HUNGRY JACK pancake mixes, while PILLSBURY ready-to-spread frostings are expected to be in full production at the plant by May 2003.

ANNUAL FINANCIAL DATA:

FISCAL YEAR	TOT. REVS. ($mill.)	NET INC. ($mill.)	TOT. ASSETS ($mill.)	OPER. PROFIT %	NET PROFIT %	RET. ON EQUITY %	RET. ON ASSETS %	CURR. RATIO	EARN. PER SH.$	CASH FL. PER SH.$	TANG. BK. VAL.$	DIV. PER SH.$	PRICE RANGE	AVG. P/E RATIO	AVG. YIELD %
3/02/02	2,849.1	③ 9.6	1,124.7	1.6	0.3	3.5	0.9	1.7	③ 0.50	1.95	1.14	0.20	24.67 - 15.89	40.6	1.0
3/03/01	2,524.9	① 21.2	764.6	2.2	0.8	8.3	2.8	1.3	① 1.12	2.47	9.29	0.80	23.31 - 9.81	14.8	4.8
2/29/00	2,384.7	①② 24.7	736.2	2.2	1.0	9.7	3.4	1.3	①② 1.31	2.49	9.08	0.80	27.25 - 11.63	14.8	4.1
2/28/99	2,296.6	①② 6.8	696.9	1.0	0.3	2.6	1.0	1.3	①② 0.36	1.53	9.49	0.80	31.44 - 15.13	64.7	3.4
2/28/98	2,611.8	① 20.0	827.4	1.7	0.8	5.6	2.4	1.6	① 1.08	2.72	11.98	0.80	32.44 - 17.25	23.0	3.2
2/28/97	2,595.9	① 2.8	915.3	0.9	0.1	1.0	0.3	1.5	① 0.15	1.86	11.21	0.80	21.38 - 15.13	121.6	4.4
2/29/96	2,523.2	① 24.1	822.3	2.0	1.0	8.0	2.9	1.7	① 1.33	2.98	11.10	0.80	23.88 - 17.63	15.6	3.9
2/28/95	2,295.1	① 57.0	846.7	3.8	2.5	19.6	6.7	1.5	① 3.16	4.67	10.14	0.80	19.13 - 15.13	5.4	4.7
2/28/94	2,224.7	① d13.4	773.7	3.1	...	...	...	1.5	① d0.72	0.87	9.67	0.80	27.50 - 17.25	...	3.6
2/28/93	2,223.9	41.2	803.5	3.4	1.9	12.8	5.1	1.4	2.13	3.63	12.19	0.80	29.25 - 23.25	12.3	3.4

Statistics are as originally reported. ① Incl. $3.5 mil pre-tax gain, 2001; $519,000 pre-tax gain, 2000; $18.7 mil after-tax chg., 1999; $3.2 mil ($0.17/sh) after-tax chg., 1998; $14.8 mil ($0.83/sh) after-tax chg., 1997; $500,000 ($0.02/sh) net after-tax gain, 1996; $29 mil ($1.61/sh) after-tax gain, 1995; $48.9 mil ($2.58/sh) after-tax chg., 1994. ② Bef. $19.6 mil ($1.04/sh) loss fr. discont. opers., 2000; $138.7 mil ($7.34/sh) loss fr. discont. opers., 1999. ③ Bef. $500,000 (0.02/sh) extraord. chg. & incl. $200,000 after-tax chg.

OFFICERS:
G. E. Costley, Chmn., C.E.O.
D. C. Swander, Pres., C.O.O.
J. E. Byom, V.P., C.F.O.

INVESTOR CONTACT: Jill Schmidt, Investor Relations, (952) 594-3385

PRINCIPAL OFFICE: 110 Cheshire Lane, Suite 300, Minnetonka, MN 55305

TELEPHONE NUMBER: (952) 594-3300
FAX: (952) 594-3343
WEB: www.multifoods.com
NO. OF EMPLOYEES: 4,680
SHAREHOLDERS: 3,998 (record).
ANNUAL MEETING: In June
INCORPORATED: DE, July, 1963; reincorp., Dec., 1969

INSTITUTIONAL HOLDINGS:
No. of Institutions: 101
Shares Held: 13,381,028
% Held: 70.0

INDUSTRY: Packaged frozen foods (SIC: 5142)

REGISTRAR(S): Wells Fargo Shareowner Services, South St. Paul, MN

INTERNATIONAL PAPER COMPANY

EXCH.	SYM.	REC. PRICE	P/E RATIO	YLD.	MKT. CAP.	RANGE (52-WK.)	'02 Y/E PR.
NYSE	IP	35.03 (2/28/03)	...	2.9%	$16.78 bill.	46.20 - 31.35	34.97

LOWER MEDIUM GRADE. THE COMPANY OUTLINED A THREE-YEAR STRATGEY TO IMPROVE PROFITABILITY.

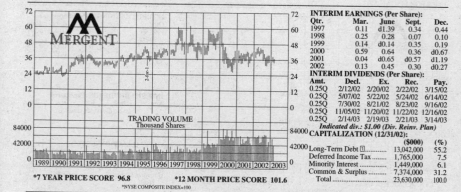

*7 YEAR PRICE SCORE 96.8   *12 MONTH PRICE SCORE 101.6
*NYSE COMPOSITE INDEX=100

INTERIM EARNINGS (Per Share):

Qtr.	Mar.	June	Sept.	Dec.
1997	0.11	d1.39	0.34	0.44
1998	0.25	0.28	0.07	0.10
1999	0.14	d0.14	0.35	0.19
2000	0.59	0.64	0.36	d0.67
2001	0.04	d0.65	d0.57	d1.19
2002	0.13	0.45	0.30	d0.27

INTERIM DIVIDENDS (Per Share):

Amt.	Decl.	Ex.	Rec.	Pay.
0.25Q	2/12/02	2/20/02	2/22/02	3/15/02
0.25Q	5/07/02	5/22/02	5/24/02	6/14/02
0.25Q	7/30/02	8/21/02	8/23/02	9/16/02
0.25Q	11/05/02	11/20/02	11/22/02	12/16/02
0.25Q	2/14/03	2/19/03	2/21/03	3/14/03

Indicated div.: $1.00 (Div. Reinv. Plan)

CAPITALIZATION (12/31/02):

	($000)	(%)
Long-Term Debt [1]	13,042,000	55.2
Deferred Income Tax	1,765,000	7.5
Minority Interest	1,449,000	6.1
Common & Surplus	7,374,000	31.2
Total	23,630,000	100.0

BUSINESS:

International Paper Company is a global paper and forest products company with an extensive distribution system. IP's businesses include paper, packaging and forest products. As of 2/20/03, IP had operations in over 40 countries and exported its products to more than 120 nations. IP's primary markets and manufacturing and distribution operations are in the U.S., Canada, Europe, the Pacific Rim and South America. IP produces printing and writing papers, pulp, tissue, paperboard and packaging and wood products. IP manufactures specialty chemicals and specialty panels and laminated products. On 4/30/99, IP acquired Union Camp Corp. On 6/19/00, IP acquired Champion International.

RECENT DEVELOPMENTS:

For the year ended 12/31/02, income amounted to $295.0 million, before an accounting change charge of $1.18 billion, compared with a loss of $1.14 billion, before an accounting change charge of $16.0 million, in 2001. The improvement in earnings was primarily attributed to cost controls and product mix improvements. Results for 2002 and 2001 included net cumulative charges of $245.0 million and $1.40 billion, respectively. Net sales declined 5.3% to $24.98 billion from $26.36 billion a year earlier. Operating income rose 8.3% to $1.94 billion.

PROSPECTS:

Going forward, IP will continue to focus on improving its three core businesses, paper, packaging and forest products and divesting its non-core operations. Moreover, IP will continue to strengthen its core businesses through a rationalization and realignment program. IP plans to grow the top line with higher volumes and a better product mix. This strategy, along with operational improvements, lower selling, general and administrative expenses and improvement to the supply chain should improve IP's results by $1.50 billion by the end of 2005. However, the mix of higher than anticipated energy costs, bad weather that has affected fiber costs and operational performance, combined with weakening demand, may negatively affect earnings in the near term.

ANNUAL FINANCIAL DATA:

FISCAL YEAR	TOT. REVS. ($mill.)	NET INC. ($mill.)	TOT. ASSETS ($mill.)	OPER. PROFIT %	NET PROFIT %	RET. ON EQUITY %	RET. ON ASSETS %	CURR. RATIO	EARN. PER SH. $	CASH FL. PER SH. $	TANG. BK. VAL.$	DIV. PER SH. $	PRICE RANGE	AVG. P/E RATIO	AVG. YIELD %
p12/31/02	24,976.0	[8] 295.0	33,792.0	...	...	...	...	1.5	[8] 0.61	1.51	7.78	1.00	46.20 - 31.35	63.6	2.6
12/31/01	26,363.0	[6][7] d1,142.0	37,158.0	...	...	...	...	1.5	[6][7] d2.37	1.89	11.89	1.00	43.31 - 30.70	...	2.7
12/31/00	28,180.0	[2][6] 368.0	42,109.0	5.5	1.3	3.1	0.9	1.4	[2][6] 0.32	5.08	11.89	1.00	60.00 - 26.31	134.8	2.3
12/31/99	24,573.0	[5][6] 199.0	30,268.0	4.0	0.8	1.9	0.7	1.7	[5][6] 0.44	4.13	18.65	1.00	59.50 - 39.50	112.5	2.0
12/31/98	19,541.0	[5] 236.0	26,356.0	4.6	1.2	2.7	0.9	1.7	[5] 0.77	4.64	20.44	1.00	61.75 - 35.50	63.1	2.1
12/31/97	20,096.0	[5] d151.0	26,754.0	2.5	...	...	...	1.2	[5] d0.50	3.68	20.36	1.00	61.00 - 38.63	...	2.0
12/31/96	20,143.0	[3][4] d881.0	28,252.0	0.7	...	...	...	1.0	[3][4] 1.04	1.04	22.59	1.00	44.63 - 35.63	38.6	2.5
12/31/95	19,797.0	[3] 1,153.0	23,977.0	12.7	5.8	14.0	4.8	1.2	[3] 4.50	8.74	24.68	0.92	45.69 - 34.13	8.9	2.3
12/31/94	14,966.0	432.0	17,836.0	7.1	2.9	6.6	2.4	1.2	1.73	5.27	22.82	0.84	40.25 - 30.31	20.4	2.4
12/31/93	13,685.0	[2] 289.0	16,631.0	5.9	2.1	4.6	1.7	1.1	[2] 1.17	4.83	22.06	0.84	34.94 - 28.31	27.0	2.7

Statistics are as originally reported. Adj. for stock split: 2-for-1, 9/95. [1] Incl. deb. conv. into common. [2] Incl. chrg. of $25 mill., 1993; $969.0 mill., 2000. [3] Bef. a $75 mill. acctg. chrg. of $70 mill., 1995; & $515 mill., 1996. [4] Incl. $592 mill. gain. [5] Incl. net after-tax loss for special items of $461.0 mill., 1997; $95.0 mill., 1998; & $593.0 mill., 1999. [6] Excl. extraord. chrg. of $16.0 mill., 1999; $226.0 mill., 2000; $46.0 mill., 2001. [7] Excl. acct. change chrg. of $16.0 mill., but incl. net nonrecurr. pretax. chrg. of $1.77 bill. [8] Bef. an acctg. chg. chrg. of $1.18 bill., but incl. net cumulative charges of $245.0 mill.

OFFICERS:
J. T. Dillon, Chmn., C.E.O.
J. V. Faraci, Pres.
J. P. Melican, Exec. V.P.
INVESTOR CONTACT: Investor Relations, (203) 541-8000
PRINCIPAL OFFICE: 400 Atlantic Street, Stamford, CT 06921

TELEPHONE NUMBER: (203) 541-8000
FAX: (203) 541-8225
WEB: www.internationalpaper.com
NO. OF EMPLOYEES: 100,000 (avg.)
SHAREHOLDERS: 39,653
ANNUAL MEETING: In May
INCORPORATED: NY, June, 1941

INSTITUTIONAL HOLDINGS:
No. of Institutions: 548
Shares Held: 412,531,108
% Held: 86.0

INDUSTRY: Paper mills (SIC: 2621)

TRANSFER AGENT(S): Mellon Investor Services, LLC, Ridgefield Park, NJ

INTERNATIONAL RECTIFIER CORP.

EXCH.	SYM.	REC. PRICE	P/E RATIO	YLD.	MKT. CAP.	RANGE (52-WK.)	'02 Y/E PR.
NYSE	IRF	22.35 (2/28/03)	...	...	$1.42 bill.	50.50 - 10.65	18.46

MEDIUM GRADE. THE COMPANY IS ON TRACK TO ACHIEVE ITS TARGETED REVENUE GROWTH OF 17.0% TO 23.0% FOR FISCAL 2003.

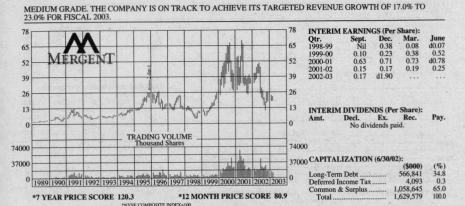

*7 YEAR PRICE SCORE 120.3   ***12 MONTH PRICE SCORE 80.9**

*NYSE COMPOSITE INDEX=100

INTERIM EARNINGS (Per Share):

Qtr.	Sept.	Dec.	Mar.	June
1998-99	Nil	0.38	0.08	d0.07
1999-00	0.10	0.23	0.38	0.52
2000-01	0.63	0.71	0.73	d0.78
2001-02	0.15	0.17	0.19	0.25
2002-03	0.17	d1.90	...	...

INTERIM DIVIDENDS (Per Share):

Amt.	Decl.	Ex.	Rec.	Pay.
		No dividends paid.		

CAPITALIZATION (6/30/02):

	($000)	(%)
Long-Term Debt	566,841	34.8
Deferred Income Tax	4,093	0.3
Common & Surplus	1,058,645	65.0
Total	1,629,579	100.0

BUSINESS:

International Rectifier Corp. is a global supplier of power management products and metal oxide semiconductor field effect transistors (MOSFETs) designed to increase system efficiency, allow more compact end products, improve features and functionality and extend battery life. IRF's products are used in a range of end-markets, including consumer electronics, information technology, automotive, aerospace and defense, communications and industrial. For the year ended 6/30/02, IRF's revenues by region were derived: North America, 34.2%; Europe, 21.8%; and Asia Pacific and Japan, 44.0%. IRF has manufacturing facilities in North America, Europe and Asia.

RECENT DEVELOPMENTS:

For the second quarter ended 12/31/02, the Company reported a net loss of $121.3 million compared with net income of $10.8 million in the equivalent 2001 quarter. Results for 2002 and 2001 included amortization of acquisition-related intangibles of $1.3 million and $971,000, respectively. Results for 2002 also included asset impairment, restructuring and severance charges of $179.8 mil-lion. Revenues advanced 21.8% to $209.5 million from $172.1 million a year earlier, primarily due to strong demand in the consumer, defense and personal computer sectors. Orders grew 33.0% year over year, reflecting continued strength of IRF's proprietary products. Gross profit rose 2.5% to $62.1 million from $60.6 million the year before.

PROSPECTS:

The Company's current restructuring actions will concentrate resources on proprietary products, reduce development and manufacturing cycle times and improve cost structure. Over the next several quarters, IRF plans to upgrade equipment and processes in designated facilities and close down a number of other facilities. IRF anticipates that its accelerated transition to proprietary products will result in stepping up their contribution by 5.0% to between 65.0% and 70.0% of total sales by the end of fiscal 2004. Separately, for fiscal 2003, the Company is on track to achieve its targeted revenue growth of 17.0% to 23.0%.

ANNUAL FINANCIAL DATA:

FISCAL YEAR	TOT. REVS. ($mill.)	NET INC. ($mill.)	TOT. ASSETS ($mill.)	OPER. PROFIT %	NET PROFIT %	RET. ON EQUITY %	RET. ON ASSETS %	CURR. RATIO	EARN. PER SH. $	CASH FL. PER SH. $	TANG. BK. VAL. $	PRICE RANGE	AVG. P/E RATIO
6/30/02	720.2	48.7	1,813.2	8.0	6.8	4.6	2.7	4.3	0.75	1.73	13.64		
6/30/01	978.6	④ 87.6	1,746.5	9.7	9.0	8.9	5.0	6.2	④ 1.35	2.45	14.13	69.50 - 24.05	34.6
6/30/00	753.3	③ 73.1	1,026.0	14.1	9.7	8.7	7.1	3.9	③ 1.27	2.24	13.70	67.44 - 23.50	35.8
6/30/99	545.4	② 20.4	709.1	...	3.7	5.1	2.9	2.2	② 0.39	1.28	7.65	26.00 - 6.25	41.3
6/30/98	551.9	16.5	735.8	5.9	3.0	4.1	2.2	2.1	0.32	1.07	7.78	14.75 - 4.25	29.7
6/30/97	486.1	① d43.2	679.8	...	...	...	...	2.8	① d0.84	d0.12	7.48	23.75 - 10.88	...
6/30/96	576.8	66.5	629.1	16.8	11.5	15.8	10.6	2.2	1.29	1.88	7.97	27.00 - 11.25	14.8
6/30/95	429.0	39.4	496.2	11.3	9.2	11.4	7.9	2.2	0.84	1.34	6.85	26.00 - 11.06	22.1
6/30/94	328.9	15.7	330.6	7.2	4.8	7.7	4.8	1.7	0.38	0.83	4.99	12.19 - 6.50	24.6
6/30/93	281.7	d3.0	278.4	0.8	...	...	...	1.8	d0.07	0.34	4.60	7.50 - 4.81	...

Statistics are as originally reported. Adj. for 2-for-1 split, 12/95. ① Incl. $58.6 mill. after-tax chg. for impairment & restr. ② Incl. $24.5 mill. restr. chgs. & excl. $26.2 mill. cumulative effect acct. chg. ③ Excl. $4.8 mill. net extraord. chg. ④ Incl. $48.0 mill. impair. of assets & restr. chg.

OFFICERS:
E. Lidow, Chmn.
A. Lidow, C.E.O.
M. P. McGee, Exec. V.P., C.F.O.

INVESTOR CONTACT: Steve Harrison, (310) 252-7731

PRINCIPAL OFFICE: 233 Kansas Street, El Segundo, CA 90245

TELEPHONE NUMBER: (310) 726-8000
FAX: (310) 322-3332
WEB: www.irf.com
NO. OF EMPLOYEES: 5,900 (approx.)
SHAREHOLDERS: 1,778,000 (approx.)
ANNUAL MEETING: In Nov.
INCORPORATED: CA, Aug., 1947; reincorp., DE, Oct., 1979

INSTITUTIONAL HOLDINGS:
No. of Institutions: 221
Shares Held: 45,959,845
% Held: 72.0

INDUSTRY: Semiconductors and related devices (SIC: 3674)

TRANSFER AGENT(S): Mellon Investor Services, Los Angeles, CA

INTERPUBLIC GROUP OF COMPANIES, INC.

EXCH.	SYM.	REC. PRICE	P/E RATIO	YLD.	MKT. CAP.	RANGE (52-WK.)	'02 Y/E PR.
NYSE	IPG	9.65 (2/28/03)	17.2	3.9%	$3.65 bill.	34.98 - 8.60	14.08

MEDIUM GRADE. FOR FULL-YEAR 2003, REVENUES ARE EXPECTED TO DECLINE BETWEEN 1.0% AND 4.0%, AND EARNINGS PER SHARE ARE ANTICIPATED TO RANGE FROM $0.68 TO $0.72.

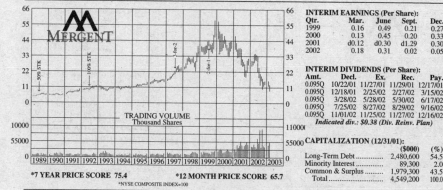

INTERIM EARNINGS (Per Share):

Qtr.	Mar.	June	Sept.	Dec.
1999	0.16	0.49	0.21	0.27
2000	0.13	0.45	0.20	0.33
2001	d0.12	d0.30	d1.29	0.30
2002	0.18	0.31	0.02	0.05

INTERIM DIVIDENDS (Per Share):

Amt.	Decl.	Ex.	Rec.	Pay.
0.095Q	10/22/01	11/27/01	11/29/01	12/17/01
0.095Q	12/18/01	2/25/02	2/27/02	3/15/02
0.095Q	3/28/02	5/28/02	5/30/02	6/17/02
0.095Q	7/25/02	8/27/02	8/29/02	9/16/02
0.095Q	11/01/02	11/25/02	11/27/02	12/16/02

Indicated div.: $0.38 (Div. Reinv. Plan)

TRADING VOLUME
Thousand Shares

*7 YEAR PRICE SCORE 75.4   ***12 MONTH PRICE SCORE 65.7**
NYSE COMPOSITE INDEX=100

CAPITALIZATION (12/31/01):

	($000)	(%)
Long-Term Debt	2,480,600	54.5
Minority Interest	89,300	2.0
Common & Surplus	1,979,300	43.5
Total	4,549,200	100.0

BUSINESS:

Interpublic Group of Companies, Inc. is a large organization of advertising agencies and marketing services companies. Its four global operating groups are McCann-Erickson WorldGroup, The Partnership, FCB Group and Interpublic Sports and Entertainment Group. Major global brands include Draft Worldwide, Foote, Cone & Belding Worldwide, Golin/Harris International, NFO WorldGroup, Initiative Media, Lowe & Partners Worldwide, McCann-Erickson, Octagon, Universal McCann, and Weber Shandwick. IPG also offers advertising agency services through association arrangements with local agencies in various parts of the world. Other activities conducted by the Company within the area of marketing communications include public relations, graphic design and market research. On 6/22/01, the Company acquired True North Communications, Inc.

RECENT DEVELOPMENTS:

For the year ended 12/31/02, IPG reported net income of $99.5 million versus a net loss of $534.5 million the year before. Earnings for 2002 and 2001 included net charges related to various items of $178.9 million and $1.16 million, and amortization of intangible assets of $13.0 million and $173.1 million, respectively. Total revenue decreased 8.7% to $6.20 billion, primarily due to softness in the advertising and marketing industries, as well as poor performance at Octagon Motor Sports and McCann-Erickson WorldGroup. Comparisons were made with restated prior-year figures.

PROSPECTS:

New business in 2002 was strong, reflecting major new or additional assignments for Bank of America, Burger King, Club Med, Levi Strauss, and Novartis. Other significant new assignments won during the fourth quarter of 2002 included Astra Zeneca's Symbicort, the Internal Revenue Service, Merck's Ezetrik and Qwest. For full-year 2003, revenues are expected to decline between 1.0% and 4.0% as a result of continued weakness in demand for advertising and marketing services, and earnings per share are anticipated to range from $0.68 to $0.72.

ANNUAL FINANCIAL DATA:

FISCAL YEAR	TOT. REVS. ($mil.)	NET INC. ($mil.)	TOT. ASSETS ($mil.)	OPER. PROFIT %	NET PROFIT %	RET. ON EQUITY %	RET. ON ASSETS %	CURR. RATIO	EARN. PER SH. $	CASH FL. PER SH. $	TANG. BK. VAL. $	DIV. PER SH. $	PRICE RANGE	AVG. P/E RATIO	AVG. YIELD %
p12/31/02	6,203.6	⑧ 99.5	...	...	...	...	...	...	⑧ 0.26	...	...	0.38	34.98 - 9.85	86.2	1.7
12/31/01	6,726.8	⑤⑦ d505.3	11,514.7	...	...	...	...	1.0	⑤⑦ d1.37	d0.15	...	0.38	47.44 - 18.25	...	1.2
12/31/00	5,625.8	⑤⑥ 358.7	10,238.2	12.0	6.4	17.5	3.5	1.0	⑤⑥ 1.15	2.11	...	0.37	57.69 - 32.69	39.3	0.8
12/31/99	4,427.3	⑤ 321.9	8,727.3	11.7	7.3	19.8	3.7	1.0	⑤ 1.11	1.86	...	0.33	58.38 - 34.41	41.8	0.7
12/31/98	3,844.3	309.9	6,942.8	12.9	8.1	24.5	4.5	1.0	1.11	1.74	...	0.29	40.31 - 22.56	28.4	0.9
12/31/97	2,997.2	239.1	5,702.5	12.1	8.0	21.6	4.2	1.1	0.95	1.43	0.32	0.25	26.50 - 15.67	22.2	1.2
12/31/96	2,430.5	④ 205.2	4,765.1	12.0	8.4	23.5	4.3	1.1	④ 0.85	1.28	0.50	0.22	16.75 - 13.21	17.6	1.5
12/31/95	2,093.8	③ 129.8	4,259.8	9.9	6.2	17.3	3.0	1.1	③ 0.55	0.94	0.47	0.20	14.46 - 10.58	22.6	1.6
12/31/94	1,916.4	② 115.2	3,793.4	8.7	6.0	17.7	3.0	1.0	② 0.51	0.84	0.21	0.18	11.96 - 9.17	20.7	1.7
12/31/93	1,739.8	① 125.3	2,869.8	11.7	7.2	22.2	4.4	1.1	① 0.56	0.87	0.32	0.16	11.88 - 7.96	17.8	1.6

Statistics are as originally reported. Adj. for stk. splits: 2-for-1, 7/99; 3-for-2, 7/97. ① Bef. acct. chrg. $512,000. ② Incl. acctg. chrg. of $21.8 mill. & restruct. chrg. of $25.7 mill. ③ Incl. aft.-tax chrg. of $38.2 mill. for write-down of assets. ④ Incl. $8.1 mill. gain from sale of a portion of IPG's interest in CKS Group, Inc. ⑤ Incl. pre-tax restruct. & other merger-rel. chrgs. of $645.6 mill., 2001; $116.1 mill. 2000; $84.2 mill., 1999. ⑥ Incl. pre-tax non-recurr. transaction costs of $44.7 mill. ⑦ Incl. costs of $303.1 mill. rel. to goodwill & oth. asset impairments. ⑧ Incl. non-recurr. net chrgs. of $178.9 mill.

OFFICERS:
D. A. Bell, Chmn., C.E.O.
S. F. Orr, Exec. V.P., C.F.O.

INVESTOR CONTACT: Susan V. Watson, Sr. V.P.-Inv. Rel., (212) 399-8208

PRINCIPAL OFFICE: 1271 Avenue of the Americas, New York, NY 10020

TELEPHONE NUMBER: (212) 399-8000
FAX: (212) 399-8130
WEB: www.interpublic.com

NO. OF EMPLOYEES: 54,100 (approx.)

SHAREHOLDERS: 17,872 (approx.)

ANNUAL MEETING: In May

INCORPORATED: DE, Sept., 1930

INSTITUTIONAL HOLDINGS:
No. of Institutions: 417
Shares Held: 340,400,044
% Held: 88.3

INDUSTRY: Advertising agencies (SIC: 7311)

TRANSFER AGENT(S): First Chicago Trust Company, Jersey City, NJ

INTERSTATE BAKERIES CORPORATION

EXCH.	SYM.	REC. PRICE	P/E RATIO	YLD.	MKT. CAP.	RANGE (52-WK.)	'02 Y/E PR.
NYSE	IBC	9.59 (2/28/03)	5.9	2.9%	$420.3 mill.	29.22 - 8.60	15.25

UPPER MEDIUM GRADE. THE COMPANY IS TAKING STEPS EXPECTED TO HELP BOOST SALES AND IMPROVE PROFITABILITY.

TRADING VOLUME
Thousand Shares

*7 YEAR PRICE SCORE 109.3   ***12 MONTH PRICE SCORE 64.0**
*NYSE COMPOSITE INDEX=100

INTERIM EARNINGS (Per Share):

Qtr.	Aug.	Nov.	Feb.	May
1997-98	0.40	0.46	0.40	0.46
1998-99	0.47	0.44	0.41	0.42
1999-00	0.47	0.40	0.30	0.12
2000-01	0.41	0.22	0.15	0.30
2001-02	0.19	0.41	0.32	0.45
2002-03	0.60	0.26	...	...

INTERIM DIVIDENDS (Per Share):

Amt.	Decl.	Ex.	Rec.	Pay.
0.07Q	3/27/02	4/11/02	4/15/02	5/01/02
0.07Q	6/26/02	7/11/02	7/15/02	8/01/02
0.07Q	9/24/02	10/10/02	10/15/02	11/01/02
0.07Q	12/12/02	1/13/03	1/15/03	2/03/03
0.07Q	3/26/03	4/11/03	4/15/03	5/01/03

Indicated div.: $0.28 (Div. Reinv. Plan)

CAPITALIZATION (6/1/02):

	($000)	(%)
Long-Term Debt	581,438	56.5
Deferred Income Tax	147,139	14.3
Common & Surplus	301,230	29.3
Total	1,029,807	100.0

BUSINESS:

Interstate Bakeries Corporation, through its wholly-owned operating subsidiary, Interstate Brands Corporation, is a baker and distributor of fresh bakery products in the United States. The Company produces, markets, distributes and sells a wide range of breads, rolls, snack cakes, donuts, sweet goods and related products. These products are sold under several national brand names, including WONDER®, HOSTESS®, ROMAN MEAL®, SUN-MAID®, and HOME PRIDE®, as well as regional brand names, including DOLLY MADISON®, BUTTERNUT®, SWEETHEART®, MERITA®, MARIE CALLENDERS®, and DRAKE'S®. In July 1995, IBC acquired Continental Baking Company from Ralston Purina Company. In March 1997, IBC acquired the assets of the San Francisco French Bread Company.

RECENT DEVELOPMENTS:

For the 12 weeks ended 11/16/02, net income totaled $11.6 million compared with $21.2 million in the corresponding period the previous year. Results for 2002 included a pre-tax non-recurring charge of $5.0 million related to the closure of the Company's Tampa, Florida bakery and a common stock award to IBC's former Chief Executive Officer.

Net sales slipped 0.3% to $823.2 million from $826.1 million a year earlier. As a percentage of net sales, gross profit slid to 51.5% versus 52.3% the year before. Operating income was $27.9 million, down 33.0% from $41.6 million in the prior year.

PROSPECTS:

Results are being negatively affected by rising costs for certain ingredients, primarily cocoa and sweeteners, and higher medical and pension expenses. In response, the Company is taking steps to drive top-line growth through the launch of new products and in-store merchandising initiatives for both bread and sweet goods. In addition, IBC is focused on minimizing product costs and reducing manufacturing and distribution costs. Separately, IBC expects to open a new bakery in Las Vegas, Nevada in the spring of 2003. This new bakery should help boost sales in the rapidly growing Las Vegas area, as well as supply needed capacity for the Company's West Coast markets.

ANNUAL FINANCIAL DATA:

FISCAL YEAR	TOT. REVS. ($Mill.)	NET INC. ($Mill.)	TOT. ASSETS ($Mill.)	OPER. PROFIT %	NET PROFIT %	RET. ON EQUITY %	RET. ON ASSETS %	CURR. RATIO	EARN. PER SH. $	CASH FL. PER SH. $	TANG. BK. VAL. $	DIV. PER SH. $	PRICE RANGE	AVG. P/E RATIO	AVG. YIELD %
6/01/02	3,532.4	③ 69.8	1,602.9	4.2	2.0	23.2	4.4	0.9	③ 1.36	3.23	...	0.28	25.95 - 13.27	14.4	1.4
6/02/01	3,496.5	61.1	1,623.5	4.2	1.7	15.6	3.8	1.0	1.13	3.17	...	0.28	20.38 - 10.50	13.7	1.8
6/03/00	3,522.9	② 89.4	1,651.9	4.8	2.5	15.1	5.4	1.0	② 1.31	2.94	2.53	0.28	27.00 - 16.19	16.5	1.3
5/29/99	3,459.4	126.2	1,680.8	6.5	3.6	20.9	7.5	1.0	1.74	3.26	2.49	0.28	38.00 - 23.38	17.6	0.9
5/30/98	3,265.8	127.9	1,550.0	7.1	3.9	22.6	8.3	0.9	1.71	3.08	2.73	0.27	36.88 - 21.63	17.1	0.9
5/31/97	3,212.4	97.2	1,493.1	6.0	3.0	18.0	6.5	0.9	1.28	2.63	2.37	0.26	24.81 - 10.19	13.7	1.5
6/01/96	2,878.2	24.5	1,486.5	2.7	0.8	5.3	1.6	0.9	0.35	1.80	1.47	0.25	11.69 - 6.69	26.2	2.7
6/03/95	1,222.8	20.7	598.4	4.7	1.7	10.5	3.5	1.1	0.53	1.38	...	0.25	7.56 - 5.81	12.7	3.7
5/28/94	1,142.7	15.8	574.8	4.1	1.4	8.4	2.7	1.1	0.39	1.17	...	0.24	10.00 - 6.88	21.6	2.9
5/29/93	1,165.6	① 30.8	586.8	6.1	2.6	15.2	5.2	1.0	① 0.73	1.48	...	0.23	10.56 - 7.19	12.2	2.5

Statistics are as originally reported. Adj. for 2-for-1 stk. split, 11/97. ① Bef. $14.1 mil ($0.34/sh) chg. for acctg. change. ② Incl. $23.6 mil ($0.22/sh) non-recurr. chg. related to a work stoppage, workers' comp. costs and bakery start-up costs. ③ Incl. $25.7 mil ($0.31/sh) non-recurr. chg. related to the closure of the Company's Detroit bakery and a litigation settlement.

OFFICERS:
C. A. Sullivan, Chmn.
J. R. Elsesser, C.E.O.
M. D. Kafoure, Pres., C.O.O.
F. W. Coffey, Sr. V.P., C.F.O.

INVESTOR CONTACT: Frank W. Coffey, Sr. V.P. & C.F.O., (816) 502-4000

PRINCIPAL OFFICE: 12 East Armour Boulevard, Kansas City, MO 64141

TELEPHONE NUMBER: (816) 502-4000
FAX: (816) 502-4126
WEB: www.interstatebakeriescorp.com

NO. OF EMPLOYEES: 35,000 (approx.)

SHAREHOLDERS: 2,154 (approx.)

ANNUAL MEETING: In Sept.

INCORPORATED: DE, 1987

INSTITUTIONAL HOLDINGS:
No. of Institutions: 171
Shares Held: 41,517,655
% Held: 93.9

INDUSTRY: Bread, cake, and related products (SIC: 2051)

TRANSFER AGENT(S): United Missouri Bank, N.A., Kansas City, MO

INVESTMENT TECHNOLOGY GROUP, INC.

EXCH.	SYM.	REC. PRICE	P/E RATIO	YLD.	MKT. CAP.	RANGE (52-WK.)	'02 Y/E PR.
NYSE	ITG	12.59 (2/28/03)	8.3	...	$0.61 bill.	54.41 - 12.27	22.36

UPPER MEDIUM GRADE. THE COMPANY WILL REDUCE ITS WORKFORCE BY APPROXIMATELY 10.0%, WHICH SHOULD RESULT IN ANNUALIZED COST SAVINGS OF APPROXIMATELY $12.0 MILLION BEGINNING IN 2003.

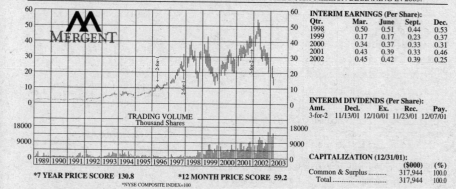

*7 YEAR PRICE SCORE 130.8   ***12 MONTH PRICE SCORE 59.2**

*NYSE COMPOSITE INDEX=100

INTERIM EARNINGS (Per Share):

Qtr.	Mar.	June	Sept.	Dec.
1998	0.50	0.51	0.44	0.53
1999	0.17	0.17	0.23	0.37
2000	0.34	0.37	0.33	0.31
2001	0.43	0.39	0.33	0.46
2002	0.45	0.42	0.39	0.25

INTERIM DIVIDENDS (Per Share):

Amt.	Decl.	Ex.	Rec.	Pay.
3-for-2	11/13/01	12/10/01	11/23/01	12/07/01

CAPITALIZATION (12/31/01):

	($000)	(%)
Common & Surplus	317,944	100.0
Total	317,944	100.0

BUSINESS:

Investment Technology Group, Inc. provides technology-based equity trading services and transaction research to institutional investors and brokers. ITG offers, among other services, POSIT, an electronic stock crossing system through which clients enter buy and sell orders to trade single stocks and portfolios of equity securities in a confidential environment; QuantEX, an advanced tool for technologically sophisticated clients transacting large volumes of orders; SmartServers, which allow clients to send orders to a computer for execution using a designated trading strategy; and the Electronic Trading Desk, a full-service agency execution group that specializes in the use of the Company's proprietary products. On 4/27/99, the Company was separated from Jefferies Group, Inc. Net sales for 2002 were derived as follows: POSIT, 40.0%; Client Site, 28.7%; Electronic Trading Desk, 28.8%; and other, 2.4%.

RECENT DEVELOPMENTS:

For the quarter ended 12/31/02, net income decreased 64.5% to $73.8 million compared with $78.9 million the year before. Earnings for 2002 included restructuring charges of $5.9 million. Earnings for 2001 included a net gain on long-term investments of $309,000. Total revenues increased 2.7% to $387.6 million from $377.4 million in the prior year. Electronic trading desk commissions advanced 24.5% to $111.7 million, and client-site trading products commissions rose 18.4% to $111.3 million. However, POSIT commissions declined 16.7% to $155.1 million from $186.1 million the year before.

PROSPECTS:

On 12/5/02, the Company announced that it is reducing its workforce by approximately 10.0% to align its infrastructure with expected continuation of weak institutional trading volumes in the first half of 2003. The Company anticipates the cuts to result in annualized cost savings of approximately $12.0 million beginning in 2003. Separately, despite difficult trading conditions in most overseas capital markets, ITG's international expansion continues to progress, with the opening of operations in Hong Kong during 2002.

ANNUAL FINANCIAL DATA:

FISCAL YEAR	TOT. REVS. ($mill.)	NET INC. ($mill.)	TOT. ASSETS ($mill.)	OPER. PROFIT %	NET PROFIT %	RET. ON EQUITY %	RET. ON ASSETS %	CURR. RATIO	EARN. PER SH.$	CASH FL. PER SH.$	TANG. BK. VAL.$	DIV. PER SH.$	PRICE RANGE	AVG. P/E RATIO	AVG. YIELD %
p12/31/02	387.6	⑤73.8	594.3						⑤1.51				54.41 - 20.40	24.8	...
12/31/01	377.4	④78.9	418.5	36.1	20.9	24.8	18.9	2.6	④1.62	1.96	5.95	...	44.10 - 24.38	21.1	...
12/31/00	310.4	④63.6	281.7	36.4	20.5	30.2	22.6	3.0	④1.35	1.63	4.34	...	35.13 - 18.13	19.8	...
12/31/99	232.0	③④45.4	179.5	35.7	19.6	39.3	25.3	1.8	③④0.95	1.22	2.23	0.03	43.34 - 11.88	29.1	0.1
12/31/98	798.7	③④69.7	2,683.6	17.3	8.7	20.8	2.6	4.1	③④1.97	2.71	10.51	0.13	39.67 - 11.04	12.9	0.5
12/31/97	764.5	63.6	2,099.5	15.2	8.3	26.2	3.0	1.1	1.87	2.39	7.98	0.08	32.00 - 12.92	12.0	0.4
12/31/96	540.8	43.6	1,568.1	15.4	8.1	22.3	2.8	1.1	2.45	3.26	12.57	0.06	13.58 - 7.42	4.3	0.6
12/31/95	419.7	28.5	1,537.0	12.7	6.8	15.3	1.9	1.1	1.59	2.13	11.03	0.03	8.08 - 4.75	4.0	0.5
12/31/94	316.1	②20.2	1,557.3	9.7	6.4	12.4	1.3	1.1	②1.08	1.52	9.71	0.03	7.63 - 4.75	5.7	0.5
12/31/93	318.1	①27.6	1,388.4	14.9	8.7	19.1	2.0	1.1	①1.79	2.22	11.39	0.03	6.75 - 3.13	2.8	0.7

Statistics are as originally reported. Figures prior to and including 12/31/98 reflect Jefferies Group, Inc. (old). Adj. for 3-for-2 stk. split, 12/01. ① Bef. acctg. gain of $1.4 mill. ② Incl. pre-tax gain of $8.3 mill. on IPO. ③ Incl. spin-off costs of $6.5 mill., 1999; $1.9 mill., 1998. ④ Incl. pre-tax net gain on lg.-tm. investments of $309,000, 12/01; loss $5.3 mill., 12/00; loss $2.7 mill., 12/99; loss $204,000, 12/98. ⑤ Incl. restructuring chrgs. of $5.9 mill.

OFFICERS:
R. L. Killian Jr., Chmn., Pres.
R. J. Russell, C.E.O.
H. C. Naphtali, C.F.O.

INVESTOR CONTACT: Howard C. Naphtali,
C.F.O., (212) 444-6160

PRINCIPAL OFFICE: 380 Madison Avenue,
New York, NY 10017

TELEPHONE NUMBER: (212) 588-4000
FAX: (212) 444-6490
WEB: www.itginc.com

NO. OF EMPLOYEES: 588 (avg.)

SHAREHOLDERS: 9,300 (approx.)

ANNUAL MEETING: In May

INCORPORATED: DE, Aug., 1983

INSTITUTIONAL HOLDINGS:
No. of Institutions: 171
Shares Held: 38,907,361
% Held: 81.2

INDUSTRY: Security brokers and dealers
(SIC: 6211)

TRANSFER AGENT(S): First Chicago Trust
Company of New York, New York, NY

IRON MOUNTAIN INC.

EXCH.	SYM.	REC. PRICE	P/E RATIO	YLD.	MKT. CAP.	RANGE (52-WK.)	'02 Y/E PR.
NYSE	IRM	35.20 (2/28/03)	45.1	...	$2.97 bill.	35.25 - 20.14	33.01

LOWER MEDIUM GRADE. ON 2/12/03, IRM ANNOUNCED THE EXPANSION OF ITS SECURE SHREDDING SERVICES FOOTPRINT WITH THE ACQUISITION OF SHREDCO, INC.

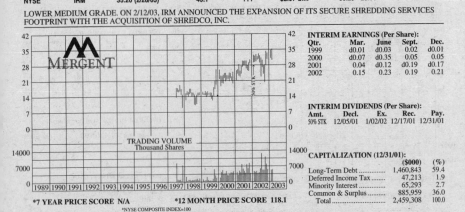

INTERIM EARNINGS (Per Share):

Qtr.	Mar.	June	Sept.	Dec.
1999	d0.01	d0.03	0.02	d0.01
2000	d0.07	d0.35	0.05	0.05
2001	0.04	d0.12	d0.19	d0.17
2002	0.15	0.23	0.19	0.21

INTERIM DIVIDENDS (Per Share):

Amt.	Decl.	Ex.	Rec.	Pay.
50% STK	12/05/01	1/02/02	12/17/01	12/31/01

CAPITALIZATION (12/31/01):

	($000)	(%)
Long-Term Debt	1,460,843	59.4
Deferred Income Tax	47,213	1.9
Minority Interest	65,293	2.7
Common & Surplus	885,959	36.0
Total	2,459,308	100.0

*7 YEAR PRICE SCORE N/A   ***12 MONTH PRICE SCORE 118.1**

*NYSE COMPOSITE INDEX=100

BUSINESS:

Iron Mountain Inc. is a global full-service provider of records, information management and related services to more than 150,000 customer accounts throughout the U.S., Canada, Europe and Latin America as of 2/27/03. The Company provides storage and management services for all types of media, including paper, computer disks and tapes, microfilm and microfiche, master audio and video tapes, film and optical disks, X-rays and blueprints. IRM's principal services include courier pickup and delivery, filing, retrieval and destruction of records, database management, customized reporting and disaster recovery support. From 1999 through 2002, IRM made 56 acquisitions, including the purchase of Pierce Leahy Inc. on 2/1/00 for $1.00 billion.

RECENT DEVELOPMENTS:

For the year ended 12/31/02, IRM reported income of $67.0 million, before a gain from discontinued operations of $1.1 million and an accounting change charge of $6.4 million, versus a loss of $32.2 million in 2001. Results for 2002 and 2001 included merger-related charges of $796,000 and $3.7 million, and excluded extraordinary charges of $3.5 million and $11.8 million, respectively. Total revenues advanced 11.2% to $1.32 billion from $1.19 billion a year earlier. Storage revenues increased 9.4% to $759.5 million, while service and storage material sales climbed 13.8% to $559.0 million. Operating income jumped 74.7% to $253.2 million.

PROSPECTS:

For 2003, the Company has revised its guidance in order to reflect its new reporting format, which includes the results of its digital business, and to incorporate certain recent acquisitions. Revenues for 2003 are expected to be in the range of $1.44 billion to $1.48 billion, up from the previous guidance of $1.41 billion to $1.45 billion. Capital expenditures for the year are expected to be between $190.0 million and $215.0 million, including at least $15.0 million associated with IRM's digital business. Separately, on 2/12/03, IRM announced that it had expanded its Secure Shredding services footprint with the acquisition of Shredco, Inc. Terms of the transaction were not disclosed.

ANNUAL FINANCIAL DATA:

FISCAL YEAR	TOT. REVS. ($mill.)	NET INC. ($mill.)	TOT. ASSETS ($mill.)	OPER. PROFIT %	NET PROFIT %	RET. ON EQUITY %	RET. ON ASSETS %	CURR. RATIO	EARN. PER SH. $	CASH FL. PER SH. $	PRICE RANGE
p12/31/02	1,318.5	9 67.0							9 0.78		34.20 - 20.14
12/31/01	1,171.1	8 d32.2	2,859.9	12.4	...	...	...	0.9	8 d0.39	1.51	30.47 - 21.08
12/31/00	986.4	7 d24.9	2,659.1	10.7	...	...	...	0.8	7 d0.31	1.31	26.06 - 18.50
5 12/31/99	519.5	6 d1.1	1,317.2	12.4	...	...	...	1.0	6 d0.02	1.33	26.21 - 12.16
12/31/98	270.3	4 4.8	666.5	18.9	1.8	7.6	0.7	0.8	4 d0.26	1.01	17.50 - 10.15
12/31/97	183.5	3 d7.8	394.7	15.8	...	...	...	0.7	3 d0.28	0.45	19.17 - 8.98
12/31/96	129.7	2 2.5	234.8	15.2	1.9	...	1.1	0.5	...	...	...
12/31/95	95.4	1 5.3	131.3	15.7	5.6	...	4.1	0.7	...	...	...
12/31/94	82.6	1 1.2	...	10.2	1.5	...	...	...	...	...	...

Statistics are as originally reported. Adj. for 50% stk. div., 12/01 ① Bef. extraord. loss $3.3 mill., 1995; $6.4 mill., 1994. ② Bef. extraord. loss $2.0 mill.; incl. non-recurr. chrg. $3.3 mill. ③ Bef. extraord. loss $6.0 mill. & incl. spec. chrg. $2.5 mill. ④ Incl. non-recurr. chrg. $7.9 mill. ⑤ Results for 1999 and prior reflect the results of Pierce Leahy. ⑥ Bef. loss from disc. opers. of $13.3 mill. ⑦ Incl. nonrecurr. chrg. of $9.1 mill. & a non-cash chrg. of $15.1 mill. ⑧ Bef. extroad. chrg. of $11.8 mill.; incl. pre-tax merger-related chrg. of $3.7 mill. ⑨ Bef. gain fr. disc. ops. $1.1 mill., extraord. chrg. $3.5 mill., acctg. change chrg. $6.4 mill.; incl. merger-relat. chrg. $796,000.

OFFICERS:
C. R. Reese, Chmn., Pres., C.E.O.
J. F. Kenny Jr., Exec. V.P., C.F.O.

INVESTOR CONTACT: Stephen P. Golden, (617) 535-4799

PRINCIPAL OFFICE: 745 Atlantic Avenue, Boston, MA 02111

TELEPHONE NUMBER: (617) 535-4766
FAX: (617) 350-7881
WEB: www.ironmountain.com
NO. OF EMPLOYEES: 11,300 (approx.)
SHAREHOLDERS: 603 (record); 9,400 (approx. beneficial)
ANNUAL MEETING: In May
INCORPORATED: PA, March, 1997

INSTITUTIONAL HOLDINGS:
No. of Institutions: 146
Shares Held: 72,671,377
% Held: 85.6
INDUSTRY: General warehousing and storage (SIC: 4225)
TRANSFER AGENT(S): EquiServe Trust Company, Providence, RI

IRWIN FINANCIAL CORP.

EXCH.	SYM.	REC. PRICE	P/E RATIO	YLD.	MKT. CAP.	RANGE (52-WK.)	'02 Y/E PR.	DIV. ACH.
NYSE	IFC	18.10 (2/28/03)	9.7	1.5%	$385.6 mill.	20.60 - 13.20	16.50	13 yrs.

MEDIUM GRADE. THE COMPANY IS PROJECTING FULL-YEAR 2003 EARNINGS IN THE RANGE OF $1.90 TO $2.10 PER SHARE.

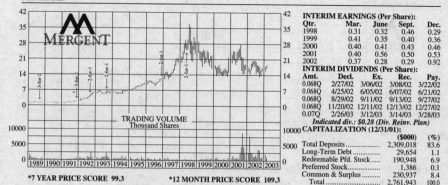

*7 YEAR PRICE SCORE 99.3　　***12 MONTH PRICE SCORE 109.3**

*NYSE COMPOSITE INDEX=100

INTERIM EARNINGS (Per Share):

Qtr.	Mar.	June	Sept.	Dec.
1998	0.31	0.32	0.46	0.29
1999	0.41	0.35	0.40	0.36
2000	0.40	0.41	0.43	0.46
2001	0.40	0.56	0.50	0.53
2002	0.37	0.28	0.29	0.92

INTERIM DIVIDENDS (Per Share):

Amt.	Decl.	Ex.	Rec.	Pay.
0.068Q	2/27/02	3/06/02	3/08/02	3/22/02
0.068Q	4/25/02	6/05/02	6/07/02	6/21/02
0.068Q	8/29/02	9/11/02	9/13/02	9/27/02
0.068Q	11/20/02	12/11/02	12/13/02	12/27/02
0.07Q	2/26/03	3/12/03	3/14/03	3/28/03

Indicated div.: $0.28 (Div. Reinv. Plan)

CAPITALIZATION (12/31/01):

	($000)	(%)
Total Deposits	2,309,018	83.6
Long-Term Debt	29,654	1.1
Redeemable Pfd. Stock	190,948	6.9
Preferred Stock	1,386	0.1
Common & Surplus	230,937	8.4
Total	2,761,943	100.0

BUSINESS:

Irwin Financial Corp. is a diversified financial services company with $4.88 billion in assets at 12/31/02. The Company operates five major lines of business through its direct and indirect subsidiaries. IFC's major lines of business are: mortgage banking, commercial banking, home equity lending, commercial finance and venture capital. Direct and indirect major subsidiaries include Irwin Mortgage Corporation, a mortgage banking company; Irwin Home Equity Corporation, a consumer home equity lending company; Irwin Union Bank and Trust, a community bank; Irwin Union Bank, F.S.B., a federal savings bank specializing in full banking and financial solutions for owner-operated businesses, entrepreneurs and professional clients; Irwin Commercial Finance, which comprises IFC's commercial finance line of business; and Irwin Ventures LLC, a venture capital company.

RECENT DEVELOPMENTS:

For the year ended 12/31/02, income was $52.8 million compared with income of $45.3 million the previous year. Results for 2002 and 2001 excluded accounting change gains of $495,000 and $175,000, respectively. Earnings were driven in part by improved mortgage banking profits, reflecting strong loan originations, the results of favorable interest rate conditions and branch expansions. Also, earnings benefited from higher commercial banking results. Net interest income climbed 45.1% to $213.6 million from $147.2 million a year earlier. Provision for loan losses was $44.0 million versus $17.5 million in 2001. Non-interest income fell 5.1% to $257.4 million.

PROSPECTS:

Strong mortgage banking results, coupled with continued growth from IFC's commercial banking and home equity lending business, strengthen the Company's near-term outlook. Moreover, improvement in IFC's commercial finance credit quality and the positioning of the Company's mortgage servicing portfolio should further enhance results. Accordingly, IFC is projecting full-year 2003 earnings in the range of $1.90 to $2.10 per share.

ANNUAL FINANCIAL DATA:

FISCAL YEAR	NET INT. INC. ($mill.)	NON-INT. INC. ($mill.)	NET INC. ($mill.)	TOT. LOANS ($mill.)	TOT. ASSETS ($mill.)	TOT. DEP. ($mill.)	RET. ON EQUITY %	RET. ON ASSETS %	EQUITY/ ASSETS %	EARN. PER SH.$	TANG. BK. VAL.$	DIV. PER SH.$	PRICE RANGE	AVG. P/E RATIO	AVG. YIELD %
p12/31/02	213.6		② 52.8							② 1.89		0.27	20.66 - 13.20	9.0	1.6
12/31/01	147.1	271.4	② 45.3	2,195.5	3,439.8	2,309.0	19.5	1.3	6.8	② 1.99	10.84	0.26	27.70 - 14.49	10.6	1.4
12/31/00	91.0	211.7	35.7	1,266.4	2,422.4	1,443.3	18.8	1.5	7.8	1.67	8.97	0.24	22.00 - 13.25	10.6	1.4
12/31/99	71.8	204.1	37.9	733.9	1,680.8	870.3	23.8	2.3	9.5	1.51	7.5	0.20	28.88 - 16.88	15.1	0.9
12/31/98	63.2	243.7	① 35.1	558.2	1,946.2	1,009.2	24.2	1.8	7.5	① 1.38	6.70	0.16	37.00 - 19.50	20.5	0.6
12/31/97	54.9	174.6	28.9	626.3	1,496.8	719.6	22.6	1.9	8.6	1.08	5.82	0.14	21.56 - 12.00	15.6	0.8
12/31/96	47.8	153.6	22.4	540.1	1,303.9	640.2	18.9	1.7	9.1	0.97	2.26	0.12	12.38 - 8.94	11.0	1.1
12/31/95	35.6	115.8	20.1	423.5	1,038.3	564.0	20.2	1.9	9.6	0.88	2.24	0.11	10.13 - 6.88	9.7	1.3
12/31/94	31.6	87.1	18.2	319.1	659.7	439.9	22.5	2.8	12.3	0.78	2.77	0.09	7.00 - 5.13	7.8	1.4
12/31/93	32.4	88.6	15.6	266.7	881.9	500.4	22.2	1.8	7.9	0.67	2.52	0.07	6.81 - 5.16	9.0	1.2

Statistics are as originally reported. Adj. for stk. splits: 2-for-1, 5/98 & 12/96. ① Incl. gain from sale of leasing assets of $5.2 mill. ② Bef. acctg. chge. gain of $495,000, 12/02; $175,000, 12/01.

OFFICERS:
W. I. Miller, Chmn.
J. A. Nash, Pres.
G. F. Ehlinger, Sr. V.P., C.F.O.

INVESTOR CONTACT: Gregory F. Ehlinger, Sr. V.P., C.F.O., (812) 376-1935

PRINCIPAL OFFICE: 500 Washington Street, Columbus, IN 47201

TELEPHONE NUMBER: (812) 376-1909
FAX: (812) 376-1709
WEB: www.irwinfinancial.com

NO. OF EMPLOYEES: 2,941 (avg.)

SHAREHOLDERS: 1,805 (approx.)

ANNUAL MEETING: In Apr.

INCORPORATED: IN, May, 1972

INSTITUTIONAL HOLDINGS:
No. of Institutions: 90
Shares Held: 12,656,914
% Held: 45.6

INDUSTRY: State commercial banks (SIC: 6022)

TRANSFER AGENT(S): National City Bank, Cleveland, OH

ISTAR FINANCIAL INC.

EXCH.	SYM.	REC. PRICE	P/E RATIO	YLD.	MKT. CAP.	RANGE (52-WK.)	'02 Y/E PR.
NYSE	SFI	28.40 (2/28/03)	13.2	8.9%	$2.48 bill.	31.80 - 23.98	28.05

MEDIUM GRADE. THE COMPANY ENTERS 2003 WITH VERY STRONG CAPITAL RESOURCES AND LIQUIDITY AND A SOLID BALANCE SHEET.

TRADING VOLUME Thousand Shares

*7 YEAR PRICE SCORE N/A   *12 MONTH PRICE SCORE 108.4

*NYSE COMPOSITE INDEX=100

INTERIM EARNINGS (Per Share):

Qtr.	Mar.	June	Sept.	Dec.
1999	------- 0.25 -------			
2000	0.50	0.52	0.54	0.54
2001	0.52	0.56	0.54	0.56
2002	0.53	0.59	0.47	0.56

INTERIM DIVIDENDS (Per Share):

Amt.	Decl.	Ex.	Rec.	Pay.
0.613Q	12/03/01	12/13/01	12/17/01	12/31/01
0.63Q	4/01/02	4/11/02	4/15/02	4/29/02
0.63Q	7/01/02	7/11/02	7/15/02	7/29/02
0.63Q	10/01/02	10/10/02	10/15/02	10/29/02
0.63Q	12/02/02	12/12/02	12/16/02	12/30/02

Indicated div.: $2.52

CAPITALIZATION (12/31/01):

	($000)	(%)
Long-Term Debt	2,495,369	58.3
Preferred Stock	11	0.0
Common & Surplus	1,787,767	41.7
Total	4,283,147	100.0

BUSINESS:

iStar Financial Inc. (formerly Starwood Financial Inc.) is a finance company that focuses on the commercial real estate industry. The Company offers structured financing to private and corporate owners of real estate nationwide, including senior and junior mortgage debt, corporate and mezzanine lending, and corporate net lease financing. The Company also provides financing solutions for a wide variety of commercial property types, including central business district and suburban office buildings, warehouse/distribution facilities, world class resorts and full service hotels, high-end multifamily properties, regional malls and mixed-use assets. Net sales for 2001 were derived as follows: real estate lending, 58.1% and corporate tenant leasing, 41.9%.

RECENT DEVELOPMENTS:

For the year ended 12/31/02, SFI reported income from continuing operations of $223.1 million, before an extraordinary loss of $12.2 million, versus income of $225.4 million, before an extraordinary loss of $1.6 million and an accounting charge of $282,000, the year before. Results for 2002 and 2001 included equity in earnings from joint ventures and unconsolidated subsidiaries of $1.2 million and $7.4 million, respectively. Results for 2002 and 2001 excluded net gains of $4.3 million and $6.4 million, respectively, from discontinued operations. Total revenue increased 11.6% to $525.7 million. Interest income rose 0.6% to $255.6 million, while interest expense grew 9.1% to $185.4 million. Provision for loan losses increased 17.9% to $8.3 million.

PROSPECTS:

SFI enters 2003 with very strong capital resources and liquidity and a solid balance sheet. Meanwhile, SFI continues to focus on its core business strategy of originating structured financing transactions for high-end real estate borrowers and corporate customers. For instance, during the fourth quarter of 2002, SFI closed 15 new financing commitments for a total of $469.1 million, of which $428.2 million was funded during the quarter. Also, SFI funded $3.7 million under four pre-existing commitments and received $196.7 million in principal repayments.

ANNUAL FINANCIAL DATA:

FISCAL YEAR	TOT. INC. ($mill.)	NET INC. ($mill.)	TOT. ⁵ASSETS ($mill.)	NET INC. + DEPR./ ASSETS %	RET. ON EQUITY %	RET. ON ASSETS %	EARN. PER SH.$	TANG. BK. VAL.$	DIV. PER SH.$	DIV. PAYOUT %	PRICE RANGE	AVG. P/E RATIO	AVG. YIELD %
p12/31/02	525.7	③223.1	5,611.7				1.93	20.46	2.52	130.6	31.80 - 23.98	14.5	9.0
12/31/01	484.2	①②231.8	4,378.6	6.1	13.0	5.3	①②2.19	20.86	2.43	111.0	28.60 - 19.19	10.9	12.8
12/31/00	471.8	①218.3	4,034.8	6.3	12.2	5.4	①2.10	20.86	2.37	112.9	22.50 - 16.00	9.2	12.3
12/31/99	264.8	38.9	3,813.6	1.3	2.2	1.0	0.25	21.20	1.70	679.7	20.67 - 16.50	74.3	9.1
④12/31/98	128.1	59.9	2,059.6	3.1	6.2	2.9	1.36	18.52	0.73	53.7	... ...	...	...
12/31/97	1.9	...	13.4	0.1	0.2	0.1	...	0.14	...	...	... ...	...	...
12/31/96	0.5	d0.6	5.7	...	...	...	d0.04	0.10	...	...	... ...	...	...
12/31/95	0.1	d0.1	2.2	...	...	...	d0.01	0.14	...	...	... ...	...	...
12/31/94	0.3	d0.3	2.4	...	...	...	d0.02	0.15	...	...	... ...	...	...
12/31/93	4.7	3.7	2.7	139.9	148.8	139.9	0.24	0.16	...	...	... ...	...	...

Statistics are as originally reported. ① Bef. extraord. loss of $1.6 mill., 2001; $705,000, 2000; incl. gain on sale of corp. tenant lease assets of $1.1 mill., 2001; $2.9 mill., 2000. ② Bef. acctg. change chrg. of $282,000. ③ Bef. a net gain from disc. opers. of $4.3 mill. & extraord. loss of $12.2 mill. ④ During 1998, Co. completed two significant transactions with Starwood Mezzanine Investors, L.P. and Lazard Freres Real Estate Fund II, L.P. involving the issuance of shares and the acquisition of new assets.

OFFICERS:
J. Sugarman, Chmn., C.E.O.
S. B. Haber, Pres., Sec.
C. D. Rice, C.F.O.

INVESTOR CONTACT: Catherine D. Rice, Investor Relations, (212) 930-9400

PRINCIPAL OFFICE: 1114 Avenue of the Americas, New York, NY 10036

TELEPHONE NUMBER: (212) 930-9400
FAX: (212) 930-9494
WEB: www.istarfinancial.com
NO. OF EMPLOYEES: 134
SHAREHOLDERS: 2,025
ANNUAL MEETING: In May
INCORPORATED: CA, April, 1988; reincorp., MD, June, 1998

INSTITUTIONAL HOLDINGS:
No. of Institutions: 188
Shares Held: 47,178,756
% Held: 52.4

INDUSTRY: Real estate investment trusts (SIC: 6798)

TRANSFER AGENT(S): EquiServe, Inc., Jersey City, NJ

ITT INDUSTRIES INC.

EXCH.	SYM.	REC. PRICE	P/E RATIO	YLD.	MKT. CAP.	RANGE (52-WK.)	'02 Y/E PR.
NYSE	ITT	56.23 (2/28/03)	13.9	1.1%	$4.99 bill.	70.85 - 53.91	60.69

UPPER MEDIUM GRADE. LOOKING AHEAD, THE COMPANY ANTICIPATES FIRST QUARTER EARNINGS OF BETWEEN $0.78 AND $0.82 PER SHARE.

MERGENT

TRADING VOLUME
Thousand Shares

1989 1990 1991 1992 1993 1994 1995 1996 1997 1998 1999 2000 2001 2002 2003

*7 YEAR PRICE SCORE 171.6   *12 MONTH PRICE SCORE 97.9
NYSE COMPOSITE INDEX=100

INTERIM EARNINGS (Per Share):

Qtr.	Mar.	June	Sept.	Dec.
1999	0.45	0.70	0.60	0.80
2000	0.57	0.78	0.72	0.87
2001	0.65	0.84	0.75	0.15
2002	0.77	0.99	1.28	1.01

INTERIM DIVIDENDS (Per Share):

Amt.	Decl.	Ex.	Rec.	Pay.
0.15Q	2/05/02	3/13/02	3/15/02	4/01/02
0.15Q	5/07/02	5/22/02	5/24/02	7/01/02
0.15Q	7/30/02	8/28/02	8/30/02	10/01/02
0.15Q	10/29/02	11/20/02	11/22/02	1/01/03
0.16Q	2/11/03	3/12/03	3/14/03	4/01/03

Indicated div.: $0.64

CAPITALIZATION (12/31/01):

	($000)	(%)
Long-Term Debt	456,400	24.9
Common & Surplus	1,375,800	75.1
Total	1,832,200	100.0

BUSINESS:

ITT Industries Inc. is comprised of four major businesses. Fluid Technology (39.3% of revenues in 2002) supplies mixers, heat exchangers and related products as well as name brand pumps. Defense Electronics & Services (30.3%) serves the military and government agencies with products such as air traffic control systems, jamming devices, digital combat radios, night vision devices and satellite instruments. Motion & Flow Control (18.7%) produces engineered valves and switches, products for the marine and leisure markets, fluid handling materials and specialty shock absorbers and friction materials. Electronic Components (11.7%) consist of products marketed under the CANNON® brand, which include connectors, switches and cabling.

RECENT DEVELOPMENTS:

For the year ended 12/31/02, ITT reported net income of $379.9 million versus income from continuing operations of $216.7 million in the previous year. Results included a credit of $3.5 million and charge of $97.7 million from restructuring and asset impairments in 2002 and 2001, respectively. Total revenues increased 6.6% to $4.99 billion from $4.68 billion a year earlier. Fluid Technology segment revenues advanced 7.0% to $1.96 billion, while Defense Electronics and Services segment revenues rose 16.0% to $1.51 billion. Motion & Flow Control segment revenues grew 4.0% to $935.5 million, while Electronics Components segment revenues decreased 10.0% to $583.5 million.

PROSPECTS:

Looking ahead, the Company anticipates first quarter earnings of between $0.78 and $0.82 per share. Full-year 2003 earnings are expected in the range of $3.70 to $3.90 per share. Separately, the Company recently acquired the business and assets of the Biopharm Manufacturing division of Martin Petersen Company, Inc., a manufacturer of process systems for the biopharmaceutical industry. Additionally, the Company has acquired PCI Membranes from Thames Water. The PCI Membrane products should complement the Fluid Technology segment's pumps, mixers, aeration equipment and wastewater process systems. Terms of the transactions were not disclosed.

ANNUAL FINANCIAL DATA:

FISCAL YEAR	TOT. REVS. ($mill.)	NET INC. ($mill.)	TOT. ASSETS ($mill.)	OPER. PROFIT %	NET PROFIT %	RET. ON EQUITY %	RET. ON ASSETS %	CURR. RATIO	EARN. PER SH. $	CASH FL. PER SH. $	TANG. BK. VAL. $	DIV. PER SH. $	PRICE RANGE	AVG. P/E RATIO	AVG. YIELD
p12/31/02	4,985.3	⑨ 379.9							⑨ 4.06			0.60	70.85 - 45.80	14.4	1.0
12/31/01	4,675.7	⑧ 216.7	4,508.4	8.5	4.6	15.8	4.8	0.8	⑧ 2.39	4.74	...	0.60	52.00 - 35.55	18.3	1.4
12/31/00	4,829.4	264.5	4,611.4	10.2	5.5	21.8	5.7	0.7	2.94	5.18	...	0.60	39.63 - 22.38	10.5	1.9
12/31/99	4,632.2	⑦ 232.9	4,529.8	9.0	5.0	19.4	5.1	0.8	⑦ 2.53	4.50	...	0.60	41.50 - 30.50	14.2	1.7
⑤12/31/98	4,492.7	⑥ d97.6	5,048.8	...	...	...	...	1.1	⑥ d0.86	0.87	4.53	0.60	40.88 - 28.13	...	1.7
12/31/97	8,777.1	④ 113.7	6,220.5	3.3	1.3	13.8	1.8	0.7	④ 0.94	4.55	...	0.60	33.69 - 22.13	29.7	2.2
12/31/96	8,718.1	222.6	5,491.2	5.8	2.6	27.9	4.1	0.9	1.85	5.45	3.80	0.45	28.63 - 21.50	13.5	1.8
12/31/95	8,884.0	② 21.0	5,879.0	5.0	0.2	0.3	0.4	0.9	② 0.03	3.96	2.26	1.49	24.00 - 21.25	751.7	6.6
12/31/94	23,620.0	① 852.0	100,854.0	6.4	3.6	15.6	0.8	1.8	① 7.10	12.60	45.32	1.98	...	...	...
12/31/93	22,762.0	③ 910.0	70,560.0	5.8	4.0	11.9	1.3	3.5	③ 7.29	12.38	59.63	1.95	...	...	...

Statistics are as originally reported. Results prior to 1995 reflect ITT Corp. ① Bef. disc. ops. gain $828.0 mill. & extraord. chrg. $50.0 mill.; incl. aft.-tax non-recurr. chrg. $164.0 mill. ② Bef. disc. ops. gain $994.0 mill. & extraord. loss $307.0 mill.; incl. aft.-tax non-recurr. chrg. $18.0 mill. ③ Bef. disc. ops. gain $831.0 mill. & acctg. change chrg. $11.0 mill. & Incl. non-recurr. credit $3.0 mill. ④ Inc. non-recurr. after-tax chrg. $145.8 mill & Bef. acctg. change chrg. $5.6 mill. ⑤ Refl. the sale of ITT Automotive ⑥ Bef. gain $1.63 bill. fr. disc. ops. ⑦ Bef. non-recurr. after-tax net cr. $2.9 mill. ⑧ Bef. gain fr. discont. ops. $60.0 mill.; incl. a restr. chrg. $63.5 mill. ⑨ Incl. restr. credit $3.5 mill.

OFFICERS:
L. J. Giuliano, Chmn., Pres., C.E.O.
D. J. Anderson, Sr. V.P., C.F.O.
D. E. Foley, Sr. V.P., Treas.
INVESTOR CONTACT: Theodore Economou, Investor Relations Dir., (914) 641-2030
PRINCIPAL OFFICE: 4 West Red Oak Lane, White Plains, NY 10604

TELEPHONE NUMBER: (914) 641-2000
FAX: (914) 696-2950
WEB: www.ittind.com
NO. OF EMPLOYEES: 38,000 (avg.)
SHAREHOLDERS: 34,869
ANNUAL MEETING: In May
INCORPORATED: IN, 1995

INSTITUTIONAL HOLDINGS:
No. of Institutions: 341
Shares Held: 79,768,892
% Held: 86.9
INDUSTRY: Fluid power pumps and motors (SIC: 3594)
TRANSFER AGENT(S): The Bank of New York, New York, NY

JABIL CIRCUIT, INC.

EXCH.	SYM.	REC. PRICE	P/E RATIO	YLD.	MKT. CAP.	RANGE (52-WK.)	'02 Y/E PR.
NYSE	JBL	17.50 (3/31/03)	102.9	...	$3.46 bill.	25.50 - 11.13	17.92

MEDIUM GRADE. THE COMPANY PLANS TO RECORD BETWEEN $60.0 MILLION AND $80.0 MILLION IN RESTRUC-TURING CHARGES OVER THE COURSE OF FISCAL 2003.

MERGENT

TRADING VOLUME
Thousand Shares

1989 1990 1991 1992 1993 1994 1995 1996 1997 1998 1999 2000 2001 2002 2003

*7 YEAR PRICE SCORE 99.5   ***12 MONTH PRICE SCORE 96.8**

*NYSE COMPOSITE INDEX=100

INTERIM EARNINGS (Per Share):

Qtr.	Nov.	Feb.	May	Aug.
1998-99	0.13	0.14	0.15	0.15
1999-00	0.15	0.18	0.21	0.24
2000-01	0.24	0.21	0.09	0.06
2001-02	0.04	0.02	0.10	0.01
2002-03	0.04	...	...	...

INTERIM DIVIDENDS (Per Share):

Amt.	Decl.	Ex.	Rec.	Pay.
		No dividends paid.		

CAPITALIZATION (8/31/02):

	($000)	(%)
Long-Term Debt	354,668	18.6
Deferred Income Tax	41,323	2.2
Common & Surplus	1,506,966	79.2
Total	1,902,957	100.0

BUSINESS:

Jabil Circuit, Inc. is an electronic manufacturing services provider for international electronics companies in the automotive, computing and storage, consumer, instrumentation and medical, networking, peripheral and telecommunications markets. JBL offers circuit design, board design from schematic, prototype assembly, volume board assem-bly, system assembly, repair and warranty services. The Company operates facilities throughout North America, Europe, Asia and Latin America. Major customers include Cisco Systems, Inc., Dell Computer Corporation, Hewlett-Packard Company, Johnson Controls, Inc., Lucent Technologies and Marconi plc.

RECENT DEVELOPMENTS:

For the first quarter ended 11/30/02, the Company reported net income of $8.4 million, flat versus the corresponding prior-year quarter. Results for 2002 and 2001 included after-tax restructuring charges of $16.5 million and $10.1 million, and acquisition-related charges of $2.3 million and $1.3 million, respectively. Results for 2002 and 2001 also included amortization of intangibles of $6.2 million and $2.8 million, respectively. Net revenue advanced 20.8% to $1.07 billion from $884.6 million a year earlier. Gross profit climbed 19.5% to $97.5 million from $81.6 million the year before. Operating income amounted to $2.9 million versus $11.1 million in the 2001 quarter. Net interest and other income was $795,000 compared with net interest expense of $612,000 in the prior-year period.

PROSPECTS:

The Company's goals for 2003 are to reduce costs and diversify through acquisitions and new business wins. JBL's cost reduction activities are on track and the Company plans to record between $60.0 million and $80.0 million in restructuring charges over the course of fiscal 2003. Meanwhile, for the second quarter of fiscal 2003, JBL expects revenue in the range of $1.10 billion to $1.20 billion. Core earnings, which exclude amortization charges, restructuring charges and other income, are expected to be $0.15 to $0.17 per share in the second quarter. On 11/18/02, JBL announced that it has completed the acquisition of six manufacturing plants as part of its previously announced agreement with Royal Philips Electronics.

ANNUAL FINANCIAL DATA:

FISCAL YEAR	TOT. REVS. ($mill.)	NET INC. ($mill.)	TOT. ASSETS ($mill.)	OPER. PROFIT %	NET PROFIT %	RET. ON EQUITY %	RET. ON ASSETS %	CURR. RATIO	EARN. PER SH. $	CASH FL. PER SH. $	TANG. BK. VAL. $	PRICE RANGE	AVG. P/E RATIO
8/31/02	3,545.5	⑤ 34.7	2,547.9	1.4	1.0	2.3	1.4	2.7	⑤ 0.17	1.11	6.63	26.79 - 11.13	111.5
8/31/01	4,330.7	② 118.5	2,357.6	3.8	2.7	8.4	5.0	2.9	② 0.59	1.35	6.43	40.99 - 14.00	46.6
8/31/00	3,558.3	① 145.6	2,018.2	6.0	4.1	11.5	7.2	2.0	① 0.78	1.31	6.68	68.00 - 18.63	55.5
8/31/99	2,000.3	91.5	920.7	7.1	4.6	16.8	9.9	1.8	0.56	0.90	3.32	38.97 - 14.25	47.5
8/31/98	1,277.4	① 56.9	526.7	6.7	4.5	22.9	10.8	1.6	① 0.37	0.60	1.67	18.72 - 5.75	33.1
8/31/97	978.1	52.5	405.9	8.4	5.4	28.9	12.9	1.6	0.34	0.50	1.23	5.69 - 3.84	31.8
8/31/96	863.3	24.3	299.9	5.3	2.8	19.6	8.1	2.0	0.17	0.29	0.87	5.33 - 0.64	17.8
8/31/95	559.5	7.3	281.0	2.9	1.3	12.2	2.6	1.2	0.06	0.15	0.50	2.88 - 0.47	28.3
8/31/94	375.8	2.6	174.3	2.2	0.7	5.0	1.5	1.3	0.02	0.10	0.45	1.17 - 0.44	38.1
8/31/93	334.7	8.1	115.8	5.0	2.4	17.1	7.0	1.6	0.07	0.13	0.43	1.25 - 0.72	13.3

Statistics are as originally reported. Adj. for stk. split: 100.0%, 3/00; 2-for-1, 2/99; 2-for-1, 7/97. ① Incl. nonrecurr. chrg. of $5.2 mill., 2000; $20.8 mill., 1998 ② Incl. acq. & merg. exps. of $6.6 mill. & restr. and other chrgs. of $27.4 mill. ③ Incl. after-tax acquis. chrg. of $4.8 mill. and after-tax restr. chrg. of $40.2 mill.

OFFICERS:
W. D. Morean, Chmn.
T. A. Sansone, Vice-Chmn.
T. L. Main, Pres., C.E.O.
INVESTOR CONTACT: Lisa Allison, (727) 803-3314
PRINCIPAL OFFICE: 10560 Ninth Street North, St. Petersburg, FL 33716

TELEPHONE NUMBER: (727) 577-9749
FAX: (727) 579-8529
WEB: www.jabil.com
NO. OF EMPLOYEES: 20,000 (approx.)
SHAREHOLDERS: 3,837 (record)
ANNUAL MEETING: In Jan.
INCORPORATED: MI, 1969; reincorp., DE, Feb., 1992

INSTITUTIONAL HOLDINGS:
No. of Institutions: 300
Shares Held: 131,587,623
% Held: 66.4

TRANSFER AGENT(S): EquiServe Trust Company, N.A., Boston MA

JACOBS ENGINEERING GROUP INC.

EXCH.	SYM.	REC. PRICE	P/E RATIO	YLD.	MKT. CAP.	RANGE (52-WK.)	'02 Y/E PR.
NYSE	JEC	37.98 (2/28/03)	18.6	...	$2.08 bill.	42.90 - 26.10	35.60

UPPER MEDIUM GRADE. THE COMPANY SHOULD CONTINUE TO BENEFIT FROM A STRONG BACKLOG.

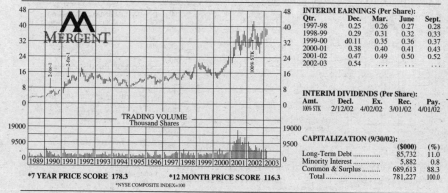

*7 YEAR PRICE SCORE 178.3   ***12 MONTH PRICE SCORE 116.3**
*NYSE COMPOSITE INDEX=100

INTERIM EARNINGS (Per Share):

Qtr.	Dec.	Mar.	June	Sept.
1997-98	0.25	0.26	0.27	0.28
1998-99	0.29	0.31	0.32	0.33
1999-00	d0.11	0.35	0.36	0.37
2000-01	0.38	0.40	0.41	0.43
2001-02	0.47	0.49	0.50	0.52
2002-03	0.54	...	...	...

INTERIM DIVIDENDS (Per Share):

Amt.	Decl.	Ex.	Rec.	Pay.
100% STK	2/12/02	4/02/02	3/01/02	4/01/02

CAPITALIZATION (9/30/02):

	($000)	(%)
Long-Term Debt	85,732	11.0
Minority Interest	5,882	0.8
Common & Surplus	689,613	88.3
Total	781,227	100.0

BUSINESS:

Jacobs Engineering Group Inc. is a major global engineering, architecture, technology, and construction firm, specializing in project services, 43.4% of 2002 revenues; construction services, 42.4%; operations and maintenance services, 10.3%; and process, scientific and systems consulting services, 3.9%. JEC has offices and subsidiaries located in the United States, Europe, Asia, Mexico, Chile and Australia. JEC has clients in the following industry groups and markets: chemicals and polymers; federal programs; buildings; pharmaceuticals and biotechnology; exploration, production and refining; infrastructure; technology and manufacturing; and pulp and paper.

RECENT DEVELOPMENTS:

For the quarter ended 12/31/02, net income increased 16.5% to $30.1 million compared with $25.9 million in the equivalent 2001 quarter. Revenues advanced 18.5% to $1.22 billion from $1.03 billion a year earlier. Total costs and expenses increased 18.7% to $1.17 billion from $987.2 million in the prior-year quarter. Operating income grew 14.2% to $46.8 million from $41.0 million the year before.

PROSPECTS:

Going forward, the Company should benefit from its strong balance sheet and healthy backlog. Backlog at 12/31/02 increased 4.4% to $6.68 billion from $6.40 billion at 12/31/01. Included in this amount was $3.10 billion of technical, professional services backlog, an increase of 19.7% from $2.59 billion at 12/31/01. Backlog at 12/31/02 reflects removal of about $140.0 million of future construction revenues on a project, which is now being performed by a corporate entity jointly owned by JEC and a partner. Field Services backlog declined 6.1% to $3.57 billion at 12/31/02.

ANNUAL FINANCIAL DATA:

FISCAL YEAR	TOT. REVS. ($mill.)	NET INC. ($mill.)	TOT. ASSETS ($mill.)	OPER. PROFIT %	NET PROFIT %	RET. ON EQUITY %	RET. ON ASSETS %	CURR. RATIO	EARN. PER SH.$	CASH FL. PER SH.$	TANG. BK. VAL.$	PRICE RANGE	AVG. P/E RATIO
9/30/02	4,555.7	109.7	1,674.0	3.8	2.4	15.9	6.6	1.3	1.98	2.61	5.45	42.90 — 26.10	17.4
9/30/01	3,957.0	87.8	1,557.0	3.6	2.2	14.8	5.6	1.4	1.61	2.32	5.10	37.85 — 21.13	18.3
9/30/00	3,418.9	②51.0	1,384.4	3.6	1.5	10.3	3.7	1.2	②0.97	1.72	4.29	24.59 — 13.09	19.5
9/30/99	2,875.0	65.4	1,220.2	3.8	2.3	14.6	5.4	1.2	1.24	1.83	3.89	21.38 — 14.63	14.6
9/30/98	2,101.1	54.4	807.5	4.1	2.6	14.6	6.7	1.5	1.04	1.48	5.74	20.38 — 12.38	15.7
9/30/97	1,780.6	46.9	744.2	4.1	2.6	14.5	6.3	1.5	0.90	1.28	4.83	16.28 — 11.63	15.5
9/30/96	1,799.0	40.4	572.5	3.6	2.2	14.2	7.0	1.7	0.78	1.13	4.72	14.69 — 9.81	15.7
9/30/95	1,723.1	32.2	533.9	3.1	1.9	13.5	6.0	1.4	0.64	0.92	3.86	12.88 — 8.63	16.9
9/30/94	1,165.8	①18.8	504.4	2.7	1.7	9.4	3.7	1.4	①0.38	0.60	3.22	13.44 — 8.44	29.2
9/30/93	1,142.9	28.7	351.0	4.0	2.3	16.5	8.2	1.6	0.58	0.75	3.21	14.94 — 10.00	21.7

Statistics are as originally reported. Adj. for 2-for-1 stk. split, 4/1/02. ① Incl. a nonrecur. chrg. of $8.6 mill. rel. to wrtdwns and a chrg. of $1.6 mill. for the settlement of litigation. ② Incl. nonrecurr. chrg. of $38.0 mill. for the settlement of litigation.

OFFICERS:
J. J. Jacobs, Chmn.
N. G. Watson, C.E.O.
C. L. Martin, Pres.
J. W. Prosser, Jr., Sr. V.P., Treas.

INVESTOR CONTACT: John W. Prosser, Jr., Sr. V.P., (626) 578-6803

PRINCIPAL OFFICE: 1111 South Arroyo Parkway, P.O. Box 7084, Pasadena, CA 91105

TELEPHONE NUMBER: (626) 578-3500
FAX: (626) 578-6967
WEB: www.jacobs.com

NO. OF EMPLOYEES: 35,000 (approx.)

SHAREHOLDERS: 986

ANNUAL MEETING: In Feb.

INCORPORATED: CA, July, 1974; reincorp., DE, Mar., 1987

INSTITUTIONAL HOLDINGS:
No. of Institutions: 227
Shares Held: 41,791,304
% Held: 76.8

INDUSTRY: Heavy construction, nec (SIC: 1629)

TRANSFER AGENT(S): Mellon Investor Services LLC, South Hackensack, NJ

JANUS CAPITAL GROUP, INC.

EXCH.	SYM.	REC. PRICE	P/E RATIO	YLD.	MKT. CAP.	RANGE (52-WK.)	'02 Y/E PR.
NYSE	JNS	11.83 (2/28/03)	39.4	0.3%	$2.63 bill.	27.08 - 8.97	13.07

LOWER MEDIUM GRADE. STILLWELL FINANCIAL, INC. COMPLETED ITS MERGER WITH JANUS CAPITAL CORPO-
RATION, FORMING JANUS CAPITAL GROUP, INC.

TRADING VOLUME
Thousand Shares

*7 YEAR PRICE SCORE N/A   *12 MONTH PRICE SCORE 85.6

*NYSE COMPOSITE INDEX=100

INTERIM EARNINGS (Per Share):

Qtr.	Mar.	June	Sept.	Dec.
2000	0.83	0.67	0.73	0.66
2001	0.48	0.39	0.11	0.32
2002	0.42	0.30	d0.60	0.18

INTERIM DIVIDENDS (Per Share):

Amt.	Decl.	Ex.	Rec.	Pay.
0.01Q	4/10/01	4/11/01	4/16/01	4/30/01
0.01Q	5/10/01	7/12/01	7/16/01	7/31/01
0.01Q	10/04/01	10/11/01	10/15/01	10/31/01
0.01Q	12/05/01	1/11/02	1/15/02	1/31/02
0.04A	5/09/02	7/11/02	7/15/02	7/31/02

Indicated div.: $0.04

CAPITALIZATION (12/31/01):

	($mill.)	(%)
Long-Term Debt	399.5	16.4
Deferred Income Tax	679.9	27.8
Common & Surplus	1,363.3	55.8
Total	2,442.7	100.0

BUSINESS:

Janus Capital Group, Inc. (formerly Stilwell Financial, Inc.) was formed through the merger of Janus Capital Corp. and Stilwell Financial Inc. on 1/1/03. Stilwell was spun off from Kansas City Southern Industries Inc. on 7/12/00. As of 1/30/03, JNS, an asset manager offering individual investors and isntitutional clients complementary asset management discipline, consists of Janus Capital Management LLC, Berger Financial Group LLC, Enhanced Investment Technologies, LLC and Bay Isle Financial LLC. JNS also owns approximately 81.0% of Nelson Money Managers Plc and approximately 33.0% of DST Systems, Inc. Nelson provides investment management services in the U.K. to retirees. DST Systems provides information processing and software to the mutual fund industry. Net sales for 2002 were derived as follows: investment management fees, 82.0%; shareowner servicing fees, 13.1%; and other, 4.9%.

RECENT DEVELOPMENTS:

For the year ended 12/31/02, net income dropped 72.0% to $84.7 million from $302.3 million the year before. Earnings included a one-time net loss of $300,000 in 2002 and a one-time net gain of $21.5 million in 2001 related to various items. Total revenues decreased 26.4% to $1.14 billion.

Investment management fees declined 26.3% to $939.3 million, while shareowner servicing fees fell 30.8% to $149.8 million. Average assets under management fell 23.4% to $164.0 billion.

PROSPECTS:

On 1/1/03, Stilwell Financial, Inc. completed its merger with Janus Capital Corp., creating Janus Capital Group, Inc., which will market and distribute its investment products globally under the Janus brand name. The Company is trading under the ticker symbol ''JNS.'' As part of the transaction, JNS announced plans to take a 30.0% ownership stake in value manager Perkins, Wolf, McDonnell and Co. Separately, effective 3/13/03, all outstanding employee-held shares of Janus Capital Management LLC, a subsidiary of JNS, were converted into shares of JNS stock. The conversion is expected to be modestly accretive to JNS' diluted earnings per share in 2003 and in future years. Meanwhile, JNS expects to start realizing $40.0 million in annual merger-related cost savings in 2003.

ANNUAL FINANCIAL DATA:

FISCAL YEAR	TOT. REVS. ($mill.)	NET INC. ($mill.)	TOT. ASSETS ($mill.)	OPER. PROFIT %	NET PROFIT %	RET. ON EQUITY %	RET. ON ASSETS %	CURR. RATIO	EARN. PER SH.$	CASH FL. PER SH.$	TANG. BK. VAL.$	DIV. PER SH.$	PRICE RANGE		AVG. P/E RATIO	AVG. YIELD %
p12/31/02	1,144.8	③ 84.7	3,321.7	34.1	19.4	22.2	8.9	0.5	③ 0.31	...	...	0.04	29.24 -	8.97	61.6	0.2
12/31/01	1,555.7	② 302.3	3,391.6	46.1	29.5	22.2	9.0	...	② 1.31	1.93	...	0.04	46.63 -	18.20	24.7	0.1
12/31/00	2,248.1	① 663.7	1,581.0	46.1	29.5	62.7	42.0	3.3	② 2.90	3.30	3.50	0.01	54.50 -	30.75	14.7	...
12/31/99	1,212.3	313.1	1,231.5	42.8	25.8	38.4	25.4	3.2	1.23	1.56	2.93	...	...		...	...
12/31/98	670.8	152.2	822.9	41.8	22.7	28.2	18.5	3.6	0.60	0.76	1.76	...	...		...	...
12/31/97	485.1	118.0	...	41.1	24.3	...	...	...	0.47	0.59	...	...	...		...	...

Statistics are as originally reported. ① Incl. a net after-tax nonrecurring gain of $52.9 mill. ② Incl. severance, facility closing & oth. costs of $82.7 mill. & a gain on the sale of DST Systems, Inc. of $28.8 mill. ③ Incl. severance, facility closing & oth. costs of $69.4 mill.

OFFICERS:
L. H. Rowland, Chmn.
M. Whiston, Pres., C.E.O.
Loren Starr, V.P., C.F.O.
INVESTOR CONTACT: Jane Ingalls, Investor Relations, (303) 394-7311
PRINCIPAL OFFICE: 920 Main Street, 21st Floor, Kansas City, MO 64105

TELEPHONE NUMBER: (816) 218-2400

NO. OF EMPLOYEES: 1,450 (approx.)

SHAREHOLDERS: 5,004

ANNUAL MEETING: In May

INCORPORATED: MO, Jan., 1998

INSTITUTIONAL HOLDINGS:
No. of Institutions: 38
Shares Held: 12,316,835
% Held: 0.0
INDUSTRY: Management services (SIC: 8741)
TRANSFER AGENT(S): UMB Bank, N.A., Kansas City, MO

JEFFERSON-PILOT CORP.

EXCH.	SYM.	REC. PRICE	P/E RATIO	YLD.	MKT. CAP.	RANGE (52-WK.)	'02 Y/E PR.	DIV. ACH.
NYSE	JP	37.70 (2/28/03)	12.4	3.5%	$5.66 bill.	53.00 - 36.35	38.11	35 yrs.

INVESTMENT GRADE. CHALLENGING CONDITIONS IN THE LIFE AND ANNUITY BUSINESSES ARE EXPECTED TO CONTINUE.

*7 YEAR PRICE SCORE 116.7   ***12 MONTH PRICE SCORE 97.8**
*NYSE COMPOSITE INDEX=100

INTERIM EARNINGS (Per Share):

Qtr.	Mar.	June	Sept.	Dec.
1998	0.69	0.63	0.68	0.60
1999	0.79	0.73	0.73	0.69
2000	0.89	0.83	0.83	0.73
2001	0.96	0.87	0.87	0.64
2002	0.92	0.84	0.81	0.46

INTERIM DIVIDENDS (Per Share):

Amt.	Decl.	Ex.	Rec.	Pay.
0.302Q	2/11/02	5/22/02	5/24/02	6/05/02
0.302Q	5/06/02	8/21/02	8/23/02	9/05/02
0.302Q	8/05/02	11/20/02	11/22/02	12/05/02
0.302Q	11/04/02	2/19/03	2/21/03	3/05/03
0.33Q	2/10/03	5/21/03	5/23/03	6/05/03

Indicated div.: $1.32 (Div. Reinv. Plan)

CAPITALIZATION (12/31/01):

	($000)	(%)
Long-Term Debt	150,000	3.9
Deferred Income Tax	291,000	7.6
Common & Surplus	3,391,000	88.5
Total	3,832,000	100.0

BUSINESS:

Jefferson-Pilot Corp. is a holding company that conducts insurance, investment, broadcasting and other business through its subsidiaries. Jefferson-Pilot Life Insurance Company offers both group and individual life insurance, health insurance, annuity and pension products. Other subsidiaries provide fire and casualty insurance, title insurance and mutual fund sales and management services. As of

2/3/03, Jefferson-Pilot Communications Company provided information and entertainment services through three network television and 17 radio stations, and produced and syndicated sports programming. Contributions to revenues in 2002 were as follows: net investment income, 46.4%; premiums & other, 44.6%; communications sales, 6.0%; broker-dealer concessions and other, 3.0%.

RECENT DEVELOPMENTS:

For the year ended 12/31/02, net income dropped 11.7% to $474.8 million from $537.4 million the previous year. Total revenue increased 4.4% to $3.48 billion from $3.32 billion in the prior year. Revenue included a realized investment loss of $22.0 million in 2002 versus a gain of $65.5 million in 2001. Revenue from premiums and other considerations

grew 9.3% to $841.1 million from $769.6 million in 2001. Revenue from universal life & investment product charges climbed 10.5% to $722.9 million. Net investment income improved 5.7% to $1.62 billion versus $1.54 billion a year earlier.

PROSPECTS:

Challenging conditions persist for JP's life and annuity businesses due to lower investment yields, reduced interest spreads, and a difficult credit market. As a result, JP is taking several proactive steps to combat these conditions, including maintaining good asset quality, strengthening the recoverability of deferred acquisition costs on its variable

products and recording charges against its investment portfolio. Meanwhile, JP's core individual life insurance business should continue to deliver solid sales growth. Moreover, JP's communications business is expected to perform well throughout the year.

ANNUAL FINANCIAL DATA:

FISCAL YEAR	PREM. INC. ($mill.)	NET INVST. INC. ($mill.)	TOT. REVS. ($mill.)	NET INC. ($mill.)	TOT. ASSETS ($mill.)	TOT. INVST. ($mill.)	RET. ON REVS. %	RET. ON EQUITY %	RET. ON ASSETS %	EARN. PER SH.$	TANG. BK. VAL.$	AVG. YIELD %	DIV. PER SH.$	PRICE RANGE	AVG. P/E RATIO
p12/31/02	1,564.1		3,480.0	474.8						3.04		2.6	1.18	53.00 - 36.35	14.7
12/31/01	1,424.0	1,533.0	3,330.0	① 537.0	28,996.0	22,135.0	16.1	15.8	1.9	① 3.34	20.53	2.4	1.07	49.67 - 38.00	13.1
12/31/00	1,365.0	1,430.0	3,238.0	537.0	27,321.0	20,499.0	16.6	17.0	2.0	3.29	18.38	2.3	0.96	50.59 - 33.25	12.8
12/31/99	903.0	1,272.0	2,561.0	495.0	26,446.0	19,536.0	19.3	18.0	1.9	2.95	15.80	1.8	0.86	53.09 - 40.79	15.9
12/31/98	1,049.0	1,202.0	2,610.0	444.0	24,338.0	18,978.0	17.0	14.5	1.8	2.61	17.77	1.8	0.77	52.25 - 32.45	16.2
12/31/97	1,135.0	1,103.0	2,578.0	396.0	23,131.0	18,094.0	15.4	14.5	1.7	2.31	15.73	2.3	0.69	38.56 - 22.89	13.3
12/31/96	994.0	893.0	2,125.0	294.0	17,562.0	14,143.0	13.8	12.8	1.7	1.82	13.89	2.7	0.62	26.50 - 20.06	12.8
12/31/95	810.0	540.8	1,569.4	② 255.3	16,478.0	13,168.1	16.3	11.8	1.5	② 1.58	13.02	3.0	0.55	21.45 - 14.96	11.5
12/31/94	655.3	375.2	1,268.8	② 229.9	6,140.3	5,220.7	18.1	13.3	3.7	② 1.40	10.26	3.4	0.50	16.33 - 12.85	10.4
12/31/93	669.8	369.6	1,246.6	① 219.3	5,640.6	4,916.9	17.6	12.7	3.9	① 1.29	10.15	2.9	0.45	17.15 - 13.48	11.9

Statistics are as originally reported. Adj. for stk. splits: 3-for-2, 4/01; 4/98; 12/95 ① Bef. acctg. gain $1.0 mill., 12/01; chrg. $24.1 mill., 12/93 ② Bef. disc. oper gain $18.5 mill.12/95; $9.3 mill., 12/94

OFFICERS:
D. A. Stonecipher, Chmn., C.E.O.
K. C. Mlekush, Vice-Chmn.
D. R. Glass, Pres., C.O.O.

INVESTOR CONTACT: Investor Relations, (336) 691-3379

PRINCIPAL OFFICE: 100 North Greene Street, Greensboro, NC 27401

TELEPHONE NUMBER: (336) 691-3000
FAX: (336) 691-3938
WEB: www.jpc.com

NO. OF EMPLOYEES: 3,000 (avg.)

SHAREHOLDERS: 9,310

ANNUAL MEETING: In May

INCORPORATED: NC, Jan., 1968

INSTITUTIONAL HOLDINGS:
No. of Institutions: 352
Shares Held: 73,817,233
% Held: 51.4

INDUSTRY: Life insurance (SIC: 6311)

TRANSFER AGENT(S): Wachovia Bank, N.A., Charlotte, NC

JOHN HANCOCK FINANCIAL SERVICES, INC.

EXCH.	SYM.	REC. PRICE	P/E RATIO	YLD.	MKT. CAP.	RANGE (52-WK.)	'02 Y/E PR.
NYSE	JHF	28.10 (2/28/03)	16.1	1.1%	$8.09 bill.	40.90 - 25.40	27.90

UPPER MEDIUM GRADE. IN 2003, THE COMPANY EXPECTS NET OPERATING EARNINGS PER SHARE GROWTH TO RANGE FROM 7.0% TO 11.0%, REFLECTING EQUITY MARKET APPRECIATION.

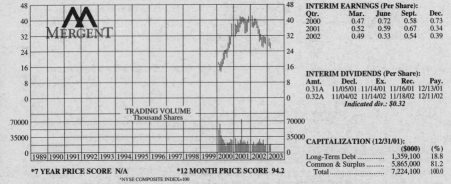

*7 YEAR PRICE SCORE N/A   *12 MONTH PRICE SCORE 94.2
*NYSE COMPOSITE INDEX=100

INTERIM EARNINGS (Per Share):

Qtr.	Mar.	June	Sept.	Dec.
2000	0.47	0.72	0.58	0.73
2001	0.52	0.59	0.67	0.34
2002	0.49	0.33	0.54	0.39

INTERIM DIVIDENDS (Per Share):

Amt.	Decl.	Ex.	Rec.	Pay.
0.31A	11/05/01	11/14/01	11/16/01	12/13/01
0.32A	11/04/02	11/14/02	11/18/02	12/11/02

Indicated div.: $0.32

CAPITALIZATION (12/31/01):

	($000)	(%)
Long-Term Debt	1,359,100	18.8
Common & Surplus	5,865,000	81.2
Total	7,224,100	100.0

BUSINESS:

John Hancock Financial Services, Inc. provides insurance and investment products and services to retail and institutional customers, primarily in North America. JHF offers variable life, universal life, whole life, term life, and individual and group long-term care insurance products, along with variable and fixed, deferred and immediate annuities, and mutual funds. In addition, JHF offers a variety of spread-based and fee-based investment products and services, most provide the customer with some form of guaranteed return, and investment management services and products marketed to institutions. As of 12/31/02, JHF and its subsidiaries had total assets under management of $127.60 billion. Net sales for 2002 were derived as follows: protection, 40.3%; guaranteed and structured financial products, 23.2%; asset gathering, 12.6%; investment management, 1.5%; and corporate and other, 22.4%.

RECENT DEVELOPMENTS:

For the year ended 12/31/02, the Company reported net income of $516.2 million versus income of $611.5 million, before an accounting change credit of $7.2 million, the year before. Earnings for 2002 and 2001 included after-tax restructuring charges of $10.5 million and $20.2 million, and net realized investment losses, on an after-tax basis, of $280.0 million and $160.7 million, respectively. Earnings also included after-tax expenses of $19.5 million related to a class action lawsuit for both 2002 and 2001. In addition, earnings for 2001 included a surplus tax of $13.4 million. Total revenues decreased 4.8% to $8.91 billion from $9.36 billion a year earlier.

PROSPECTS:

In 2003, the Company expects net operating earnings per share growth to range from 7.0% to 11.0%, reflecting equity market appreciation of approximately 2.0% per quarter and a modest improvement in the credit markets. In addition, the Company expects gross capital bond losses in 2003 to decline significantly from $582.0 million in 2002. However, credit losses are likely to remain above average due to the slower-than-expected recovery in the economy, and mortgage loan performance is anticipated to deteriorate.

ANNUAL FINANCIAL DATA:

FISCAL YEAR	PREM. INC. ($mill.)	TOT. REVS. ($mill.)	NET INC. ($mill.)	TOT. ASSETS ($mill.)	TOT. INVST. ($mill.)	RET. ON REVS. %	RET. ON EQUITY %	RET. ON ASSETS %	EARN. PER SH. $	TANG. BK. VAL. $	AVG. YIELD %	DIV. PER SH. $	PRICE RANGE	AVG. P/E RATIO
p12/31/02	3,377.1	8,910.7	③ 516.2	97,864.1					③ 1.76		0.9	0.32	42.30 - 25.84	19.4
12/31/01	3,851.3	9,109.0	②③ 611.5	91,144.2	57,681.1	6.7	10.4	0.7	②③ 1.99	19.73	0.8	0.31	42.00 - 31.50	18.5
12/31/00	2,587.1	7,598.1	① 838.9	87,353.3	40,738.4	11.0	14.5	1.0	① 2.51	18.52	1.2	0.30	38.25 - 13.44	10.3
12/31/99	2,717.5	7,857.5	① 256.5	84,455.7	46,887.8	3.3	5.4	0.3	...	...	...	...	...	...
12/31/98	2,197.9	6,902.0	① 460.2	76,966.7	43,777.5	6.7	9.3	0.6	...	...	...	...	...	...
12/31/97	2,473.6	6,946.3	483.3	71,417.5	42,441.7	7.0	10.3	0.7	...	...	...	...	...	...
12/31/96	2,922.5	7,704.8	420.5	...	...	5.5	...	...	...	...	...	...	...	...

Statistics are as originally reported. ① Bef. $10.2 mill. extraord. chrg. & incl. after-tax net chrg. of $5.8 mill., 2000; bef. $93.6 mill. extraord. chrg. & $9.7 mil acctg. chrg., 1999; bef. $11.7 mil extraord. chg., 1998. ② Bef. an acctg. cred. of $7.2 mill. ③ Incl. after-tax restruct. chrgs. of $10.5 mill., 12/02 & $27.4 mill.; 12/01; after-tax net realized investment losses of $280.0 mill., 12/02 & $160.7 mill., 12/01; and an after-tax exp. rel. to a class action lawsuit of $19.5 mill., 12/02 & $19.5 mill., 12/01.

OFFICERS:
D. F. D'Alessandro, Chmn., Pres., C.E.O.
T. E. Moloney, Sr. Exec. V.P., C.F.O.
W. A. Budd, Exec. V.P., Gen. Couns.

INVESTOR CONTACT: Jean Peters, Investor Relations, (617) 572-9282

PRINCIPAL OFFICE: John Hancock Place, 200 Clarendon Street, Boston, MA 02117

TELEPHONE NUMBER: (617) 572-6000
FAX: (617) 572-9799
WEB: www.jhancock.com

NO. OF EMPLOYEES: 7,962

SHAREHOLDERS: 611,196 (approx.)

ANNUAL MEETING: In May

INCORPORATED: DE, Jan., 1999

INSTITUTIONAL HOLDINGS:
No. of Institutions: 316
Shares Held: 142,300,702
% Held: 49.4

INDUSTRY: Life insurance (SIC: 6311)

TRANSFER AGENT(S): EquiServe Trust Company, N.A., Providence, RI

JOHNSON & JOHNSON

EXCH.	SYM.	REC. PRICE	P/E RATIO	YLD.	MKT. CAP.	RANGE (52-WK.)	'02 Y/E PR.	DIV. ACH.
NYSE	JNJ	52.45 (2/28/03)	23.7	1.6%	$159.83 bill.	65.89 - 41.40	53.71	40 yrs.

HIGH GRADE. THE COMPANY SHOULD CONTINUE TO BENEFIT FROM SALES GROWTH IN ITS PHARMACEUTICAL AND MEDICAL DEVICE SEGMENTS.

*7 YEAR PRICE SCORE 141.7   ***12 MONTH PRICE SCORE 102.6**
*NYSE COMPOSITE INDEX=100

INTERIM EARNINGS (Per Share):

Qtr.	Mar.	June	Sept.	Dec.
1998	0.37	0.37	0.35	0.25
1999	0.41	0.42	0.40	0.27
2000	0.47	0.47	0.45	0.32
2001	0.53	0.48	0.49	0.36
2002	0.59	0.54	0.60	0.48

INTERIM DIVIDENDS (Per Share):

Amt.	Decl.	Ex.	Rec.	Pay.
0.18Q	1/02/02	2/14/02	2/19/02	3/12/02
0.205Q	4/25/02	5/17/02	5/21/02	6/11/02
0.205Q	7/15/02	8/16/02	8/20/02	9/10/02
0.205Q	10/15/02	11/15/02	11/19/02	12/10/02
0.205Q	1/06/03	2/13/03	2/18/03	3/11/03

Indicated div.: $0.82 (Div. Reinv. Plan)

CAPITALIZATION (12/30/01):

	($000)	(%)
Long-Term Debt	2,217,000	8.2
Deferred Income Tax	493,000	1.8
Common & Surplus	24,233,000	89.9
Total	26,943,000	100.0

BUSINESS:

Johnson & Johnson is engaged in the manufacture and sale of a broad range of products in health care and other fields. The Pharmaceutical segment, (47.3% of 2002 sales), consists of prescription drugs in the antifungal, anti-infective, cardiovascular, dermatology, gastrointestinal, hematology, immunology, neurology, oncology, pain management, psychotropic and women's health fields. The Medical Devices and Diagnostics segment, (34.6%), includes a broad range of products used by or under the direction of health care professionals. The Consumer segment, (18.1%), consists of personal care and hygienic products. JNJ acquired ALZA Corp. on 6/22/01.

RECENT DEVELOPMENTS:

For the year ended 12/31/02, net earnings advanced 17.3% to $6.65 billion compared with $5.67 billion the previous year. Results for 2002 and 2001 included after-tax special charges of $189.0 million and $231.0 million, respectively, for costs associated with acquisitions. Sales increased 12.3% to $36.30 billion from $32.32 billion the prior year. Consumer segment sales grew 3.9% to $6.56 billion from $6.32 billion, while Pharmaceutical segment sales climbed 15.5% to $17.15 billion from $14.85 billion a year earlier. Sales in the Medical Device and Diagnostics segment improved 12.9% to $12.58 billion from $11.15 billion the year before.

PROSPECTS:

In 2003, JNJ will focus on capitalizing on the synergies of its broad-based businesses. Meanwhile, on 1/16/03, the Company and 3-Dimensional Pharmaceuticals, Inc. (3DP) announced that they have signed a definitive agreement under which JNJ will acquire 3DP, a technology company focused on the discovery and development of therapeutic small molecules, in a transaction valued at $88.0 million. The transaction is expected to close during the first half of the second quarter of 2003. Separately, the Company received FDA approval to market the VICRYL Plus Antibacterial Suture, designed with an agent to reduce bacterial colonization on the suture.

ANNUAL FINANCIAL DATA:

FISCAL YEAR	TOT. REVS. ($mill.)	NET INC. ($mill.)	TOT. ASSETS ($mill.)	OPER. PROFIT %	NET PROFIT %	RET. ON EQUITY %	RET. ON ASSETS %	CURR. RATIO	EARN. PER SH.$	CASH FL.PER SH.$	TANG. BK. VAL.$	DIV. PER SH.$	PRICE RANGE	AVG. P/E RATIO	AVG. YIELD %
p12/31/02	36,298.0	⑤ 6,651.0							⑤ 2.18			0.80	65.89 - 41.40	24.6	1.5
12/30/01	33,004.0	④ 5,668.0	38,488.0	25.0	17.2	23.4	14.7	2.3	④ 1.84	2.35	4.97	0.70	60.97 - 40.25	27.5	1.4
12/31/00	29,139.0	③ 4,800.0	31,321.0	23.5	16.5	25.5	15.3	2.2	③ 1.70	2.23	4.15	0.62	52.97 - 33.06	25.3	1.4
1/02/00	27,471.0	② 4,167.0	29,163.0	22.5	15.2	25.7	14.3	1.8	② 1.47	1.98	3.11	0.55	53.44 - 38.50	31.3	1.2
1/03/99	23,657.0	① 3,059.0	26,211.0	18.0	12.9	22.5	11.7	1.4	① 1.12	1.57	2.37	0.48	44.88 - 31.69	34.3	1.3
12/28/97	22,629.0	3,303.0	21,453.0	20.4	14.6	26.7	15.4	2.0	1.21	1.60	3.38	0.42	33.66 - 24.31	24.1	1.5
12/29/96	21,620.0	3,464.0	20,010.0	19.9	16.0	32.0	17.3	1.8	1.09	1.68	2.90	0.37	27.00 - 20.78	22.0	1.5
12/31/95	18,842.0	2,403.0	17,873.0	18.6	12.8	26.6	13.4	1.8	0.93	1.26	2.36	0.32	23.09 - 13.41	19.6	1.8
1/01/95	15,734.0	2,006.0	15,668.0	17.8	12.7	28.2	12.8	1.6	0.78	1.06	1.83	0.28	14.13 - 9.00	14.8	2.4
1/02/94	14,138.0	1,787.0	12,242.0	16.9	12.6	32.1	14.6	1.6	0.69	0.92	1.81	0.25	12.59 - 8.91	15.7	2.3

Statistics are as originally reported. Adjusted for 2-for-1 stock split, 6/96 & 6/01. ① Incl. a pre-tax in-process R&D chrg. $164.0 mill. and a pre-tax restruct. chrg. $613.0 mill. ② Incl. nonrecurr. after-tax chrg. $42.0 mill. ③ Incl. pre-tax chrg. of $54.0 mill. for in-proc. res. & devel. ④ Incl. pre-tax chrg. of $105.0 mill. for in-proc. res. & devel. ⑤ Incl. after-tax spec. chrg. of $189.0 mill. in-processed R&D costs.

OFFICERS:
W. C. Weldon, Chmn., C.E.O.
J. T. Lenehan, Vice-Chmn.

INVESTOR CONTACT: Helen E. Short, V.P.,
(800) 950-5089

PRINCIPAL OFFICE: One Johnson & Johnson Plaza, New Brunswick, NJ 08933

TELEPHONE NUMBER: (732) 524-0400
FAX: (732) 214-0332
WEB: www.jnj.com

NO. OF EMPLOYEES: 103,300 (approx.)

SHAREHOLDERS: 164,158

ANNUAL MEETING: In Apr.

INCORPORATED: NJ, Nov., 1887

INSTITUTIONAL HOLDINGS:
No. of Institutions: 1,330
Shares Held: 1,819,816,816
% Held: 61.3

INDUSTRY: Pharmaceutical preparations
(SIC: 2834)

TRANSFER AGENT(S): First Chicago Trust Company a Division of EquiServe, Jersey City, NJ

JOHNSON CONTROLS, INC.

EXCH.	SYM.	REC. PRICE	P/E RATIO	YLD.	MKT. CAP.	RANGE (52-WK.)	'02 Y/E PR.	DIV. ACH.
NYSE	JCI	77.96 (2/28/03)	11.9	1.8%	$6.93 bill.	93.20 - 69.10	80.17	27 yrs.

UPPER MEDIUM GRADE. THE COMPANY EXPECTS SALES IN FISCAL 2003 TO GROW BETWEEN 5.0% TO 10.0% OVER THE PRIOR YEAR.

TRADING VOLUME
Thousand Shares

*7 YEAR PRICE SCORE 147.7   ***12 MONTH PRICE SCORE 106.6**
*NYSE COMPOSITE INDEX=100

INTERIM EARNINGS (Per Share):

Qtr.	Dec.	Mar.	June	Sept.
1998-99	0.86	1.05	1.19	1.38
1999-00	1.06	0.95	1.45	1.63
2000-01	1.10	0.89	1.45	1.67
2001-02	1.27	1.21	1.85	2.02
2002-03	1.48	...	...	...

INTERIM DIVIDENDS (Per Share):

Amt.	Decl.	Ex.	Rec.	Pay.
0.33Q	1/23/02	3/06/02	3/08/02	3/29/02
0.33Q	5/22/02	6/12/02	6/14/02	6/28/02
0.33Q	7/24/02	9/11/02	9/13/02	9/30/02
0.36Q	11/20/02	12/11/02	12/13/02	1/02/03
0.36Q	1/22/03	3/12/03	3/14/03	3/31/03

Indicated div.: $1.44 (Div. Reinv. Plan)

CAPITALIZATION (9/30/02):

	($000)	(%)
Long-Term Debt	1,826,600	33.1
Minority Interest	189,000	3.4
Preferred Stock	103,800	1.9
Common & Surplus	3,395,900	61.6
Total	5,515,300	100.0

BUSINESS:

Johnson Controls, Inc. operates in two business segments. The Automotive segment is engaged in the design and manufacture of complete seat systems, seating components and interior trim systems for North American and European manufacturers of cars, vans and light trucks. The Controls segment is a worldwide supplier of control systems, services and products providing energy management, temperature and ventilation control, security and fire safety for non-residential buildings. Revenues (and operating income) for fiscal 2002 were derived: Automotive Systems Group, 74.7% (76.9%); and Controls Group, 25.3% (23.1%).

RECENT DEVELOPMENTS:

For the three months ended 12/31/02, net income rose 17.1% to $140.4 million compared with $119.9 million in the corresponding quarter of 2001. Net income benefited from a decrease in the effective income tax rate to 31.0% from 35.9%. Net sales were $5.18 billion, up 7.6% from $4.82 billion in the prior-year period. Sales from the Automotive Systems Group grew 7.8% to $3.94 billion from $3.66 billion due to higher revenues in Europe. Sales from the Controls Group rose 6.9% to $1.24 billion from $1.16 billion a year earlier, primarily due to an increase in revenues related to controls installation contracts for the new construction market, technical services and facility management services. Operating income climbed 3.9% to $247.9 million compared with $238.5 million a year earlier.

PROSPECTS:

On 1/8/03, the Company reaffirmed its expectations for consolidated sales in fiscal 2003 to increase by 5.0% to 10.0% over the prior year. Assuming North American light vehicle production decreases a slight percentage from units produced in 2002, the Company expects sales growth in the Automotive Systems Group to range from 5.0% to 10.0%. In addition, operating margin for the Automotive Systems Group is anticipated to be at the same level as in 2002 of approximately 5.7%. The Controls Group is anticipated to achieve sales growth of approximately 5.0% and a slight increase in operating margin from the level of 5.1% in fiscal 2002.

ANNUAL FINANCIAL DATA:

FISCAL YEAR	TOT. REVS. ($mill.)	NET INC. ($mill.)	TOT. ASSETS ($mill.)	OPER. PROFIT %	NET PROFIT %	RET. ON EQUITY %	RET. ON ASSETS %	CURR. RATIO	EARN. PER SH. $	CASH FL. PER SH. $	TANG. BK. VAL.$	DIV. PER SH. $	PRICE RANGE	AVG. P/E RATIO	AVG. YIELD %
9/30/02	20,103.4	600.5	11,165.3	5.6	3.0	17.2	5.4	1.0	6.35	11.79	4.48	1.32	93.20 - 69.10	12.8	1.6
9/30/01	18,427.2	478.3	9,911.5	5.2	2.6	16.0	4.8	1.0	5.11	10.60	7.03	1.24	82.70 - 51.94	13.2	1.8
9/30/00	17,154.6	472.4	9,428.0	5.6	2.8	18.3	5.0	0.9	5.09	10.06	3.65	1.12	65.13 - 45.81	10.9	2.0
9/30/99	16,139.4	⑤419.6	8,614.2	5.3	2.6	18.5	4.9	0.9	⑤4.48	9.25	0.45	1.00	76.69 - 49.00	14.0	1.6
9/30/98	12,586.8	④337.7	7,942.1	5.3	2.7	17.4	4.3	0.8	④3.63	7.78	...	0.92	61.88 - 40.50	14.1	1.8
9/30/97	11,145.4	③220.6	5,948.6	4.7	2.0	13.1	3.7	0.9	③2.48	6.67	...	0.86	51.00 - 35.38	17.4	2.0
9/30/96	9,210.0	②222.7	4,991.2	5.2	2.4	14.8	4.5	1.3	②2.66	6.49	0.70	0.82	42.69 - 31.25	13.9	2.2
9/30/95	8,330.3	195.8	4,320.9	5.4	2.4	14.6	4.5	1.4	2.27	5.76	8.04	0.78	34.88 - 22.88	12.7	2.7
9/30/94	6,870.5	165.2	3,806.9	5.3	2.4	13.7	4.3	1.2	1.90	5.05	6.69	0.72	30.88 - 22.44	14.0	2.7
9/30/93	6,181.7	①137.9	3,230.8	4.8	2.2	12.8	4.3	1.2	①0.09	4.50	7.60	0.68	29.56 - 21.50	300.0	2.7

Statistics are as originally reported. Adj. for 100% stk. div., 3/97. ① Bef. $122.0 mill. ($2.99/sh) acct. chg. ② Bef. $12.0 mill. chg. fr. disc. ops. ③ Bef. $67.9 mill. disc. ops. ④ Incl. $35.0 mill. after-tax gain fr. sale of bus. ⑤ Incl. $32.5 mill. net one-time gain on sale of bus.

OFFICERS:
J. H. Keyes, Chmn.
J. M. Barth, Pres., C.E.O.
S. A. Roell, Sr. V.P., C.F.O.

INVESTOR CONTACT: Shareholder Services, (414) 524-2363

PRINCIPAL OFFICE: 5757 N. Green Bay Avenue, Milwaukee, WI 53201

TELEPHONE NUMBER: (414) 524-1200
FAX: (414) 524-3200
WEB: www.johnsoncontrols.com

NO. OF EMPLOYEES: 111,000 (approx.)

SHAREHOLDERS: 57,138

ANNUAL MEETING: In Jan.

INCORPORATED: WI, July, 1900

INSTITUTIONAL HOLDINGS:
No. of Institutions: 399
Shares Held: 59,305,374
% Held: 66.7

INDUSTRY: Public building & related furniture (SIC: 2531)

TRANSFER AGENT(S): Firstar Trust Company, Milwaukee, WI

JONES APPAREL GROUP, INC.

EXCH.	SYM.	REC. PRICE	P/E RATIO	YLD.	MKT. CAP.	RANGE (52-WK.)	'02 Y/E PR.
NYSE	JNY	28.36 (2/28/03)	11.5	...	$3.56 bill.	41.68 - 26.18	35.44

INVESTMENT GRADE. JNY ANNOUNCED PLANS TO CONSOLIDATE AND REBRAND SOME OF ITS OPERATIONS.

*7 YEAR PRICE SCORE 135.8   ***12 MONTH PRICE SCORE 101.3**
*NYSE COMPOSITE INDEX=100

INTERIM EARNINGS (Per Share):

Qtr.	Mar.	June	Sept.	Dec.
1997	0.28	0.18	0.45	0.23
1998	0.37	0.24	0.57	0.30
1999	0.51	0.28	0.59	0.22
2000	0.58	0.46	0.93	0.52
2001	0.75	0.43	0.41	0.25
2002	0.63	0.49	0.95	0.39

INTERIM DIVIDENDS (Per Share):

Amt.	Decl.	Ex.	Rec.	Pay.
		No dividends paid.		

CAPITALIZATION (12/31/01):

	($000)	(%)
Long-Term Debt	949,500	32.0
Capital Lease Obligations..	27,100	0.9
Deferred Income Tax	80,800	2.7
Common & Surplus	1,905,400	64.3
Total	2,962,800	100.0

BUSINESS:

Jones Apparel Group, Inc. is a designer and marketer of branded apparel, footwear and accessories. JNY's nationally recognized brands include: JONES NEW YORK; LAUREN by Ralph Lauren, RALPH by Ralph Lauren, and POLO JEANS COMPANY, which are licensed from Polo Ralph Lauren Corporation; EVAN-PICONE, RENA ROWAN, NORTON MCNAUGHTON, ERIKA, I.E.I., GLORIA VANDERBILT, ENERGIE, CURRANTS, JAMIE SCOTT, TODD OLDHAM, NINE WEST, EASY SPIRIT, ENZO ANGIOLINI, BANDOLINO, NAPIER and JUDITH JACK. JNY also markets costume jewelry under the TOMMY HILFIGER brand licensed from Tommy Hilfiger Corp. and the GIVENCHY brand licensed from Givenchy Corp. and footwear and accessories under the ESPRIT brand licensed from Espirit Europe, B.V. On 10/2/99, JNY acquired Sun Apparel, Inc. On 6/15/99, acquired Nine West Group Inc. for about $1.40 billion.

RECENT DEVELOPMENTS:

For the year ended 12/31/02, the Company reported income of $332.3 million, before an accounting change charge of $13.8 million, versus net income of $236.2 million the previous year. Earnings for 2002 and 2001 included non-recurring items that resulted in net after-tax charges of $53.8 million and $64.5 million, respectively. Results in 2001 also included goodwill amortization of $44.2 million. Total revenues increased 5.9% to $4.34 billion. Income from operations grew to $590.6 million from $479.9 million the year before.

PROSPECTS:

On 1/16/03, the Company announced plans to consolidate and rebrand some of its operations. Specifically, JNY will close certain Sun Apparel manufacturing and warehousing facilities and consolidate these operations into existing l.e.i. facilities. In addition, the Company plans to rebrand 20 of its underperforming Enzo Angiolini retail stores under its moderate-priced Bandolino retail name. Going forward, JNY expects its strategy of continued diversification in distribution channels, new product offerings and target consumers to contribute to growth throughout 2003. JNY noted that in 2003 it plans to introduce new BANDOLINO apparel, GLORIA VANDERBILT sportswear, ESPRIT footwear and handbags, and GLORIA VANDERBILT footwear and handbags.

ANNUAL FINANCIAL DATA:

FISCAL YEAR	TOT. REVS. ($mill.)	NET INC. ($mill.)	TOT. ASSETS ($mill.)	OPER. PROFIT %	NET PROFIT %	RET. ON EQUITY %	RET. ON ASSETS %	CURR. RATIO	EARN. PER SH. $	CASH FL. PER SH. $	TANG. BK. VAL. $	PRICE RANGE	AVG. P/E RATIO
p12/31/02	4,340.9	④ 332.3		11.8	5.8	12.4	7.0	3.0	④ 2.46	2.75	0.03	41.68 - 26.18	13.8
12/31/01	4,073.1	②③ 236.1	3,373.5	14.6	7.3	20.4	10.1	1.3	②③ 1.82	3.37	0.16	47.43 - 23.75	19.6
12/31/00	4,142.7	② 301.9	2,979.2	14.6	6.0	15.2	6.7	1.7	② 2.48	2.24	...	35.00 - 20.13	11.1
① 12/31/99	3,150.7	188.4	2,792.0	12.0	8.8	26.1	13.0	3.6	1.60	1.68	2.33	35.88 - 21.50	17.9
12/31/98	1,685.2	154.9	1,188.7	15.5	9.2	26.1	13.0	3.6	1.47	1.68	2.33	37.75 - 15.88	18.2
12/31/97	1,387.5	121.7	580.8	14.2	8.8	27.9	21.0	4.0	1.13	1.26	3.96	28.72 - 16.06	19.8
12/31/96	1,021.0	80.9	488.1	12.8	7.9	21.5	16.6	4.1	0.76	0.84	3.37	18.69 - 8.91	18.3
12/31/95	776.4	63.5	401.0	13.0	8.2	20.2	15.8	4.7	0.60	0.66	2.76	9.91 - 5.66	13.0
12/31/94	633.3	54.9	318.3	13.9	8.7	22.1	17.3	4.8	0.52	0.56	2.13	8.94 - 5.50	13.9
12/31/93	541.2	48.4	266.6	14.6	8.9	25.6	18.1	4.0	0.46	0.50	1.55	10.25 - 4.66	16.1

Statistics are as originally reported. Adj. for stk. split: 2-for-1, 6/98, 10/96 ① Incl. Nine West Group., acquired 6/15/99 ② Incl. purchased inventory chrg. $17.7 mill., 12/01; $3.1 mill., 12/00 ③ Incl. inventory write-down chrg. $86.8 mill. ④ Excl. acctg. chng. chrg. $13.8 mill.; Incl. purchased invent. chrg. of $23.1 mill, consolid. chrgs. of $6.9 mill., trademark writedown of $24.4 mill. & exec. comp. chrg. of $31.9 mill.

OFFICERS:
S. Kimmel, Chmn., C.E.O.
P. Boneparth,, Pres., C.E.O.
W. R. Card, C.F.O., C.O.O.
INVESTOR CONTACT: Anita Britt, Exec. V.P., Inv. Relations, (215) 785-4000
PRINCIPAL OFFICE: 250 Rittenhouse Circle, Keystone Park, Bristol, PA 19007

TELEPHONE NUMBER: (215) 785-4000
FAX: (215) 785-1228
WEB: www.jny.com
NO. OF EMPLOYEES: 16,690 (approx.)
SHAREHOLDERS: 379
ANNUAL MEETING: In May
INCORPORATED: PA, 1975

INSTITUTIONAL HOLDINGS:
No. of Institutions: 362
Shares Held: 119,297,287
% Held: 92.6
INDUSTRY: Women's & misses' blouses & shirts (SIC: 2331)
TRANSFER AGENT(S): Bank of New York, New York, NY

KANSAS CITY SOUTHERN INDUSTRIES, INC.

EXCH.	SYM.	REC. PRICE	P/E RATIO	YLD.	MKT. CAP.	RANGE (52-WK.)	'02 Y/E PR.
NYSE	KSU	12.15 (2/28/03)	13.4	...	$0.72 bill.	17.50 - 11.20	12.00

MEDIUM GRADE. THE COMPANY'S TOP LINE IS BEING HURT BY LOWER COAL AND INTERMODAL AND AUTO-MOTIVE REVENUES.

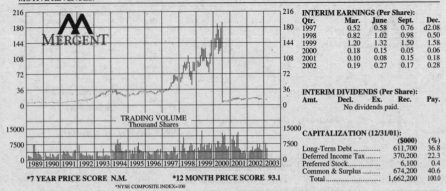

INTERIM EARNINGS (Per Share):

Qtr.	Mar.	June	Sept.	Dec.
1997	0.52	0.58	0.76	d2.08
1998	0.82	1.02	0.98	0.50
1999	1.20	1.32	1.50	1.58
2000	0.18	0.15	0.05	0.06
2001	0.10	0.08	0.15	0.18
2002	0.19	0.27	0.17	0.28

INTERIM DIVIDENDS (Per Share):

Amt.	Decl.	Ex.	Rec.	Pay.
		No dividends paid.		

CAPITALIZATION (12/31/01):

	($000)	(%)
Long-Term Debt	611,700	36.8
Deferred Income Tax	370,200	22.3
Preferred Stock	6,100	0.4
Common & Surplus	674,200	40.6
Total	1,662,200	100.0

TRADING VOLUME
Thousand Shares

*7 YEAR PRICE SCORE N.M.   *12 MONTH PRICE SCORE 93.1
*NYSE COMPOSITE INDEX=100

BUSINESS:

Kansas City Southern Industries, Inc. operates a railroad system that provides shippers with rail freight service in key commercial and industrial markets of the U.S. and Mexico. As of 9/30/02, the transportation segment included: The Kansas City Southern Railway (KCSR); Grupo Transportacion Ferroviaria Mexicana, S.A. de C.V. (Grupo TFM), a 46.6%-owned affiliate; Southern Capital Corporation, LLC, a 50.0%-owned affiliate; and Panama

Canal Railway Company, a 50.0%-owned affiliate. As of 12/31/01, KCSR owned and operated approximately 3,100 miles of main and branch lines and 1,340 miles of other tracks in a ten-state region that included Missouri, Kansas, Arkansas, Oklahoma, Mississippi, Alabama, Tennessee, Louisiana, Texas and Illinois. On 7/12/00, KSU completed the spin-off of its wholly-owned subsidiary, Stilwell Financial, Inc.

RECENT DEVELOPMENTS:

For the year ended 12/31/02, net income was $54.2 million versus income of $31.1 million, before an accounting change charge of $400,000, the previous year. Results for 2002 included a gain of $4.4 million on the sale of Mexrail, Inc., mostly offset by debt retirement costs of $4.3 million. Equity in net earnings of unconsolidated affiliates rose

50.2% to $42.8 million. Other income totaled $17.6 million versus $4.2 million in 2001. Revenues fell 2.9% to $566.2 million from $583.2 million, primarily as a result of lower coal and automotive revenue, partially offset by higher revenue for all other major commodity groups.

PROSPECTS:

KSU's outlook is mixed. On the positive side, the Company's KCSR unit has recently reported higher traffic volumes, increased length of haul and price improvements in key traffic lanes from several commodity groups, including chemical and petroleum products, paper and forest products and agriculture and mineral products. Also, future

results should benefit from KSU's increased ownership in Grupo TFM, which has performed well as trade between the U.S. and Mexico has expanded despite the difficult economic environment. However, these improvements are being offset by lower revenues for coal and intermodal and automotive business.

ANNUAL FINANCIAL DATA:

FISCAL YEAR	TOT. REVS. ($mill.)	NET INC. ($mill.)	TOT. ASSETS ($mill.)	OPER. PROFIT %	NET PROFIT %	RET. ON EQUITY %	RET. ON ASSETS %	CURR. RATIO	EARN. PER SH.$	CASH FL. PER SH.$	TANG. BK. VAL.$	PRICE RANGE	AVG. P/E RATIO
p12/31/02	566.2	⑥ 54.2							⑥ 0.87			17.50 - 11.70	16.8
12/31/01	577.3	⑤ 31.1	2,010.9	9.6	5.4	4.6	1.5	1.0	⑤ 0.51	1.46	11.38	16.75 - 9.00	25.2
④ 12/31/00	572.2	③ 25.4	1,944.5	10.1	4.4	3.9	1.3	0.9	③ 0.43	1.40	10.24	191.50 - 5.13	228.6
12/31/99	1,813.7	323.3	3,088.9	32.1	17.8	25.2	10.5	1.8	5.58	7.29	19.55	150.00 - 75.00	20.2
12/31/98	1,284.3	190.2	2,619.7	30.7	14.8	20.4	7.3	1.6	3.32	4.66	10.20	114.88 - 46.00	24.2
12/31/97	1,058.3	① d14.1	2,434.2	10.1	...	...	...	0.9	① d0.26	1.14	7.45	70.25 - 29.17	...
12/31/96	847.3	① 150.9	2,084.1	24.1	17.8	21.1	7.2	1.2	① 2.61	3.94	8.65	34.50 - 25.67	11.5
12/31/95	775.2	① 236.7	2,039.6	20.5	30.5	34.0	11.6	0.9	① 3.61	4.75	8.26	32.42 - 20.67	7.4
12/31/94	1,097.9	104.9	2,230.8	18.4	9.6	15.7	4.7	1.1	1.55	3.31	6.73	35.08 - 19.92	17.8
12/31/93	961.1	② 97.0	1,917.0	22.1	10.1	17.2	5.1	1.2	② 1.44	2.89	4.70	34.33 - 15.63	17.3

Statistics are as originally reported. Adj. for stk. splits: 1-for-2, 7/12/00; 3-for-1, 9/97. ① Incl. chrg. 12/31/97, $196.4 mill.; cr. 12/31/96, $47.7 mill.; net cr. 12/31/95, $118.7 mill. ② Bef. acctg. adj. chge. of $6.5 mill. ③ Bef. inc. fr. disc. ops. of $363.8 mill. ($6.14/sh.) & extraord. chrg. of $8.7 mill. ($0.15/sh.) ④ Refl. spin-off of Stilwell Financial, Inc. ⑤ Excl. acctg. chge. of $400,000. ⑥ Incl. gain of $4.4 mill. on sale of Mexrail, Inc. & debt retirement costs of $4.3 mill.

OFFICERS:
M. R. Haverty, Chmn., Pres., C.E.O.
R. G. Russ, Exec. V.P., C.F.O.
P. J. Weyandt, V.P., Treas.
INVESTOR CONTACT: William Galligan, Investor Relations, (816) 983-1551
PRINCIPAL OFFICE: 114 West 11th Street, Kansas City, MO 64105

TELEPHONE NUMBER: (816) 983-1303
FAX: (816) 556-0297
WEB: www.kcsi.com
NO. OF EMPLOYEES: 2,695 (approx.)
SHAREHOLDERS: 5,852 (record)
ANNUAL MEETING: In May
INCORPORATED: DE, Jan., 1962

INSTITUTIONAL HOLDINGS:
No. of Institutions: 158
Shares Held: 41,538,600
% Held: 68.1
INDUSTRY: Railroads, line-haul operating (SIC: 4011)
TRANSFER AGENT(S): UMB Bank, N.A., Kansas City, MO

KAYDON CORPORATION

EXCH.	SYM.	REC. PRICE	P/E RATIO	YLD.	MKT. CAP.	RANGE (52-WK.)	'02 Y/E PR.
NYSE	KDN	18.00 (2/28/03)	21.2	2.7%	$0.55 bill.	29.27 - 17.20	21.21

MEDIUM GRADE. IN LIGHT OF CURRENT MARKET CONDITIONS, THE COMPANY IS FOCUSED ON PERMANENT REDUCTIONS IN ITS OPERATING COST STRUCTURE.

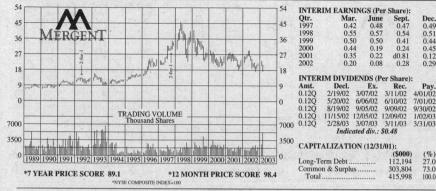

INTERIM EARNINGS (Per Share):

Qtr.	Mar.	June	Sept.	Dec.
1997	0.42	0.48	0.47	0.49
1998	0.55	0.57	0.54	0.51
1999	0.50	0.50	0.41	0.44
2000	0.44	0.19	0.24	0.24
2001	0.35	0.22	d0.81	0.12
2002	0.20	0.08	0.28	0.29

INTERIM DIVIDENDS (Per Share):

Amt.	Decl.	Ex.	Rec.	Pay.
0.12Q	2/19/02	3/07/02	3/11/02	4/01/02
0.12Q	5/20/02	6/06/02	6/10/02	7/01/02
0.12Q	8/19/02	9/05/02	9/09/02	9/30/02
0.12Q	11/15/02	12/05/02	12/09/02	1/02/03
0.12Q	2/28/03	3/07/03	3/11/03	3/31/03

Indicated div.: $0.48

*7 YEAR PRICE SCORE 89.1   ***12 MONTH PRICE SCORE 98.4**

*NYSE COMPOSITE INDEX=100

CAPITALIZATION (12/31/01):

	($000)	(%)
Long-Term Debt	112,194	27.0
Common & Surplus	303,804	73.0
Total	415,998	100.0

BUSINESS:

Kaydon Corporation manufactures complex and standard metal products used in medical, aerospace, defense, electronic, material handling, construction, marine equipment and other industrial applications. Principal products include anti-friction bearings, split roller bearings, specialty balls, linear deceleration products, metal retaining devices, engine rings, sealing rings, shaft seals, slip-rings, slip-ring assemblies, video and data multiplexers, fiber optic rotary joints, filter elements, filtration systems, metal alloys, machine tool components, presses, dies and benders used in a variety of industrial applications. On 12/31/01, the Company sold the assets of its Fluid Power Products Group. The Company operates through three operating segments: specialty metal formed products (58.9% of 2001 sales); ring, seal and filtration products (31.2%); and other metal products (9.9%).

RECENT DEVELOPMENTS:

For the year ended 12/31/02, income, before an accounting change charge of $13.2 million, declined 10.7% to $25.4 million, compared with income of $28.5 million, before a loss from discontinued operations of $32.5 million, in 2001. Results for 2002 included an unusual litigation-related charge of $7.5 million. Net sales slid 2.2% to $279.4 million from $285.6 million a year earlier. The decline in sales reflected soft demand in certain key markets and cautious capital spending programs by KDN's customers.

PROSPECTS:

Near-term results remain clouded by economic and geopolitical uncertainties. In light of the current economic environment, KDN will continue to focus on permanent reductions in its operating cost structure while continuing to make strategic business investments in an effort to generate earnings growth and improve cash flow performance. In the long-term, the Company is optimistic about improved results, which should stem from a recovery in the manufacturing economy reflecting productivity gains, fiscal stimulus and increased defense spending.

ANNUAL FINANCIAL DATA:

FISCAL YEAR	TOT. REVS. ($000)	NET INC. ($000)	TOT. ASSETS ($000)	OPER. PROFIT %	NET PROFIT %	RET. ON EQUITY %	RET. ON ASSETS %	CURR. RATIO	EARN. PER SH.$	CASH FL. PER SH.$	TANG. BK. VAL.$	DIV. PER SH.$	PRICE RANGE	AVG. P/E RATIO	AVG. YIELD %
p12/31/02	279,410	④ 25,426	477,147						④ 0.85			0.48	29.27 - 17.20	27.3	2.1
12/31/01	285,603	③ 28,480	497,798	15.9	10.0	9.4	5.7	8.3	③ 0.95	1.46	5.98	0.48	28.25 - 17.80	24.2	2.1
12/31/00	339,246	② 39,347	475,552	16.8	11.6	12.2	8.3	4.0	② 1.30	1.88	7.22	0.44	29.31 - 19.94	18.9	1.8
12/31/99	325,696	58,779	406,749	27.4	18.0	18.5	14.5	3.9	1.85	2.34	7.78	0.40	41.06 - 23.00	17.3	1.2
12/31/98	376,172	71,184	413,808	29.3	18.9	22.8	17.2	3.2	2.17	2.59	7.68	0.36	45.94 - 22.81	15.8	1.0
12/31/97	329,036	61,666	383,985	29.1	18.7	21.7	16.1	3.0	1.86	2.24	6.57	0.28	34.94 - 20.88	15.0	1.0
12/31/96	290,670	50,521	331,538	27.2	17.4	21.8	15.2	2.8	1.53	1.88	5.42	0.24	24.75 - 14.44	12.8	1.2
12/31/95	229,924	38,203	267,675	25.8	16.6	20.3	14.3	3.1	1.14	1.47	3.91	0.22	15.81 - 11.38	11.9	1.6
12/31/94	204,695	① 31,226	243,584	24.3	15.3	18.7	12.8	3.1	① 0.94	1.25	3.69	0.20	12.63 - 9.88	12.0	1.8
12/31/93	184,060	27,695	217,422	24.1	15.0	19.3	12.7	3.1	0.80	1.10	3.00	0.18	16.00 - 8.75	15.5	1.5

Statistics are as originally reported. Adj. for stk. split: 2-for-1, 10/97. ① Bef. acctg. change chrg. $2.0 mill. ($0.06/sh.). ② Incl. nonrecurr. pre-tax chrg. of $21.7 mill. for special litigation-related charges. ③ Bef. loss of $32.5 mill. from disc. opers.; incl. net special charge of $37.9 mill. ④ Incl. unus. litigation related chrg. of $7.5 mill., but excl. acctg. change chrg. of $13.2 mill.

OFFICERS:
B. P. Campbell, Chmn., Pres., C.E.O., C.F.O.
J. F. Brocci, V.P., Sec.

INVESTOR CONTACT: Brian P. Campbell, Chmn., Pres., C.E.O., C.F.O., (734) 747-7025 ext. 129

PRINCIPAL OFFICE: 315 East Eisenhower Parkway, Suite 300, Ann Arbor, MI 48108

TELEPHONE NUMBER: (734) 747-7025
FAX: (734) 747-6565
WEB: www.kaydon.com

NO. OF EMPLOYEES: 1,850 (avg.)

SHAREHOLDERS: 1,151 (record)

ANNUAL MEETING: In May

INCORPORATED: DE, Oct., 1983

INSTITUTIONAL HOLDINGS:
No. of Institutions: 125
Shares Held: 22,237,535
% Held: 74.0

INDUSTRY: Ball and roller bearings (SIC: 3562)

TRANSFER AGENT(S): Continental Stock Transfer and Trust Company, New York, NY

KB HOME

EXCH.	SYM.	REC. PRICE	P/E RATIO	YLD.	MKT. CAP.	RANGE (52-WK.)	'02 Y/E PR.
NYSE	KBH	46.90 (2/28/03)	6.5	0.6%	$2.25 bill.	54.39 - 39.31	42.85

UPPER MEDIUM GRADE. GOING FORWARD, THE COMPANY SHOULD CONTINUE TO BENEFIT FROM AN INCREASE IN COMMUNITY COUNTS AND CONTINUED EXPANSION OF ITS OPERATING MARGINS.

INTERIM EARNINGS (Per Share):

Qtr.	Feb.	May	Aug.	Nov.
1996-97	0.11	0.27	0.38	0.69
1997-98	0.20	0.42	0.68	1.02
1998-99	0.35	0.58	0.78	1.36
1999-00	1.47	0.68	1.14	2.00
2000-01	0.70	1.07	1.58	2.03
2001-02	0.95	1.42	1.95	- 2.92

INTERIM DIVIDENDS (Per Share):

Amt.	Decl.	Ex.	Rec.	Pay.
0.075Q	12/06/01	2/08/02	2/12/02	2/26/02
0.075Q	4/11/02	5/10/02	5/14/02	5/28/02
0.075Q	7/11/02	8/12/02	8/14/02	8/28/02
0.075Q	10/03/02	11/08/02	11/13/02	11/27/02
0.075Q	12/05/02	2/10/03	2/12/03	2/26/03

Indicated div.: $0.30

CAPITALIZATION (11/30/02):

	($000)	(%)
Long-Term Debt	1,688,706	55.6
Minority Interest	74,266	2.4
Common & Surplus	1,274,351	42.0
Total	3,037,323	100.0

| 1989 | 1990 | 1991 | 1992 | 1993 | 1994 | 1995 | 1996 | 1997 | 1998 | 1999 | 2000 | 2001 | 2002 | 2003 |

TRADING VOLUME
Thousand Shares

*7 YEAR PRICE SCORE 185.7   ***12 MONTH PRICE SCORE 107.4**

*NYSE COMPOSITE INDEX=100

BUSINESS:

KB Home (formerly Kaufman & Broad Home Corp.) is a builder of single-family homes with domestic operations in seven states, and international operations in France. Domestically, the Company is the largest homebuilder west of the Mississippi River, delivering more single-family homes than any other builder in the region. KBH builds homes that cater primarily to first-time and first move-up homebuyers, generally in medium-sized developments close to major metropolitan areas. In France, the Company also builds commercial projects and high-density residential properties, such as condominium and apartment complexes. KBH provides mortgage banking services to domestic homebuyers through its wholly-owned subsidiary, KB Home Mortgage Company.

RECENT DEVELOPMENTS:

For the year ended 11/30/02, net income jumped 46.7% to $314.4 million compared with $214.2 million in 2001. Total revenues advanced 10.0% to $5.03 billion from $4.57 billion a year earlier. The increase in revenues was bolstered by higher unit deliveries, which grew 2.8% to 25,565 units from 24,868 units in 2001, and higher average sales prices, which advanced 7.2% to $190,800. Revenues from construction climbed 9.7% to $4.94 billion, while revenues from mortgage banking grew 26.8% to $91.9 million. Operating margin rose 170 basis points to 10.1% for 2002 from 8.4% for 2001.

PROSPECTS:

Going forward, the Company should continue to benefit from an increase in community counts and continued expansion of its operating margins. Selling prices should continue to increase in most of the Company's geographic regions, with the strongest increase occurring in the West Coast region due to a statewide shortage of housing in California. KBH's mortgage banking operation should continue to report higher pretax income as a result of an increase in the average loan size and a more favorable interest rate spread. Moreover, KBH should benefit from a 22.8% improvement in its backlog to $2.35 billion at 11/30/02.

ANNUAL FINANCIAL DATA:

FISCAL YEAR	TOT. REVS. ($mill.)	NET INC. ($mill.)	TOT. ASSETS ($mill.)	OPER. PROFIT %	NET PROFIT %	RET. ON EQUITY %	RET. ON ASSETS %	CURR. RATIO	EARN. PER SH.$	CASH FL. PER SH.$	TANG. BK. VAL.$	DIV. PER SH.$	PRICE RANGE	AVG. P/E RATIO	AVG. YIELD %
11/30/02	**5,030.8**	**314.4**	**4,025.5**	**10.1**	**6.2**	**24.7**	**7.8**	**6.7**	**7.15**	**7.59**	**22.51**	**0.30**	**54.39 - 37.13**	**6.4**	**0.7**
11/30/01	4,574.2	214.2	3,692.9	8.4	4.7	19.6	5.8	6.8	5.50	6.66	17.40	0.30	41.44 - 24.67	6.0	0.9
11/30/00	3,930.9	② 210.0	2,828.9	7.9	5.3	32.1	7.4	7.5	② 5.24	6.30	10.19	0.30	38.31 - 16.81	5.3	1.1
11/30/99	3,836.3	147.5	2,664.2	7.2	3.8	21.8	5.5	6.5	3.08	3.91	9.79	0.30	30.25 - 16.75	7.6	1.3
11/30/98	2,449.4	95.3	1,860.2	6.9	3.9	20.1	5.1	7.5	2.32	2.76	10.73	0.30	35.00 - 17.13	11.2	1.2
11/30/97	1,876.3	58.2	1,419.0	6.2	3.1	15.2	4.1	7.7	1.45	1.81	9.02	0.30	23.13 - 12.75	12.4	1.7
11/30/96	1,787.0	① d61.2	1,243.5	6.2	...	...	...	7.1	① d1.54	d1.23	7.75	0.30	16.88 - 11.25	...	2.1
11/30/95	1,396.5	29.1	1,574.2	5.4	2.1	7.0	1.8	9.0	0.73	0.93	12.37	0.30	16.00 - 10.88	18.4	2.2
11/30/94	1,336.3	46.6	1,454.5	7.1	3.5	11.5	3.2	8.9	1.16	1.31	12.46	0.30	25.50 - 12.13	16.2	1.6
11/30/93	1,237.9	39.9	1,339.4	7.6	3.2	9.0	3.0	8.0	0.96	1.26	12.76	0.30	24.75 - 16.00	21.2	1.5

Statistics are as originally reported. ① Incl. non-recurr. chrg. $170.8 mill. ② Incl. non-recurr. gain $39.6 mill.

OFFICERS:
B. Karatz, Chmn., Pres., C.E.O.
B. P. Pachino, Sr. V.P., Gen. Couns.
J. T. Mezger, Exec. V.P., C.O.O.

INVESTOR CONTACT: Clen Teng, Director, Inv. Rel., (310) 231-4000

PRINCIPAL OFFICE: 10990 Wilshire Boulevard, Los Angeles, CA 90024

TELEPHONE NUMBER: (310) 231-4000
FAX: (310) 231-4222
WEB: www.kbhome.com

NO. OF EMPLOYEES: 4,500 (approx.)

SHAREHOLDERS: 1,132

ANNUAL MEETING: In Apr.

INCORPORATED: DE, May, 1986

INSTITUTIONAL HOLDINGS:
No. of Institutions: 251
Shares Held: 40,613,672
% Held: 101.6

INDUSTRY: Single-family housing construction (SIC: 1521)

TRANSFER AGENT(S): Mellon Investor Services LLC, South Hackensack, NJ

KELLOGG COMPANY

EXCH.	SYM.	REC. PRICE	P/E RATIO	YLD.	MKT. CAP.	RANGE (52-WK.)	'02 Y/E PR.
NYSE	K	29.57 (2/28/03)	16.9	3.4%	$12.06 bill.	37.00 - 29.35	34.27

UPPER MEDIUM GRADE. IN 2003, THE COMPANY PLANS TO FOCUS ON RESTORING GROWTH IN ITS SNACK BUSINESS.

*7 YEAR PRICE SCORE 105.8   ***12 MONTH PRICE SCORE 105.1**
*NYSE COMPOSITE INDEX=100

INTERIM EARNINGS (Per Share):

Qtr.	Mar.	June	Sept.	Dec.
1996	0.48	0.19	0.38	0.21
1997	0.39	0.40	0.50	0.08
1998	0.42	0.35	0.35	0.11
1999	0.29	0.38	d0.08	0.25
2000	0.40	0.37	0.45	0.23
2001	0.23	0.28	0.37	0.31
2002	0.37	0.42	0.49	0.47

INTERIM DIVIDENDS (Per Share):

Amt.	Decl.	Ex.	Rec.	Pay.
0.253Q	2/22/02	2/28/02	3/04/02	3/15/02
0.253Q	4/26/02	5/29/02	5/31/02	6/14/02
0.253Q	7/26/02	8/28/02	8/30/02	9/13/02
0.253Q	10/28/02	11/26/02	11/29/02	12/13/02
0.253Q	2/21/03	2/27/03	3/03/03	3/14/03

Indicated div.: $1.01 (Div. Reinv. Plan)

CAPITALIZATION (12/31/01):

	($000)	(%)
Long-Term Debt	5,619,000	86.6
Common & Surplus	871,500	13.4
Total	6,490,500	100.0

BUSINESS:

Kellogg Company is a producer of ready-to-eat cereal products and convenience foods such as cookies, crackers, toaster pastries, cereal bars, frozen waffles, meat alternatives, pie crusts, and ice cream cones. Brand names include KELLOGG'S, KEEBLER, POP-TARTS, EGGO, CHEEZ-IT, NUTRI-GRAIN, RICE KRISPIES, MURRAY, AUSTIN, MORNINGSTAR FARMS, FAMOUS AMOS, CARR'S, READY CRUST, PLANTATION, and KASHI. Products are manufactured in 19 countries and distributed in 160 countries in Asia, Australia, Europe, Africa and Latin America. Contributions to sales (and operating profit) in 2002 were: United States, 66.5% (67.1%); Europe, 17.7% (15.8%); Latin America, 7.6% (10.6%); and Other, 8.2% (6.5%). On 3/26/01, K acquired Keebler Foods Co. for $4.56 billion.

RECENT DEVELOPMENTS:

For the year ended 12/28/02, net earnings totaled $720.9 million, up 49.6% compared with earnings of $482.0 million, before a $7.4 million extraordinary charge and a $1.0 million accounting change charge, a year earlier. Results for 2001 included a pre-tax restructuring charge of $33.3 million. Net sales grew 10.0% to $8.30 billion from $7.55 billion the previous year. Net sales in the U.S. and Europe climbed 13.0% and 8.0% to $5.53 billion and $1.47 billion, respectively, while net sales in Latin America slipped 2.9% to $631.1 million. Operating profit advanced 29.1% to $1.51 billion from $1.17 billion the year before.

PROSPECTS:

Looking ahead to 2003, a major priority for the Company will be to restore growth in its snacks business. Meanwhile, the Company anticipates first-quarter 2003 earnings of $0.38 to $0.40 per share. For the full-year 2003, the Company is targeting low single-digit net sales growth, mid single-digit operating profit growth, and earnings of between $1.86 and $1.90 per share. Higher sales, an improved sales mix and productivity gains are expected to more than offset higher commodity costs and increased employee benefits expenses.

ANNUAL FINANCIAL DATA:

FISCAL YEAR	TOT. REVS. ($mill.)	NET INC. ($mill.)	TOT. ASSETS ($mill.)	OPER. PROFIT %	NET PROFIT %	RET. ON EQUITY %	RET. ON ASSETS %	CURR. RATIO	EARN. PER SH.$	CASH FL. PER SH.$	TANG. BK. VAL.$	DIV. PER SH.$	PRICE RANGE	AVG. P/E RATIO	AVG. YIELD
p12/31/02	8,304.1	720.9							1.75			1.01	37.00 - 29.02	18.9	3.1
12/31/01	8,853.3	④ 482.0	10,368.6	13.2	5.4	55.3	4.6	0.9	④ 1.18	2.26	2.14	1.01	34.00 - 24.25	24.7	3.5
12/31/00	6,954.7	② 587.7	4,896.3	14.2	8.5	65.5	12.0	0.6	② 1.45	2.17	2.21	0.99	32.00 - 20.75	18.2	3.8
12/31/99	6,984.2	② 338.3	4,808.7	11.9	4.8	41.6	7.0	1.0	② 0.83	1.54	2.01	0.96	42.25 - 30.00	43.5	2.7
12/31/98	6,762.1	② 502.6	5,051.5	13.2	7.4	56.5	9.9	0.9	② 1.23	1.91	2.20	0.92	50.19 - 28.50	32.0	2.3
12/31/97	6,830.1	②③ 564.0	4,877.6	14.8	8.3	56.5	11.6	0.9	②③ 1.36	2.06	2.43	0.87	50.50 - 32.00	30.3	2.1
12/31/96	6,676.6	① 531.0	5,050.0	14.4	8.0	41.4	10.5	0.7	① 1.25	1.84	3.06	0.81	40.31 - 31.00	28.5	2.3
12/31/95	7,003.7	① 490.3	4,414.6	12.0	7.0	30.8	11.1	1.1	① 1.12	1.71	3.67	0.75	39.75 - 26.25	29.5	2.3
12/31/94	6,562.0	② 705.4	4,467.3	17.7	10.7	39.0	15.8	1.2	② 1.58	2.14	4.08	0.70	30.38 - 23.69	17.2	2.6
12/31/93	6,295.4	② 680.7	4,237.1	17.0	10.8	39.7	16.1	1.0	② 1.47	2.04	3.63	0.66	33.94 - 23.63	19.6	2.3

Statistics are as originally reported. Adj. for 2-for-1 stk. split, 8/97. ① Incl. discont. opers. loss $120.1 mil, 1996; & loss $271.3 mil, 1995. ② Incl. $64.2 mil ($0.16/sh) after-tax restr. chg., 2000; $244.6 mil pre-tax non-recur. chg. & $168.5 mil pre-tax disposition-related chgs., 1999; $46.3 mil ($0.12/sh) after-tax, 1998; $140.5 mil ($0.34/sh) chg., 1997; net gain $200,000, 1994; & net gain $5.3 mil, 1993. ③ Bef. $18.0 mil ($0.04/sh) chg. for acctg. change. ④ Bef. $7.4 mil extraord. chg., $1.0 mil chg. for acctg. change & incl. $33.3 mil restr. chg.

OFFICERS:
C. M. Gutierrez, Chmn., Pres., C.E.O.
J. A. Bryant, Sr. V.P., C.F.O.
J. L. Kelly, Exec. V.P., Sec., Gen. Couns.

INVESTOR CONTACT: John P. Renwick, (616) 961-6365

PRINCIPAL OFFICE: One Kellogg Square, Battle Creek, MI 49016-3599

TELEPHONE NUMBER: (616) 961-2000
FAX: (616) 961-2871
WEB: www.kelloggs.com

NO. OF EMPLOYEES: 26,424 (approx.)

SHAREHOLDERS: 46,126 (record)

ANNUAL MEETING: In Apr.

INCORPORATED: DE, Dec., 1922

INSTITUTIONAL HOLDINGS:
No. of Institutions: 383
Shares Held: 332,399,898
% Held: 81.4

INDUSTRY: Cereal breakfast foods (SIC: 2043)

TRANSFER AGENT(S): Wells Fargo Shareowner Services, South St. Paul, MN

KELLWOOD COMPANY

EXCH.	SYM.	REC. PRICE	P/E RATIO	YLD.	MKT. CAP.	RANGE (52-WK.)	'02 Y/E PR.
NYSE	KWD	25.60 (2/28/03)	15.2	2.5%	$0.59 bill.	32.50 - 19.70	26.00

MEDIUM GRADE. EARNINGS FOR FISCAL 2003 ARE EXPECTED IN THE RANGE OF $2.70 TO $2.80 PER SHARE.

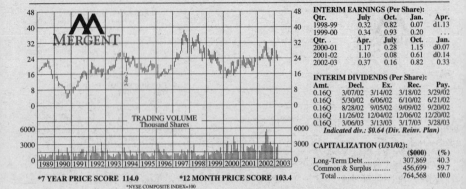

*7 YEAR PRICE SCORE 114.0   ***12 MONTH PRICE SCORE 103.4**

*NYSE COMPOSITE INDEX=100

INTERIM EARNINGS (Per Share):

Qtr.	July	Oct.	Jan.	Apr.
1998-99	0.32	0.82	0.07	d1.13
1999-00	0.34	0.93	0.20	...

Qtr.	Apr.	July	Oct.	Jan.
2000-01	1.17	0.28	1.15	d0.07
2001-02	1.10	0.08	0.61	d0.14
2002-03	0.37	0.16	0.82	0.33

INTERIM DIVIDENDS (Per Share):

Amt.	Decl.	Ex.	Rec.	Pay.
0.16Q	3/07/02	3/14/02	3/18/02	3/29/02
0.16Q	5/30/02	6/06/02	6/10/02	6/21/02
0.16Q	8/28/02	9/05/02	9/09/02	9/20/02
0.16Q	11/26/02	12/04/02	12/06/02	12/20/02
0.16Q	3/06/03	3/13/03	3/17/03	3/28/03
Indicated div.: $0.64 (Div. Reinv. Plan)				

CAPITALIZATION (1/31/02):

	($000)	(%)
Long-Term Debt	307,869	40.3
Common & Surplus	456,699	59.7
Total	764,568	100.0

BUSINESS:

Kellwood Company manufactures and markets apparel and related soft goods. The Company products include diversified lines of men's and women's sportswear, as well as intimate apparel and recreation products. The Company's brands include Sag Harbor®, Koret®, Jax®, David Dart®, Gerber® Democracy®, David Meister™, Dorby™, My Michelle®, Briggs™, Vintage Blue™, Emme®, Bill Burns®, David Brooks®, Kelty®, and Sierra Designs®. Sales to Sears, Roebuck & Co. and J.C. Penny Company, Inc. accounted for 7.0% and 11.0%, respectively, of total sales in fiscal year 2001. On 6/21/02, the Company acquired Gerber Childrenswear, Inc.

RECENT DEVELOPMENTS:

For the year ended 2/1/03, net income increased 11.3% to $42.0 million from $37.7 million the previous year. Results for 2002 included an after-tax charge of $9.7 million for business and facility realignments. The increase in earnings was attributed to higher gross margins, lower interest expense and the June 2002 acquisition of Gerber Childrenswear. Total net sales declined 3.4% to $2.20 billion from $2.28 billion the previous year. Sales of women's sportswear slid 13.1% to $1.32 billion. The dress market was exceptionally weak in 2002, with most retailers cutting their open-to-buy orders for this category by 25.0%. Sales of men's sportswear increased 23.7% to $430.2 million, while sales of other soft goods improved 9.2% to $457.7 million.

PROSPECTS:

On 2/4/03, the Company announced the acquisition of Briggs New York Corp, a manufacturer of moderately-priced women's pants and skirts. The acquisition of Briggs, which achieved sales of over $200.0 million in 2002, should provide the Company with a well-recognized name and further fortify its position in the moderately-priced retail segment. Going forward, KWD should benefit from steps recently taken to streamline its operating and warehousing and distribution and improve its sourcing. Additionally, KWD has invested in several new marketing initiatives, which should insure positive internal sales growth in 2003 and 2004. KWD expects earnings in fiscal year 2003 to be in the range of $73.0 million to $76.0 million, or $2.70 to $2.80 per share.

ANNUAL FINANCIAL DATA:

FISCAL YEAR	TOT. REVS. ($mill.)	NET INC. ($mill.)	TOT. ASSETS ($mill.)	OPER. PROFIT %	NET PROFIT %	RET. ON EQUITY %	RET. ON ASSETS %	CURR. RATIO	EARN. PER SH.$	CASH FL. PER SH.$	TANG. BK. VAL.$	DIV. PER SH.$	PRICE RANGE	AVG. P/E RATIO	AVG. YIELD %
p2/01/03	2,204.7	⑤ 42.0							⑤ 1.69			0.64	32.45 - 19.70	15.4	2.5
1/31/02	2,281.8	37.7	1,044.4	4.1	1.7	8.3	3.6	3.2	1.65	3.06	14.85	0.64	25.50 - 17.30	13.0	3.0
1/31/01	2,362.2	④ 60.8	1,265.7	5.4	2.6	14.1	4.8	2.5	④ 2.57	3.72	17.44	0.64	23.25 - 13.75	7.2	3.5
③ 1/31/00	1,565.3	41.0	1,097.9	5.4	2.6	9.2	3.7	3.3	1.48	2.17	14.43	0.64	28.88 - 16.25	15.2	2.8
4/30/99	2,151.1	② 2.0	1,054.2	6.3	0.1	0.4	0.2	2.4	② 0.07	1.28	15.98	0.64	36.69 - 22.50	422.2	2.2
4/30/98	1,781.6	42.7	1,015.5	5.7	2.4	11.1	4.2	2.2	1.95	3.30	12.96	0.63	38.56 - 19.63	14.9	2.2
4/30/97	1,521.0	37.6	874.6	5.6	2.5	10.8	4.3	1.7	1.78	3.12	11.08	0.61	20.88 - 13.63	9.7	3.5
4/30/96	1,466.0	28.0	796.7	4.7	1.9	8.6	3.5	1.8	1.32	2.66	9.65	0.60	22.88 - 16.50	14.9	3.0
4/30/95	1,364.8	① 11.1	768.1	3.3	0.8	3.6	1.4	1.9	① 0.53	1.87	8.36	0.60	26.92 - 19.13	43.4	2.6
4/30/94	1,203.1	① 35.6	641.9	5.9	3.0	11.6	5.5	2.7	① 1.71	2.91	9.51	0.53	27.17 - 15.83	12.6	2.5

Statistics are as originally reported. Adj. for stk. split: 3-for-2, 2/94 ① Incl. non-recurr. chrg. 1995, $13.9 mill.; gain 1994, $3.0 mill. ② Incl. special chrgs. totaling $62.3 mill. ③ Results for 9 months transition period due to year-end change. ④ Incl. pension termination gain of $5.9 mill. ⑤ Incl. after-tax chrg. of $9.7 mill. for bus. realign.

OFFICERS:
H. J. Upbin, Chmn., Pres., C.E.O.
J. C. Jacobsen, Vice-Chmn.
W. L. Crapps III, V.P., C.F.O.
INVESTOR CONTACT: Investor Relations, (314) 576-3100
PRINCIPAL OFFICE: 600 Kellwood Parkway, P.O. Box 14374, St. Louis, MO 63178

TELEPHONE NUMBER: (314) 576-3100
FAX: (314) 576-3462
WEB: www.kellwood.com
NO. OF EMPLOYEES: 23,000 (approx.)
SHAREHOLDERS: 3,346 (approx.)
ANNUAL MEETING: In May
INCORPORATED: DE, Aug., 1961

INSTITUTIONAL HOLDINGS:
No. of Institutions: 152
Shares Held: 20,922,530
% Held: 81.8
INDUSTRY: Men's and boys' clothing, nec (SIC: 2329)
TRANSFER AGENT(S): American Stock Transfer & Trust Company, New York, NY

KEMET CORPORATION

EXCH.	SYM.	REC. PRICE	P/E RATIO	YLD.	MKT. CAP.	RANGE (52-WK.)	'02 Y/E PR.
NYSE	KEM	7.98 (2/28/03)	...	...	$0.69 bill.	22.40 - 6.13	8.74

LOWER MEDIUM GRADE. ON 1/6/03, THE COMPANY ANNOUNCED ADDITIONAL WORKFORCE REDUCTIONS THROUGH EARLY RETIREMENT PROGRAMS AND LAYOFFS.

TRADING VOLUME
Thousand Shares

*7 YEAR PRICE SCORE 94.2   ***12 MONTH PRICE SCORE 66.7**
*NYSE COMPOSITE INDEX=100

INTERIM EARNINGS (Per Share):

Qtr.	June	Sept.	Dec.	Mar.
1998-99	0.02	0.01	0.02	0.03
1999-00	0.06	0.11	0.22	0.44
2000-01	0.90	1.08	1.10	0.90
2001-02	0.15	0.01	d0.31	d0.17
2002-03	0.04	d0.13	d0.37	...

INTERIM DIVIDENDS (Per Share):

Amt.	Decl.	Ex.	Rec.	Pay.
		No dividends paid.		

CAPITALIZATION (3/31/02):

	($000)	(%)
Long-Term Debt	100,000	9.9
Deferred Income Tax	55,358	5.5
Common & Surplus	855,045	84.6
Total	1,010,403	100.0

BUSINESS:

KEMET Corporation manufactures and sells solid tantalum, multi-layered ceramic and organic polymer capacitors in the global market under the KEMET brand name. The Company's capacitors are used in a variety of electronic applications, including communication systems, data processing equipment, personal computers, cellular phones, automotive electronic systems and military and aerospace systems. The Company has manufacturing plants in South Carolina, North Carolina and Mexico. In addition, the Company has several wholly-owned foreign subsidiaries that market KEM's products in foreign markets. Geographic revenues for the year ended 3/31/02 were derived: U.S., 45.5%; Asia Pacific, 18.5%; Mexico, 8.9%; Germany, 7.1%; and other countries, 20.0%.

RECENT DEVELOPMENTS:

For the quarter ended 12/31/02, KEM reported a net loss of $31.7 million versus a net loss of $26.9 million in the equivalent 2001 quarter. Results for 2002 and 2001 included pre-tax non-recurring charges of $42.6 million and $15.3 million, respectively. Net sales declined 11.6% to $103.7 million from $117.3 million a year earlier. Cost of goods sold fell 22.8% to $92.2 million from $119.5 million the year before. Operating loss amounted to $50.5 million versus an operating loss of $36.8 million in 2001. Overall results were negatively affected by the continued decline in shipments of electronic infrastructure, such as corporate information technology and telecommunication equipment.

PROSPECTS:

Average selling prices decreased about 6.0% sequentially during the third quarter and a similar decline is expected in the fourth quarter. However, fourth quarter net sales are expected to rise 5.0% from the preceding quarter. Looking ahead, as industry unit volumes increase once end-demand improves, the decline in average selling prices should moderate to a more typical rate of 6.0% to 8.0% per year. Separately, on 1/6/03, the Company announced additional workforce reductions through early retirement programs and layoffs. KEM expects a pre-tax charge of $11.0 million related to these reductions. Annual cost-savings are expected to be approximately $16.0 million.

ANNUAL FINANCIAL DATA:

FISCAL YEAR	TOT. REVS. ($mill.)	NET INC. ($mill.)	TOT. ASSETS ($mill.)	OPER. PROFIT %	NET PROFIT %	RET. ON EQUITY %	RET. ON ASSETS %	CURR. RATIO	EARN. PER SH.$	CASH FL. PER SH.$	TANG. BK. VAL.$	PRICE RANGE	AVG. P/E RATIO
3/31/02	⑤ 508.6	④ d27.3	1,171.7	...	...	...	...	5.0	④ d0.32	d0.32	9.46	23.31 - 13.85	...
3/31/01	1,406.1	352.3	1,366.5	40.3	25.1	39.8	25.8	2.6	4.00	4.72	9.79	44.22 - 13.75	7.2
3/31/00	822.1	70.1	927.3	15.1	8.5	12.8	7.6	2.4	0.85	1.53	5.76	22.69 - 4.94	16.2
3/31/99	565.6	6.2	663.7	4.0	1.1	2.0	0.9	1.8	0.08	0.67	3.50	11.03 - 4.38	96.2
3/31/98	667.7	③ 49.2	642.1	12.3	7.4	16.1	7.7	1.3	③ 0.63	1.12	3.31	15.69 - 8.63	19.4
3/31/97	555.3	② 37.2	543.2	11.2	6.7	14.7	6.8	1.6	② 0.48	0.90	2.62	14.63 - 7.63	23.4
3/31/96	634.2	65.2	489.8	19.0	10.3	30.8	13.3	1.3	0.84	1.32	1.92	18.06 - 6.44	14.7
3/31/95	473.2	① 31.0	387.5	13.3	6.5	22.3	8.0	1.3	① 0.40	0.74	0.96	7.44 - 3.50	13.7
3/31/94	385.1	① 16.7	362.1	9.5	4.3	15.4	4.6	1.6	① 0.23	0.56	0.66	5.00 - 3.25	18.3
3/31/93	347.7	① 11.1	353.4	11.2	3.2	21.1	3.1	1.3	① 0.22	0.72	...	3.63 - 2.88	14.8

Statistics are as originally reported. Adj. for 2-for-1 stk. split, 9/95 & 6/00. ① Bef. extraord. chrg., $1.1 mill., 1995; $4.3 mill., 1994; $1.4 mill., 1993. ② Incls. early retire. costs of $15.4 mill. ③ Incl. $10.5 mill. non-recurr. chrg. ④ Incl. pre-tax non-recurr. chrg. of $66.6 mill. ⑤ Reflects a significant reduction in capacitor consumption across several markets combined with lower capacitor orders as a result of high customer inventories.

OFFICERS:
D. E. Maguire, Chmn., C.E.O.
J. A. Graves, Pres., C.O.O.
D. R. Cash, Sr. V.P., C.F.O., Asst. Sec.
M. W. Boone, Sec., Treas., Dir., Fin.

INVESTOR CONTACT: John Warner, Dir., Inv. & Public Rel., (864) 963-6640

PRINCIPAL OFFICE: 2835 Kemet Way, Simpsonville, SC 29681

TELEPHONE NUMBER: (864) 963-6300
FAX: (864) 963-6322
WEB: www.kemet.com

NO. OF EMPLOYEES: 6,900 (approx.)

SHAREHOLDERS: 42,800 (approx.)

ANNUAL MEETING: In July

INCORPORATED: DE, July, 1990

INSTITUTIONAL HOLDINGS:
No. of Institutions: 166
Shares Held: 52,660,797
% Held: 61.1

INDUSTRY: Electronic capacitors (SIC: 3675)

TRANSFER AGENT(S): Boston EquiServe, Canton, MA

KENNAMETAL INC.

EXCH.	SYM.	REC. PRICE	P/E RATIO	YLD.	MKT. CAP.	RANGE (52-WK.)	'02 Y/E PR.
NYSE	KMT	29.92 (2/28/03)	23.4	2.3%	$0.92 bill.	43.00 - 27.73	34.48

MEDIUM GRADE. THE COMPANY EXPECTS SALES FOR THE THIRD QUARTER OF FISCAL 2003 TO GROW 18.0% TO 20.0%.

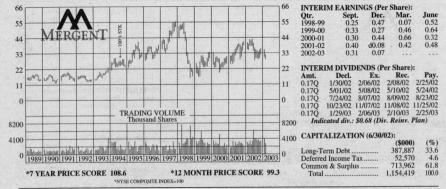

INTERIM EARNINGS (Per Share):

Qtr.	Sept.	Dec.	Mar.	June
1998-99	0.25	0.47	0.07	0.52
1999-00	0.33	0.27	0.46	0.64
2000-01	0.30	0.44	0.66	0.32
2001-02	0.40	d0.08	0.42	0.48
2002-03	0.31	0.07	...	...

INTERIM DIVIDENDS (Per Share):

Amt.	Decl.	Ex.	Rec.	Pay.
0.17Q	1/30/02	2/06/02	2/08/02	2/25/02
0.17Q	5/01/02	5/08/02	5/10/02	5/24/02
0.17Q	7/24/02	8/07/02	8/09/02	8/23/02
0.17Q	10/23/02	11/07/02	11/08/02	11/25/02
0.17Q	1/29/03	2/06/03	2/10/03	2/25/03

Indicated div.: $0.68 (Div. Reinv. Plan)

CAPITALIZATION (6/30/02):

	($000)	(%)
Long-Term Debt	387,887	33.6
Deferred Income Tax	52,570	4.6
Common & Surplus	713,962	61.8
Total	1,154,419	100.0

*7 YEAR PRICE SCORE 108.6   ***12 MONTH PRICE SCORE 99.3**
*NYSE COMPOSITE INDEX=100

BUSINESS:

Kennametal Inc. manufactures, purchases, and distributes a broad range of tools, tooling systems, supplies and services for the metalworking, mining and highway construction industries. KMT specializes in developing and manufacturing metalcutting tools and wear-resistant parts using a specialized type of powder metallurgy. KMT manufactures a complete line of toolholders, toolholding systems and rotary cutting tools by machining and fabricating steel bars and other metal alloys. Through its 99.4%-owned subsidi-

ary, JLK Direct Distribution Inc., KMT sells a broad range of metalworking consumables and related products. KMT also distributes a broad range of industrial supplies used in the metalworking industry. The Company's operations are divided into four business segments, including the Metalworking Solutions and Services Group (56.6% of 2002 sales), Advanced Materials Solutions Group (19.4%), J&L Industry Supply (14.3%), and Full Service Supply (9.7%).

RECENT DEVELOPMENTS:

For the quarter ended 12/31/02, net income amounted to $2.5 million compared with a net loss of $2.5 million in the equivalent 2001 quarter. Results for 2002 and 2001 included restructuring and asset impairment charges of $8.6 million and $17.1 million, respectively. Results for 2002

and 2001 included amortization of intangibles of $1.3 million and $689,000, respectively. Net sales rose 13.5% to $431.7 million from $380.3 million a year earlier, mainly due to the 8/31/02 acquisition of Widia Group. Operating income increased 116.8% to $11.9 million.

PROSPECTS:

Looking ahead, the Company expects sales for the third quarter of fiscal 2003 to grow 18.0% to 20.0%, with diluted earnings between $0.47 and $0.52 per share, excluding special charges. KMT anticipates year ended June 2003 sales to grow 12.0% to 14.0% and diluted earnings per

share are expected to range from $1.65 to $1.80, excluding special charges. This lowered projection is based on flat capacity utilization rates of 75.0%, and the forecast of softer industrial production growth in the U.S. and Europe during the first half of the current calendar year.

ANNUAL FINANCIAL DATA:

FISCAL YEAR	TOT. REVS. ($mill.)	NET INC. ($mill.)	TOT. ASSETS ($mill.)	OPER. PROFIT %	NET PROFIT %	RET. ON EQUITY %	RET. ON ASSETS %	CURR. RATIO	EARN. PER SH.$	CASH FL. PER SH.$	TANG. BK. VAL.$	DIV. PER SH.$	PRICE RANGE	AVG. P/E RATIO	AVG. YIELD %
6/30/02	1,583.7	⑤ 38.5	1,523.6	5.8	2.4	5.4	2.5	2.4	⑤ 1.22	3.55	9.94	0.68	43.00 - 27.73	29.0	1.9
6/30/01	1,807.9	⑤ 53.9	1,825.4	8.7	3.0	6.8	3.0	2.3	⑤ 1.75	4.92	5.58	0.68	41.37 - 25.30	19.0	2.0
6/30/00	1,853.7	③④ 52.0	1,982.9	8.6	2.8	6.7	2.6	2.1	③④ 1.71	5.06	3.90	0.68	33.81 - 19.13	15.5	2.6
6/30/99	1,902.9	③ 39.1	2,043.6	7.8	2.1	5.2	1.9	2.0	③ 1.31	4.51	1.98	0.68	33.88 - 16.38	19.2	2.7
6/30/97	1,678.4	71.2	2,139.0	11.7	4.2	9.7	3.3	2.2	2.58	5.02	0.97	0.68	54.75 - 15.63	13.6	1.9
6/30/96	1,156.3	72.0	869.3	11.0	6.2	15.7	8.3	1.6	2.71	4.27	15.69	0.68	55.69 - 33.13	16.4	1.5
6/30/96	1,080.0	69.7	799.5	11.3	6.5	15.9	8.7	2.0	2.62	4.13	15.17	0.62	39.00 - 27.75	12.7	1.9
6/30/95	983.9	68.3	781.6	12.9	6.9	17.4	8.7	1.8	2.58	4.06	13.53	0.60	41.13 - 23.00	12.4	1.9
② 6/30/94	802.5	① 10.9	697.5	4.7	1.4	3.4	1.6	1.6	① 0.45	2.23	11.03	0.59	29.56 - 21.06	56.2	2.3
6/30/93	598.5	20.1	448.3	7.2	3.4	7.9	4.5	2.4	0.93	2.35	10.28	0.58	24.00 - 14.00	20.0	3.1

Statistics are as originally reported. Adj. for stk. split: 2-for-1, 8/94. ① Incl. a restruct. chrg. of $24.7 mill. and bef. net acctg. chrg. of d$15.0 mill. (d$0.62/sh.). ② Incl. results of Hertel AG, acq. in Aug. 1993. ③ Incl. nonrecur. chrgs. of $13.9 mill., 1999; $18.5 mill., 2000. ④ Bef. extraord. loss of $267,000. ⑤ Incls. restr. & asset impairment chrg. of $27.3 mill., 2002; $9.5 mill., 2001; bef. acct. change chrg. of $250.4 mill., 2002; $599,000, 2001.

OFFICERS:
M. I. Tambakeras, Chmn., Pres., C.E.O.
F. N. Grasberger, III, V.P., C.F.O.
J. E. Morrison, V.P., Treas.

INVESTOR CONTACT: Investor Relations, (724) 539-5000

PRINCIPAL OFFICE: World Headquarters, 1600 Technology Way, P.O. Box 231, Latrobe, PA 15650-0231

TELEPHONE NUMBER: (724) 539-5000
FAX: (724) 539-4710
WEB: www.kennametal.com

NO. OF EMPLOYEES: 11,600 (approx.)

SHAREHOLDERS: 3,206 (record)

ANNUAL MEETING: In Oct.

INCORPORATED: PA, June, 1943

INSTITUTIONAL HOLDINGS:
No. of Institutions: 153
Shares Held: 29,556,124
% Held: 84.2

INDUSTRY: Machine tools, metal cutting types (SIC: 3541)

TRANSFER AGENT(S): Mellon Investor Services, LLC, Ridgefield Park, NJ

KERR-MCGEE CORPORATION

EXCH.	SYM.	REC. PRICE	P/E RATIO	YLD.	MKT. CAP.	RANGE (52-WK.)	'02 Y/E PR.
NYSE	KMG	41.24 (2/28/03)	...	4.4%	$4.13 bill.	63.58 - 38.02	44.30

MEDIUM GRADE. THE COMPANY'S EXPLORATION PROGRAM FOR 2003 WILL BE FOCUSED ON GROWING ITS CORE AREAS, PARTICULARLY THE DEEPWATER GULF OF MEXICO.

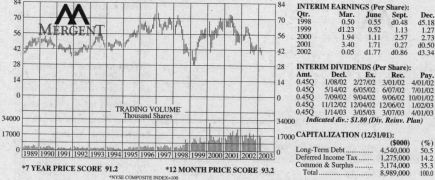

*7 YEAR PRICE SCORE 91.2　　***12 MONTH PRICE SCORE 93.2**

*NYSE COMPOSITE INDEX=100

INTERIM EARNINGS (Per Share):

Qtr.	Mar.	June	Sept.	Dec.
1998	0.50	0.55	d0.48	d5.18
1999	d1.23	0.52	1.13	1.27
2000	1.94	1.11	2.57	2.73
2001	3.40	1.71	0.27	d0.50
2002	0.05	d1.77	d1.20	d3.34

INTERIM DIVIDENDS (Per Share):

Amt.	Decl.	Ex.	Rec.	Pay.
0.45Q	1/08/02	2/27/02	3/01/02	4/01/02
0.45Q	5/14/02	6/05/02	6/07/02	7/01/02
0.45Q	7/09/02	9/04/02	9/06/02	10/01/02
0.45Q	11/12/02	12/04/02	12/06/02	1/02/03
0.45Q	1/14/03	3/05/03	3/07/03	4/01/03

Indicated div.: $1.80 (Div. Reinv. Plan)

CAPITALIZATION (12/31/01):

	($000)	(%)
Long-Term Debt	4,540,000	50.5
Deferred Income Tax	1,275,000	14.2
Common & Surplus	3,174,000	35.3
Total	8,989,000	100.0

BUSINESS:

Kerr-McGee Corporation is an energy and chemical company with worldwide operations. KMG explores for, develops, produces and markets crude oil and natural gas, and its chemical operations primarily produce and market titanium dioxide pigment. The exploration and production unit produces and explores for oil and gas in the U.S., the United Kingdom sector of the North Sea, Indonesia, China, and Ecuador. Exploration efforts also extend to Australia, Benin, Brazil, Gabon, Morocco, Canada, Thailand, Yemen and the Danish sector of the North Sea. As of 12/31/01, proven developed and undeveloped reserves for crude oil, condensate and natural gas liquids and natural gas were 841.0 million barrels and 4,007 billion cubic feet, respectively. In 2002, revenues were derived: exploration and production, 67.7%; and chemicals, 32.3%. In August 2001, KMG acquired HS Resources, Inc.

RECENT DEVELOPMENTS:

For the year ended 12/31/02, KMG posted a loss from continuing operations of $601.6 million versus income from continuing operations of $476.3 million the previous year. Results for 2002 and 2001 included asset impairment charges of $821.1 million and $76.2 million, respectively, and provisions for environmental remediation and restoration, net of reimbursements, of $80.1 million and $82.1 million. Sales rose 3.8% to $3.70 billion. Separately, on 2/5/03, KMG announced that its subsidiaries have agreed to sell their interests in Kazakhstan to Shell Kazakhstan Development, in a transaction valued at $165.0 million. Net proceeds will be used to reduce debt.

PROSPECTS:

KMG's capital budget for its 2003 oil and gas operations is $860.0 million, which includes an exploration program focused on growing its core areas, chiefly the deepwater Gulf of Mexico. KMG's capital budget will also fund ongoing projects, including deepwater Gulf of Mexico developments at the Gunnison and Red Hawk fields and the development of block 4/36 in Bohai Bay, China. First production at Gunnison is expected during the quarter ended 3/31/04, with peak production achieved in 2005. Initial production from Red Hawk is expected by 6/30/04, with peak production reached during the quarter ended 9/30/04. Initial production in Bohai Bay is expected by 12/31/04.

ANNUAL FINANCIAL DATA:

FISCAL YEAR	TOT. REVS. ($mill.)	NET INC. ($mill.)	TOT. ASSETS ($mill.)	OPER. PROFIT %	NET PROFIT %	RET. ON EQUITY %	RET. ON ASSETS %	CURR. RATIO	EARN. PER SH.$	CASH FL. PER SH.$	TANG. BK. VAL.$	DIV. PER SH.$	PRICE RANGE	AVG. P/E RATIO	AVG. YIELD %
p12/31/02	3,700.0	⑧d601.6							⑧d5.99			1.80	63.58 - 38.02		3.5
12/31/01	3,638.0	⑦506.0	10,961.0	15.6	13.9	15.9	4.6	1.2	⑦4.93	12.00	28.13	1.80	74.10 - 46.94	12.3	3.0
12/31/00	4,121.0	842.0	7,666.0	30.1	20.4	32.0	11.0	1.0	⑥8.37	15.14	27.87	1.80	71.19 - 39.88	6.6	3.2
⑤12/31/99	2,696.0	④146.0	5,899.0	8.0	5.4	9.8	2.5	1.4	1.69	9.18	17.25	1.80	62.00 - 28.50	26.8	4.0
12/31/98	1,396.0	①d227.0	3,341.0	...	...	...	...	1.4	①d4.78	1.51	28.36	1.80	73.19 - 36.19	...	3.3
12/31/97	1,711.0	194.0	3,096.0	10.9	11.3	13.5	6.3	1.3	4.04	9.69	30.00	1.76	75.00 - 55.50	16.2	2.7
12/31/96	1,931.0	②220.0	3,124.0	16.7	11.4	16.1	7.0	1.7	②4.43	10.54	27.90	1.64	74.13 - 55.75	14.7	2.5
12/31/95	1,801.0	③d24.0	3,232.0	...	...	...	...	1.3	③d0.47	6.10	27.76	1.52	64.00 - 44.00	...	2.8
12/31/94	3,353.0	90.0	3,698.0	3.3	2.7	5.8	2.4	1.1	1.74	8.37	30.25	1.52	51.00 - 40.00	26.1	3.3
12/31/93	3,281.0	77.0	3,547.0	3.0	2.3	5.1	2.2	1.1	1.57	8.12	29.08	1.52	56.00 - 41.75	31.1	3.1

Statistics are as originally reported. ① Incl. chrg. of $446.0 mill.; bef. loss fr. disc. ops. of $277.4 mill. ② Incl. chrgs. of $9.7 mill. ③ Incl. chrg. of $227.0 mill.; bef. disc. ops. loss of $7.1 mill. ④ Incl. chgs. of $150.0 mill.; bef. acctg. chrg. of $4.1 mill. ⑤ Incl. rev. of Oryx Energy Co. ⑥ Incl. after-tax chrgs. of $95.0 mill. ⑦ Incl. asset impair. chrg. of $76.2 mill. & environ. remed. prov. of $82.1 mill.; bef. acctg. chrg. of $20.3 mill. ⑧ Incl. asset impair. chrg. of $821.0 mill. & environ. remed. prov. of $80.1 mill.; bef. disc. ops. inc. of $125.7 mill.

OFFICERS:
L. R. Corbett, Chmn., C.E.O.
R. M. Wohleber, Sr. V.P., C.F.O.
E. T. Wilkinson, V.P., Treas.
INVESTOR CONTACT: R. C. Buterbaugh,
V.P., Inv. Rel. & Comm., (405) 270-3561
PRINCIPAL OFFICE: Kerr-McGee Center,
Oklahoma City, OK 73125

TELEPHONE NUMBER: (405) 270-1313
FAX: (405) 270-3123
WEB: www.kerr-mcgee.com
NO. OF EMPLOYEES: 4,638 (avg.)
SHAREHOLDERS: 30,000 (approx.)
ANNUAL MEETING: In May
INCORPORATED: DE, Nov., 1932

INSTITUTIONAL HOLDINGS:
No. of Institutions: 343
Shares Held: 88,545,058
% Held: 88.2
INDUSTRY: Crude petroleum and natural gas
(SIC: 1311)
TRANSFER AGENT(S): UMB Bank, N.A.,
Kansas City, MO

KEYCORP

EXCH.	SYM.	REC. PRICE	P/E RATIO	YLD.	MKT. CAP.	RANGE (52-WK.)	'02 Y/E PR.	DIV. ACH.
NYSE	KEY	23.73 (2/28/03)	10.5	5.1%	$10.1 mill.	29.40 - 20.98	25.14	23 yrs.

UPPER MEDIUM GRADE. THE COMPANY EXPECTS TO CONTINUE TO BE SOMEWHAT NEGATIVELY AFFECTED BY THE WEAK ECONOMY.

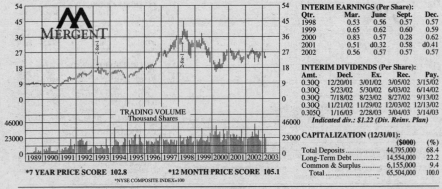

*7 YEAR PRICE SCORE 102.8 ***12 MONTH PRICE SCORE 105.1**
*NYSE COMPOSITE INDEX=100

INTERIM EARNINGS (Per Share):

Qtr.	Mar.	June	Sept.	Dec.
1998	0.53	0.56	0.57	0.57
1999	0.65	0.62	0.60	0.59
2000	0.83	0.57	0.28	0.62
2001	0.51	d0.32	0.58	d0.41
2002	0.56	0.57	0.57	0.57

INTERIM DIVIDENDS (Per Share):

Amt.	Decl.	Ex.	Rec.	Pay.
0.30Q	12/20/01	3/01/02	3/05/02	3/15/02
0.30Q	5/23/02	5/30/02	6/03/02	6/14/02
0.30Q	7/18/02	8/23/02	8/27/02	9/13/02
0.30Q	11/21/02	11/29/02	12/03/02	12/13/02
0.305Q	1/16/02	2/28/02	3/04/03	3/14/02

Indicated div.: $1.22 (Div. Reinv. Plan)

CAPITALIZATION (12/31/01):

	($000)	(%)
Total Deposits	44,795,000	68.4
Long-Term Debt	14,554,000	22.2
Common & Surplus	6,155,000	9.4
Total	65,504,000	100.0

BUSINESS:

KeyCorp (formerly Society Corporation) is a multi-line financial services company, with assets of $85.20 billion as of 12/31/02. The Company provides investment management, retail and commercial banking, retirement, consumer finance, and investment banking products and services to individuals and companies throughout the U.S. and, for certain businesses, internationally. The Company operates throughout the U.S. with a network of 2,165 ATMs, a Web site named Key.com, and telephone banking centers. In October 1998, the Company acquired McDonald & Company Investments, Inc. On 1/31/00, the Company sold its credit card business.

RECENT DEVELOPMENTS:

For the year ended 12/31/02, the Company reported net income of $976.0 million compared with income of $157.0 million, before an accounting change charge of $25.0 million, the year before. Earnings for 2002 and 2001 included amortization of intangibles of $11.0 million and $245.0 million, respectively. Net interest income slipped 2.7% to $2.75 billion from $2.83 billion the year before, reflecting a decrease in average earning assets. Provision for loan losses fell 59.0% to $553.0 million. Total non-interest income increased 2.6% to $1.77 billion due to a decrease in losses from principal investing. Total non-interest expense declined 9.8% to $2.65 billion.

PROSPECTS:

On 12/12/02, the Company announced that it has completed the acquisition of Union Bankshares, Ltd. in a cash transaction valued at approximately $61.0 million. Union Bankshares, with assets of $476.0 million, owns seven offices in Denver, Ohio. Looking ahead, the Company expects results to continue to be somewhat negatively affected by the weak economy. KEY also expects seasonal factors to lead to a decline in first quarter earnings of 2003 compared with the fourth quarter of 2002. However, long-term results should be favorably affected by restructuring initiatives implemented in 2001.

ANNUAL FINANCIAL DATA:

FISCAL YEAR	NET INT. INC. ($mill.)	NON-INT. INC. ($mill.)	NET INC. ($mill.)	TOT. LOANS ($mill.)	TOT. ASSETS ($mill.)	TOT. DEP. ($mill.)	RET. ON EQUITY %	RET. ON ASSETS %	EQUITY/ ASSETS %	EARN. PER SH. $	TANG. BK. VAL.$	DIV. PER SH. $	PRICE RANGE	AVG. P/E RATIO
p12/31/02	2,749.0	1,769.0	976.0							2.27		1.20	29.40 - 20.98	11.1
12/31/01	2,825.0	1,725.0	⑥ 157.0	63,309.0	80,938.0	44,795.0	2.6	0.2	7.6	⑥ 0.37	11.85	1.18	29.25 - 20.49	67.2
12/31/00	2,730.0	2,194.0	⑤ 1,002.0	66,905.0	87,270.0	48,649.0	15.1	1.1	7.6	⑤ 2.30	12.42	1.12	28.50 - 15.56	9.6
12/31/99	2,787.0	2,294.0	④ 1,107.0	64,222.0	83,395.0	43,233.0	17.3	1.3	7.7	④ 2.45	11.14	1.04	38.13 - 21.00	12.1
12/31/98	2,684.0	1,575.0	③ 996.0	62,012.0	80,020.0	42,583.0	16.2	1.2	7.7	③ 2.23	10.30	0.94	44.88 - 23.38	15.3
12/31/97	2,794.0	1,306.0	③ 919.0	53,380.0	73,699.0	45,073.0	17.7	1.2	7.0	③ 2.07	9.14	0.84	36.59 - 23.94	14.6
12/31/96	2,717.0	1,087.0	① 783.0	49,235.0	67,621.0	45,317.0	16.0	1.2	7.2	① 1.69	7.97	0.76	27.13 - 16.69	13.0
12/31/95	2,636.7	933.0	789.2	47,691.7	66,339.1	47,281.9	15.3	1.2	7.8	1.65	8.77	0.72	18.63 - 12.38	9.4
12/31/94	2,693.2	882.6	853.5	46,224.6	66,798.1	48,564.2	18.2	1.3	7.0	1.73	8.20	0.64	16.88 - 11.81	8.3
② 12/31/93	1,199.0	509.8	347.2	17,897.6	27,007.3	19,880.7	17.0	1.3	7.5	1.47	7.77	0.56	18.63 - 13.63	11.0

Statistics are as originally reported. Adj. for 2-for-1 splits 3/98 & 3/93. ① Incl. pre-tax SAIF chg. & restr. chgs. totaling $17.0 mill. ② Reflects pooling of interests for merger of KeyCorp (old) into and with Society Corp., 3/1/94. ③ Incl. pre-tax gain fr. sale of branch: $148.0 mill., 1999; $89.0 mill., 1998; $151.0 mill., 1997. ④ Incl. various pre-tax net gains of $448.0 mill. & restr. chgs. of $98.0 mill. ⑤ Incl. pre-tax gains from divest. of $332.0 mill. & pre-tax restr. chgs. of $102.0 mill. ⑥ Bef. acctg. chrg. of $25.0 mill.; incl. pre-tax restr. gains of $4.0 mill.

OFFICERS:
H. L. Meyer III, Chmn., Pres, C.E.O.
T. Stevens, Vice-Chmn., C.A.O., Sec.
J. B. Weeden, C.F.O.

INVESTOR CONTACT: Bernon L. Patterson, Investor Relations, (216) 689-4520

PRINCIPAL OFFICE: 127 Public Square, Cleveland, OH 44114-1306

TELEPHONE NUMBER: (216) 689-6300
FAX: (216) 689-0519
WEB: www.key.com

NO. OF EMPLOYEES: 20,437

SHAREHOLDERS: 45,340

ANNUAL MEETING: In May

INCORPORATED: OH, Dec., 1958

INSTITUTIONAL HOLDINGS:
No. of Institutions: 408
Shares Held: 242,575,374
% Held: 57.1

INDUSTRY: National commercial banks (SIC: 6021)

TRANSFER AGENT(S): Computershare Investor Services, Chicago, IL

KEYSPAN CORPORATION

EXCH.	SYM.	REC. PRICE	P/E RATIO	YLD.	MKT. CAP.	RANGE (52-WK.)	'02 Y/E PR.
NYSE	KSE	31.97 (2/28/03)	12.2	5.6%	$5.08 bill.	38.20 - 27.41	35.24

MEDIUM GRADE. THE COMPANY CONTINUES TO ASSESS POTENTIAL OPPORTUNITIES FOR THE SALE OR MONETIZATION OF ITS NON-CORE ASSETS.

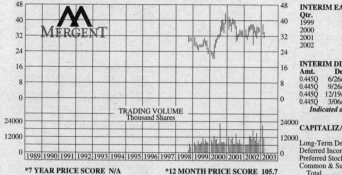

*7 YEAR PRICE SCORE N/A   *12 MONTH PRICE SCORE 105.7
*NYSE COMPOSITE INDEX=100

INTERIM EARNINGS (Per Share):

Qtr.	Mar.	June	Sept.	Dec.
1999	0.94	0.10	Nil	0.56
2000	1.22	0.35	0.10	0.44
2001	1.61	d0.06	d0.26	0.28
2002	1.51	0.06	0.03	1.03

INTERIM DIVIDENDS (Per Share):

Amt.	Decl.	Ex.	Rec.	Pay.
0.445Q	6/26/02	7/16/02	7/18/02	8/01/02
0.445Q	9/26/02	10/10/02	10/15/02	11/01/02
0.445Q	12/19/02	1/13/03	1/15/03	2/01/03
0.445Q	3/06/03	4/14/03	4/16/03	5/01/03

Indicated div.: $1.78 (Div. Reinv. Plan)

CAPITALIZATION (12/31/01):

	($000)	(%)
Long-Term Debt	4,697,649	29.5
Deferred Income Tax	598,072	3.8
Preferred Stock.................	84,077	0.5
Common & Surplus	10,562,930	66.3
Total	15,942,728	100.0

BUSINESS:

KeySpan Corporation (formerly KeySpan Energy Corporation) is a distributor of natural gas in the Northeast, with 2.5 million gas customers as of 1/28/03. KSE also operates Long Island's electric system under contract with the Long Island Power Authority for its 1.1 million customers. KSE manages a portfolio of service companies. These companies include KeySpan Energy Delivery, a group of regulated natural gas utilities; KeySpan Home Energy Services,

a group of energy product, repair and services companies for residential and small commercial business customers; and KeySpan Business Solutions, a full-service group of energy product, repair and services companies for larger business customers. The Company also has strategic investments in natural gas exploration and production, pipeline transportation, distribution and storage, Canadian gas processing and fiber-optic cable.

RECENT DEVELOPMENTS:

For the year ended 12/31/02, income from continuing operations advanced 63.1% to $397.4 million compared with income of $243.7 million the previous year, largely due to continued solid performance in the electric business, profitability in the energy services business and the recent

increase in gas commodity prices realized by KSE's gas exploration and production operations. Results for 2002 and 2001 excluded losses of $19.7 million and $19.4 million, respectively, from discontinued operations. Total revenues declined 10.0% to $5.97 billion.

PROSPECTS:

Going forward, the Company expects earnings per share to be in the range of $2.45 to $2.60 for 2003. In addition, the Company continues to assess potential opportunities for the sale or monetization of its non-core assets to further improve its balance and remain focused on growing its core businesses. On a segment basis, the Company's aggressive

marketing campaigns should add $64.0 million in new gross margin to KSE's gas business. The electric business should continue to benefit from new peaking units that were added in early 2003 and more than 97.0% availability of its New York and Long Island generation plants during the summer peak period.

ANNUAL FINANCIAL DATA:

FISCAL YEAR	TOT. REVS. ($mil.)	NET INC. ($mil.)	TOT. ASSETS ($mil.)	OPER. PROFIT %	NET PROFIT %	RET. ON EQUITY %	RET. ON ASSETS %	CURR. RATIO	EARN. PER SH. $	CASH FL. PER SH. $	TANG. BK. VAL. $	DIV. PER SH. $	PRICE RANGE	AVG. P/E RATIO	AVG. YIELD
p12/31/02	5,970.7	⑧397.4							⑧2.75			1.78	38.20 - 27.41	31.8	5.4
12/31/01	6,633.1	⑦243.7	11,789.6	12.1	3.7	2.3	2.1	0.8	⑦1.56	5.72	55.28	1.78	41.94 - 29.10	22.8	5.0
12/31/00	5,121.5	⑥300.8	11,550.1	14.3	5.9	3.0	2.6	0.8	2.10	4.60	59.42	1.78	43.63 - 20.19	15.2	5.6
⑤12/31/99	2,954.6	258.6	6,730.7	16.3	8.8	3.6	3.8	0.8	1.62	3.45	51.85	1.78	31.31 - 22.50	16.6	6.6
③12/31/98	1,721.9	②d166.9	6,895.1	0.8	...	...	...	1.6	②d1.34	0.41	60.66	0.74	32.25 - 28.69	...	2.4
3/31/98	3,124.1	362.2	11,900.7	24.6	11.6	3.3	3.0	0.8	2.56	3.87	84.40	...	...	...	...
①3/31/97	851.2	87.7	4,457.0	22.3	10.3	1.1	2.0	...	0.62	1.06	...	...	...	...	...
④12/31/96	3,150.7	316.5	4,456.8	23.4	10.0	4.1	7.1	...	2.20	4.22	...	...	...	...	...

Statistics are as originally reported. ① For 3 mos. due to fiscal year-end change. ② Incl. a net chg. of $108.0 mill. rel. to the LIPA transaction, a net chg. of $83.0 mill. assoc./with the merger with LILCO, & a non-cash net impair. chg. for the write-down of gas res. assets. ③ For 9 mos. due to fiscal year end change. ④ As reported from the 12/31/98 10K. ⑤ Reflects full-year results of LILCO. ⑥ Excl. loss of $1.9 mill. from disc. ops. & incl. after-tax nonrecurr. chrg. of $41.1 mill. ⑦ Excl. loss of $19.4 mill. from disc. ops.; incl. net after-tax chrg. of $106.3 mill. ⑧ Excl. loss of $19.7 mill. from disc. ops.

OFFICERS:
R. B. Catell, Chmn., C.E.O.
C. Matthews, Vice-Chmn., C.O.O.
G. Luterman, Exec. V.P., C.F.O.

INVESTOR CONTACT: Michael J. Taunton, Investor Relations, (718) 403-3265

PRINCIPAL OFFICE: 175 East Old Country Road, Hicksville, NY 11801

TELEPHONE NUMBER: (718) 403-3196
FAX: (718) 545-2293
WEB: www.keyspanenergy.com
NO. OF EMPLOYEES: 13,000 (approx.)
SHAREHOLDERS: 82,321 (approx.)
ANNUAL MEETING: In May
INCORPORATED: NY, Apr., 1998

INSTITUTIONAL HOLDINGS:
No. of Institutions: 307
Shares Held: 90,691,049
% Held: 63.9

INDUSTRY: Natural gas distribution (SIC: 4924)

TRANSFER AGENT(S): EquiServe Trust Company, NA, Jersey City, NJ

KIMBERLY-CLARK CORPORATION

EXCH.	SYM.	REC. PRICE	P/E RATIO	YLD.	MKT. CAP.	RANGE (52-WK.)	'02 Y/E PR.	DIV. ACH.
NYSE	KMB	45.46 (3/31/03)	14.0	3.0%	$23.68 bill.	66.79 - 42.92	47.47	28 yrs.

HIGH GRADE. IN 2003, THE COMPANY PLANS TO REDUCE COSTS IN THE RANGE OF $175.0 MILLION TO $200.0 MILLION.

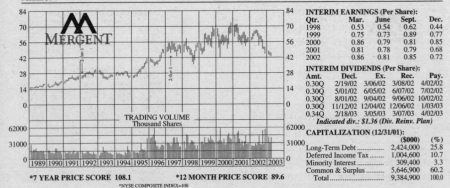

INTERIM EARNINGS (Per Share):

Qtr.	Mar.	June	Sept.	Dec.
1998	0.53	0.54	0.62	0.44
1999	0.75	0.73	0.89	0.77
2000	0.86	0.79	0.81	0.85
2001	0.81	0.78	0.79	0.68
2002	0.86	0.81	0.85	0.72

INTERIM DIVIDENDS (Per Share):

Amt.	Decl.	Ex.	Rec.	Pay.
0.30Q	2/19/02	3/06/02	3/08/02	4/02/02
0.30Q	5/01/02	6/05/02	6/07/02	7/02/02
0.30Q	8/01/02	9/04/02	9/06/02	10/02/02
0.30Q	11/12/02	12/04/02	12/06/02	1/03/03
0.34Q	2/18/03	3/05/03	3/07/03	4/02/03

Indicated div.: $1.36 (Div. Reinv. Plan)

CAPITALIZATION (12/31/01):

	($000)	(%)
Long-Term Debt	2,424,000	25.8
Deferred Income Tax	1,004,600	10.7
Minority Interest	309,400	3.3
Common & Surplus	5,646,900	60.2
Total	9,384,900	100.0

*7 YEAR PRICE SCORE 108.1   *12 MONTH PRICE SCORE 89.6

*NYSE COMPOSITE INDEX=100

BUSINESS:

Kimberly-Clark Corporation is a global manufacturer of consumer products. The Company's global personal care, tissue and health care brands include HUGGIES, PULL-UPS, LITTLE SWIMMERS, GOODNITES, KOTEX, LIGHTDAYS, DEPEND, POISE, KLEENEX, SCOTT, COTTONELLE, VIVA, ANDREX, SCOTTEX, PAGE, KIMBERLY-CLARK, KIMWIPES, WYPALL, SURPASS, SAFESKIN, TECNOL, POPEE and KIMBEES. Kimberly-Clark is also a major producer of premium business, correspondence and technical papers. KMB had manufacturing operations in 42 countries and sells its products in more than 150 countries as of 1/27/03. In fiscal 2002, net sales (and operating profit) were derived as follows: personal care, 37.2% (39.6%); consumer tissue, 36.6% (35.0%); and business-to-business, 26.2% (25.4%).

RECENT DEVELOPMENTS:

For the year ended 12/31/02, income climbed 4.7% to $1.69 billion, before an accounting change charge of $11.4 million, compared with net income of $1.61 billion in 2001. Earnings for 2002 and 2001 included nonrecurring items that resulted in net charges of $95.5 million and $206.3 million, respectively. Earnings for 2001 also included goodwill amortization of $89.4 million. Net sales increased 2.1% to $13.57 billion from $13.29 billion a year earlier. Sales reflected strong performance in the consumer tissue and personal care businesses. Gross profit rose 3.1% to $4.82 billion from $4.67 billion a year earlier. Operating income rose 5.4% to $2.46 billion versus $2.34 billion the year before.

PROSPECTS:

Going forward, the Company will focus on cutting costs in the range of $175.0 million to $200.0 million for full-year 2003. KMB expects sales to rise in the low-to-mid-single digits. Furthermore, KMB plans to improve sales volume between 3.0% and 5.0% through new products and strategic promotional spending. Pension expense in 2003 is expected to increase $145.0 million year over year or $0.20 per share. KMB expects first quarter 2003 earnings per share, before unusual items, to be flat to slightly higher quarter over quarter.

ANNUAL FINANCIAL DATA:

FISCAL YEAR	TOT. REVS. ($mill.)	NET INC. ($mill.)	TOT. ASSETS ($mill.)	OPER. PROFIT %	NET PROFIT %	RET. ON EQUITY %	RET. ON ASSETS %	CURR. RATIO	EARN. PER SH. $	CASH FL. PER SH. $	TANG. BK. VAL. $	DIV. PER SH. $	PRICE RANGE	AVG. P/E RATIO	AVG. YIELD %
p12/31/02	13,566.3	⑤⑦1,674.6							⑤⑦3.24			1.18	66.79 - 45.30	17.3	2.1
12/31/01	14,524.4	⑦1,609.9	15,007.6	16.1	11.1	28.5	10.7	0.9	⑦3.02	4.41	7.10	1.11	72.19 - 52.06	20.6	1.8
12/31/00	13,982.0	1,800.6	14,479.8	18.8	12.9	31.2	12.4	0.8	3.31	4.55	7.04	1.07	73.25 - 42.00	17.4	1.8
12/31/99	13,006.8	⑥1,668.1	12,815.5	18.7	12.8	32.8	13.0	0.9	⑥3.09	4.25	7.12	1.03	69.56 - 44.81	18.5	1.8
12/31/98	12,297.8	⑤1,177.0	11,510.3	13.6	9.6	30.3	10.2	0.9	⑤2.13	3.11	6.13	0.99	59.44 - 35.88	22.4	2.1
12/31/97	12,546.6	④884.0	11,266.0	10.4	7.0	21.4	7.8	0.9	④1.58	2.49	6.36	0.95	56.88 - 43.25	31.7	1.9
12/31/96	13,149.1	①1,403.8	11,845.7	15.6	10.7	31.3	11.9	1.0	①2.49	3.48	7.96	0.92	49.81 - 34.31	16.9	2.2
②12/31/95	13,373.0	③33.2	11,439.2	1.6	0.2	0.9	0.3	1.0	③0.06	1.10	6.11	0.90	41.50 - 23.63	541.8	2.7
12/31/94	7,364.2	①535.1	6,715.7	11.1	7.3	20.6	8.0	0.9	①1.67	2.69	0.88	30.00 - 23.50	16.1	3.3
12/31/93	6,972.9	①510.9	6,380.7	11.4	7.3	20.8	8.0	1.0	①1.59	2.51	7.64	0.85	31.00 - 22.31	16.8	3.2

Statistics are as originally reported. Adj. for stk. split: 2-for-1, 4/97. ① Incl. gain $9.4 mill., 1993; $62.5 mill., 1994; $72.6 mill., 1996. ② Refl. acq. of Scott Paper Co. on 12/15/95. ③ Incl. $1.44 bill. chrg. for merger & incl. $40.0 mill. gain. ④ Bef. extraord. cr. $17.5 mill. & incl. restruct. chrg. $481.1 mill. ⑤ Bef. acctg. chrg. of $11.4 mill., 2002; $11.2 mill., 1998. ⑥ Incl. restruct. cr. $27.0 mill. ⑦ Incl. net chrg. of $95.5 mill., 2002; $179.7 mill., 2001.

OFFICERS:
W. R. Sanders, Chmn.
T. J. Falk, Pres., C.E.O.
M. A. Buthman, Sr. V.P., C.F.O.

INVESTOR CONTACT: Investor Relations, (972) 281-1200

PRINCIPAL OFFICE: P.O. Box 619100, Dallas, TX 75261-9100

TELEPHONE NUMBER: (972) 281-1200
FAX: (972) 281-1435
WEB: www.kimberly-clark.com

NO. OF EMPLOYEES: 64,200 (avg.)

SHAREHOLDERS: 45,812

ANNUAL MEETING: In Apr.

INCORPORATED: DE, June, 1928

INSTITUTIONAL HOLDINGS:
No. of Institutions: 828
Shares Held: 372,472,503
% Held: 72.4

INDUSTRY: Paper mills (SIC: 2621)

TRANSFER AGENT(S): Bank Boston, N.A., Boston, MA

KIMCO REALTY CORP.

EXCH.	SYM.	REC. PRICE	P/E RATIO	YLD.	MKT. CAP.	RANGE (52-WK.)	'02 Y/E PR.	DIV. ACH.
NYSE	KIM	33.70 (2/28/03)	15.4	6.4%	$3.48 bill.	34.00 - 25.96	30.64	10 yrs.

MEDIUM GRADE. THE COMPANY CONTINUES TO HAVE SUCCESS LEASING AND DISPOSING OF VACANCIES RESULTING FROM THE KMART BANKRUPTCY.

*7 YEAR PRICE SCORE 129.4 ***12 MONTH PRICE SCORE 110.9**

*NYSE COMPOSITE INDEX=100

INTERIM EARNINGS (Per Share):

Qtr.	Mar.	June	Sept.	Dec.
1998	0.34	0.33	0.33	0.35
1999	0.36	0.39	0.43	0.47
2000	0.46	0.48	0.47	0.49
2001	0.51	0.55	0.54	0.56
2002	0.53	0.53	0.53	0.60

INTERIM DIVIDENDS (Per Share):

Amt.	Decl.	Ex.	Rec.	Pay.
0.52Q	3/15/02	4/01/02	4/03/02	4/15/02
0.52Q	6/17/02	7/01/02	7/03/02	7/15/02
0.52Q	9/16/02	10/01/02	10/03/02	10/15/02
0.54Q	10/28/02	12/30/02	1/02/03	1/15/03
0.54Q	3/17/03	4/01/03	4/03/03	4/15/03

Indicated div.: $2.16 (Div. Reinv. Plan)

CAPITALIZATION (12/31/01):

	($000)	(%)
Long-Term Debt	292,829	13.4
Preferred Stock	992	0.0
Common & Surplus	1,889,092	86.5
Total	2,182,913	100.0

BUSINESS:

Kimco Realty Corp. is an owner and operator of neighborhood and community shopping centers. As of 2/13/03, the Company had interests in 606 properties totaling approximately 90.0 million square feet of leaseable space located in 41 states, Canada and Mexico. The Company's portfolio includes properties relating to the Kimco Income REIT, a joint venture arrangement with institutional investors established for the purpose of investing in retail properties financed primarily with individual non-recourse mortgages debt. Through its wholly-owned subsidiary, Kimco Developers Inc., KIM is engaged in the ground-up development of neighborhood and community shopping centers and sales thereof upon completion.

RECENT DEVELOPMENTS:

For the year ended 12/31/02, income from continuing operations was $248.6 million versus income of $226.2 million the previous year. Results for 2002 included a net gain of $34.9 million on the sale of development properties and the early extinguishment of debt and a loss of $12.5 million from the adjustment of property carrying values. Results for 2001 included a net gain of $16.5 million on the disposition of properties. Also, results for 2002 and 2001 excluded a loss of $2.9 million and a gain of $10.3 million, respectively, from discontinued operations. Revenues from rental property inched up to $450.8 million from $450.4 million the prior year.

PROSPECTS:

On 1/14/03, the Company announced that it has acquired interests in 11 shopping centers and two development projects for an aggregate cost of approximately $175.3 million and has 14 additional shopping center investments and developments committed or under contract totaling approximately $280.6 million. Separately, Kmart Corporation announced that it would close it stores at nine KIM locations and three stores in an equity in which KIM owns a 43.3% interest. Nevertheless, the Company continues to have success leasing and disposing of vacancies resulting from the Kmart bankruptcy.

ANNUAL FINANCIAL DATA:

FISCAL YEAR	TOT. INC. ($mill.)	NET INC. ($mill.)	TOT. ASSETS ($mill.)	NET INC. +DEPR./ ASSETS %	RET. ON EQUITY %	RET. ON ASSETS %	EARN. PER SH. $	TANG. BK. VAL. $	DIV. PER SH. $	DIV. PAYOUT %	PRICE RANGE	AVG. P/E RATIO	AVG. YIELD %
p12/31/02	450.8	③ 248.6	3,756.9				③ 2.19		2.08	95.0	33.88 - 25.96	13.7	7.0
12/31/01	468.6	② 236.5	3,384.8	7.0	12.5	7.0	② 2.16	18.28	1.92	88.9	34.07 - 27.17	14.2	6.3
12/31/00	459.4	② 205.0	3,171.3	8.7	12.0	6.5	② 1.91	17.98	1.77	93.0	29.83 - 21.83	13.5	6.9
12/31/99	433.9	176.8	3,007.5	8.1	11.0	5.9	1.64	17.59	1.58	96.3	27.17 - 20.58	14.6	6.6
12/31/98	338.8	① 127.2	3,051.2	5.9	8.0	4.2	① 1.35	17.56	1.31	97.5	27.75 - 22.29	18.6	5.2
12/31/97	198.9	85.8	1,343.9	8.6	11.5	6.4	1.19	12.25	1.15	96.6	23.79 - 20.17	18.5	5.2
12/31/96	168.1	73.8	1,022.6	9.9	12.2	7.2	1.07	11.13	1.04	96.9	23.25 - 16.83	18.7	5.2
12/31/95	143.1	51.9	884.2	8.8	11.6	5.9	0.89	8.83	0.96	108.2	18.78 - 15.72	19.4	5.6
12/31/94	125.3	① 41.1	736.7	8.8	12.8	5.6	① 0.78	7.10	0.89	113.7	17.28 - 14.67	20.4	5.6
12/31/93	98.9	① 35.2	652.8	8.4	10.5	5.4	① 0.78	7.45	0.84	106.8	17.45 - 13.56	19.8	5.4

Statistics are as originally reported. Adj. for 3-for-2 stk. spl., 12/01, 12/95 ① Excl. extraord. chrg., 1998, $4.9 mill.; 1994, $825,000; 1993, $586,000. ② Incl. gain on sales of shopping center prop. of $16.4 mill., 2001; $4.0 mill., 2000 ③ Bef. loss from disc. oper. of $2.9 mill. & incl. net gains of $22.4 mill.

OFFICERS:
M. Cooper, Chmn., C.E.O.
M. J. Flynn, Vice-Chmn., Pres., C.O.O.
D. B. Henry, Vice-Chmn., C.I.O.

INVESTOR CONTACT: Scott G. Onufrey, Investor Relations, (516) 869-7190

PRINCIPAL OFFICE: 3333 New Hyde Park Road, New Hyde Park, NY 11042-0020

TELEPHONE NUMBER: (516) 869-9000
FAX: (516) 869-9001
WEB: www.kimcorealty.com
NO. OF EMPLOYEES: 305
SHAREHOLDERS: 1,715 (record)
ANNUAL MEETING: In May
INCORPORATED: DE, 1973; reincorp., MD, Aug., 1994

INSTITUTIONAL HOLDINGS:
No. of Institutions: 208
Shares Held: 55,367,278
% Held: 53.0

INDUSTRY: Real estate investment trusts (SIC: 6798)

TRANSFER AGENT(S): Bank Boston, Boston, MA

KINDER MORGAN, INC.

EXCH.	SYM.	REC. PRICE	P/E RATIO	YLD.	MKT. CAP.	RANGE (52-WK.)	'02 Y/E PR.
NYSE	KMI	45.53 (2/28/03)	18.1	1.3%	$5.64 bill.	52.62 - 30.05	42.27

MEDIUM GRADE. THE COMPANY HAS RAISED ITS FULL-YEAR 2003 EARNINGS EXPECTATION TO $3.18 PER SHARE.

7 YEAR PRICE SCORE 131.2   **12 MONTH PRICE SCORE 117.1**
*NYSE COMPOSITE INDEX=100

INTERIM EARNINGS (Per Share):

Qtr.	Mar.	June	Sept.	Dec.
1998	0.42	0.25	0.36	d0.05
1999	0.10	d0.04	d0.02	1.02
2000	0.41	0.21	0.23	0.73
2001	0.47	0.41	0.49	0.60
2002	0.71	0.59	0.66	0.55

INTERIM DIVIDENDS (Per Share):

Amt.	Decl.	Ex.	Rec.	Pay.
0.05Q	1/17/02	1/29/02	1/31/02	2/14/02
0.05Q	4/17/02	4/26/02	4/30/02	5/15/02
0.10Q	7/17/02	7/29/02	7/31/02	8/14/02
0.10Q	10/16/02	10/29/02	10/31/02	11/14/02
0.15Q	1/15/03	1/29/03	1/31/03	2/14/03

Indicated div.: $0.60 (Div. Reiny. Plan)

CAPITALIZATION (12/31/01):

	($000)	(%)
Long-Term Debt	2,404,967	29.4
Deferred Income Tax	2,428,504	29.7
Minority Interest	817,513	10.0
Redeemable Pfd. Stock	275,000	3.4
Common & Surplus	2,259,997	27.6
Total	8,185,981	100.0

BUSINESS:

Kinder Morgan, Inc. (formerly K N Energy, Inc.) is an energy and related services provider. As of 1/15/03, KMI operated more than 35,000 miles of natural gas and products pipelines and, through its general partner interest, operated Kinder Morgan Energy Partners, L.P., which is a pipeline master limited partnership. KMI's Natural Gas Pipeline Company of America segment includes an interstate natural gas pipeline system with about 10,000 miles of pipelines and associated storage facilities. The Retail Natural Gas Distribution segment includes a retail natural gas distribution business serving about 240,000 customers in Colorado, Nebraska and Wyoming. The Power Generation and Other segment involves the construction and operation of natural gas-fired electric generation facilities. On 10/7/99, K N Energy, Inc. and Kinder Morgan completed their merger through the acquisition of Kinder by K N Energy. As of 12/31/01, KMI owned about 18.7% of the outstanding units of Kinder Morgan Energy Partners, L.P.

RECENT DEVELOPMENTS:

For the year ended 12/31/02, income from continuing operations was $309.2 million compared with $238.6 million a year earlier. Results for 2002 included a pre-tax charge of $134.5 million related to the revaluation of power investments. Earnings were fueled by a 41.3% increase in equity in earnings from Kinder Morgan Energy Partners, L.P. (KMP) to $392.1 million, driven by internal growth from its pipeline and terminal assets, along with contributions from acquired assets. The Company's total operating revenues decreased 3.8% to $1.02 billion.

PROSPECTS:

In January 2003, KMI announced an increase in its full-year 2003 earnings expectation to $3.18 per share from $3.11 per share. The Company noted that this expectation includes contributions only from assets currently owned by KMI and KMP and do not include the benefit of future acquisitions. However, KMI stated that it is optimistic about its chances for making accretive acquisitions in 2003.

ANNUAL FINANCIAL DATA:

FISCAL YEAR	TOT. REVS. ($mill.)	NET INC. ($mill.)	TOT. ASSETS ($mill.)	OPER. PROFIT %	NET PROFIT %	NET INC./ NET PROP. %	NET INC./ TOT. CAP. %	RET. ON EQUITY %	ACCUM. DEPR./ GROSS PROP. %	EARN. PER SH.$	TANG. BK. VAL.$	DIV. PER SH.$	DIV. PAYOUT %	PRICE RANGE	AVG. P/E RATIO	AVG. YIELD %
p12/31/02	1,015.3	⑩309.2								⑩2.50		0.30	12.0	57.50 - 30.05	17.5	0.7
⑧12/31/01	1,054.9	⑧238.6	9,533.1	36.4	22.6	4.2	2.9	10.6	6.2	⑨1.97	18.24	0.20	10.2	60.00 - 42.88	26.1	0.4
12/31/00	2,713.7	⑦183.7	8,418.1	14.6	6.8	3.2	2.7	10.2	6.7	⑦1.60	15.70	0.20	12.5	54.25 - 19.88	23.2	0.5
⑤12/31/99	1,745.5	⑥154.7	9,540.3	17.5	8.9	2.7	2.1	9.3	6.1	⑥1.92	14.79	0.65	33.9	24.69 - 12.19	9.6	3.5
③12/31/98	4,387.8	④60.0	9,612.2	7.9	1.4	0.9	0.9	4.9	9.6	④0.92	17.74	0.76	82.6	40.34 - 22.33	34.1	2.4
12/31/97	2,145.1	77.5	2,305.8	6.6	3.6	5.5	5.2	12.6	27.9	1.63	12.63	0.73	44.5	35.75 - 24.08	18.3	2.4
12/31/96	1,443.2	63.8	1,629.7	9.3	4.4	6.2	5.8	12.1	33.5	1.43	11.44	0.70	49.1	27.50 - 18.00	15.9	3.1
12/31/95	1,103.4	52.5	1,257.5	10.3	4.8	6.1	6.0	12.1	36.3	1.12	10.13	0.67	55.2	20.17 - 13.50	13.8	4.0
①12/31/94	1,083.1	②15.3	1,172.4	5.0	1.4	1.8	1.8	3.8	35.2	②0.35	9.50	0.65	186.3	17.92 - 13.83	45.7	4.1
12/31/93	493.3	24.3	731.3	11.9	4.9	4.8	4.8	11.6	42.2	1.05	8.94	0.61	58.6	20.00 - 12.45	15.5	3.8

Statistics are as originally reported. Adj. for 3-for-2 stk. split, 1/99. ① Refl. acq. of American Oil and Gas Corp. ② Incl. chrgs. of $19.3 mill. ③ Refl. 1/30/98 acq. of MidCon Corp. ④ Incl. pre-tax chrgs. of $5.8 mill. ⑤ Refl. 10/7/99 acq. of Kinder Morgan & disp. & discont. of non-core ops. ⑥ Incl. $37.4 mill. chrg.; bef. $396.1 mill. loss fr. disc. ops. ⑦ Bef. loss on disp. of disc. ops. of $31.7 mill. ($0.28/sh.) ⑧ Refl. transf. of several assets to Kinder Morgan Energy Partners, incl. Kinder Morgan Texas Pipeline. ⑨ Bef. extraord. loss of $13.6 mill. ($0.11/sh.) ⑩ Incl. revalu. of power invest. chrg. of $134.5 mill.; bef. loss of $5.0 mill. on disp. of disc. ops. & extraord. loss of $1.5 mill.

OFFICERS:
R. D. Kinder, Chmn., C.E.O.
M. C. Morgan, Pres.
C. Park Shaper, C.F.O.

INVESTOR CONTACT: Twardowski Broussard, Investor Relations, (713) 369-9490

PRINCIPAL OFFICE: 500 Dallas, Suite 1000, Houston, TX 77002

TELEPHONE NUMBER: (713) 369-9000
FAX: (713) 495-2817
WEB: www.kindermorgan.com

NO. OF EMPLOYEES: 4,937 (avg.)

SHAREHOLDERS: 32,000 (approx.)

ANNUAL MEETING: In Mar.

INCORPORATED: KS, May, 1927

INSTITUTIONAL HOLDINGS:
No. of Institutions: 277
Shares Held: 66,752,081
% Held: 54.8

INDUSTRY: Gas transmission and distribution (SIC: 4923)

TRANSFER AGENT(S): EquiServe, Jersey City, NJ

KING PHARMACEUTICALS, INC.

EXCH.	SYM.	REC. PRICE	P/E RATIO	YLD.	MKT. CAP.	RANGE (52-WK.)	'02 Y/E PR.
NYSE	KG	16.75 (2/28/03)	16.0	...	$4.15 bill.	37.30 - 13.15	17.19

UPPER MEDIUM GRADE. THE COMPANY AND ELAN CORPORATION, PLC SIGNED A DEFINITIVE AGREEMENT FOR KG TO ACQUIRE ELAN'S PRIMARY CARE BUSINESS UNIT IN THE U.S. AND PUERTO RICO.

INTERIM EARNINGS (Per Share):

Qtr.	Mar.	June	Sept.	Dec.
1999	0.06	0.11	0.16	0.14
2000	0.07	0.19	d0.13	0.29
2001	0.20	0.25	0.27	0.23
2002	0.29	0.24	0.35	0.17

INTERIM DIVIDENDS (Per Share):

Amt.	Decl.	Ex.	Rec.	Pay.
4-for-3	6/21/01	7/20/01	7/03/01	7/19/01

TRADING VOLUME
Thousand Shares

CAPITALIZATION (12/31/01):

	($000)	(%)
Long-Term Debt	346,397	15.1
Deferred Income Tax	37,021	1.6
Common & Surplus	1,908,284	83.3
Total	2,291,702	100.0

*7 YEAR PRICE SCORE N/A   ***12 MONTH PRICE SCORE 78.7**

*NYSE COMPOSITE INDEX=100

BUSINESS:

King Pharmaceuticals, Inc. is a vertically integrated pharmaceutical company that researches, develops, manufactures, markets and sells primarily branded prescription pharmaceutical products. KG markets its branded pharmaceutical products to general/family practitioners, internal medicine physicians, cardiologists, endocrinologists, pediatricians and hospitals. KG's pharmaceutical products can be divided into five therapeutic areas: cardiovascular, anti-infectives, vaccines and biologicals, thyroid-disorder drugs and women's health. KG also provides contract manufacturing for a number of pharmaceutical and biotechnology companies. In February 2000, KG acquired Medco Research, Inc., which has been renamed King Pharmaceutical Research and Development. In July 2000 , KG acquired American Home Products. In August 2000, KG acquired Jones Pharma Incorporated.

RECENT DEVELOPMENTS:

For the year ended 12/31/02, net income was $255.1 million compared with income of $232.9 million, before an extraordinary charge of $14.4 million and an accounting change charge of $545,000, the previous year. The 2002 results included an in-process research and development charge of $12.0 million, an intangible asset impairment charge of $51.2 million, and a valuation charge of $35.6 million for convertible notes held by KG. The 2001 results included a special license rights research and development charge of $3.0 million. Results for 2002 and 2001 also included merger and restructuring charges of $5.9 million and $4.1 million, and charges for inventory write-offs of $15.2 million and $2.1 million, respectively. Total revenues jumped 35.2% to $1.18 billion.

PROSPECTS:

On 1/30/03, the Company and Elan Corporation, plc. announced that they have signed a definitive agreement for KG to acquire Elan's primary care business unit in the U.S. and Puerto Rico, which includes two branded prescription pharmaceutical products and rights to potential new formulations of the products, for $850.0 million. The transaction is expected to close by the end of April 2003. Meanwhile, KG expects revenues in the range of $1.65 billion to $1.85 billion and diluted earnings per share from $1.60 to $1.78 for full-year 2003.

ANNUAL FINANCIAL DATA:

FISCAL YEAR	TOT. REVS. ($000)	NET INC. ($000)	TOT. ASSETS ($000)	OPER. PROFIT %	NET PROFIT %	RET. ON EQUITY %	RET. ON ASSETS %	CURR. RATIO	EARN. PER SH.$	CASH FL.PER SH.$	TANG. BK. VAL.$	PRICE RANGE	AVG. P/E RATIO
p12/31/02	1,179,518	④ 255,112							① 1.04			37.30 - 15.00	25.1
12/31/01	872,262	③ 232,864	2,506,611	42.0	26.7	12.2	9.3	8.2	③ 0.99	1.21	3.51	46.05 - 24.79	35.8
12/31/00	620,243	② 104,581	1,282,395	34.4	16.9	10.6	8.2	3.0	② 0.47	0.68	1.16	41.63 - 14.81	59.6
12/31/99	348,271	45,654	805,689	36.8	13.1	30.8	5.7	1.5	① 0.47	0.78	...	34.00 - 6.46	43.0
12/31/98	163,463	① 25,321	668,171	33.9	15.5	25.0	3.8	1.7	① 0.28	0.39	...	9.58 - 3.54	23.4
12/31/97	47,909	6,612	104,863	27.9	13.8	22.5	6.3	1.0	0.08	0.11	...	...	...
12/31/96	20,457	d240	39,279	...	...	...	...	2.3	d0.01	0.02	0.12	...	...
12/31/95	25,441	9,334	- ...	11.5	36.7	...	...	...	0.24	0.28	...	...	...

Statistics are as originally reported. Adj. for stk. splits: 4-for-3, 7/01; 3-for-2, 11/11/99; 6/21/00. ① Bef. extraord. chrg. $705,000, 12/99; $4.4 mill., 12/98. ② Bef. extraord. chrg. of $40.1 mill., incl. non-recurr. chrgs. of $70.7 mill. ③ Bef. extraord. chrg. of $14.4 mill. and acctg. chng. of $545,000; incl. pre-tax merger & restruct. costs of $4.1 mill. ④ Incl. merger & restr. chrgs. of $5.9 mill., in-proc R&D chrg of $12.0 mill., & intang. asset impair. of $51.2 mill.

OFFICERS:
J. M. Gregory, Chmn.
J. R. Gregory, Vice-Chmn.
R. C. Williams, Vice-Chmn.

INVESTOR CONTACT: Kyle P. Macione, Pres., Inv. Rel., (423) 989-8077

PRINCIPAL OFFICE: 501 Fifth Street, Bristol, TN 37620

TELEPHONE NUMBER: (423) 989-8000
FAX: (423) 274-8677
WEB: www.kingpharm.com
NO. OF EMPLOYEES: 1,545
SHAREHOLDERS: 1,300 (approx. record)
ANNUAL MEETING: In June
INCORPORATED: TN, 1993

INSTITUTIONAL HOLDINGS:
No. of Institutions: 349
Shares Held: 189,706,176
% Held: 78.8

INDUSTRY: Pharmaceutical preparations (SIC: 2834)

TRANSFER AGENT(S): American Stock Transfer & Trust Company, New York, NY

KNIGHT RIDDER

EXCH.	SYM.	REC. PRICE	P/E RATIO	YLD.	MKT. CAP.	RANGE (52-WK.)	'02 Y/E PR.
NYSE	KRI	63.81 (2/28/03)	19.2	1.7%	$5.21 bill.	70.20 - 51.35	63.25

INVESTMENT GRADE. THE COMPANY EXPECTS TO ACHIEVE EARNINGS PER SHARE OF APPROXIMATELY $3.84 IN 2003.

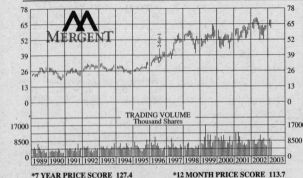

7 YEAR PRICE SCORE 127.4   **12 MONTH PRICE SCORE 113.7**
NYSE COMPOSITE INDEX=100

INTERIM EARNINGS (Per Share):

Qtr.	Mar.	June	Sept.	Dec.
1997	1.85	0.61	0.69	1.04
1998	1.02	0.68	0.58	0.83
1999	0.65	0.88	0.78	1.18
2000	1.74	1.08	0.87	d0.29
2001	0.47	0.16	0.65	0.88
2002	0.60	0.90	0.67	1.16

INTERIM DIVIDENDS (Per Share):

Amt.	Decl.	Ex.	Rec.	Pay.
0.25Q	1/22/02	2/04/02	2/06/02	2/18/02
0.25Q	4/23/02	5/06/02	5/08/02	5/20/02
0.25Q	7/23/02	8/05/02	8/07/02	8/19/02
0.27Q	10/22/02	11/04/02	11/06/02	11/18/02
0.27Q	1/28/03	2/10/03	2/12/03	2/24/03

Indicated div.: $1.08 (Div. Reinv. Plan)

CAPITALIZATION (12/30/01):

	($000)	(%)
Long-Term Debt	1,573,255	46.4
Deferred Income Tax	255,266	7.5
Common & Surplus	1,560,288	46.0
Total	3,388,809	100.0

BUSINESS:

Knight Ridder (formerly Knight-Ridder, Inc.) is a U.S. newspaper publisher, with products in print and on-line. KRI publishes 32 daily newspapers in 28 U.S. markets, with a readership of 8.5 million daily and 12.1 million on Sunday. KRI also has investments in a variety of Internet and technology companies and two newsprint companies. The Company's Internet operation, Knight Ridder Digital, creates and maintains a range of on-line services, including RealCities.com, a national network of city and regional destination sites in 56 U.S. markets. Some of the larger newspapers include THE MIAMI HERALD, THE PHILADELPHIA INQUIRER, THE KANSAS CITY STAR, SAN JOSE MERCURY NEWS, FORT WORTH STAR-TELEGRAM and THE CHARLOTTE OBSERVER.

RECENT DEVELOPMENTS:

For the year ended 12/29/02, income jumped 52.4% to $281.7 million, before an accounting change charge of $24.3 million, compared with net income of $184.8 million in 2001. Total operating revenue was $2.84 billion, down 2.0% from $2.90 billion in the prior year. Total advertising revenue slipped 2.1% to $2.21 billion from $2.25 billion a year earlier. Circulation revenues declined 4.8% to $487.7 million from $512.3 million the previous year. Operating income increased 31.1% to $605.4 million compared with $462.8 million the year before, reflecting a 19.8% decrease in newsprint, ink and supplements and tight controls with respect to labor and other operating costs.

PROSPECTS:

Results are benefiting from growth in retail and general advertising revenue, and increased growth of daily and Sunday subscriptions in eight of the largest markets the Company serves. This trend is expected to continue into 2003 with operating results also benefiting from decreased newsprint costs, ongoing cost-reduction initiatives and an anticipated gradual improvement of global economic conditions. As a result, the Company expects to achieve its earnings per share projection for 2003 of $3.84.

ANNUAL FINANCIAL DATA:

FISCAL YEAR	TOT. REVS. ($mill.)	NET INC. ($mill.)	TOT. ASSETS ($mill.)	OPER. PROFIT %	NET PROFIT %	RET. ON EQUITY %	RET. ON ASSETS %	CURR. RATIO	EARN. PER SH. $	CASH FL. PER SH. $	TANG. BK. VAL.$	DIV. PER SH. $	PRICE RANGE	AVG. P/E RATIO	AVG. YIELD %
p12/29/02	2,841.6	⑧ 281.7							⑧ 3.33			1.02	70.20 — 51.35	18.3	1.7
12/30/01	2,900.2	184.8	4,213.4	15.9	6.4	11.8	4.4	1.1	2.16	4.31	...	1.00	65.50 — 50.20	26.8	1.7
12/31/00	3,211.8	⑦ 314.4	4,243.5	20.8	9.8	20.4	7.4	1.1	⑦ 3.53	5.63	...	0.92	59.75 — 44.13	14.7	1.8
12/26/99	3,228.2	⑥ 339.9	4,192.3	19.3	10.5	19.1	8.1	1.1	⑥ 3.49	5.43	...	0.89	65.00 — 46.00	15.9	1.6
12/27/98	3,091.9	⑤ 305.6	4,257.1	16.3	9.9	18.4	7.2	0.8	⑤ 3.11	5.03	...	0.80	59.63 — 40.50	16.1	1.6
12/28/97	2,876.8	④ 396.5	4,355.1	17.6	13.8	25.6	9.1	1.1	④ 4.08	5.46	...	0.80	57.13 — 35.75	11.4	1.7
12/29/96	2,774.8	③ 267.9	2,900.3	12.1	10.4	23.7	9.2	1.0	③ 2.75	4.45	2.29	0.77	42.00 — 29.88	13.1	2.1
12/31/95	2,751.8	①② 167.4	3,005.7	8.7	6.5	15.1	5.6	1.1	①② 1.67	3.18	1.51	0.74	33.31 — 25.25	17.5	2.5
12/25/94	2,649.0	170.9	2,447.2	12.5	6.5	14.0	7.0	1.0	1.58	2.95	4.88	0.72	30.50 — 23.25	17.1	2.7
12/26/93	2,451.3	148.1	2,431.4	11.6	6.0	11.9	6.1	1.0	1.34	2.62	4.92	0.70	32.50 — 25.31	21.6	2.4

Statistics are as originally reported. Adj. for 2-for-1 split, 7/31/96. ① Incl. $53.8 mill. after-tax gain & $20.0 mill. non-recur. chg. ② Bef. $7.3 mill. acct. adj. loss. ③ Incl. $90.9 mill. gain on sale of Knight-Ridder Financial. ④ Excl. $15.3 mill. net gain & $1.3 mill. income fr. sale of disc. BIS ops. ⑤ Incl. $60.2 mill. gain fr. disc. ops., non-recur. items & relocation costs. ⑥ Incl. $2.9 mill. severance chg. & $21.4 mill. ($0.22/sh.) net gain fr. sale of stock. ⑦ Incl. $168.0 mill. pre-tax chg. fr. write-down of investments & $17.2 mill. pre-tax chg. fr. severance costs. ⑧ Excl. $24.3 mill. acctg. change chg.

OFFICERS:
P. A. Ridder, Chmn., C.E.O.
G. R. Effren, Sr. V.P., C.F.O.
A. B. Silverglat, V.P., Treas.

INVESTOR CONTACT: Polk Laffoon IV, Corp., Rel. Manager, (408) 938-7838

PRINCIPAL OFFICE: 50 W. San Fernando Street, Suite 1500, San Jose, CA 95113

TELEPHONE NUMBER: (408) 938-7700
FAX: (408) 938-7755
WEB: www.kri.com

NO. OF EMPLOYEES: 19,000 (approx.)

SHAREHOLDERS: 8,720 (record)

ANNUAL MEETING: In Apr.

INCORPORATED: OH, 1941; reincorp., FL, 1976

INSTITUTIONAL HOLDINGS:
No. of Institutions: 278
Shares Held: 65,330,180
% Held: 79.3

INDUSTRY: Newspapers (SIC: 2711)

TRANSFER AGENT(S): Mellon Investor Services, Ridgefield Park, NJ

KOHL'S CORPORATION

EXCH.	SYM.	REC. PRICE	P/E RATIO	YLD.	MKT. CAP.	RANGE (52-WK.)	'02 Y/E PR.
NYSE	KSS	48.90 (2/28/03)	26.1	...	$16.39 bill.	78.83 - 44.00	55.95

INVESTMENT GRADE. THE COMPANY PLANS TO OPEN 80 STORES IN 2003, AND BETWEEN 95 TO 100 STORES IN 2004.

TRADING VOLUME
Thousand Shares

*7 YEAR PRICE SCORE 175.6   *12 MONTH PRICE SCORE 88.7

*NYSE COMPOSITE INDEX=100

INTERIM EARNINGS (Per Share):

Qtr.	Apr.	July	Oct.	Jan.
1995-96	0.04	0.04	0.03	0.15
1996-97	0.05	0.05	0.08	0.18
1997-98	0.05	0.07	0.11	0.23
1998-99	0.09	0.10	0.13	0.29
1999-00	0.12	0.14	0.16	0.36
2000-01	0.16	0.19	0.23	0.52
2001-02	0.22	0.25	0.29	0.68
2002-03	0.31	0.36	0.39	0.81

INTERIM DIVIDENDS (Per Share):

Amt.	Decl.	Ex.	Rec.	Pay.
		No dividends paid.		

CAPITALIZATION (2/2/02):

	($000)	(%)
Long-Term Debt	1,095,420	27.4
Deferred Income Tax	114,228	2.9
Common & Surplus	2,791,406	69.8
Total	4,001,054	100.0

BUSINESS:

Kohl's Corporation operates family-oriented, specialty department stores. As of 2/1/03, KSS operated 457 stores in 33 states. The Company's stores feature quality, national brand merchandise including moderately-priced apparel, shoes, accessories, soft home products and housewares targeted to middle-income customers shopping for their families and homes. In the fiscal year ended 2/2/02, sales were derived as follows: Women's, 31.3%; Men's, 20.1%; Home, 18.5%; Children's, 12.8%; Footwear, 8.8%; and Accessories, 8.5%.

RECENT DEVELOPMENTS:

For the 52 weeks ended 2/1/03, net income advanced 29.8% to $643.4 million from $495.7 million in the corresponding period a year earlier. Net sales climbed 21.8% to $9.12 billion from $7.49 billion the year before. Comparable-store sales increased 5.3% year over year. Gross profit totaled $3.14 billion, or 34.4% of net sales, compared with $2.57 billion, or 34.3% of net sales, in the prior year. Operating income grew 28.3% to $1.09 billion from $850.0 million the previous year.

PROSPECTS:

The Company is targeting first-quarter 2003 earnings in the range of $0.36 and $0.40 per share, and comparable-store sales growth in the low-to-mid single digits. Meanwhile, KSS plans to continue its aggressive store expansion program during the current fiscal year. In 2003, 80 new stores are scheduled to open, with about 35 stores opening in the first quarter, including the Company's entry into the Los Angeles, California market with 28 stores. During fall 2003, KSS plans to open 45 new stores, including entries into the Phoenix, Tucson and Flagstaff, Arizona and Las Vegas, Nevada markets. Looking ahead, the Company expects to open between 95 and 100 stores in 2004, with expansion into new California markets, including Sacramento, San Diego and Fresno.

ANNUAL FINANCIAL DATA:

FISCAL YEAR	TOT. REVS. ($mill.)	NET INC. ($mill.)	TOT. ASSETS ($mill.)	OPER. PROFIT %	NET PROFIT %	RET. ON EQUITY %	RET. ON ASSETS %	CURR. RATIO	EARN. PER SH. $	CASH FL. PER SH. $	TANG. BK. VAL. $	PRICE RANGE	AVG. P/E RATIO
p2/01/03	9,120.3	643.4							1.87			78.83 - 44.00	32.8
2/02/02	7,488.7	495.7	4,929.6	11.4	6.6	17.8	10.1	2.8	1.45	1.92	7.78	72.24 - 41.95	39.4
2/03/01	6,152.0	372.1	3,855.2	10.6	6.0	16.9	9.7	2.7	1.10	1.49	6.21	66.50 - 33.50	45.5
1/29/00	4,557.1	258.1	2,914.7	9.8	5.7	15.3	8.9	2.2	0.77	1.04	4.70	40.63 - 28.63	45.0
1/30/99	3,681.8	192.7	1,936.1	9.2	5.2	16.6	10.0	2.5	0.59	0.81	3.55	30.75 - 16.20	39.8
1/31/98	3,060.1	142.0	1,619.7	8.5	4.6	14.9	8.8	2.8	0.46	0.64	2.88	18.84 - 9.06	30.7
2/01/97	2,388.2	102.9	1,122.4	7.9	4.3	19.9	9.2	2.0	0.35	0.50	1.57	10.50 - 6.33	24.2
2/03/96	1,925.7	①72.8	804.9	7.1	3.8	17.7	9.0	2.1	①0.25	0.36	1.19	6.89 - 4.75	23.5
1/28/95	1,554.1	68.7	658.7	8.0	4.4	20.5	10.4	1.7	0.23	0.33	0.90	6.91 - 4.89	25.2
1/29/94	1,305.7	②57.2	469.3	7.9	4.4	21.8	12.2	1.8	②0.19	0.28	0.63	6.52 - 3.27	25.7

Statistics are as originally reported. Adj. for stk. split: 2-for-1, 4/00, 4/98 & 4/96. ① Incl. $14.1 mil non-recurr. pre-tax chrg. ② Bef. $1.8 mil ($0.01/sh) extraord. chrg.

OFFICERS:
R. L. Montgomery, Chmn., C.E.O.
K. Mansell, Pres.
P. Johnson, Exec. V.P., C.F.O.

INVESTOR CONTACT: Patti Johnson, Investor Relations, (262) 703-1893

PRINCIPAL OFFICE: N56 W17000 Ridgewood Drive, Menomonee Falls, WI 53051

TELEPHONE NUMBER: (262) 703-7000
FAX: (262) 703-6373
WEB: www.kohls.com

NO. OF EMPLOYEES: 17,500 full-time (approx.); 42,500 part-time (approx.)

SHAREHOLDERS: ‹6,238

ANNUAL MEETING: In May

INCORPORATED: WI, Oct., 1988

INSTITUTIONAL HOLDINGS:
No. of Institutions: 519
Shares Held: 298,449,561
% Held: 88.5

INDUSTRY: Department stores (SIC: 5311)

TRANSFER AGENT(S): The Bank of New York, New York, NY

KRAFT FOODS, INC.

EXCH.	SYM.	REC. PRICE	P/E RATIO	YLD.	MKT. CAP.	RANGE (52-WK.)	'02 Y/E PR.
NYSE	KFT	29.61 (2/28/03)	15.1	2.0%	$51.23 bill.	43.95 - 29.00	38.93

UPPER MEDIUM GRADE. THE COMPANY IS TARGETING EARNINGS PER SHARE OF $2.10 TO $2.15 IN 2003.

7 YEAR PRICE SCORE N/A   **12 MONTH PRICE SCORE 93.9**
*NYSE COMPOSITE INDEX=100

INTERIM EARNINGS (Per Share):

Qtr.	Mar.	June	Sept.	Dec.
2000	0.32	0.39	0.38	0.29
2001	0.22	0.33	0.29	0.32
2002	0.40	0.52	0.50	0.54

INTERIM DIVIDENDS (Per Share):

Amt.	Decl.	Ex.	Rec.	Pay.
0.13Q	3/05/02	3/13/02	3/15/02	4/05/02
0.13Q	6/14/02	6/26/02	6/28/02	7/08/02
0.15Q	8/27/02	9/12/02	9/16/02	10/07/02
0.15Q	12/05/02	12/19/02	12/23/02	1/06/03
0.15Q	3/04/03	3/12/03	3/14/03	4/04/03

Indicated div.: $0.60

CAPITALIZATION (12/31/01):

	($000)	(%)
Long-Term Debt	13,134,000	31.5
Deferred Income Tax	5,031,000	12.1
Common & Surplus	23,478,000	56.4
Total	41,643,000	100.0

BUSINESS:

Kraft Foods, Inc. is a holding company, which manufactures and markets branded foods and beverages through its wholly-owned subsidiaries, Kraft Foods North America, Inc. and Kraft Foods International, Inc. As of 1/28/03, the Company had operations in 68 countries and sold its products in more than 145 countries. KFT's products include KRAFT cheese, JACOBS and MAXWELL HOUSE coffees, NABISCO cookies and crackers, PHILADELPHIA cream cheese, OSCAR MAYER meats, POST cereals and MILKA chocolates. As of 1/28/03, Altria Group, Inc. owned approximately 83.9% of the Company's outstanding common stock. Revenues in 2001 were derived as follows: snacks, 29.9%; beverages, 19.4%; cheese, 18.4%; convenient meals, 16.3%; and grocery, 16.0%.

RECENT DEVELOPMENTS:

For the twelve months ended 12/31/02, net earnings jumped 80.3% to $3.39 billion from $1.88 billion in the corresponding prior-year period. Results for 2002 included pre-tax charges of $142.0 million from separation programs, $111.0 million related to the integration of Nabisco, partially offset by an $80.0 million pre-tax gain from sales of businesses. Results for 2001 included net pre-tax charges of $74.0 million. Net revenue totaled $29.72 billion, up 1.7% compared with $29.23 billion a year earlier. Gross profit was $12.00 billion, or 40.4% of net revenue, versus $11.67 billion, or 39.9% of net revenue, the year before. Operating income rose 4.1% to $6.28 billion from $6.04 billion the previous year.

PROSPECTS:

Top-line growth is being positively affected by new product introductions, expansion in developing markets and strategic acquisitions. Looking ahead, KFT anticipates volume growth of approximately 3.0% in 2003. However, bottom-line growth is expected to be constrained by higher benefit costs and stock-based compensation expenses, along with weak economic conditions and higher commodity prices. The Company is targeting full-year 2003 earnings in the range of $2.10 to $2.15 per share.

ANNUAL FINANCIAL DATA:

FISCAL YEAR	TOT. REVS. ($mill.)	NET INC. ($mill.)	TOT. ASSETS ($mill.)	OPER. PROFIT %	NET PROFIT %	RET. ON EQUITY %	RET. ON ASSETS %	CURR. RATIO	EARN. PER SH.$	CASH FL. PER SH.$	DIV. PER SH.$	PRICE RANGE	AVG. P/E RATIO	AVG. YIELD %
p12/31/02	29,723.0	① 3,394.0							① 1.96		0.54	43.95 - 32.50	19.5	1.4
12/31/01	33,875.0	1,882.0	55,798.0	14.4	5.6	8.0	3.4	0.8	1.17	2.19	0.13	35.57 - 29.76	27.9	0.4
12/31/00	26,532.0	2,001.0	52,071.0	15.1	7.5	14.2	3.8	0.9	1.38	2.09	...	...	...	...
12/31/99	26,797.0	1,753.0	30,336.0	13.4	6.5	13.0	5.8	1.1	1.20	1.91	...	...	...	...
12/31/98	27,311.0	1,632.0	...	12.9	6.0	...	...	...	1.12	1.84	...	...	...	...

Statistics are as originally reported. ① Incl. $142.0 mil pre-tax chg. fr. separation programs, $111.0 mil chg. related to the integration of Nabisco, & a $80.0 mil gain fr. sales of businesses.

OFFICERS:
L. C. Camilleri, Chmn.
R. K. Deromedi, Co-C.E.O.
B. D. Holden, Co-C.E.O.
J. P. Dollive, Sr. V.P., C.F.O.
INVESTOR CONTACT: Mark Magnesen, (847) 646-3194
PRINCIPAL OFFICE: Three Lakes Drive, Northfield, IL 60093

TELEPHONE NUMBER: (847) 646-2000
FAX: (847) 646-6005
WEB: www.kraft.com
NO. OF EMPLOYEES: 114,000 (approx.)
SHAREHOLDERS: 1,500 (approx.)
ANNUAL MEETING: In Apr.
INCORPORATED: VA, 2000

INSTITUTIONAL HOLDINGS:
No. of Institutions: 434
Shares Held: 216,540,168
% Held: 12.5

INDUSTRY: Groceries, general line (SIC: 5141)

TRANSFER AGENT(S): EquiServe Trust Company, N.A., Jersey City, NJ

KRISPY KREME DOUGHNUTS, INC.

EXCH.	SYM.	REC. PRICE	P/E RATIO	YLD.	MKT. CAP.	RANGE (52-WK.)	'02 Y/E PR.
NYSE	KKD	32.85 (2/28/03)	58.7	...	$1.78 bill.	44.02 - 26.42	33.77

UPPER MEDIUM GRADE. THE COMPANY SIGNED A DEFINITIVE AGREEMENT TO ACQUIRE MONTANA MILLS BREAD CO., INC.

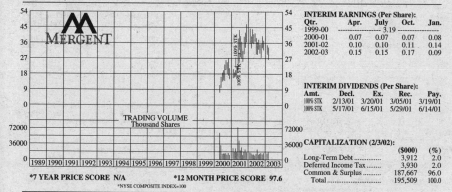

*7 YEAR PRICE SCORE N/A   ***12 MONTH PRICE SCORE 97.6**
*NYSE COMPOSITE INDEX=100

INTERIM EARNINGS (Per Share):

Qtr.	Apr.	July	Oct.	Jan.
1999-00	----------	3.19	----------	
2000-01	0.07	0.07	0.07	0.08
2001-02	0.10	0.10	0.11	0.14
2002-03	0.15	0.15	0.17	0.09

INTERIM DIVIDENDS (Per Share):

Amt.	Decl.	Ex.	Rec.	Pay.
100% STK	2/13/01	3/20/01	3/05/01	3/19/01
100% STK	5/17/01	6/15/01	5/29/01	6/14/01

CAPITALIZATION (2/3/02):

	($000)	(%)
Long-Term Debt	3,912	2.0
Deferred Income Tax	3,930	2.0
Common & Surplus	187,667	96.0
Total	195,509	100.0

BUSINESS:

Krispy Kreme Doughnuts, Inc. is a retailer of more than 20 varieties of doughnuts, including the Company's signature HOT ORIGINAL GLAZED, as well as coffee and other beverages and bakery items. As of 3/18/03, KKD operated 278 Company-owned and franchised stores in 37 states and Canada. Each of the Company's stores has the capacity, depending on equipment size, to produce from 4,000 dozen to over 10,000 dozen doughnuts daily. In addition, KKD sells fresh doughnuts, both packaged and unpackaged, to a variety of retail customers, such as supermarkets, convenience stores and other food service and institutional accounts.

RECENT DEVELOPMENTS:

For the 52 weeks ended 2/2/03, net income climbed 26.9% to $33.5 million from $26.4 million in the corresponding 53-week period the year before. Results for the recent period included a $9.1 million pre-tax charge related to an arbitration award stemming from a dispute over ownership rights of one of KKD's franchisees. Total revenues rose 24.6% to $491.5 million from $394.4 million the previous year. Company-owned store sales grew 20.1% to $319.6 million, while sales at franchised stores more than doubled to $19.3 million from $9.0 million a year earlier. Manufacturing and distribution sales advanced 33.7% to $152.7 million. On a comparable-store basis, systemwide store sales increased 11.8% year over year. Income from operations jumped 42.8% to $59.8 million.

PROSPECTS:

On 1/24/03, the Company announced it has signed a definitive agreement to acquire Montana Mills Bread Co., Inc., a Rochester, NY-based operator of a small chain of upscale bread stores located in New York, Ohio, Pennsylvania and Connecticut. The transaction is expected to be completed in the second quarter of 2003. Meanwhile, KKD is targeting fiscal 2003 earnings of about $0.88 per share, along with systemwide comparable-store sales growth of approximately 10.0%. Separately, the Company anticipates opening 77 new factory stores in 17 new markets during fiscal 2003, along with ten combination doughnut and coffee shops and/or satellite format stores.

ANNUAL FINANCIAL DATA:

FISCAL YEAR	TOT. REVS. ($000)	NET INC. ($000)	TOT. ASSETS ($000)	OPER. PROFIT %	NET PROFIT %	RET. ON EQUITY %	RET. ON ASSETS %	CURR. RATIO	EARN. PER SH.$	CASH FL. PER SH.$	TANG. BK. VAL.$	PRICE RANGE	AVG. P/E RATIO
p2/02/03	491,549	① 33,478	255,376	10.6	6.7	14.1	10.3	1.9	① 0.56	0.59	3.15	44.36 - 27.40	64.1
2/03/02	394,354	26,378	171,493	7.8	4.9	11.7	8.6	1.8	0.28	0.39	2.42	46.90 - 15.13	68.9
1/28/01	300,715	14,725	104,958	4.9	2.7	12.5	5.7	1.4	3.19	5.35	25.56	27.13 - 7.25	62.5
1/30/00	220,243	5,956	93,312	...	...	...	...	1.3	① d1.92	0.67	22.62	... ...	...
1/31/99	180,880	① d3,167	...	3.4	1.7	...	...	1.3	1.86	4.32	...	... ...	...
2/01/98	158,743	2,714											

Statistics are as originally reported. Adj. for stk. splits: 100%, 6/01 & 3/01. ① Incl. $9.1 mil pre-tax chg. related to an arbitration award, 2003; $9.5 mil pre-tax restr. chg., 1999.

OFFICERS:
S. A. Livengood, Chmn., Pres., C.E.O.
J. N. McAleer, Vice-Chmn., Exec. V.P.
J. W. Tate, C.O.O.
R. S. Casstevens, Sr. V.P., C.F.O.

INVESTOR CONTACT: Michelle Parman, Sr. V.P.-Corp. Devel., (336) 733-3762

PRINCIPAL OFFICE: 370 Knollwood Street, Suite 500, Winston-Salem, NC 27103

TELEPHONE NUMBER: (336) 725-2981
FAX: (336) 733-3794
WEB: www.krispykreme.com

NO. OF EMPLOYEES: 3,632 (avg.)

SHAREHOLDERS: 146 (approx.)

ANNUAL MEETING: In June

INCORPORATED: NC, Dec., 1999

INSTITUTIONAL HOLDINGS:
No. of Institutions: 165
Shares Held: 29,446,295
% Held: 52.4

INDUSTRY: Retail bakeries (SIC: 5461)

TRANSFER AGENT(S): Branch Banking & Trust Company, Wilson, NC

KROGER COMPANY (THE)

EXCH.	SYM.	REC. PRICE	P/E RATIO	YLD.	MKT. CAP.	RANGE (52-WK.)	'02 Y/E PR.
NYSE	KR	13.22 (2/28/03)	8.4	...	$11.82 bill.	23.81 - 11.00	15.45

MEDIUM GRADE. EARNINGS IN 2003 ARE EXPECTED TO BE HURT BY WEAK ECONOMIC CONDITIONS, INCREASED COMPETITION AND HIGHER HEALTHCARE AND PENSION COSTS.

*7 YEAR PRICE SCORE 96.0   *12 MONTH PRICE SCORE 91.1

*NYSE COMPOSITE INDEX=100

INTERIM EARNINGS (Per Share):

Qtr	Mar.	June	Sept.	Dec.
1997	0.18	0.21	0.18	0.28
1998	0.10	0.18	0.24	0.34
Qtr.	**May**	**Aug.**	**Nov.**	**Jan.**
1999-00	0.33	0.06	0.15	0.29
2000-01	0.12	0.26	0.24	0.44
2001-02	0.36	0.31	0.16	0.43
2002-03	0.47	0.34	0.33	...

INTERIM DIVIDENDS (Per Share):

Amt.	Decl.	Ex.	Rec.	Pay.
		No dividends paid.		

CAPITALIZATION (2/2/02):

	($000)	(%)
Long-Term Debt	8,412,000	70.6
Common & Surplus	3,502,000	29.4
Total	11,914,000	100.0

BUSINESS:

The Kroger Company operated 2,461 supermarkets in 32 states as of 11/9/02, principally under the Kroger, Fred Meyer, Ralphs, Smith's, King Soopers, Dillon, Fry's and Fry's Marketplace, City Market, Food 4 Less and QFC banners. Most stores operate under the combination food and drug store format, which includes floral, seafood, pharmacy, bakery and other specialty departments. KR operates 783 convenience stores under the names: Kwik Shop, Quick Stop, Tom Thumb, Turkey Hill Minit Markets, Loaf 'N Jug, and Mini-Mart. KR also operates 441 fine jewelry stores, under the banners of Fred Meyer, Merksamer, Fox's, Littman, and Barclay Jewelers, 341 supermarket fuel centers, and 41 food processing plants. On 5/27/99, KR acquired Fred Meyer, Inc.

RECENT DEVELOPMENTS:

For the quarter ended 11/9/02, net earnings totaled $254.6 million compared with $133.1 million in the corresponding prior-year period. Results included after-tax charges of $8.4 million and $125.5 million in 2002 and 2001, respectively, primarily related to restructuring and acquisitions. Sales rose 2.8% to $11.70 billion from $11.38 billion a year earlier. Identical food-store sales, including fuel, declined 0.6% year over year. Comparable food-store sales, which include relocations and expansions, increased 0.2% year over year. During the quarter, KR opened, expanded, relocated or acquired 29 food stores.

PROSPECTS:

The Company anticipates fourth-quarter 2002 earnings per share will be equal to or slightly higher than the earnings of $0.43 per share reported in the fourth quarter of 2001. Looking ahead, earnings in 2003 are expected to be essentially flat compared with earnings in 2002. In 2003, results will likely continue to be hampered by weak economic conditions, product cost deflation, and increased competition, along with significantly higher healthcare and pension costs in 2003.

ANNUAL FINANCIAL DATA:

FISCAL YEAR	TOT. REVS. ($Mill.)	NET INC. ($Mill.)	TOT. ASSETS ($Mill.)	OPER. PROFIT %	NET PROFIT %	RET. ON EQUITY %	RET. ON ASSETS %	CURR. RATIO	EARN. PER SH.$	CASH FL. PER SH.$	PRICE RANGE	AVG. P/E RATIO
2/02/02	50,098.0	⑤ 1,043.0	19,087.0	4.7	2.1	29.8	5.5	1.0	⑤ 1.26	2.57	27.66 - 19.60	18.8
2/03/01	49,000.0	③ 880.0	18,190.0	4.5	1.8	28.5	4.8	1.0	③ 1.04	2.23	27.94 - 14.06	20.2
④ 1/29/00	45,352.0	①③ 638.0	17,966.0	3.9	1.4	23.8	3.6	0.8	①③ 0.74	1.86	34.91 - 14.88	33.6
1/02/99	28,203.3	①③ 449.9	6,700.1	3.5	1.6	...	6.7	0.8	①③ 0.85	1.69	30.41 - 17.00	27.9
12/27/97	26,567.3	① 444.0	6,301.3	3.8	1.7	...	7.0	0.9	① 0.85	1.59	18.66 - 11.34	17.7
12/28/96	25,170.9	① 352.7	5,825.4	3.4	1.4	...	6.1	0.9	① 0.67	1.35	11.88 - 8.38	15.1
12/30/95	23,937.8	① 318.9	5,044.7	3.4	1.3	...	6.3	0.8	① 0.66	1.34	9.44 - 5.84	11.5
12/31/94	22,959.1	① 421.4	4,707.7	3.3	1.8	...	9.0	0.9	① 0.59	1.57	6.72 - 4.84	9.7
1/01/94	22,384.3	② 170.8	4,480.5	3.1	0.8	...	3.8	1.0	② 0.40	1.20	5.44 - 3.50	11.2
1/02/93	22,144.6	① 101.2	4,303.1	2.9	0.5	...	2.4	1.0	① 0.28	1.30	5.28 - 2.81	14.6

Statistics are as originally reported. Adj. for 2-for-1 stk. split, 6/99 & 4/97. ① Bef. extraord. chg. $10.0 mil, 1/00; $39.1 mil ($0.08/sh), 1997; $32.4 mil ($0.07/sh), 1997; $2.8 mil ($0.01/sh), 1996; $16.1 mil ($0.04/sh), 1995; $26.7 mil ($0.06/sh), 1994; $107.1 mil ($0.30/sh), 1992. ② Bef. $23.8 mil ($0.06/sh) extraord. chg., $159.2 mil ($0.38/sh) chg. for acctg. change & incl. $15 mil non-recur. chg. ③ Bef. $3.2 mil extraord. chg. & incl. $350.3 mil pre-tax one-time chgs., 2/01; $468.0 mil pre-tax merger-related chg., 1/00; & $88.1 mil ($0.17/sh) after-tax chg., 1998. ④ Incl. results of Fred Meyer, Inc., acq. on 5/27/99. ⑤ Bef. $200,000 extraord. chg. & incl. $284.5 mil pre-tax one-time chgs.

OFFICERS:
J. A. Pichler, Chmn., C.E.O.
D. B. Dillon, Pres., C.O.O.
J. M. Schlotman, Group V.P., C.F.O.
S. Henderson, Treas.

INVESTOR CONTACT: Kathy Kelly, (513) 762-4969

PRINCIPAL OFFICE: 1014 Vine Street, Cincinnati, OH 45202

TELEPHONE NUMBER: (513) 762-4000
FAX: (513) 762-1400
WEB: www.kroger.com

NO. OF EMPLOYEES: 288,000 (approx.)

SHAREHOLDERS: 54,124 (record)

ANNUAL MEETING: In June

INCORPORATED: OH, Apr., 1902

INSTITUTIONAL HOLDINGS:
No. of Institutions: 514
Shares Held: 525,040,228
% Held: 68.8

INDUSTRY: Grocery stores (SIC: 5411)

TRANSFER AGENT(S): The Bank of New York, New York, NY

L-3 COMMUNICATIONS HOLDINGS, INC.

EXCH.	SYM.	REC. PRICE	P/E RATIO	YLD.	MKT. CAP.	RANGE (52-WK.)	'02 Y/E PR.
NYSE	LLL	36.12 (2/28/03)	16.0	...	$2.84 bill.	66.78 - 35.00	44.91

MEDIUM GRADE. THE COMPANY EXPECTS FULL-YEAR 2003 DILUTED EARNINGS OF BETWEEN $2.67 AND $2.72 PER SHARE.

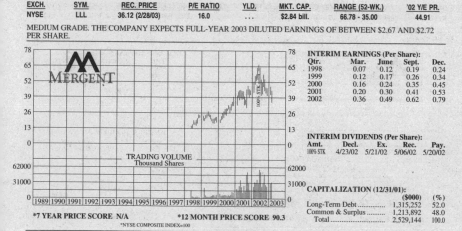

*7 YEAR PRICE SCORE N/A   *12 MONTH PRICE SCORE 90.3

*NYSE COMPOSITE INDEX=100

INTERIM EARNINGS (Per Share):

Qtr.	Mar.	June	Sept.	Dec.
1998	0.07	0.12	0.19	0.24
1999	0.12	0.17	0.26	0.34
2000	0.16	0.24	0.35	0.45
2001	0.20	0.30	0.41	0.53
2002	0.36	0.49	0.62	0.79

INTERIM DIVIDENDS (Per Share):

Amt.	Decl.	Ex.	Rec.	Pay.
100% STK	4/23/02	5/21/02	5/06/02	5/20/02

CAPITALIZATION (12/31/01):

	($000)	(%)
Long-Term Debt	1,315,252	52.0
Common & Surplus	1,213,892	48.0
Total	2,529,144	100.0

BUSINESS:

L-3 Communications Holdings, Inc. produces intelligence, surveillance, and reconnaissance (ISR) products, secure communications systems and products, training products, avionics and ocean products, microwave components and telemetry, instrumentation, space and wireless products and guidance and fuze products. LLL's systems and specialized products are used to connect a variety of airborne, space, ground-and-sea-based communication systems and are used in the transmission, processing, recording, monitoring and dissemination functions of these communication systems. LLL's customers include the U.S. Department of Defense (DoD), certain U.S. Government intelligence agencies, major aerospace and defense contractors, and commercial telecommunications and wireless customers. For the year ended 12/31/01, direct and indirect sales to the DoD provided 64.7% of LLL's sales. On 3/8/02, LLL acquired Aircraft Integration Systems for $1.13 billion.

RECENT DEVELOPMENTS:

For the year ended 12/31/02, income was $212,4 million, before an extraordinary loss of $9.9 million and an accounting change charge of $24.4 million, compared with net income of $115.5 million a year earlier. Sales climbed 70.9% to $4.01 billion from $2.35 billion the previous year. Excluding acquisitions, sales rose 14.8%. Operating income was $454.0 million, 64.9% higher than the year before. Separately, on 1/29/03, LLL announced that it has agreed to acquire Goodrich Avionics Systems, a division of Goodrich Corp., for $188.0 million.

PROSPECTS:

On 2/19/03, LLL announced that it continues to expect that it will achieve its goal of 20.0% annual growth for sales and earnings, including 8.0% to 10.0% growth excluding acquisitions, in 2003. Including acquisitions that the Company completed through 12/31/02, LLL expects total sales growth in 2003 of over 16.0% and 2003 diluted earnings per share of between $2.67 and $2.72. LLL noted that it appears well positioned to benefit from higher defense and homeland security spending as U.S. military forces continue to modernize and upgrade their existing assets. Meanwhile, LLL will continue to pursue acquisitions that complement its existing product base.

ANNUAL FINANCIAL DATA:

FISCAL YEAR	TOT. REVS. ($mill.)	NET INC. ($mill.)	TOT. ASSETS ($mill.)	OPER. PROFIT %	NET PROFIT %	RET. ON EQUITY %	RET. ON ASSETS %	CURR. RATIO	EARN. PER SH.$	CASH FL. PER SH.$	PRICE RANGE	AVG. P/E RATIO
p12/31/02	4,011.2	③ 212.4		11.7	4.9	9.5	3.5	2.4	③ 2.29		66.78 - 40.60	23.4
12/31/01	2,347.4	② 115.5	3,335.4	11.7	4.3	11.9	3.4	1.8	② 1.48	2.44	49.04 - 30.35	26.9
12/31/00	1,910.1	82.7	2,463.5	11.7	4.3	11.9	3.4	1.8	1.19	2.33	39.66 - 17.84	24.3
12/31/99	1,405.5	58.7	1,633.8	10.7	4.2	10.1	3.6	1.8	0.88	1.74	27.13 - 17.13	25.3
12/31/98	1,037.0	32.6	1,285.4	9.7	3.1	10.9	2.5	1.6	0.63	1.46	24.75 - 12.78	29.8
12/31/97	546.5	① 12.3	703.4	9.4	2.3	10.8	1.7	2.0	① 0.31	0.90	...	...
12/31/96	543.1	11.7	593.3	8.0	2.2	2.5	2.0	2.0	...	...	...	...
12/31/95	166.8	d1.0	...	2.8	...	...	...	...	...	...	...	...

Statistics are as originally reported. Adj. for 2-for-1 stk. split, 5/20/02. ① Incl. non-recurr. chrg. of $4.4 mill. ② Incl. net non-recurr. gain of $400,000. ③ Bef. extraord. loss of $9.9 mill. & acctg. chge. chrg. of $24.4 mill.

OFFICERS:
F. C. Lanza, Chmn., C.E.O.
R. V. LaPenta, Pres., C.F.O.
C. C. Cambria, Sr. V.P., Gen. Couns., Sec.
INVESTOR CONTACT: Cynthia Swain, V.P., Corp. Comm., (212) 697-1111
PRINCIPAL OFFICE: 600 Third Avenue, New York, NY 10016

TELEPHONE NUMBER: (212) 697-1111
FAX: (212) 805-5353
WEB: www.L-3Com.com
NO. OF EMPLOYEES: 18,000 (avg.)
SHAREHOLDERS: 144 (record)
ANNUAL MEETING: In Apr.
INCORPORATED: DE, Apr., 1997

INSTITUTIONAL HOLDINGS:
No. of Institutions: 411
Shares Held: 93,015,844
% Held: 98.5
INDUSTRY: Radio & TV communications equipment (SIC: 3663)
TRANSFER AGENT(S): First Chicago Trust Company of New York, Jersey City, NJ

LABOR READY, INC.

EXCH.	SYM.	REC. PRICE	P/E RATIO	YLD.	MKT. CAP.	RANGE (52-WK.)	'02 Y/E PR.
NYSE	LRW	5.40 (2/28/03)	21.6	...	$219.3 mill.	9.43 - 4.75	6.42

MEDIUM GRADE. FOR 2003, THE COMPANY ANTICIPATES EARNINGS WILL BE IN THE RANGE OF $0.30 TO $0.35 PER SHARE.

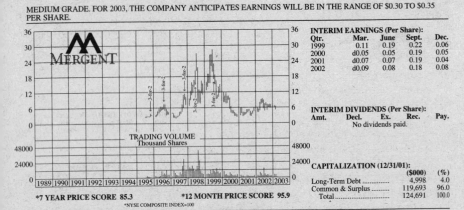

*7 YEAR PRICE SCORE 85.3   ***12 MONTH PRICE SCORE 95.9**
*NYSE COMPOSITE INDEX=100

INTERIM EARNINGS (Per Share):

Qtr.	Mar.	June	Sept.	Dec.
1999	0.11	0.19	0.22	0.06
2000	d0.05	0.05	0.19	0.05
2001	d0.07	0.07	0.19	0.04
2002	d0.09	0.08	0.18	0.08

INTERIM DIVIDENDS (Per Share):

Amt.	Decl.	Ex.	Rec.	Pay.
	No dividends paid.			

CAPITALIZATION (12/31/01):

	($000)	(%)
Long-Term Debt	4,998	4.0
Common & Surplus	119,693	96.0
Total	124,691	100.0

BUSINESS:

Labor Ready, Inc. is a national provider of temporary workers for manual labor jobs. The Company's customers are primarily businesses in the construction, freight handling, warehousing, landscaping, light manufacturing and other light industrial markets. These businesses require workers for lifting, hauling, cleaning, assembling, digging, painting and other types of manual work. Over the past several years, LRW has been diversifying its customer base to include more customers in the retail, wholesale, sanitation, printing, and hospitality industries. The Company's dispatch offices are locations where workers as well as prospective workers report prior to being assigned jobs. As of 2/4/03, LRW operated more than 750 branch offices throughout the U.S., Canada, Puerto Rico and the U.K.

RECENT DEVELOPMENTS:

For the year ended 12/31/02, net income advanced 25.7% to $11.6 million compared with $9.2 million in the previous year. Revenues from services decreased 5.9% to $862.7 million from $917.0 million a year earlier. Gross profit declined 9.1% to $250.1 million from $275.1 million the year before. Selling, general and administrative expenses fell 12.9% to $220.2 million, or 25.5% of revenues, from $252.7 million, or 27.6% of revenues, in the prior year. Income from operations jumped 46.8% to $20.7 million from $14.1 million a year earlier.

PROSPECTS:

Despite difficult economic conditions in 2002, the Company improved its income from operations, generated free cash flow and strengthened its balance sheet. LRW has significant operating leverage as a result of solid expense controls and is in a position to capitalize on increasing demand for temporary labor once the economy improves. Meanwhile, the Company plans to launch new strategic and marketing initiatives. In addition, the Company plans to open approximately 40 new branch offices, including about 15 in the U.K. and about 25 in smaller markets in the U.S. and Canada during 2003. Separately, the Company anticipates revenues for 2003 between $900.0 million and $920.0 million and net income to be in the range of $0.30 to $0.35 per share.

ANNUAL FINANCIAL DATA:

FISCAL YEAR	TOT. REVS. ($000)	NET INC. ($000)	TOT. ASSETS ($000)	OPER. PROFIT %	NET PROFIT %	RET. ON EQUITY %	RET. ON ASSETS %	CURR. RATIO	EARN. PER SH.$	CASH FL. PER SH.$	TANG. BK. VAL.$	PRICE RANGE	AVG. P/E RATIO
p12/31/02	862,733	11,586							0.28			9.43 - 4.20	24.3
12/31/01	916,965	9,215	214,030	1.5	1.0	7.7	4.3	2.5	0.23	0.43	2.95	6.12 - 2.62	19.0
12/31/00	976,573	10,059	205,423	1.7	1.0	9.0	4.9	2.7	0.24	0.41	2.70	12.00 - 2.38	29.9
12/31/99	850,873	② 24,577	174,481	4.9	2.9	22.1	14.1	3.6	② 0.53	0.68	2.53	28.42 - 9.31	35.6
12/31/98	606,895	19,799	130,736	5.5	3.3	24.6	15.1	3.0	0.46	0.60	1.89	27.00 - 6.78	36.7
12/31/97	335,409	6,963	80,367	3.2	2.1	12.0	8.7	4.2	0.17	0.26	1.37	11.45 - 1.93	40.5
12/31/96	163,450	① 1,922	64,331	2.1	1.2	3.7	3.0	4.2	① 0.05	0.10	1.17	7.41 - 2.67	100.5
12/31/95	94,362	2,062	26,182	4.3	2.2	24.2	7.9	2.5	0.07	0.09	0.17	3.75 - 2.29	44.4
12/31/94	38,951	852	8,912	4.2	2.2	28.8	9.6	1.3	0.04	0.05	0.08	...	...
12/31/93	15,659	③ 221	3,160	3.9	1.4	33.0	7.0	1.4	③ 0.01	0.01	...	...	...

Statistics are as originally reported. Adj. for stk. splits: 3-for-2, 7/12/99, 6/9/98, 10/31/97, 8/9/96, 11/28/95 ① Bef. extraord. loss 12/31/96: $1.2 mill.; credit 12/31/93: $47,821 ② Bef. acctg. change chrg. of $1.5 mill.

OFFICERS:
R. Sullivan, Chmn.
J. P. Sambataro Jr., Pres., C.E.O.
S. C. Cooper, Exec. V.P., C.F.O.

INVESTOR CONTACT: Steve Cooper, Exec. V.P., C.F.O., (253) 680-8213

PRINCIPAL OFFICE: 1015 A Street, Tacoma, WA 98402

TELEPHONE NUMBER: (253) 383-9101
FAX: (253) 383-9311
WEB: www.laborready.com

NO. OF EMPLOYEES: 2,850 (approx.)

SHAREHOLDERS: 654

ANNUAL MEETING: In June

INCORPORATED: WA, March, 1985

INSTITUTIONAL HOLDINGS:
No. of Institutions: 111
Shares Held: 31,889,621
% Held: 77.7

INDUSTRY: Help supply services (SIC: 7363)

TRANSFER AGENT(S): Computershare Trust Company, Golden, CO

LABORATORY CORPORATION OF AMERICA HOLDINGS INC.

EXCH.	SYM.	REC. PRICE	P/E RATIO	YLD.	MKT. CAP.	RANGE (52-WK.)	'02 Y/E PR.
NYSE	LH	27.77 (2/28/03)	15.7	...	$1.96 bill.	52.38 - 18.51	23.24

UPPER MEDIUM GRADE. ON 1/17/03, THE COMPANY ACQUIRED DIANON SYSTEMS INC. FOR APPROXIMATELY $598.4 MILLION.

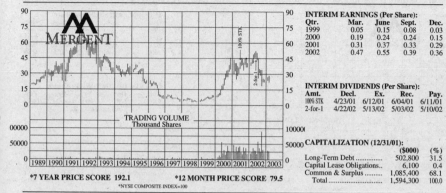

TRADING VOLUME
Thousand Shares

7 YEAR PRICE SCORE 192.1   *12 MONTH PRICE SCORE 79.5*
NYSE COMPOSITE INDEX=100

INTERIM EARNINGS (Per Share):

Qtr.	Mar.	June	Sept.	Dec.
1999	0.05	0.15	0.08	0.03
2000	0.19	0.24	0.24	0.15
2001	0.31	0.37	0.33	0.29
2002	0.47	0.55	0.39	0.36

INTERIM DIVIDENDS (Per Share):

Amt.	Decl.	Ex.	Rec.	Pay.
100% STK	4/23/01	6/12/01	6/04/01	6/11/01
2-for-1	4/22/02	5/13/02	5/03/02	5/10/02

CAPITALIZATION (12/31/01):

	($000)	(%)
Long-Term Debt	502,800	31.5
Capital Lease Obligations	6,100	0.4
Common & Surplus	1,085,400	68.1
Total	1,594,300	100.0

BUSINESS:

Laboratory Corporation of America Holdings Inc. is an independent clinical laboratory organization with annualized revenues of about $2.51 billion. As of 2/18/03, LH offered more than 4,000 different clinical tests that are used by the medical profession in routine testing, patient diagnosis, and in the monitoring and treatment of disease. The Company's operations include a network of 24 primary testing facilities and approximately 1,200 service sites consisting of branches, patient service centers and STAT laboratories, serving clients in 50 states. LH services more than 200,000 clients worldwide, including physicians, state and federal government, managed care organizations, hospitals, clinics pharmaceuticals and other clinical laboratories.

RECENT DEVELOPMENTS:

For the year ended 12/31/02, net earnings was $254.6 million compared with income of $182.8 million, before an extraordinary loss of $3.2 million, the previous year. The improvement in earnings was primarily attributed to the acquisition of Dynacare on 7/25/02. Results for 2002 included pre-tax restructuring and other special charges of $17.5 million. Net sales climbed 14.0% to $2.51 billion from $2.20 billion the year before. Testing volume, measured by accessions, increased 10.7% and price per accession increased 3.3% compared to 2001.

PROSPECTS:

On 1/17/03, the Company acquired DIANON Systems Inc., a U.S. provider of anatomic pathology and oncology testing services, for approximately $598.4 million. The Company anticipates that the acquisition will be accretive to its 2003 diluted earnings per share by approximately $0.05 and expects to realize an estimated $35.0 million in annual cost savings synergies by year-end 2005. Separately, the Company expects 2003 earnings per share growth of 22.5% over 2002. LH also expects revenue to grow 22.0% to $3.06 billion for the full-year 2003.

ANNUAL FINANCIAL DATA:

FISCAL YEAR	TOT. REVS. ($mill.)	NET INC. ($mill.)	TOT. ASSETS ($mill.)	OPER. PROFIT %	NET PROFIT %	RET. ON EQUITY %	RET. ON ASSETS %	CURR. RATIO	EARN. PER SH. $	CASH FL. PER SH. $	TANG. BK. VAL. $	PRICE RANGE	AVG. P/E RATIO
p12/31/02	2,507.7	⑨ 254.6							⑨ 1.77			52.38 - 18.51	20.0
12/31/01	2,199.8	⑧ 182.7	1,929.6	16.7	8.3	16.8	9.5	3.1	⑧ 1.30	2.03	0.83	45.68 - 24.88	27.2
12/31/00	1,919.3	⑦ 112.1	1,666.9	12.8	5.8	12.8	6.7	1.6	⑦ 0.81	1.74	0.08	45.75 - 7.81	33.3
12/31/99	1,698.7	⑥ 65.4	1,590.2	8.8	3.9	37.3	4.1	2.0	⑥ 0.30	1.93	...	9.69 - 3.13	21.3
12/31/98	1,612.6	68.8	1,640.9	7.9	4.3	44.6	4.2	2.1	0.50	2.17	...	6.88 - 2.81	9.7
12/31/97	1,579.9	⑤ d106.9	1,658.5	...	...	...	...	2.7	⑤ d2.65	d0.89	...	10.00 - 3.28	...
12/31/96	1,607.7	④ d153.5	1,917.0	...	...	...	...	2.9	④ d3.12	d1.40	...	23.44 - 5.94	...
12/31/95	1,432.0	③ d4.0	1,837.2	4.7	...	...	...	1.7	③ d0.07	1.55	...	38.75 - 20.31	...
② 12/31/94	872.5	② 30.1	1,012.7	10.2	3.4	18.1	3.0	1.4	② 0.90	2.20	...	39.38 - 26.56	36.6
12/31/93	760.5	① 112.7	585.5	24.4	14.8	80.0	19.2	1.5	① 3.15	4.05	...	48.75 - 30.00	12.5

Statistics are as originally reported. Adj. for 1-for-10 reverse stock split, 5/3/00; 2-for-1, 4/23/01. ① Incl. one-time pre-tax chrgs. of $24.9 mill., 1994; gain $15.3 mill., 1993. ② Results prior to 1995 reflect the operations of National Health Laboratories Holdings Inc., which was the surviving company in a merger with Roche holding Ltd. ③ Incl. pre-tax spec. chrg. of $90.0 mill. & bef. extraord. net chrg. of $8.3 mill. ④ Incl. spec. chrgs. of $218.0 mill. ⑤ Incl. pre-tax chrgs. of $160.0 mill. for dbtfl. accts. & $22.7 mill. for restruct. certain laboratory exps. ⑥ Incl. loss on sale of assets of $1.7 mill. ⑦ Incl. pre-tax nonrecurr. chrg. of $4.5 mill. ⑧ Incl. pre-tax chrg. of $8.9 mill. for term. of int. rate swap agree. ⑨ Incl. pre-tax restruct. & other spec. chrgs. of $17.5 mill.

OFFICERS:
T. P. Mac Mahon, Chmn., Pres., C.E.O.
W. R. Elingburg, Exec. V.P., C.F.O., Treas.

INVESTOR CONTACT: Pamela J. Sherry, V.P. Inv. Rel., (336) 436-4855

PRINCIPAL OFFICE: 358 South Main Street, Burlington, NC 27215

TELEPHONE NUMBER: (336) 229-1127
FAX: (336) 229-7717
WEB: www.labcorp.com
NO. OF EMPLOYEES: 24,000 (approx.)
SHAREHOLDERS: 653
ANNUAL MEETING: In May
INCORPORATED: DE, Mar., 1991; reincorp., DE, June, 1994

INSTITUTIONAL HOLDINGS:
No. of Institutions: 287
Shares Held: 147,840,889
% Held: 100.0

INDUSTRY: Medical laboratories (SIC: 8071)

TRANSFER AGENT(S): American Stock Transfer & Trust Company, Brooklyn, NY

LABRANCHE & CO., INC.

EXCH.	SYM.	REC. PRICE	P/E RATIO	YLD.	MKT. CAP.	RANGE (52-WK.)	'02 Y/E PR.
NYSE	LAB	20.32 (2/28/03)	15.2	1.6%	$1.19 bill.	34.15 - 16.25	26.64

INVESTMENT GRADE. THE DIFFICULT GLOBAL MARKET AND ECONOMIC CONDITIONS THAT EXISTED DURING 2001 CONTINUED THROUGHOUT 2002, ADVERSELY AFFECTING LAB'S SPECIALIST OPERATIONS.

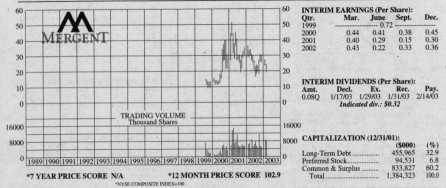

*7 YEAR PRICE SCORE N/A   *12 MONTH PRICE SCORE 102.9
*NYSE COMPOSITE INDEX=100

INTERIM EARNINGS (Per Share):

Qtr.	Mar.	June	Sept.	Dec.
1999		-------- 0.72 --------		
2000	0.44	0.41	0.38	0.45
2001	0.40	0.29	0.15	0.30
2002	0.43	0.22	0.33	0.36

INTERIM DIVIDENDS (Per Share):

Amt.	Decl.	Ex.	Rec.	Pay.
0.08Q	1/17/03	1/29/03	1/31/03	2/14/03

Indicated div.: $0.32

CAPITALIZATION (12/31/01):

	($000)	(%)
Long-Term Debt	455,965	32.9
Preferred Stock	94,531	6.8
Common & Surplus	833,827	60.2
Total	1,384,323	100.0

BUSINESS:

LaBranche & Co., Inc. is a holding company that owns all the outstanding stock of Henderson Brothers, Inc., which is a clearing broker for customers of several introducing brokers and provides direct access floor brokerage services to institutional customers. As a NYSE specialist, the Company's role is to maintain a fair and orderly market in its specialist stocks. As of 12/31/02, the Company is the specialist for more than 650 companies, nine of which are in the Dow Jones Industrial Average, 30 of which are in the S&P 100 Index and 101 of which are S&P 500 Index companies. LAB also acts as the specialist in over 120 options. The Company's Dow stocks are American Express Company, AT&T, DuPont, Eastman Kodak, Exxon Mobil, Merck, Minnesota Mining & Manufacturing, Phillip Morris and SBC Communications. Net sales for 2002 were derived as follows: net gain on principal transactions, 75.6%; commission, 20.3%; and other, 4.1%.

RECENT DEVELOPMENTS:

For the year ended 12/31/02, net income increased 21.8% to $87.2 million from $71.6 million the year before. Earnings for 2002 and 2001 included depreciation and amortization of intangibles of $13.4 million and $39.5 million, respectively. Total revenues rose 6.8% to $452.8 million from $424.1 million the year before. Net gain on principal transactions grew slightly to $342.4 million from $340.8 million in the prior year. Revenue from commissions improved 46.4% to $92.0 million. Other revenues declined 10.1% to $18.4 million.

PROSPECTS:

During 2002, LAB's net gain on principal transactions increased as a result of higher share volumes in its specialist stocks traded on the NYSE. However, despite the increases in NYSE share volume, the difficult global market and economic conditions that existed during 2001 continued throughout 2002, adversely affecting LAB's specialist operations. Looking ahead, weak corporate earnings, uncertainty about the strength and pace of the global economic recovery, continued terrorist threats and increased geopolitical tensions may continue to undermine investor confidence and adversely affect the equity markets.

ANNUAL FINANCIAL DATA:

FISCAL YEAR	TOT. REVS. ($mill.)	NET INC. ($mill.)	TOT. ASSETS ($mill.)	OPER. PROFIT %	NET PROFIT %	RET. ON EQUITY %	RET. ON ASSETS %	CURR. RATIO	EARN. PER SH. $	CASH FL. PER SH. $	TANG. BK. VAL. $	PRICE RANGE	AVG. P/E RATIO
p12/31/02	452.8	87.2	1,912.8	49.2	16.9	7.7	3.6	1.5	1.34	1.98	...	36.41 - 16.25	19.6
12/31/01	424.1	71.6	2,000.8	60.5	23.8	22.1	8.2	2.4	1.13	2.13	...	51.45 - 19.11	31.2
12/31/00	344.8	81.9	1,004.1	43.1	14.4	11.5	5.7	4.3	① 0.72	0.85	1.78	40.00 - 11.13	15.1
12/31/99	201.0	① 29.0	505.1	28.8	22.9	25.3	10.6	2.1	...	...	...	14.88 - 9.06	16.6
12/31/98	126.4	29.0	272.2	28.5	23.4	27.1	10.0	2.1	...	...	...	...	...
12/31/97	67.6	15.8	157.7	19.7	15.9	...	...	...	...	...	...	...	...
12/31/96	49.9	7.9	...										

Statistics are as originally reported. ① Incl. a loss of $25.3 mill. from limited partners' interest in earnings of a subsidiary.

OFFICERS:
G. M. LaBranche IV, Chmn., Pres., C.E.O.
H. S. Traison, Sr. V.P., C.F.O.

INVESTOR CONTACT: Nancy G. Kominsky, Director, Corporate Relations, (212) 425-1144

PRINCIPAL OFFICE: One Exchange Plaza, New York, NY 10006

TELEPHONE NUMBER: (212) 425-1144
FAX: (212) 344-1469
WEB: www.labranche.com
NO. OF EMPLOYEES: 545
SHAREHOLDERS: 150 (approx.)
ANNUAL MEETING: In May
INCORPORATED: DE, 1924

INSTITUTIONAL HOLDINGS:
No. of Institutions: 133
Shares Held: 26,389,217
% Held: 44.4
INDUSTRY: Security brokers and dealers (SIC: 6211)
TRANSFER AGENT(S): Firstar Bank, N.A., Milwaukee, WI

LAFARGE NORTH AMERICA, INC.

EXCH.	SYM.	REC. PRICE	P/E RATIO	YLD.	MKT. CAP.	RANGE (52-WK.)	'02 Y/E PR.
NYSE	LAF	28.28 (2/28/03)	7.8	2.1%	$1.92 bill.	45.15 - 25.90	32.85

UPPER MEDIUM GRADE. THE COMPANY EXPECTS RESULTS TO BE STRAINED BY WEAKNESS IN THE U.S. CONSTRUCTION SECTOR.

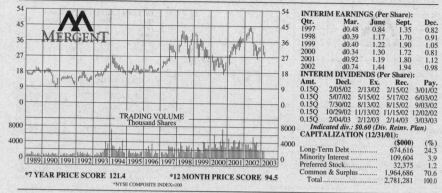

*7 YEAR PRICE SCORE 121.4   ***12 MONTH PRICE SCORE 94.5**
*NYSE COMPOSITE INDEX=100

INTERIM EARNINGS (Per Share):

Qtr.	Mar.	June	Sept.	Dec.
1997	d0.48	0.84	1.35	0.82
1998	d0.39	1.17	1.70	0.91
1999	d0.40	1.22	1.90	1.05
2000	d0.34	1.30	1.72	0.81
2001	d0.92	1.19	1.80	1.12
2002	d0.74	1.44	1.94	0.98

INTERIM DIVIDENDS (Per Share):

Amt.	Decl.	Ex.	Rec.	Pay.
0.15Q	2/05/02	2/13/02	2/15/02	3/01/02
0.15Q	5/07/02	5/15/02	5/17/02	6/03/02
0.15Q	7/30/02	8/13/02	8/15/02	9/03/02
0.15Q	10/29/02	11/13/02	11/15/02	12/02/02
0.15Q	2/04/03	2/12/03	2/14/03	3/03/03

Indicated div.: $0.60 (Div. Reinv. Plan)

CAPITALIZATION (12/31/01):

	($000)	(%)
Long-Term Debt	674,616	24.3
Minority Interest	109,604	3.9
Preferred Stock.................	32,375	1.2
Common & Surplus	1,964,686	70.6
Total	2,781,281	100.0

BUSINESS:

Lafarge North America, Inc. (formerly Lafarge Corporation) is one of North America's largest diversified suppliers of construction materials. The Company's products include construction aggregate, ready-mixed concrete, asphalt, cement, slag, fly ash and associated blended products, and gypsum drywall and related products. As of 2/4/03, the Company operated five gypsum drywall manufacturing plants. The Company's products are used in residential, commercial, institutional and public works construction in 46 states and Canada. The Company's majority shareholder is Lafarge S.A. of Paris, France. Net sales (and operating profit) for 2002 were derived from the following: construction materials, 57.2% (40.1%); cement and cement-related products, 35.9% (63.3%); and gypsum, 6.9% (d3.4%).

RECENT DEVELOPMENTS:

For the year ended 12/31/02, net income grew 14.7% to $268.4 million compared with $234.1 million in 2001. Earnings for 2002 and 2001 included gains of $30.8 million and $23.3 million, respectively, on divestitures of non-strategic businesses and other assets. Earnings for 2001 included goodwill amortization expense of $20.6 million. Total net sales slid 2.2% to $3.25 billion from $3.32 billion a year earlier. Construction materials net sales fell 6.3% to $1.94 billion, while cement and cement-related products sales declined 1.6% to $1.22 billion.

PROSPECTS:

In 2003, the Company intends to maintain its emphasis on mitigating the effects of lower demand through performance improvements, including price improvement wherever possible and further cost-reduction measures. Meanwhile, LAF may benefit from an expected recovery of paving construction activity in Ontario, Canada and full federal funding in fiscal 2003 of the TEA-21 highway construction program in the U.S. Budget constraints at the state level; however will influence the actual level of public works activity that is tendered in 2003. Separately, the Company continues to maintain a solid balance sheet with net indebtedness at 12/31/02 of $433.8 million down 34.2% from $659.4 million in 2001.

ANNUAL FINANCIAL DATA:

FISCAL YEAR	TOT. REVS. ($mill.)	NET INC. ($mill.)	TOT. ASSETS ($mill.)	OPER. PROFIT %	NET PROFIT %	RET. ON EQUITY %	RET. ON ASSETS %	CURR. RATIO	EARN. PER SH. $	CASH FL. PER SH. $	TANG. BK. VAL. $	DIV. PER SH. $	PRICE RANGE	AVG. P/E RATIO	AVG. YIELD %
p12/31/02	3,251.6	② 268.4	4,234.2	12.0	7.0	11.7	5.7	1.4	② 3.64	5.87	21.95	0.60	45.15 — 27.73	10.0	1.6
12/31/01	3,323.0	234.1	4,117.6	14.4	9.2	13.6	6.6	1.5	3.21	5.80	21.03	0.60	39.08 — 22.44	9.6	2.0
12/31/00	2,787.6	257.4	3,902.6	17.8	10.4	16.0	8.3	2.2	3.51	6.08	18.50	0.60	28.25 — 16.69	6.4	2.7
12/31/99	2,654.4	275.4	3,304.2	16.9	9.6	16.6	8.1	2.3	3.77	5.40	16.47	0.60	40.75 — 25.69	8.8	1.8
12/31/98	2,448.2	235.5	2,904.8	17.2	10.1	14.5	9.6	2.8	3.24	4.02	16.37	0.51	42.13 — 23.75	10.2	1.5
12/31/97	1,806.4	182.0	1,899.1	14.7	8.5	12.7	7.8	2.2	2.54	3.46	16.37	0.42	34.31 — 20.13	10.7	1.5
12/31/96	1,649.3	140.9	1,813.0	12.4	5.2	13.2	7.6	2.2	2.02	3.25	14.85	0.38	21.88 — 18.13	9.9	2.0
12/31/95	1,472.2	129.6	1,713.9	9.3	0.4	9.6	4.9	2.7	1.88	2.70	12.76	0.30	22.25 — 16.63	10.3	1.9
12/31/94	1,563.3	80.6	1,651.4	4.6				2.3	1.18				27.25 — 16.25	18.4	1.4
12/31/93	1,494.5	① 5.9	1,673.7				0.4	2.2	① 0.10	1.96	12.18	0.30	22.88 — 14.50	186.7	1.6

Statistics are as originally reported. ① Incl. net restruct. chrg. of $16.4 mill. ② Incl. a gain of $30.8 million on divest. of non-strategic businesses and other assets.

OFFICERS:
B. P. Collomb, Chmn.
B. L. Kasriel, Vice-Chmn.
P. R. Rollier, Pres., C.E.O.
L. J. Waisanen, Exec. V.P., C.F.O.

INVESTOR CONTACT: Investor Relations, (703) 480-3600

PRINCIPAL OFFICE: 12950 Worldgate Dr., Suite 500, Herndon, VA 20170

TELEPHONE NUMBER: (703) 480-3600
FAX: (703) 796-2214
WEB: www.lafargenorthamerica.com

NO. OF EMPLOYEES: 83,000 (approx.)

SHAREHOLDERS: 3,510 (record)

ANNUAL MEETING: In May

INCORPORATED: MD, Apr., 1977

INSTITUTIONAL HOLDINGS:
No. of Institutions: 138
Shares Held: 27,235,036
% Held: 37.3

INDUSTRY: Cement, hydraulic (SIC: 3241)

TRANSFER AGENT(S): Wachovia Bank of North Carolina, N.A., Boston, MA

LANDAMERICA FINANCIAL GROUP, INC.

EXCH.	SYM.	REC. PRICE	P/E RATIO	YLD.	MKT. CAP.	RANGE (52-WK.)	'02 Y/E PR.
NYSE	LFG	37.70 (2/28/03)	4.7	0.7%	$0.70 bill.	39.45 - 25.25	35.45

MEDIUM GRADE. GOING FORWARD, EARNINGS SHOULD CONTINUE TO BENEFIT FROM A FAVORABLE REAL ESTATE MARKET.

*7 YEAR PRICE SCORE 118.7 ***12 MONTH PRICE SCORE 120.1**
NYSE COMPOSITE INDEX=100

INTERIM EARNINGS (Per Share):

Qtr.	Mar.	June	Sept.	Dec.
1998	0.35	1.42	1.51	1.42
1999	0.73	0.86	0.48	0.70
2000	d0.30	0.97	0.43	d7.88
2001	0.36	1.54	1.01	0.32
2002	0.93	1.38	2.15	3.61

INTERIM DIVIDENDS (Per Share):

Amt.	Decl.	Ex.	Rec.	Pay.
0.05Q	2/20/02	2/27/02	3/01/02	3/15/02
0.05Q	4/25/02	5/29/02	5/31/02	6/14/02
0.07Q	7/24/02	8/28/02	8/30/02	9/13/02
0.07Q	10/23/02	11/26/02	11/29/02	12/13/02
0.07Q	2/19/03	2/26/03	2/28/03	3/14/03

Indicated div.: $0.28

CAPITALIZATION (12/31/01):

	($000)	(%)
Common & Surplus	727,493	100.0
Total	727,493	100.0

BUSINESS:

Landamerica Financial Group, Inc. is engaged in the business of issuing title insurance policies and performing other real estate-related services for both residential and commercial real estate transactions. The Company issues title insurance policies through its various title underwriting subsidiaries. As of 2/19/03, LFG served its residential and commercial customers from more than 700 offices and a network of 10,000 agents throughout the U.S., Canada, Mexico, the Caribbean, Central and South America. The Company's three principal title underwriting subsidiaries are Commonwealth Land Title Insurance Company, Lawyers Title Insurance Corporation and Transnation Title Insurance Company. The Company also offers a full range of residential real estate services to the national and regional mortgage lending community through its LandAmerica OneStop operation.

RECENT DEVELOPMENTS:

For the year ended 12/31/02, net income soared to $149.4 million from $60.3 million in the previous year. Results for 2002 included an after-tax charge of $8.7 million related to exit and termination costs associated with the residential appraisal operations, while results for 2001 included an after-tax charges of $34.0 million for intangibles and exit and termination costs. Total revenues climbed 19.2% to $2.59 billion from $2.17 billion the year before. Revenues included gains on the sale of investments of $1.3 million and $214,000, respectively. Total title and other operating revenues rose 19.5% to $2.53 billion from $2.12 billion a year earlier.

PROSPECTS:

Prospects for the first half of 2003 appear bright, reflecting near-record low mortgage rates and continued solid demand for the Company's real estate-related products and services. Meanwhile, despite an emphasis to control costs, the Company is continuing to pursue growth opportunities. On 1/7/03, LFG announced a joint venture with three agencies from Salt Lake City, Utah to create a title production center to serve the greater Salt Lake City area. On 2/3/03, LFG announced the acquisitions of New York Land Services, Inc. and Land Title Agency Inc. The transactions significantly enhances the Company's presence in the New York City commercial market

ANNUAL FINANCIAL DATA:

FISCAL YEAR	PREM. INC. ($mill.)	TOT. REVS. ($mill.)	NET INC. ($mill.)	TOT. ASSETS ($mill.)	TOT. INVST. ($mill.)	RET. ON REVS. %	RET. ON EQUITY %	RET. ON ASSETS %	EARN. PER SH.$	TANG. BK. VAL.$	AVG. YIELD %	DIV. PER SH.$	PRICE RANGE	AVG. P/E RATIO
p12/31/02	2,533.5	2,586.6	④ 149.4						④ 8.04		0.8	0.24	38.30 - 25.25	4.0
12/31/01	2,119.5	2,170.5	③ 60.3	1,707.5	1,009.0	2.8	8.3	3.5	③ 3.24	28.88	0.5	0.20	50.45 - 23.20	11.4
12/31/00	1,751.3	1,802.4	① d80.8	1,619.0	890.7	...	...	...	① d6.60	20.05	0.7	0.20	42.94 - 16.06	...
12/31/99	2,000.0	2,048.0	54.3	1,657.9	853.1	2.7	7.4	3.3	2.79	15.19	0.5	0.20	58.94 - 15.56	13.4
12/31/98	1,799.5	1,848.9	② 93.0	1,692.4	895.5	5.0	12.1	5.5	② 5.05	16.14	0.4	0.20	65.00 - 31.00	9.5
12/31/97	622.8	639.1	26.2	554.7	297.6	4.1	8.9	4.7	2.84	26.18	0.8	0.20	33.69 - 16.75	8.9
12/31/96	456.4	594.2	36.5	521.0	292.1	6.1	13.9	7.0	4.11	22.78	1.0	0.20	22.38 - 16.00	4.7
12/31/95	385.9	482.8	17.1	475.8	266.6	3.5	7.2	3.6	1.92	20.79	1.2	0.18	19.25 - 10.50	7.7
12/31/94	413.9	501.0	6.8	525.9	308.8	1.4	3.4	1.3	0.80	17.53	0.8	0.12	19.50 - 9.75	18.3
12/31/93	405.1	503.9	29.0	485.3	302.3	5.7	14.4	6.0	4.31	20.26	0.4	0.06	21.75 - 9.83	3.7

Statistics are as originally reported. Adj. for 3-for-2 stk. spl., 5/93 ① Incl. exit and termination costs of $3.1 mill. and write-off of intangibles of $177.8 mill. ② Incl. assimilation costs of $11.5 mill. ③ Incl. non-cash after-tax chrg. of $7.2 mill. ④ Incl. after-tax chrg. of $8.7 mill.

OFFICERS:
C. H. Foster, Jr., Chmn., C.E.O.
J. A. Alpert, Pres.
G. W. Evans, Exec. V.P., C.F.O.
INVESTOR CONTACT: G. William Evans, Exec. V.P., C.F.O., (804) 267-8114
PRINCIPAL OFFICE: 101 Gateway Centre Parkway, Richmond, VA 23235-5153

TELEPHONE NUMBER: (804) 267-8000
FAX: (804) 267-8833
WEB: www.landam.com
NO. OF EMPLOYEES: 8,981
SHAREHOLDERS: 1,381 (approx.)
ANNUAL MEETING: In May
INCORPORATED: VA, June, 1991

INSTITUTIONAL HOLDINGS:
No. of Institutions: 137
Shares Held: 14,825,106
% Held: 81.4

INDUSTRY: Title insurance (SIC: 6361)

TRANSFER AGENT(S): EquiServe Trust Company, N.A., Providence, RI

LA-Z-BOY INCORPORATED

EXCH.	SYM.	REC. PRICE	P/E RATIO	YLD.	MKT. CAP.	RANGE (52-WK.)	'02 Y/E PR.	DIV. ACH.
NYSE	LZB	17.75 (2/28/03)	10.8	2.3%	...	30.94 - 17.09	23.98	21 yrs.

INVESTMENT GRADE. THE COMPANY EXPECTS FOURTH QUARTER DILUTED EARNINGS IN THE RANGE OF $0.43 TO $0.48 PER SHARE.

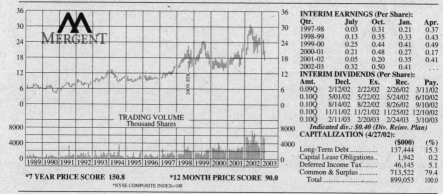

*7 YEAR PRICE SCORE 150.8   ***12 MONTH PRICE SCORE 90.0**
*NYSE COMPOSITE INDEX=100

INTERIM EARNINGS (Per Share):

Qtr.	July	Oct.	Jan.	Apr.
1997-98	0.03	0.31	0.21	0.37
1998-99	0.13	0.35	0.33	0.43
1999-00	0.25	0.44	0.41	0.49
2000-01	0.21	0.48	0.27	0.17
2001-02	0.05	0.20	0.35	0.41
2002-03	0.32	0.50	0.41	...

INTERIM DIVIDENDS (Per Share):

Amt.	Decl.	Ex.	Rec.	Pay.
0.09Q	2/12/02	2/22/02	2/26/02	3/11/02
0.10Q	5/01/02	5/22/02	5/24/02	6/10/02
0.10Q	8/14/02	8/22/02	8/26/02	9/10/02
0.10Q	11/11/02	11/21/02	11/25/02	12/10/02
0.10Q	2/11/03	2/20/03	2/24/03	3/10/03

Indicated div.: $0.40 (Div. Reinv. Plan)

CAPITALIZATION (4/27/02):

	($000)	(%)
Long-Term Debt	137,444	15.3
Capital Lease Obligations..	1,942	0.2
Deferred Income Tax	46,145	5.1
Common & Surplus	713,522	79.4
Total	899,053	100.0

BUSINESS:

La-Z-Boy Incorporated (formerly La-Z-Boy Chair Company) is one of the largest furniture manufacturers in the U.S. The Company is comprised of two business groups: upholstery and casegoods. The upholstery segment includes recliners, sofas, occasional chairs, reclining sofas and office and health care seating. The casegoods segment includes dining room tables and chairs, bed frames and bed boards, dressers, coffee tables and end tables manufactured using hardwood or hardwood veneer, as well as hospitality and assisted-living furniture. Brand names include LA-Z-BOY, ENGLAND, SAM MOORE, BAUHAUS, CENTURION, PENNSYLVANIA HOUSE, CLAYTON MARCUS, KINCAID, HAMMARY, ALEXVALE, AMERICAN DREW, LA-Z-BOY CONTRACT FURNITURE, AMERICAN OF MARTINSVILLE, and LEA. As of 2/11/03, LZB operated 310 La-Z-Boy Furniture Galleries® and 319 in-store galleries.

RECENT DEVELOPMENTS:

For the quarter ended 1/25/03, net income grew 6.9% to $23.2 million compared with $21.7 million in the equivalent 2002 quarter. Results for 2002 included a loss of $11.7 million on divestiture. Sales declined 6.1% to $510.5 million from $543.5 million a year earlier. The decrease in sales was primarily attributed to a decline in demand for the Company's casegoods segment and flat sales for the upholstery segment. Gross profit amounted to $118.3 million compared with $127.3 million in the prior year period. Operating income jumped 54.1% to $39.6 million from $25.7 million the year before.

PROSPECTS:

Looking ahead, the Company expects fourth quarter sales in the mid-single digit percentage range, excluding the effect of HICKORYMARK, and diluted earnings in the range of $0.43 to $0.48 per share. This is based on continuing consumer caution, weak retail sales, rising energy costs and geopolitical uncertainties. For the year ended 4/26/03, the Company expects diluted net income per share, before the cumulative effect of any accounting changes, to range from $1.65 to $1.70 with sales ranging from slightly reduced to flat.

ANNUAL FINANCIAL DATA:

FISCAL YEAR	TOT. REVS. ($mill.)	NET INC. ($mill.)	TOT. ASSETS ($mill.)	OPER. PROFIT %	NET PROFIT %	RET. ON EQUITY %	RET. ON ASSETS %	CURR. RATIO	EARN. PER SH. $	CASH FL. PER SH. $	TANG. BK. VAL.$	DIV. PER SH. $	PRICE RANGE	AVG. P/E RATIO	AVG. YIELD %
4/27/03												0.39	30.94 - 19.25		1.6
4/27/02	2,154.0	③ 61.8	1,160.8	4.5	2.9	8.7	5.3	3.0	③ 1.01	1.73	8.15	0.36	23.30 - 14.70	18.8	1.9
4/28/01	2,256.2	② 68.3	1,222.5	5.4	3.0	9.8	5.6	2.8	② 1.13	1.88	7.40	0.34	17.81 - 13.00	13.6	2.2
4/29/00	1,717.4	87.6	1,218.3	8.4	5.1	13.2	7.2	2.9	1.60	2.15	6.70	0.32	24.56 - 15.38	12.5	1.6
4/24/99	1,287.6	66.1	629.8	8.3	5.1	15.9	10.5	3.2	1.24	1.66	7.03	0.30	22.63 - 14.08	14.8	1.6
4/25/98	1,108.0	49.9	580.4	7.0	4.5	12.9	8.6	3.5	0.93	1.32	6.33	0.28	14.96 - 9.88	13.3	2.3
4/26/97	1,005.8	45.3	528.4	7.4	4.5	12.6	8.6	3.5	0.83	1.21	5.97	0.25	11.33 - 8.96	12.2	2.5
4/27/96	947.3	39.3	517.5	7.1	4.1	11.4	7.6	3.5	0.71	1.07	5.49	0.24	11.17 - 8.54	13.9	2.4
4/29/95	850.3	36.3	503.8	7.4	4.3	11.2	7.2	3.7	0.67	0.95	5.06	0.23	13.33 - 8.42	16.2	2.1
4/30/94	804.9	① 34.7	430.3	7.5	4.3	11.9	8.1	4.1	① 0.63	0.89	4.92	0.21	12.96 - 8.38	16.8	1.9

Statistics are as originally reported. Adj. for stk split: 200%, 9/98. ① Bef. acctg. change credit $3.4 mill. ② Incl. restruct. chrg. of $11.2 mill. ③ Incl. a loss of $11.7 mill. on divestiture.

OFFICERS:
P. H. Norton, Chmn.
G. L. Kiser, Pres., C.E.O.
D. M. Risley, Sr. V.P., C.F.O.

INVESTOR CONTACT: Gene M. Hardy, Sec., Treas., (737) 241-4414

PRINCIPAL OFFICE: 1284 North Telegraph Road, Monroe, MI 48162

TELEPHONE NUMBER: (734) 241-4414
FAX: (734) 241-4422
WEB: www.la-z-boy.com

NO. OF EMPLOYEES: 17,850 (approx.)

SHAREHOLDERS: 33,000 (approx.)

ANNUAL MEETING: In Aug.

INCORPORATED: MI, May, 1941

INSTITUTIONAL HOLDINGS:
No. of Institutions: 157
Shares Held: 27,585,625
% Held: 48.6

INDUSTRY: Wood household furniture (SIC: 2511)

TRANSFER AGENT(S): American Stock Transfer & Trust Company, New York, NY

LEAR CORPORATION

EXCH.	SYM.	REC. PRICE	P/E RATIO	YLD.	MKT. CAP.	RANGE (52-WK.)	'02 Y/E PR.
NYSE	LEA	37.98 (2/28/03)	8.2	...	$2.44 bill.	53.84 - 32.70	33.28

MEDIUM GRADE. THE COMPANY EXPECTS NEAR-TERM NET SALES TO BENEFIT FROM THE ADDITION OF NEW BUSINESS AND A STRONGER EURO.

*7 YEAR PRICE SCORE 116.1   ***12 MONTH PRICE SCORE 98.4**
NYSE COMPOSITE INDEX=100

INTERIM EARNINGS (Per Share):

Qtr.	Mar.	June	Sept.	Dec.
1999	0.75	1.10	0.58	1.37
2000	0.93	1.53	0.59	1.12
2001	0.23	0.69	0.35	d0.74
2002	0.70	1.27	0.91	1.76

INTERIM DIVIDENDS (Per Share):

Amt.	Decl.	Ex.	Rec.	Pay.
		No dividends paid.		

CAPITALIZATION (12/31/01):

	($000)	(%)
Long-Term Debt	2,293,900	59.5
Common & Surplus	1,559,100	40.5
Total	3,853,000	100.0

BUSINESS:

Lear Corporation is a worldwide supplier of complete automotive interior systems. The Company engineers, develops, manufactures and markets automotive interior products including seating systems, floor and acoustic systems, door panels, headliners, and instrument panels. LEA also is a supplier of automotive electronic and electrical distribution systems. The Company offers its customers design, engineering and project management support for the entire automotive interior. LEA's major customers include General Motors, Ford, DaimlerChrysler, BMW, Fiat, Volkswagen, Peugeot, Renault, Toyota and Subaru. The Company operates three reportable segments: Seating, Interior and Electronic and Electrical. In April 2002, LEA acquired a 29.0% stake in Hanyil Company Limited.

RECENT DEVELOPMENTS:

For the year ended 12/31/02, the Company reported income of $311.5 million, before an accounting change charge of $298.5 million, compared with net income of $26.3 million, respectively. Results for 2001 included net after-tax nonrecurring charges of $133.8 million and goodwill amortization of $90.2 million. Net sales advanced 5.9% to $14.42 billion from $13.62 billion a year earlier, reflecting higher vehicle production in North America and the addition of new business globally, partially offset by lower production levels in Western Europe and South America. LEA's cost of goods sold increased 4.6% to $13.16 billion from $12.59 billion the year before. Comparisons were made with restated prior-year results.

PROSPECTS:

The Company expects near-term net sales to benefit from the addition of new business and a stronger Euro. For full-year 2003, LEA estimates net sales of approximately $15.00 billion versus $14.42 billion in 2002. For 2003, LEA expects lower vehicle production in North America of 16.0 million units and essentially flat production in Western Europe at 16.0 million units. Given this industry outlook, the Company expects earnings in the range of $5.20 to $5.40 per share in 2003. Full-year capital spending is anticipated at approximately $300.0 million and free cash flow is estimated to be about $400.0 million.

ANNUAL FINANCIAL DATA:

FISCAL YEAR	TOT. REVS. ($mill.)	NET INC. ($mill.)	TOT. ASSETS ($mill.)	OPER. PROFIT %	NET PROFIT %	RET. ON EQUITY %	RET. ON ASSETS %	CURR. RATIO	EARN. PER SH. $	CASH FL. PER SH. $	PRICE RANGE	AVG. P/E RATIO
p12/31/02	14,424.6	⑥ 311.5							⑥ 4.65		53.84 - 32.70	9.3
12/31/01	13,624.7	⑤ 34.2	7,579.2	3.2	0.3	2.2	0.5	0.7	⑤ 0.52	6.53	42.40 - 22.60	62.5
12/31/00	14,072.8	④ 274.7	8,375.5	5.9	2.0	17.2	3.3	0.8	④ 4.17	10.13	36.25 - 19.25	6.7
12/31/99	12,428.8	③ 257.1	8,717.6	5.7	2.1	17.5	2.9	0.9	③ 3.80	8.83	53.94 - 28.75	10.9
12/31/98	9,059.4	115.5	5,677.3	3.8	1.3	8.9	2.0	0.9	1.70	4.93	57.75 - 29.81	25.8
12/31/97	7,342.9	② 208.2	4,459.1	6.6	2.8	17.2	4.7	0.9	② 3.05	5.75	51.69 - 33.25	13.9
12/31/96	6,249.1	151.9	3,816.8	6.0	2.4	14.9	4.0	0.9	2.38	4.67	39.25 - 25.25	13.5
12/31/95	4,714.4	② 94.2	3,061.3	5.2	2.0	16.2	3.1	0.9	② 1.79	3.60	32.50 - 16.63	13.7
12/31/94	3,147.5	59.8	1,715.1	5.4	1.9	28.0	3.5	0.8	1.26	2.49	22.13 - 16.00	15.1
① 12/31/93	1,005.2	d23.0	1,114.3	2.2	...	...	...	0.9	d0.65	...	...	...

Statistics are as originally reported. ① For six month period due to fiscal year change ② Bef. extraord. chrg. for early retire of debt. $1.0 mill., 1997; $2.6 mill., 1995. ③ Incl. restruct. credit of $4.4 mill. ④ Incl. gain of $36.6 mill. fr. sale of assets. ⑤ Bef. extraord. chrg. of $7.9 mill.; incl. restr. chrg. of $110.2 mill. and net non-recurring chrg. of $15.7 mill. ⑥ Bef. acctg. change chrg. of $298.5 mill.

OFFICERS:
R. E. Rossiter, Chmn., C.E.O.
J. H. Vandenberghe, Vice-Chmn.
D. C. Wajsgras, Sr. V.P., C.F.O.
INVESTOR CONTACT: Investor Relations, (800) 413-5327
PRINCIPAL OFFICE: 21557 Telegraph Road, Southfield, MI 48086-5008

TELEPHONE NUMBER: (248) 447-1500
FAX: (248) 447-7782
WEB: www.lear.com
NO. OF EMPLOYEES: 115,000 (approx.)
SHAREHOLDERS: 1,087
ANNUAL MEETING: In May
INCORPORATED: DE, Jan., 1987

INSTITUTIONAL HOLDINGS:
No. of Institutions: 248
Shares Held: 64,048,365
% Held: 97.4
INDUSTRY: Motor vehicle supplies and new parts (SIC: 5013)
TRANSFER AGENT(S): The Bank of New York, New York, NY

LEE ENTERPRISES, INC.

EXCH.	SYM.	REC. PRICE	P/E RATIO	YLD.	MKT. CAP.	RANGE (52-WK.)	'02 Y/E PR.
NYSE	LEE	32.05 (2/28/03)	16.6	2.1%	$1.42 bill.	40.09 - 28.90	33.52

UPPER MEDIUM GRADE. NEAR-TERM RESULTS ARE EXPECTED TO BENEFIT FROM IMPROVED ADVERTISING REVENUE AND CONTRIBUTIONS FROM ACQUISITIONS.

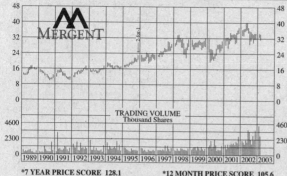

*7 YEAR PRICE SCORE 128.1   ***12 MONTH PRICE SCORE 105.6**
*NYSE COMPOSITE INDEX=100

INTERIM EARNINGS (Per Share):

Qtr.	Dec.	Mar.	June	Sept.
1997-98	0.36	0.28	0.40	0.33
1998-99	0.44	0.27	0.43	0.38
1999-00	0.68	0.27	0.36	0.36
2000-01	0.48	0.30	0.36	0.22
2001-02	0.41	0.30	0.69	0.43
2002-03	0.51	...	...	...

INTERIM DIVIDENDS (Per Share):

Amt.	Decl.	Ex.	Rec.	Pay.
0.17Q	1/23/02	2/27/02	3/01/02	4/01/02
0.17Q	5/16/02	5/30/02	6/03/02	7/01/02
0.17Q	8/05/02	8/28/02	8/30/02	10/01/02
0.17Q	11/14/02	11/27/02	12/02/02	1/02/03
0.17Q	1/22/03	2/27/03	3/03/03	4/01/03

Indicated div.: $0.68 (Div. Reinv. Plan)

CAPITALIZATION (9/30/02):

	($000)	(%)
Long-Term Debt	394,700	29.3
Deferred Income Tax	210,475	15.6
Common & Surplus	741,256	55.1
Total	1,346,431	100.0

BUSINESS:

Lee Enterprises, Inc. owns 38 daily newspapers and a joint interest in six others. The Company's 45 new newspapers have combined circulation of 1.1 million daily and 1.2 million Sunday in 18 states. The Company also owns weekly newspapers, shoppers and more than 175 classified and specialty publications. In addition, the Company's daily newspapers operate an expanding array of on-line services. As of 1/21/03, the Company owned 50.0% of the capital stock of Madison Newspapers, Inc. In fiscal 2002, revenues were as follows: advertising, 67.4%; circulation, 20.1%; and other, 12.5%.

RECENT DEVELOPMENTS:

For the three months ended 12/31/02, income from continuing operations rose 27.6% to $22.5 million compared with $17.6 million in the corresponding quarter of 2001. Earnings benefited from continued improvement in advertising revenue. Results for 2002 and 2001 excluded losses of $20,000 and $37,000, respectively, from discontinued operations. Total operating revenue was $170.5 million, up 58.9% from $107.4 million in the prior-year period. Adver- tising operating revenue jumped 65.7% to $118.8 million from $71.7 million, while circulation operating revenue leapt 64.6% to $33.6 million from $20.4 million in 2001. Other operating revenues rose 18.8% to $18.1 million from $15.3 million a year earlier. Operating income increased 44.2% to $40.1 million compared with $27.8 million the year before.

PROSPECTS:

The Company expects near-term results to continue to ben- efit from improved advertising revenue and strong perform- ances by the 16 newspapers it acquired in 2002. Going forward, the Company will continue to focus on driving revenue, improving readership and circulation, emphasiz- ing strong local news, continuing on-line growth and exer- cising strict control on costs. Separately, in 2003, the Com- pany began expensing employee stock option grants. This will reduce earnings per share for 2003 by about $0.05 to $0.07. In addition, LEE plans to restate prior years, which will lower previously reported annual 2002 results by $0.05 per share.

ANNUAL FINANCIAL DATA:

FISCAL YEAR	TOT. REVS. ($000)	NET INC. ($000)	TOT. ASSETS ($000)	OPER. PROFIT %	NET PROFIT %	RET. ON EQUITY %	RET. ON ASSETS %	CURR. RATIO	EARN. PER SH. $	CASH FL. PER SH. $	TANG. BK. VAL. $	DIV. PER SH. $	PRICE RANGE	AVG. P/E RATIO	AVG. YIELD %
9/30/02	525,896	⑤ 81,029	1,463,830	23.2	15.4	10.9	5.5	1.0	⑤ 1.83	2.62	...	0.68	40.09 - 28.90	18.8	2.0
9/30/01	441,153	③④ 59,457	1,000,397	19.5	13.5	8.7	4.3	1.9	③④ 1.35	2.08	8.42	0.68	37.60 - 26.94	23.9	2.1
9/30/00	431,513	③ 69,875	746,233	23.7	16.2	17.7	9.4	2.1	③ 1.58	2.51	1.42	0.64	31.56 - 19.69	16.2	2.5
9/30/99	536,333	67,973	679,513	21.8	12.7	19.2	10.0	1.3	1.52	2.40	...	0.60	32.25 - 26.13	19.2	2.1
9/30/98	517,293	62,233	660,585	21.8	12.0	19.5	9.4	1.0	1.37	2.19	...	0.56	33.88 - 21.81	20.3	2.0
9/30/97	446,686	② 62,745	650,963	23.3	14.0	19.6	9.6	0.4	② 1.33	1.95	...	0.52	30.50 - 22.25	19.8	2.0
9/30/96	427,369	① 53,670	527,416	22.2	12.6	16.5	10.2	1.5	① 1.12	1.79	1.51	0.44	24.50 - 19.00	19.4	2.2
9/30/95	443,188	58,459	559,929	23.3	13.2	18.8	10.4	0.9	1.24	1.80	...	0.44	23.13 - 16.75	16.1	2.2
9/30/94	402,551	50,854	474,701	23.7	12.6	21.0	10.7	1.4	1.09	1.59	0.16	0.42	19.13 - 15.75	16.0	2.4
9/30/93	372,907	41,236	482,317	21.8	11.1	18.5	8.5	1.5	0.88	1.41	...	0.40	17.50 - 13.50	17.6	2.6

Statistics are as originally reported. Adj. for 2-for-1 stock split, 12/95. ① Excl. $7.7 mill. income fr. disc. ops. ② Excl. $1.0 mill. income fr. disc. ops. ③ Excl. $13.8 mill. net income fr. disc. ops., 2000; $250.9 mill., 2001. ④ Incl. $15.8 mill. amort. of intang. and excl. $254.8 mill. gain fr. disc. ops. ⑤ Excl. $946,000 gain fr. disc. ops.

OFFICERS:
M. E. Junck, Chmn., Pres., C.E.O.
C. G. Schmidt, V.P., C.F.O., Treas.
G. Wahlig, V.P., C.A.O.
INVESTOR CONTACT: Dan Hayes, (563) 383-2163
PRINCIPAL OFFICE: 215 N. Main St., Davenport, IA 52801-1924

TELEPHONE NUMBER: (563) 383-2100
FAX: (563) 326-2972
WEB: www.lee.net
NO. OF EMPLOYEES: 6,700 (approx.)
SHAREHOLDERS: 2,830 (common); 1,868 (class B common)
ANNUAL MEETING: In Jan.
INCORPORATED: DE, Sept. 1950

INSTITUTIONAL HOLDINGS:
No. of Institutions: 170
Shares Held: 26,140,486
% Held: 59.0

INDUSTRY: Newspapers (SIC: 2711)

TRANSFER AGENT(S): EquiServe Trust Company, Jersey City, NJ

LEGG MASON, INC.

EXCH.	SYM.	REC. PRICE	P/E RATIO	YLD.	MKT. CAP.	RANGE (52-WK.)	'02 Y/E PR.	DIV. ACH.
NYSE	LM	49.23 (2/28/03)	18.0	0.9%	$3.17 bill.	57.15 - 37.11	48.54	19 yrs.

INVESTMENT GRADE. ASSETS UNDER MANAGEMENT CONTINUE TO INCREASE DUE TO MARKET APPRECIATION.

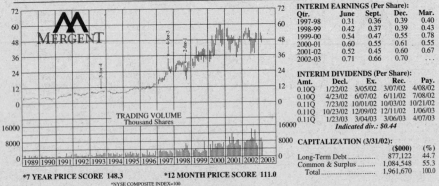

INTERIM EARNINGS (Per Share):

Qtr.	June	Sept.	Dec.	Mar.
1997-98	0.31	0.36	0.39	0.40
1998-99	0.42	0.37	0.39	0.43
1999-00	0.54	0.47	0.55	0.78
2000-01	0.60	0.55	0.61	0.55
2001-02	0.52	0.45	0.60	0.67
2002-03	0.71	0.66	0.70	...

INTERIM DIVIDENDS (Per Share):

Amt.	Decl.	Ex.	Rec.	Pay.
0.10Q	1/22/02	3/05/02	3/07/02	4/08/02
0.10Q	4/23/02	6/07/02	6/11/02	7/08/02
0.11Q	7/23/02	10/01/02	10/03/02	10/21/02
0.11Q	10/23/02	12/09/02	12/11/02	1/06/03
0.11Q	1/23/03	3/04/03	3/06/03	4/07/03

Indicated div.: $0.44

CAPITALIZATION (3/31/03):

	($000)	(%)
Long-Term Debt	877,122	44.7
Common & Surplus	1,084,548	55.3
Total	1,961,670	100.0

*7 YEAR PRICE SCORE 148.3   ***12 MONTH PRICE SCORE 111.0**

*NYSE COMPOSITE INDEX=100

BUSINESS:

Legg Mason, Inc. provides securities brokerage, investment advisory, corporate and public finance, and mortgage banking services to individuals, institutions, corporations and municipalities. As an investment advisor, the Company managed approximately $184.70 billion in assets as of 12/31/02. LM's mortgage-banking subsidiaries have direct and master servicing responsibility for commercial mortgages. For the fiscal year ended 3/31/02, revenues were derived as follows: investment advisory and related fees, 49.5%; commissions, 21.0%; principal transactions, 8.8%; investment banking, 6.5%, interest, 10.6%; and other, 3.6%. On 12/31/86, LM acquired Western Asset Management Co. On 5/26/00, LM acquired Perigee, Inc. During 2001, LM acquired Private Capital Management and Royce & Associates.

RECENT DEVELOPMENTS:

For the quarter ended 12/31/02, net income increased 16.5% to $47.9 million from $41.1 million the year before. Total revenues slid to $401.0 million from $403.8 million in the prior year. Investment advisory and related fees increased 3.8% to $215.9 million from $208.0 million a year earlier. Principal transactions revenues improved 5.2% to $39.8 million, primarily due to increased fixed income transaction volume. However, commissions revenues slipped 1.4% to $79.7 million due to a decrease in listed commission on retail trades, partially offset by an increase in annuity revenues. Investment banking revenues decreased 4.3% to $23.4 million as a result of a decline in corporate banking revenues, which more than offset higher municipal banking revenues.

PROSPECTS:

Going forward, LM should continue to benefit from increased investment advisory and related fees as a result of higher revenues at Western Asset Management, Royce & Associates and Private Capital Management. Assets under management, which were $184.7 billion as of 12/31/02, should continue to increase due to market appreciation. In addition, LM should benefit from an increase in total client assets, which aggregated $241.80 billion at 12/31/02.

ANNUAL FINANCIAL DATA:

FISCAL YEAR	TOT. REVS. ($mill.)	NET INC. ($mill.)	TOT. ASSETS ($mill.)	OPER. PROFIT %	NET PROFIT %	RET. ON EQUITY %	RET. ON ASSETS %	CURR. RATIO	EARN. PER SH.$	CASH FL. PER SH.$	TANG. BK. VAL.$	DIV. PER SH.$	PRICE RANGE	AVG. P/E RATIO	AVG. YIELD %
3/31/02	1,578.6	152.9	5,939.6	24.6	9.7	14.1	2.6	1.2	2.24	3.05	2.28	0.37	56.99 - 34.25	20.4	0.8
3/31/01	1,536.3	156.2	4,687.6	25.6	10.2	16.8	3.3	1.2	2.30	2.84	12.38	0.33	60.25 - 30.69	19.8	0.7
3/31/00	1,370.8	142.5	4,785.1	25.5	10.4	19.0	3.0	1.1	2.33	2.83	10.60	0.28	42.88 - 26.44	14.9	0.8
3/31/99	1,046.0	89.3	3,473.7	32.7	8.5	16.1	2.6	1.0	1.55	1.92	8.83	0.23	32.28 - 17.31	16.0	0.9
3/31/98	889.1	76.1	2,832.3	30.7	8.6	15.2	2.7	1.0	1.32	1.69	7.97	0.20	33.97 - 14.16	18.3	0.8
3/31/97	639.7	56.6	1,879.0	30.8	8.8	13.5	3.0	1.1	1.17	1.53	7.33	0.18	14.77 - 9.94	10.5	1.5
3/31/96	516.0	37.9	1,314.5	28.5	7.3	12.7	2.9	1.2	0.93	1.28	5.64	0.17	11.77 - 7.69	10.5	1.7
3/31/95	371.6	☐ 16.3	816.7	25.2	4.4	7.2	2.0	1.2	☐ 0.49	0.80	4.71	0.15	9.47 - 6.80	16.7	1.9
3/31/94	397.5	36.0	811.5	28.4	9.1	17.0	4.4	1.3	1.12	1.37	6.01	0.13	9.47 - 7.28	7.5	1.5
3/31/93	336.3	30.2	640.5	27.7	9.0	17.1	4.7	1.4	0.98	1.25	6.30	0.11	8.10 - 5.70	7.0	1.4

Statistics are as originally reported. Adj. for 2-for-1 split, 9/98; 4-for-3 split, 9/97; 5-for-4 splits, 9/93. ☐ Incl. $2.0 mill. ($0.06 sh.) pre-tax chg. for litigation.

OFFICERS:
R. A. Mason, Chmn., Pres., C.E.O.
C. J. Daley Jr., Sr. V.P., C.F.O., Treas.
R. F. Price, Sr. V.P., Sec., Gen. Couns.

INVESTOR CONTACT: F. Barry Bilson, Investor Relations, (410) 539-0000

PRINCIPAL OFFICE: 100 Light Street, Baltimore, MD 21202

TELEPHONE NUMBER: (410) 539-0000
FAX: (410) 539-8010
WEB: www.leggmason.com

NO. OF EMPLOYEES: 5,290 (approx.)

SHAREHOLDERS: 2,008

ANNUAL MEETING: In July

INCORPORATED: MD, 1981

INSTITUTIONAL HOLDINGS:
No. of Institutions: 224
Shares Held: 45,730,318
% Held: 70.6

INDUSTRY: Security brokers and dealers (SIC: 6211)

TRANSFER AGENT(S): First Union National Bank, Charlotte, NC

LEGGETT & PLATT, INCORPORATED

EXCH.	SYM.	REC. PRICE	P/E RATIO	YLD.	MKT. CAP.	RANGE (52-WK.)	'02 Y/E PR.	DIV. ACH.
NYSE	LEG	19.06 (2/28/03)	16.3	2.7%	$3.71 bill.	27.40 - 18.55	22.44	33 yrs.

INVESTMENT GRADE. THE COMPANY'S OUTLOOK REMAINS BRIGHT.

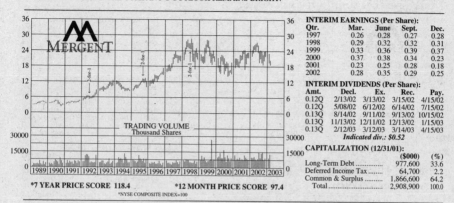

*7 YEAR PRICE SCORE 118.4   ***12 MONTH PRICE SCORE 97.4**

*NYSE COMPOSITE INDEX=100

INTERIM EARNINGS (Per Share):

Qtr.	Mar.	June	Sept.	Dec.
1997	0.26	0.28	0.27	0.28
1998	0.29	0.32	0.32	0.31
1999	0.33	0.36	0.39	0.37
2000	0.37	0.38	0.34	0.23
2001	0.23	0.25	0.28	0.18
2002	0.28	0.35	0.29	0.25

INTERIM DIVIDENDS (Per Share):

Amt.	Decl.	Ex.	Rec.	Pay.
0.12Q	2/13/02	3/13/02	3/15/02	4/15/02
0.12Q	5/08/02	6/12/02	6/14/02	7/15/02
0.13Q	8/14/02	9/11/02	9/13/02	10/15/02
0.13Q	11/13/02	12/11/02	12/13/02	1/15/03
0.13Q	2/12/03	3/12/03	3/14/03	4/15/03

Indicated div.: $0.52

CAPITALIZATION (12/31/01):

	($000)	(%)
Long-Term Debt	977,600	33.6
Deferred Income Tax	64,700	2.2
Common & Surplus	1,866,600	64.2
Total	2,908,900	100.0

BUSINESS:

Leggett & Platt, Incorporated is primarily engaged in the manufacture and distribution of metal stamping, forming, casting, machining, coating, welding, wire drawing, and assembly. The Company is an independent manufacturer of components for residential furniture and bedding; retail store fixtures and point of purchase displays; components for office furniture; non-automotive aluminum die castings; drawn steel wire; automotive seat support and lumbar systems; and bedding industry machinery for wire forming, sewing and quilting. Primary raw materials include steel and aluminum, followed by smaller amounts of chemicals, wood, and plastics. LEG's international division is involved primarily in the sale of machinery and equipment designed to manufacture LEG's MiraCoil innersprings. As of 1/29/03, LEG was composed of 29 business units and more than 300 facilities located in 18 countries.

RECENT DEVELOPMENTS:

For the year ended 12/31/02, net income advanced 24.0% to $233.1 million compared with $187.6 million in 2001 on essentially flat same location sales. The improvement in earnings was primarily attributed to reduced costs, increased market share and improved efficiency. Results for 2002 and 2001 included restructuring costs of $15.0 million and $18.0 million, respectively. Net sales climbed 3.8% to $4.27 billion from $4.11 billion a year earlier.

PROSPECTS:

Going forward, the Company plans to focus on improving its cost structure and pursuing additional market share. Moreover, the Company anticipates significant growth opportunities in its worldwide markets. LEG is predicting sales growth between zero and 5.0% for the full year and earnings per share in the range of $1.20 to $1.45. The Company completed eight acquisitions in 2002 that should add about $70.0 million to annual revenues. LEG also divested three firms, which will reduce annual revenue in the Aluminum Products segment by about $40.0 million.

ANNUAL FINANCIAL DATA:

FISCAL YEAR	TOT. REVS. ($mill.)	NET INC. ($mill.)	TOT. ASSETS ($mill.)	OPER. PROFIT %	NET PROFIT %	RET. ON EQUITY %	RET. ON ASSETS %	CURR. RATIO	EARN. PER SH.$	CASH FL. PER SH.$	TANG. BK. VAL.$	DIV. PER SH.$	PRICE RANGE	AVG. P/E RATIO	AVG. YIELD %
p12/31/02	4,271.8	③ 233.1							③ 1.17			0.49	27.40 - 18.60	19.7	2.1
12/31/01	4,113.8	③ 187.6	3,412.9	8.8	4.6	10.1	5.5	3.1	③ 0.94	1.92	4.81	0.47	24.45 - 16.85	22.0	2.3
12/31/00	4,276.3	② 264.1	3,373.2	11.4	6.2	14.7	7.8	2.9	② 1.32	2.18	4.58	0.40	22.56 - 14.19	13.9	2.2
12/31/99	3,779.0	290.5	2,977.5	13.2	7.7	17.6	9.8	2.9	1.45	2.19	4.50	0.35	28.31 - 18.63	16.2	1.5
12/31/98	3,370.4	248.0	2,535.3	12.7	7.4	17.3	9.8	2.8	1.24	1.87	4.59	0.30	28.75 - 16.88	18.4	1.3
12/31/97	2,909.2	208.3	2,106.3	12.4	7.2	17.7	9.9	2.5	1.08	1.62	3.88	0.26	23.88 - 15.75	18.3	1.3
12/31/96	2,466.2	① 153.0	1,712.9	12.3	6.2	16.3	8.9	2.6	① 0.84	1.34	3.37	0.22	17.38 - 10.31	16.6	1.6
12/31/95	2,059.3	134.9	1,218.3	11.5	6.6	18.4	11.1	2.5	0.80	1.19	3.45	0.18	13.44 - 8.50	13.8	1.6
12/31/94	1,858.1	115.4	1,119.9	10.9	6.2	18.5	8.4	2.3	0.70	1.04	2.90	0.12	12.38 - 8.31	14.9	1.1
12/31/93	1,526.7	85.9	901.9	10.3	5.6	16.7	7.8	2.6	0.52	0.80	2.46	0.14	12.53 - 8.19	19.9	1.3

Statistics are as originally reported. Adj. for stk. split: 2-for-1, 9/95 and 6/98. ① Bef. extraord. chrg. $12.5 mill. ② Incl. pre-tax chrg. of $6.2 mill. for plant closures. ③ Incl. nonrecurr. chrg. of 2002, $15.0 mill.; 2001, $18.0 mill.

OFFICERS:
F. E. Wright, Chmn., C.E.O.
D. S. Haffner, Pres., C.O.O.
E. C. Jett, V.P., Sec., Gen. Couns.

INVESTOR CONTACT: David M. DeSonier, V.P., (417) 358-8131

PRINCIPAL OFFICE: No. 1 Leggett Road, Carthage, MO 64836

TELEPHONE NUMBER: (417) 358-8131
FAX: (417) 358-8449
WEB: www.leggett.com

NO. OF EMPLOYEES: 32,000 (approx.)

SHAREHOLDERS: 16,356

ANNUAL MEETING: In May

INCORPORATED: MO, 1901

INSTITUTIONAL HOLDINGS:
No. of Institutions: 252
Shares Held: 118,894,119
% Held: 61.1

INDUSTRY: Mattresses and bedsprings (SIC: 2515)

TRANSFER AGENT(S): U.M.B. Bank, Kansas City, MO

LEHMAN BROTHERS HOLDINGS INC.

EXCH.	SYM.	REC. PRICE	P/E RATIO	YLD.	MKT. CAP.	RANGE (52-WK.)	'02 Y/E PR.
NYSE	LEH	55.37 (2/28/03)	16.0	0.9%	$12.80 bill.	67.33 - 42.47	53.29

INVESTMENT GRADE. IN JANUARY 2003, THE COMPANY ACQUIRED THE FIXED INCOME INVESTMENT MANAGEMENT BUSINESS OF LINCOLN CAPITAL MANAGEMENT.

TRADING VOLUME
Thousand Shares

*7 YEAR PRICE SCORE 153.2   *12 MONTH PRICE SCORE 105.2
*NYSE COMPOSITE INDEX=100

INTERIM EARNINGS (Per Share):

Qtr.	Feb.	May	Aug.	Nov.
1997-98	0.72	1.06	0.55	0.26
1998-99	0.79	1.05	1.10	1.14
1999-00	1.85	1.39	1.69	1.46
2000-01	1.39	1.38	1.14	0.46
2001-02	0.99	1.08	0.70	0.69

INTERIM DIVIDENDS (Per Share):

Amt.	Decl.	Ex.	Rec.	Pay.
0.09Q	1/25/02	2/13/02	2/15/02	2/28/02
0.09Q	5/03/02	5/13/02	5/15/02	5/31/02
0.09Q	8/03/02	8/13/02	8/15/02	8/31/02
0.09Q	11/03/02	11/13/02	11/15/02	11/30/02
0.12Q	1/24/03	2/12/03	2/14/03	2/28/03

Indicated div.: $0.48 (Div. Reinv. Plan)

CAPITALIZATION (11/30/02):

	($000)	(%)
Long-Term Debt	38,678,000	81.2
Preferred Stock	700,000	1.5
Common & Surplus	8,242,000	17.3
Total	47,620,000	100.0

BUSINESS:

Lehman Brothers Holdings Inc., with assets of $260.00 billion as of 11/30/02, is a holding company engaged in global investment banking. LEH provides services for institutions, corporations, governments and high-net-worth individual clients and customers. The Company provides debt and equity underwriting, merchant banking, strategic advisory services, foreign exchange trading, security trading and derivative and commodities trading. On 5/31/94, LEH was spun off from American Express Company and began trading on the New York Stock Exchange. Net sales for 2002 were derived as follows: Interest and dividends revenues, 69.9%; principal transactions revenues, 11.6%; investment banking revenues, 10.5%; commissions revenues, 7.7%; and other, 0.3%.

RECENT DEVELOPMENTS:

For the year ended 11/30/02, net income fell 22.3% to $975.0 million from $1.26 billion the year before. Earnings for 2002 included an after-tax one-time net gain of $23.0 million related to various items and an after-tax settlement charge of $56.0 million. Earnings for 2001 included an after-tax charge of $42.0 million associated with the loss stemming from the events of September 11. Total revenues declined 25.1% to $16.78 billion. Interest and dividends revenues decreased 30.1% to $11.73 billion, while principal transactions revenue dropped 29.8% to $1.95 billion. Investment banking revenue declined 11.5% to $1.78 billion. However, commissions rose 17.9% to $1.29 billion.

PROSPECTS:

The Company is expanding its asset management activities to focus on the strategic development of a comprehensive asset management platform. These responsibilities include LEH's recently established asset management initiatives, such as Lehman Brothers Alternative Investment Management, which is its joint venture with Ehrenkranz & Ehrenkranz, and its investment in the U.K.'s Edgeworth Capital. Separately, in January 2003, LEH acquired the fixed income investment management business of Lincoln Capital Management, which will become its U.S. institutional fixed income management platform for large institutional investors.

ANNUAL FINANCIAL DATA:

FISCAL YEAR	TOT. REVS. ($mill.)	NET INC. ($mill.)	TOT. ASSETS ($mill.)	OPER. PROFIT %	NET PROFIT %	RET. ON EQUITY %	RET. ON ASSETS %	CURR. RATIO	EARN. PER SH.$	CASH FL. PER SH.$	TANG. BK. VAL.$	DIV. PER SH.$	PRICE RANGE	AVG. P/E RATIO	AVG. YIELD %
11/30/02	16,781.0	⑥ 975.0	260,336.0	8.0	5.8	10.9	0.4	0.9	⑥ 3.47	6.64	34.74	0.36	69.90 — 42.47	16.2	0.6
11/30/01	22,392.0	⑤ 1,255.0	247,816.0	7.8	5.6	14.8	0.5	1.0	⑤ 4.38	7.44	31.96	0.28	86.20 — 43.50	14.8	0.4
11/30/00	26,447.0	④ 1,775.0	224,720.0	9.8	6.7	22.8	0.8	1.0	④ 6.38	8.71	29.19	0.22	80.13 — 30.31	8.7	0.4
11/30/99	18,989.0	1,132.0	192,244.0	8.6	6.0	18.0	0.6	1.0	4.08	5.75	22.75	0.18	42.78 — 21.91	7.9	0.6
11/30/98	19,894.0	736.0	153,890.0	5.3	3.7	13.6	0.5	1.0	2.60	3.84	19.04	0.15	42.50 — 11.31	10.4	0.6
11/30/97	16,883.0	647.0	151,705.0	5.5	3.8	14.3	0.4	1.0	2.36	2.72	16.51	0.12	28.25 — 14.25	9.0	0.6
11/30/96	14,260.0	③ 416.0	128,596.0	4.5	2.9	10.7	0.3	1.0	③ 1.62	2.01	15.97	0.10	16.25 — 10.31	8.2	0.8
11/30/95	13,476.0	② 242.0	115,303.0	2.7	1.8	6.5	0.2	1.0	② 0.88	1.34	13.38	0.10	12.31 — 7.25	11.1	1.0
⑪ 11/30/94	9,190.0	126.0	109,947.0	2.1	1.4	3.7	0.1	1.0	0.41	0.94	11.90	0.09	10.44 — 6.88	21.4	1.0
12/31/93	10,586.0	d291.0	80,474.0	0.3				1.2		3.04					

Statistics are as originally reported. Adj. for 2-for-1 stk. split, 10/00. ⑪ Results for 11 months only to reflect change in fiscal year to end 11/30. ② Incl. pre-tax restr. chgs. of $97.0 mill. & pre-tax gain of $79.9 mill. from the sale of Omnitel. ③ Incl. pre-tax $84.0 mill. severance costs. ④ Incl. a gain of $150.0 mill. fr. the sale of interest in an Internet company. ⑤ Incl. special chrgs. of $127.0 mill. rel. to the events of 9/11/01. ⑥ Incl. an aft.-tax settlement chrg. of $56.0 mill. & an aft.-tax one-time net gain of $23.0 mill. rel. to various items.

OFFICERS:
R. S. Fuld Jr., Chmn., C.E.O.
D. Goldfarb, Exec. C.F.O.

INVESTOR CONTACT: Shaun Butler, Investor Investor, (212) 526-8381

PRINCIPAL OFFICE: 745 Seventh Avenue, New York, NY 10019

TELEPHONE NUMBER: (212) 526-7000
FAX: (212) 526-3738
WEB: www.lehman.com

NO. OF EMPLOYEES: 12,343

SHAREHOLDERS: 22,677

ANNUAL MEETING: In April

INCORPORATED: DE, Dec., 1983

INSTITUTIONAL HOLDINGS:
No. of Institutions: 452
Shares Held: 171,557,705
% Held: 72.3

INDUSTRY: Security brokers and dealers (SIC: 6211)

TRANSFER AGENT(S): The Bank of New York, New York, NY

LENNAR CORPORATION

EXCH.	SYM.	REC. PRICE	P/E RATIO	YLD.	MKT. CAP.	RANGE (52-WK.)	'02 Y/E PR.
NYSE	LEN	53.99 (2/28/03)	6.6	0.1%	$3.50 bill.	63.97 - 43.20	51.60

UPPER MEDIUM GRADE. IN JANUARY 2003, THE COMPANY ACQUIRED A SOUTH CAROLINA HOMEBUILDER.

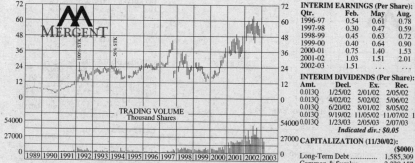

*7 YEAR PRICE SCORE 180.6   ***12 MONTH PRICE SCORE 108.9**

*NYSE COMPOSITE INDEX=100

INTERIM EARNINGS (Per Share):

Qtr.	Feb.	May	Aug.	Nov.
1996-97	0.54	0.61	0.78	0.19
1997-98	0.30	0.47	0.59	1.06
1998-99	0.45	0.63	0.72	0.95
1999-00	0.40	0.64	0.90	1.59
2000-01	0.75	1.40	1.53	2.32
2001-02	1.03	1.51	2.01	3.16
2002-03	1.51	...	...	...

INTERIM DIVIDENDS (Per Share):

Amt.	Decl.	Ex.	Rec.	Pay.
0.013Q	1/25/02	2/01/02	2/05/02	2/15/02
0.013Q	4/02/02	5/02/02	5/06/02	5/16/02
0.013Q	6/20/02	8/01/02	8/05/02	8/15/02
0.013Q	9/19/02	11/05/02	11/07/02	11/17/02
0.013Q	1/23/03	2/05/03	2/07/03	2/17/03

Indicated div.: $0.05

CAPITALIZATION (11/30/02):

	($000)	(%)
Long-Term Debt	1,585,309	41.6
Common & Surplus	2,229,157	58.4
Total	3,814,466	100.0

BUSINESS:

Lennar Corporation is a diversified national real estate company. LEN has homebuilding operations (94.2% of 2002 revenues) in 16 states and is a major builder of homes, building a variety of move-up and retirement homes. LEN builds homes under the LENNAR HOMES, U.S. HOME, GREYSTONE HOMES, VILLAGE BUILDERS, RENAISSANCE HOMES, ORRIN THOMPSON HOMES, LUNDGREN BROS., WINNCREST HOMES, SUNSTAR COMMUNITIES, DON GALLOWAY HOMES, PATRIOT HOMES, NuHOMES, BARRY ANDREWS HOMES, CONCORD HOMES, SUMMIT HOMES,

CAMBRIDGE HOMES, SEPPALA HOMES, GENESEE and RUTENBERG HOMES brand names. The Company's active adult communities are primarily marketed under the HERITAGE and GREENBRIAR brand names. LEN's financial services division (5.8%) provides residential mortgage services, title, closing and other ancillary services for its homebuyers and other customers. LEN's strategic technologies division provides high-speed Internet access, cable television and alarm monitoring services for Lennar homebuyers and other customers.

RECENT DEVELOPMENTS:

For the quarter ended 2/28/03, net income surged 47.9% to $106.3 million compared with $71.9 million in the equivalent 2002 quarter. Total revenues climbed 29.6% to $1.62 billion from $1.25 billion a year earlier, reflecting a

17.8% increase in home deliveries to 5,642 and a 10.0% year-over-year improvement in the average sales price. Total operating income advanced 42.6% to $222.7 million from $156.2 million the year before.

PROSPECTS:

On 1/30/03, the Company announced that it has completed the acquisition of Seppala Homes, which operates in the Greenville/Spartanburg, Charleston, Columbia and Myrtle Beach metropolitan areas. Seppala Homes delivered about 400 homes in 2002 at an average sales price of $104,000.

Seppala Homes currently owns or controls about 2,500 homesites. Separately, due to its solid backlog of $3.50 billion and assuming general economic stability, the Company expects earnings of about $8.50 per share in fiscal 2003 and about $10.00 per share in fiscal 2004.

ANNUAL FINANCIAL DATA:

FISCAL YEAR	TOT. REVS. ($mill.)	NET INC. ($mill.)	TOT. ASSETS ($mill.)	OPER. PROFIT %	NET PROFIT %	RET. ON EQUITY %	RET. ON ASSETS %	CURR. RATIO	EARN. PER SH.$	CASH FL. PER SH.$	TANG. BK. VAL.$	DIV. PER SH.$	PRICE RANGE	AVG. P/E RATIO	AVG. YIELD %
11/30/02	7,319.8	545.1	5,755.6	14.0	7.4	24.5	9.5	...	7.72	8.65	34.34	0.05	63.97 - 43.20	6.9	0.1
11/30/01	6,029.3	417.8	4,714.4	13.3	6.9	25.2	8.9	...	6.01	6.89	25.92	0.05	49.88 - 31.04	6.7	0.1
11/30/00	4,707.0	229.1	3,777.9	10.1	4.9	18.7	6.1	...	3.64	4.46	19.58	0.05	39.38 - 15.25	7.5	0.2
11/30/99	3,118.5	172.7	2,057.6	10.7	5.5	19.6	8.4	...	2.74	3.39	15.22	0.05	27.88 - 13.06	7.5	0.2
11/30/98	2,416.9	144.1	1,917.8	11.9	6.0	20.1	7.5	37.6	2.49	2.87	12.31	0.05	36.19 - 14.88	10.3	0.2
11/30/97	1,303.1	② 50.6	1,343.3	8.5	3.9	11.5	3.8	39.5	② 1.34	1.57	8.26	0.09	44.69 - 15.81	22.6	0.3
11/30/96	1,181.2	88.0	1,703.3	14.8	7.4	12.7	5.2	27.3	2.43	2.76	19.33	0.10	27.25 - 21.63	10.1	0.4
11/30/95	870.5	70.4	1,371.6	15.5	8.1	11.6	5.1	19.7	1.95	2.24	16.95	0.10	25.50 - 15.25	10.4	0.5
11/30/94	817.9	① 68.2	1,242.7	15.5	8.3	12.8	5.5	19.3	① 1.89	2.12	14.93	0.10	25.17 - 14.25	10.4	0.5
11/30/93	666.9	52.5	1,141.1	12.3	7.9	11.2	4.6	18.1	1.51	1.51	13.09	0.08	24.00 - 18.00	13.9	0.4

Statistics are as originally reported. Adj. for stk. split: 3-for-2, 4/94. ① Bef. acctg. change cr. of $961,000. ② Bef. inc. fr. discont. oper. of $33.8 mill. ($0.89/sh.).

OFFICERS:
L. Miller, Chmn.
R. J. Strudler, Vice-Chmn., C.O.O.
S. A. Miller, Pres., C.E.O.
B. E. Gross, V.P., C.F.O.

INVESTOR CONTACT: Investor Relations, (305) 559-4000

PRINCIPAL OFFICE: 700 Northwest 107th Avenue, Miami, FL 33172

TELEPHONE NUMBER: (305) 559-4000
FAX: (305) 227-7115
WEB: www.lennar.com

NO. OF EMPLOYEES: 9,419 (avg.)

SHAREHOLDERS: 1,600 (approx.)

ANNUAL MEETING: In Apr.

INCORPORATED: DE, Nov., 1969

INSTITUTIONAL HOLDINGS:
No. of Institutions: 290
Shares Held: 58,174,518
% Held: 89.7

INDUSTRY: Single-family housing construction (SIC: 1521)

TRANSFER AGENT(S): BankBoston, N.A. and EquiServe, L.P., Canton, MA

LENNOX INTERNATIONAL INC.

EXCH.	SYM.	REC. PRICE	P/E RATIO	YLD.	MKT. CAP.	RANGE (52-WK.)	'02 Y/E PR.
NYSE	LII	13.36 (2/28/03)	13.5	2.8%	$0.77 bill.	18.42 - 11.20	12.55

MEDIUM GRADE. IN 2003, THE COMPANY EXPECTS REVENUES TO BE RELATIVELY FLAT.

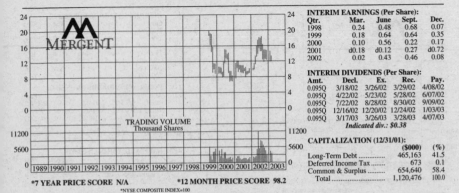

*7 YEAR PRICE SCORE N/A ***12 MONTH PRICE SCORE 98.2**
*NYSE COMPOSITE INDEX=100

INTERIM EARNINGS (Per Share):

Qtr.	Mar.	June	Sept.	Dec.
1998	0.24	0.48	0.68	0.07
1999	0.18	0.64	0.64	0.35
2000	0.10	0.56	0.22	0.17
2001	d0.18	d0.12	0.27	d0.72
2002	0.02	0.43	0.46	0.08

INTERIM DIVIDENDS (Per Share):

Amt.	Decl.	Ex.	Rec.	Pay.
0.095Q	3/18/02	3/26/02	3/29/02	4/08/02
0.095Q	4/22/02	5/23/02	5/28/02	6/07/02
0.095Q	7/22/02	8/28/02	8/30/02	9/09/02
0.095Q	12/16/02	12/20/02	12/24/02	1/03/03
0.095Q	3/17/03	3/26/03	3/28/03	4/07/03

Indicated div.: $0.38

CAPITALIZATION (12/31/01):

	($000)	(%)
Long-Term Debt	465,163	41.5
Deferred Income Tax	673	0.1
Common & Surplus	654,640	58.4
Total	1,120,476	100.0

BUSINESS:

Lennox International Inc. is a global provider of climate control services. LII designs, manufactures and markets products for the heating, ventilation, air conditioning and refrigeration markets. LII's products are sold under brand names including LENNOX, ARMSTRONG AIR, DUCANE, BOHN, LARKIN, ADVANCED DISTRIBUTOR PRODUCTS, HEATCRAFT, SERVICE EXPERTS, and others. LII also manufactures heat transfer products, such as evaporator coils and condenser coils. In addition, LII markets hearth products including pre-fabricated fireplaces and related products. The Company operates through five operating segments: Residential Heating & Cooling (39.9% of 2002 sales); Commercial Heating & Cooling (14.1%); Service Experts (30.2%); Refrigeration (11.6%) and Corporate and other (4.2%).

RECENT DEVELOPMENTS:

For the year ended 12/31/02, income amounted to $58.8 million, before an accounting change charge of $249.2 million, compared with a net loss of $42.4 million in 2001. Results for 2002 and 2001 included restructuring charges of $7.8 million and $65.3 million, respectively. Results for 2002 also included nonrecurring gains of $7.9 million. Net sales declined 2.8% to $3.03 billion from $3.11 billion a year earlier. The decline in sales was primarily attributed to soft demand from commercial customers for heating, cooling, and refrigeration equipment and services, partially offset by solid growth in LII's domestic residential businesses due to favorable weather conditions. Gross profit increased 4.1% to $951.7 million from $914.4 million in 2001. Operating income amounted to $125.6 million versus an operating loss of $696,000 the year before.

PROSPECTS:

Looking ahead, revenues for the full-year 2003 are expected to be relatively flat in 2003. However, earnings are anticipated to improve based on continued focus on cost reduction initiatives and the full-year effects of other actions taken in 2002. Earnings per share are anticipated to be in the range of $1.10 to $1.20. Continued strength in free cash flow is expected, with 2003 free cash flow approximately equal to net income.

ANNUAL FINANCIAL DATA:

FISCAL YEAR	TOT. REVS. ($mil.)	NET INC. ($mil.)	TOT. ASSETS ($mil.)	OPER. PROFIT %	NET PROFIT %	RET. ON EQUITY %	RET. ON ASSETS %	CURR. RATIO	EARN. PER SH. $	CASH FL. PER SH. $	TANG. BK. VAL. $	DIV. PER SH. $	PRICE RANGE	AVG. P/E RATIO	AVG. YIELD %
p12/31/02	3,025.8	② 58.8	1,521.7	…	…	…	…	1.3	② 1.00	…	…	0.38	18.42 - 9.67	14.0	2.7
12/31/01	3,119.7	① d42.4	1,794.0	…	…	…	…	1.3	① d0.75	0.71	…	0.38	12.15 - 7.56	…	3.9
12/31/00	3,247.4	59.1	2,055.0	4.9	1.8	7.9	2.9	1.5	1.05	2.55	0.06	0.28	15.13 - 6.81	10.4	2.6
12/31/99	2,361.7	73.2	1,683.7	6.6	3.1	12.2	4.3	1.9	1.81	3.22	4.53	0.18	19.88 - 8.88	7.9	1.3
12/31/98	1,821.8	52.5	1,153.0	5.9	2.9	14.0	4.6	1.6	1.47	2.69	6.22	…	…	…	…
12/31/97	1,444.4	d26.1	970.9	…	…	…	…	2.0	d0.99	0.22	8.22	…	…	…	…
12/31/96	1,364.5	54.7	…	7.4	4.0	…	…	…	1.62	2.64	…	…	…	…	…

Statistics are as originally reported. ① Incl. restruct. and impairment chrg. of $73.2 mill. ② Incl. restruct. chrg. of $7.8 mill. and nonrecurring gains of $7.9 mill., excl. an acctg. change chrg. of $249.2 mill.

OFFICERS:
J. W. Norris, Jr., Chmn.
R. E. Schjerven, C.E.O.
R. A. Smith, Exec. V.P., C.F.O.
INVESTOR CONTACT: Bill Moltner, V.P., Investor Relations, (972) 497-6670
PRINCIPAL OFFICE: 2140 Lake Park Blvd., Richardson, TX 75080

TELEPHONE NUMBER: (972) 497-5000
FAX: (972) 497-5292
WEB: www.lennoxinternational.com
NO. OF EMPLOYEES: 21,000 (approx.)
SHAREHOLDERS: 12,900 (approx.)
ANNUAL MEETING: In May
INCORPORATED: 1904; reincorp., DE, 1991

INSTITUTIONAL HOLDINGS:
No. of Institutions: 128
Shares Held: 27,550,077
% Held: 47.7
INDUSTRY: Refrigeration and heating equipment (SIC: 3585)
TRANSFER AGENT(S): Mellon Investor Services, South Hackensack, NJ

LEUCADIA NATIONAL CORPORATION

EXCH.	SYM.	REC. PRICE	P/E RATIO	YLD.	MKT. CAP.	RANGE (52-WK.)	'02 Y/E PR.
NYSE	LUK	33.62 (2/28/03)	23.8	0.7%	$1.86 bill.	40.27 - 27.62	37.31

MEDIUM GRADE. THE COMPANY CONTINUES TO EXPAND THROUGH STRATEGIC ACQUISITIONS.

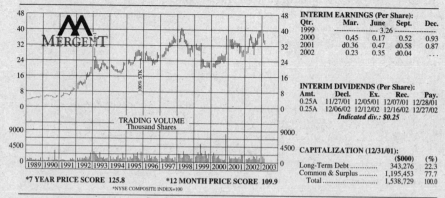

*7 YEAR PRICE SCORE 125.8   ***12 MONTH PRICE SCORE 109.9**
*NYSE COMPOSITE INDEX=100

INTERIM EARNINGS (Per Share):

Qtr.	Mar.	June	Sept.	Dec.
1999	------------ 3.26 ------------			
2000	0.45	0.17	0.52	0.93
2001	d0.36	0.47	d0.58	0.87
2002	0.23	0.35	d0.04	...

INTERIM DIVIDENDS (Per Share):

Amt.	Decl.	Ex.	Rec.	Pay.
0.25A	11/27/01	12/05/01	12/07/01	12/28/01
0.25A	12/06/02	12/12/02	12/16/02	12/27/02

Indicated div.: $0.25

CAPITALIZATION (12/31/01):

	($000)	(%)
Long-Term Debt	343,276	22.3
Common & Surplus	1,195,453	77.7
Total	1,538,729	100.0

BUSINESS:

Leucadia National Corporation, as of 11/13/02, is a holding company engaged in a variety of businesses, including banking and lending, principally through American Investment Bank, N.A.; manufacturing, through its plastics division; winery operations, real estate activities, and development of a copper mine, through its 72.8% interest in MK Gold Company; and property and casualty insurance and reinsurance. The Company also currently has equity interests of more than 5.0% in the following domestic public companies: AmeriKing, Inc. (6.8%), Carmike Cinemas, Inc. (11.1%); GFSI Holdings, Inc. (6.9%), Jackson Products, Inc. (8.8%), Jordan Industries, Inc. (10.1%), and WilTel Communications Group, Inc. (47.4%). Net sales for 2001 were derived as follows: finance, 30.6%; manufacturing, 14.5%; and investment and other income, 54.9%. In December 2001, LUK liquidated its Empire Group's property and casualty insurance operations.

RECENT DEVELOPMENTS:

For the quarter ended 9/30/02, LUK reported a net loss of $2.5 million versus a loss from continuing operations of $25.0 million in the prior-year quarter. Results included a gain of $21.8 million in 2002 and a loss of $77.0 million in 2001, respectively, from equity in associated companies.

Results also included net securities losses of $13.8 million in 2002 and net securities gains of $10.5 million in 2001. Results for 2001 excluded a loss of $7.0 million from discontinued operations. Revenues surged to $74.2 million from $36.7 million in 2001.

PROSPECTS:

The Company continues to expand through strategic acquisitions. For instance, on 1/6/03, LUK entered into an agreement to acquire over 80.% of the outstanding common stock of WebLink Wireless, Inc. Additionally, LUK acquired over 94.0% of WebLink outstanding secured notes. WebLink owns and operates a state of the art nationwide ReFLEX network that supports over 1.0 million customers throughout the U.S., with roaming partners in Canada, Mexico, the Caribbean, and Central and South America. Separately, on 12/2/02, LUK acquired 44.0% of the outstanding equity of WilTel Communications Group, Inc. in a transaction valued at $330.0 million.

ANNUAL FINANCIAL DATA:

FISCAL YEAR	PREM. INC. ($mill.)	TOT. REVS. ($mill.)	NET INC. ($mill.)	TOT. ASSETS ($mill.)	TOT. INVST. ($mill.)	RET. ON REVS. %	RET. ON EQUITY %	RET. ON ASSETS %	EARN. PER SH.$	TANG. BK. VAL.$	AVG. YIELD %	DIV. PER SH.$	PRICE RANGE	AVG. P/E RATIO
⑤ 12/31/01	...	375.3	②③ 64.8	2,577.2	1,165.1	17.3	5.4	2.5	②③ 1.17	21.61	0.8	0.25	35.70 — 26.31	26.5
12/31/00	108.5	715.5	① 115.0	3,143.6	1,253.0	16.1	9.6	3.7	① 2.07	21.78	0.9	0.25	37.50 — 20.63	14.0
12/31/99	145.2	706.6	①② 193.4	3,070.2	1,244.5	27.4	17.2	6.3	①② 3.26	19.75	50.8	13.58	33.38 — 20.13	8.2
12/31/98	228.6	530.5	② 46.2	3,959.0	1,942.6	8.7	2.5	1.2	② 0.73	29.90	...	0.25	41.13 — 26.25	46.1
④ 12/31/97	280.0	643.5	①② d22.6	4,500.4	2,163.7	...	...	...	①② d0.36	36.63	0.8	0.25	36.63 — 25.75	...
12/31/96	1,002.4	1,506.6	① 55.5	5,193.9	2,996.5	3.7	5.0	1.1	① 0.91	18.51	1.0	0.25	29.00 — 21.63	27.8
12/31/95	982.4	1,558.3	107.5	5,107.9	3,064.6	6.9	9.7	2.1	1.81	18.47	1.0	0.25	29.63 — 21.44	14.1
12/31/94	918.9	1,384.4	70.8	4,674.0	2,651.0	5.1	8.0	1.5	1.22	15.72	0.6	0.13	23.13 — 17.31	16.6
12/31/93	893.9	1,408.1	116.3	4,689.3	2,778.8	8.3	12.8	2.5	1.98	16.27	0.6	0.13	25.63 — 18.00	11.0
12/31/92	932.9	1,573.0	130.6	4,330.6	2,749.7	8.3	21.1	3.0	2.68	11.06	0.7	0.10	20.50 — 9.16	5.5

Statistics are as originally reported. Adj. for 2-for-1 stk. split, 11/95 & 1/93 ① Bef. extraord. gain, 2000, $983,000; loss, 1999, $2.6 million, 1997, $2.1 million, 1996, $6.8 mill. ② Bef. gain from disc. opers., 2001, $72.7 mill.; 1999, $24.2 mill.; 1998, $8.1 mill.; 1997, $686.5 mill. ③ Bef. acctg. credit of $411,000. ④ Reflects the sale of the Colonial Penn insurance companies. ⑤ Refl. liquidation of the Empire Group's prop. & cas. insur. opers.

OFFICERS:
I. M. Cumming, Chmn.
J. S. Steinberg, Pres.
J. A. Orlando, V.P., C.F.O.
INVESTOR CONTACT: Laura Ulbrandth, Investor Relations, (212) 460-1900
PRINCIPAL OFFICE: 315 Park Avenue South, New York, NY 10010-3607

TELEPHONE NUMBER: (212) 460-1900
FAX: (212) 598-4869
WEB: www.leucadia-nyc.com
NO. OF EMPLOYEES: 1,066
SHAREHOLDERS: 3,148 (approx.)
ANNUAL MEETING: In June
INCORPORATED: NY, 1968

INSTITUTIONAL HOLDINGS:
No. of Institutions: 149
Shares Held: 21,739,543
% Held: 39.3
INDUSTRY: National commercial banks (SIC: 6021)
TRANSFER AGENT(S): American Stock Transfer & Trust Company, New York, NY

LEXMARK INTERNATIONAL, INC.

EXCH.	SYM.	REC. PRICE	P/E RATIO	YLD.	MKT. CAP.	RANGE (52-WK.)	'02 Y/E PR.
NYSE	LXK	62.41 (2/28/03)	22.3	...	$8.14 bill.	69.50 - 41.94	60.50

UPPER MEDIUM GRADE. COST-CONTROL INITIATIVES ARE BEING IMPLEMENTED TO HELP OFFSET SLUGGISH CORPORATE AND CONSUMER SPENDING AND INCREASED COMPETITION.

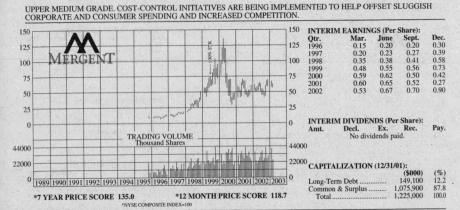

INTERIM EARNINGS (Per Share):

Qtr.	Mar.	June	Sept.	Dec.
1996	0.15	0.20	0.20	0.30
1997	0.20	0.23	0.27	0.39
1998	0.35	0.38	0.41	0.58
1999	0.48	0.55	0.56	0.73
2000	0.59	0.62	0.50	0.42
2001	0.60	0.65	0.52	0.27
2002	0.53	0.67	0.70	0.90

INTERIM DIVIDENDS (Per Share):

Amt.	Decl.	Ex.	Rec.	Pay.
		No dividends paid.		

CAPITALIZATION (12/31/01):

	($000)	(%)
Long-Term Debt	149,100	12.2
Common & Surplus	1,075,900	87.8
Total	1,225,000	100.0

*7 YEAR PRICE SCORE 135.0   ***12 MONTH PRICE SCORE 118.7**

*NYSE COMPOSITE INDEX=100

BUSINESS:

Lexmark International, Inc. (formerly Lexmark International Group, Inc.) is a global developer, manufacturer and supplier of laser and inkjet printers and associated consumable supplies for the office and home markets. The Company also sells dot matrix printers for printing single and multi-part forms by business users. In addition, LXK develops, manufactures and markets a broad line of other office imaging products, including supplies for IBM-branded printers, aftermarket supplies for original equipment manufacturer products, and typewriters and typewriter supplies that are sold under the IBM trademark. The Company sells its products to dealers, retailers and distributors in over 150 countries in North and South America, Europe, the Middle East, Africa, Asia, the Pacific Rim and the Caribbean.

RECENT DEVELOPMENTS:

For the twelve months ended 12/31/02, net earnings totaled $366.7 million compared with $273.6 million in the corresponding period a year earlier. Results for 2002 included a pre-tax gain of $5.9 million from the reversal of a restructuring charge, while results for 2001 included a $58.4 million pre-tax restructuring charge. Revenue grew 6.1% to $4.36 billion from $4.10 billion the year before. Laser and inkjet supplies revenue climbed 19.3% to $2.34 billion from $1.96 billion the year before, while laser and inkjet printer revenue rose 0.5% to $1.63 billion from $1.62 billion the previous year. Gross profit was $1.37 billion, or 31.5% of revenue, versus $1.24 billion, or 30.2% of revenue, the prior year. Operating income advanced 49.8% to $510.8 million from $341.0 million in 2001.

PROSPECTS:

The Company is taking steps to control costs in an effort to offset sluggish corporate and consumer spending and increased competition. LXK is projecting low to mid-single digit revenue growth in the first quarter of 2003, while earnings are expected to range between $0.62 and $0.72 per share. Meanwhile, the Company anticipates capital expenditures of about $125.0 million in 2003, up from approximately $112.0 million spent in 2002. These expenditures, primarily for infrastructure support and new product development, will mainly be funded through cash from operations.

ANNUAL FINANCIAL DATA:

FISCAL YEAR	TOT. REVS. ($mill.)	NET INC. ($mill.)	TOT. ASSETS ($mill.)	OPER. PROFIT %	NET PROFIT %	RET. ON EQUITY %	RET. ON ASSETS %	CURR. RATIO	EARN. PER SH. $	CASH FL. PER SH. $	TANG. BK. VAL. $	PRICE RANGE	AVG. P/E RATIO
p12/31/02	4,356.4	②366.7	2,449.9	8.2	6.6	25.4	11.2	1.6	②2.79		8.25	69.50 - 41.94	20.0
12/31/01	4,142.8	②273.6	2,073.2	8.2	6.6	25.4	11.2	1.6	②2.05	2.98	8.25	70.75 - 40.81	27.2
12/31/00	3,807.0	②285.4	2,073.2	10.9	7.5	36.7	13.8	1.3	②2.13	2.80	7.89	135.88 - 28.75	38.6
12/31/99	3,452.3	318.5	1,702.6	13.8	9.2	48.3	18.7	1.5	2.32	2.90	6.42	104.00 - 42.09	31.5
12/31/98	3,020.6	243.0	1,483.4	12.7	8.0	42.0	16.4	1.7	1.70	2.23	4.41	51.00 - 17.50	20.1
12/31/97	2,493.5	①163.0	1,208.2	11.0	6.5	32.6	13.5	1.4	①1.08	1.60	3.71	18.63 - 9.56	13.0
12/31/96	2,377.6	127.8	1,221.5	9.7	5.4	23.7	10.5	1.8	0.84	1.29	3.72	13.88 - 6.69	12.2
12/31/95	2,157.8	①48.1	1,142.9	5.0	2.2	12.3	4.2	1.5	①0.32	0.98	2.78	11.19 - 7.75	29.6
12/31/94	1,852.3	44.6	960.9	6.2	2.4	15.1	4.6	1.7	d0.23	0.80	1.90	... ...	...
12/31/93	1,675.7	d9.4	1,215.0	4.2	...	...	...	1.7	d0.17	0.96	...	... ...	...

Statistics are as originally reported. Adj. for 2-for-1 stk. split, 6/99. ① Bef. $14 mil ($0.10/sh) net extraord. loss, 1997; & $6.4 mil ($0.11/sh) loss, 1995. ② Incl. $5.9 mil pre-tax gain fr. restr. chg. reversal, 2002; $88.0 mil pre-tax non-recur. chg. related to restr. and inventory write-offs, 2001; $41.3 mil ($0.22/sh) pre-tax restr. chg., 2000.

OFFICERS:
P. J. Curlander, Chmn., C.E.O.
G. E. Morin, Exec. V.P., C.F.O.
K. M. Braun, Treas.
INVESTOR CONTACT: Mark D. Sisk, (859) 232-5934
PRINCIPAL OFFICE: One Lexmark Centre Drive, Lexington, KY 40550

TELEPHONE NUMBER: (859) 232-2000
FAX: (859) 232-3120
WEB: www.lexmark.com
NO. OF EMPLOYEES: 12,700 (approx.)
SHAREHOLDERS: 1,911
ANNUAL MEETING: In Apr.
INCORPORATED: DE, 1990

INSTITUTIONAL HOLDINGS:
No. of Institutions: 395
Shares Held: 128,848,324
% Held: 92.3
INDUSTRY: Computer peripheral equipment, nec (SIC: 3577)
TRANSFER AGENT(S): Mellon Investor Services, Ridgefield Park, NJ

LIBERTY PROPERTY TRUST

EXCH.	SYM.	REC. PRICE	P/E RATIO	YLD.	MKT. CAP.	RANGE (52-WK.)	'02 Y/E PR.
NYSE	LRY	31.22 (2/28/03)	15.9	7.7%	$2.30 bill.	35.40 - 26.05	31.94

MEDIUM GRADE. OPERATING RESULTS ARE BEING ADVERSELY AFFECTED BY THE OVERALL WEAKNESS OF THE REAL ESTATE MARKET.

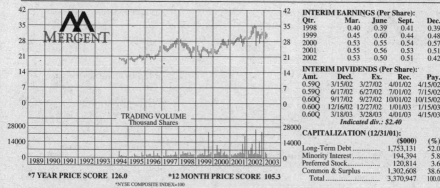

*7 YEAR PRICE SCORE 126.0   ***12 MONTH PRICE SCORE 105.3**

*NYSE COMPOSITE INDEX=100

INTERIM EARNINGS (Per Share):

Qtr.	Mar.	June	Sept.	Dec.
1998	0.40	0.39	0.41	0.39
1999	0.45	0.60	0.44	0.48
2000	0.53	0.55	0.54	0.57
2001	0.55	0.56	0.53	0.51
2002	0.53	0.50	0.51	0.42

INTERIM DIVIDENDS (Per Share):

Amt.	Decl.	Ex.	Rec.	Pay.
0.59Q	3/15/02	3/27/02	4/01/02	4/15/02
0.59Q	6/17/02	6/27/02	7/01/02	7/15/02
0.60Q	9/17/02	9/27/02	10/01/02	10/15/02
0.60Q	12/16/02	12/27/02	1/01/03	1/15/03
0.60Q	3/18/03	3/28/03	4/01/03	4/15/03

Indicated div.: $2.40

CAPITALIZATION (12/31/01):

	($000)	(%)
Long-Term Debt	1,753,131	52.0
Minority Interest	194,394	5.8
Preferred Stock	120,814	3.6
Common & Surplus	1,302,608	38.6
Total	3,370,947	100.0

BUSINESS:

Liberty Property Trust is a self-administered and self-managed Maryland real estate investment trust company. LRY provides leasing, property management, development, acquisition, construction management, design management and other related services for a portfolio of industrial and office properties. The Company has properties in Pennsylvania, New Jersey, Virginia, the Carolinas, Florida, Michigan, Maryland, Minnesota, and the United Kingdom. As of 12/31/02, LRY owned or held an interest in 652 industrial and office properties totaling about 51.1 million of leasable square feet. In addition, LRY had nine properties under development.

RECENT DEVELOPMENTS:

For the year ended 12/31/02, LRY reported income of $154.2 million, before income from discontinued operations of $7.4 million, versus income of $165.0 million, before income from discontinued operations of $1.6 million, the prior year. Results included a loss on the sale of properties of $9.3 million in 2002 and a gain of $2.1 million in 2001. Total revenue grew 4.0% to $606.0 million from $582.9 million in the year-earlier period. Revenue for 2002 included equity in earnings of unconsolidated joint ventures of $255,000. Rental revenue increased 4.6% to $435.6 million from $416.5 million in 2001. Operating expense reimbursement rose 1.2% to $161.8 million. Funds from operations were $276.2 million, up 5.1% from $262.8 million the year prior.

PROSPECTS:

Operating performance is being adversely affected by the overall weakness of the real estate market, much of which is the result of the difficult economic climate in the U.S. At year end, LRY's in-service portfolio of 51.0 million square feet was 90.7% occupied, down from 94.1% at the end of 2001. Going forward, overall occupancy is likely to remain under pressure as new properties become recognized in LRY's in-service portfolio. In addition, given the challenging economic environment, further lease terminations may lead to flattening rental rates, additional supplies of sublease space, and fewer development opportunities throughout the year.

ANNUAL FINANCIAL DATA:

FISCAL YEAR	TOT. INC. ($mill.)	NET INC. ($mill.)	TOT. ASSETS ($mill.)	NET INC. +DEPR./ ASSETS %	RET. ON EQUITY %	RET. ON ASSETS %	EARN. PER SH.$	TANG. BK. VAL.$	DIV. PER SH.$	DIV. PAYOUT %	PRICE RANGE	AVG. P/E RATIO	AVG. YIELD %
p12/31/02	606.0	② 154.2					② 1.92		2.37	123.4	35.40 — 26.05	16.0	7.7
12/31/01	587.2	166.5	3,552.8	7.6	11.7	4.7	2.15	17.68	2.30	107.0	31.20 — 25.60	13.2	8.1
12/31/00	533.0	① 161.4	3,396.4	7.5	12.2	4.8	① 2.20	17.59	2.13	96.8	29.13 — 22.00	11.6	8.3
12/31/99	472.5	① 142.5	3,118.1	7.3	11.0	4.6	① 1.97	17.53	1.87	94.9	25.94 — 20.25	11.7	8.1
12/31/98	387.1	108.6	2,933.4	6.0	8.6	3.7	1.59	17.46	1.71	107.5	28.75 — 20.13	15.4	7.0
12/31/97	232.5	60.4	2,094.3	4.8	6.3	2.9	1.38	15.84	1.65	119.6	29.38 — 23.13	19.0	6.3
12/31/96	154.3	33.7	1,152.6	5.4	9.0	2.9	1.14	11.96	1.61	141.2	25.88 — 19.38	19.8	7.1
12/31/95	117.0	19.5	898.1	4.7	5.8	2.2	0.89	11.84	1.60	179.8	21.75 — 18.38	22.5	8.0
12/31/94	46.6	③ 3.2	603.0	1.9	1.4	0.5	③ 0.46	10.86	0.43	93.5	20.38 — 17.38	41.0	2.3
12/31/93	75.4	d7.6	413.6	...	...	...	...	...	...	...	...	...	...

Statistics are as originally reported. ① Excl. extraord. chrg., $2.1 mill., 12/00; $1.1 mill., 12/99; credit $52.7 mill., 12/94 ② Excl. income fr. disc. opers. of $7.4 mill.

OFFICERS:
W. G. Rouse III, Chmn.
J. P. Denny, Vice-Chmn.
W. P. Hanowsky, Pres., C.E.O.
G. J. Alburger Jr., Exec. V.P., C.F.O., Treas.
INVESTOR CONTACT: Jeanne A. Leonard, Inv. Rel., (610) 648-1704
PRINCIPAL OFFICE: 65 Valley Stream Parkway, Suite 100, Malvern, PA 19355

TELEPHONE NUMBER: (610) 648-1700
FAX: (610) 644-4129
WEB: www.libertyproperty.com
NO. OF EMPLOYEES: 355
SHAREHOLDERS: 1,296
ANNUAL MEETING: In May
INCORPORATED: MD, March, 1994

INSTITUTIONAL HOLDINGS:
No. of Institutions: 183
Shares Held: 61,725,459
% Held: 80.8
INDUSTRY: Real estate investment trusts (SIC: 6798)
TRANSFER AGENT(S): EquiServe Shareholder Services, Providence, RI

LILLY (ELI) & COMPANY

EXCH.	SYM.	REC. PRICE	P/E RATIO	YLD.	MKT. CAP.	RANGE (52-WK.)	'02 Y/E PR.	DIV. ACH.
NYSE	LLY	56.56 (2/28/03)	22.6	2.4%	$63.49 bill.	81.09 - 43.75	63.50	35 yrs.

HIGH GRADE. THE COMPANY IS REVIEWING ITS WORLDWIDE MANUFACTURING ACTIVITIES TO LOOK FOR AREAS TO IMPROVE OPERATING PERFORMANCE.

INTERIM EARNINGS (Per Share):

Qtr.	Mar.	June	Sept.	Dec.
1999	0.40	0.52	0.67	0.73
2000	0.77	0.61	0.71	0.70
2001	0.74	0.76	0.54	0.54
2002	0.58	0.61	0.63	0.68

INTERIM DIVIDENDS (Per Share):

Amt.	Decl.	Ex.	Rec.	Pay.
0.31Q	4/15/02	5/13/02	5/15/02	6/10/02
0.31Q	6/24/02	8/13/02	8/15/02	9/10/02
0.31Q	10/21/02	11/13/02	11/15/02	12/10/02
0.335Q	12/16/02	2/12/03	2/14/03	3/10/03

Indicated div.: $1.34 (Div. Reinv. Plan)

TRADING VOLUME
Thousand Shares

*7 YEAR PRICE SCORE 101.1   ***12 MONTH PRICE SCORE 107.2**
*NYSE COMPOSITE INDEX=100

CAPITALIZATION (12/31/01):

	($000)	(%)
Long-Term Debt	3,132,100	30.6
Common & Surplus	7,104,000	69.4
Total	10,236,100	100.0

BUSINESS:

Eli Lilly & Company discovers, develops, manufactures and markets pharmaceuticals and animal health products. Neuroscience products, (46.2% of 2001 sales), include PROZAC®, ZYPREXA®, DARVON®, PERMAX® and SARAFEM™. Endocrine products, (26.9%), include HUM-ULIN®, HUMALOG®, ILETIN®, ACTOS®, EVISTA® and HUMATROPE®. Anti-infective products, (6.5%), include CECLOR®, KEFLEX®, KEFTAB®, LORABID®, DYNABAC®, NEBCIN®, TAZIDIME®, KEFUROX®, KEFZOL® and VANCOCIN®. Animal Health products, (5.9%), include TYLAN®, RUMENSIN®, COBAN®, MONTEBAN®, MAX-IBAN®, APRALAN®, MICOTIL®, PULMOTIL® and PAYLEAN®. Cardiovascular products, (5.1%), consist primarily of REOPRO® and DOBUTREX®. Oncology products, (6.4%), include GEMZAR®, ONCOVIN®, VELBAN® and ELDISINE®, and other pharmaceutical products, (3.0%).

RECENT DEVELOPMENTS:

For the year ended 12/31/02, net income was $2.71 billion compared with income of $2.81 billion, before an extraordinary loss of $29.4 million, the previous year. The decline in operating results was largely due to lower PROZAC sales, coupled with increased costs associated with manufacturing improvements. Results for 2002 and 2001 included pre-tax acquired in-process research and development charges of $84.0 million and $190.5 million, respectively. Also, the 2001 results included asset impairment and other site charges of $121.4 million. Net sales decreased 4.0% to $11.08 billion from $11.54 billion the year before.

PROSPECTS:

In December 2002, LLY initiated a plan of eliminating about 700 positions worldwide in order to streamline its operations. Expenses associated with this plan will be recorded in the first quarter of 2003 and potentially in the second quarter as costs are incurred. Separately, as a part of LLY's on-going strategic review of its worldwide manufacturing activities, it is likely that decisions made in the first quarter of 2003 will result in the impairment of certain manufacturing assets, primarily in the U.S. However, this should not result in the closure of any facilities.

ANNUAL FINANCIAL DATA:

FISCAL YEAR	TOT. REVS. ($mill.)	NET INC. ($mill.)	TOT. ASSETS ($mill.)	OPER. PROFIT %	NET PROFIT %	RET. ON EQUITY %	RET. ON ASSETS %	CURR. RATIO	EARN. PER SH.$	CASH FL.PER SH.$	TANG. BK. VAL.$	DIV. PER SH.$	PRICE RANGE	AVG. P/E RATIO	AVG. YIELD %
p12/31/02	11,077.5	⑩ 2,707.9	19,042.0						⑩ 2.50			1.24	81.09 – 43.75	25.0	2.0
12/31/01	11,542.5	② 2,809.4	16,434.1	30.7	24.3	39.5	17.1	1.3	② 2.58	2.99	6.32	1.12	95.00 – 70.01	32.0	1.4
12/31/00	10,862.2	⑧ 3,057.8	14,690.8	32.8	28.2	50.6	20.8	1.6	⑧ 2.79	3.18	5.37	1.04	109.00 – 54.00	29.2	1.3
12/31/99	10,002.9	⑦ 2,546.7	12,825.2	33.6	25.5	50.8	19.9	1.8	⑦ 2.30	2.70	4.49	0.92	97.75 – 60.56	34.4	1.2
12/31/98	9,236.8	⑥ 2,096.3	12,595.5	29.2	22.7	47.3	16.6	1.2	⑥ 1.87	2.31	2.86	0.80	91.31 – 57.69	39.8	1.1
12/31/97	8,517.6	⑤ d385.1	12,577.4	28.9	...	...	...	1.3	⑤ d0.35	0.11	2.79	0.74	70.31 – 35.56	...	1.4
12/31/96	7,346.6	1,523.5	14,307.2	27.9	20.7	25.0	10.6	0.9	1.39	1.89	1.87	0.69	40.19 – 24.69	23.3	2.1
12/31/95	6,763.8	② 1,306.6	14,412.5	29.3	19.3	24.1	9.1	0.8	② 1.15	1.63	1.21	0.66	28.50 – 15.63	19.2	3.0
12/31/94	5,711.6	②③④ 1,185.1	14,507.4	29.2	20.7	22.1	8.2	0.7	②③④ 1.03	1.40	0.81	0.63	16.56 – 11.78	13.8	4.4
12/31/93	6,452.4	③ 491.1	9,623.6	10.1	7.6	10.7	5.1	1.3	③ 0.42	0.76	3.56	0.60	15.50 – 10.91	31.6	4.6

Statistics are as originally reported. Adj. for 2-for-1 stock split, 10/97 & 12/95. ① Bef. acctg. chg. of $10.9 mill. ② Bef. inc. fr. dis. ops. of $984.3 mill., 1995; $1.19 bill., 1994. ③ Incl. nonrecurr. chgs. of $66.0 mill., 1994; $856.0 mill., 1993. ④ Ref. divest. in the Medical Devices & Diagnostic bus. ⑤ Incl. net gain of $631.8 mill. & non-cash chg. of approx. $2.40 bill. ⑥ Excl. net gain of $1.6 mill. fr. disc. opers.; incl. pre-tax chg. of $127.5 mill. ⑦ Incl. net gain of $30.4 mill.; excl. net gain of $174.3 mill. fr. disc. opers. ⑧ Incl. net one-time gain of $214.4 mill. fr. sale of Kinetra. ⑨ Bef extraord. chrg. of $29.4 mill., incl. net chrgs. of $311.9 mill. ⑩ Incl. pre-tax acq. in-proc. R&D chrg. of $84.0 mill.

OFFICERS:
S. Taurel, Chmn., Pres., C.E.O.
C. E. Golden, Exec. V.P., C.F.O.
R. O. Kendall, Sr. V.P., Gen. Couns.
INVESTOR CONTACT: Terra L. Fox, Investor Relations, (317) 276-5795
PRINCIPAL OFFICE: Lilly Corporate Center, Indianapolis, IN 46285

TELEPHONE NUMBER: (317) 276-2000
FAX: (317) 276-6331
WEB: www.lilly.com
NO. OF EMPLOYEES: 41,100 (approx.)
SHAREHOLDERS: 57,700
ANNUAL MEETING: In Apr.
INCORPORATED: IN, Jan., 1901; reincorp., IN, Jan., 1936

INSTITUTIONAL HOLDINGS:
No. of Institutions: 799
Shares Held: 751,701,008
% Held: 66.9
INDUSTRY: Pharmaceutical preparations (SIC: 2834)
TRANSFER AGENT(S): Wells Fargo Share-owner Services, South St. Paul, MN

LIMITED BRANDS

EXCH.	SYM.	REC. PRICE	P/E RATIO	YLD.	MKT. CAP.	RANGE (52-WK.)	'02 Y/E PR.
NYSE	LTD	11.88 (2/28/03)	12.4	2.5%	$5.10 bill.	22.34 - 10.88	13.93

UPPER MEDIUM GRADE. NEAR-TERM EARNINGS ARE EXPECTED TO BE HURT BY CONTINUED WEAK ECONOMIC CONDITIONS.

TRADING VOLUME
Thousand Shares

*7 YEAR PRICE SCORE 113.2   *12 MONTH PRICE SCORE 83.3
*NYSE COMPOSITE INDEX=100

INTERIM EARNINGS (Per Share):

Qtr.	Apr.	July	Oct.	Jan.
1997-98	0.05	0.05	0.08	0.16
1998-99	0.14	3.47	0.09	0.54
1999-00	0.07	0.11	0.09	0.71
2000-01	0.14	0.17	0.11	0.54
2001-02	0.07	0.16	0.21	0.75
2002-03	0.10	0.16	0.03	0.67

INTERIM DIVIDENDS (Per Share):

Amt.	Decl.	Ex.	Rec.	Pay.
0.075Q	2/04/02	3/06/02	3/08/02	3/19/02
0.075Q	5/20/02	6/05/02	6/07/02	6/18/02
0.075Q	8/16/02	9/04/02	9/06/02	9/17/02
0.075Q	11/08/02	12/04/02	12/06/02	12/17/02
0.10Q	2/03/03	3/05/03	3/07/03	3/18/03

Indicated div.: $0.40 (Div. Reinv. Plan)

CAPITALIZATION (2/2/02):

	($000)	(%)
Long-Term Debt	250,000	7.9
Minority Interest	177,000	5.6
Common & Surplus	2,744,000	86.5
Total	3,171,000	100.0

BUSINESS:

Limited Brands (formerly The Limited, Inc.) operated 4,036 specialty retail stores as of 2/27/03. The Company's stores sell a wide variety of women's and men's apparel and personal care products under the names Victoria's Secret, Bath & Body Works, Express, Express Men's (Structure), Limited Stores, White Barn Candle Co. and Henri Bendel. As of 2/2/02, the Company owned approxi-

mately 24% of Galyan's Trading Co., which offers merchandise for sports enthusiasts. LTD spun off its interest in Abercrombie and Fitch Co. in May 1998, and Too, Inc., formerly named Limited Too, Inc., in August 1999. In August 2001, the Company sold its Lane Bryant, Inc. subsidiary. In November 2002, LTD sold its Lerner New York subsidiary.

RECENT DEVELOPMENTS:

For the 52 weeks ended 2/1/03, income from continuing operations totaled $496.2 million compared with income from continuing operations of $506.2 million in the corresponding prior-year period. Results for fiscal 2002 included a $33.8 million pre-tax non-recurring charge, partially offset by a one-time pre-tax gain of $6.1 million. Results for fiscal 2001 included one-time pre-tax gains totaling $232.1

million. Net sales were $8.44 billion versus $8.42 billion a year earlier. Comparable-store sales were up 3.0% year over year. Gross profit was $3.09 billion, or 36.6% of net sales, compared with $3.02 billion, or 35.8% of net sales, the previous year. Operating income slipped 6.5% to $837.9 million from $895.9 million the year before.

PROSPECTS:

Economic weakness and sluggish consumer spending are expected to persist over the near term resulting in a decline in earnings per share of between 10.0% and 20.0% during the first half of the current fiscal year. The Company anticipates full-year 2003 earnings per share in the range of flat

to an increase of 5.0%. Separately, LTD expects to remodel approximately 100 existing stores in 2003. The Company is focusing on expanding its Victoria's Secret store space, opening new Express locations, and decreasing the store size of its existing Limited clothing stores.

ANNUAL FINANCIAL DATA:

FISCAL YEAR	TOT. REVS. ($mill.)	NET INC. ($mill.)	TOT. ASSETS ($mill.)	OPER. PROFIT %	NET PROFIT %	RET. ON EQUITY %	RET. ON ASSETS %	CURR. RATIO	EARN. PER SH. $	CASH FL. PER SH. $	TANG. BK. VAL. $	DIV. PER SH. $	PRICE RANGE	AVG. P/E RATIO	AVG. YIELD %
p2/01/03	8,444.7	④ 496.2							④ 0.95			0.30	22.34 - 12.53	18.4	1.7
2/02/02	9,363.0	③ 519.0	4,719.0	9.8	5.5	18.9	11.0	2.0	③ 1.19	1.83	6.40	0.30	21.29 - 9.00	12.7	2.0
2/03/01	10,104.6	① 427.9	4,088.1	8.6	4.2	18.5	10.5	2.1	① 0.96	1.58	5.44	0.30	27.88 - 14.44	22.0	1.4
1/29/00	9,723.3	① 460.8	4,087.7	9.5	4.7	21.5	11.3	1.8	① 1.00	1.61	4.99	0.30	25.31 - 13.75	19.5	1.5
1/30/99	9,346.9	① 2,053.6	4,549.7	26.1	22.0	92.0	45.1	1.9	① 4.16	4.75	4.93	0.26	18.25 - 10.25	3.4	1.8
1/31/98	9,188.8	② 217.4	4,300.8	5.2	2.4	10.6	5.1	1.9	② 0.40	0.97	3.73	0.24	12.88 - 8.25	26.7	2.3
2/01/97	8,644.8	① ② 434.2	4,120.0	7.4	5.0	22.6	10.5	1.7	① ② 0.77	1.28	3.55	0.20	11.25 - 7.63	12.3	2.1
2/03/96	7,881.4	① 961.5	4,915.0	7.8	12.2	30.0	19.6	3.9	① 1.34	1.74	4.50	0.20	11.63 - 7.94	7.3	2.0
1/28/95	7,320.8	448.3	4,570.1	10.9	6.1	16.2	9.8	3.2	0.63	1.00	3.86	0.18	11.19 - 8.38	15.6	1.8
1/29/94	7,245.1	391.0	4,135.1	9.7	5.4	16.0	9.5	3.1	0.54	0.91	3.41	0.18	15.00 - 8.31	21.6	1.5

Statistics are as originally reported. Adj. for 2-for-1 stk. split, 5/00. ① Incl. $9.9 mil pre-tax chg., 2001; $34.5 mil pre-tax gain, 2000; $1.74 bil pre-tax gain, 1999; $118.2 mil ($0.21/sh) net gain, 1997; & $649.5 mil ($1.19/sh) gain, 1996. ② Incl. $123.8 mil net non-recur. chg., 1998; & $122 mil pre-tax chg., 1997. ③ Incl. $170.0 mill. pre-tax gain from the sale of Lane Bryant, Inc. & $62.1 mill. pre-tax gain from the initial public offerings of Alliance Data Systems Corp and Galyan's Trading Co. ④ Bef. $5.6 mil ($0.01/sh) gain fr. discont. opers. & incl $33.8 mil pre-tax non-recurr. chg. and $6.1 mil one-time pre-tax invest. gain.

OFFICERS:
L. H. Wexner, Chmn., Pres., C.E.O.
L. A. Schlesinger, Exec. V.P., C.O.O.
V. A. Hailey, Exec. V.P., C.F.O.
INVESTOR CONTACT: T. J. Katzenmeyer, Vice-Pres., (614) 479-7000
PRINCIPAL OFFICE: Three Limited Parkway, P.O. Box 16000, Columbus, OH 43216

TELEPHONE NUMBER: (614) 415-7000
FAX: (614) 479-7440
WEB: www.limited.com
NO. OF EMPLOYEES: 100,300 (approx.)
SHAREHOLDERS: 67,000 (approx.)
ANNUAL MEETING: In May
INCORPORATED: OH, 1963; reincorp., DE, June, 1982

INSTITUTIONAL HOLDINGS:
No. of Institutions: 336
Shares Held: 406,655,083
% Held: 77.7
INDUSTRY: Women's clothing stores (SIC: 5621)
TRANSFER AGENT(S): First Chicago Trust Company of New York, Jersey City, NJ

LINCOLN NATIONAL CORPORATION

EXCH.	SYM.	REC. PRICE	P/E RATIO	YLD.	MKT. CAP.	RANGE (52-WK.)	'02 Y/E PR.	DIV. ACH.
NYSE	LNC	28.33 (2/28/03)	60.3	4.7%	$5.02 bill.	53.65 - 25.11	31.58	19 yrs.

UPPER MEDIUM GRADE. THE COMPANY ANNOUNCED PLANS TO REALIGN ITS LIFE INSURANCE OPERATIONS.

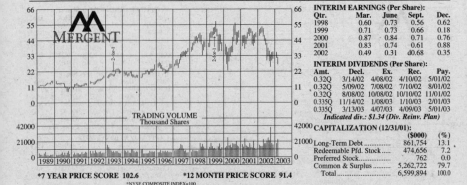

*7 YEAR PRICE SCORE 102.6   ***12 MONTH PRICE SCORE 91.4**

*NYSE COMPOSITE INDEX=100

INTERIM EARNINGS (Per Share):

Qtr.	Mar.	June	Sept.	Dec.
1998	0.60	0.73	0.56	0.62
1999	0.71	0.73	0.66	0.18
2000	0.87	0.84	0.71	0.76
2001	0.83	0.74	0.61	0.88
2002	0.49	0.31	d0.68	0.35

INTERIM DIVIDENDS (Per Share):

Amt.	Decl.	Ex.	Rec.	Pay.
0.32Q	3/14/02	4/08/02	4/10/02	5/01/02
0.32Q	5/09/02	7/08/02	7/10/02	8/01/02
0.32Q	8/08/02	10/08/02	10/10/02	11/01/02
0.335Q	11/14/02	1/08/03	1/10/03	2/01/03
0.335Q	3/13/03	4/07/03	4/09/03	5/01/03

Indicated div.: $1.34 (Div. Reinv. Plan)

CAPITALIZATION (12/31/01):

	($000)	(%)
Long-Term Debt	861,754	13.1
Redeemable Pfd. Stock	474,656	7.2
Preferred Stock	762	0.0
Common & Surplus	5,262,722	79.7
Total	6,599,894	100.0

BUSINESS:

Lincoln National Corporation operates multiple insurance and investment management businesses, divided into four business segments. The Lincoln Retirement segment (38.6% of 2002 revenues) provides fixed and variable annuities products to the individual annuities and employer-sponsored markets. The Life Insurance segment (38.5%) provides life insurance products designed specifically for the high net-worth and affluent markets. The Investment Management segment (8.6%) provides investment products and services to both individual and institutional investors. The Lincoln UK segment (6.0%) provides life insurance products in the United Kingdom. Corporate and other operations accounted for 8.3% of 2002 revenues. In January 1998, LNC acquired the individual life insurance and annuities business of CIGNA Corp. for $1.40 billion. On 12/7/01, LNC sold Lincoln Re for $2.00 billion.

RECENT DEVELOPMENTS:

For the year ended 12/31/02, net income was $91.6 million versus income of $605.7 million, before an accounting change charge of $15.6 million, the previous year. Results for 2002 included a charge of $208.5 million related to the sale of the reinsurance unit and a restructuring charge of $2.1 million. Results for 2001 included a gain on the sale of a subsidiary of $15.0 million and a restructuring gain of $24.7 million. Total revenue slid 27.3% to $4.64 billion from $6.38 billion the year before. Revenue from insurance premiums dropped 81.5% to $315.9 million from $1.70 billion a year earlier. Net investment income decreased 2.7% to $2.61 billion.

PROSPECTS:

Although earnings may continue to be hampered by weak equity markets, LNC's exposure should be somewhat mitigated by its commitment to produce positive net flows, grow deposits and premiums, enforce rigorous expense controls, and maintain effective capital management. On 1/29/02, LNC announced that it will realign its life segment operations in Hartford Connecticut and Schaumburg, Illinois to enhance productivity, efficiency and scalability. LNC expects to begin seeing some savings in the second half of 2003, with the bulk of the savings realized in 2004. As a result, LNC expects to reduce its operating and administrative expense run rate between $15.0 million and $20.0 million on a pre-tax basis.

ANNUAL FINANCIAL DATA:

FISCAL YEAR	PREM. INC. ($mill.)	TOT. REVS. ($mill.)	NET INC. ($mill.)	TOT. ASSETS ($mill.)	TOT. INVST. ($mill.)	RET. ON REVS. %	RET. ON EQUITY %	RET. ON ASSETS %	EARN. PER SH.$	TANG. BK. VAL.$	AVG. YIELD %	DIV. PER SH.$	PRICE RANGE	AVG. P/E RATIO
p12/31/02	...	4,635.5	⑤ 91.6						⑤ 0.49		3.3	1.28	53.65 - 25.11	80.4
12/31/01	1,704.0	6,380.6	①②④ 605.8	98,001.3	36,121.2	9.5	11.4	0.6	①②④ 3.05	14.11	2.7	1.22	52.75 - 38.00	14.9
12/31/00	1,813.1	6,851.9	① 621.8	99,844.1	35,375.0	9.1	12.5	0.6	① 3.19	11.06	2.9	1.16	56.38 - 22.63	12.4
12/31/99	1,881.5	6,803.7	① 454.6	103,095.7	35,604.2	6.8	10.8	0.4	① 2.30	5.59	2.4	1.10	57.50 - 36.00	20.3
12/31/98	1,620.6	6,087.1	509.8	93,836.3	37,948.3	8.4	9.5	0.5	2.51	10.16	2.5	1.04	49.44 - 33.50	16.5
12/31/97	1,328.7	4,898.5	③ 22.2	77,174.7	29,839.8	0.5	0.4	...	③ 0.11	19.38	3.1	0.98	38.56 - 24.50	300.0
12/31/96	3,182.0	6,721.3	513.6	71,713.4	34,066.2	7.6	11.5	0.7	2.46	15.97	3.8	0.92	28.50 - 20.38	10.0
12/31/95	3,253.8	6,633.3	① 482.2	63,257.7	31,942.0	7.3	11.0	0.8	① 2.32	16.20	3.9	0.86	26.88 - 17.31	9.5
12/31/94	4,444.1	6,984.4	① 349.9	49,330.1	27,068.2	5.0	11.5	0.4	① 1.69	13.68	4.2	0.82	22.19 - 17.31	11.7
12/31/93	5,356.8	8,289.8	①② 415.3	48,380.4	29,731.9	5.0	10.2	0.9	①② 2.03	18.75	3.7	0.76	24.13 - 17.34	10.2

Statistics are as originally reported. Adj. for stk. split: 2-for-1, 6/99 & 6/93. ① Incl. non-recur. chrg. $24.6 mill., 12/01; $80.2 mill., 12/00; $18.9 mill., 12/99; credit $54.2 mill., 12/95; credit $48.8 mill.12/94; chrg. $98.5 mill., 12/93. ② Bef. acctg. change chrg. $15.6 mill., 12/01; $96.4 mill., 12/93. ③ Bef. disc. oper. gain $911.8 mill. ④ Incl. gain fr. sale of subsidiaries of $12.8 mill. ⑤ Incl. net non-recurr. chrg. of $24.5 mill., chrgs. of $$208.5 mill. related to sale of reinsurance unit and resturct. chrgs. of $2.1 mill.

OFFICERS:
J. A. Boscia, Chmn., C.E.O.
R. C. Vaughan, Exec. V.P., C.F.O., Treas.
INVESTOR CONTACT: Priscilla Brown, V.P., Investor Relations, (215) 448-1422
PRINCIPAL OFFICE: 1500 Market Street, 39th Floor, Philadelphia, PA 19102-2112

TELEPHONE NUMBER: (215) 448-1400
FAX: (215) 448-6916
WEB: www.lfg.com
NO. OF EMPLOYEES: 6,780 (avg.)
SHAREHOLDERS: 10,609
ANNUAL MEETING: In May
INCORPORATED: IN, Jan., 1968

INSTITUTIONAL HOLDINGS:
No. of Institutions: 372
Shares Held: 125,692,778
% Held: 71.0
INDUSTRY: Life insurance (SIC: 6311)
TRANSFER AGENT(S): First Chicago Trust Company of New York, Jersey City, NJ

LITHIA MOTORS, INC.

EXCH.	SYM.	REC. PRICE	P/E RATIO	YLD.	MKT. CAP.	RANGE (52-WK.)	'02 Y/E PR.
NYSE	LAD	12.60 (2/28/03)	6.8	...	$163.0 mill.	31.20 - 11.80	15.69

UPPER MEDIUM GRADE. THE COMPANY IS TARGETING FULL-YEAR 2003 EARNINGS IN THE RANGE OF $1.83 AND $1.95 PER DILUTED SHARE.

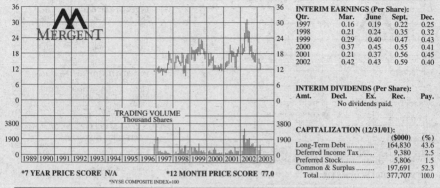

*7 YEAR PRICE SCORE N/A   ***12 MONTH PRICE SCORE 77.0**
*NYSE COMPOSITE INDEX=100

INTERIM EARNINGS (Per Share):

Qtr.	Mar.	June	Sept.	Dec.
1997	0.16	0.19	0.22	0.25
1998	0.21	0.24	0.35	0.32
1999	0.29	0.40	0.47	0.43
2000	0.37	0.45	0.55	0.41
2001	0.21	0.37	0.56	0.45
2002	0.42	0.43	0.59	0.40

INTERIM DIVIDENDS (Per Share):

Amt.	Decl.	Ex.	Rec.	Pay.
	No dividends paid.			

CAPITALIZATION (12/31/01):

	($000)	(%)
Long-Term Debt	164,830	43.6
Deferred Income Tax	9,380	2.5
Preferred Stock	5,806	1.5
Common & Surplus	197,691	52.3
Total	377,707	100.0

BUSINESS:

Lithia Motors, Inc. is an operator of automotive franchises and a retailer of new and used vehicles and services. As of 2/26/03, the Company owned 132 franchises in California, Oregon, Washington, Nevada, Colorado, Idaho, South Dakota, Alaska, Texas and Nebraska. LAD sells 24 brands of new vehicles at 71 stores and over the Internet. LAD sells new and used cars and light trucks and replacement parts, provides vehicle maintenance, warranty, paint and repair services, and arranges related financing and insurance for its automotive customers.

RECENT DEVELOPMENTS:

For the twelve months ended 12/31/02, net income advanced 48.6% to $32.3 million from $21.8 million in the corresponding prior-year period. Total revenues climbed 26.9% to $2.38 billion from $1.87 billion the previous year. New vehicle sales increased 29.3% to $1.28 billion from $993.6 million the year before. Used vehicle sales were up 26.1% to $738.1 million from $585.4 million the prior year.

Revenues from service, body and parts sales grew 22.5% to $230.0 million, while finance and insurance revenues rose 23.2% to $81.1 million. Gross profit totaled $374.8 million, or 15.8% of total revenues, versus $306.5 million, or 16.4% of total revenues, in 2001. Income from operations was $70.9 million, up 21.8% from $58.2 million a year earlier.

PROSPECTS:

The Company is targeting full-year 2003 revenue in the range of $2.60 billion to $2.80 billion, along with earnings in the range of $1.83 and $1.95 per diluted share. Results should benefit from continued aggressive acquisition activity during 2003. In 2002, LAD's acquisitions added approximately $455.0 million in annualized revenues. The Company anticipates acquiring franchises with annual revenues of between $350.0 million and $450.0 million in 2003. In February 2003, LAD completed the acquisition of Richardson Chevrolet in Salinas, California, which generates about $35.0 million in annual revenues.

ANNUAL FINANCIAL DATA:

FISCAL YEAR	TOT. REVS. ($mill.)	NET INC. ($mill.)	TOT. ASSETS ($mill.)	OPER. PROFIT %	NET PROFIT %	RET. ON EQUITY %	RET. ON ASSETS %	CURR. RATIO	EARN. PER SH.$	CASH FL. PER SH.$	TANG. BK. VAL.$	PRICE RANGE	AVG. P/E RATIO
p12/31/02	2,377.0	32.3							1.84			31.20 - 15.64	12.7
12/31/01	1,873.4	21.8	662.9	3.1	1.2	10.7	3.3	1.4	1.60	2.28	3.16	21.38 - 11.85	10.4
12/31/00	1,658.6	24.3	628.0	3.9	1.5	13.4	3.9	1.3	1.76	2.31	3.12	18.19 - 11.25	8.4
12/31/99	1,242.7	19.2	506.4	3.8	1.5	12.3	3.8	1.3	1.60	2.06	3.25	23.75 - 15.00	12.1
12/31/98	714.7	10.8	294.4	3.7	1.5	11.8	3.7	1.4	1.14	1.51	4.75	18.25 - 9.25	12.1
12/31/97	319.8	6.0	166.5	3.6	1.9	15.7	3.6	1.2	0.82	1.16	1.96	19.00 - 9.50	17.4
12/31/96	142.8	4.0	63.8	2.7	2.8	16.3	6.3	1.7	0.40	1.17	3.12	11.50 - 10.94	28.0
12/31/95	114.2	3.4	39.2	3.8	3.0	396.6	8.6	1.3	0.33	1.08	...	...	...
12/31/94	109.4	3.5	36.7	3.6	3.2	125.4	9.6	1.2	...	...	...	...	...
12/31/93	92.2	1.6	...	2.5	1.7	...	...	...	...	...	...	...	...

Statistics are as originally reported.

OFFICERS:
S. B. DeBoer, Chmn., C.E.O., Sec.
M. D. Heimann, Pres., C.O.O.
J. B. DeBoer, Sr. V.P., C.F.O.

INVESTOR CONTACT: Jeff DeBoer, Sr. V.P., C.F.O., (541) 776-6868

PRINCIPAL OFFICE: 360 E. Jackson Street, Medford, OR 97501

TELEPHONE NUMBER: (541) 776-6899
FAX: (541) 776-6362
WEB: www.lithia.com

NO. OF EMPLOYEES: 3,800 (approx.)

SHAREHOLDERS: 1,692 (record); (class A); 4,300 (approx. beneficial holders)

ANNUAL MEETING: In May

INCORPORATED: OR, 1946

INSTITUTIONAL HOLDINGS:
No. of Institutions: 70
Shares Held: 11,830,362
% Held: 65.6

INDUSTRY: New and used car dealers (SIC: 5511)

TRANSFER AGENT(S): Computershare Trust Company, Lakewood, CO

LIZ CLAIBORNE, INC.

EXCH.	SYM.	REC. PRICE	P/E RATIO	YLD.	MKT. CAP.	RANGE (52-WK.)	'02 Y/E PR.
NYSE	LIZ	28.20 (2/28/03)	13.1	0.8%	$2.97 bill.	33.25 - 23.55	29.65

UPPER MEDIUM GRADE. THE COMPANY ANNOUNCED A RESTRUCTURING OF ITS SPECIALTY RETAILER STRATEGY.

*7 YEAR PRICE SCORE 140.9   ***12 MONTH PRICE SCORE 107.5**
*NYSE COMPOSITE INDEX=100

INTERIM EARNINGS (Per Share):

Qtr.	Mar.	June	Sept.	Dec.
1997	0.30	0.21	0.48	0.35
1998	0.35	0.24	0.48	0.23
1999	0.35	0.25	0.54	0.43
2000	0.42	0.29	0.63	0.38
2001	0.44	0.31	0.69	0.39
2002	0.48	0.36	0.78	0.54

INTERIM DIVIDENDS (Per Share):

Amt.	Decl.	Ex.	Rec.	Pay.
0.056Q	3/14/02	5/16/02	5/20/02	6/10/02
0.056Q	7/25/02	8/15/02	8/19/02	9/09/02
0.056Q	10/10/02	11/14/02	11/18/02	12/09/02
0.056Q	1/29/03	2/20/03	2/24/03	3/17/03
0.056Q	3/12/03	5/29/03	6/02/03	6/16/03

Indicated div.: $0.23 (Div. Reinv. Plan)

CAPITALIZATION (12/29/01):

	($000)	(%)
Long-Term Debt	387,345	26.2
Deferred Income Tax	37,314	2.5
Common & Surplus	1,056,161	71.3
Total	1,480,820	100.0

BUSINESS:

Liz Claiborne, Inc. designs and markets an extensive range of branded women and men's apparel, accessories and fragrance products. Liz Claiborne Inc.'s brands include AXCESS, BORA BORA, CLAIBORNE, CRAZY HORSE, CURVE, DANA BUCHMAN, ELISABETH, ELLEN TRACY, EMMA JAMES, FIRST ISSUE, LAUNDRY BY SHELLI SEGAL, LIZ CLAIBORNE, LUCKY BRAND, MAMBO, MARVELLA, MEXX, MONET, MONET 2, RUSS, SIGRID OLSEN, TRIFARI and VIL-LAGER. In addition, LIZ holds certain licenses for men's and women's sportswear, jeanswear and activewear under the DKNY® JEANS and DKNY® ACTIVE trademarks, women's sportswear under the CITY DKNY® trademarks and women's apparel products under the KENNETH COLE NEW YORK, UNLISTED.COM and REACTION KENNETH COLE trademarks.

RECENT DEVELOPMENTS:

For the year ended 12/28/02, net income advanced 20.4% to $231.2 million from $192.1 million in the prior year. Results were enhanced by LIZ's multi-brand, multi-channel, multi-geography diversification strategy. Performance during 2002 was strong in the apparel businesses, particularly in SIGRID OLSEN, LUCKY BRAND AND DKNY Men's, in the costume jewelry business and in all aspects of the international operation, as LIZ made considerable progress in its sourcing and significant investment in technology. Results for 2002 and 2001 included after-tax restructuring charges of $4.5 million and $9.6 million, respectively. Net sales increased 7.8% to $3.72 billion.

PROSPECTS:

Looking ahead, LIZ remains optimistic that it can achieve a sales increase in 2003 of 9.0% to 11.0% and earnings per share in the range of $2.47 to $2.52. Separately, LIZ announced the restructuring of its specialty retailer strategy, which includes the closure of all 22 LIZ CLAIBORNE brand specialty stores in the U.S. by the second quarter, of which five will be converted to either a MEXX or SIGRID OLSEN format. These changes build upon the retail competencies established with LUCKY BRAND in the U.S. and with MEXX in Europe and in Canada. The changes also reflect LIZ's intent to continue to diversify its portfolio among brands, channels and geographies.

ANNUAL FINANCIAL DATA:

FISCAL YEAR	TOT. REVS. ($mill.)	NET INC. ($mill.)	TOT. ASSETS ($mill.)	OPER. PROFIT %	NET PROFIT %	RET. ON EQUITY %	RET. ON ASSETS %	CURR. RATIO	EARN. PER SH.$	CASH FL. PER SH.$	TANG. BK. VAL.$	DIV. PER SH.$	PRICE RANGE	AVG. P/E RATIO	AVG. YIELD %
p12/31/02	3,717.5	③ 231.2							③ 2.16			0.23	33.25 - 23.55	13.1	0.8
12/29/01	3,448.5	③ 192.1	1,951.3	9.6	5.6	18.2	9.8	2.5	③ 1.83	2.79	5.71	0.23	27.48 - 18.00	12.4	1.0
12/30/00	3,104.1	③ 184.6	1,512.2	9.8	5.9	22.1	12.2	2.5	③ 1.72	2.43	5.45	0.23	24.16 - 15.47	11.6	1.1
1/01/00	2,806.5	192.4	1,411.8	10.7	6.9	21.3	13.6	2.4	1.56	2.11	5.95	0.23	20.34 - 15.44	11.5	1.3
1/02/99	2,535.3	① 169.4	1,392.8	10.2	6.7	17.3	12.2	3.0	① 1.29	1.71	7.30	0.23	27.44 - 12.50	15.5	1.1
1/03/98	2,412.6	184.6	1,305.3	11.5	7.7	20.0	14.1	3.2	1.32	1.64	6.97	0.23	28.97 - 19.06	18.3	0.9
12/28/96	2,217.5	155.7	1,382.8	10.6	7.0	15.3	11.3	3.5	1.08	1.37	7.19	0.23	22.56 - 13.13	16.6	1.3
12/30/95	2,081.6	126.9	1,329.2	9.1	6.1	12.8	9.5	3.5	0.85	1.11	6.71	0.23	15.00 - 7.19	13.1	2.0
12/31/94	2,162.9	② 82.8	1,289.7	5.6	3.8	8.4	6.4	3.4	① 0.53	0.75	6.38	0.23	13.31 - 7.69	19.8	2.1
12/25/93	2,204.3	② 125.3	1,236.3	8.3	5.7	12.8	10.1	3.9	② 0.77	0.97	6.20	0.22	21.44 - 9.00	19.8	1.4

Statistics are as originally reported. Adj. for stk. split: 100% div., 1/02 ① Incl. non-recurr. chrg. $27.0 mill., 12/98; $30.0 mill., 12/94 ② Bef. acctg. change chrg. $1.6 mill. ③ Incl. restruc. chrgs. of $7.1 mill., 12/02; $15.1 mill., 12/01; $21.0 mill., 12/00

OFFICERS:
P. R. Charron, Chmn., C.E.O.
M. Scarpa, V.P., C.F.O.
E. H. Goodell, V.P., Contr.
INVESTOR CONTACT: Investor Relations, (212) 354-4900
PRINCIPAL OFFICE: 1441 Broadway, New York, NY 10018

TELEPHONE NUMBER: (212) 354-4900
FAX: (212) 626-1800
WEB: www.lizclaiborne.com
NO. OF EMPLOYEES: 10,400 (approx.)
SHAREHOLDERS: 7,232 (approx.)
ANNUAL MEETING: In May
INCORPORATED: NY, Jan., 1976; reincorp., DE, April, 1976

INSTITUTIONAL HOLDINGS:
No. of Institutions: 317
Shares Held: 100,228,087
% Held: 93.8
INDUSTRY: Women's and misses' outerwear, nec (SIC: 2339)
TRANSFER AGENT(S): First Chicago Trust Company of New York, Jersey City, NJ

LOCKHEED MARTIN CORPORATION

EXCH.	SYM.	REC. PRICE	P/E RATIO	YLD.	MKT. CAP.	RANGE (52-WK.)	'02 Y/E PR.
NYSE	LMT	45.72 (2/28/03)	38.7	1.0%	$20.16 bill.	71.52 - 44.34	57.75

MEDIUM GRADE. IN 2003, THE COMPANY EXPECTS EARNINGS PER SHARE FROM CONTINUING OPERATIONS TO RANGE FROM $2.15 TO $2.20.

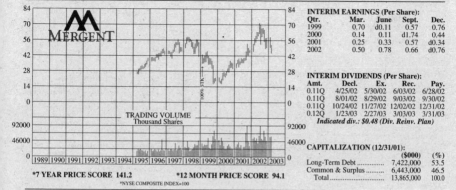

INTERIM EARNINGS (Per Share):

Qtr.	Mar.	June	Sept.	Dec.
1999	0.70	d0.11	0.57	0.76
2000	0.14	0.11	d1.74	0.44
2001	0.25	0.33	0.57	d0.34
2002	0.50	0.78	0.66	d0.76

INTERIM DIVIDENDS (Per Share):

Amt.	Decl.	Ex.	Rec.	Pay.
0.11Q	4/25/02	5/30/02	6/03/02	6/28/02
0.11Q	8/01/02	8/29/02	9/03/02	9/30/02
0.11Q	10/24/02	11/27/02	12/02/02	12/31/02
0.12Q	1/23/03	2/27/03	3/03/03	3/31/03

Indicated div.: $0.48 (Div. Reinv. Plan)

TRADING VOLUME Thousand Shares

*7 YEAR PRICE SCORE 141.2 ***12 MONTH PRICE SCORE 94.1**

*NYSE COMPOSITE INDEX=100

CAPITALIZATION (12/31/01):

	($000)	(%)
Long-Term Debt	7,422,000	53.5
Common & Surplus	6,443,000	46.5
Total	13,865,000	100.0

BUSINESS:

Lockheed Martin Corporation was created on 3/15/95 through a merger of equals between Lockheed Corp. and Martin Marietta Corp. LMT designs, develops, manufactures and integrates advanced technology systems, products, and services for government and commercial customers worldwide. Business areas include aeronautics, space, systems integration, and technology services. LMT is the world's largest defense, Department of Energy, and NASA contractor. Net sales for 2002 were derived as follows: systems integration, 36.1%; space systems, 27.8%; aeronautics, 24.3%; technology services, 11.7%; and corporate and other, 0.1%. In August 2000, LMT acquired the remaining 51.0% of COMSAT stock that it did not own.

RECENT DEVELOPMENTS:

For the year ended 12/31/02, LMT reported income from continuing operations of $533.0 million versus income of $43.0 million the year before. Earnings for 2002 and 2001 excluded losses of $33.0 million and $1.09 billion, respectively, from discontinued operations. Net sales grew 10.8% to $26.58 billion. On a segment basis, systems integration sales advanced 6.5% to $9.60 billion, while space systems sales improved 8.0% to $7.38 billion. Aeronautics sales rose 20.8% to $6.47 billion. Technology services sales grew 12.3% to $3.10 billion.

PROSPECTS:

In 2003, the Company expects earnings per share from continuing operations in the range of $2.15 to $2.20, sales growth between 8.0% and 12.0%, profit from operating segments of $2.30 billion to $2.40 billion, unallocated corporate net expense of $325.0 million to $375.0 million, and interest expense of approximately $535.0 million. Free cash flow is expected to be at least $800.0 million in 2003 and at least $1.80 billion over the two-year period from 2003 through 2004. In 2004, the Company anticipates sales growth of about 5.0% and profit from operating segments to range from $2.50 billion to $2.60 billion. Separately, on 1/28/03, LMT was awarded a $595.0 million contract by the U.S. Navy to build submarine-launched Trident-2 ballistic missile systems.

ANNUAL FINANCIAL DATA:

FISCAL YEAR	TOT. REVS. ($mill.)	NET INC. ($mill.)	TOT. ASSETS ($mill.)	OPER. PROFIT %	NET PROFIT %	RET. ON EQUITY %	RET. ON ASSETS %	CURR. RATIO	EARN. PER SH.$	CASH FL. PER SH.$	TANG. BK. VAL.$	DIV. PER SH.$	PRICE RANGE	AVG. P/E RATIO	AVG. YIELD %
p12/31/02	26,578.0	⑤ 533.0	25,789.0	...	...	...	...	...	⑤ 1.18	...	...	0.44	71.52 — 45.85	49.7	0.7
12/31/01	23,990.0	⑤ 79.0	27,654.0	6.4	0.3	1.2	0.3	1.1	⑤ 0.18	2.09	...	0.44	52.98 — 31.00	233.1	1.0
12/31/00	25,329.0	④ d424.0	30,349.0	6.4	...	...	...	1.1	④ d1.05	1.36	...	0.44	37.58 — 16.50	...	1.6
12/31/99	25,530.0	③ 737.0	30,261.0	6.5	2.9	11.6	2.4	1.2	③ 1.92	4.44	...	0.88	46.00 — 16.38	16.2	2.8
12/31/98	26,266.0	1,001.0	28,744.0	9.0	3.8	16.3	3.5	1.0	2.63	5.26	...	0.82	58.94 — 41.00	19.0	1.6
12/31/97	28,069.0	① 1,300.0	28,361.0	8.2	4.6	25.1	4.6	1.1	① 3.05	5.51	...	0.80	56.72 — 39.13	15.7	1.7
12/31/96	26,875.0	② 1,347.0	29,257.0	8.5	5.0	19.6	4.6	1.1	② 3.40	6.73	...	0.80	48.31 — 36.50	12.5	1.9
12/31/95	22,853.0	⑥ 682.0	17,648.0	5.6	3.0	10.6	3.9	1.5	⑥ 1.64	4.24	2.03	0.53	39.75 — 25.00	19.7	1.6
12/31/94	22,906.0	1,055.0	18,049.0	7.8	4.6	17.3	5.8	1.4	2.66	5.33	0.71	...	...	...	...
12/31/93	9,436.0	450.0	7,745.0	8.4	4.8	15.6	5.8	1.4	2.13	4.66	...	...	...	...	...

Statistics are as originally reported. All fin'l info. for 1994 is unaudit. & pro forma using the pool. of ints. acctg. method. Fin'l data for 12/31/93 & earlier are for Martin Marietta Corp. Adj. for 2-for-1 split, 12/98. ① Incl. aft-tax one-time net gain of $8.0 mill., 12/93; chrgs. $436.0 mill., 12/95. ② Incl. a one-time net gain of $340.0 mill. ③ Bef. acctg. chrg. $355.0 mill. & incl. various gains of $249.0 mill. ④ Bef. extraord. loss of $95.0 mill. & incl. a net nonrecur. loss of $539.0 mill. ⑤ Bef. an extraord. loss of $36.0 mill., 12/01 & a loss fr. disc. opers. of $33.0 mill., 12/02; $1.1 mill., 12/01; incl. losses rel. to nonrecurr. unusual items, $632.0 mill., 12/02; $615.0 mill., 12/01.

OFFICERS:
V. D. Coffman, Chmn., C.E.O.
R. J. Stevens, Pres., C.O.O.

INVESTOR CONTACT: Randa Middleton, Dir.-Inv. Rel., (301) 897-6455

PRINCIPAL OFFICE: 6801 Rockledge Drive, Bethesda, MD 20817-1877

TELEPHONE NUMBER: (301) 897-6000
FAX: (301) 897-6083
WEB: www.lockheedmartin.com
NO. OF EMPLOYEES: 125,000 (approx.)
SHAREHOLDERS: 49,425 (approx.)
ANNUAL MEETING: In April
INCORPORATED: MD, Oct., 1961; reincorp., MD, Aug., 1994

INSTITUTIONAL HOLDINGS:
No. of Institutions: 534
Shares Held: 493,166,287
% Held: 108.1
INDUSTRY: Guided missiles and space vehicles (SIC: 3761)
TRANSFER AGENT(S): First Chicago Trust Company of New York, Jersey City, NJ

LOEWS CORPORATION

EXCH.	SYM.	REC. PRICE	P/E RATIO	YLD.	MKT. CAP.	RANGE (52-WK.)	'02 Y/E PR.
NYSE	LTR	43.71 (2/28/03)	9.7	1.4%	$8.37 bill.	62.30 - 37.50	44.46

LOWER MEDIUM GRADE. THE UPGRADE BY DIAMOND OFFSHORE OF THE OCEAN ROVER IN SINGAPORE IS
EXPECTED TO BE COMPLETED IN THE THIRD QUARTER OF 2003.

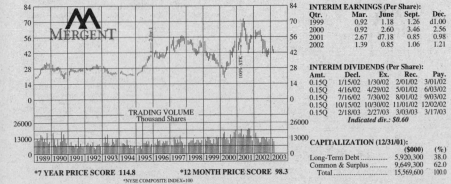

INTERIM EARNINGS (Per Share):

Qtr.	Mar.	June	Sept.	Dec.
1999	0.92	1.18	1.26	d1.00
2000	0.92	2.60	3.46	2.56
2001	2.67	d7.18	0.85	0.98
2002	1.39	0.85	1.06	1.21

INTERIM DIVIDENDS (Per Share):

Amt.	Decl.	Ex.	Rec.	Pay.
0.15Q	1/15/02	1/30/02	2/01/02	3/01/02
0.15Q	4/16/02	4/29/02	5/01/02	6/03/02
0.15Q	7/16/02	7/30/02	8/01/02	9/03/02
0.15Q	10/15/02	10/30/02	11/01/02	12/02/02
0.15Q	2/18/03	2/27/03	3/03/03	3/17/03

Indicated div.: $0.60

CAPITALIZATION (12/31/01):

	($000)	(%)
Long-Term Debt	5,920,300	38.0
Common & Surplus	9,649,300	62.0
Total	15,569,600	100.0

*7 YEAR PRICE SCORE 114.8   ***12 MONTH PRICE SCORE 98.3**

*NYSE COMPOSITE INDEX=100

BUSINESS:

Loews Corporation is a highly diversified company that operates primarily in the cigarette and insurance businesses. The Company produces and sells cigarettes through its wholly-owned subsidiary Lorillard, Inc. Brand names include NEWPORT, KENT and TRUE. As of 9/30/02, the Company owned 90% of CNA Financial Corporation, which has operations in property and casualty insurance. Another wholly-owned subsidiary is Loews Hotels Holding

Corporation, which owns and operates 18 Loews Hotels. LTR also holds a 97% interest in Bulova Corporation and a 54% interest in Diamond Offshore Drilling Inc., which operates 45 offshore drilling rigs. Net sales for 2002 were derived as follows: CNA Financial, 70.8%; Lorillard, 21.7%; Diamond Offshore, 4.5%; Loews Hotel, 1.7%; and investment income, including watch and clock operations, 1.3%.

RECENT DEVELOPMENTS:

For the year ended 12/31/02, LTR reported income from continuing operations of $982.6 million, before an accounting charge of $39.6 million, compared with a loss of $543.2 million, before an accounting charge of $53.3 million, the year before. Results excluded a loss of $31.0 million in 2002 and a gain of $9.4 million in 2001 from discontinued

operations. Total revenues decreased 6.8% to $17.50 billion from $18.77 billion a year earlier. Insurance premiums and net investment income fell 7.1% to $11.87 billion, while manufactured products revenue slipped 1.2% to $3.96 billion. Other revenue declined 15.9% to $1.66 billion. Comparisons were made with restated prior-year figures.

PROSPECTS:

CNA Financial Corporation is obligated to make future payments totaling $470.0 million for non-cancelable operating leases expiring from 2002 through 2014 primarily for office space and data processing, office and transportation equipment. Separately, the remaining estimated cost of

upgrades by Diamond Offshore of the Ocean Rover in Singapore is anticipated to be about $200.0 million in addition to the $125.0 million that was spent in 2002. The upgrade is expected to take about 19 months to complete with delivery estimated in the third quarter of 2003.

ANNUAL FINANCIAL DATA:

FISCAL YEAR	TOT. REVS. ($mill.)	NET INC. ($mill.)	TOT. ASSETS ($mill.)	OPER. PROFIT %	NET PROFIT %	RET. ON EQUITY %	RET. ON ASSETS %	CURR. RATIO	EARN. PER SH.$	CASH FL. PER SH.$	TANG. BK. VAL.$	DIV. PER SH.$	PRICE RANGE	AVG. P/E RATIO	AVG. YIELD %
p12/31/02	17,495.4	⑧ 982.6							⑧ 4.49			0.60	62.30 — 37.50	11.1	1.2
12/31/01	19,417.2	③⑦ d535.8	75,251.1	...	...	...	...	7.5	③⑦ d2.75	d2.44	48.70	0.57	72.50 — 41.05	...	1.0
12/31/00	21,337.8	⑥ 1,876.7	70,877.1	16.7	8.8	16.8	2.6	17.2	⑥ 9.44	9.37	54.82	0.50	52.47 — 19.13	3.8	1.4
12/31/99	21,465.2	⑤ 521.1	69,463.7	6.0	2.4	5.2	0.8	18.4	⑤ 2.40	3.77	45.79	0.50	52.25 — 29.25	17.0	1.2
12/31/98	21,208.3	③ 464.8	70,906.4	6.8	2.2	4.6	0.7	22.1	③ 2.03	2.99	43.13	0.50	54.13 — 39.00	22.9	1.1
12/31/97	20,138.8	③④ 793.6	69,577.1	9.5	3.9	8.2	1.1	22.4	③④ 3.45	4.44	38.76	0.50	57.81 — 42.75	14.6	1.0
12/31/96	20,442.4	③④ 1,383.9	67,683.0	13.3	6.8	15.9	2.0	9.9	③④ 5.96	6.42	35.52	0.50	47.94 — 36.25	7.1	1.2
12/31/95	18,677.4	②③ 1,765.7	65,516.9	16.7	9.5	21.4	2.7	12.8	②③ 7.49	7.85	32.91	0.31	39.94 — 21.66	4.1	1.0
12/31/94	13,515.2	①③ 267.8	50,336.0	3.3	2.0	5.0	0.5	5.8	①③ 1.11	1.28	22.52	0.25	25.69 — 21.13	21.1	1.1
12/31/93	13,686.8	①③ 594.1	45,849.8	6.2	4.3	9.7	1.3	15.8	①③ 2.32	2.47	24.90	0.25	30.06 — 21.69	11.2	1.0

Statistics are as originally reported. Adj. for 2-for-1 split, 3/01 & 10/95. ① Incl. loss of $255.7 mill., 12/94; $270.1 mill., 12/93. ② Incl. ops. of Continental Corp., acq. 5/95. ③ Incl. invest. gain (loss): cr$1.39 bill., 2001; cr$149.7 mill., 1998; d$237.9 mill., 1997; cr$491.3 mill., 1996; cr$192.9 mill., 1995; d$447.0 mill., 1994; cr$862.8 mill., 1993. ④ Incl. one-time gain of $124.3 mill., 1997; $186.6 mill., 1996. ⑤ Bef. an acctg. chrg. of $157.9 mill. & incl. a pre-tax invest. loss of $158.2 mill. ⑥ Incl. a pre-tax invest. gain of $1.31 bill. & aft.-tax tobacco litig. chrgs. of $642.3 mill. ⑦ Incl. one-time loss of $200.0 mill. ⑧ Bef. a loss of $31.0 mill. fr. disc. opers. & acctg. chrg. of $39.6 mill.

OFFICERS:
L. A. Tisch, Co-Chmn.
P. R. Tisch, Co-Chmn.
J. S. Tisch, Pres., C.E.O.
INVESTOR CONTACT: Joshua E. Kahn, Sr.
V.P. & Sec., (212) 521-2788
PRINCIPAL OFFICE: 667 Madison Ave., New York, NY 10021-8087

TELEPHONE NUMBER: (212) 521-2000
FAX: (212) 521-2498
WEB: www.loews.com
NO. OF EMPLOYEES: 27,820 (approx.)
SHAREHOLDERS: 2,100 (approx.) 5 (record, Carolina Group stock)
ANNUAL MEETING: In May
INCORPORATED: DE, Nov., 1969

INSTITUTIONAL HOLDINGS:
No. of Institutions: 302
Shares Held: 122,675,833
% Held: 66.2
INDUSTRY: Fire, marine, and casualty insurance (SIC: 6331)
TRANSFER AGENT(S): Mellon Investor Services, LLC, New York, NY

LONGS DRUG STORES CORPORATION

EXCH.	SYM.	REC. PRICE	P/E RATIO	YLD.	MKT. CAP.	RANGE (52-WK.)	'02 Y/E PR.
NYSE	LDG	13.81 (2/28/03)	16.6	4.1%	$0.52 bill.	32.25 - 13.05	20.74

UPPER MEDIUM GRADE. THE COMPANY IS TARGETING EARNINGS OF BETWEEN $0.89 AND $0.96 PER SHARE FOR THE CURRENT FISCAL YEAR.

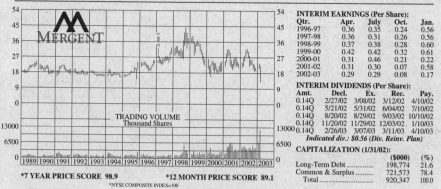

*7 YEAR PRICE SCORE 98.9　　***12 MONTH PRICE SCORE 89.1**

NYSE COMPOSITE INDEX=100

INTERIM EARNINGS (Per Share):

Qtr.	Apr.	July	Oct.	Jan.
1996-97	0.36	0.35	0.24	0.56
1997-98	0.36	0.31	0.26	0.56
1998-99	0.37	0.38	0.28	0.60
1999-00	0.42	0.42	0.32	0.61
2000-01	0.31	0.46	0.21	0.22
2001-02	0.31	0.30	0.07	0.58
2002-03	0.29	0.29	0.08	0.17

INTERIM DIVIDENDS (Per Share):

Amt.	Decl.	Ex.	Rec.	Pay.
0.14Q	2/27/02	3/08/02	3/12/02	4/10/02
0.14Q	5/21/02	5/31/02	6/04/02	7/10/02
0.14Q	8/20/02	8/29/02	9/03/02	10/10/02
0.14Q	11/20/02	11/29/02	12/03/02.	1/10/03
0.14Q	2/26/03	3/07/03	3/11/03	4/10/03

Indicated div.: $0.56 (Div. Reinv. Plan)

CAPITALIZATION (1/31/02):

	($000)	(%)
Long-Term Debt	198,774	21.6
Common & Surplus	721,573	78.4
Total	920,347	100.0

BUSINESS:

Longs Drug Stores Corporation operated a chain of 457 drug stores, as of 2/26/03, located in California, Hawaii, Washington, Nevada, Colorado, and Oregon. The Company's stores, which range in size from 15,000 to 30,000 square feet, sell both nationally advertised brand-name merchandise and LDG's private-label merchandise. Prescription drugs and "front end" merchandise, including over-the-counter medications, health care products, photo and photo processing, cosmetics and greeting cards are the Company's core merchandise segments.

RECENT DEVELOPMENTS:

For the 52 weeks ended 1/30/03, the Company reported income of $31.3 million, before a $24.6 million accounting change charge, compared with net income of $47.2 million in the corresponding 53-week period the year before. Results for fiscal 2003 and fiscal 2002 included a $10.8 million charge and a $1.7 million gain, respectively, from store closures and asset impairment. Results also included charges of $469,000 in fiscal 2003 and $860,000 in fiscal 2002 from legal settlements. Sales rose 2.8% to $4.43 billion from $4.30 billion the previous year. Same-store sales, on a comparative 52-week basis, were up 2.8% year over year, fueled by a 5.8% increase in pharmacy same-store sales and a 0.5% increase in front-end same-store sales. Gross profit totaled $1.16 billion, or 26.2% of sales, versus $1.10 billion, or 25.6% of sales, a year earlier. Operating income slid 35.4% to $57.7 million.

PROSPECTS:

The Company is aggressively implementing initiatives to help boost profitability. On 2/26/03, LDG announced that it is eliminating approximately 170 positions, primarily in its California offices, and abandoning an inefficient pharmacy technology information system. The Company expects to incur charges of about $9.0 million in the current fiscal year related to these initiatives. Meanwhile, LDG is targeting full fiscal-2004 sales growth in the range of 3.0% to 5.0% and earnings, including the aforementioned charges, of between $0.89 and $0.96 per share. Separately, LDG plans to open about 20 new stores and remodel approximately 20 existing stores during the current fiscal year.

ANNUAL FINANCIAL DATA:

FISCAL YEAR	TOT. REVS. ($mill.)	NET INC. ($mill.)	TOT. ASSETS ($mill.)	OPER. PROFIT %	NET PROFIT %	RET. ON EQUITY %	RET. ON ASSETS %	CURR. RATIO	EARN. PER SH.$	CASH FL. PER SH.$	TANG. BK. VAL.$	DIV. PER SH.$	PRICE RANGE	AVG. P/E RATIO	AVG. YIELD %
p1/30/03	4,426.3	③ 31.3							④ 0.82			0.56	32.25 - 19.25	31.4	2.2
1/31/02	4,304.7	② 47.2	1,411.6	2.1	1.1	6.5	3.3	1.5	② 1.25	3.37	15.75	0.56	32.00 - 19.90	20.8	2.2
1/25/01	4,027.1	② 44.9	1,353.7	2.1	1.1	6.6	3.3	1.4	② 1.19	3.08	14.70	0.56	26.00 - 15.94	17.6	2.7
1/27/00	3,672.4	69.0	1,270.3	3.2	1.9	9.8	5.4	1.7	1.76	1.84	14.37	0.56	39.50 - 22.25	17.5	1.8
1/28/99	3,266.9	③ 63.4	1,025.1	3.2	1.9	9.9	6.2	1.5	③ 1.64	1.70	16.40	0.56	44.50 - 26.00	21.5	1.6
1/29/98	2,952.9	57.7	946.3	3.2	2.0	9.4	6.1	1.5	1.49	1.54	15.12	0.56	32.75 - 22.63	18.6	2.0
1/30/97	2,828.3	58.6	879.6	3.4	2.1	10.6	6.7	1.6	1.49	1.53	14.21	0.56	25.19 - 18.94	14.8	2.5
1/25/96	2,644.4	② 46.2	853.6	3.4	1.7	8.8	5.4	1.6	② 1.15	1.18	13.19	0.56	24.13 - 14.13	16.6	2.9
1/26/95	2,558.3	48.7	828.0	3.2	1.9	9.3	5.9	1.7	1.18	1.22	12.75	0.56	19.94 - 15.13	14.9	3.2
1/27/94	2,499.2	① 49.8	794.8	3.3	2.0	10.0	6.3	1.6	① 1.21	1.24	12.09	0.56	18.94 - 15.63	14.3	3.2

Statistics are as originally reported. Adj. for 2-for-1 stk. split, 1/97. ① Incl. $1.0 mil pre-tax chg. & bef. $3.0 mil ($0.08/sh) cr. for acctg. change. ② Incl. $1.4 mil ($0.04/sh) after-tax chg., 1/02; $12.3 mil ($0.33/sh) after-tax chgs., 1/01; $8.4 mil chg., 1/96. ③ Incl. exp. of $5.5 million relating to remediation of Year 2000 issues. ④ Bef. $24.6 mil ($0.64/sh) acctg. chg., incl. $10.8 mil net pre-tax chg. for store closures and asset impair. and a $469,000 chg. fr. legal settle.

OFFICERS:
R. M. Long, Chmn.
H. R. Somerset, Vice-Chmn.
W. F. Bryant, Pres., C.E.O.
S. F. McCann, Sr. V.P., C.F.O., Treas.

INVESTOR CONTACT: Investor Relations, (925) 937-1170

PRINCIPAL OFFICE: 141 North Civic Drive, Walnut Creek, CA 94596

TELEPHONE NUMBER: (925) 937-1170
FAX: (925) 210-6886
WEB: www.longs.com
NO. OF EMPLOYEES: 22,200 (avg.)
SHAREHOLDERS: 18,996 (approx.)
ANNUAL MEETING: In May
INCORPORATED: CA, Oct., 1946; reincorp., MD, May, 1985

INSTITUTIONAL HOLDINGS:
No. of Institutions: 137
Shares Held: 21,779,436
% Held: 56.6

INDUSTRY: Drug stores and proprietary stores (SIC: 5912)

TRANSFER AGENT(S): Mellon Investor Services, Ridgefield Park, NJ

LOUISIANA-PACIFIC CORPORATION

EXCH.	SYM.	REC. PRICE	P/E RATIO	YLD.	MKT. CAP.	RANGE (52-WK.)	'02 Y/E PR.
NYSE	LPX	8.71 (2/28/03)	...	...	$0.91 bill.	12.55 - 5.35	8.06

LOWER MEDIUM GRADE. THE DISPOSAL OF ASSETS VALUED BETWEEN $600.0 MILLION AND $700.0 MILLION IS ON SCHEDULE.

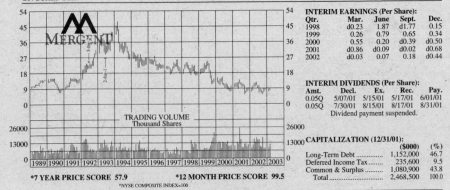

*7 YEAR PRICE SCORE 57.9   *12 MONTH PRICE SCORE 99.5
*NYSE COMPOSITE INDEX=100

INTERIM EARNINGS (Per Share):

Qtr.	Mar.	June	Sept.	Dec.
1998	d0.23	1.87	d1.77	0.15
1999	0.26	0.79	0.65	0.34
2000	0.55	0.20	d0.39	d0.50
2001	d0.86	d0.09	d0.02	d0.68
2002	d0.03	0.07	0.18	d0.44

INTERIM DIVIDENDS (Per Share):

Amt.	Decl.	Ex.	Rec.	Pay.
0.05Q	5/07/01	5/15/01	5/17/01	6/01/01
0.05Q	7/30/01	8/15/01	8/17/01	8/31/01
	Dividend payment suspended.			

CAPITALIZATION (12/31/01):

	($000)	(%)
Long-Term Debt	1,152,000	46.7
Deferred Income Tax	235,600	9.5
Common & Surplus	1,080,900	43.8
Total	2,468,500	100.0

BUSINESS:

Louisiana-Pacific Corporation is a manufacturer and distributor of building materials. As of 12/31/01, the Company operated 59 facilities in the U.S., and Canada, one facility in Chile, and one facility in Ireland. LPX also owned 935,000 acres of timberland in the U.S., predominantly in the south, and managed approximately 49.0 million acres of timberland in Canada. The Oriented Strand Board-North America (OSB) segment (36.8% of 2002 revenues) manufactures and distributes OSB. The Composite Wood Products segment (20.4%) produces and markets wood siding and related accessories, interior hardboard products and specialty OSB. The Plastic Building Products segment (7.8%) produces and markets vinyl siding and related accessories, plastic moldings and composite decking. The Structural Framing Products segment (30.4%) manufactures and distributes structural lumber and engineered wood products (EWP), including laminated veneer lumber (LVL) and I-Joists. The Other Products segment (4.5%) is comprised of other products that are not individually significant. During 2001, LPX exited the pulp (0.1%) business.

RECENT DEVELOPMENTS:

For the year ended 12/31/02, loss from continuing operations was $21.5 million compared with $135.4 million in 2001. Results for 2002 and 2001 included a credit of $35.6 million and a charge of $37.4 million, respectively, on the sale or impairment of long lived assets. Results also included nonrecurring net charges of $29.5 million and $15.7 million in 2002 and 2001, respectively. In addition, results for 2001 included a loss of $42.5 million related to assets and liabilities transferred under contractual arrangement. Net sales increased 4.0% to $1.94 billion.

PROSPECTS:

The disposal of assets valued between $600.0 million and $700.0 million is on schedule. Separately, in 2003, LPX expects cash funding requirements for pension plans to increase to $36.0 million from $27.0 million in 2002. Moreover, LPX anticipates pension expense for 2003 to be about $15.0 million. On 2/24/03, LPX announced the sale of its Missoula, Montana particleboard mill to Roseburg Forest Products for about $20.0 million, including inventories.

ANNUAL FINANCIAL DATA:

FISCAL YEAR	TOT. REVS. ($mill.)	NET INC. ($mill.)	TOT. ASSETS ($mill.)	OPER. PROFIT %	NET PROFIT %	RET. ON EQUITY %	RET. ON ASSETS %	CURR. RATIO	EARN. PER SH.$	CASH FL. PER SH.$	TANG. BK. VAL.$	DIV. PER SH.$	PRICE RANGE	AVG. P/E RATIO	AVG. YIELD %
p12/31/02	1,942.7	⑥ d21.5							⑥ d0.21			...	12.55 - 5.35	...	...
12/31/01	2,359.7	⑤ d171.6	3,016.8	...	...	...	...	1.6	⑤ d1.64	0.23	7.48	0.24	13.95 - 5.46	...	2.5
12/31/00	2,932.8	④ d13.8	3,374.7	1.0	...	...	...	1.7	④ d0.13	2.13	9.28	0.56	15.81 - 7.06	...	4.9
12/31/99	2,878.6	④ 216.8	3,488.2	12.8	7.5	15.9	6.2	3.2	④ 2.04	3.94	9.64	0.56	24.88 - 11.38	8.9	3.1
12/31/98	2,297.1	④ 2.0	2,519.1	1.2	0.1	0.2	0.1	1.7	④ 0.02	1.73	10.84	0.56	25.88 - 16.38	N.M.	2.8
12/31/97	2,402.5	③ d101.8	2,578.4	...	...	...	...	1.9	③ d0.94	0.76	11.02	0.56	25.88 - 17.00	...	2.6
12/31/96	2,486.0	④ d200.7	2,588.7	...	...	...	...	1.7	④ d1.87	d0.08	12.70	0.56	28.13 - 19.63	...	2.3
12/31/95	2,843.2	② d51.7	2,805.4	...	...	...	...	1.4	② d0.48	1.41	15.12	0.55	30.50 - 20.88	...	2.1
12/31/94	3,039.5	346.9	2,716.2	18.4	11.4	18.8	12.8	4.6	3.15	4.94	16.51	0.48	48.00 - 25.75	11.7	1.3
12/31/93	2,511.3	① 254.4	2,466.3	17.2	10.1	16.2	10.3	3.7	① 2.32	3.99	14.26	0.43	42.13 - 28.75	15.3	1.2

Statistics are as originally reported. ① Bef. acctg. adj. chrg. of $10.4 mill. ② Incl. chrg. of $221.8 mill. rel. to class action settlements. ③ Incl. after-tax chrg. of $94.3 mill. ($0.87/sh.) for settlement & other unusual items. ④ Incl. nonrecurr. chrgs. of $70.5 mill., 2000; $5.1 mill., 1999; $36.1 mill., 1998; $215.0 mill., 1996. ⑤ Incl. nonrecurr. chrg. of $42.5 mill. rel. to transfer of assets and liab. ⑥ Excl. dis. ops. loss of $36.7 mill., acctg. change chrg. of $3.8 mill., but incl. impairment credit of $35.6 mill., and non-recurr. chrg. of $29.5 mill.

OFFICERS:
M. A. Suwyn, Chmn., C.E.O.
C. M. Stevens, Exec. V.P., C.F.O., Treas.

INVESTOR CONTACT: William L. Herbert, (503) 821-5100

PRINCIPAL OFFICE: 805 SW Broadway, Suite 1200, Portland, OR 97205-3303

TELEPHONE NUMBER: (503) 821-5100
FAX: (503) 821-5204
WEB: www.lpcorp.com
NO. OF EMPLOYEES: 9,700 (approx.)
SHAREHOLDERS: 14,583
ANNUAL MEETING: In May
INCORPORATED: DE, July, 1972

INSTITUTIONAL HOLDINGS:
No. of Institutions: 210
Shares Held: 55,767,599
% Held: 72.4
INDUSTRY: Sawmills and planing mills, general (SIC: 2421)
TRANSFER AGENT(S): First Chicago Trust Company of New York, Jersey City, NJ

LOWE'S COMPANIES, INC.

EXCH.	SYM.	REC. PRICE	P/E RATIO	YLD.	MKT. CAP.	RANGE (52-WK.)	'02 Y/E PR.	DIV. ACH.
NYSE	LOW	39.30 (2/28/03)	21.1	0.3%	$30.49 bill.	49.99 - 32.50	37.50	41 yrs.

HIGH GRADE. THE COMPANY EXPECTS DILUTED EARNINGS PER SHARE OF $2.16 TO $2.20 FOR THE FISCAL YEAR ENDING 1/30/04.

7 YEAR PRICE SCORE 182.4   **12 MONTH PRICE SCORE 97.4**

*NYSE COMPOSITE INDEX=100

INTERIM EARNINGS (Per Share):

Qtr.	Apr.	July	Oct.	Jan.
1997-98	0.11	0.19	0.13	0.11
1998-99	0.14	0.24	0.17	0.15
1999-00	0.17	0.30	0.22	0.20
2000-01	0.25	0.37	0.27	0.19
2001-02	0.29	0.42	0.32	0.28
2002-03	0.44	0.59	0.43	0.40

INTERIM DIVIDENDS (Per Share):

Amt.	Decl.	Ex.	Rec.	Pay.
0.02Q	1/03/02	1/16/02	1/18/02	2/01/02
0.02Q	4/09/02	4/17/02	4/19/02	5/03/02
0.02Q	5/31/02	7/17/02	7/19/02	8/02/02
0.02Q	9/30/02	10/16/02	10/18/02	11/01/02
0.025Q	12/06/02	1/15/03	1/17/03	1/31/03

Indicated div.: $0.10 (Div. Reinv. Plan)

CAPITALIZATION (2/1/02):

	($000)	(%)
Long-Term Debt	3,734,011	35.9
Common & Surplus	6,674,442	64.1
Total	10,408,453	100.0

BUSINESS:

Lowe's Companies, Inc. is a specialty retailer that combines the merchandise, sales and service of a home improvement center, a building materials supplier and a consumer-durables retailer to serve the do-it-yourself home improvement and construction markets. As of 1/31/03, LOW operated 854 stores in 44 states representing 94.7 million square feet of selling space. Each store is stocked with more than 40,000 separate items, while the Company's special order program features more than 400,000 additional items. On 4/2/99, the Company acquired Eagle Hardware & Garden, Inc.

RECENT DEVELOPMENTS:

For the year ended 1/31/03, net earnings advanced 43.8% to $1.47 billion from $1.02 billion the year before. Earnings for 2003 and 2002 included store opening costs of $128.7 million and $139.9 million, respectively. Net sales climbed 19.8% to $26.49 billion from $22.11 billion the previous year. Comparable-store sales increased 5.6% year over year. Gross margin totaled $8.03 billion, or 30.3% of net sales, compared with $6.37 billion, or 28.8% of net sales, a year earlier. During the quarter, the Company opened 37 new stores, including six relocations.

PROSPECTS:

Looking ahead to fiscal year 2003, the Company expects to open 130 stores, reflecting total square footage growth of 15.0% to 16.0%. Total sales are expected to increase approximately 16.0% to 17.0% for the year. The Company expects to report a comparable-store sales increase of approximately 4.0% to 5.0%. Operating margin is expected to increase approximately 20 basis points. Store opening costs are expected to be approximately $140.0 million. Diluted earnings per share of $2.16 to $2.20 are expected for the fiscal year ending 1/30/04.

ANNUAL FINANCIAL DATA:

FISCAL YEAR	TOT. REVS. ($mill.)	NET INC. ($mill.)	TOT. ASSETS ($mill.)	OPER. PROFIT %	NET PROFIT %	RET. ON EQUITY %	RET. ON ASSETS %	CURR. RATIO	EARN. PER SH. $	CASH FL. PER SH. $	TANG. BK. VAL.$	DIV. PER SH.$	PRICE RANGE	AVG. P/E RATIO	AVG. YIELD %
p1/31/03	26,490.9	☑1,471.5	16,108.5						☑1.85			0.08	49.99 - 32.50	22.3	0.2
2/01/02	22,111.1	*1,023.3	13,736.2	8.1	4.6	15.3	7.4	1.6	1.30	1.96	8.60	0.075	48.88 - 21.88	27.2	0.2
2/02/01	18,778.6	809.9	11,375.8	7.5	4.3	14.7	7.1	1.4	1.06	1.59	7.17	0.07	33.63 - 17.13	24.0	0.3
1/28/00	15,905.6	☐672.8	9,012.3	7.2	4.2	14.3	7.5	1.6	☐0.88	1.32	6.14	0.06	33.22 - 21.50	31.3	0.2
1/29/99	12,244.9	482.4	6,344.7	6.8	3.9	15.4	7.6	1.5	0.68	1.07	4.45	0.058	26.09 - 10.80	27.1	0.3
1/30/98	10,136.9	357.5	5,219.3	6.2	3.5	13.7	6.8	1.5	0.52	0.86	3.71	0.055	12.28 - 7.91	19.6	0.5
1/31/97	8,600.2	292.2	4,435.0	5.8	3.4	13.2	6.6	1.4	0.44	0.73	3.20	0.05	10.88 - 7.16	20.7	0.6
1/31/96	7,075.4	226.0	3,556.4	5.5	3.2	13.6	6.4	1.7	0.35	0.59	2.57	0.047	9.72 - 6.50	23.0	0.6
1/31/95	6,110.5	223.6	3,106.0	6.1	3.7	15.7	7.2	1.6	0.36	0.54	2.23	0.046	10.34 - 6.64	23.6	0.5
1/31/94	4,538.0	131.8	2,201.6	4.8	2.9	15.1	6.0	1.6	0.22	0.36	1.48	0.043	7.48 - 3.02	23.5	0.8

Statistics are as originally reported. Adj. for 2-for-1 stk. split, 6/01, 6/98 & 3/94. ☐ Incl. $24.4 mil pre-tax, non-recur. chg. ☑ Incl. store opening costs of $128.7 mill.

OFFICERS:
R. L. Tillman, Chmn., C.E.O.
R. A. Niblock, Exec. V.P., C.F.O.
S. A. Hellrung, Sr. V.P., Sec., Gen. Couns.

INVESTOR CONTACT: Marshall Croom, (336) 658-4022

PRINCIPAL OFFICE: 1605 Curtis Bridge Road, Wilkesboro, NC 28697

TELEPHONE NUMBER: (336) 658-4000
FAX: (336) 658-4766
WEB: www.lowes.com

NO. OF EMPLOYEES: 81,000 full-time (approx.); 21,000 part-time (approx.)

SHAREHOLDERS: 19,277

ANNUAL MEETING: In May

INCORPORATED: NC, Aug., 1952

INSTITUTIONAL HOLDINGS:
No. of Institutions: 725
Shares Held: 621,766,357
% Held: 79.6

INDUSTRY: Lumber and other building materials (SIC: 5211)

TRANSFER AGENT(S): EquiServe Trust Company, NA, Boston, MA

LSI LOGIC CORPORATION

EXCH.	SYM.	REC. PRICE	P/E RATIO	YLD.	MKT. CAP.	RANGE (52-WK.)	'02 Y/E PR.
NYSE	LSI	4.44 (2/28/03)	...	...	$1.64 bill.	18.60 - 3.78	5.77

SPECULATIVE GRADE. RECENT ORDER STRENGTH FROM THE COMPANY'S STORAGE BUSINESSES IS BEING OFFSET BY DECLINES IN SEMICONDUCTOR ORDERS FROM THE CONSUMER AND COMMUNICATIONS MARKETS.

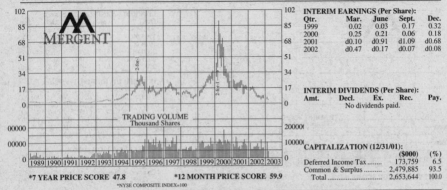

*7 YEAR PRICE SCORE 47.8   ***12 MONTH PRICE SCORE 59.9**
*NYSE COMPOSITE INDEX=100

INTERIM EARNINGS (Per Share):

Qtr.	Mar.	June	Sept.	Dec.
1999	0.02	0.03	0.17	0.32
2000	0.25	0.21	0.06	0.18
2001	d0.10	d0.91	d1.09	d0.68
2002	d0.47	d0.17	d0.07	d0.08

INTERIM DIVIDENDS (Per Share):

Amt.	Decl.	Ex.	Rec.	Pay.
		No dividends paid.		

CAPITALIZATION (12/31/01):

	($000)	(%)
Deferred Income Tax	173,759	6.5
Common & Surplus	2,479,885	93.5
Total	2,653,644	100.0

BUSINESS:

LSI Logic Corporation is a designer, developer, manufacturer and marketer of high performance application-specific integrated circuits (ASICs) and storage systems. The Company's integrated circuits are used in a range of communication devices, including devices used for wireless, broadband, data networking and set-top-box applications. The Company's semiconductor segment uses advanced process technology and design methodology to design and develop highly complex ASICs and other integrated circuits. The Company's Storage Area Networks (SAN) segment designs and manufactures enterprise storage systems through LSI Logic Storage Systems, Inc., a wholly-owned subsidiary, under the MetaStor® brand name.

RECENT DEVELOPMENTS:

For the year ended 12/31/02, the Company reported a net loss of $292.4 million compared with a net loss of $992.0 million a year earlier. Results for 2002 and 2001 excess inventory and related charges of $45.5 million and $210.6 million, and acquired in-process research and development charges of $2.9 million and $96.6 million, respectively. Results for 2002 and 2001 also included restructuring and other non-recurring charges of $67.1 million and $219.6 million, and amortization of acquisition-related items of $155.9 million and $292.9 million, respectively. Revenues increased 1.8% to $1.82 billion from $1.78 billion a year earlier.

PROSPECTS:

Recent order strength from the Company's storage businesses is being offset by declines in semiconductor orders from the consumer and communications markets. As a result, first quarter revenues are expected in the range of $370.0 million to $390.0 million. Looking ahead, orders are expected to improve substantially for the second quarter of 2003. Consumer, storage components and storage systems are expected to be the drivers for the second quarter improvement. However, in the communications market, LSI believes that the enterprise sector is stabilizing while the wide area network sector is unlikely to demonstrate improvement until late 2003 or 2004.

ANNUAL FINANCIAL DATA:

FISCAL YEAR	TOT. REVS. ($mill.)	NET INC. ($mill.)	TOT. ASSETS ($mill.)	OPER. PROFIT %	NET PROFIT %	RET. ON EQUITY %	RET. ON ASSETS %	CURR. RATIO	EARN. PER SH.$	CASH FL. PER SH.$	TANG. BK. VAL.$	PRICE RANGE		AVG. P/E RATIO
p12/31/02	1,816.9	⑥ d292.4	...	...	...	...	...	...	⑥ d0.79	...	...	18.60 - 3.97		...
12/31/01	1,784.9	⑤ d992.0	4,625.8	...	...	...	...	3.5	⑤ d2.84	d1.02	3.15	26.10 - 9.70		...
12/31/00	2,737.7	④ 236.6	4,197.5	10.6	8.6	9.5	5.6	3.3	④ 0.70	1.92	5.96	90.38 - 16.30		76.2
12/31/99	2,089.4	③ 158.9	3,206.6	9.5	7.6	8.6	5.0	2.7	③ 0.51	1.62	5.21	35.69 - 8.06		42.9
12/31/98	1,490.7	② d131.6	2,800.0	...	...	...	...	1.4	② d0.46	0.33	4.16	14.69 - 5.25		...
12/31/97	1,290.3	① 160.7	2,126.9	15.1	12.5	10.3	7.6	2.0	① 0.56	1.14	5.59	23.44 - 9.31		29.2
12/31/96	1,238.7	147.2	1,952.7	15.5	11.9	11.2	7.5	3.0	0.56	1.12	5.10	19.81 - 8.50		25.3
12/31/95	1,267.7	238.1	1,849.6	25.1	18.8	19.6	12.9	2.9	0.93	1.46	4.70	31.25 - 9.13		21.7
12/31/94	901.8	108.7	1,270.4	17.5	12.1	20.0	8.6	2.4	0.50	0.97	2.38	11.34 - 3.88		15.4
12/31/93	718.8	53.8	852.7	11.7	7.5	18.4	6.3	2.3	0.27	0.60	1.47	4.81 - 2.56		13.7

Statistics are as originally reported. Adj. for 2-for-1 split, 2/00 & 6/95. ① Bef. $1.4 mill. acct. chrg. ② Incl. $146.0 mill. in-process R&D chrg., $75.4 mill. restr. chrg., & $9.1 mill. spl. exp. chrgs. ③ Bef. $91.8 mill. acct. chrg.; incl. $2.1 mill. restr. gain, $4.6 mill. acq. in-process R&D, $48.4 mill. gain on sale of eq. secs. ④ Incl. $2.8 mill. non-recur. chrgs., $77.5 mill. in-process R&D chrg., $113.8 mill. amort. chrg. & $80.1 mill. gain fr. sale of sec. ⑤ Incl. excess inv. chrg. $210.6 mill., restr. chrge. $219.6 mill., acquired in-process R&D charge $96.6 mill. and a gain on sale of eq. securs. $5.3 mill. ⑥ Incl. excess inv. chrg. $45.5 mill., acq. in-process R&D $2.9 mill. and restr. & oth. chrg. $67.1 mill.

OFFICERS:
W. J. Corrigan, Chmn., C.E.O.
B. Look, Exec. V.P., C.F.O.
D. G. Pursel, V.P., Sec., Gen. Couns.
INVESTOR CONTACT: Diana Matley, Investor Relations, (408) 433-4365
PRINCIPAL OFFICE: 1621 Barber Lane, Milpitas, CA 95035

TELEPHONE NUMBER: (408) 433-8000
FAX: (408) 433-3220
WEB: www.lsilogic.com
NO. OF EMPLOYEES: 6,737
SHAREHOLDERS: 4,408 (approx. record)
ANNUAL MEETING: In May
INCORPORATED: CA, Nov., 1980; reincorp., DE, June, 1987

INSTITUTIONAL HOLDINGS:
No. of Institutions: 326
Shares Held: 202,027,263
% Held: 54.3
INDUSTRY: Semiconductors and related devices (SIC: 3674)
TRANSFER AGENT(S): EquiServe Trust Company, Canton, MA

LUBRIZOL CORPORATION

EXCH.	SYM.	REC. PRICE	P/E RATIO	YLD.	MKT. CAP.	RANGE (52-WK.)	'02 Y/E PR.
NYSE	LZ	28.93 (2/28/03)	11.9	3.6%	$1.48 bill.	36.36 - 26.20	30.50

UPPER MEDIUM GRADE. EARNINGS FOR 2003 ARE EXPECTED TO RANGE FROM $2.20 TO $2.30 PER SHARE.

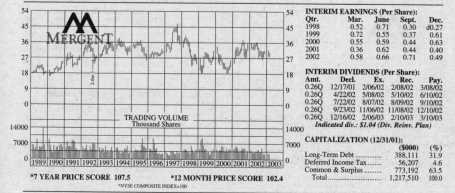

INTERIM EARNINGS (Per Share):

Qtr.	Mar.	June	Sept.	Dec.
1998	0.52	0.71	0.30	d0.27
1999	0.72	0.55	0.37	0.61
2000	0.55	0.59	0.44	0.63
2001	0.36	0.62	0.44	0.40
2002	0.58	0.66	0.71	0.49

INTERIM DIVIDENDS (Per Share):

Amt.	Decl.	Ex.	Rec.	Pay.
0.26Q	12/17/01	2/06/02	2/08/02	3/08/02
0.26Q	4/22/02	5/08/02	5/10/02	6/10/02
0.26Q	7/22/02	8/07/02	8/09/02	9/10/02
0.26Q	9/23/02	11/06/02	11/08/02	12/10/02
0.26Q	12/16/02	2/06/03	2/10/03	3/10/03

Indicated div.: $1.04 (Div. Reinv. Plan)

CAPITALIZATION (12/31/01):

	($000)	(%)
Long-Term Debt	388,111	31.9
Deferred Income Tax	56,207	4.6
Common & Surplus	773,192	63.5
Total	1,217,510	100.0

*7 YEAR PRICE SCORE 107.5   ***12 MONTH PRICE SCORE 102.4**

*NYSE COMPOSITE INDEX=100

BUSINESS:

The Lubrizol Corporation is a global fluid technology company that develops, produces and sells high-performance chemicals, systems and services for industry and transportation. The Company creates these products, including specialty additive packages and related equipment, for use in transportation and industrial lubricants and other markets. The Company groups its product lines into two operating segments: fluid technologies for transportation (79.4% of revenues for 2002), which is comprised of additives for lubricating engine oils, additives for driveline oils, and additives for fuel products and refinery and oil field chemicals; and fluid technologies for industry (19.3%), which includes industrial additives, performance chemicals, and performance systems.

RECENT DEVELOPMENTS:

For the twelve months ended 12/31/02, income advanced 34.2% to $126.3 million, before an accounting change charge of $7.8 million, compared with net income of $94.1 million in 2001. Net income benefited from increased shipment volumes, contributions from acquisitions and organic growth. Total revenues were $1.98 billion, up 7.5% from $1.84 billion in the prior year. Revenue from the fluid technologies for transportation segment grew 3.6% to $1.58 billion, while revenue from the fluid technologies for industry segment rose 27.4% to $382.4 million. Operating income increased 19.4% to $372.1 million from $311.8 million the year before.

PROSPECTS:

The Company remains optimistic that the introduction of new products will contribute to the growth of its businesses. Also, contributions from acquisitions completed in 2002 should further enhance operating performance. Looking ahead, the Company expects earnings per share for the first quarter of 2003 in the range of the high-$0.50's to low-$0.60's. Moreover, earnings for full-year 2003 are expected to range from $2.20 to $2.30 per share, given the continued challenges that LZ faces in the marketplace and ongoing growth in earnings from the fluid technologies for industry segment.

ANNUAL FINANCIAL DATA:

FISCAL YEAR	TOT. REVS. ($mill.)	NET INC. ($mill.)	TOT. ASSETS ($mill.)	OPER. PROFIT %	NET PROFIT %	RET. ON EQUITY %	RET. ON ASSETS %	CURR. RATIO	EARN. PER SH.$	CASH FL.PER SH.$	TANG. BK. VAL.$	DIV. PER SH.$	PRICE RANGE	AVG. P/E RATIO	AVG. YIELD %
p12/31/02	1,983.9	⑧ 126.3							⑧ 2.44			1.04	36.36 – 26.20	12.8	3.3
12/31/01	1,844.6	94.1	1,662.3	8.6	5.1	12.2	5.7	2.9	1.83	3.75	11.86	1.04	37.69 – 24.13	16.9	3.4
12/31/00	1,775.8	⑦ 118.0	1,659.5	10.1	6.6	15.7	7.1	2.6	⑦ 2.22	4.11	11.34	1.04	33.88 – 18.25	11.7	4.0
12/31/99	1,748.0	⑥ 123.0	1,682.4	12.9	7.0	15.6	7.3	2.5	⑥ 2.25	4.07	11.75	1.04	31.38 – 18.00	11.0	4.2
12/31/98	1,617.9	⑤ 71.2	1,643.2	9.5	4.4	9.3	4.3	2.5	⑤ 1.27	2.84	11.04	1.04	40.19 – 22.38	24.6	3.3
12/31/97	1,673.8	154.9	1,462.3	13.9	9.3	19.0	10.6	2.5	2.66	4.16	14.31	1.01	46.94 – 30.38	14.5	2.6
12/31/96	1,597.6	① 169.8	1,402.1	12.2	10.6	20.7	12.1	2.6	① 2.80	4.13	14.00	0.97	37.38 – 26.50	10.5	3.3
12/31/95	1,663.6	①③ 151.6	1,492.0	11.7	9.1	17.9	10.2	2.4	①③ 2.37	3.54	13.49	0.93	37.38 – 25.50	13.3	3.0
12/31/94	1,599.0	② 175.6	1,394.4	12.6	11.0	21.1	12.6	2.5	② 2.67	3.67	12.83	0.89	38.63 – 28.50	12.6	2.7
12/31/93	1,525.5	②④ 85.0	1,182.6	10.7	5.6	11.6	7.2	2.5	②④ 1.25	2.17	11.00	0.85	36.38 – 26.63	25.2	2.7

Statistics are as originally reported. ① Incl. $53.3 mill. gain on sale of invest., 1996; $38.5 mill, 1995. ② Incl. $11.5 mill. gain fr. sale of Genentech shs.. 1994; $42.4 mill. & $86.3 mill. chg. for restr., 1993. ③ Incl. $9.5 mill. asset impairment chgs. ④ Bef. d$51.5 mill. acct. adj. ⑤ Incl. $10.5 mill. gain fr. settlement of litigation & $25.8 mill. after-tax spl. chgs. for restr. plan & write-off. ⑥ Incl. $10.9 mill. net gain fr. litigation & $13.2 mill. net spl. chg. ⑦ Incl. $14.9 mill. litigation settlement gain & $4.5 mill. net spl. gain fr. adjustment of prev. chgs. ⑧ Excl. $7.8 mill. acctg. chg.

OFFICERS:
W. G. Bares, Chmn., C.E.O.
J. L. Hambrick, Pres.
C. P. Cooley, V.P., C.F.O.
INVESTOR CONTACT: Investor Relations, (440) 943-4200
PRINCIPAL OFFICE: 29400 Lakeland Blvd., Wickliffe, OH 44092-2298

TELEPHONE NUMBER: (440) 943-4200
FAX: (440) 943-5337
WEB: www.lubrizol.com
NO. OF EMPLOYEES: 4,530 (avg.)
SHAREHOLDERS: 4,628 (record)
ANNUAL MEETING: In Apr.
INCORPORATED: OH, July, 1928; reincorp., Jan. 2000

INSTITUTIONAL HOLDINGS:
No. of Institutions: 200
Shares Held: 38,078,070
% Held: 74.0
INDUSTRY: Gum and wood chemicals (SIC: 2861)
TRANSFER AGENT(S): American Stock Transfer & Trust Company, New York, NY

LUCENT TECHNOLOGIES INC.

EXCH.	SYM.	REC. PRICE	P/E RATIO	YLD.	MKT. CAP.	RANGE (52-WK.)	'02 Y/E PR.
NYSE	LU	1.64 (2/28/03)	...	...	$5.72 bill.	6.68 - 0.55	1.26

SPECULATIVE GRADE. THE COMPANY CONTINUES TO WORK TOWARD A RETURN TO PROFITABILITY IN LATE 2003.

TRADING VOLUME
Thousand Shares

1989 1990 1991 1992 1993 1994 1995 1996 1997 1998 1999 2000 2001 2002 2003

*7 YEAR PRICE SCORE N/A   *12 MONTH PRICE SCORE 71.5
*NYSE COMPOSITE INDEX=100

INTERIM EARNINGS (Per Share):

Qtr.	Dec.	Mar.	June	Sept.
1997-98	0.31	0.01	d0.09	0.15
1998-99	1.00	0.16	0.24	0.30
1999-00	0.34	0.19	Nil	d0.01
2000-01	d0.47	d1.00	d0.55	d2.16
2001-02	d0.14	d0.19	d2.35	d0.84
2002-03	d0.11	...	...	...

INTERIM DIVIDENDS (Per Share):

Amt.	Decl.	Ex.	Rec.	Pay.
Last dist. $0.02Q, 6/02/01.				

CAPITALIZATION (9/30/02):

	($000)	(%)
Long-Term Debt	3,236,000	1284.1
Redeemable Pfd. Stock	1,750,000	694.4
Common & Surplus	d4,734,000	-1878.6
Total	252,000	100.0

BUSINESS:

Lucent Technologies Inc. is a global company with two reportable business segments. The Integrated Network Solutions segment (INS) targets wireline customers, while the Mobility Solutions segment targets wireless customers. Lucent Worldwide Services, which provides planning and design, consulting and integration support services as well as network engineering, provisioning (allocating data transmission or bandwidth capacity), installation and warranty support, supports both the INS and Mobility segments. LU's research and development activities are conducted through Bell Laboratories. In April 1996, LU, which was formed as a result of AT&T's planned restructuring, implemented an initial public offering (IPO). AT&T spun off its remaining 82.4% interest in Lucent Technologies to shareholders on 9/30/96. LU spun off to shareholders Avaya Inc. on 9/30/00, and its Agere business unit on 6/1/02.

RECENT DEVELOPMENTS:

For the three months ended 12/31/02, LU posted a net loss of $264.0 million compared with a net loss of $423.0 million in the corresponding year-earlier period. Results for 2002 and 2001 included net business restructuring reversals and asset impairment credits of $19.0 million and $79.0 million and amortization of goodwill and other acquired intangibles of $5.0 million and $74.0 million, respectively.

Results also included a recovery of $91.0 million for 2002 and a provision of $451.0 million for 2001 for bad debts and customer financings. Revenue fell 42.0% to $2.08 billion from $3.58 billion the previous year, primarily due to continuing reductions in capital spending by service providers. However, gross margin as a percentage of total revenues improved to 21.9% versus 12.2% the year before.

PROSPECTS:

LU's outlook remains difficult as market conditions are not expected to improve over the near term. On the positive side, LU expects its ongoing actions to reduce the Company's cost and expense structure will allow it to achieve earnings per share breakeven at $2.50 billion of quarterly revenue by the end of fiscal 2003. In addition, LU reiterated that it continues to work toward a return to profitability in late fiscal 2003.

ANNUAL FINANCIAL DATA:

FISCAL YEAR	TOT. REVS. ($mill.)	NET INC. ($mill.)	TOT. ASSETS ($mill.)	OPER. PROFIT %	NET PROFIT %	RET. ON EQUITY %	RET. ON ASSETS %	CURR. RATIO	EARN. PER SH.$	CASH FL. PER SH.$	TANG. BK. VAL.$	DIV. PER SH.$	PRICE RANGE	AVG. P/E RATIO	AVG. YIELD %
9/30/02	12,321.0	⑦d11,826.0	17,791.0	...	...	...	...	1.4	⑦d3.51	d3.08	...	...	7.50 - 0.55	...	...
9/30/01	21,294.0	⑥d14,170.0	33,664.0	...	...	...	...	1.6	⑥d4.18	d3.43	2.80	0.04	21.13 - 5.00	...	0.3
9/30/00	33,813.0	⑤1,681.0	48,792.0	8.8	5.0	6.4	3.4	2.0	⑤0.51	1.20	4.59	0.08	77.50 - 12.19	87.9	0.2
9/30/99	38,303.0	④3,458.0	38,775.0	14.1	9.0	25.5	8.9	1.9	④1.52	1.67	4.27	0.08	84.19 - 47.00	59.6	0.1
9/30/98	30,147.0	③970.0	26,720.0	8.2	3.2	17.5	3.6	1.4	③0.37	0.86	1.99	0.08	56.94 - 18.36	103.1	0.2
9/30/97	26,360.0	①541.0	23,811.0	6.2	2.1	16.0	2.3	1.2	①0.21	0.77	1.20	0.07	22.69 - 11.19	80.6	0.4
②9/30/96	15,859.0	224.0	22,626.0	3.1	1.4	8.3	1.0	1.2	0.10	0.40	0.91	0.04	13.28 - 7.44	108.9	0.4
12/31/95	21,413.0	d867.0	19,722.0	...	...	...	...	1.0	d0.41	0.30	...	...	...	...	...
12/31/94	19,765.0	482.0	17,340.0	4.9	2.4	19.5	2.8	1.0	...	...	...	...	...	...	...
12/31/93	17,734.0	③430.0	16,330.0	3.8	2.4	...	...	...	...	...	...	...	...	...	...

Statistics are as originally reported. Adj. for 2-for-1 stk. splits, 4/99 & 4/98. ① Incl. non-recurr. pre-tax chrgs. of $1.42 bill., 9/98; $1.02 bill., 9/97 ② Results are for the nine months ended 9/30/96 due to fiscal year changed. ③ Bef. acctg. adj. chrg. of $4.2 mill. ④ Incl. non-recurr. chrg. $375.0 mill.; bef. acctg. chge. cr. $1.31 bill. ⑤ Bef. loss of $462.0 mill. fr. disc. ops. ⑥ Incl. restr. & asset impairmnt. chrgs. of $10.16 bill.; bef. loss of $3.17 bill. fr. disc. ops., extraord. gain of $1.18 bill. & acctg. chge. chrg. of $38.0 mill. ⑦ Incl. net restr. & asset impairmnt. chrgs. of $2.25 bill.; bef. inc. of $73.0 mill. fr. disc. ops.

OFFICERS:
P. F. Russo, Chmn., Pres., C.E.O.
F. D'Amelio, Exec. V.P., C.F.O.
R. J. Rawson, Sr. V.P., Sec., Gen. Couns.

INVESTOR CONTACT: (888) 458-2368

PRINCIPAL OFFICE: 600 Mountain Avenue, Murray Hill, NJ 07974

TELEPHONE NUMBER: (908) 582-8500
FAX: (908) 582-7826
WEB: www.lucent.com
NO. OF EMPLOYEES: 47,000 (approx.)
SHAREHOLDERS: 1,476,691 (approx.)
ANNUAL MEETING: In Feb.
INCORPORATED: DE, Nov., 1995

INSTITUTIONAL HOLDINGS:
No. of Institutions: 614
Shares Held: 1,295,433,212
% Held: 35.9
INDUSTRY: Telephone communications, exc. radio (SIC: 4813)
TRANSFER AGENT(S): First Chicago Trust Company of New York, Jersey City, NJ

LYONDELL CHEMICAL COMPANY

EXCH.	SYM.	REC. PRICE	P/E RATIO	YLD.	MKT. CAP.	RANGE (52-WK.)	'02 Y/E PR.
NYSE	LYO	11.91 (2/28/03)	...	7.6%	$1.40 bill.	17.59 - 10.33	12.64

LOWER MEDIUM GRADE. LYONDELL AND EQUISTAR INCREASED PRICES FOR THE MAJORITY OF THEIR PRODUCTS TO OFFSET THE EFFECTS OF HIGHER ENERGY AND RAW MATERIAL COSTS.

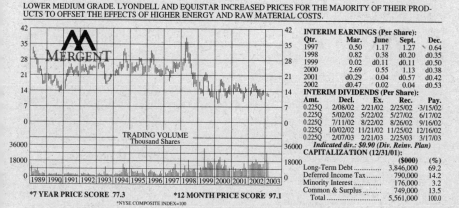

INTERIM EARNINGS (Per Share):

Qtr.	Mar.	June	Sept.	Dec.
1997	0.50	1.17	1.27	0.64
1998	0.82	0.38	d0.20	d0.35
1999	0.02	d0.11	d0.11	d0.50
2000	2.69	0.55	1.13	d0.38
2001	d0.29	0.04	d0.57	d0.42
2002	d0.47	0.02	0.04	d0.53

INTERIM DIVIDENDS (Per Share):

Amt.	Decl.	Ex.	Rec.	Pay.
0.225Q	2/08/02	2/21/02	2/25/02	3/15/02
0.225Q	5/02/02	5/22/02	5/27/02	6/17/02
0.225Q	7/11/02	8/22/02	8/26/02	9/16/02
0.225Q	10/02/02	11/21/02	11/25/02	12/16/02
0.225Q	2/07/03	2/21/03	2/25/03	3/17/03

Indicated div.: $0.90 (Div. Reinv. Plan)

CAPITALIZATION (12/31/01):

	($000)	(%)
Long-Term Debt	3,846,000	69.2
Deferred Income Tax	790,000	14.2
Minority Interest	176,000	3.2
Common & Surplus	749,000	13.5
Total	5,561,000	100.0

TRADING VOLUME
Thousand Shares

1989 1990 1991 1992 1993 1994 1995 1996 1997 1998 1999 2000 2001 2002 2003

*7 YEAR PRICE SCORE 77.3   ***12 MONTH PRICE SCORE 97.1**

*NYSE COMPOSITE INDEX=100

BUSINESS:

Lyondell Chemical Company (formerly Lyondell Petrochemical Co.) is a global chemical and refining company that operates in five business segments: intermediate chemicals and derivatives, petrochemicals, polymers, refining, and methanol. LYO manufactures petrochemicals, including propylene oxide and derivatives; olefins (ethylene, propylene, butadiene, and butylenes); polyolefins (polypropylene and high- and low-density polyethylene);

methanol; methyl tertiary butyl ether and aromatics. As of 1/30/03, LYO held a 58.75% participation interest in Lyondell-Citgo Refining Co. Ltd., which produces refined petroleum products, including gasoline, heating fuel, jet fuel, aromatics and lubricants, and a 70.5% interest in Equistar Chemicals, L.P. Lyondell Methanol Company, L.P. is a wholly-owned subsidiary of LYO. On 8/1/98, LYO acquired ARCO Chemical Company.

RECENT DEVELOPMENTS:

For the twelve months ended 12/31/02, net loss amounted to $133.0 million, before an after-tax extraordinary loss of $15.0 million, compared with a loss of $145.0 million, before an after-tax extraordinary loss of $5.0 million, in 2001. Results were negatively affected by unfavorable eco-

nomic conditions, higher energy costs, and weak supply and demand balances in the chemical industry. Results for 2001 included amortization of goodwill of $30.0 million. Sales and other operating revenues climbed 2.2% to $3.26 billion from $3.19 billion in the prior year.

PROSPECTS:

Energy and raw material costs have been higher and more volatile in the first quarter of 2003 than in the fourth quarter of 2002. As a result, Lyondell and Equistar increased their prices for the majority of intermediate chemicals and derivatives and Equistar products. Benefits from these

increases are expected to be realized in the first quarter. In addition, earnings for the first quarter are expected to be hampered by the prolonged oil situation in Venezuela. However, the Company has acquired crude oil from alternate sources.

ANNUAL FINANCIAL DATA:

FISCAL YEAR	TOT. REVS. ($mill.)	NET INC. ($mill.)	TOT. ASSETS ($mill.)	OPER. PROFIT %	NET PROFIT %	RET. ON EQUITY %	RET. ON ASSETS %	CURR. RATIO	EARN. PER SH.$	CASH FL. PER SH.$	TANG. BK. VAL.$	DIV. PER SH.$	PRICE RANGE	AVG. P/E RATIO	AVG. YIELD %
p12/31/02	3,262.0	9 d133.0							9 d0.99			0.90	17.59 - 10.33	...	6.4
12/31/01	3,226.0	8 d185.0	6,703.0	3.5	...	...	...	2.2	8 d1.24	0.71	...	0.90	17.95 - 9.45	...	6.6
12/31/00	4,036.0	7 470.0	7,047.0	8.4	11.6	41.0	6.7	1.8	7 3.99	6.36	...	0.90	19.50 - 8.44	3.5	6.4
12/31/99	3,693.0	6 d80.0	9,498.0	10.9	...	...	...	1.8	6 d0.77	2.42	...	0.90	22.50 - 11.25	...	5.3
12/31/98	1,477.0	5 52.0	9,225.0	19.9	3.1	9.1	0.6	0.6	5 0.67	2.44	...	0.90	38.13 - 15.88	39.6	3.4
12/31/97	4 3,010.0	3 286.0	1,559.0	17.7	9.5	46.2	18.3	0.3	3 3.58	4.62	7.74	0.90	27.38 - 18.63	6.4	3.9
12/31/96	5,052.0	2 126.0	3,276.0	5.5	2.5	29.2	3.8	1.1	2 1.58	2.95	5.39	0.90	32.25 - 20.38	16.7	3.4
12/31/95	4,936.0	389.0	2,606.0	14.3	7.9	102.4	14.9	0.9	4.86	5.94	4.75	0.90	29.13 - 21.13	5.2	3.6
12/31/94	3,857.0	223.0	1,663.0	11.0	5.8	354.0	13.4	1.6	2.78	3.60	0.91	0.79	33.00 - 20.63	9.6	3.4
12/31/93	3,850.0	1 4.0	1,231.0	2.4	0.1	...	0.3	1.7	1 0.06	0.78	...	1.35	29.50 - 16.75	384.8	5.8

Statistics are as originally reported. ① Bef. cr$22.0 mill. acct. adj. ② Incl. $20.0 mill. after-tax gain on sale of assets. ③ Incl. $25.0 mill. non-recur. after-tax chg. ④ Refl. chg. in reporting of LCR fr. consol. to equity method. ⑤ Incl. $48.0 mill. in after-tax non-recur. chgs. & $6.0 mill. in after-tax charges rel. to formation of Equistar joint venture. ⑥ Excl. d$35.0 mill. net extraord. chg. ⑦ Incl. $400.0 mill. net gain fr. sale of bus. & excl. $33.0 mill. net extraord. chg. ⑧ Incl. $99.0 mill. amort. of intang., $63.0 mill. unusual chg. & excl. $5.0 mill. extraord. loss. ⑨ Excl. $15.0 mill. net extraord. loss.

OFFICERS:
W. T. Butler, Chmn.
D. F. Smith, Pres., C.E.O.
T. K. DeNicola, Sr. V.P., C.F.O.

INVESTOR CONTACT: Doug Pike, Dir. of
Investor Relations, (713) 652-7200

PRINCIPAL OFFICE: 1221 McKinney St.,
Suite 700, Houston, TX 77010

TELEPHONE NUMBER: (713) 652-7200
FAX: (713) 652-4563
WEB: www.lyondell.com

NO. OF EMPLOYEES: 3,300 (approx.)

SHAREHOLDERS: 1,789 (approx.)

ANNUAL MEETING: In May

INCORPORATED: DE, 1985

INSTITUTIONAL HOLDINGS:
No. of Institutions: 186
Shares Held: 107,527,321
% Held: 67.3

INDUSTRY: Petroleum refining (SIC: 2911)

TRANSFER AGENT(S): American Stock
Transfer & Trust Company, New York, NY

M&T BANK CORPORATION

EXCH.	SYM.	REC. PRICE	P/E RATIO	YLD.	MKT. CAP.	RANGE (52-WK.)	'02 Y/E PR.	DIV. ACH.
NYSE	MTB	79.02 (2/28/03)	15.6	1.5%	$7.40 bill.	90.05 - 67.70	79.35	22 yrs.

UPPER MEDIUM GRADE. THE COMPANY CONTINUES TO BENEFIT FROM GROWTH IN ITS CONSUMER LOAN PORTFOLIO AND A STRONG NET INTEREST MARGIN.

TRADING VOLUME
Thousand Shares

1989 1990 1991 1992 1993 1994 1995 1996 1997 1998 1999 2000 2001 2002 2003

*7 YEAR PRICE SCORE 163.9   ***12 MONTH PRICE SCORE 107.4**

*NYSE COMPOSITE INDEX=100

INTERIM EARNINGS (Per Share):

Qtr.	Mar.	June	Sept.	Dec.
1999	0.83	0.80	0.83	0.82
2000	0.86	0.97	0.94	0.76
2001	1.14	0.94	0.98	1.05
2002	1.25	1.26	1.23	1.33

INTERIM DIVIDENDS (Per Share):

Amt.	Decl.	Ex.	Rec.	Pay.
0.25Q	2/20/02	2/26/02	2/28/02	3/29/02
0.25Q	4/16/02	5/30/02	6/03/02	6/28/02
0.25Q	7/16/02	8/29/02	9/03/02	9/30/02
0.30Q	10/15/02	11/27/02	12/02/02	12/31/02
0.30Q	2/18/03	2/27/03	3/03/03	3/31/03

Indicated div.: $1.20 (Div. Reinv. Plan)

CAPITALIZATION (12/31/01):

	($000)	(%)
Total Deposits	21,580,400	77.1
Long-Term Debt	3,461,769	12.4
Common & Surplus	2,939,451	10.5
Total	27,981,620	100.0

BUSINESS:

M&T Bank Corporation, with assets of $33.17 billion as of 12/31/02, is a bank holding company with two wholly-owned bank subsidiaries, Manufacturers and Traders Trust Company and M&T Bank, National Association. The banks collectively offer commercial banking, trust and investment services to their customers. The Company's five reportable segments are Commercial Banking (20.7% of net interest income and 10.9% of non-interest income as of 12/31/01), Commercial Real Estate (13.6% and 1.4%), Discretionary Portfolio (4.4% and 9.3%), Residential Mortgage Banking (5.2% and 36.6%) and Retail Banking (56.1% and 41.7%). On 2/10/01, the Company acquired Premier National Bancorp, Inc.

RECENT DEVELOPMENTS:

For the year ended 12/31/02, net income increased 28.3% to $485.1 million compared with $378.1 million the year before. Earnings for 2001 included amortization of goodwill of $61.8 million. Interest income declined 12.4% to $1.84 billion from $2.10 billion in the prior year. Interest expense fell 37.0% to $594.5 million from $943.6 million a year earlier. Net interest income grew 7.7% to $1.25 billion from $1.16 billion the year before. Provision for credit losses rose 17.9% to $122,000. Total other income improved 7.2% to $511.9 million, while total other expense decreased 2.9% to $921.0 million.

PROSPECTS:

The Company continues to benefit from growth in its consumer loan portfolio, principally in home equity lines of credit and automobile loans, and a strong net interest margin. Diluted earnings per share for 2003 are expected to range from $5.25 to $5.35, excluding the acquisition of Allfirst Financial Inc. The acquisition has been approved by the shareholders of the Company and Allied Irish Banks, p.l.c., the parent company of Allfirst, but needs approval by various regulatory agencies. The transaction is anticipated to close in the first quarter of 2003.

ANNUAL FINANCIAL DATA:

FISCAL YEAR	NET INT. INC. ($mill.)	NON-INT. INC. ($mill.)	NET INC. ($mill.)	TOT. LOANS ($mill.)	TOT. ASSETS ($mill.)	TOT. DEP. ($mill.)	RET. ON EQUITY %	RET. ON ASSETS %	EQUITY/ ASSETS %	EARN. PER SH.$	TANG. BK. VAL.$	DIV. PER SH.$	PRICE RANGE	AVG. P/E RATIO
p12/31/02	1,247.6	511.9	485.1		33,174.2		15.2	1.5		5.07		1.05	90.05 - 67.70	15.6
12/31/01	1,158.3	477.4	☐ 378.1	25,395.5	31,450.2	21,580.4	12.9	1.2	9.3	☐ 3.82	17.84	1.00	82.11 - 59.80	18.6
12/31/00	854.2	324.7	☐ 286.2	22,970.3	28,949.5	20,232.7	10.6	1.0	9.3	☐ 3.44	16.10	0.63	68.42 - 35.70	15.1
12/31/99	759.4	282.4	☐ 265.6	17,572.9	22,409.1	15,373.6	14.8	1.2	8.0	☐ 3.28	14.88	0.45	58.25 - 40.60	15.1
12/31/98	664.3	270.6	☐ 208.0	16,005.7	20,583.9	14,737.2	13.0	1.0	7.8	☐ 2.62	13.72	0.38	58.20 - 40.00	18.8
12/31/97	556.9	193.1	176.2	11,765.5	14,002.9	11,163.2	17.1	1.3	7.4	2.53	15.59	0.32	45.50 - 28.10	14.6
12/31/96	531.0	170.2	151.1	11,120.2	12,943.9	10,514.5	16.7	1.2	7.0	2.13	13.55	0.28	28.96 - 20.90	11.7
12/31/95	486.4	149.5	131.0	9,873.7	11,955.9	9,469.6	15.5	1.1	7.1	1.88	12.53	0.25	21.80 - 13.60	9.4
12/31/94	468.1	123.7	117.3	8,447.1	10,528.6	8,243.1	16.3	1.1	6.8	1.69	9.95	0.22	16.50 - 13.45	8.9
12/31/93	470.8	110.5	102.0	7,439.1	10,365.0	7,353.3	14.1	1.0	7.0	1.43	9.94	0.19	15.90 - 13.03	10.1

Statistics are as originally reported. Adj. for 10-for-1 stk. split, 10/5/00. ☐ Incl. after-tax nonrecurr. merger & acq. chrgs.: $4.8 mill., 2001; $16.4 mill., 2000; $3.0 mill., 12/31/99; $14.0 mill., 12/31/98.

OFFICERS:
R. G. Wilmers, Chmn., Pres., C.E.O.
C. L. Campbell, Vice-Chmn.
M. P. Pinto, Exec. V.P., C.F.O.

INVESTOR CONTACT: M. S. Piemonte,
Shldr. Rel./Corp. Fin. Dept., (716) 842-5138

PRINCIPAL OFFICE: One M&T Plaza, 5th Floor, Buffalo, NY 14203

TELEPHONE NUMBER: (716) 842-5445
FAX: (716) 842-5177
WEB: www.mandtbank.com

NO. OF EMPLOYEES: 8,139 full-time; 1,152 part-time

SHAREHOLDERS: 12,565

ANNUAL MEETING: In April
INCORPORATED: NY, Nov., 1969

INSTITUTIONAL HOLDINGS:
No. of Institutions: 259
Shares Held: 51,738,906
% Held: 56.3

INDUSTRY: State commercial banks (SIC: 6022)

TRANSFER AGENT(S): BankBoston, N.A. c/o Equiserve, Boston, MA

MACK-CALI REALTY CORPORATION

EXCH.	SYM.	REC. PRICE	P/E RATIO	YLD.	MKT. CAP.	RANGE (52-WK.)	'02 Y/E PR.
NYSE	CLI	28.90 (2/28/03)	11.9	8.7%	$1.64 bill.	35.73 - 26.64	30.30

MEDIUM GRADE. GOING FORWARD, THE COMPANY EXPECTS FUNDS FROM OPERATIONS PER DILUTED SHARE TO RANGE FROM $3.52 TO $3.66 FOR FISCAL 2003.

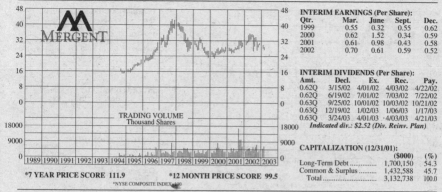

INTERIM EARNINGS (Per Share):

Qtr.	Mar.	June	Sept.	Dec.
1999	0.55	0.32	0.55	0.62
2000	0.62	1.52	0.34	0.59
2001	0.61	0.98	0.43	0.58
2002	0.70	0.61	0.59	0.52

INTERIM DIVIDENDS (Per Share):

Amt.	Decl.	Ex.	Rec.	Pay.
0.62Q	3/15/02	4/01/02	4/03/02	4/22/02
0.62Q	6/19/02	7/01/02	7/03/02	7/22/02
0.63Q	9/25/02	10/01/02	10/03/02	10/21/02
0.63Q	12/19/02	1/02/03	1/06/03	1/17/03
0.63Q	3/24/03	4/01/03	4/03/03	4/21/03

Indicated div.: $2.52 (Div. Reinv. Plan)

TRADING VOLUME
Thousand Shares

1989 1990 1991 1992 1993 1994 1995 1996 1997 1998 1999 2000 2001 2002 2003

*7 YEAR PRICE SCORE 111.9   ***12 MONTH PRICE SCORE 99.5**

*NYSE COMPOSITE INDEX=100

CAPITALIZATION (12/31/01):

	($000)	(%)
Long-Term Debt	1,700,150	54.3
Common & Surplus	1,432,588	45.7
Total	3,132,738	100.0

BUSINESS:

Mack-Cali Realty Corporation is a fully-integrated, self-administered and self-managed real estate investment trust that owns and operates a portfolio comprised of office and office/flex properties located primarily in the Northeast. CLI performs commercial real estate leasing, management, acquisition, development and construction services on an in-house basis. As of 12/31/02, CLI owned or had interests in 265 properties, totaling about 29.3 million square feet, plus developable land. The properties were comprised of:

150 office buildings and 95 office/flex buildings totaling about 26.7 million square feet, six industrial/warehouse buildings totaling 387,400 square feet two stand-alone retail properties and three land lease; and six office builds and one office/flex buildings aggregating 2.1 million square feet, one stand-alone retail property aggregating approximately 100,740 square feet and a 350-room hotel, owned by unconsolidated joint ventures in which CLI has investment interests.

RECENT DEVELOPMENTS:

For the year ended 12/31/02, net income climbed 6.1% to $139.7 million compared with $131.7 million in the equivalent period of the previous year. Results for 2002 and 2001 included a realized gain of $2.8 million and an unrealized loss of $11.9 million, respectively, on the disposition

of rental property. Total revenues slipped to $569.6 million from $575.3 million in the prior-year quarter. Revenues from base rents decreased 2.8% to $492.4 million from $506.6 million, while revenues from escalations and recoveries from tenants grew 1.7% to $57.1 million.

PROSPECTS:

The Company should continue to benefit from solid occupancy levels and a high-quality cash flow stream. Moreover, recent acquisitions should further enhance CLI's strong Northeast presence. Based on existing market conditions, rental rates, occupancy levels and other projections, CLI expects funds from operations to range from $3.52 to $3.66

for fiscal 2003. Separately, on 1/2/03, CLI announced that it acquired two class A office buildings totaling 188,103 square feet in suburban Philadelphia for $34.0 million. Also, on 12/16/02, CLI announced that it acquired a 174,124 square-foot class A office property in suburban Philadelphia for $26.3 million.

ANNUAL FINANCIAL DATA:

FISCAL YEAR	TOT. INC. ($mill.)	NET INC. ($mill.)	TOT. ASSETS ($mill.)	NET INC. + DEPR./ ASSETS %	RET. ON EQUITY %	RET. ON ASSETS %	EARN. PER SH. $	TANG. BK. VAL. $	DIV. PER SH. $	DIV. PAYOUT %	PRICE RANGE	AVG. P/E RATIO	AVG. YIELD %
p12/31/02	569.6	⑥ 139.7					2.43		2.49	102.5	35.73 - 26.64	12.8	8.0
12/31/01	584.3	131.7	3,746.8	6.0	9.2	3.5	2.32	25.26	2.45	105.6	32.20 - 25.49	12.4	8.5
12/31/00	576.2	②④ 185.3	3,677.0	7.5	12.8	5.0	②④ 3.10	24.64	2.35	75.8	28.88 - 22.75	8.3	9.1
12/31/99	551.5	①② 119.7	3,629.6	5.7	8.3	3.3	①② 2.04	24.67	2.23	109.3	33.63 - 23.13	13.9	7.9
12/31/98	493.7	③ 119.0	3,452.2	5.7	8.4	3.4	③ 2.11	24.86	1.55	73.5	41.38 - 26.13	16.0	4.6
12/31/97	249.8	①③ 5.0	2,593.4	1.6	0.4	0.2	①③ 0.12	23.22	...	...	43.00 - 28.38	297.1	...
12/31/96	95.5	②③ 32.4	1,026.3	4.7	4.6	3.2	②③ 1.76	...	...	...	31.00 - 20.50	14.6	...
12/31/95	62.3	13.6	363.9	7.1	7.3	3.7	1.23	12.30	...	...	22.00 - 15.38	15.2	...
12/31/94	16.8	3.9	225.3	3.4	3.6	1.7	0.38	10.32	...	...	17.38 - 14.88	42.4	...
⑤ 12/31/93	47.9	d1.1	208.8	...	...	...	...	...	...	...	...	...	...

Statistics are as originally reported. ① Incl. non-recurr. merger-related chrg., 1999, $16.5 mill.; 1997, $46.5 mill. ② Incl. gain on sale of rental property, 2000, $75.0 mill.; 1999, $2.0 mill.; 1996, $5.7 mill. ③ Excl. extraord. chrg., 1998, $2.4 mill.; 1997, $3.6 mill.; 1996, $475,000. ④ Incl. non-recurr. chrg., $32.7 mill. ⑤ Combined financial statements of Cali Group ⑥ Incl. real. gain of $2.8 mill. on disp. of rental prop.

OFFICERS:
W. L. Mack, Chmn.
M. E. Hersh, C.E.O.
B. Lefkowitz, Exec. V.P., C.F.O.
INVESTOR CONTACT: Barry Leftowitz, Investor Relations, (908) 272-8000
PRINCIPAL OFFICE: 11 Commerce Drive, Cranford, NJ 07016-3501

TELEPHONE NUMBER: (908) 272-8000
FAX: (908) 272-6755
WEB: www.mack-cali.com
NO. OF EMPLOYEES: 380 (approx.)
SHAREHOLDERS: 528
ANNUAL MEETING: In May
INCORPORATED: MD, May, 1994

INSTITUTIONAL HOLDINGS:
No. of Institutions: 183
Shares Held: 42,796,967
% Held: 74.4
INDUSTRY: Real estate investment trusts (SIC: 6798)
TRANSFER AGENT(S): EquiServe, Inc., Jersey City, NJ

MANDALAY RESORT GROUP

EXCH.	SYM.	REC. PRICE	P/E RATIO	YLD.	MKT. CAP.	RANGE (52-WK.)	'02 Y/E PR.
NYSE	MBG	25.24 (2/28/03)	15.6	...	$1.73 bill.	37.00 - 23.19	30.61

MEDIUM GRADE. MANDALAY BAY CONTINUES CONSTRUCTION ON A NEW TOWER OF 1,122 SUITES, WHICH IS EXPECTED TO OPEN IN NOVEMBER 2003.

TRADING VOLUME
Thousand Shares

*7 YEAR PRICE SCORE 131.5   ***12 MONTH PRICE SCORE 98.1**
*NYSE COMPOSITE INDEX=100

INTERIM EARNINGS (Per Share):

Qtr.	Apr.	July	Oct.	Jan.
1998-99	0.23	0.27	0.25	0.16
1999-00	d0.05	0.26	0.31	d0.06
2000-01	0.58	0.48	0.38	0.04
2001-02	0.61	0.40	0.32	d0.66
2002-03	0.68	0.41	0.47	0.06

INTERIM DIVIDENDS (Per Share):

Amt.	Decl.	Ex.	Rec.	Pay.
		No dividends paid.		

CAPITALIZATION (1/31/02):

	($000)	(%)
Long-Term Debt	2,482,087	68.5
Deferred Income Tax	199,478	5.5
Common & Surplus	940,609	26.0
Total	3,622,174	100.0

BUSINESS:

Mandalay Resort Group (formerly Circus Circus Enterprises, Inc.), as of 3/6/03, owned and operated eleven properties in Nevada: Mandalay Bay, Luxor, Excalibur, Circus Circus, and Slots-A-Fun in Las Vegas; Circus Circus-Reno; Colorado Belle and Edgewater in Laughlin; Gold Strike and Nevada Landing in Jean and Railroad Pass in Henderson. MBG also owns and operates Gold Strike, a hotel/casino in Tunica County, Mississippi. MBG owns a 50% interest in Silver Legacy in Reno, and a 50% interest

in and operates Monte Carlo in Las Vegas. MBG owns a 50% interest in and operates Grand Victoria, a riverboat casino in Elgin, Illinois, and owns a 53.5% interest in and operates MotorCity in Detroit, Michigan. MBG caters to high volume business by providing moderately-priced rooms, food and alternative entertainment with gaming activity for family-oriented vacationers. Net sales for 2001 were derived as follows: casino, 47.6%; rooms, 23.0%; food and beverage, 16.2%; and other, 13.2%.

RECENT DEVELOPMENTS:

For the year ended 1/31/03, the Company reported income of $117.5 million, before an accounting charge of $1.9 million, compared with net income of $53.0 million the year before. Earnings for 2002 and 2001 included pre-tax pre-opening expenses of $4.6 million and $2.2 million, and

impairment losses of $5.4 million and $52.0 million, respectively. Earnings for 2002 also included a pre-tax write-off of $13.0 million for intangible assets. Revenues slipped to $2.34 billion from $2.35 billion a year earlier.

PROSPECTS:

Mandalay Bay continues to benefit from its recently opened convention center, with total show attendance in January 2003 exceeding 65,000. Mandalay expects to host approximately 60 shows in fiscal 2003. Meanwhile, Mandalay

continues construction on a new tower of 1,122 suites, which is expected to open in November 2003. These suites will complement the above-mentioned convention center and should contribute to higher results in fiscal 2003.

ANNUAL FINANCIAL DATA:

FISCAL YEAR	TOT. REVS. ($mill.)	NET INC. ($mill.)	TOT. ASSETS ($mill.)	OPER. PROFIT %	NET PROFIT %	RET. ON EQUITY %	RET. ON ASSETS %	CURR. RATIO	EARN. PER SH. $	CASH FL. PER SH. $	TANG. BK. VAL. $	PRICE RANGE	AVG. P/E RATIO
p1/31/03	2,343.2	⑤⑦ 117.5							⑥⑦ 1.65			37.00 - 21.12	17.6
1/31/02	2,461.8	⑤⑥ 53.0	4,037.0	14.3	2.2	5.6	1.3	0.9	⑤⑥ 0.71	3.61	13.10	27.89 - 13.90	29.4
1/31/01	2,524.2	⑤ 119.7	4,248.3	17.1	4.7	11.2	2.8	1.0	⑤ 1.50	4.24	8.98	28.38 - 12.88	13.7
1/31/00	2,050.9	④ 64.2	4,329.5	13.3	3.1	5.4	1.5	1.2	④ 0.70	2.57	8.81	26.31 - 11.56	27.1
1/31/99	1,479.8	85.2	3,869.7	16.4	5.8	7.4	2.2	0.7	0.90	2.40	8.72	26.50 - 7.13	18.7
1/31/98	1,354.5	③ 89.9	3,263.5	17.5	6.6	8.0	2.8	0.9	③ 0.94	2.31	7.87	36.50 - 20.00	30.0
1/31/97	1,334.3	① 100.7	2,729.1	16.7	7.5	10.4	3.7	1.2	① 0.99	2.01	6.23	44.63 - 27.63	36.5
1/31/96	1,299.6	② 128.9	2,211.9	19.3	9.9	10.5	5.8	1.3	② 1.33	2.34	7.38	36.13 - 23.50	22.4
1/31/95	1,170.2	136.3	1,507.1	21.9	11.6	19.9	9.0	1.3	1.59	2.55	7.88	40.75 - 19.75	19.0
1/31/94	954.9	116.2	1,297.9	21.1	12.2	20.7	9.0	1.0	1.34	2.01	6.64	49.75 - 27.58	28.9

Statistics are as originally reported. Adj. for stk. splits: 3-for-2, 7/93. ① Incl. $48.3 mill. chrg. for write-offs rel. to construct. projects. ② Incl. $45.1 mill. chrg. for write-off of certain assets. ③ Incl. a net loss of $5.4 mill. rel. to various items. ④ Bef. an acctg. chrg. of $22.0 mill.; incl. one-time pre-tax net loss of $54.5 mill. ⑤ Incl. a pre-tax pre-open. exp. of $4.6 mill., 1/03; $2.2 mill., 1/02; $1.8 mill., 1/01. ⑥ Incl. an impairment loss of $52.0 mill. ⑦ Incl. an impairment loss of $5.4 mill. & write-off of intang. asset of $13.0 mill.

OFFICERS:
M. S. Ensign, Chmn., C.E.O., C.O.O.
W. A. Richardson, Vice-Chmn.
G. Schaeffer, Pres., C.F.O., Treas.

INVESTOR CONTACT: Glenn Schaeffer, Pres. & C.F.O., (702) 632-6708

PRINCIPAL OFFICE: 3950 Las Vegas Blvd. South, Las Vegas, NV 89119

TELEPHONE NUMBER: (702) 632-6700
FAX: (702) 634-3450
WEB: www.mandalayresortgroup.com

NO. OF EMPLOYEES: 33,300 (approx.)

SHAREHOLDERS: 2,966

ANNUAL MEETING: In June

INCORPORATED: NV, Feb., 1974

INSTITUTIONAL HOLDINGS:
No. of Institutions: 187
Shares Held: 49,296,276
% Held: 74.7

INDUSTRY: Amusement and recreation, nec (SIC: 7999)

TRANSFER AGENT(S): Wells Fargo Shareowner Services, St. Paul, MN

MANITOWOC COMPANY, INC.

EXCH.	SYM.	REC. PRICE	P/E RATIO	YLD.	MKT. CAP.	RANGE (52-WK.)	'02 Y/E PR.
NYSE	MTW	18.17 (2/28/03)	10.9	1.5%	$437.0 mill.	44.39 - 17.85	25.50

MEDIUM GRADE. THE COMPANY IS TARGETING FULL-YEAR 2003 EARNINGS PER SHARE RANGE THAT IS FLAT TO 10.0% HIGHER THAN THE PRIOR YEAR, BEFORE SPECIAL ITEMS.

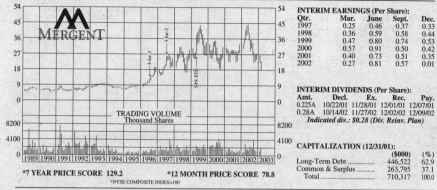

INTERIM EARNINGS (Per Share):

Qtr.	Mar.	June	Sept.	Dec.
1997	0.25	0.46	0.37	0.33
1998	0.36	0.59	0.58	0.44
1999	0.47	0.80	0.74	0.53
2000	0.57	0.91	0.50	0.42
2001	0.40	0.73	0.51	0.35
2002	0.27	0.81	0.57	0.01

INTERIM DIVIDENDS (Per Share):

Amt.	Decl.	Ex.	Rec.	Pay.
0.225A	10/22/01	11/28/01	12/01/01	12/07/01
0.28A	10/14/02	11/27/02	12/02/02	12/09/02

Indicated div.: $0.28 (Div. Reinv. Plan)

CAPITALIZATION (12/31/01):

	($000)	(%)
Long-Term Debt	446,522	62.9
Common & Surplus	263,795	37.1
Total	710,317	100.0

TRADING VOLUME
Thousand Shares

*7 YEAR PRICE SCORE 129.2   ***12 MONTH PRICE SCORE 78.8**

*NYSE COMPOSITE INDEX=100

BUSINESS:

Manitowoc Company, Inc. is a diversified industrial manufacturer with positions in three principal markets: cranes; foodservice equipment; and marine services in the Great Lakes region. The cranes and related products segment (51.5% of 2002 revenues) provides lifting equipment for the global construction industry, including lattice-boom cranes, tower cranes, mobile telescopic cranes, boom trucks, and aerial work platforms. The foodservice segment (32.9%) designs, manufactures and markets full product lines of ice making machines, walk-in and reach-in refrigerator/freezers, fountain beverage delivery systems and other foodservice refrigeration products for the restaurant, lodging, convenience store and institutional foodservice markets. The marine service segment (15.6%) provides ship building, repair and maintenance services in the U.S. Great Lakes region. On 5/9/01, MTW acquired Potain SA, for $424.8 million. In August 2002, MTW acquired Grove Investors, Inc. for $271.0 million.

RECENT DEVELOPMENTS:

For the year ended 12/31/02, earnings from continuing operations was $40.2 million versus $48.7 million a year earlier. Results for 2002 and 2001 included amortization of $2.0 million and $11.1 million, respectively. Results for 2002 also included a plant consolidation charge of $3.9 million and a restructuring charge of $7.7 million. Net sales rose 34.4% to $1.41 billion, primarily due to the Grove Investors, Inc. and Potain SA acquisitions.

PROSPECTS:

MTW is projecting full-year 2003 consolidated sales growth of approximately 20.0%, primarily due to a full year effect of Grove, which was acquired in August 2002, and gains from the Company's foodservice segment. Internal sales for full-year 2003 are expected to be flat versus the previous year. MTW is targeting a full-year earnings per share range that is flat to 10.0% higher than the prior year, before special items. Separately, on 2/17/03, MTW announced that it has sold its Femco Machine Company business to a group of private investors. Also, in January 2003, MTW completed the sale of Manitowoc Boom Trucks, Inc. to Quantum Heavy Equipment, LLC. The sale was required by the Department of Justice in order for the Company to acquire Grove Worldwide.

ANNUAL FINANCIAL DATA:

FISCAL YEAR	TOT. REVS. ($000)	NET INC. ($000)	TOT. ASSETS ($000)	OPER. PROFIT %	NET PROFIT %	RET. ON EQUITY %	RET. ON ASSETS %	CURR. RATIO	EARN. PER SH. $	CASH FL. PER SH. $	TANG. BK. VAL.$	DIV. PER SH. $	PRICE RANGE	AVG. P/E RATIO	AVG. YIELD %
p12/31/02	1,406,577	⑥ 40,179							⑥ 1.56			0.28	44.39 - 22.10	21.3	0.8
⑤ 12/31/01	1,116,580	④ 48,872	1,080,812	10.6	4.4	18.5	4.5	1.1	④ 1.99	3.48	...	0.30	32.84 - 22.30	13.9	1.1
12/31/00	873,272	60,268	642,530	12.9	6.9	25.8	9.4	0.9	2.40	3.14	...	0.30	34.88 - 17.63	10.9	1.1
12/31/99	805,491	66,784	530,240	14.8	8.3	28.8	12.6	1.0	2.55	3.21	...	0.30	43.75 - 24.21	13.3	0.9
12/31/98	694,822	51,380	481,014	13.3	7.4	29.8	10.7	1.0	1.97	2.54	...	0.30	31.33 - 16.33	12.1	1.3
12/31/97	545,864	36,423	396,368	11.9	6.7	28.3	9.2	0.9	1.39	1.86	...	0.30	27.13 - 14.83	15.1	1.4
12/31/96	500,465	25,643	317,710	10.2	5.1	25.6	8.1	1.2	0.99	1.44	0.24	0.30	19.56 - 8.19	14.0	2.1
12/31/95	313,149	① 14,569	324,915	7.4	4.7	17.8	4.5	1.2	① 0.56	0.83	...	0.30	9.07 - 6.22	13.6	3.9
7/02/94	275,380	② 14,043	185,848	7.7	5.1	15.0	7.6	1.8	② 0.48	0.69	3.26	0.30	9.59 - 6.37	16.7	3.7
7/03/93	278,558	③ 6,317	208,011	3.0	2.3	5.3	3.0	2.5	③ 0.19	3.77	3.77	0.30	9.85 - 7.26	44.3	3.5

Statistics are as originally reported. Refls. 3-for-2 stk. splits, 3/99, 6/97 & 7/96. ① Incl. non-recurr. chrg. of $1.8 mill. ② Incl. non-recurr. chrg. of $14.0 mill. ③ Bef. acctg. adj. chrg. of $10.2 mill. ④ Bef. extraord. loss of $3.3 mill. ⑤ Refl. the 11/00 acq. of Marinette Marine & 5/01 acq. of Potain SA. ⑥ Incl. plant consol. costs of $3.9 mill. & restruct. chrgs. of $7.7 mill.; bef. inc. fr. disc. ops. of $1.6 mill., loss on sale of disc. ops. of $25.5 mill. & acctg. chge. chrg. of $36.8 mill.

MANOR CARE, INC.

EXCH.	SYM.	REC. PRICE	P/E RATIO	YLD.	MKT. CAP.	RANGE (52-WK.)	'02 Y/E PR.
NYSE	HCR	18.33 (2/28/03)	13.8	...	$1.88 bill.	27.01 - 16.20	18.61

MEDIUM GRADE. RESULTS ARE BENEFITING FROM HIGHER OCCUPANCY AS WELL AS THE COMPANY'S COST CONTROL AND GROWTH INITIATIVES.

INTERIM EARNINGS (Per Share):

Qtr.	Mar.	June	Sept.	Dec.
1999	0.37	0.30	0.31	d1.59
2000	d0.01	d0.03	0.20	0.22
2001	0.24	0.29	0.30	d0.03
2002	0.33	0.38	0.38	0.24

INTERIM DIVIDENDS (Per Share):

Amt.	Decl.	Ex.	Rec.	Pay.
		No dividends paid.		

TRADING VOLUME
Thousand Shares

*7 YEAR PRICE SCORE 90.8　　***12 MONTH PRICE SCORE 95.7**

*NYSE COMPOSITE INDEX=100

CAPITALIZATION (12/31/01):

	($000)	(%)
Long-Term Debt	715,830	38.4
Deferred Income Tax	103,095	5.5
Common & Surplus	1,046,538	56.1
Total	1,865,463	100.0

BUSINESS:

Manor Care, Inc. (formerly HCR Manor Care, Inc.) was formed upon the merger of Manor Care, Inc. and Health Care & Retirement Corp. on 9/25/98. HCR provides a range of health care services, including skilled nursing care, assisted living, subacute medical and rehabilitation care, rehabilitation therapy, home health care, hospice care and management services for subacute care and rehabilitation therapy. The most significant portion of HCR's business is long-term care, including skilled nursing care and assisted living. The Company provides care through a network of more than 500 centers under the Manor Care, Heartland and Arden Courts names.

RECENT DEVELOPMENTS:

For the year ended 12/31/02, income was $131.9 million, before an accounting change charge of $1.3 million, compared with net income of $68.5 million the previous year. Results for 2002 and 2001 included a gain of $30.7 million and a loss of $445,000, respectively. The 2002 results also included a pre-tax asset impairment charge of $33.6 million. Revenues climbed 7.8% to $2.91 billion from $2.69 billion the year before. The improvement in revenues was primarily attributed to higher skilled nursing center occupancy.

PROSPECTS:

Going forward, the Company should continue to benefit from its growth strategies even in the midst of Medicare reimbursement uncertainties. The Company is working to restore Medicare funding care for the elderly and those in need of subacute and shorter-term care. Meanwhile, the Company's results should continue to benefit from its focus on occupancy, controlling indirect costs, growing its businesses outside its skilled nursing centers and emphasizing its ability to serve a broader spectrum of patients and clients through its specialty services. Moreover, the Company will continue to aggressively market its services, fill recently completed expansions and meet the needs of a diverse patient/client base.

ANNUAL FINANCIAL DATA:

FISCAL YEAR	TOT. REVS. ($mill.)	NET INC. ($mill.)	TOT. ASSETS ($mill.)	OPER. PROFIT %	NET PROFIT %	RET. ON EQUITY %	RET. ON ASSETS %	CURR. RATIO	EARN. PER SH.$	CASH FL. PER SH.$	TANG. BK. VAL.$	PRICE RANGE	AVG. P/E RATIO
p12/31/02	2,905.4	⑤ 131.9							⑤ 1.33			27.01 - 16.20	16.2
12/31/01	2,694.1	68.5	2,424.1	6.6	2.5	6.5	2.8	1.5	0.66	1.90	9.28	34.50 - 17.31	39.2
12/31/00	2,380.6	39.1	2,358.5	5.8	1.6	3.9	1.7	1.1	0.38	1.55	8.86	21.19 - 6.44	36.3
12/31/99	2,135.3	④ d55.2	2,280.9	10.8	...	...	...	1.1	④ d0.51	0.56	8.71	33.50 - 12.75	...
12/31/98	2,209.1	① d46.2	2,715.1	...	...	...	...	0.8	① d0.42	0.67	10.85	47.88 - 23.50	...
③ 12/31/97	892.0	70.1	936.4	12.7	7.9	16.2	7.5	1.4	1.51	2.32	6.78	42.50 - 25.00	22.3
12/31/96	782.0	59.4	802.8	12.0	7.6	15.1	7.4	1.2	1.24	1.91	7.06	29.25 - 21.75	20.6
12/31/95	713.5	50.6	729.2	11.4	7.1	13.5	6.9	1.1	1.03	1.60	7.10	24.08 - 16.75	19.8
12/31/94	615.1	42.0	657.3	11.5	6.8	12.2	6.4	1.2	0.84	1.30	7.27	20.17 - 14.17	20.4
12/31/93	559.3	② 34.1	636.0	11.1	6.1	10.8	5.4	1.1	② 0.69	1.10	6.57	14.83 - 8.33	16.9

Statistics are as originally reported. Adj. for stk. splits 2-for-1, 3/93, 3-for-2, 6/96. ① Incl. a non-recurr charge of $278.3 million but excl. a gain of $67.9 million from discontinued operations, an extraord. chrg. of $19.0 mill. and an acctg. chrg. of $5.6 mill. ② Bef. an acctg. change chrg. of $1.4 mill. ③ Results for 12/31/97 and prior are for Health Care & Retirement Corp. prior to the merger with Manor Care, Inc. ④ Incl. a non-recurr. chrg. totaling $14.8 mill. but excl. a net extraord. gain of $11.5 mill. ⑤ Bef. an acctg. chng. chrg. of $1.3 mill. & incl. pre-tax gain of $30.7 mill. on sale of assets & pre-tax asset impair. chrg. of $33.6 mill.

OFFICERS:
P. A. Ormond, Chmn., Pres., C.E.O.
G. G. Meyers, Exec. V.P., C.F.O.
M. K. Weikel, Sr., Exec. V.P., C.O.O.
R. J. Bixler, V.P., Gen. Couns., Sec.

INVESTOR CONTACT: Geoffrey G. Meyers, (419) 252-5545

PRINCIPAL OFFICE: 333 N. Summit Street, Toledo, OH 43604-2617

TELEPHONE NUMBER: (419) 252-5500
FAX: (419) 247-1364
WEB: www.hcr-manorcare.com
NO. OF EMPLOYEES: 61,000 (avg.)
SHAREHOLDERS: 3,090 (of record); 20,000 (approx. beneficial)
ANNUAL MEETING: In May
INCORPORATED: DE, Aug., 1991

INDUSTRY: Skilled nursing care facilities (SIC: 8051)

TRANSFER AGENT(S): Computershare Investor Services, Chicago, IL

MANPOWER INC.

EXCH.	SYM.	REC. PRICE	P/E RATIO	YLD.	MKT. CAP.	RANGE (52-WK.)	'02 Y/E PR.
NYSE	MAN	30.37 (2/28/03)	20.8	0.7%	$2.31 bill.	43.30 - 24.99	31.90

MEDIUM GRADE. EARLY IN 2003, THE COMPANY CONTINUES TO GAIN STRENGTH THROUGHOUT ALL OF ITS MAJOR OPERATIONS.

TRADING VOLUME
Thousand Shares

*7 YEAR PRICE SCORE 109.9   ***12 MONTH PRICE SCORE 100.3**
*NYSE COMPOSITE INDEX=100

INTERIM EARNINGS (Per Share):

Qtr.	Mar.	June	Sept.	Dec.
1999	0.26	0.40	0.63	0.63
2000	0.33	0.49	0.70	0.70
2001	0.35	0.45	0.48	0.34
2002	0.09	0.33	0.52	0.52

INTERIM DIVIDENDS (Per Share):

Amt.	Decl.	Ex.	Rec.	Pay.
0.10S	5/02/01	5/30/01	6/01/01	6/14/01
0.10S	10/30/01	11/29/01	12/03/01	12/14/01
0.10S	5/03/02	5/30/02	6/03/02	6/14/02
0.10S	10/29/02	11/29/02	12/03/02	12/16/02

Indicated div.: $0.20 (Div. Reinv. Plan)

CAPITALIZATION (12/31/01):

	($000)	(%)
Long-Term Debt	811,100	49.9
Common & Surplus	814,300	50.1
Total	1,625,400	100.0

BUSINESS:

Manpower Inc. is engaged primarily in temporary staffing services, contract services, and training and testing of temporary and permanent workers. As of 2/27/03, the Company operated 3,900 offices in 63 countries. The largest operations, based on revenues, are located in the United States, France and the United Kingdom. The Company provides employment services to a wide variety of customers, none of which individually comprise a significant portion of revenues within a given geographic region or for the Company as a whole. In France, the Company's largest market, MAN conducts operations under the names Manpower and Supplay.

RECENT DEVELOPMENTS:

For the year ended 12/31/02, net earnings declined 9.1% to $113.2 million versus $124.5 million in the prior year. Results for 2001 included after-tax amortization of intangibles of $14.8 million. Systemwide sales, including sales at franchise offices, slipped to $11.76 billion from $11.78 billion in 2001. Revenue from services increased 1.2% to $10.61 billion from $10.48 billion a year earlier. Gross profit decreased 2.4% to $1.91 billion from $1.96 billion the year before. Operating profit fell 1.2% to $234.8 million from $237.6 million the previous year. For the fourth quarter ended 12/31/02, net earnings advanced 54.9% to $40.1 million from $26.0 million in the corresponding prior-year quarter. Revenues from services climbed 11.9% to $2.84 billion from $2.54 billion in the year-earlier quarter.

PROSPECTS:

In 2002, MAN strengthened its position in the marketplace through expansion of offices in the specialty services areas and the launch of new services. The Company continues to gain strength throughout all of its major operations. France, MAN's largest operation, has performed particularly well recently, given the weak economic conditions. Results are also benefiting from favorable foreign currency gains. Earnings for the first quarter of 2003 are expected to be in the range of $0.16 to $0.20 per share.

ANNUAL FINANCIAL DATA:

FISCAL YEAR	TOT. REVS. ($mill.)	NET INC. ($mill.)	TOT. ASSETS ($mill.)	OPER. PROFIT %	NET PROFIT %	RET. ON EQUITY %	RET. ON ASSETS %	CURR. RATIO	EARN. PER SH. $	CASH FL. PER SH. $	TANG. BK. VAL. $	DIV. PER SH. $	PRICE RANGE	AVG. P/E RATIO	AVG. YIELD %
p12/31/02	10,610.9	113.2							1.46			0.20	43.30 - 24.99	23.4	0.6
12/31/01	10,483.8	124.5	3,238.6	2.3	1.2	15.3	3.8	1.8	1.62	2.66	4.38	0.20	38.00 - 23.39	18.9	0.7
12/31/00	10,842.8	171.2	3,041.6	2.9	1.6	23.1	5.6	1.6	2.22	3.09	6.50	0.20	40.25 - 25.50	14.8	0.6
12/31/99	9,770.1	② 150.0	2,718.7	2.4	1.5	23.1	5.5	1.6	② 1.91	2.72	7.39	0.20	39.50 - 20.25	15.6	0.7
12/31/98	8,814.3	① 75.7	2,381.1	1.5	0.9	11.3	3.2	1.5	① 0.93	1.64	8.48	0.19	45.75 - 18.25	34.4	0.6
12/31/97	7,258.5	163.9	2,047.0	3.5	2.3	26.5	8.0	1.7	1.97	2.46	7.69	0.17	50.38 - 29.50	20.3	0.4
12/31/96	6,079.9	162.3	1,752.3	3.7	2.7	27.0	9.3	1.8	1.95	2.38	7.41	0.15	43.00 - 23.63	17.1	0.5
12/31/95	5,484.2	128.0	1,517.8	3.9	2.3	28.1	8.4	1.6	1.65	2.01	5.61	0.13	34.25 - 24.13	17.7	0.4
12/31/94	4,296.4	68.7	1,203.7	3.2	1.6	33.8	5.7	1.5	1.12	1.28	2.69	0.11	29.88 - 16.88	20.9	0.5
12/31/93	3,180.4	① d61.2	833.3	...	...	...	...	1.4	① d0.66	0.48	1.29	...	17.88 - 13.50	...	...

Statistics are as originally reported. ① Incl. non-recurr. chrg. 1998, $92.1 mill.; 1993, $20.0 mill. ② Incl. one-time after-tax charges totaling $700,000.

OFFICERS:
J. A. Joerres, Chmn., Pres., C.E.O.
M. J. Van Handel, Exec. V.P., C.F.O., Sec.

INVESTOR CONTACT: Mike Van Handel, C.F.O., (414) 906-6305

PRINCIPAL OFFICE: 5301 N. Ironwood Road, Milwaukee, WI 53217

TELEPHONE NUMBER: (414) 961-1000
FAX: (414) 961-7081
WEB: www.manpower.com

NO. OF EMPLOYEES: 21,400 (approx.)

SHAREHOLDERS: 7,474 (record)

ANNUAL MEETING: In April

INCORPORATED: WI, April, 1990

INSTITUTIONAL HOLDINGS:
No. of Institutions: 236
Shares Held: 74,369,955
% Held: 96.9

INDUSTRY: Help supply services (SIC: 7363)

TRANSFER AGENT(S): Mellon Investor Services, LLC, South Hackensack, NJ

MARATHON OIL CORPORATION

EXCH.	SYM.	REC. PRICE	P/E RATIO	YLD.	MKT. CAP.	RANGE (52-WK.)	'02 Y/E PR.
NYSE	MRO	23.09 (2/28/03)	14.2	4.0%	$7.14 bill.	30.00 - 18.85	21.29

MEDIUM GRADE. THE COMPANY APPROVED A 2003 CAPITAL, INVESTMENT AND EXPLORATION EXPENDITURE BUDGET OF $1.96 BILLION, 8.2% HIGHER THAN THE PREVIOUS YEAR.

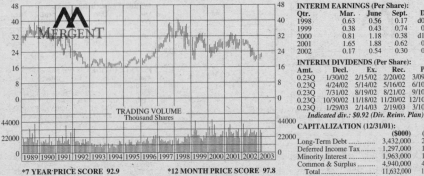

TRADING VOLUME
Thousand Shares

*7 YEAR PRICE SCORE 92.9   *12 MONTH PRICE SCORE 97.8
*NYSE COMPOSITE INDEX=100

INTERIM EARNINGS (Per Share):

Qtr.	Mar.	June	Sept.	Dec.
1998	0.63	0.56	0.17	d0.29
1999	0.38	0.43	0.74	0.55
2000	0.81	1.36	0.38	d1.00
2001	1.65	1.88	0.62	0.17
2002	0.17	0.54	0.30	0.62

INTERIM DIVIDENDS (Per Share):

Amt.	Decl.	Ex.	Rec.	Pay.
0.23Q	1/30/02	2/15/02	2/20/02	3/09/02
0.23Q	4/24/02	5/14/02	5/16/02	6/10/02
0.23Q	7/31/02	8/19/02	8/21/02	9/10/02
0.23Q	10/30/02	11/18/02	11/20/02	12/10/02
0.23Q	1/29/03	2/14/03	2/19/03	3/10/03

Indicated div.: $0.92 (Div. Reinv. Plan)

CAPITALIZATION (12/31/01):

	($000)	(%)
Long-Term Debt	3,432,000	29.5
Deferred Income Tax	1,297,000	11.2
Minority Interest	1,963,000	16.9
Common & Surplus	4,940,000	42.5
Total	11,632,000	100.0

BUSINESS:

Marathon Oil Corporation (formerly USX-Marathon Group) is engaged in worldwide exploration and production of crude oil and natural gas; domestic refining, marketing and transportation of petroleum products primarily through its 62.0%-owned subsidiary, Marathon Ashland Petroleum LLC; and other energy-related businesses. MRO began trading as a standalone company on 1/2/02 following final action by USX Corporation to separate the Marathon Group and the U.S. Steel Group into two independent companies. Net estimated developed and undeveloped proved reserves as of 12/31/01 were: liquid hydrocarbons, 570.0 million barrels; natural gas, 2.86 trillion cubic feet.

RECENT DEVELOPMENTS:

For the year ended 12/31/02, income was $536.0 million, before an extraordinary loss of $33.0 million and an accounting change gain of $13.0 million, versus income from continuing operations of $1.32 billion a year earlier. Earnings included a credit of $72.0 million for 2002 and charges of $72.0 million for 2001, both related to inventory market valuation. MRO's earnings were especially effected by lower refining, marketing and transportation operating profits. Total revenues and other income fell 4.2% to $31.72 billion and included net gains of $65.0 million on the disposal of assets.

PROSPECTS:

On 2/6/03, MRO announced it has approved a 2003 capital, investment and exploration expenditure budget of $1.96 billion, 8.2% higher than the previous year, excluding acquisitions. The budget includes exploration and production spending of $1.10 billion and $732.0 million for refining, marketing and transportation projects. MRO also announced that it plans to sell about $400.0 million in non-core assets during 2003. The budget reflects MRO's continuing emphasis on expanding the development of its international upstream portfolio with assets that will enable it to realize long-term value-added growth. The budget will also allow MRO to continue investing in its U.S. downstream operations as well as its core domestic upstream business.

ANNUAL FINANCIAL DATA:

FISCAL YEAR	TOT. REVS. ($mill.)	NET INC. ($mill.)	TOT. ASSETS ($mill.)	OPER. PROFIT %	NET PROFIT %	RET. ON EQUITY %	RET. ON ASSETS %	CURR. RATIO	EARN. PER SH. $	CASH FL. PER SH. $	TANG. BK. VAL. $	DIV. PER SH. $	PRICE RANGE	AVG. P/E RATIO	AVG. YIELD %
p12/31/02	31,720.0	⑧ 536.0							⑧ 1.72			0.92	30.30 - 18.85	14.3	3.7
12/31/01	33,066.0	⑦ 1,318.0	16,129.0	8.9	4.0	26.7	8.2	1.3	⑦ 4.26	8.25	15.97	0.92	33.73 - 24.95	6.9	3.1
12/31/00	33,859.0	⑥ 432.0	15,232.0	4.9	1.3	8.9	2.8	1.2	⑥ 1.39	5.38	15.72	0.88	30.38 - 20.69	18.4	3.4
12/31/99	24,327.0	⑥ 654.0	15,705.0	7.0	2.7	13.6	4.2	1.3	⑤ 2.11	5.18	15.50	0.84	33.44 - 19.63	12.6	3.2
12/31/98	22,075.0	④ 310.0	14,544.0	4.2	1.4	7.2	2.1	1.1	④ 1.05	4.27	13.95	0.84	40.50 - 25.00	31.2	2.6
12/31/97	15,754.0	① 456.0	10,565.0	5.9	2.9	12.6	4.3	0.9	① 1.58	3.85	12.52	0.76	38.88 - 23.75	19.8	2.4
12/31/96	16,332.0	① 671.0	10,151.0	7.6	4.1	20.1	6.6	1.0	① 2.33	4.74	11.60	0.70	25.50 - 17.25	9.2	3.3
12/31/95	13,871.0	② d83.0	10,109.0	0.8	...	...	...	0.9	② d0.31	2.54	10.01	0.68	21.50 - 15.75	...	3.7
12/31/94	12,757.0	321.0	10,951.0	4.6	2.5	9.9	2.9	1.0	1.10	3.61	11.02	0.68	19.13 - 15.63	15.8	3.9
12/31/93	11,962.0	⑥ d6.0	10,806.0	1.4	...	...	...	1.0	⑥ d0.04	2.49	...	0.68	20.63 - 16.38	...	3.7

Statistics are as originally reported. Chart prices prior to May, 1991 are for USX Corp. ① Incl. nonrecur. chrg. 12/31/97, $284.0 mill.; cr. 12/31/96, $137.0 mill. ② Bef. acctg. adj. chrg. of $659.0 mill. ③ Incl. nonrecur. chrg. of $241.0 mill.; bef. acctg. adj. chrg. of $23.0 mill. ④ Incl. invent. mkt. valuation cr. of $267.0 mill. ⑤ Incl. net after-tax gain of $220.0 mill. ⑥ Incl. net after-tax nonrecur. chrgs. of $876.0 mill. ⑦ Incl. invent. mkt. valuation chrgs. of $72.0 mill.; bef. inc. fr. disc. ops. of $169.0 mill., loss on disp. of U.S. Steel Corp. of $984.0 mill. & acctg. chge. chrg. of $8.0 mill. ⑧ Incl. invent. mkt. valuation cr. of $72.0 mill.; bef. extraord. loss of $33.0 mill. & acctg chge. gain of $13.0 mill.

OFFICERS:
C. P. Cazalot, Jr., Pres., C.E.O.
J. T. Mills, Sr. V.P., C.F.O
W. F. Schwind, Jr., V.P., Gen. Counsel, Sec.
INVESTOR CONTACT: Kenneth L. Matheny, V.P., Inv. Rel., (713) 296-4114
PRINCIPAL OFFICE: 5555 San Felipe Road, Houston, TX 77056-2723

TELEPHONE NUMBER: (713) 629-6600
WEB: www.marathon.com
NO. OF EMPLOYEES: 30,671
SHAREHOLDERS: 69,264
ANNUAL MEETING: In Apr.
INCORPORATED: DE, 1965

INSTITUTIONAL HOLDINGS:
No. of Institutions: 401
Shares Held: 248,606,759
% Held: 80.2
INDUSTRY: Oil and gas exploration services (SIC: 1382)
TRANSFER AGENT(S): National City Bank, Cleveland, OH

MARKEL CORPORATION

EXCH.	SYM.	REC. PRICE	P/E RATIO	YLD.	MKT. CAP.	RANGE (52-WK.)	'02 Y/E PR.
NYSE	MKL	213.66 (2/28/03)	28.0	...	$2.10 bill.	222.03 - 175.00	205.50

MEDIUM GRADE. THE COMPANY IS BENEFITING FROM IMPROVEMENTS IN UNDERWRITING RESULTS.

*7 YEAR PRICE SCORE 136.7   *12 MONTH PRICE SCORE 113.3
*NYSE COMPOSITE INDEX=100

INTERIM EARNINGS (Per Share):

Qtr.	Mar.	June	Sept.	Dec.
2000	2.44	d2.44	d2.15	d1.84
2001	1.04	0.09	d10.58	d4.78
2002	1.73	2.36	0.88	2.67

INTERIM DIVIDENDS (Per Share):

Amt.	Decl.	Ex.	Rec.	Pay.
	No dividends paid.			

CAPITALIZATION (12/31/01):

	($000)	(%)
Long-Term Debt	381,020	23.6
Redeemable Pfd. Stock	150,000	9.3
Common & Surplus	1,085,108	67.1
Total	1,616,128	100.0

BUSINESS:

Markel Corporation is an insurance holding company, that writes specialty insurance products and programs for a variety of niche markets through its insurance subsidiaries. The Company competes in four distinct areas of the specialty insurance market. Markel North America competes domestically in the Excess and Surplus Lines Market (E&S Market) and the Specialty Admitted Market. Markel International competes in the London Company Market and the Lloyd's Market. Markel International writes specialty property, casualty, marine and aviation insurance on a direct and reinsurance basis. In March 2000, the Company acquired Terra Nova (Bermuda) Holdings Ltd., which was renamed as Markel International.

RECENT DEVELOPMENTS:

For the year ended 12/31/02, net income was $75.3 million versus a net loss of $125.7 million the year before. The increase in earnings was attributable to minimal catastrophe losses and lower underwriting losses in discontinued lines, partially offset by reserve increases related primarily to asbestos exposures. Total operating revenues increased 26.7% to $1.77 billion from $1.40 billion the previous year. Revenues for 2002 and 2001 included net realized investment gains of $51.0 million and $20.0 million, respectively. Earned premiums climbed 28.4% to $1.55 billion from $1.21 billion in 2001. Loss and loss adjustment expenses rose 6.2% to $1.11 billion. The combined ratio, a key measure of underwriting profitability, improved 21.0 basis points to 103.0% from 124.0% a year earlier.

PROSPECTS:

The Company anticipates that all segments of its specialty insurance business will continue to enjoy favorable market conditions in the coming year. For 2003, MKL expects gross premium growth for its specialty insurance of 15.0%, with domestic operations slightly higher than its international operations. Meanwhile, the Company is intent on strengthening Markel International's operating performance and balance sheet through a focus on expense control, and underwriting discipline, which includes improved risk selection, pricing and the appropriate use of reinsurance.

ANNUAL FINANCIAL DATA:

FISCAL YEAR	PREM. INC. ($mill.)	NET INVST. INC. ($mill.)	TOT. REVS. ($mill.)	NET INC. ($mill.)	TOT. ASSETS ($mill.)	TOT. INVST. ($mill.)	RET. ON REVS. %	RET. ON EQUITY %	RET. ON ASSETS %	EARN. PER SH. $	TANG. BK. VAL. $	PRICE RANGE	AVG. P/E RATIO
p12/31/02	1,549.0		1,770.2	75.3						7.65		222.03 - 171.10	25.7
12/31/01	1,206.7	170.7	1,397.4	d125.7	6,440.6	3,294.4	...	...	...	d14.73	72.61	213.25 - 159.75	...
12/31/00	938.5	154.2	1,094.5	d27.6	5,473.2	2,885.8	...	...	...	d3.99	47.66	183.25 - 111.50	...
12/31/99	437.2	87.7	524.3	40.6	2,455.3	1,623.1	7.7	10.6	1.7	7.20	52.07	193.00 - 143.25	23.4
12/31/98	333.3	71.0	426.0	57.3	1,921.3	1,481.1	13.4	13.5	3.0	10.17	70.63	187.00 - 132.00	15.7
12/31/97	332.9	68.7	419.0	50.4	1,870.1	1,408.3	12.0	14.1	2.7	8.92	58.36	161.13 - 89.00	14.0
12/31/96	307.5	51.2	366.7	☐46.7	1,605.3	1,130.8	12.7	17.4	2.9	☐8.58	41.96	94.50 - 72.50	9.7
12/31/95	285.1	43.0	343.6	34.5	1,314.5	908.6	10.0	16.2	2.6	6.15	31.68	75.50 - 40.75	9.5
12/31/94	243.1	29.1	279.7	18.6	1,162.5	611.7	6.6	13.4	1.6	3.33	17.34	44.50 - 37.50	12.3
12/31/93	192.6	23.5	234.9	23.6	1,177.4	597.0	10.1	15.7	2.0	4.23	18.02	40.50 - 30.75	8.4

Statistics are as originally reported. ☐ Incl. $10.4 mill. loss on building.

OFFICERS:
A. I. Kirshner, Chmn., C.E.O.
S. A. Markel, Vice-Chmn.
A. F. Markel, Pres., C.O.O.

INVESTOR CONTACT: Bruce Kay, V.P., Inv. Rel., (800) 446-6671

PRINCIPAL OFFICE: 4521 Highwoods Parkway, Glen Allen, VA 23060-6148

TELEPHONE NUMBER: (804) 747-0136
FAX: (804) 965-1600
WEB: www.markelcorp.com

NO. OF EMPLOYEES: 1,622 (avg.)
SHAREHOLDERS: 507
ANNUAL MEETING: In May
INCORPORATED: VA, 1930

INSTITUTIONAL HOLDINGS:
No. of Institutions: 136
Shares Held: 7,405,774
% Held: 75.3

INDUSTRY: Fire, marine, and casualty insurance (SIC: 6331)

TRANSFER AGENT(S): Wachovia Bank, N.A., Charlotte, NC

MARRIOTT INTERNATIONAL, INC.

EXCH.	SYM.	REC. PRICE	P/E RATIO	YLD.	MKT. CAP.	RANGE (52-WK.)	'02 Y/E PR.
NYSE	MAR	30.22 (2/28/03)	17.5	0.9%	$7.13 bill.	46.45 - 26.25	32.87

UPPER MEDIUM GRADE. THE COMPANY EXPECTS TO ADD BETWEEN 25,000 AND 30,000 HOTEL ROOMS ANNU-ALLY IN BOTH 2003 AND 2004 TO ITS LODGING PORTFOLIO.

MERGENT

TRADING VOLUME
Thousand Shares

*7 YEAR PRICE SCORE N/A   *12 MONTH PRICE SCORE 95.4

*NYSE COMPOSITE INDEX=100

INTERIM EARNINGS (Per Share):

Qtr.	Mar.	June	Sept.	Dec.
1999	0.38	0.42	0.36	0.44
2000	0.37	0.50	0.43	0.59
2001	0.47	0.50	0.39	d0.48
2002	0.32	0.49	0.45	0.47

INTERIM DIVIDENDS (Per Share):

Amt.	Decl.	Ex.	Rec.	Pay.
0.065Q	2/07/02	4/02/02	4/04/02	4/26/02
0.07Q	5/03/02	6/25/02	6/27/02	7/19/02
0.07Q	8/01/02	9/23/02	9/25/02	10/11/02
0.07Q	11/07/02	12/23/02	12/26/02	1/08/03
0.07Q	2/06/03	3/31/03	4/02/03	4/30/03

Indicated div.: $0.28 (Div. Reinv. Plan)

CAPITALIZATION (1/3/03):

	($000)	(%)
Long-Term Debt	1,553,000	30.3
Common & Surplus	3,573,000	69.7
Total	5,126,000	100.0

BUSINESS:

Marriott International, Inc. is a worldwide operator and franchisor of hotels and related lodging facilities with 2,557 hotels and timeshare resorts in the U.S. and 66 other countries as of 1/3/03. MAR operates and franchises full-service hotels (64.8% of 2002 sales) under the Marriot, JW Marriot, The Ritz-Carlton, Renaissance, Ramada International, and Bvlgari brands; Timeshare (14.3%) under the Marriot Vacation Club International, Horizons, The Ritz-Carlton Club and Marriot Grand Residence Club brands; select service lodging (11.5%) under the Courtyard, Fairfield Inn and SpringHill Suites brands; and extending stay lodging (7.1%) under the Residence Inn, TownePlace Suites, Marriot ExecuStay and Mariott Executive Apartments brands. MAR is also in the synthetic fuel business (2.3%). On 3/27/98, MAR was spun off to shareholders of the former company and renamed Marriott International, Inc.

RECENT DEVELOPMENTS:

For the 53 weeks ended 1/3/03, income was $439.0 million versus $269.0 million in 2001. Results for 2002 included a pre-tax gain on the sale of an investment of $44.0 million and a write-down of acquisition goodwill of $50.0 million. Results for 2001 included a restructuring charge of $62.0 million. Earnings excluded losses on discontinued operations of $162.0 million in 2002 and $33.0 million in 2001.

Total revenues advanced 8.4% to $8.44 billion from $7.79 billion a year earlier. Revenues for 2002 included synthetic fuel revenues of $193.0 million. Total lodging revenues increased 5.9% to $8.25 billion. In 2002, MAR added 188 hotels and timeshare resorts, with 31,605 rooms, to its lodging portfolio, while 25 properties, with 4,663 rooms, exited the portfolio.

PROSPECTS:

MAR expects to add between 25,000 and 30,000 hotel rooms annually in both 2003 and 2004 to its lodging portfolio. At 1/3/03, MAR's pipeline of properties under construction, awaiting conversion, or approved for development exceeded 50,000 rooms. Due to continuing soft demand trends, revenue per available room for 2003 is expected to be roughly flat versus 2002 levels. As a result, hotel house profit margins are likely to decline reflecting higher casualty insurance and medical benefits costs. Separately, MAR estimates earnings per share from continuing operations to range from $1.85 to $1.95 per share in 2003, including contributions from its synthetic fuel operations.

ANNUAL FINANCIAL DATA:

FISCAL YEAR	TOT. REVS. ($mill.)	NET INC. ($mill.)	TOT. ASSETS ($mill.)	OPER. PROFIT %	NET PROFIT %	RET. ON EQUITY %	RET. ON ASSETS %	CURR. RATIO	EARN. PER SH. $	CASH FL. PER SH. $	TANG. BK. VAL. $	DIV. PER SH. $	PRICE RANGE	AVG. P/E RATIO	AVG. YIELD
1/03/03	8,441.0	④ 439.0	8,296.0	5.3	5.2	12.3	5.3	0.8	④ 1.74	2.46	9.14	0.27	46.45 — 26.25	20.9	0.7
12/28/01	10,152.0	③ 236.0	9,107.0	4.4	2.3	6.8	2.6	1.2	③ 0.92	1.78	7.12	0.25	50.50 — 27.30	42.3	0.6
12/29/00	10,017.0	② 479.0	8,237.0	8.0	4.8	14.7	5.8	0.7	② 1.89	2.65	5.95	0.23	43.50 — 26.13	18.4	0.7
12/31/99	8,739.0	400.0	7,324.0	7.6	4.6	13.8	5.5	0.9	1.51	2.27	4.42	0.21	44.50 — 29.00	24.3	0.6
1/01/99	7,968.0	390.0	6,233.0	7.9	4.9	15.2	6.3	0.9	1.46	1.94	3.36	0.14	37.94 — 19.38	19.6	0.5
1/02/98	9,046.0	324.0	5,557.0	5.8	3.6	12.5	5.8	0.8	① 1.19	1.62	4.45	...	...	...	...
1/03/97	7,267.0	270.0	4,198.0	6.0	3.7	18.7	6.4	0.7	① 1.06	1.41	...	...	...	...	...
12/29/95	6,255.0	219.0	...	5.3	3.5	...	...	...	① 0.88	1.14	...	...	...	...	...

Statistics are as originally reported. ① Pro forma ② Incl. pre-tax non-recurr. chrg. of $15.0 mill. ③ Incl. after-tax restr. chrg. of $79.0 mill. and other after-tax non-recurr. chrgs. of $93.0 mill. ④ Bef. a loss fr. disc. ops. $162.0 mill.; incl. pre-tax gain on inv. $44.0 mill. and pre-tax writedown of goodwill amort. $50.0 mill.

OFFICERS:
J. W. Marriott Jr., Chmn., C.E.O.
W. J. Shaw, Pres., C.O.O.
INVESTOR CONTACT: Tom Marder, (301) 380-2553
PRINCIPAL OFFICE: 10400 Fernwood Road, Bethesda, MD 20817

TELEPHONE NUMBER: (301) 380-3000
FAX: (301) 380-3967
WEB: www.marriott.com
NO. OF EMPLOYEES: 144,000 (approx.)
SHAREHOLDERS: 55,122
ANNUAL MEETING: In May
INCORPORATED: DE, 1998

INSTITUTIONAL HOLDINGS:
No. of Institutions: 291
Shares Held: 151,108,688
% Held: 63.6
INDUSTRY: Hotels and motels (SIC: 7011)
TRANSFER AGENT(S): EquiServe, First Chicago Trust Division, Jersey City, NJ

MARSH & MCLENNAN COMPANIES, INC.

EXCH.	SYM.	REC. PRICE	P/E RATIO	YLD.	MKT. CAP.	RANGE (52-WK.)	'02 Y/E PR.	DIV. ACH.
NYSE	MMC	40.70 (2/28/03)	16.5	2.8%	$22.33 bill.	57.30 - 34.61	46.21	41 yrs.

INVESTMENT GRADE. THE COMPANY'S RISK AND INSURANCE SERVICES BUSINESS SHOULD CONTINUE TO FACE CHALLENGING MARKET CONDITIONS IN THE COMING YEAR.

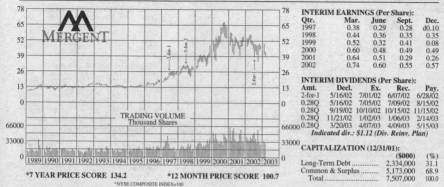

*7 YEAR PRICE SCORE 134.2   ***12 MONTH PRICE SCORE 100.7**
*NYSE COMPOSITE INDEX=100

INTERIM EARNINGS (Per Share):

Qtr.	Mar.	June	Sept.	Dec.
1997	0.38	0.29	0.28	d0.10
1998	0.44	0.36	0.35	0.35
1999	0.52	0.32	0.41	0.08
2000	0.60	0.48	0.49	0.49
2001	0.64	0.51	0.29	0.26
2002	0.74	0.60	0.55	0.57

INTERIM DIVIDENDS (Per Share):

Amt.	Decl.	Ex.	Rec.	Pay.
2-for-1	5/16/02	7/01/02	6/07/02	6/28/02
0.28Q	5/16/02	7/05/02	7/09/02	8/15/02
0.28Q	9/19/02	10/10/02	10/15/02	11/15/02
0.28Q	11/21/02	1/02/03	1/06/03	2/14/03
0.28Q	3/20/03	4/07/03	4/09/03	5/15/03

Indicated div.: $1.12 (Div. Reinv. Plan)

CAPITALIZATION (12/31/01):

	($000)	(%)
Long-Term Debt	2,334,000	31.1
Common & Surplus	5,173,000	68.9
Total	7,507,000	100.0

BUSINESS:

Marsh & McLennan Companies, Inc. is engaged in the worldwide business of providing retail and wholesale insurance services, principally as a broker or consultant for insurers, insurance underwriters and other brokers. MMC subsidiaries include Marsh Inc., a risk and insurance services firm; Putnam Investments, one of the largest investment management companies in the U.S.; and Mercer Inc.,

a major global provider of consulting services. Other subsidiaries render advisory services in the area of employee benefits and compensation consulting, management consulting, economic consulting and environmental consulting. Contributions to revenues by type of service in 2002 were as follows: risk and insurance services, 56.7%; consulting, 22.6%; and investment management, 20.7%.

RECENT DEVELOPMENTS:

For the year ended 12/31/02, net income climbed 40.1% to $1.37 billion from $974.0 million the previous year. Results reflect increased activity in MMC's risk and insurance services business, partially offset by a decline in assets under management in the investment management segment. Results for 2001 included charges related to the events of

9/11/01 and special credits of $174.0 million. Total revenue grew 5.8% to $10.44 billion from $9.87 billion a year earlier. Risk and insurance services revenue grew 14.7% to $5.91 billion from $5.15 billion the year before. Consulting revenue rose 2.4% to $2.36 billion, while investment management revenue slid 10.1% to $2.17 billion.

PROSPECTS:

MMC's risk and insurance services business should continue to face difficult market conditions in the coming year. Moreover, Putnam Investments continues to manage through prolonged downturn in equity markets, making adjustments to strengthen its operations. Assets under management, which dropped 18.2% year-over-year to $251.00

billion at the end of 2002, were up 5.5% from $238.00 billion in the third quarter. Meanwhile, trends in consulting revenues should continue to improve as retirement consulting and administration practices, which represent almost half of the Company's consulting business, showed sustained growth through the end of the year.

ANNUAL FINANCIAL DATA:

FISCAL YEAR	TOT. REVS. ($mill.)	NET INC. ($mill.)	TOT. ASSETS ($mill.)	TOT. INVST. ($mill.)	RET. ON REVS. %	RET. ON EQUITY %	RET. ON ASSETS %	EARN. PER SH. $	TANG. BK. VAL. $	AVG. YIELD %	DIV. PER SH. $	PRICE RANGE	AVG. P/E RATIO
p12/31/02	10,440.0	1,365.0						2.45		2.4	1.09	57.30 - 34.61	18.8
12/31/01	9,943.0	① 974.0	13,293.0	826.0	9.8	18.8	7.3	① 1.70	...	2.1	1.03	59.03 - 39.50	29.1
12/31/00	10,157.0	1,181.0	13,769.0	976.0	11.6	22.6	8.6	2.05	...	1.8	0.95	67.84 - 35.25	25.1
12/31/99	9,157.0	③ 726.0	13,021.0	687.0	7.9	17.4	5.6	③ 1.31	...	2.2	0.85	48.38 - 28.56	29.4
12/31/98	7,190.0	796.0	11,871.0	828.0	11.1	21.8	6.7	1.49	...	2.7	0.73	32.16 - 21.69	18.1
12/31/97	6,008.6	① 399.4	7,914.2	720.2	6.6	12.5	5.0	① 0.80	1.53	2.9	0.63	26.67 - 17.10	27.5
12/31/96	4,149.0	459.3	4,545.2	573.3	11.1	24.3	10.1	1.06	3.10	3.3	0.55	19.15 - 14.04	15.7
12/31/95	3,770.3	402.9	4,329.5	411.8	10.7	24.2	9.3	0.92	2.14	3.6	0.50	15.02 - 12.69	15.0
12/31/94	3,435.0	② 382.0	3,830.6	282.8	11.1	26.2	10.0	② 0.87	1.73	3.5	-0.47	14.79 - 11.88	15.4
12/31/93	3,163.4	332.4	3,546.6	363.6	10.5	24.3	9.4	0.75	1.59	3.1	0.45	16.27 - 12.83	19.3

Statistics are as originally reported. Adj. for stk. split: 2-for-1, 7/02; 3-for-2, 6/98; 2-for-1, 6/97 ① Incl. non-recurr. chrg. 2001, $396.0 mill.; 1997, $296.8 mill. ② Bef. acctg. change chrg. $10.5 mill. ③ Incl. special chrg. $337.0 mill.

OFFICERS:
J. W. Greenberg, Chmn., Pres., C.E.O.
M. Cabiallavetta, Vice-Chmn.
C. A. Davis, Vice-Chmn.
S. S. Wijnberg, Sr. V.P., C.F.O.
INVESTOR CONTACT: Mike Bischoff, Investor Relations, (212) 345-5470
PRINCIPAL OFFICE: 1166 Avenue of the Americas, New York, NY 10036-2774

TELEPHONE NUMBER: (212) 345-5000
FAX: (212) 345-4809
WEB: www.mmc.com
NO. OF EMPLOYEES: 57,800 (approx.)
SHAREHOLDERS: 10,927
ANNUAL MEETING: In May
INCORPORATED: DE, March, 1969

INSTITUTIONAL HOLDINGS:
No. of Institutions: 653
Shares Held: 353,971,610
% Held: 65.9
INDUSTRY: Insurance agents, brokers, & service (SIC: 6411)
TRANSFER AGENT(S): The Bank of New York, New York, NY

MARSHALL & ILSLEY CORPORATION

EXCH.	SYM.	REC. PRICE	P/E RATIO	YLD.	MKT. CAP.	RANGE (52-WK.)	'02 Y/E PR.	DIV. ACH.
NYSE	MI	26.57 (2/28/03)	12.3	2.4%	$6.01 bill.	32.12 - 23.11	27.38	29 yrs.

UPPER MEDIUM GRADE. THE COMPANY EXPECTS NET INTEREST INCOME TO INCREASE DUE TO INTERNAL GROWTH AND ACQUISITIONS.

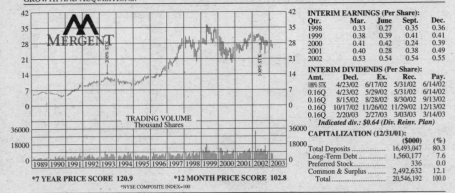

*7 YEAR PRICE SCORE 120.9   *12 MONTH PRICE SCORE 102.8
*NYSE COMPOSITE INDEX=100

INTERIM EARNINGS (Per Share):

Qtr.	Mar.	June	Sept.	Dec.
1998	0.33	0.27	0.35	0.36
1999	0.38	0.39	0.41	0.41
2000	0.41	0.42	0.24	0.39
2001	0.40	0.28	0.38	0.49
2002	0.53	0.54	0.54	0.55

INTERIM DIVIDENDS (Per Share):

Amt.	Decl.	Ex.	Rec.	Pay.
100% STK.	4/23/02	6/17/02	5/31/02	6/14/02
0.16Q	4/23/02	5/29/02	5/31/02	6/14/02
0.16Q	8/15/02	8/28/02	8/30/02	9/13/02
0.16Q	10/17/02	11/26/02	11/29/02	12/13/02
0.16Q	2/20/03	2/27/03	3/03/03	3/14/03

Indicated div.: $0.64 (Div. Reinv. Plan)

CAPITALIZATION (12/31/01):

	($000)	(%)
Total Deposits	16,493,047	80.3
Long-Term Debt	1,560,177	7.6
Preferred Stock	336	0.0
Common & Surplus	2,492,632	12.1
Total	20,546,192	100.0

BUSINESS:

Marshall & Ilsley Corporation, a multibank holding company with assets of $29.20 billion as of 12/31/02, is headquartered in Milwaukee, Wisconsin. The Company's principal subsidiary is Metavante Corporation (formerly MI's M&I Data Services Division), a provider of integrated financial transaction processing, outsourcing services, software, and consulting services. The Company has 214 banking offices in Wisconsin, 24 locations throughout Arizona, 10 offices in Minneapolis/St. Paul, Minnesota, and locations in Las Vegas, Nevada and Naples, Florida. The Company also provides trust and investment management, equipment leasing, mortgage banking, financial planning, investments, and insurance services from offices throughout the U.S. and on the Internet.

RECENT DEVELOPMENTS:

For the year ended 12/31/02, net income amounted to $480.3 million. Results included amortization of intangibles of $25.1 million. Interest income was $1.60 billion and interest expense was $561.0 million. Net interest income totaled $1.04 billion. Loan loss provision was $74.4 million. Total non-interest revenue amounted to $1.08 billion, while total non-interest expense was $1.30 billion. For the fourth quarter ended 12/31/02, net income rose 15.4% to $125.0 million compared with $108.3 million in the same period of 2001. Net interest income grew 10.6% to $271.3 million from $245.2 million the year before. Loan loss provision increased 16.4% to $23.4 million from $20.1 million a year earlier. Total non-interest revenues climbed 9.5% to $287.0 million, while total non-interest expense rose 8.4% to $334.6 million.

PROSPECTS:

The Company expects net interest margin to continue to decline in the first quarter of 2003 and net interest income to increase due to internal growth and acquisitions. The current level of lower interest rates and higher level of prepayments has reduced the expected life of many of the Company's financial assets. As a result, the Company plans to actively manage the re-pricing of its interest bearing liabilities in an attempt to minimize the long-term effect on net interest income. MI also expects home equity loans and lines to continue to drive results in its consumer operations.

ANNUAL FINANCIAL DATA:

FISCAL YEAR	NET INT. INC. ($Mill.)	NON-INT. INC. ($Mill.)	NET INC. ($Mill.)	TOT. LOANS ($Mill.)	TOT. ASSETS ($Mill.)	TOT. DEP. ($Mill.)	RET. ON EQUITY %	RET. ON ASSETS %	EQUITY/ ASSETS %	EARN. PER SH. $	TANG. BK. VAL. $	DIV. PER SH. $	PRICE RANGE	AVG. P/E RATIO
p12/31/02	1,038.5	1,082.7	480.3	19,295.4	27,253.7	16,493.0				2.16	9.16	0.63	32.12 - 23.11	12.8
12/31/01	842.8	1,002.8	②③ 337.9	19,295.4	27,253.7	16,493.0	13.6	1.2	9.1	②③ 1.55	9.16	0.57	32.12 - 23.54	18.0
12/31/00	673.0	928.4	②③ 317.4	17,587.1	26,077.7	19,248.6	14.2	1.2	8.6	②③ 1.46	9.22	0.52	31.13 - 19.13	17.3
12/31/99	705.3	845.8	354.5	16,335.1	24,369.7	16,435.2	16.7	1.5	8.7	1.57	8.27	0.47	36.38 - 27.19	20.2
12/31/98	676.1	1,424.2	③ 301.3	13,996.2	21,566.3	15,919.9	13.4	1.4	10.4	③ 1.31	8.99	0.43	31.13 - 19.69	19.5
12/31/97	564.0	598.9	245.1	12,542.3	19,477.5	14,356.0	12.8	1.3	9.9	1.21	9.45	0.39	30.25 - 16.19	19.2
12/31/96	505.7	503.3	203.4	9,301.9	14,763.3	10,952.4	16.1	1.4	8.5	1.04	7.12	0.36	17.81 - 12.19	14.5
12/31/95	491.5	424.2	193.3	8,868.9	13,343.1	10,280.8	15.4	1.4	9.4	0.98	6.72	0.32	13.25 - 9.00	11.4
12/31/94	491.2	361.5	①③ 94.4	8,792.5	12,612.9	9,499.1	8.9	0.7	8.4	①③ 0.48	5.73	0.29	12.00 - 8.88	22.0
12/31/93	309.2	299.9	125.5	5,371.1	7,970.2	6,195.9	16.7	1.6	9.4	-0.94	5.65	0.27	13.00 - 10.46	12.5

Statistics are as originally reported. Adj. for stk. splits: 2-for-1, 6/02; 3-for-1, 6/93. ① Bef. extraord. credit $11.5 mill. ② Bef. acctg. change chrg., $436,000, 2001; $2.3 mill., 2000. ③ Incl. non-recur. net chrgs. of $68.1 mill., 2001; $16.7 mill., 2000; $23.4 mill., 1998; $75.2 mill.; 1994.

OFFICERS:
J. B. Wigdale, Chmn.
D. J. Kuester, Pres., C.E.O.
M. F. Furlong, Exec. V.P., C.F.O.
INVESTOR CONTACT: M.A. Hatfield, Secretary, (414) 765-7801
PRINCIPAL OFFICE: 770 North Water Street, Milwaukee, WI 53202

TELEPHONE NUMBER: (414) 765-7801
FAX: (414) 765-8026
WEB: www.micorp.com
NO. OF EMPLOYEES: 11,657 (approx.)
SHAREHOLDERS: 19,311 (approx.)
ANNUAL MEETING: In Apr.
INCORPORATED: WI, Feb., 1959

INSTITUTIONAL HOLDINGS:
No. of Institutions: 268
Shares Held: 77,066,225
% Held: 35.3
INDUSTRY: National commercial banks (SIC: 6021)
TRANSFER AGENT(S): BankBoston, N.A., Boston, MA

MARTIN MARIETTA MATERIALS, INC.

EXCH.	SYM.	REC. PRICE	P/E RATIO	YLD.	MKT. CAP.	RANGE (52-WK.)	'02 Y/E PR.
NYSE	MLM	27.58 (2/28/03)	13.8	2.2%	$1.34 bill.	43.97 - 27.06	30.66

MEDIUM GRADE. IN 2003, THE COMPANY EXPECTS FULL-YEAR DILUTED EARNINGS IN THE RANGE OF $1.95 TO $2.25 PER SHARE.

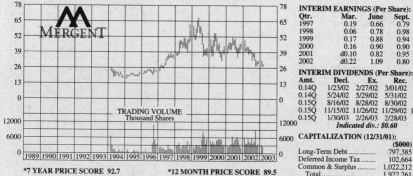

*7 YEAR PRICE SCORE 92.7   *12 MONTH PRICE SCORE 89.5

*NYSE COMPOSITE INDEX=100

INTERIM EARNINGS (Per Share):

Qtr.	Mar.	June	Sept.	Dec.
1997	0.19	0.66	0.79	0.50
1998	0.06	0.78	0.98	0.66
1999	0.17	0.88	0.94	0.70
2000	0.16	0.90	0.90	0.44
2001	d0.10	0.82	0.95	0.52
2002	d0.22	1.09	0.80	0.33

INTERIM DIVIDENDS (Per Share):

Amt.	Decl.	Ex.	Rec.	Pay.
0.14Q	1/23/02	2/27/02	3/01/02	3/29/02
0.14Q	5/24/02	5/29/02	5/31/02	6/28/02
0.15Q	8/16/02	8/28/02	8/30/02	9/30/02
0.15Q	11/15/02	11/26/02	11/29/02	12/31/02
0.15Q	1/30/03	2/26/03	2/28/03	3/31/03

Indicated div.: $0.60

CAPITALIZATION (12/31/01):

	($000)	(%)
Long-Term Debt	797,385	41.5
Deferred Income Tax	102,664	5.3
Common & Surplus	1,022,212	53.2
Total	1,922,261	100.0

BUSINESS:

Martin Marietta Materials, Inc. is a producer of aggregates for the construction industry, including highways, infrastructure, commercial and residential. MLM's Aggregates division processes and sells granite, sandstone, limestone, shell and other aggregates products. MLM's Magnesia Specialties division manufactures and markets magnesia-based products, including heat-resistant refractory products for the steel industry, chemicals products for industrial, agricultural and environmental uses, and dolomitic lime. MLM was spun off from Lockheed Martin Corp. in October 1996 to be the successor to substantially all of the assets and liabilities of the materials group of Martin Marietta Corporation and its subsidiaries. In 2002, MLM's Aggregates business accounted for 95.0% of total revenues and MLM's Magnesia Specialties segment accounted for 5.0%. In 1998, MLM acquired Redland Stone Products Company. In 2000, MLM acquired the remaining equity interest in Meridian Aggregates Company.

RECENT DEVELOPMENTS:

For the year ended 12/31/02, income, before an accounting change charge of $11.5 million, declined 7.2% to $97.8 million from $105.4 million in 2001. Earnings for 2001 included goodwill amortization of $22.4 million. Total revenues slid 1.5% to $1.69 billion from $1.72 billion a year earlier. Results reflected a reduction in production and the resultant under-absorption of fixed costs, which adversely affected margins, partially offset by price increases.

PROSPECTS:

The Company's new structural composites business recently announced the opening of a manufacturing facility for its composite products in Sparta, North Carolina. The 185,000 square-foot facility is a key growth initiative for this business. Also, MLM announced the recent installation of two additional composite bridge decks in Pennsylvania and Ohio as well as plans to install composite decks in three European countries in 2003. MLM's future earnings will reflect the timing and amount of the final appropriation for federal transportation funding. MLM currently estimates full-year net earnings in the range of $1.95 to $2.25 per diluted share. Meanwhile, MLM is focused on productivity improvement and cash generation.

ANNUAL FINANCIAL DATA:

FISCAL YEAR	TOT. REVS. ($mill.)	NET INC. ($mill.)	TOT. ASSETS ($mill.)	OPER. PROFIT %	NET PROFIT %	RET. ON EQUITY %	RET. ON ASSETS %	CURR. RATIO	EARN. PER SH. $	CASH FL. PER SH. $	TANG. BK. VAL. $	DIV. PER SH. $	PRICE RANGE	AVG. P/E RATIO	AVG. YIELD %
p12/31/02	1,692.4	① 97.8							② 2.00			0.58	49.33 - 27.30	19.2	1.5
12/31/01	1,718.1	105.4	2,224.6	11.5	6.1	10.3	4.7	2.6	2.19	5.41	8.55	0.56	51.60 - 34.75	19.7	1.3
12/31/00	1,517.5	112.0	1,841.4	13.3	7.4	13.0	6.1	2.2	2.39	5.29	9.70	0.54	55.25 - 31.65	18.2	1.2
12/31/99	1,258.8	125.8	1,742.6	15.0	8.8	16.3	7.2	2.2	2.68	5.34	7.86	0.52	68.13 - 35.25	19.3	1.0
12/31/98	1,057.7	③ 115.6	1,588.6	18.6	10.9	17.3	7.3	2.4	③ 2.49	4.59	6.25	0.50	62.19 - 35.81	19.7	1.0
12/31/97	900.9	98.5	1,105.7	18.1	10.9	17.5	8.9	3.0	2.13	3.86	8.37	0.48	38.50 - 23.00	14.4	1.6
12/31/96	721.9	78.6	768.9	16.7	10.9	16.3	10.2	3.1	1.71	3.03	9.07	0.46	25.75 - 19.50	13.2	2.0
12/31/95	664.4	67.6	789.4	16.2	10.2	15.9	8.6	1.8	1.47	2.67	7.86	0.44	22.13 - 16.50	13.1	2.4
12/31/94	501.7	58.3	593.9	18.3	11.6	15.5	9.8	3.4	② 1.30	2.25	7.30	0.22	25.88 - 17.00	16.5	1.0
12/31/93	452.9	① 48.0	484.4	17.4	10.6	33.0	9.9	2.6	...	...		...	...	...	...

Statistics are as originally reported. ① Bef. net acctg. change chrg. $11.5 mill., 2002; $17.5 mill., 1993. ② Bef. extraord. loss of $4.6 million (d$0.01/sh.). ③ Incl. a write-down of $1.9 mill.

OFFICERS:
S. P. Zelnak, Jr., Chmn., Pres., C.E.O.
P. J. Sipling, Exec. V.P.
J. K. Henry, Sr. V.P., C.F.O.
INVESTOR CONTACT: Janice K. Henry, Investor Relations, (919) 783-4658
PRINCIPAL OFFICE: 2710 Wycliff Road, Raleigh, NC 27607-3033

TELEPHONE NUMBER: (919) 781-4550
FAX: (919) 783-4552
WEB: www.martinmarietta.com
NO. OF EMPLOYEES: 6,900 (approx.)
SHAREHOLDERS: 1,331 (approx. record)
ANNUAL MEETING: In May
INCORPORATED: NC, Nov., 1993

INSTITUTIONAL HOLDINGS:
No. of Institutions: 181
Shares Held: 44,878,831
% Held: 91.9
INDUSTRY: Highway and street construction (SIC: 1611)
TRANSFER AGENT(S): First Union National Bank, Charlotte, NC

MASCO CORPORATION

EXCH.	SYM.	REC. PRICE	P/E RATIO	YLD.	MKT. CAP.	RANGE (52-WK.)	'02 Y/E PR.	DIV. ACH.
NYSE	MAS	18.38 (2/28/03)	13.6	3.0%	$8.44 bill.	29.43 - 16.80	21.05	44 yrs.

MEDIUM GRADE. THE COMPANY EXPECTS EARNINGS PER SHARE FOR THE FULL-YEAR 2003 IN THE RANGE OF $1.65 TO $1.70.

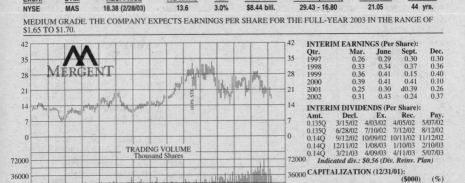

7 YEAR PRICE SCORE 106.6   **12 MONTH PRICE SCORE 89.6**
NYSE COMPOSITE INDEX=100

INTERIM EARNINGS (Per Share):

Qtr.	Mar.	June	Sept.	Dec.
1997	0.26	0.29	0.30	0.30
1998	0.33	0.34	0.37	0.36
1999	0.36	0.41	0.15	0.40
2000	0.39	0.41	0.41	0.10
2001	0.25	0.30	d0.39	0.26
2002	0.31	0.43	0.24	0.37

INTERIM DIVIDENDS (Per Share):

Amt.	Decl.	Ex.	Rec.	Pay.
0.135Q	3/15/02	4/03/02	4/05/02	5/07/02
0.135Q	6/28/02	7/10/02	7/12/02	8/12/02
0.14Q	9/12/02	10/09/02	10/11/02	11/12/02
0.14Q	12/11/02	1/08/03	1/10/03	2/10/03
0.14Q	3/21/03	4/09/03	4/11/03	5/07/03

Indicated div.: $0.56 (Div. Reinv. Plan)

CAPITALIZATION (12/31/01):

	($000)	(%)
Long-Term Debt	3,627,630	46.8
Preferred Stock	20	0.0
Common & Surplus	4,119,810	53.2
Total	7,747,460	100.0

BUSINESS:

Masco Corporation manufactures faucets, cabinets, architectural coatings, locks and other consumer brand-name home improvement and building products. MAS' principal product and service categories are kitchen and bathroom cabinets, faucets, other kitchen and bath products, architectural coatings, builders' hardware products and other specialty products and services. Brand-names include MERIL-LAT, KRAFTMAID, and QUALITY CABINETS kitchen and bathroom cabinets; DELTA and PEERLESS faucets; WEISER and BALDWIN locks; and BEHR architectural coatings. Sales in 2001 were derived as follows: cabinets and related products, 30.9%; plumbing products, 21.0%; installation and other services, 20.2%; decorative architectural products, 18.1%; and other specialty products, 9.8%.

RECENT DEVELOPMENTS:

For the year ended 12/31/02, income amounted to $682.1 million, before an accounting change charge of $92.4 million, compared with net income of $198.5 million in 2001. Results for 2002 included a litigation settlement charge of $146.8 million and the reversal of a charge for the planned disposition of a business of $15.6 million. Results for 2001 included goodwill amortization of $93.2 million. Net sales increased 13.7% to $9.42 billion from $8.28 billion a year earlier primarily due to acquisitions.

PROSPECTS:

In December 2002, MAS increased its ownership of Hansgrohe AG from 27.0% to approximately 64.0%. Hansgrohe, based in Schiltach, Germany, is a manufacturer of kitchen and bath faucets, hand-held and fixed showers, luxury shower systems and whirlpool tubs, which are sold throughout Europe, Asia and the United States. In early 2003, MAS acquired PowerShot Tool Company, Inc., a manufacturer of fastening products. Combined annualized sales for Hansgrohe and PowerShot approximate $400.0 million. Total consideration for both transactions approximated $190.0 million. Favorable company sales performance has continued in early 2003, and, based on current business trends, MAS expects earnings for the full-year 2003 in the range of $1.65 to $1.70 per common share.

ANNUAL FINANCIAL DATA:

FISCAL YEAR	TOT. REVS. ($mill.)	NET INC. ($mill.)	TOT. ASSETS ($mill.)	OPER. PROFIT %	NET PROFIT %	RET. ON EQUITY %	RET. ON ASSETS %	CURR. RATIO	EARN. PER SH. $	CASH FL. PER SH. $	TANG. BK. VAL. $	DIV. PER SH. $	PRICE RANGE	AVG. P/E RATIO	AVG. YIELD %
p12/31/02	9,419.4	[7] 682.1							[7] 1.15			0.545	29.43 - 17.25	20.3	2.3
12/31/01	8,358.0	[6] 198.5	9,183.3	12.4	2.4	4.8	2.2	2.1	[6] 0.42	0.99	1.30	0.53	26.94 - 17.76	53.2	2.3
12/31/00	7,243.0	[5] 591.7	7,744.0	13.3	8.2	17.3	7.6	2.1	[5] 1.31	1.84	2.78	0.49	27.00 - 14.50	15.8	2.4
12/31/99	6,307.0	[4] 569.6	6,634.9	14.5	9.0	18.2	8.6	2.5	[4] 1.28	1.78	3.14	0.45	33.69 - 22.50	21.9	1.6
12/31/98	4,345.0	476.0	5,167.4	15.7	11.0	17.4	9.2	2.2	1.39	1.78	4.99	0.43	33.00 - 20.75	19.3	1.6
12/31/97	3,760.0	382.4	4,333.8	15.6	10.2	17.2	8.8	2.6	1.15	1.48	4.53	0.41	26.91 - 16.88	19.0	1.9
12/31/96	3,237.0	295.2	3,701.7	14.8	9.1	16.0	8.0	2.8	0.92	1.23	4.30	0.39	18.44 - 13.25	17.2	2.4
[3] 12/31/95	2,927.0	[2] 200.1	3,778.6	13.7	6.8	12.1	5.3	2.2	[2] 0.63	0.91	4.09	0.36	15.75 - 11.25	21.6	2.7
12/31/94	4,468.0	[1] 193.7	4,390.0	11.4	4.3	9.2	4.4	3.1	[1] 0.61	0.99	4.48	0.34	19.94 - 10.63	25.0	2.3
12/31/93	3,886.0	221.1	4,021.1	10.4	5.7	11.1	5.5	3.4	0.73	1.10	4.56	0.33	19.44 - 12.75	22.2	2.0

Statistics are as originally reported. Adj. for stk. split: 2-for-1, 7/98. [1] Incl. non-recurr. chrg. $79.3 mill. [2] Incl. non-recurr. chrg. $47.9 mill.; bef. discont. oper. loss $641.7 mill. [3] Reflects the sale of the Masco Home Furnishings Group businesses. [4] Incl. aftertax non-recurr. chrg. of approx. $126.0 mill. [5] Incl. pre-tax chrg. of $55.0 mill. for the write-down of assets and $90.0 mill. for the planned dispos. of assets. [6] Incl. a pretax, noncash write-down charge of $530.0 mill. [7] Incl. chrg. of $146.8 mill. for litigation settlement and gain of $15.6 mill. for rever. of the planned dispos. of business; Bef. acctg. change chrg. of $92.4 mill.

OFFICERS:
R. A. Manoogian, Chmn., C.E.O.
T. Wadhams, V.P., C.F.O.
R. B. Rosowski, V.P., Treas., Contr.

INVESTOR CONTACT: Investor Relations, (313) 274-7400

PRINCIPAL OFFICE: 21001 Van Born Road, Taylor, MI 48180

TELEPHONE NUMBER: (313) 274-7400
FAX: (313) 792-6135
WEB: www.masco.com
NO. OF EMPLOYEES: 55,400 (approx.)
SHAREHOLDERS: 6,000 (approx.)
ANNUAL MEETING: In May
INCORPORATED: MI, Dec., 1929; reincorp., DE, 1968

INSTITUTIONAL HOLDINGS:
No. of Institutions: 412
Shares Held: 408,167,766
% Held: 83.0
INDUSTRY: Plumbing fixture fittings and trim (SIC: 3432)
TRANSFER AGENT(S): Bank of New York, New York, NY

MASSEY ENERGY COMPANY

EXCH.	SYM.	REC. PRICE	P/E RATIO	YLD.	MKT. CAP.	RANGE (52-WK.)	'02 Y/E PR.
NYSE	MEE	9.32 (2/28/03)	...	1.7%	$0.69 bill.	18.70 - 4.55	9.72

LOWER MEDIUM GRADE. THE COMPANY PROJECTS 2003 SALES IN THE RANGE OF 40.0 MILLION TO 45.0 MILLION TONS OF COAL.

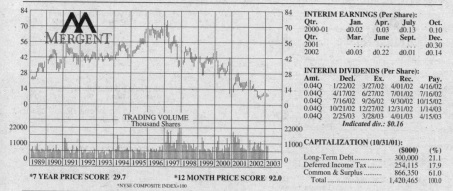

*7 YEAR PRICE SCORE 29.7   ***12 MONTH PRICE SCORE 92.0**
NYSE COMPOSITE INDEX=100

INTERIM EARNINGS (Per Share):

Qtr.	Jan.	Apr.	July	Oct.
2000-01	d0.02	0.03	d0.13	0.10
Qtr.	Mar.	June	Sept.	Dec.
2001	...	...	...	d0.30
2002	d0.03	d0.22	d0.01	d0.14

INTERIM DIVIDENDS (Per Share):

Amt.	Decl.	Ex.	Rec.	Pay.
0.04Q	1/22/02	3/27/02	4/01/02	4/16/02
0.04Q	4/17/02	6/27/02	7/01/02	7/16/02
0.04Q	7/16/02	9/26/02	9/30/02	10/15/02
0.04Q	10/21/02	12/27/02	12/31/02	1/14/03
0.04Q	2/25/03	3/28/03	4/01/03	4/15/03

Indicated div.: $0.16

CAPITALIZATION (10/31/01):

	($000)	(%)
Long-Term Debt	300,000	21.1
Deferred Income Tax	254,115	17.9
Common & Surplus	866,350	61.0
Total	1,420,465	100.0

BUSINESS:

Massey Energy Company was created on 11/30/00 as a result of a reverse spin-off transaction by Flour Corporation, wherein two publicly-traded companies were created: Massey Energy Company and a "new" Fluor Corporation. The Company produces, processes and sells bituminous, low-sulfur coal of steam and metallurgical grades through processing and shipping centers, called "resource complexes." As of 9/30/02, MEE operated 18 resource complexes that serve over 200 utility, industrial and metallurgical customers worldwide. The Company operates coal mines in West Virginia, Kentucky, Tennessee and Virginia. MEE's steam coal is primarily purchased by utilities and industrial clients as fuel for power plants. MEE's metallurgical coal is used to make coke for the manufacture of steel.

RECENT DEVELOPMENTS:

For the year ended 12/31/02, MEE reported a net loss of $30.0 million compared with a net loss of $16.5 million in 2001. Results for 2002 included pre-tax charges of $25.6 million related to the Harman jury verdict and $10.6 million related to the Duke arbitration. Total revenues increased 10.4% to $1.63 billion from $1.48 billion a year earlier. Revenues for 2002 included bond repurchase income of $3.3 million. Produced coal revenue rose 6.4% to $1.32 billion, while purchased coal revenue surged 94.5% to $117.1 million. Other revenue climbed 56.7% to $78.8 million, while freight and handling revenue fell 11.7% to $112.0 million.

PROSPECTS:

Weak coal market conditions persisted through the fourth quarter of 2002 due to slow economic conditions in the U.S., tight cash management by utilities and increased electricity generation by gas-fired production plants. However, demand for coal is expected to accelerate in early 2003 due to inventory shrinkage at utilities and the comparatively cold winter as well as production declines by producers throughout central Appalachia. MEE projects 2003 sales in the range of 40.0 million to 45.0 million tons of coal. The Company has sales commitment for calendar 2003 of 36.0 million tons of coal at an average expected price of $30.80 per ton.

ANNUAL FINANCIAL DATA:

FISCAL YEAR	TOT. REVS. ($mill.)	NET INC. ($mill.)	TOT. ASSETS ($mill.)	OPER. PROFIT %	NET PROFIT %	RET. ON EQUITY %	RET. ON ASSETS %	CURR. RATIO	EARN. PER SH. $	CASH FL. PER SH. $	TANG. BK. VAL. $	DIV. PER SH. $	PRICE RANGE	AVG. P/E RATIO	AVG. YIELD %
③ p12/31/02	1,629.7	② d30.0		1.3	...	...	...	0.8	② d0.40			0.16	22.41 - 4.55	...	1.2
10/31/01	1,253.8	d1.0	2,268.7	1.3	...	...	...	0.8	d0.01	2.44	11.62	0.16	28.95 - 11.25	...	0.8
① 10/31/00	1,140.7	78.8	2,161.1	8.5	6.9	5.7	3.6	1.4	1.07	3.39	18.70	1.00	48.50 - 9.94	27.3	3.4
10/31/99	12,417.4	104.2	4,886.1	1.5	0.8	6.6	2.1	0.9	1.37	5.56	19.27	0.80	46.50 - 26.19	26.5	2.2
10/31/98	13,504.8	235.3	5,019.2	2.7	1.7	15.4	4.7	0.9	2.97	6.62	18.35	0.80	52.50 - 34.13	14.6	1.8
10/31/97	14,298.5	146.2	4,998.3	1.8	1.0	8.4	2.9	1.1	1.73	4.67	18.90	0.76	75.88 - 33.50	31.6	1.4
10/31/96	11,015.2	268.1	3,954.7	3.8	2.4	16.1	6.8	1.1	3.17	5.47	18.92	0.68	71.88 - 57.75	20.4	1.0
10/31/95	9,301.4	231.8	3,231.8	3.9	2.5	16.2	7.2	1.1	2.78	4.54	16.80	0.60	68.00 - 42.75	19.9	1.1
10/31/94	8,485.3	192.4	2,849.1	3.6	2.3	15.8	6.8	1.2	2.32	3.70	14.65	0.52	56.25 - 40.13	20.8	1.1
10/31/93	7,850.2	166.8	2,588.9	3.1	2.1	16.0	6.4	1.1	2.03	3.39	12.72	0.48	46.13 - 38.00	20.7	1.1

Statistics are as originally reported. ① Reflects spin-off of Fluor Corporation. ② Incl. pre-tax Harman litig. chrg. $25.6 mill. and pre-tax Duke arbitration chrg. $10.6 mill. ③ Reflects year-end change.

OFFICERS:
D. L. Blankenship, Chmn., Pres., C.E.O.
K. J. Stockel, Sr. V.P., C.F.O.
B. F. Phillips Jr., V.P., Treas.

INVESTOR CONTACT: Katharine W. Kenny, Investor Relations, (804) 788-1824

PRINCIPAL OFFICE: 4 North 4th Street, Richmond, VA 23219

TELEPHONE NUMBER: (804) 788-1800
FAX: (804) 788-1870
WEB: www.masseyenergyco.com

NO. OF EMPLOYEES: 4,552

SHAREHOLDERS: 10,503 (approx.)

ANNUAL MEETING: In April

INCORPORATED: DE, Jan., 1978

INSTITUTIONAL HOLDINGS:
No. of Institutions: 167
Shares Held: 67,906,938
% Held: 90.2

INDUSTRY: Bituminous coal and lignite "surface (SIC: 1221)

TRANSFER AGENT(S): Mellon Investor Services, LLC, Ridgefield Park, NJ

MATTEL, INC.

EXCH.	SYM.	REC. PRICE	P/E RATIO	YLD.	MKT. CAP.	RANGE (52-WK.)	'02 Y/E PR.
NYSE	MAT	21.32 (2/28/03)	20.9	0.2%	$9.19 bill.	22.36 - 15.05	19.15

MEDIUM GRADE. THE COMPANY ANNOUNCED THE CONSOLIDATION OF ITS GIRLS AND BOYS/ENTERTAINMENT BUSINESS UNITS INTO ONE DIVISION, RENAMED MATTEL BRANDS.

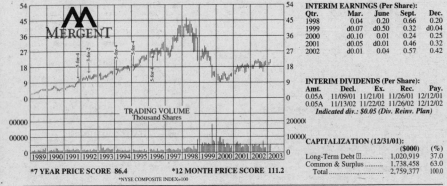

INTERIM EARNINGS (Per Share):

Qtr.	Mar.	June	Sept.	Dec.
1998	0.04	0.20	0.66	0.20
1999	d0.07	d0.50	0.32	d0.04
2000	d0.10	0.01	0.24	0.25
2001	d0.05	d0.01	0.46	0.32
2002	d0.01	0.04	0.57	0.42

INTERIM DIVIDENDS (Per Share):

Amt.	Decl.	Ex.	Rec.	Pay.
0.05A	11/09/01	11/21/01	11/26/01	12/12/01
0.05A	11/13/02	11/22/02	11/26/02	12/12/02

Indicated div.: $0.05 (Div. Reinv. Plan)

TRADING VOLUME Thousand Shares

CAPITALIZATION (12/31/01):

	($000)	(%)
Long-Term Debt 1	1,020,919	37.0
Common & Surplus	1,738,458	63.0
Total	2,759,377	100.0

*7 YEAR PRICE SCORE 86.4   *12 MONTH PRICE SCORE 111.2

*NYSE COMPOSITE INDEX=100

BUSINESS:

Mattel, Inc. is the largest toy maker in the world in terms of revenues. MAT's four principal product lines are BARBIE fashion dolls, doll clothing and accessories; AMERICAN GIRL collection of books, dolls and accessories based on American heroines; FISHERPRICE toys and juvenile products; and HOT WHEELS. Additional principal product lines include large dolls; preschool toys; including SEE N SAY talking toys; and the UNO and SKIPBO games. In November of 1993, Fisher-Price, Inc. became a wholly-owned subsidiary. As of 2/3/03, MAT had offices and facilities in about 36 foreign countries and sold its products in more than 150 nations throughout the world. MAT acquired Tyco Toys, Inc. in 3/97. In 2000, MAT sold The Learning Company.

RECENT DEVELOPMENTS:

For the year ended 12/31/02, income was $455.0 million, before an accounting change charge of $252.2 million and a gain of $27.3 million from discontinued operations, compared with income of $310.9 million, before an accounting change charge of $12.0 million, the previous year. Results for 2002 and 2001 included pre-tax restructuring charges of $24.6 million and $15.7 million, respectively. Net sales rose 4.2% to $4.89 billion from $4.69 billion the year before. Operating income increased 25.7% to $735.4 million versus $585.1 million the prior year.

PROSPECTS:

On 2/28/03, the Company announced the consolidation of its Girls and Boys/Entertainment business units into one division, renamed Mattel Brands. The new global division includes the BARBIE® and HOT WHEELS® brands, as well as licensed entertainment properties. Separately, the Company should continue to benefit from strong growth in its core brands. MAT continues to expect revenues to grow in the mid-single-digit range and earnings per share growth ranging from the low double-digits to the mid-teens. In addition, MAT is on target to deliver initial cumulative cost savings of at least $200.0 million from its financial realignment plan by year end 2003.

ANNUAL FINANCIAL DATA:

FISCAL YEAR	TOT. REVS. ($mill.)	NET INC. ($mill.)	TOT. ASSETS ($mill.)	OPER. PROFIT %	NET PROFIT %	RET. ON EQUITY %	RET. ON ASSETS %	CURR. RATIO	EARN. PER SH.$	CASH FL.PER SH.$	TANG. BK. VAL.$	DIV. PER SH.$	PRICE RANGE	AVG. P/E RATIO	AVG. YIELD %
p12/31/02	4,885.3	10 455.0							10 1.03			0.05	22.36 - 15.05	18.2	0.3
12/31/01	4,804.1	9 310.9	4,540.6	12.5	6.5	17.9	6.8	1.3	9 0.71	1.31	1.46	0.05	19.92 - 13.52	23.5	0.3
12/31/00	4,669.9	8 170.2	4,313.4	8.1	3.6	12.1	3.9	1.2	8 0.40	1.00	0.62	0.36	15.13 - 8.94	30.1	3.0
12/31/99	5,515.0	7 d82.4	5,127.0	0.5	...	...	...	1.3	7 d0.21	0.51	1.35	0.34	30.31 - 11.69	...	1.6
12/31/98	4,781.9	6 332.3	4,262.2	13.1	6.9	18.3	7.8	1.6	6 1.10	1.78	1.98	0.30	46.56 - 21.25	30.8	0.9
12/31/97	4,834.6	5 289.8	3,803.8	11.4	6.0	15.9	7.6	2.1	5 0.94	1.59	4.38	0.26	42.25 - 23.38	34.9	0.8
12/31/96	3,786.0	4 211.6	2,893.5	17.1	5.6	14.6	7.3	1.8	4 1.36	1.30	3.84	0.23	32.50 - 21.63	19.9	0.8
12/31/95	3,638.8	204.5	2,695.5	16.5	5.6	16.0	7.6	2.0	1.26	1.19	3.09	0.18	24.90 - 15.76	16.1	0.9
12/31/94	3,205.0	2 119.4	2,459.0	14.9	3.7	11.0	4.9	1.7	2 0.90	0.85	2.37	0.15	18.88 - 13.25	17.8	0.9
12/31/93	2,704.4	2 135.9	2,000.1	11.5	5.0	16.6	6.8	1.9	3 0.62	1.04	3.23	0.11	15.74 - 10.50	21.3	0.9

Statistics are as originally reported. Adj. for 5-for-4 stock split, 3/96, 1/95 & 1/94. 1 Incl. debs. conv. into com. 2 Incl. $75.0 mill. restruct. chg. 3 Bef. acctg. adj. chg. of $4.0 mill., extraord. chg. of $14.7 mill., & incl. chg. of $90.4 mill. 4 Incl. after-tax chg. of $15.1 mill. & after-tax refund accrual of $8.0 mill. 5 Incl. a pre-tax integrat./restruct. chg. of $275.0 mill. & excl. an after-tax extraord. chg. of $4.6 mill. 6 Inc. a net chg. of $27.0 mill. & an addit. $4.0 mill. net nonrecurr. chrg. 7 Incl. net restruct. chrgs. of $265.0 mill. 8 Incl. pre-tax nonrecurr. chrgs. of $179.0 mill. & excl. loss of $601.1 mill. fr. disc. opers. 9 Bef. acctg chng. chrg. of $12.0 mill. & incl. pre-tax restruct. & other chrgs. of $15.7 mill. 10 Bef. acctg. chrg. of $252.2 mill. & gain of $27.3 mill. fr. disc. ops. & incl. restruct. chrg. of $24.6 mill.

OFFICERS:
R. A. Eckert, Chmn., C.E.O.
K. M. Farr, C.F.O.

INVESTOR CONTACT: Investor Relations, (310) 252-2000

PRINCIPAL OFFICE: 333 Continental Boulevard, El Segundo, CA 90245-5012

TELEPHONE NUMBER: (310) 252-2000
FAX: (310) 252-3671
WEB: www.mattel.com
NO. OF EMPLOYEES: 27,000 (approx.)
SHAREHOLDERS: 49,000 (approx.)
ANNUAL MEETING: In May
INCORPORATED: CA, Mar., 1948; reincorp., DE, Mar., 1968

INSTITUTIONAL HOLDINGS:
No. of Institutions: 427
Shares Held: 366,633,329
% Held: 83.9
INDUSTRY: Dolls and stuffed toys (SIC: 3942)
TRANSFER AGENT(S): Fleet National Bank, Boston, MA

MAVERICK TUBE CORPORATION

EXCH.	SYM.	REC. PRICE	P/E RATIO	YLD.	MKT. CAP.	RANGE (52-WK.)	'02 Y/E PR.
NYSE	MVK	17.44 (2/28/03)	174.4	...	$0.57 bill.	19.15 - 8.21	13.03

MEDIUM GRADE. THE COMPANY ANTICIPATES HIGHER DRILLING LEVELS IN 2003.

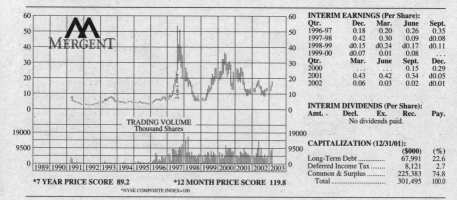

INTERIM EARNINGS (Per Share):

Qtr.	Dec.	Mar.	June	Sept.
1996-97	0.18	0.20	0.26	0.35
1997-98	0.42	0.30	0.09	d0.08
1998-99	d0.15	d0.24	d0.17	d0.11
1999-00	d0.07	0.01	0.08	...

Qtr.	Mar.	June	Sept.	Dec.
2000	...	...	0.15	0.29
2001	0.43	0.42	0.34	d0.05
2002	0.06	0.03	0.02	d0.01

INTERIM DIVIDENDS (Per Share):

Amt.	Decl.	Ex.	Rec.	Pay.
No dividends paid.				

CAPITALIZATION (12/31/01):

	($000)	(%)
Long-Term Debt	67,991	22.6
Deferred Income Tax	8,121	2.7
Common & Surplus	225,383	74.8
Total	301,495	100.0

*7 YEAR PRICE SCORE 89.2   ***12 MONTH PRICE SCORE 119.8**

*NYSE COMPOSITE INDEX=100

BUSINESS:

Maverick Tube Corporation and its subsidiaries, Maverick Tube, L.P. and Prudential Steel Ltd., manufacture tubular steel products used in the energy industry in drilling, production, well servicing and line pipe applications as well as industrial tubing products (HSS, and standard pipe) used in various industrial applications. The Company manufactures its products at three facilities in Conroe, Texas, Hickman, Arkansas, and Calgary, Alberta, Canada. On 9/22/00, MVK acquired Prudential Steel Ltd. On 3/29/02, MVK sold its Cold Drawn Tubular Business. On 4/1/02, MVK acquired Precision Tube Holding Corp. On 12/31/02, MVK acquired the tubular business of the LTV Steel Corporation.

RECENT DEVELOPMENTS:

For the year ended 12/31/02, income plunged 92.1% to $3.1 million, before income of $518,000 from discontinued operations and an extraordinary loss of $227,000, compared with $39.2 million, before a loss of $11.2 million from discontinued operations, in 2001. The decrease in income was primarily due to sharply higher steel costs. Results for 2002 and 2001 included restructuring charges of $1.5 million and $8.1 million, respectively. Also, results for 2002 included a benefit of $2.7 million from a partial trade case recovery, while results for 2001 included start-up costs of $1.1 million. Net sales declined 17.0% to $439.0 million from $528.6 million a year earlier. Average U.S. rig count declined 28.2% to 831, while average Canadian rig count decreased 22.2% to 266.

PROSPECTS:

Looking ahead, the Company anticipates higher drilling levels, supported by the considerably improved oil and gas prices experienced in recent months. MVK's strong start to the winter drilling season in Canada, coupled with anticipated benefits from reduced raw material costs, has lead the Company to be optimistic about an improved business environment in 2003. Separately, on 3/3/03, the Company announced that it had acquired SeaCAT Corporation, a producer and seller of specialized coiled tubing products. For the two years ended 9/30/02, SeaCAT's annual revenues averaged over $17.0 million.

ANNUAL FINANCIAL DATA:

FISCAL YEAR	TOT. REVS. ($000)	NET INC. ($000)	TOT. ASSETS ($000)	OPER. PROFIT %	NET PROFIT %	RET. ON EQUITY %	RET. ON ASSETS %	CURR. RATIO	EARN. PER SH.$	CASH FL.PER SH.$	TANG. BK. VAL.$	PRICE RANGE	AVG. P/E RATIO
p12/31/02	439,004	④ 3,113	595,012	...	...	...	...	...	④ 0.08	...	...	19.15 - 8.21	171.0
12/31/01	528,606	③ 39,238	357,447	12.0	7.4	17.4	11.0	3.7	③ 1.15	1.59	6.87	27.20 - 8.47	15.5
② 12/31/00	560,382	① 16,565	389,029	7.9	3.0	7.8	4.3	2.2	① 0.48	0.88	6.33	36.50 - 12.38	50.9
12/31/99	129,616	1,547	323,255	2.7	1.2	0.8	0.5	...	0.05	0.15	...	26.75 - 5.38	320.6
9/30/99	172,417	① d10,449	160,148	...	...	...	...	2.1	① d0.68	d0.20	5.16	26.75 - 5.38	...
9/30/98	265,389	11,385	156,885	7.0	4.3	12.6	7.3	3.3	0.73	1.13	5.83	26.88 - 5.03	21.9
9/30/97	291,060	14,885	162,064	8.3	5.1	19.1	9.2	1.7	0.97	1.35	5.05	53.87 - 6.13	30.9
9/30/96	204,182	7,538	125,556	5.8	3.7	13.2	6.0	1.8	0.51	0.85	3.83	8.25 - 3.69	11.8
9/30/95	167,896	d2,334	106,494	...	...	...	...	2.3	d0.15	0.16	3.33	5.25 - 3.06	...
9/30/94	124,843	429	99,434	1.4	0.3	0.8	0.4	2.0	0.04	0.30	3.48	5.38 - 3.38	124.6

Statistics are as originally reported. ① Incl. non-recurr. chrg. $13.2 mill., 12/00; $3.5 mill., 9/99. ② Refls. fiscal year-end chg. to 12/30; & the acq. of Prudential Steel Ltd. ③ Incl. start-up costs of $1.1 mill. and restruct. chrg. of $8.1 mill., but bef. loss of $11.2 mill. from discont. oper. ④ Excl. dis. ops. inc. of $518,000, extraord. loss of $227,000, but incl. restruct. chrg. of $1.5 mill. and benefit of $2.7 mill. fr. a partial trade case recov.

OFFICERS:
G. M. Eisenberg, Chmn., Pres., C.E.O.
P. G. Boone, V.P., C.F.O., Treas., Sec.
J. Cowan, Exec. V.P., C.O.O.
INVESTOR CONTACT: Pamela G. Boone,
V.P., C.F.O., Treas., Sec., (636) 733-1600
PRINCIPAL OFFICE: 16401 Swingley Ridge Road, Seventh Floor, Suite 700, Chesterfield, MO 63017

TELEPHONE NUMBER: (636) 733-1600
FAX: (636) 537-1363
WEB: www.maverick-tube.com
NO. OF EMPLOYEES: 1,569 (avg.)
SHAREHOLDERS: 155 (record); 7 (exchangeable)
ANNUAL MEETING: In May
INCORPORATED: MO, 1977; reincorp., DE, 1987

INSTITUTIONAL HOLDINGS:
No. of Institutions: 142
Shares Held: 34,102,100
% Held: 83.3

INDUSTRY: Steel pipe and tubes (SIC: 3317)

TRANSFER AGENT(S): Computershare Investor Service, Chicago IL

MAY DEPARTMENT STORES COMPANY (THE)

EXCH.	SYM.	REC. PRICE	P/E RATIO	YLD.	MKT. CAP.	RANGE (52-WK.)	'02 Y/E PR.	DIV. ACH.
NYSE	MAY	19.62 (2/28/03)	11.1	4.9%	$5.63 bill.	37.75 - 18.69	22.98	27 yrs.

INVESTMENT GRADE. THE COMPANY PLANS TO OPEN ELEVEN NEW DEPARTMENT STORES AND 30 NEW DAVID'S BRIDAL STORES IN 2003.

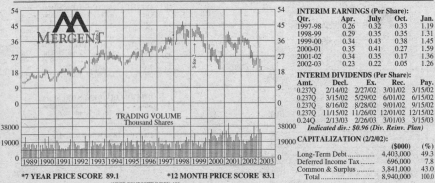

INTERIM EARNINGS (Per Share):

Qtr.	Apr.	July	Oct.	Jan.
1997-98	0.26	0.32	0.33	1.19
1998-99	0.29	0.35	0.35	1.31
1999-00	0.34	0.43	0.38	1.45
2000-01	0.35	0.41	0.27	1.59
2001-02	0.34	0.35	0.17	1.36
2002-03	0.23	0.22	0.05	1.26

INTERIM DIVIDENDS (Per Share):

Amt.	Decl.	Ex.	Rec.	Pay.
0.237Q	2/14/02	2/27/02	3/01/02	3/15/02
0.237Q	3/15/02	5/29/02	6/01/02	6/15/02
0.237Q	8/16/02	8/28/02	9/01/02	9/15/02
0.237Q	11/15/02	11/26/02	12/01/02	12/15/02
0.24Q	2/13/03	2/26/03	3/01/03	3/15/03

Indicated div.: $0.96 (Div. Reinv. Plan)

CAPITALIZATION (2/2/02):

	($000)	(%)
Long-Term Debt	4,403,000	49.3
Deferred Income Tax	696,000	7.8
Common & Surplus	3,841,000	43.0
Total	8,940,000	100.0

*7 YEAR PRICE SCORE 89.1   ***12 MONTH PRICE SCORE 83.1**

*NYSE COMPOSITE INDEX=100

BUSINESS:

The May Department Stores Company operated 443 department stores in 45 states, the District of Columbia and Puerto Rico as of 2/6/03 under the following names: Lord & Taylor, Hecht's, Strawbridge's, Foley's, Robinsons-May, Filene's, Kaufmann's, Famous-Barr, L.S. Ayers, The Jones Store and Meier & Frank. In addition, MAY operated 180 David's Bridal stores, 235 After Hours stores and ten Priscilla of Boston stores. Thalhimers was acquired for $317.0 million in 1990, and was consolidated with the Hecht's division in January 1992. On 5/4/96, the Company completed its spin-off of Payless ShoeSource, Inc. On 8/11/00, MAY acquired David's Bridal, Inc.

RECENT DEVELOPMENTS:

For the 52 weeks ended 2/1/03, net earnings totaled $542.0 million, down 22.9% compared with $703.0 million in the corresponding prior-year period. Results for 2002 included an after-tax charge of $76.0 million stemming from the combination of certain divisions and an after-tax charge of $6.0 million related to the early redemption of debt. Net sales slipped 2.8% to $13.49 billion from $13.88 billion the year before. Comparable-store sales declined 5.3% year-over-year. Earnings before income taxes slid 28.0% to $820.0 million from $1.14 billion the previous year. In 2002, MAY opened eleven new department stores, which added 1.7 million square feet of retail space, and 30 new David's Bridal stores.

PROSPECTS:

The Company anticipates opening eleven new department stores and 30 new David's Bridal stores in 2003. Meanwhile, MAY is taking aggressive steps to streamline its operations to help reduce costs and improve profitability. In 2002, the Company completed the Filene's/Kaufmann's and Robinson-May/Meier & Frank division combinations, which are expected to generate cost savings of about $60.0 million annually. In January 2003, MAY announced plans to close its credit center in Arizona and consolidate its data centers into an existing facility in Lorian, Ohio.

ANNUAL FINANCIAL DATA:

FISCAL YEAR	TOT. REVS. ($mill.)	NET INC. ($mill.)	TOT. ASSETS ($mill.)	OPER. PROFIT %	NET PROFIT %	RET. ON EQUITY %	RET. ON ASSETS %	CURR. RATIO	EARN. PER SH.$	CASH FL. PER SH.$	TANG. BK. VAL.$	DIV. PER SH.$	PRICE RANGE	AVG. P/E RATIO	AVG. YIELD %
p2/01/03	13,491.0	④ 542.0	11,936.0			13.4	4.5		① 1.76			0.95	38.86 - 20.10	16.8	3.2
2/02/02	14,175.0	① 706.0	11,920.0	10.5	5.0	18.4	5.9	1.9	① 2.22	3.98	7.76	0.94	41.25 - 27.00	15.4	2.8
2/03/01	14,511.0	858.0	11,574.0	12.0	5.9	22.3	7.4	2.4	2.62	4.18	8.53	0.93	33.94 - 19.19	10.1	3.5
1/29/00	13,866.0	927.0	10,935.0	13.1	6.7	22.7	8.5	2.1	2.60	3.93	9.51	0.89	45.38 - 29.19	14.3	2.4
1/30/99	13,413.0	849.0	10,533.0	12.5	6.3	22.1	8.1	2.4	2.30	3.51	8.67	0.85	47.25 - 33.17	17.5	2.1
1/31/98	12,685.0	① 779.0	9,930.0	12.4	6.1	20.5	7.8	2.6	① 2.07	3.19	8.82	0.80	38.09 - 29.08	16.2	2.4
2/01/97	12,000.0	① 749.0	10,059.0	12.6	6.2	20.5	7.4	2.6	① 1.96	3.01	8.09	0.77	34.84 - 26.67	15.7	2.5
③ 2/03/96	10,952.0	② 700.0	10,122.0	12.9	6.4	15.3	6.9	3.2	② 1.82	2.75	10.48	0.74	30.25 - 21.92	14.3	2.8
1/28/95	12,223.0	782.0	9,472.0	12.5	6.4	18.9	8.3	2.6	2.04	3.10	9.50	0.67	30.08 - 21.50	12.6	2.6
1/29/94	11,529.0	711.0	8,800.0	12.3	6.2	19.5	7.1	2.6	1.85	2.82	8.12	0.60	31.00 - 22.29	14.4	2.2

Statistics are as originally reported. Adj. for 3-for-2 stk. split, 3/99. ① Bef. $3 mil ($0.01/sh) extraord. loss, 2002; $4 mil extraord. loss, 1997; & bef. $5 mil extraord. loss & cr$11 mil from discont. opers., 1996. ② Bef. discont. opers. cr$55 mil; bef. $3 mil extraord. loss; & incl. $44 mil non-recur. chg. ③ Excl. results of spun-off PayLess ShoeSource, Inc. ④ Incl. $76.0 mil ($0.24/sh) after-tax chg. for division combinations & $6.0 mil after-tax chg. fr. early debt redemption.

OFFICERS:
E. S. Kahn, Chmn., C.E.O.
J. L. Dunham, Pres.
T. D. Fingleton, Exec. V.P., C.F.O.

INVESTOR CONTACT: Sharon L. Bateman, Investor Relations, (314) 342-6494

PRINCIPAL OFFICE: 611 Olive Street, St. Louis, MO 63101

TELEPHONE NUMBER: (314) 342-6300
FAX: (314) 342-6497
WEB: www.maycompany.com
NO. OF EMPLOYEES: 60,000 full-time (approx.); 67,000 part-time (approx.)
SHAREHOLDERS: 41,000 (approx.)
ANNUAL MEETING: In May
INCORPORATED: NY, June, 1910; reincorp., DE, May, 1996

INSTITUTIONAL HOLDINGS:
No. of Institutions: 398
Shares Held: 226,015,667
% Held: 78.4

INDUSTRY: Department stores (SIC: 5311)

TRANSFER AGENT(S): The Bank of New York, New York, NY

MAYTAG CORPORATION

EXCH.	SYM.	REC. PRICE	P/E RATIO	YLD.	MKT. CAP.	RANGE (52-WK.)	'02 Y/E PR.
NYSE	MYG	24.10 (2/28/03)	9.9	3.0%	$1.89 bill.	47.94 - 18.84	28.50

UPPER MEDIUM GRADE. THE COMPANY BEGAN 2003 WITH AN AGGRESSIVE PRODUCT LAUNCH PROGRAM.

*7 YEAR PRICE SCORE 98.3   ***12 MONTH PRICE SCORE 85.1**

*NYSE COMPOSITE INDEX=100

INTERIM EARNINGS (Per Share):

Qtr.	Mar.	June	Sept.	Dec.
1998	0.75	0.71	0.85	0.75
1999	0.95	0.97	0.92	0.82
2000	0.89	0.92	0.74	d0.12
2001	0.96	0.32	d0.32	0.31
2002	0.75	0.86	0.78	0.05

INTERIM DIVIDENDS (Per Share):

Amt.	Decl.	Ex.	Rec.	Pay.
0.18Q	2/13/02	2/27/02	3/01/02	3/15/02
0.18Q	5/09/02	5/29/02	5/31/02	6/14/02
0.18Q	8/08/02	8/28/02	8/30/02	9/16/02
0.18Q	11/14/02	11/27/02	12/02/02	12/16/02
0.18Q	2/13/03	2/26/03	2/28/03	3/14/03

Indicated div.: $0.72 (Div. Reinv. Plan)

CAPITALIZATION (12/31/01):

	($000)	(%)
Long-Term Debt	932,065	86.2
Deferred Income Tax	25,100	2.3
Minority Interest	100,142	9.3
Common & Surplus	23,546	2.2
Total	1,080,853	100.0

BUSINESS:

Maytag Corporation is a manufacturer of home and commercial appliances. MYG's Home Appliances segment (94.8% of 2002 net sales) includes washers, dryers, and electric ranges, ovens, refrigerators, dishwashers and floor care products sold under the DIXIE-NARCO and PITCO FRIALATOR brands to distributors, soft drink bottlers and restaurant chains. MYG acquired Jade Range in 1999 and Amana Appliances in 2001. On 12/21/01, MYG sold its Blodgett commercial foodservice equipment business. During the third quarter of 2002, MYG disposed of its 50.5% interest in the Rongshida-Maytag joint venture in China.

care products sold under the MAYTAG, MAGIC CHEF, HOOVER, JENN-AIR, and ADMIRAL brand names to retailers in North America. The Commercial Appliances segment (5.2%) includes commercial cooking and vending equipment sold primarily under the DIXIE-NARCO and PITCO

RECENT DEVELOPMENTS:

For the year ended 12/31/02, MYG reported income from continuing operations of $191.4 million versus $167.5 million the year before. Results for 2002 and 2001 included pre-tax special charges of $67.1 million and $9.8 million, respectively. Results for 2002 and 2001 excluded losses of $2.6 million and $110.9 million, respectively, from discon-

tinued operations. Results for 2001 also excluded an extraordinary charge of $5.2 million and an accounting charge of $3.7 million and included a loss on securities of $7.2 million. Net sales grew 11.5% to $4.67 billion. Home appliance sales advanced 11.8% to $4.42 billion, while commercial appliance sales rose 6.3% to $244.7 million.

PROSPECTS:

The Company began 2003 with an aggressive product launch program, including cooking, small household appliances, refrigeration and air purifier introductions. The Company plans to introduce new or redesigned products in every quarter of 2003. This includes a new laundry plat-

form, several new floor care products and a newly designed vending unit. In 2003, the Company expects revenue growth of approximately 7.0%, as well as earnings per share from continuing operations of $0.70 in the first quarter and between $3.10 and $3.20 for the full year.

ANNUAL FINANCIAL DATA:

FISCAL YEAR	TOT. REVS. ($mill.)	NET INC. ($mill.)	TOT. ASSETS ($mill.)	OPER. PROFIT %	NET PROFIT %	RET. ON EQUITY %	RET. ON ASSETS %	CURR. RATIO	EARN. PER SH.$	CASH FL. PER SH.$	TANG. BK. VAL.$	DIV. PER SH.$	PRICE RANGE	AVG. P/E RATIO	AVG. YIELD %
p12/31/02	4,666.0	⑥ 191.4	3,104.2						⑥ 2.44			0.72	47.94 - 18.84	13.7	2.2
12/31/01	4,323.7	⑤ 167.5	3,156.2	6.7	3.9	711.5	5.3	1.3	⑤ 2.13	4.16	...	0.72	37.40 - 22.25	14.0	2.4
12/31/00	4,247.5	① 201.0	2,668.9	9.8	4.7	927.1	7.5	1.1	① 2.44	4.38	...	0.72	47.75 - 25.00	14.9	2.0
12/31/99	4,323.7	328.5	2,636.5	13.3	7.6	76.9	12.5	1.2	3.66	5.30	...	0.72	74.81 - 31.25	14.5	1.4
12/31/98	4,069.3	③ 286.5	2,587.7	12.8	7.0	56.4	11.1	1.2	③ 3.05	4.63	0.23	0.68	64.50 - 35.38	16.4	1.4
12/31/97	3,407.9	② 183.5	2,514.2	10.5	5.4	29.8	7.3	1.6	② 1.87	3.28	1.56	0.64	37.56 - 19.75	15.3	2.2
12/31/96	3,001.7	③③ 138.0	2,329.9	9.0	4.6	24.0	5.9	1.6	③③ 1.36	2.45	1.85	0.56	22.88 - 17.50	14.8	2.8
12/31/95	3,039.5	④ d15.0	2,125.1	9.5	...	...	...	2.5	④ d0.14	0.90	2.33	0.52	21.50 - 14.50	...	2.9
12/31/94	3,372.5	①② 151.1	2,504.3	9.6	4.5	20.7	6.0	2.1	①② 1.42	2.53	3.14	0.50	20.13 - 14.00	12.0	2.9
12/31/93	2,987.1	① 51.3	2,469.5	5.3	1.7	8.7	2.1	1.6	① 0.48	1.53	2.46	0.50	18.63 - 13.00	32.9	3.2

Statistics are as originally reported. ① Incl. non-recur. chrg. of $31.2 mill., 2000; $24 mill., 1996; $16.4 mill., 1994; $30.0 mill., 1993. ② Bef. $3.2 mill. acctg. chrg. & $20 mill. tax benefit. ③ Bef. extraord. chrg. $5.9 mill., 1998; $3.2 mill., 1997; $1.5 mill., 1996. ④ Bef. extraord. chrge. $5.5 mill.; incl. $149.8 mill. loss fr. disc. ops. & $9.9 mill. chrg. for lawsuit settlement. ⑤ Incl. pre-tax spec. chrgs. of $9.8 mill.; bef. loss of $110.9 mill. fr. disc. opers.; extraord. loss of $5.2 mill. & acctg. chrg. of $3.7 mill. ⑥ Bef. loss of $2.6 mill. fr. disc. opers.; incl. pre-tax spec. chrgs. of $67.1 mill.

OFFICERS:
R. F. Hake, Chmn., C.E.O.
L. A. Hadley, Pres.

INVESTOR CONTACT: John P. Tolson, Inv. Rel., (641) 787-8136

PRINCIPAL OFFICE: 403 West Fourth Street North, Newton, IA 50208

TELEPHONE NUMBER: (641) 792-7000
FAX: (641) 787-8376
WEB: www.maytagcorp.com
NO. OF EMPLOYEES: 21,581 (avg.)
SHAREHOLDERS: 21,114
ANNUAL MEETING: In May
INCORPORATED: DE, Aug., 1925

INSTITUTIONAL HOLDINGS:
No. of Institutions: 273
Shares Held: 50,710,253
% Held: 65.0
INDUSTRY: Household appliances, nec (SIC: 3639)
TRANSFER AGENT(S): Computershare Investor Services, Chicago, IL

MBIA INC.

EXCH.	SYM.	REC. PRICE	P/E RATIO	YLD.	MKT. CAP.	RANGE (52-WK.)	'02 Y/E PR.	DIV. ACH.
NYSE	MBI	38.13 (2/28/03)	9.7	2.1%	$5.66 bill.	60.11 - 34.93	43.86	15 yrs.

INVESTMENT GRADE. GOING FORWARD, THE COMPANY EXPECTS CONTINUED ROBUST DEMAND FOR ITS FINANCIAL GUARANTEE PRODUCTS.

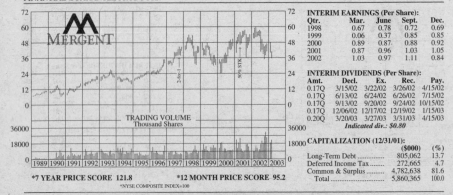

*7 YEAR PRICE SCORE 121.8   ***12 MONTH PRICE SCORE 95.2**

*NYSE COMPOSITE INDEX=100

INTERIM EARNINGS (Per Share):

Qtr.	Mar.	June	Sept.	Dec.
1998	0.67	0.78	0.72	0.69
1999	0.06	0.37	0.85	0.85
2000	0.89	0.87	0.88	0.92
2001	0.87	0.96	1.03	1.05
2002	1.03	0.97	1.11	0.84

INTERIM DIVIDENDS (Per Share):

Amt.	Decl.	Ex.	Rec.	Pay.
0.17Q	3/15/02	3/22/02	3/26/02	4/15/02
0.17Q	6/13/02	6/24/02	6/26/02	7/15/02
0.17Q	9/13/02	9/24/02	9/24/02	10/15/02
0.17Q	12/06/02	12/17/02	12/19/02	1/15/03
0.20Q	3/20/03	3/27/03	3/31/03	4/15/03

Indicated div.: $0.80

CAPITALIZATION (12/31/01):

	($000)	(%)
Long-Term Debt	805,062	13.7
Deferred Income Tax	272,665	4.7
Common & Surplus	4,782,638	81.6
Total	5,860,365	100.0

BUSINESS:

MBIA Inc. is the holding company of MBIA Insurance Corporation, a major company in the municipal bond and structured finance insurance business. MBIA's principal business is to guarantee timely payment of principal and interest for new municipal bond issues, asset-backed securities, bonds traded in the secondary market and those held in unit investment trusts and mutual funds. In addition, it provides equity and fixed-income investment services for the public and private sectors. MBIA serves state and local governments and other agencies, issuers of asset-backed securities, financial advisors, investment banking firms, bond traders, sponsors of unit investment trusts and mutual funds and the investing public. MBI's operations take place in North America, Europe, Asia and Australia. MBI acquired CapMAC Holdings, Inc. on 2/17/98 and 1838 Investment Advisors on 7/31/98.

RECENT DEVELOPMENTS:

For the year ended 12/31/02, income was $586.8 million compared with $583.2 million a year earlier. Results for 2002 and 2001 included net realized gains of $15.4 million and $8.9 million, respectively, and charges related to the change in fair value of derivative instruments of $81.9 million and $3.9 million. Results for 2002 and 2001 excluded accounting change charges of $7.7 million and $13.1 million, respectively. Total revenues increased 7.2% to $1.22 billion. Total insurance revenues rose 9.9% to $1.07 billion. Revenues from investment management services decreased 11.9% to $110.9 million, while municipal services revenues declined 8.2% to $24.8 million.

PROSPECTS:

In the near-term, the difficult economic climate is expected to persist. Nevertheless, the Company should continue to benefit from new business activity in its insurance operations due to robust demand for its financial guarantee products. In addition, the Company should benefit from the ongoing resilience of its credit portfolio. However, MBI's asset management business may continue to be negatively affected by the severe drop in the equity markets. Moreover, MBI will continue to be challenged by its ability to close transactions on terms and prices that meet its underwriting and return standards.

ANNUAL FINANCIAL DATA:

FISCAL YEAR	PREM. INC. ($mill.)	NET INVST. INC. ($mill.)	TOT. REVS. ($mill.)	NET INC. ($mill.)	TOT. ASSETS ($mill.)	TOT. INVST. ($mill.)	RET. ON REVS. %	RET. ON EQUITY %	RET. ON ASSETS %	EARN. PER SH.$	TANG. BK. VAL.$	AVG. YIELD %	DIV. PER SH.$	PRICE RANGE	AVG. P/E RATIO
p12/31/02	588.5	432.9	1,217.4	① 586.8						① 3.92		1.4	0.66	60.11 - 34.93	12.1
12/31/01	523.9	412.8	1,135.8	① 583.2	16,199.7	14,516.2	51.3	12.2	3.6	① 3.82	31.56	1.3	0.59	57.49 - 36.00	12.2
12/31/00	446.4	394.0	1,024.6	528.6	13,894.3	12,547.6	51.6	12.5	3.8	3.55	27.86	1.5	0.55	50.79 - 24.21	10.6
12/31/99	442.8	359.5	964.4	③ 320.5	12,263.9	10,954.8	33.2	9.1	2.6	③ 2.13	22.79	1.4	0.53	47.92 - 30.08	18.3
12/31/98	424.6	331.8	921.0	② 432.7	11,258.3	10,080.5	47.0	11.4	3.7	② 2.88	24.59	1.2	0.52	53.96 - 30.71	14.7
12/31/97	297.4	281.5	654.0	374.2	9,810.8	8,943.4	57.2	12.3	3.8	2.81	21.82	1.4	0.51	44.84 - 30.29	13.4
12/31/96	251.7	247.6	545.5	322.2	8,562.0	7,865.2	59.1	13.0	3.8	2.48	18.28	1.6	0.47	34.88 - 23.33	11.7
12/31/95	215.1	219.9	462.2	...	7,267.5	6,607.3	...	...	...	2.14	16.88	1.9	0.42	25.83 - 18.46	10.3
12/31/94	218.3	193.9	439.5	260.2	5,456.4	4,866.8	59.2	15.3	4.8	2.06	12.76	1.9	0.36	21.75 - 15.75	9.1
12/31/93	231.3	178.9	429.0	① 246.1	4,106.3	3,544.3	57.4	15.4	6.0	① 1.93	11.80	1.3	0.30	27.08 - 18.42	11.8

Statistics are as originally reported. Adj. for stk. splits: 3-for-2, 4/01; 2-for-1, 10/97. ① Bef. acctg. chrg. $7.7 mill., 12/02; $3.9 mill., 12/01; credit $12.9 mill., 12/93. ② Incl. non-recurr. chrg. of $36.1 mill. ③ Incl. non-recurr. chrg. of $105.0 mill.

OFFICERS:
J. W. Brown, Jr., Chmn., C.E.O.
G. C. Dunton, Pres.
N. G. Budnick, V.P., C.F.O.
INVESTOR CONTACT: Michael C. Ballinger, Inv. Rel., (914) 765-3893
PRINCIPAL OFFICE: 113 King Street, Armonk, NY 10504

TELEPHONE NUMBER: (914) 273-4545
FAX: (914) 765-3163
WEB: www.mbia.com
NO. OF EMPLOYEES: 601
SHAREHOLDERS: 851
ANNUAL MEETING: In May
INCORPORATED: CT, Nov., 1986

INSTITUTIONAL HOLDINGS:
No. of Institutions: 435
Shares Held: 132,704,931
% Held: 91.5

INDUSTRY: Surety insurance (SIC: 6351)

TRANSFER AGENT(S): Mellon Investor Services, LLC, Ridgefield Park, NJ

MBNA CORPORATION

EXCH.	SYM.	REC. PRICE	P/E RATIO	YLD.	MKT. CAP.	RANGE (52-WK.)	'02 Y/E PR.	DIV.' ACH.
NYSE	KRB	13.85 (2/28/03)	10.3	2.3%	$17.70 bill.	26.30 - 12.95	19.02	11 yrs.

UPPER MEDIUM GRADE. DURING 2002, THE COMPANY ADDED 14.2 MILLION NEW CUSTOMERS AND 12.0 MILLION NEW ACCOUNTS.

*7 YEAR PRICE SCORE 132.5   ***12 MONTH PRICE SCORE 89.4**

*NYSE COMPOSITE INDEX=100

INTERIM EARNINGS (Per Share):

Qtr.	Mar.	June	Sept.	Dec.
1999	0.15	0.18	0.23	0.25
2000	0.19	0.23	0.29	0.32
2001	0.23	0.29	0.36	0.40
2002	0.28	0.35	0.30	0.41

INTERIM DIVIDENDS (Per Share):

Amt.	Decl.	Ex.	Rec.	Pay.
0.10Q	4/11/02	6/12/02	6/14/02	7/01/02
50% STK	6/06/02	7/16/02	7/01/02	7/15/02
0.07Q	7/16/02	9/12/02	9/16/02	10/01/02
0.07Q	10/17/02	12/11/02	12/13/02	1/01/03
0.08Q	1/23/03	3/12/03	3/15/03	4/01/03

Indicated div.: $0.32

CAPITALIZATION (12/31/01):

	($000)	(%)
Total Deposits	27,094,745	64.9
Long-Term Debt	6,867,033	16.4
Preferred Stock	86	0.0
Common & Surplus	7,798,632	18.7
Total	41,760,496	100.0

BUSINESS:

MBNA Corporation is a registered bank holding company, with assets of $52.86 billion as of 12/31/02. The Company is the parent of MBNA America Bank, N.A., which has two wholly-owned foreign bank subsidiaries, MBNA Europe Bank Limited, located in the United Kingdom, and MBNA Canada Bank. MBNA America Bank is also the parent of MBNA.com, a provider of credit card, consumer loan, retail deposit, travel and shopping services. The Company is an independent credit card lender and an issuer of affinity credit cards, marketed primarily to members of associations and customers of financial institutions. In addition to its credit card lending, the Company also makes other consumer loans and offers insurance and deposit products.

RECENT DEVELOPMENTS:

For the year ended 12/31/02, net income increased 4.2% to $1.77 billion compared with $1.69 billion in the previous year. Earnings for 2002 included a one-time after-tax charge of $167.2 million related to the implementation of the Federal Financial Institutions Examination Council guidance for uncollectible accrued interest and fees. Net interest income advanced 25.2% to $2.07 billion from $1.66 billion the year before. Provision for possible credit losses fell 17.5% to $1.34 billion from $1.14 billion a year earlier. Other operating income rose 1.2% to $6.75 billion, while other operating expense climbed 5.1% to $4.70 billion.

PROSPECTS:

As of 12/31/02, total managed loans increased 10.0% to $107.26 billion compared with $97.50 billion in the prior year. In addition, during 2002, the Company added 14.2 million new customers and 12.0 million new accounts. Meanwhile, the Company is continuing to benefit from its on-line service MBNA.com. Separately, the Company's affinity credit card business acquired 405 new endorsements and renewed more than 1,100 group contracts during 2002.

ANNUAL FINANCIAL DATA:

FISCAL YEAR	NET INT. INC. ($mill.)	NON-INT. INC. ($mill.)	NET INC. ($mill.)	TOT. LOANS ($mill.)	TOT. ASSETS ($mill.)	TOT. DEP. ($mill.)	RET. ON EQUITY %	RET. ON ASSETS %	EQUITY/ ASSETS %	EARN. PER SH.$	TANG. BK. VAL.$	DIV. PER SH.$	PRICE RANGE	AVG. P/E RATIO
p12/31/02	2,074.6	6,752.9	④ 1,766.0	17,696.9	52,856.7	30,616.2	19.4	3.3		④ 1.34		0.27	26.30 - 12.95	14.6
12/31/01	1,391.0	6,939.6	1,694.3	14,703.6	45,447.9	27,094.7	21.7	3.7	17.2	1.28	4.08	0.23	26.38 - 15.62	16.4
12/31/00	1,084.0	5,093.2	1,312.5	11,682.9	38,678.1	24,343.6	19.8	3.4	17:1	1.02	3.03	0.21	26.75 - 13.00	19.5
12/31/99	933.8	4,207.8	1,024.4	7,971.1	30,859.1	18,714.8	24.4	3.3	13.6	0.81	3.49	0.18	22.17 - 13.88	22.3
12/31/98	742.3	3,229.0	776.3	11,776.1	25,806.3	15,407.0	13.6	3.0	9.3	0.65	2.12	0.16	17.25 - 9.00	20.3
12/31/97	692.4	2,812.9	622.5	8,261.9	21,305.5	12,913.2	31.6	2.9	9.2	0.51	1.75	0.14	13.59 - 7.96	21.1
12/31/96	640.5	1,895.9	② 474.5	7,659.1	17,035.3	10,151.7	27.8	2.8	10.0	② 0.39	1.51	0.12	8.64 - 4.48	16.6
12/31/95	544.2	1,424.6	② 353.1	4,967.5	13,228.9	8,608.9	27.9	2.7	9.6	② 0.30	1.12	0.11	5.74 - 2.95	14.3
12/31/94	532.1	1,013.6	③ 266.6	3,408.0	9,671.9	6,632.5	29.0	2.8	9.5	③ 0.23	0.82	0.09	3.60 - 2.53	13.2
12/31/93	474.3	740.0	① 207.8	3,725.5	7,319.8	5,241.9	27.0	2.8	10.5	① 0.12	0.45	0.08	3.32 - 1.88	21.5

Statistics are as originally reported. Adj. for 3-for-2 splits: 10/98, 10/97, 2/97, 2/96 & 2/94. ① Incl. pre-tax exp. fr. termination of mktg. agreement: $54.3 mill., 1996; $150.0 mill., 1993. ② Incl. pre-tax gain on invest. securities sold, $39,000. ③ Incl. $74,000 pre-tax loss on invest. securities sold. ④ Incl. aft-tax chrg. of $167.2 mill. rel. to implementation of the Federal Financial Institutions Examination Council for uncollectible interest and fees.

OFFICERS:
R. D. Lerner, Chmn.
C. M. Cawley, Pres., C.E.O.
M. S. Kaufman, Exec. V.P., C.F.O., Treas.

INVESTOR CONTACT: Brian D. Dalphon,
Dir., Investor Relations, (302) 432-1251

PRINCIPAL OFFICE: 1100 North King Street,
Wilmington, DE 19884-0141

TELEPHONE NUMBER: (302) 456-8588
FAX: (302) 456-8541
WEB: www.mbna.com

NO. OF EMPLOYEES: 28,000 (approx.)

SHAREHOLDERS: 2,723

ANNUAL MEETING: In May

INCORPORATED: MD, Dec., 1990

INSTITUTIONAL HOLDINGS:
No. of Institutions: 638
Shares Held: 927,876,987
% Held: 72.6

INDUSTRY: National commercial banks
(SIC: 6021)

TRANSFER AGENT(S): National City Bank,
Cleveland, OH

MCCLATCHY COMPANY (THE)

EXCH.	SYM.	REC. PRICE	P/E RATIO	YLD.	MKT. CAP.	RANGE (52-WK.)	'02 Y/E PR.
NYSE	MNI	54.22 (2/28/03)	19.1	0.8%	$2.47 bill.	65.55 - 51.50	56.73

UPPER MEDIUM GRADE. ADVERTISING REVENUE GROWTH FOR 2003 IS EXPECTED TO BE IN THE LOW TO MID SINGLE-DIGIT RANGE.

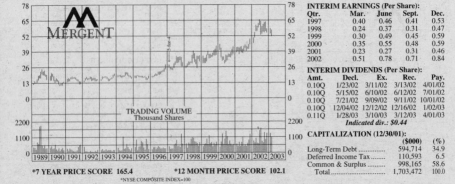

*7 YEAR PRICE SCORE 165.4   ***12 MONTH PRICE SCORE 102.1**
*NYSE COMPOSITE INDEX=100

INTERIM EARNINGS (Per Share):

Qtr.	Mar.	June	Sept.	Dec.
1997	0.40	0.46	0.41	0.53
1998	0.24	0.37	0.31	0.47
1999	0.30	0.49	0.45	0.59
2000	0.35	0.55	0.48	0.59
2001	0.23	0.27	0.31	0.46
2002	0.51	0.78	0.71	0.84

INTERIM DIVIDENDS (Per Share):

Amt.	Decl.	Ex.	Rec.	Pay.
0.10Q	1/23/02	3/11/02	3/13/02	4/01/02
0.10Q	5/15/02	6/10/02	6/12/02	7/01/02
0.10Q	7/21/02	9/09/02	9/11/02	10/01/02
0.10Q	12/04/02	12/12/02	12/16/02	1/02/03
0.11Q	1/28/03	3/10/03	3/12/03	4/01/03

Indicated div.: $0.44

CAPITALIZATION (12/30/01):

	($000)	(%)
Long-Term Debt	594,714	34.9
Deferred Income Tax	110,593	6.5
Common & Surplus	998,165	58.6
Total	1,703,472	100.0

BUSINESS:

The McClatchy Company (formerly McClatchy Newspapers, Inc.) owns and publishes 11 daily and 13 non-daily newspapers with a combined circulation of 1.4 million daily and 1.9 million Sunday. MNI has operations in the following regions: California, the Northwest, the Carolinas, and Minnesota. The Company's newspapers range from large dailies serving metropolitan areas to non-daily newspapers serving small communities. Other businesses include: Nando Media, the Raleigh News & Observer's on-line service; The Newspaper Network, a distributor of preprinted advertising inserts and run-of-press advertising; and commercial printing operations in California and North Carolina. Revenues for 2002 were derived: advertising, 82.2%; circulation, 15.5%; and other, 2.3%.

RECENT DEVELOPMENTS:

For the year ended 12/29/02, net income more than doubled to $131.2 million compared with $58.0 million in 2001. Net revenues were relatively flat at $1.08 billion compared with the prior year. Advertising revenues climbed 0.7% to $877.8 million from $871.4 million, while circulation revenues slipped 1.4% to $166.1 million from $168.5 million a year earlier. Other revenues declined 9.1% to $24.7 million from $27.1 million in 2001. Operating income jumped 40.9% to $245.0 million compared with $173.8 million the year before. Overall results benefited from revenue growth coupled with continued cost controls.

PROSPECTS:

In 2003, results may be hampered by uncertainty surrounding the geopolitical and economic climate as well as tough year-over-year comparisons. Nevertheless, employment advertising trends are improving and the retail sector is stabilizing. As a result, the Company expects advertising revenue growth for 2003 to be in the low to mid single-digit range. Moreover, the Company will continue to focus on controlling overall expense growth in the low to mid single-digit range, despite expense increases in newsprint prices, retirement costs and medical care expenses.

ANNUAL FINANCIAL DATA:

FISCAL YEAR	TOT. REVS. ($mill.)	NET INC. ($mill.)	TOT. ASSETS ($mill.)	OPER. PROFIT %	NET PROFIT %	RET. ON EQUITY %	RET. ON ASSETS %	CURR. RATIO	EARN. PER SH. $	CASH FL. PER SH. $	TANG. BK. VAL. $	DIV. PER SH. $	PRICE RANGE	AVG. P/E RATIO	AVG. YIELD %
p12/29/02	1,081.9	131.2							2.84			0.40	65.55 – 45.95	19.6	0.7
12/30/01	1,080.1	58.0	2,104.2	16.1	5.4	5.8	2.8	0.8	1.27	3.72	...	0.40	49.60 – 36.50	33.9	0.9
12/31/00	1,142.1	88.9	2,165.7	20.5	7.8	9.3	4.1	1.0	1.97	4.44	...	0.40	45.13 – 28.75	18.7	1.1
12/26/99	1,087.9	82.5	2,204.0	20.7	7.6	9.4	3.7	0.9	1.83	4.28	...	0.38	43.75 – 29.00	19.9	1.0
12/27/98	968.7	④61.1	⑤2,246.7	18.7	6.3	7.6	2.7	0.9	④1.41	3.64	...	0.38	39.56 – 24.94	22.9	1.2
12/31/97	642.0	③68.8	853.8	18.0	10.7	12.2	8.1	1.2	③1.80	3.20	4.50	0.38	35.19 – 23.38	16.3	1.3
12/31/96	624.2	44.5	875.7	13.7	7.1	8.8	5.1	1.2	1.18	2.58	2.43	0.30	28.10 – 17.40	19.3	1.3
12/31/95	540.9	②33.6	893.0	11.5	6.2	7.2	3.8	1.1	②0.90	2.07	0.97	0.30	19.30 – 15.30	19.2	1.7
12/31/94	471.4	①46.6	586.6	15.2	9.9	10.5	8.0	2.3	①1.26	2.30	8.74	0.25	21.80 – 16.30	15.1	1.3
12/31/93	449.1	31.8	525.2	14.5	7.1	8.3	6.1	1.8	0.88	1.87	7.18	0.30	20.50 – 14.50	19.9	1.2

Statistics are as originally reported. Adj. for 5-for-4 split, 1/97. ① Incl. $768,000 pre-tax restr. chg. ② Incl. $2.7 mill. ($0.04/sh.) pre-tax chg. for early retirement program. ③ Incl. $6.6 mill. gain on sale of newspaper ops. ④ Incl. $1.5 mill. income fr. a partnership & $111,000 loss on the sale of certain business ops. ⑤ Incl. amort. of goodwill of $929.0 mill. rel. to the acq. of Cowles Media Co. in 3/98.

OFFICERS:
G. B. Pruitt, Chmn., Pres., C.E.O.
P. J. Talamantes, V.P., C.F.O.
R. W. Berger, Asst. Treas., Contr.

INVESTOR CONTACT: R. Elaine Lintcum, Inv. Rel. Mgr., (916) 321-1846

PRINCIPAL OFFICE: 2100 Q Street, Sacramento, CA 95816

TELEPHONE NUMBER: (916) 321-1846
FAX: (916) 321-1964
WEB: www.mcclatchy.com
NO. OF EMPLOYEES: 9,570 (avg.)
SHAREHOLDERS: 1,782 (Class A com.); 24(Class B com.)
ANNUAL MEETING: In May
INCORPORATED: CA, June, 1930; reincorp., DE, Aug., 1987

INSTITUTIONAL HOLDINGS:
No. of Institutions: 131
Shares Held: 16,369,538
% Held: 35.6

INDUSTRY: Newspapers (SIC: 2711)

TRANSFER AGENT(S): Mellon Investor Services, Ridgefield Park, NJ

MCCORMICK & COMPANY, INC.

EXCH.	SYM.	REC. PRICE	P/E RATIO	YLD.	MKT. CAP.	RANGE (52-WK.)	'02 Y/E PR.	DIV. ACH.
NYSE	MKC	23.13 (2/28/03)	18.2	1.9%	$3.20 bill.	27.25 - 20.70	23.20	16 yrs.

UPPER MEDIUM GRADE. THE COMPANY IS TARGETING FULL-YEAR 2003 SALES GROWTH OF 3.0% TO 7.0% AND EARNINGS PER SHARE GROWTH OF BETWEEN 9.0% AND 11.0%.

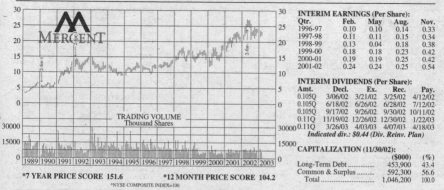

INTERIM EARNINGS (Per Share):

Qtr.	Feb.	May	Aug.	Nov.
1996-97	0.10	0.10	0.14	0.33
1997-98	0.11	0.11	0.15	0.34
1998-99	0.13	0.04	0.18	0.38
1999-00	0.18	0.18	0.23	0.42
2000-01	0.19	0.19	0.25	0.42
2001-02	0.24	0.24	0.25	0.54

INTERIM DIVIDENDS (Per Share):

Amt.	Decl.	Ex.	Rec.	Pay.
0.105Q	3/06/02	3/21/02	3/25/02	4/12/02
0.105Q	6/18/02	6/26/02	6/28/02	7/12/02
0.105Q	9/17/02	9/26/02	9/30/02	10/11/02
0.11Q	11/19/02	12/26/02	12/30/02	1/22/03
0.11Q	3/26/03	4/03/03	4/07/03	4/18/03

Indicated div.: $0.44 (Div. Reinv. Plan)

TRADING VOLUME Thousand Shares

*7 YEAR PRICE SCORE 151.6   *12 MONTH PRICE SCORE 104.2

*NYSE COMPOSITE INDEX=100

CAPITALIZATION (11/30/02):

	($000)	(%)
Long-Term Debt	453,900	43.4
Common & Surplus	592,300	56.6
Total	1,046,200	100.0

BUSINESS:

McCormick & Company, Inc. is a diversified specialty food company primarily engaged in the manufacture of spices, seasonings, flavors and other specialty food products. The Company operates in three business segments: consumer, industrial, and packaging. The consumer segment (47.2% of 2002 revenues) sells spices, herbs, extracts, proprietary seasoning blends, sauces and marinades to the consumer food market under a variety of brands, including the McCormick brand, the Club House brand in Canada, and the Schwartz brand in the U.K. The industrial segment (45.5%) sells spices, herbs, extracts, proprietary seasonings, condiments, coatings and compound flavors to food processors, restaurant chains, distributors, warehouse clubs and institutional operations. The packaging segment (7.3%) sells plastic packaging products to the food, personal care and other industries, primarily in the U.S.

RECENT DEVELOPMENTS:

For the year ended 11/30/02, net income totaled $179.8 million, up 22.7% compared with $146.6 million a year earlier. Results included one-time pre-tax special charges of $8.0 million and $10.8 million in 2002 and 2001, respectively. Net sales rose 4.6% to $2.32 billion from $2.22 billion the year before. Gross profit was $856.6 million, or 36.9% of net sales, versus $797.5 million, or 35.9% of net sales, the prior year. Operating income climbed 15.4% to $277.7 million from $240.6 million the previous year.

PROSPECTS:

The Company is targeting full-year 2003 sales growth of 3.0% to 7.0% and earnings per share growth of between 9.0% and 11.0%. Separately, on 1/9/03, the Company announced that its McCormick (UK) Ltd. subsidiary has completed its acquisition of UniqSauces, a condiment business based in Europe, from Uniq Plc for approximately $19.0 million in cash. Meanwhile, the Company continues to pursue strategic acquisitions that will help broaden its selection of consumer and industrial products.

ANNUAL FINANCIAL DATA:

FISCAL YEAR	TOT. REVS. ($mill.)	NET INC. ($mill.)	TOT. ASSETS ($mill.)	OPER. PROFIT %	NET PROFIT %	RET. ON EQUITY %	RET. ON ASSETS %	CURR. RATIO	EARN. PER SH. $	CASH FL. PER SH. $	TANG. BK. VAL. $	DIV. PER SH. $	PRICE RANGE	AVG. P/E RATIO	AVG. YIELD %
11/30/02	2,320.0	⑴ 179.8	1,930.8	12.0	7.8	30.4	9.3	1.1	⑴ 1.26	1.73	0.62	0.42	27.25 - 20.70	19.0	1.8
11/30/01	2,372.3	⑴ 146.6	1,772.0	10.1	6.2	31.7	8.3	0.9	⑴ 1.05	1.57	...	0.40	23.27 - 17.00	19.3	2.0
11/30/00	2,123.5	⑴ 137.5	1,659.9	10.6	6.5	38.3	8.3	0.6	⑴ 0.99	1.43	...	0.38	18.88 - 11.88	15.5	2.5
11/30/99	2,006.9	⑴ 103.3	1,188.8	8.8	5.1	27.0	8.7	1.0	⑴ 0.72	1.12	1.70	0.34	17.31 - 13.31	21.4	2.2
11/30/98	1,881.1	⑴ 103.8	1,259.1	9.7	5.5	26.7	8.2	1.0	⑴ 0.71	1.07	1.57	0.32	18.22 - 13.53	22.5	2.0
11/30/97	1,801.0	② 97.4	1,256.2	9.5	5.4	24.8	7.8	1.0	② 0.65	0.97	1.59	0.30	14.19 - 11.31	19.8	2.4
11/30/96	1,732.5	③ 43.5	1,326.6	5.4	2.5	9.7	3.3	1.1	③ 0.27	0.67	1.82	0.28	12.69 - 9.44	41.0	2.5
11/30/95	1,858.7	① 97.5	1,614.3	11.0	5.2	18.8	6.0	1.0	① 0.54	2.08	2.08	0.26	13.31 - 9.06	20.9	2.3
11/30/94	1,694.8	② 61.2	1,568.7	7.6	3.6	12.5	3.9	1.1	② 0.38	0.76	1.81	0.24	12.38 - 8.88	28.3	2.3
11/30/93	1,556.6	④ 99.7	1,313.2	11.6	6.4	21.4	7.6	1.4	④ 0.61	0.93	2.08	0.22	14.88 - 10.00	20.4	1.8

Statistics are as originally reported. Adj. for 2-for-1 stk. split, 4/02. ⑴ Incl. $8.0 mill. pre-tax chrg., 2002; $10.8 mill. pre-tax chrg., 2001; $1.1 mil pre-tax chrg., 2000; $18.4 mill. after-tax chrg., 1999; $2.3 mill. pre-tax chrg., 1998; $3.9 mill. pre-tax credit, 1995; $70.4 mil pre-tax chrg., 1994 ② Bef. $1.0 mill. disc. oper. gain & incl. $3.2 mill. pre-tax credit. ③ Bef. $7.8 mill. extraord. chrg., $6.2 mill. disc. oper. gain & incl. $58.1 mill. pre-tax chrg. ④ Bef. $26.6 mill. acctg. change chrg.

OFFICERS:
R. J. Lawless, Chmn., Pres., C.E.O.
F. A. Contino, Exec. V.P., C.F.O.
C. J. Kurtzman, V.P., Treas.

INVESTOR CONTACT: Chris Kurtzman, V.P., Treas., (410) 771-7244

PRINCIPAL OFFICE: 18 Loveton Circle, P.O Box 6000, Sparks, MD 21152

TELEPHONE NUMBER: (410) 771-7301
FAX: (410) 771-7462
WEB: www.mccormick.com

NO. OF EMPLOYEES: 9,000 (approx.)

SHAREHOLDERS: 2,200 (approx. common); 9,900 (approx. non-voting common)

ANNUAL MEETING: In Mar.

INCORPORATED: MD, Nov., 1915

INSTITUTIONAL HOLDINGS:
No. of Institutions: 262
Shares Held: 91,760,297
% Held: 65.6

INDUSTRY: Food preparations, nec (SIC: 2099)

TRANSFER AGENT(S): Wells Fargo Shareowner Services, South St. Paul, MN

MCDERMOTT INTERNATIONAL, INC.

EXCH.	SYM.	REC. PRICE	P/E RATIO	YLD.	MKT. CAP.	RANGE (52-WK.)	'02 Y/E PR.
NYSE	MDR	4.30 (2/28/03)	...	...	$265.4 mill.	17.29 - 2.35	4.38

SPECULATIVE GRADE. THE COMPANY'S OUTLOOK IS CLOUDED BY UNCERTAINTY AT ITS J. RAY MCDERMOTT SEGMENT.

TRADING VOLUME
Thousand Shares

1989 1990 1991 1992 1993 1994 1995 1996 1997 1998 1999 2000 2001 2002 2003

*7 YEAR PRICE SCORE 44.5   *12 MONTH PRICE SCORE 57.3
*NYSE COMPOSITE INDEX=100

INTERIM EARNINGS (Per Share):

Qtr.	June	Sept.	Dec.	Mar.
1998-99	1.88	0.85	0.71	d1.06
1999-00	0.33	0.06	d0.39	...
Qtr.	**Mar.**	**June**	**Sept.**	**Dec.**
2000	0.13	d0.17	0.09	d0.42
2001	d0.07	0.13	0.31	d0.70
2002	d0.03	d3.81	d5.88	d2.94

INTERIM DIVIDENDS (Per Share):

Amt.	Decl.	Ex.	Rec.	Pay.
		No dividends paid.		

CAPITALIZATION (12/31/01):

	($000)	(%)
Long-Term Debt	100,393	11.5
Common & Surplus	770,110	88.5
Total	870,503	100.0

BUSINESS:

McDermott International, Inc. operates in three business segments. The Marine Construction Services segment (65.6% of 2002 revenues) includes the operations of J. Ray McDermott, which supplies worldwide services to the offshore oil and gas exploration and production and hydrocar-bon processing industries. The Government Operations segment (31.7%) is the sole supplier of nuclear fuel assemblies and major reactor components for certain U.S. Government programs. The Power Generation Systems segment (2.7%) includes Babcock & Wilcox Volund ApS.

RECENT DEVELOPMENTS:

For the year ended 12/31/02, MDR posted a loss from continuing operations of $786.2 million versus a loss of $24.4 million in 2001. Results for 2002 and 2001 included net losses on asset disposals and impairments of $7.8 million and $3.7 million, respectively. Results for 2002 also included a loss of $224.7 million on the write-off of MDR's investment in The Babcock & Wilcox Co. (B&W), a charge of $313.0 million related to an impairment of J. Ray McDermott, S.A. goodwill, and a charge of $86.4 million related to the estimated loss on the B&W bankruptcy settlement. Results for 2001 included a nonrecurring gain of $28.0 million. Revenues slid 7.8% to $1.75 billion.

PROSPECTS:

MDR's outlook is clouded by uncertainty at its J. Ray McDermott segment. The Company noted that due primarily to the losses incurred on the EPIC spar projects, it expects J. Ray to experience negative cash flows during 2003. J. Ray intends to fund its cash needs through borrowings under its credit facility, intercompany loans from MDR and sales of non-strategic assets. However, if J. Ray experiences additional significant costs of the spar projects or any other projects that are unanticipated, MDR may be unable to fund all of its anticipated operating and capital needs and may have to pursue other financing options that may or may not be available to the Company.

ANNUAL FINANCIAL DATA:

FISCAL YEAR	TOT. REVS. ($mill.)	NET INC. ($mill.)	TOT. ASSETS ($mill.)	OPER. PROFIT %	NET PROFIT %	RET. ON EQUITY %	RET. ON ASSETS %	CURR. RATIO	EARN. PER SH.$	CASH FL. PER SH.$	TANG. BK. VAL.$	DIV. PER SH.$	PRICE RANGE	AVG. P/E RATIO	AVG. YIELD
p12/31/02	1,748.7	⑧ d786.2							⑧ d12.71				17.29 - 2.35	...	...
12/31/01	⑥ 1,969.8	⑦ d20.9	2,103.8	4.1	...	...	...	0.8	⑦ d0.34	0.68	7.12	...	16.85 - 7.31	...	...
12/31/00	⑥ 1,877.8	④ d22.1	2,025.1	0.4	...	...	...	0.9	④ d0.37	0.70	7.03	0.15	13.56 - 7.19	...	1.4
⑤ 12/31/99	1,891.1	0.4	3,874.9	4.5	...	0.1	...	1.1	0.01	1.14	5.83	0.20	32.50 - 7.25	N.M.	1.0
3/31/99	3,150.0	③ 192.1	4,305.5	6.6	6.1	24.2	4.5	1.1	③ 3.16	4.76	11.30	0.20	43.94 - 19.25	10.0	0.6
3/31/98	3,674.6	215.7	4,501.1	7.3	5.9	31.7	4.8	1.1	3.48	5.48	9.73	0.20	40.13 - 16.00	8.1	0.7
3/31/97	3,150.9	③ d206.1	4,599.5	...	...	...	...	1.1	③ d3.95	d1.16	0.20	1.00	23.25 - 16.00	...	5.1
3/31/96	3,279.1	② 20.6	4,387.3	0.8	0.6	3.0	0.5	1.2	② 0.23	...	4.06	1.00	29.13 - 15.38	96.7	4.5
3/31/95	3,043.7	① 10.9	4,751.7	0.2	0.4	1.5	0.2	1.0	① 0.05	2.36	6.05	1.00	27.50 - 19.38	467.8	4.3
3/31/94	3,059.9	① 90.0	4,223.6	1.3	2.9	16.6	2.1	1.1	① 1.57	3.58	7.26	1.00	32.88 - 22.25	17.6	3.6

Statistics are as originally reported. ① Bef. acctg. chrg. 3/31/95, $1.8 mil.; chrg. 3/31/94, $100.8 mil. ② Incl. cr. of $34.8 mil. & chrg. of $12.6 mil. ③ Incl. cr. 3/31/99, $17.9 mil.; cr. 3/31/97, $79.1 mil. ④ Incl. net loss of $2.8 mil. fr. asset disp. & impair. and restruct. chgs. of $4.1 mil. ⑤ Results for 9 months only to refl. chge. in fiscal year fr. 3/31 to 12/31. ⑥ Excl. ops. of Babcock & Wilcox Co. and its subs., which filed for reorg. under chapter 11 on 2/22/00. ⑦ Incl. net loss of $3.7 mil. fr. asset disp. & impair., nonrecur. tax prov. of $85.4 mil. and aft.-tax gain of $25.6 mil. on sale of business; bef. extraord. gain of $875,000. ⑧ Incl. net loss of $7.8 mil. fr. asset disp. & impair., $224.7 mil. loss on write-off of invest. in The Babcock & Wilcox Co. (B&W), chrg. of $313.0 mil. on impair. of J. Ray McDermott, S.A. goodwill, and chrg. of $86.4 mil. on est. loss on B&W bankruptcy settlmnt.; bef. inc. fr. disc. ops. of $9.5 mil. & extraord. gain of $341,000.

OFFICERS:
B. W. Wilkinson, Chmn., C.E.O.
F. S. Kalman, Exec. V.P., C.F.O.
J. R. Easter, V.P., Treas.
INVESTOR CONTACT: D. Washington, Inv. Rel., (504) 587-4080
PRINCIPAL OFFICE: 1450 Poydras Street, New Orleans, LA 70112-6050

TELEPHONE NUMBER: (504) 587-5400
FAX: (504) 587-6153
WEB: www.mcdermott.com
NO. OF EMPLOYEES: 13,300 (approx.)
SHAREHOLDERS: 3,934 (approx.)
ANNUAL MEETING: In May
INCORPORATED: Panama, 1959

INSTITUTIONAL HOLDINGS:
No. of Institutions: 144
Shares Held: 39,239,067
% Held: 61.5
INDUSTRY: Motors and generators (SIC: 3621)
TRANSFER AGENT(S): First Chicago Trust Company, Jersey City, NJ

MCDONALD'S CORPORATION

EXCH.	SYM.	REC. PRICE	P/E RATIO	YLD.	MKT. CAP.	RANGE (52-WK.)	'02 Y/E PR.	DIV. ACH.
NYSE	MCD	13.61 (2/28/03)	17.7	1.7%	$17.43 bill.	30.68 - 12.77	16.08	26 yrs.

INVESTMENT GRADE. IN 2003, THE COMPANY PLANS TO OPEN ABOUT 850 TRADITIONAL RESTAURANTS, 380 SATELLITE RESTAURANTS AND 150 PARTNER BRAND RESTAURANTS.

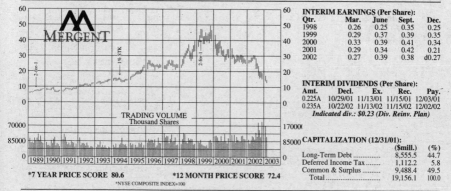

*7 YEAR PRICE SCORE 80.6   *12 MONTH PRICE SCORE 72.4

*NYSE COMPOSITE INDEX=100

INTERIM EARNINGS (Per Share):

Qtr.	Mar.	June	Sept.	Dec.
1998	0.26	0.25	0.35	0.25
1999	0.29	0.37	0.39	0.35
2000	0.33	0.39	0.41	0.34
2001	0.29	0.34	0.42	0.21
2002	0.27	0.39	0.38	d0.27

INTERIM DIVIDENDS (Per Share):

Amt.	Decl.	Ex.	Rec.	Pay.
0.225A	10/29/01	11/13/01	11/15/01	12/03/01
0.235A	10/22/02	11/13/02	11/15/02	12/02/02

Indicated div.: $0.23 (Div. Reinv. Plan)

CAPITALIZATION (12/31/01):

	($mill.)	(%)
Long-Term Debt	8,555.5	44.7
Deferred Income Tax	1,112.2	5.8
Common & Surplus	9,488.4	49.5
Total	19,156.1	100.0

BUSINESS:

McDonald's Corporation develops, licenses, leases and services a worldwide system of restaurants. Units serve a standardized menu of moderately priced food consisting of hamburgers, cheeseburgers, chicken sandwiches, salads, desserts and beverages. As of 12/31/02, there were 17,864 units operated by franchisees, 9,000 units operated by the Company, and 4,244 units operated by affiliates. MCD included in its restaurant units 662 Boston Markets, 232 Chipotle Mexican Grills, 181 Donatos Pizzas, and 8 Fazoli's. Systemwide sales in 2002 were derived from: franchised restaurants, 61.9%; Company-owned units' sales, 27.7%; and affiliated restaurants, 10.4%. On 5/26/00, MCD acquired approximately 750 Boston Market restaurants from Boston Chicken, Inc. In March 2002, MCD sold its Aroma Cafe business in the U.K.

RECENT DEVELOPMENTS:

For the year ended 12/31/02, the Company reported income of $992.1 million, before an accounting change charge of $98.6 million, compared with net income of $1.64 billion the year before. Results for 2002 and 2001 included net after-tax charges of $699.9 million and $142.5 million, respectively. Systemwide sales improved 2.2% to $41.53 billion from $40.63 billion in 2001. Total revenues increased 3.6% to $15.41 billion from $14.87 billion a year earlier. The improvement in revenues primarily reflected restaurant expansion. Sales by Company-operated restaurants climbed 4.2% to $11.50 billion, while revenues from franchised and affiliated restaurants rose 2.0% to $3.91 billion. Operating income fell 21.7% to $2.11 billion from $2.70 billion the year before.

PROSPECTS:

In December 2002, the Company and Fazoli's, a fast-casual Italian restaurant concept, formed a joint venture to develop 20 to 30 Fazoli's restaurants in three U.S. markets. Going forward, the Company plans to open about 850 traditional restaurants, 380 satellite restaurants and 150 partner brand restaurants in 2003. MCD expects sales from new McDonald's restaurants to add approximately three percentage points to sales growth in 2003. Additionally, MCD plans to close about 400 traditional restaurants and 200 satellite restaurants, primarily in the U.S. and Japan.

ANNUAL FINANCIAL DATA:

FISCAL YEAR	TOT. REVS. ($mill.)	NET INC. ($mill.)	TOT. ASSETS ($mill.)	OPER. PROFIT %	NET PROFIT %	RET. ON EQUITY %	RET. ON ASSETS %	CURR. RATIO	EARN. PER SH. $	CASH FL. PER SH. $	TANG. BK. VAL. $	DIV. PER SH. $	PRICE RANGE	AVG. P/E RATIO	AVG. YIELD %
p12/31/02	15,405.7	⚁⚂ 992.1							⚁⚂ 0.77			0.235	30.68 - 15.17	29.8	1.0
12/31/01	14,870.0	⚁ 1,636.6	22,534.5	18.1	11.0	17.2	7.3	0.8	⚁ 1.25	2.08	6.30	0.225	35.06 - 24.75	23.9	0.8
12/31/00	14,243.0	1,977.3	21,683.5	23.4	13.9	21.5	9.1	0.7	1.46	2.20	5.95	0.215	43.63 - 26.38	24.0	0.6
12/31/99	13,259.3	⚁ 1,947.9	20,983.2	25.0	14.7	20.2	9.3	0.5	⚁ 1.39	2.07	6.20	0.20	49.56 - 35.94	30.8	0.5
12/31/98	12,421.4	⚁ 1,550.1	19,784.4	22.2	12.5	16.4	7.8	0.5	⚁ 1.10	1.73	6.26	0.18	39.75 - 22.31	28.2	0.6
12/31/97	11,408.8	1,642.5	18,241.5	24.6	14.4	18.6	9.0	0.4	1.15	1.73	4.83	0.16	27.44 - 21.06	21.2	0.7
12/31/96	10,686.5	1,572.6	17,386.0	24.6	14.7	18.0	9.0	0.5	1.11	1.66	5.48	0.15	27.13 - 20.50	21.5	0.6
12/31/95	9,794.5	1,427.3	15,414.6	26.6	14.6	18.2	9.3	0.5	0.99	1.52	4.98	0.13	24.00 - 14.31	19.4	0.7
12/31/94	8,320.8	1,224.4	13,591.9	26.9	14.7	17.8	9.0	0.3	0.84	1.32	4.13	0.12	15.69 - 12.78	16.9	0.8
12/31/93	7,408.1	1,082.5	12,035.2	26.8	14.6	17.3	9.0	0.6	0.73	1.16	3.66	0.11	14.78 - 11.38	18.0	0.8

Statistics are as originally reported. Adj. for stk. splits: 2-for-1, 3/99, 5/94. ⚀ Incl. after-tax non-recurr. chrg. of $699.9 mill., 2002; $18.9 mill., 1999; $321.6 mill., 1998. ⚁ Incl. an after-tax gain on McDonald's Japan initial public offering of $137.1 million and after-tax non-recurring chrgs. totaling $279.6 mill. ⚂ Bef. acctg. change chrg. of $98.6 mill.

OFFICERS:
J. R. Cantalupo, Chmn., C.E.O.
C. Bell, Pres., C.O.O.

INVESTOR CONTACT: Investor Relations
Service Center, (630) 623-7428

PRINCIPAL OFFICE: McDonald's Plaza, Oak Brook, IL 60523

TELEPHONE NUMBER: (630) 623-3000
FAX: (630) 623-5027
WEB: www.mcdonalds.com
NO. OF EMPLOYEES: 395,000 (approx.)
SHAREHOLDERS: 1,027,000 (approx.)
ANNUAL MEETING: In May
INCORPORATED: DE, Mar., 1965

INSTITUTIONAL HOLDINGS:
No. of Institutions: 766
Shares Held: 821,309,602
% Held: 64.7

INDUSTRY: Eating places (SIC: 5812)

TRANSFER AGENT(S): EquiServe Trust Company, N.A., Jersey City, NJ

MCGRAW-HILL COMPANIES, INC. (THE)

EXCH.	SYM.	REC. PRICE	P/E RATIO	YLD.	MKT. CAP.	RANGE (52-WK.)	'02 Y/E PR.	DIV. ACH.
NYSE	MHP	56.24 (2/28/03)	19.0	1.9%	$10.79 bill.	69.70 - 50.71	60.44	29 yrs.

INVESTMENT GRADE. IN 2003, EARNINGS PER SHARE GROWTH IS EXPECTED TO RANGE FROM 7.0% TO 9.0%, REFLECTING CONTINUED STRENGTH IN KEY MARKETS AND IMPROVEMENT IN ADVERTISING.

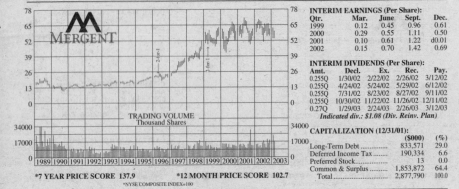

INTERIM EARNINGS (Per Share):

Qtr.	Mar.	June	Sept.	Dec.
1999	0.12	0.45	0.96	0.61
2000	0.29	0.55	1.11	0.50
2001	0.10	0.61	1.22	d0.01
2002	0.15	0.70	1.42	0.69

INTERIM DIVIDENDS (Per Share):

Amt.	Decl.	Ex.	Rec.	Pay.
0.255Q	1/30/02	2/22/02	2/26/02	3/12/02
0.255Q	4/24/02	5/24/02	5/29/02	6/12/02
0.255Q	7/31/02	8/23/02	8/27/02	9/11/02
0.255Q	10/30/02	11/22/02	11/26/02	12/11/02
0.27Q	1/29/03	2/24/03	2/26/03	3/12/03

Indicated div.: $1.08 (Div. Reinv. Plan)

CAPITALIZATION (12/31/01):

	($000)	(%)
Long-Term Debt	833,571	29.0
Deferred Income Tax	190,334	6.6
Preferred Stock	13	0.0
Common & Surplus	1,853,872	64.4
Total	2,877,790	100.0

*7 YEAR PRICE SCORE 137.9   *12 MONTH PRICE SCORE 102.7

*NYSE COMPOSITE INDEX=100

BUSINESS:

McGraw-Hill Companies, Inc., a multimedia publishing and information services company, serves worldwide markets in education, finance and business information. As of 12/31/02, MHP operated more than 350 offices in 33 countries. The Company provides information in print through books, newsletters, and magazines, including Business Week; on-line over electronic networks; over the air by television, satellite and FM sideband; and on software, videotape, facsimile and compact disks. Among the Company's business units are Standard & Poor's Financial Information Services and Standard & Poor's Ratings Services divisions. Net sales for 2002 were derived as follows: McGraw-Hill Education, 49.2%; Financial Services, 33.9%; and Information and Media Services, 16.9%.

RECENT DEVELOPMENTS:

For the year ended 12/31/02, net income grew 53.0% to $576.8 million from $377.0 million the year before. Earnings for 2002 included a pre-tax loss of $14.5 million from the sale of MMS International. Earnings for 2001 included a net non-recurring pre-tax loss of $143.3 million related to various items. Operating revenue rose 3.1% to $4.79 billion. On a segment basis, revenue from McGraw-Hill Education rose 1.5% to $2.36 billion, while revenue from Financial Services grew 9.7% to $1.62 billion. Revenue from Information and Media Services decreased 4.3% to $809.4 million. Operating income grew 38.4% to $927.6 million from $670.1 million in 2001. Results were enhanced by improvement in advertising and effective cost controls.

PROSPECTS:

In 2003, earnings per share growth is expected to range from 7.0% to 9.0%, reflecting continued strength in key markets and improvement in advertising. The estimated earnings per share growth includes an accounting change charge of $0.05. Separately, on 1/16/03, MHP announced that it signed an agreement to sell S&P ComStock Inc., the real-time market data unit of Standard & Poor's, to Interactive Data Corporation in a cash transaction valued at $115.0 million. The divestiture is anticipated to close in the first quarter of 2003.

ANNUAL FINANCIAL DATA:

FISCAL YEAR	TOT. REVS. ($mill.)	NET INC. ($mill.)	TOT. ASSETS ($mill.)	OPER. PROFIT %	NET PROFIT %	RET. ON EQUITY %	RET. ON ASSETS %	CURR. RATIO	EARN. PER SH. $	CASH FL. PER SH. $	TANG. BK. VAL. $	DIV. PER SH. $	PRICE RANGE	AVG. P/E RATIO	AVG. YIELD %
p12/31/02	4,787.7	⑤ 576.8							⑤ 2.96			1.02	69.70 - 50.71	20.3	1.7
12/31/01	4,645.5	④ 377.0	5,161.2	14.4	8.1	20.3	7.3	1.0	④ 1.92	4.07	0.18	0.98	70.87 - 48.70	31.1	1.6
12/31/00	4,281.0	③ 471.9	4,931.4	19.2	11.0	26.8	9.6	1.0	③ 2.41	4.25	0.33	0.94	67.69 - 41.88	22.7	1.7
12/31/99	3,992.0	⑪ 425.8	4,088.8	18.5	10.7	25.2	10.4	1.0	⑪ 2.14	3.70	2.24	0.86	63.13 - 47.13	25.8	1.6
12/31/98	3,729.1	② 341.9	3,788.1	16.3	9.2	22.0	9.0	1.1	② 1.71	3.22	1.48	0.78	51.66 - 34.25	25.1	1.8
12/31/97	3,534.1	⑪ 290.7	3,724.5	14.8	8.2	20.3	7.8	1.2	⑪ 1.46	2.93	0.64	0.72	37.38 - 22.44	20.6	2.4
12/31/96	3,074.7	⑪ 495.7	3,642.2	28.1	16.1	36.4	13.6	1.1	⑪ 2.48	3.67	0.28	0.66	24.63 - 18.63	8.7	3.1
12/31/95	2,935.3	227.2	3,104.4	15.7	7.7	21.9	7.3	1.2	1.14	2.30	0.38	0.60	21.91 - 15.91	16.6	3.2
12/31/94	2,760.9	203.1	3,008.5	14.4	7.4	22.2	6.8	1.1	1.03	2.19	...	0.58	19.31 - 15.63	17.0	3.3
12/31/93	2,195.5	⑪ 11.4	3,084.2	4.7	0.5	1.4	0.4	1.1	⑪ 0.06	0.77	...	0.57	18.81 - 13.81	280.8	3.5

Statistics are as originally reported. Adj. for 2-for-1 splits, 3/8/99 & 4/96. ⑪ Incl. a non-recurr. net gain of $24.2 mill., 1999; gain $40.1 mill., 1997; gain $260.6 mill., 1996; and loss $160.8 mill., 1993. ② Bef. extraord. chrg. of $8.7 mill. ③ Bef. acctg. chrg. of $68.1 mill.; incl. a gain of $10.2 mill. fr. the sale of Tower Group Int'l. ④ Incl. a prov. of $159.0 mill. for restruct. & asset write-down & a pre-tax net chrg. of $7.1 mill. rel. to various one-time items. ⑤ Incl. a loss of $14.5 mill. fr. sale of MMS Int'l.

OFFICERS:
H. McGraw III, Chmn., Pres., C.E.O.
R. J. Bahash, Exec. V.P., C.F.O.
F. D. Penglase, Sr. V.P.

INVESTOR CONTACT: Donald S. Rubin, Sr. V.P.-Inv. Rel., (212) 512-4321

PRINCIPAL OFFICE: 1221 Avenue Of The Americas, New York, NY 10020

TELEPHONE NUMBER: (212) 512-2000
FAX: (212) 512-2305
WEB: www.mcgraw-hill.com

NO. OF EMPLOYEES: 17,135

SHAREHOLDERS: 5,122 (approx.)

ANNUAL MEETING: In April

INCORPORATED: NY, Dec., 1925

INSTITUTIONAL HOLDINGS:
No. of Institutions: 493
Shares Held: 136,468,122
% Held: 70.4

INDUSTRY: Book publishing (SIC: 2731)

TRANSFER AGENT(S): Mellon Investor Services, South Hackensack, NJ

MCKESSON CORPORATION

EXCH.	SYM.	REC. PRICE	P/E RATIO	YLD.	MKT. CAP.	RANGE (52-WK.)	'02 Y/E PR.
NYSE	MCK	26.64 (2/28/03)	15.8	…	$7.67 bill.	42.09 - 23.50	27.03

MEDIUM GRADE. REVENUE GROWTH IS BEING FUELED BY INCREASED SALES OF GENERIC DRUGS AND SOFTWARE.

TRADING VOLUME
Thousand Shares

*7 YEAR PRICE SCORE 86.9   ***12 MONTH PRICE SCORE 94.4**

NYSE COMPOSITE INDEX=100

INTERIM EARNINGS (Per Share):

Qtr.	June	Sept.	Dec.	Mar.
1998-99	0.43	0.52	0.40	d0.27
1999-00	0.25	0.21	0.56	d0.31
2000-01	0.22	0.22	0.03	d0.62
2001-02	0.36	0.27	0.37	0.42
2002-03	0.39	0.42	0.46	…

INTERIM DIVIDENDS (Per Share):

Amt.	Decl.	Ex.	Rec.	Pay.
0.06Q	5/29/02	6/06/02	6/10/02	7/01/02
0.06Q	7/31/02	8/28/02	9/02/02	10/01/02
0.06Q	10/25/02	11/27/02	12/02/02	1/02/03
0.06Q	1/29/03	2/27/03	3/03/03	4/01/03

Indicated div.: $0.24(Div. Reinv. Plan)

CAPITALIZATION (3/31/02):

	($000)	(%)
Long-Term Debt	1,288,400	23.8
Redeemable Pfd. Stock	196,100	3.6
Common & Surplus	3,940,100	72.6
Total	5,424,600	100.0

BUSINESS:

McKesson Corporation (formerly McKesson HBOC, Inc.) operates in three segments. The Company, through its Pharmaceutical Solutions segment (93.0% of revenue in fiscal 2002), distributes ethical and proprietary drugs and health and beauty care products principally to chain and independent drug stores, hospitals, alternate care sites, food stores and mass merchandisers. The Medical-Surgical Solutions segment (5.0%) offers a full range of supplies, equipment, logistics and related services to healthcare providers. The Information Solutions segment (2.0%) provides software, support and services to healthcare organizations throughout the United States and certain foreign countries. On 1/12/99, the Company acquired HBO & Co.

RECENT DEVELOPMENTS:

For the three months ended 12/31/02, net income was $134.3 million, up 22.0% compared with income from continuing operations of $110.1 million in the corresponding quarter a year earlier. Total revenues grew 13.1% to $14.92 billion from $13.19 billion the year before. Gross profit totaled $727.6 million, or 4.9% of total revenues, versus $686.5 million, or 5.2% of total revenues, the previous year. Operating income climbed 10.7% to $209.8 million from $189.5 million in the prior year.

PROSPECTS:

Revenue growth is being fueled by strong sales in the Pharmaceutical Solutions segment, reflecting increased sales of generic drugs in the U.S., along with robust sales in the Information Solutions segment, driven by sharply higher sales of software. Meanwhile, the Company continues to consolidate operations in the Medical-Surgical Solutions segment in an effort to increase efficiencies. MCK expects to complete the consolidation of its distribution network during the current fiscal year, and will consolidate the information systems in fiscal 2003.

ANNUAL FINANCIAL DATA:

FISCAL YEAR	TOT. REVS. ($mill.)	NET INC. ($mill.)	TOT. ASSETS ($mill.)	OPER. PROFIT %	NET PROFIT %	RET. ON EQUITY %	RET. ON ASSETS %	CURR. RATIO	EARN. PER SH.$	CASH FL. PER SH.$	TANG. BK. VAL.$	DIV. PER SH.$	PRICE RANGE	AVG. P/E RATIO	AVG. YIELD %
3/31/02	50,006.0	⑧418.6	13,324.0	1.4	0.8	10.6	3.1	1.4	⑧1.43	2.10	9.81	0.24	41.50 – 23.40	22.7	0.7
3/31/01	42,010.0	⑦d42.7	11,529.9	0.2	…	…	…	1.4	⑦d0.15	0.72	8.55	0.24	37.00 – 16.00	…	0.9
3/31/00	36,734.2	⑥184.6	10,372.9	0.4	0.5	5.2	1.8	1.6	⑥0.66	1.37	8.47	0.30	89.75 – 18.56	82.0	0.6
⑤3/31/99	30,382.3	③84.9	9,081.6	1.1	0.3	2.9	0.9	1.4	③0.31	0.98	5.88	0.50	96.25 – 47.88	232.4	0.7
3/31/98	20,857.3	③154.9	5,607.5	1.7	0.7	11.0	2.8	1.6	③1.59	2.39	7.02	0.50	56.88 – 25.88	26.0	1.2
3/31/97	12,886.7	④5.1	5,172.8	0.7	…	0.4	0.1	1.4	④0.06	0.86	5.73	0.50	28.50 – 19.50	399.3	2.1
3/31/96	13,716.4	③135.4	3,503.9	2.0	1.0	12.7	3.9	1.5	③1.45	2.22	9.80	0.38	26.63 – 15.94	14.7	1.8
3/31/95	13,189.1	②d193.2	3,479.2	…	…	…	…	1.6	②d2.25	d1.42	9.01	…	16.75 – 15.06	…	…
3/31/94	12,251.4	①126.5	2,835.0	1.7	1.0	18.6	4.5	1.3	①1.47	2.37	3.35	…	…	…	…
3/31/93	11,555.7	95.1	2,603.6	1.8	0.8	15.4	3.7	1.2	1.10	2.04	…	…	…	…	…

Statistics are as originally reported. Adj. for 100% stk. div., 1/98. ① Bef. $4.2 mil extraord. loss & $15.8 mil chg. for acctg. adj.; & incl. $37.4 mil pre-tax gain. ② Bef. $21 mil cr. fr disc. ops. & $576.7 mil gain fr sale of PCS Health Sys. ③ Incl. $293.9 mil ($1.02/sh) after-tax chg., 1999; $20.8 mil after-tax chg., 1998; & $11.2 mil pre-tax gain, 1996. ④ Incl. $109.5 mil after-tax chg. & bef. $120.2 mil gain fr sale of Armor All. ⑤ Restated to refl corrections of improper acctg practices in MCK's Healthcare Info. Tech. segment, formerly HBO & Co. ⑥ Bef. $539.1 mil ($1.91/sh) gain fr. discont. opers. & incl. $80.4 mil ($0.28/sh) after-tax chg. ⑦ Bef. $5.6 mil ($0.02/sh) loss fr. discont. opers. & incl. $61.5 mil ($0.21/sh) after-tax chg. ⑧ Incl. $88.5 mil ($0.06/sh) pre-tax chg. fr. asset impairments.

OFFICERS:
J. H. Hammergren, Chmn., Pres., C.E.O.
W. R. Graber, Sr. V.P., C.F.O.
I. D. Meyerson, V.P., Gen. Couns., Sec.

INVESTOR CONTACT: Ana Schrank, Dir., Inv. Rel., (415) 983-7153

PRINCIPAL OFFICE: One Post Street, San Francisco, CA 94104

TELEPHONE NUMBER: (415) 983-8300
FAX: (415) 983-8453
WEB: www.mckhboc.com

NO. OF EMPLOYEES: 24,000 (approx.)

SHAREHOLDERS: 15,100 (approx. record)

ANNUAL MEETING: In July

INCORPORATED: DE, July, 1994

INSTITUTIONAL HOLDINGS:
No. of Institutions: 376
Shares Held: 221,530,296
% Held: 76.1

INDUSTRY: Drugs, proprietaries, and sundries (SIC: 5122)

TRANSFER AGENT(S): First Chicago Trust Co. of New York, Jersey City, NJ

MDU RESOURCES GROUP, INC.

EXCH.	SYM.	REC. PRICE	P/E RATIO	YLD.	MKT. CAP.	RANGE (52-WK.)	'02 Y/E PR.	DIV. ACH.
NYSE	MDU	26.97 (2/28/03)	13.0	3.6%	$1.88 bill.	33.45 - 18.00	25.81	12 yrs.

MEDIUM GRADE. THE COMPANY ENTERED INTO AN AGREEMENT TO PURCHASE A 66.6-MEGAWATT MOUNTAIN VIEW WIND POWERED ELECTRIC GENERATION FACILITY IN CALIFORNIA FOR $102.5 MILLION CASH.

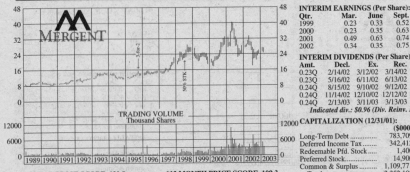

*7 YEAR PRICE SCORE 120.8   *12 MONTH PRICE SCORE 109.3
*NYSE COMPOSITE INDEX=100

INTERIM EARNINGS (Per Share):

Qtr.	Mar.	June	Sept.	Dec.
1999	0.23	0.33	0.52	0.42
2000	0.23	0.35	0.63	0.56
2001	0.49	0.63	0.74	0.42
2002	0.34	0.35	0.75	0.63

INTERIM DIVIDENDS (Per Share):

Amt.	Decl.	Ex.	Rec.	Pay.
0.23Q	2/14/02	3/12/02	3/14/02	4/01/02
0.23Q	5/16/02	6/11/02	6/13/02	7/01/02
0.24Q	8/15/02	9/10/02	9/12/02	10/01/02
0.24Q	11/14/02	12/10/02	12/12/02	1/01/03
0.24Q	2/13/03	3/11/03	3/13/03	4/01/03

Indicated div.: $0.96 (Div. Reinv. Plan)

CAPITALIZATION (12/31/01):

	($000)	(%)
Long-Term Debt	783,709	34.8
Deferred Income Tax	342,412	15.2
Redeemable Pfd. Stock	1,400	0.1
Preferred Stock	14,900	0.7
Common & Surplus	1,109,771	49.3
Total	2,252,192	100.0

BUSINESS:

MDU Resources Group, Inc. is a diversified natural resource company. Through its public utility division, Montana-Dakota Utilities Co., MDU generates, transmits and distributes electricity, distributes natural gas and provides related value-added products and services in North Dakota, Montana, South Dakota and Wyoming. Great Plains Natural Gas Co., another public utility division of the company, distributes natural gas in southeastern North Dakota and western Minnesota. In addition, MDU, through its wholly-owned subsidiary, Centennial Energy Holdings, Inc., owns WBI Holdings, Inc., a provider of pipeline and energy services and a natural gas and oil producer; Knife River Corporation, a producer of construction materials; Utility Services, Inc., a utility infrastructure company; and Centennial Holdings Capital Corp., which invests in new growth opportunities. MDU invests in projects outside the U.S. through its MDU Resources International, Inc. subsidiary.

RECENT DEVELOPMENTS:

For the year ended 12/31/02, net income fell 4.8% to $148.4 million compared with $155.9 million a year earlier. Operating revenues slid 8.6% to $2.03 billion. Operating earnings decreased 2.6% to $266.1 million, reflecting lower results from Company's electric, natural gas distribution, utility services, and natural gas and oil production segments. These declines were partially offset by increased operating profits from MDU's construction materials and mining, as well as pipeline and energy services segments.

PROSPECTS:

MDU's near-term outlook appears moderately positive. The Company should benefit from its diverse collection of business assets, which will help to offset the effects of the sluggish U.S. economy. Accordingly, MDU is maintaining its full-year 2003 earnings guidance of between $1.80 and $2.05 per diluted share, before the cumulative effect of an accounting change. Separately, on 12/20/02, MDU entered into an agreement to purchase a 66.6-megawatt Mountain View wind powered electric generation facility in California from an affiliate of PG&E National Energy Group for $102.5 million cash. Closing is expected to occur in early 2003.

ANNUAL FINANCIAL DATA:

FISCAL YEAR	TOT. REVS. ($mill.)	NET INC. ($mill.)	TOT. ASSETS ($mill.)	OPER. PROFIT %	NET PROFIT %	NET INC./ NET PROP. %	NET INC./ TOT. CAP. %	RET. ON EQUITY %	ACCUM. DEPR./ GROSS PROP. %	EARN. PER SH.$	TANG. BK. VAL.$	DIV. PER SH.$	DIV. PAYOUT %	PRICE RANGE	AVG. P/E RATIO	AVG. YIELD %
p12/31/02	2,031.5	148.4								2.07		0.93	44.9	33.45 - 18.00	12.4	3.6
12/31/01	2,223.6	155.8	2,623.1	12.3	7.0	8.6	6.9	13.9	34.4	2.29	15.90	0.89	38.9	40.37 - 22.38	13.7	2.8
12/31/00	1,873.7	111.0	2,313.0	11.6	5.9	6.9	5.8	12.4	35.9	1.80	13.55	0.85	47.2	33.00 - 17.63	14.1	3.4
12/31/99	1,279.8	84.1	1,766.3	12.5	6.6	6.7	5.7	12.3	38.9	1.52	11.74	0.81	53.3	27.19 - 18.81	15.1	3.5
12/31/98	896.6	①34.1	1,452.8	7.9	3.8	3.1	3.0	6.0	40.1	①0.66	10.39	0.78	117.4	28.88 - 18.83	36.1	3.2
12/31/97	607.7	54.6	1,113.9	18.4	9.0	6.5	6.7	13.6	44.4	1.24	8.84	0.75	60.2	22.33 - 14.00	14.6	4.1
12/31/96	514.7	45.5	1,205.4	21.7	8.8	6.0	5.9	12.4	45.1	1.05	8.21	0.73	69.7	15.67 - 13.25	13.8	5.0
12/31/95	464.2	41.6	1,056.5	19.5	9.0	5.8	5.9	11.8	44.3	0.95	7.90	0.71	75.0	15.39 - 11.45	14.1	5.3
12/31/94	449.5	39.8	1,004.7	17.4	8.9	5.8	5.9	11.6	43.9	0.92	7.66	0.70	76.3	14.33 - 11.28	14.0	5.4
12/31/93	439.6	38.8	1,041.1	19.1	8.8	5.8	5.7	11.7	43.0	0.89	7.45	0.67	74.6	14.72 - 11.50	14.7	5.1

Statistics are as originally reported. Adj. for 50% stk. div., 7/98; 3-for-2 stk. split, 10/95. ① Incl. chrg. of $66.0 mill. related to write-downs of oil & gas prop.

OFFICERS:
M. A. White, Chmn., Pres., C.E.O.
W. L. Robinson, Exec. V.P., Treas., C.F.O.
L. H. Loble, II, V.P., Gen. Couns. & Sec.
INVESTOR CONTACT: Cathi Christopherson, (701) 222-7959
PRINCIPAL OFFICE: Schuchart Building, 918 East Divide Avenue, Bismarck, ND 58506

TELEPHONE NUMBER: (701) 222-7900
FAX: (701) 222-7607
WEB: www.mdu.com
NO. OF EMPLOYEES: 6,568
SHAREHOLDERS: 14,000 (approx.)
ANNUAL MEETING: In Apr.
INCORPORATED: DE, Mar., 1924

INSTITUTIONAL HOLDINGS:
No. of Institutions: 170
Shares Held: 22,791,040
% Held: 30.9
INDUSTRY: Gas and other services combined (SIC: 4932)
TRANSFER AGENT(S): Wells Fargo Shareowner Services, St. Paul, MN

MEADWESTVACO CORPORATION

EXCH.	SYM.	REC. PRICE	P/E RATIO	YLD.	MKT. CAP.	RANGE (52-WK.)	'02 Y/E PR.
NYSE	MWV	23.19 (2/28/03)	…	4.0%	$4.64 bill.	36.50 - 15.57	24.71

LOWER MEDIUM GRADE. THE COMPANY PLANS TO IMPROVE PROFITABILITY IN 2003.

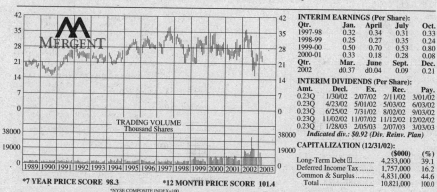

*7 YEAR PRICE SCORE 98.3   *12 MONTH PRICE SCORE 101.4

*NYSE COMPOSITE INDEX=100

INTERIM EARNINGS (Per Share):

Qtr.	Jan.	April	July	Oct.
1997-98	0.32	0.34	0.31	0.33
1998-99	0.25	0.27	0.35	0.24
1999-00	0.50	0.70	0.53	0.80
2000-01	0.33	0.18	0.28	0.08
Qtr.	Mar.	June	Sept.	Dec.
2002	d0.37	d0.04	0.09	0.21

INTERIM DIVIDENDS (Per Share):

Amt.	Decl.	Ex.	Rec.	Pay.
0.23Q	1/30/02	2/07/02	2/11/02	3/01/02
0.23Q	4/23/02	5/01/02	5/03/02	6/03/02
0.23Q	6/25/02	7/31/02	8/02/02	9/03/02
0.23Q	11/02/02	11/07/02	11/12/02	12/02/02
0.23Q	1/28/03	2/05/03	2/07/03	3/03/03

Indicated div.: $0.92 (Div. Reinv. Plan)

CAPITALIZATION (12/31/02):

	($000)	(%)
Long-Term Debt ☐	4,233,000	39.1
Deferred Income Tax	1,757,000	16.2
Common & Surplus	4,831,000	44.6
Total	10,821,000	100.0

BUSINESS:

MeadWestvaco Corporation (formerly Westvaco Corporation) was formed through the acquisition of The Mead Corporation by Westvaco Corporation on 1/29/02. MWV is a global producer of packaging, coated and specialty papers, consumer and office products, and specialty chemicals. The principal markets for MWV's products are in the U.S., Canada, Latin America, Europe and Asia. As of 10/22/02, MWV operated in 33 countries and served customers in about 100 nations. The Company serves customers that are engaged in the automotive, beverage, consumer products, healthcare, media and entertainment, and publishing markets. MWV's consumer and office brands include AT-A-GLANCE®, CAMBRIDGE®, COLUMBIAN®, FIVE STAR® and MEAD®. Using sustainable forestry practices, MWV manages 3.4 million acres of forests.

RECENT DEVELOPMENTS:

For the year ended 12/31/02, MWV incurred a loss of $3.0 million, before a loss from discontinued operations of $34.0 million and an accounting change charge of $352.0 million, compared with net income of $41.0 million in 2001. Results for 2002 included restructuring and merger related expenses of $95.0 million, a charge for early retirement of debt of $4.0 million, goodwill impairment of $352.0 mil-lion, and gains on sales of timberland of $65.0 million. Sales increased 85.4% to $7.24 billion. MWV's financial results for 2002 include twelve months of operations for Westvaco Corporation and eleven months for the Mead Corporation, while results for 2001 reflect only Westvaco Corporation.

PROSPECTS:

Due to restruction actions taken thus far, MWV is better positioned to improve profitability in 2003. Profits should also be enhanced by disciplined capital spending, continued synergy realization and ongoing timber divestitures, and reducing debt while building financial flexibility through an improved cash flow. Meanwhile, MWV is raising its 2003 savings goal from the acquisition of the Mead Corporation by Westvaco Corporation on 1/29/02 to $360.0 million. MWV expects to attain its full merger integration synergies a year ahead of its original plans of 2002.

ANNUAL FINANCIAL DATA:

FISCAL YEAR	TOT. REVS. ($mill.)	NET INC. ($mill.)	TOT. ASSETS ($mill.)	OPER. PROFIT %	NET PROFIT %	RET. ON EQUITY %	RET. ON ASSETS %	CURR. RATIO	EARN. PER SH. $	CASH FL. PER SH. $	TANG. BK. VAL. $	DIV. PER SH. $	PRICE RANGE	AVG. P/E RATIO	AVG. YIELD %
p12/31/02	7,242.0	⑦d3.0	12,921.0	2.6	…	…	…	1.5	⑦d0.01	3.49	20.44	0.92	36.50 - 15.57	…	3.5
⑥12/31/01	600.4	d21.7	6,828.3	…	…	…	…	1.4	d0.21	0.38	17.00	0.88	32.10 - 22.68	…	3.3
10/31/01	3,983.6	④⑤88.2	6,787.0	8.2	2.2	3.8	1.3	1.4	④⑤0.87	4.29	17.21	0.88	32.10 - 22.68	31.5	3.2
10/31/00	3,719.9	③④254.7	6,569.9	16.0	6.8	10.9	3.9	1.9	③④2.53	5.63	23.17	0.88	34.75 - 24.06	11.6	3.0
10/31/99	2,831.2	④111.2	4,896.7	9.6	3.9	5.1	2.3	1.7	④1.11	3.90	21.65	0.88	33.50 - 20.81	24.5	3.2
10/31/98	2,904.7	132.0	5,008.7	10.8	4.5	5.9	2.6	1.6	1.30	4.06	22.39	0.88	34.13 - 21.00	21.2	3.2
10/31/97	3,011.0	162.7	4,898.8	11.3	5.4	7.1	3.3	2.0	1.60	4.21	22.35	0.88	37.50 - 25.00	19.5	2.8
10/31/96	3,074.5	212.4	4,437.5	13.9	6.9	9.6	4.8	1.7	2.09	4.45	22.35	0.88	33.13 - 25.38	14.0	3.0
10/31/95	3,302.7	③283.4	4,252.7	17.3	8.6	13.6	6.7	1.8	③2.80	5.08	20.49	0.77	31.67 - 24.08	10.0	2.8
10/31/94	2,613.2	②103.6	3,984.4	10.4	4.0	5.6	2.6	1.7	②1.03	3.21	18.48	0.73	26.50 - 19.75	22.4	3.2

Statistics are as originally reported. ☐ Incl. capital lease obligations. ② Incl. net gains of $6.0 mill. from sale of assets. ③ Bef. extraord. chrg. $8.8 mill., 2000; $2.6 mill., 1995. ④ Incl. restruct. chrg. of $51.7 mill., 2001; $16.1 mill., 2000; $80.5 mill., 1999. ⑤ Incl. after-tax gains of $21.5 mill. ($0.21/sh.) from land sales. ⑥ For two months due to fiscal year-end change. ⑦ Bef. loss fr. disc. oper. of $34.0 & acctg. chg. chrg. of $352.0 mill., but incl. restr. chrg. of $95.0 mill., early debt ret. of $4.0 mill., goodwill impair. of $352.0 mill.

OFFICERS:
J. A. Luke, Jr., Chmn., Pres., C.E.O.
K. R. Osar, Sr. V.P., C.F.O.
W. L. Willkie II, Sr. V.P., Gen. Couns., Sec.
INVESTOR CONTACT: Roger A. Holmes, Investor Relations, (203) 461-7537
PRINCIPAL OFFICE: One High Ridge Park, Stamford, CT 06905

TELEPHONE NUMBER: (203) 461-7400
FAX: (203) 461-7490
WEB: www.westvaco.com
NO. OF EMPLOYEES: 30,700 (approx.)
SHAREHOLDERS: 37,200
ANNUAL MEETING: In Apr.
INCORPORATED: DE, Jan., 2002

INSTITUTIONAL HOLDINGS:
No. of Institutions: 294
Shares Held: 155,365,398
% Held: 77.7

INDUSTRY: Paper mills (SIC: 2621)

TRANSFER AGENT(S): The Bank of New York, New York, NY

MEDIA GENERAL, INC.

EXCH.	SYM.	REC. PRICE	P/E RATIO	YLD.	MKT. CAP.	RANGE (52-WK.)	'02 Y/E PR.
NYSE	MEG	50.10 (2/28/03)	21.8	1.5%	$1.15 bill.	69.49 - 46.55	59.95

MEDIUM GRADE. FOR THE FULL-YEAR 2003, THE COMPANY EXPECTS EARNINGS PER SHARE IN THE AREA OF $2.50 OR BETTER.

*7 YEAR PRICE SCORE 133.3   ***12 MONTH PRICE SCORE 103.4**
*NYSE COMPOSITE INDEX=100

INTERIM EARNINGS (Per Share):

Qtr.	Mar.	June	Sept.	Dec.
1998	0.48	0.80	0.54	0.82
1999	0.26	0.44	0.96	0.96
2000	0.55	0.64	0.36	0.91
2001	0.15	0.33	d0.03	0.34
2002	0.26	0.70	0.41	0.93

INTERIM DIVIDENDS (Per Share):

Amt.	Decl.	Ex.	Rec.	Pay.
0.18Q	3/27/02	5/29/02	5/31/02	6/15/02
0.18Q	8/01/02	8/28/02	8/30/02	9/15/02
0.18Q	9/26/02	11/26/02	11/29/02	12/15/02
0.19Q	1/29/03	2/26/03	2/28/03	3/15/03
0.19Q	3/28/03	5/28/03	5/30/03	6/15/03

Indicated div.: $0.76 (Div. Reinv. Plan)

CAPITALIZATION (12/30/01):

	($000)	(%)
Long-Term Debt	777,662	33.9
Deferred Income Tax	350,854	15.3
Common & Surplus	1,163,668	50.8
Total	2,292,184	100.0

BUSINESS:

Media General, Inc. is an independent, publicly-owned communications company with interests in newspapers, television stations, interactive media, and diversified information services. MEG's publishing assets include THE TAMPA TRIBUNE, the RICHMOND TIMES-DIS-PATCH, the WINSTON-SALEM JOURNAL, and 22 other daily newspapers in Virginia, North Carolina, Florida, Alabama and South Carolina, as well as nearly 100 other periodicals and a 20.0%

interest in THE DENVER POST. MEG's 26 network-affiliated television stations reach more than 30.0% of the television households in the Southeast, and nearly 8.0% of those in the U.S. MEG's interactive media offerings include more than 50 on-line enterprises. Revenues for 2002 were derived: publishing, 63.0%; broadcast, 35.6%; and interactive media, 1.4%.

RECENT DEVELOPMENTS:

For the year ended 12/29/02, income soared to $53.4 million, before an accounting change charge of $126.3 million, compared with income from continuing operations of $17.9 million in 2001. Results for 2001 excluded a gain of $280,000 on the disposition of discontinued operations. Total revenues climbed 3.7% to $836.8 million from

$807.2 million a year earlier. The improvement in revenues was primarily attributed to increases of 15.9% and 28.0% in the Company's Broadcast and Interactive Media divisions, respectively. The improvement was partially offset by a 2.5% decline in Publishing division revenues.

PROSPECTS:

For the first quarter of 2003, the Publishing division expects moderate revenue growth of 3.0% to 4.0% with improvement in all categories. Employment linage is expected to be slightly below the first quarter of 2002, but should be offset by gains in automotive and other classified categories. Revenues for the Broadcast division is expected

to grow 5.0% over the first quarter of 2002. Moreover, higher operating costs will offset revenue increases, but overall results should benefit from lower interest expense. MEG expects first-quarter earnings per share to be in the range of $0.32 to $0.35, and full-year 2003 earnings per share of $2.50 or better.

ANNUAL FINANCIAL DATA:

FISCAL YEAR	TOT. REVS. ($mill.)	NET INC. ($mill.)	TOT. ASSETS ($mill.)	OPER. PROFIT %	NET PROFIT %	RET. ON EQUITY %	RET. ON ASSETS %	CURR. RATIO	EARN. PER SH. $	CASH FL. PER SH. $	TANG. BK. VAL. $	DIV. PER SH. $	PRICE RANGE	AVG. P/E RATIO	AVG. YIELD
p12/29/02	836.8	⑥ 53.4							⑥ 2.30			0.72	69.49 - 46.55	25.2	1.2
12/30/01	807.2	⑤ 17.9	2,534.1	9.0	2.2	1.5	0.7	1.6	⑤ 0.78	5.74	...	0.68	53.50 - 34.06	56.1	1.6
12/31/00	830.6	④ 63.6	2,561.3	14.9	2.5	5.4	2.5	1.5	④ 2.63	6.98	...	0.64	54.75 - 33.65	16.8	1.4
12/26/99	795.4	③ 69.9	2,340.4	13.9	8.8	5.3	3.0	1.3	③ 2.60	6.23	11.92	0.60	59.50 - 44.31	20.0	1.2
12/27/98	974.0	70.9	1,917.3	16.0	7.3	14.8	3.7	1.2	2.63	6.36	...	0.56	53.50 - 33.88	16.6	1.3
12/28/97	910.0	② 52.5	1,814.2	14.2	5.8	12.6	2.9	1.3	② 1.97	5.65	...	0.53	44.63 - 28.38	18.5	1.5
12/29/96	765.1	70.5	1,025.5	13.4	9.2	16.1	6.9	1.1	2.65	5.10	6.12	0.50	39.50 - 27.63	12.7	1.5
12/31/95	707.8	① 53.2	1,016.7	10.3	7.5	14.1	5.2	1.2	① 2.01	4.30	4.90	0.48	38.38 - 27.25	16.3	1.5
12/25/94	626.2	① 117.0	787.2	10.6	18.7	35.1	14.9	1.1	① 4.45	6.56	11.00	0.44	30.25 - 21.38	5.8	1.7
12/26/93	600.8	25.7	745.2	10.0	4.3	11.4	3.4	1.1	0.98	3.16	6.86	0.44	31.63 - 17.50	25.1	1.8

Statistics are as originally reported. ① Incl. cr$2.5 mill. ($0.09/sh.) after-tax non-recur., 1995; cr$83.3 mill. ($3.17/sh.), 1994. ② Bef. extraord. chrg. $63.0 mill. ($2.37/sh.). ③ Incl. non-recurr. gain $31 mill.; Excl. gain from disc. oper. $812.7 mill. ($30.23/sh.); Excl. extraord. chrg. $1.3 mill. ($0.05/sh.). ④ Bef. disc. oper. loss of $4.4 mill. & loss on sale of operations $5.5 mill. ⑤ Bef. after-tax gain of $160,000 from disc. oper. ⑥ Excl. $126.3 mill. acctg. chg.

OFFICERS:
J. S. Bryan III, Chmn., C.E.O.
R. Ashe, Pres., C.O.O.
M. N. Morton, Vice-Chmn., C.F.O.
INVESTOR CONTACT: Investor Relations, (804) 649-6000
PRINCIPAL OFFICE: 333 East Franklin Street, Richmond, VA 23219

TELEPHONE NUMBER: (804) 649-6000
FAX: (804) 649-6898
WEB: www.mediageneral.com
NO. OF EMPLOYEES: 7,700 (approx.)
SHAREHOLDERS: 1,930 (approx. class A); 12 (approx. class B)
ANNUAL MEETING: In May
INCORPORATED: VA, Aug., 1969

INSTITUTIONAL HOLDINGS:
No. of Institutions: 157
Shares Held: 15,788,472
% Held: 68.1

INDUSTRY: Newspapers (SIC: 2711)

TRANSFER AGENT(S): American Stock Transfer & Trust Company, New York, NY

MEDTRONIC, INC.

EXCH.	SYM.	REC. PRICE	P/E RATIO	YLD.	MKT. CAP.	RANGE (52-WK.)	'02 Y/E PR.	DIV. ACH.
NYSE	MDT	44.70 (2/28/03)	38.5	0.6%	$54.32 bill.	49.48 - 32.50	45.60	25 yrs.

INVESTMENT GRADE. THE COMPANY IS BENEFITING FROM GROWTH IN ITS CARDIAC RHYTHM MANAGEMENT AND SPINAL BUSINESSES.

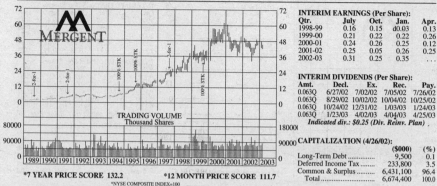

*7 YEAR PRICE SCORE 132.2   *12 MONTH PRICE SCORE 111.7
*NYSE COMPOSITE INDEX=100

INTERIM EARNINGS (Per Share):

Qtr.	July	Oct.	Jan.	Apr.
1998-99	0.16	0.15	d0.03	0.13
1999-00	0.21	0.22	0.22	0.26
2000-01	0.24	0.26	0.25	0.12
2001-02	0.25	0.05	0.26	0.25
2002-03	0.31	0.25	0.35	...

INTERIM DIVIDENDS (Per Share):

Amt.	Decl.	Ex.	Rec.	Pay.
0.063Q	6/27/02	7/02/02	7/05/02	7/26/02
0.063Q	8/29/02	10/02/02	10/04/02	10/25/02
0.063Q	10/24/02	12/31/02	1/03/03	1/24/03
0.063Q	1/23/03	4/02/03	4/04/03	4/25/03

Indicated div.: $0.25 (Div. Reinv. Plan)

CAPITALIZATION (4/26/02):

	($000)	(%)
Long-Term Debt	9,500	0.1
Deferred Income Tax	233,800	3.5
Common & Surplus	6,431,100	96.4
Total	6,674,400	100.0

BUSINESS:

Medtronic, Inc. is a medical technology company operating in five operating segments that manufacture and sell device-based medical therapies. Cardiac Rhythm Management (45.9% of 2002 revenues) offers physicians and their patients a product line to treat bradycardia, tachyarrhythmias and heart failure. Cardiac Surgery (8.1%) offers a broad range of products for use by cardiac surgeons in the operating room. The Vascular segment (14.1%) offers minimally invasive products for the treatment of coronary vascular disease as well as diseases and conditions of the peripheral arteries. The Neurological and Diabetes segment (16.0%) offers products for the treatment of neurological disorders, diabetes, gastroenterology and urology conditions. The Spinal and Ear, Nose & Throat segment (15.9%) offers a range of products and therapies to treat a variety of disorders of the cranium, spine, ear, nose and throat.

RECENT DEVELOPMENTS:

For the three months ended 1/24/03, net earnings jumped 35.8% to $427.7 million compared with $314.9 million in the equivalent quarter of the previous year. Results for 2002 included a purchased in-process research and development charge of $32.7 million and a non-recurring special charge of $30.4 million. Net sales advanced 20.1% to $1.91 billion from $1.59 billion in the year-earlier period. Revenues for the Cardiac Rhythm Management segment increased 24.0% to $905.0 million, while Neurological and Diabetes segment revenues climbed 19.0% to $343.5 million. Revenues for the Spinal and Ear, Nose & Throat segment soared 36.0% to $344.5 million, while cardiac surgery segment revenues rose 8.0% to $137.7 million. Vascular segment revenues fell 4.0% to $181.8 million.

PROSPECTS:

The Company announced an agreement under which Medtronic Sofamor Danek, the spinal business of MDT, will exclusively promote in Europe recombinant human bone morphogenetic protein, the genetically engineered version of a naturally occurring human protein that forms new bone. Separately, the Company announced that it has started enrollment for its pivotal clinical to evaluate the safety and performance of its Exponent self-expanding carotid stent system.

ANNUAL FINANCIAL DATA:

FISCAL YEAR	TOT. REVS. ($mill.)	NET INC. ($mill.)	TOT. ASSETS ($mill.)	OPER. PROFIT %	NET PROFIT %	RET. ON EQUITY %	RET. ON ASSETS %	CURR. RATIO	EARN. PER SH. $	CASH FL. PER SH. $	TANG. BK. VAL.$	DIV. PER SH. $	PRICE RANGE	AVG. P/E RATIO	AVG. YIELD %
4/26/02	6,410.8	⑥ 984.0	10,904.5	24.4	15.3	15.3	9.0	0.9	⑥ 0.80	1.07	1.10	0.21	60.81 — 36.64	60.9	0.4
4/27/01	5,551.8	②⑤ 1,046.0	7,038.9	27.7	18.8	19.0	14.9	2.8	②⑤ 0.85	1.10	3.53	0.18	62.00 — 32.75	55.7	0.4
4/30/99	5,014.6	④ 1,098.5	5,669.4	32.2	21.9	24.5	19.4	3.0	④ 0.90	1.10	2.61	0.14	44.63 — 29.94	41.4	0.4
4/30/99	4,134.1	③ 468.4	4,870.3	19.3	11.3	12.8	9.6	2.4	③ 0.40	0.57	1.99	0.12	38.38 — 22.72	77.3	0.4
4/30/98	2,604.8	② 457.4	2,774.7	27.8	17.6	22.4	16.5	2.7	② 0.48	0.63	1.68	0.10	26.38 — 14.41	42.5	0.5
4/30/97	2,438.2	530.0	2,409.2	32.2	21.7	30.4	22.0	2.4	0.56	0.68	1.34	0.08	17.47 — 11.13	25.8	0.6
4/30/96	2,169.1	437.8	2,503.3	29.8	20.2	24.5	17.5	2.6	0.47	0.59	1.41	0.06	15.00 — 6.55	22.9	0.6
4/30/95	1,742.4	294.0	1,946.7	25.0	16.9	22.0	15.1	2.4	0.32	0.43	1.05	0.05	6.98 — 4.32	17.7	0.8
4/30/94	1,390.9	① 232.4	1,623.3	23.9	16.7	22.1	14.3	1.9	① 0.25	0.34	0.74	0.04	5.97 — 3.23	18.2	0.8
4/30/93	1,328.2	211.6	1,286.5	20.9	15.9	25.1	16.4	2.2	0.22	0.30	0.76	0.03	6.53 — 3.95	23.5	0.6

Statistics are as originally reported. Adj. for 2-for-1 stk split, 9/99, 9/97, 9/95, 9/94. ① Incl. pre-tax gain of $14.0 mill., 1994; $50.0 mill., 1992 ② Incl. a pre-tax chrg. of $169.3 mill., 1998; $338.8 mill., 2001. ③ Incl. a pre-tax nonrecur. chg. of $371.3 mill. & a pre-tax chg. of $150.9 mill. for pchsd. in-process R&D. ④ Incl. a pre-tax nonrecur. chrg. of $14.7 mill. for the Xomed acquis. ⑤ Incl. pre-tax spec. chrg. of $338.8 mill. ⑥ Incl. purch. in-process res. & dev. chrg. of $293.0 mill. & spec. chrg. of $290.8 mill.

OFFICERS:
A. D. Collins Jr., Chmn., Pres., C.E.O.
G. D. Nelson, Vice-Chmn.

INVESTOR CONTACT: Rachael Scherer, Investor Relations, (763) 505-2694

PRINCIPAL OFFICE: 710 Medtronic Parkway, Minneapolis, MN 55432

TELEPHONE NUMBER: (763) 514-4000
FAX: (763) 514-4000
WEB: www.medtronic.com
NO. OF EMPLOYEES: 28,000 (approx.)
SHAREHOLDERS: 48,500 (approx. record)
ANNUAL MEETING: In Aug.
INCORPORATED: MN, 1957

INSTITUTIONAL HOLDINGS:
No. of Institutions: 970
Shares Held: 898,354,327
% Held: 73.6
INDUSTRY: Electromedical equipment (SIC: 3845)
TRANSFER AGENT(S): Wells Fargo Bank Minnesota N.A., St. Paul, MN

MELLON FINANCIAL CORPORATION

EXCH.	SYM.	REC. PRICE	P/E RATIO	YLD.	MKT. CAP.	RANGE (52-WK.)	'02 Y/E PR.
NYSE	MEL	22.51 (2/28/03)	14.6	2.3%	$10.05 bill.	40.62 - 20.42	26.11

UPPER MEDIUM GRADE. THE COMPANY LAUNCHED ITS IN-HOUSE UNITED KINGDOM CUSTODY OPERATION.

TRADING VOLUME
Thousand Shares

*7 YEAR PRICE SCORE 99.4   ***12 MONTH PRICE SCORE 85.6**
*NYSE COMPOSITE INDEX=100

INTERIM EARNINGS (Per Share):

Qtr.	Mar.	June	Sept.	Dec.
1998	0.39	0.41	0.41	0.42
1999	0.53	0.45	0.45	0.48
2000	0.50	0.50	0.51	0.52
2001	0.54	0.21	0.38	d0.09
2002	0.47	0.25	0.44	0.38

INTERIM DIVIDENDS (Per Share):

Amt.	Decl.	Ex.	Rec.	Pay.
0.12Q	1/15/02	1/29/02	1/31/02	2/15/02
0.12Q	4/16/02	4/26/02	4/30/02	5/15/02
0.12Q	7/16/02	7/29/02	7/31/02	8/15/02
0.13Q	10/15/02	10/29/02	10/31/02	11/15/02
0.13Q	1/15/03	1/29/03	1/31/03	2/14/03

Indicated div.: $0.52 (Div. Reinv. Plan)

CAPITALIZATION (12/31/01):

	($000)	(%)
Total Deposits	20,715,000	70.9
Long-Term Debt	4,045,000	13.8
Redeemable Pfd. Stock	991,000	3.4
Common & Surplus	3,482,000	11.9
Total	29,233,000	100.0

BUSINESS:

Mellon Financial Corporation (formerly Mellon Bank Corporation), with assets of $36.23 billion as of 12/31/02, is a provider of wealth management and global asset management for individual and institutional investors, as well as global investment services for businesses and institutions. Mellon also offers an array of banking services for individuals and small, mid-size and large businesses and institu-

tions in selected geographies. Its asset management companies, which include The Dreyfus Corp. and Founders Asset Management, LLC in the U.S. and Newton Management Ltd. in the U.K., provide investment products. In addition, Mellon is a global provider of custody, retirement and benefits consulting services through its Mellon Trust and Buck Consultants affiliates.

RECENT DEVELOPMENTS:

For the year ended 12/31/02, MEL reported income from continuing operations of $667.0 million versus income of $436.0 million the year before. Earnings for 2002 included gains on sales of securities of $59.0 million, while earnings for 2001 included amortization of goodwill of $73.0 million. Earnings for 2002 and 2001 also included equity

investment losses of $28.0 million and $380.0 million, and excluded gains from discontinued operations of $15.0 million and $882.0 million, respectively. Net interest revenue increased 6.3% to $610.0 million. Provision for credit losses amounted to $172.0 million versus a loss of $4.0 million.

PROSPECTS:

The Company expects its performance program, initiated in the third quarter of 2001, to be fully implemented by the second quarter of 2003. The program is anticipated to produce $300.0 million in pre-tax revenue enhancements and expense savings, annually. Separately, on 12/9/02, MEL announced the launch of its in-house U.K. custody opera-

tion. This new service will administer approximately $45.70 billion in assets held in the U.K. on behalf of the Company's global custody client base. The operation should reinforce MEL's presence in the U.K. and throughout Europe.

ANNUAL FINANCIAL DATA:

FISCAL YEAR	NET INT. INC. ($mill.)	NON-INT. INC. ($mill.)	NET INC. ($mill.)	TOT. LOANS ($mill.)	TOT. ASSETS ($mill.)	TOT. DEP. ($mill.)	RET. ON EQUITY %	RET. ON ASSETS %	EQUITY/ ASSETS %	EARN. PER SH. $	TANG. BK. VAL. $	DIV. PER SH. $	PRICE RANGE	AVG. P/E RATIO
p12/31/02	610.0	3,681.0	⑥667.0		36,231.0		12.5	1.3	10.1	⑥1.52		0.49	40.80 – 20.42	20.1
12/31/01	⑥574.0	2,658.0	⑤436.0	8,540.0	34,360.0	20,715.0	12.5	1.3	10.1	⑤2.76	3.66	0.82	51.63 – 27.75	14.4
12/31/00	1,501.0	3,150.0	1,007.0	26,369.0	50,364.0	36,890.0	24.3	2.0	8.2	2.03	4.34	0.86	51.94 – 26.81	19.4
12/31/99	1,430.0	3,227.0	④989.0	30,248.0	47,946.0	33,421.0	24.6	2.1	8.4	④1.90	3.72	0.78	40.19 – 31.31	18.8
12/31/98	1,491.0	2,922.0	③870.0	32,093.0	50,777.0	34,383.0	19.2	1.7	8.9	③1.63	2.05	0.70	40.19 – 22.50	19.3
12/31/97	1,467.0	2,418.0	771.0	29,142.0	44,892.0	31,305.0	20.1	1.7	8.6	1.44	2.27	0.65	32.41 – 17.25	17.2
12/31/96	1,478.0	2,023.0	733.0	27,393.0	42,596.0	31,374.0	19.6	1.7	8.8	1.29	2.80	0.59	18.69 – 12.06	11.9
12/31/95	1,548.0	1,676.0	691.0	27,690.0	43,165.0	29,261.0	17.2	1.6	9.3	1.13	3.56	0.50	14.13 – 7.66	9.7
12/31/94	1,508.0	1,647.0	②433.0	26,733.0	41,888.0	27,570.0	10.5	1.0	9.8	②0.61	3.91	0.39	10.08 – 7.50	14.5
12/31/93	1,307.0	1,276.0	①361.0	24,473.0	38,235.0	27,538.0	10.9	0.9	8.7	①0.77	3.73	0.25	11.23 – 8.54	12.8

Statistics are as originally reported. Adj. for 2-for-1 stk. split, 5/99, 5/97 & 3-for-2 stk. split, 11/94. ① Incl. restruct. chrgs. of $175.0 mill. ② Incl. pre-tax merger-rel. chrgs. (Dreyfus Corp.) of $104.0 mill. & one-time pre-tax chrg. of $223.0 mill. for repos. of secur. lending port. ③ Incl. gain of $35.0 mill. fr. the sale of Co.'s merchant card process. bus. ④ Bef. acctg. chrg. of $26.0 mill. & incl. pre-tax gain of $127.0 mill. fr. divestitures. ⑤ Bef. gain fr. disc. ops. of $15.0 mill,. 12/02; $882.0 mill., 12/01. ⑥ Reflects sale of Co.'s mid-Atlantic regional consumer banking, small business banking & certain middle market banking ops. to Citizens Fin'l Group, Inc.

OFFICERS:
M. G. McGuinn, Chmn., C.E.O.
S. G. Elliott, Sr. Vice-Chmn.
M. A. Bryson, C.F.O.
INVESTOR CONTACT: Investor Relations,
(412) 234-5601
PRINCIPAL OFFICE: One Mellon Center,
Pittsburgh, PA 15258-0001

TELEPHONE NUMBER: (412) 234-5000
FAX: (412) 234-6283
WEB: www.mellon.com
NO. OF EMPLOYEES: 21,300 (approx.)
SHAREHOLDERS: 23,377
ANNUAL MEETING: In April
INCORPORATED: PA, Aug., 1971

INSTITUTIONAL HOLDINGS:
No. of Institutions: 522
Shares Held: 331,831,457
% Held: 77.0
INDUSTRY: National commercial banks
(SIC: 6021)
TRANSFER AGENT(S): Mellon Investor Services, Ridgefield, NJ

MEN'S WEARHOUSE, INC. (THE)

EXCH.	SYM.	REC. PRICE	P/E RATIO	YLD.	MKT. CAP.	RANGE (52-WK.)	'02 Y/E PR.
NYSE	MW	14.20 (2/28/03)	13.5	...	$0.58 bill.	28.72 - 9.61	17.15

UPPER MEDIUM GRADE. THE COMPANY IS TARGETING EARNINGS OF BETWEEN $1.22 AND $1.28 PER SHARE FOR THE CURRENT FISCAL YEAR.

*7 YEAR PRICE SCORE 90.4   ***12 MONTH PRICE SCORE 80.8**
*NYSE COMPOSITE INDEX=100

INTERIM EARNINGS (Per Share):

Qtr.	Apr.	July	Oct.	Jan.
1996-97	0.15	0.19	0.18	0.49
1997-98	0.19	0.25	0.25	0.60
1998-99	0.20	0.23	0.21	0.53
1999-00	0.07	0.21	0.31	0.72
2000-01	0.32	0.38	0.40	0.90
2001-02	0.31	0.25	0.10	0.39
2002-03	0.25	0.19	0.11	0.50

INTERIM DIVIDENDS (Per Share):

Amt.	Decl.	Ex.	Rec.	Pay.
	No dividends paid.			

CAPITALIZATION (2/2/02):

	($000)	(%)
Long-Term Debt	37,740	6.9
Common & Surplus	509,883	93.1
Total	547,623	100.0

BUSINESS:

The Men's Wearhouse, Inc. is a specialty retailer of men's tailored business attire. As of 2/1/03, the Company operated 575 stores in the U.S. under the names Men's Wearhouse and K&G, as well as 114 Moores, Clothing for Men stores in Canada. MW's stores offer a selection of designer, brand name and private label merchandise, including suits, sport coats, slacks, business casual, sportswear, outerwear, dress shirts, shoes and accessories, at prices typically 20.0% to 30.0% below the regular prices found at traditional department and specialty stores. On 2/10/99, MW completed the acquisition of Moores Retail Group. On 6/2/99, the Company acquired K&G Men's Center Inc.

RECENT DEVELOPMENTS:

For the twelve months ended 2/1/03, net earnings slipped 2.0% to $42.4 million from $43.3 million in the corresponding period a year earlier. Net sales totaled $1.30 billion, up 1.7% compared with $1.27 billion the previous year. U.S. comparable-store sales decreased 3.1%, while Canadian comparable-store sales were down 2.1% versus the year before. Gross profit was $454.3 million, or 35.1% of net sales, versus $451.1 million, or 35.4% of net sales, the year before. Operating income slid 6.0% to $69.4 million from $73.8 million in the prior year.

PROSPECTS:

The Company is targeting full-year fiscal 2003 earnings per share in the range of $1.22 to $1.28, reflecting anticipated earnings of between $0.31 and $0.33 per share in the first quarter. In addition, MW anticipates full-year fiscal 2003 net sales in the range of $1.34 billion and $1.35 billion, along with comparable-store sales growth in the low single-digits for its U.S. and Canadian stores. Meanwhile, the Company plans to open 10 new Men's Wearhouse stores and seven new K&G locations during the current fiscal year. Five existing K&G stores are scheduled to be closed during the first quarter of 2003.

ANNUAL FINANCIAL DATA:

FISCAL YEAR	TOT. REVS. ($000)	NET INC. ($000)	TOT. ASSETS ($000)	OPER. PROFIT %	NET PROFIT %	RET. ON EQUITY %	RET. ON ASSETS %	CURR. RATIO	EARN. PER SH.$	CASH FL. PER SH.$	TANG. BK. VAL.$	PRICE RANGE	AVG. P/E RATIO
p2/01/03	1,295,049	42,412							1.04			28.72 - 9.61	18.4
2/02/02	1,273,154	43,276	717,869	5.8	3.4	8.5	6.0	3.0	1.04	2.06	12.44	33.07 - 17.00	24.1
2/03/01	1,333,501	84,661	707,734	10.6	6.3	17.1	12.0	3.1	2.00	2.81	11.80	34.00 - 17.25	12.8
1/29/00	1,186,748	①55,957	611,195	8.5	4.7	13.7	9.2	3.0	①1.32	2.03	9.76	34.94 - 19.50	20.6
1/30/99	767,922	②40,920	403,732	9.3	5.3	13.7	10.1	2.8	②1.17	1.73	8.55	36.88 - 14.00	21.7
1/31/98	631,110	28,883	379,415	8.2	4.6	13.1	7.6	2.9	0.87	1.29	6.64	27.50 - 15.33	24.5
2/01/97	483,547	21,143	295,478	7.9	4.4	13.3	7.2	2.9	0.67	1.06	5.07	25.67 - 10.83	27.4
2/03/96	406,343	16,508	204,105	7.5	4.1	12.1	8.1	2.6	0.55	0.86	4.39	20.17 - 8.00	25.7
1/28/95	317,127	12,108	160,494	7.1	3.8	14.3	7.5	2.5	0.42	0.67	2.98	15.45 - 7.00	26.6
1/29/94	240,394	8,739	112,176	6.6	3.6	15.1	7.8	2.1	0.32	0.53	2.13	14.56 - 4.74	30.1

Statistics are as originally reported. Adj. for stk. splits: 50% div., 6/98 & 11/95. ① Bef. $2.9 mil ($0.07/sh) extraord. chg. & incl. $7.7 mil one-time transaction chg., $6.1 mil. store closing chg., and $930,000 litigation chg. ② Bef. $701,000 ($0.02/sh) extraord. chg.

OFFICERS:
G. Zimmer, Chmn., C.E.O.
D. H. Edwab, Vice-Chmn.
E. J. Lane, Pres., C.O.O.
N. P. Davis, Exec. V.P., C.F.O., Treas.

INVESTOR CONTACT: Claudia Pruitt, (713) 592-7200

PRINCIPAL OFFICE: 5803 Glenmont Drive, Houston, TX 77081-1701

TELEPHONE NUMBER: (713) 592-7200
FAX: (713) 657-0872
WEB: www.menswearhouse.com
NO. OF EMPLOYEES: 8,300 full-time (approx.); 2,500 part-time (approx.).
SHAREHOLDERS: 1,280 (approx. record); 7,100 (approx. beneficial).
ANNUAL MEETING: In June
INCORPORATED: TX, May, 1974

INSTITUTIONAL HOLDINGS:
No. of Institutions: 136
Shares Held: 30,604,053
% Held: 77.1

INDUSTRY: Men's & boys' clothing stores (SIC: 5611)

TRANSFER AGENT(S): American Stock Transfer & Trust Company, New York, NY

MERCK & CO., INC.

EXCH.	SYM.	REC. PRICE	P/E RATIO	YLD.	MKT. CAP.	RANGE (52-WK.)	'02 Y/E PR.	DIV. ACH.
NYSE	MRK	52.75 (2/28/03)	16.8	2.7%	$119.89 bill.	64.50 - 38.50	56.61	19 yrs.

HIGH GRADE. ON 1/9/03, THE COMPANY ANNOUNCED THAT IT WILL LAUNCH A TENDER OFFER TO PURCHASE THE REMAINING 49.0% OF BANYU PHARMACEUTICAL CO., LTD. FOR ABOUT $1.52 BILLION.

TRADING VOLUME
Thousand Shares

*7 YEAR PRICE SCORE 94.2   ***12 MONTH PRICE SCORE 112.8**
*NYSE COMPOSITE INDEX=100

INTERIM EARNINGS (Per Share):

Qtr.	Mar.	June	Sept.	Dec.
1998	0.48	0.54	0.56	0.58
1999	0.54	0.61	0.64	0.66
2000	0.63	0.73	0.78	0.75
2001	0.71	0.78	0.84	0.81
2002	0.71	0.77	0.83	0.83

INTERIM DIVIDENDS (Per Share):

Amt.	Decl.	Ex.	Rec.	Pay.
0.35Q	2/26/02	3/06/02	3/08/02	4/01/02
0.35Q	5/28/02	6/05/02	6/07/02	7/01/02
0.36Q	7/23/02	9/04/02	9/06/02	10/01/02
0.36Q	11/26/02	12/04/02	12/06/02	1/02/03
0.36Q	2/25/03	3/05/03	3/07/03	4/01/03

Indicated div.: $1.44 (Div. Reinv. Plan)

CAPITALIZATION (12/31/01):

	($000)	(%)
Long-Term Debt	4,798,600	18.7
Minority Interest	4,837,500	18.8
Common & Surplus	16,050,100	62.5
Total	25,686,200	100.0

BUSINESS:

Merck & Co., Inc. is a research pharmaceutical company that discovers, develops, manufactures and markets human and animal health products, directly and through its joint ventures, and provides pharmaceutical benefit services through Merck-Medco Managed Care LLC. The Merck Pharmaceuticals segment (41.4% of 2002 sales) consists of therapeutic and preventive agents, generally sold by prescription, for the treatment of human disorders. Human health products include ZOCOR, a cholesterol-lowering medicine, FOSAMAX, a treatment for osteoporosis, VIOXX, a prescription arthritis medicine, SINGULAIR, for the treatment of chronic asthma, and COZAAR and HYZAAR for the treatment of high blood pressure. The Medco Health Solutions, Inc. segment (58.6%) includes sales of non-Merck products and Merck-Medco pharmaceutical benefit services for more than 65.0 million customers.

RECENT DEVELOPMENTS:

For the year ended 12/31/02, net income slipped 1.8% to $7.15 billion compared with $7.28 billion in the previous year. Sales climbed 8.5% to $51.79 billion from $47.72 billion the year before. The improvement in sales was largely due to a 14.0% year-over-year aggregate sales increase of ZOCOR, FOSAMAX, COZAAR, SINGULAIR and VIOXX. Materials and production expenses grew 14.1% to $33.05 billion from $28.98 billion in 2001, due to sales growth of 14.0% in the Medco Health Solutions, Inc. business.

PROSPECTS:

On 1/9/03, the Company announced that it will launch a tender offer to purchase the remaining 49.0% of the common shares of Banyu Pharmaceutical Co., Ltd. that it does not already own for approximately $1.52 billion. The tender offer process should close on 3/6/03. Separately, the Company anticipates earnings per share to range from $3.40 to $3.47 for the full year 2003. The full year estimate reflects MRK's expectation for double digit earnings per share growth in the core pharmaceuticals business and includes a full year of net income from Medco Health Solutions, Inc. However, MRK's intention to separate the Medco Health business in mid-2003 remains unchanged.

ANNUAL FINANCIAL DATA:

FISCAL YEAR	TOT. REVS. ($mill.)	NET INC. ($mill.)	TOT. ASSETS ($mill.)	OPER. PROFIT %	NET PROFIT %	RET. ON EQUITY %	RET. ON ASSETS %	CURR. RATIO	EARN. PER SH. $	CASH FL. PER SH. $	TANG. BK. VAL. $	DIV. PER SH. $	PRICE RANGE	AVG. P/E RATIO	AVG. YIELD
p12/31/02	51,790.3	7,149.5							3.14			1.41	64.50 - 38.50	16.4	2.7
12/31/01	47,715.7	7,281.8	44,006.7	21.1	15.3	45.4	16.5	1.1	3.14	3.77	3.77	1.37	95.25 - 56.80	24.2	1.8
12/31/00	40,363.2	6,821.7	39,910.4	23.3	16.9	46.0	17.1	1.4	2.90	3.44	3.23	1.21	96.69 - 52.00	25.6	1.6
12/31/99	32,714.0	④ 5,890.5	35,634.9	24.0	18.0	44.5	16.5	1.3	②2.45	2.93	2.43	1.10	87.38 - 60.94	30.3	1.5
12/31/98	26,898.2	③ 5,248.2	31,853.4	20.8	19.5	41.0	16.5	1.7	③2.15	2.57	1.91	0.94	80.88 - 50.69	30.6	1.4
12/31/97	23,636.9	② 4,614.1	25,811.9	24.8	19.5	36.6	17.9	1.5	②1.87	2.21	2.44	0.84	60.31 - 39.00	26.6	1.7
12/31/96	19,828.7	4,122.1	24,293.1	26.1	20.8	34.4	17.0	1.6	1.60	2.00	2.17	0.71	42.13 - 28.25	22.0	2.0
12/31/95	16,681.1	① 3,641.5	23,831.8	26.5	21.8	31.0	15.3	1.5	①1.35	1.74	2.00	0.62	33.63 - 18.19	19.2	2.4
12/31/94	14,969.8	3,229.8	21,856.6	30.7	21.6	29.0	14.8	1.3	1.19	1.56	1.57	0.57	19.75 - 14.06	14.2	3.4
12/31/93	10,498.2	① 2,202.4	19,927.5	29.9	21.0	22.0	11.1	1.0	①0.94	1.12	1.35	0.52	22.06 - 14.31	19.4	2.8

Statistics are as originally reported. Adj. for 2-for-1 stock split, 2/99. ① Inc. a net pre-tax gain of $169.4 mill., 1995; & a chg. of $775.0 mill., 1993. ② Inc. a nonrecurr. pre-tax gain of $213.0 mill. & non-recurr. pre-tax chgs. totaling $207.0 mill. ③ Incl. a pre-tax gain of $2.15 bill. from the sale of businesses, and a pre-tax charge of $1.04 bill. for acquired research and development. ④ Incl. a pre-tax chg. of $51.1 mill. for acquired research.

OFFICERS:
R. V. Gilmartin, Chmn., Pres., C.E.O.
J. C. Lewent, Exec. V.P., C.F.O.
C. Dorsa, V.P., Treas.

INVESTOR CONTACT: Mark Stejbach, Investor Relations, (908) 423-5185

PRINCIPAL OFFICE: One Merck Drive, Whitehouse Station, NJ 08889-0100

TELEPHONE NUMBER: (908) 423-1000
FAX: (908) 735-1500
WEB: www.merck.com

NO. OF EMPLOYEES: 78,100 (avg.)

SHAREHOLDERS: 256,200

ANNUAL MEETING: In Apr.

INCORPORATED: NJ, June, 1927

INDUSTRY: Pharmaceutical preparations (SIC: 2834)

TRANSFER AGENT(S): Wells Fargo Shareowner Services, South St. Paul, MN

MERCURY GENERAL CORPORATION

EXCH.	SYM.	REC. PRICE	P/E RATIO	YLD.	MKT. CAP.	RANGE (52-WK.)	'02 Y/E PR.	DIV. ACH.
NYSE	MCY	36.21 (2/28/03)	29.9	3.6%	$1.97 bill.	51.15 - 33.50	37.58	16 yrs.

MEDIUM GRADE. GOING FORWARD, THE COMPANY SHOULD CONTINUE TO BENEFIT FROM ITS CONSERVATIVE
UNDERWRITING APPROACH AND PRICING STRATEGIES.

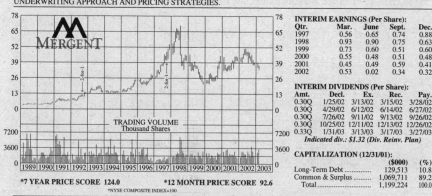

*7 YEAR PRICE SCORE 124.0   ***12 MONTH PRICE SCORE 92.6**
*NYSE COMPOSITE INDEX=100

INTERIM EARNINGS (Per Share):

Qtr.	Mar.	June	Sept.	Dec.
1997	0.56	0.65	0.74	0.88
1998	0.93	0.90	0.75	0.63
1999	0.73	0.60	0.51	0.60
2000	0.55	0.48	0.51	0.48
2001	0.45	0.49	0.59	0.41
2002	0.53	0.02	0.34	0.32

INTERIM DIVIDENDS (Per Share):

Amt.	Decl.	Ex.	Rec.	Pay.
0.30Q	1/25/02	3/13/02	3/15/02	3/28/02
0.30Q	4/29/02	6/12/02	6/14/02	6/27/02
0.30Q	7/26/02	9/11/02	9/13/02	9/26/02
0.30Q	10/25/02	12/11/02	12/13/02	12/26/02
0.33Q	1/31/03	3/13/03	3/17/03	3/27/03

Indicated div.: $1.32 (Div. Reinv. Plan)

CAPITALIZATION (12/31/01):

	($000)	(%)
Long-Term Debt	129,513	10.8
Common & Surplus	1,069,711	89.2
Total	1,199,224	100.0

BUSINESS:

Mercury General Corporation, through its subsidiaries, engages primarily in writing all risk classifications of automobile insurance in a number of states, principally in California. The Company offers automobile policyholders the following types of coverage: bodily injury liability, under-insured and uninsured motorist, personal injury protection, property damage liability, comprehensive, collision and other hazards specified in the policy. The Company sells its policies through independent agents in California, Florida, Georgia, Illinois, New York, Oklahoma, Texas and Virginia. In addition, MCY writes other lines of insurance in various states, including mechanical breakdown and homeowners insurance. During 2002, approximately 85.1% of MCV's net premiums written were derived from California.

RECENT DEVELOPMENTS:

For the year ended 12/31/02, net income decreased 37.2% to $66.1 million from $105.3 million the previous year. Earnings were hampered by higher paid losses and loss adjustment expense and higher incurred losses. Also, 2002 results were affected by a net realized investment loss of $45.8 million versus a gain of $4.2 million in 2001. Net premiums written increased 29.3% to $1.87 billion from $1.44 billion in the prior year. Net premiums earned increased 26.1% to $1.74 billion versus $1.38 billion in 2001. Incurred losses grew 25.5% to $1.27 billion from $1.10 billion a year earlier. The combined ratio, a key measure of underwriting profitability, improved to 98.8% versus 99.6% for 2001.

PROSPECTS:

Near-term results should continue to benefit from the Company's conservative underwriting approach and pricing strategies. In California, the Company has implemented and is continuing to seek rate increases to offset the effects of loss cost inflation in its personal auto business. Meanwhile, the Company is beginning to see improvement in many of its non-California operations. The Company's operations located in Florida, Texas, New York and the American Mercury operations located in Oklahoma and Texas all showed significant premium growth and posted notable underwriting improvements.

ANNUAL FINANCIAL DATA:

FISCAL YEAR	PREM. INC. ($mill.)	NET INVST. INC. ($mill.)	TOT. REVS. ($mill.)	NET INC. ($mill.)	TOT. ASSETS ($mill.)	TOT. INVST. ($mill.)	RET. ON REVS. %	RET. ON EQUITY %	RET. ON ASSETS %	EARN. PER SH.$	TANG. BK. VAL.$	AVG. YIELD %	DIV. PER SH.$	PRICE RANGE	AVG. P/E RATIO
p12/31/02	1,741.5	113.1		66.1						1.22		2.7	1.20	51.15 — 37.25	36.2
12/31/01	1,380.6	114.5	1,507.0	105.3	2,316.5	1,936.2	7.0	9.8	4.5	1.94	19.71	2.8	1.06	44.50 — 32.00	19.7
12/31/00	1,249.3	106.5	1,366.0	109.4	2,142.3	1,795.0	8.0	10.6	5.1	2.02	19.06	2.9	0.96	44.88 — 21.06	16.3
12/31/99	1,188.3	99.4	1,280.7	133.7	1,906.4	1,575.5	10.4	14.7	7.0	2.44	16.71	2.5	0.84	45.50 — 20.94	13.6
12/31/98	1,121.6	96.2	1,222.1	177.5	1,877.0	1,590.6	14.5	19.4	9.5	3.21	16.78	1.4	0.70	70.00 — 33.00	16.0
12/31/97	1,031.3	86.8	1,127.9	156.3	1,725.5	1,448.2	13.9	19.5	9.1	2.82	14.51	1.4	0.58	54.44 — 26.13	14.3
12/31/96	754.7	70.2	825.0	105.8	1,419.9	1,168.3	12.8	16.5	7.4	1.93	11.66	2.0	0.48	29.13 — 19.88	12.7
12/31/95	616.3	63.0	683.7	90.3	1,081.7	923.2	13.2	16.0	8.3	1.66	10.30	2.1	0.40	24.88 — 14.13	11.8
12/31/94	529.4	54.6	577.2	66.3	911.7	751.6	11.5	14.5	7.3	1.22	8.34	2.5	0.35	15.75 — 12.75	11.7
12/31/93	474.1	54.1	533.8	96.2	864.0	740.5	18.0	21.4	11.1	1.76	8.22	1.8	0.30	19.75 — 13.06	9.3

Statistics are as originally reported. Adj. for 2-for-1 stk. split, 10/97.

OFFICERS:
G. Joseph, Chmn., C.E.O.
G. Tirador, Pres., C.O.O.
T. R. Stalick, V.P., C.F.O.
INVESTOR CONTACT: Investor Relations,
(323) 857-4973
PRINCIPAL OFFICE: 4484 Wilshire
Boulevard, Los Angeles, CA 90010

TELEPHONE NUMBER: (323) 937-1060
FAX: (323) 857-7116
WEB: www.mercuryinsurance.com
NO. OF EMPLOYEES: 2,800 (approx.)
SHAREHOLDERS: 241 (approx.)
ANNUAL MEETING: In May
INCORPORATED: CA, 1961

INSTITUTIONAL HOLDINGS:
No. of Institutions: 132
Shares Held: 21,460,811
% Held: 39.5
INDUSTRY: Fire, marine, and casualty insurance (SIC: 6331)
TRANSFER AGENT(S): The Bank of New York, New York, NY

MEREDITH CORPORATION

EXCH.	SYM.	REC. PRICE	P/E RATIO	YLD.	MKT. CAP.	RANGE (52-WK.)	'02 Y/E PR.
NYSE	MDP	39.12 (2/28/03)	18.2	1.0%	$1.94 bill.	47.75 - 33.42	41.11

UPPER MEDIUM GRADE. THE COMPANY COMPLETED THE ACQUISITION OF AMERICAN BABY MAGAZINE AND ITS RELATED PROPERTIES FROM PRIMEDIA, INC. IN A TRANSACTION VALUED AT $115.0 MILLION.

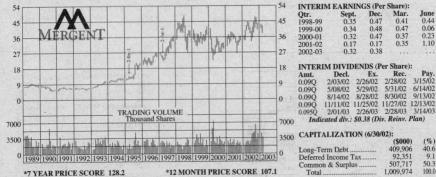

INTERIM EARNINGS (Per Share):

Qtr.	Sept.	Dec.	Mar.	June
1998-99	0.35	0.47	0.41	0.44
1999-00	0.34	0.48	0.47	0.06
2000-01	0.32	0.47	0.37	0.23
2001-02	0.17	0.17	0.35	1.10
2002-03	0.32	0.38	...	...

INTERIM DIVIDENDS (Per Share):

Amt.	Decl.	Ex.	Rec.	Pay.
0.09Q	2/03/02	2/26/02	2/28/02	3/15/02
0.09Q	5/08/02	5/29/02	5/31/02	6/14/02
0.09Q	8/14/02	8/28/02	8/30/02	9/13/02
0.09Q	11/11/02	11/25/02	11/27/02	12/13/02
0.095Q	2/01/03	2/26/03	2/28/03	3/14/03

Indicated div.: $0.38 (Div. Reinv. Plan)

CAPITALIZATION (6/30/02):

	($000)	(%)
Long-Term Debt	409,906	40.6
Deferred Income Tax	92,351	9.1
Common & Surplus	507,717	50.3
Total	1,009,974	100.0

TRADING VOLUME Thousand Shares

*7 YEAR PRICE SCORE 128.2   ***12 MONTH PRICE SCORE 107.1**

*NYSE COMPOSITE INDEX=100

BUSINESS:

Meredith Corporation is a diversified media company involved in magazine and book publishing, television broadcasting, and interactive integrated marketing. As of 1/28/03, the Company published sixteen subscription magazines, including Ladies' Home Journal, Better Homes and Gardens, and American Baby, and approximately 170 special interest publications. MDP owns eleven television stations in the U.S., and has nearly 300 books in print. The

Company also has established marketing partnerships with companies such as The Home Depot, Daimler/Chrysler, and Carnival Cruise Lines. In addition, MDP has an extensive Internet presence, including 24 Web sites and branded anchor tenant positions on America Online. On 7/1/98, MDP sold its residential real estate franchising operations. Net sales for fiscal 2002 were derived as follows: publishing, 74.2%, and broadcasting, 25.8%.

RECENT DEVELOPMENTS:

For the quarter ended 12/31/02, net income more than doubled to $19.3 million compared with $8.7 million the year before. Total revenues increased 10.4% to $251.7 million from $228.0 million the year before. Publishing seg-

ment revenues grew 7.5% to $170.9 million, while broadcasting segment revenues advanced 17.1% to $80.8 million. Income from operations advanced 96.3% to $38.3 million from $19.5 million in the prior year.

PROSPECTS:

On 12/5/02, the Company acquired American Baby magazine and its related properties from Primedia, Inc. in a transaction valued at $115.0 million. The acquisition is expected to be accretive to earnings per share beginning with the second half of fiscal 2003, and in subsequent years. Separately, the Company's publishing segment continues to benefit from most of its magazine operations, its

book business, and its interactive media operations. Looking ahead, in fiscal 2003, earnings per share are expected to be $0.48 for the third quarter, and range from $1.65 to $1.75 for the full year. Additionally, publishing advertising revenues are anticipated to be in the low teens, while broadcast revenues are expected to be in the low double-digits for the third quarter of fiscal 2003.

ANNUAL FINANCIAL DATA:

FISCAL YEAR	TOT. REVS. ($mill.)	NET INC. ($mill.)	TOT. ASSETS ($mill.)	OPER. PROFIT %	NET PROFIT %	RET. ON EQUITY %	RET. ON ASSETS %	CURR. RATIO	EARN. PER SH.$	CASH FL. PER SH.$	TANG. BK. VAL.$	DIV. PER SH.$	PRICE RANGE	AVG. P/E RATIO	AVG. YIELD %
6/30/02	987.8	91.4	1,460.3	11.9	9.3	18.0	6.3	0.9	1.79	3.64	...	0.36	47.75 - 33.42	22.6	0.9
6/30/01	1,053.2	⑧⑦71.3	1,437.7	12.0	6.8	15.9	5.0	0.8	⑧⑦1.39	3.25	...	0.34	38.97 - 26.50	23.5	1.0
6/30/00	1,097.2	⑥71.0	1,439.8	14.7	6.5	18.7	4.9	0.8	⑥1.35	3.01	...	0.32	41.06 - 22.38	23.5	1.0
6/30/99	1,036.1	⑤89.7	1,423.4	16.5	8.7	24.9	6.3	0.7	⑤1.67	3.20	...	0.30	42.00 - 30.63	21.7	0.8
6/30/98	1,009.9	⑤79.9	1,066.6	15.1	7.9	22.8	7.5	0.7	⑤1.46	2.64	...	0.28	48.50 - 26.69	25.7	0.7
6/30/97	855.2	④67.6	760.9	13.4	7.9	20.7	8.9	1.2	④1.22	1.95	1.01	0.26	36.94 - 22.13	24.2	0.9
6/30/96	867.1	③54.7	733.8	11.2	6.3	20.9	7.4	0.8	③0.97	1.75	...	0.22	26.94 - 19.56	24.0	0.9
6/30/95	884.6	①②39.8	882.3	8.6	4.5	16.5	4.5	0.9	①②0.72	1.70	...	0.20	21.25 - 11.31	22.6	1.2
6/30/94	799.5	②27.2	864.5	6.2	3.4	10.5	3.1	1.1	②0.48	1.48	...	0.18	12.28 - 9.69	23.0	1.6
6/30/93	768.8	18.6	900.8	5.3	2.4	6.6	2.1	1.0	0.31	1.28	...	0.16	10.88 - 6.56	28.6	1.8

Statistics are as originally reported. Adj. for 2-for-1 stk. split 3/95 & 3/97. ① Bef. acct. change of cr$7.3 mill., 1992; d$46.2 mill., 1995. ② Incl. gain of $4.7 mill., 1995; $5.6 mill., 1994. ③ Incl. net gain of $3.4 mill. from disp. of book clubs. ④ Bef. gain of $27.7 mill. from the sale of cable ops. ⑤ Incl. gain on sale of BH&G Real Estate Service of $2.4 mill., 6/99; $1.4 mill., 6/98. ⑥ Incl. a non-recurr. chrg. of $25.3 mill., 6/01; $19.1 mill., 6/00. ⑦ Incl. a gain from disposition of $21.5 mill.

OFFICERS:
W. T. Kerr, Chmn., C.E.O.
S. V. Radia, V.P., C.F.O.

INVESTOR CONTACT: Jennifer S. McCoy, Mgr. Inv. Commun., (800) 284-4236

PRINCIPAL OFFICE: 1716 Locust Street, Des Moines, IA 50309-3023

TELEPHONE NUMBER: (515) 284-3000
FAX: (515) 284-2700
WEB: www.meredith.com
NO. OF EMPLOYEES: 2,434 full-time; 135 part-time
SHAREHOLDERS: 1,800 (cl A); 1100 (cl B)
ANNUAL MEETING: In Nov.
INCORPORATED: IA, Nov. 1905

INSTITUTIONAL HOLDINGS:
No. of Institutions: 216
Shares Held: 38,090,234
% Held: 76.8

INDUSTRY: Periodicals (SIC: 2721)

TRANSFER AGENT(S): Boston EquiServe, Boston, MA

MERRILL LYNCH & CO., INC.

EXCH.	SYM.	REC. PRICE	P/E RATIO	YLD.	MKT. CAP.	RANGE (52-WK.)	'02 Y/E PR.
NYSE	MER	34.08 (2/28/03)	12.7	1.9%	$28.75 bill.	56.60 - 28.21	37.95

UPPER MEDIUM GRADE. THE COMPANY CONTINUES TO FOCUS ON REVENUE ENHANCEMENTS AND COST REDUCTIONS.

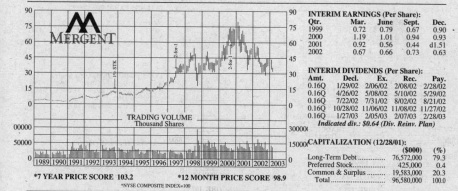

INTERIM EARNINGS (Per Share):

Qtr.	Mar.	June	Sept.	Dec.
1999	0.72	0.79	0.67	0.90
2000	1.19	1.01	0.94	0.93
2001	0.92	0.56	0.94	d1.51
2002	0.67	0.66	0.73	0.63

INTERIM DIVIDENDS (Per Share):

Amt.	Decl.	Ex.	Rec.	Pay.
0.16Q	1/29/02	2/06/02	2/08/02	2/28/02
0.16Q	4/26/02	5/08/02	5/10/02	5/29/02
0.16Q	7/22/02	7/31/02	8/02/02	8/21/02
0.16Q	10/28/02	11/06/02	11/08/02	11/27/02
0.16Q	1/27/03	2/05/03	2/07/03	2/28/03

Indicated div.: $0.64 (Div. Reinv. Plan)

CAPITALIZATION (12/28/01):

	($000)	(%)
Long-Term Debt	76,572,000	79.3
Preferred Stock	425,000	0.4
Common & Surplus	19,583,000	20.3
Total	96,580,000	100.0

*7 YEAR PRICE SCORE 103.2   ***12 MONTH PRICE SCORE 98.9**
*NYSE COMPOSITE INDEX=100

BUSINESS:

Merrill Lynch & Co., Inc. provides investment, financing, insurance and related services. Merrill Lynch, Pierce, Fenner & Smith, Inc. (MLPF&S), its largest subsidiary, is one of the largest securities firms in the world. MLPF&S is a broker and a dealer in various financial instruments, and an investment banker. MER is also engaged in asset management, investment counseling, and is a dealer in U.S. government and federal agency obligations. As of 12/27/02, client assets totaled $1.30 trillion, including $462.00 billion under management. Net sales for 2002 were derived as follows: Private Client Group, 44.7%; Global Markets and Investment Banking Group, 46.8%; and Merrill Lynch Investment Managers, 8.5%.

RECENT DEVELOPMENTS:

For the year ended 12/27/02, net income surged to $2.58 billion versus $573.0 million the year before. Earnings included an after-tax net gain of $25.0 million in 2002 and an after-tax net charge of $1.78 billion in 2001. Earnings for 2001 also included goodwill amortization of $207.0 million. Total net revenues declined 15.0% to $18.61 billion. Interest and dividend revenues decreased 34.6% to $13.18 billion. Commissions revenue fell 12.2% to $4.63 billion, while asset management and portfolio service fees declined 8.2% to $4.91 billion. Principal transactions revenue dropped 40.5% to $2.34 billion, and investment banking revenue decreased 30.9% to $2.44 billion. Comparisons were made with restated 2001 figures.

PROSPECTS:

The Company's Global Markets and Investment Banking Group continues to improve its pre-tax operating profit margins despite the downturn in the economy, due in part to the strength of MER's debt markets business, which had a record year in 2002 for net revenues and profits. Separately, the Private Client segment (GPC) continues to focus on individual client relationships and the expansion of its product offerings while increasing its fee-based and recurring revenue sources. GPC's business in the U.S. continues to focus on diversifying revenues, with current high mortgage origination volumes and increased sales of annuity products.

ANNUAL FINANCIAL DATA:

FISCAL YEAR	TOT. REVS. ($mill.)	NET INC. ($mill.)	TOT. ASSETS ($mill.)	OPER. PROFIT %	NET PROFIT %	RET. ON EQUITY %	RET. ON ASSETS %	CURR. RATIO	EARN. PER SH. $	CASH FL. PER SH. $	TANG. BK. VAL. $	DIV. PER SH. $	PRICE RANGE	AVG. P/E RATIO	AVG. YIELD %
p12/31/02	18,608.0	③ ④ 2,577.0							③ ④ 2.69			0.64	59.32 - 28.21	16.3	1.5
12/28/01	38,757.0	③ 573.0	419,419.0	3.6	1.5	2.9	0.1	1.2	③ 0.57	2.93	18.39	0.64	80.00 - 33.50	99.6	1.1
12/29/00	44,872.0	3,784.0	407,200.0	12.7	8.4	20.7	0.9	1.3	4.11	5.83	16.67	0.60	74.63 - 36.31	13.5	1.1
12/31/99	34,879.0	2,618.0	328,071.0	11.7	7.5	20.4	0.8	1.3	3.09	4.70	10.09	0.53	51.25 - 31.00	13.3	1.3
12/25/98	35,853.0	② 1,259.0	299,804.0	5.8	3.5	12.4	0.4	1.3	② 1.50	2.50	6.09	0.46	54.56 - 17.88	24.1	1.3
12/26/97	31,731.0	1,906.0	292,819.0	9.6	6.0	22.9	0.7	0.8	2.42	2.99	3.65	0.38	39.09 - 19.63	12.2	1.3
12/27/96	25,011.0	1,619.0	213,016.0	10.3	6.5	23.5	0.8	0.7	2.05	2.58	9.47	0.29	21.28 - 12.34	8.2	1.7
12/29/95	21,513.0	1,114.0	176,857.0	8.4	5.2	18.1	0.6	0.7	1.36	1.83	7.87	0.25	16.19 - 8.66	9.1	2.0
12/30/94	18,233.1	1,016.8	163,749.3	9.5	5.6	17.5	0.6	0.7	1.19	1.57	6.92	0.22	11.41 - 8.06	8.2	2.3
12/31/93	16,588.2	① 1,394.4	152,910.4	14.6	8.4	25.4	0.9	0.7	① 1.54	1.87	5.60	0.17	12.80 - 7.00	6.4	1.8

Statistics are as originally reported. Adj. for 2-for-1 stk. split, 8/00 & 5/97. ① Bef. acct. chrg. $35.4 mill. ② Incl. after-tax provision of $430.0 million for costs related to staff reductions. ③ Incl. after-tax restruct. benefits of $42.0 mill., 12/02; chrgs. $1.73 bill., 12/01 & after-tax recoveries rel. to 9/11/01 events of $126.0 mill., 12/02; exps. $83.0 mill., 12/01. ④ Incl. after-tax research rel. exps. of $143.0 mill.

OFFICERS:
D. H. Komansky, Chmn.
E. S. O'Neal, C.E.O.
A. Fakahany, Exec. V.P., C.F.O.
INVESTOR CONTACT: Martin Wise, Investor Relations, (866) 607-1234
PRINCIPAL OFFICE: 4 World Financial Center, New York, NY 10080

TELEPHONE NUMBER: (212) 449-1000
FAX: (212) 449-7461
WEB: www.ml.com
NO. OF EMPLOYEES: 50,900
SHAREHOLDERS: 13,955 (approx.)
ANNUAL MEETING: In April
INCORPORATED: DE, May, 1973

INSTITUTIONAL HOLDINGS:
No. of Institutions: 629
Shares Held: 653,589,876
% Held: 75.6
INDUSTRY: Security brokers and dealers (SIC: 6211)
TRANSFER AGENT(S): Mellon Investor Services, LLC, New York, NY

METLIFE, INC.

EXCH.	SYM.	REC. PRICE	P/E RATIO	YLD.	MKT. CAP.	RANGE (52-WK.)	'02 Y/E PR.
NYSE	MET	26.17 (2/28/03)	16.6	0.8%	$18.72 bill.	34.85 - 20.60	27.04

MEDIUM GRADE. MET EXPECTS 2003 OPERATING EARNINGS IN THE RANGE OF $2.80 TO $2.90 PER SHARE.

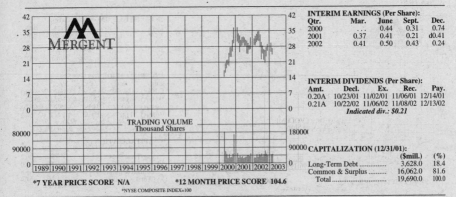

INTERIM EARNINGS (Per Share):

Qtr.	Mar.	June	Sept.	Dec.
2000	...	0.44	0.31	0.74
2001	0.37	0.41	0.21	d0.41
2002	0.41	0.50	0.43	0.24

INTERIM DIVIDENDS (Per Share):

Amt.	Decl.	Ex.	Rec.	Pay.
0.20A	10/23/01	11/02/01	11/06/01	12/14/01
0.21A	10/22/02	11/06/02	11/08/02	12/13/02

Indicated div.: $0.21

CAPITALIZATION (12/31/01):

	($mill.)	(%)
Long-Term Debt	3,628.0	18.4
Common & Surplus	16,062.0	81.6
Total	19,690.0	100.0

*7 YEAR PRICE SCORE N/A   ***12 MONTH PRICE SCORE 104.6**

*NYSE COMPOSITE INDEX=100

BUSINESS:

MetLife, Inc. is a provider of insurance and financial services to individual and institutional customers. As of 11/5/02, MET provided individual insurance, annuities and investment products to approximately 10.0 million households in the U.S. Also, MET provided group insurance and retirement and savings products and services to companies and institutions with approximately 33.0 million employees and members. The Company is organized into six major businesses: Individual Business, Reinsurance, Institutional Business, Asset Management, Auto & Home and International. As of 11/5/02, MET had international insurance operations in 13 countries with a focus on the Asia/Pacific region, Latin America and selected European countries. On 1/6/00, the Company acquired GenAmerica Corp. for about $1.20 billion. On 4/7/00, Metropolitan Life converted from a mutual to a stock company.

RECENT DEVELOPMENTS:

For the year ended 12/31/02, income was $1.16 billion, before income from discontinued operations of $450.0 million, versus income of $387.0 million, before income from discontinued operations of $86.0 million, in 2001. Results for 2002 included an after-tax charge of $169.0 million related to asbestos litigation. Results for 2002 and 2001 included several one-time items that resulted in a net gain of $37.0 million in 2002 and a net charge of $233.0 million in 2001. Results for 2001 included an after-tax charge of $330.0 million for business realignment. Also, results for 2001 included after-tax losses of $208.0 million associated with 9/11/01. Total revenues grew 6.0% to $33.15 billion.

PROSPECTS:

The Company's outlook is positive, reflecting recent actions taken to enhance MET's long-term financial strength and to improve its overall risk-adjusted capital, including recent capital contributions and the sale of real estate assets. Moreover, through improved operating fundamentals, including year-over-year rate increases of 11.0% and 26.0% in the automobile and homeowners lines, respectively, combined with strategic acquisitions in Mexico and Chile, should provide opportunities for continued growth. Separately, MET expects 2003 operating earnings in the range of $2.80 to $2.90 per diluted share.

ANNUAL FINANCIAL DATA:

FISCAL YEAR	PREM. INC. ($mill.)	TOT. REVS. ($mill.)	NET INC. ($mill.)	TOT. ASSETS ($mill.)	TOT. INVST. ($mill.)	RET. ON REVS. %	RET. ON EQUITY %	RET. ON ASSETS %	EARN. PER SH.$	TANG. BK. VAL.$	AVG. YIELD %	DIV. PER SH.$	PRICE RANGE	AVG. P/E RATIO
p12/31/02	21,225.0	33,147.0	④ 1,155.0	...	...	...	...	...	④ 1.58	...	0.8	0.21	34.85 - 20.60	17.5
12/31/01	19,101.0	31,928.0	③ 473.0	256,898.0	162,222.0	1.5	2.9	0.2	③ 0.62	22.45	0.7	0.20	36.63 - 24.70	49.4.
12/31/00	18,137.0	31,947.0	② 953.0	253,928.0	156,527.0	3.0	5.8	0.4	② 1.49	22.31	0.8	0.20	36.50 - 14.31	17.1
12/31/99	13,526.0	25,426.0	① 842.0	141,159.0	...	3.3	6.2	0.6	...	18.11	...	...	...	...
12/31/98	12,863.0	27,106.0	① 1,347.0	141,973.0	...	5.0	9.1	0.9	...	...	...	...	...	...

Statistics are as originally reported. ① Bef. extraord. chrg. $225.0 mill, 12/99; $4.0 mill., 12/98. ② Incls. net realized invest. losses of $236.0 mill., a one-time payout to transferred Canadian policyholders of $327.0 mill., demutalization expenses of $170.0 million and a surplus tax credit of $145.0 million. ③ Incl. litig. set. chrg. $159.0 mill., chrgs. of $208.0 mill fr. events of 9/11/01, & other non-recurr. chrgs. of $404.0 mill. ④ Bef. inc. fr. disc. opers. $450.0 mill.; incl. chrg. of $169.0 mill. for asbestos litig. & other one-time gains of $37.0 mill.

OFFICERS:
R. H. Benmosche, Chmn., Pres., C.E.O.
G. Clark, Vice-Chmn., C.I.O.
S. G. Nagler, Vice-Chmn., C.F.O.
INVESTOR CONTACT: Kevin Helmintoller, Investor Relations, (212) 578-5140
PRINCIPAL OFFICE: One Madison Avenue, New York, NY 10010-3690

TELEPHONE NUMBER: (212) 578-2211
FAX: (212) 578-3320
WEB: www.metlife.com
NO. OF EMPLOYEES: 46,000 (approx.)
SHAREHOLDERS: 35,327
ANNUAL MEETING: In April
INCORPORATED: DE, Aug., 1999

INSTITUTIONAL HOLDINGS:
No. of Institutions: 357
Shares Held: 286,019,429
% Held: 40.8
INDUSTRY: Insurance agents, brokers, & service (SIC: 6411)
TRANSFER AGENT(S): Mellon Investor Services, South Hackensack, NJ

METRIS COMPANIES, INC.

EXCH.	SYM.	REC. PRICE	P/E RATIO	YLD.	MKT. CAP.	RANGE (52-WK.)	'02 Y/E PR.
NYSE	MXT	1.50 (2/28/03)	...	...	$95.1 mill.	27.05 - 1.25	2.47

SPECULATIVE GRADE. THE COMPANY EXPECTS TO RETURN TO PROFITABILITY IN 2003.

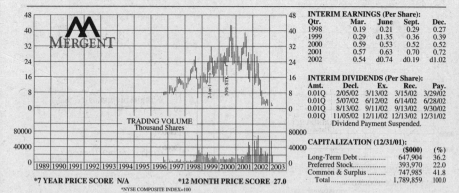

*7 YEAR PRICE SCORE N/A ***12 MONTH PRICE SCORE 27.0**

*NYSE COMPOSITE INDEX=100

INTERIM EARNINGS (Per Share):

Qtr.	Mar.	June	Sept.	Dec.
1998	0.19	0.21	0.29	0.27
1999	0.29	d1.35	0.36	0.39
2000	0.59	0.53	0.52	0.52
2001	0.57	0.63	0.70	0.72
2002	0.54	d0.74	d0.19	d1.02

INTERIM DIVIDENDS (Per Share):

Amt.	Decl.	Ex.	Rec.	Pay.
0.01Q	2/05/02	3/13/02	3/15/02	3/29/02
0.01Q	5/07/02	6/12/02	6/14/02	6/28/02
0.01Q	8/13/02	9/11/02	9/13/02	9/30/02
0.01Q	11/05/02	12/11/02	12/13/02	12/31/02

Dividend Payment Suspended.

CAPITALIZATION (12/31/01):

	($000)	(%)
Long-Term Debt	647,904	36.2
Preferred Stock	393,970	22.0
Common & Surplus	747,985	41.8
Total	1,789,859	100.0

BUSINESS:

Metris Companies, Inc. is a direct marketer of consumer credit products and fee-based services primarily to moderate-income consumers. The Company's consumer credit products are primarily unsecured credit cards issued by its subsidiary, Direct Merchants Credit Card Bank, N.A. Customers and prospects include individuals for whom credit bureau information is available and existing customers of a former affiliate, Fingerhut Corporation. The Company markets its fee-based services to its credit card customers and customers of third parties. The Company has operations in Champaign, Illinois; Jacksonville and Orlando, Florida; Scottsdale, Arizona; Tulsa, Oklahoma; Duluth, Minnesota; and White Marsh, Maryland.

RECENT DEVELOPMENTS:

For the year ended 12/31/02, net loss was $33.9 million versus income of $260.3 million, before an accounting change charge of $14.5 million, the previous year. Results for 2002 included a pre-tax charge of $18.0 million for the write-down of excess property, equipment and operating leases and a one-time, pre-tax marketing charge of $7.0 million. Total interest income slid 24.3% to $527.4 million. Net interest income dropped 20.1% to $423.8 million from $530.7 million in 2001. Provision for loan losses rose 4.4% to $573.5 million versus $549.1 million a year earlier. Other non-interest income fell 25.7% to $858.1 million. Other non-interest expenses grew 6.2% to $758.2 million.

PROSPECTS:

The Company is conducting a broad review of its business and operations so that it can restore the Company to profitability in 2003. On 1/22/03, the Company announced that it will take a $4.9 million charge in the first quarter of 2003 for a workforce reduction. The elimination of approximately 180 positions will result in approximately $20.8 million in annual savings. Going forward, the Company may continue to experience a higher charge-off rate due to the weak economic environment, higher bankruptcies and a declining receivable base. Moreover, the Company plans to slow account growth, utilize tighter underwriting standards, and implement more stringent credit line management strategies.

ANNUAL FINANCIAL DATA:

FISCAL YEAR	TOT. REVS. ($000)	NET INC. ($000)	TOT. ASSETS ($000)	OPER. PROFIT %	NET PROFIT %	RET. ON EQUITY %	RET. ON ASSETS %	CURR. RATIO	EARN. PER SH. $	CASH FL. PER SH. $	TANG. BK. VAL. $	DIV. PER SH. $	PRICE RANGE	AVG. P/E RATIO	AVG. YIELD %
p12/31/02	1,385,420	④ d33,851							④ d1.20			0.04	27.90 - 1.43	...	0.3
12/31/01	1,851,447	③ 260,291	4,228,686	22.8	14.1	22.8	6.2	0.3	③ 2.62	3.34	10.30	0.04	39.10 - 13.50	10.0	0.2
12/31/00	1,438,565	③ 198,591	3,736,025	22.4	13.8	22.5	5.3	0.3	③ 2.15	1.75	4.58	0.03	42.94 - 13.58	13.1	0.1
12/31/99	859,941	② 115,363	2,045,082	22.2	13.4	18.5	5.6	0.5	② d0.19	1.11	3.63	0.02	31.67 - 12.43	...	0.1
12/31/98	426,169	57,348	945,719	21.9	13.5	13.2	6.1	4.5	0.94	1.75	2.60	0.02	26.92 - 5.17	17.1	0.1
12/31/97	255,871	38,058	673,221	24.2	14.9	21.6	5.7	0.2	0.63	0.87	2.42	0.01	16.33 - 7.00	18.6	0.1
12/31/96	156,416	20,016	286,616	20.8	12.8	14.4	7.0	0.3	0.39	0.65	2.41	...	8.58 - 6.71	19.6	...
12/31/95	58,699	4,581	174,428	12.7	7.8	6.4	2.6	0.8	① 0.09	0.09	1.49	...	...	...	...
12/31/94	14,725	2,198	9,856	23.8	14.9	32.6	22.3	...	① 0.05	0.05	0.14	...	...	...	...
12/31/93	10,332	1,262	...	19.3	12.2	...	...	...	① 0.03	0.03	...	...	...	...	...

Statistics are as originally reported. Adj. for 3-for-2 stk. spl., 6/00; 2-for-1 stk. spl., 6/99 ① Pro forma ② Excl. extra. loss of $50.8 mill. ③ Excl. cum. effect of acctg. change chrg., $14.5 mill., 12/01; $3.4 mill., 12/00 ④ Incl. pre-tax chrg. of $18.0 mill. for write-down of excess prop., equip. & leases & a one-time pre-tax marketing chrg. of $7.0 mill.

OFFICERS:
D. Wesselink, Chmn., C.E.O.
B. Woo, C.F.O.

INVESTOR CONTACT: Mark Van Ert, V.P., Investor Relations, (952) 525-5092

PRINCIPAL OFFICE: 10900 Wayzata Blvd., Minnetonka, MN 55305-1534

TELEPHONE NUMBER: (952) 525-5020
FAX: (952) 595-0519
WEB: www.metriscompanies.com
NO. OF EMPLOYEES: 3,700 (approx.)
SHAREHOLDERS: 350
ANNUAL MEETING: In May
INCORPORATED: DE, Aug., 1996

INSTITUTIONAL HOLDINGS:
No. of Institutions: 129
Shares Held: 54,438,182
% Held: 94.5
INDUSTRY: Personal credit institutions (SIC: 6141)
TRANSFER AGENT(S): Computershare Investor Services, Chicago, IL

METRO-GOLDWYN-MAYER INC.

EXCH.	SYM.	REC. PRICE	P/E RATIO	YLD.	MKT. CAP.	RANGE (52-WK.)	'02 Y/E PR.
NYSE	MGM	10.01 (2/28/03)	...	...	$2.49 bill.	18.70 - 9.00	13.00

LOWER MEDIUM GRADE. THE COMPANY'S GOAL IS TO PRODUCE OR CO-PRODUCE AND DISTRIBUTE SEVEN TO TEN MOTION PICTURES ANNUALLY.

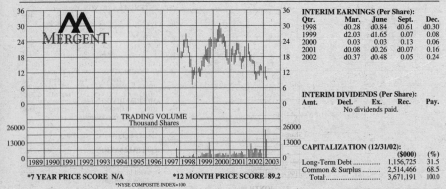

*7 YEAR PRICE SCORE N/A   *12 MONTH PRICE SCORE 89.2

*NYSE COMPOSITE INDEX=100

INTERIM EARNINGS (Per Share):

Qtr.	Mar.	June	Sept.	Dec.
1998	d0.28	d0.84	d0.61	d0.30
1999	d2.03	d1.65	0.07	0.08
2000	0.03	0.03	0.13	0.06
2001	d0.08	d0.26	d0.07	0.16
2002	d0.37	d0.48	0.05	0.24

INTERIM DIVIDENDS (Per Share):

Amt.	Decl.	Ex.	Rec.	Pay.
	No dividends paid.			

CAPITALIZATION (12/31/02):

	($000)	(%)
Long-Term Debt	1,156,725	31.5
Common & Surplus	2,514,466	68.5
Total	3,671,191	100.0

BUSINESS:

Metro-Goldwyn-Mayer Inc. is an entertainment content company engaged in the production and distribution of motion pictures, television programming, home video, interactive media, music, and licensed merchandise. The Company's film library includes approximately 4,000 titles. MGM's operating units include MGM Pictures, United Artists Corporation, MGM Television Entertainment, MGM Networks, MGM Distribution Company, MGM Worldwide Television Distribution, MGM Home Entertainment, MGM On Stage, MGM Consumer Products, MGM Music, MGM Interactive, and MGM Online. As of 2/05/03, MGM owned a 20.0% equity interest in American Movie Classics, The Independent Film Channel and WE: Women's Entertainment.

RECENT DEVELOPMENTS:

For the year ended 12/31/02, the Company reported a net loss of $142.2 million compared with a loss of $55.7 million, before an accounting change charge of $382.3 million, the previous year. Results for 2002 included a gain of $32.5 million from the sale of equity interest in cable channel. Total revenues increased 19.2% to $1.65 billion from $1.39 billion the year before. Revenues from feature films advanced 16.3% to $1.42 billion from $1.22 billion, while television programming revenues advanced 24.1% to $171.2 million from $138.0 million a year earlier. Other income more than doubled to $65.9 million from $31.6 million the prior year. Operating loss was $101.1 million versus operating income of $3.0 million in 2001.

PROSPECTS:

Going forward, MGM will look to produce new motion pictures and television episodes, develop new distribution channels and further penetrate emerging international markets. The Company's goal is to produce or co-produce and distribute seven to ten motion pictures annually through MGM Pictures across a variety of genres. Separately, MGM Worldwide Television Distribution, a unit of MGM, announced that it has entered into an agreement with UPC Nederland B.V., a cable operator, to launch the MGM Channel for the first time in the Netherlands.

ANNUAL FINANCIAL DATA:

FISCAL YEAR	TOT. REVS. ($mill.)	NET INC. ($mill.)	TOT. ASSETS ($mill.)	OPER. PROFIT %	NET PROFIT %	RET. ON EQUITY %	RET. ON ASSETS %	CURR. RATIO	EARN. PER SH.$	CASH FL. PER SH.$	TANG. BK. VAL.$	PRICE RANGE	AVG. P/E RATIO
12/31/02	1,654.1	③ d142.2	4,269.0	...	...	...	...	2.3	③ d0.57	2.79	8.03	23.25 - 9.00	...
12/31/01	1,387.5	② d55.7	3,923.2	0.2	...	...	...	1.0	② d0.24	2.30	8.23	23.37 - 13.19	...
12/31/00	1,237.4	① 51.0	3,548.2	8.3	4.1	2.2	1.4	1.2	① 0.24	3.57	8.58	31.06 - 14.88	95.7
12/31/99	1,142.4	d530.9	3,424.4	...	...	...	...	1.3	d3.36	2.24	7.80	25.50 - 10.25	...
12/31/98	1,240.7	d157.6	3,159.0	...	...	...	...	1.1	d2.08	8.23	9.01	27.00 - 7.13	...
12/31/97	831.3	d128.1	2,822.7	...	...	...	...	0.7	d4.47	11.32	12.22	22.19 - 19.75	...
12/31/96	228.7	0.2	1,774.7	5.9	0.1	...	...	1.0	0.01	5.26	35.95	...	...

Statistics are as originally reported. ① Incl. pre-tax chrg. of $3.7 mill. for sever. & rel. recov. ② Bef. acctg. chrg. of $382.3 mill. ③ Incl. gain of $32.5 mill. on sale of equity int. in cable channel.

OFFICERS:
A. Yemenidjian, Chmn., C.E.O.
C. J. McGurk, Vice-Chmn., C.O.O.
D. J. Taylor, Sr. Exec. V.P., C.F.O.
W. A. Jones, Sr. Exec. V.P., Sec.

INVESTOR CONTACT: Joseph Fitzgerald, Investor Relations, (310) 449-3600

PRINCIPAL OFFICE: 2500 Broadway Street, Santa Monica, CA 90404

TELEPHONE NUMBER: (310) 449-3000
FAX: (310) 449-8750
WEB: www.mgm.com

NO. OF EMPLOYEES: 1,150 (avg.)

SHAREHOLDERS: 2,000 (approx. beneficial)

ANNUAL MEETING: In May

INCORPORATED: DE, July, 1996

INSTITUTIONAL HOLDINGS:
No. of Institutions: 99
Shares Held: 50,614,580
% Held: 20.3

INDUSTRY: Motion picture & video production (SIC: 7812)

TRANSFER AGENT(S): Mellon Shareholder Services, Ridgefield Park, NJ

METTLER-TOLEDO INTERNATIONAL INC.

EXCH.	SYM.	REC. PRICE	P/E RATIO	YLD.	MKT. CAP.	RANGE (52-WK.)	'02 Y/E PR.
NYSE	MTD	29.86 (2/28/03)	13.5	…	$1.32 bill.	48.25 - 24.85	32.06

MEDIUM GRADE. RESULTS FOR 2003 SHOULD BENEFIT FROM THE COMPANY'S RESTRUCTURING EFFORTS.

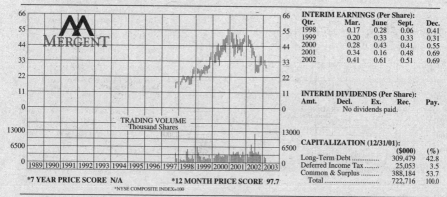

*7 YEAR PRICE SCORE N/A   *12 MONTH PRICE SCORE 97.7

*NYSE COMPOSITE INDEX=100

INTERIM EARNINGS (Per Share):

Qtr.	Mar.	June	Sept.	Dec.
1998	0.17	0.28	0.06	0.41
1999	0.20	0.33	0.33	0.31
2000	0.28	0.43	0.41	0.55
2001	0.34	0.16	0.48	0.69
2002	0.41	0.61	0.51	0.69

INTERIM DIVIDENDS (Per Share):

Amt.	Decl.	Ex.	Rec.	Pay.
	No dividends paid.			

CAPITALIZATION (12/31/01):

	($000)	(%)
Long-Term Debt	309,479	42.8
Deferred Income Tax	25,053	3.5
Common & Surplus	388,184	53.7
Total	722,716	100.0

BUSINESS:

Mettler-Toledo International Inc. is a global supplier of precision instruments. The Company manufactures and markets weighing instruments for use in laboratory, industrial and food retailing applications, and is a major provider of automated chemistry systems used in drug and chemical compound discovery and development. The Company's analytical instruments include titrators, thermal analysis systems and other analytical instruments. Also, the Company is a manufacturer and marketer of metal detection systems used in the production and packaging of goods in industries such as food processing, pharmaceutical, cosmetics, chemicals and other industries. Geographically, revenues for 2001 were derived: Europe, 44.6%; the Americas, 42.8%; and the rest of the world, 12.6%. In 2000, the Company acquired Berger Instruments, Thornton Inc. and AVS.

RECENT DEVELOPMENTS:

For the year ended 12/31/02, net earnings jumped 39.0% to $100.4 million versus $72.3 million in 2001. Results benefited from better than expected sales growth, driven by drug discovery, packaging, process analysis and U.S. food retailing businesses. MTD's Asian operations also reported strong sales growth. Results for 2002 and 2001 included amortization of $9.3 million and $14.1 million, respectively. Results also included a non-recurring charge and a non-recurring gain of $3.1 million and $14.6 million, respectively. Net sales climbed 5.7% to $1.21 billion from $1.15 billion the year before. The results for 2002 included Ranin Instrument, which was acquired in 2001.

PROSPECTS:

The Company made progress in several key areas that should improve results in 2003. Over the last several years, MTD has made significant investments in research and development and plans to introduce several new products in 2003. The Company also plans to grow its service business due to its expanded regulatory compliance offering. In addition, MTD expects sales growth in Asia to be strong, primarily due to robust demand in China due to immense capital investment taking place in the region. Moreover, near-term results should benefit from restructuring initiatives, including the transferring of production to China from two recently-closed facilities.

ANNUAL FINANCIAL DATA:

FISCAL YEAR	TOT. REVS. ($mill.)	NET INC. ($mill.)	TOT. ASSETS ($mill.)	OPER. PROFIT %	NET PROFIT %	RET. ON EQUITY %	RET. ON ASSETS %	CURR. RATIO	EARN. PER SH. $	CASH FL. PER SH. $	PRICE RANGE	AVG. P/E RATIO
p12/31/02	1,213.7	④ 100.4							④ 2.21		51.85 - 24.85	17.4
12/31/01	1,148.0	③ 72.3	1,189.4	13.1	6.3	18.6	6.1	1.2	③ 1.68	2.54	53.92 - 36.50	26.9
12/31/00	1,095.5	70.1	887.6	12.0	6.4	39.2	7.9	1.2	1.66	2.45	56.00 - 30.00	25.9
12/31/99	1,065.5	48.1	821.0	10.5	4.5	42.9	5.9	1.2	1.16	2.02	39.50 - 19.63	…
12/31/98	935.7	② 37.6	820.4	8.9	4.0	69.9	4.6	1.2	② 0.92	1.72	28.94 - 16.25	…
12/31/97	878.4	①② d23.9	749.3	4.6	…	…	…	1.2	①② d0.76	0.25	18.75 - 14.00	…
12/31/96	186.9	② d159.0	771.9	…	…	…	…	1.3	② d5.18	d4.89	…	…
10/14/96	662.2	14.5	…	5.7	2.2	…	…	…	…	…	…	…
12/31/95	850.4	18.3	724.1	4.3	2.1	9.4	2.5	1.3	…	…	…	…
12/31/94	769.1	13.5	…	3.7	1.8	…	…	…	…	…	…	…

Statistics are as originally reported. ① Bef. extraord. loss, $41.2 mill. ② Incls. one-time chrg. of $10.0 mill., 12/98; $30.0 mill., 12/97; $114.1 mill., 12/96. ③ Incl. $14.6 mill. after-tax non-recur. chg. & $600.00 tax benefit. ④ Incl. $11.5 mill. after-tax non-recur. chg.

OFFICERS:
R. F. Spoerry, Chmn., Pres., C.E.O.
D. Braun, C.F.O.

INVESTOR CONTACT: Mary T. Finnegan, Treas., Investor Relations, (614) 438-4748

PRINCIPAL OFFICE: Im Langacher, P.O. Box MT-100, Greifensee, Switzerland

TELEPHONE NUMBER: (614) 438-4748
FAX: (614) 438-4646
WEB: www.mt.com
NO. OF EMPLOYEES: 8,500 (approx.)
SHAREHOLDERS: 246 (record)
ANNUAL MEETING: In May
INCORPORATED: DE, Dec., 1991

INSTITUTIONAL HOLDINGS:
No. of Institutions: 136
Shares Held: 38,516,975
% Held: 86.8
INDUSTRY: Analytical instruments (SIC: 3826)
TRANSFER AGENT(S): Mellon Investor Services, Ridgefield Park, NJ

MGIC INVESTMENT CORPORATION

EXCH.	SYM.	REC. PRICE	P/E RATIO	YLD.	MKT. CAP.	RANGE (52-WK.)	'02 Y/E PR.
NYSE	MTG	39.46 (2/28/03)	6.5	0.3%	$4.19 bill.	74.40 - 33.60	41.30

UPPER MEDIUM GRADE. EARNINGS ARE BEING NEGATIVELY AFFECTED BY AN INCREASE IN LOAN LOSSES.

TRADING VOLUME
Thousand Shares

*7 YEAR PRICE SCORE 114.6   ***12 MONTH PRICE SCORE 84.8**
*NYSE COMPOSITE INDEX=100

INTERIM EARNINGS (Per Share):

Qtr.	Mar.	June	Sept.	Dec.
1997	0.61	0.67	0.72	0.75
1998	0.81	0.82	0.86	0.91
1999	0.91	1.02	1.11	1.25
2000	1.19	1.27	1.36	1.23
2001	1.46	1.49	1.47	1.50
2002	1.58	1.61	1.47	1.37

INTERIM DIVIDENDS (Per Share):

Amt.	Decl.	Ex.	Rec.	Pay.
0.025Q	1/24/02	2/06/02	2/08/02	3/01/02
0.025Q	5/02/02	5/14/02	5/16/02	6/03/02
0.025Q	7/18/02	8/07/02	8/09/02	9/04/02
0.025Q	10/24/02	11/06/02	11/11/02	12/02/02
0.025Q	1/23/03	2/06/03	2/10/03	3/03/03

Indicated div.: $0.10

CAPITALIZATION (12/31/01):

	($000)	(%)
Long-Term Debt	472,102	13.5
Common & Surplus	3,020,187	86.5
Total	3,492,289	100.0

BUSINESS:

MGIC Investment Corporation is a holding company which, through its subsidiary, Mortgage Guaranty Insurance Corp., is a provider of private mortgage insurance coverage in the United States to mortgage bankers, savings institutions, commercial banks, mortgage brokers, credit unions and other lenders. Private mortgage insurance covers residential first mortgage loans and expands home ownership opportunities. Private mortgage insurance also facilitates the sale of low down-payment mortgage loans in the secondary mortgage market, principally to the Federal Home Loan Mortgage Corporation and the Federal National Mortgage Association. In addition, MTG provides various underwriting and contract services related to home mortgage lending. As of 12/31/02, the Company had about $196.99 billion in primary insurance in force covering approximately 1.7 million mortgages. MTG is licensed in all 50 states of the United States, the District of Columbia and Puerto Rico.

RECENT DEVELOPMENTS:

For the year ended 12/31/02, net income decreased 1.6% to $629.2 million from $639.1 million in the previous year. The decrease in earnings was primarily due to increased losses resulting from bad loans. Total revenues grew 15.3% to $1.57 billion from $1.36 billion in the prior year. Revenues for 2002 and 2001 included realized gains of $29.1 million and $37.4 million, respectively. Net premiums written increased 13.7% to $1.18 billion. Net premiums earned grew 13.4% to $1.18 billion from $1.04 billion a year earlier. Investment income rose 1.5% to $207.5 million. Losses incurred jumped to $365.8 million versus $160.8 million the year before.

PROSPECTS:

Looking ahead, 2003 is expected to be a tough year for the Company as the economic downturn means increasing defaults on mortgage repayments and additional claims. Accordingly, MTG lowered its earnings per share guidance for 2003 to a range of $5.85 to $6.10, excluding realized gains and losses. The Company's 2003 earnings expectation is built on assumptions that include a decline in refinance volume in the mortgage origination market, with purchase money volume continuing to remain strong; improving persistency due to lower refinances; lower growth in earned premiums; lower underwriting expenses due to lower refinances; and higher incurred losses.

ANNUAL FINANCIAL DATA:

FISCAL YEAR	PREM. INC. ($mill.)	TOT. REVS. ($mill.)	NET INC. ($mill.)	TOT. ASSETS ($mill.)	TOT. INVST. ($mill.)	RET. ON REVS. %	RET. ON EQUITY %	RET. ON ASSETS %	EARN. PER SH. $	TANG. BK. VAL. $	AVG. YIELD %	DIV. PER SH. $	PRICE RANGE	AVG. P/E RATIO
p12/31/02	1,182.1	1,565.8	629.2						6.04		0.2	0.10	74.40 - 33.60	8.9
12/31/01	1,042.3	1,357.8	639.1	4,567.0	4,231.1	47.1	21.2	14.0	5.93	28.47	0.2	0.10	77.31 - 50.56	10.8
12/31/00	890.1	1,110.3	⬚ 542.0	3,857.8	3,611.0	48.8	22.0	14.0	⬚ 5.05	23.07	0.2	0.10	71.50 - 31.94	10.2
12/31/99	792.6	996.8	470.2	3,104.4	2,891.3	47.2	26.5	15.1	4.30	16.79	0.2	0.10	62.75 - 30.13	10.8
12/31/98	763.5	971.7	385.5	3,050.5	2,855.0	39.7	23.5	12.6	3.39	15.05	0.2	0.10	74.50 - 24.25	14.6
12/31/97	708.7	868.3	323.8	2,617.7	2,446.1	37.3	21.8	12.4	2.75	13.07	0.2	0.10	66.00 - 34.94	18.4
12/31/96	617.0	745.6	258.0	2,222.3	2,036.2	34.6	18.9	11.6	2.17	11.59	0.2	0.08	38.88 - 25.25	14.8
12/31/95	506.5	617.9	207.6	1,874.7	1,687.2	33.6	18.5	11.1	1.75	9.89	0.3	0.08	31.00 - 16.38	13.5
12/31/94	404.0	502.2	159.5	1,476.3	1,293.0	31.8	19.0	10.8	1.35	7.18	0.5	0.08	17.13 - 12.50	11.0
12/31/93	299.3	403.5	127.3	1,343.2	1,099.6	31.5	17.9	9.5	1.08	6.11	0.5	0.07	17.84 - 14.12	14.0

Statistics are as originally reported. Adj. for stk. splits: 2-for-1, 6/97 & 12/93. ⬚ Incl. litigation settlement chrg. of $23.2 mill

OFFICERS:
C. S. Culver, Pres., C.E.O.
J. M. Lauer, Exec. V.P., C.F.O.
INVESTOR CONTACT: Shareholder Services, (414) 347-6596
PRINCIPAL OFFICE: 250 E. Kilbourn Ave., Milwaukee, WI 53202

TELEPHONE NUMBER: (414) 347-6480
FAX: (414) 347-6696
WEB: www.mgic.com
NO. OF EMPLOYEES: 1,223 (avg.)
SHAREHOLDERS: 244
ANNUAL MEETING: In May
INCORPORATED: WI, 1984

MGM MIRAGE

EXCH.	SYM.	REC. PRICE	P/E RATIO	YLD.	MKT. CAP.	RANGE (52-WK.)	'02 Y/E PR.
NYSE	MGG	25.62 (2/28/03)	14.1	...	$4.03 bill.	42.03 - 24.09	32.97

UPPER MEDIUM GRADE. CAPITAL EXPENDITURES ARE EXPECTED TO RANGE FROM $375.0 MILLION TO $425.0 MILLION IN 2003.

*7 YEAR PRICE SCORE 145.7   ***12 MONTH PRICE SCORE 88.2**

*NYSE COMPOSITE INDEX=100

INTERIM EARNINGS (Per Share):

Qtr.	Mar.	June	Sept.	Dec.
1998	0.14	0.13	0.16	0.21
1999	0.17	0.19	0.11	0.36
2000	0.38	d0.13	0.45	0.42
2001	0.53	0.47	d0.09	0.15
2002	0.51	0.63	0.43	0.25

INTERIM DIVIDENDS (Per Share):

Amt.	Decl.	Ex.	Rec.	Pay.
		No dividends paid.		

CAPITALIZATION (12/31/01):

	($000)	(%)
Long-Term Debt	5,352,561	55.7
Deferred Income Tax	1,746,272	18.2
Common & Surplus	2,510,700	26.1
Total	9,609,533	100.0

BUSINESS:

MGM Mirage (formerly MGM Grand, Inc.) is an entertainment, hotel and gaming company, which owns and/or operates 15 casino properties located in Nevada, Mississippi and Michigan as of 12/31/02. MGG's U.S. holdings include: Bellagio, the MGM Grand Hotel and Casino-The City of Entertainment, The Mirage, Treasure Island, New York-New York Hotel and Casino, the Boardwalk Hotel and Casino, 50% of Monte Carlo, and The Golden Nugget, all located in Las Vegas; Whiskey Pete's, Buffalo Bill's and the Primm Valley Resort in Primm, Nevada; two championship golf courses in CA; a golf course in Las Vegas; the Golden Nugget in Nevada; the Beau Rivage resort in Mississippi; MGM Grand Detroit Casino; and the MGM Grand Hotel and Casino in Darwin, Australia. Net sales for 2002 were derived as follows: casino, 49.1%; rooms, 18.9%; food and beverage, 17.0%; and entertainment, retail and other, 15.0%. On 5/31/00, MGG acquired Mirage Resorts, Inc.

RECENT DEVELOPMENTS:

For the year ended 12/31/02, the Company reported income of $292.8 million, before an extraordinary loss of $328,000, compared with income of $170.6 million, before an extraordinary loss of $778,000, the year before. Earnings for 2002 and 2001 included net charges of $19.2 million and $76.8 million, respectively, related to various items. Revenues, net of promotional allowances, increased 1.5% to $4.03 billion from $3.97 billion a year earlier.

PROSPECTS:

For 2003, the Company will continue to repay debt and invest in its premier properties. Capital expenditures for the coming year are expected to range from $375.0 million to $425.0 million, including development expenditures related to the Bellagio expansion, EZ Pay™ system, and theatres for the two new Cirque du Soleil shows. During the quarter, MGG entered into an agreement with Turnberry Associates to jointly develop a luxury condominium-hotel complex at MGM Grand Las Vegas. Additionally, MGG began installation of International Game Technology's EZ-Pay™ cashless gaming system at its resorts, with conversion of almost all of its slot machines expected by mid-2003.

ANNUAL FINANCIAL DATA:

FISCAL YEAR	TOT. REVS. ($mill.)	NET INC. ($mill.)	TOT. ASSETS ($mill.)	OPER. PROFIT %	NET PROFIT %	RET. ON EQUITY %	RET. ON ASSETS %	CURR. RATIO	EARN. PER SH. $	CASH FL. PER SH. $	TANG. BK. VAL.$	DIV. PER SH. $	PRICE RANGE	AVG. P/E RATIO	AVG. YIELD %
p12/31/02	4,031.3	⑤ 292.8							⑤ 1.83				42.03 - 27.80	19.1	...
12/31/01	4,009.6	⑤ 170.6	10,497.4	15.7	4.3	6.8	1.6	0.7	⑤ 1.06	3.68	15.30	...	32.85 - 16.19	23.1	...
⑥ 12/31/00	3,232.6	⑤ 166.2	10,734.6	16.6	5.1	7.0	1.5	0.6	⑤ 1.13	3.32	14.63	0.10	38.81 - 18.44	25.3	0.3
12/31/99	1,391.7	④ 95.1	2,760.7	15.1	6.8	9.2	3.4	0.9	④ 0.80	1.86	8.76	...	27.28 - 13.56	25.5	...
12/31/98	773.9	68.9	1,773.8	17.0	8.9	7.1	3.9	1.1	0.61	1.31	8.91	...	19.94 - 11.28	25.6	...
12/31/97	827.6	③ 115.3	1,398.4	23.1	13.9	10.5	8.2	0.9	③ 0.98	1.54	9.17	...	23.44 - 16.06	20.2	...
12/31/96	804.8	② 74.5	1,287.7	16.1	9.3	7.7	5.8	1.2	② 0.69	1.28	8.07	...	24.38 - 11.38	26.1	...
12/31/95	721.8	46.6	1,282.2	14.4	6.5	8.0	3.6	1.8	0.48	1.08	5.58	...	16.19 - 11.38	28.7	...
12/31/94	742.2	① 73.5	1,140.8	17.5	9.9	13.9	6.4	1.8	① 0.75	1.24	5.51	...	19.81 - 11.31	20.7	...
12/31/93	57.8	d117.6	1,160.1	...	...	...	...	1.6	d1.23	d1.12	4.92	...	24.88 - 9.50	...	...

Statistics are as originally reported. Adj. for 2-for-1 stk. split, 2/10/00. ① Bef. income from disc. ops. of $1.0 mill. ② Incl. various chrgs. of $80.2 mill. ③ Incl. $28.6 mill. chg. for asset disp. & excl. extraord. chrg. of $4.2 mill. ④ Incl. pre-open. & oth. exps. of $71.5 mill.; excl. extraord. chrg. of $898,000 & acctg. chrg. of $8.2 mill. ⑤ Bef. extraord. loss of $328,000, 2002; $778,000, 2001; $5.4 million, 2000; incl. various items resulting in a net loss of $19.2 mill., 2002; $76.8 mill., 2001; $131.3 mill., 2000. ⑥ Reflects the acq. of Mirage Resorts, Inc. on 5/31/00.

OFFICERS:
J. T. Lanni, Chmn., C.E.O.
D. M. Wade, Vice-Chmn.
J. J. Murren, Pres., C.F.O., Treas.
INVESTOR CONTACT: Scott Langsner, Sr. V.P., Sec. & Treas., (702) 891-3333
PRINCIPAL OFFICE: 3600 Las Vegas Boulevard South, Las Vegas, NV 89109

TELEPHONE NUMBER: (702) 693-7120
FAX: (702) 693-8626
WEB: www.mgmmirage.com
NO. OF EMPLOYEES: 34,000 full-time (approx.); 8,000 part-time (approx.)
SHAREHOLDERS: 4,460 (approx.)
ANNUAL MEETING: In Mar.
INCORPORATED: DE, Jan., 1986

INSTITUTIONAL HOLDINGS:
No. of Institutions: 206
Shares Held: 80,269,920
% Held: 51.8

INDUSTRY: Amusement parks (SIC: 7996)

TRANSFER AGENT(S): Mellon Investor Services, Ridgefield Park, NJ

MICHAELS STORES, INC.

EXCH.	SYM.	REC. PRICE	P/E RATIO	YLD.	MKT. CAP.	RANGE (52-WK.)	'02 Y/E PR.
NYSE	MIK	23.50 (2/28/03)	11.1	...	$1.54 bill.	49.33 - 22.26	31.30

MEDIUM GRADE. THE COMPANY ANNOUNCED PLANS TO LAUNCH A NEW SCRAPBOOKING RETAIL BUSINESS IN THE COMING MONTHS.

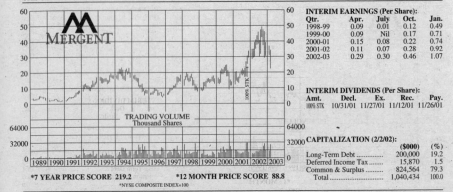

INTERIM EARNINGS (Per Share):

Qtr.	Apr.	July	Oct.	Jan.
1998-99	0.09	0.01	0.12	0.49
1999-00	0.09	Nil	0.17	0.71
2000-01	0.15	0.08	0.22	0.74
2001-02	0.11	0.07	0.28	0.92
2002-03	0.29	0.30	0.46	1.07

INTERIM DIVIDENDS (Per Share):

Amt.	Decl.	Ex.	Rec.	Pay.
100% STK	10/31/01	11/27/01	11/12/01	11/26/01

CAPITALIZATION (2/2/02):

	($000)	(%)
Long-Term Debt	200,000	19.2
Deferred Income Tax	15,870	1.5
Common & Surplus	824,564	79.3
Total	1,040,434	100.0

*7 YEAR PRICE SCORE 219.2   ***12 MONTH PRICE SCORE 88.8**

*NYSE COMPOSITE INDEX=100

BUSINESS:

Michaels Stores, Inc. is a national specialty retailer providing arts, crafts, framing, floral, decorative wall decor and seasonal merchandise for the hobbyist and do-it-yourself home decorator. As of 3/12/03, the Company owned and operated 765 Michaels stores in 48 states and Canada, 153 Aaron Brothers stores, located primarily on the West Coast, and Star Wholesale located in Dallas, Texas, offers merchandise primarily to interior decorators/designers, wedding/event planners, florists, hotels, restaurants and commercial display companies. The average square feet of selling space for Star Wholesale, Michaels, and Aaron Brothers is 50,000, 18,100, and 5,900, respectively.

RECENT DEVELOPMENTS:

For the year ended 2/1/03, income surged 65.9% to $147.7 million, before an accounting change charge of $7.4 million, compared with net income of $89.0 million in 2001. Results for 2002 and 2001 included store opening costs of $8.6 million and $10.4 million, respectively. Results for 2001 included litigation settlement expenses of $8.2 million. Net sales rose 12.9% to $2.86 billion from $2.53 billion a year earlier. Comparable-store sales increased 4.0%. Gross profit advanced 21.0% to $1.05 billion from $897.0 million the year before. Operating income increased 50.1% to $269.8 million from $179.7 million in 2001.

PROSPECTS:

On 3/13/03, MIK announced that it will launch a new scrapbooking retail business in the coming months. The stores, to be known as Recollections, will provide merchandise and accessories in a community learning environment to assist crafters with all their scrapbook making needs. MIK expects to open two test stores in the Dallas-Fort Worth, Texas area by summer 2003. The stores will average between 5,000 and 6,000 square feet and hold more than 10,000 SKU's of scrapbooking and paper crafting products, including local interest SKU's like school and team logos and colors. The stores will feature two large classrooms and offer a variety of scrapbook support services. Separately, MIK continues to implement its perpetual inventory and automated replenishment initiatives.

ANNUAL FINANCIAL DATA:

FISCAL YEAR	TOT. REVS. ($mill.)	NET INC. ($mill.)	TOT. ASSETS ($mill.)	OPER. PROFIT %	NET PROFIT %	RET. ON EQUITY %	RET. ON ASSETS %	CURR. RATIO	EARN. PER SH.$	CASH FL. PER SH.$	TANG. BK. VAL.$	PRICE RANGE	AVG. P/E RATIO
p2/1/03	2,856.4	⑤ 147.7	1,561.0	...	...	...	...	...	⑤ 2.09	...	...	49.33 - 28.50	18.6
2/02/02	2,530.7	94.3	1,414.6	7.1	3.7	11.4	6.7	2.7	1.41	2.45	10.79	33.70 - 12.13	16.2
2/03/01	2,249.4	①②80.4	1,158.4	6.6	3.6	11.4	6.9	2.5	①②1.18	2.14	9.16	24.81 - 9.00	14.4
1/29/00	1,882.5	②④62.3	1,096.7	6.6	3.3	11.0	5.7	2.7	②④1.00	1.84	7.35	17.94 - 8.00	13.0
1/30/99	1,574.0	②43.6	962.7	5.7	2.8	9.1	4.5	2.7	②0.72	1.53	6.17	19.96 - 7.75	19.4
1/31/98	1,456.5	30.1	908.5	4.7	2.1	6.8	3.3	2.7	0.53	1.32	5.25	18.50 - 5.66	23.0
2/01/97	1,378.3	d31.2	784.4	...	...	...	...	2.2	d0.67	0.23	4.05	9.94 - 4.03	...
1/28/96	1,294.9	d20.4	739.8	...	...	...	...	2.2	d0.47	0.24	4.47	18.50 - 5.50	...
1/29/95	994.6	③35.6	686.0	6.4	3.6	10.0	5.2	2.2	③0.89	1.41	5.59	23.25 - 14.75	21.5
1/30/94	619.7	26.3	397.8	6.7	4.2	14.2	6.6	2.7	0.77	1.13	4.85	19.50 - 12.63	21.0

Statistics are as originally reported. Adj. for stk. split: 100%, 11/01. ① Excl. acctg. change chrg. of $1.9 mill. ② Incl. store pre-opening costs of $10.2 mill., 2001; $11.1 mill. 2000; $7.9 mill. 1999. ③ Incl. store closing & conversion costs of $7.1 mill. ④ Incl. litigation settlement chrg. of $1.5 mill. ⑤ Incl. store opening costs of $8.6 mill., bef. acctg. change chrg. of $7.4 mill.

OFFICERS:
C. J. Wyly, Jr., Chmn.
S. Wyly, Vice-Chmn.
R. M. Rouleau, Pres., C.E.O.

INVESTOR CONTACT: Investor Relation, (972) 409-1300

PRINCIPAL OFFICE: 800 Bent Branch Drive, Irving, TX 75063

TELEPHONE NUMBER: (972) 409-1300
FAX: (972) 409-1555
WEB: www.michaels.com
NO. OF EMPLOYEES: 12,300 full-time (approx.); 25,400 part-time (approx.)
SHAREHOLDERS: 617 (record).
ANNUAL MEETING: In June
INCORPORATED: CO, 1962; reincorp., DE, 1983

INSTITUTIONAL HOLDINGS:
No. of Institutions: 255
Shares Held: 59,234,963
% Held: 87.8

INDUSTRY: Hobby, toy, and game shops (SIC: 5945)

TRANSFER AGENT(S): Computershare Investor Services, LLC, Chicago, IL

MICRON TECHNOLOGY, INC.

EXCH.	SYM.	REC. PRICE	P/E RATIO	YLD.	MKT. CAP.	RANGE (52-WK.)	'02 Y/E PR.
NYSE	MU	7.99 (2/28/03)	...	...	$4.78 bill.	39.50 - 6.60	9.74

SPECULATIVE GRADE. THE COMPANY'S WORLDWIDE PRODUCTION CONTINUES TO SHIFT TO 0.13 MICRON PROCESS.

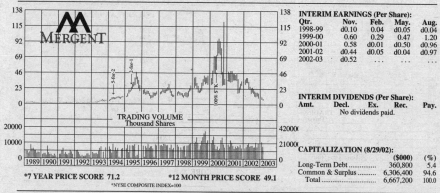

*7 YEAR PRICE SCORE 71.2   *12 MONTH PRICE SCORE 49.1

*NYSE COMPOSITE INDEX=100

INTERIM EARNINGS (Per Share):

Qtr.	Nov.	Feb.	May.	Aug.
1998-99	d0.10	0.04	d0.05	d0.05
1999-00	0.60	0.29	0.47	1.20
2000-01	0.58	d0.01	d0.50	d0.96
2001-02	d0.44	d0.05	d0.04	d0.97
2002-03	0.52	...	...	...

INTERIM DIVIDENDS (Per Share):

Amt.	Decl.	Ex.	Rec.	Pay.
		No dividends paid.		

CAPITALIZATION (8/29/02):

	($000)	(%)
Long-Term Debt	360,800	5.4
Common & Surplus	6,306,400	94.6
Total	6,667,200	100.0

BUSINESS:

Micron Technology, Inc. designs, develops, manufactures, and markets semiconductor memory products. MU's products include Dynamic Random Access Memory chips (DRAMs), including Double Data Rate Synchronous DRAMs and Synchronous DRAMs, as well as Static RAMs. These products store digital information and provide high-speed storage and retrieval of data. MU's semiconductor products also include flash memory devices used in networking applications, workstations, servers, personal computers, and handheld electronic devices and complementary metal-oxide semiconductor imaging sensors used in miniature cellular phone cameras, digital cameras, consumable pill cameras for medical use, automotive headlight dimming and motion tracking systems. On 4/30/01, MU acquired the remaining 75.0% interest in KMT Semiconductor Limited.

RECENT DEVELOPMENTS:

For the first quarter ended 11/28/02, the Company reported a net loss of $315.9 million compared with a net loss of $265.9 million in the corresponding prior-year quarter. Results for 2002 and 2001 included inventory write-down charges of $103.0 million and $173.0 million, respectively. Also, results for 2002 included a net loss on write-downs and disposals of semiconductor equipment of $7.0 million. Net sales jumped 61.6% to $685.1 million from $423.9 million a year earlier. Operating loss narrowed to $296.6 million from $452.0 million the year before. Net interest income amounted to $1.5 million versus $14.8 million in the 2001 quarter.

PROSPECTS:

MU is in the midst of transitions to both double data rate (DDR) devices and 0.13 micron line-width processes in light of increasing demand. As of 11/28/02, approximately 40.0% of MU's worldwide production had shifted to 0.13 micron process. Meanwhile, the transition from trench technology used in its recently acquired Manassas, Virginia facility to stack technology should be completed in the first calendar quarter of 2003. Separately, MU may benefit from any duty imposed by the U.S. Department of Commerce on imported products from the Korean DRAM industry.

ANNUAL FINANCIAL DATA:

FISCAL YEAR	TOT. REVS. ($mill.)	NET INC. ($mill.)	TOT. ASSETS ($mill.)	OPER. PROFIT %	NET PROFIT %	RET. ON EQUITY %	RET. ON ASSETS %	CURR. RATIO	EARN. PER SH.$	CASH FL. PER SH.$	TANG. BK. VAL.$	DIV. PER SH.$	PRICE RANGE		AVG. P/E RATIO	AVG. YIELD %
8/29/02	2,589.0	⑦ d907.0	7,555.4	...	...	...	...	2.8	⑦ d1.51	0.45	9.93	...	39.50 -	9.50	...	...
8/30/01	3,935.9	⑥ d521.2	8,363.2	...	...	...	...	4.6	⑥ d0.88	1.00	11.59	...	49.61 -	16.39	...	...
8/31/00	7,336.3	⑤ 1,504.2	9,631.5	31.3	20.5	23.4	15.6	3.0	⑤ 2.56	4.13	10.96	...	122.06 -	28.00	29.3	...
9/02/99	3,764.0	④ d68.9	6,965.2	...	...	...	...	3.1	④ d0.13	1.49	7.44	...	42.50 -	17.13	...	...
9/03/98	3,011.9	③ d233.7	4,688.3	...	...	...	...	2.0	③ d0.55	0.88	6.11	...	27.81 -	10.03	...	...
8/28/97	3,515.5	③ 320.3	4,851.3	11.3	9.1	11.1	6.6	2.6	③ 0.77	1.81	6.70	0.05	30.03 -	11.00	26.6	...
8/29/96	3,653.8	② 586.0	3,751.5	25.8	16.0	23.4	15.6	1.5	② 1.38	2.21	5.89	0.05	22.00 -	8.31	11.0	0.3
8/31/95	2,952.7	① 839.2	2,774.9	43.9	28.4	44.3	30.2	2.1	① 1.98	2.43	4.49	0.05	47.38 -	10.63	14.7	0.3
9/01/94	1,628.6	397.9	1,529.7	38.1	24.4	37.9	26.0	2.9	0.96	1.28	2.46	0.04	11.47 -	4.46	8.3	0.5
9/02/93	828.3	104.1	965.7	20.0	12.6	16.3	10.8	2.1	0.26	0.54	1.42	0.01	6.36 -	1.81	15.7	0.1

Statistics are as originally reported. Adj. for stk. splits: 100%, 5/00; 5-for-2, 4/94; 2-for-1, 5/95 ① Incl. nonrecurr. pre-tax gain $29.0 mill. on merger of subs. with ZEOS. ② Incl. nonrecurr. chrg. $29.6 mill. for restr. ③ Incl. nonrecurr. gain after-tax $211.0, 1997; pre-tax $157.7 mill., 1998. ④ Incl. nonrecurr. pre-tax loss of $47.0 mill. & pre-tax gain of $10.0 mill. ⑤ Incl. nonrecurr. pre-tax loss of $23.0 mill. & pre-tax gain of $56.0 mill. ⑥ Incl. nonrecurr. pre-tax loss of $732.0 mill. but excl. loss from disc. oper. $103.0 mill. ⑦ Incl. inventory write-downs and oth. nonrecurr. chrgs. of $403.0 mill.

OFFICERS:
S. R. Appleton, Chmn., Pres., C.E.O.
W. G. Stover Jr., V.P., C.F.O.
R. W. Lewis, V.P., Sec., Gen. Couns.

INVESTOR CONTACT: David T. Parker, Investor Relations, (208) 368-5584

PRINCIPAL OFFICE: 8000 S. Federal Way, P.O. Box 6, Boise, ID 83707-0006

TELEPHONE NUMBER: (208) 368-4000
FAX: (208) 368-4435
WEB: www.micron.com
NO. OF EMPLOYEES: 18,700 (approx.)
SHAREHOLDERS: 3,841
ANNUAL MEETING: In Nov.
INCORPORATED: DE, Oct., 1978

INSTITUTIONAL HOLDINGS:
No. of Institutions: 369
Shares Held: 441,723,283
% Held: 73.0
INDUSTRY: Semiconductors and related devices (SIC: 3674)
TRANSFER AGENT(S): Wells Fargo Shareowner Services, South St. Paul, MN

MID ATLANTIC MEDICAL SERVICES, INC.

EXCH.	SYM.	REC. PRICE	P/E RATIO	YLD.	MKT. CAP.	RANGE (52-WK.)	'02 Y/E PR.
NYSE	MME	35.75 (2/28/03)	15.3	...	$1.71 bill.	43.20 - 25.80	32.40

UPPER MEDIUM GRADE. THE COMPANY SHOULD CONTINUE TO BENEFIT FROM PRODUCT DIVERSITY, IMPROVED CUSTOMER SERVICE AND DISCIPLINED PRICING.

*7 YEAR PRICE SCORE 209.9   ***12 MONTH PRICE SCORE 106.3**
NYSE COMPOSITE INDEX=100

INTERIM EARNINGS (Per Share):

Qtr.	Mar.	June	Sept.	Dec.
1998	0.14	0.08	d0.15	0.13
1999	0.14	0.11	0.17	0.22
2000	0.22	0.19	0.28	0.31
2001	0.32	0.30	0.36	0.43
2002	0.45	0.44	0.54	0.91

INTERIM DIVIDENDS (Per Share):

Amt.	Decl.	Ex.	Rec.	Pay.
		No dividends paid.		

CAPITALIZATION (12/31/01):

	($000)	(%)
Common & Surplus	281,471	100.0
Total	281,471	100.0

BUSINESS:

Mid Atlantic Medical Services, Inc. is a regional holding company for healthcare organizations. As of 9/30/02, MME offered service coverage to Washington D.C., Maryland, West Virginia, Delaware, North Carolina, Virginia and Pennsylvania with a network of providers and hospitals. MME owns and operates three licensed health maintenance organizations: M.D.-Individual Practice Association, Inc., Optimum Choice, Inc. and Optimum Choice of the Carolinas, Inc. MME also offers access to preferred provider network (PPOs) through Alliance PPO, LLC. In addition, MAMSI Life and Health Insurance Company, is a wholly-owned life and health insurance company. MME operates a coordination of benefits company through Alliance Recovery Services, LLC. MME also operates home care companies such as HomeCall, Inc., FirstCall, Inc. and HomeCall Pharmaceutical Services, Inc. As of 12/31/02, membership totaled approximately 2.0 million covered lives.

RECENT DEVELOPMENTS:

For the year ended 12/31/02, net income soared 70.3% to $97.4 million compared with $57.2 million the previous year. The improvement in earnings was primarily attributed to strong membership growth and increased health premiums and a reduction in administrative expenses as a percentage of total revenue. Total revenue jumped 28.8% to $2.33 billion from $1.81 billion the year before. Health premium revenues improved 29.8% to $2.26 billion from $1.74 billion, while fee and other revenues grew 5.5% to $22.4 million from $21.2 million the prior year. Home health services revenues fell 3.3% to $22.0 million from $22.7 million, while life and short-term disability revenues increased 12.6% to $9.1 million from $8.1 million in 2001.

PROSPECTS:

The recent improvement in operating performance is being supported by product diversity, improved customer service and disciplined pricing. Meanwhile, the Company believes it can meet its goals in fiscal 2003 by continuing to pursue strategic, profitable growth in the mid-Atlantic region. Moreover, the Company expects full-year 2003 earnings to range from $2.32 to $2.38 per share.

ANNUAL FINANCIAL DATA:

FISCAL YEAR	TOT. REVS. ($mill.)	NET INC. ($mill.)	TOT. ASSETS ($mill.)	OPER. PROFIT %	NET PROFIT %	RET. ON EQUITY %	RET. ON ASSETS %	CURR. RATIO	EARN. PER SH.$	CASH FL. PER SH.$	TANG. BK. VAL.$	PRICE RANGE	AVG. P/E RATIO
p12/31/02	2,328.0	97.4							2.34			43.20 - 22.30	14.0
12/31/01	1,807.7	57.2	594.2	4.7	3.2	20.3	9.6	1.6	1.41	1.68	5.88	23.18 - 14.69	13.4
12/31/00	1,484.5	③ 39.4	467.0	3.8	2.7	17.4	8.4	1.6	③ 1.00	1.26	4.65	21.88 - 7.50	14.7
12/31/99	1,317.3	26.3	388.6	3.0	2.0	14.1	6.8	1.6	0.64	0.89	3.78	13.13 - 5.13	14.3
12/31/98	1,187.9	② 9.0	362.8	1.0	0.8	4.7	2.5	1.7	② 0.20	0.44	3.85	14.00 - 4.44	46.1
12/31/97	1,111.7	14.5	342.8	1.9	1.3	7.0	4.2	2.0	0.31	0.53	3.81	17.06 - 10.00	43.6
12/31/96	1,133.7	d2.8	334.7	...	...	...	...	1.8	d0.06	0.11	3.37	24.88 - 9.75	...
12/31/95	955.4	61.1	354.2	10.1	6.4	28.1	17.3	2.1	1.28	1.40	4.66	26.13 - 16.50	16.6
12/31/94	749.9	54.5	268.5	11.5	7.3	38.6	20.3	1.8	1.15	1.24	3.10	30.25 - 12.06	18.4
12/31/93	646.8	① 25.5	189.6	6.2	3.9	35.4	13.5	1.4	① 0.57	0.65	1.63	14.00 - 4.25	16.1

Statistics are as originally reported. Adj. for 100% stk. split, 8/94 and 3-for-2, 11/93. ① Bef. an acctg. adj. chrg. of $663,000 ($0.03/sh.) ② Incl. nonrecurr. chgs. of $10.9 mill. ③ Incl. one-time tax adj. of $1.3 mill.

OFFICERS: M. D. Groban, Chmn. T. P. Barbera, Vice-Chmn., Pres., C.E.O. R. E. Foss, Sr. Exec. V.P., C.F.O. **INVESTOR CONTACT:** Deborah V. Robinson, Investor Relation, (301) 545-5256 **PRINCIPAL OFFICE:** 4 Taft Court, Rockville, MD 20850	**TELEPHONE NUMBER:** (301) 294-5140 **FAX:** (301) 762-0658 **WEB:** www.mamsi.com **NO. OF EMPLOYEES:** 2,801 full-time; 347 part-time **SHAREHOLDERS:** 665 (approx.) **ANNUAL MEETING:** In Apr. **INCORPORATED:** DE, Oct., 1986	**INSTITUTIONAL HOLDINGS:** No. of Institutions: 218 Shares Held: 31,306,669 % Held: 65.4 **INDUSTRY:** Hospital and medical service plans (SIC: 6324) **TRANSFER AGENT(S):** Bank of New York, New York, NY

MILACRON, INC.

EXCH.	SYM.	REC. PRICE	P/E RATIO	YLD.	MKT. CAP.	RANGE (52-WK.)	'02 Y/E PR.
NYSE	MZ	4.70 (2/28/03)	…	0.9%	$157.3 mill.	15.29 - 3.10	5.95

SPECULATIVE GRADE. THE COMPANY PLANS TO FOCUS ON COST REDUCTIONS, EFFICIENCY IMPROVEMENTS AND BETTER MANAGEMENT OF WORKING CAPITAL.

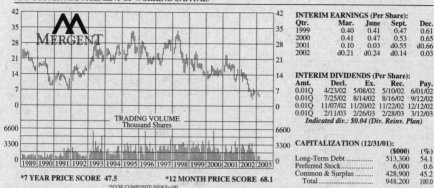

*7 YEAR PRICE SCORE 47.5   *12 MONTH PRICE SCORE 68.1
*NYSE COMPOSITE INDEX=100

INTERIM EARNINGS (Per Share):

Qtr.	Mar.	June	Sept.	Dec.
1999	0.40	0.41	0.47	0.61
2000	0.41	0.47	0.53	0.65
2001	0.10	0.03	d0.55	d0.66
2002	d0.21	d0.24	d0.14	0.03

INTERIM DIVIDENDS (Per Share):

Amt.	Decl.	Ex.	Rec.	Pay.
0.01Q	4/23/02	5/08/02	5/10/02	6/01/02
0.01Q	7/25/02	8/14/02	8/16/02	9/12/02
0.01Q	11/07/02	11/20/02	11/22/02	12/12/02
0.01Q	2/11/03	2/26/03	2/28/03	3/12/03

Indicated div.: $0.04 (Div. Reinv. Plan)

CAPITALIZATION (12/31/01):

	($000)	(%)
Long-Term Debt	513,300	54.1
Preferred Stock	6,000	0.6
Common & Surplus	428,900	45.2
Total	948,200	100.0

BUSINESS:

Milacron, Inc. (formerly Cincinnati Milacron) is engaged in plastics technologies and industrial fluids. MZ has major manufacturing facilities in North America, Europe and Asia. Milacron's plastics technologies segment includes injection molding machines, blow molding equipment, extrusion systems and wear items, mold bases, mold-making equipment and mold components, as well as aftermarket and maintenance, repair and operating parts and services. MZ sold its machine tools segment on 10/2/98 for $187.0 million. On 12/31/99, MZ sold its European plastics extrusion systems business for $47.0 million. On 8/9/02, MZ sold its North American metalcutting tool business for $175.0 million. On 8/30/02, MZ sold its overseas metalcutting tool business for $184.0 million.

RECENT DEVELOPMENTS:

For the year ended 12/31/02, MZ reported a loss of $18.4 million, before an accounting change charge of $187.7 million and a loss of $16.8 million from discontinued operations, versus a loss of $28.7 million, before a loss of $7.0 million from discontinued operations, in 2002. Results for 2002 and 2001 included pre-tax restructuring charges of $12.0 million and $14.4 million, respectively. Sales declined 8.2% to $693.2 million. Plastic technologies segment sales fell 9.2% to $597.2 million, while sales from the industrial fluids segment rose 3.4% to $96.0 million.

PROSPECTS:

The Company remains committed to achieving further gains in operating results in 2003. The Company will so by focusing on areas it can control, namely cost reductions, efficiency improvements and better working capital management, to compensate for factors beyond its control, such as the economy, increased insurance costs and a decline in pension income. Given the seasonality of MZ's business, it is likely to record modest losses in the first half of 2003 to be offset by comparable or greater earnings in the second half of the year.

ANNUAL FINANCIAL DATA:

FISCAL YEAR	TOT. REVS. ($mill.)	NET INC. ($mill.)	TOT. ASSETS ($mill.)	OPER. PROFIT %	NET PROFIT %	RET. ON EQUITY %	RET. ON ASSETS %	CURR. RATIO	EARN. PER SH.$	CASH FL. PER SH.$	TANG. BK. VAL.$	DIV. PER SH.$	PRICE RANGE	AVG. P/E RATIO	AVG. YIELD %
p12/31/02	693.2	⑨ d18.4							⑨ d0.56			0.04	16.60 - 3.10	…	0.4
12/31/01	1,262.7	⑧ d35.7	1,512.3	…	…	…	…	1.9	⑧ d1.08	…	1.88	0.37	22.94 - 10.82	…	2.2
12/31/00	1,584.2	⑦ 72.3	1,464.9	8.8	4.6	14.9	4.9	1.6	⑦ 2.06	3.73	1.94	0.48	18.25 - 12.06	7.4	3.2
12/31/99	1,624.7	⑥ 70.1	1,536.7	8.4	4.3	14.3	4.6	1.3	⑥ 1.89	3.47	1.77	0.48	24.50 - 13.50	10.1	2.5
⑤ 12/31/98	1,514.7	④ 75.4	1,557.1	9.1	5.0	15.8	4.8	1.3	④ 1.91	3.38	1.93	0.48	33.75 - 14.63	12.7	2.0
12/27/97	1,896.7	80.6	1,392.5	6.7	4.2	17.1	5.8	1.8	2.01	3.36	5.93	0.42	29.88 - 17.88	11.9	1.8
12/28/96	1,729.7	66.3	1,336.3	6.4	3.8	14.9	5.0	1.8	1.73	3.13	5.28	0.36	29.25 - 18.38	13.8	1.5
12/31/95	1,649.3	③ 105.6	1,197.1	9.6	6.4	39.0	8.8	2.0	③ 3.04	4.39	7.2	0.36	33.63 - 19.88	8.8	1.3
12/31/94	1,197.1	37.7	787.6	5.4	3.1	23.9	4.8	1.4	1.10	1.97	4.50	0.36	27.63 - 18.63	21.0	1.6
1/01/94	1,029.4	② d45.4	729.6	…	…	…	…	1.3	② d1.41	d0.60	3.53	0.36	29.63 - 16.25	…	1.6
1/02/93	578.9	① 16.1	578.9	5.5	2.0	12.0	2.8	1.8	① 0.58	1.34	4.67	0.36	18.25 - 10.88	25.1	2.5

Statistics are as originally reported. ① Bef. extraord. chrg. $4.0 mill. and Bef. extraord. credit $5.4 mill ($0.19/sh.) ② Bef. acctg. chrg. $52.1 mill. ($1.72/sh.); Bef. extraord. chrg. $4.4 mill. ($0.14/sh.); Incl. non-recurr chrg. $61.8 mill. ③ Incl. non-recurr. credit $56.4 mill. ($1.63/sh.) and Incl. non-recurr. chrg. $7.8 mill. ($0.23/sh.) ④ Bef. disc. opers. loss of $33.9 mill. ⑤ Reflects the sale of the Company's machine tools business. ⑥ Incl. net. non-recurr. chrg. $3.1 mill. ⑦ Incl. after-tax restruct. chrg. of $1.9 mill. and a gain on divest. of bus. of $800,000. ⑧ Incl. after-tax restruct. chrg. of $19.1 mill. ⑨ Bef. loss from disc. ops. of $16.8 mill. & acctg. chng. chrg. of $187.7 mill., incl. after-tax restruct. chrg. of $8.8 mill.

OFFICERS:
R. D. Brown, Chmn., C.E.O.
H. J. Faig, Pres., C.O.O.
R. P. Lienesch, V.P., C.F.O.

INVESTOR CONTACT: Al Beaupre, Investor Relations, (513) 487-5918

PRINCIPAL OFFICE: 2090 Florence Avenue, Cincinnati, OH 45206

TELEPHONE NUMBER: (513) 487-5000
FAX: (513) 841-8991
WEB: www.milacron.com

NO. OF EMPLOYEES: 4,000
SHAREHOLDERS: 4,495 (approx.)
ANNUAL MEETING: In Apr.
INCORPORATED: DE, Apr., 1983

INSTITUTIONAL HOLDINGS:
No. of Institutions: 96
Shares Held: 23,867,432
% Held: 70.7

INDUSTRY: Machine tools, metal cutting types (SIC: 3541)

TRANSFER AGENT(S): Mellon Investor Services, Ridgefield, NJ

MILLENNIUM CHEMICALS INC.

EXCH.	SYM.	REC. PRICE	P/E RATIO	YLD.	MKT. CAP.	RANGE (52-WK.)	'02 Y/E PR.
NYSE	MCH	10.91 (2/28/03)	34.1	4.9%	$0.69 bill.	15.80 - 7.79	9.52

LOWER MEDIUM GRADE. THE COMPANY EXPECTS SEQUENTIAL INCREASES IN SALES VOLUMES FOR ITS CORE TITANITUM DIOXIDE, ACETYLS, AND SPECIALTY CHEMICALS BUSINESSES.

7 YEAR PRICE SCORE N/A *12 MONTH PRICE SCORE 93.3*
NYSE COMPOSITE INDEX=100

INTERIM EARNINGS (Per Share):

Qtr.	Mar.	June	Sept.	Dec.
1997	0.26	1.07	0.87	0.21
1998	0.66	0.57	0.42	0.52
1999	0.12	0.68	0.67	d5.86
2000	0.37	0.74	0.55	0.22
2001	d0.24	d0.37	d0.20	0.13
2002	d0.49	0.01	0.10	0.70

INTERIM DIVIDENDS (Per Share):

Amt.	Decl.	Ex.	Rec.	Pay.
0.135Q	1/31/02	3/11/02	3/13/02	3/29/02
0.135Q	5/02/02	6/10/02	6/12/02	6/30/02
0.135Q	7/31/02	9/10/02	9/12/02	9/30/02
0.135Q	10/30/02	12/06/02	12/10/02	12/31/02
0.135Q	1/30/03	3/10/03	3/12/03	3/31/03

Indicated div.: $0.54

CAPITALIZATION (12/31/01):

	($000)	(%)
Long-Term Debt	1,172,000	57.2
Common & Surplus	878,000	42.8
Total	2,050,000	100.0

BUSINESS:

Millennium Chemicals Inc. is an international chemicals concern with market positions in a broad range of commodity, industrial, performance and specialty chemicals. The Company conducts business through its operating subsidiaries: Millennium Inorganic Chemicals Inc., the second largest producer of titanium dioxide (TiO2) in the world; Millennium Specialty Chemicals Inc., a major producer of terpene-based fragrance and flavor chemicals; and Millennium Petrochemicals Inc., the second largest manufacturer of acetic acid and vinyl acetate monomer in North America. As of 1/30/03, MCH also owned a 29.5% interest in Equistar Chemicals L.P., a producer of ethylene and polyethylene, and an 85.0% interest in La Porte Methanol Company, L.P., a limited partnership. Revenues for 2002 were derived: titanium dioxide, 72.7%; acetyls, 21.5%; and specialty chemicals, 5.8%.

RECENT DEVELOPMENTS:

For the year ended 12/31/02, income amounted to $21.0 million, before an accounting change charge of $305.0 million, compared with a net loss of $47.0 million in 2001. Results for 2001 included reorganization and plant closure charges of $36.0 million. Net sales were $1.55 billion, down 2.3% from $1.59 billion in the prior year. Operating income increased 24.0% to $93.0 million compared with $75.0 million the year before, due to cost reduction and containment programs.

PROSPECTS:

Titanium dioxide sales volume in the first quarter of 2003 is anticipated to be comparable to the fourth quarter of 2002, approximately 142,000 metric tons, which is in line with seasonal demand trends. In addition, recent price increases are expected to result in improved average pricing and profitability. Also, first quarter results for the acetyls segment is expected to be similar to results in the fourth quarter, assuming higher natural gas and ethylene costs are offset by favorable pricing. Meanwhile, first quarter results for the specialty chemicals segment are expected to improve from the fourth quarter of 2002 due to an anticipated increase in sales volumes.

ANNUAL FINANCIAL DATA:

FISCAL YEAR	TOT. REVS. ($mill.)	NET INC. ($mill.)	TOT. ASSETS ($mill.)	OPER. PROFIT %	NET PROFIT %	RET. ON EQUITY %	RET. ON ASSETS %	CURR. RATIO	EARN. PER SH.$	CASH FL. PER SH.$	TANG. BK. VAL.$	DIV. PER SH.$	PRICE RANGE	AVG. P/E RATIO	AVG. YIELD %
p12/31/02	1,554.0	⑧ 21.0							⑧ 0.33			0.54	15.80 - 7.79	35.7	4.6
12/31/01	1,590.0	⑦ d43.0	3,004.0	2.9	...	...	...	2.0	⑦ d0.68	1.07	7.90	0.58	19.00 - 9.00		4.2
12/31/00	1,793.0	122.0	3,220.0	11.9	6.8	12.4	3.8	1.2	1.89	3.55	9.23	0.60	22.88 - 12.69	9.4	3.4
12/31/99	1,589.0	⑥ d326.0	3,250.0	10.6	...	...	...	1.7	⑥ d4.71	d3.08	8.95	0.60	28.38 - 16.56	...	2.7
⑤ 12/31/98	1,597.0	④ 163.0	4,100.0	12.8	10.2	10.3	4.0	2.5	④ 2.17	3.57	14.95	0.60	37.13 - 18.25	12.8	2.2
12/31/97	3,048.0	③ 185.0	4,326.0	14.7	6.1	12.6	4.3	1.8	③ 2.47	5.48	12.94	0.60	24.50 - 16.63	8.3	2.9
12/31/96	3,040.0	② 141.0	5,601.0	9.3	4.6	10.7	2.5	1.9	② 1.84	4.62	...	...	26.38 - 17.25	11.9	...
12/31/95	3,800.0	331.0	10,043.0	22.2	8.7	6.9	3.3	6.2	5.10	7.63	36.30	...	...	...	...
① 12/31/94	908.0	84.0	10,024.0	22.4	9.3	1.7	0.8	1.9	...	...	...	...	...	...	...
9/30/94	3,288.0	66.0	...	10.5	2.0	...	...	...	...	...	...	...	...	...	...

Statistics are as originally reported. ① For 3 mos. due to fiscal year-end change. ② Excl. loss fr. disc. opers. of $2.84 billion ($37.17 per share). ③ Incl. $37.0 mill. after-tax chg. rel. to formation of Equistar. ④ Incl. $10.0 mill. after-tax chg. fr. ins. settlements, $42.0 mill. tax benefit fr. prev. yrs. & $3.0 mill. chg. for MCH's sh. of Equistar's transition costs. ⑤ Results reflected MCH's decision to reduce prod. of TiO2 due to low demand. ⑥ Incl. $400.0 mill. net chg. fr. loss in value of Equistar investment & excl. $38.0 mill. net gain fr. disc. ops. ⑦ Incl. $36.0 mill. reorg. & plant closing chgs. ⑧ Excl. $305.0 mill. acctg. chg.

OFFICERS:
W. M. Landuyt, Chmn., Pres., C.E.O.
J. E. Lushefski, Sr. V.P., C.F.O.
C. W. Carmean, Sr. V.P., Sec., Gen. Couns.
INVESTOR CONTACT: A. Mickey Foster, V.P., Investor Relations, (732) 933-5140
PRINCIPAL OFFICE: 230 Half Mile Road, Red Bank, NJ 07701

TELEPHONE NUMBER: (732) 933-5000
FAX: (732) 933-5240
WEB: www.millenniumchem.com
NO. OF EMPLOYEES: 3,875 (approx.)
SHAREHOLDERS: 19,351
ANNUAL MEETING: In May
INCORPORATED: DE, Apr., 1996

INSTITUTIONAL HOLDINGS:
No. of Institutions: 115
Shares Held: 53,544,038
% Held: 84.9
INDUSTRY: Plastics materials and resins (SIC: 2821)
TRANSFER AGENT(S): First Chicago Trust Company of New York, Jersey City, NJ

MINERALS TECHNOLOGIES INC.

EXCH.	SYM.	REC. PRICE	P/E RATIO	YLD.	MKT. CAP.	RANGE (52-WK.)	'02 Y/E PR.
NYSE	MTX	38.07 (2/28/03)	14.5	0.3%	$0.75 bill.	54.90 - 32.00	43.15

UPPER MEDIUM GRADE. THE COMPANY CONTINUES TO ENJOY SOLID GROWTH IN SALES.

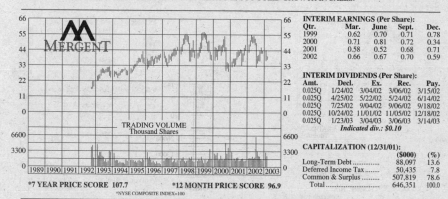

*7 YEAR PRICE SCORE 107.7   ***12 MONTH PRICE SCORE 96.9**
NYSE COMPOSITE INDEX=100

INTERIM EARNINGS (Per Share):

Qtr.	Mar.	June	Sept.	Dec.
1999	0.62	0.70	0.71	0.78
2000	0.71	0.81	0.72	0.34
2001	0.58	0.52	0.68	0.71
2002	0.66	0.67	0.70	0.59

INTERIM DIVIDENDS (Per Share):

Amt.	Decl.	Ex.	Rec.	Pay.
0.025Q	1/24/02	3/04/02	3/06/02	3/15/02
0.025Q	4/25/02	5/22/02	5/24/02	6/14/02
0.025Q	7/25/02	9/04/02	9/06/02	9/18/02
0.025Q	10/24/02	11/01/02	11/05/02	12/18/02
0.025Q	1/23/03	3/04/03	3/06/03	3/14/03

Indicated div.: $0.10

CAPITALIZATION (12/31/01):

	($000)	(%)
Long-Term Debt	88,097	13.6
Deferred Income Tax	50,435	7.8
Common & Surplus	507,819	78.6
Total	646,351	100.0

BUSINESS:

Minerals Technologies Inc. is a resource- and technology-based corporation that develops, produces and markets worldwide a range of specialty mineral, mineral-based and synthetic mineral products. MTX has two operating segments. The Specialty Materials segment (69.1% of net sales in 2002) produces and sells the synthetic mineral product precipitated calcium carbonate (PCC) and the processed mineral product quicklime, and mines, processes and sells the natural mineral products limestone and talc. Specialty materials products are used in the paper, building materials, paint and coatings, glass, ceramic, polymer, food and pharmaceutical industries. The Refractories segment (30.9%) produces and markets monolithic and shaped refractory materials and specialty products and services used primarily by the steel, cement and glass industries.

RECENT DEVELOPMENTS:

For the year ended 12/31/02, net income advanced 8.0% to $53.8 million compared with $49.8 million in 2001. Results for 2002 included a writedown of impaired assets of $750,000. Results for 2001 included goodwill amortization of $1.3 million and a restructuring charge of $3.9 million. Net sales climbed 10.0% to $752.7 million from $684.4 million a year earlier. Specialty Minerals segment sales increased 7.6% to $520.1 million, primarily due to an 8.0% increase in PCC volumes to 3.4 million tons. Refractories segment sales jumped 15.7% to $232.6 million, primarily due to the 2001 acquisitions of the Martin Maretta refractories business and Rijnstaal. B.V.

PROSPECTS:

Despite economic uncertainty, MTX continues to enjoy solid growth in sales. However, recent profitability is being adversely affected by a number of factors including the bankruptcy filing of one of MTX's paper company customers. On 1/10/03, Great Northern Paper Inc. filed a petition for bankruptcy protection. MTX owns and operates a satellite PCC plant that supplies filler grade PCC to Great Northern's two paper mills in Millinocket and East Millinocket, Maine. As a precaution, MTX increased its bad debt reserve by approximately $3.0 million, and will continue to evaluate the prospects for its Millinocket plant.

ANNUAL FINANCIAL DATA:

FISCAL YEAR	TOT. REVS. ($000)	NET INC. ($000)	TOT. ASSETS ($000)	OPER. PROFIT %	NET PROFIT %	RET. ON EQUITY %	RET. ON ASSETS %	CURR. RATIO	EARN. PER SH.$	CASH FL. PER SH.$	TANG. BK. VAL.$	DIV. PER SH.$	PRICE RANGE	AVG. P/E RATIO	AVG. YIELD %
p12/31/02	752,680	③ 53,752							③ 2.61			0.10	54.90 - 32.00	16.6	0.2
12/31/01	684,419	② 49,793	847,810	11.8	7.3	9.8	5.9	1.5	② 2.48	5.80	25.89	0.10	48.00 - 32.00	16.1	0.3
12/31/00	670,917	① 54,208	799,832	12.6	8.1	11.2	6.8	1.6	① 2.58	5.48	24.22	0.10	54.06 - 28.94	16.1	0.2
12/31/99	637,519	62,116	769,131	15.3	9.7	11.6	8.1	1.9	2.80	5.45	20.85	0.11	57.00 - 36.75	16.7	0.2
12/31/98	609,193	57,224	760,912	15.2	9.4	11.7	7.5	2.2	2.50	4.81	22.42	0.10	55.56 - 35.88	18.3	0.2
12/31/97	602,335	50,312	741,407	13.3	8.4	10.8	6.8	2.4	2.18	4.47	20.72	0.10	46.13 - 32.13	17.9	0.3
12/31/96	555,988	43,097	713,861	12.1	7.8	9.6	6.0	2.3	1.91	3.95	19.83	0.10	41.38 - 30.25	18.7	0.3
12/31/95	524,451	39,529	649,144	11.2	7.5	9.5	6.1	1.9	1.75	3.53	18.37	0.10	43.25 - 27.25	20.1	0.3
12/31/94	472,637	33,346	588,124	11.1	7.1	8.7	5.7	3.2	1.48	3.06	16.86	0.10	31.38 - 24.00	18.7	0.4
12/31/93	428,313	28,973	549,160	10.8	6.8	8.4	5.3	2.7	1.25	2.69	15.19	0.10	32.00 - 22.00	21.6	0.4

Statistics are as originally reported. ① Incl. special chrgs. totaling $10.5 mill. ② Incl. restr. chrg. $3.4 mill. ③ Incl. write-down of impair. assets $750,000.

OFFICERS:
P. R. Saueracker, Chmn., Pres., C.E.O.
J. A. Sorel, Sr. V.P., C.F.O., Treas.
S. G. Gray, V.P., Gen. Couns., Sec.
INVESTOR CONTACT: Rick B. Honey, V.P., Inv. Rel. & Corp. Comm., (212) 878-1831
PRINCIPAL OFFICE: The Chrysler Bldg., 405 Lexington Ave., New York, NY 10174-1901

TELEPHONE NUMBER: (212) 878-1800
FAX: (212) 878-1801
WEB: www.mineralstech.com
NO. OF EMPLOYEES: 2,305 (approx.)
SHAREHOLDERS: 225 (approx.)
ANNUAL MEETING: In May
INCORPORATED: DE, Feb., 1968

INSTITUTIONAL HOLDINGS:
No. of Institutions: 141
Shares Held: 20,691,812
% Held: 102.7
INDUSTRY: Industrial organic chemicals, nec (SIC: 2869)
TRANSFER AGENT(S): EquiServe Trust Company, Providence, RI

MIRANT CORP.

EXCH.	SYM.	REC. PRICE	P/E RATIO	YLD.	MKT. CAP.	RANGE (52-WK.)	'02 Y/E PR.
NYSE	MIR	1.35 (2/28/03)	...	...	$0.54 bill.	15.05 - 1.06	1.87

SPECULATIVE GRADE. THE COMPANY EXPECTS EARNINGS PER SHARE FOR FULL-YEAR 2002 TO RANGE BETWEEN $1.00 TO $1.05.

*7 YEAR PRICE SCORE N/A   *12 MONTH PRICE SCORE 39.8
*NYSE COMPOSITE INDEX=100

INTERIM EARNINGS (Per Share):

Qtr.	Mar.	June	Sept.	Dec.
1999	0.29	0.26	0.57	0.25
2000	0.37	0.34	0.36	0.23
2001	0.51	0.36	0.67	0.09
2002	d0.09	d0.38	Nil	...

INTERIM DIVIDENDS (Per Share):

Amt.	Decl.	Ex.	Rec.	Pay.
	No dividends paid.			

CAPITALIZATION (12/31/01):

	($000)	(%)
Long-Term Debt	2,073,000	25.0
Deferred Income Tax	109,000	1.3
Minority Interest	282,000	3.4
Redeemable Pfd. Stock	345,000	4.2
Common & Surplus	5,498,000	66.2
Total	8,307,001	100.0

BUSINESS:

Mirant Corp. develops, constructs, owns and operates power plants, and sells wholesale electricity, gas and other energy-related commodity products. The Company has operations in North America, Europe and Asia. The Company owns or controls more than 22,000 megawatts of electric generating capacity around the world, with approximately another 6,800 megawatts under development.

Southern Company sold 19.7% of MIR's stock through an initial public offering in September 2000, and spun off the remaining 80.3% to Southern shareholders on 4/2/01. On 8/10/00, the Company acquired Vastar Resources, Inc.'s 40.0% interest in Mirant Americas Energy Marketing for $250.0 million.

RECENT DEVELOPMENTS:

For the three months ended 9/30/02, the Company reported a loss from continuing operations of $3.0 million compared with income of $230.0 million in the same period of 2001. Results for 2002 and 2001 included impairment losses of $204.0 million and $3.0 million, and a gain of $1.0 million and a loss of $1.0 million from the sale of assets, respectively. Results for 2002 also included a restructuring charge

of $8.0 million and an impairment loss of $18.0 million on minority-owned affiliates. Results for 2002 and 2001 excluded income of $2.0 million and $4.0 million, respectively, from discontinued operations. Operating revenues slipped 9.1% to $2.26 billion from $2.48 billion in the prior-year period. Operating income was $156.0 million versus $448.0 million a year earlier.

PROSPECTS:

The Company lowered its guidance for 2002 due to continued adverse market conditions in North America, a decrease in MIR's gas operations to lower collateral requirements, and a higher effective tax rate on earnings of its businesses in Asia. As a result, the Company expects

earnings per share for full-year 2002 to range between $1.00 to $1.05. Separately, on 12/31/02, the Company completed the sale of its 33.0% economic interest in the Shajiao C power plant in China to China Resources Power Holding Co. Ltd. for $300.0 million.

ANNUAL FINANCIAL DATA:

FISCAL YEAR	TOT. REVS. ($mill.)	NET INC. ($mill.)	TOT. ASSETS ($mill.)	OPER. PROFIT %	NET PROFIT %	RET. ON EQUITY %	RET. ON ASSETS %	CURR. RATIO	EARN. PER SH.$	CASH FL. PER SH.$	TANG. BK. VAL.$	PRICE RANGE	AVG. P/E RATIO
12/31/01	④ 31,537.0	③ 563.0	22,754.0	3.2	1.8	10.2	2.5	0.8	③ 1.62	2.77	3.45	47.20 - 13.16	18.6
② 12/31/00	13,315.0	① 332.0	24,136.0	5.0	2.5	8.0	1.4	0.9	① 1.15	2.30	0.31	...	...
12/31/99	2,268.0	① 362.0	13,863.0	19.6	16.0	11.7	2.6	0.4	① 1.33	...	...	...	...
12/31/98	1,819.0	① d12.0	12,054.0	...	...	...	...	0.5	① d0.04	...	...	...	...
12/31/97	3,750.0	① d24.0	5,812.0	7.3	...	...	...	0.5	① d0.09	...	...	...	...

Statistics are as originally reported. ① Bef. discont. oper., 2000, $27.0 mill.; 1999, $10.0 mill.; 1998, $12.0 mill.; 1997, $8.0 mill. ② Incls. the acq. of Vastar's 40% int. in Mirant Americas Energy Marketing. ③ Incl. $94.0 mill. impairment loss & excl. $5.0 mill. income fr. disc. ops. ④ Revs. benefited fr. MIR's business plan & strategic acqs.

OFFICERS:
A. W. Dahlberg, Chmn.
S. M. Fuller, Pres., C.E.O.
H. A. Wagner, Exec. V.P., C.F.O.

INVESTOR CONTACT: Hank Pennington, Investor Relations, (678) 579-7592

PRINCIPAL OFFICE: 1155 Perimeter Center West, Suite 100, Atlanta, GA 30338-5416

TELEPHONE NUMBER: (678) 579-5000
FAX: (678) 579-5001
WEB: www.mirant.com

NO. OF EMPLOYEES: 10,000 (approx.)

SHAREHOLDERS: 64 (approx.)

ANNUAL MEETING: In Apr.

INCORPORATED: DE, Apr., 1993

INSTITUTIONAL HOLDINGS:
No. of Institutions: 305
Shares Held: 187,587,724
% Held: 46.6

INDUSTRY: Electric and other services combined (SIC: 4931)

TRANSFER AGENT(S): Mellon Investor Services, Ridgefield Park, NJ

MOHAWK INDUSTRIES, INC.

EXCH.	SYM.	REC. PRICE	P/E RATIO	YLD.	MKT. CAP.	RANGE (52-WK.)	'02 Y/E PR.
NYSE	MHK	49.38 (2/28/03)	11.4	...	$2.60 bill.	70.60 - 40.25	56.95

INVESTMENT GRADE. THE COMPANY'S INTEGRATION OF DAL-TILE, WHICH WAS ACQUIRED ON 3/20/02, IS PROGRESSING ACCORDING TO PLAN.

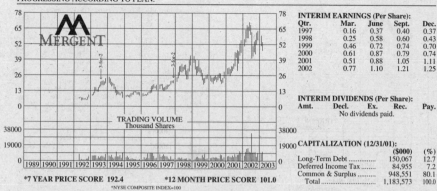

*7 YEAR PRICE SCORE 192.4   *12 MONTH PRICE SCORE 101.0
*NYSE COMPOSITE INDEX=100

INTERIM EARNINGS (Per Share):

Qtr.	Mar.	June	Sept.	Dec.
1997	0.16	0.37	0.40	0.37
1998	0.25	0.58	0.60	0.43
1999	0.46	0.72	0.74	0.70
2000	0.61	0.87	0.79	0.74
2001	0.51	0.88	1.05	1.11
2002	0.77	1.10	1.21	1.25

INTERIM DIVIDENDS (Per Share):

Amt.	Decl.	Ex.	Rec.	Pay.
		No dividends paid.		

CAPITALIZATION (12/31/01):

	($000)	(%)
Long-Term Debt	150,067	12.7
Deferred Income Tax	84,955	7.2
Common & Surplus	948,551	80.1
Total	1,183,573	100.0

BUSINESS:

Mohawk Industries, Inc. and its primary operating subsidiaries, Mohawk Carpet Corporation, Aladdin Manufacturing Corporation and Dal-Tile International Inc., produce flooring products for residential and commercial applications in the United States. The Company produces woven and tufted broadloom carpet, rugs and ceramic tile. MHK distributes brand names such as MOHAWK, ALADDIN, BIGELOW COMMERCIAL, CUSTOM WEAVE, DURKAN, GALAXY, HELIOS, HORIZON, KARASTAN, MOHAWK COMMERCIAL, WORLD, and WUNDAWEVE. MHK offers a broad line of home products including rugs, throws, pillows and bedspreads under the brand names ALADDIN, GOODWIN WEAVERS, KARASTAN, MOHAWK HOME and NEWMARK. The Company manufactures and distributes ceramic tile and natural stone products under the brand names DAL-TILE, MOHAWK and AMERICAN OLEAN. The Company also offers products including laminate, wood and vinyl flooring and carpet padding under the MOHAWK brand name. The Company markets its products primarily through retailers and dealers.

RECENT DEVELOPMENTS:

For the year ended 12/31/02, net income grew 50.8% to $284.5 million compared with $188.6 million in 2001. The improvement in earnings was attributed to the Dal-Tile merger, internal growth of Mohawk products, and manufacturing cost improvements. Net sales climbed 31.2% to $4.52 billion from $3.45 billion a year earlier. Operating income advanced 58.7% to $519.1 million.

PROSPECTS:

The Company's integration of Dal-Tile, which was acquired on 3/20/02, is progressing according to plan. Meanwhile, the Dal-Tile segment continues to expand its market share as it broadens its customer base and increases its product offering. As of 12/31/02, about 30.0% of MHK's total sales were derived from hard surface products. As a result, the Company plans to increase its market share of ceramic tile, wood, laminate and vinyl floorcovering products. The Company believes there is pent up demand as consumers defer purchases due to the slowdown in the economy and tensions in the Middle East.

ANNUAL FINANCIAL DATA:

FISCAL YEAR	TOT. REVS. ($mill.)	NET INC. ($mill.)	TOT. ASSETS ($mill.)	OPER. PROFIT %	NET PROFIT %	RET. ON EQUITY %	RET. ON ASSETS %	CURR. RATIO	EARN. PER SH. $	CASH FL. PER SH. $	TANG. BK. VAL. $	PRICE RANGE	AVG. P/E RATIO
p12/31/02	4,522.3	284.5	3,596.7						4.39			70.60 - 41.90	12.8
12/31/01	3,445.9	188.6	1,768.5	9.5	5.5	19.9	10.7	1.8	3.55	5.13	15.93	55.55 - 25.50	11.4
12/31/00	3,255.8	162.6	1,792.6	9.5	5.0	21.6	9.1	1.7	3.00	4.51	14.42	29.13 - 18.94	8.0
12/31/99	3,083.3	157.2	1,682.9	9.6	5.1	22.7	9.3	2.5	2.61	4.35	12.21	42.00 - 18.38	11.6
12/31/98	2,639.2	② 107.6	1,331.4	8.8	4.1	18.3	8.1	2.1	② 1.86	3.03	10.22	42.44 - 20.50	16.9
12/31/97	1,901.4	68.0	961.0	7.4	3.6	16.8	7.1	2.2	1.30	2.43	7.78	21.75 - 12.92	13.3
12/31/96	1,795.1	① 49.1	955.8	6.7	2.7	14.7	5.1	2.3	① 0.95	2.01	5.41	18.58 - 8.33	14.2
12/31/95	1,648.5	① 6.4	903.2	2.9	0.4	2.3	0.7	1.9	① 0.13	1.19	4.43	12.83 - 7.25	79.0
12/31/94	1,437.5	② 33.0	854.8	6.8	2.3	12.5	3.9	2.8	② 0.66	1.65	5.42	24.33 - 7.17	23.9
12/31/93	734.0	22.7	561.3	6.7	3.1	14.2	4.0	2.2	0.77	1.56	5.64	23.17 - 8.78	20.7

Statistics are as originally reported. Adj. for 3-for-2 stk. spl., 12/97 & 8/93 ① Incl. restruct. costs, 1996, $700,000; 1995, $8.4 mill. ② Incl. acq. costs, 1998, $17.7 mill.; 1994, $10.2 mill.

OFFICERS:
D. L. Kolb, Chmn.
J. S. Lorberbaum, Pres., C.E.O.
J. D. Swift, V.P., C.F.O., Asst. Sec.
INVESTOR CONTACT: John D. Swift, V.P., C.F.O., Asst. Sec., (706) 624-2247
PRINCIPAL OFFICE: P.O. Box 12069, 160 S. Industrial Blvd., Calhoun, GA 30701

TELEPHONE NUMBER: (706) 629-7721
FAX: (706) 625-3851
WEB: www.mohawkind.com
NO. OF EMPLOYEES: 31,350 (approx.)
SHAREHOLDERS: 360 (record, approx.)
ANNUAL MEETING: In May
INCORPORATED: DE, Dec., 1988

INSTITUTIONAL HOLDINGS:
No. of Institutions: 245
Shares Held: 56,101,768
% Held: 84.6

INDUSTRY: Carpets and rugs (SIC: 2273)

TRANSFER AGENT(S): First Union National Bank, Charlotte, NC

MONACO COACH CORPORATION

EXCH.	SYM.	REC. PRICE	P/E RATIO	YLD.	MKT. CAP.	RANGE (52-WK.)	'02 Y/E PR.
NYSE	MNC	11.12 (2/28/03)	7.4	...	$318.4 mill.	30.70 - 10.60	16.55

UPPER MEDIUM GRADE. THE COMPANY EXPECTS FULL-YEAR 2003 REVENUE GROWTH OF 8.0% TO 12.0%.

*7 YEAR PRICE SCORE 179.2   ***12 MONTH PRICE SCORE 71.4**
NYSE COMPOSITE INDEX=100

INTERIM EARNINGS (Per Share):

Qtr.	Mar.	June	Sept.	Dec.
1998	0.15	0.16	0.22	0.27
1999	0.34	0.39	0.39	0.39
2000	0.45	0.39	0.34	0.30
2001	0.18	0.19	0.23	0.26
2002	0.33	0.37	0.40	0.41

INTERIM DIVIDENDS (Per Share):

Amt.	Decl.	Ex.	Rec.	Pay.
50% STK	8/06/01	9/10/01	8/20/01	9/07/01

CAPITALIZATION (12/29/01):

	($000)	(%)
Long-Term Debt	30,000	11.9
Deferred Income Tax	8,312	3.3
Common & Surplus	213,130	84.8
Total	251,442	100.0

BUSINESS:

Monaco Coach Corporation is a manufacturer of premium Class A motor coaches, Class C motor coaches and towable recreational vehicles. As of 12/28/02, the Company manufactured 33 motor coaches and seven towable models (fifth wheel trailers and travel trailers) with suggested retail prices typically ranging from $70,000 to $1.1 million for motor coaches, and $25,000 to $65,000 for towables. As of 12/28/02, MNC's products were sold under the MONACO,
HOLIDAY RAMBLER, ROYALE COACH, BEAVER, SAFARI, and MCKENZIE TOWABLES brand names. As of 12/28/02, MNC's products were sold through a network of 420 dealerships located primarily in the U.S. and Canada. Fiscal 2002 motorhome sales totaled 8,005 units and towable recreational vehicles totaled 3,206 units. MNC operates facilities in Oregon and Indiana. MNC's motor coach products generated 89.6% of total revenues for fiscal 2002.

RECENT DEVELOPMENTS:

For the year ended 12/28/02, net income soared 78.6% to $44.5 million compared with $24.9 million in 2001. Results for 2001 included goodwill amortization expense of $645,000. Net sales grew 30.5% to $1.22 billion from
$937.1 million a year earlier. Unit sales of MNC's products rose 18.1% to 11,211 reflecting careful balancing of production levels with demand. Operating income climbed 78.0% to $75.9 million from $42.7 million in 2001.

PROSPECTS:

Looking ahead, the Company is focused on product development and gaining market share in the gasoline and diesel-powered motorhome and towable market segments. MNC's towable production expansion project remains on track, and MNC should have additional towable production capacity available by mid-year 2003. In addition, MNC plans to be more aggressive with retail sales promotions
designed to increase market share and ensure that its models are turning on dealer lots. In 2003, the Company expects revenue growth of 8.0% to 12.0%. The Company continues to invest in Outdoor Resorts of America with the purpose of developing two luxury recreational vehicle resorts. MNC expects to close the sale of undeveloped property in Naples, Florida in the second quarter of 2003.

ANNUAL FINANCIAL DATA:

FISCAL YEAR	TOT. REVS. ($000)	NET INC. ($000)	TOT. ASSETS ($000)	OPER. PROFIT %	NET PROFIT %	RET. ON EQUITY %	RET. ON ASSETS %	CURR. RATIO	EARN. PER SH. $	CASH FL. PER SH. $	TANG. BK. VAL. $	PRICE RANGE	AVG. P/E RATIO
p12/28/02	1,222,689	44,515	547,417						1.51			30.70 - 14.30	14.9
12/29/01	937,073	24,919	427,098	4.6	2.7	11.7	5.8	1.4	0.85	1.11	5.46	23.25 - 10.48	19.8
12/30/00	901,890	42,521	321,610	7.7	4.7	22.8	13.2	1.5	1.47	1.69	5.91	17.04 - 7.21	8.3
1/01/00	780,815	② 43,761	246,727	9.3	5.6	30.5	17.7	1.4	② 1.51	1.71	4.38	20.63 - 10.08	10.2
1/02/99	594,802	22,669	190,127	6.7	3.8	23.1	11.9	1.3	0.79	0.90	2.76	11.78 - 4.74	10.4
1/03/98	441,895	12,436	159,832	5.1	2.8	16.6	7.8	1.1	0.47	0.60	2.36	5.27 - 3.06	8.8
12/28/96	365,638	5,909	135,368	3.8	1.6	13.5	4.4	1.1	0.25	0.39	0.95	3.26 - 1.68	9.8
12/30/95	141,611	4,898	68,502	5.9	3.5	12.9	7.2	1.2	0.21	0.27	0.84	3.31 - 1.58	11.3
12/31/94	107,300	5,941	48,219	9.0	5.5	18.0	12.3	1.4	0.26	0.30	0.59	3.33 - 2.52	11.1
1/01/94	65,964	① 2,302	40,052	7.8	3.5	8.5	5.7	1.2	① 0.13	0.17	0.30	3.16 - 1.98	19.3

Statistics are as originally reported. Adj. for stk. splits: 50% div., 11/30/98; 50% div., 4/16/98; 3-for-2, 7/99; 50% div., 9/7/01. ① Bef. extraord. chrg. $558,000. ② Incl. nonrecurr. gain of $1.2 mill. and incl. nonrecurr. loss of $639,000.

OFFICERS:
K. L. Toolson, Chmn., C.E.O.
J. W. Nepute, Pres.
P. M. Daley, V.P., C.F.O.

INVESTOR CONTACT: Mike Duncan, Investor Relations, (541) 686-8011

PRINCIPAL OFFICE: 91320 Industrial Way, Coburg, OR 97408

TELEPHONE NUMBER: (541) 686-8011
FAX: (541) 686-8084
WEB: www.monaco-online.com

NO. OF EMPLOYEES: 4,822

SHAREHOLDERS: 697 (approx.)

ANNUAL MEETING: In May

INCORPORATED: DE, Dec., 1992

INSTITUTIONAL HOLDINGS:
No. of Institutions: 127
Shares Held: 23,148,341
% Held: 80.2

INDUSTRY: Motor vehicles and car bodies (SIC: 3711)

TRANSFER AGENT(S): Wells Fargo Shareowner Services, N.A., St. Paul, MN

MONSANTO COMPANY

EXCH.	SYM.	REC. PRICE	P/E RATIO	YLD.	MKT. CAP.	RANGE (52-WK.)	'02 Y/E PR.
NYSE	MON	16.42 (2/28/03)	33.5	2.9%	$4.24 bill.	33.99 - 13.20	19.25

LOWER MEDIUM GRADE. THE COMPANY EXPECTS EARNINGS FOR 2003 TO RANGE FROM $1.20 TO $1.40 PER SHARE, BEFORE UNUSUAL ITEMS.

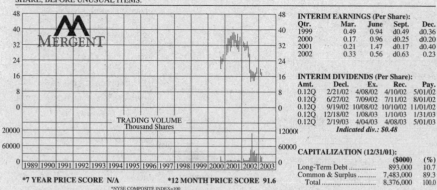

INTERIM EARNINGS (Per Share):

Qtr.	Mar.	June	Sept.	Dec.
1999	0.49	0.94	d0.49	d0.36
2000	0.17	0.96	d0.25	d0.20
2001	0.21	1.47	d0.17	d0.40
2002	0.33	0.56	d0.63	0.23

INTERIM DIVIDENDS (Per Share):

Amt.	Decl.	Ex.	Rec.	Pay.
0.12Q	2/21/02	4/08/02	4/10/02	5/01/02
0.12Q	6/27/02	7/09/02	7/11/02	8/01/02
0.12Q	9/19/02	10/08/02	10/10/02	11/01/02
0.12Q	12/18/02	1/08/03	1/10/03	1/31/03
0.12Q	2/19/03	4/04/03	4/08/03	5/01/03

Indicated div.: $0.48

TRADING VOLUME
Thousand Shares

*7 YEAR PRICE SCORE N/A   *12 MONTH PRICE SCORE 91.6

*NYSE COMPOSITE INDEX=100

CAPITALIZATION (12/31/01):

	($000)	(%)
Long-Term Debt	893,000	10.7
Common & Surplus	7,483,000	89.3
Total	8,376,000	100.0

BUSINESS:

Monsanto Company is a global provider of technology-based applications and agricultural products for growers and downstream customers, such as grain processors, food companies and consumers, in agricultural markets. MON is comprised of the operations, assets and liabilities that were previously the agricultural division of Pharmacia. On 9/1/00, the assets and liabilities of the agricultural business were transferred from Pharmacia to MON. The Company has two segments, agricultural productivity and seeds and genomics. Agricultural productivity products (66.1% of 2002 revenues) include herbicides such as ROUNDUP®, HARNESS®, LASSO®, PERMIT® and AVADEX®, as well as POSILAC® bovine somatotropin for increased milk production in diary and DEKALB Choice Genetics™ for increased productivity of swine. Seeds and genomics products (33.9%) include several types of crops tolerant to herbicides and/or resistant to certain insects.

RECENT DEVELOPMENTS:

For the year ended 12/31/02, income fell 56.3% to $129.0 million, before an accounting change charge of $1.82 billion, versus net income of $295.0 million in 2001. Results for 2002 and 2001 included net restructuring charges of $103.0 million and $122.0 million, respectively. Results for 2001 also included amortization and adjustments of goodwill of $121.0 million. Net sales declined 14.4% to $4.67 billion from $5.46 billion a year earlier, primarily due to competitive pricing pressures on ROUNDUP in the U.S. and actions taken with customers to reduce the risk of doing business in Latin America.

PROSPECTS:

Actions taken by the Company in 2002 to reduce its risk of doing business in Latin America should position MON well for a return to more normal operations in that area in the future. Meanwhile, higher revenues and gross profits from seeds and traits should help offset the estimated decline in gross profit from ROUNDUP herbicide. Separately, the Company expects earnings for full-year 2003 to range from $1.20 to $1.40 per share, excluding accounting change charges. Moreover, free cash flow is expected to range from $350.0 million to $400.0 million.

ANNUAL FINANCIAL DATA:

FISCAL YEAR	TOT. REVS. ($mill.)	NET INC. ($mill.)	TOT. ASSETS ($mill.)	OPER. PROFIT %	NET PROFIT %	RET. ON EQUITY %	RET. ON ASSETS %	CURR. RATIO	EARN. PER SH.$	CASH FL. PER SH.$	TANG. BK. VAL.$	DIV. PER SH.$	PRICE RANGE	AVG. P/E RATIO	AVG. YIELD %
p12/31/02	4,673.0	④ 129.0							④ 0.49			0.48	33.99 - 13.20	48.2	2.0
12/31/01	5,462.0	③ 297.0	11,429.0	12.1	5.4	4.0	2.6	2.0	③ 1.13	...	15.67	0.45	38.80 - 23.50	29.1	1.4
12/31/00	5,493.0	② 175.0	11,726.0	10.3	3.2	2.4	1.5	1.8	② 0.68	2.79	14.47	...	27.38 - 19.75	34.6	...
12/31/99	5,248.0	② 150.0	11,101.0	11.6	2.9	3.2	1.4	2.4	② 0.58	1.10	0.99	...	...	...	...
12/31/98	4,448.0	① d125.0	10,891.0	1.2	...	...	...	2.0	① d0.48	...	...	...	...	...	...
12/31/97	3,673.0	31.0	...	0.4	0.8	...	...	...	...	...	...	...	...	...	...

Statistics are as originally reported. Figures for 12/31/00 and prior are pro-forma. ① Incl. chg. of $402.0 mill. for acq. in-process R&D and net restr. chg. of $94.0 mill. ② Incl. net restr. chgs. of $103.0 mill., 2000; $22.0 mill., 1999. ③ Incl. $121.0 mill. amort. of goodwill & $122.0 mill. net restr. chgs. and excl. $2.0 mill. net extraord. chg. ④ Incl. $103.0 mill. net restr. chg. & excl. $1.82 bill. acctg. chg. chrg.

OFFICERS:
F. V. Atlee III, Chmn., Interim C.E.O.
T. K. Crews, Exec. V.P., C.F.O.
C. W. Burson, Exec. V.P., Sec., Gen. Couns.
INVESTOR CONTACT: Investor Relations, (314) 694-1000
PRINCIPAL OFFICE: 800 North Lindbergh Boulevard, St. Louis, MO 63167

TELEPHONE NUMBER: (314) 694-1000
FAX: (314) 694-1057
WEB: www.monsanto.com
NO. OF EMPLOYEES: 14,600 (approx.)
SHAREHOLDERS: 154 (approx.)
ANNUAL MEETING: In Apr.
INCORPORATED: Feb., 2000

INSTITUTIONAL HOLDINGS:
No. of Institutions: 376
Shares Held: 215,593,613
% Held: 82.5
INDUSTRY: Agricultural chemicals, nec (SIC: 2879)
TRANSFER AGENT(S): Mellon Investor Services, Ridgefield Park, NJ

MONY GROUP INC. (THE)

EXCH.	SYM.	REC. PRICE	P/E RATIO	YLD.	MKT. CAP.	RANGE (52-WK.)	'02 Y/E PR.
NYSE	MNY	21.40 (2/28/03)	...	2.1%	$1.03 bill.	41.99 - 20.43	23.94

MEDIUM GRADE. FOR 2003, MNY EXPECTS OPERATING EARNINGS IN THE RANGE OF $0.30 TO $0.35 PER SHARE.

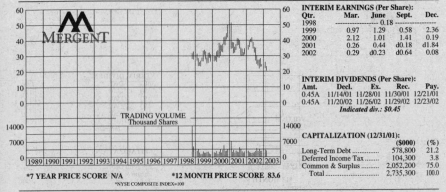

TRADING VOLUME
Thousand Shares

*7 YEAR PRICE SCORE N/A   ***12 MONTH PRICE SCORE 83.6**
NYSE COMPOSITE INDEX=100

INTERIM EARNINGS (Per Share):
Qtr.	Mar.	June	Sept.	Dec.
1998		0.18		
1999	0.97	1.29	0.58	2.36
2000	2.12	1.01	1.41	0.19
2001	0.26	0.44	d0.18	d1.84
2002	0.29	d0.23	d0.64	0.08

INTERIM DIVIDENDS (Per Share):
Amt.	Decl.	Ex.	Rec.	Pay.
0.45A	11/14/01	11/28/01	11/30/01	12/21/01
0.45A	11/20/02	11/26/02	11/29/02	12/23/02

Indicated div.: $0.45

CAPITALIZATION (12/31/01):
	($000)	(%)
Long-Term Debt	578,800	21.2
Deferred Income Tax	104,300	3.8
Common & Surplus	2,052,200	75.0
Total	2,735,300	100.0

BUSINESS:

The MONY Group Inc. is a financial services firm that manages a portfolio of member companies. These companies include MONY Life Insurance Company (formerly The Mutual Life Insurance Company of New York), a stock life insurance company that converted from a mutual fund structure in 1998, The Advest Group, Inc., Matrix Capital Markets Group, Inc., Enterprise Capital Management, Inc., U.S. Financial Life Insurance Company,

Lebenthal, a division of Advest, Inc. These companies manufacture and distribute protection, asset accumulation and retail brokerage products and services to individuals, corporations and institutions through advisory and wholesale distribution channels. As of 2/6/03, MNY had approximately $57.00 billion in assets under management. On 1/31/01, MNY acquired Advest Inc.

RECENT DEVELOPMENTS:

For the year ended 12/31/02, the Company reported a loss of $20.8 million, before a loss from discontinued operations of $2.5 million, versus a net loss of $60.8 million, the previous year. Earnings for 2002 and 2001 included restructuring and related charges of $5.0 million and $81.9 million, respectively. Also, earnings included a venture

capital gain of $3.6 million in 2002 and a venture capital loss of $9.1 million 2001. In addition, earnings for 2002 included a litigation-related charge of $4.5 million and a gain of $31.3 million related to a final payment from a transferred pension business. Total revenues slipped to $2.09 billion from $2.10 billion a year earlier.

PROSPECTS:

For 2003, MNY expects continued growth in life insurance and annuity production as it further expands distribution through the brokerage community. MNY is also striving for further efficiencies and increased productivity from its career system and more competitive products and services by its manufacturing units. Meanwhile, MNY's mutual

fund and retail brokerage may be positively affected when the economy and markets begin to stabilize. MNY is targeting $2.40 billion in sales, and 10.0% increases in life insurance and retail brokerage revenues. MNY expects operating earnings in the range of $0.30 to $0.35 per share, excluding venture capital income.

ANNUAL FINANCIAL DATA:

FISCAL YEAR	PREM. INC. ($mill.)	TOT. REVS. ($mill.)	NET INC. ($mill.)	TOT. ASSETS ($mill.)	TOT. INVST. ($mill.)	RET. ON REVS. %	RET. ON EQUITY %	RET. ON ASSETS %	EARN. PER SH. $	TANG. BK. VAL.$	AVG. YIELD %	DIV. PER SH. $	PRICE RANGE	AVG. P/E RATIO
p12/31/02	690.4	2,094.5	⑥ d20.8						⑥ d0.49			0.45	41.99 - 21.79	...
⑤ 12/31/01	695.3	2,103.6	④ d60.8	25,652.3	11,038.0	...	...	...	④ d1.25	42.66	1.1	0.45	51.38 - 29.91	...
② 12/31/00	118.1	1,251.8	③ 262.3	24,575.3	4,747.9	21.0	12.9	1.1	③ 5.49	44.22	1.2	0.45	50.00 - 26.19	6.9
② 12/31/99	96.3	1,245.6	③ 250.6	24,753.4	4,926.0	20.1	13.7	1.0	③ 5.20	38.68	1.4	0.40	33.81 - 23.25	5.5
12/31/97	621.7	1,856.2	① 191.2	24,956.0	4,638.6	10.3	10.8	0.8	① 0.18	37.66	...	...	32.75 - 27.56	167.4
12/31/96	838.6	1,976.4	① 130.4	23,611.3	8,965.2	6.6	9.9	0.6	...	...	...	...	...	...
12/31/96	859.8	1,965.0	56.5	22,143.5	8,579.6	2.9	4.8	0.3	...	...	...	...	...	...
12/31/95	875.9	1,859.6	40.4	...	...	2.2	...	...	...	...	...	...	...	...

Statistics are as originally reported. ① Excl. extraord. chrgs. in connection with the plan of reorganization: $13.3 mill., 1997; $27.2 mill., 1998; $2.0 mill., 1999. ② Excl. revenues set aside to fund certain policies affected by the conversion of MNY from a mutual to a stock-based Co. of $582.4 mill., 12/00; $620.8 mill., 12/99 ③ Excl. extraord. chrg. of $37.7 mill., ④ Incl. one-time chrgs. of $8.1 mill. ⑤ Reflects acq. of Advest Inc. on 1/31/01. ⑥ Excl. loss fr. disc. opers. of $2.5 mill.; incl. net one-time gains of $25.4 mill.

OFFICERS:
M. I. Roth, Chmn., C.E.O.
S. J. Foti, Pres., C.O.O.
R. Daddario, Exec. V.P., C.F.O.
INVESTOR CONTACT: Jay Davis, Investor Relations, (212) 708-2917
PRINCIPAL OFFICE: 1740 Broadway, New York, NY 10019

TELEPHONE NUMBER: (212) 708-2000
FAX: (212) 206-3425
WEB: www.mony.com
NO. OF EMPLOYEES: 4,173 (avg.)
SHAREHOLDERS: 581,632
ANNUAL MEETING: In May
INCORPORATED: DE, 1998

INSTITUTIONAL HOLDINGS:
No. of Institutions: 134
Shares Held: 16,774,037
% Held: 35.8

INDUSTRY: Life insurance (SIC: 6311)

TRANSFER AGENT(S): EquiServe Trust Company N.A., Jersey City, NJ

MOODY'S CORPORATION

EXCH.	SYM.	REC. PRICE	P/E RATIO	YLD.	MKT. CAP.	RANGE (52-WK.)	'02 Y/E PR.
NYSE	MCO	44.10 (2/28/03)	24.1	0.4%	$6.81 bill.	52.40 - 36.90	41.29

UPPER MEDIUM GRADE. FOR 2003, THE COMPANY EXPECTS STRONG GROWTH IN ITS RESEARCH BUSINESS AND ITS MOODY'S KMV BUSINESS.

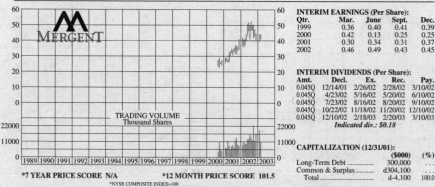

*7 YEAR PRICE SCORE N/A   ***12 MONTH PRICE SCORE 101.5**

*NYSE COMPOSITE INDEX=100

INTERIM EARNINGS (Per Share):

Qtr.	Mar.	June	Sept.	Dec.
1999	0.36	0.40	0.41	0.39
2000	0.42	0.13	0.25	0.25
2001	0.30	0.34	0.31	0.37
2002	0.46	0.49	0.43	0.45

INTERIM DIVIDENDS (Per Share):

Amt.	Decl.	Ex.	Rec.	Pay.
0.045Q	12/14/01	2/26/02	2/28/02	3/10/02
0.045Q	4/23/02	5/16/02	5/20/02	6/10/02
0.045Q	7/23/02	8/16/02	8/20/02	9/10/02
0.045Q	10/22/02	11/18/02	11/20/02	12/10/02
0.045Q	12/10/02	2/18/03	2/20/03	3/10/03

Indicated div.: $0.18

CAPITALIZATION (12/31/01):

	($000)	(%)
Long-Term Debt	300,000	...
Common & Surplus	d304,100	...
Total	d-4,100	100.0

BUSINESS:

Moody's Corporation (formerly Dun & Bradstreet Corp.) is a global credit ratings, research and analysis firm that, through its Moody's Investor Service subsidiary, publishes credit opinions, research and ratings on fixed-income securities, issuers of securities and other credit obligations. As of 12/31/02, MCO had provided credit rating and analysis on more than $30.00 trillion of debt, covering approximately 85,000 corporate and government securities, 73,000 public finance obligations, 4,300 corporate relationships and 100 sovereign nations. Moody's KMV, a wholly-owned subsidiary, provides financial software, credit training and both quantitative and judgmental risk assessment models. On 9/30/00, MCO spun off its credit information and receivables management services as a new company, The Dun & Bradstreet Corp. On 4/12/02 MCO acquired KMV for $210.0 million.

RECENT DEVELOPMENTS:

For the year ended 12/31/02, net income advanced 36.1% to $288.9 million versus $212.2 million in 2001. Total revenue increased 28.4% to $1.02 billion from $796.7 million a year earlier. Total ratings revenue rose 22.1% to $848.2 million, driven by strength in U.S. and European structured finance, global financial institutions, and U.S. public finance. Global research revenue climbed 30.9% to $93.6 million. Revenue from Moody's KMV more than doubled to $81.5 million from $30.8 million in 2001, primarily due to the KMV acquisition.

PROSPECTS:

MCO expects strong growth in its research business and its Moody's KMV business during 2003. In 2003, MCO expects modest revenue growth from its structured and corporate finance ratings businesses and expects a modest decline in revenues from its public finance ratings business. Overall for 2003, MCO expects that percent revenue growth will be in the high single digits. In addition, with the impact of a lower effective tax rate and share repurchases, MCO anticipates diluted earnings per share growth for 2003 in the low double digits, before the impact of expensing stock options and a non-recurring insurance recovery gain of $13.6 million.

ANNUAL FINANCIAL DATA:

FISCAL YEAR	TOT. REVS. ($mill.)	NET INC. ($mill.)	TOT. ASSETS ($mill.)	OPER. PROFIT %	NET PROFIT %	RET. ON EQUITY %	RET. ON ASSETS %	CURR. RATIO	EARN. PER SH. $	CASH FL. PER SH. $	TANG. BK. VAL.$	DIV. PER SH. $	PRICE RANGE	AVG. P/E RATIO	AVG. YIELD %
p12/31/02	1,023.3	288.9							1.83			0.18	51.74 - 35.80	23.9	0.4
12/31/01	796.7	212.2	505.4	50.0	26.6	...	42.0	1.0	1.32	1.43	...	0.18	41.10 - 25.56	25.3	0.5
12/31/00	602.3	158.5	398.3	47.9	26.3	...	39.8	1.1	0.97	1.07	...	0.60	28.88 - 22.63	26.5	2.3
12/31/99	1,971.8	⑥ 256.0	1,785.7	22.3	13.0	...	14.3	0.6	⑥ 1.56	2.42	...	0.74	...	...	...
12/31/98	1,934.5	⑤ 246.4	1,789.2	21.7	12.7	...	13.8	0.6	⑤ 1.44	2.26	...	0.37	...	...	...
12/31/97	2,154.4	④ 311.0	2,151.9	25.4	14.4	...	14.5	0.6	④ 1.80	2.69	...	...	...	...	...
12/31/96	2,159.2	③ d27.3	2,294.2	9.2	...	...	...	0.5	③ d0.16	0.77	...	...	...	...	...
12/31/95	5,415.1	② 320.8	5,515.8	9.6	5.9	27.1	5.8	0.8	② 1.89	4.69	...	...	...	...	...
12/31/94	4,895.7	629.5	5,463.9	18.9	12.9	47.7	11.5	0.9	3.70	6.18	...	...	...	...	...
12/31/93	4,710.4	① 428.7	5,170.4	11.7	9.1	38.6	8.3	1.0	① 2.42	4.53	...	...	...	...	...

Statistics are as originally reported. Results for 1995 and earlier include the operations of Cognizant Corp. and ACNielsen Corp. Results for 12/31/99 and prior are for the Dun & Bradstreet Corp. & subsidaries. ① Bef. acctg. change chrg. $390.6 mill.; incl. reorg. cost $277.5 mill. ② Incl. reorg. credit $120.3 ③ Bef. disc. oper. loss $171.1 mill.; incl. reorg. cost $161.2 mill. ④ Bef. acctg. change chrg. $150.6 mill. ⑤ Bef. disc. oper. gain $33.7 mill. ⑥ Incl. restruct. chrg. of $41.2 mill. and after-tax gain of $5.1 mill. from the sale of financial information services business.

OFFICERS:
C. L. Alexander Jr., Chmn.
J. Rutherfurd Jr., Pres., C.E.O.
J. M. Dering, Sr. V.P., C.F.O.
INVESTOR CONTACT: Michael Courtain, Investor Relations, (212) 553-7194
PRINCIPAL OFFICE: 99 Church Street, New York, NY 10007

TELEPHONE NUMBER: (212) 553-0300
FAX: (212) 553-4820
WEB: www.moodys.com
NO. OF EMPLOYEES: 1,700 (approx.)
SHAREHOLDERS: 5,754
ANNUAL MEETING: In April
INCORPORATED: DE, 1933

INSTITUTIONAL HOLDINGS:
No. of Institutions: 392
Shares Held: 132,705,755
% Held: 86.5
INDUSTRY: Credit reporting services (SIC: 7323)
TRANSFER AGENT(S): The Bank of New York, New York, NY

MORGAN (J.P.) CHASE & COMPANY

EXCH.	SYM.	REC. PRICE	P/E RATIO	YLD.	MKT. CAP.	RANGE (52-WK.)	'02 Y/E PR.	DIV. ACH.
NYSE	JPM	22.68 (2/28/03)	28.7	6.0%	$45.33 bill.	38.75 - 15.26	24.00	11 yrs.

MEDIUM GRADE. THE COMPANY'S CONSUMER-RELATED OPERATIONS SHOULD CONTINUE TO CONTRIBUTE TO REVENUE GROWTH IN THE NEAR TERM.

TRADING VOLUME
Thousand Shares

*7 YEAR PRICE SCORE 73.0   *12 MONTH PRICE SCORE 96.9

*NYSE COMPOSITE INDEX=100

INTERIM EARNINGS (Per Share):

Qtr.	Mar.	June	Sept.	Dec.
1999	0.88	1.07	0.91	1.32
2000	1.06	0.85	0.66	0.34
2001	0.58	0.18	0.22	d0.18
2002	0.48	0.50	0.01	d0.20

INTERIM DIVIDENDS (Per Share):

Amt.	Decl.	Ex.	Rec.	Pay.
0.34Q	3/19/02	4/03/02	4/05/02	4/30/02
0.34Q	5/21/02	7/02/02	7/05/02	7/31/02
0.34Q	9/17/02	10/02/02	10/05/02	10/31/02
0.34Q	12/17/02	1/02/03	1/06/03	1/31/03
0.34Q	3/18/03	4/02/03	4/04/03	4/30/03

Indicated div.: $1.36 (Div. Reinv. Plan)

CAPITALIZATION (12/31/01):

	($000)	(%)
Total Deposits	293,650,000	77.5
Long-Term Debt	43,622,000	11.5
Redeemable Pfd. Stock	550,000	0.1
Preferred Stock	1,009,000	0.3
Common & Surplus	40,090,000	10.6
Total	378,921,000	100.0

BUSINESS:

J.P. Morgan Chase & Company (formerly Chase Manhattan Corp.) is a global financial services firm with assets of $758.80 billion at 12/31/02. On 3/31/96, Chase Manhattan Corp. was acquired by Chemical Banking Corp., which then changed its name to Chase Manhattan Corp. (CMC) JPM's present name was adopted as a result of the acquisi-tion of J.P. Morgan & Co. Inc. by CMC on 12/31/00. JPM conducts financial services businesses through various bank and non-bank subsidiaries. As of 1/22/03, JPM served more than 30.0 million customers throughout the U.S., and had offices in more than 50 countries. On 12/10/99, JPM acquired Hambrecht & Quist Group, Inc.

RECENT DEVELOPMENTS:

For the year ended 12/31/02, JPM reported net income of $1.66 billion compared with income of $1.72 billion, before an accounting change charge of $25.0 million, in the previous year. Results for 2002 and 2001 included merger and restructuring charges of $1.21 billion and $2.52 billion, respectively. Results for 2002 also included a charge of $1.30 billion related to the settlement of the Enron surety litigation and the establishment of a litigation reserve. Net interest income increased 6.7% to $11.53 billion from $10.80 billion a year earlier. Provision for loan losses jumped 36.1% to $4.33 billion from $3.18 in 2001. Total non-interest revenue declined 2.4% to $18.09 billion, while total non-interest expense fell 3.5% to $22.76 million.

PROSPECTS:

Due to the low interest rate environment, JPM is experienc-ing continued revenue growth from its mortgage origina-tion operations, its auto finance portfolio, and its managed credit cards reflecting both organic growth and the acquisi-tion of the $8.20 billion Providian credit card portfolio. Separately, investment banking operations are benefiting from higher investment banking fees and improved trading revenues. Meanwhile, for 2003, higher operating expenses are expected due to increased pension funding and occu-pancy costs, the expensing of stock options and perform-ance stock and growth at retail and treasury and securities services operations.

ANNUAL FINANCIAL DATA:

FISCAL YEAR	NET INT. INC. ($mill.)	NON-INT. INC. ($mill.)	NET INC. ($mill.)	TOT. LOANS ($mill.)	TOT. ASSETS ($mill.)	TOT. DEP. ($mill.)	RET. ON EQUITY %	RET. ON ASSETS %	EQUITY/ ASSETS %	EARN. PER SH. $	TANG. BK. VAL. $	DIV. PER SH. $	PRICE RANGE	AVG. P/E RATIO
p12/31/02	11,526.0	18,088.0	7 1,663.0		758,800.0	304,753.0				7 0.80		1.36	39.68 - 15.26	34.3
12/31/01	10,802.0	18,248.0	1 2 1,719.0	217,444.0	693,575.0	293,650.0	4.2	0.2	5.9	1 2 0.80	12.54	1.34	57.33 - 29.04	54.0
6 12/31/00	9,512.0	23,422.0	1 5,727.0	216,050.0	715,348.0	279,365.0	13.5	0.8	5.9	1 2.86	12.96	1.23	67.17 - 32.38	17.4
5 12/31/99	8,744.0	13,473.0	1 5,446.0	176,159.0	406,105.0	241,745.0	23.1	1.3	5.8	4 4.18	18.29	1.06	60.75 - 43.88	12.5
12/31/98	8,566.0	10,301.0	3,782.0	172,754.0	365,875.0	212,437.0	15.9	1.0	6.5	2.83	17.93	0.93	51.71 - 23.71	13.3
12/31/97	8,158.0	8,625.0	3,708.0	170,066.0	365,521.0	193,688.0	17.1	1.0	5.9	2.68	15.84	0.81	42.19 - 28.21	13.1
12/31/96	8,340.0	7,512.0	2,461.0	156,465.0	336,099.0	180,921.0	11.7	0.7	6.2	1.67	14.19	0.73	31.96 - 17.38	14.7
12/31/95	4,689.0	3,766.0	2 3 1,816.0	82,628.0	182,926.0	98,417.0	15.2	1.0	6.5	2 3 2.26	14.16	0.63	21.58 - 11.92	7.4
12/31/94	4,674.0	3,597.0	1,294.0	79,227.0	171,423.0	96,506.0	12.1	0.8	6.2	1.55	12.60	0.53	14.04 - 11.21	8.2
12/31/93	4,636.0	4,024.0	1 2 1,569.0	75,858.0	149,888.0	98,277.0	14.1	1.0	7.4	1 2 1.86	12.58	0.43	15.46 - 11.67	7.3

Statistics are as originally reported. Adj. for 3-for-2 split, 6/00; 2-for-1 split, 6/98. 1 Incl. restr. chrg.: $2.52 bill., 2001; $1.43 bill., 2000; $48.0 mill., 1999; $192.0 mill., 1997; $1.81 bill., 1996; $48.0 mill., 1994; and $43.0 mill., 1993. 2 Bef. acctg. chrg. $25.0 mill., 2001; $110.0 mill., 1995 and $35.0 mill., 1993. 3 Incl. $76.0 mill. gain on the sale of assets. 4 Incl. restr. chrgs. of $529.0 mill. & prov. for risk mgmt. instrument cr. losses of $211.0 mill. 5 Results are for Chase Manhattan Corp for 1999 and earlier. 6 Reflects merger with J.P. Morgan & Co. 7 Incl. surety settlement and litigation chrg. of $1.30 billion and a merger & restr. chrg. of $1.21 billion

OFFICERS:
W. B. Harrison Jr., Chmn., C.E.O.
D. Dublon, C.F.O.
W. H. McDavid, Gen. Couns.
INVESTOR CONTACT: Ann Borowiec, (212) 270-7318
PRINCIPAL OFFICE: 270 Park Avenue, New York, NY 10017

TELEPHONE NUMBER: (212) 270-6000
FAX: (212) 270-1648
WEB: www.jpmorganchase.com
NO. OF EMPLOYEES: 95,812 (avg.)
SHAREHOLDERS: 135,359
ANNUAL MEETING: In May
INCORPORATED: DE, 1968

INSTITUTIONAL HOLDINGS:
No. of Institutions: 919
Shares Held: 1,359,783,498
% Held: 68.1
INDUSTRY: National commercial banks (SIC: 6021)
TRANSFER AGENT(S): Mellon Investor Ser-vices, L.L.C., Ridgefield Park, NJ

MORGAN STANLEY

EXCH.	SYM.	REC. PRICE	P/E RATIO	YLD.	MKT. CAP.	RANGE (52-WK.)	'02 Y/E PR.
NYSE	MWD	36.85 (2/28/03)	13.6	2.5%	$39.85 bill.	58.27 - 28.80	39.92

INVESTMENT GRADE. EARNINGS ARE BEING ADVERSELY AFFECTED BY WEAK INVESTMENT CONDITIONS.

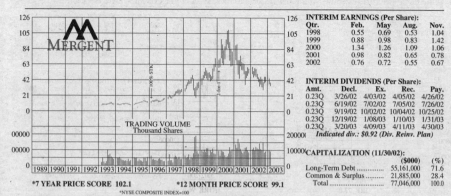

*7 YEAR PRICE SCORE 102.1   ***12 MONTH PRICE SCORE 99.1**

*NYSE COMPOSITE INDEX=100

INTERIM EARNINGS (Per Share):

Qtr.	Feb.	May	Aug.	Nov.
1998	0.55	0.69	0.53	1.04
1999	0.88	0.98	0.83	1.42
2000	1.34	1.26	1.09	1.06
2001	0.98	0.82	0.65	0.78
2002	0.76	0.72	0.55	0.67

INTERIM DIVIDENDS (Per Share):

Amt.	Decl.	Ex.	Rec.	Pay.
0.23Q	3/26/02	4/03/02	4/05/02	4/26/02
0.23Q	6/19/02	7/02/02	7/05/02	7/26/02
0.23Q	9/19/02	10/02/02	10/04/02	10/25/02
0.23Q	12/19/02	1/08/03	1/10/03	1/31/03
0.23Q	3/20/03	4/09/03	4/11/03	4/30/03

Indicated div.: $0.92 (Div. Reinv. Plan)

CAPITALIZATION (11/30/02):

	($000)	(%)
Long-Term Debt	55,161,000	71.6
Common & Surplus	21,885,000	28.4
Total	77,046,000	100.0

BUSINESS:

Morgan Stanley (formerly Morgan Stanley Dean Witter & Co.) was formed on June 2, 1997 resulting from a merger between Dean Witter, Discover & Co. and Morgan Stanley Group Inc., with Dean Witter, Discover & Co. as the surviving corporation. MWD is engaged in four business. The Institutional Securities business (48.5% of 2002 net revenues) includes securities underwriting and distribution, financial advisory services, sales, trading, financing and market-making activities in equity and fixed income securities, principal investing and aircraft financing activities.

MWD's Individual Investor Group (20.8%) provides financial planning and investment advisory services. MWD's Investment Management business (12.1%) provides global asset management products and services for individual and institutional investors. The Company's Credit Services business (18.6%) offers DISCOVER®-branded cards and other consumer finance products and services and includes the operation of Discover Business Services, a network of merchant and cash access locations primarily in the U.S.

RECENT DEVELOPMENTS:

For the year ended 11/30/02, net income was $2.99 billion versus income of $3.61 billion, before an accounting change charge of $59.0 million and an extraordinary loss of $30.0 million the previous year. Earnings for 2002 included an after-tax restructuring charge of $152.0 million. Total revenues slid 26.1% to $32.42 billion. Revenues from commissions, which rose to $3.28 billion from $3.16 billion in 2001, were offset by a 26.2% drop in investment banking revenues to $2.53 billion and a 51.1% reduction in trading revenue to $2.69 billion.

PROSPECTS:

Industry-wide declines in the level of activity significantly depressed revenues in its securities and asset management business. However, the Company was able to generate a 14.0% return on equity due to record profits generated by its Discover Card business and MWD's focus on its cost structure. Going forward, MWD intends to mitigate the potential effects of market downturns by diversification of its revenue sources, enhancement of its global franchise, and management of costs and its capital structure.

ANNUAL FINANCIAL DATA:

FISCAL YEAR	TOT. REVS. ($mill.)	NET INC. ($mill.)	TOT. ASSETS ($mill.)	OPER. PROFIT %	NET PROFIT %	RET. ON EQUITY %	RET. ON ASSETS %	CURR. RATIO	EARN. PER SH.$	CASH FL.PER SH.$	TANG. BK. VAL.$	DIV. PER SH.$	PRICE RANGE	AVG. P/E RATIO	AVG. YIELD %
11/30/02	32,415.0	⑤ 2,988.0	529,499.0	14.6	9.2	13.7	0.6	0.8	⑤ 2.69	3.40	18.90	0.92	60.02 — 28.80	16.5	2.1
11/30/01	43,727.0	④ 3,610.0	482,628.0	13.0	8.3	17.4	0.7	0.8	④ 3.19	3.84	18.64	0.92	90.49 — 35.75	19.8	1.5
11/30/00	45,413.0	③ 5,456.0	426,794.0	18.7	12.0	28.3	1.3	0.8	③ 4.73	5.37	16.91	0.80	110.00 — 58.63	17.8	0.9
11/30/99	33,928.0	4,791.0	366,967.0	22.8	14.1	28.2	1.3	0.8	4.10	4.56	14.80	0.48	71.44 — 35.41	13.0	0.9
11/30/98	31,131.0	3,393.0	317,590.0	15.1	10.9	24.0	1.1	0.8	2.76	3.23	11.88	0.40	48.75 — 18.25	12.1	1.2
11/30/97	27,132.0	② 2,586.0	302,287.0	15.8	9.5	18.5	0.9	0.9	② 2.13	2.40	11.00	0.34	29.75 — 16.38	10.9	1.5
① 12/31/96	9,028.6	951.4	42,413.6	17.1	10.5	18.4	2.2	0.5	1.40	1.52	8.08	0.35	17.19 — 11.25	10.2	2.5
12/31/95	7,934.4	856.4	38,208.2	17.6	10.8	17.7	2.2	0.6	1.22	1.32	6.92	0.24	14.56 — 8.38	9.4	2.1
12/31/94	6,602.6	740.9	31,859.4	18.4	11.2	18.0	2.3	0.7	1.07	1.15	5.84	0.30	10.78 — 7.88	8.7	3.2
12/31/93	5,821.6	603.6	27,662.3	17.1	10.4	17.4	2.2	0.8	0.91	0.98	4.84	0.27	11.63 — 7.66	10.7	2.8

Statistics are as originally reported. Adj. for stk split: 2-for-1, 1/00 & 1/97 ① Figures prior to 1997 are for Dean Witter, Discover & Co. ② Incl. non-recurr. chrg. $74.0 mill. ③ Incl. gain on the sale of a business of $35.0 mill. ④ Bef. acctg. chrg. $59.0 mill. & extraord. chrg. $30.0 mill. ⑤ Incl. after-tax restruct. chrg. of $152.0 mill.

OFFICERS:
P. J. Purcell, Chmn., C.E.O.
R. G. Scott, Pres., C.O.O.

INVESTOR CONTACT: William Pike, Investor Relations, (212) 761-0008

PRINCIPAL OFFICE: 1585 Broadway, New York, NY 10036

TELEPHONE NUMBER: (212) 761-4000
FAX: (212) 761-0086
WEB: www.msdw.com
NO. OF EMPLOYEES: 55,726 (avg.)
SHAREHOLDERS: 141,000 (approx.)
ANNUAL MEETING: In April
INCORPORATED: DE, 1981

INSTITUTIONAL HOLDINGS:
No. of Institutions: 710
Shares Held: 716,266,444
% Held: 66.0
INDUSTRY: National commercial banks (SIC: 6021)
TRANSFER AGENT(S): Mellon Investor Services, South Hackensack, NJ

MOTOROLA, INC.

EXCH.	SYM.	REC. PRICE	P/E RATIO	YLD.	MKT. CAP.	RANGE (52-WK.)	'02 Y/E PR.
NYSE	MOT	8.42 (2/28/03)	…	1.9%	$18.98 bill.	17.11 - 7.30	8.65

LOWER MEDIUM GRADE. ON 1/13/03, THE COMPANY ANNOUNCED THAT IT PLANS TO MAKE A TENDER OFFER FOR ALL OF THE OUTSTANDING SHARES OF ITS SUBSIDIARY, NEXT LEVEL COMMUNICATIONS, INC.

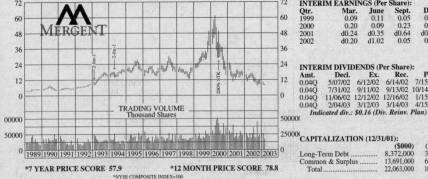

INTERIM EARNINGS (Per Share):

Qtr.	Mar.	June	Sept.	Dec.
1999	0.09	0.11	0.05	0.19
2000	0.20	0.09	0.23	0.06
2001	d0.24	d0.35	d0.64	d0.55
2002	d0.20	d1.02	0.05	0.08

INTERIM DIVIDENDS (Per Share):

Amt.	Decl.	Ex.	Rec.	Pay.
0.04Q	5/07/02	6/12/02	6/14/02	7/15/02
0.04Q	7/31/02	9/11/02	9/13/02	10/14/02
0.04Q	11/06/02	12/12/02	12/16/02	1/15/03
0.04Q	2/04/03	3/12/03	3/14/03	4/15/03

Indicated div.: $0.16 (Div. Reinv. Plan)

CAPITALIZATION (12/31/01):

	($000)	(%)
Long-Term Debt	8,372,000	37.9
Common & Surplus	13,691,000	62.1
Total	22,063,000	100.0

*7 YEAR PRICE SCORE 57.9   *12 MONTH PRICE SCORE 78.8
*NYSE COMPOSITE INDEX=100

BUSINESS:

Motorola, Inc. provides electronic equipment, systems components and services for worldwide markets. MOT operates through six primary business segments. The Personal Communications segment includes sales of digital phones, wireless telephones and paging products. The Global Telecom Solutions segment designs, manufactures, sells, installs and services wireless cellular and personal communication infrastructure equipment. The Commercial, Government and Industrial Solutions segment provides integrated information and communications solutions for commercial, government and industrial customers worldwide. The Semiconductor Products segment designs and produces integrated semiconductors and software services. The Broadband Communications segment focuses on services that deliver interactive television, the Internet and cable modem business. The Integrated Electronic Systems segment designs, manufactures and sells automotive and industrial electronics systems and services.

RECENT DEVELOPMENTS:

For the year ended 12/31/02, MOT reported a net loss of $2.49 billion compared with a net loss of $3.94 billion the previous year. Earnings for 2002 and 2001 included non-recurring items that resulted in net after-tax charges of $2.8 million and $3.26 billion, respectively. Net sales decreased 10.7% to $26.68 billion from $29.87 billion a year earlier. Gross margin advanced 21.2% to $8.74 billion from $7.21 billion the year before. Operating loss narrowed to $1.81 billion from $5.80 billion the prior year.

PROSPECTS:

On 1/13/03, the Company announced that it plans to make a tender offer for all of the outstanding publicly held shares of its subsidiary, Next Level Communications, Inc. MOT currently owns 74.0% of the outstanding common stock of Next Level. The aggregate consideration for the outstanding Next Level share would be approximately $30.0 million. Separately, the Company expects sales of about $27.50 billion with earnings of approximately $0.40 per diluted share for full-year 2003. The Company also expects each of its major segments to have positive operating earnings in 2003 and to generate positive operating cash flow.

ANNUAL FINANCIAL DATA:

FISCAL YEAR	TOT. REVS. ($mill.)	NET INC. ($mill.)	TOT. ASSETS ($mill.)	OPER. PROFIT %	NET PROFIT %	RET. ON EQUITY %	RET. ON ASSETS %	CURR. RATIO	EARN. PER SH.$	CASH FL.PER SH.$	TANG. BK. VAL.$	DIV. PER SH.$	PRICE RANGE	AVG. P/E RATIO	AVG. YIELD %
p12/31/02	26,679.0	⑤ d2,485.0		…	…	…	…	1.8	⑤ d1.09			0.16	17.11 - 7.30	…	1.3
12/31/01	30,004.0	④ d3,937.0	33,398.0	…	…	…	…	1.8	④ d1.78	d0.63	6.07	0.16	25.13 - 10.50	…	0.9
12/31/00	37,580.0	1,318.0	42,343.0	2.4	3.5	7.1	3.1	1.2	0.58	1.70	8.49	0.16	61.54 - 15.81	66.7	0.4
12/31/99	33,075.0	③ 891.0	40,489.0	4.3	2.7	4.8	2.2	1.4	③ 0.41	1.43	8.74	0.16	49.83 - 20.85	86.8	0.5
12/31/98	29,398.0	② d962.0	28,728.0	…	…	…	…	1.2	② d0.54	0.69	6.78	0.16	21.96 - 12.79	…	0.9
12/31/97	29,794.0	① 1,180.0	27,278.0	6.5	4.0	8.9	4.3	1.5	① 0.65	1.92	7.41	0.16	30.16 - 18.00	37.2	0.7
12/31/96	27,973.0	1,154.0	24,076.0	7.0	4.1	9.8	4.8	1.4	0.63	1.90	6.63	0.15	22.83 - 14.71	29.6	0.8
12/31/95	27,037.0	1,781.0	22,738.0	10.8	6.6	16.2	7.8	1.3	0.98	2.03	6.20	0.13	27.50 - 17.16	22.9	0.6
12/31/94	22,245.0	1,560.0	17,536.0	11.6	7.0	17.2	8.9	1.5	0.89	1.75	5.16	0.09	20.37 - 14.04	19.4	0.5
12/31/93	16,963.0	1,022.0	13,498.0	9.8	6.0	15.9	7.6	1.5	0.59	1.27	3.83	0.07	17.91 - 8.12	22.0	0.6

Statistics are as originally reported. Adj. for stk. splits: 2-for-1, 1/93, 4/94; 3-for-1, 6/00. ① Incl. non-recurr. pre-tax chrg. $170.0 mill. for exiting DRAM business & pre-tax chrg. $95.0 mill. for exiting MacOS computer system business. ② Incl. non-recurr. chrg. $1.98 bill. fr. restruc. ③ Incl. non-recurr. credit $236.0 million rel. to special items. ④ Incl. pre-tax chrgs. of $5.19 bill. & incl. gains on sales of invest. and bus. of $1.93 bill. ⑤ Incl. net non-recurr. chrgs. of $1.68 bill.

OFFICERS:
C. B. Galvin, Chmn., C.E.O.
R. Growney, Vice-Chmn.
M. Zafirovski, Pres., C.O.O.
INVESTOR CONTACT: Scott Wyman, Investor Relations, (847) 576-2246
PRINCIPAL OFFICE: 1303 E. Algonquin Road, Schaumburg, IL 60196

TELEPHONE NUMBER: (847) 576-5000
FAX: (847) 576-3477
WEB: www.motorola.com
NO. OF EMPLOYEES: 111,000 (avg.)
SHAREHOLDERS: 54,836 (record)
ANNUAL MEETING: In May
INCORPORATED: IL, Sept., 1928; reincorp., DE, May, 1973

MPS GROUP, INC.

EXCH.	SYM.	REC. PRICE	P/E RATIO	YLD.	MKT. CAP.	RANGE (52-WK.)	'02 Y/E PR.
NYSE	MPS	4.91 (2/28/03)	. . .	. . .	$482.7 mill.	9.80 - 4.35	5.54

SPECULATIVE GRADE. THE COMPANY EXPECTS ITS ENTRY INTO HEALTHCARE STAFFING WILL PROVIDE OPPORTUNITIES FOR FUTURE GROWTH.

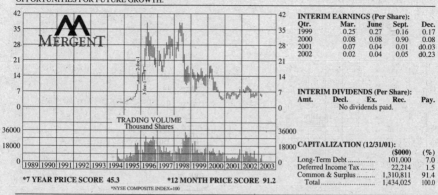

*7 YEAR PRICE SCORE 45.3   *12 MONTH PRICE SCORE 91.2
*NYSE COMPOSITE INDEX=100

INTERIM EARNINGS (Per Share):

Qtr.	Mar.	June	Sept.	Dec.
1999	0.25	0.27	0.16	0.17
2000	0.08	0.08	0.90	0.08
2001	0.07	0.04	0.01	d0.03
2002	0.02	0.04	0.05	d0.23

INTERIM DIVIDENDS (Per Share):

Amt.	Decl.	Ex.	Rec.	Pay.
		No dividends paid.		

CAPITALIZATION (12/31/01):

	($000)	(%)
Long-Term Debt	101,000	7.0
Deferred Income Tax	22,214	1.5
Common & Surplus	1,310,811	91.4
Total	1,434,025	100.0

BUSINESS:

MPS Group, Inc. (formerly Modis Professional Services, Inc.) is a global provider of professional staffing, e-business services, information technology (IT) project support and career management consulting. MPS provides services in the areas of IT, law, accounting and finance, e-business, retained executive search, engineering, human capital auto-mation and workforce consulting. MPS operates through the IT Services division (49.8% of revenue in 2002), operating under the Modis brand, the Professional Services division (42.9%), and the e-Business Solutions division (7.3%), operating under the Idea Integration brand.

RECENT DEVELOPMENTS:

For the year ended 12/31/02, MPS reported a loss of $12.6 million, before an accounting change charge of $553.7 million, versus net income of $8.3 million in the previous year. Results for 2002 and 2001 included depreciation and amortization charges of $21.0 million and $60.1 million, respectively. Results for 2002 also included an investment impairment charge of $16.1 million, a lease restructuring charge of $9.7 million and a proposed IRS audit adjustment that increased the income tax provision by $8.7 million. Total revenue fell 25.4% to $1.15 billion from $1.55 billion a year earlier. Information technology services revenue declined 25.4% to $575.3 million, while professional services revenue decreased 18.7% to $495.2 million. E-business solutions revenue dropped 49.9% to $84.5 million.

PROSPECTS:

On 3/11/03, the Company outlined its long-term strategy for growing its healthcare staffing business unit, which will operate under the new Soliant Health brand name. Soliant will focus on travel healthcare staffing. MPS entered the healthcare staffing space due to the long-term trends in healthcare and the overall imbalance in supply and demand for healthcare professionals. Demand continues to rise for nurses and other healthcare professionals, while graduation rates in these fields continue to decline Separately, for the first quarter of 2003 MPS expects revenue to range from $265.0 million to $275.0 million and earnings in the range of $0.02 to $0.04 per diluted share.

ANNUAL FINANCIAL DATA:

FISCAL YEAR	TOT. REVS. ($mill.)	NET INC. ($mill.)	TOT. ASSETS ($mill.)	OPER. PROFIT %	NET PROFIT %	RET. ON EQUITY %	RET. ON ASSETS %	CURR. RATIO	EARN. PER SH. $	CASH FL. PER SH. $	TANG. BK. VAL. $	PRICE RANGE	AVG. P/E RATIO
p12/31/02	1,155.0	⑦ d12.6							⑦ d0.12			9.80 - 4.35	. . .
12/31/01	1,548.5	8.3	1,543.6	1.6	0.5	0.6	0.5	3.1	0.08	0.70	1.47	8.20 - 3.65	74.0
12/31/00	1,827.7	⑥ 119.8	1,653.6	4.3	6.6	9.2	7.2	3.0	⑥ 1.23	1.78	1.07	18.69 - 3.38	9.0
⑤ 12/31/99	592.5	④ 18.6	1,490.3	5.4	3.1	1.6	1.2	1.9	④ 0.19	0.33	9.00	17.50 - 7.00	64.4
③ 12/31/98	1,702.1	② 68.9	1,571.9	7.7	4.0	6.4	4.4	1.0	② 0.61	0.91	0.47	38.06 - 9.94	39.3
12/31/97	2,424.8	① 102.0	1,479.5	7.7	4.2	12.6	6.9	2.7	① 0.93	1.22	. . .	32.00 - 15.75	25.7
12/31/96	1,448.6	27.9	897.1	6.6	1.9	4.3	3.1	3.0	0.31	0.46	1.84	38.00 - 11.58	79.9
12/31/95	267.6	8.7	141.7	5.3	3.3	7.9	6.1	2.8	0.22	0.27	0.92	14.75 - 2.23	38.6
1/01/95	137.1	3.0	35.4	3.7	2.2	11.4	8.5	4.2	0.12	0.14	0.72	2.44 - 1.77	18.0
1/02/94	89.1	0.7	14.2	1.7	0.8	17.5	5.0	2.9	0.03	0.05	0.12	. . .	. . .

Statistics are as originally reported. Adj. for stk. splits: 3-for-1, 3/96; 2-for-1, 11/95 ① Incl. non-recurr. chrg. $5.0 mill. ② Bef. disc. ops. gain $260.6 mill. & extr. loss $5.6 mill. ③ Refl. sale of commercial staffing business. ④ Incl. asset write-down $25.0 mill. & restr. credit $2.3 mill; bef. disc. ops. gain $78.5 mill. ⑤ Excl. results of Information Technology division, which was reported as a disc. oper. Including this division, rev. and earns. were $1.94 bill. and $97.1 mill., respectively. ⑥ Incl. pre-tax canceled IPO and separation chrgs. $7.3 mill. & asset write-down $13.1 mill. ⑦ Bef. acctg. change chrg. $80.0 mill.; incl. invest. impair. chrg. $16.1 mill. and lease restr. chrg. $9.7 mill.

OFFICERS:
D. E. Dewan, Chmn.
T. D. Payne, Pres. C.E.O.
R. P. Crouch, Sr. V.P., C.F.O., Treas.
INVESTOR CONTACT: Tyra Tutor, V.P., Corp. Devel. (904) 360-2500
PRINCIPAL OFFICE: 1 Independent Drive, Jacksonville, FL 32202

TELEPHONE NUMBER: (904) 360-2000
FAX: (904) 360-2814
WEB: www.mpsgroup.com
NO. OF EMPLOYEES: 14,200 (approx.)
SHAREHOLDERS: 851 (approx.)
ANNUAL MEETING: In Oct.
INCORPORATED: FL, May, 1992

INSTITUTIONAL HOLDINGS:
No. of Institutions: 143
Shares Held: 86,970,775
% Held: 84.8
INDUSTRY: Help supply services (SIC: 7363)
TRANSFER AGENT(S): Sun Trust Bank, Atlanta, GA

MSC INDUSTRIAL DIRECT CO., INC.

EXCH.	SYM.	REC. PRICE	P/E RATIO	YLD.	MKT. CAP.	RANGE (52-WK.)	'02 Y/E PR.
NYSE	MSM	17.85 (2/28/03)	30.3	...	$1.19 bill.	24.36 - 9.30	17.75

MEDIUM GRADE. THE COMPANY IS IMPLEMENTING INITIATIVES EXPECTED TO DRIVE SALES GROWTH THROUGH AN EXPANDED CUSTOMER BASE.

*7 YEAR PRICE SCORE 101.4   ***12 MONTH PRICE SCORE 114.3**
*NYSE COMPOSITE INDEX=100

INTERIM EARNINGS (Per Share):

Qtr.	Nov.	Feb.	May	Aug.
1996-97	0.11	0.13	0.16	0.13
1997-98	0.14	0.17	0.21	0.17
1998-99	0.18	0.22	0.18	0.14
1999-00	0.16	0.20	0.24	0.18
2000-01	0.20	0.21	0.04	0.15
2001-02	0.11	0.12	0.15	0.13
2002-03	0.19	...	...	...

INTERIM DIVIDENDS (Per Share):

Amt.	Decl.	Ex.	Rec.	Pay.
		No dividends paid.		

CAPITALIZATION (8/31/02):

	($000)	(%)
Long-Term Debt	1,308	0.3
Deferred Income Tax	15,329	3.1
Common & Surplus	474,679	96.6
Total	491,316	100.0

BUSINESS:

MSC Industrial Direct Co., Inc. is a direct marketer of a broad range of industrial products to small and mid-sized industrial customers throughout the United States. The Company distributes a full line of industrial products, such as cutting tools, abrasives, measuring instruments, machine tool accessories, safety equipment, fasteners and welding and electrical supplies. As of 1/9/03, the Company offered over 500,000 stock-keeping units through its master catalog and weekly, monthly and quarterly specialty and promotional catalogs, newspapers and brochures and services its customers from approximately 90 branch offices and four distribution centers. Most of the Company's products are carried in stock, and orders for these products are typically fulfilled the day on which the order is received.

RECENT DEVELOPMENTS:

For the 13 weeks ended 11/30/02, net income totaled $12.5 million, up 57.3% compared with $7.9 million in the corresponding period a year earlier. Net sales climbed 11.6% to $210.7 million from $188.9 million in the prior year. Gross profit was $94.5 million, or 44.9% of net sales, versus $82.3 million, or 43.6% of net sales, the previous year. Income from operations advanced 57.6% to $20.4 million from $12.9 million the year before. Income before taxes rose 57.4% to $20.6 million from $13.1 million in 2001.

PROSPECTS:

Earnings growth is being fueled by a more favorable product sales mix, modest price increases and improved purchasing. Going forward, sales should benefit from initiatives focused on increasing the Company's customer base. MSM is taking steps to provide next-day ground delivery in new markets, increase circulation and the number of products offered in the Company's master catalog, as well as expand its targeted mail campaign. In addition, the Company is taking steps expected to boost the productivity and increase the size of its direct sales operations.

ANNUAL FINANCIAL DATA:

FISCAL YEAR	TOT. REVS. ($mill.)	NET INC. ($mill.)	TOT. ASSETS ($mill.)	OPER. PROFIT %	NET PROFIT %	RET. ON EQUITY %	RET. ON ASSETS %	CURR. RATIO	EARN. PER SH.$	CASH FL. PER SH.$	TANG. BK. VAL.$	PRICE RANGE	AVG. P/E RATIO
8/31/02	794.0	☑ 36.4	562.9	7.6	4.6	7.7	6.5	5.2	☑ 0.51	0.74	6.17	24.36 - 9.30	33.0
9/01/01	869.2	☑ 40.5	553.9	10.1	4.7	8.6	7.3	5.5	☑ 0.58	0.83	5.96	20.49 - 13.90	29.6
8/26/00	792.9	52.9	581.0	11.8	6.7	12.6	9.1	4.8	0.78	0.99	5.25	23.25 - 11.31	22.2
8/28/99	651.5	48.9	514.4	12.6	7.5	13.7	9.5	4.1	0.72	0.85	4.31	26.25 - 7.50	23.4
8/29/98	583.0	47.3	401.7	13.1	8.1	14.7	11.8	3.6	0.69	0.80	3.88	33.50 - 12.25	33.1
8/30/97	438.0	36.0	334.8	13.4	8.2	13.1	10.8	4.5	0.53	0.61	3.56	23.06 - 13.88	34.8
8/31/96	305.3	☐ 28.5	265.5	11.3	9.3	16.5	10.7	4.4	☐ 0.34	0.52	2.54	19.63 - 12.25	47.6

Statistics are as originally reported. Adj. for stk. splits: 100%, 5/26/98. ☐ Incls. one-time chrg. of $8.6 mill. ☑ Incl. nonrecurr. chrg. of $700,000, 2002; $10.3 mill., 2001.

OFFICERS:
M. Jacobson, Chmn., Pres., C.E.O.
S. Jacobson, Vice-Chmn.
C. A. Boehlke, Jr., Exec. V.P., C.F.O.

INVESTOR CONTACT: Shelly Boxer, Investor Relations, (212) 812-2000

PRINCIPAL OFFICE: 75 Maxess Road, Melville, NY 11747

TELEPHONE NUMBER: (516) 812-2000
FAX: (516) 349-7096
WEB: www.mscdirect.com

NO. OF EMPLOYEES: 2,830 full-time (approx.); 110 part-time (approx.)

SHAREHOLDERS: 660 (approx. class A com.); 11 (class B com.)

ANNUAL MEETING: In Jan.

INCORPORATED: NY, Oct., 1995

INSTITUTIONAL HOLDINGS:
No. of Institutions: 93
Shares Held: 32,690,544
% Held: 49.2

INDUSTRY: Industrial machinery and equipment (SIC: 5084)

TRANSFER AGENT(S): American Stock Transfer & Trust Co., New York, NY

MURPHY OIL CORPORATION

EXCH.	SYM.	REC. PRICE	P/E RATIO	YLD.	MKT. CAP.	RANGE (52-WK.)	'02 Y/E PR.
NYSE	MUR	43.03 (2/28/03)	39.8	1.9%	$3.90 bill.	49.73 - 31.90	42.85

MEDIUM GRADE. THE COMPANY ANNOUNCED A CAPITAL PROGRAM OF $952.0 MILLION FOR 2003, AN INCREASE OF 9.8% FROM 2002.

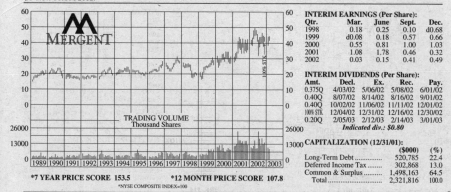

*7 YEAR PRICE SCORE 153.5   *12 MONTH PRICE SCORE 107.8
*NYSE COMPOSITE INDEX=100

INTERIM EARNINGS (Per Share):

Qtr.	Mar.	June	Sept.	Dec.
1998	0.18	0.25	0.10	d0.68
1999	d0.08	0.18	0.57	0.66
2000	0.55	0.81	1.00	1.03
2001	1.08	1.78	0.46	0.32
2002	0.03	0.15	0.41	0.49

INTERIM DIVIDENDS (Per Share):

Amt.	Decl.	Ex.	Rec.	Pay.
0.375Q	4/03/02	5/06/02	5/08/02	6/01/02
0.40Q	8/07/02	8/14/02	8/16/02	9/01/02
0.40Q	10/02/02	11/06/02	11/11/02	12/01/02
100% STK	12/04/02	12/31/02	12/16/02	12/30/02
0.20Q	2/05/03	2/12/03	2/14/03	3/01/03

Indicated div.: $0.80

CAPITALIZATION (12/31/01):

	($000)	(%)
Long-Term Debt	520,785	22.4
Deferred Income Tax	302,868	13.0
Common & Surplus	1,498,163	64.5
Total	2,321,816	100.0

BUSINESS:

Murphy Oil Corporation is an international oil and gas company. MUR produces oil and natural gas in the U.S., Canada, the United Kingdom, and Ecuador, and conducts exploration activities worldwide. As of 12/31/01, the Company had a 5.0% interest in a Canadian synthetic oil operation, operated two oil refineries in the U.S. and owned a 30.0% interest in a U.K. refinery. MUR markets petroleum products under various brand names to unbranded wholesale customers in the U.S. and the United Kingdom. As of 12/31/01, estimated net proved reserves were: crude oil, condensate and natural gas liquids, 377.9 million barrels; and natural gas, 740.1 billion cubic feet.

RECENT DEVELOPMENTS:

For the year ended 12/31/02, income from continuing operations was $97.5 million versus income of $328.4 million a year earlier. Results for 2002 and 2001 included gains of $14.7 million and $8.9 million from the settlement of tax matters and a tax rate change, gains of $13.0 million and $71.1 million from the sale of assets, and charges of $20.6 million and $6.8 million from the impairment of properties, respectively. Results for 2002 also included a charge of $3.3 million for storm-related damages in the Gulf of Mexico, while results for 2001 included a provision for environmental matters of $5.5 million. Total revenues rose 1.5% to $3.92 billion.

PROSPECTS:

MUR announced a capital program of $952.0 million for 2003, an increase of 9.8% from 2002. Exploration expenditures are expected to be $248.0 million versus $249.0 million the prior year, while development expenditures are expected to rise 27.2% to $486.0 million. Fueling this increase are deepwater Gulf of Mexico projects at Front Runner, Medusa, and Habanero, the West Patricia development in shallow-water Malaysia, and the Phase III expansion of the Syncrude operation. Capital expenditures for refining and marketing operations are budgeted to be $216.0 million in 2003 and include the continuing build out of the Murphy USA program at Wal-Mart stores and completion of a clean fuels project at MUR's refinery in Meraux, Louisiana.

ANNUAL FINANCIAL DATA:

FISCAL YEAR	TOT. REVS. ($mill.)	NET INC. ($mill.)	TOT. ASSETS ($mill.)	OPER. PROFIT %	NET PROFIT %	RET. ON EQUITY %	RET. ON ASSETS %	CURR. RATIO	EARN. PER SH. $	CASH FL. PER SH. $	TANG. BK. VAL. $	DIV. PER SH. $	PRICE RANGE	AVG. P/E RATIO	AVG. YIELD %
p12/31/02	3,923.3	⑨ 97.5							⑨ 1.06			0.78	49.73 - 31.90	38.5	1.9
12/31/01	4,478.5	⑧ 328.4	3,259.1	11.7	7.4	22.1	10.2	1.1	⑧ 3.63	6.43	15.97	0.75	43.93 - 27.63	9.9	2.1
12/31/00	4,639.2	⑦ 305.6	3,134.4	10.4	6.6	24.3	9.7	1.1	⑦ 3.38	5.89	13.44	0.70	34.53 - 24.09	8.7	2.5
12/31/99	2,041.2	⑥ 119.7	2,445.5	9.7	5.9	11.3	4.9	1.2	⑥ 1.33	3.72	11.75	0.70	30.81 - 16.44	17.8	3.0
12/31/98	1,698.8	⑤ d14.4	2,164.4	0.6	...	...	...	1.1	⑤ d0.16	2.21	10.88	0.70	27.22 - 17.25	...	3.1
12/31/97	2,137.8	⑤ 132.4	2,238.3	9.9	6.2	12.3	5.9	1.1	⑤ 1.47	3.92	12.02	0.68	31.28 - 21.50	18.0	2.6
12/31/96	2,022.2	③ 126.0	2,243.8	10.8	6.2	12.3	5.6	1.1	③ 1.40	3.54	11.45	0.65	28.25 - 20.31	17.3	2.7
12/31/95	1,631.8	② d127.9	2,098.5	...	...	...	...	1.2	② d1.42	1.17	12.28	0.65	22.69 - 18.75	...	3.1
12/31/94	1,768.5	④ 106.6	2,312.0	9.0	6.0	8.4	4.6	1.2	④ 1.19	3.62	14.17	0.65	24.56 - 18.94	18.4	3.0
12/31/93	1,671.1	① 86.8	2,168.9	8.1	5.2	7.1	4.0	1.3	① 0.97	3.07	13.64	0.65	23.94 - 16.50	20.8	3.1

Statistics are as originally reported. Adj. for 100% stk. div., 12/30/02. ① Incl. chrg. of $87.4 mill.; ② Incl. net chrg. 12/31/97, $94.2 mill.; chrg. 12/31/95, $160.2 mill. ③ Bef. inc. fr. disc. ops. of $11.9 mill. ④ Bef. extraord. cr. of $20.3 mill. ⑤ Bef. acctg. adj. cr. of $15.3 mill. ⑥ Incl. chrg. of $953,000. ⑦ Incl. prop. impair. chrg. of $27.9 mill.; bef. acctg. chg. chrg. of $8.7 mill. ⑧ Incl. gain on sale of assets of $71.1 mill., inc. tax ben. of $8.9 mill., prop. impair. chrg. of $6.8 mill. & chrg. of $5.5 mill. for environ. matters. ⑨ Incl. gain on sale of assets of $2.3 mill., inc. tax ben. of $14.7 mill., prop. impair. chrg. of $20.6 mill. & chrg. of $3.3 mill. rel. to storm-rel. dmgs.; bef. inc. fr. disc. ops. of $14.0 mill.

OFFICERS:
W. C. Nolan, Jr., Chmn.
C. P. Deming, Pres., C.E.O.
K. G. Fitzgerald, Treas.

INVESTOR CONTACT: Mindy K. West, Dir., Investor Relations, (870) 864-6315

PRINCIPAL OFFICE: 200 Peach Street, P.O. Box 7000, El Dorado, AR 71731-7000

TELEPHONE NUMBER: (870) 862-6411
FAX: (870) 864-3673
WEB: www.murphyoilcorp.com
NO. OF EMPLOYEES: 1,863 (full-time)
SHAREHOLDERS: 2,991 (of record)
ANNUAL MEETING: In May
INCORPORATED: LA, May, 1950; reincorp., DE, May, 1963

INSTITUTIONAL HOLDINGS:
No. of Institutions: 239
Shares Held: 57,908,528
% Held: 126.4

INDUSTRY: Petroleum refining (SIC: 2911)

TRANSFER AGENT(S): Computershare Investor Services, L.L.C., Chicago, IL

MYERS INDUSTRIES, INC.

EXCH.	SYM.	REC. PRICE	P/E RATIO	YLD.	MKT. CAP.	RANGE (52-WK.)	'02 Y/E PR.	DIV. ACH.
NYSE	MYE	9.70 (2/28/03)	12.3	2.1%	$289.2 mill.	14.48 - 9.50	10.70	26 yrs.

MEDIUM GRADE. RISING RAW MATERIAL PRICES COULD NEGATIVELY AFFECT RESULTS FOR THE COMPANY'S MANUFACTURING SEGMENT IN THE NEAR TERM.

TRADING VOLUME
Thousand Shares

*7 YEAR PRICE SCORE 114.3   ***12 MONTH PRICE SCORE 94.1**
*NYSE COMPOSITE INDEX=100

INTERIM EARNINGS (Per Share):

Qtr.	Mar.	June	Sept.	Dec.
1997	0.16	0.17	0.12	0.27
1998	0.23	0.26	0.17	0.30
1999	0.27	0.30	0.13	0.33
2000	0.28	0.27	0.11	0.15
2001	0.30	0.12	0.06	0.08
2002	0.34	0.22	0.10	0.13

INTERIM DIVIDENDS (Per Share):

Amt.	Decl.	Ex.	Rec.	Pay.
0.06Q	4/25/02	6/12/02	6/14/02	7/01/02
5-for-4	6/26/02	9/03/02	8/09/02	8/30/02
0.05Q	6/26/02	9/04/02	9/06/02	10/01/02
0.05Q	9/19/02	12/04/02	12/06/02	1/02/03
0.05Q	2/13/03	3/05/03	3/07/03	4/01/03

Indicated div.: $0.20 (Div. Reinv. Plan)

CAPITALIZATION (12/31/01):

	($000)	(%)
Long-Term Debt	247,145	51.8
Deferred Income Tax	12,596	2.6
Common & Surplus	217,526	45.6
Total	477,267	100.0

BUSINESS:

Myers Industries, Inc. is comprised of two segments: the manufacturing business (75.0% of 2001 sales) and the distribution business (25.0%). The manufacturing business designs, manufactures and markets plastic and rubber products for the industrial, agricultural, automotive, commercial and consumer markets. As of 2/13/03, MYE operated 25 manufacturing facilities in Europe and North America and marketed reusable plastics under the brand names NESTIER, AKROBINS and BUCKHORN. MYE also manufactures and sells molded rubber products and other materials used primarily in the tire and tire repair industries and for various other uses. As of 2/13/03, the distribution business, primarily conducted by the Myers Tire Supply division through 43 U.S. and five international branches, was engaged in the distribution of tools, equipment and supplies used for tire servicing and automotive underbody repair.

RECENT DEVELOPMENTS:

For the year ended 12/31/02, net income jumped 57.7% to $24.0 million compared with $15.2 million in 2001. The improvement in earnings was primarily attributed to steady demand and lower interest expense as the Company worked to mitigate the effects of weak end-use markets and rising raw material costs by developing new sales channels and maintaining productivity. Net sales were flat at $608.0 million compared with 2001. Gross profit declined 1.7% to $201.4 million. Operating income rose 13.6% to $52.2 million from $45.9 million in 2001.

PROSPECTS:

Going forward, MYE will continue to develop new products and markets, as well as expand customer relationships. In addition, the Company plans to continue to improve its balance sheet and strengthen internal processes for more profitable operations. Meanwhile, raw material prices remain on an upward trend, fueled by rising energy costs and world tension. Consequently, near-term results for the Company's manufacturing segment will be negatively affected. However, the Company's distribution segment should continue to benefit from steady dmenad for consumable service supplies.

ANNUAL FINANCIAL DATA:

FISCAL YEAR	TOT. REVS. ($000)	NET INC. ($000)	TOT. ASSETS ($000)	OPER. PROFIT %	NET PROFIT %	RET. ON EQUITY %	RET. ON ASSETS %	CURR. RATIO	EARN. PER SH.$	CASH FL.PER SH.$	TANG. BK. VAL.$	DIV. PER SH.$	PRICE RANGE	AVG. P/E RATIO	AVG. YIELD %
p12/31/02	607,991	23,960	602,482						0.80			0.194	14.48 - 9.20	14.8	1.6
12/31/01	607,950	15,191	582,166	7.6	2.5	7.0	2.6	1.9	0.51	1.99	0.90	0.18	11.66 - 8.01	15.4	1.8
12/31/00	652,660	①24,001	624,797	9.7	3.7	11.2	3.8	1.9	①0.81	2.24	0.56	0.16	10.73 - 7.00	8.8	1.8
12/31/99	580,761	31,176	600,410	12.0	5.4	15.0	5.2	2.0	1.03	2.25	0.28	0.15	18.18 - 8.43	10.4	1.1
12/31/98	392,020	28,679	306,708	12.6	7.3	14.1	9.4	3.0	0.94	1.52	5.35	0.13	17.24 - 9.84	11.5	0.9
12/31/97	339,626	22,339	224,078	11.3	6.6	12.6	10.0	2.7	0.73	1.16	5.06	0.11	11.27 - 8.20	10.7	1.2
12/31/96	320,944	21,003	207,122	11.2	6.5	12.9	10.1	2.9	0.68	1.04	4.71	0.09	11.61 - 7.85	11.5	1.0
12/31/95	300,699	15,969	193,604	9.3	5.3	11.0	8.2	3.1	0.52	0.86	4.05	0.08	9.15 - 6.52	12.1	1.0
12/31/94	274,054	17,831	172,027	11.2	6.5	13.6	10.4	2.8	0.58	0.89	3.84	0.07	9.14 - 6.40	10.7	0.9
12/31/93	245,136	15,395	152,386	10.8	6.3	13.4	10.1	3.2	0.52	0.78	3.32	0.07	10.13 - 7.59	13.6	0.8

Statistics are as originally reported. Adj. for stk. splits: 10% div., 8/01, 8/00, 8/99, 8/97 & 8/95; 5-for-4, 8/02. ① Incl. an after-tax restructuring chrg. of $1.9 mill.

OFFICERS:
S. E. Myers, Pres., C.E.O.
J. C. Orr, C.O.O.
G. J. Stodnick, V.P., C.F.O.
M. I. Wiskind, Sr. V.P., Sec.

INVESTOR CONTACT: Gregory J. Stodnick, V.P., C.F.O., (330) 253-5592
PRINCIPAL OFFICE: 1293 South Main Street, Akron, OH 44301

TELEPHONE NUMBER: (330) 253-5592
FAX: (330) 761-6156
WEB: www.myersind.com
NO. OF EMPLOYEES: 4,300 (approx.)
SHAREHOLDERS: 2,200 (approx.)
ANNUAL MEETING: In Apr.
INCORPORATED: OH, Jan., 1955

INSTITUTIONAL HOLDINGS:
No. of Institutions: 97
Shares Held: 15,548,825
% Held: 51.7

INDUSTRY: Plastics products, nec (SIC: 3089)

TRANSFER AGENT(S): First Chicago Trust Company of New York, New York, NY

MYLAN LABORATORIES INC.

EXCH.	SYM.	REC. PRICE	P/E RATIO	YLD.	MKT. CAP.	RANGE (52-WK.)	'02 Y/E PR.
NYSE	MYL	28.55 (2/28/03)	20.2	0.5%	$5.41 bill.	28.66 - 16.73	23.27

UPPER MEDIUM GRADE. THE COMPANY SHOULD CONTINUE TO BENEFIT FROM EXISTING PRODUCT GROWTH, AS WELL AS VOLUME INCREASES AND STABLE PRICING.

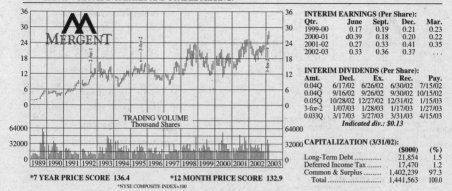

7 YEAR PRICE SCORE 136.4   *12 MONTH PRICE SCORE 132.9*

NYSE COMPOSITE INDEX=100

INTERIM EARNINGS (Per Share):

Qtr.	June	Sept.	Dec.	Mar.
1999-00	0.17	0.19	0.21	0.23
2000-01	d0.39	0.18	0.20	0.22
2001-02	0.27	0.33	0.41	0.35
2002-03	0.33	0.36	0.37	...

INTERIM DIVIDENDS (Per Share):

Amt.	Decl.	Ex.	Rec.	Pay.
0.04Q	6/17/02	6/26/02	6/30/02	7/15/02
0.04Q	9/16/02	9/26/02	9/30/02	10/15/02
0.05Q	10/28/02	12/27/02	12/31/02	1/15/03
3-for-2	1/07/03	1/28/03	1/17/03	1/27/03
0.033Q	3/17/03	3/27/03	3/31/03	4/15/03

Indicated div.: $0.13

CAPITALIZATION (3/31/02):

	($000)	(%)
Long-Term Debt	21,854	1.5
Deferred Income Tax	17,470	1.2
Common & Surplus	1,402,239	97.3
Total	1,441,563	100.0

BUSINESS:

Mylan Laboratories Inc. is engaged in the development, licensing, manufacturing, marketing and distribution of generic and branded pharmaceutical products for resale by others. The Company's generic operations (88.0% of fiscal 2002 revenues) consists of two principal business units, Mylan Pharmaceuticals Inc., MYL's primary generic pharmaceutical development, manufacturing, marketing and distribution division, and UDL Laboratories, Inc., which

packages and markets generic products obtained from Mylan Pharmaceuticals or third parties. The Company's branded operations (12.0%) are conducted through, Bertek Pharmaceuticals Inc. and Mylan Technologies Inc., and focus on pharmaceutical products that have patent protection, have achieved brand recognition in the marketplace, or represent branded generic pharmaceutical products that are responsive to promotional offers.

RECENT DEVELOPMENTS:

For the three months ended 12/31/02, net income decreased 12.5% to $68.4 million compared with $78.2 million in the corresponding quarter of the previous year. Net revenues climbed 7.9% to $320.5 million from $297.2 million in the year-earlier period. Net revenues in the generic segment declined 2.8% to $253.9 million in the

prior-year quarter, reflecting the loss of exclusivity on buspirone in February 2002. Net revenues in the Company's brand segment rocketed 85.8% to $66.6 million, due to increased revenues from three existing products, including DIGITEK®, phenytoin and ACTICIN®. Operating income dropped 14.4% to $102.7 million.

PROSPECTS:

The Company anticipates diluted earnings per share to range from $0.34 to $0.37 for the fourth quarter of fiscal 2003, and increased its guidance for fiscal 2003 to a range of $1.39 to $1.42 per diluted share. Moreover, the Company estimates fiscal 2004 diluted earnings per share to a

range of $1.59 to $1.69, reflecting net revenue growth of 9.0% to 11.0%. Meanwhile, the Company should continue to benefit from the launch of Amnesteem™, for the treatment of severe recalcitrant nodular acne.

ANNUAL FINANCIAL DATA:

FISCAL YEAR	TOT. REVS. ($000)	NET INC. ($000)	TOT. ASSETS ($000)	OPER. PROFIT %	NET PROFIT %	RET. ON EQUITY %	RET. ON ASSETS %	CURR. RATIO	EARN. PER SH.$	CASH FL. PER SH.$	TANG. BK. VAL.$	DIV. PER SH.$	PRICE RANGE	AVG. P/E RATIO	AVG. YIELD %
3/31/02	1,104,050	260,251	1,616,710	35.8	23.6	18.6	16.1	6.1	1.36	1.60	5.96	0.11	25.41 - 13.43	14.3	0.5
3/31/01	846,696	37,128	1,465,973	2.3	4.4	3.3	2.5	3.0	0.19	0.42	4.46	0.11	21.50 - 10.67	83.3	0.7
3/31/00	790,145	③ 154,246	1,341,230	28.2	19.5	12.8	11.5	7.8	③ 0.79	0.97	4.49	0.11	21.33 - 11.38	20.8	0.7
3/31/99	721,123	② 115,409	1,206,661	23.4	16.0	10.9	9.6	6.0	② 0.61	0.75	3.71	0.11	23.96 - 11.38	29.1	0.6
3/31/98	555,423	100,777	847,753	22.4	18.1	13.5	11.9	6.3	0.55	0.66	3.36	0.11	16.88 - 7.67	22.4	0.9
3/31/97	440,192	63,127	777,580	13.2	14.3	9.6	8.1	4.8	0.35	0.44	2.85	0.11	15.58 - 9.33	35.9	0.9
3/31/96	392,860	① 102,325	692,009	25.5	26.0	16.6	14.8	7.8	① 0.57	0.65	2.97	0.14	16.33 - 11.00	23.8	1.0
3/31/95	396,120	120,869	546,201	34.8	30.5	25.0	22.1	5.9	0.68	0.75	2.54	0.08	13.28 - 6.95	14.9	0.7
3/31/94	251,773	73,067	403,325	22.0	29.0	19.2	18.1	11.7	0.41	0.47	1.95	0.06	16.72 - 8.72	30.8	0.5
3/31/93	211,964	70,621	351,105	34.1	33.3	23.9	20.1	6.8	0.41	0.44	1.46	0.05	14.17 - 7.00	26.0	0.4

Statistics are as originally reported. Adjusted for 3-for-2 stock split, 8/95 & 1/03. ① Incl. an after-tax charge of $800,000 resulting from the sale of certain assets. ② Incl. a pre-tax charge of $29.0 million for acquired research and development associated with the acquisition of Penederm, Inc. ③ Incl. litig. settle. chrg. of $147.0 mill.

OFFICERS:
M. Puskar, Chmn.
R. J. Coury, Vice-Chmn., C.E.O.
C. B. Todd, Pres., C.O.O.
INVESTOR CONTACT: Kris King, Investor, Relations, (412) 232-0100
PRINCIPAL OFFICE: 130 Seventh Street, 1030 Century Building, Pittsburgh, PA 15222

TELEPHONE NUMBER: (412) 232-0100
FAX: (412) 232-0123
WEB: www.mylan.com
NO. OF EMPLOYEES: 2,200 (approx.)
SHAREHOLDERS: 99,021 (approx.)
ANNUAL MEETING: In July
INCORPORATED: PA, 1970

INSTITUTIONAL HOLDINGS:
No. of Institutions: 346
Shares Held: 119,584,896
% Held: 97.6

INDUSTRY: Pharmaceutical preparations (SIC: 2834)

TRANSFER AGENT(S): American Stock Transfer & Trust Company, New York, NY

NACCO INDUSTRIES, INC.

EXCH.	SYM.	REC. PRICE	P/E RATIO	YLD.	MKT. CAP.	RANGE (52-WK.)	'02 Y/E PR.	DIV. ACH.
NYSE	NC	44.85 (2/28/03)	7.4	2.2%	$367.6 mill.	76.20 - 36.39	43.77	19 yrs.

MEDIUM GRADE. THE COMPANY EXPECTS GENERALLY IMPROVED MARKET PROSPECTS FOR ITS BUSINESSES IN 2003.

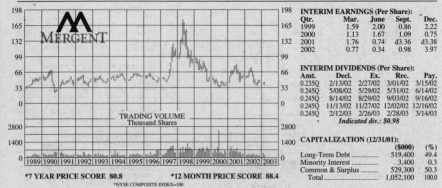

INTERIM EARNINGS (Per Share):

Qtr.	Mar.	June	Sept.	Dec.
1999	1.59	2.00	0.86	2.22
2000	1.13	1.67	1.09	0.75
2001	1.76	0.74	d3.36	d3.38
2002	0.77	0.34	0.98	3.97

INTERIM DIVIDENDS (Per Share):

Amt.	Decl.	Ex.	Rec.	Pay.
0.235Q	2/13/02	2/27/02	3/01/02	3/15/02
0.245Q	5/08/02	5/29/02	5/31/02	6/14/02
0.245Q	8/14/02	8/29/02	9/03/02	9/16/02
0.245Q	11/13/02	11/27/02	12/02/02	12/16/02
0.245Q	2/12/03	2/26/03	2/28/03	3/14/03

Indicated div.: $0.98

CAPITALIZATION (12/31/01):

	($000)	(%)
Long-Term Debt	519,400	49.4
Minority Interest	3,400	0.3
Common & Surplus	529,300	50.3
Total	1,052,100	100.0

*7 YEAR PRICE SCORE 80.8   *12 MONTH PRICE SCORE 88.4
*NYSE COMPOSITE INDEX=100

BUSINESS:

Nacco Industries, Inc. is a holding company with three principal businesses. NACCO Materials Handling Group (NMHG) (62.3% of 2002 revenue) designs, engineers, manufactures and sells a full line of lift trucks and replacement parts marketed worldwide under the HYSTER™ and YALE™ brand names. NACCO Housewares Group (24.0%) consists of Hamilton Beach/Procter-Silex, Inc., a manufacturer and marketer of small household appliances and commercial products for restaurants, bars and hotels, and The Kitchen Collection, Inc., a national specialty retailer of brand-name kitchenware and electrical appliances. The North American Coal Corporation (13.7%) mines and markets lignite coal primarily as fuel for power generators.

RECENT DEVELOPMENTS:

For the year ended 12/31/02, NC reported income of $49.6 million, before an extraordinary loss of $7.2 million, compared with a loss of $34.7 million, before an accounting change charge of $1.3 million, the previous year. Total revenues declined 3.4% to $2.55 billion from $2.64 billion a year earlier. Materials Handling Group revenue fell 5.0% to $1.59 billion, reflecting lower lift truck volumes and the sale of Hyster Germany dealerships in 2001. Housewares group revenues decreased 3.4% to $610.3 million, primarily due to NC's exit of selected low-margin opening price point business and lower sales of TrueAir™ home health products, partially offset by higher sales of General Electric branded products and increased sales at Kitchen Collection. North American Coal Corporation revenues increased 4.8% to $349.3 million. Operating profit amounted to $131.8 million versus $5.7 million in 2001.

PROSPECTS:

NC expects generally improved market prospects for its businesses in 2003. In December 2002, NC announced that NMHG expects to close a manufacturing facility in Lenoir, North Carolina, which employs about 310 people, and restructure the operations of its Irvine, Scotland facility, which employs approximately 450 people. Separately, NMHG completed the sale of its wholly-owned U.S. retail operations to M.H. Logistics, an independent Hyster dealer.

ANNUAL FINANCIAL DATA:

FISCAL YEAR	TOT. REVS. ($mill.)	NET INC. ($mill.)	TOT. ASSETS ($mill.)	OPER. PROFIT %	NET PROFIT %	RET. ON EQUITY %	RET. ON ASSETS %	CURR. RATIO	EARN. PER SH.$	CASH FL. PER SH.$	TANG. BK. VAL.$	DIV. PER SH.$	PRICE RANGE	AVG. P/E RATIO	AVG. YIELD %
p12/31/02	2,548.1	⑥ 49.6							⑥ 6.05			0.97	76.20 - 36.39	9.3	1.7
12/31/01	2,637.9	②⑤ d34.7	2,161.9	0.2	...	...	...	0.9	②⑤ d4.24	10.12	12.37	0.93	82.80 - 42.50	...	1.5
12/31/00	2,871.3	①④ 37.8	2,193.9	4.1	1.3	6.2	1.7	1.3	①④ 4.63	17.62	20.01	0.89	55.75 - 33.56	9.6	2.0
12/31/99	2,602.8	③ 54.3	2,013.0	5.0	2.1	9.7	2.7	1.3	③ 6.66	19.41	11.51	0.85	97.00 - 44.50	10.6	1.2
12/31/98	2,536.2	③ 102.3	1,898.3	7.8	4.0	19.7	5.4	1.3	③ 12.53	23.43	9.52	0.81	177.00 - 76.25	10.1	0.6
12/31/97	2,246.9	② 61.8	1,729.1	5.9	2.8	14.5	3.6	1.2	② 7.55	18.37	...	0.77	127.00 - 44.38	11.3	0.9
12/31/96	2,273.2	50.6	1,708.1	5.8	2.2	13.3	3.0	1.4	5.67	15.22	...	0.74	64.00 - 43.13	9.4	1.4
12/31/95	2,204.5	① 65.5	1,833.8	6.9	3.0	17.7	3.6	1.4	① 7.31	16.13	...	0.71	64.00 - 46.88	7.6	1.3
12/31/94	1,864.9	① 45.3	1,694.3	7.2	2.4	16.2	2.7	1.2	① 5.06	14.02	...	0.68	64.00 - 45.75	10.8	1.2
12/31/93	1,549.4	① 11.6	1,642.5	6.0	0.7	4.9	0.7	1.3	① 1.30	10.03	...	0.66	58.25 - 42.00	38.6	1.3

Statistics are as originally reported. ① Bef. extra. gain of $29.9 mill., 2000; gain $28.9 mill., 1995; chrg. $3.2 mill., 1994; chrg. $3.3 mill., 1993. ② Incl. restruct. chrgs. $21.5 mill., 2001; $1.6 mill., 1998; $8.0 mill., 1997. ③ Bef. acctg. chrg. of $1.2 mill. & incl. chrg. of $1.9 mill. rel. to the proposed acq. of Nissan Motor Co., Ltd.'s global lift truck business. ④ Incl. an after-tax restruct. chrg. of $8.3 mill. & an after-tax write-off of assets of $1.5 mill. ⑤ Incl. loss on sale of dealers of $10.4 mill. & ins. recovery of $8.0 mill.; bef. acctg. chrg. of $1.3 mill. ⑥ Bef. extraord. loss of $7.2 mill.

OFFICERS:
A. M. Rankin Jr., Chmn., Pres., C.E.O.
J. C. Butler Jr., V.P., Treas.
C. A. Bittenbender, V.P., Gen. Couns., Sec.
INVESTOR CONTACT: Ira Gamm, Manager,
Investor Relations, (440) 449-9676
PRINCIPAL OFFICE: 5875 Landerbrook
Drive, Mayfield Heights, OH 44124-4017

TELEPHONE NUMBER: (440) 449-9600
FAX: (440) 449-9607
WEB: www.naccoind.com
NO. OF EMPLOYEES: 13,300 (approx.)
SHAREHOLDERS: 500 (cl. A com.); 400 (cl. B com.)
ANNUAL MEETING: In May
INCORPORATED: DE, 1986

INSTITUTIONAL HOLDINGS:
No. of Institutions: 64
Shares Held: 3,374,775
% Held: 41.2
INDUSTRY: Industrial trucks and tractors (SIC: 3537)
TRANSFER AGENT(S): National City Bank, Cleveland, OH

NATIONAL CITY CORPORATION

EXCH.	SYM.	REC. PRICE	P/E RATIO	YLD.	MKT. CAP.	RANGE (52-WK.)	'02 Y/E PR.	DIV. ACH.
NYSE	NCC	27.62 (2/28/03)	10.7	4.4%	$16,775.14 bill.	33.70 - 24.60	27.32	10 yrs.

UPPER MEDIUM GRADE. MORTGAGE ACTIVITY IS ANTICIPATED TO REMAIN STRONG DURING THE FIRST HALF OF 2003 AS INTEREST RATES CONTINUE TO BE LOW.

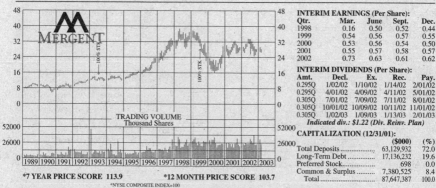

*7 YEAR PRICE SCORE 113.9   *12 MONTH PRICE SCORE 103.7
*NYSE COMPOSITE INDEX=100

INTERIM EARNINGS (Per Share):

Qtr.	Mar.	June	Sept.	Dec.
1998	0.16	0.50	0.52	0.44
1999	0.54	0.56	0.57	0.55
2000	0.53	0.56	0.54	0.50
2001	0.55	0.57	0.58	0.57
2002	0.73	0.63	0.61	0.62

INTERIM DIVIDENDS (Per Share):

Amt.	Decl.	Ex.	Rec.	Pay.
0.295Q	1/02/02	1/10/02	1/14/02	2/01/02
0.295Q	4/01/02	4/09/02	4/11/02	5/01/02
0.305Q	7/01/02	7/09/02	7/11/02	8/01/02
0.305Q	10/01/02	10/09/02	10/11/02	11/01/02
0.305Q	1/02/03	1/09/03	1/13/03	2/01/03

Indicated div.: $1.22 (Div. Reinv. Plan)

CAPITALIZATION (12/31/01):

	($000)	(%)
Total Deposits	63,129,932	72.0
Long-Term Debt	17,136,232	19.6
Preferred Stock	698	0.0
Common & Surplus	7,380,525	8.4
Total	87,647,387	100.0

BUSINESS:

National City Corporation is a bank holding company, with total assets of $118.3 billion as of 12/31/02, providing financial services principally in Ohio, Pennsylvania, Kentucky, Michigan, Illinois, and Indiana. Its principal banking subsidiaries are National City Bank, Cleveland; BancOhio National Bank, Columbus; First National Bank of Louisville; and Merchants National Bank & Trust Co. of Indian-apolis. NCC's primary businesses include commercial and retail banking, consumer finance, asset management, mortgage financing and servicing, and payment processing. As of 12/31/02, NCC owned 85.0% of National Processing Inc. In March 1998, NCC acquired Fort Wayne Corp. and First of America Bank Corp. On 9/1/99, NCC acquired First Franklin Financial Cos., Inc.

RECENT DEVELOPMENTS:

For the year ended 12/31/02, net income increased 14.8% to $1.59 billion from $1.39 billion a year earlier. Earnings for 2002 and 2001 included net gains from mortgage servicing asset hedging activities of $231.7 million and $36.8 million, respectively. Net interest income improved 16.2% to $4.04 billion. Provision for loan losses rose 12.8% to $681.9 million. Total fees and other income advanced 7.6% to $2.73 billion, while total non-interest expense increased 11.5% to $3.73 billion. Net interest margin grew to 4.34% from 4.09% in the prior year, reflecting a more favorable asset mix and lower funding costs, combined with strong core deposit growth.

PROSPECTS:

Mortgage activity is anticipated to remain strong during the first half of 2003 as interest rates continue to be low. Additionally, deposit growth is expected to continue at a pace equal to or exceeding 2002's. However, deposit margins may be compressed by the cumulative effects of low interest rates. Meanwhile, corporate loan demand is likely to continue to be weak, and credit costs are anticipated to be significantly lower. As a result, NCC will be aggressively seeking ways to reduce overhead expenditures. Looking ahead, the Company expects earnings per share of about $2.61 for 2003.

ANNUAL FINANCIAL DATA:

FISCAL YEAR	NET INT. INC. ($mill.)	NON-INT. INC. ($mill.)	NET INC. ($mill.)	TOT. LOANS ($mill.)	TOT. ASSETS ($mill.)	TOT. DEP. ($mill.)	RET. ON EQUITY %	RET. ON ASSETS %	EQUITY/ ASSETS %	EARN. PER SH.$	TANG. BK. VAL.$	DIV. PER SH.$	PRICE RANGE	AVG. P/E RATIO
p12/31/02	4,035.7	2,700.0	1,593.6							2.59		1.20	33.70 - 24.60	11.3
12/31/01	3,438.8	2,677.8	④ 1,388.1	68,040.6	105,816.7	63,129.9	18.8	1.3	7.0	④ 2.27	12.15	1.16	32.70 - 23.69	12.4
12/31/00	2,958.4	2,484.2	1,302.4	65,604.4	88,534.6	55,256.4	19.2	1.5	7.6	2.13	11.06	1.14	29.75 - 16.00	10.7
12/31/99	3,000.0	2,380.8	③ 1,405.5	60,203.9	87,121.5	50,066.3	24.5	1.6	6.6	③ 2.22	9.39	1.06	37.81 - 22.13	13.5
② 12/31/98	2,911.6	2,314.1	① 1,070.7	58,011.2	88,245.6	58,246.9	15.3	1.2	7.9	① 1.61	10.69	0.94	38.75 - 28.47	20.9
12/31/97	1,942.8	1,375.9	① 807.4	38,442.2	54,883.5	36,861.1	18.9	1.5	7.8	① 1.83	10.14	0.83	33.78 - 21.25	15.0
12/31/96	1,942.6	1,273.0	① 736.6	35,495.3	50,855.8	35,999.7	16.6	1.4	8.7	① 1.65	9.93	0.73	23.63 - 15.31	11.8
12/31/95	1,321.1	916.8	465.1	26,055.3	36,199.0	25,200.5	15.9	1.3	8.1	1.52	9.40	0.65	16.88 - 12.63	9.7
12/31/94	1,236.8	863.4	429.4	22,992.7	32,114.0	24,471.9	16.5	1.3	8.1	1.35	8.18	0.59	14.50 - 11.88	9.8
12/31/93	1,200.1	811.7	404.0	20,777.0	31,067.7	23,063.0	14.6	1.3	8.9	1.21	8.08	0.53	14.03 - 11.56	10.6

Statistics are as originally reported. Adj. for stk. split: 2-for-1, 7/99 & 8/93. ① Incl. pre-tax merger-related chgs. totaling: $379.4 mill., 1998; $65.9 mill, 1997; $74.7 mill., 1996. ② Results reflect the consummation of the 3/31/98 merger with First of America Bank Corporation. ③ Incl. an after-tax non-recurring gain of $1.3 mill. ④ Incl. net ineffective hedge & oth. derivative gains of $362.9 mill. & write-downs to automobile lease residual values of $67.4 mill.

OFFICERS:
D. A. Daberko, Chmn., C.E.O.
W. E. MacDonald III, Vice-Chmn.
R. G. Siefers, Vice-Chmn.
J. D. Kelly, Exec. V.P., C.F.O.
INVESTOR CONTACT: Derek Green, V.P., Investor Relations, (800) 622-4204
PRINCIPAL OFFICE: 1900 East Ninth Street, Cleveland, OH 44114-3484

TELEPHONE NUMBER: (216) 222-2000
FAX: (216) 575-2353
WEB: www.nationalcity.com
NO. OF EMPLOYEES: 32,360
SHAREHOLDERS: 34,631
ANNUAL MEETING: In April
INCORPORATED: DE, Aug., 1972

INSTITUTIONAL HOLDINGS:
No. of Institutions: 467
Shares Held: 298,669,133
% Held: 48.8

INDUSTRY: National commercial banks (SIC: 6021)

TRANSFER AGENT(S): National City Bank Corporate Trust Operations, Cleveland, OH

NATIONAL COMMERCE FINANCIAL CORPORATION

EXCH.	SYM.	REC. PRICE	P/E RATIO	YLD.	MKT. CAP.	RANGE (52-WK.)	'02 Y/E PR.	DIV. ACH.
NYSE	NCF	24.28 (2/28/03)	15.6	2.8%	$4.98 bill.	29.60 - 21.27	23.85	28 yrs.

UPPER MEDIUM GRADE. ON 12/13/02, THE COMPANY ANNOUNCED THAT IT HAS ACQUIRED BANCMORTGAGE FINANCIAL CORP.

*7 YEAR PRICE SCORE 140.7　***12 MONTH PRICE SCORE 102.4**

*NYSE COMPOSITE INDEX=100

INTERIM EARNINGS (Per Share):

Qtr.	Mar.	June	Sept.	Dec.
1998	0.19	0.20	0.21	0.22
1999	0.23	0.24	0.26	0.26
2000	0.29	0.29	d0.05	0.04
2001	0.25	0.27	0.28	0.29
2002	0.36	0.39	0.40	0.41

INTERIM DIVIDENDS (Per Share):

Amt.	Decl.	Ex.	Rec.	Pay.
0.15Q	1/15/02	3/06/02	3/08/02	4/01/02
0.15Q	4/24/02	6/05/02	6/07/02	7/01/02
0.17Q	7/16/02	9/11/02	9/13/02	10/01/02
0.17Q	10/17/02	12/04/02	12/06/02	1/02/03
0.17Q	1/14/03	3/05/03	3/07/03	4/01/03

Indicated div.: $0.68 (Div. Reinv. Plan)

CAPITALIZATION (12/31/01):

	($000)	(%)
Total Deposits	12,619,479	71.4
Long-Term Debt	2,588,572	14.7
Common & Surplus	2,455,331	13.9
Total	17,663,382	100.0

BUSINESS:

National Commerce Financial Corporation is a bank holding company with assets of $21.47 billion as of 12/31/02. The Company's banking subsidiaries, National Bank of Commerce (NBC) and NBC Bank, Federal Savings Bank (FSB), provide commercial and retail banking, savings and trust services through its Central Carolina Bank offices located in North Carolina and South Carolina and its National Bank of Commerce offices located in Tennessee, Mississippi, Arkansas, Georgia, Virginia and West Virginia. NBC Bank operates offices in DeSoto County, Mississippi. The Company also provides trust services through a subsidiary in Florida. As of 1/16/03, NCF owned 49.0% of First Market Bank, FSB. In addition to its banking subsidiaries, the Company operates several other non-banking financial businesses. In July 2000, the Company acquired CCB Financial Corporation. In 2001 NCF acquired SouthBanc Shares, Inc. and First Vantage-Tennessee.

RECENT DEVELOPMENTS:

For the year ended 12/31/02, net income advanced 43.6% to $323.6 million versus $225.3 million in the prior year. Results for 2002 and 2001 included pre-tax acquisition charges of $4.9 million and $11.4 million, respectively. Net interest income climbed 12.7% to $733.6 million from $651.1 million the year before. Provision for loan losses rose 10.8% to $32.3 million from $29.2 million the previous year. Total non-interest income grew 20.3% to $391.0 million, while total non-interest expense increased 5.1% to $618.2 million.

PROSPECTS:

The Company is aggressively expanding its operations in Atlanta, Georgia through strategic acquisitions. On 12/13/02, the Company announced that it has completed its acquisition of BancMortgage Financial Corp., an Atlanta-based provider of mortgage origination products and services. The acquisition of BancMortgage, which originated more than $1.40 billion in loans in 2001, is expected to approximately double NCF's existing loan origination business.

ANNUAL FINANCIAL DATA:

FISCAL YEAR	NET INT. INC. ($mill.)	NON-INT. INC. ($mill.)	NET INC. ($mill.)	TOT. LOANS ($mill.)	TOT. ASSETS ($mill.)	TOT. DEP. ($mill.)	RET. ON EQUITY %	RET. ON ASSETS %	EQUITY/ ASSETS %	EARN. PER SH. $	TANG. BK. VAL. $	DIV. PER SH. $	PRICE RANGE	AVG. P/E RATIO
p12/31/02	733.6	391.0	☒ 323.6							☒ 1.55		0.62	29.60 - 21.27	16.4
12/31/01	651.1	324.9	☒ 225.3	11,991.7	19,273.7	12,619.5	9.2	1.2	12.7	☒ 1.09	6.13	0.54	27.88 - 20.00	22.0
☐ 12/31/00	585.7	247.5	☒ 117.5	11,050.2	16,553.5	11,982.3	9.2	0.7	7.7	☒ 0.57	6.23	0.45	25.19 - 15.19	35.4
12/31/99	236.5	92.5	107.2	3,988.6	6,806.2	4,495.9	19.2	1.6	8.2	0.99	5.15	0.36	26.50 - 17.50	22.2
12/31/98	192.6	84.9	85.1	3,200.1	5,811.1	3,947.3	20.8	1.5	7.0	0.83	4.03	0.29	27.38 - 13.38	24.5
12/31/97	162.8	82.4	69.8	2,611.2	4,692.0	3,251.2	19.8	1.5	7.5	0.69	3.60	0.22	17.88 - 8.94	19.4
12/31/96	135.5	70.9	57.5	2,348.0	4,200.4	2,976.4	18.4	1.4	7.5	0.58	3.21	0.19	9.75 - 6.38	14.0
12/31/95	120.0	53.9	49.0	1,933.0	3,695.0	2,574.8	16.5	1.3	8.0	0.49	2.99	0.17	6.81 - 5.69	12.9
12/31/94	110.0	49.9	44.3	1,594.7	3,005.8	2,154.4	19.8	1.5	7.5	0.44	2.29	0.15	6.06 - 5.13	12.6
12/31/93	100.4	52.3	39.4	1,396.3	2,620.8	1,919.6	16.8	1.5	9.0	0.40	2.41	0.10	6.19 - 4.71	13.8

Statistics are as originally reported. Adj. for stock splits: 2-for-1, 7/98 & 5/97. ☐ Reflects the 7/00 acquisition of CCB Financial Corp. ☒ Incl. pre-tax acquisition chrg. of $4.9 mill., 2002; $11.4 mill., 2001; $122.9 mill., 2000.

OFFICERS:
E. C. Roessler, Chmn., Pres., C.E.O.
S. M. Fox, C.F.O.
D. T. Popwell, Exec. V.P., Sec.
W. R. Reed, Jr., C.O.O.
INVESTOR CONTACT: Jekka Pinckney, (901) 523-3525
PRINCIPAL OFFICE: One Commerce Square, Memphis, TN 38150

TELEPHONE NUMBER: (901) 523-3434
FAX: (901) 523-3310
WEB: www.ncbccorp.com
NO. OF EMPLOYEES: 5,490
SHAREHOLDERS: 17,800
ANNUAL MEETING: In Apr.
INCORPORATED: TN, Feb., 1966

INSTITUTIONAL HOLDINGS:
No. of Institutions: 241
Shares Held: 87,630,995
% Held: 42.7

INDUSTRY: National commercial banks (SIC: 6021)

TRANSFER AGENT(S): Bank of New York, New York, NY

NATIONAL FUEL GAS COMPANY

EXCH.	SYM.	REC. PRICE	P/E RATIO	YLD.	MKT. CAP.	RANGE (52-WK.)	'02 Y/E PR.	DIV. ACH.
NYSE	NFG	19.54 (2/28/03)	12.0	5.3%	$1.55 bill.	25.70 - 15.61	20.73	31 yrs.

INVESTMENT GRADE. THE COMPANY'S PROPOSED ACQUISITION OF THE EMPIRE STATE PIPELINE CONTINUES TO MOVE FORWARD.

TRADING VOLUME
Thousand Shares

1989 1990 1991 1992 1993 1994 1995 1996 1997 1998 1999 2000 2001 2002 2003

*7 YEAR PRICE SCORE 99.9   ***12 MONTH PRICE SCORE 104.7**
NYSE COMPOSITE INDEX=100

INTERIM EARNINGS (Per Share):

Qtr.	Dec.	Mar.	June	Sept.
1998-99	0.49	0.79	0.15	0.06
1999-00	0.57	0.91	0.12	0.03
2000-01	0.66	0.94	0.45	d1.24
2001-02	0.41	0.77	0.22	0.06
2002-03	0.58	...	...	...

INTERIM DIVIDENDS (Per Share):

Amt.	Decl.	Ex.	Rec.	Pay.
0.253Q	3/14/02	3/26/02	3/29/02	4/15/02
0.26Q	6/13/02	6/26/02	6/28/02	7/15/02
0.26Q	9/12/02	9/26/02	9/30/02	10/15/02
0.26Q	12/12/02	12/27/02	12/31/02	1/15/03
0.26Q	3/17/03	3/27/03	3/31/03	4/15/03

Indicated div.: $1.04 (Div. Reinv. Plan)

CAPITALIZATION (9/30/02):

	($000)	(%)
Long-Term Debt	1,145,341	45.1
Deferred Income Tax	356,220	14.0
Minority Interest	28,785	1.1
Common & Surplus	1,006,858	39.7
Total	2,537,204	100.0

BUSINESS:

National Fuel Gas Company is a diversified energy company consisting of six business segments. The Utility segment operations (53.1% of 2002 revenues) are carried out by National Fuel Gas Distribution Corporation, which sells natural gas or provides natural gas transportation services to about 732,000 customers, as of 9/30/02, through a local distribution system located in western New York and northwestern Pennsylvania. The Exploration and Production segment operations (21.3%) are carried out by Seneca

Resources Corporation. The Energy Marketing segment operations (10.4%) are carried out by National Fuel Resources, Inc. The International segment operations (6.5%) are carried out by Horizon Energy Development. The Pipeline and Storage segment operations (5.5%) are carried out by National Fuel Gas Supply Corporation. The Timber segment operations (3.2%) are carried out by Highland Forest Resources, Inc. and by a division of Seneca known as its Northeast Division.

RECENT DEVELOPMENTS:

For the three months ended 12/31/02, income was $46.9 million, before an accounting change charge of $638,000, versus net income of $33.2 million in the same period a year earlier. Operating revenues advanced 22.3% to $479.7 million. Operating profit rose 22.5% to $72.0 million versus $59.0 million the year before. NFG attributed the

improved profits to higher commodity prices that resulted in increased Exploration and Production earnings, colder weather in the Utility segment's Pennsylvania service territory, and increased harvesting in the Timber segment. International segment profits were also higher, aided by higher heating rates and greater electric volumes.

PROSPECTS:

NFG's proposed acquisition of the Empire State Pipeline from a subsidiary of Duke Energy, which was announced in October 2002, continues to move forward. The transaction has cleared FTC review under the Hart Scott Rodino Antitrust Improvements Act. NFG stated that assuming the Pub-

lic Service Commission of the State of New York issues an order that is satisfactory to the Company, the Empire acquisition should close during the second quarter of fiscal 2003. Separately, NFG has re-affirmed its full-year fiscal 2003 earnings guidance of between $1.60 and $1.70 per share.

ANNUAL FINANCIAL DATA:

FISCAL YEAR	TOT. REVS. ($mill.)	NET INC. ($mill.)	TOT. ASSETS ($mill.)	OPER. PROFIT %	NET PROFIT %	NET INC./ NET PROP. %	NET INC./ TOT. CAP. %	RET. ON EQUITY %	ACCUM. DEPR./ GROSS PROP. %	EARN. PER SH. $	TANG. BK. VAL. $	DIV. PER SH. $	DIV. PAYOUT %	PRICE RANGE	AVG. P/E RATIO	AVG. YIELD %
9/30/02	1,464.5	③ 117.7	3,401.3	15.8	8.0	4.1	4.6	11.7	37.0	③ 1.46	12.44	1.02	70.2	25.70 - 15.61	14.1	5.0
9/30/01	2,100.4	② 65.5	3,445.6	7.6	3.1	2.4	2.7	6.5	34.9	② 0.82	12.63	0.98	120.1	31.59 - 21.95	32.6	3.7
9/30/00	1,425.3	127.2	3,236.9	15.3	8.9	4.7	5.6	12.9	29.9	1.61	12.55	0.94	58.9	32.25 - 19.69	16.2	3.6
9/30/99	1,263.3	115.0	2,842.6	15.2	9.1	4.9	5.6	12.2	30.4	1.48	12.09	0.92	62.0	26.47 - 18.75	15.3	4.0
9/30/98	1,248.0	32.3	2,684.5	6.7	2.6	1.4	1.7	3.7	29.5	0.42	11.38	0.89	210.7	24.81 - 19.81	53.1	4.0
9/30/97	1,265.8	114.7	2,267.3	13.3	9.1	6.3	6.4	12.5	31.8	1.51	12.02	0.85	56.8	24.44 - 19.69	14.7	3.9
9/30/96	1,208.0	104.7	2,149.8	13.0	8.7	6.1	6.1	12.2	30.8	1.39	11.31	0.82	59.3	22.06 - 15.69	13.6	4.4
9/30/95	975.5	75.9	2,038.3	12.8	7.8	4.6	4.9	9.5	29.0	1.02	10.69	0.80	78.8	16.94 - 12.50	14.5	5.4
9/30/94	1,141.3	① 82.4	1,981.7	11.0	7.2	5.3	5.4	10.6	28.7	① 1.12	10.47	0.78	69.9	18.13 - 12.63	13.8	5.1
9/30/93	1,020.4	75.2	1,801.5	12.0	7.4	5.1	5.4	10.2	27.5	1.08	10.04	0.76	70.7	18.44 - 14.38	15.3	4.6

Statistics are as originally reported. Adj. for 2-for-1 stk. split, 9/01. ① Bef. acctg. change credit $3.2 mill. ② Incl. after-tax impairment chrg. of $104.0 mill. ③ Incl. impairment of invest. in partnership chrg. of $15.2 mill.

OFFICERS:
P. C. Ackerman, Chmn., Pres., C.E.O.
W. E. DeForest, Sr. V.P.
J. P. Pawlowski, Treas.
INVESTOR CONTACT: Margaret M. Suto, Director, Investor Relations, (716) 857-6987
PRINCIPAL OFFICE: 10 Lafayette Square, Buffalo, NY 14203

TELEPHONE NUMBER: (716) 857-7000
FAX: (716) 857-7229
WEB: www.nationalfuelgas.com
NO. OF EMPLOYEES: 3,177
SHAREHOLDERS: 20,004
ANNUAL MEETING: In Feb.
INCORPORATED: NJ, Dec., 1902

INSTITUTIONAL HOLDINGS:
No. of Institutions: 182
Shares Held: 34,061,344
% Held: 42.3
INDUSTRY: Natural gas distribution (SIC: 4924)
TRANSFER AGENT(S): Mellon Investor Services, South Hackensack, NJ

NATIONAL SEMICONDUCTOR CORPORATION

EXCH.	SYM.	REC. PRICE	P/E RATIO	YLD.	MKT. CAP.	RANGE (52-WK.)	'02 Y/E PR.
NYSE	NSM	17.13 (2/28/03)	...	...	$3.09 bill.	37.30 - 9.95	15.01

LOWER MEDIUM GRADE. ON 2/20/03, THE COMPANY ANNOUNCED A SERIES OF STRATEGIC PROFIT-IMPROVEMENT ACTIONS.

MERGENT

TRADING VOLUME
Thousand Shares

1989 1990 1991 1992 1993 1994 1995 1996 1997 1998 1999 2000 2001 2002 2003

*7 YEAR PRICE SCORE 83.5   ***12 MONTH PRICE SCORE 75.3**

*NYSE COMPOSITE INDEX=100

INTERIM EARNINGS (Per Share):

Qtr.	Aug.	Nov.	Feb.	May
1998-99	d0.63	d0.57	d0.16	d4.65
1999-00	0.25	0.49	1.68	0.78
2000-01	0.74	0.56	0.21	d0.26
2001-02	d0.31	d0.26	d0.21	0.09
2002-03	0.01	0.03	d0.20	...

INTERIM DIVIDENDS (Per Share):

Amt.	Decl.	Ex.	Rec.	Pay.
		No dividends paid.		

CAPITALIZATION (5/26/02):

	($000)	(%)
Long-Term Debt	20,400	1.1
Common & Surplus	1,781,100	98.9
Total	1,801,500	100.0

BUSINESS:

National Semiconductor Corporation provides a variety of semiconductor products. The Analog segment (75.4% of fiscal 2002 sales) includes a range of building block products such as high-performance operational amplifiers, power management circuits, data acquisition circuits, interface circuits and circuits targeted towards monitor applications such as ultra-thin flat panel displays. The Analog segment's wireless circuits are used primarily for handset and base station applications in the cellular and cordless telephone markets. The Information Appliance (13.3%) segment provides component and system products to the information appliance market, including application-specific integrated microprocessors based on NSM's GEODE™ technology, software and hardware products and diverse advanced input/output controllers. All other segments accounted for 11.3% of 2002 sales.

RECENT DEVELOPMENTS:

For the quarter ended 2/23/03, NSM reported a net loss of $36.4 million versus a net loss of $37.8 million in the equivalent 2002 quarter. Results for 2003 and 2002 included a net loss of $6.3 million and a net gain of $900,000, respectively, on investments. Results for 2003 also included a charge for writedown of technology licenses of $13.8 million and a workforce reduction charge of $17.0 million. Net sales advanced 9.4% to $404.3 million from $369.5 million a year earlier. Operating loss narrowed to $31.0 million from $41.5 million in 2002.

PROSPECTS:

On 2/20/03, the Company announced a series of strategic profit-improvement actions that are designed to accelerate NSM's return on investments and streamline its cost structure. As a key part of this effort, the Company is seeking to sell its Information Appliance unit, consisting primarily of the GEODE™ family of products, as well as its cellular baseband business. NSM has also entered into a new long-term technology and manufacturing agreement with Taiwan Semiconductor Manufacturing Corporation. In addition, NSM will realign some manufacturing, product development, and support personnel and reduce its workforce by approximately 500 positions.

ANNUAL FINANCIAL DATA:

FISCAL YEAR	TOT. REVS. ($mill.)	NET INC. ($mill.)	TOT. ASSETS ($mill.)	OPER. PROFIT %	NET PROFIT %	RET. ON EQUITY %	RET. ON ASSETS %	CURR. RATIO	EARN. PER SH. $	CASH FL. PER SH. $	TANG. BK. VAL. $	PRICE RANGE	AVG. P/E RATIO
5/26/02	1,494.8	⑤ d121.9	2,288.8	...	...	...	...	2.7	⑤ d0.69	0.61	8.91	35.10 - 19.70	...
5/27/01	2,112.6	④ 245.7	2,362.3	10.5	11.6	13.9	10.4	2.7	④ 1.30	2.60	9.39	85.94 - 17.13	39.6
5/28/00	2,139.9	③ 627.6	2,382.2	16.0	29.3	38.2	26.3	2.3	③ 3.27	4.65	9.25	51.88 - 8.88	9.3
5/30/99	1,956.8	① d1,009.9	2,044.3	...	...	...	...	1.5	① d6.04	d3.62	5.33	28.25 - 7.44	...
5/31/98	2,536.7	① d98.6	3,100.7	...	...	...	...	1.6	① d0.60	1.27	11.23	42.88 - 21.63	...
5/25/97	2,507.3	① d53.7	2,914.1	...	...	...	...	2.0	① 0.19	1.24	12.05	27.63 - 13.00	106.9
5/26/96	2,623.1	① 185.4	2,658.0	8.2	7.1	11.8	7.0	1.9	① 1.36	3.11	11.52	33.63 - 16.50	18.4
5/28/95	2,379.4	① 264.2	2,235.7	13.2	11.1	18.8	11.8	1.7	① 2.02	3.50	11.45	25.00 - 14.38	9.7
5/29/94	2,295.4	259.1	1,747.7	12.7	11.3	23.4	14.8	1.8	1.98	3.41	9.04	21.75 - 10.13	8.0
5/30/93	2,013.7	② 130.3	1,476.5	7.3	6.5	15.6	8.8	1.7	② 0.98	2.36	7.63	14.13 - 6.38	10.5

Statistics are as originally reported. ① Incl. non-recurr. chrg. $700.9 mill., 1999; $196.7 mill., 1998; $134.2 mill., 1997; $166.2 mill., 1996; $30.7 mill., 1995. ② Bef. acctg. change chrg. $4.9 mill. ③ Incl. spec. pre-tax gain of $26.8 mill. for sale of Cyrix PC bus.; excl. $6.8 mill. extraord. chrg. for debt exiting and one-time gain $270.7 mill. from the sale of Fairchild Semiconductor stock. ④ Incl. a spec. pre-tax in process R&D chrg. of $16.2 mill. and a spec. pre-tax restruct. chrg. of $2.3 mill. ⑤ Incl. spec. pre-tax chrg. of $9.3 mill.

OFFICERS:
B. L. Halla, Chmn., Pres., C.E.O.
L. Chew, Sr. V.P., C.F.O.
D. Macleod, Exec. V.P., C.O.O.

INVESTOR CONTACT: Jim Foltz, Investor Relations, (408) 721-5693

PRINCIPAL OFFICE: 2900 Semiconductor Dr., P.O. Box 58090, Santa Clara, CA 95052-8090

TELEPHONE NUMBER: (408) 721-5000
FAX: (408) 739-9803
WEB: www.national.com

NO. OF EMPLOYEES: 10,000 (approx.)

SHAREHOLDERS: 8,194 (approx. record)

ANNUAL MEETING: In Oct.

INCORPORATED: DE, May, 1959

INSTITUTIONAL HOLDINGS:
No. of Institutions: 275
Shares Held: 157,527,821
% Held: 87.1

INDUSTRY: Semiconductor and related devices (SIC: 3674)

TRANSFER AGENT(S): EquiServe Trust Company, N.A., Providence, RI

NATIONAL-OILWELL, INC.

EXCH.	SYM.	REC. PRICE	P/E RATIO	YLD.	MKT. CAP.	RANGE (52-WK.)	'02 Y/E PR.
NYSE	NOI	22.50 (2/28/03)	25.0	...	$1.82 bill.	28.81 - 15.19	21.84

MEDIUM GRADE. THE COMPANY HAS ACQUIRED THE MONO PUMPING PRODUCTS BUSINESS FROM HALLIBURTON ENERGY SERVICES.

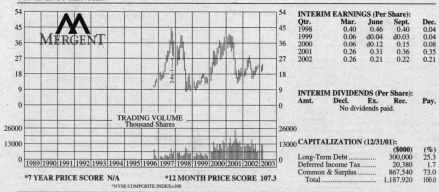

INTERIM EARNINGS (Per Share):

Qtr.	Mar.	June	Sept.	Dec.
1998	0.40	0.46	0.40	0.04
1999	0.06	d0.04	d0.03	0.04
2000	0.06	d0.12	0.15	0.08
2001	0.26	0.31	0.36	0.35
2002	0.26	0.21	0.22	0.21

INTERIM DIVIDENDS (Per Share):

Amt.	Decl.	Ex.	Rec.	Pay.
		No dividends paid.		

TRADING VOLUME
Thousand Shares

*7 YEAR PRICE SCORE N/A   ***12 MONTH PRICE SCORE 107.3**

*NYSE COMPOSITE INDEX=100

CAPITALIZATION (12/31/01):

	($000)	(%)
Long-Term Debt	300,000	25.3
Deferred Income Tax	20,380	1.7
Common & Surplus	867,540	73.0
Total	1,187,920	100.0

BUSINESS:

National-Oilwell, Inc. is a designer, manufacturer and seller of systems and components used in oil and gas drilling and production, and also provides supply chain integration services to the oil and gas industry. The Company manufactures and assembles drilling machinery, including drawworks, mud pumps and top drives, which are the major mechanical components of drilling rigs, as well as masts, derricks and substructures. The Company also provides electrical power systems, computer control systems and automation systems for drilling rigs. NOI's products and technology segment also designs and manufactures drilling motors and specialized downhole tools for rent and sale. The Company's distribution services segment offers supply chain integration services through its network of approximately 150 distribution service centers.

RECENT DEVELOPMENTS:

For the year ended 12/31/02, net income declined 29.8% to $73.1 million compared with $104.1 million a year earlier. Revenues slid 12.9% to $1.52 billion, reflecting lower drilling activity. Products and technology group revenue decreased 18.2% to $917.3 million and operating profit slid 25.7% to $127.0 million. Distribution services group revenue slipped 3.1% to $686.2 million, while operating profit dropped 36.5% to $18.1 million.

PROSPECTS:

On 1/17/03, NOI announced that it has acquired the Mono pumping products business from Halliburton Energy Services through the purchase of all the outstanding stock of Monoflo, Inc. in the United States and Mono Group in the United Kingdom. Mono is a worldwide manufacturer of power sections for downhole drilling motors, downhole artificial lift pumps, progressive cavity fluid transfer pumps, grinders and screens and services the oilfield, industrial and agricultural markets. Consideration for the acquisition included $22.7 million in cash and 3.2 million shares of NOI common stock. NOI expects to contribute significant additional volume to the Mono business, which generated revenues of approximately $80.0 million in 2002, and believes the acquisition will be accretive by more than $0.05 per share to 2003 earnings.

ANNUAL FINANCIAL DATA:

FISCAL YEAR	TOT. REVS. ($mill.)	NET INC. ($mill.)	TOT. ASSETS ($mill.)	OPER. PROFIT %	NET PROFIT %	RET. ON EQUITY %	RET. ON ASSETS %	CURR. RATIO	EARN. PER SH. $	CASH FL. PER SH. $	TANG. BK. VAL. $	PRICE RANGE	AVG. P/E RATIO
p12/31/02	1,521.9	73.1							0.89			28.81 - 15.19	24.7
12/31/01	1,747.5	104.1	1,471.7	10.8	6.0	12.0	7.1	3.3	1.27	1.75	6.37	41.24 - 12.40	21.1
12/31/00	1,149.9	☑13.1	1,278.9	4.2	1.1	1.7	1.0	2.8	☑0.16	0.60	5.44	39.69 - 14.00	167.7
12/31/99	745.2	☑1.5	782.3	2.9	0.2	0.4	0.2	2.7	☑0.03	0.42	3.79	18.50 - 8.50	448.5
12/31/98	1,172.0	☑68.9	818.0	10.3	5.9	17.8	8.4	2.6	☑1.30	1.66	4.31	40.44 - 7.63	18.5
12/31/97	1,005.6	☐☑51.3	567.5	8.7	5.1	18.5	9.0	2.2	☐☑0.99	1.27	4.91	44.44 - 14.00	29.5
12/31/96	648.6	☑0.2	266.7	1.8	...	0.2	0.1	2.3	☑0.01	0.13	2.88	15.38 - 10.00	N.M.
12/31/95	545.8	③17.6	288.6	4.1	3.2	9.9	6.1	3.0	...	...	...	...	...
12/31/94	562.1	☑23.9	268.3	5.2	4.2	14.8	8.9	2.7	...	...	...	...	...
12/31/03	627.3	☑d17.5	...	...	...	...	...	...	...	...	...	...	...

Statistics are as originally reported. Adj. for 2-for-1 stk. split, 11/97. ☐ Bef. extraord. chrg. of $623,000. ☑ Incl. special chrgs.: 2000, $29.8 mill.; 1999, $1.8 mill.; 1998, $16.4 mill.; 1997, $10.7 mill.; 1996, $23.0 mill.; 1993, $8.6 mill. ③ Incl. non-recurr. charge: 1995, $8.5 mill.; 1994, $13.9 mill.

OFFICERS: M. A. Miller, Jr., Chmn., Pres., C.E.O. J. Gjedebo, Exec. V.P., Chief Tech. Off. S. W. Krablin, V.P., C.F.O. **INVESTOR CONTACT:** Steve Krablin, V.P., C.F.O., (713) 346-7773 **PRINCIPAL OFFICE:** 10000 Richmond Avenue, 4th Floor, Houston, TX 77042-4200	**TELEPHONE NUMBER:** (713) 346-7500 **FAX:** (713) 960-5212 **WEB:** www.natoil.com **NO. OF EMPLOYEES:** 6,200 (avg.) **SHAREHOLDERS:** 506 **ANNUAL MEETING:** In May **INCORPORATED:** DE, Jan., 1996	**INSTITUTIONAL HOLDINGS:** No. of Institutions: 215 Shares Held: 69,573,931 % Held: 85.9 **INDUSTRY:** Industrial machinery and equipment (SIC: 5084) **TRANSFER AGENT(S):** American Stock Transfer & Trust Company, New York, NY

NATIONWIDE FINANCIAL SERVICES, INC.

EXCH.	SYM.	REC. PRICE	P/E RATIO	YLD.	MKT. CAP.	RANGE (52-WK.)	'02 Y/E PR.
NYSE	NFS	24.30 (2/28/03)	27.6	2.1%	$3.13 bill.	45.65 - 21.80	28.65

MEDIUM GRADE. THE COMPANY EXPECTS NET OPERATING INCOME PER SHARE FOR 2003 IN THE RANGE OF $2.75 TO $2.95.

MERGENT

TRADING VOLUME
Thousand Shares

1989 1990 1991 1992 1993 1994 1995 1996 1997 1998 1999 2000 2001 2002 2003

*7 YEAR PRICE SCORE N/A   ***12 MONTH PRICE SCORE 89.5**
*NYSE COMPOSITE INDEX=100

INTERIM EARNINGS (Per Share):

Qtr.	Mar.	June	Sept.	Dec.
1997	0.63	0.43	0.51	0.59
1998	0.67	0.65	0.61	0.66
1999	0.68	0.71	0.80	0.77
2000	0.82	0.81	0.91	0.85
2001	0.87	0.88	1.03	0.45
2002	0.80	0.62	d1.18	0.64

INTERIM DIVIDENDS (Per Share):

Amt.	Decl.	Ex.	Rec.	Pay.
0.12Q	2/27/02	3/27/02	4/01/02	4/15/02
0.13Q	5/08/02	6/27/02	7/01/02	7/15/02
0.13Q	8/08/02	9/27/02	10/01/02	10/15/02
0.13Q	12/11/02	12/30/02	1/02/03	1/15/03
0.13Q	3/05/03	3/28/03	4/01/03	4/15/03

Indicated div.: $0.52 (Div. Reinv. Plan)

CAPITALIZATION (12/31/01):

	($000)	(%)
Long-Term Debt	597,000	13.8
Preferred Stock	300,000	6.9
Common & Surplus	3,443,300	79.3
Total	4,340,300	100.0

BUSINESS:

Nationwide Financial Services, Inc. was formed in 1996 as the holding company for Nationwide Life Insurance Company and the other companies within the Nationwide Insurance Enterprise that offer or distribute long-term savings and retirement products. NFS develops and sells a diverse range of products including individual annuities, private and public pension plans, life insurance and mutual funds as well as investment management and administrative services. NFS' life insurance segment is composed of a wide range of variable universal life insurance, whole life insurance, term life insurance and corporate-owned life insurance products. As of 2/3/03, NFS was 63.0%-owned by Nationwide Corporation.

RECENT DEVELOPMENTS:

For the year ended 12/31/02, income from continuing operations was $140.8 million, before income from discontinued operations of $3.4 million, versus income of $424.3 million, before an accounting change charge of $7.1 million and a loss from discontinued operations of $4.4 million, the previous year. Earnings for 2002 and 2001 included amortization of deferred policy acquisition costs of $678.1 million and $348.1 million, respectively. Also, results for 2002 included amortization of value of business acquired of $15.2 million. Total operating revenues increased 7.1% to $3.29 billion. Revenues from policy charges rose 0.9% to $1.03 billion. Revenues from life insurance premiums climbed 20.4% to $302.3 million, while net investment income grew 10.5% to $1.92 billion.

PROSPECTS:

The Company's prospects appear positive, due in part to progress made to improve its competitive position in the retirement savings market. During 2002, NFS expanded its distribution network, completed the demutualization of Provident Mutual Life Insurance Company, took steps to improve the competitiveness of its product portfolio and gained share in selected markets. These strengths, along with NFS' strong capital position, should enable NFS to continue to grow despite the current challenging operating environment. For 2003, NFS expects revenue growth to be between 18.0% to 20.0% and net operating income per share in the range of $2.75 to $2.95.

ANNUAL FINANCIAL DATA:

FISCAL YEAR	TOT. REVS. ($mill.)	NET INC. ($mill.)	TOT. ASSETS ($mill.)	OPER. PROFIT %	NET PROFIT %	RET. ON EQUITY %	RET. ON ASSETS %	CURR. RATIO	EARN. PER SH.$	CASH FL.PER SH.$	TANG. BK. VAL.$	DIV. PER SH.$	PRICE RANGE	AVG. P/E RATIO	AVG. YIELD %
p12/31/02	3,287.8	③ 140.8							③ 1.06			0.50	45.65 - 21.80	31.8	1.5
12/31/01	3,179.0	② 419.9	91,960.9	17.7	13.2	12.2	0.5	...	② 3.20	5.81	26.73	0.48	47.94 - 31.50	12.4	1.2
12/31/00	3,170.3	434.9	93,178.6	19.7	13.7	14.5	0.5	139.2	3.38	6.10	23.29	0.44	51.44 - 19.50	10.5	1.2
12/31/99	2,803.3	381.3	93,054.0	20.4	13.6	15.3	0.4	...	2.96	5.15	19.35	0.36	54.13 - 26.75	13.7	0.9
12/31/98	2,511.7	332.4	74,671.2	20.1	13.2	13.6	0.4	...	2.58	4.20	19.05	0.28	55.84 - 28.25	16.3	0.7
12/31/97	2,238.4	265.2	59,892.9	18.2	11.8	12.5	0.4	...	2.14	3.48	16.53	0.12	38.25 - 23.38	14.4	0.4
12/31/96	2,016.6	① 212.3	47,770.2	16.3	10.5	10.0	0.4	24.5	① 1.69	2.82	20.35	...	...	...	...
12/31/95	1,837.0	① 184.9	38,506.1	15.3	10.1	7.1	0.5	346.1	...	...	...	...	...	...	...
12/31/94	1,634.1	① 157.9	...	14.7	9.7	...	...	...	...	...	...	...	...	...	...

Statistics are as originally reported. ① Before inc. from disc. opers. of $11.3 mill., 1996; $24.7 mill., 1995; $20.5 mill., 1994. ② Bef. acctg. chrg. $7.1 mill. ③ Bef. inc. fr. disc. opers. of $3.4 mill.; incl. deferred policy acquisition costs of $678.1 mill. & amort. of value of business acq. of $15.2 mill.

OFFICERS:
W. G. Jurgensen, Chmn., C.E.O.
J. J. Gasper, Pres., C.O.O.
M. R. Thresher, Sr. V.P., C.F.O.
INVESTOR CONTACT: Kevin G. O'Brien,
V.P., Inv. Rel., (614) 677-5331
PRINCIPAL OFFICE: One Nationwide Plaza,
Columbus, OH 43215

TELEPHONE NUMBER: (614) 249-7111
FAX: (614) 249-9071
WEB: www.nationwide.com
NO. OF EMPLOYEES: 3,700 (approx.)
SHAREHOLDERS: 2,398 (approx. class A)
ANNUAL MEETING: In May
INCORPORATED: DE, Nov., 1996

INSTITUTIONAL HOLDINGS:
No. of Institutions: 152
Shares Held: 30,753,800
% Held: 20.2

INDUSTRY: Life insurance (SIC: 6311)

TRANSFER AGENT(S): Mellon Investor Services, South Hackensack, NJ

NAVISTAR INTERNATIONAL CORPORATION

EXCH.	SYM.	REC. PRICE	P/E RATIO	YLD.	MKT. CAP.	RANGE (52-WK.)	'02 Y/E PR.
NYSE	NAV	23.63 (2/28/03)	...	...	$1.43 bill.	47.38 - 14.77	24.31

LOWER MEDIUM GRADE. THE COMPANY EXPECTS TO RETURN TO PROFITABILITY IN THE THIRD AND FOURTH QUARTERS OF FISCAL 2003.

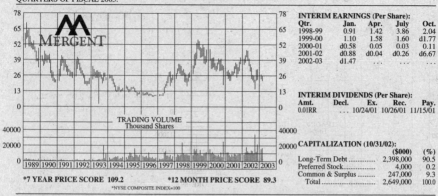

*7 YEAR PRICE SCORE 109.2   *12 MONTH PRICE SCORE 89.3
*NYSE COMPOSITE INDEX=100

INTERIM EARNINGS (Per Share):

Qtr.	Jan.	Apr.	July	Oct.
1998-99	0.91	1.42	3.86	2.04
1999-00	1.10	1.58	1.60	d1.77
2000-01	d0.58	0.05	0.03	0.11
2001-02	d0.88	d0.04	d0.26	d6.67
2002-03	d1.47	...	...	...

INTERIM DIVIDENDS (Per Share):

Amt.	Decl.	Ex.	Rec.	Pay.
0.01RR	...	10/24/01	10/26/01	11/15/01

CAPITALIZATION (10/31/02):

	($000)	(%)
Long-Term Debt	2,398,000	90.5
Preferred Stock	4,000	0.2
Common & Surplus	247,000	9.3
Total	2,649,000	100.0

BUSINESS:

Navistar International Corporation operates in three principal industry segments: truck (69.5% of fiscal 2002 revenues), engine (26.4%) and financial services (4.1%). NAV's subsidiary, International Truck and Engine Corporation produces mid-range diesel engines, medium trucks, heavy trucks, severe service vehicles, and provides parts and services under the International® brand. IC Corporation, a wholly-owned subsidiary, produces school buses. NAV is also a private label designer and manufacturer of diesel engines for the pickup truck, van and SUV markets. Navistar Financial is engaged in the wholesale, retail and lease financing of new and used trucks sold by Navistar and its dealers in the U.S. NAV has significant operations in the U.S., Canada, Mexico, Brazil and Argentina.

RECENT DEVELOPMENTS:

For the first quarter ended 1/31/03, the Company reported a loss from continuing operations of $98.0 million compared with a loss of $53.0 million in the corresponding prior-year quarter. Results for 2002 included a loss on the sale of business of $1.0 million. Earnings for 2003 and 2002 excluded losses from discontinued operations of $1.0 million and $3.0 million, respectively. Total sales and revenues increased 7.7% to $1.58 billion from $1.47 billion a year earlier. Sales of manufactured products climbed 7.2% to $1.48 billion, while finance and insurance revenue advanced 19.5% to $92.0 million. Other income decreased 16.7% to $5.0 million. Cost of products and services sold grew 13.8% to $1.42 billion, or 90.0% of revenues, from $1.25 billion, or 85.2% of revenues, in the previous year.

PROSPECTS:

The Company anticipates a second quarter loss of $0.25 to $0.30 per share if there is a favorable resolution of negotiations with Ford Motor Company in regard to the delay of its V-6 engine program. However, NAV expects to return to profitability in the third and fourth quarters and be profitable for the full year as a result of improved industry demand, increased truch and engine shipments, rationalization of fixed costs and resolution of the Ford V-6 issues. Meanwhile, NAV has realigned its manufacturing facilities to deliver scale for focused products and has invested to make its plants more efficient. Moreover, NAV is projecting cost reductions of $100.0 million in 2003.

ANNUAL FINANCIAL DATA:

FISCAL YEAR	TOT. REVS. ($mill.)	NET INC. ($mill.)	TOT. ASSETS ($mill.)	OPER. PROFIT %	NET PROFIT %	RET. ON EQUITY %	RET. ON ASSETS %	CURR. RATIO	EARN. PER SH. $	CASH FL. PER SH. $	TANG. BK. VAL. $	DIV. PER SH. $	PRICE RANGE	AVG. P/E RATIO
10/31/02	6,784.0	⑥ d476.0	6,943.0	...	...	...	...	1.1	⑥ d7.88	d4.25	4.08	...	47.38 - 14.77	...
10/31/01	6,722.0	⑤ d23.0	7,067.0	2.2	...	...	...	1.2	⑤ d0.39	3.26	18.91	0.01	41.20 - 21.78	...
10/31/00	8,451.0	④ 159.0	6,945.0	5.4	1.9	2.3	2.3	1.0	④ 2.58	5.82	22.05	...	48.00 - 18.25	12.8
10/31/99	8,647.0	544.0	6,928.0	9.3	6.3	42.1	7.9	1.1	8.20	10.81	20.36	...	56.25 - 27.13	5.1
10/31/98	7,885.0	299.0	6,178.0	7.5	3.8	38.9	4.8	2.9	4.11	6.39	8.55	...	35.88 - 17.00	6.4
10/31/97	6,371.0	150.0	5,516.0	5.9	2.4	14.7	2.7	2.9	1.66	3.30	7.79	...	29.50 - 9.00	11.6
10/31/96	5,754.0	③ 65.0	5,326.0	4.5	1.1	7.1	1.2	3.7	③ 0.49	1.91	4.90	...	12.13 - 8.38	20.9
10/31/95	6,342.0	164.0	5,566.0	5.5	2.6	18.9	2.9	3.5	1.83	2.92	4.14	...	17.50 - 9.00	7.2
10/31/94	5,337.0	① 102.0	4,956.0	4.4	1.9	12.5	2.1	1.7	① 0.99	1.93	3.57	...	26.63 - 12.25	19.6
10/31/93	4,694.0	② d273.0	5,060.0	...	...	...	...	2.0	② d8.63	d6.49	2.53	...	33.75 - 2.38	...

Statistics are as originally reported. ① Bef. disc. opers. gain $20.0 mill. ② Bef. acctg. change chrg. $228.0 mill. and disc. opers. loss $47.0 mill. ③ Incl. non-recurr chrg. $35.0 mill. ④ Incl. pre-tax restr. chrg. $286.0 mill. ⑤ Incl. after-tax restr. chrg. $1.0 mill. ⑥ Bef. disc. opers. loss $60.0 mill.; incl. after-tax restr. and oth. chrg. $344.0 mill.

OFFICERS:
J. R. Horne, Chmn., C.E.O.
R. C. Lannert, Vice-Chmn., C.F.O.
D. C. Ustian, Pres., C.O.O.
INVESTOR CONTACT: Ramona Long, (630) 753-2406
PRINCIPAL OFFICE: 4201 Winfield Road, P.O.Box 1488, Warrenville, IL 60555

TELEPHONE NUMBER: (630) 753-5000
FAX: (630) 753-3982
WEB: www.navistar.com
NO. OF EMPLOYEES: 16,500 (avg.)
SHAREHOLDERS: 30,900 (approx.)
ANNUAL MEETING: In Feb.
INCORPORATED: DE, Dec., 1965

INSTITUTIONAL HOLDINGS:
No. of Institutions: 186
Shares Held: 71,486,411
% Held: 104.8
INDUSTRY: Motor vehicles and car bodies (SIC: 3711)
TRANSFER AGENT(S): Mellon Investor Services, South Hackensack, NJ

NCR CORPORATION

EXCH.	SYM.	REC. PRICE	P/E RATIO	YLD.	MKT. CAP.	RANGE (52-WK.)	'02 Y/E PR.
NYSE	NCR	19.45 (2/28/03)	14.4	...	$1.89 bill.	45.49 - 16.92	23.74

MEDIUM GRADE. TOTAL REVENUE GROWTH FOR FULL-YEAR 2003 IS EXPECTED TO BE FLAT, PARTICULARLY IN THE FINANCIAL SELF SERVICE, SYSTEMEDIA, AND PAYMENT AND IMAGING SEGMENTS.

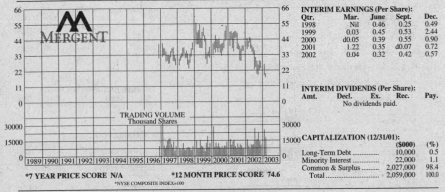

INTERIM EARNINGS (Per Share):

Qtr.	Mar.	June	Sept.	Dec.
1998	Nil	0.46	0.25	0.49
1999	0.03	0.45	0.53	2.44
2000	d0.05	0.39	0.55	0.90
2001	1.22	0.35	d0.07	0.72
2002	0.04	0.32	0.42	0.57

INTERIM DIVIDENDS (Per Share):

Amt.	Decl.	Ex.	Rec.	Pay.
	No dividends paid.			

CAPITALIZATION (12/31/01):

	($000)	(%)
Long-Term Debt	10,000	0.5
Minority Interest	22,000	1.1
Common & Surplus	2,027,000	98.4
Total	2,059,000	100.0

*7 YEAR PRICE SCORE N/A   *12 MONTH PRICE SCORE 74.6

*NYSE COMPOSITE INDEX=100

BUSINESS:

NCR Corporation provides consulting services, value-added software customer support services, consumable and media products, and hardware. Its areas of focus include Teradata® warehouses, automated teller machines and retail store automation. NCR provides applications for the retail and financial industries, as well as telecommunications, transportation, insurance, utilities and electronic commerce. Revenues for 2002 were derived: data warehousing, 21.2%; financial self service, 18.9%; retail store automation, 12.3%; systemedia, 9.0%; payment and imaging, 2.6%; customer services, 31.0%; and other, 5.0%. NCR was acquired by AT&T in 1991 and spun off to AT&T shareholders in 1996.

RECENT DEVELOPMENTS:

For the twelve months ended 12/31/02, income fell 42.1% to $128.0 million, before an accounting change charge of $348.0 million, versus income of $221.0 million, before an accounting change charge of $4.0 million, in 2001. Declines in the retail store automation and customer services segments negatively affected results. Total revenues were $5.59 billion, down 5.6% from $5.92 billion in the prior year. Products revenues declined 5.3% to $2.89 billion from $3.05 billion, while services revenues slid 5.9% to $2.70 billion from $2.87 billion. Income from operations climbed 1.6% to $189.0 million versus $186.0 million the year before.

PROSPECTS:

The Company expects loss per share for the first quarter of 2003 to be in the range of $0.45 to $0.50. Looking ahead, the Company expects to generate positive free cash flow of approximately $50.0 million to $100.0 million in 2003. Total revenue growth for full-year 2003 is expected to be flat, particularly in the financial self service, systemedia, and payment and imaging segments. Revenue growth for the data warehousing segment for 2003 is anticipated to range from zero to 5.0%, while revenue growth for the retail store automation to range from 10.0% to 15.0%.

ANNUAL FINANCIAL DATA:

FISCAL YEAR	TOT. REVS. ($mill.)	NET INC. ($mill.)	TOT. ASSETS ($mill.)	OPER. PROFIT %	NET PROFIT %	RET. ON EQUITY %	RET. ON ASSETS %	CURR. RATIO	EARN. PER SH.$	CASH FL. PER SH.$	TANG. BK. VAL.$	PRICE RANGE	AVG. P/E RATIO
p12/31/02	5,585.0	④ 128.0							④ 1.27			45.49 - 18.80	25.3
12/31/01	5,917.0	④ 221.0	4,855.0	3.1	3.7	10.9	4.6	1.3	④ 2.22	6.47	20.81	50.00 - 28.59	17.7
12/31/00	5,959.0	③ 178.0	5,106.0	3.4	3.0	10.1	3.5	1.2	③ 1.82	5.50	18.47	53.69 - 32.38	23.6
12/31/99	6,196.0	② 337.0	4,895.0	1.3	5.4	21.1	6.9	1.5	② 3.35	6.91	17.05	55.75 - 26.69	12.3
12/31/98	6,505.0	① 122.0	4,892.0	1.6	1.9	8.4	2.5	1.5	① 1.20	4.76	14.66	41.88 - 23.50	27.2
12/31/97	6,589.0	7.0	5,293.0	...	0.1	0.5	0.1	1.7	0.07	3.82	13.11	41.38 - 25.88	479.7
12/31/96	6,963.0	d109.0	5,280.0	1.9	...	...	...	1.7	d0.11	0.27	1.38	40.75 - 30.88	...
12/31/95	8,162.0	d2,280.0	5,256.0	...	...	...	...	1.1	d2.26	d2.68	0.50	...	...
12/31/94	8,461.0	d203.0	5,836.0	...	...	...	...	1.8	...	...	2.35	...	...
12/31/93	7,265.0	d418.0	4,664.0	...	...	...	...	58.8	...	...	...	...	...

Statistics are as originally reported. ① Incl. $50.0 mill. non-recur. pension chg. ② Incl. $125.0 mill. restr. chg., $98.0 mill. gain fr. dispositions & $232.0 mill. gain fr. favorable tax valuation. ③ Incl. $38.0 mill. restr. chg., $25.0 mill. R&D chg. & $2.0 mill. one-time chg. ④ Excl. $348.0 mill. acctg. chg. 2002; $4.0 mill., 2001.

OFFICERS:
L. Nyberg, Chmn.
M. V. Hurd, Pres., C.E.O.
E. Shanks, Sr. V.P., C.F.O.

INVESTOR CONTACT: Gregg Swearingen, Investor Relations, (937) 445-4700

PRINCIPAL OFFICE: 1700 South Patterson Blvd., Dayton, OH 45479

TELEPHONE NUMBER: (937) 445-5000
FAX: (937) 445-5541
WEB: www.ncr.com
NO. OF EMPLOYEES: 30,445 (avg.)
SHAREHOLDERS: 213,000 (approx.)
ANNUAL MEETING: In Apr.
INCORPORATED: OH, 1884; reincorp., MD, 1926

INSTITUTIONAL HOLDINGS:
No. of Institutions: 265
Shares Held: 76,440,894
% Held: 78.4

INDUSTRY: Calculating and accounting equipment (SIC: 3578)

TRANSFER AGENT(S): American Stock Transfer & Trust Co., New York, NY

NEIMAN MARCUS GROUP, INC. (THE)

EXCH.	SYM.	REC. PRICE	P/E RATIO	YLD.	MKT. CAP.	RANGE (52-WK.)	'02 Y/E PR.
NYSE	NMGA	27.08 (2/28/03)	10.1	...	$1.30 bill.	39.80 - 23.75	30.39

UPPER MEDIUM GRADE. EARNINGS ARE BEING POSITIVELY AFFECTED BY DECREASED PROMOTIONAL SELL-ING.

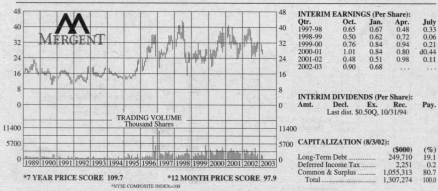

*7 YEAR PRICE SCORE 109.7　　***12 MONTH PRICE SCORE 97.9**

*NYSE COMPOSITE INDEX=100

INTERIM EARNINGS (Per Share):

Qtr.	Oct.	Jan.	Apr.	July
1997-98	0.65	0.67	0.48	0.33
1998-99	0.50	0.62	0.72	0.06
1999-00	0.76	0.84	0.94	0.21
2000-01	1.01	0.84	0.80	d0.44
2001-02	0.48	0.51	0.98	0.11
2002-03	0.90	0.68	...	...

INTERIM DIVIDENDS (Per Share):

Amt.	Decl.	Ex.	Rec.	Pay.
Last dist. $0.50Q, 10/31/94				

CAPITALIZATION (8/3/02):

	($000)	(%)
Long-Term Debt	249,710	19.1
Deferred Income Tax	2,251	0.2
Common & Surplus	1,055,313	80.7
Total	1,307,274	100.0

BUSINESS:

The Neiman Marcus Group, Inc. operates specialty retail stores, consisting of 35 Neiman Marcus stores and two Bergdorf Goodman stores as of 11/7/02. Neiman Marcus stores offer women's, men's and children's apparel, fashion accessories, shoes, cosmetics, furs, precious and designer jewelry, decorative home accessories, fine china, crystal and silver, gourmet food products and gift items. Bergdorf Goodman stores primarily sell high-end women's apparel and unique fashion accessories. In addition, the Company's direct marketing business offers women's apparel under the Neiman Marcus name and, through its Horchow catalogue, offers quality home furnishings, tabletop, linens and decorative accessories. The Company offers more modestly-priced items through its Grand Finale catalogue and annually publishes the Neiman Marcus Christmas Book.

RECENT DEVELOPMENTS:

For the 13 weeks ended 2/1/03, net earnings totaled $32.5 million, up 33.6% compared with $24.3 million in the corresponding prior-year period. Results for 2002 included a $2.0 million pre-tax impairment charge. Revenues climbed 3.3% to $938.5 million from $908.1 million the year before. Comparable-store revenues were up 0.5% year over year. Specialty retail store revenues rose 1.3% to $756.0 million, while direct marketing revenues grew 11.8% to $161.0 million. Operating earnings advanced 30.3% to $58.4 million from $44.8 million a year earlier.

PROSPECTS:

Earnings are being positively affected by decreased promotional selling stemming from the Company's efforts to introduce new merchandise. Meanwhile, sales growth continues to be constrained by sluggish economic growth in the U.S. and lower consumer spending levels. Third-quarter 2003 sales will likely be hurt by inclement weather conditions in the eastern U.S. during February. The Company is targeting comparable-store sales of between a decline of 1.0% and an increase of 1.0% in the third quarter of fiscal 2003.

ANNUAL FINANCIAL DATA:

FISCAL YEAR	TOT. REVS. ($mill.)	NET INC. ($mill.)	TOT. ASSETS ($mill.)	OPER. PROFIT %	NET PROFIT %	RET. ON EQUITY %	RET. ON ASSETS %	CURR. RATIO	EARN. PER SH. $	CASH FL. PER SH. $	TANG. BK. VAL. $	DIV. PER SH. $	PRICE RANGE	AVG. P/E RATIO	AVG. YIELD %
8/03/02	2,948.3	④ 99.6	1,907.5	6.0	3.4	9.4	5.2	2.2	④ 2.08	3.80	22.00	...	39.80 - 23.75	15.3	...
7/28/01	3,015.5	②③ 107.5	1,785.9	6.4	3.6	11.4	6.0	2.1	②③ 2.26	3.92	17.19	...	41.01 - 23.53	14.3	...
7/29/00	2,854.6	134.0	1,762.1	8.7	4.7	16.2	7.6	2.2	2.75	4.16	14.69	...	39.63 - 19.38	10.7	...
7/31/99	2,553.4	94.8	1,502.2	7.1	3.7	12.9	6.3	2.2	1.90	3.22	15.01	...	32.00 - 21.13	14.0	...
8/01/98	2,373.3	106.3	1,437.8	8.4	4.5	16.2	7.4	2.1	2.13	3.33	13.20	...	43.44 - 15.00	13.7	...
8/02/97	2,209.9	91.2	1,287.9	8.2	4.1	16.4	7.1	2.2	1.32	2.59	9.20	...	35.88 - 19.00	20.8	...
8/03/96	2,075.0	77.4	1,252.4	7.7	3.7	102.4	6.2	1.8	1.26	2.74	...	...	36.25 - 17.13	21.2	...
7/29/95	1,888.2	① 67.3	1,108.4	7.9	3.6	253.6	6.1	1.7	① 1.01	2.28	...	...	23.50 - 13.00	18.1	...
7/30/94	2,092.9	② 15.9	1,323.1	2.8	0.8	428.6	1.2	1.8	② d0.35	1.26	0.10	0.20	18.75 - 13.00	...	1.3
7/31/93	2,016.9	③ 58.6	1,278.6	5.4	2.9	240.5	4.6	2.0	③ 0.78	2.36	0.64	0.20	19.50 - 13.88	21.4	1.2

Statistics are as originally reported. ① Bef. $11.7 mil ($0.31/sh) loss fr. discont. opers. ② Incl. $9.8 mil non-recur. pre-tax impair. chg., 2001; $48.4 mil pre-tax restr. chg., 1994. ③ Bef. $1.9 mil ($0.04/sh) acctg. chg., 2001; $11.2 mil ($0.30/sh), 1993. ④ Incl. $16.6 mil pre-tax gain fr. a vacation policy change and a $13.2 mil pre-tax impair. chg.

OFFICERS:
R. A. Smith, Chmn.
B. M. Tansky, Pres., C.E.O.
J. E. Skinner, Sr. V.P., C.F.O.

INVESTOR CONTACT: James E. Skinner, Sr. V.P. & C.F.O., (214) 743-7625

PRINCIPAL OFFICE: 1618 Main Street, Dallas, TX 75201

TELEPHONE NUMBER: (214) 741-6911
FAX: (214) 741-6857
WEB: www.neimanmarcusgroup.com

NO. OF EMPLOYEES: 14,300 (approx.)

SHAREHOLDERS: 9,902 (class A); 3,596 (class B)

ANNUAL MEETING: In Jan.

INCORPORATED: DE, June, 1987

INSTITUTIONAL HOLDINGS:
No. of Institutions: 145
Shares Held: 28,785,459
% Held: 60.0

INDUSTRY: Department stores (SIC: 5311)

TRANSFER AGENT(S): EquiServe, Boston, MA

NETWORKS ASSOCIATES, INC.

EXCH.	SYM.	REC. PRICE	P/E RATIO	YLD.	MKT. CAP.	RANGE (52-WK.)	'02 Y/E PR.
NYSE	NET	14.80 (2/28/03)	43.5	…	$2.08 bill.	29.95 - 8.14	16.09

LOWER MEDIUM GRADE. GOING FORWARD, NET REVENUE FOR 2003 IS EXPECTED IN THE RANGE OF $1.00 BILLION TO $1.03 BILLION.

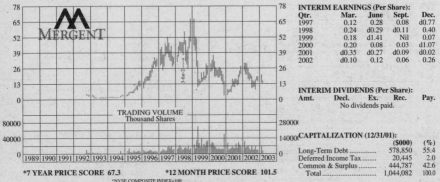

*7 YEAR PRICE SCORE 67.3   ***12 MONTH PRICE SCORE 101.5**

*NYSE COMPOSITE INDEX=100

INTERIM EARNINGS (Per Share):

Qtr.	Mar.	June	Sept.	Dec.
1997	0.12	0.28	0.08	d0.77
1998	0.24	d0.29	d0.11	0.40
1999	0.18	d1.41	Nil	0.07
2000	0.20	0.08	0.03	d1.07
2001	d0.35	d0.27	d0.09	d0.02
2002	d0.10	0.12	0.06	0.26

INTERIM DIVIDENDS (Per Share):

Amt.	Decl.	Ex.	Rec.	Pay.
		No dividends paid.		

CAPITALIZATION (12/31/01):

	($000)	(%)
Long-Term Debt	578,850	55.4
Deferred Income Tax	20,445	2.0
Common & Surplus	444,787	42.6
Total	1,044,082	100.0

BUSINESS:

Networks Associates, Inc. (formerly McAfee Associates, Inc.) is a supplier of network security and network management services. The Company is organized into five business segments: McAfee Security, which primarily markets the McAfee Active Virus Defense product suite; Sniffer Technologies, which primarily markets the Sniffer Total Network Visibility product suite; Magic Solutions, which primarily markets the Magic Total Support Desk product suite; Expert Services, which offers network and security consulting and educational services; and McAfee Consumer group, which incorporates McAfee retail products and McAfee.com on-line services. In addition, the Company operates myCIO, a wholly-owned subsidiary and a business applications service provider.

RECENT DEVELOPMENTS:

For the year ended 12/31/02, income was $90.2 million, before an extraordinary gain of $26,000, versus a loss of $102.4 million, before an extraordinary gain of 1.7 million, the previous year. Earnings were boosted by the Company's acquisition of McAfee.com. Results for 2002 and 2001 included several non-recurring items that resulted in net after-tax charges of $45.4 million and $137.2 million, respectively. Net revenues rose 1.6% to $941.9 million from $812.5 million the year before. Gross profit was $784.4 million versus $652.9 million a year earlier.

PROSPECTS:

The McAfee Consumer Group continues to aggressively target the consumer and small and home office markets. During the fourth quarter, McAfee's on-line subscriber base added 133,000 new subscribers, reaching over 2.3 million active subscriptions at 12/31/02. Meanwhile, McAfee Consumer Group bolstered its roster of partners in the service provider and the hardware manufacturer markets via an agreement with America Online, Inc., which offers on-line anti-virus services to AOL members and users of AOL Web properties. Additionally, Dell Computer Corp. began offering McAfee's anti-virus on-line services to their consumer and small business customers. Separately, NET acquired Bysupport S.A., a large security services reseller in Latin America. Going forward, NET expects net revenue for 2003 in the range of $1.00 billion to $1.03 billion.

ANNUAL FINANCIAL DATA:

FISCAL YEAR	TOT. REVS. ($mill.)	NET INC. ($mill.)	TOT. ASSETS ($mill.)	OPER. PROFIT %	NET PROFIT %	RET. ON EQUITY %	RET. ON ASSETS %	CURR. RATIO	EARN. PER SH.$	CASH FL.PER SH.$	TANG. BK. VAL.$	PRICE RANGE		AVG. P/E RATIO
p12/31/02	941.9	③ 90.2		…	…	…	…		③ 0.57			30.50	8.14	33.9
12/31/01	834.5	② d102.4	1,627.1	…	…	…	…	2.0	② d0.74	0.04	1.85	27.84	3.56	…
12/31/00	745.7	d102.7	1,384.8	…	…	…	…	1.5	d0.72	0.09	3.76	37.19	3.25	…
12/31/99	683.7	① d159.9	1,479.4	…	…	…	…	1.7	① d1.15	0.057	4.73	67.50	10.06	…
12/31/98	990.0	① 36.4	1,536.7	12.1	3.7	9.3	5.0	2.5	① 0.26	0.81	5.27	67.69	25.50	179.1
12/31/97	612.2	① d28.4	601.9	3.0	…	…	…	1.9	① d0.27	d0.03	3.43	52.33	24.33	…
12/31/96	181.1	① 39.0	194.5	37.1	21.5	26.1	20.1	4.0	① 0.49	0.56	2.03	35.22	9.26	45.7
12/31/95	90.1	① 14.9	104.0	26.9	16.6	23.5	14.3	2.5	① 0.20	0.24	0.87	15.67	2.96	46.6
12/31/94	32.9	① 1.4	56.4	5.1	4.2	6.0	2.5	1.8	① 0.03	0.05	0.38	4.00	1.28	105.3
12/31/93	17.9	7.3	39.1	64.5	40.8	39.8	18.7	2.4	0.14	0.14	0.36	4.00	0.89	18.0

Statistics are as originally reported. Adj. for stk. splits: 3-for-2, 5/29/98; 3-for-2, 10/17/96; 3-for-2, 5/16/96 ① Incl. non-recurr. credit $3.2 mill., 12/99; chgs. $135.6 mill., 12/98; $175.8 mill., 12/97; $11.2 mill., 12/96; $12.8 mill., 12/95; $12.8 mill., 12/94 ② Incl. gain on invest. $1.0 mill & loss on write-down of strategic and other invest. ③ Excl. extraord. gain of $26,000; Incl. non-recurr. chrgs. totaling $45.4 mill.

OFFICERS:
G. Samenuk, Chmn., C.E.O.
G. Hodges, Pres.
S. C. Richards, C.F.O., C.O.O.
INVESTOR CONTACT: Investor Relations, (877) 346-3575
PRINCIPAL OFFICE: 3965 Freedom Circle, Santa Clara, CA 95054

TELEPHONE NUMBER: (408) 988-3832
FAX: (408) 970-9727
WEB: www.nai.com
NO. OF EMPLOYEES: 3,659
SHAREHOLDERS: 1,083
ANNUAL MEETING: In May
INCORPORATED: DE, Aug., 1992

INSTITUTIONAL HOLDINGS:
No. of Institutions: 259
Shares Held: 148,809,451
% Held: 95.1
INDUSTRY: Prepackaged software (SIC: 7372)
TRANSFER AGENT(S): Boston EquiServe, Boston, MA

NEUBERGER BERMAN INC.

EXCH.	SYM.	REC. PRICE	P/E RATIO	YLD.	MKT. CAP.	RANGE (52-WK.)	'02 Y/E PR.
NYSE	NEU	26.64 (2/28/03)	15.7	1.1%	$1.88 bill.	48.67 - 22.83	33.49

UPPER MEDIUM GRADE. THE COMPANY COMPLETED THE ACQUISITION OF THE ASSETS OF LIBERTYVIEW CAPITAL MANAGEMENT, INC. ON 12/31/02.

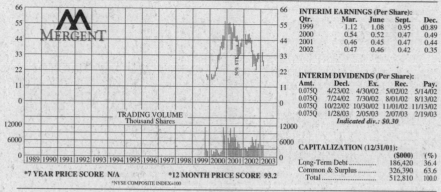

*7 YEAR PRICE SCORE N/A   ***12 MONTH PRICE SCORE 93.2**
*NYSE COMPOSITE INDEX=100

INTERIM EARNINGS (Per Share):

Qtr.	Mar.	June	Sept.	Dec.
1999	1.12	1.08	0.95	d0.89
2000	0.54	0.52	0.47	0.49
2001	0.46	0.45	0.47	0.44
2002	0.47	0.46	0.42	0.35

INTERIM DIVIDENDS (Per Share):

Amt.	Decl.	Ex.	Rec.	Pay.
0.075Q	4/23/02	4/30/02	5/02/02	5/14/02
0.075Q	7/24/02	7/30/02	8/01/02	8/13/02
0.075Q	10/22/02	10/30/02	11/01/02	11/13/02
0.075Q	1/28/03	2/05/03	2/07/03	2/19/03

Indicated div.: $0.30

CAPITALIZATION (12/31/01):

	($000)	(%)
Long-Term Debt	186,420	36.4
Common & Surplus	326,390	63.6
Total	512,810	100.0

BUSINESS:

Neuberger Berman Inc. is the holding company of Neuberger Berman, LLC and Neuberger Berman Management Inc., which are investment advisory firms that provide discretionary money management for individuals, institutions and mutual funds. As of 12/31/02, NEU had $56.10 billion in assets under management. NEU is segregated into three business segments: private asset management (49.4% of net revenues after interest expense for 2002), which provides investment management services to high net-worth individuals, families and smaller institutions, and had $21.56 billion in assets under management at 12/31/02; mutual fund and institutional (36.3%), which provides advisory services to mutual funds and institutional clients; and professional securities services segment (14.2%), formerly a partnership, which markets services to third-party investment advisers and professional investors, including investor clearing services and research sales.

RECENT DEVELOPMENTS:

For the year ended 12/31/02, net income declined 10.2% to $119.1 million versus $132.7 million the year before. Earnings for 2002 included an after-tax charge of $2.7 million, primarily for severance and severance-related expenses. Gross revenues fell 11.6% to $650.8 million. Net revenues after interest expense slid 1.6% to $603.4 million. Investment advisory and administrative fees decreased 1.1% to $418.0 million, while interest income dropped 57.8% to $66.6 million. However, commissions improved 0.4% to $145.2 million from $145.0 million in 2001.

PROSPECTS:

NUE acquired substantially all of the assets of LibertyView Capital Management, Inc., which held about $1.00 billion in assets under management. LibertyView is an alternative investment manager with both multi-strategy and single strategy funds that focus on equity, credit, volatility and mortgage-backed arbitrage and investing. Separately, NEU's mutual fund and institutional segment continues to diversify its product mix as well as expand its capabilities in high-yield bonds. Additionally, NEU recently entered the closed-end fund business and raised over $800.0 million in three closed-end municipal bond funds and a real estate income fund during the fourth quarter of 2002.

ANNUAL FINANCIAL DATA:

FISCAL YEAR	TOT. REVS. ($mill.)	NET INC. ($mill.)	TOT. ASSETS ($mill.)	OPER. PROFIT %	NET PROFIT %	RET. ON EQUITY %	RET. ON ASSETS %	CURR. RATIO	EARN. PER SH.$	CASH FL. PER SH.$	TANG. BK. VAL.$	DIV. PER SH.$	PRICE RANGE	AVG. P/E RATIO	AVG. YIELD %
p12/31/02	650.8	③ 119.1		31.1	18.0	40.6	3.0	1.1	③ 1.69			0.23	48.67 - 22.83	21.2	0.6
12/31/01	736.4	132.7	4,382.5	31.1	18.0	40.6	3.0	1.1	1.82	2.03	4.64	0.28	56.33 - 31.10	24.0	0.6
12/31/00	799.8	② 150.4	4,421.8	30.9	18.8	42.9	3.4	1.1	② 2.02	2.16	4.78	0.27	57.13 - 15.88	18.1	0.7
12/31/99	697.6	① 135.6	3,847.6	17.7	19.4	54.5	3.5	1.1	① 2.03	2.19	3.34	...	21.50 - 15.75	9.2	...
12/31/98	711.5	320.1	3,829.4	45.0	45.0	293.1	8.4	1.0	...	...	5.75	...	...	...	...
12/31/97	627.1	298.7	2,410.2	47.6	47.6	187.8	12.4	1.0	...	...	8.48	...	...	...	...
12/31/96	535.9	229.1	...	42.8	42.8	...	...	...	...	...	...	...	...	...	...

Statistics are as originally reported. Adj. for 50% stk. div., 8/01. ① Incl. $98.2 mill. after-tax one-time chg. fr. IPO. ② Incl. $750,000 pre-tax chg. for sever. payments & excl. $9.6 mill. tax benefit. ③ Incl. an after-tax chrg. of $2.7 million, primarily for severance exps.

OFFICERS:
L. Zicklin, Chmn.
R. A. Cantor, Vice-Chmn.
M. C. Schwartz, Vice-Chmn.
INVESTOR CONTACT: Robert Matza, Exec. V.P. & C.A.O., (212) 476-9808
PRINCIPAL OFFICE: 605 Third Avenue, New York, NY 10158

TELEPHONE NUMBER: (212) 476-9000
FAX: (212) 476-9890
WEB: www.nb.com
NO. OF EMPLOYEES: 1,268 (avg.)
SHAREHOLDERS: 99 (approx.)
ANNUAL MEETING: In May
INCORPORATED: DE, Aug., 1998

INSTITUTIONAL HOLDINGS:
No. of Institutions: 133
Shares Held: 20,606,026
% Held: 29.5

INDUSTRY: Investment advice (SIC: 6282)

TRANSFER AGENT(S): American Stock Transfer & Trust Company, Brooklyn, NY

NEW YORK TIMES COMPANY

EXCH.	SYM.	REC. PRICE	P/E RATIO	YLD.	MKT. CAP.	RANGE (52-WK.)	'02 Y/E PR.
NYSE	NYT	46.46 (2/28/03)	24.1	1.2%	$7.04 bill.	53.00 - 38.60	45.73

UPPER MEDIUM GRADE. THE COMPANY PURCHASED THE REMAINING 50.0% INTEREST IT DID NOT OWN IN THE INTERNATIONAL HERALD TRIBUNE FROM THE WASHINGTON POST COMPANY.

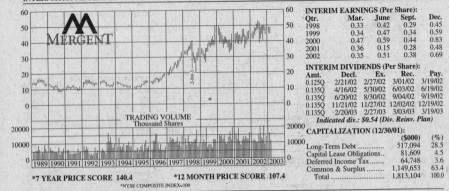

TRADING VOLUME
Thousand Shares

*7 YEAR PRICE SCORE 140.4   ***12 MONTH PRICE SCORE 107.4**

NYSE COMPOSITE INDEX=100

INTERIM EARNINGS (Per Share):

Qtr.	Mar.	June	Sept.	Dec.
1998	0.33	0.42	0.29	0.45
1999	0.34	0.47	0.34	0.59
2000	0.47	0.59	0.44	0.83
2001	0.36	0.15	0.28	0.48
2002	0.35	0.51	0.38	0.69

INTERIM DIVIDENDS (Per Share):

Amt.	Decl.	Ex.	Rec.	Pay.
0.125Q	2/21/02	2/27/02	3/01/02	3/19/02
0.135Q	4/16/02	5/30/02	6/03/02	6/19/02
0.135Q	6/20/02	8/30/02	9/04/02	9/19/02
0.135Q	11/21/02	11/27/02	12/02/02	12/19/02
0.135Q	2/20/03	2/27/03	3/03/03	3/19/03

Indicated div.: $0.54 (Div. Reinv. Plan)

CAPITALIZATION (12/30/01):

	($000)	(%)
Long-Term Debt	517,094	28.5
Capital Lease Obligations..	81,609	4.5
Deferred Income Tax	64,748	3.6
Common & Surplus	1,149,653	63.4
Total	1,813,104	100.0

BUSINESS:

New York Times Company is a diversified communications corporation organized into two segments. The Newspaper segment includes THE NEW YORK TIMES, THE BOSTON GLOBE, THE INTERNATIONAL HERALD TRIBUNE, 16 regional newspapers, newspaper distributors, and certain related businesses. The Broadcasting segment is made up of eight network-affiliated television stations, two New York City radio stations and more than 40 Web sites. NYT's equity interests include a newsprint company and a partnership in a supercalendered paper mill. In April 2001, the Company sold its golf properties, including GolfDigest.com. Revenues in 2002 were derived: newspapers, 92.6%; broadcasting, 5.0%; and New York Times Digital, 2.4%.

RECENT DEVELOPMENTS:

For the twelve months ended 12/29/02, net income jumped 48.2% to $299.7 million compared with income from continuing operations of $202.2 million in 2001. Results for both 2002 and 2001 included income of $5.0 million related to a non-compete agreement. Results for 2002 and 2001 also included a net loss of $13.0 million and net income of $7.7 million, respectively, from joint ventures. Results for 2001 excluded net gains of $242.5 million from discontinued operations. Revenues climbed 2.1% to $3.08 billion from $3.02 billion in the prior year due to growth across all business segments. Operating profit increased 45.5% to $544.9 million compared with $374.4 million in the previous year.

PROSPECTS:

On 1/2/03, the Company completed the purchase of the 50.0% interest it did not already own in THE INTERNATIONAL HERALD TRIBUNE from The Washington Post Company for $65.0 million. The transaction should strengthen the Company's position in the markets outside of the U.S. Going forward, the Company will continue to focus on cost-reduction efforts and growth strategies, which should lead to improved earnings in 2003. NYT expects earnings per share growth for 2003 to range from the mid-single digits to low-double digits.

ANNUAL FINANCIAL DATA:

FISCAL YEAR	TOT. REVS. ($mill.)	NET INC. ($mill.)	TOT. ASSETS ($mill.)	OPER. PROFIT %	NET PROFIT %	RET. ON EQUITY %	RET. ON ASSETS %	CURR. RATIO	EARN. PER SH.$	CASH FL. PER SH.$	TANG. BK. VAL.$	DIV. PER SH.$	PRICE RANGE	AVG. P/E RATIO	AVG. YIELD %
p12/29/02	3,079.0	⑧ 299.7							⑧ 1.94			0.53	53.00 - 38.60	23.6	1.2
12/30/01	3,016.0	⑦ 202.2	3,438.7	12.4	6.7	17.6	5.9	0.7	⑦ 1.26	2.48	...	0.49	47.98 - 35.48	33.1	1.2
12/31/00	3,489.5	⑥ 397.5	3,606.7	18.2	11.4	31.0	11.0	0.7	⑥ 2.32	3.65	...	0.45	49.98 - 32.63	17.8	1.2
12/26/99	3,130.6	⑤ 310.2	3,495.8	18.2	9.9	21.4	8.9	0.9	⑤ 1.73	2.83	0.83	0.41	40.69 - 26.50	22.1	1.1
12/27/98	2,936.7	④ 286.6	3,465.1	17.5	9.8	18.7	8.3	0.8	④ 1.49	2.46	1.12	0.37	40.69 - 20.50	20.5	1.2
12/28/97	2,866.4	262.3	3,639.0	15.9	9.2	15.2	7.2	0.9	1.33	2.21	1.81	0.32	33.25 - 18.19	19.3	1.2
12/29/96	2,615.0	①② 84.5	3,539.9	6.6	3.2	5.2	2.4	0.7	①② 0.44	1.19	0.95	0.28	19.94 - 12.88	37.7	1.7
12/31/95	2,409.4	③ 135.9	3,376.7	9.5	5.6	8.4	4.0	0.9	③ 0.70	1.42	1.10	0.28	15.44 - 10.06	18.2	2.2
12/31/94	2,357.6	① 213.3	3,137.6	9.0	9.0	13.8	6.8	0.9	① 1.03	1.75	0.83	0.28	14.75 - 10.63	12.4	2.2
12/31/93	2,019.7	⑥ 6.1	3,215.2	6.3	0.3	0.4	0.2	0.9	⑥ 0.04	0.80	0.83	0.28	15.63 - 11.19	382.5	2.1

Statistics are as originally reported. Adj. for 2-for-1 split, 7/98. ① Incl. $32.9 mill. p-tax gain fr. sale of assets & $31.5 mill. p-tax chg. rel. to workforce reduc. 1996; $11.3 mill. p-tax gain & $10.1 mill. p-tax chg., 1995; $205.1 mill. p-tax gain, 1994. ② Incl. $94.5 mill. after-tax loss impair. of long-lived assets. ③ Incl. $47.0 mill. after-tax chg & $35.4 mill. p-tax gain. ④ Incl. $12.6 mill. in p-tax gains, $5.4 mill. p-tax chg. for sev. costs, & excl. $7.7 mill. after-tax extraord. item. ⑤ Incl. $3.1 mill. net chg. ⑥ Incl. $85.3 mill. gain fr. disp. of assets. ⑦ Incl. $5.0 mill. gain fr. disp. of assets and excl. $242.5 mill. gain fr. disc. ops. ⑧ Incl. $13.0 mill. net loss fr. jt. vent. & $5.0 mill. inc. fr. agreement.

OFFICERS:
A. Sulzberger Jr., Chmn.
M. Golden, Vice-Chmn., Sr. V.P.
R. T. Lewis, Pres., C.E.O.

INVESTOR CONTACT: Catherine J. Mathis, Dir., Investor Relations, (212) 556-1981

PRINCIPAL OFFICE: 229 West 43rd Street, New York, NY 10036

TELEPHONE NUMBER: (212) 556-1234
FAX: (212) 556-4647
WEB: www.nytco.com
NO. OF EMPLOYEES: 12,050 (approx.)
SHAREHOLDERS: 10,373 (class A common); 35 (class B common)
ANNUAL MEETING: In Apr.
INCORPORATED: NY, Aug., 1896

INSTITUTIONAL HOLDINGS:
No. of Institutions: 347
Shares Held: 118,800,676
% Held: 78.4

INDUSTRY: Newspapers (SIC: 2711)

TRANSFER AGENT(S): First Chicago Trust Company of New York, Jersey City, NJ

NEWELL RUBBERMAID INC.

EXCH.	SYM.	REC. PRICE	P/E RATIO	YLD.	MKT. CAP.	RANGE (52-WK.)	'02 Y/E PR.
NYSE	NWL	28.20 (2/28/03)	22.9	3.0%	$7.96 bill.	36.70 - 26.65	30.33

UPPER MEDIUM GRADE. AS A RESULT OF THE ACQUISITION OF AMERICAN SAW & MFG. COMPANY, NEWELL RAISED ITS FULL-YEAR 2003 EARNINGS PER SHARE GUIDANCE.

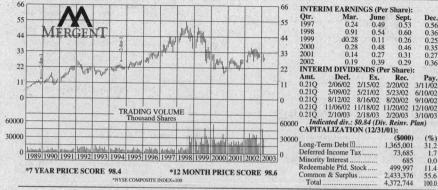

*7 YEAR PRICE SCORE 98.4   *12 MONTH PRICE SCORE 98.6

*NYSE COMPOSITE INDEX=100

INTERIM EARNINGS (Per Share):

Qtr.	Mar.	June	Sept.	Dec.
1997	0.24	0.49	0.53	0.56
1998	0.91	0.54	0.60	0.36
1999	d0.28	0.11	0.26	0.25
2000	0.28	0.48	0.46	0.35
2001	0.14	0.27	0.31	0.27
2002	0.19	0.39	0.29	0.36

INTERIM DIVIDENDS (Per Share):

Amt.	Decl.	Ex.	Rec.	Pay.
0.21Q	2/06/02	2/15/02	2/20/02	3/11/02
0.21Q	5/09/02	5/21/02	5/23/02	6/10/02
0.21Q	8/12/02	8/16/02	8/20/02	9/10/02
0.21Q	11/06/02	11/18/02	11/20/02	12/10/02
0.21Q	2/10/03	2/18/03	2/20/03	3/10/03

Indicated div.: $0.84 (Div. Reinv. Plan)

CAPITALIZATION (12/31/01):

	($000)	(%)
Long-Term Debt 🔢	1,365,001	31.2
Deferred Income Tax	73,685	1.7
Minority Interest	685	0.0
Redeemable Pfd. Stock	499,997	11.4
Common & Surplus	2,433,376	55.6
Total	4,372,744	100.0

BUSINESS:

Newell Rubbermaid Inc. (formerly Newell Company) is a multi-national manufacturer and marketer of high-volume, long life cycle, branded consumer products. NWL reports its results in the following five business segments: Rubbermaid, including RUBBERMAID™ indoor and outdoor organization, storage and cleaning products, and GOODY® hair accessories; Parker/Eldon, including markers and writing instruments and office storage and organization businesses, including PAPER MATE®, PARKER®, and SHARPIE® businesses; Levolor/Hardware, including window furnishings, cabinet hardware, decorative trim, paint brushes and rollers and propane torches; Calphalon/WearEver, including branded cookware, bakeware and serving products; Little Tikes/Graco, including high chairs, strollers and outdoor play equipment. NWL acquired Rubbermaid, Inc. in March 1999 and American Tool Companies, Inc. in April 2002.

RECENT DEVELOPMENTS:

For the year ended 12/31/02, income increased 17.7% to $311.5 million, before an accounting change charge of $514.9 million, compared with net income of $264.6 million in 2001. Results for 2002 and 2001 included restructuring costs of $122.7 million and $66.7 million, respectively.

Results for 2001 also included goodwill amortization expense of $57.0 million. Net sales grew 7.9% to $7.45 billion from $6.91 billion a year earlier. Internal sales growth was 3.3% with sales growth across all four of NWL's business segments.

PROSPECTS:

On 1/6/03, NWL acquired American Saw & Mfg. Company, a manufacturer of linear edge power tool accessories, hand tools and band saw blades marketed under the Lenox® brand, for $450.0 million in cash. The purchase is expected to contribute $0.04 to NWL's 2003 earnings per share. As a result, NWL raised its full-year 2003 guidance

and now expects diluted earnings per share, excluding charges, to be in the range of $1.77 to $1.87. NWL anticipates pre-tax restructuring charges and other one-time charges for 2003 to be between $125.0 million and $150.0 million. In addition, NWL expects full-year 2003 internal sales growth of 2.0% to 4.0%.

ANNUAL FINANCIAL DATA:

FISCAL YEAR	TOT. REVS. ($mill.)	NET INC. ($mill.)	TOT. ASSETS ($mill.)	OPER. PROFIT %	NET PROFIT %	RET. ON EQUITY %	RET. ON ASSETS %	CURR. RATIO	EARN. PER SH.$	CASH FL.PER SH.$	TANG. BK. VAL.$	DIV. PER SH.$	PRICE RANGE	AVG. P/E RATIO	AVG. YIELD %
p12/31/02	7,453.9	⑥ 311.5	7,388.9						⑧ 1.16			0.84	36.70 - 26.11	27.1	2.7
12/31/01	6,909.3	② 264.6	7,266.1	8.3	3.8	10.9	3.6	1.1	② 0.99	2.22	0.41	0.84	29.50 - 20.50	25.2	3.4
⑥ 12/31/00	6,934.7	② 421.6	7,261.9	12.0	6.1	17.2	5.8	1.9	② 1.57	2.57	0.92	0.84	31.88 - 15.63	16.0	3.4
④⑤ 12/31/99	6,413.1	③ 95.4	7,294.7	5.4	1.5	3.5	1.3	1.7	③ 0.34	1.30	2.38	0.80	50.63 - 25.25	111.5	2.1
12/31/98	3,720.0	② 396.2	4,327.8	14.4	10.6	19.9	9.2	1.9	② 2.38	3.14	2.06	0.72	55.19 - 35.69	19.1	1.6
12/31/97	3,234.3	290.4	3,943.8	17.7	9.0	16.5	7.4	2.1	1.82	2.62	2.48	0.64	43.81 - 30.13	20.3	1.7
12/31/96	2,872.8	256.5	3,005.0	16.9	8.9	17.0	8.5	1.7	1.62	2.35	3.68	0.56	33.75 - 25.00	18.1	1.9
12/31/95	2,498.4	222.5	2,939.0	16.8	8.9	17.0	7.6	1.7	1.41	2.05	2.64	0.46	27.25 - 20.25	16.8	1.9
12/31/94	2,074.9	195.6	2,488.3	17.2	9.4	17.2	7.9	1.2	1.24	1.70	2.76	0.39	23.88 - 18.81	17.2	1.8
12/31/93	1,645.0	165.3	1,952.9	17.4	10.1	16.7	8.5	1.1	1.05	1.46	2.88	0.34	21.50 - 15.38	17.6	1.9

Statistics are as originally reported. Adj. for stk. split: 2-for-1, 9/94. 🔢 Incl. debs. conv. into common. ② Incl. non-recurr. chrg. of $66.7 mill., 2001; $48.6 mill., 2000; $56.5 mill., 1998. ③ Incl. non-recurr. after-tax chrg. of $369.6 mill. ④ Incl. results of Rubbermaid, Inc., acqd. 3/99. ⑤ Results were reclassified to incl. freight exp. as a cost of products sold. ⑥ Excl. acctg. change chrg. of $514.9 mill., but incl. restruct. costs of $122.7 mill.

OFFICERS:
W. P. Sovey, Chmn.
J. Galli, Jr., Pres., C.E.O.
W. T. Alldredge, Pres., C.F.O.
INVESTOR CONTACT: Investor Relations,
(815) 235-4171
PRINCIPAL OFFICE: Newell Center, 29 East
Stephenson Street, Freeport, IL 61032-0943

TELEPHONE NUMBER: (815) 235-4171
FAX: (815) 233-8060
WEB: www.newellco.com
NO. OF EMPLOYEES: 48,000 (approx.)
SHAREHOLDERS: 24,868
ANNUAL MEETING: In May
INCORPORATED: DE, 1970

INSTITUTIONAL HOLDINGS:
No. of Institutions: 417
Shares Held: 215,436,350
% Held: 80.6

INDUSTRY: Glass containers (SIC: 3221)

TRANSFER AGENT(S): First Chicago Trust
Company of New York, Jersey City, NJ

NEWFIELD EXPLORATION CO.

EXCH.	SYM.	REC. PRICE	P/E RATIO	YLD.	MKT. CAP.	RANGE (52-WK.)	'02 Y/E PR.
NYSE	NFX	34.10 (2/28/03)	21.4	...	$1.50 bill.	39.24 - 27.16	36.05

MEDIUM GRADE. THE COMPANY EXPECTS 2003 PRODUCTION TO RANGE BETWEEN 215 BILLION CUBIC FEET EQUIVALENT (BCFE) AND 225 BCFE, AN INCREASE OF 16.8% TO 22.2% OVER 2002 LEVELS.

7 YEAR PRICE SCORE 126.6　　　　**12 MONTH PRICE SCORE 105.1**

*NYSE COMPOSITE INDEX=100

INTERIM EARNINGS (Per Share):

Qtr.	Mar.	June	Sept.	Dec.
1997	0.34	0.32	0.24	0.34
1998	0.18	0.10	0.02	d1.71
1999	Nil	0.10	0.29	0.39
2000	0.35	0.60	0.95	1.01
2001	1.32	1.18	0.91	d0.89
2002	0.37	0.36	0.21	0.65

INTERIM DIVIDENDS (Per Share):

Amt.	Decl.	Ex.	Rec.	Pay.
	No dividends paid.			

CAPITALIZATION (12/31/01):

	($000)	(%)
Long-Term Debt	428,631	31.8
Deferred Income Tax	207,880	15.4
Common & Surplus	709,978	52.7
Total	1,346,489	100.0

BUSINESS:

Newfield Exploration Co. is an independent oil company engaged in the exploration, development and acquisition of crude oil and natural gas properties. The Company's operations are focused in the Gulf of Mexico and the Anadarko Basin of Oklahoma, along with the U.S. onshore Gulf Coast, offshore northwest Australia, and the Bohai Bay, offshore China. As of 12/31/02, NFX had proved reserves of 1.20 trillion cubic feet equivalent. Total reserves were 81.0% natural gas. On 1/23/01, the Company acquired Lariat Petroleum for approximately $333.0 million.

RECENT DEVELOPMENTS:

For the twelve months ended 12/31/02, net income was $73.8 million versus income of $123.7 million, before an accounting charge of $4.8 million, the previous year. Results included unrealized commodity derivative expense of $29.1 million for 2002, and income of $24.8 million for 2001. Results for 2001 also included a ceiling test writedown of $106.0 million. Revenues fell 11.7% to $661.8 million from $749.4 million in 2001. Production volumes for 2002 increased 5.1% to 184.1 billion cubic feet equivalent (Bcfe). NFX noted that production was negatively affected by two factors, including approximately 4 Bcfe that was shut-in during the second half of 2002 due to storms in the Gulf of Mexico, and, in February 2002, about 1 Bcf that was curtailed in response to low gas prices.

PROSPECTS:

NFX has announced a 2003 capital spending budget of $450.0 million, an increase of 34.0% from the 2002 level. The program includes $200.0 million for exploration. Drilling plans call for between 25 to 35 wells in the Gulf of Mexico, including 7 to 10 deep shelf wells and 2 to 3 deepwater wells; 45 to 50 wells onshore Gulf Coast; 40 to 50 wells in the Mid-Continent; and one to three wells overseas. Separately, NFX expects its 2003 production to be in the range of 215 billion Bcfe to 225 billion Bcfe, an gain of 16.8% to 22.2% over 2002 production of 184.1 Bcfe.

ANNUAL FINANCIAL DATA:

FISCAL YEAR	TOT. REVS. ($mill.)	NET INC. ($mill.)	TOT. ASSETS ($mill.)	OPER. PROFIT %	NET PROFIT %	RET. ON EQUITY %	RET. ON ASSETS %	CURR. RATIO	EARN. PER SH. $	CASH FL. PER SH. $	TANG. BK. VAL. $	PRICE RANGE	AVG. P/E RATIO
p12/31/02	661.8	④ 73.8							④ 1.61			39.24 - 27.16	20.6
12/31/01	749.4	③ 123.7	1,663.4	25.5	16.5	17.4	7.4	1.4	③ 2.66	8.31	16.10	47.75 - 26.25	13.9
12/31/00	526.6	①② 134.7	1,023.3	42.0	25.6	20.3	13.2	1.3	①② 2.98	6.90	12.19	50.25 - 24.50	12.5
12/31/99	282.0	33.2	781.6	23.1	11.8	6.4	4.2	1.4	0.81	4.39	8.99	35.00 - 14.88	30.8
12/31/98	195.7	① d57.7	629.3	...	...	...	...	0.8	① d1.55	1.75	8.01	27.69 - 15.44	...
12/31/97	199.4	① 40.6	553.6	32.4	20.4	13.9	7.3	1.0	① 1.07	3.54	8.12	33.00 - 16.88	23.3
12/31/96	149.3	38.5	395.9	39.4	25.8	16.0	9.7	1.2	1.03	2.76	6.81	26.50 - 12.50	18.9
12/31/95	94.6	16.3	277.4	25.6	17.2	8.4	5.9	1.4	0.45	1.83	5.63	16.06 - 9.00	27.8
12/31/94	69.7	14.4	215.6	30.4	20.7	8.5	6.7	1.4	0.40	1.35	5.08	13.00 - 8.69	27.1
12/31/93	60.2	14.0	183.7	34.9	23.3	9.2	7.6	4.9	0.49	1.36	4.62	9.25 - 7.88	17.5

Statistics are as originally reported. Adj. for 2-for-1 split, 12/96. ① Incl. ceiling test write-down chrg. of $4.2 mill., 1997; $105.0 mill., 1998; $503,000, 2000. ② Bef. acctg. chrg. of $2.4 mill. ③ Incl. ceiling test write-down chrg. of $106.0 mill. & unrealized commodity derivative inc. of $24.8 mill.; bef. acctg. chge. chrg. of $4.8 mill. ④ Incl. unrealized commodity derivative exp. of $29.1 mill.

OFFICERS:
D. A. Trice, Pres., C.E.O.
T. W. Rathert, V.P., C.F.O., Sec.
S. G. Riggs, Treas.

INVESTOR CONTACT: Steve Campbell, Investor Relations, (281) 847-6081

PRINCIPAL OFFICE: 363 N. Sam Houston Pkwy. East, Ste. 2020, Houston, TX 77060

TELEPHONE NUMBER: (281) 847-6000
FAX: (281) 847-6006
WEB: www.newfld.com

NO. OF EMPLOYEES: 410 (avg.)

SHAREHOLDERS: 300 (approx.)

ANNUAL MEETING: In May

INCORPORATED: DE, Dec., 1988

INSTITUTIONAL HOLDINGS:
No. of Institutions: 218
Shares Held: 43,054,829
% Held: 96.8

INDUSTRY: Crude petroleum and natural gas (SIC: 1311)

TRANSFER AGENT(S): Mellon Investor Services LLC, Ridgefield Park, NJ

NEWMONT MINING CORPORATION

EXCH.	SYM.	REC. PRICE	P/E RATIO	YLD.	MKT. CAP.	RANGE (52-WK.)	'02 Y/E PR.
NYSE	NEM	27.33 (2/28/03)	97.6	0.6%	$5.36 bill.	32.75 - 20.80	29.03

MEDIUM GRADE. FOR 2003, THE COMPANY EXPECTS TO SELL APPROXIMATELY 7.1 MILLION EQUITY OUNCES OF GOLD.

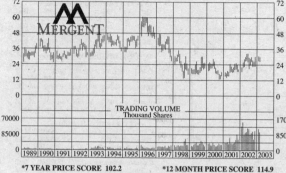

*7 YEAR PRICE SCORE 102.2   ***12 MONTH PRICE SCORE 114.9**
NYSE COMPOSITE INDEX=100

INTERIM EARNINGS (Per Share):

Qtr.	Mar.	June	Sept.	Dec.
1999	0.06	0.04	d0.23	0.28
2000	0.04	d0.10	d0.11	0.12
2001	d0.20	d0.17	0.11	0.10
2002	d0.04	0.16	0.06	...

INTERIM DIVIDENDS (Per Share):

Amt.	Decl.	Ex.	Rec.	Pay.
0.03Q	5/15/02	6/03/02	6/05/02	6/19/02
0.03Q	8/06/02	8/30/02	9/04/02	9/18/02
0.03Q	11/20/02	12/02/02	12/04/02	12/18/02
0.04Q	1/29/03	3/03/03	3/05/03	3/19/03

Indicated div.: $0.16 (Div. Reinv. Plan)

CAPITALIZATION (12/31/01):

	($000)	(%)
Long-Term Debt	1,089,718	40.3
Deferred Income Tax	133,621	4.9
Preferred Stock	11,500	0.4
Common & Surplus	1,468,548	54.3
Total	2,703,387	100.0

BUSINESS:

Newmont Mining Corporation is engaged in the production of gold, the development of gold properties, the exploration for gold and the acquisition of gold properties worldwide. NEM produces gold from operations in Nevada and California, as well as in Australia, Bolivia, Canada, Indonesia, Mexico, New Zealand, Peru, Turkey and the Central Asian Republic of Uzbekistan. In 2002, Newmont Mining sold about 7.6 million ounces of gold. On 5/5/97, NEM acquired Santa Fe Pacific Gold Corp. On 1/10/01, NEM acquired Battle Mountain Gold Company. In February 2002, NEM acquired Franco-Nevada Mining Corporation Limited and Normandy Mining Limited of Australia.

RECENT DEVELOPMENTS:

The Company has requested pre-clearance from the Securities and Exchange Commission regarding NEM's methodology used to allocate the purchase price of Normandy Mining Limited and Franco-Nevada Mining Corporation Limited under new business combination rules. Financial statements will be finalized and released once the SEC's concurrence is received. For the quarter ended 9/30/02, net income increased 16.5% to $24.0 million compared with $20.6 million in the corresponding prior-year quarter. Results included a loss of $11.2 million in 2002 and a gain of $900,000 in 2001 on derivative instruments. Total revenues advanced 73.0% to $728.3 million from $421.1 million a year earlier. Comparisons were made with restated results for the prior year.

PROSPECTS:

On 1/31/03, the Company completed the sale of its TCX-Newmont joint venture for $180.0 million in cash. In early 2003, the Company converted its 45.0% equity interest in Echo Bay to a non-equity accounted 13.8% interest in Kinross Gold Corporation. For 2003, the Company expects to sell approximately 7.1 million equity ounces of gold with average production costs of about $195.00 per ounce. Meanwhile, in accordance with NEM's no-hedging philosophy, the Company continues to reduce gold hedge books from the Normandy acquisition.

ANNUAL FINANCIAL DATA:

FISCAL YEAR	TOT. REVS. ($mill.)	NET INC. ($mill.)	TOT. ASSETS ($mill.)	OPER. PROFIT %	NET PROFIT %	RET. ON EQUITY %	RET. ON ASSETS %	CURR. RATIO	EARN. PER SH. $	CASH FL. PER SH. $	TANG. BK. VAL. $	DIV. PER SH. $	PRICE RANGE	AVG. P/E RATIO	AVG. YIELD %
p12/31/02												0.12	32.75 - 18.52		0.5
12/31/01	1,664.1	③ d23.3	4,062.4	...	...	...	...	1.5	d0.16	1.63	7.49	0.12	25.23 - 14.00	...	0.6
12/31/00	1,566.7	⑦ d10.5	3,510.7	4.9	...	...	...	1.8	⑦ d0.06	2.40	8.58	0.12	28.38 - 12.75	...	0.6
12/31/99	1,431.6	⑥ 24.8	3,383.4	11.7	1.7	1.7	0.7	2.0	⑥ 0.15	1.91	8.66	0.12	30.06 - 16.38	154.7	0.5
12/31/98	1,474.9	⑤ d360.5	3,186.8	...	...	...	...	2.4	⑤ d2.27	d0.12	8.61	0.12	34.88 - 13.25	...	0.5
④ 12/31/97	1,628.0	③ 68.4	3,614.0	8.1	4.2	4.3	1.9	1.6	③ 0.44	2.49	10.17	0.39	47.50 - 26.56	84.1	1.1
12/31/96	794.9	41.1	2,081.1	...	5.2	4.0	2.0	2.0	0.86	1.67	10.30	0.48	60.75 - 43.88	60.8	0.9
12/31/95	791.6	② 76.2	1,773.8	9.7	9.6	10.3	4.3	1.5	② 1.17	1.98	7.89	0.48	46.25 - 33.13	33.9	1.2
12/31/94	619.7	66.3	1,656.7	4.7	10.7	9.8	4.0	2.4	0.70	1.68	7.66	0.48	48.08 - 33.88	58.5	1.2
12/31/93	683.9	① 94.7	1,186.4	17.5	13.8	16.0	8.0	2.1	① 0.92	2.21	7.17	0.48	47.18 - 29.65	41.7	1.3

Statistics are as originally reported. Adj. for 1.2481-for-1 stock split 4/94. ① Bef. actg. adj. of $38.5 mill.; incl. net invest. disp. gain of $19.5 mill. ② Incl. net gain on sale of equity invest. of $72.0 mill. & a $37.1 million prop. write-off chg. ③ Incl. pre-tax asset write-offs of $162.7 mill. ④ Inc. results of Santa Fe Pacific Gold Corp. ⑤ Bef actg. chg. of $32.9 mill.; incl. pre-tax aset write-down chg. of $614.9 mill. ⑥ Incl. net non-recurr. chg. of $41.9 mill. ⑦ Bef. actg. chg. of $8.4 mill.; incl. pre-tax gain of $26.8 mill. on call opts., pre-tax chg. of $42.2 mill. for acq. settlement. ⑧ Incl. after-tax merger and non-cash chgs. of $44.5 mill.

OFFICERS:
W. W. Murdy, Chmn., C.E.O.
P. Lassonde, Pres.
B. D. Hansen, Sr. V.P., C.F.O.

INVESTOR CONTACT: Russell Ball, (303) 837-5927

PRINCIPAL OFFICE: 1700 Lincoln Street, Denver, CO 80203

TELEPHONE NUMBER: (303) 863-7414
FAX: (303) 837-5837
WEB: www.newmont.com

NO. OF EMPLOYEES: 10,600 (avg.)

SHAREHOLDERS: 26,193 (approx. record)

ANNUAL MEETING: In May

INCORPORATED: DE, May, 1921

INSTITUTIONAL HOLDINGS:
No. of Institutions: 382
Shares Held: 275,419,279
% Held: 78.2

INDUSTRY: Gold ores (SIC: 1041)

TRANSFER AGENT(S): Mellon Investor Services, LLC, Ridgefield, NJ

NICOR INC.

EXCH.	SYM.	REC. PRICE	P/E RATIO	YLD.	MKT. CAP.	RANGE (52-WK.)	'02 Y/E PR.	DIV. ACH.
NYSE	GAS	30.09 (2/28/03)	10.3	6.2%	$1.34 bill.	49.00 - 17.25	34.03	15 yrs.

UPPER MEDIUM GRADE. LOOKING AHEAD, HIGHER OPERATING COSTS AND THE EFFECTS OF A WEAK ECONOMY SHOULD PLACE NEAR-TERM PRESSURE ON EARNINGS.

INTERIM EARNINGS (Per Share):

Qtr.	Mar.	June	Sept.	Dec.
1999	0.82	0.56	0.42	0.83
2000	0.83	0.66	d1.37	0.87
2001	0.85	0.59	0.73	1.01
2002	0.90	0.46	0.68	0.89

INTERIM DIVIDENDS (Per Share):

Amt.	Decl.	Ex.	Rec.	Pay.
0.46Q	3/21/02	3/26/02	3/28/02	5/01/02
0.46Q	4/18/02	6/26/02	6/28/02	8/01/02
0.46Q	7/18/02	9/26/02	9/30/02	11/01/02
0.46Q	11/21/02	12/27/02	12/31/02	2/01/03
0.465Q	3/20/03	3/27/03	3/31/03	5/01/03

Indicated div.: $1.86 (Div. Reinv. Plan)

CAPITALIZATION (12/31/01):

	($000)	(%)
Long-Term Debt	446,400	28.3
Deferred Income Tax	395,100	25.1
Redeemable Pfd. Stock	6,100	0.4
Common & Surplus	727,600	46.2
Total	1,575,200	100.0

*7 YEAR PRICE SCORE 103.6   ***12 MONTH PRICE SCORE 98.8**

*NYSE COMPOSITE INDEX=100

BUSINESS:

NICOR Inc. is engaged in the purchase, storage, distribution, transportation, sale, and gathering of natural gas. The Company's natural gas unit, Northern Illinois Gas, is the largest gas distribution company in Illinois and one of the biggest in the nation. As of 12/31/01, Northern Illinois served more than 2.0 million customers in the northern third of the state, generally outside of Chicago. NICOR also owns Tropical Shipping Co., a containerized shipping business serving 26 Caribbean ports from the Port of Palm Beach in Florida. In 2002, operating revenues were derived: 83.1% gas distribution, 13.9% shipping and 3.0% other energy ventures.

RECENT DEVELOPMENTS:

For the year ended 12/31/02, net income climbed 4.8% to $128.0 million compared with $122.1 million the previous year. Results for 2002 and 2001 included pre-tax gains of $4.1 million and $3.9 million, respectively, from the sale of property. Earnings growth was largely due to significant insurance recoveries, positive adjustments in the Company's gas distribution segment, lower net interest expense and operating income improvements in GAS' shipping segment. Operating revenues decreased 19.8% to $1.90 billion from $2.37 billion the year before. Gas distribution revenues decreased 23.9% to $1.59 billion from $2.09 billion, while shipping operating revenues increased 15.5% to $266.0 million from $230.3 million a year earlier. Comparisons were made with restated prior-year figures.

PROSPECTS:

Looking ahead, higher operating costs and the effects of a weak economy should place near-term pressure on earnings. Despite the challenge, the Company should be well-positioned to build upon its strong financial position, strategic location and customer base. Meanwhile, the Company expects fiscal 2003 diluted earnings to range from $2.40 to $2.60 per share, assuming normal weather. The reduction in estimated financial earnings reflects lower anticipated operating results in the gas distribution segment, Nicor Gas.

ANNUAL FINANCIAL DATA:

FISCAL YEAR	TOT. REVS. ($mill.)	NET INC. ($mill.)	TOT. ASSETS ($mill.)	OPER. PROFIT %	NET PROFIT %	NET INC./ NET PROP. %	NET INC./ TOT. CAP. %	RET. ON EQUITY %	ACCUM. DEPR./ GROSS PROP. %	EARN. PER SH. $	TANG. BK. VAL. $	DIV. PER SH. $	DIV. PAYOUT %	PRICE RANGE	AVG. P/E RATIO	AVG. YIELD %
p12/31/02	1,897.4	④ 128.0								④ 2.88	1.91	1.82	63.2	49.00 — 17.25	11.5	5.5
12/31/01	2,544.1	143.7	2,574.8	9.6	5.6	8.1	9.1	19.7	d52.6	3.17	16.39	1.74	54.7	42.38 — 34.00	12.0	4.5
12/31/00	2,298.1	③ 46.7	2,885.4	4.1	2.0	2.7	3.3	6.6	d51.6	③ 1.00	15.56	1.64	163.5	43.88 — 29.38	36.6	4.5
12/31/99	1,615.2	② 124.4	2,451.8	13.1	7.7	7.2	7.9	15.8	d50.2	② 2.62	16.80	1.54	58.8	42.94 — 31.19	14.1	4.1
12/31/98	1,465.1	116.4	2,364.6	14.2	7.9	6.7	7.1	15.3	d48.8	2.42	15.97	1.46	60.3	44.44 — 37.13	16.9	3.6
12/31/97	1,992.6	127.9	2,394.6	11.5	6.4	7.4	8.0	17.2	d46.9	2.61	15.43	1.37	52.5	42.94 — 30.00	14.0	3.8
12/31/96	1,850.7	① 121.2	2,438.6	12.6	6.5	6.8	7.8	16.6	d44.5	① 2.42	14.74	1.31	54.1	37.13 — 25.38	12.9	4.2
12/31/95	1,480.1	99.8	2,259.1	12.8	6.7	5.6	6.8	14.5	d42.8	1.96	13.67	1.27	65.0	28.50 — 21.75	12.8	5.1
12/31/94	1,609.4	109.5	2,209.9	11.8	6.8	6.4	7.8	16.0	d41.8	2.07	13.26	1.25	60.4	29.25 — 21.88	12.3	4.9
12/31/93	1,673.9	109.4	2,222.1	11.8	6.5	6.6	7.6	15.5	d42.6	1.97	13.05	1.21	61.4	31.63 — 24.13	14.1	4.3

Statistics are as originally reported. ① Bef. inc. fr. dis. ops. of $150.0 mill. ② Incl. a pre-tax gain of $3.8 million on the sale of the Company's interest in QuickTrade. ③ Excls. one-time after-tax chrg. of $89.7 mill. ④ Incl. pre-tax gain of $4.1 mill. from the sale of prop.

OFFICERS:
T. L. Fisher, Chmn., C.E.O.
R. M. Strobel, Pres.
K. L. Halloran, Exec. V.P., C.F.O.
G. M. Behrens, V.P., Treas.

INVESTOR CONTACT: Mark Knox, Investor Relations, (630) 983-9500 ext.2529

PRINCIPAL OFFICE: 1844 Ferry Road, Naperville, IL 60563-9600

TELEPHONE NUMBER: (630) 305-9500
FAX: (630) 983-9328
WEB: www.nicorinc.com

NO. OF EMPLOYEES: 2,300 (approx.)

SHAREHOLDERS: 27,500 (approx.)

ANNUAL MEETING: In Mar.

INCORPORATED: IL, 1976

INSTITUTIONAL HOLDINGS:
No. of Institutions: 225
Shares Held: 23,457,525
% Held: 53.3

INDUSTRY: Natural gas distribution (SIC: 4924)

TRANSFER AGENT(S): Computershare Investor Services, Chicago, IL

NIKE, INC.

EXCH.	SYM.	REC. PRICE	P/E RATIO	YLD.	MKT. CAP.	RANGE (52-WK.)	'02 Y/E PR.
NYSE	NKE	46.37 (2/28/03)	17.8	1.2%	$12.34 bill.	64.28 - 38.53	44.47

INVESTMENT GRADE. LOOKING AHEAD, NKE EXPECTS U.S. REVENUES TO CONTINUE TO BE HAMPERED BY DECLINING SALES AT FOOT LOCKER.

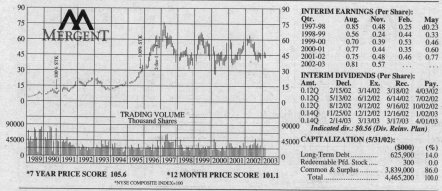

*7 YEAR PRICE SCORE 105.6　　***12 MONTH PRICE SCORE 101.1**
NYSE COMPOSITE INDEX=100

INTERIM EARNINGS (Per Share):

Qtr.	Aug.	Nov.	Feb.	May
1997-98	0.85	0.48	0.25	d0.23
1998-99	0.56	0.24	0.44	0.33
1999-00	0.70	0.39	0.53	0.46
2000-01	0.77	0.44	0.35	0.60
2001-02	0.75	0.48	0.46	0.77
2002-03	0.81	0.57	...	...

INTERIM DIVIDENDS (Per Share):

Amt.	Decl.	Ex.	Rec.	Pay.
0.12Q	2/15/02	3/14/02	3/18/02	4/03/02
0.12Q	5/13/02	6/12/02	6/14/02	7/02/02
0.12Q	8/12/02	9/12/02	9/16/02	10/02/02
0.14Q	11/25/02	12/12/02	12/16/02	1/02/03
0.14Q	2/14/03	3/13/03	3/17/03	4/01/03

Indicated div.: $0.56 (Div. Reinv. Plan)

CAPITALIZATION (5/31/02):

	($000)	(%)
Long-Term Debt	625,900	14.0
Redeemable Pfd. Stock	300	0.0
Common & Surplus	3,839,000	86.0
Total	4,465,200	100.0

BUSINESS:

Nike, Inc. designs, manufactures and markets worldwide athletic footwear and apparel products. The Company sells its products to approximately 19,700 retail accounts, including department stores, footwear stores, sporting good stores, tennis and golf shops and other outlets. The Company's major products consist of an extensive line of athletic shoes for men, women and children for competitive and recreational use. Substantially all of the Company's footwear products are designed as athletic shoes for specific sports. However, a large percentage of the shoes are purchased and worn for casual or leisure purposes. Nike also offers active sports apparel.

RECENT DEVELOPMENTS:

For the quarter ended 11/30/02, net income climbed 17.6% to $152.0 million from $129.3 million in the corresponding 2001 quarter. Earnings were fueled by margin expansion, tight inventory controls and continued strength in international markets. Total revenues increased 7.6% to $2.51 billion from $2.34 billion the previous year. U.S. athletic footwear revenues dropped 13.0% to $596.0 million, while U.S. apparel revenues slipped 1.0% to $370.0 million. Revenues in the Europe, Middle East and Africa group surged 35.0% to $781.0 million. Asia Pacific revenues increased 13.0% to $134.0 million. Revenues in the Latin American region declined 13.0% to $134.0 million.

PROSPECTS:

Looking ahead, NKE expects U.S. revenues to continue to be hampered by declining sales at Foot Locker through at least the beginning of the second quarter of fiscal 2004. Although NKE expects that Foot Locker will continue to be a significant business partner, Foot Locker will no longer be a primary distribution point for NKE's high-end footwear products nor will it distribute the Company's U.S. elite and statement level products and will not participate in the NKE's key U.S. footwear product launches after February 2003. NKE will continue to pursue incremental sales with other retailers, in order to offset the decline in revenues from Foot Locker. Although NKE does not expect to fully offset the revenue loss from Foot Locker in the short term, the Company expects that the realignment of its U.S. distribution will enable it to meet demand and generate profitable revenue growth.

ANNUAL FINANCIAL DATA:

FISCAL YEAR	TOT. REVS. ($mill.)	NET INC. ($mill.)	TOT. ASSETS ($mill.)	OPER. PROFIT %	NET PROFIT %	RET. ON EQUITY %	RET. ON ASSETS %	CURR. RATIO	EARN. PER SH.$	CASH FL. PER SH.$	TANG. BK. VAL.$	DIV. PER SH.$	PRICE RANGE	AVG. P/E RATIO	AVG. YIELD %
5/31/02	9,893.0	② 668.3	6,443.0	10.8	6.8	17.4	10.4	2.3	② 2.46	3.47	12.78	0.48	60.06 - 35.50	19.4	1.0
5/31/01	9,488.8	589.7	5,819.6	10.7	6.2	16.9	10.1	2.0	2.16	2.94	11.53	0.48	57.00 - 25.81	19.2	1.2
5/31/00	8,995.1	① 579.1	5,856.9	10.9	6.4	18.5	9.9	1.7	① 2.07	2.87	10.11	0.48	66.94 - 38.75	25.5	0.9
5/31/99	8,776.9	① 451.4	5,247.7	9.8	5.1	13.5	8.6	2.3	① 1.57	2.36	10.30	0.48	52.69 - 31.00	26.7	1.1
5/31/98	9,553.1	① 399.6	5,397.4	9.0	4.2	12.3	7.4	2.1	① 1.35	2.15	9.85	0.40	76.38 - 37.75	42.3	0.7
5/31/97	9,186.5	795.8	5,361.2	15.0	8.7	25.2	14.8	2.1	2.68	3.25	9.30	0.30	64.00 - 31.75	17.9	0.6
5/31/96	6,470.6	553.2	3,951.6	15.1	8.5	22.8	14.0	1.9	1.88	2.33	6.81	0.25	35.19 - 17.19	13.9	1.0
5/31/95	4,760.8	385.0	3,142.7	14.4	8.1	19.6	12.2	1.8	1.36	1.60	5.14	0.20	19.13 - 11.56	11.3	1.3
5/31/94	3,789.7	298.8	2,373.8	13.6	7.9	17.2	12.6	3.2	0.99	1.23	5.18	0.20	22.31 - 10.78	16.7	1.2
5/31/93	3,931.0	365.0	2,187.5	15.8	9.3	22.2	16.7	3.6	0.59	0.71	2.45	0.15	22.56 - 13.75	30.6	0.8

Statistics are as originally reported. Adj. for stk. splits: 2-for-1, 10/96 & 10/95 ① Incl. non-recurr. chrg. $300,000, 2000; $45.1 mill., 1999; $129.9 mill., 1998. ② Bef. acctg. chng. chrg. $5.0 mill.

OFFICERS:
P. H. Knight, Chmn, Pres., C.E.O.
D. W. Blair, V.P., C.F.O.
L. D. Stewart, V.P., Asst. Sec.
INVESTOR CONTACT: Investor Relations, (503) 671-6453
PRINCIPAL OFFICE: One Bowerman Drive, Beaverton, OR 97005-6453

TELEPHONE NUMBER: (503) 671-6453
FAX: (503) 671-6300
WEB: www.nikebiz.com
NO. OF EMPLOYEES: 22,700 (approx.)
SHAREHOLDERS: 19,500 (class B); 27 (class A)
ANNUAL MEETING: In Sept.
INCORPORATED: OR, 1968

INSTITUTIONAL HOLDINGS:
No. of Institutions: 349
Shares Held: 148,279,131
% Held: 55.9
INDUSTRY: Rubber and plastics footwear (SIC: 3021)
TRANSFER AGENT(S): Equiserve Trust Company, N.A., Jersey City, NJ

99 CENTS ONLY STORES

EXCH.	SYM.	REC. PRICE	P/E RATIO	YLD.	MKT. CAP.	RANGE (52-WK.)	'02 Y/E PR.
NYSE	NDN	22.28 (2/28/03)	27.9	...	$1.55 bill.	33.00 - 20.26	26.86

MEDIUM GRADE. IN 2003, THE COMPANY EXPECTS TO GROW SQUARE FOOTAGE BY AT LEAST 25.0% AND INCREASE EARNINGS BY 20.0%.

TRADING VOLUME
Thousand Shares

*7 YEAR PRICE SCORE N/A   *12 MONTH PRICE SCORE 105.9

*NYSE COMPOSITE INDEX=100

INTERIM EARNINGS (Per Share):

Qtr.	Mar.	June	Sept.	Dec.
2000	------------------ 0.56 ------------------			
2001	0.11	0.12	0.16	0.23
2002	0.14	0.19	0.19	0.28

INTERIM DIVIDENDS (Per Share):

Amt.	Decl.	Ex.	Rec.	Pay.
3-for-2	2/28/01	3/21/01	3/14/01	3/20/01
4-for-3	3/12/02	4/04/02	3/25/02	4/03/02

CAPITALIZATION (12/31/01):

	($000)	(%)
Capital Lease Obligations..	1,637	0.5
Common & Surplus	319,643	99.5
Total	321,280	100.0

BUSINESS:

99 Cents Only Stores is a deep-discount retailer of primarily name-brand, consumable general merchandise. The Company's stores offer a wide assortment of regularly available consumer goods and a broad range of first-quality, close-out merchandise. As of 2/4/03, the Company operated 153 retail stores in southern and central California, Las Vegas, Nevada and Phoenix, Arizona. These stores have an average size of approximately 20,000 square feet. The Company's 99 Cents Only Stores generated average net sales per estimated saleable square foot of $309.00 and average net sales per store of $4.8 million for stores open the full year in 2002. The Company also sells merchandise through its Bargain Wholesale division at prices generally below normal wholesale levels to local, regional, and national discount, drug and grocery store chains and independent retailers, distributors, and exporters. Revenues for 2002 were derived: 99 Cents Only Stores, 93.0%; and Bargain Wholesale, 7.0%.

RECENT DEVELOPMENTS:

For the year ended 12/31/02, net income rose 21.7% to $59.0 million versus $48.4 million in 2001. Earnings benefited from the rollout of milk in the second half of 2002 to NDN's California stores and the success of the newly introduced gourmet food sections. Net sales were $713.9 million, up 23.5% from $578.3 million in the prior year. Gross profit jumped 25.8% to $286.6 million from $227.8 million the year before, primarily due to a higher retail versus wholesale sales mix. Operating income rose 22.4% to $90.5 million versus $74.0 million in 2001.

PROSPECTS:

In 2003, the Company expects to grow square footage by at least 25.0% and increase earnings by 20.0%. In addition, the Company is accelerating its entry into Texas from early 2004 to June 2003. On 1/28/03, the Company purchased a large distribution center in the Houston, Texas area where the initial cluster of stores will be located. As a result, the Company has revised the timing of its new store openings in the first half of 2003, but plans to meet its annual target of 38 new stores. Approximately 15 of the new 38 stores planned for 2003 will be located in Houston, Texas.

ANNUAL FINANCIAL DATA:

FISCAL YEAR	TOT. REVS. ($000)	NET INC. ($000)	TOT. ASSETS ($000)	OPER. PROFIT %	NET PROFIT %	RET. ON EQUITY %	RET. ON ASSETS %	CURR. RATIO	EARN. PER SH.$	CASH FL. PER SH.$	TANG. BK. VAL.$	PRICE RANGE	AVG. P/E RATIO
p12/31/02	713,942	58,974						0.83				33.00 - 20.26	32.1
12/31/01	578,269	48,443	352,158	12.8	8.4	15.2	13.8	7.7	0.69	0.87	4.60	31.50 - 12.91	32.2
12/31/00	451,947	② 38,858	277,285	13.3	8.6	15.3	14.0	8.7	② 0.56	0.69	3.71	27.69 - 10.13	33.8
12/31/99	359,958	① 34,138	224,015	15.4	9.5	17.5	15.2	7.3	① 0.50	0.59	2.96	19.69 - 9.38	29.1
12/31/98	323,273	26,693	198,123	13.8	8.3	16.2	13.5	6.2	0.41	0.48	2.51	18.52 - 7.95	32.3
12/31/97	230,855	18,950	119,443	13.5	8.2	19.7	15.9	6.8	0.30	0.35	1.56	9.39 - 3.84	21.8
12/31/96	183,643	13,702	98,997	12.5	7.5	17.9	13.8	6.4	0.23	0.27	1.24	4.20 - 3.12	15.7
12/31/95	152,827	9,594	57,598	11.0	6.3	27.0	16.7	3.8	0.18	0.21	0.86	... ...	...
12/31/94	131,737	8,004	51,419	8.4	6.1	26.0	15.6	3.6	...	...	0.74	... ...	...
12/31/93	122,949	5,866		7.6	4.8				...	...	...	... ...	...

Statistics are as originally reported. Adj. for 4-for-3 split, 4/02; 3-for-2 split, 3/01; 4-for-3 split, 2/00; 5-for-4 split, 11/98; and 5-for-4 split, 11/97. ① Excl. $3.2 mill. loss fr. disc. ops. & $9.0 mill. loss fr. disposal of disc. ops. ② Excl. $1.1 mill. loss fr. disc. ops.

OFFICERS:
D. Gold, Chmn., C.E.O.
E. Schiffer, Pres.
A. Farina, C.F.O.

INVESTOR CONTACT: Investor Relations, (323) 980-8145

PRINCIPAL OFFICE: 4000 Union Pacific Avenue, City of Commerce, CA 90023

TELEPHONE NUMBER: (323) 980-8145
FAX: (323) 980-8160
WEB: www.99only.com
NO. OF EMPLOYEES: 5,674 (avg.)
SHAREHOLDERS: 13,642 (approx.)
ANNUAL MEETING: In June
INCORPORATED: CA, 1982

INSTITUTIONAL HOLDINGS:
No. of Institutions: 149
Shares Held: 34,678,317
% Held: 49.5

INDUSTRY: Variety stores (SIC: 5331)

TRANSFER AGENT(S): American Stock Transfer & Trust Company, New York, NY

NISOURCE, INC.

EXCH.	SYM.	REC. PRICE	P/E RATIO	YLD.	MKT. CAP.	RANGE (52-WK.)	'02 Y/E PR.
NYSE	NI	16.94 (2/28/03)	8.6	6.8%	$3.48 bill.	24.99 - 14.51	20.00

UPPER MEDIUM GRADE. GAS WILL FOCUS ON MAXIMIZING PRODUCTION FROM ITS EXISTING ASSETS.

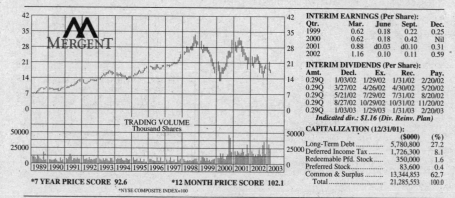

*7 YEAR PRICE SCORE 92.6 ***12 MONTH PRICE SCORE 102.1**

*NYSE COMPOSITE INDEX=100

INTERIM EARNINGS (Per Share):

Qtr.	Mar.	June	Sept.	Dec.
1999	0.62	0.18	0.22	0.25
2000	0.62	0.18	0.42	Nil
2001	0.88	d0.03	d0.10	0.31
2002	1.16	0.10	0.11	0.59

INTERIM DIVIDENDS (Per Share):

Amt.	Decl.	Ex.	Rec.	Pay.
0.29Q	1/03/02	1/29/02	1/31/02	2/20/02
0.29Q	3/27/02	4/26/02	4/30/02	5/20/02
0.29Q	5/21/02	7/29/02	7/31/02	8/20/02
0.29Q	8/27/02	10/29/02	10/31/02	11/20/02
0.29Q	1/03/03	1/29/03	1/31/03	2/20/03

Indicated div.: $1.16 (Div. Reinv. Plan)

CAPITALIZATION (12/31/01):

	($000)	(%)
Long-Term Debt	5,780,800	27.2
Deferred Income Tax	1,726,300	8.1
Redeemable Pfd. Stock	350,000	1.6
Preferred Stock	83,600	0.4
Common & Surplus	13,344,853	62.7
Total	21,285,553	100.0

BUSINESS:

NiSource, Inc. (formerly NIPSCO Industries, Inc.) is an energy-based holding company that provides electricity, natural gas and other products and services to 3.7 million customers from the Gulf Coast through the Midwest to New England as of 12/31/02. The Company's principal subsidiaries include Columbia Energy Resources, Inc., a natural gas distribution, transmission, storage and exploration and production holding company; Northern Indiana Public Service Company, a gas and electric company providing service to customers in northern Indiana; and Bay State Gas Company, a natural gas distribution company serving customers in New England. NI provides non-regulated energy marketing and services through its wholly-owned subsidiary, EnergyUSA, Inc. and develops power projects through its subsidiary, Primary Energy, Inc. In February 1999, NI acquired Bay State Gas Company. In November 2000, NI acquired Columbia Energy Group for approximately $6.00 billion.

RECENT DEVELOPMENTS:

For the year ended 12/31/02, income was $425.7 million, before a loss of $53.2 million from discontinued operations, compared with income of $226.4 million, before an accounting change charge of $4.0 million and loss of $14.2 million from discontinued operations, the previous year. Results for 2002 and 2001 included gains of $27.2 million and $100,000, respectively, on the sale or impairment of assets. Gross revenues dropped 31.4% to $6.49 billion from $9.46 billion the year before. Gas distribution revenues decreased 24.9% to $2.89 billion from $3.85 billion a year earlier. Operating income increased 16.4% to $1.20 billion versus $1.03 billion the prior year.

PROSPECTS:

On 1/28/03, the Company announced that its subsidiary Columbia Natural Resources, Inc. sold its interest in a natural gas exploration and production joint venture in New York state for approximately $95.0 million to an undisclosed buyer. As a result, GAS will no longer invest in exploratory drilling and will focus on maximizing production from its existing assets. Meanwhile, GAS should continue to benefit from its strategy to focus on its core regulated, asset-based businesses and its commitment to reducing operation and maintenance expenses.

ANNUAL FINANCIAL DATA:

FISCAL YEAR	TOT. REVS. ($mill.)	NET INC. ($mill.)	TOT. ASSETS ($mill.)	OPER. PROFIT %	NET PROFIT %	NET INC./ NET PROP. %	NET INC./ TOT. CAP. %	RET. ON EQUITY %	ACCUM. DEPR./ GROSS PROP. %	EARN. PER SH.$	TANG. BK. VAL.$	DIV. PER SH.$	DIV. PAYOUT %	PRICE RANGE	AVG. P/E RATIO	AVG. YIELD %
p12/31/02	6,492.3	④ 425.7		10.7	2.2	2.2	1.0	2.2	47.4	④ 2.00		1.16	58.0	24.20 – 14.51	9.7	6.0
12/31/01	9,458.7	③ 212.1	13,904.7	10.7	2.2	2.2	1.0	2.2	47.4	③ 1.01	1.16	126.2	32.55 – 18.25	24.7	4.6
② 12/31/00	6,030.7	① 147.1	19,696.8	9.4	2.4	1.5	1.3	4.2	43.6	① 1.08	...	1.08	100.0	31.50 – 12.75	20.5	4.9
12/31/99	3,144.6	160.4	6,835.2	14.7	5.1	3.1	4.6	22.5	41.8	1.27	...	1.02	80.3	30.94 – 16.38	18.6	4.3
12/31/98	2,932.8	193.9	4,986.5	14.4	6.6	6.6	5.3	15.7	44.8	1.59	9.23	0.96	60.4	33.75 – 24.66	18.4	3.3
12/31/97	2,586.5	190.8	4,937.0	15.9	7.4	7.4	5.1	14.1	43.0	1.53	8.10	0.90	58.8	24.94 – 19.00	14.4	4.1
12/31/96	1,821.6	176.7	4,274.3	15.7	9.7	9.7	5.9	15.0	44.4	1.44	9.20	0.84	58.3	20.13 – 17.63	13.1	4.5
12/31/95	1,722.3	175.5	3,999.5	16.5	10.2	10.2	5.7	14.6	42.5	1.36	8.99	0.78	57.3	19.25 – 14.63	12.5	4.6
12/31/94	1,676.4	164.0	3,947.1	21.4	9.8	9.8	5.4	13.7	40.5	1.24	8.67	0.72	58.1	16.50 – 13.06	11.9	4.9
12/31/93	1,677.9	156.1	3,912.3	21.4	9.3	9.3	5.1	13.1	38.8	1.02	8.31	0.66	65.0	17.44 – 13.06	15.0	4.3

Statistics are as originally reported. Adj. for stk. split 2-for-1: 2/98 ① Excl. inc. from disc. oper. of $9.8 mill., but incl. loss on asset impair. of $65.8 mill. ② Results for 2000 reflect the acq. of Columbia Energy Group on 11/1/00. ③ Bef. acctg. chng. cr. of $4.0 mill. & excl. gain of $100,000 from disc. ops., but incl. loss on impair. of $9.2 mill. ④ Bef. losses of $53.2 mill. from disc. ops. & incl. a gain of $27.2 mill. on sale or impair. of assets.

OFFICERS:
G. L. Neale, Chmn., Pres., C.E.O.
S. P. Adik, Vice-Chmn.
M. O'Donnell, Exec. V.P., C.F.O.
INVESTOR CONTACT: Dennis Senchak, V.P.
Inv. Rel., (219) 647-5200
PRINCIPAL OFFICE: 801 East 86th Avenue, Merrillville, IN 46410

TELEPHONE NUMBER: (219) 647-5200
FAX: (219) 647-6085
WEB: www.nisource.com
NO. OF EMPLOYEES: 12,501
SHAREHOLDERS: 49,389
ANNUAL MEETING: In May
INCORPORATED: IN, Sept., 1987; reincorp. in DE, Nov., 2000

INSTITUTIONAL HOLDINGS:
No. of Institutions: 340
Shares Held: 180,578,216
% Held: 86.9
INDUSTRY: Electric and other services combined (SIC: 4931)
TRANSFER AGENT(S): Computershare Investor Services, Chicago, IL

NL INDUSTRIES, INC.

EXCH.	SYM.	REC. PRICE	P/E RATIO	YLD.	MKT. CAP.	RANGE (52-WK.)	'02 Y/E PR.
NYSE	NL	15.40 (2/28/03)	20.3	5.2%	$0.76 bill.	18.80 - 13.07	17.00

MEDIUM GRADE. THE COMPANY EXPECTS FULL-YEAR 2003 SALES VOLUME TO BE COMPARABLE TO 2002 AND AVERAGE SELLING PRICES TO BE HIGHER THAN LAST YEAR.

*7 YEAR PRICE SCORE 110.5   ***12 MONTH PRICE SCORE 111.6**
*NYSE COMPOSITE INDEX=100

INTERIM EARNINGS (Per Share):

Qtr.	Mar.	June	Sept.	Dec.
1997	d0.79	d0.07	0.08	0.19
1998	0.31	0.45	0.60	0.36
1999	0.27	2.16	0.33	0.33
2000	0.46	1.25	0.60	0.75
2001	0.69	0.51	0.41	0.83
2002	0.13	0.29	0.18	0.16

INTERIM DIVIDENDS (Per Share):

Amt.	Decl.	Ex.	Rec.	Pay.
0.20Q	5/08/02	6/12/02	6/14/02	6/24/02
0.20Q	7/30/02	9/06/02	9/10/02	9/24/02
0.20Q	10/22/02	12/05/02	12/09/02	12/23/02
2.50Sp	11/14/02	11/21/02	11/25/02	12/06/02
0.20Q	2/05/03	3/12/03	3/14/03	3/26/03
	Indicated div.: $0.80			

CAPITALIZATION (12/31/01):

	($000)	(%)
Long-Term Debt	195,465	26.9
Deferred Income Tax	143,256	19.7
Common & Surplus	386,943	53.3
Total	725,664	100.0

BUSINESS:

NL Industries, Inc. conducts its operations through its wholly-owned subsidiary, Kronos, Inc. Kronos is the world's fifth largest producer of titanium dioxide pigments (TiO2), with an estimated 12.0% share of worldwide sales volume in 2002. TiO2 is a white pigment used to impart whiteness, brightness and opacity to a wide range of products including paints, plastics, paper, fibers and ceramics. Kronos serves more than 4,000 domestic and international customers with a majority of sales in Europe and North America. Net sales for 2002 were derived: Germany, 34.3%; U.S., 24.8%; Canada, 13.4%; Belgium, 10.4%; Norway, 9.5%; and other, 7.6%.

RECENT DEVELOPMENTS:

For the year ended 12/31/02, net income fell 69.7% to $36.8 million compared with $121.4 million in 2001. Results for 2002 and 2001 included litigation settlement gains, net, and other income of $9.3 million and $16.3 million, respectively. Results for 2002 also included a currency transaction gain of $6.3 million, while results for 2001 included a net insurance recovery of $17.5 million. Total revenues and other income were $876.0 million, up 3.6% from $845.9 million in the prior year. The increase in revenues was due in part to higher sales volumes, which were up to 455,000 metric tons. Operating income dropped 43.0% to $96.5 million compared with $169.2 million the previous year, primarily due to 9.0% lower average selling prices, partially offset by 13.0% increased sales volume and 7.0% higher production yield.

PROSPECTS:

Prices for titanium dioxide pigments, which continue to trend upward, have been raised again by the Company. Nevertheless, the Company expects full-year 2003 sales volume to be comparable to 2002 and average selling prices to be higher than last year. Based on these assumptions, the Company expects increased year over year operating income in 2003. However, due to economic uncertainties, the Company is unable to report projections for full-year 2003.

ANNUAL FINANCIAL DATA:

FISCAL YEAR	TOT. REVS. ($mill.)	NET INC. ($mill.)	TOT. ASSETS ($mill.)	OPER. PROFIT %	NET PROFIT %	RET. ON EQUITY %	RET. ON ASSETS %	CURR. RATIO	EARN. PER SH.$	CASH FL.PER SH.$	TANG. BK. VAL.$	DIV. PER SH.$	PRICE RANGE	AVG. P/E RATIO	AVG. YIELD %
p12/31/02	876.0	⑥ 36.8	1,151.1	20.8	13.7	31.4	10.5	1.9	⑥ 0.76			0.80	17.54 - 11.20	18.9	5.6
12/31/01	887.4	⑤ 121.4	1,120.8	1.6	15.3	45.1	13.9	1.9	⑤ 2.44	3.03	7.89	0.80	24.31 - 11.60	7.4	4.5
12/31/00	1,015.1	④ 155.3	1,120.8	1.6	15.3	45.1	13.9	1.9	④ 3.06	3.65	6.88	0.65	25.00 - 13.00	6.2	3.4
12/31/99	932.0	③ 159.8	1,056.2	1.5	17.2	58.9	15.1	1.9	③ 3.08	3.73	5.29	0.14	15.44 - 8.75	3.9	1.2
12/31/98	920.2	② 89.9	1,155.0	1.9	9.8	59.0	7.8	1.8	② 1.73	2.39	2.94	0.09	27.06 - 12.75	11.5	0.5
12/31/97	856.6	① d29.9	1,098.2	0.5	...	...	...	1.6	① d0.58	0.10	...	...	17.31 - 9.13	...	...
12/31/96	1,016.6	10.8	1,221.4	0.7	1.1	...	...	1.7	0.21	0.39	...	0.30	15.38 - 7.63	54.7	2.6
12/31/95	1,046.2	85.6	1,271.7	1.5	8.2	...	5.0	1.8	1.66	1.99	...	...	17.50 - 10.88	8.5	...
12/31/94	932.8	d24.0	1,162.4	0.3	...	...	...	2.1	d0.47	d0.67	...	...	13.25 - 4.38	...	...
12/31/93	827.4	d83.2	1,206.5	0.1	...	...	...	2.0	d1.63	d1.16	...	...	6.13 - 3.38	...	...

Statistics are as originally reported. ① Incl. $30.0 mill. ($0.59/sh.) acct. chg. for environ. remediation liabs. & excl. $20.4 mill. disc. ops. fr. sale of Rheox. ② Excl. inc. of $287.4 mill. from disc. ops. of Rheox & d$10.6 extraord. item. ③ Incl. $64.6 mill. net income tax benefit. ④ Incl. $73.7 mill. net gain fr. litigation settlement & excl. $700,000 extraord. loss. ⑤ Incl. $17.5 mill. net gain fr. ins. recovery & $16.3 mill. gain fr. litigation settlement. ⑥ Incl. $9.3 mill. litigation settlement & $6.3 mill. currency trans. gains.

OFFICERS:
H. C. Simmons, Chmn.
J. L. Martin, Pres., C.E.O.
R. D. Hardy, V.P., C.F.O., Treas., Contr.

INVESTOR CONTACT: Investor Relations, (281) 423-3332

PRINCIPAL OFFICE: 16825 Northchase Drive, Suite 1200, Houston, TX 77060-2544

TELEPHONE NUMBER: (281) 423-3300
FAX: (281) 423-3216
WEB: www.nl-ind.com

NO. OF EMPLOYEES: 2,500 (approx.)

SHAREHOLDERS: 6,000 (approx.)

ANNUAL MEETING: In May

INCORPORATED: NJ, Dec., 1891

INSTITUTIONAL HOLDINGS:
No. of Institutions: 66
Shares Held: 3,734,532
% Held: 7.8

INDUSTRY: Inorganic pigments (SIC: 2816)

TRANSFER AGENT(S): First Chicago Trust Company of New York, Jersey City, NJ

NOBLE CORPORATION

EXCH.	SYM.	REC. PRICE	P/E RATIO	YLD.	MKT. CAP.	RANGE (52-WK.)	'02 Y/E PR.
NYSE	NE	36.30 (2/28/03)	23.0	...	$4.79 bill.	45.95 - 27.00	35.15

MEDIUM GRADE. THE COMPANY HAS ACQUIRED TWO JACKUP DRILLING UNITS FROM A SUBSIDIARY OF SCHLUMBERGER LIMITED FOR AN AGGREGATE PURCHASE PRICE OF $95.0 MILLION.

MERGENT

TRADING VOLUME
Thousand Shares

1989 1990 1991 1992 1993 1994 1995 1996 1997 1998 1999 2000 2001 2002 2003

7 YEAR PRICE SCORE N/A   **12 MONTH PRICE SCORE N/A**

*NYSE COMPOSITE INDEX=100

INTERIM EARNINGS (Per Share):

Qtr.	Mar.	June	Sept.	Dec.
1997	0.17	1.20	0.25	0.35
1998	0.35	0.38	0.25	0.25
1999	0.20	0.21	0.19	0.12
2000	0.19	0.32	0.33	0.38
2001	0.40	0.50	0.58	0.48
2002	0.39	0.43	0.37	0.39

INTERIM DIVIDENDS (Per Share):

Amt.	Decl.	Ex.	Rec.	Pay.
	No dividends paid.			

CAPITALIZATION (12/31/01):

	($000)	(%)
Long-Term Debt	550,131	21.8
Deferred Income Tax	202,646	8.0
Minority Interest	d4,934	-0.2
Common & Surplus	1,778,319	70.4
Total	2,526,162	100.0

BUSINESS:

Noble Corporation (formerly Noble Drilling Corporation) is a provider of diversified services for the oil and gas industry. As of 1/30/03, contract drilling services were performed with a fleet of 55 offshore drilling units located in markets worldwide. The Company's fleet of floating deepwater units consists of 13 semisubmersibles and three drillships, seven of which are designed to operate in water depths greater than 5,000 feet. NE's fleet of 36 independent leg, cantilever jackup rigs includes 22 units that operate in water depths of 300 feet and greater, four of which operate in water depths of 360 feet and greater, and 11 units that operate in water depths of 250 feet. In addition, NE's fleet includes three submersible units. As of 1/30/03, about 67.0% of the fleet was deployed in international markets. NE also provides labor contract drilling services, well site and project management services, and engineering services.

RECENT DEVELOPMENTS:

For the year ended 12/31/02, net income declined 20.3% to $209.5 million compared with $262.9 million a year earlier. Operating revenues decreased 4.2% to $986.4 million from $1.03 billion the previous year, due in part to weak market conditions in the U.S. Gulf of Mexico. Operating income slid 28.4% to $275.0 million versus $384.3 million the year before. Operating costs and expenses climbed to 72.1% of revenues from 62.7% in 2001.

PROSPECTS:

NE's near-term outlook appears challenging, reflecting continued soft market conditions in the U.S. Gulf of Mexico. For instance, the average dayrate for the Company's domestic jackup rigs during the quarter ended 12/31/02 was $29,927, 33.5% lower than the previous year. However, NE noted that utilization on these rigs increased to 82.0% from 65.0% the year before, which could signal the start of a pick-up in demand that should lead to higher average dayrates. Separately, on 12/12/02, NE announced that it has acquired two jackup drilling units, the TRIDENT III and the DHABI II, from a subsidiary of Schlumberger Limited for an aggregate purchase price of $95.0 million in an all cash transaction.

ANNUAL FINANCIAL DATA:

FISCAL YEAR	TOT. REVS. ($mill.)	NET INC. ($mill.)	TOT. ASSETS ($mill.)	OPER. PROFIT %	NET PROFIT %	RET. ON EQUITY %	RET. ON ASSETS %	CURR. RATIO	EARN. PER SH.$	CASH FL. PER SH.$	TANG. BK. VAL.$	PRICE RANGE	AVG. P/E RATIO
p12/31/02	986.4	209.5							1.57			49.95 - 27.00	21.3
12/31/01	1,002.3	⑥263.9	2,750.7	38.3	26.3	14.8	9.6	2.4	⑥1.97	3.02	13.47	54.00 - 20.80	19.0
12/31/00	882.6	165.6	2,595.5	30.4	18.8	10.5	6.4	1.8	1.22	2.04	11.80	53.50 - 27.25	33.1
12/31/99	705.9	⑤95.3	2,432.3	21.2	13.5	6.8	3.9	1.2	⑤0.72	1.39	10.60	32.88 - 12.00	31.2
12/31/98	788.2	162.0	2,178.6	29.1	20.6	12.4	7.4	1.3	1.23	1.77	10.00	34.69 - 10.75	18.5
12/31/97	713.2	④263.9	1,505.8	53.5	37.0	23.0	17.5	1.7	④1.98	2.56	8.77	38.19 - 15.50	13.6
12/31/96	514.3	③79.3	1,367.4	21.9	15.4	8.6	5.8	2.6	③0.66	1.19	7.01	22.00 - 8.00	22.7
12/31/95	328.0	1.6	741.4	3.2	0.5	0.3	0.2	2.2	d0.08	0.34	5.50	9.13 - 5.00	...
12/31/94	352.0	②21.5	739.9	5.2	6.1	4.1	2.9	2.9	②0.11	0.63	6.69	9.13 - 5.25	65.3
12/31/93	194.9	①19.1	499.7	12.1	9.8	5.8	3.8	2.8	①0.32	0.86	6.86	11.13 - 3.63	23.0

Statistics are as originally reported. ① Bef. extraord. gain of $1.8 mill. ($0.05/sh.) ② Incl. restruct. chrgs. of $3.7 mill. & one-time gain of $8.9 mill. ③ Incl. gain of $36.1 mill.; bef. extraord. chrg. of $660,000. ④ Incl. gain on sale of prop. & equip. of $197.7 mill.; bef. extraord. chrg. of $6.7 mill. ($0.05/sh.) ⑤ Incl. restruct. chrgs. of $7.5 mill.; bef. extraord. chrg. of $10.8 mill. ($0.08/sh.) ⑥ Bef. extraord. chrg. of $988,000 ($0.01/sh.)

OFFICERS:
J. C. Day, Chmn., C.E.O.
R. D. Campbell, Pres.
M. A. Jackson, Sr. V.P., C.F.O.

INVESTOR CONTACT: John Rynd, V.P., Investor Relations, (281) 276-6100

PRINCIPAL OFFICE: 13135 South Dairy Ashford, Suite 800, Sugar Land, TX 77478

TELEPHONE NUMBER: (281) 276-6100
FAX: (281) 491-2091
WEB: www.noblecorp.com
NO. OF EMPLOYEES: 3,774 (avg.)
SHAREHOLDERS: 1,765
ANNUAL MEETING: In Apr.
INCORPORATED: DE, 1939; reincorp., Cayman Islands, April, 2002

INSTITUTIONAL HOLDINGS:
No. of Institutions: N/A
Shares Held: N/A
% Held: N/A

INDUSTRY: Drilling oil and gas wells (SIC: 1381)

TRANSFER AGENT(S): UMB Bank N.A., Kansas City, MO

NOBLE ENERGY, INC.

EXCH.	SYM.	REC. PRICE	P/E RATIO	YLD.	MKT. CAP.	RANGE (52-WK.)	'02 Y/E PR.
NYSE	NBL	35.30 (2/28/03)	113.9	0.5%	$2.01 bill.	40.76 - 26.65	37.55

MEDIUM GRADE. THE COMPANY ANNOUNCED BUDGETED CAPITAL EXPENDITURES OF $510.0 MILLION FOR 2003.

*7 YEAR PRICE SCORE 104.9   *12 MONTH PRICE SCORE 108.1

*NYSE COMPOSITE INDEX=100

INTERIM EARNINGS (Per Share):

Qtr.	Mar.	June	Sept.	Dec.
1998	0.24	0.21	d0.44	d2.89
1999	d0.16	0.16	0.48	0.38
2000	0.47	0.65	1.01	1.26
2001	1.84	0.89	0.07	d0.48
2002	d0.26	0.30	0.02	0.29

INTERIM DIVIDENDS (Per Share):

Amt.	Decl.	Ex.	Rec.	Pay.
0.04Q	1/29/02	2/07/02	2/11/02	2/25/02
0.04Q	4/22/02	5/02/02	5/06/02	5/20/02
0.04Q	7/23/02	8/01/02	8/05/02	8/19/02
0.04Q	10/29/02	11/06/02	11/11/02	11/25/02
0.04Q	1/28/03	2/06/03	2/10/03	2/24/03

Indicated div.: $0.16

CAPITALIZATION (12/31/01):

	($000)	(%)
Long-Term Debt	837,177	41.4
Deferred Income Tax	176,259	8.7
Common & Surplus	1,010,198	49.9
Total	2,023,634	100.0

BUSINESS:

Noble Energy, Inc. (formerly Noble Affiliates, Inc.), is principally engaged in the exploration, production and marketing of oil and gas. NBL's wholly-owned subsidiary, Samedan Oil Corporation, investigates potential oil and gas properties, seeks to acquire exploration rights in areas of interest and conducts exploration activities. Domestically, Samedan has exploration, exploitation and production operations in the Gulf of Mexico and California, the Gulf Coast Region, the Mid-Continent Region, and the Rocky Mountain Region. International areas of operations include Argentina, China, Ecuador, Equatorial Guinea, the Mediterranean Sea, the North Sea and Vietnam. NBL's wholly-owned subsidiary, Noble Gas Marketing, Inc., markets the majority of NBL's natural gas as well as third-party gas. NBL's wholly-owned subsidiary, Noble Trading, Inc., markets a portion of its oil as well as third-party oil.

RECENT DEVELOPMENTS:

For the year ended 12/31/02, net income fell 86.8% to $17.7 million compared with $133.6 million a year earlier. NBL attributed the drop in earnings primarily to lower production volumes and realized natural gas prices. Total production volumes for 2002 decreased 2.4% to 101,068 barrels of oil equivalent per day (Boepd), reflecting lower domestic production caused by reduced domestic drilling levels, natural decline rates for natural gas properties in the Gulf of Mexico and the onshore Gulf Coast region, as well as hurricanes-related shut-ins of over 1,000 Boepd. Total revenues slid 9.1% to $1.44 billion from $1.59 billion the previous year.

PROSPECTS:

NBL announced budgeted capital expenditures of $510.0 million for 2003, 15.7% lower than 2002. About 30.0% of the 2003 capital budget has been allocated for exploration opportunities, and 70.0% has been dedicated to production and development projects. Domestic spending is budgeted for $235.0 million and international expenditures are budgeted for $275.0 million. Planned international expenditure allocations include the four regions where NBL is most active, including Equatorial Guinea, $180.0 million; Israel, $60.0 million; North Sea, $22.0 million; and Latin America and Far East, $13.0 million.

ANNUAL FINANCIAL DATA:

FISCAL YEAR	TOT. REVS. ($mill.)	NET INC. ($mill.)	TOT. ASSETS ($mill.)	OPER. PROFIT %	NET PROFIT %	RET. ON EQUITY %	RET. ON ASSETS %	CURR. RATIO	EARN. PER SH. $	CASH FL. PER SH. $	TANG. BK. VAL. $	DIV. PER SH. $	PRICE RANGE	AVG. P/E RATIO	AVG. YIELD %
p12/31/02	1,443.7	17.7							0.31			0.16	40.76 - 26.65	108.7	0.5
12/31/01	1,572.3	133.6	2,479.8	15.9	8.5	13.2	5.4	0.9	2.33	7.59	17.72	0.16	51.09 - 27.50	16.9	0.4
12/31/00	1,393.6	191.6	1,879.3	23.8	13.7	22.5	10.2	0.8	3.38	7.73	15.15	0.16	48.38 - 19.19	10.0	0.5
12/31/99	909.8	49.5	1,450.4	13.3	5.4	7.2	3.4	0.8	0.86	5.47	11.98	0.16	35.00 - 19.13	31.5	0.6
12/31/98	911.6	① d164.0	1,686.1	...	...	...	...	1.4	① d2.88	2.76	11.27	0.16	46.19 - 21.94	...	0.5
12/31/97	1,116.6	99.3	1,875.5	18.3	8.9	12.2	5.3	1.2	1.73	7.10	14.29	0.16	50.00 - 32.19	23.8	0.4
12/31/96	887.2	83.9	1,956.9	19.5	9.5	11.6	4.3	1.1	1.63	6.29	12.68	0.16	49.00 - 26.88	23.3	0.4
12/31/95	487.0	4.1	989.2	5.5	0.8	1.0	0.4	1.2	0.08	4.23	8.21	0.16	30.50 - 21.25	323.0	0.6
12/31/94	358.4	3.2	933.5	6.4	0.9	0.8	0.3	1.4	0.06	2.77	8.24	0.16	32.25 - 22.50	455.5	0.6
12/31/93	286.6	12.6	1,068.0	12.6	4.4	3.0	1.2	1.8	0.26	2.74	8.32	0.16	31.00 - 15.75	89.9	0.7

Statistics are as originally reported. ① Incl. impairment of oper. assets chrg. of $223.3 mill.

OFFICERS:
C. Davidson, Chmn., Pres., C.E.O.
J. L. McElvany, Sr. V.P., C.F.O.
A. D. Hoppe, Sr. V.P., Sec., Gen., Couns.
INVESTOR CONTACT: William R. McKown III, Asst. Treas., (281) 872-3140
PRINCIPAL OFFICE: 350 Glenborough Drive, Suite 100, Houston, TX 77067

TELEPHONE NUMBER: (281) 872-3100
FAX: (281) 872-3111
WEB: www.nobleaff.com
NO. OF EMPLOYEES: 610 (avg.)
SHAREHOLDERS: 1,125
ANNUAL MEETING: In Apr.
INCORPORATED: DE, Dec., 1969

INSTITUTIONAL HOLDINGS:
No. of Institutions: 221
Shares Held: 51,520,460
% Held: 89.9
INDUSTRY: Crude petroleum and natural gas (SIC: 1311)
TRANSFER AGENT(S): First Union National Bank, Charlotte, NC

NORDSTROM, INC.

EXCH.	SYM.	REC. PRICE	P/E RATIO	YLD.	MKT. CAP.	RANGE (52-WK.)	'02 Y/E PR.
NYSE	JWN	17.01 (2/28/03)	14.9	2.4%	$2.29 bill.	26.87 - 15.06	18.97

UPPER MEDIUM GRADE. THE COMPANY IS TARGETING FULL FISCAL-2003 EARNINGS OF BETWEEN $1.33 AND $1.39 PER SHARE.

MERGENT

TRADING VOLUME
Thousand Shares

*7 YEAR PRICE SCORE 88.1   *12 MONTH PRICE SCORE 93.6

*NYSE COMPOSITE INDEX=100

INTERIM EARNINGS (Per Share):

Qtr.	Apr.	July	Oct.	Jan.
1997-98	0.21	0.38	0.24	0.38
1998-99	0.22	0.47	0.27	0.47
1999-00	0.22	0.51	0.25	0.50
2000-01	0.25	0.35	d0.03	0.20
2001-02	0.18	0.29	0.08	0.38
2002-03	0.22	0.34	0.14	0.44

INTERIM DIVIDENDS (Per Share):

Amt.	Decl.	Ex.	Rec.	Pay.
0.09Q	2/26/02	2/26/02	2/28/02	3/15/02
0.09Q	5/21/02	5/29/02	5/31/02	6/14/02
0.10Q	8/20/02	8/28/02	8/31/02	9/16/02
0.10Q	11/18/02	11/26/02	11/30/02	12/16/02
0.10Q	2/18/03	2/26/03	2/28/03	3/14/03

Indicated div.: $0.40

CAPITALIZATION (1/31/02):

	($000)	(%)
Long-Term Debt	1,351,044	50.7
Common & Surplus	1,314,488	49.3
Total	2,665,532	100.0

BUSINESS:

Nordstrom, Inc. operated a total of 142 stores as of 2/20/03, including large specialty stores, in 27 states, selling a wide selection of apparel, shoes and accessories for women, men and children. Included in the total number of stores are 47 Nordstrom Racks, which serve as outlets for clearance merchandise from the Company's large specialty stores. The Racks also purchase merchandise directly from manufac-turers. The remaining stores include 88 full-line stores, five Faconnable boutiques, one free-standing shoe store and one clearance store. In addition, JWN operates 23 Faconnable boutiques throughout Europe. The Company also sells merchandise online, through its Nordstrom Direct subsidiary, and through its direct-mail catalogs.

RECENT DEVELOPMENTS:

For the year ended 1/31/03, the Company reported earnings of $103.6 million, before an accounting change charge of $13.4 million, compared with net earnings of $124.7 million in the prior year. Results for the recent period included a $48.2 million after-tax charge from the purchase of a minority interest in Nordstrom.com and associated reintegration costs, and a $9.5 million after-tax charge for the write-down of an information technology investment. Net sales grew 6.1% to $5.98 billion from $5.63 billion a year earlier. Comparable-store sales were up 1.3% year over year. Gross profit was $2.00 billion, or 33.5% of net sales, versus $1.87 billion, or 33.2% of net sales, the year before. Operating income climbed 30.3% to $189.7 million from $145.6 million the previous year.

PROSPECTS:

For the first quarter of fiscal 2003, the Company anticipates earnings in the range of $0.23 to $0.27 per share. Looking ahead, JWN is targeting full fiscal-2003 earnings of between $1.33 and $1.39 per share and flat to low single-digit comparable-store sales growth. Meanwhile, the Company expects fiscal 2003 square-footage growth of about 4.0%, down from 8.0% square-footage growth in fiscal 2002 when JWN opened eight full-line stores, four Nordstrom Rack stores and one U.S. Faconnable boutique.

ANNUAL FINANCIAL DATA:

FISCAL YEAR	TOT. REVS. ($mill.)	NET INC. ($mill.)	TOT. ASSETS ($mill.)	OPER. PROFIT %	NET PROFIT %	RET. ON EQUITY %	RET. ON ASSETS %	CURR. RATIO	EARN. PER SH. $	CASH FL. PER SH. $	TANG. BK. VAL. $	DIV. PER SH. $	PRICE RANGE	AVG. P/E RATIO	AVG. YIELD %
p1/31/03	5,975.1	② 103.6							② 0.66			0.38	26.87 - 15.06	31.8	1.8
1/31/02	5,634.1	124.7	4,048.8	2.6	2.2	9.5	3.1	2.2	0.93	2.49	8.75	0.36	22.97 - 13.80	19.8	2.0
1/31/01	5,528.5	① 101.9	3,608.5	2.4	1.8	8.3	2.8	1.9	① 0.78	2.24	8.12	0.35	34.50 - 14.13	31.2	1.4
1/31/00	5,124.2	202.6	3,062.1	5.3	4.0	17.1	6.6	1.8	1.46	2.82	8.96	0.32	44.81 - 21.69	22.8	1.0
1/31/99	5,027.9	206.7	3,115.4	5.5	4.1	15.7	6.6	2.2	1.41	2.61	9.26	0.30	40.38 - 21.43	21.9	1.0
1/31/98	4,851.6	186.2	2,865.2	4.8	3.8	12.6	6.5	1.7	1.20	2.27	9.93	0.27	34.09 - 16.94	21.3	1.0
1/31/97	4,453.1	147.5	2,702.5	3.4	3.3	10.0	5.5	1.9	0.91	1.88	9.25	0.25	26.75 - 17.13	24.1	1.1
1/31/96	4,113.5	165.1	2,732.6	4.5	4.0	11.6	6.0	1.9	1.01	1.83	8.77	0.25	22.63 - 17.50	19.9	1.2
1/31/95	3,894.5	203.0	2,396.8	7.0	5.2	15.1	8.4	2.0	1.24	1.91	8.17	0.19	24.88 - 15.50	16.3	1.0
1/31/94	3,589.9	140.4	2,177.5	5.0	3.9	12.0	6.4	2.1	0.86	1.49	7.11	0.17	21.75 - 12.63	20.1	1.0

Statistics are as originally reported. Adj. for 2-for-1 stk. split, 6/98. ① Incl. $56.0 mil. ($0.26/sh) one-time pre-tax chg. fr. an investment write-down, estimated severance costs and the write-off of certain information technology investments. ② Bef. $13.4 mil acctg. chg. and incl. $57.7 mil after-tax chg. fr. purch. of a minority int. in Nordstrom.com & the write-down of an information technology investment.

OFFICERS:
B. A. Nordstrom, Chmn.
B. W. Nordstrom, Pres.
M. G. Koppel, Exec. V.P., C.F.O., Contr.

INVESTOR CONTACT: Stephanie Allen, Investor Relations, (206) 303-3262

PRINCIPAL OFFICE: 1617 Sixth Avenue, Suite 500, Seattle, WA 98101-1742

TELEPHONE NUMBER: (206) 628-2111
FAX: (206) 628-1795
WEB: www.nordstrom.com

NO. OF EMPLOYEES: 43,000 (approx.)

SHAREHOLDERS: 76,000 (approx.)

ANNUAL MEETING: In May

INCORPORATED: WA, 1946

INSTITUTIONAL HOLDINGS:
No. of Institutions: 224
Shares Held: 74,863,447
% Held: 55.3

INDUSTRY: Family clothing stores (SIC: 5651)

TRANSFER AGENT(S): Mellon Investor Services, South Hackensack, NJ

NORFOLK SOUTHERN CORPORATION

EXCH.	SYM.	REC. PRICE	P/E RATIO	YLD.	MKT. CAP.	RANGE (52-WK.)	'02 Y/E PR.
NYSE	NSC	19.06 (2/28/03)	16.2	1.5%	$7.35 bill.	26.98 - 17.20	19.99

UPPER MEDIUM GRADE. THE COMPANY'S INTERMODAL SEGMENT IS BENEFITING FROM THE INTRODUCTION OF NEW SERVICES.

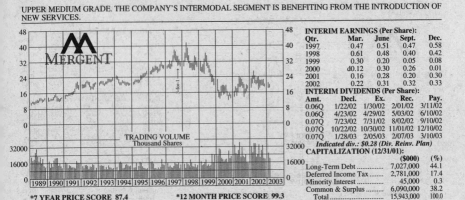

INTERIM EARNINGS (Per Share):

Qtr.	Mar.	June	Sept.	Dec.
1997	0.47	0.51	0.47	0.58
1998	0.61	0.48	0.40	0.42
1999	0.30	0.20	0.05	0.08
2000	d0.12	0.30	0.26	0.01
2001	0.16	0.28	0.20	0.30
2002	0.22	0.31	0.32	0.33

INTERIM DIVIDENDS (Per Share):

Amt.	Decl.	Ex.	Rec.	Pay.
0.06Q	1/22/02	1/30/02	2/01/02	3/11/02
0.06Q	4/23/02	4/29/02	5/03/02	6/10/02
0.07Q	7/23/02	7/31/02	8/02/02	9/10/02
0.07Q	10/22/02	10/30/02	11/01/02	12/10/02
0.07Q	1/28/03	2/05/03	2/07/03	3/10/03

Indicated div.: $0.28 (Div. Reinv. Plan)

CAPITALIZATION (12/31/01):

	($000)	(%)
Long-Term Debt	7,027,000	44.1
Deferred Income Tax	2,781,000	17.4
Minority Interest	45,000	0.3
Common & Surplus	6,090,000	38.2
Total	15,943,000	100.0

*7 YEAR PRICE SCORE 87.4   ***12 MONTH PRICE SCORE 99.3**

*NYSE COMPOSITE INDEX=100

BUSINESS:

Norfolk Southern Corporation is a holding company engaged principally in the transportation of freight by rail. Operations are conducted through NSC's wholly-owned subsidiary, Norfolk Southern Railway Company. As of 12/31/02, NSC operated approximately 21,500 miles of track in 22 states, the District of Columbia and the Province of Ontario, Canada. NSC's rail freight largely consists of raw materials, intermediate products and finished goods classified in the following groups: coal (23.0% of 2002 railway operating revenues); intermodal (18.8%); automotive (15.3%); chemicals (12.3%); metals/construction (11.0%); agricultural/consumer products/government (10.0%); and paper/clay/forest products (9.6%). Through a jointly-owned entity, NSC and CSX Corporation own the stock of Conrail Inc., which owns the major Northeast freight railroad. As of 12/31/02, NSC had a 58.0% economic and 50.0% voting interest in the jointly-owned entity.

RECENT DEVELOPMENTS:

For the year ended 12/31/02, net income was $460.0 million compared with income from continuing operations of $362.0 million a year earlier. Total railway operating revenues increased 1.6% to $6.27 billion from $6.17 billion the previous year. General merchandise revenue rose 3.5% to $3.65 billion, while intermodal revenues advanced 5.2% to $1.18 billion. However, coal revenues decreased 5.3% to $1.44 billion, reflecting lower demand for utility coal. Total railway operating expenses were $5.11 billion versus $5.16 billion the year before.

PROSPECTS:

NSC's near-term prospects appear good, reflecting favorable general merchandise and intermodal railway revenue trends. The Company attributed the improvement of the latter to the introduction of new services that enabled conversion of highway movements to rail as well as gains in on-time reliability and service. Also, NSC has been able to improve its efficiency, which is key in the current economic environment that has resulted in sluggish top-line growth. For example, for the year ended 12/31/02, NSC's railway operating ratio, which measures the percentage of railway operating revenues consumed by railway operating expenses, improved to 81.5% versus 83.7% the prior year.

ANNUAL FINANCIAL DATA:

FISCAL YEAR	TOT. REVS. ($mill.)	NET INC. ($mill.)	TOT. ASSETS ($mill.)	OPER. PROFIT %	NET PROFIT %	RET. ON EQUITY %	RET. ON ASSETS %	CURR. RATIO	EARN. PER SH. $	CASH FL. PER SH. $	TANG. BK. VAL. $	DIV. PER SH. $	PRICE RANGE	AVG. P/E RATIO	AVG. YIELD %
p12/31/02	6,270.0	460.0							1.18			0.26	26.98 - 17.20	18.7	1.2
12/31/01	6,170.0	⑦ 362.0	19,418.0	16.3	5.9	5.9	1.9	0.4	⑦ 0.94	2.30	15.78	0.24	24.11 - 13.41	20.0	1.3
12/31/00	6,159.0	⑥ 172.0	18,976.0	10.3	2.8	3.0	0.9	0.4	⑥ 0.45	1.80	15.16	0.80	22.75 - 11.94	38.5	4.6
12/31/99	5,195.0	⑤ 239.0	19,250.0	13.8	4.6	4.0	1.2	0.7	⑤ 0.63	1.91	15.50	0.80	36.44 - 19.63	44.5	2.9
12/31/98	4,221.0	① 630.0	18,180.0	24.9	14.9	10.6	3.5	0.8	① 1.65	2.83	15.61	0.80	41.75 - 27.44	21.0	2.3
12/31/97	4,223.0	② 699.0	17,350.0	28.7	16.6	12.8	4.0	1.0	② 1.84	2.98	14.44	0.80	38.13 - 28.21	18.0	2.4
12/31/96	4,770.0	770.4	11,416.4	25.1	16.2	15.5	6.7	1.2	2.03	3.12	13.26	0.75	32.21 - 25.46	14.2	2.6
12/31/95	4,668.0	③ 712.7	10,904.8	23.3	15.3	14.8	6.5	1.1	③ 1.81	2.84	12.47	0.69	27.21 - 20.17	13.1	2.9
12/31/94	4,581.3	667.8	10,587.8	23.3	14.6	14.3	6.3	1.2	1.63	2.62	11.73	0.64	24.92 - 19.50	13.6	2.9
12/31/93	4,460.1	④ 548.7	10,519.8	19.3	12.3	11.9	5.2	1.3	④ 1.31	2.28	11.12	0.62	24.13 - 19.75	16.7	2.8

Statistics are as originally reported. Adj. for 3-for-1 stk. split, 10/97. ① Incl. non-recurr. chrgs. of $156.0 mill.; Bef. disc. ops. cr. of $104.0 mill. ② Bef. disc. oper. gain of $22.0 mill. & incl. one-time Conrail-related chrg. of $107.0 mill. ③ Incl. non-recurr. chrg. of $20.4 mill. ④ Bef. acctg. change cr. of $223.0 mill. ⑤ Incl. special chrg. of $49.0 mill. ⑥ Incl. aft-tax workforce reduct. chrg. of $101.0 mill. ($0.26/sh.) & aft-tax gain fr. sale of timber prop. of $46.0 mill. ($0.12/sh.) ⑦ Bef. disc. ops. gain of $13.0 mill.

OFFICERS:
D. R. Goode, Chmn., Pres., C.E.O.
L. I. Prillaman, Vice-Chmn., C.M.O.
S. C. Tobias, Vice-Chmn., C.O.O.
INVESTOR CONTACT: Henry C. Wolf, Vice-Chmn. & C.F.O., (757) 629-2650
PRINCIPAL OFFICE: Three Commercial Place, Norfolk, VA 23510-2191

TELEPHONE NUMBER: (757) 629-2680
FAX: (757) 629-2345
WEB: www.nscorp.com
NO. OF EMPLOYEES: 30,894 (avg.)
SHAREHOLDERS: 53,042
ANNUAL MEETING: In May
INCORPORATED: VA, July, 1980

INSTITUTIONAL HOLDINGS:
No. of Institutions: 432
Shares Held: 267,877,949
% Held: 68.9
INDUSTRY: Railroads, line-haul operating (SIC: 4011)
TRANSFER AGENT(S): The Bank of New York, New York, NY

NORTH FORK BANCORPORATION, INC.

EXCH.	SYM.	REC. PRICE	P/E RATIO	YLD.	MKT. CAP.	RANGE (52-WK.)	'02 Y/E PR.
NYSE	NFB	32.24 (2/28/03)	12.5	3.3%	$5.25 bill.	42.74 - 31.07	33.74

UPPER MEDIUM GRADE. THE COMPANY'S EXPANSION INTO NEW YORK CITY CONTINUES TO PROVIDE NFB WITH COMMERCIAL LOAN OPPORTUNITIES, WHICH HAVE SHORTER TERMS AND HIGHER YIELDS.

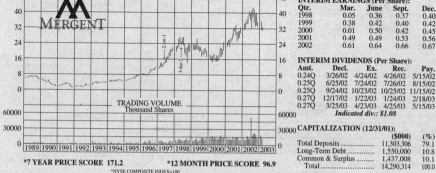

TRADING VOLUME
Thousand Shares

*7 YEAR PRICE SCORE 171.2   ***12 MONTH PRICE SCORE 96.9**

*NYSE COMPOSITE INDEX=100

INTERIM EARNINGS (Per Share):

Qtr.	Mar.	June	Sept.	Dec.
1998	0.05	0.36	0.37	0.40
1999	0.38	0.42	0.40	0.42
2000	0.01	0.50	0.42	0.45
2001	0.49	0.49	0.53	0.56
2002	0.61	0.64	0.66	0.67

INTERIM DIVIDENDS (Per Share):

Amt.	Decl.	Ex.	Rec.	Pay.
0.24Q	3/26/02	4/24/02	4/26/02	5/15/02
0.25Q	6/25/02	7/24/02	7/26/02	8/15/02
0.25Q	9/24/02	10/23/02	10/25/02	11/15/02
0.27Q	12/17/02	1/22/03	1/24/03	2/18/03
0.27Q	3/25/03	4/23/03	4/25/03	5/15/03

Indicated div.: $1.08

CAPITALIZATION (12/31/01):

	($000)	(%)
Total Deposits	11,303,306	79.1
Long-Term Debt	1,550,000	10.8
Common & Surplus	1,437,008	10.1
Total	14,290,314	100.0

BUSINESS:

North Fork Bancorporation, Inc. is a bank holding company with assets of $21.41 billion as of 12/31/02. NFB operates through its primary subsidiary North Fork Bank and its investment management and broker/dealer subsidiaries, Compass Investment Services Corp. and Amivest Corporation, providing a variety of banking and financial services to middle market and small business organizations, local governmental units, and retail customers. As of 12/31/02, North Fork Bank operated 171 full-service retail banking facilities located in the New York metropolitan area. The Company's other bank subsidiary, Superior Savings of New England, a Connecticut chartered savings bank located in the Connecticut county of New Haven, operates from one location where it currently conducts a telebanking operation focused on gathering deposits throughout the New England region. On 11/9/01, the Company acquired Commercial Bank of New York.

RECENT DEVELOPMENTS:

For the year ended 12/31/02, net income increased 25.8% to $416.9 million from $331.5 million the year before. Results for 2002 and 2001 included amortization of intangibles of $3.8 million and $22.1 million, respectively. Net interest income improved 26.4% to $841.8 million, benefiting from growth in average interest earning assets, particularly in bankwide deposit balances. Provision for loan losses grew 40.8% to $25.0 million. Total non-interest income rose 14.0% to $124.1 million, while total non-interest expense increased 21.6% to $305.2 million.

PROSPECTS:

The Company's expansion into New York City continues to provide NFB with commercial loan opportunities, which have shorter terms and higher yields that were previously unattainable in suburban markets. During 2002, the Company opened a total of ten new branches, including five in Manhattan. Additionally, the Company plans to open more branches in 2003, including at least three in Manhattan. A branch will be established in New Jersey, where NFB recently received regulatory approval to enter the state. Separately, non-interest income continues to benefit from the Company's expanded and diverse customer base and multiple product offerings.

ANNUAL FINANCIAL DATA:

FISCAL YEAR	NET INT. INC. ($mill.)	NON-INT. INC. ($mill.)	NET INC. ($mill.)	TOT. LOANS ($mill.)	TOT. ASSETS ($mill.)	TOT. DEP. ($mill.)	RET. ON EQUITY %	RET. ON ASSETS %	EQUITY/ ASSETS %	EARN. PER SH. $	TANG. BK. VAL. $	DIV. PER SH. $	PRICE RANGE	AVG. P/E RATIO
p12/31/02	841.8	124.1	③ 416.9		21,413.1					③ 2.58		0.98	42.74 - 31.22	14.3
12/31/01	686.5	108.9	331.5	10,413.8	17,232.1	11,303.3	23.1	1.9	8.3	2.05	6.20	0.81	33.73 - 22.31	13.7
12/31/00	592.0	102.5	① 234.8	9,409.8	14,841.0	9,169.2	19.3	1.6	8.2	① 1.39	5.39	0.72	25.00 - 14.44	14.2
12/31/99	449.3	73.0	220.4	6,630.5	12,108.1	6,544.8	35.6	1.8	5.1	1.62	4.20	0.72	26.75 - 17.13	13.5
12/31/98	424.6	64.3	① 168.0	5,731.4	10,679.6	6,427.6	20.2	1.6	7.8	① 1.18	5.29	0.47	27.54 - 14.13	17.7
12/31/97	278.4	41.6	119.3	3,714.7	6,829.4	4,637.2	19.8	1.7	8.8	1.20	5.07	0.37	22.21 - 11.25	13.9
12/31/96	230.9	31.1	①② 62.4	3,194.1	5,750.5	4,469.5	13.6	1.1	8.0	①② 0.65	3.86	0.25	12.08 - 7.54	15.2
12/31/95	141.2	27.3	52.2	1,985.0	3,303.3	2,535.5	16.9	1.6	9.4	0.71	3.80	0.17	8.42 - 4.50	9.1
12/31/94	132.5	9.8	① 29.7	1,831.5	2,717.8	2,342.9	11.6	1.1	9.4	① 0.42	3.37	0.08	5.63 - 4.17	11.7
12/31/93	77.4	18.0	15.1	1,029.8	1,883.9	1,442.3	9.8	0.8	8.2	0.35	3.43	...	4.46 - 2.54	10.0

Statistics are as originally reported. Adj. for 2-for-1 stk. split, 5/97; 3-for-2, 5/98. ① Incl. one-time chrgs. of $64.0 mill., 2000; $52.5 mill., 1998; $21.6 mill., 1996; $14.3 mill., 1994. ② Incl. SAIF recapitalization chrg. $8.4 mill. ③ Incl. a gain of sale of branch facilities of $3.3 mill.

OFFICERS:
J. A. Kanas, Chmn., Pres., C.E.O.
J. Bohlsen, Vice-Chmn.
D. M. Healy, Exec. V.P., C.F.O.
INVESTOR CONTACT: Linda Bishop, Investor Relations, (631) 501-4618
PRINCIPAL OFFICE: 275 Broadhollow Road, Melville, NY 11747

TELEPHONE NUMBER: (631) 844-1004
FAX: (631) 694-1536
WEB: www.northforkbank.com
NO. OF EMPLOYEES: 2,540
SHAREHOLDERS: 8,803
ANNUAL MEETING: In April
INCORPORATED: DE, 1980

INSTITUTIONAL HOLDINGS:
No. of Institutions: 388
Shares Held: 100,953,861
% Held: 62.5
INDUSTRY: State commercial banks (SIC: 6022)
TRANSFER AGENT(S): First Chicago Trust Company of New York, Jersey City, NJ

NORTHEAST UTILITIES

EXCH.	SYM.	REC. PRICE	P/E RATIO	YLD.	MKT. CAP.	RANGE (52-WK.)	'02 Y/E PR.
NYSE	NU	14.00 (2/28/03)	11.9	3.9%	$1.82 bill.	20.70 - 12.66	15.17

LOWER MEDIUM GRADE. THE COMPANY EXPECTS EARNINGS PER SHARE FOR 2003 OF BETWEEN $1.10 AND $1.30.

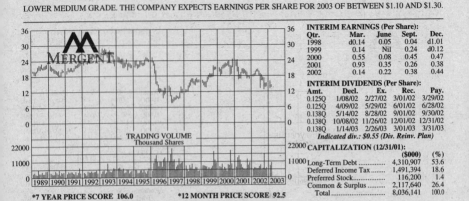

*7 YEAR PRICE SCORE 106.0 *12 MONTH PRICE SCORE 92.5
*NYSE COMPOSITE INDEX=100

INTERIM EARNINGS (Per Share):

Qtr.	Mar.	June	Sept.	Dec.
1998	d0.14	0.05	0.04	d1.01
1999	0.14	Nil	0.24	d0.12
2000	0.55	0.08	0.45	0.47
2001	0.93	0.35	0.26	0.38
2002	0.14	0.22	0.38	0.44

INTERIM DIVIDENDS (Per Share):

Amt.	Decl.	Ex.	Rec.	Pay.
0.125Q	1/08/02	2/27/02	3/01/02	3/29/02
0.125Q	4/09/02	5/29/02	6/01/02	6/28/02
0.138Q	5/14/02	8/28/02	9/01/02	9/30/02
0.138Q	10/08/02	11/26/02	12/01/02	12/31/02
0.138Q	1/14/03	2/26/03	3/01/03	3/31/03

Indicated div.: $0.55 (Div. Reinv. Plan)

CAPITALIZATION (12/31/01):

	($000)	(%)
Long-Term Debt	4,310,907	53.6
Deferred Income Tax	1,491,394	18.6
Preferred Stock	116,200	1.4
Common & Surplus	2,117,640	26.4
Total	8,036,141	100.0

BUSINESS:

Northeast Utilities is the parent company of Northeast Utilities Systems, which is comprised of the following subsidiaries: Connecticut Light and Power, Western Massachusetts Electric Co., Holyoke Water Power Co., Public Service Co. of New Hampshire, NU Enterprises, Inc., Northeast Generation Company, and Northeast Generation Services Company. In 2001, electric operating revenues were 24.2% residential; 21.1% commercial; 8.9% industrial; 43.2% other utilities; 0.7% streetlighting and railroads; and 1.9% miscellaneous. Non-utility subsidiaries include: Charter Oak Energy. Inc., HEC Inc., Select Energy, Inc., and Mode 1 Communications, Inc. On 3/1/00, NU acquired Yankee Energy System, Inc.

RECENT DEVELOPMENTS:

For the twelve months ended 12/31/02, net income dropped 42.8% to $152.1 million compared with income of $265.9 million, before an accounting change charge of $22.4 million, in 2001. The decrease in earnings was primarily attributed to the weak performance of NU's competitive energy businesses due to difficult market conditions, natural gas trading losses, and unfavorable natural gas and electricity supply contracts. Results for 2002 and 2001 included gains on the sale of utility plants of $187.1 million and $642.0 million, respectively. Operating revenues were $5.03 billion, down 15.6% from $5.97 billion in the prior year.

PROSPECTS:

In 2003, regulated company earnings are expected to decline to between $1.05 and $1.15 per share due to the elimination of operating earnings related to the Seabrook nuclear station, lower investment tax credits and lower projected pension income at NU's regulated businesses. However, NU is forecasting a significant recovery in its competitive energy businesses in 2003, projecting earnings in the range of $0.15 to $0.25 per share. Overall, the Company expects earnings per share for 2003 of between $1.10 and $1.30. Meanwhile, the Company plans to expand and improve its energy delivery system in 2003 by making significant investments to enhance service reliability and energy choices in NU's three-state regulated service area.

ANNUAL FINANCIAL DATA:

FISCAL YEAR	TOT. REVS. ($mill.)	NET INC. ($mill.)	TOT. ASSETS ($mill.)	OPER. PROFIT %	NET PROFIT %	NET INC./ NET PROP. %	NET INCJ/ TOT. CAP. %	RET. ON EQUITY %	ACCUM. DEPR./ GROSS PROP. %	EARN. PER SH. $	TANG. BK. VAL.$	DIV. PER SH.$	DIV. PAYOUT %	PRICE RANGE	AVG. P/E RATIO	AVG. YIELD %
p12/31/02	5,034.9	⑥152.1								⑥1.18		0.53	44.9	20.70 - 12.66	14.1	3.2
12/31/01	6,873.8	⑤265.9	10,241.4	7.8	3.9	7.0	3.3	11.9	47.2	⑤1.96	16.27	0.45	23.0	24.35 - 16.59	10.4	2.2
12/31/00	5,876.6	④205.3	10,217.1	7.9	3.5	5.8	3.3	8.7	66.5	④1.45	15.43	0.40	27.6	24.56 - 18.00	14.7	1.9
12/31/99	4,471.3	③34.2	9,688.1	7.7	0.8	0.9	0.5	1.5	62.7	③0.26	15.91	0.10	38.4	22.00 - 13.56	68.4	0.6
12/31/98	3,767.7	②d146.8	10,387.4	6.0	...	...	...	...	42.1	②d1.12	15.63	...	...	17.25 - 11.69	...	...
12/31/97	3,834.8	d135.7	10,414.4	4.8	...	...	...	...	41.7	d1.05	16.34	0.25	...	14.25 - 7.63	...	2.3
12/31/96	3,792.1	1.8	10,741.7	7.2	...	...	...	0.1	38.9	0.01	17.73	1.38	...	25.25 - 9.50	...	7.9
12/31/95	3,750.6	282.4	10,559.6	15.8	7.5	4.0	3.1	10.9	36.1	2.24	19.08	1.76	78.6	25.38 - 21.00	10.4	7.6
12/31/94	3,642.7	286.9	10,584.9	15.0	7.9	4.3	3.2	11.3	33.3	2.30	18.48	1.76	76.5	25.75 - 20.38	10.0	7.6
12/31/93	3,629.1	①198.3	10,668.2	12.4	5.5	3.0	2.2	8.0	31.2	①1.60	17.89	1.76	110.0	28.88 - 22.00	15.9	6.9

Statistics are as originally reported. ① Bef. $51.7 mill. ($0.39/sh.) chg. from acct. adj. ② Incl. $163.2 mill. write-off fr. investment & Argentine power plant and $1.7 mill. gain for Mode 1 shs. ③ Incl. $308.9 mill. gain fr. sale of utility plant. ④ Bef. extraord. chg. of $225.0 mill.; incls. $11.7 mill. one-time chg. for settlement & $10.4 mill. one-time after-tax gain fr. investment. ⑤ Incl. $642.0 mill. gain fr. sale of plant & excl. $22.4 mill. gain fr. acctg. change. ⑥ Incl. $187.1 mill. gain fr. sale of utility plant.

OFFICERS:
M. G. Morris, Chmn., Pres., C.E.O.
J. H. Forsgren, Exec. V.P., C.F.O.
G. B. Butler, V.P., Sec., Gen. Couns.
INVESTOR CONTACT: Jeff Kotkin, Inv. Rel., (413) 655-5154
PRINCIPAL OFFICE: 174 Brush Hill Avenue, West Springfield, MA 01090-2010

TELEPHONE NUMBER: (413) 785-5871
FAX: (413) 665-3652
WEB: www.nu.com
NO. OF EMPLOYEES: 7,520 (approx.)
SHAREHOLDERS: 76,028
ANNUAL MEETING: In May
INCORPORATED: MA, Jan., 1927

INSTITUTIONAL HOLDINGS:
No. of Institutions: 166
Shares Held: 81,356,611
% Held: 63.3

INDUSTRY: Electric services (SIC: 4911)

TRANSFER AGENT(S): The Bank of New York, New York, NY

NORTHROP GRUMMAN CORPORATION

EXCH.	SYM.	REC. PRICE	P/E RATIO	YLD.	MKT. CAP.	RANGE (52-WK.)	'02 Y/E PR.
NYSE	NOC	86.70 (2/28/03)	15.2	...	$9.41 bill.	135.00 - 86.05	97.00

MEDIUM GRADE. NOC COMPLETED THE ACQUISITION OF TRW, INC. IN A STOCK-FOR-STOCK TRANSACTION VALUED AT APPROXIMATELY $7.80 BILLION, INCLUDING DEBT.

TRADING VOLUME
Thousand Shares

1989 1990 1991 1992 1993 1994 1995 1996 1997 1998 1999 2000 2001 2002 2003

*7 YEAR PRICE SCORE 131.9 ***12 MONTH PRICE SCORE 91.4**

*NYSE COMPOSITE INDEX=100

INTERIM EARNINGS (Per Share):

Qtr.	Mar.	June	Sept.	Dec.
1999	1.50	1.64	1.83	1.96
2000	2.47	2.50	2.11	1.99
2001	1.42	1.28	1.28	1.28
2002	1.27	1.53	1.17	1.72

INTERIM DIVIDENDS (Per Share):

Amt.	Decl.	Ex.	Rec.	Pay.
0.40Q	2/20/02	2/28/02	3/04/02	3/16/02
0.40Q	5/15/02	5/23/02	5/28/02	6/08/02
0.40Q	8/21/02	8/29/02	9/03/02	9/14/02
0.40Q	11/20/02	11/27/02	12/02/02	12/14/02
0.40Q	2/19/03	2/27/03	3/03/03	3/15/03

Indicated div.: $1.60 (Div. Reinv. Plan)

CAPITALIZATION (12/31/01):

	($000)	(%)
Long-Term Debt	5,033,000	38.1
Deferred Income Tax	669,000	5.1
Minority Interest	122,000	0.9
Common & Surplus	7,391,000	55.9
Total	13,215,000	100.0

BUSINESS:

Northrop Grumman Corporation (formerly Northrop Grumman.) is a technology co. operating in six sectors: Electronic Systems (30.4% of net sales for 2002), which designs, develops and manufactures a wide variety of defense electronics and systems, airspace management systems, and precision weapons; Information Technology (24.2%), which provides advanced information technologies, systems and services; Integrated Systems (18.6%), which designs and produces airborne early warning, electronic warfare and surveillance and battlefield management systems; and Ships (26.8%), which is engaged in the building of large multimission non-nuclear surface ships for the U.S. Navy, and other government and commercial customers. On 4/2/01, NNG, Inc. acquired Northrop Grumman Corp. and adopted its name. On 5/30/01, NOC acquired Litton Industries, Inc. for $5.10 billion. On 1/18/02, NOC acquired Newport News Shipbuilding, Inc. On 12/11/02, NOC acquired TRW, Inc. for $7.80 billion.

RECENT DEVELOPMENTS:

For the year ended 12/31/02, NOC reported earnings from continuing operations of $697.0 million, before an accounting charge of $432.0 million, versus net income of $642.0 million in 2001. Earnings for 2002 excluded a loss of $201.0 million from discontinued operations. Earnings for 2001 included goodwill amortization of $183.0 million. Net sales increased 32.2% to $17.21 billion. Electronic Systems segment sales advanced 16.4% to $5.34 billion, while sales for the Information Technology segment grew 12.0% to $4.24 billion. Ships segment sales more than doubled to $4.71 billion. Comparisons were made with restated 2001 figures.

PROSPECTS:

On 12/11/02, NOC acquired TRW, Inc. in a transaction valued at approximately $7.80 billion, including debt. As a result of the acquisition, NOC expects sales to range from $25.00 billion to $26.00 billion in 2003 and foresees double-digit sales growth in 2004 and 2005. Earnings per share are anticipated to be between $4.00 to $4.50 in 2003. On 3/3/03, NOC sold the TRW Automotive unit to the Blackstone Group in a transaction valued at $4.70 billion, including debt. The sale allows NOC to focus on TRW's space, electronics and systems businesses.

ANNUAL FINANCIAL DATA:

FISCAL YEAR	TOT. REVS. ($mill.)	NET INC. ($mill.)	TOT. ASSETS ($mill.)	OPER. PROFIT %	NET PROFIT %	RET. ON EQUITY %	RET. ON ASSETS %	CURR. RATIO	EARN. PER SH.$	CASH FL. PER SH.$	TANG. BK. VAL.$	DIV. PER SH.$	PRICE RANGE	AVG. P/E RATIO	AVG. YIELD %
p12/31/02	17,206.0	③⑥ 697.0	39,791.0						③⑥ 5.72			1.60	135.0 — 87.20	19.4	1.4
⑦ 12/31/01	13,558.0	427.0	20,886.0	7.4	3.1	5.8	2.0	0.9	4.80	5.01	...	1.60	110.56 — 76.40	19.5	1.7
12/31/00	7,618.0	⑥ 625.0	9,622.0	14.4	8.2	15.9	6.5	0.9	⑥ 8.82	8.82	...	1.60	93.88 — 42.63	7.7	2.3
12/31/99	8,995.0	⑤ 483.0	9,285.0	10.8	5.4	14.8	5.2	1.1	⑤ 6.93	12.58	...	1.60	75.94 — 47.00	8.9	2.6
12/31/98	7,367.0	④⑤ 193.0	9,536.0	10.2	2.6	6.8	2.0	1.3	④⑤ 2.78	8.43	...	1.60	139.00 — 59.31	35.7	1.6
12/31/97	9,153.0	407.0	9,677.0	9.6	4.4	15.5	4.2	1.1	5.98	12.35	...	1.60	127.88 — 71.38	16.7	1.6
12/31/96	8,071.0	234.0	9,422.0	8.2	2.9	11.0	2.5	1.0	4.33	11.13	...	1.60	84.25 — 57.75	16.4	2.3
12/31/95	6,818.0	252.0	5,455.0	7.9	3.7	17.3	4.6	1.2	5.11	10.83	...	1.60	64.25 — 39.75	10.2	3.1
12/31/94	6,711.0	② 35.0	6,047.0	3.0	0.5	2.7	0.6	1.2	② 0.72	6.18	...	1.60	47.38 — 34.50	56.8	3.9
12/31/93	5,063.0	① 96.0	2,939.0	4.3	1.9	7.3	3.3	1.4	① 1.99	6.44	27.03	1.60	42.63 — 30.50	18.4	4.4

Statistics are as originally reported. ① Incl. loss on disposition of property, plant & equipment: $26.0 mill., 1993; $11.0 mill., 1992 ② Incl. $282.0 mill. from special termination benefit. ③ Bef. acctg. chrg. $432.0 mill., 2002; $16.0 mill., 1999. ④ Incl. non-recurr. pre-tax chgs. of $186.0 mill. ⑤ Incl. investment loss of $30.0 mill. ⑥ Bef. a net loss from disc. opers. of $201.0 mill., 2002; $17.0 mill., 2000. ⑦ Refl. the acqs. of Litton Industries, Newport News Shipbuilding & the electronics & info. systems group of Aerojet-General Corp.

OFFICERS:
K. Kresa, Chmn., C.E.O.
R. D. Sugar, Pres., C.O.O.
R. B. Waugh, Jr., Corp. V.P., Pres., C.F.O.
INVESTOR CONTACT: Gaston Kent, V.P.,
Investor Relations, (310) 553-6262
PRINCIPAL OFFICE: 1840 Century Park East,
Los Angeles, CA 90067-2199

TELEPHONE NUMBER: (310) 553-6262
FAX: (310) 553-2076
WEB: www.northropgrumman.com
NO. OF EMPLOYEES: 120,000 (avg.)
SHAREHOLDERS: 17,880
ANNUAL MEETING: In May
INCORPORATED: CA, May, 1939; reincorp.,
DE, June, 1985

INSTITUTIONAL HOLDINGS:
No. of Institutions: 529
Shares Held: 175,748,901
% Held: 155.3
INDUSTRY: Search and navigation equipment (SIC: 3812)
TRANSFER AGENT(S): EquiServe, Inc.,
Jersey City, NJ

NORTHWEST NATURAL GAS COMPANY

EXCH.	SYM.	REC. PRICE	P/E RATIO	YLD.	MKT. CAP.	RANGE (52-WK.)	'02 Y/E PR.
NYSE	NWN	24.50 (2/28/03)	15.2	5.1%	$0.62 bill.	30.70 - 23.46	27.06

MEDIUM GRADE. LONG-TERM RESULTS SHOULD BENEFIT FROM RAPID GROWTH IN ITS INTERSTATE GAS STORAGE MARKET, RESIDENTIAL AND COMMERCIAL CUSTOMER GROWTH AND EFFECTIVE COST CONTROL.

TRADING VOLUME Thousand Shares

*7 YEAR PRICE SCORE 118.4   *12 MONTH PRICE SCORE 102.3
*NYSE COMPOSITE INDEX=100

INTERIM EARNINGS (Per Share):

Qtr.	Mar.	June	Sept.	Dec.
1999	0.93	0.40	d0.17	0.53
2000	1.22	0.07	d0.22	0.80
2001	0.99	0.17	d0.22	0.99
2002	1.32	d0.14	d0.26	0.69

INTERIM DIVIDENDS (Per Share):

Amt.	Decl.	Ex.	Rec.	Pay.
0.315Q	4/05/02	4/26/02	4/30/02	5/15/02
0.315Q	7/05/02	7/29/02	7/31/02	8/15/02
0.315Q	10/03/02	10/29/02	10/31/02	11/15/02
0.315Q	1/03/03	1/29/03	1/31/03	2/15/03

Indicated div.: $1.26 (Div. Reinv. Plan)

CAPITALIZATION (12/31/01):

	($000)	(%)
Long-Term Debt	378,377	37.4
Deferred Income Tax	130,424	12.9
Redeemable Pfd. Stock	9,000	0.9
Preferred Stock	25,000	2.5
Common & Surplus	468,161	46.3
Total	1,010,962	100.0

BUSINESS:

Northwest Natural Gas Company is principally engaged in the distribution of natural gas to customers in western Oregon, including the Portland metropolitan area, most of the Willamette Valley and the coastal area from Astoria to Coos Bay. NWN also holds exclusive rights to serve portions of three Washington counties bordering the Columbia River. In addition, NWN operates NNG Financial Corporation, which holds financial investments as a limited partner in three solar electric generating plants, four windpower electric generation projects and a hydroelectric project, all located in California, and in two low-income housing projects in Portland. NNG Financial Corporation also holds interests in certain gas producing properties in the western United States. In January 2000, the Company sold its interest in Canor Energy Ltd.

RECENT DEVELOPMENTS:

For the year ended 12/31/02, net income decreased 12.7% to $43.8 million compared with $50.2 million the previous year. Earnings were adversely affected by an extremely warm December and the changes relating to the termination of the Company's contract to acquire Portland General Electric Company. Gross operating revenues declined 1.4% to $641.4 million from $650.3 million the year before. Operating margin, which is gross revenues less the cost of gas, grew 4.2% to $287.5 million from $276.0 million a year earlier. Operating income climbed 5.5% to $116.3 million from $110.2 million the prior year.

PROSPECTS:

Long-term results should benefit from rapid growth in NWN's interstate gas storage market, residential and commercial customer growth, effective cost control and advantageous gas purchasing early in fiscal 2002. For full-year 2003, the Company continues to expect earnings to range from $1.70 to $1.85 per share. The Company noted that this expectation is based on average weather conditions and cautioned that the El Nino weather that affected the western U.S. in December 2002 is continuing in early 2003.

ANNUAL FINANCIAL DATA:

FISCAL YEAR	TOT. REVS. ($mill.)	NET INC. ($mill.)	TOT. ASSETS ($mill.)	OPER. PROFIT %	NET PROFIT %	NET INC./ NET PROP. %	NET INC./ TOT. CAP. %	RET. ON EQUITY %	ACCUM. DEPR./ GROSS PROP. %	EARN. PER SH. $	TANG. BK. VAL. $	DIV. PER SH. $	DIV. PAYOUT %	PRICE RANGE	AVG. P/E RATIO	AVG. YIELD %
p12/31/02	641.4	43.8								1.62		1.26	77.8	30.70 - 23.46	16.7	4.7
12/31/01	650.3	50.2	1,435.0	16.9	7.7	5.3	5.0	10.2	35.1	1.88	18.56	1.25	66.2	26.75 - 21.65	12.9	5.1
12/31/00	532.1	① 47.8	1,278.7	19.6	9.0	5.1	4.6	10.0	34.0	① 1.79	17.92	1.24	69.3	27.50 - 17.75	12.6	5.5
12/31/99	455.8	② 44.9	1,244.4	20.8	9.9	5.0	4.5	9.9	32.8	② 1.69	17.12	1.23	72.5	27.88 - 19.50	14.0	5.2
12/31/98	416.7	27.3	1,191.7	19.1	6.6	3.3	2.8	6.2	32.6	1.02	16.59	1.22	119.6	30.75 - 24.25	27.0	4.4
12/31/97	361.8	43.1	1,111.6	24.9	11.9	5.4	4.8	11.0	31.5	1.76	16.02	1.21	68.5	31.25 - 23.00	15.4	4.4
12/31/96	380.3	46.8	988.9	24.4	12.3	6.5	6.0	12.6	31.9	1.97	15.37	1.20	60.9	25.88 - 20.83	11.9	5.1
12/31/95	356.3	38.1	929.3	21.2	10.7	5.8	5.0	10.9	31.9	1.61	14.55	1.18	73.2	22.83 - 18.33	12.8	5.7
12/31/94	368.3	35.5	889.3	19.6	9.6	5.6	4.9	11.8	30.7	1.63	13.63	1.17	72.1	24.33 - 18.83	13.3	5.4
12/31/93	358.7	37.6	849.0	23.4	10.5	6.4	5.5	13.2	30.4	1.74	13.08	1.17	67.0	25.83 - 19.00	12.9	5.2

Statistics are as originally reported. Adj. for stk. split: 3-for-2, 9/6/96 ① Bef. inc. from disc. opers. $2.4 mill., 2000; $355,000, 1999.

OFFICERS:
R. G. Reiten, Chmn.
M. S. Dodson, Pres., C.E.O., C.O.O.
B. R. DeBolt, Sr. V.P., C.F.O.
S. P. Feltz, Treas., Contr.

INVESTOR CONTACT: James R. Boehlke, Investor Relations, (800) 422-4012 ext.2451

PRINCIPAL OFFICE: 220 N.W. Second Avenue, Portland, OR 97209

TELEPHONE NUMBER: (503) 226-4211
FAX: (503) 273-4824
WEB: www.nwnatural.com

NO. OF EMPLOYEES: 1,284 (avg.)

SHAREHOLDERS: 10,359

ANNUAL MEETING: In May

INCORPORATED: OR, Jan., 1910

INSTITUTIONAL HOLDINGS:
No. of Institutions: 134
Shares Held: 10,775,346
% Held: 42.2

INDUSTRY: Natural gas distribution (SIC: 4924)

TRANSFER AGENT(S): The Company

NORTHWESTERN CORPORATION

EXCH.	SYM.	REC. PRICE	P/E RATIO	YLD.	MKT. CAP.	RANGE (52-WK.)	'02 Y/E PR.	DIV. ACH.
NYSE	NOR	2.64 (2/28/03)	1.7	...	$71.9 mill.	23.64 - 2.50	5.08	19 yrs.

SPECULATIVE GRADE. THE COMPANY OUTLINED A PLAN DESIGNED TO RETURN ITS FOCUS TO ITS CORE
ELECTRIC AND NATURAL GAS UTILITY BUSINESS.

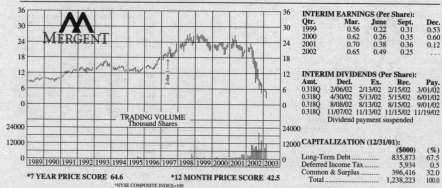

*7 YEAR PRICE SCORE 64.6   ***12 MONTH PRICE SCORE 42.5**

*NYSE COMPOSITE INDEX=100

INTERIM EARNINGS (Per Share):

Qtr.	Mar.	June	Sept.	Dec.
1999	0.56	0.22	0.31	0.53
2000	0.62	0.26	0.35	0.60
2001	0.70	0.38	0.36	0.12
2002	0.65	0.49	0.25	...

INTERIM DIVIDENDS (Per Share):

Amt.	Decl.	Ex.	Rec.	Pay.
0.318Q	2/06/02	2/13/02	2/15/02	3/01/02
0.318Q	4/30/02	5/13/02	5/15/02	6/01/02
0.318Q	8/08/02	8/13/02	8/15/02	9/01/02
0.318Q	11/07/02	11/13/02	11/15/02	11/19/02
Dividend payment suspended				

CAPITALIZATION (12/31/01):

	($000)	(%)
Long-Term Debt	835,873	67.5
Deferred Income Tax	5,934	0.5
Common & Surplus	396,416	32.0
Total	1,238,223	100.0

BUSINESS:

NorthWestern Corporation (formerly Northwestern Public Service Company) provides energy and communications services to more than 2.0 million residential and business customers nationwide as of 11/7/02. NOR's partner entities include Expanets, Inc., a provider of integrated communication and data services to small and medium-sized businesses; NorthWestern Services Group, a provider of electric, natural gas and communications services to customers in the upper Midwest; Blue Dot Services, Inc. a provider of air conditioning, heating, plumbing and related services; and CornerStone Propane Partners L.P., a publicly-held retail propane distributor for more than 480,000 residential, commercial, industrial and agricultural customers in 34 states. NorthWestern Growth Corporation, a wholly-owned subsidiary, is the development and investment capital arm of NOR. On 2/15/02, NOR acquired The Montana Power Company's energy transmission and distribution business for $1.09 billion.

RECENT DEVELOPMENTS:

For the quarter ended 9/30/02, income from continuing operations was $14.6 million compared with income from continuing operations of $14.1 million in the corresponding period of the previous year. Results for 2002 and 2001 excluded losses of $55.9 million and $3.8 million, respectively, from discontinued operations. Operating revenues jumped 27.7% to $509.3 million from $398.7 million in the year-earlier quarter. Gross margin advanced 50.1% to $248.6 million from $165.6 million in the prior-year period. Operating income was $45.5 million versus an operating loss of $12.1 million the year before.

PROSPECTS:

On 2/19/03, NOR outlined a plan designed to return its focus to its core electric and natural gas utility business and review strategic options for its non-regulated businesses. The Company also addressed its need to improve liquidity and financial controls and reduce corporate overhead. NOR is targeting debt reduction of at least $200.0 million in the next 12 months by suspending common stock dividends and selling non-core assets. Meanwhile, NOR's utility business expects improved results in 2003 due to the benefit of full-year results from the Montana operations.

ANNUAL FINANCIAL DATA:

FISCAL YEAR	TOT. REVS. ($mill.)	NET INC. ($mill.)	TOT. ASSETS ($mill.)	OPER. PROFIT %	NET PROFIT %	NET INC./ NET PROP. %	NET INC./ TOT. CAP. %	RET. ON EQUITY %	ACCUM. DEPR./ GROSS PROP. %	EARN. PER SH. $	TANG. BK. VAL. $	DIV. PER SH. $	DIV. PAYOUT %	PRICE RANGE	AVG. P/E RATIO	AVG. YIELD %
12/31/01	4,237.8	44.5	2,617.4	...	1.1	5.4	3.6	11.2	30.0	1.53	...	1.21	79.1	26.75 - 18.25	14.7	5.4
③ 12/31/00	7,132.1	② 50.6	2,898.1	0.6	0.7	7.3	2.1	15.9	29.0	② 1.87	...	1.13	60.4	23.94 - 19.13	11.5	5.2
12/31/99	3,004.3	44.7	1,956.8	2.6	1.5	6.6	2.8	14.9	25.8	1.62	...	1.05	64.8	27.13 - 20.63	14.7	4.4
12/31/98	1,187.2	30.4	1,736.8	6.2	2.6	4.8	2.1	10.8	23.8	1.44	...	0.98	68.4	27.38 - 20.25	16.5	4.1
12/31/97	918.1	26.3	1,375.1	6.4	2.9	4.8	2.0	15.8	24.3	1.31	...	0.93	71.2	23.50 - 16.94	15.4	4.6
12/31/96	344.0	① 26.1	1,113.7	14.7	7.6	5.0	3.0	15.9	23.9	① 1.28	...	0.89	69.5	18.25 - 13.38	12.4	5.6
12/31/95	205.0	19.3	558.7	18.6	9.4	5.7	4.3	12.6	30.9	1.11	5.81	0.86	77.2	14.19 - 12.13	11.9	6.5
12/31/94	157.3	15.4	359.1	19.3	9.8	6.2	5.5	13.5	35.7	1.00	7.27	0.83	83.5	14.81 - 12.25	13.5	6.2
12/31/93	153.3	15.2	343.6	13.2	9.9	6.4	5.6	13.9	35.4	0.98	7.14	0.81	83.2	16.75 - 13.13	15.2	5.5
12/31/92	119.2	13.7	313.5	16.4	11.5	6.0	5.4	12.8	34.7	0.89	6.98	0.80	89.8	14.38 - 11.75	14.8	6.1

Statistics are as originally reported. Adj. for 2-for-1 stock split, 5/97. ① Incl. a non-recurr., one-time gain of $0.09 a share. ② Excl. acctg. chrg. of $1.0 mill. ($0.04/sh.) ③ Results reflect the purch. of Lucent Technologies' Growing and Emerging Markets business on 4/1/00.

OFFICERS:
G. G. Drook, Interim C.E.O.
R. R. Hylland, Pres., C.O.O.
K. D. Orme, V.P., C.F.O.
INVESTOR CONTACT: Elizabeth Evans, Investor Relations, (605) 978-2904
PRINCIPAL OFFICE: 125 South Dakota Avenue, Sioux Falls, SD 57104

TELEPHONE NUMBER: (605) 978-2908
FAX: (605) 353-7631
WEB: www.northwestern.com
NO. OF EMPLOYEES: 10,251 (avg.)
SHAREHOLDERS: 10,322
ANNUAL MEETING: In May
INCORPORATED: DE, Nov., 1923

INSTITUTIONAL HOLDINGS:
No. of Institutions: 141
Shares Held: 19,715,988
% Held: 52.7
INDUSTRY: Electric and other services combined (SIC: 4931)
REGISTRAR(S): Wells Fargo Shareowner Services, South St. Paul, MN

NSTAR

EXCH.	SYM.	REC. PRICE	P/E RATIO	YLD.	MKT. CAP.	RANGE (52-WK.)	'02 Y/E PR.
NYSE	NST	40.42 (2/28/03)	13.3	5.3%	$2.14 bill.	48.20 - 34.00	44.39

MEDIUM GRADE. EARNINGS PER SHARE FOR 2003 ARE EXPECTED IN THE RANGE OF $3.35 TO $3.45.

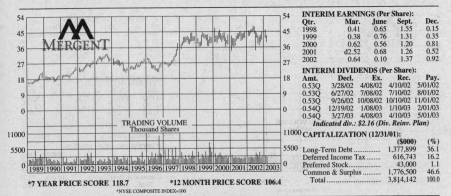

INTERIM EARNINGS (Per Share):

Qtr.	Mar.	June	Sept.	Dec.
1998	0.41	0.65	1.55	0.15
1999	0.38	0.76	1.31	0.35
2000	0.62	0.56	1.20	0.81
2001	d2.52	0.68	1.26	0.52
2002	0.64	0.10	1.37	0.92

INTERIM DIVIDENDS (Per Share):

Amt.	Decl.	Ex.	Rec.	Pay.
0.53Q	3/28/02	4/08/02	4/10/02	5/01/02
0.53Q	6/27/02	7/08/02	7/10/02	8/01/02
0.53Q	9/26/02	10/08/02	10/10/02	11/01/02
0.54Q	12/19/02	1/08/03	1/10/03	2/01/03
0.54Q	3/27/03	4/08/03	4/10/03	5/01/03

Indicated div.: $2.16 (Div. Reinv. Plan)

CAPITALIZATION (12/31/01):

	($000)	(%)
Long-Term Debt	1,377,899	36.1
Deferred Income Tax	616,743	16.2
Preferred Stock	43,000	1.1
Common & Surplus	1,776,500	46.6
Total	3,814,142	100.0

*7 YEAR PRICE SCORE 118.7   ***12 MONTH PRICE SCORE 106.4**

NYSE COMPOSITE INDEX=100

BUSINESS:

NSTAR was formed through the merger of BEC Energy and Commonwealth Energy System on August 25, 1999. As of 1/23/03, the Company provided regulated electric and gas utility services to about 1.3 million customers, including 1.1 million electric customers in 81 communities and 247,000 gas customers in 51 communities throughout Massachusetts. The Company's utility subsidiaries include Boston Edison, Cambridge Electric Light Company, Commonwealth Electric Company, and NSTAR Gas Company. NSTAR's non-utility operations include telecommunications, district heating and cooling operations and liquefied natural gas services.

RECENT DEVELOPMENTS:

For the year ended 12/31/02, net income soared to $163.7 million compared with $3.2 million in 2001. Results for 2002 and 2001 included net impairment charges related to the RCN Corporation investment of $17.7 million and $173.9 million, respectively. Results for 2001 also included an after-tax charge of $4.9 million related to the shutdown of a district energy facility. Earnings benefited from increases in electric sales and gas sales due to very cold weather versus a mild winter in 2001. Heating degree days were greater than last year and greater than normal conditions. In addition, a decrease in operations and maintenance expense and a lower preferred dividend requirement contributed to the increase in earnings, offset by higher interest costs. Operating revenues declined 14.8% to $2.72 billion from $3.19 billion in the prior year.

PROSPECTS:

Based on challenging economic conditions, the Company expects unit sales of electricity to grow at approximately 1.0% during 2003. Total operations and maintenance expense is expected to remain flat in spite of an estimated $10.0 million increase in pension and postretirement benefits expense. In addition, capital investments are expected to be approximately $300.0 million. Meanwhile, earnings per share for the year are expected to be in the range of $3.35 to $3.45.

ANNUAL FINANCIAL DATA:

FISCAL YEAR	TOT. REVS. ($mill.)	NET INC. ($mill.)	TOT. ASSETS ($mill.)	OPER. PROFIT %	NET PROFIT %	NET INC./ NET PROP. %	NET INC./ TOT. CAP. %	RET. ON EQUITY %	ACCUM. DEPR./ GROSS PROP. %	EARN. PER SH. $	TANG. BK. VAL. $	DIV. PER SH. $	DIV. PAYOUT %	PRICE RANGE	AVG. P/E RATIO	AVG. YIELD %
p12/31/02	2,719.2	③ 163.7								③ 3.03		2.12	70.0	48.20 - 34.00	13.6	5.2
12/31/01	3,191.8	② 3.2	5,328.2	11.0	0.1	0.1	0.1	0.2	33.1	② d0.05	24.76	2.06	...	45.24 - 33.94	...	5.2
12/31/00	2,699.5	181.0	5,569.5	14.4	6.7	6.9	4.4	9.2	33.1	3.18	27.35	2.00	62.9	47.00 - 36.38	13.1	4.8
12/31/99	1,851.4	146.5	5,482.9	14.2	7.9	5.5	3.8	6.4	33.8	2.76	29.35	0.48	17.6	44.63 - 36.44	14.7	1.2
① 12/31/98	1,622.5	141.0	3,203.0	15.0	8.7	7.6	5.8	12.3	33.5	2.75	22.29	...	...	44.94 - 35.06	14.5	...
12/31/97	1,778.5	144.6	...	14.4	8.1	...	...	...	...	2.71	...	...	...	38.38 - 24.63	11.6	...

Statistics are as originally reported. ① Results for 12/98 and earlier are for BEC Energy prior to the merger with Commonwealth Energy System. ② Incl. following one-time after-tax items: $2.4 mill. chg. for serv. quality plan; $4.9 mill. chg. for shutdown of energy facility; $2.9 mill. gain for receipt of equity securities; and $173.9 mill. chg. for invest. ③ Incl. $17.7 mill. net impair. chg. rel. to RCN Corp. invest.

OFFICERS:
T. J. May, Chmn., C.E.O.
J. J. Judge, Sr. V.P., C.F.O., Treas.
D. S. Horan, Sr. V.P., Gen. Couns.

INVESTOR CONTACT: John F. Gavin, Manager, Investor Relations, (617) 424-2562

PRINCIPAL OFFICE: 800 Boylston Street, Boston, MA 02199

TELEPHONE NUMBER: (617) 424-2000
FAX: (617) 424-4032
WEB: www.nstaronline.com
NO. OF EMPLOYEES: 3,300 (approx.)
SHAREHOLDERS: 29,890
ANNUAL MEETING: In May
INCORPORATED: MA, Jan., 1886; reincorp., MA, Aug., 1999

INSTITUTIONAL HOLDINGS:
No. of Institutions: 191
Shares Held: 75,236,918
% Held: 141.9

INDUSTRY: Electric services (SIC: 4911)

TRANSFER AGENT(S): Boston EquiServe, Boston, MA

NUCOR CORPORATION

EXCH.	SYM.	REC. PRICE	P/E RATIO	YLD.	MKT. CAP.	RANGE (52-WK.)	'02 Y/E PR.	DIV. ACH.
NYSE	NUE	41.60 (2/28/03)	20.1	1.9%	$3.23 bill.	70.15 - 35.03	41.30	30 yrs.

UPPER MEDIUM GRADE. NEAR-TERM RESULTS ARE EXPECTED TO BE HAMPERED BY CONTINUING WEAK ECONOMIC CONDITIONS AND SEVERELY DEPRESSED LEVELS OF NON-RESIDENTIAL CONSTRUCTION.

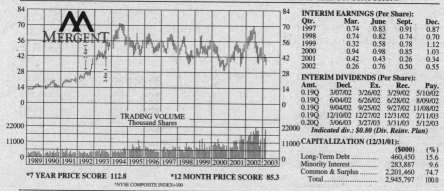

INTERIM EARNINGS (Per Share):

Qtr.	Mar.	June	Sept.	Dec.
1997	0.74	0.83	0.91	0.87
1998	0.74	0.82	0.74	0.70
1999	0.32	0.58	0.78	1.12
2000	0.94	0.98	0.85	1.03
2001	0.42	0.43	0.26	0.34
2002	0.26	0.76	0.50	0.55

INTERIM DIVIDENDS (Per Share):

Amt.	Decl.	Ex.	Rec.	Pay.
0.19Q	3/07/02	3/26/02	3/29/02	5/10/02
0.19Q	6/04/02	6/26/02	6/28/02	8/09/02
0.19Q	9/04/02	9/25/02	9/27/02	11/08/02
0.19Q	12/10/02	12/27/02	12/31/02	2/11/03
0.20Q	3/06/03	3/27/03	3/31/03	5/12/03

Indicated div.: $0.80 (Div. Reinv. Plan)

CAPITALIZATION (12/31/01):

	($000)	(%)
Long-Term Debt	460,450	15.6
Minority Interest	283,887	9.6
Common & Surplus	2,201,460	74.7
Total	2,945,797	100.0

*7 YEAR PRICE SCORE 112.8   ***12 MONTH PRICE SCORE 85.3**

*NYSE COMPOSITE INDEX=100

BUSINESS:

Nucor Corporation is a recycler of steel in the U.S. As of 2/6/03, NUE and affiliates manufactured steel products, with operating facilities in 14 states. The Company's manufactured products include carbon and alloy steel, for use in bars, beams, sheet and plate; steel joists and joist girders; steel deck; cold finished steel; steel fasteners; metal building systems; and light gauge steel framing. The primary raw material is ferrous scrap, which is acquired from numerous sources throughout the U.S. Hot-rolled and cold-rolled sheet steel are produced to customer orders. Other hot-rolled steel, cold-rolled steel, cold-finished steel and steel fasteners are manufactured in standard sizes and inventories are maintained. Steel joists, joist girders and steel deck are sold to general contractors and fabricators throughout the U.S. In December 2002, NUE acquired Birmingham Steel Corporation.

RECENT DEVELOPMENTS:

For the year ended 12/31/02, net income increased 43.5% to $162.1 million compared with $113.0 million in 2001. Net sales advanced 10.4% to $4.57 billion from $4.14 billion a year earlier. The improvement in sales reflected a less than 1.0% year-over-year increase in average sales price per ton and a 10.7% increase in total tons shipped to outside customers. Pre-operating, start-up and acquisition expenses decreased 10.7% to $87.8 million versus $98.3 million in 2001. Cost of products sold as a percentage of net sales amounted to 89.3% versus 89.8% a year earlier.

PROSPECTS:

Near-term results are expected to be hampered by continuing weak economic conditions and severely depressed levels of non-residential construction. Shrinking margins are anticipated due to lower selling prices and higher scrap prices. Accordingly, NUE expects first quarter 2003 earnings per share in the range of $0.20 to $0.25. However, NUE expects business conditions and profitability to measurably improve as 2003 progresses. Meanwhile, NUE's new facility, Nucor Steel Decatur, LLC, is slated to produce 1.5 million tons of steel in 2003. Separately, in December 2002, NUE completed the purchase of substantially all of the assets of Birmingham Steel Corporation for $615.0 million, including $116.9 million in inventory and receivables.

ANNUAL FINANCIAL DATA:

FISCAL YEAR	TOT. REVS. ($mill.)	NET INC. ($mill.)	TOT. ASSETS ($mill.)	OPER. PROFIT %	NET PROFIT %	RET. ON EQUITY %	RET. ON ASSETS %	CURR. RATIO	EARN. PER SH. $	CASH FL. PER SH. $	TANG. BK. VAL. $	DIV. PER SH. $	PRICE RANGE	AVG. P/E RATIO	AVG. YIELD %
p12/31/02	4,568.3	☐ 162.1							☐ 2.07	·		0.74	70.15 - 36.00	25.6	1.4
12/31/01	4,139.2	☐ 113.0	3,759.3	4.4	2.7	5.1	3.0	2.8	☐ 1.45	5.17	28.33	0.66	56.50 - 33.45	31.0	1.5
12/31/00	4,586.1	310.9	3,721.8	10.4	6.8	14.6	8.4	2.5	3.80	6.97	27.47	0.58	56.44 - 29.50	11.3	1.3
12/31/99	4,009.3	244.6	3,729.8	9.3	6.1	10.8	6.6	2.9	2.80	5.74	25.93	0.51	61.81 - 41.63	18.5	1.0
12/31/98	4,151.2	263.7	3,226.5	9.9	6.4	12.7	8.2	2.3	3.00	5.88	23.73	0.46	60.63 - 35.25	16.0	1.0
12/31/97	4,184.5	294.5	2,984.4	11.0	7.0	15.7	9.9	2.1	3.34	5.84	21.32	0.38	62.94 - 44.75	16.1	0.7
12/31/96	3,647.0	248.2	2,619.5	10.6	6.8	15.4	9.5	1.8	2.83	4.91	18.33	0.31	63.00 - 45.13	19.1	0.6
12/31/95	3,462.0	274.5	2,296.1	12.5	7.9	19.9	12.0	1.9	3.14	5.13	15.78	0.26	63.25 - 42.00	16.8	0.5
12/31/94	2,975.6	226.6	2,001.9	12.4	7.6	20.2	11.3	1.7	2.60	4.41	12.85	0.17	72.00 - 48.75	23.2	0.3
12/31/93	2,253.7	123.5	1,829.3	8.9	5.5	13.7	6.8	1.3	1.42	2.83	10.36	0.15	57.25 - 38.00	33.5	0.3

Statistics are as originally reported. Adj. for stk. splits: 2-for-1, 10/92 & 9/93. ☐ Incl. chrg. of 2002, $87.8 mill.; 2001, $97.8 mill. for pre-operating and start-up costs of new facilities.

OFFICERS:
P. C. Browning, Chmn.
D. R. DiMicco, Vice-Chmn., Pres., C.E.O.
T. S. Lisenby, Exec. V.P., C.F.O., Treas.
INVESTOR CONTACT: Terry S. Lisenby, Vice Pres., (704) 366-7000
PRINCIPAL OFFICE: 2100 Rexford Road, Charlotte, NC 28211

TELEPHONE NUMBER: (704) 366-7000
FAX: (704) 362-4208
WEB: www.nucor.com
NO. OF EMPLOYEES: 8,400
SHAREHOLDERS: 47,000
ANNUAL MEETING: In May
INCORPORATED: MI, Jan., 1940; reincorp., DE, Mar., 1958

INSTITUTIONAL HOLDINGS:
No. of Institutions: 304
Shares Held: 56,929,772
% Held: 72.8
INDUSTRY: Blast furnaces and steel mills (SIC: 3312)
TRANSFER AGENT(S): American Stock Transfer & Trust Company, New York, NY

NUVEEN INVESTMENTS, INC.

EXCH.	SYM.	REC. PRICE	P/E RATIO	YLD.	MKT. CAP.	RANGE (52-WK.)	'02 Y/E PR.	DIV. ACH.
NYSE	JNC	22.27 (2/28/03)	17.3	2.3%	$1.06 bill.	31.05 - 20.12	25.35	10 yrs.

UPPER MEDIUM GRADE. RESULTS ARE BENEFITING FROM INCREASED SALES OF CLOSED-END FUNDS INVESTING IN MUNICIPAL BONDS AND PREFERRED STOCKS.

*7 YEAR PRICE SCORE 175.4   ***12 MONTH PRICE SCORE 101.3**

*NYSE COMPOSITE INDEX=100

INTERIM EARNINGS (Per Share):

Qtr.	Mar.	June	Sept.	Dec.
1998	0.19	0.19	0.20	0.23
1999	0.23	0.24	0.24	0.26
2000	0.26	0.26	0.26	0.27
2001	0.27	0.28	0.28	0.30
2002	0.30	0.31	0.33	0.35

INTERIM DIVIDENDS (Per Share):

Amt.	Decl.	Ex.	Rec.	Pay.
0.24Q	2/08/02	2/27/02	3/01/02	3/15/02
0.24Q	5/09/02	5/30/02	6/03/02	6/17/02
100% STK	5/09/02	6/25/02	6/03/02	6/24/02
0.13Q	8/09/02	8/29/02	9/03/02	9/16/02
0.13Q	11/08/02	11/27/02	12/02/02	12/16/02

Indicated div.: $0.52

CAPITALIZATION (12/31/01):

	($000)	(%)
Common & Surplus	406,265	100.0
Total	406,265	100.0

BUSINESS:

Nuveen Investments, Inc. (formerly The John Nuveen Company) is engaged in asset management and related research, as well as the development, marketing and distribution of investment products and services primarily targeted at affluent, high net-worth individuals and institutional markets. As of 12/31/02, total assets under management was approximately $79.72 billion. The Company distributes its investment products and services, including mutual funds, exchange-traded funds, defined portfolios and separately managed accounts through unaffiliated intermediary firms, including broker/dealers, commercial banks, affiliates of insurance providers, financial planners, accountants, consultants and investment advisors. The St. Paul Companies, Inc. owned approximately 77.0% of the Company's common stock as of 12/31/01.

RECENT DEVELOPMENTS:

For the year ended 12/31/02, net income increased 10.0% to $126.2 million from $114.7 million in the previous year. Total operating revenues rose 6.8% to $396.4 million from $371.1 million a year earlier. Investment advisory fees from assets under management grew 7.5% to $355.5 million from $330.6 million the year before. Product distribution revenues fell 38.1% to $12.1 million from $19.5 million in 2001, while other revenue/performance fees jumped 61.5% to $29.0 million from $18.0 million the prior year. Operating income totaled $211.8 million, up 12.2% versus $188.8 million the previous year.

PROSPECTS:

Earnings growth is being fueled by increased sales of the Company's new closed-end funds. In 2002, the Company boosted its assets by about $6.00 billion through 21 initial public offerings of closed-end funds investing in municipal bonds and preferred stocks. These investments should continue to attract risk-adverse investors if equity market conditions continue to deteriorate. However, if market conditions begin to improve, the Company stands to benefit from the wide selection of funds it offers.

ANNUAL FINANCIAL DATA:

FISCAL YEAR	TOT. REVS. ($mill.)	NET INC. ($mill.)	TOT. ASSETS ($mill.)	OPER. PROFIT %	NET PROFIT %	RET. ON EQUITY %	RET. ON ASSETS %	CURR. RATIO	EARN. PER SH. $	CASH FL. PER SH. $	TANG. BK. VAL.$	DIV. PER SH. $	PRICE RANGE	AVG. P/E RATIO	AVG. YIELD %
p12/31/02	396.4	126.2							1.29			0.50	31.05 - 20.12	19.8	2.0
12/31/01	371.1	114.7	696.6	50.9	30.9	28.2	16.5	0.7	1.13	1.27	0.01	0.47	27.15 - 16.73	19.4	2.1
12/31/00	358.4	106.7	607.0	46.9	29.8	24.6	17.6	3.8	1.05	1.16	2.40	0.41	19.44 - 11.17	14.6	2.7
12/31/99	338.8	97.3	541.0	44.3	28.7	28.1	18.0	2.9	0.95	1.07	1.58	0.38	14.56 - 11.44	13.7	2.9
12/31/98	307.5	83.6	468.0	45.6	27.2	27.5	17.9	2.0	0.81	0.93	1.07	0.33	13.92 - 10.52	15.1	2.7
12/31/97	268.9	74.2	492.2	46.8	27.6	27.2	15.1	1.2	0.71	0.79	0.67	0.29	12.58 - 8.75	15.0	2.7
12/31/96	232.5	72.5	355.3	51.5	31.2	26.7	20.4	4.5	0.66	0.72	2.74	0.26	9.58 - 7.92	13.3	3.0
12/31/95	236.2	70.6	402.5	49.3	29.9	21.9	17.5	5.9	0.62	0.72	2.78	0.23	9.04 - 6.83	12.7	2.9
12/31/94	220.3	58.2	348.8	44.1	26.4	20.4	16.7	6.6	0.51	0.62	2.56	0.21	9.13 - 6.33	15.2	2.8
12/31/93	245.7	72.5	410.6	47.2	29.5	26.3	17.6	1.2	0.59	0.70	2.37	0.19	13.88 - 7.75	18.4	1.7

Statistics are as originally reported. Adj. for 100% stk. div., 6/25/02; 50% stk. div., 9/28/01.

OFFICERS:
T. R. Schwertfeger, Chmn., C.E.O.
J. P. Amboian, Pres.
A. G. Berkshire, Sr. V.P., Gen. Couns.

INVESTOR CONTACT: Laurel O'Brien, (312) 917-8254

PRINCIPAL OFFICE: 333 West Wacker Drive, Chicago, IL 60606

TELEPHONE NUMBER: (312) 917-7700
FAX: (312) 917-8049
WEB: www.nuveen.com

NO. OF EMPLOYEES: 597

SHAREHOLDERS: 2,700 (approx.)

ANNUAL MEETING: In May

INCORPORATED: DE, Mar., 1992

INSTITUTIONAL HOLDINGS:
No. of Institutions: 107
Shares Held: 11,636,513
% Held: 12.5

INDUSTRY: Security brokers and dealers (SIC: 6211)

TRANSFER AGENT(S): The Bank of New York, New York, NY

OAKLEY, INC.

EXCH.	SYM.	REC. PRICE	P/E RATIO	YLD.	MKT. CAP.	RANGE (52-WK.)	'02 Y/E PR.
NYSE	OO	7.99 (2/28/03)	13.5	...	$0.55 bill.	20.09 - 7.67	10.27

UPPER MEDIUM GRADE. THE COMPANY ANNOUNCED PLANS TO RESTRUCTURE ITS EUROPEAN SALES AND DISTRIBUTION OPERATIONS.

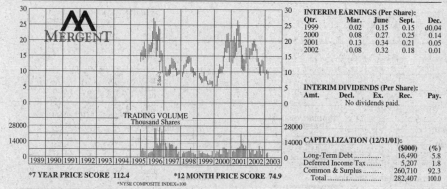

*7 YEAR PRICE SCORE 112.4   ***12 MONTH PRICE SCORE 74.9**

*NYSE COMPOSITE INDEX=100

INTERIM EARNINGS (Per Share):

Qtr.	Mar.	June	Sept.	Dec.
1999	0.02	0.15	0.15	d0.04
2000	0.08	0.27	0.25	0.14
2001	0.13	0.34	0.21	0.05
2002	0.08	0.32	0.18	0.01

INTERIM DIVIDENDS (Per Share):

Amt.	Decl.	Ex.	Rec.	Pay.
		No dividends paid.		

CAPITALIZATION (12/31/01):

	($000)	(%)
Long-Term Debt	16,490	5.8
Deferred Income Tax	5,207	1.8
Common & Surplus	260,710	92.3
Total	282,407	100.0

BUSINESS:

Oakley, Inc. designs, manufactures and distributes consumer products that include high-performance eyewear, footwear, watches, apparel and accessories under the OAKLEY brand name. The Company sells its OAKLEY eyewear in the U.S. through a selected base of approximately 8,600 active accounts as of 12/31/01, with approximately 12,000 locations comprised of optical stores, sunglass retailers and specialty sport stores, including bike, surf, ski and golf shops, motorcycle, running and sporting goods stores. The Company's products are also sold in over 70 countries outside the U.S. OO's designs and innovations are protected by approximately 600 legal patents worldwide. In June 1997, OO acquired One Xcel, Inc., a company that designs, markets, and distributes protective face shields available for use with sports helmets.

RECENT DEVELOPMENTS:

For the year ended 12/31/02, net income dropped 19.3% to $40.6 million from $50.4 million the previous year. Earnings were hampered by production and distribution delays, difficult retail conditions and lower consumer spending in several of the Company's major markets, principally in its sunglass business. Results for 2002 included an after-tax restructuring charge of $1.8 million. Net sales grew 14.0% to $489.6 million from $429.3 million the prior year. Total domestic net sales increased 19.2% to $254.0 million, while international net sales rose 9.0% to $235.5 million. Gross profit as a percentage of sales dropped to 56.7% from 59.4% a year earlier.

PROSPECTS:

On 12/5/02, OO announced plans to restructure its European operations. The restructuring includes modifying and terminating relationships with several outside sales agents. Changes will also be implemented to rationalize other warehousing and distribution functions within the European markets. Separately, the Company has begun implementing cost control initiatives to reduce 2003 budgeted expenses by at least $5.0 million and to minimize future increases in operating expenses. Approximately one-half of the savings are targeted to come from advertising and marketing, with the remainder generated from reductions in planned new personnel, travel and other discretionary expenses.

ANNUAL FINANCIAL DATA:

FISCAL YEAR	TOT. REVS. ($mill.)	NET INC. ($mill.)	TOT. ASSETS ($mill.)	OPER. PROFIT %	NET PROFIT %	RET. ON EQUITY %	RET. ON ASSETS %	CURR. RATIO	EARN. PER SH.$	CASH FL. PER SH.$	TANG. BK. VAL.$	PRICE RANGE	AVG. P/E RATIO
p12/31/02	489.6	② 40.6							② 0.59			20.09 - 8.87	24.5
12/31/01	429.3	50.4	362.8	17.3	11.7	19.3	13.9	2.3	0.72	1.06	3.79	26.56 - 10.26	25.6
12/31/00	363.5	51.1	303.0	22.4	14.0	24.5	16.8	2.1	0.73	1.02	3.03	22.50 - 5.31	19.0
12/31/99	257.9	19.8	239.4	12.6	7.7	11.2	8.3	2.5	0.28	0.55	2.54	9.88 - 5.31	27.1
12/31/98	231.9	24.1	225.8	17.8	10.4	14.9	10.7	2.1	0.34	0.57	2.29	15.00 - 8.25	34.2
12/31/97	194.0	19.6	181.3	17.0	10.1	14.3	10.8	2.9	0.28	0.46	1.94	14.38 - 8.38	40.6
12/31/96	218.6	46.0	158.2	33.8	21.0	37.9	29.1	2.0	0.64	0.77	1.70	27.19 - 9.50	28.7
12/31/95	172.8	① 45.2	97.7	30.8	26.1	55.3	46.2	3.4	① 0.48	0.78	1.14	19.63 - 13.06	34.4
12/31/94	124.0	13.5	49.7	11.3	10.9	40.9	27.2	1.6	0.12	0.31	0.51	...	...
12/31/93	92.7	13.3	43.6	14.8	14.4	40.7	30.6	3.8	...	...	...	...	...

Statistics are as originally reported. Adj. for 2-for-1 stk. spl., 9/96 ① Incl. gain on disposition of prop., plant & equip., $4.8 mill. ② Incl. after-tax restruct. chrg. of $1.8 mill.

OFFICERS:
J. Jannard, Chmn., C.E.O.
C. Baden, Pres.
T. George, C.F.O.
INVESTOR CONTACT: Gar Jackson, Investor Relations, (949) 672-6985
PRINCIPAL OFFICE: One Icon, Foothill Ranch, CA 92610

TELEPHONE NUMBER: (949) 951-0991
FAX: (949) 951-8326
WEB: www.oakley.com
NO. OF EMPLOYEES: 1,685 (avg.)
SHAREHOLDERS: 474
ANNUAL MEETING: In June
INCORPORATED: CA, 1987; reincorp., WA, Mar., 1994

INSTITUTIONAL HOLDINGS:
No. of Institutions: 91
Shares Held: 21,702,918
% Held: 31.7

INDUSTRY: Ophthalmic goods (SIC: 3851)

TRANSFER AGENT(S): American Stock Transfer & Trust Company, New York, NY

OCCIDENTAL PETROLEUM CORPORATION

EXCH.	SYM.	REC. PRICE	P/E RATIO	YLD.	MKT. CAP.	RANGE (52-WK.)	'02 Y/E PR.
NYSE	OXY	29.90 (2/28/03)	9.8	3.5%	$11.21 bill.	30.75 - 22.98	28.45

UPPER MEDIUM GRADE. THE COMPANY INDICATED THAT IT REMAINS ON TRACK TO MEET OR EXCEED ITS COMBINED CRUDE OIL AND NATURAL GAS PRODUCTION TARGETS FOR 2003.

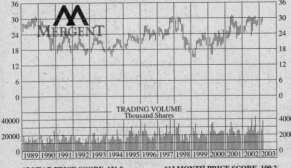

INTERIM EARNINGS (Per Share):

Qtr.	Mar.	June	Sept.	Dec.
1998	0.38	0.51	0.10	d0.12
1999	d0.17	0.03	0.35	1.33
2000	0.74	1.53	1.09	0.90
2001	1.37	1.26	1.18	d0.65
2002	0.33	0.63	1.25	0.84

INTERIM DIVIDENDS (Per Share):

Amt.	Decl.	Ex.	Rec.	Pay.
0.25Q	5/02/02	6/06/02	6/10/02	7/15/02
0.25Q	7/18/02	9/06/02	9/10/02	10/15/02
0.25Q	9/12/02	12/06/02	12/10/02	1/15/03
0.26Q	12/10/02	3/06/03	3/10/03	4/15/03

Indicated div.: $1.04 (Div. Reinv. Plan)

CAPITALIZATION (12/31/01):

	($000)	(%)
Long-Term Debt	4,065,000	30.1
Deferred Income Tax	1,103,000	8.2
Minority Interest	2,224,000	16.5
Redeemable Pfd. Stock	463,000	3.4
Common & Surplus	5,634,000	41.8
Total	13,489,000	100.0

*7 YEAR PRICE SCORE 121.9   ***12 MONTH PRICE SCORE 109.2**

NYSE COMPOSITE INDEX=100

BUSINESS:

Occidental Petroleum Corporation principal businesses constitute two industry segments. The oil and gas segment (63.2% of 2002 revenues and 86.1% of earnings) explores for, develops, produces and markets crude oil and natural gas. The chemicals segment (36.8%, 13.9%) manufactures and markets basic chemicals, vinyls, and performance chemicals. Net proved developed reserves at 12/31/02 were as follows: oil, 1.54 billion barrels, and gas, 1.74 trillion cubic feet. On 4/19/00, OXY acquired Altura Energy Ltd. for about $3.60 billion. On 8/22/02, OXY sold its 29.5% equity interest in Equistar to Lyondell Chemical Company for 34.0 million shares of Lyondell common stock.

RECENT DEVELOPMENTS:

For the twelve months ended 12/31/02, income from continuing operations was $1.16 billion compared with $1.18 billion a year earlier. Results for 2002 and 2001 included environmental remediation charges of $23.0 million and $109.0 million, respectively. Results for 2002 also included a net gain of $164.0 million related to the sale of the Company's Equistar chemical investment. Results for 2001 included a non-recurring gain of $399.0 million, offset by an investment write-down of $412.0 million. Lastly, results for 2001 included an after-tax loss of $272.0 million on the sale of a pipeline-owning entity. Total revenues declined 10.1% to $7.49 billion from $8.34 billion the previous year.

PROSPECTS:

OXY's near-term outlook is promising, due in part to the recent improvement in worldwide crude oil and natural gas prices as well as higher production volumes. For instance, oil and gas production for the quarter ended 12/31/02 averaged 518,000 barrels of oil equivalent (BOE) per day, an increase of 7.5% from the previous year. Accordingly, OXY has indicated that it remains on target to meet or exceed its 2003 forecast of 525,000 BOE per day. OXY achieved total worldwide production of 515,000 BOE per day during fiscal 2002.

ANNUAL FINANCIAL DATA:

FISCAL YEAR	TOT. REVS. ($mill.)	NET INC. ($mill.)	TOT. ASSETS ($mill.)	OPER. PROFIT %	NET PROFIT %	RET. ON EQUITY %	RET. ON ASSETS %	CURR. RATIO	EARN. PER SH. $	CASH FL. PER SH. $	TANG. BK. VAL. $	DIV. PER SH. $	PRICE RANGE	AVG. P/E RATIO	AVG. YIELD %
p12/31/02	⑨ 7,491.0	⑨ 1,163.0							⑨ 3.07			1.00	30.75 - 22.98	8.8	3.7
12/31/01	14,126.0	⑥ 1,186.0	17,850.0	13.4	8.4	21.1	6.6	0.8	⑧ 3.09	5.78	15.06	1.00	31.10 - 21.88	8.6	3.8
⑦ 12/31/00	14,543.0	⑥ 1,569.0	19,414.0	22.0	10.8	32.9	8.1	0.8	④ 4.26	6.71	12.90	1.00	25.56 - 15.75	4.8	4.8
12/31/99	8,551.0	⑤ 568.0	14,125.0	14.7	6.6	16.1	4.0	0.9	1.58	3.88	9.58	1.00	24.56 - 14.63	12.4	5.1
12/31/98	7,381.0	① 325.0	15,252.0	9.3	4.4	9.7	2.1	1.0	① 0.88	3.32	8.97	1.00	30.44 - 16.63	26.7	4.2
12/31/97	8,101.0	②③ 217.0	15,282.0	6.5	2.7	5.1	1.4	1.0	②③ 0.39	2.87	5.16	1.00	30.75 - 21.75	67.3	3.8
12/31/96	10,898.0	②④ 698.0	17,634.0	10.6	6.4	13.6	4.0	0.9	②④ 1.86	4.48	7.34	1.00	27.25 - 20.13	12.7	4.2
12/31/95	10,694.0	① 511.0	17,815.0	8.5	4.8	11.0	2.9	0.9	1.31	4.31	10.36	1.00	24.38 - 18.00	16.2	4.7
12/31/94	9,416.0	d36.0	17,989.0	1.1	...	...	...	0.9	d0.36	2.52	9.88	1.00	22.38 - 15.13	...	5.3
12/31/93	8,544.0	74.0	17,123.0	2.5	0.9	1.9	0.4	0.9	0.12	3.09	11.06	1.00	23.50 - 16.88	168.1	5.0

Statistics are as originally reported. ① Bef. disc. ops. inc. of $38.0 mil. ② Incl. non-recur. chrgs. 12/31/97, $474.0 mil.; cr. 12/31/96, $11.0 mil.; chrgs. 12/31/95, $132.0 mil. ③ Bef. disc. ops. loss of $390.0 mil. ④ Bef. extraord. chrg. of $30.0 mil. ⑤ Bef. acctg. chrg. of $13.0 mil. & extraord. loss of $107.0 mil. ⑥ Incl. asset disp. gain of $639.0 mil. & asset write-down chrg. of $180.0 mil.; bef. extraord. gain of $1.0 mil. ⑦ Refl. incr. commodity prices & acqs. ⑧ Incl. environ. remed. chrgs. of $109.0 mil. & aft.-tax non-recur. loss of $272.0 mil.; bef. extraord. loss of $8.0 mil. & acctg. chrg. of $24.0 mil. ⑨ Incl. environ. remed. chrgs. of $23.0 mil. & gain of $164.0 mil. on sale of Equistar invest.; bef. disc. ops. loss of $79.0 mill. & acctg. chg. chrg. of $95.0 mill. ⑩ Refl. adoption of certain prov. of Emerging Issues Task Force Issue No. 02-3. As a result, OXY now refl. rev. fr. trading activs. on a net basis.

OFFICERS:
R. R. Irani, Chmn., C.E.O.
D. R. Laurance, Pres.
S. I. Chazen, Exec. V.P., C.F.O.

INVESTOR CONTACT: Kenneth J. Huffman, Investor Relations, (212) 603-8111

PRINCIPAL OFFICE: 10889 Wilshire Boulevard, Los Angeles, CA 90024

TELEPHONE NUMBER: (310) 208-8800
FAX: (310) 443-6690
WEB: www.oxy.com
NO. OF EMPLOYEES: 8,235 (avg.)
SHAREHOLDERS: 59,853 (approx.)
ANNUAL MEETING: In May
INCORPORATED: DE, Apr., 1986

INSTITUTIONAL HOLDINGS:
No. of Institutions: 385
Shares Held: 299,564,205
% Held: 79.5

INDUSTRY: Crude petroleum and natural gas (SIC: 1311)

TRANSFER AGENT(S): Mellon Investor Services, Ridgefield Park, NJ

OCEAN ENERGY, INC.

EXCH.	SYM.	REC. PRICE	P/E RATIO	YLD.	MKT. CAP.	RANGE (52-WK.)	'02 Y/E PR.
NYSE	OEI	20.07 (2/28/03)	25.7	0.8%	$3.46 bill.	22.85 - 15.80	19.97

MEDIUM GRADE. THE COMPANY HAS ENTERED INTO AN AGREEMENT TO BE ACQUIRED BY DEVON ENERGY CORPORATION.

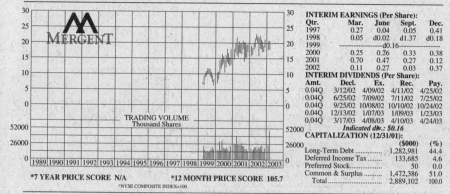

*7 YEAR PRICE SCORE N/A   *12 MONTH PRICE SCORE 105.7
*NYSE COMPOSITE INDEX=100

INTERIM EARNINGS (Per Share):

Qtr.	Mar.	June	Sept.	Dec.
1997	0.27	0.04	0.05	0.41
1998	0.05	d0.02	d1.37	d0.18
1999	---------------d0.16---------------			
2000	0.25	0.26	0.33	0.38
2001	0.70	0.47	0.27	0.12
2002	0.11	0.27	0.03	0.37

INTERIM DIVIDENDS (Per Share):

Amt.	Decl.	Ex.	Rec.	Pay.
0.04Q	3/12/02	4/09/02	4/11/02	4/25/02
0.04Q	6/25/02	7/09/02	7/11/02	7/25/02
0.04Q	9/25/02	10/08/02	10/10/02	10/24/02
0.04Q	12/13/02	1/07/03	1/09/03	1/23/03
0.04Q	3/17/03	4/08/03	4/10/03	4/24/03

Indicated div.: $0.16

CAPITALIZATION (12/31/01):

	($000)	(%)
Long-Term Debt	1,282,981	44.4
Deferred Income Tax	133,685	4.6
Preferred Stock	50	0.0
Common & Surplus	1,472,386	51.0
Total	2,889,102	100.0

BUSINESS:

Ocean Energy, Inc. is an independent oil and gas exploration and production company. The Company's North American operations include the shelf and deepwater areas of the Gulf of Mexico, the Rocky Mountains, Permian Basin, Anadarko, East Texas, North Louisiana and the Gulf Coast regions. Internationally, OEI holds a major position among U.S. independents in West Africa with oil and gas activities in Equatorial Guinea, Angola and Cote d'Ivoire. The Company also conducts operations in Egypt, Tatarstan, Brazil, and Indonesia. As of 12/31/01, total estimated proved reserves were 601.0 million barrels of oil equivalent. On 3/30/99, the Company acquired Seagull Energy Corp.

RECENT DEVELOPMENTS:

For the year ended 12/31/02, net income was $135.2 million compared with $273.8 million a year earlier. Results included and an impairment of oil and gas properties charge of $76.4 million. Revenues declined 7.4% to $1.16 billion from $1.26 billion the previous year. Average daily production was 82,000 barrels of oil, up 9.3% from the prior year, and 426.0 million cubic feet of natural gas, 3.8% lower than the year before.

PROSPECTS:

On 2/24/03, OEI and Devon Energy Corporation announced an agreement under which Devon will acquire OEI. Under the terms of the agreement, the Company's shareholders will receive 0.414 shares of Devon common stock for each common share of OEI. The aggregate value of the transaction, including the assumption of OEI's debt and other obligations, is approximately $5.30 billion. Completion of the transaction is expected in the second or third quarter of 2003. The combined company, expected to be named Devon Energy Corporation, will have approximately 2.20 billion barrels of oil equivalent proved reserves, with 84.0% in North America. 90.0% of Devon's worldwide production will be from North America, of which 69.0% will be natural gas.

ANNUAL FINANCIAL DATA:

FISCAL YEAR	TOT. REVS. ($mill.)	NET INC. ($mill.)	TOT. ASSETS ($mill.)	OPER. PROFIT %	NET PROFIT %	RET. ON EQUITY %	RET. ON ASSETS %	CURR. RATIO	EARN. PER SH.$	CASH FL. PER SH.$	TANG. BK. VAL.$	DIV. PER SH.$	PRICE RANGE	AVG. P/E RATIO	AVG. YIELD %
p12/31/02	1,162.1	⑤ 135.2							⑤ 0.74			0.16	22.85 - 15.80	26.1	0.8
12/31/01	1,255.5	④ 277.8	3,469.2	45.2	22.1	18.9	8.0	0.7	④ 1.55	3.50	8.55	0.16	21.72 - 14.00	11.5	0.9
12/31/00	1,073.6	① 213.2	2,890.4	42.5	19.9	18.5	7.4	0.8	① 1.22	2.98	6.89	...	18.13 - 7.00	10.3	...
12/31/99	735.5	①②③ d21.6	2,783.1	18.0	...	...	...	0.8	①②③ d0.16	1.99	5.69	...	11.81 - 6.31	...	...
12/31/98	426.2	③④ d95.7	1,416.1	...	...	...	...	0.7	③④ d1.51	1.20	8.68	...		...	...
12/31/97	549.4	④ 49.1	1,411.1	20.1	8.9	7.6	3.5	1.0	0.77	3.49	10.27	...		...	...
12/31/96	518.6	①④ 29.0	1,515.1	20.3	5.6	4.8	1.9	1.0	①④⑤ 0.45	2.94	9.53	...		...	...
12/31/95	336.3	④ 0.6	1,198.8	...	0.2	0.1	0.1	1.3	④ 0.02	3.63	12.35	...		...	...
12/31/94	408.1	3.2	1,299.6	15.2	0.8	0.7	0.2	0.9	0.09	4.19	12.22	...		...	...
12/31/93	377.2	27.2	1,118.3	20.1	7.2	6.2	2.4	0.9	0.76	4.22	12.19	...		...	...

Statistics are as originally reported. ① Incl. merger expenses, 2000, $3.3 mill.; 1999, $49.6 mill.; 1996, $10.0 mill. ② Bef. inc. fr. disc. opers. of $1.1 mill. ③ Bef. extraord. chrg., 2001, $4.0 mill.; 1999, $23.4 mill.; 1998, $1.0 mill. ④ Incl. net gain on sale of assets, 1998, $127,000; 1997, $11.3 mill.; 1996, $1.1 mill.; 1995, $83.6 mill. ⑤ Incl. impairment chrg. of $76.4 mill.

OFFICERS:
J. T. Hackett, Chmn., Pres., C.E.O.
W. L. Transier, Exec. V.P., C.F.O.
R. K. Reeves, Exec. V.P., Sec., Gen. Couns.

INVESTOR CONTACT: Bruce Busmire, (713) 265-6161

PRINCIPAL OFFICE: 1001 Fannin Street, Suite 1600, Houston, TX 77002-6794

TELEPHONE NUMBER: (713) 265-6000
FAX: (713) 265-8001
WEB: www.oceanenergy.com
NO. OF EMPLOYEES: 1,100
SHAREHOLDERS: 2,898 (approx.)
ANNUAL MEETING: In May
INCORPORATED: TX, 1973; reincorp., DE, May, 2001

INSTITUTIONAL HOLDINGS:
No. of Institutions: 305
Shares Held: 146,754,604
% Held: 83.2

INDUSTRY: Gas transmission and distribution (SIC: 4923)

TRANSFER AGENT(S): EquiServe Trust, Providence, RI

OFFICE DEPOT, INC.

EXCH.	SYM.	REC. PRICE	P/E RATIO	YLD.	MKT. CAP.	RANGE (52-WK.)	'02 Y/E PR.
NYSE	ODP	11.74 (2/28/03)	12.0	...	$3.62 bill.	21.96 - 10.60	14.76

UPPER MEDIUM GRADE. THE COMPANY PLANS TO OPEN ITS FIRST RETAIL STORES IN SPAIN IN APRIL 2003.

*7 YEAR PRICE SCORE 116.4   ***12 MONTH PRICE SCORE 92.6**

*NYSE COMPOSITE INDEX=100

INTERIM EARNINGS (Per Share):

Qtr.	Mar.	June	Sept.	Dec.
1995	0.14	0.12	0.16	0.15
1996	0.14	0.12	0.13	0.15
1997	0.16	0.13	0.18	0.19
1998	0.22	0.18	0.04	0.18
1999	0.25	0.19	Nil	0.24
2000	0.32	0.18	0.16	d0.57
2001	0.19	0.14	0.20	0.13
2002	0.32	0.18	0.27	0.21

INTERIM DIVIDENDS (Per Share):

Amt.	Decl.	Ex.	Rec.	Pay.
		No dividends paid.		

CAPITALIZATION (12/29/01):

	($000)	(%)
Long-Term Debt	317,552	14.7
Common & Surplus	1,848,438	85.3
Total	2,165,990	100.0

BUSINESS:

Office Depot, Inc. operates the largest chain of high-volume retail office supply stores in the U.S. ODP's stores utilize a warehouse format and carry large inventories of merchandise. Products include general office supplies, business machines, business supplies, computers and accessories, and office furniture. As of 12/28/02, ODP operated 867 stores in the United States and Canada, in addition to a national business-to-business delivery network supported by 24 delivery centers, more than 60 local sales offices and thirteen regional call centers. In addition, ODP sells products and services in 20 countries outside the U.S. and Canada, including 37 stores in France and thirteen in Japan that are owned and operated by the Company. The Company also operates 121 stores under joint venture and licensing agreements in seven foreign countries. On 8/26/98, ODP acquired Viking Office Products, Inc.

RECENT DEVELOPMENTS:

For the 52 weeks ended 12/28/02, earnings from continuing operations totaled $311.5 million, up 54.5% compared with earnings from continuing operations of $201.7 million in the corresponding prior-year period. Sales grew 2.5% to $11.36 billion from $11.08 billion a year earlier. Comparable-store sales were essentially flat in 2002. Gross profit climbed 6.1% to $3.33 billion, or 29.4% of sales, from $3.14 billion, or 28.4% of sales, the previous year. Operating profit advanced 41.4% to $499.7 million from $353.4 million the year before. In 2002, ODP opened 21 new stores in North America, relocated eight existing stores, and closed 13 under-performing stores. The Company also opened 28 net new stores outside North America during 2002.

PROSPECTS:

The Company anticipates full-year 2003 earnings per share growth of between 5.0% and 10.0%. In 2003, ODP plans to open approximately 40 new retail stores in North America, along with five to ten new retail stores in France and Japan. In addition, the Company plans to open its first retail stores in Spain in April 2003, with six new stores opening in Madrid and the surrounding area by mid 2003. Separately, on 1/6/03, ODP announced that it has completed the sale of its Viking Office Products Inc. operations in Australia to Officeworks Superstores Pty, Ltd.

ANNUAL FINANCIAL DATA:

FISCAL YEAR	TOT. REVS. ($mill.)	NET INC. ($mill.)	TOT. ASSETS ($mill.)	OPER. PROFIT %	NET PROFIT %	RET. ON EQUITY %	RET. ON ASSETS %	CURR. RATIO	EARN. PER SH.$	CASH FL. PER SH.$	TANG. BK. VAL.$	PRICE RANGE	AVG. P/E RATIO
p12/28/02	11,356.6	①311.5							②0.98			21.96 - 10.60	16.6
12/29/01	11,154.1	①201.0	4,331.6	3.2	1.8	10.9	4.6	1.3	②0.66	1.27	5.28	18.70 - 7.13	19.6
12/30/00	11,569.7	③49.3	4,196.3	1.0	0.4	3.1	1.2	1.4	③0.16	0.82	4.66	14.88 - 5.88	64.8
12/25/99	10,263.3	②257.6	4,276.2	4.0	2.5	13.5	6.0	1.4	②0.69	1.08	5.06	26.00 - 9.00	25.4
12/26/98	8,997.7	②233.2	4,113.0	4.4	2.6	11.5	5.7	1.8	②0.61	0.93	4.86	24.83 - 10.58	29.2
12/27/97	6,717.5	②159.7	2,981.1	4.5	2.4	12.0	5.4	1.8	②0.65	1.07	4.82	16.00 - 8.42	18.9
12/28/96	6,068.6	129.0	2,740.3	3.9	2.1	11.2	4.7	1.6	0.54	0.89	4.09	17.08 - 8.58	23.8
12/30/95	5,313.2	132.4	2,531.2	4.6	2.5	13.2	5.2	1.7	0.57	0.85	3.46	21.42 - 12.67	30.1
12/31/94	4,266.2	105.0	1,904.0	4.5	2.5	14.7	5.5	1.6	0.46	0.68	2.30	18.00 - 12.58	33.2
12/25/93	2,579.5	63.4	1,463.9	4.4	2.5	11.4	4.3	1.8	0.30	0.44	1.67	15.95 - 7.93	40.0

Statistics are as originally reported. Adj. for 3-for-2 stk. split, 4/99 & 6/94. ① Bef. $775,000 loss fr. discont. opers. ② Incl. one-time pre-tax chgs. of $49.3 mil, 2001; $33.3 mil, 1999; $119.1 mil pre-tax merger costs, 1998; $16.1 mil, 1997. ③ Incl. $260.6 mil one-time net pre-tax chgs. fr. asset disposals, store closures, severance costs and restructuring, and investment write-off.

OFFICERS:
M. B. Nelson, Chmn., C.E.O.
P. B. Morrison, Exec. V.P., Chief Info. Off.
C. Brown, C.F.O.
INVESTOR CONTACT: Eileen H. Dunn, V.P., Inv. Rel., (561) 438-4930
PRINCIPAL OFFICE: 2200 Old Germantown Road, Delray Beach, FL 33445

TELEPHONE NUMBER: (561) 438-4800
FAX: (561) 265-4406
WEB: www.officedepot.com
NO. OF EMPLOYEES: 45,000 (approx.)
SHAREHOLDERS: 3,872
ANNUAL MEETING: In Apr.
INCORPORATED: FL, Mar., 1986; reincorp., DE, Sept., 1986

INSTITUTIONAL HOLDINGS:
No. of Institutions: 342
Shares Held: 245,169,999
% Held: 79.5

INDUSTRY: Office equipment (SIC: 5044)

TRANSFER AGENT(S): Mellon Investor Services, Ridgefield Park, NJ

OFFICEMAX, INC.

EXCH.	SYM.	REC. PRICE	P/E RATIO	YLD.	MKT. CAP.	RANGE (52-WK.)	'02 Y/E PR.
NYSE	OMX	4.79 (2/28/03)	8.1	...	$0.64 bill.	8.06 - 3.05	5.00

LOWER MEDIUM GRADE. THE COMPANY IS TARGETING FISCAL-2003 EARNINGS OF BETWEEN $0.28 AND $0.30 PER SHARE.

TRADING VOLUME
Thousand Shares

*7 YEAR PRICE SCORE 60.9   *12 MONTH PRICE SCORE 98.4
*NYSE COMPOSITE INDEX=100

INTERIM EARNINGS (Per Share):

Qtr.	Apr.	July	Oct.	Jan.
1996-97	0.10	0.02	0.19	0.24
1997-98	0.13	0.02	0.25	0.32
1998-99	0.15	0.02	0.27	d0.06
1999-00	0.19	d0.22	d0.33	0.20
2000-01	d0.02	d0.22	d0.20	d0.76
2001-02	d0.15	d0.22	d0.23	d1.95
2002-03	0.51	d0.27	0.13	0.22

INTERIM DIVIDENDS (Per Share):

Amt.	Decl.	Ex.	Rec.	Pay.
	No dividends paid.			

CAPITALIZATION (1/26/02):

	($000)	(%)
Long-Term Debt	1,530	0.2
Common & Surplus	705,949	99.8
Total	707,479	100.0

BUSINESS:

OfficeMax, Inc. operated about 1,000 office product superstores in 49 states, Puerto Rico and the U.S. Virgin Islands as of 3/4/03, as well as a joint venture partnership in Mexico. In addition, the Company operates three distribution facilities, 18 delivery centers and two national call centers. The typical superstore is approximately 20,000 to 23,500 square feet and features CopyMax and FurnitureMax, in-store modules devoted exclusively to print-for-pay services and office furniture. Additionally, the Company also offers more than 40,000 items through its e-commerce site, OfficeMax.com, its direct-mail catalogs and its outside sales force.

RECENT DEVELOPMENTS:

For the 52 weeks ended 1/25/03, net income totaled $73.7 million compared with a net loss of $309.5 million a year earlier. Results for the recent period included a pre-tax charge of $2.5 million for store closures and asset impairment. Results for 2001 included one-time pre-tax charges totaling $260.9 million. Sales rose 3.2% to $4.78 billion from $4.63 billion the previous year. Comparable-store sales were up 3.0% year over year. Gross profit climbed 10.2% to $1.20 billion, or 25.1% of sales, from $1.09 billion, or 23.5% of sales, the year before. Operating income was $24.6 million compared with an operating loss of $201.9 million in the prior year.

PROSPECTS:

The Company anticipates full fiscal-2003 sales of more than $5.00 billion, comparable-store sales growth in the mid single-digit range, and earnings of between $0.28 and $0.30 per share. Meanwhile, results are being positively affected by the development and installation of supply chain management and computer systems, increased training for OMX's sales staff, and a more focused marketing program. Separately, the Company is shifting its focus from expanding its store base to remodeling existing stores. OMX anticipates remodeling more than 250 locations during the current fiscal year.

ANNUAL FINANCIAL DATA:

FISCAL YEAR	TOT. REVS. ($mil.)	NET INC. ($mil.)	TOT. ASSETS ($mil.)	OPER. PROFIT %	NET PROFIT %	RET. ON EQUITY %	RET. ON ASSETS %	CURR. RATIO	EARN. PER SH. $	CASH FL. PER SH. $	TANG. BK. VAL. $	PRICE RANGE	AVG. P/E RATIO
p1/25/03	4,775.6	⑥ 73.7							⑥ 0.59			8.06 - 3.05	9.4
1/26/02	4,636.0	⑤ d309.5	1,755.0	...	...	...	...	1.3	⑤ d2.72	d1.79	3.09	4.95 - 2.50	...
1/27/01	5,156.4	④ d133.2	2,293.3	...	...	...	...	1.4	④ d1.20	d0.28	5.46	7.63 - 1.50	...
1/22/00	4,842.7	③ 10.0	2,275.0	0.7	0.2	0.9	0.4	1.4	③ 0.09	0.87	7.18	12.50 - 4.44	94.0
1/23/99	4,337.8	② 48.6	2,231.9	2.0	1.1	4.3	2.2	1.5	② 0.39	0.99	7.05	19.63 - 6.63	33.6
1/24/98	3,765.4	89.6	1,906.0	3.9	2.4	7.7	4.7	1.8	0.72	1.25	6.73	16.31 - 9.88	18.2
1/25/97	3,179.3	68.8	1,867.3	3.3	2.2	6.5	3.7	1.7	0.55	0.96	5.90	19.25 - 10.13	26.7
1/27/96	2,542.5	① 125.8	1,587.9	3.4	4.9	12.7	7.9	1.9	① 1.04	1.38	5.25	17.67 - 9.72	13.2
1/21/95	1,841.2	30.4	1,257.5	3.0	1.6	4.1	2.4	1.4	0.27	0.57	3.45	11.78 - 9.61	40.0
1/22/94	1,421.8	10.8	1,009.7	1.4	0.8	1.8	1.1	1.3	0.09	0.33	4.69	...	...

Statistics are as originally reported. Adj. for 3-for-2 stk. split, 7/96 & 7/95. ① Incl. $69.1 mil ($0.57/sh) gain from sale of Corporate Express, Inc. ② Incl. $80.0 mil ($0.41/sh) one-time chg. from realignment of Computer Business Segment. ③ Incl. $77.4 mil pre-tax inventory markdown chg. ④ Incl. $117.8 mil pre-tax chg. for store closings, asset impairments and inventory liquidations & a $19.5 mil pre-tax litigation chg. ⑤ Incl. $80.4 mil pre-tax chg. for store closings, asset impairments and inventory liquidations & a $165.2 mil pre-tax chg. for deferred tax assets. ⑥ Incl. $2.5 mil pre-tax chg. for store closings and asset impairments.

OFFICERS:
M. Feuer, Chmn., C.E.O.
G. J. Peterson, Pres., C.O.O.
M. F. Killeen, Sr. Exec. V.P., C.F.O.

INVESTOR CONTACT: M. W. Weisbarth,
Div. V.P., Inv. Rel., (216) 295-6698

PRINCIPAL OFFICE: 3605 Warrensville
Center Road, Shaker Heights, OH 44122

TELEPHONE NUMBER: (216) 471-6900
FAX: (216) 471-4040
WEB: www.officemax.com

NO. OF EMPLOYEES: 16,500 full-time
(approx.); 14,000 part-time (approx.)
SHAREHOLDERS: 3,837 (approx.)
ANNUAL MEETING: In May
INCORPORATED: OH, July, 1988

INSTITUTIONAL HOLDINGS:
No. of Institutions: 142
Shares Held: 74,653,096
% Held: 60.1

INDUSTRY: Stationery stores (SIC: 5943)

TRANSFER AGENT(S): EquiServe, Jersey
City, NJ

OGE ENERGY CORP.

EXCH.	SYM.	REC. PRICE	P/E RATIO	YLD.	MKT. CAP.	RANGE (52-WK.)	'02 Y/E PR.
NYSE	OGE	17.37 (2/28/03)	15.8	7.7%	$1.35 bill.	24.24 - 13.70	17.60

MEDIUM GRADE. THE COMPANY EXPECTS FULL-YEAR 2003 EARNINGS TO RANGE BETWEEN $1.35 AND $1.45 PER SHARE.

*7 YEAR PRICE SCORE 93.0   *12 MONTH PRICE SCORE 97.6

*NYSE COMPOSITE INDEX=100

INTERIM EARNINGS (Per Share):

Qtr.	Mar.	June	Sept.	Dec.
1997	d0.11	0.76	2.20	0.29
1998	d0.03	0.59	1.33	0.13
1999	0.14	0.49	1.16	0.16
2000	0.01	0.41	1.38	0.09
2001	d0.19	0.32	1.25	d0.09
2002	d0.08	0.36	1.24	d0.42

INTERIM DIVIDENDS (Per Share):

Amt.	Decl.	Ex.	Rec.	Pay.
0.333Q	3/20/02	4/08/02	4/10/02	4/30/02
0.333Q	5/16/02	7/08/02	7/10/02	7/30/02
0.333Q	9/18/02	10/08/02	10/10/02	10/30/02
0.333Q	11/20/02	1/08/03	1/10/03	1/30/03
0.333Q	3/26/03	4/08/03	4/10/03	4/30/03

Indicated div.: $1.33 (Div. Reinv. Plan)

CAPITALIZATION (12/31/01):

	($000)	(%)
Long-Term Debt	1,526,303	47.7
Deferred Income Tax	634,946	19.8
Common & Surplus	1,040,569	32.5
Total	3,201,818	100.0

BUSINESS:

OGE Energy Corp. (formerly Oklahoma Gas & Electric Company) is an energy services provider that operates through electric utility and energy supply business segments. The operations of the electric utility segment are conducted through Oklahoma Gas and Electric Company (OG&E), which has 718,513 retail customers in Oklahoma and western Arkansas, as of 12/31/02. Electricity comes from eight OGE-owned power plants that are either coal or natural gas-fired, plus some purchased power. Power is delivered across an interconnected transmission and distribution system that spans 30,000 square miles. Enogex Inc., handles OGE's gas production, gathering, transportation, processing and energy marketing business, with interest in about 9,700 miles of pipeline and 11 gas processing plants, as of 12/31/01. On 7/1/99, OGE acquired Tejas Transok Holdings, L.L.C., for $701.3 million.

RECENT DEVELOPMENTS:

For the twelve months ended 12/31/02, income from continuing operations was $81.0 million compared with income of $93.9 million a year earlier. Results for 2002 included a charge of $50.1 million for the impairment of assets. Results for 2002 and 2001 excluded income of $9.8 million and $6.7 million, respectively, from discontinued operations. Operating revenues slipped 1.3% to $3.02 billion from $3.06 billion the previous year. Revenues from the Company's Oklahoma Gas and Electric Company segment decreased 4.7% to $1.39 billion, while Enogex revenues increased 2.1% to $1.68 billion.

PROSPECTS:

On 2/24/03, OGE announced that its Enogex Products Corp. subsidiary has closed the sale of its interest in the NuStar joint venture in Texas to Benedum Gas Partners, L.P. NuStar is engaged in the extraction and sale of natural gas liquids. Proceeds of $37.0 million from the sale will be used to pay down debt in keeping with the Company's focus on reducing leverage and commodity exposure at Enogex. Separately, OGE expects full-year 2003 earnings to range between $1.35 and $1.45 per share, which reflects the rate recent reduction of OG&E and improved results from Enogex.

ANNUAL FINANCIAL DATA:

FISCAL YEAR	TOT. REVS. ($mill.)	NET INC. ($mill.)	TOT. ASSETS ($mill.)	OPER. PROFIT %	NET PROFIT %	NET INC./ NET PROP. %	NET INC./ TOT. CAP. %	RET. ON EQUITY %	ACCUM. DEPR./ GROSS PROP. %	EARN. PER SH.$	TANG. BK. VAL.$	DIV. PER SH.$	DIV. PAYOUT %	PRICE RANGE	AVG. P/E RATIO	AVG. YIELD %
p12/31/02	3,023.9	③ 81.0								③ 1.04		1.33	128.1	24.24 - 13.70	18.2	7.0
12/31/01	3,182.4	100.6	3,996.6	8.7	3.2	3.1	3.1	9.7	41.2	1.29	13.34	1.33	103.1	24.69 - 20.00	17.3	6.0
12/31/00	3,298.7	147.0	4,319.6	10.6	4.5	4.6	4.4	13.8	40.1	1.89	13.66	1.33	70.4	24.75 - 16.50	10.9	6.4
12/31/99	2,172.4	151.3	3,891.3	15.6	7.0	4.7	5.6	15.3	38.4	1.94	12.71	1.33	68.6	29.06 - 18.44	12.2	5.6
12/31/98	1,617.7	165.9	2,983.9	14.3	10.3	6.6	6.6	15.9	43.1	2.04	12.91	1.33	65.2	30.00 - 25.63	13.6	4.8
12/31/97	1,472.3	132.6	2,765.9	13.2	9.0	5.6	5.6	12.8	43.3	1.62	12.19	1.33	82.1	27.31 - 20.25	14.7	5.6
12/31/96	1,200.3	② 116.9	2,421.2	14.8	9.7	5.7	5.8	13.1	43.3	② 1.42	10.41	1.33	93.7	21.81 - 18.44	14.2	6.6
12/31/95	1,302.0	125.3	2,754.9	15.5	9.6	5.3	5.4	12.7	40.4	1.53	11.61	1.33	86.9	21.81 - 16.28	12.5	7.0
12/31/94	1,355.2	① 123.8	2,782.6	14.8	9.1	5.3	5.6	12.7	39.0	① 1.51	11.41	1.33	88.1	18.63 - 14.69	11.1	8.0
12/31/93	1,447.3	114.3	2,731.4	13.5	7.9	4.9	5.0	11.9	37.1	1.39	11.24	1.33	95.7	19.31 - 16.44	12.9	7.4

Statistics are as originally reported. Adj. for stk. split: 2-for-1, 6/98. ① Incl. restr. chrg. $21.0 mill. ② Bef. disc. opers gain $16.5 mill. ③ Incl. impairment of assets chrg. of $50.1 mill.; bef. inc. fr. disc. ops. of $9.8 mill.

OFFICERS:
S. E. Moore, Chmn., Pres., C.E.O.
J. R. Hatfield, Sr. V.P., C.F.O.
E. B. Weekes, Treas.
INVESTOR CONTACT: Jim Hatfield, Sr. V.P., C.F.O., (405) 553-3984
PRINCIPAL OFFICE: 321 North Harvey, Oklahoma City, OK 73101-0321

TELEPHONE NUMBER: (405) 553-3000
FAX: (405) 553-3760
WEB: www.oge.com
NO. OF EMPLOYEES: 3,255 (avg.)
SHAREHOLDERS: 33,748
ANNUAL MEETING: In May
INCORPORATED: OK, Feb., 1902; reincorp., OK, Aug., 1995

INSTITUTIONAL HOLDINGS:
No. of Institutions: 181
Shares Held: 24,004,165
% Held: 30.6
INDUSTRY: Natural gas transmission (SIC: 4922)
TRANSFER AGENT(S): Mellon Investor Services, South Hackensack, NJ

OLD NATIONAL BANCORP

EXCH.	SYM.	REC. PRICE	P/E RATIO	YLD.	MKT. CAP.	RANGE (52-WK.)	'02 Y/E PR.	DIV. ACH.
NYSE	ONB	21.88 (2/28/03)	12.4	3.5%	$1.34 bill.	25.24 - 21.24	23.14	19 yrs.

MEDIUM GRADE. THE AMOUNT OF RESIDENTIAL MORTGAGE LOANS CONTINUES TO INCREASE, REFLECTING HIGH LEVELS OF REFINANCINGS.

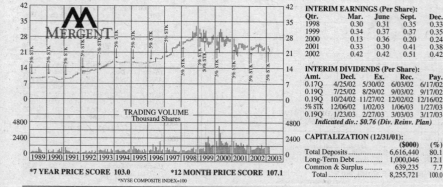

*7 YEAR PRICE SCORE 103.0   ***12 MONTH PRICE SCORE 107.1**
*NYSE COMPOSITE INDEX=100

INTERIM EARNINGS (Per Share):

Qtr.	Mar.	June	Sept.	Dec.
1998	0.30	0.31	0.35	0.33
1999	0.34	0.37	0.37	0.35
2000	0.13	0.36	0.20	0.24
2001	0.33	0.30	0.41	0.38
2002	0.42	0.42	0.51	0.42

INTERIM DIVIDENDS (Per Share):

Amt.	Decl.	Ex.	Rec.	Pay.
0.17Q	4/25/02	5/30/02	6/03/02	6/17/02
0.19Q	7/25/02	8/29/02	9/03/02	9/17/02
0.19Q	10/24/02	11/27/02	12/02/02	12/16/02
5% STK	12/06/02	1/02/03	1/06/03	1/27/03
0.19Q	1/23/03	2/27/03	3/03/03	3/17/03

Indicated div.: $0.76 (Div. Reinv. Plan)

CAPITALIZATION (12/31/01):

	($000)	(%)
Total Deposits	6,616,440	80.1
Long-Term Debt	1,000,046	12.1
Common & Surplus	639,235	7.7
Total	8,255,721	100.0

BUSINESS:

Old National Bancorp, with total assets of $9.61 billion as of 12/31/02, is a financial holding company headquartered in Evansville, Indiana with banking activity in Indiana, Illinois, Kentucky, Missouri, Tennessee, and Ohio. As of 9/30/02, the Company had 252 automatic teller machines and 133 banking offices serving customers in both urban and rural markets. The Company's banking centers provide a wide range of financial services, such as commercial, real estate, and consumer loans; lease financing; checking, savings, time deposits and other depository accounts; letters of credit; cash management services; credit life, accident and health insurance; safe deposit facilities; investments and brokerage products; debit cards and other electronically accessed banking services; and Internet banking. The Company's non-bank affiliates provide additional financial or support services incidental to its operations, including issuance and reinsurance of credit life, accident, health, life, property, and casualty insurance; investment services; fiduciary and trust services; and property ownership.

RECENT DEVELOPMENTS:

For the year ended 12/31/02, net income advanced 26.7% to $117.9 million versus $93.0 million the year before. Earnings for 2002 included an after-tax gain on branch sales of $8.3 million. Earnings for 2001 included an after-tax restructuring charge of $5.9 million. Net interest income grew to $314.6 million from $312.6 million in 2001. Provision for loan losses increased 16.7% to $33.5 million. Total non-interest income climbed 19.8% to $129.6 million, while other expense rose 5.2% to $257.8 million.

PROSPECTS:

Total assets continue to benefit from growth in ONB's investment portfolio due to strong demand for residential mortgage loans, reflecting high levels of refinancings. ONB is also benefiting from the restructuring of its mortgage lending operations, which improved operational efficien-cies and enhanced product development. During 2002, the Company originated $1.10 billion in mortgage loans, generating mortgage revenues of $14.5 million compared with $9.7 million in 2001.

ANNUAL FINANCIAL DATA:

FISCAL YEAR	NET INT. INC. ($mill.)	NON-INT. INC. ($mill.)	NET INC. ($mill.)	TOT. LOANS ($mill.)	TOT. ASSETS ($mill.)	TOT. DEP. ($mill.)	RET. ON EQUITY %	RET. ON ASSETS %	EQUITY/ ASSETS %	EARN. PER SH. $	TANG. BK. VAL. $	DIV. PER SH. $	PRICE RANGE	AVG. P/E RATIO
p12/31/02	314.6	129.6	② 117.9							② 1.71	...	0.69	25.24 - 21.21	13.5
12/31/01	291.3	113.0	① 93.0	6,132.9	9,080.5	6,616.4	14.6	1.0	7.0	① 1.42	9.95	0.62	27.50 - 19.39	16.5
12/31/00	269.9	101.7	① 61.7	6,350.8	8,767.7	6,583.9	9.9	0.7	7.1	① 0.93	9.42	0.59	31.75 - 20.92	28.2
12/31/99	238.4	67.5	82.7	4,841.3	6,982.9	5,071.3	16.8	1.2	7.1	1.44	9.00	0.55	31.82 - 23.43	19.1
12/31/98	214.8	54.6	71.7	4,162.2	6,166.0	4,443.5	14.5	1.2	8.0	1.32	9.46	0.48	32.98 - 24.68	21.8
12/31/97	219.2	47.1	60.7	3,730.2	5,688.2	4,298.7	12.7	1.1	8.4	1.11	9.53	0.46	25.99 - 18.94	20.3
12/31/96	203.8	44.8	60.2	3,523.3	5,366.6	4,268.0	13.1	1.1	8.5	1.10	8.52	0.44	19.53 - 16.23	16.5
12/31/95	181.2	39.2	51.7	3,037.7	4,822.6	3,973.7	12.1	1.1	8.9	0.95	8.13	0.42	17.00 - 15.99	17.4
12/31/94	159.4	32.7	46.0	2,561.1	4,152.1	3,268.9	12.6	1.1	8.8	0.94	7.54	0.40	17.08 - 16.25	17.7
12/31/93	144.1	29.7	42.5	2,172.8	3,714.5	3,045.5	13.5	1.1	8.5	0.91	6.69	0.34	17.08 - 13.20	16.7

Statistics are as originally reported. Adj. for 5% stk. div.: 1/03, 1/02, 1/01; 1/00; 1/98, 1/97, 2/96, and 1/95; 50% div., 5/24/99. ① Incl. after-tax merger and restruct. costs of $5.9 mill., 2001; $25.7 mill., 2000. ② Incl. after-tax gain of $8.3 mill. on branch sales.

OFFICERS:
J. A. Risinger, Chmn., Pres., C.E.O.
J. S. Poelker, Exec. V.P., C.F.O.

INVESTOR CONTACT: Lynell J. Walton, Asst. V.P., (812) 464-1366

PRINCIPAL OFFICE: 420 Main Street, Evansville, IN 47708

TELEPHONE NUMBER: (812) 464-1200
FAX: (812) 464-1567
WEB: www.oldnational.com
NO. OF EMPLOYEES: 3,000 (approx.)
SHAREHOLDERS: 24,838
ANNUAL MEETING: In April
INCORPORATED: IN, June, 1982

INSTITUTIONAL HOLDINGS:
No. of Institutions: 85
Shares Held: 14,808,983
% Held: 24.5
INDUSTRY: National commercial banks (SIC: 6021)
TRANSFER AGENT(S): Old National Bancorp, Evansville, IN

OLD REPUBLIC INTERNATIONAL CORPORATION

EXCH.	SYM.	REC. PRICE	P/E RATIO	YLD.	MKT. CAP.	RANGE (52-WK.)	'02 Y/E PR.	DIV. ACH.
NYSE	ORI	27.30 (2/28/03)	8.5	2.3%	$3.34 bill.	35.00 - 24.40	28.00	21 yrs.

UPPER MEDIUM GRADE. GOING FORWARD, THE COMPANY SHOULD CONTINUE TO BENEFIT FROM ITS DISCI-PLINED UNDERWRITING APPROACH.

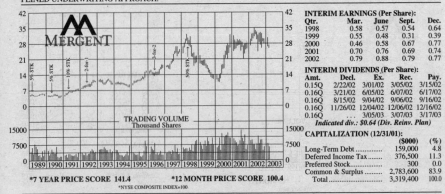

*7 YEAR PRICE SCORE 141.4   ***12 MONTH PRICE SCORE 100.4**

*NYSE COMPOSITE INDEX=100

INTERIM EARNINGS (Per Share):

Qtr.	Mar.	June	Sept.	Dec.
1998	0.58	0.57	0.54	0.64
1999	0.55	0.48	0.31	0.39
2000	0.46	0.58	0.67	0.77
2001	0.70	0.76	0.69	0.74
2002	0.79	0.88	0.77	0.77

INTERIM DIVIDENDS (Per Share):

Amt.	Decl.	Ex.	Rec.	Pay.
0.15Q	2/22/02	3/01/02	3/05/02	3/15/02
0.16Q	3/21/02	6/05/02	6/07/02	6/17/02
0.16Q	8/15/02	9/04/02	9/06/02	9/16/02
0.16Q	11/26/02	12/04/02	12/06/02	12/16/02
0.16Q	...	3/05/03	3/07/03	3/17/03

Indicated div.: $0.64 (Div. Reinv. Plan)

CAPITALIZATION (12/31/01):

	($000)	(%)
Long-Term Debt	159,000	4.8
Deferred Income Tax	376,500	11.3
Preferred Stock	300	0.0
Common & Surplus	2,783,600	83.9
Total	3,319,400	100.0

BUSINESS:

Old Republic International Corporation is a multiple line insurance holding company with assets of approximately $8.71 billion and total capitalization of $3.29 billion as of 1/28/03. The Company's subsidiaries market, underwrite, and manage a wide range of specialty and general insurance programs in the property & liability, title, mortgage guaranty insurance and life & disability businesses. The Company primarily serves the insurance and related needs of major financial services and industrial corporations, with an emphasis on energy services, construction and forest products, transportation and housing industries. In 2002, revenues were derived as follows: general insurance, 50.2%; title insurance, 30.5%; mortgage guaranty, 17.0%; life and health insurance, 2.1% and other, 0.2%.

RECENT DEVELOPMENTS:

For the year ended 12/31/02, net income grew 13.3% to $392.9 million from $346.9 million the previous year. Earnings benefited from greater underwriting and service income in the Company's three largest segments. Results for 2002 included special after-tax charges of $13.8 million. Total revenues increased 16.1% to $2.76 billion from $2.37 billion in the prior year. Revenues for 2002 and 2001 included realized investment gains of $13.9 million and $29.7 million, respectively. On a segment basis, operating income for the general insurance group increased 28.8% to $182.1 million. Operating income in the mortgage guaranty group rose 2.2% to $267.7 million, while operating income for the title insurance group climbed 31.0% to $97.8 million.

PROSPECTS:

On 1/15/03, ORI's wholly-owned subsidiary, Old Republic Insurance Company, reached a definitive agreement to purchase the renewal rights to certain large risk national accounts of the Kemper Insurance Companies. The accounts, which total about $140.0 million in gross premium volume on an annualized basis, are part of ORI's commitment to the large account risk management business. Going forward, the Company will continue to focus on the achievement of underwriting profitability through disaplined pricing and risk selection.

ANNUAL FINANCIAL DATA:

FISCAL YEAR	PREM. INC. ($mill.)	NET INVST. INC. ($mill.)	TOT. REVS. ($mill.)	NET INC. ($mill.)	TOT. ASSETS ($mill.)	TOT. INVST. ($mill.)	RET. ON REVS. %	RET. ON EQUITY %	RET. ON ASSETS %	EARN. PER SH. $	TANG. BK. VAL. $	AVG. YIELD %	DIV. PER SH. $	PRICE RANGE	AVG. P/E RATIO
p12/31/02			2,756.4	③ 392.9						③ 3.23		2.1	0.63	35.00 — 24.40	9.2
12/31/01	1,786.8	274.7	2,373.2	346.9	7,919.8	5,472.9	14.6	12.5	4.4	2.88	22.78	2.2	0.59	31.56 — 21.20	9.2
12/31/00	1,550.3	273.9	2,070.3	297.4	7,280.9	5,038.9	14.4	12.2	4.1	2.47	20.08	2.6	0.55	32.06 — 10.63	8.6
12/31/99	1,567.2	263.2	2,101.9	226.8	6,938.4	4,739.4	10.8	7.4	3.3	1.75	19.65	2.8	0.49	22.75 — 12.06	9.9
12/31/98	1,568.1	273.1	2,171.5	323.8	7,019.7	4,854.2	14.9	14.0	4.6	2.33	17.27	1.5	0.39	32.25 — 17.94	10.8
12/31/97	1,464.6	270.8	1,962.6	297.6	6,922.8	4,720.1	15.2	13.8	4.3	2.10	15.59	1.5	0.33	26.79 — 16.42	10.3
12/31/96	1,360.4	260.5	1,803.6	② 234.6	6,655.7	4,414.0	13.0	12.3	3.5	② 1.64	14.57	1.7	0.28	18.50 — 13.50	9.8
12/31/95	1,251.7	251.9	1,695.7	212.7	6,592.8	4,325.8	12.5	12.8	3.2	1.61	13.58	1.8	0.23	15.78 — 9.33	7.8
12/31/94	1,282.9	227.5	1,678.8	151.2	6,262.5	3,810.7	9.0	10.9	2.4	1.13	11.46	2.2	0.21	10.89 — 8.39	8.5
12/31/93	1,246.0	220.7	1,736.1	① 166.4	6,097.8	3,618.2	9.6	12.6	2.7	① 1.26	10.77	1.8	0.19	12.28 — 9.56	8.7

Statistics are as originally reported. Adj. for stk. splits: 50% div., 5/98; 3-for-2, 5/96; 2-for-1, 5/92. ① Bef. acctg. change credit $8.6 mill. ② Bef. extraord. chrg. $4.4 mill. ③ Incl. spec. after-tax chrg. $13.8 mill.

OFFICERS:
A. C. Zucaro, Chmn., Pres., C.E.O.
J. S. Adams, Sr. V.P., C.F.O., Treas.
S. LeRoy III, Sr. V.P., Gen. Couns., Sec.

INVESTOR CONTACT: A. C. Zucaro, Chmn., Pres. & C.E.O., (312) 346-8100

PRINCIPAL OFFICE: 307 N. Michigan Ave., Chicago, IL 60601

TELEPHONE NUMBER: (312) 346-8100
FAX: (312) 726-0309
WEB: www.oldrepublic.com

NO. OF EMPLOYEES: 6,135 (approx.)

SHAREHOLDERS: 3,120

ANNUAL MEETING: In May

INSTITUTIONAL HOLDINGS:
No. of Institutions: 274
Shares Held: 86,475,193
% Held: 71.7

INDUSTRY: Surety insurance (SIC: 6351)

TRANSFER AGENT(S): EquiServe, Jersey City, NJ

OLIN CORPORATION

EXCH.	SYM.	REC. PRICE	P/E RATIO	YLD.	MKT. CAP.	RANGE (52-WK.)	'02 Y/E PR.
NYSE	OLN	16.50 (2/28/03)	...	4.8%	$0.72 bill.	22.60 - 13.90	15.55

LOWER MEDIUM GRADE. THE COMPANY PLANS TO RECORD A PRE-TAX RESTRUCTURING CHARGE OF $50.0 MILLION IN THE FIRST QUARTER OF 2003.

*7 YEAR PRICE SCORE 68.0   ***12 MONTH PRICE SCORE 98.7**
*NYSE COMPOSITE INDEX=100

INTERIM EARNINGS (Per Share):

Qtr.	Mar.	June	Sept.	Dec.
1998	0.46	0.37	d0.24	0.19
1999	0.05	0.05	0.06	0.20
2000	0.43	0.52	0.52	0.34
2001	0.06	0.15	d0.45	0.02
2002	d0.26	d0.15	d0.02	d0.21

INTERIM DIVIDENDS (Per Share):

Amt.	Decl.	Ex.	Rec.	Pay.
0.20Q	1/31/02	2/07/02	2/11/02	3/11/02
0.20Q	4/25/02	5/08/02	5/10/02	6/10/02
0.20Q	7/25/02	8/07/02	8/09/02	9/10/02
0.20Q	10/31/02	11/06/02	11/11/02	12/10/02
0.20Q	1/30/03	2/06/03	2/10/03	3/10/03

Indicated div.: $0.80 (Div. Reinv. Plan)

CAPITALIZATION (12/31/01):

	($000)	(%)
Long-Term Debt	329,000	49.0
Deferred Income Tax	72,000	10.7
Common & Surplus	271,000	40.3
Total	672,000	100.0

BUSINESS:

Olin Corporation is a manufacturer concentrated in three business segments: chlor alkali products, metals, and winchester. Chlor alkali products include chlorine and caustic soda, sodium hydrosulfite and high strength bleach products. Metals products include copper and copper alloy sheet, strip, welded tube, and fabricated parts. Winchester products include sporting ammunition, canister powder, reloading components, and small caliber military ammunition. Revenues in 2002 were derived: metals, 53.5%; chlor alkali products, 24.7%; and winchester, 21.8%. On 2/8/99, the Company completed the spin-off of Arch Chemicals, Inc.

RECENT DEVELOPMENTS:

For the twelve months ended 12/31/02, the Company reported a net loss of $31.3 million compared with a net loss of $9.5 million in 2001. The loss was primarily due to soft economic conditions, which hampered sales to electronics customers served by OLN's metals business. Results for 2002 and 2001 included losses for non-consolidated affiliates of $7.3 million and $7.6 million, respectively. Results for 2001 also included a restructuring charge of $39.0 million. Sales were $1.30 billion, up 2.4% from $1.27 billion the year before. Sales for the metals segment grew 12.8% to $696.8 million, while sales for the winchester segment climbed 5.3% to $283.7 million. However, sales for the chlor alkali products segment declined 16.4% to $320.8 million.

PROSPECTS:

On 1/10/03, the Company announced that it plans to close its manufacturing plant in Indianapolis, Indiana, which manufactures copper and copper alloy sheet and strip products. Production at the mill will be consolidated within OLN's facility in East Alton, Illinois. As a result of the closure, the Company plans to record a pre-tax restructuring charge of about $50.0 million in the first quarter of 2003. Meanwhile, the Company expects to return to profitability in the first quarter of 2003 with earnings per share of approximately $0.10.

ANNUAL FINANCIAL DATA:

FISCAL YEAR	TOT. REVS. ($mill.)	NET INC. ($mill.)	TOT. ASSETS ($mill.)	OPER. PROFIT %	NET PROFIT %	RET. ON EQUITY %	RET. ON ASSETS %	CURR. RATIO	EARN. PER SH. $	CASH FL. PER SH. $	TANG. BK. VAL. $	DIV. PER SH. $	PRICE RANGE	AVG. P/E RATIO	AVG. YIELD %
p12/31/02	1,301.3	⑦ d31.3	...	...	...	...	...	...	⑦ d0.63	...	...	0.80	22.60 - 13.85	...	4.4
12/31/01	1,271.0	⑥ d9.0	1,219.0	...	...	...	...	1.8	⑥ d0.22	1.79	6.24	0.80	22.75 - 12.05	...	4.6
12/31/00	1,549.0	81.0	1,123.0	9.0	5.2	24.6	7.2	1.9	1.80	3.60	7.48	0.80	23.19 - 14.19	10.4	4.3
12/31/99	1,315.0	⑤ 16.2	1,063.0	3.9	1.3	5.5	1.6	2.0	⑤ 0.36	2.14	6.86	0.90	29.25 - 9.50	53.8	4.6
12/31/98	1,426.0	④ 38.0	1,577.0	9.3	2.7	4.8	2.4	1.8	④ 0.79	2.43	17.21	1.20	49.31 - 23.88	46.3	3.3
12/31/97	2,410.0	153.0	1,946.0	9.5	6.3	17.4	7.9	1.8	3.00	5.45	18.01	1.20	51.38 - 35.38	14.5	2.8
12/31/96	2,638.0	①② 288.0	2,339.0	9.8	10.9	30.4	12.3	1.6	①② 5.52	8.30	18.12	1.20	48.00 - 34.88	7.5	2.9
12/31/95	3,150.0	140.0	2,272.0	7.8	4.4	16.6	6.2	1.4	2.75	5.75	12.86	1.20	38.56 - 24.19	11.4	3.8
12/31/94	2,658.0	91.0	2,047.0	6.3	3.4	12.1	4.5	1.4	1.83	4.87	12.52	1.10	30.06 - 23.00	14.5	4.1
12/31/93	2,423.0	③ d92.0	1,930.0	...	...	...	...	1.2	③ d2.26	0.91	10.18	1.10	25.25 - 19.94	...	4.9

Statistics are as originally reported. Adj. for 2-for-1 split, 10/96. ① Incl. $115.3 mill. ($2.20/sh.) after-tax gain on sale of TDI & ADI isocyanates bus. ② Bef. $7.9 mill. ($0.18/sh.) loss fr. disc. ops. ③ Incl. $131.7 mill. restr. chg. ④ Incl. $26.2 mill. after-tax chg. on sale of bus. & restr. chgs., $15.4 mill. after-tax non-recur. chg. for spin-off of Arch Chemicals, Inc., & excl. $40.0 mill. after-tax income fr. disc. ops. ⑤ Excl. $4.4 mill. income fr. disc. ops. ⑥ Incl. $39.0 mill. restr. chg. ⑦ Incl. $7.3 mill. loss of non-consol. affiliates.

OFFICERS:
D. W. Griffin, Chmn.
J. D. Rupp, Pres., C.E.O.
A. Ruggiero, Exec. V.P., C.F.O.

INVESTOR CONTACT: Richard E. Koch,
V.P., Investor Relations, (203) 750-3254

PRINCIPAL OFFICE: 501 Merritt 7, Norwalk, CT 06856

TELEPHONE NUMBER: (203) 750-3000
FAX: (203) 750-3205
WEB: www.olin.com

NO. OF EMPLOYEES: 5,900 (approx.)

SHAREHOLDERS: 7,500 (approx.)

ANNUAL MEETING: In Apr.

INCORPORATED: VA, Aug., 1892

INSTITUTIONAL HOLDINGS:
No. of Institutions: 168
Shares Held: 39,154,242
% Held: 68.3

INDUSTRY: Alkalies and chlorine (SIC: 2812)

TRANSFER AGENT(S): Mellon Investor Services, Ridgefield Park, NJ

OM GROUP, INC.

EXCH.	SYM.	REC. PRICE	P/E RATIO	YLD.	MKT. CAP.	RANGE (52-WK.)	'02 Y/E PR.
NYSE	OMG	8.46 (2/28/03)	...	...	$204.2 mill.	73.70 - 4.00	6.88

LOWER MEDIUM GRADE. THE COMPANY ANNOUNCED A RESTRUCTURING PROGRAM DESIGNED TO IMPROVE CASH FLOW AND STRENGTHEN ITS BALANCE SHEET.

TRADING VOLUME
Thousand Shares

1989 1990 1991 1992 1993 1994 1995 1996 1997 1998 1999 2000 2001 2002 2003

*7 YEAR PRICE SCORE 103.7   ***12 MONTH PRICE SCORE 22.5**

*NYSE COMPOSITE INDEX=100

INTERIM EARNINGS (Per Share):

Qtr.	Mar.	June	Sept.	Dec.
1998	----	2.05	----	
1999	0.54	0.58	0.59	0.60
2000	0.63	0.76	0.77	0.79
2001	0.81	0.83	0.84	0.81
2002	0.85	0.89	d2.52	d6.53

INTERIM DIVIDENDS (Per Share):

Amt.	Decl.	Ex.	Rec.	Pay.
0.13Q	8/06/01	8/15/01	8/17/01	8/31/01
0.13Q	11/05/01	11/14/01	11/17/01	11/30/01
0.14Q	2/11/02	2/19/02	2/21/02	2/28/02
0.14Q	4/12/02	5/15/02	5/17/02	5/31/02
0.14Q	8/05/02	8/14/02	8/16/02	8/30/02

Dividend payment suspended.

CAPITALIZATION (12/31/01):

	($000)	(%)
Long-Term Debt	1,300,507	64.4
Deferred Income Tax	76,366	3.8
Minority Interest	74,564	3.7
Common & Surplus	569,533	28.2
Total	2,020,970	100.0

BUSINESS:

OM Group, Inc. is an international producer and marketer of value-added, metal-based specialty chemicals. The Company supplies customers in 50 countries with more than 3,000 product offerings, primarily organics, inorganics, powders and metals. The Company's organic, inorganic and powder products serve more than 30 large industries, including aerospace, appliance, automotive, catalysts, ceramics, coatings, electronics, fuel cells, hard metal tools, magnetic tapes, petrochemical, plastics, rechargeable batteries, rubber, stainless steel and other specialty chemicals. The Company operates manufacturing facilities in North America, Europe, Asia, Africa and Australia. Revenues for 2001 were derived: base metal chemistry, 33.5%; precious metal chemistry, 24.7%; and metal management, 41.8%.

RECENT DEVELOPMENTS:

For the twelve months ended 12/31/02, loss from continuing operations was $198.3 million versus income of $90.4 million, before an extraordinary loss of $4.6 million, in 2001. Results for 2002 included a write-down of inventories of $108.2 million and restructuring and other unusual charges of $162.7 million. Results for 2002 and 2001 excluded losses of $129.6 million and $10.2 million, respectively, from discontinued operations. Net sales more than doubled to $4.91 billion from $2.24 billion, primarily due to the acquisition of the precious metals business of dmc2 in August 2001.

PROSPECTS:

The Company recently initiated a restructuring program designed to improve cash flow and strengthen its balance sheet. The program includes generating up to $100.0 million from the sale of non-core assets; reducing workforce expenses by approximately $35.0 million in 2003, or by approximately $45.0 million on an annualized basis beginning in 2004; and lowering manufacturing and administra- tive costs by about $30.0 million in 2003, or by about $40.0 million on an annualized basis starting in 2004. As a result of the program, the Company incurred a restructuring charge of approximately $335.0 million in the fourth quarter of 2002. Looking ahead, the Company expects sales for 2003 to range from $5.00 billion to $5.20 billion.

ANNUAL FINANCIAL DATA:

FISCAL YEAR	TOT. REVS. ($mill.)	NET INC. ($mill.)	TOT. ASSETS ($mill.)	OPER. PROFIT %	NET PROFIT %	RET. ON EQUITY %	RET. ON ASSETS %	CURR. RATIO	EARN. PER SH.$	CASH FL.PER SH.$	TANG. BK. VAL.$	DIV. PER SH.$	PRICE RANGE		AVG. P/E RATIO	AVG. YIELD %
p12/31/02	4,909.4	③ d198.3							③ d7.07			0.42	73.70 -	4.00	...	1.1
12/31/01	② 2,367.4	① 80.2	2,541.2	7.1	3.4	14.1	3.2	3.4	① 3.28	5.87	14.76	0.52	67.00 -	46.25	17.3	0.9
12/31/00	887.7	71.5	1,357.5	15.6	8.1	14.1	5.3	3.0	2.95	4.57	13.17	0.44	57.00 -	33.75	15.4	1.0
12/31/99	507.0	55.8	1,017.9	19.5	11.0	12.4	5.5	4.0	2.30	3.40	11.15	0.40	42.50 -	26.50	15.0	1.2
12/31/98	521.2	48.4	870.7	16.7	9.3	12.0	5.6	3.5	2.05	3.13	9.09	0.36	46.00 -	25.00	17.3	1.0
12/31/97	487.3	38.4	601.1	14.5	7.9	12.8	6.4	3.2	1.78	2.76	8.36	0.32	42.06 -	25.00	18.8	1.0
12/31/96	388.0	30.0	438.6	13.3	7.7	16.2	6.9	2.8	1.56	2.38	8.72	0.29	28.75 -	21.67	16.2	1.2
12/31/95	361.0	25.9	358.0	12.2	7.2	16.1	7.2	2.7	1.36	2.07	7.39	0.24	22.33 -	14.50	13.5	1.3
12/31/94	251.3	20.7	278.0	14.0	8.3	14.7	7.5	2.1	1.11	1.64	6.50	0.19	16.50 -	12.50	13.1	1.3
12/31/93	179.5	15.4	217.3	14.0	8.6	12.3	7.1	3.1	0.95	1.55	5.55	...	14.00 -	9.33	12.2	...

Statistics are as originally reported. ① Excl. $4.6 mill. extraord. chg. ② Reflects acq. of Degussa Metals Catalysts Cerdec in 8/01. ③ Incl. $108.2 mill. write-down of inventories & excl. $129.6 mill. loss fr. disc. ops.

OFFICERS:
J. P. Mooney, Chmn., C.E.O.
T. R. Miklich, C.F.O.
M. J. Scott, V.P., Sec., Gen. Couns., C.A.O.
INVESTOR CONTACT: Investor Relations, (216) 781-0083
PRINCIPAL OFFICE: 50 Public Square, Suite 3500, Cleveland, OH 44113

TELEPHONE NUMBER: (216) 781-0083
FAX: (216) 781-1502
WEB: www.omgi.com
NO. OF EMPLOYEES: 5,210
SHAREHOLDERS: 11,000 (approx.)
ANNUAL MEETING: In May
INCORPORATED: DE, 1991

INSTITUTIONAL HOLDINGS:
No. of Institutions: 117
Shares Held: 15,036,550
% Held: 53.4
INDUSTRY: Industrial inorganic chemicals, nec (SIC: 2819)
TRANSFER AGENT(S): National City Bank, Cleveland, OH

OMNICARE, INC.

EXCH.	SYM.	REC. PRICE	P/E RATIO	YLD.	MKT. CAP.	RANGE (52-WK.)	'02 Y/E PR.
NYSE	OCR	25.28 (2/28/03)	19.0	0.4%	$2.39 bill.	28.83 - 17.51	23.83

MEDIUM GRADE. ON 1/18/03, THE COMPANY ANNOUNCED THAT IT COMPLETED THE ACQUISITION OF NCS HEALTHCARE, INC. IN A TRANSACTION VALUED AT APPROXIMATELY $460.0 MILLION.

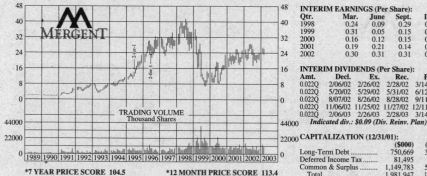

*7 YEAR PRICE SCORE 104.5   ***12 MONTH PRICE SCORE 113.4**
NYSE COMPOSITE INDEX=100

INTERIM EARNINGS (Per Share):

Qtr.	Mar.	June	Sept.	Dec.
1998	0.24	0.09	0.29	0.29
1999	0.31	0.05	0.15	0.12
2000	0.16	0.12	0.15	0.11
2001	0.19	0.21	0.14	0.25
2002	0.30	0.31	0.31	0.41

INTERIM DIVIDENDS (Per Share):

Amt.	Decl.	Ex.	Rec.	Pay.
0.022Q	2/06/02	2/26/02	2/28/02	3/14/02
0.022Q	5/20/02	5/29/02	5/31/02	6/12/02
0.022Q	8/07/02	8/26/02	8/28/02	9/11/02
0.022Q	11/06/02	11/25/02	11/27/02	12/11/02
0.022Q	2/06/03	2/26/03	2/28/03	3/14/03

Indicated div.: $0.09 (Div. Reinv. Plan)

CAPITALIZATION (12/31/01):

	($000)	(%)
Long-Term Debt	750,669	37.9
Deferred Income Tax	81,495	4.1
Common & Surplus	1,149,783	58.0
Total	1,981,947	100.0

BUSINESS:

Omnicare, Inc. is a provider of pharmacy services to long-term care institutions such as skilled nursing facilities, assisted living communities and other institutional health care facilities. OCR purchases, repackages and dispenses pharmaceuticals, both prescription and non-prescription, and provides computerized medical record-keeping and third-party billing for residents in such facilities. OCR also provides consultant pharmacist services, including evaluating residents' drug therapy, monitoring the control, distribution and administration of drugs and assisting in compliance with state and federal regulations. Additionally, OCR provides ancillary services, such as infusion therapy, distributes medical supplies and offers clinical and financial software information systems to its client nursing facilities.

RECENT DEVELOPMENTS:

For the year ended 12/31/02, net income advanced 69.5% to $125.9 million compared with $74.3 million the previous year. Results for 2002 and 2001 included after-tax restructuring charges of $14.4 million, respectively. Total net sales increased 20.6% to $2.63 billion from $2.18 billion the year before. Sales improved 20.7% to $2.61 billion from $2.16 billion, while reimbursements received for out-of-pockets expenses climbed 10.3% to $26.3 million from $23.9 million a year earlier. Gross profit grew 19.3% to $691.1 million from $579.4 million in 2001. Operating income jumped 47.9% to $256.6 million from $173.5 million the prior year.

PROSPECTS:

On 1/18/03, the Company announced that it completed the acquisition of NCS Healthcare, Inc. in a transaction valued at approximately $460.0 million. The transaction expands OCR's presence in the long-term care market, increasing the residents it serves by 27.0% to about 945,000 and annualized revenues by 24.0% to approximately $3.30 billion. Meanwhile, the Company believes it is on track to achieve both top and bottom line growth in 2003 due to productivity and consolidation initiatives and the integration of acquisitions.

ANNUAL FINANCIAL DATA:

FISCAL YEAR	TOT. REVS. ($mill.)	NET INC. ($mill.)	TOT. ASSETS ($mill.)	OPER. PROFIT %	NET PROFIT %	RET. ON EQUITY %	RET. ON ASSETS %	CURR. RATIO	EARN. PER SH. $	CASH FL. PER SH. $	TANG. BK. VAL.$	DIV. PER SH. $	PRICE RANGE	AVG. P/E RATIO	AVG. YIELD %
p12/31/02	2,632.8	⑥ 125.9							⑥ 1.33			0.09	28.83 - 17.51	17.4	0.4
12/31/01	2,159.1	⑥ 74.3	2,290.3	8.0	3.4	6.5	3.2	3.4	⑥ 0.79	1.58	0.27	0.09	26.00 - 16.88	27.1	0.4
12/31/00	1,971.3	⑥ 48.8	2,210.2	6.6	2.5	4.6	2.2	3.2	⑥ 0.53	1.33	...	0.09	23.00 - 8.00	29.2	0.4
12/31/99	1,861.9	⑤ 57.7	2,168.0	7.3	3.1	5.6	2.7	2.3	⑥ 0.63	1.39	...	0.09	36.19 - 6.88	34.2	0.4
⑦ 12/31/98	1,517.4	⑤ 80.4	1,903.8	10.3	5.3	8.3	4.2	2.6	⑤ 0.90	1.43	...	0.08	41.56 - 25.00	37.0	0.2
12/31/97	895.7	③④ 55.7	1,289.6	10.9	6.2	7.2	4.3	3.7	③④ 0.69	1.01	0.99	0.07	34.56 - 22.38	41.3	0.2
12/31/96	536.6	③ 43.5	721.7	12.0	8.1	6.8	6.0	6.3	③ 0.64	0.87	4.87	0.06	32.50 - 19.13	40.3	0.2
12/31/95	399.6	③ 24.8	360.8	10.9	6.2	11.5	6.9	2.9	③ 0.47	0.68	1.08	0.05	22.69 - 10.22	35.0	0.3
12/31/94	275.7	② 13.4	305.8	9.7	4.9	7.5	4.4	4.4	② 0.30	0.47	1.21	0.04	11.31 - 6.72	29.7	0.5
12/31/93	159.6	① 8.7	218.8	9.6	5.5	9.0	4.0	3.3	① 0.24	0.35	0.18	0.04	8.03 - 3.31	24.1	0.7

Statistics are as originally reported. Adj. for 2-for-1 stk. split 6/95 & 6/96. ① Bef. cr$280,000 fr. an acctg. adj. ② Incl. nonrecur. chgs. of $1.9 mill. ③ Incl. a net chg. of $989,000, 1995; $534,000, 1996; $3.1 mill., 1997. ④ Incl. a net non-recur. chg. of $6.0 mill. ⑤ Incl. a net chg. of $13.9 mill. for trans-rel. exps. in the CompScript and IBAH acqs. & a nonrecur. net restruct. chg. of $2.7 mill. ⑥ Incl. an after-tax net restruct. chg. of $17.2 mill., 1999; $17.1 mill. ($0.19/sh.), 2000; $11.4 mill., 2001; $14.4 mill., 2002. ⑦ Incl. the results of CompScript, Inc. and IBAH, Inc.

OFFICERS:
E. L. Hutton, Chmn.
J. F. Gemunder, Pres., C.E.O.
D. W. Froesel Jr., Sr. V.P., C.F.O.

INVESTOR CONTACT: Investor Relations Dept., (859) 392-3331

PRINCIPAL OFFICE: 1600 Rivercenter II, 100 East Rivercenter Blvd., Covington, KY 41011

TELEPHONE NUMBER: (859) 392-3300
FAX: (859) 392-3333
WEB: www.omnicare.com

NO. OF EMPLOYEES: 5,800 full-time (approx.); 3,200 part-time (approx.)

SHAREHOLDERS: 2,468

ANNUAL MEETING: In May
INCORPORATED: DE, May, 1981

INSTITUTIONAL HOLDINGS:
No. of Institutions: 214
Shares Held: 101,466,158
% Held: 107.6

INDUSTRY: Drug stores and proprietary stores (SIC: 5912)

TRANSFER AGENT(S): First Chicago Trust Company of New York, Jersey City, NJ

OMNICOM GROUP, INC.

EXCH.	SYM.	REC. PRICE	P/E RATIO	YLD.	MKT. CAP.	RANGE (52-WK.)	'02 Y/E PR.
NYSE	OMC	52.98 (2/28/03)	15.4	1.5%	$10.10 bill.	97.35 - 36.50	64.60

INVESTMENT GRADE. OMC EXPECTS TO CONTINUE TO BENEFIT FROM ITS CLIENTS' EXPANDING THE FOCUS OF THEIR BRAND STRATEGIES FROM NATIONAL MARKETS TO THE GLOBAL MARKET.

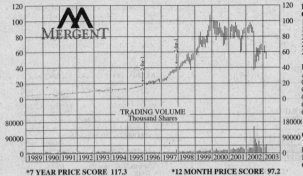

INTERIM EARNINGS (Per Share):

Qtr.	Mar.	June	Sept.	Dec.
1998	0.31	0.50	0.32	0.55
1999	0.37	0.59	0.39	0.66
2000	0.78	0.70	0.48	0.78
2001	0.52	0.81	0.50	0.87
2002	0.68	1.00	0.68	1.08

INTERIM DIVIDENDS (Per Share):

Amt.	Decl.	Ex.	Rec.	Pay.
0.20Q	1/28/02	3/06/02	3/08/02	4/04/02
0.20Q	5/21/02	6/05/02	6/07/02	7/05/02
0.20Q	9/10/02	9/18/02	9/20/02	10/04/02
0.20Q	12/10/02	12/18/02	12/20/02	1/03/03
0.20Q	2/04/03	-3/05/03	3/07/03	4/04/03

Indicated div.: $0.80 (Div. Reinv. Plan)

CAPITALIZATION (12/31/01):

	($000)	(%)
Long-Term Debt	1,340,105	36.4
Minority Interest	158,123	4.3
Common & Surplus	2,178,419	59.3
Total	3,676,647	100.0

*7 YEAR PRICE SCORE 117.3   *12 MONTH PRICE SCORE 97.2

*NYSE COMPOSITE INDEX=100

BUSINESS:

Omnicom Group, Inc. is a provider of marketing communications and advertising services. The Omnicom Group companies service clients through worldwide, national and regional independent agency brands. These brands include BBDO Worldwide, DDB Worldwide and TBWA Worldwide. Omincom also includes Diversified Agency Services (DAS), which operates branded independent agencies in public relations, specialty advertising, and direct response

and promotional marketing; Omnicom Media Group, which includes two international media buying and planning agencies, OMD and PhD; and Communicade, which manages investments in Internet and digital media development companies. In January 1998, OMC acquired Fleishman-Hillard, Inc., GPC International Holdings, Inc., and Palmer Jarvis, Inc. Net sales for 2002 were derived as follows: domestic, 56.9% and international, 43.1%.

RECENT DEVELOPMENTS:

For the year ended 12/31/02, net income advanced 27.9% to $643.5 million from $503.1 million the year before. Earnings for 2002 and 2001 included losses from equity in affiliates of $54.5 million and $40.1 million, respectively. Total revenue improved 9.4% to $7.54 billion from $6.89 billion a year earlier. Domestic revenues grew 15.3% to

$4.28 billion from $3.72 billion in the prior year. International revenues rose 2.5% to $3.25 billion from $3.17 billion in the previous year. For the quarter ended 12/31/02, net income increased 22.7% to $201.5 million, while total revenue advanced 11.1% to $2.12 billion.

PROSPECTS:

OMC expects to continue to benefit from several long-term trends, including its clients' increasingly expanding the focus of their brand strategies from national markets to the global market. Additionally, in an effort to gain greater efficiency from their marketing dollars, clients are increasingly requiring greater coordination of their advertising and

marketing activities and concentrating these activities with a smaller number of service providers. Meanwhile, international business continues to be favorably affected by the relatively stronger Euro and British Pound against the U.S. dollar, partially offset by the strengthening of the U.S. dollar against the Brazilian Real.

ANNUAL FINANCIAL DATA:

FISCAL YEAR	TOT. REVS. ($mill.)	NET INC. ($mill.)	TOT. ASSETS ($mill.)	OPER. PROFIT %	NET PROFIT %	RET. ON EQUITY %	RET. ON ASSETS %	CURR. RATIO	EARN. PER SH. $	CASH FL. PER SH. $	DIV. PER SH. $	PRICE RANGE	AVG. P/E RATIO	AVG. YIELD %
p12/31/02	7,536.3	643.5		14.1	7.3	23.1	4.7	0.8	3.44		0.80	97.35 - 36.50	19.5	1.2
12/31/01	6,889.4	503.1	10,617.4	14.3	7.3	23.1	4.7	0.8	2.70	4.00	0.75	98.20 - 59.10	29.1	1.0
12/31/00	6,154.2	②498.8	9,891.5	14.3	8.1	32.2	5.0	0.8	②2.73	3.83	0.70	100.94 - 68.13	31.0	0.8
12/31/99	5,130.5	362.9	9,017.6	14.1	7.1	23.4	4.0	0.8	2.01	2.94	0.60	107.50 - 55.94	40.7	0.7
12/31/98	4,092.0	285.1	6,910.1	13.7	7.0	26.2	4.1	0.8	1.68	2.50	0.50	58.50 - 37.00	28.4	1.0
12/31/97	3,124.8	222.4	4,965.7	12.9	7.1	25.7	4.5	0.8	1.37	2.02	0.42	41.50 - 22.25	23.3	1.3
12/31/96	2,641.7	176.3	4,055.9	12.4	6.7	22.0	4.3	0.8	1.15	1.79	0.45	26.06 - 17.75	19.1	2.1
12/31/95	2,257.5	140.0	3,527.7	12.0	6.2	25.4	4.0	0.8	0.95	1.51	0.32	18.75 - 12.47	16.4	2.1
12/31/94	1,756.2	①108.1	2,852.2	11.7	6.2	20.0	3.8	0.8	①0.79	1.27	0.31	13.44 - 10.94	15.4	2.5
12/31/93	1,516.5	85.3	2,289.9	11.2	5.6	21.2	3.7	0.8	0.67	1.14	0.31	11.88 - 9.25	15.8	2.9

Statistics are as originally reported. Adjusted for 2-for-1 stock split, 1/98 & 12/95. ① Bef. acct. chrg. of $28.0 mill. ② Incl. a pre-tax realized gain on the sale of an investment of $110.0 mill.

OFFICERS:
B. Crawford, Chmn.
J. D. Wren, Pres., C.E.O.
R. J. Weisenburger, Exec. V.P., C.F.O.
INVESTOR CONTACT: Randall Weisenburger, Exec. V.P., C.F.O., (212) 415-3393
PRINCIPAL OFFICE: 437 Madison Ave, New York, NY 10022

TELEPHONE NUMBER: (212) 415-3600
FAX: (212) 415-3393
WEB: www.omnicomgroup.com
NO. OF EMPLOYEES: 57,000 (approx.)
SHAREHOLDERS: 3,756
ANNUAL MEETING: In May
INCORPORATED: NY, Mar., 1944; reincorp., NY, Aug., 1986

INSTITUTIONAL HOLDINGS:
No. of Institutions: 467
Shares Held: 172,950,280
% Held: 92.0
INDUSTRY: Advertising agencies (SIC: 7311)
TRANSFER AGENT(S): Mellon Investor Services, L.L.C., Ridgefield Park, NJ

ONEIDA LTD.

EXCH.	SYM.	REC. PRICE	P/E RATIO	YLD.	MKT. CAP.	RANGE (52-WK.)	'02 Y/E PR.
NYSE	OCQ	11.01 (2/28/03)	19.7	0.7%	$181.9 mill.	19.75 - 10.14	11.03

MEDIUM GRADE. IN THE NEAR-TERM, THE COMPANY ANTICIPATES SEQUENTIAL IMPROVEMENT IN SALES AND SUBSTANTIAL GAINS ON ITS BALANCE SHEET.

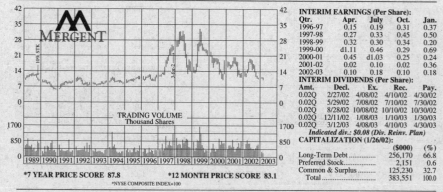

TRADING VOLUME
Thousand Shares

*7 YEAR PRICE SCORE 87.8   *12 MONTH PRICE SCORE 83.1
*NYSE COMPOSITE INDEX=100

INTERIM EARNINGS (Per Share):

Qtr.	Apr.	July	Oct.	Jan.
1996-97	0.15	0.19	0.31	0.37
1997-98	0.27	0.33	0.45	0.50
1998-99	0.32	0.30	0.34	0.20
1999-00	d1.11	0.46	0.29	0.69
2000-01	0.45	d1.03	0.25	0.24
2001-02	0.02	0.10	0.02	0.36
2002-03	0.10	0.18	0.10	0.18

INTERIM DIVIDENDS (Per Share):

Amt.	Decl.	Ex.	Rec.	Pay.
0.02Q	2/27/02	4/08/02	4/10/02	4/30/02
0.02Q	5/29/02	7/08/02	7/10/02	7/30/02
0.02Q	8/28/02	10/08/02	10/10/02	10/30/02
0.02Q	12/11/02	1/08/03	1/10/03	1/30/03
0.02Q	3/12/03	4/08/03	4/10/03	4/30/03

Indicated div.: $0.08 (Div. Reinv. Plan)

CAPITALIZATION (1/26/02):

	($000)	(%)
Long-Term Debt	256,170	66.8
Preferred Stock	2,151	0.6
Common & Surplus	125,230	32.7
Total	383,551	100.0

BUSINESS:

Oneida Ltd. is a manufacturer and marketer of tableware products. OCQ's principal industry segments are grouped around the manufacture and distribution of three major product categories: metalware, dinnerware and glassware. Metalware (64.9% of fiscal 2001 revenues) is comprised of stainless steel, silverplated and sterling silver flatware, stainless steel and silverplated holloware, cutlery and cookware. Dinnerware (27.5%) includes domestic and imported china, porcelain and stoneware plates, bowls, cups, mugs and a variety of serving pieces. OCQ's glassware segment (6.5%) includes glass and crystal stemware, barware, serveware, giftware and decorative pieces. Other tabletop accessories (1.1%) include ceramic and plastic serveware, kitchen and table linens, picture frames and decorative pieces distributed primarily by OCQ's Encore Promotions and Kenwood Silver subsidiaries.

RECENT DEVELOPMENTS:

For the year ended 1/25/03, net income advanced 31.4% to $9.2 million compared with $7.0 million the year before. Earnings for fiscal 2002 included a gain of $1.6 million from insurance proceeds. Earnings for fiscal 2001 included a gain of $5.1 million from marketable securities. Net sales slipped 3.8% to $480.1 million from $499.2 million a year earlier. Gross profit was $153.6 million, or 32.0% of net sales, versus $161.9 million, or 32.4% of net sales, in the prior year. Operating income declined 7.6% to $25.6 million from $27.7 million in the previous year. Comparisons were made with restated fiscal 2001 figures.

PROSPECTS:

Looking ahead, the Company should continue to benefit from a sequential improvement in sales and substantial gains on its balance sheet despite the weak economy and declining consumer confidence. In addition, the Company should continue to experience solid growth in its higher-end bridal flatware, as well as modest improvement in its foodservice unit. Going forward, the Company will continue to seek to gain market share within all of its divisions, which should be attainable due to its strong product offering and significant brand awareness.

ANNUAL FINANCIAL DATA:

FISCAL YEAR	TOT. REVS. ($000)	NET INC. ($000)	TOT. ASSETS ($000)	OPER. PROFIT %	NET PROFIT %	RET. ON EQUITY %	RET. ON ASSETS %	CURR. RATIO	EARN. PER SH. $	CASH FL. PER SH. $	TANG. BK. VAL. $	DIV. PER SH. $	PRICE RANGE	AVG. P/E RATIO	AVG. YIELD %
p1/25/03	480,100	④ 9,200	527,800						⑤ 0.55			0.08	19.75 - 10.60	27.6	0.5
1/26/02	500,750	8,501	546,135	6.0	1.7	6.7	1.6	3.4	0.51	1.55	...	0.25	20.35 - 11.25	31.0	1.6
1/27/01	521,988	④ d1,300	610,573	3.9	...	...	...	2.9	④ d0.09	0.87	...	0.30	22.88 - 10.06	...	1.8
1/29/00	495,917	④ 5,511	449,238	4.9	1.1	4.1	1.2	2.1	④ 0.32	1.16	6.23	0.40	33.06 - 13.06	72.0	1.7
1/30/99	466,738	④ 19,750	442,068	8.6	4.2	-14.1	4.5	2.0	④ 1.16	2.11	5.95	0.50	32.19 - 12.81	19.4	2.2
1/31/98	442,866	③ 26,135	363,586	11.4	5.9	19.3	7.2	2.3	③ 1.55	2.38	5.67	0.45	25.92 - 11.50	12.1	2.4
② 1/25/97	376,923	① 17,276	350,228	9.5	4.6	14.6	4.9	2.3	① 1.03	1.72	5.11	0.35	12.58 - 9.42	10.7	3.2
1/27/96	514,281	18,088	344,363	7.7	3.5	17.0	5.3	2.3	1.09	2.03	6.29	0.32	11.75 - 8.58	9.4	3.1
1/28/95	493,422	13,493	336,030	6.4	2.7	14.2	4.0	2.3	0.83	1.72	5.68	0.32	11.33 - 8.08	11.7	3.3
1/29/94	455,669	10,662	318,505	5.9	2.3	12.4	3.3	2.3	0.67	1.59	5.21	0.32	9.67 - 7.33	12.6	3.8

Statistics are as originally reported. Adj. for 3-for-2 stk. split, 12/97. ① Bef. loss of $304,000 from discont. opers. ② Excl. results of Camden Wire subsid. ③ Excl. a gain of $2.6 mill. sale of subsid. ④ Incl. pre-tax restr. chrg. of $39.0 mill., 1/01; $44.3 mill., 1/00; $5.0 mill., 1/99. ⑤ Incl. gain from insur. proceeds of $1.6 mill.

OFFICERS:
P. J. Kallet, Chmn., Pres., C.E.O.
G. R. Denny, C.F.O.
C. H. Suttmeier, V.P., Gen. Couns., Sec.

INVESTOR CONTACT: Gregg Denny, C.F.O., (315) 361-3138

PRINCIPAL OFFICE: 163-181 Kenwood Avenue, Oneida, NY 13421-2899

TELEPHONE NUMBER: (315) 361-3636
FAX: (315) 361-3399
WEB: www.oneida.com
NO. OF EMPLOYEES: 3,970 (approx.)
SHAREHOLDERS: 3,790
ANNUAL MEETING: In May
INCORPORATED: NY, Nov., 1880

INSTITUTIONAL HOLDINGS:
No. of Institutions: 60
Shares Held: 11,259,208
% Held: 68.1

INDUSTRY: Silverware and plated ware (SIC: 3914)

TRANSFER AGENT(S): American Stock Transfer & Trust Co., New York, NY

ONEOK INC.

EXCH.	SYM.	REC. PRICE	P/E RATIO	YLD.	MKT. CAP.	RANGE (52-WK.)	'02 Y/E PR.
NYSE	OKE	17.23 (2/28/03)	13.3	3.6%	$1.03 bill.	23.14 - 14.62	19.20

UPPER MEDIUM GRADE. THE COMPANY EXPECTS FULL-YEAR 2003 EARNINGS OF BETWEEN $2.40 AND $2.45 PER SHARE.

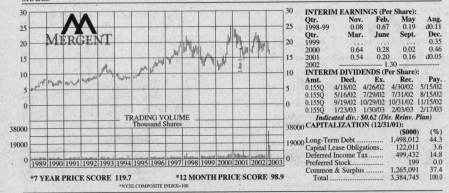

INTERIM EARNINGS (Per Share):

Qtr.	Nov.	Feb.	May	Aug.
1998-99	0.08	0.67	0.19	d0.11
Qtr.	Mar.	June	Sept.	Dec.
1999	...	...	...	0.35
2000	0.64	0.28	0.02	0.46
2001	0.54	0.20	0.16	d0.05
2002	---------------- 1.30 ----------------			

INTERIM DIVIDENDS (Per Share):

Amt.	Decl.	Ex.	Rec.	Pay.
0.155Q	4/18/02	4/26/02	4/30/02	5/15/02
0.155Q	5/16/02	7/29/02	7/31/02	8/15/02
0.155Q	9/19/02	10/29/02	10/31/02	11/15/02
0.155Q	1/23/03	1/30/03	2/03/03	2/17/03

Indicated div.: $0.62 (Div. Reinv. Plan)

CAPITALIZATION (12/31/01):

	($000)	(%)
Long-Term Debt	1,498,012	44.3
Capital Lease Obligations	122,011	3.6
Deferred Income Tax	499,432	14.8
Preferred Stock	199	0.0
Common & Surplus	1,265,091	37.4
Total	3,384,745	100.0

*7 YEAR PRICE SCORE 119.7   ***12 MONTH PRICE SCORE 98.9**

*NYSE COMPOSITE INDEX=100

BUSINESS:

ONEOK Inc. is a diversified energy company involved primarily in oil and gas production, natural gas processing, gathering, storage and transmission in the mid-continent areas of the U.S. As of 2/26/03, OKE's energy marketing and trading operations provided service to customers in 33 states. OKE is also a major distributor of natural gas, serving 1.9 million customers in Kansas, Oklahoma, and Texas.

In 2002, net revenues were derived: distribution, 42.6%, marketing, 22.0%; gathering and processing, 20.0%; transportation and storage, 12.1%; and production, 3.3%. In January 2003, OKE purchased the Texas gas distribution assets of Southern Union Company for $420.0 million, and sold certain natural gas and oil producing properties to Chesapeake Energy for $300.0 million in cash.

RECENT DEVELOPMENTS:

For the year ended 12/31/02, income from continuing operations was $156.0 million versus income from continuing operations of $78.8 million the previous year. Operating revenues climbed 9.8% to $2.10 billion vs $1.92 billion a year earlier. Operating income rose 45.3% to $371.5 million. Separately, on 1/31/03, OKE announced that it has

closed on the sale of certain natural gas and oil properties to Chesapeake Energy for $300.0 million in cash. The Company estimates that annual production of its retained properties will be about 8.00 billion cubic feet of natural gas and 370,000 barrels of oil. This represents approximately 33.3% of OKE's previous annual production.

PROSPECTS:

On 1/3/03, OKE announced that it has closed on the purchase of the Texas gas distribution assets of Southern Union Company for $420.0 million. In addition to the gas distribution assets, the acquisition included 125 miles of natural gas transmission system as well as other energy-related assets involved in gas marketing, retail propane, and

natural gas distribution investments in Mexico. Also, on 12/13/02, OKE announced that it has closed the sale of certain midstream assets to an affiliate of Mustang Fuel Corporation for $92.5 million. Separately, OKE expects full-year 2003 earnings of between $2.40 and $2.45 per share, excluding accounting changes.

ANNUAL FINANCIAL DATA:

FISCAL YEAR	TOT. REVS. ($mill.)	NET INC. ($mill.)	TOT. ASSETS ($mill.)	OPER. PROFIT %	NET PROFIT %	NET INC./ NET PROP. %	NET INC./ TOT. CAP. %	RET. ON EQUITY %	ACCUM. DEPR./ GROSS PROP. %	EARN. PER SH.$	TANG. BK. VAL.$	DIV. PER SH.$	DIV. PAYOUT %	PRICE RANGE	AVG. P/E RATIO	AVG. YIELD %
12/31/02	⑥ 2,104.3	⑤ 156.0								⑤ 1.30		0.62	47.7	23.14 - 14.62	14.5	3.3
12/31/01	6,803.1	④ 103.7	5,879.2	4.3	1.5	3.2	3.1	8.2	27.4	④ 0.85	19.19	0.62	72.9	24.34 - 14.17	22.7	3.2
③ 12/31/00	6,642.9	② 143.5	7,369.1	5.0	2.2	4.6	4.7	11.7	26.4	② 1.48	19.12	0.62	41.9	25.31 - 10.88	12.2	3.4
① 12/31/99	2,071.0	106.9	3,239.6	11.5	5.2	5.0	4.7	9.3	32.5	1.05	18.11	0.62	59.3	18.59 - 12.25	14.8	4.0
8/31/98	1,835.4	101.8	2,422.5	7.5	5.5	6.0	5.7	8.7	35.2	1.12	8.28	0.61	54.3	22.13 - 14.88	16.6	3.3
8/31/97	1,161.9	59.3	1,237.4	8.1	5.1	7.0	6.1	12.8	41.0	1.07	8.24	0.60	56.3	20.34 - 12.94	15.6	3.6
8/31/96	1,224.3	52.8	1,219.9	7.2	4.3	6.6	5.6	12.5	40.5	0.97	7.61	0.59	61.7	15.19 - 10.00	13.0	4.7
8/31/95	949.9	42.8	1,169.5	8.4	4.5	5.6	4.6	10.8	40.0	0.79	7.19	0.57	71.5	12.41 - 8.56	13.3	5.4
8/31/94	792.4	36.2	1,137.0	9.0	4.6	4.9	3.9	9.5	39.4	0.67	6.94	0.55	83.5	10.19 - 7.88	13.5	6.2
8/31/93	789.1	38.4	1,104.5	9.6	4.9	5.3	4.1	10.3	39.7	0.72	6.82	0.54	75.5	13.13 - 8.81	15.3	4.9

Statistics are as originally reported. Adj. for 2-for-1 stk. split, 6/01. ① Refl. change in fiscal year from 8/31 to 12/31. ② Bef. acctg. chg. credit of $2.1 mill. ③ Refl. the acquisition of mid-stream assets from Dynergy Inc. and Kinder Morgan, Inc. ④ Incl. pre-tax chrgs. of $34.6 mill. for outstg. gas costs & $37.4 mill. rel. to Enron bankruptcy; bef. acctg. chg. chrg. of $2.2 mill. ⑤ Bef. inc. fr. disc. ops. of $10.6 mill. ⑥ Refl. adoption of certain prov. of Emerging Issues Task Force Issue No. 02-3. EITF 02-3 provides that all mark-to-market gains and losses on energy trading contracts should be presented on a net basis.

OFFICERS:
D. L. Kyle, Chmn., Pres., C.E.O.
J. C. Kneale, Sr. V.P., C.F.O., Treas.
J. A. Gaberino, Jr., Sr. V.P., Gen. Couns.
INVESTOR CONTACT: Weldon Watson, V.P., Investor Relations, (918) 588-7158
PRINCIPAL OFFICE: 100 West Fifth Street, Tulsa, OK 74103

TELEPHONE NUMBER: (918) 588-7000
FAX: (918) 588-7273
WEB: www.oneok.com
NO. OF EMPLOYEES: 4,520 (avg.)
SHAREHOLDERS: 14,454
ANNUAL MEETING: In May
INCORPORATED: DE, Nov., 1933; reincorp., OK, May, 1997

INSTITUTIONAL HOLDINGS:
No. of Institutions: 163
Shares Held: 31,846,353
% Held: 52.7
INDUSTRY: Gas transmission and distribution (SIC: 4923)
TRANSFER AGENT(S): UMB Bank, N.A., Kansas City, MO

ORTHODONTIC CENTERS OF AMERICA, INC.

EXCH.	SYM.	REC. PRICE	P/E RATIO	YLD.	MKT. CAP.	RANGE (52-WK.)	'02 Y/E PR.
NYSE	OCA	10.17 (2/28/03)	9.0	...	$0.52 bil.	29.65 - 7.80	10.91

MEDIUM GRADE. THE COMPANY'S HAS A SOUND BUSINESS MODEL AND SOLID GROWTH STRATEGY FOR 2003 AND BEYOND.

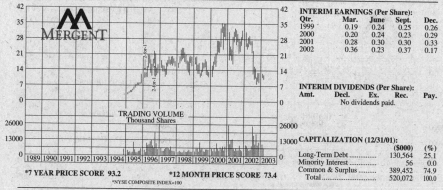

INTERIM EARNINGS (Per Share):

Qtr.	Mar.	June	Sept.	Dec.
1999	0.19	0.24	0.25	0.26
2000	0.20	0.24	0.23	0.29
2001	0.28	0.30	0.30	0.33
2002	0.36	0.23	0.37	0.17

INTERIM DIVIDENDS (Per Share):

Amt.	Decl.	Ex.	Rec.	Pay.
		No dividends paid.		

CAPITALIZATION (12/31/01):

	($000)	(%)
Long-Term Debt	130,564	25.1
Minority Interest	56	0.0
Common & Surplus	389,452	74.9
Total	520,072	100.0

TRADING VOLUME
Thousand Shares

*7 YEAR PRICE SCORE 93.2   ***12 MONTH PRICE SCORE 73.4**

NYSE COMPOSITE INDEX=100

BUSINESS:

Orthodontic Centers of America, Inc. provides integrated business services to orthodontic and pediatric dental practices throughout the U.S. and in Japan, Mexico, Spain and Puerto Rico. The Company provides a range of services to its affiliated practices, including marketing and advertising, management information systems, staffing, supplies and inventory, scheduling, billing, financial reporting, account-

ing and other administrative and business services. These services are provided under long-term agreements with affiliated orthodontists and pediatric dentists and/or their wholly-owned professional corporation and other entity. On 11/9/01, the Company acquired OrthAlliance, Inc., a provider of practice management and consulting services to orthodontic and pediatric dentistry practices in the U.S.

RECENT DEVELOPMENTS:

For the year ended 12/31/02, net income slipped 4.8% to $58.2 million compared with $61.1 million in 2001. Results for 2002 included asset impairments of $2.8 million and a non-recurring recruiting expense of $12.8 million. Fee revenue jumped 25.3% to $439.6 million from $351.0 million

in the prior year, primarily due to an increase in new patient contracts. Operating income amounted to $99.5 million, down 4.3% from $104.0 million the year before. Record patient case starts rose 21.0% to 242,332 in 2002 from 200,281 in 2001.

PROSPECTS:

Going forward, the Company will continue to implement steps to position itself for future growth in earnings and increased cash flow. There are several factors that are expected to drive growth in the coming years, including assisting affiliated practices in becoming larger, more efficient and more profitable, as well as continuing to expand

internationally. In addition, OCA will begin to offer a portion of its services to general dentists for a monthly fee and engage in certain new affiliations in key growth areas. The Company should benefit from its sound business model and solid growth strategy in 2003 and beyond.

ANNUAL FINANCIAL DATA:

FISCAL YEAR	TOT. REVS. (Smill.)	NET INC. (Smill.)	TOT. ASSETS (Smill.)	OPER. PROFIT %	NET PROFIT %	RET. ON EQUITY %	RET. ON ASSETS %	CURR. RATIO	EARN. PER SH.$	CASH FL. PER SH.$	TANG. BK. VAL.$	PRICE RANGE	AVG. P/E RATIO
p12/31/02	439.6	☑ 58.2							1.13			31.33 - 7.80	17.3
12/31/01	351.0	☑ 61.1	580.5	29.6	17.4	15.7	10.5	1.9	☑ 1.21	1.61	1.74	32.98 - 16.80	20.6
12/31/00	268.8	☑ 47.7	367.9	29.8	17.8	16.6	13.0	2.8	☑ 0.96	1.26	1.91	35.31 - 11.06	24.2
12/31/99	226.3	☑ 46.5	367.0	34.0	20.6	16.7	12.7	6.4	☑ 0.96	1.21	2.32	20.13 - 10.81	16.1
12/31/98	171.3	33.8	296.8	31.7	19.7	14.6	11.4	3.2	0.70	0.89	1.65	24.06 - 11.75	25.6
12/31/97	117.3	22.6	229.0	30.6	19.3	11.9	9.9	5.1	0.50	0.62	1.91	20.25 - 11.00	31.2
12/31/96	71.3	14.4	145.1	30.4	20.2	12.5	9.9	3.5	0.34	0.41	1.42	22.63 - 10.38	48.5
12/31/95	41.6	9.0	92.6	29.4	21.7	11.7	9.8	5.1	0.24	0.27	1.71	12.06 - 2.91	31.8
12/31/94	25.4	2.0	37.5	34.5	8.0	7.9	5.4	3.6	...	...	0.78	3.13 - 2.75	...
12/31/93	18.8	6.1	12.5	35.4	32.5	80.3	49.0	2.7	...	...	...	...	...

Statistics are as originally reported. ☐ Excl. acctg. change chg., $50.6 mill., 12/00; $678,000, 12/99. ☑ Incl. loss of $56,000 non-controlling int. in sub. ☑ Incl. $2.8 mill. asset impair. & $12.8 mill. non-recur. recruiting exp.

OFFICERS:
B. F. Palmisano Sr., Chmn., Pres., C.E.O.
T. J. Sandeman, C.F.O.
B. F. Palmisano Jr., C.O.O.

INVESTOR CONTACT: Cory B. Armand,
V.P., Investor Relations, (866) 765-8583

PRINCIPAL OFFICE: 3850 N. Causeway
Blvd., Suite 800, Metairie, LA 70002

TELEPHONE NUMBER: (504) 834-4392
FAX: (504) 834-3663
WEB: www.4braces.com

NO. OF EMPLOYEES: 2,699 full-time; 798 part-time

SHAREHOLDERS: 235 (approx.)

ANNUAL MEETING: In May

INCORPORATED: DE, July, 1994

INSTITUTIONAL HOLDINGS:
No. of Institutions: 149
Shares Held: 38,259,625
% Held: 74.8

INDUSTRY: Specialty outpatient clinics, nec
(SIC: 8093)

TRANSFER AGENT(S): EquiServe Trust
Company N.A., Jersey City, NJ

OUTBACK STEAKHOUSE, INC.

EXCH.	SYM.	REC. PRICE	P/E RATIO	YLD.	MKT. CAP.	RANGE (52-WK.)	'02 Y/E PR.
NYSE	OSI	32.20 (2/28/03)	15.8	1.5%	$2.48 bill.	39.80 - 24.90	34.44

UPPER MEDIUM GRADE. OSI PLANS TO GROW REVENUES IN 2003 BY OPENING ADDITIONAL RESTAURANTS AND INCREASING COMPARABLE-STORE SALES AND AVERAGE UNIT VOLUMES IN ALL BRANDS.

TRADING VOLUME
Thousand Shares

*7 YEAR PRICE SCORE 136.8   *12 MONTH PRICE SCORE 108.0
*NYSE COMPOSITE INDEX=100

INTERIM EARNINGS (Per Share):

Qtr.	Mar.	June	Sept.	Dec.
1998	0.30	0.33	0.33	0.35
1999	0.37	0.40	0.40	0.38
2000	0.45	0.48	0.45	0.41
2001	0.49	0.47	0.32	0.43
2002	0.52	0.53	0.46	0.53

INTERIM DIVIDENDS (Per Share):

Amt.	Decl.	Ex.	Rec.	Pay.
0.12Q	10/23/02	11/20/02	11/22/02	12/06/02
0.12Q	1/23/03	2/19/03	2/21/03	3/07/03

Indicated div.: $0.48

CAPITALIZATION (12/31/01):

	($000)	(%)
Long-Term Debt	13,830	1.4
Deferred Income Tax	22,878	2.3
Common & Surplus	941,844	96.2
Total	978,552	100.0

BUSINESS:

Outback Steakhouse, Inc., through its subsidiaries and affiliates, develops, franchises and operates 961 full-service restaurants as of 2/13/03, including 783 Outback Steakhouses, 124 Carrabba's Italian Grills, 18 Fleming's Prime Steakhouse and Wine Bars, 17 Roy's Restaurants, 17 Bonefish Grills, one Lee Roy Selmon's, and and one Cheeseburger in Paradise in 50 states and 21 countries.

Outback Steakhouses feature steaks, prime rib, pork chops, ribs, chicken, seafood and pasta. Carrabba's features a limited menu of Italian dishes including pastas, seafood, and wood-fired pizza. Fleming's features prime cuts of beef, fresh seafood, pork, veal and chicken entrees as well as an extensive selection of wine. Roy's features Euro-Asian cuisine. Lee Roy's features southern cuisine.

RECENT DEVELOPMENTS:

For the year ended 12/31/02, the Company reported income of $160.8 million, before an accounting charge of $4.4 million, compared with net income $133.4 million the year before. Results for 2002 and 2001 included provisions for impaired assets and restaurant closings of $5.3 million and $4.6 million, respectively. Also, results for 2001 included a one-time charge of $7.0 million. Total revenues increased

11.0% to $2.36 billion from $2.13 billion a year earlier. Restaurant sales rose 11.2% to $2.34 billion, while other revenues slipped 2.8% to $19.3 million. System-wide sales grew 11.0% to $2.91 billion. Comparable-store sales for the fourth quarter improved 1.4% and 1.1% for domestic Outback Steakhouses and Carrabba's Italian Grills, respectively, versus the corresponding prior-year period.

PROSPECTS:

The Company plans to grow revenues in 2003 by opening additional restaurants and increasing comparable-store sales and average unit volumes in all brands. Also, the Company expects to increase its advertising expenditures in

2003 as a percentage of sales for both Outback and Carrabba's Italian Grill. For 2003, the Company anticipates opening 40 to 47 Outback Steakouses, 22 to 25 Carrabba's Italian Grills and 11 to 17 Bonefish Grills.

ANNUAL FINANCIAL DATA:

FISCAL YEAR	TOT. REVS. ($mill.)	NET INC. ($mill.)	TOT. ASSETS ($mill.)	OPER. PROFIT %	NET PROFIT %	RET. ON EQUITY %	RET. ON ASSETS %	CURR. RATIO	EARN. PER SH.$	CASH FL. PER SH.$	TANG. BK. VAL.$	DIV. PER SH.$	PRICE RANGE	AVG. P/E RATIO	AVG. YIELD %
p12/31/02	2,362.1	② 160.8							② 2.03			0.12	39.80 - 24.90	15.9	0.4
12/31/01	2,127.1	① 133.4	1,237.7	11.1	6.3	13.6	10.8	1.1	① 1.70	2.58	12.25	...	35.62 - 22.19	17.0	...
12/31/00	1,906.0	141.1	1,022.5	13.1	7.4	17.5	13.8	1.1	1.78	2.51	10.54	...	34.44 - 21.50	15.7	...
12/31/99	1,646.0	① 124.3	852.3	13.5	7.6	17.9	14.6	1.1	① 1.57	2.22	8.95	...	40.13 - 19.81	19.1	...
12/31/98	1,358.9	97.2	705.2	12.7	7.2	17.8	13.8	1.1	1.29	1.81	7.37	...	28.08 - 15.58	16.9	...
12/31/97	1,151.6	① 61.5	592.8	10.2	5.3	14.1	10.4	0.9	① 0.84	1.46	5.97	...	21.58 - 11.92	19.9	...
12/31/96	937.4	71.6	469.8	14.0	7.6	20.9	15.2	0.6	0.97	1.45	4.76	...	27.17 - 14.25	21.4	...
12/31/95	664.0	54.7	343.8	14.9	8.2	21.4	15.9	0.8	0.77	1.13	3.77	...	25.25 - 15.25	26.4	...
12/31/94	451.9	39.3	228.5	16.0	8.7	22.8	17.2	1.0	0.59	0.82	2.68	...	21.33 - 15.08	30.7	...
12/31/93	271.2	37.0	141.2	15.9	13.7	30.4	26.2	2.1	0.38	0.74	2.04	...	17.45 - 10.33	36.5	...

Statistics are as originally reported. Adj. for stk. splits: 3-for-2, 3/99; 3-for-2, 2/94. ① Incl. non-recurr. chrgs. $11.6 mill., 2001; $26.0 mill., 1997; $5.5 mill., 1995. ② Bef. acctg. chrg. of $4.4 mill.; incl. non-recurr. chrg. of $5.3 mill.

OFFICERS:
C. T. Sullivan, Chmn., C.E.O.
R. D. Basham, Pres., C.O.O.
R. S. Merritt, Sr. V.P., C.F.O., Treas.

INVESTOR CONTACT: Robert S. Merritt, Sr.
V.P. & C.F.P., (813) 282-1225

PRINCIPAL OFFICE: 2202 North West Shore Boulevard, 5th Floor, Tampa, FL 33607

TELEPHONE NUMBER: (813) 282-1225
FAX: (813) 282-1209
WEB: www.outback.com

NO. OF EMPLOYEES: 54,000 (approx.)

SHAREHOLDERS: 1,900 (approx.)

ANNUAL MEETING: In April

INCORPORATED: FL, Oct., 1987; reincorp., DE, April, 1991

INSTITUTIONAL HOLDINGS:
No. of Institutions: 221
Shares Held: 57,993,923
% Held: 76.5

INDUSTRY: Eating places (SIC: 5812)

TRANSFER AGENT(S): Bank of New York, New York, NY

OWENS & MINOR, INC.

EXCH.	SYM.	REC. PRICE	P/E RATIO	YLD.	MKT. CAP.	RANGE (52-WK.)	'02 Y/E PR.
NYSE	OMI	16.30 (2/28/03)	12.9	2.0%	$0.55 bill.	20.90 - 13.00	16.42

UPPER MEDIUM GRADE. THE COMPANY ANTICIPATES SALES GROWTH OF 3.0% TO 6.0% AND EARNINGS PER SHARE GROWTH OF BETWEEN 6.0% AND 10.0% IN 2003.

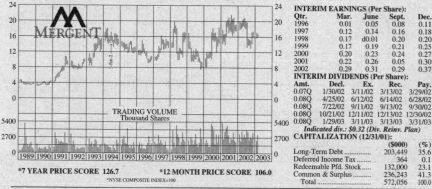

*7 YEAR PRICE SCORE 126.7   ***12 MONTH PRICE SCORE 106.0**
*NYSE COMPOSITE INDEX=100

INTERIM EARNINGS (Per Share):

Qtr.	Mar.	June	Sept.	Dec.
1996	0.01	0.05	0.08	0.11
1997	0.12	0.14	0.16	0.18
1998	0.17	d0.01	0.20	0.20
1999	0.17	0.19	0.21	0.25
2000	0.20	0.23	0.24	0.27
2001	0.22	0.26	0.05	0.30
2002	0.29	0.31	0.29	0.37

INTERIM DIVIDENDS (Per Share):

Amt.	Decl.	Ex.	Rec.	Pay.
0.07Q	1/30/02	3/11/02	3/13/02	3/29/02
0.08Q	4/25/02	6/12/02	6/14/02	6/28/02
0.08Q	7/22/02	9/11/02	9/13/02	9/30/02
0.08Q	10/21/02	12/11/02	12/13/02	12/30/02
0.08Q	1/29/03	3/11/03	3/13/03	3/31/03

Indicated div.: $0.32 (Div. Reinv. Plan)

CAPITALIZATION (12/31/01):

	($000)	(%)
Long-Term Debt	203,449	35.6
Deferred Income Tax	364	0.1
Redeemable Pfd. Stock	132,000	23.1
Common & Surplus	236,243	41.3
Total	572,056	100.0

BUSINESS:

Owens & Minor, Inc. is a distributor of medical/surgical supplies in the U.S. OMI distributes more than 120,000 finished medical/surgical products to hospitals and alternate care facilities such as nursing homes, clinics, surgery centers, rehabilitation facilities, physicians' offices and home healthcare. Most of OMI's sales consist of disposable gloves, dressings, endoscopic products, intravenous prod-

ucts, needles and syringes, sterile procedure trays, surgical products and gowns, urological products and wound closure products. Owens & Minor has 44 distribution centers serving all 50 states and the District of Columbia. In May 1994, OMI acquired Stuart Medical, Inc., a medical/surgical supplies distributor. On 7/30/99, OMI acquired Medix, Inc., a distributor of medical/surgical supplies.

RECENT DEVELOPMENTS:

For the year ended 12/31/02, the Company reported income of $47.2 million, before a $50,000 extraordinary gain, compared with income of $30.1 million, before a $7.1 million extraordinary charge, in the prior year. Results included pre-tax restructuring credits of $487,000 and $1.5 million in 2002 and 2001, respectively. Results for 2001 also

included a $1.1 million pre-tax charge for impairment loss on an investment. Net sales rose 3.8% to $3.96 billion from $3.81 billion a year earlier. Gross margin amounted to $419.9 million, or 10.6% of net sales, versus $408.2 million, or 10.7% of net sales, the previous year.

PROSPECTS:

The Company anticipates full-year 2003 sales growth of 3.0% to 6.0% and earnings per share growth of between 6.0% and 10.0%. On 11/20/02, OMI launched a series of initiatives expected to help boost sales and earnings. The Company will establish a supply chain management con-

sulting business focused on implementing cost reduction and operational improvement for hospital customers. In addition, OMI is developing a third-party logistics service for the healthcare industry.

ANNUAL FINANCIAL DATA:

FISCAL YEAR	TOT. REVS. ($mill.)	NET INC. ($mill.)	TOT. ASSETS ($mill.)	OPER. PROFIT %	NET PROFIT %	RET. ON EQUITY %	RET. ON ASSETS %	CURR. RATIO	EARN. PER SH.$	CASH FL. PER SH.$	TANG. BK. VAL.$	DIV. PER SH.$	PRICE RANGE	AVG. P/E RATIO	AVG. YIELD %
p12/31/02	3,959.8	⑤ 47.2							⑤ 1.26			0.31	20.90 - 13.00	13.5	1.8
12/31/01	3,815.0	④ 30.1	953.9	2.3	0.8	12.7	3.2	1.8	④ 0.85	1.30	1.12	0.27	21.69 - 13.92	20.9	1.5
12/31/00	3,503.6	③ 33.1	867.5	2.5	0.9	15.6	3.8	1.6	③ 0.94	1.38	0.24	0.25	18.38 - 8.13	14.1	1.9
12/31/99	3,186.4	③ 28.0	865.0	2.3	0.9	15.3	3.2	1.6	③ 0.82	1.21	...	0.23	17.00 - 7.56	15.0	1.9
12/31/98	3,082.1	③ 20.1	717.8	2.2	0.7	12.5	2.8	1.9	③ 0.56	1.12	0.09	0.20	19.88 - 10.00	26.7	1.3
12/31/97	3,116.8	24.3	712.6	2.1	0.8	9.4	3.4	1.9	0.60	1.15	...	0.18	16.25 - 9.75	21.7	1.4
12/31/96	3,019.0	13.0	679.5	1.6	0.4	5.3	1.9	1.7	0.25	0.75	...	0.18	15.00 - 9.13	48.2	1.5
12/31/95	2,976.5	③ d11.3	857.8	0.9	...	...	...	2.1	③ d0.53	d0.03	...	0.18	14.88 - 11.63	...	1.4
12/31/94	2,395.8	② 7.9	868.6	2.3	0.3	3.1	0.9	1.8	② 0.15	0.57	...	0.17	18.17 - 13.25	104.7	1.1
12/31/93	1,397.0	① 18.5	334.3	2.3	1.3	13.5	5.5	2.0	① 0.60	0.84	3.93	0.13	15.58 - 8.33	19.9	1.1

Statistics are as originally reported. Adj. for 3-for-2 stk. split, 3/94. ① Bef. $911,000 ($0.03/sh) income from discont. opers. & $706,000 ($0.02/sh) gain from acctg. adj. ② From recur. opers. ③ Incl. $750,000 pre-tax restr. credit, 2000; $1.0 mil pre-tax restr. credit,1999; $6.6 mil after-tax restr. chg., 1998; $16.7 mil restr. chg. & $3.5 mil consol. chgs., 1995. ④ Bef. $7.1 mil ($0.17/sh) extraord. chg., incl. $1.1 mil impair. loss on invest. & $1.5 mil restr. credit. ⑤ Bef. $50,000 ($0.01/sh) extraord. gain & incl. $487,000 restr. credit.

OFFICERS:
G. G. Minor, III, Chmn., C.E.O.
C. R. Smith, Pres., C.O.O.
J. Kaczka, Sr. V.P., C.F.O.

INVESTOR CONTACT: Shareholder Relations, (800) 524-4458

PRINCIPAL OFFICE: 4800 Cox Road, Glen Allen, VA 23060

TELEPHONE NUMBER: (804) 747-9794
FAX: (804) 270-7281
WEB: www.owens-minor.com

NO. OF EMPLOYEES: 2,937 (avg.)

SHAREHOLDERS: 15,000 (approx.)

ANNUAL MEETING: In Apr.

INCORPORATED: VA, Dec., 1926

INSTITUTIONAL HOLDINGS:
No. of Institutions: 142
Shares Held: 31,269,572
% Held: 91.7

INDUSTRY: Medical and hospital equipment (SIC: 5047)

TRANSFER AGENT(S): The Bank of New York, New York, NY

OWENS-ILLINOIS, INC.

EXCH.	SYM.	REC. PRICE	P/E RATIO	YLD.	MKT. CAP.	RANGE (52-WK.)	'02 Y/E PR.
NYSE	OI	9.00 (2/28/03)	...	...	$1.32 bill.	19.19 - 8.68	14.58

LOWER MEDIUM GRADE. THE COMPANY WILL BUILD A NEW GLASS CONTAINER MANUFACTURING PLANT TO BE THE PRIMARY SUPPLIER TO THE ANHEUSER-BUSCH, INC. BREWERY IN FORT COLLINS, COLORADO.

MERGENT

TRADING VOLUME
Thousand Shares

1989 1990 1991 1992 1993 1994 1995 1996 1997 1998 1999 2000 2001 2002 2003

*7 YEAR PRICE SCORE 69.8   *12 MONTH PRICE SCORE 90.1

*NYSE COMPOSITE INDEX=100

INTERIM EARNINGS (Per Share):

Qtr.	Mar.	June	Sept.	Dec.
1998	0.56	0.75	0.69	d1.24
1999	0.41	0.67	0.46	0.24
2000	0.36	0.57	d3.12	0.18
2001	0.30	1.61	0.44	d0.07
2002	d1.67	0.62	0.63	0.32

INTERIM DIVIDENDS (Per Share):

Amt.	Decl.	Ex.	Rec.	Pay.
	No dividends paid.			

CAPITALIZATION (12/31/01):

	($000)	(%)
Long-Term Debt	5,329,700	67.1
Deferred Income Tax	465,200	5.9
Preferred Stock	452,500	5.7
Common & Surplus	1,699,300	21.4
Total	7,946,700	100.0

BUSINESS:

Owens-Illinois, Inc. is a manufacturer of packaging products. In addition to being the largest manufacturer of glass containers in North America, South America, Australia, and New Zealand, and one of the largest in Europe, the Company is a major manufacturer in North America of plastic containers, plastic closures, and plastic prescription containers. The Company also has plastics packaging operations in South America, Australia, Europe, and New Zealand. In 2002, contributions to total sales from the Glass Containers segment and Plastics Packaging segment were 68.7% and 31.3%, respectively.

RECENT DEVELOPMENTS:

For the year ended 12/31/02, the Company reported income of $9.4 million, before an extraordinary loss of $9.6 million and an accounting charge of $460.0 million, compared with income of $360.7 million, before an extraordinary loss of $4.1 million, the year before. Earnings for 2002 included an after-tax charge of $308.8 for estimated future asbestos-related costs. Total revenues slid 4.2% to $5.76 billion from $6.01 billion a year earlier. Net sales in the glass containers segment grew 8.5% to $3.88 billion, while net sales in the plastics packaging segment declined 3.3% to $1.77 billion.

PROSPECTS:

On 2/7/03, OI announced that as part of a new, expanded contract with Anheuser-Busch, Inc., it will build a new glass container manufacturing plant to be the primary supplier to the Anheuser-Busch brewery in Fort Collins, Colorado. The plant is expected to start production in early 2005, and upon reaching full capacity, is anticipated to produce over 1.00 billion bottles annually. Separately, OI collected $24.8 million in asbestos-related insurance proceeds during 2002. The remaining receivable for asbestos-related insurance is about $12.0 million, which the Company expects to receive over the next two years. Looking ahead, OI expects to be negatively affected by lower pension income and higher interest expense in 2003. Pension credits are anticipated to decrease by about $55.0 million in 2003 due to the declines in the stock market. Interest expense is expected to increase by about $25.0 million, reflecting increased debt refinance activity.

ANNUAL FINANCIAL DATA:

FISCAL YEAR	TOT. REVS. ($mill.)	NET INC. ($mill.)	TOT. ASSETS ($mill.)	OPER. PROFIT %	NET PROFIT %	RET. ON EQUITY %	RET. ON ASSETS %	CURR. RATIO	EARN. PER SH. $	CASH FL. PER SH. $	TANG. BK. VAL. $	PRICE RANGE	AVG. P/E RATIO
p12/31/02	5,760.1	①⑥ 9.4							①⑥ d0.08	6.21		19.19 - 9.55	...
12/31/01	6,013.3	①⑤ 360.7	10,106.6	18.3	6.0	16.8	3.6	1.6	①⑤ 2.33	1.92		10.08 - 3.62	2.9
12/31/00	5,814.8	④ d269.7	10,343.2	1.6	...	...	...	1.6	④ d2.00	5.44		24.88 - 2.50	...
12/31/99	5,786.7	③ 299.1	10,756.3	16.0	5.2	12.7	2.8	1.7	③ 1.79	3.88		33.44 - 19.31	14.7
12/31/98	5,499.3	① 122.1	11,060.7	10.7	2.2	4.9	1.1	1.6	① 0.71	4.54	0.19	49.00 - 23.75	51.2
12/31/97	4,828.4	① 272.4	6,845.1	15.6	5.6	20.3	4.0	1.6	① 2.01	3.85		37.13 - 21.50	14.6
12/31/96	3,976.2	191.1	6,105.3	15.8	4.8	26.2	3.1	1.4	1.58	3.41		22.75 - 13.63	11.5
12/31/95	3,881.0	169.1	5,439.2	15.7	4.4	31.8	3.1	1.4	1.40	2.62		14.75 - 10.13	8.9
12/31/94	3,652.9	78.3	5,317.6	12.3	2.1	20.8	1.5	1.2	0.64	0.26		13.63 - 10.25	18.6
12/31/93	3,662.1	② d200.8	4,901.4	...	...	...	...	1.3	② d1.70			12.38 - 9.00	...

Statistics are as originally reported. ① Bef. extra. loss of $9.6 mill. & acctg. chrg. of $460.0 mill., 2002; $4.1 mill., 2001; $14.1 mill., 1998; & $104.5 mill., 1997. ② Incl. non-recurring chgs. of $322.4 mill. & bef. extra. chg. of $12.7 mill. ③ Incl. non-recurr. after-tax gains of $23.6 mill. & after-tax restruct. chrgs. & write-offs of assets in Europe and South America of $14.0 mill. ④ Incl. unusual after-tax chrgs. of $513.1 mill. & a tax benefit of $9.3 mill. ⑤ Incl. non-recurr. after-tax net gain of $170.5 mill. ⑥ Incl. after-tax asbestos-related costs of $308.8 mill.

OFFICERS:
J. H. Lemieux, Chmn., C.E.O.
R. S. Trumbull, Exec. V.P., C.F.O.
J. A. Denker, Treas.
INVESTOR CONTACT: Jim Weber, Dir., Investor Relations, (419) 247-2400
PRINCIPAL OFFICE: One SeaGate, Toledo, OH 43666

TELEPHONE NUMBER: (419) 247-5000
FAX: (419) 247-2839
WEB: www.o-i.com
NO. OF EMPLOYEES: 29,700 (approx.)
SHAREHOLDERS: 1,284
ANNUAL MEETING: In May
INCORPORATED: DE, 1907; reincorp., DE, 1987

INSTITUTIONAL HOLDINGS:
No. of Institutions: 156
Shares Held: 102,571,143
% Held: 69.6

INDUSTRY: Glass containers (SIC: 3221)

TRANSFER AGENT(S): First Chicago Trust Co. of New York, Jersey City, NJ

OXFORD HEALTH PLANS, INC.

EXCH.	SYM.	REC. PRICE	P/E RATIO	YLD.	MKT. CAP.	RANGE (52-WK.)	'02 Y/E PR.
NYSE	OHP	28.00 (2/28/03)	11.4	...	$2.96 bill.	51.94 - 27.00	36.45

MEDIUM GRADE. THE COMPANY IS FOCUSING ON DEVELOPING NEW PRODUCTS AND BENEFIT DESIGNS.

7 YEAR PRICE SCORE 128.3   **12 MONTH PRICE SCORE 91.9**

*NYSE COMPOSITE INDEX=100

INTERIM EARNINGS (Per Share):

Qtr.	Mar.	June	Sept.	Dec.
1998	d0.57	d6.41	d0.58	d0.23
1999	0.04	d0.16	0.34	3.05
2000	0.34	0.45	0.81	0.59
2001	0.65	0.73	0.85	1.00
2002	0.78	0.58	0.26	0.84

INTERIM DIVIDENDS (Per Share):

Amt.	Decl.	Ex.	Rec.	Pay.
	No dividends paid.			

CAPITALIZATION (12/31/02):

	($000)	(%)
Long-Term Debt	96,250	16.1
Capital Lease Obligations	5,749	1.0
Common & Surplus	496,917	83.0
Total	598,916	100.0

BUSINESS:

Oxford Health Plans, Inc. is a managed-care company that provides health-benefit plans in New York, New Jersey and Connecticut. The Company's product line includes its point-of-service plans, health maintenance organizations, preferred provider organization plans, third-party administration of employer-funded benefits and Medicare plans. The Company currently offers its products through its HMO subsidiaries, Oxford Health Plans (New York), Inc., Oxford Health Plans (New Jersey), Inc. and Oxford Health Plans (Connecticut), Inc., MedSpan Health Options, Inc. and through Oxford Health Insurance, Inc. and Investors Guaranty Life Insurance Company, the Company's health insurance subsidiaries.

RECENT DEVELOPMENTS:

For the year ended 12/31/02, net income dropped 31.2% to $222.0 million compared with $322.4 million the previous year. Results for 2002 included a pre-tax litigation charge of $151.3 million for estimated settlement. Total revenues advanced 12.3% to $4.96 billion from $4.42 billion the year before. Premiums earned increased 12.5% to $4.85 billion from $4.31 billion, while revenues from third-party administration improved 28.7% to $17.7 million from $13.8 million a year earlier. Net investment and other income slipped to $94.7 million from $95.0 million the prior year. Total membership grew 6.1% to 1.6 million versus 1.5 million in 2001.

PROSPECTS:

The Company's strategy for 2003 will be to focus on developing new products and benefit designs to meet the changing needs of customers in its markets. Additionally, the Company will focus on modest geographic expansion, primarily to contiguous markets and continuing efforts to impact health care affordability by managing health care costs through a variety of initiatives. Moreover, OHP will look to achieve administrative efficiencies by increasing the level of electronic transactions and automation throughout its businesses.

ANNUAL FINANCIAL DATA:

FISCAL YEAR	TOT. REVS. ($mill.)	NET INC. ($mill.)	TOT. ASSETS ($mill.)	OPER. PROFIT %	NET PROFIT %	RET. ON EQUITY %	RET. ON ASSETS %	CURR. RATIO	EARN. PER SH. $	CASH FL. PER SH. $	TANG. BK. VAL. $	PRICE RANGE	AVG. P/E RATIO
p12/31/02	4,963.4	③ 222.0							③ 2.45			51.94 - 28.64	16.4
12/31/01	4,421.2	322.4	1,576.7	11.6	7.3	69.6	20.4	1.5	3.21	3.42	4.61	39.56 - 21.90	9.6
12/31/00	4,111.8	② 285.4	1,444.6	11.8	6.9	62.2	19.8	1.3	② 2.24	2.60	4.67	42.75 - 12.06	12.2
12/31/99	4,197.8	319.9	1,686.9	3.9	7.6	324.0	19.0	1.5	3.26	3.91	1.20	24.25 - 9.75	5.2
12/31/98	4,719.4	① d596.8	1,637.8	...	...	...	...	1.2	① d7.79	d6.96	...	22.00 - 5.81	...
12/31/97	4,240.1	① d291.3	1,398.0	...	...	...	...	1.1	① d3.70	d2.93	4.39	89.00 - 13.75	...
12/31/96	3,075.0	99.6	1,346.7	5.7	3.2	16.7	7.4	1.6	1.24	1.78	7.73	62.25 - 27.69	36.3
12/31/95	1,765.4	52.4	608.8	5.4	3.0	23.8	8.6	1.3	0.71	1.03	3.20	41.88 - 19.25	43.0
12/31/94	721.0	28.2	314.8	7.1	3.9	22.2	9.0	1.4	0.43	0.54	2.00	20.88 - 9.88	35.7
12/31/93	311.8	14.9	165.6	8.3	4.8	16.4	9.0	1.8	0.23	0.26	1.46	14.00 - 3.91	39.8

Statistics are as originally reported. Adj. for stk. splits: 2-for-1, 4/1/96; 2-for-1, 3/27/95; 2-for-1, 10/27/93 ① Incl. net non-recurr. chrgs. 12/31/98: $183.8 mill.; 12/31/97: $17.6 mill. ($0.22/sh.) ② Bef. extraord. chrg. of $20.3 mill. ③ Incl. pre-tax litig. chrg. of $151.3 mill.

OFFICERS:
K. J. Thiry, Chmn.
C. G. Berg, Pres., C.E.O., C.O.O.
K. Thompson, Exec. V.P., C.F.O.

INVESTOR CONTACT: Investor Relations Dept., (203) 459-6838

PRINCIPAL OFFICE: 48 Monroe Turnpike, Trumbull, CT 06611

TELEPHONE NUMBER: (203) 459-6000
FAX: (203) 851-2464
WEB: www.oxfordhealth.com

NO. OF EMPLOYEES: 3,500 (approx.)

SHAREHOLDERS: 895 (record)

ANNUAL MEETING: In May

INCORPORATED: DE, Sept., 1984

INSTITUTIONAL HOLDINGS:
No. of Institutions: 258
Shares Held: 83,574,078
% Held: 95.6

INDUSTRY: Hospital and medical service plans (SIC: 6324)

TRANSFER AGENT(S): EquiServe Trust Company, N.A., Canton, MA

PACKAGING CORPORATION OF AMERICA

EXCH.	SYM.	REC. PRICE	P/E RATIO	YLD.	MKT. CAP.	RANGE (52-WK.)	'02 Y/E PR.
NYSE	PKG	17.25 (2/28/03)	37.5	...	$1.82 bill.	21.10 - 16.20	18.24

MEDIUM GRADE. EARNINGS WERE ADVERSELY AFFECTED BY LOWER PRICES FOR CONTAINERBOARD AND CORRUGATED PRODUCTS.

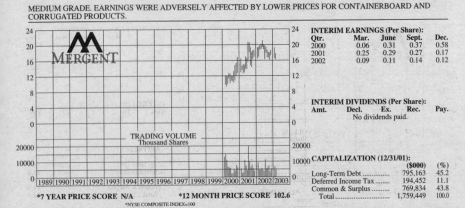

INTERIM EARNINGS (Per Share):

Qtr.	Mar.	June	Sept.	Dec.
2000	0.06	0.31	0.37	0.58
2001	0.25	0.29	0.27	0.17
2002	0.09	0.11	0.14	0.12

INTERIM DIVIDENDS (Per Share):

Amt.	Decl.	Ex.	Rec.	Pay.
		No dividends paid.		

CAPITALIZATION (12/31/01):

	($000)	(%)
Long-Term Debt	795,163	45.2
Deferred Income Tax	194,452	11.1
Common & Surplus	769,834	43.8
Total	1,759,449	100.0

*7 YEAR PRICE SCORE N/A   *12 MONTH PRICE SCORE 102.6

*NYSE COMPOSITE INDEX=100

BUSINESS:

Packaging Corporation of America was formed in April 1999 following the sale of Pactiv Corporation's former containerboard and corrugated products business to Madison Dearborn Partners, LLC, a private equity investment firm. The Company is a producer of containerboard and corrugated products in the United States, including kraft linerboard and corrugating medium. PKG's converting operations produce a range of corrugated packaging products, including conventional shipping containers used to protect and transport manufactured goods. PKG also produces multi-color boxes and displays that help to merchandise the packaged product in retail locations. In addition, PKG is a producer of meat boxes and wax-coated boxes for the agricultural industry. PKG operated four paper mills and 64 corrugated product plants in 25 states across the country as of 1/23/03. In 2001, PKG produced about 2.1 million tons of containerboard and shipped about 26.10 billion square feet of corrugated products.

RECENT DEVELOPMENTS:

For the year ended 12/31/02, net income declined 55.2% to $48.2 million compared with income of $107.5 million, before an extraordinary loss of $600,000 and an accounting change charge of $500,000, in 2001. The decline in earnings was primarily attributed to lower prices for containerboard and corrugated products. Also, higher volume and lower interest expense was partially offset by increased recycled fiber and medical costs and higher depreciation. Net sales decreased 3.0% to $1.74 billion from $1.79 billion a year earlier. Operating income fell 41.8% to $145.3 million from $249.5 million the year before.

PROSPECTS:

During the first quarter of 2003, the Company will take downtime at its two linerboard mills, Counce and Valdosta, for annual maintenance outages, which should reduce production by approximately 26,000 tons compared with the fourth quarter of 2002 and also increase mill operating costs. In addition, PKG expects seasonally higher fuel and wood costs in the first quarter. Based on these factors, and in light of current economic and pricing conditions, the Company expects first quarter 2003 earnings to be $0.04 lower than the fourth quarter of 2002.

ANNUAL FINANCIAL DATA:

FISCAL YEAR	TOT. REVS. ($Mill.)	NET INC. ($Mill.)	TOT. ASSETS ($Mill.)	OPER. PROFIT %	NET PROFIT %	RET. ON EQUITY %	RET. ON ASSETS %	CURR. RATIO	EARN. PER SH. $	CASH FL. PER SH. $	TANG. BK. VAL. $	PRICE RANGE	AVG. P/E RATIO
p12/31/02	1,735.9	48.2	1,971.8	13.9	6.0	14.0	5.5	2.3	0.45 ④ 0.99	2.33	7.25	21.10 - 16.20	41.4
12/31/01	1,790.0	② ④ 107.5	1,942.1	21.1	9.0	25.2	8.9	1.8	② ③ 1.43	2.81	6.45	20.70 - 12.65	16.8
12/31/00	1,921.9	② ③ 173.0	2,153.2	14.6	3.6	11.4	2.2	1.8	② 0.39	1.56	4.39	16.81 - 9.25	9.1
① 12/31/99	1,317.3	② 47.4										...	...

Statistics are as originally reported. ① From 4/12/99, date of inception. ② Bef. extraord. charge of $600,000, 2001; $11.1 mill., 2000; $6.9 mill., 12/31/99. ③ Incl. nonrecurr. gain of $60.4 mill. on timberland sales. ④ Excl. acctg. change chrg. of $500,000.

OFFICERS:
P. T. Stecko, Chmn., C.E.O.
R. B. West, Sr. V.P., C.F.O., Sec.

INVESTOR CONTACT: Investor Relations, (847) 454-2509

PRINCIPAL OFFICE: 1900 West Field Court, Lake Forest, IL 60045

TELEPHONE NUMBER: (847) 482-3000
FAX: (847) 482-3020
WEB: www.packagingcorp.com
NO. OF EMPLOYEES: 7,900 (avg.)
SHAREHOLDERS: 72
ANNUAL MEETING: In May
INCORPORATED: DE, Jan., 1999

INSTITUTIONAL HOLDINGS:
No. of Institutions: 140
Shares Held: 56,950,540
% Held: 54.5
INDUSTRY: Corrugated and solid fiber boxes (SIC: 2653)
TRANSFER AGENT(S): First Chicago Trust Company of New York, Jersey City, NJ

PACTIV CORPORATION

EXCH.	SYM.	REC. PRICE	P/E RATIO	YLD.	MKT. CAP.	RANGE (52-WK.)	'02 Y/E PR.
NYSE	PTV	19.76 (2/28/03)	14.3	...	$3.15 bill.	24.47 - 15.35	21.86

UPPER MEDIUM GRADE. THE COMPANY ANTICIPATES FULL-YEAR 2003 EARNINGS PER SHARE IN THE RANGE OF $1.40 TO $1.46, INCLUDING A PRE-TAX NON-CASH CHARGE FOR PENSION INCOME OF $60.0 MILLION.

INTERIM EARNINGS (Per Share):

Qtr.	Mar.	June	Sept.	Dec.
1998	0.11	0.30	0.09	d0.01
1999	0.03	0.28	0.01	d1.00
2000	0.17	0.24	0.24	0.05
2001	0.18	0.28	0.28	0.29
2002	0.26	0.38	0.37	0.37

INTERIM DIVIDENDS (Per Share):

Amt.	Decl.	Ex.	Rec.	Pay.
		No dividends paid.		

CAPITALIZATION (12/31/01):

	($000)	(%)
Long-Term Debt	1,211,000	34.6
Deferred Income Tax	594,000	17.0
Minority Interest	8,000	0.2
Common & Surplus	1,689,000	48.2
Total	3,502,000	100.0

*7 YEAR PRICE SCORE N/A   ***12 MONTH PRICE SCORE 110.7**
*NYSE COMPOSITE INDEX=100

BUSINESS:

Pactiv Corporation (formerly Tenneco Packaging Inc.) is a global supplier of consumer and specialty packaging products. The Company manufactures, markets, and sells consumer products, such as plastic storage bags for food and household items, plastic waste bags, foam and molded fiber tableware, and aluminum cookware. Well-known brands include HEFTY®, BAGGIES®, HEFTY ONEZIP®, KORDITE®, and E-Z FOIL®. The Company's protective packaging products are used to protect and cushion various commercial and industrial products from the point of manufacture to the point of delivery or pick-up, and principally serves the electronics, automotive, furniture, and e-commerce markets. The Company's flexible packaging products are mainly used in food, medical, pharmaceutical, chemical, and hygiene applications. PTV operated 72 facilities in 13 countries as of 1/22/03. On 11/4/99, PTV was spun off to shareholders of Tenneco Inc.

RECENT DEVELOPMENTS:

For the year ended 12/31/02, income increased 33.3% to $220.0 million, before an accounting change charge of $72.0 million, compared with income of $165.0 million, before income from discontinued operations of $28.0 million, in 2001. Results for 2002 included an unusual charge of $4.0 million. Sales rose 2.4% to $2.88 billion. During the year, volume grew 7.7% with 5.3% coming from base business and 2.4% from acquisitions.

PROSPECTS:

Going forward, strong volume growth from the Company's base business and improved efficiency stemming from productivity initiatives are expected to fuel results for 2003. The Company anticipates full-year 2003 earnings per share in the range of $1.40 to $1.46, including a pre-tax non-cash charges for pension income of $60.0 million. PTV expects free cash flow for 2003 in the range of $240.0 million to $260.0 million.

ANNUAL FINANCIAL DATA:

FISCAL YEAR	TOT. REVS. ($mill.)	NET INC. ($mill.)	TOT. ASSETS ($mill.)	OPER. PROFIT %	NET PROFIT %	RET. ON EQUITY %	RET. ON ASSETS %	CURR. RATIO	EARN. PER SH.$	CASH FL. PER SH.$	TANG. BK. VAL.$	PRICE RANGE	AVG. P/E RATIO
p12/31/02	2,880.0	⑦ 220.0	3,412.0						⑦ 1.37			24.47 - 15.35	14.5
12/31/01	2,812.0	⑥ 165.0	4,060.0	14.1	5.9	9.8	4.1	1.6	⑥ 1.03	2.14	4.90	18.10 - 11.26	14.3
12/31/00	3,134.0	⑤ 113.0	4,341.0	10.7	3.6	7.3	2.6	1.8	⑤ 0.70	1.84	3.79	13.31 - 7.50	14.9
12/31/99	2,913.0	④ d112.0	4,588.0	...	...	...	...	0.9	④ d0.67	0.43	2.19	14.50 - 9.31	...
12/31/98	2,788.0	③ 82.0	4,798.0	10.2	2.9	4.6	1.7	0.8	③ 0.49	1.52	...	...	...
12/31/97	2,569.0	② 106.0	4,618.0	11.9	4.1	5.8	2.3	1.2	② 0.63	1.57	...	...	...
12/31/96	2,036.0	① 65.0	...	11.5	3.2	...	...	...	① 0.38	1.16	...	...	...

Statistics are as originally reported. ① Bef. $71.0 mil ($0.42/sh) gain fr. disc. opers., $2.0 mil ($0.01/sh) extraord. chg. & incl. $15.0 mil gain fr. sale of assets. ② Bef. $21.0 mil ($0.12/sh) gain fr. disc. opers & $38.0 mil ($0.23/sh) acctg. chg. ③ Bef. $57.0 mil ($0.34/sh) inc. fr. disc. opers. & incl. $9.0 mil chg. fr. sale of assets. ④ Bef. $193.0 mil ($1.15/sh) loss fr. disc. opers., $7.0 mil ($0.04/sh) extraord. loss, $32.0 mil ($0.19/sh) acctg. chg. & incl. one-time pre-tax chgs. of $195.0 mil fr. restr. and sale of assets. ⑤ Bef. $134.0 mil ($0.83/sh) gain fr. disc. opers. & incl. $70.0 mil pre-tax restr. chg. and a net pre-tax gain of $26.0 mil fr. the sale of a business and spin-off transaction. ⑥ Bef. $28.0 mil ($0.17/sh) gain fr. disc. opers. & incl. $12.0 mil pre-tax restr. chg. and a net pre-tax gain of $12.0 mil fr. spin-off transaction. ⑦ Excl. an acctg. change chrg. of $72.0 mill., but incl. an unus. chrg. of $4.0 mill.

OFFICERS:
R. L. Wambold, Chmn., Pres., C.E.O.
A. A. Campbell, Sr. V.P., C.F.O.
J. V. Faulkner, Jr., V.P., Gen. Couns.

INVESTOR CONTACT: Christine Hanneman, Inv. Rel., (847) 482-2429

PRINCIPAL OFFICE: 1900 West Field Court, Lake Forest, IL 60045

TELEPHONE NUMBER: (847) 482-2000
FAX: (847) 482-4548
WEB: www.pactiv.com
NO. OF EMPLOYEES: 13,000 (approx.)
SHAREHOLDERS: 49,959 (approx.)
ANNUAL MEETING: In May
INCORPORATED: DE, 1965

INSTITUTIONAL HOLDINGS:
No. of Institutions: 301
Shares Held: 129,249,026
% Held: 81.6

INDUSTRY: Plastics products, nec (SIC: 3089)

TRANSFER AGENT(S): First Chicago Trust Company of New York, Jersey City, NJ

PALL CORPORATION

EXCH.	SYM.	REC. PRICE	P/E RATIO	YLD.	MKT. CAP.	RANGE (52-WK.)	'02 Y/E PR.
NYSE	PLL	16.14 (2/28/03)	47.5	2.2%	$1.98 bill.	23.42 - 14.68	16.68

UPPER MEDIUM GRADE. THE COMPANY EXPECTS FISCAL 2003 EARNINGS IN THE RANGE OF $1.02 TO $1.12 PER SHARE.

7 YEAR PRICE SCORE 88.0   **12 MONTH PRICE SCORE 93.9**
*NYSE COMPOSITE INDEX=100

INTERIM EARNINGS (Per Share):

Qtr.	Oct.	Jan.	Apr.	July
1996-97	0.14	0.23	d0.18	0.34
1997-98	0.15	0.22	0.06	0.32
1998-99	0.12	0.15	d0.23	0.40
1999-00	0.20	0.27	0.34	0.37
2000-01	0.21	0.24	0.30	0.21
2001-02	0.16	0.15	0.21	0.07
2002-03	d0.19	0.25	...	...

INTERIM DIVIDENDS (Per Share):

Amt.	Decl.	Ex.	Rec.	Pay.
0.17Q	1/16/02	1/30/02	2/01/02	2/13/02
0.09Q	4/17/02	5/01/02	5/03/02	5/17/02
0.09Q	7/16/02	7/30/02	8/01/02	8/15/02
0.09Q	10/04/02	10/22/02	10/24/02	11/06/02
0.09Q	1/15/03	1/30/03	2/03/03	2/17/03

Indicated div.: $0.36 (Div. Reinv. Plan)

CAPITALIZATION (8/3/02):

	($000)	(%)
Long-Term Debt	619,705	41.9
Deferred Income Tax	38,261	2.6
Common & Surplus	819,720	55.5
Total	1,477,686	100.0

BUSINESS:

Pall Corporation is a supplier of fine filters mainly made by the Company using its proprietary filter media, and other fluid clarification and separations equipment for the removal of solid, liquid and gaseous contaminants from a wide variety of liquids and gases. The Company provides products for use in biotechnology; pharmaceuticals; transfusion medicine; semiconductors; municipal drinking water; and aerospace. PLL is comprised of two operating segments: Life Sciences and Industrial. The Industrial sub-segments (53.1% of 2002 revenues) are General Industrial, Aerospace, and Microelectronics. The Life Sciences segment (46.9%) is comprised of two sub-segments: Medical and BioPharmaceuticals. PLL has operations in more than 30 countries.

RECENT DEVELOPMENTS:

For the quarter ended 2/1/03, net income leapt 70.4% to $31.4 million compared with $18.4 million in the equivalent 2002 quarter. Earnings benefited from internal growth, boosted by continuing cost-reduction programs, as well as contributions from the Filtration and Separations Group (FSG), acquired in April 2002. Results for 2002 included restructuring and other charges of $924,000. Net sales jumped 36.1% to $388.5 million from $285.4 million a year earlier. Gross profit increased 34.6% to $188.4 million from $140.0 million the year before.

PROSPECTS:

Looking ahead, the Company expects fiscal 2003 earnings in the range of $1.02 to $1.12 per share, an increase of $0.02 from the mid-point of its prior guidance. PLL expects fiscal third quarter earnings in the range of $0.28 to $0.33 per share. The integration of FSG remains on track. Furthermore, during the first quarter of fiscal 2003, PLL reorganized its Life Science business such that the Company's hospital and medical original equipment manufacturing sub-segments were combined with the Blood segment to form a new segment called Pall Medical. This action is expected to reduce costs and result in the termination of approximately 105 employees globally.

ANNUAL FINANCIAL DATA:

FISCAL YEAR	TOT. REVS. ($mill.)	NET INC. ($mill.)	TOT. ASSETS ($mill.)	OPER. PROFIT %	NET PROFIT %	RET. ON EQUITY %	RET. ON ASSETS %	CURR. RATIO	EARN. PER SH.$	CASH FL.PER SH.$	TANG. BK. VAL.$	DIV. PER SH.$	PRICE RANGE	AVG. P/E RATIO	AVG. YIELD %
8/03/02	1,290.8	⑥ 73.2	2,027.2	8.9	5.7	8.9	3.6	2.1	⑥ 0.59	1.19	4.21	0.44	24.48 - 14.68	33.2	2.2
7/28/01	1,235.4	⑤ 118.0	1,548.5	13.5	9.6	15.3	7.6	2.5	⑤ 0.95	1.53	6.29	0.68	26.25 - 17.50	23.0	3.1
7/29/00	1,224.1	146.6	1,507.3	16.5	12.0	19.3	9.7	1.7	1.18	1.75	6.18	0.66	25.00 - 17.13	17.8	3.1
7/31/99	1,147.1	② 51.5	1,488.3	6.3	4.5	7.0	3.5	1.3	② 0.41	1.01	5.88	0.64	26.19 - 15.75	51.1	3.1
8/01/98	1,087.3	④ 93.6	1,346.9	13.1	8.6	12.2	7.0	1.5	④ 0.75	1.33	6.18	0.62	26.63 - 19.38	30.7	2.7
8/02/97	1,062.0	③ 67.3	1,265.6	8.4	6.3	8.2	5.3	2.0	③ 0.53	1.03	6.48	0.56	26.13 - 19.50	43.0	2.5
8/03/96	967.4	138.5	1,185.0	21.5	14.3	18.9	11.7	1.8	1.21	1.67	6.37	0.49	29.38 - 19.63	20.2	2.0
7/29/95	829.3	① 119.2	1,074.9	21.4	14.4	18.3	11.1	1.8	① 1.04	1.43	5.70	0.42	27.88 - 18.38	22.2	1.8
7/30/94	706.1	② 98.9	959.6	20.1	14.0	16.8	10.3	1.8	② 0.86	1.20	5.09	0.37	20.25 - 13.63	19.7	2.2
7/31/93	691.9	⑥ 78.3	902.3	16.3	11.3	14.4	8.7	1.7	⑥ 0.68	1.00	4.68	0.32	21.63 - 15.63	27.4	1.7

Statistics are as originally reported. ① Bef. acctg. change chrg. $780,000. ② Incl. restruct. chrg. $17.3 mill. (d$0.15/sh.), 1993; $2.3 mill., 1994; $89.4 mill., 1999; $9.9 mill., 2000. ③ Incl. merger (Gelman Sciences) restruct. chrgs. & other one-time chrgs. of $95.9 mill. ④ Incl. non-recurr. income of $5.0 mill. from litigation settlement & a chrg. of $27.0 mill. acq. related Rochem chrg. ⑤ Incl. restruct. & other chrgs. of $17.2 mill. ⑥ Incl. restruct. and other chrg. of $26.8 mill. and non-recurr. chrg. $6.0 million

OFFICERS:
E. Krasnoff, Chmn., C.E.O.
J. Hayward-Surry, Pres.
C. Stevens, C.O.O.
J. Adamovich, Jr., Group V.P., C.F.O., Treas.

INVESTOR CONTACT: Diane Foster, Investor Relations, (516) 801-9102

PRINCIPAL OFFICE: 2200 Northern Boulevard, East Hills, NY 11548

TELEPHONE NUMBER: (516) 484-5400
FAX: (516) 484-3649
WEB: www.pall.com

NO. OF EMPLOYEES: 10,700 (approx.)

SHAREHOLDERS: 5,300 (approx.)

ANNUAL MEETING: In Nov.

INCORPORATED: NY, July, 1946

INSTITUTIONAL HOLDINGS:
No. of Institutions: 273
Shares Held: 109,278,846
% Held: 88.9

INDUSTRY: General industrial machinery, nec (SIC: 3569)

TRANSFER AGENT(S): EquiServe, L.P., Providence, RI

PARK PLACE ENTERTAINMENT CORPORATION

EXCH.	SYM.	REC. PRICE	P/E RATIO	YLD.	MKT. CAP.	RANGE (52-WK.)	'02 Y/E PR.
NYSE	PPE	7.20 (2/28/03)	14.1	...	$2.17 bill.	12.93 - 6.06	8.40

MEDIUM GRADE. THE COMPANY PLANS TO EXPAND ROOM CAPACITY AT CERTAIN OF ITS PROPERTIES.

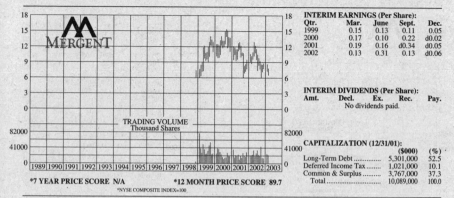

7 YEAR PRICE SCORE N/A *12 MONTH PRICE SCORE 89.7*
*NYSE COMPOSITE INDEX=100

INTERIM EARNINGS (Per Share):

Qtr.	Mar.	June	Sept.	Dec.
1999	0.15	0.13	0.11	0.05
2000	0.17	0.10	0.22	d0.02
2001	0.19	0.16	d0.34	d0.05
2002	0.13	0.31	0.13	d0.06

INTERIM DIVIDENDS (Per Share):

Amt.	Decl.	Ex.	Rec.	Pay.
	No dividends paid.			

CAPITALIZATION (12/31/01):

	($000)	(%)
Long-Term Debt	5,301,000	52.5
Deferred Income Tax	1,021,000	10.1
Common & Surplus	3,767,000	37.3
Total	10,089,000	100.0

BUSINESS:

Park Place Entertainment Corporation is primarily engaged in the ownership, operation and development of gaming facilities, and conducts its operations under the Caesars, Bally's, Paris, Flamingo, Grand, Hilton, and Conrad brands. As of 12/31/02, the Company operated a total of 27 casino hotels, including 17 located in the U.S., of which eight are located in Nevada, four are located in Atlantic City, New Jersey, and five are located in Mississippi. As of 6/30/02, PPE had a 49.9%-owned and managed riverboat casino in New Orleans, an 82.0%-owned and managed riverboat casino in Harrison County, Indiana, the casino operations of Caesars Palace at Sea, and two partially owned and managed casinos in Nova Scotia, Canada. The Company partially owns and manages two casino investments internationally. The Company also provides management services to two casinos internationally and the slot operations at the Dover Downs racetrack in Delaware. Net sales for 2001 were derived as follows: casino, 70.6%; rooms, 12.0%; food and beverage, 9.8%; and other revenue, 7.6%.

RECENT DEVELOPMENTS:

For the year ended 12/31/02, PPE reported income of $158.0 million, before an accounting charge of $979.0 million, versus a net loss of $24.0 million in 2001. Earnings for 2002 and 2001 included pre-opening expenses of $1.0 million and $2.0 million, one-time expenses of $62.0 million and $143.0 million, and equity in earnings of unconsolidated affiliates of $29.0 million and $50.0 million, respectively. Earnings also included an investment gain of $44.0 million in 2002 and an investment loss of $32.0 million in 2001. Net revenue rose 1.5% to $4.65 billion.

PROSPECTS:

The Company is reviewing plans to increase room capacity at Caesars Palace in Las Vegas and Caesars Atlantic City. Preliminary costs for the Caesars Palace project total $350.0 million, to be spent in the second half of 2003 through the end of 2004. Preliminary cost estimates for the Caesars Atlantic City project are $200.0 million, to be spent beginning in the fourth quarter of 2003 through the second half of 2005. Looking ahead, in 2003, earnings per share are expected to range from $0.13 to $0.15 in the first quarter and between $0.52 and $0.57 for the full year.

ANNUAL FINANCIAL DATA:

FISCAL YEAR	TOT. REVS. ($mill.)	NET INC. ($mill.)	TOT. ASSETS ($mill.)	OPER. PROFIT %	NET PROFIT %	RET. ON EQUITY %	RET. ON ASSETS %	CURR. RATIO	EARN. PER SH. $	CASH FL. PER SH. $	TANG. BK. VAL. $	PRICE RANGE	AVG. P/E RATIO
p12/31/02	4,652.0	④⑤ 158.0			...	...	...		④⑤ d2.70			12.93 - 6.06	...
12/31/01	4,631.0	④ d24.0	10,808.0	8.8	...	...	...	1.3	④ d0.08	1.71	6.49	12.93 - 6.00	...
12/31/00	4,896.0	④ 143.0	10,995.0	14.2	2.9	3.8	1.3	1.3	④ 0.46	2.16	6.52	15.38 - 9.88	27.4
12/31/99	3,176.0	②③ 138.0	11,151.0	12.6	4.3	3.7	1.2	1.2	②③ 0.45	1.46	6.01	14.00 - 6.06	22.3
12/31/98	2,305.0	109.0	7,174.0	13.1	4.7	3.0	1.5	1.4	0.42	1.28	7.63	7.44 - 6.00	16.0
12/31/97	2,572.0	67.0	5,689.0	7.8	2.6	2.0	1.2	1.3	0.25	1.04	7.22	...	...
12/31/96	1,415.0	① 36.0	5,447.0	6.5	2.5	1.1	0.7	1.3	① 0.18	0.74	...	...	...
12/31/95	1,284.0	85.0	...	12.9	6.6	...	...	...	0.44	0.84	...	...	...

Statistics are as originally reported. ① Bef. extraord. loss of $74.0 mill. ② Incl. impair. losses & oth. exp. of $26.0 mill., 1999; $29.0 mill., 1998. ③ Bef. acctg. chrg. of $2.0 mill.; incl. pre-open. exp. of $47.0 mill. ④ Incl. pre-tax pre-open. exp. of $1.0 mill., 2002; $2.0 mill., 2001; $3.0 mill., 2000 & pre-tax net nonrecurr. chrgs. of $18.0 mill., 2002; $175.0 mill., 2001; $45.0 mill., 2000. ⑤ Bef. acctg. chrg. of $979.0 mill.

OFFICERS:
S. F. Bollenbach, Chmn.
W. R. Barr, Pres., C.E.O.
H. C. Hagerty, Exec. V.P., C.F.O., Treas.
INVESTOR CONTACT: Josh Hirsburg, Investor Relations, (702) 699-5269
PRINCIPAL OFFICE: 3930 Howard Hughes Parkway, Las Vegas, NV 89109

TELEPHONE NUMBER: (702) 699-5000
FAX: (702) 699-5121
WEB: www.parkplace.com
NO. OF EMPLOYEES: 55,000 (approx.)
SHAREHOLDERS: 11,000 (approx.)
ANNUAL MEETING: In May
INCORPORATED: DE, Dec., 1998

INSTITUTIONAL HOLDINGS:
No. of Institutions: 230
Shares Held: 203,869,656
% Held: 67.8

INDUSTRY: Hotels and motels (SIC: 7011)

TRANSFER AGENT(S): Wells Fargo Shareowner Services, South St. Paul, MN

PARKER-HANNIFIN CORP.

EXCH.	SYM.	REC. PRICE	P/E RATIO	YLD.	MKT. CAP.	RANGE (52-WK.)	'02 Y/E PR.
NYSE	PH	40.31 (2/28/03)	33.9	1.9%	$4.76 bill.	54.88 - 34.52	46.13

MEDIUM GRADE. THE COMPANY NOW EXPECTS FULL-YEAR FISCAL 2003 EARNINGS OF BETWEEN $2.10 AND $2.30 PER SHARE, EXCLUDING REALIGNMENT COSTS.

TRADING VOLUME
Thousand Shares

*7 YEAR PRICE SCORE 117.3   *12 MONTH PRICE SCORE 103.4
*NYSE COMPOSITE INDEX=100

INTERIM EARNINGS (Per Share):

Qtr.	Sept.	Dec.	Mar.	June
1997-98	0.70	0.63	0.75	0.80
1998-99	0.71	0.58	0.92	0.84
1999-00	0.67	0.68	0.97	0.99
2000-01	1.09	0.68	0.42	0.42
2001-02	0.52	0.25	0.45	d0.10
2002-03	0.52	0.32	...	...

INTERIM DIVIDENDS (Per Share):

Amt.	Decl.	Ex.	Rec.	Pay.
0.18Q	1/31/02	2/12/02	2/14/02	3/01/02
0.18Q	4/18/02	5/21/02	5/23/02	6/07/02
0.18Q	7/11/02	8/20/02	8/22/02	9/06/02
0.18Q	10/23/02	11/18/02	11/20/02	12/06/02
0.19Q	1/30/03	2/18/03	2/20/03	3/07/03

Indicated div.: $0.76 (Div. Reinv. Plan)

CAPITALIZATION (6/30/02):

	($000)	(%)
Long-Term Debt	1,088,883	29.0
Deferred Income Tax	76,955	2.1
Common & Surplus	2,583,516	68.9
Total	3,749,354	100.0

BUSINESS:

Parker-Hannifin Corp. is a worldwide producer of motion control products, including fluid power systems, electromechanical controls and related components. The Industrial segment, (66.2% of fiscal 2002 sales), includes several business units that produce motion-control and fluid power system components for builders and users of various types of manufacturing, packaging, processing, transportation, agricultural, construction and military machinery, vehicles and equipment. The Aerospace segment, (19.1%), produces hydraulic, pneumatic and fuel systems and components that are utilized on domestic commercial, military and general aviation aircraft. The Other segment, (14.7%), consists of several business units that produce motion-control and fluid power system components for use primarily in the transportation industry. On 7/21/01, PH acquired Wynn's International, Inc. for about $497.0 million.

RECENT DEVELOPMENTS:

For the quarter ended 12/31/02, net income increased 29.2% to $37.6 million compared with $29.1 million in the same period a year earlier. Net sales climbed 5.6% to $1.52 billion from $1.44 billion the previous year. PH's North American Industrial operations reported a sales gain of 3.6% to $669.9 million, while operating profits grew 16.3% to $27.4 million. International Industrial sales and operating income climbed 28.7% and 69.0% to $373.9 million and $22.3 million, respectively, aided by recent acquisitions and currency. Sales and operating profit from the Aerospace segment slipped 4.5% to $275.4 million and operating income slid 8.2% to $42.7 million.

PROSPECTS:

PH's near-term prospects are mixed. On the positive side, the Company has indicated that it is in the final stages of its planned realignment activities, which should enable it to capitalize on the eventual industrial economic recovery. In addition, PH noted that it is seeing some stability from its commercial aviation segment; however, the Company expects that this segment will have to contend with margin pressure into the foreseeable future. Consequently, PH now expects full-year fiscal 2003 earnings of between $2.10 and $2.30 per share, down from its previous guidance that ranged from $2.20 to $2.50 per share. Both projections exclude realignment costs.

ANNUAL FINANCIAL DATA:

FISCAL YEAR	TOT. REVS. ($mill.)	NET INC. ($mill.)	TOT. ASSETS ($mill.)	OPER. PROFIT %	NET PROFIT %	RET. ON EQUITY %	RET. ON ASSETS %	CURR. RATIO	EARN. PER SH.$	CASH FL. PER SH.$	TANG. BK. VAL.$	DIV. PER SH.$	PRICE RANGE	AVG. P/E RATIO	AVG. YIELD %
6/30/02	6,149.1	④ 130.2	5,752.6	5.0	2.1	5.0	2.3	1.6	④ 1.12	3.55	12.27	0.72	54.88 - 34.52	39.9	1.6
6/30/01	5,979.6	①③ 344.2	5,337.7	9.6	5.8	13.6	6.4	1.6	①③ 2.99	5.29	13.43	0.72	50.10 - 30.40	13.5	1.8
6/30/00	5,355.3	368.2	4,646.3	11.6	6.9	15.9	7.9	1.8	3.31	5.17	14.94	0.68	54.00 - 31.00	12.8	1.6
6/30/99	4,958.8	310.5	3,705.9	10.9	6.3	16.7	8.4	2.4	2.83	4.67	12.62	0.68	51.44 - 29.50	14.3	1.7
6/30/98	4,633.0	① 323.2	3,524.8	11.9	7.0	19.2	9.2	1.8	① 2.88	4.52	11.74	0.60	52.63 - 26.56	13.7	1.5
6/30/97	4,091.1	274.0	2,998.9	11.3	6.7	17.7	9.1	2.1	2.46	3.98	11.32	0.57	51.25 - 24.92	15.5	1.5
6/30/96	3,586.4	239.7	2,887.1	11.3	6.7	17.3	8.3	1.8	2.15	3.42	9.55	0.48	29.42 - 21.25	11.8	1.9
6/30/95	3,214.4	218.2	2,302.2	11.9	6.8	18.3	9.5	1.9	1.97	3.06	9.75	0.47	27.67 - 18.39	11.7	2.1
6/30/94	2,576.3	①② 52.2	1,912.8	6.4	2.0	5.4	2.7	2.0	①② 0.48	1.51	8.31	0.44	20.95 - 15.11	37.9	2.5
6/30/93	2,489.3	65.1	1,963.6	6.1	2.6	7.0	3.3	2.3	0.60	1.64	7.96	0.43	16.95 - 12.45	24.7	2.9

Statistics are as originally reported. Adj. for 3-for-2 stk. split, 9/97 & 6/95. ① Bef. extraord. chrg. 6/30/01, $3.4 mill.; chrg. 6/30/98, $3.7 mill.; chrg. 6/30/94, $4.5 mill. ② Incl. non-recurr. pre-tax chrg. of $56.5 mill. ③ Incl. $47.7 mill. gain on disp. of assets. ④ Incl. goodwill impairment loss of $39.5 mill. & loss on disp. of assets of $8.5 mill.

OFFICERS:
D. E. Collins, Chmn.
D. E. Washkewicz, Pres., C.E.O.
M. J. Hiemstra, Exec. V.P., C.F.O.
INVESTOR CONTACT: Lorrie Paul Crum, V.P., Corp. Comm., (216) 896-2750
PRINCIPAL OFFICE: 6035 Parkland Blvd., Cleveland, OH 44124-4141

TELEPHONE NUMBER: (216) 896-3000
FAX: (216) 383-9414
WEB: www.parker.com
NO. OF EMPLOYEES: 48,176 (approx.)
SHAREHOLDERS: 53,000 (approx. benef.)
ANNUAL MEETING: In Oct.
INCORPORATED: OH, Dec., 1938

PAYLESS SHOESOURCE INC.

EXCH.	SYM.	REC. PRICE	P/E RATIO	YLD.	MKT. CAP.	RANGE (52-WK.)	'02 Y/E PR.
NYSE	PSS	15.54 (Adj.; 2/28/03)	10.1	…	$1.04 bill.	21.57 - 13.73	17.16

MEDIUM GRADE. THE COMPANY IS TARGETING EARNINGS OF $1.55 TO $1.75 PER SHARE FOR FISCAL 2003.

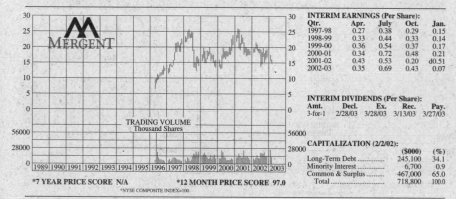

*7 YEAR PRICE SCORE N/A   ***12 MONTH PRICE SCORE 97.0**

NYSE COMPOSITE INDEX=100

INTERIM EARNINGS (Per Share):

Qtr.	Apr.	July	Oct.	Jan.
1997-98	0.27	0.38	0.29	0.15
1998-99	0.33	0.44	0.33	0.14
1999-00	0.36	0.54	0.37	0.17
2000-01	0.34	0.72	0.48	0.21
2001-02	0.43	0.53	0.20	d0.51
2002-03	0.35	0.69	0.43	0.07

INTERIM DIVIDENDS (Per Share):

Amt.	Decl.	Ex.	Rec.	Pay.
3-for-1	2/28/03	3/28/03	3/13/03	3/27/03

CAPITALIZATION (2/2/02):

	($000)	(%)
Long-Term Debt	245,100	34.1
Minority Interest	6,700	0.9
Common & Surplus	467,000	65.0
Total	718,800	100.0

BUSINESS:

Payless ShoeSource Inc. is a retailer of family footwear. As of 2/1/03, PSS operated a total of 4,992 stores located in 50 states, the District of Columbia, Puerto Rico, the U.S. Virgin Islands, Guam, Saipan, Canada, Costa Rica, El Salvador, Guatemala, Trinadad and Tobago, and the Dominican Republic. Payless ShoeSource® stores, which average about 3,300 square feet, feature footwear for men, women and children, including athletic, casual, dress, sandals, work boots and slippers. In addition, PSS operates stores under the Parade name, which average about 2,400 square feet, that sell women's footwear and accessories at moderate prices. In March 1997, PSS purchased inventory, property and trademarks, and assumed leases on 186 stores of the Parade division from J. Baker, Inc. for about $28.0 million.

RECENT DEVELOPMENTS:

For the 52 weeks ended 2/1/03, net earnings more than doubled to $105.8 million from $45.4 million in the corresponding prior-year period. Results for fiscal 2003 included a one-time pre-tax gain of $2.8 million stemming from the reversal of a restructuring charge reported in the fourth quarter of 2001. Results for fiscal 2002 included a $65.6 million one-time pre-tax restructuring charge. Net retail sales slipped 1.2% to $2.88 billion from $2.91 billion the previous year. Same-store sales decreased 3.2% year over year. Gross profit was $871.9 million, or 30.3% of net sales, versus $881.4 million, or 30.3% of net sales, a year earlier. Operating profit advanced 78.3% to $178.1 million.

PROSPECTS:

For the first quarter of fiscal 2003, PSS anticipates earnings in the range of $0.38 to $0.42 per share. Looking ahead, the Company is targeting full fiscal-2003 earnings of between $1.55 and $1.75 per share and low single-digit comparable-store sales growth. Meanwhile, PSS expects total capital expenditures for fiscal 2003 to be about $130.0 million, including a $7.0 million contribution from the Company's joint venture partners in Latin America. During fiscal 2003, PSS plans to expand its store base by 50 to 60 net new stores. The Company anticipates opening between 25 and 30 new stores in Central America, 10 to 15 stores in South America, and approximately ten net new stores in Canada in fiscal 2003.

ANNUAL FINANCIAL DATA:

FISCAL YEAR	TOT. REVS. ($mill.)	NET INC. ($mill.)	TOT. ASSETS ($mill.)	OPER. PROFIT %	NET PROFIT %	RET. ON EQUITY %	RET. ON ASSETS %	CURR. RATIO	EARN. PER SH. $	CASH FL. PER SH. $	TANG. BK. VAL. $	PRICE RANGE	AVG. P/E RATIO
p2/01/03	2,878.0	① 105.8							① 1.55			21.57 - 13.73	11.4
2/02/02	2,913.7	① 45.4	1,069.2	3.4	1.6	9.7	4.2	1.8	① 0.67	2.25	7.00	26.07 - 17.17	32.3
2/03/01	2,948.4	② 124.2	1,002.8	7.7	4.2	30.3	12.4	1.9	② 1.72	3.14	6.22	23.90 - 12.92	10.7
1/29/00	2,730.1	136.5	1,074.6	8.3	5.0	19.4	12.7	2.9	1.45	2.51	7.92	19.94 - 13.33	11.5
1/30/99	2,615.5	135.0	1,017.9	8.3	5.2	19.2	13.3	2.5	1.26	2.17	7.22	25.67 - 12.33	15.1
1/31/98	2,566.9	128.9	1,073.0	8.0	5.0	15.4	12.0	3.2	1.10	1.92	7.47	22.63 - 11.46	15.4
2/01/97	2,333.7	107.7	1,091.8	7.4	4.6	12.6	9.9	3.1	0.89	1.71	7.12	13.92 - 6.50	11.4
2/03/96	2,330.3	① 54.0	1,014.3	3.9	2.3	7.2	5.3	2.1	① 0.45	1.23	6.27	…	…
1/28/95	2,116.4	131.5	1,019.8	10.3	6.2	16.6	12.9	2.3	…	…	…	…	…
1/31/94	1,966.5	132.8	…	11.3	6.8	…	…	…	…	…	…	…	…

Statistics are as originally reported. Adj. for stk. split: 3-for-1, 3/03. ① Incl. $2.8 mill. non-recurr. gain, 2003; $65.6 mill. chg., 2002; $71.8 mill. chg., 1996. ② Bef. $3.6 mill. ($0.05/sh.) extraord. chg. & incl. $8.0 mill. non-recurr. chg.

OFFICERS:
S. J. Douglass, Chmn., C.E.O.
D. L. Cantrell, Pres.
U. E. Porzig, Sr. V.P., C.F.O., Treas.
INVESTOR CONTACT: Investor Relations,
(800) 626-3204
PRINCIPAL OFFICE: 3231 South East Sixth Avenue, Topeka, KS 66607-2207

TELEPHONE NUMBER: (785) 233-5171
FAX: (785) 295-6049
WEB: www.paylessshoesource.com
NO. OF EMPLOYEES: 14,900 full-time (approx.); 13,100 part-time (approx.)
SHAREHOLDERS: 16,000 (approx.)
ANNUAL MEETING: In May
INCORPORATED: DE, June, 1988

INSTITUTIONAL HOLDINGS:
No. of Institutions: 174
Shares Held: 74,065,827 (Adj.)
% Held: 98.9

INDUSTRY: Shoe stores (SIC: 5661)

TRANSFER AGENT(S): UMB Bank, Kansas City, MO

PEABODY ENERGY CORP.

EXCH.	SYM.	REC. PRICE	P/E RATIO	YLD.	MKT. CAP.	RANGE (52-WK.)	'02 Y/E PR.
NYSE	BTU	28.58 (2/28/03)	14.6	1.4%	$1.49 bill.	30.75 - 17.50	29.23

LOWER MEDIUM GRADE. EARNINGS FOR 2003 ARE EXPECTED TO BENEFIT FROM DEMAND IMPROVEMENTS IN THE SECOND HALF OF 2003, NEW MINES INSTALLED IN 2002 AND 2003 AND OPERATING COST INITIATIVES.

TRADING VOLUME
Thousand Shares

1989 1990 1991 1992 1993 1994 1995 1996 1997 1998 1999 2000 2001 2002 2003

*7 YEAR PRICE SCORE N/A   *12 MONTH PRICE SCORE 111.0

*NYSE COMPOSITE INDEX=100

INTERIM EARNINGS (Per Share):

Qtr.	June	Sept.	Dec.	Mar.
1999-00	d0.27	d0.20	d0.18	4.08
2000-01	d0.25	d0.33	d0.06	3.60
2001-02	0.22	0.08	0.10	...
Qtr.	Mar.	June	Sept.	Dec.
2002	0.42	0.45	0.54	0.55

INTERIM DIVIDENDS (Per Share):

Amt.	Decl.	Ex.	Rec.	Pay.
0.10Q	1/29/02	2/08/02	2/12/02	3/06/02
0.10Q	4/18/02	4/30/02	5/02/02	5/23/02
0.10Q	7/23/02	7/31/02	8/02/02	8/23/02
0.10Q	10/22/02	11/01/02	11/05/02	11/26/02
0.10Q	1/28/03	2/07/03	2/11/03	3/05/03

Indicated div.: $0.40

CAPITALIZATION (12/31/01):

	($000)	(%)
Long-Term Debt	984,568	38.1
Deferred Income Tax	564,764	21.8
Common & Surplus	1,035,472	40.1
Total	2,584,804	100.0

BUSINESS:

Peabody Energy Corp. (formerly P&L Coal Holdings Corporation) is a coal-mining company. BTU owns majority interests in coal operations located throughout all major U.S. coal producing regions, including mines in Arizona, Colorado, Montana, New Mexico, Wyoming, Illinois, Indiana, Kentucky and West Virginia. In addition to its mining operations, the Company markets and trades coal and emission allowances and is expanding into energy-related businesses, including coalbed methane production, transportation-related services, third-party coal contract restructuring and participation in the development of coal-based generating plants. For 2002, BTU sold approximately 197.9 million tons of coal. BTU's coal products fuel more than 9.0% of all U.S. electricity generation.

RECENT DEVELOPMENTS:

For the year ended 12/31/02, BTU reported net income of $105.5 million versus income of $143.7 million, before a gain from discontinued operations of $1.1 million and an extraordinary charge of $37.5 million, in the previous year. Earnings were negatively affected by cost increases from operating certain mines below capacity and higher revenue-based royalties and taxes. Results for 2001 included a gain on the sale of Peabody Resources Limited of $171.7 mil-

lion. Total revenues increased 4.1% to $2.72 billion from $2.61 billion a year earlier, driven by improved pricing and a 2.0% increase in sales volume. Results included Australian mining operations revenue of $9.9 million in 2002 and other revenue of $18.7 million. Revenue from U.S. mining operations rose 6.1% to $2.48 billion, while trading and brokerage revenue declined 7.2% to $205.0 million.

PROSPECTS:

The Company expects normal weather patterns and high natural gas prices to positively impact coal-fueled generation and increase coal demand approximately 2.0% in 2003, while financial concerns for certain producers may negatively affect industry production. BTU believes a sustained

economic recovery, severe weather or natural gas shortages could strain generating capacity and coal supplies. Earnings for 2003 are expected to benefit from demand improvements in the second half of 2003, new mines installed in 2002 and 2003 and operating cost initiatives.

ANNUAL FINANCIAL DATA:

FISCAL YEAR	TOT. REVS. ($mill.)	NET INC. ($mill.)	TOT. ASSETS ($mill.)	OPER. PROFIT %	NET PROFIT %	RET. ON EQUITY %	RET. ON ASSETS %	CURR. RATIO	EARN. PER SH. $	CASH FL. PER SH. $	TANG. BK. VAL. $	DIV. PER SH. $	PRICE RANGE	AVG. P/E RATIO	AVG. YIELD %
p12/31/02	2,717.1	[7] 105.5							[7] 1.96			0.40		12.3	1.7
[8] 12/31/01	2,026.8	[5] 19.3	5,150.9	5.7	1.0	1.9	0.4	0.8	[5] 0.38	4.02	19.91	0.20	30.75 - 17.50	79.1	0.7
3/31/01	2,669.7	[4] 102.7	5,209.5	12.8	3.8	16.3	2.0	0.8	[4] 2.97	12.17	22.86	...	37.95 - 22.20	...	...
3/31/00	2,710.5	[3] 118.6	5,826.8	7.1	4.4	23.3	2.0	0.9	[3] 3.43	14.04	18.45	...	...	...	...
3/31/99	2,056.8	[2] d5.4		7.6		...	...	...	[2] d0.16	7.08	...	...	...	...	...
5/19/98	290.7	[1] 1.6	...	3.0	0.5	...	...	...	...	1.06	...	...	...	...	...

Statistics are as originally reported. [1] Bef. loss fr. disc. oper. $1.7 mill.; incl. pre-tax net gain on asset disp. $328,000. [2] Bef. inc.fr. disc. oper. $6.4 mill. [3] Bef. loss fr. disc. oper. $12.1 mill.; incl. incl. pre-tax net gain on asset disp. $6.4 mill. [4] Bef. extr. chrg. $8.5 mill. & gain fr. disc. oper. $12.9 mill.; incl. pre-tax gain on sale of Australian oper. $171.7 mill. and pre-tax net gain on asset disp. $5.7 mill. [5] Bef. extr. chrg. $29.0 mill.; incl. net pre-tax gain on asset sale $14.3 mill. [6] For 9 months. [7] Incl. litig. chrg. $17.2 mill. and restr. chrg. $13.0 mill.

OFFICERS:
I. F. Engelhardt, Chmn., C.E.O.
R. A. Navarre, Exec. V.P., C.F.O.
S. F. Schaab, V.P., Treas.
INVESTOR CONTACT: Vic Svec, (314) 342-7768
PRINCIPAL OFFICE: 701 Market Street, St. Louis, MO 63101-1826

TELEPHONE NUMBER: (314) 342-3400
WEB: www.peabodyenergy.com
NO. OF EMPLOYEES: 6,500 (approx.)
SHAREHOLDERS: 243
ANNUAL MEETING: In May
INCORPORATED: DE, 1998

INSTITUTIONAL HOLDINGS:
No. of Institutions: 132
Shares Held: 46,601,481
% Held: 89.1
INDUSTRY: Coal mining services (SIC: 1241)
TRANSFER AGENT(S): EquiServe Trust Company, Canton, MA

PENNEY (J.C.) COMPANY, INC.

EXCH.	SYM.	REC. PRICE	P/E RATIO	YLD.	MKT. CAP.	RANGE (52-WK.)	'02 Y/E PR.
NYSE	JCP	19.85 (2/28/03)	16.3	2.5%	$5.24 bill.	25.70 - 14.07	23.01

LOWER MEDIUM GRADE. THE COMPANY IS TARGETING FULL FISCAL-2003 EARNINGS OF BETWEEN $1.50 AND $1.70 PER SHARE.

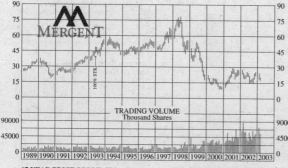

*7 YEAR PRICE SCORE 57.2　　***12 MONTH PRICE SCORE 108.3**

*NYSE COMPOSITE INDEX=100

INTERIM EARNINGS (Per Share):

Qtr.	Apr.	July	Oct.	Jan.
1997-98	0.53	0.32	0.40	0.85
1998-99	0.64	0.08	0.68	0.77
1999-00	0.61	0.12	0.51	d0.08
2000-01	d0.48	0.06	d0.15	d1.11
2001-02	0.13	d0.23	0.09	0.32
2002-03	0.29	d0.05	0.30	0.68

INTERIM DIVIDENDS (Per Share):

Amt.	Decl.	Ex.	Rec.	Pay.
0.125Q	3/22/02	4/08/02	4/10/02	5/01/02
0.125Q	5/17/02	7/08/02	7/10/02	8/01/02
0.125Q	9/20/02	10/08/02	10/10/02	11/01/02
0.125Q	12/11/02	1/08/03	1/10/03	2/01/03
0.125Q	3/21/03	4/08/03	4/10/03	5/01/03

Indicated div.: $0.50 (Div. Reinv. Plan)

CAPITALIZATION (1/26/02):

	($000)	(%)
Long-Term Debt	5,179,000	41.3
Deferred Income Tax	1,231,000	9.8
Preferred Stock	363,000	2.9
Common & Surplus	5,766,000	46.0
Total	12,539,000	100.0

BUSINESS:

J.C. Penney Company, Inc. is a major department store, drugstore, catalog and e-commerce retailer. As of 1/25/03, the Company operated 1,049 JCPenney department stores that sell family apparel, shoes, jewelry, accessories, and home furnishings in all 50 states, Puerto Rico and Mexico. Virtually all domestic stores feature JCPenney Catalog departments. The Company also operated 54 Renner department stores in Brazil and 2,686 Eckerd drug stores. Revenues in 2002 were derived as follows: Department Stores and Catalog, 54.7% and Drugstores, 45.3%. The Company acquired Eckerd Corp. on 2/27/97. On 3/1/99, JCP acquired Genovese Drug Stores, Inc.

RECENT DEVELOPMENTS:

For the 52 weeks ended 1/25/03, income from continuing operations totaled $371.0 million versus income from continuing operations of $114.0 million in the corresponding prior-year period. Results for fiscal 2002 and fiscal 2001 included pre-tax charges of $42.0 million and $121.0 million, respectively, primarily related to acquisition amortization. Total retail sales rose 1.1% to $32.35 billion from $32.00 billion a year earlier. Comparable-store sales for department stores increased 2.6% year over year, while comparable-store sales for Eckerd climbed 5.2%. Gross profit increased 6.1% to $9.77 billion, or 30.2% of total sales, from $9.22 billion, or 28.8% of total sales, the year before.

PROSPECTS:

The Company is targeting full-year fiscal 2003 earnings of between $1.50 and $1.70 per share. In an effort to boost profitability, JCP is taking steps to restructure its catalog operations. The Company will eliminate approximately 2,000 full and part-time positions through the closure of a catalog fulfillment center in Atlanta, Georgia, as well as telemarketing centers located in Atlanta and Lenexa, Kansas, by the end of the second quarter of 2003. JCP expects these actions will result in charges of about $40.0 million in the first half of the current fiscal year, and will generate annual cost savings of about $30.0 million, beginning in 2004.

ANNUAL FINANCIAL DATA:

FISCAL YEAR	TOT. REVS. ($mill.)	NET INC. ($mill.)	TOT. ASSETS ($mill.)	OPER. PROFIT %	NET PROFIT %	RET. ON EQUITY %	RET. ON ASSETS %	CURR. RATIO	EARN. PER SH.$	CASH FL. PER SH.$	TANG. BK. VAL.$	DIV. PER SH.$	PRICE RANGE	AVG. P/E RATIO	AVG. YIELD %
p1/25/03	32,347.0	⑧ 371.0							⑧ 1.25			0.50	27.75 - 14.07	16.7	2.4
1/26/02	32,004.0	⑤ 114.0	18,048.0	1.9	0.4	1.9	0.6	1.9	⑤ 0.32	3.11	11.46	0.50	29.50 - 10.50	62.5	2.5
1/27/01	31,846.0	④ d568.0	19,742.0	0.1	...	...	...	1.7	④ d2.29	0.48	11.37	0.99	22.50 - 8.63	...	6.3
1/29/00	32,510.0	③ 336.0	20,888.0	3.1	1.0	4.6	1.6	1.9	③ 1.16	3.67	14.28	2.19	54.44 - 17.69	31.1	6.1
1/30/99	30,678.0	① 594.0	23,638.0	5.0	1.9	8.3	2.5	1.9	② 2.19	4.54	15.04	2.17	78.75 - 42.63	27.7	3.6
1/31/98	30,546.0	② 566.0	23,493.0	6.7	1.9	7.7	2.4	1.9	② 2.10	4.27	15.50	2.13	68.25 - 44.88	26.9	3.8
1/25/97	23,649.0	③ 565.0	22,088.0	6.6	2.4	9.5	2.6	2.8	③ 2.29	4.11	15.73	2.04	57.00 - 44.00	22.1	4.0
1/27/96	21,419.0	② 838.0	17,102.0	7.1	3.9	14.2	4.9	5.8	② 3.48	5.17	23.58	1.86	50.00 - 39.88	12.9	4.1
1/28/95	21,082.0	1,057.0	16,202.0	8.5	5.0	18.8	6.5	4.3	4.29	5.84	21.96	1.62	59.00 - 41.13	11.7	3.2
1/29/94	19,578.0	② 944.0	14,788.0	8.3	4.8	17.6	6.4	4.9	② 3.79	5.47	19.99	1.41	56.38 - 35.38	12.1	3.1

Statistics are as originally reported. ① Incl. $22 mil ($0.05/sh) pre-tax gain, 1999; & $67 mil net gain, 1996. ② Bef. $55 mil extraord. chg. & bef. $51 mil acctg. cr. ③ Incl. $169 mil ($0.53/sh) chg., 2000; $447 mil chg., 1998; $207 mil ($0.84/sh) chg., 1997. ④ Bef. $159.0 mil ($0.61/sh) inc. fr. disc opers., $296.0 mil ($1.13/sh) loss on sale of disc. opers. & incl. $488.0 mil non-recur. chg. ⑤ Bef. $16.0 mil loss fr. disc. opers. & incl. $36.0 mil ($0.07/sh) non-recur. chg. ⑧ Bef. $34.0 mil gain fr. disc. opers.

OFFICERS:
A. I. Questrom, Chmn., C.E.O.
R. B. Cavanaugh, Exec. V.P., C.F.O.
C. R. Lotter, Exec. V.P., Sec., Gen. Couns.
V. J. Castagna, Exec. V.P., C.O.O.
INVESTOR CONTACT: Eli Akresh, (972) 431-2207
PRINCIPAL OFFICE: 6501 Legacy Drive, Plano, TX 75024-3698

TELEPHONE NUMBER: (972) 431-1000
FAX: (972) 431-1362
WEB: www.jcpenney.com
NO. OF EMPLOYEES: 250,000 (avg.)
SHAREHOLDERS: 53,000 (approx.)
ANNUAL MEETING: In May
INCORPORATED: DE, Dec., 1924

INSTITUTIONAL HOLDINGS:
No. of Institutions: 338
Shares Held: 246,040,048
% Held: 91.7

INDUSTRY: Department stores (SIC: 5311)

TRANSFER AGENT(S): Mellon Investor Services, South Hackensack, NJ

PENTAIR, INC.

EXCH.	SYM.	REC. PRICE	P/E RATIO	YLD.	MKT. CAP.	RANGE (52-WK.)	'02 Y/E PR.	DIV. ACH.
NYSE	PNR	36.35 (2/28/03)	13.9	2.3%	$1.79 bill.	49.84 - 29.02	34.55	26 yrs.

UPPER MEDIUM GRADE. THE COMPANY EXPECTS FULL-YEAR 2003 EARNINGS OF BETWEEN $2.90 AND $3.05 PER SHARE.

*7 YEAR PRICE SCORE 120.4   ***12 MONTH PRICE SCORE 97.0**

*NYSE COMPOSITE INDEX=100

INTERIM EARNINGS (Per Share):

Qtr.	Mar.	June	Sept.	Dec.
1998	0.54	0.56	0.64	0.76
1999	0.05	0.66	0.69	0.90
2000	0.69	0.79	0.58	d0.38
2001	0.42	0.58	0.50	d0.33
2002	0.43	0.86	0.75	0.57

INTERIM DIVIDENDS (Per Share):

Amt.	Decl.	Ex.	Rec.	Pay.
0.18Q	4/11/02	4/24/02	4/26/02	5/10/02
0.19Q	6/25/02	7/24/02	7/26/02	8/09/02
0.19Q	10/10/02	10/23/02	10/25/02	11/08/02
0.19Q	1/09/03	1/22/03	1/24/03	2/07/03
0.21Q	2/26/03	4/23/03	4/25/03	5/09/03

Indicated div.: $0.84 (Div. Reinv. Plan)

CAPITALIZATION (12/31/01):

	($000)	(%)
Long-Term Debt	714,977	40.5
Deferred Income Tax	34,128	1.9
Common & Surplus	1,015,002	57.5
Total	1,764,107	100.0

BUSINESS:

Pentair, Inc. is a diversified manufacturer operating in three segments on a global basis. The Tools segment (42.3% of 2002 sales), manufactures and markets tool products, including woodworking machinery, portable power tools, compressors, generators, and pressure washers. The Water segment (36.1%), manufactures and markets water and wastewater pumps, control valves, pumps and pumping stations for thick fluid transfer applications, storage tanks, filtration systems, and pool and spa accessories. The Enclosures segment (21.6%), designs, manufactures, and markets customized and standard metal and composite enclosures. Products include metallic and composite enclosures, cabinets, cases, subracks, thermal management backplanes and power supplies.

RECENT DEVELOPMENTS:

For the year ended 12/31/02, net income was $129.9 million versus income from continuing operations of $57.5 million a year earlier. Results for 2001 included a restructuring charge of $40.1 million, a write-off of investment charge of $3.0 million and goodwill amortization of $36.1 million. Net sales slipped to $2.58 billion from $2.57 billion the previous year. Gross profit improved 1.6% to $615.7 million, or 23.9% of net sales, versus $606.1 million, or 23.5% of net sales, the year before. Operating income rose 49.6% $236.0 million.

PROSPECTS:

Slower sell-through at PNR's major retail and industrial accounts, coupled with continued constrained spending in machine tool, capital goods and technology markets, temper the Company's near-term outlook. However, PNR's future prospects hold promise. For instance, the Company is executing plans designed to spur organic growth that include exploring new business platforms within existing operations, expanding product lines, adding new channels, and entering new geographic markets. Future acquisitions could also contribute to growth. Accordingly, PNR has indicated that assuming there is no change in the business environment in 2003, the Company expects full-year 2003 earnings of between $2.90 and $3.05 per share.

ANNUAL FINANCIAL DATA:

FISCAL YEAR	TOT. REVS. ($mill.)	NET INC. ($mill.)	TOT. ASSETS ($mill.)	OPER. PROFIT %	NET PROFIT %	RET. ON EQUITY %	RET. ON ASSETS %	CURR. RATIO	EARN. PER SH. $	CASH FL. PER SH. $	TANG. BK. VAL. $	DIV. PER SH. $	PRICE RANGE	AVG. P/E RATIO	AVG. YIELD %
p12/31/02	2,580.8	129.9							2.61			0.74	49.84 — 29.02	15.1	1.9
12/31/01	2,615.9	④57.5	2,372.2	6.0	2.2	5.7	2.4	2.0	④1.17	3.28	...	0.70	39.60 — 21.88	26.3	2.3
12/31/00	2,748.0	③81.9	2,644.0	7.4	3.0	8.1	3.1	1.7	③1.68	3.72	...	0.66	44.63 — 20.63	19.4	2.0
12/31/99	2,367.8	103.3	2,803.0	9.1	4.4	10.4	3.7	1.5	2.33	4.33	...	0.64	49.44 — 29.88	17.0	1.6
12/31/98	1,937.6	106.8	1,554.7	10.0	5.5	15.1	6.9	1.9	2.46	3.96	4.71	0.60	46.25 — 26.75	14.8	1.6
12/31/97	1,839.1	①91.6	1,472.9	9.2	5.0	14.5	6.2	1.8	①2.11	3.59	3.71	0.54	39.88 — 27.25	15.9	1.6
12/31/96	1,567.1	①74.5	1,289.0	9.1	4.8	13.2	5.8	2.0	①1.83	3.40	5.39	0.50	32.25 — 22.88	15.1	1.8
12/31/95	1,402.9	②60.5	1,252.5	8.3	4.3	12.0	4.8	1.6	②1.48	2.79	4.18	0.40	26.50 — 19.88	15.7	1.7
12/31/94	1,649.2	53.6	1,281.5	7.2	3.3	12.4	4.2	2.0	1.31	3.05	5.28	0.36	22.38 — 16.13	14.7	1.9
12/31/93	1,328.2	46.6	958.8	7.4	3.5	12.6	4.9	2.0	1.13	2.53	5.86	0.34	20.63 — 13.00	14.9	2.0

Statistics are as originally reported. Adj. for 2-for-1 stk. split, 2/96. ① Incl. non-recurr. credit 12/31/97: $10.3 mill.; credit 12/31/96: $12.1 mill. ② Bef. disc. oper. gain $4.7 mill. ③ Incl. restruct. chrg. of $24.8 mill.; bef. loss fr. disc. ops. of $24.8 mill. ($0.51/sh.) & acctg. change chrg. of $1.2 mill. ($0.02/sh.) ④ Incl. restruct. chrg. of $40.1 mill.; bef. loss on sale of disc. ops. of $24.6 mill. ($0.50/sh.)

OFFICERS:
R. J. Hogan, Chmn., Pres., C.E.O.
D. D. Harrison, Exec. V.P., C.F.O.
L. L. Ainsworth, Sr. V.P., Gen. Couns., Sec.

INVESTOR CONTACT: Mark Cain, Investor Relations, (651) 639-5278

PRINCIPAL OFFICE: 1500 Country Road B2 West, Suite 400, St. Paul, MN 55113

TELEPHONE NUMBER: (651) 636-7920
FAX: (651) 639-5203
WEB: www.pentair.com

NO. OF EMPLOYEES: 12,000 (approx.)

SHAREHOLDERS: 4,229

ANNUAL MEETING: In May

INCORPORATED: MN, Aug., 1966

INSTITUTIONAL HOLDINGS:
No. of Institutions: 207
Shares Held: 33,594,327
% Held: 68.2

INDUSTRY: Woodworking machinery (SIC: 3553)

TRANSFER AGENT(S): Wells Fargo Shareowner Services, South St. Paul, MN

PEOPLES ENERGY CORPORATION

EXCH.	SYM.	REC. PRICE	P/E RATIO	YLD.	MKT. CAP.	RANGE (52-WK.)	'02 Y/E PR.	DIV. ACH.
NYSE	PGL	35.80 (2/28/03)	14.3	5.9%	$1.27 bill.	40.41 - 27.80	38.65	19 yrs.

UPPER MEDIUM GRADE. ON 11/26/02, PGL'S OIL AND GAS PRODUCTION SUBSIDIARY, PEOPLES ENERGY PRODUCTION, PURCHASED AN INTEREST IN FIVE PROPERTIES FOR ABOUT $33.0 MILLION.

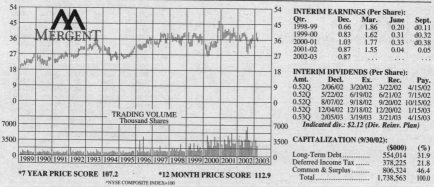

TRADING VOLUME
Thousand Shares

*7 YEAR PRICE SCORE 107.2   ***12 MONTH PRICE SCORE 112.9**
*NYSE COMPOSITE INDEX=100

INTERIM EARNINGS (Per Share):

Qtr.	Dec.	Mar.	June	Sept.
1998-99	0.66	1.86	0.20	d0.11
1999-00	0.83	1.62	0.31	d0.32
2000-01	1.03	1.77	0.33	d0.38
2001-02	0.87	1.55	0.04	0.05
2002-03	0.87	...	...	...

INTERIM DIVIDENDS (Per Share):

Amt.	Decl.	Ex.	Rec.	Pay.
0.52Q	2/06/02	3/20/02	3/22/02	4/15/02
0.52Q	5/22/02	6/19/02	6/21/02	7/15/02
0.52Q	8/07/02	9/18/02	9/20/02	10/15/02
0.52Q	12/04/02	12/18/02	12/20/02	1/15/03
0.53Q	2/05/03	3/19/03	3/21/03	4/15/03

Indicated div.: $2.12 (Div. Reinv. Plan)

CAPITALIZATION (9/30/02):

	($000)	(%)
Long-Term Debt	554,014	31.9
Deferred Income Tax	378,225	21.8
Common & Surplus	806,324	46.4
Total............................	1,738,563	100.0

BUSINESS:

Peoples Energy Corporation is a diversified energy company comprised of five primary business segment: gas distribution, power generation, midstream services, oil and gas production, and retail energy services. As of 9/30/02, these utilities distribute natural and synthetic gas to approximately 1.0 million customers in Chicago and northeastern Illinois. Other operations are conducted through PGL's subsidiaries engaged in non-regulated diversified energy operations. These subsidiaries consists of: Peoples District Energy Corp., a provider of district energy services; Peoples Energy Services, a provider of nonregulated retail energy sales; Peoples Energy Resources, a provider of gas-fired electric generation; Peoples NGV, a fueling station for natural gas-fueled vehicles; and Peoples Energy Production Company, which acquires investments in oil and gas production properties.

RECENT DEVELOPMENTS:

For the three months ended 12/31/02, net income remained flat at $31.0 million compared with net income in the corresponding quarter of the previous year. Results reflect a return to more normal weather for PGL's core gas distribution business, partially offset by a reduction in pension credits and an increase in the provision of uncollectibles.

Operating revenues advanced 45.4% to $549.1 million from $377.5 million in the year-earlier period. Revenue growth was largely due to strong results in PGL's diversified energy businesses. Operating income declined 5.9% to $60.6 million versus $64.3 million in the prior-year period.

PROSPECTS:

On 11/26/02, PGL's oil and gas production subsidiary, Peoples Energy Production, purchased an interest in five properties in south Texas and the upper Texas gulf coast area from a subsidiary of Magnum Hunter Resources Inc. for about $33.0 million. The acquisition of additional reserves should bolster year-over-year results of the diversified energy businesses. Meanwhile, colder year-over-year weather should benefit PGL's gas distribution, but this improvement may be offset by reduction of $0.35 to $0.40 per share in pension credits for 2003.

ANNUAL FINANCIAL DATA:

FISCAL YEAR	TOT. REVS. ($mill.)	NET INC. ($mill.)	TOT. ASSETS ($mill.)	OPER. PROFIT %	NET PROFIT %	NET INC./ NET PROP. %	NET INC./ TOT. CAP. %	RET. ON EQUITY %	ACCUM. DEPR./ GROSS PROP. %	EARN. PER SH. $	TANG. BK. VAL. $	DIV. PER SH. $	DIV. PAYOUT %	PRICE RANGE	AVG. P/E RATIO	AVG. YIELD %
9/30/02	1,482.5	☐ 89.1	2,723.6	11.6	6.0	5.0	5.1	11.0	36.5	☐ 2.51	22.74	2.07	82.5	40.41 - 27.80	13.6	6.1
9/30/01	2,270.2	☐ 97.1	2,994.1	7.1	4.3	5.5	5.4	12.0	35.1	☐ 2.74	22.66	2.03	74.1	44.63 - 34.35	14.4	5.1
9/30/00	1,417.5	86.4	2,501.9	11.2	6.1	5.3	5.6	11.1	34.6	2.44	21.86	1.99	81.6	46.94 - 26.19	15.0	5.4
9/30/99	1,194.4	92.6	2,100.2	13.1	7.8	6.1	5.8	12.1	34.8	2.61	21.66	1.95	74.7	40.25 - 31.75	13.8	5.4
9/30/98	1,138.1	79.4	1,904.5	10.0	7.0	5.5	5.2	10.7	34.5	2.25	20.94	1.91	84.9	40.13 - 32.13	16.1	5.3
9/30/97	1,274.4	98.4	1,820.8	10.5	7.7	7.0	6.6	13.7	33.8	2.81	20.43	1.87	66.5	39.88 - 31.25	12.7	5.3
9/30/96	1,198.7	103.4	1,783.8	11.0	8.6	7.5	7.2	15.2	32.5	2.96	19.48	1.83	61.8	37.38 - 29.63	11.3	5.5
9/30/95	1,033.4	62.2	1,822.5	10.5	6.0	4.5	4.2	9.7	34.2	1.78	18.38	1.80	101.1	32.00 - 24.25	15.8	6.4
9/30/94	1,279.5	74.4	1,809.3	8.0	5.8	5.5	5.1	11.6	33.5	2.13	18.39	1.79	84.3	32.13 - 23.31	13.0	6.5
9/30/93	1,258.9	73.4	1,765.9	9.1	5.8	5.6	5.4	11.7	32.4	2.11	18.05	1.77	84.1	35.00 - 27.50	14.8	5.7

Statistics are as originally reported. ☐ Incls. special charges of $14.7 mill., 9/01; $17.0 mill., 9/02.

OFFICERS:
R. E. Terry, Chmn., C.E.O.
T. M. Patrick, Pres., C.O.O.
T. A. Nardi, Sr. V.P., C.F.O.

INVESTOR CONTACT: Mary Ann Wall, Manager, Investor Relations, (312) 240-7534

PRINCIPAL OFFICE: 130 East Randolph Drive, 24th Floor, Chicago, IL 60601-6207

TELEPHONE NUMBER: (312) 240-4000
FAX: (312) 240-4220
WEB: www.pecorp.com

NO. OF EMPLOYEES: 2,479

SHAREHOLDERS: 21,550

ANNUAL MEETING: In Feb.

INCORPORATED: IL, 1967

INSTITUTIONAL HOLDINGS:
No. of Institutions: 206
Shares Held: 16,257,993
% Held: 45.9

INDUSTRY: Natural gas distribution (SIC: 4924)

TRANSFER AGENT(S): Computershare Investor Services, Chicago, IL

PEP BOYS-MANNY, MOE & JACK

EXCH.	SYM.	REC. PRICE	P/E RATIO	YLD.	MKT. CAP.	RANGE (52-WK.)	'02 Y/E PR.
NYSE	PBY	9.03 (2/28/03)	11.3	3.0%	$484.2 mill.	19.39 - 8.64	11.60

LOWER MEDIUM GRADE. RESULTS ARE BEING HURT BY SHARPLY LOWER SALES OF REPLACEMENT TIRES.

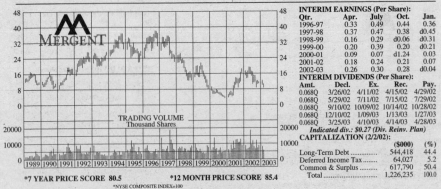

*7 YEAR PRICE SCORE 80.5   ***12 MONTH PRICE SCORE 85.4**

*NYSE COMPOSITE INDEX=100

INTERIM EARNINGS (Per Share):

Qtr.	Apr.	July	Oct.	Jan.
1996-97	0.33	0.49	0.44	0.36
1997-98	0.37	0.47	0.38	d0.45
1998-99	0.16	0.29	d0.06	d0.31
1999-00	0.20	0.39	0.20	d0.21
2000-01	0.09	0.07	d1.24	0.03
2001-02	0.18	0.24	0.21	0.07
2002-03	0.26	0.30	0.28	d0.04

INTERIM DIVIDENDS (Per Share):

Amt.	Decl.	Ex.	Rec.	Pay.
0.068Q	3/26/02	4/11/02	4/15/02	4/29/02
0.068Q	5/29/02	7/11/02	7/15/02	7/29/02
0.068Q	9/10/02	10/09/02	10/14/02	10/28/02
0.068Q	12/10/02	1/09/03	1/13/03	1/27/03
0.068Q	3/25/03	4/10/03	4/14/03	4/28/03

Indicated div.: $0.27 (Div. Reinv. Plan)

CAPITALIZATION (2/2/02):

	($000)	(%)
Long-Term Debt	544,418	44.4
Deferred Income Tax	64,027	5.2
Common & Surplus	617,790	50.4
Total	1,226,235	100.0

BUSINESS:

Pep Boys-Manny, Moe & Jack operate a chain of 629 specialty retail stores that sell a full range of brand name and private label automotive parts and accessories at discount prices and offer automotive maintenance and service and the installation of parts. PBY's stores are located in 36 states, mainly in the middle Atlantic, Southwest and South-east regions of the United States, the District of Columbia, and Puerto Rico. The Supercenter stores contain automotive merchandise along with a full-service maintenance center. The PartsUSA stores do not provide service bays, nor do they stock tires.

RECENT DEVELOPMENTS:

For the 52 weeks ended 2/1/03, the Company reported earnings of $43.8 million, including a $239,000 charge from the early retirement of debt, compared with earnings of $35.3 million, including a $765,000 charge from the early retirement of debt, in the corresponding period the year before. Results for the recent period also included a $3.3 million after-tax non-recurring charge from the non-renewal of the Chairman & CEO's employment agreement and related search fees. Total revenues slipped 0.6% to $2.17 billion from $2.18 billion the previous year. Comparable-store sales were down 0.7% year over year.

PROSPECTS:

Results are being negatively affected by weaker demand for replacement tires and reduced consumer spending, due to uncertain economic conditions, partially offset by higher merchandise and service center margins, along with effective cost-control initiatives. Meanwhile, results for the first quarter of fiscal 2003 will likely be hampered by unusually harsh winter weather conditions in the eastern U.S. during February. Separately, the Company anticipates free cash flow of approximately $100.0 million for the current fiscal year.

ANNUAL FINANCIAL DATA:

FISCAL YEAR	TOT. REVS. ($mill.)	NET INC. ($mill.)	TOT. ASSETS ($mill.)	OPER. PROFIT %	NET PROFIT %	RET. ON EQUITY %	RET. ON ASSETS %	CURR. RATIO	EARN. PER SH.$	CASH FL. PER SH.$	TANG. BK. VAL.$	DIV. PER SH.$	PRICE RANGE	AVG. P/E RATIO	AVG. YIELD %
p2/01/03	2,172.5	⑤43.8							⑤0.82			0.27	19.39 - 8.75	17.2	1.9
2/02/02	2,183.7	④36.1	1,812.7	4.7	1.7	5.8	2.0	1.2	④0.69	2.32	11.52	0.27	18.49 - 3.75	16.1	2.4
2/03/01	2,418.5	③d53.1	1,906.2	...	...	...	...	1.2	③d1.04	0.90	11.13	0.27	9.38 - 3.31	...	4.3
1/29/00	2,394.5	29.3	2,072.7	3.9	1.2	4.5	1.4	1.3	0.58	2.48	12.38	0.27	21.63 - 8.06	25.6	1.8
1/30/99	2,398.7	②5.0	2,096.1	2.3	0.2	0.6	0.2	1.5	②0.08	1.65	12.71	0.26	26.69 - 12.38	243.8	1.3
1/31/98	2,056.5	②49.6	2,161.4	5.4	2.4	6.0	2.3	1.2	②0.80	2.15	12.92	0.23	35.63 - 22.00	36.0	0.8
2/01/97	1,828.5	100.8	1,818.4	10.2	5.5	13.0	5.5	1.1	1.62	2.58	12.33	0.20	38.25 - 23.88	19.2	0.7
2/03/96	1,594.3	81.5	1,500.0	10.0	5.1	12.2	5.4	1.1	1.34	2.16	10.72	0.18	34.75 - 21.88	21.1	0.7
1/28/95	1,407.0	①80.0	1,291.0	10.6	5.7	13.6	6.2	1.4	①1.32	2.05	9.53	0.17	36.88 - 25.13	23.5	0.6
1/29/94	1,241.1	65.5	1,078.5	9.7	5.3	12.0	6.1	1.4	1.06	1.78	9.11	0.15	27.38 - 19.88	22.3	0.6

Statistics are as originally reported. ① Bef. $4.3 mil ($0.07/sh) chg. for acctg. adj. ② Incl. $20.1 mil ($0.33/sh) net non-recur. chg., 1999; $18.4 mil ($0.30/sh) net non-recur. chg., 1998. ③ Bef. $2.1 mil ($0.04/sh) extraord. gain fr. the repurchase of a portion of the Company's Liquid Yield Option Notes & incl. one-time pre-tax chgs. of $96.5 mil fr. store closings, asset write-downs, severance payments and reserve increases. ④ Bef. $765,000 ($0.01/sh) extraord. chg. ⑤ Incl. $239,000 extraord. chg fr. debt retirement and a $3.3 mil after-tax non-recur. chg.

OFFICERS:
M. G. Leibovitz, Chmn., C.E.O.
G. Babich, Jr., Pres., C.F.O.
F. A. Stampone, Sr. V.P., C.A.O., Sec.

INVESTOR CONTACT: George Babich, Pres. & C.F.O., (215) 430-9720

PRINCIPAL OFFICE: 3111 West Allegheny Avenue, Philadelphia, PA 19132

TELEPHONE NUMBER: (215) 430-9000
FAX: (215) 227-4067
WEB: www.pepboys.com

NO. OF EMPLOYEES: 16,049 full-time; 6,152 part-time

SHAREHOLDERS: 3,214

ANNUAL MEETING: In May

INCORPORATED: PA, Jan., 1925

INSTITUTIONAL HOLDINGS:
No. of Institutions: 157
Shares Held: 36,704,444
% Held: 71.2

INDUSTRY: Auto and home supply stores (SIC: 5531)

TRANSFER AGENT(S): American Stock & Transfer Company, New York, NY

PEPCO HOLDINGS, INC.

EXCH.	SYM.	REC. PRICE	P/E RATIO	YLD.	MKT. CAP.	RANGE (52-WK.)	'02 Y/E PR.
NYSE	POM	17.95 (2/28/03)	11.1	5.6%	$2.31 bill.	23.83 - 15.37	19.39

MEDIUM GRADE. GOING FORWARD, THE COMPANY EXPECTS ITS CORE REGULATED DELIVERY BUSINESSES TO PROVIDE OVER 70.0% OF EARNINGS.

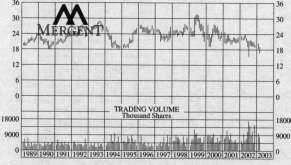

*7 YEAR PRICE SCORE 93.0 ***12 MONTH PRICE SCORE 97.9**
*NYSE COMPOSITE INDEX=100

INTERIM EARNINGS (Per Share):

Qtr.	Mar.	June	Sept.	Dec.
1998	0.03	0.46	1.23	d0.02
1999	0.20	0.61	1.25	d0.09
2000	0.07	0.47	1.04	1.43
2001	0.57	0.45	0.64	d0.16
2002	0.22	0.43	0.80	0.16

INTERIM DIVIDENDS (Per Share):

Amt.	Decl.	Ex.	Rec.	Pay.
0.25Q	4/25/02	6/06/02	6/10/02	6/28/02
0.003Sp	7/08/02	7/29/02	7/31/02	8/15/02
0.166Sp	8/01/02	9/06/02	9/10/02	9/30/02
0.25Q	10/24/02	12/06/02	12/10/02	12/31/02
0.25Q	1/23/03	3/06/03	3/10/03	3/31/03

Indicated div.: $1.00 (Div. Reinv. Plan)

CAPITALIZATION (12/31/01):

	($000)	(%)
Long-Term Debt	1,722,400	40.5
Deferred Income Tax	501,600	11.8
Redeemable Pfd. Stock	209,800	4.9
Common & Surplus	1,823,200	42.8
Total	4,257,000	100.0

BUSINESS:

Pepco Holdings, Inc. (formerly Potomac Electric Power Company) is a holding company that was formed on 8/1/02 through the acquisition by Potomac Electric Power Company (PEP) of Conectiv. POM is the largest electricity delivery company in the mid-Atlantic region with a transmission network serving more than 1.8 million customers in a 10,000 square-mile area. PEP, based in Washington, and Conectiv, based in Wilmington, DE, will continue to operate as separate companies. PEP delivers electricity to more than 700,000 customers in Washington, D.C. and the Maryland suburbs. Conectiv is focused on two core energy businesses. Conectiv Power Delivery provides energy to more than one million customers in New Jersey, Delaware, Maryland and Virginia. Conectiv Energy manages a growing portfolio of power plants designed to respond quickly to changes in the demand for power from the Pennsylvania-New Jersey-Maryland power pool.

RECENT DEVELOPMENTS:

For the year ended 12/31/02, net income rose 28.8% to $210.5 million versus $163.4 million in 2001. Results for 2002 included Pepco and its pre-merger subsidiaries for a full 12 months consolidated with results from Conectiv and its subsidiaries for the five post merger months of August through December. Results for 2002 and 2001 included corporate and other non-recurring charges of $17.5 million and $35.0 million, respectively. Operating revenues soared 80.1% to $4.32 billion from $2.40 billion in the prior year.

PROSPECTS:

On 2/27/03, Pepco Energy Services, a subsidiary of the Company, agreed to purchase the federal government business unit of CMS Viron, an engineering-based energy services company. The acquisition will give POM access to numerous federal contract opportunities. Furthermore, the transaction is expected to be accretive to earnings in 2003 and will strengthen the Company's position in the marketplace. Separately, POM's core regulated delivery businesses, Pepco and Conectiv Power Delivery, are expected to provide over 70.0% of earnings going forward. Additionally, POM's unregulated energy-related business should continue to benefit from improved performance.

ANNUAL FINANCIAL DATA:

FISCAL YEAR	TOT. REVS. ($mill.)	NET INC. ($mill.)	TOT. ASSETS ($mill.)	OPER. PROFIT %	NET PROFIT %	RET. ON EQUITY %	RET. ON ASSETS %	CURR. RATIO	EARN. PER SH.$	CASH FL.PER SH.$	TANG. BK. VAL.$	DIV. PER SH.$	PRICE RANGE	AVG. P/E RATIO	AVG. YIELD %
⑧ p12/31/02	4,324.5	⑥ 210.5							⑤ 1.61			⑦ 0.92	23.83 - 15.37	12.2	4.7
12/31/01	2,502.9	⑤ 168.4	5,285.9	14.6	6.7	9.2	3.2	1.2	⑤ 1.50	3.07	17.00	1.17	24.90 - 20.08	15.0	5.2
12/31/00	3,047.7	④ 352.0	7,027.3	23.0	11.5	18.9	5.0	1.2	④ 2.96	5.02	16.82	1.66	27.88 - 19.06	7.9	7.1
12/31/99	2,476.0	③ 247.1	6,910.6	15.0	10.0	12.9	3.6	1.1	③ 1.98	4.31	16.12	1.66	31.75 - 21.25	13.4	6.3
12/31/98	2,063.9	② 226.3	6,654.8	17.2	11.0	3.8	3.4	1.4	② 1.73	3.61	49.69	1.66	27.81 - 23.06	14.7	6.5
12/31/97	1,863.5	181.9	6,707.6	17.5	9.8	3.0	2.7	1.4	1.38	3.20	49.74	1.66	26.81 - 21.00	17.3	6.9
12/31/96	2,010.3	237.0	6,891.9	17.3	11.8	4.0	3.3	1.4	1.86	3.74	49.06	1.66	27.38 - 23.63	13.7	6.5
12/31/95	1,876.1	① 94.4	7,118.2	18.5	5.0	1.6	1.3	1.3	① 0.65	2.39	49.19	1.66	26.25 - 18.38	34.3	7.4
12/31/94	1,823.1	227.2	6,965.8	17.8	12.5	3.8	3.3	1.7	1.79	3.31	49.92	1.66	26.63 - 18.25	12.5	7.4
12/31/93	1,725.2	241.6	6,701.9	18.8	14.0	4.1	3.6	1.3	1.95	3.36	49.00	1.64	28.88 - 23.88	13.5	6.2

Statistics are as originally reported. ① Incl. $122.2 mill. after-tax non-recur. chg. ② Incl. a net charge of $4.7 mill. assoc. with POM's sev. program. ③ Incl. gain of $14.2 mill. contract term. fee. ④ Incl. $423.8 mill. gain fr. a divest. ⑤ Incl. $29.3 mill. gain fr. divest. of gen. assets & impair. loss of $65.5 mill. ⑥ Incl. $17.5 mill. corp. & other non-recur. chg. ⑦ Incl. spl. div. of $0.16848. ⑧ Incl. Pepco & its pre-merg. subs. for a full 12 mon. consol. w/ results fr. Conectiv & its subs. for 5 post merg. mon. of Aug.- Dec. 2002.

OFFICERS:
J. M. Derrick Jr., Chmn., C.E.O.
D. R. Wraase, Pres., C.O.O.
A. W. Williams, Sr. V.P., C.F.O.
INVESTOR CONTACT: Ernest J. Bourscheid, Mgr. Investor Rel., (202) 872-2797
PRINCIPAL OFFICE: 701 Ninth Street, N.W., Washington, DC 20068

TELEPHONE NUMBER: (202) 872-2000
FAX: (202) 331-6874
WEB: www.pepco.com
NO. OF EMPLOYEES: 2,449
SHAREHOLDERS: 55,343
ANNUAL MEETING: In Apr.
INCORPORATED: DC, Dec., 1896; reincorp., VA, 1949

INSTITUTIONAL HOLDINGS:
No. of Institutions: 238
Shares Held: 78,246,352
% Held: 46.4
INDUSTRY: Communication services, nec (SIC: 4899)
TRANSFER AGENT(S): Mellon Investor Services, Ridgefield Park, NJ

PEPSI BOTTLING GROUP INC.

EXCH.	SYM.	REC. PRICE	P/E RATIO	YLD.	MKT. CAP.	RANGE (52-WK.)	'02 Y/E PR.
NYSE	PBG	23.25 (2/28/03)	15.8	0.2%	$6.54 bill.	34.80 - 22.90	25.70

UPPER MEDIUM GRADE. THE COMPANY EXPECTS TO ACHIEVE FULL-YEAR 2003 EARNINGS OF BETWEEN $1.68 AND $1.74 PER SHARE.

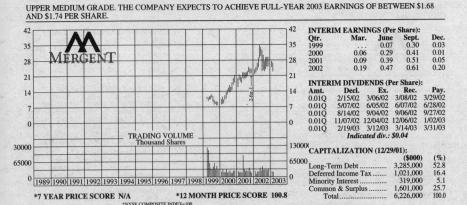

INTERIM EARNINGS (Per Share):

Qtr.	Mar.	June	Sept.	Dec.
1999	...	0.07	0.30	0.03
2000	0.06	0.29	0.41	0.01
2001	0.09	0.39	0.51	0.05
2002	0.19	0.47	0.61	0.20

INTERIM DIVIDENDS (Per Share):

Amt.	Decl.	Ex.	Rec.	Pay.
0.01Q	2/15/02	3/06/02	3/08/02	3/29/02
0.01Q	5/07/02	6/05/02	6/07/02	6/28/02
0.01Q	8/14/02	9/04/02	9/06/02	9/27/02
0.01Q	11/07/02	12/04/02	12/06/02	1/02/03
0.01Q	2/19/03	3/12/03	3/14/03	3/31/03

Indicated div.: $0.04

CAPITALIZATION (12/29/01):

	($000)	(%)
Long-Term Debt	3,285,000	52.8
Deferred Income Tax	1,021,000	16.4
Minority Interest	319,000	5.1
Common & Surplus	1,601,000	25.7
Total	6,226,000	100.0

*7 YEAR PRICE SCORE N/A   ***12 MONTH PRICE SCORE 100.8**

*NYSE COMPOSITE INDEX=100

BUSINESS:

Pepsi Bottling Group Inc. manufactures, sells and distributes Pepsi-Cola beverages. Pepsi-Cola beverages sold by PBG include PEPSI-COLA, DIET PEPSI, PEPSI ONE, PEPSI TWIST, MOUNTAIN DEW, MOUNTAIN DEW CODE RED, AMP, LIPTON'S ICED TEA, SLICE, MUG, AQUAFINA, STARBUCKS FRAPPUCCINO, FRUITWORKS, SIERRA MIST, DOLE, SOBE, and outside the U.S., 7UP, PEPSI MAX, MIRINDA and KAS. PBG has the exclusive right to manufacture, sell and distribute Pepsi-Cola beverages in all or a portion of 41 states, the District of Columbia, eight Canadian provinces, Spain, Greece, Russia and Turkey. PBG was incorporated to effect the separation of most of PepsiCo's company-owned bottling businesses and became a publicly-traded company on 3/31/99. In November 2002, PBG acquired Mexican bottler Pepsi-Gemex, S.A. de C.V. As of 2/21/02, PepsiCo's ownership represented 42.9% of the voting power of all classes of PBG's voting stock.

RECENT DEVELOPMENTS:

For the 52 weeks ended 12/28/02, net income was $428.0 million versus $305.0 million a year earlier. Results for 2001 included a tax benefit of $25.0 million. Net revenue rose 9.2% to $9.22 billion, due in part to acquisitions. Worldwide and U.S. physical case volume (which measures the number of units produced, distributed and sold regardless of package configuration) on a constant territory basis rose 2.0% and 1.0%, respectively, year over year.

PROSPECTS:

Despite some expected near-term weakness due in part to severe weather conditions that affected more than half of the Company's U.S. territories, PBG's prospects appear solid. For instance, PBG noted that the pricing environment in the U.S. remains encouraging, owing to recent price hikes that are holding. The Company should also continue to experience growth from its newly acquired territories, notably in Turkey and Mexico. However, as a result of the recent shortfall in U.S. volume and profitability, PBG has lowered its constant territory U.S. volume growth projection to a range of flat to 1.0% for 2003. PBG expects constant territory worldwide volume growth for 2003 will be 2.0% to 3.0%. Accordingly, PBG now sees full-year 2003 earnings of between $1.61 and $1.67 per share.

ANNUAL FINANCIAL DATA:

FISCAL YEAR	TOT. REVS. ($mill.)	NET INC. ($mill.)	TOT. ASSETS ($mill.)	OPER. PROFIT %	NET PROFIT %	RET. ON EQUITY %	RET. ON ASSETS %	CURR. RATIO	EARN. PER SH. $	CASH FL. PER SH. $	DIV. PER SH. $	PRICE RANGE	AVG. P/E RATIO	AVG. YIELD %
p12/28/02	9,216.0	428.0	7,857.0	8.0	3.6	19.1	3.9	1.4	1.46	2.77	0.04	34.80 - 21.65	19.3	0.1
12/29/01	8,443.0	③ 305.0	7,736.0	7.4	2.9	13.9	3.0	1.6	③ 1.03	2.35	0.04	25.00 - 15.81	19.8	0.2
12/30/00	7,982.0	229.0	7,619.0	5.5	1.6	7.5	1.5	1.6	0.77	2.43	0.04	21.25 - 8.13	19.2	0.3
12/25/99	7,505.0	② 118.0	7,322.0	0.8	1.6	...	1.6	1.3	② 0.46	2.96	0.02	12.63 - 7.75	22.1	0.2
12/26/98	7,041.0	① d146.0	7,188.0	5.1	...	...	...	1.3	① d1.32	4.53	...	...	...	...
12/27/97	6,592.0	59.0	...	5.6	0.9	...	0.8	1.2	0.54	4.31	...	...	...	...
12/28/96	6,603.0	49.0	...		0.7	...			0.45		...	...	...	...

Statistics are as originally reported. Adj. for 2-for-1 stk. split, 12/01. ① Incls. non-recurr. impair. & oth. charges of $222.0 mill. ② Incls. non-recurr. credit of $16.0 mill. ③ Incls. income rate chge. benefit of $25.0 mill., due to Canadian income tax rate reduction.

OFFICERS:
J. T. Cahill, Chmn., Pres.
A. H. Drewes, Sr. V.P., C.F.O.

INVESTOR CONTACT: Mary Winn Settino, Director, Inv. Rel., (914) 767-7216

PRINCIPAL OFFICE: One Pepsi Way, Somers, NY 10589

TELEPHONE NUMBER: (914) 767-6000
FAX: (914) 767-1313
WEB: www.pbg.com
NO. OF EMPLOYEES: 37,000 (approx.)
SHAREHOLDERS: 44,033 (approx.)
ANNUAL MEETING: In May
INCORPORATED: DE, Jan., 1999

INSTITUTIONAL HOLDINGS:
No. of Institutions: 307
Shares Held: 165,851,946
% Held: 59.1
INDUSTRY: Bottled and canned soft drinks (SIC: 2086)
TRANSFER AGENT(S): The Bank of New York, New York, NY

PEPSIAMERICAS, INC.

EXCH.	SYM.	REC. PRICE	P/E RATIO	YLD.	MKT. CAP.	RANGE (52-WK.)	'02 Y/E PR.
NYSE	PAS	12.22 (2/28/03)	13.9	0.3%	$1.88 bill.	15.94 - 11.12	13.43

MEDIUM GRADE. THE COMPANY EXPECTS TO ACHIEVE FULL-YEAR 2003 EARNINGS PER SHARE GROWTH OF BETWEEN 9.0% AND 11.0%.

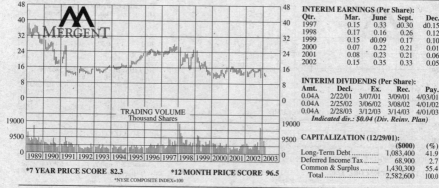

*7 YEAR PRICE SCORE 82.3   *12 MONTH PRICE SCORE 96.5
*NYSE COMPOSITE INDEX=100

INTERIM EARNINGS (Per Share):

Qtr.	Mar.	June	Sept.	Dec.
1997	0.15	0.33	d0.30	d0.15
1998	0.17	0.16	0.26	0.12
1999	0.15	d0.09	0.17	0.10
2000	0.07	0.22	0.21	0.01
2001	0.08	0.23	0.21	0.06
2002	0.15	0.35	0.33	0.05

INTERIM DIVIDENDS (Per Share):

Amt.	Decl.	Ex.	Rec.	Pay.
0.04A	2/22/01	3/07/01	3/09/01	4/03/01
0.04A	2/25/02	3/06/02	3/08/02	4/01/02
0.04A	2/28/03	3/12/03	3/14/03	4/01/03

Indicated div.: $0.04 (Div. Reinv. Plan)

CAPITALIZATION (12/29/01):

	($000)	(%)
Long-Term Debt	1,083,400	41.9
Deferred Income Tax	68,900	2.7
Common & Surplus	1,430,300	55.4
Total	2,582,600	100.0

BUSINESS:

PepsiAmericas, Inc. (formerly Whitman Corporation) is the number two anchor bottler in the Pepsi system, with operations in an 18-state region, primarily in the Midwest. Outside the U.S., PAS serves Central European and Caribbean markets, including Poland, Hungary, the Czech Republic, the Republic of Slovakia, Puerto Rico, Jamaica, the Bahamas, Barbados, and Trinidad and Tobago. PAS manufactures, distributes and markets a broad portfolio of Pepsi-Cola, Cadbury, and other national and regional brands. On 1/30/98, PAS completed the spin-off of its refrigeration and equipment business and its automotive services business. On 5/20/99, the Company's shareholders approved the merger with Heartland Territories Holdings, Inc., a subsidiary of Pepsico, Inc., which established a new business relationship between PAS and Pepsico. On 11/30/00, PAS completed its acquisition of PepsiAmericas, Inc. As of 1/28/03, Pepsico maintained an approximate 38.8% ownership interest in PAS.

RECENT DEVELOPMENTS:

For the year ended 12/31/02, income from continuing operations was $135.7 million compared with income from continuing operations of $90.1 million a year earlier. Results for 2002 and 2001 included net special charges of $2.6 million and $13.8 million, respectively. Results for 2001 also included amortization expense of $50.0 million and a gain of $8.9 million on pension curtailment. Net sales increased 3.0% to $3.24 billion. Total volume rose 3.5%, and included domestic volume growth of 1.9% and international volume growth of 8.8%.

PROSPECTS:

Recent weakness from PAS's domestic operations, due in part to a negative shift in channel and packaging mix, tempers the Company's near-term outlook. Meanwhile, PAS has stated that in fiscal 2003 it expects to achieve earnings per share growth of 9.0% to 11.0%, and worldwide volume growth of 2.0% to 3.0%. Also, PAS expects net price increases in the range of 2.5% to 3.5% and cost increases in the mid-single digits.

ANNUAL FINANCIAL DATA:

FISCAL YEAR	TOT. REVS. ($mil.)	NET INC. ($mil.)	TOT. ASSETS ($mil.)	OPER. PROFIT %	NET PROFIT %	RET. ON EQUITY %	RET. ON ASSETS %	CURR. RATIO	EARN. PER SH.$	CASH FL.PER SH.$	TANG. BK. VAL.$	DIV. PER SH.$	PRICE RANGE	AVG. P/E RATIO	AVG. YIELD %
p12/31/02	3,239.8	⑨ 135.7							⑨ 0.89			0.04	15.94 - 11.12	15.2	0.3
12/29/01	3,170.7	⑧ 90.1	3,419.3	8.5	2.8	6.3	2.6	0.7	⑧ 0.58	2.11	...	0.04	16.95 - 12.25	25.2	0.3
12/30/00	2,527.6	⑦ 71.5	3,335.6	8.8	2.8	4.9	2.1	0.5	⑦ 0.51	1.71	...	0.05	16.44 - 10.38	26.3	0.4
12/31/99	2,138.2	⑥ 42.9	2,864.3	8.5	2.0	3.8	1.5	0.7	⑥ 0.35	1.36	...	0.02	24.94 - 12.19	53.0	0.1
12/31/98	1,635.0	⑤ 62.5	1,569.3	12.5	3.8	19.1	4.0	1.8	⑤ 0.61	1.36	...	...	26.63 - 14.88	34.0	...
④12/31/97	1,557.5	③ 15.8	2,029.7	8.4	1.0	2.9	0.8	1.1	③ 0.15	0.87	0.76	...	28.13 - 21.63	165.7	...
12/31/96	3,111.3	139.4	2,409.4	11.8	4.5	21.7	5.8	1.6	1.31	2.40	0.80	...	25.75 - 21.75	18.1	...
12/31/95	2,946.5	133.5	2,363.3	11.6	4.5	21.3	5.6	1.5	1.26	2.28	0.56	...	23.38 - 15.63	15.5	...
12/31/94	2,658.8	② 106.4	2,135.4	12.3	4.0	19.3	5.0	1.5	② 1.00	1.92	0.27	...	18.00 - 14.75	16.4	...
12/31/93	2,529.7	① 106.4	2,103.2	12.1	4.2	20.6	5.1	1.5	① 0.99	1.88	...	...	17.00 - 12.75	15.0	...

Statistics are as originally reported. ① Bef. extra. loss of $4.2 mil. & acctg. chrg. of $24.0 mil. ② Incl. net chrg. of $15.5 mil. fr. unreal. invest. loss; bef. disc. ops. loss of $3.2 mil. ③ Incl. spec. chrg. of $173.2 mil.; bef. disc. ops. loss of $11.7 mil. ④ Refl. divest. of Midas Inc. & Hussmann Corp. ⑤ Bef. extra. loss of $18.3 mil. & disc. ops. loss of $500,000 ⑥ Incl. aft.-tax chrgs. of $54.9 mil. & aft.-tax gain of $7.8 mil. fr. sale of franch.; bef. loss fr. disc. ops. of $51.7 mil. ⑦ Incl. aft.-tax spec. chrg. of $13.2 mil.; bef. inc. fr. disc. ops. of $8.9 mil. ⑧ Incl. spec. chrgs. of $13.8 mil. & pension curtail. gain of $8.9 mil.; bef. loss fr. disc. ops. of $71.2 mil. ⑨ Incl. spec. chrgs. of $2.6 mil.; bef. loss fr. disc. ops. of $6.0 mil.

OFFICERS:
R. C. Pohlad, Chmn., C.E.O.
K. E. Keiser, Pres., C.O.O.
G. M. Durkin, Jr., Sr. V.P., C.F.O.
INVESTOR CONTACT: John F. Bierbaum, (612) 661-3830
PRINCIPAL OFFICE: 3501 Algonquin Road, Rolling Meadows, IL 60008

TELEPHONE NUMBER: (847) 483-5000
FAX: (847) 483-6880
WEB: www.pepsiamericas.com
NO. OF EMPLOYEES: 15,400 (approx.)
SHAREHOLDERS: 13,408 (record)
ANNUAL MEETING: In Apr.
INCORPORATED: DE, Aug., 1962

INSTITUTIONAL HOLDINGS:
No. of Institutions: 168
Shares Held: 59,847,574
% Held: 39.8
INDUSTRY: Bottled and canned soft drinks (SIC: 2086)
TRANSFER AGENT(S): Wells Fargo Shareowner Services, South St. Paul, MN

PEPSICO INC.

EXCH.	SYM.	REC. PRICE	P/E RATIO	YLD.	MKT. CAP.	RANGE (52-WK.)	'02 Y/E PR.	DIV. ACH.
NYSE	PEP	38.32 (2/28/03)	20.7	1.6%	$67.3 mill.	53.50 - 35.01	42.22	31 yrs.

INVESTMENT GRADE. THE COMPANY IS STRIVING TO SUSTAINABLY GROW VOLUME AND NET REVENUES IN THE MID-SINGLE DIGITS AND EARNINGS PER SHARE IN THE LOW DOUBLE-DIGITS OVER THE LONG RUN.

INTERIM EARNINGS (Per Share):

Qtr.	Mar.	June	Sept.	Dec.
1998	0.24	0.33	0.50	0.24
1999	0.22	0.49	0.32	0.33
2000	0.29	0.38	0.40	0.41
2001	0.32	0.44	0.34	0.37
2002	0.36	0.49	0.54	0.46

INTERIM DIVIDENDS (Per Share):

Amt.	Decl.	Ex.	Rec.	Pay.
0.15Q	5/01/02	6/05/02	6/07/02	6/28/02
0.15Q	7/18/02	9/04/02	9/06/02	9/27/02
0.15Q	11/22/02	12/04/02	12/06/02	1/02/03
0.15Q	1/30/03	3/12/03	3/14/03	3/31/03

Indicated div.: $0.60 (Div. Reinv. Plan)

TRADING VOLUME
Thousand Shares

CAPITALIZATION (12/29/01):

	($000)	(%)
Long-Term Debt	2,651,000	20.7
Deferred Income Tax	1,496,000	11.7
Common & Surplus	8,648,000	67.6
Total	12,795,000	100.0

*7 YEAR PRICE SCORE 120.1 ***12 MONTH PRICE SCORE 100.1**

NYSE COMPOSITE INDEX=100

BUSINESS:

PepsiCo Inc. is a worldwide consumer products company. Worldwide snacks (57.1% of 2002 division net sales and 56.4% of operating profit) manufactures, markets, sells and distributes primarily salty, sweet and grain-based snacks including such brands as LAY'S, DORITOS, CHEETOS, ROLD GOLD, SABRITAS and WALKERS. Worldwide beverages (36.9%, 34.6%) includes such brands as PEPSI, DIET PEPSI, MOUNTAIN DEW, MUG, AQUAFINA, SOBE, TROPICANA PURE PREMIUM, GATORADE and MIRINDA and 7-UP internationally. Quaker Foods North America (6.0%, 9.1%) manufactures, markets and sells a variety of food products. PEP also has various ownership interests in a number of bottling concerns. In August 2001, PEP acquired The Quaker Oats Company.

RECENT DEVELOPMENTS:

For the 52 weeks ended 12/28/02, net income was $3.31 billion compared with $2.66 billion a year earlier. Results for 2002 and 2001 included pre-tax merger-related charges of $224.0 million and $356.0 million, respectively. Results for 2001 also included other impairment and restructuring charges of $31.0 million. PEP's earnings were fueled by sales and operating profit gains from across each of its operating units, cost savings associated with the Company's August 2001 acquisition of The Quaker Oats Company, as well as productivity gains. Net sales increased 6.8% to $25.11 billion from $23.51 billion the previous year. Operating earnings rose 17.6% to $4.73 billion.

PROSPECTS:

PEP has indicated that over the long term it believes that the Company can sustainably grow volume and net revenues in the mid-single digits and earnings per share in the low double-digits. Meanwhile, the integration of The Quaker Oats Company is proceeding ahead of schedule. According to PEP, the Company realized approximately $250.0 million in cost savings from the acquisition in fiscal year 2002. PEP expects to realize $400.0 million in annual cost savings from the transaction by the end of 2004.

ANNUAL FINANCIAL DATA:

FISCAL YEAR	TOT. REVS. ($mill.)	NET INC. ($mill.)	TOT. ASSETS ($mill.)	OPER. PROFIT %	NET PROFIT %	RET. ON EQUITY %	RET. ON ASSETS %	CURR. RATIO	EARN. PER SH.$	CASH FL PER SH.$	TANG. BK. VAL.$	DIV. PER SH.$	PRICE RANGE	AVG. P/E RATIO	AVG. YIELD
p12/28/02	25,112.0	⑧ 3,313.0							⑧ 1.85			0.59	53.50 - 35.01	23.9	1.3
12/29/01	26,935.0	⑧ 2,662.0	21,695.0	14.9	9.9	30.7	12.3	1.2	⑥ 1.47	2.07	2.17	0.57	50.46 - 40.25	30.9	1.3
12/30/00	20,438.0	2,183.0	18,339.0	15.8	10.7	30.1	11.9	1.2	1.48	2.13	1.91	0.55	49.94 - 29.69	26.9	1.4
12/25/99	20,367.0	⑤ 2,050.0	17,551.0	13.8	10.1	29.8	11.7	1.1	⑤ 1.37	2.06	1.47	0.53	42.56 - 30.13	26.5	1.5
12/26/98	22,348.0	④ 1,993.0	22,660.0	11.6	8.9	31.1	8.8	0.6	④ 1.31	2.12	...	0.51	44.81 - 27.56	27.6	1.4
⑦ 12/27/97	20,917.0	① 1,491.0	20,101.0	12.7	7.1	21.5	7.4	1.5	① 0.95	1.65	0.72	0.48	41.31 - 28.25	36.6	1.4
12/28/96	31,645.0	② 1,149.0	24,512.0	8.0	3.6	17.3	4.7	1.0	② 0.72	1.79	...	0.43	35.88 - 27.25	43.8	1.4
12/30/95	30,421.0	② 1,606.0	25,432.0	9.8	5.3	22.0	6.3	1.1	② 1.00	2.08	...	0.38	29.38 - 16.94	23.2	1.6
12/31/94	28,472.4	③ 1,784.0	24,792.0	11.2	6.3	26.0	7.2	1.0	③ 1.11	2.09	...	0.34	20.56 - 14.63	15.8	1.9
12/25/93	25,020.7	1,754.5	23,705.8	11.6	7.0	27.7	7.4	0.8	0.98	1.97	...	0.29	21.81 - 17.25	19.9	1.5

Statistics are as originally reported. Adj. for 2-for-1 stk. split, 5/96. ① Incl. non-recurr. chrgs. of $290.0 mill.; bef. disc. oper. gain of $651.0 mill. ② Incl. non-recurr. chrgs. 1/31/96, $716.0 mill.; non-cash chrg. 12/31/95, $520.0 mill. ③ Bef. acctg. change chrg. of $32.0 mill. ④ Incl. non-recurr. chrg. of $288.0 mill. ⑤ Incl. non-recurr. chrg. of $65.0 mill. ⑥ Incl. after-tax merger-rel. chrgs. of $322.0 mill. and oth. asset impairmnt. & restruct. chrgs. of $19.0 mill. ⑦ Refl. 10/6/97 spin-off of TRICON Global Restaurants. ⑧ Incl. merger-rel. chrgs. of $224.0 mill.

OFFICERS:
S. S. Reinemund, Chmn., C.E.O.
I. K. Nooyi, Pres., C.F.O.
D. R. Andrews, Sr. V.P., Sec., Gen. Couns.

INVESTOR CONTACT: Kathleen Luke, V.P., Inv. Rel., (914) 253-3691

PRINCIPAL OFFICE: 700 Anderson Hill Road, Purchase, NY 10577-1444

TELEPHONE NUMBER: (914) 253-2000
FAX: (914) 253-2070
WEB: www.pepsico.com

NO. OF EMPLOYEES: 143,000 (approx.)

SHAREHOLDERS: 227,000 (approx.)

ANNUAL MEETING: In May

INCORPORATED: DE, Sept., 1919; reincorp., NC, Dec., 1986

INSTITUTIONAL HOLDINGS:
No. of Institutions: 1,098
Shares Held: 1,113,934,504
% Held: 64.5

INDUSTRY: Bottled and canned soft drinks (SIC: 2086)

TRANSFER AGENT(S): The Bank of New York, Newark, NJ

PERKINELMER, INC.

EXCH.	SYM.	REC. PRICE	P/E RATIO	YLD.	MKT. CAP.	RANGE (52-WK.)	'02 Y/E PR.
NYSE	PKI	8.48 (2/28/03)	...	3.3%	$1.05 bill.	23.00 - 4.28	8.25

LOWER MEDIUM GRADE. THE COMPANY EXPECTS EARNINGS PER SHARE FROM CONTINUING OPERATIONS FOR FULL-YEAR 2003 IN THE RANGE OF $0.37 TO $0.43.

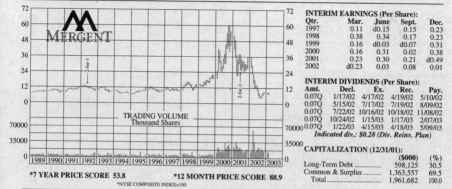

*7 YEAR PRICE SCORE 53.8 ***12 MONTH PRICE SCORE 88.9**

*NYSE COMPOSITE INDEX=100

INTERIM EARNINGS (Per Share):

Qtr.	Mar.	June	Sept.	Dec.
1997	0.11	d0.15	0.15	0.23
1998	0.38	0.34	0.17	0.23
1999	0.16	d0.03	d0.07	0.31
2000	0.16	0.31	0.02	0.38
2001	0.23	0.30	0.21	d0.49
2002	d0.23	0.03	0.08	0.01

INTERIM DIVIDENDS (Per Share):

Amt.	Decl.	Ex.	Rec.	Pay.
0.07Q	1/17/02	4/17/02	4/19/02	5/10/02
0.07Q	5/15/02	7/17/02	7/19/02	8/09/02
0.07Q	7/22/02	10/16/02	10/18/02	11/08/02
0.07Q	10/24/02	1/15/03	1/17/03	2/07/03
0.07Q	1/22/03	4/15/03	4/18/03	5/09/03

Indicated div.: $0.28 (Div. Reinv. Plan)

CAPITALIZATION (12/31/01):

	($000)	(%)
Long-Term Debt	598,125	30.5
Common & Surplus	1,363,557	69.5
Total	1,961,682	100.0

BUSINESS:

PerkinElmer, Inc. (formerly EG&G, Inc.) is a technology company that operates three business units. The Life and Analytical Sciences segment offers drug discovery tools for customers engaged in pharmaceutical, biotechnology and academic laboratory research, and genetic disease screening software, reagents and analysis tools to test for a number of inherited disorders. This segment also manufactures and markets products for measurement and testing applica-

tions for research laboratories, academia, medical institutions, government agencies and a wide range of industrial applications. The Optoelectronics segment provides telecommunications, specialty lighting, sensor and digital imaging to customers in the health sciences, communications and industrial markets. The Fluid Sciences segment provides sealing applications and advanced fluid containment technologies.

RECENT DEVELOPMENTS:

For the twelve months ended 12/29/02, loss was $4.1 million, before an accounting change charge of $117.8 million, compared with income from continuing operations of $41.5 million in 2001. Results for 2002 and 2001 included restructuring charges of $35.7 million and $7.0 million, gains on dispositions of $5.2 million and $33.2 million, and

amortization of intangibles of $28.3 million and $43.9 million, respectively. Results for 2002 and 2001 excluded losses of $30.0 million and $7.0 million, respectively, from discontinued operations. Sales slipped 1.3% to $1.50 billion from $1.53 billion in the prior year.

PROSPECTS:

Looking ahead, POM expects earnings per share from continuing operations in 2003 in the range of $0.37 to $0.43, including the negative effect of intangibles amortization of $0.15 per share. For the first quarter of 2003, the Company

projects earnings per share from continuing operations between $0.02 and $0.05, including intangibles amortization. Meanwhile, POM plans to continue its strategy of driving cost productivity and introducing new products.

ANNUAL FINANCIAL DATA:

FISCAL YEAR	TOT. REVS. ($mill.)	NET INC. ($mill.)	TOT. ASSETS ($mill.)	OPER. PROFIT %	NET PROFIT %	RET. ON EQUITY %	RET. ON ASSETS %	CURR. RATIO	EARN. PER SH. $	CASH FL. PER SH. $	TANG. BK. VAL. $	DIV. PER SH. $	PRICE RANGE	AVG. P/E RATIO	AVG. YIELD %
p12/29/02	1,505.0	⑩ d4.1							⑩ d0.03			0.28	36.30 - 4.28	...	1.4
12/31/01	1,330.1	⑨ d0.6	2,919.1	4.8	...	...	...	1.4	⑨ d0.01	0.81	...	0.28	52.31 - 21.28	...	0.8
12/31/00	1,695.3	⑧ 86.1	2,260.2	11.0	5.1	11.8	3.8	1.2	⑧ 0.84	1.70	...	0.28	60.50 - 19.00	47.3	0.7
1/02/00	1,363.1	⑦ 28.4	1,714.6	4.9	2.1	5.2	1.7	1.0	⑦ 0.31	1.01	...	0.28	22.50 - 12.75	57.8	1.6
1/03/99	1,407.9	⑥ 102.0	1,184.9	11.0	7.2	25.5	8.6	1.1	⑥ 1.11	1.66	0.92	0.28	16.88 - 9.44	11.9	2.1
12/28/97	1,460.8	④⑤ 30.6	832.1	4.1	2.1	9.3	3.7	1.7	④⑤ 0.34	0.82	2.75	0.28	12.31 - 9.00	31.8	2.6
12/29/96	1,427.3	④⑤ 54.5	822.9	6.1	3.8	14.9	6.6	1.8	④⑤ 0.58	1.01	2.75	0.28	12.56 - 8.13	18.0	2.7
12/31/95	1,419.6	④ 54.3	803.9	5.8	3.8	14.8	6.8	1.9	④ 0.53	0.91	2.56	0.28	12.25 - 6.50	17.9	3.0
③ 1/01/95	1,332.6	② d32.1	793.1	...	...	...	...	1.7	② d0.29	0.04	2.88	0.28	9.50 - 6.88	...	3.4
1/02/94	2,697.9	① 79.6	768.8	4.5	2.9	16.7	10.3	2.0	① 0.71	1.04	3.01	0.26	12.25 - 7.88	14.3	2.6

Statistics are as originally reported. Adj. for 2-for-1 split 6/01. ① Excl. $20.5 mil acct chg. ② Incl. $40.3 mil goodwill write-down, $30.4 mil restr chg & excl $26.5 mil fr disc ops. ③ Results no longer reflect disc. DOE support segment. ④ Excl. $3.0 mil inc fr disc ops, 1997; $5.7 mil, 1996; $13.7 mil, 1995. ⑤ Incl. $26.7 0 mil net assets write-down chg, 1997; $4.2 mil prov fr infring settlemnt, 1996. ⑥ Incl. $2.3 mil R&D chgs, $54.5 mil restr chgs, $7.4 mil asset impair chgs & $125.8 mil gain on dispos. ⑦ Incl. $42.2 mil net chgs & excl $125.9 mil net gain fr disc ops. ⑧ Incl. $13.4 mil non-recur chgs & excl $4.5 mil gain fr disc ops. ⑨ Bef. $2.4 mil gain fr disc ops.; Incl $80.0 mil one-time chg & $26.6 mil gain fr dispos. ⑩ Incl. $35.7 mil restr chg, $5.2 mil gain on disp, and excl $30.0 mil loss fr disc ops & $117.8 mil acct chg.

OFFICERS:
G. L. Summe, Chmn., Pres., C.E.O.
R. F. Friel, Sr. V.P., C.F.O.
T. L. Carlson, Sr. V.P., Gen. Couns.

INVESTOR CONTACT: Dan Sutherby, Investor Relations, (781) 431-4306

PRINCIPAL OFFICE: 45 William Street, Wellesley, MA 02481

TELEPHONE NUMBER: (781) 237-5100
FAX: (781) 431-4255
WEB: www.perkinelmer.com
NO. OF EMPLOYEES: 10,800 (approx.)
SHAREHOLDERS: 9,200 (approx.)
ANNUAL MEETING: In Apr.
INCORPORATED: MA, Nov., 1947

INSTITUTIONAL HOLDINGS:
No. of Institutions: 239
Shares Held: 86,883,279
% Held: 68.8

INDUSTRY: Analytical instruments (SIC: 3826)

TRANSFER AGENT(S): Mellon Investor Services, LLC, Ridgefield Park, NJ

PEROT SYSTEMS CORPORATION

EXCH.	SYM.	REC. PRICE	P/E RATIO	YLD.	MKT. CAP.	RANGE (52-WK.)	'02 Y/E PR.
NYSE	PER	10.01 (2/28/03)	14.7	...	$1.02 bill.	20.20 - 8.21	10.72

MEDIUM GRADE. THE COMPANY DOUBLED THE SIZE OF ITS GOVERNMENT SERVICES SEGMENT WITH THE ACQUISITION OF SOZA & COMPANY, LTD.

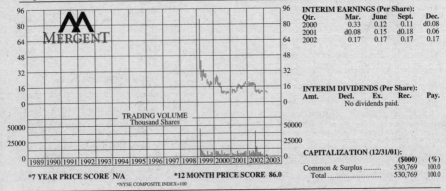

INTERIM EARNINGS (Per Share):

Qtr.	Mar.	June	Sept.	Dec.
2000	0.33	0.12	0.11	d0.08
2001	d0.08	0.15	d0.18	0.06
2002	0.17	0.17	0.17	0.17

INTERIM DIVIDENDS (Per Share):

Amt.	Decl.	Ex.	Rec.	Pay.
		No dividends paid.		

CAPITALIZATION (12/31/01):

	($000)	(%)
Common & Surplus	530,769	100.0
Total	530,769	100.0

*7 YEAR PRICE SCORE N/A ***12 MONTH PRICE SCORE 86.0**
*NYSE COMPOSITE INDEX=100

BUSINESS:

Perot Systems Corporation is a global provider of information technology services and business applications to clients in the financial services, healthcare, energy, travel and transportation, communications and media, insurance, and manufacturing industries. The Company offers services under three primary lines of business. The Information Technology Solutions division, PER's largest line of business, provides services to customers primarily under long-term contracts, including technology and business process outsourcing, as well as industry domain-based, short-term

project and consulting capabilities. The Consulting line of business includes Solutions Consulting and the Global Software Services group and includes services related to the design and implementation of business and software solutions, business and technical expertise and intellectual property, primarily under short-term contracts. The Government Services segment was formed in the third quarter of 2002 following the acquisition of ADI Technology Corporation and provides applications for the defense, intelligence and law enforcement communities.

RECENT DEVELOPMENTS:

For the twelve months ended 12/31/02, net income jumped to $78.3 million compared with a net loss of $2.7 million in 2001. Total revenue amounted to $1.33 billion, up 10.6% from $1.20 billion in the prior year. PER's revenue from the healthcare market grew 43.0%, while revenue for the

consulting segment rose 13.0% for the year. Gross profit increased 22.1% to $311.3 million from $255.0 million the year before. Separately, during the twelve months ended 12/31/02, PER signed new contracts valued at more than $1.00 billion in revenues.

PROSPECTS:

On 2/25/03, PER completed the acquisition of Soza & Company, Ltd., a government information technology company, for $75.0 million in cash and up to $32.0 million in cash and stock if certain performance targets are met. The acquisition is strategically in line with PER's growth strat-

egy and doubles the size of its government services group. The transaction also expands PER's presence in the government agency area, particularly in homeland security initiatives. Separately, PER expects revenue for the first quarter of 2003 to range from $335.0 million to $350.0 million.

ANNUAL FINANCIAL DATA:

FISCAL YEAR	TOT. REVS. ($mill.)	NET INC. ($mill.)	TOT. ASSETS ($mill.)	OPER. PROFIT %	NET PROFIT %	RET. ON EQUITY %	RET. ON ASSETS %	CURR. RATIO	EARN. PER SH.$	CASH FL. PER SH.$	TANG. BK. VAL.$	PRICE RANGE	AVG. P/E RATIO
p12/31/02	1,332.1	78.3							0.68			20.75 - 8.21	21.3
12/31/01	1,204.7	d2.7	757.6	...	...	...	...	2.3	d0.03	0.33	3.96	21.11 - 9.19	
12/31/00	1,105.9	③ 55.5	673.2	3.1	5.0	11.1	8.2	2.8	③ 0.49	0.74	4.29	27.94 - 7.81	36.5
12/31/99	1,151.6	75.5	614.0	9.3	6.6	19.3	12.3	2.5	0.67	0.91	4.22	85.75 - 15.31	75.4
12/31/98	993.6	40.5	382.1	6.2	4.1	28.4	10.6	1.3	0.42	0.80	1.76	...	...
12/31/97	781.6	② 11.2	267.1	2.3	1.4	12.0	4.2	1.0	② 0.12	0.49	1.00	...	...
12/31/96	599.4	① 20.5	232.2	6.9	3.4	29.0	8.8	1.1	① 0.27	0.53	0.80	...	...
12/31/95	342.3	10.8	...	6.1	3.2	...	...	...	0.16	0.40	...	...	...

Statistics are as originally reported. ① Incl. $3.9 mill. purch. R&D chg. ② Incl. $2.0 mill. purch. R&D chg. and $3.9 mill. write-down of non-market. equity sec. ③ Incl. $22.1 mill. compensation chg. rel. to acq.

OFFICERS:
R. Perot, Chmn.
R. Perot Jr., Pres., C.E.O.
R. Freeman, V.P., C.F.O.
INVESTOR CONTACT: Investor Relations, (877) 737-6973
PRINCIPAL OFFICE: 2300 West Plano Parkway, Plano, TX 75075

TELEPHONE NUMBER: (972) 577-0000
WEB: www.perotsystems.com
NO. OF EMPLOYEES: 8,100 (approx.)
SHAREHOLDERS: 3,418 (approx. class A common)
ANNUAL MEETING: In May
INCORPORATED: TX, 1988; reincorp., DE, Dec., 1995

INSTITUTIONAL HOLDINGS:
No. of Institutions: 95
Shares Held: 46,338,010
% Held: 42.8
INDUSTRY: Computer programming services (SIC: 7371)
TRANSFER AGENT(S): Mellon Investor Services, Ridgefield Park, NJ

PFIZER INC.

EXCH.	SYM.	REC. PRICE	P/E RATIO	YLD.	MKT. CAP.	RANGE (52-WK.)	'02 Y/E PR.	DIV. ACH.
NYSE	PFE	29.82 (2/28/03)	20.0	2.0%	$187.18 bill.	41.90 - 25.13	30.57	35 yrs.

HIGH GRADE. THE COMPANY AGREED TO SELL ITS ADAMS CONFECTIONERY BUSINESS AND SCHICK-WILKINSON SWORD SHAVING PRODUCTS BUSINESS FOR $4.20 BILLION AND $930.0 MILLION, RESPECTIVELY.

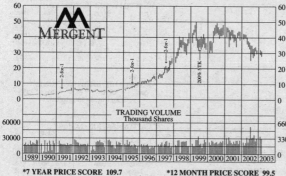

*7 YEAR PRICE SCORE 109.7   *12 MONTH PRICE SCORE 99.5
*NYSE COMPOSITE INDEX=100

INTERIM EARNINGS (Per Share):

Qtr.	Mar.	June	Sept.	Dec.
1998	0.18	0.16	0.13	0.08
1999	0.16	0.19	0.18	0.25
2000	0.31	0.18	0.21	0.23
2001	0.30	0.29	0.33	0.30
2002	0.37	0.32	0.38	0.42

INTERIM DIVIDENDS (Per Share):

Amt.	Decl.	Ex.	Rec.	Pay.
0.13Q	12/18/01	2/13/02	2/15/02	3/07/02
0.13Q	4/25/02	5/15/02	5/17/02	6/06/02
0.13Q	6/27/02	8/14/02	8/16/02	9/05/02
0.13Q	10/24/02	11/13/02	11/15/02	12/05/02
0.15Q	12/16/02	1/15/03	1/17/03	2/14/03

Indicated div.: $0.60 (Div. Reinv. Plan)

CAPITALIZATION (12/31/01):

	($000)	(%)
Long-Term Debt	2,609,000	12.2
Deferred Income Tax	452,000	2.1
Common & Surplus	18,293,000	85.7
Total	21,354,000	100.0

BUSINESS:

Pfizer Inc. is a research-based, global pharmaceutical company that discovers, develops, manufactures and markets medicines for humans and animals. The products include NORVASC, a once-a-day calcium channel blocker for treatment of angina and hypertension, ZYRTEC, an anti-allergy medicine, VIAGRA, an oral medication for the treatment of erectile dysfunction, ZOLOFT, a selective serotonin reuptake inhibitor for the treatment of depression, ZITHROMAX, an oral or injectable antibiotic, DIFLUCAN, used to treat various fugal infections, as well as non-prescription self-medications. The animal health segment includes anti-parasitic, anti-infective and anti-inflammatory medicines, and vaccines. Revenues for 2002 were derived as follows: pharmaceutical segment, 92.2% and consumer product segment, 7.8%. PFE acquired Warner-Lambert Co. on 6/19/00.

RECENT DEVELOPMENTS:

For the year ended 12/31/02, income from continuing operations was $9.18 billion compared with $7.54 billion the previous year. Results for 2002 and 2001 included pre-tax merger-related costs of $630.0 million and $819.0 million, respectively. Results for 2002 excluded a gain of $77.0 million from the sale of discontinued operations. Revenues advanced 11.5% to $32.37 billion from $29.02 billion the year before. Sales in the pharmaceutical segment increased 11.9% to $29.84 from $26.67 billion, while consumer products segment sales climbed 7.5% to $2.53 billion from $2.35 billion a year earlier.

PROSPECTS:

On 12/17/02, the Company agreed to sell its Adams confectionery business for approximately $4.20 billion in cash to Cadbury Schweppes plc. Separately, on 1/21/03, the Company announced its decision to sell its Schick-Wilkinson Sword shaving products business for about $930.0 million to Energizer Holdings, Inc. Both transactions are expected to close in the first half of 2003. Meanwhile, shareholders of both companies approved the acquisition of Pharmacia by PFE, and it is now awaiting clearance by the U.S. and European regulatory authorities. The Company expects diluted earnings per share to be $1.80 for fiscal 2003. 2003.

ANNUAL FINANCIAL DATA:

FISCAL YEAR	TOT. REVS. ($mill.)	NET INC. ($mill.)	TOT. ASSETS ($mill.)	OPER. PROFIT %	NET PROFIT %	RET. ON EQUITY %	RET. ON ASSETS %	CURR. RATIO	EARN. PER SH. $	CASH FL. PER SH. $	TANG. BK. VAL. $	DIV. PER SH. $	PRICE RANGE	AVG. P/E RATIO	AVG. YIELD %
p12/31/02	32,373.0	5 9,181.0							5 1.47			0.52	42.46 - 25.13	23.0	1.5
12/31/01	32,259.0	5 7,752.0	39,153.0	32.0	24.0	42.4	19.8	1.4	5 1.22	1.39	2.64	0.44	46.75 - 34.00	33.1	1.1
12/31/00	29,574.0	5 3,718.0	33,510.0	19.5	12.6	23.1	11.1	1.4	5 0.59	0.74	2.26	0.36	49.25 - 30.00	67.1	0.9
12/31/99	16,204.0	4 3,199.0	20,574.0	27.5	19.7	36.0	15.5	1.2	4 0.82	0.96	2.11	0.31	50.04 - 31.54	49.7	0.8
12/31/98	13,544.0	3 1,950.0	18,302.0	19.2	14.4	22.1	10.7	1.4	3 0.49	0.62	2.06	0.25	42.98 - 23.69	68.0	0.8
12/31/97	12,504.0	2,213.0	15,336.0	24.7	17.7	27.9	14.4	1.3	0.57	0.69	1.71	0.23	26.66 - 13.44	35.4	1.1
12/31/96	11,306.0	1,929.0	14,667.0	24.8	17.1	27.7	13.2	1.1	0.50	0.61	1.43	0.20	15.21 - 10.04	25.3	1.6
12/31/95	10,021.4	2 1,554.2	12,729.3	22.9	15.5	28.2	12.2	1.2	2 0.41	0.51	1.12	0.17	11.14 - 6.21	21.1	2.0
12/31/94	8,281.3	1,298.4	11,098.5	22.5	15.7	30.0	11.7	1.2	0.35	0.43	1.06	0.16	6.61 - 4.43	15.8	2.8
12/31/93	7,477.7	1 657.5	9,330.9	12.2	8.8	17.0	7.0	1.4	1 0.17	0.24	0.94	0.14	6.30 - 4.37	31.2	2.6

Statistics are as originally reported. Adj. for stock splits: 200% div., 6/30/99; 2-for-1, 9/97, 6/95. 1 Incl. chg. for restruct. & unus. items of $750.0 mill. 2 Excl. gain of $18.8 mill. for dis. ops. 3 Incl. unus. & nonrecurr. pre-tax chrg. total. $1.06 bill.; excl. a $1.40 bill. gain from disc. opers. 4 Incl. a one-time after-tax chrg. of $1.37 bill. for TROVAN inv. 5 Bef. inc. from disc. opers. of $355.0 mill., 2002; $36.0 mill., 2001; $8.0 mill., 2000 & incl. merger-rel. costs of $630.0 mill., 2002; $839.0 mill., 2001; $3.26 bill, 2000.

OFFICERS:
H. A. McKinnell, Chmn., Pres., C.E.O.
J. F. Niblack, Vice-Chmn.
D. Shedlarz, Exec. V.P., C.F.O.
INVESTOR CONTACT: Investor Relations, (212) 573-2323
PRINCIPAL OFFICE: 235 East 42nd Street, New York, NY 10017-5755

TELEPHONE NUMBER: (212) 573-2323
FAX: (212) 573-2641
WEB: www.pfizer.com
NO. OF EMPLOYEES: 90,000 (approx.)
SHAREHOLDERS: 210,095
ANNUAL MEETING: In Apr.
INCORPORATED: DE, 1942

INSTITUTIONAL HOLDINGS:
No. of Institutions: 1,383
Shares Held: 3,818,175,563
% Held: 62.0
INDUSTRY: Pharmaceutical preparations (SIC: 2834)
TRANSFER AGENT(S): EquiServe Trust Company, N.A., Jersey City, NJ

PG&E CORPORATION

EXCH.	SYM.	REC. PRICE	P/E RATIO	YLD.	MKT. CAP.	RANGE (52-WK.)	'02 Y/E PR.
NYSE	PCG	12.75 (2/28/03)	...	...	$4.87 bill.	23.75 - 8.00	13.90

LOWER MEDIUM GRADE. THE COMPANY'S EMPHASIS REMAINS ON REACHING A CONSENSUAL RESTRUCTUR-
ING AGREEMENT WITH THE CREDITORS OF PG&E NATIONAL ENERGY GROUP.

*7 YEAR PRICE SCORE 71.2   *12 MONTH PRICE SCORE 95.9

*NYSE COMPOSITE INDEX=100

INTERIM EARNINGS (Per Share):

Qtr.	Mar.	June	Sept.	Dec.
1997	0.42	0.49	0.62	0.22
1998	0.36	0.46	0.55	0.51
1999	0.39	0.50	0.54	d1.49
2000	0.77	0.68	0.67	d11.28
2001	d2.62	2.07	2.12	1.42
2002	1.69	0.75	1.17	d3.72

INTERIM DIVIDENDS (Per Share):

Amt.	Decl.	Ex.	Rec.	Pay.
		Last Dist. $0.30Q, 10/15/00		

CAPITALIZATION (12/31/02):

	($000)	(%)
Long-Term Debt	5,505,000	49.9
Deferred Income Tax	1,439,000	13.0
Redeemable Pfd. Stock	480,000	4.3
Common & Surplus	3,613,000	32.7
Total	11,037,000	100.0

BUSINESS:

PG&E Corporation is an energy-based holding company that conducts its business through two principal subsidiaries: Pacific Gas and Electric Company (PG&E) and PG&E National Energy Group, Inc. (PG&E NEG). PG&E is engaged principally in the business of providing electricity and natural gas distribution and transmission services throughout most of northern and central California. PG&E NEG is engaged in power generation, wholesale energy marketing and trading, risk management and natural gas transmission. The Company has three operating segments:

utility, integrated energy and marketing and interstate pipeline operations. The utility segment provides natural gas and electric service in northern and central California. The integrated energy and marketing activities segment is engaged in the generation, transport, marketing and trading of electricity, various fuels and other energy-related commodities throughout North America. PCG's interstate pipeline operations own, operate and develop interstate natural gas transmission pipeline facilities which run from the Canada/U.S. border to the California/Oregon border.

RECENT DEVELOPMENTS:

For the year ended 12/31/02, PCG reported a loss of $57.0 million, before a loss from discontinued operations of $756.0 million and an accounting change charge of $61.0 million, versus income of $983.0 million, before income from discontinued operations of $107.0 million and an

accounting gain of $9.0 million, the year before. Earnings for 2002 included impairments and other costs of $2.77 billion. Also, results for 2002 and 2001 included reorganization and professional fees and expenses of $155.0 million and $97.0 million, respectively.

PROSPECTS:

PCG's national wholesale energy business, PG&E National Energy Group, is continuing its efforts to reach an agreement with lenders and debt holders on a global restructuring plan to address financial obligations the company cannot meet, including amounts due under credit facilities and

equity commitments for various power plant construction projects. Meanwhile, the Company's California utility business, PG&E, continues to perform well and provides a solid foundation for the Company to move forward with the utility's proposed plan of reorganization.

ANNUAL FINANCIAL DATA:

FISCAL YEAR	TOT. REVS. ($mill.)	NET INC. ($mill.)	TOT. ASSETS ($mill.)	OPER. PROFIT %	NET PROFIT %	NET INC./ NET PROP. %	NET INC./ TOT. CAP. %	RET. ON EQUITY %	ACCUM. DEPR./ GROSS PROP. %	EARN. PER SH.$	TANG. BK. VAL.$	DIV. PER SH.$	DIV. PAYOUT %	PRICE RANGE	AVG. P/E RATIO	AVG. YIELD %
12/31/02	12,495.0	④ d57.0	33,696.0	9.1	...	...	...	45.7	④ d0.15	9.47	...	...	23.75 - 8.00	...	...
12/31/01	22,959.0	③ 1,090.0	35,862.0	11.9	4.7	5.7	7.0	25.2	41.9	③ 2.99	11.87	...	...	20.94 - 6.50	4.6	...
12/31/00	26,232.0	② d3,324.0	35,291.0	...	...	...	...	...	41.7	② d9.18	8.73	1.20	...	31.81 - 17.00	...	4.9
12/31/99	20,820.0	13.0	29,715.0	4.2	0.1	0.1	0.2	0.2	40.2	0.04	19.10	1.20	N.M.	34.00 - 20.25	676.4	4.4
12/31/98	19,942.0	719.0	33,234.0	10.1	3.6	4.0	3.2	8.9	40.3	1.88	21.08	1.20	63.8	35.06 - 29.06	17.1	3.7
12/31/97	15,400.0	① 716.0	30,557.0	11.2	4.6	3.5	3.0	7.7	43.9	① 1.75	21.28	1.20	68.6	30.94 - 20.88	14.8	4.6
12/31/96	9,610.0	755.2	26,129.9	19.7	7.9	4.0	3.6	8.6	42.9	1.75	20.73	1.96	112.0	28.38 - 19.50	13.7	8.2
12/31/95	9,621.8	1,338.9	26,850.3	28.7	13.9	7.1	6.3	14.9	41.3	2.99	20.77	1.96	65.5	30.63 - 24.25	9.2	7.1
12/31/94	10,447.4	1,007.5	27,708.6	15.6	9.6	5.2	4.6	10.8	38.7	2.21	20.07	1.94	87.8	35.00 - 21.38	12.8	6.9
12/31/93	10,582.4	1,065.5	27,162.5	16.7	10.1	5.4	4.7	11.5	36.3	2.33	19.77	1.85	79.4	36.75 - 31.75	14.7	5.4

Statistics are as originally reported. ① Incl. non-recurr gains of $0.28/sh. fr. sale of assets ② Incl. after-tax chrg. of $4.10 bill.; excl. loss from disc. oper. of $40.0 mill. ③ Bef. acctg. change gain $9.0 mill.; incl. net non-recurr. chrg. $9.0 mill. ④ Bef. loss fr. disc. opers. of $756.0 mill. & acctg. chrg. of $61.0 mill.; incl. chrgs. of $2.77 bill. for impair., write-offs & other chrgs. & non-recurring expenses of $155.0 mill.

OFFICERS:
R. D. Glynn Jr., Chmn., Pres., C.E.O.
P. Darbee, Sr. V.P., C.F.O., Treas.
L. H. Everett, V.P., Corp. Sec.

INVESTOR CONTACT: Gabriel B. Togneri,
V.P., Inv. Rel., (415) 267-7080

PRINCIPAL OFFICE: One Mkt., Spear Twr.,
Suite 2400, San Francisco, CA 94105

TELEPHONE NUMBER: (415) 267-7000
FAX: (415) 267-7267
WEB: www.pgecorp.com
NO. OF EMPLOYEES: 22,619 (avg.)
SHAREHOLDERS: 124,405
ANNUAL MEETING: In April
INCORPORATED: CA, Oct., 1905; reincorp.,
CA, 1995

INSTITUTIONAL HOLDINGS:
No. of Institutions: 287
Shares Held: 226,819,721
% Held: 56.0
INDUSTRY: Electric and other services combined (SIC: 4931)
TRANSFER AGENT(S): First Interstate Bank of California, San Francisco, CA

PHARMACIA CORPORATION

EXCH.	SYM.	REC. PRICE	P/E RATIO	YLD.	MKT. CAP.	RANGE (52-WK.)	'02 Y/E PR.
NYSE	PHA	41.32 (2/28/03)	22.5	1.3%	$53.65 bill.	46.64 - 30.36	41.80

INVESTMENT GRADE. PHA ANNOUNCED THAT ITS SHAREHOLDERS VOTED TO APPROVE THE SALE OF THE COMPANY TO PFIZER INC.

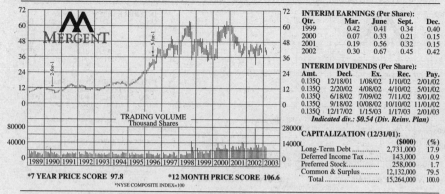

*7 YEAR PRICE SCORE 97.8　　　***12 MONTH PRICE SCORE 106.6**

*NYSE COMPOSITE INDEX=100

INTERIM EARNINGS (Per Share):

Qtr.	Mar.	June	Sept.	Dec.
1999	0.42	0.41	0.34	0.40
2000	0.07	0.33	0.21	0.15
2001	0.19	0.56	0.32	0.15
2002	0.30	0.67	0.45	0.42

INTERIM DIVIDENDS (Per Share):

Amt.	Decl.	Ex.	Rec.	Pay.
0.135Q	12/18/01	1/08/02	1/10/02	2/01/02
0.135Q	2/20/02	4/08/02	4/10/02	5/01/02
0.135Q	6/18/02	7/09/02	7/11/02	8/01/02
0.135Q	9/18/02	10/08/02	10/10/02	11/01/02
0.135Q	12/17/02	1/15/03	1/17/03	2/01/03

Indicated div.: $0.54 (Div. Reinv. Plan)

CAPITALIZATION (12/31/01):

	($000)	(%)
Long-Term Debt	2,731,000	17.9
Deferred Income Tax	143,000	0.9
Preferred Stock	258,000	1.7
Common & Surplus	12,132,000	79.5
Total	15,264,000	100.0

BUSINESS:

Pharmacia Corporation was formed as a result of the merger between Monsanto Company and Pharmacia & Upjohn, Inc. on 3/31/00. PHA is a global pharmaceutical group engaged in the research, development, manufacture and sale of pharmaceutical and healthcare products. The Company's core business includes both prescription and non-prescription products for humans and animals, bulk pharmaceutical and contract manufacturing. The Company's major pharmaceutical brands include CELEBREX, XALATAN, DETROL, CAMPTOSAR, GENOTROPIN, AMBIEN, NICORETTE, MEDROL and CLEOCIN. The Company has research, manufacturing, and administration and sales operations in more than 60 countries. On 8/15/02, PHA spun off its remaining ownership in Monsanto Co.

RECENT DEVELOPMENTS:

For the year ended 12/31/02, income from continuing operations was $2.44 billion, before an extraordinary gain of $653.0 million and an accounting change charge of $1.54 billion, compared with income of $1.29 billion, before an extraordinary charge of $12.0 million and an accounting change credit of $1.0 million, the previous year. Results for 2002 and 2001 included after-tax merger and restructuring charges of $54.0 million and $418.0 million, respectively. Net sales grew 1.1% to $13.99 billion from $13.84 billion the year before. Sales and continuing earnings reflect only the results of the Company's pharmaceutical business.

PROSPECTS:

During the quarter, PHA announced that its shareholders voted to approve the sale of the Company to Pfizer Inc. The two companies continue to make progress in obtaining other approvals necessary to complete the transaction, which is expected to close in 2003. Separately, PHA announced the submission of a new drug application for celecoxib in Japan for the treatment of several indications including rheumatoid arthritis and osteoarthritis.

ANNUAL FINANCIAL DATA:

FISCAL YEAR	TOT. REVS. ($mill.)	NET INC. ($mill.)	TOT. ASSETS ($mill.)	OPER. PROFIT %	NET PROFIT %	RET. ON EQUITY %	RET. ON ASSETS %	CURR. RATIO	EARN. PER SH. $	CASH FL. PER SH. $	TANG. BK. VAL. $	DIV. PER SH. $	PRICE RANGE	AVG. P/E RATIO	AVG. YIELD %
p12/31/02	13,993.0	⑦2,437.0							⑦1.84			0.54	46.64 - 30.36	20.9	1.4
12/31/01	13,837.0	⑥1,291.0	22,377.0	11.5	9.3	10.4	5.8	1.5	⑦0.97	1.44	8.19	0.51	60.94 - 36.50	50.2	1.0
12/31/00	18,144.0	⑤984.0	26,656.0	8.9	5.4	8.3	3.7	1.9	⑤0.75	1.72	4.94	0.28	64.00 - 33.75	65.2	0.6
12/31/99	9,146.0	④503.0	16,535.0	12.7	5.5	9.4	3.0	1.5	④0.77	1.90	1.07	0.12	50.81 - 32.75	54.3	0.3
12/31/98	8,648.0	d250.0	16,724.0	1.3	...	...	...	1.5	d0.41	0.64	...	0.12	63.94 - 33.75	...	0.2
12/31/97	7,514.0	②294.0	10,774.0	6.6	3.9	7.2	2.7	1.2	②0.48	1.32	2.13	0.50	52.31 - 34.75	90.7	1.1
12/31/96	9,262.0	①385.0	11,191.0	6.4	4.2	10.4	3.4	1.3	①0.64	1.63	2.61	0.59	43.25 - 23.08	51.8	1.8
12/31/95	8,962.0	①739.0	10,611.0	11.0	8.2	19.8	7.0	1.5	①1.26	2.33	3.07	0.54	24.95 - 13.65	15.3	2.8
12/31/94	8,272.0	622.0	8,891.0	11.2	7.5	21.1	7.0	1.6	1.06	2.02	3.24	0.49	17.30 - 13.30	14.4	3.2
12/31/93	7,902.0	494.0	8,640.0	10.3	6.3	17.3	5.7	1.6	0.82	1.78	2.87	0.46	15.00 - 9.78	15.1	3.7

Statistics are as originally reported. Stk. price, div. and fin. for 1999 and prior years reflect Monsanto Company. ① Incl. a restruct. and mgr. costs of $241.6 mill., 1995; $436.0 mill., 1996 ② Incl. pre-tax exps. of $73.0 mill. rel. to the Biotech mgr. and $316.0 mill. for restruct. chrgs. ③ Incl. after-tax nonrecurr. chg. of $41.0 mill. ④ Incl. a pre-tax chg. of $61.0 mill. & $70.0 mill. for org. restruct. ⑤ Incl. a pre-tax mgr. and restruct. chrg. of $1.08 bill. & excl. discont. oper. of $37.0 mill. ⑥ Incl. a after-tax mgr. and restruct. chrg. of $418.0 mill. & excl. discont. oper. of $8.0 mill., extraord. chrg. of $12.0 mill. & acctg. chng. credit of $1.0 mill. ⑦ Bef. gain of $952.0 mill. from the disp. of disc. ops., extraord. gain of $653.0 mill. & acctg. chng. chrg. of $1.54 bill.; incl. after-tax merger & restruct. chrg. of $54.0 mill.

OFFICERS:
F. Hassan, Chmn., C.E.O.
C. J. Coughlin, Exec. V.P., C.F.O.

INVESTOR CONTACT: Investor Relations, (888) 768-5501

PRINCIPAL OFFICE: 100 Route 206 North, Peapack, NJ 07977

TELEPHONE NUMBER: (908) 901-8000
FAX: (908) 901-8379
WEB: www.pharmacia.com

NO. OF EMPLOYEES: 45,000 (avg.)

SHAREHOLDERS: 72,007

ANNUAL MEETING: In Apr.

INCORPORATED: DE, Apr., 1933

INSTITUTIONAL HOLDINGS:
No. of Institutions: 800
Shares Held: 1,047,121,461
% Held: 81.0

INDUSTRY: Organic fibers, noncellulosic (SIC: 2824)

TRANSFER AGENT(S): Mellon Investor Services, South Hackensack, NJ

PHELPS DODGE CORPORATION

EXCH.	SYM.	REC. PRICE	P/E RATIO	YLD.	MKT. CAP.	RANGE (52-WK.)	'02 Y/E PR.
NYSE	PD	35.96 (2/28/03)	...	...	$2.83 bill.	42.51 - 22.90	31.65

LOWER MEDIUM GRADE. THE COMPANY'S PERFORMANCE IMPROVEMENT PROGRAM SHOULD DELIVER ANNUAL OPERATING INCOME IMPROVEMENTS OF $400.0 MILLION BY THE END OF 2003.

TRADING VOLUME
Thousand Shares

1989 1990 1991 1992 1993 1994 1995 1996 1997 1998 1999 2000 2001 2002 2003

*7 YEAR PRICE SCORE 66.4　　***12 MONTH PRICE SCORE 110.1**

*NYSE COMPOSITE INDEX=100

INTERIM EARNINGS (Per Share):

Qtr.	Mar	June	Sept.	Dec.
1998	2.80	0.69	0.49	d0.72
1999	0.01	d0.99	0.27	d2.91
2000	0.25	d0.48	0.50	0.10
2001	0.21	d1.41	d1.28	d1.00
2002	d0.06	d0.48	d0.37	d2.54

INTERIM DIVIDENDS (Per Share):

Amt.	Decl.	Ex.	Rec.	Pay.
0.50Q	2/07/01	2/14/01	2/16/01	3/09/01
0.125Q	5/03/01	5/16/01	5/18/01	6/08/01
0.125Q	6/20/01	8/15/01	8/17/01	9/07/01
	Dividend payment suspended.			

CAPITALIZATION (12/31/01):

	($000)	(%)
Long-Term Debt	2,522,000	44.5
Deferred Income Tax	441,800	7.8
Common & Surplus	2,707,200	47.7
Total	5,671,000	100.0

BUSINESS:

Phelps Dodge Corporation is among the world's largest producers of copper and molybdenum. Using copper from its own production and copper purchased from others, the Company's Phelps Dodge Mining Company (PD Mining) subsidiary (66.8% of 2002 revenues) produces continuous cast copper rod, the basic feed for the electrical wire and cable industry. In 2002, PD Mining produced 1.0 million tons of copper. The Phelps Dodge Industries segment (33.2%) is comprised of a group of companies that manufacture engineered products principally for the transportation, energy and telecommunications sectors worldwide. This business segment includes PD's carbon black operations and its U.S. and international wire and cable and specialty conductor operations.

RECENT DEVELOPMENTS:

For the year ended 12/31/02, PD reported a loss of $292.1 million, before an extraordinary charge of $26.6 million, compared with a loss of $273.0 million in the previous year. Results included net non-recurring after-tax charges of $238.4 million in 2002 and a net after-tax non-recurring gain of $11.9 million in 2001. Earnings for 2002 and 2001 excluded accounting change charges of $22.9 million and $2.0 million, respectively. Sales and operating revenues declined 7.0% to $3.72 billion from $4.00 billion a year earlier. Phelps Dodge Mining Company revenues decreased 6.2% to $2.49 billion, while Phelps Dodge Industries revenues fell 8.6% to $1.24 billion. Operating loss amounted to $227.5 million versus an operating loss of $44.9 million in 2001.

PROSPECTS:

The Company's performance improvement program achieved approximately $250.0 million in annual operating income improvements during 2002. The program is expected to deliver annual operating income improvements of $400.0 million by the of 2003. These operating improvements, together with PD's substantial production capacity, should benefit results greatly as copper prices rise.

ANNUAL FINANCIAL DATA:

FISCAL YEAR	TOT. REVS. ($mill.)	NET INC. ($mill.)	TOT. ASSETS ($mill.)	OPER. PROFIT %	NET PROFIT %	RET. ON EQUITY %	RET. ON ASSETS %	CURR. RATIO	EARN. PER SH.$	CASH FL. PER SH.$	TANG. BK. VAL.$	DIV. PER SH.$	PRICE RANGE	AVG. P/E RATIO	AVG. YIELD %
p12/31/02	3,722.0	⑨ d292.1							⑨ d3.58				42.51 — 22.90	...	...
12/31/01	4,002.4	⑧ d273.0	7,618.8	...	...	...	...	1.5	⑧ d3.47	2.45	34.40	0.75	55.69 — 25.74	...	1.8
12/31/00	4,525.1	⑦ 29.0	7,830.8	5.2	0.6	0.9	0.4	1.1	⑦ 0.37	6.26	39.45	2.00	73.00 — 36.06	147.3	3.7
12/31/99	3,114.4	⑥ d254.3	8,229.0	...	...	...	...	1.2	⑥ d4.13	1.21	41.64	2.00	70.63 — 41.88	...	3.6
12/31/98	3,063.4	⑤ 190.9	5,036.5	13.8	6.2	7.4	3.8	1.5	⑤ 3.26	8.28	44.69	2.00	71.75 — 43.88	17.7	3.5
12/31/97	3,914.3	④ 408.5	4,965.2	15.6	10.4	16.3	8.2	1.5	④ 6.63	11.24	39.68	2.00	89.63 — 59.88	11.3	2.7
12/31/96	3,786.6	③ 461.8	4,816.4	18.8	12.2	16.8	9.6	2.1	③ 6.97	10.73	40.19	1.95	77.63 — 54.63	9.5	2.9
12/31/95	4,185.4	② 746.6	4,646.0	26.3	17.8	27.9	16.1	2.6	② 10.65	13.84	36.96	1.80	70.50 — 51.88	5.7	2.9
12/31/94	3,289.2	① 271.0	4,133.8	12.2	8.2	12.4	6.6	1.9	① 3.81	6.56	28.87	1.69	65.00 — 47.63	14.8	3.0
12/31/93	2,596.0	187.0	3,720.9	12.1	7.2	9.2	5.0	1.8	2.66	5.27	28.48	1.65	55.63 — 39.13	17.8	3.5

Statistics are as originally reported. ① Incl. a net chg. $91.7 mill. ② Incl. a gain $26.8 mill. ③ Incl. an after-tax chg. $10.0 mill. for prov. of reclaim. costs. ④ Incl. after-tax chgs. $31.6 mill. ⑤ Incl. $131.1 mill. after-tax gain fr. the disposal of Accuride Corp. & an after-tax loss $32.0 mill. fr. sale & costs rel. to its mining co. ⑥ Incl. $455.4 mill. non-recur. chg. & excl. loss $3.5 mill. fr. cumulative effect. ⑦ Incl. $51.8 mill. net non-recur. chg. ⑧ Bef. an acctg. change chrg. $2.0 mill.; incl. net non-recur. gain $31.6 mill. and an investment loss $12.9 mill. ⑨ Bef. an acctg. change chrg. $22.9 mill. and extr. chrg. $26.6 mill.; incl. net restr., impair., eviron., litig. chrgs. of $238.4 mill.

OFFICERS:
J. S. Whisler, Chmn.,Pres., C.E.O.
R. G. Peru, Sr. V.P., C.F.O.
S. D. Colton, Sr. V.P., Gen. Couns., Sec.

INVESTOR CONTACT: Stanton K. Rideout, (602) 366-8589

PRINCIPAL OFFICE: 1 North Central Avenue, Phoenix, AZ 85004-2306

TELEPHONE NUMBER: (602) 366-8100
FAX: (602) 366-7314
WEB: www.phelpsdodge.com

NO. OF EMPLOYEES: 13,500 (approx.)

SHAREHOLDERS: 28,853 (record)

ANNUAL MEETING: In April

INCORPORATED: NY, Aug., 1885

INSTITUTIONAL HOLDINGS:
No. of Institutions: 252
Shares Held: 78,628,206
% Held: 88.4

INDUSTRY: Primary copper (SIC: 3331)

TRANSFER AGENT(S): Mellon Investor Services, Ridgefield Park, NJ

PHILADELPHIA SUBURBAN CORPORATION

EXCH.	SYM.	REC. PRICE	P/E RATIO	YLD.	MKT. CAP.	RANGE (52-WK.)	'02 Y/E PR.	DIV. ACH.
NYSE	PSC	20.93 (2/28/03)	21.8	2.7%	$1.43 bill.	25.00 - 16.02	20.60	11 yrs.

MEDIUM GRADE. THE COMPANY IS BENEFITING FROM RATE RELIEF IN ITS VARIOUS OPERATING DIVISIONS.

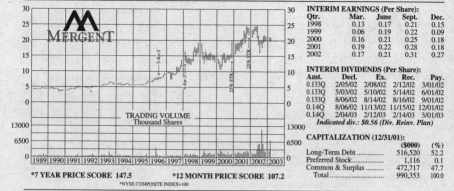

*7 YEAR PRICE SCORE 147.5   ***12 MONTH PRICE SCORE 107.2**
*NYSE COMPOSITE INDEX=100

INTERIM EARNINGS (Per Share):

Qtr.	Mar.	June	Sept.	Dec.
1998	0.13	0.17	0.21	0.15
1999	0.06	0.19	0.22	0.09
2000	0.16	0.21	0.25	0.18
2001	0.19	0.22	0.28	0.18
2002	0.17	0.21	0.31	0.27

INTERIM DIVIDENDS (Per Share):

Amt.	Decl.	Ex.	Rec.	Pay.
0.133Q	2/05/02	2/08/02	2/12/02	3/01/02
0.133Q	5/03/02	5/10/02	5/14/02	6/01/02
0.133Q	8/06/02	8/14/02	8/16/02	9/01/02
0.14Q	8/06/02	11/13/02	11/15/02	12/01/02
0.14Q	2/04/03	2/12/03	2/14/03	3/01/03

Indicated div.: $0.56 (Div. Reinv. Plan)

CAPITALIZATION (12/31/01):

	($000)	(%)
Long-Term Debt	516,520	52.2
Preferred Stock	1,116	0.1
Common & Surplus	472,717	47.7
Total	990,353	100.0

BUSINESS:

Philadelphia Suburban Corporation is a holding company for regulated utilities providing water or wastewater services to approximately 2.0 million people in Pennsylvania, Illinois, Ohio, New Jersey, Maine, and North Carolina as of 2/5/03. PSC's two primary subsidiaries are Pennsylvania Suburban Water Company, a regulated public utility that provides water or wastewater services to about 1.3 million residents in the suburban areas north and west of the City of Philadelphia and in ten other counties in Pennsylvania, and Consumers Water Company, a holding company for several regulated public utility companies that provide water or wastewater service to about 700,000 residents in various communities in four states. In addition, PSC provides water and wastewater service to about 35,000 people through operating and maintenance contracts with municipal authorities and other parties close to its operating companies' service territories. Some of PSC's subsidiaries provide wastewater collection, treatment and disposal services, primarily residential, to about 40,000 people in Pennsylvania, Illinois, New Jersey and North Carolina.

RECENT DEVELOPMENTS:

For the year ended 12/31/02, net income increased 11.8% to $67.2 million compared with $60.1 million in 2001. Results for 2002 and 2001 included a gain of the sale of other assets of $2.1 million and $3.4 million, respectively. Also, results for 2002 included a gain on the sale of a water system of $5.7 million. Operating revenues rose 4.8% to $322.0 million from $307.3 million a year earlier. The improvement in revenues was primarily attributed to rate relief in PSC's various operating divisions aided by continued customer growth due to acquisitions, partially offset by a decrease in overall water consumption in PSC's largest operating division.

PROSPECTS:

The Company received regulatory approval from Sarasota County Florida concerning its proposed acquisition of the water and wastewater systems of AquaSource, Inc., a subsidiary of DQE, Inc. Upon completion of the transaction, the states where AquaSource's utilities operate will add more than 20.0% to PSC's customer base. As of 3/18/03, the Company had nine of the 12 regulatory approvals required. The transaction is expected to close in mid-2003.

ANNUAL FINANCIAL DATA:

FISCAL YEAR	TOT. REVS. ($mill.)	NET INC. ($mill.)	TOT. ASSETS ($mill.)	OPER. PROFIT %	NET PROFIT %	NET INC./ NET PROP. %	NET INC./ TOT. CAP. %	RET. ON EQUITY %	ACCUM. DEPR./ GROSS PROP. %	EARN. PER SH.$	TANG. BK. VAL.$	DIV. PER SH.$	DIV. PAYOUT %	PRICE RANGE	AVG. P/E RATIO	AVG. YIELD %
p12/31/02	322.0	⑥ 67.2								⑥ 0.97		0.54	55.4	25.00 - 16.02	21.1	2.6
12/31/01	307.3	② 60.1	1,560.3	43.7	19.6	4.4	6.1	12.7	18.4	② 0.87	6.93	0.50	58.0	24.64 - 15.65	23.2	2.5
12/31/00	275.5	③ 52.9	1,414.0	42.9	19.2	4.2	5.9	12.2	18.5	③ 0.81	8.05	0.47	58.1	19.95 - 10.56	18.9	3.1
12/31/99	257.3	⑤ 36.4	1,280.8	39.3	14.1	3.2	4.7	9.9	18.5	⑤ 0.56	8.99	0.45	79.6	19.04 - 12.64	28.1	2.8
12/31/98	151.0	28.8	701.5	44.2	19.1	4.7	5.8	12.3	18.2	0.66	5.34	0.43	64.6	19.24 - 12.08	23.8	2.7
12/31/97	136.2	23.2	618.5	41.7	17.0	4.3	5.5	11.9	18.5	0.56	4.46	0.40	70.8	13.77 - 7.32	18.7	3.8
12/31/96	122.5	④ 19.8	582.9	40.2	16.1	3.9	5.0	11.0	17.9	④ 0.67	5.98	0.38	57.0	9.54 - 6.56	12.1	4.7
12/31/95	117.0	④ 18.0	518.1	39.4	15.4	4.1	5.4	11.5	17.5	④ 0.64	5.49	0.36	57.0	6.88 - 5.56	9.7	5.9
12/31/94	108.6	15.6	458.2	37.6	14.4	4.1	5.3	10.9	16.6	0.58	5.35	0.35	61.1	6.28 - 5.48	10.2	6.0
12/31/93	101.2	13.8	439.7	37.0	13.7	3.8	10.2	10.2	15.5	0.54	5.07	0.34	63.2	6.64 - 5.00	10.7	5.9

Statistics are as originally reported. Adj. for stk. splits: 25% div., 11/01 & 12/00; 4-for-3, 1/98; 3-for-2, 7/96. ① Incl. restruct. recovery costs of $3.8 mill. ② Incl. gain on the sale of other assets of $3.4 mill. ③ Incl. restruct. recovery gain of $1.1 mill., merger transaction recovery costs of $2.9 mill., gain on the sale of other assets of $5.1 mill. ④ Incl. reversal of reserve for discont. oper. of $965,000, 1996; $370,000, 1995. ⑤ Incl. merger transaction costs of $6.3 mill. ⑥ Incl. a net gain on sale of water system & other assets of $7.8 mill.

OFFICERS:
N. DeBenedictis, Chmn., Pres.
D. P. Smeltzer, Sr. V.P., C.F.O.
R. H. Stahl, Exec. V.P., Gen. Couns.
INVESTOR CONTACT: Keya W. Epps, Investor Relations, (610) 645-1084
PRINCIPAL OFFICE: 762 W. Lancaster Ave., Bryn Mawr, PA 19010-3489

TELEPHONE NUMBER: (610) 527-8000
FAX: (610) 527-1061
WEB: www.suburbanwater.com
NO. OF EMPLOYEES: 951
SHAREHOLDERS: 21,056 (approx.)
ANNUAL MEETING: In May
INCORPORATED: PA, May, 1969

INSTITUTIONAL HOLDINGS:
No. of Institutions: 168
Shares Held: 24,165,208
% Held: 35.6

INDUSTRY: Water supply (SIC: 4941)

TRANSFER AGENT(S): EquiServe, L.P., Canton, MA

PHILLIPS-VAN HEUSEN CORPORATION

EXCH.	SYM.	REC. PRICE	P/E RATIO	YLD.	MKT. CAP.	RANGE (52-WK.)	'02 Y/E PR.
NYSE	PVH	11.95 (2/28/03)	11.1	1.3%	$330.1 mill.	16.25 - 10.80	11.56

LOWER MEDIUM GRADE. PVH COMPLETED THE ACQUISITION OF CALVIN KLEIN, INC. FOR ABOUT $430.0 MILLION.

*7 YEAR PRICE SCORE 120.0   ***12 MONTH PRICE SCORE 95.1**

*NYSE COMPOSITE INDEX=100

INTERIM EARNINGS (Per Share):

Qtr.	Apr.	July	Oct.	Jan.
1997-98	d0.17	d1.23	0.54	0.20
1998-99	d0.16	0.10	0.51	0.02
1999-00	d0.17	0.13	0.56	0.10
2000-01	d0.07	0.22	0.71	0.24
2001-02	0.02	0.25	0.45	d0.34
2002-03	d0.03	0.28	0.63	0.20

INTERIM DIVIDENDS (Per Share):

Amt.	Decl.	Ex.	Rec.	Pay.
0.037Q	3/06/02	3/15/02	3/19/02	3/25/02
0.037Q	4/25/02	5/28/02	5/30/02	6/17/02
0.037Q	8/07/02	8/28/02	8/30/02	9/13/02
0.037Q	11/01/02	11/13/02	11/15/02	12/16/02
0.037Q	3/06/03	3/14/03	3/18/03	3/28/03

Indicated div.: $0.15

CAPITALIZATION (2/3/02):

	($000)	(%)
Long-Term Debt	248,935	48.4
Common & Surplus	265,727	51.6
Total	514,662	100.0

BUSINESS:

Phillips-Van Heusen Corporation is a vertically-integrated manufacturer and marketer of a broad range of men's and women's apparel and women's and children's footwear. The Company's products include shirts, sweaters and shoes and, to a lesser extent, neckwear, furnishings, bottoms, outerwear and leather and canvas accessories. PVH's brands includes VAN HEUSEN®; BASS®, men's, women's and children's casual footwear; GEOFFREY BEENE®, designer dress shirt label; and three sportswear brands, IZOD®, VAN HEUSEN® and GEOFFREY BEENE®. In addition, PVH licenses CK CALVIN KLEIN®, DKNY®, Kenneth Cole®, ARROW®, FUBU® AND REGIS™ by the Van Heusen Company and JOHN HENRY® for dress shirts and ARROW® for sportswear. In 2/99, PVH sold its Gant apparel brand.

RECENT DEVELOPMENTS:

For the year ended 2/2/03, net income soared to $30.4 million from $10.7 million the previous year. Earnings benefited from the strong performance of the Company's wholesale sportswear and dress shirt businesses. Results for 2001 included after-tax restructuring charges of $13.4 million. Net sales declined 1.9% to $1.40 billion from $1.43 billion in 2001. Gross margin improved to 37.8% from 35.7% a year earlier. Gross margin benefited from tight management of PVH's inventory, which eliminated a significant amount of clearance markdowns.

PROSPECTS:

On 2/12/03, PVH acquired Calvin Klein, Inc. for about $430.0 million. Key opportunities to grow the Calvin Klein business include the launch of better men's and women's sportswear and accessories lines, global expansion through a strategic plan together with Calvin Klein's licensing partners, global expansion through Calvin Klein retail stores, and additional growth opportunities in Europe and Asia.

PVH anticipates the acquisition will be somewhat dilutive in 2003, but should make a positive contribution to annual earnings by 2004. During 2003, due to normal integration and transition costs, operating earnings per share are expected to be in a range of $0.45 to $0.55. Earnings per share for fiscal 2004 and beyond are expected to grow at an annual rate of 15.0% to 20.0%.

ANNUAL FINANCIAL DATA:

FISCAL YEAR	TOT. REVS. ($mill.)	NET INC. ($mill.)	TOT. ASSETS ($mill.)	OPER. PROFIT %	NET PROFIT %	RET. ON EQUITY %	RET. ON ASSETS %	CURR. RATIO	EARN. PER SH. $	CASH FL. PER SH. $	TANG. BK. VAL. $	DIV. PER SH. $	PRICE RANGE	AVG. P/E RATIO	AVG. YIELD %
2/02/03	**1,405.0**	**30.4**							**1.08**			**0.15**	**16.25 - 10.35**	**12.3**	**1.1**
2/03/02	1,431.9	③ 10.7	708.9	2.9	0.7	4.0	1.5	3.5	③ 0.38	1.30	5.53	0.15	18.74 - 8.32	35.6	1.1
2/04/01	1,455.5	30.1	724.4	4.8	2.1	11.2	4.2	3.2	1.10	1.83	5.67	0.15	13.88 - 5.81	8.9	1.5
1/30/00	1,271.5	① 16.9	673.7	3.8	1.3	7.0	2.5	3.4	① 0.62	1.33	5.79	0.15	10.63 - 5.38	12.9	1.9
1/31/99	1,303.1	①② 12.9	674.3	3.3	1.0	5.6	1.9	2.8	①② 0.47	1.40	4.23	0.15	15.13 - 6.50	23.0	1.4
2/01/98	1,350.0	① d66.6	660.5	...	...	...	...	1.4	① d2.46	d1.52	3.82	0.15	15.88 - 11.50	...	1.1
2/02/97	1,359.6	18.5	657.4	3.5	1.4	6.4	2.8	3.0	0.69	1.55	6.28	0.15	15.13 - 9.50	17.8	1.2
1/28/96	1,464.1	① 0.3	749.1	1.4	...	0.1	...	2.4	① 0.01	0.99	5.76	0.19	18.00 - 9.13	...	1.4
1/29/95	1,255.5	① 30.0	596.3	4.0	2.4	10.9	5.0	3.8	① 1.11	1.81	9.69	0.15	39.00 - 14.00	23.9	0.6
1/30/94	1,152.4	② 43.3	554.8	7.0	3.8	17.5	7.8	3.8	② 1.60	2.30	8.64	0.15	37.50 - 25.75	19.8	0.5

Statistics are as originally reported. ① Incl. non-recurr. chrg. 1/30/00, $8.5 mill.; 1/31/99, $8.5 mill.; 2/1/98, $86.7 mill.; 1/28/96, $27.0 mill.; 1/29/95, $7.0 mill. ② Bef. extraord. chrg. 1/31/99, $1.1 mill.; 1/30/94, $11.4 mill. ③ Incl. restruc. chrgs. $13.4 mill.

OFFICERS:
B. J. Klatsky, Chmn., C.E.O.
A. E. Sirkin, Vice-Chmn.
M. Weber, Pres., C.O.O.
INVESTOR CONTACT: Emanuel Chirico, Exec. V.P., C.F.O., (212) 381-3503
PRINCIPAL OFFICE: 200 Madison Avenue, New York, NY 10016

TELEPHONE NUMBER: (212) 381-3500
FAX: (212) 247-5309
WEB: www.pvh.com
NO. OF EMPLOYEES: 8,800 (approx.)
SHAREHOLDERS: 1,160 (approx.)
ANNUAL MEETING: In June
INCORPORATED: NY, July, 1914; reincorp., DE, April, 1976

INSTITUTIONAL HOLDINGS:
No. of Institutions: 112
Shares Held: 19,344,557
% Held: 69.6
INDUSTRY: Men's & boys' clothing stores (SIC: 5611)
TRANSFER AGENT(S): The Bank of New York, New York, NY

PIEDMONT NATURAL GAS COMPANY, INC.

EXCH.	SYM.	REC. PRICE	P/E RATIO	YLD.	MKT. CAP.	RANGE (52-WK.)	'02 Y/E PR.	DIV. ACH.
NYSE	PNY	34.41 (2/28/03)	14.5	4.8%	$1.14 bill.	38.00 - 27.35	35.35	23 yrs.

UPPER MEDIUM GRADE. THE COMPANY EXPECTS EARNINGS FOR FISCAL 2003 TO RANGE FROM $2.05 TO $2.15 PER DILUTED SHARE.

TRADING VOLUME
Thousand Shares

1989 1990 1991 1992 1993 1994 1995 1996 1997 1998 1999 2000 2001 2002 2003

*7 YEAR PRICE SCORE 118.9   ***12 MONTH PRICE SCORE 107.6**

NYSE COMPOSITE INDEX=100

INTERIM EARNINGS (Per Share):

Qtr.	Jan.	Apr.	July	Oct.
1998-99	1.32	1.12	d0.26	d0.28
1999-00	1.40	1.18	d0.32	d0.23
2000-01	1.56	1.23	d0.52	d0.24
2001-02	1.26	1.27	d0.27	d0.36
2002-03	1.74	...	...	...

INTERIM DIVIDENDS (Per Share):

Amt.	Decl.	Ex.	Rec.	Pay.
0.40Q	2/22/02	3/21/02	3/25/02	4/15/02
0.40Q	5/31/02	6/20/02	6/24/02	7/15/02
0.40Q	8/23/02	9/20/02	9/24/02	10/15/02
0.40Q	12/13/02	12/20/02	12/24/02	1/15/03
0.415Q	2/28/03	3/21/03	3/25/03	4/15/03

Indicated div.: $1.66 (Div. Reinv. Plan)

CAPITALIZATION (10/31/02):

	($000)	(%)
Long-Term Debt	462,000	38.2
Deferred Income Tax	158,275	13.1
Common & Surplus	589,596	48.7
Total	1,209,871	100.0

BUSINESS:

Piedmont Natural Gas Company, Inc. is engaged in the transportation, distribution and sale of natural gas to over 740,000 residential, commercial and industrial customers in North Carolina, South Carolina and Tennessee. Non-utility subsidiaries and divisions are involved in the exploration, development, marketing and transportation of natural gas, oil, and propane. PNY's utility operations are subject to regulation by the North Carolina Utilities Commission, the Tennessee Public Service Commission and the Public Service Commission of South Carolina. PNY also owns Tennessee Natural Resources, Inc., and its subsidiaries.

RECENT DEVELOPMENTS:

For the quarter ended 1/31/03, net income advanced 40.9% to $58.0 million compared with $41.2 million in the corresponding period of the previous year. Earnings growth was primarily attributed higher sales and transportation deliveries due to continued customer growth and weather that was colder than the prior year. Operating revenues soared 70.9% to $493.5 million from $288.8 million in the year-earlier quarter. Margin (revenues less the cost of gas) jumped 31.2% to $161.7 million from $123.2 million the year before. Operating income surged 40.9% to $65.7 million versus $46.6 million in 2001. System throughput leapt 53.0% to 63.6 million dekatherms.

PROSPECTS:

The Company's recently announced agreement to purchase the stock of North Carolina Natural Gas is expected to close in mid-2003, granted regulatory approval. Upon completion, the transaction is expected to be dilutive by $0.05 to $0.07 per share during fiscal 2003, but accretive to earnings in fiscal 2004, the first full year following closing. Meanwhile, the Company expects earnings for fiscal 2003 in the range of $2.05 to $2.15 per diluted share. Moreover, the Company anticipates customer growth of about 3.5% during fiscal 2003 and utility capital expenditures totaling around $85.0 million to fund this growth.

ANNUAL FINANCIAL DATA:

FISCAL YEAR	TOT. REVS. ($mill.)	NET INC. ($mill.)	TOT. ASSETS ($mill.)	OPER. PROFIT %	NET PROFIT %	NET INC./ NET PROP. %	NET INC./ TOT. CAP. %	RET. ON EQUITY %	ACCUM. DEPR./ GROSS PROP. %	EARN. PER SH. $	TANG. BK. VAL. $	DIV. PER SH. $	DIV. PAYOUT %	PRICE RANGE	AVG. P/E RATIO	AVG. YIELD %
10/31/02	832.0	62.2	1,445.1	10.8	7.5	5.4	5.1	10.6	33.1	1.89	17.82	1.58	83.9	38.00 - 27.35	17.3	4.9
10/31/01	1,107.9	65.5	1,393.7	8.5	5.9	5.9	5.4	11.7	31.5	2.02	17.26	1.52	75.2	38.00 - 29.19	16.6	4.5
10/31/00	830.4	64.0	1,445.0	10.8	7.7	6.0	5.7	12.1	30.2	2.01	16.52	1.44	71.6	39.44 - 23.69	15.7	4.6
10/31/99	686.5	58.2	1,288.7	13.4	8.5	5.6	5.6	11.8	29.1	1.86	15.71	1.36	73.1	36.63 - 28.63	17.5	4.2
10/31/98	765.3	60.3	1,162.8	11.9	7.9	6.1	6.4	13.2	28.4	1.96	14.91	1.28	65.3	36.13 - 27.88	16.3	4.0
10/31/97	775.5	① 54.1	1,098.2	10.8	7.0	5.7	6.0	12.9	27.2	① 1.81	13.90	1.21	66.6	36.44 - 22.00	16.1	4.1
10/31/96	685.1	48.6	1,064.9	10.9	7.1	5.5	5.6	12.6	26.2	1.67	13.07	1.15	68.6	25.75 - 20.50	13.8	5.0
10/31/95	505.2	40.3	964.9	12.9	8.0	4.9	5.0	11.4	25.4	1.45	12.31	1.08	74.8	24.88 - 18.25	14.9	5.0
10/31/94	575.4	35.5	887.8	9.7	6.2	4.7	5.2	11.8	24.9	1.35	11.36	1.02	75.9	23.38 - 18.00	15.3	5.0
10/31/93	552.8	37.5	796.5	10.2	6.8	5.5	5.8	13.2	25.4	1.45	10.90	0.96	66.5	26.38 - 18.81	15.6	4.3

Statistics are as originally reported. ① Incl. pre-tax restruct. chg. of $1.8 mill.

OFFICERS:
J. H. Maxheim, Chmn.
T. E. Skains, Pres., & C.O.O.
D. J. Dzuricky, Sr. V.P., & C.F.O.

INVESTOR CONTACT: Stephen D. Connor, Investor Relations, (704) 364-3483 ext.6205

PRINCIPAL OFFICE: 1915 Rexford Road, Charlotte, NC 28211

TELEPHONE NUMBER: (704) 364-3120
FAX: (704) 365-8515
WEB: www.piedmontng.com

NO. OF EMPLOYEES: 1,715 (avg.)

SHAREHOLDERS: 16,186 (record)

ANNUAL MEETING: In Feb.

INCORPORATED: NY, May, 1950; reincorp., NC, Mar., 1994

INSTITUTIONAL HOLDINGS:
No. of Institutions: 143
Shares Held: 9,359,459
% Held: 28.4

INDUSTRY: Natural gas distribution (SIC: 4924)

TRANSFER AGENT(S): Wachovia Bank of North Carolina, NA, Boston, MA

PIER 1 IMPORTS, INC.

EXCH.	SYM.	REC. PRICE	P/E RATIO	YLD.	MKT. CAP.	RANGE (52-WK.)	'02 Y/E PR.	DIV. ACH.
NYSE	PIR	15.97 (2/28/03)	12.3	1.5%	$1.49 bill.	24.35 - 14.35	18.93	11 yrs.

UPPER MEDIUM GRADE. THE COMPANY'S BALANCE SHEET CONTINUES TO BE STRONG, REFLECTING INCREASED FREE CASH FLOW GENERATION AND ACCELERATED OPENINGS OF PIER 1 AND CARGOKIDS STORES.

TRADING VOLUME
Thousand Shares

*7 YEAR PRICE SCORE 172.5   *12 MONTH PRICE SCORE 98.1
*NYSE COMPOSITE INDEX=100

INTERIM EARNINGS (Per Share):

Qtr.	May	Aug.	Nov.	Feb.
1996-97	0.09	0.11	0.10	0.17
1997-98	0.13	0.21	0.16	0.24
1998-99	0.15	0.17	0.19	0.27
1999-00	0.13	0.12	0.16	0.34
2000-01	0.17	0.18	0.24	0.38
2001-02	0.13	0.14	0.26	0.51
2002-03	0.23	0.23	0.33	...

INTERIM DIVIDENDS (Per Share):

Amt.	Decl.	Ex.	Rec.	Pay.
0.05Q	4/05/02	5/06/02	5/08/02	5/22/02
0.05Q	6/27/02	8/05/02	8/07/02	8/21/02
0.05Q	9/26/02	11/04/02	11/06/02	11/20/02
0.06Q	12/05/02	2/03/03	2/05/03	2/19/03
0.06Q	3/27/03	5/05/03	5/07/03	5/21/03

Indicated div.: $0.24 (Div. Reinv. Plan)

CAPITALIZATION (3/2/02):

	($000)	(%)
Long-Term Debt	25,356	4.1
Common & Surplus	585,656	95.9
Total	611,012	100.0

BUSINESS:

Pier 1 Imports, Inc. is a retailer of decorative home furnishings, furniture, dining and kitchen goods, bath and bedding accessories and other specialty items for the home imported from over 40 countries. As of 2/28/03, PIR operated more than 1,000 stores in 50 states, Canada, Puerto Rico, the United Kingdom and Mexico. The Company's stores operate under the "Pier 1 Imports" and "Cargokids!" names, as well as under the name "The Pier" in the United King-

dom. Also, PIR supplies merchandise and licenses the Pier 1 Imports name to Sears Mexico and Sears Puerto Rico, which sell Pier 1 merchandise in a "store-within-a-store" format in 16 Sears Mexico stores and in seven Sears Puerto Rico stores. In 1997, PIR acquired a national bank and its assets in Omaha, Nebraska, which operates under the name of Pier 1 National Bank and holds the credit card accounts for the Company's proprietary credit card.

RECENT DEVELOPMENTS:

For the three months ended 11/30/02, net income climbed 24.2% to $31.1 million from $25.0 million in the corresponding prior-year period. Net sales totaled $438.5 million, up 13.2% compared with $387.4 million the previous year. Comparable-store sales were up 4.6% year over year.

Cost of sales, including buying and store occupancy, increased 11.2% to $246.7 million from $222.0 million the year before. Operating income advanced 24.3% to $49.3 million from $39.7 million a year earlier.

PROSPECTS:

The Company's balance sheet continues to be strong, reflecting increased free cash flow generation and accelerated openings of Pier 1 and Cargokids stores. As of 2/28/03, PIR expects to increase its number of stores to 1,500 from approximately 1,000 by 2010. Looking ahead,

the Company expects earnings per share to range from $0.55 to $0.57 in its fiscal fourth quarter, as sales are likely to benefit from winter clearance sales, partially offset by the chilly weather in the East and the Columbia space shuttle disaster, which kept shoppers at home.

ANNUAL FINANCIAL DATA:

FISCAL YEAR	TOT. REVS. ($mill.)	NET INC. ($mill.)	TOT. ASSETS ($mill.)	OPER. PROFIT %	NET PROFIT %	RET. ON EQUITY %	RET. ON ASSETS %	CURR. RATIO	EARN. PER SH. $	CASH FL. PER SH. $	TANG. BK. VAL. $	DIV. PER SH. $	PRICE RANGE		AVG. P/E RATIO	AVG. YIELD %
3/02/02	1,548.6	100.2	862.7	10.3	6.5	17.1	11.6	2.9	1.04	1.49	6.27	0.16	18.30 -	7.97	12.6	1.2
3/03/01	1,411.5	94.7	735.7	10.7	6.7	17.8	12.9	3.3	0.97	1.41	5.53	0.14	14.50 -	5.88	10.5	1.4
2/26/00	1,231.1	74.7	670.7	10.0	6.1	17.0	11.1	2.4	0.75	1.11	4.70	0.12	12.38 -	5.25	11.7	1.4
2/27/99	1,138.6	80.4	654.0	11.8	7.1	19.9	12.3	2.9	0.77	1.02	4.14	0.11	20.75 -	6.06	17.4	0.8
2/28/98	1,075.4	①78.0	653.4	11.3	7.3	19.9	11.9	3.3	①0.72	0.90	3.86	0.08	15.96 -	7.22	16.1	0.7
3/01/97	947.1	③48.2	570.3	9.5	5.1	14.9	8.5	2.6	③0.49	0.69	3.19	0.07	7.95 -	4.61	12.8	1.1
3/02/96	810.7	②10.0	531.1	9.0	1.2	4.4	1.9	3.5	②0.11	0.30	2.56	0.05	5.50 -	3.45	40.6	1.2
2/25/95	712.0	②24.9	488.7	7.8	3.5	11.0	5.1	4.1	②0.28	0.46	2.66	0.04	4.50 -	3.02	13.4	1.2
2/26/94	685.4	②5.9	463.3	4.0	0.9	3.0	1.3	3.5	②0.07	0.24	2.38	0.04	5.56 -	3.49	64.5	0.8
2/27/93	629.2	23.0	460.5	8.1	3.7	11.5	5.0	3.4	0.26	0.43	2.27	0.02	5.56 -	2.81	16.1	0.5

Statistics are as originally reported. Adj. for 3-for-2 stk. split, 7/98 & 7/97; & 5% stk. div., 5/95. ① Incl. $9.1 mil ($0.08/sh) gain. ② Incl. $9.6 mil non-recur. chg., 3/2/96; $7.5 mil non-cash chg., 2/25/95; & $21.3 mil non-recur. chg., 2/26/94. ③ Bef. $4.1 mil extraord. chg.

OFFICERS:
M. J. Girouard, Chmn., C.E.O.
C. H. Turner, Exec. V.P., Fin., C.F.O., Treas.
J. R. Lawrence, Exec. V.P., Sec.

INVESTOR CONTACT: Cary Turner, Investor Relations, (817) 252-8400

PRINCIPAL OFFICE: 301 Commerce Street, Suite 600, Fort Worth, TX 76102

TELEPHONE NUMBER: (817) 252-8000
FAX: (817) 334-0191
WEB: www.pier1.com
NO. OF EMPLOYEES: 8,000 full-time (approx.); 9,100 part-time (approx.)
SHAREHOLDERS: 40,000 (approx.)
ANNUAL MEETING: In June
INCORPORATED: GA, May, 1978; reincorp., DE, Apr., 1979

INSTITUTIONAL HOLDINGS:
No. of Institutions: 266
Shares Held: 74,295,829
% Held: 80.0

INDUSTRY: Furniture stores (SIC: 5712)

TRANSFER AGENT(S): Mellon Investor Services, Ridgefield Park, NJ

PINNACLE WEST CAPITAL CORP.

EXCH.	SYM.	REC. PRICE	P/E RATIO	YLD.	MKT. CAP.	RANGE (52-WK.)	'02 Y/E PR.
NYSE	PNW	30.54 (2/28/03)	12.0	5.6%	$2.59 bill.	46.68 - 21.70	34.09

UPPER MEDIUM GRADE. GOING FORWARD, RESULTS SHOULD BE ENHANCED BY SOLID CUSTOMER GROWTH.

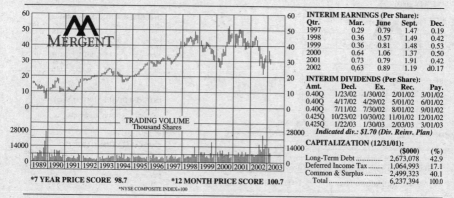

*7 YEAR PRICE SCORE 98.7   ***12 MONTH PRICE SCORE 100.7**

*NYSE COMPOSITE INDEX=100

INTERIM EARNINGS (Per Share):

Qtr.	Mar.	June	Sept.	Dec.
1997	0.29	0.79	1.47	0.19
1998	0.36	0.57	1.49	0.42
1999	0.36	0.81	1.48	0.53
2000	0.64	1.06	1.37	0.50
2001	0.73	0.79	1.91	0.42
2002	0.63	0.89	1.19	d0.17

INTERIM DIVIDENDS (Per Share):

Amt.	Decl.	Ex.	Rec.	Pay.
0.40Q	1/23/02	1/30/02	2/01/02	3/01/02
0.40Q	4/17/02	4/29/02	5/01/02	6/01/02
0.40Q	7/11/02	7/30/02	8/01/02	9/01/02
0.425Q	10/23/02	10/30/02	11/01/02	12/01/02
0.425Q	1/22/03	1/30/03	2/03/03	3/01/03

Indicated div.: $1.70 (Div. Reinv. Plan)

CAPITALIZATION (12/31/01):

	($000)	(%)
Long-Term Debt	2,673,078	42.9
Deferred Income Tax	1,064,993	17.1
Common & Surplus	2,499,323	40.1
Total	6,237,394	100.0

BUSINESS:

Pinnacle West Capital Corp. is a holding company whose principal asset is Arizona Public Service (APS), the state's largest utility with more than 874,000 customers as of 12/30/01, which provides wholesale and retail electric service to the entire state of Arizona, with the exception of Tuscon and about one-half of the Phoenix area. The Company is engaged in the generation and distribution of elec-

tricity, real estate development, and venture capital investments. The Company also owns SunCor Development Company, a major real estate developer engaged in owning, development, and sale of real estate property, including homebuilding, and El Dorado Investment, which makes equity investments in other companies.

RECENT DEVELOPMENTS:

For the year ended 12/31/02, the Company reported income of $215.2 million, before an accounting change charge of $65.7 million, versus income of $327.4 million, before an accounting change charge of $15.2 million, the previous year. Results for 2002 included a charge of $21.8 million for a voluntary workforce reduction, a charge of $29.7 million resulting from the cancellation of Redhawk Units 3

and 4 and a charge of $35.5 million related to an investment in NAC International. Total operating revenues dropped 22.2% to $2.64 billion from $3.39 billion the year before. Operating revenues from the regulated electricity segment declined 21.4% to $2.01 billion, while operating revenues from the marketing and trading segment slid 63.7% to $325.9 million.

PROSPECTS:

PNW's retail service territory, which is experiencing solid customer growth, expanded 3.1% year-over-year, or about three times the national average. Moreover, PNW may continue to benefit from lower replacement power costs for plant outages and the absence of costs for temporary gener-

ating units. However, lower market prices and margins resulting from the collapse of the western wholesale electricity market, continued milder weather, and a 1.5% decline in retail electricity prices, which took effect on 7/1/02, may negatively affect future results.

ANNUAL FINANCIAL DATA:

FISCAL YEAR	TOT. REVS. ($mill.)	NET INC. ($mill.)	TOT. ASSETS ($mill.)	OPER. PROFIT %	NET PROFIT %	RET. ON EQUITY %	RET. ON ASSETS %	CURR. RATIO	EARN. PER SH.$	CASH FL. PER SH.$	TANG. BK. VAL.$	DIV. PER SH.$	PRICE RANGE	AVG. P/E RATIO	AVG. YIELD %
p12/31/02	2,637.4	⑥ 215.2							⑥ 2.53			1.63	46.68 - 21.70	13.5	4.8
12/31/01	4,551.4	⑤ 327.4	7,981.7	14.8	7.2	13.1	4.1	0.7	⑤ 3.85	9.23	29.46	1.52	50.70 - 37.65	11.5	3.5
12/31/00	3,690.2	302.3	7,149.2	18.3	8.2	12.7	4.2	0.7	3.56	8.56	28.09	1.43	52.69 - 25.69	11.0	3.6
12/31/99	2,423.4	④ 269.8	6,608.5	23.9	11.1	12.2	4.1	1.0	④ 3.17	8.08	26.00	1.32	43.38 - 30.19	11.6	3.6
12/31/98	2,130.6	242.9	6,824.5	26.6	11.4	11.2	3.6	0.7	2.85	7.68	25.50	1.23	49.25 - 39.38	15.5	2.8
12/31/97	1,995.0	235.9	6,850.4	27.9	11.8	11.6	3.4	0.9	2.74	7.41	23.90	1.13	42.75 - 27.63	12.8	3.2
12/31/96	1,817.8	③ 211.1	6,989.3	29.9	11.6	10.7	3.0	0.8	③ 2.41	6.24	22.51	1.02	32.25 - 26.25	12.1	3.5
12/31/95	1,669.8	② 199.6	6,997.1	33.7	12.0	10.6	2.9	0.9	② 2.28	5.44	21.49	0.93	28.88 - 19.63	10.6	3.8
12/31/94	1,685.4	200.6	6,909.8	31.7	11.9	11.3	2.9	0.8	2.30	5.40	20.32	0.82	22.88 - 16.00	8.5	4.2
12/31/93	1,718.5	① 170.0	6,956.8	31.0	9.9	10.3	2.4	0.9	① 1.95	4.91	18.87	0.20	25.25 - 19.63	11.5	0.9

Statistics are as originally reported. ① Bef. acctg change chrg. $19.3 mill. ② Bef. extraord. charge $11.6 mill. ③ Bef extraord. chrg. $31.9 mill fr. early retire. of debt & Bef. disc. opers. loss $9.5 mill. ④ Bef. income $38.0 mill. from disc. ops. & extraord. chrg. $139.9 mill. ⑤ Bef. acctg. change chrg. $15.2 mill.; incl. non-recurr. chrg. $13.0 mill. ⑥ Bef. acctg. change chrg. $66.7 mill.; incl. non-recurr. chrgs. of $87.0 mill.

OFFICERS:
W. J. Post, Chmn., C.E.O.
J. E. Davis, Pres.
D. E. Brandt, C.F.O.

INVESTOR CONTACT: Rebecca L. Hickman, Dir. Inv. Rel., (602) 250-5668

PRINCIPAL OFFICE: 400 East Van Buren Street, P.O. Box 52132, Phoenix, AZ 85072

TELEPHONE NUMBER: (602) 379-2500
FAX: (602) 379-2625
WEB: www.pinnaclewest.com

NO. OF EMPLOYEES: 7,600 (avg.)

SHAREHOLDERS: 38,021 (approx.)

ANNUAL MEETING: In May

INCORPORATED: AZ, Feb., 1985

INSTITUTIONAL HOLDINGS:
No. of Institutions: 228
Shares Held: 72,838,212
% Held: 80.6

INDUSTRY: Electric services (SIC: 4911)

TRANSFER AGENT(S): BankBoston, N.A., Boston, MA

PIONEER NATURAL RESOURCES COMPANY

EXCH.	SYM.	REC. PRICE	P/E RATIO	YLD.	MKT. CAP.	RANGE (52-WK.)	'02 Y/E PR.
NYSE	PXD	26.15 (2/28/03)	62.3	...	$2.72 bill.	27.50 - 19.45	25.25

LOWER MEDIUM GRADE. THE COMPANY EXPECTS AVERAGE DAILY PRODUCTION TO RISE APPROXIMATELY 45.0% IN 2003.

TRADING VOLUME
Thousand Shares

*7 YEAR PRICE SCORE N/A   *12 MONTH PRICE SCORE 113.5
*NYSE COMPOSITE INDEX=100

INTERIM EARNINGS (Per Share):

Qtr.	Mar.	June	Sept.	Dec.
1997	0.53	0.21	d0.18	d11.43
1998	d0.27	d0.33	d0.44	d6.41
1999	d0.02	d0.74	0.46	0.08
2000	0.15	d0.04	0.69	0.85
2001	0.68	0.28	0.24	d0.16
2002	d0.02	0.12	0.16	0.16

INTERIM DIVIDENDS (Per Share):

Amt.	Decl.	Ex.	Rec.	Pay.
	No dividends paid.			

CAPITALIZATION (12/31/01):

	($000)	(%)
Long-Term Debt	1,577,304	54.8
Deferred Income Tax	13,768	0.5
Common & Surplus	1,285,389	44.7
Total	2,876,461	100.0

BUSINESS:

Pioneer Natural Resources Company is an oil and gas exploration and production company with ownership interests in oil and gas properties located principally in the Mid Continent, Southwestern and onshore and offshore Gulf Coast regions of the United States and in Argentina, Canada, South Africa, Gabon and Tunisia. Proved reserves as of 12/31/02 totaled 736.7 million barrels of oil equivalent, comprised of 380.8 million barrels of oil and natural gas liquids and 2.14 trillion cubic feet of natural gas. The Company was formed as a result of the 8/7/97 merger between Parker & Parsley Petroleum Company and MESA Inc.

RECENT DEVELOPMENTS:

For the year ended 12/31/02, income was $49.1 million compared with $103.7 million a year earlier. Earnings for 2002 and 2001 excluded extraordinary charges of $22.3 million and $3.8 million, respectively. Total revenues declined 18.1% to $717.4 million from $876.5 million the previous year. Revenues for 2002 and 2001 included gains of $4.4 million and $7.7 million, respectively, on the net disposition of assets.

PROSPECTS:

PXD has established a 2003 capital budget of between $450.0 million and $550.0 million for its planned development and exploration activities. Development activities account for approximately 65.0% of expected capital expenditures, while exploration drilling capital represents about 25.0% of the budget. Seismic and other items represent the remaining 10.0% of the budget. PXD noted that it plans to drill approximately 450 wells during 2003, up from 229 in 2002. Meanwhile, the Company expects average daily production in 2003 to rise approximately 45.0%, reflecting the anticipated second quarter 2003 start-up of its Falcon and Sable projects. Moreover, production is expected to rise at least 10.0% to 15.0% in 2004 due to the effect of a full year of production from the Company's Falcon, Sable and Devils Tower fields, the latter of which is expected to achieve first production in early 2004.

ANNUAL FINANCIAL DATA:

FISCAL YEAR	TOT. REVS. ($mill.)	NET INC. ($mill.)	TOT. ASSETS ($mill.)	OPER. PROFIT %	NET PROFIT %	RET. ON EQUITY %	RET. ON ASSETS %	CURR. RATIO	EARN. PER SH.$	CASH FL. PER SH.$	TANG. BK. VAL.$	DIV. PER SH.$	PRICE RANGE	AVG. P/E RATIO	AVG. YIELD %
p12/31/02	717.4	⑧49.1							⑧0.43				27.50 - 16.10	50.7	...
12/31/01	876.5	⑦103.7	3,271.1	27.4	11.8	8.1	3.2	1.1	⑦1.04	3.27	12.37	...	23.05 - 12.62	17.1	...
12/31/00	912.7	⑥164.5	2,954.4	35.1	18.0	18.2	5.6	0.9	⑥1.65	3.82	9.19	...	20.63 - 6.75	8.3	...
12/31/99	710.1	⑤d22.5	2,929.5	20.7	...	...	...	0.9	⑤d0.22	2.13	7.72	...	13.19 - 5.00	...	...
12/31/98	721.5	④d746.4	3,481.3	...	...	...	...	0.4	④d7.46	d4.09	7.87	0.10	30.00 - 7.75	...	0.5
①12/31/97	546.0	②③d877.3	3,946.6	...	...	...	...	1.2	②③d16.88	③d11.86	15.33	0.05	44.38 - 25.63	...	0.1
12/31/96	535.3	140.2	1,199.9	46.0	26.2	26.4	11.7	1.3	3.92	7.06	15.12	...			
12/31/95	513.7	②③d104.1	1,319.2	...	...	...	...	1.3	②③d2.95	③1.56	11.62	...			
12/31/94	496.2	d14.0	...	6.1	...	...	...	...	d0.47	4.37	...			
12/31/93	356.1	31.4	...	20.1	8.8	...	...	...	1.13	4.00	...			

Statistics are as originally reported. ① Results prior to 12/31/97 refl. ops. of Parker & Parsley Petroleum Company. ② Bef. extraord. chrg., 12/31/97, $13.4 mill.; cr. 12/31/95, $4.3 mill. ③ Incl. pre-tax chrg. 12/31/97, $1.35 bill.; pre-tax chrg. 12/31/95, $130.5 mill. for impairmt. of oil & gas props. ④ Incl. chrg. of $445,000 ⑤ Incl. chrg. of $24.2 mill. ⑥ Bef. extraord. chrg. of $12.3 mill.; incl. net gain on disp. of assets of $34.2 mill. ⑦ Bef. extraord. chrg. of $3.8 mill.; incl. net gain on disp. of assets of $7.7 mill. ⑧ Bef. extraord. chrg. of $22.3 mill.; incl. net gain on disp. of assets of $4.4 mill.

OFFICERS:
S. D. Sheffield, Chmn., Pres., C.E.O.
T. L. Dove, Exec. V.P., C.F.O.
M. L. Winthrow, Exec. V.P., Couns., Sec.

INVESTOR CONTACT: Susan Spratlen, V.P., Inv. Rel. & Comm., (972) 444-9001

PRINCIPAL OFFICE: 5205 N. O'Connor Blvd., Suite 1400, Irving, TX 75039

TELEPHONE NUMBER: (972) 444-9001
FAX: (972) 969-3559
WEB: www.pioneernrc.com

NO. OF EMPLOYEES: 926 (avg.)

SHAREHOLDERS: 38,866 (approx. record)

ANNUAL MEETING: In May

INCORPORATED: DE, Apr., 1997

INSTITUTIONAL HOLDINGS:
No. of Institutions: 245
Shares Held: 88,494,920
% Held: 75.6

INDUSTRY: Crude petroleum and natural gas (SIC: 1311)

TRANSFER AGENT(S): Continental Stock Transfer & Trust Company, New York, NY

PITNEY BOWES INC.

EXCH.	SYM.	REC. PRICE	P/E RATIO	YLD.	MKT. CAP.	RANGE (52-WK.)	'02 Y/E PR.	DIV. ACH.
NYSE	PBI	31.04 (2/28/03)	17.1	3.9%	$7.31 bill.	44.41 - 28.55	32.66	19 yrs.

UPPER MEDIUM GRADE. THE COMPANY IS TARGETING FULL-YEAR 2003 PROFORMA EARNINGS PER SHARE FROM CONTINUING OPERATIONS IN THE RANGE OF $2.38 TO $2.45, EXCLUDING ONE-TIME CHARGES.

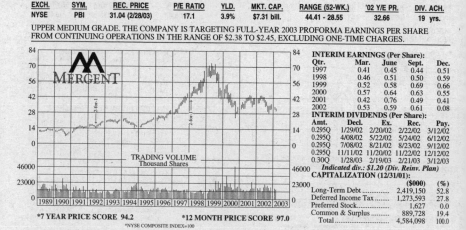

*7 YEAR PRICE SCORE 94.2   *12 MONTH PRICE SCORE 97.0
*NYSE COMPOSITE INDEX=100

INTERIM EARNINGS (Per Share):

Qtr.	Mar.	June	Sept.	Dec.
1997	0.41	0.45	0.44	0.51
1998	0.46	0.51	0.50	0.59
1999	0.52	0.58	0.69	0.66
2000	0.57	0.64	0.63	0.55
2001	0.42	0.76	0.49	0.41
2002	0.53	0.59	0.61	0.08

INTERIM DIVIDENDS (Per Share):

Amt.	Decl.	Ex.	Rec.	Pay.
0.295Q	1/29/02	2/20/02	2/22/02	3/12/02
0.295Q	4/08/02	5/22/02	5/24/02	6/12/02
0.295Q	7/08/02	8/21/02	8/23/02	9/12/02
0.295Q	11/11/02	11/20/02	11/22/02	12/12/02
0.30Q	1/28/03	2/19/03	2/21/03	3/12/03

Indicated div.: $1.20 (Div. Reinv. Plan)

CAPITALIZATION (12/31/01):

	($000)	(%)
Long-Term Debt	2,419,150	52.8
Deferred Income Tax	1,273,593	27.8
Preferred Stock	1,627	0.0
Common & Surplus	889,728	19.4
Total	4,584,098	100.0

BUSINESS:

Pitney Bowes Inc. and its subsidiaries operate within three industry segments: Global Mailing, Enterprise Solutions, and Capital Services. Global Mailing, 68.3% of 2002 revenue (84.9% of operating profit), includes the sale, rental, and financing of mail finishing, mail creation and shipping equipment, related supplies and services, postal payment services, and software. Enterprise Solutions, 27.6% (7.9%),

includes facilities management, through Pitney Bowes Management Services, Inc., and sales, service and financing of high-speed, software-enabled production mail systems, sorting equipment, incoming mail systems, electronic statement, billing and payment services, and mailing software. Capital Services, 4.1% (7.2%), includes large-ticket financing programs for a broad range of products.

RECENT DEVELOPMENTS:

For the year ended 12/31/02, income from continuing operations totaled $437.7 million compared with income from continuing operations of $514.3 million in the prior year. Results for 2002 included pre-tax charges totaling $213.2 million to increase credit reserves and write down investments. Results for 2001 included a pre-tax restructuring charge of $116.1 million, a $268.3 million pre-tax charge related to new mailing technology and a $338.1 million pre-tax gain from litigation settlement. Total revenue grew 7.0% to $4.41 billion from $4.12 billion a year earlier.

PROSPECTS:

Results are being positively affected by strong demand for the Company's networked mailing systems in the U.S. and its global mailing systems in the U.K. and Canada. In 2003, PBI plans to begin implementing restructuring initiatives that are expected to result in after-tax charges of approxi-

mately $100.0 million over a two-year period. Separately, the Company is targeting full-year 2003 revenue growth in the range of 2.0% to 4.0% and proforma earnings per share from continuing operations of between $2.38 and $2.45, excluding restructuring charges.

ANNUAL FINANCIAL DATA:

FISCAL YEAR	TOT. REVS. ($mill.)	NET INC. ($mill.)	TOT. ASSETS ($mill.)	OPER. PROFIT %	NET PROFIT %	RET. ON EQUITY %	RET. ON ASSETS %	CURR. RATIO	EARN. PER SH.$	CASH FL.PER SH.$	TANG. BK. VAL.$	DIV. PER SH.$	PRICE RANGE	AVG. P/E RATIO	AVG. YIELD
p12/31/02	4,409.8	☑ 437.7							☑ 1.83			1.18	44.41 — 28.55	20.2	3.2
12/31/01	4,122.5	⑥ 514.3	8,318.5	14.9	12.5	57.7	6.2	0.8	⑥ 2.08	3.36	1.05	1.16	44.70 — 32.00	18.4	3.0
12/31/00	3,880.9	⑤ 563.1	7,901.3	25.6	14.5	43.8	7.1	0.9	⑤ 2.18	3.42	4.34	1.14	54.13 — 24.00	17.9	2.9
12/31/99	4,432.6	① 659.2	8,222.7	25.1	14.9	40.5	8.0	1.2	① 2.42	3.94	5.28	1.02	73.31 — 40.88	23.6	1.8
12/31/98	4,220.5	① 567.9	7,661.0	24.0	13.5	34.5	7.4	0.9	① 2.03	3.32	5.26	0.90	66.38 — 42.22	26.7	1.7
12/31/97	4,100.5	526.0	7,893.4	24.5	12.8	28.1	6.7	0.7	1.80	2.82	5.96	0.80	45.75 — 26.81	20.2	2.2
12/31/96	3,858.6	④ 469.4	8,155.7	22.8	12.2	21.0	5.8	0.7	④ 1.56	2.51	6.86	0.69	30.69 — 20.94	16.5	2.7
12/31/95	3,554.8	② 407.7	7,844.6	23.6	11.5	19.7	5.2	0.6	② 1.34	2.25	6.20	0.60	24.13 — 15.00	14.6	3.1
12/31/94	3,270.6	①③ 348.4	7,399.7	22.3	10.7	20.0	4.7	0.5	①③ 1.11	1.97	5.02	0.52	23.19 — 14.63	17.1	2.8
12/31/93	3,542.9	353.2	6,793.8	21.2	10.0	18.9	5.2	0.6	1.11	1.89	5.18	0.45	21.25 — 18.13	18.2	2.2

Statistics are as originally reported. Adj. for 2-for-1 stk. split, 1/98. ① Bef. discont. opers. chg. $22.9 mil ($0.08/sh), 1999; $8.5 mil ($0.03/sh), 1998; & cr.$32.5 mil, 1994. ② Bef. discont. opers. cr$174.4 mil & incl. $155 mil non-recur. gain. ③ Bef. $119.5 mil chg. for acctg. adj. ④ Incl. $30 mil restr. chg. ⑤ Bef. $64.1 mil ($0.25/sh) discont. oper. gain & $4.7 mil ($0.02/sh) acctg. chg. ⑥ Bef. $26.0 mil ($0.10/sh) discont. oper. chg. & incl. $268.3 mil chg for new mailing technology, $116.1 mil restr. chg. and $338.1 mil gain fr. a lawsuit settlement. ☑ Bef. $38.0 mil ($0.16/sh) discont. oper. gain & incl. $213.2 mil non-recur. chg.

OFFICERS:
M. J. Critelli, Chmn., C.E.O.
B. P. Nolop, Exec V.P., C.F.O.
G. E. Buoncontri, Sr. V.P., Chief Info. Off.

INVESTOR CONTACT: Charles F. McBride, Exec. Dir., Invest. Rel., (203) 351-6349

PRINCIPAL OFFICE: One Elmcroft Road, Stamford, CT 06926-0700

TELEPHONE NUMBER: (203) 356-5000
FAX: (203) 351-7336
WEB: www.pb.com

NO. OF EMPLOYEES: 32,724 (avg.)

SHAREHOLDERS: 27,849

ANNUAL MEETING: In May

INCORPORATED: DE, Apr., 1920

INSTITUTIONAL HOLDINGS:
No. of Institutions: 470
Shares Held: 178,422,834
% Held: 75.4

INDUSTRY: Office machines, nec (SIC: 3579)

TRANSFER AGENT(S): EquiServe, Jersey City, NJ

PITTSTON COMPANY (THE)

EXCH.	SYM.	REC. PRICE	P/E RATIO	YLD.	MKT. CAP.	RANGE (52-WK.)	'02 Y/E PR.
NYSE	PZB	14.17 (2/28/03)	10.8	0.7%	$0.77 bill.	28.92 - 12.90	18.48

MEDIUM GRADE. THE COMPANY WILL CONTINUE TO FOCUS ON GROWING AND IMPROVING THE FINANCIAL PERFORMANCE OF ITS CORE BUSINESSES.

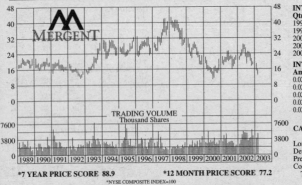

*7 YEAR PRICE SCORE 88.9   ***12 MONTH PRICE SCORE 77.2**

*NYSE COMPOSITE INDEX=100

INTERIM EARNINGS (Per Share):

Qtr.	Mar.	June	Sept.	Dec.
1998	0.44	0.52	0.51	0.55
1999	0.26	0.32	0.48	d0.37
2000	0.21	d0.03	0.15	0.05
2001	0.17	0.07	0.17	0.46
2002	0.37	0.36	0.41	0.17

INTERIM DIVIDENDS (Per Share):

Amt.	Decl.	Ex.	Rec.	Pay.
0.025Q	2/01/02	2/13/02	2/15/02	3/01/02
0.025Q	5/03/02	5/13/02	5/15/02	6/03/02
0.025Q	7/12/02	8/13/02	8/15/02	9/03/02
0.025Q	10/31/02	11/13/02	11/15/02	12/02/02
0.025Q	2/07/03	2/13/03	2/18/03	3/03/03

Indicated div.: $0.10

CAPITALIZATION (12/31/01):

	($000)	(%)
Long-Term Debt	252,900	33.7
Deferred Income Tax	20,700	2.8
Preferred Stock	200	0.0
Common & Surplus	475,900	63.5
Total	749,700	100.0

BUSINESS:

The Pittston Company (formerly Pittston Brink's Group) is comprised of three operating segments. BAX Global Inc. (49.6% of 2002 revenues) is a transportation and supply chain management company offering multi-modal freight forwarding to business-to-business shippers through a global network. The major activities of Brink's, Incorporated (41.8%) are contract-carrier armored car, ATM, air courier, coin wrapping, and currency and deposit processing services. Brink's Home Security, Inc. (7.5%) is engaged in marketing, selling, installing, servicing and monitoring electronic security systems primarily in owner-occupied, single-family residences. The other operations segment contributed 1.1% to 2002 revenues.

RECENT DEVELOPMENTS:

For the year ended 12/31/02, income increased 50.7% to $69.0 million, before a loss from discontinued operations of $42.9 million, compared with income of $45.8 million, before a loss from discontinued operations of $29.2 million, in 2001. Results for 2002 included a gain of $5.9 million from the receipt of a Stabilization Act compensation claim and an impairment charge of $26.3 million. Results for 2001 included a restructuring gain of $200,000. Revenues rose 4.2% to $3.78 billion due to strong revenue growth at BAX Global in the Asia Pacific region.

PROSPECTS:

The Company plans to concentrate on improving its core businesses. BAX Global is expected to report strong returns as global economic conditions improve. At Brink's, Incorporated, the Company also plans to develop new business opportunities while effectively managing the risks inherent in the business. Meanwhile, Brink's Home Security will attempt to raise the cash generating capacity of its business, while adhering to its traditional operating, service and value creation standards.

ANNUAL FINANCIAL DATA:

FISCAL YEAR	TOT. REVS. ($mill.)	NET INC. ($mill.)	TOT. ASSETS ($mill.)	OPER. PROFIT %	NET PROFIT %	RET. ON EQUITY %	RET. ON ASSETS %	CURR. RATIO	EARN. PER SH. $	CASH FL. PER SH. $	TANG. BK. VAL. $	DIV. PER SH. $	PRICE RANGE	AVG. P/E RATIO	AVG. YIELD %
p12/31/02	3,776.7	④ 69.0	2,459.9						④ 1.30			0.10	28.92 - 17.50	17.9	0.4
12/31/01	3,624.2	③ 45.8	2,394.0	2.4	1.3	9.6	1.9	0.9	③ 0.88	4.66	4.62	0.10	25.31 - 15.75	23.3	0.5
12/31/00	3,834.1	③ 2.7	2,478.7	0.9	0.1	0.6	0.1	0.9	③ 0.05	3.80	4.69	0.10	22.19 - 10.69	329.4	0.6
② 12/31/99	4,089.2	① 34.7	2,468.6	1.4	0.8	4.6	1.4	1.1	① d4.74	2.90	6.28	0.10	31.81 - 18.13	. . .	0.4
12/31/98	3,746.9	66.1	2,331.1	2.8	1.8	9.0	2.8	1.0	0.92	3.25	5.49	0.10	42.88 - 28.00	38.5	0.3
12/31/97	3,394.4	110.2	1,995.9	5.1	3.2	16.1	5.5	1.1	3.61	3.52	5.48	0.10	42.13 - 25.25	9.3	0.3
12/31/96	3,106.6	104.2	1,812.9	4.8	3.4	17.2	5.7	1.1	4.46	3.32	4.10	0.10	33.00 - 22.38	6.2	0.4
12/31/95	2,926.1	98.0	1,807.4	4.1	3.3	18.8	5.4	1.1	4.53	3.12	2.73	0.20	32.63 - 22.50	6.1	0.7
12/31/94	2,667.3	26.9	1,737.8	0.7	1.0	6.0	1.5	1.0	d4.37	1.49	1.65	0.20	31.25 - 21.38	. . .	0.8
12/31/93	2,256.1	14.1	1,361.5	0.6	0.6	4.0	1.0	1.0	d2.77	1.67	2.12	0.25	29.75 - 13.63	. . .	1.2

Statistics are as originally reported. Price chart reflects the The Pittston Company as a whole. ① Incl. restruct. charge of $1.5 mill. ② Results for 1999 and after are for The Pittston Co. as a whole, while prior years represent Pittston Brink's Group only. ③ Incl. pre-tax restruct. credit of $200,000, 2001; chrg. of $57.5 mill., 2000, but excl. loss fr. discont. oper. of $29.2 mill., 2001; $207.4 mill. & acctg. chrg. of $52.0 mill., 2000. ④ Excl. discont. oper. loss of $42.9 mill., but incl. impair. chrgs. $26.3 mill. & non-recurr. gain of $5.9 mill. related to a payment received under the Air Transpor. Safety and System Stabilization.

OFFICERS:
M. T. Dan, Chmn., Pres., C.E.O.
R. T. Ritter, V.P., C.F.O.
J. B. Hartough, V.P., Treas.
A. F. Reed, V.p., Gen. Couns., Sec.

INVESTOR CONTACT: Investor Relations, (804) 289-9709

PRINCIPAL OFFICE: 1801 Bayberry Court, Richmond, VA 23226-8100

TELEPHONE NUMBER: (804) 289-9600
FAX: (804) 289-9770
WEB: www.pittston.com

NO. OF EMPLOYEES: 50,000 (approx.)

SHAREHOLDERS: 4,000 (approx.)

ANNUAL MEETING: In May

INCORPORATED: DE, Jan., 1930; reincorp., VA, Dec., 1986

INSTITUTIONAL HOLDINGS:
No. of Institutions: 166
Shares Held: 43,354,563
% Held: 79.9

INDUSTRY: Minerals, ground or treated (SIC: 3295)

TRANSFER AGENT(S): Fleet National Bank, Providence, RI

PLAINS ALL AMERICAN PIPELINE, L.P.

EXCH.	SYM.	REC. PRICE	P/E RATIO	YLD.	MKT. CAP.	RANGE (52-WK.)	'02 Y/E PR.
NYSE	PAA	25.21 (2/28/03)	18.8	8.5%	$0.84 bill.	27.30 - 19.50	24.40

LOWER MEDIUM GRADE. THE COMPANY HAS ANNOUNCED THE COMPLETION OF TWO PIPELINE ACQUISITIONS THUS FAR IN 2003.

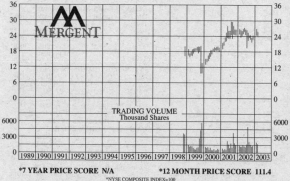

*7 YEAR PRICE SCORE N/A   ***12 MONTH PRICE SCORE 111.4**

NYSE COMPOSITE INDEX=100

INTERIM EARNINGS (Per Share):

Qtr.	Mar.	June	Sept.	Dec.
1999	d0.33	d0.29	d1.88	d0.69
2000	1.83	0.49	0.13	0.19
2001	0.36	0.19	0.38	0.20
2002	0.31	0.37	0.33	0.33

INTERIM DIVIDENDS (Per Share):

Amt.	Decl.	Ex.	Rec.	Pay.
0.512Q	1/17/02	1/31/02	2/04/02	2/14/02
0.525Q	4/22/02	5/02/02	5/06/02	5/15/02
0.537Q	7/23/02	8/01/02	8/05/02	8/14/02
0.537Q	10/24/02	10/31/02	11/04/02	11/14/02
0.537Q	1/24/03	1/31/03	2/04/03	2/14/03

Indicated div.: $2.15

CAPITALIZATION (12/31/01):

	($000)	(%)
Long-Term Debt	351,677	46.6
Common & Surplus	402,797	53.4
Total	754,474	100.0

BUSINESS:

Plains All American Pipeline, L.P. is engaged in interstate and intrastate marketing, transportation and terminalling of crude oil and liquefied petroleum gas. PAA conducts its operations through its wholly-owned operating limited partnerships Plains Marketing, L.P., All American Pipeline, L.P., and Plains Marketing Canada, L.P. PAA's operations are concentrated in Texas, Oklahoma, California, Louisiana and the Canadian provinces of Alberta, Saskatchewan and Manitoba. The Company was formed in September 1998 to acquire and operate the mid-stream crude oil business and assets of Plains Resources Inc. as a separate, publicly traded master limited partnership. As of 12/31/02, Plains Resources Inc.'s effective ownership in PAA totaled approximately 25.0%. In May 2001, PAA acquired substantially all of Murphy Oil Company Ltd.'s Canadian mid-stream operations for approximately $161.0 million.

RECENT DEVELOPMENTS:

For the year ended 12/31/02, net income was $65.3 million versus income of $43.7 million, before an accounting change gain of $508,000, a year earlier. Results for 2002 and 2001 included net unusual or nonrecurring charges of $1.9 million and $12.5 million, respectively. Revenues increased 22.1% to $8.38 billion, reflecting recent acquisitions and expansion projects. Gross profit climbed 22.5% to $174.3 million versus $142.3 million in 2001. Operating income was $94.6 million, 32.5% higher than the previous year.

PROSPECTS:

On 3/4/03, PAA announced that it has acquired a West Texas crude oil gathering system from Navajo Refining Company, L.P. for approximately $24.0 million. The assets are located in the Permian Basin in West Texas and consist of about 367 miles of crude oil gathering lines. Also during the first quarter of 2003, PAA acquired a 347-mile crude oil pipeline that originates at Sabine Station in East Texas and terminates near Cushing, Oklahoma. PAA anticipates making approximately $15.0 million in capital expenditures on the assets acquired in the two transactions, with about half being spent in 2003 and half in 2004.

ANNUAL FINANCIAL DATA:

FISCAL YEAR	TOT. REVS. ($Mill.)	NET INC. ($Mill.)	TOT. ASSETS ($Mill.)	OPER. PROFIT %	NET PROFIT %	RET. ON EQUITY %	RET. ON ASSETS %	CURR. RATIO	EARN. PER SH. $	CASH FL. PER SH. $	TANG. BK. VAL. $	DIV. PER SH. $⑨	PRICE RANGE	AVG. P/E RATIO	AVG. YIELD %
p12/31/02	8,384.2	⑨ 65.3							⑨ 1.34			2.11	27.30 - 19.50	17.5	9.0
12/31/01	6,868.2	⑧ 43.7	1,261.3	1.0	0.6	10.8	3.5	1.1	⑧ 1.12	1.81	12.12	1.95	29.65 - 19.06	21.7	8.0
12/31/00	6,641.2	⑦ 92.6	885.8	0.9	1.4	43.3	10.5	1.1	⑦ 2.64	3.41	6.22	1.82	20.06 - 13.00	6.3	11.0
③ 12/31/99	4,701.9	⑥ d101.8	1,223.0	...	...	...	...	1.2	①② d3.16	d2.67	5.61	1.59	20.25 - 9.63	...	10.6
④ 12/31/98	176.4	4.2	610.2	3.1	2.4	1.5	· 0.7	1.1	0.14	0.18	9.23	...	20.19 - 16.25	130.0	...
⑤ 11/22/98	953.2	7.0	...	2.3	0.7	...	...	...	0.40	0.66	...	...	20.19 - 16.25	45.5	...
12/31/97	752.5	2.1	149.6	1.0	0.3	35.8	1.4	1.0	0.12	0.19	...	...	...	...	...
12/31/96	531.7	1.2	...	1.0	0.2	...	...	...	0.07	0.14	...	...	...	...	...

Statistics are as originally reported. ① Bef. extraord. loss of $1.5 mill. ② Incl. restruct. chrg. of $1.4 mill. ③ Results refl. acquisitions & internal develop. ④ 1 month only refl. formation of the Company; prior periods refl. predecessor company. ⑤ 11 months only. ⑥ Per limited partner unit. ⑦ Incl. asset sale gain of $48.2 mill.; bef. extraord. loss of $15.2 mill. ⑧ Incl. inv. valuation adj. chrg. of $5.0 mill.; bef. acctg. chg. credit of $508,000 ⑨ Incl. nonrecurr. chrg. of $1.9 mill.

OFFICERS:
G. L. Armstrong, Chmn., C.E.O.
H. N. Pefanis, Pres., C.O.O.
P. D. Kramer, Exec. V.P., C.F.O.
INVESTOR CONTACT: Carolyn F. Tice, Admin. of Inv. Rel., (713) 646-4491
PRINCIPAL OFFICE: 333 Clay Street, Suite 1600, Houston, TX 77210

TELEPHONE NUMBER: (713) 646-4100
FAX: (713) 646-4572
WEB: www.plainsallamerican.com
NO. OF EMPLOYEES: 1,000 (approx.)
SHAREHOLDERS: 17,300 (approx. beneficial)
ANNUAL MEETING: N/A
INCORPORATED: DE, Sept., 1998

INSTITUTIONAL HOLDINGS:
No. of Institutions: 65
Shares Held: 8,211,130
% Held: 16.6

INDUSTRY: Pipelines, nec (SIC: 4619)

TRANSFER AGENT(S): American Stock Transfer & Trust Co., New York, NY

PLUM CREEK TIMBER COMPANY, INC.

EXCH.	SYM.	REC. PRICE	P/E RATIO	YLD.	MKT. CAP.	RANGE (52-WK.)	'02 Y/E PR.
NYSE	PCL	21.70 (2/28/03)	17.2	6.5%	$3.99 bill.	31.25 - 18.92	23.60

UPPER MEDIUM GRADE. THE COMPANY EXPECTS FULL-YEAR 2003 EARNINGS IN THE RANGE OF $1.00 TO $1.25 PER SHARE.

TRADING VOLUME Thousand Shares

*7 YEAR PRICE SCORE 98.7   ***12 MONTH PRICE SCORE 92.2**

*NYSE COMPOSITE INDEX=100

INTERIM EARNINGS (Per Share):

Qtr.	Mar.	June	Sept.	Dec.
1997	0.43	0.42	0.52	0.35
1998	0.28	0.17	0.16	0.29
1999	0.20	0.30	0.72	0.38
2000	1.16	0.30	0.14	0.30
2001	0.74	0.25	0.24	1.25
2002	0.30	0.29	0.38	0.29

INTERIM DIVIDENDS (Per Share):

Amt.	Decl.	Ex.	Rec.	Pay.
0.57Q	12/07/01	12/13/01	12/17/01	12/28/01
0.57Q	4/23/02	5/13/02	5/15/02	5/30/02
0.57Q	7/23/02	8/14/02	8/16/02	8/30/02
0.35Q	10/17/02	11/08/02	11/13/02	11/27/02
0.35Q	1/28/03	2/12/03	2/14/03	2/28/03

Indicated div.: $1.40

CAPITALIZATION (12/31/01):

	($000)	(%)
Long-Term Debt	1,647,000	41.7
Capital Lease Obligations..	20,000	0.5
Deferred Income Tax	38,000	1.0
Common & Surplus	2,247,000	56.9
Total	3,952,000	100.0

BUSINESS:

Plum Creek Timber Company, Inc. (formerly Plum Creek Timber Company, L.P.), is a real estate investment trust (REIT). As of 1/23/03, the Company and its subsidiaries owned, managed, and operated over 8.1 million acres of timberlands in every significant timber-growing region in the United States. PCL also operated ten wood product mills in the Northwest. On 7/1/99, the Company converted from a Master Limited Partnership to a REIT. On 10/06/01, the Company completed the acquisition of The Timber Company for $4.00 billion.

RECENT DEVELOPMENTS:

For the year ended 12/31/02, net income decreased 31.1% to $233.0 million compared with $338.0 million in 2001. Results for 2001 included merger-related charges of $183.0 million. Total revenues jumped 90.1% to $1.14 billion from $598.0 million a year earlier. Operating income grew 35.2% to $338.0 million from $250.0 million the year before. Results for the full-year 2002 reflected the performance of the combined operations of Plum Creek and The Timber Company as of 10/6/01 and are not directly comparable to the results reported for the full-year 2001.

PROSPECTS:

Looking ahead, the Company expects full-year 2003 earnings to be in the range of $1.00 to $1.25 per share, with the first quarter contributing between $0.12 and $0.17 per share. Meanwhile, PCL expects timber markets in 2003 to be challenging. Although demand has been consistent, oversupply in the lumber markets has kept log prices depressed. As a result, the Company anticipates reducing its Southern harvest as much as 500,000 tons. The reductions are expected to come in the first quarter of the year. Separately, manufacturing prices and volume may improve in the latter part of the first quarter as customers begin to purchase for the spring and summer building season. Meanwhile, PCL expects 2003 real estate revenue in the range of $80.0 million to $100.0 million.

ANNUAL FINANCIAL DATA:

FISCAL YEAR	TOT. INC. ($mill.)	NET INC. ($mill.)	TOT. ASSETS ($mill.)	NET INC. +DEPR./ ASSETS %	RET. ON EQUITY %	RET. ON ASSETS %	EARN. PER SH.$	TANG. BK. VAL.$	DIV. PER SH.$	DIV. PAYOUT %	PRICE RANGE	AVG. P/E RATIO	AVG. YIELD %
p12/31/02	1,137.0	233.0					1.26		1.49	118.2	36.45 - 23.75	23.0	4.9
12/31/01	598.0	⑤338.0	4,122.0	8.2	15.0	8.2	2.58	12.22	2.85	110.5	30.00 - 23.30	10.3	10.7
⑥12/31/00	209.1	②③131.9	1,250.1	10.6	13.0	10.6	②③1.91	14.64	2.28	119.4	29.81 - 21.50	13.4	8.9
④12/31/99	460.6	①②113.4	1,250.8	9.1	10.6	9.1	①②1.94	15.55	1.14	58.8	32.13 - 23.13	14.2	4.1
12/31/98	699.4	①②75.4	1,438.2	5.2	18.6	5.2	①②0.90	8.75	2.26	251.1	34.88 - 23.44	32.4	7.8
12/31/97	725.6	223.4	1,300.9	17.2	47.5	17.2	1.72	10.15	2.16	125.6	36.00 - 25.75	17.9	7.0
12/31/96	633.7	223.6	413.8	54.0	45.5	54.0	4.71	10.61	2.00	42.5	27.75 - 22.88	5.4	7.9
12/31/95	585.1	110.7	358.1	30.9	47.3	30.9	2.17	5.76	1.90	87.6	26.75 - 19.88	10.7	8.2
12/31/94	578.7	112.2	327.8	34.2	50.3	34.2	2.36	5.49	1.62	68.6	32.50 - 19.63	11.0	6.2
12/31/93	501.0	91.4	289.8	31.6	47.5	31.6	1.92	4.74	1.30	80.2	26.75 - 14.67	10.8	6.3

Statistics are as originally reported. Adj. for stk. split: 3-for-1, 12/93. ① Incls. reorg. costs of $4.8 mill., 1998; $5.1 mill., 1999. ② Incl. loss on disposition of assets of $805,000, 1998; gain of $3.7 mill., 1999; gain of $49.6 mill., 2000. ③ Incl. merger expenses of $3.8 mill. ④ Reflects conversion from an L.P. to a REIT effective 7/1/99. ⑤ Incl. nonrecur. merger-related items resulting in a chrg. of $183.0 mill. ⑥ Results reflect the operations of Plum Creek Timber Company, Inc. prior to the merger with The Timber Company on 10/6/01.

OFFICERS:
D. D. Leland, Chmn.
R. R. Holley, Pres., C.E.O.
W. R. Brown, Exec. V.P., C.F.O.
D. W. Lambert, V.P., Treas.

INVESTOR CONTACT: John Hobbs, (800) 858-5347

PRINCIPAL OFFICE: 999 Third Avenue, Seattle, WA 98104-4096

TELEPHONE NUMBER: (206) 467-3600
FAX: (206) 467-3795
WEB: www.plumcreek.com

NO. OF EMPLOYEES: 775 full-time (approx.); 1,300 part-time (approx.)

SHAREHOLDERS: 30,808 (approx.)

ANNUAL MEETING: In May

INCORPORATED: DE, June, 1989

INSTITUTIONAL HOLDINGS:
No. of Institutions: 366
Shares Held: 81,133,302
% Held: 43.9

INDUSTRY: Logging (SIC: 2411)

TRANSFER AGENT(S): Fleet National Bank, Providence, RI

PMI GROUP, INC. (THE)

EXCH.	SYM.	REC. PRICE	P/E RATIO	YLD.	MKT. CAP.	RANGE (52-WK.)	'02 Y/E PR.
NYSE	PMI	27.10 (2/28/03)	7.2	0.4%	$2.42 bill.	44.00 - 24.82	30.04

UPPER MEDIUM GRADE. FOR 2003, PMI'S INTERNATIONAL AND STRATEGIC INVESTMENTS ARE EXPECTED TO PROVIDE A SIGNIFICANT CONTRIBUTION TO OVERALL PROFITABILITY.

INTERIM EARNINGS (Per Share):

Qtr.	Mar.	June	Sept.	Dec.
1998	0.47	0.49	0.58	0.49
1999	0.48	0.55	0.61	0.63
2000	0.67	0.73	0.77	0.73
2001	0.80	0.83	0.86	0.88
2002	1.02	0.88	0.97	1.00

INTERIM DIVIDENDS (Per Share):

Amt.	Decl.	Ex.	Rec.	Pay.
100% STK	5/16/02	6/18/02	5/31/02	6/17/02
0.025Q	5/16/02	6/26/02	6/28/02	7/15/02
0.025Q	9/19/02	9/26/02	9/30/02	10/15/02
0.025Q	11/21/02	12/27/02	12/31/02	1/15/03
0.025Q	2/21/03	3/27/03	3/31/03	4/15/03

Indicated div.: $0.10

CAPITALIZATION (12/31/01):

	($000)	(%)
Long-Term Debt	422,950	18.6
Deferred Income Tax	63,852	2.8
Common & Surplus	1,786,688	78.6
Total	2,273,490	100.0

*7 YEAR PRICE SCORE 145.9   ***12 MONTH PRICE SCORE 93.5**

*NYSE COMPOSITE INDEX=100

BUSINESS:

The PMI Group, Inc. is a holding company that conducts its residential mortgage insurance business through PMI Mortgage Insurance Co., Residential Guaranty Co., Residential Insurance Co., TPG Insurance Co., PMI Mortgage Guaranty Co., TPG Segregated Portfolio Company, and PMI Mortgage Insurance Ltd. PMI also conducts title insurance business through its subsidiary American Pioneer Title Insurance Company. In addition, PMI owns PMI Mortgage Services Co., which is engaged in the contract underwriting. PMI has operations in Australia, New Zealand, Europe and Hong Kong.

RECENT DEVELOPMENTS:

For the year ended 12/31/02, income was $339.0 million, before an accounting gain of $7.2 million, versus income of $312.0 million, before an extraordinary loss of $4.8 million, the previous year. Results for 2002 included an after-tax litigation charge of $7.9 million. Total revenues advanced 19.7% to $1.12 billion from $937.0 million the prior year. Revenues for 2002 and 2001 included net realized investment gains of $1.3 million and $11,000, respectively. Also, revenues for 2002 and 2001 included equity in earnings of unconsolidated subsidiaries of $44.2 million and $18.8 million, respectively. Premiums earned climbed 19.8% to $904.5 million from $754.8 million a year earlier.

PROSPECTS:

Going forward, PMI's international and strategic investments are expected to continue to provide a significant and growing contribution to overall profitability. PMI anticipates these operations will account for between 26.0% and 30.0% of consolidated net operating income in 2003. Meanwhile, the Company is anticipating another strong year for the U.S. mortgage market, with approximately $1.60 to $2.00 trillion in mortgage originations in 2003. However, PMI's loss and loss adjustment expense in its U.S. mortgage insurance portfolio are expected to increase approximately $45.0 million to $55.0 million above 2002 levels. PMI is targeting 2003 income, before one-time items, at $4.08 to $4.30 per share.

ANNUAL FINANCIAL DATA:

FISCAL YEAR	PREM. INC. ($mill.)	TOT. REVS. ($mill.)	NET INC. ($mill.)	TOT. ASSETS ($mill.)	TOT. INVST. ($mill.)	RET. ON REVS. %	RET. ON EQUITY %	RET. ON ASSETS %	EARN. PER SH. $	TANG. BK. VAL. $	AVG. YIELD %	DIV. PER SH. $	PRICE RANGE	AVG. P/E RATIO
p12/31/02	904.5	1,121.4	③ 339.0						③ 3.79	1.01	0.3	0.09	44.00 - 24.82	9.1
12/31/01	754.8	937.0	② 312.0	2,990.0	2,582.8	33.3	17.5	10.4	② 3.44	20.04	0.3	0.08	37.25 - 24.19	8.9
12/31/00	634.4	762.6	260.2	2,392.7	2,078.2	34.1	17.4	10.9	2.89	16.92	0.3	0.08	37.47 - 16.75	9.4
12/31/99	558.6	670.1	204.5	2,100.8	1,817.3	30.5	16.8	9.7	2.26	13.62	0.3	0.07	27.75 - 13.33	9.1
12/31/98	491.2	620.9	190.4	1,777.9	1,532.2	30.7	17.3	10.7	2.01	12.08	0.3	0.07	28.50 - 11.00	9.8
12/31/97	453.9	564.6	175.3	1,686.6	1,490.6	31.0	16.5	10.4	1.74	10.90	0.3	0.07	24.67 - 15.92	11.6
12/31/96	412.7	501.4	157.9	1,509.9	1,291.7	31.5	16.0	10.5	1.50	9.53	0.4	0.07	20.00 - 13.29	11.1
12/31/95	328.8	405.0	135.2	1,304.4	1,133.0	33.4	15.5	10.4	1.28	8.29	0.2	0.03	17.83 - 12.00	11.6
12/31/94	296.3	360.0	106.1	1,116.7	960.5	29.5	15.4	9.5	1.01	6.54	...	...	...	...
12/31/93	268.6	315.5	① 88.7	985.1	848.1	28.1	15.4	9.0	① 0.84	5.48	...	...	...	...

Statistics are as originally reported. Adj. for stk splits: 100% div., 6/02; 3-for-2, 8/99. ① Bef. loss fr. disc. opers. of $28.9 mill. ② Bef. extraord. loss $4.8 mill. ③ Bef. acctg. gain $7.2 mill; Incl. after-tax litigation chrg. $7.9 mill

OFFICERS:
W. R. Haughton, Chmn., C.E.O.
L. S. Smith, Pres., C.O.O.
J. M. Lorenzen Jr., Exec. V.P., C.F.O., Asst. Sec.

INVESTOR CONTACT: Matt Nichols, Investor Relations, (925) 658-6618

PRINCIPAL OFFICE: 3003 Oak Road, Walnut Creek, CA 94597-2098

TELEPHONE NUMBER: (925) 658-7878
FAX: (925) 658-6931
WEB: www.pmigroup.com

NO. OF EMPLOYEES: 1,235 (avg.)

SHAREHOLDERS: 39 (approx.)

ANNUAL MEETING: In May

INCORPORATED: DE, Dec., 1972

INSTITUTIONAL HOLDINGS:
No. of Institutions: 240
Shares Held: 87,567,553
% Held: 97.0

INDUSTRY: Surety insurance (SIC: 6351)

TRANSFER AGENT(S): Continental Stock Transfer & Trust Company, New York, NY

PNC FINANCIAL SERVICES GROUP, INC.

EXCH.	SYM.	REC. PRICE	P/E RATIO	YLD.	MKT. CAP.	RANGE (52-WK.)	'02 Y/E PR.
NYSE	PNC	44.93 (2/28/03)	10.7	4.3	$12.72 bill.	62.53 - 32.70	41.90

UPPER MEDIUM GRADE. THE COMPANY CONTINUES TO STRENGTHEN ITS BALANCE SHEET WITH AN INCREASE IN LOAN LOSS RESERVES AND CORE DEPOSIT FUNDING.

INTERIM EARNINGS (Per Share):

Qtr.	Mar.	June	Sept.	Dec.
1998	0.87	0.90	0.91	0.92
1999	1.05	1.03	1.06	1.01
2000	1.03	1.06	1.01	1.06
2001	0.89	1.00	1.02	d1.15
2002	1.11	1.12	1.00	0.97

INTERIM DIVIDENDS (Per Share):

Amt.	Decl.	Ex.	Rec.	Pay.
0.48Q	10/03/01	10/10/01	10/12/01	10/24/01
0.48Q	1/03/02	1/09/02	1/11/02	1/24/02
0.48Q	4/02/02	4/10/02	4/12/02	4/24/02
0.48Q	7/02/02	7/10/02	7/12/02	7/24/02
0.48Q	10/13/02	10/09/02	10/11/02	10/24/02
0.48Q	1/03/03	1/09/03	1/13/03	1/24/03

Indicated div.: $1.92 (Div. Reinv. Plan)

CAPITALIZATION (12/31/02):

	($000)	(%)
Total Deposits	44,982,000	74.8
Long-Term Debt	8,264,000	13.7
Common & Surplus	6,859,000	11.4
Total	60,105,000	100.0

*7 YEAR PRICE SCORE 99.4　　***12 MONTH PRICE SCORE 101.5**

*NYSE COMPOSITE INDEX=100

BUSINESS:

PNC Financial Services Group, Inc. (formerly PNC Bank Corporation) is one of the largest diversified financial services companies in the nation with $66.38 billion in total assets as of 12/31/02. PNC operates seven major businesses engaged in regional community banking, corporate banking, real estate finance, asset-based lending, wealth management, asset management and global fund services. The Company provides products and services nationally and in PNC's primary geographic markets in Pennsylvania, New Jersey, Delaware, Ohio and Kentucky. On 12/31/95, PNC acquired Midlantic Corp. On 12/1/98, PNC acquired Hilliard-Lyons, Inc. As of 12/31/02, assets under management totaled $313.00 billion. Net sales for 2002 were derived as follows: Regional Community Banking, 40.4%; PFPC, 15.7%; PNC Advisors, 12.7%; BlackRock, 11.1%; Corporate Banking, 12.1%; PNC Real Estate Finance, 4.3%; and PNC Business Credit, 3.7%.

RECENT DEVELOPMENTS:

For the year ended 12/31/02, the Company reported income from continuing operations of $1.20 billion versus income of $377.0 million, before an accounting change charge of $5.0 million, the year before. Earnings excluded a loss of $16.0 million in 2002 and a gain of $5.0 million in 2001 from discontinued operations. Net interest income slipped 2.9% to $2.20 billion from $2.30 billion the year before, due to a decline in average earning assets. Total non-interest income improved 20.6% to $3.20 billion. Net interest margin totaled 3.87% compared with 3.88% a year earlier.

PROSPECTS:

During the quarter, asset quality remained relatively stable as nonperforming assets increased $9.0 million, or 2.0% year over year. Additionally, the Company continues to strengthen its balance sheet with an increase in loan loss reserves and core deposit funding. Moreover, the Company's results should benefit from capital management and efficiency initiatives, including investments in its businesses and the resumption of its share repurchase program.

ANNUAL FINANCIAL DATA:

FISCAL YEAR	NET INT. INC. ($mill.)	NON-INT. INC. ($mill.)	NET INC. ($mill.)	TOT. LOANS ($mill.)	TOT. ASSETS ($mill.)	TOT. DEP. ($mill.)	RET. ON EQUITY %	RET. ON ASSETS %	EQUITY/ ASSETS %	EARN. PER SH.$	TANG. BK. VAL.$	DIV. PER SH.$	PRICE RANGE	AVG. P/E RATIO
12/31/02	2,197.0	3,197.0	⑥ 1,200.0	36,525.0	66,377.0	44,982.0	17.5	1.8	10.3	⑥ 4.20	14.78	1.92	62.80 - 32.70	11.4
12/31/01	2,262.0	2,543.0	⑦ 377.0	39,138.0	69,568.0	47,304.0	6.5	0.5	8.4	⑦ 1.26	12.19	1.92	75.81 - 51.14	50.4
12/31/00	2,164.0	2,891.0	⑥ 1,214.0	51,600.0	69,844.0	47,664.0	18.2	1.7	9.5	⑥ 4.09	14.42	1.83	75.00 - 36.00	13.6
12/31/99	2,433.0	2,745.0	⑤ 1,264.0	50,770.0	75,413.0	46,668.0	21.3	1.7	7.9	⑤ 4.15	6.20	1.68	62.00 - 43.00	12.7
12/31/98	2,573.0	2,302.0	1,115.0	58,204.0	77,207.0	47,496.0	18.5	1.4	7.8	3.60	11.49	1.58	66.75 - 38.75	14.7
12/31/97	2,495.0	1,775.0	1,052.0	54,657.0	75,120.0	47,649.0	19.5	1.4	7.2	3.28	12.47	1.50	58.75 - 36.50	14.5
12/31/96	2,444.0	1,395.0	④ 992.0	52,183.0	73,260.0	45,676.0	16.9	1.4	8.0	④ 2.90	18.09	1.42	39.75 - 27.50	11.6
12/31/95	2,141.9	960.4	③ 408.1	49,056.0	73,404.0	46,899.0	7.1	0.6	7.9	③ 1.19	17.06	1.40	32.38 - 21.13	22.5
12/31/94	1,910.0	823.0	② 612.0	35,647.0	64,145.0	35,011.0	13.9	1.0	6.9	② 2.57	18.85	1.31	31.63 - 20.00	10.0
12/31/93	1,829.0	946.0	① 747.0	33,530.0	62,080.0	33,115.0	17.3	1.2	7.0	① 3.14	18.40	1.18	36.38 - 27.00	10.1

Statistics are as originally reported. ① Bef. acct. change chrg. of $19.4 mill. ② Incl. $79.0 mill. loss on sale of fixed incm. sec. & $31.4 mill. restr. chg. ③ Incl. after-tax merger-rel. & restr. chgs. totaling $380.2 mill. ④ Incl. pre-tax SAIF chg. of $35.1 mill. ⑤ Incl. various nonrecurr. after-tax net gains of $280.0 mill. ⑥ Excl. a loss fr. disc. ops. of $16.0 mill., 2002; gain $65.0 mill., 2000 ⑦ Bef. acctg. chrg. of $5.0 mill. & a gain of $5.0 mill. fr. disc. ops.; incl. an after-tax strategic repositioning cost of $615.0 mill.

OFFICERS:
J. E. Rohr, Chmn., C.E.O.
W. S. Demchak, Vice-Chmn., C.F.O.
J. C. Guyaux, Pres.

INVESTOR CONTACT: William H. Callihan, VP, Investor Relations, (412) 762-8257

PRINCIPAL OFFICE: One PNC Plaza, 249 Fifth Avenue, Pittsburgh, PA 15265

TELEPHONE NUMBER: (412) 762-1553
FAX: (412) 762-5798
WEB: www.pnc.com

NO. OF EMPLOYEES: 23,900 (avg.)

SHAREHOLDERS: 51,754

ANNUAL MEETING: In April

INCORPORATED: PA, Jan., 1983

INSTITUTIONAL HOLDINGS:
No. of Institutions: 481
Shares Held: 184,063,343
% Held: 64.8

INDUSTRY: National commercial banks (SIC: 6021)

TRANSFER AGENT(S): Mellon Investor Services, Ridgefield Park, NJ

POLARIS INDUSTRIES INC.

EXCH.	SYM.	REC. PRICE	P/E RATIO	YLD.	MKT. CAP.	RANGE (52-WK.)	'02 Y/E PR.
NYSE	PII	48.40 (2/28/03)	11.0	2.6%	$1.11 bill.	77.00 - 46.85	58.60

UPPER MEDIUM GRADE. THE COMPANY ANTICIPATES CONTINUED GROWTH IN SALES AND EARNINGS DRIVEN BY NEW PRODUCT INTRODUCTIONS AND CONTINUED GROSS MARGIN IMPROVEMENT.

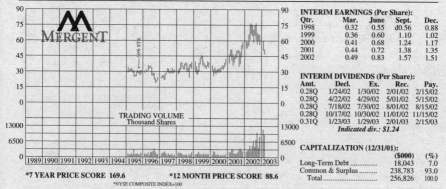

*7 YEAR PRICE SCORE 169.6   ***12 MONTH PRICE SCORE 88.6**
*NYSE COMPOSITE INDEX=100

INTERIM EARNINGS (Per Share):

Qtr.	Mar.	June	Sept.	Dec.
1998	0.32	0.55	d0.56	0.88
1999	0.36	0.60	1.10	1.02
2000	0.41	0.68	1.24	1.17
2001	0.44	0.72	1.38	1.35
2002	0.49	0.83	1.57	1.51

INTERIM DIVIDENDS (Per Share):

Amt.	Decl.	Ex.	Rec.	Pay.
0.28Q	1/24/02	1/30/02	2/01/02	2/15/02
0.28Q	4/22/02	4/29/02	5/01/02	5/15/02
0.28Q	7/18/02	7/30/02	8/01/02	8/15/02
0.28Q	10/17/02	10/30/02	11/01/02	11/15/02
0.31Q	1/23/03	1/29/03	2/01/03	2/15/03

Indicated div.: $1.24

CAPITALIZATION (12/31/01):

	($000)	(%)
Long-Term Debt	18,043	7.0
Common & Surplus	238,783	93.0
Total	256,826	100.0

BUSINESS:

Polaris Industries Inc. designs, engineers and manufactures snowmobiles, all-terrain vehicles (ATVs), motorcycles and personal watercraft and markets them, together with related replacement parts, garments and accessories, through dealers and distributors in the U.S., Canada and Europe, and on the Internet. PII's full line of snowmobiles range from youth to economy models to performance and competition models. PII's line of ATVs include sport and four-wheel drive utility models. PII has a six-wheel off-road utility vehicle and the Polaris RANGER, a six-wheel off-road side-by-side utility and recreational vehicle. The Company also manufactures a V-twin cruiser motorcycle, the Victory V92C. The Polaris Professional Series, a line of heavy duty Workmobiles™ targeted at lawn and landscape companies, equipment rental companies and construction operations, marks PII's expansion into the commercial equipment marketplace.

RECENT DEVELOPMENTS:

For the year ended 12/31/02, net income increased 13.3% to $103.6 million compared with $91.4 million in 2001. The improvement in earnings was primarily attributed to higher gross margins of 120 basis points. Sales rose 2.3% to $1.52 billion from $1.49 billion a year earlier. Income from financial services climbed 2.0% to $152.9 million. Operating income grew 6.1% to $152.9 million from $144.2 million the year before.

PROSPECTS:

Looking ahead, the Company anticipates growth in results driven by new product introductions and continued gross margin improvement. Meanwhile, on 2/3/03, the Company and Mercury Marine, a division of Brunswick Corporation, announced a distribution agreement for selling the Polaris Watercraft™ brand through select Mercury Marine branch operations in Asia and Latin America, including Japan, China, Brazil, and other markets. Separately, on 1/23/03, PII announced its entry into the sport boat market with the Polaris EX2100 Sport Boat™ line, through a strategic alliance with Mercury Marine and Baja Marine, a high-performance boat manufacturer.

ANNUAL FINANCIAL DATA:

FISCAL YEAR	TOT. REVS. ($mill.)	NET INC. ($mill.)	TOT. ASSETS ($mill.)	OPER. PROFIT %	NET PROFIT %	RET. ON EQUITY %	RET. ON ASSETS %	CURR. RATIO	EARN. PER SH.$	CASH FL.PER SH.$	TANG. BK. VAL.$	DIV. PER SH.$	PRICE RANGE	AVG. P/E RATIO	AVG. YIELD %
p12/31/02	1,521.3	103.6							4.39			1.12	77.00 - 52.05	14.7	1.7
12/31/01	1,512.0	91.4	565.2	8.6	6.0	38.3	16.2	1.0	3.88	6.11	10.41	1.00	58.70 - 35.10	12.1	2.1
12/31/00	1,425.7	82.8	490.2	8.5	5.8	40.4	16.9	1.0	3.50	5.48	7.77	0.88	42.06 - 25.56	9.7	2.6
12/31/99	1,321.1	76.3	442.0	8.6	5.8	45.4	17.3	0.9	3.07	4.64	6.03	0.80	45.69 - 27.00	11.8	2.2
12/31/98	1,175.5	② 153.8	378.7	8.5	13.1	100.4	40.6	0.9	② 1.19	7.31	5.14	0.72	39.38 - 24.00	26.6	2.3
12/31/97	1,048.3	65.4	384.7	8.9	6.2	38.6	17.0	1.1	2.45	3.69	5.60	0.64	33.63 - 21.88	11.3	2.3
12/31/96	1,191.9	62.3	351.7	8.2	5.2	40.1	17.7	1.2	2.24	3.33	4.85	0.60	36.25 - 18.75	12.3	2.2
12/31/95	1,113.9	60.8	314.4	9.1	5.5	51.3	19.3	0.9	2.19	3.00	3.42	4.27	34.33 - 25.00	13.5	14.4
12/31/94	826.3	① 64.0	331.2	9.2	7.7	37.7	19.3	1.3	① 2.97	3.17	5.29	...	34.58 - 34.08	...	...
12/31/93	528.0	① 45.8	180.5	10.1	8.7	55.5	25.4	1.1	① 1.50	2.71	2.30	...	...	...	...

Statistics are as originally reported. Adj. for stk. split: 3-for-2, 1995. ① Incl. conversion costs of $12.3 mill., 1994; $43,000, 1993. ② Incl. prov. for litigation loss of $61.4 mill.

OFFICERS:
W. H. Wendel, Jr., Chmn.
T. C. Tiller, Pres., C.E.O.
M. W. Malone, V.P, C.F.O., Sec.

INVESTOR CONTACT: Richard Edwards,
(763) 513-3477

PRINCIPAL OFFICE: 2100 Highway 55,
Medina, MN 55340

TELEPHONE NUMBER: (763) 542-0500
FAX: (763) 542-0599
WEB: www.polarisindustries.com
NO. OF EMPLOYEES: 3,550
SHAREHOLDERS: 2,592 (record)
ANNUAL MEETING: In May
INCORPORATED: DE, Apr., 1987; reincorp.,
MN, Dec., 1994

INSTITUTIONAL HOLDINGS:
No. of Institutions: 196
Shares Held: 15,028,758
% Held: 66.2

INDUSTRY: Transportation equipment, nec
(SIC: 3799)

TRANSFER AGENT(S): Wells Fargo Shareowner Services, South St. Paul, MN

POLO RALPH LAUREN CORPORATION

EXCH.	SYM.	REC. PRICE	P/E RATIO	YLD.	MKT. CAP.	RANGE (52-WK.)	'02 Y/E PR.
NYSE	. RL	20.19 (2/28/03)	13.5	...	$1.98 bill.	30.82 - 16.49	21.76

MEDIUM GRADE. THE COMPANY EXPECTS THE CONSOLIDATION OF ITS EUROPEAN OPERATIONS TO BE COMPLETED IN THE FOURTH QUARTER OF THE CURRENT FISCAL YEAR.

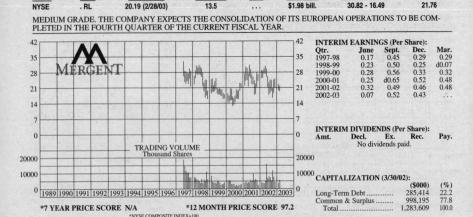

*7 YEAR PRICE SCORE N/A   ***12 MONTH PRICE SCORE 97.2**

*NYSE COMPOSITE INDEX=100

INTERIM EARNINGS (Per Share):

Qtr.	June	Sept.	Dec.	Mar.
1997-98	0.17	0.45	0.29	0.29
1998-99	0.23	0.50	0.25	d0.07
1999-00	0.28	0.56	0.33	0.32
2000-01	0.25	d0.65	0.52	0.48
2001-02	0.32	0.49	0.46	0.48
2002-03	0.07	0.52	0.43	...

INTERIM DIVIDENDS (Per Share):

Amt.	Decl.	Ex.	Rec.	Pay.
		No dividends paid.		

CAPITALIZATION (3/30/02):

	($000)	(%)
Long-Term Debt	285,414	22.2
Common & Surplus	998,195	77.8
Total	1,283,609	100.0

BUSINESS:

Polo Ralph Lauren Corporation is engaged in the design, marketing and distribution of premium lifestyle products. Brand names include POLO BY RALPH LAUREN, RALPH LAUREN PURPLE LABEL, RALPH LAUREN, RALPH, LAUREN, POLO JEANS CO., RL, CHAPS and CLUBMONACO, among others. RL offers broad lifestyle product collections in four categories: apparel, home, accessories and fragrance. Apparel products include extensive collections of menswear, womenswear and children's clothing. The Ralph Lauren Home Collection offers coordinated products for the home, including bedding and bath products, interior decor, furniture and tabletop and gift items. Accessories include footwear, eyewear, jewelry and leather goods. Fragrance and skin care products are sold under the Company's POLO, LAUREN, ROMANCE, SAFARI and POLO SPORT brands, among others.

RECENT DEVELOPMENTS:

For the quarter ended 12/28/02, net income declined 6.1% to $42.8 million from $45.6 million in the equivalent 2001 quarter. Results for 2002 included an after-tax charge of $5.1 million related to restructuring of RL's European operations. Net revenues increased 3.6% to $639.2 million from $617.1 million the previous year, as increases in the Company's European businesses helped offset a decrease in sales in its men's domestic wholesale business and the elimination of the women's RL Sport line. Retail net sales advanced 12.4% to $315.1 million, while wholesale net sales declined 4.2% to $268.3 million. Operating income dropped 6.6% to $69.5 million.

PROSPECTS:

During the next twelve months, RL's major efforts in Europe include consolidating its headquarters into Geneva, centralizing its logistics operations in Italy, and migrating to information systems throughout Western Europe. Meanwhile, RL expects the final phase of the process, related to its back office functions in France, to be completed during the fourth quarter of fiscal 2003. Earnings per share for fiscal 2004 are expected in the range of $1.95 and $2.05, driven by low single digit revenue growth and ongoing improvements in operating margins.

ANNUAL FINANCIAL DATA:

FISCAL YEAR	TOT. REVS. ($mill.)	NET INC. ($mill.)	TOT. ASSETS ($mill.)	OPER. PROFIT %	NET PROFIT %	RET. ON EQUITY %	RET. ON ASSETS %	CURR. RATIO	EARN. PER SH.$	CASH FL. PER SH.$	TANG. BK. VAL.$	PRICE RANGE	AVG. P/E RATIO
3/30/02	2,363.7	⑤ 172.5	1,749.5	12.4	7.3	17.3	9.9	2.6	⑤ 1.75	2.60	7.38	31.34 — 17.80	14.0
3/31/01	2,225.8	④ 59.3	1,626.1	5.3	2.7	7.3	3.6	2.1	④ 0.61	1.41	5.76	23.25 — 12.75	29.5
4/01/00	1,955.5	③ 147.5	1,620.6	13.5	7.5	19.1	9.1	2.1	③ 1.49	2.16	5.07	25.38 — 16.06	13.9
4/03/99	1,726.9	② 90.6	1,104.6	9.0	5.2	13.7	8.2	2.0	② 0.91	1.37	6.60	31.38 — 15.88	26.0
3/28/98	① 1,470.9	147.6	825.1	13.6	10.0	25.3	17.9	2.8	1.20	1.75	5.84	33.00 — 21.75	22.8
3/29/97	① 1,180.4	117.3	576.7	13.3	9.9	45.0	20.3	1.9	0.88	1.41	...	...	...
3/30/96	1,019.9	98.8	563.7	12.5	9.7	41.6	17.5	2.3	...	...	...	...	...
4/01/95	846.6	80.2	...	13.0	9.5	...	...	...	...	...	...	...	...

Statistics are as originally reported. ① Pro forma ② Incl. non-recurr. chrgs. $34.7 mill. ③ Bef. acctg. change chrg. $4.0 mill. ($0.04 a sh.) ④ Incl. net after-tax non-recurr. chrg. $107.3 mill. ⑤ Incl. restruct. & spec. chrgs. $16.0 mill.

OFFICERS:
R. Lauren, Chmn., C.E.O.
F. L. Isham, Vice-Chmn
R. N. Farah, Pres., C.O.O.

INVESTOR CONTACT: Nancy S. Murray, Investor Relations, (212) 813-7862

PRINCIPAL OFFICE: 650 Madison Avenue, New York, NY 10022

TELEPHONE NUMBER: (212) 318-7000
FAX: (212) 888-5780
WEB: www.doublerl.com
NO. OF EMPLOYEES: 10,100 (approx.)
SHAREHOLDERS: 1,270 (class A); 5 (class B); 5 (class C)
ANNUAL MEETING: In Aug.
INCORPORATED: DE, March, 1997

INSTITUTIONAL HOLDINGS:
No. of Institutions: 143
Shares Held: 34,614,792
% Held: 33.7

INDUSTRY: Men's and boys' clothing, nec (SIC: 2329)

TRANSFER AGENT(S): The Bank of New York, New York, NY

POLYONE CORPORATION

EXCH.	SYM.	REC. PRICE	P/E RATIO	YLD.	MKT. CAP.	RANGE (52-WK.)	'02 Y/E PR.
NYSE	POL	3.83 (2/28/03)	...	6.5%	$348.5 mill.	13.40 - 3.03	3.92

LOWER MEDIUM GRADE. THE COMPANY PLANS TO LOWER SELLING AND ADMINISTRATIVE COSTS BETWEEN $30.0 MILLION AND $35.0 MILLION PRE-TAX ANNUALLY, BEGINNING WITH THE SECOND QUARTER OF 2003.

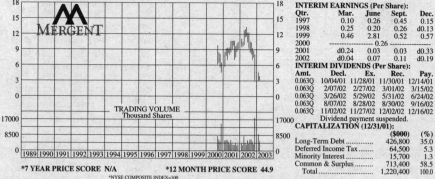

INTERIM EARNINGS (Per Share):

Qtr.	Mar.	June	Sept.	Dec.
1997	0.10	0.26	0.45	0.15
1998	0.25	0.20	0.26	d0.13
1999	0.46	2.81	0.52	0.57
2000	------------------ 0.26 ------------------			
2001	d0.24	0.03	0.03	d0.33
2002	d0.04	0.07	0.11	d0.19

INTERIM DIVIDENDS (Per Share):

Amt.	Decl.	Ex.	Rec.	Pay.
0.063Q	10/04/01	11/28/01	11/30/01	12/14/01
0.063Q	2/07/02	2/27/02	3/01/02	3/15/02
0.063Q	3/26/02	5/29/02	5/31/02	6/24/02
0.063Q	8/07/02	8/28/02	8/30/02	9/16/02
0.063Q	11/02/02	11/27/02	12/02/02	12/16/02

Dividend payment suspended.

CAPITALIZATION (12/31/01):

	($000)	(%)
Long-Term Debt	426,800	35.0
Deferred Income Tax	64,500	5.3
Minority Interest	15,700	1.3
Common & Surplus	713,400	58.5
Total	1,220,400	100.0

*7 YEAR PRICE SCORE N/A   *12 MONTH PRICE SCORE 44.9

*NYSE COMPOSITE INDEX=100

BUSINESS:

PolyOne Corporation (formerly The Geon Company) is an international polymer services company with operations in thermoplastic compounds, specialty resins, specialty polymer formulations, engineered films, color and additive systems, elastomer compounding and thermoplastic resin distribution. The Company operates manufacturing sites in North America, Europe, Asia and Australia, and joint ventures in North America, South America, Europe, Asia and Australia. POL was formed on 8/31/00 as a result of the consolidation of The Geon Company and M.A. Hanna Company.

RECENT DEVELOPMENTS:

For the year ended 12/31/02, loss was $6.6 million, before an accounting change charge of $53.7 million, compared with a loss from continuing operations of $47.1 million in 2001. Results for 2002 and 2001 included employee separation and plant phase-out charges of $1.1 million and $36.1 million, and losses on the divestiture of an equity investment of $5.1 million and $9.5 million, respectively. Results for 2001 also included merger and integration costs of $5.9 million. Results for 2002 and 2001 excluded income of $1.4 million and $1.0 million, respectively, from discontinued operations. Sales slipped 3.2% to $2.50 billion from $2.58 billion in the prior year.

PROSPECTS:

On 1/14/03, the Company announced a series of actions designed to improve profitability by lowering POL's cost structure. These actions include the elimination of about 400 salaried positions, primarily in administrative functions, which should lower selling and administrative costs between $30.0 million and $35.0 million pre-tax annually beginning with the second quarter of 2003. In addition, POL will implement about $5.0 million to $10.0 million in reductions of non-personnel costs. Separately, the Company expects loss per share for the first quarter of 2003 in the range of $0.03 to $0.07. POL anticipates higher operating income from its resins and intermediates segment, due primarily to improved customer demand.

ANNUAL FINANCIAL DATA:

FISCAL YEAR	TOT. REVS. ($mill.)	NET INC. ($mill.)	TOT. ASSETS ($mill.)	OPER. PROFIT %	NET PROFIT %	RET. ON EQUITY %	RET. ON ASSETS %	CURR. RATIO	EARN. PER SH.$	CASH FL. PER SH.$	TANG. BK. VAL.$	DIV. PER SH.$	PRICE RANGE		AVG. P/E RATIO	AVG. YIELD %
p12/31/02	2,498.2	⑥ d6.6		...	...	...	...		⑧ d0.07			0.25	13.40 -	3.03	...	3.0
12/31/01	2,654.6	⑤ d46.1	2,061.2	...	...	...	...	1.0	⑧ d0.51	0.50	1.94	0.25	10.70 -	4.81	...	3.1
12/31/00	1,887.8	④ 15.9	2,460.7	3.4	0.8	1.9	0.6	1.1	④ 0.26	1.18	3.06	0.06	9.88 -	4.56	27.8	0.9
③ 12/31/99	1,261.2	② 106.2	1,162.6	7.9	8.4	31.7	9.1	0.8	② 4.37	6.20	6.37	...	...	...	...	...
12/31/98	1,284.4	13.8	802.0	3.2	1.1	6.4	1.7	0.9	0.58	3.04	5.67	...	...	...	...	...
12/31/97	1,250.0	① 22.5	872.9	4.2	1.8	10.4	2.6	1.0	① 0.95	3.21	9.65	...	...	...	...	...

Statistics are as originally reported. ① Incl. a pretax spec. chrg. of $15.0 mill. ($0.39/sh.) related to employee separation, 1997; & $14.6 mill., 1998. ② Bef. an acctg. adj. chrg. of $1.5 mill., but incl. gain of $93.5 mill. for formation of joint ventures and $500,000 chrg. for employee separation and plant phase-out. ③ Results for 12/31/99 and earlier represent only the operations of The Geon Company. ④ Incl. non-recurr. chrg. of $2.8 mill. ⑤ Incl. $36.1 mill. employee sep. chg. & $5.9 mill. merger and integration chg. ⑥ Incl. $1.1 mill. employee sep. chg. & $5.1 mill. loss on divest. of invest. and excl. $1.4 mill. gain fr. disc. ops. & $53.7 mill. acct. chg.

OFFICERS:
T. A. Waltermire, Chmn., Pres., C.E.O.
W. D. Wilson, V.P., C.F.O.
J. L. Rastetter, Treas.
INVESTOR CONTACT: Dennis Cocco, Investor Relations, (216) 589-4018
PRINCIPAL OFFICE: 200 Public Square, Suite 36-5000, Cleveland, OH 44114-2304

TELEPHONE NUMBER: (216) 589-4000
FAX: (216) 589-4077
WEB: www.polyone.com
NO. OF EMPLOYEES: 8,000 (avg.)
SHAREHOLDERS: 3,582 (approx.)
ANNUAL MEETING: In May
INCORPORATED: OH, Feb., 1993

INSTITUTIONAL HOLDINGS:
No. of Institutions: 147
Shares Held: 83,764,876
% Held: 91.4
INDUSTRY: Plastics materials and resins (SIC: 2821)
TRANSFER AGENT(S): Equiserve Trust Company, Jersey City, NJ

POTLATCH CORPORATION

EXCH.	SYM.	REC. PRICE	P/E RATIO	YLD.	MKT. CAP.	RANGE (52-WK.)	'02 Y/E PR.
NYSE	PCH	20.64 (2/28/03)	...	2.9%	$0.58 bill.	36.45 - 19.35	23.88

LOWER MEDIUM GRADE. THE COMPANY SOLD ITS BRAINERD, MINNESOTA PAPER MILL AND RELATED ASSETS FOR $4.4 MILLION.

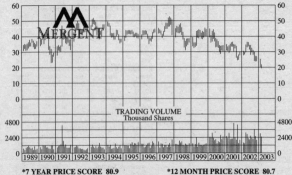

*7 YEAR PRICE SCORE 80.9   ***12 MONTH PRICE SCORE 80.7**
*NYSE COMPOSITE INDEX=100

INTERIM EARNINGS (Per Share):

Qtr.	Mar.	June	Sept.	Dec.
1997	0.22	0.34	0.49	0.20
1998	0.37	0.35	0.43	0.13
1999	0.02	0.33	0.77	0.29
2000	0.08	d0.25	d0.37	d0.55
2001	d1.11	d0.35	d0.23	d1.12
2002	d0.54	d0.23	d0.36	d0.67

INTERIM DIVIDENDS (Per Share):

Amt.	Decl.	Ex.	Rec.	Pay.
0.15Q	3/01/02	5/06/02	5/08/02	6/03/02
0.15Q	7/25/02	8/07/02	8/09/02	9/03/02
0.15Q	9/23/02	11/04/02	11/06/02	12/03/02
0.15Q	1/23/03	2/06/03	2/10/03	3/03/03
0.15Q	3/07/03	5/07/03	5/09/03	6/02/03

Indicated div.: $0.60 (Div. Reinv. Plan)

CAPITALIZATION (12/31/01):

	($000)	(%)
Long-Term Debt	1,017,522	52.6
Deferred Income Tax	210,610	10.9
Common & Surplus	707,304	36.5
Total	1,935,436	100.0

BUSINESS:

Potlatch Corporation is an integrated forest products company with approximately 1.5 million acres of timberlands in Arkansas, Idaho and Minnesota, as of 12/31/02. In addition, the Company operates 15 manufacturing facilities. The Company is engaged principally in the growing and harvesting of timber and the manufacture and sale of wood products. PCH's manufacturing facilities convert wood fiber into two main lines of products: wood products (lumber, plywood, oriented strand board, particleboard) and bleached fiber products (bleached kraft pulp, paperboard, and consumer tissue). Contributions to sales in 2002 were: pulp and paper, 44.2%; wood products, 31.1%; and resource, 24.7%.

RECENT DEVELOPMENTS:

For the year ended 12/31/02, PCH incurred a loss of $50.9 million compared with a loss of $56.6 million in 2001. The loss reflected poor market conditions for PCH's wood products and paperboard. Results for 2002 included debt extinguishment costs of $15.4 million. Earnings for 2002 and 2001 included restructuring and other charges of $9.0 million and $2.8 million, respectively. Earnings for 2002 and 2001 excluded losses from discontinued operations of $418.0 million and $52.1 million, respectively. Net sales inched up 0.9% to $1.29 billion.

PROSPECTS:

In the near-term, the Company should continue to benefit from improved shipments for pulp and paperboard. However, wood products segment results will likely be adversely affected by the poor market conditions for wood products that have been ongoing since the second half of 2000. Meanwhile, beginning in the first quarter of 2003, results for consumer tissue products will be reported as a stand-alone segment, separate from pulp and paperboard, due to management changes effective in January 2003. Moreover, results for the new segment may be negatively affected by competitive market conditions. Separately, on 2/28/03, the Company announced that it has sold its Brainerd, Minnesota, paper mill and related assets to Missota Paper Company LLC for $4.4 million in cash.

ANNUAL FINANCIAL DATA:

FISCAL YEAR	TOT. REVS. ($mill.)	NET INC. ($mill.)	TOT. ASSETS ($mill.)	OPER. PROFIT %	NET PROFIT %	RET. ON EQUITY %	RET. ON ASSETS %	CURR. RATIO	EARN. PER SH.$	CASH FL. PER SH.$	TANG. BK. VAL.$	DIV. PER SH.$	PRICE RANGE	AVG. P/E RATIO	AVG. YIELD %
p12/31/02	1,286.2	⑦ d50.9							⑦ d1.79			0.60	36.45 - 23.75	...	2.0
12/31/01	1,752.0	⑥ d79.4	2,487.1	...	...	...	...	1.4	⑥ d2.81	d2.81	24.98	1.17	36.51 - 24.50	...	3.8
⑥ 12/31/00	1,808.8	⑤ d33.2	2,542.4	0.5	...	...	...	1.1	⑤ d1.16	d1.16	28.69	1.74	48.88 - 28.56	...	4.7
12/31/99	1,676.8	④ 40.9	2,446.5	6.7	2.4	4.4	1.7	1.1	④ 1.41	1.41	31.79	1.74	45.50 - 32.50	27.7	4.5
12/31/98	1,565.9	37.2	2,377.3	6.3	2.4	4.0	1.6	1.3	1.28	1.28	32.19	1.74	48.38 - 31.00	31.0	4.4
12/31/97	1,568.9	36.1	2,365.1	5.9	2.3	3.8	1.5	1.4	1.24	1.24	32.82	1.71	52.75 - 39.00	37.0	3.7
12/31/96	1,554.4	③ 61.5	2,265.7	7.9	4.0	6.4	2.7	1.5	③ 2.13	2.13	33.06	1.67	44.88 - 35.13	18.8	4.2
12/31/95	1,605.2	108.5	2,265.3	13.7	6.8	11.3	4.8	1.4	3.72	3.72	33.23	1.61	44.13 - 37.13	10.9	4.0
12/31/94	1,471.3	② 49.0	2,081.2	8.7	3.3	5.3	2.4	1.6	② 1.68	1.68	31.49	1.57	49.50 - 35.50	25.3	3.7
12/31/93	1,368.9	① 38.3	2,066.8	7.1	2.8	4.2	1.9	1.7	① 1.31	1.31	31.50	1.51	51.88 - 38.25	34.4	3.4

Statistics are as originally reported. ① Bef. acctg. change chrg. $31.7 mill. ($0.43/sh.). ② Incl. pre-tax chrg. of $10 mill. ($0.21/sh.) for early retirement programs. ③ Bef. extraord. chrg. $3.4 mill. for loss from early exting. of debt. ④ Incl. nonrecur. pre-tax chrg. of $7.5 mill. ⑤ Incl. nonrecur. pre-tax chrg. of $2.8 mill., 2001; $46.4 mill., 2000. ⑥ Net sales were reclassified to include freight costs. ⑦ Incl. restruct. chrg. of $9.0 mill., debt exting. costs of $15.4 mill.; excl. dis. ops. loss of $300.7 mill.

OFFICERS:
L. P. Siegel, Chmn., C.E.O.
R. L. Paulson, Pres., C.O.O.
G. L. Zuehlke, V.P., C.F.O., Treas.

INVESTOR CONTACT: Gerald L. Zuehlke, (509) 835-1550

PRINCIPAL OFFICE: 601 West Riverside Avenue, Suite 1100, Spokane, WA 99201

TELEPHONE NUMBER: (509) 835-1500
FAX: (509) 835-1555
WEB: www.potlatchcorp.com
NO. OF EMPLOYEES: 6,200 full-time (approx.); 100 part-time (avg.)
SHAREHOLDERS: 2,900 (approx.)
ANNUAL MEETING: In May
INCORPORATED: DE, 1903

INSTITUTIONAL HOLDINGS:
No. of Institutions: 118
Shares Held: 15,092,303
% Held: 52.9

INDUSTRY: Paper mills (SIC: 2621)

TRANSFER AGENT(S): Computershare Investor Services, LLC, Chicago, IL

PPG INDUSTRIES, INC.

EXCH.	SYM.	REC. PRICE	P/E RATIO	YLD.	MKT. CAP.	RANGE (52-WK.)	'02 Y/E PR.	DIV. ACH.
NYSE	PPG	46.40 (2/28/03)	...	3.7%	$7.86 bill.	62.86 - 41.39	50.15	31 yrs.

INVESTMENT GRADE. THE COMPANY PLANS TO CONTINUE EFFORTS TO LOWER MANUFACTURING AND OVER-HEAD COSTS AND REDUCE DEBT.

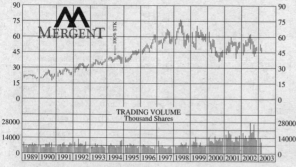

*7 YEAR PRICE SCORE 101.5 ***12 MONTH PRICE SCORE 102.6**

*NYSE COMPOSITE INDEX=100

INTERIM EARNINGS (Per Share):

Qtr.	Mar.	June	Sept.	Dec.
1998	1.08	1.11	1.39	0.91
1999	0.70	1.05	0.56	0.92
2000	0.79	1.17	0.86	0.75
2001	0.33	0.92	0.55	0.49
2002	0.25	d2.03	0.87	0.55

INTERIM DIVIDENDS (Per Share):

Amt.	Decl.	Ex.	Rec.	Pay.
0.42Q	1/17/02	2/14/02	2/19/02	3/12/02
0.42Q	4/18/02	5/08/02	5/10/02	6/12/02
0.43Q	7/18/02	8/08/02	8/12/02	9/12/02
0.43Q	10/17/02	11/07/02	11/12/02	12/12/02
0.43Q	1/16/03	2/13/03	2/18/03	3/12/03

Indicated div.: $1.72 (Div. Reinv. Plan)

CAPITALIZATION (12/31/01):

	($000)	(%)
Long-Term Debt	1,699,000	31.9
Deferred Income Tax	552,000	10.4
Common & Surplus	3,080,000	57.8
Total	5,331,000	100.0

BUSINESS:

PPG Industries, Inc. is a supplier of products for manufacturing, construction, automotive, chemical processing and numerous other world industries. The diversified global manufacturer makes protective and decorative coatings, flat glass, fabricated glass products, continuous-strand fiberglass, and industrial and specialty chemicals. As of 12/31/02, PPG operated 170 manufacturing facilities in countries including Canada, China, England, France, Germany, Ireland, Italy, Mexico, the Netherlands, Portugal, Spain, Taiwan, and the U.S. In 2002, revenues (and operating income) were derived: coatings, 55.6% (69.4%); glass, 25.7% (16.4%); and chemicals, 18.8% (14.2%).

RECENT DEVELOPMENTS:

For the twelve months ended 12/31/02, loss amounted to $60.0 million, before an accounting change charge of $9.0 million, compared with net income of $387.0 million in 2001. Results for 2002 and 2001 included amortization of $32.0 million and $72.0 million, and business realignment expenses of $77.0 million and $103.0 million, respectively. Results for 2002 also included an asbestos settlement gain of $755.0 million. Net sales slipped 1.2% to $8.07 billion from $8.17 billion the year before. Net sales in the coatings segment grew 1.6% to $4.48 billion from $4.41 billion due to stronger volumes in the architectural and industrial markets and the strength of foreign currencies. Sales in the glass segment declined 7.4% to $2.07 billion from $2.24 billion, while sales in the chemicals segment slipped 0.6% to $1.51 billion from $1.52 billion.

PROSPECTS:

The Company expects the global economic environment to continue to be challenging in 2003. As a result, the Company plans to continue efforts to further improve its cost structure and cash flow. These initiatives include lowering manufacturing and overhead costs and reducing debt. Meanwhile, near-term results should continue to benefit from strong volumes in architectural and industrial coatings and improved manufacturing efficiencies. This may be partially offset by increased energy costs, higher selling prices and increased pension and retiree medical costs.

ANNUAL FINANCIAL DATA:

FISCAL YEAR	TOT. REVS. ($mill.)	NET INC. ($mill.)	TOT. ASSETS ($mill.)	OPER. PROFIT %	NET PROFIT %	RET. ON EQUITY %	RET. ON ASSETS %	CURR. RATIO	EARN. PER SH.$	CASH FL. PER SH.$	TANG. BK. VAL.$	DIV. PER SH.$	PRICE RANGE	AVG. P/E RATIO	AVG. YIELD %
p12/31/02	8,067.0	⑩ d0.60							⑩ d0.36			1.70	62.86 - 41.39	...	3.3
12/31/01	8,169.0	⑨ 387.0	8,452.0	12.2	4.7	12.6	4.6	1.4	⑨ 2.29	4.96	9.12	1.68	59.75 - 38.99	21.6	3.4
12/31/00	⑧ 8,629.0	⑦ 620.0	9,125.0	14.8	7.2	20.0	6.8	1.2	⑦ 3.57	6.19	8.61	1.60	65.06 - 36.00	14.2	3.2
12/31/99	7,757.0	⑥ 568.0	8,914.0	14.9	7.3	18.3	6.4	1.3	⑥ 3.23	5.62	8.30	1.52	70.75 - 47.94	18.4	2.6
12/31/98	7,510.0	⑤ 801.0	7,387.0	17.0	10.7	27.8	10.8	1.4	⑤ 4.48	6.63	13.17	1.42	76.63 - 49.13	14.0	2.3
12/31/97	7,379.0	④ 714.0	6,812.0	17.8	9.7	28.5	10.5	1.6	④ 3.94	5.91	21.29	1.33	67.50 - 48.63	14.7	2.3
12/31/96	7,218.1	744.0	6,441.4	17.9	10.3	30.0	11.6	1.3	3.96	5.89	13.55	1.26	62.25 - 42.88	13.3	2.4
12/31/95	7,057.7	③ 767.6	6,194.3	18.4	10.9	29.9	12.4	1.4	③ 3.80	5.54	13.21	1.18	47.88 - 34.88	10.9	2.9
12/31/94	6,331.2	② 684.6	5,893.9	16.0	10.8	26.8	11.6	1.5	② 2.43	4.81	12.35	1.12	42.13 - 33.75	15.6	3.0
12/31/93	5,753.9	① 547.8	5,651.5	12.5	9.5	22.2	9.7	5.6	① 1.39	4.22	11.57	1.04	38.13 - 29.69	24.4	3.1

Statistics are as originally reported. Adj for 2-1 split, 6/94. ① Bef dr$363.2 mil acct adj & incl $126.4 mil restr. chg & $44.2 mil a-tx chg sale med elec bus. ② Incl $51.9 mil a-tx chg dvst med elec bus. ③ Incl $24.2 mil a-tax nonrecur. gain. ④ Incl $102 mil nonrecur. p-tx chg & $59 mil p-tx gain dvst chem busn. ⑤ Incl $85.0 mill. p-tax gain fr. sale of bus. & $27.0 mill. p-tax restr. chg. and oth. chgs. ⑥ Incl. $110.0 mill. in p-tax chgs. ⑦ Incl. $5.0 mill. one-time chg. fr. bus. divestiture & realignments. ⑧ Bef outgoing freight costs. Prior years' revs are net of these costs. ⑨ Incl $103.0 mil bus. alignments. ⑩ Incl $755.0 mil net asbestos settlmt, $77.0 mil bus align. & excl $9.0 mil acctg chg.

OFFICERS:
R. W. LeBoeuf, Chmn., C.E.O.
J. C. Diggs, Sr. V.P., Gen. Couns.
W. H. Hernandez, Sr. V.P., C.F.O.
INVESTOR CONTACT: D. B. Atkinson, Investor Relations, (412) 434-2120
PRINCIPAL OFFICE: One PPG Place, Pittsburgh, PA 15272

TELEPHONE NUMBER: (412) 434-3131
FAX: (412) 434-2571
WEB: www.ppg.com
NO. OF EMPLOYEES: 34,900 (avg.)
SHAREHOLDERS: 29,005
ANNUAL MEETING: In Apr.
INCORPORATED: PA, Nov., 1883; reincorp., PA, Nov., 1920

INSTITUTIONAL HOLDINGS:
No. of Institutions: 441
Shares Held: 94,098,468
% Held: 55.5
INDUSTRY: Paints and allied products (SIC: 2851)
TRANSFER AGENT(S): Mellon Investor Services, Ridgefield Park, NJ

PPL CORPORATION

EXCH.	SYM.	REC. PRICE	P/E RATIO	YLD.	MKT. CAP.	RANGE (52-WK.)	'02 Y/E PR.
NYSE	PPL	35.17 (2/28/03)	24.8	4.4%	$5.16 bill.	39.95 - 26.00	34.68

LOWER MEDIUM GRADE. THE COMPANY EXPECTS EARNINGS PER SHARE FROM CORE OPERATIONS IN 2003 TO RANGE BETWEEN $3.45 AND $3.75.

TRADING VOLUME
Thousand Shares

*7 YEAR PRICE SCORE 123.9   *12 MONTH PRICE SCORE 112.0

*NYSE COMPOSITE INDEX=100

INTERIM EARNINGS (Per Share):

Qtr.	Mar.	June	Sept.	Dec.
1998	0.60	0.32	0.81	0.47
1999	0.70	0.40	1.07	1.02
2000	0.99	0.64	0.94	0.87
2001	1.52	0.80	1.04	d2.12
2002	d0.02	d0.18	0.80	0.82

INTERIM DIVIDENDS (Per Share):

Amt.	Decl.	Ex.	Rec.	Pay.
0.36Q	1/29/02	3/06/02	3/08/02	4/01/02
0.36Q	5/24/02	6/06/02	6/10/02	7/01/02
0.36Q	8/23/02	9/06/02	9/10/02	10/01/02
0.36Q	11/22/02	12/06/02	12/10/02	1/01/03
0.385Q	2/28/03	3/06/03	3/10/03	4/01/03

Indicated div.: $1.54 (Div. Reinv. Plan)

CAPITALIZATION (12/31/01):

	($000)	(%)
Long-Term Debt	5,081,000	64.5
Minority Interest	38,000	0.5
Redeemable Pfd. Stock	825,000	10.5
Preferred Stock	82,000	1.0
Common & Surplus	1,857,000	23.6
Total	7,883,000	100.0

BUSINESS:

PPL Corporation (formerly PP&L Resources, Inc.) delivers electricity and natural gas to more than 1.3 million customers in Pennsylvania; markets wholesale or retail energy in 42 U.S. states and Canada; provides energy services for businesses in the Mid-Atlantic and Northeastern U.S.; generates electricity at power plants in Pennsylvania, Maine and Montana; delivers electricity to 2.4 million customers in southwest Great Britain; and delivers electricity to about 1.8 million customers in Chile, Bolivia, El Salvador and Brazil. Revenues for 2002 were derived: utility, 67.7%; wholesale energy marketing, 18.3%; and energy-related and other businesses, 10.6%; and unregulated retail electric and gas, 3.4%.

RECENT DEVELOPMENTS:

For the twelve months ended 12/31/02, income surged 92.3% to $425.0 million, before an accounting change charge of $150.0 million, compared with income of $221.0 million, before an accounting change gain of $10.0 million, in 2001. Results for 2002 and 2001 included amortization of recoverable transition costs of $226.0 million and $251.0 million, and a charge for the write-down of international energy projects of $113.0 million and $336.0 million, respectively. Results also included a write-down charge of $44.0 million for generation assets and a charge for $75.0 million for workforce reductions in 2002, as well as a cancellation charge of $150.0 million for generation projects in 2001. Total operating revenues increased 6.9% to $5.43 billion from $5.08 billion a year earlier.

PROSPECTS:

The Company anticipates earnings of between $3.75 and $4.05 per share, including unusual items for full-year 2003. This forecast, which excludes any impact from exiting its Brazilian investment, reflects the planned issuance of additional common stock in 2003, a continuation of current wholesale electricity prices, and decreased pension income. In addition, the Company expects to report 5.0% to 8.0% compound annual growth in core earnings from operations based on 2002 earnings from core operations.

ANNUAL FINANCIAL DATA:

FISCAL YEAR	TOT. REVS. ($Mill.)	NET INC. ($Mill.)	TOT. ASSETS ($Mill.)	OPER. PROFIT %	NET PROFIT %	NET INC./ NET PROP. %	NET INC./ TOT. CAP. %	RET. ON EQUITY %	ACCUM. DEPR./ GROSS PROP. %	EARN. PER SH. $	TANG. BK. VAL. $	DIV. PER SH. $	DIV. PAYOUT %	PRICE RANGE	AVG. P/E RATIO	AVG. YIELD %
p12/31/02	5,429.0	⑦425.0								⑦3.54		1.44	40.7	39.95 - 26.00	9.3	4.4
12/31/01	5,725.0	⑥221.0	12,574.0	14.9	3.9	3.6	2.8	11.4	...	⑥1.15	12.67	1.06	25.1	62.36 - 30.99	40.6	2.3
12/31/00	5,683.0	⑤513.0	12,360.0	21.2	9.0	8.6	7.5	21.5	...	⑤3.28	12.96	1.06	32.3	46.13 - 18.38	9.8	3.3
12/31/99	4,590.0	④504.0	11,174.0	19.0	11.0	8.4	8.2	24.3	...	④3.14	12.96	1.00	42.6	32.00 - 20.38	8.3	3.8
12/31/98	3,786.0	③404.0	9,607.0	21.8	10.7	9.0	7.7	18.9	60.5	③2.29	12.96	1.50	65.6	28.94 - 20.88	10.9	6.0
12/31/97	3,049.0	320.0	9,485.0	17.9	10.5	4.7	4.1	11.4	35.1	1.80	18.32	1.67	92.8	24.25 - 19.00	12.0	7.7
12/31/96	2,910.0	357.0	9,636.0	19.1	12.3	5.1	4.4	13.0	33.4	2.05	16.88	1.67	81.5	26.00 - 21.63	11.6	7.0
12/31/95	2,751.8	②350.4	9,491.7	30.4	12.7	4.9	4.4	13.5	29.6	②2.05	16.29	0.83	40.7	26.50 - 17.88	10.8	3.8
12/31/94	2,725.1	①244.3	9,371.7	18.4	9.0	3.4	3.1	10.0	27.5	①1.41	15.79	...	...	27.25 - 18.63	16.3	...
12/31/93	2,727.0	348.1	9,454.1	20.6	12.8	4.9	4.5	14.3	14.3	2.07	15.95	...	...	31.00 - 26.13	13.8	...

Statistics are as originally reported. ① Incl. $83.0 mill. after-tax chgs. ② Incl. $0.21 per sh. gain fr. adjust. rel. to a rate decision, $0.12 per sh. gain fr. sale of Greene Hill reserves. & $0.11 per sh. chg. fr. employ. reductions. ③ Excl. $948.0 mill. net extraord. loss rel. to settlement of restr. cas with PA Public Utility Comm. ④ Excl. $46.0 mill. extraord. loss fr. repurchase of first mortgage bonds. ⑤ Excl. $11.0 mill. net extraord. gain. ⑥ Incl. $336.0 mill. write-down & $150.0 mill chg.; Bef. $10.0 mill. acctg. chge. benefit ⑦ Incl. $113.0 mill. write-down of proj., $44.0 mill. write-down of gener. assets, $75.0 mill. workforce reduct. chg. & excl. $150.0 acctg. change chg.

OFFICERS:
W. F. Hecht, Chmn., Pres., C.E.O.
J. R. Biggar, Exec. V.P., C.F.O.
R. J. Grey, Sr. V.P., Sec., Gen. Couns.
INVESTOR CONTACT: George I. Kline, Manager, Investor Services, (800) 345-3085
PRINCIPAL OFFICE: Two North Ninth Street, Allentown, PA 18101-1179

TELEPHONE NUMBER: (610) 774-5151
FAX: (610) 774-5106
WEB: www.pplweb.com
NO. OF EMPLOYEES: 12,496
SHAREHOLDERS: 87,796
ANNUAL MEETING: In Apr.
INCORPORATED: PA, Mar., 1994

INSTITUTIONAL HOLDINGS:
No. of Institutions: 292
Shares Held: 83,623,598
% Held: 50.9

INDUSTRY: Electric services (SIC: 4911)

TRANSFER AGENT(S): Wells Fargo Shareowner Services, South St. Paul, MN

PRAXAIR, INC.

EXCH.	SYM.	REC. PRICE	P/E RATIO	YLD.	MKT. CAP.	RANGE (52-WK.)	'02 Y/E PR.	DIV. ACH.
NYSE	PX	52.85 (2/28/03)	15.9	1.6%	$8.58 bill.	61.11 - 44.55	57.77	10 yrs.

UPPER MEDIUM GRADE. THE COMPANY EXPECTS SALES AND EARNINGS TO GROW IN 2003 DESPITE UNCERTAINTY REGARDING THE PACE OF ECONOMIC RECOVERY.

TRADING VOLUME
Thousand Shares

*7 YEAR PRICE SCORE 127.1   ***12 MONTH PRICE SCORE 107.9**
*NYSE COMPOSITE INDEX=100

INTERIM EARNINGS (Per Share):

Qtr.	Mar.	June	Sept.	Dec.
1997	0.62	0.65	0.65	0.61
1998	0.66	0.66	0.66	0.66
1999	0.67	0.66	0.69	0.70
2000	0.71	0.76	0.76	0.03
2001	0.77	0.77	0.38	0.72
2002	0.77	0.91	0.80	0.85

INTERIM DIVIDENDS (Per Share):

Amt.	Decl.	Ex.	Rec.	Pay.
0.19Q	1/23/02	3/05/02	3/07/02	3/15/02
0.19Q	4/23/02	6/05/02	6/07/02	6/17/02
0.19Q	7/23/02	9/04/02	9/06/02	9/16/02
0.19Q	10/22/02	12/04/02	12/06/02	12/16/02
0.215Q	1/28/03	3/05/03	3/07/03	3/17/03

Indicated div.: $0.86 (Div. Reinv. Plan)

CAPITALIZATION (12/31/01):

	($000)	(%)
Long-Term Debt	2,725,000	52.4
Common & Surplus	2,477,000	47.6
Total	5,202,000	100.0

BUSINESS:

Praxair, Inc. is one of the largest suppliers of industrial gases worldwide, particularly in North and South America. PX serves industries through the production, sale and distribution of industrial gases and high-performance surface coatings, along with related services, materials and systems. Praxair's primary products are atmospheric gases (oxygen, nitrogen, argon, and rare gases) and process gases (carbon dioxide, helium, hydrogen, electronics gases, and acetylene). PX also designs, engineers, and supervises construction of cryogenic and non-cryogenic supply systems. PX's surface technology applies metallic and ceramic coatings and powders to metal surfaces in order to resist wear, high temperatures, and corrosion. Sales in North America accounted for 65.3% of revenues in 2002.

RECENT DEVELOPMENTS:

For the year ended 12/31/02, income rose 26.9% to $548.0 million, before an accounting change charge of $139.0 million, versus income of $432.0 million, before an accounting change charge of $2.0 million, in 2001. Sales slipped 0.6% to $5.13 billion from $5.16 billion in the prior year, primarily due to weak global economic conditions. Operating profit increased 15.4% to $923.0 million compared with $800.0 million the year before due to pricing initiatives and cost controls. Overall results benefited from the Company's cost-reduction initiatives, productivity improvements and new business developments.

PROSPECTS:

PX's focus in the short term will be to drive its growth programs in healthcare, refinery hydrogen, electronics, technology licensing and China. These programs, combined with PX's focus on productivity and capital discipline, should deliver solid results in 2003. For the full-year 2003, PX anticipates sales and operating profit growth of 2.0% to 4.0%. Full-year 2003 diluted earnings per share are estimated in the range of $3.40 to $3.60. Full-year capital expenditures are expected to be approximately $600.0 million.

ANNUAL FINANCIAL DATA:

FISCAL YEAR	TOT. REVS. ($mill.)	NET INC. ($mill.)	TOT. ASSETS ($mill.)	OPER. PROFIT %	NET PROFIT %	RET. ON EQUITY %	RET. ON ASSETS %	CURR. RATIO	EARN. PER SH. $	CASH FL. PER SH. $	TANG. BK. VAL. $	DIV. PER SH. $	PRICE RANGE	AVG. P/E RATIO	AVG. YIELD %
p12/31/02	5,128.0	⑦ 548.0							⑦ 3.33			0.76	61.11 - 44.55	15.9	1.4
12/31/01	5,124.0	⑦ 432.0	7,715.0	15.6	8.4	17.4	5.6	1.1	⑦ 2.64	5.69	15.28	0.68	55.92 - 36.50	17.5	1.5
12/31/00	5,043.0	⑥ 363.0	7,762.0	14.0	7.2	15.4	4.7	0.9	⑥ 2.25	5.18	14.79	0.62	54.94 - 30.31	18.9	1.5
12/31/99	4,639.0	⑤ 441.0	7,722.0	17.9	9.5	19.3	5.7	0.8	⑤ 2.72	5.46	14.40	0.56	58.13 - 32.00	16.6	1.2
12/31/98	4,833.0	④ 425.0	8,096.0	17.7	8.8	18.2	5.2	1.1	④ 2.60	5.46	14.80	0.50	53.88 - 30.69	16.3	1.2
12/31/97	4,735.0	③ 416.0	7,810.0	17.7	8.8	19.6	5.3	1.1	③ 2.53	5.24	13.48	0.44	58.00 - 39.25	19.2	0.9
12/31/96	4,449.0	② 282.0	7,161.4	14.5	6.3	13.8	3.9	0.7	② 1.77	4.41	5.56	0.38	50.13 - 31.50	23.1	0.9
12/31/95	3,146.0	262.0	4,134.0	17.4	8.3	23.4	6.3	0.9	1.82	3.75	6.74	0.32	34.13 - 19.75	14.8	1.2
12/31/94	2,711.0	203.0	3,520.0	16.5	7.5	19.4	5.8	0.9	1.45	3.40	6.94	0.28	24.63 - 16.25	14.1	1.4
12/31/93	2,438.0	① 143.0	3,255.0	14.0	5.9	17.9	4.4	0.8	① 1.06	3.00	5.44	0.25	18.63 - 14.13	15.4	1.5

Statistics are as originally reported. ① Bef. an acctg. chg. of $25.0 mill. ② Incl. CBI integra. chg. of $53.0 mill. ③ Incl. $10.0 mill. pre-tax chg. for restr. & $11.0 mill. pre-tax profit from settlement. ④ Incl. $8.0 mill. chg. for exps. rel. to acq. & $29.0 mill. spl chgs. for impair. loss & prov. loss fr. sale of plant equip. ⑤ Incl. $14.0 mill. after-tax non-recur. gain & excl. d$10.0 mill. acct. chg. ⑥ Incl. $117.0 mill. after-tax chg. for reposit. program, $44.0 mill. chg. for consol. costs, & $67.0 mill. write-off of assets. ⑦ Excl. $139.0 mill. acctg. change chg., 2002; $2.0 mill., 2001.

OFFICERS:
D. H. Reilley, Chmn., Pres., C.E.O.
J. S. Sawyer, V.P.,C.F.O.
D. H. Chaifetz, V.P., Gen Couns., Sec.

INVESTOR CONTACT: Elizabeth T. Hirsch, Director, Inv. Rel., (203) 837-2354

PRINCIPAL OFFICE: 39 Old Ridgebury Rd., Danbury, CT 06810-5113

TELEPHONE NUMBER: (203) 837-2000
FAX: (203) 837-2450
WEB: www.praxair.com

NO. OF EMPLOYEES: 24,271

SHAREHOLDERS: 20,448

ANNUAL MEETING: In Apr.

INCORPORATED: DE, Oct., 1988

INSTITUTIONAL HOLDINGS:
No. of Institutions: 419
Shares Held: 132,511,837
% Held: 81.9

INDUSTRY: Industrial gases (SIC: 2813)

TRANSFER AGENT(S): The Bank of New York, New York, NY

PRECISION CASTPARTS CORP.

EXCH.	SYM.	REC. PRICE	P/E RATIO	YLD.	MKT. CAP.	RANGE (52-WK.)	'02 Y/E PR.
NYSE	PCP	23.60 (2/28/03)	7.4	0.5%	$1.23 bill.	38.00 - 16.85	24.25

UPPER MEDIUM GRADE. SALES ARE BEING ADVERSELY AFFECTED BY THE CONTINUED WEAKNESS IN AERO-SPACE AND INDUSTRIAL GAS TURBINE MARKETS.

TRADING VOLUME
Thousand Shares

*7 YEAR PRICE SCORE 111.2   ***12 MONTH PRICE SCORE 100.3**

NYSE COMPOSITE INDEX=100

INTERIM EARNINGS (Per Share):

Qtr.	June	Sept.	Dec.	Mar.
1998-99	0.50	0.52	0.53	0.57
1999-00	0.46	0.48	0.26	0.55
2000-01	0.57	0.61	0.51	0.75
2001-02	0.77	0.23	d1.14	0.93
2002-03	0.78	0.78	0.69	...

INTERIM DIVIDENDS (Per Share):

Amt.	Decl.	Ex.	Rec.	Pay.
0.03Q	2/13/02	3/06/02	3/08/02	4/04/02
0.03Q	6/05/02	6/05/02	6/07/02	7/01/02
0.03Q~	8/14/02	9/04/02	9/06/02	9/30/02
0.03Q	11/12/02	12/04/02	12/06/02	1/02/03
0.03Q	2/12/03	3/05/03	3/07/03	3/31/03

Indicated div.: $0.12

CAPITALIZATION (3/31/02):

	($000)	(%)
Long-Term Debt	697,000	42.3
Common & Surplus	951,800	57.7
Total	1,648,800	100.0

BUSINESS:

Precision Castparts Corp. is a worldwide manufacturer of metal components and products, including large, complex structural investment castings, airfoil castings and forged components used in jet aircraft engines and industrial gas turbines. In addition, the Company serves the fluid management, metalworking tools and machines, pulp and paper, advanced metalforming technologies, airframe and military components, and other metal products markets. The Company's operations are classified into four reportable business segments. Investment Cast Products include the PCC Structurals, PCC Airfoils and Wyman-Gordon Castings businesses. Forged Products comprises all of the forging businesses of Wyman-Gordon. Fluid Management Products is the Company's PCC Flow Technologies operation. The Industrial Products segment includes PCC Specialty Products, Inc., J&L Fiber Services, Inc., Advanced Forming Technology and STW Composites.

RECENT DEVELOPMENTS:

For the quarter ended 12/29/02, income from continuing operations amounted to $37.4 million compared with a loss of $24.5 million in the equivalent 2001 quarter. Results for 2001 included a provision for restructuring of $10.5 million and impairment of long-lived assets of $57.8 million.

Results for 2002 and 2001 excluded charges of $1.2 million and $34.6 million, respectively, for discontinued operations. Net sales declined 18.4% to $501.6 million from $614.6 million a year earlier, reflecting continued weakness in the aerospace and industrial gas turbine markets.

PROSPECTS:

The Company continues to focus on maintaining its tight control of costs due to continued weakness in the marketplace. Accordingly, ongoing efforts to reduce expenses, consolidate resources and exploit synergies have led to improved operating margins. PCP's intention moving forward is to maintain its improved operating performance as well as position the Company for long-term growth and an eventual recovery in its major markets. The Company is making considerable progress in finalizing long-term agreements with major customers.

ANNUAL FINANCIAL DATA:

FISCAL YEAR	TOT. REVS. ($mill.)	NET INC. ($mill.)	TOT. ASSETS ($mill.)	OPER. PROFIT %	NET PROFIT %	RET. ON EQUITY %	RET. ON ASSETS %	CURR. RATIO	EARN. PER SH.$	CASH FL.PER SH.$	TANG. BK. VAL.$	DIV. PER SH.$	PRICE RANGE	AVG. P/E RATIO	AVG. YIELD %
3/31/02	2,557.4	③ 42.4	2,564.9	12.9	1.7	4.5	1.7	1.2	③ 0.81	2.74	...	0.12	49.50 — 18.00	41.7	0.4
4/01/01	2,326.3	② 124.9	2,572.9	12.4	5.4	13.9	4.9	1.3	② 2.45	4.47	...	0.12	45.56 — 11.84	11.7	0.4
4/02/00	1,673.7	② 85.3	2,415.7	10.8	5.1	11.0	3.5	1.3	② 1.74	3.24	...	0.12	23.63 — 11.72	10.2	0.7
3/28/99	1,471.9	② 103.3	1,449.6	12.1	7.0	14.8	7.1	1.8	② 2.11	3.21	3.50	0.12	32.13 — 16.31	11.5	0.5
3/29/98	1,316.7	② 86.1	1,274.6	11.8	6.5	14.5	6.8	1.9	② 1.77	2.66	2.96	0.12	33.84 — 24.00	16.4	0.4
3/30/97	972.8	56.5	1,070.1	11.6	5.8	11.2	5.3	1.8	1.30	2.10	2.60	0.12	25.63 — 16.69	16.3	0.6
3/31/96	556.8	② 41.1	450.5	11.5	7.4	13.6	9.1	2.3	② 1.01	1.57	5.41	0.12	20.00 — 9.81	14.8	0.8
4/02/95	436.4	29.0	406.7	10.4	6.6	11.2	7.1	1.9	0.73	1.32	4.47	0.09	13.75 — 9.00	15.7	0.8
4/03/94	420.4	25.1	342.9	9.2	6.0	11.3	7.3	2.5	0.64	1.38	5.67	0.04	9.67 — 5.79	12.0	0.5
3/28/93	461.4	① 1.8	433.3	2.0	0.4	0.4	0.9	1.9	① 0.03	0.41	5.21	0.04	12.00 — 5.58	257.8	0.5

Statistics are as originally reported. Adj. for stk. split: 3-for-2, 8/94; 100%, 9/00. ① Bef. an acctg. change of $2.9 mill. & incl. a tax benefit of $2.4 mill. ② Incl. restruct. chrg. of $9.4 mill., 2001; $11.0 mill., 2000; $13.1 mill., 1999; $8.6 mill., 1998; $3.4 mill., 1996. ③ Incl. impairment of long-lived assets of $129.1 mill. & restr. chrg. of $16.3 mill.

OFFICERS:
W. C. McCormick, Chmn., C.E.O.
M. Donegan, Pres., C.O.O.
W. D. Larsson, Sr. V.P., C.F.O.
INVESTOR CONTACT: Dwight E. Weber, Dir., Comm., (503) 417-4855
PRINCIPAL OFFICE: 4650 S.W. Macadam Avenue, Suite 440, Portland, OR 97239-4252

TELEPHONE NUMBER: (503) 417-4800
FAX: (503) 417-4817
WEB: www.precast.com
NO. OF EMPLOYEES: 13,813
SHAREHOLDERS: 6,143
ANNUAL MEETING: In Aug.
INCORPORATED: OR, 1956

INSTITUTIONAL HOLDINGS:
No. of Institutions: 205
Shares Held: 39,643,834
% Held: 75.8

INDUSTRY: Steel investment foundries (SIC: 3324)

TRANSFER AGENT(S): The Bank of New York, New York, NY

PREMCOR INC.

EXCH.	SYM.	REC. PRICE	P/E RATIO	YLD.	MKT. CAP.	RANGE (52-WK.)	'02 Y/E PR.
NYSE	PCO	25.11 (2/28/03)	...	...	$0.8 mill.	28.25 - 13.00	22.23

LOWER MEDIUM GRADE. THE COMPANY EXPECTS TURNAROUND MAINTENANCE ACTIVITY AT ITS REFINERIES WILL BE MINIMAL IN 2003.

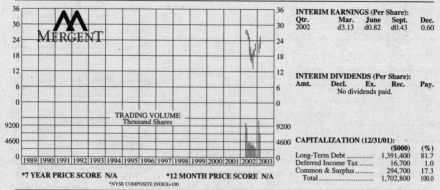

INTERIM EARNINGS (Per Share):

Qtr.	Mar.	June	Sept.	Dec.
2002	d3.13	d0.82	d0.43	0.60

INTERIM DIVIDENDS (Per Share):

Amt.	Decl.	Ex.	Rec.	Pay.
	No dividends paid.			

CAPITALIZATION (12/31/01):

	($000)	(%)
Long-Term Debt	1,391,400	81.7
Deferred Income Tax	16,700	1.0
Common & Surplus	294,700	17.3
Total	1,702,800	100.0

*7 YEAR PRICE SCORE N/A   ***12 MONTH PRICE SCORE N/A**

*NYSE COMPOSITE INDEX=100

BUSINESS:

Premcor Inc. is an independent petroleum refiner and supplier of unbranded transportation fuels, heating oil, petrochemical feedstocks, petroleum coke and other petroleum products in the United States. As of 9/30/02, PCO owned and operated two refineries with a combined crude oil throughput capacity of 420,000 barrels per day. The refineries are located in Port Arthur, Texas and Lima, Ohio. The Company sells its products on an unbranded basis to approximately 600 distributors and chain retailers through its own product distribution system and an extensive third-party-owned product distribution system, as well as in the spot market. On 5/3/02, PCO completed an IPO of 20.7 million shares of common stock. Prior to the IPO, the Company's common equity was privately held and controlled by Blackstone Capital Partners III Merchant Banking Fund L.P. and its affiliates. As a result of the IPO and other restructuring actions, Blackstone's ownership was reduced to about 48.0% as of 9/30/02.

RECENT DEVELOPMENTS:

For the twelve months ended 12/31/02, PCO reported a net loss of $127.1 million compared with income from continuing operations of $171.0 million a year earlier. Results for 2002 and 2001 included pre-tax restructuring and other charges of $172.9 million and $176.2 million, respectively. Also, results included a loss of $19.5 million for 2002 and a gain of $8.7 million for 2001 on the extinguishment of long-term debt. Operating revenues increased 5.5% to $6.77 billion from $6.42 billion the previous year. Gross margin was down 42.5% to $671.0 million.

PROSPECTS:

PCO's near-term outlook appears to be brightening. For instance, the Company should benefit from recently completed restructuring actions, including the closure of its Hartford refinery. In addition, PCO has stated that turnaround maintenance activity at its refineries in 2003 will be minimal, including that associated with the Memphis refinery, which the Company expects to acquire from The Williams Companies during the first quarter of 2003.

ANNUAL FINANCIAL DATA:

FISCAL YEAR	TOT. REVS. ($mill.)	NET INC. ($mill.)	TOT. ASSETS ($mill.)	OPER. PROFIT %	NET PROFIT %	RET. ON EQUITY %	RET. ON ASSETS %	CURR. RATIO	EARN. PER SH.$	CASH FL. PER SH.$	TANG. BK. VAL.$	PRICE RANGE	AVG. P/E RATIO
p12/31/02	6,772.8	③ d127.1							③ d2.65			28.25 - 13.00	...
12/31/01	6,417.5	② 165.4	2,509.8	5.7	2.6	56.1	6.6	1.8	② 4.49	7.49	9.26		...
12/31/00	7,301.7	89.7	2,469.1	2.0	1.2	59.0	3.6	1.5	2.55	5.17	4.78		...
12/31/99	4,520.5	① d69.0	...	0.2	...	...	...	...	① d3.59	d0.32	...		...

Statistics are as originally reported. ① Incl. inv. recovery of $105.8 mill. fr. mkt. write-down; bef. loss fr. disc. ops. of $4.3 mill. & gain on disposal of disc. ops. of $36.9 mill. ② Incl. refinery restruct. & other pre-tax chrgs. of $176.2 mill.; bef. loss fr. disc. ops. of $18.0 mill. & extraord. gain of $5.6 mill. ③ Incl. restruct. & other chrgs. of $172.9 mill. & loss of $19.5 mill. on exting. of long-term debt.

OFFICERS:
T. D. O'Malley, Chmn., C.E.O.
H. M. Kuchta, Pres., C.O.O.
W. E. Hantke, Exec. V.P., C.F.O.

INVESTOR CONTACT: Joe Watson, Investor Relations, (203) 698-7510

PRINCIPAL OFFICE: 1700 E. Putnam Avenue, Suite 500, Old Greenwich, CT 06870

TELEPHONE NUMBER: (203) 698-7500
WEB: www.premcorinc.com

NO. OF EMPLOYEES: 1,862 (approx.)

SHAREHOLDERS: 8

ANNUAL MEETING: N/A

INCORPORATED: DE, Apr., 1999

INSTITUTIONAL HOLDINGS:
No. of Institutions: 87
Shares Held: 21,232,063
% Held: 36.7

INDUSTRY: Petroleum refining (SIC: 2911)

TRANSFER AGENT(S): American Stock Transfer & Trust Company, New York, NY

PRIDE INTERNATIONAL, INC.

EXCH.	SYM.	REC. PRICE	P/E RATIO	YLD.	MKT. CAP.	RANGE (52-WK.)	'02 Y/E PR.
NYSE	PDE	14.50 (2/28/03)	...	...	$1.93 bill.	19.70 - 10.80	14.90

LOWER MEDIUM GRADE. THE COMPANY RELOCATED SEVERAL RIGS TO TAKE ADVANTAGE OF SIGNIFICANTLY HIGHER PREVAILING DAY RATES.

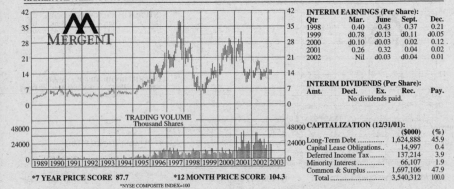

*7 YEAR PRICE SCORE 87.7   ***12 MONTH PRICE SCORE 104.3**
*NYSE COMPOSITE INDEX=100

INTERIM EARNINGS (Per Share):

Qtr	Mar.	June	Sept.	Dec.
1998	0.40	0.43	0.37	0.21
1999	d0.78	d0.13	d0.11	d0.05
2000	d0.10	d0.03	0.02	0.12
2001	0.26	0.32	0.04	0.02
2002	Nil	d0.03	d0.04	0.01

INTERIM DIVIDENDS (Per Share):

Amt.	Decl.	Ex.	Rec.	Pay.
		No dividends paid.		

CAPITALIZATION (12/31/01):

	($000)	(%)
Long-Term Debt	1,624,888	45.9
Capital Lease Obligations..	14,997	0.4
Deferred Income Tax	137,214	3.9
Minority Interest	66,107	1.9
Common & Surplus	1,697,106	47.9
Total	3,540,312	100.0

BUSINESS:

Pride International Inc. is an international provider of contract drilling and related services, operating both offshore and on land. As of 2/27/03, PDE operated in more than 20 countries and marine provinces through a global fleet of 327 rigs, including two ultra-deepwater drillships, 11 semisubmersible rigs, 35 jackup rigs, 29 tender-assisted, barge and platform rigs and 250 land rigs. PDE also designs specialized drilling equipment and provides turnkey, project management and other engineering services. On 9/13/01, PDE acquired Marine Drilling Companies, Inc.

RECENT DEVELOPMENTS:

For the twelve months ended 12/31/02, PDE posted a loss of $8.1 million, before an extraordinary loss of $798,000, versus income of $89.9 million, before an extraordinary gain of $1.3 million, a year earlier. Results for 2001 included merger and pooling charges of $35.8 million. Revenues fell 16.1% to $1.27 billion from $1.51 billion the previous year. PDE attributed the lower results primarily to weak conditions in the U.S. Gulf of Mexico jackup market. Average utilization of the Company's Gulf of Mexico jackup fleet during 2002 was 45.0% compared with 80.0% in 2001. Results for PDE's international land and exploration and production services also declined, reflecting reduced activity, particularly in Argentina and Venezuela, due to economic and political instability in those countries.

PROSPECTS:

PDE's focus on long-term contracts for its rigs, due to the Company's belief that rates in 2003 for most rig types will remain under pressure, appears to be well timed. PDE noted that it has moved 11 of its 27 Gulf of Mexico jackups and four of its 11 floaters to new markets. Nine jackups were moved to Mexico and one each to Nigeria and India pursuant to contract ranging from two to four years. PDE relocated these rigs to take advantage of significantly higher prevailing day rates versus those achievable in the depressed U.S. Gulf of Mexico jackup market. Accordingly, revenues and cashflows from these rigs are expected to greatly enhance the Company's performance in 2003 and beyond. Meanwhile, PDE's remaining available jackup capacity in the U.S. Gulf of Mexico should allow the Company to benefit from an eventual upturn in that market.

ANNUAL FINANCIAL DATA:

FISCAL YEAR	TOT. REVS. ($mill.)	NET INC. ($mill.)	TOT. ASSETS ($mill.)	OPER. PROFIT %	NET PROFIT %	RET. ON EQUITY %	RET. ON ASSETS %	CURR. RATIO	EARN. PER SH. $	CASH FL. PER SH. $	TANG. BK. VAL. $	PRICE RANGE	AVG. P/E RATIO
p12/31/02	1,269.8	5 d8.1							5 d0.06			19.70 - 10.80	...
4 12/31/01	1,512.9	3 89.9	4,205.7	18.2	5.9	5.3	2.1	1.2	3 0.67	2.18	12.29	32.66 - 9.68	31.6
12/31/00	909.0	0.7	2,676.9	10.3	0.1	0.1	...	1.2	0.01	2.10	13.39	29.63 - 13.25	N.M.
12/31/99	619.4	2 d55.8	2,388.7	...	...	...	...	1.5	2 d1.06	0.97	13.66	18.31 - 4.81	...
12/31/98	835.6	77.5	2,192.2	16.9	9.3	10.2	3.5	1.3	1.39	2.71	15.08	27.50 - 6.13	12.1
12/31/97	699.8	104.0	1,541.5	15.5	14.9	15.2	6.7	1.5	2.16	3.31	13.62	37.75 - 16.25	12.5
12/31/96	407.2	22.7	542.1	9.9	5.6	11.3	4.2	1.7	0.81	1.84	6.97	23.25 - 9.13	20.0
12/31/95	263.6	15.4	257.6	10.0	5.8	11.7	6.0	1.7	0.60	1.26	5.14	11.00 - 4.75	13.1
12/31/94	182.3	6.2	205.2	4.4	3.4	5.6	3.0	1.8	0.30	0.76	4.49	6.25 - 4.63	18.1
12/31/93	127.1	1 2.1	110.0	2.2	1.7	3.0	1.9	1.9	1 0.13	0.52	4.17	7.50 - 3.50	42.3

Statistics are as originally reported. 1 Bef. acctg. change credit of $3.8 mill. 2 Incl. restruct. chrg. of $36.6 mill.; bef. extraord. gain of $3.9 mill. 3 Incl. pooling & merger costs of $35.8 mill.; bef. extraord. gain of $1.3 mill. 4 Refl. acq. of Marine Drilling Companies, Inc. 5 Bef. extraord. loss of $798,000.

OFFICERS:
R. L. Barbanell, Chmn.
P. A. Bragg, Pres., C.E.O.
E. W. McNiel, V.P., C.F.O.
INVESTOR CONTACT: Nicolas J. Evanoff, (713) 789-1400
PRINCIPAL OFFICE: 5847 San Felipe, Suite 3300, Houston, TX 77057

TELEPHONE NUMBER: (713) 789-1400
FAX: (713) 789-1430
WEB: www.prde.com
NO. OF EMPLOYEES: 9,500 (approx.)
SHAREHOLDERS: 1,642 (record)
ANNUAL MEETING: In May
INCORPORATED: LA, Dec., 1968; reincorp., DE, Sept. 2001

INSTITUTIONAL HOLDINGS:
No. of Institutions: 212
Shares Held: 112,534,879
% Held: 83.7
INDUSTRY: Oil and gas field services, nec (SIC: 1389)
TRANSFER AGENT(S): American Stock Transfer & Trust Company, New York, NY

PRINCIPAL FINANCIAL GROUP, INC.

EXCH.	SYM.	REC. PRICE	P/E RATIO	YLD.	MKT. CAP.	RANGE (52-WK.)	'02 Y/E PR.
NYSE	PFG	27.57 (2/28/03)	15.6	0.9%	$9.93 bill.	31.50 - 22.50	30.13

MEDIUM GRADE. THE COMPANY EXPECTS FULL-YEAR 2003 OPERATING EARNINGS OF BETWEEN $2.25 AND $2.40 PER DILUTED SHARE.

INTERIM EARNINGS (Per Share):

Qtr.	Mar.	June	Sept.	Dec.
2002	0.68	0.33	0.12	0.64

INTERIM DIVIDENDS (Per Share):

Amt.	Decl.	Ex.	Rec.	Pay.
0.25A	10/25/02	11/06/02	11/08/02	12/09/02

Indicated div.: $0.25

*7 YEAR PRICE SCORE N/A ***12 MONTH PRICE SCORE 110.3**
*NYSE COMPOSITE INDEX=100

CAPITALIZATION (12/31/01):

	($000)	(%)
Long-Term Debt	1,378,400	15.2
Deferred Income Tax	894,600	9.8
Common & Surplus	6,820,300	75.0
Total	9,093,300	100.0

BUSINESS:

The Principal Financial Group, Inc. is a provider of retirement savings, investment and insurance products and services with $111.1 billion in assets under management and about 13.0 million customers worldwide as of 12/31/02. PFG's U.S. and international operations concentrate primarily on asset management and accumulation. PFG also offers a range of individual and group life insurance, group health insurance, individual and group disability insurance and residential mortgage loan origination and servicing. PFG is organized into four operating segments: U.S. Asset Management and Accumulation; International Asset Management and Accumulation; Life and Health Insurance; and Mortgage Banking. Effective 10/26/01, Principal Mutual Holding Company was converted from a mutual insurance holding company to a stock company and subsequently became a wholly owned subsidiary of PFG.

RECENT DEVELOPMENTS:

For the year ended 12/31/02, income from continuing operations was $619.9 million versus $380.7 million a year earlier. Total revenues rose 2.7% to $8.82 billion, due to higher Mortgage Banking revenues. Revenues from premiums and other considerations fell 5.8% to $3.88 billion, while fees and other revenues grew 24.4% to $1.99 billion. Net investment income slipped 2.3% to $3.30 billion.

PROSPECTS:

In February 2003, Principal Residential Mortgage, a company of PFG, entered into a definitive agreement to sell its retail mortgage lending branches to American Home Mortgage, Inc. (AHMH). AHMH will pay Principal Residential Mortgage a guaranteed profit margin on its current application pipeline, purchase the assets of the branch network, and assume related liabilities. The sale agreement follows PFG's January 2003 announcement that it would focus its retail consumer loan origination business within its Mortgage Direct operation, which originates loans across the nation via phone and online. Separately, PFG expects full-year 2003 operating earnings of between $2.25 and $2.40 per diluted share, including the effect of expensing employee stock options, estimated at $0.04 a share in 2003 and additional pension benefit expense of $0.11 a share in 2003.

ANNUAL FINANCIAL DATA:

FISCAL YEAR	TOT. REVS. ($mill.)	NET INC. ($mill.)	TOT. ASSETS ($mill.)	OPER. PROFIT %	NET PROFIT %	RET. ON EQUITY %	RET. ON ASSETS %	CURR. RATIO	EARN. PER SH. $	CASH FL. PER SH. $	TANG. BK. VAL. $	DIV PER SH. $	PRICE RANGE	AVG. P/E RATIO	AVG. YIELD %
p12/31/02	8,822.5	② 619.9							② 1.77			0.25	31.50 - 22.00	15.1	0.9
12/31/01	8,817.5	① 369.5	88,350.5	5.1	4.2	5.4	0.4	63.7	① 1.02	3.02	10.59	...	24.75 - 20.40	22.1	...
12/31/00	8,884.9	620.2	84,404.9	9.7	7.0	9.9	0.7	52.0	...	...	...	...	...	...	...
12/31/99	8,701.4	742.1	83,953.2	12.2	8.5	13.4	0.9	37.0	...	...	...	...	...	...	...
12/31/98	8,196.9	693.0	...	9.0	8.5	...	...	...	...	...	...	...	...	...	...

Statistics are as originally reported. ① Bef. acctg. chge. chrg. of $10.7 mill. ② Bef. loss fr. disc. ops. of $196.7 mill. & acctg. chge. chrg. of $280.9 mill.

OFFICERS:
J. B. Griswell, Chmn., Pres., C.E.O.
M. H. Gersie, Exec. V.P., C.F.O.
J. N. Hoffman, Sr. V.P., Sec.
INVESTOR CONTACT: Tom Graf, Investor Relations, (515) 235-9500
PRINCIPAL OFFICE: 711 High Street, Des Moines, IA 50392

TELEPHONE NUMBER: (515) 247-5111
FAX: (515) 235-1959
WEB: www.principal.com
NO. OF EMPLOYEES: 17,138 (avg.)
SHAREHOLDERS: 635,001
ANNUAL MEETING: In May
INCORPORATED: DE, 2001

INSTITUTIONAL HOLDINGS:
No. of Institutions: 297
Shares Held: 161,826,642
% Held: 48.0

INDUSTRY: Life insurance (SIC: 6311)

TRANSFER AGENT(S): Mellon Investor Services LLC, Ridgefield Park, NJ

PROCTER & GAMBLE COMPANY (THE)

EXCH.	SYM.	REC. PRICE	P/E RATIO	YLD.	MKT. CAP.	RANGE (52-WK.)	'02 Y/E PR.	DIV. ACH.
NYSE	PG	81.86 (2/28/03)	23.5	2.0%	$106.48 bill.	94.75 - 74.08	85.94	49 yrs.

INVESTMENT GRADE. PG EXPECTS EARNINGS PER SHARE TO GROW BETWEEN 12.0% AND 13.0% FOR FISCAL 2003.

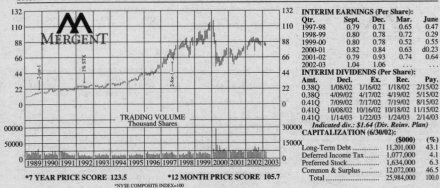

INTERIM EARNINGS (Per Share):

Qtr.	Sept.	Dec.	Mar.	June
1997-98	0.79	0.71	0.65	0.47
1998-99	0.80	0.78	0.72	0.29
1999-00	0.80	0.78	0.52	0.55
2000-01	0.82	0.84	0.63	d0.23
2001-02	0.79	0.93	0.74	0.64
2002-03	1.04	1.06	...	...

INTERIM DIVIDENDS (Per Share):

Amt.	Decl.	Ex.	Rec.	Pay.
0.38Q	1/08/02	1/16/02	1/18/02	2/15/02
0.38Q	4/09/02	4/17/02	4/19/02	5/15/02
0.41Q	7/09/02	7/17/02	7/19/02	8/15/02
0.41Q	10/08/02	10/16/02	10/18/02	11/15/02
0.41Q	1/14/03	1/22/03	1/24/03	2/14/03

Indicated div.: $1.64 (Div. Reinv. Plan)

CAPITALIZATION (6/30/02):

	($000)	(%)
Long-Term Debt	11,201,000	43.1
Deferred Income Tax	1,077,000	4.1
Preferred Stock	1,634,000	6.3
Common & Surplus	12,072,000	46.5
Total	25,984,000	100.0

*7 YEAR PRICE SCORE 123.5   *12 MONTH PRICE SCORE 105.7
*NYSE COMPOSITE INDEX=100

BUSINESS:

The Procter & Gamble Company manufactures and markets nearly 300 brands of consumer products including laundry, cleaning and personal-care products, pharmaceuticals, foods and beverages, and business and industrial products. Leading brands are: DOWNY and TIDE cleansing compounds, BOUNTY paper towels, CREST toothpastes, ALWAYS sanitary napkins, HEAD AND SHOULDERS and PANTENE PROV shampoos. Other products include VICK'S cough and cold remedies, WHISPER sanitary pads, LENOR fabric conditioner, CHARMIN toilet tissue, PAMPERS diapers, OIL OF OLAY skin products, FOLGER'S coffee, PRINGLES potato chips, ACTONEL, a post-menopausal drug, and IAMS pet food, and CLAIROL NICE 'N EASY hair coloring products. As of 1/28/03, PG had operations in over 80 countries and marketed to consumers in more than 160 countries. On 11/15/01, PG acquired the Clairol hair care business for $4.95 billion.

RECENT DEVELOPMENTS:

For the quarter ended 12/31/02, net income increased 15.0% to $1.49 billion from $1.30 billion in the equivalent 2001 quarter. Results for 2002 and 2001 included after-tax restructuring charges of $98.0 million and $146.0 million, respectively. Net sales increased 5.8% to $11.01 billion from $10.40 billion the previous year. Gross margin was 50.1% in 2002 versus 48.7% in 2001. Overall results benefited from unit volume growth of 8.0%, double-digit growth in the health and beauty care businesses and strength in the baby and family-care business.

PROSPECTS:

Going forward, the Company will continue to focus on the core categories of laundry, hair care, diapers and feminine-protection. In addition, PG will concentrate on its leading brands, large developed and key developing markets, and driving higher-growth, higher-margin businesses. For the fiscal year, sales growth is expected to be at the top-end of PG's 4.0% to 6.0% target range, and earnings per share are anticipated to range between 12.0% and 13.0%. Moreover, the Company has set capital expenditures for the fiscal year at or below 4.5% of expected sales.

ANNUAL FINANCIAL DATA:

FISCAL YEAR	TOT. REVS. ($mill.)	NET INC. ($mill.)	TOT. ASSETS ($mill.)	OPER. PROFIT %	NET PROFIT %	RET. ON EQUITY %	RET. ON ASSETS %	CURR. RATIO	EARN. PER SH. $	CASH FL. PER SH. $	TANG. BK. VAL. $	DIV. PER SH. $	PRICE RANGE	AVG. P/E RATIO	AVG. YIELD %
6/30/02	40,238.0	③ 4,352.0	40,776.0	16.6	10.8	31.8	10.7	1.0	③ 3.09	4.21	...	1.58	94.75 - 74.08	27.3	1.9
6/30/01	39,244.0	② 2,922.0	34,387.0	12.1	7.4	24.3	8.5	1.1	③ 2.07	3.61	1.55	1.46	81.72 - 55.96	33.3	2.1
6/30/00	39,951.0	③ 3,542.0	34,194.0	14.9	8.9	28.8	10.4	1.0	③ 2.47	3.94	1.35	1.34	118.38 - 52.75	34.6	1.6
6/30/99	38,125.0	③ 3,763.0	32,113.0	16.4	9.9	31.2	11.7	1.1	③ 2.59	4.01	2.62	1.21	115.63 - 82.00	38.2	1.2
6/30/98	37,154.0	3,780.0	30,966.0	16.3	10.2	30.9	12.2	1.1	2.56	3.60	2.55	1.07	94.81 - 65.13	31.2	1.3
6/30/97	35,764.0	3,415.0	27,544.0	15.3	9.5	28.3	12.4	1.4	2.43	3.60	4.59	0.95	83.44 - 51.81	27.8	1.4
6/30/96	35,284.0	3,046.0	27,730.0	13.6	8.6	26.0	11.0	1.4	2.15	3.21	4.05	0.85	55.50 - 39.69	22.2	1.8
6/30/95	33,434.0	2,645.0	28,125.0	12.5	7.9	25.0	9.4	1.3	1.86	2.84	2.99	0.75	44.75 - 30.31	20.2	2.0
6/30/94	30,296.0	2,211.0	25,535.0	11.8	7.3	25.0	8.7	1.2	1.55	2.45	2.29	0.66	32.31 - 25.63	18.7	2.3
6/30/93	30,433.0	① ② 269.0	24,935.0	1.5	0.9	3.6	1.1	1.2	① ② 0.13	1.04	1.25	0.58	29.44 - 22.63	208.1	1.2

Statistics are as originally reported. Adj. for stk. splits: 2-for-1, 9/97. ① Bef. acctg. change chrg. $925.0 mill. ② Incl. non-recurr. chrg. $2.7 mill. ③ Incl. after-tax chrg. for organization 2005, $706.0 mill., 6/02; $1.48 billion, 6/01; $688.0 mill., 6/00; $385.0 mill., 6/99

OFFICERS:
A. G. Lafley, Chmn., Pres., C.E.O.
B. Byrnes, Vice-Chmn.
R. K. Clark, Vice-Chmn.

INVESTOR CONTACT: Shareholder Services, (513) 983-3034

PRINCIPAL OFFICE: One Procter & Gamble Plaza, Cincinnati, OH 45202

TELEPHONE NUMBER: (513) 983-1100
FAX: (513) 983-2062
WEB: www.pg.com

NO. OF EMPLOYEES: 102,000 (approx.)

SHAREHOLDERS: 1,004,000 (approx.)

ANNUAL MEETING: In Oct.

INCORPORATED: OH, May, 1905

INSTITUTIONAL HOLDINGS:
No. of Institutions: 1,106
Shares Held: 710,421,253
% Held: 54.7

INDUSTRY: Soap and other detergents (SIC: 2841)

TRANSFER AGENT(S): The Procter and Gamble Company, Cincinnati, OH

PROGRESS ENERGY, INC.

EXCH.	SYM.	REC. PRICE	P/E RATIO	YLD.	MKT. CAP.	RANGE (52-WK.)	'02 Y/E PR.	DIV. ACH.
NYSE	PGN	38.90 (2/28/03)	15.3	5.8%	$8.51 bill.	52.60 - 32.84	43.35	14 yrs.

UPPER MEDIUM GRADE. THE COMPANY REBRANDED CAROLINA POWER & LIGHT AND FLORIDA POWER CORPORATION UNDER THE PROGRESS NAME.

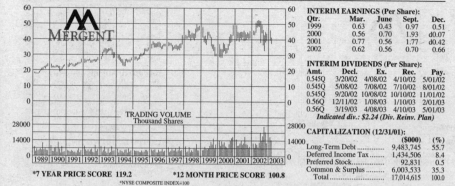

*7 YEAR PRICE SCORE 119.2   ***12 MONTH PRICE SCORE 100.8**
*NYSE COMPOSITE INDEX=100

INTERIM EARNINGS (Per Share):

Qtr.	Mar.	June	Sept.	Dec.
1999	0.63	0.43	0.97	0.51
2000	0.56	0.70	1.93	d0.07
2001	0.77	0.56	1.77	d0.42
2002	0.62	0.56	0.70	0.66

INTERIM DIVIDENDS (Per Share):

Amt.	Decl.	Ex.	Rec.	Pay.
0.545Q	3/20/02	4/08/02	4/10/02	5/01/02
0.545Q	5/08/02	7/08/02	7/10/02	8/01/02
0.545Q	9/20/02	10/08/02	10/10/02	11/01/02
0.56Q	12/11/02	1/08/03	1/10/03	2/01/03
0.56Q	3/19/03	4/08/03	4/10/03	5/01/03

Indicated div.: $2.24 (Div. Reinv. Plan)

CAPITALIZATION (12/31/01):

	($000)	(%)
Long-Term Debt	9,483,745	55.7
Deferred Income Tax	1,434,506	8.4
Preferred Stock	92,831	0.5
Common & Surplus	6,003,533	35.3
Total	17,014,615	100.0

BUSINESS:

Progress Energy, Inc. (formerly CP&L Energy, Inc.) is a full-service utility holding company with more than 21,800 megawatts of generating capacity. PGN's diverse portfolio includes two major electric utility companies, Progress Energy Carolinas, Inc. and Progress Energy Florida, Inc., as well as Progress Telecommunications Corporation, Progress Rail Services Corporation and Progress Ventures, Inc.

Progress Ventures manages fuel extraction, manufacturing and delivery; merchant generation; and energy marketing and trading. PGN's electric utilities serve 2.7 million customers in North Carolina, South Carolina and Florida. On 11/30/00, the Company acquired Progress Energy Florida for approximately $5.40 billion.

RECENT DEVELOPMENTS:

For the year ended 12/31/02, income from continuing operations increased 2.2% to $552.2 million compared with $540.4 million the previous year. Results for 2002 and 2001 included impairment of assets of $305.0 million and $44.8 million, and impairment on investments of $25.0 million and $164.2 million, respectively. Earnings excluded a loss of $23.8 million in 2002 and a gain of $1.2 million in

2001 from discontinued operations. Total operating revenues decreased 1.7% to $8.00 billion from $8.14 billion a year earlier. Revenues from diversified businesses fell 11.3% to $1.40 billion, while electric revenues inched up 0.7% to $6.60 billion. Operating income declined 18.3% to $1.00 billion from $1.23 billion in the prior year.

PROSPECTS:

On 1/8/03, PGN announced it will reduce the scope of its marketing and trading operations and power plant operations in response to the soft wholesale energy market. As a result, PGN will eliminate approximately 50 jobs at Progress Ventures. Separately, the previously announced agreement to sell North Carolina Natural Gas to Piedmont

Natural Gas remains on schedule to close by summer 2003. Additionally, the Company changed the names of Carolina Power & Light to Progress Energy Carolinas, Inc. and Florida Power Corporation to Progress Energy Florida, Inc. The total re-brand of the two electric utilities will be completed in phases over two years.

ANNUAL FINANCIAL DATA:

FISCAL YEAR	TOT. REVS. ($mill.)	NET INC. ($mill.)	TOT. ASSETS ($mill.)	OPER. PROFIT %	NET PROFIT %	NET INC./ NET PROP. %	NET INC./ TOT. CAP. %	RET. ON EQUITY %	ACCUM. DEPR./ GROSS PROP. %	EARN. PER SH.$	TANG. BK. VAL.$	DIV. PER SH.$	DIV. PAYOUT %	PRICE RANGE	AVG. P/E RATIO	AVG. YIELD %
p12/31/02	8,004.7	⑤552.2	21,845.1							⑤2.53		2.18	86.2	52.60 - 32.84	16.9	5.1
12/31/01	8,461.5	④541.6	20,739.8	14.7	6.4	5.0	3.2	8.9	48.1	④2.64	10.58	2.12	80.3	49.25 - 38.78	16.7	4.8
12/31/00	4,118.9	③478.4	20,091.0	17.5	11.6	4.6	3.6	8.7	47.3	③3.03	8.60	2.06	68.0	49.38 - 28.25	12.0	4.7
12/31/99	3,357.6	②382.3	9,494.0	25.0	11.4	5.7	8.1	643.8	42.4	②2.55	...	2.00	78.4	47.88 - 29.25	15.1	5.3
12/31/98	3,130.0	399.2	8,347.4	28.7	12.8	6.3	5.5	13.3	41.7	2.75	19.49	1.94	70.5	49.63 - 39.19	16.1	5.2
12/31/97	3,024.1	388.3	8,220.4	26.3	12.8	6.2	5.5	13.5	39.9	2.66	18.63	1.88	70.7	42.69 - 32.75	14.2	4.4
12/31/96	2,995.7	391.3	8,369.2	26.2	13.1	6.1	5.4	13.8	37.2	2.66	17.77	1.82	68.4	38.75 - 33.75	13.6	5.0
12/31/95	3,006.6	372.6	8,227.1	26.3	12.4	5.9	5.3	13.7	35.6	2.48	16.93	1.76	71.0	34.63 - 26.13	12.2	5.0
12/31/94	2,876.6	①313.2	8,211.2	22.3	10.9	4.9	4.5	11.5	33.5	①2.03	16.54	1.70	83.7	30.00 - 22.50	12.9	5.8
12/31/93	2,895.4	346.5	8,194.0	22.7	12.0	5.4	5.0	12.5	31.1	2.10	16.38	1.64	78.1	34.63 - 27.00	14.7	5.5

Statistics are as originally reported. Adj. for stk. split: 2-for-1, 2/93. ① Incl. non-recurr. chrg. $20.6 mill. ② Incl. one-time chrg. of $29.0 mill. related to storm damage. ③ Incl. after-tax nonrecurr. chrg. of $118.3 mill. & an after-tax gain of $121.1 mill. fr. sale of an investment. ④ Incl. non-recurr. impair. chrg. of $209.0 mill. ⑤ Incl. asset impair. chrg. of $305.0 mill. & invest. impair. chrg. of $25.0 mill.; bef. a loss of $25.8 mill. from disc. ops.

OFFICERS:
W. Cavanaugh III, Chmn., C.E.O.
R. B. McGehee, Pres., C.O.O.
P. M. Scott III, Exec. V.P., C.F.O.

INVESTOR CONTACT: Investor Relations, (800) 662-7232

PRINCIPAL OFFICE: 410 South Wilmington Street, Raleigh, NC 27601-1748

TELEPHONE NUMBER: (919) 546-6111
FAX: (919) 546-7678
WEB: www.progress-energy.com
NO. OF EMPLOYEES: 16,200
SHAREHOLDERS: 218,727,139
ANNUAL MEETING: In May
INCORPORATED: NC, April, 1926

INSTITUTIONAL HOLDINGS:
No. of Institutions: 381
Shares Held: 121,497,228
% Held: 51.2

INDUSTRY: Electric services (SIC: 4911)

TRANSFER AGENT(S): EquiServe Trust Company, N.A., Providence, RI

PROGRESSIVE CORPORATION (THE)

EXCH.	SYM.	REC. PRICE	P/E RATIO	YLD.	MKT. CAP.	RANGE (52-WK.)	'02 Y/E PR.	DIV. ACH.
NYSE	PGR	52.01 (2/28/03)	17.5	0.2%	$11.45 bill.	60.49 - 44.75	49.63	33 yrs.

UPPER MEDIUM GRADE. RESULTS ARE BENEFITING FROM HIGHER PREMIUMS.

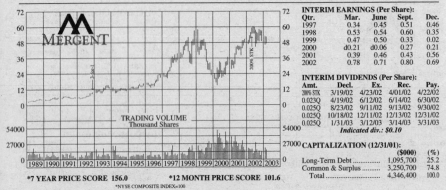

*7 YEAR PRICE SCORE 156.0   ***12 MONTH PRICE SCORE 101.6**

NYSE COMPOSITE INDEX=100

INTERIM EARNINGS (Per Share):

Qtr.	Mar.	June	Sept.	Dec.
1997	0.34	0.45	0.51	0.46
1998	0.53	0.54	0.60	0.35
1999	0.47	0.50	0.33	0.02
2000	d0.21	d0.06	0.27	0.21
2001	0.39	0.46	0.43	0.56
2002	0.78	0.71	0.80	0.69

INTERIM DIVIDENDS (Per Share):

Amt.	Decl.	Ex.	Rec.	Pay.
200% STK	3/19/02	4/23/02	4/01/02	4/22/02
0.023Q	4/19/02	6/12/02	6/14/02	6/30/02
0.025Q	8/23/02	9/11/02	9/13/02	9/30/02
0.025Q	10/18/02	12/11/02	12/13/02	12/31/02
0.025Q	1/31/03	3/12/03	3/14/03	3/31/03

Indicated div.: $0.10

CAPITALIZATION (12/31/01):

	($000)	(%)
Long-Term Debt	1,095,700	25.2
Common & Surplus	3,250,700	74.8
Total	4,346,400	100.0

BUSINESS:

The Progressive Corporation, through its subsidiaries and affiliates, provides personal automobile insurance and other specialty property-casualty insurance and related services throughout the United States. PGR's personal lines business units write insurance for private passenger automobiles and recreation vehicles. PGR's commercial auto business unit writes insurance for automobiles and trucks owned by small businesses for primary liability, physical damage and other auto-related insurance coverages. PGR's

other businesses primarily include writing lenders' collateral protection and directors' and officers' liability insurance and providing insurance-related services, primarily processing business for Commercial Auto Insurance Procedures, which are state supervised plans serving the involuntary market. The Company ranks fourth in the nation for auto insurance based on premiums written, offering its products by phone, on-line and through more than 30,000 independent insurance agencies.

RECENT DEVELOPMENTS:

For the year ended 12/31/02, net income climbed 62.2% to $667.3 million from $411.4 million in the previous year. Total revenues grew 24.1% to $9.29 billion from $7.49 billion in the prior year. Revenues for 2002 and 2001 included net realized security losses of $78.6 million and $111.9 million respectively. Net premiums written

increased 30.2% to $9.45 billion from $7.26 billion in 2001. Premiums earned grew 24.0% to $8.88 billion versus $7.16 billion a year earlier. Investment income rose 10.1% to $455.2 million. Losses and loss adjustment expenses jumped 19.7% to $6.30 billion from $5.26 billion the year before.

PROSPECTS:

Looking ahead, the Company is well positioned for growth based on a number of initiatives, including recent aggressive premium rate increases, shortened policy terms, and reduced expense levels. For the year, the combined loss and expense ratio, a key measurement of underwriting profit-

ability, improved to 92.4% in 2002 compared with 95.2% for 2001. Meanwhile, the Company should continue to benefit from its multiple channel distribution platform and the utilization of underwriting and claims handling technology to improve its pricing and underwriting capabilities.

ANNUAL FINANCIAL DATA:

FISCAL YEAR	PREM. INC. ($mill.)	TOT. REVS. ($mill.)	NET INC. ($mill.)	TOT. ASSETS ($mill.)	TOT. INVST. ($mill.)	RET. ON REVS. %	RET. ON EQUITY %	RET. ON ASSETS %	EARN. PER SH. $	TANG. BK. VAL. $	AVG. YIELD %	DIV. PER SH. $	PRICE RANGE	AVG. P/E RATIO
p12/31/02	8,883.5	9,294.4	667.3						2.99		0.2	0.10	60.49 - 44.75	17.6
12/31/01	7,161.8	7,488.2	411.4	11,122.4	8,226.3	5.5	12.7	3.7	1.83	13.32	0.2	0.09	50.59 - 27.37	21.3
12/31/00	6,348.4	6,771.0	①46.1	10,051.6	6,983.3	0.7	1.6	0.5	①0.21	11.61	0.3	0.09	37.00 - 15.00	125.5
12/31/99	5,683.6	6,124.2	295.2	9,704.7	6,427.7	4.8	10.7	3.0	1.32	10.99	0.2	0.09	58.08 - 22.83	30.6
12/31/98	4,948.0	5,292.4	456.7	8,463.1	5,674.3	8.6	17.9	5.4	2.04	10.38	0.2	0.08	57.33 - 31.33	21.8
12/31/97	4,189.5	4,608.2	400.0	7,559.6	5,270.4	8.7	18.7	5.3	1.77	8.65	0.3	0.08	39.75 - 20.50	17.0
12/31/96	3,199.3	3,478.4	313.7	6,183.9	4,450.6	9.0	18.7	5.1	1.38	6.88	0.4	0.08	24.08 - 13.46	13.6
12/31/95	2,727.2	3,011.9	250.5	5,352.5	3,768.0	8.3	17.0	4.7	1.09	5.60	0.5	0.07	16.50 - 11.58	12.9
12/31/94	2,191.1	2,415.3	274.3	4,675.1	3,180.0	11.4	23.8	5.9	1.20	4.23	0.6	0.07	13.50 - 9.25	9.5
12/31/93	1,668.7	1,954.8	275.3	4,011.3	2,786.4	14.1	27.6	6.9	1.20	3.63	0.5	0.07	15.37 - 9.17	10.2

Statistics are as originally reported. Adj. for stk. split: 200% div., 4/02 ① Incl. non-recurr. chrg. $4.2 mill.

OFFICERS:
P. B. Lewis, Chmn.
G. M. Renwick, Pres., C.E.O.
W. T. Forrester, C.F.O., Treas.
INVESTOR CONTACT: Investor Relations, (440) 446-2851
PRINCIPAL OFFICE: 6300 Wilson Mills Road, Mayfield Village, OH 44143

TELEPHONE NUMBER: (440) 461-5000
FAX: (440) 446-7168
WEB: www.progressive.com
NO. OF EMPLOYEES: 22,000 (approx.)
SHAREHOLDERS: 3,586
ANNUAL MEETING: In April
INCORPORATED: OH, Feb., 1965

INSTITUTIONAL HOLDINGS:
No. of Institutions: 324
Shares Held: 151,278,017
% Held: 69.5
INDUSTRY: Fire, marine, and casualty insurance (SIC: 6331)
TRANSFER AGENT(S): National City Bank, Cleveland, OH

PROLOGIS

EXCH.	SYM.	REC. PRICE	P/E RATIO	YLD.	MKT. CAP.	RANGE (52-WK.)	'02 Y/E PR.
NYSE	PLD	24.78 (2/28/03)	20.7	5.7%	$4.36 bill.	26.00 - 21.70	25.15

MEDIUM GRADE. RESULTS BENEFITED FROM BUILD-TO-SUIT DEMAND AND NETWORK RECONFIGURATION ACTIVITY.

INTERIM EARNINGS (Per Share):

Qtr.	Mar.	June	Sept.	Dec.
1998	0.23	0.19	d0.07	0.16
1999	0.20	0.80	0.44	d0.62
2000	0.28	0.12	0.29	0.27
2001	0.25	0.26	0.28	d0.27
2002	0.31	0.31	0.14	0.44

INTERIM DIVIDENDS (Per Share):

Amt.	Decl.	Ex.	Rec.	Pay.
0.345Q	5/01/01	5/10/01	5/14/01	5/25/01
0.345Q	8/01/01	8/08/01	8/10/01	8/24/01
0.345Q	11/01/01	11/07/01	11/12/01	11/23/01
0.355Q	12/14/01	2/12/02	2/14/02	2/28/02
0.355Q	5/01/02	5/13/02	5/15/02	5/29/02

Indicated div.: $1.42 (Div. Reinv. Plan)

CAPITALIZATION (12/31/01):

	($000)	(%)
Long-Term Debt	2,202,465	44.7
Minority Interest	45,639	0.9
Preferred Stock	400,000	8.1
Common & Surplus	2,275,999	46.2
Total	4,924,103	100.0

*7 YEAR PRICE SCORE 117.5   *12 MONTH PRICE SCORE 109.5

*NYSE COMPOSITE INDEX=100

BUSINESS:

ProLogis (formerly ProLogis Trust) is a global provider of integrated distribution facilities and services with 226.6 million square feet in 1,760 distribution facilities, which were owned, operated or under development in 70 markets in North America, Europe and Japan. The Property Operations segment (75.7% of 2002 total income) is engaged in long-term ownership, management and leasing of industrial distribution facilities. The Corporate Distribution Facilities Services segment (CDFS) (23.3%) is engaged in the development of industrial distribution facilities to be disposed of to unaffiliated customers or entities in which PLD has an ownership interest or for a development fee for unaffiliated customers. During 2002, PLD sold its North American temperature-controlled logistics business (1.0%).

RECENT DEVELOPMENTS:

For the year ended 12/31/02, net income surged 94.2% to $248.9 million compared with $128.1 million in 2001. Results for 2002 and 2001 included gains of $6.6 million and $10.0 million from the gain on the disposition of non-CDFS assets. Total revenues rose 29.0% to $675.0 million from $523.0 million the year before. Rental expense, net of recoveries, amounted to $32.6 million from $28.7 million in 2001. During 2002, PLD reported a record $956.0 million in development starts, reflecting solid build-to-suit demand and network reconfiguration activity.

PROSPECTS:

On 2/26/03, the Company announced that the ProLogis European Properties Fund has entered into a sale-lease back agreement with logistics company Geodis Teisa for a 123,677 square foot distribution facility at Centro de Trasportes Coslada in Madrid, Spain. Geodis Teisa uses the location as its main parcel sorting and distribution facility for the greater Madrid area. Meanwhile, the success of PLD's CDFS business continues to reflect its ability to capitalize on distribution inefficiencies, and continuing demand from build-to-suit facilities across all of its markets.

ANNUAL FINANCIAL DATA:

FISCAL YEAR	TOT. INC. ($mill.)	NET INC. ($mill.)	TOT. ASSETS ($mill.)	NET INC. + DEPR./ ASSETS %	RET. ON EQUITY %	RET. ON ASSETS %	EARN. PER SH. $	TANG. BK. VAL. $	DIV. PER SH. $	DIV. PAYOUT %	PRICE RANGE	AVG. P/E RATIO	AVG. YIELD %
p12/31/02	675.0	⑤ 248.9	5,923.5				⑤ 1.20		1.42	118.3	26.00 - 20.96	19.6	6.0
12/31/01	519.4	④ 128.1	5,603.9	4.8	4.8	2.3	④ 0.52	12.94	1.38	265.3	23.30 - 19.35	41.0	6.5
12/31/00	625.6	214.5	5,946.3	6.2	7.3	3.6	0.96	13.53	1.34	139.6	24.69 - 17.56	22.0	6.3
12/31/99	550.6	① 182.3	5,848.0	5.7	6.2	3.1	① 0.82	13.86	1.30	158.5	22.19 - 16.75	23.7	6.7
12/31/98	372.8	② 111.3	4,330.7	4.9	4.9	2.6	② 0.51	12.83	1.24	243.1	26.50 - 19.75	45.3	5.4
12/31/97	302.5	③ 39.7	3,034.0	3.8	2.0	1.3	③ 0.04	13.14	1.07	N.M.	25.50 - 18.88	553.3	4.8
12/31/96	233.5	79.4	2,462.3	5.7	5.0	3.2	0.63	12.42	1.01	160.3	22.50 - 16.50	30.9	5.2
12/31/95	158.5	48.7	1,834.0	4.8	4.3	2.7	0.61	12.30	0.94	153.3	17.75 - 14.50	26.4	5.8
12/31/94	71.7	25.1	1,194.9	3.6	3.2	2.1	0.57	12.04	0.64	111.8	18.25 - 13.50	27.8	4.0
12/31/93	10.3	4.4	401.9	1.7	2.1	1.1	0.47	10.60	...	...	... - ...	...	...

Statistics are as originally reported. ① Bef. acctg. chrg. of $1.4 mill., but incl. int. hedge expend. of $945,000. ② Incl. int. hedge expend. of $26.1 mill. ③ Incl. a chrg. of $75.4 mill. for acq. of mgmt. companies. ④ Incl. writedwn of oper. assets & other impairment chrgs. of $53.3 mill. for the North American temperature-controlled operations (CSI) and $35.1 for Frigoscandia and nonrecurr. chrgs. of $5.8 mill. ⑤ Incl. gains of $6.6 on the disposition of non-CDFS assets.

OFFICERS:
K. D. Brooksher, Chmn., C.E.O.
I. F. Lyons, III, Vice-Chmn., C.I.O.
W. C. Rakowich, C.F.O.
M. G. Keiser, Jr., Sr. V.P., Treas.

INVESTOR CONTACT: Investor Relations, (303) 375-9292

PRINCIPAL OFFICE: 14100 East 35th Place, Aurora, CO 80011

TELEPHONE NUMBER: (303) 375-9292
FAX: (303) 375-8581
WEB: www.prologis.com

NO. OF EMPLOYEES: 650 (approx.)

SHAREHOLDERS: 10,380 (approx.)

ANNUAL MEETING: In June

INCORPORATED: MD, Mar., 1993

INSTITUTIONAL HOLDINGS:
No. of Institutions: 225
Shares Held: 149,369,247
% Held: 83.8

INDUSTRY: Real estate agents and managers (SIC: 6531)

TRANSFER AGENT(S): Boston EquiServe, Boston, MA

PROTECTIVE LIFE CORPORATION

EXCH.	SYM.	REC. PRICE	P/E RATIO	YLD.	MKT. CAP.	RANGE (52-WK.)	'02 Y/E PR.	DIV. ACH.
NYSE	PL	27.12 (2/28/03)	10.5	2.2%	$1.86 bill.	33.90 - 25.70	27.52	13 yrs.

MEDIUM GRADE. THE STRONG FINISH IN 2002 BODES WELL FOR IMPROVING OVERALL PERFORMANCE AND GROWTH IN 2003 AND BEYOND.

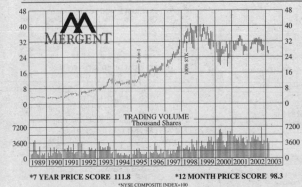

TRADING VOLUME
Thousand Shares

*7 YEAR PRICE SCORE 111.8 ***12 MONTH PRICE SCORE 98.3**

*NYSE COMPOSITE INDEX=100

INTERIM EARNINGS (Per Share):

Qtr.	Mar.	June	Sept.	Dec.
1998	0.47	0.52	0.52	0.53
1999	0.56	0.54	0.57	0.62
2000	0.65	0.59	0.52	0.56
2001	0.67	0.38	0.61	0.38
2002	0.59	0.77	0.73	0.50

INTERIM DIVIDENDS (Per Share):

Amt.	Decl.	Ex.	Rec.	Pay.
0.14Q	2/04/02	2/13/02	2/15/02	3/01/02
0.15Q	5/06/02	5/15/02	5/17/02	5/31/02
0.15Q	8/12/02	8/21/02	8/23/02	9/03/02
0.15Q	11/04/02	11/13/02	11/15/02	12/02/02
0.15Q	2/03/03	2/12/03	2/14/03	2/28/03

Indicated div.: $0.60 (Div. Reinv. Plan)

CAPITALIZATION (12/31/01):

	($000)	(%)
Long-Term Debt	376,211	19.8
Deferred Income Tax	127,230	6.7
Common & Surplus	1,400,144	73.6
Total	1,903,585	100.0

BUSINESS:

Protective Life Corporation is a holding company that provides financial services through the production, distribution and administration of insurance and investment products. The Company operates several divisions whose strategic focuses can be grouped into three segments: life insurance, specialty insurance products and retirement savings and investment products. The life insurance segment (86.4% of 2002 pre-tax operating income) includes the individual life, West Coast and acquisitions divisions. The retirement savings and the investment products segment (22.7%) includes the Stable Value products division, which markets guaranteed investment contracts, and investment products division, which sells variable annuities. The specialty insurance products segment (-9.1%) includes the financial institutions divisions, which markets credit life and disability insurance products.

RECENT DEVELOPMENTS:

For the year ended 12/31/02, PL reported income of $178.8 million, before an extraordinary loss of $1.4 million, compared with income of $141.1 million, before an accounting change charge of $7.6 million and a loss from discontinued operations of $30.5 million, the previous year. Results for 2002 and 2001 included realized gains of $2.7 million and realized losses of $13.8 million, respectively. Life insurance sales jumped 37.1% to $224.1 million from $163.5 million, and sales from retirement savings and investment products rose 5.5% to $2.11 billion from $2.00 billion in the prior year. Sales from specialty insurance products decreased 6.0% to $490.3 million from $521.5 million the year before.

PROSPECTS:

The Company is benefiting from strong performances in its core life insurance, acquisitions, and stable value lines of business. In addition, the Company is enjoying the solid performance in its investment portfolios. Meanwhile, the Company continues to take aggressive action in the asset protection segment to improve results. The Company believes that the reserve strengthening, combining with the exit from ancillary lines of business and focus on expense and claims management, should allow the segment to contribute to earnings in 2003.

ANNUAL FINANCIAL DATA:

FISCAL YEAR	PREM. INC. ($mill.)	NET INVST. INC. ($mill.)	TOT. REVS. ($mill.)	NET INC. ($mill.)	TOT. ASSETS ($mill.)	TOT. INVST. ($mill.)	RET. ON REVS. %	RET. ON EQUITY %	RET. ON ASSETS %	EARN. PER SH. $	TANG. BK. VAL. $	AVG. YIELD %	DIV. PER SH. $	PRICE RANGE	AVG. P/E RATIO
p12/31/02			③ 178.8							③ 2.50		2.0	0.59	33.90 - 26.00	12.0
12/31/01	618.7	884.0	1,614.2	② 141.1	19,718.8	13,317.7	8.7	10.1	0.7	② 2.01	19.72	1.8	0.55	35.00 - 24.80	14.9
12/31/00	833.7	737.3	1,734.0	153.5	15,145.6	10,241.4	8.9	13.8	1.0	2.32	13.38	2.0	0.51	32.25 - 19.00	11.0
12/31/99	761.3	676.4	1,533.9	① 153.1	12,994.2	8,722.0	10.0	17.7	1.2	① 2.32	10.03	1.4	0.47	40.75 - 27.81	14.8
12/31/98	662.8	636.4	1,366.4	130.8	11,989.5	8,606.6	9.6	13.9	1.1	2.04	11.51	1.2	0.43	41.25 - 28.00	17.0
12/31/97	522.3	591.4	1,147.3	112.0	10,511.6	8,049.4	9.8	14.8	1.1	1.78	12.30	1.5	0.39	32.75 - 18.81	14.5
12/31/96	494.2	517.5	1,038.0	89.0	8,263.2	6,552.2	8.6	14.5	1.1	1.47	9.99	2.0	0.35	20.81 - 15.06	12.2
12/31/95	432.6	475.9	921.9	76.7	7,231.3	6,025.1	8.3	14.6	1.1	1.34	9.15	2.4	0.31	15.69 - 10.69	9.8
12/31/94	402.8	417.8	848.4	70.4	6,130.3	5,301.9	8.3	26.0	1.1	1.28	4.93	2.6	0.28	12.16 - 9.22	8.3
12/31/93	370.8	362.1	759.6	56.6	5,316.0	4,766.7	7.4	15.7	1.1	1.04	6.59	2.5	0.25	13.09 - 6.88	9.6

Statistics are as originally reported. Adj. for 100% stk. split, 4/98, 2-for-1, 6/95. ① Bef. extraord. loss of $1.8 mill. ② Bef. acctg. change chrg. $7.6 mill. & loss fr. disc. opers. of $30.5 mill. ③ Bef. extraord. loss of $1.4 mill. & incl. realized invest. gain of $2.7 mill.

OFFICERS:
J. D. Johns, Chmn., Pres., C.E.O.
A. Ritchie, Exec. V.P., C.F.O.

INVESTOR CONTACT: Allen Ritchie, Exec. V.P., C.F.O., (205) 868-3500

PRINCIPAL OFFICE: 2801 Highway 280 South, Birmingham, 35223

TELEPHONE NUMBER: (205) 879-9230
FAX: (205) 868-3541
WEB: www.protective.com
NO. OF EMPLOYEES: 2,524 (approx.)
SHAREHOLDERS: 2,300 (approx.)
ANNUAL MEETING: In May
INCORPORATED: DE, Feb., 1981

INSTITUTIONAL HOLDINGS:
No. of Institutions: 230
Shares Held: 52,344,206
% Held: 76.2

INDUSTRY: Life insurance (SIC: 6311)

TRANSFER AGENT(S): Bank of New York, New York, NY

PROVIDIAN FINANCIAL CORP.

EXCH.	SYM.	REC. PRICE	P/E RATIO	YLD.	MKT. CAP.	RANGE (52-WK.)	'02 Y/E PR.
NYSE	PVN	6.10 (2/28/03)	11.7	...	$1.74 bill.	8.49 - 2.50	6.49

SPECULATIVE GRADE. THE COMPANY IS MAKING SOLID PROGRESS TOWARDS IMPROVED FINANCIAL STABILITY.

*7 YEAR PRICE SCORE 22.8   *12 MONTH PRICE SCORE 119.9
*NYSE COMPOSITE INDEX=100

INTERIM EARNINGS (Per Share):

Qtr.	Mar.	June	Sept.	Dec.
1997	0.16	0.16	0.17	0.19
1998	0.20	0.22	0.29	0.33
1999	0.39	0.44	0.52	0.55
2000	0.60	0.22	0.68	0.73
2001	0.80	0.82	0.20	d1.39
2002	0.02	0.31	0.15	0.04

INTERIM DIVIDENDS (Per Share):

Amt.	Decl.	Ex.	Rec.	Pay.
0.03Q	5/09/01	5/30/01	6/01/01	6/15/01
0.03Q	8/08/01	8/29/01	9/03/01	9/17/01
	Dividend payment suspended.			

CAPITALIZATION (12/31/01):

	($000)	(%)
Total Deposits	15,318,165	84.2
Long-Term Debt	959,281	5.3
Common & Surplus	1,907,511	10.5
Total	18,184,957	100.0

BUSINESS:

Providian Financial Corp. is a provider of lending and deposit products to customers throughout the United States. PVN serves a broad, diversified market with its loan products, which include credit cards, home equity loans, secured cards and membership services. The Company's lending and deposit-taking activities are conducted primarily through Providian National Bank (PNB) and Providian Bank (PB). Providian Bankcorp Services performs a variety of servicing activities in support of PNB, PB and other affiliates. PVN, formerly Providian Bancorp, was spun off from Providian Corp. in June, 1997. As of 12/31/02, the Company had more than $19.60 billion in managed receivables and more than 12.0 million customers.

RECENT DEVELOPMENTS:

For the year ended 12/31/02, income was $151.0 million, before income from discontinued operations of $67.2 million, versus income of $141.4 million, before a loss from discontinued operations of $118.3 million, an extraordinary gain of $13.9 million and an accounting change benefit of $1.8 million, the previous year. Total interest income declined 34.6% to $1.69 billion. Net interest income slid 44.4% to $919.3 million from $1.65 billion a year earlier. Provision for credit losses amounted to $1.29 billion, down 35.9% from $2.01 billion in 2001. Total non-interest income decreased 19.1% to $2.38 billion. Total non-interest expense dropped 22.9% to $1.81 billion.

PROSPECTS:

PVN successfully completed several key financial objectives in 2002, including the sale of more than $10.00 billion in managed loans receivable. Moreover, PVN strengthened the capitalization of its banking subsidiaries, accessed the capital markets for over $1.80 billion in new securitization funding and built a stronger liquidity position, all while reducing deposits by $2.60 billion. Going forward, while earnings could come under greater pressure in the near-term as credit costs for more established accounts increase, the actions PVN has taken over the past year should provide a solid foundation for long-term stability.

ANNUAL FINANCIAL DATA:

FISCAL YEAR	NET INT. INC. ($mill.)	NON-INT. INC. ($mill.)	NET INC. ($mill.)	TOT. LOANS ($mill.)	TOT. ASSETS ($mill.)	TOT. DEP. ($mill.)	RET. ON EQUITY %	RET. ON ASSETS %	EQUITY/ ASSETS %	EARN. PER SH.$	TANG. BK. VAL.$	DIV. PER SH.$	PRICE RANGE	AVG. P/E RATIO
p12/31/02	919.3		② 151.0							② 0.52		...	8.49 - 2.50	10.6
12/31/01	1,653.4	2,942.2	① 141.4	11,559.1	19,938.2	15,318.2	7.4	0.7	9.6	① 0.49	6.70	0.09	64.06 - 2.00	67.4
12/31/00	1,824.8	3,248.3	651.8	13,770.2	18,055.3	13,113.4	32.1	3.6	11.3	2.23	7.11	0.10	67.00 - 29.06	21.5
12/31/99	1,175.2	2,412.5	550.3	11,610.0	14,340.9	10,538.1	41.3	3.8	9.3	1.89	4.72	0.10	69.00 - 34.75	27.4
12/31/98	595.3	1,266.2	296.4	5,741.1	7,231.2	4,672.3	36.9	4.1	11.1	1.02	2.83	0.07	37.84 - 14.19	25.5
12/31/97	399.4	634.6	191.5	2,815.4	4,449.4	3,212.8	32.2	4.3	13.4	0.67	2.09	0.03	20.21 - 9.71	22.4
12/31/96	405.6	412.0	159.8	2,956.3	4,326.7	3,390.1	33.1	3.7	11.2	0.57	.г.	...	18.46 - 12.71	27.3
12/31/95	321.1	335.8	135.5	3,096.5	3,611.1	2,157.8	38.8	3.8	9.7	0.47	...	...	14.29 - 10.29	26.1
12/31/94	242.1	269.3	110.1	...	...	...	...	...	...	0.37	...	...	12.71 - 9.54	30.1

Statistics are as originally reported. Adj. for stk. split: 2-for-1, 11/00; 3-for-2, 12/98. Per share figures prior to 1997 are pro forma. ① Excl. extraord. gain $13.9 mill., discontin. loss of $118.3 mill. & acctg. credit of $1.8 mill. ② Bef. loss fr. disc. opers. of $67.2 mill.

OFFICERS:
J. Saunders, Chmn., Pres., C.E.O.
A. Vuoto, Vice-Chmn., C.F.O.
E. Richey, Vice-Chmn., Gen. Couns., Sec.

INVESTOR CONTACT: Investor Relations,
(415) 278-4492

PRINCIPAL OFFICE: 201 Mission Street,
28th Floor, San Francisco, CA 94105

TELEPHONE NUMBER: (415) 543-0404
FAX: (415) 278-6028
WEB: www.providian.com

NO. OF EMPLOYEES: 6,261

SHAREHOLDERS: 9,331 (approx.)

ANNUAL MEETING: In May

INCORPORATED: DE, 1984

INSTITUTIONAL HOLDINGS:
No. of Institutions: 299
Shares Held: 191,104,581
% Held: 66.1

INDUSTRY: Short-term business credit (SIC: 6153)

REGISTRAR(S): EquiServe Trust Company, N.A., Jersey City, NJ

PRUDENTIAL FINANCIAL, INC.

EXCH.	SYM.	REC. PRICE	P/E RATIO	YLD.	MKT. CAP.	RANGE (52-WK.)	'02 Y/E PR.
NYSE	PRU	30.03 (2/28/03)	24.0	1.3%	$17.59 bill.	36.00 - 25.25	31.74

MEDIUM GRADE. THE COMPANY AND WACHOVIA CORP. ANNOUNCED THAT THEY ARE COMBINING RETAIL BROKERAGE OPERATIONS.

TRADING VOLUME
Thousand Shares

7 YEAR PRICE SCORE N/A   *12 MONTH PRICE SCORE 110.0*

NYSE COMPOSITE INDEX=100

INTERIM EARNINGS (Per Share):

① Qtr.	Mar.	June	Sept.	Dec.
2001	...	...	...	0.07
2002	0.46	0.19	0.70	d0.10

INTERIM DIVIDENDS (Per Share):

Amt.	Decl.	Ex.	Rec.	Pay.
0.40A	11/12/02	11/21/02	11/25/02	12/18/02

Indicated div.: $0.40

CAPITALIZATION (12/31/01):

	($000)	(%)
Long-Term Debt	5,304,000	20.6
Common & Surplus	20,453,000	79.4
Total	25,757,000	100.0

BUSINESS:

Prudential Financial, Inc. was formed through the conversion of The Prudential Insurance Company of America (TPICA) from a mutual life insurance company, effective 12/18/01. PRU, with $555.60 billion in total assets under management and administration as of 12/31/02, serves individual and institutional customers worldwide. PRU offers a variety of products and services, including life insurance, property and casualty insurance, mutual funds, annuities, pension and retirement related services and administration, asset management, securities brokerage, banking and trust services, real estate brokerage franchises and relocation services. PRU conducts its principal businesses through three divisions: the Insurance Division (41.6% of 2002 revenue), the Investment Division (30.0%) and the International Insurance and Investments Division (26.4%). Corporate and other operations accounted for 2.0% of revenue.

RECENT DEVELOPMENTS:

For the year ended 12/31/02, PRU reported income of $256.0 million, before a loss from discontinued operations of $62.0 milion, versus a loss of $107.0 million, before a loss from discontinued operations of $47.0 million, in 2001. Total revenues were $26.68 billion, down 1.5% from $27.07 billion a year earlier. Income from continuing operations from the financial services businesses surged 112.3% to $741.0 million, while closed block business net loss widened to $485.0 million from $456.0 million in 2001. Results for 2001 included demutualization charges of $588.0 million. Total financial services revenue climbed 4.7% to $20.44 billion. Premiums rose 15.6% to $9.51 billion, while net investment income slipped 0.6% to $5.19 billion. Policy charges and fee income fell 8.3% to $1.65 billion, and commissions, investment management fees and other income decreased 4.3% to $4.08 billion.

PROSPECTS:

On 2/19/03, the Company and Wachovia Corp. announced that they are joining retail brokerage operations to create the third largest brokerage firm in the U.S., based on combined client assets. The firm will have more than 3,500 brokerage locations, including 791 dedicated retail offices in 48 states and the District of Columbia. Under terms of the agreement Wachovia will have a 62.0% ownership interest in the firm, and PRU will own the remaining 38.0%. After-tax annual cost savings of approximately $220.0 million are expected by 2005.

ANNUAL FINANCIAL DATA:

FISCAL YEAR	PREM. INC. ($mill.)	TOT. REVS. ($mill.)	NET INC. ($mill.)	TOT. ASSETS ($mill.)	TOT. INVST. ($mill.)	RET. ON REVS. %	RET. ON EQUITY %	RET. ON ASSETS %	PRICE RANGE
p12/31/02		26,675.0	⑥ 256.0						36.00 - 25.25
12/31/01	12,477.0	27,177.0	⑤ d170.0	293,030.0	156,203.0	...	...	...	...
12/31/00	10,221.0	26,544.0	④ 321.0	272,753.0	139,262.0	1.2	1.6	0.1	...
12/31/99	9,528.0	26,568.0	③ 1,213.0	285,094.0	137,860.0	4.6	6.3	0.4	...
12/31/98	9,048.0	27,024.0	② 1,627.0	...	...	6.0	...	...	...

Statistics are as originally reported. 12/31/01 and prior periods are bef. demutualization on 12/18/01. ① For financial services business, excludes closed block business results. ② Bef. loss fr. disc. opers. $521.0 mill.; incl. demut. chrg. $24.0 mill. and oth. non-rec. chrg. $1.15 bill. ③ Bef. loss fr. disc. opers. $400.0 mill.; incl. demut. chrg. $75.0 mill. and oth. non-rec. chrg. $100.0 mill. ④ Bef. inc. fr. disc. opers. $77.0 mill.; incl. demut. chrg. $143.0 mill. ⑤ Bef. inc. fr. disc. opers. $16.0 mill.; incl. demut. chrg. $588.0 mill. ⑥ Bef. loss fr. disc. oper. $62.0 mill.

OFFICERS:
A. F. Ryan, Chmn., Pres., C.E.O.
R. J. Carbone, Sr. V.P., C.F.O.
INVESTOR CONTACT: Bob DeFilippo, (973) 802-4149
PRINCIPAL OFFICE: 751 Broad Street, Newark, NJ 07102

TELEPHONE NUMBER: (973) 802-6000
FAX: (973) 367-6476
WEB: www.prudential.com
NO. OF EMPLOYEES: 60,792 (avg.)
SHAREHOLDERS: 4,675,234 (class A)
ANNUAL MEETING: In June
INCORPORATED: NJ, Dec., 1999

INSTITUTIONAL HOLDINGS:
No. of Institutions: 381
Shares Held: 245,143,835
% Held: 43.1
INDUSTRY: Life insurance (SIC: 6311)
TRANSFER AGENT(S): EquiServe Trust Company, N.A., Providence, RI

PUBLIC SERVICE ENTERPRISE GROUP INC.

EXCH.	SYM.	REC. PRICE	P/E RATIO	YLD.	MKT. CAP.	RANGE (52-WK.)	'02 Y/E PR.
NYSE	PEG	34.63 (2/28/03)	17.7	6.2%	$7.13 bill.	47.25 - 20.00	32.10

MEDIUM GRADE. THE COMPANY PLANS TO LOWER ITS DEBT RATIO TO THE HIGH 50.0% RANGE BY THE END OF THE YEAR.

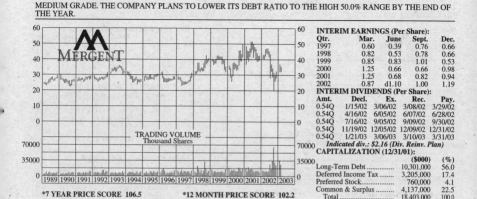

INTERIM EARNINGS (Per Share):

Qtr.	Mar.	June	Sept.	Dec.
1997	0.60	0.39	0.76	0.66
1998	0.82	0.53	0.78	0.66
1999	0.85	0.83	1.01	0.53
2000	1.25	0.66	0.66	0.98
2001	1.25	0.68	0.82	0.94
2002	0.87	d1.10	1.00	1.19

INTERIM DIVIDENDS (Per Share):

Amt.	Decl.	Ex.	Rec.	Pay.
0.54Q	1/15/02	3/06/02	3/08/02	3/29/02
0.54Q	4/16/02	6/05/02	6/07/02	6/28/02
0.54Q	7/16/02	9/05/02	9/09/02	9/30/02
0.54Q	11/19/02	12/05/02	12/09/02	12/31/02
0.54Q	1/21/03	3/06/03	3/10/03	3/31/03

Indicated div.: $2.16 (Div. Reinv. Plan)

CAPITALIZATION (12/31/01):

	($000)	(%)
Long-Term Debt	10,301,000	56.0
Deferred Income Tax	3,205,000	17.4
Preferred Stock	760,000	4.1
Common & Surplus	4,137,000	22.5
Total	18,403,000	100.0

*7 YEAR PRICE SCORE 106.5   ***12 MONTH PRICE SCORE 102.2**

*NYSE COMPOSITE INDEX=100

BUSINESS:

Public Service Enterprise Group Inc. is the holding company of four wholly-owned subsidiaries. Public Service Electric and Gas Co. (PSE&G) supplies electric and gas service in areas of New Jersey in which approximately 5.5 million people reside. PSEG Power LLC is a multi-regional generating and energy trading company established to acquire, own and operate the electric generation-related business of PSE&G. PSEG Energy Holdings is the parent company for the Company's non-utility businesses, which includes diversified investments, energy-related engineering, consulting and mechanical contracting services, debt financing and real estate investment. PSEG Services Corporation provides management and administrative services for PEG and its subsidiaries. Revenues for 2002 were derived: PSE&G, 70.5%; PSEG Power, 43.7%; PSEG Energy Holdings, 9.0%; and other, d23.2%.

RECENT DEVELOPMENTS:

For the twelve months ended 12/31/02, income from continuing operations fell 46.4% to $416.0 million, before an accounting change charge of $120.0 million, compared with income of $776.0 million, before an accounting change credit of $9.0 million, in 2001. Results for 2002 and 2001 included write-downs of project investments of $497.0 million and $7.0 million, respectively. Results for 2002 and 2001 excluded losses of $51.0 million and $15.0 million, respectively, from discontinued operations. Operating revenues rose 18.9% to $8.39 billion from $7.06 billion a year earlier. Operating income decreased 20.4% to $1.53 billion compared with $1.92 billion the year before.

PROSPECTS:

PSEG Energy Holdings has ceased making new capital investments at two of its subsidiaries, PSEG Resources and PSEG Global, through 2004. These actions will lower the Company's capital requirements by about $500.0 million in 2003. Meanwhile, PEG has reduced its debt ratio to the low 60.0% range and expects this ratio to decline into the high 50.0% range by the end of the year. Looking ahead, the Company anticipates earnings per share from ongoing operations for 2003 to be in the range of $3.70 to $3.90.

ANNUAL FINANCIAL DATA:

FISCAL YEAR	TOT. REVS. ($mill.)	NET INC. ($mill.)	TOT. ASSETS ($mill.)	OPER. PROFIT %	NET PROFIT %	NET INC./ NET PROP. %	NET INC./ TOT. CAP. %	RET. ON EQUITY %	ACCUM. DEPR./ GROSS PROP. %	EARN. PER SH. $	TANG. BK. VAL.$	DIV. PER SH. $	DIV. PAYOUT %	PRICE RANGE		AVG. P/E RATIO	AVG. YIELD %
p12/31/02	8,390.0	⑦ 416.0								⑦ 1.99		2.16	108.5	47.25	20.00	16.9	6.4
12/31/01	9,815.0	⑥ 763.0	25,397.0	19.3	7.8	7.6	4.1	15.6	32.4	⑥ 3.67	16.95	2.16	58.9	51.55 – 36.88		12.0	4.9
12/31/00	6,848.0	764.0	20,796.0	27.6	11.2	9.9	5.0	13.2	35.6	3.55	27.82	2.16	60.8	50.00 – 25.69		10.7	5.7
12/31/99	6,497.0	⑤ 723.0	19,015.0	28.3	11.1	10.2	5.7	17.7	36.6	⑤ 3.29	18.46	2.16	65.7	42.63 – 32.00		11.3	5.8
12/31/98	5,931.0	644.0	17,997.0	20.0	10.9	5.9	4.4	12.4	39.3	2.79	22.49	2.16	77.4	42.75 – 30.31		13.1	5.9
12/31/97	6,370.0	④ 560.0	17,943.0	17.5	8.8	5.1	3.9	10.6	36.9	④ 2.41	22.47	2.16	89.6	31.25 – 22.88		11.2	8.0
12/31/96	6,041.2	③ 587.4	16,915.3	17.5	9.7	5.2	4.3	11.0	34.5	③ 2.42	22.33	2.16	89.3	32.13 – 25.13		11.8	7.5
12/31/95	6,164.2	662.3	17,171.4	18.8	10.7	5.6	4.6	11.5	32.7	2.71	22.25	2.16	79.7	30.63 – 26.00		10.4	7.6
12/31/94	5,915.8	679.0	16,717.4	19.7	11.5	5.8	4.8	11.9	31.7	2.78	21.70	2.16	77.7	32.00 – 23.88		10.0	7.7
12/31/93	5,705.6	①② 595.5	16,305.2	19.4	10.4	5.2	4.3	10.7	30.6	①② 2.48	21.07	2.16	87.1	36.13 – 30.00		13.3	6.5

Statistics are as originally reported. ① Incl. $77.6 mill. pre-tax chg. fr. write-down of prop. ② Bef. $5.4 mill. acct. adj. ③ Excl. $10.7 mill. inc. fr. disc. ops. & $13.5 mill. gain on disp. of ops.; incl. $18.5 mill. pre-tax gain on pfd. stk. redemp. ④ Incl. $62.0 mill. non-recur. chg. rel. to litigation settlement. ⑤ Excl. $804.0 mill. net extra. loss fr. the refinement of estimates in the impair. analysis of elec. gen. assets stemming fr. the NJ Board of Public Utilities' restr. decision in its Energy Master Plan proceedings. ⑥ Bef. $2.0 mill. extraord. chg. & $9.0 mill. acctg. chge. benefit. ⑦ Incl. $497.0 mill. write-down of invest. and excl. $51.0 mill. loss fr. disc. ops. & $120.0 mill. acct. chg.

OFFICERS:
E. J. Ferland, Chmn., Pres., C.E.O.
T. M. O'Flynn, Exec. V.P., C.F.O.
R. E. Selover, V.P., Gen. Couns.
INVESTOR CONTACT: Investor Relations, (877) 773-4111
PRINCIPAL OFFICE: 80 Park Plaza, P.O. Box 1171, Newark, NJ 07101-1171

TELEPHONE NUMBER: (973) 430-7000
FAX: (973) 430-5983
WEB: www.pseg.com
NO. OF EMPLOYEES: 13,391 (avg.)
SHAREHOLDERS: 119,944
ANNUAL MEETING: In Apr.
INCORPORATED: NJ, July, 1985

INSTITUTIONAL HOLDINGS:
No. of Institutions: 338
Shares Held: 111,579,304
% Held: 50.2
INDUSTRY: Electric and other services combined (SIC: 4931)
TRANSFER AGENT(S): EquiServe First Chicago Trust Division, Jersey City, NJ

PUBLIC STORAGE, INC.

EXCH.	SYM.	REC. PRICE	P/E RATIO	YLD.	MKT. CAP.	RANGE (52-WK.)	'02 Y/E PR.
NYSE	PSA	33.00 (2/28/03)	27.7	5.5%	$4.02 bill.	39.29 - 27.98	32.31

UPPER MEDIUM GRADE. DURING THE FOURTH QUARTER, THE COMPANY OPENED TWO NEWLY DEVELOPED SELF-STORAGE FACILITIES AT A TOTAL COST OF APPROXIMATELY $12.7 MILLION.

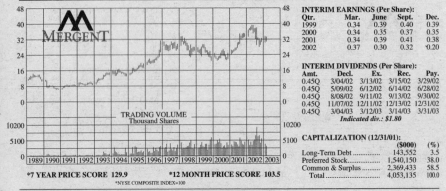

*7 YEAR PRICE SCORE 129.9 ***12 MONTH PRICE SCORE 103.5**
*NYSE COMPOSITE INDEX=100

INTERIM EARNINGS (Per Share):

Qtr.	Mar.	June	Sept.	Dec.
1999	0.34	0.39	0.40	0.39
2000	0.34	0.35	0.37	0.35
2001	0.34	0.39	0.41	0.38
2002	0.37	0.30	0.32	0.20

INTERIM DIVIDENDS (Per Share):

Amt.	Decl.	Ex.	Rec.	Pay.
0.45Q	3/04/02	3/13/02	3/15/02	3/29/02
0.45Q	5/09/02	6/12/02	6/14/02	6/28/02
0.45Q	8/08/02	9/11/02	9/13/02	9/30/02
0.45Q	11/07/02	12/11/02	12/13/02	12/31/02
0.45Q	3/04/03	3/12/03	3/14/03	3/31/03

Indicated div.: $1.80

CAPITALIZATION (12/31/01):

	($000)	(%)
Long-Term Debt	143,552	3.5
Preferred Stock	1,540,150	38.0
Common & Surplus	2,369,433	58.5
Total	4,053,135	100.0

BUSINESS:

Public Storage, Inc. is a fully integrated, self-administered and self-managed real estate investment trust that acquires, develops, owns and operates self-storage facilities. As of 12/31/02, the Company owned and operated storage space in 37 states, with direct and indirect equity investments in 1,409 facilities. The Company's self-storage operations are by far the largest component of its business, representing approximately 86.5% of total revenues generated in fiscal 2001. On 4/19/02, the Company acquired PS Partners V, Ltd.

RECENT DEVELOPMENTS:

For the year ended 12/31/02, income from continuing operations was $332.7 million compared with income of $321.3 million the previous year. Results for 2002 and 2001 excluded a net loss of $13.9 million and net gain of $2.9 million, respectively, from discontinued operations. The decline in earnings was largely due to a decrease in same-store property operations, increased depreciation expense resulting primarily from new property additions, and special charges relating to the closure of certain containerized storage facilities. This was partially offset by an increase in earnings generated by the acquisition of additional real estate investments in 2002 and 2001, earnings generated by the tenant reinsurance business, which was acquired at the end of 2001, and reduced general and administrative expenses. Total revenues rose 5.8% to $763.3 million from $721.7 million the year before. Revenues for self-storage facilities climbed 7.6% to $841.5 million from $782.2 million a year earlier.

PROSPECTS:

During the fourth quarter, the Company opened two newly developed self-storage facilities at a total cost of approximately $12.7 million. As of 12/31/02, there were 38 projects that were in construction or expected to begin construction generally by 6/30/03, which include new developments and expansions to existing self-storage facilities. Meanwhile, the Company expects to continue promotional discounting and television advertising during 2003, which will likely continue to have an adverse effect on its net operating income.

ANNUAL FINANCIAL DATA:

FISCAL YEAR	TOT. INC. ($mill.)	NET INC. ($mill.)	TOT. ASSETS ($mill.)	NET INC. + DEPR./ ASSETS %	RET. ON EQUITY %	RET. ON ASSETS %	EARN. PER SH. $	TANG. BK. VAL. $	DIV. PER SH. $	DIV. PAYOUT %	PRICE RANGE	AVG. P/E RATIO	AVG. YIELD %
p12/31/02	841.5	② 332.7					② 1.19		1.80	151.3	39.29 - 27.98	28.3	5.4
12/31/01	834.6	① 320.1	4,625.9	10.6	8.2	6.9	① 1.51	17.77	1.69	111.9	35.15 - 24.13	19.6	5.7
12/31/00	757.3	① 293.3	4,513.9	9.8	7.9	6.5	① 1.41	18.24	1.48	105.0	26.94 - 20.88	17.0	6.2
12/31/99	676.7	① 285.7	4,214.4	10.0	7.7	6.8	① 1.52	17.50	0.88	57.9	29.38 - 20.81	16.5	3.5
12/31/98	582.2	227.0	3,403.9	9.8	7.3	6.7	1.30	16.65	0.88	67.7	33.63 - 22.63	21.6	3.1
12/31/97	470.8	178.6	3,311.6	8.2	6.3	5.4	0.91	16.31	0.88	96.7	30.88 - 25.88	31.2	3.1
12/31/96	341.1	153.5	2,572.2	8.5	6.7	6.0	1.10	14.14	0.88	80.0	31.38 - 18.75	22.8	3.5
12/31/95	212.7	70.4	1,937.5	5.7	4.3	3.6	0.95	11.04	0.88	92.6	19.75 - 13.50	17.5	5.3
12/31/94	147.2	42.1	820.3	8.6	7.2	5.1	1.05	12.66	0.85	80.9	16.75 - 13.00	14.2	5.7
12/31/93	114.7	28.0	666.1	8.0	7.5	4.2	1.96	11.93	0.84	42.9	15.00 - 8.88	6.1	7.0

Statistics are as originally reported. ① Bef. after-tax gain of disposition of real estate $4.1 mill., 2001; $3.8 mill., 2000; $2.2 mill., 1999 ② Bef. net loss of $13.9 mill. from disc. ops.

OFFICERS:
B. W. Hughes, Chmn.
R. L. Havner, Vice-Chmn. C.E.O.
H. Lenkin, Pres. & C.O.O.
J. Reyes, Sr. V.P., C.F.O.
INVESTOR CONTACT: Harvey Lenkin, Pres. & C.O.O., (818) 244-8080
PRINCIPAL OFFICE: 701 Western Avenue, Glendale, CA 91201-2349

TELEPHONE NUMBER: (818) 244-8080
FAX: (818) 244-0581
WEB: www.publicstorage.com
NO. OF EMPLOYEES: 4,400 (approx.)
SHAREHOLDERS: 20,022 (approx.)
ANNUAL MEETING: In May
INCORPORATED: CA, July, 1980

INSTITUTIONAL HOLDINGS:
No. of Institutions: 197
Shares Held: 52,912,149
% Held: 42.5
INDUSTRY: Real estate investment trusts (SIC: 6798)
TRANSFER AGENT(S): BankBoston, NA, Boston, MA

PUGET ENERGY, INC.

EXCH.	SYM.	REC. PRICE	P/E RATIO	YLD.	MKT. CAP.	RANGE (52-WK.)	'02 Y/E PR.
NYSE	PSD	20.24 (2/28/03)	16.3	4.9%	$1.76 bill.	23.30 - 16.63	22.05

UPPER MEDIUM GRADE. THE COMPANY IS TARGETING EARNINGS FOR 2003 IN THE RANGE OF $1.50 TO $1.60 PER SHARE.

*7 YEAR PRICE SCORE 91.9   ***12 MONTH PRICE SCORE 106.2**

*NYSE COMPOSITE INDEX=100

INTERIM EARNINGS (Per Share):

Qtr.	Mar.	June	Sept.	Dec.
1997	0.29	0.33	0.11	0.52
1998	0.74	0.19	0.21	0.71
1999	0.79	0.33	0.26	0.68
2000	0.89	0.29	0.20	0.78
2001	0.98	0.26	0.05	0.07
2002	0.28	0.34	0.07	0.55

INTERIM DIVIDENDS (Per Share):

Amt.	Decl.	Ex.	Rec.	Pay.
0.46Q	1/07/02	1/16/02	1/18/02	2/15/02
0.25Q	3/21/02	4/17/02	4/19/02	5/15/02
0.25Q	7/09/02	7/17/02	7/19/02	8/15/02
0.25Q	10/08/02	10/16/02	10/18/02	11/15/02
0.25Q	1/06/03	1/15/03	1/17/03	2/15/03

Indicated div.: $1.00 (Div. Reinv. Plan)

CAPITALIZATION (12/31/01):

	($000)	(%)
Long-Term Debt	2,127,054	47.2
Deferred Income Tax	605,315	13.4
Redeemable Pfd. Stock	350,662	7.8
Preferred Stock................	60,000	1.3
Common & Surplus	1,362,724	30.2
Total	4,505,755	100.0

BUSINESS:

Puget Energy, Inc. (formerly Puget Sound Energy Inc.) is a public utility holding company. Through its subsidiaries, the Company provides electric and gas service in a territory covering approximately 6,000 square miles, principally in the Puget Sound region of Washington. As of 12/31/02, the Company had approximately 950,052 electric customers, consisting of 839,878 residential, 104,273 commercial, 3,953 industrial, 16 transportation customers and 1,932 other customers; and approximately 614,418 gas customers, consisting of 565,003 residential, 46,523 commercial, 2,770 industrial and 122 transportational. In 2002, revenues were 57.1% electric; 29.1% natural gas; and 13.8% other.

RECENT DEVELOPMENTS:

For the year ended 12/31/02, the Company posted net income of $117.9 million compared with income of $121.6 million, before an accounting change charge of $14.7 million the previous year. Earnings were hampered by lower electric and gas revenues, partially offset by decreased fuel costs and general tariff rate increases that took effect on 7/1/02. Total operating revenues dropped 17.1% to $2.39 billion from $2.87 billion the previous year. Electric operating revenues slid 26.8% to $1.37 billion from the prior year. Gas operating revenues fell 14.5% to $697.2 million, while other operating revenues surged 59.6% to $329.3 million.

PROSPECTS:

Looking ahead, persistent drought conditions in the Pacific Northwest associated with El Nino weather conditions may hamper hydroelectric production and related power costs at its electricity supply and transmission business, forcing PSD to purchase more costly replacement power. The Company estimates that the resulting increase in power costs could reduce its earnings by about $0.25 per share in 2003. However, given that PSD expects to reach the cumulative cap allowed under the power cap adjustment (PCA) mechanism by the end of 2003, the Company should be insulated from significant increases in power costs starting in 2004. The Company is targeting earnings for 2003 in the range of $1.50 to $1.60 per share.

ANNUAL FINANCIAL DATA:

FISCAL YEAR	TOT. REVS. ($mill.)	NET INC. ($mill.)	TOT. ASSETS ($mill.)	OPER. PROFIT %	NET PROFIT %	NET INC./ NET PROP. %	NET INC./ TOT. CAP. %	RET. ON EQUITY %	ACCUM. DEPR./ GROSS PROP. %	EARN. PER SH.$	TANG. BK. VAL.$	DIV. PER SH.$	DIV. PAYOUT %	PRICE RANGE	AVG. P/E RATIO	AVG. YIELD %
p12/31/02	2,392.3	117.9								1.24		1.21	97.6	23.60 - 16.63	16.2	6.0
12/31/01	3,374.0	⑤ 121.6	5,547.0	8.8	3.6	3.1	2.7	8.5	36.1	⑤ 1.31	14.55	1.84	140.4	27.75 - 18.51	17.7	8.0
12/31/00	3,441.7	193.8	5,556.7	10.6	5.6	5.0	4.4	13.0	34.6	2.16	16.61	1.84	85.2	28.00 - 18.94	10.9	7.8
12/31/99	2,066.6	④ 185.6	5,145.6	15.0	9.0	4.9	4.6	12.9	33.6	④ 2.06	16.24	1.84	89.3	28.38 - 18.63	11.4	7.8
12/31/98	1,907.3	169.6	4,720.7	15.7	8.9	4.9	4.6	11.7	33.4	1.85	16.00	1.84	99.5	30.25 - 24.06	14.7	6.8
12/31/97	1,676.9	③ 125.7	4,493.4	12.9	7.5	3.9	3.4	8.6	33.2	③ 1.28	16.06	1.84	143.7	30.19 - 23.50	21.0	6.9
12/31/96	1,198.8	② 135.4	3,187.3	16.7	11.3	5.9	5.4	11.5	34.2	② 1.89	18.53	1.84	97.3	26.00 - 22.13	12.7	7.6
12/31/95	1,179.3	135.7	3,269.0	18.2	11.5	5.9	5.2	11.5	32.9	1.89	18.48	1.84	97.3	24.00 - 20.13	11.7	8.3
12/31/94	1,194.1	① 120.1	3,463.8	16.2	10.1	5.3	4.5	10.2	31.4	① 1.64	18.43	1.84	112.2	24.88 - 16.50	12.6	8.9
12/31/93	1,112.9	138.3	3,341.1	19.0	12.4	6.4	5.0	11.7	31.3	2.00	18.65	1.83	91.5	29.75 - 23.50	13.3	6.9

Statistics are as originally reported. ① Inc. non-recurr. after-tax chrg. $16.3 mill. ② Bef. disc. opers. $41.0 mill. fr. sale of invest. in conservation assets to a grantor trust in June 1995 ③ Incl. non-reucrr. pre-tax chrg. $55.8 mill. fr. merger ④ Incl. gain $7.8 mill. fr. sale of Homeguard Security Services, Inc. and investment in Cabot Oil & Gas Corp. ⑤ Bef. acctg. chrg. $14.9 mill.

OFFICERS:
D. P. Beighle, Chmn.
S. P. Reynolds, Pres., C.E.O.
R. L. Hawley, V.P., C.F.O.

INVESTOR CONTACT: Durga D. Waite,
Investor Relations, (425) 462-3808

PRINCIPAL OFFICE: 411-108th Avenue N.E.,
Bellevue, WA 98009

TELEPHONE NUMBER: (425) 454-6363
FAX: (425) 454-3300
WEB: www.pugetsoundenergy.com
NO. OF EMPLOYEES: 3,972
SHAREHOLDERS: 48,700
ANNUAL MEETING: In May
INCORPORATED: WA, Nov., 1960;
reincorp., WA, 1999

INSTITUTIONAL HOLDINGS:
No. of Institutions: 191
Shares Held: 34,907,379
% Held: 37.7

INDUSTRY: Electric services (SIC: 4911)

TRANSFER AGENT(S): Mellon Investor Services, Ridgefield Park, NJ

PULITZER INC.

EXCH.	SYM.	REC. PRICE	P/E RATIO	YLD.	MKT. CAP.	RANGE (52-WK.)	'02 Y/E PR.
NYSE	PTZ	42.64 (2/28/03)	26.5	1.7%	$0.90 bill.	55.80 - 40.12	44.95

MEDIUM GRADE. THE COMPANY EXPECTS BOTH ADVERTISING AND TOTAL REVENUE IN 2003 TO GROW IN THE RANGE OF 4.0% TO 5.5%.

*7 YEAR PRICE SCORE N/A   *12 MONTH PRICE SCORE 102.1
*NYSE COMPOSITE INDEX=100

INTERIM EARNINGS (Per Share):

Qtr.	Mar.	June	Sept.	Dec.
1998	0.26	0.30	0.29	0.34
1999	d0.38	0.43	0.45	0.52
2000	0.45	0.50	0.23	0.43
2001	0.10	0.19	0.07	0.14
2002	0.32	0.32	0.40	0.57

INTERIM DIVIDENDS (Per Share):

Amt.	Decl.	Ex.	Rec.	Pay.
0.175Q	3/14/02	4/04/02	4/08/02	5/01/02
0.175Q	5/14/02	7/03/02	7/08/02	8/01/02
0.175Q	9/10/02	10/07/02	10/09/02	11/01/02
0.18Q	1/06/03	1/14/03	1/16/03	2/03/03
0.18Q	3/11/03	4/07/03	4/09/03	5/01/03

Indicated div.: $0.72

CAPITALIZATION (12/30/01):

	($000)	(%)
Long-Term Debt	306,000	27.7
Common & Surplus	797,237	72.3
Total	1,103,237	100.0

BUSINESS:

Pulitzer Inc. is a newspaper publishing company with related Internet operations in 14 U.S. markets. PTZ's newspaper operations include two major metropolitan newspapers, the ST LOUIS POST-DISPATCH and The ARIZONA DAILY STAR, and 12 other daily newspapers, primarily serving smaller markets in the West and Midwest. The Company also owns the Suburban Journals of Greater St. Louis, a group of 37 weekly papers and various niche publications. PTZ's news media and interactive Web sites include STLtoday.com in St. Louis and azstarnet.com in Tucson. On 3/18/99, Pulitzer Inc., consisting of publishing and new media companies, was spun off from Pulitzer Publishing Company.

RECENT DEVELOPMENTS:

For the twelve months ended 12/29/02, net income more than doubled to $34.7 million compared with income from continuing operations of $12.3 million in 2001. Results benefited from efforts to strengthen editorial products, emphasis on cross selling and creative initiatives, and an ongoing focus on cost reductions. Results for 2002 and 2001 included net losses of $8.0 million and $5.0 million, respectively, on marketable securities and investments. Results for 2001 excluded a loss of $1.6 million from discontinued operations. Total operating revenues climbed 0.6% to $416.0 million from $413.5 million a year earlier. Operating income soared 91.0% to $82.9 million compared with $43.4 million the year before.

PROSPECTS:

Looking ahead to the coming year, the Company expects both advertising and total revenue in 2003 to grow in the range of 4.0% to 5.5%, assuming stability in the economy. In addition, the Company expects an increase in newsprint costs of between 5.0% to 10.0% and an increase of less than 3.0% in non-newsprint costs, including labor. Moreover, the combination of revenue growth and cost-reduction efforts should increase operating income margin by 1.0% to 2.0%. Meanwhile, the Company reiterated its earnings per share for 2003 forecast of at least $1.95.

ANNUAL FINANCIAL DATA:

FISCAL YEAR	TOT. REVS. ($000)	NET INC. ($000)	TOT. ASSETS ($000)	OPER. PROFIT %	NET PROFIT %	RET. ON EQUITY %	RET. ON ASSETS %	CURR. RATIO	EARN. PER SH. $	CASH FL. PER SH. $	TANG. BK. VAL. $	DIV. PER SH. $	PRICE RANGE	AVG. P/E RATIO	AVG. YIELD %
p12/31/02	415,960	⑤ 34.7							⑤ 1.62			0.70	55.80 - 40.12	29.6	1.5
12/30/01	413,506	② 12,286	1,288,783	10.5	3.0	1.5	1.0	5.4	④ 0.58	2.47	...	0.68	57.00 - 41.25	84.7	1.4
12/31/00	407,541	③ 34,902	1,282,873	15.3	8.6	4.4	2.7	5.3	③ 1.60	3.15	...	0.64	47.70 - 32.81	25.2	1.6
12/31/99	391,383	② 22,957	978,287	4.9	5.9	2.8	2.3	16.0	② 1.02	1.77	28.42	0.45	48.56 - 36.25	41.6	1.1
12/31/98	372,924	① 27,016	546,393	11.5	7.2	7.0	4.9	3.9	① 1.19	1.81	8.35	...	...	...	...
12/31/97	357,969	① 25,759	464,311	11.6	7.2	8.3	5.5	3.0	① 1.15	1.73	5.66	...	...	...	...
12/31/96	309,096	① 14,792	...	8.7	4.8	...	...	...	① 0.67	1.07	...	...	...	...	...

Statistics are as originally reported. ① Bef. disc oper. gain $49.3 mill., 1998; $40.3 mill., 1997; $42.7 mill., 1996. ② Bef. disc. oper. loss $21.4 mill. & incl. exps. of $26.7 mill. from stk. option cash-outs & bonuses. ③ Incl. pre-tax loss of $8.1 mill. for newspaper transactions, a pre-tax chrg. of $607,000 for workforce reductions & a $1.2 mill. chrg. for non-oper. invest. losses. ④ Excl. $1.6 mill. loss fr. disc. ops. ⑤ Incl. $8.0 mill. net loss on market sec. & invest.

OFFICERS:
M. E. Pulitzer, Chmn.
R. C. Woodworth, Pres., C.E.O.

INVESTOR CONTACT: James V. Maloney, Sec., (314) 340-8402

PRINCIPAL OFFICE: 900 North Tucker Boulevard, St. Louis, MO 63101

TELEPHONE NUMBER: (314) 340-8000
FAX: (314) 340-3125
WEB: www.pulitzerinc.com
NO. OF EMPLOYEES: 4,000 full-time (approx.); 1,200 part-time (approx.)
SHAREHOLDERS: 381 (approx. record); 27 (class B common)
ANNUAL MEETING: In May
INCORPORATED: DE, 1998

PULTE HOMES, INC.

EXCH.	SYM.	REC. PRICE	P/E RATIO	YLD.	MKT. CAP.	RANGE (52-WK.)	'02 Y/E PR.
NYSE	PHM	50.83 (2/28/03)	7.1	0.3%	$3.11 bill.	59.75 - 36.21	47.87

UPPER MEDIUM GRADE. THE COMPANY PLANS TO EXPAND THE DEL WEBB BRAND INTO A NUMBER OF NEW DOMESTIC MARKETS.

*7 YEAR PRICE SCORE 182.4   ***12 MONTH PRICE SCORE 112.9**
*NYSE COMPOSITE INDEX=100

INTERIM EARNINGS (Per Share):

Qtr.	Mar.	June	Sept.	Dec.
1998	0.25	0.54	0.64	0.87
1999	0.54	0.85	1.08	1.60
2000	0.57	1.15	1.47	2.01
2001	0.91	1.40	1.53	1.99
2002	1.12	1.45	1.83	2.78

INTERIM DIVIDENDS (Per Share):

Amt.	Decl.	Ex.	Rec.	Pay.
0.04Q	3/06/02	3/14/02	3/18/02	4/01/02
0.04Q	5/15/02	6/12/02	6/14/02	7/01/02
0.04Q	9/12/02	9/19/02	9/23/02	10/01/02
0.04Q	12/12/02	12/19/02	12/23/02	1/02/03
0.04Q	2/05/03	3/14/03	3/18/03	4/01/03

Indicated div.: $0.16

CAPITALIZATION (12/31/01):

	($000)	(%)
Long-Term Debt [1]	1,737,869	43.3
Common & Surplus	2,276,665	56.7
Total	4,014,534	100.0

BUSINESS:

Pulte Homes, Inc. (formerly Pulte Corporation) is engaged in the homebuilding and financial services businesses. As of 1/28/03, the Company had operations in 44 markets across the United States, Argentina, Puerto Rico and Mexico, where it was the fifth-largest builder. Through its Del Webb operations, PHM is also a builder of active adult communities for people age 55 and older. PHM has two operating segments: Homebuilding (98.6% of 2002 revenues), which includes the domestic, international and active adult markets, and Financial Services (1.4%), which consists principally of the mortgage banking operations of Pulte Mortgage Corporation. During 1994, PHM sold its banking operation, First Heights Bank. On 7/31/01, PHM acquired Del Webb Corporation for $1.70 billion.

RECENT DEVELOPMENTS:

For the year ended 12/31/02, income increased 47.0% to $444.6 million, before income from discontinued operations of $9.0 million, compared with income of $302.4 million, before a loss from discontinued operations of $1.0 million, in 2001. The improvement in earnings was attributed to growth throughout PHM's operations and the 2001 acquisition of Del Webb Corporation. Total revenues advanced 38.6% to $7.47 billion. Homebuilding segment revenues improved 38.7% to $7.36 billion, reflecting a 26.1% jump in closings to 28,903 homes and an 7.6% increase in the average sales price per home to $242,000. Financial services segment revenues grew 38.1% to $106.6 million, reflecting a 21.3% rise in loan originations to 23,074 and improved secondary marketing gains.

PROSPECTS:

Looking ahead, the Company plans to expand its penetration of the first time, first and second-move up and active adult segments within the markets PHM operates. Also, PHM plans to expand the Del Webb brand into a number of new domestic markets. Meanwhile, the Company's strong cash position of over $600.0 million as of 12/31/02 should provide PHM with a solid financial base and flexibility.

ANNUAL FINANCIAL DATA:

FISCAL YEAR	TOT. REVS. ($mill.)	NET INC. ($mill.)	TOT. ASSETS ($mill.)	OPER. PROFIT %	NET PROFIT %	RET. ON EQUITY %	RET. ON ASSETS %	CURR. RATIO	EARN. PER SH.$	CASH FL. PER SH.$	TANG. BK. VAL.$	DIV. PER SH.$	PRICE RANGE	AVG. P/E RATIO	AVG. YIELD %
p12/31/02	7,471.8	④ 444.6							④ 7.20			0.16	59.75 - 36.21	6.7	0.3
12/31/01	5,381.9	⑥ 302.4	5,714.3	9.0	5.6	13.3	5.3	2.3	⑥ 6.01	6.66	30.54	0.16	50.24 - 26.10	6.4	0.4
12/31/00	4,159.1	④ 218.4	2,886.5	8.4	5.3	17.5	7.6	2.2	④ 5.18	5.52	30.02	0.16	45.00 - 15.25	5.8	0.5
12/31/99	3,730.3	⑧ 178.3	2,596.8	7.5	4.8	16.3	6.9	2.1	⑧ 4.07	4.38	25.27	0.16	31.25 - 16.75	5.9	0.7
12/31/98	2,866.5	④ 101.1	2,349.8	5.8	3.5	11.0	4.3	2.0	④ 2.30	2.42	21.35	0.14	36.19 - 19.94	12.2	0.5
12/31/97	2,524.0	④⑤ 49.8	2,150.8	3.2	2.0	6.1	2.3	2.2	④⑤ 1.14	1.31	19.10	0.12	21.25 - 13.63	15.4	0.7
12/31/96	2,384.3	④ 63.2	1,985.1	4.3	2.7	7.6	3.2	2.1	④ 1.26	1.40	17.82	0.12	17.31 - 12.00	11.6	0.8
12/31/95	2,029.1	④ 48.8	2,048.5	4.0	2.4	6.4	2.4	2.2	④ 0.90	1.01	14.08	0.12	17.31 - 10.06	15.3	0.9
12/31/94	1,755.9	③ 62.4	1,941.4	5.9	3.6	8.8	3.2	1.4	③ 1.12	1.36	12.94	0.12	19.31 - 9.06	12.7	0.8
12/31/93	1,490.8	② 55.5	3,810.9	6.1	3.7	10.0	1.5	0.3	② 1.39	1.02	10.10	0.12	20.69 - 11.75	11.7	0.7

Statistics are as originally reported. Adj. for stk. split: 100%, 6/98. ① Incl. sub. deb. conv. into com. ② Bef. acctg. adj. $5.0 mill. & extraord. chrg. of $3.4 mill. ③ Excl. extraord chrg. of $2.6 mill., tax benefit of $72.0 mill. and inc. fr. discont. oper. of $103 mill. ④ Bef. inc. fr. discont. oper. of $9.0 mill., 2002; $29.9 mill, 2000; $1.0 mill., 1998; $1.0mill., 1997; $116.4 mill., 1996; $9.5 mill., 1995.$9.5 mill., 1995. ⑤ Incl. restruct. costs of $20.0 mill. ⑥ Bef. loss fr. discont. oper. of $1.0 mill., 2001; $122,000, 1999.

OFFICERS:
W. J. Pulte, Chmn.
M. J. O'Brien, Pres., C.E.O.
R. J. Dugas, C.O.O.
R. A. Cregg, Sr. V.P., C.F.O.

INVESTOR CONTACT: James P. Zeumer, V.P., Corp. Comm., (248) 433-4597

PRINCIPAL OFFICE: 33 Bloomfield Hills Parkway, Suite 200, Bloomfield Hills, MI 48304

TELEPHONE NUMBER: (248) 647-2750
FAX: (248) 433-4598
WEB: www.pulte.com

NO. OF EMPLOYEES: 9,400 (approx.)

SHAREHOLDERS: 1,684 (record)

ANNUAL MEETING: In May

INCORPORATED: MI, Sept., 1987

INSTITUTIONAL HOLDINGS:
No. of Institutions: 247
Shares Held: 45,006,914
% Held: 73.5

INDUSTRY: Operative builders (SIC: 1531)

TRANSFER AGENT(S): State Street Bank and Trust Company, a division of EquiServe, Canton, MA

QUAKER CHEMICAL CORPORATION

EXCH.	SYM.	REC. PRICE	P/E RATIO	YLD.	MKT. CAP.	RANGE (52-WK.)	'02 Y/E PR.	DIV. ACH.
NYSE	KWR	20.00 (2/28/03)	13.2	4.2%	$182.7 mill.	25.50 - 18.07	23.20	31 yrs.

MEDIUM GRADE. THE INCREASE IN CRUDE OIL PRICES IS EXPECTED TO HAMPER SHORT-TERM RAW MATERIAL PRICES.

*7 YEAR PRICE SCORE 131.8   *12 MONTH PRICE SCORE 103.4

*NYSE COMPOSITE INDEX=100

INTERIM EARNINGS (Per Share):

Qtr.	Mar.	June	Sept.	Dec.
1998	0.33	0.39	0.40	0.08
1999	0.34	0.42	0.48	0.51
2000	0.49	0.53	0.53	0.39
2001	0.45	0.45	0.12	d0.17
2002	0.26	0.35	0.45	0.46

INTERIM DIVIDENDS (Per Share):

Amt.	Decl.	Ex.	Rec.	Pay.
0.21Q	3/13/02	4/12/02	4/16/02	4/30/02
0.21Q	5/08/02	7/15/02	7/17/02	7/31/02
0.21Q	9/25/02	10/15/02	10/17/02	10/31/02
0.21Q	11/20/02	1/15/03	1/17/03	1/31/03
0.21Q	3/19/03	4/14/03	4/16/03	4/30/03

Indicated div.: $0.84 (Div. Reinv. Plan)

CAPITALIZATION (12/31/01):

	($000)	(%)
Long-Term Debt	19,380	19.1
Deferred Income Tax	1,233	1.2
Common & Surplus	80,899	79.7
Total	101,512	100.0

BUSINESS:

Quaker Chemical Corporation develops, produces, and markets a wide range of formulated chemical specialty products for various heavy industrial and manufacturing applications and, in addition, offers and markets chemical management services. The Company operates in three segments: metalworking process chemicals; coatings; and other chemical products. KWR's principal product lines include rolling lubricants, corrosion preventives, hydraulic fluids, machining and grinding compounds, forming compounds, chemical milling maskants, metal finishing compounds, technology for the removal of hydrogen sulfides, construction products and programs to provide chemical management services. In 2002, KWR acquired The United Lubricants Corporation and Epmar Corporation.

RECENT DEVELOPMENTS:

For the twelve months ended 12/31/02, net income soared 86.5% to $14.3 million compared with $7.7 million in 2001. Results for 2001 included restructuring charges totaling $5.9 million for facility rationalization, severance, and acquisition-related charges. Net sales were $274.5 million, up 9.3% from $251.1 million in the prior year. The improvement was attributed to the acquisitions of The United Lubricants in March 2002 and Epmar Corporation in April 2002, as well as the purchase of a controlling interest in KWR's South African joint venture. Operating income jumped 68.9% to $24.0 million compared with $14.2 million the year before.

PROSPECTS:

Looking ahead to fiscal 2003, the Company anticipates continued sales growth, supported by further penetration into its core steel and metalworking markets. However, KWR expects the uncertain global business environment will likely place pressure on industrial production demand and earnings. Additionally, the Company expects higher crude oil prices to negatively affect its raw materials prices, especially in the short term. The higher raw material prices, coupled with increased selling, general and administrative expenses, are expected to reduce operating results by approximately $0.35 per share in the coming year.

ANNUAL FINANCIAL DATA:

FISCAL YEAR	TOT. REVS. ($000)	NET INC. ($000)	TOT. ASSETS ($000)	OPER. PROFIT %	NET PROFIT %	RET. ON EQUITY %	RET. ON ASSETS %	CURR. RATIO	EARN. PER SH. $	CASH FL. PER SH. $	TANG. BK. VAL. $	DIV. PER SH. $	PRICE RANGE	AVG. P/E RATIO	AVG. YIELD %
p12/31/02	274,521	14,297							1.51			0.84	25.50 - 18.22	14.5	3.8
12/31/01	251,074	⑤ 7,665	178,823	5.7	3.1	9.5	4.3	2.1	⑤ 0.84	1.54	7.06	0.82	22.30 - 16.12	22.9	4.3
12/31/00	267,570	④ 17,163	188,161	9.4	6.4	20.2	9.1	2.1	④ 1.93	2.70	7.63	0.79	19.25 - 13.38	8.5	4.8
12/31/99	258,461	③ 15,651	182,213	10.6	6.1	19.3	8.6	2.2	③ 1.74	2.52	7.30	0.77	18.38 - 13.50	9.2	4.8
12/31/98	257,100	③ 10,650	189,903	6.7	4.1	12.7	5.6	1.9	③ 1.20	2.00	7.01	0.73	21.00 - 13.00	14.2	4.3
12/31/97	241,534	② 12,611	170,640	6.6	5.2	16.7	7.4	2.1	② 1.45	2.28	7.01	0.70	19.81 - 15.00	12.0	4.1
12/31/96	240,251	① d7,599	165,608	...	...	...	...	1.4	① d0.88	0.13	6.00	0.69	17.25 - 11.75	...	4.7
12/31/95	229,128	6,688	185,408	5.9	2.9	7.1	3.6	1.4	0.76	1.77	8.52	0.68	19.00 - 11.00	19.7	4.5
12/31/94	196,929	9,402	170,172	8.0	4.8	10.0	5.5	1.9	1.03	1.89	9.15	0.62	19.50 - 14.75	16.6	3.6
12/31/93	196,425	d1,758	170,985	...	...	...	...	2.0	d0.19	0.63	8.32	0.60	24.63 - 14.25	...	3.1

Statistics are as originally reported. ① Incl. $16.9 mill. aft-tax spl. chg. ② Incl. $1.7 mill. aft-tax gain fr. sale of European bus. & $1.3 mill. aft-tax chg. for litigation. ③ Incl. $5.3 mill. aft-tax chgs. for reposit. and integration, 1998; $314,000, 1999. ④ Incl. $27,000 non-recur. gain. ⑤ Incl. $5.9 mill. restr. chg. & environmental chg. of $500,000.

OFFICERS:
R. J. Naples, Chmn., C.E.O.
J. W. Bauer, Pres., C.O.O.
M. F. Barry, V.P., C.F.O., Treas.

INVESTOR CONTACT: Michael F. Barry, V.P., C.F.O., Treas., (610) 832-8500

PRINCIPAL OFFICE: One Quaker Park, 901 Hector Street, Conshohocken, PA 19428

TELEPHONE NUMBER: (610) 832-4000
FAX: (610) 832-8682
WEB: www.quakerchem.com

NO. OF EMPLOYEES: 955
SHAREHOLDERS: 810
ANNUAL MEETING: In May
INCORPORATED: PA, 1930

INSTITUTIONAL HOLDINGS:
No. of Institutions: 66
Shares Held: 4,964,546
% Held: 53.3

INDUSTRY: Lubricating oils and greases (SIC: 2992)

TRANSFER AGENT(S): American Stock Transfer & Trust Company, New York, NY

QUANEX CORPORATION

EXCH.	SYM.	REC. PRICE	P/E RATIO	YLD.	MKT. CAP.	RANGE (52-WK.)	'02 Y/E PR.
NYSE	NX	31.60 (2/28/03)	9.0	2.2%	$0.52 bill.	44.20 - 27.93	33.50

MEDIUM GRADE. THE COMPANY IS ENCOURAGED BY STRONG DEMAND FOR ITS TARGET MARKETS.

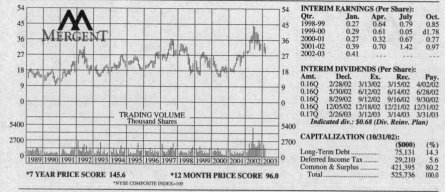

*7 YEAR PRICE SCORE 145.6   ***12 MONTH PRICE SCORE 96.0**

*NYSE COMPOSITE INDEX=100

INTERIM EARNINGS (Per Share):

Qtr.	Jan.	Apr.	July	Oct.
1998-99	0.27	0.64	0.79	0.85
1999-00	0.29	0.61	0.05	d1.78
2000-01	0.27	0.32	0.67	0.77
2001-02	0.39	0.70	1.42	0.97
2002-03	0.41	...	...	...

INTERIM DIVIDENDS (Per Share):

Amt.	Decl.	Ex.	Rec.	Pay.
0.16Q	2/28/02	3/13/02	3/15/02	4/02/02
0.16Q	5/30/02	6/12/02	6/14/02	6/28/02
0.16Q	8/29/02	9/12/02	9/16/02	9/30/02
0.16Q	12/05/02	12/18/02	12/21/02	12/31/02
0.17Q	2/26/03	3/12/03	3/14/03	3/31/03

Indicated div.: $0.68 (Div. Reinv. Plan)

CAPITALIZATION (10/31/02):

	($000)	(%)
Long-Term Debt	75,131	14.3
Deferred Income Tax	29,210	5.6
Common & Surplus	421,395	80.2
Total	525,736	100.0

BUSINESS:

Quanex Corporation (formerly Michigan Seamless Tube Company) is a manufacturer of engineered carbon and alloy steel bars, aluminum flat-rolled products, and precision-formed metal and wood products, which primarily serves the vehicular products and building products markets. The Company's growth strategy is focused on the continued penetration of these target markets and growing its two core business, MACSTEEL and Engineered Products, which serve those markets. The Building Products segment accounted for 53.8% of 2002 sales and the Vehicular Products segment accounted for 46.2% of sales. The Company operated 18 manufacturing facilities in ten states as of 10/31/02.

RECENT DEVELOPMENTS:

For the quarter ended 1/31/03, net income increased 24.2% to $6.8 million compared with $5.5 million in the equivalent 2002 quarter. Earnings benefited from an improved product mix, share gains, lower interest costs and some price relief. Net sales grew 12.4% to $229.5 million from $204.2 million a year earlier. Sales for the Vehicular Products segment rose 6.3% to $108.9 million, while the Building Products segment grew 11.8% to $120.6 million. Operating income climbed 2.8% to $10.1 million from $9.8 million in 2001.

PROSPECTS:

The Company is benefiting from solid demand in its target markets due to by original equipment manufacturer incentives and favorable interest rates. The Company's Vehicular Products segment may be hindered by rising scrap prices, which are up about $20.00 per ton year over year. New light vehicle builds for 2003 are expected to be about 15.8 million to 16.0 million units, down from 16.5 million units in 2002. Within the Building Products segment, rising scrap prices are an issue at Nichols Aluminum. New housing starts for 2003 are expected to be down 5.0% from last year while remodeling expenditures are expected to be in line with 2002.

ANNUAL FINANCIAL DATA:

FISCAL YEAR	TOT. REVS. ($mill.)	NET INC. ($mill.)	TOT. ASSETS ($mill.)	OPER. PROFIT %	NET PROFIT %	RET. ON EQUITY %	RET. ON ASSETS %	CURR. RATIO	EARN. PER SH. $	CASH FL. PER SH. $	TANG. BK. VAL. $	DIV. PER SH. $	PRICE RANGE	AVG. P/E RATIO	AVG. YIELD %
10/31/02	994.4	55.5	689.1	8.4	5.6	13.2	8.1	1.7	3.52	6.13	21.45	0.64	44.20 - 28.04	10.3	1.8
10/31/01	924.4	28.8	697.6	6.2	3.1	10.3	4.1	1.8	④ 2.05	4.71	16.41	0.64	29.50 - 17.35	11.4	2.7
10/31/00	934.2	① ④ d10.0	645.9	...	...	...	...	1.8	① ④ d0.73	2.80	16.35	0.64	26.56 - 14.38	...	3.1
10/31/99	810.1	① 39.3	690.4	8.9	4.9	13.1	5.7	1.6	① 2.56	5.08	17.66	0.64	29.00 - 15.38	8.7	2.9
10/31/98	797.5	③ d3.9	674.3	0.3	...	...	...	1.4	③ d0.27	2.72	15.50	0.64	33.81 - 15.63	...	2.6
10/31/97	746.1	② 27.7	685.7	7.4	3.7	10.3	4.0	1.4	② 2.01	4.75	12.62	0.62	36.50 - 23.38	14.9	2.1
10/31/96	895.7	① 32.9	718.2	7.4	3.7	16.9	4.6	1.7	① 2.41	5.22	8.12	0.60	29.13 - 18.75	9.9	2.5
10/31/95	891.2	① 33.9	546.7	7.5	3.8	19.9	6.2	1.5	① 2.20	4.59	10.27	0.60	26.63 - 18.00	10.1	2.7
10/31/94	699.3	18.9	564.0	5.9	2.7	8.1	3.3	1.9	0.96	3.07	8.45	0.56	27.25 - 17.00	23.0	2.5
10/31/93	616.1	8.4	528.9	3.8	1.4	3.7	1.6	2.6	0.18	2.35	7.93	0.56	21.25 - 14.00	97.9	3.2

Statistics are as originally reported. ① Bef. an extraord. loss of $2.0 mill., 1995; loss of $2.5 mill., 1996; gain of $415,000, 1999; gain of $358,000, 2000; gain of $372,000, 2001. ② Bef. $41.5 mill. discont. oper. ③ Excl. gain of $13.0 mill. for sale of discont. oper., but incl. pre-tax restruct. chrg. of $58.5 mill. ④ Incl. unusual chrgs. of $70.6 mill.

OFFICERS:
R. A. Jean, Chmn., Pres., C.E.O.
T. M. Murphy, V.P., C.F.O.

INVESTOR CONTACT: Investor Relations,
(800) 231-8176

PRINCIPAL OFFICE: 1900 West Loop South,
Suite 1500, Houston, TX 77027

TELEPHONE NUMBER: (713) 961-4600
FAX: (713) 877-5333
WEB: www.quanex.com

NO. OF EMPLOYEES: 3,476

SHAREHOLDERS: 5,006 (record).

ANNUAL MEETING: In Feb.

INCORPORATED: MI, Apr., 1927; reincorp.,
DE, June, 1968

INSTITUTIONAL HOLDINGS:
No. of Institutions: 133
Shares Held: 13,712,351
% Held: 83.4

INDUSTRY: Blast furnaces and steel mills
(SIC: 3312)

TRANSFER AGENT(S): American Stock
Transfer & Trust Company, New York, NY

QUANTA SERVICES, INC.

EXCH.	SYM.	REC. PRICE	P/E RATIO	YLD.	MKT. CAP.	RANGE (52-WK.)	'02 Y/E PR.
NYSE	PWR	3.30 (2/28/03)	...	...	$200.5 mill.	18.90 - 1.75	3.50

SPECULATIVE GRADE. THE COMPANY EXPECTS FULL-YEAR 2003 REVENUE IN THE RANGE OF $1.65 BILLION TO $1.70 BILLION.

*7 YEAR PRICE SCORE N/A   ***12 MONTH PRICE SCORE 52.7**
*NYSE COMPOSITE INDEX=100

INTERIM EARNINGS (Per Share):

Qtr.	Mar.	June	Sept.	Dec.
1997	d0.67	0.13	0.25	0.57
1998	0.27	0.11	0.20	d0.21
1999	0.09	0.11	0.35	0.45
2000	0.28	0.42	0.53	0.20
2001	0.38	0.21	0.34	0.17
2002	0.13	d2.26	d0.11	d0.08

INTERIM DIVIDENDS (Per Share):

Amt.	Decl.	Ex.	Rec.	Pay.
		No dividends paid.		

CAPITALIZATION (12/31/01):

	($000)	(%)
Long-Term Debt	500,274	29.3
Common & Surplus	1,206,751	70.7
Total	1,707,025	100.0

BUSINESS:

Quanta Services, Inc. is a provider of specialty contracting services, delivering end-to-end network products and services for electric power, gas, telecommunications and cable television industries. The Company's services include the designing, installation, repair and maintenance of electric power transmission and distribution lines and telecommunication and cable television lines, the construction of electric substations, the erection of cellular telephone, PCS® and microwave towers, the installation of highway lighting and traffic control systems, design and engineering services and the provision of specialty contracting services for electric, video, security, fire, voice and data systems.

RECENT DEVELOPMENTS:

For the year ended 12/31/02, the Company reported a loss of $174.1 million, before an accounting change charge of $445.4 million, compared with net income of $85.8 million in 2001. Results for 2002 included goodwill impairment of $166.6 million, while results for 2001 included goodwill amortization of $26.0 million. Earnings also included non-recurring items that resulted in a net after-tax charge of $65.8 million and $20.5 million in 2002 and 2001, respectively. Revenues slid 13.1% to $1.75 billion from $2.01 billion a year earlier. Gross profit declined to $236.8 million from $413.8 million on the year before. Loss from operations amounted to $155.5 million compared with income from operations of $193.3 million the prior year.

PROSPECTS:

The Company expects first quarter 2003 revenue in the range of $350.0 million to $370.0 million. The Company also expects first quarter 2003 earnings per share to be approximately breakeven. Moreover, PWR expects full-year 2003 revenues in the range of $1.65 billion to $1.70 billion, with earnings per share ranging between $0.28 and $0.36. Separately, the Company secured a $99.0 million investment in exchange from 37.0% of PWR's voting stock from a private equity fund managed by First Reserve Corporation.

ANNUAL FINANCIAL DATA:

FISCAL YEAR	TOT. REVS. ($mill.)	NET INC. ($mill.)	TOT. ASSETS ($mill.)	OPER. PROFIT %	NET PROFIT %	RET. ON EQUITY %	RET. ON ASSETS %	CURR. RATIO	EARN. PER SH. $	CASH FL. PER SH. $	TANG. BK. VAL. $	PRICE RANGE	AVG. P/E RATIO
p12/31/02	1,750.7	② d174.1	1,364.8						② d2.26	2.10	2.79	18.90 - 1.78	...
12/31/01	2,014.9	85.8	2,042.9	9.6	4.3	7.1	4.2	2.4	1.10	2.10	2.79	37.50 - 9.94	21.6
12/31/00	1,793.3	① 105.7	1,874.1	12.4	5.9	9.9	5.6	2.4	① 1.42	2.12	2.80	63.13 - 17.92	28.5
12/31/99	925.7	① 53.9	1,159.6	12.6	5.8	7.1	4.7	2.0	① 1.00	1.58	2.41	29.58 - 13.42	21.5
12/31/98	309.2	① 15.2	335.0	10.0	4.9	8.9	4.5	2.1	① 0.37	0.61	0.40	15.33 - 7.33	30.4
12/31/97	76.2	2.5	35.7	7.4	3.3	22.5	7.1	1.2	0.28	0.66	0.68	...	...
12/31/96	71.3	1.8	...	5.9	2.5	...	...	...	0.20	0.52	...	...	...

Statistics are as originally reported. Adj. for stk. split: k50%, 4/00. ① Incl. merger and special charges of $28.6 mill., 2000; $6.6 mill., 1999; $231,000, 1998. ② Bef. acctg. chg. chrg. of $445.4 mill., incl. goodwill impair. of $166.6 mill., one-time item chrgs. of $65.8 mill.

OFFICERS:
J. R. Colson, Chmn., C.E.O.
J. H. Haddox, C.F.O.
P. T. Dameris, Exec. V.P., C.O.O.

INVESTOR CONTACT: James H. Haddox, Investor Relations, (713) 629-7600

PRINCIPAL OFFICE: 1360 Post Oak Boulevard, Suite 2100, Houston, TX 77056

TELEPHONE NUMBER: (713) 629-7600
FAX: (713) 629-7676
WEB: www.quantaservices.com

NO. OF EMPLOYEES: 13,487 (avg.)

SHAREHOLDERS: 311 (record); 31 (limited vote common); 1 (series A convert pfd)

ANNUAL MEETING: In May

INCORPORATED: DE, Aug., 1997

INSTITUTIONAL HOLDINGS:
No. of Institutions: 123
Shares Held: 23,985,458
% Held: 34.5

INDUSTRY: Electrical work (SIC: 1731)

TRANSFER AGENT(S): American Stock Transfer & Trust Company, New York, NY

QUEST DIAGNOSTICS, INCORPORATED

EXCH.	SYM.	REC. PRICE	P/E RATIO	YLD.	MKT. CAP.	RANGE (52-WK.)	'02 Y/E PR.
NYSE	DGX	52.76 (2/28/03)	16.3	...	$5.17 bill.	96.14 - 47.36	56.90

UPPER MEDIUM GRADE. ON 2/26/03, THE COMPANY ANNOUNCED THAT IT ACQUIRED UNILAB CORPORATION.

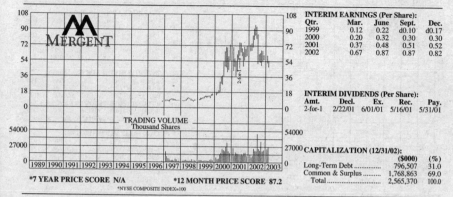

INTERIM EARNINGS (Per Share):

Qtr.	Mar.	June	Sept.	Dec.
1999	0.12	0.22	d0.10	d0.17
2000	0.20	0.32	0.30	0.30
2001	0.37	0.48	0.51	0.52
2002	0.67	0.87	0.87	0.82

INTERIM DIVIDENDS (Per Share):

Amt.	Decl.	Ex.	Rec.	Pay.
2-for-1	2/22/01	6/01/01	5/16/01	5/31/01

TRADING VOLUME
Thousand Shares

***7 YEAR PRICE SCORE N/A**   ***12 MONTH PRICE SCORE 87.2**
*NYSE COMPOSITE INDEX=100

CAPITALIZATION (12/31/02):

	($000)	(%)
Long-Term Debt	796,507	31.0
Common & Surplus	1,768,863	69.0
Total	2,565,370	100.0

BUSINESS:

Quest Diagnostics, Incorporated is a provider of diagnostic testing, information and services. DGX offers clinical laboratory testing services used by physicians in the detection, diagnosis, evaluation, monitoring and treatment of diseases and other medical conditions. DGX maintained a national network of approximately 30 full-service laboratories, 140 rapid response laboratories and more than 1,700 patient service centers as of 12/31/02. DGX is also involved in clinical laboratory testing, and esoteric testing, as well as anatomic pathology services and testing for drugs of abuse. DGX's clinical trials business provides testing to support clinical trials of new pharmaceuticals worldwide. DGX also collects and analyzes laboratory, pharmaceutical and other data through its Quest Informatics division in order to help pharmaceutical companies with their marketing and disease management efforts, as well as help large healthcare customers better manage the health of their patients.

RECENT DEVELOPMENTS:

For the year ended 12/31/02, net income was $322.2 million versus income of $183.9 million, before an extraordinary loss of $21.6 million, the previous year. Results for 2001 included pre-tax provisions for restructuring and other special charges of $6.0 million. Net revenues increased 13.2% to $4.11 billion from $3.63 billion a year earlier, reflecting the acquisition of American Medical Laboratories on 4/1/02. Revenue growth was also due to clinical testing volume, measured by the number of requisitions, which increased 10.4% compared with the prior year.

PROSPECTS:

On 2/26/03, the Company announced that it acquired Unilab Corporation by accepting for payment all shares of Unilab common stock that were tendered. The Company acquired all of Unilab's operations, including three-full service laboratories, 35 rapid-response laboratories, and 367 patient service centers. Going forward, the Company anticipates diluted earnings to range from $4.00 to $4.20 per share on revenue growth of approximately 8.0% to 10.0%, excluding the effect of the Unilab acquisition, in 2003.

ANNUAL FINANCIAL DATA:

FISCAL YEAR	TOT. REVS. ($mill.)	NET INC. ($mill.)	TOT. ASSETS ($mill.)	OPER. PROFIT %	NET PROFIT %	RET. ON EQUITY %	RET. ON ASSETS %	CURR. RATIO	EARN. PER SH. $	CASH FL. PER SH. $	TANG. BK. VAL. $	PRICE RANGE	AVG. P/E RATIO
12/31/02	4,108.1	322.2	3,324.2	14.1	7.8	18.2	9.7	1.3	3.23	4.54	...	96.14 - 49.09	22.5
12/31/01	3,627.8	② 183.9	2,930.6	10.9	5.1	13.8	6.3	1.3	② 1.88	3.40	...	75.75 - 36.60	29.9
12/31/00	3,421.2	② 104.9	2,864.5	9.0	3.1	10.2	3.7	1.0	② 1.11	2.54	...	73.13 - 14.56	39.5
12/31/99	2,205.2	① ② d1.3	2,878.5	-3.3	...	...	...	1.2	① ② d0.02	1.28	...	16.47 - 8.88	...
12/31/98	1,458.6	26.9	1,360.2	6.3	1.8	4.7	2.0	1.9	0.45	1.58	1.20	11.53 - 7.25	21.1
12/31/97	1,528.7	① d22.3	1,400.9	1.6	...	...	...	1.9	① d0.38	0.93	0.45	10.44 - 7.13	...
12/31/96	1,616.3	① d626.0	1,395.1	...	...	...	...	2.0	...	...	...	7.88 - 6.63	...
12/31/95	1,629.4	① d52.1	318.3	1.9	...	...	...	...	...	...	...	...	...

Statistics are as originally reported. Adj. for stock split, 2-for-1, 5/31/01 ① Incl. pre-tax provision for restruct. & other spec. chrgs. $6.0 mill., 2001; $2.1 mill, 2000; $73.4 mill., 1999; $48.7 mill., 1997; $668.5 mill., 1996; $50.6 mill., 1995 ② Bef. extraord. loss of $21.6 mill., 2001; $2.9 mill., 2000; $2.1 mill., 1999

OFFICERS:
K. W. Freeman, Chmn., C.E.O.
S. N. Mohapatra Ph.D., Pres., C.O.O.
R. A. Hagemann, V.P., C.F.O.

INVESTOR CONTACT: Cathy Doherty, Investor Relations, (201) 393-5030

PRINCIPAL OFFICE: One Malcolm Avenue, Teterboro, NJ 07608

TELEPHONE NUMBER: (201) 393-5000
FAX: (201) 462-4169
WEB: www.questdiagnostics.com

NO. OF EMPLOYEES: 33,400 (approx.)

SHAREHOLDERS: 6,200 (approx. record).

ANNUAL MEETING: In May

INCORPORATED: DE, 1980

INSTITUTIONAL HOLDINGS:
No. of Institutions: 378
Shares Held: 96,053,486
% Held: 98.2

INDUSTRY: Medical laboratories (SIC: 8071)

TRANSFER AGENT(S): Computershare Investor Services, Chicago, IL

QUESTAR CORPORATION

EXCH.	SYM.	REC. PRICE	P/E RATIO	YLD.	MKT. CAP.	RANGE (52-WK.)	'02 Y/E PR.	DIV. ACH.
NYSE	STR	27.88 (2/28/03)	13.5	2.7%	$2.27 bill.	29.45 - 18.01	27.82	23 yrs.

INVESTMENT GRADE. THE COMPANY IS STRIVING TO GROW ITS NONREGULATED PRODUCTION BY 5.0% TO 10.0% IN 2003.

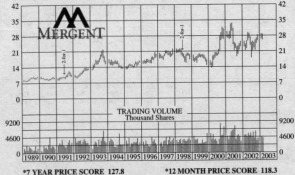

*7 YEAR PRICE SCORE 127.8   *12 MONTH PRICE SCORE 118.3

*NYSE COMPOSITE INDEX=100

INTERIM EARNINGS (Per Share):

Qtr.	Mar.	June	Sept.	Dec.
1998	0.50	0.19	0.10	0.14
1999	0.52	0.28	0.18	0.21
2000	0.62	0.33	0.34	0.65
2001	0.85	0.30	0.27	0.52
2002	0.61	0.36	0.28	0.82

INTERIM DIVIDENDS (Per Share):

Amt.	Decl.	Ex.	Rec.	Pay.
0.18Q	5/21/02	5/29/02	5/31/02	6/17/02
0.18Q	8/13/02	8/21/02	8/23/02	9/16/02
0.185Q	10/24/02	11/20/02	11/22/02	12/16/02
0.185Q	2/11/03	2/19/03	2/21/03	3/17/03

Indicated div.: $0.74 (Div. Reinv. Plan)

CAPITALIZATION (12/31/01):

	($000)	(%)
Long-Term Debt	997,423	41.2
Deferred Income Tax	324,309	13.4
Minority Interest	19,805	0.8
Common & Surplus	1,080,781	44.6
Total	2,422,318	100.0

BUSINESS:

Questar Corporation is a diversified energy services holding company with two divisions. Market Resources engages in energy development and production; gas gathering and processing; and wholesale gas and hydrocarbon liquids marketing, risk management, and storage. Regulated Services, through two subsidiaries, conducts interstate gas transmission and storage activities and retail gas distribution services. The Company is also involved in providing integrated information and communication services.

RECENT DEVELOPMENTS:

For the twelve months ended 12/31/02, income was $170.9 million, before an accounting change charge of $15.3 million, compared with net income of $158.2 million the previous year. Total revenues decreased 16.6% to $1.20 billion from $1.44 billion a year earlier. Operating income rose to $274.2 million versus $274.1 million the year before. Nonregulated proved reserves as of 12/31/02 were approximately 1,113.00 billion cubic feet equivalent (bcfe), reflecting asset sales, additions, revisions and production, compared with 1,184.00 bcfe a year earlier.

PROSPECTS:

STR is projecting full-year 2003 earnings of between $1.95 and $2.10 per share, based on the Company's hedge positions, and anticipated prices for its unhedged gas and oil production, based on forward price curves at the close of business 2/11/03. The guidance excludes gains and losses on asset sales and the effects of accounting changes. STR stated that its goal is to grow nonregulated production by 5.0% to 10.0% in 2003, assuming no further asset sales and no price-related curtailments. Separately, on 12/4/02, STR announced that it has completed the sale of its interest in the TransColorado Pipeline to a Kinder Morgan affiliate. Under the sales agreement, which was effective 10/1/02, Kinder Morgan paid the Company $105.5 million.

ANNUAL FINANCIAL DATA:

FISCAL YEAR	TOT. REVS. ($mill.)	NET INC. ($mill.)	TOT. ASSETS ($mill.)	OPER. PROFIT %	NET PROFIT %	NET INC./ NET PROP. %	NET INC./ TOT. CAP. %	RET. ON EQUITY %	ACCUM. DEPR./ GROSS PROP. %	EARN. PER SH.$	TANG. BK. VAL.$	DIV. PER SH.$	DIV. PAYOUT %	PRICE RANGE	AVG. P/E RATIO	AVG. YIELD %
p12/31/02	1,200.7	⑤ 170.9								⑤ 2.07		0.73	35.3	29.45 - 18.01	11.5	3.1
12/31/01	1,439.4	② 158.2	3,235.7	19.0	11.0	6.2	6.5	14.6	37.3	④ 1.94	12.14	0.70	36.3	33.75 - 18.58	13.5	2.7
12/31/00	1,266.2	③ 156.7	2,539.0	20.5	12.4	8.0	8.0	15.8	44.9	③ 1.94	12.01	0.69	35.3	31.88 - 13.56	11.7	3.0
12/31/99	924.2	① 98.8	2,238.0	19.5	10.7	5.5	5.3	10.7	45.2	① 1.20	11.37	0.67	55.8	19.94 - 14.75	14.5	3.9
12/31/98	906.3	② 76.9	2,161.3	14.7	8.5	4.4	4.5	8.8	43.7	② 0.93	10.62	0.65	70.2	22.38 - 15.81	20.5	3.4
12/31/97	933.3	104.8	1,945.0	18.2	11.2	6.8	6.5	12.4	44.2	1.26	10.30	0.62	49.2	22.31 - 17.13	15.6	3.1
12/31/96	818.0	98.1	1,816.2	21.0	12.0	6.6	6.4	12.7	42.6	1.20	9.41	0.59	49.8	20.69 - 15.44	15.1	3.3
12/31/95	649.3	83.8	1,584.6	21.9	12.9	6.4	6.3	11.8	43.8	1.03	8.76	0.58	56.6	16.88 - 13.06	14.6	3.9
12/31/94	670.3	① 49.4	1,585.6	23.1	7.4	3.8	3.8	7.6	42.2	① 0.61	8.08	0.56	93.4	17.63 - 13.31	25.6	3.7
12/31/93	660.4	84.5	1,417.7	22.5	12.8	7.3	7.4	14.0	43.1	1.05	7.49	0.55	51.9	22.00 - 12.69	16.5	3.1

Statistics are as originally reported. Adj. for 2-for-1 stk. split, 6/98. ① Incl. write-down of invst. in partnerships of $49.7 mill., 1999; $61.7 mill., 1994. ② Incl. $34.00 mill. write-down of oil & gas prop. ③ Incl. after-tax gain of $16.3 mill. ($0.20/sh.) on sale of securities. ④ Incl. after-tax loss of $905,000 on sale of securities & after-tax gain of $13.5 mill. on sales of nonstrategic properties. ⑤ Bef. acctg. chge. chrg. of $15.3 mill.

OFFICERS:
R. D. Cash, Chmn.
K. O. Rattie, Pres., C.E.O.
C. C. Holbrook, Sr. V.P., Gen. Coun., Corp. Sec.

INVESTOR CONTACT: Stephen E. Parks, Sr. V.P., Treas., C.F.O., (801) 324-5497

PRINCIPAL OFFICE: 180 East 100 South Street, Salt Lake City, UT 84145-0433

TELEPHONE NUMBER: (801) 324-5000
FAX: (801) 324-5483
WEB: www.questar.com

NO. OF EMPLOYEES: 2,221 (avg.)

SHAREHOLDERS: 11,299 (record); 30,000-35,000 (approx. beneficial)

ANNUAL MEETING: In May

INCORPORATED: UT, Oct., 1984

INSTITUTIONAL HOLDINGS:
No. of Institutions: 232
Shares Held: 50,171,415
% Held: 61.3

INDUSTRY: Gas transmission and distribution (SIC: 4923)

TRANSFER AGENT(S): Questar Corp., Salt Lake City, UT

QWEST COMMUNICATIONS INTERNATIONAL, INC.

EXCH.	SYM.	REC. PRICE	P/E RATIO	YLD.	MKT. CAP.	RANGE (52-WK.)	'02 Y/E PR.
NYSE	Q	3.58 (2/28/03)	...	...	$5.96 bill.	10.29 - 1.07	5.00

SPECULATIVE GRADE. THE COMPANY'S TOP LINE HAS BEEN HAMPERED BY COMPETITIVE PRESSURES IN LOCAL AND LONG-DISTANCE VOICE SERVICES.

7 YEAR PRICE SCORE N/A   **12 MONTH PRICE SCORE 115.4**
*NYSE COMPOSITE INDEX=100

INTERIM EARNINGS (Per Share):

Qtr.	Mar.	June	Sept.	Dec.
1997	d0.01	d0.01	0.03	0.03
1998	d0.01	d1.67	d0.01	d0.03
1999	0.01	0.02	Nil	0.56
2000	0.45	d0.14	d0.15	d0.07
2001	0.01	d1.99	d0.09	d0.32
2002	----------------d9.84----------------			

INTERIM DIVIDENDS (Per Share):

Amt.	Decl.	Ex.	Rec.	Pay.
Last dist. $0.05A, 6/29/01				

CAPITALIZATION (12/31/01):

	($000)	(%)
Long-Term Debt	20,197,000	34.2
Deferred Income Tax	2,194,000	3.7
Common & Surplus	36,655,000	62.1
Total	59,046,000	100.0

BUSINESS:

Qwest Communications International, Inc. provides local telecommunications and related services, wireless services and directory services in the 14-state local service area of Arizona, Colorado, Idaho, Iowa, Minnesota, Montana, Nebraska, New Mexico, North Dakota, Oregon, South Dakota, Utah, Washington and Wyoming, as of 12/31/01. The Company also provides secure broadband data, voice and image communications globally. Qwest's principal asset is its telecommunications network, which consists of both its traditional telephone communications network and the Qwest Macro Capacity™ Fiber Network. As of 12/31/01, the Company offered high-speed, high-capacity connectivity to six continents with a total network footprint of more than 190,000 route-miles. The North American portion of the fiber optic broadband network, including both in and out of the Company's local service area, reaches over 32,000 route-miles. On 6/30/00, Qwest acquired U S West, Inc. for approximately $40.00 billion.

RECENT DEVELOPMENTS:

For the twelve months ended 12/31/02, Q reported a loss from continuing operations of $16.55 billion versus a loss from continuing operations of $5.26 billion a year earlier. Results for 2002 and 2001 included goodwill and other intangible amortization of $186.0 million and $1.34 billion, restructuring, merger-related and other charges of $171.0 million and $1.21 billion, and investment write-downs of $1.20 billion and $3.29 billion, respectively. Results also included asset impairments of $18.42 billion in 2002 and non-recurring gains of $68.0 million in 2001. Total operating revenues fell 7.5% to $15.49 billion. Comparisons were made with restated 2001 figures.

PROSPECTS:

Q's near-term outlook appears unfavorable. The Company noted that access lines are expected to continue to face pressure from wireless and broadband substitution, competition, and a declining regional economy. In addition, Q expects demand for data and internet protocol services to remain relatively flat in 2003. Capital expenditures are expected in the range of 15.0% to 20.0% of revenue.

ANNUAL FINANCIAL DATA:

FISCAL YEAR	TOT. REVS. ($mill.)	NET INC. ($mill.)	TOT. ASSETS ($mill.)	OPER. PROFIT %	NET PROFIT %	RET. ON EQUITY %	RET. ON ASSETS %	CURR. RATIO	EARN. PER SH.$	CASH FL. PER SH.$	TANG. BK. VAL.$	DIV. PER SH.$	PRICE RANGE	AVG. P/E RATIO	AVG. YIELD %
p12/31/02	15,487.0	⑥ d16,500.0	...	...	...	...	...	...	⑥ d9.84	...	...	...	15.19 - 1.07	...	...
12/31/01	19,695.0	⑤ d3,958.0	73,781.0	4.2	...	...	...	0.6	⑤ d2.38	0.83	1.28	0.05	48.19 - 11.08	...	0.2
④ 12/31/00	16,610.0	③ d81.0	73,501.0	11.0	...	...	...	0.5	③ d0.06	2.56	5.37	...	66.00 - 32.13	...	...
12/31/99	3,927.6	② 458.5	11,058.1	8.2	11.7	6.5	4.1	1.4	② 0.60	1.13	4.95	...	52.38 - 25.03	64.5	...
12/31/98	2,242.7	① d844.0	8,067.6	...	...	...	...	1.2	① d1.51	d1.15	1.20	...	25.66 - 11.00	...	...
12/31/97	696.7	14.5	1,398.1	3.4	2.1	3.8	1.0	2.3	0.04	0.09	0.92	...	17.22 - 6.59	339.2	...
12/31/96	231.0	d7.0	262.6	...	...	...	...	0.4	d0.02	0.03	...	...	...	...	...
12/31/95	125.1	d25.1	184.2	...	...	...	...	1.0	d0.08	d0.04	0.05	...	...	...	...
12/31/94	70.9	d6.9	...	...	...	...	...	...	d0.02	d0.01	...	...	...	...	...

Statistics are as originally reported. Adj. for stk. splits: 2-for-1, 5/24/99 & 2/24/98. ① Incl. non-recurr. chrg. of $86.5 mill. ② Incl. non-recurr. chrg. of $31.5 mill. ③ Incl. merger-rel. & oth. chrgs. of $1.75 bill. and gain on sales of invest. of $327.0 mill. ④ Refls. acq. of U S West, Inc. ⑤ Incl. restruct., merger-rel. & oth. chrgs. of $1.20 bill., non-recurr. gain of $77.0 mill., and invest. write-down of $3.29 bill.; bef. extraord. chrg. of $65.0 mill. ⑥ Incl. asset impair. chrg. of $18.42 bill., restruct., merger-rel. & oth. chrgs. of $171.0 mill. & invest. write-down of $1.20 bill.; bef. net inc. fr. disc. ops. of $2.09 bill., extraord. gain of $1.07 bill. & acctg. chge. chrg. of $22.52 bill.

OFFICERS:
R. C. Notebaert, Chmn., C.E.O.
O. G. Shaffer, Vice-Chmn., C.F.O.
R. Baer, Exec. V.P., Couns.
INVESTOR CONTACT: Investor Relations, (877) 877-7978
PRINCIPAL OFFICE: 1801 California Street, Denver, CO 80202

TELEPHONE NUMBER: (303) 992-5109
FAX: (303) 291-1724
WEB: www.qwest.com
NO. OF EMPLOYEES: 61,000 (approx.)
SHAREHOLDERS: 438,000 (approx. record)
ANNUAL MEETING: In June
INCORPORATED: DE, 1997

RADIAN GROUP INC.

EXCH.	SYM.	REC. PRICE	P/E RATIO	YLD.	MKT. CAP.	RANGE (52-WK.)	'02 Y/E PR.
NYSE	RDN	34.87 (2/28/03)	7.9	0.2%	$3.28 bill.	55.56 - 29.40	37.15

UPPER MEDIUM GRADE. THE COMPANY SHOULD CONTINUE TO BENEFIT FROM GROWTH IN ITS CORE MORTGAGE INSURANCE BUSINESS.

TRADING VOLUME
Thousand Shares

*7 YEAR PRICE SCORE 155.5   *12 MONTH PRICE SCORE 93.6

*NYSE COMPOSITE INDEX=100

INTERIM EARNINGS (Per Share):

Qtr.	Mar.	June	Sept.	Dec.
1999	0.49	0.32	0.49	0.63
2000	0.77	0.80	0.83	0.83
2001	0.96	0.97	0.96	1.00
2002	1.08	1.12	1.07	1.14

INTERIM DIVIDENDS (Per Share):

Amt.	Decl.	Ex.	Rec.	Pay.
0.02Q	2/01/02	2/15/02	2/20/02	3/20/02
0.02Q	5/07/02	5/20/02	5/22/02	6/19/02
0.02Q	8/06/02	8/19/02	8/21/02	9/18/02
0.02Q	11/05/02	11/18/02	11/20/02	12/18/02
0.02Q	2/03/03	2/12/03	2/17/03	3/19/03

Indicated div.: $0.08

CAPITALIZATION (12/31/01):

	($000)	(%)
Long-Term Debt	324,076	10.6
Deferred Income Tax	432,098	14.1
Common & Surplus	2,306,328	75.3
Total	3,062,502	100.0

BUSINESS:

Radian Group Inc. was formed on June 9, 1999 from the acquisition by CMAC Investment Corporation of Amerin Corporation. Through its subsidiaries, RDN provides products and services through three business lines: financial guaranty, mortgage insurance and mortgage services. In the mortgage insurance business (accounting for 68.4% of revenues in 2002), RDN provides private mortgage insurance coverage in the United States on residential first mortgage loans. Private mortgage insurance protects mortgage lenders and investors from default-related losses on residential first mortgage loans made primarily to home buyers who make down payments of less than 20.0% of the home's purchase price. In the financial guaranty insurance business (22.5%), the Company provides insurance to the holder of a debt obligation. Through RDN's acquisition of ExpressClose.com, Inc., its mortgage services business (9.1%) provides lenders and consumers with mortgage processing, closing and settlement services through the Internet.

RECENT DEVELOPMENTS:

For the year ended 12/31/02, net income increased 18.5% to $427.2 million from $360.4 million the previous year. Total revenues climbed 21.6% to $1.15 billion from $947.2 million in 2001. Revenues for 2002 and 2001 included equity in net income of affiliates of $81.7 million and $41.3 million, respectively. Net premiums written grew 21.9% to $954.9 million. Mortgage insurance accounted for 70.0% of this total, while the financial guaranty business represented 30.0%. Premiums earned increased 18.3% to $847.1 million.

PROSPECTS:

Going forward, RDN should continue to benefit from revenue and earnings growth in its core mortgage insurance business. During the fourth quarter, the Company signed $15.30 billion in new primary mortgage insurance, including $5.00 billion of structured mortgage insurance. In addition, primary mortgage insurance-in-force was $110.30 billion at 12/31/02 versus $107.90 billion a year ago. Meanwhile, the Company's financial guaranty business should continue to benefit from a favorable environment as well as significant new writings in the direct municipal, reinsurance and structured product areas.

ANNUAL FINANCIAL DATA:

FISCAL YEAR	PREM. INC. ($mill.)	TOT. REVS. ($mill.)	NET INC. ($mill.)	TOT. ASSETS ($mill.)	TOT. INVST. ($mill.)	RET. ON REVS. %	RET. ON EQUITY %	RET. ON ASSETS %	EARN. PER SH.$	TANG. BK. VAL.$	AVG. YIELD %	DIV. PER SH.$	PRICE RANGE	AVG. P/E RATIO
p12/31/02	847.1	1,152.1	⑤427.2						⑤4.41		0.2	0.08	55.56 — 29.40	9.6
12/31/01	715.9	947.2	④360.4	4,438.6	3,546.9	38.1	15.6	8.1	④3.88	24.54	0.2	0.07	43.87 — 26.91	9.1
12/31/00	520.9	615.4	248.9	2,272.8	1,750.5	40.4	18.3	11.0	3.22	17.97	0.2	0.06	38.50 — 17.13	8.6
③12/31/99	472.6	552.8	②148.1	1,776.7	1,388.7	26.8	14.0	8.3	②1.92	14.17	0.3	0.06	27.97 — 16.66	11.7
12/31/98	282.2	333.0	91.1	968.2	736.3	27.3	17.4	9.4	1.86	11.52	0.3	0.06	35.00 — 12.69	12.8
12/31/97	237.7	277.3	75.0	704.6	596.9	27.0	17.4	10.6	1.53	9.54	0.3	0.06	30.94 — 15.81	15.3
12/31/96	187.9	222.6	62.2	592.7	513.2	28.0	17.5	10.5	1.28	7.96	0.4	0.05	19.38 — 11.00	11.9
12/31/95	137.1	165.6	50.8	499.1	437.5	30.7	17.0	10.2	1.05	6.71	0.5	0.05	13.94 — 7.19	10.1
12/31/94	106.1	130.5	41.1	410.2	358.7	31.5	17.2	10.0	0.85	5.46	0.7	0.05	7.72 — 5.81	7.9
12/31/93	81.6	107.2	①34.1	375.1	327.0	31.8	16.0	9.1	①0.70	4.85	0.7	0.05	8.78 — 5.75	10.5

Statistics are as originally reported. Adj. for 2-for-1 stk. spl., 6/01 ① Bef. acctg. change credit, $1.7 mill. ② Incl. merger expenses, $37.8 mill. ③ Figures for '98 & earlier are for CMAC Investment Corporation ④ Incl. chrg. of $5.8 mill. rel. to a chng. in the fair value of derivatives ⑤ Incl. chrg. of $13.0 mill. rel. to a chng. in the fair value of derivatives.

OFFICERS:
F. P. Filipps, Chmn., C.E.O.
R. J. Kasmar, Pres., C.O.O.
C. R. Quint, C.F.O., Exec. V.P.
INVESTOR CONTACT: Investor Relations, (215) 564-6600
PRINCIPAL OFFICE: 1601 Market Street, Philadelphia, PA 19103

TELEPHONE NUMBER: (215) 564-6600
FAX: (215) 564-0129
WEB: www.radiangroupinc.com
NO. OF EMPLOYEES: 1,194 (approx.)
SHAREHOLDERS: 10,500 (approx.)
ANNUAL MEETING: In May
INCORPORATED: DE, Dec., 1991

INSTITUTIONAL HOLDINGS:
No. of Institutions: 269
Shares Held: 88,593,655
% Held: 94.8

INDUSTRY: Surety insurance (SIC: 6351)

TRANSFER AGENT(S): Bank of New York, New York, NY

RADIOSHACK CORPORATION

EXCH.	SYM.	REC. PRICE	P/E RATIO	YLD.	MKT. CAP.	RANGE (52-WK.)	'02 Y/E PR.
NYSE	RSH	19.64 (2/28/03)	13.4	1.1%	$3.47 bill.	36.21 - 16.99	18.74

MEDIUM GRADE. THE COMPANY ANTICIPATES SALES GROWTH OF 2.0% TO 3.0% AND EARNINGS OF AT LEAST $1.60 PER SHARE IN 2003.

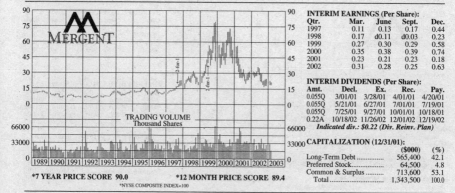

INTERIM EARNINGS (Per Share):

Qtr.	Mar.	June	Sept.	Dec.
1997	0.11	0.13	0.17	0.44
1998	0.17	d0.11	d0.03	0.23
1999	0.27	0.30	0.29	0.58
2000	0.35	0.38	0.39	0.74
2001	0.23	0.21	0.23	0.18
2002	0.31	0.28	0.25	0.63

INTERIM DIVIDENDS (Per Share):

Amt.	Decl.	Ex.	Rec.	Pay.
0.055Q	3/01/01	3/28/01	4/01/01	4/20/01
0.055Q	5/21/01	6/27/01	7/01/01	7/19/01
0.055Q	7/25/01	9/27/01	10/01/01	10/18/01
0.22A	10/18/02	11/26/02	12/01/02	12/19/02

Indicated div.: $0.22 (Div. Reinv. Plan)

TRADING VOLUME
Thousand Shares

*7 YEAR PRICE SCORE 90.0   ***12 MONTH PRICE SCORE 89.4**
*NYSE COMPOSITE INDEX=100

CAPITALIZATION (12/31/01):

	($000)	(%)
Long-Term Debt	565,400	42.1
Preferred Stock	64,500	4.8
Common & Surplus	713,600	53.1
Total	1,343,500	100.0

BUSINESS:

RadioShack Corporation (formerly Tandy Corporation) is one of America's largest retailers of name-brand and private label consumer electronics and personal computers. As of 2/20/03, the Company's retail operations included more than 7,200 Company-owned and dealer/franchise RadioShack® stores. The Company also designs, installs and maintains cabling systems for the transmission of video, voice and data, primarily for home use, through its wholly-owned subsidiary, AmeriLink Corporation. Private-label brands owned by RSH include Tandy®, Optimus®, Realistic®, DUoFONE, and Archer. The Company's Incredible Universe division ceased operations in 1997. On 8/31/98, RSH sold its Computer City, Inc. subsidiary.

RECENT DEVELOPMENTS:

For the twelve months ended 12/31/02, net income advanced 58.0% to $263.4 million from $166.7 million in the corresponding prior-year period. Results for 2002 included a $5.6 million after-tax gain stemming from a litigation settlement and a contract termination, partially offset by an impairment charge. Results for 2001 included after-tax charges totaling $125.1 million. Net sales and operating revenues slipped 4.2% to $4.58 billion from $4.78 billion the year before. Comparable-store sales were down 1.0% year over year. Gross profit totaled $2.24 billion, or 48.9% of net sales and operating revenues, versus $2.30 billion, or 48.1% of net sales and operating revenues, a year earlier. Operating income climbed 18.4% to $425.4 million from $359.3 million in 2001.

PROSPECTS:

The Company is targeting earnings of approximately $0.33 per share for the first quarter of 2003. RSH anticipates full-year 2003 sales growth of between 2.0% and 3.0%, along with earnings per share of at least $1.60. Results are expected to benefit from RSH's efforts to remodel existing stores and include an expanded selection of higher-profit items, such as computer accessories, and digital cameras. In 2003, the Company plans to open about 70 new stores and close up to 120 existing locations.

ANNUAL FINANCIAL DATA:

FISCAL YEAR	TOT. REVS. ($mill.)	NET INC. ($mill.)	TOT. ASSETS ($mill.)	OPER. PROFIT %	NET PROFIT %	RET. ON EQUITY %	RET. ON ASSETS %	CURR. RATIO	EARN. PER SH. $	CASH FL. PER SH. $	TANG. BK. VAL. $	DIV. PER SH. $	PRICE RANGE	AVG. P/E RATIO	AVG. YIELD %
p12/31/02	4,577.2	⑤ 263.4							⑤ 1.45			0.22	36.21 - 16.99	18.3	0.8
12/31/01	4,775.7	④ 166.7	2,245.1	7.5	3.5	21.4	7.4	2.1	④ 0.85	1.41	4.04	0.22	56.50 - 20.10	45.1	0.6
12/31/00	4,794.7	368.0	2,576.5	13.1	7.7	41.8	14.3	1.5	1.84	2.38	4.37	0.22	72.94 - 35.06	29.3	0.4
12/31/99	4,126.2	297.9	2,142.0	12.1	7.2	35.9	13.9	1.5	1.43	1.87	4.08	0.20	79.50 - 20.59	35.0	0.4
12/31/98	4,787.9	② 61.3	1,993.6	2.8	1.3	7.2	3.1	1.5	② 0.27	0.73	3.86	0.20	31.94 - 15.19	87.2	0.8
12/31/97	5,372.2	186.9	2,317.5	6.3	3.5	17.7	8.1	1.8	0.82	1.24	4.68	0.20	23.00 - 10.16	20.3	1.2
12/31/96	6,285.5	③ d91.6	394.5	...	...	...	...	1.6	③ d0.41	0.04	...	0.20	14.78 - 8.53	...	1.7
12/31/95	5,839.1	212.0	2,722.1	5.7	3.6	13.2	7.8	2.1	0.78	1.13	6.03	0.18	16.09 - 9.13	16.2	1.4
12/31/94	4,943.7	② 224.3	3,243.8	6.3	4.5	12.1	6.9	2.1	② 0.73	1.01	5.61	0.15	12.66 - 7.69	14.0	1.5
12/31/93	4,102.6	① 195.6	3,219.1	7.0	4.8	10.0	6.1	2.1	① 0.63	0.95	5.55	0.15	12.69 - 6.16	15.1	1.6

Statistics are as originally reported. Adj. for 2-for-1 stk. split, 6/99 & 9/97. ① Bef. $13 mil ($0.05/sh) cr. for acctg. adj. & $111.8 mil ($0.37/sh) loss from discont. opers. ② Incl. $190.8 mil pre-tax, non-recur. chg., 1998; & $89.1 mil restr. chgs., 1994. ③ Incl. $112.8 mil pre-tax impair. chg. & $162.1 mil restr. chg. ④ Incl. $57.2 mil loss fr. asset sale, $39.8 mil chg. fr. asset impair., $18.3 mil employ. separation chg. & $30.0 mil loss fr. internet-related invest. ⑤ Incl. $18.5 mil gain fr. contract term., $8.1 mil chg. fr. asset impair. & $1.3 mil litigation chg.

OFFICERS:
L. R. Roberts, Chmn., C.E.O.
D. J. Edmondson, Pres., C.O.O.
M. Newman, Sr. V.P., C.F.O.
M. C. Hill, Sr. V.P., Sec., Gen. Couns.

INVESTOR CONTACT: Investor Relations, (817) 415-6675

PRINCIPAL OFFICE: 100 Throckmorton Street, Suite 1800, Fort Worth, TX 76102

TELEPHONE NUMBER: (817) 415-3700
FAX: (817) 878-4887
WEB: www.radioshack.com

NO. OF EMPLOYEES: 41,400 (approx.)

SHAREHOLDERS: 31,671

ANNUAL MEETING: In May

INCORPORATED: NJ, May, 1899; reincorp., DE, Dec., 1967

INSTITUTIONAL HOLDINGS:
No. of Institutions: 266
Shares Held: 129,482,644
% Held: 76.9

INDUSTRY: Radio, TV, & electronic stores (SIC: 5731)

TRANSFER AGENT(S): Fleet National Bank c/o EquiServe, Boston, MA

RAYMOND JAMES FINANCIAL, INC.

EXCH.	SYM.	REC. PRICE	P/E RATIO	YLD.	MKT. CAP.	RANGE (52-WK.)	'02 Y/E PR.
NYSE	RJF	25.48 (2/28/03)	16.8	1.4%	$1.24 bill.	37.30 - 22.75	29.58

UPPER MEDIUM GRADE. THE COMPANY ANTICIPATES WEAKER RESULTS FOR THE NEXT THREE QUARTERS OF FISCAL 2003.

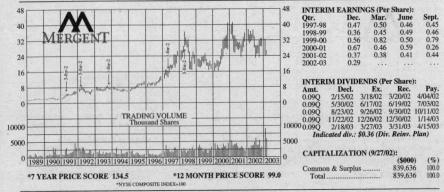

*7 YEAR PRICE SCORE 134.5   ***12 MONTH PRICE SCORE 99.0**
*NYSE COMPOSITE INDEX=100

INTERIM EARNINGS (Per Share):

Qtr.	Dec.	Mar.	June	Sept.
1997-98	0.47	0.50	0.46	0.45
1998-99	0.36	0.45	0.49	0.46
1999-00	0.56	0.82	0.50	0.79
2000-01	0.67	0.46	0.59	0.26
2001-02	0.37	0.38	0.41	0.44
2002-03	0.29	...	...	...

INTERIM DIVIDENDS (Per Share):

Amt.	Decl.	Ex.	Rec.	Pay.
0.09Q	2/15/02	3/18/02	3/20/02	4/04/02
0.09Q	5/30/02	6/17/02	6/19/02	7/03/02
0.09Q	8/23/02	9/26/02	9/30/02	10/11/02
0.09Q	11/22/02	12/26/02	12/30/02	1/14/03
0.09Q	2/18/03	3/27/03	3/31/03	4/15/03

Indicated div.: $0.36 (Div. Reinv. Plan)

CAPITALIZATION (9/27/02):

	($000)	(%)
Common & Surplus	839,636	100.0
Total	839,636	100.0

BUSINESS:

Raymond James Financial, Inc., with assets totaling $6.16 billion as of 12/27/02, is a holding company primarily engaged in investment and financial planning, including securities brokerage, investment banking and asset management; banking and cash management; trust services; and life insurance. RJF's two broker/dealer subsidiaries, Raymond James & Associates and Raymond James Financial Services, serve more than 1.0 million accounts. RJF operates from the following segments: retail (65.6% of revenues as of 12/27/02), capital markets (22.0%), asset management (8.5%), RJBank (2.1%), and other (1.8%). RJF's asset management subsidiaries manage approximately $16.02 billion in financial assets for individuals, pension plans and municipalities. RJF operates from more than 2,100 locations in the U.S., Canada and abroad. On 12/29/00, RJF acquired Vancouver-based brokerage Raymond James Ltd., formerly Goepel McDermid.

RECENT DEVELOPMENTS:

For the quarter ended 12/27/02, net income decreased 20.3% to $14.4 million from $18.1 million in the corresponding period of the previous year. Total revenues declined 5.4% to $344.6 million compared with $364.1 million a year earlier. Securities commissions and fees revenue declined 5.5% to $237.8 million from $251.7 million the year before. Interest revenue dropped 23.7% to $34.6 million, while investment advisory fees slipped 5.3% to $26.3 million. However, investment banking revenue rose 3.5% to $11.2 million.

PROSPECTS:

Revenues and earnings are being adversely affected by lower gross interest income, as well as a decrease in commission and lending fees. Looking ahead, the Company anticipates weak results for the next three quarters of fiscal 2003 as market conditions should continue to be volatile. Furthermore, the current market environment is likely to adversely affect commission activity and investment banking volume as investors remain cautious and customers are less likely to borrow money to invest.

ANNUAL FINANCIAL DATA:

FISCAL YEAR	TOT. REVS. ($mill.)	NET INC. ($mill.)	TOT. ASSETS ($mill.)	OPER. PROFIT %	NET PROFIT %	RET. ON EQUITY %	RET. ON ASSETS %	CURR. RATIO	EARN. PER SH. $	CASH FL. PER SH. $	TANG. BK. VAL. $	DIV. PER SH. $	PRICE RANGE	AVG. P/E RATIO	AVG. YIELD %
9/27/02	1,515.9	79.3	6,040.3	8.7	5.2	9.4	1.3	1.0	1.60	2.06	16.02	0.36	37.50 - 22.75	18.8	1.2
9/28/01	1,657.8	③ 96.4	6,372.1	9.5	5.8	12.5	1.5	1.0	③ 1.98	2.64	14.71	0.36	41.35 - 23.36	16.3	1.1
9/29/00	1,698.6	③ 125.2	6,308.8	12.0	7.4	19.2	2.0	1.0	③ 2.67	3.18	13.35	0.30	41.00 - 16.00	10.7	1.1
9/24/99	1,232.2	85.1	5,030.7	11.2	6.9	15.2	1.7	1.0	1.76	2.17	11.08	0.28	25.19 - 16.69	11.9	1.3
9/25/98	1,082.9	② 92.7	3,852.7	13.9	8.6	18.2	2.4	1.0	② 1.86	2.18	10.56	0.24	36.50 - 16.75	14.3	0.9
9/26/97	927.6	① 98.9	3,278.6	17.3	10.7	23.4	3.0	1.0	① 2.04	2.32	8.87	0.21	26.50 - 12.45	9.5	1.1
9/27/96	721.8	· 66.0	2,566.4	15.0	9.1	20.2	2.6	1.0	1.40	1.63	6.67	0.17	13.67 - 8.45	7.9	1.5
9/29/95	554.1	46.1	2,012.7	13.4	8.3	17.3	2.3	1.0	0.99	1.20	5.74	0.16	11.22 - 6.11	8.7	1.8
9/30/94	507.1	42.1	1,698.3	13.3	8.3	18.5	2.5	1.0	0.88	1.02	4.65	0.14	8.33 - 5.83	8.1	2.0
9/24/93	451.7	49.3	1,447.6	17.8	10.9	24.0	3.4	1.1	1.01	1.12	4.29	0.09	9.00 - 6.04	7.4	1.5

Statistics are as originally reported. Adj for 3-for-2 stock split, 4/98, 4/97 & 11/93. ① Incl. $30.6 mill. gain fr. the sale of Liberty Investment Management, Inc. & a $2.5 mill. gin fr. the sale of the Company's former headquarters building. ② Incl. $1.7 mill. gain related to the sale of the real estate portfolio and property management subsidiaries & $2.4 mill. gain from the sale of the Company's specialist operations on the Chicago Exchange. ③ Incl. a pre-tax credit related to changes in litigation reserves of $16.0 mill., 9/01; d$20.0 mill., 9/00.

OFFICERS:
T. A. James, Chmn., C.E.O.
F. S. Gobold, Vice-Chmn.
C. Helck, Pres., C.O.O.
J. P. Julien, Sr. V.P., C.F.O.

INVESTOR CONTACT: Lawrence Silver, V.P., (727) 573-3800

PRINCIPAL OFFICE: 880 Carillon Parkway, St. Petersburg, FL 33716

TELEPHONE NUMBER: (727) 567-1000
FAX: (727) 573-8365
WEB: www.raymondjames.com

NO. OF EMPLOYEES: 5,651

SHAREHOLDERS: 13,000 (approx.)

ANNUAL MEETING: In Feb.

INCORPORATED: FL, 1974

INSTITUTIONAL HOLDINGS:
No. of Institutions: 168
Shares Held: 24,138,179
% Held: 49.5

INDUSTRY: Security brokers and dealers (SIC: 6211)

TRANSFER AGENT(S): Mellon Investor Services, LLP, Ridgefield Park, NJ

RAYONIER INC.

EXCH.	SYM.	REC. PRICE	P/E RATIO	YLD.	MKT. CAP.	RANGE (52-WK.)	'02 Y/E PR.
NYSE	RYN	42.52 (2/28/03)	21.7	3.4%	$1.16 bill.	58.67 - 36.70	45.25

MEDIUM GRADE. THE COMPANY EXPECTS NEAR TERM RESULTS TO BE ADVERSELY AFFECTED BY THE WEAK TIMBER MARKET AND HIGHER RAW MATERIAL AND ENERGY COSTS.

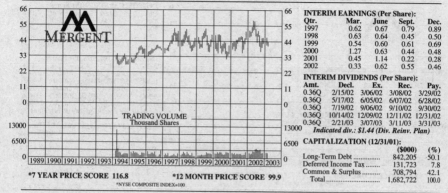

*7 YEAR PRICE SCORE 116.8   *12 MONTH PRICE SCORE 99.9
*NYSE COMPOSITE INDEX=100

INTERIM EARNINGS (Per Share):

Qtr.	Mar.	June	Sept.	Dec.
1997	0.62	0.67	0.79	0.89
1998	0.63	0.64	0.45	0.50
1999	0.54	0.60	0.61	0.69
2000	1.27	0.63	0.44	0.48
2001	0.45	1.14	0.22	0.28
2002	0.33	0.62	0.55	0.46

INTERIM DIVIDENDS (Per Share):

Amt.	Decl.	Ex.	Rec.	Pay.
0.36Q	2/15/02	3/06/02	3/08/02	3/29/02
0.36Q	5/17/02	6/05/02	6/07/02	6/28/02
0.36Q	7/19/02	9/06/02	9/10/02	9/30/02
0.36Q	10/14/02	12/09/02	12/11/02	12/31/02
0.36Q	2/21/03	3/07/03	3/11/03	3/31/03

Indicated div.: $1.44 (Div. Reinv. Plan)

CAPITALIZATION (12/31/01):

	($000)	(%)
Long-Term Debt	842,205	50.1
Deferred Income Tax	131,723	7.8
Common & Surplus	708,794	42.1
Total	1,682,722	100.0

BUSINESS:

Rayonier Inc. is an international forest products company that is primarily engaged in the production and sale of cellulose fibers and activities associated with timber and land management, including the sale of timber and land. As of 1/21/03, Rayonier owned and operated two performance fiber mills in the U.S. and, owned, leased or controlled approximately 2.2 million acres of timberland located in the U.S. and New Zealand. RYN also engages in the manufacturing of logs and wood products, and has lumber manufacturing facilities in the United States and a medium-density fiberboard plant in New Zealand. RYN operates in three reportable business segments: Performance Fibers (46.7% of 2002 sales); Wood Products and Trading, (31.4%); and Timber and Land, (21.9%). Performance Fibers includes two business units, Cellulose Specialties and Absorbent Materials. Specialty cellulose products are used in dissolving chemical applications. Fiber materials are used for absorbent hygiene products.

RECENT DEVELOPMENTS:

For the year ended 12/31/02, income declined 3.5% to $54.9 million, before a loss of $700,000 from discontinued operations, compared with income of $56.9 million, before a gain of $700,000 from discontinued operations, in 2001. Results for 2002 included a provision for dispositions of $2.7 million. Sales were flat at $1.12 billion compared with the prior year. Performance Fibers segment sales decreased 3.8% to $526.1 million, while Wood Products and Trading segment sales advanced 11.7% to $353.6 million. Timber and Land segment sales fell 9.3% to $247.1 million. Comparisons were made with restated results.

PROSPECTS:

RYN expects to post lower first quarter 2003 earnings year over year due to the timing of both land sales and performance fibers' shipments, as well as weaker timber markets and higher raw material and energy costs. However, continued strong demand for the Company's cellulose specialty products and anticipated land sales should provide a solid earnings base for the year. Furthermore, RYN plans to capture appreciating timber and land values by annually selling 2.0% to 4.0% of its holdings, opportunistically timely purchasing timberlands.

ANNUAL FINANCIAL DATA:

FISCAL YEAR	TOT. REVS. ($mill.)	NET INC. ($mill.)	TOT. ASSETS ($mill.)	OPER. PROFIT %	NET PROFIT %	RET. ON EQUITY %	RET. ON ASSETS %	CURR. RATIO	EARN. PER SH. $	CASH FL. PER SH. $	TANG. BK. VAL. $	DIV. PER SH. $	PRICE RANGE	AVG. P/E RATIO	AVG. YIELD %
p12/31/02	1,117.4	⑤ 54.9							⑤ 1.95			1.44	58.67 — 36.70	24.4	3.0
12/31/01	1,164.9	57.6	2,025.0	12.9	4.9	8.1	2.8	1.5	2.09	8.50	25.92	1.44	50.98 — 35.80	20.8	3.3
12/31/00	1,226.9	④ 78.2	2,162.3	15.4	6.4	11.5	3.6	1.4	④ 2.82	9.21	25.09	1.44	48.88 — 31.25	14.2	3.6
12/31/99	1,035.9	③ 68.7	2,280.2	13.1	6.6	10.5	3.0	1.4	③ 2.44	6.18	23.82	1.29	52.88 — 36.25	18.3	2.9
12/31/98	1,008.6	63.6	1,600.9	12.3	6.3	10.0	4.0	1.6	2.22	5.76	23.01	1.24	52.50 — 36.63	20.1	2.8
12/31/97	1,104.2	③ 87.3	1,595.6	15.0	7.9	13.8	5.5	1.5	③ 2.97	7.21	22.36	1.20	53.00 — 35.25	14.9	2.7
12/31/96	1,178.0	② d0.2	1,597.7	2.9	...	...	...	1.6	② d3.28	4.14	21.27	1.16	41.25 — 33.13	...	3.1
12/31/95	1,260.5	① 142.3	1,647.9	18.5	11.3	18.5	8.6	1.9	① 4.75	8.95	25.91	1.00	40.63 — 28.25	7.2	2.9
12/31/94	1,069.5	70.0	1,511.2	15.8	6.5	10.7	4.6	1.7	2.36	6.49	22.14	0.72	35.00 — 26.75	13.1	2.3
12/31/93	936.3	52.5	1,474.8	13.6	5.6	8.7	3.6	0.9	1.77	5.18	20.48	...	...	...	...

Statistics are as originally reported. ① Incl. non-recurr. gain of $34.8 mill. ② Bef. disc. oper. loss of $98.2 mill., incl. provision for despositions of $124.6 mill. ③ Incl. gains from sale of assets of $7.7 mill., 1999; $8.4 mill., 1997. ④ Incl. $15.0 mill. provisions for dispositions and gains from sale of assets of $7.6 mill. ⑤ Bef. disc. oper. loss of $700,000, incl. provision for despositions of $2.7 mill.

OFFICERS:
W. L. Nutter, Chmn., Pres., C.E.O.
G. J. Pollack, Sr. V.P., C.F.O.
J. Witter, V.P., Gen. Couns.
INVESTOR CONTACT: Parag Bhansali, (904) 357-9155
PRINCIPAL OFFICE: 50 North Laura Street, Jacksonville, FL 32202

TELEPHONE NUMBER: (904) 357-9100
FAX: (904) 357-9101
WEB: www.rayonier.com
NO. OF EMPLOYEES: 2,300 (avg.)
SHAREHOLDERS: 15,426 (approx.)
ANNUAL MEETING: In May
INCORPORATED: DE, 1937; reincorp., NC, Dec., 1937

INSTITUTIONAL HOLDINGS:
No. of Institutions: 162
Shares Held: 24,207,752
% Held: 87.3

INDUSTRY: Logging (SIC: 2411)

TRANSFER AGENT(S): The Bank of New York, New York, NY

RAYTHEON COMPANY

EXCH.	SYM.	REC. PRICE	P/E RATIO	YLD.	MKT. CAP.	RANGE (52-WK.)	'02 Y/E PR.
NYSE	RTN	27.08 (2/28/03)	14.6	3.0%	$10.71 bill.	45.70 - 26.30	30.75

MEDIUM GRADE. FOR 2003, THE COMPANY EXPECTS NET SALES GROWTH TO RANGE FROM 6.0% TO 7.0%.

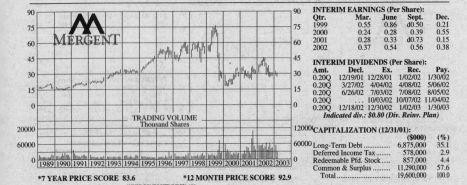

INTERIM EARNINGS (Per Share):

Qtr.	Mar.	June	Sept.	Dec.
1999	0.55	0.86	d0.50	0.21
2000	0.24	0.28	0.39	0.55
2001	0.28	0.33	d0.73	0.15
2002	0.37	0.54	0.56	0.38

INTERIM DIVIDENDS (Per Share):

Amt.	Decl.	Ex.	Rec.	Pay.
0.20Q	12/19/01	12/28/01	1/02/02	1/30/02
0.20Q	3/27/02	4/04/02	4/08/02	5/06/02
0.20Q	6/26/02	7/03/02	7/08/02	8/05/02
0.20Q	...	10/03/02	10/07/02	11/04/02
0.20Q	12/18/02	12/30/02	1/02/03	1/30/03

Indicated div.: $0.80 (Div. Reinv. Plan)

CAPITALIZATION (12/31/01):

	($000)	(%)
Long-Term Debt	6,875,000	35.1
Deferred Income Tax	578,000	2.9
Redeemable Pfd. Stock	857,000	4.4
Common & Surplus	11,290,000	57.6
Total	19,600,000	100.0

*7 YEAR PRICE SCORE 83.6   *12 MONTH PRICE SCORE 92.9

*NYSE COMPOSITE INDEX=100

BUSINESS:

Raytheon Company, which operates throughout the U.S., provides products and services in the areas of defense, government and commercial electronics, and business and special mission aircraft. The electronics group designs, manufactures and services electronics devices, equipment and systems for both government and commercial customers. The aircraft group markets and supports piston-powered aircraft, jet props and light and medium jets for the world's commercial, regional airlines and military aircraft markets. On 12/17/97, RTN merged with HE Holdings, Inc. The operations and assets of HE Holdings consisted of the defense business of Hughes Electronics Corp. On 7/7/00, RTN sold its Raytheon Engineers and Constructors unit. Net sales for 2002 were derived as follows: Electronic Systems, 50.4%; Command, Control, Communication and Information Systems, 23.2%; Aircraft, 12.1%; Technical Services, 11.9%; and Commercial Electronics, 2.4%.

RECENT DEVELOPMENTS:

For the year ended 12/31/02, RTN reported income from continuing operations of $755.0 million, before an extraordinary gain of $1.0 million, versus income of $18.0 million, before an extraordinary loss of $16.0 million, the year before. Earnings for 2002 included a net charge of $146.0 million related to various items. Earnings for 2002 and 2001 excluded losses of $834.0 million and $757.0 million, respectively, from discontinued operations. Net sales increased 4.6% to $16.76 billion. Comparisons were made with restated 2002 figures.

PROSPECTS:

For 2003, the Company expects net sales growth to range from 6.0% to 7.0%, diluted earnings per share from continuing operations between $1.70 and $1.80, and cash flow from continuing operations in the range of $950 million to $1.05 billion. For 2004, RTN expects year-over-year net sales growth to range from 6.0% to 7.0% and diluted earnings per share from continuing operations between $1.60 and $1.70 versus 2003. Separately, the Company continues to win strategic contracts, including a $265.8 million U.S. Army contract modification.

ANNUAL FINANCIAL DATA:

FISCAL YEAR	TOT. REVS. ($mill.)	NET INC. ($mill.)	TOT. ASSETS ($mill.)	OPER. PROFIT %	NET PROFIT %	RET. ON EQUITY %	RET. ON ASSETS %	CURR. RATIO	EARN. PER SH.$	CASH FL. PER SH.$	TANG. BK. VAL.$	DIV. PER SH.$	PRICE RANGE	AVG. P/E RATIO	AVG. YIELD %
p12/31/02	16,760.0	②⑦755.0	23,427.0						②⑦1.85			0.80	45.70 - 26.30	19.5	2.2
12/31/01	16,867.0	⑤5.0	26,636.0	4.5	...	...	...	1.5	⑦0.01	2.03	...	0.80	37.44 - 23.95	307.0	2.6
12/31/00	16,895.0	⑥498.0	26,777.0	9.6	2.9	4.6	1.9	1.6	⑥1.46	3.49	...	0.80	35.81 - 17.50	18.3	3.0
12/31/99	19,841.0	④457.0	28,110.0	7.7	2.3	4.2	1.6	1.1	⑤d0.15	3.47	...	0.80	76.56 - 22.19	...	1.6
12/31/98	19,530.0	④864.0	27,939.0	10.4	4.4	8.0	3.1	1.3	④2.53	4.75	...	0.80	60.75 - 40.69	20.0	1.6
12/31/97	13,673.0	①527.0	28,598.0	7.9	3.9	5.1	1.8	0.8	①2.18	4.07	30.76	...	60.56 - 41.75	23.5	...
12/31/96	12,330.5	③761.2	11,126.1	9.7	6.2	16.6	6.8	1.2	③3.21	4.76	12.80	...	56.13 - 43.38	15.5	...
12/31/95	11,715.6	②792.5	9,840.9	9.3	6.8	18.5	8.1	1.4	②3.25	4.77	7.25	...	47.25 - 31.44	12.1	...
12/31/94	10,012.9	①596.9	7,422.0	8.3	6.0	15.2	8.1	1.5	①2.26	3.40	12.92	...	34.44 - 30.25	14.3	...
12/31/93	9,201.2	693.0	7,367.2	10.0	7.5	16.1	9.4	1.6	2.56	3.58	15.89	...	34.25 - 25.25	11.6	...

Statistics are as originally reported. Stk. prices reflect Cl. B shares prior to the reclassif. of Cl. A & Cl. B shares into a single class of new com. stk. on 5/14/01; adj. for 2-for-1 splits 10/95. ① Incl. after-tax restruct. chg. of $321.7 mill., 1997; $162.3 mill., 1994. ② Incl. one-time net chrg. of $716.0 mill., 2002; gain of $8.0 mill., 1995. ③ Incl. $34.0 mill. pre-tax chg. & $75.0 mill. tax credit. ④ Incl. pre-tax restruct. & spec. chgs. of $252.0 mill. ⑤ Bef. acctg. chrg. of $53.0 mill. ⑥ Excl. disc. opers. loss of $357.0 mill. ⑦ Bef. loss fr. disc. ops. of $834.0 mill., 2002; $692.0 mill., 2001 & extraord. gain $1.0 mill, 2002; loss $16.0 mill., 2001.

OFFICERS:
D. P. Burnham, Chmn., C.E.O.
W. H. Swanson, Pres.

INVESTOR CONTACT: Timothy C. Oliver, V.P., Investor Relations, (781) 860-2303

PRINCIPAL OFFICE: 141 Spring Street, Lexington, MA 02421

TELEPHONE NUMBER: (781) 862-6600
FAX: (781) 860-2811
WEB: www.raytheon.com
NO. OF EMPLOYEES: 76,400
SHAREHOLDERS: 76,041
ANNUAL MEETING: In April
INCORPORATED: DE, May, 1928

INSTITUTIONAL HOLDINGS:
No. of Institutions: 529
Shares Held: 303,125,891
% Held: 74.7
INDUSTRY: Search and navigation equipment (SIC: 3812)
TRANSFER AGENT(S): EquiServe, Canton, MA

READER'S DIGEST ASSOCIATION, INC. (THE)

EXCH.	SYM.	REC. PRICE	P/E RATIO	YLD.	MKT. CAP.	RANGE (52-WK.)	'02 Y/E PR.
NYSE	RDA	10.81 (2/28/03)	11.8	1.9%	$1.08 bill.	25.10 - 10.31	15.10

MEDIUM GRADE. THE COMPANY EXPECTS EARNINGS PER SHARE TO RANGE FROM $1.08 TO $1.18 FOR FISCAL 2003, EXCLUDING RECAPITALIZATION EXPENSES.

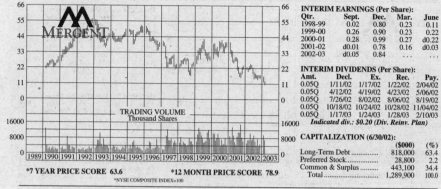

INTERIM EARNINGS (Per Share):

Qtr.	Sept.	Dec.	Mar.	June
1998-99	0.02	0.80	0.23	0.11
1999-00	0.26	0.90	0.23	0.22
2000-01	0.28	0.99	0.27	d0.22
2001-02	d0.01	0.78	0.16	d0.03
2002-03	d0.05	0.84	...	...

INTERIM DIVIDENDS (Per Share):

Amt.	Decl.	Ex.	Rec.	Pay.
0.05Q	1/11/02	1/17/02	1/22/02	2/04/02
0.05Q	4/12/02	4/19/02	4/23/02	5/06/02
0.05Q	7/26/02	8/02/02	8/06/02	8/19/02
0.05Q	10/18/02	10/24/02	10/28/02	11/04/02
0.05Q	1/17/03	1/24/03	1/28/03	2/10/03

Indicated div.: $0.20 (Div. Reinv. Plan)

CAPITALIZATION (6/30/02):

	($000)	(%)
Long-Term Debt	818,000	63.4
Preferred Stock	28,800	2.2
Common & Surplus	443,100	34.4
Total	1,289,900	100.0

*7 YEAR PRICE SCORE 63.6   ***12 MONTH PRICE SCORE 78.9**

*NYSE COMPOSITE INDEX=100

BUSINESS:

The Reader's Digest Association, Inc. is a global publisher and direct mail marketer of magazines, books, music, videos, and other products, including financial services. As of 6/30/02, Reader's Digest magazine had a circulation of about 23.0 million and over 100.0 million readers each month. Reader's Digest is published in 48 editions and 19 languages. RDA also publishes Reader's Digest Condensed Books, book series, books of general interest and home entertainment products. Contributions to sales as of 6/30/02 were as follows: international businesses, 45.2%; North America books and home entertainment, 28.3%; and U.S. magazines, 26.5%.

RECENT DEVELOPMENTS:

For the quarter ended 12/31/02, net income increased 6.9% to $84.2 million compared with $78.8 million in the corresponding prior-year period. Total revenues increased 5.9% to $830.6 million, primarily driven by the addition of Reiman Publications LLC, as well as revenue growth at Books Are Fun and growth at QSP Inc. International businesses revenues slid 7.6% to $289.5 million, reflecting a weaker-than-expected performance, especially in Europe, due to softness in the economy. U.S. magazines revenues advanced 39.9% to $341.8 million. North America books and home entertainment revenues fell 12.0% to $199.3 million.

PROSPECTS:

Looking ahead, RDA expects continued strength in its U.S. businesses and weakness internationally for the remainder of fiscal 2003. As a result, RDA will focus on cutting costs overseas and reducing mailing quantities. Additionally, several of RDA's international businesses are investing in new initiatives, including the international expansion of Books Are Fun, QSP Inc., and Reiman Publications LLC. Moreover, RDA expects earnings per share of $0.02 to $0.07 in the third quarter of fiscal 2003 and between $1.08 to $1.18 for the full year, excluding recapitalization expenses. Separately, RDA announced a new global organizational structure of four groups: Reader's Digest International, Reader's Digest North America, Consumer Business Services, and QSP.

ANNUAL FINANCIAL DATA:

FISCAL YEAR	TOT. REVS. ($mill.)	NET INC. ($mill.)	TOT. ASSETS ($mill.)	OPER. PROFIT %	NET PROFIT %	RET. ON EQUITY %	RET. ON ASSETS %	CURR. RATIO	EARN. PER SH.$	CASH FL. PER SH.$	TANG. BK. VAL.$	DIV. PER SH.$	PRICE RANGE	AVG. P/E RATIO	AVG. YIELD %
6/30/02	2,368.6	91.2	2,702.7	6.7	3.9	19.3	3.4	0.9	0.89	1.26	...	0.20	25.10 - 13.76	21.8	1.0
6/30/01	2,518.2	132.1	1,675.1	9.1	5.2	29.0	7.9	0.9	1.26	1.82	0.17	0.20	40.50 - 15.25	22.1	0.7
6/30/00	2,553.7	173.8	1,758.8	9.9	6.8	34.5	9.9	0.9	1.61	2.07	0.64	0.20	41.88 - 28.38	21.8	0.6
6/30/99	2,532.2	①126.6	1,710.5	5.1	5.0	33.2	7.4	1.2	①1.15	1.58	2.22	0.20	42.50 - 24.75	29.2	0.6
6/30/98	2,633.7	③17.9	1,564.0	1.1	0.7	6.9	1.1	1.0	③0.16	0.60	1.91	0.72	29.19 - 16.25	141.9	3.2
6/30/97	2,839.0	③133.5	1,643.8	6.8	4.7	38.6	8.1	0.9	③1.24	1.69	2.70	1.35	41.00 - 21.00	25.0	4.4
6/30/96	3,098.1	②80.6	1,904.1	3.5	2.6	16.8	4.2	1.1	②0.73	1.20	3.90	1.80	51.38 - 34.00	58.5	4.2
6/30/95	3,068.5	264.0	1,958.7	12.8	8.6	41.2	13.5	1.1	2.35	2.76	4.94	1.65	52.00 - 38.25	19.2	3.7
6/30/94	2,806.4	①272.1	2,049.4	14.0	9.7	34.4	13.3	1.2	①2.34	2.72	6.08	1.45	49.38 - 39.88	19.1	3.2
6/30/93	2,868.6	③258.3	1,872.4	12.3	9.0	32.0	13.8	1.2	③2.16	2.56	6.02	1.25	55.88 - 36.13	21.3	2.7

Statistics are as originally reported. ① Bef. acctg. change credit $25.3 mill., 6/99; chrg. $25.8 mill., 6/94; chrg. $50.9 mill., 6/93. ② Incl. after-tax restr. chg. of $169.8 mill. ③ Incl. pre-tax restr. chg.: $70.0 mill., 6/98; $35.0 mill., 6/97.

OFFICERS:
T. O. Ryder, Chmn., C.E.O.
M. S. Geltzeiler, Sr. V.P., C.F.O.
M. A. Brizel, V.P., General Couns.

INVESTOR CONTACT: Richard Clark, V.P.-Inv. Rel., (914) 244-5425

PRINCIPAL OFFICE: Reader's Digest Road, Pleasantville, NY 10570-7000

TELEPHONE NUMBER: (914) 238-1000
FAX: (914) 238-4559
WEB: www.readersdigest.com
NO. OF EMPLOYEES: 5,000 (approx.)
SHAREHOLDERS: 1,804 (approx. cl A); 173 (approx. cl B)
ANNUAL MEETING: In Nov.
INCORPORATED: NY, 1926; reincorp., DE, 1951

INSTITUTIONAL HOLDINGS:
No. of Institutions: 180
Shares Held: 71,604,682
% Held: 69.2

INDUSTRY: Book publishing (SIC: 2731)

TRANSFER AGENT(S): Mellon Investor Services, Ridgefield Park, NJ

REEBOK INTERNATIONAL, LTD.

EXCH.	SYM.	REC. PRICE	P/E RATIO	YLD.	MKT. CAP.	RANGE (52-WK.)	'02 Y/E PR.
NYSE	RBK	31.25 (2/28/03)	15.2	...	$1.84 bill.	32.14 - 21.25	29.40

LOWER MEDIUM GRADE. THE COMPANY IS TARGETING SALES GROWTH FOR 2003 IN THE MID-TO HIGH-SINGLE DIGIT RANGE AND EARNINGS PER SHARE GROWTH OF ABOUT 15.0%.

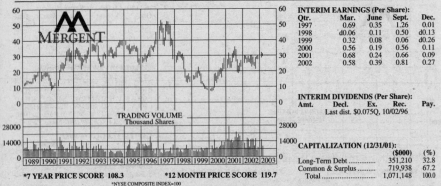

INTERIM EARNINGS (Per Share):

Qtr.	Mar.	June	Sept.	Dec.
1997	0.69	0.35	1.26	0.01
1998	d0.06	0.11	0.50	d0.13
1999	0.32	0.08	0.06	d0.26
2000	0.56	0.19	0.56	0.11
2001	0.68	0.24	0.66	0.09
2002	0.58	0.39	0.81	0.27

INTERIM DIVIDENDS (Per Share):

Amt.	Decl.	Ex.	Rec.	Pay.
Last dist. $0.075Q, 10/02/96				

TRADING VOLUME
Thousand Shares

1989 1990 1991 1992 1993 1994 1995 1996 1997 1998 1999 2000 2001 2002 2003

*7 YEAR PRICE SCORE 108.3   ***12 MONTH PRICE SCORE 119.7**

*NYSE COMPOSITE INDEX=100

CAPITALIZATION (12/31/01):

	($000)	(%)
Long-Term Debt	351,210	32.8
Common & Surplus	719,938	67.2
Total	1,071,148	100.0

BUSINESS:

Reebok International, Ltd. is a worldwide company engaged primarily in the design and marketing of sports and fitness products, including footwear and apparel, as well as the design and marketing of footwear and apparel for casual use. The Company has four major brand groups. The Reebok Division designs, produces and markets sports, fitness and casual footwear, apparel and accessories under the REEBOK® brand. The Rockport Company designs, produces and distributes specially-engineered comfort footwear for men and women worldwide under the ROCKPORT® brand. Ralph Lauren Footwear Co., Inc., a subsidiary of the Company, is responsible for footwear and certain apparel sold under the RALPH LAUREN® and POLO SPORT® brands. The Greg Norman Division produces a range of men's apparel and accessories marketed under the GREG NORMAN name and logo.

RECENT DEVELOPMENTS:

For the year ended 12/31/02, the Company reported income of $131.5 million, before an accounting change charge of $5.1 million, versus net income of $102.8 million the previous year. Earnings were driven by strong sales of Company-branded apparel products, including NFL and NBA jerseys. Net sales increased 4.5% to $3.13 billion from $2.99 billion the prior year. Worldwide footwear sales declined 0.4% to $1.58 billion. Worldwide apparel sales amounted to $1.01 billion, up 19.1% from $851.1 million the year before.

PROSPECTS:

Going forward, given the recent success of RBK apparel products in the U.S., the Company intends to introduce this category into its international markets during 2003. In addition, the Company plans on expanding its line of sports licensed products by introducing new product and marketing initiatives designed to enhance the prominence of the Reebok vector logo. Meanwhile, RBK plans to continue to focus on expanding its Rockport product offerings to service new channels of distribution. In particular, RBK plans to develop Rockport's women's business into a meaningful long-term revenue and profit contributor. RBK is targeting sales growth for 2003 in the mid-to high-single digit range and earnings per share growth of about 15.0%

ANNUAL FINANCIAL DATA:

FISCAL YEAR	TOT. REVS. ($mill.)	NET INC. ($mill.)	TOT. ASSETS ($mill.)	OPER. PROFIT %	NET PROFIT %	RET. ON EQUITY %	RET. ON ASSETS %	CURR. RATIO	EARN. PER SH. $	CASH FL. PER SH. $	TANG. BK. VAL. $	DIV. PER SH. $	PRICE RANGE		AVG. P/E RATIO	AVG. YIELD %
p12/31/02	3,127.9	② 131.5							② 2.04	2.13	10.90	...	30.25	21.25	12.6	...
12/31/01	2,992.9	102.7	1,543.2	6.2	3.4	14.3	6.7	2.9	1.66	2.20	9.45	...	35.75	18.50	16.3	...
12/31/00	2,865.2	80.9	1,463.0	5.9	2.8	13.3	5.5	2.5	1.40	2.20	6.94	...	28.33	6.94	12.6	...
12/31/99	2,891.2	① 11.0	1,564.1	4.5	0.4	2.1	0.7	2.0	① 0.20	1.06	8.17	...	22.75	7.81	76.4	...
12/31/98	3,205.4	① 23.9	1,739.6	3.8	0.7	4.6	1.4	2.2	① 0.42	1.26	8.05	...	33.19	12.56	54.5	...
12/31/97	3,637.4	① 135.1	1,756.1	7.4	3.7	26.6	7.7	2.5	① 2.32	3.13	8.27	...	52.88	27.63	17.3	...
12/31/96	3,482.9	139.0	1,786.2	7.7	4.0	36.4	7.8	2.8	2.00	2.65	5.58	0.30	45.25	25.38	17.7	0.8
12/31/95	3,484.6	① 164.8	1,656.2	10.5	4.7	18.4	10.0	3.1	① 2.07	2.57	11.11	0.30	39.63	24.13	15.4	0.9
12/31/94	3,287.6	254.5	1,649.5	13.0	7.7	25.7	15.4	2.6	3.02	3.46	11.05	0.30	40.25	28.38	11.4	0.9
12/31/93	2,893.9	① 223.4	1,391.7	13.6	7.7	26.4	16.1	2.8	① 2.53	2.93	8.99	0.30	38.63	23.00	12.2	1.0

Statistics are as originally reported. ① Incl. non-recurr. chrg. 1999, $61.6 mill.; 1998, $35.0 mill.; 1997, $58.2 mill.; 1995, $72.1 mill.; 1993, $8.4 mill. ② Bef. acctg. chng. chrg. $5.1 mill.

OFFICERS:
P. B. Fireman, Chmn., C.E.O.
J. Margolis, Pres., C.O.O.
K. I. Watchmaker, Exec. V.P., C.F.O.
INVESTOR CONTACT: Neil Kerman, Investor Relations, (781) 401-7152
PRINCIPAL OFFICE: 1895 J.W. Foster Boulevard, Canton, MA 02021

TELEPHONE NUMBER: (781) 401-5000
FAX: (781) 401-7402
WEB: www.reebok.com
NO. OF EMPLOYEES: 6,700 (approx.)
SHAREHOLDERS: 6,082
ANNUAL MEETING: In May
INCORPORATED: MA, July, 1979

INSTITUTIONAL HOLDINGS:
No. of Institutions: 225
Shares Held: 46,149,153
% Held: 77.0
INDUSTRY: Rubber and plastics footwear (SIC: 3021)
TRANSFER AGENT(S): American Stock Transfer & Trust Company, New York, NY

REGAL ENTERTAINMENT GROUP

EXCH.	SYM.	REC. PRICE	P/E RATIO	YLD.	MKT. CAP.	RANGE (52-WK.)	'02 Y/E PR.
NYSE	RGC	20.00 (2/28/03)	...	3.0%	...	25.10 - 16.00	21.42

MEDIUM GRADE. THE COMPANY'S PROPOSED ACQUISITION WILL GIVE REGAL THEATRE REPRESENTATION IN BOSTON, WHICH IS THE ONLY TOP 10 DESIGNATED MARKET WHERE IT HAS NO THEATRES.

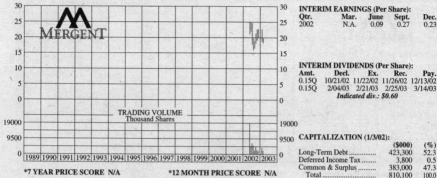

INTERIM EARNINGS (Per Share):

Qtr.	Mar.	June	Sept.	Dec.
2002	N.A.	0.09	0.27	0.23

INTERIM DIVIDENDS (Per Share):

Amt.	Decl.	Ex.	Rec.	Pay.
0.15Q	10/21/02	11/22/02	11/26/02	12/13/02
0.15Q	2/04/03	2/21/03	2/25/03	3/14/03

Indicated div.: $0.60

TRADING VOLUME
Thousand Shares

*7 YEAR PRICE SCORE N/A   ***12 MONTH PRICE SCORE N/A**

*NYSE COMPOSITE INDEX=100

CAPITALIZATION (1/3/02):

	($000)	(%)
Long-Term Debt	423,300	52.3
Deferred Income Tax	3,800	0.5
Common & Surplus	383,000	47.3
Total	810,100	100.0

BUSINESS:

Regal Entertainment Group is a motion picture exhibitor operating the largest theatre circuit in the United States, based on the number of screens. As of 2/4/03, the Company's nationwide theatre circuit, included Regal Cinemas, Inc., United Artists Theatre Company and Edwards Theatres, Inc. RGC operated 5,663 screens in 524 theatres in 36 states as of 2/4/03. RGC's theatres are primarily multis-creen complexes typically containing 10 to 18 screens with auditoriums ranging from 100 to 500 seats each. The Company's geographically diverse circuit includes theatres in 41 of the top 50 U.S. demographic markets as well as prime locations in growing suburban markets. RGC is approximately 77.5%-owned by Anschutz Company.

RECENT DEVELOPMENTS:

For the year ended 12/26/02, net income was $118.7 million, before an extraordinary charge of $1.5 million, compared with $4.9 million in 2001. Results for 2002 included merger and restructuring expenses of $18.9 million. Results for 2002 and 2001 also included losses on the disposal and impairment of operating assets of $6.4 million and $300,000, respectively. Total revenues were $2.14 billion versus $556.0 million a year earlier. Operating income amounted to $283.6 million compared with $34.1 million in 2001. The historical combined operating results for the 2001 period reflects the operations of United Artists Theatre Group and exclude the operating results of Regal Cinemas Corporation and Edwards Theatres.

PROSPECTS:

On 2/4/03, the Company announced that it has entered into a definitive stock purchase agreement wherein RGC will acquire certain assets of Hoyts Cinemas Corporation. The transaction will be for a combination of cash and stock valued at about $200.0 million and the assumption of certain capital leases. The Company anticipates acquiring 52 of the 97 Hoyts theatres representing 554 screens. The proposed acquisition would enhance RGC's presence in the northeast United States and provide the Company with representation in the Boston designated market area, which was the only top 10 DMA where RGC had no theatres.

ANNUAL FINANCIAL DATA:

FISCAL YEAR	TOT. REVS. ($mill.)	NET INC. ($mill.)	TOT. ASSETS ($mill.)	OPER. PROFIT %	NET PROFIT %	RET. ON EQUITY %	RET. ON ASSETS %	CURR. RATIO	EARN. PER SH. $
p12/26/02	2,140.2	118.7		5.7	0.9	1.3	0.4	0.7	② 0.79
① 1/03/02	556.9	4.9	1,122.7						...

Statistics are as originally reported. ① Includes results from United Artists from 3/2/01, and Edwards Theatres from 10/1/01. ② Bef. extraord. chrg. of $1.5 mill., but incl. merger and restruct. chrg. of $18.9 mill. and loss on disposal and impairment of operations assets of $6.4 mill.

OFFICERS:
P. F. Anschutz, Non-Exec. Chmn.
M. L. Campbell, Co-Chmn., Co-C.E.O.
K. C. Hall, Co-Chmn., Co-C.E.O.
INVESTOR CONTACT: Investor Relations, 1-866-REGAL-EG
PRINCIPAL OFFICE: 9110 East Nichols Avenue, Suite 200, Centennial, CO 80112

TELEPHONE NUMBER: (303) 792-3600
WEB: www.regalcinemas.com
NO. OF EMPLOYEES: 23,815 (avg.)
SHAREHOLDERS: N/A
ANNUAL MEETING: In May
INCORPORATED: DE, 2001

INSTITUTIONAL HOLDINGS:
No. of Institutions: 110
Shares Held: 32,939,429
% Held: 25.1
INDUSTRY: Motion picture theaters, ex drive-in (SIC: 7832)
TRANSFER AGENT(S): Wells Fargo Shareowner Services, St. Paul, MN

REGIONS FINANCIAL CORPORATION

EXCH.	SYM.	REC. PRICE	P/E RATIO	YLD.	MKT. CAP.	RANGE (52-WK.)	'02 Y/E PR.	DIV. ACH.
NYSE	RF	32.38 (2/28/03)	11.9	3.7%	$7.45 bill.	38.40 - 27.10	33.36	31 yrs.

UPPER MEDIUM GRADE. RESULTS ARE BENEFITING FROM STRONG MORTGAGE BANKING ACTIVITY.

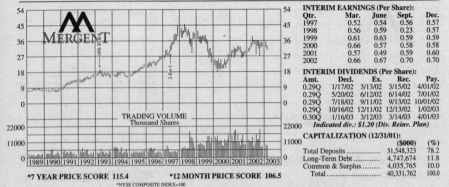

INTERIM EARNINGS (Per Share):

Qtr.	Mar.	June	Sept.	Dec.
1997	0.52	0.54	0.56	0.57
1998	0.56	0.59	0.23	0.57
1999	0.61	0.63	0.59	0.59
2000	0.66	0.57	0.58	0.58
2001	0.57	0.49	0.59	0.60
2002	0.66	0.67	0.70	0.70

INTERIM DIVIDENDS (Per Share):

Amt.	Decl.	Ex.	Rec.	Pay.
0.29Q	1/17/02	3/13/02	3/15/02	4/01/02
0.29Q	5/20/02	6/12/02	6/14/02	7/01/02
0.29Q	7/18/02	9/11/02	9/13/02	10/01/02
0.29Q	10/16/02	12/11/02	12/13/02	1/02/03
0.30Q	1/16/03	3/12/03	3/14/03	4/01/03

Indicated div.: $1.20 (Div. Reinv. Plan)

CAPITALIZATION (12/31/01):

	($000)	(%)
Total Deposits	31,548,323	78.2
Long-Term Debt	4,747,674	11.8
Common & Surplus	4,035,765	10.0
Total	40,331,762	100.0

*7 YEAR PRICE SCORE 115.4   ***12 MONTH PRICE SCORE 106.5**

*NYSE COMPOSITE INDEX=100

BUSINESS:

Regions Financial Corporation (formerly First Alabama Bancshares, Inc.) is a regional financial holding company with assets of $47.94 billion as of 12/31/02. Serving customers throughout the South, RF provides traditional commercial and retail banking services and other financial services in the fields of investment banking, asset management, trust, mutual funds, securities brokerage, insurance, leasing and mortgage banking. RF's banking affiliate, Regions Bank, offers banking services from more than 680 full-service banking offices in Alabama, Arkansas, Florida, Georgia, Louisiana, North Carolina, South Carolina, Tennessee and Texas. RF also provides investment and brokerage services from more than 140 offices of Morgan Keegan & Company, Inc., which was acquired in March 2001. Morgan Keegan is one of the South's largest investment firms. On 4/2/02, RGBK acquired Brookhollow Bancshares, Inc.

RECENT DEVELOPMENTS:

For the year ended 12/31/02, net income increased 21.8% to $619.9 million from $508.9 million in the corresponding prior-year period. Net interest income rose 5.1% to $1.50 billion from $1.43 billion the year before. Provision for loan losses declined 22.9% to $127.5 million from $165.4 million the previous year. Total non-interest income advanced 25.3% to $1.26 billion from $1.00 billion a year earlier. Total non-interest expense climbed 13.8% to $1.76 billion from $1.55 billion in 2001.

PROSPECTS:

Results are being positively affected by strong mortgage banking activity, particularly single-family residential mortgage loan production, which is being driven by increased levels of refinancings. Meanwhile, earnings are benefiting from higher commissions and fees in the fixed-income, investment advisory and private client operations of Morgan Keegan. Going forward, results should continue to benefit from significant growth in loans from the Company's community banking franchise.

ANNUAL FINANCIAL DATA:

FISCAL YEAR	NET INT. INC. ($mill.)	NON-INT. INC. ($mill.)	NET INC. ($mill.)	TOT. LOANS ($mill.)	TOT. ASSETS ($mill.)	TOT. DEP. ($mill.)	RET. ON EQUITY %	RET. ON ASSETS %	EQUITY/ ASSETS %	EARN. PER SH.$	TANG. BK. VAL.$	DIV. PER SH.$	PRICE RANGE	AVG. P/E RATIO
p12/31/02	1,497.6		619.9							2.72		1.15	38.40 - 27.10	12.0
12/31/01	1,425.5	981.9	508.9	31,137.0	45,382.7	31,548.3	12.6	1.1	8.9	2.24	17.54	1.11	32.99 - 25.73	13.1
12/31/00	1,388.8	601.2	527.5	31,472.7	43,688.3	32,022.5	15.3	1.2	7.9	2.38	15.73	1.06	28.00 - 18.31	9.7
12/31/99	1,425.9	537.1	525.4	28,221.2	42,714.4	29,989.1	17.1	1.2	7.2	2.35	13.89	0.98	41.63 - 23.19	13.8
12/31/98	1,324.8	474.7	① 421.7	24,430.1	36,831.9	28,350.1	14.1	1.1	8.1	① 1.88	13.61	0.89	45.63 - 28.88	19.8
12/31/97	828.9	258.6	299.7	16,427.6	23,034.2	17,750.9	15.7	1.3	8.3	2.15	13.99	0.78	45.00 - 25.69	16.4
12/31/96	700.5	220.7	① 229.7	13,335.5	18,930.2	15,048.3	14.4	1.2	8.4	① 1.85	12.76	0.69	27.00 - 20.25	12.8
12/31/95	497.3	159.8	172.8	9,564.4	13,708.6	10,896.1	15.4	1.3	8.2	1.88	12.37	0.65	22.50 - 15.50	10.1
12/31/94	435.6	143.4	145.9	9,043.5	12,839.3	10,093.1	14.4	1.1	7.9	1.70	11.26	0.58	18.38 - 14.88	9.8
12/31/93	342.1	132.0	112.0	6,869.5	10,476.3	8,770.7	13.2	1.1	8.1	1.51	10.37	0.49	19.19 - 14.81	11.3

Statistics are as originally reported. Adj. for stk. splits: 2-for-1, 6/13/97. ① Incl. merger and assessment expenses of $121.4 mill., 1998; $30.5 mill., 1996.

OFFICERS:
C. E. Jones, Jr., Chmn., Pres., C.E.O.
R. D. Horsley, Vice-Chmn., C.F.O.

INVESTOR CONTACT: Kenneth Till, Investor Relations, (205) 326-7605

PRINCIPAL OFFICE: 417 North 20th Street, Birmingham, AL 35203

TELEPHONE NUMBER: (205) 944-1300
FAX: (205) 326-7459
WEB: www.regionsbank.com

NO. OF EMPLOYEES: 15,921

SHAREHOLDERS: 54,512 (record)

ANNUAL MEETING: In May

INCORPORATED: DE, June, 1970

INSTITUTIONAL HOLDINGS:
No. of Institutions: 266
Shares Held: 64,524,701
% Held: 29.2

INDUSTRY: National commercial banks (SIC: 6021)

TRANSFER AGENT(S): First Chicago Trust Company of New York, Jersey City, NJ

REINSURANCE GROUP OF AMERICA, INC.

EXCH.	SYM.	REC. PRICE	P/E RATIO	YLD.	MKT. CAP.	RANGE (52-WK.)	'02 Y/E PR.
NYSE	RGA	26.43 (2/28/03)	10.4	0.9%	$1.31 bill.	33.25 - 24.00	27.08

MEDIUM GRADE. THE COMPANY IS TARGETING OPERATING EARNINGS FOR 2003 IN THE RANGE OF $2.95 TO $3.15 PER SHARE.

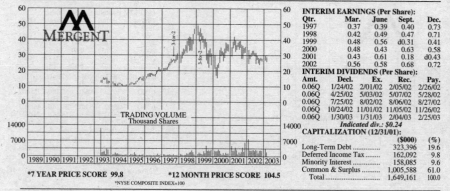

*7 YEAR PRICE SCORE 99.8   ***12 MONTH PRICE SCORE 104.5**
*NYSE COMPOSITE INDEX=100

INTERIM EARNINGS (Per Share):

Qtr.	Mar.	June	Sept.	Dec.
1997	0.37	0.39	0.40	0.73
1998	0.42	0.49	0.47	0.71
1999	0.48	0.56	d0.31	0.41
2000	0.48	0.43	0.63	0.58
2001	0.43	0.61	0.18	d0.43
2002	0.56	0.58	0.68	0.72

INTERIM DIVIDENDS (Per Share):

Amt.	Decl.	Ex.	Rec.	Pay.
0.06Q	1/24/02	2/01/02	2/05/02	2/26/02
0.06Q	4/25/02	5/03/02	5/07/02	5/28/02
0.06Q	7/25/02	8/02/02	8/06/02	8/27/02
0.06Q	10/24/02	11/01/02	11/05/02	11/26/02
0.06Q	1/30/03	1/31/03	2/04/03	2/25/03

Indicated div.: $0.24

CAPITALIZATION (12/31/01):

	($000)	(%)
Long-Term Debt	323,396	19.6
Deferred Income Tax	162,092	9.8
Minority Interest	158,085	9.6
Common & Surplus	1,005,588	61.0
Total	1,649,161	100.0

BUSINESS:

Reinsurance Group of America, Inc., is an insurance holding company primarily engaged in life reinsurance, accident and health insurance, and international life and disability on a direct and reinsurance basis. RGA has five main operational segments: U.S., Canada, Latin America, Asia Pacific, and Europe and other international operations. The U.S. operations provide traditional life reinsurance and non-traditional reinsurance. The Canada operations provide insurers with traditional reinsurance as well as capital management. The Latin America operations include traditional reinsurance and reinsurance of pension products in Argentina. Asia Pacific operations provide life reinsurance. Other international operations include traditional business from Europe and South Africa. Metropolitan Life Insurance Co. is the beneficial owner of approximately 59.0% of RGA's common shares as of 1/30/03.

RECENT DEVELOPMENTS:

For the year ended 12/31/02, income was $128.5 million, before a loss from discontinued operations of $5.7 million, versus income of $39.9 million, before a loss from discontinued operations of $6.9 million, the previous year. Earnings reflected higher premium rates and improved mortality experience. Total revenues climbed 21.0% to $2.38 billion from $1.97 billion the prior year. Revenues for 2002 and 2001 included net realized investment losses of $14.7 million and $68.4 million, respectively. Net premiums climbed 19.2% to $1.98 billion from $1.66 billion a year earlier.

PROSPECTS:

The Company appears to be well positioned for continued earnings growth. Business activity in the U.S. surged during the fourth quarter of 2002 as direct life insurance companies sought reinsurance services to manage their risk profile and to control their capital levels. Moreover, RGA executed two large fixed annuity transactions as well as several small-to medium-sized in-force transactions, adding $700.0 million in assets to RGA's balance sheet. Meanwhile, operations in Asia Pacific, Europe and South Africa continue to grow at a strong pace, with net premiums increasing 95.0% to $134.9 million during the fourth quarter. Going forward, RGA is targeting operating earnings for 2003 in a range of $2.95 to $3.15 per share.

ANNUAL FINANCIAL DATA:

FISCAL YEAR	PREM. INC. ($mill.)	TOT. REVS. ($mill.)	NET INC. ($mill.)	TOT. ASSETS ($mill.)	TOT. INVST. ($mill.)	RET. ON REVS. %	RET. ON EQUITY %	RET. ON ASSETS %	EARN. PER SH. $	TANG. BK. VAL. $	AVG. YIELD %	DIV. PER SH. $	PRICE RANGE	AVG. P/E RATIO
p12/31/02	1,980.7	2,382.0	① 128.5						① 2.59		0.8	0.24	33.65 - 24.00	11.1
12/31/01	1,661.8	1,968.3	① 39.9	6,894.3	5,088.4	2.0	4.0	0.6	① 0.80	20.30	0.7	0.24	42.15 - 27.95	43.8
12/31/00	1,404.1	1,725.7	① 105.8	6,061.9	4,560.2	6.1	12.3	1.7	2.12	17.51	0.9	0.24	38.38 - 15.38	12.7
12/31/99	1,315.6	1,607.1	① 53.0	5,123.7	3,811.9	3.3	7.2	1.0	1.15	14.68	0.6	0.22	49.17 - 22.13	31.0
12/31/98	1,016.4	1,344.5	① 89.7	6,318.6	5,129.4	6.7	12.0	1.4	2.08	16.52	0.5	0.17	47.09 - 25.08	17.3
12/31/97	835.5	1,071.5	54.6	4,673.6	3,634.0	5.1	10.9	1.2	1.42	13.21	0.6	0.15	31.13 - 19.67	17.9
12/31/96	674.9	830.0	55.1	2,893.7	2,272.0	6.6	12.9	1.9	1.44	11.14	0.7	0.13	22.22 - 15.06	12.9
12/31/95	570.0	668.1	47.3	1,989.9	1,405.5	7.1	12.5	2.4	1.25	9.96	0.9	0.12	16.28 - 10.61	10.8
12/31/94	451.7	525.8	40.4	1,394.3	1,016.6	7.7	14.6	2.9	1.05	7.28	0.9	0.11	12.83 - 9.72	10.8
12/31/93	379.9	446.5	34.1	1,249.6	920.6	7.6	12.2	2.7	1.00	7.15	0.4	0.05	15.50 - 11.50	13.6

Statistics are as originally reported. ① Excl. loss on disc. opers. $5.7 mill., 12/02; $6.9 mill., 12/01; $28.1 mill., 12/00; $12.2 mill., 12/99; $27.6 mill., 12/98.

OFFICERS:
R. A. Liddy, Chmn.
A. G. Woodring, Pres., C.E.O.
J. B. Lay, Exec. V.P., C.F.O.
INVESTOR CONTACT: Jack B. Lay, Dir., Inv. Rel., (636) 736-7439
PRINCIPAL OFFICE: 1370 Timberlake Manor Parkway, Chesterfield, MO 63017

TELEPHONE NUMBER: (636) 736-7439
FAX: (636) 453-7307
WEB: www.rgare.com
NO. OF EMPLOYEES: 678 (avg.)
SHAREHOLDERS: 106
ANNUAL MEETING: In May
INCORPORATED: MO, Dec., 1992

INSTITUTIONAL HOLDINGS:
No. of Institutions: 89
Shares Held: 27,052,935
% Held: 54.8
INDUSTRY: Accident and health insurance (SIC: 6321)
TRANSFER AGENT(S): Mellon Investor Services, Ridgefield Park, NJ

RELIANCE STEEL & ALUMINUM CO.

EXCH.	SYM.	REC. PRICE	P/E RATIO	YLD.	MKT. CAP.	RANGE (52-WK.)	'02 Y/E PR.
NYSE	RS	16.35 (2/28/03)	17.2	1.5%	$0.52 bill.	34.25 - 15.17	20.84

MEDIUM GRADE. THE COMPANY CONTINUES TO EXPAND THROUGH OPENING NEW FACILITIES IN LAS VEGAS AND BELGIUM.

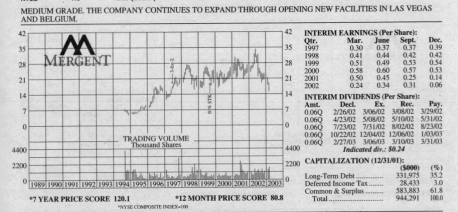

*7 YEAR PRICE SCORE 120.1   *12 MONTH PRICE SCORE 80.8

*NYSE COMPOSITE INDEX=100

INTERIM EARNINGS (Per Share):

Qtr.	Mar.	June	Sept.	Dec.
1997	0.30	0.37	0.37	0.39
1998	0.41	0.44	0.42	0.42
1999	0.51	0.49	0.53	0.54
2000	0.58	0.60	0.57	0.53
2001	0.50	0.45	0.25	0.14
2002	0.24	0.34	0.31	0.06

INTERIM DIVIDENDS (Per Share):

Amt.	Decl.	Ex.	Rec.	Pay.
0.06Q	2/26/02	3/06/02	3/08/02	3/29/02
0.06Q	4/23/02	5/08/02	5/10/02	5/31/02
0.06Q	7/23/02	7/31/02	8/02/02	8/23/02
0.06Q	10/22/02	12/04/02	12/06/02	1/03/03
0.06Q	2/27/03	3/06/03	3/10/03	3/31/03

Indicated div.: $0.24

CAPITALIZATION (12/31/01):

	($000)	(%)
Long-Term Debt	331,975	35.2
Deferred Income Tax	28,433	3.0
Common & Surplus	583,883	61.8
Total	944,291	100.0

BUSINESS:

Reliance Steel & Aluminum Co. is a metals service center company. The Company has 15 subsidiaries operating metals service centers, with 99 processing and distribution facilities, excluding American Steel, L.L.C., in 27 states, France and South Korea as of 2/20/03. Through this network, RS provides value-added metals processing services and distributes a full line of more than 85,000 metal products, including carbon, alloy, stainless and specialty steel, aluminum, brass and copper products to more than 75,000 customers in a broad range of industries. Some of these metals service centers provide processing services for specialty metals only. On 5/16/02, RS obtained a majority interest in American Steel, L.L.C., which operates two metals service centers in the Pacific Northwest.

RECENT DEVELOPMENTS:

For the year ended 12/31/02, net income declined 17.0% to $30.2 million compared with $36.3 million in 2001. Results for 2002 included a gain of $800,000 related to the sale of real estate. Results for 2001 included goodwill amortization expense of $7.1 million. Revenues grew 5.3% to $1.75 billion from $1.66 billion. The improvement in revenues was primarily attributed to an increase in tons sold, partially offset by a decrease in the average selling price per ton. Lower earnings reflected a 6.1% rise in total costs and expenses to $1.70 billion.

PROSPECTS:

In February 2003, the Company's subsidiary, PDM Steel Service Centers, Inc., opened a sales and distribution facility in Las Vegas, Nevada to better service and expand its customer base in this region. Separately, RS' subsidiary, Phoenix Metals Company, relocated its Nashville, Tennessee service center to a newly constructed facility at the end of 2002. Meanwhile, during the fourth quarter of 2002, RS' subsidiary, AMI Metals, Inc., expanded into Europe with the opening of a facility on the Aeropole site in Gosselies, Belgium. This European operation adds to AMI's six existing strategic locations in the U.S. designed to meet the demands of the aerospace industry.

ANNUAL FINANCIAL DATA:

FISCAL YEAR	TOT. REVS. ($mill.)	NET INC. ($mill.)	TOT. ASSETS ($mill.)	OPER. PROFIT %	NET PROFIT %	RET. ON EQUITY %	RET. ON ASSETS %	CURR. RATIO	EARN. PER SH.$	CASH FL. PER SH.$	TANG. BK. VAL.$	DIV. PER SH.$	PRICE RANGE	AVG. P/E RATIO	AVG. YIELD %
p12/31/02	1,748.3	② 30.2	1,139.2						② 0.95				0.24	34.25 - 18.99	28.0	0.9
12/31/01	1,660.8	36.3	1,082.3	5.2	2.2	6.2	3.4	3.8	1.28	2.41	10.57	0.23	30.75 - 20.50	20.0	0.9
12/31/00	1,730.1	62.3	997.2	7.3	3.6	15.5	6.2	3.4	2.28	3.31	6.80	0.21	26.06 - 16.88	9.4	1.0
12/31/99	1,517.4	① 57.6	900.0	7.6	3.8	14.4	6.4	2.8	① 2.07	2.98	6.66	0.17	26.75 - 16.83	10.5	0.8
12/31/98	1,355.8	47.7	841.4	6.8	3.5	13.8	5.7	3.3	1.69	2.37	6.10	0.14	27.50 - 16.08	12.9	0.7
12/31/97	965.1	② 34.2	583.9	6.5	3.5	10.9	5.9	3.0	② 1.43	1.99	8.71	0.10	21.79 - 11.56	11.6	0.6
12/31/96	658.4	② 29.8	391.2	7.3	4.5	15.5	7.6	2.8	② 1.90	2.44	11.39	0.08	18.06 - 8.00	6.9	0.6
12/31/95	563.7	22.7	260.5	6.6	4.0	13.8	8.7	2.5	1.45	1.79	10.64	0.07	9.22 - 5.06	4.9	0.9
12/31/94	448.7	14.4	199.4	5.9	3.2	9.6	7.2	3.1	1.17	1.48	9.20	...	7.28 - 4.67	5.1	...
12/31/93	373.1	9.2	163.4	4.6	2.5	10.2	5.7	2.7	0.82	1.14	8.18	...	... - ...	...	...

Statistics are as originally reported. Adj. for stk. splits: 50%, 9/24/99; 3-for-2, 6/27/97. ① Incl. gain of $2.3 mill. from a life insur. policy in conection with RS' supplemental exec. retirement plan. ② Incl. gain on sale of real estate of $800,000, 2002; $1.0 mill., 1997; $1.5 mill., 1996.

OFFICERS:
J. D. Crider, Chmn.
G. J. Mollins, Pres., C.O.O.
D. H. Hannah, C.E.O.
K. R. McDowell, Exec. V.P., C.F.O.

INVESTOR CONTACT: Kim P. Feazle, Investor Relations, (213) 576-2428

PRINCIPAL OFFICE: 350 South Grand Avenue, Suite 5100, Los Angeles, CA 90071

TELEPHONE NUMBER: (213) 687-7700
FAX: (213) 687-7701
WEB: www.rsac.com

NO. OF EMPLOYEES: 4,300 (approx.)

SHAREHOLDERS: 293 (record)

ANNUAL MEETING: In May

INCORPORATED: CA, Feb., 1939

INSTITUTIONAL HOLDINGS:
No. of Institutions: 101
Shares Held: 19,456,622
% Held: 61.3

INDUSTRY: Metals service centers and offices (SIC: 5051)

TRANSFER AGENT(S): EquiServe Trust Company, N.A., Jersey City, NJ

RELIANT RESOURCES, INC.

EXCH.	SYM.	REC. PRICE	P/E RATIO	YLD.	MKT. CAP.	RANGE (52-WK.)	'02 Y/E PR.
NYSE	RRI	4.05 (2/28/03)	5.4	...	$1.21 bill.	17.45 - 0.99	3.20

SPECULATIVE GRADE. THE COMPANY RECENTLY AGREED TO SELL ITS EUROPEAN BUSINESS TO NV NUON.

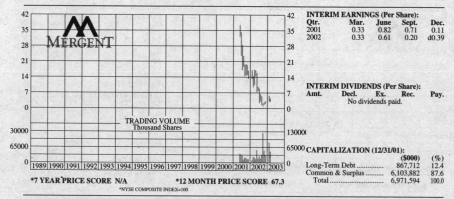

INTERIM EARNINGS (Per Share):

Qtr.	Mar.	June	Sept.	Dec.
2001	0.33	0.82	0.71	0.11
2002	0.33	0.61	0.20	d0.39

INTERIM DIVIDENDS (Per Share):

Amt.	Decl.	Ex.	Rec.	Pay.
		No dividends paid.		

TRADING VOLUME
Thousand Shares

*7 YEAR PRICE SCORE N/A   *12 MONTH PRICE SCORE 67.3

*NYSE COMPOSITE INDEX=100

CAPITALIZATION (12/31/01):

	($000)	(%)
Long-Term Debt	867,712	12.4
Common & Surplus	6,103,882	87.6
Total	6,971,594	100.0

BUSINESS:

Reliant Resources, Inc. is a provider of electricity and energy services to wholesale and retail customers in the U.S. and Europe, marketing those services under the Reliant Energy brand name. As of 1/30/03, RRI had approximately 21,000 megawatts of power generation capacity in operation, under construction or advanced development, or under contract in the U.S. RRI also markets both electricity and natural gas in North America. At the retail level, RRI provides energy products and services to more than 1.7 million electricity customers in Texas. In May 2001, RRI completed its initial public offering. On 2/19/02, RRI acquired Orion Power Holdings, Inc. On 9/30/02, CenterPoint Energy, Inc. spun off its remaining equity interest in RRI to Centerpoint shareholders.

RECENT DEVELOPMENTS:

For the year ended 12/31/02, RRI reported income of $221.0 million versus $554.4 million in 2001. Earnings for 2002 and 2001 included non-recurring items that resulted in net after-tax charges of $137.0 million and $51.0 million, respectively. Earnings excluded a charge of $233.6 million in 2002 and a credit of $3.1 million in 2001 from accounting changes. Total revenues advanced 79.5% to $11.65 billion from $6.49 billion a year earlier. Retail Energy segment revenues surged to $4.35 billion from $188.0 million as a result of the Texas retail electricity market deregulation in January 2002. Meanwhile, Wholesale Energy segment revenues climbed 17.4% to $6.67 billion, and European Energy segment revenues rose 2.9% to $632.0 million.

PROSPECTS:

RRI recently agreed to sell its European business to nv Nuon, an electricity distributor based in The Netherlands, in a transaction valued at approximately $1.30 billion. Proceeds will be used to pay off the Eruo 600.0 million bank term loan at Reliant Energy Capital Europe and improve RRI's liquidity. Meanwhile, RRI has decided to exit its proprietary natural gas trading operations. For 2003, RRI expects earnings of $0.80 to $1.00 per share, before one-time items.

ANNUAL FINANCIAL DATA:

FISCAL YEAR	TOT. REVS. ($mill.)	NET INC. ($mill.)	TOT. ASSETS ($mill.)	OPER. PROFIT %	NET PROFIT %	RET. ON EQUITY %	RET. ON ASSETS %	CURR. RATIO	EARN. PER SH.$	CASH FL. PER SH.$	TANG. BK. VAL.$	PRICE RANGE	AVG. P/E RATIO
p12/31/02	⑥ 11,653.7	⑤ 221.0							⑤ 0.76			17.45 - 0.99	12.1
12/31/01	④ 36,545.7	① 554.4	12,253.6	2.1	1.5	9.1	4.5	1.3	① 2.00	2.89	16.48	37.50 - 13.20	12.7
① 12/31/00	19,791.9	② 202.5	13,591.7	2.2	1.0	8.7	1.5	0.8	② 1.31	1.65	3.57	...	...
① 12/31/99	7,956.1	③ 24.0	5,623.6	0.2	0.3	3.2	0.4	0.7	...	...	...	...	...
① 12/31/98	4,370.8	21.1	...	0.9	0.5	...	...	...	...	...	...	...	...

Statistics are as originally reported. ① Proforma ② Incl. net invest. gain $22.0 mill., 2001; $16.0 mill., 1999 ③ Bef. extraord. gain $7.4 mill.; incl. net invest. loss $16.5 mill. and gain on sale of devel. proj. $18.0 mill. ④ Reflects increased volumes for natural gas and power sales. ⑤ Bef. acctg. change chrg. $233.6 mill.; incl. aft.-tax CenterPoint payment chrg. $80.0 mill., impair. chrg. $54.0 mill. and pension and post-retire. benef. chrg. of $29.0 mill. ⑥ Reflects change to reporting mark-to-market gains and losses on energy trading contracts net of expenses.

OFFICERS:
R. S. Letbetter, Chmn., C.E.O.
S. W. Naeve, Pres., C.O.O.
M. M. Jacobs, Exec. V.P., C.F.O.

INVESTOR CONTACT: Dennis Barber (713) 497-3042

PRINCIPAL OFFICE: 1111 Louisiana St., Houston, TX 77002

TELEPHONE NUMBER: (713) 497-3000
FAX: (713) 497-3169
WEB: www.reliantresources.com
NO. OF EMPLOYEES: 5,052
SHAREHOLDERS: 41 (approx. record); 15,000 (approx. benef.)
ANNUAL MEETING: In June
INCORPORATED: DE, Aug., 2000

INSTITUTIONAL HOLDINGS:
No. of Institutions: 214
Shares Held: 146,706,396
% Held: 50.5

INDUSTRY: Electric services (SIC: 4911)

TRANSFER AGENT(S): CenterPoint Energy, Inc., Houston, TX

REPUBLIC SERVICES, INC.

EXCH.	SYM.	REC. PRICE	P/E RATIO	YLD.	MKT. CAP.	RANGE (52-WK.)	'02 Y/E PR.
NYSE	RSG	19.07 (2/28/03)	13.3	...	$3.24 bill.	21.77 - 16.26	20.98

MEDIUM GRADE. THE COMPANY ANTICIPATES 2003 EARNINGS IN THE RANGE OF $1.49 TO $1.51 PER SHARE.

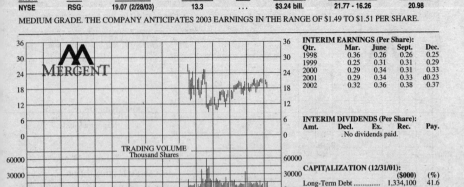

INTERIM EARNINGS (Per Share):

Qtr.	Mar.	June	Sept.	Dec.
1998	0.36	0.26	0.26	0.25
1999	0.25	0.31	0.31	0.29
2000	0.29	0.34	0.31	0.33
2001	0.29	0.34	0.33	d0.23
2002	0.32	0.36	0.38	0.37

INTERIM DIVIDENDS (Per Share):

Amt.	Decl.	Ex.	Rec.	Pay.
		No dividends paid.		

CAPITALIZATION (12/31/01):

	($000)	(%)
Long-Term Debt	1,334,100	41.6
Deferred Income Tax	118,700	3.7
Common & Surplus	1,755,900	54.7
Total	3,208,700	100.0

*7 YEAR PRICE SCORE N/A　　***12 MONTH PRICE SCORE 110.1**

*NYSE COMPOSITE INDEX=100

BUSINESS:

Republic Services, Inc. is a provider of domestic non-hazardous solid waste collection and disposal services for commercial, industrial, municipal and residential customers in high growth domestic markets. RSG provides solid waste collection services through 145 collection companies in 22 states. RSG also owns or operates 90 transfer stations and 54 solid waste landfills. RSG generates revenue primarily from its solid waste collection operations (75.3% of 2002 revenues) with remaining revenue obtained from net transfer and disposal (18.0%) and other services (6.7%), including recycling, remediation and composting operations. RSG was formerly a subsidiary of AutoNation, Inc. RSG completed its initial public offering of common stock in June, 1998, and secondary offering in May, 1999.

RECENT DEVELOPMENTS:

For the year ended 12/31/02, net income grew 90.9% to $239.6 million compared with $125.5 million in 2001. Results for 2002 included a pre-tax gain of $5.6 million related to the sale of certain assets for amounts exceeding estimates originally made during the three months ended 12/31/01. Results for 2001 included pre-tax charges of $99.6 million related to exiting certain markets and non-core businesses. Revenues climbed 4.8% to $2.37 billion from $2.26 billion a year earlier. Internal growth from operations amounted to 3.8% and reflected an increase in price and volume of 1.8% and 2.0%, respectively.

PROSPECTS:

The Company's objectives for 2003 once again focus on increasing its free cash flow, which RSG intends to use to repurchase stock under its $150.0 million share repurchase program, approved in October 2002. The Company anticipates free cash flow of approximately 90.0% of net income for the full year. Also, earnings for 2003 are expected to range from $1.49 to $1.51 per share, excluding one-time non-cash costs. Moreover, the Company believes internal growth for the year will be approximately 2.0% to 3.0%, with 1.0% to 1.5% from price increases and 1.0% to 1.5% from volume growth. Capital spending for 2003 should be approximately $260.0 million.

ANNUAL FINANCIAL DATA:

FISCAL YEAR	TOT. REVS. ($mill.)	NET INC. ($mill.)	TOT. ASSETS ($mill.)	OPER. PROFIT %	NET PROFIT %	RET. ON EQUITY %	RET. ON ASSETS %	CURR. RATIO	EARN. PER SH.$	CASH FL. PER SH.$	TANG. BK. VAL.$	PRICE RANGE	AVG. P/E RATIO
p12/31/02	2,365.1	⑤ 239.6							⑤ 1.44			21.77 - 16.26	13.2
12/31/01	2,257.5	④ 125.5	3,856.3	12.6	5.6	7.1	3.3	0.8	④ 0.73	1.99	1.20	20.90 - 13.75	23.7
12/31/00	2,103.3	③ 221.0	3,561.5	20.6	10.5	13.2	6.2	1.1	③ 1.26	2.39	1.37	17.50 - 9.63	10.8
12/31/99	1,838.5	② 200.8	3,288.3	21.2	10.9	13.4	6.1	0.9	② 1.14	2.07	1.17	25.50 - 8.88	15.1
12/31/98	1,369.1	② 153.7	2,812.1	20.8	11.2	11.8	5.5	1.0	② 1.13	1.92	7.41	27.44 - 13.38	18.1
12/31/97	1,127.7	116.2	1,348.0	17.9	10.3	15.5	8.6	0.4	...	...	...	...	...
12/31/96	953.3	51.8	1,090.3	11.1	5.4	10.5	4.8	0.5	...	...	...	...	...
12/31/95	805.0	49.4	...	11.7	6.1	...	...	...	...	...	...	...	...

Statistics are as originally reported. ① Incl. pre-tax chrg. of $6.4 mill. for costs related to the Company's separation from its former parent company, AutoNation, Inc. ② Incl. pre-tax charges of $15.0 mill. for AutoNation overhead charges. ③ Incl. pre-tax nonrec. chrg. of $6.7 mill. ④ Incl. an after-tax, non-cash chrg. of $86.1 million to exit certain markets and non-core businesses. ⑤ Incl. a pre-tax gain of $5.6 mill. for real estate assets.

OFFICERS:
J. E. O'Connor, Chmn., Pres., C.E.O.
H. W. Hudson, Vice-Chmn., Sec.

INVESTOR CONTACT: Investor Relations, (954) 769-2400

PRINCIPAL OFFICE: 110 S.E. 6th Street, 28th Floor, Ft. Lauderdale, FL 33301

TELEPHONE NUMBER: (954) 769-2400
FAX: (954) 769-6416
WEB: www.republicservices.com
NO. OF EMPLOYEES: 12,700 (approx.)
SHAREHOLDERS: 97 (approx. record)
ANNUAL MEETING: In May
INCORPORATED: DE, 1998

INSTITUTIONAL HOLDINGS:
No. of Institutions: 254
Shares Held: 147,268,734
% Held: 89.9

INDUSTRY: Refuse systems (SIC: 4953)

TRANSFER AGENT(S): First Union National Bank, Charlotte, NC

REYNOLDS AND REYNOLDS COMPANY (THE)

EXCH.	SYM.	REC. PRICE	P/E RATIO	YLD.	MKT. CAP.	RANGE (52-WK.)	'02 Y/E PR.
NYSE	REY	24.45 (2/28/03)	15.0	1.8%	$2.06 bill.	31.55 - 19.74	25.47

MEDIUM GRADE. ON 1/22/03, THE COMPANY ACQUIRED THE MSN AUTOS DEALERPOINT AUTOMOTIVE LEAD MANAGEMENT SERVICE.

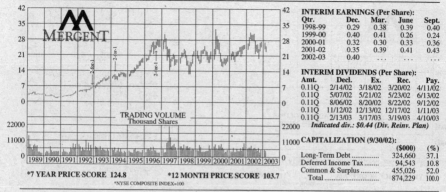

*7 YEAR PRICE SCORE 124.8   *12 MONTH PRICE SCORE 103.7

*NYSE COMPOSITE INDEX=100

INTERIM EARNINGS (Per Share):

Qtr.	Dec.	Mar.	June	Sept.
1998-99	0.29	0.38	0.39	0.40
1999-00	0.40	0.41	0.26	0.24
2000-01	0.32	0.30	0.33	0.36
2001-02	0.35	0.39	0.41	0.43
2002-03	0.40	...	...	...

INTERIM DIVIDENDS (Per Share):

Amt.	Decl.	Ex.	Rec.	Pay.
0.11Q	2/14/02	3/18/02	3/20/02	4/11/02
0.11Q	5/07/02	5/21/02	5/23/02	6/13/02
0.11Q	8/06/02	8/20/02	8/22/02	9/12/02
0.11Q	11/12/02	12/13/02	12/17/02	1/11/03
0.11Q	2/13/03	3/17/03	3/19/03	4/10/03

Indicated div.: $0.44 (Div. Reinv. Plan)

CAPITALIZATION (9/30/02):

	($000)	(%)
Long-Term Debt	324,660	37.1
Deferred Income Tax	94,543	10.8
Common & Surplus	455,026	52.0
Total	874,229	100.0

BUSINESS:

Reynolds & Reynolds Company operates in four business segments: Software Solutions, Transformation Solutions, Documents and Financial Services. The Software Solutions segment (63.2% of fiscal 2002 net sales and revenues, 71.3% of operating profit) provides integrated computer systems products and related services. The Documents segment (18.5%, 20.9%) manufactures and distributes printed business forms to automotive retailers. The Transformation Solutions segment (14.1%, -5.1%) provides specialized training, Web services and customer relationship management products and services. The Financial Services segment (4.2%, 12.9%) provides financing for REY's computer systems products through its wholly-owned subsidiary, Reyna Capital Corp. On 8/4/00, REY sold its document outsourcing and customer relationship management business to The Carlyle Group for $360.0 million.

RECENT DEVELOPMENTS:

For the three months ended 12/31/02, net income totaled $28.2 million, up 11.2% compared with income of $25.4 million, before a $36.6 million accounting change charge, in the corresponding period the year before. Net sales and revenues grew 2.7% to $246.6 million from $240.1 million a year earlier. Higher sales in the Software Solutions segment were partially offset by lower sales in the Transformation Solutions, Documents and Financial Services segments. Gross profit was $139.3 million, or 56.5% of net sales and revenues, versus $140.6 million, or 58.6% of net sales and revenues, the previous year. Operating income rose 5.1% to $45.8 million from $43.5 million in 2001.

PROSPECTS:

On 1/22/03, the Company announced that it has acquired the MSN Autos Dealerpoint automotive lead management service, which is used to deliver sales leads to more than 4,000 Ford, Lincoln Mercury, Honda, Acura and Isuzu dealers. The leads originate from multiple sources, including the car companies themselves and on-line third-party buying services. Separately, the Company anticipates full fiscal-year 2003 earnings of about $1.70 per share, along with operating margins of approximately 19.0%.

ANNUAL FINANCIAL DATA:

FISCAL YEAR	TOT. REVS. ($mill.)	NET INC. ($mill.)	TOT. ASSETS ($mill.)	OPER. PROFIT %	NET PROFIT %	RET. ON EQUITY %	RET. ON ASSETS %	CURR. RATIO	EARN. PER SH.$	CASH FL. PER SH.$	TANG. BK. VAL.$	DIV. PER SH.$	PRICE RANGE	AVG. P/E RATIO	AVG. YIELD %
9/30/02	992.4	① 115.6	1,137.2	18.0	11.6	25.4	10.2	2.0	① 1.58	2.00	3.52	0.44	31.55 - 19.74	16.2	1.7
9/30/01	1,004.0	⑤ 97.9	1,142.4	17.1	9.8	20.5	8.6	1.9	⑤ 1.31	1.97	3.07	0.44	26.00 - 18.24	16.9	2.0
9/30/00	④ 924.4	③ 88.4	1,217.3	16.8	9.6	17.7	7.3	2.0	③ 1.11	1.60	4.12	0.44	33.00 - 15.94	22.0	1.8
9/30/99	1,563.0	③ 116.9	1,262.1	13.1	7.5	25.2	9.3	2.2	③ 1.46	2.04	3.88	0.40	25.31 - 17.31	14.6	1.9
9/30/98	1,486.0	③ 113.6	1,157.7	13.7	7.6	28.1	9.8	1.9	③ 1.40	2.13	3.12	0.36	24.00 - 12.63	13.1	2.0
9/30/97	1,385.7	② 59.2	1,102.5	9.1	4.3	16.3	5.4	1.6	② 0.70	1.43	2.50	0.32	30.63 - 14.38	32.1	1.4
9/30/96	1,100.4	93.7	923.6	15.0	8.5	25.1	10.1	1.6	1.10	1.62	2.50	0.25	28.25 - 18.19	21.1	1.1
9/30/95	910.9	78.6	755.5	15.0	8.6	23.6	10.4	1.5	0.92	1.36	1.99	0.20	19.81 - 11.44	17.0	1.3
9/30/94	808.8	66.2	634.7	12.1	8.2	22.6	10.4	1.9	0.76	1.16	1.83	0.17	13.31 - 9.88	15.4	1.4
9/30/93	697.0	① 52.5	570.6	13.1	7.5	19.9	9.2	1.9	① 0.60	0.89	1.50	0.13	11.47 - 6.03	14.6	1.5

Statistics are as originally reported. Adj. for 2-for-1 stk. split, 9/96 & 3/94. ① Bef. $36.6 mil ($0.50/sh) chg. for acctg. adj., 2002; $19.1 mil ($0.22/sh), 1993. ② Incl. $34.1 mil ($0.41/sh) non-recur. after-tax chg. ③ Bef. disc. oper. gain of $28.2 mil ($0.36/sh) & incl. $10.6 mil ($0.08/sh) restr. chg., 2000; $5.8 mil ($0.07/sh), 1999; loss $10.4 mil ($0.13/sh), 1998. ④ Reflects the sale of the Information Solutions Group. ⑤ Bef. $1.6 mil ($0.02/sh) disc. oper. gain.

OFFICERS:
L. G. Waterhouse, Chmn., Pres., C.E.O.
D. L. Medford, Exec. V.P., C.F.O.
M. J. Gapinski, Treas., Asst. Sec.

INVESTOR CONTACT: John Shave, Investor Relations, (937) 485-2633

PRINCIPAL OFFICE: 115 South Ludlow Street, Dayton, OH 45402

TELEPHONE NUMBER: (937) 485-2000
FAX: (937) 449-4213
WEB: www.reyrey.com
NO. OF EMPLOYEES: 4,602
SHAREHOLDERS: 3,170 (approx. class A); 1 (class B).
ANNUAL MEETING: In Feb.
INCORPORATED: OH, 1889

REYNOLDS (R.J.) TOBACCO HOLDINGS, INC.

EXCH.	SYM.	REC. PRICE	P/E RATIO	YLD.	MKT. CAP.	RANGE (52-WK.)	'02 Y/E PR.
NYSE	RJR	39.91 (2/28/03)	8.9	9.5%	$3.76 bill.	71.90 - 34.83	42.11

MEDIUM GRADE. THE COMPANY EXPECTS FULL-YEAR 2003 EARNINGS OF BETWEEN $4.85 AND $5.60 PER DILUTED SHARE.

TRADING VOLUME
Thousand Shares

7 YEAR PRICE SCORE N/A *12 MONTH PRICE SCORE 86.7*

NYSE COMPOSITE INDEX=100

INTERIM EARNINGS (Per Share):

Qtr.	Mar.	June	Sept.	Dec.
1998	d0.10	d0.44	0.45	d1.83
1999	0.22	d0.39	0.88	1.00
2000	0.77	1.07	1.16	0.45
2001	0.98	1.26	1.31	0.93
2002	1.79	2.29	1.56	d1.16

INTERIM DIVIDENDS (Per Share):

Amt.	Decl.	Ex.	Rec.	Pay.
0.95Q	6/05/02	6/14/02	6/18/02	7/01/02
0.95Q	8/29/02	9/06/02	9/10/02	10/01/02
0.95Q	12/10/02	12/18/02	12/20/02	1/02/03
0.95Q	2/05/03	3/07/03	3/11/03	4/01/03

Indicated div.: $3.80 (Div. Reinv. Plan)

CAPITALIZATION (12/31/01):

	($000)	(%)
Long-Term Debt	1,631,000	14.3
Deferred Income Tax	1,726,000	15.2
Common & Surplus	8,026,000	70.5
Total	11,383,000	100.0

BUSINESS:

R.J. Reynolds Tobacco Holdings, Inc. (formerly RJR Nabisco, Inc.) was formed through a reorganization and spun off from its parent, Nabisco Group Holdings Corp. (NGH), formerly RJR Nabisco Holdings Corp., on 6/15/99. As a part of the spin-off, RJR transferred its 80.5% interest in NGH and nearly $1.60 billion in net proceeds from the sale of its international tobacco business to NGH. RJR is presently the holding company of R.J. Reynolds Tobacco Company, the second-largest manufacturer of cigarettes in the U.S. Major cigarette brands include CAMEL, WINSTON, SALEM, and DORAL. On 12/11/00, RJR acquired its former parent, NGH, a non-operating public shell company with no material assets or liabilities, at the time of the acquisition, other than $11.80 billion in cash, for $9.80 billion.

RECENT DEVELOPMENTS:

For the year ended 12/31/02, income from continuing operations was $418.0 million versus income from continuing operations of $444.0 million a year earlier. Results for 2002 included restructuring and asset impairment charges of $224.0 million and a trademark impairment charge of $13.0 million. Results for 2001 included amortization of trademarks and goodwill of $362.0 million. Net sales slipped to $6.21 billion from $6.27 billion in 2001, due to increased discounting and a less-favorable full-price/savings brand mix, partially offset by higher pricing.

PROSPECTS:

Higher promotional spending, growth in deep-discount brands as well as the effects of increased cigarette excise taxes are hampering RJR's results. In response, RJR has cut its cost structure, sought to maintain competitive pricing levels and is seeking buyers for two non-tobacco businesses. Meanwhile, the re-launch of RJR's SALEM brand is slated to begin in the second quarter of 2003 with new packaging and expansion of the slide-box styles into additional markets. Consequently, RJR expects full-year 2003 earnings of between $4.85 and $5.60 per diluted share.

ANNUAL FINANCIAL DATA:

FISCAL YEAR	TOT. REVS. ($mill.)	NET INC. ($mill.)	TOT. ASSETS ($mill.)	OPER. PROFIT %	NET PROFIT %	RET. ON EQUITY %	RET. ON ASSETS %	CURR. RATIO	EARN. PER SH. $	CASH FL. PER SH. $	DIV. PER SH. $	PRICE RANGE	AVG. P/E RATIO	AVG. YIELD %
p12/31/02	⑪ 6,211.0	⑩ 418.0							⑩ 4.64		3.65	71.90 - 34.83	11.5	6.8
12/31/01	8,585.0	⑨ 444.0	15,050.0	10.7	5.2	5.5	3.0	1.4	⑨ 4.48	9.45	3.20	62.70 - 44.19	11.9	6.0
12/31/00	8,167.0	⑧ 352.0	15,554.0	10.1	4.3	4.2	2.3	1.4	⑧ 3.46	8.22	3.10	50.25 - 15.75	9.5	9.4
12/31/99	7,567.0	⑦ 195.0	14,377.0	9.5	2.6	2.8	1.4	0.8	⑦ 1.80	6.24	0.78	34.00 - 16.00	13.9	3.1
12/31/98	17,037.0	⑥ d516.0	28,863.0	2.3	...	...	...	1.0	...	...	...	...	...	...
12/31/97	17,057.0	② 454.0	30,657.0	11.9	2.7	4.1	1.5	1.2	...	...	...	...	...	...
12/31/96	17,063.0	⑤ 666.0	31,260.0	13.2	3.9	5.7	2.1	1.2	...	...	...	...	...	...
12/31/95	16,008.0	④ 638.0	31,508.0	14.6	4.0	5.2	2.0	1.1	...	...	...	...	...	...
12/31/94	15,366.0	③ 762.0	31,393.0	16.7	5.0	6.7	2.4	0.8	...	...	...	...	...	...
12/31/93	15,104.0	⑥ d4.0	31,272.0	9.2	...	...	...	1.1	...	...	...	...	...	...

Statistics are as originally reported. Results prior to 1999 refl. ops. of RJR Nabisco, Inc. ① Incl. chrg. of $2.03 bill. ② Incl. chrg. of $660.0 mill.; bef. extr. chrg. of $21.0 mill. ③ Incl. chrgs. of $428.0 mill. ④ Incl. chrgs. of $154.0 mill.; bef. extr. chrg. of $16.0 mill. ⑤ Bef. extr. chrg. of $245.0 mill. ⑥ Incl. chrg. of $730.0 mill.; bef. extr. chrg. of $135.0 mill. ⑦ Incl. tobacco setlmt. chrgs. & rel. exp. of $2.20 bill.; bef. gain of $2.40 bill. fr. disc. ops. & extr. chrg. of $250.0 mill. ⑧ Incl. tobacco setlmt. chrgs. & rel. exp. of $2.33 bill. and impair. chrg. of $89.0 mill.; bef. extra. gain of $1.48 bill. on acq. of Nabisco Group Holdings Corp. ⑨ Bef. loss fr. disc. ops. of $9.0 mill. ⑩ Incl. restruct. & asset impair. chrgs. of $224.0 mill. and trademark impair. chrg. of $13.0 mill.; bef. sale gain adj. of $40.0 mill. & acctg. chge. chrg. of $502.0 mill. ⑪ Refl. adopt. of emerg. issues task force issue No. 00-25. Thus, certain sales incent. hist. incl. in SG&A exp. are now incl. as a reduct. of rev.

OFFICERS:
A. J. Schindler, Chmn., C.E.O.
L. J. Beasley, Pres., C.O.O.
R. H. Bogan, Exec. V.P., C.F.O.
INVESTOR CONTACT: Office of Investor Relations, (336) 741-5165
PRINCIPAL OFFICE: 401 North Main Street, Winston-Salem, NC 27101-2866

TELEPHONE NUMBER: (336) 741-5500
FAX: (336) 741-5511
WEB: www.rjrt.com
NO. OF EMPLOYEES: 8,200 full-time (approx.); 1,100 part-time (approx.)
SHAREHOLDERS: 38,000 (approx.)
ANNUAL MEETING: In Apr.
INCORPORATED: DE, Mar., 1970

INSTITUTIONAL HOLDINGS:
No. of Institutions: 235
Shares Held: 72,888,613
% Held: 82.6

INDUSTRY: Cigarettes (SIC: 2111)

TRANSFER AGENT(S): The Bank of New York, New York, NY

RITE AID CORPORATION

EXCH.	SYM.	REC. PRICE	P/E RATIO	YLD.	MKT. CAP.	RANGE (52-WK.)	'02 Y/E PR.
NYSE	RAD	2.40 (2/28/03)	...	...	$1.24 bill.	4.25 - 1.65	2.45

SPECULATIVE GRADE. THE COMPANY ANTICIPATES SALES OF BETWEEN $16.60 BILLION AND $16.80 IN FISCAL 2004, WHICH ENDS ON 2/28/04.

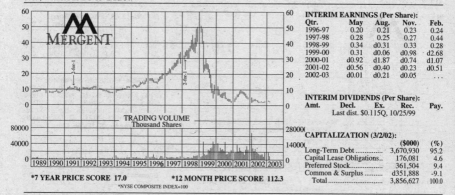

INTERIM EARNINGS (Per Share):

Qtr.	May	Aug.	Nov.	Feb.
1996-97	0.20	0.21	0.23	0.24
1997-98	0.28	0.25	0.27	0.44
1998-99	0.34	d0.31	0.33	0.28
1999-00	0.31	d0.06	d0.98	d2.68
2000-01	d0.92	d1.87	d0.74	d1.07
2001-02	d0.56	d0.40	d0.23	d0.51
2002-03	d0.01	d0.21	d0.05	...

INTERIM DIVIDENDS (Per Share):

Amt.	Decl.	Ex.	Rec.	Pay.
Last dist. $0.115Q, 10/25/99				

CAPITALIZATION (3/2/02):

	($000)	(%)
Long-Term Debt	3,670,930	95.2
Capital Lease Obligations..	176,081	4.6
Preferred Stock.................	361,504	9.4
Common & Surplus	d351,888	-9.1
Total	3,856,627	100.0

*7 YEAR PRICE SCORE 17.0   ***12 MONTH PRICE SCORE 112.3**

*NYSE COMPOSITE INDEX=100

BUSINESS:

Rite Aid Corporation operates the third largest retail drugstore chain in the U.S. based on store count. As of 1/25/03, RAD operated 3,406 drugstores in 28 states and the District of Columbia. The Company's stores sell prescription drugs and a wide assortment of general merchandise including prescription health and personal care items, cosmetics, household items, beverages, convenience foods, greeting cards, one-hour photo development and seasonal and other convenience products. The sales mix for fiscal 2002 was as follows: prescription drugs, 61.3%; general merchandise and other, 23.2%; over-the-counter and personal care, 10.2%; and health and beauty aids, 5.3%. On 10/2/00, RAD completed the sale of its pharmacy benefits management subsidiary, PCS Health Systems, Inc.

RECENT DEVELOPMENTS:

For the 13 weeks ended 11/30/02, the Company reported a net loss of $16.4 million compared with a net loss of $112.8 million in the corresponding prior-year period. Results for 2002 included a store closing and impairment charge of $2.9 million, a $2.6 million stock-based compen- sation charge, and a $775,000 net gain on the sale of assets and investments. Earnings for 2001 included one-time items that resulted in a gain of $2.9 million. Revenues grew 4.0% to $3.88 billion from $3.73 billion a year earlier. Same-store sales were up 6.7% year over year.

PROSPECTS:

Results are being positively affected by strong sales of prescription drugs, along with lower overall interest rates and the Company's efforts to reduce debt levels. During the third quarter of the current fiscal year, RAD opened one new store, remodeled 45 stores, relocated four stores and closed 34 existing stores. Looking ahead, the Company anticipates sales of between $16.60 billion and $16.80 in fiscal 2004, which ends on 2/28/04. Same-store sales are expected to increase between 6.0% and 7.0% in fiscal 2004, while EBITDA is projected to be in the range of $675.0 million to $725.0 million.

ANNUAL FINANCIAL DATA:

FISCAL YEAR	TOT. REVS. ($mill.)	NET INC. ($mill.)	TOT. ASSETS ($mill.)	OPER. PROFIT %	NET PROFIT %	RET. ON EQUITY %	RET. ON ASSETS %	CURR. RATIO	EARN. PER SH.$	CASH FL. PER SH.$	TANG. BK. VAL.$	DIV. PER SH.$	PRICE RANGE	AVG. P/E RATIO	AVG. YIELD %
3/02/02	15,171.1	⑥ d761.1	6,479.2	...	...	...	...	1.9	⑥ d1.68	d0.94	...	...	9.99 — 2.25	...	...
3/03/01	14,516.9	⑤ d1,431.8	7,913.9	...	...	...	...	2.2	⑤ d5.15	d3.33	...	...	12.25 — 1.75	...	...
2/26/00	14,681.4	④ d1,115.8	10,807.9	...	...	...	...	1.3	④ d4.34	d2.37	...	0.46	51.13 — 4.50	...	1.7
2/27/99	12,731.9	③ 143.7	10,421.7	3.1	1.1	4.9	1.4	1.0	③ 0.54	1.69	...	0.43	50.38 — 29.22	73.7	1.1
2/28/98	11,375.1	316.4	7,655.3	6.1	2.8	10.8	4.1	1.9	1.22	2.41	3.68	0.40	34.19 — 18.81	21.7	1.5
3/01/97	6,970.2	② 160.5	6,417.0	5.1	2.3	6.5	2.5	2.4	② 0.87	1.78	3.44	0.38	20.44 — 13.63	19.6	2.2
3/02/96	5,446.0	158.9	2,842.0	6.0	2.9	14.4	5.6	2.3	0.95	1.66	4.56	0.34	17.19 — 11.00	14.8	2.4
3/04/95	4,533.9	141.3	2,472.6	6.0	3.1	14.0	5.7	2.4	0.84	1.41	4.50	0.30	12.00 — 7.88	11.9	3.0
2/26/94	4,058.7	① 26.2	1,989.1	1.8	0.6	2.7	1.3	3.1	① 0.15	0.75	4.82	0.30	10.75 — 7.63	61.2	3.3
2/27/93	4,085.1	132.4	1,875.2	6.1	3.2	12.8	7.1	3.9	0.76	1.31	4.93	0.28	12.06 — 9.63	14.4	2.5

Statistics are as originally reported. Adj. for 2-for-1 stk. split, 2/98. ① Bef. $16.9 mil loss from discont. opers. & incl. $90.6 mil restr. chg. ② Bef. $45.2 mil ($0.25/sh) extraord. loss & incl. $42.4 mil ($0.20/sh) non-recur. chg. ③ Incl. $176.9 mil ($0.67/sh) after-tax, non-recur. chg. ④ Bef. $27.3 mil ($0.11/sh) acctg. chg. & incl. $80.1 mil pre-tax gain fr. sale of stores. ⑤ Bef. $157.5 mil ($0.50/sh) loss from discont. opers. & incl. $645.8 mil non-recur. chg. ⑥ Bef. $66.6 mil ($0.14/sh) extraord. chg. & incl. $417.5 mil non-recur. chg.

OFFICERS:
R. G. Miller, Chmn., C.E.O.
M. F. Sammons, Pres., C.O.O.
C. Hall, Exec. V.P., C.F.O.

INVESTOR CONTACT: Dave Jessick, Investor Relations, (717) 975-5750

PRINCIPAL OFFICE: 30 Hunter Lane, Camp Hill, PA 17011

TELEPHONE NUMBER: (717) 761-2633
FAX: (717) 975-5905
WEB: www.riteaid.com

NO. OF EMPLOYEES: 75,000

SHAREHOLDERS: 11,982 (approx. record)

ANNUAL MEETING: In June

INCORPORATED: PA, 1958; reincorp., DE, Apr., 1968

INSTITUTIONAL HOLDINGS:
No. of Institutions: 166
Shares Held: 164,561,338
% Held: 31.9

INDUSTRY: Drug stores and proprietary stores (SIC: 5912)

TRANSFER AGENT(S): Computershare Investor Services, Chicago, IL

RLI CORP.

EXCH.	SYM.	REC. PRICE	P/E RATIO	YLD.	MKT. CAP.	RANGE (52-WK.)	'02 Y/E PR.	DIV. ACH.
NYSE	RLI	25.93 (2/28/03)	13.2	1.4%	$257.0 mill.	30.20 - 23.05	27.90	26 yrs.

UPPER MEDIUM GRADE. STRENGTH IN THE COMPANY'S PROPERTY SEGMENT IS OFFSETTING WEAKNESS IN ITS SURETY SEGMENT.

INTERIM EARNINGS (Per Share):

Qtr.	Mar.	June	Sept.	Dec.
1999	0.32	0.44	0.42	0.37
2000	0.33	0.35	0.37	0.39
2001	0.36	0.37	0.40	0.39
2002	0.45	0.49	0.28	0.54

INTERIM DIVIDENDS (Per Share):

Amt.	Decl.	Ex.	Rec.	Pay.
0.17Q	5/03/02	6/26/02	6/28/02	7/15/02
0.18Q	8/29/02	9/26/02	9/30/02	10/15/02
2-for-1	8/29/02	10/16/02	9/30/02	10/15/02
0.09Q	12/19/02	12/27/02	12/31/02	1/15/03

Indicated div.: $0.36 (Div. Reinv. Plan)

*7 YEAR PRICE SCORE 153.8   *12 MONTH PRICE SCORE 110.0

*NYSE COMPOSITE INDEX=100

CAPITALIZATION (12/31/01):

	($000)	(%)
Deferred Income Tax	43,151	11.4
Common & Surplus	335,432	88.6
Total	378,583	100.0

BUSINESS:

RLI Corp. is a holding company composed primarily of four main insurance companies. RLI Insurance Company, the principal subsidiary, writes multiple lines of insurance on an admitted basis in all 50 states, the District of Columbia and Puerto Rico. Mt. Hawley Insurance Company, a subsidiary of RLI Insurance Company, writes surplus lines of insurance in all 50 states, the District of Columbia, Puerto Rico, the Virgin Islands and Guam. Underwriters Indemnity Company, a subsidiary of RLI Insurance Company, has authority to write multiple lines of insurance on an admitted basis in 33 states and the District of Colombia and surplus lines of insurance in Ohio. Planet Indemnity Company, a subsidiary of Mt. Hawley, has authority to write multiple lines of insurance on an admitted basis in 40 states and the District of Columbia. Other companies in the RLI Insurance Group include: Replacement Lens Inc., RLI Insurance Agency, Ltd., RLI Insurance Ltd., Underwriters Indemnity General Agency, Inc., and Safe Fleet Insurance Services, Inc.

RECENT DEVELOPMENTS:

For the twelve months ended 12/31/02, net income was $35.9 million compared with income of $30.2 million, before an accounting change credit of $800,000, the previous year. Total revenue increased 23.5% to $382.2 million from $309.4 million the prior year. Net premiums earned advanced 27.5% to $348.1 million from $273.0 million, while net investment income climbed 17.0% to $37.6 million from $32.2 million a year earlier. Net realized investment loss was $3.6 million versus net realized investment gains of $4.2 million in 2001.

PROSPECTS:

Solid results in the Company's property segment reflect fewer significant losses, firming prices, and the benefits of a more focused underwriting strategy. Casualty segment results also benefited from a favorable premium rate environment that is expected to continue through 2003. Meanwhile, the Company experienced losses in its contract surety business, where reserves were strengthened by $3.9 million in the fourth quarter of 2002.

ANNUAL FINANCIAL DATA:

FISCAL YEAR	PREM. INC. ($000)	NET INVST. INC. ($000)	TOT. REVS. ($000)	NET INC. ($000)	TOT. ASSETS ($000)	TOT. INVST. ($000)	RET. ON REVS. %	RET. ON EQUITY %	RET. ON ASSETS %	EARN. PER SH. $	TANG. BK. VAL. $	AVG. YIELD %	DIV. PER SH. $	PRICE RANGE	AVG. P/E RATIO
p12/31/02	348,065	37,640	382,153	35,851						1.75			0.34	30.20 - 22.23	15.0
12/31/01	273,008	32,178	309,354	③ 30,247	1,390,970	814,435	9.8	9.0	2.2	③ 1.51	15.36	1.5	0.31	23.08 - 19.38	14.1
12/31/00	231,603	29,046	263,496	28,693	1,281,323	774,159	10.9	8.8	2.2	1.45	14.99	1.6	0.29	22.53 - 13.13	12.3
12/31/99	195,274	26,015	225,756	31,451	1,170,363	706,314	13.9	10.7	2.7	1.54	13.11	1.6	0.27	19.41 - 13.94	10.8
12/31/98	142,324	23,937	168,114	28,239	1,012,685	690,751	16.8	9.6	2.8	1.33	14.12	1.3	0.25	22.81 - 15.34	14.4
12/31/97	141,884	24,558	169,424	③ 30,171	911,741	617,472	17.8	11.3	3.3	① 1.67	15.44	1.4	0.23	20.10 - 12.20	9.7
12/31/96	130,656	23,681	155,354	① 25,696	845,474	546,917	16.5	12.8	3.0	① 1.30	10.23	1.9	0.22	13.40 - 8.95	8.6
12/31/95	133,468	22,029	190,549	7,950	814,647	474,590	4.2	5.0	1.0	0.40	8.08	2.4	0.20	10.00 - 6.52	20.4
12/31/94	140,184	20,133	171,902	d5,001	752,301	416,533	...	...	...	d0.27	6.88	2.4	0.18	8.88 - 6.36	...
12/31/93	125,989	16,857	155,125	② 14,132	668,921	403,582	9.1	10.1	2.1	② 0.77	7.53	2.0	0.17	9.16 - 7.72	10.9

Statistics are as originally reported. Adjusted for 5-for-4 stock split 6/95; 2-for-1, 10/02. ① Incl. net realized gains of $0.21 per share, 1997; $0.07 per share, 1996. ② Excl. $1.7 mill. gain from acctg. changes. ③ Bef. acctg. credit of $800,000

OFFICERS:
G. D. Stephens, Chmn.
J. E. Michael, Pres., C.E.O.
J. E. Dondanville, V.P., C.F.O.

INVESTOR CONTACT: Mike Price, Treasurer, (309) 693-5880

PRINCIPAL OFFICE: 9025 North Lindbergh Drive, Peoria, IL 61615

TELEPHONE NUMBER: (309) 692-1000
FAX: (309) 692-1068
WEB: www.rlicorp.com
NO. OF EMPLOYEES: 488 full-time; 67 part-time
SHAREHOLDERS: 4,168
ANNUAL MEETING: In May
INCORPORATED: DE, May, 1984; reincorp., IL, May, 1993

INSTITUTIONAL HOLDINGS:
No. of Institutions: 100
Shares Held: 5,622,501
% Held: 22.8

INDUSTRY: Fire, marine, and casualty insurance (SIC: 6331).

TRANSFER AGENT(S): Wells Fargo Shareowner Services, South St. Paul, MN

ROBERT HALF INTERNATIONAL, INC.

EXCH.	SYM.	REC. PRICE	P/E RATIO	YLD.	MKT. CAP.	RANGE (52-WK.)	'02 Y/E PR.
NYSE	RHI	13.39 (2/28/03)	1339.0	...	$2.34 bill.	30.90 - 11.94	16.11

MEDIUM GRADE. THE COMPANY BELIEVES THAT IT IS WELL-POSITIONED TO TAKE ADVANTAGE OF ANY IMPROVEMENT IN THE JOB MARKET RESULTING FROM A STRENGTHENING ECONOMY.

TRADING VOLUME
Thousand Shares

*7 YEAR PRICE SCORE 105.0   ***12 MONTH PRICE SCORE 79.6**
*NYSE COMPOSITE INDEX=100

INTERIM EARNINGS (Per Share):

Qtr.	Mar.	June	Sept.	Dec.
1998	0.16	0.17	0.19	0.19
1999	0.19	0.19	0.19	0.21
2000	0.24	0.25	0.26	0.26
2001	0.26	0.21	0.13	0.07
2002	0.05	0.02	d0.02	d0.04

INTERIM DIVIDENDS (Per Share):

Amt.	Decl.	Ex.	Rec.	Pay.
	No dividends paid.			

CAPITALIZATION (12/31/01):

	($000)	(%)
Long-Term Debt	2,480	0.3
Common & Surplus	805,696	99.7
Total	808,176	100.0

BUSINESS:

Robert Half International, Inc. is a specialized provider of temporary, permanent and project personnel in the field of accounting and finance through its ACCOUNTEMPS® (44.1% of 2002 revenue), ROBERT HALF® MANAGEMENT RESOURCES (11.2%) and ROBERT HALF® FINANCE & ACCOUNTING (5.3%) divisions. In addition, OFFICETEAM® (25.6%) provides skilled temporary administrative support personnel. ROBERT HALF® TECHNOLOGY (11.6%) provides temporary and contract placement for information technology professionals. THE AFFILIATES® places temporary and regular employees in paralegal, legal administrative and other legal support positions. THE CREATIVE GROUP® provides project staffing in the advertising, marketing and Web design fields. RHI's Protiviti subsidiary (2.2%) provides independent business risk consulting and internal auditing services.

RECENT DEVELOPMENTS:

For the year ended 12/31/02, RHI reported net income of $2.2 million versus $121.1 million in the previous year. Results for 2002 and 2001 included amortization of intangibles of $6.3 million and $5.3 million, respectively. Earnings for 2002 were negatively affected by weak hiring activity among businesses. Net service revenues fell 22.3% to $1.90 billion from $2.45 billion a year earlier. Results for 2002 included Protiviti revenues of $41.7 million. Accountemps revenue decreased 22.8% to $840.1 million, while OfficeTeam revenue was down 18.8% to $488.7 million. Robert Half Technology revenue dropped 29.0% to $220.7 million, and Robert Half Management Resources revenue dipped 18.7% to $213.7 million. Robert Half Finance & Accounting revenue declined 47.0% to $100.0 million.

PROSPECTS:

Going forward, economic uncertainty continues to negatively affect the hiring plans of businesses. Meanwhile, the Company continues to generate strong after-tax cash flows even in a difficult economy. In addition, the Company believes that it is well-positioned to take advantage of any improvement in the job market resulting from a strengthening economy. Separately, RHI continues to make progress in meeting Protiviti Inc.'s back office and technology infrastructure requirements.

ANNUAL FINANCIAL DATA:

FISCAL YEAR	TOT. REVS. ($Mill.)	NET INC. ($Mill.)	TOT. ASSETS ($Mill.)	OPER. PROFIT %	NET PROFIT %	RET. ON EQUITY %	RET. ON ASSETS %	CURR. RATIO	EARN. PER SH. $	CASH FL. PER SH. $	TANG. BK. VAL. $	PRICE RANGE	AVG. P/E RATIO
p12/31/02	1,905.0	2.2							0.01			30.90 - 11.94	N.M.
12/31/01	2,452.9	121.1	994.2	7.7	4.9	15.0	12.2	3.9	0.67	1.07	3.69	30.90 - 18.50	36.9
12/31/00	2,699.3	186.1	971.0	10.8	6.9	25.9	19.2	2.8	1.00	1.30	3.13	38.63 - 12.34	25.5
12/31/99	2,081.3	141.4	777.2	11.0	6.8	24.6	18.2	2.8	0.77	0.98	2.27	24.19 - 10.22	22.5
12/31/98	1,793.0	131.6	703.7	12.0	7.3	25.2	18.7	2.8	0.70	0.82	1.89	30.13 - 14.50	32.1
12/31/97	1,302.9	93.7	561.4	11.9	7.2	22.4	16.7	2.7	0.50	0.59	1.32	21.53 - 11.13	32.6
12/31/96	898.6	61.1	416.0	11.3	6.8	19.8	14.7	2.5	0.35	0.41	0.75	13.83 - 6.50	29.5
12/31/95	628.5	40.3	301.1	10.9	6.4	17.7	13.4	2.4	0.24	0.28	0.42	7.44 - 3.27	22.8
12/31/94	446.3	26.1	227.8	10.5	5.9	14.8	11.5	2.3	0.15	0.20	0.14	4.46 - 2.13	21.5
12/31/93	306.2	11.7	204.6	8.3	3.8	8.8	5.7	2.1	0.08	0.12	...	2.50 - 1.05	23.0

Statistics are as originally reported. Adj. for stk. splits: 2-for-1, 6/00, 6/96 & 8/94; and 3-for-2, 9/97.

OFFICERS:
H. M. Messmer Jr., Chmn., Pres., C.E.O.
M. K. Waddell, Vice-Chmn., C.F.O., Treas.
INVESTOR CONTACT: Investor Relations, (650) 234-6000
PRINCIPAL OFFICE: 2884 Sand Hill Road, Suite 200, Menlo Park, CA 94025

TELEPHONE NUMBER: (650) 234-6000
FAX: (650) 234-6999
WEB: www.rhii.com
NO. OF EMPLOYEES: 6,300 (approx.)
SHAREHOLDERS: 2,220 (approx.)
ANNUAL MEETING: In May
INCORPORATED: DE, June, 1987

INSTITUTIONAL HOLDINGS:
No. of Institutions: 231
Shares Held: 140,677,215
% Held: 81.2
INDUSTRY: Help supply svcs. (SIC: 7363)
TRANSFER AGENT(S): Mellon Investor Services, San Francisco, CA

ROCKWELL AUTOMATION

EXCH.	SYM.	REC. PRICE	P/E RATIO	YLD.	MKT. CAP.	RANGE (52-WK.)	'02 Y/E PR.
NYSE	ROK	23.01 (2/28/03)	18.3	...	$4.28 bill.	23.87 - 14.71	20.71

MEDIUM GRADE. RESULTS CONTINUE TO REFLECT THE STRENGTH OF THE COMPANY'S CONTROL SYSTEMS BUSINESS SEGMENT.

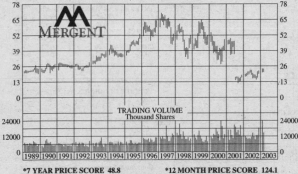

*7 YEAR PRICE SCORE 48.8   ***12 MONTH PRICE SCORE 124.1**
*NYSE COMPOSITE INDEX=100

INTERIM EARNINGS (Per Share):

Qtr.	Dec.	Mar.	June	Sept.
1998-99	0.70	0.74	0.77	0.80
1999-00	0.81	0.85	0.90	0.78
2000-01	0.38	0.38	d0.15	0.09
2001-02	0.16	0.31	0.47	0.26
2002-03	0.22	...	...	...

INTERIM DIVIDENDS (Per Share):

Amt.	Decl.	Ex.	Rec.	Pay.
0.165Q	4/05/02	5/09/02	5/13/02	6/03/02
0.165Q	6/05/02	8/08/02	8/12/02	9/03/02
0.165Q	11/06/02	11/14/02	11/18/02	12/09/02
0.165Q	2/05/03	2/13/03	2/18/03	3/10/03

Indicated div.: $0.66 (Div. Reinv. Plan)

CAPITALIZATION (9/30/02):

	($000)	(%)
Long-Term Debt	767,000	30.3
Deferred Income Tax	158,000	6.2
Common & Surplus	1,609,000	63.5
Total	2,534,000	100.0

BUSINESS:

Rockwell Automation (formerly Rockwell International) is a provider of industrial automation power, control and information services that help customers meet manufacturing productivity objectives. ROK brings together major brands in industrial automation for automation services, including Dodge® mechanical power transmission products, Reliance Electric™ motors and drives, Allen-Bradley® controls and engineered services and Rockwell Software® factory management software. ROK's other business segment includes the FirstPoint Contact business and the Science Center. On 9/30/97, ROK completed the spin-off of its Automotive Component Systems business. On 12/31/98, ROK spun off of its semiconductor business, Conexant Systems, Inc. In June 2001, ROK spun off its communications and aviation electronics business, Rockwell Collins.

RECENT DEVELOPMENTS:

For the three months ended 12/31/02, net income was $42.0 million compared with income of $29.0 million, before an accounting change charge of $108.0 million, in the corresponding quarter of the previous year. The improvement in earnings was due to strong customer demand. Total sales rose 4.8% to $984.0 million from $939.0 million in the year-earlier period. Control systems sales climbed 8.9% to $787.0 million from $723.0 million, while power systems sales declined 3.1% to $171.0 million from $178.0 million in the prior-year quarter. FirstPoint Contact sales dropped 31.6% to $26.0 million from $38.0 million the year before.

PROSPECTS:

Results continue to reflect the strength of the Company's control systems business segment, which is benefiting from growth in the automotive, food and beverage, and life sciences industries. Meanwhile, ROK expects earnings per share to range from $0.23 to $0.26 for the second quarter of fiscal 2003, due to slow customer demand and a modestly lower sales run rate. Moreover, ROK estimates fiscal 2003 earnings to be approximately $1.10 per share, based on the assumption that markets will remain generally stable and sales will be up 2.0% to 4.0% over last year.

ANNUAL FINANCIAL DATA:

FISCAL YEAR	TOT. REVS. ($mill.)	NET INC. ($mill.)	TOT. ASSETS ($mill.)	OPER. PROFIT %	NET PROFIT %	RET. ON EQUITY %	RET. ON ASSETS %	CURR. RATIO	EARN. PER SH. $	CASH FL. PER SH. $	TANG. BK. VAL.$	DIV. PER SH. $	PRICE RANGE	AVG. P/E RATIO	AVG. YIELD %
9/30/02	3,909.0	⑧ 226.0	4,024.0	7.2	5.8	14.0	5.6	1.8	⑧ 1.20	2.29	2.61	0.17	22.79 - 14.71	15.6	0.9
⑦ 9/30/01	4,323.0	⑥ 125.0	4,074.0	5.8	2.9	7.8	3.1	2.0	⑥ 0.68	2.14	2.22	0.84	49.45 - 11.78	45.0	2.7
9/30/00	7,220.0	⑤ 636.0	6,390.0	14.1	8.8	23.8	10.0	1.8	⑤ 3.35	5.29	6.90	1.02	54.50 - 27.69	12.3	2.5
9/30/99	7,151.0	④ 582.0	6,704.0	13.6	8.1	22.1	8.7	1.7	④ 3.01	4.75	5.76	1.02	64.94 - 39.94	17.4	1.9
9/30/98	6,840.0	③ d109.0	7,170.0	1.2	...	...	...	2.1	③ d0.55	1.00	8.85	1.02	61.63 - 32.13	...	2.2
9/30/97	7,882.0	② 586.0	7,971.0	12.1	7.4	12.2	7.4	1.9	② 2.74	5.00	14.61	1.13	70.63 - 44.31	21.0	2.0
9/30/96	10,542.0	① 555.0	10,065.0	8.8	5.3	13.0	5.5	1.3	① 2.55	5.04	19.48	...	64.63 - 47.50	22.0	...
9/30/95	13,099.0	742.0	12,505.0	10.7	5.7	19.6	5.9	1.4	3.42	6.05	8.13	...	53.00 - 35.00	12.9	...
9/30/94	11,204.7	634.1	9,860.8	10.0	5.7	18.9	6.4	1.6	2.87	5.12	11.79	...	44.13 - 33.50	13.5	...
9/30/93	10,920.9	561.9	9,885.1	9.2	5.1	19.0	5.7	1.7	2.55	4.79	9.71	...	38.50 - 27.88	13.0	...

Statistics are as originally reported. ① Bef. disc. oper. credit $171.0 mill., but incl. non-recurr. chrg. $122.0 mill. ② Bef. disc. oper. credit $58.0 mill. ③ Bef. disc. oper. loss $301.0 mill. & acctg. change chrg. $17.0 mill. ④ Bef. disc. oper. loss $20.0 mill. ⑤ Bef. disc. oper. gain $292.0 mill. and incl. pre-tax gain of $14.0 mill. from the sale of a bus. ⑥ Bef. disc. oper. gain $180.0 mill. and incl. pre-tax spec. chrg. of $73.0 mill. ⑦ Ref. spin-off of comm. & aviation electronics bus. in June 2001. ⑧ Bef. disc. oper. credit $3.0 mill.

OFFICERS:
D. H. Davis Jr., Chmn., C.E.O.
M. A. Bless, Sr. V.P., C.F.O.

INVESTOR CONTACT: Steve Smith, Investor Relations, (414) 382-5580

PRINCIPAL OFFICE: 777 East Wisconsin Avenue, Suite 1400, Milwaukee, WI 53202

TELEPHONE NUMBER: (414) 212-5299
FAX: (414) 212-5212
WEB: www.rockwellautomation.com

NO. OF EMPLOYEES: 22,000 (approx.)

SHAREHOLDERS: 43,628

ANNUAL MEETING: In Feb.

INCORPORATED: DE, Dec., 1928

INSTITUTIONAL HOLDINGS:
No. of Institutions: 321
Shares Held: 105,395,368
% Held: 56.7

INDUSTRY: Relays and industrial controls (SIC: 3625)

TRANSFER AGENT(S): Mellon Investor Services, South Hackensack, NJ

ROHM & HAAS COMPANY

EXCH.	SYM.	REC. PRICE	P/E RATIO	YLD.	MKT. CAP.	RANGE (52-WK.)	'02 Y/E PR.	DIV. ACH.
NYSE	ROH	28.54 (2/28/03)	28.8	2.9%	$6.31 bill.	42.60 - 27.53	32.48	25 yrs.

UPPER MEDIUM GRADE. SALES GROWTH FOR 2003 IS EXPECTED IN THE HIGH SINGLE-DIGIT RANGE DUE TO THE COMPANY'S MARKET POSITION AND THE INTRODUCTION OF NEW PRODUCTS.

MERGENT

2009% STK.

TRADING VOLUME
Thousand Shares

| 1989 | 1990 | 1991 | 1992 | 1993 | 1994 | 1995 | 1996 | 1997 | 1998 | 1999 | 2000 | 2001 | 2002 | 2003 |

*7 YEAR PRICE SCORE 115.3   ***12 MONTH PRICE SCORE 94.9**

*NYSE COMPOSITE INDEX=100

INTERIM EARNINGS (Per Share):

Qtr.	Mar.	June	Sept.	Dec.
1998	0.58	0.96	0.50	0.44
1999	0.64	d0.06	0.26	0.41
2000	0.56	0.35	0.38	0.32
2001	0.29	d0.94	0.24	0.17
2002	0.38	0.42	0.35	d0.16

INTERIM DIVIDENDS (Per Share):

Amt.	Decl.	Ex.	Rec.	Pay.
0.20Q	2/05/02	2/13/02	2/15/02	3/01/02
0.20Q	5/06/02	5/15/02	5/17/02	6/01/02
0.21Q	7/22/02	7/31/02	8/02/02	9/01/02
0.21Q	10/17/02	11/06/02	11/08/02	12/01/02
0.21Q	2/03/03	2/12/03	2/14/03	3/01/03

Indicated div.: $0.84 (Div. Reinv. Plan)

CAPITALIZATION (12/31/01):

	($000)	(%)
Long-Term Debt	2,720,000	34.7
Deferred Income Tax	1,278,000	16.3
Minority Interest	18,000	0.2
Common & Surplus	3,815,000	48.7
Total	7,831,000	100.0

BUSINESS:

Rohm & Haas Company is a multinational producer of specialty polymers and biologically active compounds. Products range from basic petrochemicals such as propylene, acetone and styrene to differentiated specialty products. ROH has developed acrylic plastics, a field that it pioneered with its development of plexiglas, which is used in outdoor signs, industrial lighting, skylights, and boat windshields. Other products include polymers, resins and monomers geared toward a wide variety of industrial applications. ROH also manufactures industrial chemicals. Contributions to sales in 2002 were as follows: coatings, 29.4%; performance chemicals, 19.2%; electronic materials, 15.6%; monomers, 15.4%; salt, 11.1%; and adhesives and sealants, 9.3%.

RECENT DEVELOPMENTS:

For the twelve months ended 12/31/02, earnings from continuing operations amounted to $218.0 million compared with a loss from continuing operations of $70.0 million in 2001. Results for 2002 and 2001 included amortization of goodwill and other intangibles of $69.0 million and $156.0 million, and restructuring and asset impairment charges of $177.0 million and $320.0 million, respectively. Results for 2002 and 2001 excluded extraordinary losses of $8.0 million and $1.0 million, respectively, and accounting change charges of $773.0 million and $2.0 million, respectively. Results for 2002 and 2001 also excluded a loss of $7.0 million and a gain of $468.0 million, respectively, from discontinued operations. Net sales climbed 1.1% to $5.73 billion from $5.67 billion the year before.

PROSPECTS:

The Company is cautious about the global recovery in 2003 due to continued economic and geo-political uncertainty. Raw material and gas prices are expected to be significantly higher than levels in 2002 due to instability in the Middle East and Venezuela. However, sales growth for 2003 is expected in the high single-digit range, reflecting ROH's market position and new products. In addition, recent acquisitions are anticipated to contribute about 2.0% to sales growth. Moreover, increased selling prices should help mitigate the effect of rising global costs.

ANNUAL FINANCIAL DATA:

FISCAL YEAR	TOT. REVS. ($mill.)	NET INC. ($mill.)	TOT. ASSETS ($mill.)	OPER. PROFIT %	NET PROFIT %	RET. ON EQUITY %	RET. ON ASSETS %	CURR. RATIO	EARN. PER SH. $	CASH FL. PER SH. $	TANG. BK. VAL. $	DIV. PER SH. $	PRICE RANGE	AVG. P/E RATIO	AVG. YIELD
p12/31/02	5,727.0	⑨ 218.0		1.6	...	...	1.5	⑨ 0.98			0.82	42.60 - 30.19	37.1	2.3
12/31/01	5,666.0	⑦ d70.0	10,350.0	...	...	...	1.5	⑦ d0.31	2.23	...	0.80	38.70 - 24.90	...	2.5
12/31/00	6,879.0	⑥ 354.0	11,267.0	11.0	5.1	9.7	3.1	1.3	⑥ 1.61	4.39	...	0.78	49.44 - 24.38	22.9	2.1
⑧ 12/31/99	5,339.0	⑤ 249.0	11,256.0	11.8	4.7	7.2	2.2	1.0	⑤ 1.27	3.19	...	0.74	49.25 - 28.13	30.5	1.9
12/31/98	3,720.0	④ 453.0	3,648.0	16.7	12.2	29.0	12.4	1.5	④ 2.52	4.02	9.66	0.69	38.88 - 26.00	12.9	2.1
12/31/97	3,999.0	410.0	3,900.0	15.4	10.3	22.8	10.5	1.6	2.13	3.55	9.15	0.63	33.75 - 23.54	13.4	2.2
12/31/96	3,982.0	③ 363.0	3,933.0	14.2	9.1	21.0	9.2	1.6	③ 1.82	3.15	8.44	0.57	27.50 - 18.29	12.6	2.5
12/31/95	3,884.0	② 292.0	3,916.0	13.2	7.5	16.4	7.5	1.7	② 1.41	2.60	8.16	0.52	21.63 - 16.50	13.5	2.7
12/31/94	3,534.0	264.0	3,861.0	13.2	7.5	16.3	6.8	1.5	1.26	2.40	7.32	0.48	22.83 - 17.75	16.1	2.4
12/31/93	3,269.0	① 126.0	3,524.0	9.2	3.9	8.7	3.6	1.7	① 0.58	1.70	6.43	0.45	20.67 - 15.75	31.4	2.5

Statistics are as originally reported. Adj. for 3-for-1 split, 9/98. ① Incl. $6.0 mill. aft-tax non-recur. chgs. ② Bef. dr$19.0 mill. acct. adj. ③ Incl. $17.0 mill. chg. for cleanup. ④ Excl. $13.0 mill. aft-tax extraord. loss. ⑤ Incl. $105.0 mill. in-proc. R&D chg., $22.0 mill. loss fr. disp. of joint vent. & $36.0 mill. restr. chg. ⑥ Incl. $13.0 mill. purch. in-proc. R&D chg. & $13.0 mill. restr. chg. ⑦ Incl. $320.0 mill. restr. chg.; Bef. gain of $468.0 mill. fr. disc. ops., $1.0 mill. extraord. loss & $2.0 mill. acctg. chg. chrg. ⑧ Results benefited fr. acqs. of Morton International & LeaRonal. ⑨ Incl. $177.0 mill. restr. chg. and excl. $7.0 mill. gain fr. disc. ops., $8.0 mill. extraord. loss & $773.0 mill. acctg. chg. chrg.

OFFICERS:
R. L. Gupta, Chmn., C.E.O.
J. M. Fitzpatrick, Pres., C.O.O.
B. J. Bell, Sr. V.P., C.F.O.
INVESTOR CONTACT: Laura L. Hadden, Mgr. Bus. & Fin., (215) 592-3052
PRINCIPAL OFFICE: 100 Independence Mall West, Philadelphia, PA 19106

TELEPHONE NUMBER: (215) 592-3000
FAX: (215) 592-3377
WEB: www.rohmhaas.com
NO. OF EMPLOYEES: 18,210 (avg.)
SHAREHOLDERS: 9,234
ANNUAL MEETING: In May
INCORPORATED: DE, Apr., 1917

INSTITUTIONAL HOLDINGS:
No. of Institutions: 303
Shares Held: 171,269,966
% Held: 77.5
INDUSTRY: Plastics materials and resins (SIC: 2821)
TRANSFER AGENT(S): EquiServe, LP, Boston, MA

ROPER INDUSTRIES, INC.

EXCH.	SYM.	REC. PRICE	P/E RATIO	YLD.	MKT. CAP.	RANGE (52-WK.)	'02 Y/E PR.	DIV. ACH.
NYSE	ROP	28.85 (2/28/03)	15.3	1.2%	$0.89 bill.	51.90 - 27.25	36.60	10 yrs.

MEDIUM GRADE. FOR FISCAL 2003, THE COMPANY ANTICIPATES RESULTS WILL BENEFIT FROM COMPLETED ACQUISITIONS AND NEW BUSINESS OFFERINGS.

TRADING VOLUME
Thousand Shares

*7 YEAR PRICE SCORE 132.0   *12 MONTH PRICE SCORE 97.8
*NYSE COMPOSITE INDEX=100

INTERIM EARNINGS (Per Share):

Qtr.	Jan.	April	July	Oct.
1998-99	0.26	0.39	0.41	0.47
1999-00	0.31	0.44	0.36	0.48
2000-01	0.38	0.44	0.41	0.54
2001-02	0.46	0.55	0.47	0.60
2002-03	0.26	...	...	...

INTERIM DIVIDENDS (Per Share):

Amt.	Decl.	Ex.	Rec.	Pay.
0.083Q	2/21/02	4/12/02	4/16/02	4/30/02
0.083Q	5/23/02	7/12/02	7/16/02	7/31/02
0.083Q	9/03/02	10/10/02	10/15/02	10/31/02
0.087Q	11/20/02	1/15/03	1/17/03	1/31/03
0.087Q	3/24/03	4/14/03	4/16/03	4/30/03

Indicated div.: $0.35

CAPITALIZATION (10/31/02):

	($000)	(%)
Long-Term Debt	311,590	45.3
Common & Surplus	376,012	54.7
Total	687,602	100.0

BUSINESS:

Roper Industries, Inc. produces specialty industrial controls, fluid handling and analytical instrumentation products. The Instrumentation segment provides primarily test, inspection and measurement products for oil and gas, research and industrial markets under brands such as Acton Research, Antek, Gatan, Logitech, Struers and Uson. The industrial technology segment provides services for industrial, energy, commercial refrigeration, and water/wastewater markets under the brands, Abel Pump,

AMOT Controls, Cornell Pump, Flow Technology, Fluid Metering, and Hansen. The Energy Systems and Controls segment provides control, monitoring and and inspection systems for energy markets under the brands Compressor Controls, Petrotech, Metrix amd Zetec. The Scientific and Industrial Imaging segment provides high-performance digital imaging products and equipment for industrial, medical and science applications under the brands Media Cybernetics, QImaging, Redlake, and Roper Scientific.

RECENT DEVELOPMENTS:

For the first quarter ended 1/31/03, the Company reported earnings from continuing operations of $8.4 million compared with $14.7 million, before an accounting change charge of $26.0 million, in the corresponding prior-year quarter. Earnings excluded losses from discontinued opera-

tions of $369,000 and $187,000 in 2003 and 2002, respectively. Net sales decreased 5.6% to $138.3 million from $146.5 million a year earlier. Gross profit fell 9.1% to $71.4 million from $78.5 million the year before. Income from operations dropped 36.4% to $15.9 million.

PROSPECTS:

The Company's goals for 2003 include pursuing internal growth, capitalizing on synergies that exist among its businesses, improving working capital efficiency, and continuing with a disciplined acquisition process. Separately, based on first quarter bookings and expected net sales to

Gazprom, the Company expects second quarter earnings from continuing operations in the range of $0.52 to $0.57 per share. Earnings from continuing operations for fiscal 2003 are expected to be between $2.11 and $2.26 per share.

ANNUAL FINANCIAL DATA:

FISCAL YEAR	TOT. REVS. ($000)	NET INC. ($000)	TOT. ASSETS ($000)	OPER. PROFIT %	NET PROFIT %	RET. ON EQUITY %	RET. ON ASSETS %	CURR. RATIO	EARN. PER SH.$	CASH FL.PER SH.$	TANG. BK. VAL.$	DIV. PER SH.$	PRICE RANGE	AVG. P/E RATIO	AVG. YIELD %
10/31/02	627,030	① 66,023	828,973	18.3	10.5	17.6	8.0	1.9	① 2.08	2.55	...	0.33	52.91 - 27.25	19.3	0.8
10/31/01	586,506	55,839	762,122	16.8	9.5	17.3	7.3	2.2	1.77	2.64	...	0.30	52.25 - 31.00	23.5	0.7
10/31/00	503,813	49,278	596,902	17.5	9.8	18.2	8.3	2.5	1.58	2.30	...	0.28	37.94 - 24.00	19.6	0.9
10/31/99	407,256	47,346	420,163	19.1	11.6	20.4	11.3	2.2	1.53	2.04	0.56	0.26	38.56 - 19.63	19.0	0.9
10/31/98	389,170	39,316	381,533	17.0	10.1	20.0	10.3	2.4	1.24	1.69	...	0.24	34.06 - 13.31	19.1	1.0
10/31/97	298,236	36,350	329,320	20.4	12.2	20.4	11.0	2.9	1.16	1.52	0.76	0.20	34.88 - 18.56	23.0	0.7
10/31/96	225,651	28,857	242,953	20.9	12.8	21.0	11.9	2.1	0.94	1.19	0.32	0.16	36.38 - 17.50	23.5	0.7
10/31/95	175,421	23,271	155,381	21.3	13.3	22.0	15.0	2.4	0.77	0.97	3.53	0.11	20.25 - 10.50	20.0	0.7
10/31/94	147,683	20,862	121,982	22.3	14.1	25.2	17.1	2.6	0.70	0.87	2.80	0.07	17.00 - 9.00	18.7	0.5
10/31/93	132,530	19,058	87,820	22.9	14.4	30.5	21.7	2.4	0.65	0.82	0.68	0.04	19.50 - 4.44	18.6	0.4

Statistics are as originally reported. Adj. for stk. splits: 2-for-1, 8/97 & 9/93. ① Bef. acctg. change chrg. of $26.0 mill.; incl. Euro debt currency exchange loss of $4.1 mill.

OFFICERS:
D. N. Key, Chmn.
B. D. Jellison, Pres., C.E.O.
M. S. Headley, V.P., C.F.O.

INVESTOR CONTACT: Christopher M. Hix, Dir., Invest. Rel., (706) 369-7170

PRINCIPAL OFFICE: 160 Ben Burton Road, Bogart, GA 30622

TELEPHONE NUMBER: (706) 369-7170
FAX: (706) 353-6496
WEB: www.roperind.com

NO. OF EMPLOYEES: 2,950 (approx.)

SHAREHOLDERS: 215

ANNUAL MEETING: In March

INCORPORATED: DE, 1981

INSTITUTIONAL HOLDINGS:
No. of Institutions: 158
Shares Held: 27,760,494
% Held: 88.6

INDUSTRY: Pumps and pumping equipment (SIC: 3561)

TRANSFER AGENT(S): SunTrust Bank, Atlanta, GA

ROUSE COMPANY (THE)

EXCH.	SYM.	REC. PRICE	P/E RATIO	YLD.	MKT. CAP.	RANGE (52-WK.)	'02 Y/E PR.	DIV. ACH.
NYSE	RSE	33.36 (2/28/03)	22.7	5.0%	$2.31 bill.	33.71 - 27.47	31.70	10 yrs.

MEDIUM GRADE. THE COMPANY EXPECTS RESULTS FROM RETAIL AND COMMUNITY DEVELOPMENT OPERATIONS WILL BE STRONG IN 2003.

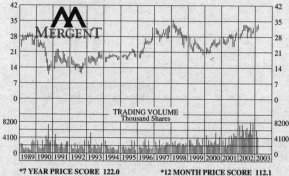

*7 YEAR PRICE SCORE 122.0   *12 MONTH PRICE SCORE 112.1

*NYSE COMPOSITE INDEX=100

INTERIM EARNINGS (Per Share):

Qtr.	Mar.	June	Sept.	Dec.
1998	0.46	0.37	0.27	0.24
1999	0.34	0.37	0.32	0.73
2000	0.40	0.44	0.96	0.41
2001	0.41	0.34	0.37	0.93
2002	0.20	1.04	0.33	d0.10

INTERIM DIVIDENDS (Per Share):

Amt.	Decl.	Ex.	Rec.	Pay.
0.39Q	2/21/02	3/13/02	3/15/02	3/29/02
0.39Q	5/09/02	6/12/02	6/14/02	6/28/02
0.39Q	5/09/02	9/12/02	9/16/02	9/30/02
0.39Q	12/05/02	12/11/02	12/13/02	12/23/02
0.42Q	2/20/03	3/12/03	3/14/03	3/28/03

Indicated div.: $1.68 (Div. Reinv. Plan)

CAPITALIZATION (12/31/01):

	($000)	(%)
Long-Term Debt	3,488,820	81.5
Redeemable Pfd. Stock	136,965	3.2
Preferred Stock	41	0.0
Common & Surplus	655,319	15.3
Total	4,281,145	100.0

BUSINESS:

The Rouse Company operated, as of 12/31/02, more than 175 properties encompassing retail, office, research and development, hotel and industrial space in 22 states. RSE owns and/or operates 52 regional retail centers and three community centers, with more than 45.0 million square feet and including about 137 nationally known department stores and 7,000 small merchants. RSE also owns and/or operates six mixed-use projects and an additional 2.7 million square feet of office/industrial space, mainly located either in the Baltimore-Washington corridor or in Las Vegas, Nevada. RSE, through its affiliates, is the developer of the cities of Columbia, Maryland and Summerlin, Nevada.

RECENT DEVELOPMENTS:

For the twelve months ended 12/31/02, net earnings rose 26.3% to $139.9 million compared with $110.7 million in 2001. Results for 2002 and 2001 included a net gain of $37.0 million and a net loss of $432,000 on operating properties, and net losses from the early extinguishment of debt of $8.2 million and $696,000, respectively. Results for 2002 also included a restructuring charge of $21.8 million and an impairment loss of $11.6 million, while results for 2001 included an accounting change charge of $411.0 million. Revenues grew 15.3% to $1.22 billion compared with $1.06 billion the year before. Operating income increased 16.5% to $650.5 million compared with $558.5 million the year before, primarily due to assets acquired from Rodamco, N.A. in May 2002.

PROSPECTS:

The Company's properties located in Columbia, Maryland and Summerlin, Nevada have been recognized as strong communities for living, working and shopping due to their amenities, facilities and programs. In addition, the new Fairwood, Maryland community is progressing along a similar path as Columbia and Summerlin. As a result, solid performance from these markets bode well for long-term profitability.

ANNUAL FINANCIAL DATA:

FISCAL YEAR	TOT. REVS. ($mill.)	NET INC. ($mill.)	TOT. ASSETS ($mill.)	OPER. PROFIT %	NET PROFIT %	RET. ON EQUITY %	RET. ON ASSETS %	EARN. PER SH.$	CASH FL. PER SH.$	TANG. BK. VAL.$	DIV. PER SH.$	PRICE RANGE	AVG. P/E RATIO	AVG. YIELD %
p12/31/02	1,221.7	⑩ 139.9						⑩ 1.47			1.56	33.50 - 27.25	20.7	5.1
12/31/01	966.3	⑨ 112.5	4,880.4	34.9	11.6	17.1	2.3	⑨ 1.42	3.41	9.45	1.42	30.16 - 23.59	18.9	5.3
12/31/00	633.7	⑧ 168.3	4,175.5	38.3	26.6	26.7	4.0	⑧ 2.21	3.72	9.29	1.32	27.13 - 20.13	10.7	5.6
12/31/99	715.7	⑦ 108.9	4,427.2	38.7	15.2	17.1	2.5	⑦ 1.77	3.37	9.03	1.20	27.75 - 19.75	13.4	5.1
12/31/98	692.6	⑥ 116.3	5,154.6	36.1	16.8	18.5	2.3	⑥ 1.34	2.61	8.71	1.12	35.69 - 23.13	21.9	3.8
12/31/97	916.8	⑤ 189.9	3,589.8	32.5	20.7	40.8	5.3	⑤ 2.59	3.45	6.96	1.00	33.00 - 25.75	11.3	3.4
12/31/96	831.9	④ 17.9	3,643.5	33.6	2.1	10.1	0.5	④ 0.14	1.57	2.65	0.88	32.25 - 18.25	180.2	3.5
12/31/95	672.8	③ 5.9	2,985.6	37.0	0.9	13.7	0.2	③ d0.18	1.34	0.89	0.80	22.63 - 17.63	...	4.0
12/31/94	671.2	② 6.6	2,915.9	35.0	1.0	7.0	0.2	② d0.14	1.42	2.00	0.68	20.00 - 16.25	...	3.8
12/31/93	646.8	① d1.3	2,875.0	34.0	...	...	...	① d0.27	1.21	2.38	0.62	21.25 - 15.00	...	3.4

Statistics are as originally reported. ① Bef. $8.1 mil extraord. chg. & incl. $5.8 mil non-recurr. chg. ② Bef. $4.4 mil extraord. chg. & incl. $7.9 mil non-recur. chg. ③ Bef. $8.6 mil extraord. chg. & incl. $25.7 mil non-recur. chg. ④ Bef. $1.5 mil extraord. chg. & incl. $15.9 mil non-recur. chg. ⑤ Bef. $21.3 mil extraord. chg. and $1.2 mil acctg. chg. & incl. $23.5 mil non-recurr. chg. ⑥ Bef. $4.4 mil extraord. gain and $4.6 mil acctg. chg. & incl. $11.2 mil non-recur. chg. ⑦ Bef. $5.9 mil extraord. chg. & incl. $32.6 mil non-recur. gain. ⑧ Bef. $2.2 mil extraord. gain & incl. $33.2 mil non-recur. gain. ⑨ Incl. $1.2 mil loss on oper. prop. and excl. $696,000 extraord. loss & $411,000 acctg. chg. ⑩ Incl. $21.8 mill. restr. chg., $11.6 mill. impair. loss, $8.2 mill. net loss fr. exting. of debt, & $37.0 mill. net gain fr. sale of prop.

OFFICERS:
A. W. Deering, Chmn., Pres., C.E.O.
T. J. DeRosa, Vice-Chmn., C.F.O.
J. D. Smalley, Vice-Chmn., C.O.O.
INVESTOR CONTACT: David L. Tripp, Investor Relations, (410) 992-6546
PRINCIPAL OFFICE: 10275 Little Patuxent Parkway, Columbia, MD 21044-3456

TELEPHONE NUMBER: (410) 992-6000
FAX: (410) 992-6363
WEB: www.therousecompany.com
NO. OF EMPLOYEES: 3,396 (avg.)
SHAREHOLDERS: 2,391
ANNUAL MEETING: In May
INCORPORATED: MD, Oct., 1956

INSTITUTIONAL HOLDINGS:
No. of Institutions: 172
Shares Held: 75,372,656
% Held: 86.8
INDUSTRY: Nonresidential building operators (SIC: 6512)
TRANSFER AGENT(S): The Bank of New York, New York, NY

ROWAN COMPANIES, INC.

EXCH.	SYM.	REC. PRICE	P/E RATIO	YLD.	MKT. CAP.	RANGE (52-WK.)	'02 Y/E PR.
NYSE	RDC	19.63 (2/28/03)	21.6	...	$1.84 bill.	27.03 - 16.36	22.70

MEDIUM GRADE. THE COMPANY IS EXPERIENCING WEAK UTILIZATION RATES FROM BOTH ITS OFFSHORE AND LAND DRILLING OPERATIONS.

TRADING VOLUME
Thousand Shares

*7 YEAR PRICE SCORE 104.8   *12 MONTH PRICE SCORE 107.0
*NYSE COMPOSITE INDEX=100

INTERIM EARNINGS (Per Share):

Qtr.	Mar.	June	Sept.	Dec.
1997	0.09	0.47	0.63	0.53
1998	0.48	0.50	0.38	0.06
1999	d0.12	d0.03	0.01	0.03
2000	0.07	0.12	0.27	0.29
2001	0.33	0.36	0.22	d0.10
2002	0.92	d0.09	0.11	d0.03

INTERIM DIVIDENDS (Per Share):

Amt.	Decl.	Ex.	Rec.	Pay.
0.25Sp	4/26/02	5/14/02	5/16/02	6/06/02

CAPITALIZATION (12/31/01):

	($000)	(%)
Long-Term Debt	438,484	26.2
Deferred Income Tax	127,952	7.6
Common & Surplus	1,108,087	66.2
Total	1,674,523	100.0

BUSINESS:

Rowan Companies, Inc. provides international and domestic contract drilling and aviation services. Drilling operations are conducted through RDC's offshore mobile fleet of 23 self-elevating deep-water drilling platforms and 17 deep-well land rigs and one mobile offshore floating platform, as of 3/28/02. Other operations include LeTourneau, Inc., which operates a mini-steel mill, a manufacturing facility that produces heavy equipment for mining, timber, and transportation industries, and a drilling products group that designs and builds mobile offshore jack-up drilling rigs. Era Aviation, Inc. provides charter and contract helicopter and fixed-wing aircraft services in Alaska, the coastal areas of Louisiana and Texas, and the western U.S. Revenues in 2002 were: drilling services, 57.9%; manufacturing sales and services, 19.1%; aviation services, 23.0%.

RECENT DEVELOPMENTS:

For the year ended 12/31/02, net income was $86.3 million compared with $77.0 million the year before. Earnings for 2002 included net proceeds of $157.1 million from the settlement of a contract dispute. Excluding the effects of the contract settlement, RDC's results would have been a net loss of about $16.0 million. Total revenues fell 15.6% to $617.3 million. Loss from operations was $12.9 million versus income from operations of $124.6 million in 2001. Drilling services revenues slid 26.5% to $357.2 million, while aviation services slipped to $141.9 million from $142.6 million the previous year. Manufacturing sales and services rose 15.6% to $118.1 million.

PROSPECTS:

Ongoing weakness in RDC's offshore and land drilling markets, as evidenced by the decline in rig utilization rates to 88.0% and 68.0% for the quarter ended 12/31/02 versus 93.0% and 76.0%, respectively, in the previous quarter, temper the Company's near-term outlook. However, RDC anticipates year-over-year improvement in industry conditions as 2003 develops. Specifically, RDC expects that its commitment to natural gas in the Gulf of Mexico, coupled with anticipated projects offshore eastern Canada and in the North Sea, will result in a strong recovery for its drilling division. Also, RDC sees its manufacturing and aviation divisions adding to its improved financial results.

ANNUAL FINANCIAL DATA:

FISCAL YEAR	TOT. REVS. ($mill.)	NET INC. ($mill.)	TOT. ASSETS ($mill.)	OPER. PROFIT %	NET PROFIT %	RET. ON EQUITY %	RET. ON ASSETS %	CURR. RATIO	EARN. PER SH.$	CASH FL. PER SH.$	TANG. BK. VAL.$	PRICE RANGE	AVG. P/E RATIO
p12/31/02	617.3	②86.3							②0.90			27.03 - 16.04	
12/31/01	731.1	77.0	1,939.0	17.0	10.5	6.9	4.0	2.5	0.80	1.52	11.84	33.89 - 11.10	28.1
12/31/00	646.0	70.2	1,678.4	17.3	10.9	6.7	4.2	4.6	0.74	1.33	11.17	34.25 - 19.06	36.0
12/31/99	460.6	d9.7	1,356.1	...	...	...	...	1.6	d0.12	0.50	8.69	21.69 - 8.50	...
12/31/98	706.4	124.5	1,249.1	25.8	17.6	17.0	10.0	4.6	1.43	1.96	8.77	32.50 - 9.00	14.5
12/31/97	695.3	①156.4	1,122.1	26.2	22.5	24.0	13.9	5.1	①1.76	2.24	7.53	43.94 - 16.75	17.2
12/31/96	571.2	61.3	899.3	13.8	10.7	12.4	6.8	3.7	0.70	...	5.80	24.50 - 8.88	23.8
12/31/95	471.3	d18.4	802.5	...	...	...	...	3.8	d0.22	...	4.97	10.00 - 5.38	...
12/31/94	438.2	d23.0	805.2	...	...	...	...	4.4	d0.27	...	5.25	9.25 - 5.75	...
12/31/93	353.2	d13.3	765.3	2.1	...	...	...	4.9	d0.17	...	5.49	10.75 - 6.63	...

Statistics are as originally reported. ① Bef. extraord. chrg. of $9.8 mill. ② Incl. non-recurring gain of $157.1 mill. from contract dispute settlement.

OFFICERS:
C. R. Palmer, Chmn., Pres., C.E.O.
E. E. Thiele, Sr. V.P., Treas.
M. H. Hay, Sec., Asst. Treas.
INVESTOR CONTACT: William C. Provine, V.P., (713) 960-7575
PRINCIPAL OFFICE: 2800 Post Oak Blvd., Suite 5450, Houston, TX 77056-6127

TELEPHONE NUMBER: (713) 621-7800
FAX: (713) 960-7660
WEB: www.rowancompanies.com
NO. OF EMPLOYEES: 5,085
SHAREHOLDERS: 2,300 (approx. record)
ANNUAL MEETING: In Apr.
INCORPORATED: DE, Dec., 1947

INSTITUTIONAL HOLDINGS:
No. of Institutions: 233
Shares Held: 79,374,828
% Held: 84.9
INDUSTRY: Drilling oil and gas wells (SIC: 1381)
TRANSFER AGENT(S): Computershare Trust Company, Inc., Golden, CO

RPM INTERNATIONAL INC.

EXCH.	SYM.	REC. PRICE	P/E RATIO	YLD.	MKT. CAP.	RANGE (52-WK.)	'02 Y/E PR.	DIV. ACH.
NYSE	RPM	10.00 (2/28/03)	10.0	5.2%	$1.02 bill.	17.87 - 9.29	15.28	29 yrs.

MEDIUM GRADE. THE COMPANY EXPECTS MODEST GROWTH IN INDUSTRIAL VOLUME AND SOME CHALLENGE TO THE RECENT GROWTH RATES WITHIN ITS CONSUMER SEGMENT.

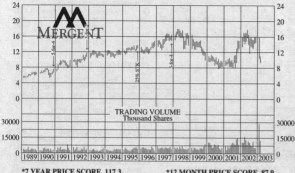

*7 YEAR PRICE SCORE 117.3   ***12 MONTH PRICE SCORE 87.9**

*NYSE COMPOSITE INDEX=100

INTERIM EARNINGS (Per Share):

Qtr.	Aug.	Nov.	Feb.	May
1997-98	0.29	0.22	0.06	0.33
1998-99	0.29	0.20	0.06	0.32
1999-00	0.07	0.19	0.04	0.09
2000-01	0.28	0.17	d0.07	0.24
2001-02	0.36	0.24	0.03	0.33
2002-03	0.38	0.26	...	...

INTERIM DIVIDENDS (Per Share):

Amt.	Decl.	Ex.	Rec.	Pay.
0.125Q	1/04/02	1/10/02	1/14/02	1/31/02
0.125Q	4/01/02	4/10/02	4/12/02	4/30/02
0.125Q	7/01/02	7/10/02	7/12/02	7/31/02
0.13Q	10/11/02	10/17/02	10/21/02	10/31/02
0.13Q	1/09/03	1/09/03	1/13/03	1/31/03

Indicated div.: $0.52 (Div. Reinv. Plan)

CAPITALIZATION (5/31/02):

	($000)	(%)
Long-Term Debt	707,921	43.8
Deferred Income Tax	50,204	3.1
Common & Surplus	858,106	53.1
Total	1,616,231	100.0

BUSINESS:

RPM International Inc. (formerly RPM, Inc.) is a manufacturer of specialty coatings, with manufacturing facilities in the United States, Argentina, Belgium, Brazil, Canada, China, Colombia, Germany, Italy, Malaysia, Mexico, New Zealand, the Netherlands, Poland, South Africa, the United Arab Emirates and the United Kingdom. RPM participates in two broad market categories worldwide: industrial and consumer. As of 5/31/02, approximately 53.0% of RPM's

sales were derived from the industrial market sectors, with the remainder in consumer products. RPM's industrial brands consists of Stonhard, Tremco, Carboline, Day-Glo, Euco and Dryvit. The major product brand line groupings comprising RPM's consumer division include Zinsser, Rust-Oleum, DAP, Varathane, Bondo and Testors. On 8/31/99, RPM acquired DAP Products Inc. and DAP Canada Corp.

RECENT DEVELOPMENTS:

For the quarter ended 11/30/02, net income increased 21.0% to $29.6 million compared with $24.5 million in the equivalent 2001 quarter. Net sales advanced 6.2% to $518.0 million from $487.9 million a year earlier. Unit volume growth was solid while pricing remained flat. The

improvement in sales was primarily attributed continued strong demand for consumer/do-it-yourself products and slightly improved sales of industrial products and services. Gross profit rose 5.5% to $234.1 million versus $222.0 million in 2001.

PROSPECTS:

The Company continues to experience rapid growth of its recently-acquired Tremco services business, whose products carry lower margins than its average industrial product margin. However, the Company has not seen signs of any overall improvement in the industrial and manufacturing

sectors it serves. Consequently, the Company anticipates only modest growth in industrial volume and expects some challenge to the recent growth rates within its consumer segment for the balance of fiscal 2003.

ANNUAL FINANCIAL DATA:

FISCAL YEAR	TOT. REVS. ($mill.)	NET INC. ($mill.)	TOT. ASSETS ($mill.)	OPER. PROFIT %	NET PROFIT %	RET. ON EQUITY %	RET. ON ASSETS %	CURR. RATIO	EARN. PER SH. $	CASH FL. PER SH. $	TANG. BK. VAL. $	DIV. PER SH. $	PRICE RANGE		AVG. P/E RATIO	AVG. YIELD %
5/31/02	1,986.1	101.6	2,036.4	9.8	5.1	11.8	5.0	2.2	0.97	1.52	0.01	0.50	15.05 -	7.91	11.8	4.4
5/31/01	2,007.8	☐ 63.0	2,078.5	8.3	3.1	9.8	3.0	2.2	☐ 0.62	1.41	...	0.49	11.31 -	7.75	15.4	5.2
5/31/00	1,954.1	☐ 41.0	2,099.2	9.0	2.1	6.3	2.0	2.1	☐ 0.38	1.12	...	0.47	16.50 -	9.94	34.8	3.6
5/31/99	1,712.2	94.5	1,737.2	11.2	5.5	12.7	5.4	2.3	0.86	1.41	0.77	0.45	18.00 -	12.75	17.9	2.9
5/31/98	1,615.3	87.8	1,683.3	11.5	5.4	15.5	5.2	2.4	0.84	1.30	...	0.42	16.80 -	12.50	17.4	2.9
5/31/97	1,350.5	78.3	1,633.2	12.5	5.8	15.9	4.8	3.0	0.80	1.32	...	0.39	14.90 -	11.50	16.5	3.0
5/31/96	1,136.4	68.9	1,155.1	12.8	6.1	15.5	6.0	2.5	0.72	1.17	0.18	0.36	13.80 -	11.36	17.5	2.9
5/31/95	1,017.0	61.1	964.0	12.8	6.0	17.6	6.3	2.8	0.86	1.37	0.71	0.34	12.56 -	10.40	13.4	3.0
5/31/94	815.6	52.6	660.8	12.4	6.5	16.7	8.0	3.2	0.74	1.11	2.50	0.31	12.40 -	10.40	15.3	2.8
5/31/93	625.7	39.4	584.6	12.7	6.3	16.5	6.7	2.4	0.66	1.02	1.69	0.29	11.84 -	8.05	15.0	3.0

Statistics are as originally reported. Adj. for stk. splits: 5-for-4, 12/8/97; 25% div., 12.8/95; 3-for-2, 12/7/92. ☐ Incl. restruct. chrg. of $52.0 million, 5/01; $45.0 mill., 5/00.

OFFICERS:
T. C. Sullivan, Chmn.
F. C. Sullivan, Pres., C.E.O., C.O.O.
R. L. Matejka, V.P., C.F.O., Contr.

INVESTOR CONTACT: Glenn R. Hasman,
V.P.-Fin., (330) 273-8820

PRINCIPAL OFFICE: P.O. Box 777, 2628
Pearl Road, Medina, OH 44258

TELEPHONE NUMBER: (330) 273-5090
FAX: (330) 225-8743
WEB: www.rpminc.com

NO. OF EMPLOYEES: 7,687 (avg.)

SHAREHOLDERS: 40,230 (approx.)

ANNUAL MEETING: In Oct.

INCORPORATED: OH, May, 1947

INSTITUTIONAL HOLDINGS:
No. of Institutions: 258
Shares Held: 68,903,182
% Held: 60.0

INDUSTRY: Paints and allied products (SIC: 2851)

TRANSFER AGENT(S): Computershare Investor Services, Chicago, IL

RUBY TUESDAY, INC.

EXCH.	SYM.	REC. PRICE	P/E RATIO	YLD.	MKT. CAP.	RANGE (52-WK.)	'02 Y/E PR.
NYSE	RI	18.63 (2/28/03)	19.2	0.2%	$1.20 bill.	27.15 - 14.24	17.29

MEDIUM GRADE. RI EXPECTS DILUTED EARNINGS PER SHARE TO RANGE FROM $0.38 TO $0.39 FOR THE THIRD QUARTER AND EARNINGS PER SHARE GROWTH RANGING FROM 15.0% TO 16.0% FOR THE FULL YEAR.

*7 YEAR PRICE SCORE 181.0   *12 MONTH PRICE SCORE 99.6
*NYSE COMPOSITE INDEX=100

INTERIM EARNINGS (Per Share):

Qtr.	Aug.	Nov.	Feb.	May
1999-00	0.16	0.13	0.22	0.07
2000-01	0.20	0.17	0.28	0.26
2001-02	0.26	0.23	0.07	0.32
2002-03	0.31	0.27	. . .	. . .

INTERIM DIVIDENDS (Per Share):

Amt.	Decl.	Ex.	Rec.	Pay.
0.022S	7/09/01	7/19/01	7/23/01	8/06/01
0.022S	1/10/02	1/23/02	1/25/02	2/08/02
0.022S	7/08/02	7/18/02	7/22/02	8/05/02
0.022S	1/09/03	1/22/03	1/24/03	2/07/03

Indicated div.: $0.04

CAPITALIZATION (6/4/02):

	($000)	(%)
Long-Term Debt	7,626	2.1
Deferred Income Tax	24,255	6.6
Common & Surplus	334,406	91.3
Total	366,287	100.0

BUSINESS:

Ruby Tuesday, Inc. (formerly Morrison Restaurants Inc.) owned and operated 421 full-service, casual restaurants under the name Ruby Tuesday®, as of 12/3/02. The restaurants are located primarily in the southeast, northeast, mid-Atlantic and midwest regions of the United States. Ruby Tuesday® restaurants offer a variety of entrees and sandwiches in the price range of $5.49 to $15.99. In addition, the Company franchised 187 domestic and 19 international Ruby Tuesday® restaurants as of 12/3/02. On 11/20/00, the Company sold its American Cafe® and Tia's® restaurant divisions for about $59.0 million.

RECENT DEVELOPMENTS:

For the 13 weeks ended 12/3/02, net income advanced 16.6% to $17.6 million from $15.1 million in the corresponding prior-year quarter. Total system-wide sales increased 9.1% to $297.8 million from $272.8 million in 2001. Total operating revenues climbed 6.3% to $211.5 million. Company restaurant revenues grew 6.3% to $208.1 million, while franchise income rose 5.9% to $3.4 million. Company-owned freestanding restaurants same-store sales slipped 0.1% over year, while Company-owned mall restaurants same-store sales decreased 1.6%. Year-over-year average unit volumes increased 1.5% at Company-owned Ruby Tuesday restaurants.

PROSPECTS:

For the third quarter of fiscal 2003, RI estimates that if same-store sales are approximately flat, diluted earnings per share will likely range between $0.38 and $0.39. If same-store sales are approximately flat for the fourth quarter, RI anticipates annual fiscal 2003 earnings per share growth to range from 15.0% to 16.0%. This estimate excludes the non-recurring charge recorded in fiscal 2002 to fully reserve the Specialty Restaurant Group, LLC note receivable. Separately, during the quarter, RI exercised its right to acquire an additional 49.0% interest in three of its franchise partners. RI now has a 50.0% interest in nine franchise partners collectively operating 91 franchised Ruby Tuesday restaurants.

ANNUAL FINANCIAL DATA:

FISCAL YEAR	TOT. REVS. ($mill.)	NET INC. ($mill.)	TOT. ASSETS ($mill.)	OPER. PROFIT %	NET PROFIT %	RET. ON EQUITY %	RET. ON ASSETS %	CURR. RATIO	EARN. PER SH.$	CASH FL. PER SH.$	TANG. BK. VAL.$	DIV. PER SH.$	PRICE RANGE	AVG. P/E RATIO	AVG. YIELD %
6/04/02	833.2	⑤ 58.3	520.3	13.2	7.0	17.4	11.2	1.0	⑤ 0.88	1.40	5.09	0.04	21.65 - 13.25	19.8	0.3
6/05/01	789.6	59.2	445.7	11.2	7.5	20.8	13.3	0.7	0.91	1.45	4.37	0.04	16.63 - 7.84	13.4	0.4
6/04/00	797.5	④ 36.5	439.2	9.3	4.6	15.9	8.3	0.6	④ 0.57	1.22	3.59	0.04	11.03 - 8.16	16.8	0.5
6/06/99	722.3	36.5	430.8	8.3	5.1	16.5	8.5	0.6	0.54	1.13	3.17	0.04	10.63 - 6.03	15.4	0.5
6/06/98	711.4	29.1	409.6	6.9	4.1	13.7	7.1	0.6	0.42	1.00	2.93	. . .	7.16 - 4.16	13.5	. . .
5/31/97	655.4	25.0	418.9	6.5	3.8	11.2	6.0	0.5	0.35	0.90	2.89	0.02	5.75 - 3.19	12.8	0.5
③ 6/01/96	620.1	① d0.7	381.1	4.5	. . .	. . .	. . .	0.5	① d0.01	0.48	2.52	0.09	6.97 - 3.13	. . .	1.8
6/03/95	1,035.1	62.2	536.1	7.6	6.0	25.3	11.6	0.6	0.87	1.42	3.16	0.08	7.44 - 5.22	7.3	1.3
6/04/94	1,213.4	44.7	418.0	5.9	3.7	20.2	10.7	0.6	0.60	1.14	2.81	0.08	6.56 - 3.96	8.8	1.5
6/05/93	1,099.8	② 38.2	411.4	5.6	3.5	17.4	9.3	1.0	② 0.51	0.88	2.69	0.08	4.96 - 2.83	7.7	2.0

Statistics are as originally reported. Adj. for stk. splits: 2-for-1, 5/00, 5/98; 3-for-2, 11/93; 5/92 ① Bef. disc. oper. loss, $2.2 mill. & incl. non-recurr. chrg. $5.3 mill. ② Bef. acctg. change chrg. $184,000 ③ On 3/9/96, the Company was spun off from Morrisons Restaurants Inc. ④ Incl. a net loss of $10.1 mill. related to the sale of American Cafe® and Tia's® Tex Mex restaurants. ⑤ Incl. a loss of $28.9 mill. on a note receivable; bef. acctg. change chrg. of $58,000.

OFFICERS:
S. E. Beall III, Chmn., C.E.O.
R. D. McClenagan, Pres.

INVESTOR CONTACT: Price Cooper, V.P., Inv. Rel., (865) 379-5700

PRINCIPAL OFFICE: 150 West Church Avenue, Maryville, TN 37801

TELEPHONE NUMBER: (865) 379-5700
FAX: (865) 379-6817
WEB: www.rubytuesday.com
NO. OF EMPLOYEES: 11,900 full-time (approx.); 19,500 part-time (approx.)
SHAREHOLDERS: 5,701 (approx.)
ANNUAL MEETING: In Oct.
INCORPORATED: LA, July, 1928; reincorp., GA, Mar., 1996

INSTITUTIONAL HOLDINGS:
No. of Institutions: 178
Shares Held: 54,458,273
% Held: 85.3

INDUSTRY: Eating places (SIC: 5812)

TRANSFER AGENT(S): The Bank of New York, New York, NY

RUDDICK CORPORATION

EXCH.	SYM.	REC. PRICE	P/E RATIO	YLD.	MKT. CAP.	RANGE (52-WK.)	'02 Y/E PR.
NYSE	RDK	12.21 (2/28/03)	10.4	2.9%	$0.57 bill.	17.97 - 11.95	13.69

UPPER MEDIUM GRADE. THE COMPANY PLANS TO OPEN FIVE NEW HARRIS TEETER STORES AND REMODEL 15 EXISTING LOCATIONS DURING THE CURRENT FISCAL YEAR.

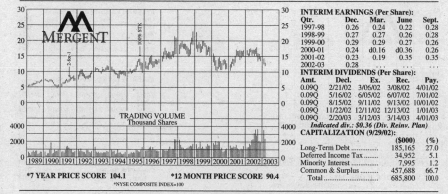

*7 YEAR PRICE SCORE 104.1   *12 MONTH PRICE SCORE 90.4
*NYSE COMPOSITE INDEX=100

INTERIM EARNINGS (Per Share):

Qtr.	Dec.	March	June	Sept.
1997-98	0.26	0.24	0.22	0.28
1998-99	0.27	0.27	0.26	0.28
1999-00	0.29	0.29	0.27	0.26
2000-01	0.24	d0.16	d0.36	0.26
2001-02	0.23	0.19	0.35	0.35
2002-03	0.28	...	...	...

INTERIM DIVIDENDS (Per Share):

Amt.	Decl.	Ex.	Rec.	Pay.
0.09Q	2/21/02	3/06/02	3/08/02	4/01/02
0.09Q	5/16/02	6/05/02	6/07/02	7/01/02
0.09Q	8/15/02	9/11/02	9/13/02	10/01/02
0.09Q	11/22/02	12/11/02	12/13/02	1/01/03
0.09Q	2/20/03	3/12/03	3/14/03	4/01/03

Indicated div.: $0.36 (Div. Reinv. Plan)

CAPITALIZATION (9/29/02):

	($000)	(%)
Long-Term Debt	185,165	27.0
Deferred Income Tax	34,952	5.1
Minority Interest	7,995	1.2
Common & Surplus	457,688	66.7
Total	685,800	100.0

BUSINESS:

Ruddick Corporation is a diversified holding company that is engaged in two primary businesses. As of 12/29/02, Harris Teeter, Inc. operated a chain of 141 supermarkets in North Carolina, South Carolina, Virginia, Georgia, Tennessee, and Florida. American & Efird, Inc. manufactures and distributes industrial and consumer sewing thread and sales yarn. The Company was created through the consolidation of the predecessor companies of American & Efird and Ruddick Investment Company. In 1969, Ruddick acquired Harris Teeter. Sales (and operating profit) in fiscal 2002 were derived as follows: Harris Teeter, 88.9% (87.7%) and American & Efird, 11.1% (12.3%).

RECENT DEVELOPMENTS:

For the three months ended 12/29/02, net income totaled $13.0 million, up 23.3% compared with $10.5 million in the corresponding quarter a year earlier. Net sales increased 3.9% to $678.4 million from $653.2 million the previous year. Harris Teeter's net sales rose 3.4% to $607.8 million from $587.5 million the year before. Comparable-store sales were down 0.5% year over year. American & Efird's net sales grew 7.5% to $70.6 million from $65.7 million the prior year. Gross profit was $191.8 million, or 28.3% of net sales, versus $181.0 million, or 27.7% of net sales, a year earlier.

PROSPECTS:

Higher sales at the Company's Harris Teeter stores are being fueled by RDK's ongoing store expansion program. During the current fiscal year, the Company plans to open five new stores and remodel 15 existing locations. Meanwhile, comparable-store sales are being hampered by increased competition from other supermarkets, as well as other non-food retailers, and weak overall economic conditions. Separately, results at American & Efird are being positively affected by strong sales in Latin America and China. Going forward, American & Efird will continue to expand its presence internationally through joint ventures and other investments.

ANNUAL FINANCIAL DATA:

FISCAL YEAR	TOT. REVS. ($mill.)	NET INC. ($mill.)	TOT. ASSETS ($mill.)	OPER. PROFIT %	NET PROFIT %	RET. ON EQUITY %	RET. ON ASSETS %	CURR. RATIO	EARN. PER SH.$	CASH FL. PER SH.$	TANG. BK. VAL.$	DIV. PER SH.$	PRICE RANGE	AVG. P/E RATIO	AVG. YIELD %
9/29/02	2,644.2	③ 52.0	1,038.9	3.8	2.0	11.4	5.0	1.6	③ 1.12	2.74	9.85	0.36	17.97 - 13.40	14.0	2.3
9/30/01	2,743.3	③ d0.7	940.0	1.9	...	...	...	1.5	③ d0.02	1.72	9.61	0.36	17.20 - 10.44	...	2.6
10/01/00	2,682.8	51.0	1,021.0	4.0	1.9	10.8	5.0	1.6	1.10	2.76	10.23	0.36	15.94 - 10.25	11.9	2.7
10/03/99	2,624.8	50.7	970.1	4.0	1.9	11.4	5.2	1.5	1.08	2.60	9.55	0.33	22.75 - 15.13	17.5	1.7
9/27/98	2,487.4	46.8	931.6	3.8	1.9	11.4	5.0	1.4	1.00	2.41	8.82	0.32	23.00 - 15.00	19.0	1.7
9/28/97	2,300.1	47.7	885.2	4.1	2.1	12.5	5.4	1.4	1.02	2.29	8.17	0.32	21.38 - 13.25	17.0	1.8
9/29/96	2,142.5	① 42.8	801.7	3.9	2.0	12.3	5.3	1.3	① 0.92	2.03	7.47	0.26	15.38 - 10.63	14.1	2.0
10/01/95	2,070.8	39.3	721.9	3.8	1.9	12.4	5.4	1.3	0.84	1.78	6.82	0.25	14.13 - 9.38	14.0	2.1
10/02/94	1,908.4	31.8	640.8	3.4	1.7	10.9	5.0	1.5	0.67	1.52	6.28	0.21	11.50 - 7.81	14.4	2.2
10/03/93	1,732.5	② 30.0	586.8	3.6	1.7	10.9	5.1	1.6	② 0.63	1.41	5.96	0.18	11.94 - 9.31	16.9	1.7

Statistics are as originally reported. Adj. for 100% stk. div., 10/95. ① Bef. $76,000 of income from discont. opers. ② Bef. $3.9 mil ($0.08/sh) gain from acctg. adj. ③ Incl. $7.1 mil pre-tax non-recur. chg., 2002; $47.1 mil chg., 2001.

OFFICERS:
A. T. Dickson, Chmn.
T. W. Dickson, Pres., C.E.O.
J. B. Woodlief, V.P., C.F.O.

INVESTOR CONTACT: Katherine W. Kenny, V.P., Inv. Rel., (704) 372-5404

PRINCIPAL OFFICE: 301 S. Tryon St., Suite 1800, Charlotte, NC 28202

TELEPHONE NUMBER: (704) 372-5404
FAX: (704) 372-6409
WEB: www.ruddickcorp.com

NO. OF EMPLOYEES: 8,154 full-time (approx.); 6,481 part-time (approx.)

SHAREHOLDERS: 5,867 (record)

ANNUAL MEETING: In Feb.

INCORPORATED: NC, Oct., 1968

INSTITUTIONAL HOLDINGS:
No. of Institutions: 128
Shares Held: 23,642,908
% Held: 50.8

INDUSTRY: Grocery stores (SIC: 5411)

TRANSFER AGENT(S): First Union National Bank, Charlotte, NC

RUSS BERRIE & COMPANY, INC.

EXCH.	SYM.	REC. PRICE	P/E RATIO	YLD.	MKT. CAP.	RANGE (52-WK.)	'02 Y/E PR.
NYSE	RUS	31.05 (2/28/03)	13.8	3.6%	$0.63 bill.	37.65 - 26.30	33.78

MEDIUM GRADE. THE COMPANY EXPECTS SALES AND EARNINGS GROWTH FOR 2003 TO RANGE FROM 6.0% TO 9.0%, REFLECTING THE FULL-YEAR EFFECT OF THE SASSY, INC. ACQUISITION.

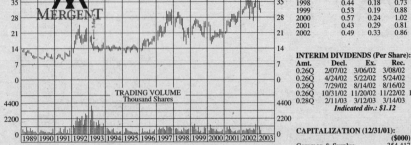

INTERIM EARNINGS (Per Share):

Qtr.	Mar.	June	Sept.	Dec.
1998	0.44	0.18	0.73	0.46
1999	0.53	0.19	0.88	0.11
2000	0.57	0.24	1.02	0.53
2001	0.43	0.29	0.81	0.45
2002	0.49	0.33	0.86	0.57

INTERIM DIVIDENDS (Per Share):

Amt.	Decl.	Ex.	Rec.	Pay.
0.26Q	2/07/02	3/06/02	3/08/02	3/22/02
0.26Q	4/24/02	5/22/02	5/24/02	6/07/02
0.26Q	7/29/02	8/14/02	8/16/02	8/30/02
0.26Q	10/31/02	11/20/02	11/22/02	12/06/02
0.28Q	2/11/03	3/12/03	3/14/03	3/28/03

Indicated div.: $1.12

TRADING VOLUME Thousand Shares

*7 YEAR PRICE SCORE 140.2   *12 MONTH PRICE SCORE 105.5
*NYSE COMPOSITE INDEX=100

CAPITALIZATION (12/31/01):

	($000)	(%)
Common & Surplus	354,417	100.0
Total	354,417	100.0

BUSINESS:

Russ Berrie & Company, Inc. designs, manufactures through third parties, and markets a wide variety of gift products to retail stores throughout the U.S. and most countries throughout the world. RUS's product line of approximately 6,000 items are marketed under the trade name and trademark RUSS®. Products include heirloom bears, stuffed animals, baby gifts, picture frames, candles, figurines and home decor gifts based on current fashions and trends. The Company maintains product depth in categories such as Birthday, Anniversaries, Over-The-Hill, Fun 'N Games, Gifted Moments, Inspirational Gifts, Lifestyles, Home Styles, Gentlemen's Gifts, Collectibles and Baby Products. Extensive seasonal lines include products for all the major holidays.

RECENT DEVELOPMENTS:

For the year ended 12/31/02, net income increased 14.6% to $46.0 million compared with $40.2 million the previous year. The improvement in results was attributable in part to the inclusion of operations of Sassy, Inc., acquired on 7/26/02, partially offset by higher selling, general and administrative expenses. Net sales climbed 9.2% to $321.4 million from $294.3 million the year before, reflecting year-over-year growth of 3.4% in the Company's core segment and the aforementioned acquisition. Gross profit advanced 9.0% to $176.3 million from $161.7 million a year earlier. Net investment and other income slipped to $8.5 million from $8.6 million the prior year.

PROSPECTS:

The Company expects the retail environment to remain difficult in the coming year as a result of the continued weak global economy and uncertainty over possible military action. Consequently, the Company expects sales and earnings growth for 2003 to range from 6.0% to 9.0%, reflecting the full-year effect of the Sassy, Inc. acquisition. Furthermore, the Company expects fiscal 2003 sales in its core business to be flat versus the prior year. Meanwhile, the Company should be well-positioned for future growth once market conditions improve, evidenced by its strong debt-free balance sheet.

ANNUAL FINANCIAL DATA:

FISCAL YEAR	TOT. REVS. ($000)	NET INC. ($000)	TOT. ASSETS ($000)	OPER. PROFIT %	NET PROFIT %	RET. ON EQUITY %	RET. ON ASSETS %	CURR. RATIO	EARN. PER SH.$	CASH FL. PER SH.$	TANG. BK. VAL.$	DIV. PER SH.$	PRICE RANGE	AVG. P/E RATIO	AVG. YIELD %
p12/31/02	321,355	46,020							2.24			1.04	37.65 - 26.30	14.3	3.3
12/31/01	294,291	⑧ 40,174	386,644	16.7	13.7	11.3	10.4	11.0	⑧ 1.99	2.19	17.52	1.46	30.91 - 20.56	12.9	5.7
12/31/00	300,801	47,941	367,009	20.2	15.9	14.3	13.1	10.4	2.37	2.56	16.85	0.88	25.94 - 15.88	8.8	4.2
12/31/99	277,516	⑦ 36,436	355,420	16.4	13.1	11.4	10.3	9.0	⑦ 1.72	1.95	15.53	0.80	27.50 - 18.94	13.5	3.4
12/31/98	270,511	40,596	378,456	18.3	15.0	11.8	10.7	9.7	⑥ 1.81	1.93	15.46	0.76	30.50 - 15.75	12.8	3.3
12/31/97	271,336	⑤ 37,265	353,445	17.5	13.7	11.8	10.5	8.8	⑤ 1.67	1.80	14.35	0.68	31.56 - 17.63	14.7	2.8
12/31/96	226,243	③④ 26,699	276,966	13.9	11.8	10.7	9.6	7.6	③④ 1.23	1.39	13.13	0.60	19.50 - 12.51	13.1	3.7
12/31/95	348,474	16,540	265,163	6.8	4.7	7.4	6.2	4.8	0.77	1.10	8.77	0.60	15.88 - 12.00	18.1	4.3
12/31/94	278,105	5,327	254,826	1.7	1.9	2.4	2.1	5.2	0.25	0.57	8.49	0.60	15.63 - 12.75	56.7	4.2
12/31/93	279,111	①② 13,182	259,115	5.4	4.7	5.9	5.1	6.1	①② 0.61	0.91	9.69	0.60	19.83 - 12.38	26.4	3.7

Statistics are as originally reported. Adjusted for 3-for-2 split 4/93. ① Incl. a net charge of $3.2 mill. ② Incl. a net gain of $2.0 mill. fr. the sale of an office facility. ③ Incl. a $3.0 mill. after-tax gain on the sale of Papel/Freelance and $2.8 mill. for the reversal of a litig. prov. ④ Bef. inc. from disc. opers. of $5.0 mill. ⑤ Excl. a pre-tax gain of $46.7 mill. from the sale of assets and a pre-tax loss of $1.3 mill. fr. disc. opers. & incl. a net prov. to close all remaining retail opers. of $945,000. ⑥ Incl. an after-tax charge of $1.2 million for the completion of a transaction agreement related to the sale of Papel/Freelance, Inc. ⑦ Incls. an after-tax chrg. of $6.5 mill. ⑧ Incl. an after-tax gain of $900,000.

OFFICERS:
J. Weston, Acting Chmn.
A. Berrie, C.E.O.
J. D. Wille, V.P., C.F.O.
INVESTOR CONTACT: John Willis, V.P. & C.F.O., (201) 337-9000
PRINCIPAL OFFICE: 111 Bauer Drive, Oakland, NJ 07436

TELEPHONE NUMBER: (201) 337-9000
FAX: (201) 337-7909
WEB: www.russberrie.com
NO. OF EMPLOYEES: 1,563 (avg.)
SHAREHOLDERS: 510 (record)
ANNUAL MEETING: In Apr.
INCORPORATED: NJ, 1966

INSTITUTIONAL HOLDINGS:
No. of Institutions: 105
Shares Held: 9,694,293
% Held: 47.3
INDUSTRY: Dolls and stuffed toys (SIC: 3942)
TRANSFER AGENT(S): First City Transfer Company, Iselin, NJ

RUSSELL CORPORATION

EXCH.	SYM.	REC. PRICE	P/E RATIO	YLD.	MKT. CAP.	RANGE (52-WK.)	'02 Y/E PR.
NYSE	RML	16.15 (2/28/03)	11.1	1.0%	$0.52 bill.	19.55 - 13.14	16.74

LOWER MEDIUM GRADE. THE COMPANY ACQUIRED BIKE ATHLETIC COMPANY FOR $16.3 MILLION.

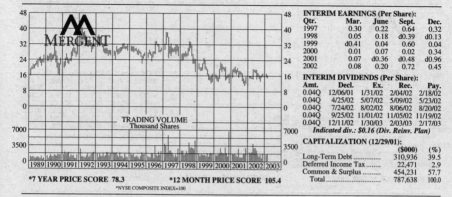

*7 YEAR PRICE SCORE 78.3   *12 MONTH PRICE SCORE 105.4
*NYSE COMPOSITE INDEX=100

INTERIM EARNINGS (Per Share):

Qtr.	Mar.	June	Sept.	Dec.
1997	0.30	0.22	0.64	0.32
1998	0.05	0.18	d0.39	d0.13
1999	d0.41	0.04	0.60	0.04
2000	0.01	0.07	0.02	0.34
2001	0.07	d0.36	d0.48	d0.96
2002	0.08	0.20	0.72	0.45

INTERIM DIVIDENDS (Per Share):

Amt.	Decl.	Ex.	Rec.	Pay.
0.04Q	12/06/01	1/31/02	2/04/02	2/18/02
0.04Q	4/25/02	5/07/02	5/09/02	5/23/02
0.04Q	7/24/02	8/02/02	8/06/02	8/20/02
0.04Q	9/25/02	11/01/02	11/05/02	11/19/02
0.04Q	12/11/02	1/30/03	2/03/03	2/17/03
Indicated div.: $0.16 (Div. Reinv. Plan)				

CAPITALIZATION (12/29/01):

	($000)	(%)
Long-Term Debt	310,936	39.5
Deferred Income Tax	22,471	2.9
Common & Surplus	454,231	57.7
Total	787,638	100.0

BUSINESS:

Russell Corporation is an international branded apparel company specializing in activewear, casualwear and athletic uniforms. RML's major brands include RUSSELL ATHLETIC®, JERZEES®, MOSSY OAK®, CROSS CREEK®, DISCUS®, MOVING COMFORT® and Bike®. RML designs and merchandises a variety of leisure and sports apparel marketed to sporting goods dealers, department and specialty stores, mass merchandisers, golf pro shops, college bookstores, screen printers and embroiderers, distributors, mail order houses and other apparel manufacturers. Products are derived from a combination of internally produced products, contractors and third-party sources.

RECENT DEVELOPMENTS:

For the 53 weeks ended 1/4/03, the Company reported income of $46.9 million, before an extraordinary charge of $12.6 million, versus a net loss of $55.5 million the previous year. Results for 2001 included a bad debt reserve charge of $6.2 million and restructuring charges of $91.9 million. Net sales were relatively flat versus the prior year at $1.16 billion. Cost of goods sold declined 7.6% to $825.8 million from $894.0 million a year earlier. Gross margins improved to 29.1% from 23.0% the year before due to continued sorcing and manufacturing improvements, increased volumes and a better product mix.

PROSPECTS:

For the full-year 2003, RML is forecasting sales to increase 4.0% to 6.0% over 2002 levels, and earnings per share in the range of $1.60 to $1.75, including a $0.07 to $0.08 impact from the changes in accounting for stock compensation and revised pension plan assumptions. Separately, on 2/13/03, RML announced that it has completed the acquisition of Bike Athletic Company for $16.3 million. The acquisition is expected to enhance the Company's position in the team uniform business, while placing RML in new categories, such as men's performance underwear and protective gear. Bike had sales of approximately $35.0 million in 2002.

ANNUAL FINANCIAL DATA:

FISCAL YEAR	TOT. REVS. ($mill.)	NET INC. ($mill.)	TOT. ASSETS ($mill.)	OPER. PROFIT %	NET PROFIT %	RET. ON EQUITY %	RET. ON ASSETS %	CURR. RATIO	EARN. PER SH.$	CASH FL. PER SH.$	TANG. BK. VAL.$	DIV. PER SH.$	PRICE RANGE	AVG. P/E RATIO	AVG. YIELD %
p1/04/03	1,164.3	④ 46.9							④ 1.45				0.16	19.55 - 13.14	11.3	1.0
12/29/01	1,160.9	③ d55.5	995.2	...	...	...	...	3.3	③ d1.74	d0.19	14.19	0.46	20.84 - 11.02	...	2.9
12/30/00	1,217.6	② 14.5	1,153.2	5.4	1.2	2.8	1.3	3.8	② 0.44	2.12	16.49	0.56	22.94 - 12.13	39.8	3.2
1/01/00	1,142.2	② 8.4	1,153.1	4.2	0.7	1.5	0.7	4.0	② 0.25	2.13	16.74	0.56	25.13 - 12.13	74.5	3.0
1/02/99	1,180.1	d10.4	1,153.6	1.5	...	...	...	3.9	d0.29	1.77	17.31	0.56	33.88 - 18.00	...	2.2
1/03/98	1,228.2	54.4	1,248.0	9.5	4.4	8.2	4.4	4.4	1.47	3.48	18.25	0.53	38.50 - 25.00	21.6	1.7
1/04/97	1,244.2	81.6	1,195.2	12.5	6.6	12.0	6.8	3.2	2.11	3.98	17.87	0.50	33.75 - 23.13	13.5	1.8
12/30/95	1,152.6	54.1	1,118.2	9.5	4.7	8.6	4.8	4.5	1.38	3.11	16.34	0.48	31.25 - 22.00	19.3	1.8
⑤ 12/31/94	1,098.3	78.8	1,046.6	13.4	7.2	12.5	7.5	2.5	1.96	3.63	15.84	0.42	32.63 - 24.00	14.4	1.5
1/01/94	930.8	49.3	1,017.0	10.5	5.3	8.4	4.8	2.4	1.19	2.80	14.54	0.39	36.88 - 26.00	26.4	1.2

Statistics are as originally reported. ① Incl. results of The Game Inc., acquired in Dec. 1993. ② Incl. restruct., asset impairment and other chrg. $47.6 mill., 12/00; $46.6 mill., 1/00 ③ Incl. restruct. & other chrgs. of $91.9 mill. & asset write-off of $3.8 mill. ④ Bef. extraord. loss $12.6 mill.

OFFICERS:
J. F. Ward, Chmn., C.E.O.
J. R. Letzler, Pres., C.O.O.
R. D. Martin, Sr. V.P., C.F.O.
E. Zakas, V.P., Treas.

INVESTOR CONTACT: Robert D. Martin, Sr.
V.P., C.F.O., (678) 742-8100

PRINCIPAL OFFICE: 755 Lee Street, P.O.
Box 272, Alexander City, AL 35011-0272

TELEPHONE NUMBER: (256) 500-4000
FAX: (256) 500-4474
WEB: www.russellcorp.com

NO. OF EMPLOYEES: 13,130 (avg.)

SHAREHOLDERS: 8,800 (approx.)

ANNUAL MEETING: In April

INCORPORATED: AL, 1902

INSTITUTIONAL HOLDINGS:
No. of Institutions: 118
Shares Held: 20,168,895
% Held: 62.7

INDUSTRY: Knit outerwear mills (SIC: 2253)

TRANSFER AGENT(S): SunTrust Bank,
Atlanta, Atlanta, GA

RYDER SYSTEM, INC.

EXCH.	SYM.	REC. PRICE	P/E RATIO	YLD.	MKT. CAP.	RANGE (52-WK.)	'02 Y/E PR.
NYSE	R	22.69 (2/28/03)	12.6	2.6%	$1.42 bill.	31.09 - 21.05	22.44

MEDIUM GRADE. EARNINGS PER SHARE FOR 2003 ARE EXPECTED TO BE IN THE RANGE OF $1.95 TO $2.00.

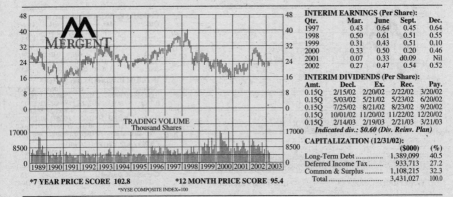

*7 YEAR PRICE SCORE 102.8   ***12 MONTH PRICE SCORE 95.4**

*NYSE COMPOSITE INDEX=100

INTERIM EARNINGS (Per Share):

Qtr.	Mar.	June	Sept.	Dec.
1997	0.43	0.64	0.45	0.64
1998	0.50	0.61	0.51	0.55
1999	0.31	0.43	0.51	0.10
2000	0.33	0.50	0.20	0.46
2001	0.07	0.33	d0.09	Nil
2002	0.27	0.47	0.54	0.52

INTERIM DIVIDENDS (Per Share):

Amt.	Decl.	Ex.	Rec.	Pay.
0.15Q	2/15/02	2/20/02	2/22/02	3/20/02
0.15Q	5/03/02	5/21/02	5/23/02	6/20/02
0.15Q	7/25/02	8/21/02	8/23/02	9/20/02
0.15Q	10/01/02	11/20/02	11/22/02	12/20/02
0.15Q	2/14/03	2/19/03	2/21/03	3/21/03

Indicated div.: $0.60 (Div. Reinv. Plan)

CAPITALIZATION (12/31/02):

	($000)	(%)
Long-Term Debt	1,389,099	40.5
Deferred Income Tax	933,713	27.2
Common & Surplus	1,108,215	32.3
Total	3,431,027	100.0

BUSINESS:

Ryder System, Inc. provides a continuum of logistics, supply chain, transportation and fleet management services worldwide. R's product offerings range from full-service leasing, commercial rental and programmed maintenance of vehicles to integrated services such as dedicated contract carriage and carrier management. In addition, R offers supply chain services, consulting, lead logistics management services and e-commerce services that support clients'

entire supply chains. The Company serves customers throughout North America, Latin America, Europe and Asia. Revenues for 2002 were derived as follows: fleet management solutions, 62.5%; supply chain solutions, 27.3%; and dedicated contract carriage, 10.2%. As of 12/31/02, Ryder and its subsidiaries held a fleet of 161,400 vehicles. On 9/13/99, R sold its public transportation subsidiary.

RECENT DEVELOPMENTS:

For the twelve months ended 12/31/02, earnings jumped to $112.6 million, before an accounting change charge of $18.9 million, compared with net earnings of $18.7 million in 2001. Earnings benefited from the Company's strategic process improvement and cost management actions. Results for 2002 and 2001 included gains from sales of

vehicles of $14.2 million and $12.0 million, and restructuring and other charges of $4.2 million and $116.6 million, respectively. Revenue slipped 4.6% to $4.78 billion from $5.01 billion in the previous year, primarily due to challenging economic conditions.

PROSPECTS:

The Company expects soft economic conditions to continue in 2003, with prospects for modest improvement during the second half of the year. As a result, the Company is forecasting overall revenues for 2003 to be essentially unchanged from 2002, despite some anticipated improve-

ment in certain areas of the business such as commercial truck rental and the Company's European operations. Moreover, the Company expects earnings per share for 2003 to be in the range of $1.95 to $2.00.

ANNUAL FINANCIAL DATA:

FISCAL YEAR	TOT. REVS. ($mill.)	NET INC. ($mill.)	TOT. ASSETS ($mill.)	OPER. PROFIT %	NET PROFIT %	RET. ON EQUITY %	RET. ON ASSETS %	CURR. RATIO	EARN. PER SH. $	CASH FL. PER SH. $	TANG. BK. VAL. $	DIV. PER SH. $	PRICE RANGE	AVG. P/E RATIO	AVG. YIELD %
12/31/02	4,776.3	⑩ 112.6	4,767.0	5.5	2.4	10.2	2.4	1.2	⑩ 1.80	10.63	17.75	0.60	31.09 - 21.05	14.5	2.3
12/31/01	5,006.1	⑨ 18.7	4,923.6	5.3	0.4	1.5	0.4	1.0	⑨ 0.31	10.80	20.24	0.60	23.19 - 16.06	63.3	3.1
12/31/00	5,336.8	⑧ 89.0	5,474.9	6.3	1.7	7.1	1.6	0.7	⑧ 1.49	11.75	20.86	0.60	25.13 - 14.81	13.4	3.0
12/31/99	4,952.2	⑦⑦ 72.9	5,770.5	8.0	1.5	6.1	1.3	0.8	⑦⑦ 1.06	9.69	20.29	0.60	28.75 - 18.81	22.4	2.5
12/31/98	5,188.7	③ 159.1	5,708.6	8.8	3.1	14.5	2.8	0.8	② 2.16	10.40	15.37	0.60	40.56 - 19.44	13.9	2.0
12/31/97	4,893.9	② 160.2	5,509.1	9.1	3.3	15.1	2.9	1.0	② 2.05	9.74	14.39	0.60	37.13 - 27.13	15.7	1.9
12/31/96	5,519.4	⑥ d31.3	5,645.4	3.0	...	...	...	1.0	⑥ d0.39	8.39	14.19	0.60	31.13 - 22.63	...	2.2
12/31/95	5,167.4	⑤ 155.4	5,893.8	8.8	3.0	12.5	2.6	0.8	④ 1.96	10.33	15.64	0.60	26.13 - 21.00	12.0	2.5
12/31/94	4,685.6	153.5	5,014.5	8.7	3.3	13.6	3.1	0.7	1.95	9.46	14.33	0.60	28.00 - 19.88	12.3	2.5
12/31/93	4,217.0	④ 114.7	4,258.4	7.9	2.7	11.6	2.7	0.6	① 1.43	8.44	12.81	0.60	33.50 - 24.75	20.4	2.1

Statistics are as originally reported. ① Incl. $23.6 mill. after-tax chg. for Year 2000 costs, 1998; $24.0 mill. chg., 1999. ② Bef. $15.5 mill. inc. fr. disc. op. ③ Bef. $25.4 mill. acct. chg. & $150.7 mill. loss fr. disc. ops. ④ Refl. spin-off of Availl. ⑤ Bef. $7.8 mill. chg. fr. change in acct. ⑥ Bef. $10.0 mill. extraord. loss, incl. $163.9 mill. restr. chgs. & $15.1 mill. gain on Consumer Truck sale. ⑦ Bef. gain of $351.0 mill. fr. disc. ops. and extra. loss of $4.4 mill. & incl. non-recur. chgs. of $76.1 mill. ⑧ Incl. $42.0 mill. restr. & other chgs. ⑨ Incl. $12.0 mill. gain fr. vehicle sales & $116.5 mill. restr. chg. ⑩ Incl. $14.2 mill. gain fr. vehicle sales, $4.2 mill. restr. chg. & excl. $18.9 mill. acct. chg.

OFFICERS:
G. T. Swienton, Chmn., Pres., C.E.O.
C. J. Nelson, Sr. Exec. V.P., C.F.O.
V. O'Meara, Exec. V.P., Gen. Couns., Sec.
INVESTOR CONTACT: Robert S. Brunn, Dir., Investor Relations, (305) 500-4053
PRINCIPAL OFFICE: 3600 N.W. 82nd Avenue, Miami, FL 33166

TELEPHONE NUMBER: (305) 500-3726
FAX: (305) 500-4129
WEB: www.ryder.com
NO. OF EMPLOYEES: 27,800 (approx.)
SHAREHOLDERS: 13,157 (record)
ANNUAL MEETING: In May
INCORPORATED: FL, Mar., 1955

INSTITUTIONAL HOLDINGS:
No. of Institutions: 232
Shares Held: 54,631,582
% Held: 87.6
INDUSTRY: Transportation services, nec (SIC: 4789)
TRANSFER AGENT(S): Fleet National Bank, c/o EquiServe, LP, Providence, RI

RYERSON TULL, INC.

EXCH.	SYM.	REC. PRICE	P/E RATIO	YLD.	MKT. CAP.	RANGE (52-WK.)	'02 Y/E PR.
NYSE	RT	6.33 (2/28/03)	...	3.2%	$156.9 mill.	11.76 - 5.60	6.10

LOWER MEDIUM GRADE. THE COMPANY IS ATTEMPTING TO STIMULATE GROWTH BY IMPROVING EFFICIENCY AND REDUCING COSTS.

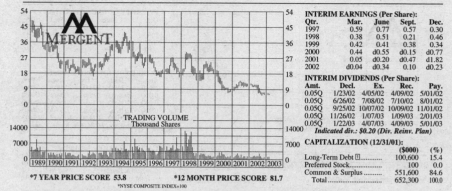

*7 YEAR PRICE SCORE 53.8   ***12 MONTH PRICE SCORE 81.7**
*NYSE COMPOSITE INDEX=100

INTERIM EARNINGS (Per Share):

Qtr.	Mar.	June	Sept.	Dec.
1997	0.59	0.77	0.57	0.30
1998	0.38	0.51	0.21	0.46
1999	0.42	0.41	0.38	0.34
2000	0.44	d0.55	d0.15	d0.77
2001	0.05	d0.20	d0.47	d1.82
2002	d0.04	d0.34	0.10	d0.23

INTERIM DIVIDENDS (Per Share):

Amt.	Decl.	Ex.	Rec.	Pay.
0.05Q	1/23/02	4/05/02	4/09/02	5/01/02
0.05Q	6/26/02	7/08/02	7/10/02	8/01/02
0.05Q	9/25/02	10/07/02	10/09/02	11/01/02
0.05Q	11/26/02	1/07/03	1/09/03	2/01/03
0.05Q	1/22/03	4/07/03	4/09/03	5/01/03

Indicated div.: $0.20 (Div. Reinv. Plan)

CAPITALIZATION (12/31/01):

	($000)	(%)
Long-Term Debt ⑪............	100,600	15.4
Preferred Stock.................	100	0.0
Common & Surplus	551,600	84.6
Total......................	652,300	100.0

BUSINESS:

Ryerson Tull, Inc. (formerly Inland Steel Industries, Inc.) conducts its materials distribution operations in the U.S. through its operating subsidiaries, Ryerson and Tull; in Canada through Ryerson Tull Canada, Inc.; in Mexico through an arrangement with G. Collado S.A. de C.V.; and in India through Tata Ryerson Limited. RT distributes and processes metals and other materials throughout the continental U.S., and is among the largest purchasers of steel in the U.S. On 2/1/99, RT acquired Washington Specialty Metals. On 2/25/99, Ryerson Tull (old) was merged into Inland Steel Industries. Following the merger, RT's name was changed to Ryerson Tull (new).

RECENT DEVELOPMENTS:

For the year ended 12/31/02, RT incurred a loss from continuing operations of $12.4 million versus a net loss of $60.2 million in 2001. Results for 2002 and 2001 included gains of $10.9 million and $1.3 million, respectively, on the sale of assets. Results for 2002 also included a loss of $8.5 million on an adjustment to a gain on the sale of Inland Engineered Materials Corp. Results for 2002 and 2001 also included restructuring and plant closure costs of $2.7 million and $19.4 million, respectively. Results for 2002 included a gain of $4.1 million and for 2001 included a loss of $3.2 million on the sale of foreign interests. Net sales slid 6.6% to $2.10 billion from $2.24 billion a year earlier, reflecting a 7.3% fall in tons shipped, partially offset by a 0.9% increase in the average selling price per ton.

PROSPECTS:

Looking ahead, assuming no improvement in underlying metals industry conditions, RT will seek to stimulate growth by improving efficiencies and reducing costs. During the fourth quarter of 2003, RT completed the consolidation of two of its Chicago service centers, capturing $10.0 million in annualized fixed-cost savings. Moreover, RT has completed its cost cutting and organization realignment program that began in 2000, thereby reducing its annual fixed-cost structure by a total of $75.0 million.

ANNUAL FINANCIAL DATA:

FISCAL YEAR	TOT. REVS. ($mill.)	NET INC. ($mill.)	TOT. ASSETS ($mill.)	OPER. PROFIT %	NET PROFIT %	RET. ON EQUITY %	RET. ON ASSETS %	CURR. RATIO	EARN. PER SH.$	CASH FL. PER SH.$	TANG. BK. VAL.$	DIV. PER SH.$	PRICE RANGE		AVG. P/E RATIO	AVG. YIELD %
p12/31/02	2,096.5	⑨ d12.4	...	...	...	...	...	...	⑨ 0.44	...	...	0.20	12.49	— 5.60	...	2.2
12/31/01	2,243.5	⑧ d60.2	1,009.9	...	...	...	...	3.8	⑧ d2.44	d0.98	18.24	0.20	13.99	— 8.19	...	1.8
12/31/00	2,862.4	② d25.1	1,372.1	...	...	...	...	1.9	② d1.03	0.26	22.81	0.20	20.19	— 6.94	...	1.5
12/31/99	2,763.5	⑦ 38.4	1,387.2	3.5	1.4	5.5	2.8	3.2	⑦ 1.56	2.86	23.80	0.20	25.06	— 14.00	12.5	1.0
⑥ 12/31/98	2,782.7	⑤ 47.7	1,343.9	3.4	1.7	2.8	3.5	3.1	⑤ 0.99	1.77	22.10	0.20	30.50	— 14.13	22.5	0.9
12/31/97	5,046.8	④ 119.3	3,646.5	5.7	2.4	12.9	3.3	2.1	④ 2.13	5.17	17.20	0.20	27.50	— 15.88	10.2	0.9
12/31/96	4,584.1	③ 69.0	3,541.6	3.6	1.5	8.4	1.9	2.3	③ 1.23	4.36	14.71	0.20	29.00	— 16.00	18.3	0.9
12/31/95	4,781.5	146.8	3,558.3	6.9	3.1	18.7	4.1	2.0	2.69	5.72	13.41	0.15	36.75	— 21.25	10.8	0.5
12/31/94	4,497.0	107.4	3,353.4	5.5	2.4	19.6	3.2	1.9	1.81	5.00	11.65	...	42.00	— 29.38	19.7	...
12/31/93	3,888.2	② d37.6	3,435.8	0.7	...	...	...	1.8	② d1.93	1.75	6.94	...	35.00	— 20.00	...	...

Statistics are as originally reported. ⑪ Incl. cap. lease oblig. ② Incl. nonrecurr. net chrg. $11.7 mill. & excl. dis. oper. loss of $4.8 mill., 2000; pretax net chrg. of $4.5 mill., 1993. ③ Excl. extraord. chrg. of $23.3 mill. & incl. nonrecurr. $31.4 mill. pretax gain and a loss of $26.3 mill. ④ Incl. pretax nonrecur. gain of $17.2 mill. ⑤ Bef. discont. oper. inc. of $524.6 mill. & extraord. loss of $21.4 mill. ⑥ Figures for 1998 and prior are for Inland Steel Industries, Inc. prior to the merger with Ryerson Tull. ⑦ Incl. pretax gain of $1.8 mill. and excl. a net gain of $17.3 mill. fr. dis. ops. ⑧ Incl. net nonrecurr. chrgs. of $22.4 mill. ⑨ Incl. net nonrecurr. gain of $3.8 mill., excl. loss of $1.7 mill. fr. dis. ops. and acctg. change chrg. of $82.2 mill.

OFFICERS:
N. S. Novich, Chmn., Pres., C.E.O.
J. M. Gratz, Exec. V.P., C.F.O.
J. E. Mims, V.P., Gen. Couns.

INVESTOR CONTACT: Terence R. Rogers, Treas., (773) 788-3206

PRINCIPAL OFFICE: 2621 West 15th Place, Chicago, IL 60608

TELEPHONE NUMBER: (773) 762-2121
FAX: (773) 762-3311
WEB: www.ryersontull.com
NO. OF EMPLOYEES: 3,800 (approx.)
SHAREHOLDERS: 9,989
ANNUAL MEETING: In May
INCORPORATED: DC, Feb., 1917; reincorp., DE, Feb. 1986

INSTITUTIONAL HOLDINGS:
No. of Institutions: 91
Shares Held: 19,704,196
% Held: 79.4

INDUSTRY: Blast furnaces and steel mills (SIC: 3312)

TRANSFER AGENT(S): Computershare Investor Services, Chicago, IL

RYLAND GROUP, INC. (THE)

EXCH.	SYM.	REC. PRICE	P/E RATIO	YLD.	MKT. CAP.	RANGE (52-WK.)	'02 Y/E PR.
NYSE	RYL	41.30 (2/28/03)	6.2	0.2%	$1.09 bill.	58.40 - 31.00	33.35

UPPER MEDIUM GRADE. THE COMPANY EXPECTS EARNINGS PER SHARE TO EXCEED $7.25 IN 2003.

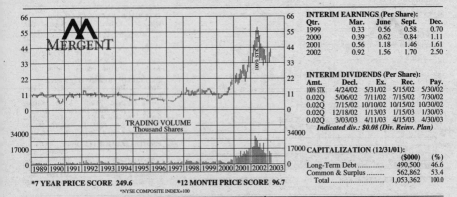

INTERIM EARNINGS (Per Share):

Qtr.	Mar.	June	Sept.	Dec.
1999	0.33	0.56	0.58	0.70
2000	0.39	0.62	0.84	1.11
2001	0.56	1.18	1.46	1.61
2002	0.92	1.56	1.70	2.50

INTERIM DIVIDENDS (Per Share):

Amt.	Decl.	Ex.	Rec.	Pay.
100% STK	4/24/02	5/31/02	5/15/02	5/30/02
0.02Q	5/06/02	7/11/02	7/15/02	7/30/02
0.02Q	7/15/02	10/10/02	10/15/02	10/30/02
0.02Q	12/18/02	1/13/03	1/15/03	1/30/03
0.02Q	3/03/03	4/11/03	4/15/03	4/30/03

Indicated div.: $0.08 (Div. Reinv. Plan)

*7 YEAR PRICE SCORE 249.6   *12 MONTH PRICE SCORE 96.7
*NYSE COMPOSITE INDEX=100

CAPITALIZATION (12/31/01):

	($000)	(%)
Long-Term Debt	490,500	46.6
Common & Surplus	562,862	53.4
Total	1,053,362	100.0

BUSINESS:

The Ryland Group, Inc. is a national homebuilder and mortgage-related financial services firm. The Company builds homes in 25 markets across the country. For the year ended 12/31/02, the Company's average closing price was $210,000. RYL's homebuilding segment specializes in the sale and construction of single-family attached and detached housing. The financial services segment, whose business is conducted through Ryland Mortgage Company and its subsidiaries, complements the Company's homebuilding activities by providing various mortgage-related products and services for retail customers including loan origination, title and escrow services, and by conducting investment activities. In the second quarter of 1995, RYL sold its mortgage securities administration business to Norwest Bank Minnesota. Contributions to 2002 revenues were as follows: homebuilding, 97.5%; and financial services, 2.5%.

RECENT DEVELOPMENTS:

For the year ended 12/31/02, net income advanced 40.5% to $185.6 million compared with $132.1 million the year before. Revenues rose 4.7% to $2.88 billion from $2.75 billion a year earlier. Homebuilding revenues rose 4.5% to $2.81 billion, reflecting an increase in average closing price to $210,000 from $208,000, a 3.6% rise in closings to 13,145 homes, and an increase in the number of active communities in which RYL operates. Financial services revenue rose 14.4% to $72.2 million, due to an increase in loan sales volume, higher origination volume, and increased profitability as a result of the recent interest rate environment.

PROSPECTS:

The Company continues to perform well and should be primed for further growth in the coming year with a record backlog of 5,368 outstanding contracts at 12/31/02. Additionally, new orders were 13,936 for the 12 months ended 12/31/02 versus 13,095 the year before. The Company enters 2003 with cash and cash equivalents of $269.4 million, and no borrowings outstanding against its $300.0 million revolving credit facility. Moreover, the Company's net debt-to-capital ratio was 24.8% at 12/31/02 compared with 25.8% at 12/31/01. Looking ahead, RYL expects earnings per share to exceed $7.25 in 2003.

ANNUAL FINANCIAL DATA:

FISCAL YEAR	TOT. REVS. ($mill.)	NET INC. ($mill.)	TOT. ASSETS ($mill.)	OPER. PROFIT %	NET PROFIT %	RET. ON EQUITY %	RET. ON ASSETS %	CURR. RATIO	EARN. PER SH.$	CASH FL. PER SH.$	TANG. BK. VAL.$	DIV. PER SH.$	PRICE RANGE	AVG. P/E RATIO	AVG. YIELD %
p12/31/02	2,877.2	185.6	1,657.8						6.64			0.08	58.90 - 31.00	6.8	0.2
12/31/01	2,741.8	② 136.5	1,510.9	10.3	5.0	24.2	9.0	3.5	② 4.79	6.08	20.61	0.08	37.92 - 17.67	5.8	0.3
12/31/00	2,331.6	82.3	1,361.3	8.2	3.5	18.1	6.0	2.7	2.96	3.96	16.36	0.08	21.19 - 7.59	4.9	0.6
12/31/99	3,968.1	66.7	1,248.3	7.7	3.3	17.3	5.3	2.2	2.15	3.03	13.16	0.08	15.22 - 9.88	5.8	0.6
12/31/98	3,460.0	② 43.6	1,215.4	7.1	2.5	12.6	-3.6	1.4	② 1.40	2.19	10.78	0.08	15.81 - 9.72	9.2	0.6
12/31/97	3,207.1	21.9	1,283.4	5.6	1.3	7.2	1.7	1.0	0.66	1.68	9.53	0.19	13.00 - 5.56	14.1	2.0
12/31/96	3,053.5	15.8	1,338.5	5.4	1.0	5.1	1.2	0.9	0.44	1.44	8.80	0.30	8.56 - 5.63	16.1	4.2
12/31/95	3,043.2	④ d25.5	1,580.8	1.5	...	...	...	0.7	④ d0.89	0.22	10.68	0.30	8.75 - 6.13	...	4.0
12/31/94	1,642.8	③ 22.5	1,704.5	9.7	1.4	7.2	1.3	0.7	③ 0.65	1.47	8.93	0.30	12.81 - 6.44	14.9	3.1
12/31/93	1,474.4	① d2.7	2,315.7	11.7	...	...	...	0.3	① d0.17	0.68	8.28	0.30	12.25 - 7.94	...	3.0

Statistics are as originally reported. Adj. for stk. split: 2-for-1, 5/02. ① Incl. non-recur. chrg. of $45.0 mill. ② Bef. extraord. loss of $4.4 mill., 2001; $3.3 mill., 1998. ③ Bef. an acctg. chrg. of $2.1 mill. ④ Incl. net chrg. of $27.0 mill. from write-down of inventories, bef. gain from discont. oper. of $22.9 mill.

OFFICERS:
R. C. Dreier, Chmn., Pres., C.E.O.
G. A. Milne, Exec. V.P., C.F.O.
INVESTOR CONTACT: Investor Relations, (818) 223-7500
PRINCIPAL OFFICE: 24025 Park Sorrento, Suite 400, Calabasas, CA 91302

TELEPHONE NUMBER: (818) 223-7500
WEB: www.ryland.com
NO. OF EMPLOYEES: 2,302
SHAREHOLDERS: 2,814
ANNUAL MEETING: In April
INCORPORATED: MD, Mar., 1967

INSTITUTIONAL HOLDINGS:
No. of Institutions: 176
Shares Held: 22,406,366
% Held: 87.3
INDUSTRY: Operative builders (SIC: 1531)
TRANSFER AGENT(S): EquiServe Trust Company NA, Jersey City, NJ

SABRE HOLDING CORPORATION

EXCH.	SYM.	REC. PRICE	P/E RATIO	YLD.	MKT. CAP.	RANGE (52-WK.)	'02 Y/E PR.
NYSE	TSG	16.56 (2/28/03)	10.9	...	$2.36 bill.	49.98 - 14.85	18.11

MEDIUM GRADE. IN 2003, THE COMPANY IS PROJECTING SOLID GROWTH IN REVENUES AND EARNINGS PER SHARE.

*7 YEAR PRICE SCORE N/A   *12 MONTH PRICE SCORE 68.5

*NYSE COMPOSITE INDEX=100

INTERIM EARNINGS (Per Share):

Qtr.	Mar.	June	Sept.	Dec.
1998	0.55	0.52	0.55	0.16
1999	0.71	0.48	0.55	0.75
2000	0.48	0.46	0.34	d0.23
2001	Nil	0.04	0.13	d0.52
2002	0.64	0.47	0.40	0.01

INTERIM DIVIDENDS (Per Share):

Amt.	Decl.	Ex.	Rec.	Pay.
		No dividends paid.		

CAPITALIZATION (12/31/01):

	($000)	(%)
Long-Term Debt	400,375	24.1
Minority Interest	219,716	13.2
Common & Surplus	1,041,776	62.7
Total	1,661,867	100.0

BUSINESS:

Sabre Holding Corporation is a provider of technology, distribution and marketing services for the travel industry. TSG provides products that enable travel commerce and services, and enhance airline/supplier operations. As of 1/16/03, TSG owned 100.0% of Travelocity.com, an on-line travel site. TSG also owns GetThere, a provider of Web-based travel reservation systems for corporations and travel suppliers. At 12/31/02, total bookings were $397.2 million. Revenues for 2002 were derived: travel marketing and distribution, 73.6%; Travelocity, 14.4%; GetThere, 2.4%; and airline solutions, 9.6%. On 3/1/00, AMR Corp., parent of American Airlines, spun off its 83.0% stake in TSG to shareholders.

RECENT DEVELOPMENTS:

For the twelve months ended 12/31/02, net earnings surged to $214.1 million compared with a loss of $47.0 million, before income from discontinued operations of $75.1 million and an accounting credit of $3.1 million, in 2001. Earnings benefited from the Company's buy in of Travelocity, purchase of Site59, and acceleration of merchant model and on-line technology initiatives. Total revenues declined 3.5% to $2.03 billion from $2.10 billion in the previous year, primarily due to the continued downturn in the travel industry. Operating income jumped to $317.5 million compared with an operating loss of $8.7 million the year before.

PROSPECTS:

For the full-year 2003, the Company is projecting earnings per share in the range of $1.54 to $1.64, representing three to nine percent growth, year over year. Excluding special items, earnings per share are expected to be between $1.78 to $1.88, zero to five percent growth, year over year. In 2003, special non-cash and one-time charges, net of tax and minority interests, are expected to be $34.0 million, which includes amortization of intangible assets and stock compensation expenses associated with strategic acquisitions. Additionally, TSG is forecasting revenue in the range of $2.10 billion to $2.20 billion, four to nine percent growth, year over year. Operating earnings are expected to grow in the mid-teens.

ANNUAL FINANCIAL DATA:

FISCAL YEAR	TOT. REVS. (Smill.)	NET INC. (Smill.)	TOT. ASSETS (Smill.)	OPER. PROFIT %	NET PROFIT %	RET. ON EQUITY %	RET. ON ASSETS %	CURR. RATIO	EARN. PER SH.$	CASH FL. PER SH.$	TANG. BK. VAL.$	DIV. PER SH.$	PRICE RANGE	AVG. P/E RATIO	AVG. YIELD %
p12/31/02	2,029.5	214.1							1.50			...	49.98 - 14.85	21.6	...
12/31/01	2,103.1	② d47.0	2,376.0	...	...	...	...	1.9	② d0.35	2.95	2.84	...	54.98 - 21.22	...	...
12/31/00	2,617.4	① 144.1	2,650.4	9.6	5.5	18.2	5.4	0.5	① 1.11	3.77	...	5.20	53.50 - 22.31	34.1	13.7
12/31/99	2,434.6	331.9	1,951.2	15.3	13.6	26.3	17.0	1.9	2.54	4.52	9.72	...	72.00 - 38.25	21.7	...
12/31/98	2,306.4	231.9	1,926.8	15.2	10.1	24.3	12.0	2.4	1.78	3.68	7.35	...	44.88 - 23.00	19.1	...
12/31/97	1,783.5	199.9	1,524.0	17.3	11.2	26.4	13.1	2.8	1.53	2.94	5.79	...	37.00 - 23.25	19.7	...
12/31/96	1,622.0	186.6	1,287.1	20.1	11.5	32.8	14.5	2.4	1.43	2.94	4.36	...	33.38 - 25.63	20.6	...
12/31/95	1,529.6	225.9	729.4	24.9	14.8	52.3	31.0	1.2	1.73	3.84	...	...	...	...	...
12/31/94	1,406.7	197.2	873.5	24.9	14.0	68.1	22.6	0.8	...	...	...	...	...	...	...
12/31/93	1,258.1	100.0	...	20.2	7.9	...	...	...	...	...	...	...	...	...	...

Statistics are as originally reported. ① Incl. $158.4 mill. special chgs. ② Excl. $36.3 mill. inc. fr. disc. ops., $38.8 mill. gain fr. sale of assets & $3.1 mill. acctg. credit.

OFFICERS:
W. J. Hannigan, Chmn., Pres., C.E.O.
J. M. Jackson, Exec. V.P., C.F.O., Treas.
D. A. Schwarte, Exec. V.P., Gen. Couns.
INVESTOR CONTACT: Investor Relations, (817) 358-1700
PRINCIPAL OFFICE: 3150 Sabre Drive, Southlake, TX 76092

TELEPHONE NUMBER: (682) 605-1000
WEB: www.sabre.com
NO. OF EMPLOYEES: 6,500 (approx.)
SHAREHOLDERS: 10,731 (approx.)
ANNUAL MEETING: In May
INCORPORATED: DE, June, 1996

INSTITUTIONAL HOLDINGS:
No. of Institutions: 241
Shares Held: 131,444,727
% Held: 92.1
INDUSTRY: Data processing and preparation (SIC: 7374)
TRANSFER AGENT(S): First Chicago Trust Company of New York, Jersey City, NJ

SAFEWAY INC.

EXCH.	SYM.	REC. PRICE	P/E RATIO	YLD.	MKT. CAP.	RANGE (52-WK.)	'02 Y/E PR.
NYSE	SWY	19.89 (2/28/03)	17.8	...	$9.71 bill.	46.90 - 18.45	23.36

UPPER MEDIUM GRADE. IN 2003, THE COMPANY PLANS TO OPEN 50 TO 55 NEW STORES AND REMODEL BETWEEN 100 AND 125 EXISTING STORES.

*7 YEAR PRICE SCORE 85.3   ***12 MONTH PRICE SCORE 84.1**

*NYSE COMPOSITE INDEX=100

INTERIM EARNINGS (Per Share):

Qtr.	Mar.	June	Sept.	Dec.
1996	0.20	0.22	0.22	0.32
1997	0.26	0.27	0.30	0.43
1998	0.33	0.38	0.38	0.50
1999	0.40	0.46	0.44	0.59
2000	0.48	0.55	0.53	0.58
2001	0.55	0.59	0.60	0.76
2002	0.67	0.63	0.60	d0.78

INTERIM DIVIDENDS (Per Share):

Amt.	Decl.	Ex.	Rec.	Pay.
		No dividends paid.		

CAPITALIZATION (12/29/01):

	($000)	(%)
Long-Term Debt	6,236,800	47.6
Capital Lease Obligations..	475,500	3.6
Deferred Income Tax	498,100	3.8
Common & Surplus	5,889,600	45.0
Total	13,100,000	100.0

BUSINESS:

Safeway Inc. operated 1,695 stores in the United States and Canada as of 2/6/03 that offer a wide selection of both food and general merchandise. U.S. retail operations are located in California, Oregon, Washington, Alaska, Colorado, Arizona, Texas, the Chicago metropolitan area and the Mid-Atlantic region. Canadian retail operations are located principally in British Columbia, Alberta and Manitoba/Saskatchewan. The Vons Companies, Inc., which operates 336 grocery stores located mainly in southern California, became a wholly-owned subsidiary on 4/8/97. In November, 1998, SWY acquired Dominick's Supermarkets, Inc., which operates 114 grocery stores in the Chicago area. In April 1999, SWY acquired Carr-Gottstein Foods Co., which operates 49 food stores in Alaska. As of 12/29/01, SWY held a 49% interest in Casa Ley, S.A. de C.V., which operates 99 stores in western Mexico.

RECENT DEVELOPMENTS:

For the 52 weeks ended 12/28/02, income from continuing operations totaled $565.0 million, before a $700.0 million accounting change charge, versus income from continuing operations of $1.29 billion in the corresponding period a year earlier. Results for 2002 included a $704.2 million pre-tax impairment charge and a $58.9 million pre-tax restructuring charge. Results for 2001 included goodwill amortization of $101.0 million. Sales grew 1.9% to $32.40 billion from $31.80 billion the previous year. Gross profit was $10.10 billion, or 31.2% of sales, versus $9.85 billion, or 31.0% of sales, the year before. Operating profit slid 34.4% to $1.67 billion from $2.54 billion in the prior year.

PROSPECTS:

The Company is taking aggressive steps to reduce costs in an effort to offset higher wage and employee benefit costs and pension expenses. Meanwhile, SWY is continuing to aggressively expand its store base. During 2002, the Company opened 71 new stores, closed 32 stores and remodeled 191 existing locations. SWY anticipates spending between $1.10 billion and $1.30 billion to open 50 to 55 new stores and remodel between 100 and 125 existing stores in 2003. Separately, in late 2002, SWY decided to sell its Dominick's supermarkets and exit the Chicago market due to union labor issues.

ANNUAL FINANCIAL DATA:

FISCAL YEAR	TOT. REVS. ($mill.)	NET INC. ($mill.)	TOT. ASSETS ($mill.)	OPER. PROFIT %	NET PROFIT %	RET. ON EQUITY %	RET. ON ASSETS %	CURR. RATIO	EARN. PER SH. $	CASH FL. PER SH. $	TANG. BK. VAL. $	PRICE RANGE	AVG. P/E RATIO
p12/28/02	32,399.2	③ 565.0							③ 1.19			46.90 - 18.45	27.5
12/29/01	34,301.0	② 1,253.9	17,462.6	7.5	3.7	21.3	7.2	0.9	② 2.44	4.29	1.67	61.38 - 37.44	20.2
12/30/00	31,976.9	1,091.9	15,965.3	7.1	3.4	20.3	6.8	0.9	2.13	3.77	1.35	62.69 - 30.75	21.9
1/01/00	28,859.9	970.9	14,900.3	6.9	3.4	23.8	6.5	0.9	1.88	3.24	...	62.44 - 29.31	24.4
1/02/99	24,484.2	806.7	11,389.6	6.5	3.3	26.2	7.1	0.8	1.59	2.63	...	61.38 - 30.50	28.9
1/03/98	22,483.8	① 621.5	8,493.9	5.7	2.8	28.9	7.3	0.8	① 1.25	2.17	0.68	31.66 - 21.06	21.1
12/28/96	17,269.0	460.6	5,545.2	5.2	2.7	38.8	8.3	0.8	0.97	1.68	1.97	22.69 - 11.22	17.5
12/30/95	16,397.5	① 328.3	5,194.3	4.4	2.0	41.3	6.3	0.8	① 0.68	1.38	1.10	12.88 - 7.66	15.1
12/31/94	15,626.6	① 250.2	5,022.1	3.9	1.6	38.9	5.0	0.8	① 0.63	1.19	0.75	7.97 - 4.81	10.2
1/01/94	15,214.5	123.3	5,074.7	2.9	0.8	32.2	2.4	0.9	0.26	0.94	0.09	5.69 - 2.72	16.5

Statistics are as originally reported. Adj. for 2-for-1 stk. split, 2/98 & 1/96. ① Bef. $64.1 mil ($0.13/sh) extraord. loss, 1997; $2 mil loss, 1995; & $10.5 mil loss, 1994. ② Incl. $42.7 mil pre-tax chg. fr. bankruptcies of Furr's and Homeland & $30.1 mil pre-tax chg. fr. GroceryWorks impairment. ③ Bef. $693.1 mil ($1.46/sh) loss fr. discont. opers., $700.0 mil (1.48/sh) acctg. change chg. & incl. $763.1 mil pre-tax restr. and impair. chgs.

OFFICERS:
S. A. Burd, Chmn., Pres., C.E.O.
V. M. Prabhu, Exec. V.P., C.F.O.
R. A. Gordon, Sr. V.P., Gen. Couns.
INVESTOR CONTACT: Julie Hong, Investor Relations, (925) 467-3832
PRINCIPAL OFFICE: 5918 Stoneridge Mall Rd., Pleasanton, CA 94588

TELEPHONE NUMBER: (925) 467-3000
FAX: (925) 467-3323
WEB: www.safeway.com
NO. OF EMPLOYEES: 193,000 (approx.)
SHAREHOLDERS: 18,197
ANNUAL MEETING: In May
INCORPORATED: DE, July, 1986

INSTITUTIONAL HOLDINGS:
No. of Institutions: 488
Shares Held: 357,311,595
% Held: 81.0

INDUSTRY: Grocery stores (SIC: 5411)

TRANSFER AGENT(S): EquiServe Trust Compnay, N.A., Jersey City, NJ

SAKS INCORPORATED

EXCH.	SYM.	REC. PRICE	P/E RATIO	YLD.	MKT. CAP.	RANGE (52-WK.)	'02 Y/E PR.
NYSE	SKS	7.69 (2/28/03)	16.4	...	$1.11 bill.	15.75 - 7.50	11.74

MEDIUM GRADE. THE COMPANY ENTERED INTO AN AGREEMENT UNDER WHICH FAO, INC. WILL OPERATE LICENSED DEPARTMENTS IN SKS' STORES.

TRADING VOLUME
Thousand Shares

*7 YEAR PRICE SCORE 65.6   ***12 MONTH PRICE SCORE 85.3**
*NYSE COMPOSITE INDEX=100

INTERIM EARNINGS (Per Share):

Qtr.	Apr.	July	Oct.	Jan.
1997-98	0.15	0.09	0.18	0.38
1998-99	0.19	0.02	d0.74	0.68
1999-00	0.23	0.13	0.18	0.84
2000-01	0.24	d0.04	d0.06	0.39
2001-02	0.11	d0.44	d0.17	0.38
2002-03	0.13	d0.14	0.01	0.47

INTERIM DIVIDENDS (Per Share):

Amt.	Decl.	Ex.	Rec.	Pay.
		No dividends paid.		

CAPITALIZATION (2/2/02):

	($000)	(%)
Long-Term Debt	1,356,580	37.4
Common & Surplus	2,271,437	62.6
Total	3,628,017	100.0

BUSINESS:

Saks Incorporated (formerly Proffitt's, Inc.) operates in two business segments. The Saks Department Store Group segment (60.5% of fiscal 2003 net sales) includes 244 stores in 24 states as of 3/5/03 operating under the names Younkers, Parisian, Herberger's, Carson Pirie Scott, McRae's, Proffitt's, Bergner's and Boston Store. These stores are principally anchor stores in malls that sell fashion apparel, shoes, accessories, jewelry, cosmetics, and decorative home furnishings, as well as furniture in selected locations. The Saks Fifth Avenue Enterprises segment (39.5%) includes 60 Saks Fifth Avenue stores in 24 states and 52 Off 5th Saks Fifth Avenue Outlet stores in 23 states.

RECENT DEVELOPMENTS:

For the year ended 2/1/03, SKS reported income of $69.8 million, before a $45.6 million accounting change charge, compared with net income of $322,000 the year before. Results for fiscal 2002 and fiscal 2001 included gains from the early extinguishment of debt of $709,000 and $26.1 million, respectively. Results also included pre-tax integration charges of $10.0 million and $1.5 million, and pre-tax losses from long-lived assets of $19.5 million and $32.6 million in fiscal 2002 and fiscal 2001, respectively. Net sales slipped 2.6% to $5.91 billion from $6.07 billion a year earlier. Comparable-store sales were down 1.4% year over year. Gross profit totaled $2.17 billion, or 36.7% of net sales, versus $2.11 billion, or 34.8% of net sales, the previous year.

PROSPECTS:

On 2/24/03, the Company announced that it has entered into an agreement with FAO, Inc., an operator of stores under the FAO Schwartz, The Right Start and Zany Brainy names, under which SKS will sell FAO's educational products, toys, games, books, multimedia products and candy in most of its department stores, beginning in the second half of 2003. Separately, SKS is targeting full-year fiscal 2003 earnings per share growth in the mid single-digit range. The Company anticipates spending approximately $200.0 million in fiscal 2003, primarily related to opening six new stores and upgrading several existing locations.

ANNUAL FINANCIAL DATA:

FISCAL YEAR	TOT. REVS. ($mill.)	NET INC. ($mill.)	TOT. ASSETS ($mill.)	OPER. PROFIT %	NET PROFIT %	RET. ON EQUITY %	RET. ON ASSETS %	CURR. RATIO	EARN. PER SH.$	CASH FL.PER SH.$	TANG. BK. VAL.$	PRICE RANGE	AVG. P/E RATIO
p2/01/03	5,911.1	⑤ 69.8							⑤ 0.48			15.75 - 8.55	25.3
2/02/02	6,070.6	④ d15.7	4,595.5	1.7	...	...	...	2.2	④ d0.11	1.44	13.27	14.23 - 4.60	...
2/03/01	6,581.2	② 75.2	5,050.6	4.0	1.1	3.3	1.5	2.3	② 0.53	2.03	12.56	16.25 - 7.63	22.5
1/29/00	6,423.8	①② 198.9	5,099.0	7.1	3.1	9.0	3.9	2.4	①② 1.36	2.59	11.40	39.50 - 14.63	19.9
1/30/99	6,219.9	①② 25.0	5,189.0	2.5	0.4	1.2	0.5	2.0	①② 0.17	1.23	9.95	44.44 - 16.38	178.8
1/31/98	3,544.7	①② 72.1	2,224.9	2.8	2.0	6.6	3.2	2.5	①② 0.81	1.51	9.19	32.44 - 15.63	29.7
2/01/97	1,889.8	② 37.4	1,403.8	3.3	2.0	6.9	2.7	2.4	② 0.66	1.49	4.68	21.38 - 10.75	24.5
2/03/96	1,333.5	①② d6.4	815.7	...	...	...	...	2.3	①② d0.21	0.72	7.20	17.13 - 10.38	...
1/28/95	617.4	16.1	540.1	4.5	2.6	8.9	3.0	2.3	0.73	1.69	5.38	12.88 - 7.38	13.9
1/29/94	200.9	③ 5.7	259.9	2.8	2.9	4.6	2.2	7.6	③ 0.31	0.67	6.67	18.38 - 10.13	46.0

Statistics are as originally reported. Adj. for 2-for-1 stk. split, 10/28/97. ① Bef. $9.3 mil ($0.06/sh) extraord. chg., 1/00; $25.9 mil ($0.18/sh), 1/99; $9.3 mil ($0.10/sh), 1/98; $2.1 mil ($0.06/sh), 2/96. ② Incl. $57.5 mil ($0.40/sh) after-tax non-recurr. chg., 2/01; $35.7 mil pre-tax chg., 1/00; $111.3 mil, 1/99; $43.5 mil, 1/98; $15.9 mil, 2/97; $20.8 mil, 2/96. ③ Bef. $333,000 ($0.02/sh) acctg. chg., 1/00. ④ Bef. $16.1 mil ($0.11/sh) extraord. gain & incl. $23.5 mil ($0.17/sh) after-tax net chg. ⑤ Bef. $45.6 mil acctg. chg. & Incl. $709,000 gain on extinguish. of debt, $19.5 mil loss fr. long-lived assets and $10.0 mil integration chg.

OFFICERS:
R. B. Martin, Chmn., C.E.O.
J. A. Coggin, Pres., Chief Admin. Off.
D. E. Coltharp, Exec. V.P., C.F.O.
INVESTOR CONTACT: Julia Bentley, Sr. V.P., Inv. Rel., (865) 981-6243
PRINCIPAL OFFICE: 750 Lakeshore Parkway, Birmingham, AL 35211

TELEPHONE NUMBER: (205) 940-4000
FAX: (205) 940-4987
WEB: www.saksincorporated.com
NO. OF EMPLOYEES: 31,800 full-time (approx.); 21,200 part-time (approx.)
SHAREHOLDERS: 2,500 (approx.)
ANNUAL MEETING: In June
INCORPORATED: TN, 1919

INSTITUTIONAL HOLDINGS:
No. of Institutions: 170
Shares Held: 83,502,747
% Held: 58.6

INDUSTRY: Department stores (SIC: 5311)

TRANSFER AGENT(S): The Bank of New York, New York, NY

SALTON, INC.

EXCH.	SYM.	REC. PRICE	P/E RATIO	YLD.	MKT. CAP.	RANGE (52-WK.)	'02 Y/E PR.
NYSE	SFP	10.13 (2/28/03)	5.2	...	$111.4 mill.	23.60 - 7.61	9.62

LOWER MEDIUM GRADE. THE COMPANY SHOULD CONTINUE TO BENEFIT FROM THE LAUNCH OF A NUMBER OF NEW PRODUCTS.

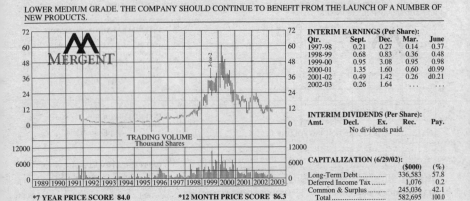

*7 YEAR PRICE SCORE 84.0   ***12 MONTH PRICE SCORE 86.3**
*NYSE COMPOSITE INDEX=100

INTERIM EARNINGS (Per Share):

Qtr.	Sept.	Dec.	Mar.	June
1997-98	0.21	0.27	0.14	0.37
1998-99	0.68	0.83	0.36	0.48
1999-00	0.95	3.08	0.95	0.98
2000-01	1.35	1.60	0.60	d0.99
2001-02	0.49	1.42	0.26	d0.21
2002-03	0.26	1.64	...	...

INTERIM DIVIDENDS (Per Share):

Amt.	Decl.	Ex.	Rec.	Pay.
		No dividends paid.		

CAPITALIZATION (6/29/02):

	($000)	(%)
Long-Term Debt	336,583	57.8
Deferred Income Tax	1,076	0.2
Common & Surplus	245,036	42.1
Total	582,695	100.0

BUSINESS:

Salton, Inc. (formerly Salton/Maxim Housewares, Inc.) designs, markets and distributes a broad range of small appliances under brand names including SALTON®, GEORGE FOREMAN™, TOASTMASTER®, KENMORE®, BREADMAN®, JUICEMAN®, WHITE-WESTINGHOUSE®, FARBERWARE®, MELITTA®, RUSSELL HOBBS®, TOWER®, HADEN®, MAXIM®, and WESTINGHOUSE®. SFP also designs and markets tabletop products, time products, light-

ing products and personal care and wellness products under brand names such as BLOCK CHINA®, CALVIN KLEIN®, INGRAHAM®, WESTCLOX®, STIFFEL®, ULTRASONEX™, RELAXOR®, CARMEN®, PIFCO®, and REJUVENIQUE®. Net sales for fiscal 2002 were derived as follows: small appliances, 87.6%; Salton at home, 9.3%; and personal care and wellness products, 3.1%.

RECENT DEVELOPMENTS:

For the quarter ended 12/28/02, net income increased 17.9% to $25.0 million from $21.2 million in the corresponding prior-year period. Earnings for 2002 included a fair market value adjustment on derivatives of $1.0 million.

Net sales grew 6.5% to $339.3 million, reflecting the strength of the Company's product diversification and the success of SFP's international expansion. Gross profit slipped 2.1% to $111.4 million.

PROSPECTS:

The Company should continue to benefit from the launch of a number of new products that has been well received in the marketplace. For instance, SFP introduced the Melitta One:One™ single-cup pod-operated coffee maker and the Westinghouse Unplugged upright vacuum cleaner. Separately, on 2/12/03, SFP announced that its wholly-owned subsidiary, Salton Hong Kong Ltd., has offered to increase

its 30.8% interest in Amalgamated Appliance Holdings Ltd. to 52.0% in a transaction valued at about $6.0 million. Amalgamated is a manufacturer of appliances and electrical accessories, primarily to the South African market. Looking ahead, SFP expects sales to range from $360.0 million to $400.0 million and diluted earnings per share between breakeven to $0.35 for the second half of 2003.

ANNUAL FINANCIAL DATA:

FISCAL YEAR	TOT. REVS. ($000)	NET INC. ($000)	TOT. ASSETS ($000)	OPER. PROFIT %	NET PROFIT %	RET. ON EQUITY %	RET. ON ASSETS %	CURR. RATIO	EARN. PER SH.$	CASH FL. PER SH.$	TANG. BK. VAL.$	PRICE RANGE	AVG. P/E RATIO
6/29/02	922,479	☐ 30,147	825,568	9.9	3.3	12.3	3.7	2.2	☐ 2.00	4.04	7.69	23.60 - 7.61	7.8
6/30/01	792,114	☐ 46,154	722,884	14.1	5.8	21.8	6.4	3.4	☐ 2.87	4.34	6.98	23.00 - 7.96	5.4
7/01/00	837,302	91,816	564,276	21.0	11.0	52.8	16.3	2.1	5.91	7.14	4.12	60.88 - 16.56	6.6
6/26/99	506,116	50,061	328,316	13.7	9.9	98.7	15.2	2.7	2.37	3.94	0.79	39.44 - 14.00	11.3
6/27/98	305,599	☐ 19,981	141,397	9.7	6.5	34.6	14.1	1.5	☐ 0.99	1.20	2.68	17.17 - 5.33	11.4
6/28/97	182,806	4,399	102,343	5.7	2.4	11.4	4.3	1.3	0.23	0.39	1.73	7.33 - 3.75	24.4
6/29/96	99,202	4,595	59,481	5.1	4.6	23.1	7.7	1.3	0.47	0.70	1.66	5.83 - 1.50	7.8
7/01/95	76,991	651	41,121	4.8	0.8	4.2	1.6	1.4	0.07	0.30	1.20	3.00 - 1.08	27.9
7/02/94	48,807	d2,944	38,635	...	...	...	...	1.4	d0.39	d0.18	1.00	2.33 - 0.83	...
6/26/93	50,661	d3,151	35,797	...	...	...	...	1.5	d0.43	d0.19	1.77	2.42 - 0.50	...

Statistics are as originally reported. Adj. for stk. split, 3-for-2, 7/99. ☐ Incl. pre-tax non-recurr. chg. of $14.8 mill., 6/02; $15.3 mill., 6/01; $1.1 mil., 6/98.

OFFICERS:
D. C. Sabin, Chmn.
L. Dreimann, C.E.O.
W. B. Rue, Pres., C.O.O.

INVESTOR CONTACT: William B. Rue,
Investor Relations, (847) 803-4600

PRINCIPAL OFFICE: 1955 Field Court, Lake Forest, IL 60045

TELEPHONE NUMBER: (847) 803-4600
FAX: (847) 803-1186
WEB: www.saltoninc.com

NO. OF EMPLOYEES: 1,400 (approx.)

SHAREHOLDERS: 337 (approx.)

ANNUAL MEETING: In Dec.

INCORPORATED: DE, Aug., 1991

INSTITUTIONAL HOLDINGS:
No. of Institutions: 85
Shares Held: 7,057,228
% Held: 64.2

INDUSTRY: Electric housewares and fans (SIC: 3634)

TRANSFER AGENT(S): UMB Bank, Kansas City, MO

SARA LEE CORPORATION

EXCH.	SYM.	REC. PRICE	P/E RATIO	YLD.	MKT. CAP.	RANGE (52-WK.)	'02 Y/E PR.	DIV. ACH.
NYSE	SLE	19.80 (2/28/03)	12.9	3.1%	$15.54 bill.	23.84 - 16.15	22.51	26 yrs.

INVESTMENT GRADE. APPAREL SALES SHOULD BENEFIT FROM THE LAUNCH OF THE COMPANY'S NEW RETAIL STORES CALLED INNER SELF.

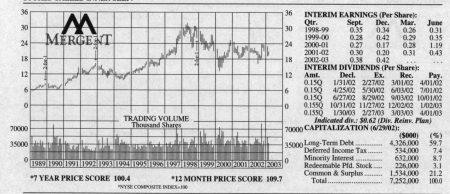

INTERIM EARNINGS (Per Share):

Qtr.	Sept.	Dec.	Mar.	June
1998-99	0.35	0.34	0.26	0.31
1999-00	0.28	0.42	0.29	0.35
2000-01	0.27	0.17	0.28	1.19
2001-02	0.30	0.20	0.31	0.43
2002-03	0.38	0.42	...	...

INTERIM DIVIDENDS (Per Share):

Amt.	Decl.	Ex.	Rec.	Pay.
0.15Q	1/31/02	2/27/02	3/01/02	4/01/02
0.15Q	4/25/02	5/30/02	6/03/02	7/01/02
0.15Q	6/27/02	8/29/02	9/03/02	10/01/02
0.155Q	10/31/02	11/27/02	12/02/02	1/02/03
0.155Q	1/30/03	2/27/03	3/03/03	4/01/03

Indicated div.: $0.62 (Div. Reinv. Plan)

CAPITALIZATION (6/29/02):

	($000)	(%)
Long-Term Debt	4,326,000	59.7
Deferred Income Tax	534,000	7.4
Minority Interest	632,000	8.7
Redeemable Pfd. Stock	226,000	3.1
Common & Surplus	1,534,000	21.2
Total	7,252,000	100.0

TRADING VOLUME Thousand Shares

*7 YEAR PRICE SCORE 100.4   ***12 MONTH PRICE SCORE 109.7**
*NYSE COMPOSITE INDEX=100

BUSINESS:

Sara Lee Corporation is a global manufacturer and marketer of brand-name foods and consumer products. Intimates & Underwear (36.6% of fiscal 2002 sales) is comprised of SLE's intimates, knit products, legwear and accessories businesses. Well-known brands include BALI, HANES HER WAY, and PLAYTEX. Sara Lee Meats (21.0%) such brands as HILLSHIRE FARM, JIMMY DEAN, BALL PARK, and BRYAN. Sara Lee Bakery (16.9%) includes products sold under the EARTH GRAINS brand. Beverage (14.4%) includes such brands as HILLS BROS., CHOCK FULL O'NUTS, DOUWE EGBERTS, PICKWICK and MARCILLA. Household Products (11.1%) is comprised of shoe care, body care, insecticides, air fresheners, and SLE's direct sales operations. On 12/4/00, SLE sold PYA/Monarch, its U.S. foodservice distributor. On 8/7/01, SLE acquired The Earthgrains Company.

RECENT DEVELOPMENTS:

For the quarter ended 12/28/02, net income more than doubled to $348.0 million versus $160.0 million a year earlier. Earnings benefited from cost savings generated by SLE's restructuring efforts, partially offset by increased advertising and promotional spending. Results included a pre-tax gain of $3.0 million and a charge of $188.0 million in 2002 and 2001, respectively, primarily related to business dispositions. Net sales grew 1.9% to $4.78 billion from $4.69 billion the year before. Operating income advanced 91.5% to $471.0 million from $246.0 million the previous year.

PROSPECTS:

The Company hopes to bolster sales of apparel through the launch of a new chain of retail stores called Inner Self. As of 1/3/02, SLE operated four Inner Self stores, which sell lingerie primarily to women between the ages of 25 and 55. The Company expects to have ten inner self stores open by the end of June 2003. Separately, SLE is targeting sales growth of approximately 2.0%, excluding acquisitions, in the current fiscal year, along with earnings in the range of $1.54 to $1.60 per share.

ANNUAL FINANCIAL DATA:

FISCAL YEAR	TOT. REVS. ($mill.)	NET INC. ($mill.)	TOT. ASSETS ($mill.)	OPER. PROFIT %	NET PROFIT %	RET. ON EQUITY %	RET. ON ASSETS %	CURR. RATIO	EARN. PER SH.$	CASH FL. PER SH.$	DIV. PER SH.$	PRICE RANGE	AVG. P/E RATIO	AVG. YIELD %
6/29/02	17,628.0	⑥ 1,010.0	13,753.0	8.9	5.7	65.8	7.3	0.9	⑥ 1.23	1.95	0.60	23.84 - 16.15	16.3	3.0
6/30/01	17,747.0	⑤ 1,603.0	10,167.0	9.0	9.0	142.9	15.8	1.0	⑤ 1.87	2.58	0.58	24.75 - 18.26	11.5	2.7
7/01/00	17,511.0	④ 1,158.0	11,611.0	10.0	6.6	93.8	10.0	0.9	④ 1.27	1.92	0.54	25.31 - 13.38	15.2	2.8
7/03/99	20,012.0	② 1,191.0	10,521.0	8.7	6.0	94.1	11.3	0.8	② 1.26	1.83	0.50	28.75 - 21.06	19.8	2.0
6/27/98	20,011.0	d523.0	10,989.0	8.9	...	...	...	0.9	③ d0.57	0.09	0.46	31.81 - 22.16	...	1.7
6/28/97	19,734.0	1,009.0	12,953.0	8.3	5.1	23.6	7.8	1.1	1.02	1.71	0.42	28.91 - 18.25	23.2	1.8
6/29/96	18,624.0	916.0	12,602.0	8.3	4.9	21.2	7.3	1.1	0.92	1.57	0.38	20.25 - 14.94	19.2	2.2
7/01/95	17,719.0	804.0	12,431.0	7.9	4.5	20.4	6.5	1.0	0.81	1.44	0.34	16.88 - 12.13	17.9	2.3
7/02/94	15,536.0	① 234.0	11,665.0	8.1	1.5	7.0	2.0	0.9	① 0.22	0.81	0.32	13.00 - 9.69	51.5	2.8
7/03/93	14,580.0	704.0	10,862.0	8.0	4.8	19.8	6.5	1.0	0.70	1.24	0.29	15.56 - 10.50	18.6	2.2

Statistics are as originally reported. Adj. for 2-for-1 stk. split, 12/98. ① Bef. $35 mil ($0.04/sh) chg. for acctg. adj. & incl. $495 mil ($0.52/sh) net non-recur. chg. ② Incl. $50 mil ($0.05/sh) net chg. from product recall & incl. $97 mil ($0.10/sh) net gain on sale of int'l tobacco opers. ③ Incl. $1.60 bil ($1.72/sh) after-tax restr. chg. ④ Bef. $64.0 mil ($0.07/sh) income fr. disc. oper. ⑤ Bef. $663 mil ($0.78/sh) gain fr. disc. opers., incl. $967 mil pre-tax gain fr. disposal of Coach business, and $554 mil of other one-time pre-tax chgs. ⑥ Incl. $170 mil pre-tax chg.

OFFICERS:
C. S. McMillan, Chmn., Pres., C.E.O.
L. M. de Kool, Exec. V.P., C.F.O.
R. A. Palmore, Sr. V.P., Sec., Gen. Couns.

INVESTOR CONTACT: Janet Bergman, Sr. V.P., Corp. Rel., (312) 558-8651

PRINCIPAL OFFICE: Three First National Plaza, Suite 4600, Chicago, IL 60602-4260

TELEPHONE NUMBER: (312) 726-2600
FAX: (312) 558-4913
WEB: www.saralee.com

NO. OF EMPLOYEES: 154,900 (approx.)

SHAREHOLDERS: 74,500 (approx.)

ANNUAL MEETING: In Oct.

INCORPORATED: MD, Sept., 1941

INSTITUTIONAL HOLDINGS:
No. of Institutions: 598
Shares Held: 459,660,784
% Held: 59.0

INDUSTRY: Sausages and other prepared meats (SIC: 2013)

TRANSFER AGENT(S): Sara Lee Corp., Chicago, IL

SBC COMMUNICATIONS INC.

EXCH.	SYM.	REC. PRICE	P/E RATIO	YLD.	MKT. CAP.	RANGE (52-WK.)	'02 Y/E PR.	DIV. ACH.
NYSE	SBC	24.44 (1/31/03)	10.6	4.4%	$81.98 bill.	39.56 - 19.57	27.11	18 yrs.

UPPER MEDIUM GRADE. THE COMPANY ANTICIPATES LOW SINGLE-DIGIT PERCENTAGE DECLINES IN CONSOLIDATED REVENUE FOR FULL-YEAR 2003.

TRADING VOLUME
Thousand Shares

*7 YEAR PRICE SCORE 80.2   ***12 MONTH PRICE SCORE 99.5**

*NYSE COMPOSITE INDEX=100

INTERIM EARNINGS (Per Share):

Qtr.	Mar.	June	Sept.	Dec.
1997	0.43	d0.43	0.45	0.32
1998	0.49	0.52	0.65	2.05
1999	0.56	0.59	0.64	0.50
2000	0.53	0.54	0.88	0.38
2001	0.54	0.61	0.61	0.37
2002	0.51	0.55	0.53	0.71

INTERIM DIVIDENDS (Per Share):

Amt.	Decl.	Ex.	Rec.	Pay.
0.256Q	12/14/01	1/08/02	1/10/02	2/01/02
0.27Q	3/22/02	4/08/02	4/10/02	5/01/02
0.27Q	6/28/02	7/08/02	7/10/02	8/01/02
0.27Q	9/27/02	10/08/02	10/10/02	11/01/02
0.27Q	12/13/02	1/08/03	1/10/03	2/03/03

Indicated div.: $1.08 (Div. Reinv. Plan)

CAPITALIZATION (12/31/01):

	($000)	(%)
Long-Term Debt	17,133,000	29.4
Deferred Income Tax	8,578,000	14.7
Common & Surplus	32,491,000	55.8
Total	58,202,000	100.0

BUSINESS:

SBC Communications Inc. (formerly Southwestern Bell) is one of seven regional holding companies divested by AT&T in 1984. SBC offers a variety of products and services under the SBC Ameritech, SBC Nevada Bell, SBC Pacific Bell, SBC SNET, and SBC Southwestern Bell brands, including local and long-distance voice, Internet services, telecommunications equipment, messaging, paging, directory advertising and publishing. As of 1/28/03,

SBC had 57.0 million network access lines in service and maintained a 60.0% equity interest in Cingular Wireless, which was formed in April 2000 and serves more than 22.0 million wireless customers. Internationally, SBC has telecommunications investments in 27 countries. On 4/1/97, SBC acquired Pacific Telesis Group. On 10/26/98, SBC acquired Southern New England Telecommunications Corporation. On 10/8/99, SBC acquired Ameritech Corp.

RECENT DEVELOPMENTS:

For the twelve months ended 12/31/02, income was $7.47 billion, before an accounting change charge of $1.82 billion, versus income of $7.03 billion, before an extraordinary loss of $18.0 million, the previous year. Total operating revenues fell 6.0% to $43.14 billion from $45.91 billion

a year earlier, reflecting a weak economy and competitive pressures. Operating income declined 17.9% to $8.62 billion versus $10.51 billion in 2001. Comparisons were made with restated prior-year figures.

PROSPECTS:

For 2003, SBC expects a continuation of competitive and economic trends that may result in continued negative access line trends, with long-distance entry in additional states and expansion of the Company's bundling initiative helping to slow the rate of decline as the year progresses.

Also, SBC sees continued solid digital subscriber line growth, modest growth in data traffic, and modest subscriber and revenue growth at Cingular Wireless. Overall, SBC anticipates low single-digit percentage declines in consolidated revenue for full-year 2003.

ANNUAL FINANCIAL DATA:

FISCAL YEAR	TOT. REVS. ($mill.)	NET INC. ($mill.)	TOT. ASSETS ($mill.)	OPER. PROFIT %	NET PROFIT %	RET. ON EQUITY %	RET. ON ASSETS %	CURR. RATIO	EARN. PER SH. $	CASH FL. PER SH. $	TANG. BK. VAL. $	DIV. PER SH. $	PRICE RANGE	AVG. P/E RATIO	AVG. YIELD %
p12/31/02	43,138.0	⑨ 7,473.0							⑨ 2.23			1.07	40.99 - 19.57	13.6	3.5
12/31/01	45,908.0	⑧ 7,260.0	96,322.0	23.7	15.8	22.3	7.5	0.5	⑧ 2.14	4.80	8.62	1.02	53.06 - 36.50	20.9	2.3
12/31/00	51,476.0	⑦ 7,967.0	98,651.0	20.9	15.5	26.2	8.1	0.8	⑦ 2.32	5.14	7.38	1.00	59.00 - 34.81	20.2	2.1
12/31/99	49,489.0	⑥ 6,573.0	83,215.0	23.4	13.3	24.6	7.9	0.6	⑥ 1.90	4.35	5.87	0.96	59.94 - 44.06	27.4	1.9
12/31/98	28,777.0	④ 4,068.0	45,066.0	23.9	14.1	31.8	9.0	0.8	④ 2.05	4.62	4.95	0.93	54.88 - 35.00	21.9	2.1
① 12/31/97	24,856.0	②③ 1,474.0	42,132.0	12.8	5.9	14.9	3.5	0.7	②③ 0.80	3.42	3.61	0.89	38.06 - 24.63	39.2	2.8
12/31/96	13,898.0	2,101.0	23,449.0	25.6	15.1	30.7	9.0	0.7	1.73	3.55	3.62	0.85	30.13 - 23.00	15.4	3.2
12/31/95	12,670.0	1,889.0	22,002.0	24.0	14.9	30.2	8.6	0.7	1.55	3.30	2.94	0.82	29.25 - 19.81	15.8	3.3
12/31/94	11,618.5	1,648.7	26,005.3	24.0	14.2	19.7	6.3	0.7	1.37	3.01	4.68	0.78	22.19 - 18.38	14.8	3.9
12/31/93	10,690.3	③⑤ 1,435.2	24,307.5	22.3	13.4	18.9	5.9	0.8	③⑤ 1.20	2.81	5.38	0.75	23.50 - 17.09	17.0	3.7

Statistics are as originally reported. Adj. 100% stk. div., 3/98. ① Incl. ops. of Pacific Telesis Group, acq. 4/97. ② Incl. nonrecur. chrgs. $1.89 bil. ③ Bef. extraord. chrg. 12/31/97: $2.82 bil.; chrg. 12/31/93: $153.0 mill. ④ Bef. extraord. loss of $60.0 mill.; bef. acctg. chg. cr. of $15.0 mill. ⑤ Bef. acctg. chg. chrg. of $2.13 bil. ⑥ Bef. extraord. gain of $1.38 bil. & acctg. chg. cr. of $207.0 mill.; incl. nonrecur. chrgs. of $866.0 mill. ⑦ Incl. nonrecur. chrgs. of $659.0 mill. ⑧ Bef. extraord. chrg. of $18.0 mill.; incl. nonrecur. chrgs. of $1.14 mill. ⑨ Bef. acctg. chg. chrg. of $1.82 bil.

OFFICERS:
E. E. Whitacre, Jr., Chmn., C.E.O.
W. M. Daley, Pres.
S. Stephenson, Sr., Exec. V.P., C.F.O.

INVESTOR CONTACT: Larry L. Solomon, Investor Relations, (210) 351-3990

PRINCIPAL OFFICE: 175 E. Houston, P.O. Box 2933, San Antonio, TX 78205-2933

TELEPHONE NUMBER: (210) 821-4105
FAX: (210) 351-3553
WEB: www.sbc.com
NO. OF EMPLOYEES: 192,550 (approx.)
SHAREHOLDERS: 1,086,775
ANNUAL MEETING: In Apr.
INCORPORATED: DE, Oct., 1983

INSTITUTIONAL HOLDINGS:
No. of Institutions: 1,013
Shares Held: 1,626,416,249
% Held: 49.0

INDUSTRY: Telephone communications, exc. radio (SIC: 4813)

TRANSFER AGENT(S): EquiServe Trust Company, N.A., Jersey City, NJ

SCANA CORPORATION

EXCH.	SYM.	REC. PRICE	P/E RATIO	YLD.	MKT. CAP.	RANGE (52-WK.)	'02 Y/E PR.
NYSE	SCG	29.99 (2/28/03)	36.6	4.6%	$3.14 bill.	32.70 - 23.50	30.96

MEDIUM GRADE. SCG'S ELECTRIC SALES MARGINS SHOULD CONTINUE TO BENEFIT FROM CUSTOMER GROWTH, LOWER INTEREST EXPENSE AND IMPROVED RESULTS FROM ITS NON-REGULATED BUSINESSES.

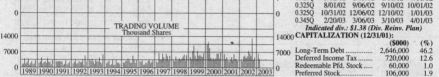

*7 YEAR PRICE SCORE 111.8   ***12 MONTH PRICE SCORE 112.5**

NYSE COMPOSITE INDEX=100

INTERIM EARNINGS (Per Share):

Qtr.	Mar.	June	Sept.	Dec.
1998	0.60	0.40	0.82	0.30
1999	0.36	0.23	0.65	0.49
2000	1.00	0.27	0.56	0.57
2001	0.75	3.67	0.61	0.12
2002	d0.68	0.38	0.74	0.38

INTERIM DIVIDENDS (Per Share):

Amt.	Decl.	Ex.	Rec.	Pay.
0.325Q	2/21/02	3/06/02	3/08/02	4/01/02
0.325Q	5/02/02	6/05/02	6/10/02	7/01/02
0.325Q	8/01/02	9/06/02	9/10/02	10/01/02
0.325Q	10/31/02	12/06/02	12/10/02	1/01/03
0.345Q	2/20/03	3/06/03	3/10/03	4/01/03

Indicated div.: $1.38 (Div. Reinv. Plan)

CAPITALIZATION (12/31/01):

	($000)	(%)
Long-Term Debt	2,646,000	46.2
Deferred Income Tax	720,000	12.6
Redeemable Pfd. Stock	60,000	1.0
Preferred Stock	106,000	1.9
Common & Surplus	2,194,000	38.3
Total	5,726,000	100.0

BUSINESS:

SCANA Corporation is a public utility holding company. Through its wholly-owned subsidiaries, SCG is engaged mainly in the generation and sale of electricity and in the purchase, sale and transportation of natural gas to wholesale and retail customers in South Carolina. Regulated utilities include South Carolina Electric & Gas Co. (SCE&G), South Carolina Fuel Co., Inc., South Carolina Generating Co., Inc. (GENCO), and South Carolina Pipeline Corp. SCANA is also engaged in other energy-related businesses, including natural gas marketing, oil and natural gas production and power plant operations maintenance. In addition, the Company has investments in telecommunications companies and provides fiber optic communications in South Carolina.

RECENT DEVELOPMENTS:

For the year ended 12/31/02, income plummeted to $88.0 million, before an accounting change charge of $230.0 million, compared with net income of $539.0 million the previous year. Results for 2002 included a non-cash writedown of $189.0 million related to SCG's telecommunication investment and a gain of $25.0 million from asset sales. Results for 2001 include a net one-time gain of $314.0 million. Total operating revenues decreased 14.4% to $2.95 billion from $3.45 billion the year before. Revenues from electric operations inched up to $1.38 billion from $1.37 billion, while revenues from regulated gas operations declined 13.5% to $878.0 million from $1.02 billion in 2001. Revenues from nonregulated gas operations dropped 34.8% to $696.0 million.

PROSPECTS:

The Company's electric sales margins should continue to benefit from strong customer growth, lower interest expense and improved results from its non-regulated businesses. Meanwhile, the Company's focus will continue to center on growing its core businesses, strengthening its balance sheet, and increasing dividends to shareholders. The Company expects earnings from ongoing operations to range from $2.50 to $2.60 per share in 2003. This guidance reflects the impact of a 5.8% increase in retail electric base rates approved by the South Carolina Public Service Commission that was placed into effect on 2/1/03.

ANNUAL FINANCIAL DATA:

FISCAL YEAR	TOT. REVS. ($mill.)	NET INC. ($mill.)	TOT. ASSETS ($mill.)	OPER. PROFIT %	NET PROFIT %	NET INC./ NET PROP. %	NET INC./ TOT. CAP. %	RET. ON EQUITY %	ACCUM. DEPR./ GROSS PROP. %	EARN. PER SH.$	TANG. BK. VAL.$	DIV. PER SH.$	DIV. PAYOUT %	PRICE RANGE	AVG. P/E RATIO	AVG. YIELD %
12/31/02	2,954.0	⑤ 88.0	7,822.0	15.3	15.6	10.2	9.4	23.4	33.2	⑤ 0.83		1.30	156.6	32.15 - 23.50	33.5	4.6
12/31/01	3,451.0	③ 539.0	7,420.0	16.1	15.6	10.4	8.9	24.1	33.4	③ 5.15	20.95	1.19	23.1	30.00 - 24.25	5.3	4.4
12/31/00	3,433.0	② 516.0	7,420.0	16.1	15.0	10.4	8.9	24.1	33.4	② 2.12	19.40	0.86	40.7	31.13 - 22.00	12.5	3.2
12/31/99	1,650.0	① 464.0	6,011.0	18.8	28.1	12.0	10.0	21.0	32.6	① 1.73	20.27	1.43	82.7	32.56 - 21.13	15.5	5.3
12/31/98	1,632.0	485.0	5,281.0	21.1	29.7	12.8	11.6	26.2	31.8	2.12	16.86	1.53	72.2	37.25 - 27.88	15.4	4.7
12/31/97	1,523.0	① 469.0	4,932.0	20.6	30.8	12.9	11.3	24.8	31.2	① 2.06	16.68	1.50	72.8	29.94 - 23.38	12.9	5.6
12/31/96	1,512.8	465.8	4,759.3	20.7	30.8	13.2	11.9	27.2	30.5	2.05	15.86	1.46	71.2	28.63 - 25.25	13.1	5.4
12/31/95	1,353.0	395.7	4,534.4	21.3	29.3	11.4	10.5	25.0	28.7	1.70	15.00	1.43	84.1	28.63 - 20.56	14.5	5.8
12/31/94	1,322.1	386.3	4,393.1	19.6	29.2	11.7	10.7	26.9	29.3	1.60	14.69	1.40	87.5	25.06 - 20.50	14.3	6.1
12/31/93	1,264.2	397.7	4,040.5	19.4	31.5	13.2	11.7	29.3	29.9	1.86	14.30	1.36	73.1	26.13 - 20.06	12.4	5.9

Statistics are as originally reported. Adj. for stk. splits: 2-for-1, 5/95 ① Incl. non-recur. gain $39.0 mill, 1999; incl. non-recur. gain $18.0 mill. ($0.16/sh.), 1997. ② Excl. non-recur. credit of $29.0 mill. ③ Incls. gains totaling $553.0 million from the sale of assets & invests. & chrg. of $62.0 mill. for impairment of invests. ④ Ref. the acq. of PSNC on 2/10/00. ⑤ Bef. acctg. chng. chrg. of $230.0 mill., incl. a non-cash writedown of $189.0 mill. & a gain of $25.0 mill.

OFFICERS:
W. B. Timmerman, Chmn., Pres., C.E.O.
K. B. Marsh, Sr. V.P., C.F.O.
H. T. Arthur II, Sr. V.P., Gen. Couns.
INVESTOR CONTACT: H. John Winn, III, Mgr.-Inv. Rel., (803) 217-9240
PRINCIPAL OFFICE: 1426 Main Street, Columbia, SC 29201

TELEPHONE NUMBER: (803) 217-9000
FAX: (803) 343-2389
WEB: www.scana.com
NO. OF EMPLOYEES: 5,369
SHAREHOLDERS: 41,677 (record)
ANNUAL MEETING: In May
INCORPORATED: SC, Oct., 1984

INSTITUTIONAL HOLDINGS:
No. of Institutions: 235
Shares Held: 42,816,747
% Held: 38.7

INDUSTRY: Electric and other services combined (SIC: 4931)

TRANSFER AGENT(S): SCANA Corporation

SCHERING-PLOUGH CORPORATION

EXCH.	SYM.	REC. PRICE	P/E RATIO	YLD.	MKT. CAP.	RANGE (52-WK.)	'02 Y/E PR.	DIV. ACH.
NYSE	SGP	18.02 (2/28/03)	12.8	3.8%	$26.40 bill.	36.25 - 16.10	22.20	17 yrs.

INVESTMENT GRADE. THE COMPANY SHOULD CONTINUE TO BENEFIT FROM NEW PRODUCT LAUNCHES AND INCREASED MARKET PENETRATION.

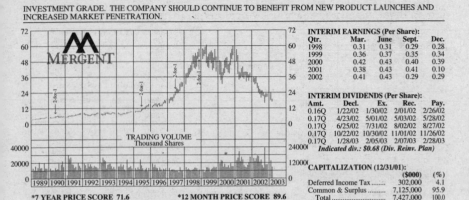

INTERIM EARNINGS (Per Share):

Qtr.	Mar.	June	Sept.	Dec.
1998	0.31	0.31	0.29	0.28
1999	0.36	0.37	0.35	0.34
2000	0.42	0.43	0.40	0.39
2001	0.38	0.43	0.41	0.10
2002	0.41	0.43	0.29	0.29

INTERIM DIVIDENDS (Per Share):

Amt.	Decl.	Ex.	Rec.	Pay.
0.16Q	1/22/02	1/30/02	2/01/02	2/26/02
0.17Q	4/23/02	5/01/02	5/03/02	5/28/02
0.17Q	6/25/02	7/31/02	8/02/02	8/27/02
0.17Q	10/22/02	10/30/02	11/01/02	11/26/02
0.17Q	1/28/03	2/05/03	2/07/03	2/28/03

Indicated div.: $0.68 (Div. Reinv. Plan)

*7 YEAR PRICE SCORE 71.6   ***12 MONTH PRICE SCORE 89.6**

*NYSE COMPOSITE INDEX=100

CAPITALIZATION (12/31/01):

	($000)	(%)
Deferred Income Tax	302,000	4.1
Common & Surplus	7,125,000	95.9
Total	7,427,000	100.0

BUSINESS:

Schering-Plough Corporation is a global company primarily engaged in the development, manufacturing and marketing of pharmaceutical and consumer products. Pharmaceutical products include prescription drugs, over-the-counter medicines, vision-care products and animal health products promoted to the medical and allied professions. Prescription products include: CELESTAMINE, CLARINEX, CLARITIN, CLARITIN-D, CLARITIN SYRUP NASONEX, POLARAMINE, PROVENTIL, and VANCERIL. The healthcare product segment consists of over-the-counter foot care products, including DR. SHOLLS, and sun care products, including COPPERTONE and BAIN DE SOLEIL. Healthcare products are sold primarily in the United States. In 2002, contributions to sales were pharmaceutical products, 85.9%; and healthcare products, 14.1%.

RECENT DEVELOPMENTS:

For the twelve months ended 12/31/02, net income climbed 7.5% to $2.09 billion compared with $1.94 million the previous year. Results for 2002 included a pre-tax gain of $80.0 million from the sale of U.S. marketing rights for SUBOXONE and SUBOXONE sublingual tablets, while results for 2001 included a one-time provision of $500.0 million for a consent decree payment. Net sales rose 4.3% to $10.18 billion from $9.76 billion in 2001. Worldwide pharmaceuticals sales grew 4.6% to $8.75 billion from $8.36 billion the prior year. However, U.S. pharmaceutical sales fell 5.9% to $4.80 billion from $5.10 billion a year earlier, due primarily to lower sales of CLARITIN, which lost its market exclusivity in December 2002.

PROSPECTS:

Looking ahead, SGP estimates full-year 2003 earnings per share in the range of $1.00 to $1.15. Meanwhile, SGP should continue to benefit from new product launches and increased market penetration. Separately, in January 2003, SGP announced that its ASMANEX inhaled asthma drug and device received marketing approval in Europe and was subsequently launched in the U.K. Separately, SGP announced that it has received marketing authorization in Europe for CAELYX® as monotherapy for metastatic breast cancer in patients who are at increased cardiac risk.

ANNUAL FINANCIAL DATA:

FISCAL YEAR	TOT. REVS. ($mill.)	NET INC. ($mill.)	TOT. ASSETS ($mill.)	OPER. PROFIT %	NET PROFIT %	RET. ON EQUITY %	RET. ON ASSETS %	CURR. RATIO	EARN. PER SH. $	CASH FL. PER SH. $	TANG. BK. VAL. $	DIV. PER SH. $	PRICE RANGE	AVG. P/E RATIO	AVG. YIELD %
p12/31/02	10,180.0	④ 2,089.0	12,174.0	25.7	19.8	27.3	16.0	1.7	④ 1.42	1.54	4.41	0.67	36.25 - 16.10	18.4	2.6
12/31/01	9,802.0	③ 1,943.0	12,174.0	25.7	19.8	27.3	16.0	1.7	③ 1.32	1.54	4.41	0.62	57.25 - 32.35	33.9	1.4
12/31/00	9,815.0	2,423.0	10,805.0	32.5	24.7	39.6	22.4	1.6	1.64	1.84	3.75	0.55	60.00 - 30.50	27.6	1.2
12/31/99	9,176.0	2,110.0	9,375.0	30.5	23.0	40.9	22.5	1.5	1.42	1.60	3.11	0.48	60.81 - 40.25	35.6	1.0
12/31/98	8,077.0	1,756.0	7,840.0	28.8	21.7	43.9	22.4	1.3	1.18	1.34	2.33	0.42	57.75 - 30.34	37.3	1.0
12/31/97	6,778.0	1,444.0	6,507.0	28.2	21.3	51.2	22.2	1.0	0.97	1.11	1.60	0.37	32.00 - 15.88	24.7	1.5
12/31/96	5,656.0	1,213.0	5,398.1	29.1	21.4	58.9	22.5	0.7	0.83	0.94	1.41	0.32	18.28 - 12.63	18.7	2.1
12/31/95	5,104.0	① 1,053.0	4,664.6	28.4	20.6	64.9	22.6	0.6	① 0.71	0.82	1.11	0.28	15.19 - 8.88	16.9	2.3
12/31/94	4,657.1	922.0	4,325.7	26.8	19.8	58.6	21.3	0.6	0.60	0.71	1.06	0.25	9.48 - 6.81	13.5	3.0
12/31/93	4,341.3	② 825.0	4,316.9	25.5	19.0	52.2	19.1	0.9	② 0.53	0.62	0.90	0.22	8.88 - 6.47	14.5	2.8

Statistics are as originally reported. Adjusted for 2-for-1 stock split, 12/98, 8/97 & 6/95. ① Bef. dis. opers. loss of $166.4 mill. ② Bef. acctg. adj. loss of $94.2 mill. ③ Incl. $500.0 mill. provision for a consent decree payment. ④ Incl. pre-tax gain of $80.0 mill.

OFFICERS:
R. Osborne, Chmn.
R. J. Kogan, Pres., C.E.O.
J. L. Wyszomierski, Exec. V.P., C.F.O.
INVESTOR CONTACT: Geraldine U. Foster, Sr. V.P., (908) 298-4000
PRINCIPAL OFFICE: 2000 Galloping Hill Road, Kenilworth, NJ 07033

TELEPHONE NUMBER: (908) 298-4000
FAX: (908) 298-7082
WEB: www.schering-plough.com
NO. OF EMPLOYEES: 29,800 (approx.)
SHAREHOLDERS: 47,900 (approx.)
ANNUAL MEETING: In Apr.
INCORPORATED: NJ, July, 1970

INSTITUTIONAL HOLDINGS:
No. of Institutions: 864
Shares Held: 1,024,724,001
% Held: 69.9
INDUSTRY: Pharmaceutical preparations (SIC: 2834)
TRANSFER AGENT(S): The Bank of New York, New York, NY

SCHLUMBERGER LIMITED

EXCH.	SYM.	REC. PRICE	P/E RATIO	YLD.	MKT. CAP.	RANGE (52-WK.)	'02 Y/E PR.
NYSE	SLB	41.61 (2/28/03)	...	1.8%	...	62.43 - 33.40	42.09

UPPER MEDIUM GRADE. THE COMPANY'S CUSTOMERS HAVE NOT INCREASED SPENDING DESPITE HIGH COMMODITY PRICES DUE TO A LACK OF GROWTH IN ENERGY DEMAND.

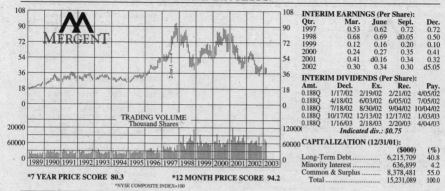

*7 YEAR PRICE SCORE 80.3   ***12 MONTH PRICE SCORE 94.2**
*NYSE COMPOSITE INDEX=100

INTERIM EARNINGS (Per Share):

Qtr.	Mar.	June	Sept.	Dec.
1997	0.53	0.62	0.72	0.72
1998	0.68	0.69	d0.05	0.50
1999	0.12	0.16	0.20	0.10
2000	0.24	0.27	0.35	0.41
2001	0.41	d0.16	0.34	0.32
2002	0.30	0.34	0.30	d5.05

INTERIM DIVIDENDS (Per Share):

Amt.	Decl.	Ex.	Rec.	Pay.
0.188Q	1/17/02	2/19/02	2/21/02	4/05/02
0.188Q	4/18/02	6/03/02	6/05/02	7/05/02
0.188Q	7/18/02	8/30/02	9/04/02	10/04/02
0.188Q	10/17/02	12/13/02	12/17/02	1/03/03
0.188Q	1/16/03	2/18/03	2/20/03	4/04/03

Indicated div.: $0.75

CAPITALIZATION (12/31/01):

	($000)	(%)
Long-Term Debt	6,215,709	40.8
Minority Interest	636,899	4.2
Common & Surplus	8,378,481	55.0
Total	15,231,089	100.0

BUSINESS:

Schlumberger Limited is a global technology services company consisting of two business segments. The Oilfield Services segment supplies services and technology to the international petroleum industry. SchlumbergerSema is an information technology services company providing consulting and systems integration services, and network and infrastructure services to the energy, oil and gas, telecommunications, finance and public sector markets.

SchlumbergerSema was formed through the combination of certain businesses of Schlumberger Test & Transactions and Resource Management Services, and the acquisition of Sema plc on 4/6/01. On 12/31/99, SLB completed the spin-off of its offshore contract drilling business, Sedco Forex, to its stockholders. As of 12/10/02, SLB owned 70.0% of WesternGeco, a seismic joint venture that was formed with Baker Hughes on 11/30/00.

RECENT DEVELOPMENTS:

For the year ended 12/31/02, SLB posted a loss from continuing operations of $2.42 billion versus income from continuing operations of $490.6 million a year earlier. Results for 2002 included charges of $3.17 billion, including a goodwill impairment charge of $2.64 billion and other nonrecurring charges totaling $587.0 million. Results for 2002 also included a gain of $87.0 million on the sale of two

drilling rigs. SLB noted that the impairment of goodwill mainly reflected the current difficulties of the telecommunications industry and the severely depressed market values of the information technology companies serving the sector. Total operating revenue declined 4.2% to $13.47 billion, primarily due to reduced oilfield activity in North America and Latin America.

PROSPECTS:

SLB's outlook appears lackluster, reflecting political uncertainty in the Middle East, the ongoing effects of the oil strike in Venezuela, and reduced oil company investment in Europe and Africa. Moreover, SLB noted that its customers have not increased spending despite high commodity prices

due to a lack of energy demand. Separately, SLB has announced an updated strategy for its SchlumbergerSema business segment that includes focusing on information technology consulting, systems integration and network and infrastructure solutions, primarily in global energy.

ANNUAL FINANCIAL DATA:

FISCAL YEAR	TOT. REVS. ($mill.)	NET INC. ($mill.)	TOT. ASSETS ($mill.)	OPER. PROFIT %	NET PROFIT %	RET. ON EQUITY %	RET. ON ASSETS %	CURR. RATIO	EARN. PER SH.$	CASH FL. PER SH.$	TANG. BK. VAL.$	DIV. PER SH.$	PRICE RANGE	AVG. P/E RATIO	AVG. YIELD %
p12/31/02	13,473.7	⑥ d2,417.5							⑥ d4.18			0.75	62.43 - 33.40	...	1.6
12/31/01	13,988.1	⑤ 522.2	22,326.5	8.1	3.7	6.2	2.3	1.2	⑤ 0.91	0.90	2.27	0.75	82.81 - 40.84	67.9	1.2
12/31/00	10,034.7	734.6	17,172.7	9.6	7.3	8.9	4.3	1.9	1.27	1.27	17.34	0.75	88.88 - 53.50	56.0	1.1
12/31/99	8,751.7	③ 329.3	15,081.2	5.4	3.8	4.3	2.2	2.5	③ 0.58	0.58	13.64	0.75	70.69 - 45.44	100.1	1.3
12/31/98	11,997.3	② 1,014.2	16,077.9	11.0	8.5	12.5	6.3	2.2	② 1.81	1.81	15.02	0.75	86.44 - 40.06	34.9	1.2
12/31/97	10,754.4	1,295.7	12,096.7	15.5	12.0	19.4	10.7	1.7	2.52	2.52	13.44	0.75	94.44 - 49.00	28.5	1.0
12/31/96	9,025.7	④ 1,184.6	10,325.1	11.2	13.1	21.1	11.5	1.5	④ 1.74	2.42	9.13	0.75	54.13 - 32.69	24.9	1.7
12/31/95	7,713.2	649.2	8,910.1	10.0	8.4	13.1	7.3	1.5	1.35	1.33	10.23	0.68	35.25 - 25.06	25.5	2.2
12/31/94	6,780.7	536.1	8,322.1	9.1	7.9	11.7	6.4	1.4	1.11	1.10	9.58	0.60	31.50 - 25.00	22.8	2.1
12/31/93	6,804.3	① 582.8	7,916.9	9.8	8.6	13.2	7.4	1.4	① 1.20	1.20	9.20	0.60	34.44 - 27.69	25.9	1.9

Statistics are as originally reported. All figures are in U.S. dollars unless otherwise noted. Adj. for 2-for-1 stk. split, 7/97. ① Bef. acctg. chg. of $248.0 mill. ② Bef. disc. oper. gain of $396.2 mill. ③ Bef. disc. oper. gain of $37.4 mill., incl. non-recurr. chrgs. $129.0 mill. ④ Incl. unusual chrg. of $333.0 mill. ⑤ Incl. net nonrecurr. items and chrgs. totaling $297.0 mill. ⑥ Incl. net nonrecurr. items and chrgs. totaling $3.08 bill.; bef. inc. fr. disc. ops. of $97.5 mill.

OFFICERS:
E. Baird, Chmn.,C.E.O.
A. Gould, Pres., C.O.O.
J. Perraud, Exec. V.P., C.F.O., C.A.O.
INVESTOR CONTACT: Christian Lang, Investor Relations, (212) 350-9432
PRINCIPAL OFFICE: 153 East 53rd Street, 57th Floor, New York, NY

TELEPHONE NUMBER: (212) 350-9400
FAX: (212) 350-8129
WEB: www.slb.com
NO. OF EMPLOYEES: 81,000 (avg.)
SHAREHOLDERS: 23,000 (approx.)
ANNUAL MEETING: In Apr.
INCORPORATED: Nov. 6, 1956, Netherlands

INSTITUTIONAL HOLDINGS:
No. of Institutions: 805
Shares Held: 436,019,777
% Held: 75.1
INDUSTRY: Crude petroleum and natural gas (SIC: 1311)
TRANSFER AGENT(S): Fleet National Bank c/o EquiServe, Providence, RI

SCHWAB (CHARLES) CORPORATION

EXCH.	SYM.	REC. PRICE	P/E RATIO	YLD.	MKT. CAP.	RANGE (52-WK.)	'02 Y/E PR.
NYSE	SCH	7.90 (2/28/03)	112.9	0.6%	$10.81 bill.	15.80 - 7.02	10.85

MEDIUM GRADE. THE COMPANY PLANS TO IMPLEMENT A SERIES OF EXPENSE REDUCTION MEASURES TARGETED TO REDUCE QUARTERLY EXPENSES BY ABOUT $40.0 MILLION.

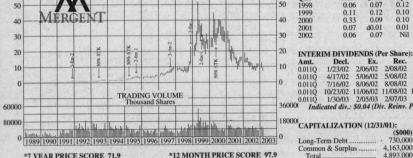

*7 YEAR PRICE SCORE 71.9   ***12 MONTH PRICE SCORE 97.9**

*NYSE COMPOSITE INDEX=100

INTERIM EARNINGS (Per Share):

Qtr.	Mar.	June	Sept.	Dec.
1998	0.06	0.07	0.12	0.09
1999	0.11	0.12	0.10	0.13
2000	0.33	0.09	0.10	0.10
2001	0.07	d0.01	0.01	d0.01
2002	0.06	0.07	Nil	d0.06

INTERIM DIVIDENDS (Per Share):

Amt.	Decl.	Ex.	Rec.	Pay.
0.011Q	1/23/02	2/06/02	2/08/02	2/22/02
0.011Q	4/17/02	5/06/02	5/08/02	5/22/02
0.011Q	7/16/02	8/06/02	8/08/02	8/22/02
0.011Q	10/23/02	11/06/02	11/08/02	11/22/02
0.011Q	1/30/03	2/05/03	2/07/03	2/21/03

Indicated div.: $0.04 (Div. Reinv. Plan)

CAPITALIZATION (12/31/01):

	($000)	(%)
Long-Term Debt	730,000	14.9
Common & Surplus	4,163,000	85.1
Total	4,893,000	100.0

BUSINESS:

The Charles Schwab Corporation and its subsidiaries provide brokerage and related investment services to 8.0 million active investor accounts, with $765.00 billion in client assets as of 12/31/02. The Company's principal subsidiary, Charles Schwab & Co. Inc., is a securities broker-dealer with 388 domestic branch offices in 48 states, as well as branches in the Commonwealth of Puerto Rico and the U.S. Virgin Islands. U.S. Trust Corp. is a wealth management firm that provides fiduciary services and private banking services through 34 offices in 12 states. Other subsidiaries include Charles Schwab Investment Management, Inc., the investment advisor for SCH's proprietary mutual funds; Schwab Capital Markets L.P., a market maker in Nasdaq and other securities providing trade execution services; and CyberTrader, Inc., an electronic trading technology and brokerage firm. Net sales for 2002 were derived as follows: asset management and administration fees, 42.6%; commissions, 29.2%; net interest revenue, 20.3%; principal transactions, 4.4%; and other, 3.5%.

RECENT DEVELOPMENTS:

For the year ended 12/31/02, income dropped 24.4% to $97.0 million, before an extraordinary gain of $12.0 million, versus $78.0 million, before an extraordinary gain of $121.0 million, in 2001. Earnings for 2002 and 2001 included non-recurring net charges of $434.0 million and $419.0 million, respectively, related to various items. Revenues slipped 5.0% to $4.14 billion. Asset management and administration fees rose 5.1% to $1.76 billion.

PROSPECTS:

On 3/13/03, the Company announced that it plans to implement a series of expense reduction measures, including a postponement of some of its planned marketing investments, reductions in discretionary expenses, further restrictions on hiring, and adjustments to certain employee benefits. These measures are targeted to reduce quarterly expenses by about $40.0 million, largely beginning in the second quarter of 2003. Separately, SCH agreed to sell its 50.0% ownership interest in Glasgow, Scotland-based Aitken Campbell to its joint venture partner, TD Waterhouse Group, Inc. The transaction should result in a tax benefit of about $10.0 million in the first quarter of 2003.

ANNUAL FINANCIAL DATA:

FISCAL YEAR	TOT. REVS. ($mill.)	NET INC. ($mill.)	TOT. ASSETS ($mill.)	OPER. PROFIT %	NET PROFIT %	RET. ON EQUITY %	RET. ON ASSETS %	CURR. RATIO	EARN. PER SH. $	CASH FL. PER SH. $	TANG. BK. VAL. $	DIV. PER SH. $	PRICE RANGE		AVG. P/E RATIO	AVG. YIELD %
p12/31/02	4,135.0	[1][3] 97.0							[1][3] 0.07			0.04	19.00 -	7.22	187.3	0.3
12/31/01	4,353.0	[4] 78.0	40,464.0	3.1	1.8	1.9	0.2	1.0	[4] 0.06	0.34	2.58	0.04	33.00 -	8.13	342.8	0.2
12/31/00	5,787.7	[3] 718.1	38,154.0	21.3	12.4	17.0	1.9	1.0	[3] 0.51	0.73	2.69	0.04	44.75 -	22.46	65.9	0.1
12/31/99	3,944.8	588.9	29,299.1	24.6	14.9	25.9	2.0	1.1	0.47	0.59	1.81	0.04	51.67 -	16.96	73.5	0.1
12/31/98	2,736.2	348.5	22,264.4	21.1	12.7	24.4	1.6	1.0	0.28	0.39	1.15	0.04	22.83 -	6.17	51.2	0.2
12/31/97	2,298.8	[2] 270.3	16,481.7	19.5	11.8	23.6	1.6	1.0	[2] 0.22	0.32	0.90	0.03	9.83 -	4.50	32.6	0.4
12/31/96	1,850.9	233.8	13,778.8	21.3	12.6	27.4	1.7	1.0	0.19	0.28	0.66	0.03	4.87 -	2.67	19.5	0.7
12/31/95	1,419.9	172.6	10,552.0	19.5	12.2	27.3	1.6	1.0	0.14	0.20	0.47	0.02	4.30 -	1.64	20.6	0.7
12/31/94	1,064.6	135.3	7,917.9	21.1	12.7	29.0	1.7	1.0	0.11	0.16	0.38	0.01	1.83 -	1.17	13.1	0.9
12/31/93	965.0	[1] 124.4	6,896.5	21.4	12.9	32.8	1.8	1.0	[1] 0.10	0.14	0.30	0.01	1.90 -	0.82	13.2	0.7

Statistics are as originally reported. Tot. revs. incl. int. inc., net of int. exp.; adj. for 3-for-2 split: 5/00, 12/98, 9/97, 3/95 & 6/93; 2-for-1 split: 7/99 & 9/95. [1] Bef. extra. gain of $12.0 mill., 2002; chrg. $6.7 mill., 1993. [2] Incl. $23.6 mill. chg. for litigation settlement. [3] Incl. a non-recurr. net chrg. rel. to various items. of $244.0 mill., 2002; $131.0 mill., 2000. [4] Bef. $121.0 mill. extraord. gain & incl. $419.0 mill. restr. & other chgs.

OFFICERS:
C. R. Schwab, Chmn.
D. S. Pottruck, Pres., C.E.O.
C. V. Dodds, Exec. V.P., C.F.O.
INVESTOR CONTACT: Richard Fowler,
Investor Relations, (415) 636-9869
PRINCIPAL OFFICE: 101 Montgomery Street,
San Francisco, CA 94104

TELEPHONE NUMBER: (415) 627-7000
FAX: (415) 627-8894
WEB: www.schwab.com
NO. OF EMPLOYEES: 19,600
SHAREHOLDERS: 12,918
ANNUAL MEETING: In May
INCORPORATED: DE, Nov., 1986

INSTITUTIONAL HOLDINGS:
No. of Institutions: 460
Shares Held: 714,605,968
% Held: 53.2
INDUSTRY: Security brokers and dealers
(SIC: 6211)
TRANSFER AGENT(S): Wells Fargo Bank
Minnesota, N.A., St. Paul, MN

SCIENTIFIC-ATLANTA INC.

EXCH.	SYM.	REC. PRICE	P/E RATIO	YLD.	MKT. CAP.	RANGE (52-WK.)	'02 Y/E PR.
NYSE	SFA	13.13 (2/28/03)	26.3	0.3%	$2.06 bill.	27.00 - 10.10	11.86

UPPER MEDIUM GRADE. THE COMPANY ACQUIRED THE ASSETS OF CHANNELOGICS, AN ATLANTA-BASED SOFTWARE COMPANY.

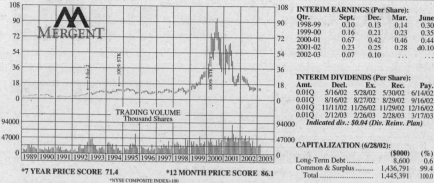

*7 YEAR PRICE SCORE 71.4   *12 MONTH PRICE SCORE 86.1
*NYSE COMPOSITE INDEX=100

INTERIM EARNINGS (Per Share):

Qtr.	Sept.	Dec.	Mar.	June
1998-99	0.10	0.13	0.14	0.30
1999-00	0.16	0.21	0.23	0.35
2000-01	0.67	0.42	0.46	0.44
2001-02	0.23	0.25	0.46	d0.10
2002-03	0.07	0.10	...	...

INTERIM DIVIDENDS (Per Share):

Amt.	Decl.	Ex.	Rec.	Pay.
0.01Q	5/16/02	5/28/02	5/30/02	6/14/02
0.01Q	8/16/02	8/27/02	8/29/02	9/16/02
0.01Q	11/11/02	11/26/02	11/29/02	12/16/02
0.01Q	2/12/03	2/26/03	2/28/03	3/17/03

Indicated div.: $0.04 (Div. Reinv. Plan)

CAPITALIZATION (6/28/02):

	($000)	(%)
Long-Term Debt	8,600	0.6
Common & Surplus	1,436,791	99.4
Total	1,445,391	100.0

BUSINESS:

Scientific-Atlanta, Inc. provides its customers with content distribution networks, broadband transmission networks, digital interactive subscriber systems and worldwide customer service and support. The Company's broadband segment includes modulators, demodulators and signal processors for video and audio receiving stations, products for distributing communications signals by coaxial cable and fiber optics from head-end systems to subscribers and ana-

log channels transmitted by cable television system operators. The products also include receivers, transmitters, distribution amplifiers, taps and passives, signal encoders and decoders, controllers, optical amplifiers, source lasers, digital video compression and transmission equipment and fiber optic distribution equipment. On 4/25/00, SFA sold its satellite network business to ViaSat, Inc.

RECENT DEVELOPMENTS:

For the quarter ended 12/27/02, net income fell 61.5% to $15.1 milion compared with $39.2 million in the equivalent period of the previous year. Earnings for 2002 included non-recurring items that resulted in a net after-tax charge of $10.2 million. Results for 2001 included an after-tax restructuring charge of $18.7 million. Sales declinced

15.8% to $352.0 million from $418.20 million in the prior-year quarter. This was partially attributed to lower sales of subscriber transmission products. Total bookings dropped 30.3% to $333.1 million from $478.3 million in the year-earlier period. At 12/27/02, backlog was $382.7 million, a decrease of 47.0% from the second quarter in 2001.

PROSPECTS:

During the quarter, the Company announced the PRISMA® G1 Cable Modem Termination System, which is expected to strengthen its data infrastructure offerings. Separately, the Company acquired the assets of ChanneLogics, an

Atlanta-based software company with products that provide management and monitoring capabilities for high speed data networks.

ANNUAL FINANCIAL DATA:

FISCAL YEAR	TOT. REVS. ($mil.)	NET INC. ($mil.)	TOT. ASSETS ($mil.)	OPER. PROFIT %	NET PROFIT %	RET. ON EQUITY %	RET. ON ASSETS %	CURR. RATIO	EARN. PER SH. $	CASH FL. PER SH. $	TANG. BK. VAL. $	DIV. PER SH. $	PRICE RANGE	AVG. P/E RATIO	AVG. YIELD %
6/28/02	1,671.1	⑥ 104.4	1,914.6	8.2	6.2	7.3	5.5	3.9	⑥ 0.66	1.04	7.61	0.04	28.18 - 10.10	29.0	0.1
6/29/01	2,512.0	⑤ 333.7	2,002.8	16.2	13.3	22.1	16.7	3.9	⑤ 1.99	2.39	8.70	0.04	65.80 - 15.75	20.5	0.1
6/30/00	1,715.4	155.8	1,779.5	11.8	9.1	12.8	8.8	3.0	0.94	1.25	7.58	0.04	94.00 - 24.41	63.0	0.1
7/02/99	1,243.5	102.3	1,062.3	6.1	8.2	13.9	9.6	3.1	0.65	0.94	4.72	0.03	33.25 - 11.06	34.1	0.1
6/26/98	1,181.4	④ 80.8	940.1	2.5	6.8	12.8	8.6	2.8	④ 0.51	0.81	3.94	0.03	13.97 - 5.88	19.5	0.3
6/27/97	1,168.2	③ 60.6	823.6	7.2	5.2	11.4	7.4	2.4	③ 0.39	0.66	3.35	0.03	12.47 - 7.13	25.1	0.3
6/28/96	1,047.9	① 7.2	763.3	3.6	0.7	1.5	0.9	2.1	① 0.05	0.29	2.97	0.03	10.19 - 6.00	179.5	0.4
6/30/95	1,146.5	63.5	785.3	7.8	5.5	13.4	8.1	2.2	0.42	0.61	3.04	0.03	12.44 - 5.69	21.8	0.3
7/01/94	811.6	35.0	640.2	8.2	4.3	8.9	5.5	2.5	0.23	0.37	2.57	0.03	11.63 - 6.22	38.8	0.3
7/02/93	730.6	② 24.7	524.2	4.1	3.4	7.0	4.7	3.1	② 0.17	0.29	2.32	0.03	9.72 - 4.44	42.9	0.4

Statistics are as originally reported. Adj. for stk. splits: 2-for-1, 10/94; 100%, 3/00. ① Bef. disc. opers. loss $13.2 mill. ($0.17/sh.) & Incl. chrg. $14.6 mill. ② Bef. acctg. change chrg. $4.17 mill ($0.13/sh.) ③ Bef. disc. opers. gain $3.4 mill. ④ Incl. non-recurr. chrg. $23.4 mill. fr. restruc. ⑤ Incl. an after-tax net gain of $49.5 mill. fr. sale of a port. of invest. and one-time chrg. of $7.1 mill. rel. to the tender of shrs. of PowerTV. ⑥ Incl. pre-tax restruct. chrg. of $28.2 mill.

OFFICERS:
J. F. McDonald, Chmn., Pres., C.E.O.
W. G. Haislip, Sr. V.P., C.F.O., Treas.
C. J. Wredberg, Sr. V.P., C.O.O.
W. E. Eason, Jr., Sr. V.P., Sec., Gen. Couns.

INVESTOR CONTACT: Thomas B. Robey, V.P., Investor Relations, (770) 903-4608

PRINCIPAL OFFICE: 5030 Sugarloaf Parkway, Lawrenceville, GA 30044

TELEPHONE NUMBER: (770) 903-5000
FAX: (770) 903-4775
WEB: www.scientificatlanta.com

NO. OF EMPLOYEES: 5,700 (approx.)

SHAREHOLDERS: 5,995 (approx.)

ANNUAL MEETING: In Nov.

INCORPORATED: GA, Oct., 1951

INSTITUTIONAL HOLDINGS:
No. of Institutions: 298
Shares Held: 113,874,647
% Held: 73.8

INDUSTRY: Radio & TV communications equipment (SIC: 3663)

TRANSFER AGENT(S): The Bank of New York, New York, NY

SCOTTS COMPANY (THE)

EXCH.	SYM.	REC. PRICE	P/E RATIO	YLD.	MKT. CAP.	RANGE (52-WK.)	'02 Y/E PR.
NYSE	SMG	50.35 (2/28/03)	16.4	...	$1.52 bill.	55.75 - 34.80	49.04

MEDIUM GRADE. FOR 2003, COMPANY-WIDE SALES ARE EXPECTED TO INCREASE BETWEEN 7.0% AND 9.0%.

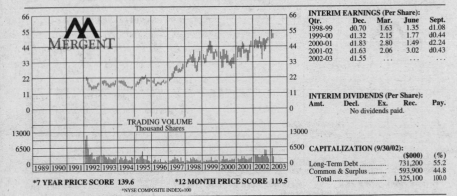

*7 YEAR PRICE SCORE 139.6   ***12 MONTH PRICE SCORE 119.5**
*NYSE COMPOSITE INDEX=100

INTERIM EARNINGS (Per Share):
Qtr.	Dec.	Mar.	June	Sept.
1998-99	d0.70	1.63	1.35	d1.08
1999-00	d1.32	2.15	1.77	d0.44
2000-01	d1.83	2.80	1.49	d2.24
2001-02	d1.63	2.06	3.02	d0.43
2002-03	d1.55	...	...	...

INTERIM DIVIDENDS (Per Share):
Amt.	Decl.	Ex.	Rec.	Pay.
		No dividends paid.		

CAPITALIZATION (9/30/02):
	($000)	(%)
Long-Term Debt	731,200	55.2
Common & Surplus	593,900	44.8
Total	1,325,100	100.0

BUSINESS:

The Scotts Company provides products for lawns, gardens, professional turf and horticulture. Products include: lawn fertilizers, lawn fertilizer combination products and lawn control products, garden tools, walk-behind and riding mowers, grass seed, lawn spreaders and lawn and garden carts; garden and indoor plant care products; potting soils and other growing media products; and pesticides (including herbicides, insecticides and fungicides). SMG operates in four principle business segments: the North American Consumer Business Group (71.3% of fiscal 2002 consolidated sales), includes products of the Consumer Lawns, Consumer Gardens, Consumer Growing Media and Consumer Ortho groups, sold in the United States and Canada; the International Consumer Group (14.1%); the Global Professional Business Group (10.3%); and LawnService (4.3%), a provider of full-service lawn care.

RECENT DEVELOPMENTS:

For the first quarter ended 12/28/02, SMG reported a net loss of $46.8 million versus a loss of $46.9 million, before an accounting change charge of $18.5 million, in the corresponding prior-year quarter. Results for 2002 and 2001 included after-tax restructuring and other one-time charges of $3.9 million and $900,000, and amortization of goodwill and other intangibles of $2.0 million and $1.8 million, respectively. Net sales advanced 12.0% to $180.8 million from $161.4 million a year earlier. On a segment basis, North American Consumer sales increased 11.3% to $84.8 million, while LawnService sales jumped 75.9% to $15.3 million. International Consumer sales rose 7.7% to $43.2 million, and Global professional sales grew 3.0% to $37.5 million.

PROSPECTS:

For 2003, company-wide sales are expected to increase between 7.0% and 9.0% and sales at SMG's core North American Consumer segment are expected to rise 6.0% to 8.0%. Meanwhile, both the International Consumer and the Global Professional segments are being adversely affected by customers moving shipments closer to consumer takeaway. Going forward, SMG anticipates lower net income, before one-time items, due to investments in its business development and North American sales groups, information services and European integration.

ANNUAL FINANCIAL DATA:

FISCAL YEAR	TOT. REVS. ($mill.)	NET INC. ($mill.)	TOT. ASSETS ($mill.)	OPER. PROFIT %	NET PROFIT %	RET. ON EQUITY %	RET. ON ASSETS %	CURR. RATIO	EARN. PER SH.$	CASH FL.PER SH.$	TANG. BK. VAL.$	PRICE RANGE	AVG. P/E RATIO
9/30/02	1,760.6	⑤ 101.0	1,901.4	13.6	5.7	17.0	5.3	1.6	⑤ 3.19	4.56	...	50.75 — 34.80	13.4
9/30/01	1,747.7	④ 15.5	1,843.0	6.7	0.9	3.1	0.8	1.6	④ 0.51	2.60	...	47.77 — 33.20	79.4
9/30/00	1,764.3	73.1	1,761.4	11.9	4.1	15.3	4.2	1.6	2.25	4.49	...	42.00 — 28.25	15.6
9/30/99	1,648.3	①③ 69.1	1,769.6	11.9	4.2	15.6	3.9	1.7	①③ 2.27	3.92	...	48.00 — 31.94	17.6
9/30/98	1,113.0	①③ 37.0	1,035.2	8.5	3.3	9.2	3.6	1.4	①③ 1.22	2.15	...	41.63 — 26.00	27.7
9/30/97	900.8	39.5	787.6	10.7	4.4	10.1	5.0	2.1	1.60	2.05	...	31.75 — 19.50	16.0
9/30/96	751.9	② d2.5	731.7	3.7	...	...	...	2.6	② d0.65	0.91	...	21.50 — 16.13	...
9/30/95	732.8	25.1	807.4	9.1	3.4	6.5	3.1	2.9	1.11	2.24	...	24.00 — 15.63	17.8
9/30/94	606.3	② 23.9	528.6	9.8	3.9	14.2	4.5	2.3	② 1.27	2.44	1.86	20.25 — 14.50	13.7
9/30/93	466.0	21.0	321.6	9.5	4.5	14.7	6.5	2.4	1.07	1.99	4.38	20.50 — 15.25	16.7

Statistics are as originally reported. ① Bef. loss on early extinguish. of debt of $992,000, 1994; $700,000, 1998; $5.9 mill., 1999; ② Incl. pre-tax unusual chrgs. of $17.7 mill. ③ Incl. pre-tax restruct. & other chrgs. of $15.4 mill., 1998; $1.4 mill., 1999. ④ Incl. restr. chrg. of $75.7 mill. ⑤ Bef. acctg. change chrg. of $18.5 mill.; incl. after-tax restr. chrg. of $6.9 mill. and after-tax gain on sale of assets of $3.6 mill.

OFFICERS:
J. Hagedorn, Chmn., Pres., C.E.O.
C. Nagel, Exec. V.P., C.F.O.
D. Aronowitz, Exec. V.P., Gen Couns., Sec.
INVESTOR CONTACT: Jim King, Dir., Investor Relations, (937) 578-5622
PRINCIPAL OFFICE: 14111 Scottslawn Rd., Marysville, OH 43041

TELEPHONE NUMBER: (937) 644-0011
FAX: (937) 578-5754
WEB: www.scotts.com
NO. OF EMPLOYEES: 3,411
SHAREHOLDERS: 9,040 (approx.)
ANNUAL MEETING: In Jan.
INCORPORATED: DE, Jan., 1992; reincorp., OH, Sept., 1994

INSTITUTIONAL HOLDINGS:
No. of Institutions: 177
Shares Held: 19,690,599
% Held: 64.8
INDUSTRY: Agricultural chemicals, nec (SIC: 2879)
TRANSFER AGENT(S): National City Bank, Cleveland, OH

SCRIPPS (E.W.) COMPANY (THE)

EXCH.	SYM.	REC. PRICE	P/E RATIO	YLD.	MKT. CAP.	RANGE (52-WK.)	'02 Y/E PR.
NYSE	SSP	80.10 (2/28/03)	34.2	0.7%	$6.34 bill.	87.50 - 65.13	76.95

UPPER MEDIUM GRADE. EARNINGS PER SHARE FROM CORE OPERATIONS FOR THE FIRST QUARTER OF 2003 ARE EXPECTED TO BE BETWEEN $0.60 AND $0.70.

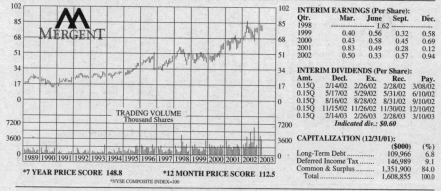

*7 YEAR PRICE SCORE 148.8   ***12 MONTH PRICE SCORE 112.5**

*NYSE COMPOSITE INDEX=100

INTERIM EARNINGS (Per Share):

Qtr.	Mar.	June	Sept.	Dec.
1998		1.62		
1999	0.40	0.56	0.32	0.58
2000	0.43	0.58	0.45	0.69
2001	0.83	0.49	0.28	0.12
2002	0.50	0.33	0.57	0.94

INTERIM DIVIDENDS (Per Share):

Amt.	Decl.	Ex.	Rec.	Pay.
0.15Q	2/14/02	2/26/02	2/28/02	3/08/02
0.15Q	5/17/02	5/29/02	5/31/02	6/10/02
0.15Q	8/16/02	8/28/02	8/31/02	9/10/02
0.15Q	11/15/02	11/26/02	11/30/02	12/10/02
0.15Q	2/14/03	2/26/03	2/28/03	3/10/03

Indicated div.: $0.60

CAPITALIZATION (12/31/01):

	($000)	(%)
Long-Term Debt	109,966	6.8
Deferred Income Tax	146,989	9.1
Common & Surplus	1,351,900	84.0
Total	1,608,855	100.0

BUSINESS:

The E.W. Scripps Company is a diversified media company operating in three business segments: newspapers, cable television networks (referred to as Scripps Networks) and broadcast television. The newspapers segment includes 21 daily newspapers in the U.S. Scripps Networks consists of four national television networks distributed by cable and satellite television, including Home & Garden Television, Food Network, Fine Living and Do It Yourself, and the Company's 12.0% interest in FOX SportsSOUTH, a regional television network. The broadcast television segment includes 10 television stations, nine of which are affiliated with national television networks. The Company also operates Scripps Howard News Service, United Media, the worldwide licensing and syndication home of PEANUTS and DILBERT, and 31 Web sites, including hgtv.com, foodtv.com, diynet.com, fineliving.com and comics.com.

RECENT DEVELOPMENTS:

For the twelve months ended 12/31/02, net income jumped 36.5% to $188.3 million compared with $138.0 million in 2001. Results reflected strong growth at Home & Garden Television and the Food Network, strong political advertising, and modest improvement in advertising revenue. Results for 2002 and 2001 included investment writedowns of $55.6 million and $3.8 million, respectively. Results for 2002 also included a gain on the sale of real estate of $2.4 million and a prior-year tax liability adjustment of $9.8 million. Results for 2001 included an employee workforce reduction charge of $10.1 million and amortization of goodwill and intangible assets of $28.1 million. Operating revenues rose 11.5% to $1.61 billion from $1.44 billion in the previous year.

PROSPECTS:

The Company anticipates advertising revenue for the first quarter of 2003 at Scripps Network to be up about 30.0% year-over-year based on advance advertising sales. Affiliate revenue is expected to increase about 20.0%, net of distribution fee amortization. In addition, earnings per share from core operations for the first quarter of 2003 are expected to be between $0.60 and $0.70. Planned capital expenditures for 2003 are up 13.0% to $100.0 million.

ANNUAL FINANCIAL DATA:

FISCAL YEAR	TOT. REVS. ($Mil.)	NET INC. ($Mil.)	TOT. ASSETS ($Mil.)	OPER. PROFIT %	NET PROFIT %	RET. ON EQUITY %	RET. ON ASSETS %	CURR. RATIO	EARN. PER SH.$	CASH FL.PER SH.$	TANG. BK. VAL.$	DIV. PER SH.$	PRICE RANGE	AVG. P/E RATIO	AVG. YIELD %
p12/31/02	1,609.3	⑤ 188.3							⑤ 2.34			0.60	87.50 - 65.13	32.6	0.8
12/31/01	1,437.1	138.0	2,643.8	19.1	9.6	10.2	5.2	0.5	1.73	2.96	1.88	0.60	71.70 - 54.70	36.5	0.9
12/31/00	1,719.4	④ 163.5	2,572.9	20.1	9.5	12.8	6.4	1.0	④ 2.06	3.44	0.87	0.56	63.25 - 42.38	25.6	1.1
12/31/99	1,571.3	146.9	2,520.2	18.9	9.4	12.6	5.8	0.8	1.86	3.18	...	0.56	53.00 - 40.50	25.1	1.2
12/31/98	1,454.6	131.2	2,345.1	19.0	9.0	12.3	5.6	0.8	1.62	2.90	...	0.54	58.50 - 38.50	29.9	1.1
12/31/97	1,242.0	① 157.7	2,280.8	20.2	12.7	15.0	6.9	0.9	① 1.93	2.88	...	0.52	48.50 - 32.25	20.9	1.3
12/31/96	1,121.9	①②③ 130.1	1,468.7	18.3	11.6	13.8	8.9	1.0	①②③ 1.62	2.48	4.38	0.13	52.38 - 32.75	26.3	0.3
12/31/95	1,030.4	② 93.6	1,655.6	17.6	9.1	7.9	5.7	1.3	② 1.17	2.00	8.69	...	40.63 - 26.75	28.8	...
12/31/94	964.6	①② 92.8	...	19.0	9.6	...	...	...	①② 1.22	1.99	...	.:.	31.00 - 23.00	22.1	...

Statistics are as originally reported. ① Incl. non-recur. gain of $44.9 mill., 1997; $21.5 mill., 1996; and $14.7 mill., 1994. ② Excl. gain fr. disc. opers. of $39.5 mill., 1996; $39.8 mill., 1995; and $29.9 mill., 1994. ③ Excl. loss of $12.3 mill. fr. cost of cable transaction. ④ Incl. net gain on divested opers. of $6.2 mill. ⑤ Incl. $55.6 mill. invest. write-down, $2.4 mill. gain fr. sale of real estate & $9.8 mill. tax liabil. adj.

OFFICERS:
W. R. Burleigh, Chmn.
K. W. Lowe, Pres., C.E.O.
J. G. NeCastro, Sr. V.P., C.F.O.

INVESTOR CONTACT: Tim Stautberg, Investor Relations, (513) 977-3826

PRINCIPAL OFFICE: 312 Walnut Street, Cincinnati, OH 45202

TELEPHONE NUMBER: (513) 977-3000
FAX: (513) 977-3721
WEB: www.scripps.com
NO. OF EMPLOYEES: 7,400 (approx.)
SHAREHOLDERS: 11,500 (approx. class A); 18 (common voting)
ANNUAL MEETING: In May
INCORPORATED: OH; 1878; reincorp., DE, 1994

INSTITUTIONAL HOLDINGS:
No. of Institutions: 181
Shares Held: 33,463,535
% Held: 41.8

INDUSTRY: Newspapers (SIC: 2711)

TRANSFER AGENT(S): The Fifth Third Bank, Cincinnati, OH

SEALED AIR CORPORATION

EXCH.	SYM.	REC. PRICE	P/E RATIO	YLD.	MKT. CAP.	RANGE (52-WK.)	'02 Y/E PR.
NYSE	SEE	36.27 (2/28/03)	...	...	$3.04 bill.	48.39 - 12.70	37.30

UPPER MEDIUM GRADE. THE COMPANY IS WELL-POSITIONED FOR GROWTH IN 2003.

*7 YEAR PRICE SCORE 77.0   *12 MONTH PRICE SCORE 123.0
*NYSE COMPOSITE INDEX=100

INTERIM EARNINGS (Per Share):

Qtr.	Mar.	June	Sept.	Dec.
1998	0.22	0.21	d0.85	0.56
1999	0.34	0.40	0.43	0.50
2000	0.45	0.44	0.46	0.56
2001	0.25	0.30	0.37	0.30
2002	0.56	0.61	0.62	d6.13

INTERIM DIVIDENDS (Per Share):

Amt.	Decl.	Ex.	Rec.	Pay.
		No dividends paid.		

CAPITALIZATION (12/31/01):

	($000)	(%)
Long-Term Debt	788,111	42.6
Deferred Income Tax	210,830	11.4
Common & Surplus	850,152	46.0
Total	1,849,093	100.0

BUSINESS:

Sealed Air Corporation is engaged in the manufacture and sale of a wide range of food, protective and specialty packaging materials and systems throughout the world. SEE's Food Packaging (61.1% of 2002 revenues) products are flexible materials and related systems marketed primarily under CRYOVAC™ for a broad range of perishable food applications, as well as rigid packaging including foam and solid trays and containers used by food processors, distributors and food service businesses, and absorbent pads used for the retail packaging of meat, fish and poultry. SEE's Protective and Specialty Packaging (38.9%) products include protective packaging products, engineered products and shrink packaging products used principally for non-food packaging. In April 1998, after W.R. Grace spun off its specialty chemical business it acquired Sealed Air Corporation. The "old" W.R. Grace, consisting of the Cryovac business, and the "old" Sealed Air then changed its name to Sealed Air Corporation.

RECENT DEVELOPMENTS:

For the year ended 12/31/02, SEE incurred a net loss of $309.1 million compared with net income of $156.7 million in 2001. Results included a gain of $1.3 million in 2002 and a loss of $32.8 million in 2001 from restructuring and other items. Results for 2002 and 2001 also included asbestos settlement and related costs of $850.1 million and $12.0 million, respectively. In addition, results for 2001 included goodwill amortization of $57.0 million. Total net sales rose 4.5% to $3.20 billion, reflecting higher sales volumes for certain products, partially offset by unfavorable changes in product price/mix. Operating income advanced 33.3% to $516.4 million.

PROSPECTS:

Looking ahead, the Company should continue to benefit from its strategic growth initiatives, including case ready, vertical pouch packaging and inflatable packaging. Also, SEE's sales force continues to find new customers and applications for its existing products. Meanwhile, the Company remains focused on continuous improvement in all of its business processes with particular emphasis on asset utilization.

ANNUAL FINANCIAL DATA:

FISCAL YEAR	TOT. REVS. ($mill.)	NET INC. ($mill.)	TOT. ASSETS ($mill.)	OPER. PROFIT %	NET PROFIT %	RET. ON EQUITY %	RET. ON ASSETS %	CURR. RATIO	EARN. PER SH.$	CASH FL.PER SH.$	TANG. BK. VAL.$	PRICE RANGE	AVG. P/E RATIO
p12/31/02	3,204.3	⑤⑥ d309.1							⑤⑥ d4.30			48.39 - 12.70	...
12/31/01	3,067.5	④ 156.7	3,907.9	12.6	5.1	18.4	4.0	1.2	④ 1.22	3.94	...	47.10 - 28.80	31.1
12/31/00	3,067.7	⑤ 225.3	4,048.1	15.3	7.3	29.9	5.6	1.3	⑤ 1.93	4.85	...	61.88 - 26.38	22.9
12/31/99	2,839.6	211.5	3,855.2	15.9	7.4	38.4	5.5	1.4	1.68	4.34	...	68.44 - 44.50	33.6
12/31/98	2,506.8	⑤ 73.0	4,039.9	10.3	2.9	16.7	1.8	1.6	⑤ 0.02	2.71	...	70.00 - 27.38	...
12/31/97	842.8	③ 79.9	498.4	16.4	9.5	31.1	16.0	1.5	③ 1.88	2.41	4.80	62.75 - 39.75	27.3
12/31/96	789.6	69.3	467.1	16.5	8.8	37.1	14.8	1.4	1.63	2.57	2.98	44.13 - 26.00	21.5
12/31/95	723.1	52.7	443.5	15.1	7.3	49.6	11.9	1.3	1.25	2.09	1.24	30.75 - 17.94	19.5
12/31/94	519.2	② 37.2	331.1	16.2	7.2	338.0	11.2	1.1	② 0.94	1.52	...	18.13 - 13.31	16.7
12/31/93	451.7	① 25.9	279.8	16.4	5.7	...	9.3	1.4	① 0.66	1.29	...	16.00 - 10.50	20.1

Statistics are as originally reported. Adj. for stk. split: 100% stk. div., 9/95. Figures are for the "old" Sealed Air Corp. prior to 3/31/98 acquisition of Sealed Air Corp. ① Excl. acctg. change chrg. of $1.5 mill. ② Bef. $5.6 mill. chrg. for early retirement of debt. ($0.04/sh.). ③ Incl. transaction exp. of $8.4 mill. rel. to pending merger with the packaging business of W.R. Grace & Co. ④ Incl. restruct. chrg. of $32.8 mill., goodwill amort. exp. of $57.0 mill., 2001, and asbestos settlement costs of $12.0 mill. ⑤ Incl. restruct. credit of $1.3 mill., 2002; $1.2 mill., 2000; chrg. of $87.5 mill., 1998. ⑥ Incl. asbestos settlement costs of $850.1 mill.

OFFICERS:
T. J. Dermot Dunphy, Chmn.
W. V. Hickey, Pres., C.E.O.
D. H. Kelsey, V.P., C.F.O.
INVESTOR CONTACT: Philip H. Cook, (201) 791-7600
PRINCIPAL OFFICE: Park 80 East, Saddle Brook, NJ 07663-5291

TELEPHONE NUMBER: (201) 791-7600
FAX: (201) 703-4205
WEB: www.sealedair.com
NO. OF EMPLOYEES: 17,700 (approx.)
SHAREHOLDERS: 9,592 (approx.)
ANNUAL MEETING: In May
INCORPORATED: DE, Feb., 1969

INSTITUTIONAL HOLDINGS:
No. of Institutions: 290
Shares Held: 80,273,337
% Held: 95.6
INDUSTRY: Unsupported plastics film & sheet (SIC: 3081)
TRANSFER AGENT(S): Mellon Investor Services LLC, South Hackensack, NJ

SEARS, ROEBUCK & CO.

EXCH.	SYM.	REC. PRICE	P/E RATIO	YLD.	MKT. CAP.	RANGE (52-WK.)	'02 Y/E PR.
NYSE	S	21.78 (2/28/03)	3.9	4.2%	...	59.90 - 19.71	23.95

MEDIUM GRADE. THE COMPANY IS TARGETING FIRST-QUARTER 2003 EARNINGS OF BETWEEN $0.50 TO $0.65 PER SHARE.

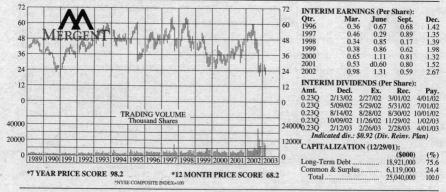

*7 YEAR PRICE SCORE 98.2   ***12 MONTH PRICE SCORE 68.2**

NYSE COMPOSITE INDEX=100

INTERIM EARNINGS (Per Share):

Qtr.	Mar.	June	Sept.	Dec.
1996	0.36	0.67	0.68	1.42
1997	0.46	0.29	0.89	1.35
1998	0.34	0.85	0.17	1.39
1999	0.38	0.86	0.62	1.98
2000	0.65	1.11	0.81	1.32
2001	0.53	d0.60	0.80	1.52
2002	0.98	1.31	0.59	2.67

INTERIM DIVIDENDS (Per Share):

Amt.	Decl.	Ex.	Rec.	Pay.
0.23Q	2/13/02	2/27/02	3/01/02	4/01/02
0.23Q	5/09/02	5/29/02	5/31/02	7/01/02
0.23Q	8/14/02	8/28/02	8/30/02	10/01/02
0.23Q	10/09/02	11/26/02	11/29/02	1/02/03
0.23Q	2/12/03	2/26/03	2/28/03	4/01/03

Indicated div.: $0.92 (Div. Reinv. Plan)

CAPITALIZATION (12/29/01):

	($000)	(%)
Long-Term Debt	18,921,000	75.6
Common & Surplus	6,119,000	24.4
Total	25,040,000	100.0

BUSINESS:

Sears, Roebuck and Co. is a retailer of apparel, home and automotive products and related services. At 12/28/02, the Company operated 872 full-line department stores and 1,305 specialty format stores, including National Tire & Battery automotive stores and neighborhood hardware stores operating under the Sears Hardware and Orchard Supply Hardware names. In addition, S provides various financial, credit and related insurance products. In 1995, the Company spun off The Allstate Corporation and divested its real estate concern, Homart Development Co. The Company sold PRODIGY, its joint venture on-line service, in May 1996. On 11/2/98, S sold its Western Auto subsidiary. The Company acquired Lands' End, Inc. in June 2002.

RECENT DEVELOPMENTS:

For the 52 weeks ended 12/28/02, the Company reported income of $1.58 billion, before a $208.0 million accounting change charge, compared with net income of $735.0 million in the corresponding period the year before. Results included pre-tax special charges and impairments of $111.0 million and $542.0 million in 2002 and 2001, respectively. Results for 2001 also included a provision of $522.0 mil- lion for previously-securitized receivables. Total revenues rose 0.9% to $41.37 billion from $40.99 billion the previous year. Merchandise sales and services revenue slipped to $35.70 billion from $35.76 billion a year earlier, while credit and financial products revenue grew 8.3% to $5.67 billion from $5.24 billion the previous year. Operating income totaled $2.08 billion versus $1.18 billion in 2001.

PROSPECTS:

Top-line growth stemming from the June 2002 acquisition of Lands' End, Inc. is being partially offset by weak sales of big-ticket items such as appliances, home electronics and lawn and garden products. Meanwhile, the Company expects reduced profits from its credit operations reflecting increased provisions for uncollectible accounts due to higher levels of bankruptcy filings by customers. The Com- pany anticipates first-quarter 2003 earnings of between $0.50 and $0.65 per share. Looking ahead, S is targeting full-year 2003 earnings growth in the low to mid-single digit percentage range.

ANNUAL FINANCIAL DATA:

FISCAL YEAR	TOT. REVS. ($mill.)	NET INC. ($mill.)	TOT. ASSETS ($mill.)	OPER. PROFIT %	NET PROFIT %	RET. ON EQUITY %	RET. ON ASSETS %	CURR. RATIO	EARN. PER SH. $	CASH FL. PER SH. $	TANG. BK. VAL.$	DIV. PER SH. $	PRICE RANGE	AVG. P/E RATIO	AVG. YIELD %
p12/28/02	41,366.0	① 1,584.0							① 4.94			0.92	59.90 - 19.71	8.1	2.3
12/29/01	41,078.0	② 735.0	44,317.0	2.9	1.8	12.0	1.7	2.3	② 2.24	2.24	19.10	0.92	48.93 - 29.90	17.6	2.3
12/30/00	40,937.0	③ 1,343.0	36,899.0	5.3	3.3	19.8	3.6	1.8	③ 3.88	3.88	20.32	0.92	43.50 - 25.25	8.9	2.7
1/01/00	41,071.0	③ 1,453.0	36,954.0	5.9	3.5	21.2	3.9	2.1	③ 3.81	3.81	18.53	0.92	53.19 - 26.69	10.5	2.3
1/02/99	41,322.0	⑥ 1,072.0	37,675.0	4.5	2.6	17.7	2.8	2.1	⑥ 2.74	2.74	15.82	0.92	65.00 - 39.06	19.0	1.8
1/03/98	41,296.0	⑤ 1,188.0	38,700.0	4.8	2.9	20.3	3.1	1.9	⑤ 2.99	2.99	15.00	0.92	65.25 - 38.75	17.4	1.8
12/28/96	38,236.0	③ 1,271.0	36,167.0	5.4	3.3	25.7	3.5	1.9	③ 3.12	3.18	12.63	0.92	53.88 - 38.25	14.8	2.0
⑦ 12/30/95	34,925.0	③ 1,025.0	33,130.0	4.9	2.9	23.4	3.1	1.8	③ 2.53	2.60	10.40	1.43	61.25 - 30.38	18.1	3.1
12/31/94	54,559.0	③ 1,244.0	91,896.0	3.1	2.3	11.5	1.4	1.9	③ 3.12	3.20	26.27	1.60	55.13 - 42.13	15.6	3.3
12/31/93	50,837.5	④ 2,409.1	90,807.8	4.1	4.7	20.7	2.7	2.0	④ 6.22	6.29	28.80	1.70	60.13 - 42.00	8.2	3.3

Statistics are as originally reported. ① Bef. $208.0 mil ($0.65/sh) acctg. change chg. & incl. $111.0 mil pre-tax non-recur. chg. ② Incl. $542.0 mil pre-tax restr. chg., 2001; $251.0 mil, 2000; $41.0 mil, 1999; & $10.0 mil, 1996. ③ Bef. cr$776 mil from discont. opers. ④ Bef. $176.1 mil gain from discont. opers. & $210.8 mil extraord. chg. ⑤ Incl. $115.0 mil ($0.28/sh) net chg., 1997; & $1.42 bil non-recur. chg., 1994. ⑥ Bef. extraord. chg. of $24.0 mil ($0.06/sh.) & incl. $228.0 mil ($0.58/sh) net chg. ⑦ Results reflect the spin-off of Allstate Corp.

OFFICERS:
A. J. Lacy, Chmn., Pres., C.E.O.
G. R. Richter, Sr. V.P., C.F.O.
A. D. Kelly, Sr. V.P., Gen. Couns.
INVESTOR CONTACT: Investor Relations, (847) 286-7385
PRINCIPAL OFFICE: 3333 Beverly Road, Hoffman Estates, IL 60179

TELEPHONE NUMBER: (847) 286-2500
FAX: (847) 875-0658
WEB: www.sears.com
NO. OF EMPLOYEES: 310,000 (approx.)
SHAREHOLDERS: 162,848
ANNUAL MEETING: In May
INCORPORATED: NY, June, 1906

INSTITUTIONAL HOLDINGS:
No. of Institutions: 423
Shares Held: 267,035,852
% Held: 84.4

INDUSTRY: Department Stores (SIC: 5311)

TRANSFER AGENT(S): First Chicago Trust Company of New York, Jersey City, NJ

SEMPRA ENERGY

EXCH.	SYM.	REC. PRICE	P/E RATIO	YLD.	MKT. CAP.	RANGE (52-WK.)	'02 Y/E PR.
NYSE	SRE	23.20 (2/28/03)	8.3	4.3%	$4.74 bill.	26.25 - 15.50	23.65

MEDIUM GRADE. THE COMPANY REAFFIRMED ITS FULL-YEAR 2003 EARNINGS OUTLOOK OF BETWEEN $2.60 AND $2.80 PER SHARE.

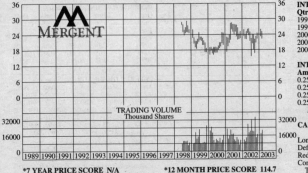

INTERIM EARNINGS (Per Share):

Qtr.	Mar.	June	Sept.	Dec.
1998	0.47	0.13	0.38	0.36
1999	0.42	0.35	0.45	0.44
2000	0.49	0.55	0.55	0.47
2001	0.88	0.66	0.46	0.52
2002	0.71	0.71	0.73	0.65

INTERIM DIVIDENDS (Per Share):

Amt.	Decl.	Ex.	Rec.	Pay.
0.25Q	6/04/02	6/19/02	6/21/02	7/15/02
0.25Q	9/10/02	9/18/02	9/20/02	10/15/02
0.25Q	12/04/02	12/19/02	12/23/02	1/15/03
0.25Q	2/18/03	3/18/03	3/20/03	4/15/03

Indicated div.: $1.00 (Div. Reinv. Plan)

CAPITALIZATION (12/31/01):

	($000)	(%)
Long-Term Debt	3,596,000	47.7
Deferred Income Tax	847,000	11.2
Redeemable Pfd. Stock	404,000	5.4
Common & Surplus	2,692,000	35.7
Total	7,539,000	100.0

TRADING VOLUME Thousand Shares

*7 YEAR PRICE SCORE N/A   *12 MONTH PRICE SCORE 114.7
*NYSE COMPOSITE INDEX=100

BUSINESS:

Sempra Energy is an energy services company whose principal utility subsidiaries are Southern California Gas Company (46.3% of 2001 revenues), a natural gas distribution utility serving customers in southern and central California, and San Diego Gas & Electric (28.8%), which provides electric and natural gas service in San Diego County and southern Orange County. Together, the two utilities serve about 21.0 million customers. Other subsidiaries (12.8%) include Sempra Energy Resources, which develops power

plants and natural gas storage, production and transportation facilities in the U.S. and Mexico; Sempra Energy International; Sempra Energy Solutions; and Sempra Energy Financial. Another subsidiary, Sempra Energy Trading (12.5%), is engaged in the wholesale trading and marketing of natural gas, power, petroleum and other commodities. Intersegment revenues (-0.4%) comprise the balance. SRE was formed with the merger of Pacific Enterprises and Enova Corp. on 6/26/98.

RECENT DEVELOPMENTS:

For the year ended 12/31/02, income was $575.0 million, before an extraordinary gain of $16.0 million, versus net income of $518.0 million a year earlier. Earnings were aided by improved results from SRE's San Diego Gas &

Electric and Southern California utilities operations. Total operating revenues decreased 22.1% to $6.02 billion from $7.73 billion a year earlier. Operating income slipped 1.0% to $987.0 million versus $997.0 million the year before.

PROSPECTS:

In February 2003, SRE signed an agreement to acquire the proposed Hackberry, Louisiana, liquefied natural gas (LNG) project from Dynegy Midstream Services L.P. for an initial payment of $20.0 million, with additional contingent payments based on the performance of the project. The Hackberry LNG project has received preliminary regulatory approval and a final decision is expected later in 2003.

Pending approval, SRE will build a LNG receiving facility capable of processing up to 1.50 billion cubic feet per day of natural gas. The total cost for developing the project is expected to be about $700.0 million. It is anticipated that the project will begin commercial operations in early 2007. Separately, SRE has reaffirmed its full-year 2003 earnings outlook of between $2.60 and $2.80 per share.

ANNUAL FINANCIAL DATA:

FISCAL YEAR	TOT. REVS. ($mill.)	NET INC. ($mill.)	TOT. ASSETS ($mill.)	OPER. PROFIT %	NET PROFIT %	NET INC./ NET PROP. %	NET INC./ TOT. CAP. %	RET. ON EQUITY %	ACCUM. DEPR./ GROSS PROP. %	EARN. PER SH.$	TANG. BK. VAL.$	DIV. PER SH.$	DIV. PAYOUT %	PRICE RANGE	AVG. P/E RATIO	AVG. YIELD %
p12/31/02	6,020.0	④ 575.0								④ 2.79		1.00	35.8	26.25 - 15.50	7.5	4.8
12/31/01	8,029.0	518.0	15,156.0	12.4	6.5	8.3	6.9	19.2	51.5	2.52	13.17	1.00	39.7	28.61 - 17.31	9.1	4.4
12/31/00	7,143.0	429.0	15,612.0	14.2	6.0	7.5	6.1	17.2	51.8	③ 2.06	12.35	1.14	55.3	24.88 - 16.19	10.0	5.6
12/31/99	5,435.0	② 394.0	11,270.0	15.0	7.2	7.3	5.9	13.2	51.5	② 1.66	12.58	1.56	94.0	26.00 - 17.13	13.0	7.2
12/31/98	5,525.0	① 294.0	10,456.0	11.8	5.3	5.4	4.5	10.1	51.6	① 1.24	12.14	0.39	31.4	29.31 - 23.75	21.4	1.5
12/31/97	5,127.0	432.0	10,751.0	18.7	8.4	7.1	6.0	14.6	49.2	1.82	12.54	...	...	... - ...	...	...
12/31/96	4,524.0	427.0	9,762.0	21.0	9.4	6.7	6.3	14.6	46.4	1.77	12.21	...	...	... - ...	...	...
12/31/95	4,201.0	401.0	....	21.8	9.5	...	...	...	...	1.67	...	...	...	... - ...	...	...

Statistics are as originally reported. ① Incl. after-tax business combination chrgs. of $85.0 mill. ② Incl. net busines combination costs of $13.0 million related to the proposed merger with KN Energy, which was terminated by both companies 6/20/99. ③ Incl. non-recurr. chrgs. of $40.0 mill. ④ Bef. extraord. gain of $16.0 mill.

OFFICERS:
S. L. Baum, Chmn., Pres., C.E.O.
N. E. Schmale, Exec. V.P., C.F.O.
J. Light, Exec. V.P., Gen. Couns.
INVESTOR CONTACT: Clem Teng, Dir., Investor Relations, (619) 696-2901
PRINCIPAL OFFICE: 101 Ash Street, San Diego, CA 92101-3017

TELEPHONE NUMBER: (619) 696-2000
FAX: (619) 696-2374
WEB: www.sempra.com
NO. OF EMPLOYEES: 11,511 (avg.)
SHAREHOLDERS: 70,000
ANNUAL MEETING: In May
INCORPORATED: CA, June, 1998

INSTITUTIONAL HOLDINGS:
No. of Institutions: 279
Shares Held: 107,633,935
% Held: 52.5
INDUSTRY: Gas and other services combined (SIC: 4932)
TRANSFER AGENT(S): First Chicago Trust Company of New York, Jersey City, NJ

SENSIENT TECHNOLOGIES CORPORATION

EXCH.	SYM.	REC. PRICE	P/E RATIO	YLD.	MKT. CAP.	RANGE (52-WK.)	'02 Y/E PR.
NYSE	SXT	20.70 (2/28/03)	12.2	2.7%	$0.98 bill.	25.84 - 17.95	22.47

UPPER MEDIUM GRADE. THE COMPANY IS TARGETING EARNINGS FROM CONTINUING OPERATIONS OF BETWEEN $1.80 AND $1.84 PER SHARE IN 2003.

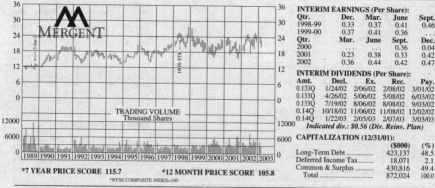

*7 YEAR PRICE SCORE 115.7　　　***12 MONTH PRICE SCORE 105.8**

*NYSE COMPOSITE INDEX=100

INTERIM EARNINGS (Per Share):

Qtr.	Dec.	Mar.	June	Sept.
1998-99	0.33	0.37	0.41	0.46
1999-00	0.37	0.41	0.36	...

Qtr.	Mar.	June	Sept.	Dec.
2000	...	...	0.36	0.04
2001	0.23	0.38	0.33	0.42
2002	0.36	0.44	0.42	0.47

INTERIM DIVIDENDS (Per Share):

Amt.	Decl.	Ex.	Rec.	Pay.
0.133Q	1/24/02	2/06/02	2/08/02	3/01/02
0.133Q	4/26/02	5/06/02	5/08/02	6/03/02
0.133Q	7/19/02	8/06/02	8/08/02	9/03/02
0.14Q	10/18/02	11/06/02	11/08/02	12/02/02
0.14Q	1/22/03	2/05/03	2/07/03	3/03/03

Indicated div.: $0.56 (Div. Reinv. Plan)

CAPITALIZATION (12/31/01):

	($000)	(%)
Long-Term Debt	423,137	48.5
Deferred Income Tax	18,071	2.1
Common & Surplus	430,816	49.4
Total	872,024	100.0

BUSINESS:

Sensient Technologies Corporation (formerly Universal Foods Corporation) is an international manufacturer and marketer of value-added food products and ingredients. The Company's major customers are food processors and the food service industry. SXT's Flavors and Fragrances segment (62.3% of 2002 revenue, 51.4% of operating profit) manufactures flavors, flavor enhancers and dehydrated vegetables for the food, beverage and dairy industries. The Color segment (37.7%, 48.6%) produces synthetic color products used in food, beverages, cosmetics, pharmaceuticals, specialty inks and a variety of other applications. The Company also develops and markets products in the Pacific Rim that appeal to regional preferences. In August 1994, SXT sold its frozen foods business to Conagra, Inc.

RECENT DEVELOPMENTS:

For the twelve months ended 12/31/02, net earnings totaled $80.7 million, up 24.2% versus earnings from continuing operations of $65.0 million in the corresponding prior-year period. Revenue climbed 15.0% to $939.9 million from $816.9 million the year before. Flavors and Fragrances segment revenue grew 8.8% to $572.2 million from $525.7 million the previous year. Revenue for the Color segment advanced 25.5% to $346.5 million from $276.0 million a year earlier. Operating income was $146.5 million, up 20.6% compared with $121.5 million in 2001.

PROSPECTS:

The Company is targeting first-quarter 2003 earnings of approximately $0.40 per share. Looking ahead, SXT anticipates full-year 2003 earnings from continuing operations of between $1.80 and $1.84 per share. Strong revenue growth in the Color segment is being fueled by recent acquisitions, along with increased sales of the Company's natural color, pharmaceutical and cosmetic products. Meanwhile, results in the Flavors and Fragrances segment are benefiting from SXT's traditional flavor products, with especially strong demand for beverage flavors.

ANNUAL FINANCIAL DATA:

FISCAL YEAR	TOT. REVS. ($mill.)	NET INC. ($mill.)	TOT. ASSETS ($mill.)	OPER. PROFIT %	NET PROFIT %	RET. ON EQUITY %	RET. ON ASSETS %	CURR. RATIO	EARN. PER SH.$	CASH FL. PER SH.$	TANG. BK. VAL.$	DIV. PER SH.$	PRICE RANGE	AVG. P/E RATIO	AVG. YIELD %
p12/31/02	939.9	80.7							1.69			0.54	25.84 - 17.95	13.0	2.5
12/31/01	816.9	⑧65.0	1,104.8	14.9	8.0	15.1	5.9	2.2	⑧1.36	2.32	2.65	0.53	23.99 - 15.55	14.5	2.7
④12/31/00	809.2	⑦56.3	1,164.2	13.9	7.0	13.5	4.8	1.9	⑦1.15	2.07	2.54	0.53	23.19 - 16.00	17.0	2.7
9/30/99	920.2	80.1	1,142.7	15.8	8.7	18.6	7.0	1.7	1.57	2.53	3.04	0.53	27.38 - 18.25	14.5	2.3
9/30/98	856.8	72.6	991.2	15.0	8.5	17.9	7.3	1.7	1.40	2.25	3.69	0.53	27.75 - 19.44	16.9	2.2
9/30/97	825.7	⑤64.7	887.7	13.0	7.8	17.0	7.3	1.9	⑤1.27	2.00	3.89	0.52	21.47 - 16.00	14.8	2.8
9/30/96	806.4	④44.2	780.5	10.4	5.5	12.6	5.7	2.0	④0.86	1.51	4.12	0.51	20.19 - 14.00	19.9	3.0
9/30/95	793.0	③66.1	776.9	16.4	8.3	18.3	8.5	1.8	③1.27	1.93	4.08	0.48	20.63 - 13.63	13.5	2.8
9/30/94	929.9	①50.9	763.7	10.4	5.5	15.6	6.7	1.7	①0.98	1.67	3.45	0.47	17.19 - 13.06	15.5	3.1
9/30/93	891.6	②56.6	730.0	11.9	6.3	18.6	7.8	1.8	②1.08	1.74	3.75	0.45	18.63 - 15.19	15.7	2.6

Statistics are as originally reported. Adj. for 100% stk. div., 5/98. ① Incl. non-recur. chg. $4.6 mil, 1997; $16.7 mil chg., 1996; & $12.1 mil chg., 1994. ② Bef. $23.6 mil chg. for acctg. adj. ③ Incl. non-recur. chg. $49.6 mil gain & $22.8 mil chg. ④ For the 12 mos. ended 12/31/00, refl. a fiscal year-end change to 12/31 fr. 9/30. ⑤ Bef. $3.3 mil gain fr. discont. opers. & $2.4 mil acctg. change chg.; Incls. a $19.0 mil pre-tax special chg. rel. to mfg. facility consol. in the U.S. and Europe. ⑧ Bef. $8.6 mil ($0.18/sh) gain fr. discont. opers.

OFFICERS:
K. P. Manning, Chmn., Pres., C.E.O.
R. F. Hobbs, V.P., C.F.O., Treas.
J. L. Hammond, V.P., Sec., Gen. Couns.

INVESTOR CONTACT: Dick Hobbs, (414) 347-3836

PRINCIPAL OFFICE: 777 East Wisconsin Avenue, Milwaukee, WI 53202-5304

TELEPHONE NUMBER: (414) 271-6755
FAX: (414) 347-4794
WEB: www.sensient-tech.com

NO. OF EMPLOYEES: 3,454 (avg.)

SHAREHOLDERS: 4,593 (record)

ANNUAL MEETING: In Mar.

INCORPORATED: WI, Dec., 1882

SEQUA CORPORATION

EXCH.	SYM.	REC. PRICE	P/E RATIO	YLD.	MKT. CAP.	RANGE (52-WK.)	'02 Y/E PR.
NYSE	SQAA	35.25 (2/28/03)	52.6	...	$366.2 mill.	65.99 - 32.39	39.11

LOWER MEDIUM GRADE. DEPENDING ON CHANGES IN THE CONDITION OF THE COMMERCIAL AIRLINE INDUSTRY, CHROMALLOY MAY IMPLEMENT FURTHER RESTRUCTURING ACTIONS DURING 2003.

*7 YEAR PRICE SCORE 101.4 *12 MONTH PRICE SCORE 78.5

*NYSE COMPOSITE INDEX=100

INTERIM EARNINGS (Per Share):

Qtr.	Mar.	June	Sept.	Dec.
1999	0.53	1.00	0.57	0.38
2000	0.36	0.47	0.44	0.85
2001	d0.08	3.36	d0.32	d2.51
2002	d0.35	0.30	0.16	0.56

INTERIM DIVIDENDS (Per Share):

Amt.	Decl.	Ex.	Rec.	Pay.
		No dividends paid.		

CAPITALIZATION (12/31/01):

	($000)	(%)
Long-Term Debt	707,986	51.4
Deferred Income Tax	24,277	1.8
Preferred Stock	797	0.1
Common & Surplus	643,665	46.8
Total	1,376,725	100.0

BUSINESS:

Sequa Corporation has operations in the following segments: Aerospace (40.0% of 2002 sales) consists of Chromalloy Gas Turbine, which repairs and manufactures components for jet aircraft engines; Propulsion (18.1%) consists of Atlantic Research Corporation, a supplier of solid rocket fuel; Metal Coatings (13.9%) consists of Precoat Metals, which is engaged in the application of protective and decorative coatings to continuous steel and aluminum coils; The Specialty Chemicals group (9.5%) consists of Warwick International, which produces detergent additives; Other Products (18.5%) include group professional consulting services, automotive products, food cans and men's apparel.

RECENT DEVELOPMENTS:

For the year ended 12/31/02, the Company reported income from continuing operations of $9.2 million, before an accounting charge of $114.8 million, compared with net income of $8.0 million the year before. Earnings for 2002 excluded loss from discontinued operations of $11.0 million. Total sales slid 3.8% to $1.69 billion, reflecting a decrease in sales at the Company's largest business unit, Chromalloy Gas Turbine, and at MEGTEC Systems, the Company's equipment supplier. Sales in the Aerospace segment declined 10.3% to $675.2 million. Metal Coating segment sales slipped 2.6% to $234.8 million, while other products sales decreased 5.9% to $311.6 million. Conversely, sales in the Propulsion segment grew 6.4% to $306.1 million, while Specialty Chemicals segment sales improved 11.9% to $160.8 million. Operating income jumped to $61.2 million from $25.9 million a year earlier.

PROSPECTS:

Results from Chromalloy Gas Turbine are not expected to return to its pre-September 11 performance level in 2003. Moreover, depending on changes in the condition of the commercial airline industry, Chromalloy may implement further restructuring actions during 2003. Meanwhile, operating results in the Propulsion segment continue to benefit from productivity gains, partially due to lower operating expenses. Also, propulsion sales continue to increase under tactical weapons programs and the initiation of development work on contracts for air breathing rocket systems.

ANNUAL FINANCIAL DATA:

FISCAL YEAR	TOT. REVS. ($mill.)	NET INC. ($mill.)	TOT. ASSETS ($mill.)	OPER. PROFIT %	NET PROFIT %	RET. ON EQUITY %	RET. ON ASSETS %	CURR. RATIO	EARN. PER SH.$	CASH FL. PER SH.$	TANG. BK. VAL.$	DIV. PER SH.$	PRICE RANGE	AVG. P/E RATIO	AVG. YIELD %
p12/31/02	1,688.5	⑥ 9.2							⑥ 0.68			...	65.99 - 36.30	75.2	...
12/31/01	1,755.8	⑤ 8.0	1,835.8	1.5	0.5	1.2	0.4	2.4	⑤ 0.58	10.07	33.25	...	54.22 - 33.88	75.9	...
12/31/00	1,773.1	④ 24.0	1,731.1	5.8	1.4	3.6	1.4	2.1	④ 2.12	10.66	35.02	...	54.06 - 30.25	19.9	...
12/31/99	1,699.5	① 27.8	1,671.7	5.6	1.6	4.2	1.7	2.3	① 2.48	10.89	32.14	...	72.75 - 44.00	23.5	...
12/31/98	1,802.4	③ 63.9	1,624.1	5.9	3.5	9.6	3.9	2.1	③ 5.87	13.86	32.69	...	75.88 - 45.75	10.4	...
12/31/97	1,595.1	② 19.6	1,591.7	5.3	1.2	3.2	1.2	1.9	② 1.66	10.22	30.15	...	67.94 - 36.25	31.4	...
12/31/96	1,459.0	① 9.6	1,548.2	4.5	0.7	1.7	0.6	2.0	① 0.65	9.92	26.35	...	46.50 - 29.50	58.5	...
12/31/95	1,414.1	8.8	1,622.0	4.8	0.6	1.5	0.5	1.9	0.57	10.35	25.68	...	32.13 - 21.88	47.4	...
12/31/94	1,419.6	① d24.7	1,648.2	2.8	...	...	...	1.9	① d2.87	7.79	24.97	...	39.75 - 17.63	...	...
12/31/93	1,697.0	d55.5	1,803.5	0.9	...	...	...	1.8	d6.07	5.33	26.91	0.30	34.50 - 17.88	...	1.1

Statistics are as originally reported. ① Bef. an extraord. loss of $5.7 mill., 1999; $369,000, 1996; $1.1 mill., 1994. ② Incl. restruct. chrgs. of $7.2 mill. & a $6.5 mill. gain from the sale of Kollsman opers. ③ Incl. a pre-tax gain of $56.5 mill. fr. the sale of bus. ④ Incl. a prov. of $3.2 mill. to cover the cost of an early retirement program. ⑤ Incl. a tax settlement of $36.0 mill. ⑥ Bef. acctg. chrg. of $114.8 mill. & loss from disc. opers. of $11.0 mill.

OFFICERS:
N. E. Alexander, Chmn., C.E.O.
J. J. Quicke, Pres., C.O.O.

INVESTOR CONTACT: Linda G. Kyriakou, V.P. Corp. Comm., (212) 986-5500

PRINCIPAL OFFICE: 200 Park Avenue, New York, NY 10166

TELEPHONE NUMBER: (212) 986-5500
FAX: (212) 370-1969
WEB: www.sequa.com
NO. OF EMPLOYEES: 10,700 (approx.)
SHAREHOLDERS: 2,075 (approx. class A common); 430 (approx. class B common)
ANNUAL MEETING: In May
INCORPORATED: DE, Mar., 1929

INSTITUTIONAL HOLDINGS:
No. of Institutions: 74
Shares Held: 3,423,127
% Held: 32.8
INDUSTRY: Aircraft engines and engine parts (SIC: 3724)
TRANSFER AGENT(S): Bank of New York, New York, NY

SERVICEMASTER COMPANY (THE)

EXCH.	SYM.	REC. PRICE	P/E RATIO	YLD.	MKT. CAP.	RANGE (52-WK.)	'02 Y/E PR.	DIV. ACH.
NYSE	SVM	9.77 (2/28/03)	...	4.3%	$2.94 bill.	15.50 - 8.89	11.10	32 yrs.

MEDIUM GRADE. FOR 2003, THE COMPANY EXPECTS TO ACHIEVE MID SINGLE-DIGIT EARNINGS GROWTH.

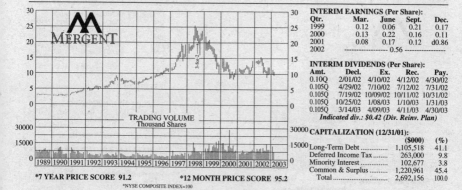

*7 YEAR PRICE SCORE 91.2   ***12 MONTH PRICE SCORE 95.2**
*NYSE COMPOSITE INDEX=100

INTERIM EARNINGS (Per Share):

Qtr.	Mar.	June	Sept.	Dec.
1999	0.12	0.06	0.21	0.17
2000	0.13	0.22	0.16	0.11
2001	0.08	0.17	0.12	d0.86
2002	---------------- 0.56 ----------------			

INTERIM DIVIDENDS (Per Share):

Amt.	Decl.	Ex.	Rec.	Pay.
0.10Q	2/01/02	4/10/02	4/12/02	4/30/02
0.105Q	4/29/02	7/10/02	7/12/02	7/31/02
0.105Q	7/19/02	10/09/02	10/11/02	10/31/02
0.105Q	10/25/02	1/08/03	1/10/03	1/31/03
0.105Q	3/14/03	4/09/03	4/11/03	4/30/03

Indicated div.: $0.42 (Div. Reinv. Plan)

CAPITALIZATION (12/31/01):

	($000)	(%)
Long-Term Debt	1,105,518	41.1
Deferred Income Tax	263,000	9.8
Minority Interest	102,677	3.8
Common & Surplus	1,220,961	45.4
Total	2,692,156	100.0

BUSINESS:

The ServiceMaster Company (formerly ServiceMaster L.P.) provides services to residential and commercial customers worldwide. The TruGreen segment (38.3% of 2002 revenue) includes lawn care operations performed under the TruGreen ChemLawn and landscaping services provided under the TruGreen LandCare brands. The Terminix segment (25.8%) includes domestic termite and pest control services. The American Residential Services and American Mechanical Services (ARS/AMS) segment (20.0%) pro-

vides heating, ventilation, air conditioning and plumbing services under the ARS, AMS and Rescue Rooter brands. The American Home Shield segment (11.7%) offers warranty contracts on home systems and appliances and home inspection services through AmeriSpec. The Other Operations segment (4.2%) includes ServiceMaster Clean, Merry Maids and Furniture Medic franchise operations. On 11/30/01, SVM sold its management services business to ARAMARK Corp. for about $800.0 million.

RECENT DEVELOPMENTS:

For the year ended 12/31/02, SVM reported income from continuing operations of $170.0 million versus a loss from continuing operations of $168.0 million in the prior year. Results for 2002 and 2001 included intangible amortization of $7.4 million and $70.8 million, and a credit of $2.0 million and a charge of $393.9 million for asset impairments, respectively. Earnings for 2002 and 2001 excluded a

net loss of $3.9 million and a net gain of $288.7 million from discontinued operations, and extraordinary losses of $9.2 million and $3.4 million, respectively. Total revenues increased 0.9% to $3.59 billion. Notably, Terminix segment revenues climbed 9.3% to $924.4 million, and ARS/AMS segment revenue fell 12.3% to $718.9 million. Comparisons were made with restated prior-year results.

PROSPECTS:

For 2003, SVM expects to achieve mid single-digit earnings growth. Throughout 2003, SVM will maintain a strong focus on top-line sales, increased retention, controlling expenses and continued strong cash flow. Meanwhile, the

TruGreen, Terminix and American Home Shield segments should continue to benefit from new marketing strategies, higher customer renewals and strong increases in sales through the real estate and direct-to-consumer channels.

ANNUAL FINANCIAL DATA:

FISCAL YEAR	TOT. REVS. ($mill.)	NET INC. ($mill.)	TOT. ASSETS ($mill.)	OPER. PROFIT %	NET PROFIT %	RET. ON EQUITY %	RET. ON ASSETS %	CURR. RATIO	EARN. PER SH.$	CASH FL. PER SH.$	DIV. PER SH.$	PRICE RANGE		AVG. P/E RATIO	AVG. YIELD %
p12/31/02	3,587.3	② 170.0							⑥ 0.56		0.41	15.50 -	8.89	21.8	3.3
⑤ 12/31/01	3,601.4	④ d171.8	3,674.7	...	...	...	...	1.4	④ d0.54	d0.14	0.40	14.20 -	9.84	...	3.3
12/31/00	5,970.6	② 185.0	3,967.7	7.0	3.1	15.9	4.7	1.2	② 0.61	1.12	0.38	14.94 -	8.25	19.0	3.3
12/31/99	5,703.5	③ 173.6	3,870.2	6.7	3.0	14.4	4.5	1.1	③ 0.55	0.99	0.36	22.00 -	10.13	29.2	2.2
12/31/98	4,724.1	318.8	2,914.9	8.4	6.7	33.3	10.9	0.9	0.64	1.42	0.33	25.50 -	16.00	32.4	1.6
12/31/97	3,961.5	264.1	2,475.2	8.7	6.7	50.4	10.7	1.1	0.55	1.19	0.31	19.67 -	10.95	28.0	2.0
12/31/96	3,458.3	245.1	1,846.8	8.5	7.1	30.8	13.3	1.2	0.76	0.99	0.29	11.83 -	8.63	13.5	2.9
12/31/95	3,202.5	172.0	1,649.9	7.9	5.4	23.0	10.4	1.1	0.65	0.88	0.28	9.00 -	6.37	11.9	3.6
12/31/94	2,985.2	139.9	1,230.8	7.2	4.7	45.5	11.4	1.1	0.33	0.76	0.27	8.41 -	6.37	22.4	3.7
12/31/93	2,758.9	① 145.9	1,122.5	6.3	5.3	50.5	13.0	1.2	① 0.56	0.76	0.26	9.19 -	5.24	12.8	3.6

Statistics are as originally reported. Adj. for stk. splits: 3-for-2, 8/98, 6/97, 6/96. On 12/26/97, SVM converted from a publicly traded partnership to a taxable corporation. Prior to that date, net income was not subject to federal and state taxes. ① Incl. non-recurr. credit $30.2 mill. ② Bef. acctg. change chrg. $11.2 mill. ③ Incl. non-recurr. chrg. $85.5 mill. ④ Bef. income from disc. oper. $330.2 mill. and extr. chrg. $3.4 mill.; incl. impair. and oth. chrg. $396.7 mill. ⑤ Refl. the sale of management services business, certain European pest control subsidiaries and TruGreen LandCare Construction. ⑥ Bef. net disc. oper. loss $3.9 mill. and extr. loss $9.2 mill.; incl. impair. credit of $2.0 mill.

OFFICERS:
J. P. Ward, Chmn., C.E.O.
E. J. Mrozek, Pres., C.O.O.
INVESTOR CONTACT: Bruce J. Byots, V.P.,
Investor Relations (630) 663-2906
PRINCIPAL OFFICE: 2300 Warrenville Rd.,
Downers Grove, IL 60515-1700

TELEPHONE NUMBER: (630) 271-1300
FAX: (630) 271-2710
WEB: www.servicemaster.com
NO. OF EMPLOYEES: 37,000 (approx.)
SHAREHOLDERS: 50,000 (approx.)
ANNUAL MEETING: In May
INCORPORATED: DE, Oct., 1986

INSTITUTIONAL HOLDINGS:
No. of Institutions: 245
Shares Held: 152,279,068
% Held: 50.5
INDUSTRY: Management svcs. (SIC: 8741)
TRANSFER AGENT(S): Computershare Investor Services, Chicago, IL

7-ELEVEN, INC.

EXCH.	SYM.	REC. PRICE	P/E RATIO	YLD.	MKT. CAP.	RANGE (52-WK.)	'02 Y/E PR.
NYSE	SE	7.03 (2/28/03)	17.6	…	$0.74 bill.	11.15 - 6.65	7.50

MEDIUM GRADE. THE COMPANY IS PROJECTING FULL-YEAR 2003 EARNINGS OF BETWEEN $0.70 AND $0.75 PER SHARE.

*7 YEAR PRICE SCORE 73.5   *12 MONTH PRICE SCORE 100.6
*NYSE COMPOSITE INDEX=100

INTERIM EARNINGS (Per Share):

Qtr.	Mar.	June	Sept.	Dec.
1996	0.10	0.35	0.40	0.20
1997	0.05	0.30	0.35	0.05
1998	d0.15	0.30	0.35	0.05
1999	0.05	0.30	0.40	0.15
2000	0.16	0.32	0.35	0.12
2001	0.02	0.28	0.35	0.16
2002	d0.05	0.30	0.25	d0.10

INTERIM DIVIDENDS (Per Share):

Amt.	Decl.	Ex.	Rec.	Pay.
	No dividends paid.			

CAPITALIZATION (12/31/01):

	($000)	(%)
Long-Term Debt	1,663,907	91.6
Common & Surplus	152,475	8.4
Total	1,816,382	100.0

BUSINESS:

7-Eleven, Inc. (formerly The Southland Corporation) is a major specialty retailer, operating more than 24,000 Company-owned, franchised and licensed convenience stores, principally under the name 7-Eleven. As of 12/31/02, the Company operated or franchised 5,823 convenience stores in the U.S. and Canada. Another 19,000 7-Eleven stores are operated by area licensees and affiliates in 17 other countries. IYG Holding Company, a wholly-owned subsidiary of Ito-Yokado Co., Ltd. and Seven-Eleven Japan Co., Ltd., has had a majority interest in the Company since 1991. Seven-Eleven Japan operates about 9,000 7-Eleven stores under an area license agreement.

RECENT DEVELOPMENTS:

For the twelve months ended 12/31/02, earnings from continuing operations totaled $52.5 million, before a $28.1 million accounting change charge, compared with earnings from continuing operations of $100.6 million, before a $9.8 million accounting change charge, a year earlier. Total revenues rose 4.9% to $10.21 billion from $9.73 billion the prior year. Merchandise sales grew 5.4% to $7.28 billion from $6.91 billion the year before, while gasoline sales increased 4.3% to $2.83 billion from $2.71 billion the previous year. U.S. same-store merchandise sales were up 3.3% year over year.

PROSPECTS:

The Company is projecting full-year 2003 earnings of between $0.70 and $0.75 per share, along with a year-over-year same-store sales increase in the range of 4.0% to 5.0%. Meanwhile, SE expects capital expenditures ranging from $335.0 million to $365.0 million in 2003. SE plans to open about 100 new stores in the U.S. and Canada during the year. SE also plans to expand its selection of fresh foods in 2003. The Company anticipates completing the installation of its Vcom™ kiosks, which provide check-cashing services, money order transactions and ATM services, into 1,000 stores throughout the U.S. by the end of the second quarter of 2003.

ANNUAL FINANCIAL DATA:

FISCAL YEAR	TOT. REVS. ($mil.)	NET INC. ($mil.)	TOT. ASSETS ($mil.)	OPER. PROFIT %	NET PROFIT %	RET. ON EQUITY %	RET. ON ASSETS %	CURR. RATIO	EARN. PER SH. $	CASH FL. PER SH. $	TANG. BK. VAL. $	PRICE RANGE	AVG. P/E RATIO
p12/31/02	10,212.8	④ 52.5							④ 0.48			12.20 - 6.65	19.6
12/31/01	9,894.1	③ 93.6	2,902.8	2.2	0.9	61.4	3.2	0.8	③ 0.83	2.86	1.45	14.00 - 8.25	13.4
12/31/00	9,451.0	① 106.5	2,742.3	2.5	1.1	129.7	3.9	0.7	① 0.97	2.85	0.78	21.25 - 8.00	15.1
12/31/99	8,349.5	① 78.8	2,685.7	2.7	0.9	…	2.9	0.6	① 0.85	2.76	…	13.75 - 7.97	12.8
12/31/98	7,349.8	① 50.7	2,415.8	2.4	0.7	…	2.1	0.7	① 0.60	2.41	…	15.16 - 7.82	19.1
12/31/97	7,060.6	70.0	2,090.1	2.9	1.0	…	3.4	0.5	0.80	2.76	…	18.44 - 8.60	16.9
12/31/96	6,955.3	89.5	2,039.1	3.2	1.3	…	4.4	0.5	1.00	2.85	…	24.69 - 12.19	18.4
12/31/95	6,816.8	① 167.6	2,081.1	2.7	2.5	…	8.1	0.5	① 2.00	4.01	…	23.60 - 14.38	9.5
12/31/94	6,759.8	92.0	2,000.6	2.7	1.4	…	4.6	0.4	1.10	3.11	…	33.75 - 19.07	24.0
12/31/93	6,814.2	①② d11.3	1,998.7	1.3	…	…	…	0.3	①② d0.15	1.75	…	38.44 - 14.85	…

Statistics are as originally reported. Adj. for stk. split: 1-for-5, 5/1/00. ① Bef. extraord. credit $1.8 mill., 2000; $4.3 mill., 1999; $23.3 mill., 1998; $103.2 mill., 1995; $99.0 mill., 1993. ② Bef. acctg. change chrg. $16.5 mill. ③ Bef. $9.8 mill. ($0.08/sh) acctg. chg. and incl. $9.3 mill. after-tax gain related to SFAS No. 133 and $3.2 mill. after-tax store closing chg. ④ Bef. $28.1 mil ($0.25/sh) acctg. chg. and $11.6 mil ($0.10/sh) loss fr. discont. opers.

OFFICERS:
M. Ito, Chmn.
J. W. Keyes, Pres., C.E.O.
E. W. Moneypenny, Sr. V.P., C.F.O.

INVESTOR CONTACT: Carole Davidson, Investor Relations Manager, (214) 828-7021

PRINCIPAL OFFICE: 2711 North Haskell Ave., Dallas, TX 75204-2906

TELEPHONE NUMBER: (214) 828-7011
FAX: (214) 841-6799
WEB: www.7-eleven.com

NO. OF EMPLOYEES: 33,313 (avg.)

SHAREHOLDERS: 1,973 (record)

ANNUAL MEETING: In Apr.

INCORPORATED: DE, 1934; reincorp., TX, Nov., 1961

INSTITUTIONAL HOLDINGS:
No. of Institutions: 63
Shares Held: 8,715,539
% Held: 8.3

INDUSTRY: Grocery stores (SIC: 5411)

TRANSFER AGENT(S): Computershare Investor Services, Chicago, IL

SHAW GROUP INC. (THE)

EXCH.	SYM.	REC. PRICE	P/E RATIO	YLD.	MKT. CAP.	RANGE (52-WK.)	'02 Y/E PR.
NYSE	SGR	9.59 (2/28/03)	4.3	...	$391.7 mill.	36.09 - 8.90	16.45

UPPER MEDIUM GRADE. THE COMPANY IS ENCOURAGED BY STRONG BIDDING ACTIVITY AND STEADY BOOK-INGS OF NEW WORK.

MERGENT

TRADING VOLUME
Thousand Shares

1989 1990 1991 1992 1993 1994 1995 1996 1997 1998 1999 2000 2001 2002 2003

*7 YEAR PRICE SCORE 123.2   ***12 MONTH PRICE SCORE 73.0**

*NYSE COMPOSITE INDEX=100

INTERIM EARNINGS (Per Share):

Qtr.	Nov.	Feb.	May	Aug.
1998-99	0.12	0.18	0.22	0.22
1999-00	0.21	0.22	0.23	0.33
2000-01	0.31	0.28	0.42	0.45
2001-02	0.45	0.51	0.61	0.70
2002-03	0.42	...	...	...

INTERIM DIVIDENDS (Per Share):

Amt.	Decl.	Ex.	Rec.	Pay.
		No dividends paid.		

CAPITALIZATION (8/31/02):

	($000)	(%)
Long-Term Debt	521,190	42.4
Capital Lease Obligations..	957	0.1
Deferred Income Tax	15,452	1.3
Common & Surplus	692,257	56.3
Total	1,229,856	100.0

BUSINESS:

Shaw Group Inc. (The) is a vertically-integrated provider of comprehensive engineering, procurement, pipe fabrication, construction and maintenance services. The Company operates primarily in the United States, the Far East/Pacific Rim, Europe, South America and the Middle East for customers in the power generation, process (including petrochemical, chemical and refining) and other industries and the environmental and infrastructure sector. SGR offers comprehensive design and engineering services, piping system fabrication, industrial construction and maintenance services, manufacturing and sale of specialty pipe fittings and design and fabrication of pipe support systems. SGR's operations are conducted primarily through wholly-owned subsidiaries and joint ventures.

RECENT DEVELOPMENTS:

For the quarter ended 11/30/02, net income rose 13.2% to $16.4 million compared with $18.9 million in the equivalent 2001 quarter. Sales increased 119.8% to $996.9 million from $453.6 million a year earlier. Operating income climbed 2.3% to $32.5 million. SGR's backlog advanced 11.1% to $5.00 billion versus $4.50 billion at 11/30/01. The backlog benefited from contributions of approximately $457.0 million in new awards booked during the quarter, including about $220.0 million from SGR's environmental and infrastructure division.

PROSPECTS:

The Company is encouraged by strong bidding activity and steady bookings of new work. Meanwhile, on 1/9/03, SGR announced that its Shaw Environmental & Infrastructure Division was awarded a contract by the Naval Facilities Engineering Command, Atlantic Division, for environmental remediation services. The award is for a base period of one year with four one-year option periods. The five-year contract has a potential value of up to $125.0 million. Separately, on 1/13/03, SGR announced that its subsidiary, Shaw Constructors, Inc., was awarded a contract with the Dow Chemical Company for the construction of a Polymeric Methylene Diisocyanate facility in Freeport, Texas.

ANNUAL FINANCIAL DATA:

FISCAL YEAR	TOT. REVS. ($mill.)	NET INC. ($mill.)	TOT. ASSETS ($mill.)	OPER. PROFIT %	NET PROFIT %	RET. ON EQUITY %	RET. ON ASSETS %	CURR. RATIO	EARN. PER SH. $	CASH FL. PER SH. $	TANG. BK. VAL. $	PRICE RANGE	AVG. P/E RATIO
8/31/02	3,170.7	98.4	2,304.2	5.2	3.1	14.2	4.3	1.4	2.26	2.82	4.73	36.09 - 8.90	10.0
8/31/01	1,538.9	① 61.2	1,701.9	7.0	4.0	10.2	3.6	1.9	① 1.46	2.55	5.60	63.48 - 19.76	28.5
8/31/00	762.7	①② 30.4	1,335.1	6.9	4.0	8.1	2.3	1.2	①② 0.99	1.53	2.68	50.50 - 11.38	31.4
8/31/99	494.0	18.1	407.1	6.8	3.7	10.4	4.5	1.8	0.74	1.27	6.05	12.75 - 4.09	11.5
8/31/98	501.6	16.2	389.8	6.2	3.2	9.5	4.2	2.1	0.63	1.03	5.17	13.97 - 3.19	13.6
8/31/97	338.4	14.0	262.5	7.8	4.2	10.2	5.4	2.2	0.61	0.92	5.52	13.38 - 6.25	16.2
8/31/96	222.0	8.8	205.4	7.2	4.0	12.0	4.3	1.5	0.47	0.69	3.85	18.50 - 4.38	24.3
8/31/95	135.3	4.3	106.4	7.1	3.2	7.9	4.0	2.0	0.25	0.38	3.17	5.38 - 1.94	14.6
8/31/94	113.2	3.0	91.5	4.4	2.7	6.0	3.3	1.8	0.20	0.29	2.92	13.25 - 1.38	37.5
8/31/93	120.7	4.2	67.4	7.0	3.5	34.0	6.3	1.2	0.32	0.39	0.96	9.75 - 7.50	27.4

Statistics are as originally reported. ① Excl. extraord. chrg. of $215,000, 2001; $553,000, 2000. ② Excl. acctg. chrg. $320,000.

OFFICERS:
J. M. Bernhard, Jr., Chmn., Pres., C.E.O.
R. L. Belk, Exec. V.P., C.F.O.
R. F. Gill, Exec. V.P., C.O.O.
G. P. Graphia, Sec.

INVESTOR CONTACT: Christine R. Noel, Dir., Inv. Rel., (225) 932-2500

PRINCIPAL OFFICE: 4171 Essen Lane, Baton Rouge, LA 70809

TELEPHONE NUMBER: (225) 932-2500
FAX: (225) 296-1199
WEB: www.shawgrp.com

NO. OF EMPLOYEES: 17,000 (approx.)

SHAREHOLDERS: 163

ANNUAL MEETING: In Jan.

INCORPORATED: LA, Aug., 1987

INSTITUTIONAL HOLDINGS:
No. of Institutions: 178
Shares Held: 30,828,781
% Held: 81.8

INDUSTRY: Fabricated pipe and fittings (SIC: 3498)

TRANSFER AGENT(S): Wachovia Bank, N.A., Charlotte, NC

SHERWIN-WILLIAMS COMPANY

EXCH.	SYM.	REC. PRICE	P/E RATIO	YLD.	MKT. CAP.	RANGE (52-WK.)	'02 Y/E PR.	DIV. ACH.
NYSE	SHW	26.64 (1/31/03)	13.1	2.3%	$4.10 bill.	33.24 - 21.75	28.25	23 yrs.

UPPER MEDIUM GRADE. THE COMPANY IS PROJECTING FULL-YEAR 2003 SALES GROWTH IN THE RANGE OF 3.0% TO 5.0%.

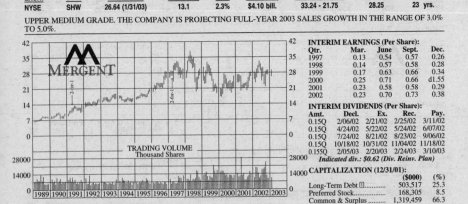

*7 YEAR PRICE SCORE 108.8   ***12 MONTH PRICE SCORE 109.9**
*NYSE COMPOSITE INDEX=100

INTERIM EARNINGS (Per Share):

Qtr.	Mar.	June	Sept.	Dec.
1997	0.13	0.54	0.57	0.26
1998	0.14	0.57	0.58	0.28
1999	0.17	0.63	0.66	0.34
2000	0.25	0.71	0.66	d1.55
2001	0.23	0.58	0.58	0.29
2002	0.23	0.70	0.73	0.38

INTERIM DIVIDENDS (Per Share):

Amt.	Decl.	Ex.	Rec.	Pay.
0.15Q	2/06/02	2/21/02	2/25/02	3/11/02
0.15Q	4/24/02	5/22/02	5/24/02	6/07/02
0.15Q	7/24/02	8/21/02	8/23/02	9/06/02
0.15Q	10/18/02	10/31/02	11/04/02	11/18/02
0.155Q	2/05/03	2/20/03	2/24/03	3/10/03

Indicated div.: $0.62 (Div. Reinv. Plan)

CAPITALIZATION (12/31/01):

	($000)	(%)
Long-Term Debt ⬚	503,517	25.3
Preferred Stock	168,305	8.5
Common & Surplus	1,319,459	66.3
Total	1,991,281	100.0

BUSINESS:

Sherwin-Williams Company is engaged in the manufacture, distribution and sale of coatings and related products. The Paint Stores' division (63.7% of 2002 net sales) consisted of 2,643 company-operated specialty paint stores in the U.S., Canada, the Virgin Islands, Puerto Rico and Mexico, as of 12/31/02. The Consumer segment (22.8%) develops, manufactures and distributes a variety of paint, coatings and related products to third party customers and the Paint

stores segment. The Automotive Finishes segment (8.8%) develops, manufactures and distributes motor vehicle finish products throughout North and South America, the Caribbean Islands and Italy. The International Coatings segment (4.7%) develops, licenses, manufactures and distributes a variety of paint, coatings and related products worldwide. SHW's brands include SHERWINWILLIAMS®, DUTCH BOY®, and KRYLON®.

RECENT DEVELOPMENTS:

For the year ended 12/31/02, income increased 18.1% to $310.7 million, before an accounting change charge of $183.1 million, compared with net income of $263.2 million in 2001. Net sales rose 2.3% to $5.18 billion from $5.07 billion a year earlier. The increase in sales was due to strong domestic architectural paint sales, an increasingly

favorable do-it-yourself market and aggressive promotion of new products and color palettes. Gross profit as a percentage of net sales rose to 45.1% from 43.8% in 2001 due to moderating raw material costs earlier in the year, manufacturing volume gains and other operational efficiencies.

PROSPECTS:

Looking ahead, the Company expects 2003 will be a low-growth, challenging year due to uncertain worldwide economic conditions, the pending war with Iraq and the slow, long-term recovery expected in the domestic economy. SHW expects sales growth for 2003 in the range of 3.0% to

5.0%, and diluted earnings per share, before an accounting change, of between $2.17 and $2.29. The Company expects first quarter 2003 sales growth in the range of about 2.5% to 4.5% year-over-year, and diluted earnings per share, before an accounting change, of between $0.24 and $0.27.

ANNUAL FINANCIAL DATA:

FISCAL YEAR	TOT. REVS. (Smill.)	NET INC. (Smill.)	TOT. ASSETS (Smill.)	OPER. PROFIT %	NET PROFIT %	RET. ON EQUITY %	RET. ON ASSETS %	CURR. RATIO	EARN. PER SH.$	CASH FL. PER SH.$	TANG. BK. VAL.$	DIV. PER SH.$	PRICE RANGE	AVG. P/E RATIO	AVG. YIELD %
p12/31/02	5,184.8	③ 310.7							③ 2.04			0.60	33.24 - 21.75	13.5	2.2
12/31/01	5,066.0	263.2	3,627.9	9.7	5.2	17.7	7.3	1.3	1.68	2.62	2.59	0.58	28.23 - 19.73	14.3	2.4
12/31/00	5,211.6	② 16.0	3,750.7	4.1	0.3	1.1	0.4	1.4	② 0.10	1.08	3.18	0.54	27.63 - 17.13	223.5	2.4
12/31/99	5,003.8	303.9	4,052.1	11.5	6.1	17.9	7.5	1.3	1.80	2.72	2.32	0.48	32.88 - 18.75	14.3	1.9
12/31/98	4,934.4	272.9	4,065.5	10.8	5.5	15.9	6.7	1.4	1.57	2.42	1.76	0.45	37.88 - 19.44	18.3	1.6
12/31/97	4,881.1	260.6	4,035.8	10.7	5.3	16.4	6.5	1.4	1.50	2.30	0.70	0.40	33.38 - 24.13	19.2	1.4
12/31/96	4,132.9	224.9	2,994.6	10.1	5.4	16.1	7.5	1.3	1.34	1.92	3.65	0.35	28.88 - 19.50	18.0	1.4
12/31/95	3,273.8	200.7	2,141.1	9.8	6.1	16.6	9.4	2.0	1.18	1.62	5.85	0.32	20.75 - 16.00	15.6	1.7
12/31/94	3,100.1	186.8	1,962.0	10.0	6.0	17.7	9.5	2.0	1.08	1.51	5.39	0.28	17.88 - 14.75	15.1	1.7
12/31/93	2,949.3	165.2	1,914.7	9.2	5.6	16.0	8.6	2.0	0.93	1.31	4.96	0.25	18.75 - 14.94	18.2	1.5

Statistics are as originally reported. Adj. for stk. splits: 2-for-1, 3/97. ① Incl. debentures conv. into common. ② Incl. impairment of long-lived assets chrg. of $352.0 mill. ③ Excl. acctg. change chrg. of $183.1 mill.

OFFICERS:
C. M. Connor, Chmn., C.E.O.
J. M. Scaminace, Pres., C.O.O.
S. P. Hennessy, Sr. V.P., C.F.O., Treas.

INVESTOR CONTACT: Conway G. Ivy, Sr. V.P., (216) 566-2102

PRINCIPAL OFFICE: 101 Prospect Avenue N.W., Cleveland, OH 44115-1075

TELEPHONE NUMBER: (216) 566-2000
FAX: (216) 566-3310
WEB: www.sherwin.com

NO. OF EMPLOYEES: 25,789 (avg.)

SHAREHOLDERS: 10,229

ANNUAL MEETING: In Apr.

INCORPORATED: OH, July, 1884

INSTITUTIONAL HOLDINGS:
No. of Institutions: 327
Shares Held: 107,438,664
% Held: 71.7

INDUSTRY: Paints and allied products (SIC: 2851)

TRANSFER AGENT(S): The Bank of New York, New York, NY

SHOPKO STORES, INC.

EXCH.	SYM.	REC. PRICE	P/E RATIO	YLD.	MKT. CAP.	RANGE (52-WK.)	'02 Y/E PR.
NYSE	SKO	10.95 (2/28/03)	7.7	...	$314.5 mill.	22.80 - 9.71	12.45

LOWER MEDIUM GRADE. THE COMPANY IS TARGETING FULL FISCAL-YEAR 2003 EARNINGS OF BETWEEN $1.40 AND $1.50 PER SHARE.

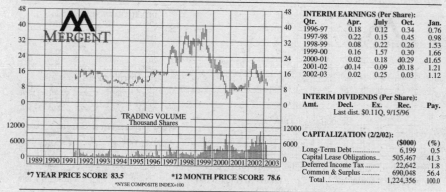

INTERIM EARNINGS (Per Share):

Qtr.	Apr.	July	Oct.	Jan.
1996-97	0.18	0.12	0.34	0.76
1997-98	0.22	0.15	0.45	0.98
1998-99	0.08	0.22	0.26	1.53
1999-00	0.16	1.57	0.30	1.66
2000-01	0.02	0.18	d0.29	d1.65
2001-02	d0.14	0.09	d0.18	1.21
2002-03	0.02	0.25	0.03	1.12

INTERIM DIVIDENDS (Per Share):

Amt.	Decl.	Ex.	Rec.	Pay.
Last dist. $0.11Q, 9/15/96				

*7 YEAR PRICE SCORE 83.5   ***12 MONTH PRICE SCORE 78.6**

*NYSE COMPOSITE INDEX=100

CAPITALIZATION (2/2/02):

	($000)	(%)
Long-Term Debt	6,199	0.5
Capital Lease Obligations..	505,467	41.3
Deferred Income Tax	22,642	1.8
Common & Surplus	690,048	56.4
Total	1,224,356	100.0

BUSINESS:

ShopKo Stores, Inc. operated, as of 3/13/03, 364 retail stores in 23 states, primarily in the Midwest, Western Mountain and Pacific Northwest regions of the U.S. Retail operations include 141 specialty discount stores operating under the ShopKo name in mid-sized and larger cities, and 223 Pamida discount stores in smaller, rural communities. On 7/6/99, the Company acquired Pamida Holdings Corporation. On 6/16/00, the Company sold its healthcare benefits management subsidiary, ProVantage Health Services, Inc.

RECENT DEVELOPMENTS:

For the 52 weeks ended 2/1/03, earnings totaled $41.2 million, before a $186.1 million accounting change charge, compared with net earnings of $28.2 million in the corresponding period a year earlier. Results for the recent period included a $6.0 million pre-tax restructuring charge. Total revenues slipped 4.0% to $3.25 billion from $3.39 billion the year before. Net sales for ShopKo stores declined 3.3% to $2.46 billion, while net sales for Pamida stores fell 6.1% to $784.1 million. Consolidated comparable-store sales were down 2.0% year over year, reflecting comparable-store sales declines of 4.8% and 1.1% at Pamida and ShopKo stores, respectively. Gross margin was $833.3 million, or 25.6% of total revenues, versus $806.1 million, or 23.8% of total revenues, in the prior year. Income from operations rose 4.4% to $120.6 million from $115.6 million the previous year.

PROSPECTS:

The Company anticipates a loss of between $0.05 per share to breakeven for the first quarter of the current fiscal year. Looking ahead, SKO is targeting full fiscal-year 2003 earnings in the range of $1.40 to $1.50 per share. Despite weaker sales due primarily to unfavorable economic conditions, results are benefiting from improved merchandise margin rates and decreased shrink expenses, or costs related to theft or damaged products, from the Company's Pamida operations. In addition, results are being positively affected by lower interest expense stemming from SKO's aggressive efforts to reduce debt levels.

ANNUAL FINANCIAL DATA:

FISCAL YEAR	TOT. REVS. ($mill.)	NET INC. ($mill.)	TOT. ASSETS ($mill.)	OPER. PROFIT %	NET PROFIT %	RET. ON EQUITY %	RET. ON ASSETS %	CURR. RATIO	EARN. PER SH. $	CASH FL. PER SH. $	TANG. BK. VAL. $	DIV. PER SH. $	PRICE RANGE	AVG. P/E RATIO	AVG. YIELD %
p2/01/03	3,252.8	⑤ 41.2							⑤ 1.41			...	22.80 - 8.76	11.2	...
2/02/02	3,387.0	28.2	1,820.0	3.4	0.8	4.1	1.6	1.2	0.98	4.16	16.78	...	11.00 - 4.81	8.1	...
2/03/01	3,530.5	④ d50.0	1,984.5	...	...	...	...	1.3	④ d1.72	1.52	15.60	...	23.00 - 3.00	...	...
1/29/00	3,911.9	①② 106.0	2,083.3	4.4	2.7	15.3	5.1	1.1	①② 3.70	6.66	14.27	...	40.75 - 18.50	8.0	...
1/30/99	2,993.8	② 55.6	1,373.5	4.3	1.9	12.1	4.1	1.4	② 2.10	4.65	14.72	...	37.00 - 21.38	13.9	...
③ 1/31/98	2,459.6	② 48.8	1,250.8	4.5	2.0	12.3	3.9	1.4	② 1.71	3.75	12.59	...	29.94 - 14.38	13.0	...
2/22/97	2,346.5	44.9	1,233.9	4.5	1.9	9.8	3.6	1.7	1.40	3.26	12.45	0.33	17.13 - 10.88	10.0	2.4
2/24/96	1,981.9	38.4	1,118.0	4.9	1.9	9.1	3.4	1.8	1.20	2.96	12.55	0.44	14.00 - 8.63	9.4	3.9
2/25/95	1,865.4	37.8	1,109.8	4.9	2.0	9.5	3.4	1.7	1.18	2.85	12.41	0.44	12.13 - 8.75	8.8	4.2
2/26/94	1,750.6	32.1	953.0	4.2	1.8	8.6	3.4	1.5	1.00	2.48	11.67	0.44	16.00 - 9.75	12.9	3.4

Statistics are as originally reported. ① Bef. $3.8 mil ($0.13/sh) extraord. chg. ② Incl. $48.7 mil pre-tax non-recur. gain, 10/99; $5.7 mil chg., 1/99; & $2.8 mil chg., 1/98. ③ For 49 weeks due to fiscal year-end change. ④ Bef. $32.6 mil ($1.12/sh) gain on sale of discont. opers and $1.6 mil ($0.05/sh) inc. fr. discont. opers. & incl. $75.9 mil ($2.62/sh) after-tax restr. chg. ⑤ Bef. $186.1 mil ($6.36/sh) acctg. chg. & incl. $6.0 mil ($0.12/sh) pre-tax restr. chg.

OFFICERS:
J. W. Eugster, Chmn.
J. C. Girard, Vice-Chmn.
S. K. Duncan, Pres., C.E.O.
B. W. Bender, Sr. V.P., C.F.O.

INVESTOR CONTACT: Vicki Shamion, Investor Relations, (920) 429-7039

PRINCIPAL OFFICE: 700 Pilgrim Way, Green Bay, WI 54304

TELEPHONE NUMBER: (920) 429-2211
FAX: (920) 496-4225
WEB: www.shopko.com
NO. OF EMPLOYEES: 13,000 full-time (approx.); 13,000 part-time (approx.)
SHAREHOLDERS: 2,629
ANNUAL MEETING: In May
INCORPORATED: MN, 1961; reincorp., WI, May, 1998

INSTITUTIONAL HOLDINGS:
No. of Institutions: 144
Shares Held: 29,462,709
% Held: 99.9

INDUSTRY: Variety stores (SIC: 5331)

TRANSFER AGENT(S): Wells Fargo Shareowner Services, South St. Paul, MN

SIERRA PACIFIC RESOURCES

EXCH.	SYM.	REC. PRICE	P/E RATIO	YLD.	MKT. CAP.	RANGE (52-WK.)	'02 Y/E PR.
NYSE	SRP	2.99 (2/28/03)	...	...	$305.3 mill.	16.85 - 2.88	6.50

SPECULATIVE GRADE. THE COMPANY IS TAKING ACTIONS TO IMPROVE ITS BALANCE SHEET AND OVERALL FINANCIAL STRENGTH.

TRADING VOLUME Thousand Shares

*7 YEAR PRICE SCORE N/A   *12 MONTH PRICE SCORE 72.3
*NYSE COMPOSITE INDEX=100

INTERIM EARNINGS (Per Share):

Qtr.	Mar.	June	Sept.	Dec.
1997		---- 2.40 ----		
1998	0.69	0.50	0.68	0.62
1999	0.09	0.23	0.93	d0.42
2000	0.23	d0.26	d0.29	d0.23
2001	d1.07	0.35	0.89	0.06
2002	d2.98	d0.41	0.78	d0.05

INTERIM DIVIDENDS (Per Share):

Amt.	Decl.	Ex.	Rec.	Pay.
0.20Q	7/20/01	8/22/01	8/24/01	9/15/01
0.20Q	11/06/01	11/19/01	11/21/01	12/15/01
0.20Q	2/06/02	2/20/02	2/22/02	3/15/02

Dividend Payment Suspended.

CAPITALIZATION (12/31/01):

	($000)	(%)
Long-Term Debt	3,376,105	56.0
Deferred Income Tax	719,967	11.9
Redeemable Pfd. Stock	188,872	3.1
Preferred Stock	50,000	0.8
Common & Surplus	1,695,336	28.1
Total	6,030,280	100.0

BUSINESS:

Sierra Pacific Resources is a holding company whose principal subsidiaries are Sierra Pacific Power Company and Nevada Power Company. The Company was created from the merger between Sierra Pacific Resources (old) and Nevada Power Company. As of 12/31/01, the Company served 953,914 electric customers in southern and northern Nevada and the Lake Tahoe area of California and 119,471 natural gas customers in Reno and Sparks, Nevada. Nevada Power Company is engaged in the electricity utility business in the City of Las Vegas and the vicinity in Southern Nevada. As of 12/31/01, Sierra Pacific Power Company provided electricity to customers in Northern Nevada and the Lake Tahoe area in California. Other subsidiaries include the Tuscarora Gas Pipeline Company, which owns a 50.0% interest in an interstate natural gas transmission partnership and Sierra Pacific Communications, a telecommunications company.

RECENT DEVELOPMENTS:

For the year ended 12/31/02, SRP posted a net loss of $307.5 million compared with net income of $56.7 million the year prior. Results for 2002 included pre-tax charges of $527.0 million for the disallowance of deferred energy and related carrying costs. Total operating revenues slid 34.8% to $2.99 billion from $4.59 billion the prior year.

Operating revenues from Sierra Pacific Power Company dropped 30.1% to $1.08 billion, while operating revenues from Nevada Power Company fell 37.2% to $1.90 billion. Total operating expenses amounted to $3.02 billion, down 30.8% from $4.37 billion the year before.

PROSPECTS:

The Company is continuing to take steps to restore and rebuild its financial health. On 2/3/03, the Company announced it had reached agreements to exchange 30.0% of its mandatorily convertible securities into common stock, reducing the Company's outstanding debt by approximately $105.0 million and its future interest expense by approximately $26.0 million through 2005. Meanwhile, on 2/12/03, the Company issued $300.0 million of convertible debt to retire floating rate notes due in April 2003, leaving SRP with an additional $50.0 million of added liquidity.

ANNUAL FINANCIAL DATA:

FISCAL YEAR	TOT. REVS. ($mill.)	NET INC. ($mill.)	TOT. ASSETS ($mill.)	OPER. PROFIT %	NET PROFIT %	NET INC./NET PROP. %	NET INC./TOT. CAP. %	RET. ON EQUITY %	ACCUM. DEPR./GROSS PROP. %	EARN. PER SH.$	TANG. BK. VAL.$	DIV. PER SH.$	DIV. PAYOUT %	PRICE RANGE	AVG. P/E RATIO	AVG. YIELD %
p12/31/02	2,991.7	[5]d307.5	...	...	...	...	...	...	...	[5]d3.01	...	0.20	...	16.85 — 4.65	...	...
12/31/01	4,588.7	[4]29.9	8,181.3	4.9	0.7	0.7	0.5	1.7	30.2	[4]0.34	13.55	0.65	191.1	17.18 — 10.56	40.8	4.7
12/31/00	2,334.3	[3]d49.4	5,639.5	5.5	...	...	...	...	29.1	[3]d0.63	13.25	1.00	...	19.44 — 12.13	...	6.3
12/31/99	1,309.1	[2]51.8	5,247.4	13.1	4.0	1.3	1.4	3.4	27.8	[2]0.83	14.66	0.50	60.2	26.44 — 16.88	26.1	2.3
[1]12/31/98	741.8	77.3	2,041.4	16.7	10.4	4.6	4.9	10.4	30.3	2.49	21.72	...	...	...	...	
12/31/97	663.2	74.4	1,935.9	17.9	11.2	4.7	4.8	10.5	29.3	2.40	20.49	...	...	...	...	
12/31/96	627.7	66.9	...	17.3	10.7	...	...	...	...	2.19	...	...	...	...	...	

Statistics are as originally reported. [1] Results for 1998 and prior are for Sierra Pacific Resources (old). [2] Incl. pre-tax chrg. $56.0 mill. for the disallowance of energy expenses. [3] Bef. inc. from disc. opers. of $9.6 mill. [4] Excl. $18.0 mill. net gain fr. sale of water business & one-time net chrgs. of $42.4 mill. [5] Incl. pre-tax chrg. of $527.0 mill. for deferred energy & other rel. chrgs.

OFFICERS:
W. M. Higgins, Chmn., Pres., C.E.O.
R. K. Atkinson, V.P., C.F.O.
C. S. Hunterton, Gen. Couns., Sec.
INVESTOR CONTACT: Shareholder Relations, (800) 662-7575
PRINCIPAL OFFICE: 6100 Neil Road, P.O. Box 30150, Reno, NV 89520-3150

TELEPHONE NUMBER: (775) 834-4011
WEB: www.sierrapacific.com
NO. OF EMPLOYEES: 3,333
SHAREHOLDERS: 25,019
ANNUAL MEETING: In May
INCORPORATED: NV, Dec., 1983

INSTITUTIONAL HOLDINGS:
No. of Institutions: 144
Shares Held: 70,309,049
% Held: 68.8
INDUSTRY: Electric and other services combined (SIC: 4931)
TRANSFER AGENT(S): Computershare Investor Services, Chicago IL

SIMON PROPERTY GROUP, INC.

EXCH.	SYM.	REC. PRICE	P/E RATIO	YLD.	MKT. CAP.	RANGE (52-WK.)	'02 Y/E PR.
NYSE	SPG	34.64 (2/28/03)	17.9	6.9%	$6.02 bill.	36.95 - 29.40	34.07

MEDIUM GRADE. THE COMPANY INTENDS TO ACQUIRE THE REMAINING OWNERSHIP INTEREST IN THE FORUM SHOPS AT CAESARS IN LAS VEGAS.

*7 YEAR PRICE SCORE 124.2   ***12 MONTH PRICE SCORE 107.1**

*NYSE COMPOSITE INDEX=100

INTERIM EARNINGS (Per Share):

Qtr.	Mar.	June	Sept.	Dec.
1999	0.21	0.22	0.25	0.32
2000	0.21	0.24	0.24	0.44
2001	0.19	0.21	0.21	0.25
2002	0.17	0.91	0.33	0.52

INTERIM DIVIDENDS (Per Share):

Amt.	Decl.	Ex.	Rec.	Pay.
0.525Q	2/07/02	2/13/02	2/15/02	2/28/02
0.55Q	5/08/02	5/15/02	5/17/02	5/31/02
0.55Q	7/31/02	8/14/02	8/16/02	8/30/02
0.55Q	10/31/02	11/13/02	11/15/02	11/29/02
0.60Q	2/06/03	2/13/03	2/18/03	2/28/03

Indicated div.: $2.40 (Div. Reinv. Plan)

CAPITALIZATION (12/31/01):

	($000)	(%)
Long-Term Debt	8,841,378	73.3
Preferred Stock	877,468	7.3
Common & Surplus	2,337,223	19.4
Total	12,056,069	100.0

BUSINESS:

Simon Property Group, Inc. is a self-administered and self-managed real estate investment trust company. SPG is engaged in the ownership, operation, management, leasing, acquisition, expansion and development of real estate properties, primarily regional malls, community shopping centers and specialty retail centers. As of 2/6/03, SPG owned or held an interest in 242 income-producing properties containing an aggregate 183.0 million square feet of gross leasable space in 36 states, and eight additional assets in Europe and Canada, as well as ownership interests in other real estate assets.

RECENT DEVELOPMENTS:

For the year ended 12/31/02, SPG reported income of $547.3 million versus income of $282.3 million, before an accounting charge of $1.7 million, a year earlier. Earnings benefited from higher occupancy rates, the acquisition of profitable assets from Rodamco North America N.V. and lower mortgage interest rates. Results for 2002 and 2001 included net gains on asset sales of $162.0 million and $2.6 million, and net losses from MerchantWired LLC of $32.7 million and $18.1 million, respectively. Results for 2001 also included an investment property impairment charge of $47.0 million. Total revenue increased 6.7% to $2.19 billion from $2.05 billion in 2001. Minimum rent revenue rose 5.3% to $1.34 billion, and tenant reimbursements revenue climbed 8.6% to $658.9 million.

PROSPECTS:

On 1/9/03, SPG sold mall properties in Wisconsin and Indiana for total consideration of $34.0 million. Meanwhile on 2/6/03, SPG announced plans to acquire the remaining ownership interest in The Forum Shops at Caesars in Las Vegas for about $174.0 million in cash. Meanwhile, a 175,000 square foot expansion affronting Las Vegas Boulevard is scheduled to open in the fall of 2004 adding a multilevel luxury retail, restaurant, and entertainment complex to the project. Separately, SPG expects funds from operations of approximately $4.01 per share in 2003.

ANNUAL FINANCIAL DATA:

FISCAL YEAR	TOT. INC. ($mill.)	NET INC. ($mill.)	TOT. ASSETS ($mill.)	NET INC. +DEPR./ ASSETS %	RET. ON EQUITY %	RET. ON ASSETS %	EARN. PER SH.$	TANG. BK. VAL.$	DIV. PER SH.$	DIV. PAYOUT %	PRICE RANGE	AVG. P/E RATIO	AVG. YIELD %
p12/31/02	2,185.8	⑥ 547.3					⑥ 1.93		2.18	112.7	36.95 - 28.00	16.8	6.7
12/31/01	2,048.8	⑤ 200.7	13,811.0	4.7	6.2	1.5	⑤ 0.86	13.23	2.08	241.8	30.97 - 23.75	31.8	7.6
12/31/00	2,012.7	④ 241.9	13,911.4	4.8	7.9	1.7	④ 1.16	14.23	2.02	174.1	27.13 - 21.50	21.0	8.3
12/31/99	1,895.0	③ 221.7	14,199.3	4.3	6.8	1.6	③ 0.99	15.95	2.02	204.0	30.94 - 20.44	25.9	7.9
12/31/98	1,405.1	① 159.8	13,269.1	3.2	4.7	1.2	① 1.01	15.70	2.02	200.0	34.88 - 25.81	30.0	6.7
12/31/97	1,054.2	① 137.2	7,662.7	4.4	8.8	1.8	① 1.08	11.11	2.01	185.9	34.38 - 27.88	28.8	6.4
12/31/96	747.7	① 88.8	5,895.9	3.8	6.8	1.5	① 1.02	10.45	2.12	208.0	31.00 - 21.13	25.5	8.1
12/31/95	553.7	① 62.6	2,556.4	6.1	26.9	2.4	① 1.08	2.28	1.95	180.8	26.00 - 22.50	22.5	8.1
12/31/94	473.7	② 41.4	2,316.9	5.1	72.2	1.8	② 0.71	1.18	1.43	200.7	28.00 - 22.50	35.6	5.6
12/31/93	18.4	① 19.1	1,756.7	1.2	64.8	1.1	① 0.11	...	...	...	... 102.7		

Statistics are as originally reported. ① Bef. extr. credit, 1998, $7.2 mill.; credit, 1997, $58,000.; chrg., 1996, $3.5 mill.; chrg., 1995, $3.3 mill.; chrg., 1993, $30.5 mill. ② Bef. extr. chrg. $18.0 mill.; incl. non-recurr. interest exp., $27.2 mill. ③ Bef. unusual chrg. $12.0 mill. and extr. chrg. $6.7 mill. ④ Bef. extr. chrg. $649,000 & acctg. change chrg., $12.3 mill.; incl. gain $9.1 mill. on the sale of real estate. ⑤ Bef. extr. gain $163,000 & acctg. change chrg. $1.7 mill.; incl. gain $2.6 mill. on the sale of real estate & impair. chrg. $47.0 mill. on invest. prop. ⑥ Bef. extr. gain $14.3 mill.; incl. net loss fr. Merchant Wired LLC $32.7 mill. & net gain on sale of assets $162.0 mill.

OFFICERS:
M. Simon, Co-Chmn.
H. Simon, Co-Chmn.
H. C. Mautner, Vice-Chmn.
D. Simon, C.E.O.

INVESTOR CONTACT: Shelly Doran, (317) 685-7330

PRINCIPAL OFFICE: 115 W. Washington St., Suite 15 East, Indianapolis, IN 46204

TELEPHONE NUMBER: (317) 636-1600
FAX: (317) 685-7222
WEB: www.shopsimon.com
NO. OF EMPLOYEES: 2,580 full-time (approx.); 1,590 part-time (approx.)
SHAREHOLDERS: 2,455
ANNUAL MEETING: In May
INCORPORATED: MD, Sept., 1993; reincorp., DE, Sept., 1998

INSTITUTIONAL HOLDINGS:
No. of Institutions: 319
Shares Held: 146,856,717
% Held: 77.5

INDUSTRY: Real estate investment trusts (SIC: 6798)

TRANSFER AGENT(S): Mellon Investor Services LLC, South Hackensack, NJ

SIMPSON MANUFACTURING CO., INC.

EXCH.	SYM.	REC. PRICE	P/E RATIO	YLD.	MKT. CAP.	RANGE (52-WK.)	'02 Y/E PR.
NYSE	SSD	33.80 (2/28/03)	16.1	...	$0.82 bill.	36.56 - 25.33	32.90

UPPER MEDIUM GRADE. FUTURE ACQUISITIONS ARE EXPECTED TO COMPLEMENT THE COMPANY'S SIMPSON STRONG-TIE LINE OF CONNECTORS.

INTERIM EARNINGS (Per Share):

Qtr.	Mar.	June	Sept.	Dec.
1998	0.24	0.35	0.39	0.33
1999	0.32	0.41	0.45	0.39
2000	0.38	0.46	0.47	0.26
2001	0.37	0.52	0.49	0.28
2002	0.40	0.60	0.67	0.43

INTERIM DIVIDENDS (Per Share):

Amt.	Decl.	Ex.	Rec.	Pay.
2-for-1	7/30/02	8/19/02	8/08/02	8/16/02

TRADING VOLUME
Thousand Shares

*7 YEAR PRICE SCORE 155.6   ***12 MONTH PRICE SCORE 113.8**
*NYSE COMPOSITE INDEX=100

CAPITALIZATION (12/31/01):

	($000)	(%)
Long-Term Debt	5,687	1.9
Common & Surplus	288,117	98.1
Total............................	293,804	100.0

BUSINESS:

Simpson Manufacturing Co., Inc., through its subsidiary, Simpson Strong-Tie Company Inc., designs, engineers and manufactures wood-to-wood, wood-to-concrete and wood-to-masonry connectors and shearwalls. Simpson Strong-Tie also offers a full line of adhesives, mechanical anchors and powder actuated tools for concrete, masonry and steel.

Through its subsidiary, Simpson Dura-Vent Company, Inc., the Company designs, engineers and manufactures venting systems for gas and wood-burning appliances. SSD markets its products to the residential construction, light industrial and commercial construction, remodeling and do-it-yourself markets.

RECENT DEVELOPMENTS:

For the year ended 12/31/02, net income climbed 28.2% to $51.9 million compared with $40.5 million in 2001. Net sales grew 11.9% to $465.5 million from $415.9 million a year earlier, supported by solid growth throughout North America and Europe. The growth in the United States was strongest in California and the southern and eastern portion

of the country. Sales of Simpson Strong-Tie increased 14.2% year over year, while sales of Simpson Dura-Vent inched up 0.7%. Gross profit rose 19.5% to $188.9 million from $158.1 million in 2001. Operating income increased 30.8% to $86.1 million from $65.8 million the year before.

PROSPECTS:

On 2/21/03, the Company announced that its Canadian subsidiary, Simpson Strong-Tie Canada Limited, signed a letter of intent to purchase 100.0% of the equity of MGA Construction Hardware & Steel Fabricating Limited (MGA) and MGA Connectors Limited (MGA), for approximately $8.8 million in cash. MGA manufactures and distributes a line of connectors used in construction throughout Canada and portions of the United States. The MGA

product line would be complementary and additive to Simpson Strong-Tie's line of connectors, and is expected to give Simpson Strong-Tie Canada's customers additional cost-effective products. Subject to negotiation of a definitive purchase and sale agreement and satisfaction of usual closing conditions, including regulatory and other approvals, the transaction should close in the second quarter of 2003.

ANNUAL FINANCIAL DATA:

FISCAL YEAR	TOT. REVS. ($mill.)	NET INC. ($mill.)	TOT. ASSETS ($mill.)	OPER. PROFIT %	NET PROFIT %	RET. ON EQUITY %	RET. ON ASSETS %	CURR. RATIO	EARN. PER SH. $	CASH FL. PER SH. $	TANG. BK. VAL. $	PRICE RANGE	AVG. P/E RATIO
p12/31/02	465.5	51.9	396.4					2.09				36.56 - 25.33	14.8
12/31/01	415.9	40.5	329.6	15.8	9.7	14.1	12.3	6.4	1.65	2.28	11.84	30.50 - 23.20	16.3
12/31/00	369.1	38.4	279.5	16.2	10.4	15.7	13.7	6.1	1.56	2.09	10.18	26.50 - 19.09	14.6
12/31/99	328.4	38.5	247.3	19.0	11.7	18.3	15.6	5.2	1.57	2.02	8.76	27.47 - 16.38	14.0
12/31/98	279.1	31.1	191.6	18.4	11.2	19.3	16.3	4.9	1.29	1.64	6.96	21.50 - 12.63	13.2
12/31/97	246.1	26.0	150.8	17.6	10.6	20.2	17.2	5.0	1.09	1.37	5.60	21.00 - 10.75	14.6
12/31/96	202.4	19.7	123.6	16.2	9.7	19.3	16.0	4.6	0.84	1.14	4.47	12.00 - 6.50	11.0
12/31/95	168.0	14.1	97.6	13.6	8.4	17.3	14.5	4.5	0.62	0.85	3.59	7.69 - 4.69	10.1
12/31/94	151.3	5.5	81.6	9.3	3.6	8.2	6.7	4.3	0.26	0.45	2.95	6.38 - 4.88	22.1
12/31/93	113.9	8.0	58.3	12.8	7.0	24.5	13.7	2.3	0.45	0.59	1.81	... - ...	...

Statistics are as originally reported. Adj. for stk. split: 2-for-1, 8/02.

OFFICERS:
B. Simpson, Chmn.
T. J. Fitzmyers, Pres., C.E.O.
M. J. Herbert, C.F.O., Treas., Sec.
INVESTOR CONTACT: Investor Relations, (925) 560-9000
PRINCIPAL OFFICE: 4120 Dublin Blvd., Suite 400, Dublin, CA 94568

TELEPHONE NUMBER: (925) 560-9000
FAX: (925) 833-1496
WEB: www.simpsonmfg.com
NO. OF EMPLOYEES: 1,895
SHAREHOLDERS: 3,350 (approx. beneficial)
ANNUAL MEETING: In May
INCORPORATED: CA, 1994; reincorp., DE, June, 1999

INSTITUTIONAL HOLDINGS:
No. of Institutions: 107
Shares Held: 12,649,591
% Held: 51.6

INDUSTRY: Hardware, nec (SIC: 3429)

TRANSFER AGENT(S): Fleet National Bank c/o Boston Equiserve, Boston, MA

SIX FLAGS, INC.

EXCH.	SYM.	REC. PRICE	P/E RATIO	YLD.	MKT. CAP.	RANGE (52-WK.)	'02 Y/E PR.
NYSE	PKS	5.40 (2/28/03)	...	...	$499.1 mill.	18.69 - 3.00	5.71

LOWER MEDIUM GRADE. THE COMPANY EXPERIENCED A 7.8% DECLINE IN ATTENDANCE IN 2002, PARTLY OFFSET BY A 7.6% INCREASE IN PER CAPITA SPENDING.

MERGENT

TRADING VOLUME
Thousand Shares

1989 1990 1991 1992 1993 1994 1995 1996 1997 1998 1999 2000 2001 2002 2003

*7 YEAR PRICE SCORE 55.7   *12 MONTH PRICE SCORE 63.1*
NYSE COMPOSITE INDEX=100

INTERIM EARNINGS (Per Share):

Qtr.	Mar.	June	Sept.	Dec.
1997	d0.31	0.15	0.73	d0.19
1998	d0.39	0.19	1.24	d0.78
1999	d1.16	0.38	1.29	d0.55
2000	d1.53	0.12	1.49	d1.19
2001	d1.65	0.08	1.39	d1.02
2002	d1.23	d0.08	1.31	d0.82

INTERIM DIVIDENDS (Per Share):

Amt.	Decl.	Ex.	Rec.	Pay.
		No dividends paid.		

CAPITALIZATION (12/31/01):

	($000)	(%)
Long-Term Debt	2,222,442	54.8
Deferred Income Tax	109,926	2.7
Redeemable Pfd. Stock	278,867	6.9
Common & Surplus	1,446,622	35.6
Total	4,057,857	100.0

BUSINESS:

Six Flags, Inc. (formerly Premier Park, Inc.) is the largest regional theme park operator in the world. The 37 parks it operates has annual attendance of approximately 44.2 million in 2002. These parks include 15 of the 50 highest-attendance theme parks in North America, the largest paid admission theme park in Mexico and eight theme parks in Europe. Each theme park is individually themed and provides a complete family-oriented entertainment experience. The theme parks generally offer a broad selection of state-of-the-art and traditional thrill rides, water attractions, themed areas, concerts and shows, restaurants, game venues and merchandise outlets.

RECENT DEVELOPMENTS:

For the year ended 12/31/02, the Company reported a loss of $26.1 million, before an extraordinary loss of $18.5 million and an accounting change charge of $61.1 million, compared with a loss of $49.6 million, before an extraordinary loss of $8.5 million, in 2001. Results for 2002 and 2001 included amortization of $1.4 million and $57.8 million, respectively. Revenues slid 0.8% to $1.04 billion from $1.05 billion a year earlier. The decline in revenues was primarily attributed to a 7.8% decline in attendance at the consolidated parks, partially offset by a 7.6% increase in total per capita spending at those parks. Operating income advanced 25.3% to $187.7 million from $149.7 million the year before.

PROSPECTS:

The Company expects same-park consolidated revenue growth in the range of 4.0% and 5.0% reflecting an expected increase in attendance between 3.5% and 4.0% and a per capita spending increase in the range of 1.0% to 5.0%. As a result, the Company expects full-year 2003 earnings before interest, taxes, depreciation and amortization of about $410.0 million. The aforementioned expectations should result from a rebound in performance of the parks that had disappointing seasons in 2002 and the grand opening of Six Flags New Orleans.

ANNUAL FINANCIAL DATA:

FISCAL YEAR	TOT. REVS. ($mill.)	NET INC. ($mill.)	TOT. ASSETS ($mill.)	OPER. PROFIT %	NET PROFIT %	RET. ON EQUITY %	RET. ON ASSETS %	CURR. RATIO	EARN. PER SH.$	CASH FL. PER SH.$	TANG. BK. VAL.$	PRICE RANGE	AVG. P/E RATIO
p12/31/02	1,037.9	②d26.1	...	...	...	...	...	...	②d0.52	...	...	18.69 - 3.00	...
12/31/01	1,046.0	①d49.6	4,246.1	14.3	...	...	...	1.0	①d0.85	1.79	2.52	23.73 - 10.34	...
12/31/00	1,007.0	d52.0	4,191.3	17.5	...	...	...	1.1	d0.96	1.73	4.23	28.88 - 13.38	...
12/31/99	927.0	①d19.2	4,161.6	16.4	...	...	...	1.6	①d0.55	1.53	4.54	41.63 - 23.38	...
12/31/98	792.7	①35.6	4,052.5	21.5	4.5	2.2	0.9	1.9	①0.26	1.95	4.55	33.69 - 14.00	91.7
12/31/97	193.9	14.1	611.3	17.1	7.3	4.4	2.3	3.0	0.38	0.97	7.36	21.75 - 12.50	45.1
12/31/96	93.4	1.8	304.8	15.5	1.9	1.6	0.6	0.8	0.07	0.62	3.63	16.44 - 5.63	169.5
12/31/95	41.5	①d1.0	173.3	9.5	...	...	...	3.0	①d0.08	d0.02	1.89	10.00 - 1.25	...
12/31/94	24.9	0.1	45.5	10.2	0.4	0.6	0.2	1.2	0.03	0.39	2.69	...	...
12/31/93	21.8	1.4	36.7	13.2	6.2	10.3	3.7	1.6	0.25	0.60	2.48	...	...

Statistics are as originally reported. Adj. for stk. split: 2-for-1, 8/10/98. ① Bef. extraord. loss of $8.5 mill., 2001; $11.3 mill., 1999; $788,000, 1998; $140,000, 1995. ② Bef. extraord. loss of $18.5 mill. & acctg. chg. chrg. of $61.1 mill., but incl. goodwill imparment of $61.1 mill.

OFFICERS:
K. E. Burke, Chmn., C.E.O.
G. Story, Pres., C.O.O.
J. F. Dannhauser, C.F.O.
W. S. Hawrylak, V.P., Sec.

INVESTOR CONTACT: Joseph Mansi, (212) 682-6300

PRINCIPAL OFFICE: 11501 Northeast Expressway, Oklahoma City, OK 73131

TELEPHONE NUMBER: (405) 475-2500
FAX: (405) 475-2555
WEB: www.sixflags.com

NO. OF EMPLOYEES: 3,000 full-time (approx.); 44,000 part-time (approx.)

SHAREHOLDERS: 790

ANNUAL MEETING: In June

INCORPORATED: DE, 1981

INSTITUTIONAL HOLDINGS:
No. of Institutions: 137
Shares Held: 78,972,789
% Held: 85.3

INDUSTRY: Amusement parks (SIC: 7996)

TRANSFER AGENT(S): The Bank of New York, New York, NY

SLM CORPORATION

EXCH.	SYM.	REC. PRICE	P/E RATIO	YLD.	MKT. CAP.	RANGE (52-WK.)	'02 Y/E PR.	DIV. ACH.
NYSE	SLM	108.95 (2/28/03)	22.1	0.9%	$16.94 bill.	110.53 - 79.75	103.86	22 yrs.

INVESTMENT GRADE. THE COMPANY CONTINUES TO BENEFIT FROM INCREASED DEMAND FOR COLLEGE LOANS.

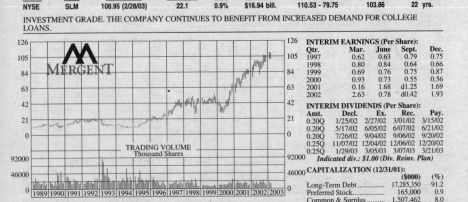

INTERIM EARNINGS (Per Share):

Qtr.	Mar.	June	Sept.	Dec.
1997	0.62	0.63	0.79	0.75
1998	0.80	0.84	0.64	0.66
1999	0.69	0.76	0.75	0.87
2000	0.93	0.73	0.55	0.56
2001	0.16	1.68	d1.25	1.69
2002	2.63	0.78	d0.42	1.93

INTERIM DIVIDENDS (Per Share):

Amt.	Decl.	Ex.	Rec.	Pay.
0.20Q	1/25/02	2/27/02	3/01/02	3/15/02
0.20Q	5/17/02	6/05/02	6/07/02	6/21/02
0.20Q	7/26/02	9/04/02	9/06/02	9/20/02
0.25Q	11/07/02	12/04/02	12/06/02	12/20/02
0.25Q	1/29/03	3/05/03	3/07/03	3/21/03

Indicated div.: $1.00 (Div. Reinv. Plan)

CAPITALIZATION (12/31/01):

	($000)	(%)
Long-Term Debt	17,285,350	91.2
Preferred Stock	165,000	0.9
Common & Surplus	1,507,462	8.0
Total	18,957,812	100.0

*7 YEAR PRICE SCORE 195.7   ***12 MONTH PRICE SCORE 118.4**

*NYSE COMPOSITE INDEX=100

BUSINESS:

SLM Corporation (formerly USA Education, Inc.) is a provider of education funding, managing nearly $78.00 billion in student loans for more than seven million borrowers. The Company primarily provides federally guaranteed student loans originated under the Federal Family Education Loan Program, and offers comprehensive information and resources to help guide students, parents and guidance professionals through the financial aid process. Through its subsidiaries and divisions, the Company also provides an array of consumer credit loans, including those for lifelong learning and K-12 education, and business and technical outsourcing services for colleges and universities. On 7/7/00, the Company acquired Student Loan Funding Resources, Inc. On 7/31/00, the Company acquired USA Group's guarantee servicing, student loan servicing and secondary market operations for $770.0 million.

RECENT DEVELOPMENTS:

For the year quarter ended 12/31/02, net income surged 106.3% to $792.0 million from $384.0 million the previous year. Results included a derivative market value loss of $203.9 million and $452.4 million for 2002 and 2001, respectively. Total interest income dropped 26.2% to $2.21 billion from $3.00 billion the year before. Net interest income increased 15.5% to $1.01 billion from $873.4 million in the prior year. Provision for loan losses jumped 76.7% to $116.6 million from $66.0 million a year earlier. Total other income leapt 97.2% to $1.02 billion from $517.6 million the year before. Operating expenses declined 2.5% to $689.8 million.

PROSPECTS:

The Company continues to benefit from increased demand for college loans. For instance, SLM's preferred channel loan originations, a key measure of SLM's market success and a predictable indicator of future loan volume, grew 18.0% during calendar year 2002 to $11.90 billion. Separately, on 12/11/02, the Company announced that it had completed the purchase of First Trust Financial, a mortgage banking company, for an undisclosed amount. The acquisition is intended to supplement in-house, fee-based mortgage origination activities as well as expand SLM's presence in New England.

ANNUAL FINANCIAL DATA:

FISCAL YEAR	NET INT. INC. ($mill.)	NON-INT. INC. ($mill.)	NET INC. ($mill.)	TOT. LOANS ($mill.)	TOT. ASSETS ($mill.)	RET. ON EQUITY %	RET. ON ASSETS %	EQUITY/ ASSETS %	EARN. PER SH. $	TANG. BK. VAL. $	DIV. PER SH. $	PRICE RANGE	AVG. P/E RATIO	AVG. YIELD %
p12/31/02	1,009.1	1,020.7	④ 792.0						④ 4.93		0.85	106.95 - 77.00	18.7	0.9
12/31/01	873.4	517.6	④ 384.0	42,769.0	52,874.0	23.0	0.7	3.2	④ 2.28	9.69	0.73	87.99 - 55.88	31.5	1.0
12/31/00	641.8	687.6	⑤ 465.0	39,485.8	48,791.8	32.9	1.0	2.9	③ 2.76	7.62	0.66	68.25 - 27.81	17.4	1.4
12/31/99	693.8	450.8	500.8	35,879.3	44,024.8	59.6	1.1	1.9	3.06	4.29	0.61	53.94 - 39.50	15.3	1.3
12/31/98	662.7	477.0	501.5	31,005.6	37,210.0	76.7	1.3	1.8	2.95	3.98	0.57	51.38 - 27.50	13.4	1.4
12/31/97	757.7	500.9	② 511.2	32,764.3	39,908.8	75.8	1.3	1.7	② 2.80	3.67	0.52	47.18 - 25.43	13.0	1.4
12/31/96	866.4	146.9	② 413.5	38,016.3	47,629.9	49.6	0.9	1.8	② 2.13	3.63	0.47	28.07 - 18.07	10.8	2.0
12/31/95	673.0	...	①② 371.2	39,513.5	50,001.7	34.3	0.7	2.2	①② 2.14	6.01	0.43	20.25 - 9.39	6.9	2.9
12/31/94	709.1	...	② 412.1	39,351.2	52,960.8	28.0	0.8	2.8	② 2.01	4.06	0.41	14.25 - 8.93	5.8	3.5
12/31/93	936.8	...	② 567.4	35,543.7	46,508.7	44.3	1.2	2.8	② 2.56	5.07	0.36	21.50 - 11.39	6.4	2.2

Statistics are as originally reported. Adj. for stk split: 7-for-2, 1/98 ① Bef. acctg. change chrg. of $130.1 mill. ② Bef. chrgs. on debt extinguished, $3.3 mill., 12/97; $4.8 mill., 12/96; $4.9 mill., 12/95; $9.3 mill., 12/94; $137.4 mill., 12/93 ③ Incl. one-time integration chrg. $53.0 mill. ④ Incl. derivative mkt. value adjust. loss $203.9 mill., 12/02; $505.7 mill., 12/01.

OFFICERS:
E. A. Fox, Chmn.
A. L. Lord, Vice-Chmn., C.E.O.
T. J. Fitzpatrick, Pres., C.O.O.
J. F. Remondi, Exec. V.P., C.F.O.

PRINCIPAL OFFICE: 11600 Sallie Mae Drive, Reston, VA 20193

TELEPHONE NUMBER: (703) 810-3000
FAX: (703) 810-5074
WEB: www.salliemae.com
NO. OF EMPLOYEES: 6,011 (avg.)
SHAREHOLDERS: 554 (approx.)
ANNUAL MEETING: In May
INCORPORATED: DE, Feb., 1997

INSTITUTIONAL HOLDINGS:
No. of Institutions: 375
Shares Held: 139,836,495
% Held: 91.1
INDUSTRY: Personal credit institutions (SIC: 6141)
TRANSFER AGENT(S): The Bank of New York, New York, NY

SMITH (A.O.) CORPORATION

EXCH.	SYM.	REC. PRICE	P/E RATIO	YLD.	MKT. CAP.	RANGE (52-WK.)	'02 Y/E PR.	DIV. ACH.
NYSE	AOS	25.78 (2/28/03)	13.7	2.2%	$0.61 bill.	32.75 - 20.56	27.01	10 yrs.

UPPER MEDIUM GRADE. THE COMPANY'S OPERATING UNITS WILL CONTINUE TO AGGRESSIVELY MANAGE COSTS IN 2003.

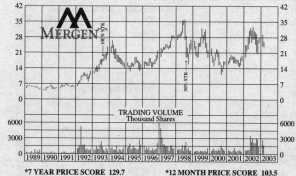

TRADING VOLUME
Thousand Shares

*7 YEAR PRICE SCORE 129.7 ***12 MONTH PRICE SCORE 103.5**
*NYSE COMPOSITE INDEX=100

INTERIM EARNINGS (Per Share):

Qtr.	Mar.	June	Sept.	Dec.
1999	0.48	0.59	0.52	0.20
2000	0.60	0.74	0.31	0.11
2001	0.36	0.45	0.02	d0.21
2002	0.50	0.66	0.34	0.38

INTERIM DIVIDENDS (Per Share):

Amt.	Decl.	Ex.	Rec.	Pay.
0.13Q	1/15/02	1/29/02	1/31/02	2/15/02
0.13Q	4/09/02	4/26/02	4/30/02	5/15/02
0.14Q	7/09/02	7/29/02	7/31/02	8/15/02
0.14Q	10/11/02	10/29/02	10/31/02	11/15/02
0.14Q	1/15/03	1/29/03	1/31/03	2/18/03

Indicated div.: $0.56 (Div. Reinv. Plan)

CAPITALIZATION (12/31/01):

	($000)	(%)
Long-Term Debt	390,385	43.2
Deferred Income Tax	62,154	6.9
Common & Surplus	451,878	50.0
Total	904,417	100.0

BUSINESS:

A.O. Smith Corporation consists of two platforms, Electric Motor Technologies (53.8% of total 2002 net sales) and Water Systems Technologies (46.2%). The Electric Motor Technologies segment consists of A.O. Smith Electrical Products Company, which manufactures and markets hermetic motors directly to original equipment manufacturers and through a distributor network. The Water Systems Technologies segment consists of A.O. Smith Water Products Company, which manufactures residential and commercial gas and electric water heating systems and copper tube boilers. The Company markets its gas and water heaters through a network of plumbing wholesalers in the U.S. and Canada. On 12/28/01, AOS acquired State Industries, Inc. for $117.2 million.

RECENT DEVELOPMENTS:

For the year ended 12/31/02, AOS reported net income of $51.3 million compared with $14.5 million in the previous year. Results for 2002 and 2001 included amortization of intangibles of $282,000 and $7.0 million, respectively. Results for 2001 also included restructuring and other charges of $9.4 million. Net sales advanced 27.6% to $1.47 billion from $1.15 billion a year earlier. Water systems sales surged 94.8% to $678.7 million, primarily due to the acquisition of State Industries, as well as higher water heater sales volumes and sales growth in China. Electrical products sales decreased 1.5% to $790.4 million. Gross profit grew 48.1% to $299.8 million, or 20.4% of net sales, from $202.3 million, or 17.6% of net sales, in the prior year.

PROSPECTS:

The Company's overall cost structure improved significantly during 2002 due to cost reduction actions in its electrical motor business and integration efforts in its water heater business. Going forward, AOS' operating units will continue to aggressively manage costs. Consequently, the Company expects full-year 2003 earnings in the range of $2.05 to $2.25 per share. Higher pension, employee medical and liability insurance costs in 2003 should be offset by incremental operating improvements from the motor repositioning programs, integration activities and new water heater products. For the first quarter of 2003, AOS expects earnings in the range of $0.41 to $0.45 per share.

ANNUAL FINANCIAL DATA:

FISCAL YEAR	TOT. REVS. ($mill.)	NET INC. ($mill.)	TOT. ASSETS ($mill.)	OPER. PROFIT %	NET PROFIT %	RET. ON EQUITY %	RET. ON ASSETS %	CURR. RATIO	EARN. PER SH.$	CASH FL. PER SH.$	TANG. BK. VAL.$	DIV. PER SH.$	PRICE RANGE	AVG. P/E RATIO	AVG. YIELD %
p12/31/02	1,469.1	51.3	1,224.9		3.5	10.0	4.2		1.86			0.54	32.75 - 19.00	13.9	2.1
12/31/01	1,151.2	④ 14.5	1,293.9	4.1	1.3	3.2	1.1	1.9	④ 0.61	2.57	6.30	0.52	20.10 - 14.67	28.5	3.0
12/31/00	1,247.9	③ 41.7	1,059.2	7.6	3.3	9.3	3.9	2.4	③ 1.76	3.66	8.64	0.50	23.13 - 11.19	9.7	2.9
12/31/99	1,039.3	② 50.3	1,064.0	9.3	4.8	11.7	4.7	2.3	② 2.11	3.68	7.69	0.48	32.00 - 18.81	12.0	1.9
12/31/98	917.6	44.5	767.4	8.8	4.8	11.1	5.8	2.2	1.84	3.13	10.93	0.47	35.88 - 15.81	14.0	1.8
12/31/97	832.9	① 37.6	716.5	7.6	4.5	9.4	5.2	2.9	① 1.33	2.26	10.69	0.45	28.92 - 19.08	18.0	1.9
12/31/96	781.2	① 25.2	885.0	7.6	3.2	5.9	2.9	1.7	① 0.81	1.52	13.52	0.44	22.00 - 13.92	22.3	2.5
12/31/95	1,544.8	61.4	952.9	7.1	4.0	16.5	6.4	1.6	1.96	3.73	11.87	0.39	19.08 - 12.75	8.1	2.4
12/31/94	1,373.5	57.3	847.9	7.5	4.2	18.3	6.8	1.5	1.83	3.40	9.61	0.33	26.67 - 14.08	11.1	1.6
12/31/93	1,193.9	42.7	823.1	6.9	3.6	15.8	5.2	1.4	1.39	2.77	8.69	0.45	23.83 - 11.58	12.8	2.5

Statistics are as originally reported. Adj. for stk. split: 3-for-2, 8/98. ① Bef. disc. opers. gain $15.2 mill. & gain of $101.0 mill. on disposition, 1997; $109.8 mill. ($5.80/sh.), 1996. ② Bef. loss from disc. opers. of $890,000 & loss of $7.0 mill. ($0.29/sh.) on disposition. ③ Bef. net loss of $11.9 mill. fr. disc. opers. ④ Incl. restr. chrg. of $9.4 mill.

OFFICERS:
R. J. O'Toole, Chmn., C.E.O.
K. W. Krueger, Sr. V.P., C.F.O.
W. D. Romoser, V.P., Sec., Gen. Couns.
INVESTOR CONTACT: Craig Watson, Director of Investor Relations, (414) 359-4009
PRINCIPAL OFFICE: 11270 West Park Place, P.O. Box 245008, Milwaukee, WI 53224

TELEPHONE NUMBER: (414) 359-4000
FAX: (414) 359-4180
WEB: www.aosmith.com
NO. OF EMPLOYEES: 14,800 (approx.)
SHAREHOLDERS: 1,186 (common); 501 (class A common)
ANNUAL MEETING: In April
INCORPORATED: DE, Oct., 1986

INSTITUTIONAL HOLDINGS:
No. of Institutions: 131
Shares Held: 17,604,916
% Held: 60.8
INDUSTRY: Motors and generators (SIC: 3621)
TRANSFER AGENT(S): Wells Fargo Shareowner Services, South St. Paul, MN

SMITH INTERNATIONAL, INC.

EXCH.	SYM.	REC. PRICE	P/E RATIO	YLD.	MKT. CAP.	RANGE (52-WK.)	'02 Y/E PR.
NYSE	SII	34.86 (2/28/03)	43.0	...	$3.44 bill.	38.73 - 25.79	32.62

MEDIUM GRADE. THE COMPANY HAS ACQUIRED THE OILFIELD CHEMICAL OPERATIONS OF FINLAND-BASED DYNEA INTERNATIONAL.

TRADING VOLUME
Thousand Shares

1989 1990 1991 1992 1993 1994 1995 1996 1997 1998 1999 2000 2001 2002 2003

*7 YEAR PRICE SCORE 127.8   ***12 MONTH PRICE SCORE 108.7**

*NYSE COMPOSITE INDEX=100

INTERIM EARNINGS (Per Share):

Qtr.	Mar.	June	Sept.	Dec.
1997	0.27	0.30	0.35	0.38
1998	0.38	d0.08	0.25	d0.17
1999	0.07	d0.03	0.48	0.07
2000	0.12	0.15	0.21	0.26
2001	0.34	0.38	0.42	0.39
2002	0.29	0.14	0.20	0.18

INTERIM DIVIDENDS (Per Share):

Amt.	Decl.	Ex.	Rec.	Pay.
100% STK	6/06/02	7/09/02	6/20/02	7/08/02

CAPITALIZATION (12/31/01):

	($000)	(%)
Long-Term Debt	538,842	26.7
Deferred Income Tax	40,504	2.0
Minority Interest	490,292	24.3
Common & Surplus	949,159	47.0
Total	2,018,797	100.0

BUSINESS:

Smith International, Inc. is a worldwide supplier of premium products and services to the oil and gas exploration and production industry, the petrochemical industry and other industrial markets. SII provides a comprehensive line of products and engineering services, including drilling and completion fluid systems, solids-control equipment, waste-management services, three-cone and diamond drill bits, fishing services, drilling tools, underreamers, casing exit and multilateral systems, packers and liner hangers. SII also offers supply-chain management solutions through an extensive branch network providing pipe, valve, tool, safety and other maintenance products. Operations are conducted through SII's four business units, which consists of M-I (49.2% of 2002 revenues), Wilson Industries (28.0%), Smith Services (12.6%), and Smith Bits (10.2%).

RECENT DEVELOPMENTS:

For the year ended 12/31/02, net income was $93.2 million compared with $152.1 million a year earlier. Results for 2001 included goodwill amortization of $15.7 million. Revenues fell 10.7% to $3.17 billion. SII attributed the majority of the revenue decline to the reduction in natural gas-directed drilling in North America, which negatively affected demand for the Company's products and services. Oilfield products and services revenues slid 5.8% to $2.28 billion and operating profit fell 24.8% to $266.7 million. Distribution revenues dropped 21.3% to $887.2 million and the unit posted an operating loss of $4.0 million versus an operating profit of $22.9 million the year before.

PROSPECTS:

SII believes that the strengthening fundamentals for North American natural gas drilling, which should result in higher exploration and production spending by customers as 2003 unfolds, will lead to improved results for 2003. Separately, on 1/29/03, the Company's M-I business unit announced the acquisition of the oilfield chemical operations of Finland-based Dynea International. In connection with the transaction, M-I acquired substantially all of the net assets of Dynea's production chemical business in exchange for cash consideration of approximately Euro 76.0 million.

ANNUAL FINANCIAL DATA:

FISCAL YEAR	TOT. REVS. ($mill.)	NET INC. ($mill.)	TOT. ASSETS ($mill.)	OPER. PROFIT %	NET PROFIT %	RET. ON EQUITY %	RET. ON ASSETS %	CURR. RATIO	EARN. PER SH.$	CASH FL. PER SH.$	TANG. BK. VAL.$	PRICE RANGE	AVG. P/E RATIO
p12/31/02	3,170.1	93.2							0.93			38.73 - 23.19	33.3
12/31/01	3,551.2	152.1	2,735.8	10.5	4.3	16.0	5.6	2.3	1.52	2.44	3.79	42.26 - 16.15	19.3
12/31/00	2,761.0	72.8	2,295.3	7.2	2.6	8.9	3.2	2.0	0.73	1.53	3.65	44.25 - 22.50	46.0
12/31/99	1,806.2	②56.7	1,894.6	8.3	3.1	7.9	3.0	2.3	②0.58	1.35	3.79	26.03 - 12.00	33.1
12/31/98	2,118.7	①34.1	1,759.0	5.9	5.4	1.9	1.4	1.4	①0.35	1.08	3.58	32.25 - 8.63	58.4
12/31/97	1,563.1	102.4	1,396.0	13.9	6.5	21.8	7.3	2.3	1.28	1.85	3.28	43.94 - 19.25	24.8
12/31/96	1,156.7	64.4	1,074.6	11.5	5.6	17.5	6.0	2.2	0.81	1.20	2.59	24.00 - 9.94	20.9
12/31/95	874.5	45.6	702.8	9.9	5.2	15.2	6.5	2.6	0.58	0.90	3.28	11.94 - 5.50	15.0
12/31/94	653.9	35.9	619.8	9.2	5.5	14.2	5.8	2.6	0.46	0.74	2.76	8.81 - 4.19	14.1
12/31/93	220.7	d4.0	348.4	8.4	...	...	...	3.2	d0.06	0.09	2.77	5.75 - 3.88	...

Statistics are as originally reported. Adj. for 100% stk. div., 7/8/02. ① Incls. one-time pre-tax chrgs. of $82.5 mill. ② Incls. one-time pre-tax credit of $84.0 mill.

OFFICERS:
D. L. Rock, Chmn., C.E.O.
M. K. Dorman, Sr. V.P., C.F.O., Treas.
N. S. Sutton, Sr. V.P., Sec., Gen. Couns.

INVESTOR CONTACT: Margaret K. Dorman, Sr. V.P., C.F.O., Treas., (281) 443-3370

PRINCIPAL OFFICE: 411 North Sam Houston Parkway, Suite 600, Houston, TX 77060

TELEPHONE NUMBER: (281) 443-3370
FAX: (281) 233-5199
WEB: www.smith.com
NO. OF EMPLOYEES: 11,494
SHAREHOLDERS: 2,302
ANNUAL MEETING: In Apr.
INCORPORATED: CA, Jan., 1937; reincorp., DE, May, 1983

INSTITUTIONAL HOLDINGS:
No. of Institutions: 259
Shares Held: 98,186,466
% Held: 96.7

INDUSTRY: Chemical preparations, nec (SIC: 2899)

TRANSFER AGENT(S): First Chicago Trust Company of New York, Jersey City, NJ

SMUCKER (J.M.) COMPANY

EXCH.	SYM.	REC. PRICE	P/E RATIO	YLD.	MKT. CAP.	RANGE (52-WK.)	'02 Y/E PR.
NYSE	SJM	34.25 (2/28/03)	19.1	2.3%	$1.70 bill.	42.25 - 28.71	39.81

MEDIUM GRADE. THE COMPANY IS EXPANDING ITS SMUCKER'S UNCRUSTABLES PRODUCTS INTO NEW MARKETS.

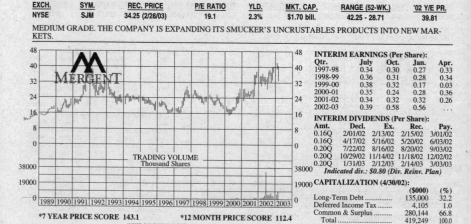

*7 YEAR PRICE SCORE 143.1   ***12 MONTH PRICE SCORE 112.4**

*NYSE COMPOSITE INDEX=100

INTERIM EARNINGS (Per Share):

Qtr.	July	Oct.	Jan.	Apr.
1997-98	0.34	0.30	0.27	0.33
1998-99	0.36	0.31	0.28	0.34
1999-00	0.38	0.32	0.17	0.03
2000-01	0.35	0.24	0.28	0.36
2001-02	0.34	0.32	0.32	0.26
2002-03	0.39	0.58	0.56	...

INTERIM DIVIDENDS (Per Share):

Amt.	Decl.	Ex.	Rec.	Pay.
0.16Q	2/01/02	2/13/02	2/15/02	3/01/02
0.16Q	4/17/02	5/16/02	5/20/02	6/03/02
0.20Q	7/22/02	8/16/02	8/20/02	9/03/02
0.20Q	10/29/02	11/14/02	11/18/02	12/02/02
0.20Q	1/31/03	2/12/03	2/14/03	3/03/03

Indicated div.: $0.80 (Div. Reinv. Plan)

CAPITALIZATION (4/30/02):

	($000)	(%)
Long-Term Debt	135,000	32.2
Deferred Income Tax	4,105	1.0
Common & Surplus	280,144	66.8
Total	419,249	100.0

BUSINESS:

The J.M. Smucker Company manufactures and markets food products, including fruit spreads, dessert toppings, peanut butter, industrial fruit products, fruit and vegetable juices, juice beverages, syrups, condiments, shortening and oils. Well-recognized brand names include: SMUCKER'S, JIF, CRISCO, DICKINSON'S, MAGIC SHELL and GOOBER. Products are sold primarily through brokers to chain, wholesale, cooperative, independent grocery accounts, as well as through food service distributors and chains including hotels, restaurants, and institutions, and to other food manufacturers. Distribution outside of the U.S. is principally in Canada, Australia, Mexico, Latin America, the Pacific Rim, and Greater Europe, although products are exported to other countries as well. During fiscal 2002, international sales represented approximately 14.1% of SJM's consolidated sales.

RECENT DEVELOPMENTS:

For the three months ended 1/31/03, net income totaled $28.0 million compared with $7.9 million in the corresponding prior-year period. Results included pre-tax merger and integration charges of $1.5 million and $914,000 in 2003 and 2002, respectively. Net sales more than doubled to $340.8 million from $168.4 million a year earlier, driven by sales of $167.6 million from JIF and CRISCO branded products. Gross profit was $122.9 million, or 36.1% of net sales, versus $55.0 million, or 32.7% of net sales, the previous year. Operating income amounted to $49.5 million compared with $14.3 million in the prior year.

PROSPECTS:

On 12/20/02, the Company announced plans to build a new facility in Scottsville, Kentucky that will produce SMUCKER'S UNCRUSTABLES, a line of thaw-'n-serve peanut butter and jelly sandwiches. The facility, which is expected to be operational in the spring 2004, will help support SJM's expansion of the UNCRUSTABLES products into new markets, primarily in the northeast U.S. Meanwhile, the Company is targeting full fiscal-2003 earnings, excluding one-time merger-related charges, in the range of $2.10 to $2.14 per share.

ANNUAL FINANCIAL DATA:

FISCAL YEAR	TOT. REVS. ($000)	NET INC. ($000)	TOT. ASSETS ($000)	OPER. PROFIT %	NET PROFIT %	RET. ON EQUITY %	RET. ON ASSETS %	CURR. RATIO	EARN. PER SH.$	CASH FL. PER SH.$	TANG. BK. VAL.$	DIV. PER SH.$	PRICE RANGE	AVG. P/E RATIO	AVG. YIELD %
4/30/02	687,148	④ 30,851	524,892	8.0	4.5	11.0	5.9	3.5	④ 1.24	2.39	9.32	0.64	37.73 - 22.61	24.3	2.1
4/30/01	651,242	⑤ 31,659	470,469	8.4	4.9	12.8	6.7	3.4	⑤ 1.23	2.28	8.27	0.63	29.00 - 15.00	17.9	2.9
4/30/00	632,486	④ 26,357	475,384	6.5	4.2	8.4	5.5	3.4	④ 0.92	1.83	9.29	0.59	25.75 - 18.38	24.0	2.7
4/30/99	602,457	37,763	433,883	9.8	6.3	11.6	8.7	2.1	1.29	2.09	9.04	0.55	28.19 - 20.63	18.9	2.3
4/30/98	565,476	① 36,348	407,973	10.1	6.4	12.0	8.9	2.4	① 1.24	2.01	8.91	0.52	30.00 - 16.00	18.5	2.3
4/30/97	542,602	30,935	384,773	9.8	5.7	10.6	8.0	2.5	1.06	1.81	8.44	0.52	22.50 - 16.13	18.2	2.7
② 4/30/96	528,576	③ 29,453	424,952	10.2	5.6	10.7	6.9	3.2	③ 1.01	1.61	7.96	0.52	24.50 - 17.25	20.7	2.5
4/30/95	628,279	36,303	421,017	9.9	5.8	14.1	8.6	2.4	1.25	...	6.08	0.49	26.00 - 20.50	18.6	2.1
4/30/94	511,525	30,498	378,641	9.9	6.0	13.0	8.1	2.1	1.05	...	5.99	0.45	32.38 - 20.25	25.1	1.7
4/30/93	491,309	① 37,399	294,811	12.2	7.6	17.0	12.7	3.0	① 1.27	...	...	...	39.00 - 24.50	25.0	1.3

Statistics are as originally reported. On 8/29/00, the Company combined its Cl. A and Cl. B shs. into a new class of com. stk. ① Bef. $3.0 mil ($0.10/sh) acctg. chg., 1998; & $4.5 mil ($0.15/sh) chg., 1993. ② Reflects disposition of Mrs. Smith's frozen pie business. ③ Bef. $140,000 loss from discont. oprs. ④ Incl. $5.0 mil pre-tax non-recur. acquisition-related chg., 2002; $9.6 mil ($0.34/sh) after-tax non-recur. chg. related to the impairment of certain long-lived assets, 2000. ⑤ Bef. $992,000 ($0.04/sh) chg. for acctg. adj. & incl. $2.2 mil ($0.05/sh) pre-tax non-recur. chg. fr. sale of real estate.

OFFICERS:
T. P. Smucker, Chmn., Co-C.E.O.
R. K. Smucker, Pres., Co-C.E.O.
S. J. Ellcessor, V.P., C.F.O., Sec.
M. R. Belgya, Treas.

PRINCIPAL OFFICE: One Strawberry Lane, Orrville, OH 44667-0280

TELEPHONE NUMBER: (330) 682-3000
FAX: (330) 682-3370
WEB: www.smuckers.com
NO. OF EMPLOYEES: 2,700 (approx.)
SHAREHOLDERS: 148,652
ANNUAL MEETING: In Aug.
INCORPORATED: OH, Sept., 1921

INSTITUTIONAL HOLDINGS:
No. of Institutions: 286
Shares Held: 23,846,679
% Held: 48.0
INDUSTRY: Canned fruits and vegetables (SIC: 2033)
TRANSFER AGENT(S): Computershare Investor Services, Chicago, IL

SNAP-ON INCORPORATED

EXCH.	SYM.	REC. PRICE	P/E RATIO	YLD.	MKT. CAP.	RANGE (52-WK.)	'02 Y/E PR.
NYSE	SNA	24.99 (2/28/03)	14.2	4.0%	$1.60 bill.	35.15 - 20.71	28.11

UPPER MEDIUM GRADE. THE COMPANY EXPECTS A SUBSTANTIAL PART OF ITS FULL-YEAR 2003 EARNINGS GROWTH TO OCCUR IN THE SECOND HALF OF 2003.

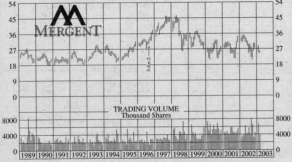

*7 YEAR PRICE SCORE 91.6　　　***12 MONTH PRICE SCORE 98.4**

*NYSE COMPOSITE INDEX=100

INTERIM EARNINGS (Per Share):

Qtr.	Mar.	June	Sept.	Dec.
1997	0.56	0.64	0.58	0.68
1998	0.56	0.38	d1.24	0.21
1999	0.55	0.42	0.72	0.47
2000	0.58	0.75	0.46	0.24
2001	0.51	0.15	0.01	d0.30
2002	0.37	0.50	0.33	0.56

INTERIM DIVIDENDS (Per Share):

Amt.	Decl.	Ex.	Rec.	Pay.
0.24Q	1/25/02	2/13/02	2/15/02	3/08/02
0.24Q	4/26/02	5/16/02	5/20/02	6/10/02
0.24Q	6/28/02	8/16/02	8/20/02	9/10/02
0.25Q	10/25/02	11/15/02	11/19/02	12/10/02
0.25Q	1/24/03	2/12/03	2/17/03	3/10/03

Indicated div.: $1.00 (Div. Reinv. Plan)

CAPITALIZATION (12/29/01):

	($000)	(%)
Long-Term Debt	445,500	35.8
Deferred Income Tax	24,700	2.0
Common & Surplus	775,800	62.3
Total	1,246,000	100.0

BUSINESS:

Snap-on Incorporated is a global developer, manufacturer and marketer of tool, diagnostic and equipment applications for professional technicians, shop owners, franchised and chain vehicle service centers, vehicle and equipment manufacturers, and commercial industrial tool and equipment users worldwide. Product lines include hand and power tools, diagnostics and shop equipment, tool storage products, diagnostics software and other tools for the vehicle service, industrial, government and agricultural customers and other commercial applications, including construction and electrical. SNA's three business segments are The Snap-on Dealer Group (43.6% of 2002 sales), the Commercial and Industrial Group (42.6%), and the Diagnostics and Information Group (13.8%). Products are sold through SNA's franchised dealer vans, Company-direct sales and distributor channels, as well as over the Internet. SNA also offers extended-credit financing for the purchase of its products. On 9/30/99, SNA acquired the Sandvik Saws and Tools business, which was renamed Bahco Group AB.

RECENT DEVELOPMENTS:

For the year ended 12/28/03, income was $103.2 million versus income of $21.5 million in 2001. Results for 2002 and 2001 included after-tax restructuring charges of $3.3 million and $46.1 million, respectively. Earnings also included nonrecurring items that resulted in a net after-tax gain of $1.3 million in 2002 and an after-tax charge of $39.1 million in 2001. Net sales grew 0.6% to $2.11 billion. Snap-on Dealer Group net sales rose 0.4% to $1.06 billion, while Commercial and Industrial Group net sales climbed 1.2% to $1.03 billion.

PROSPECTS:

Looking ahead, SNA expects retirement and insurance costs to increase approximately $22.0 million year over year. Meanwhile, SNA will continue to invest in product development and continue to incur costs to implement business and process improvements identified through the adoption of lean operating practices and other rationalization activities. SNA also expects to continue to experience U.S. dealer inventory reductions through the first half of 2003. For full-year 2003, SNA expects earnings per share to grow in the range of 10.0% to 15.0% year over year.

ANNUAL FINANCIAL DATA:

FISCAL YEAR	TOT. REVS. ($mill.)	NET INC. ($mill.)	TOT. ASSETS ($mill.)	OPER. PROFIT %	NET PROFIT %	RET. ON EQUITY %	RET. ON ASSETS %	CURR. RATIO	EARN. PER SH. $	CASH FL. PER SH. $	TANG. BK. VAL.$	DIV. PER SH. $	PRICE RANGE	AVG. P/E RATIO	AVG. YIELD %
p12/31/02	2,109.1	⑥ 103.2	1,994.1						⑥ 1.77			0.97	35.15 - 20.71	15.8	3.5
12/29/01	2,095.7	⑤⑤ 21.5	1,974.3	4.1	1.0	2.8	1.1	2.1	⑤⑤ 0.37	1.54	6.01	0.96	34.40 - 21.15	75.0	3.5
12/30/00	2,175.7	④ 123.1	2,050.4	10.6	5.7	14.6	6.0	2.2	④ 2.10	3.23	13.99	0.94	32.44 - 20.88	12.7	3.5
1/01/00	1,945.6	③ 127.2	2,149.8	10.9	6.5	15.4	5.9	2.7	③ 2.16	3.10	12.65	0.90	37.81 - 26.44	14.9	2.8
1/02/99	1,772.6	② d4.8	1,674.9	1.9	…	…	…	2.4	② d0.08	0.68	11.61	0.86	46.44 - 25.50	…	2.4
1/03/98	1,672.2	150.4	1,641.4	15.9	9.0	16.9	9.2	2.9	2.44	3.06	14.74	0.82	46.31 - 34.25	16.5	2.0
12/28/96	1,485.3	131.5	1,520.8	14.8	8.9	15.9	8.6	3.0	2.16	2.68	13.62	0.76	38.25 - 27.33	15.2	2.3
12/30/95	1,292.1	113.3	1,361.0	14.6	8.8	15.1	8.3	2.8	1.84	2.36	12.35	0.72	31.50 - 20.67	14.2	2.8
12/31/94	1,194.3	① 98.3	1,234.9	13.3	8.2	12.8	8.0	3.7	① 1.53	1.99	11.92	0.72	29.58 - 19.33	16.0	2.9
1/01/94	1,132.0	85.8	1,218.9	13.0	7.6	12.2	7.0	2.8	1.35	1.85	10.99	0.72	29.67 - 20.33	18.6	2.9

Statistics are as originally reported. Adj. for stk. split: 3-for-2, 9/96. ① Incl. net gain of $2.2 mill. from sale of Systems Control, Inc. ② Incl. pre-tax chrgs. of $149.9 mill. ③ Incl. nonrecurr. chrgs. of $49.4 mill., 2001; $20.6 mill., 1/1/00. ④ Incl. nonrecurr. chrg. of $21.8 mill., excl. acctg. chrg. of $25.4 mill. ⑤ Excl. acctg. change chrg. of $2.5 mill. ⑥ Excl. acctg. change credit of $2.8 mill., but incl. after-tax restruct. chrg. of $3.3 milll. and special items of an after-tax credit of $1.3 mill.

OFFICERS:
D. F. Elliot, Chmn., Pres., C.E.O.
S. F. Marrinan, V.P., Sec., Gen. Counsel
M. M. Ellen, Sr. V.P., C.F.O.
INVESTOR CONTACT: Bill Pfund, Investor Contact, (262) 656-6488
PRINCIPAL OFFICE: 10801 Corporate Drive, Pleasant Prairie, WI 53158-1603

TELEPHONE NUMBER: (262) 656-5200
FAX: (262) 656-5577
WEB: www.snapon.com
NO. OF EMPLOYEES: 13,500 (approx.)
SHAREHOLDERS: 10,819
ANNUAL MEETING: In Apr.
INCORPORATED: WI, Apr., 1920; reincorp., DE, Apr., 1930

INSTITUTIONAL HOLDINGS:
No. of Institutions: 217
Shares Held: 47,141,901
% Held: 80.7
INDUSTRY: Instruments to measure electricity (SIC: 3825)
TRANSFER AGENT(S): First Chicago Trust Company of New York, Jersey City, NJ

SOLECTRON CORPORATION

EXCH.	SYM.	REC. PRICE	P/E RATIO	YLD.	MKT. CAP.	RANGE (52-WK.)	'02 Y/E PR.
NYSE	SLR	3.15 (2/28/03)	...	...	$2.60 bill.	10.68 - 1.39	3.55

SPECULATIVE GRADE. THE COMPANY ACQUIRED INTERNATIONAL BUSINESS MACHINE CORPORATION'S GLOBAL ASSET RECOVERY OPERATIONS IN RALEIGH, NORTH CAROLINA.

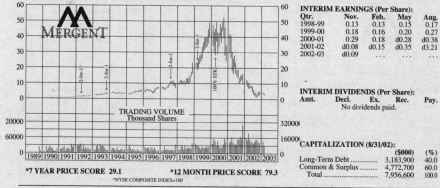

INTERIM EARNINGS (Per Share):

Qtr.	Nov.	Feb.	May	Aug.
1998-99	0.13	0.13	0.15	0.17
1999-00	0.18	0.16	0.20	0.27
2000-01	0.29	0.18	d0.28	d0.38
2001-02	d0.08	d0.15	d0.35	d3.21
2002-03	d0.09	...	...	...

INTERIM DIVIDENDS (Per Share):

Amt.	Decl.	Ex.	Rec.	Pay.
		No dividends paid.		

CAPITALIZATION (8/31/02):

	($000)	(%)
Long-Term Debt	3,183,900	40.0
Common & Surplus	4,772,700	60.0
Total	7,956,600	100.0

*7 YEAR PRICE SCORE 29.1   ***12 MONTH PRICE SCORE 79.3**

*NYSE COMPOSITE INDEX=100

BUSINESS:

Solectron Corporation is a global, provider of customized, integrated manufacturing services to electronic original equipment manufacturers. SLR furnishes integrated supply-chain services that span the entire product life cycle from technology to manufacturing to global services. SLR's manufacturing services include advanced building block design services, product design and testing, new product introduction management, materials purchasing and management, prototyping, printed circuit board and systems assembly, distribution, product repair and warranty services. Segments include: Global Operations (83.8% of fiscal 2002 sales), Technology Solutions (7.0%), Global Services (6.7%) and MicroSystems (2.5%) segments. On 12/3/01, SLR acquired C-MAC Industries Inc.

RECENT DEVELOPMENTS:

For the quarter ended 11/30/02, SLR reported a net loss of $70.9 million versus a net loss of $52.5 million in the equivalent 2001 quarter. Results for 2002 and 2001 included after-tax charges of $85.4 million and $51.7 million for restructuring and impairments, and $5.5 million and $14.5 million for intangible asset amortization, respectively. Results also included an after-tax gain of $21.3 million in 2002 and a loss of $2.0 million in 2001. Net sales slipped 0.5% to $3.14 billion from $3.15 billion a year earlier. On a segment basis, Global Operations sales fell 12.6% to $2.50 billion, while Technology Solutions sales jumped 83.6% to $283.6 million. Global Services sales climbed 77.3% to $251.4 million, and MicroSystem sales were $105.9 million in 2002.

PROSPECTS:

On 2/19/03, SLR acquired IBM's Global Asset Recovery operations in Raleigh, North Carolina. The transaction expands SLR's relationship with IBM through a three-year supply agreement. In addition, the acquisition bolsters SLR's North American network of asset-recovery centers, which provide de-manufacturing, remanufacturing, recycling and disposal services to customers. Separately, SLR reached a manufacturing and supply agreement with Hewlett-Packard to produce printed circuit boards and memory modules for mid- and high-end enterprise servers. At anticipated production levels, the contract would generate about $1.40 billion in sales over five years.

ANNUAL FINANCIAL DATA:

FISCAL YEAR	TOT. REVS. ($mill.)	NET INC. ($mill.)	TOT. ASSETS ($mill.)	OPER. PROFIT %	NET PROFIT %	RET. ON EQUITY %	RET. ON ASSETS %	CURR. RATIO	EARN. PER SH.$	CASH FL. PER SH.$	TANG. BK. VAL.$	PRICE RANGE	AVG. P/E RATIO
8/31/02	12,276.2	④ d3,110.2	11,014.0	...	...	...	...	2.2	④ d3.98	d3.50	3.16	12.42 - 1.39	...
8/31/01	18,692.3	① d123.5	12,930.4	...	...	...	...	3.2	① d0.19	0.64	4.81	41.95 - 9.65	...
③ 8/31/00	14,137.5	② 500.7	10,375.6	5.0	3.5	13.2	4.8	2.7	② 0.80	1.21	6.28	52.63 - 24.54	48.2
8/31/99	8,391.4	293.9	4,834.7	5.2	3.5	10.5	6.1	3.6	0.57	0.91	5.15	49.00 - 18.64	59.8
8/31/98	5,288.3	198.8	2,410.6	5.7	3.8	16.8	8.2	2.2	0.41	0.64	2.51	23.38 - 8.86	39.0
8/31/97	3,694.4	① 158.1	1,852.4	6.4	4.3	17.2	8.5	2.7	① 0.34	0.57	2.01	11.86 - 5.89	25.9
8/31/96	2,817.2	114.2	1,452.2	6.2	4.1	16.3	7.9	3.2	0.27	0.48	1.67	7.52 - 3.63	20.3
8/31/95	2,065.6	79.5	940.9	6.0	3.9	14.8	8.5	2.0	0.23	0.40	1.36	5.64 - 2.77	18.4
8/31/94	1,456.8	55.5	766.4	6.1	3.8	16.8	7.2	2.1	0.17	0.30	1.00	4.25 - 2.92	21.7
8/31/93	836.3	30.6	603.3	6.4	3.7	11.7	5.1	2.3	0.10	0.19	0.80	3.72 - 2.07	28.9

Statistics are as originally reported. Adj. for stk. split: 2-for-1, 3/00; 2/99; 8/97; 10/93. ① Incl. non-recurr. pre-tax chrg. $492.0 mill., 2001; $4.0 mill., 8/97. ② Excl. acctg. chrg. of $3.5 mill. and incl. non-recurr. chrgs. of $37.9 mill. ③ Revs. reflected strategic acqs. & robust global demand. ④ Incl. acquis. and impair. chrg. of $3.31 billion and a gain of $75.7 mill. on the retirement of debt.

OFFICERS:
W. A. Hasler, Chmn.
M. R. Cannon, Pres., C.E.O.
K. Patel, Exec. V.P., C.F.O.
INVESTOR CONTACT: Perry Hayes, (408) 956-7543
PRINCIPAL OFFICE: 777 Gibraltar Drive, Milpitas, CA 95035

TELEPHONE NUMBER: (408) 957-8500
FAX: (408) 957-6056
WEB: www.solectron.com
NO. OF EMPLOYEES: 73,000 (approx.)
SHAREHOLDERS: 9,600 (approx.)
ANNUAL MEETING: In Jan.
INCORPORATED: CA, Aug., 1977; reincorp., DE, Feb., 1997

INSTITUTIONAL HOLDINGS:
No. of Institutions: 377
Shares Held: 696,036,644
% Held: 84.3
INDUSTRY: Printed circuit boards (SIC: 3672)
TRANSFER AGENT(S): EquiServe Trust Company, N.A., Providence, RI

SOLUTIA INC.

EXCH.	SYM.	REC. PRICE	P/E RATIO	YLD.	MKT. CAP.	RANGE (52-WK.)	'02 Y/E PR.
NYSE	SOI	2.68 (2/28/03)	...	1.5%	$280.0 mill.	9.00 - 2.38	3.63

SPECULATIVE GRADE. THE COMPANY COMPLETED THE SALE OF ITS RESINS, ADDITIVES AND ADHESIVES BUSINESSES TO UCB S.A. FOR $500.0 MILLION IN CASH.

TRADING VOLUME
Thousand Shares

*7 YEAR PRICE SCORE N/A   *12 MONTH PRICE SCORE 65.9
*NYSE COMPOSITE INDEX=100

INTERIM EARNINGS (Per Share):

Qtr.	Mar.	June	Sept.	Dec.
1997	0.54	0.51	0.44	0.06
1998	0.51	0.58	0.47	0.46
1999	0.20	0.61	0.53	0.46
2000	0.46	0.04	0.74	d0.81
2001	0.21	0.12	0.07	d0.97
2002	d1.46	0.22	Nil	d0.20

INTERIM DIVIDENDS (Per Share):

Amt.	Decl.	Ex.	Rec.	Pay.
0.04A	10/24/01	11/13/01	11/15/01	12/12/01
0.04A	10/23/02	11/13/02	11/15/02	12/12/02

Indicated div.: $0.04 (Div. Reinv. Plan)

CAPITALIZATION (12/31/01):

	($000)	(%)
Long-Term Debt	627,000	122.0
Common & Surplus	d113,000	-22.0
Total	514,000	100.0

BUSINESS:

Solutia Inc., spun off from Monsanto Co. on 9/1/97, operates in two business segments. The Performance Films segment (42.2% of 2002 revenues) is comprised of SOI's performance film product line and specialties, which consists of industrial products and pharmaceutical services. The performance films product line manufactures SAFLEX® plastic interlayer, which is used to make laminated glass for windshields, and VANCEA™, which is used for side and rear windows. The Integrated Nylon segment (57.8%) produces an integrated family of nylon products, including VYDYNE® and ASCEND® nylon polymers; nylon fibers such as WEAR-DATED® and ULTRON® brands used in carpet; and ACRILAN® acrylic fibers. On 1/31/03, SOI sold its specialty products business to UCB S.A.

RECENT DEVELOPMENTS:

For the twelve months ended 12/31/02, loss amounted to $8.0 million, before an accounting change charge of $167.0 million, compared with a loss from continuing operations of $81.0 million in 2001. Results benefited from lower raw material and energy costs, cost-reduction efforts and reduced amortization expense, partially offset by decreased average selling prices and higher interest expense. Results for 2002 and 2001 included amortization expenses of $3.0 million and $12.0 million, respectively. Results for 2002 and 2001 excluded income of $24.0 million and $22.0 million, respectively, from discontinued ops. Net sales slipped 1.2% to $2.24 billion from $2.27 billion in the prior year. Operating income jumped to $38.0 million compared with an operating loss of $36.0 million a year earlier.

PROSPECTS:

On 1/31/03, the Company completed the sale of its resins, additives and adhesives businesses to UCB S.A. for $500.0 million in cash. The proceeds from the sale, which was strategically in line with the Company's plans to realign its businesses into two operating segments, will be used to reduce debt. In addition, the sale is anticipated to be accretive to earnings in 2003 and SOI expects to save approximately $40.0 million in cash interest in 2003. Separately, the Company expects uncertain economic conditions to result in near-term volatility in raw material and energy costs.

ANNUAL FINANCIAL DATA:

FISCAL YEAR	TOT. REVS. ($mill.)	NET INC. ($mill.)	TOT. ASSETS ($mill.)	OPER. PROFIT %	NET PROFIT %	RET. ON EQUITY %	RET. ON ASSETS %	CURR. RATIO	EARN. PER SH.$	CASH FL. PER SH.$	DIV. PER SH.$	PRICE RANGE	AVG. P/E RATIO	AVG. YIELD %
p12/31/02	2,241.0	⑤ d8.0	...	...	...	...	...	0.7	⑤ d1.44	...	0.04	13.89 — 2.67	...	0.5
12/31/01	2,817.0	d59.0	3,408.0	...	...	...	...	0.8	d0.57	1.07	0.04	15.32 — 10.90	...	0.3
12/31/00	3,185.0	④ 49.0	3,581.0	0.8	1.5	...	1.4	0.8	④ 0.46	2.12	0.04	17.25 — 10.19	29.8	0.3
12/31/99	2,830.0	② 206.0	3,770.0	10.4	7.3	251.2	5.5	0.8	② 1.80	3.03	0.04	26.31 — 13.50	11.1	0.2
12/31/98	2,835.0	① 249.0	2,765.0	13.6	8.8	...	9.0	1.4	① 2.03	3.17	0.04	32.00 — 18.69	12.5	0.2
12/31/97	2,969.0	192.0	2,768.0	9.8	6.5	...	6.9	1.1	1.55	2.70	0.01	27.75 — 18.69	15.0	...
12/31/96	2,977.0	③ 32.0	2,483.0	1.1	1.1	4.9	1.3	1.2	③ 0.27	1.71	...	...	...	...
12/31/95	2,964.0	③ 147.0	2,462.0	8.7	5.4	21.1	6.5	1.4	③ 1.27	2.82	...	...	...	...
12/31/94	3,097.0	③ 149.0	2,435.0	8.3	4.8	...	6.1	...	...	...	...	...	...	...

Statistics are as originally reported. ① Incl. reversal of $6.0 mill. after-tax chg. rel. to closing of some facilities & an employment reduct. plan. ② Incl. $40.0 mill. net special chgs. ③ Incl. restr. chgs. $192.0 mill., 1996; $53.0 mill., 1995; $34.0 mill., 1994. ④ Incl. $90.0 mill. net closing & sev. costs, $4.0 mill. net impair. chg., $15.0 mill. net chg. fr. jt. ventures, $16.0 mill. net write-down of equity invest. & $82.0 mill. net gain fr. sale of assets. ⑤ Excl. $24.0 mill. gain fr. disc. ops. & $167.0 mill. acct. chg.

OFFICERS:
J. C. Hunter III, Chmn., Pres., C.E.O.
R. A. Clausen, Vice-Chmn., C.F.O.
J. N. Quinn, Sr. V.P., Sec., Gen. Couns.
INVESTOR CONTACT: Liesl Livingston, Director, Inv. Rel., (314) 674-7777
PRINCIPAL OFFICE: 575 Maryville Centre Dr., P.O. Box 66760, St. Louis, MO 63166

TELEPHONE NUMBER: (314) 674-1000
FAX: (314) 674-7625
WEB: www.solutia.com
NO. OF EMPLOYEES: 9,170 (approx.)
SHAREHOLDERS: 34,367
ANNUAL MEETING: In Apr.
INCORPORATED: DE, Apr., 1997

INSTITUTIONAL HOLDINGS:
No. of Institutions: 156
Shares Held: 77,817,537
% Held: 74.3
INDUSTRY: Chemical preparations, nec (SIC: 2899)
TRANSFER AGENT(S): EquiServe, First Chicago Trust Division, Jersey City, NJ

SONIC AUTOMOTIVE, INC.

EXCH.	SYM.	REC. PRICE	P/E RATIO	YLD.	MKT. CAP.	RANGE (52-WK.)	'02 Y/E PR.
NYSE	SAH	15.22 (2/28/03)	6.1	...	$0.62 bill.	39.75 - 13.31	14.87

UPPER MEDIUM GRADE. THE COMPANY IS TARGETING EARNINGS OF BETWEEN $2.70 AND $2.80 PER SHARE IN 2003.

MERGENT

TRADING VOLUME
Thousand Shares

17000

8500

| 1989 | 1990 | 1991 | 1992 | 1993 | 1994 | 1995 | 1996 | 1997 | 1998 | 1999 | 2000 | 2001 | 2002 | 2003 |

*7 YEAR PRICE SCORE N/A   ***12 MONTH PRICE SCORE 75.1**

*NYSE COMPOSITE INDEX=100

INTERIM EARNINGS (Per Share):

Qtr.	Mar.	June	Sept.	Dec.
1998	0.09	0.20	0.21	0.24
1999	0.24	0.30	0.33	0.38
2000	0.39	0.51	0.51	0.29
2001	0.33	0.55	0.53	0.51
2002	0.53	0.69	0.74	0.53

INTERIM DIVIDENDS (Per Share):

Amt.	Decl.	Ex.	Rec.	Pay.
		No dividends paid.		

CAPITALIZATION (12/31/01):

	($000)	(%)
Long-Term Debt	517,713	48.7
Deferred Income Tax	28,199	2.7
Common & Surplus	517,261	48.7
Total	1,063,173	100.0

BUSINESS:

Sonic Automotive, Inc., the second largest automotive retailer in the United States based on total revenue, operated 187 dealership franchises and 45 collision repair centers in 15 states as of 3/4/03. The Company's franchises provide comprehensive services including sales of both new and used cars and light trucks, replacement parts and vehicle maintenance, warranty, paint and repair services.

The Company also offers extended warranty contracts and financing and insurance for its customers. In 2002, revenues were derived as follows: new vehicle sales, 60.4%; used vehicle sales, 17.2%; parts, service, and collision repair, 12.9%; wholesale vehicle sales, 6.7%; and finance and insurance, 2.8%.

RECENT DEVELOPMENTS:

For the twelve months ended 12/31/02, income from continuing operations totaled $108.5 million, up 32.0% compared with income from continuing operations of $82.2 million a year earlier. Results for 2001 included goodwill amortization of $17.6 million. Total revenues climbed 20.3% to $7.07 billion from $5.88 billion the year before.

New vehicle sales advanced 21.2% to $4.27 billion, while used vehicle sales increased 13.2% to $1.21 billion. Gross profit was $1.09 billion, or 15.4% of total revenue, versus $904.7 million, or 15.4% of total revenue, in the prior year. Operating income rose 17.5% to $235.2 million from $200.2 million a year earlier.

PROSPECTS:

The Company is targeting earnings of between $2.70 and $2.80 per share in 2003. SAH is taking steps to reduce its inventory of new vehicles in response to decreased demand, primarily at the Company's domestic-branded franchises. Meanwhile, SAH continues to seek strategic acquisitions and expects to announce agreements to acquire

dealerships with at least $500.0 million in annual revenues during 2003. Recently, SAH entered into an agreement to acquire Larry Miller Toyota in Denver, Colorado and was awarded a Mitsubishi franchise for an existing facility in the Denver area. These two new franchises are expected to add approximately $100.0 million in annual revenues.

ANNUAL FINANCIAL DATA:

FISCAL YEAR	TOT. REVS. ($mill.)	NET INC. ($mill.)	TOT. ASSETS ($mill.)	OPER. PROFIT %	NET PROFIT %	RET. ON EQUITY %	RET. ON ASSETS %	CURR. RATIO	EARN. PER SH.$	CASH FL. PER SH.$	TANG. BK. VAL.$	PRICE RANGE	AVG. P/E RATIO
p12/31/02	7,071.0	② 108.5							② 2.51			39.75 - 13.31	10.6
12/31/01	6,337.4	79.3	1,805.9	3.2	1.3	15.3	4.4	1.3	1.91	2.53	...	23.98 - 6.00	7.8
12/31/00	① 6,052.5	74.2	1,789.2	3.5	1.2	16.4	4.1	1.3	1.69	2.21	...	12.25 - 5.69	5.3
12/31/99	3,350.8	44.6	1,501.1	3.5	1.3	11.1	3.0	1.3	1.27	1.60	...	18.94 - 7.69	10.5
12/31/98	1,603.7	18.6	576.1	3.3	1.2	13.0	3.2	1.3	0.74	0.93	...	18.44 - 4.84	15.7
12/31/97	536.0	3.7	291.5	2.8	0.7	4.4	1.3	1.3	0.27	0.36	0.44	6.19 - 4.69	20.5
12/31/96	376.6	3.0	111.0	2.9	0.8	11.3	2.7	1.3	0.24	0.32	1.76	... ...	...
12/31/95	311.0	3.2	79.5	3.2	1.0	19.9	4.1	1.3	...	...	...	... ...	...
12/31/94	267.1	3.7	...	3.2	1.4	...	...	...	...	...	...	... ...	...

Statistics are as originally reported. Adj. for 2-for-1 stk. split, 1/99. ① Revenue growth reflects multiple acquisitions of dealerships. ② Bef. $1.9 mil ($0.04/sh) loss fr. disc. opers.

OFFICERS:
O. B. Smith, Chmn., C.E.O.
B. S. Smith, Vice-Chmn.
T. M. Wright, Pres., C.F.O.
J. C. Rachor, Exec. V.P., C.O.O.

INVESTOR CONTACT: Todd Atenhan, Investor Relations, (888) 766-4218

PRINCIPAL OFFICE: 5401 East Independence Boulevard, Charlotte, NC 28212

TELEPHONE NUMBER: (704) 566-2400
FAX: (704) 536-5116
WEB: www.sonicautomotive.com
NO. OF EMPLOYEES: 10,000 (approx.)
SHAREHOLDERS: 97 (class A common); 4 (class B common)
ANNUAL MEETING: In May
INCORPORATED: DE, Feb., 1997

INSTITUTIONAL HOLDINGS:
No. of Institutions: 115
Shares Held: 24,491,017
% Held: 59.0

INDUSTRY: New and used car dealers (SIC: 5511)

TRANSFER AGENT(S): First Union National Bank of North Carolina, Charlotte, NC

SONOCO PRODUCTS COMPANY

EXCH.	SYM.	REC. PRICE	P/E RATIO	YLD.	MKT. CAP.	RANGE (52-WK.)	'02 Y/E PR.	DIV. ACH.
NYSE	SON	20.75 (2/28/03)	14.8	4.0%	$1.99 bill.	29.70 - 19.45	22.93	19 yrs.

MEDIUM GRADE. THE COMPANY'S OBJECTIVE OVER THE NEXT FOUR YEARS IS TO GROW ANNUAL SALES TO $4.00 BILLION.

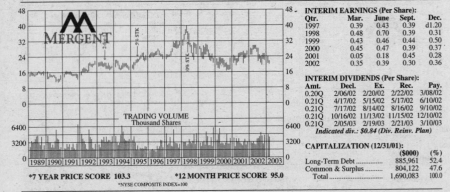

INTERIM EARNINGS (Per Share):

Qtr.	Mar.	June	Sept.	Dec.
1997	0.39	0.43	0.39	d1.20
1998	0.48	0.70	0.39	0.31
1999	0.43	0.46	0.44	0.50
2000	0.45	0.47	0.39	0.37
2001	0.05	0.18	0.45	0.28
2002	0.35	0.39	0.30	0.36

INTERIM DIVIDENDS (Per Share):

Amt.	Decl.	Ex.	Rec.	Pay.
0.20Q	2/06/02	2/20/02	2/22/02	3/08/02
0.21Q	4/17/02	5/15/02	5/17/02	6/10/02
0.21Q	7/17/02	8/14/02	8/16/02	9/10/02
0.21Q	10/16/02	11/13/02	11/15/02	12/10/02
0.21Q	2/05/03	2/19/03	2/21/03	3/10/03

Indicated div.: $0.84 (Div. Reinv. Plan)

CAPITALIZATION (12/31/01):

	($000)	(%)
Long-Term Debt	885,961	52.4
Common & Surplus	804,122	47.6
Total	1,690,083	100.0

*7 YEAR PRICE SCORE 103.3 ***12 MONTH PRICE SCORE 95.0**
*NYSE COMPOSITE INDEX=100

BUSINESS:

Sonoco Products Company is a multinational manufacturer of industrial and consumer packaging products. SON is also vertically integrated into paperboard production and recovered-paper collection. The paperboard utilized in SON's packaging products is produced substantially from recovered paper. As of 1/29/03, SON operated approximately 300 facilities in 32 countries serving customers in some 85 nations. The industrial packaging segment (50.1% of 2002 sales) includes engineered carriers (paper and plastic tubes and cores), paper (paper manufacturing and recovered paper operations) and protective packaging (designed interior packaging and protective reels). The consumer packaging segment (49.9%) includes composite cans; flexible packaging (printing flexibles, high density bags and film products); and packaging services and specialty products (e-marketplace/supply chain management, graphics management, folding cartons, and paper glass covers and coasters).

RECENT DEVELOPMENTS:

For the year ended 12/31/02, net income increased 47.7% to $135.3 million compared with $91.6 million in 2001. Results for 2002 and 2001 included restructuring charges of $12.6 million and $53.6 million, respectively. Results for 2001 included goodwill amortization of $12.1 million and a nonrecurring gain of $226,000. Sales grew 7.9% to $2.81 billion from $2.61 billion a year earlier, reflecting contributions from acquisitions made in 2001 and, to a lesser extent, additional volume in the consumer segment.

PROSPECTS:

SON's objective over the next four years is to grow annual sales to $4.00 billion through new product development, geographical expansions and strategic acquisitions. SON expects to drive growth through continued strong cash flow production and by maintaining a healthy balance sheet. SON anticipates productivity improvements in 2003 between $40.0 million and $50.0 million.

ANNUAL FINANCIAL DATA:

FISCAL YEAR	TOT. REVS. ($mill.)	NET INC. ($mill.)	TOT. ASSETS ($mill.)	OPER. PROFIT %	NET PROFIT %	RET. ON EQUITY %	RET. ON ASSETS %	CURR. RATIO	EARN. PER SH. $	CASH FL. PER SH. $	TANG. BK. VAL. $	DIV. PER SH. $	PRICE RANGE	AVG. P/E RATIO	AVG. YIELD %
p12/31/02	2,812.2	③ 135.3							⑤ 1.39			0.83	29.70 - 19.45	17.7	3.4
12/31/01	2,606.3	③ 91.6	2,352.2	8.6	3.5	11.4	3.9	1.4	③ 0.96	2.61	4.64	0.80	26.88 - 19.20	24.0	3.5
12/31/00	2,711.5	③ 166.3	2,212.6	12.0	6.1	20.7	7.5	1.6	③ 1.66	3.17	5.94	0.79	23.50 - 16.56	12.1	3.9
12/31/99	2,546.7	187.8	2,297.0	13.2	7.4	20.8	8.2	1.7	1.83	3.25	6.37	0.75	30.50 - 20.69	14.0	2.9
12/31/98	2,557.9	② 192.0	2,083.0	15.2	7.5	23.4	9.2	1.5	② 1.84	3.24	6.40	0.70	40.00 - 22.13	16.9	2.3
12/31/97	2,847.8	① 2.6	2,176.9	4.1	0.1	0.3	0.1	2.0	① Nil	1.43	6.69	0.64	32.27 - 22.61	...	2.3
12/31/96	2,788.1	170.9	2,387.5	11.8	6.1	18.6	7.2	1.6	1.64	3.08	3.49	0.59	28.07 - 22.61	15.5	2.3
12/31/95	2,706.2	164.5	2,115.4	11.5	6.1	17.9	7.8	1.5	1.56	2.82	3.34	0.53	26.14 - 17.37	13.9	2.4
12/31/94	2,300.1	129.8	1,835.1	10.6	5.6	15.6	7.1	1.6	1.22	2.34	3.00	0.48	22.30 - 17.10	16.2	2.4
12/31/93	1,947.2	118.8	1,707.1	10.9	6.1	15.1	7.0	1.7	1.17	2.12	2.73	0.46	21.54 - 17.10	16.5	2.4

Statistics are as originally reported. Adj. for stk. splits: 2-for-1, 6/93; 5% div., 6/95; 10%, 6/98. ① Incl. non-recurr. after-tax chrg. $174.5 mill. for asset write-down. ② Bef. exraord. loss of $11.8 mill. and net gain on sale of divested assets of $85.4 mill. ③ Incl. nonrecurr. chrg. of $12.6 mill., 2002; $53.3 mill., 2001; $5.5 mill., 2000.

OFFICERS:
C. W. Coker, Chmn.
H. E. DeLoach, Jr., Pres., C.E.O.
C. J. Hupfer, V.P., C.F.O.

INVESTOR CONTACT: Allan V. Cecil, V.P.
Inv. Rel. & Corp. Affairs, (843) 383-7524

PRINCIPAL OFFICE: One North Second Street, Post Office Box 160, Hartsville, SC 29551-0160

TELEPHONE NUMBER: (843) 383-7000
FAX: (843) 383-7008
WEB: www.sonoco.com

NO. OF EMPLOYEES: 17,900 (approx.)

SHAREHOLDERS: 43,000 (approx.)

ANNUAL MEETING: In Apr.

INCORPORATED: SC, May, 1899

INSTITUTIONAL HOLDINGS:
No. of Institutions: 207
Shares Held: 49,066,730
% Held: 50.8

INDUSTRY: Paperboard mills (SIC: 2631)

TRANSFER AGENT(S): EquiServe, Providence, RI

SOUTHERN COMPANY (THE)

EXCH.	SYM.	REC. PRICE	P/E RATIO	YLD.	MKT. CAP.	RANGE (52-WK.)	'02 Y/E PR.
NYSE	SO	28.21 (2/28/03)	15.2	4.9%	$19.72 bill.	31.14 - 23.22	28.39

UPPER MEDIUM GRADE. THE COMPANY PLANS TO COMPLETE APPROXIMATELY 4,000 MEGAWATTS OF ADDITIONAL COMPETITIVE ELECTRIC GENERATING CAPACITY BY 2005.

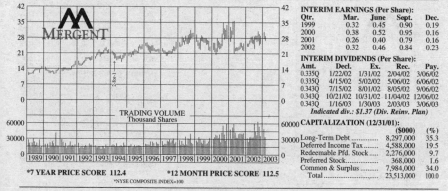

INTERIM EARNINGS (Per Share):

Qtr.	Mar.	June	Sept.	Dec.
1999	0.32	0.45	0.90	0.19
2000	0.38	0.52	0.95	0.16
2001	0.26	0.40	0.79	0.16
2002	0.32	0.46	0.84	0.23

INTERIM DIVIDENDS (Per Share):

Amt.	Decl.	Ex.	Rec.	Pay.
0.335Q	1/22/02	1/31/02	2/04/02	3/06/02
0.335Q	4/15/02	5/03/02	5/06/02	6/06/02
0.343Q	7/15/02	8/01/02	8/05/02	9/06/02
0.343Q	10/21/02	10/31/02	11/04/02	12/06/02
0.343Q	1/16/03	1/30/03	2/03/03	3/06/03

Indicated div.: $1.37 (Div. Reinv. Plan)

CAPITALIZATION (12/31/01):

	($000)	(%)
Long-Term Debt	8,297,000	35.3
Deferred Income Tax	4,588,000	19.5
Redeemable Pfd. Stock	2,276,000	9.7
Preferred Stock	368,000	1.6
Common & Surplus	7,984,000	34.0
Total	23,513,000	100.0

TRADING VOLUME Thousand Shares

*7 YEAR PRICE SCORE 112.4   *12 MONTH PRICE SCORE 112.5

*NYSE COMPOSITE INDEX=100

BUSINESS:

The Southern Company is an energy company with 4.0 million customers and nearly 37,000 megawatts of electric generating capacity in the Southeast as of 1/27/03. The Company is one of the largest producers of electricity in the U.S. The Southern Company is the parent firm of the following electric utilities in the Southeast: Alabama Power, Georgia Power, Gulf Power, Mississippi Power and Savannah Electric. SO also owns Southern Nuclear, Southern

Management Development, Southern Company Services, Southern LINC, Southern Telecom, Southern Power and Southern Company Gas LLC. Southern Power was formed in 2001 to construct, own and manage wholesale generating assets in the Southeast. On 4/2/01, the Company completed the spin-off of its 80.3% ownership interest in Mirant Corporation.

RECENT DEVELOPMENTS:

For the year ended 12/31/02, net income advanced 17.7% to $1.32 billion compared with income from continuing operations of $1.12 billion in the previous year. Regulated retail business earnings increased 11.4% to $1.11 billion, while competitive generation earnings grew 22.6% to $168.0 million. Total revenues increased 3.9% to $10.55

billion from $10.16 billion a year earlier. Retail revenue rose 3.4% to $8.73 billion, while wholesale revenue slipped 0.5% to $1.17 billion. Other operating revenues jumped 21.1% to $655.0 million. Operating income climbed 8.7% to $2.60 billion from $2.39 billion the year before.

PROSPECTS:

The Company plans to complete approximately 4,000 megawatts of additional competitive electric generating capacity by 2005 to serve rapid demand growth in the southeast U.S. Meanwhile, the Company's long-term earnings per share growth target is at least 5.0% annually. For

2003, the Company expects earnings of approximately $1.84 per share. Separately, SO is planning to increase its annual dividend by half the rate of earnings per share growth until the payout declines to between 70.0% and 75.0% of earnings, which will probably happen by 2004.

ANNUAL FINANCIAL DATA:

FISCAL YEAR	TOT. REVS. ($Mill.)	NET INC. ($Mill.)	TOT. ASSETS ($Mill.)	OPER. PROFIT %	NET PROFIT %	NET INC./ NET PROP. %	NET INC./ TOT. CAP. %	RET. ON EQUITY %	ACCUM. DEPR./ GROSS PROP. %	EARN. PER SH. $	TANG. BK. VAL. $	DIV. PER SH. $	DIV. PAYOUT %	PRICE RANGE	AVG. P/E RATIO	AVG. YIELD %
p12/31/02	10,549.0	1,318.0								1.86		1.36	72.9	31.14 - 23.22	14.6	5.0
12/31/01	10,155.0	⑥ 1,119.0	29,824.0	23.5	11.0	4.8	4.8	13.4	39.4	⑥ 1.61	11.42	1.34	83.2	35.72 - 20.89	17.6	4.7
12/31/00	10,066.0	⑤ 994.0	31,362.0	23.9	9.9	4.6	3.9	9.0	39.9	③ 1.52	15.67	1.34	88.2	35.00 - 20.38	18.2	4.8
12/31/99	11,585.0	④ 1,276.0	38,396.0	24.0	11.0	5.2	4.3	13.3	36.4	④ 1.86	13.82	1.34	72.0	29.63 - 22.06	13.9	5.2
12/31/98	11,403.0	③ 977.0	36,192.0	15.4	8.6	4.0	3.4	9.6	35.4	③ 1.40	14.14	1.34	95.7	31.56 - 23.94	19.8	4.8
12/31/97	12,611.0	② 972.0	35,271.0	15.4	7.7	4.1	3.5	9.6	33.5	② 1.42	13.92	1.30	91.5	26.25 - 19.88	16.2	5.6
12/31/96	10,358.0	1,127.0	30,292.0	17.9	10.9	4.8	4.6	11.1	31.9	1.68	13.59	1.26	75.0	25.88 - 21.13	14.0	5.4
12/31/95	9,180.0	1,103.0	30,554.0	20.5	12.0	4.8	4.5	10.8	30.4	1.66	13.09	1.22	73.5	25.00 - 19.38	13.4	5.5
12/31/94	8,297.0	① 989.0	27,042.0	20.7	11.9	4.7	4.4	10.3	31.2	① 1.52	12.46	1.18	77.6	22.06 - 17.00	12.8	6.0
12/31/93	8,489.0	1,072.0	25,911.0	20.8	11.8	5.0	4.7	11.1	30.9	1.57	12.06	1.14	72.6	23.63 - 18.44	13.4	5.4

Statistics are as originally reported. Adj. for stk. splits: 2-for-1, 3/94. ① Incl. a $61.0 mill. chrg. for workforce reduction programs ② Incl. non-recurr. chrg. $111.0 mill. ($0.16/sh.) for UK windfall profit tax ③ Incl. non-recurr. chrg. of $342.0 mill. for the write-down of assets and a gain of $59.0 mill. on assets sales. ④ Incl. non-recurr. chrg. of $69.0 mill. and a gain of $315.0 mill. on asset sales. ⑤ Bef. income from disc. opers. of $319.0 mill.; incl. non-recurr. chrg. of $90.0 mill. & a gain of $8.0 mill. fr. a litigation settlement. ⑥ Bef. income from disc. opers. of $142.0 mill. and acctg. change gain of $1.0 mill.

OFFICERS:
H. A. Franklin, Chmn., Pres., C.E.O.
G. K. Klappa, Exec. V.P., C.F.O., Treas.

INVESTOR CONTACT: Glen Kundert, Dir., Investor Relations, (404) 506-5135

PRINCIPAL OFFICE: 270 Peachtree St., N.W., Atlanta, GA 30303

TELEPHONE NUMBER: (404) 506-5000
FAX: (404) 506-0455
WEB: www.southerncompany.com
NO. OF EMPLOYEES: 26,122
SHAREHOLDERS: 500,000 (approx.)
ANNUAL MEETING: In May
INCORPORATED: DE, Nov., 1945

INSTITUTIONAL HOLDINGS:
No. of Institutions: 508
Shares Held: 285,226,592
% Held: 40.0

INDUSTRY: Electric services (SIC: 4911)

TRANSFER AGENT(S): SCS Stockholder Services, Atlanta, GA

SOUTHWEST AIRLINES CO.

EXCH.	SYM.	REC. PRICE	P/E RATIO	YLD.	MKT. CAP.	RANGE (52-WK.)	'02 Y/E PR.
NYSE	LUV	12.07 (2/28/03)	40.2	0.1%	$9.37 bill.	21.41 - 10.90	13.90

UPPER MEDIUM GRADE. THE COMPANY IS TAKING AGGRESSIVE STEPS TO REDUCE COSTS.

*7 YEAR PRICE SCORE 136.4   ***12 MONTH PRICE SCORE 93.2**

*NYSE COMPOSITE INDEX=100

INTERIM EARNINGS (Per Share):

Qtr.	Mar.	June	Sept.	Dec.
1996	0.05	0.11	0.08	0.04
1997	0.07	0.12	0.12	0.10
1998	0.09	0.17	0.17	0.13
1999	0.12	0.19	0.16	0.12
2000	0.12	0.24	0.23	0.19
2001	0.16	0.22	0.19	0.08
2002	0.03	0.13	0.09	0.05

INTERIM DIVIDENDS (Per Share):

Amt.	Decl.	Ex.	Rec.	Pay.
0.004Q	1/17/02	2/27/02	3/01/02	3/26/02
0.004Q	5/15/02	6/03/02	6/05/02	6/26/02
0.004Q	7/18/02	8/30/02	9/04/02	9/25/02
0.004Q	11/21/02	12/09/02	12/11/02	1/10/03
0.004Q	1/16/03	3/04/03	3/06/03	3/27/03

Indicated div.: $0.02

CAPITALIZATION (12/31/02):

	($000)	(%)
Long-Term Debt	1,552,781	21.6
Deferred Income Tax	1,227,475	17.0
Common & Surplus	4,421,617	61.4
Total	7,201,873	100.0

BUSINESS:

Southwest Airlines Co. provides single-class, high-frequency, point-to-point, air transport service to 58 cities in 30 states as of 2/13/03. Southwest principally concentrates on short-haul markets and emphasizes high aircraft utilization and high employee productivity. Primary hubs include Dallas Love Field, Houston Hobby Airport and Phoenix Sky Harbor International. Southwest acquired Morris Air Corporation on 12/31/93 and completed the integration of Morris' operations with its own by March 1995. At 12/31/02, Southwest operated 375 Boeing 737 aircraft.

RECENT DEVELOPMENTS:

For the twelve months ended 12/31/02, net income totaled $241.0 million, down 52.9% compared with $511.1 million in the corresponding period a year earlier. Results included one-time gains of $48.0 million in 2002 and $235.0 million in 2001, respectively, related to the Air Transportation Safety and System Stabilization Act. Results for 2001 also included a $48.0 million pre-tax charge stemming from the terrorist attacks on 9/11/01. Total operating revenues slipped 0.6% to $5.52 billion from $5.56 billion in the prior year. Passenger revenues slid 0.7% to $5.34 billion, while freight revenues fell 7.2% to $84.7 million. Other revenue climbed 12.4% to $95.7 million. Operating income dropped 33.9% to $417.3 million from $631.1 million in 2001. The passenger load factor, or percentage of seats filled, decreased to 65.9% compared with 68.1% a year earlier.

PROSPECTS:

Results are being negatively affected by weak overall demand for air travel and sharply higher labor and jet fuel costs. The Company is taking steps to limit its exposure to jet fuel price increases through an aggressive hedging program. LUV has hedged approximately 87.0% of its second-quarter fuel requirement, as well as about 75.0% of it second-half 2003 fuel requirement, to protect against further price increases. In 2003, LUV anticipates net deliveries of eleven new airplanes and plans to increase seat capacity by 4.0%. Meanwhile, near-term prospects remain uncertain due to an increased threat of war with Iraq.

ANNUAL FINANCIAL DATA:

FISCAL YEAR	TOT. REVS. ($mill.)	NET INC. ($mill.)	TOT. ASSETS ($mill.)	OPER. PROFIT %	NET PROFIT %	RET. ON EQUITY %	RET. ON ASSETS %	CURR. RATIO	EARN. PER SH.$	CASH FL. PER SH.$	TANG. BK. VAL.$	DIV. PER SH.$	PRICE RANGE	AVG. P/E RATIO	AVG. YIELD %
12/31/02	5,521.8	④ 241.0	8,953.8	7.6	4.4	5.4	2.7	1.6	④ 0.30	0.78	5.69	0.02	22.00 - 10.90	54.8	0.1
12/31/01	5,555.2	③ 511.1	8,997.1	11.4	9.2	12.7	5.7	1.1	③ 0.63	1.06	5.23	0.02	23.32 - 11.25	27.4	0.1
12/31/00	5,649.6	② 625.2	6,669.6	18.1	11.1	18.1	9.4	0.6	② 0.79	1.16	4.56	0.01	23.33 - 10.00	21.2	0.1
12/31/99	4,735.6	474.4	5,652.1	16.5	10.0	16.7	8.4	0.7	0.59	0.92	4.21	0.01	15.72 - 9.58	21.3	0.1
12/31/98	4,164.0	433.4	4,716.0	16.4	10.4	18.1	9.2	0.7	0.55	0.84	3.21	0.01	10.56 - 6.81	15.9	0.1
12/31/97	3,816.8	317.8	4,246.2	13.7	8.3	15.8	7.5	0.9	0.42	0.68	2.69	0.01	7.78 - 4.20	14.4	0.2
12/31/96	3,406.2	207.3	3,723.5	10.3	6.1	12.6	5.6	1.0	0.27	0.51	2.24	0.01	6.57 - 4.07	19.6	0.2
12/31/95	2,872.8	182.6	3,256.1	10.9	6.4	12.8	5.6	0.8	0.24	0.44	1.96	0.01	5.90 - 3.23	18.8	0.2
12/31/94	2,591.9	179.3	2,823.1	12.2	6.9	14.5	6.4	0.6	0.24	0.41	1.71	0.01	7.70 - 3.06	22.3	0.1
① 12/31/93	2,296.7	① 154.3	2,576.0	12.7	6.7	14.6	6.0	0.9	② 0.21	0.34	1.46	0.01	7.43 - 3.59	26.6	0.2

Statistics are as originally reported. Adj. for all stk. div. & splits through 2/01. ① Incl. results of Morris Air Corp. acqd. 12/31/93. ② Bef. $22.1 mil ($0.03/sh.) acctg. chrg., 2000; $15.3 mil ($0.02/sh.) cr. from acctg. adj., 1993. ③ Incl. $235.0 mil pre-tax gain from airline stabilization act & $48.0 mil pre-tax chg related to the 9/11/01 terrorist attacks. ④ Incl. $48.0 mil pre-tax gain from airline stabilization act.

OFFICERS:
H. D. Kelleher, Chmn.
J. F. Parker, Vice-Chmn., C.E.O.
C. C. Barrett, Pres., C.O.O.
G. C. Kelly, Exec. V.P., C.F.O.

INVESTOR CONTACT: Investor Relations,
(214) 792-4908

PRINCIPAL OFFICE: 2702 Love Field Drive,
P.O. Box 36611, Dallas, TX 75235-1611

TELEPHONE NUMBER: (214) 792-4000
FAX: (214) 792-5015
WEB: www.southwest.com

NO. OF EMPLOYEES: 33,705 (avg.)

SHAREHOLDERS: 11,858 (record)

ANNUAL MEETING: In May

INCORPORATED: TX, Mar., 1967

INSTITUTIONAL HOLDINGS:
No. of Institutions: 438
Shares Held: 606,042,476
% Held: 78.2

INDUSTRY: Air transportation, scheduled
(SIC: 4512)

TRANSFER AGENT(S): Continental Stock
Transfer & Trust Co., New York, NY

SOVEREIGN BANCORP, INC.

EXCH.	SYM.	REC. PRICE	P/E RATIO	YLD.	MKT. CAP.	RANGE (52-WK.)	'02 Y/E PR.
NYSE	SOV	13.58 (2/28/03)	11.0	0.7%	$3.43 bill.	15.90 - 11.20	14.05

MEDIUM GRADE. THE COMPANY EXPECTS EARNINGS FOR 2003 TO RANGE FROM $1.40 TO $1.45 PER SHARE.

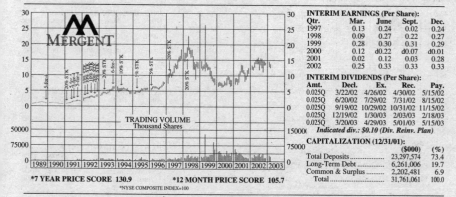

INTERIM EARNINGS (Per Share):

Qtr.	Mar.	June	Sept.	Dec.
1997	0.13	0.24	0.02	0.24
1998	0.09	0.27	0.22	0.27
1999	0.28	0.30	0.31	0.29
2000	0.12	d0.22	d0.07	d0.01
2001	0.02	0.12	0.03	0.28
2002	0.25	0.33	0.33	0.33

INTERIM DIVIDENDS (Per Share):

Amt.	Decl.	Ex.	Rec.	Pay.
0.025Q	3/22/02	4/26/02	4/30/02	5/15/02
0.025Q	6/20/02	7/29/02	7/31/02	8/15/02
0.025Q	9/19/02	10/29/02	10/31/02	11/15/02
0.025Q	12/19/02	1/30/03	2/03/03	2/18/03
0.025Q	3/20/03	4/29/03	5/01/03	5/15/03

Indicated div.: $0.10 (Div. Reinv. Plan)

CAPITALIZATION (12/31/01):

	($000)	(%)
Total Deposits	23,297,574	73.4
Long-Term Debt	6,261,006	19.7
Common & Surplus	2,202,481	6.9
Total	31,761,061	100.0

*7 YEAR PRICE SCORE 130.9   ***12 MONTH PRICE SCORE 105.7**

*NYSE COMPOSITE INDEX=100

BUSINESS:

Sovereign Bancorp, Inc. (formerly Penn Savings Bank, F.S.B.), the parent company for Sovereign Bank, is a $40.00 billion financial institution with approximately 530 community banking offices, approximately 1,000 ATMs and about 7,500 team members in Pennsylvania, New Jersey, Connecticut, New Hampshire, New York, Rhode Island and Massachusetts. The Company's primary business consists of attracting deposits from its network of community banking offices, and originating small business and middle market commercial and asset-based loans, consumer and residential mortgage loans and home equity lines of credit in the communities it serves. On 3/8/02, the Company completed the acquisition of Main Street Bancorp, Inc.

RECENT DEVELOPMENTS:

For the year ended 12/31/02, net income more than doubled to $342.0 million compared with income of $123.4 million, before an extraordinary loss of $6.5 million, in 2001. Results for 2002 and 2001 included amortization of goodwill and other intangibles of $80.3 million and $133.6 million, gains on the sale of investments and related derivative transactions of $51.4 million and $15.5 million, and merger-related and integration charges of $15.9 million and $8.5 million, respectively. Also, results for 2001 included non-solicitation and restructuring expenses of $243.2 million. Net interest income rose 10.0% to $1.16 billion compared with $1.05 billion the year before. Provision for loan losses jumped 50.9% to $146.5 million versus $97.1 million in 2001. Total non-interest income grew 4.4% to $432.5 million, while total non-interest expense declined 19.9% to $979.1 million.

PROSPECTS:

The Company is faced with challenging business conditions as a result of the adverse economic climate. Nevertheless, SOV continues to perform quite well, supported by a higher level of earning assets and solid revenue growth in both its commercial and consumer banking businesses. Also, the Company is encouraged by its sizable reduction in non-performing loans and improved credit quality in recent months. For 2003, the Company expects full-year earnings in the range of $1.40 to $1.45 per share, and first quarter earnings of $0.32 to $0.33 per share.

ANNUAL FINANCIAL DATA:

FISCAL YEAR	NET INT. INC. ($mill.)	NON-INT. INC. ($mill.)	NET INC. ($mill.)	TOT. LOANS ($mill.)	TOT. ASSETS ($mill.)	TOT. DEP. ($mill.)	RET. ON EQUITY %	RET. ON ASSETS %	EQUITY/ ASSETS %	EARN. PER SH. $	TANG. BK. VAL.$	DIV. PER SH. $	PRICE RANGE	AVG. P/E RATIO
p12/31/02	1,159.6	432.5	4 342.0							4 1.23		0.10	15.90 - 11.20	11.0
12/31/01	1,054.3	426.1	3 123.4	20,399.6	35,474.8	23,297.6	5.6	0.3	6.2	3 0.48	3.40	0.10	13.50 - 7.16	21.5
12/31/00	854.8	108.6	2 d41.0	21,912.2	33,457.8	24,498.9	...	...	5.8	2 d0.18	2.14	0.10	9.97 - 6.25	...
12/31/99	614.7	130.3	179.3	14,226.5	26,607.1	11,719.6	9.8	0.7	6.8	1.01	6.03	0.10	26.25 - 7.00	16.5
12/31/98	493.6	105.6	1 136.5	11,285.8	21,912.9	12,322.7	11.3	0.6	5.5	0.85	4.87	0.08	22.75 - 8.75	18.5
12/31/97	340.8	38.5	1 77.6	9,923.5	14,336.3	7,889.9	10.0	0.5	5.4	0.63	5.05	0.07	18.44 - 7.45	20.5
12/31/96	216.7	26.7	51.5	6,156.3	9,433.2	5,052.4	10.8	0.5	5.0	0.60	3.50	0.06	8.03 - 5.31	11.1
12/31/95	174.2	25.8	56.4	4,674.4	8,078.3	5,039.1	13.2	0.7	5.3	0.69	3.17	0.06	5.99 - 4.07	7.2
12/31/94	155.4	14.6	46.4	4,350.9	6,564.1	4,027.1	15.3	0.7	4.6	0.63	3.65	0.06	6.38 - 4.07	8.4
12/31/93	115.4	14.5	37.5	2,726.0	4,495.4	2,842.3	17.0	0.8	4.9	0.45	2.86	0.06	6.38 - 3.36	10.9

Statistics are as originally reported. Adj. for stk. splits: 6-for-5, 1/22/98; 6-for-5, 1/16/97; 5% div., 2/15/96; 5% div., 4/11/95; 10% div., 5/16/94. 1 Incl. merger-related exps. of $50.4 mill., 1998; $29.3 mill., 1997 2 Bef. extraord. gain of $10.8 mill., incls. restr. chrgs. of $18.5 mill. 3 Incl. $15.5 mill. gain fr. sale of investments & derivatives. 4 Incl. $51.4 mill. gain fr. invest. & related deriv. trans. and $15.9 mill. merg.-rel. & intergra. chg.

OFFICERS:
J. S. Sidhu, Chmn., Pres., C.E.O.
J. D. Hogan, C.F.O.
L. M. Thompson Jr., C.A.O.
INVESTOR CONTACT: Dawn B. Heart, Investor Relations, (800) 628-2673
PRINCIPAL OFFICE: 1500 Market Street, Philadelphia, PA 19103

TELEPHONE NUMBER: (215) 557-4630
FAX: (215) 320-8448
WEB: www.sovereignbank.com
NO. OF EMPLOYEES: 6,147 full-time; 956 part-time
SHAREHOLDERS: 15,055
ANNUAL MEETING: In Apr.
INCORPORATED: PA, Dec., 1987

INSTITUTIONAL HOLDINGS:
No. of Institutions: 279
Shares Held: 175,166,019
% Held: 67.1
INDUSTRY: Federal savings institutions (SIC: 6035)
TRANSFER AGENT(S): Mellon Investor Services, Pittsburgh, PA

SPHERION CORPORATION

EXCH.	SYM.	REC. PRICE	P/E RATIO	YLD.	MKT. CAP.	RANGE (52-WK.)	'02 Y/E PR.
NYSE	SFN	6.07 (2/28/03)	...	...	$354.3 mill.	12.84 - 4.59	6.70

SPECULATIVE GRADE. THE COMPANY ESTIMATES CAPITAL EXPENDITURES WILL BE APPROXIMATELY $55.0 MILLION TO $65.0 MILLION IN 2003.

*7 YEAR PRICE SCORE 50.4   *12 MONTH PRICE SCORE 75.4
*NYSE COMPOSITE INDEX=100

INTERIM EARNINGS (Per Share):

Qtr.	Mar.	June	Sept.	Dec.
1999	0.33	0.40	0.21	0.35
2000	0.37	0.42	0.37	d0.01
2001	d0.38	2.83	0.79	d0.09
2002	d0.06	d0.01	0.06	d4.60

INTERIM DIVIDENDS (Per Share):

Amt.	Decl.	Ex.	Rec.	Pay.
	No dividends paid.			

CAPITALIZATION (12/28/01):

	($000)	(%)
Long-Term Debt	215,751	14.3
Common & Surplus	1,294,978	85.7
Total	1,510,729	100.0

BUSINESS:

Spherion Corporation (formerly Interim Services Inc.) provides staffing and personnel management to businesses, professional and service organizations, governmental agencies and individuals. SFN operates through offices in North America, Europe, Australia, and Asia. SFN's Recruitment segment (68.5% of revenue and 26.2% of income in 2002) provides staffing services and permanent placement of personnel in office, clerical and administrative, light industrial, accounting/finance, engineering, sales/marketing, human resources and law positions. SFN's Technology segment (16.0%, 15.4%) delivers information technology staffing and managed services focused on both technology applications and infrastructure. SFN's Outsourcing segment (15.5%, 58.4%) provides outsourcing services in the areas of call center and administrative outsourcing services. SFN disposed of its interest in Michael Page on 4/2/01.

RECENT DEVELOPMENTS:

For the year ended 12/27/02, SFN reported a loss from continuing operations of $273.3 million versus earnings from continuing operations of $115.3 million in the previous year. Results for 2002 and 2001 included amortization of intangibles of $321,000 and $34.3 million, and restructuring and asset impairment charges of $10.4 million and $137.3 million, respectively. Results for 2002 also included a goodwill impairment charge of $291.5 million and other gains of $10.5 million. Results for 2001 also included one-time gains of $308.1 million. Total revenues fell 20.7% to $2.12 billion from $2.67 billion a year earlier. Results for 2001 included Michael Page revenues of $179.6 million. Gross profit dropped 30.7% to $527.3 million from $760.9 million in 2001.

PROSPECTS:

Going forward, the Company will continue to make investments in sales and technology initiatives designed to improve productivity and profitability in 2003. For the first quarter of 2003, the Company expects revenues of between $480.0 million and $500.0 million and anticipates a loss from continuing operations to range from $0.07 to $0.12 per share. Meanwhile, SFN estimates capital expenditures will be approximately $55.0 million to $65.0 million in 2003, including between $35.0 million and $40.0 million for investment in enterprise-wide information systems.

ANNUAL FINANCIAL DATA:

FISCAL YEAR	TOT. REVS. ($mill.)	NET INC. ($mill.)	TOT. ASSETS ($mill.)	OPER. PROFIT %	NET PROFIT %	RET. ON EQUITY %	RET. ON ASSETS %	CURR. RATIO	EARN. PER SH.$	CASH FL.PER SH.$	TANG. BK. VAL.$	PRICE RANGE	AVG. P/E RATIO
12/27/02	2,116.1	⑦d273.3		...					⑦d4.60	2.67	4.81	12.84 — 5.35	...
12/28/01	2,713.1	⑥108.1	1,868.3	...	4.0	8.3	5.8	2.6	⑥1.73	2.67	4.81	12.52 — 5.83	5.3
12/29/00	3,740.8	⑤74.5	2,483.2	4.7	2.0	6.3	3.0	1.0	⑤1.16	2.23	...	28.38 — 9.69	16.4
12/31/99	3,168.0	④70.8	2,438.9	5.2	2.2	6.1	2.9	1.1	④1.27	2.24	...	24.81 — 13.75	15.2
12/25/98	1,890.1	④58.6	1,613.4	6.8	3.1	7.9	3.6	1.3	④1.29	2.13	...	34.25 — 13.25	18.4
12/26/97	1,608.3	③42.5	1,091.7	6.2	2.6	9.0	3.9	1.3	③1.05	1.92	...	31.13 — 13.50	21.2
12/27/96	1,147.2	②23.0	512.5	5.2	2.0	5.5	4.5	2.8	②0.69	1.25	6.16	25.13 — 17.00	30.5
12/29/95	780.9	17.5	406.6	4.3	2.2	8.9	4.3	1.3	0.75	1.34	1.08	17.75 — 11.31	19.4
①12/30/94	634.4	14.2	260.7	4.3	2.2	7.9	5.4	1.7	0.62	1.12	3.78	14.13 — 10.06	19.5
3/25/94	539.8	11.7	233.9	4.3	2.2	7.0	5.0	1.8	0.54	1.11	...	...	...

Statistics are as originally reported. Adj. for stk. splits: 2-for-1, 9/97. ① For twelve months, fiscal year change. ② Incl. $8.6 mill. merger exp. ③ Incl. $5.3 mill. gain on sale of HealthCare business. ④ Bef. extr. chrg. $2.8 mill. ⑤ Incl. one-time chrg. $24.8 mill., 2000; $33.9 mill., 1999. ⑥ Bef. acctg. change chrg. $1.1 mill.; incl. net one-time. gain $168.0 mill. ⑦ Bef. loss fr. disc. oper. $14.4 mill. & acctg. change chrg. $615.6 mill.; incl. restr. & impair. chrg. $10.4 mill., goodwill impair. chrg. $291.5 mill. & gain on repurch. of debt instr. $10.5 mill.

OFFICERS:
S. S. Elbaum, Chmn.
C. A. Hallman, Pres., C.E.O.
R. G. Krause, Exec. V.P., C.F.O.
INVESTOR CONTACT: Terri Miller, (954) 308-8216
PRINCIPAL OFFICE: 2050 Spectrum Boulevard, Fort Lauderdale, FL 33309

TELEPHONE NUMBER: (954) 308-7600
FAX: (954) 351-8117
WEB: www.spherion.com
NO. OF EMPLOYEES: 5,000 full-time (approx.)
SHAREHOLDERS: 2,424 (approx.)
ANNUAL MEETING: In May
INCORPORATED: DE, 1946

INSTITUTIONAL HOLDINGS:
No. of Institutions: 113
Shares Held: 49,475,096
% Held: 83.9
INDUSTRY: Help supply services (SIC: 7363)
TRANSFER AGENT(S): The Bank of New York, New York, NY

SPRINT CORPORATION FON GROUP

EXCH.	SYM.	REC. PRICE	P/E RATIO	YLD.	MKT. CAP.	RANGE (52-WK.)	'02 Y/E PR.
NYSE	FON	12.70 (2/28/03)	10.9	3.9%	$11.29 bill.	17.53 - 6.65	14.48

LOWER MEDIUM GRADE. FON IS PROJECTING FULL-YEAR 2003 EARNINGS OF BETWEEN $1.40 AND $1.45 PER SHARE.

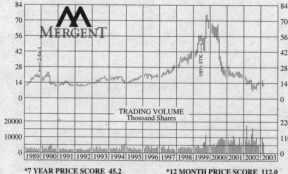

*7 YEAR PRICE SCORE 45.2 ***12 MONTH PRICE SCORE 112.0**
*NYSE COMPOSITE INDEX=100

INTERIM EARNINGS (Per Share):

Qtr.	Mar.	June	Sept.	Dec.
1998	---------------- 1.78 ----------------			
1999	0.47	0.44	0.41	0.49
2000	0.50	0.41	0.43	0.11
2001	0.36	0.33	0.18	d1.02
2002	0.27	0.07	0.54	0.28

INTERIM DIVIDENDS (Per Share):

Amt.	Decl.	Ex.	Rec.	Pay.
0.125Q	2/04/02	3/06/02	3/08/02	3/29/02
0.125Q	4/16/02	6/05/02	6/07/02	6/28/02
0.125Q	8/05/02	9/05/02	9/09/02	9/30/02
0.125Q	10/08/02	12/05/02	12/09/02	12/30/02
0.125Q	2/11/03	3/06/03	3/10/03	3/31/03

Indicated div.: $0.50 (Div. Reinv. Plan)

CAPITALIZATION (12/31/01):

	($000)	(%)
Long-Term Debt	16,501,000	56.7
Common & Surplus	12,616,000	43.3
⑨ Total.......................	29,117,000	100.0

BUSINESS:

Sprint Corporation is a global telecommunications company whose principal businesses are divided into two groups: The FON Group is comprised of the Global Markets segment, which includes domestic and international long distance communications, broadband fixed wireless services and certain other ventures; and the Local Services segment, which includes local exchange communications and consumer long distance services used by customers within Sprint's local franchise territories. The FON Group also includes other businesses consisting primarily of wholesale distribution of telecommunication products. The PCS Group consists of Sprint's wireless personal communications services operations. On 3/3/03, Sprint closed on the sale of its directory publishing business to R.H. Donnelley for $2.23 billion in cash.

RECENT DEVELOPMENTS:

For the year ended 12/31/02, income from continuing operations was $1.05 billion versus a loss from continuing operations of $296.0 million a year earlier. Results for 2002 and 2001 included restructuring and asset impairment charges of $251.0 million and $1.80 billion, respectively. Net operating revenues fell 7.2% to $15.18 billion. Global Market segment revenue slid 9.8% to $8.94 billion, reflecting the weak pricing environment for long-distance services as well as the sluggish economy. Local Services revenues were $6.21 billion versus $6.25 billion in 2001.

PROSPECTS:

FON is projecting full-year 2003 earnings of between $1.40 and $1.45 per share. Included in this estimate are increased pension costs, which the Company estimates will reduce earnings by $0.11 per share versus no effect in 2002. Revenues are expected to decline at a low single-digit rate. Global Markets division revenues are expected to decline at a mid-single-digit rate, while Local Telecommunications division revenue is expected to be flat.

ANNUAL FINANCIAL DATA:

FISCAL YEAR	TOT. REVS. ($mill.)	NET INC. ($mill.)	TOT. ASSETS ($mill.)	OPER. PROFIT %	NET PROFIT %	RET. ON EQUITY %	RET. ON ASSETS %	CURR. RATIO	EARN. PER SH. $	CASH FL. PER SH. $	TANG. BK. VAL. $	DIV. PER SH. $	PRICE RANGE	AVG. P/E RATIO	AVG. YIELD %
p12/31/02	15,182.0	⑧ 1,046.0							⑧ 1.18			0.50	20.47 - 6.65	11.5	3.7
12/31/01	16,924.0	⑦ d146.0	24,164.0	...	...	...	...	0.6	⑦ d0.16	2.60	11.40	0.50	29.31 - 18.50	...	2.1
12/31/00	17,688.0	⑥ 1,292.0	23,649.0	13.8	7.3	10.5	5.5	0.9	⑥ 1.45	4.04	12.65	0.50	67.81 - 19.63	30.2	1.1
12/31/99	17,016.0	⑤ 1,736.0	21,803.0	17.2	10.2	12.8	8.0	1.0	⑤ 1.97	4.36	11.59	0.50	75.94 - 36.88	28.6	1.1
12/31/98	16,016.9	⑤ 1,540.1	19,274.8	17.2	9.6	17.1	8.0	1.2	⑤ 1.78	4.14	12.59	0.50	42.69 - 27.63	19.8	1.4
12/31/97	14,873.9	⑦ 952.5	18,184.8	16.5	6.4	10.6	5.2	1.2	⑦ 1.09	3.07	10.50	0.50	30.31 - 19.19	22.7	2.0
12/31/96	14,044.7	② 1,190.9	16,953.0	16.1	8.5	14.0	7.0	1.3	② 1.40	3.26	9.90	0.50	22.75 - 17.25	14.3	2.5
12/31/95	12,765.1	③ 946.1	15,195.9	14.4	7.4	20.4	6.2	0.7	③ 1.35	3.44	6.65	0.50	20.56 - 12.94	12.5	3.0
12/31/94	12,661.8	① 883.7	14,936.3	14.1	7.0	19.5	5.9	0.7	① 1.27	3.39	5.48	0.50	20.06 - 13.06	13.1	3.0
12/31/93	11,367.8	④ 480.6	14,148.9	11.0	4.2	12.3	3.4	0.6	④ 0.70	2.67	4.63	0.50	20.13 - 12.75	23.6	3.0

Statistics are as originally reported. Refl. ops. of FON Group only as of 12/31/98. Adj. for 2-for-1 stk. split, 5/13/99 ① Incl. nonrecur. cr. 12/31/97, $31.0 mil.; cr. 12/31/94, $22.0 mil. ② Incl. nonrecur. chrg. of $36.0 mil.; bef. disc. ops. cr. of $2.6 mil. & extraord. chrg. of $4.5 mil. ③ Bef. acctg. adj. chg. of $565.3 mil. & disc. ops. cr. of $14.5 mil. ④ Bef. acctg. adj. chg. of $384.5 mil., extraord. item of $29.2 mil. & disc. ops. of $12.3 mil. ⑤ Bef. extraord. chrg. 12/31/99, $39.0 mil.; chrg. 12/31/98, $5.0 mil. ⑥ Incl. merger-rel. costs of $401.0 mil.; bef. inc. fr. disc. ops. of $675.0 mil., extraord. loss of $1.0 mil. & acctg. chge. chrg. of $2.0 mil. ⑦ Incl. restruct. & asset impair. chrg. of $1.80 bil.; bef. extraord. loss of $1.0 mil. ⑧ Incl. restruct. & asset impair. chrg. of $251.0 mil.; bef. net inc. fr. disc. ops. of $159.0 mil. & extraord. gain of $3.0 mil. ⑨ Sprint consolidated balance sheet data.

OFFICERS:
W. T. Esrey, Chmn.
G. D. Forsee, C.E.O.
R. T. LeMay, Pres., C.O.O.

INVESTOR CONTACT: Don A. Jensen, V.P., Sec., (913) 624-2541

PRINCIPAL OFFICE: P.O. Box 11315, Kansas City, MO 64112

TELEPHONE NUMBER: (913) 624-3000
FAX: (913) 624-3496
WEB: www.sprint.com
NO. OF EMPLOYEES: 75,000 (approx.)
SHAREHOLDERS: 67,800 (FON)
ANNUAL MEETING: In Apr.
INCORPORATED: KS, 1938

INSTITUTIONAL HOLDINGS:
No. of Institutions: 455
Shares Held: 703,995,688
% Held: 71.8

INDUSTRY: Telephone communications, exc. radio (SIC: 4813)

TRANSFER AGENT(S): UMB Bank, Kansas City, MO

SPX CORPORATION

EXCH.	SYM.	REC. PRICE	P/E RATIO	YLD.	MKT. CAP.	RANGE (52-WK.)	'02 Y/E PR.
NYSE	SPW	36.38 (2/28/03)	10.9	...	$2.94 bill.	75.72 - 35.13	37.45

MEDIUM GRADE. THE COMPANY CONTINUES TO MAKE SELECTIVE ACQUISITIONS THAT SHOULD ENHANCE OR COMPLEMENT THE CURRENT PRODUCTS AND SERVICES OFFERED BY ITS SUBSIDIARIES.

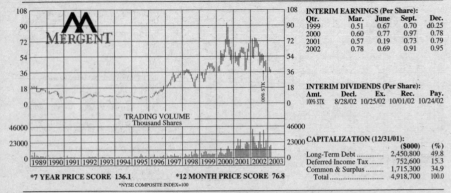

*7 YEAR PRICE SCORE 136.1   ***12 MONTH PRICE SCORE 76.8**
*NYSE COMPOSITE INDEX=100

INTERIM EARNINGS (Per Share):

Qtr.	Mar.	June	Sept.	Dec.
1999	0.51	0.67	0.70	d0.25
2000	0.60	0.77	0.97	0.78
2001	0.57	0.19	0.73	0.79
2002	0.78	0.69	0.91	0.95

INTERIM DIVIDENDS (Per Share):

Amt.	Decl.	Ex.	Rec.	Pay.
100% STK	8/28/02	10/25/02	10/01/02	10/24/02

CAPITALIZATION (12/31/01):

	($000)	(%)
Long-Term Debt	2,450,800	49.8
Deferred Income Tax	752,600	15.3
Common & Surplus	1,715,300	34.9
Total	4,918,700	100.0

BUSINESS:

SPX Corporation is a global multi-industry company. The Company's segments include Industrial Products and Services (31.8% of 2002 revenues), Flow Technology (27.5%), Technical Products and Systems (26.5%) and Service Solutions (14.2%). The Company offers a diverse collection of products, which include networking and switching products, fire detection and building life-safety products, television and radio broadcast antennas and towers, life science products and services, transformers, compaction equipment, high-integrity castings, dock products and systems, cooling towers, air filtration products, valves, back-flow protection and fluid-handling devices, and metering and mixing applications. Products and services also include specialty service tools, diagnostic systems, service equipment and technical information services. SPX acquired United Dominion Industries Ltd. on 5/24/01.

RECENT DEVELOPMENTS:

For the year ended 12/31/02, SPW reported income of $276.0 million, before an accounting change charge of $148.6 million, versus net income of $173.0 million in 2001. Results for 2002 and 2001 included special charges of $99.0 million and $87.9 million, and goodwill and intangible amortization of $8.2 million and $69.4 million, respectively. Total revenues advanced 22.6% to $5.05 billion. Technical Products & Systems revenue climbed 17.5% to $1.34 billion, while Industrial Products & Services revenue rose 15.2% to $1.60 billion. Flow Technology revenues jumped 51.9% to $1.39 billion. Service Solutions revenue increased 7.0% to $719.5 million.

PROSPECTS:

The Company continues to make selective acquisitions that should enhance and/or complement the current products and services offered by its subsidiaries. Recent acquisitions include Flash Technology, a provider of aviation obstruction lighting systems; Hankinson International, a manufacturer of compressed air dehydration and filtration products; and IDenticard Systems Inc. and IDenticam Systems Canada Ltd., providers of identification systems.

ANNUAL FINANCIAL DATA:

FISCAL YEAR	TOT. REVS. ($mill.)	NET INC. ($mill.)	TOT. ASSETS ($mill.)	OPER. PROFIT %	NET PROFIT %	RET. ON EQUITY %	RET. ON ASSETS %	CURR. RATIO	EARN. PER SH. $	CASH FL. PER SH. $	TANG. BK. VAL.$	DIV. PER SH. $	PRICE RANGE	AVG. P/E RATIO	AVG. YIELD %
p12/31/02	5,045.8	[12] 276.0							[12] 3.33				75.73 - 35.90	16.8	...
[11] 12/31/01	4,114.3	[10] 173.0	7,080.1	10.2	4.2	10.1	2.4	1.6	[10] 2.34	4.69	...	...	68.99 - 37.50	22.8	...
12/31/00	2,678.9	[9] 198.3	3,164.6	10.3	7.4	32.6	6.3	1.7	[9] 3.13	4.87	...	...	93.00 - 37.00	20.8	...
12/31/99	2,712.3	[8] 107.5	2,846.0	11.6	4.0	19.5	3.8	1.3	[8] 1.73	3.43	...	...	47.00 - 24.38	20.6	...
[7] 12/31/98	1,825.4	[6] d41.7	2,968.3	...	...	...	...	1.4	[6] d0.97	0.64	...	...	39.63 - 18.03	...	...
12/31/97	922.3	[5] d3.4	538.0	...	...	...	...	1.6	[5] d0.13	0.85	...	0.05	35.31 - 18.69	...	0.2
12/31/96	1,109.4	[4] d55.6	616.0	...	...	...	...	2.3	[4] d1.99	d0.53	1.60	0.20	20.25 - 6.81	...	1.5
12/31/95	1,098.1	[3] d1.4	831.4	2.8	...	...	...	1.7	[3] d0.05	1.60	...	0.20	8.69 - 5.38	...	2.8
12/31/94	1,092.7	[2] 14.1	931.7	5.9	1.3	8.7	1.5	1.8	[2] 0.55	2.05	...	0.20	9.25 - 6.94	14.7	2.5
12/31/93	756.1	[1] 25.1	1,024.4	4.7	3.3	17.1	2.4	1.3	[1] 0.60	1.96	...	0.20	9.44 - 7.50	14.1	2.4

Statistics are as originally reported. Adj. for 2-for-1 stk. split, 10/02. [1] Incl. special items $33.5 mill.; bef. acctg. chrg. $31.8 mill. & extr. loss $24.0 mill. [2] Incl. non-recurr gain $1.3 mill. [3] Bef. disc. oper. loss $4.2 mill. & extr. chrg. $1.1 mill.; incl. non-recurr. chrg. $7.0 mill. [4] Inc. after-tax non-recurr. chrg. of $87.9 mill. & bef. extr. loss $6.63 mill. [5] Bef. after-tax extr. chrg. $10.3 mill. & incl. non-recurr. chrg. $116.5 mill. [6] Incl. special chrg. $101.7 mill. [7] Incl. General Signal Corp. results following acq. on 10/6/98. [8] Bef. extr. chrg. $6.0 mill.; incl. non-recurr. chrg. $38.4 mill. [9] Bef. extr. chrg. $8.8 mill.; incl. net non-recurr. gain $10.6 mill. [10] Incl. pre-tax restr. chrg. $87.9 mill. [11] Incl. results of United Dominion Industries, Ltd. from 5/24/01. [12] Bef. acctg. chng. chrg. $148.6 mill.; incl. spec. chrg. $99.0 mill.

OFFICERS:
J. B. Blystone, Chmn., Pres., C.E.O.
P. J. O'Leary, V.P., C.F.O., Treas.
C. J. Kearney, V.P., Gen Couns., Sec.
INVESTOR CONTACT: Charles A. Bowman, (704) 752-4400
PRINCIPAL OFFICE: 13515 Ballantyne Corporate Place, Charlotte, NC 28277

TELEPHONE NUMBER: (704) 752-4400
FAX: (704) 752-7415
WEB: www.spx.com
NO. OF EMPLOYEES: 23,431 (approx.)
SHAREHOLDERS: 5,577 (approx.)
ANNUAL MEETING: In April
INCORPORATED: MI, Jan., 1911; reincorp., DE, April, 1968

INSTITUTIONAL HOLDINGS:
No. of Institutions: 283
Shares Held: 65,852,735
% Held: 81.8
INDUSTRY: Machine tools, metal cutting types (SIC: 3541)
TRANSFER AGENT(S): EquiServe Trust Company, N.A., Providence, RI

ST. JOE COMPANY (THE)

EXCH.	SYM.	REC. PRICE	P/E RATIO	YLD.	MKT. CAP.	RANGE (52-WK.)	'02 Y/E PR.
NYSE	JOE	28.26 (2/28/03)	13.3	0.3%	$2.25 bill.	33.74 - 24.35	30.00

UPPER MEDIUM GRADE. PRE-TAX INCOME FROM CONTINUING OPERATIONS FOR ST. JOE COMMERCIAL AND ARVIDA COMMUNITY DEVELOPMENT IS EXPECTED TO CONTINUE TO GROW IN 2003.

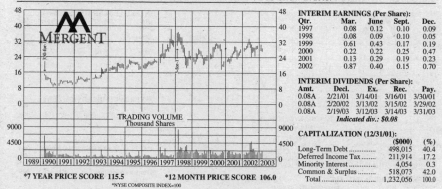

*7 YEAR PRICE SCORE 115.5   ***12 MONTH PRICE SCORE 106.0**
*NYSE COMPOSITE INDEX=100

INTERIM EARNINGS (Per Share):

Qtr.	Mar.	June	Sept.	Dec.
1997	0.08	0.12	0.10	0.09
1998	0.08	0.09	0.10	0.05
1999	0.61	0.43	0.17	0.19
2000	0.22	0.22	0.25	0.47
2001	0.13	0.29	0.19	0.23
2002	0.87	0.40	0.15	0.70

INTERIM DIVIDENDS (Per Share):

Amt.	Decl.	Ex.	Rec.	Pay.
0.08A	2/21/01	3/14/01	3/16/01	3/30/01
0.08A	2/20/02	3/13/02	3/15/02	3/29/02
0.08A	2/19/03	3/12/03	3/14/03	3/31/03

Indicated div.: $0.08

CAPITALIZATION (12/31/01):

	($000)	(%)
Long-Term Debt	498,015	40.4
Deferred Income Tax	211,914	17.2
Minority Interest	4,054	0.3
Common & Surplus	518,073	42.0
Total	1,232,056	100.0

BUSINESS:

The St. Joe Company is a real estate operating concern primarily engaged in community residential, commercial, hospitality and leisure resort development, along with residential and commercial real estate services and land sales. The Company also has significant interests in timber and owns the Apalachicola Northern Railroad Company, a short-line railroad operating between Port St. Joe and Chattahoochee, Florida. The majority of the Company's real estate operations are principally in Florida. JOE's forestry operations are in both Florida and Georgia. The Company conducts business in the following operating segments: residential real estate services (31.9% of 2001 revenues), community residential development (30.4%), commercial real estate (24.3%), land sales (8.8%), forestry (4.3%), transportation (0.2%) and other (0.1%). On 10/9/00, JOE spun off its 54.0% interest in Florida East Coast Industries, Inc.

RECENT DEVELOPMENTS:

For the year ended 12/31/02, income more than doubled to $151.2 million, before income from discontinued operations of $23.2 million, compared with income of $59.2 million, before income from discontinued operations of $11.0 million, in 2001. Results benefited from favorable contributions across JOE's business units. Total revenues climbed 9.4% to $646.4 million from $590.9 million in the prior year, primarily due to increased sales at Arvida Community Development and higher land and building sales by St. Joe Commercial. Operating profit increased 20.4% to $121.5 million compared with $100.9 million the year before. Comparisons were made with restated prior-year figures.

PROSPECTS:

During 2003, St. Joe Commercial will continue to focus on the development and sale of retail and commercial properties in Northwest Florida. JOE expects to make significant progress in 2003 in the planning and entitlement of communities in Gulf, Bay and Franklin counties in Northwest Florida, although they will not contribute to 2003 earnings. This progress will position JOE for solid earnings growth in the future. Meanwhile, JOE will continue to grow its portfolio of multi-tenant buildings. Net operating income is expected to increase by more than 20.0% in 2003.

ANNUAL FINANCIAL DATA:

FISCAL YEAR	TOT. REVS. ($mill.)	NET INC. ($mill.)	TOT. ASSETS ($mill.)	OPER. PROFIT %	NET PROFIT %	RET. ON EQUITY %	RET. ON ASSETS %	CURR. RATIO	EARN. PER SH. $	CASH FL. PER SH. $	TANG. BK. VAL. $	DIV. PER SH. $	PRICE RANGE	AVG. P/E RATIO	AVG. YIELD %
p12/31/02	646.4	① 151.2							① 1.86			0.08	33.74 - 24.35	15.6	0.3
12/31/01	868.4	70.2	1,340.6	13.5	8.1	13.6	5.2	0.9	0.83	1.18	4.71	0.08	29.75 - 20.90	30.5	0.3
12/31/00	880.8	100.3	1,115.0	18.0	11.4	17.6	9.0	1.2	1.15	1.75	5.20	0.08	31.38 - 17.69	21.3	0.3
12/31/99	750.4	77.6	1,821.6	11.7	10.3	8.3	4.3	1.5	1.34	1.43	9.28	0.02	28.56 - 20.06	18.1	0.1
12/31/98	392.2	26.1	1,604.3	12.6	6.7	3.0	1.6	1.8	0.28	0.70	8.52	0.08	37.00 - 18.50	99.1	0.3
12/31/97	346.3	35.5	1,546.6	15.2	10.2	3.9	2.3	6.0	0.38	0.73	9.89	3.74	38.50 - 21.04	78.3	12.6
12/31/96	431.2	91.9	1,806.2	34.4	21.3	7.7	5.1	11.1	1.00	. . .	13.08	0.07	23.17 - 17.88	20.5	0.3
12/31/95	334.9	29.4	1,531.0	14.1	8.8	2.9	1.9	11.2	0.32	. . .	11.10	0.07	22.67 - 17.50	62.7	0.3
12/31/94	330.9	37.9	1,449.4	18.1	11.4	4.0	2.6	7.1	0.46	. . .	10.24	0.07	20.88 - 16.38	40.5	0.4
12/31/93	312.5	26.7	1,491.3	17.6	8.6	3.0	1.8	3.0	0.29	0.58	9.87	0.07	18.33 - 12.50	53.1	0.4

Statistics are as originally reported. Adj. for stk. split: 3-for-1, 1/98. ① Excl. $23.2 mill. gain fr. disc. ops.

OFFICERS:
P. S. Rummell, Chmn., C.E.O.
K. Twomey, Pres., C.F.O., C.O.O.

INVESTOR CONTACT: Steve Swartz, Investor Relations, (904) 858-5295

PRINCIPAL OFFICE: 1650 Prudential Drive, Suite 400, Jacksonville, FL 32207

TELEPHONE NUMBER: (904) 396-6600
FAX: (904) 396-4042
WEB: www.joe.com
NO. OF EMPLOYEES: 2,339 (approx.)
SHAREHOLDERS: 24,500 (approx., beneficial)
ANNUAL MEETING: In May
INCORPORATED: FL, 1936

INSTITUTIONAL HOLDINGS:
No. of Institutions: 139
Shares Held: 23,262,303
% Held: 30.3

INDUSTRY: Paperboard mills (SIC: 2631)

TRANSFER AGENT(S): First Union National Bank, Charlotte, NC

ST. JUDE MEDICAL, INC.

EXCH.	SYM.	REC. PRICE	P/E RATIO	YLD.	MKT. CAP.	RANGE (52-WK.)	'02 Y/E PR.
NYSE	STJ	45.68 (2/28/03)	30.3	...	$7.97 bill.	45.76 - 30.52	39.72

INVESTMENT GRADE. THE COMPANY EXPECTS TO CLOSE THE ACQUISITION OF GETZ BROS. CO., LTD. DURING THE SECOND QUARTER OF 2003.

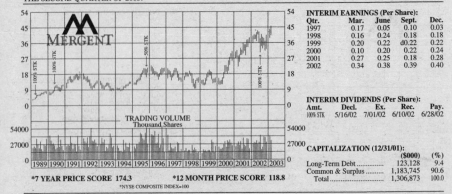

*7 YEAR PRICE SCORE 174.3   ***12 MONTH PRICE SCORE 118.8**

*NYSE COMPOSITE INDEX=100

INTERIM EARNINGS (Per Share):

Qtr.	Mar.	June	Sept.	Dec.
1997	0.17	0.05	0.10	0.03
1998	0.16	0.24	0.18	0.18
1999	0.20	0.22	d0.22	0.22
2000	0.10	0.20	0.22	0.24
2001	0.27	0.25	0.18	0.28
2002	0.34	0.38	0.39	0.40

INTERIM DIVIDENDS (Per Share):

Amt.	Decl.	Ex.	Rec.	Pay.
100% STK	5/16/02	7/01/02	6/10/02	6/28/02

CAPITALIZATION (12/31/01):

	($000)	(%)
Long-Term Debt	123,128	9.4
Common & Surplus	1,183,745	90.6
Total	1,306,873	100.0

BUSINESS:

St. Jude Medical, Inc. develops, manufactures and distributes medical devices and provides services for the cardiovascular segment of the medical device industry. STJ operates through a heart valve division and a cardiac rhythm management division. The Company's products are distributed worldwide through a combination of direct sales personnel, independent manufacturers' representatives and distribution organizations. The main markets for the Company's products are the U.S., Western Europe and Japan. On 3/16/99, STJ acquired the Angio-Seal business of Tyco International Ltd. On 9/27/99, STJ acquired Vascular Science, Inc.

RECENT DEVELOPMENTS:

For the year ended 12/31/02, net income climbed 60.1% to $276.3 million from $172.6 million the previous year. Results for 2001 included non-recurring charges of $30.5 million. Net sales increased 18.0% to $1.59 billion from $1.35 billion the prior year. Tachycardia sales climbed 50.7% to $303.0 million, reflecting favorable market acceptance of the St. Jude Medical Atlas™ implantable cardioverter defibrillator (ICD) and the availability of the Riata™ ICD lead family. Low-voltage or pacing sales grew 9.1% to $752.0 million. Sales of STJ's Medical Angio-Seal™ vascular closure products climbed 54.0% to $156.0 million, while sales of cardiac surgery products rose 1.0% to $251.0 million. Operating income was $370.0 million, up 56.9% from $235.8 million the year before.

PROSPECTS:

The Company's outlook for 2003 continues to be positive. Sales and earnings growth is being fueled by the introduction of new products, which is expected to accelerate in the coming year. Moreover, STJ expects operating margins to continue to improve on a comparable basis and research and development to increase in 2003. Separately, STJ expects to close the acquisition of Getz Bros. Co., Ltd. during the second quarter. This acquisition represents a substantial opportunity for growth as it allows STJ to establish a major presence in Japan, the second largest health care market in the world.

ANNUAL FINANCIAL DATA:

FISCAL YEAR	TOT. REVS. ($mill.)	NET INC. ($mill.)	TOT. ASSETS ($mill.)	OPER. PROFIT %	NET PROFIT %	RET. ON EQUITY %	RET. ON ASSETS %	CURR. RATIO	EARN. PER SH. $	CASH FL. PER SH. $	TANG. BK. VAL. $	DIV. PER SH. $	PRICE RANGE	AVG. P/E RATIO	AVG. YIELD %
p12/31/02	1,589.9	⑥ 276.3							⑥ 1.51			...	43.13 - 30.52	24.4	...
12/31/01	1,347.4	⑤ 172.6	1,628.7	17.5	12.8	14.6	10.6	2.5	⑤ 0.97	1.47	4.55	...	39.04 - 22.23	31.7	...
12/31/00	1,178.8	⑤ 129.1	1,532.7	17.2	11.0	13.7	8.4	2.4	⑤ 0.76	1.29	2.99	...	31.25 - 11.81	28.5	...
12/31/99	1,114.5	④ 24.2	1,554.0	8.0	2.2	3.1	1.6	2.4	④ 0.15	0.65	2.04	...	20.38 - 11.47	109.7	...
12/31/98	1,016.0	129.1	1,384.6	19.1	12.7	16.0	9.3	3.4	0.75	1.15	4.79	...	19.84 - 9.59	19.6	...
12/31/97	994.4	②③ 54.7	1,458.6	8.7	5.5	5.5	3.8	3.0	②③ 0.30	0.66	5.37	...	21.47 - 13.50	59.2	...
12/31/96	808.8	①② 92.2	1,301.4	15.7	11.4	11.0	7.1	2.3	①② 0.56	0.84	5.16	...	23.00 - 14.81	33.8	...
12/31/95	723.5	129.4	1,015.9	26.8	17.9	18.4	12.7	2.7	0.91	1.19	5.02	...	21.63 - 11.83	18.4	...
12/31/94	359.6	① 79.2	919.9	27.6	22.0	14.3	8.6	3.9	① 0.57	0.68	3.96	0.10	13.67 - 8.25	19.4	0.9
12/31/93	252.6	109.6	526.8	52.0	43.4	22.6	20.8	11.0	0.78	0.83	3.48	0.13	14.08 - 8.33	14.5	1.2

Statistics are as originally reported. Adj. for stk splits: 100% stk. div., 6/28/02; 50% stk. div., 11/16/95. ① Incl. a pre-tax chg. for purch. res. & dev. of $40.4 mill., 1996; $40.8 mill., 1994. ② Incl. a pre-tax spec. chg. of $58.7 mill., 12/97; $47.8 mill., 12/96. ③ Bef. acctg. chrg. of $1.6 mill. ④ Incl. a pre-tax in-process res. & devel. chrg. of $115.2 mill. rel. to the acquisitions of Angio-Seal & Vascular Science, Inc. & pre-tax spec. chrgs. of $9.8 mill. assoc. w/ restruct. int'l. opers. ⑤ Incl. pre-tax pur. res. & dev. exp. of $10.0 million, 2001; $5.0 mill., 2000 & spec. chrgs. of $11.2 mill., 2001; $26.1 mill., 2000. ⑥ Incl. after-tax non-recurr. chrgs. of $30.5 mill.

OFFICERS:
T. L. Shepherd, Chmn., C.E.O.
D. J. Starks, Pres., & C.O.O.
J. C. Heinmiller, V.P., C.F.O., Treas.
INVESTOR CONTACT: Laura Merriam, Dir., Inv. Rel., (651) 766-3029
PRINCIPAL OFFICE: One Lillehei Plaza, St. Paul, MN 55117

TELEPHONE NUMBER: (651) 483-2000
FAX: (651) 482-8318
WEB: www.sjm.com
NO. OF EMPLOYEES: 5,568
SHAREHOLDERS: 3,451
ANNUAL MEETING: In May
INCORPORATED: MN, May, 1976

INSTITUTIONAL HOLDINGS:
No. of Institutions: 344
Shares Held: 161,622,965
% Held: 91.0
INDUSTRY: Electromedical equipment (SIC: 3845)
TRANSFER AGENT(S): EquiServe Trust Company, N.A., Providence, RI

ST. PAUL COMPANIES, INC. (THE)

EXCH.	SYM.	REC. PRICE	P/E RATIO	YLD.	MKT. CAP.	RANGE (52-WK.)	'02 Y/E PR.	DIV. ACH.
NYSE	SPC	30.86 (2/28/03)	32.8	3.8%	$6.41 bill.	50.60 - 23.00	34.05	16 yrs.

UPPER MEDIUM GRADE. THE COMPANY IS FOCUSING ON REDUCING COSTS AND COMPLETING ITS RESTRUC-TURING INITIATIVES.

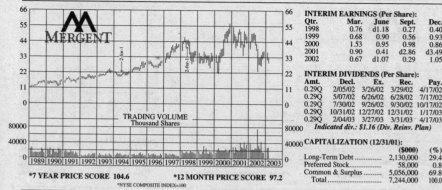

INTERIM EARNINGS (Per Share):

Qtr.	Mar.	June	Sept.	Dec.
1998	0.76	d1.18	0.27	0.40
1999	0.68	0.90	0.56	0.93
2000	1.53	0.95	0.98	0.86
2001	0.90	0.41	d2.86	d3.49
2002	0.67	d1.07	0.29	1.05

INTERIM DIVIDENDS (Per Share):

Amt.	Decl.	Ex.	Rec.	Pay.
0.29Q	2/05/02	3/26/02	3/29/02	4/17/02
0.29Q	5/07/02	6/26/02	6/28/02	7/17/02
0.29Q	7/30/02	9/26/02	9/30/02	10/17/02
0.29Q	10/31/02	12/27/02	12/31/02	1/17/03
0.29Q	2/04/03	3/27/03	3/31/03	4/17/03

Indicated div.: $1.16 (Div. Reinv. Plan)

TRADING VOLUME
Thousand Shares

*7 YEAR PRICE SCORE 104.6   ***12 MONTH PRICE SCORE 97.2**
*NYSE COMPOSITE INDEX=100

CAPITALIZATION (12/31/01):

	($000)	(%)
Long-Term Debt	2,130,000	29.4
Preferred Stock	58,000	0.8
Common & Surplus	5,056,000	69.8
Total	7,244,000	100.0

BUSINESS:

The St. Paul Companies, Inc. is a management company principally engaged in two industry segments: commercial property-liability insurance and nonlife reinsurance products and services. The Company also has a presence in the asset management industry through its 77.0% majority ownership of Nuveen Investments, Inc. As a management company, SPC oversees the operations of its subsidiaries and provides those subsidiaries with capital, management and administrative services. The primary business of the

Company is underwriting, which produced 95.4% of consolidated revenues in 2002. The Company's investment banking-asset management operations accounted for 4.4% of consolidated revenues in 2002. In May 1997, the Company sold its insurance brokerage operation, The Minet Group. In April 1998, SPC acquired USF&G Corporation. In May 1997, the Company sold its insurance brokerage operation, The Minet Group. In April 1998, SPC acquired USF&G Corporation.

RECENT DEVELOPMENTS:

For the year ended 12/31/02, the Company reported income of $249.1 million, before a loss from discontinued operations of $25.3 million an an accounting change charge of $6.0 million, compared with a loss of $1.01 billion, before a loss from discontinued operations of $79.6 million, in the previous year. Results for 2002 and 2001 included after-tax

catastrophe losses of $43.4 million versus $838.3 million in 2001. Results for 2002 also included an after-tax settlement charge of $306.8 million. Total revenues were unchanged versus the prior year at $8.92 billion. Revenues for 2002 and 2001 included realized investment losses of $164.6 million and $94.4 million, respectively.

PROSPECTS:

Results are benefiting from SPC's initiatives to reposition its business and improve profitability. During the fourth quarter, the Company completed the transfer of its reinsurance operations to Platinum Underwriters Holdings Ltd., a new reinsurer based in Bermuda. SPC also completed the

refocusing of its International operations by selling St. Paul Holdings, the immediate parent of its Spanish operations, as well as operations in Argentina and Mexico. In addition, SPC exceeded its goal of reducing corporate and insurance expenses by $125.0 million in 2002.

ANNUAL FINANCIAL DATA:

FISCAL YEAR	PREM. INC. ($mill.)	NET INVST. INC. ($mill.)	TOT. REVS. ($mill.)	NET INC. ($mill.)	TOT. ASSETS ($mill.)	TOT. INVST. ($mill.)	RET. ON REVS. %	RET. ON EQUITY %	RET. ON ASSETS %	EARN. PER SH. $	TANG. BK. VAL.$	AVG. YIELD %	DIV. PER SH. $	PRICE RANGE	AVG. P/E RATIO
p12/31/02	7,390.0		8,917.7	①⑤ 249.1						①⑤ 0.94		3.1	1.15	50.60 - 23.00	39.1
12/31/01	7,296.0	1,217.0	8,943.0	①④ d1,009.0	38,321.0	22,178.0	...	...	...	④ d4.84	21.03	2.5	1.11	54.44 - 34.00	...
12/31/00	5,898.0	1,616.0	8,608.0	① 1,013.0	41,075.0	27,099.0	11.8	14.0	2.5	4.32	30.54	2.7	1.07	57.00 - 21.31	9.1
12/31/99	5,290.0	1,557.0	7,569.0	③ 779.0	38,873.0	26,252.0	10.3	12.0	2.0	3.19	26.42	3.3	1.03	37.06 - 25.38	9.8
12/31/98	6,944.6	1,585.0	9,108.4	② 89.3	38,322.7	27,222.7	1.0	1.3	0.2	② 0.32	25.79	2.6	0.98	47.19 - 28.06	117.5
12/31/97	4,616.5	886.2	6,219.3	① 773.2	21,500.7	15,166.3	12.4	16.7	3.6	① 4.20	25.09	2.6	0.93	42.75 - 28.81	8.5
12/31/96	4,448.2	807.3	5,734.2	① 557.9	20,681.0	14,509.2	9.7	13.9	2.7	① 3.25	22.87	3.1	0.86	30.38 - 25.06	8.5
12/31/95	3,971.3	771.6	5,409.6	521.2	19,738.1	13,316.6	9.6	13.7	2.6	3.00	20.76	3.1	0.79	29.69 - 21.75	8.6
12/31/94	3,412.1	694.6	4,701.3	442.8	17,495.8	11,310.6	9.4	16.2	2.5	2.56	14.57	3.5	0.74	22.75 - 18.84	8.1
12/31/93	3,178.3	661.1	4,460.2	427.6	17,149.2	11,562.2	9.6	14.2	2.5	2.46	16.06	3.2	0.69	24.50 - 18.75	8.8

Statistics are as originally reported. Adj. for stk. splits: 2-for-1, 5/98 & 6/94 ① Bef. disc. oper. loss $25.3 mill., 12/02; $79.6 mill., 12/01; $19.3 mill., 12/00; $67.8 mill., 12/97; $107.8 mill., 12/96 ② Incl. non-recurr. chrg. $221.0 mill. ③ Bef. acctg. change chrg. $29.9 mill. and excl. from disc. oper. $85.1 mill. ④ Incl. pre-tax restr. & goodwill chrgs. of $126.5 mill. ⑤ Bef. acctg. chrg. $6.0 mill.; Incl. an after-tax settlement charge of $306.8 million.

OFFICERS:
J. S. Fishman, Chmn., C.E.O.
T. A. Bradley, Sr. V.P., C.F.O.

INVESTOR CONTACT: Laura Gagon, Investor Relations, (651) 310-7696

PRINCIPAL OFFICE: 385 Washington Street, Saint Paul, MN 55102

TELEPHONE NUMBER: (651) 310-7911
FAX: (651) 310-3386
WEB: www.stpaul.com
NO. OF EMPLOYEES: 10,200 (approx.)
SHAREHOLDERS: 17,467
ANNUAL MEETING: In May
INCORPORATED: MN, May, 1853

STANCORP FINANCIAL GROUP, INC.

EXCH.	SYM.	REC. PRICE	P/E RATIO	YLD.	MKT. CAP.	RANGE (52-WK.)	'02 Y/E PR.
NYSE	SFG	49.75 (2/28/03)	13.3	0.8%	$1.48 bill.	61.20 - 45.14	48.85

UPPER MEDIUM GRADE. SFG EXPECTS CONTINUED GROWTH IN ITS EMPLOYEE BENEFITS SEGMENT.

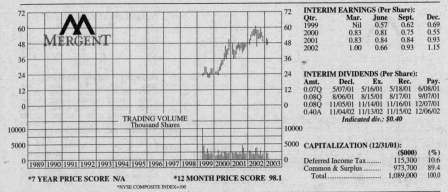

*7 YEAR PRICE SCORE N/A   ***12 MONTH PRICE SCORE 98.1**
*NYSE COMPOSITE INDEX=100

INTERIM EARNINGS (Per Share):

Qtr.	Mar.	June	Sept.	Dec.
1999	Nil	0.57	0.62	0.69
2000	0.83	0.81	0.75	0.55
2001	0.83	0.84	0.84	0.93
2002	1.00	0.66	0.93	1.15

INTERIM DIVIDENDS (Per Share):

Amt.	Decl.	Ex.	Rec.	Pay.
0.07Q	5/07/01	5/16/01	5/18/01	6/08/01
0.08Q	8/06/01	8/15/01	8/17/01	9/07/01
0.08Q	11/05/01	11/14/01	11/16/01	12/07/01
0.40A	11/04/02	11/13/02	11/15/02	12/06/02

Indicated div.: $0.40

CAPITALIZATION (12/31/01):

	($000)	(%)
Deferred Income Tax	115,300	10.6
Common & Surplus	973,700	89.4
Total	1,089,000	100.0

BUSINESS:

StanCorp Financial Group, Inc., through its subsidiaries, Standard Insurance Company; The Standard Life Insurance Company of New York; StanCorp Mortgage Investors, LLC; and StanCorp Investment Advisers, Inc., is a provider of employee benefits products and services. SFG's largest subsidiary, SIC, underwrites group and individual disability and annuity products, and life and dental insurance for groups. The Standard Life Insurance Company of New York provides short-term and long-term disability insur-

ance products for groups in New York. StanCorp Mortgage Investors, LLC is engaged in originating and servicing small commercial mortgage loans. StanCorp Investment Advisers, Inc. is a registered investment adviser providing performance analysis, fund selection support and model portfolios to SIC's retirement plan clients. In 1999, SFG was formed as a holding company for Standard Insurance Company, which converted from a mutual life insurance company to a stock life insurance company.

RECENT DEVELOPMENTS:

For the year ended 12/31/02, net income grew 4.7% to $111.0 million from $106.0 million the previous year. Earnings for 2002 benefited from premium growth and favorable claims experience in SFG's employees benefits insurance segment. Total revenues increased 10.4% to

$1.75 billion from $1.59 billion the prior year. Revenues for 2002 included net capital losses of $19.7 million. Total premiums climbed 12.3% to $1.38 billion from $1.23 billion a year earlier. Net investment income rose 9.2% to $380.8 million.

PROSPECTS:

Going forward, SFG expects continued growth in its employees benefits segment. Total premiums are expected to grow by 10.0% to 12.0% in 2003, with operating income per diluted share, excluding stock-based compensation, rising 12.0% to 15.0%. SFG is targeting an operating return on average equity of 13.0% to 14.0% by the end of 2003,

and 14.0% to 15.0% by the end of 2005. Separately, SFG announced that the integration of the Teachers Insurance and Annuity Association (TIAA) business should be completed by mid-2003. SFG expects TIAA to add about $0.15 to $0.20 per diluted share to earnings in 2003, with most of the benefits occurring during the second half.

ANNUAL FINANCIAL DATA:

FISCAL YEAR	PREM. INC. ($mill.)	TOT. REVS. ($mill.)	NET INC. ($mill.)	TOT. ASSETS ($mill.)	TOT. INVST. ($mill.)	RET. ON REVS. %	RET. ON EQUITY %	RET. ON ASSETS %	EARN. PER SH.$	TANG. BK. VAL.$	AVG. YIELD %	DIV. PER SH.$	PRICE RANGE	AVG. P/E RATIO
p12/31/02	1,383.3	1,750.3	111.0						3.73		0.8	0.40	61.20 - 45.14	14.3
12/31/01	1,231.7	1,585.4	② 106.0	7,277.0	4,781.0	6.7	10.9	1.5	② 3.44	32.69	0.7	0.30	48.50 - 35.60	12.2
12/31/00	1,102.0	1,462.7	94.7	6,859.6	4,836.7	6.5	10.2	1.4	2.95	29.29	0.7	0.27	51.00 - 23.00	12.5
12/31/99	914.4	1,234.5	① 84.4	5,857.1	3,962.8	6.8	10.0	1.4	① 2.37	25.68	0.5	0.12	30.00 - 20.94	10.7
12/31/98	890.9	1,232.6	① 75.6	5,278.8	4,197.5	6.1	9.0	1.4	60.29		...	...	...	...
12/31/97	1,085.0	1,391.2	88.1	4,524.6	3,926.6	6.3	29.1	1.9	...	...	...	...	...	...
12/31/96	971.2	1,262.7	59.7	4,111.7	3,661.8	4.7	22.5	1.5	...	...	...	...	...	...
12/31/95	869.1	1,166.3	60.5	3,749.3	3,437.2	5.2	23.6	1.6	...	...	...	...	...	...
12/31/94	816.9	1,095.1	12.1	3,391.0	3,170.9	1.1	6.0	0.4	...	...	...	...	...	...
12/31/93	796.7	1,062.7	10.7	3,049.1	2,888.7	1.0	5.3	0.4	...	...	...	...	...	...

Statistics are as originally reported. ① Bef. extraord. chrg., $4.5 mill., 12/99; $6.1 mill., 12/98. ② Incl. pre-tax chrgs. of $5.0 mill. rel to evenues of 9/11/01

OFFICERS:
R. E. Timpe, Chmn.
E. E. Parsons, Pres., C.E.O., C.O.O.
C. J. McPike, V.P., C.F.O.
INVESTOR CONTACT: Scott Hibbs, Asst. V.P., Inv. Rel., (503) 321-7529
PRINCIPAL OFFICE: 1100 S.W. Sixth Avenue, Portland, OR 97204

TELEPHONE NUMBER: (503) 321-7000
FAX: (503) 321-6776
WEB: www.stancorpfinancial.com
NO. OF EMPLOYEES: 2,465
SHAREHOLDERS: 58,108
ANNUAL MEETING: In May
INCORPORATED: OR, Feb., 1906

INSTITUTIONAL HOLDINGS:
No. of Institutions: 175
Shares Held: 17,007,044
% Held: 57.9

INDUSTRY: Life insurance (SIC: 6311)

TRANSFER AGENT(S): Mellon Investor Services, South Hackensack, NJ

STANDARD COMMERCIAL CORP.

EXCH.	SYM.	REC. PRICE	P/E RATIO	YLD.	MKT. CAP.	RANGE (52-WK.)	'02 Y/E PR.
NYSE	STW	16.80 (2/28/03)	5.3	1.5%	$224.6 mill.	23.00 - 14.50	18.10

LOWER MEDIUM GRADE. THE COMPANY HAS BEGUN CONSTRUCTION OF A NEW PROCESSING FACILITY IN INDONESIA.

*7 YEAR PRICE SCORE 160.4   ***12 MONTH PRICE SCORE 100.6**

*NYSE COMPOSITE INDEX=100

INTERIM EARNINGS (Per Share):

Qtr.	June	Sept.	Dec.	Mar.
1997-98	0.17	0.41	0.62	0.79
1998-99	0.16	0.31	0.06	0.13
1999-00	0.10	0.17	0.20	0.34
2000-01	0.13	0.38	0.42	0.51
2001-02	0.28	0.91	0.43	0.89
2002-03	0.41	1.05	0.83	...

INTERIM DIVIDENDS (Per Share):

Amt.	Decl.	Ex.	Rec.	Pay.
0.05Q	2/14/02	2/26/02	2/28/02	3/15/02
0.05Q	6/12/02	6/26/02	6/28/02	7/15/02
0.063Q	8/13/02	8/28/02	8/30/02	9/16/02
0.063Q	11/13/02	11/26/02	11/29/02	12/13/02
0.063Q	2/10/03	2/26/03	2/28/03	3/14/03

Indicated div.: $0.25

CAPITALIZATION (3/31/02):

	($000)	(%)
Long-Term Debt	146,812	42.9
Deferred Income Tax	5,000	1.5
Common & Surplus	190,653	55.7
Total	342,465	100.0

BUSINESS:

Standard Commercial Corp. is primarily engaged in the purchasing, processing and selling of leaf tobacco and wool. The Company's tobacco operations, which accounted for 82.8% of revenues for the year ended 3/31/02, consist of purchasing, processing, storing, selling and shipping leaf tobacco grown in over 30 countries, servicing cigarette manufacturers from 25 processing facilities strategically located throughout the world. The Company's nontobacco operations, 17.2% of revenues, is comprised of STW's wool operations, which are concentrated on the core sourcing, processing and sales markets of Australia and Europe and the carpet sector of the wool industry.

RECENT DEVELOPMENTS:

For the quarter ended 12/31/02, income from continuing operations surged 95.3% to $12.1 million compared with income from continuing operations of $6.2 million in the corresponding period a year earlier. Total sales rose 11.9% to $263.0 million from $235.0 million the previous year. Tobacco sales advanced 7.9% to $211.5 million and nontobacco sales, mainly comprised of STW's wool operations, grew 32.2% to $51.5 million. However, STW noted that the increase in revenues in the wool division were offset by higher raw material and processing costs. Gross profit climbed 22.0% to $38.8 million, or 14.7% of total sales, versus $31.8 million, or 13.5% of total sales, the year before. STW attributed the improvement in gross margin mainly to increased fee income and improved efficiencies at both Wilson, North Carolina tobacco processing facilities.

PROSPECTS:

STW announced that it has recently begun construction of a new processing facility in Indonesia. The facility will be a joint venture in which the Company has a 55.0% ownership. Completion of the facility, which STW expects will be accretive in its first full year of operation, is expected in the Company's fiscal third quarter of 2004. Meanwhile, STW noted that it continues to make progress in restructuring its wool operations. As of 2/4/03, STW has sold its New Zealand operations, substantially liquidated its Argentinean and Dutch subsidiaries and is winding down its South African operations.

ANNUAL FINANCIAL DATA:

FISCAL YEAR	TOT. REVS. ($mill.)	NET INC. ($mill.)	TOT. ASSETS ($mill.)	OPER. PROFIT %	NET PROFIT %	RET. ON EQUITY %	RET. ON ASSETS %	CURR. RATIO	EARN. PER SH. $	CASH FL. PER SH. $	TANG. BK. VAL. $	DIV. PER SH. $	PRICE RANGE	AVG. P/E RATIO	AVG. YIELD %
3/31/02	942.3	⑧ 36.2	650.6	6.4	3.8	19.0	5.6	1.6	⑦ 2.55	3.67	14.26	0.20	21.15 - 6.00	5.3	1.5
3/31/01	1,116.9	⑧ 19.5	692.9	4.3	1.7	11.5	2.8	1.6	⑦ 1.47	2.52	12.84	0.20	6.81 - 2.75	3.3	4.2
3/31/00	1,105.7	10.3	820.8	2.4	0.9	6.9	1.3	1.5	0.80	2.07	11.48	0.20	9.25 - 2.75	7.5	3.3
3/31/99	1,102.8	8.4	878.4	1.5	0.8	5.6	1.0	1.4	0.66	2.09	11.69	0.10	17.50 - 6.38	18.1	0.8
3/31/98	1,492.8	26.9	839.5	2.9	1.8	18.0	3.2	1.5	2.05	3.22	11.68	...	21.08 - 14.25	8.6	...
3/31/97	1,354.3	16.9	735.7	2.4	1.3	18.8	2.3	1.3	1.76	3.98	9.34	...	20.34 - 7.07	7.8	...
① 3/31/96	1,359.5	② d9.4	782.8	...	...	...	...	1.1	② d1.06	1.54	6.69	...	13.97 - 8.71	...	...
③ 3/31/95	773.5	④ d27.9	608.4	...	...	...	...	1.2	④ d3.08	d1.85	7.78	0.27	17.31 - 10.19	...	2.0
3/31/94	1,042.0	④ ⑤ d36.5	890.8	...	...	...	...	1.1	④ ⑤ d3.95	d2.22	10.96	0.49	29.76 - 11.77	...	2.4
3/31/93	1,239.5	⑥ 20.7	926.4	2.9	1.7	13.7	2.2	1.3	⑥ 2.20	3.99	16.23	0.47	31.57 - 24.33	12.7	1.7

Statistics are as originally reported. Adj. for all stk. splits & divs. thru 6/97. ① Refl. reinstat. of wool bus. as cont. ops. ② Incl. non-recurr. chrg. of $12.5 mill.; bef. revers. of $10.1 mill. in provs. ③ Refl. wool bus. as disc. ops. ④ Bef. disc. ops. loss 3/31/95, $10.1 mill.; inc. 3/31/94, $689,000. ⑤ Bef. acctg. adj. cr. of $23,000. ⑥ Bef. extraord. cr. of $503,000. ⑦ Bef. extraord. gain of $3.2 mill. ⑧ Bef. disc. ops. loss of $15.3 mill. & extraord. loss of $1.1 mill.

OFFICERS:
J. A. G. Murray, Chmn.
R. E. Harrison, Pres., C.E.O.
R. A. Sheets, V.P., C.F.O.
INVESTOR CONTACT: Henry C. Babb, V.P., Gen. Couns., Sec., (252) 291-5507
PRINCIPAL OFFICE: 2201 Miller Road, Wilson, NC 27893

TELEPHONE NUMBER: (252) 291-5507
FAX: (252) 237-0018
WEB: www.sccgroup.com
NO. OF EMPLOYEES: 2,648 (approx.)
SHAREHOLDERS: 571 (record)
ANNUAL MEETING: In Aug.
INCORPORATED: NY, 1913; reincorp., NC, Mar., 1983

INSTITUTIONAL HOLDINGS:
No. of Institutions: 66
Shares Held: 9,003,594
% Held: 66.8
INDUSTRY: Farm-product raw materials, nec (SIC: 5159)
TRANSFER AGENT(S): First Union National Bank, Charlotte, NC

STANLEY WORKS

EXCH.	SYM.	REC. PRICE	P/E RATIO	YLD.	MKT. CAP.	RANGE (52-WK.)	'02 Y/E PR.	DIV. ACH.
NYSE	SWK	25.81 (2/28/03)	12.0	4.0%	$2.19 bill.	52.00 - 23.84	34.58	35 yrs.

UPPER MEDIUM GRADE. THE COMPANY HAS COMPLETED THE ACQUISITION OF BEST ACCESS SYSTEMS FOR APPROXIMATELY $310.0 MILLION.

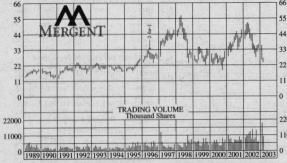

TRADING VOLUME
Thousand Shares

*7 YEAR PRICE SCORE 113.3   *12 MONTH PRICE SCORE 83.1

*NYSE COMPOSITE INDEX=100

INTERIM EARNINGS (Per Share):

Qtr.	Mar.	June	Sept.	Dec.
1998	0.40	0.47	0.37	0.29
1999	0.34	0.28	0.56	0.49
2000	0.54	0.58	0.56	0.54
2001	0.54	0.58	0.62	0.07
2002	0.56	0.72	0.62	0.25

INTERIM DIVIDENDS (Per Share):

Amt.	Decl.	Ex.	Rec.	Pay.
0.24Q	1/24/02	2/28/02	3/04/02	3/22/02
0.24Q	4/24/02	5/30/02	6/03/02	6/28/02
0.255Q	7/17/02	8/29/02	9/03/02	9/24/02
0.255Q	10/16/02	11/20/02	11/22/02	12/27/02
0.255Q	1/24/03	3/06/03	3/10/03	3/28/03

Indicated div.: $1.02 (Div. Reinv. Plan)

CAPITALIZATION (12/29/01):

	($000)	(%)
Long-Term Debt	196,800	19.1
Common & Surplus	832,300	80.9
Total	1,029,100	100.0

BUSINESS:

Stanley Works is a worldwide producer of tools and door products for professional, industrial and consumer use. The Tools segment (75.4% of 2002 sales) manufactures and markets carpenters', mechanics', pneumatic and hydraulic tools as well as tool sets. SWK markets its carpenters' tools under the STANLEY®, FATMAX™, MAXGRIP™, POWERLOCK®, INTELLITOOLS™, CONTRACTOR GRADE™, DYNAGRIP®, ACCUSCAPE®, and GOLDBLATT® brands. The Doors segment (24.6%) manufactures and markets commercial and residential doors as well as closet doors and systems, home decor and door and consumer hardware. Products in the Doors segment include residential insulated steel, reinforced fiberglass and wood entrance door systems. Door products are marketed under the STANLEY®, MAGICDOOR®, WELCOMEWATCH®, STANLEY-ACME TRACK™, MONARCH™ and ACME® brands. A substantial portion of SWK's products are sold through home centers and mass merchant distribution channels in the U.S.

RECENT DEVELOPMENTS:

For the year ended 12/28/02, net income grew 19.3% to $188.8 million compared with $158.3 million in 2001. Results for 2001 included a restructuring charge of $72.4 million. Net sales slid 0.5% to $2.59 billion from $2.61 billion lead by a 2.0% decline in internal operations, which are exclusive of the effects of acquisitions. The Tools segment sales fell 2.7% to $1.95 billion, while the Doors segment sales advanced 6.7% to $638.9 million.

PROSPECTS:

On 11/25/02, the Company announced that it had completed the acquisition of Best Access Systems for approximately $310.0 million. Best is a global provider of security access control systems with $250.0 million in annual sales. SWK expects the acquisition to be immediately accretive to earnings and to generate a return that covers the Company's cost of capital in the first year of ownership. Integration plans have been developed and will begin to be implemented before year-end. Looking ahead, the Company expects first quarter 2003 earnings in the range of $0.44 to $0.46 per share, and full-year 2003 earnings per share to grow by a low double-digit percentage.

ANNUAL FINANCIAL DATA:

FISCAL YEAR	TOT. REVS. ($mill.)	NET INC. ($mill.)	TOT. ASSETS ($mill.)	OPER. PROFIT %	NET PROFIT %	RET. ON EQUITY %	RET. ON ASSETS %	CURR. RATIO	EARN. PER SH. $	CASH FL. PER SH. $	TANG. BK. VAL. $	DIV. PER SH. $	PRICE RANGE	AVG. P/E RATIO	AVG. YIELD %
p12/28/02	2,593.5	188.8							2.14			0.99	52.00 - 27.31	18.5	2.5
12/29/01	2,624.4	⑤ 158.3	2,055.7	9.8	6.0	19.0	7.7	1.4	⑤ 1.81	2.76	7.04	0.94	46.97 - 28.06	20.7	2.5
12/30/00	2,748.9	194.4	1,884.8	12.4	7.1	26.4	10.3	1.5	2.22	3.17	6.58	0.90	31.88 - 18.44	11.3	3.6
1/01/00	2,751.8	④ 150.0	1,890.6	9.3	5.5	20.4	7.9	1.6	④ 1.67	2.62	6.19	0.87	35.00 - 22.00	17.1	3.1
1/02/99	2,729.1	③ 137.8	1,932.9	9.2	5.0	20.6	7.1	1.5	③ 1.53	2.41	5.32	0.83	57.25 - 23.50	26.4	2.1
1/03/98	2,669.5	② d41.9	1,758.7	0.7	...	...	...	1.6	② d0.47	0.34	5.67	0.77	47.38 - 28.00	...	2.0
12/28/96	2,670.8	② 96.9	1,659.6	8.2	3.6	12.4	5.8	2.4	② 1.09	1.93	7.68	0.73	32.81 - 23.63	25.9	2.6
12/30/95	2,624.3	② 59.1	1,670.0	6.0	2.3	8.0	3.5	2.4	② 0.67	1.58	6.79	0.71	26.69 - 17.81	33.5	3.2
12/31/94	2,510.9	125.3	1,701.1	10.6	5.0	16.8	7.4	2.1	1.40	2.31	6.52	0.69	22.44 - 17.44	14.2	3.5
1/01/94	2,273.1	① 92.6	1,576.9	9.1	4.1	13.6	5.9	2.1	① 1.03	1.93	5.70	0.67	23.94 - 18.94	20.8	3.5

Statistics are as originally reported. Adj. for stk. split: 2-for-1, 6/96. ① Incl. a gain of $29 mill. from sale of investment, Max, Co. Ltd.; a fine fee of $5.0 mill.; and a chrg. of $23 mill. for contingency reserves related to litigation & bef. acctg. change chrg. of $8.5 mill. ② Incl. pretax restruct chrgs. of $238.5 mill., 1997; $47.8 mill. 1996; & $85.8 mill., 1995. ③ Incl. restruct. chrg. of $27.8 mill. ④ Incl. restruct. credit of $21.3 mill. ⑤ Incl. restruct. chrg. and asset write-offs of $72.4 mill.

OFFICERS:
J. M. Trani, Chmn., C.E.O.
J. M. Loree, V.P., Fin., C.F.O.
S. S. Weddle, V.P., Gen. Couns.

INVESTOR CONTACT: Gerard J. Gould, Dir., Investor Relations, (860) 827-3833

PRINCIPAL OFFICE: 1000 Stanley Drive, P.O. Box 7000, New Britain, CT 06053

TELEPHONE NUMBER: (860) 225-5111
FAX: (860) 827-3895
WEB: www.stanleyworks.com

NO. OF EMPLOYEES: 14,400 (approx.)

SHAREHOLDERS: 15,290

ANNUAL MEETING: In Apr.

INCORPORATED: CT, July, 1852

INSTITUTIONAL HOLDINGS:
No. of Institutions: 230
Shares Held: 57,317,991
% Held: 64.9

INDUSTRY: Hand and edge tools, nec (SIC: 3423)

TRANSFER AGENT(S): EquiServe Limited Partnership, Boston, MA

STARWOOD HOTELS & RESORTS WORLDWIDE, INC.

EXCH.	SYM.	REC. PRICE	P/E RATIO	YLD.	MKT. CAP.	RANGE (52-WK.)	'02 Y/E PR.
NYSE	HOT	22.61 (2/28/03)	18.7	3.7%	$4.51 bill.	39.94 - 19.00	23.74

LOWER MEDIUM GRADE. THE COMPANY EXPECTS NET PROCEEDS OF AT LEAST $500.0 MILLION FROM DOMESTIC AND INTERNATIONAL ASSET SALES BY THE END OF 2003.

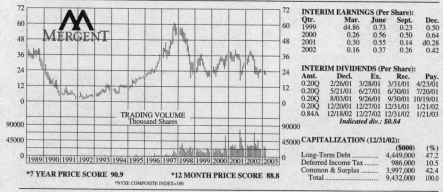

INTERIM EARNINGS (Per Share):

Qtr.	Mar.	June	Sept.	Dec.
1999	d4.86	0.73	0.23	0.50
2000	0.26	0.56	0.50	0.64
2001	0.30	0.55	0.14	d0.28
2002	0.16	0.37	0.26	0.42

INTERIM DIVIDENDS (Per Share):

Amt.	Decl.	Ex.	Rec.	Pay.
0.20Q	2/26/01	3/28/01	3/31/01	4/23/01
0.20Q	5/21/01	6/27/01	6/30/01	7/20/01
0.20Q	8/03/01	9/26/01	9/30/01	10/19/01
0.20Q	12/20/01	12/27/01	12/31/01	1/21/02
0.84A	12/18/02	12/27/02	12/31/02	1/21/03

Indicated div.: $0.84

CAPITALIZATION (12/31/02):

	($000)	(%)
Long-Term Debt	4,449,000	47.2
Deferred Income Tax	986,000	10.5
Common & Surplus	3,997,000	42.4
Total	9,432,000	100.0

*7 YEAR PRICE SCORE 90.9   ***12 MONTH PRICE SCORE 88.8**
*NYSE COMPOSITE INDEX=100

BUSINESS:

Starwood Hotels & Resorts Worldwide, Inc., (formerly Starwood Lodging), is a hotel and leisure company that operates directly and through its subsidiary, ITT Sheraton Corporation. The Company offers luxury and upscale full-service hotels under the following brand names: Sheraton®, Westin®, The Luxury Collection®, St. Regis®, W® brands and Four Points® by Sheraton. As of 1/29/03, the Company's portfolio of owned, managed and franchised hotels totaled more than 750 properties in over 80 countries. HOT's subsidiary, Starwood Vacation Ownership, Inc., offers vacation ownership interest in 11 resort locations.

RECENT DEVELOPMENTS:

For the year ended 12/31/02, HOT reported income from continuing operations of $246.0 million versus net income of $145.0 million in 2001. Results included a restructuring credit of $7.0 million and a charge of $50.0 million, and an asset disposition gain of $3.0 million and a charge of $57.0 million, in 2002 and 2001, respectively. Results for 2002 and 2001 also included early debt extinguishment charges of $30.0 million and $9.0 million, respectively. Total revenues slipped 1.0% to $4.66 billion from $4.71 billion a year earlier. Revenues from owned, leased and consolidated joint venture hotels decreased 3.3% to $3.23 billion, while other hotel and leisure revenues rose 3.7% to $647.0 million. Other managed and franchised properties revenues climbed 5.4% to $780.0 million.

PROSPECTS:

Including 10 management and franchise contracts representing 4,000 rooms signed during the fourth quarter, HOT expects 31 new full-service hotels and resorts around the world, with 9,000 rooms to commence operations in 2003. HOT also expects net proceeds of at least $500.0 million from domestic and international asset sales by the end of 2003. Separately, HOT anticipates total capital expenditures in 2003 to range from $400.0 million to $450.0 million. Full-year earnings per share growth is expected in the range of flat to up 10.0%, before one-time items.

ANNUAL FINANCIAL DATA:

FISCAL YEAR	TOT. REVS. ($mill.)	NET INC. ($mill.)	TOT. ASSETS ($mill.)	OPER. PROFIT %	NET PROFIT %	RET. ON EQUITY %	RET. ON ASSETS %	CURR. RATIO	EARN. PER SH.$	CASH FL.PER SH.$	TANG. BK. VAL.$	DIV. PER SH.$	PRICE RANGE	AVG. P/E RATIO	AVG. YIELD %
12/31/02	4,659.0	⑦ 246.0	12,259.0	12.6	5.3	6.2	2.0	0.4	⑦ 1.20	3.69	7.15	0.20	39.94 - 19.00	24.6	0.7
12/31/01	3,967.0	⑥ 151.0	12,461.0	15.5	3.8	4.0	1.2	0.6	⑥ 0.73	3.37	2.35	0.77	40.89 - 17.10	39.7	2.7
12/31/00	4,345.0	⑤ 401.0	12,660.0	23.7	9.2	10.4	3.2	0.6	⑤ 1.96	4.36	4.99	0.67	37.50 - 19.75	14.6	2.3
12/31/99	3,862.0	④ d638.0	12,923.0	2.0	. . .	. . .	. . .	0.5	④ d3.41	d0.77	4.32	0.45	37.75 - 19.50	. . .	1.6
③ 12/31/98	4,700.0	② d254.0	11,214.0	3.3	. . .	. . .	. . .	0.5	② d1.37	1.04	. . .	. . .	57.88 - 18.75	. . .	. . .
12/31/97	933.6	① 60.2	3,009.5	13.4	6.4	5.9	2.0	0.6	① 0.85	3.82	9.95	. . .	61.50 - 33.50	55.9	. . .
12/31/96	428.5	① 36.1	1,312.7	13.9	8.4	6.1	2.8	0.7	① 0.86	3.07	7.39	. . .	36.92 - 19.67	32.9	. . .
12/31/95	161.7	① 18.1	460.0	19.3	11.2	8.4	3.9	1.2	① 0.95	2.88	5.20	. . .	20.08 - 9.98	15.8	. . .
12/31/94	114.0	d4.7	184.0	11.4	. . .	. . .	. . .	0.3	d1.54	1.15	2.87	. . .	13.47 - 5.99	. . .	. . .
12/31/93	117.2	d7.0	195.4	7.0	. . .	. . .	. . .	0.3	d2.32	0.73	4.33	. . .	13.47 - 3.99	. . .	. . .

Statistics are as originally reported. Adj. for stk. splits: 3-for-2, 1/97; 1-for-6, 6/95. ① Bef. extr. chg. 1997, $3.5 mil.; cr. 1996, $1.1 mil.; chg. 1995, $2.2 mil. ② Incl. pre-tax restr. & oth. chg. $204.0 mil. & a pre-tax gain $55.0 mil. from asset sales; excl. a disc. oper. gain $1.11 bill. ③ Results of ITT Corp. for the yr. ended 12/31/98 and the results of Starwood Hotels & Resorts, Starwood Hotels & Resorts Worldwide, Inc., inclusive of Westin, fr. the close of the ITT merger (2/23/98) through 12/31/98. ④ Incl. pre-tax gain $191.0 mill. and pre-tax restr. chg. $3.0 mill.; bef. disc. oper. loss $71.0 mill.& extraord. loss $32.0 mill. ⑤ Bef. extr. chg. $3.0 mill. & disc. oper. gain $5.0 mill.; incl. net invest. sale gain $2.0 mill. ⑥ Bef. extr. chg. $6.0 mill.; incl. net restr. and oth. spec. chg. $50.0 mill. and a loss on asset dispos. $57.0 mill. ⑦ Bef. disc. oper. gain $109.0 mill.; incl. restr. credit $7.0 mill., gain on asset dispos. $3.0 mill. and debt extinguish. chg. $30.0 mill.

OFFICERS:
B. S. Sternlicht, Chmn., C.E.O.
R. C. Brown, Exec., V.P., C.F.O.
INVESTOR CONTACT: David Matheson, (914) 640-5204
PRINCIPAL OFFICE: 1111 Westchester Avenue, White Plains, NY 10604

TELEPHONE NUMBER: (914) 640-8100
FAX: (914) 640-8310
WEB: www.starwoodhotels.com
NO. OF EMPLOYEES: 105,000 (approx.)
SHAREHOLDERS: 19,000 (approx. record)
ANNUAL MEETING: In May
INCORPORATED: MD, 1969

INSTITUTIONAL HOLDINGS:
No. of Institutions: 295
Shares Held: 186,496,814
% Held: 93.5
INDUSTRY: Hotels and motels (SIC: 7011)
TRANSFER AGENT(S): Mellon Investor Services, South Hackensack, NJ

STATE STREET CORPORATION

EXCH.	SYM.	REC. PRICE	P/E RATIO	YLD.	MKT. CAP.	RANGE (52-WK.)	'02 Y/E PR.	DIV. ACH.
NYSE	STT	36.85 (2/28/03)	11.9	1.4%	$11.97 bill.	58.36 - 32.11	39.00	22 yrs.

UPPER MEDIUM GRADE. THE COMPANY COMPLETED THE SALE OF ITS CORPORATE TRUST BUSINESS IN A
TRANSACTION VALUED AT APPROXIMATELY $725.0 MILLION.

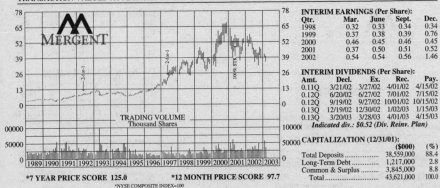

*7 YEAR PRICE SCORE 125.0   *12 MONTH PRICE SCORE 97.7

*NYSE COMPOSITE INDEX=100

INTERIM EARNINGS (Per Share):

Qtr.	Mar.	June	Sept.	Dec.
1998	0.32	0.33	0.34	0.34
1999	0.37	0.38	0.39	0.76
2000	0.46	0.45	0.46	0.45
2001	0.37	0.50	0.51	0.52
2002	0.54	0.54	0.56	1.46

INTERIM DIVIDENDS (Per Share):

Amt.	Decl.	Ex.	Rec.	Pay.
0.11Q	3/21/02	3/27/02	4/01/02	4/15/02
0.12Q	6/20/02	6/27/02	7/01/02	7/15/02
0.12Q	9/19/02	9/27/02	10/01/02	10/15/02
0.13Q	12/19/02	12/30/02	1/02/03	1/15/03
0.13Q	3/20/03	3/28/03	4/01/03	4/15/03

Indicated div.: $0.52 (Div. Reinv. Plan)

CAPITALIZATION (12/31/01):

	($000)	(%)
Total Deposits	38,559,000	88.4
Long-Term Debt	1,217,000	2.8
Common & Surplus	3,845,000	8.8
Total	43,621,000	100.0

BUSINESS:

State Street Corporation (formerly State Street Boston Corporation), as of 12/31/02, is a bank holding company with $85.79 billion in assets that conducts business worldwide principally through its subsidiary, State Street Bank and Trust Company. The Company has two lines of business: services for institutional investors and investment management. Services for institutional investors are primarily accounting, custody and other services for large pools of assets. Investment management offers index and active

equity strategies, short-term investment funds and fixed income products. As of 12/31/02, STT had $763.00 billion in assets under management. On 10/1/99, the Company sold its commercial lending business. On 2/8/01, STT acquired a majority interest in Bel Air Investment Advisors LLC. On 7/3/01, STT acquired DST Systems, Inc.'s portfolio accounting service business. On 12/31/02, STT sold its corporate trust business.

RECENT DEVELOPMENTS:

For the year ended 12/31/02, net income increased 61.6% to $1.02 billion from $628.0 million the year before. Earnings included a net gain of $571 million in 2002 and a net loss of $16.0 million in 2001, related to various items. Net interest revenue declined 4.5% to $979.0 million. Provision for loan losses decreased 60.0% to $4.0 million. Total fee

revenue grew 2.9% to $2.85 billion. Servicing fees rose 4.1% to $1.72 billion and management fees grew 1.9% to $526.0 million, both reflecting strong new business success. Foreign exchange trading revenue fell 18.5% to $300.0 million due to low currency volatility. Processing fees and other revenue advanced 24.3% to $184.0 million.

PROSPECTS:

On 12/31/02, the Company announced that it completed the sale of its corporate trust business to U.S. Bank, N.A., a subsidiary of U.S. Bancorp, in a transaction valued at approximately $725.0 million. The sale will enable STT to focus on its core businesses. Separately, the Company

remains on schedule with the acquisition of Deutsche Bank's Global Securities Services business. Meanwhile, the Company continues to benefit from new client wins, an expanded product range, and controlled expense growth.

ANNUAL FINANCIAL DATA:

FISCAL YEAR	NET INT. INC. ($mill.)	NON-INT. INC. ($mill.)	NET INC. ($mill.)	TOT. LOANS ($mill.)	TOT. ASSETS ($mill.)	TOT. DEP. ($mill.)	RET. ON EQUITY %	RET. ON ASSETS %	EQUITY/ ASSETS %	EARN. PER SH. $	TANG. BK. VAL. $	DIV. PER SH. $	PRICE RANGE	AVG. P/E RATIO
p12/31/02	979.0	2,850.0	☑ 1,015.0		85,794.0					☑ 3.10		0.46	58.36 - 32.11	14.6
12/31/01	1,025.0	2,782.0	628.0	5,341.0	69,896.0	38,559.0	16.3	0.9	5.5	1.90	11.88	0.39	63.93 - 36.25	26.4
12/31/00	894.0	2,665.0	595.0	5,273.0	69,298.0	37,937.0	18.2	0.9	4.7	1.82	10.09	0.33	68.40 - 31.22	27.4
12/31/99	781.0	2,537.0	① 619.0	4,293.0	60,896.0	34,145.0	23.3	1.0	4.4	① 1.89	8.31	0.29	47.63 - 27.75	19.9
12/31/98	745.0	1,997.0	436.0	6,309.0	47,082.0	27,539.0	18.9	0.9	4.9	1.33	7.19	0.25	37.16 - 23.94	23.0
12/31/97	641.0	1,673.0	380.0	5,562.0	37,975.0	24,878.0	19.0	1.0	5.3	1.16	5.97	0.21	31.84 - 15.66	20.5
12/31/96	551.0	1,302.0	293.0	4,713.0	31,524.0	19,519.0	16.5	0.9	5.6	0.90	5.47	0.18	17.13 - 10.44	15.3
12/31/95	429.4	1,119.1	247.1	3,986.1	25,785.2	16,647.2	15.6	1.0	6.2	0.75	4.82	0.17	11.56 - 7.00	12.5
12/31/94	367.2	981.0	207.4	3,233.2	21,729.5	13,902.7	16.8	1.0	5.9	0.68	4.03	0.14	10.78 - 6.91	13.1
12/31/93	317.6	833.4	179.8	2,680.2	18,720.1	13,017.9	16.3	1.0	5.9	0.59	3.64	0.13	12.28 - 7.31	16.6

Statistics are as originally reported. Adj. for 2-for-1 stock splits, 5/01 & 5/97. ① Incl. pre-tax net gain on the sale of Co.'s commercial banking business of $282.0 mill. ☑ Incl. a net gain of 571.0 million related to various items.

OFFICERS:
D. A. Spina, Chmn., C.E.O
R. E. Logue, Pres., C.O.O.
R. L. O'Kelley, Exec. V.P., C.F.O., Treas.
INVESTOR CONTACT: S. Kelley MacDonald,
Sr. V.P.-Inv. Rel., (617) 664-3477
PRINCIPAL OFFICE: 225 Franklin Street,
Boston, MA 02110

TELEPHONE NUMBER: (617) 786-3000
FAX: (617) 985-8055
WEB: www.statestreet.com
NO. OF EMPLOYEES: 19,105 full-time; 648 part-time
SHAREHOLDERS: 5,648
ANNUAL MEETING: In April
INCORPORATED: MA, Oct., 1969

INSTITUTIONAL HOLDINGS:
No. of Institutions: 545
Shares Held: 234,475,420
% Held: 72.3
INDUSTRY: State commercial banks (SIC: 6022)
TRANSFER AGENT(S): State Street Bank and Trust Company, Boston, MA

STEELCASE INC.

EXCH.	SYM.	REC. PRICE	P/E RATIO	YLD.	MKT. CAP.	RANGE (52-WK.)	'02 Y/E PR.
NYSE	SCS	9.21 (2/28/03)	...	2.6%	$1.36 bill.	18.00 - 7.95	10.96

LOWER MEDIUM GRADE. THE COMPANY PLANS TO LAUNCH NEW FURNITURE, ARCHITECTURE, AND TECHNOLOGY PRODUCTS IN AN EFFORT TO WIN NEW BUSINESS.

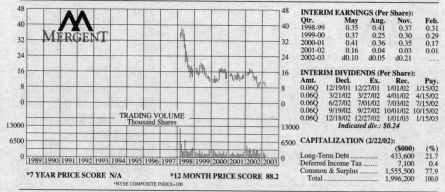

*7 YEAR PRICE SCORE N/A ***12 MONTH PRICE SCORE 88.2**
*NYSE COMPOSITE INDEX=100

INTERIM EARNINGS (Per Share):

Qtr.	May	Aug.	Nov.	Feb.
1998-99	0.35	0.41	0.37	0.31
1999-00	0.37	0.25	0.30	0.29
2000-01	0.41	0.36	0.35	0.17
2001-02	0.16	0.04	0.03	0.01
2002-03	d0.10	d0.05	d0.21	...

INTERIM DIVIDENDS (Per Share):

Amt.	Decl.	Ex.	Rec.	Pay.
0.06Q	12/19/01	12/27/01	1/01/02	1/15/02
0.06Q	3/21/02	3/27/02	4/01/02	4/15/02
0.06Q	6/27/02	7/01/02	7/03/02	7/15/02
0.06Q	9/19/02	9/27/02	10/01/02	10/15/02
0.06Q	12/18/02	12/27/02	1/01/03	1/15/03

Indicated div.: $0.24

CAPITALIZATION (2/22/02):

	($000)	(%)
Long-Term Debt	433,600	21.7
Deferred Income Tax	7,100	0.4
Common & Surplus	1,555,500	77.9
Total	1,996,200	100.0

BUSINESS:

Steelcase Inc. provides products and services that enable customers and their consultants to create work environments that integrate architecture, furniture and technology. SCS' product portfolio includes interior architectural products, furniture systems, technology products, seating, lighting, storage and related products and services. The North America business segment includes SCS' STEELCASE and TURNSTONE brands, and consolidated dealers in the U.S. and Canada. The Steelcase Design Partnership segment includes SCS' Brayton, Designtex Group, Details, Metro and Vecta subsidiaries. The International furniture segment includes the rest of the world, with the major portion of operations in Europe. The Financial Services business segment includes customer leasing and dealer financing services. The Other business segment includes SCS' PolyVision, IDEO and Attwood subsidiaries, other ventures and unallocated corporate expenses.

RECENT DEVELOPMENTS:

For the quarter ended 11/22/02, the Company reported a net loss of $31.1 million compared with net income of $4.9 million in the equivalent 2001 quarter. The loss was due to unusually high-after tax charges associated with an increase in reserves for workers compensation costs, lease credit issues and dealer transition financing, partially offset by better than anticipated operating performance. Results for 2002 and 2001 included restructuring costs of $29.3 million and $7.4 million, respectively. Total revenues declined 11.6% to $646.7 million from $731.4 million in 2001.

PROSPECTS:

Looking ahead, the Company expects a modest decrease in fourth quarter shipments versus the third quarter due to continued volatile order and bid activity. However, SCS is taking steps across its businesses that should help to stimulate additional demand and win new business. For example, SCS is in the process of launching new furniture, architecture, and technology products. This launch includes enhancements to two of SCS' fastest-growing systems furniture lines. However, given lower anticipated volume in the fourth quarter, SCS expects a loss, before non-recurring charges, in the range of $0.05 to $0.10 per share.

ANNUAL FINANCIAL DATA:

FISCAL YEAR	TOT. REVS. ($mill.)	NET INC. ($mill.)	TOT. ASSETS ($mill.)	OPER. PROFIT %	NET PROFIT %	RET. ON EQUITY %	RET. ON ASSETS %	CURR. RATIO	EARN. PER SH. $	CASH FL. PER SH. $	TANG. BK. VAL. $	DIV. PER SH. $	PRICE RANGE	AVG. P/E RATIO	AVG. YIELD %
2/22/02	3,089.5	③ 1.0	2,967.5	0.6	...	0.1	...	1.3	③ 0.01	...	6.89	0.44	16.00 - 11.25	...	3.2
2/23/01	3,885.8	② 193.7	3,157.0	7.9	5.0	11.8	6.1	1.4	② 1.29	2.38	8.34	0.44	18.44 - 10.25	11.1	3.1
2/25/00	3,316.1	① 184.2	3,037.6	8.2	5.6	11.8	6.1	1.2	① 1.21	2.13	7.54	0.44	20.75 - 11.00	13.1	2.8
2/26/99	2,742.5	221.4	2,182.5	11.6	8.1	14.8	10.1	1.7	1.44	2.14	9.12	0.30	38.38 - 12.75	17.8	1.2
2/27/98	2,760.0	217.0	2,007.2	11.5	7.9	16.3	10.8	1.8	1.40	2.02	8.26	...	...	...	...
2/28/97	2,408.4	27.7	1,922.1	5.9	1.2	2.0	1.4	2.4	d2.29	0.78	...	...	...	...	...
2/23/96	2,155.9	123.5	1,884.5	7.6	5.7	8.9	6.6	2.5	...	...	...	...	...	...	...
2/28/95	2,048.7	64.2	...	3.8	3.1	...	...	...	...	...	...	...	...	...	...

Statistics are as originally reported. ① Incl. net nonrecur. after-tax chrg. of $5.7 mill. ② Incl. net nonrecur. after-tax chrg. of $9.9 mill. ③ Incl. restruct. and other non-recurr. chrgs. of $50.3 mill.

OFFICERS:
E. D. Holton, Chmn.
J. P. Hackett, Pres., C.E.O.
J. P. Keane, Sr. V.P., C.F.O.
INVESTOR CONTACT: Perry Grueber, (616) 247-2200
PRINCIPAL OFFICE: 901 44th Street, Grand Rapids, MI 49508

TELEPHONE NUMBER: (616) 247-2710
FAX: (616) 475-2270
WEB: www.steelcase.com
NO. OF EMPLOYEES: 17,000 (approx.)
SHAREHOLDERS: 12,461 (class A record); 206 (class B record)
ANNUAL MEETING: In June
INCORPORATED: MI, 1912

INSTITUTIONAL HOLDINGS:
No. of Institutions: 89
Shares Held: 29,028,696
% Held: 19.7
INDUSTRY: Office furniture, except wood (SIC: 2522)
TRANSFER AGENT(S): Bank of Boston, NA, Boston, MA

STEPAN COMPANY

EXCH.	SYM.	REC. PRICE	P/E RATIO	YLD.	MKT. CAP.	RANGE (52-WK.)	'02 Y/E PR.	DIV. ACH.
NYSE	SCL	24.31 (2/28/03)	11.8	3.1%	...	29.60 - 20.55	25.00	36 yrs.

MEDIUM GRADE. THE UNCERTAIN ECONOMY AND INCREASED INTERNAL SURFACTANT PRODUCTION CAPACITY AMONG SOME U.S. CUSTOMERS MAY HINDER THE COMPANY'S GROWTH PROSPECTS IN 2003.

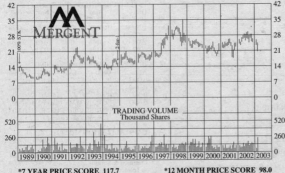

*7 YEAR PRICE SCORE 117.7   ***12 MONTH PRICE SCORE 98.0**

NYSE COMPOSITE INDEX=100

INTERIM EARNINGS (Per Share):

Qtr.	March	June	Sept.	Dec.
1998	0.52	0.64	0.45	0.51
1999	0.57	0.75	d0.02	0.76
2000	0.41	0.64	0.61	d0.25
2001	0.36	0.61	0.44	0.18
2002	0.39	0.84	0.58	0.25

INTERIM DIVIDENDS (Per Share):

Amt.	Decl.	Ex.	Rec.	Pay.
0.182Q	2/12/02	2/26/02	2/28/02	3/15/02
0.182Q	4/30/02	5/29/02	5/31/02	6/14/02
0.182Q	8/06/02	8/28/02	8/30/02	9/13/02
0.19Q	11/01/02	11/26/02	11/29/02	12/13/02
0.19Q	2/11/03	2/26/03	2/28/03	3/14/03

Indicated div.: $0.76

CAPITALIZATION (12/31/01):

	($000)	(%)
Long-Term Debt	109,588	36.0
Deferred Income Tax	35,040	11.5
Preferred Stock	14,581	4.8
Common & Surplus	145,148	47.7
Total	304,357	100.0

BUSINESS:

The Stepan Company is a producer of specialty and intermediate chemicals that are used in a variety of end products. The Company operates in three business segments: surfactants (80.0% of 2002 net sales), polymers (17.0%), and specialty products (3.0%). Surfactants are a principal ingredient in consumer and industrial cleaning products such as detergents, shampoos, lotions, toothpastes and cosmetics. Other applications include lubricating ingredients and emulsifiers for agricultural products, plastics and composites. Polymer products include phthalic anhydride, polyurethane systems and polyurethane polyols, which are used in construction materials and components of automotive, boating and other consumer products. Polyurethane systems provide thermal insulation. Polyurethane polyols are used in manufacturing laminate board. Specialty products include chemicals used in food, flavoring and pharmaceutical applications.

RECENT DEVELOPMENTS:

For the year ended 12/31/02, net income advanced 25.2% to $20.1 million compared with $16.1 million in 2001. Earnings benefited from global growth, particularly from the 2001 U.K. acquisition and the Philippine joint venture. Net sales increased 5.2% to $748.5 million from $711.5 million a year earlier. Gross profit climbed 14.3% to $122.5 million, or 16.4% of net sales, from $107.2 million, or 15.1% of net sales, the year before. Administrative costs jumped 24.9% to $35.8 million, primarily due to higher systems implementation costs, legal fees, auditing fees and the full year addition of Stepan U.K. Comparisons were made with restated results for the previous year.

PROSPECTS:

The uncertainty surrounding the economy and the impact it may have on raw material costs, coupled with increased internal surfactant production capacity among some U.S. customers may provide a challenge for 2003 earnings growth prospects. However, SCL is seeing increased interest in its fabric softener technology, which should be commercialized during 2003. Going forward, the Company will continue to pursue profitable global niche opportunities that compliment or enhance SCL's global capabilities.

ANNUAL FINANCIAL DATA:

FISCAL YEAR	TOT. REVS. ($000)	NET INC. ($000)	TOT. ASSETS ($000)	OPER. PROFIT %	NET PROFIT %	RET. ON EQUITY %	RET. ON ASSETS %	CURR. RATIO	EARN. PER SH. $	CASH FL. PER SH. $	TANG. BK. VAL. $	DIV. PER SH. $	PRICE RANGE	AVG. P/E RATIO	AVG. YIELD %
p12/31/02	748,539	20,129			2.7				2.05			0.74	29.60 - 23.44	12.9	2.8
12/31/01	711,517	16,152	435,488	4.4	2.3	10.1	3.7	1.7	1.59	5.54	15.41	0.71	26.38 - 17.65	13.8	3.2
12/31/00	698,937	15,008	415,049	4.6	2.1	9.7	3.6	1.6	1.47	5.30	15.47	0.66	25.00 - 18.50	14.8	3.0
12/31/99	666,784	① 22,129	414,576	6.3	3.3	14.3	5.3	1.7	① 2.08	5.79	14.28	0.61	26.69 - 22.19	11.7	2.5
12/31/98	610,451	23,454	404,361	7.4	3.8	15.8	5.8	1.7	2.12	5.51	13.24	0.56	35.13 - 23.13	13.7	1.9
12/31/97	581,949	20,410	374,936	7.6	3.5	14.8	5.4	1.8	1.86	5.08	12.16	0.51	32.38 - 18.00	13.5	2.0
12/31/96	536,635	19,067	381,012	7.5	3.6	14.5	5.0	1.8	1.80	5.12	11.38	0.48	20.50 - 15.75	10.1	2.6
12/31/95	528,218	16,119	362,527	6.2	3.1	13.2	4.4	1.8	1.51	4.66	10.25	0.45	20.88 - 14.75	11.8	2.5
12/31/94	443,948	13,845	324,948	6.7	3.1	12.4	4.3	1.6	1.29	4.31	9.18	0.42	17.69 - 12.38	11.7	2.8
12/31/93	438,825	10,776	300,934	6.2	2.5	10.3	3.6	1.7	0.98	3.89	8.56	0.41	18.94 - 12.56	16.1	2.6

Statistics are as originally reported. Adj. for stk. splits: 2-for-1, 12/94 ① Incl. after-tax chrg. of $6.3 mill. related to a lawsuit settlement.

OFFICERS:
F. Q. Stepan, Chmn., C.E.O.
F. Q. Stepan Jr., Pres., C.O.O.
F. S. Eberts III, V.P., Gen Couns., Sec.
INVESTOR CONTACT: James E. Hurlbutt,
. (847) 446-7500
PRINCIPAL OFFICE: Edens & Winnetka
Road, Northfield, IL 60093

TELEPHONE NUMBER: (847) 446-7500
FAX: (847) 501-2443
WEB: www.stepan.com
NO. OF EMPLOYEES: 1,491 (avg.)
SHAREHOLDERS: 1,231
ANNUAL MEETING: In April
INCORPORATED: IL, Jan., 1940; reincorp.,
DE, 1959

INSTITUTIONAL HOLDINGS:
No. of Institutions: 41
Shares Held: 3,088,132
% Held: 34.8
INDUSTRY: Surface active agents (SIC: 2843)
TRANSFER AGENT(S): Computershare Investor Services, Chicago, IL

STERIS CORPORATION

EXCH.	SYM.	REC. PRICE	P/E RATIO	YLD.	MKT. CAP.	RANGE (52-WK.)	'02 Y/E PR.
NYSE	STE	25.25 (2/28/03)	25.3	...	$1.75 bill.	27.30 - 16.30	24.25

UPPER MEDIUM GRADE. THE COMPANY EXPECTS THAT DEMAND WILL REMAIN STRONG RESULTING IN OVERALL REVENUE GROWTH OF APPROXIMATELY 11.0% FOR FISCAL YEAR 2003.

TRADING VOLUME
Thousand Shares

1989 1990 1991 1992 1993 1994 1995 1996 1997 1998 1999 2000 2001 2002 2003

*7 YEAR PRICE SCORE 124.3   ***12 MONTH PRICE SCORE 118.2**
*NYSE COMPOSITE INDEX=100

INTERIM EARNINGS (Per Share):

Qtr.	June	Sept.	Dec.	Mar.
1996-97	d1.08	0.17	0.19	0.23
1997-98	0.17	0.22	0.26	0.29
1998-99	0.21	0.27	0.33	0.41
1999-00	0.14	0.21	0.16	d0.36
2000-01	0.01	0.10	0.15	d0.24
2001-02	0.06	0.13	0.20	0.26
2002-03	0.18	0.26	0.30	...

INTERIM DIVIDENDS (Per Share):

Amt.	Decl.	Ex.	Rec.	Pay.
		No dividends paid.		

CAPITALIZATION (3/31/02):

	($000)	(%)
Long-Term Debt	115,228	18.5
Deferred Income Tax	19,381	3.1
Common & Surplus	487,145	78.4
Total	621,754	100.0

BUSINESS:

STERIS Corporation is a worldwide provider of infection prevention, contamination prevention, microbial reduction, and surgical support systems, products, services, and technologies to health care, scientific, research, and industrial customers. The Company's customer support facilities are located in major global market centers with production operations in the United States, Canada, Germany, Finland, Sweden, and Australia. STERIS SYSTEM 1™, the Company's site-of-care sterile processing system, enables health care professionals to safely and economically sterilize immersible surgical and diagnostic devices between patient procedures in less than thirty minutes. On 5/13/96, the Company acquired Amsco International, Inc. Revenes for fiscal 2002 were comprised of the following: Healthcare Group, 68.5%; and Scientific and Industrial Group, 31.5%.

RECENT DEVELOPMENTS:

For the three months ended 12/31/02, net income advanced 53.4% to $21.5 million compared with $14.0 million in the corresponding quarter of the previous year. The improvement in earnings was largely due to strong customer growth and increased manufacturing capacity. Net revenues increased 11.7% to $244.3 million from $218.6 million the year before. Revenue growth was primarily attributed to net revenue increases of 7.9% and 20.7% in the Healthcare and Scientific and Industrial Groups, respectively. Gross profit improved 17.0% to $103.9 million from $88.8 million a year earlier. Operating income soared 44.7% to $34.0 million versus $23.5 million the year before.

PROSPECTS:

Going forward, the Company expects that demand will remain strong resulting in overall revenue growth of approximately 11.0% for the full fiscal year ending 3/31/03. This ongoing revenue growth, combined with improvement in operating margins, leads STE to a current earnings guidance of $1.10 to $1.12 per diluted share for the year. Looking beyond the 2003 fiscal year to the next two fiscal years, the Company is targeting average annual growth from its current core businesses of 10.0% in revenues and 15.0% for earnings.

ANNUAL FINANCIAL DATA:

FISCAL YEAR	TOT. REVS. ($000)	NET INC. ($000)	TOT. ASSETS ($000)	OPER. PROFIT %	NET PROFIT %	RET. ON EQUITY %	RET. ON ASSETS %	CURR. RATIO	EARN. PER SH.$	CASH FL. PER SH.$	TANG. BK. VAL.$	DIV. PER SH.$	PRICE RANGE	AVG. P/E RATIO	AVG. YIELD %
3/31/02	866,697	46,202	841,572	9.3	5.3	9.5	5.5	1.9	0.65	1.32	4.27	...	24.91 - 11.60	28.1	...
3/31/01	800,087	③ 1,317	844,980	3.0	0.2	0.3	0.2	2.2	③0.02	0.69	3.44	...	17.19 - 7.94	625.0	...
3/31/00	760,626	③ 10,485	903,574	3.9	1.4	2.5	1.2	2.5	③0.15	0.73	3.21	...	35.06 - 9.44	148.2	...
3/31/99	797,611	84,854	865,996	17.1	10.6	19.5	9.8	2.5	1.20	1.67	3.35	2.00	35.94 - 18.50	22.7	7.3
3/31/98	719,656	65,496	732,325	15.6	9.1	18.2	8.9	2.0	0.94	1.28	2.72	...	25.13 - 11.31	19.5	...
3/31/97	587,852	① d30,606	539,455	...	...	...	...	1.9	① d0.45	d0.21	2.58	...	22.00 - 12.50	...	...
3/31/96	91,192	12,794	85,367	22.2	14.0	20.5	15.0	2.7	0.33	0.37	1.42	...	22.50 - 7.44	45.3	...
3/31/95	64,272	8,736	54,893	20.6	13.6	19.6	15.9	4.1	0.23	0.26	1.18	...	10.00 - 4.19	30.8	...
3/31/94	45,822	② 5,146	42,715	17.4	11.2	14.6	12.0	5.2	②0.14	0.16	1.00	...	5.31 - 3.19	30.3	...
3/31/93	26,662	2,508	30,863	8.5	9.4	9.3	8.1	7.3	0.08	0.09	0.77	...	4.50 - 1.81	40.4	...

Statistics are as originally reported. Adj. for stk. splits: 2-for-1, 8/24/98; 2-for-1, 8/24/95 ① Incl. non-recurr. after-tax chrg. $81.3 mill. ② Bef. acctg. change credit $1.2 mill. ③ Incl. pre-tax non-recurr. chrg. of $39.7 mill., 2000; $41.5 mill., 2001.

OFFICERS:
J. E. Robertson, Chmn.
L. C. Vinney, Pres., C.E.O.
L. Brlas, Sr. V.P., C.F.O.

PRINCIPAL OFFICE: 5960 Heisley Road, Mentor, OH 44060-1834

TELEPHONE NUMBER: (440) 354-2600
WEB: www.steris.com

NO. OF EMPLOYEES: 4,496

SHAREHOLDERS: 1,832 (approx. record)

ANNUAL MEETING: In July

INCORPORATED: OH, 1985

INSTITUTIONAL HOLDINGS:
No. of Institutions: 228
Shares Held: 53,616,352
% Held: 77.3

INDUSTRY: Surgical appliances and supplies (SIC: 3842)

TRANSFER AGENT(S): National City Bank, Cleveland, OH

STORAGE TECHNOLOGY CORPORATION

EXCH.	SYM.	REC. PRICE	P/E RATIO	YLD.	MKT. CAP.	RANGE (52-WK.)	'02 Y/E PR.
NYSE	STK	23.13 (2/28/03)	22.5	...	$2.47 bill.	25.82 - 9.66	21.42

MEDIUM GRADE. THE COMPANY EXPECTS NET INCOME FOR 2003 OF BETWEEN $125.0 MILLION AND $135.0 MILLION AND EARNINGS PER SHARE RANGING FROM $1.17 TO $1.26.

TRADING VOLUME Thousand Shares

*7 YEAR PRICE SCORE 92.0   *12 MONTH PRICE SCORE 139.5

*NYSE COMPOSITE INDEX=100

INTERIM EARNINGS (Per Share):

Qtr.	Mar.	June	Sept.	Dec.
1996	0.33	0.35	0.33	0.58
1997	0.32	0.44	0.44	0.75
1998	0.74	0.50	0.48	0.52
1999	0.06	d0.38	d0.16	d0.26
2000	d0.39	0.01	0.06	0.30
2001	d0.03	0.12	0.17	0.38
2002	0.06	0.18	0.22	0.57

INTERIM DIVIDENDS (Per Share):

Amt.	Decl.	Ex.	Rec.	Pay.
	No dividends paid.			

CAPITALIZATION (12/28/01):

	($000)	(%)
Long-Term Debt	9,523	0.9
Common & Surplus	1,034,820	99.1
Total	1,044,343	100.0

BUSINESS:

Storage Technology Corporation designs, develops, manufactures, and markets a range of information storage products and provides maintenance and consulting services. The Company is organized into two business segments: storage products and storage services. The Company's storage product offerings include tape, disk and network products. The storage services segment is divided into two categories: maintenance services and consulting services. The Company provides maintenance services for both StorageTek products and third-party products. The storage consulting services segment primarily supports sales of STK's hardware and software products, particularly for the Virtual Storage Manager®, a software-driven data storage management application, and its storage networking products. Revenues for 2002 were derived: storage products, 62.6%; and storage services, 37.4%.

RECENT DEVELOPMENTS:

For the year ended 12/27/02, net income advanced 63.7% to $110.0 million compared with $67.2 million in 2001. Earnings benefited from market share gains in tape, disk, networking and storage services. Results for 2002 and 2001 included non-recurring gains of $10.5 million and $2.2 million, respectively. Total revenue slipped 0.3% to $2.04 billion from $2.05 billion the year before. Storage products revenue declined 6.1% to $1.28 billion from $1.36 billion in 2001. Meanwhile, storage services revenue increased 11.3% to $763.7 million from $686.0 million a year earlier. Gross profit climbed 1.6% to $914.5 million from $900.5 million in the previous year. Operating profit jumped 40.3% to $138.2 million compared with $98.5 million the year before.

PROSPECTS:

Near-term results are expected to benefit from an increase in telemarketing, a larger sales force and higher advertising spending. Looking ahead, the Company anticipates reporting revenue growth across all of its product and service offerings due to continuing efforts to strengthen STK's business model. Revenue growth for 2003 is estimated to be in the low-to-mid-single digit range versus 2002. As a result, the Company projects net income for 2003 of between $125.0 million and $135.0 million and earnings per share ranging from $1.17 to $1.26.

ANNUAL FINANCIAL DATA:

FISCAL YEAR	TOT. REVS. ($mill.)	NET INC. ($mill.)	TOT. ASSETS ($mill.)	OPER. PROFIT %	NET PROFIT %	RET. ON EQUITY %	RET. ON ASSETS %	CURR. RATIO	EARN. PER SH.$	CASH FL. PER SH.$	TANG. BK. VAL.$	PRICE RANGE	AVG. P/E RATIO
p12/27/02	2,039.6	⑥ 110.0							⑥ 1.02			25.65 - 9.66	17.3
12/28/01	2,045.3	⑤ 67.2	1,758.9	4.8	3.3	6.5	3.8	1.8	⑤ 0.64	1.66	9.87	23.24 - 9.00	25.2
12/29/00	2,060.2	④ d1.8	1,653.6	0.2	...	...	...	1.7	④ d0.02	1.37	9.11	18.75 - 8.50	...
12/31/99	2,368.2	③ d74.5	1,735.5	...	...	...	...	1.6	③ d0.75	0.69	9.13	41.63 - 14.25	...
12/25/98	2,258.2	198.2	1,842.9	13.9	8.8	19.8	10.8	1.7	1.86	3.02	9.97	51.13 - 20.13	19.2
12/26/97	2,144.7	231.8	1,740.0	13.6	10.8	20.8	13.3	2.1	1.90	2.81	10.39	33.50 - 16.63	13.2
12/27/96	2,039.6	170.8	1,884.3	11.1	8.4	14.5	9.1	2.4	1.50	3.03	10.16	26.00 - 11.00	12.3
12/29/95	1,929.5	② d142.3	1,888.6	...	...	...	...	1.8	② d1.45	0.52	9.03	16.63 - 8.94	...
12/30/94	1,625.0	41.4	1,890.0	3.5	2.6	3.9	2.2	2.1	0.33	2.65	12.07	20.75 - 12.50	50.4
12/31/93	1,404.8	① d117.8	1,793.0	...	...	...	...	2.2	① d1.49	0.26	11.81	22.50 - 9.00	...

Statistics are as originally reported. Adj. for 2-for-1 split, 6/98. ① Incl. $212.2 mill. restr. chg. ② Incl. $74.8 mill. restr. chg. & excl. $40.0 mill. acct. credit. ③ Incl. $43.3 mill. restr. chg. & $103.6 mill. litigation expense. ④ Incl. $27.2 mill. restr. chgs. ⑤ Incl. $3.3 mill. credit fr. litigation & other special items. ⑥ Incl. $10.5 mill. non-recur. gain.

OFFICERS:
P. J. Martin, Chmn., Pres., C.E.O.
R. S. Kocol, Corp. V.P., C.F.O.

INVESTOR CONTACT: Bill Watts, Investor Relations, (303) 673-5020

PRINCIPAL OFFICE: One StorageTek Drive, Louisville, CO 80028-4309

TELEPHONE NUMBER: (303) 673-5151
FAX: (303) 673-5019
WEB: www.storagetek.com
NO. OF EMPLOYEES: 7,800 (approx.)
SHAREHOLDERS: 10,693 (record)
ANNUAL MEETING: In May
INCORPORATED: DE, Aug., 1969

INSTITUTIONAL HOLDINGS:
No. of Institutions: 210
Shares Held: 91,578,268
% Held: 86.0
INDUSTRY: Computer storage devices (SIC: 3572)
TRANSFER AGENT(S): American Stock Transfer & Trust Company, New York, NY

STRYKER CORPORATION

EXCH.	SYM.	REC. PRICE	P/E RATIO	YLD.	MKT. CAP.	RANGE (52-WK.)	'02 Y/E PR.	DIV. ACH.
NYSE	SYK	65.20 (2/28/03)	38.4	0.2%	$12.92 bill.	69.00 - 43.85	67.12	10 yrs.

UPPER MEDIUM GRADE. THE COMPANY IS BENEFITING FROM STRONG DEMAND FOR ITS ORTHOPAEDIC IMPLANTS PRODUCTS.

MERGENT

TRADING VOLUME
Thousand Shares

*7 YEAR PRICE SCORE 180.9   ***12 MONTH PRICE SCORE 119.4**

*NYSE COMPOSITE INDEX=100

INTERIM EARNINGS (Per Share):

Qtr.	Mar.	June	Sept.	Dec.
1998	0.19	0.18	0.18	d0.34
1999	d0.11	d0.02	Nil	0.22
2000	0.26	0.26	0.25	0.33
2001	0.32	0.32	0.30	0.40
2002	0.40	0.42	0.36	0.52

INTERIM DIVIDENDS (Per Share):

Amt.	Decl.	Ex.	Rec.	Pay.
0.08A	12/15/00	12/29/00	12/31/00	1/31/01
0.10A	12/21/01	12/27/01	12/31/01	1/31/02
0.12A	12/03/02	12/27/02	12/31/02	1/31/03

Indicated div.: $0.12

CAPITALIZATION (12/31/01):

	($000)	(%)
Long-Term Debt	720,900	40.6
Common & Surplus	1,056,200	59.4
Total	1,777,100	100.0

BUSINESS:

Stryker Corporation and its subsidiaries develop, manufacture and market specialty surgical and medical products, including orthopaedic reconstructive, trauma, spinal and craniomaxillofacial implants, power surgical instruments, endoscopic systems, patient care and handling equipment for the global market and provides outpatient physical therapy services in the U.S. The Company, through its subsidiary, develops, builds, and markets video communications hardware and software for medical education. Revenues for 2002 were derived as follows: 56.6% from orthopaedic implants, 36.7% from MedSurg equipment, and 6.7% from physical therapy services. On 12/4/98, SYK acquired Howmedica, Inc., which was the orthopaedic division of Pfizer Inc.

RECENT DEVELOPMENTS:

For the year ended 12/31/02, the Company reported net income of $345.6 million compared with income of $271.8 million, before an extraordinary loss of $4.8 million, in the previous year. Results for 2002 and 2001 included after-tax restructuring and acquisition-related items of $11.5 million and $400,000, respectively. Net sales increased 15.7% to $3.01 billion from $2.60 billion in the prior year. Orthopaedic implant sales climbed 17.8% to $1.70 billion from $1.45 billion in the year-earlier period. MedSurg equipment sales advanced 13.5% to $1.11 billion, while physical therapy services sales rose 11.4% to $201.5 million.

PROSPECTS:

The Company is benefiting from its strong market position in the orthopaedic implants market and positive industry growth trends from its MedSurg equipment, as well as higher contributions from its physical therapy services operations in the U.S. Separately, on 2/3/03, the Company received approval by the USDA to market a new ceramic-on-ceramic hip replacement implant, the TRIDENT® CERAMIC ACETABULAR INSERT, which is designed to reduce the wear and tear of traditional hip implants. Going forward, future sales and profits should continue to grow as demand for artificial hip and knee implants needed by the aging population increases.

ANNUAL FINANCIAL DATA:

FISCAL YEAR	TOT. REVS. ($mill.)	NET INC. ($mill.)	TOT. ASSETS ($mill.)	OPER. PROFIT %	NET PROFIT %	RET. ON EQUITY %	RET. ON ASSETS %	CURR. RATIO	EARN. PER SH.$	CASH FL.PER SH.$	TANG. BK. VAL.$	DIV. PER SH.$	PRICE RANGE	AVG. P/E RATIO	AVG. YIELD
p12/31/02	3,011.6	⑥ 345.6							⑥ 1.70			0.10	67.47 - 43.85	32.7	0.2
12/31/01	2,602.3	④⑤ 271.8	2,423.6	19.6	10.4	25.7	11.2	1.9	④⑤ 1.34	2.19	1.29	0.08	63.20 - 43.30	39.7	0.2
12/31/00	2,289.4	④ 221.0	2,430.8	20.4	9.7	25.9	9.1	1.6	④ 1.10	1.94	0.08	0.07	57.75 - 24.44	37.4	0.2
12/31/99	2,103.7	③ 19.4	2,580.5	8.6	0.9	2.9	0.8	1.7	③ 0.10	0.92	...	0.06	36.63 - 22.22	293.9	0.2
12/31/98	1,103.2	② 39.6	2,885.9	5.0	3.6	6.1	1.4	1.9	② 0.20	0.39	...	0.06	27.88 - 15.50	108.4	0.3
12/31/97	980.1	125.3	985.1	18.8	12.8	20.5	12.7	2.5	0.64	0.81	2.95	0.05	22.66 - 12.13	27.2	0.3
12/31/96	910.1	① d17.7	993.5	3.4	...	...	...	3.0	① 0.54	0.09	2.51	0.02	16.06 - 9.94	24.1	0.2
12/31/95	872.0	87.0	854.9	18.0	10.0	19.2	10.2	3.6	0.45	0.60	2.25	0.02	14.63 - 9.03	26.3	0.2
12/31/94	681.9	72.4	768.0	17.7	10.6	20.2	9.4	3.0	0.38	0.48	1.76	0.02	9.38 - 5.94	20.4	0.2
12/31/93	557.3	60.2	454.2	16.5	10.8	20.9	13.3	2.6	0.31	0.39	1.45	0.01	9.94 - 5.25	24.3	0.2

Statistics are as originally reported. Adjusted for a 2-for-1 stock split 6/10/96 & 5/12/00. ① Incl. a pre-tax charge of $41.8 mill. & a pre-tax gain of $61.1 mill. on a patent. ② Incl. a pre-tax chg. of $83.3 mill. for purchased research and development & a pre-tax chg. of $49.9 mill. for acquisition-related expenses. ③ Incl. net nonrecurr. chrgs. of $141.1 mill. ④ Incl. pre-tax restruct. chrg. of $600,000, 2001; credit of $1.0 mill., 2000. ⑤ Bef. extraord. loss of $4.8 mill.; incl. pre-tax restruct. chrgs. of $600,000 ⑥ Incl. pre-tax restruct. chrgs. of $11.5 mill.

OFFICERS:
J. W. Brown, Chmn., Pres., C.E.O.
D. J. Simpson, Exec. V.P.
D. H. Bergy, V.P., C.F.O., Sec.

INVESTOR CONTACT: Dean H. Bergy, V.P., C.F.O., & Sec., (269) 385-2600

PRINCIPAL OFFICE: P.O. Box 4085, Kalamazoo, MI 49003-4085

TELEPHONE NUMBER: (269) 385-2600
FAX: (269) 385-1062
WEB: www.strykercorp.com

NO. OF EMPLOYEES: 12,839

SHAREHOLDERS: 2,988

ANNUAL MEETING: In April

INCORPORATED: MI, Feb., 1946

INSTITUTIONAL HOLDINGS:
No. of Institutions: 410
Shares Held: 132,468,270
% Held: 66.9

INDUSTRY: Surgical and medical instruments (SIC: 3841)

TRANSFER AGENT(S): National City Bank, Cleveland, OH

STUDENT LOAN CORP. (THE)

EXCH.	SYM.	REC. PRICE	P/E RATIO	YLD.	MKT. CAP.	RANGE (52-WK.)	'02 Y/E PR.
NYSE	STU	94.30 (2/28/03)	10.8	3.3%	$1.89 bill.	102.00 - 73.30	97.80

UPPER MEDIUM GRADE. STRONG OVERALL DEMAND FOR STUDENT LOANS CONTINUES TO DRIVE EARNINGS.

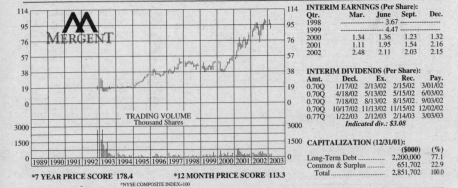

*7 YEAR PRICE SCORE 178.4   *12 MONTH PRICE SCORE 113.3
*NYSE COMPOSITE INDEX=100

INTERIM EARNINGS (Per Share):

Qtr.	Mar.	June	Sept.	Dec.
1998		3.67		
1999		4.47		
2000	1.34	1.36	1.23	1.32
2001	1.11	1.95	1.54	2.16
2002	2.48	2.11	2.03	2.15

INTERIM DIVIDENDS (Per Share):

Amt.	Decl.	Ex.	Rec.	Pay.
0.70Q	1/17/02	2/13/02	2/15/02	3/01/02
0.70Q	4/18/02	5/13/02	5/15/02	6/03/02
0.70Q	7/18/02	8/13/02	8/15/02	9/03/02
0.70Q	10/17/02	11/13/02	11/15/02	12/02/02
0.77Q	1/22/03	2/12/03	2/14/03	3/03/03

Indicated div.: $3.08

CAPITALIZATION (12/31/01):

	($000)	(%)
Long-Term Debt	2,200,000	77.1
Common & Surplus	651,702	22.9
Total	2,851,702	100.0

BUSINESS:

The Student Loan Corp. originates, holds and services federally insured student loans through a trust agreement with Citibank (New York State), an indirect wholly-owned subsidiary of Citigroup Inc. The Company is an originator and holder of student loans guaranteed under the Federal Family Education Loan Program, and authorized by the United States Department of Education. STU also holds student loans not insured under the Federal Higher Education Act of 1965, including CitiAssist Loans. The Company's portfolio is comprised primarily of loans, including subsidized Federal Stafford Loans, unsubsidized Federal Stafford Loans, PLUS Loans and Federal Consolidation Loans. STU also owns a portfolio of Health Education Assistance Loans (HEAL Loans), comprised of guaranteed student loans in designated health professions, which are administered by the United States Department of Health and Human Services. As of 1/22/03, Citibank owned approximately 80.0% of the Company's shares.

RECENT DEVELOPMENTS:

For the year ended 12/31/02, net income increased 29.6% to $175.5 million from $135.4 million the previous year. The increase in earnings was primarily attributed to solid portfolio growth, higher net interest margin and strict management of expenses, net of investments. Results for 2002 included a gain of $4.1 million from student loan securitization. Net interest income advanced 24.3% to $393.3 million from $316.5 million in the prior year. Provision for loan losses increased 53.4% to $11.2 million. Fee and other income climbed 71.7% to $18.2 million.

PROSPECTS:

The Company's outlook continues to brighten, reflecting strong overall demand for student loans and benefits from STU's strategic focus to diversify its marketing channels. As of 12/31/02, STU's student loan assets amounted to $20.50 billion, up 12.6% from $18.20 billion at 12/31/01. Combined Federal Family Education Loan Program (FFELP) Stafford and PLUS Loan disbursements and new CitiAssist Loan commitments grew 21.5% during 2002 to $3.15 billion. Meanwhile, STU's secondary market loan program continued to enjoy solid growth, adding $2.04 billion of FFELP loans to the Company's student loan portfolio during the year.

ANNUAL FINANCIAL DATA:

FISCAL YEAR	NET INT. INC. ($mill.)	NON-INT. INC. ($mill.)	NET INC. ($mill.)	TOT. LOANS ($mill.)	TOT. ASSETS ($mill.)	RET. ON EQUITY %	RET. ON ASSETS %	EQUITY/ ASSETS %	EARN. PER SH.$	TANG. BK. VAL.$	DIV. PER SH.$	PRICE RANGE	AVG. P/E RATIO
p12/31/02	393.3	18.2	③175.5	18,237.0	18,717.1	20.8	0.7	3.5	③8.77		2.80	102.00 - 80.13	10.4
12/31/01	316.5	10.6	135.4	15,774.3	16,243.2	18.3	0.6	3.5	6.77	32.59	2.80	83.68 - 52.63	10.1
12/31/00	258.3	6.4	104.9	15,774.3	16,243.2	18.3	0.8	4.6	5.24	28.61	2.40	56.13 - 37.13	8.9
12/31/99	225.8	3.8	①89.5	10,865.0	11,196.5	17.4	0.8	4.6	①4.47	25.76	1.95	50.50 - 37.38	9.8
12/31/98	192.3	2.3	①73.4	8,636.3	8,903.1	15.8	0.8	5.2	①3.67	23.23	0.60	51.06 - 40.00	12.4
12/31/97	175.9	- 3.3	①51.7	7,625.2	7,873.1	12.8	0.7	5.1	①2.58	20.16	0.54	54.25 - 35.50	17.4
12/31/96	175.2	...	64.9	6,894.3	7,118.3	17.9	0.9	5.1	3.25	18.10	0.30	41.75 - 32.00	11.3
12/31/95	161.9	0.1	60.6	6,169.8	6,387.4	20.0	0.9	4.7	3.03	15.15	0.24	35.63 - 18.38	8.9
12/31/94	144.5	1.6	②55.4	5,171.4	5,365.1	22.4	1.0	4.6	②2.77	12.36	0.24	20.88 - 18.13	7.0
12/31/93	146.9	0.9	64.7	4,184.2	4,346.9	32.8	1.5	4.5	3.23	9.85	0.18	30.50 - 14.25	6.9

Statistics are as originally reported. ① Incl. restructuring gain $2.2 mill., 12/99; $7.5 mill., 12/98; chrg. $20.5 mill., 12/97 ② Bef. acctg. chng. chrg. $512,000 ③ Incl. gain fr. student loan securitization of $4.1 mill.

OFFICERS:
B. Beckmann, Chmn.
Y. Zographakis, C.E.O.
S. F. Roberts, Pres.
INVESTOR CONTACT: Bradley D. Svalberg, Dir., Inv. Rel., (203) 975-6292
PRINCIPAL OFFICE: 750 Washington Blvd., Stamford, CT 06901

TELEPHONE NUMBER: (203) 975-6292
FAX: (203) 975-6299
WEB: www.studentloan.com
NO. OF EMPLOYEES: 360 (approx.)
SHAREHOLDERS: 48 (approx.)
ANNUAL MEETING: In May
INCORPORATED: DE, Nov., 1992

INSTITUTIONAL HOLDINGS:
No. of Institutions: 79
Shares Held: 19,044,996
% Held: 95.2
INDUSTRY: Misc. business credit institutions (SIC: 6159)
TRANSFER AGENT(S): Citibank N.A., New York, NY

SUNGARD DATA SYSTEMS INC.

EXCH.	SYM.	REC. PRICE	P/E RATIO	YLD.	MKT. CAP.	RANGE (52-WK.)	'02 Y/E PR.
NYSE	SDS	19.68 (2/28/03)	17.6	…	$5.53 bill.	35.10 - 14.70	23.56

UPPER MEDIUM GRADE. THE COMPANY COMPLETED ITS CASH TENDER OFFER FOR THE OUTSTANDING COMMON SHARES OF H.T.E., INC. FOR $7.00 PER SHARE.

TRADING VOLUME
Thousand Shares

*7 YEAR PRICE SCORE N/A   *12 MONTH PRICE SCORE 91.5

*NYSE COMPOSITE INDEX=100

INTERIM EARNINGS (Per Share):

Qtr.	Mar.	June	Sept.	Dec.
1998	0.10	0.14	0.15	0.17
1999	d0.08	0.16	0.14	0.17
2000	0.16	0.20	0.21	0.23
2001	0.20	0.22	0.22	0.23
2002	0.24	0.28	0.27	0.33

INTERIM DIVIDENDS (Per Share):

Amt.	Decl.	Ex.	Rec.	Pay.
2-for-1	5/14/01	6/19/01	5/25/01	6/18/01

CAPITALIZATION (12/31/01):

	($000)	(%)
Long-Term Debt	355,474	16.5
Common & Surplus	1,793,856	83.5
Total	2,149,330	100.0

BUSINESS:

SunGard Data Systems Inc. is engaged in integrated information technology and "eProcessing" for financial services. The Company serves more than 20,000 clients in over 50 countries, including 47 of the world's 50 largest financial services institutions. The Company offers integrated, Web-enabled services and software for the management, trading, processing and accounting of financial assets and offers high-availability infrastructure, outsourcing and hosting for on-line and other operations. The Company's products and services generally are delivered and supported through individual business units that offer product-specific development and customer support.

RECENT DEVELOPMENTS:

For the year ended 12/31/02, net income jumped 32.3% to $325.6 million compared with $246.1 million in 2001. Results reflected the Company's focus on operational efficiency. Results for 2002 and 2001 included amortization of acquisition-related intangible assets of $65.1 million and $66.9 million, and merger costs of $12.5 million and $7.2 million, respectively. Product and service revenues amounted to $2.53 billion, up 31.2% from $1.93 billion the year before. Revenue from services rose 36.2% to $2.34 billion, while revenue from license and resale fees declined 8.8% to $195.2 million. Reimbursed expenses rose to $62.9 million from $53.2 million in the prior year. Income from operations increased 37.1% to $547.2 million compared with $399.2 million in the previous year.

PROSPECTS:

On 3/17/03, the Company announced that it has completed its cash tender offer for the outstanding common shares of H.T.E., Inc., a provider of a range of innovative software applications, for $7.00 per share, or approximately $121.0 million. Separately, on 1/21/03, the Company announced that it has reached a definitive agreement to acquire all the shares of Caminus Corporation, an integrated software applications provider for the energy industry, for $9.00 per share. The transaction has an aggregate value of approximately $159.0 million. Caminus will become an operating unit within SDS' trading and risk systems.

ANNUAL FINANCIAL DATA:

FISCAL YEAR	TOT. REVS. ($mill.)	NET INC. ($mill.)	TOT. ASSETS ($mill.)	OPER. PROFIT %	NET PROFIT %	RET. ON EQUITY %	RET. ON ASSETS %	CURR. RATIO	EARN. PER SH. $	CASH FL. PER SH. $	TANG. BK. VAL. $	PRICE RANGE	AVG. P/E RATIO
p12/31/02	2,593.2	④325.6							④1.12			35.10 - 14.70	22.2
12/31/01	1,928.7	④246.1	2,898.2	20.7	12.8	13.7	8.5	1.5	④0.86	1.48	2.50	32.49 - 20.00	30.5
12/31/00	1,660.7	②213.0	1,845.2	20.2	12.8	14.8	11.5	2.3	②0.79	1.32	3.25	27.50 - 11.50	24.8
12/31/99	1,444.5	①②73.2	1,564.8	12.2	5.1	6.0	4.7	2.3	①②0.40	0.75	3.09	20.97 - 8.44	36.7
12/31/98	1,159.7	118.9	1,075.3	17.5	10.3	15.6	11.1	1.9	0.55	1.05	2.52	20.00 - 10.84	28.0
12/31/97	862.2	77.5	786.3	15.5	9.0	13.9	9.9	1.4	0.44	0.96	1.82	15.72 - 9.25	28.7
12/31/96	670.3	34.9	679.9	8.9	5.2	7.5	5.1	1.1	0.20	0.62	1.40	11.88 - 6.88	46.2
12/31/95	532.6	48.7	579.7	15.0	9.1	11.5	8.4	1.9	0.31	0.65	1.61	8.13 - 4.44	20.4
12/31/94	437.2	43.1	485.7	16.1	9.9	12.0	8.9	2.0	0.28	0.58	1.60	5.13 - 3.94	16.2
12/31/93	381.4	③38.5	418.1	15.6	10.1	12.1	9.2	2.1	③0.27	0.52	1.36	5.34 - 3.50	16.5

Statistics are as originally reported. Adj. for 2-for-1 stk. spl., 6/01, 9/97 & 7/95. ① Bef. extraord. gain, $10.7 mill. ② Incl. $13.2 mill. in merger costs, 2000; $99.2 mill., 1999. ③ Incl. $4.1 mill. gain on sale of product line. ④ Incl. $12.5 mill. merger costs, 2002; $7.2 mill., 2001.

OFFICERS:
J. L. Mann, Chmn.
C. I. Conde, Pres., C.E.O.
M. J. Ruane, Sr. V.P., C.F.O., Treas.

INVESTOR CONTACT: Michael J. Ruane, (610) 341-8709

PRINCIPAL OFFICE: 1285 Drummers Lane, Wayne, PA 19087

TELEPHONE NUMBER: (610) 341-8700
FAX: (610) 341-8739
WEB: www.sungard.com

NO. OF EMPLOYEES: 8,700 (approx.)

SHAREHOLDERS: 6,600 (approx. record)

ANNUAL MEETING: In May

INCORPORATED: DE, 1982

INSTITUTIONAL HOLDINGS:
No. of Institutions: 447
Shares Held: 244,206,333
% Held: 86.2

INDUSTRY: Data processing and preparation (SIC: 7374)

TRANSFER AGENT(S): Wells Fargo Shareowner Services, South St. Paul, MN

SUNOCO, INC.

EXCH.	SYM.	REC. PRICE	P/E RATIO	YLD.	MKT. CAP.	RANGE (52-WK.)	'02 Y/E PR.
NYSE	SUN	35.39 (2/28/03)	...	2.8%	$2.67 bill.	42.25 - 27.02	33.18

MEDIUM GRADE. THE COMPANY HAS SIGNED A DEFINITIVE AGREEMENT TO PURCHASE 193 OF SPEEDWAY SUPERAMERICA'S DIRECT RETAIL SITES FOR $140.0 MILLION PLUS INVENTORY.

TRADING VOLUME Thousand Shares

*7 YEAR PRICE SCORE 107.8   ***12 MONTH PRICE SCORE 104.8**
*NYSE COMPOSITE INDEX=100

INTERIM EARNINGS (Per Share):

Qtr.	Mar.	June	Sept.	Dec.
1997	0.10	1.29	1.38	0.25
1998	0.58	0.97	0.85	0.55
1999	0.21	0.28	0.15	0.42
2000	0.75	2.44	d0.29	1.80
2001	1.24	2.35	1.14	0.05
2002	d1.41	0.12	d0.13	0.79

INTERIM DIVIDENDS (Per Share):

Amt.	Decl.	Ex.	Rec.	Pay.
0.25Q	1/03/02	2/06/02	2/08/02	3/08/02
0.25Q	4/04/02	5/08/02	5/10/02	6/10/02
0.25Q	7/02/02	8/07/02	8/09/02	9/10/02
0.25Q	10/03/02	11/06/02	11/08/02	12/10/02
0.25Q	1/02/03	2/05/03	2/07/03	3/07/03

Indicated div.: $1.00 (Div. Reinv. Plan)

CAPITALIZATION (12/31/01):

	($000)	(%)
Long-Term Debt	1,142,000	34.2
Deferred Income Tax	551,000	16.5
Common & Surplus	1,642,000	49.2
Total	3,335,000	100.0

BUSINESS:

Sunoco, Inc. (formerly Sun Company, Inc.) is principally a petroleum refiner and marketer and chemicals manufacturer with interests in logistics and cokemaking. SUN's petroleum refining and marketing operations include the manufacturing and marketing of a full range of petroleum products, including fuels, lubricants and petrochemicals. SUN's chemical operations comprise the manufacturing, distribution and marketing of commodity and intermediate petro-chemicals. The petroleum refining and marketing, chemicals and logistics operations are conducted mainly in the eastern half of the U.S. As of 12/31/02, SUN operated four refineries and a network of 4,328 retail outlets in 23 states. Also, as of 12/31/02, SUN owned a 75.3% interest in Sunoco Logistics Partners L.P., which operates its transportation functions, including its crude oil and product terminals, rail and tank car transport and marine operations.

RECENT DEVELOPMENTS:

For the year ended 12/31/02, SUN posted a net loss of $47.0 million compared with net income of $398.0 million a year earlier. Results for 2002 and 2001 included charges of $34.0 million and $6.0 million, respectively, related to the write-down of assets and other matters. SUN attributed the net loss primarily to significantly lower margins from its refining and supply and retail marketing businesses. Revenues rose 1.7% to $14.38 billion.

PROSPECTS:

On 2/7/03, SUN announced that it has signed a definitive agreement with Speedway SuperAmerica LLC, a subsidiary of Marathon Ashland Petroleum LLC, to purchase 193 of Speedway SuperAmerica's direct retail sites in the Southeast U.S. for $140.0 million plus inventory. All of the sites are company-operated locations with convenience stores, with 115 sites located in Florida, 62 in South Carolina, 13 in North Carolina, and 3 in Georgia. The sites will be re-branded to Sunoco gasoline and APlus® convenience stores. Sun expects that the acquisition will be immediately accretive to earnings and cash flow. Separately, SUN announced a 2003 capital program of $519.0 million, including $89.0 million for refinery turnarounds and $70.0 million for various income improvement projects.

ANNUAL FINANCIAL DATA:

FISCAL YEAR	TOT. REVS. ($mill.)	NET INC. ($mill.)	TOT. ASSETS ($mill.)	OPER. PROFIT %	NET PROFIT %	RET. ON EQUITY %	RET. ON ASSETS %	CURR. RATIO	EARN. PER SH.$	CASH FL. PER SH.$	TANG. BK. VAL.$	DIV. PER SH.$	PRICE RANGE	AVG. P/E RATIO	AVG. YIELD
p12/31/02	14,384.0	⑧d47.0							⑧d0.62			1.00	42.25 — 27.02	...	2.9
12/31/01	14,143.0	⑦398.0	5,932.0	4.9	2.8	24.2	6.7	0.8	⑦4.85	8.77	21.74	1.00	42.73 — 29.13	7.4	2.8
12/31/00	14,300.0	⑥411.0	5,426.0	4.7	2.9	24.1	7.6	1.0	⑥4.70	8.10	20.06	1.00	34.56 — 21.94	6.0	3.5
12/31/99	10,068.0	⑤97.0	5,196.0	2.3	1.0	6.4	1.9	0.8	⑤1.07	4.10	16.77	1.00	39.44 — 22.88	29.1	3.2
12/31/98	8,583.0	④280.0	4,849.0	5.4	3.3	18.5	5.8	0.9	④2.95	5.44	16.82	1.00	44.31 — 29.50	12.5	2.7
12/31/97	10,531.0	263.0	4,667.0	4.3	2.5	18.0	5.6	0.9	2.70	4.91	10.41	1.00	46.38 — 24.00	13.0	2.8
12/31/96	11,300.0	①d281.0	5,025.0	...	...	...	...	0.8	①d4.43	d0.80	9.45	1.00	32.63 — 21.88	...	3.7
12/31/95	10,441.0	②266.0	5,375.0	4.4	2.5	15.7	4.9	1.0	②2.24	d6.67	12.82	1.40	32.88 — 24.75	12.9	4.9
12/31/94	9,919.0	③97.0	6,465.0	2.5	1.0	5.2	1.5	0.8	③0.91	d4.26	17.41	1.80	35.25 — 25.13	33.2	6.0
12/31/93	9,417.0	283.0	5,549.0	5.6	3.0	14.3	5.1	0.8	2.65	5.95	18.54	1.80	32.75 — 22.25	10.4	6.5

Statistics are as originally reported. ① Bef. disc. ops. cr. of $166.0 mill. ② Incl. chrg. of $96.0 mill.; bef. acctg. adj. chrg. of $87.0 mill. ③ Bef. acctg. adj. chrg. 12/31/94, $7.0 mill.; cr. 12/31/93, $5.0 mill. ④ Incl. aft.-tax benefit of $13.0 mill. ⑤ Incl. aft.-tax cr. of $46.0 mill. ⑥ Incl. aft.-tax chrg. of $147.0 mill. & non-recurr. gain of $131.0 mill.; bef. disc. ops. of $11.0 mill. ($0.12/sh.) ⑦ Incl. prov. for write-down of assets & oth. of $23.0 mill. ⑧ Incl. prov. for write-down of assets & oth. of $34.0 mill.

OFFICERS:
J. G. Drosdick, Chmn., Pres., C.E.O.
T. W. Hofmann, Sr. V.P., C.F.O.
M. S. Kuritzkes, Sr. V.P., Gen. Counsel

INVESTOR CONTACT: T. P. Delaney, Mgr., Investor Relations, (215) 977-6106

PRINCIPAL OFFICE: Ten Penn Center, 1801 Market Street, Philadelphia, PA 19103-1699

TELEPHONE NUMBER: (215) 977-3000
FAX: (215) 977-3409
WEB: www.sunocoinc.com

NO. OF EMPLOYEES: 14,200 (approx.)

SHAREHOLDERS: 27,500 (approx.)

ANNUAL MEETING: In May

INCORPORATED: PA, 1971

INSTITUTIONAL HOLDINGS:
No. of Institutions: 237
Shares Held: 56,729,710
% Held: 74.3

INDUSTRY: Petroleum refining (SIC: 2911)

TRANSFER AGENT(S): EquiServe Trust Company, N.A., Jersey City, NJ

SUNTRUST BANKS, INC.

EXCH.	SYM.	REC. PRICE	P/E RATIO	YLD.	MKT. CAP.	RANGE (52-WK.)	'02 Y/E PR.	DIV. ACH.
NYSE	STI	56.25 (2/28/03)	12.1	3.2%	$15.92 bill.	70.20 - 51.48	56.92	17 yrs.

INVESTMENT GRADE. THE COMPANY SIGNED A DEFINITIVE AGREEMENT TO ACQUIRE LIGHTHOUSE FINANCIAL SERVICES, INC. FOR $130.0 MILLION.

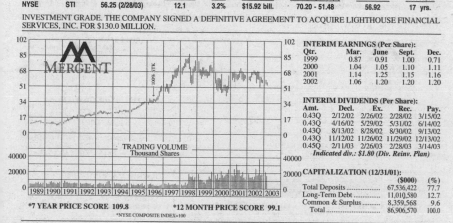

*7 YEAR PRICE SCORE 109.8　　　　***12 MONTH PRICE SCORE 99.1**

NYSE COMPOSITE INDEX=100

INTERIM EARNINGS (Per Share):

Qtr.	Mar.	June	Sept.	Dec.
1999	0.87	0.91	1.00	0.71
2000	1.04	1.05	1.10	1.11
2001	1.14	1.25	1.15	1.16
2002	1.06	1.20	1.20	1.20

INTERIM DIVIDENDS (Per Share):

Amt.	Decl.	Ex.	Rec.	Pay.
0.43Q	2/12/02	2/26/02	2/28/02	3/15/02
0.43Q	4/16/02	5/29/02	5/31/02	6/14/02
0.43Q	8/13/02	8/28/02	8/30/02	9/13/02
0.43Q	11/12/02	11/26/02	11/29/02	12/13/02
0.45Q	2/11/03	2/26/03	2/28/03	3/14/03

Indicated div.: $1.80 (Div. Reinv. Plan)

CAPITALIZATION (12/31/01):

	($000)	(%)
Total Deposits	67,536,422	77.7
Long-Term Debt	11,010,580	12.7
Common & Surplus	8,359,568	9.6
Total	86,906,570	100.0

BUSINESS:

SunTrust Banks, Inc., through its primary subsidiary, SunTrust Bank, provides deposit, credit, trust and investment services to a broad range of retail, business and institutional clients. Other subsidiaries provide mortgage banking, credit-related insurance, asset management, brokerage and capital market services. At 12/31/02, STI had total assets of $117.32 billion. The Company serves clients through its network of traditional and in-store branches and ATMs located in Alabama, Florida, Georgia, Maryland, Tennessee, Virginia and the District of Columbia. In addition, STI provides customers with a full range of technology-based banking channels including Internet, personal computer and telephone banking.

RECENT DEVELOPMENTS:

For the year ended 12/31/02, net income was $1.33 billion, down 2.7% compared with income of $1.37 billion, before an extraordinary gain of $6.3 million, in the corresponding prior-year period. Results for 2002 included an after-tax merger-related charge of $10.4 million. Net interest income slipped 0.3% to $3.24 billion from $3.25 billion the previous year. Provision for loan losses grew 70.7% to $469.8 million from $275.2 million a year earlier. Total non-interest income climbed 10.9% to $2.39 billion from $2.16 billion in 2001, while total non-interest expense rose 7.3% to $3.34 billion from $3.11 billion the prior year.

PROSPECTS:

Higher mortgage-origination fees are being offset by a decline in mortgage-servicing fees and investment banking income. Meanwhile, earnings are being negatively affected by increased expenses stemming from higher default levels on consumer loans. Separately, STI is taking steps to expand into fast-growing markets. On 1/22/03, the Company announced it has signed a definitive agreement to acquire Hilton Head Island, South Carolina-based Lighthouse Financial Services, Inc. for $130.0 million. The transaction is expected to close in the summer of 2003.

ANNUAL FINANCIAL DATA:

FISCAL YEAR	NET INT. INC. ($mill.)	NON-INT. INC. ($mill.)	NET INC. ($mill.)	TOT. LOANS ($mill.)	TOT. ASSETS ($mill.)	TOT. DEP. ($mill.)	RET. ON EQUITY %	RET. ON ASSETS %	EQUITY/ ASSETS %	EARN. PER SH. $	TANG. BK. VAL. $	DIV. PER SH. $	PRICE RANGE	AVG. P/E RATIO
p12/31/02	3,243.7		① 1,331.8							① 4.66		1.72	70.20 - 51.48	13.1
12/31/01	3,252.6	2,155.8	② 1,369.2	68,959.2	104,740.6	67,536.4	16.4	1.3	8.0	② 4.70	26.67	1.60	72.35 - 57.29	13.8
12/31/00	3,108.4	1,773.6	① 1,294.1	72,239.8	103,496.4	69,533.3	15.7	1.3	8.0	① 4.30	25.07	1.48	68.06 - 41.63	12.8
12/31/99	3,145.5	1,660.0	①② 1,124.0	66,002.8	95,390.0	60,100.5	14.7	1.2	8.0	①② 3.50	23.24	1.38	79.81 - 60.44	20.0
12/31/98	2,929.1	1,716.2	① 971.0	61,540.6	93,169.9	59,033.3	11.9	1.0	8.8	① 3.04	22.99	1.00	87.75 - 54.00	23.3
12/31/97	1,894.4	934.2	667.3	40,135.5	57,982.7	38,197.5	12.8	1.2	9.0	3.13	23.38	0.93	75.25 - 44.13	19.1
12/31/96	1,784.2	818.0	616.6	35,404.2	52,468.2	36,890.4	12.6	1.2	9.3	2.76	20.87	0.82	52.50 - 32.00	15.3
12/31/95	1,676.4	713.1	565.5	31,301.4	46,471.5	33,183.2	13.2	1.2	9.2	2.47	17.71	0.74	35.44 - 23.63	12.0
12/31/94	1,619.9	699.9	522.7	28,548.9	42,709.1	32,218.4	15.1	1.2	8.1	2.25	13.90	0.66	25.69 - 21.75	10.5
12/31/93	1,571.7	726.5	473.7	25,347.6	40,728.4	30,485.8	13.1	1.2	8.9	1.89	13.89	0.58	24.81 - 20.69	12.1

Statistics are as originally reported. Adj. for 2-for-1 stk. split, 5/96. ① Incl. pre-tax merger-related chrg.: $16.0 mill. 2002; $42.4 mill., 2000; $45.6 mill., 1999; $119.4 mill., 1998. ② Bef. extraord. gain of $6.3 mill., 2001; $202.6 mill., 1999.

OFFICERS:
L. P. Humann, Chmn., Pres., C.E.O.
J. W. Spiegal, Vice-Chmn., C.F.O.
T. J. Hoepner, Vice-Chmn.

INVESTOR CONTACT: Gary Peacock, Jr., Dir. of Inv. Rel., (404) 658-4879

PRINCIPAL OFFICE: 303 Peachtree Street N.E., Atlanta, GA 30308

TELEPHONE NUMBER: (404) 588-7711
FAX: (404) 827-6173
WEB: www.suntrust.com

NO. OF EMPLOYEES: 28,391

SHAREHOLDERS: 38,439

ANNUAL MEETING: In Apr.

INCORPORATED: GA, July, 1985

INSTITUTIONAL HOLDINGS:
No. of Institutions: 463
Shares Held: 136,377,274
% Held: 48.1

INDUSTRY: National commercial banks (SIC: 6021)

TRANSFER AGENT(S): SunTrust Bank Atlanta, Atlanta, GA

SUPERIOR INDUSTRIES INTERNATIONAL, INC.

EXCH.	SYM.	REC. PRICE	P/E RATIO	YLD.	MKT. CAP.	RANGE (52-WK.)	'02 Y/E PR.	DIV. ACH.
NYSE	SUP	38.74 (2/28/03)	13.3	1.3%	$1.00 bill.	53.80 - 35.79	41.36	17 yrs.

UPPER MEDIUM GRADE. THE COMPANY PLANS TO INCREASE ITS ANNUAL ALUMINUM WHEEL CAPACITY BY 25.0% OVER THE NEXT TWO YEARS.

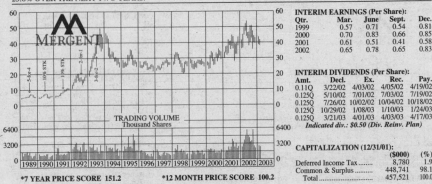

*7 YEAR PRICE SCORE 151.2   *12 MONTH PRICE SCORE 100.2
*NYSE COMPOSITE INDEX=100

INTERIM EARNINGS (Per Share):

Qtr.	Mar.	June	Sept.	Dec.
1999	0.57	0.71	0.54	0.81
2000	0.70	0.83	0.66	0.85
2001	0.61	0.51	0.41	0.58
2002	0.65	0.78	0.65	0.83

INTERIM DIVIDENDS (Per Share):

Amt.	Decl.	Ex.	Rec.	Pay.
0.11Q	3/22/02	4/03/02	4/05/02	4/19/02
0.125Q	5/10/02	7/01/02	7/03/02	7/19/02
0.125Q	7/26/02	10/02/02	10/04/02	10/18/02
0.125Q	10/29/02	1/08/03	1/10/03	1/24/03
0.125Q	3/21/03	4/01/03	4/03/03	4/17/03

Indicated div.: $0.50 (Div. Reinv. Plan)

CAPITALIZATION (12/31/01):

	($000)	(%)
Deferred Income Tax	8,780	1.9
Common & Surplus	448,741	98.1
Total	457,521	100.0

BUSINESS:

Superior Industries International, Inc. designs and manufactures automotive parts and accessories for original equipment manufacturers (OEMs) and for the automotive aftermarket. The OEM cast aluminum road wheels, the Company's primary product, are sold to General Motors, Ford, DaimlerChrysler, BMW, Volkswagen, Audi, Land Rover, MG Rover, Toyota, Mazda, Mitsubishi, Nissan, Subaru and Isuzu, for factory installation as optional or

standard equipment on selected vehicle models. SUP also manufactures aluminum suspension components, as well as aftermarket accessories including bed mats, exhaust extensions, license frames, lug nuts, springs and suspension products, steering wheel covers and other miscellaneous accessories. The Company operates manufacturing facilities in the U.S., Mexico and Hungary.

RECENT DEVELOPMENTS:

For the year ended 12/31/02, net income advanced 41.4% to $78.3 million compared with $55.4 million in the previous year. Results for 2002 and 2001 included start-up and pre-production costs of $8.5 million and $9.7 million, respectively. Earnings benefited from SUP's increased share in the aluminum road wheel market, as well as

growth in OEM aluminum wheel installation rates on new cars and light trucks. Net sales increased 21.6% to $782.6 million from $643.4 million a year earlier. Year-over-year unit wheel shipments climbed 22.0% to 14.5 million. Income from operations jumped 43.8% to $109.5 million from $76.1 million in 2001.

PROSPECTS:

The Company has invested heavily in expanding and improving its manufacturing capabilities, adding new plants and expanding and updating existing facilities. SUP has increased its North American manufacturing capacity by over 20.0% in the past two years. Meanwhile, due to continuing growth of the aluminum wheel market, SUP

plans to increase its annual capacity by an additional 25.0% over the next two years. Separately, SUP's new aluminum components business recently began manufacturing the lower crankcase bed plate for GM's 4-cylinder engine, small-car platforms, including those of Chevrolet, Pontiac, and Saturn.

ANNUAL FINANCIAL DATA:

FISCAL YEAR	TOT. REVS. ($000)	NET INC. ($000)	TOT. ASSETS ($000)	OPER. PROFIT %	NET PROFIT %	RET. ON EQUITY %	RET. ON ASSETS %	CURR. RATIO	EARN. PER SH.$	CASH FL. PER SH.$	TANG. BK. VAL.$	DIV. PER SH.$	PRICE RANGE	AVG. P/E RATIO	AVG. YIELD %
p12/31/02	782,599	③ 78,275	645,796		10.0	14.8	12.1		③ 2.91	3.18	17.30	0.47	53.80 - 35.79	15.4	1.0
12/31/01	643,395	② 55,354	540,838	11.8	8.6	12.3	10.2	3.9	② 2.10	3.18	17.30	0.42	44.85 - 28.00	17.3	1.2
12/31/00	644,899	① 79,937	491,664	18.8	12.4	20.0	16.3	3.3	① 3.04	4.07	15.45	0.38	36.00 - 22.94	9.7	1.3
12/31/99	571,782	70,808	460,468	18.4	12.4	20.1	15.4	3.0	2.62	3.67	13.35	0.34	29.38 - 22.75	9.9	1.3
12/31/98	539,431	52,319	427,430	14.9	9.7	16.8	12.2	2.6	1.88	2.84	11.42	0.30	33.88 - 20.06	14.3	1.1
12/31/97	549,131	55,389	382,679	16.1	10.1	19.3	14.5	3.1	1.96	2.92	10.30	0.26	29.50 - 22.13	13.2	1.0
12/31/96	504,241	46,850	357,590	16.2	9.3	18.7	13.1	2.1	1.63	2.58	8.87	0.22	28.38 - 21.63	15.3	0.9
12/31/95	521,997	53,064	341,770	18.0	10.2	23.2	15.5	1.7	1.78	2.70	7.89	0.19	35.75 - 23.88	16.7	0.6
12/31/94	456,638	56,315	357,683	20.2	12.3	28.1	15.7	1.5	1.85	2.73	6.76	0.15	46.25 - 24.25	19.1	0.4
12/31/93	393,033	45,177	310,123	19.0	11.5	25.5	14.6	1.9	1.47	2.18	5.88	0.11	49.38 - 18.58	23.1	0.3

Statistics are as originally reported. ① Incl. non-recurr. chrg. $2.5 mill. ② Incl. non-recurr. start-up chrg. of $9.7 mill. ③ Incl. non-recurr. pre-production costs of $8.5 mill.

OFFICERS:
L. L. Borick, Chmn., C.E.O.
S. J. Borick, Pres., C.O.O.
R. J. Ornstein, V.P., C.F.O.
INVESTOR CONTACT: Investor Relations, (818) 902-2701
PRINCIPAL OFFICE: 7800 Woodley Avenue, Van Nuys, CA 91406

TELEPHONE NUMBER: (818) 781-4973
FAX: (818) 780-3500
WEB: www.supind.com
NO. OF EMPLOYEES: 6,200 (approx.)
SHAREHOLDERS: 878 (approx.)
ANNUAL MEETING: In May
INCORPORATED: DE, June, 1969; reincorp., CA, June, 1994

INSTITUTIONAL HOLDINGS:
No. of Institutions: 165
Shares Held: 18,906,238
% Held: 71.1
INDUSTRY: Motor vehicle parts and accessories (SIC: 3714)
TRANSFER AGENT(S): Registrar and Transfer Company, Cranford, NJ

SUPERVALU INC.

EXCH.	SYM.	REC. PRICE	P/E RATIO	YLD.	MKT. CAP.	RANGE (52-WK.)	'02 Y/E PR.	DIV. ACH.
NYSE	SVU	13.92 (2/28/03)	8.2	4.1%	$1.85 bill.	30.81 - 13.50	16.51	30 yrs.

UPPER MEDIUM GRADE. RESULTS SHOULD BENEFIT FROM THE COMPANY'S EFFORTS TO EXPAND ITS RETAIL STORE NETWORK.

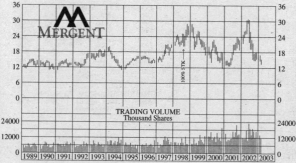

INTERIM EARNINGS (Per Share):

Qtr.	May	Aug.	Nov.	Feb.
1997-98	0.37	0.72	0.34	0.43
1998-99	0.43	0.33	0.37	0.45
1999-00	0.55	0.37	0.42	0.52
2000-01	0.53	0.43	0.36	d0.70
2001-02	0.45	0.39	0.44	0.26
2002-03	0.57	0.44	0.43	...

INTERIM DIVIDENDS (Per Share):

Amt.	Decl.	Ex.	Rec.	Pay.
0.14Q	12/12/01	2/27/02	3/01/02	3/15/02
0.14Q	4/10/02	5/30/02	6/03/02	6/17/02
0.142Q	6/25/02	8/28/02	9/01/02	9/16/02
0.142Q	10/09/02	11/26/02	12/01/02	12/16/02
0.142Q	2/12/03	2/26/03	2/28/03	3/17/03

Indicated div.: $0.57 (Div. Reinv. Plan)

CAPITALIZATION (2/23/02):

	($000)	(%)
Long-Term Debt	1,342,428	34.7
Capital Lease Obligations..	533,445	13.8
Deferred Income Tax	79,750	2.1
Common & Surplus	1,916,693	49.5
Total	3,872,316	100.0

*7 YEAR PRICE SCORE 114.8   ***12 MONTH PRICE SCORE 79.0**

*NYSE COMPOSITE INDEX=100

BUSINESS:

SUPERVALU Inc. is a major food retailer and distributor to independently-owned retail food stores. The Company operates three principal store formats at retail and sells food and non-food products at wholesale. As of 11/30/02, SVU operated 1,123 Save-A-Lot limited assortment stores, including 778 licensed Save-A-Lot locations, 262 Company-owned stores and 83 Deals-Nothing Over a Dollar general merchandise stores; 208 traditional superstores under the Cub Foods, Shop 'n Save, Shoppers Food Warehouse, Metro and bigg's banners; and 60 traditional supermarkets, including Farm Fresh, Scott's Foods, and Hornbacher's stores. Additionally, SVU is the primary supplier to approximately 2,490 retail grocery stores, as well as 31 of SVU's franchised Cub Foods locations, while serving as a secondary supplier to about 1,400 stores.

RECENT DEVELOPMENTS:

For the 12 weeks ended 11/30/02, net earnings slipped 1.5% to $57.1 million from $58.0 million in the corresponding period the year before. Net sales grew 2.0% to $4.70 billion from $4.61 billion a year earlier. Food distribution net sales inched up 0.7% to $2.43 billion from $2.42 billion in 2001, while retail food net sales rose 3.5% to $2.27 billion from $2.19 billion the previous year. Operating earnings totaled $128.5 million, up 5.8% compared with $136.4 million the year before.

PROSPECTS:

The Company is targeting earnings per share of between $1.98 and $2.03 for the fiscal year ending on 2/22/03. Looking ahead, SVU anticipates capital expenditures during the following fiscal year in the range of $475.0 million to $500.0 million, including about $50.0 million in capitalized leases. Meanwhile, results should benefit from SVU's efforts to expand its retail store network and introduce general merchandise in a new Save-A-Lot store format. SVU plans to open 150 to 170 Save-A-Lot extreme value food stores and between ten and fifteen price superstores in the upcoming fiscal year.

ANNUAL FINANCIAL DATA:

FISCAL YEAR	TOT. REVS. ($mill.)	NET INC. ($mill.)	TOT. ASSETS ($mill.)	OPER. PROFIT %	NET PROFIT %	RET. ON EQUITY %	RET. ON ASSETS %	CURR. RATIO	EARN. PER SH. $	CASH FL. PER SH. $	TANG. BK. VAL. $	DIV. PER SH. $	PRICE RANGE	AVG. P/E RATIO	AVG. YIELD %
2/23/02	20,908.5	④ 205.5	5,824.8	2.5	1.0	10.7	3.5	0.9	④ 1.53	4.11	2.90	0.56	24.10 - 12.60	12.0	3.0
2/24/01	23,194.3	④ 82.0	6,407.2	1.5	0.4	4.6	1.3	0.9	④ 0.62	3.24	1.64	0.55	22.88 - 11.75	27.9	3.1
2/26/00	20,339.1	③ 242.9	6,495.4	2.9	1.2	13.3	3.7	0.9	③ 1.87	4.06	1.58	0.54	28.88 - 16.81	12.2	2.3
2/27/99	17,420.5	191.3	4,265.9	2.4	1.1	14.7	4.5	1.0	1.57	3.45	6.09	0.53	28.94 - 20.19	15.6	2.1
2/28/98	17,201.4	② 230.8	4,093.0	2.4	1.3	19.2	5.6	1.1	② 1.83	3.64	5.80	0.51	21.09 - 14.06	9.6	2.9
2/22/97	16,551.9	175.0	4,283.5	2.3	1.1	13.4	4.1	1.2	1.30	3.03	6.06	0.49	16.50 - 13.56	11.6	3.3
2/24/96	16,486.3	166.4	4,183.5	2.2	1.0	13.7	4.0	1.2	1.22	2.82	5.27	0.48	16.44 - 11.25	11.3	3.5
2/25/95	16,563.8	① 43.3	4,305.1	0.7	0.3	3.6	1.0	1.1	① 0.31	1.70	4.79	0.46	20.06 - 11.00	50.9	2.9
2/26/94	15,936.9	185.3	4,042.4	2.3	1.2	14.5	4.6	1.3	1.29	2.59	5.84	0.41	18.94 - 14.75	13.1	2.5
2/27/93	12,568.0	164.5	4,064.2	2.3	1.3	14.5	4.0	1.2	1.16	2.14	4.87	0.38	17.44 - 11.69	12.6	2.6

Statistics are as originally reported. Adj. for 100% stk. div., 8/98. ① Incl. $244 mil total non-recur. chg. ② Incl. $53.7 mil ($0.43/sh.) non-recur net gain from sale of int. in ShopKo Stores, Inc. ③ Incl. $163.7 pre-tax gain on sale of Hazelwood Farms Bakeries & incl. $103.6 pre-tax restructuring chg. ④ Incl. after-tax restr. & other chgs $35.2 mil ($0.27/sh), 2002; $153.9 mil ($1.16/sh.), 2001.

OFFICERS:
J. Noddle, Chmn., Pres., C.E.O.
P. K. Knous, Exec. V.P., C.F.O.

INVESTOR CONTACT: Yolanda Scharton, V.P., Investor Relations, (952) 828-4540

PRINCIPAL OFFICE: 11840 Valley View Road, Eden Prairie, MN 55344

TELEPHONE NUMBER: (952) 828-4000
FAX: (952) 828-8998
WEB: www.supervalu.com

NO. OF EMPLOYEES: 57,800 (approx.)

SHAREHOLDERS: 7,155

ANNUAL MEETING: In May

INCORPORATED: DE, Dec., 1925

INSTITUTIONAL HOLDINGS:
No. of Institutions: 310
Shares Held: 103,280,926
% Held: 77.3

INDUSTRY: Groceries, general line (SIC: 5141)

TRANSFER AGENT(S): Wells Fargo Shareowner Services, St. Paul, MN

SYBASE, INC.

EXCH.	SYM.	REC. PRICE	P/E RATIO	YLD.	MKT. CAP.	RANGE (52-WK.)	'02 Y/E PR.
NYSE	SY	14.69 (2/28/03)	38.7	...	$1.45 bill.	19.24 - 9.15	13.40

MEDIUM GRADE. THE COMPANY STRENGTHENED ITS POSITION IN THE MOBILE MIDDLEWARE MARKET WITH THE ACQUISITION OF AVANTGO, INC.

*7 YEAR PRICE SCORE N/A   *12 MONTH PRICE SCORE 112.9
*NYSE COMPOSITE INDEX=100

INTERIM EARNINGS (Per Share):

Qtr.	Mar.	June	Sept.	Dec.
1997	d0.08	d0.23	d0.08	d0.32
1998	d1.01	0.01	0.03	d0.18
1999	0.07	0.17	0.19	0.31
2000	0.07	0.14	0.18	0.39
2001	0.16	d0.42	d0.07	0.06
2002	0.16	0.20	0.12	d0.10

INTERIM DIVIDENDS (Per Share):

Amt.	Decl.	Ex.	Rec.	Pay.
		No dividends paid.		

CAPITALIZATION (12/31/01):

	($000)	(%)
Minority Interest	5,029	0.7
Common & Surplus	716,519	99.3
Total	721,548	100.0

BUSINESS:

Sybase, Inc. develops, markets and supports a full line of relational database management software products and services for on-line applications in networked computing environments. SY offers a broad range of relational database management system servers, application development tools and connectivity software and complements this product portfolio by providing consulting and integration services required to support enterprise-wide on-line applications. SY's business is organized into five operating divisions: Enterprise Solutions, iAnywhere Solutions, Inc., Business Intelligence, Internet Applications and Financial Fusion, Inc. iAnywhere Solutions, Inc. and Financial Fusion, Inc. are wholly-owned subsidiaries.

RECENT DEVELOPMENTS:

For the twelve months ended 12/31/02, income jumped to $37.8 million, before an accounting change charge of $132.5 million, versus a net loss of $25.5 million in 2001. Results for 2002 and 2001 included amortization of other purchased intangibles of $2.0 million in both years, stock compensation charges of $1.9 million and $1.3 million, and restructuring charges of $40.4 million and $48.8 million, respectively. Results also included a goodwill impairment loss of $12.3 million for 2002, as well as amortization of goodwill of $53.9 million, and an in-process research and development charge of $18.5 million for 2001. Total revenues declined 10.6% to $829.9 million from $927.9 million the year before, due to a 16.2% drop in license fees and a 6.5% decrease in services revenue.

PROSPECTS:

On 2/26/03, the Company completed the acquisition of AvantGo, Inc., a provider of mobile enterprise software, for approximately $1.029 per share. AvantGo will be integrated with SY's iAnywhere Solutions subsidiary and should strengthen the Company's position in the mobile middleware market. Separately, iAnywhere Solutions, Inc., a subsidiary of SY, announced a strategic relationship with Intel Corporation to drive the development of available mobile enterprise applications that extend enterprise information to mobile workers.

ANNUAL FINANCIAL DATA:

FISCAL YEAR	TOT. REVS. ($000)	NET INC. ($000)	TOT. ASSETS ($000)	OPER. PROFIT %	NET PROFIT %	RET. ON EQUITY %	RET. ON ASSETS %	CURR. RATIO	EARN. PER SH.$	CASH FL.PER SH.$	TANG. BK. VAL.$	PRICE RANGE	AVG. P/E RATIO
p12/31/02	829,861	④ 37,781		...	...	...	...		④ 0.38			19.24 - 9.15	37.4
12/31/01	926,086	③ d25,522	1,133,242	...	...	...	...	1.3	③ d0.27	1.19	2.91	26.44 - 8.35	...
12/31/00	960,458	72,125	915,040	9.4	7.5	14.7	7.9	1.4	0.78	1.95	3.53	31.00 - 15.44	29.8
12/31/99	871,633	② 62,495	737,335	10.0	7.2	18.6	8.5	1.3	② 0.74	1.81	3.71	19.81 - 5.31	17.0
12/31/98	867,469	① d93,128	696,604	...	...	...	...	1.2	① d1.15	0.18	3.27	11.25 - 4.50	...
12/31/97	903,937	d55,424	781,625	...	...	...	...	1.2	d0.70	0.63	4.09	23.63 - 11.50	...
12/31/96	1,011,545	① d79,006	751,891	...	...	...	...	1.3	① d1.05	0.25	4.25	37.38 - 13.50	...
12/31/95	956,586	① d19,502	766,292	...	...	...	...	1.4	① d0.27	0.78	4.95	55.00 - 19.88	...
12/31/94	693,806	75,207	575,597	16.8	10.8	22.3	13.1	1.7	1.38	2.11	6.30	57.00 - 35.25	33.4
12/31/93	426,698	44,146	332,510	16.3	10.3	23.2	13.3	1.9	0.86	1.33	3.82	43.50 - 22.75	38.5

Statistics are as originally reported. ① Incl. non-recur. chg. $74.2 mill., 12/31/98; $49.2 mill., 12/31/96; $44.0 mill., 12/31/95. ② Incl. restr. credit of $8.5 mill. ③ Incl. $55.9 mill. amort. of goodwill, $18.5 mill. in-process R&D chg., $1.3 mill. stock comp. expense and $48.8 mill. restr. chg. ④ Incl. $12.3 mill. goodwill impair. loss, $1.9 mill. stk. comp. exp., $40.4 mill. restr. chg. & excl. $132.5 mill. acctg. chg.

OFFICERS:
J. S. Chen, Chmn., Pres., C.E.O.
P. Van der Vorst, Sr. V.P., C.F.O.
D. R. Carl, V.P., Gen. Couns.

INVESTOR CONTACT: Scott Irey, Treas., (510) 922-3500

PRINCIPAL OFFICE: One Sybase Drive, Dublin, CA 94568

TELEPHONE NUMBER: (925) 236-5000
FAX: (925) 236-4468
WEB: www.sybase.com
NO. OF EMPLOYEES: 4,639 (avg.)
SHAREHOLDERS: 1,663
ANNUAL MEETING: In May
INCORPORATED: CA, Nov., 1984; reincorp., DE, July, 1991

INSTITUTIONAL HOLDINGS:
No. of Institutions: 189
Shares Held: 81,481,815
% Held: 86.1

INDUSTRY: Prepackaged software (SIC: 7372)

TRANSFER AGENT(S): American Stock Transfer & Trust Co., New York, NY

SYMBOL TECHNOLOGIES, INC.

EXCH.	SYM.	REC. PRICE	P/E RATIO	YLD.	MKT. CAP.	RANGE (52-WK.)	'02 Y/E PR.
NYSE	SBL	8.61 (3/31/03)	172.2	0.2%	$1.97 bill.	11.35 - 4.98	8.22

LOWER MEDIUM GRADE. FOR 2003, REVENUE GROWTH IS EXPECTED IN THE 15.0% TO 20.0% RANGE AND EARNINGS PER SHARE IN A RANGE OF $0.34 TO $0.42, BEFORE RESTRUCTURING CHARGES.

TRADING VOLUME Thousand Shares

*7 YEAR PRICE SCORE 63.9   *12 MONTH PRICE SCORE 118.3
*NYSE COMPOSITE INDEX=100

INTERIM EARNINGS (Per Share):

Qtr.	Mar.	June	Sept.	Dec.
1997	0.07	0.08	0.09	0.10
1998	0.09	0.11	0.12	0.11
1999	0.11	0.13	0.15	0.15
2000	0.15	0.17	0.19	d0.84
2001	0.12	d0.27	d0.16	0.06
2002	0.01	d0.10	0.06	0.08

INTERIM DIVIDENDS (Per Share):

Amt.	Decl.	Ex.	Rec.	Pay.
50% STK	2/26/01	4/17/01	3/26/01	4/16/01
0.01S	8/13/01	9/17/01	9/14/01	10/05/01
0.01S	2/19/02	3/07/02	3/11/02	4/05/02
0.01S	8/12/02	9/11/02	9/13/02	10/07/02
0.01S	3/10/03	4/10/03	4/14/03	4/28/03

Indicated div.: $0.02

CAPITALIZATION (12/31/01):

	($000)	(%)
Long-Term Debt	310,220	20.8
Common & Surplus	1,180,789	79.2
Total	1,491,009	100.0

BUSINESS:

Symbol Technologies, Inc. develops, manufactures, sells and services scanning products that employ laser technology to read data encoded in bar code symbols, and wireless networking and information systems that allow users to access, capture and transmit information at the point of activity over local area networks, wide area networks and the Internet. The Company is engaged in two reportable business segments, including the design, manufacture and marketing of scanner integrated mobile and wireless information management systems; and the servicing, customer support and other professional services pertaining to these systems. The Company's products are used in diverse markets such as retail, transportation and logistics, parcel delivery and postal service, warehousing and distribution, industrial, health care, hospitality, education and government.

RECENT DEVELOPMENTS:

For the year ended 12/31/02, net income amounted to $10.5 million compared with a net loss of $53.9 million in 2001. Earnings benefited from greater operating efficiencies and organizational alignments. Results for 2002 and 2001 included amortization of software development costs of $19.1 million and $17.1 million, respectively. Results for 2002 also included a compensation charge of $8.6 million and an asset impairment charge of $47.2 million, while results for 2001 included restructuring and impairment charges of $169.7 million and goodwill amortization of $16.4 million. Net revenue slipped 9.1% to $1.32 billion from $1.45 billion in the previous year.

PROSPECTS:

For 2003, the Company expects revenue growth in the 15.0% to 20.0% range and earnings per share in a range of $0.34 to $0.42, before restructuring charges. The Company anticipates the first quarter of 2003 will reflect traditional seasonality with subsequent quarters improving. However, global economic conditions, geopolitical climate and levels of corporate information technology investments may hamper these guidances. Separately, on 2/27/03, the Company acquired the software and technology assets of ImageWare Technologies, Inc.

ANNUAL FINANCIAL DATA:

FISCAL YEAR	TOT. REVS. ($mill.)	NET INC. ($mill.)	TOT. ASSETS ($mill.)	OPER. PROFIT %	NET PROFIT %	RET. ON EQUITY %	RET. ON ASSETS %	CURR. RATIO	EARN. PER SH.$	CASH FL. PER SH.$	TANG. BK. VAL.$	DIV. PER SH.$	PRICE RANGE	AVG. P/E RATIO	AVG. YIELD %
p12/31/02	1,320.1	⑥ 10.5							⑥ 0.05			0.02	17.50 — 4.98	224.8	0.2
12/31/01	1,452.7	⑤ d54.7	1,892.7	...	...	...	...	2.9	⑤ d0.24	0.18	3.20	0.02	37.34 — 9.50	...	0.1
12/31/00	1,449.5	④ d69.0	2,093.2	...	...	...	...	2.4	④ d0.33	0.06	3.49	0.01	46.03 — 17.08	...	
12/31/99	1,139.3	116.4	1,047.9	15.5	10.2	18.2	11.1	2.5	0.55	0.86	2.23	0.01	28.89 — 11.56	37.0	0.1
12/31/98	977.9	③ 93.0	838.4	14.5	9.5	17.5	11.1	2.6	③ 0.44	0.70	1.87	0.01	19.08 — 7.25	29.9	0.1
12/31/97	774.3	70.2	679.2	14.6	9.1	15.5	10.3	2.5	0.34	0.56	1.57	0.01	8.88 — 5.63	21.3	0.1
12/31/96	656.7	② 50.3	614.2	12.8	7.7	12.6	8.2	2.7	② 0.25	0.44	1.32	...	6.52 — 4.20	21.9	...
12/31/95	555.2	① 184.1	544.3	38.6	33.2	52.2	33.8	3.0	① 0.23	1.06	1.21	...	5.35 — 3.21	18.8	...
12/31/94	465.3	35.0	474.2	13.6	7.5	11.1	7.4	3.6	0.18	0.32	1.02	...	4.53 — 2.06	18.6	...
12/31/93	360.0	12.4	419.6	6.5	3.5	4.8	3.0	2.8	0.07	0.21	0.78	...	2.60 — 1.48	29.5	...

Statistics are as originally reported. Adj. for 3-for-2 split, 4/97, 9/98, & 6/99. Adj. for 50% stk. div., 4/98, 9/98, 6/99, 4/00 & 4/01. ① Incl. $2.5 mill. pre-tax chg. on mgmt. change. ② Incl. $12.3 mill. pre-tax chg. rel. to acq. costs. ③ Incl. a pre-tax charge of $3.6 million related to a terminated acq. & pre-tax gain of $500,000 on the sale of a bus. ④ Incl. $146.7 mill. restr. chg., $87.6 mill. in-process R&D chg., & $39.2 mill. merger integration chg. ⑤ Incl. $16.4 mill. chg. for amort. of excess costs; bef. $813,000 extraord. gain. ⑥ Incl. $8.6 mill. comp. chg. & $47.2 mill. asset impair. chg.

OFFICERS:
J. Swartz, Chmn.
R. Bravman, Vice-Chmn., C.E.O.
W. Nuti, Pres., C.O.O.
INVESTOR CONTACT: Nancy Tully, (631) 738-5050
PRINCIPAL OFFICE: One Symbol Plaza, Holtsville, NY 11742-1300

TELEPHONE NUMBER: (631) 738-2400
FAX: (631) 738-5990
WEB: www.symbol.com
NO. OF EMPLOYEES: 5,250 (approx.)
SHAREHOLDERS: 1,800
ANNUAL MEETING: In May
INCORPORATED: NY, 1973; reincorp., DE, Nov., 1987

INSTITUTIONAL HOLDINGS:
No. of Institutions: 296
Shares Held: 179,348,304
% Held: 77.8
INDUSTRY: Computer peripheral equipment, nec (SIC: 3577)
TRANSFER AGENT(S): Continental Stock & Transfer Company, New York, NY

SYNOVUS FINANCIAL CORPORATION

EXCH.	SYM.	REC. PRICE	P/E RATIO	YLD.	MKT. CAP.	RANGE (52-WK.)	'02 Y/E PR.	DIV. ACH.
NYSE	SNV	19.25 (2/28/03)	15.7	3.4%	$5.78 bill.	31.93 - 16.48	19.40	26 yrs.

UPPER MEDIUM GRADE. THE COMPANY IS TARGETING FULL-YEAR 2003 EARNINGS PER SHARE GROWTH IN THE RANGE OF 10.0% TO 14.0%.

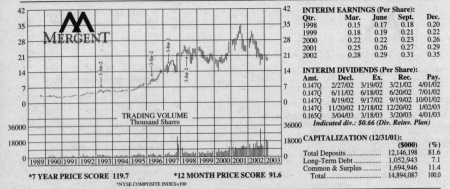

*7 YEAR PRICE SCORE 119.7   ***12 MONTH PRICE SCORE 91.6**

*NYSE COMPOSITE INDEX=100

INTERIM EARNINGS (Per Share):

Qtr.	Mar.	June	Sept.	Dec.
1998	0.15	0.17	0.18	0.20
1999	0.18	0.19	0.21	0.22
2000	0.22	0.22	0.23	0.26
2001	0.25	0.26	0.27	0.29
2002	0.28	0.29	0.31	0.35

INTERIM DIVIDENDS (Per Share):

Amt.	Decl.	Ex.	Rec.	Pay.
0.147Q	2/27/02	3/19/02	3/21/02	4/01/02
0.147Q	6/11/02	6/18/02	6/20/02	7/01/02
0.147Q	8/19/02	9/17/02	9/19/02	10/01/02
0.147Q	11/20/02	12/18/02	12/20/02	1/02/03
0.165Q	3/04/03	3/18/03	3/20/03	4/01/03

Indicated div.: $0.66 (Div. Reinv. Plan)

CAPITALIZATION (12/31/01):

	($000)	(%)
Total Deposits	12,146,198	81.6
Long-Term Debt	1,052,943	7.1
Common & Surplus	1,694,946	11.4
Total	14,894,087	100.0

BUSINESS:

Synovus Financial Corporation, with assets of $19.04 billion as of 12/31/02, is a registered bank holding company engaged in two principal business segments: banking, which encompasses commercial banking, trust services, mortgage banking, credit card banking and certain securities brokerage operations, and bankcard data processing. SNV has 37 wholly-owned subsidiaries located in Georgia,

Alabama, Florida, South Carolina, and Tennessee, offering a wide range of commercial banking services, including accepting customary types of demand and savings deposits; making individual, consumer, commercial, installment, first and second mortgage loans; and other fiduciary services. SNV also owns 81.0% of Total System Services, Inc.® (TSYS), an electronic transaction processing company.

RECENT DEVELOPMENTS:

For the year ended 12/31/02, net income advanced 17.2% to $365.3 million from $311.6 million in the corresponding period of the prior year. Earnings for 2002 included an $8.4 million pre-tax impairment loss on a private equity investment. Net interest income climbed 13.9% to $717.5 million

from $629.8 million the year before. SNV's provision for loan losses rose 26.4% to $65.3 million. Total non-interest income grew 6.1% to $1.23 billion from $1.16 billion a year earlier, while total non-interest expense increased 5.4% to $1.30 billion from $1.23 billion in 2001.

PROSPECTS:

Results are being positively affected by strong growth of home-equity and automobile loans, driven by lower interest rates, along with strong credit quality and improved net interest margin. Meanwhile, the Company continues to expand into high-growth markets. During 2002, SNV

opened eleven new banking locations in high-growth markets, while closing four locations and exiting three low-growth markets. Looking ahead, the Company is targeting full-year 2003 earnings per share growth in the range of 10.0% to 14.0%.

ANNUAL FINANCIAL DATA:

FISCAL YEAR	NET INT. INC. ($mill.)	NON-INT. INC. ($mill.)	NET INC. ($mill.)	TOT. LOANS ($mill.)	TOT. ASSETS ($mill.)	TOT. DEP. ($mill.)	RET. ON EQUITY %	RET. ON ASSETS %	EQUITY/ ASSETS %	EARN. PER SH. $	TANG. BK. VAL. $	DIV. PER SH. $	PRICE RANGE	AVG. P/E RATIO
p12/31/02	717.5		②365.3	12,439.6	16,657.9	12,146.2	18.4	1.9	10.2	②1.21	5.75	0.57	31.93 - 16.48	20.0
12/31/01	629.8	937.7	311.6	12,439.6	16,657.9	12,146.2	18.4	1.9	10.2	1.05	5.75	0.49	34.74 - 22.75	27.4
12/31/00	562.3	833.5	262.6	10,768.3	14,908.1	11,161.7	18.5	1.8	9.5	0.92	4.98	0.42	27.38 - 14.00	22.5
12/31/99	513.3	739.8	225.3	9,077.5	12,547.0	9,440.1	18.4	1.8	9.8	0.80	4.35	0.34	25.13 - 17.25	26.5
12/31/98	440.5	562.0	187.1	7,420.5	10,498.0	8,542.8	17.5	1.8	10.2	0.70	3.96	0.28	25.92 - 17.25	30.8
12/31/97	412.4	489.2	165.2	6,615.6	9,260.3	7,707.9	18.3	1.8	9.8	0.62	3.44	0.23	22.42 - 13.11	28.6
12/31/96	374.9	425.4	139.6	6,075.5	8,612.3	7,203.0	17.8	1.6	9.1	0.53	2.99	0.19	14.83 - 7.78	21.2
12/31/95	341.9	340.8	114.6	5,528.8	7,927.6	6,727.9	16.5	1.4	9.2	0.45	2.66	0.15	8.89 - 5.26	15.9
12/31/94	259.5	263.9	86.4	4,330.5	6,115.4	5,027.5	17.0	1.4	8.3	0.38	2.22	0.13	5.89 - 4.93	14.2
12/31/93	229.1	226.1	①74.1	3,848.5	5,627.4	4,673.8	15.5	1.3	8.5	①0.33	2.12	0.11	6.04 - 4.45	15.9

Statistics are as originally reported. Adj. for stk. splits: 3-for-2, 5/98; 4/97 & 4/96. ① Bef. acctg. change chrg. $2.9 mill. ② Incl. $8.4 mill. pre-tax impairment loss on a private equity investment.

OFFICERS:
J. H. Blanchard, Chmn., C.E.O.
J. D. Yancey, Pres., C.O.O.
T. J. Prescott, Exec. V.P., C.F.O.

INVESTOR CONTACT: Patrick A. Reynolds, Dir. of Inv. Rel., (706) 649-4973

PRINCIPAL OFFICE: 901 Front Avenue, P.O. Box 120, Columbus, GA 31902

TELEPHONE NUMBER: (706) 649-2401
FAX: (706) 641-6555
WEB: www.synovus.com

NO. OF EMPLOYEES: 10,166

SHAREHOLDERS: 66,060 (approx.)

ANNUAL MEETING: In Apr.

INCORPORATED: GA, June, 1972

INSTITUTIONAL HOLDINGS:
No. of Institutions: 235
Shares Held: 125,307,459
% Held: 41.8

INDUSTRY: National commercial banks (SIC: 6021)

TRANSFER AGENT(S): State Street Bank and Trust Company, Boston, MA

SYSCO CORPORATION

EXCH.	SYM.	REC. PRICE	P/E RATIO	YLD.	MKT. CAP.	RANGE (52-WK.)	'02 Y/E PR.	DIV. ACH.
NYSE	SYY	27.12 (2/28/03)	24.7	1.6%	$18.04 bill.	32.58 - 21.25	29.79	26 yrs.

INVESTMENT GRADE. RESULTS ARE BENEFITING FROM THE COMPANY'S ONGOING EFFORTS TO EXPAND ITS OPERATIONS.

*7 YEAR PRICE SCORE 169.9   ***12 MONTH PRICE SCORE 110.1**

*NYSE COMPOSITE INDEX=100

INTERIM EARNINGS (Per Share):

Qtr.	Sept.	Dec.	Mar.	June
1997-98	0.12	0.13	0.10	0.15
1998-99	0.13	0.13	0.11	0.18
1999-00	0.16	0.16	0.16	0.22
2000-01	0.21	0.21	0.21	0.26
2001-02	0.24	0.24	0.23	0.31
2002-03	0.28	0.28	...	...

INTERIM DIVIDENDS (Per Share):

Amt.	Decl.	Ex.	Rec.	Pay.
0.09Q	2/08/02	4/03/02	4/05/02	4/26/02
0.09Q	5/10/02	7/02/02	7/05/02	7/26/02
0.09Q	9/13/02	10/02/02	10/04/02	10/25/02
0.11Q	11/08/02	12/31/02	1/03/03	1/24/03
0.11Q	2/07/03	4/02/03	4/04/03	4/25/03

Indicated div.: $0.44 (Div. Reinv. Plan)

CAPITALIZATION (6/29/02):

	($000)	(%)
Long-Term Debt	1,176,307	31.4
Deferred Income Tax	441,570	11.8
Common & Surplus	2,132,519	56.9
Total	3,750,396	100.0

BUSINESS:

Sysco Corporation is a major marketer and distributor of foodservice products. Included among its customers are about 415,000 restaurants, hotels, hospitals, schools and other institutions. The Company distributes entree items, dry and canned foods, fresh produce, beverages, dairy products and certain nonfood products, including paper products and cleaning supplies. Through its SYGMA Network, Inc. subsidiary, the Company serves pizza, chicken, steak and hamburgers to fast-food chains and other limited menu chain restaurants. SYY has three Canadian facilities located in Vancouver, Edmonton and Toronto. In fiscal 2002, the foodservice sales breakdown was: 63% restaurants; 10% hospitals and nursing homes; 6% schools and colleges; 6% hotels and motels; and 15% other.

RECENT DEVELOPMENTS:

For the 13 weeks ended 12/28/02, net earnings totaled $184.6 million, up 16.4% compared with $158.5 million in the corresponding prior-year period. Sales climbed 13.6% to $6.35 billion from $5.59 billion a year earlier. Cost of sales was $5.10 billion, or 80.3% of sales, versus $4.48 billion, or 80.2% of total sales, the year before. Earnings before income taxes advanced 16.4% to $298.9 million from $256.7 million the previous year. Results benefited from acquisitions completed during the year and the Company's efforts to control costs.

PROSPECTS:

Results are benefiting from the Company's ongoing efforts to expand its operations. Construction of a new broadline fold-out operation, or foodservice distribution center, in Oxnard, California is expected to begin in the spring of 2003. The facility, which will be the Company's twelfth broadline fold-out company, is expected to be operational by the second quarter of calendar year 2004. Meanwhile, construction has begun on a new facility located in Front Royal, Virginia that will receive and redistribute food and food-related products to 14 of SYY's operating companies in the northeast U.S. This facility, which is expected to be operational by the summer of 2004, should help generate cost savings through increased supply chain efficiencies.

ANNUAL FINANCIAL DATA:

FISCAL YEAR	TOT. REVS. ($Mill.)	NET INC. ($Mill.)	TOT. ASSETS ($Mill.)	OPER. PROFIT %	NET PROFIT %	RET. ON EQUITY %	RET. ON ASSETS %	CURR. RATIO	EARN. PER SH. $	CASH FL. PER SH. $	TANG. BK. VAL. $	DIV. PER SH. $	PRICE RANGE	AVG. P/E RATIO	AVG. YIELD %
6/29/02	23,350.5	679.8	5,989.8	5.0	2.9	31.9	11.3	1.4	1.01	1.42	1.85	0.36	32.58 - 21.25	26.6	1.3
6/30/01	21,784.5	596.9	5,468.5	4.8	2.7	27.8	10.9	1.4	0.88	1.27	2.07	0.28	30.12 - 21.75	29.5	1.1
7/01/00	19,303.3	①453.6	4,814.0	4.2	2.4	25.8	9.4	1.5	①0.68	1.01	1.90	0.24	30.44 - 13.06	32.0	1.1
7/03/99	17,422.8	362.3	4,096.6	3.8	2.1	25.4	8.8	1.7	0.54	0.84	1.71	0.20	20.56 - 12.47	30.6	1.2
6/27/98	15,327.5	①324.8	3,780.2	3.9	2.1	23.9	8.6	1.6	①0.48	0.74	1.57	0.18	14.34 - 9.97	25.6	1.5
6/28/97	14,454.6	302.5	3,436.6	3.8	2.1	21.6	8.8	1.9	0.43	0.65	1.67	0.15	11.81 - 7.31	22.5	1.6
6/29/96	13,395.1	276.9	3,325.4	3.7	2.1	18.8	8.3	1.9	0.38	0.58	1.70	0.13	9.06 - 6.91	21.0	1.6
7/01/95	12,118.0	251.8	3,097.2	3.7	2.1	17.9	8.1	1.9	0.35	0.52	1.57	0.11	8.16 - 6.22	20.8	1.5
7/02/94	10,942.5	216.8	2,811.7	3.7	2.0	17.5	7.7	1.9	0.30	0.46	1.33	0.09	7.31 - 5.28	21.3	1.4
7/03/93	10,021.5	201.8	2,530.0	3.7	2.0	17.7	8.0	1.9	0.27	0.41	1.18	0.07	7.75 - 5.56	24.6	1.1

Statistics are as originally reported. Adj. for 2-for-1 stk. split, 12/00 & 3/98. ① Bef. $8.0 mil ($0.01/sh) chg. for acctg. adj., 2000; $28.1 mil ($0.04/sh), 1998.

OFFICERS:
R. J. Schnieders, Chmn., C.E.O.
T. E. Lankford, Pres., C.O.O.
J. K. Stubblefield, Exec. V.P.-Fin. & Admin.

INVESTOR CONTACT: John M. Palizza,
(281) 584-1308

PRINCIPAL OFFICE: 1390 Enclave Parkway,
Houston, TX 77077-2099

TELEPHONE NUMBER: (281) 584-1390
FAX: (281) 584-1737
WEB: www.sysco.com

NO. OF EMPLOYEES: 48,000 (approx.)

SHAREHOLDERS: 15,583

ANNUAL MEETING: In Nov.

INCORPORATED: DE, May, 1969

INSTITUTIONAL HOLDINGS:
No. of Institutions: 635
Shares Held: 444,641,769
% Held: 67.7

INDUSTRY: Groceries, general line (SIC: 5141)

TRANSFER AGENT(S): EquiServe Trust Company, N.A., Providence, RI

TALBOTS (THE), INC.

EXCH.	SYM.	REC. PRICE	P/E RATIO	YLD.	MKT. CAP.	RANGE (52-WK.)	'02 Y/E PR.
NYSE	TLB	24.92 (2/28/03)	12.4	1.4%	$1.50 bill.	41.50 - 20.59	27.53

INVESTMENT GRADE. THE COMPANY CONTINUES TO BENEFIT FROM ITS RECENTLY-LAUNCHED TALBOTS MENS PRODUCT LINE, WHICH IS PERFORMING WELL ABOVE THE COMPANY'S EXPECTATIONS.

7 YEAR PRICE SCORE 139.7   **12 MONTH PRICE SCORE 91.0**

*NYSE COMPOSITE INDEX=100

INTERIM EARNINGS (Per Share):

Qtr.	Apr.	July	Oct.	Jan.
1997-98	0.25	d0.18	0.18	d0.16
1998-99	0.23	0.02	0.20	0.13
1999-00	0.31	0.06	0.32	0.24
2000-01	0.52	0.23	0.54	0.51
2001-02	0.62	0.28	0.58	0.53
2002-03	0.57	0.33	0.63	0.48

INTERIM DIVIDENDS (Per Share):

Amt.	Decl.	Ex.	Rec.	Pay.
0.08Q	2/27/02	3/07/02	3/11/02	3/25/02
0.09Q	5/23/02	5/30/02	6/03/02	6/17/02
0.09Q	8/13/02	8/29/02	9/03/02	9/16/02
0.09Q	10/31/02	11/27/02	12/02/02	12/16/02
0.09Q	2/27/03	3/06/03	3/10/03	3/24/03

Indicated div.: $0.36

CAPITALIZATION (2/2/02):

	($000)	(%)
Long-Term Debt	100,000	15.0
Common & Surplus	567,876	85.0
Total	667,876	100.0

BUSINESS:

The Talbots, Inc. is a national specialty retailer and cataloger of women's and children's classic apparel, accessories and shoes. As of 3/12/03, the Company operated 895 stores in the U.S., Canada and the United Kingdom. The Company's stores and catalogs offer sportswear, casual wear, dresses, coats, sweaters, accessories and shoes, consisting primarily of the Company's own private-label merchandise in misses and petites sizes. Talbots Kids & Babies stores and catalogs sell an assortment of clothing and accessories for infants, toddlers, boys and girls. During 2002, the Company circulated approximately 50.0 million catalogs worldwide. At 4/18/02, AEON (U.S.A.), Inc. (formerly Jusco (U.S.A.), Inc.) owned approximately 57.9% of TLB's common stock.

RECENT DEVELOPMENTS:

For the 52 weeks ended 2/1/03, net income totaled $120.8 million, down 4.9% compared with $127.0 million the year before. Net sales slid 1.1% to $1.60 billion from $1.61 billion a year earlier. Retail store sales remained the same at $1.35 billion versus the prior year. Comparable-store sales declined 6.6% year over year. Catalog sales were down 7.2% to $247.4 million from $266.5 million in the previous year. Operating income slipped 6.6% to $196.1 million from $210.0 million in the prior year.

PROSPECTS:

The Company continues to move forward with its store expansion program. During fiscal 2002, the Company opened a total of 92 new stores. Additionally, TLB continues to benefit from its recently-launched Talbots Mens product line, in a separate catalog, which is performing well above the Company's expectations. In April 2003, TLB plans to introduce its next phase with the opening of its first Talbots Mens stores in three locations, which include Connecticut, Ohio and Pennsylvania. In the Fall of 2003, TLB will open an additional three Talbots Men stores, including one in New York. Separately, the Company introduced new print and television advertising designed to appeal to a broader range of women who favor classic styling.

ANNUAL FINANCIAL DATA:

FISCAL YEAR	TOT. REVS. ($mill.)	NET INC. ($mill.)	TOT. ASSETS ($mill.)	OPER. PROFIT %	NET PROFIT %	RET. ON EQUITY %	RET. ON ASSETS %	CURR. RATIO	EARN. PER SH. $	CASH FL. PER SH. $	TANG. BK. VAL. $	DIV. PER SH. $	PRICE RANGE	AVG. P/E RATIO	AVG. YIELD %
p2/01/03	1,595.3	120.8	871.9						2.01			0.35	41.50 - 20.59	15.4	1.1
2/02/02	1,612.5	127.0	831.1	13.0	7.9	22.4	15.3	3.3	2.00	2.84	7.56	0.31	54.99 - 22.02	19.3	0.8
2/03/01	1,595.0	115.2	858.6	12.0	7.2	20.9	13.4	2.7	1.80	2.52	6.90	0.27	54.00 - 14.13	18.9	0.8
1/29/00	1,290.9	58.5	693.9	7.9	4.5	13.6	8.4	2.6	0.93	1.61	5.05	0.23	26.97 - 11.28	20.7	1.2
1/30/99	1,142.2	36.7	657.1	5.9	3.2	9.1	5.6	2.5	0.58	1.24	4.47	0.22	15.78 - 6.75	19.6	2.0
1/31/98	1,053.8	5.8	676.4	1.6	0.6	1.5	0.9	1.7	0.09	0.71	4.24	0.21	17.19 - 8.38	141.9	1.6
2/01/97	1,018.6	63.6	621.8	10.7	6.2	14.7	10.2	2.4	0.96	1.49	4.55	0.17	20.25 - 11.94	16.8	1.1
2/03/96	981.0	62.6	572.1	11.1	6.4	15.7	10.9	2.4	0.91	1.40	3.87	0.13	21.50 - 11.75	18.3	0.8
1/28/95	879.6	54.5	532.5	10.7	6.2	14.1	10.2	2.3	0.78	1.22	3.44	0.09	18.25 - 11.63	19.1	0.6
1/29/94	736.7	35.2	485.9	8.9	4.8	10.4	7.2	1.8	0.71	1.25	2.64	...	13.88 - 10.94	17.5	...

Statistics are as originally reported. Adj. for 2-for-1 stk. split, 11/00.

OFFICERS:
A. B. Zetcher, Chmn., Pres., C.E.O.
E. L. Larsen, Sr. V.P., C.F.O., Treas.
R. T. O'Connell Jr., Sr. V.P., Sec.

INVESTOR CONTACT: Julie Lorigan, Investor Relations, (781) 741-7775

PRINCIPAL OFFICE: One Talbots Drive, Hingham, MA 02043-1586

TELEPHONE NUMBER: (781) 749-7600
FAX: (781) 741-4369
WEB: www.talbots.com

NO. OF EMPLOYEES: 3,000 full-time (approx.); 7,400 part-time (approx.)

SHAREHOLDERS: 430

ANNUAL MEETING: In May

INCORPORATED: MA, ; reincorp., DE, 1989

INSTITUTIONAL HOLDINGS:
No. of Institutions: 156
Shares Held: 21,717,283
% Held: 37.8

INDUSTRY: Women's clothing stores (SIC: 5621)

TRANSFER AGENT(S): EquiServe Shareholder Services, Boston, MA

TARGET CORPORATION

EXCH.	SYM.	REC. PRICE	P/E RATIO	YLD.	MKT. CAP.	RANGE (52-WK.)	'02 Y/E PR.	DIV. ACH.
NYSE	TGT	28.65 (2/28/03)	15.8	0.8%	$25.93 bill.	46.00 - 24.90	30.00	31 yrs.

INVESTMENT GRADE. RESULTS ARE BENEFITING FROM STRONG EARNINGS GROWTH FROM THE COMPANY'S CREDIT-CARD OPERATIONS.

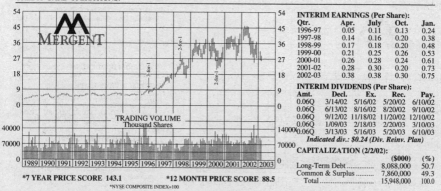

*7 YEAR PRICE SCORE 143.1   ***12 MONTH PRICE SCORE 88.5**
*NYSE COMPOSITE INDEX=100

INTERIM EARNINGS (Per Share):

Qtr.	Apr.	July	Oct.	Jan.
1996-97	0.05	0.11	0.13	0.24
1997-98	0.14	0.16	0.20	0.38
1998-99	0.17	0.18	0.20	0.48
1999-00	0.21	0.25	0.26	0.53
2000-01	0.26	0.28	0.24	0.61
2001-02	0.28	0.30	0.20	0.73
2002-03	0.38	0.38	0.30	0.75

INTERIM DIVIDENDS (Per Share):

Amt.	Decl.	Ex.	Rec.	Pay.
0.06Q	3/14/02	5/16/02	5/20/02	6/10/02
0.06Q	6/13/02	8/16/02	8/20/02	9/10/02
0.06Q	9/12/02	11/18/02	11/20/02	12/10/02
0.06Q	1/09/03	2/18/03	2/20/03	3/10/03
0.06Q	3/13/03	5/16/03	5/20/03	6/10/03

Indicated div.: $0.24 (Div. Reinv. Plan)

CAPITALIZATION (2/2/02):

	($000)	(%)
Long-Term Debt	8,088,000	50.7
Common & Surplus	7,860,000	49.3
Total	15,948,000	100.0

BUSINESS:

Target Corporation (formerly Dayton Hudson Corporation) is a diversified general merchandise retailer. As of 2/20/03, the Company operated 1,475 stores in 47 states including 1,147 Target stores, 264 Mervyn's stores and 64 Marshall Field's stores. Target (85.0% of fiscal 2002 revenue) is a national discount store chain offering low prices with stores selling hardlines and fashion softgoods; Mervyn's (8.8%) is a moderate-priced department store chain specializing in active and casual apparel and home softlines. Marshall Field's (6.2%) is a full-service, full-line department store chain offering moderate to better merchandise.

RECENT DEVELOPMENTS:

For the year ended 2/1/03, net earnings totaled $1.65 billion, up 20.9% compared with $1.37 billion a year earlier. Prior-year results included a one-time pre-tax charge of $67.0 million related to a securitization adjustment. Total revenues climbed 10.3% to $43.92 billion from $39.83 billion the previous year. Revenues from Target stores advanced 13.3% to $36.92 billion from $32.59 billion the year before. Revenues from Mervyn's slid 5.2% to $3.82 billion from $4.03 billion the prior year, while revenues from Marshall Field's slipped 3.1% to $2.69 billion from $2.78 billion a year earlier. Total comparable-store sales were up 1.1% year over year. Comparable-store sales growth of 2.2% at Target stores was partially offset by comparable-store sales declines at Mervyn's and Marshall Field's of 5.3% and 3.7%, respectively.

PROSPECTS:

Strong earnings growth from the Company's credit-card operations, driven by increased customer usage of the Target Visa card, and TGT's focus on controlling costs are more than offsetting sluggish retail sales growth due to continued weak economic conditions. Going forward, TGT is projecting fiscal 2003 earnings of about $2.05 per share. The Company remains confident that it can deliver annual earnings per share growth of 15.0% over the long term.

ANNUAL FINANCIAL DATA:

FISCAL YEAR	TOT. REVS. ($mill.)	NET INC. ($mill.)	TOT. ASSETS ($mill.)	OPER. PROFIT %	NET PROFIT %	RET. ON EQUITY %	RET. ON ASSETS %	CURR. RATIO	EARN. PER SH. $	CASH FL. PER SH. $	TANG. BK. VAL. $	DIV. PER SH. $	PRICE RANGE	AVG. P/E RATIO	AVG. YIELD %
p2/01/03	43,917.0	1,654.0							1.81			0.24	46.15 - 24.90	19.6	0.7
2/02/02	39,888.0	① 1,374.0	24,154.0	6.7	3.4	17.5	5.7	1.4	① 1.51	2.70	8.68	0.22	41.74 - 26.00	22.4	0.6
2/03/01	36,903.0	1,264.0	19,490.0	6.7	3.4	19.4	6.5	1.2	1.38	2.41	7.15	0.21	39.19 - 21.63	22.0	0.7
1/29/00	33,702.0	② 1,185.0	17,143.0	6.9	3.5	20.2	6.9	1.1	② 1.27	2.19	6.43	0.20	38.50 - 25.03	25.0	0.6
1/30/99	30,951.0	③ 962.0	15,666.0	6.3	3.1	18.1	6.1	1.2	③ 1.02	1.86	6.12	0.18	27.13 - 15.72	21.0	0.8
1/31/98	27,757.0	④ 802.0	14,191.0	6.3	2.9	18.0	5.7	1.2	④ 0.85	1.61	4.77	0.17	18.50 - 8.97	16.2	1.2
2/03/97	25,371.0	⑤ 474.0	13,389.0	4.8	1.9	12.5	3.5	1.3	⑤ 0.52	1.28	4.05	0.15	10.16 - 5.76	15.4	1.9
2/03/96	23,516.0	311.0	12,570.0	4.0	1.3	9.1	2.5	1.4	0.33	1.04	3.64	0.14	6.71 - 5.27	18.4	2.4
1/28/95	21,311.0	434.0	11,697.0	5.3	2.0	13.6	3.7	1.5	0.48	1.14	3.37	0.14	7.24 - 5.41	13.2	2.2
1/29/94	19,233.0	375.0	10,778.0	5.5	1.9	13.7	3.5	1.5	0.42	1.03	3.17	0.13	7.08 - 5.22	14.8	2.2

Statistics are as originally reported. Adj. for 2-for-1 stk. split, 7/00 & 4/98; 3-for-1 stk. split, 7/96. ① Bef. $6 mil ($0.01/sh) extraord. chg. & incl. $67 mil pre-tax chg. ② Bef. $41 mil ($0.05/sh) extraord. chg. ③ Bef. $27 mil ($0.03/sh) extraord. chg. ④ Bef. $51 mil ($0.06/sh) extraord. chg. & incl. $45 mil pre-tax gain. ⑤ Bef. $11 mil extraord. chg. & incl. $134 mil pre-tax chg.

OFFICERS:
R. J. Ulrich, Chmn., C.E.O.
G. L. Storch, Vice-Chmn.
D. A. Scovanner, Exec. V.P., C.F.O.

INVESTOR CONTACT: S.D. Kahn, V.P.-Inv. Rel., (612) 370-6736

PRINCIPAL OFFICE: 1000 Nicollet Mall, Minneapolis, MN 55403

TELEPHONE NUMBER: (612) 370-6948
FAX: (612) 370-5502
WEB: www.target.com

NO. OF EMPLOYEES: 252,000 (avg.)

SHAREHOLDERS: 15,773

ANNUAL MEETING: In May

INCORPORATED: MN, 1902

INSTITUTIONAL HOLDINGS:
No. of Institutions: 786
Shares Held: 794,488,552
% Held: 87.4

INDUSTRY: Variety stores (SIC: 5331)

TRANSFER AGENT(S): EquiServe, Jersey City, NJ

TCF FINANCIAL CORP.

EXCH.	SYM.	REC. PRICE	P/E RATIO	YLD.	MKT. CAP.	RANGE (52-WK.)	'02 Y/E PR.	DIV. ACH.
NYSE	TCB	41.94 (2/28/03)	13.3	3.1%	$3.23 bill.	54.60 - 35.10	43.69	11 yrs.

UPPER MEDIUM GRADE. THE COMPANY PLANS TO OPEN 24 NEW BRANCHES IN 2003.

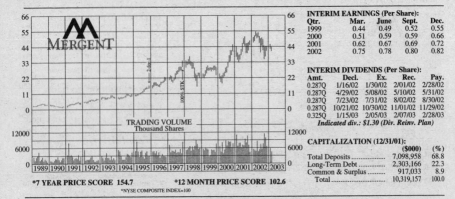

INTERIM EARNINGS (Per Share):

Qtr.	Mar.	June	Sept.	Dec.
1999	0.44	0.49	0.52	0.55
2000	0.51	0.59	0.59	0.66
2001	0.62	0.67	0.69	0.72
2002	0.75	0.78	0.80	0.82

INTERIM DIVIDENDS (Per Share):

Amt.	Decl.	Ex.	Rec.	Pay.
0.287Q	1/16/02	1/30/02	2/01/02	2/28/02
0.287Q	4/29/02	5/08/02	5/10/02	5/31/02
0.287Q	7/23/02	7/31/02	8/02/02	8/30/02
0.287Q	10/21/02	10/30/02	11/01/02	11/29/02
0.325Q	1/15/03	2/05/03	2/07/03	2/28/03

Indicated div.: $1.30 (Div. Reinv. Plan)

CAPITALIZATION (12/31/01):

	($000)	(%)
Total Deposits	7,098,958	68.8
Long-Term Debt	2,303,166	22.3
Common & Surplus	917,033	8.9
Total	10,319,157	100.0

*7 YEAR PRICE SCORE 154.7   ***12 MONTH PRICE SCORE 102.6**

*NYSE COMPOSITE INDEX=100

BUSINESS:

TCF Financial Corp., with $12.20 billion in assets as of 12/31/02, is the holding company for two national banks. As of 12/31/02, TCB operated more than 390 banking offices, including 244 full-service supermarket branches, in Illinois, Indiana, Michigan, Minnesota, Wisconsin and Colorado. The Company's primary focus is lower- and middle-income customers and small- to medium-sized businesses in its markets. TCB's branches are typically open 12 hours a day, seven days a week and on holidays. TCB's products include commercial, consumer and residential mortgage loans and deposit and equipment finance, discount brokerage and investment and insurance sales products.

RECENT DEVELOPMENTS:

For the year ended 12/31/02, net income advanced 12.4% to $232.9 million versus $207.3 million the year before. Results for 2002 and 2003 net gains on sales of both branches and securities available for sale of $13.5 million and $5.0 million, respectively. Results for 2001 included amortization of goodwill of $7.8 million. Net interest income grew 3.7% to $499.2 million from $481.2 million in the previous year due to growth in average low-cost deposits such as checking, savings and money market accounts, combined with growth in the Company's Power Assets® lending operations and lower borrowing costs. Provision for credit losses increased 5.4% to $22.0 million from $20.9 million a year earlier. Non-interest income rose 12.7% to $418.8 million, while non-interest expense climbed 7.2% to $538.4 million.

PROSPECTS:

During the fourth quarter of 2002, the Company opened twelve branches. TCF has opened 220 branches since January 1998 and currently has branches under construction in each of its markets. The Company plans to open 24 additional new branches in 2003. Meanwhile, the Company's focus on its expansion and overall convenience strategies should help spur checking account growth. During 2002, TCB added 89,000 checking accounts, increasing its total to about 1.4 million accounts.

ANNUAL FINANCIAL DATA:

FISCAL YEAR	NET INT. INC. ($mill.)	NON-INT. INC. ($mill.)	NET INC. ($mill.)	TOT. LOANS ($mill.)	TOT. ASSETS ($mill.)	TOT. DEP. ($mill.)	RET. ON EQUITY %	RET. ON ASSETS %	EQUITY/ ASSETS %	EARN. PER SH.$	TANG. BK. VAL.$	DIV. PER SH.$	PRICE RANGE	AVG. P/E RATIO
p12/31/02	499.2	418.8	5 6 232.9							5 6 3.15		1.15	54.60 - 35.10	14.2
12/31/01	481.2	354.9	5 207.3	8,244.2	11,358.7	7,099.0	22.6	1.8	8.1	5 2.70	9.91	1.00	51.12 - 32.81	15.5
12/31/00	438.5	325.2	186.2	8,546.7	11,197.5	6,891.8	20.5	1.7	8.1	2.35	9.29	0.82	45.56 - 18.00	13.5
12/31/99	424.2	306.6	166.0	7,895.7	10,661.7	6,584.8	20.5	1.6	7.6	2.00	7.78	0.72	30.69 - 21.69	13.1
12/31/98	425.7	280.3	156.2	7,141.2	10,164.6	6,715.1	18.5	1.5	8.3	1.76	7.74	0.61	37.25 - 15.81	15.1
12/31/97	393.6	215.0	145.1	7,174.9	9,744.7	6,907.3	15.2	1.5	9.8	1.61	7.94	0.47	34.38 - 18.75	15.7
12/31/96	340.1	147.8	4 85.7	5,080.1	7,091.0	4,977.6	15.6	1.2	7.8	4 1.21	7.36	0.36	22.69 - 14.81	15.5
12/31/95	319.2	126.5	1 2 3 82.7	5,350.6	7,240.2	5,191.6	15.7	1.1	7.3	1 2 3 0.86	6.84	0.38	16.69 - 9.28	15.2
12/31/94	205.1	112.3	57.4	3,102.8	5,068.7	3,819.6	17.5	1.1	6.5	1.16	6.20	0.25	10.78 - 7.13	7.7
12/31/93	184.4	115.8	2 38.0	2,758.8	5,025.5	4,102.6	12.8	0.8	5.9	2 0.76	5.36	0.17	10.00 - 6.94	11.1

Statistics are as originally reported. Adj. for 2-for-1 stk. spl., 12/97 & 12/95. ① Bef. extraord. chrg., $963,000. ② Incl. merger-related expenses, 1995, $21.7 mill.; 1993, $5.5 mill. ③ Incl. cancel. costs early termination int.-rate exchg. chrg. $4.4 mill. ④ Incl. chrg. of $34.8 mill. for FDIC special assessment ⑤ Incl. a pre-tax gain on the sale of branches of $2.0 mill., 2002; $3.3 mill., 2001. ⑥ Incl gains on sales of securities avail. for sale of $11.5 mill.

OFFICERS:
W. A. Cooper, Chmn., C.E.O.
T. A. Cusick, Vice-Chmn., C.O.O.
L. A. Nagorske, Pres.
INVESTOR CONTACT: Jason E. Korstange, Senior VP, Investor Relations, (612) 745-2755
PRINCIPAL OFFICE: 200 Lake Street East Wayzata, MN 55391-1693

TELEPHONE NUMBER: (612) 661-6500
FAX: (612) 332-1753
WEB: www.tcfbank.com
NO. OF EMPLOYEES: 5,100 full-time (approx.); 2,900 part-time (approx.)
SHAREHOLDERS: 11,400 (approx.)
ANNUAL MEETING: In May
INCORPORATED: DE, Nov., 1987

INSTITUTIONAL HOLDINGS:
No. of Institutions: 257
Shares Held: 44,875,032
% Held: 60.5
INDUSTRY: Federal savings institutions (SIC: 6035)
TRANSFER AGENT(S): BankBoston, N.A., Boston, MA

TECO ENERGY, INC.

EXCH.	SYM.	REC. PRICE	P/E RATIO	YLD.	MKT. CAP.	RANGE (52-WK.)	'02 Y/E PR.	DIV. ACH.
NYSE	TE	11.08 (2/28/03)	5.4	12.8%	$1.55 bill.	29.05 - 10.02	15.47	43 yrs.

MEDIUM GRADE. FOR 2003, EARNINGS ARE EXPECTED TO BE BETWEEN $1.75 AND $2.00 PER SHARE.

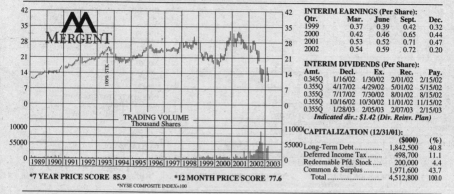

INTERIM EARNINGS (Per Share):

Qtr.	Mar.	June	Sept.	Dec.
1999	0.37	0.39	0.42	0.32
2000	0.42	0.46	0.65	0.44
2001	0.53	0.52	0.71	0.47
2002	0.54	0.59	0.72	0.20

INTERIM DIVIDENDS (Per Share):

Amt.	Decl.	Ex.	Rec.	Pay.
0.345Q	1/16/02	1/30/02	2/01/02	2/15/02
0.355Q	4/17/02	4/29/02	5/01/02	5/15/02
0.355Q	7/17/02	7/30/02	8/01/02	8/15/02
0.355Q	10/16/02	10/30/02	11/01/02	11/15/02
0.355Q	1/28/03	2/05/03	2/07/03	2/15/03

Indicated div.: $1.42 (Div. Reinv. Plan)

TRADING VOLUME
Thousand Shares

CAPITALIZATION (12/31/01):

	($000)	(%)
Long-Term Debt	1,842,500	40.8
Deferred Income Tax	498,700	11.1
Redeemable Pfd. Stock	200,000	4.4
Common & Surplus	1,971,600	43.7
Total	4,512,800	100.0

*7 YEAR PRICE SCORE 85.9   ***12 MONTH PRICE SCORE 77.6**

*NYSE COMPOSITE INDEX=100

BUSINESS:

TECO Energy, Inc. is a public utility holding company, which operates through the following segments: Tampa Electric Co. (57.6% of 2002 revenues) provides retail electric service to more than 575,000 customers in West Central Florida. Peoples Gas System (8.1%), a division of Tampa Electric, is engaged in the purchase, distribution and marketing of natural gas for more than 272,000 residential, commercial, industrial and electric power generation customers in Florida. TECO Coal Corp. (19.0%) owns mineral rights, and owns or operates surface and underground mines, synthetic fuel facilities, and coal processing and loading facilities in KY, TN and VA. TECO Power Services Corp. (8.4%) has interests in independent power projects in AK, AZ, FL, MS, TX, VA, HI and Guatemala. TECO Transport Corp. (5.2%) transports, stores and transfers coal and other dry-bulk commodities. Other diversified businesses accounted for 1.7% of 2002 revenues.

RECENT DEVELOPMENTS:

For the year ended 12/31/02, the Company reported income from continuing operations of $298.2 million compared with $273.8 million in the previous year. Results for 2002 included an after-tax debt refinancing charge of $20.9 million and an after-tax asset valuation charge of $5.8 million. Earnings excluded income from discontinued operations of $31.9 million and $29.9 million in 2002 and 2001, respectively. Income from regulated operations climbed 10.7% to $196.0 million, reflecting increased sales and customer growth at Tampa Electric and Peoples Gas System as well as lower short-term borrowing costs. Income from unregulated operations rose 5.7% to $102.2 million. Total revenues increased 7.5% to $2.68 billion from $2.49 billion a year earlier.

PROSPECTS:

The Company has completed more than two-thirds of its previously announced plan to raise cash and reduce spending by a total of $900.0 million. Accomplishments under the plan include the sale of substantially all of Teco Coalbed Methane's assets in Alabama to the Municipal Gas Authority of Georgia for proceeds of $140.0 million, reductions in capital spending of $250.0 million, and proceeds from newly issued common equity of $207.0 million. For 2003, earnings are expected to be between $1.75 and $2.00 per share.

ANNUAL FINANCIAL DATA:

FISCAL YEAR	TOT. REVS. ($mill.)	NET INC. ($mill.)	TOT. ASSETS ($mill.)	OPER. PROFIT %	NET PROFIT %	NET INC./ NET PROP. %	NET INC./ TOT. CAP. %	RET. ON EQUITY %	ACCUM. DEPR./ GROSS PROP. %	EARN. PER SH.$	TANG. BK. VAL.$	DIV. PER SH.$	DIV. PAYOUT %	PRICE RANGE	AVG. P/E RATIO	AVG. YIELD %
p12/31/02	2,675.8	⑥ 298.2		11.1						⑥ 1.95	1.41			29.05 - 10.02	10.0	7.2
12/31/01	2,648.6	⑤ 303.7	6,722.1	16.0	11.5	6.3	6.7	15.4	35.9	⑤ 2.24	12.94	1.37	61.2	32.97 - 24.75	12.9	4.7
12/31/00	2,295.1	④ 250.9	5,676.2	18.0	10.9	6.3	7.1	16.7	39.5	④ 1.97	12.63	1.33	67.5	33.19 - 17.25	12.8	5.3
12/31/99	1,983.0	②③ 200.9	4,690.1	21.4	10.1	5.5	6.4	14.2	40.2	②③ 1.53	11.19	1.28	84.0	28.00 - 18.38	15.2	5.5
12/31/98	1,958.1	②③ 200.4	4,179.3	20.2	10.2	6.1	6.1	13.3	40.9	②③ 1.52	11.42	1.23	80.6	30.63 - 24.75	18.2	4.4
12/31/97	1,862.3	② 211.4	3,960.4	22.2	11.4	6.5	7.1	14.6	39.6	② 1.61	11.04	1.17	72.4	28.00 - 22.75	15.8	4.6
12/31/96	1,473.0	200.7	3,560.7	23.3	13.6	6.8	7.4	15.7	37.4	1.71	10.73	1.10	64.6	27.00 - 23.00	14.6	4.4
12/31/95	1,392.3	186.1	3,473.4	22.8	13.4	6.5	7.1	15.2	36.0	1.60	10.00	1.05	65.5	25.75 - 20.00	14.3	4.6
12/31/94	1,350.9	② 153.2	3,312.2	20.0	11.3	5.8	6.2	14.4	36.0	② 1.32	8.65	1.00	75.6	22.63 - 18.13	15.4	4.9
12/31/93	1,283.9	② 150.3	3,127.8	22.6	11.7	6.1	5.8	12.9	35.4	② 1.30	9.62	0.95	72.9	25.88 - 20.19	17.7	4.1

Statistics are as originally reported. Adj. for stk. split: 2-for-1, 8/93 ① Bef. acctg. credit $11.2 mill. ② Incl. non-recurr. chrg. $16.1 mill. 1999; $25.9 mill., 1998; $25.0 mill., 1994 ③ Bef. disc. oper. loss $14.8 mill., 1999; gain $6.1 mill., 1998; loss $9.5 mill., 1997 ④ Incl. after-tax gain $8.3 mill. & nonrecurr. chrgs. $9.0 mill. ⑤ Incl. after-tax write-down of $6.1 mill. ⑥ Bef. gain from disc. opers. of $31.9 mill.; incl. aft.-tax chrgs. of $20.9 mill. for debt refin. and $5.8 mill. for asset valuation.

OFFICERS:
R. D. Fagan, Chmn., Pres., C.E.O.
G. L. Gillette, Sr. V.P., C.F.O.
INVESTOR CONTACT: Mark M. Kane, Investor Relations, (813) 228-1772
PRINCIPAL OFFICE: 702 N. Franklin Street, Tampa, FL 33602

TELEPHONE NUMBER: (813) 228-4111
FAX: (813) 228-1670
WEB: www.tecoenergy.com
NO. OF EMPLOYEES: 6,315
SHAREHOLDERS: 22,989
ANNUAL MEETING: In April
INCORPORATED: FL, Jan., 1981

INSTITUTIONAL HOLDINGS:
No. of Institutions: 356
Shares Held: 70,612,180
% Held: 40.2
INDUSTRY: Electric services (SIC: 4911)
TRANSFER AGENT(S): EquiServe Trust Company, N.A., Providence, RI

TEKTRONIX, INC.

EXCH.	SYM.	REC. PRICE	P/E RATIO	YLD.	MKT. CAP.	RANGE (52-WK.)	'02 Y/E PR.
NYSE	TEK	16.52 (2/28/03)	34.4	...	$1.50 bill.	26.60 - 14.64	18.19

LOWER MEDIUM GRADE. THE COMPANY EXPECTS SALES IN THE THIRD QUARTER OF FISCAL 2003 TO BE DOWN APPROXIMATELY 3.0% FROM THE SAME PERIOD OF 2002.

*7 YEAR PRICE SCORE 101.7   ***12 MONTH PRICE SCORE 98.5**
*NYSE COMPOSITE INDEX=100

INTERIM EARNINGS (Per Share):

Qtr.	Aug.	Nov.	Feb.	May
1997-98	0.27	d0.21	0.34	0.42
1998-99	d0.05	d0.91	0.16	0.27
1999-00	d0.09	0.10	d0.18	0.32
2000-01	0.28	0.38	0.43	0.37
2001-02	0.09	0.09	0.11	0.07
2002-03	0.22	0.08	...	...

INTERIM DIVIDENDS (Per Share):

Amt.	Decl.	Ex.	Rec.	Pay.
	No dividends paid.			

CAPITALIZATION (5/25/02):

	($000)	(%)
Long-Term Debt	57,302	5.8
Common & Surplus	927,156	94.2
Total	984,458	100.0

BUSINESS:

Tektronix, Inc. is a test, measurement, and monitoring company providing measurement applications to the semiconductor, computer and telecommunications industries. TEK enables its customers to design, deploy, and manage next generation global communications networks and Internet technologies. Measurement business products include general purpose test instruments, radio frequency and wireless instruments, telecommunications instruments, and television test instruments. Geographic revenues for 5/25/02 were derived: U.S., 49.8%; and international, 50.2%. In January 2000, TEK sold its color printing business to Xerox Corporation.

RECENT DEVELOPMENTS:

For the quarter ended 11/30/02, earnings from continuing operations slipped 6.1% to $6.9 million compared with $7.4 million in the same period of 2001. Earnings were hampered by difficult market conditions. Results for 2002 and 2001 included business realignment costs of $3.3 million and $4.4 million, and a gain of $492,000 and a loss of $3.4 million, respectively, from the sale of assets. Results for 2002 also included an acquisition-related charge of $1.8 million. In addition, results for 2002 and 2001 excluded a loss of $2.2 million and a gain of $577,000, respectively, from discontinued operations. Net sales declined 1.4% to $204.6 million from $207.6 million in the prior-year period. Gross profit was $101.1 million, down 2.0% from $103.1 million the previous year. Operating income increased 14.1% to $6.1 million from $5.4 million a year earlier.

PROSPECTS:

Looking ahead, the Company expects sales in the third quarter of fiscal 2003 to be down about 3.0% from the same period of 2002. Operating margins are anticipated to be in the low-to-mid single digits, excluding non-recurring items of approximately $15.0 million. The Company expects non-recurring costs in the third quarter largely associated with reductions in staffing levels in Japan. Going forward, the Company plans to continue to structure its business to drive operational efficiency and increase market share.

ANNUAL FINANCIAL DATA:

FISCAL YEAR	TOT. REVS. ($mill.)	NET INC. ($mill.)	TOT. ASSETS ($mill.)	OPER. PROFIT %	NET PROFIT %	RET. ON EQUITY %	RET. ON ASSETS %	CURR. RATIO	EARN. PER SH.$	CASH FL. PER SH.$	TANG. BK. VAL.$	DIV. PER SH.$	PRICE RANGE	AVG. P/E RATIO	AVG. YIELD %
⑥ 5/25/02	843.3	⑤ 30.5	1,384.2	3.2	3.6	3.3	2.2	2.7	⑤ 0.33	0.77	10.24	...	40.50 - 16.75	86.7	...
5/26/01	1,235.3	④ 140.1	1,522.1	15.1	11.3	13.8	9.2	3.0	④ 1.46	1.92	11.01	0.06	43.66 - 17.19	20.8	0.2
5/27/00	1,120.6	③ 12.7	1,534.6	0.4	1.1	1.3	0.8	3.4	③ 0.13	0.59	10.28	0.24	20.00 - 8.78	110.6	1.7
5/29/99	1,861.5	② d51.2	1,359.4	...	...	...	...	1.4	② d0.53	0.25	6.63	0.24	24.09 - 6.84	...	1.6
5/31/98	2,085.8	82.3	1,376.8	5.5	3.9	10.5	6.0	2.1	0.80	1.44	7.80	0.21	23.21 - 16.08	24.6	1.1
5/31/97	1,940.1	① 114.8	1,316.7	8.5	5.9	14.9	8.7	2.5	① 1.16	1.76	7.70	0.20	17.42 - 9.92	11.8	1.5
5/25/96	1,768.9	99.6	1,328.5	8.1	5.6	14.7	7.5	2.1	1.00	1.41	6.89	0.20	20.63 - 10.46	15.5	1.3
5/27/95	1,471.8	81.3	1,209.7	7.8	5.5	13.5	6.7	1.7	0.88	1.31	6.39	0.20	13.50 - 7.88	12.2	1.9
5/28/94	1,318.0	60.7	991.1	6.6	4.6	12.9	6.1	2.0	0.67	1.27	5.17	0.20	9.29 - 6.71	12.0	2.5
5/29/93	1,302.4	d58.4	984.5	...	...	...	...	1.5	d0.65	0.05	4.76	0.20	7.63 - 5.50	...	3.0

Statistics are as originally reported. Adj. for 3-for-2 split, 10/31/00 & 10/97. Fiscal year ends 5/31 of following year. ① Incl. $40.5 mill. non-recur. restr. chg. for in-process R&D. ② Incl. $84.4 mill. non-recur. chgs. ③ Incl. $31.6 mill. pre-tax chg. fr. sale of bus., $37.7 mill. non-recur. chg. & excl. $196.4 mill. fr. disc. ops. ④ Incl. $10.0 mill. in non-recur. credits, gain of $1.5 mill. fr. sale of video & networking divison and $1.8 mill. loss fr. asset dispositions. ⑤ Incl. $818,000 gain fr. sale of video & networking div. & $27.0 mill non-recur. chg.; excl. $2.2 mill. gain fr. disc. ops. ⑥ Results were hampered by the economic downturn in the optical design market and the telecommunications industry.

OFFICERS:
R. H. Wills, Chmn., Pres., C.E.O.
C. L. Slade, Sr. V.P., C.F.O.
J. F. Dalton, V.P., Sec., Gen. Couns.
INVESTOR CONTACT: Colin Slade, V.P., C.F.O., (503) 627-7727
PRINCIPAL OFFICE: 14200 S.W. Karl Braun Drive, Beaverton, OR 97077

TELEPHONE NUMBER: (503) 627-7111
FAX: (503) 685-4104
WEB: www.tektronix.com
NO. OF EMPLOYEES: 4,301 (avg.)
SHAREHOLDERS: 3,038
ANNUAL MEETING: In Sept.
INCORPORATED: OR, Jan., 1946

INSTITUTIONAL HOLDINGS:
No. of Institutions: 197
Shares Held: 74,726,584
% Held: 86.0
INDUSTRY: Instruments to measure electricity (SIC: 3825)
TRANSFER AGENT(S): Mellon Investor Services, South Hackensack, NJ

TELEFLEX INC.

EXCH.	SYM.	REC. PRICE	P/E RATIO	YLD.	MKT. CAP.	RANGE (52-WK.)	'02 Y/E PR.	DIV. ACH.
NYSE	TFX	37.20 (2/28/03)	11.8	1.9%	$1.45 bill.	59.35 - 36.58	42.89	25 yrs.

UPPER MEDIUM GRADE. THE COMPANY EXPECTS REVENUES AND EARNINGS IN 2003 TO INCREASE AT A SINGLE-DIGIT PERCENTAGE RATE.

*7 YEAR PRICE SCORE 134.9   ***12 MONTH PRICE SCORE 92.5**
*NYSE COMPOSITE INDEX=100

INTERIM EARNINGS (Per Share):

Qtr.	Mar.	June	Sept.	Dec.
1997	0.45	0.49	0.36	0.56
1998	0.52	0.55	0.42	0.66
1999	0.60	0.67	0.49	0.71
2000	0.70	0.76	0.56	0.81
2001	0.77	0.79	0.56	0.74
2002	0.77	0.84	0.66	0.88

INTERIM DIVIDENDS (Per Share):

Amt.	Decl.	Ex.	Rec.	Pay.
0.17Q	2/04/02	2/21/02	2/25/02	3/15/02
0.18Q	4/26/02	5/22/02	5/24/02	6/14/02
0.18Q	8/05/02	8/22/02	8/26/02	9/16/02
0.18Q	11/04/02	11/21/02	11/25/02	12/16/02
0.18Q	1/27/03	2/21/03	2/25/03	3/14/03

Indicated div.: $0.72 (Div. Reinv. Plan)

CAPITALIZATION (12/31/01):

	($000)	(%)
Long-Term Debt	228,180	22.7
Common & Surplus	778,143	77.3
Total	1,006,323	100.0

BUSINESS:

Teleflex Inc. operates in three segments. Commercial Products (52.3% of 2002 sales and 48.4% of operating profit) designs and manufactures proprietary mechanical controls for the automotive market; mechanical, electrical and hydraulic controls, and electronics for the pleasure marine market; and proprietary products for fluid transfer and industrial applications. Medical Products (21.6%, 35.0%)

manufactures and distributes a broad range of invasive disposable and reusable devices worldwide. Aerospace Products (26.1%, 16.6%) serves the aerospace and turbine engine markets. Its businesses design and manufacture precision controls and cargo systems for aviation; provide coating and repair services and manufactured components for users of both flight and land-based turbine engines.

RECENT DEVELOPMENTS:

For the year ended 12/29/02, net income rose 11.5% to $125.3 million compared with $112.3 million in 2001. Earnings benefited from the Company's diverse portfolio and strong performances in several of its businesses. Results for 2002 included a non-operating gain of $10.1 million, while results for 2001 included goodwill amortiza-

tion of $12.9 million. Revenues climbed 9.0% to $2.08 billion from $1.91 billion the previous year. Commercial Products segment revenue grew 19.5% to $1.09 billion, while Medical Products segment revenue climbed 4.5% to $448.7 million. Aerospace Products segment revenue declined 4.5% to $542.1 million.

PROSPECTS:

Looking ahead, the Company expects challenging business conditions to continue in 2003 for the aerospace market. In addition, the Company assumes there will be no significant change in the economy in 2003. As a result, TFX expects revenues and earnings for 2003 to increase at a single-digit percentage rate. Moreover, earnings for the first quarter of

2003 are expected to be down versus the same period of 2002, but should increase in the subsequent quarters as cost-reduction efforts take effect and new product introductions are launched. Separately, on 2/12/03, the Company acquired Megatech Electro, Inc., a designer and manufacturer of electronic and electromechanical products.

ANNUAL FINANCIAL DATA:

FISCAL YEAR	TOT. REVS. ($mill.)	NET INC. ($mill.)	TOT. ASSETS ($mill.)	OPER. PROFIT %	NET PROFIT %	RET. ON EQUITY %	RET. ON ASSETS %	CURR. RATIO	EARN. PER SH. $	CASH FL. PER SH. $	TANG. BK. VAL. $	DIV. PER SH. $	PRICE RANGE	AVG. P/E RATIO	AVG. YIELD %
p12/29/02	2,076.2	①125.3							①3.15			0.71	59.35 - 40.64	15.9	1.4
12/31/01	1,905.0	112.3	1,635.0	8.4	5.9	14.4	6.9	1.5	2.86	5.21	19.99	0.66	50.99 - 34.00	14.9	1.6
12/31/00	1,764.5	109.2	1,401.3	9.0	6.2	15.8	7.8	1.7	2.83	4.83	18.01	0.58	45.38 - 26.13	12.6	1.6
12/26/99	1,601.1	95.2	1,263.4	8.9	5.9	15.8	7.5	1.8	2.47	4.22	15.85	0.51	50.44 - 28.88	16.1	1.3
12/27/98	1,437.6	82.6	1,215.9	8.7	5.7	15.4	6.8	2.0	2.15	3.71	14.21	0.45	46.38 - 29.50	17.6	1.2
12/28/97	1,145.8	70.1	1,079.2	9.3	6.1	15.1	6.5	1.9	1.86	3.13	12.49	0.39	39.75 - 23.19	16.9	1.2
12/29/96	931.2	57.2	857.9	9.3	6.1	14.0	6.7	2.4	1.58	2.65	11.30	0.34	26.13 - 18.94	14.3	1.5
12/31/95	912.7	48.9	785.2	8.1	5.4	13.8	6.2	2.3	1.38	2.43	10.28	0.30	22.88 - 17.19	14.6	1.5
12/25/94	812.7	41.2	710.8	7.8	5.1	13.3	5.8	2.3	1.18	2.12	8.94	0.26	20.13 - 15.88	15.3	1.4
12/26/93	666.8	33.7	640.6	7.8	5.1	12.5	5.3	2.1	0.98	1.79	7.90	0.23	19.13 - 13.88	16.9	1.4

Statistics are as originally reported. Adj. for 2-for-1 split, 6/97. ① Incl. $10.1 mill. non-operating gain.

OFFICERS:
L. K. Black, Chmn.
J. P. Black, Pres., C.E.O.
H. Zuber, Jr., Exec. V.P., C.F.O.
INVESTOR CONTACT: Janine Dusossoit, V.P., Investor Relations, (610) 834-6362
PRINCIPAL OFFICE: 630 West Germantown Pike, Suite 450, Plymouth Meeting, PA 19462

TELEPHONE NUMBER: (610) 834-6301
FAX: (610) 834-8228
WEB: www.teleflex.com
NO. OF EMPLOYEES: 17,600 (approx.)
SHAREHOLDERS: 1,186
ANNUAL MEETING: In Apr.
INCORPORATED: DE, June, 1943

INSTITUTIONAL HOLDINGS:
No. of Institutions: 228
Shares Held: 24,974,419
% Held: 63.5
INDUSTRY: Surgical and medical instruments (SIC: 3841)
TRANSFER AGENT(S): American Stock Transfer & Trust Company, New York, NY

TEMPLE-INLAND INC.

EXCH.	SYM.	REC. PRICE	P/E RATIO	YLD.	MKT. CAP.	RANGE (52-WK.)	'02 Y/E PR.
NYSE	TIN	41.90 (2/28/03)	33.5	3.2%	$2.07 bill.	59.99 - 32.69	44.81

MEDIUM GRADE. THE COMPANY EXPECTS ANNUAL SAVINGS OF ABOUT $35.0 MILLION FROM ANNOUNCED CONSOLIDATION AND SUPPLY CHAIN INITIATIVES.

*7 YEAR PRICE SCORE 95.0　　　***12 MONTH PRICE SCORE 97.2**

NYSE COMPOSITE INDEX=100

INTERIM EARNINGS (Per Share):

Qtr.	Mar.	June	Sept.	Dec.
1998	0.47	0.62	0.44	d0.32
1999	0.33	0.74	1.07	1.03
2000	1.04	1.20	0.87	0.72
2001	0.24	0.58	0.90	0.54
2002	0.30	0.31	0.28	0.36

INTERIM DIVIDENDS (Per Share):

Amt.	Decl.	Ex.	Rec.	Pay.
0.32Q	2/01/02	2/27/02	3/01/02	3/15/02
0.32Q	5/03/02	5/29/02	5/31/02	6/14/02
0.32Q	8/02/02	8/28/02	8/30/02	9/13/02
0.32Q	11/01/02	11/26/02	11/29/02	12/13/02
0.34Q	2/07/03	2/26/03	2/28/03	3/14/03

Indicated div.: $1.36 (Div. Reinv. Plan)

CAPITALIZATION (12/29/01):

	($000)	(%)
Long-Term Debt	4,988,000	69.4
Deferred Income Tax	304,000	4.2
Common & Surplus	1,896,000	26.4
Total	7,188,000	100.0

BUSINESS:

Temple-Inland Inc. is a major manufacturer of corrugated packaging and building products, with financial services operations in mortgage and consumer banking. The corrugated packaging group (57.3% of 2002 revenues) manufactures corrugated packaging, and produced annual linerboard and medium mill capacity of about 3.3 million tons, as of 6/30/02. TIN's financial services group (25.3%) consists of savings bank, mortgage banking, real estate, and insurance brokerage activities. TIN's building products group (17.4%) manufactures products including lumber, particleboard, medium density fiberboard, gypsum wallboard and fiberboard. Forest resources include approximately 2.1 million acres of timberland as of 2/7/03. On 4/5/02, TIN acquired Gaylord Container Corporation for about $847.0 million.

RECENT DEVELOPMENTS:

For the year ended 12/28/02, income decreased 41.4% to $65.0 million, before a loss from discontinued operations of $1.0 million and an accounting change charge of $11.0 million, compared with income of $111.0 million, before an accounting change charge of $2.0 million, in 2001. Results for 2002 included a special after-tax charge of $14.0 million, while results for 2001 included a special after-tax gain of $9.0 million. Total revenues climbed 10.0% to $4.52 billion from $4.11 billion a year earlier. Corrugated packaging group operating income fell 27.1% to $78.0 million, while the Financial services group operating income decreased 7.1% to $171.0 million. Building products group operating income was $49.0 million, up from $13.0 million in the same period a year earlier.

PROSPECTS:

During the first half of 2003, TIN expects earnings to be adversely affected by difficult market conditions, higher pension expense and an anticipated increase in energy costs. Late in 2002, TIN announced a new initiative to improve organizational effectiveness and reduce costs, including consolidating corporate administrative functions in Austin, and implementing a shared services concept throughout the entire company. Consequently, TIN expects annual savings of about $35.0 million, with the majority of savings to be in place and to occur in 2004.

ANNUAL FINANCIAL DATA:

FISCAL YEAR	TOT. REVS. ($mill.)	NET INC. ($mill.)	TOT. ASSETS ($mill.)	OPER. PROFIT %	NET PROFIT %	RET. ON EQUITY %	RET. ON ASSETS %	CURR. RATIO	EARN. PER SH.$	CASH FL. PER SH.$	TANG. BK. VAL.$	DIV. PER SH.$	PRICE RANGE	AVG. P/E RATIO	AVG. YIELD %
p12/28/02	4,518.0	⑥ 65.0							⑥ 1.25			1.28	59.99 - 32.69	37.1	2.8
12/29/01	4,172.0	⑤ 111.0	18,687.0	6.6	2.7	5.9	0.6	0.1	⑤ 2.26	7.42	34.64	1.28	62.15 - 40.35	22.7	2.5
12/31/00	4,286.0	④ 195.0	18,142.0	9.7	4.5	10.6	1.1	0.1	④ 3.83	8.80	37.28	1.28	67.69 - 34.63	13.4	2.5
1/01/00	3,682.0	③ 191.0	16,186.0	10.5	5.2	9.9	1.2	1.8	③ 3.43	7.01	35.55	1.28	77.50 - 53.63	19.1	2.0
1/02/99	3,740.0	② 67.0	15,990.0	6.0	1.8	3.4	0.4	0.1	② 1.21	7.85	35.94	1.28	67.25 - 42.69	45.4	2.3
12/31/97	3,625.0	51.0	14,364.0	5.5	1.4	2.5	0.4	0.1	0.90	6.19	36.32	1.28	69.44 - 49.63	66.1	2.2
12/28/96	3,460.0	133.0	12,947.0	7.5	3.8	6.6	1.0	0.1	2.39	7.39	36.37	1.24	55.38 - 39.75	19.9	2.6
12/31/95	3,460.0	281.0	12,764.0	14.5	8.1	14.2	2.2	0.1	5.01	9.20	35.27	1.14	55.75 - 41.50	9.7	2.3
12/31/94	2,938.0	131.0	12,251.0	8.7	4.5	7.3	1.1	0.2	2.35	6.27	31.84	1.02	56.75 - 43.00	21.2	2.0
1/01/94	2,736.0	① 67.0	11,959.0	5.9	2.4	3.9	0.6	0.2	① 1.21	4.95	30.91	1.00	52.50 - 37.25	37.1	2.2

Statistics are as originally reported. ① Bef. extraord. cr. of $50.0 mill. ($0.90/sh.) due to acctg. changes. ② Incl. nonrecur. charges of $32.1 mill. ③ Bef. discont. oper. of the bleached paperboard operation of $92.4 mill. ④ Incl. after-tax nonrecur. chrg. of $9.0 mill., 2000. ⑤ Incl. nonrecur. credits of $9.0 mill., excl. acct. change chrg. of $2.0 mill. ⑥ Bef. loss fr. dis. op. of $1.0 mill. & acctg. change chrg. of $11.0 mill.; incl. a special after-tax charge of $14.0 mill.

OFFICERS:
K. M. Jastrow, II, Chmn., C.E.O.
R. D. Levy, C.F.O
D. W. Turpin, Treas.
INVESTOR CONTACT: Doyle R. Simmons, (512) 434-3737
PRINCIPAL OFFICE: 1300 MoPac Expressway, Austin, TX 78746

TELEPHONE NUMBER: (512) 434-5800
FAX: (512) 434-8001
WEB: www.templeinland.com
NO. OF EMPLOYEES: 16,500 (approx.)
SHAREHOLDERS: 5,560 (approx.)
ANNUAL MEETING: In May
INCORPORATED: DE, 1983

INSTITUTIONAL HOLDINGS:
No. of Institutions: 255
Shares Held: 44,657,358
% Held: 83.1
INDUSTRY: Corrugated and solid fiber boxes (SIC: 2653)
TRANSFER AGENT(S): First Chicago Trust Company of New York, Jersey City, NJ

TENET HEALTHCARE CORPORATION

EXCH.	SYM.	REC. PRICE	P/E RATIO	YLD.	MKT. CAP.	RANGE (52-WK.)	'02 Y/E PR.
NYSE	THC	18.17 (2/28/03)	7.2	...	$8.88 bill.	52.50 - 13.70	16.40

MEDIUM GRADE. THE COMPANY ANNOUNCED INITIATIVES TO REDUCE OPERATING EXPENSES.

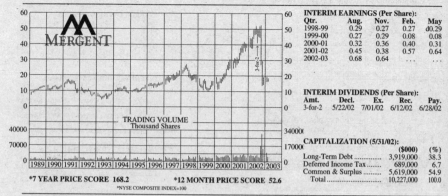

*7 YEAR PRICE SCORE 168.2   ***12 MONTH PRICE SCORE 52.6**

NYSE COMPOSITE INDEX=100

INTERIM EARNINGS (Per Share):

Qtr.	Aug.	Nov.	Feb.	May
1998-99	0.29	0.27	0.27	d0.29
1999-00	0.27	0.29	0.08	0.08
2000-01	0.32	0.36	0.40	0.31
2001-02	0.45	0.38	0.57	0.64
2002-03	0.68	0.64	...	...

INTERIM DIVIDENDS (Per Share):

Amt.	Decl.	Ex.	Rec.	Pay.
3-for-2	5/22/02	7/01/02	6/12/02	6/28/02

CAPITALIZATION (5/31/02):

	($000)	(%)
Long-Term Debt	3,919,000	38.3
Deferred Income Tax	689,000	6.7
Common & Surplus	5,619,000	54.9
Total	10,227,000	100.0

BUSINESS:

Tenet Healthcare Corporation (formerly National Medical Enterprises, Inc.) is the nation's second largest investor-owned health care services company. As of 1/13/03, THC owned and operated 114 acute care hospitals with 27,851 licensed beds in 16 states. The Company's related health care facilities included a small number of rehabilitation hospital, specialty hospitals, long-term-care facilities, a psychiatric facility and medical office buildings located on the same campus as,or nearby, its general hospitals, physician practices and various ancillary health care businesses, including outpatient surgery centers, home health care agencies, occupational and rural health care clinics and health maintenance organizations.

RECENT DEVELOPMENTS:

For the quarter ended 11/30/02, net income more than tripled to $315.0 million compared with $89.0 million in the corresponding period of the previous year. The improvement in earnings was primarily attributed to the strength of the Company's core business. Results for 2002 included a pre-tax impairment of investment securities charge of $64.0 million, while 2001 results included a pre-tax impairment of long-lived assets charge of $99.0 million and a loss of $165.0 million from the early extinguishment of debt. Net operating revenues advanced 11.3% to $3.78 billion.

PROSPECTS:

The U.S. Justice Department suing the Company for as much as $323.0 million for allegedly overcharging Medicare for certain procedures in order to inflate its revenue. Separately, THC announced that it will divest or consolidate 14 hospitals with aggregate annual revenues of approximately $933.0 million that no longer fit its core operating strategy. Meanwhile, retroactive to December 31, 2002, THC has changed from a non-standard fiscal year ending May 31 to a calendar year ended December 31.

ANNUAL FINANCIAL DATA:

FISCAL YEAR	TOT. REVS. ($mill.)	NET INC. ($mill.)	TOT. ASSETS ($mill.)	OPER. PROFIT %	NET PROFIT %	RET. ON EQUITY %	RET. ON ASSETS %	CURR. RATIO	EARN. PER SH. $	CASH FL. PER SH. $	TANG. BK. VAL. $	DIV. PER SH. $	PRICE RANGE	AVG. P/E RATIO
5/31/02	13,913.0	⑨ 1,025.0	13,814.0	15.1	7.4	18.2	7.4	1.3	⑨ 2.04	3.24	4.39	...	41.86 - 25.33	16.5
5/31/01	12,053.0	⑧ 678.0	12,995.0	12.8	5.6	13.3	5.2	1.5	⑧ 1.39	2.51	3.44	0.01	30.50 - 11.29	15.1
5/31/00	11,414.0	⑦ 340.0	13,161.0	9.2	3.0	8.4	2.6	1.9	⑦ 0.72	1.85	1.57	...	18.13 - 10.25	19.7
5/31/99	10,880.0	⑥ 249.0	13,771.0	8.6	2.3	6.4	1.8	2.0	⑥ 0.53	1.71	1.01	...	27.29 - 15.83	40.9
5/31/98	9,895.0	⑤ 378.0	12,833.0	11.4	3.8	10.6	2.9	1.6	⑤ 0.81	1.79	0.31	...	23.25 - 14.25	23.1
5/31/97	8,691.0	④ d73.0	11,705.0	4.8	...	...	...	1.3	④ d0.16	0.81	0.17	...	15.83 - 12.08	...
5/31/96	5,559.0	③ 398.0	8,332.0	12.4	7.2	15.1	4.8	1.4	④ 1.27	2.29	0.05	...	13.83 - 8.92	9.0
5/31/95	3,318.0	② 194.0	7,918.0	11.8	5.8	9.8	2.5	1.2	⑤ 0.73	1.47	...	...	13.00 - 8.33	14.6
5/31/94	2,967.0	② 216.0	3,697.0	10.6	7.3	16.4	5.8	0.9	② 0.86	1.65	4.87	...	9.58 - 4.33	8.1
5/31/93	3,762.0	160.0	4,173.0	10.6	4.3	9.1	3.8	1.2	0.64	1.44	6.16	...	12.08 - 6.42	14.5

Statistics are as originally reported. Adj. for 3-for-2 stk. split, 6/28/02. ① Incl. net. chrgs. of $353.0 mill.; excl. acctg. chrg. of $19.0 mill. ② Incl. non-recurr. chrg. $221.0 mill. & loss of $17.0 mill.; bef. extraord. chrg. $117.0 mill. ③ Incl. non-recurr. chrg. $740.0 mill. & loss on disp. $18.0 mill.; bef. disc. loss $134.0 mill. & extraord. chrg. $47.0 mill. ④ Incl. gain on disp. $329.0 mill.; bef. disc. oper. loss $25.0 mill. & extraord. chrg. $23.0 mill. ⑤ Incl. non-recurr. chrg. $37.0 mill.; bef. disc. oper. loss $9.0 mill. & extraord. chrg. $20.0 mill. ⑥ Bef. disc. oper. loss $701.0 mill. & acctg. cr$60.0 mill. ⑦ Bef. acctg. chrg. of $19.0 mill. & disc. opers. loss of $19.0 mill.; Incl. net chrg. of $344.0 mill. ⑧ Bef. extraord. chrg. $35.0 mill.; Incl. net chrgs. of $115.0 mill. ⑨ Bef. extraord. chrg. of $240.0 mill., incl. impair. & other chrgs. of $99.0 mill.

OFFICERS:
J. C. Barbakow, Chmn., C.E.O.
D. L. Dennis, Vice-Chmn., Chief Corp. Off., C.F.O.
B. P. Schochet, Vice Chmn.

INVESTOR CONTACT: Paul J. Russell, V.P. Investor Relations, (805) 563-7188

PRINCIPAL OFFICE: 3820 State Street, Santa Barbara, CA 93105

TELEPHONE NUMBER: (805) 563-7000
FAX: (888) 896-9016
WEB: www.tenethealth.com
NO. OF EMPLOYEES: 113,887 (approx.)
SHAREHOLDERS: 10,100 (approx.)
ANNUAL MEETING: In Oct.
INCORPORATED: CA, June, 1968; reincorp., NV, Dec., 1975

INSTITUTIONAL HOLDINGS:
No. of Institutions: 475
Shares Held: 421,720,055
% Held: 86.5

INDUSTRY: General medical & surgical hospitals (SIC: 8062)

TRANSFER AGENT(S): The Bank of New York, New York, NY

TENNANT COMPANY

EXCH.	SYM.	REC. PRICE	P/E RATIO	YLD.	MKT. CAP.	RANGE (52-WK.)	'02 Y/E PR.	DIV. ACH.
NYSE	TNC	33.35 (2/28/03)	35.1	2.5%	$301.4 mill.	44.00 - 26.35	32.60	30 yrs.

MEDIUM GRADE. GOING FORWARD, THE COMPANY PLANS TO FOCUS ON MARKETS WHERE DEMAND HAS BEEN LESS DAMPENED BY BUSINESS CONDITIONS.

TRADING VOLUME
Thousand Shares

1989 1990 1991 1992 1993 1994 1995 1996 1997 1998 1999 2000 2001 2002 2003

*7 YEAR PRICE SCORE 108.8   ***12 MONTH PRICE SCORE 97.3**
*NYSE COMPOSITE INDEX=100

INTERIM EARNINGS (Per Share):

Qtr.	Mar.	June	Sept.	Dec.
1998	0.54	0.70	0.67	0.76
1999	0.53	0.66	0.35	0.61
2000	0.60	0.83	0.79	0.87
2001	0.02	0.14	0.32	0.04
2002	d0.15	0.32	0.30	0.48

INTERIM DIVIDENDS (Per Share):

Amt.	Decl.	Ex.	Rec.	Pay.
0.20Q	2/21/02	2/28/02	3/04/02	3/15/02
0.20Q	5/02/02	5/29/02	5/31/02	6/14/02
0.21Q	8/15/02	8/28/02	8/30/02	9/16/02
0.21Q	11/14/02	11/26/02	11/29/02	12/16/02
0.21Q	2/20/03	2/26/03	2/28/03	3/14/03

Indicated div.: $0.84 (Div. Reinv. Plan)

CAPITALIZATION (12/31/01):

	($000)	(%)
Long-Term Debt	10,000	6.1
Common & Surplus	154,328	93.9
Total	164,328	100.0

BUSINESS:

Tennant Company is a manufacturer of nonresidential floor maintenance and outdoor cleaning equipment, floor coatings and related offerings. The Company's products include scrubbers, sweepers, extractors, buffers and other specialized floor cleaning equipment and supplies, plus an array of industrial floor coatings. The Company has manufacturing operations in Holland, Michigan and Uden, The Netherlands. TNC sells its products directly in nine countries and through distributors in 45 others. In January 1999, the Company acquired the business and assets of Paul Andra KG, a privately-owned manufacturer of commercial floor maintenance equipment in Germany.

RECENT DEVELOPMENTS:

For the year ended 12/31/02, net income increased to $8.6 million compared with $4.8 million in 2001. Results for 2002 and 2001 included restructuring charges of $4.0 million and $10.0 million, respectively. Results for 2001 also included a pension settlement gain of $5.9 million. Net sales rose 0.5% to $425.1 million from $423.0 million a year earlier. Sales for 2001 included an extra month of sales from the Company's European operations. This resulted from TNC's adjustment of its fiscal year in Europe to match the calender year. Operating income climbed 17.2% to $15.7 million from $13.4 million the year before.

PROSPECTS:

The Company expects results in 2003 to benefit from lower costs stemming from prior restructuring actions. Accordingly, the Company expects earnings per diluted share, before unusual items, in the range of $1.40 to $1.70. Meanwhile, in North America, the Company will continue to focus on markets where demand has been less dampened by business conditions. In Europe, results should benefit from favorable foreign currency exchange rates, lower costs, and prior investments. Going forward, the Company plans to continue to introduce new products.

ANNUAL FINANCIAL DATA:

FISCAL YEAR	TOT. REVS. ($000)	NET INC. ($000)	TOT. ASSETS ($000)	OPER. PROFIT %	NET PROFIT %	RET. ON EQUITY %	RET. ON ASSETS %	CURR. RATIO	EARN. PER SH. $	CASH FL. PER SH. $	TANG. BK. VAL.$	DIV. PER SH. $	PRICE RANGE	AVG. P/E RATIO	AVG. YIELD %
p12/31/02	425,100	① 8,600							① 0.95			0.82	44.00 - 26.35	37.0	2.3
12/31/01	422,970	①② 4,804	246,619	3.2	1.1	3.1	1.9	2.7	①② 0.52	2.53	15.18	0.80	49.56 - 32.80	79.2	1.9
12/31/00	454,044	28,250	263,285	9.6	6.2	18.2	10.7	2.6	3.09	5.11	15.16	0.78	53.38 - 28.25	13.2	1.9
12/31/99	429,407	① 19,693	257,533	7.3	4.6	14.5	7.6	2.2	① 2.15	4.20	13.06	0.76	45.00 - 31.44	17.8	2.0
12/31/98	389,388	25,325	239,098	9.6	6.5	19.3	10.6	2.5	2.67	4.51	12.68	0.74	45.75 - 33.00	14.7	1.9
12/31/97	372,428	24,205	232,744	9.7	6.5	18.2	10.4	2.6	2.41	4.15	12.00	0.72	27.50 - 21.25	11.6	2.2
12/31/96	344,433	21,027	177,490	9.2	6.1	16.3	11.8	16.0	2.10	3.73	11.15	0.69	27.50 - 21.25	13.6	2.2
12/31/95	325,368	19,662	215,750	9.3	6.0	17.2	9.1	2.0	1.98	3.40	9.57	0.68	29.00 - 22.25	12.9	2.7
12/31/94	281,685	15,735	210,758	8.6	5.6	12.7	7.5	1.5	1.60	2.94	10.66	0.65	24.25 - 20.47	14.0	2.9
12/31/93	221,002	① 9,126	128,634	5.1	4.1	10.9	7.1	2.4	① 0.93	2.04	8.38	0.64	24.25 - 19.75	23.7	2.9

Statistics are as originally reported. Adj. for stk. split: 2-for-1, 4/26/95 ① Incl. non-recurr. chrg. $4.0 mill., 2002; $10.0 mill., 2001; $6.7 mill, 12/99; $4.1 mill., 12/93. ② Incl. pension settlement gain of $5.9 mill.

OFFICERS:
J. M. Dolan, Pres., C.E.O.
A. T. Brausen, V.P., C.F.O., Treas.
E. A. Blanchard, V.P., Gen. Couns., Sec.

INVESTOR CONTACT: Anthony T. Brausen, V.P., C.F.O. & Treas., (763) 540-1553

PRINCIPAL OFFICE: 701 North Lilac Drive, P.O. Box 1452, Minneapolis, MN 55440

TELEPHONE NUMBER: (763) 540-1200
FAX: (763) 540-1437
WEB: www.tennantco.com

NO. OF EMPLOYEES: 2,387 (avg.)

SHAREHOLDERS: 3,700 (approx.)

ANNUAL MEETING: In May

INCORPORATED: MN, Jan., 1909

INSTITUTIONAL HOLDINGS:
No. of Institutions: 63
Shares Held: 6,345,777
% Held: 70.6

INDUSTRY: Service industry machinery, nec (SIC: 3589)

TRANSFER AGENT(S): Wells Fargo Bank Minnesota, N.A., St. Paul, MN

TENNECO AUTOMOTIVE, INC.

EXCH.	SYM.	REC. PRICE	P/E RATIO	YLD.	MKT. CAP.	RANGE (52-WK.)	'02 Y/E PR.
NYSE	TEN	2.35 (2/28/03)	3.2	...	$94.1 mill.	8.32 - 2.11	4.04

SPECULATIVE GRADE. THE COMPANY CONTINUES TO FOCUS ON GENERATING CASH TO PAY DOWN DEBT.

*7 YEAR PRICE SCORE 4.9   ***12 MONTH PRICE SCORE 71.9**
NYSE COMPOSITE INDEX=100

INTERIM EARNINGS (Per Share):

Qtr.	Mar.	June	Sept.	Dec.
1998	2.20	4.05	3.10	d1.80
1999	0.47	1.06	0.86	d4.25
2000	0.03	0.42	0.16	d1.74
2001	d0.84	0.06	d0.06	d2.53
2002	d0.05	0.45	0.13	0.21

INTERIM DIVIDENDS (Per Share):

Amt.	Decl.	Ex.	Rec.	Pay.
	Last dist. $0.05Q, 12/05/00			

CAPITALIZATION (12/31/01):

	($000)	(%)
Long-Term Debt	1,324,000	83.9
Deferred Income Tax	166,000	10.5
Minority Interest	15,000	0.9
Common & Surplus	74,000	4.7
Total	1,579,000	100.0

BUSINESS:

Tenneco Automotive, Inc. (formerly Tenneco Inc.) is a worldwide producer and marketer of ride control and exhaust systems and products, which are sold under the Monroe® and Walker® global brand names. Among its products are Sensa-Trac® and Monroe® Reflex™ shocks and struts, Rancho® shock absorbers, Walker® Quiet-Flow™ mufflers and DynoMax™ performance exhaust products, and Monroe® Clevite™ vibration control components. In addition, TEN serves original equipment manufacturers, including Ford, General Motors, Honda, Toyota, DaimlerChrysler, Volkswagen, BMW and Volvo. On 11/4/99, TEN completed the spin-off of Pactiv Corporation.

RECENT DEVELOPMENTS:

For the year ended 12/31/02, TEN reported income of $31.0 million, before an accounting change charge of $218.0 million, compared with a net loss of $130.0 million in the previous year. Results for 2002 and 2001 included net after-tax restructuring charges of $6.0 million and $43.0 million, and after-tax debt renegotiation charges of $1.0 million and $2.0 million, respectively. Results also included non-recurring after-tax gains of $13.0 million in 2002 and an after-tax environmental charge of $2.0 million in 2001. Net sales and operating revenues increased 2.8% to $3.46 billion from $3.36 billion a year earlier. Operating income surged 83.7% to $169.0 million.

PROSPECTS:

For 2003, the Company will continue to focus on generating cash to pay down debt, primarily through additional working capital improvement and strengthening margins. TEN expects to grow revenues at its businesses by leveraging its advanced technologies and brand strength and expanding into adjacent markets. Separately, on 3/11/03, TEN announced that its exhaust manufacturing joint venture in Dalian, China has expanded its operations with a new manufacturing plant in Changchun, China. The new facility is already producing components for Volkswagen. Initially, the facility will supply about 140,000 exhaust systems for 12 different engine models.

ANNUAL FINANCIAL DATA:

FISCAL YEAR	TOT. REVS. ($mill.)	NET INC. ($mill.)	TOT. ASSETS ($mill.)	OPER. PROFIT %	NET PROFIT %	RET. ON EQUITY %	RET. ON ASSETS %	CURR. RATIO	EARN. PER SH.$	CASH FL. PER SH.$	TANG. BK. VAL.$	DIV. PER SH.$	PRICE RANGE	AVG. P/E RATIO	AVG. YIELD %
p12/31/02	3,459.0	③ 31.0							⑨ 0.74			...	8.32 - 1.90	6.9	...
12/31/01	3,364.0	⑧ d130.0	2,681.0	2.7	...	...	...	1.1	⑧ d3.43	0.61	...	...	5.45 - 1.35	...	...
12/31/00	3,549.0	⑦ d41.0	2,886.0	3.4	...	...	...	1.4	⑦ d1.18	3.14	...	0.20	11.50 - 2.50	...	2.9
12/31/99	3,279.0	⑥ d63.0	2,943.0	4.5	...	...	...	1.8	⑥ d1.87	2.41	...	...	186.25 - 7.00	...	...
12/31/98	7,605.0	⑤ 255.0	8,791.0	8.4	3.4	10.2	2.9	0.9	⑤ 7.55	20.80	25.75	...	237.50 - 147.50	25.5	...
12/31/97	7,318.0	④ 361.0	8,332.0	10.4	4.9	14.3	4.3	1.3	④ 10.55	21.23	27.97	...	260.63 - 186.57	21.2	...
12/31/96	6,648.0	③ 218.0	7,587.0	9.4	3.3	8.2	2.9	1.2	③ 6.40	15.06	37.94	...	292.50 - 216.88	39.8	...
12/31/95	5,260.0	② 258.0	7,413.0	12.8	4.9	8.2	3.4	1.2	② 7.40	12.70	60.69	...	251.88 - 209.38	31.2	...
12/31/94	4,164.0	① 238.0	...	11.0	5.7	...	...	...	① 6.60	10.22	...	...	293.75 - 185.00	36.3	...

Statistics are as originally reported. Adj. for reverse 1-for-5 stk. split, 11/99. ① Bef. acctg. chng. chrg. $39.0 mill., extr. chrg. $5.0 mill. & disc. oper. gain $214.0 mill. ② Bef. disc. oper. gain $477.0 mill. ③ Bef. extr. chrg. $236.0 mill. & disc. oper. gain $428.0 mill. ④ Bef. acctg. chrg.: $46.0 mill. ⑤ Incl. net pre-tax non-recurr. gains $32.0 mill. ⑥ Bef. acctg. chrg. $134.0 mill., extr. chrg. $18.0 mill. & disc. oper. loss $208.0 mill.; incl. aft.-tax restr. chrg. of $50.0 mill. & aft.-tax spin-off costs $8.0 mill. ⑦ Bef. extr. chrg. $1.0 mill.; incl. a one-time chrg. $45.0 mill. ⑧ Incl. aft.-tax restr. & oth. chrg. $43.0 mill. ⑨ Bef. acctg. chng. chrg. $218.0 mill.; incl. aft.-tax restr. and oth. chrg. $7.0 mill. & one-time aft.-tax gains $13.0 mill.

OFFICERS:
M. P. Frissora, Chmn., Pres., C.E.O.
M. A. McCollum, Sr. V.P., C.F.O.
T. R. Donovan, Exec. V.P., Gen. Couns.
INVESTOR CONTACT: Investor Relations, (847) 482-5042
PRINCIPAL OFFICE: 500 North Field Drive, Lake Forest, IL 60045

TELEPHONE NUMBER: (847) 482-5000
FAX: (847) 482-5940
WEB: www.tenneco-automotive.com
NO. OF EMPLOYEES: 20,000 (approx.)
SHAREHOLDERS: 86,000 (approx.)
ANNUAL MEETING: In May
INCORPORATED: DE, Aug., 1996

INSTITUTIONAL HOLDINGS:
No. of Institutions: 94
Shares Held: 18,469,924
% Held: 44.7
INDUSTRY: Motor vehicle parts and accessories (SIC: 3714)
TRANSFER AGENT(S): First Union National Bank, Charlotte, NC

TEPPCO PARTNERS, L.P.

EXCH.	SYM.	REC. PRICE	P/E RATIO	YLD.	MKT. CAP.	RANGE (52-WK.)	'02 Y/E PR.	DIV. ACH.
NYSE	TPP	30.38 (2/28/03)	17.0	7.9%	$1.23 bill.	33.20 - 23.90	27.75	10 yrs.

MEDIUM GRADE. THE COMPANY EXPECTS FULL-YEAR 2003 EARNINGS TO RANGE BETWEEN $1.30 PER UNIT AND $1.55 PER UNIT.

MERGENT

TRADING VOLUME
Thousand Shares

1989 1990 1991 1992 1993 1994 1995 1996 1997 1998 1999 2000 2001 2002 2003

*7 YEAR PRICE SCORE 124.2   ***12 MONTH PRICE SCORE 108.8**

*NYSE COMPOSITE INDEX=100

INTERIM EARNINGS (Per Share):

Qtr.	Mar.	June	Sept.	Dec.
2000	0.60	0.35	0.41	0.53
2001	0.55	0.89	0.35	0.40
2002	0.46	0.39	0.48	0.46

INTERIM DIVIDENDS (Per Share):

Amt.	Decl.	Ex.	Rec.	Pay.
0.575Q	1/22/02	1/29/02	1/31/02	2/08/02
0.575Q	4/22/02	4/26/02	4/30/02	5/08/02
0.60Q	7/18/02	7/29/02	7/31/02	8/08/02
0.60Q	10/16/02	10/29/02	10/31/02	11/08/02
0.60Q	1/16/03	1/29/03	1/31/03	2/07/03

Indicated div.: $2.40

CAPITALIZATION (12/31/01):

	($000)	(%)
Long-Term Debt	730,472	53.0
Redeemable Pfd. Stock	105,630	7.7
Common & Surplus	543,181	39.4
Total	1,379,283	100.0

BUSINESS:

TEPPCO Partners, L.P. operates through three operating segments. The midstream segment, which comprised 88.2% of 2002 revenues and 15.5% of operating income, includes natural gas gathering services, and transportation and fractionation of natural gas liquids. The upstream segment (7.5%, 48.8%), includes crude oil transportation, storage, gathering and marketing activities, and distribution of lubrication oils and specialty chemicals. The downstream segment (4.3%, 35.7%) includes the transportation and storage of refined products, liquefied petroleum gases and petrochemicals. The Company, a master limited partnership formed in March 1990, operates through various subsidiaries. Texas Eastern Products Pipeline Company, LLC, a wholly-owned subsidiary of Duke Energy Field Services (DEFS), serves as the general partner of TPP. The assets of the midstream segment are managed and operated by DEFS under an agreement with TPP. In June 2002, TPP acquired the Val Verde Gathering System for $444.0 million. In March 2002, TPP acquired the Chaparral and Quanah pipelines for about $132.0 million.

RECENT DEVELOPMENTS:

For the twelve months ended 12/31/02, net income was $117.9 million compared with $109.1 million the previous year. Earnings for 2001 included net income of $18.9 million from the settlement of a canceled transportation agreement with Pennzoil-Quaker State Company related to the sale of their refinery in Shreveport, LA. Total operating revenues decreased 8.8% to $3.24 billion from $3.56 billion a year earlier. Operating income increased 12.1% to $117.9 million versus $109.1 million, due primarily to acquisitions that were completed during 2002.

PROSPECTS:

For full-year 2003, TPP expects earnings to range between $1.30 per unit and $1.55 per unit, which reflects the full year contribution of the Company's Val Verde acquisition and its Jonah Gas Gathering Company expansions. TPP also anticipates improved results from its downstream segment and a continued solid performance from its upstream segment. TPP stated that it expects to invest approximately $55.0 million in capital projects in 2003; however, this amount may increase depending on the pace of development of a number of internal growth projects.

ANNUAL FINANCIAL DATA:

FISCAL YEAR	TOT. REVS. ($mill.)	NET INC. ($mill.)	TOT. ASSETS ($mill.)	OPER. PROFIT %	NET PROFIT %	RET. ON EQUITY %	RET. ON ASSETS %	CURR. RATIO	EARN. PER SH.$	CASH FL. PER SH.$	TANG. BK. VAL.$	DIV. PER SH.$	PRICE RANGE	AVG. P/E RATIO	AVG. YIELD %
p12/31/02	3,242.2	117.9							1.79			2.35	33.25 - 23.90	16.0	8.2
12/31/01	3,556.4	③109.1	2,065.3	4.2	3.1	20.1	5.3	0.4	③2.18	3.95	6.79	2.15	36.50 - 24.38	14.0	7.1
12/31/00	3,087.9	77.4	1,622.8	3.5	2.5	24.6	4.8	1.0	1.89	3.35	8.46	1.89	27.00 - 19.00	12.2	8.7
12/31/99	1,934.9	72.1	1,041.4	5.2	3.7	31.4	6.9	1.1	1.91	2.33	6.72	1.85	28.25 - 17.13	11.9	8.2
12/31/98	429.6	②53.3	915.0	18.6	12.4	23.5	5.8	1.3	②1.61	1.07	6.56	1.75	30.69 - 23.25	16.7	6.5
12/31/97	222.1	①61.3	673.9	41.2	27.6	20.2	9.1	1.7	①1.95	2.93	10.45	1.55	28.25 - 19.81	12.3	6.4
12/31/96	216.0	58.6	671.2	40.5	27.1	20.2	8.7	2.1	1.89	2.83	10.01	1.45	21.06 - 17.13	10.1	7.6
12/31/95	203.7	46.7	669.9	37.5	22.9	16.9	7.0	2.2	1.54	2.41	9.53	1.32	18.63 - 12.63	10.1	8.5
12/31/94	197.3	46.5	665.3	40.5	23.6	17.3	7.0	2.5	1.57	2.40	10.17	1.19	15.00 - 12.56	8.8	8.6
12/31/93	183.6	37.2	655.1	39.1	20.2	14.4	5.7	2.9	1.27	2.09	9.71	1.11	14.75 - 10.88	10.1	8.7

Statistics are as originally reported. Adj. for 2-for-1 stk. split, 8/98. ① Incl. gain on sale of inventory of $2.3 mill. ② Bef. extraord. loss of $72.8 mill. ③ Incl. net income of $18.9 mill. ($0.39/unit) fr. settlement of canceled transportation contract.

OFFICERS:
J. W. Mogg, Chmn.
F. J. Fowler, Vice-Chmn.
B. R. Pearl, Pres., C.E.O., C.O.O.
INVESTOR CONTACT: Brenda Peters, Dir. of Investor Relations, (713) 759-3954
PRINCIPAL OFFICE: 2929 Allen Pkwy, P.O. Box 2521, Houston, TX 77252-2521

TELEPHONE NUMBER: (713) 759-3636
FAX: (713) 759-3957
WEB: www.teppco.com
NO. OF EMPLOYEES: 919 (avg.)
SHAREHOLDERS: 31,000 (approx. ben.)
ANNUAL MEETING: N/A
INCORPORATED: DE, Mar., 1990

INSTITUTIONAL HOLDINGS:
No. of Institutions: 104
Shares Held: 10,098,032
% Held: 18.9
INDUSTRY: Refined petroleum pipelines (SIC: 4613)
TRANSFER AGENT(S): Mellon Investor Services, L.L.C., Ridgefield Park, NJ

TERADYNE, INC.

EXCH.	SYM.	REC. PRICE	P/E RATIO	YLD.	MKT. CAP.	RANGE (52-WK.)	'02 Y/E PR.
NYSE	TER	11.59 (2/28/03)	...	...	$2.10 bill.	40.20 - 7.10	13.01

SPECULATIVE GRADE. THE COMPANY EXPECTS SALES FOR THE FIRST QUARTER OF 2003 TO BE BETWEEN $310.0 MILLION AND $340.0 MILLION.

TRADING VOLUME
Thousand Shares

*7 YEAR PRICE SCORE 73.4   ***12 MONTH PRICE SCORE 64.5**

*NYSE COMPOSITE INDEX=100

INTERIM EARNINGS (Per Share):

Qtr.	Mar.	June	Sept.	Dec.
1996	0.32	0.11	0.12	0.02
1997	0.10	0.15	0.23	0.27
1998	0.29	0.23	0.01	0.07
1999	0.10	0.20	0.35	0.42
2000	0.60	0.76	0.84	0.66
2001	0.33	d0.23	d0.59	d0.63
2002	d0.42	d0.28	d0.91	d2.31

INTERIM DIVIDENDS (Per Share):

Amt.	Decl.	Ex.	Rec.	Pay.
		No dividends paid.		

CAPITALIZATION (12/31/01):

	($000)	(%)
Long-Term Debt	451,682	20.4
Common & Surplus	1,764,384	79.6
Total	2,216,066	100.0

BUSINESS:

Teradyne, Inc. is a supplier of automatic test equipment and a provider of high performance interconnection systems and electronic manufacturing services. The Company's automatic test equipment products include systems that test semiconductors, test and inspect circuit-boards and test high speed voice and data communication. TER's interconnection systems products and services include high bandwidth backplane assemblies and associated connectors used in electronic systems and electronic manufacturing services of assemblies, which include Teradyne backplanes and connectors. The Company's four principal segments are semiconductor test systems (50.0% of revenues for 2001), connection systems (38.0%), circuit board test and inspection systems (9.0%), and other test systems (3.0%).

RECENT DEVELOPMENTS:

For the year ended 12/31/02, the Company reported a net loss of $718.5 million compared with a net loss of $202.2 million in 2001. Earnings were negatively affected by weak economic conditions, low demand for technology products and uncertain global market conditions. Results for 2002 and 2001 included restructuring and asset impairment charges of $204.2 million and $74.3 million, respectively. Net sales decreased 15.2% to $1.22 billion from $1.44 billion in the prior year. Net expenses climbed 0.9% to $1.78 billion from $1.77 billion the year before. Net orders grew 12.0% to $905.3 million from $808.2 million a year earlier.

PROSPECTS:

The near-term outlook for the Company is uncertain due to weak global market conditions and volatile global situations. As a result, the Company expects sales for the first quarter of 2003 to be between $310.0 million and $340.0 million. In addition, TER expects to report a loss per share of between $0.25 and $0.33, before any special items and assuming no tax benefit from the losses. However, the Company may benefit from the recent trend of improvement in gross orders throughout most of its product lines and businesses, particularly in the semiconductor test product line.

ANNUAL FINANCIAL DATA:

FISCAL YEAR	TOT. REVS. ($mill.)	NET INC. ($mill.)	TOT. ASSETS ($mill.)	OPER. PROFIT %	NET PROFIT %	RET. ON EQUITY %	RET. ON ASSETS %	CURR. RATIO	EARN. PER SH.$	CASH FL.PER SH.$	TANG. BK. VAL.$	PRICE RANGE	AVG. P/E RATIO
p12/31/02	1,222.2	[7] d718.5		...	...	...	...		[7] d3.93			40.20 - 7.10	...
12/31/01	1,440.6	[6] d202.2	2,542.4	...	...	...	...	4.1	[6] d1.15	d0.36	8.69	47.21 - 18.43	...
12/31/00	3,043.9	[5] 517.8	2,355.9	23.4	17.0	30.3	22.0	2.2	[5] 2.86	3.42	9.89	115.44 - 23.00	24.2
12/31/99	1,790.9	191.7	1,568.2	14.4	10.7	16.6	12.2	2.3	1.07	1.56	6.77	66.00 - 20.63	40.5
12/31/98	1,489.2	[4] 102.1	1,312.8	9.0	6.9	9.9	7.8	3.0	[4] 0.60	1.04	6.13	24.22 - 7.50	26.7
12/31/97	1,266.3	[3] 127.6	1,251.7	13.8	10.1	13.6	10.2	2.6	[3] 0.74	1.08	5.62	29.59 - 11.81	28.0
12/31/96	1,171.6	[1] 93.6	1,096.8	10.5	8.0	11.1	8.5	2.7	[1] 0.55	0.85	5.10	13.88 - 5.56	17.7
12/31/95	1,191.0	159.3	1,023.8	20.5	13.4	21.0	15.6	3.2	0.95	1.20	4.60	21.44 - 8.03	15.6
12/31/94	677.4	70.9	655.9	14.5	10.5	14.4	10.8	3.2	0.48	0.72	3.39	8.56 - 5.09	14.3
12/31/93	554.7	[2] 35.9	544.4	9.2	6.5	8.6	6.6	3.2	[2] 0.25	0.49	2.94	7.41 - 3.25	21.3

Statistics are as originally reported. Adj. for 2-for-1 split, 8/99 & 8/95. [1] Incl. $10.8 mill. chg. rel. to workforce reduct. [2] Bef. $729,000 ($0.02/sh.) extraord. item. [3] Incl. $0.04/sh. non-recur. chg. [4] Incl. $23.0 mill. pre-tax chg. for excess raw material inventory. [5] Excl. $64.1 mill. net cumulative effect of acctg. chg. [6] Incl. $7.8 mill. impair. chg. for oper. leases, $2.3 mill. chg. for duplicated invent. & $9.3 mill. pre-tax prov. for workforce reduct. [7] Incl. $204.2 mill. restr. & asset impair. chgs.

OFFICERS:
G. W. Chamillard, Chmn., Pres., C.E.O.
G. R. Beecher, V.P., C.F.O., Treas.

INVESTOR CONTACT: Tom Newman, V.P., Corp. Relations, (617) 422-2425

PRINCIPAL OFFICE: 321 Harrison Avenue, Boston, MA 02118

TELEPHONE NUMBER: (617) 482-2700
FAX: (617) 422-2910
WEB: www.teradyne.com

NO. OF EMPLOYEES: 7,200 (approx.)

SHAREHOLDERS: 891

ANNUAL MEETING: In May

INCORPORATED: MA, Sept., 1960

INSTITUTIONAL HOLDINGS:
No. of Institutions: 278
Shares Held: 169,484,932
% Held: 92.6

INDUSTRY: Instruments to measure electricity (SIC: 3825)

TRANSFER AGENT(S): BankBoston, N.A., c/o Boston EquiServe, Boston, MA

TESORO PETROLEUM CORPORATION

EXCH.	SYM.	REC. PRICE	P/E RATIO	YLD.	MKT. CAP.	RANGE (52-WK.)	'02 Y/E PR.
NYSE	TSO	5.35 (2/28/03)	...	...	$221.6 mill.	14.54 - 1.24	4.52

LOWER MEDIUM GRADE. ADDITIONAL DEBT REDUCTION REMAINS THE COMPANY'S TOP PRIORITY IN 2003.

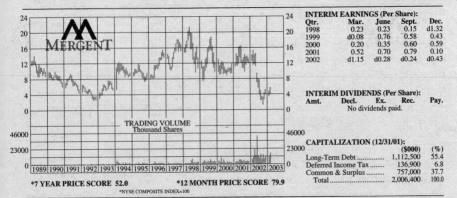

*7 YEAR PRICE SCORE 52.0   *12 MONTH PRICE SCORE 79.9
*NYSE COMPOSITE INDEX=100

INTERIM EARNINGS (Per Share):

Qtr.	Mar.	June	Sept.	Dec.
1998	0.23	0.23	0.15	d1.32
1999	d0.08	0.76	0.58	0.43
2000	0.20	0.35	0.60	0.59
2001	0.52	0.70	0.79	0.10
2002	d1.15	d0.28	d0.24	d0.43

INTERIM DIVIDENDS (Per Share):

Amt.	Decl.	Ex.	Rec.	Pay.
		No dividends paid.		

CAPITALIZATION (12/31/01):

	($000)	(%)
Long-Term Debt	1,112,500	55.4
Deferred Income Tax	136,900	6.8
Common & Surplus	757,000	37.7
Total	2,006,400	100.0

BUSINESS:

Tesoro Petroleum Corp. is an independent refiner and marketer of petroleum products and provider of marine logistics services. As of 1/29/03, TSO owned and operated six petroleum refineries in the western U.S. with a combined rated crude oil capacity of nearly 560,000 barrels per day. TSO sells its refined products to customers in the western and mid-continental U.S. and other countries on the Pacific Rim. TSO's retail business includes a network of about 660 branded retail stations. TSO also operates a network of terminals along the Texas and Louisiana Gulf Coast that provides fuel and logistical support services to the marine and offshore exploration and production industries. On 9/6/01, TSO acquired certain refining and marketing assets from BP p.l.c. for about $666.0 million. On 5/17/02, TSO acquired Valero Energy Corporation's Golden Eagle refinery and 70 associated retail sites for $945.0 million.

RECENT DEVELOPMENTS:

For the year ended 12/31/02, the Company reported a net loss of $117.0 million compared with net income of $88.0 million a year earlier. Results for 2002 and 2001 included losses of $8.4 million and $1.8 million, respectively, on the sale of assets. Lower refining margins as well as significantly higher interest and financing costs, which climbed to $166.1 million from $52.8 million partially due to the 5/17/02 Golden Eagle refinery acquisition, negatively affected earnings. Revenues increased 37.4% to $7.12 billion from $5.18 billion the previous year.

PROSPECTS:

On 12/31/02, TSO announced that it has closed an agreement with Skyline-FRI 7, TSO, L.P. to sell and lease-back 30 of the Company's retail outlets located in Alaska, Hawaii, Idaho and Utah for gross proceeds of almost $41.0 million. Additional asset sales completed in December 2002 included TSO's sale of the Northern Great Plains Products System to Kaneb Pipe Line Partners L.P. for $100.0 million, and the sale of the Company's 70 Northern California retail outlets for total proceeds of $67.0 million. Approximately 50.0% of the proceeds from the aforementioned sales were used to reduce debt. Looking ahead, TSO has indicated that further debt reduction remains its top priority with the Company striving to eliminate $500.0 million in debt by the end of 2003.

ANNUAL FINANCIAL DATA:

FISCAL YEAR	TOT. REVS. ($mill.)	NET INC. ($mill.)	TOT. ASSETS ($mill.)	OPER. PROFIT %	NET PROFIT %	RET. ON EQUITY %	RET. ON ASSETS %	CURR. RATIO	EARN. PER SH.$	CASH FL. PER SH.$	TANG. BK. VAL.$	PRICE RANGE	AVG. P/E RATIO
p12/31/02	7,119.3	⑤d117.0	2,662.3	3.8	1.7	11.6	3.3	1.6	⑤d1.93	3.33	18.28	15.29 - 1.24	...
12/31/01	5,217.8	88.0	1,543.6	3.9	1.4	11.0	4.8	1.6	2.10	2.56	16.38	16.50 - 9.70	6.2
12/31/00	5,104.4	73.4	1,486.5	4.4	1.1	5.2	2.2	1.9	1.75	1.92	14.14	13.00 - 8.94	6.3
12/31/99	3,000.3	①32.2	1,428.4	4.0	1.1	...	...	1.9	①0.62	1.70	14.14	18.81 - 7.44	21.2
12/31/98	1,490.3	②d15.0	627.8	3.1	...	...	0.4	1.9	②d0.86	1.70	12.20	21.38 - 9.56	...
12/31/97	853.1	①2.4	582.6	13.9	0.3	...	13.2	1.7	①1.14	2.66	11.51	18.19 - 10.25	12.5
12/31/96	1,039.8	③④76.8	519.2	10.6	7.4	25.3	11.1	1.7	③④2.90	4.52	8.74	15.50 - 8.00	4.1
12/31/95	1,002.9	③④57.5	484.4	5.9	5.7	26.6	4.2	1.7	③④2.29	4.05	6.59	12.00 - 7.25	4.2
12/31/94	877.2	③20.5	434.4	4.7	2.3	12.7	3.9	1.9	③④0.77	2.44	4.06	12.38 - 5.25	11.4
12/31/93	834.9	③17.0			2.0	29.0		2.7	③0.54	2.26		7.75 - 3.00	10.0

Statistics are as originally reported. ① Bef. inc. fr. disc. ops. of $42.8 mill.,1999; $28.3 mill., 1997 ② Bef. extraord. loss of $4.4 mill. ③ Incl. gain on sales of assets & oth. inc. of $4.4 mill.,1996; $32.7 mill., 1995; $2.4 mill., 1994; $60,000, 1993. ④ Bef. extraord. loss of $2.3 mill., 1996; $2.9 mill., 1995; $4.8 mill., 1994 ⑤ Incl. loss on asset sales of $8.4 mill.

OFFICERS:
B. A. Smith, Chmn., Pres., C.E.O.
G. A. Wright, Sr. V.P., C.F.O.
S. L. Layman, V.P., Treas.
INVESTOR CONTACT: John Robertson, Investor Relations, (210) 283-2682
PRINCIPAL OFFICE: 300 Concord Plaza Dr., San Antonio, TX 78216-6999

TELEPHONE NUMBER: (210) 828-8484
FAX: (210) 283-2003
WEB: www.tesoropetroleum.com
NO. OF EMPLOYEES: 3,290 (approx.)
SHAREHOLDERS: 2,700 (approx. record)
ANNUAL MEETING: In May
INCORPORATED: CA, Dec., 1939; reincorp., DE, Dec., 1968

INSTITUTIONAL HOLDINGS:
No. of Institutions: 98
Shares Held: 39,015,913
% Held: 60.4

INDUSTRY: Petroleum refining (SIC: 2911)

TRANSFER AGENT(S): Mellon Investor Services, L.L.C., Ridgefield Park, NJ

TEXAS INDUSTRIES, INC.

EXCH.	SYM.	REC. PRICE	P/E RATIO	YLD.	MKT. CAP.	RANGE (52-WK.)	'02 Y/E PR.
NYSE	TXI	19.85 (2/28/03)	35.4	1.5%	$417.4 mill.	44.85 - 19.50	24.30

MEDIUM GRADE. THE COMPANY IS LOOKING FORWARD TO IMPROVED OPERATING MARGINS DUE TO BETTER OPERATING EFFICIENCIES.

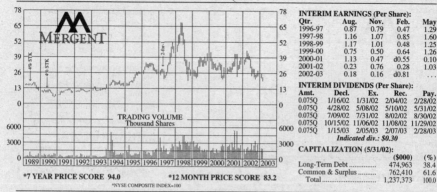

INTERIM EARNINGS (Per Share):

Qtr.	Aug.	Nov.	Feb.	May
1996-97	0.87	0.79	0.47	1.29
1997-98	1.16	1.07	0.85	1.60
1998-99	1.17	1.01	0.48	1.25
1999-00	0.75	0.50	0.64	1.26
2000-01	1.13	0.47	d0.55	0.10
2001-02	0.23	0.76	0.28	1.03
2002-03	0.18	0.16	d0.81	...

INTERIM DIVIDENDS (Per Share):

Amt.	Decl.	Ex.	Rec.	Pay.
0.075Q	1/16/02	1/31/02	2/04/02	2/28/02
0.075Q	4/28/02	5/08/02	5/10/02	5/31/02
0.075Q	7/09/02	7/31/02	8/02/02	8/30/02
0.075Q	10/15/02	11/06/02	11/08/02	11/29/02
0.075Q	1/15/03	2/05/03	2/07/03	2/28/03

Indicated div.: $0.30

CAPITALIZATION (5/31/02):

	($000)	(%)
Long-Term Debt	474,963	38.4
Common & Surplus	762,410	61.6
Total	1,237,373	100.0

*7 YEAR PRICE SCORE 94.0   ***12 MONTH PRICE SCORE 83.2**

*NYSE COMPOSITE INDEX=100

BUSINESS:

Texas Industries, Inc., directly and through subsidiaries, is a producer of steel and cement/concrete products for the construction and manufacturing industries. The Company's steel operations are conducted through its 100%-owned subsidiary, Chaparral Steel Company, located in Midlothian, Texas. This division produces beams, rebar, channels, reinforcing bars, merchant quality rounds and special bar quality rounds. A major portion of TXI's shredded steel requirements is produced at its own steel mill. Products produced and supplied by the cement/concrete segment include cement, aggregates, ready-mix, block, brick and pipe. Cement operations serve Texas and California, the largest cement markets in the nation. Structural steel products are distributed throughout North America.

RECENT DEVELOPMENTS:

For the quarter ended 2/28/03, the Company reported a net loss of $17.2 million compared with net income of $6.1 million in the equivalent 2002 quarter. Net sales decreased 9.8% to $273.6 million from $303.5 million a year earlier. The decline in results reflected soft market demand, bleak weather conditions and higher energy costs. Also, a planned maintenance shutdown for the North Texas cement plant was extended as a result of a contractor accident. Operating profit of the cement, aggregate and concrete segment plunged 67.9% to $6.7 million. Operating loss of the steel operations was $12.5 million versus operating income of $9.8 million a year earlier.

PROSPECTS:

The Company announced selling price increases to help offset rising raw material and energy costs. TXI expects operating efficiencies to enhance margins as more normal weather conditions return. Separately, TXI's decline in its earnings before interest, taxes, depreciation and amortization in the quarter ended 2/28/03 triggered a need for the Company to alter its credit agreement with its lenders. The Company secured an agreement with its lenders, which provides liquidity to TXI and modifies the leverage covenant in its revolving credit facility and extends the term of its receivables purchase agreement through late May 2003. The Company is pursuing further altered financial agreements and an increase the receivables purchase agreement beyond May 2003.

ANNUAL FINANCIAL DATA:

FISCAL YEAR	TOT. REVS. ($mill.)	NET INC. ($mill.)	TOT. ASSETS ($mill.)	OPER. PROFIT %	NET PROFIT %	RET. ON EQUITY %	RET. ON ASSETS %	CURR. RATIO	EARN. PER SH.$	CASH FL. PER SH.$	TANG. BK. VAL.$	DIV. PER SH.$	PRICE RANGE	AVG. P/E RATIO	AVG. YIELD
5/31/02	1,344.9	51.3	1,773.3	7.6	3.8	6.7	2.9	2.2	2.38	7.06	29.29	0.30	42.14 - 23.00	13.7	0.9
5/31/01	1,252.2	26.2	1,857.4	4.7	2.1	3.7	1.4	2.0	1.24	5.99	27.10	0.30	43.38 - 20.88	25.9	0.9
5/31/00	1,306.4	69.8	1,815.7	9.8	5.3	10.0	3.8	2.2	3.15	6.82	25.90	0.30	42.56 - 21.63	10.2	0.9
5/31/99	1,126.8	88.7	1,531.1	11.8	7.9	14.0	5.8	2.1	3.92	6.65	22.73	0.30	68.25 - 19.56	11.2	0.7
5/31/98	1,196.3	102.1	1,185.8	13.6	8.5	18.5	8.6	2.6	4.69	7.54	18.88	0.30	52.00 - 20.88	7.8	0.8
5/31/97	973.8	75.5	847.9	13.4	7.8	16.7	8.9	3.4	3.40	5.82	18.64	0.20	34.63 - 25.06	8.8	0.7
5/31/96	967.4	80.0	801.1	14.7	8.3	19.0	10.0	3.1	3.52	5.68	16.20	0.20	27.31 - 15.06	6.0	0.9
5/31/95	830.5	48.0	753.1	10.9	5.8	14.0	6.4	2.8	1.94	3.92	12.77	0.10	19.88 - 14.75	8.9	0.6
5/31/94	707.1	25.8	749.1	8.7	3.6	7.3	3.4	2.4	1.15	3.30	11.18	0.10	16.25 - 10.56	11.7	0.5
5/31/93	614.3	1.1	757.3	4.2	0.2	0.4	0.1	2.6	0.06	2.29	9.38	0.10	12.63 - 9.63	201.9	0.9

Statistics are as originally reported. Adj. for stk. splits and dividends: 2-for-1, 2/97. Incl. the results of Chaparral Steel on a consolidated basis.

OFFICERS:
R. D. Rogers, Pres., C.E.O.
R. M. Fowler, Exec. V.P., C.F.O.
R. C. Moore, V.P., Sec., Gen. Couns.
INVESTOR CONTACT: Investor Relations, (972) 647-6700
PRINCIPAL OFFICE: 1341 West Mockingbird Lane, Suite 700W, Dallas, TX 75247-6913

TELEPHONE NUMBER: (972) 647-6700
FAX: (972) 647-3878
WEB: www.txi.com
NO. OF EMPLOYEES: 4,400 (approx.)
SHAREHOLDERS: 3,109 (approx.)
ANNUAL MEETING: In Oct.
INCORPORATED: DE, Apr., 1951

INSTITUTIONAL HOLDINGS:
No. of Institutions: 113
Shares Held: 18,159,645
% Held: 86.3
INDUSTRY: Blast furnaces and steel mills (SIC: 3312)
TRANSFER AGENT(S): Mellon Investor Services, Ridgefield Park, NJ

TEXAS INSTRUMENTS INCORPORATED

EXCH.	SYM.	REC. PRICE	P/E RATIO	YLD.	MKT. CAP.	RANGE (52-WK.)	'02 Y/E PR.
NYSE	TXN	16.75 (2/28/03)	...	0.5%	$28.99 bill.	35.94 - 13.10	15.01

MEDIUM GRADE. FOR 2003, THE COMPANY EXPECTS CAPITAL EXPENDITURES TO BE APPROXIMATELY $800.0 MILLION.

INTERIM EARNINGS (Per Share):

Qtr.	Mar.	June	Sept.	Dec.
1999	0.15	0.20	0.24	0.26
2000	0.25	0.75	0.38	0.37
2001	0.13	d0.11	d0.07	d0.07
2002	d0.02	0.05	0.11	d0.34

INTERIM DIVIDENDS (Per Share):

Amt.	Decl.	Ex.	Rec.	Pay.
0.021Q	1/17/02	1/29/02	1/31/02	2/11/02
0.021Q	4/17/02	4/26/02	4/30/02	5/20/02
0.021Q	7/18/02	7/29/02	7/31/02	8/19/02
0.021Q	10/17/02	10/29/02	10/31/02	11/18/02
0.021Q	1/16/03	1/29/03	1/31/03	2/10/03

Indicated div.: $0.09 (Div. Reinv. Plan)

TRADING VOLUME
Thousand Shares

*7 YEAR PRICE SCORE 86.5   ***12 MONTH PRICE SCORE 77.2**

*NYSE COMPOSITE INDEX=100

CAPITALIZATION (12/31/02):

	($000)	(%)
Long-Term Debt	833,000	7.1
Deferred Income Tax	129,000	1.1
Common & Surplus	10,734,000	91.8
Total	11,696,000	100.0

BUSINESS:

Texas Instruments Incorporated is a global semiconductor company that designs and supplies digital signal processors (DSPs) and analog integrated circuits to more than 30,000 customers in commercial, industrial and consumer markets. TXN also designs and manufactures other semiconductor products including standard logic devices, application-specific integrated circuits, reduced instruction-set computing microprocessors, microcontrollers and digital imaging devices. In addition to the semiconductor business (82.7% of 2002 revenues), TXN operates two other segments, Sensors & Controls (11.4%) and Educational & Productivity Solutions (E&PS) (5.9%). Sensors & Controls sells electrical and electronic controls, sensors and radio-frequency identification systems to commercial and industrial markets. E&PS supplies educational and graphing calculators.

RECENT DEVELOPMENTS:

For the year ended 12/31/02, the Company reported a net loss of $344.0 million compared with a net loss of $201.0 million in the previous year. Results for 2002 included a write-down of investment in Micron of $638.0 million and net restructuring, acquisition and other one-time charges of $134.0 million. Net revenues increased 2.2% to $8.38 billion from $8.20 billion a year earlier. Semiconductor segment revenues rose 2.5% to $6.93 billion, primarily due to higher analog and digital signal processor shipments. Educational & Productivity Solutions segment revenue increased 6.2% to $494.0 million, while Sensors and Controls segment revenue slipped 0.1% to $954.0 million.

PROSPECTS:

During 2002, the Company's DSP revenue growth of 30.0% was more than twice as fast as the DSP market overall. The strong growth came from the wireless communications and digital consumer electronics sectors. In addition, overall DSP inventory levels appear to be in good shape. For 2003, TXN expects research and development expense of about $1.70 billion and capital expenditures of approximately $800.0 million. For the first quarter of 2003, the Company expects earnings of about $0.06 per share.

ANNUAL FINANCIAL DATA:

FISCAL YEAR	TOT. REVS. ($Mill.)	NET INC. ($Mill.)	TOT. ASSETS ($Mill.)	OPER. PROFIT %	NET PROFIT %	RET. ON EQUITY %	RET. ON ASSETS %	CURR. RATIO	EARN. PER SH. $	CASH FL. PER SH. $	TANG. BK. VAL. $	DIV. PER SH. $	PRICE RANGE	AVG. P/E RATIO	AVG. YIELD %
12/31/02	8,383.0	⑧ d344.0	14,679.0	3.4	...	...	...	3.2	⑧ d0.20	0.78	5.73	0.09	35.94 - 13.10	...	0.3
12/31/01	8,201.0	⑦ d201.0	15,779.0	...	...	...	...	3.7	⑦ d0.12	0.94	6.42	0.09	54.69 - 20.10	...	0.2
12/31/00	11,875.0	⑥ 3,087.0	17,720.0	19.7	26.0	24.5	17.4	2.9	⑥ 1.73	2.49	6.71	0.09	99.78 - 35.00	39.0	0.1
12/31/99	9,468.0	⑤ 1,406.0	15,028.0	17.9	14.9	15.2	9.4	2.3	⑤ 0.84	1.47	5.38	0.09	70.13 - 21.50	54.5	0.2
12/31/98	8,460.0	407.0	11,250.0	4.7	4.8	6.2	3.6	2.2	0.26	0.97	4.17	0.09	22.61 - 10.06	64.0	0.5
12/31/97	9,750.0	④ 302.0	10,849.0	6.3	3.1	5.1	2.8	2.4	④ 0.19	0.89	3.80	0.09	17.81 - 7.77	67.3	0.7
12/31/96	9,940.0	③ d46.0	9,360.0	...	...	...	...	1.8	③ d0.03	0.56	2.69	0.09	8.55 - 5.06	...	1.2
12/31/95	13,128.0	② 1,040.0	9,215.0	12.1	7.9	25.4	11.3	1.7	② 0.70	1.16	2.71	0.07	10.47 - 4.30	10.5	1.0
12/31/94	10,315.0	646.0	6,989.0	10.5	6.3	21.3	9.2	1.8	0.45	0.86	2.05	0.05	5.59 - 3.81	10.4	1.1
12/31/93	8,523.0	① 476.0	5,993.0	8.5	5.6	20.6	7.9	1.7	① 0.32	0.73	1.59	0.04	5.27 - 2.86	12.8	1.1

Statistics are as originally reported. Adj. for stk. splits: 2-for-1, 5/00, 8/99, 11/97, 8/95. ① Bef. acctg. chg. loss $4.0 mill. ② Incl. one-time pre-tax chrg. $132.0 mill. ③ Bef. disc. opers. chrg. $109.0 mill.; incl. $294.0 mill. chrg. for acqd. in-proc. R&D, severance chg. & asset writedowns. ④ Bef. disc. opers. gain $1.52 bill.; incl. $22.0 mill. chrg. on extinguish. of debt. ⑤ Incl. pre-tax spec. chrgs. $127.0 mill. & pre-tax invest. gains $87.0 mill. ⑥ Bef. acctg. chg. $29.0 mill.; incl. after-tax one-time gain $1.58 bill. ⑦ Incl. net special chrgs. $357.0 mill. and a gain from the sale of facilities $9.0 mill. ⑧ Incl. pre-tax write-down invest. $638.0 mill. & net restr., acq.-related and oth. one-time chrg. $134.0 mill.

OFFICERS:
T. J. Engibous, Chmn., Pres., C.E.O.
R. K. Templeton, Exec. V.P., C.O.O.
W. A. Aylesworth, Sr. V.P., C.F.O.

INVESTOR CONTACT: Investor Relations, (972) 995-3773

PRINCIPAL OFFICE: 12500 TI Boulevard, P.O. Box 660199, Dallas, TX 75266-0199

TELEPHONE NUMBER: (972) 995-3773
FAX: (972) 995-4360
WEB: www.ti.com

NO. OF EMPLOYEES: 34,589 (avg.)
SHAREHOLDERS: 26,884
ANNUAL MEETING: In April
INCORPORATED: DE, Dec., 1938

INSTITUTIONAL HOLDINGS:
No. of Institutions: 846
Shares Held: 1,169,180,587
% Held: 67.5
INDUSTRY: Semiconductors and related devices (SIC: 3674)
TRANSFER AGENT(S): Computershare Investor Services, LLC, Chicago, IL

TEXTRON INC.

EXCH.	SYM.	REC. PRICE	P/E RATIO	YLD.	MKT. CAP.	RANGE (52-WK.)	'02 Y/E PR.
NYSE	TXT	36.13 (2/28/03)	13.9	3.6%	$5.10 bill.	53.60 - 32.20	42.99

MEDIUM GRADE. THE COMPANY SOLD ITS 50.0% INTEREST IN AN ITALIAN AUTOMOTIVE JOINT VENTURE TO COLLINS & AIKMAN.

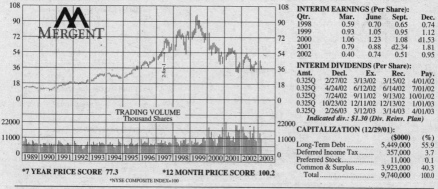

TRADING VOLUME
Thousand Shares

*7 YEAR PRICE SCORE 77.3 ***12 MONTH PRICE SCORE 100.2**
NYSE COMPOSITE INDEX=100

INTERIM EARNINGS (Per Share):

Qtr.	Mar.	June	Sept.	Dec.
1998	0.59	0.70	0.65	0.74
1999	0.93	1.05	0.95	1.12
2000	1.06	1.23	1.08	d1.53
2001	0.79	0.88	d2.34	1.81
2002	0.40	0.74	0.51	0.95

INTERIM DIVIDENDS (Per Share):

Amt.	Decl.	Ex.	Rec.	Pay.
0.325Q	2/27/02	3/13/02	3/15/02	4/01/02
0.325Q	4/24/02	6/12/02	6/14/02	7/01/02
0.325Q	7/24/02	9/11/02	9/13/02	10/01/02
0.325Q	10/23/02	12/11/02	12/13/02	1/01/03
0.325Q	2/26/03	3/12/03	3/14/03	4/01/03

Indicated div.: $1.30 (Div. Reinv. Plan)

CAPITALIZATION (12/29/01):

	($000)	(%)
Long-Term Debt	5,449,000	55.9
Deferred Income Tax	357,000	3.7
Preferred Stock	11,000	0.1
Common & Surplus	3,923,000	40.3
Total	9,740,000	100.0

BUSINESS:

Textron Inc. is a global, multi-industry company with manufacturing facilities in 40 countries as of 1/23/03. The Company operates in five industries: Aircraft (46.2% of net sales as of 12/28/02), which includes commercial and military helicopters, tiltrotor aircraft, and business jets; Industrial Products (17.3%), which includes fluid and power systems, golf, turf-care and specialty products, light construction equipment, and electrical and video tools; Fastening Systems (15.5%), which includes fasteners, fastening systems, engineered assemblies and installation tools; Industrial Components (15.1%), which includes the Fluid and Power divisions and the former divisions of Automotive Trim and Turbine Engine Components Textron; and Finance (5.9%), which provides diversified commercial lending. Among the Company's products are Bell Helicopter, Cessna Aircraft, Kautex, Lycoming, E-Z-GO golf cars, and Greenlee. In January 2002, TXT completed the sale of its automotive trim business.

RECENT DEVELOPMENTS:

For the year ended 12/31/02, TXT reported income of $364.0 million, before an accounting charge of $488.0 million, compared with net income of $166.0 million the year before. Earnings for 2002 and 2001 included net after-tax special charges of $123.0 million and $95.0 million, respectively, related to various nonrecurring items. Earnings for 2001 also included goodwill amortization of $98.0 million. Total revenues decreased 13.5% to $10.66 billion, primarily due to the divestitures of Automotive Trim and several of other businesses, as well as lower revenue in the non-aircraft segments, partially offset by higher revenues in the aircraft segment.

PROSPECTS:

On 1/21/03, the Company announced that it sold its 50.0% interest in an Italian automotive joint venture to Collins & Aikman. The transaction, which is part of the Company's strategy to divest non-core assets, will result in an after-tax gain of $12.0 million in the first quarter of 2003. Looking ahead, in 2003, TXT expects diluted earnings per share, excluding restructuring costs and the gain on the sale of the Italian automotive joint interest venture, of approximately $0.50 for the first quarter and $3.05 for the full year. Additionally, TXT anticipates free cash flow before restructuring of about $400.0 million and a cash tax benefit of approximately $100.0 million in 2003.

ANNUAL FINANCIAL DATA:

FISCAL YEAR	TOT. REVS. ($mill.)	NET INC. ($mill.)	TOT. ASSETS ($mill.)	OPER. PROFIT %	NET PROFIT %	RET. ON EQUITY %	RET. ON ASSETS %	CURR. RATIO	EARN. PER SH. $	CASH FL. PER SH. $	TANG. BK. VAL. $	DIV. PER SH. $	PRICE RANGE	AVG. P/E RATIO	AVG. YIELD %
p12/28/02	10,658.0	②⑥ 364.0	15,505.0						②⑥ 2.60			1.30	53.60 - 32.20	16.5	3.0
12/29/01	12,321.0	⑥ 166.0	16,052.0	3.4	1.6	4.2	1.0	1.3	⑥ 1.16	4.94	13.86	1.30	60.47 - 31.29	39.5	2.8
12/30/00	13,090.0	②⑦ 277.0	16,370.0	4.7	2.1	6.9	1.7	1.2	②⑦ 1.90	5.28	11.65	1.30	77.50 - 40.69	31.1	2.2
1/01/00	11,579.0	①③ 623.0	16,393.0	8.9	5.4	14.2	3.8	1.1	①③ 4.05	6.91	10.60	1.26	98.00 - 65.88	20.2	1.5
1/02/99	9,683.0	⑥ 443.0	13,721.0	8.2	4.6	14.8	3.2	1.1	⑧ 2.68	4.86	5.59	1.10	80.94 - 52.06	24.8	1.7
⑤ 1/03/98	10,544.0	558.0	18,610.0	9.0	5.3	17.3	3.0	3.7	3.29	5.84	8.97	0.97	70.75 - 45.00	17.6	1.7
12/28/96	9,274.0	③ 482.0	18,235.0	8.9	5.2	15.1	2.6	4.0	③ 2.80	5.05	9.40	0.85	48.88 - 34.56	14.9	2.0
12/31/95	9,973.0	479.0	23,172.0	8.2	4.8	14.0	2.1	5.4	2.76	5.14	10.53	0.76	38.69 - 24.31	11.4	2.4
12/31/94	9,683.0	④ 433.0	20,925.0	7.8	4.5	15.0	2.1	5.2	④ 2.40	4.62	7.96	0.68	30.31 - 23.25	11.2	2.5
12/31/93	9,078.0	379.0	19,658.0	6.8	4.2	13.6	1.9	5.0	2.11	4.46	7.54	0.60	29.44 - 20.19	11.8	2.4

Statistics are as originally reported. Adj. for 2-for-1 stk. split, 6/97. ① Bef. extraord. chrg. of $43.0 mill. ② Bef. acctg. chrg. of $488.0 mill., 2002; $59.0 mill., 12/00; $680.0 mill.,1/93. ③ Bef. disc. opers. gain $1.65 bill., 4/99; loss $229.0 mill.,12/96. ④ Incl. a pre-tax net chrg. of $483.0 mill., 12/00; $9.0 mill.,12/94. ⑤ Incl. fin. & insur. subs. ⑥ Incl. special pre-tax chrgs. of $128.0 mill., 2002; $437.0 mill., 2001; $87.0 mill., 1999 & a gain of fr. the sale of bus. of $5.0 mill., 2002; $342.0 mill., 2001; $97.0 mill., 1999. ⑦ Incl. nonrecurr. chrg. of $483.0 mill.

THERMO ELECTRON CORPORATION

EXCH.	SYM.	REC. PRICE	P/E RATIO	YLD.	MKT. CAP.	RANGE (52-WK.)	'02 Y/E PR.
NYSE	TMO	17.60 (2/28/03)	16.0	...	$3.10 bill.	21.33 - 14.33	20.12

MEDIUM GRADE. THE COMPANY IS TARGETING FULL-YEAR 2003 EARNINGS FROM CONTINUING OPERATIONS OF BETWEEN $1.07 AND $1.12 PER SHARE.

INTERIM EARNINGS (Per Share):

Qtr.	Mar.	June	Sept.	Dec.
1997	0.35	0.37	0.41	0.40
1998	0.41	0.37	0.11	0.23
1999	0.17	d1.49	0.22	0.13
2000	0.09	0.13	0.04	0.10
2001	0.12	0.05	0.14	d0.04
2002	0.34	0.28	0.23	0.25

INTERIM DIVIDENDS (Per Share):

Amt.	Decl.	Ex.	Rec.	Pay.
	No dividends paid.			

CAPITALIZATION (12/29/01):

	($000)	(%)
Long-Term Debt	727,502	27.4
Deferred Income Tax	7,907	0.3
Minority Interest	6,901	0.3
Common & Surplus	1,908,142	72.0
Total	2,650,452	100.0

*7 YEAR PRICE SCORE 73.3   ***12 MONTH PRICE SCORE 109.0**
*NYSE COMPOSITE INDEX=100

BUSINESS:

Thermo Electron Corporation reports its business in three segments: Life and Laboratory Sciences (54.4% of 2002 revenues) serves the pharmaceutical, biotechnology, academic, and other research and industrial laboratory markets, as well as the clinical laboratory and healthcare industries. Measurement and Control (29.3%) provides a range of real-time, on-line sensors, monitors, and control systems to customers in industrial markets. Optical Technologies Products (16.3%) includes lasers, photonics, and semiconductor equipment and test systems. Products within the Optical Technologies sector are used in markets such as the scientific instrument, microelectronics, industrial processes, and biomedical industries.

RECENT DEVELOPMENTS:

For the year ended 12/28/02, income from continuing operations was $195.3 million versus income from continuing operations of $49.6 million a year earlier. Results for 2002 and 2001 included restructuring and other charges of $52.1 million and $132.7 million, and amortization of intangible assets of $8.3 million and $47.1 million, respectively. Revenues decreased 4.7% to $2.09 billion. Operating income amounted to $155.5 million versus $34.2 million in 2001.

PROSPECTS:

TMO's lack of top-line growth clouds the Company's near-term outlook. On the plus side, TMO is seeing gains in its Measurement and Control segment, due in part to strong demand for its explosives trace detection equipment and expanded line of radiation-monitoring products used in security applications to protect public safety at borders. However, weakness in the worldwide semiconductor market and slow economic conditions for TMO's industrial customers have affected its entire optical sector. In response, TMO will continue to focus on productivity initiatives as well as new products and services. Accordingly, TMO is targeting full-year 2003 earnings from continuing operations of between $1.07 and $1.12 per share, excluding non-recurring and extraordinary items.

ANNUAL FINANCIAL DATA:

FISCAL YEAR	TOT. REVS. ($mill.)	NET INC. ($mill.)	TOT. ASSETS ($mill.)	OPER. PROFIT %	NET PROFIT %	RET. ON EQUITY %	RET. ON ASSETS %	CURR. RATIO	EARN. PER SH.$	CASH FL. PER SH.$	TANG. BK. VAL.$	DIV. PER SH.$	PRICE RANGE	AVG. P/E RATIO
p12/28/02	2,086.4	⑥ 195.3							⑥ 1.12			...	24.60 - 14.33	17.4
12/29/01	2,188.2	⑤ 49.6	3,825.1	1.6	2.3	2.6	1.3	1.7	⑤ 0.27	0.81	3.17	...	30.62 - 16.55	87.3
12/30/00	2,280.5	④ 62.0	4,863.0	11.7	2.7	2.4	1.3	3.4	④ 0.36	0.94	6.34	...	31.24 - 14.00	62.8
1/01/00	2,471.2	③ d14.6	5,181.8	4.0	...	...	...	2.4	③ d0.11	0.63	4.76	...	20.25 - 12.50	...
1/02/99	3,867.6	① 176.8	6,331.6	8.6	4.6	7.9	2.8	2.9	① 1.07	1.90	2.10	...	44.25 - 13.56	27.0
1/03/98	3,558.3	② 239.3	5,795.9	11.4	6.7	12.0	4.1	2.8	② 1.41	2.13	1.92	...	44.00 - 28.38	25.7
12/28/96	2,932.6	② 190.8	5,141.2	8.4	6.5	10.9	3.7	3.4	② 1.35	2.16	4.48	0.01	44.38 - 29.75	27.5
12/30/95	2,270.3	139.6	3,744.9	9.9	6.1	10.7	3.7	3.4	1.10	1.77	3.25	...	34.67 - 15.94	23.0
12/31/94	1,585.3	103.4	3,019.9	11.3	6.5	10.4	3.4	3.1	0.93	1.50	3.62	...	21.28 - 16.00	20.0
1/01/94	1,249.7	76.6	2,473.7	9.2	6.1	8.9	3.1	3.0	0.78	1.21	3.57	...	19.22 - 13.93	21.3

Statistics are as originally reported. Adj. for 3-for-2 stk. splits, 5/95 & 6/96. ① Incl. nonrecur. chrgs. of $23.6 mill.; bef. extraord. cr. of $5.1 mill. ② Incl. nonrecur. cr., 12/31/97, $78.8 mill.; cr. 12/31/96, $2.8 mill. ③ Incl. restr. & nonrecur. chrgs. of $149.6 mill.; bef. extraord. cr. of $1.5 mill. & loss fr. disc. ops. of $161.5 mill. ④ Incl. restr. & unusual gains of $67.9 mill.; bef. loss fr. disc. ops. of $85.8 mill. & extraord. gain of $532,000. ⑤ Incl. restr. & unusual chrgs. of $132.7 mill.; bef. loss on disp. of disc. ops. of $50.4 mill., extraord. gain of $1.1 mill. & acctg. chrg. of $994,000. ⑥ Incl. restr. & unusual chrgs. of $52.1 mill.; bef. gain on disp. of disc. ops. of $115.4 mill. & extraord. loss of $970,000.

OFFICERS:
R. F. Syron, Chmn.
M. E. Dekkers, Pres., C.E.O.
S. H. Hoogasian, V.P., Gen. Couns., Sec.

INVESTOR CONTACT: Tim Corcoran, (781) 622-1306

PRINCIPAL OFFICE: 81 Wyman St., P.O. Box 9046, Waltham, MA 02454-9046

TELEPHONE NUMBER: (781) 622-1000
FAX: (781) 933-4476
WEB: www.thermo.com
NO. OF EMPLOYEES: 12,000 (approx.)
SHAREHOLDERS: 13,248 (record)
ANNUAL MEETING: In May
INCORPORATED: MA, 1956; reincorp., DE, Oct., 1960

INSTITUTIONAL HOLDINGS:
No. of Institutions: 289
Shares Held: 131,210,459
% Held: 80.2

INDUSTRY: Measuring & controlling devices, nec (SIC: 3829)

TRANSFER AGENT(S): American Stock Transfer & Trust Co., New York, NY

THOMAS & BETTS CORPORATION

EXCH.	SYM.	REC. PRICE	P/E RATIO	YLD.	MKT. CAP.	RANGE (52-WK.)	'02 Y/E PR.
NYSE	TNB	15.13 (2/28/03)	...	...	$0.88 bill.	24.50 - 12.20	16.90

LOWER MEDIUM GRADE. THE COMPANY SHOULD CONTINUE TO BENEFIT FROM THE COMPLETION OF AN AGGRESSIVE MANUFACTURING RESTRUCTURING PROGRAM.

TRADING VOLUME
Thousand Shares

*7 YEAR PRICE SCORE 56.6   ***12 MONTH PRICE SCORE 101.5**
*NYSE COMPOSITE INDEX=100

INTERIM EARNINGS (Per Share):

Qtr.	Mar.	June	Sept.	Dec.
1999	0.67	0.76	0.82	0.40
2000	0.62	d2.87	0.33	d1.20
2001	d0.09	d0.09	0.78	d1.43
2002	d0.20	0.01	0.18	0.23

INTERIM DIVIDENDS (Per Share):

Amt.	Decl.	Ex.	Rec.	Pay.
0.28Q	2/07/01	3/01/01	3/05/01	4/02/01
0.28Q	5/02/01	6/13/01	6/15/01	7/02/01
	Dividend Payment Suspended			

CAPITALIZATION (12/30/01):

	($000)	(%)
Long-Term Debt	618,035	47.5
Common & Surplus	683,285	52.5
Total	1,301,320	100.0

BUSINESS:

Thomas & Betts Corporation is a designer and manufacturer of connectors and components for electrical and communication markets. TNB is also a producer of steel structures, used primarily for utility transmission, and industrial heating units. TNB classifies its products into four business segments. The Electrical segment designs, manufactures and markets electrical connectors, components and other products for electrical applications. The Steel Structures segment designs, manufactures and markets tubular steel transmission and distribution poles and lattice steel transmission towers for North American power and telecommunications companies. The Communications segment designs, manufactures and markets components, subsystems and accessories used to construct, maintain and repair cable television and telecommunications networks. The Heating, Ventilation, and Air Conditioning segment designs, manufactures and markets heating and ventilation products for commercial and industrial buildings.

RECENT DEVELOPMENTS:

For the year ended 12/28/03, loss narrowed to $8.2 million from $138.9 million in 2001. Results for 2002 included an after-tax restructuring charge of $23.8 million, an after-tax charge of $13.1 million for legal settlement, and an after-tax charge of $10.9 million for impact of changes in U.S. tax laws. Results for 2001 included net after-tax, nonrecurring charges of $101.9 million. Net sales declined 10.1% to $1.35 billion.

PROSPECTS:

Going forward, the Company should continue to benefit from the completion of an aggressive manufacturing restructuring program, tightly managed discretionary spending, and an intense focus on effectively managing working capital. However, these gains may be mitigated by weak market conditions. Meanwhile, first quarter trends indicate that 2003 will likely be difficult with little improvements in results. Nevertheless, the Company expects to produce higher net earnings for full-year 2003.

ANNUAL FINANCIAL DATA:

FISCAL YEAR	TOT. REVS. ($mill.)	NET INC. ($mill.)	TOT. ASSETS ($mill.)	OPER. PROFIT %	NET PROFIT %	RET. ON EQUITY %	RET. ON ASSETS %	CURR. RATIO	EARN. PER SH.$	CASH FL. PER SH.$	TANG. BK. VAL.$	DIV. PER SH.$	PRICE RANGE	AVG. P/E RATIO	AVG. YIELD %
12/29/02	1,345.9	7 d8.2		...	...	...	...	...	7 d0.14	...	...	...	24.50 - 12.20	...	...
12/30/01	1,497.5	6 d138.9	1,761.6	...	...	...	...	2.2	6 d2.39	d1.02	3.58	0.84	23.90 - 15.28	...	4.3
12/31/00	1,756.1	4 5 d193.4	2,087.8	...	...	...	...	2.3	4 5 d3.33	d1.70	6.34	1.12	34.38 - 13.06	...	4.7
1/02/00	2,522.0	4 148.3	2,652.7	7.6	5.9	13.6	5.6	2.3	4 2.56	4.25	8.33	1.12	53.69 - 27.56	15.9	2.8
1/03/99	2,230.4	87.5	2,499.6	6.9	3.9	8.6	3.5	1.8	1.54	3.21	6.93	1.12	64.00 - 33.31	31.6	2.3
12/28/97	2,114.7	154.9	2,038.7	12.3	7.3	15.8	7.6	1.8	2.81	4.54	8.58	1.12	59.25 - 40.38	17.7	2.2
12/29/96	1,985.1	3 59.9	2,131.2	9.6	6.1	13.9	5.7	1.9	3 1.13	2.85	6.55	1.12	47.25 - 33.25	35.6	2.8
12/31/95	1,236.8	2 80.9	1,259.4	11.1	6.5	13.5	6.4	1.9	2 2.02	3.39	7.14	1.12	38.13 - 31.00	17.1	3.2
1/01/95	1,076.2	1.9	1,208.2	2.3	0.2	0.3	0.2	1.9	0.05	1.44	5.86	1.12	35.63 - 29.06	645.6	3.5
12/31/93	1,075.9	1 54.9	1,133.2	10.9	5.1	11.4	4.8	2.4	1 1.46	2.99	4.50	1.12	36.00 - 28.50	22.2	3.5

Statistics are as originally reported. Adj. for 2-for-1 stk. split, 4/96. 1 Excl. benefit from acctg. chg. of $1.6 mill. 2 Bef. gain of $65.9 mill. fr. disc. opers.; Incl. restruct. chrg. $79.0 mill. 3 Incl. restruct. chgs., merger exps. & other spec. chgs. totaling $97.1 mill. 4 Incl. a pre-tax rec. for restruct. opers. of $449,000, 2000; $11.6 mill., 1999; pre-tax chrg. of $62.1 mill. 1998. 5 Bef. net gain of $148.8 mill. ($2.56/sh) fr. disc. oper.; Incl. $33.4 mill. impairment chgs. and a pre-tax recovery for restruct. opers. of $2.8 mill. 6 Bef. net gain of $7.5 fr. disc. oper.; Incl. net non-recurr. chrgs. of $95.0 mill. 7 Bef. acctg. chng. chrg. of $44.8 mill. & incl. an after-tax restruct. chrg. of $23.8 mill., an after-tax chrg. of $13.1 mill. for legal settle. and an after-tax chrg. of $10.9 mill. for impact of chngs. in U.S. tax laws.

OFFICERS: T. K. Dunnigan, Chmn., C.E.O. D. J. Pileggi, Pres., C.O.O. J. P. Murphy, Sr. V.P., C.F.O. **INVESTOR CONTACT:** Tricia Bergeren, Investor Relations, (901) 252-8266 **PRINCIPAL OFFICE:** 8155 T & B Boulevard, Memphis, TN 38125	**TELEPHONE NUMBER:** (901) 252-8000 **FAX:** (901) 685-1988 **WEB:** www.tnb.com **NO. OF EMPLOYEES:** 10,000 (approx.) **SHAREHOLDERS:** 3,475 (record) **ANNUAL MEETING:** In May **INCORPORATED:** NJ, 1917; reincorp., TN, May, 1996	**INSTITUTIONAL HOLDINGS:** No. of Institutions: 178 Shares Held: 52,623,643 % Held: 90.3 **INDUSTRY:** Electronic connectors (SIC: 3678) **TRANSFER AGENT(S):** First Chicago Trust Company of New York, Jersey City, NJ

THOR INDUSTRIES, INC.

EXCH.	SYM.	REC. PRICE	P/E RATIO	YLD.	MKT. CAP.	RANGE (52-WK.)	'02 Y/E-PR.
NYSE	THO	25.69 (2/28/03)	10.0	0.2%	$0.73 bill.	42.78 - 21.75	34.43

UPPER MEDIUM GRADE. DURING 2003, THE COMPANY PLANS TO EXPAND ITS ELDORADO NATIONAL CALIFORNIA BUS OPERATION.

INTERIM EARNINGS (Per Share):

Qtr.	Oct.	Jan.	April	July
1997-98	0.23	0.14	0.25	0.18
1998-99	0.29	0.23	0.37	0.39
1999-00	0.40	0.28	0.42	0.40
2000-01	0.35	0.14	0.29	0.36
2001-02	0.29	0.29	0.58	0.71
2002-03	0.73	0.54	...	...

INTERIM DIVIDENDS (Per Share):

Amt.	Decl.	Ex.	Rec.	Pay.
0.02Q	5/22/02	6/12/02	6/14/02	7/03/02
2-for-1	6/11/02	7/09/02	6/19/02	7/08/02
0.01Q	6/11/02	9/26/02	9/30/02	10/11/02
0.01Q	11/15/02	12/18/02	12/20/02	1/03/03
0.01Q	12/10/02	3/12/03	3/14/03	4/02/03

Indicated div.: $0.04

CAPITALIZATION (7/31/02):

	($000)	(%)
Common & Surplus	334,619	100.0
Total	334,619	100.0

*7 YEAR PRICE SCORE 224.4   ***12 MONTH PRICE SCORE 99.6**

*NYSE COMPOSITE INDEX=100

BUSINESS:

Thor Industries, Inc. is the largest manufacturer of recreational vehicles (RVs) in North America and the largest builder of small and mid-size buses in terms of units. The Company manufactures and sells a wide variety of RVs, as well as related parts and accessories, throughout the U.S. and Canada. At 7/31/02, the Company owned or leased about 3.3 million square feet of plant and office space.

Recreation vehicle brand names include AERO, AIRSTREAM, DUTCHMAN, FOUR WINDS, KEYSTONE, KOMFORT, THOR AMERICA, CITAIR, and THOR CALIFORNIA, while bus brand names include CHAMPION, ELDORADO CALIFORNIA, and ELDORADO KANSAS. Fiscal 2002 sales contributions were: RVs, 78.2%; bus products, 21.8%.

RECENT DEVELOPMENTS:

For the quarter ended 1/31/03, net income doubled to $15.4 million compared with $7.7 million in the equivalent 2002 quarter. Net sales advanced 23.1% to $329.9 million from $267.9 million a year earlier. Recreation vehicle sales increased 37.0% to $276.0 million, while bus sales decreased 18.9% to $53.9 million. Gross profit leapt 54.9%

to $45.2 million from $29.1 million in 2001 primarily due to increased recreational vehicle sales and lower material cost on recreation vehicles. RV price increases during the quarter averaged 1.0%, while bus pricing did not increase due to competitive pressures.

PROSPECTS:

At 1/31/03, THO's backlog of recreational vehicles was $180.7 million, up 41.3%, reflecting the continued strength of the marketplace. Meanwhile, the Company's bus vehicle order backlog was $91.6 million, down 21.7% due in part to delayed purchases and funding as a result of state and municipal budget constraints. Separately, during 2003, THO anticipates capital expenditures of about $21.0 mil-

lion in addition to about $14.1 million spent for the six months ended 1/31/03 to complete the plant expansion at its Dutchmen facility, its Four Winds facility and its Keystone facility. Also, THO plans to expand its ElDorado National California bus operations in order to increase production efficiencies and techniques and to produce 40 foot buses.

ANNUAL FINANCIAL DATA:

FISCAL YEAR	TOT. REVS. ($mill.)	NET INC. ($mill.)	TOT. ASSETS ($mill.)	OPER. PROFIT %	NET PROFIT %	RET. ON EQUITY %	RET. ON ASSETS %	CURR. RATIO	EARN. PER SH.$	CASH FL. PER SH.$	TANG. BK. VAL.$	DIV. PER SH.$	PRICE RANGE	AVG. P/E RATIO	AVG. YIELD %
7/31/02	1,245.3	·51.2	497.5	6.4	4.1	15.3	10.3	1.9	1.87	2.06	6.70	0.04	37.18 - 18.65	14.9	0.1
7/31/01	826.9	26.7	309.1	4.7	3.2	12.1	8.6	2.7	1.12	1.32	8.71	0.04	20.38 - 9.84	13.5	0.3
7/31/00	894.0	36.1	282.1	6.4	4.0	18.5	12.8	2.6	1.49	1.68	7.57	0.04	15.28 - 9.53	8.4	0.3
7/31/99	805.8	30.8	245.9	6.2	3.8	18.6	12.5	2.6	1.26	1.41	6.17	0.04	16.00 - 11.13	10.8	0.3
7/31/98	715.6	②19.4	214.0	4.5	2.7	14.0	9.1	2.3	②0.79	0.97	4.94	0.04	14.83 - 10.00	15.7	0.3
7/31/97	624.4	17.8	175.4	4.8	2.9	14.6	10.2	2.6	0.72	0.89	4.15	0.04	11.50 - 6.79	12.8	0.4
7/31/96	602.1	16.1	175.9	4.5	2.7	13.5	9.1	2.4	0.61	0.80	3.69	0.04	8.75 - 5.42	11.7	0.6
7/31/95	562.7	13.8	148.5	3.9	2.5	12.8	9.3	2.7	0.52	0.69	3.11	0.04	7.25 - 5.25	12.1	0.6
7/31/94	491.1	16.0	142.4	5.5	3.3	16.7	11.3	2.2	0.60	0.77	2.66	0.04	10.13 - 6.25	13.6	0.5
7/31/93	412.2	①11.3	122.7	4.7	2.7	13.9	9.2	2.0	①0.42	0.58	2.05	0.04	9.54 - 5.00	17.2	0.6

Statistics are as originally reported. Adj. for stk. split: 50%, 7/02; 4/98. ① Bef. an acctg. credit of $561,000. ② Incl. loss of $2.7 mill. from divestment of Thor West and a gain of $1.3 million from sale of a subsidiary.

OFFICERS:
W. F. Thompson, Chmn., Pres., C.E.O.
P. B. Orthwein, Vice-Chmn., Treas.

INVESTOR CONTACT: Investor Relations,
(937) 596-6849

PRINCIPAL OFFICE: 419 West Pike Street,
Jackson Center, OH 45334-0629

TELEPHONE NUMBER: (937) 596-6849
FAX: (937) 596-6539
WEB: www.thorindustries.com
NO. OF EMPLOYEES: 5,113 (approx.)
SHAREHOLDERS: 193 record
ANNUAL MEETING: In Dec.
INCORPORATED: NE, July, 1980; reincorp.,
DE, July, 1983

INSTITUTIONAL HOLDINGS:
No. of Institutions: 125
Shares Held: 15,077,555
% Held: 52.9

INDUSTRY: Motor homes (SIC: 3716)

TRANSFER AGENT(S): Computershare Investor Services, Chicago, IL

THORNBURG MORTGAGE, INC.

EXCH.	SYM.	REC. PRICE	P/E RATIO	YLD.	MKT. CAP.	RANGE (52-WK.)	'02 Y/E PR.
NYSE	TMA	20.20 (2/28/03)	7.8	11.6%	$1.07 bill.	21.33 - 16.20	20.10

MEDIUM GRADE. TMA IS TARGETING 15.0% TO 20.0% GROWTH IN ITS ORIGINATION BUSINESS IN 2003.

*7 YEAR PRICE SCORE 142.3   ***12 MONTH PRICE SCORE 112.4**

*NYSE COMPOSITE INDEX=100

INTERIM EARNINGS (Per Share):

Qtr.	Mar.	June	Sept.	Dec.
1998	0.42	0.27	0.14	d0.08
1999	0.14	0.25	0.26	0.24
2000	0.25	0.25	0.25	0.28
2001	0.43	0.46	0.52	0.65
2002	0.62	0.63	0.67	0.67

INTERIM DIVIDENDS (Per Share):

Amt.	Decl.	Ex.	Rec.	Pay.
0.55Q	4/23/02	5/01/02	5/03/02	5/17/02
0.57Q	7/23/02	8/01/02	8/05/02	8/16/02
0.58Q	10/21/02	11/01/02	11/05/02	11/18/02
0.585Q	12/17/02	12/27/02	12/31/02	1/24/03

Indicated div.: $2.34 (Div. Reinv. Plan)

CAPITALIZATION (12/31/01):

	($000)	(%)
Long-Term Debt	5,171,408	90.7
Preferred Stock	65,805	1.2
Common & Surplus	466,853	8.2
Total	5,704,066	100.0

BUSINESS:

Thornburg Mortgage, Inc. (formerly Thornburg Mortgage Asset Corp.) is a single-family residential mortgage origination and acquisition company that originates, acquires and invests in adjustable-rate mortgage (ARM) assets comprised of ARM securities and ARM loans. The Company generates income both from its direct investment in these assets and the difference between the yield on its assets and the cost of its borrowings. TMA is organized for tax purposes as a real estate investment trust (REIT). TMA has

five qualified REIT subsidiaries, two of which are involved in financing its mortgage loan assets. The Company's two financing subsidiaries are Thornburg Mortgage Funding Corporation and Thornburg Mortgage Acceptance Corporation. TMA also has a wholly-owned mortgage banking subsidiary, Thornburg Mortgage Home Loans, Inc., that conducts its mortgage loan acquisition and origination activities. Thornburg Mortgage Advisory Corporation carries out the Company's day-to-day operations.

RECENT DEVELOPMENTS:

For the year ended 12/31/02, the Company reported net income of $120.0 million compared with income of $58.7 million, before an accounting change charge of $202,000, in the previous year. Earnings were fueled by favorable market conditions supported by a continued low interest

rate environment. Results for 2002 and 2001 included a net gain on the sale of assets of $903,000 and $1,000, respectively. Net interest income more than doubled to $157.9 million from $78.8 million a year earlier.

PROSPECTS:

TMA's mortgage originations reached historic levels in 2002, closing $2.30 billion of loans during the year and exceeding its mortgage origination target by 34.0%. Looking ahead, origination volumes should remain strong with $728.7 million of loans in the pipeline at 12/31/02, most of which are expected to close during the first quarter of 2003.

Meanwhile, TMA will continue to focus on building direct lending relationships with financial advisors, planners and corporate affinity clients. By pursuing this strategy, TMA believes loan originations can grow between 15.0% to 20.0% and account for 40.0% of its portfolio acquisition needs in 2003.

ANNUAL FINANCIAL DATA:

FISCAL YEAR	TOT. INC. ($000)	NET INC. ($000)	TOT. ASSETS ($000)	NET INC. + DEPR./ ASSETS %	RET. ON EQUITY %	RET. ON ASSETS %	EARN. PER SH. $	TANG. BK. VAL. $	DIV. PER SH. $	DIV. PAYOUT %	PRICE RANGE	AVG. P/E RATIO	AVG. YIELD %
p12/31/02	401,967	120,016					2.59		2.25	86.9	21.33 - 16.20	7.2	12.0
12/31/01	278,594	① 58,662	5,803,648	1.0	11.0	1.0	① 2.10	14.02	1.45	69.0	21.50 - 9.13	7.3	9.5
12/31/00	289,973	29,165	4,190,167	0.7	9.2	0.7	1.05	11.67	0.94	89.5	9.81 - 7.06	8.0	11.1
12/31/99	260,365	25,584	4,375,965	0.6	8.2	0.6	0.88	11.40	0.92	104.5	11.38 - 7.44	10.7	9.8
12/31/98	287,032	22,695	4,344,633	0.5	7.3	0.5	0.75	11.45	1.41	187.3	18.50 - 5.63	16.1	11.6
12/31/97	247,721	41,402	4,691,116	0.9	11.6	0.9	1.94	14.42	1.92	99.0	24.25 - 15.88	10.3	9.6
12/31/96	151,883	25,737	2,755,358	0.9	11.6	0.9	1.73	13.70	1.58	91.3	21.50 - 14.13	10.3	8.9
12/31/95	116,049	10,452	2,017,985	1.0	6.5	0.5	0.88	13.16	0.70	79.5	15.88 - 7.38	13.2	6.0
12/31/94	85,661	11,946	1,751,832	0.7	10.0	0.7	1.02	10.19	0.99	97.0	17.38 - 6.75	11.8	8.2
12/31/93	12,168	2,572	1,364,429	0.2	1.5	0.2	0.36	14.50	0.15	41.7	17.75 - 14.50	44.8	0.9

Statistics are as originally reported. ① Excl. acctg. chrg. $202,000

OFFICERS:
G. Thornburg, Chmn., C.E.O.
L. A. Goldstone, Pres., C.O.O.
R. P. Story, Exec. V.P., C.F.O., Treas.
INVESTOR CONTACT: Leanne L. Gallagher, Investor Relations, (505) 954-5302
PRINCIPAL OFFICE: 150 Washington Avenue, Suite 302, Santa Fe, NM 87501

TELEPHONE NUMBER: (505) 989-1900
FAX: (505) 989-8156
WEB: www.thornburg.com
NO. OF EMPLOYEES: N/A
SHAREHOLDERS: 1,927
ANNUAL MEETING: In April
INCORPORATED: MD, July, 1992

INSTITUTIONAL HOLDINGS:
No. of Institutions: 111
Shares Held: 11,077,176
% Held: 21.1
INDUSTRY: Real estate investment trusts (SIC: 6798)
TRANSFER AGENT(S): American Stock Transfer & Trust Company, New York, NY

3M COMPANY

EXCH.	SYM.	REC. PRICE	P/E RATIO	YLD.	MKT. CAP.	RANGE (52-WK.)	'02 Y/E PR.	DIV. ACH.
NYSE	MMM	125.37 (2/28/03)	25.0	2.1%	$49.06 bill.	131.55 - 108.20	123.30	44 yrs.

UPPER MEDIUM GRADE. THE COMPANY EXPECTS TO BENEFIT FROM ITS RECENT BUSINESS PORTFOLIO REALIGNMENT.

INTERIM EARNINGS (Per Share):

Qtr.	Mar.	June	Sept.	Dec.
1999	0.95	1.17	1.13	1.10
2000	1.21	1.18	1.25	1.00
2001	1.13	0.50	0.99	0.96
2002	1.14	1.18	1.21	1.31

INTERIM DIVIDENDS (Per Share):

Amt.	Decl.	Ex.	Rec.	Pay.
0.60Q	11/12/01	11/20/01	11/23/01	12/12/01
0.62Q	2/11/02	2/20/02	2/22/02	3/12/02
0.62Q	5/14/02	5/22/02	5/24/02	6/12/02
0.62Q	8/12/02	8/21/02	8/23/02	9/12/02
0.62Q	11/11/02	11/20/02	11/22/02	12/12/02

Indicated div.: $2.48 (Div. Reinv. Plan)

TRADING VOLUME
Thousand Shares

*7 YEAR PRICE SCORE 137.5   *12 MONTH PRICE SCORE 111.3

*NSYE COMPOSITE INDEX=100

CAPITALIZATION (12/31/01):

	($000)	(%)
Long-Term Debt	1,520,000	20.0
Common & Surplus	6,086,000	80.0
Total	7,606,000	100.0

BUSINESS:

3M Company (formerly Minnesota Mining and Manufacturing Company) is a worldwide producer of a diverse variety of industrial and consumer products. MMM has operations in more than 60 countries and serves customers in nearly 200 countries. 3M operates in seven business sectors: Transportation Graphics and Safety (23.5% of 2002 revenues) provides reflective sheeting, high-performance graphics, respirators and optical films; Health Care (21.8%) provides skin health products, medical/surgical supplies and devices, infection control, cardiovascular systems, health care information systems, pharmaceuticals, and dental products; Industrial (19.7%) provides telecommunications products, industrial tapes, industrial abrasives, and specialty materials, including protective material for furniture and fabrics, firefighting agents and engineering fluids; Consumer and Office (17.1%) provides consumer and office products; Electro and Communications (11.7%) provides electronic and electrical products; Specialty Material (5.8%) provides specialty materials, including protective material for furniture and fabrics, firefighting agents and engineering fluids; and Corporate and Unallocated (0.4%).

RECENT DEVELOPMENTS:

For the year ended 12/31/02, net income increased 38.0% to $1.97 billion from $1.43 billion the year before. Net sales grew 1.7% to $16.33 billion from $16.05 billion a year earlier. Transportation, graphics and safety sales advanced 8.9% to $3.84 billion. Health care sales rose 7.8% to $3.56 billion, while industrial sales improved 1.0% to $3.23 billion. Operating income grew 34.0% to $3.05 billion compared with $2.27 billion in the previous year.

PROSPECTS:

The Company expects to benefit from its recent business portfolio realignment, which involved reorganizing its businesses into seven units from six in order to better focus on markets and customers. Separately, in 2003, earnings per share are anticipated between $1.38 and $1.43 in the first quarter, and range from $5.80 to $6.00 for the full year. Meanwhile, on 1/22/03, Dyneon LLC, a subsidiary of MMM, acquired Solvay Fluoropolymers, Inc., a subsidiary of Solvay America, Inc. The acquisition should contribute to Dyneon's growing fluoropolymers business.

ANNUAL FINANCIAL DATA:

FISCAL YEAR	TOT. REVS. ($mill.)	NET INC. ($mill.)	TOT. ASSETS ($mill.)	OPER. PROFIT %	NET PROFIT %	RET. ON EQUITY %	RET. ON ASSETS %	CURR. RATIO	EARN. PER SH.$	CASH FL. PER SH.$	TANG. BK. VAL.$	DIV. PER SH.$	PRICE RANGE	AVG. P/E RATIO	AVG. YIELD %
p12/31/02	16,332.0	1,974.0	15,329.0	18.7		32.9	12.9		5.06			2.48	131.55 - 100.00	22.9	2.1
12/31/01	16,079.0	⑦1,430.0	14,606.0	14.1	8.9	23.5	9.8	1.4	⑦3.58	6.30	15.55	2.40	127.00 - 85.86	29.7	2.3
12/31/00	16,724.0	⑥1,857.0	14,522.0	18.3	11.1	28.4	12.8	1.3	⑥4.64	7.21	16.49	2.32	122.94 - 78.19	21.7	2.3
12/31/99	15,659.0	⑤1,763.0	13,896.0	18.9	11.3	28.0	12.7	1.6	⑤4.34	6.55	15.77	2.24	103.38 - 69.31	19.9	2.6
12/31/98	15,021.0	④1,213.0	14,153.0	13.6	8.1	20.4	8.6	1.4	④2.97	5.10	14.80	2.20	97.88 - 65.63	27.5	2.7
12/31/97	15,070.0	②2,121.0	13,238.0	17.8	14.1	35.8	16.0	1.5	③5.06	7.14	14.63	2.12	105.50 - 80.00	18.3	2.3
12/31/96	14,236.0	1,516.0	13,364.0	17.5	10.6	24.1	11.3	1.8	3.63	5.74	15.07	1.92	85.88 - 61.25	20.3	2.6
12/31/95	13,460.0	①1,306.0	14,183.0	16.5	9.7	19.0	9.2	1.2	②3.11	5.15	16.43	1.88	69.88 - 50.75	19.4	3.1
12/31/94	15,079.0	①1,322.0	14,413.0	14.9	8.8	19.6	9.2	1.5	①3.13	5.73	16.03	1.76	57.13 - 46.38	16.5	3.4
12/31/93	14,020.0	1,263.0	12,894.0	14.0	9.0	19.4	9.8	1.6	2.91	5.39	15.14	1.66	58.50 - 48.63	18.4	3.1

Statistics are as originally reported. Adj. for 2-for-1 split, 4/94. ① Incl. pre-tax litigation chg. of $35.0 mill. ② Bef. disc. ops. loss of $330.0 mill. ① Incl $803.0 mill. gain fr. sale of outdoor adver. bus. ④ Bef. extraord. chrg. of $38.0 mill.; incl. pre-tax restruct. chrg. of $493.0 mill. & a gain on divest. of $10.0 mill. ⑤ Incl. a one-time net gain of $100.0 mill. related to various items. ⑥ Incl. a net after-tax chrg. of $15.0 mill. & excl. an acctg. chrg. of $75.0 mill. ⑦ Incl. non-recurr. net chrgs. of $504.0 mill. rel. to various items.

OFFICERS:
W. J. McNerney Jr., Chmn., C.E.O.
P. D. Campbell, Sr. V.P., C.F.O.

INVESTOR CONTACT: Matt Ginter, Director, Investor Relations, (651) 733-8206

PRINCIPAL OFFICE: 3M Center, St. Paul, MN 55144

TELEPHONE NUMBER: (651) 733-1110
FAX: (651) 737-3061
WEB: www.3m.com
NO. OF EMPLOYEES: 71,669 (avg.)
SHAREHOLDERS: 127,196
ANNUAL MEETING: In May
INCORPORATED: MN, July, 1902; reincorp., DE, June, 1929

INSTITUTIONAL HOLDINGS:
No. of Institutions: 912
Shares Held: 276,520,407
% Held: 70.9
INDUSTRY: Adhesives and sealants (SIC: 2891)
TRANSFER AGENT(S): Wells Fargo Shareowner Services, St. Paul, MN

TIDEWATER INC.

EXCH.	SYM.	REC. PRICE	P/E RATIO	YLD.	MKT. CAP.	RANGE (52-WK.)	'02 Y/E PR.
NYSE	TDW	30.62 (2/28/03)	17.6	2.0%	$1.72 bill.	45.70 - 23.38	31.10

MEDIUM GRADE. THE COMPANY ENTERED INTO AN AGREEMENT TO ACQUIRE ENSCO INTERNATIONAL INCORPORATED'S GULF OF MEXICO BASED MARINE FLEET FOR $79.0 MILLION.

TRADING VOLUME
Thousand Shares

*7 YEAR PRICE SCORE 92.1   *12 MONTH PRICE SCORE 98.3
*NYSE COMPOSITE INDEX=100

INTERIM EARNINGS (Per Share):

Qtr.	June	Sept.	Dec.	Mar.
1997-98	0.80	1.01	1.15	1.05
1998-99	1.05	0.98	0.71	0.93
1999-00	0.30	0.34	0.40	0.34
2000-01	0.15	0.47	0.40	0.53
2001-02	0.69	0.63	0.60	0.50
2002-03	0.41	0.41	0.42	...

INTERIM DIVIDENDS (Per Share):

Amt.	Decl.	Ex.	Rec.	Pay.
0.15Q	1/31/02	2/07/02	2/11/02	2/21/02
0.15Q	6/06/02	6/13/02	6/17/02	6/27/02
0.15Q	7/25/02	8/01/02	8/05/02	8/15/02
0.15Q	11/21/02	11/27/02	12/02/02	12/12/02
0.15Q	1/30/03	2/06/03	2/10/03	2/20/03

Indicated div.: $0.60

CAPITALIZATION (3/31/02):

	($000)	(%)
Long-Term Debt	54,000	3.6
Deferred Income Tax	173,422	11.5
Common & Surplus	1,285,818	85.0
Total	1,513,240	100.0

BUSINESS:

Tidewater Inc. is a major provider of offshore supply vessels and marine support services serving the energy industry. TDW, through its fleet of over 550 vessels as of 1/21/03, serves most of the world's significant oil and gas exploration and production markets and provides services supporting all phases of offshore exploration, development and production. TDW's services include: the towing of and anchor-handling of mobile drilling rigs and equipment;

transporting supplies and personnel necessary to sustain drilling, workover and production activities; assisting in offshore construction activities; and a variety of specialized services including pipe laying, cable laying and 3-D seismic work. Principal markets served by TDW include the U.S. Gulf of Mexico, the North Sea, the Persian Gulf, and areas offshore Australia, Brazil, Egypt, India, Indonesia, Malaysia, Mexico, Trinidad, Venezuela, and West Africa.

RECENT DEVELOPMENTS:

For the Company's fiscal third quarter ended 12/31/02, net earnings were $23.6 million compared with $33.5 million in the corresponding year-earlier period. Results included a pre-tax loss of $12,000 for 2002 and a pre-tax gain of

$780,000 for 2001 on the sale of assets. Total revenue decreased 10.3% to $163.1 million from $181.8 million the previous year. Total costs and expenses declined 27.5% to $34.0 million.

PROSPECTS:

On 2/20/03, TDW announced that it has entered into an agreement with ENSCO International Incorporated to acquire ENSCO's 27-vessel Gulf of Mexico based marine fleet. The five anchor handling towing-supply vessels, six modern large capacity 220-foot "stretched" platform supply vessels, 13 standard supply vessels and three utility vessels are being acquired for a cash price of $79.0 million. Also included in the agreement is a provision that gives

TDW the opportunity to provide supply, anchor handling and towing vessels to ENSCO for its Gulf of Mexico operations. The acquisition, which is expected to close in early April 2003, is intended to enhance TDW's competitive position in the business of anchor handling and towing-supply services in the Gulf of Mexico. In addition, the acquisition should help better position the Company for an upturn in the domestic market.

ANNUAL FINANCIAL DATA:

FISCAL YEAR	TOT. REVS. ($mill.)	NET INC. ($mill.)	TOT. ASSETS ($mill.)	OPER. PROFIT %	NET PROFIT %	RET. ON EQUITY %	RET. ON ASSETS %	CURR. RATIO	EARN. PER SH. $	CASH FL. PER SH. $	TANG. BK. VAL. $	DIV. PER SH. $	PRICE RANGE	AVG. P/E RATIO	AVG. YIELD %
3/31/02	729.0	⑤ 136.2	1,669.4	26.3	18.7	10.6	8.2	3.2	⑤ 2.41	3.80	17.02	0.60	52.95 — 24.13	16.0	1.6
3/31/01	616.7	⑤ 86.1	1,505.5	13.4	14.0	7.3	5.7	3.5	⑤ 1.53	2.94	15.16	0.60	49.69 — 25.19	24.5	1.6
3/31/00	574.8	⑤ 76.6	1,423.3	11.6	13.3	6.9	5.3	5.4	⑤ 1.37	2.85	12.82	0.60	36.50 — 18.31	20.0	2.2
3/31/99	969.0	① 210.7	1,394.5	27.2	21.7	19.7	15.1	3.4	① 3.68	5.33	11.90	0.60	55.19 — 17.06	9.8	1.7
3/31/98	1,060.2	② 243.0	1,492.8	34.2	22.9	24.3	16.3	1.6	② 3.99	5.49	10.80	0.60	70.50 — 35.88	13.3	1.1
3/31/97	803.0	③ 146.0	1,039.0	25.7	18.2	19.0	14.1	2.8	③ 2.34	3.67	12.40	0.55	50.00 — 29.38	17.0	1.4
3/31/96	643.4	76.2	978.2	17.7	11.8	10.3	7.8	2.4	1.23	2.55	11.57	0.45	31.63 — 16.50	19.6	1.9
3/31/95	538.8	42.6	902.2	11.2	7.9	7.3	4.7	2.0	0.80	2.42	10.43	0.40	25.00 — 18.00	26.9	1.9
3/31/94	522.1	③ 36.1	809.9	10.7	6.9	6.5	4.5	2.2	③ 0.67	2.25	10.49	0.38	27.00 — 16.38	32.4	1.7
3/31/93	475.5	④ 27.8	806.4	10.1	5.8	5.1	3.4	3.1	④ 0.53	2.04	10.36	0.15	21.00 — 11.38	30.5	0.9

Statistics are as originally reported. ① Incls. one-time gain of $5.1 mill. ② Incls. one-time credit of $16.5 mill.; bef. gain of $61.7 mill. from disc. ops. ③ Incls. one-time credit 3/97, $6.4 mill.; credit 3/94, $4.6 mill. ④ Incls. one-time credit of $3.1 mill.; bef. gain of $3.4 mill. from disc. ops. ⑤ Incls. gain on sale of assets: 3/02, $6.4 mill.; 3/01, $22.8 mill.; 3/00, $19.4 mill.

OFFICERS:
D. E. Taylor, Pres., C.E.O.
J. K. Lousteau, Sr. V.P., C.F.O., Treas.
C. F. Laborde, Exec. V.P., Gen. Couns.
INVESTOR CONTACT: Keith Lousteau, Sr. V.P., C.F.O., Treas., (504) 568-1010
PRINCIPAL OFFICE: 601 Poydras Street, Suite 1900, New Orleans, LA 70130

TELEPHONE NUMBER: (504) 568-1010
FAX: (504) 566-4582
WEB: www.tdw.com
NO. OF EMPLOYEES: 6,800 (approx.)
SHAREHOLDERS: 1,779 (approx. record)
ANNUAL MEETING: In July
INCORPORATED: DE, Feb., 1956

INSTITUTIONAL HOLDINGS:
No. of Institutions: 249
Shares Held: 45,729,731
% Held: 80.9
INDUSTRY: Towing and tugboat service (SIC: 4492)
TRANSFER AGENT(S): Fleet National Bank, c/o EquiServe L.P., Providence, RI

TIFFANY & CO.

EXCH.	SYM.	REC. PRICE	P/E RATIO	YLD.	MKT. CAP.	RANGE (52-WK.)	'02 Y/E PR.
NYSE	TIF	23.97 (2/28/03)	18.7	0.7%	$3.48 bill.	41.00 - 19.40	23.91

INVESTMENT GRADE. GOING FORWARD, THE COMPANY INTENDS TO MAINTAIN ITS NORMAL PACE OF STORE EXPANSION AND PRODUCT DEVELOPMENT.

*7 YEAR PRICE SCORE 137.4   ***12 MONTH PRICE SCORE 88.5**

*NYSE COMPOSITE INDEX=100

INTERIM EARNINGS (Per Share):

Qtr.	Apr.	July	Oct.	Jan.
1996-97	0.04	0.06	0.07	0.25
1997-98	0.07	0.08	0.08	0.30
1998-99	0.08	0.10	0.09	0.38
1999-00	0.11	0.16	0.15	0.56
2000-01	0.20	0.26	0.24	0.56
2001-02	0.20	0.24	0.16	0.55
2002-03	0.22	0.24	0.24	0.60

INTERIM DIVIDENDS (Per Share):

Amt.	Decl.	Ex.	Rec.	Pay.
0.04Q	2/20/02	3/18/02	3/20/02	4/10/02
0.04Q	5/16/02	6/18/02	6/20/02	7/10/02
0.04Q	8/13/02	9/18/02	9/20/02	10/10/02
0.04Q	11/21/02	12/18/02	12/20/02	1/10/03
0.04Q	2/20/03	3/18/03	3/20/03	4/10/03

Indicated div.: $0.16

CAPITALIZATION (1/31/02):

	($000)	(%)
Long-Term Debt	179,065	14.7
Common & Surplus	1,036,945	85.3
Total	1,216,010	100.0

BUSINESS:

Tiffany & Co. is a designer, manufacturer, retailer and distributor offering an extensive array of fine jewelry, sterling silverware, china, crystal, timepieces, stationery, writing instruments, leather goods, scarves, and fragrances. As of 11/13/02, the Company operated 135 retail stores worldwide, including 48 stores in the U.S. TIF operates three channels of distribution: U.S. Retail (49.0% of fiscal 2002 net sales) includes retail sales in Company-operated stores in the U.S.; International Retail (41.0%) includes retail sales through Company-operated stores outside the U.S, along with Internet sales and wholesale sales to independent retailers and distributors in certain international markets; and Direct Marketing (10.0%) includes business-to-business, catalog and Internet sales in the U.S.

RECENT DEVELOPMENTS:

For the year ended 1/31/03, net earnings increased 9.4% to $189.9 million from $173.6 million the year before. Net sales totaled $1.71 billion, up 6.2% versus $1.61 billion a year earlier. U.S. retail sales grew 4.0% to $819.8 million, while international retail sales rose 4.0% to $683.5 million. Direct marketing sales were up 11.0% to $179.2 million. Gross profit was $1.01 billion, or 59.3% of net sales, versus $943.5 million, or 58.7% of net sales, the year before. During 2002, the Company opened five stores, one of which replaced two hotel-based retail locations that were closed, in the U.S. Additionally, TIF opened two department-store retail locations and closed one in Japan, and opened retail locations in Korea, Taiwan and Paris.

PROSPECTS:

Going forward, the Company intends to maintain its normal pace of store expansion and product development. Looking ahead to the full-year 2003, TIF expects a low-teens percentage increase in net sales, including mid-single-digit comparable store sales increases in the U.S. and Japan, and 5.0% growth in retail store square footage. The Company also anticipates a mid-to-high single-digit increase in net earnings, or diluted earnings per share of $1.33 to $1.38 in 2003. In addition, cash flow is expected to be healthy, while capital expenditures will decelerate to about 8.0% of net sales as a result of the completion of some major projects.

ANNUAL FINANCIAL DATA:

FISCAL YEAR	TOT. REVS. ($mill.)	NET INC. ($mill.)	TOT. ASSETS ($mill.)	OPER. PROFIT %	NET PROFIT %	RET. ON EQUITY %	RET. ON ASSETS %	CURR. RATIO	EARN. PER SH.$	CASH FL. PER SH.$	TANG. BK. VAL.$	DIV. PER SH.$	PRICE RANGE	AVG. P/E RATIO	AVG. YIELD %
p1/31/03	1,706.6	189.9	1,923.6						1.28			0.16	41.00 - 19.40	23.6	0.5
1/31/02	1,606.5	173.6	1,629.9	19.3	10.8	16.7	10.7	2.8	1.15	1.58	7.15	0.16	38.25 - 19.90	25.3	0.5
1/31/01	1,668.1	190.6	1,568.3	19.6	11.4	20.6	12.2	3.0	1.26	1.56	6.34	0.14	45.38 - 27.09	28.8	0.4
1/31/00	1,461.9	145.7	1,343.6	17.6	10.0	19.2	10.8	3.2	0.98	1.25	5.22	0.10	45.00 - 12.63	29.5	0.4
1/31/99	1,169.2	90.1	1,057.0	13.8	7.7	17.4	8.5	2.8	0.63	0.83	3.72	0.08	13.00 - 6.75	15.8	0.8
1/31/98	1,017.6	72.8	827.1	13.1	7.2	16.4	8.8	2.5	0.51	0.66	3.18	0.06	12.16 - 8.44	20.4	0.6
1/31/97	922.1	②58.4	739.4	11.9	6.3	15.4	7.9	2.5	②0.42	0.57	2.70	0.04	10.56 - 6.17	20.0	0.5
1/31/96	803.3	39.2	654.3	10.0	4.9	14.8	6.0	2.3	0.31	0.45	2.02	0.04	6.86 - 3.63	17.2	0.7
1/31/95	682.8	29.3	551.4	9.5	4.3	13.2	5.3	2.4	0.23	0.36	1.71	0.04	5.45 - 3.56	19.5	0.8
1/31/94	451.5	①d10.2	504.4	…	…	…	…	2.4	①d0.08	0.03	1.51	0.04	4.75 - 3.02	…	0.9

Statistics are as originally reported. Adj. for 2-for-1 stk. splits, 7/00, 7/99 & 7/96. ① Incl. $32.7 mil ($0.26/sh) chg. ② Incl. $100,000 non-recur. net gain.

OFFICERS:
W. R. Chaney, Chmn.
M. J. Kowalski, Pres., & C.E.O.
J. N. Fernandez, Exec. V.P., C.F.O.
INVESTOR CONTACT: Mark L. Aaron, V.P., Inv. Rel., (212) 230-5301
PRINCIPAL OFFICE: 727 Fifth Avenue, New York, NY 10022

TELEPHONE NUMBER: (212) 755-8000
FAX: (212) 605-4465
WEB: www.tiffany.com
NO. OF EMPLOYEES: 5,938 (approx.)
SHAREHOLDERS: 3,416
ANNUAL MEETING: In May
INCORPORATED: DE, Aug., 1984

INSTITUTIONAL HOLDINGS:
No. of Institutions: 329
Shares Held: 141,682,587
% Held: 97.6

INDUSTRY: Jewelry stores (SIC: 5944)

TRANSFER AGENT(S): Mellon Investor Services LLC, Ridgefield Park, NJ

TIMBERLAND CO. (THE)

EXCH.	SYM.	REC. PRICE	P/E RATIO	YLD.	MKT. CAP.	RANGE (52-WK.)	'02 Y/E PR.
NYSE	TBL	38.40 (2/28/03)	16.1	...	$1.47 bill.	45.95 - 25.80	35.61

UPPER MEDIUM GRADE. THE COMPANY IS TARGETING LOW DOUBLE-DIGIT REVENUE GROWTH FOR THE FIRST HALF OF 2003.

7 YEAR PRICE SCORE 154.4 **12 MONTH PRICE SCORE 103.4**
*NYSE COMPOSITE INDEX=100

INTERIM EARNINGS (Per Share):

Qtr.	Mar.	June	Sept.	Dec.
1997	0.10	0.02	0.53	0.37
1998	0.16	0.04	0.62	0.45
1999	0.18	0.06	0.81	0.69
2000	0.34	0.26	1.35	0.96
2001	0.43	0.26	1.22	0.77
2002	0.23	0.13	1.30	0.73

INTERIM DIVIDENDS (Per Share):

Amt.	Decl.	Ex.	Rec.	Pay.
		No dividends paid.		

CAPITALIZATION (12/31/01):

	($000)	(%)
Deferred Income Tax	9,349	2.5
Common & Surplus	359,238	97.5
Total	368,587	100.0

BUSINESS:

The Timberland Company designs, engineers and markets premium quality footwear, apparel and accessories under the TIMBERLAND® brand name, and the MOUNTAIN ATHLETICS™ by Timberland and TIMBERLAND PRO™ series sub-brands. Timberland® products for men, women and children include premium boots, casual shoes, hiking boots and boat shoes, as well as outdoor-inspired apparel and accessories manufactured to withstand the elements of nature. THE MOUNTAIN ATHLETICS™ by Timberland series offers footwear and gear for the outdoor athlete, and the TIMBERLAND PRO™ series provides workboots engineered to meet the demands of the professional trades person. The Company's products can be found in better-grade department and specialty stores as well as Timberland® retail stores throughout North America, Europe, Asia, Latin America, and the Middle East.

RECENT DEVELOPMENTS:

For the year ended 12/31/02, the Company reported income of $90.2 million, before an accounting change charge of $4.9 million, versus net income of $106.7 million in the previous year. Earnings were restrained by a soft retail environment combined with higher operating costs. Revenue inched up 0.6% to $1.19 billion from $1.18 billion in 2001. Gross profit declined to $518.3 million from $520.8 million a year earlier. Selling expenses grew 5.1% to $307.0 million, while general and administrative expenses climbed 12.2% to $72.5 million. Operating income amounted to $138.8 million, down 14.9% from $163.1million the year before.

PROSPECTS:

Going forward, results should benefit from progress on key strategic fronts, including expansion of the Company's international operations, strengthening of TBL's U.S. footwear business and extension of brand recognition through ongoing development of its apparel and accessories businesses. Accordingly, the Company is targeting low double-digit revenue growth for the first half of 2003, with moderate improvements in operating margins throughout the year. Meanwhile, TBL, which continues to maintain a cautious outlook for the second half of 2003, is forecasting revenue growth in the mid single-digit range.

ANNUAL FINANCIAL DATA:

FISCAL YEAR	TOT. REVS. ($000)	NET INC. ($000)	TOT. ASSETS ($000)	OPER. PROFIT %	NET PROFIT %	RET. ON EQUITY %	RET. ON ASSETS %	CURR. RATIO	EARN. PER SH.$	CASH FL. PER SH.$	TANG. BK. VAL.$	PRICE RANGE	AVG. P/E RATIO
p12/31/02	1,190,896	③ 90,200	504,612	13.8	9.0	29.7	21.2	3.2	③ 2.49	3.20	9.00	45.95 - 25.80	14.4
12/31/01	1,183,623	106,741	476,311	16.9	11.4	39.2	26.1	2.6	2.65	3.36	7.60	74.25 - 25.65	18.8
12/31/00	1,091,478	② 124,124	493,311	12.7	8.2	27.6	15.3	3.7	② 2.91	2.25	6.17	71.00 - 18.13	15.3
12/31/99	917,216	75,247	469,467	11.0	6.9	22.2	12.6	4.0	1.26	1.64	7.05	21.94 - 7.02	11.5
12/31/98	862,168	59,156	420,003	10.5	5.9	22.0	11.3	3.5	1.01	1.44	4.27	20.72 - 9.16	14.8
12/31/97	796,458	47,321		7.4	3.0	12.3	4.5	3.6	0.45	0.93	3.20	10.03 - 4.13	15.6
12/31/96	689,973	20,419	449,586	...	...	...	...	4.8	① d0.26	0.17	2.67	9.16 - 4.38	...
12/31/95	655,138	① d11,635	421,408	6.8	2.8	11.9	3.7	3.5	0.40	0.74	2.81	15.25 - 4.97	25.6
12/31/94	637,545	17,710	473,264	9.6	5.4	17.5	7.7	3.4	0.50	0.73	2.54	21.34 - 4.72	26.0
12/31/93	418,918	22,521	290,611										

Statistics are as originally reported. Adj. for stk. splits: 2-for-1, 7/00, 9/99 ① Incl. restr. chrg. $16.0 mill. ② Bef. extraord. chrg. $2.1 mill. ③ Bef. acctg. chrg. $4.9 mill.

OFFICERS:
S. W. Swartz, Chmn.
J. B. Swartz, Pres., C.E.O.
B. P. McKeon, Sr. V.P., C.F.O.
INVESTOR CONTACT: Susan Ostrow, Investor Relations, (603) 773-1212
PRINCIPAL OFFICE: 200 Domain Drive, Stratham, NH 03885

TELEPHONE NUMBER: (603) 772-9500
FAX: (603) 773-1640
WEB: www.timberland.com
NO. OF EMPLOYEES: 5,600 (approx.)
SHAREHOLDERS: 812 (class A); 7 (class B)
ANNUAL MEETING: In May
INCORPORATED: DE, Dec., 1978

INSTITUTIONAL HOLDINGS:
No. of Institutions: 156
Shares Held: 32,730,962
% Held: 88.8
INDUSTRY: Men's footwear, except athletic (SIC: 3143)
TRANSFER AGENT(S): State Street Bank & Trust Company, Boston, MA

TIMKEN COMPANY (THE)

EXCH.	SYM.	REC. PRICE	P/E RATIO	YLD.	MKT. CAP.	RANGE (52-WK.)	'02 Y/E PR.
NYSE	TKR	16.03 (2/28/03)	19.3	3.2%	$0.96 bill.	27.41 - 14.88	19.10

MEDIUM GRADE. THE PENDING ACQUISITION OF THE TORRINGTON COMPANY IS PROCEEDING AS EXPECTED.

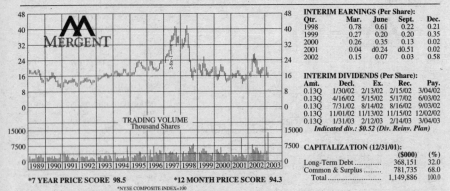

INTERIM EARNINGS (Per Share):

Qtr.	Mar.	June	Sept.	Dec.
1998	0.78	0.61	0.22	0.21
1999	0.27	0.20	0.20	0.35
2000	0.26	0.35	0.13	0.02
2001	0.04	d0.24	d0.51	0.02
2002	0.15	0.07	0.03	0.58

INTERIM DIVIDENDS (Per Share):

Amt.	Decl.	Ex.	Rec.	Pay.
0.13Q	1/30/02	2/13/02	2/15/02	3/04/02
0.13Q	4/16/02	5/15/02	5/17/02	6/03/02
0.13Q	7/31/02	8/14/02	8/16/02	9/03/02
0.13Q	11/01/02	11/13/02	11/15/02	12/02/02
0.13Q	1/31/03	2/12/03	2/14/03	3/04/03

Indicated div.: $0.52 (Div. Reinv. Plan)

TRADING VOLUME
Thousand Shares

CAPITALIZATION (12/31/01):

	($000)	(%)
Long-Term Debt	368,151	32.0
Common & Surplus	781,735	68.0
Total	1,149,886	100.0

*7 YEAR PRICE SCORE 98.5   ***12 MONTH PRICE SCORE 94.3**
*NYSE COMPOSITE INDEX=100

BUSINESS:

The Timken Company is an international manufacturer of anti-friction bearings and steel. Products fall into two industry segments. The first includes tapered roller bearings used in a multitude of applications to reduce friction and conserve energy. The second classification is steel products including low and intermediate alloy, vacuum processed alloys, tool steel, carbon grades and custom-made steel

products. Bearings are manufactured in the U.S., Brazil, Canada, France, South Africa, Australia and the U.K. Alloy mechanical tubing, alloy bars and high-alloy specialty steels are produced in the U.S. In 2002, 34.6% 33.0% and 32.4% of net sales were derived from industrial bearings, automotive bearings and steel, respectively.

RECENT DEVELOPMENTS:

For the year ended 12/31/02, income amounted to $51.5 million, before an accounting change charge of $12.7 million, compared with a net loss of $41.7 million in 2001. Results for 2002 and 2001 included impairment and restructuring charges of $32.1 million and $54.7 million, and reorganization charges of $18.4 million and $12.6 million, respectively. Results for 2001 included goodwill

amortization of $6.1 million. Results for 2002 and 2001 included receipt of Continued Dumping & Subsidy Offset Act payment of $50.2 million and $29.6 million, respectively. Net sales grew 4.2% to $2.55 billion from $2.45 billion a year earlier due to strong automotive markets in North America.

PROSPECTS:

TKR's proposed acquisition of The Torrington Company from Ingersoll Rand Company Limited for about $840.0 million is proceeding as expected. TKR received U.S. antitrust approval for the acquisition under the Hart-Scott-Rodino Act in December. The transaction is expected to close during the first quarter of 2003, pending additional

regulatory clearances outside the United States, successful completion of debt and equity financing, and customary closing conditions. In connection with the acquisition, the Company believes that it can attain pretax savings of about $80.0 million by the end of 2005 before implementation costs.

ANNUAL FINANCIAL DATA:

FISCAL YEAR	TOT. REVS. ($mill.)	NET INC. ($mill.)	TOT. ASSETS ($mill.)	OPER. PROFIT %	NET PROFIT %	RET. ON EQUITY %	RET. ON ASSETS %	CURR. RATIO	EARN. PER SH. $	CASH FL. PER SH. $	TANG. BK. VAL. $	DIV. PER SH. $	PRICE RANGE	AVG. P/E RATIO	AVG. YIELD %
p12/31/02	2,550.1	③④ 51.5	2,748.4	...	...	...	...	...	③④ 0.84	...	...	0.52	27.41 - 14.92	25.2	2.5
12/31/01	2,447.2	③ d41.7	2,533.1	...	...	...	...	1.3	③ d0.69	1.85	8.28	0.72	18.65 - 11.75	...	4.4
12/31/00	2,643.0	② 45.9	2,564.1	4.0	1.7	4.6	1.8	1.5	② 0.76	3.24	12.75	0.72	21.81 - 12.56	22.6	4.2
12/31/99	2,495.0	62.6	2,441.3	5.3	2.5	6.0	2.6	1.5	1.01	3.43	14.58	0.72	25.81 - 15.63	20.5	3.5
12/31/98	2,679.8	114.5	2,450.0	8.4	4.3	10.8	4.7	1.7	1.82	4.05	14.65	0.72	41.94 - 13.63	15.3	2.6
12/31/97	2,617.6	171.4	2,326.6	11.1	6.5	16.6	7.4	1.5	2.69	4.79	14.20	0.66	41.50 - 22.63	11.9	2.1
12/31/96	2,394.8	138.9	2,071.3	10.7	5.8	15.1	6.7	1.5	2.22	4.23	12.73	0.60	23.81 - 18.25	9.5	2.9
12/31/95	2,230.5	112.4	1,925.9	9.4	5.0	13.7	5.8	1.5	1.80	3.78	11.46	0.56	24.00 - 16.25	11.2	2.8
12/31/94	1,930.4	68.5	1,858.7	7.2	3.5	9.3	3.7	1.4	1.11	3.03	10.33	0.50	19.63 - 15.63	15.9	2.8
12/31/93	1,708.8	① d17.7	1,789.7	1.2	...	...	...	1.4	① d0.28	1.64	9.59	0.50	17.44 - 13.25	...	3.3

Statistics are as originally reported. Adj. for stk. splits: 2-for-1, 5/97. ① Bef. acctg. chg. chrg. $254.3 mill. ($4.15/sh.); Incl. $48.0 mill. chrg. fr. restruct. ② Incl. pre-tax restruct. and impair. chrgs. of $27.6 mill. ③ Incl. impairment and restruct. chrg. of $32.1 mill., 2002; $54.7 mill., 2001. ④ Bef. acctg. chrg. $12.7 mill.; incl. reorg. chrgs. of $18.4 mill. & receipt of Continued Dumping & Subsidiy Offset Act payments of $50.2 mill.

OFFICERS:
W. R. Timken, Jr., Chmn.
J. W. Griffith, Pres., C.E.O.
S. B. Bailey, Sr. V.P., Contr.
INVESTOR CONTACT: Richard J. Mertes, Mgr.-Investor Relations, (330) 471-3924
PRINCIPAL OFFICE: 1835 Dueber Ave., S.W., Canton, OH 44706-2798

TELEPHONE NUMBER: (330) 438-3000
FAX: (330) 471-3452
WEB: www.timken.com
NO. OF EMPLOYEES: 18,000 (avg.)
SHAREHOLDERS: 8,109 (approx. record)
ANNUAL MEETING: In Apr.
INCORPORATED: OH, 1904

INSTITUTIONAL HOLDINGS:
No. of Institutions: 161
Shares Held: 28,459,716
% Held: 44.9
INDUSTRY: Ball and roller bearings (SIC: 3562)
TRANSFER AGENT(S): EquiServe First Chicago Trust Division, Jersey City, NJ

TITAN CORPORATION (THE)

EXCH.	SYM.	REC. PRICE	P/E RATIO	YLD.	MKT. CAP.	RANGE (52-WK.)	'02 Y/E PR.
NYSE	TTN	7.95 (2/28/03)	...	...	$0.55 bill.	23.45 - 7.20	10.40

MEDIUM GRADE. THE COMPANY ANTICIPATES EARNINGS PER SHARE FOR 2003 OF $0.65 AND OVERALL REVENUE GROWTH OF APPROXIMATELY 15.0%.

MERGENT

TRADING VOLUME
Thousand Shares

1989 1990 1991 1992 1993 1994 1995 1996 1997 1998 1999 2000 2001 2002 2003

*7 YEAR PRICE SCORE 109.4   ***12 MONTH PRICE SCORE 78.5**

*NYSE COMPOSITE INDEX=100

INTERIM EARNINGS (Per Share):

Qtr.	Mar.	June	Sept.	Dec.
1997	0.04	0.05	0.07	0.09
1998	0.02	0.07	0.05	0.03
1999	0.08	0.12	0.15	0.44
2000	d0.25	d0.22	0.09	0.05
2001	d1.29	d0.16	0.06	0.12
2002	0.09	0.05	d0.43	0.09

INTERIM DIVIDENDS (Per Share):

Amt.	Decl.	Ex.	Rec.	Pay.
	No dividends paid.			

CAPITALIZATION (12/31/01):

	($000)	(%)
Long-Term Debt	322,799	30.6
Minority Interest	23	0.0
Redeemable Pfd. Stock	250,000	23.7
Preferred Stock	690	0.1
Common & Surplus	480,460	45.6
Total	1,053,972	100.0

BUSINESS:

The Titan Corporation is a diversified technology company operating in three business segments. The Titan Systems segment provides information technology and communications services for defense, intelligence, and other U.S. and allied government agencies. The Titan Wireless segment designs, manufactures and installs satellite communication systems and provides services that support telephony and Internet access in developing countries. The Titan Technologies segment develops medical product sterilization systems and commercial applications. On 8/5/02, the Company completed the spin-off of SureBeam Corporation.

RECENT DEVELOPMENTS:

For the year ended 12/31/02, net loss was $7.8 million, before an extraordinary loss of $5.4 million and an accounting change charge of $40.1 million, versus a loss from continuing operations of $3.5 million in 2001. Results for 2002 and 2001 included amortization of goodwill and purchased intangibles of $5.7 million and $10.0 million, and deferred compensation of $27.8 million and $4.3 million, respectively. Results for 2002 also included exit and other charges of $53.3 million, while results for 2001 included acquisition and integration charges of $27.8 million. Results for 2002 and 2001 excluded losses of $218.1 million and $95.2 million, respectively, from discontinued operations. Revenues jumped 42.9% to $1.39 billion from $974.5 million a year earlier.

PROSPECTS:

The Company is secure with its earnings per share guidance for 2003 of $0.65, which translates to earnings per share from continuing operations of $0.57, on revenues of $1.59 billion to $1.61 billion. As a result, internal revenue growth is expected to be approximately 13.5%, with overall revenue growth of approximately 15.0%. Separately, on 2/24/03, the Company was awarded a five-year, U.S. Navy contract with a potential value of $169.0 million. Under the terms of the contract, TTN will provide a wide range of technical services aboard all classes of U.S. Navy ships.

ANNUAL FINANCIAL DATA:

FISCAL YEAR	TOT. REVS. ($mill.)	NET INC. ($mill.)	TOT. ASSETS ($mill.)	OPER. PROFIT %	NET PROFIT %	RET. ON EQUITY %	RET. ON ASSETS %	CURR. RATIO	EARN. PER SH. $	CASH FL. PER SH. $	TANG. BK. VAL.$	PRICE RANGE	AVG. P/E RATIO
p12/31/02	**1,392.2**	⑨ d7.8							⑨ d0.11			20.16 — 7.15	...
12/31/01	1,132.1	⑧ d14.2	1,358.7	1.2	...	...	...	2.2	⑧ d0.32	0.48	...	29.01 — 13.20	...
12/31/00	⑦ 1,033.2	⑦ d12.5	959.4	1.3	...	...	...	2.4	⑦ d0.32	0.58	...	60.50 — 11.13	...
12/31/99	406.6	⑥ 37.2	400.8	16.7	9.2	33.6	9.3	1.6	⑥ 0.81	1.01	...	48.38 — 4.75	32.8
12/31/98	303.4	⑤ 7.2	192.6	6.0	2.4	14.2	3.7	2.1	⑤ 0.18	0.37	0.31	8.25 — 3.81	33.5
12/31/97	171.2	④ 5.5	138.1	8.0	3.2	10.3	4.0	2.5	④ 0.26	0.48	1.82	8.38 — 2.75	21.4
12/31/96	137.7	d3.4	127.8	...	...	...	...	2.4	d0.27	0.11	1.53	7.75 — 2.38	...
12/31/95	134.0	③ d3.8	95.2	...	...	...	...	1.5	③ d0.33	d0.03	2.47	10.38 — 5.38	...
12/31/94	136.2	② 6.0	81.9	7.1	4.4	15.4	7.3	1.6	② 0.40	0.65	2.59	8.00 — 2.88	13.6
12/31/93	149.3	① d9.6	93.2	...	...	...	...	1.3	① d0.87	0.65	...	4.38 — 2.00	...

Statistics are as originally reported. ① Bef. $4.7 mil extraord chg, $55,000 foreign curr loss, & $1.5 mil loss fr disc ops and incl. $39.4 mil acq-rel chg & $6.2 mil def comp chg. ② Bef. $5.6 mil loss fr disc ops & incl. $28.9 mil non-recur gain. ③ Bef. $19.5 mil acct chg, $7.4 mil loss fr disc ops & incl. $9.9 mil p-tax acq chg. ④ Bef. $343,000 loss fr disc ops. ⑤ Incl. $6.2 mil p-tax restr chg, 1995; $1.2 mil restr credit, 1994. ⑥ Bef. $1.7 mil acct gain. ⑦ Revs. incl acqs of Adv. Comm. Systems Inc. & AverStar Inc. ⑧ Incl. $36.8 mil chg for acq & integr-rel exps.; bef. $84.4 mil loss fr disc ops. ⑨ Incl. $53.3 mil exit chgs.; excl. $218.1 mil loss fr disc ops, $5.4 mil extrord loss & $40.1 mil acct chg.

OFFICERS:
G. W. Ray, Chmn., Pres., C.E.O.
M. W. Sopp, Sr. V.P., C.F.O.

INVESTOR CONTACT: Rochelle Bold, V.P., Investor Relations, (858) 552-9400

PRINCIPAL OFFICE: 3033 Science Park Road, San Diego, CA 92121-1199

TELEPHONE NUMBER: (858) 552-9500
FAX: (858) 552-9645
WEB: www.titan.com
NO. OF EMPLOYEES: 11,000 (approx.)
SHAREHOLDERS: 3,700 (approx. common); 485 (preferred)
ANNUAL MEETING: In May
INCORPORATED: IN, May, 1910; reincorp., DE, July, 1910

INSTITUTIONAL HOLDINGS:
No. of Institutions: 193
Shares Held: 54,807,390
% Held: 70.2

INDUSTRY: Computer integrated systems design (SIC: 7373)

TRANSFER AGENT(S): Bank of America N.T. & S.A., Los Angeles, CA

TJX COMPANIES, INC. (THE)

EXCH.	SYM.	REC. PRICE	P/E RATIO	YLD.	MKT. CAP.	RANGE (52-WK.)	'02 Y/E PR.
NYSE	TJX	16.07 (2/28/03)	14.9	0.7%	$8.73 bill.	22.45 - 15.30	19.52

INVESTMENT GRADE. THE COMPANY ANTICIPATES OPENING APPROXIMATELY 192 NEW STORES DURING 2003.

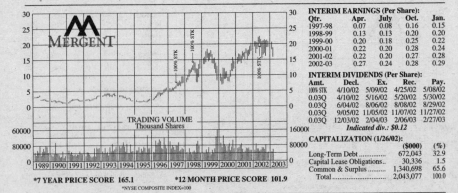

INTERIM EARNINGS (Per Share):

Qtr.	Apr.	July	Oct.	Jan.
1997-98	0.07	0.08	0.16	0.15
1998-99	0.13	0.13	0.20	0.20
1999-00	0.20	0.18	0.25	0.22
2000-01	0.22	0.20	0.28	0.24
2001-02	0.22	0.20	0.27	0.28
2002-03	0.27	0.24	0.28	0.29

INTERIM DIVIDENDS (Per Share):

Amt.	Decl.	Ex.	Rec.	Pay.
100% STK	4/10/02	5/09/02	4/25/02	5/08/02
0.03Q	4/10/02	5/16/02	5/20/02	5/30/02
0.03Q	6/04/02	8/06/02	8/08/02	8/29/02
0.03Q	9/05/02	11/05/02	11/07/02	11/27/02
0.03Q	12/03/02	2/04/03	2/06/03	2/27/03

Indicated div.: $0.12

CAPITALIZATION (1/26/02):

	($000)	(%)
Long-Term Debt	672,043	32.9
Capital Lease Obligations	30,336	1.5
Common & Surplus	1,340,698	65.6
Total	2,043,077	100.0

*7 YEAR PRICE SCORE 165.1   *12 MONTH PRICE SCORE 101.9

*NYSE COMPOSITE INDEX=100

BUSINESS:

The TJX Companies, Inc. (formerly Zayre Corp.) is a major off-price retailer of apparel and home fashions in the U.S. and worldwide. As of 1/25/03, T.J. Maxx operated 713 stores, selling brand-name family apparel and accessories, women's shoes, domestic furnishings, jewelry and giftware. Marshalls is an off-price family apparel chain, operating 629 stores. HomeGoods operated 142 off-price home fashion stores in a no-frills environment. T.K. Maxx is an off-price apparel concept operating 123 stores in the United Kingdom and Ireland. A.J. Wright operated 75 off-price family apparel stores. The Company also has 15 HomeSense stores and 146 Winners Apparel Ltd. stores in Canada. On 12/7/96, TJX sold its Chadwick's of Boston apparel mail-order catalog subsidiary to Brylane, L.P.

RECENT DEVELOPMENTS:

For the 52 weeks ended 1/25/03, net income was $578.4 million, up 7.0% versus income from continuing operations of $540.4 million a year earlier. Results for 2002 included an after-tax charge of $10.0 million from a litigation settlement. Net sales climbed 11.9% to $11.98 billion from $10.71 billion a year earlier. Net sales at the Marmaxx group, the combined entity of T.J. Maxx and Marshalls, rose 7.0% to $9.49 billion, while net sales at the Winners group, which includes TJX's HomeSense stores, grew 20.0% to $793.2 million. Net sales at T.K. Maxx advanced 38.3% to $720.1 million, while net sales at HomeGoods jumped 39.0% to $705.1 million. Net sales at A.J. Wright leapt 76.2% to $277.2 million. Consolidated comparable-store sales increased 3.0% year over year.

PROSPECTS:

Results are being positively affected by TJX's aggressive store expansion program and careful management of inventory levels. In 2003, the Company anticipates opening approximately 192 new stores, up from a net addition of 178 stores during 2002. Meanwhile, results are being hampered by weak consumer spending, reflecting uncertain economic conditions, and sharply higher insurance and employee benefits costs.

ANNUAL FINANCIAL DATA:

FISCAL YEAR	TOT. REVS. ($mill.)	NET INC. ($mill.)	TOT. ASSETS ($mill.)	OPER. PROFIT %	NET PROFIT %	RET. ON EQUITY %	RET. ON ASSETS %	CURR. RATIO	EARN. PER SH. $	CASH FL.PER SH. $	TANG. BK. VAL. $	DIV. PER SH. $	PRICE RANGE	AVG. P/E RATIO	AVG. YIELD %
p1/25/03	11,981.0	⑥ 578.4							⑥ 1.08			0.11	22.45 - 15.30	17.5	0.6
1/26/02	10,709.0	⑤ 540.4	3,595.7	8.2	5.0	40.3	15.0	1.6	⑤ 0.97	1.34	2.14	0.09	20.30 - 13.56	17.5	0.5
1/27/01	9,579.0	538.1	2,932.3	9.3	5.6	44.2	18.3	1.4	0.93	1.23	1.84	0.08	15.75 - 6.97	12.2	0.7
1/29/00	8,795.3	④ 526.8	2,805.0	9.8	6.0	47.1	18.8	1.2	④ 0.83	1.08	1.55	0.07	18.50 - 8.25	16.1	0.5
1/30/99	7,949.1	④ 433.2	2,747.8	8.9	5.4	35.5	15.8	1.3	④ 0.65	0.85	1.59	0.06	15.00 - 7.75	17.6	0.5
1/31/98	7,389.1	④ 306.6	2,609.6	7.1	4.1	26.3	11.7	1.4	④ 0.44	0.60	1.39	0.05	9.64 - 4.78	16.4	0.6
1/25/97	6,689.4	③ 213.8	2,561.2	6.0	3.2	19.0	8.3	1.4	③ 0.30	0.45	1.20	0.04	6.03 - 2.13	13.8	0.9
1/27/96	4,447.5	② 63.6	2,745.6	3.4	1.4	8.3	2.3	1.3	② 0.09	0.24	0.42	0.07	2.39 - 1.39	20.3	3.7
1/28/95	3,842.8	82.6	1,638.2	4.4	2.1	13.6	5.0	1.4	0.13	0.26	0.71	0.07	3.67 - 1.78	21.1	2.5
1/29/94	3,626.6	① 127.0	1,427.4	6.3	3.5	21.5	8.9	1.5	① 0.20	0.32	0.67	0.06	4.28 - 3.06	18.1	1.7

Statistics are as originally reported. Adj. for 2-for-1 stk. split, 5/02, 6/98 & 6/97. ① Bef. $5.2 mil acctg. chg., 1/00; $2.7 mil acctg. chg., 1/94. ② Bef. $3.3 mil ($0.02/sh) extraord. chg., $31.7 mil ($0.12/sh) loss fr disc. ops. & incl. $35 mil ($0.08/sh) pre-tax chg. ③ Bef. $154.9 mil gain fr disc. ops. & $5.6 mil ($0.02/sh) extraord. chg. ④ Incl. $3.6 mil ($0.01/sh) after-tax gain & bef. $1.8 mil ($0.01/sh) extraord. chg. ⑤ Bef. $40.0 mil ($0.07/sh) loss fr disc. ops., 2002; $9.0 mil ($0.01/sh) loss,1999. ⑥ Incl. $10.0 mil after-tax chg. fr. litigation settlement

OFFICERS:
B. Cammarata, Chmn.
E. J. English, Pres., C.E.O.
D. G. Campbell, Exec. V.P., C.F.O.

INVESTOR CONTACT: Sherry Lang, V.P., Investor Relations, (508) 390-2323

PRINCIPAL OFFICE: 770 Cochituate Road, Framingham, MA 01701

TELEPHONE NUMBER: (508) 390-1000
FAX: (508) 390-2091
WEB: www.tjx.com

NO. OF EMPLOYEES: 89,000 (approx.)

SHAREHOLDERS: 46,700 (approx.)

ANNUAL MEETING: In June

INCORPORATED: DE, Apr., 1962

INSTITUTIONAL HOLDINGS:
No. of Institutions: 420
Shares Held: 487,740,798
% Held: 92.8

INDUSTRY: Family clothing stores (SIC: 5651)

TRANSFER AGENT(S): EquiServe Limited Partnership, Boston, MA

TOLL BROTHERS, INC.

EXCH.	SYM.	REC. PRICE	P/E RATIO	YLD.	MKT. CAP.	RANGE (52-WK.)	'02 Y/E PR.
NYSE	TOL	19.37 (2/28/03)	6.6	...	$1.36 bill.	31.80 - 17.76	20.20

UPPER MEDIUM GRADE. THE COMPANY ANTICIPATES MORE THAN $2.60 BILLION IN HOME BUILDING REVENUES IN FISCAL 2003.

*7 YEAR PRICE SCORE 178.9   ***12 MONTH PRICE SCORE 92.7**

*NYSE COMPOSITE INDEX=100

INTERIM EARNINGS (Per Share):

Qtr.	Jan.	April	July	Oct.
1996-97	0.21	0.18	0.24	0.35
1997-98	0.22	0.21	0.34	0.41
1998-99	0.23	0.30	0.40	0.45
1999-00	0.31	0.38	0.50	0.76
2000-01	0.51	0.59	0.77	0.92
2001-02	0.60	0.69	0.70	0.93
2002-03	0.61	...	...	...

INTERIM DIVIDENDS (Per Share):

Amt.	Decl.	Ex.	Rec.	Pay.
100% STK	3/04/02	4/01/02	3/14/02	3/28/02

CAPITALIZATION (10/31/02):

	($000)	(%)
Long-Term Debt	1,121,853	49.8
Common & Surplus	1,129,509	50.2
Total	2,251,362	100.0

BUSINESS:

Toll Brothers, Inc. builds luxury single-family and attached home communities and master-planned luxury multi-product residential golf course communities principally on land it develops and improves. TOL serves move-up, empty-nester active-adult and second home buyers. The Company operated 172 communities in 22 states as of 1/31/03. TOL operates its own architectural, engineering, mortgage, title, land development and land sale, golf course development and management, home security, landscape, cable TV and broadband Internet delivery subsidiaries. TOL also operates its own lumber distribution, and house component assembly and manufacturing operations. The Company acquires and develops apartment and commercial properties through its affiliate, Toll Brothers Realty Trust.

RECENT DEVELOPMENTS:

For the quarter ended 1/31/03, net income increased 2.1% to $45.4 million compared with $44.5 million in the corresponding period of the previous year. Results for 2002 included expenses related to early retirement of debt of $3.9 million. Total revenues grew 15.9% to $570.3 million from $492.2 million the year before. Housing sales grew 15.6% to $557.9 million, while land sales advanced 46.9% to $9.4 million. Total closings as of 1/31/03, increased 34.0% to $1.89 billion compared with the same period a year earlier.

PROSPECTS:

The Company expects its results to be negatively affected by this winter's severe weather, particularly in the Northeast and Mid-Atlantic regions. This will cause likely delays in community openings and home deliveries and increase weather-related costs. Additionally, economic weakness and the war in Iraq has kept some buyers indoors and caused some hesitancy among others. Nevertheless, TOL anticipates more than $2.60 billion in home building revenues in fiscal 2003. Moreover, the Company expects to have approximately 185 communities open by 10/31/03.

ANNUAL FINANCIAL DATA:

FISCAL YEAR	TOT. REVS. ($mill.)	NET INC. ($mill.)	TOT. ASSETS ($mill.)	OPER. PROFIT %	NET PROFIT %	RET. ON EQUITY %	RET. ON ASSETS %	CURR. RATIO	EARN. PER SH. $	CASH FL. PER SH. $	TANG. BK. VAL. $	PRICE RANGE	AVG. P/E RATIO
10/31/02	2,329.0	☑ 219.9	2,895.4	17.7	9.4	19.5	7.6	2.7	☑ 2.91	3.05	16.09	31.80 - 17.76	8.5
10/31/01	2,229.6	213.7	2,532.2	17.8	9.6	23.4	8.4	2.6	2.76	2.88	13.12	22.95 - 12.93	6.5
10/31/00	1,814.4	145.9	2,030.3	15.3	8.0	19.6	7.2	2.4	1.95	2.06	10.38	21.38 - 8.00	7.5
10/31/99	1,464.1	① 103.0	1,668.1	13.8	7.0	16.7	6.2	2.8	① 1.38	1.46	8.32	12.19 - 7.78	7.3
10/31/98	1,210.8	① 85.8	1,254.5	14.1	7.1	16.3	6.8	2.7	① 1.13	1.19	7.12	15.81 - 8.69	10.9
10/31/97	971.7	① 67.8	1,118.6	14.1	7.0	17.6	6.1	2.7	① 0.97	1.03	5.62	13.75 - 8.75	11.6
10/31/96	760.7	53.7	837.9	14.5	7.1	17.1	6.4	2.6	0.78	0.83	4.64	11.75 - 7.31	12.2
10/31/95	646.3	49.9	692.5	15.7	7.7	19.5	7.2	3.2	0.74	0.78	3.82	11.50 - 5.00	11.2
10/31/94	504.1	36.2	586.9	14.9	7.2	17.7	6.2	3.8	0.54	0.58	3.05	9.88 - 4.56	13.4
10/31/93	397.0	27.4	476.0	15.4	6.9	16.4	5.8	3.7	0.41	0.45	2.51	8.88 - 4.44	16.2

Statistics are as originally reported. ① Bef. extraord. loss of $2.7 mill., 1997; $1.1 mill., 1998; and $1.5 mill., 1999. ☑ Incl. exps. rel. to early retirement of debt of $3.9 mill.

OFFICERS:
R. I. Toll, Chmn., C.E.O.
B. E. Toll, Vice-Chmn.
Z. Barzilay, Pres., C.O.O.
J. H. Rassman, Exec. V.P., C.F.O., Treas.

INVESTOR CONTACT: Investor Relations, (215) 938-8000

PRINCIPAL OFFICE: 3103 Philmont Avenue, Huntingdon Valley, PA 19006-4298

TELEPHONE NUMBER: (215) 938-8000
FAX: (215) 938-8023
WEB: www.tollbrothers.com

NO. OF EMPLOYEES: 2,960

SHAREHOLDERS: 744 (approx.)

ANNUAL MEETING: In Mar.

INCORPORATED: DE, May, 1986

INSTITUTIONAL HOLDINGS:
No. of Institutions: 179
Shares Held: 38,193,499
% Held: 54.4

INDUSTRY: Operative builders (SIC: 1531)

TRANSFER AGENT(S): Mellon Investor Services, L.L.C., Ridgefield Park, NJ

TOOTSIE ROLL INDUSTRIES, INC.

EXCH.	SYM.	REC. PRICE	P/E RATIO	YLD.	MKT. CAP.	RANGE (52-WK.)	'02 Y/E PR.	DIV. ACH.
NYSE	TR	27.30 (Adj.; 2/28/03)	21.8	1.0%	$1.42 bill.	45.26 - 25.66	28.92	39 yrs.

INVESTMENT GRADE. THE COMPANY'S ONGOING COST CONTAINMENT PROGRAMS SHOULD HELP MITIGATE THE NEGATIVE EFFECTS OF HIGHER INGREDIENT COSTS AND LOWER INVESTMENT INCOME.

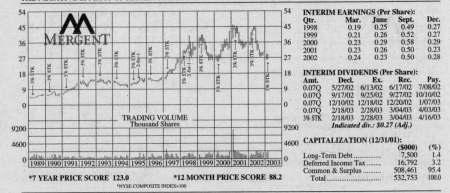

*7 YEAR PRICE SCORE 123.0   ***12 MONTH PRICE SCORE 88.2**
*NYSE COMPOSITE INDEX=100

INTERIM EARNINGS (Per Share):

Qtr.	Mar.	June	Sept.	Dec.
1998	0.19	0.25	0.49	0.27
1999	0.21	0.26	0.52	0.27
2000	0.23	0.29	0.58	0.29
2001	0.23	0.26	0.50	0.23
2002	0.24	0.23	0.50	0.28

INTERIM DIVIDENDS (Per Share):

Amt.	Decl.	Ex.	Rec.	Pay.
0.07Q	5/27/02	6/13/02	6/17/02	7/08/02
0.07Q	9/17/02	9/25/02	9/27/02	10/10/02
0.07Q	12/10/02	12/18/02	12/20/02	1/07/03
0.07Q	2/18/03	2/28/03	3/04/03	4/03/03
3% STK	2/18/03	2/28/03	3/04/03	4/16/03

Indicated div.: $0.27 (Adj.)

CAPITALIZATION (12/31/01):

	($000)	(%)
Long-Term Debt	7,500	1.4
Deferred Income Tax	16,792	3.2
Common & Surplus	508,461	95.4
Total	532,753	100.0

BUSINESS:

Tootsie Roll Industries, Inc. is engaged in the manufacture and sale of candy. The majority of the Company's products are sold under the following registered trademarks: TOOTSIE ROLL, TOOTSIE ROLL POPS, CHILD'S PLAY, CARAMEL APPLE POPS, CHARMS, BLOW-POP, BLUE RAZZ, ZIP-A-DEE-DOO-DA POPS, CELLA'S, MASON DOTS, MASON CROWS, JUNIOR MINT, CHARLESTON CHEW, SUGAR DADDY, SUGAR BABIES, ANDES and FLUFFY STUFF cotton candy. In September 1988, the Company acquired Charms Company for approximately $65.0 million. On 5/12/00, the Company acquired the assets of Andes Candies Inc. The Company has manufacturing facilities in Illinois, New York, Tennessee, Massachusetts, Wisconsin, Maryland and Mexico.

RECENT DEVELOPMENTS:

For the year ended 12/31/02, net earnings increased 1.1% to $66.4 million compared with $65.7 million in the previous year. Earnings for 2002 were adversely affected by higher ingredient costs and lower investment income. Results for 2001 included an investment capital gain of $962,000 and non-recurring charges of $1.8 million related to the closing of a small manufacturing plant and inventory adjustments. Sales increased slightly to $393.2 million from $391.8 million a year earlier. For the fourth quarter ended 12/31/02, net earnings advanced 18.5% to $14.7 million versus $12.4 million in the corresponding prior-year quarter. Sales climbed 3.8% to $90.8 million from $87.5 million in the 2001 quarter.

PROSPECTS:

The increase in recent sales is attributable to some advanced customer buy-in due to price increases that became effective in early 2003 and effective marketing programs. However, growth is being slowed by lower sales in Mexico, slower retail traffic, and retail bankruptcies, as well as overall competitive activity and the weak economic climate. Going forward, the Company's ongoing cost containment programs should help mitigate the negative effects of higher ingredient costs and lower investment income on earnings.

ANNUAL FINANCIAL DATA:

FISCAL YEAR	TOT. REVS. ($000)	NET INC. ($000)	TOT. ASSETS ($000)	OPER. PROFIT %	NET PROFIT %	RET. ON EQUITY %	RET. ON ASSETS %	CURR. RATIO	EARN. PER SH.$	CASH FL. PER SH.$	TANG. BK. VAL.$	DIV. PER SH.$	PRICE RANGE	AVG. P/E RATIO	AVG. YIELD %
p12/31/02	393,185	66,388							1.25			0.27	46.61 - 28.25	29.9	0.7
12/31/01	423,496	① 65,687	618,676	22.2	15.5	12.9	10.6	4.3	① 1.23	1.54	7.31	0.26	47.53 - 33.00	32.9	0.6
12/31/00	427,054	75,737	562,442	25.9	17.7	16.5	13.5	3.5	1.40	1.65	6.30	0.24	43.76 - 25.44	24.7	0.7
12/31/99	396,750	71,310	529,416	26.3	18.0	16.6	13.5	4.0	1.30	1.48	6.33	0.20	41.71 - 26.10	26.1	0.6
12/31/98	388,659	67,526	487,423	26.1	17.4	17.0	13.9	4.3	1.22	1.45	5.73	0.16	41.30 - 24.37	27.0	0.5
12/31/97	375,594	60,682	436,742	24.0	16.2	17.3	13.9	3.9	1.08	1.31	4.70	0.13	27.38 - 15.15	19.6	0.6
12/31/96	340,909	47,207	391,456	21.0	13.8	15.1	12.1	4.2	0.84	1.06	3.91	0.11	16.42 - 13.77	18.0	0.7
12/31/95	312,660	40,368	353,816	19.6	12.9	14.8	11.4	3.0	0.72	0.91	3.20	0.09	16.19 - 11.40	19.3	0.7
12/31/94	296,932	37,931	310,083	20.2	12.8	15.8	12.2	4.5	0.67	0.86	2.58	0.08	14.37 - 10.35	18.4	0.6
12/31/93	259,593	35,442	303,940	20.6	13.7	16.7	11.7	2.2	0.64	0.81	2.02	0.06	15.51 - 12.00	21.3	0.5

Statistics are as originally reported. Adj. for all stk. splits and divs. through 4/03. ① Incl. a nonrecurr. chrg. of $0.04 per sh. for the closing & consol. of a manufac. plant & for inventory adjustments.

OFFICERS:
M. J. Gordon, Chmn., C.E.O.
E. R. Gordon, Pres., C.O.O.
G. H. Ember Jr., V.P., C.F.O.

INVESTOR CONTACT: Investor Relations, (800) 851-9677

PRINCIPAL OFFICE: 7401 South Cicero Avenue, Chicago, IL 60629

TELEPHONE NUMBER: (773) 838-3400
FAX: (773) 838-3534
WEB: www.tootsie.com
NO. OF EMPLOYEES: 1,950 (approx.)
SHAREHOLDERS: 6,000 (approx. com. & cl. B com.)
ANNUAL MEETING: In May
INCORPORATED: VA, June, 1919

INSTITUTIONAL HOLDINGS:
No. of Institutions: 135
Shares Held: 12,248,131 (Adj.)
% Held: 23.1

INDUSTRY: Candy & other confectionery products (SIC: 2064)

TRANSFER AGENT(S): Mellon Investor Services, LLC, Ridgefield Park, NJ

TORCHMARK CORPORATION

EXCH.	SYM.	REC. PRICE	P/E RATIO	YLD.	MKT. CAP.	RANGE (52-WK.)	'02 Y/E PR.
NYSE	TMK	36.31 (2/28/03)	11.4	1.0%	$4.46 bill.	42.17 - 30.02	36.53

UPPER MEDIUM GRADE. GOING FORWARD, EARNINGS SHOULD BENEFIT FROM CONTINUED STRENGTH IN THE LIFE INSURANCE BUSINESS.

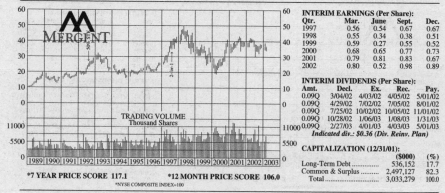

TRADING VOLUME
Thousand Shares

*7 YEAR PRICE SCORE 117.1   *12 MONTH PRICE SCORE 106.0
*NYSE COMPOSITE INDEX=100

INTERIM EARNINGS (Per Share):

Qtr.	Mar.	June	Sept.	Dec.
1997	0.56	0.54	0.67	0.67
1998	0.55	0.34	0.38	0.51
1999	0.59	0.27	0.55	0.52
2000	0.68	0.65	0.77	0.73
2001	0.79	0.81	0.83	0.67
2002	0.80	0.52	0.98	0.89

INTERIM DIVIDENDS (Per Share):

Amt.	Decl.	Ex.	Rec.	Pay.
0.09Q	3/04/02	4/03/02	4/05/02	5/01/02
0.09Q	4/29/02	7/02/02	7/05/02	8/01/02
0.09Q	7/25/02	10/02/02	10/05/02	11/01/02
0.09Q	10/28/02	1/06/03	1/08/03	1/31/03
0.09Q	2/27/03	4/01/03	4/03/03	5/01/03

Indicated div.: $0.36 (Div. Reinv. Plan)

CAPITALIZATION (12/31/01):

	($000)	(%)
Long-Term Debt	536,152	17.7
Common & Surplus	2,497,127	82.3
Total	3,033,279	100.0

BUSINESS:

Torchmark Corporation is a diversified insurance and financial services company that operates through Liberty National Life Insurance Company, Globe Life & Accident Insurance Company, United American Insurance Company and United Investors Life Insurance Company. Torchmark's insurance subsidiaries write a variety of non-participating ordinary life insurance products. These include traditional and interest-sensitive whole-life insur-ance, term life insurance, and other life insurance. TMK also offers supplemental health insurance products classified as Medicare Supplement, cancer and other health policies. Annuity products include single-premium deferred annuities, flexible-premium deferred annuities, and variable annuities. For 2001, premiums revenue accounted for 75.7% of all revenues.

RECENT DEVELOPMENTS:

For the year ended 12/31/02, income was $383.4 million versus income of $390.9 million the previous year. Earnings for 2002 excluded an extraordinary loss of $2,000, while earnings for 2001 excluded a loss from discontinued operations of $3.3 million, an extraordinary loss of $4.6 million and an accounting change charge of $26.6 million. Total revenue rose 1.1% to $2.74 billion. Revenues included realized investment losses of $61.8 million and $2.4 million, respectively. Total premium revenue increased 3.0% to $2.30 billion. Life premium revenue increased 7.0% to $1.2 billion. Health premium revenue rose 1.0% to $1.00 billion, while annuity premium revenue declined 35.0% to $39.0 million. Net investment income grew 5.3% to $522.3 million.

PROSPECTS:

Looking ahead, earnings should continue to benefit from continued strength in TMK's life insurance business. The direct response unit continued as the largest writer of new life insurance sales with $123.0 million for the year, a 10.0% increase over 2001. American Income was the fastest growing life distributor with life sales of $92.0 million, a 38.0% increase over 2001. The military distribution unit also had growth of 11.0% at $23 million for the year. Meanwhile, with respect to the health insurance business, Medicare supplement sales are expected to be hampered by increased competitive premium rate pressures in some markets.

ANNUAL FINANCIAL DATA:

FISCAL YEAR	PREM. INC. ($mill.)	TOT. REVS. ($mill.)	NET INC. ($mill.)	TOT. ASSETS ($mill.)	TOT. INVST. ($mill.)	RET. ON REVS. %	RET. ON EQUITY %	RET. ON ASSETS %	EARN. PER SH.$	TANG. BK. VAL.$	AVG. YIELD %	DIV. PER SH.$	PRICE RANGE	AVG. P/E RATIO
p12/31/02	2,279.0	2,738.0	⑤ 383.4						⑤ 3.18		1.0	0.36	42.17 - 30.02	11.4
12/31/01	2,215.2	2,707.0	① ② 390.9	12,428.2	7,104.4	14.4	15.7	3.1	① ② 3.11	17.24	0.9	0.36	43.25 - 32.56	12.2
12/31/00	2,046.2	2,515.9	③ 361.8	12,962.6	6,471.2	14.4	16.4	2.8	③ 2.82	14.34	1.2	0.36	41.19 - 18.75	10.6
12/31/99	1,884.1	2,226.9	④ 258.9	12,131.7	6,187.8	11.6	13.0	2.1	④ 1.93	12.05	1.2	0.36	38.00 - 24.56	16.2
12/31/98	1,753.6	2,157.9	③ 255.8	11,249.0	6,444.1	11.9	11.3	2.3	③ 1.81	13.48	1.4	0.58	49.81 - 31.81	22.5
12/31/97	1,678.0	2,282.5	337.7	10,967.3	6,640.7	14.8	17.5	3.1	2.39	10.05	1.7	0.58	42.81 - 25.00	14.2
12/31/96	1,609.9	2,205.8	① 318.5	9,800.8	6,027.6	14.4	19.5	3.2	① 2.24	7.80	2.5	0.58	26.06 - 20.13	10.3
12/31/95	1,546.3	2,067.5	① 271.9	9,364.1	5,855.0	13.2	17.1	2.9	① 1.90	7.21	2.8	0.56	22.63 - 17.13	10.5
12/31/94	1,388.9	1,922.6	273.2	8,017.5	5,322.0	14.2	22.0	3.3	1.86	4.70	2.7	0.56	24.75 - 16.19	11.0
12/31/93	1,492.9	2,176.8	③ 279.6	7,646.2	5,520.0	12.8	19.7	3.7	③ 1.88	8.39	2.0	0.54	32.38 - 20.56	14.1

Statistics are as originally reported. Adj. for stk. splits: 2-for-1, 8/97. ① Bef. disc. oper. loss $3.3 mill. 12/01; $7.1 mill., 12/96; $128.7 mill., 12/95 ② Bef. acctg. change chrg. $26.6 mill., 12/01; credit $18.4 mill., 12/93 ③ Bef. disc. oper. loss $6.4 mill. and extraord. loss $5.0 mill. ④ Incl. non-recurr. chrg. $13.4 mill., net chrg. $72.1 mill. and gain $3.3 mill. on sale of assets. ⑤ Excl. extraord. loss $2,000, 12/02; gain $202,000, 12/00

OFFICERS:
C. B. Hudson, Chmn., Pres., C.E.O.
G. L. Coleman, Exec. V.P., C.F.O.
INVESTOR CONTACT: Joyce L. Lane, Inv. Rel., (972) 569-3627
PRINCIPAL OFFICE: 2001 Third Ave. South, Birmingham, AL 35233

TELEPHONE NUMBER: (205) 325-4200
FAX: (205) 325-4157
WEB: www.torchmarkcorp.com
NO. OF EMPLOYEES: 1,959 (avg.)
SHAREHOLDERS: 5,749
ANNUAL MEETING: In April
INCORPORATED: DE, Nov., 1979

INSTITUTIONAL HOLDINGS:
No. of Institutions: 294
Shares Held: 83,046,571
% Held: 70.1
INDUSTRY: Life insurance (SIC: 6311)
TRANSFER AGENT(S): The Bank of New York, New York, NY

TORO COMPANY (THE)

EXCH.	SYM.	REC. PRICE	P/E RATIO	YLD.	MKT. CAP.	RANGE (52-WK.)	'02 Y/E PR.
NYSE	TTC	34.40 (Adj.; 2/28/03)	12.4	0.7%	$0.84 bill.	34.63 - 23.15	31.95

UPPER MEDIUM GRADE. THE COMPANY EXPECTS CONTINUED SALES GROWTH IN ITS PROFESSIONAL AND RESIDENTIAL SEGMENTS.

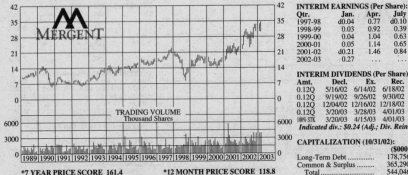

*7 YEAR PRICE SCORE 161.4   ***12 MONTH PRICE SCORE 118.8**

*NYSE COMPOSITE INDEX=100

INTERIM EARNINGS (Per Share):

Qtr.	Jan.	Apr.	July	Oct.
1997-98	d0.04	0.77	d0.10	d0.48
1998-99	0.03	0.92	0.39	d0.01
1999-00	0.04	1.04	0.63	0.04
2000-01	0.05	1.14	0.65	0.09
2001-02	d0.21	1.46	0.84	0.20
2002-03	0.27	...	...	...

INTERIM DIVIDENDS (Per Share):

Amt.	Decl.	Ex.	Rec.	Pay.
0.12Q	5/16/02	6/14/02	6/18/02	7/12/02
0.12Q	9/19/02	9/26/02	9/30/02	10/12/02
0.12Q	12/04/02	12/16/02	12/18/02	1/10/03
0.12Q	3/20/03	3/28/03	4/01/03	4/14/03
100% STK	3/20/03	4/15/03	4/01/03	4/14/03

Indicated div.: $0.24 (Adj.; Div. Reinv. Plan)

CAPITALIZATION (10/31/02):

	($000)	(%)
Long-Term Debt	178,756	32.9
Common & Surplus	365,290	67.1
Total	544,046	100.0

BUSINESS:

The Toro Company designs, manufactures and markets professional turf maintenance equipment, irrigation systems, landscaping equipment, and consumer products. Products include: gas-powered walk mowers, riding mowers, lawn and garden tractors, gas and electric snow throwers, trimmers, irrigation products, and grooming and operating equipment for golf courses, parks, landscape contractors and schools. The Company currently distributes its products worldwide with sales and/or distribution offices in the U.S., Canada, Belgium, the U.K., Australia, Singapore, Japan, China and Italy. In fiscal 2002, sales were derived as follows: professional, 61.6%; residential, 33.9%; distribution, 11.4%; and other, (6.9%).

RECENT DEVELOPMENTS:

For the quarter ended 1/31/03, net income was $7.0 million versus a loss of $5.1 million, before an accounting change charge of $24.6 million, in the equivalent prior-year quarter. Earnings benefited from demand for new products, better management of inventories, the transfer of certain production to lower cost environments and other elements of TTC's profit improvement initiatives. Results for fiscal 2003 included a one-time gain of about $2.1 million from a legal settlement, while results for fiscal 2002 included a charge of $10.0 million for restructuring and other one-time items. Net sales advanced 6.5% to $296.0 million from $277.9 million the previous year. Professional segment sales increased 10.1% to $193.4 million, while residential segment sales grew 2.7% to $94.7 million.

PROSPECTS:

Going forward, TTC expects continued sales growth in its professional and residential segments despite the volatile geopolitical situation and uncertain economic conditions. In addition, much of the margin improvement and cost containment measures that benefited TTC's first quarter results should continue during 2003. Moreover, TTC's production capacity and inventories are better aligned with demand due to recent facility rationalization and inventory management actions. Accordingly, TTC raised its net earnings guidance for fiscal 2003 to between $5.65 and $5.75 per diluted share, excluding the gain from the legal settlement.

ANNUAL FINANCIAL DATA:

FISCAL YEAR	TOT. REVS. ($mill.)	NET INC. ($mill.)	TOT. ASSETS ($mill.)	OPER. PROFIT %	NET PROFIT %	RET. ON EQUITY %	RET. ON ASSETS %	CURR. RATIO	EARN. PER SH.$	CASH FL. PER SH.$	TANG. BK. VAL.$	DIV. PER SH.$	PRICE RANGE	AVG. P/E RATIO	AVG. YIELD %
10/31/02	1,399.3	⑥ 59.9	846.1	7.2	4.3	16.4	7.1	2.0	⑥ 2.32	3.51	11.73	0.24	33.60 - 22.50	12.1	0.9
10/31/01	1,353.1	⑤ 50.4	835.7	7.0	3.7	14.8	6.0	1.9	④ 1.93	3.35	9.53	0.24	25.00 - 17.19	10.9	1.1
10/31/00	1,336.9	④ 45.3	779.4	7.3	3.4	14.3	5.8	2.0	④ 1.74	3.19	12.62	0.24	18.75 - 13.63	9.3	1.5
10/31/99	1,275.0	④ 35.1	787.2	5.9	2.7	12.5	4.5	1.7	④ 1.32	2.79	11.12	0.24	19.75 - 14.38	12.9	1.4
10/31/98	1,110.4	③ 4.1	724.0	2.1	0.4	1.6	0.6	1.9	③ 0.16	1.60	10.31	0.24	21.38 - 8.25	95.5	1.6
10/31/97	1,051.2	② 36.5	661.6	6.9	3.5	15.1	5.5	2.0	② 1.51	2.79	9.89	0.24	23.16 - 16.50	13.1	1.2
10/31/96	930.9	36.4	496.9	6.8	3.9	17.0	7.3	1.9	1.45	2.17	8.87	0.24	18.25 - 15.00	11.5	1.4
① 10/31/95	192.3	4.0	472.7	3.5	2.1	2.1	0.8	1.7	0.16	0.30	7.84	...	... - ...	...	...
7/31/95	932.9	36.7	468.3	6.9	3.9	19.8	7.8	1.8	1.41	2.07	7.70	0.24	16.44 - 12.81	10.4	1.6
7/31/94	794.3	22.2	443.6	5.4	2.8	13.2	5.0	1.9	0.86	1.58	6.71	0.24	15.25 - 10.44	15.0	1.9

Statistics are as originally reported. Adj. for stk. split: 100% div., 4/03 ① Results for 3 mos. only due to fiscal year-end change to 10/31 from 7/31. ② Bef. extraord. chrg. of $1.7 mill. ③ Incl. non-recurr. pre-tax chrgs. of $15.0 mill. ④ Incl. one-time chrgs. of $1.7 mill.; 1999: $2.0 mill.; 2000. ⑤ Incls. restruct. & other unusual inc. of $679,000. ⑥ Incls. restruct. chrg. of $8.4 mill.; bef. acctg. chge. chrg. of $24.6 mill.

OFFICERS:
K. B. Melrose, Chmn., C.E.O.
S. P. Wolfe, V.P., C.F.O., Treas.
J. L. McIntyre, V.P., Sec., Gen. Couns.
INVESTOR CONTACT: Investor Relations, (800) 468-9716
PRINCIPAL OFFICE: 8111 Lyndale Ave. South, Bloomington, MN 55420

TELEPHONE NUMBER: (952) 888-8801
FAX: (952) 887-8258
WEB: www.toro.com
NO. OF EMPLOYEES: 4,984
SHAREHOLDERS: 5,553 (approx.)
ANNUAL MEETING: In March
INCORPORATED: ND, 1928; reincorp., MI, Nov., 1935

INSTITUTIONAL HOLDINGS:
No. of Institutions: 148
Shares Held: 17,505,706 (Adj.)
% Held: 71.9
INDUSTRY: Lawn and garden equipment (SIC: 3524)
TRANSFER AGENT(S): Wells Fargo Shareowner Services, South St. Paul, MN

TOTAL SYSTEM SERVICES, INC.

EXCH.	SYM.	REC. PRICE	P/E RATIO	YLD.	MKT. CAP.	RANGE (52-WK.)	'02 Y/E PR.
NYSE	TSS	15.75 (2/28/03)	25.0	0.4%	$3.07 bill.	29.44 - 11.01	13.50

UPPER MEDIUM GRADE. THE COMPANY EXPECTS NET INCOME IN 2003 TO GROW BETWEEN 12.0% AND 15.0% YEAR OVER YEAR.

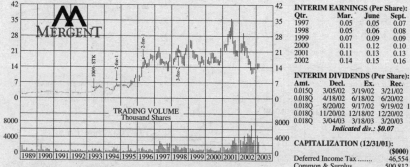

*7 YEAR PRICE SCORE 98.0   ****12 MONTH PRICE SCORE 92.9**
*NYSE COMPOSITE INDEX=100

INTERIM EARNINGS (Per Share):

Qtr.	Mar.	June	Sept.	Dec.
1997	0.05	0.05	0.07	0.08
1998	0.05	0.06	0.08	0.09
1999	0.07	0.09	0.09	0.10
2000	0.11	0.12	0.10	0.11
2001	0.11	0.13	0.13	0.15
2002	0.14	0.15	0.16	0.18

INTERIM DIVIDENDS (Per Share):

Amt.	Decl.	Ex.	Rec.	Pay.
0.015Q	3/05/02	3/19/02	3/21/02	4/01/02
0.018Q	4/18/02	6/18/02	6/20/02	7/01/02
0.018Q	8/20/02	9/17/02	9/19/02	10/01/02
0.018Q	11/20/02	12/18/02	12/20/02	1/02/03
0.018Q	3/04/03	3/18/03	3/20/03	4/01/03

Indicated div.: $0.07

CAPITALIZATION (12/31/01):

	($000)	(%)
Deferred Income Tax	46,554	8.5
Common & Surplus	500,812	91.5
Total	547,365	100.0

BUSINESS:

Total System Services, Inc. is an electronic payment processor of credit, debit, commercial stored value and retail cards. The Company provides the electronic link between buyers and sellers with a comprehensive on-line system of data processing services servicing issuing institutions throughout the United States, Canada, Mexico, Honduras and the Caribbean, representing more than 240.0 million cardholder accounts on file as of 12/31/02. TSS also offers value-added products and services, such as credit evaluation, fraud control and marketing, to support its core processing services. As of 12/31/02, Synovus Financial Corp. owned 81.1% of the Company.

RECENT DEVELOPMENTS:

For the twelve months ended 12/31/02, net income rose 20.5% to $125.8 million compared with $104.4 million in 2001. Results for 2002 and 2001 included a gain of $75,000 and a loss of $93,000, respectively, on the disposal of equipment. Total revenues climbed 7.0% to $955.1 million from $892.3 million in the prior year. Revenues before reimbursable items grew 9.8% to $724.0 million from $659.2 million the year before. Operating income increased 14.5% to $157.7 million compared with $137.7 million a year earlier. Earnings benefited from the acquisition of ProCard, Inc., which was completed on 11/1/02. As a result, the Company restated all periods prior to the acquisition to reflect the combined results of TSS and ProCard.

PROSPECTS:

The Company expects net income in 2003 to grow between 12.0% and 15.0% year over year. This estimate assumes an increase in revenues, excluding reimbursables, in the range of 9.0% to 10.0%, an internal growth rate from existing customers of approximately 11.0% and an ongoing focus on expense management. In addition, the forecast does not include any revenues or expenses related to the possibility of signing and converting a major client. Separately, on 12/17/02, Canadian Tire Financial Services, a provider of financial-related products and services to retail and petroleum customers, renewed its contract with the Company via a seven-year agreement under which TSS will be the exclusive processor for Canadian Tire's retail MasterCard and gift card programs.

ANNUAL FINANCIAL DATA:

FISCAL YEAR	TOT. REVS. ($mill.)	NET INC. ($mill.)	TOT. ASSETS ($mill.)	OPER. PROFIT %	NET PROFIT %	RET. ON EQUITY %	RET. ON ASSETS %	CURR. RATIO	EARN. PER SH. $	CASH FL. PER SH. $	TANG. BK. VAL. $	DIV. PER SH. $	PRICE RANGE	AVG. P/E RATIO	AVG. YIELD %
p12/31/02	955.1	125.8							0.64			0.07	29.44 - 11.01	31.6	0.3
12/31/01	650.4	102.9	652.3	23.5	15.8	20.5	15.8	2.0	0.53	0.82	1.69	0.06	35.84 - 18.91	51.6	0.2
12/31/00	601.3	85.6	604.4	21.3	14.2	20.9	14.2	1.4	0.44	0.70	1.35	0.04	22.75 - 14.88	42.7	0.2
12/31/99	533.9	68.6	457.3	18.8	12.8	20.5	15.0	1.7	0.35	0.61	1.21	0.04	26.25 - 14.13	57.7	0.2
12/31/98	396.2	54.8	348.9	20.0	13.8	20.3	15.7	2.0	0.28	0.47	1.05	0.04	24.19 - 14.44	69.0	0.2
12/31/97	361.5	47.5	296.9	19.2	13.1	21.2	16.0	2.2	0.25	0.39	0.92	0.03	23.08 - 12.08	71.2	0.2
12/31/96	311.6	39.4	246.8	18.9	12.7	21.8	16.0	1.9	0.21	0.32	0.72	0.03	19.83 - 7.63	66.3	0.2
12/31/95	249.7	27.7	199.0	17.2	11.1	18.9	13.9	1.9	0.14	0.25	0.54	0.03	10.54 - 4.46	52.4	0.4
12/31/94	187.6	22.5	165.0	18.7	12.0	18.3	13.6	2.3	0.12	0.20	0.43	0.03	6.58 - 3.19	41.7	0.5
12/31/93	152.1	20.2	133.3	21.4	13.3	19.8	15.2	2.7	0.10	0.18	0.38	0.02	5.50 - 2.40	38.3	0.6

Statistics are as originally reported. Adj. for 2-for-1 stk. spl., 4/96, 10/94 & 5/93; 3-for-2 stk. spl., 5/98.

OFFICERS:
R. W. Ussery, Chmn., C.E.O.
P. W. Tomlinson, Pres.
J. B. Lipham, Exec. V.P., C.F.O.
INVESTOR CONTACT: Leo S. Berard, Investor Relations Manager, (706) 649-5220
PRINCIPAL OFFICE: 1600 First Avenue, P.O. Box 1755, Columbus, GA 31902-2567

TELEPHONE NUMBER: (706) 649-2310
FAX: (706) 649-2456
WEB: www.tsys.com
NO. OF EMPLOYEES: 4,711
SHAREHOLDERS: 11,911
ANNUAL MEETING: In Apr.
INCORPORATED: GA, Dec., 1982

INSTITUTIONAL HOLDINGS:
No. of Institutions: 81
Shares Held: 13,367,560
% Held: 6.8
INDUSTRY: Data processing and preparation (SIC: 7374)
TRANSFER AGENT(S): EquiServe Trust Company NA, Providence, RI

TOWER AUTOMOTIVE, INC.

EXCH.	SYM.	REC. PRICE	P/E RATIO	YLD.	MKT. CAP.	RANGE (52-WK.)	'02 Y/E PR.
NYSE	TWR	3.35 (2/28/03)	...	...	$161.1 mill.	15.40 - 2.66	4.50

LOWER MEDIUM GRADE. IN 2003, THE COMPANY WILL CONTINUE WITH LAUNCH ACTIVITY RELATED TO SEVERAL OF THE NEW PROJECTS IN ITS BACKLOG.

INTERIM EARNINGS (Per Share):

Qtr.	Mar.	June	Sept.	Dec.
1998	0.37	0.46	0.36	0.50
1999	0.51	0.58	0.44	0.58
2000	0.65	0.68	0.21	d1.54
2001	0.28	0.35	d0.03	d6.15
2002	d0.72	0.37	0.15	0.29

INTERIM DIVIDENDS (Per Share):

Amt.	Decl.	Ex.	Rec.	Pay.
		No dividends paid.		

CAPITALIZATION (12/31/01):

	($000)	(%)
Long-Term Debt	801,068	63.9
Capital Lease Obligations..	4,620	0.4
Common & Surplus	447,408	35.7
Total	1,253,096	100.0

*7 YEAR PRICE SCORE 58.2   ***12 MONTH PRICE SCORE 48.2**

NYSE COMPOSITE INDEX=100

BUSINESS:

Tower Automotive, Inc. is a designer and producer of structural components and assemblies used by automotive original equipment manufacturers of automobiles and light trucks, including Ford, DaimlerChrysler, General Motors, Honda, Toyota, Nissan, Fiat, Hyundai/Kia, BMW and Volkswagen Group. The Company's current products include body structures and assemblies, lower vehicle frames and structures, chassis modules and systems and suspension components.

RECENT DEVELOPMENTS:

For the year ended 12/31/02, income was $15.2 million, before an accounting change charge of $112.8 million, compared with a net loss of $267.5 million the year before. Results for 2002 and 2001 included pre-tax restructuring and asset impairment charges of $61.1 million and $383.7 million, respectively. Revenues advanced 11.6% to $2.75 billion from $2.47 billion the year before. The improvement in revenues was primarily attributed to volume increases and lower capital expenditures. Gross profit climbed 7.8% to $298.9 million from $277.2 million a year earlier. Operating income was $89.8 million versus an operating loss of $270.6 million the prior year.

PROSPECTS:

In 2003, the Company will continue to move forward with launch activity related to several of the new projects in its backlog, with planned capital expenditures of approximately $200.0 million. Over the long term, the Company should benefit from improved operating results and return on capital as a result of the relatively lower capital requirements of its new platforms. Meanwhile, the Company expects sales and operating earnings for fiscal 2003 to remain relatively consistent with 2002 levels.

ANNUAL FINANCIAL DATA:

FISCAL YEAR	TOT. REVS. ($mill.)	NET INC. ($mill.)	TOT. ASSETS ($mill.)	OPER. PROFIT %	NET PROFIT %	RET. ON EQUITY %	RET. ON ASSETS %	CURR. RATIO	EARN. PER SH.$	CASH FL.PER SH.$	TANG. BK. VAL.$	PRICE RANGE	AVG. P/E RATIO
p12/31/02	2,754.5	④ 15.2		...	...	...	...	0.5	④ 0.26	d2.36		15.40 — 4.11	37.5
12/31/01	2,467.4	③ d267.5	2,533.4	...	...	...	...	1.0	③ d5.87	3.39	...	15.48 — 5.87	
12/31/00	2,532.0	②③ 16.4	2,892.7	2.8	0.6	2.3	0.6	1.0	②③ 0.34	2.94	...	17.88 — 6.94	36.5
12/31/99	2,170.0	117.1	2,552.6	10.4	5.4	16.1	4.6	1.3	2.10	3.57	3.03	28.25 — 13.38	9.9
12/31/98	1,836.5	88.0	1,936.2	9.6	4.8	14.5	4.5	1.3	1.68	2.94	4.00	27.50 — 15.50	12.8
12/31/97	1,235.8	② 48.7	1,680.1	8.9	3.9	9.4	2.9	1.6	② 1.14	2.14	2.33	24.34 — 14.88	17.2
12/31/96	399.9	20.6	398.6	9.9	5.2	11.3	5.2	2.5	0.78	1.24	3.24	16.13 — 7.19	15.0
12/31/95	222.8	12.1	211.7	9.8	5.4	14.1	5.7	2.1	0.53	0.80	2.10	8.75 — 3.69	11.8
12/31/94	165.5	7.4	1179.4	8.6	4.4	10.1	4.1	2.2	0.43	0.66	1.58	7.06 — 3.69	12.5
① 12/31/93	61.3	3.1	51.6	9.8	5.0	28.5	6.0	1.1	0.23	0.36	...	...	...

Statistics are as originally reported. Adj. for 2-for-1 split, 6/98. ① From 4/15/93 commencement of operations. ② Bef. extraord loss of $3.0 mill., 2000; $2.4 mill., 1997. ③ Incl. pre-tax restruct. chrg. of $141.3 mill., 2000; $383.7 mill., 2001. ④ Incl. pre-tax restruct. & asset impair. chrgs. of $61.1 mill.

OFFICERS:
S. A. Johnson, Chmn.
D. K. Campbell, Pres., C.E.O.
A. A. Barone, V.P., C.F.O.

INVESTOR CONTACT: Ernie Thomas, Investor Relations, (616) 802-1600

PRINCIPAL OFFICE: 5211 Cascade Road S.E., Suite 300, Grand Rapids, MI 49546

TELEPHONE NUMBER: (616) 802-1600
FAX: (612) 802-1599
WEB: www.towerautomotive.com

NO. OF EMPLOYEES: 13,000 (approx.)

SHAREHOLDERS: 2,893 (approx. record)

ANNUAL MEETING: In May

INCORPORATED: DE, Mar., 1993

INSTITUTIONAL HOLDINGS:
No. of Institutions: 124
Shares Held: 42,020,142
% Held: 74.1

INDUSTRY: Metal stampings, nec (SIC: 3469)

TRANSFER AGENT(S): EquiServe Trust Company, N.A. Jersey City, NJ

TOYS "R" US, INC.

EXCH.	SYM.	REC. PRICE	P/E RATIO	YLD.	MKT. CAP.	RANGE (52-WK.)	'02 Y/E PR.
NYSE	TOY	8.08 (2/28/03)	7.6	...	$1.59 bill.	20.75 - 7.80	10.00

LOWER MEDIUM GRADE. THE COMPANY IS IMPLEMENTING COST-CONTROL INITIATIVES TO HELP BOOST PROFITABILITY.

*7 YEAR PRICE SCORE 64.9   ***12 MONTH PRICE SCORE 73.8**

*NYSE COMPOSITE INDEX=100

INTERIM EARNINGS (Per Share):

Qtr.	Apr.	July	Oct.	Jan.
1995-96	0.06	0.06	0.08	0.34
1996-97	0.07	d0.03	0.12	1.37
1997-98	0.10	0.13	0.16	1.32
1998-99	0.07	0.06	d1.85	1.23
1999-00	0.07	0.05	0.06	0.98
2000-01	0.93	0.01	d0.32	1.23
2001-02	d0.09	d0.15	d0.22	0.78
2002-03	d0.02	d0.08	d0.13	1.30

INTERIM DIVIDENDS (Per Share):

Amt.	Decl.	Ex.	Rec.	Pay.
		No dividends paid.		

CAPITALIZATION (2/2/02):

	($000)	(%)
Long-Term Debt	1,816,000	32.0
Deferred Income Tax	395,000	7.0
Minority Interest	53,000	0.9
Common & Surplus	3,414,000	60.1
Total	5,678,000	100.0

BUSINESS:

Toys "R" Us, Inc. operated 681 toy stores in the U.S. and 544 international toy stores as of 3/5/03. These stores sell both children's and adult's toys, sporting goods, electronic and video games, books, infant and juvenile furniture, as well as educational and entertainment computer software for children. In addition, TOY operated 146 Kids "R" Us stores, which sell children's apparel. The Company also operated 183 Babies "R" Us stores, which offer everything for babies from diapers to baby furniture to clothing, 37 Imaginarium stores that sell specialty toys, and four Geoffrey stores. In addition, TOY sells merchandise through mail order catalogs and the Internet. On 2/3/97, TOY acquired Baby Superstore, Inc.

RECENT DEVELOPMENTS:

For the year ended 2/1/03, net earnings totaled $229.0 million compared with $67.0 million in the previous year. Results for the prior year included after-tax restructuring and other charges of $126.0 million. Net sales rose 2.6% to $11.31 billion from $11.02 billion a year earlier. Same-store sales for the Company's U.S. stores decreased 1.0%, while international same-store sales were up 6.0% year over year. Babies "R" Us same-store sales increased 3.0%, while Kids "R" Us same-store sales slid 10.0%. Gross profit totaled $3.51 billion, or 31.0% of net sales, versus $3.42 billion, or 31.0% of net sales, the year before. Operating earnings were $471.0 million compared with $200.0 million the previous year.

PROSPECTS:

The Company is aggressively implementing cost-control initiatives in an effort to boost profitability. On 3/5/03, TOY announced plans to eliminate approximately 200 jobs, or about 10.0% of the Company's headquarters staff. These job cuts, along with approximately 700 management and supervisory positions eliminated at TOY's U.S. stores in late January 2003, should have a positive effect on earnings in 2003. However, first-quarter results will likely be hurt by higher severance costs related to the job cuts. Meanwhile, TOY is taking steps to improve customer service by increasing the number of associates available on the sales floor.

ANNUAL FINANCIAL DATA:

FISCAL YEAR	TOT. REVS. ($mill.)	NET INC. ($mill.)	TOT. ASSETS ($mill.)	OPER. PROFIT %	NET PROFIT %	RET. ON EQUITY %	RET. ON ASSETS %	CURR. RATIO	EARN. PER SH.$	CASH FL. PER SH.$	TANG. BK. VAL.$	PRICE RANGE		AVG. P/E RATIO
p2/01/03	11,305.0	229.0							1.09			23.10 -	8.51	14.5
2/02/02	11,019.0	②67.0	8,076.0	1.8	0.6	2.0	0.8	1.3	②0.33	1.82	15.59	31.00 -	16.81	72.4
2/03/01	11,332.0	③404.0	8,003.0	3.8	3.6	11.8	5.0	1.2	③1.88	3.23	15.48	20.00 -	9.75	7.9
1/29/00	11,862.0	279.0	8,353.0	4.4	2.4	7.6	3.3	1.0	1.14	2.27	13.82	24.75 -	13.13	16.6
1/30/99	11,170.0	②d132.0	7,899.0	...	...	...	...	1.0	②d0.50	0.46	13.08	32.75 -	15.63	...
1/31/98	11,038.0	490.0	7,963.0	7.6	4.4	11.1	6.2	1.2	1.70	2.58	14.42	37.13 -	24.38	18.1
2/01/97	9,932.4	②427.4	8,023.2	7.6	4.3	10.2	5.3	1.2	②1.54	2.28	13.29	37.63 -	20.50	18.9
2/03/96	9,426.9	①148.1	6,737.5	3.7	1.6	4.3	2.2	1.2	①0.53	1.23	12.57	30.88 -	21.63	49.5
1/28/95	8,745.6	531.8	6,571.2	10.4	6.1	15.5	8.1	1.2	1.85	2.41	12.26	40.88 -	29.63	19.1
1/29/94	7,946.1	483.0	6,149.6	10.3	6.1	15.3	7.9	1.3	1.63	2.08	10.87	42.88 -	32.38	23.1

Statistics are as originally reported. ① Incl. $270 mil restr. chg. ② Incl. $126.0 mil after-tax restr. chg., 2002; $508.0 mil after-tax restr. chg., 1999; $37.8 mil ($0.14/sh) after-tax chg. related to arbitration, 1997. ③ Incl. a one-time after-tax gain of $200.0 mil ($0.93/sh) from the 4/24/00 initial public offering of the Company's Japanese subsidiary.

OFFICERS:
J. H. Eyler, Jr., Chmn., C.E.O.
L. Lipschitz, Exec. V.P., C.F.O.
C. K. Kay, Exec. V.P., Sec., Gen. Couns.
INVESTOR CONTACT: Louis Lipschitz, Exec. V.P., C.F.O., (201) 802-5548
PRINCIPAL OFFICE: 461 From Road, Paramus, NJ 07652

TELEPHONE NUMBER: (201) 262-7800
FAX: (201) 843-0973
WEB: www.toysrus.com
NO. OF EMPLOYEES: 71,000 (approx.)
SHAREHOLDERS: 20,269 (approx. record)
ANNUAL MEETING: In June
INCORPORATED: DE, 1928

INSTITUTIONAL HOLDINGS:
No. of Institutions: 289
Shares Held: 202,343,440
% Held: 95.2
INDUSTRY: Hobby, toy, and game shops (SIC: 5945)
TRANSFER AGENT(S): American Stock Transfer & Trust Company, New York, NY

TRANSATLANTIC HOLDINGS, INC.

EXCH.	SYM.	REC. PRICE	P/E RATIO	YLD.	MKT. CAP.	RANGE (52-WK.)	'02 Y/E PR.	DIV. ACH.
NYSE	TRH	66.50 (1/31/03)	20.8	0.6%	$3.48 bill.	90.10 - 60.25	66.70	12 yrs.

UPPER MEDIUM GRADE. THE COMPANY IS BENEFITING FROM FAVORABLE UNDERWRITING CONDITIONS.

*7 YEAR PRICE SCORE 137.4   ***12 MONTH PRICE SCORE 98.6**

*NYSE COMPOSITE INDEX=100

INTERIM EARNINGS (Per Share):

Qtr.	Mar.	June	Sept.	Dec.
1997	0.80	0.83	0.92	1.01
1998	0.91	1.24	1.50	1.08
1999	1.42	1.13	0.69	0.34
2000	1.07	0.97	1.02	0.97
2001	0.96	0.76	d1.49	0.12
2002	1.00	1.16	1.16	d0.12

INTERIM DIVIDENDS (Per Share):

Amt.	Decl.	Ex.	Rec.	Pay.
0.096Q	12/03/01	2/27/02	3/01/02	3/15/02
0.096Q	3/21/02	6/05/02	6/07/02	6/14/02
0.10Q	5/16/02	9/04/02	9/06/02	9/13/02
0.10Q	9/19/02	11/26/02	11/29/02	12/13/02
0.10Q	12/05/02	3/05/03	3/07/03	3/21/03

Indicated div.: $0.40

CAPITALIZATION (12/31/01):

	($000)	(%)
Common & Surplus	1,846,010	100.0
Total	1,846,010	100.0

BUSINESS:

Transatlantic Holdings, Inc., through its wholly-owned subsidiaries Transatlantic Reinsurance Company, Trans Re Zurich and Putnam Reinsurance Company, offers reinsurance capacity for a full range of property and casualty products on a treaty and facultative basis, directly and through brokers, to insurance and reinsurance companies, in both the domestic and international markets. The Company's principal lines of reinsurance include auto liability, other liability, accident and health, medical malpractice, marine and aviation, and surety and credit in the casualty lines, and fire and allied in the property lines. As of 2/3/03, the Company had operations based in Chicago, Toronto, Miami (serving Latin America and the Caribbean), Buenos Aires, Rio de Janeiro, London, Paris, Zurich, Warsaw, Johannesburg, Sydney, Hong Kong, Shanghai and Tokyo.

RECENT DEVELOPMENTS:

For the year ended 12/31/02, net income amounted to $169.3 million versus $18.9 million in the prior year. Results for 2002 included an after-tax charge of $65.0 million for an increase in reserve strengthening. Results for 2001 included an after-tax charge of $139.8 million, primarily related to the 9/11/01 terrorist attacks, and an after-tax charge of $39.0 million for Enron reinsurance exposure. Total revenues climbed 28.8% to $2.62 billion from $2.03 billion the previous year. Revenues for 2002 and 2001 included net realized capital losses of $6.0 million and $240,000, respectively. Net premiums written increased 31.2% to $2.50 billion. Net premiums earned grew 32.3% to $2.37 billion from $1.79 billion a year earlier. Net investment income rose 5.0% to $252.0 million.

PROSPECTS:

The Company continues to generate favorable results. During the year, TRH achieved record increases in premiums and operating cash flow, with contributions spread throughout virtually all of its domestic and international operations. Looking ahead, to overcome the severity of catastrophe losses in recent years and several years of declining rates, further pricing increases are expected in 2003. TRH remains confident that a higher prices, combined with a strict underwriting discipline, will have a positive effect on results in 2003 and beyond.

ANNUAL FINANCIAL DATA:

FISCAL YEAR	PREM. INC. ($mill.)	NET INVST. INC. ($mill.)	TOT. REVS. ($mill.)	NET INC. ($mill.)	TOT. ASSETS ($mill.)	TOT. INVST. ($mill.)	RET. ON REVS. %	RET. ON EQUITY %	RET. ON ASSETS %	EARN. PER SH.$	TANG. BK. VAL.$	AVG. YIELD %	DIV. PER SH.$	PRICE RANGE	AVG. P/E RATIO
p12/31/02	2,369.5	252.0	2,615.5	③169.3	7,286.5		0.9		0.3	③3.21		0.5	0.39	91.00 — 60.25	23.6
12/31/01	1,790.3	240.1	2,030.2	②18.9	6,741.3	4,880.2	0.9	1.0	0.3	②0.36	35.33	0.5	0.37	92.75 — 62.00	214.9
12/31/00	1,631.5	234.5	1,866.0	211.6	5,522.7	4,262.0	11.3	11.4	3.8	4.03	35.59	0.6	0.35	70.59 — 45.84	14.4
12/31/99	1,484.6	230.7	1,715.4	187.4	5,480.2	4,229.4	10.9	11.4	3.4	3.58	31.53	0.6	0.31	53.67 — 46.04	13.9
12/31/98	1,380.6	222.0	1,602.6	247.5	5,253.2	4,258.2	15.4	15.4	4.7	4.73	30.96	0.5	0.28	63.00 — 45.84	11.5
12/31/97	1,259.3	207.6	1,466.9	185.5	4,835.0	3,921.8	12.6	13.7	3.8	3.56	26.17	0.6	0.25	51.04 — 33.89	11.9
12/31/96	1,130.6	192.6	1,323.3	154.9	4,379.1	3,512.4	11.7	13.6	3.5	4.49	32.95	0.7	0.21	36.11 — 27.72	7.1
12/31/95	981.2	172.9	1,154.1	131.9	3,899.0	2,940.1	11.4	13.3	3.4	3.83	28.71	0.6	0.18	32.83 — 23.22	7.3
12/31/94	851.2	153.6	1,004.8	101.6	3,457.8	2,434.3	10.1	13.3	2.9	2.96	22.20	0.7	0.16	25.50 — 20.17	7.7
12/31/93	581.1	138.9	720.0	①86.7	3,169.6	2,289.2	12.0	11.2	2.7	①2.53	22.48	0.5	0.12	27.33 — 21.78	9.7

Statistics are as originally reported. Adj. for stk. splits: 50% div., 7/01; 3-for-2, 7/97 ① Bef. acctg. chg. credit of $46.4 mill. ② Incl. after-tax catastrophe losses of $139.8 mill. ③ Incl. after-tax chrg. of $65.0 mill. for increase in reserves.

OFFICERS:
M. R. Greenberg, Chmn.
R. F. Orlich, Pres., C.E.O.
S. S. Skalicky, Exec. V.P., C.F.O.
INVESTOR CONTACT: Steven S. Skalicky, Exec. V.P., C.F.O., (212) 770-2040
PRINCIPAL OFFICE: 80 Pine Street, New York, NY 10005

TELEPHONE NUMBER: (212) 770-2000
FAX: (212) 785-7230
WEB: www.transre.com
NO. OF EMPLOYEES: 400 (approx.)
SHAREHOLDERS: 23,500 (approx.)
ANNUAL MEETING: In May
INCORPORATED: DE, 1986

INSTITUTIONAL HOLDINGS:
No. of Institutions: 94
Shares Held: 50,081,642
% Held: 95.7
INDUSTRY: Fire, marine, and casualty insurance (SIC: 6331)
TRANSFER AGENT(S): American Stock Transfer & Trust Company, New York, NY

TRANSOCEAN INC.

EXCH.	SYM.	REC. PRICE	P/E RATIO	YLD.	MKT. CAP.	RANGE (52-WK.)	'02 Y/E PR.
NYSE	RIG	22.70 (2/28/03)	...	...	$7.24 bill.	39.33 - 18.10	23.20

MEDIUM GRADE. WEAK DRILLING DEMAND TEMPERS THE COMPANY'S NEAR-TERM OUTLOOK.

TRADING VOLUME
Thousand Shares

*7 YEAR PRICE SCORE N/A   *12 MONTH PRICE SCORE N/A

*NYSE COMPOSITE INDEX=100

INTERIM EARNINGS (Per Share):

Qtr.	Mar.	June	Sept.	Dec.
1997	0.27	0.28	0.39	0.46
1998	0.77	0.69	0.92	1.02
1999	0.85	0.56	0.46	d0.11
2000	0.15	0.17	0.22	d0.04
2001	0.11	0.26	0.30	0.17
2002	0.24	0.25	0.78	d8.71

INTERIM DIVIDENDS (Per Share):

Amt.	Decl.	Ex.	Rec.	Pay.
0.03Q	2/14/02	2/27/02	3/01/02	3/15/02
0.03Q	5/09/02	5/28/02	5/30/02	6/13/02
	Dividend payment suspended.			

CAPITALIZATION (12/31/01):

	($000)	(%)
Long-Term Debt	4,539,400	28.8
Deferred Income Tax	317,100	2.0
Common & Surplus	10,910,300	69.2
Total	15,766,800	100.0

BUSINESS:

Transocean Inc. (formerly Transocean Sedco Forex Inc.) is an international provider of offshore and inland marine contract drilling services for oil and gas wells. As of 1/30/03, RIG owned, had partial ownership interests in or operated more than 150 mobile offshore drilling units, inland drilling barges and other assets utilized in the support of offshore drilling activities worldwide. RIG's active fleet includes 31 high-specification semisubmersibles, 27 other floaters, and 55 jackup rigs. RIG also has a fleet of land and barge drilling rigs in Venezuela. On 12/31/99, Transocean Offshore Inc. completed its merger with Sedco Forex, which was spun off from Schlumberger Limited on 12/30/99. On 1/31/01, RIG acquired R&B Falcon Corporation in a transaction valued at $6.70 billion.

RECENT DEVELOPMENTS:

For the year ended 12/31/02, RIG posted a loss of $2.37 billion, before an accounting change charge of $1.36 billion, versus income of $271.9 million, before an extraordinary loss of $19.3 million, the previous year. Results for 2002 and 2001 included impairment losses on long-lived assets of $2.93 billion and $40.4 million, and net gains from the sale of assets of $3.7 million and $56.5 million, respectively. Results for 2001 also included goodwill amortization of $154.9 million. Operating revenues fell 5.2% to $2.67 billion. International and U.S. Floater Contract Drilling Services segment revenue of $2.49 billion was essentially flat versus the prior year. Revenue from the Gulf of Mexico Shallow and Inland Water segment slid 60.7% to $187.8 million.

PROSPECTS:

RIG has indicated that it expects utilization of its fleet of other floaters, specifically second and third generation semisubmersible rigs, to remain depressed over the near term. Additionally, RIG expects that these units will see a sequential decline in dayrates. RIG also anticipates that the utilization of its high-specification fleet will decline due in part to the deepwater drillship DISCOVERER SEVEN SEAS and semisubmersible rig JACK BATES being idle. The deepwater semisubmersible rig TRANSOCEAN RATHER should also be idle for the majority of the quarter ended 3/31/03.

ANNUAL FINANCIAL DATA:

FISCAL YEAR	TOT. REVS. ($mill.)	NET INC. ($mill.)	TOT. ASSETS ($mill.)	OPER. PROFIT %	NET PROFIT %	RET. ON EQUITY %	RET. ON ASSETS %	CURR. RATIO	EARN. PER SH.$	CASH FL. PER SH.$	TANG. BK. VAL.$	DIV. PER SH.$	PRICE RANGE	AVG. P/E RATIO	AVG. YIELD %
p12/31/02	2,673.9	d2,368.2							d7.42			0.06	39.33 - 18.10	...	0.2
12/31/01	2,820.1	271.9	17,019.8	19.5	9.6	2.5	1.6	1.5	0.86	2.84	13.94	0.12	57.69 - 23.05	46.9	0.3
12/31/00	1,229.5	107.1	6,358.8	10.8	8.7	2.7	1.7	0.9	0.50	1.73	14.08	0.12	65.50 - 29.25	94.8	0.3
12/31/99	648.2	58.1	6,140.2	7.5	9.0	1.5	0.9	1.1	0.53	1.49	13.53	0.12	32.50 - 19.63	49.2	0.3
12/31/98	1,089.6	343.4	3,250.9	42.2	31.5	17.4	10.6	1.9	3.41	4.56	12.96	0.12	59.94 - 23.00	12.2	0.3
12/31/97	892.0	141.9	2,755.1	24.4	15.9	8.8	5.2	1.7	1.38	2.38	9.29	0.12	60.50 - 26.13	31.4	0.3
12/31/96	528.9	78.0	2,443.2	20.3	14.8	4.8	3.2	1.1	1.09	1.73	8.39	0.12	35.69 - 20.56	25.9	0.4
12/31/95	322.7	46.9	542.3	16.1	14.6	12.9	8.7	3.1	0.83	1.30	6.40	0.12	24.63 - 8.88	20.3	0.7
12/31/94	243.0	12.7	493.5	8.6	5.2	4.0	2.6	2.6	0.23	0.66	5.66	0.12	10.75 - 7.81	41.2	1.3
12/31/93	271.3	24.0	472.0	8.9	8.9	7.7	5.1	2.2	0.50	0.94	5.55	0.03	11.75 - 7.63	19.4	0.3

Statistics are as originally reported. Adj. for 2-for-1 stk. split, 9/97. All figs. for 1999 & earlier are for Transocean Offshore Inc. ① Incl. ops. of Transocean ASA, acq. 9/96 ② Bef. acctg. adj. chrg. of $6.7 mil. ③ Incl. one-time cr. of $46.1 mil. ④ E.P.S. figs. are pro-forma; incl. non-recur. chrgs. of $13.4 mil. ⑤ Incl. aft.-tax chrgs. of $42.2 mil. & gain fr. sale of assets of $17.8 mil.; bef. extraord. gain of $1.4 mil. ⑥ Incl. impair. loss on long-lived assets of $40.4 mil. & gain fr. sale of assets of $56.5 mil.; bef. extraord. loss of $19.3 mil. ⑦ Incl. ops. of R&B Falcon Corp., acq. 1/01 ⑧ Incl. impair. loss on long-lived assets of $2.37 bil. & gain fr. sale of assets of $3.7 mil.; bef. acctg. chge. chrg. of $1.36 bil.

OFFICERS:
J. M. Talbert, Chmn.
R. L. Long, Pres., C.E.O.
J. P. Cahuzac, Pres., C.O.O.
INVESTOR CONTACT: Jeffrey L. Chastain, (713) 232-7551
PRINCIPAL OFFICE: 4 Greenway Plaza, Houston, TX 77046

TELEPHONE NUMBER: (713) 232-7500
FAX: (713) 850-3834
WEB: www.deepwater.com
NO. OF EMPLOYEES: 14,260 (approx.)
SHAREHOLDERS: 25,911 (approx. record)
ANNUAL MEETING: In May
INCORPORATED: DE, 1953; reincorp., Cayman Islands, May, 1999

INSTITUTIONAL HOLDINGS:
No. of Institutions: N/A
Shares Held: N/A
% Held: N/A
INDUSTRY: Drilling oil and gas wells (SIC: 1381)
TRANSFER AGENT(S): The Bank of New York, New York, NY

TRIBUNE COMPANY

EXCH.	SYM.	REC. PRICE	P/E RATIO	YLD.	MKT. CAP.	RANGE (52-WK.)	'02 Y/E PR.
NYSE	TRB	44.85 (2/28/03)	25.1	1.0%	$13.37 bill.	49.49 - 35.66	45.46

UPPER MEDIUM GRADE. GOING FORWARD, THE COMPANY WILL CONTINUE COST-REDUCTION EFFORTS.

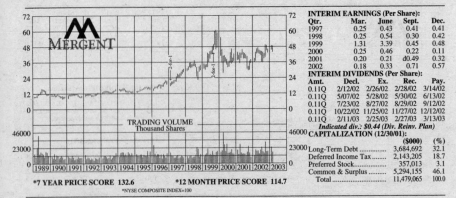

*7 YEAR PRICE SCORE 132.6   ***12 MONTH PRICE SCORE 114.7**

*NYSE COMPOSITE INDEX=100

INTERIM EARNINGS (Per Share):

Qtr.	Mar.	June	Sept.	Dec.
1997	0.25	0.43	0.41	0.41
1998	0.25	0.54	0.30	0.42
1999	1.31	3.39	0.45	0.48
2000	0.25	0.46	0.22	0.11
2001	0.20	0.21	d0.49	0.32
2002	0.18	0.33	0.71	0.57

INTERIM DIVIDENDS (Per Share):

Amt.	Decl.	Ex.	Rec.	Pay.
0.11Q	2/12/02	2/26/02	2/28/02	3/14/02
0.11Q	5/07/02	5/28/02	5/30/02	6/13/02
0.11Q	7/23/02	8/27/02	8/29/02	9/12/02
0.11Q	10/22/02	11/25/02	11/27/02	12/12/02
0.11Q	2/11/03	2/25/03	2/27/03	3/13/03

Indicated div.: $0.44 (Div. Reinv. Plan)

CAPITALIZATION (12/30/01):

	($000)	(%)
Long-Term Debt	3,684,692	32.1
Deferred Income Tax	2,143,205	18.7
Preferred Stock	357,013	3.1
Common & Surplus	5,294,155	46.1
Total	11,479,065	100.0

BUSINESS:

Tribune Company is a media company operating businesses in broadcasting, publishing and on the Internet. The Company owns and operates 24 major-market television stations and reaches more than 80.0% of U.S. television households. Broadcasting properties also include four radio stations, Tribune Entertainment and the Chicago Cubs baseball team. In addition, the Company operates 12 daily newspapers, including THE BALTIMORE SUN, THE LOS ANGELES TIMES, THE HARTFORD COURANT, THE ADVO-CATE, CHICAGO TRIBUNE, SOUTH FLORIDA SUN-SENTINEL, THE MORNING CALL, GREENWICH TIME, NEWSDAY, ORLANDO SENTINEL, and DAILY PRESS. The Company also distributes entertainment listings and syndicated content, and operates two 24-hour cable news channels. The Company's interactive segment operates news and information Web sites in 18 of the nation's top 30 markets. On 6/12/00, TRB completed the acquisition of Times Mirror for approximately $8.00 billion in cash and stock.

RECENT DEVELOPMENTS:

For the year ended 12/29/02, income amounted to $608.6 million, before an accounting change charge of $165.6 million, compared with net income of $111.1 million in 2001. Earnings reflected strength of TRB's local mass media franchises and cost-reduction efforts. Results for 2002 and 2001 included restructuring charges of $27.3 million and $151.9 million, and non-operating charges of $9.3 million and $45.7 million, respectively. Operating revenues grew 2.5% to $5.38 billion from $5.25 billion the year before.

PROSPECTS:

Looking ahead, the Company expects earnings per share in 2003 in the low double-digit range, excluding non-operating items. The Company also expects to generate free cash flow of nearly $800 million, with debt declining to about $2.50 billion at year-end 2003. Meanwhile, TRB will continue its cost-control efforts. Separately, on 12/30/02, TRB agreed to acquire KPLR-TV of St. Louis, Missouri and KWBP-TV of Portland, Oregon from ACME Communications for $275.0 million.

ANNUAL FINANCIAL DATA:

FISCAL YEAR	TOT. REVS. ($mill.)	NET INC. ($mill.)	TOT. ASSETS ($mill.)	OPER. PROFIT %	NET PROFIT %	RET. ON EQUITY %	RET. ON ASSETS %	CURR. RATIO	EARN. PER SH.$	CASH FL.PER SH.$	TANG. BK. VAL.$	DIV. PER SH.$	PRICE RANGE	AVG. P/E RATIO	AVG. YIELD %
p12/29/02	5,384.4	⑦ 608.6							⑦ 1.80			0.44	49.49 — 35.66	23.7	1.0
12/30/01	5,253.4	⑧ 111.1	14,504.7	12.4	2.1	2.0	0.8	0.9	⑧ 0.28	1.73	...	0.44	45.90 — 29.71	135.0	1.2
12/31/00	4,910.4	⑨ 310.4	14,676.2	21.0	6.3	5.3	2.1	1.0	⑨ 0.99	2.20	...	0.40	55.19 — 26.88	41.9	1.0
12/26/99	3,221.9	④ 1,483.1	8,797.7	23.9	46.0	42.7	16.9	2.4	④ 5.62	6.44	...	0.36	60.88 — 30.16	8.1	0.8
12/27/98	2,980.9	③ 414.3	5,935.6	23.6	13.9	17.6	7.0	1.1	③ 1.51	2.21	...	0.34	37.53 — 22.38	19.9	1.1
12/28/97	2,719.8	③ 393.6	4,777.6	23.6	14.5	21.6	8.2	1.2	③ 1.41	2.23	...	0.32	30.75 — 17.75	17.3	1.3
12/29/96	2,405.7	①② 282.8	3,700.9	20.4	11.8	18.4	7.6	1.3	①② 1.08	1.66	...	0.30	22.06 — 14.16	16.8	1.7
12/31/95	2,244.7	①② 245.5	3,288.3	18.1	10.9	17.8	7.5	1.0	①② 0.88	1.34	0.27	0.28	17.22 — 12.69	17.1	1.9
12/25/94	2,154.9	① 242.0	2,785.8	18.4	11.2	18.2	8.7	1.0	① 0.83	1.26	...	0.26	16.13 — 12.22	17.1	1.8
12/26/93	1,952.5	188.6	2,536.4	18.3	9.7	17.2	7.4	1.1	0.64	1.03	...	0.24	15.31 — 12.00	21.3	1.8

Statistics are as originally reported. Adj. for 2-for-1 split, 1/97 & 9/99. ① Incl. $10.0 mill. after-tax non-recur. gains, 1996; $8.7 mill., 1995; $13.0 mill., 1994. ② Bef. $89.3 mill. gain fr. disc. ops., 1996; $32.7 mill., 1995. ③ Incl. $119.1 mill. pre-tax non-recur. gains, 1998; $111.8 mill., 1997. ④ Incl. $1.76 bill. non-oper. gains & excl. d$3.1 mill. acct. chg. ⑤ Incl. a loss of $149.0 mill. from non-oper. items & excl. $86.0 mill. net loss fr. disc. ops. ⑥ Incl. $74.9 mill. net loss fr. non-oper. items & restr. chg. of $151.9 mill. ⑦ Incl. $27.3 mill. restr. chg. & $9.3 mill. net loss fr. non-oper. items.

OFFICERS:
J. W. Madigan, Chmn.
D. J. FitzSimons, Pres., C.E.O., C.O.O.
C. H. Kenney, Sr. V.P., Gen. Couns., Sec.
INVESTOR CONTACT: Ruthelyn Musil, V.P., Corp. Relations, (312) 222-3787
PRINCIPAL OFFICE: 435 North Michigan Avenue, Chicago, IL 60611

TELEPHONE NUMBER: (312) 222-9100
FAX: (312) 222-4917
WEB: www.tribune.com
NO. OF EMPLOYEES: 25,600 (avg.)
SHAREHOLDERS: 7,464
ANNUAL MEETING: In May
INCORPORATED: IL, 1861; reincorp., DE, 1968

INSTITUTIONAL HOLDINGS:
No. of Institutions: 443
Shares Held: 168,806,118
% Held: 55.4

INDUSTRY: Newspapers (SIC: 2711)

TRANSFER AGENT(S): EquiServe, First Chicago Trust Division, Jersey City, NJ

TUPPERWARE CORPORATION

EXCH.	SYM.	REC. PRICE	P/E RATIO	YLD.	MKT. CAP.	RANGE (52-WK.)	'02 Y/E PR.
NYSE	TUP	12.47 (2/28/03)	8.0	7.1%	$0.72 bill.	24.99 - 12.45	15.08

LOWER MEDIUM GRADE. FOR THE FULL-YEAR 2003, EARNINGS PER SHARE ARE EXPECTED TO BE BETWEEN $1.50 AND $1.60.

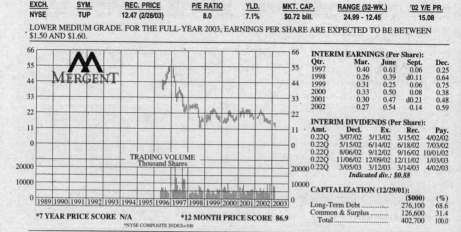

INTERIM EARNINGS (Per Share):

Qtr.	Mar.	June	Sept.	Dec.
1997	0.40	0.61	0.06	0.25
1998	0.26	0.39	d0.11	0.64
1999	0.31	0.25	0.06	0.75
2000	0.33	0.50	0.08	0.38
2001	0.30	0.47	d0.21	0.48
2002	0.27	0.54	0.14	0.59

INTERIM DIVIDENDS (Per Share):

Amt.	Decl.	Ex.	Rec.	Pay.
0.22Q	3/07/02	3/13/02	3/15/02	4/02/02
0.22Q	5/15/02	6/14/02	6/18/02	7/03/02
0.22Q	8/06/02	9/12/02	9/16/02	10/01/02
0.22Q	11/06/02	12/09/02	12/11/02	1/03/03
0.22Q	3/05/03	3/12/03	3/14/03	4/02/03

Indicated div.: $0.88

CAPITALIZATION (12/29/01):

	($000)	(%)
Long-Term Debt	276,100	68.6
Common & Surplus	126,600	31.4
Total	402,700	100.0

*7 YEAR PRICE SCORE N/A ***12 MONTH PRICE SCORE 86.9**

*NYSE COMPOSITE INDEX=100

BUSINESS:

Tupperware Corporation is a direct-selling multinational consumer products company engaged in the manufacture and sale of Tupperware products. The core of TUP's product line consists of a broad line of high-quality food storage containers that preserve freshness through the well-known Tupperware seals. TUP also has an established line of food preparation and serving containers, kitchen gadgets, children's educational toys, microwave products and gifts. As of 1/20/03, the Company had more than 1.2 million independent sales consultants worldwide. In addition, the Company is a direct-seller of premium beauty and skin care products through its BeautiControl brand in North America, Latin America, and Asia Pacific. Sales in 2002 were derived: Europe, 38.1%; North America, 24.3%; Asia Pacific, 19.0%; Latin America, 11.9%; and BeautiControl, 6.7%. The Company was spun off from Premark International, Inc. on 5/31/96.

RECENT DEVELOPMENTS:

For the year ended 12/28/02, net income grew 46.5% to $90.1 million compared with $61.5 million in 2001. Results for 2002 and 2001 included re-engineering and impairment charges of $20.8 million and $24.8 million, respectively. Total sales and other income climbed 3.3% to $1.15 billion from $1.12 billion a year earlier. The improvement in sales was primarily attributed to strong improvement in BeautiControl, in addition to modest increases in North America and Europe, partially offset by a sharp decline in Latin America and a slight decrease in Asia Pacific.

PROSPECTS:

For the full-year of 2003, recent momentum in Europe, led by Germany, is expected to continue. Additionally, many of the markets in Asia Pacific, North America and BeautiControl are expected to make progress as well. However, total company results for the first half of the year will be under significant pressure resulting in earnings below prior year due to the challenges in Mexico, Venezuela, Korea and the Philippines where improvement is not expected until the second half of 2003. The 2003 outlook is for a moderate increase in sales. Earnings per share for 2003 are expected to be in the range of $1.50 to $1.60. Expectations for the balance sheet are to keep working capital flat resulting in free cash flow equal to net income before profits on land development.

ANNUAL FINANCIAL DATA:

FISCAL YEAR	NET SALES ($mill.)	NET INC. ($mill.)	TOT. ASSETS ($mill.)	OPER. PROFIT %	NET PROFIT %	RET. ON EQUITY %	RET. ON ASSETS %	CURR. RATIO	EARN. PER SH.$	CASH FL. PER SH.$	TANG. BK. VAL.$	DIV. PER SH.$	PRICE RANGE	AVG. P/E RATIO	AVG. YIELD %
p12/28/02	1,103.5	② 90.1	835.3						② 1.54			0.88	24.99 - 14.40	12.8	4.5
12/29/01	1,114.4	② 61.5	845.7	11.7	5.5	48.6	7.3	1.0	② 1.04	1.89	1.21	0.88	26.00 - 17.70	21.0	4.0
12/30/00	1,073.1	② 74.9	849.4	12.7	7.0	60.5	8.8	1.4	② 1.29	2.19	1.14	0.88	24.50 - 14.56	15.1	4.5
12/25/99	1,063.8	② 79.0	796.1	13.3	7.4	54.4	9.9	1.2	② 1.37	2.32	2.47	0.88	25.50 - 15.06	14.8	4.3
12/26/98	1,082.8	69.1	823.4	10.5	6.4	50.9	8.4	1.3	1.18	2.27	2.36	0.88	29.00 - 11.44	17.1	4.4
12/27/97	1,229.3	① 82.0	847.2	11.0	6.7	38.3	9.7	1.3	① 1.32	2.40	3.43	0.88	54.50 - 22.50	29.2	2.3
12/28/96	1,369.3	174.7	978.5	18.6	12.8	57.2	17.9	1.4	2.70	3.80	4.90	0.22	55.50 - 38.25	17.4	0.5
12/30/95	1,359.4	171.4	944.0	16.5	12.6	41.2	18.2	1.2	2.55	3.69	...	...	...	...	...
12/31/94	1,274.6	149.2	882.6	15.0	11.7	37.8	16.9	1.2	...	...	...	...	...	...	...
12/25/93	1,171.8	117.9	...	13.8	10.1	...	...	...	...	...	...	...	...	...	...

Statistics are as originally reported. ① Incl. nonrecur. chrg. of $42.4 mill. ② Incl. re-engineering chrg. of $20.8 mill., 2002; $24.8 mill., 2001; $12.5 mill., 2000; $15.1 mill., 1999.

OFFICERS:
E. V. Goings, Chmn., C.E.O.
P. Mathur, Sr. V.P., C.F.O.
INVESTOR CONTACT: Jane Garrard V.P.,
Investor Relations, (407) 826-4522
PRINCIPAL OFFICE: 14901 South Orange
Blossom Trail, Orlando, FL 32837

TELEPHONE NUMBER: (407) 826-5050
FAX: (407) 826-8849
WEB: www.tupperware.com
NO. OF EMPLOYEES: 6,800 (approx.)
SHAREHOLDERS: 29,821
ANNUAL MEETING: In May
INCORPORATED: DE, Feb., 1996

INSTITUTIONAL HOLDINGS:
No. of Institutions: 194
Shares Held: 44,640,551
% Held: 76.5
INDUSTRY: Toilet preparations (SIC: 2844)
TRANSFER AGENT(S): Wells Fargo Bank
Shareowner Services, St. Paul, MN

21ST CENTURY INSURANCE GROUP

EXCH.	SYM.	REC. PRICE	P/E RATIO	YLD.	MKT. CAP.	RANGE (52-WK.)	'02 Y/E PR.
NYSE	TW	11.94 (2/28/03)	...	0.7%	$1.02 bill.	21.80 - 9.15	12.52

MEDIUM GRADE. THE COMPANY IS BENEFITING FROM SEVERAL NEW MARKETING CAMPAIGNS AND PRODUCTS INTRODUCED DURING 2002.

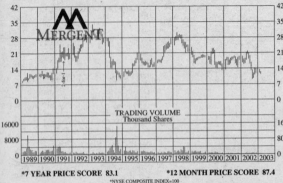

INTERIM EARNINGS (Per Share):

Qtr.	Mar.	June	Sept.	Dec.
1998	0.34	0.49	0.44	d0.06
1999	0.33	0.38	0.21	0.08
2000	0.04	0.06	0.03	0.02
2001	0.06	0.07	0.03	d0.48
2002	0.10	0.11	d0.53	0.17

INTERIM DIVIDENDS (Per Share):

Amt.	Decl.	Ex.	Rec.	Pay.
0.08Q	2/27/02	3/12/02	3/14/02	3/29/02
0.08Q	6/27/02	7/03/02	7/08/02	7/19/02
0.08Q	9/25/02	10/03/02	10/07/02	10/25/02
0.02Q	12/19/02	12/26/02	12/30/02	1/17/03
0.02Q	2/27/03	3/06/03	3/10/03	3/28/03

Indicated div.: $0.08

CAPITALIZATION (12/31/01):

	($000)	(%)
Common & Surplus	659,306	100.0
Total	659,306	100.0

*7 YEAR PRICE SCORE 83.1   ***12 MONTH PRICE SCORE 87.4**

*NYSE COMPOSITE INDEX=100

BUSINESS:

21st Century Insurance Group is an insurance holding company. The Company, through its subsidiaries, 21st Century Insurance Company and 21st Century Casualty Company, directly markets and underwrites private passenger automobile and personal umbrella insurance. The Company offers the following insurance coverages for private passenger automobiles: bodily injury liability, property damage, medical payments, uninsured and underinsured motorist, rental reimbursement, uninsured motorist property damage and collision deductible, towing, comprehensive, and collision. The Company markets personal automobile insurance in Arizona, California, Nevada, Oregon, and Washington. On 1/1/02, TW acquired American International Group, Inc.'s 51.0% interest in 21st Century Insurance Company of Arizona for $4.4 million.

RECENT DEVELOPMENTS:

For the year ended 12/31/02, net loss narrowed to $12.3 million from $27.6 million the previous year. Results for 2002 included an after-tax charge of $24.2 million for the write-off of software. Also, results for 2002 and 2001 included after-tax losses of $38.2 million and $50.4 million, respectively, related to earthquake claims. Net premiums written increased 7.4% to $998.2 million, while net premiums earned climbed 11.1% to $965.3 million. Loss and loss adjustment expenses declined 4.3% to $826.7 million versus $836.2 million a year earlier.

PROSPECTS:

Future results should continue to benefit from growth in TW's customer base, in particular, TW's expansion into the Latino market which currently represents nearly 20.0% of new customer efforts. New customers have increased from an average of over 2,000 per week in the first quarter of 2002 to over 4,000 per week in the fourth quarter of 2002. Moreover, growth has continued into 2003 with 124 new customers on New Year's Day and over 5,000 per week in January 2003. Separately, TW received approval for a 3.9% rate increase for its California auto product. This rate increase should enable TW to continue the steady improvement in its personal auto combined ratio in the face of rising loss costs. TW plans to implement this increase in March 2003.

ANNUAL FINANCIAL DATA:

FISCAL YEAR	PREM. INC. ($mill.)	NET INVST. INC. ($mill.)	TOT. REVS. ($mill.)	NET INC. ($mill.)	TOT. ASSETS ($mill.)	TOT. INVST. ($mill.)	RET. ON REVS. %	RET. ON EQUITY %	RET. ON ASSETS %	EARN. PER SH. $	TANG. BK. VAL. $	AVG. YIELD %	DIV. PER SH. $	PRICE RANGE	AVG. P/E RATIO
p12/31/02	924.6		981.3	③ d12.3	1,352.0	855.7	...	...	...	③ d0.14		1.6	0.24	21.80 - 9.15	...
12/31/01	864.1	45.9	914.1	② d27.6	1,338.1	913.1	1.5	1.8	1.0	② d0.32	7.72	1.9	0.32	19.57 - 13.44	...
12/31/00	825.5	49.3	869.8	12.9	1,338.1	913.1	1.5	1.8	1.0	0.15	8.46	2.7	0.48	23.00 - 13.13	120.3
12/31/99	770.4	62.7	832.7	87.5	1,379.3	943.5	10.5	12.1	6.3	1.00	8.39	3.2	0.64	23.56 - 16.00	19.8
12/31/98	772.9	75.1	870.7	101.1	1,593.2	1,068.6	11.6	12.9	6.3	1.19	8.97	2.3	0.58	30.38 - 20.94	21.6
12/31/97	786.0	73.5	863.5	110.9	1,482.5	1,084.5	12.8	19.0	7.5	1.37	6.93	1.1	0.25	27.75 - 16.38	16.1
12/31/96	856.6	73.2	937.1	74.1	1,513.8	1,064.6	7.9	15.2	4.9	0.92	5.09	0.3	0.05	20.63 - 14.50	19.1
12/31/95	963.8	81.7	1,055.7	69.6	1,608.9	1,127.1	6.6	14.9	4.3	0.88	4.69	...	...	21.25 - 10.38	18.0
12/31/94	1,034.0	84.8	1,180.3	d498.0	1,702.8	942.2	...	...	...	d9.69	2.29	1.7	0.32	28.13 - 8.75	...
12/31/93	989.7	97.6	1,103.8	① 108.6	1,648.1	1,422.6	9.8	16.6	6.6	② 2.11	12.74	2.2	0.64	34.00 - 25.13	14.0

Statistics are as originally reported. ① Bef. acctg. change credit of $4.0 mill. ② Incl. restr. chrgs. $13.6 mill. & earthquake claims of $70.0 mill. ③ Incl. after-tax write-off of software of $24.2 mill. & after-tax earthquake claims of $38.2 mill.

OFFICERS:
R. M. Sandler, Chmn.
B. W. Marlow, Vice-Chmn., Pres., C.E.O.
J. Lorentz, Acting C.F.O., Contr.
INVESTOR CONTACT: Doug Howell, (818) 704-3595
PRINCIPAL OFFICE: 6301 Owensmouth Ave., Suite 700, Woodland Hills, CA 91367

TELEPHONE NUMBER: (818) 704-3700
FAX: (818) 704-3485
WEB: www.i21.com
NO. OF EMPLOYEES: 2,500 (avg.)
SHAREHOLDERS: 690 (approx.)
ANNUAL MEETING: In June
INCORPORATED: CA, May, 1969

INSTITUTIONAL HOLDINGS:
No. of Institutions: 51
Shares Held: 64,071,638
% Held: 75.0
INDUSTRY: Fire, marine, and casualty insurance (SIC: 6331)
TRANSFER AGENT(S): American Stock Transfer & Trust Company, New York, NY

TXU CORPORATION

EXCH.	SYM.	REC. PRICE	P/E RATIO	YLD.	MKT. CAP.	RANGE (52-WK.)	'02 Y/E PR.
NYSE	TXU	15.97 (2/28/03)	22.5	3.1%	$4.23 bill.	57.05 - 10.10	18.68

LOWER MEDIUM GRADE. LOOKING AHEAD, TXU WILL FOCUS ON GROWING ITS NORTH AMERICAN AND AUSTRALIAN ENERGY AND ENERGY-DELIVERY BUSINESSES

INTERIM EARNINGS (Per Share):

Qtr.	Mar.	June	Sept.	Dec.
1998	0.51	0.33	1.04	0.84
1999	0.65	0.35	1.31	1.24
2000	0.71	0.87	1.25	0.61
2001	0.76	0.78	1.28	d0.29
2002	1.01	0.73	0.78	d1.81

INTERIM DIVIDENDS (Per Share):

Amt.	Decl.	Ex.	Rec.	Pay.
0.60Q	2/15/02	3/06/02	3/08/02	4/01/02
0.60Q	5/10/02	6/05/02	6/07/02	7/01/02
0.60Q	8/16/02	9/04/02	9/06/02	10/01/02
0.125Q	10/15/02	12/04/02	12/06/02	1/02/03
0.125Q	2/21/03	3/05/03	3/07/03	4/01/03

Indicated div.: $0.50

CAPITALIZATION (12/31/01):

	($000)	(%)
Long-Term Debt	16,173,000	56.6
Deferred Income Tax	3,796,000	13.3
Redeemable Pfd. Stock	665,000	2.3
Preferred Stock	300,000	1.0
Common & Surplus	7,656,000	26.8
Total	28,590,000	100.0

TRADING VOLUME Thousand Shares

*7 YEAR PRICE SCORE 99.5   ***12 MONTH PRICE SCORE 52.7**
NYSE COMPOSITE INDEX=100

BUSINESS:

TXU Corporation (formerly Texas Utilities Company) is a major energy company with operations in North America and Australia, serving over five million electricity and gas customers as of 12/31/02. The Company's North American energy business, TXU Energy, is the largest power generator and electricity retailer in Texas with approximately 19,000 megawatts of competitive generation and 2.7 mil-

lion electric customers. The Company's electricity and natural gas utilities in Texas deliver over 100.0 million megawatt hours of electricity and over 140.00 billion cubic feet of natural gas annually. TXU's business in Australia includes both electricity and natural gas delivery and energy operations, with 1,280 megawatts of generation and almost 1.0 million electricity and natural gas customers.

RECENT DEVELOPMENTS:

For the year ended 12/31/02, TXU reported income of $175.0 million, before a loss from discontinued operations of $4.21 billion and an extraordinary loss of $175.0 million, versus income of $639.0 million, before income from discontinued operations of $192.0 million and an extraordinary loss of $154.0 million, in the previous year. Results

for 2002 included an after-tax charge of $328.0 million for the write-down of projects and telecommunications investments, an after-tax charge of $120.0 million related to the restructuring of the Texas electricity market and an after-tax charge of $21.0 million for severance costs. Operating revenues declined 1.4% to $10.03 billion.

PROSPECTS:

For 2003, TXU will focus on growing its North American and Australian energy and energy-delivery businesses. Contributions from North America Energy are expected to improve substantially as TXU has targeted a net reduction of expenses of about $250.0 million. However, earnings from this segment are expected to be down slightly from 2002 as customer and usage growth and improvement in

results from gas operations are likely to be outweighed by higher amortization and interest expenses. Meanwhile, earnings for TXU's operations in Australia are expected to be slightly lower than 2002 results due to a regulatory mandated 4.0% decrease in ex-franchise small consumer electricity rates.

ANNUAL FINANCIAL DATA:

FISCAL YEAR	TOT. REVS. ($mill.)	NET INC. ($mill.)	TOT. ASSETS ($mill.)	OPER. PROFIT %	NET PROFIT %	NET INC./ NET PROP. %	NET INC./ TOT. CAP. %	RET. ON EQUITY %	ACCUM. DEPR./ GROSS PROP. %	EARN. PER SH. $	TANG. BK. VAL. $	DIV. PER SH. $	DIV. PAYOUT %	PRICE RANGE	AVG. P/E RATIO	AVG. YIELD %
⑧ p12/31/02	10,034.0	⑦ 175.0	30,887.0							⑦ 0.55		2.40	436.4	57.05 - 10.10	61.0	7.1
12/31/01	27,927.0	① 831.0	44,990.0	8.2	3.0	3.7	2.9	10.4	…	① 2.52	26.82	2.40	95.2	50.00 - 34.81	16.8	5.7
12/31/00	22,009.0	916.0	42,020.0	11.3	4.2	3.9	3.2	11.9	27.3	3.43	28.96	2.40	70.0	45.25 - 25.94	10.4	6.7
12/31/99	17,118.0	③ 985.0	40,741.0	15.2	5.8	4.2	3.3	11.6	25.7	③ 3.53	30.15	2.30	65.2	47.19 - 32.75	11.3	5.8
④ 12/31/98	14,736.0	⑤⑥ 740.0	39,514.0	16.7	5.0	3.2	2.6	8.8	24.5	⑤ 2.79	29.21	2.20	78.9	48.06 - 38.38	15.5	5.1
12/31/97	7,945.6	② 660.5	24,874.1	24.0	8.3	3.6	3.3	9.2	26.6	② 2.85	27.90	2.10	73.7	42.00 - 31.50	12.9	5.7
12/31/96	6,550.9	753.6	21,375.7	30.6	11.5	4.3	4.1	11.6	25.8	3.35	26.86	2.00	59.7	43.75 - 38.50	12.3	4.9
12/31/95	5,638.7	① d138.6	21,535.9	31.7	…	…	…	…	23.9	① d0.61	25.38	3.08	…	41.25 - 30.13	…	8.6
12/31/94	5,663.5	542.8	20,893.4	29.1	9.6	3.1	2.9	7.4	22.1	2.40	28.74	3.08	128.3	43.13 - 29.63	15.2	8.5
12/31/93	5,434.5	① 368.7	21,518.1	27.8	6.8	2.1	1.9	4.8	20.5	① 1.66	29.29	3.07	184.9	49.75 - 41.63	27.5	6.7

Statistics are as originally reported. ① Incl. after-tax non-recurr. chrg. $325.0 mill., 12/01; $31.0 mill., 12/98; $802.0 mill., 12/95; pre-tax chrg. $359.7 mill., 12/93 ② Incl. $80.0 mill. rate settlement refund, $79.0 mill. fuel reconciliation disallowance and $12.0 mill. in interest related to fuel reconciliation and disallowance ③ Incl. gain of $145.0 mill. from sale of PrimeCo & non-recurr. chrg. $48.0 mill. ④ Reflects 5/98 acq. of The Energy Group PLC ⑤ Incl. non-recurr. after-tax restr. chg. & acq. costs $50.0 mill. ⑥ Reflects the exit of TXU's European operations. ⑦ Excl. loss. fr. disc. operations of $4.21 bill. & extraord. loss of $175.0 mill.; Incl. after-tax non-recurr. chrgs. of $469.0 mill.

OFFICERS:
E. Nye, Chmn., C.E.O.
M. McNally, Exec. V.P., C.F.O.
INVESTOR CONTACT: David Anderson, Inv. Rel., (214) 812-4641
PRINCIPAL OFFICE: Energy Plaza, 1601 Bryan Street, Dallas, TX 75201-3411

TELEPHONE NUMBER: (214) 812-4600
FAX: (214) 812-4651
WEB: www.tu.com
NO. OF EMPLOYEES: 18,000 (approx.)
SHAREHOLDERS: 73,161
ANNUAL MEETING: In May
INCORPORATED: TX, Sept., 1945

TYSON FOODS, INC.

EXCH.	SYM.	REC. PRICE	P/E RATIO	YLD.	MKT. CAP.	RANGE (52-WK.)	'02 Y/E PR.
NYSE	TSN	9.20 (2/28/03)	11.1	1.7%	$3.25 bill.	15.71 - 8.95	11.22

MEDIUM GRADE. THE COMPANY IS INTRODUCING NEW BEEF AND PORK PRODUCTS UNDER ITS TYSON BRAND.

TRADING VOLUME
Thousand Shares

*7 YEAR PRICE SCORE 80.9   *12 MONTH PRICE SCORE 92.7
*NYSE COMPOSITE INDEX=100

INTERIM EARNINGS (Per Share):

Qtr.	Dec.	Mar.	June	Sept.
1997-98	0.21	0.10	0.20	d0.39
1998-99	0.24	0.28	0.30	0.18
1999-00	0.25	0.16	0.18	0.08
2000-01	0.12	d0.03	0.09	0.22
2001-02	0.36	0.18	0.30	0.24
2002-03	0.11	...	...	...

INTERIM DIVIDENDS (Per Share):

Amt.	Decl.	Ex.	Rec.	Pay.
0.04Q	1/31/02	5/29/02	6/01/02	6/15/02
0.04Q	5/03/02	8/28/02	9/01/02	9/15/02
0.04Q	8/02/02	11/26/02	12/01/02	12/15/02
0.04Q	11/15/02	2/26/03	3/01/03	3/15/03
0.04Q	2/07/03	5/28/03	6/01/03	6/15/03

Indicated div.: $0.16 (Div. Reinv. Plan)

CAPITALIZATION (9/28/02):

	($000)	(%)
Long-Term Debt	3,733,000	46.4
Deferred Income Tax	643,000	8.0
Common & Surplus	3,662,000	45.6
Total	8,038,000	100.0

BUSINESS:

Tyson Foods, Inc. operates in five reportable segments. The Beef segment (44.9% of fiscal 2002 sales) is primarily involved in the slaughter of live feed cattle and fabrication into meat cuts and case-ready products. The Chicken segment (30.9%) includes fresh, frozen and value-added chicken products, as well as TSN's chicken breeding operations. The Prepared Foods segment (13.1%) manufactures and markets frozen and refrigerated food products. The Pork segment (10.7%) includes hog slaughter and fabrication into case-ready products and related allied product processing. The Other segment (0.4%) includes the logistics group and other corporate operations. TSN's products are marketed and sold through retail grocery stores, warehouse stores, national and regional chain restaurants or their distributors, and food service operations such as plant and school cafeterias, convenience stores and hospitals. On 7/19/99, TSN sold its seafood division assets. On 9/28/01, the Company acquired IBP, Inc.

RECENT DEVELOPMENTS:

For the three months ended 12/28/02, net income totaled $39.0 million compared with $127.0 million in the corresponding prior-year period. Results for 2002 included a one-time charge of $47.0 million related to the closing of two poultry operations, partially offset by a $28.0 million gain from ongoing vitamin antitrust settlements. Sales slipped 1.1% to $5.80 billion from $5.87 billion a year earlier. Operating income was $145.0 million, down 46.9% versus $273.0 million the year before.

PROSPECTS:

On 1/21/03, TSN announced plans to introduce a wide selection of new beef and pork value-added products under the Company's TYSON brand. The introduction of these products will be supported by a $40.0 million advertising campaign. Meanwhile, earnings are being negatively affected by increased grain costs and lower market prices, due to an oversupply of meat, as well as from import restrictions and political pressures in international markets, primarily Russia and China. TSN is targeting second-quarter fiscal 2003 earnings in the range of $0.10 to $0.14 per share, excluding one-time items, and full fiscal-2003 earnings of between $0.90 and $1.00 per share.

ANNUAL FINANCIAL DATA:

FISCAL YEAR	TOT. REVS. ($mill.)	NET INC. ($mill.)	TOT. ASSETS ($mill.)	OPER. PROFIT %	NET PROFIT %	RET. ON EQUITY %	RET. ON ASSETS %	CURR. RATIO	EARN. PER SH.$	CASH FL. PER SH.$	TANG. BK. VAL.$	DIV. PER SH.$	PRICE RANGE	AVG. P/E RATIO	AVG. YIELD %
9/28/02	23,367.0	② 383.0	10,372.0	3.8	1.6	10.5	3.7	1.5	② 1.08	2.39	2.92	0.16	15.71 - 9.27	11.6	1.3
9/29/01	10,751.0	88.0	10,632.0	2.9	0.8	2.6	0.8	1.4	0.40	1.91	1.71	0.16	14.20 - 8.10	27.9	1.4
9/30/00	7,158.0	① 151.0	4,854.0	4.9	2.1	6.9	3.1	1.8	① 0.67	1.97	5.50	0.16	17.38 - 8.50	19.3	1.2
10/02/99	7,362.9	① 230.1	5,082.7	6.6	3.1	10.8	4.5	1.7	① 1.00	2.26	5.10	0.13	23.75 - 14.88	19.3	0.7
10/03/98	7,414.1	① 25.1	5,242.5	2.7	0.3	1.3	0.5	2.1	① 0.11	1.32	4.05	0.10	26.00 - 16.31	192.2	0.5
9/27/97	6,355.7	185.8	4,411.0	6.3	2.9	11.5	4.2	2.2	0.86	1.92	4.17	0.10	24.25 - 17.38	24.2	0.5
9/28/96	6,453.8	86.9	4,544.1	4.2	1.3	5.6	1.9	2.6	0.40	1.50	3.72	0.08	23.08 - 13.83	46.1	0.4
9/30/95	5,511.2	219.2	4,443.3	8.6	4.0	14.9	4.9	1.8	1.01	1.95	3.04	0.06	18.33 - 13.83	16.0	0.4
10/01/94	5,110.3	d2.1	3,668.0	3.8	...	...	...	2.3	d0.01	0.84	2.51	0.05	16.67 - 12.50	...	0.4
10/02/93	4,707.4	180.3	3,253.5	8.0	3.8	13.3	5.5	1.5	0.81	1.60	1.98	0.03	18.08 - 12.83	19.0	0.2

Statistics are as originally reported. Adj. for 3-for-2 stk. split, 2/97. ① Incl. $24.2 mil chrg. from AmeriServe reorganization, 2000; $76.9 mil chrg. fr. sale of assets, 1999; $142.2 mil asset impairment chg., 1998. ② Incl. $53.0 mil chrg. fr. restr. and discont. of the Thomas E. Wilson brand & $22.0 mil one-time gain fr. sale of Specialty Brands, Inc. subsidiary.

OFFICERS:
J. Tyson, Chmn., C.E.O.
S. Hankins, Exec. V.P., C.F.O.
G. W. Lee, Exec. V.P., C.O.O.
INVESTOR CONTACT: Louis C. Gottsponer, Jr., Dir., Investor Relations, (501) 290-4826
PRINCIPAL OFFICE: 2210 West Oaklawn Drive, Springdale, AR 72762-6999

TELEPHONE NUMBER: (479) 290-4000
FAX: (479) 290-4061
WEB: www.tysonfoodsinc.com
NO. OF EMPLOYEES: 120,000 (approx.)
SHAREHOLDERS: 41,000 (cl. A); 17 (cl. B)
ANNUAL MEETING: In Feb.
INCORPORATED: AR, Oct., 1947; reincorp., Feb., 1986

INSTITUTIONAL HOLDINGS:
No. of Institutions: 230
Shares Held: 134,397,334
% Held: 38.1
INDUSTRY: Poultry slaughtering and processing (SIC: 2015)
TRANSFER AGENT(S): EquiServe, Providence, RI

U.S. BANCORP

EXCH.	SYM.	REC. PRICE	P/E RATIO	YLD.	MKT. CAP.	RANGE (52-WK.)	'02 Y/E PR.
NYSE	USB	20.92 (2/28/03)	12.2	3.9%	$40.10 bill.	24.48 - 16.05	21.22

UPPER MEDIUM GRADE. THE COMPANY'S SUBSIDIARY, U.S. BANK, N.A., ACQUIRED THE CORPORATE TRUST BUSINESS OF STATE STREET CORPORATION.

*7 YEAR PRICE SCORE 82.7   *12 MONTH PRICE SCORE 107.1

*NYSE COMPOSITE INDEX=100

INTERIM EARNINGS (Per Share):

Qtr.	Mar.	June	Sept.	Dec.
1998	0.44	0.43	0.44	0.48
1999	0.50	0.51	0.54	0.50
2000	0.51	0.52	0.54	0.56
2001	0.21	0.29	0.02	0.36
2002	0.39	0.43	0.45	0.44

INTERIM DIVIDENDS (Per Share):

Amt.	Decl.	Ex.	Rec.	Pay.
0.195Q	3/12/02	3/26/02	3/29/02	4/15/02
0.195Q	6/18/02	6/26/02	6/28/02	7/15/02
0.195Q	9/17/02	9/26/02	9/30/02	10/15/02
0.195Q	12/17/02	12/27/02	12/31/02	1/15/03
0.205Q	3/12/03	3/27/03	3/31/03	4/15/03

Indicated div.: $0.82 (Div. Reinv. Plan)

CAPITALIZATION (12/31/02):

	($000)	(%)
Total Deposits	115,534,000	71.2
Long-Term Debt	28,588,000	17.6
Common & Surplus	18,101,000	11.2
Total	162,223,000	100.0

BUSINESS:

U.S. Bancorp, with $180.03 billion in assets as of 12/31/02, is the eighth largest banking services holding company in the U.S. As of 1/21/03, the Company operated 2,142 banking offices and 4,604 ATMs, providing a comprehensive line of banking, brokerage, insurance, investment, mortgage, trust and payment services products to consumers, businesses and institutions throughout the midwest and western U.S. USB is the parent company of U.S. Bank. On 9/20/99, USB completed the acquisition of Mercantile Bancorporation, Inc. On 2/27/01, USB completed the acquisition of Firstar Corporation.

RECENT DEVELOPMENTS:

For the year ended 12/31/02, the Company reported income of $3.33 billion, before an accounting charge of $37.2 million, compared with net income of $1.71 billion the year before. Results for 2002 and 2001 included merger and restructuring-related charges of $324.1 million and $946.4 million, respectively. Results for 2001 also included goodwill of $251.1 million. Net interest income increased 7.4% to $6.84 billion from $6.37 billion a year earlier. Provision for credit losses dropped 46.7% to $1.35 billion from $2.53 billion in 2001. Total non-interest income grew 8.7% to $5.87 billion, while total non-interest expense declined 5.3% to $6.26 billion.

PROSPECTS:

On 12/31/02, the Company announced that its subsidiary, U.S. Bank, N.A., completed the acquisition of the corporate trust business of State Street Corporation, which includes $689.00 billion in assets under administration, 20,000 new client issuances, and 365,000 bondholders. Separately, the Company's results continue to reflect strong growth in consumer banking and payment services revenue, somewhat offset by lower investment banking activity. Meanwhile, the Company anticipates charges of approximately $70.0 million in 2003 associated with the acquisition of NOVA Corporation, as well as other smaller acquisitions.

ANNUAL FINANCIAL DATA:

FISCAL YEAR	NET INT. INC. ($mill.)	NON-INT. INC. ($mill.)	NET INC. ($mill.)	TOT. LOANS ($mill.)	TOT. ASSETS ($mill.)	TOT. DEP. ($mill.)	RET. ON EQUITY %	RET. ON ASSETS %	EQUITY/ ASSETS %	EARN. PER SH.$	TANG. BK. VAL.$	DIV. PER SH.$	PRICE RANGE	AVG. P/E RATIO
p12/31/02	6,839.7	5,868.6	⑦ 3,326.4		180,027.0					⑦ 1.73		0.78	24.48 - 16.05	11.7
⑥ 12/31/01	6,408.8	5,359.4	② 1,706.5	114,405.0	171,390.0	105,219.0	10.4	1.0	9.6	② 0.88	4.64	0.56	26.06 - 16.50	24.2
12/31/00	3,471.3	3,258.4	② 1,592.0	69,091.0	87,336.0	53,257.0	18.4	1.8	9.9	② 2.13	7.11	0.86	30.50 - 16.88	11.1
12/31/99	3,260.7	2,758.7	② 1,506.5	62,885.0	81,530.0	51,530.0	19.7	1.8	9.4	② 2.06	6.07	0.78	38.06 - 21.88	14.5
12/31/98	3,060.6	2,256.6	② 1,327.4	59,122.0	76,438.0	50,034.0	22.2	1.7	7.8	② 1.78	5.50	0.70	47.31 - 25.63	20.5
① 12/31/97	3,048.1	1,615.2	②③ 838.5	54,708.0	71,295.0	49,027.0	14.2	1.2	8.3	②③ 1.11	5.96	0.62	38.88 - 22.50	27.6
12/31/96	1,533.0	1,185.7	②③ 739.8	27,128.0	36,489.0	24,379.0	24.2	2.0	8.4	②③ 1.78	7.55	0.55	24.67 - 15.33	11.2
12/31/95	1,440.2	783.1	④ 568.1	26,400.0	33,874.0	22,514.0	20.8	1.7	8.0	④ 1.40	6.86	0.483	17.92 - 10.88	10.3
12/31/94	1,419.4	628.0	②⑤ 313.5	24,550.0	34,128.0	24,256.0	12.0	0.9	7.7	②⑤ 0.74	6.21	0.387	13.00 - 9.79	15.5
12/31/93	1,134.0	569.6	299.0	18,779.0	26,385.0	21,031.0	13.3	1.1	8.5	0.80	6.05	0.333	11.38 - 8.63	12.5

Statistics are as originally reported. ① Reflects the acq. of Business and Professional Bank of Sacramento, CA on 4/30/97. ② Incl. pre-tax net merger-rel. chrgs. of $884.2 mill., 2001; $61.3 mill., 2000; $62.4 mill., 1999; $216.5 mill., 1998; $511.6 mill., 1997; $69.9 mill., 1996; $31.0 mill., 1995; $122.7 mill., 1994. ③ Incl. a pre-tax gain fr. the sale of mtge. bank opers. of $9.4 mill., 1997; $45.8 mill., 1996. ④ Incl. a pre-tax gain fr. the sale of branches of $31.0 mill. ⑤ Bef. disc. opers. loss of $8.5 mill. ⑥ Reflects the acq. of Firstar Corp. ⑦ Bef. acctg. chrg. of $37.2 mill; incl. a pre-tax merger & restruct.-rel. chrg. of $460.7 mill.

OFFICERS:
J. A. Grundhofer, Chmn., Pres., C.E.O.
D. M. Moffett, Vice-Chmn., C.F.O.

INVESTOR CONTACT: H.D. McCullough, (612) 303-0786

PRINCIPAL OFFICE: 800 Nicollet Mall, Minneapolis, MN 55402-4302

TELEPHONE NUMBER: (612) 973-1111
FAX: (612) 370-4352
WEB: www.usbank.com

NO. OF EMPLOYEES: 50,461 (avg.)

SHAREHOLDERS: 76,395

ANNUAL MEETING: In April

INCORPORATED: DE, April, 1929

INSTITUTIONAL HOLDINGS:
No. of Institutions: 726
Shares Held: 1,053,052,863
% Held: 55.0

INDUSTRY: National commercial banks (SIC: 6021)

TRANSFER AGENT(S): U.S. Bank National Association, Milwahkee, WI

UAL CORPORATION

EXCH.	SYM.	REC. PRICE	P/E RATIO	YLD.	MKT. CAP.	RANGE (52-WK.)	'02 Y/E PR.
NYSE	UAL	1.08 (2/28/03)	...	...	$59.4 mill.	17.90 - 0.64	1.43

SPECULATIVE GRADE. THE COMPANY IS AGGRESSIVELY IMPLEMENTING COST-CONTROL INITIATIVES.

*7 YEAR PRICE SCORE 13.6   *12 MONTH PRICE SCORE 19.1
*NYSE COMPOSITE INDEX=100

INTERIM EARNINGS (Per Share):

Qtr.	Mar.	June	Sept.	Dec.
1997	0.92	2.31	5.61	0.12
1998	0.34	2.44	3.71	0.27
1999	0.44	5.80	2.89	0.84
2000	0.62	2.86	d2.17	d1.40
2001	d5.82	d5.50	d21.43	d5.68
2002	d9.22	d6.08	d15.57	d20.70

INTERIM DIVIDENDS (Per Share):

Amt.	Decl.	Ex.	Rec.	Pay.
Last dist. $0.05Q, 8/1/01.				

CAPITALIZATION (12/31/01):

	($000)	(%)
Long-Term Debt	6,622,000	56.2
Capital Lease Obligations..	1,943,000	16.5
Redeemable Pfd. Stock	175,000	1.5
Common & Surplus	3,033,000	25.8
Total	11,773,000	100.0

BUSINESS:

UAL Corporation is the parent company of United Airlines, Inc., which is the world's largest airline as measured by revenue passenger miles flown. As of 12/9/02, United offered about 1,700 flights a day through its global network of major connecting airports including Chicago, Denver, San Francisco, Los Angeles, Washington, D.C., Miami, Frankfurt, London, Tokyo, and Toronto. As of 12/31/02, United operated a fleet of 567 aircraft. In October 1994, United began operating the United Shuttle® to compete with low-cost carriers on routes fewer than 750 miles.

RECENT DEVELOPMENTS:

For the year ended 12/31/02, net loss was $3.21 billion versus a loss of $2.13 billion, before an $8.0 million accounting change charge, a year earlier. Results included after-tax gains of $176.0 million and $580.0 million, related to investment sales and the Air Transportation Safety and System Stabilization Act, and net special charges of $159.0 million and $938.0 million in 2002 and 2001, respectively. Total operating revenues slid 11.5% to $14.29 billion from $16.14 billion the year before. Loss from operations was $2.84 billion versus a loss of $3.77 billion in 2001. The passenger load factor, or percentage of seats filled, rose to 73.5% from 70.8% in the prior year.

PROSPECTS:

UAL has obtained $1.50 billion in financing from several banks to help the Company to continue to operate throughout its reorganization process, which is expected to last about 18 months from its Chapter 11 bankruptcy filing on 12/9/02. Meanwhile, cost-control initiatives are being aggressively implemented in an effort to return the Company to financial stability. In January 2003, UAL closed certain reservation call centers and its 32 ticket offices in the U.S. The Company is reducing capacity in 2003 by 6.0% and plans to stop service to New Zealand in March. Separately, UAL expects to report a significant loss for the first quarter of 2003 due to reduced traffic by business travelers and weak international bookings.

ANNUAL FINANCIAL DATA:

FISCAL YEAR	TOT. REVS. ($mill.)	NET INC. ($mill.)	TOT. ASSETS ($mill.)	OPER. PROFIT %	NET PROFIT %	RET. ON EQUITY %	RET. ON ASSETS %	CURR. RATIO	EARN. PER SH. $	CASH FL. PER SH. $	TANG. BK. VAL. $	DIV. PER SH. $	PRICE RANGE	AVG. P/E RATIO	AVG. YIELD %
p12/31/02	14,286.0	⑧d3,205.0							⑧d53.55				17.90 - 0.64	...	...
12/31/01	16,138.0	⑦d2,131.0	25,197.0	...	...	...	...	0.6	⑦d39.90	d4.93	37.27	0.68	45.50 - 9.40	...	2.5
12/31/00	19,352.0	⑥271.0	24,355.0	3.4	1.4	5.2	1.1	0.7	⑥1.89	10.84	86.01	0.94	79.00 - 34.06	29.9	1.7
12/31/99	18,027.0	⑤1,243.0	20,963.0	7.7	6.9	24.1	5.9	0.5	⑤9.97	18.32	90.26	...	87.38 - 58.13	7.3	...
12/31/98	17,561.0	827.0	18,559.0	8.4	4.7	25.2	4.5	0.5	6.83	14.79	50.28	...	97.50 - 55.25	11.2	...
12/31/97	17,378.0	④963.0	15,464.0	7.2	5.5	41.2	6.2	0.6	④9.04	16.66	28.67	...	101.75 - 55.38	8.7	...
12/31/96	16,362.0	③600.0	12,677.0	6.9	3.7	60.3	4.7	0.5	③5.96	15.69	7.87	...	64.75 - 38.56	8.7	...
12/31/95	14,943.0	③378.0	11,641.0	5.5	2.5	...	3.2	0.7	③5.47	16.10	...	...	52.97 - 21.91	6.9	...
12/31/94	13,950.0	②77.0	11,764.0	3.7	0.6	...	0.7	0.7	②0.19	8.75	...	...	37.50 - 20.78	153.3	...
12/31/93	14,511.0	①d31.0	12,840.0	1.8	...	...	...	0.8	①d0.66	6.38	3.12	...	38.88 - 27.69	...	...

Statistics are as originally reported. Adj. for 4-for-1 stk. split, 5/96. ① Bef. $19 mil extraord. loss & incl. $15 mil non-recur. chg. ② Bef. $26 mil chg. for acctg. adj. & incl. $169 mil chg. ③ Bef. $67 mil loss & incl. $31 mil net chg., 1996; & $29 mil extraord. loss & incl. $13 mil chg., 1995. ④ Bef. $9 mil extraord. chg. & incl. $235 mil after-tax gain. ⑤ Bef. $3 mil extraord. loss & incl. $468 mil after-tax gain. ⑥ Bef. $209.0 mil acctg. chg., $6.0 mil extraord. chg. & incl. $200.0 mil pre-tax one-time chgs. and a $109.0 mil one-time pre-tax gain fr. invest. sales. ⑦ Bef. $8 mil acctg. chg., incl $1.48 bil special chg., $652.0 mil gain fr. airline stabilization grant & $261.0 mil gain fr. sale of invest. ⑧ Incl. $149.0 mil special chg., $10.0 mil net restr. chg., $130.0 mil gain fr. airline stabilization grant & $46.0 mil gain fr. sale of invest.

OFFICERS:
G. F. Tilton, Chmn., Pres., C.E.O.
F. F. Brace, Exec. V.P., C.F.O.
F. M. Maher, Sr. V.P., Gen. Couns., Sec.
INVESTOR CONTACT: Patricia Chaplinski, Investor Relations Dir., (847) 700-7501
PRINCIPAL OFFICE: 1200 East Algonquin Road, Elk Grove Township, IL 60007

TELEPHONE NUMBER: (847) 700-4000
FAX: (847) 700-2214
WEB: www.ual.com
NO. OF EMPLOYEES: 78,700 (avg.)
SHAREHOLDERS: 26,047 (record)
ANNUAL MEETING: In May
INCORPORATED: DE, Dec., 1968

INSTITUTIONAL HOLDINGS:
No. of Institutions: 75
Shares Held: 10,006,401
% Held: 15.1
INDUSTRY: Air transportation, scheduled (SIC: 4512)
TRANSFER AGENT(S): Computershare Investor Services, Chicago, IL

UGI CORPORATION

EXCH.	SYM.	REC. PRICE	P/E RATIO	YLD.	MKT. CAP.	RANGE (52-WK.)	'02 Y/E PR.	DIV. ACH.
NYSE	UGI	27.60 (Adj.; 2/28/03)	13.3	4.1%	$1.13 bill.	28.37 - 17.11	24.93	15 yrs.

MEDIUM GRADE. THE COMPANY IS BENEFITING FROM A RETURN TO COLDER WINTER WEATHER PATTERNS.

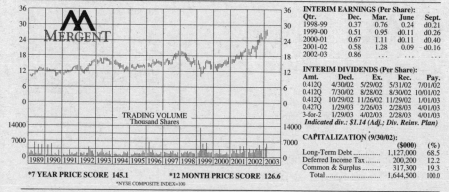

*7 YEAR PRICE SCORE 145.1   ***12 MONTH PRICE SCORE 126.6**
*NYSE COMPOSITE INDEX=100

INTERIM EARNINGS (Per Share):

Qtr.	Dec.	Mar.	June	Sept.
1998-99	0.37	0.76	0.24	d0.21
1999-00	0.51	0.95	d0.11	d0.26
2000-01	0.67	1.11	d0.11	d0.40
2001-02	0.58	1.28	0.09	d0.16
2002-03	0.86	...	...	...

INTERIM DIVIDENDS (Per Share):

Amt.	Decl.	Ex.	Rec.	Pay.
0.412Q	4/30/02	5/29/02	5/31/02	7/01/02
0.412Q	7/30/02	8/28/02	8/30/02	10/01/02
0.412Q	10/29/02	11/26/02	11/29/02	1/01/03
0.427Q	1/29/03	2/26/03	2/28/03	4/01/03
3-for-2	1/29/03	4/02/03	2/28/03	4/01/03

Indicated div.: $1.14 (Adj.; Div. Reinv. Plan)

CAPITALIZATION (9/30/02):

	($000)	(%)
Long-Term Debt	1,127,000	68.5
Deferred Income Tax	200,200	12.2
Common & Surplus	317,300	19.3
Total	1,644,500	100.0

BUSINESS:

UGI Corporation is a holding company that operates propane distribution, gas and electric utility, energy marketing and related businesses through subsidiaries. The Company's majority-owned subsidiary AmeriGas Partners, L.P. conducts a retail propane distribution business. UGI Utilities, Inc. owns and operates a natural gas distribution utility and an electricity distribution utility in eastern Pennsylvania. UGI Enterprises, Inc., conducts domestic and international energy-related businesses through subsidiaries. Enterprises operates UGI Energy Services, which markets natural gas, oil and electricity, and UGI HVAC Enterprises, Inc., a heating and cooling installation and services business in the Mid-Atlantic region. Additionally, Enterprises owns FLAGA GmbH, which is engaged in the distribution of propane in Austria, the Czech Republic, and Slovakia. Enterprises also participates in a propane distribution joint venture in China. Revenues in 2002 were derived: 59.1% propane, 22.2% gas and electric utilities, 15.0% energy services, 2.1% international propane, and 1.6% other enterprises.

RECENT DEVELOPMENTS:

For the quarter ended 12/31/02, net income rose 52.3% to $36.7 million compared with $24.1 million in the same period a year earlier. Total revenues grew 19.5% to $739.9 million. Retail propane sales volumes of 306.6 million gallons were 15.0% higher than the year before, due in part to weather than was essentially normal during the recent quarter versus weather that was about 15.0% warmer than normal in the prior year. Operating earnings climbed 45.5% to $107.4 million, driven by gains from AmeriGas Propane and UGI's gas utility.

PROSPECTS:

UGI's prospects appear positive. The Company's propane and utility operations should continue to benefit from growth and a return to colder winter weather patterns. Meanwhile, UGI is seeking additional growth opportunities at its energy marketing unit. Also, UGI's international operations should be aided by more normal unit margins in fiscal 2003 from Artargaz. UGI owns about 20.0% of Antargaz, a large propane distributor in France.

ANNUAL FINANCIAL DATA:

FISCAL YEAR	TOT. REVS. ($mill.)	NET INC. ($mill.)	TOT. ASSETS ($mill.)	OPER. PROFIT %	NET PROFIT %	RET. ON EQUITY %	RET. ON ASSETS %	CURR. RATIO	EARN. PER SH. $	CASH FL. PER SH. $	TANG. BK. VAL.$	DIV. PER SH. $	PRICE RANGE	AVG. P/E RATIO	AVG. YIELD %
9/30/02	2,213.7	75.5	2,614.4	11.4	3.4	23.8	2.9	0.9	1.80	4.03	...	1.08	26.99 - 17.11	12.3	4.9
9/30/01	2,468.1	⑤ 52.0	2,550.2	9.2	2.1	20.3	2.0	0.8	③ 1.27	3.83	...	1.05	21.02 - 15.00	14.2	5.8
9/30/00	1,761.7	44.7	2,278.8	10.9	2.5	18.1	2.0	0.8	1.09	3.48	...	1.02	16.74 - 12.13	13.6	6.9
9/30/99	1,383.6	② 55.7	2,135.9	12.7	4.0	22.4	2.6	0.7	② 1.16	3.03	...	0.98	16.46 - 10.00	11.4	7.4
9/30/98	1,439.7	40.3	2,074.6	11.8	2.8	11.0	1.9	1.1	0.81	2.58	...	0.97	19.83 - 13.67	20.6	5.8
9/30/97	1,642.0	52.1	2,151.7	12.2	3.2	13.9	2.4	1.0	1.05	2.78	...	0.95	19.92 - 14.42	16.4	5.6
9/30/96	1,557.6	39.5	2,144.9	10.3	2.5	10.5	1.8	1.0	0.79	2.52	...	0.94	16.58 - 13.33	18.9	6.3
9/30/95	877.6	① 7.9	2,164.0	8.9	0.9	2.1	0.4	1.1	① 0.16	1.40	...	0.93	14.75 - 12.58	85.4	6.8
9/30/94	762.2	37.7	1,134.7	15.3	4.9	8.9	3.2	0.8	0.78	1.65	3.69	0.91	16.33 - 11.58	17.9	6.5
9/30/93	509.5	12.8	1,167.9	13.5	2.5	3.1	1.1	1.0	0.28	1.44	3.41	0.88	17.08 - 14.33	56.1	5.6

Statistics are as originally reported. Adj. for 3-for-2 split, 4/03. Incl. results of AP Propane on a consolidated basis for all yrs. shown. ① Incl. non-recurr. chrgs. totaling $24.9 mill. ② Incl. non-recurr. chrg. of $1.6 mill. ③ Incl. non-recurr. chrg. of $8.5 mill.; bef. acctg. chge. credit of $4.5 mill.

OFFICERS:
L. R. Greenberg, Chmn., Pres., C.E.O.
A. J. Mendicino, Sr. V.P., C.F.O.
B. P. Bovaird, V.P., Gen. Couns.

INVESTOR CONTACT: Robert W. Krick, Treas., (610) 337-1000, ext. 3141

PRINCIPAL OFFICE: 460 North Gulph Road, King of Prussia, PA 19406

TELEPHONE NUMBER: (610) 337-1000
FAX: (610) 992-3254
WEB: www.ugicorp.com

NO. OF EMPLOYEES: 6,300 (approx.)

SHAREHOLDERS: 10,054 (record)

ANNUAL MEETING: In Feb.

INCORPORATED: PA, 1991

INSTITUTIONAL HOLDINGS:
No. of Institutions: 160
Shares Held: 22,363,403 (Adj.)
% Held: 53.8

INDUSTRY: Natural gas distribution (SIC: 4924)

TRANSFER AGENT(S): Mellon Investor Services, LLC, Ridgefield Park, NJ

UNION PACIFIC CORP.

EXCH.	SYM.	REC. PRICE	P/E RATIO	YLD.	MKT. CAP.	RANGE (52-WK.)	'02 Y/E PR.
NYSE	UNP	55.19 (2/28/03)	10.9	1.7%	$13.8 mill.	65.15 - 53.00	59.87

UPPER MEDIUM GRADE. THE COMPANY IS PROJECTING YEAR-OVER-YEAR RAIL REVENUE GROWTH IN ALL COMMODITY GROUPS IN 2003.

*7 YEAR PRICE SCORE 114.2   ***12 MONTH PRICE SCORE 105.2**

*NYSE COMPOSITE INDEX=100

INTERIM EARNINGS (Per Share):

Qtr.	Mar.	June	Sept.	Dec.
1998	d0.25	d0.91	0.13	d1.83
1999	0.52	0.77	0.86	0.95
2000	0.74	0.96	1.00	0.63
2001	0.72	0.95	1.04	1.06
2002	0.86	1.15	1.63	1.41

INTERIM DIVIDENDS (Per Share):

Amt.	Decl.	Ex.	Rec.	Pay.
0.20Q	2/25/02	3/11/02	3/13/02	4/01/02
0.20Q	5/30/02	6/10/02	6/12/02	7/01/02
0.20Q	7/25/02	9/09/02	9/11/02	10/01/02
0.23Q	11/21/02	12/09/02	12/11/02	1/02/03
0.23Q	2/27/03	3/10/03	3/12/03	4/01/03

Indicated div.: $0.92 (Div. Reinv. Plan)

CAPITALIZATION (12/31/02):

	($000)	(%)
Long-Term Debt	7,428,000	28.0
Deferred Income Tax	8,478,000	31.9
Common & Surplus	10,651,000	40.1
Total	26,557,000	100.0

BUSINESS:

Union Pacific Corporation is engaged primarily in rail transportation and trucking. Union Pacific Railroad operates over 33,000 route miles linking the Pacific Coast and Gulf Coast ports with the Midwest and eastern U.S. gateways and providing several north/south corridors to Mexican gateways. Major categories of freight are: agricultural products, automotive, chemicals, energy, industrial products and intermodal. The trucking segment includes the operations of Overnite and Motor Cargo. Overnite is an interstate trucking company specializing in less-than-truckload (LTL) shipments. Overnite serves all 50 states and portions of Canada and Mexico through 170 service centers providing regional, inter-regional and long haul service. Motor Cargo is a western regional LTL carrier that provides service throughout 10 western states.

RECENT DEVELOPMENTS:

For the year ended 12/31/02, net income was $1.34 billion compared with $966.0 million a year earlier. Results for 2002 included two pre-tax asset sale transactions totaling $214.0 million, and tax adjustments of $67.0 million for prior years' income tax examinations. Total operating revenues rose 4.3% to $12.49 billion. Revenues for 2002 included $142.2 million from Motor Cargo, which was acquired on 11/30/01. UNP's operating ratio for the year ended 12/31/02, excluding its Overnite's operations, improved to 79.8% versus 81.4% the year before. The operating ratio measures the percentage of operating revenues consumed by operating expenses.

PROSPECTS:

For 2003, UNP is projecting rail revenue growth across all commodity groups with the largest percentage gains seen in the intermodal, agricultural and industrial groups. In addition, UNP will continue to focus on improving service performance while developing new rail service offerings. Meanwhile, UNP's Overnite trucking unit expects to see solid revenue growth, in part due to added business resulting from the forced closure of Consolidated Freightways. Cost controls and productivity improvements should also have a positive effect on Overnite's operating expenses.

ANNUAL FINANCIAL DATA:

FISCAL YEAR	TOT. REVS. ($mill.)	NET INC. ($mill.)	TOT. ASSETS ($mill.)	OPER. PROFIT %	NET PROFIT %	RET. ON EQUITY %	RET. ON ASSETS %	CURR. RATIO	EARN. PER SH.$	CASH FL. PER SH.$	TANG. BK. VAL.$	DIV. PER SH.$	PRICE RANGE	AVG. P/E RATIO	AVG. YIELD %
12/31/02	12,491.0	⑧1,341.0	32,764.0	18.6	10.7	12.6	4.1	0.8	⑧5.05	9.20	41.99	0.80	65.15 - 53.00	11.7	1.4
12/31/01	11,973.0	966.0	31,551.0	17.3	8.1	10.1	3.1	0.6	3.77	7.87	38.26	0.80	60.70 - 43.75	13.9	1.5
12/31/00	11,878.0	⑦842.0	30,499.0	16.0	7.1	9.7	2.8	0.4	⑦3.34	7.36	35.09	0.80	52.81 - 34.25	13.0	1.8
12/31/99	11,273.0	⑧783.0	29,888.0	16.0	6.9	9.8	2.6	0.5	⑧3.12	6.92	32.29	0.80	67.88 - 39.00	17.1	1.5
12/31/98	10,553.0	⑤d633.0	29,374.0	...	...	...	...	0.5	⑤d2.57	1.78	29.93	1.03	63.75 - 37.31	...	2.0
12/31/97	11,079.0	①432.0	28,764.0	11.3	3.9	5.3	1.5	0.4	①1.74	5.95	30.79	1.72	72.98 - 56.25	37.1	2.7
②12/31/96	8,786.0	①③733.0	27,914.0	17.4	8.3	8.9	2.6	0.4	①③3.36	6.86	42.76	1.72	74.50 - 50.00	18.5	2.8
12/31/95	7,486.0	③619.0	19,446.0	17.9	8.3	9.7	3.2	0.9	③3.01	6.12	27.35	1.72	70.13 - 45.63	19.2	3.0
12/31/94	7,798.0	958.0	15,942.0	20.5	12.3	18.7	6.0	0.7	4.66	9.53	20.45	1.63	67.13 - 43.75	11.9	2.9
12/31/93	7,561.0	④705.0	11,458.0	19.7	9.3	14.4	6.2	0.7	④3.43	8.03	23.83	1.51	67.00 - 56.68	18.1	2.4

Statistics are as originally reported. ① Incl. non-recurr. chrg. 12/31/97, $555.0 mill.; chrg. 12/31/96, $2.0 mill. ② Incl. ops. of Southern Pacific Rail Corp., acq. 9/96. ③ Bef. disc. ops. inc. 12/31/96, $171.0 mill.; income 12/31/95, $327.0 mill. ④ Bef. acctg. adj. chrg. of $175.0 mill. ⑤ Incl. pre-tax merger-rel. chrgs. of $69.0 mill. & goodwill impair. of $547.0 mill. ⑥ Bef. disc. ops. gain of $27.0 mill. ⑦ Incl. after-tax workforce reduct. chrg. of $72.0 mill. ($0.27/sh.) ⑧ Incl. asset sales of $214.0 million.

OFFICERS:
R. K. Davidson, Chmn., Pres., C.E.O.
M. S. Jones, V.P., Treas.
C. W. von Bernuth, Sr. V.P., Gen. Couns., Sec.

INVESTOR CONTACT: Jennifer Hamann, Investor Relations, (402) 271-3475

PRINCIPAL OFFICE: 1416 Dodge Street, Omaha, NE 68179

TELEPHONE NUMBER: (402) 271-5777
WEB: www.up.com

NO. OF EMPLOYEES: 61,391 (avg.)

SHAREHOLDERS: 34,184 (approx.)

ANNUAL MEETING: In Apr.

INCORPORATED: UT, Feb., 1969

INSTITUTIONAL HOLDINGS:
No. of Institutions: 575
Shares Held: 222,698,944
% Held: 87.9

INDUSTRY: Railroads, line-haul operating (SIC: 4011)

TRANSFER AGENT(S): Computershare Investor Services, Chicago, IL

UNION PLANTERS CORPORATION

EXCH.	SYM.	REC. PRICE	P/E RATIO	YLD.	MKT. CAP.	RANGE (52-WK.)	'02 Y/E PR.
NYSE	UPC	27.52 (2/28/03)	10.7	4.8%	$5.67 bill.	33.80 - 23.51	28.14

UPPER MEDIUM GRADE. THE COMPANY CONTINUES TO FOCUS ON OPTIMIZING ITS BALANCE SHEET, IMPROVING PRODUCT CAPABILITIES AND INCREASING SALES TRAINING.

TRADING VOLUME Thousand Shares

*7 YEAR PRICE SCORE 108.5   ***12 MONTH PRICE SCORE 101.7**

*NYSE COMPOSITE INDEX=100

INTERIM EARNINGS (Per Share):

Qtr.	Mar.	June	Sept.	Dec.
1998	0.49	0.37	0.07	0.13
1999	0.45	0.49	0.51	0.46
2000	0.49	0.51	0.50	0.51
2001	0.51	0.53	0.54	0.55
2002	0.61	0.62	0.66	0.68

INTERIM DIVIDENDS (Per Share):

Amt.	Decl.	Ex.	Rec.	Pay.
0.50Q	4/18/02	4/29/02	5/01/02	5/15/02
50% STK	4/18/02	6/07/02	5/22/02	6/06/02
0.333Q	7/18/02	7/30/02	8/01/02	8/15/02
0.333Q	10/17/02	10/30/02	11/01/02	11/15/02
0.333Q	1/16/03	1/30/03	2/03/03	2/17/03

Indicated div.: $1.33 (Div. Reinv. Plan)

CAPITALIZATION (12/31/01):

	($000)	(%)
Total Deposits	23,430,502	79.7
Long-Term Debt	2,736,699	9.3
Preferred Stock	16,101	0.1
Common & Surplus	3,207,640	10.9
Total	29,390,942	100.0

BUSINESS:

Union Planters Corporation, with $34.14 billion in assets as of 12/31/02, is a multi-state bank holding company headquartered in Tennessee. UPC's principal banking markets are Alabama, Arkansas, Florida, Kentucky, Illinois, Indiana, Iowa, Louisiana, Mississippi, Missouri, Tennessee, and Texas. As of 12/31/02, the Company's existing market areas were served by its 762 banking offices and 965 ATMs. The mortgage operations of UPC's subsidiary, Union Planter Bank, N.A., operate offices in Alabama, Arizona, California, Colorado, Florida, Georgia, Louisiana, Mississippi, Nevada, North Carolina, Ohio, Tennessee, Texas, and Washington, in addition to mortgage production offices located in its branch banking locations. On 7/1/98, the Company acquired People's First Corporation for $1.43 billion.

RECENT DEVELOPMENTS:

For the year ended 12/31/02, net earnings advanced 19.3% to $529.0 million compared with $443.6 million the year before. Earnings for 2002 and 2001 included goodwill amortization of $5.5 million and $48.4 million, and investment securities gains of $23.0 million and $9.6 million, respectively. Net interest income grew 1.1% to $1.29 billion from $1.28 billion in the prior year. Provision for losses on loans increased 50.0% to $197.9 million compared with $132.0 million the year before. Total non-interest income rose 2.2% to $786.5 million from $769.7 million the year before. Non-interest expense declined 10.3% to $1.11 billion versus $1.24 billion in 2000.

PROSPECTS:

The Company continues to rationalize its branch network and consolidate its bank-office functions, which resulted in an efficiency ratio of 50.0% in 2002. Additionally, the Company continues to focus on optimizing its balance sheet, improving product capabilities and increasing sales training. During the quarter, nonperforming assets declined 10.0%. Meanwhile, noninterest income continues to grow, reflecting strong growth in mortgage banking revenue and solid growth in service charges on deposit accounts, bank card fees, professional employment organization net revenues, factoring commissions and fees, and investment services and insurance income.

ANNUAL FINANCIAL DATA:

FISCAL YEAR	NET INT. INC. ($mill.)	NON-INT. INC. ($mill.)	NET INC. ($mill.)	TOT. LOANS ($mill.)	TOT. ASSETS ($mill.)	TOT. DEP. ($mill.)	RET. ON EQUITY %	RET. ON ASSETS %	EQUITY/ ASSETS %	EARN. PER SH.$	TANG. BK. VAL.$	DIV. PER SH.$	PRICE RANGE	AVG. P/E RATIO
p12/31/02	1,289.4	786.5	529.0		34,144.4					2.59		1.33	33.80 - 23.51	11.0
12/31/01	1,276.0	769.7	443.6	23,184.0	33,197.6	23,430.5	13.8	1.3	9.7	2.13	10.33	1.33	31.29 - 22.50	12.6
12/31/00	1,231.1	559.4	409.3	23,982.2	34,720.7	23,113.4	14.0	1.2	8.4	2.00	9.03	1.33	26.13 - 16.83	10.7
12/31/99	1,256.5	512.7	410.0	21,474.5	33,280.4	23,372.1	14.8	1.2	8.3	1.90	7.98	1.33	33.08 - 25.50	15.4
② 12/31/98	1,207.2	568.8	225.6	19,611.2	31,692.0	24,896.5	7.6	0.7	9.4	1.05	11.61	1.33	45.29 - 26.75	34.2
12/31/97	770.4	361.6	208.8	12,687.1	18,105.1	13,440.3	12.0	1.2	9.6	1.63	12.89	1.00	44.75 - 25.50	21.5
12/31/96	606.0	226.3	133.7	10,464.2	15,222.6	11,490.3	9.9	0.9	8.9	1.30	11.86	0.72	27.67 - 18.75	17.9
12/31/95	447.4	157.7	135.4	7,100.1	11,277.1	9,447.7	14.0	1.2	8.6	1.88	11.97	0.65	21.67 - 13.67	9.4
12/31/94	388.3	93.6	58.6	5,980.6	10,015.1	8,417.8	8.0	0.6	7.3	0.83	9.84	0.59	19.25 - 13.00	19.3
12/31/93	234.6	84.8	① 61.3	2,951.9	6,318.2	5,251.4	12.8	1.0	7.6	① 1.79	11.26	0.48	20.00 - 14.92	9.7

Statistics are as originally reported. Adj. for 3-for-2 stk. split, 6/02. ① Bef. extraord. chrg. of $3.2 mill. & acctg. cr. of $5.0 mill. ② Reflects the acq. of People's First Corporation on 7/1/98.

OFFICERS:
J. W. Moore, Chmn., Pres., C.E.O.
B. L. Doxey, Sr. Exec. V.P., C.F.O.

INVESTOR CONTACT: Charles R. Boyce, Investor Relations, (901) 580-5974

PRINCIPAL OFFICE: 6200 Poplar Ave., Memphis, TN 38119

TELEPHONE NUMBER: (901) 580-6000
FAX: (901) 383-2396
WEB: www.unionplanters.com
NO. OF EMPLOYEES: 9,852 full-time; 1,945 part-time
SHAREHOLDERS: 32,300 (approx.)
ANNUAL MEETING: In April
INCORPORATED: TN, Nov., 1971

INSTITUTIONAL HOLDINGS:
No. of Institutions: 302
Shares Held: 72,022,934
% Held: 36.4
INDUSTRY: National commercial banks (SIC: 6021)
TRANSFER AGENT(S): American Stock Transfer & Trust Company, New York, NY

UNIONBANCAL CORPORATION

EXCH.	SYM.	REC. PRICE	P/E RATIO	YLD.	MKT. CAP.	RANGE (52-WK.)	'02 Y/E PR.
NYSE	UB	41.62 (2/28/03)	12.4	2.7%	$6.51 bill.	49.83 - 34.72	39.27

MEDIUM GRADE. THE COMPANY CONTINUES TO PERFORM WELL, SUPPORTED BY THE STRENGTH OF ITS COMMERCIAL AND RETAIL DEPOSIT BUSINESSES, AS WELL AS AN IMPROVED LOAN PORTFOLIO MIX.

TRADING VOLUME
Thousand Shares

*7 YEAR PRICE SCORE 146.7   *12 MONTH PRICE SCORE 102.7
*NYSE COMPOSITE INDEX=100

INTERIM EARNINGS (Per Share):

Qtr.	Mar.	June	Sept.	Dec.
1998	0.54	0.62	0.84	0.65
1999	0.69	0.69	0.43	0.83
2000	0.96	0.87	0.82	0.05
2001	0.67	0.74	0.79	0.84
2002	0.73	0.81	0.88	0.95

INTERIM DIVIDENDS (Per Share):

Amt.	Decl.	Ex.	Rec.	Pay.
0.25Q	1/23/02	3/06/02	3/08/02	4/05/02
0.28Q	4/24/02	6/05/02	6/07/02	7/05/02
0.28Q	7/24/02	9/04/02	9/06/02	10/04/02
0.28Q	10/23/02	12/04/02	12/06/02	1/03/03
0.28Q	1/29/03	3/05/03	3/07/03	4/04/03

Indicated div.: $1.12 (Div. Reinv. Plan)

CAPITALIZATION (12/31/01):

	($000)	(%)
Total Deposits	28,556,199	87.9
Long-Term Debt	400,000	1.2
Common & Surplus	3,546,242	10.9
Total	32,502,441	100.0

BUSINESS:

UnionBanCal Corporation is a commercial bank holding company based in San Francisco with consolidated assets of $40.17 billion as of 12/31/02. The Company's principal subsidiary, Union Bank of California, N.A., is the third largest commercial bank in California, based on total assets and total deposits. Union Bank of California, N.A., has 259 banking offices in California, 6 banking offices in Oregon and Washington, and 18 international facilities.

The Company provides a wide range of financial services to consumers, small businesses, middle-market companies and major corporations, primarily in California, Oregon, and Washington, but also nationally and internationally. As of 7/29/02, the Company was approximately 67.0%-owned by The Bank of Tokyo-Mitsubishi, Ltd. The Company was formed as a result of the combination of Union Bank with BanCal Tri-State Corporation on 4/1/96.

RECENT DEVELOPMENTS:

For the year ended 12/31/02, net income increased 9.7% to $527.9 million from $481.4 million the year before. Net interest income grew 2.5% to $1.56 billion from $1.53 billion in the previous year due to higher volumes of earning assets and demand deposits. Provision for credit losses decreased 38.6% to $175.0 million. Total interest income declined 15.4% to $1.86 billion. Total interest expense dropped 56.2% to $294.0 million, while total non-interest income improved 2.7% to $736.0 million. Total non-interest expense grew 8.7% to $1.35 billion.

PROSPECTS:

The Company continues to perform well, supported by the strength of its commercial and retail deposit businesses, as well as an improved loan portfolio mix, which resulted in higher asset quality. Separately, in December 2002, Union Bank of California, N.A., a subsidiary of the Company, completed the acquisition of San Diego-based John Burnham & Company, dba John Burnham Insurance Services, a privately-held commercial insurance brokerage with annual premiums in excess of $200.0 million. This transaction is part of the Company's strategy to provide its customers with a major insurance agency presence, particularly in the Southern California marketplace.

ANNUAL FINANCIAL DATA:

FISCAL YEAR	NET INT. INC. ($mill.)	NON-INT. INC. ($mill.)	NET INC. ($mill.)	TOT. LOANS ($mill.)	TOT. ASSETS ($mill.)	TOT. DEP. ($mill.)	RET. ON EQUITY %	RET. ON ASSETS %	EQUITY/ ASSETS %	EARN. PER SH. $	TANG. BK. VAL. $	DIV. PER SH. $	PRICE RANGE	AVG. P/E RATIO
p12/31/02	1,564.6	736.0	527.9		40,169.8					3.38	22.66	1.09	49.83 - 34.70	12.5
12/31/01	1,524.0	716.4	481.4	24,994.0	36,039.1	28,556.2	13.6	1.3	9.8	3.04	20.17	1.00	39.28 - 23.94	10.4
12/31/00	1,584.4	647.2	②439.9	26,010.4	35,162.5	27,283.2	13.7	1.3	9.1	②2.72	18.18	1.00	39.69 - 17.94	10.6
12/31/99	1,415.8	586.8	②441.7	25,913.0	33,684.8	26,256.6	14.8	1.3	8.9	②2.64	17.45	0.76	46.44 - 30.13	14.5
12/31/98	1,318.2	533.5	①466.5	24,296.1	32,276.3	24,507.9	15.3	1.4	9.5	①2.65	16.40	0.56	38.33 - 23.62	11.7
12/31/97	1,231.7	463.0	411.3	22,581.3	30,585.3	23,296.4	15.2	1.3	8.8	2.30	16.40	0.49	35.50 - 16.91	11.4
12/31/96	1,168.6	418.7	249.5	20,898.1	29,234.1	21,533.0	10.0	0.9	8.6	1.37	11.84	0.23	19.16 - 15.42	12.6
12/31/95	832.4	247.5	207.3	14,392.4	19,518.1	14,867.1	13.5	1.1	7.9	1.79	10.22	1.40	19.25 - 8.92	7.9
12/31/94	713.3	225.1	60.3	12,360.9	16,761.1	12,834.7	4.9	0.4	7.4	0.60	10.16	1.40	10.50 - 8.08	15.5
12/31/93	708.5	262.9	83.1	11,957.0	16,390.9	12,554.4	6.9	0.5	7.4	0.70		1.40	13.17 - 7.92	15.0

Statistics are as originally reported. Adj. for stk. split: 3-for-1, 12/21/98. ① Incl. after-tax cr. $44.8 mill. fr. red. in CA tax liab. ② Incl. restruct. credit, 2000, $19.0 mill.; chrg., 1999, $85.0 mill.

OFFICERS: K. Hayama, Chmn. N. Kanari, Pres., C.E.O. D. Matson, V.P., C.F.O.	**TELEPHONE NUMBER:** (415) 765-2969 **FAX:** (415) 765-2950 **WEB:** www.unionbancal.com	**INSTITUTIONAL HOLDINGS:** No. of Institutions: 147 Shares Held: 138,229,348 % Held: 92.0
INVESTOR CONTACT: John A. Rice, Jr., Sr. V.P. & Mgr., Inv. Rel., (415) 765-2998	**NO. OF EMPLOYEES:** 9,232 **SHAREHOLDERS:** 1,755 (approx.)	**INDUSTRY:** National commercial banks (SIC: 6021)
PRINCIPAL OFFICE: 400 California Street, San Francisco, CA 94104-1302	**ANNUAL MEETING:** In April **INCORPORATED:** CA, Feb., 1953	**TRANSFER AGENT(S):** ComputerShare Investor Services, LLC, Chicago, IL

UNISOURCE ENERGY CORPORATION

EXCH.	SYM.	REC. PRICE	P/E RATIO	YLD.	MKT. CAP.	RANGE (52-WK.)	'02 Y/E PR.
NYSE	UNS	16.77 (2/28/03)	17.3	3.6%	$0.56 bill.	20.75 - 13.70	17.29

LOWER MEDIUM GRADE. THE COMPANY IS TARGETING EARNINGS FOR 2003 IN THE RANGE OF $1.30 TO $1.50 PER SHARE.

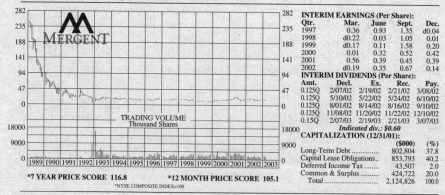

INTERIM EARNINGS (Per Share):

Qtr.	Mar.	June	Sept.	Dec.
1997	0.36	0.93	1.35	d0.04
1998	d0.22	0.03	1.05	0.01
1999	d0.17	0.11	1.58	0.20
2000	0.01	0.32	0.52	0.42
2001	0.56	0.39	0.45	0.39
2002	d0.19	0.35	0.67	0.14

INTERIM DIVIDENDS (Per Share):

Amt.	Decl.	Ex.	Rec.	Pay.
0.125Q	2/07/02	2/19/02	2/21/02	3/08/02
0.125Q	5/10/02	5/22/02	5/24/02	6/10/02
0.125Q	8/01/02	8/14/02	8/16/02	9/10/02
0.125Q	11/08/02	11/20/02	11/22/02	12/10/02
0.15Q	2/07/03	2/19/03	2/21/03	3/07/03

Indicated div.: $0.60

CAPITALIZATION (12/31/01):

	($000)	(%)
Long-Term Debt	802,804	37.8
Capital Lease Obligations..	853,793	40.2
Deferred Income Tax	43,507	2.0
Common & Surplus	424,722	20.0
Total	2,124,826	100.0

TRADING VOLUME Thousand Shares

*7 YEAR PRICE SCORE 116.8   ***12 MONTH PRICE SCORE 105.1**

*NYSE COMPOSITE INDEX=100

BUSINESS:

UniSource Energy Corporation is a holding company that conducts business through its wholly-owned subsidiaries Tucson Electric Power Company (TEP), Millennium Energy Holdings, Inc. (MEH) and UniSource Energy Development Company (UED). TEP is a regulated utility that provides electricity to over 355,000 retail customers as of 12/31/02 and to wholesale customers. TEP's retail ser-

vice territory consists of a 1,155 square mile area of Southeastern Arizona. As of 12/31/02, MEH, an unregulated energy business, owned 100.0% of Southwest Energy Solutions, Inc., 77.5% of Infinite Power Solutions, Inc., 87.0% of Global Solar Energy, Inc., and 49.0% of MicroSat Systems, Inc. UED engages in developing generating resources and other product development activities.

RECENT DEVELOPMENTS:

For the year ended 12/31/02, net income was $33.3 million versus income of $60.9 million, before an accounting gain of $470,000, the previous year. Earnings were adversely affected by reduced wholesale power prices, mild weather and lower demand from TEP's mining customers. The resulting decline in kilowatt-hour sales, as well as the

expense of a coal contract buyout and higher operating costs at some of UNS' unregulated subsidiaries also hampered earnings. Total operating revenues fell 39.6% to $856.2 million. Wholesale electric sales slid 75.7% to $177.9 million. Retail electric sales declined 0.6% to $666.0 million.

PROSPECTS:

Going forward, retail sales and revenues for Tucson Electric Power Company (TEP), UNS' primary subsidiary, may continue to be affected by its mining customers. The nationwide economic slowdown has caused many of TEP's mining customers to curtail their production and energy usage. However, TEP's core retail customer base should continue to grow. In addition, TEP's wholesale revenues

are expected to be hampered by lower wholesale power prices and softening demand. Moreover, results for Millenium Energy Holdings, parent of UNS' unregulated energy businesses, are expected to be negatively affected by higher operating costs as well as increased research and development expenses. For 2003, UNS is targeting earnings in the range of $1.30 to $1.50 per share.

ANNUAL FINANCIAL DATA:

FISCAL YEAR	TOT. REVS. ($mill.)	NET INC. ($mill.)	TOT. ASSETS ($mill.)	OPER. PROFIT %	NET PROFIT %	NET INC./ NET PROP. %	NET INC./ TOT. CAP. %	RET. ON EQUITY %	ACCUM. DEPR./ GROSS PROP. %	EARN. PER SH. $	TANG. BK. VAL. $	DIV. PER SH. $	DIV. PAYOUT %	PRICE RANGE		AVG. P/E RATIO	AVG. YIELD %
12/31/02	856.2	33.3								0.97		0.50	51.5	20.75	- 13.70	17.8	2.9
12/31/01	1,444.7	⑤ 60.9	2,735.3	17.2	4.2	3.6	2.9	14.3	49.3	⑤ 1.79	12.68	0.40	22.3	25.99	- 13.80	11.1	2.0
12/31/00	1,033.7	41.9	2,671.4	19.1	4.1	2.5	1.7	11.3	47.1	1.27	11.20	0.32	25.2	19.31	- 10.81	11.9	2.1
12/31/99	803.8	④ 56.5	2,656.3	19.6	7.0	3.3	2.4	17.4	44.9	④ 1.74	10.02	...	...	13.94	- 10.38	7.0	...
12/31/98	768.7	28.0	2,634.2	17.6	3.6	1.5	1.2	11.4	35.3	0.87	7.65	...	...	18.94	- 12.25	17.9	...
12/31/97	729.9	83.6	2,634.4	18.4	11.4	4.3	3.5	38.5	33.4	2.59	6.75	...	...	18.25	- 13.88	6.2	...
12/31/96	715.9	③ 120.9	2,568.5	16.4	16.9	6.2	5.1	90.7	31.6	③ 3.76	4.15	...	...	20.75	- 12.25	4.4	...
12/31/95	670.6	② 54.9	2,587.1	18.2	8.2	2.8	2.4	439.7	29.6	② 1.71	0.39	...	...	18.75	- 13.13	9.3	...
12/31/94	691.5	20.7	2,701.9	16.5	3.0	1.0	0.9	...	27.4	0.65	...	...	...	20.63	- 14.38	26.9	...
12/31/93	662.4	① d21.8	2,714.1	12.7	...	...	...	...	25.2	① d0.70	...	...	...	23.13	- 9.38	...	...

Statistics are as originally reported. Adj. for stk. split: 5/96 ① Bef. disc. opers. loss $4.0 mill. ② Incl. non-recurr. chrg. $12.2 mill. reduction in fuel exp. & $15.7 mill inc. tax benefit ③ Inc. one-time charge $13.6 mill. for workforce reduction ④ Bef. extraord. gain $22.6 mill.; but incl. pre-tax gain of $34.7 mill. on sale of NewEnergy. ⑤ Bef. acctg. chrg. $470,000; incl. net loss on fwrd. sales & purchases $1.3 mill.

OFFICERS:
J. S. Pignatelli, Chmn., Pres., C.E.O.
K. Larson, V.P., C.F.O.
D. R. Nelson, V.P., Gen. Couns., Sec.
INVESTOR CONTACT: Jo Smith, Investor Relations., (520) 884-3650
PRINCIPAL OFFICE: 220 West Sixth Street, Tucson, AZ 85701

TELEPHONE NUMBER: (520) 571-4000
FAX: (520) 884-3934
WEB: www.unisourceenergy.com
NO. OF EMPLOYEES: 1,157 (avg.)
SHAREHOLDERS: 20,297
ANNUAL MEETING: In May
INCORPORATED: AZ, March, 1995

INSTITUTIONAL HOLDINGS:
No. of Institutions: 120
Shares Held: 23,004,418
% Held: 68.5

INDUSTRY: Electric services (SIC: 4911)

TRANSFER AGENT(S): The Bank of New York, New York, NY

UNISYS CORPORATION

EXCH.	SYM.	REC. PRICE	P/E RATIO	YLD.	MKT. CAP.	RANGE (52-WK.)	'02 Y/E PR.
NYSE	UIS	9.26 (2/28/03)	13.6	...	$3.02 bill.	13.84 - 5.92	9.90

LOWER MEDIUM GRADE. THE COMPANY EXPECTS EARNINGS FOR 2003 TO RANGE FROM $0.77 TO $0.82 PER SHARE.

TRADING VOLUME
Thousand Shares

1989 | 1990 | 1991 | 1992 | 1993 | 1994 | 1995 | 1996 | 1997 | 1998 | 1999 | 2000 | 2001 | 2002 | 2003

*7 YEAR PRICE SCORE 62.2   ***12 MONTH PRICE SCORE 105.6**   •
*NYSE COMPOSITE INDEX=100

INTERIM EARNINGS (Per Share):

Qtr.	Mar.	June	Sept.	Dec.
1996	d0.25	d0.14	d0.09	0.15
1997	d0.06	0.08	0.14	d4.75
1998	0.14	0.24	0.26	0.42
1999	0.32	0.38	0.47	0.46
2000	0.34	0.18	0.14	0.12
2001	0.22	0.09	0.07	d0.53
2002	0.10	0.13	0.18	0.27

INTERIM DIVIDENDS (Per Share):

Amt.	Decl.	Ex.	Rec.	Pay.
		No dividends paid.		

CAPITALIZATION (12/31/01):

	($000)	(%)
Long-Term Debt	745,000	26.1
Common & Surplus	2,112,700	73.9
Total	2,857,700	100.0

BUSINESS:

Unisys Corporation is an information management company that provides information services, technology, software and customer support on a worldwide basis. The Company operates in two business segments: Services and Technology. The Services segment consists of systems integration, including industry and custom applications, outsourcing, network services and multivendor maintenance. The Technology segment provides enterprise-class servers, specialized technologies and personal computers. Unisys services banks, airlines, newspapers, telecommunications, and government agencies. Revenues in 2002 were derived: Services, 76.4%; and Technology, 23.6%.

RECENT DEVELOPMENTS:

For the year ended 12/31/02, net income soared to $223.0 million compared with a loss of $49.9 million, before an extraordinary charge of $17.2 million, in 2001. Net income benefited from the Company's cost-reduction initiatives. Revenue slipped 6.8% to $5.61 billion versus $6.02 billion in the prior year, primarily due to continued weakness in Latin America and Europe, which more than offset gains in the U.S. market. Gross profit as a percentage of net sales amounted to 30.1% compared with 27.4% a year earlier. Operating income jumped to $423.2 million versus an operating loss of $4.5 million in the previous year, reflecting UIS' focus on value-added business opportunities and continued tight cost controls.   •

PROSPECTS:

Despite challenging business conditions, the Company expects to report earnings growth in 2003, with earnings ranging $0.77 to $0.82 per share. These estimates reflect recent momentum gained through new global contracts, an expanding client base and improved margins and profits. Additionally, the Company looks for revenue growth to build through the course of 2003, leading to mid single-digit revenue growth for the full year. Moreover, UIS expects revenue for the first quarter of 2003 to be equal to the comparable period of 2001 and earnings to range from $0.11 to $0.13 per share.

ANNUAL FINANCIAL DATA:

FISCAL YEAR	TOT. REVS. ($mill.)	NET INC. ($mill.)	TOT. ASSETS ($mill.)	OPER. PROFIT %	NET PROFIT %	RET. ON EQUITY %	RET. ON ASSETS %	CURR. RATIO	EARN. PER SH. $	CASH FL. PER SH. $	TANG. BK. VAL. $	PRICE RANGE	AVG. P/E RATIO
p12/31/02	5,607.4	223.0							0.69			13.84 - 5.92	14.3
12/31/01	6,018.1	⑦ d49.9	5,769.1	...	...	...	...	0.9	⑦ d0.16	0.79	5.20	19.70 - 7.70	...
12/31/00	6,885.0	⑥ 244.8	5,717.7	6.2	3.6	11.2	4.3	1.0	⑥ 0.77	1.63	5.99	36.06 - 9.13	29.3
12/31/99	7,544.6	⑤ 522.8	5,889.7	12.7	6.9	26.8	8.9	1.1	⑤ 1.63	2.51	5.42	49.69 - 20.94	21.7
12/31/98	7,208.4	387.0	5,577.7	11.2	5.4	25.5	6.9	1.1	1.06	2.05	...	35.38 - 13.31	23.0
12/31/97	6,636.0	⑤ d853.6	5,591.3	...	...	...	...	1.1	⑤ d5.30	1.39	...	16.50 - 5.75	...
12/31/96	6,370.5	④ 61.8	6,967.1	5.1	1.0	3.8	0.9	1.3	④ d0.34	1.56	...	9.13 - 5.38	...
12/31/95	6,202.3	①② d627.3	7,113.2	...	...	...	...	1.0	①② d4.37	d2.05	...	11.75 - 5.50	...
12/31/94	7,399.7	④ 108.2	7,323.9	4.1	1.5	4.2	1.5	1.3	④ d0.07	2.54	...	16.50 - 8.25	...
12/31/93	7,742.5	③ 361.6	7,519.2	9.5	4.7	13.4	4.8	1.4	③ 1.46	4.08	...	13.88 - 9.88	8.1

Statistics are as originally reported. ① Bef. $2.7 mill. ($0.02/sh.) inc. fr. disc. ops. ② Incl. $581.9 mill. ($3.39/sh.) after-tax restr. chg. & $88.6 mill. ($0.51/sh.) after-tax chg. cov. loss prov. ③ Excl. net benefit fr. acct. chg. & $203.8 mill. ($1.23/sh.) extraord. items. ④ Excl. $12.1 mill. ($0.07/sh.) extra. loss, 1996; $7.7 mill. ($0.04/sh.), 1994. ⑤ Bef. extra. loss of $19.8 mill. ⑥ Excl. $12.1 mill. extraord. chg., 1999; $19.8 mill., 2000. ⑦ Incl. pre-tax chg. of $276.3 mill. & excl. $17.2 mill. extraord. credit.

OFFICERS:
L. A. Weinbach, Chmn., Pres., C.E.O.
J. M. Haugen, Sr. V.P., C.F.O.
N. Sundheim, Sr. V.P., Gen. Couns., Sec.

INVESTOR CONTACT: Jim Kerr, Investor Relations, (215) 986-5795

PRINCIPAL OFFICE: Unisys Way, Blue Bell, PA 19424

TELEPHONE NUMBER: (215) 986-4011
FAX: (215) 986-6850
WEB: www.unisys.com
NO. OF EMPLOYEES: 38,900 (approx.)
SHAREHOLDERS: 28,400 (approx.)
ANNUAL MEETING: In Apr.
INCORPORATED: MI, Jan., 1905; reincorp., DE, Feb., 1984

INSTITUTIONAL HOLDINGS:
No. of Institutions: 272
Shares Held: 206,103,032
% Held: 63.1

INDUSTRY: Electronic computers (SIC: 3571)

TRANSFER AGENT(S): EquiServe Trust Company, N.A., Jersey City, NJ

UNITED AUTO GROUP, INC.

EXCH.	SYM.	REC. PRICE	P/E RATIO	YLD.	MKT. CAP.	RANGE (52-WK.)	'02 Y/E PR.
NYSE	UAG	11.13 (2/28/03)	7.5	...	$219.5 mill.	32.00 - 10.56	12.47

MEDIUM GRADE. THE COMPANY IS TARGETING EARNINGS PER SHARE OF BETWEEN $1.96 AND $2.06 IN 2003.

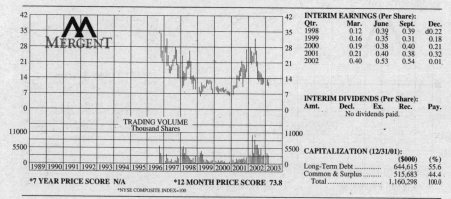

INTERIM EARNINGS (Per Share):

Qtr.	Mar.	June	Sept.	Dec.
1998	0.12	0.39	0.39	d0.22
1999	0.16	0.35	0.31	0.18
2000	0.19	0.38	0.40	0.21
2001	0.21	0.40	0.38	0.32
2002	0.40	0.53	0.54	0.01

INTERIM DIVIDENDS (Per Share):

Amt.	Decl.	Ex.	Rec.	Pay.
		No dividends paid.		

CAPITALIZATION (12/31/01):

	($000)	(%)
Long-Term Debt	644,615	55.6
Common & Surplus	515,683	44.4
Total	1,160,298	100.0

TRADING VOLUME
Thousand Shares

1989 1990 1991 1992 1993 1994 1995 1996 1997 1998 1999 2000 2001 2002 2003

*7 YEAR PRICE SCORE N/A   ***12 MONTH PRICE SCORE 73.8**
*NYSE COMPOSITE INDEX=100

BUSINESS:

United Auto Group, Inc. operated, as of 2/19/03, 129 franchised automobile and light truck dealerships located in the United States and 71 internationally, primarily in the United Kingdom. The Company's dealerships sell new and used vehicles, operate service and parts departments, as well as collision repair centers. In addition, UAG sells various aftermarket products, including finance, warranty,

extended service and insurance contracts. As of 3/26/02, the Penske investment group, which includes Penske Corp., held approximately 72.0% of UAG's common stock. In 2002, revenues were derived as follows: new vehicle sales, 59.4%; used vehicle sales, 20.0%; service and parts, 10.4%; wholesale vehicle sales, 6.3%; finance and insurance, 2.4%; and fleet sales, 1.5%.

RECENT DEVELOPMENTS:

For the twelve months ended 12/31/02, income from continuing operations totaled $61.2 million, up 39.3% compared with income from continuing operations of $44.0 million in the prior year. Total revenues climbed 26.7% to $7.43 billion from $5.87 billion a year earlier. New vehicle sales increased 23.4% to $4.42 billion from $3.58 billion the year before, while used vehicle sales jumped 38.5% to

$1.49 billion from $1.08 billion in 2001. Service and parts revenue advanced 32.1% to $772.8 million, while finance and insurance revenue rose 24.7% to $177.9 million. Gross profit was $1.06 billion, or 14.3% of total revenues, versus $815.4 million, or 13.9% of total revenues, the previous year. Operating income was up 16.7% to $180.0 million from $154.3 million in the prior year.

PROSPECTS:

Results are benefiting from strong growth of UAG's service and parts and finance and insurance businesses. Meanwhile, UAG is targeting full-year 2003 earnings in the range of $1.96 to $2.06 per share, with first-quarter earnings in the range of $0.35 to $0.40 per share. Separately, on

2/19/03, UAG announced that it has signed a definitive agreement to acquire Rhode Island-based INSKIP Autocenter, which has estimated annual revenues of about $300.0 million. Terms of the transaction, which is expected to close in the second quarter of 2003, were not disclosed.

ANNUAL FINANCIAL DATA:

FISCAL YEAR	TOT. REVS. ($mill.)	NET INC. ($mill.)	TOT. ASSETS ($mill.)	OPER. PROFIT %	NET PROFIT %	RET. ON EQUITY %	RET. ON ASSETS %	CURR. RATIO	EARN. PER SH. $	CASH FL. PER SH. $	TANG. BK. VAL. $	PRICE RANGE	AVG. P/E RATIO
p12/31/02	7,434.9	④ 61.2							④ 1.49			32.00 - 11.12	14.5
12/31/01	6,220.7	44.7	1,946.6	2.5	0.7	8.7	2.3	1.2	1.31	2.29	...	27.00 - 6.50	12.8
12/31/00	4,884.0	① 34.0	1,762.7	2.8	0.7	7.4	1.9	1.1	① 1.16	1.98	...	10.50 - 6.00	7.1
12/31/99	4,022.5	② 26.7	1,279.3	2.6	0.7	6.2	2.1	1.2	② 1.01	1.73	...	13.25 - 5.75	9.4
12/31/98	3,343.1	③ 13.4	1,184.2	1.6	0.4	3.9	1.1	1.2	③ 0.64	1.43	...	26.31 - 8.88	27.5
12/31/97	2,089.8	d10.1	975.7	0.1	...	...	...	1.3	d0.54	d0.02	...	31.75 - 13.75	...
12/31/96	1,303.8	① 7.5	523.0	1.6	0.6	2.7	1.4	1.4	① 0.69	1.41	...	35.25 - 21.38	41.0
12/31/95	806.2	d3.5	236.0	...	...	...	...	1.0	d0.63	d0.12	0.18	...	...
12/31/94	731.6	d1.7	170.3	0.5	...	...	...	0.9	d0.44	0.14	3.77	...	...
12/31/93	606.1	0.1	...	0.2	...	...	...	...	0.05	0.05	...	...	...

Statistics are as originally reported. ① Bef. $4.0 mil ($0.14/sh) extraord. chg., 2000; $5.0 mil (0.46/sh), 1996. ② Bef. $46,000 loss fr disc. ops & $732,000 extraord. gain ③ Bef. $12.9 mil loss fr disc. opers. & $1.2 mil extraord. chg. ④ Bef. $1.0 mil ($0.02/sh) gain fr. disc. opers. & incl. $13.6 mil ($0.33/sh) after-tax non-recurr. chg.

OFFICERS:
R. S. Penske, Chmn., C.E.O.
S. X. DiFeo, Pres., C.O.O.
R. H. Kurnick, Jr., Exec. V.P., Sec., Gen. Couns.
INVESTOR CONTACT: Tony Pordon, V.P., Investor Relations, (248) 648-2540
PRINCIPAL OFFICE: 2555 Telegraph Road, Bloomfield Hills, MI 48302-0954

TELEPHONE NUMBER: (248) 648-2500 .
FAX: (248) 648-2525
WEB: www.unitedauto.com
NO. OF EMPLOYEES: 8,500 (approx.)
SHAREHOLDERS: 251 (record)
ANNUAL MEETING: In May
INCORPORATED: DE, Dec., 1990

UNITED DOMINION REALTY TRUST, INC.

EXCH.	SYM.	REC. PRICE	P/E RATIO	YLD.	MKT. CAP.	RANGE (52-WK.)	'02 Y/E PR.	DIV. ACH.
NYSE	UDR	15.57 (2/28/03)	67.7	7.3%	$1.61 bill.	16.81 - 13.18	16.36	17 yrs.

MEDIUM GRADE. THE COMPANY DOES NOT SEE POSITIVE TRENDS IN SOME OF THE KEY DRIVERS OF ITS BUSINESS FOR 2003.

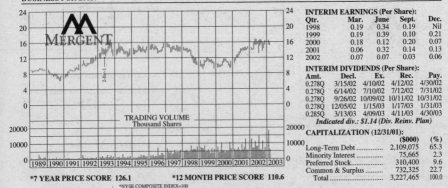

INTERIM EARNINGS (Per Share):

Qtr.	Mar.	June	Sept.	Dec.
1998	0.19	0.34	0.19	Nil
1999	0.19	0.39	0.10	0.21
2000	0.18	0.12	0.20	0.07
2001	0.06	0.32	0.14	0.13
2002	0.07	0.07	0.03	0.06

INTERIM DIVIDENDS (Per Share):

Amt.	Decl.	Ex.	Rec.	Pay.
0.278Q	3/15/02	4/10/02	4/12/02	4/30/02
0.278Q	6/14/02	7/10/02	7/12/02	7/31/02
0.278Q	9/26/02	10/09/02	10/11/02	10/31/02
0.278Q	12/05/02	1/15/03	1/17/03	1/31/03
0.285Q	3/13/03	4/09/03	4/11/03	4/30/03

Indicated div.: $1.14 (Div. Reinv. Plan)

CAPITALIZATION (12/31/01):

	($000)	(%)
Long-Term Debt	2,109,075	65.3
Minority Interest	75,665	2.3
Preferred Stock	310,400	9.6
Common & Surplus	732,325	22.7
Total	3,227,465	100.0

TRADING VOLUME
Thousand Shares

*7 YEAR PRICE SCORE 126.1   *12 MONTH PRICE SCORE 110.6
*NYSE COMPOSITE INDEX=100

BUSINESS:

United Dominion Realty Trust, Inc. is a self-administered equity real estate investment trust with activities related to the ownership, development, acquisition, renovation, management, marketing and strategic disposition of multifamily apartment communities nationwide. At 12/31/02, UDR's apartment portfolio included 260 communities located in 21 states, with a total of 74,480 completed apartment homes. In addition, the Company had 178 apartment homes under development. The Company's apartment communities consist primarily of upper- and middle-income garden and townhouse communities that make up the broadest segment of the apartment market. UDR has regional offices in Richmond, Dallas and Atlanta.

RECENT DEVELOPMENTS:

For the year ended 12/31/02, income was $50.1 million, before income from discontinued operations of $36.9 million and an extraordinary loss of $33.8 million, versus income of $53.6 million, before income from discontinued operations of $11.4 million and an extraordinary loss of $3.2 million, the previous year. Total income increased 4.6% to $596.1 million. Rental income grew 5.1% to $594.3 million. Funds from operations jumped 16.4% to $208.1 million, or $1.63 per share. Comparisons were made with restated prior-year figures.

PROSPECTS:

Looking ahead towards the balance of 2003, UDR does not see positive trends in some of the key drivers of its business, such as job growth, levels of new construction nor reduction in the flight to home ownership. The Company anticipates that funds from operations (FFO) for 2003 will be affected by international and regional economic trends and conditions, the acquisition and/or disposition of apartment communities and other factors. Given the current expectations, the company is forecasting FFO in the range of $1.51 to $1.59 per share. In addition, the Company estimates that recurring capital expenditures for 2003 will be $435.00 per apartment home or $0.025 per share.

ANNUAL FINANCIAL DATA:

FISCAL YEAR	TOT. INC. ($mill.)	NET INC. ($mill.)	TOT. ASSETS ($mill.)	NET INC. +DEPR./ ASSETS %	RET. ON EQUITY %	RET. ON ASSETS %	EARN. PER SH. $	TANG. BK. VAL.$	DIV. PER SH.$	DIV. PAYOUT %	PRICE RANGE	AVG. P/E RATIO	AVG. YIELD %
p12/31/02	596.1	①③ 50.1					①③ 0.21		1.10	523.8	16.81 - 13.18	71.4	7.3
12/31/01	623.2	①② 65.3	3,348.1	6.6	6.3	2.0	①② 0.27	7.10	1.08	398.9	14.85 - 10.56	47.0	8.5
12/31/00	622.2	① 75.8	3,454.0	6.8	6.2	2.2	① 0.41	7.91	1.07	260.3	11.75 - 9.38	25.8	10.1
12/31/99	620.7	①② 92.7	3,688.3	5.9	7.1	2.5	①② 0.54	8.59	1.06	195.8	12.06 - 9.06	19.6	10.0
12/31/98	482.1	② 72.5	3,762.9	4.7	5.3	1.9	② 0.49	9.11	1.04	212.2	14.81 - 10.06	25.4	8.4
12/31/97	387.8	①② 70.2	2,313.7	6.4	6.6	3.0	①② 0.60	9.01	1.00	166.2	16.00 - 13.38	24.5	6.8
12/31/96	243.8	①② 38.0	1,966.9	4.4	4.5	1.9	①② 0.49	9.09	0.94	192.8	15.81 - 13.13	29.5	6.5
12/31/95	195.2	33.1	1,080.6	6.8	6.4	3.1	0.50	7.30	0.87	174.0	15.38 - 13.00	28.4	6.1
12/31/94	140.0	① 19.2	911.9	5.4	5.4	2.1	① 0.41	7.09	0.76	185.3	15.88 - 12.25	34.3	5.4
12/31/93	89.1	11.2	505.8	6.2	4.3	2.2	0.29	6.24	0.69	237.8	16.88 - 11.88	49.6	4.8

Statistics are as originally reported. ① Bef. extraord. chrg. $33.8 mill., 12/02; $3.5 mill., 12/01; gain, $831,000, 12/00; gain $927,000, 12/99; chrg $138,000, 12/98; chrg. $50,000, 12/97; chrg. $23,000, 12/96; $89,000, 12/94 ② Incl. non-recurr. chrg. $10.8 mill., 12/01; $19.3 mill., 12/99; $15.6 mill., 12/98; $1.4 mill., 12/97; $290,000, 12/96 ③ Bef. income fr. disc. opers. of $36.9 mill.

OFFICERS:
R. Larson, Chmn.
T. W. Toomey, Pres., C.E.O.
C. Genry, C.F.O.

INVESTOR CONTACT: Ella Neyland, Investor Relations, (720) 283-6144

PRINCIPAL OFFICE: 1745 Shea Center Dr., Ste. 200, Highland Ranch,, CO 80129

TELEPHONE NUMBER: (720) 283-6120
FAX: (720) 283-2454
WEB: www.udrt.com

NO. OF EMPLOYEES: 1,985

SHAREHOLDERS: 7,943

ANNUAL MEETING: In May

INCORPORATED: VA, Dec., 1984

INSTITUTIONAL HOLDINGS:
No. of Institutions: 202
Shares Held: 54,180,861
% Held: 50.6

INDUSTRY: Real estate investment trusts (SIC: 6798)

TRANSFER AGENT(S): Mellon Investor Services, Pittsburg, PA

UNITED INDUSTRIAL CORPORATION

EXCH.	SYM.	REC. PRICE	P/E RATIO	YLD.	MKT. CAP.	RANGE (52-WK.)	'02 Y/E PR.
NYSE	UIC	12.35 (2/28/03)	45.7	3.2%	$140.4 mill.	26.05 - 12.28	16.00

MEDIUM GRADE. THE COMPANY SHOULD BENEFIT FROM RECENT CONTRACT WINS.

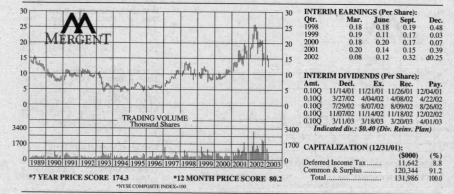

*7 YEAR PRICE SCORE 174.3   ***12 MONTH PRICE SCORE 80.2**
*NYSE COMPOSITE INDEX=100

INTERIM EARNINGS (Per Share):

Qtr.	Mar.	June	Sept.	Dec.
1998	0.18	0.18	0.19	0.48
1999	0.19	0.11	0.17	0.03
2000	0.18	0.20	0.17	0.07
2001	0.20	0.14	0.15	0.39
2002	0.08	0.12	0.32	d0.25

INTERIM DIVIDENDS (Per Share):

Amt.	Decl.	Ex.	Rec.	Pay.
0.10Q	11/14/01	11/21/01	11/26/01	12/04/01
0.10Q	3/27/02	4/08/02	4/08/02	4/22/02
0.10Q	7/29/02	8/07/02	8/09/02	8/26/02
0.10Q	11/07/02	11/14/02	11/18/02	12/02/02
0.10Q	3/11/03	3/18/03	3/20/03	4/01/03

Indicated div.: $0.40 (Div. Reinv. Plan)

CAPITALIZATION (12/31/01):

	($000)	(%)
Deferred Income Tax	11,642	8.8
Common & Surplus	120,344	91.2
Total	131,986	100.0

BUSINESS:

United Industrial Corporation designs and produces defense, training, and energy systems. UIC's products include unmanned aerial vehicles, training and simulation systems, and automated aircraft test and maintenance equipment. The Company also offers logistical/engineering services for government-owned equipment and manufactures combustion equipment for biomass and refuse fuels.

The Company's operations are conducted through two wholly-owned subsidiaries: AAI Corporation and Detroit Stoker Co. On 9/29/00, the Company sold Symtron Systems, Inc. On 7/26/02, the Company sold its transportation overhaul business. Net sales for 2002 were derived as follows: defense, 88.6% and energy, 11.4%.

RECENT DEVELOPMENTS:

For the year ended 12/31/02, the Company reported income from continuing operations of $3.9 million versus $14.6 million the year before. Earnings for 2002 included an after-tax charge of $3.1 million associated with the asbestos-related provision and the closing of UIC's foundry

operations. Earnings for 2002 and 2001 excluded losses of $42.9 million and $9.3 million, respectively, from discontinued operations. Net sales increased 8.5% to $258.8 million. Sales from defense rose 9.9% to $229.2 million, while sales from energy slipped 1.2% to $29.6 million.

PROSPECTS:

The Company should benefit from recent contract wins. For instance, on 1/16/03, UIC was awarded an $86.0 million first full rate production contract by the U.S. Army for its Tactical Unmanned Aerial Vehicle (TUAV) program. This contract provides for the production of nine TUAV systems, including spare parts, maintenance, ground and other equipment. Additionally, the Company is expanding a

number of separate contracts for additional services in support of the TUAV program. Meanwhile, UIC continues to move forward in exploring the potential sale of all or parts of the Company. However, the asbestos-related matter has complicated efforts. As a result, UIC is evaluating potential strategies to better position the Company for a sale.

ANNUAL FINANCIAL DATA:

FISCAL YEAR	TOT. REVS. ($000)	NET INC. ($000)	TOT. ASSETS ($000)	OPER. PROFIT %	NET PROFIT %	RET. ON EQUITY %	RET. ON ASSETS %	CURR. RATIO	EARN. PER SH.$	CASH FL.PER SH.$	TANG. BK. VAL.$	DIV. PER SH.$	PRICE RANGE		AVG. P/E RATIO	AVG. YIELD %
p12/31/02	258,767	⑥⑦ 3,864							⑥⑦ 0.28			0.30	26.05	12.02	68.0	1.6
12/31/01	238,495	⑥ 15,806	252,525	8.0	6.6	13.1	6.3	1.8	⑥ 1.19	1.67	10.58	0.40	19.90	10.63	12.8	2.6
12/31/00	256,358	⑤ 7,779	248,385	...	3.0	6.8	3.1	1.7	⑤ 0.62	1.36	10.95	0.40	11.63	8.13	15.9	4.1
12/31/99	216,979	6,277	201,792	4.4	2.9	5.7	3.1	1.9	0.50	1.12	9.03	0.40	12.50	7.38	19.9	4.0
12/31/98	204,305	④ 13,011	184,446	5.0	6.4	-11.9	7.1	2.4	④ 1.03	1.65	8.93	0.40	14.00	8.13	10.7	3.6
12/31/97	235,183	③ 14,825	183,291	6.6	6.3	14.5	8.1	3.0	③ 1.19	1.96	8.33	0.29	11.38	5.88	7.2	3.4
12/31/96	220,822	② 6,404	179,968	5.3	2.9	7.1	3.6	1.8	② 0.52	1.20	7.40	0.20	6.50	4.75	10.8	3.6
12/31/95	227,398	② 888	183,106	1.8	0.4	1.0	0.5	2.1	② 0.07	0.75	7.08	0.26	7.25	4.38	82.9	4.5
12/31/94	209,727	5,212	203,307	3.8	2.5	5.9	2.6	2.2	0.43	1.10	7.27	0.28	6.63	4.13	12.5	5.2
12/31/93	252,993	① d12,017	216,511	...	...	...	...	2.0	① d0.98	0.37	6.96	0.44	10.63	4.00	...	4.6

Statistics are as originally reported. ① Incl. restruct. chg. of $14.7 mill. & bef. acctg. cr. of $994,000. ② Incl. after-tax write-off of certain inventories, recognition of reserves and chgs. rel. to resolvement of a dispute with the U.S. Navy: $5.1 mill., 1995; $2.6 mill., 1996. ③ Incl. after-tax gain of $8.5 mill. from the sale of bus. & $1.8 mill. fr. litig. settle. ④ Incl. pre-tax gain of $4.9 mill. fr. sale of assets. ⑤ Incl. a gain of $3.9 mill. fr. the sale of Symtron Systems, Inc. & an insurance recovery of $2.3 mill. ⑥ Bef. loss fr. discont. opers. of $42.9 mill., 2002; $10.4 mill., 2001. ⑦ Incl. an aft.-tax chrg. of $3.1 mill. assoc. with asbestos-rel. provision & restruct.

OFFICERS:
H. S. Gelb, Chmn.
R. R. Erkeneff, Pres., C.E.O.
J. H. Perry, V.P., C.F.O., Treas.
INVESTOR CONTACT: Investor Relations, (212) 752-8787
PRINCIPAL OFFICE: 570 Lexington Avenue, New York, NY 10022

TELEPHONE NUMBER: (212) 752-8787
FAX: (212) 838-4629
WEB: www.unitedindustrial.com
NO. OF EMPLOYEES: 1,500 (approx.)
SHAREHOLDERS: 2,000 (approx.)
ANNUAL MEETING: In May
INCORPORATED: DE, Sept., 1959

INSTITUTIONAL HOLDINGS:
No. of Institutions: 56
Shares Held: 5,125,160
% Held: 39.2
INDUSTRY: Special industry machinery, nec (SIC: 3559)
TRANSFER AGENT(S): American Stock Transfer and Trust Co., New York, NY

UNITED PARCEL SERVICE, INC.

EXCH.	SYM.	REC. PRICE	P/E RATIO	YLD.	MKT. CAP.	RANGE (52-WK.)	'02 Y/E PR.
NYSE	UPS	57.54 (2/28/03)	20.0	1.5%	$64.56 bill.	67.10 - 56.00	63.08

UPPER MEDIUM GRADE. THE COMPANY CONTINUES TO REPORT STRONG RESULTS IN ITS INTERNATIONAL BUSINESS, REFLECTING ITS EXPANDED NETWORK IN ASIA.

TRADING VOLUME
Thousand Shares

1989 1990 1991 1992 1993 1994 1995 1996 1997 1998 1999 2000 2001 2002 2003

*7 YEAR PRICE SCORE N/A   *12 MONTH PRICE SCORE 107.1
*NYSE COMPOSITE INDEX=100

INTERIM EARNINGS (Per Share):

Qtrs.	Mar.	June	Sept.	Dec.
1999	0.44	d0.77	0.52	0.56
2000	0.67	0.60	0.60	0.63
2001	0.48	0.55	0.50	0.57
2002	0.50	0.54	0.51	1.32

INTERIM DIVIDENDS (Per Share):

Amt.	Decl.	Ex.	Rec.	Pay.
0.19Q	2/14/02	2/25/02	2/27/02	3/08/02
0.19Q	5/15/02	5/23/02	5/28/02	6/07/02
0.19Q	8/14/02	8/22/02	8/26/02	9/10/02
0.19Q	11/13/02	11/21/02	11/25/02	1/06/03
0.21Q	2/13/03	2/20/03	2/24/03	3/11/03

Indicated div.: $0.84

CAPITALIZATION (12/31/01):

	($000)	(%)
Long-Term Debt	4,648,000	31.2
Common & Surplus	10,248,000	68.8
Total	14,896,000	100.0

BUSINESS:

United Parcel Service provides express delivery and logistics services, including comprehensive management of supply chains, for 1.8 million shipping customers per day throughout the United States and in over 200 other countries and territories. As of 12/31/02, the UPS airline reported 257 aircraft owned, 326 aircraft leased or chartered, 77 aircraft on order, and 60 aircraft under option.

On 11/9/99, the Company brought to market an initial public offering of 109.4 million shares of Class B common stock at $50 per share. On 5/24/01, UPS acquired Fritz Companies. On 8/7/01, UPS acquired First International Bancorp. Net sales for 2002 were derived as follows: U.S. domestic package, 76.5%; international package, 15.0%; and non-package, 8.5%.

RECENT DEVELOPMENTS:

For the year ended 12/31/02, the Company reported income of $3.25 billion, before an accounting change charge of $72.0 million, compared with income of $2.43 billion, before an accounting change charge of $26.0 million, the year before. Earnings for 2002 included a gain of $1.02 billion from a tax assessment reversal and a net gain of

$91.0 million related to various nonrecurring items. Total revenue improved 3.1% to $31.27 billion from $30.32 billion in the prior year. U.S. domestic package revenue slid to $23.92 billion from $24.00 billion a year earlier. International package revenue advanced 10.2% to $4.68 billion, while non-package revenue rose 28.3% to $2.67 billion.

PROSPECTS:

The Company continues to report strong results in its international business, reflecting its expanded network in Asia, combined with increased service through more than 100 additional Asian flights. Additionally, the European export market continues to experience double-digit growth. Separately, in 2003, the Company expects diluted earnings per share to range from $0.48 to $0.53 in the first quarter and

earnings per share growth between 10.0% and 15.0% for the full year. The Company anticipates results will begin to strengthen in the second quarter of 2003 due to an improving economy and more favorable comparisons to the periods in 2002 when labor negotiations slowed the U.S. package business. Meanwhile, capital expenditures are anticipated to total approximately $2.00 billion in 2003.

ANNUAL FINANCIAL DATA:

FISCAL YEAR	TOT. REVS. ($mill.)	NET INC. ($mill.)	TOT. ASSETS ($mill.)	OPER. PROFIT %	NET PROFIT %	RET. ON EQUITY %	RET. ON ASSETS %	CURR. RATIO	EARN. PER SH. $	CASH FL. PER SH. $	TANG. BK. VAL. $	DIV. PER SH. $	PRICE RANGE	AVG. P/E RATIO	AVG. YIELD %
p12/31/02	31,272.0	①④ 3,254.0							①④ 2.81			0.76	67.10 - 54.25	21.6	1.3
12/31/01	30,646.0	③ 2,425.0	24,636.0	12.9	7.9	23.7	9.8	1.6	③ 2.12	3.34	9.15	0.74	62.50 - 46.15	25.6	1.4
12/31/00	29,771.0	② 2,934.0	21,662.0	15.2	9.9	30.1	13.5	1.6	② 2.50	3.50	8.58	0.81	69.75 - 49.50	23.8	1.4
12/31/99	27,052.0	① 883.0	23,043.0	14.7	3.3	7.1	3.8	2.7	① 0.77	1.77	10.50	...	76.94 - 61.00	89.6	...
12/31/98	24,788.0	1,741.0	17,067.0	12.5	7.0	24.3	10.2	1.5	1.57	2.57	6.42	...	...	...	...
12/31/97	22,458.0	909.0	15,912.0	7.6	4.0	14.9	5.7	1.3	0.81	1.77	5.42	...	...	...	...

Statistics are as originally reported. Adj. for 2-for-1 merger exchange ratio as effected in connection with Co.'s initial public offering in 11/99. ① Incl. tax assessment credit of $1.02 bill. 2002; chrg. $1.79 bill., 1999. ② Incl. a net gain of $139.0 mill. from nonrecurr. items. ③ Bef. an acctg. chrg. of $26.0 mill., 2001. ④ Bef. an acctg. chrg. of $72.0 mill. & one-time net gain of $91 mill. rel. to various items.

OFFICERS:
M. L. Eskew, Chmn., C.E.O.
D. S. Davis, Sr. V.P., C.F.O., Treas.

INVESTOR CONTACT: Kurt Kuehn, Investor Relations, (404) 828-6977

PRINCIPAL OFFICE: 55 Glenlake Parkway, NE, Atlanta, GA 30328

TELEPHONE NUMBER: (404) 828-6000
FAX: (404) 828-6562
WEB: www.ups.com
NO. OF EMPLOYEES: 371,000
SHAREHOLDERS: 138,783 (class A); 12,760 (class B)
ANNUAL MEETING: In May
INCORPORATED: DE, July, 1999

INSTITUTIONAL HOLDINGS:
No. of Institutions: 557
Shares Held: 384,269,742
% Held: 34.4
INDUSTRY: Courier services, except by air (SIC: 4215)
TRANSFER AGENT(S): First Union National Bank, Charlotte, NC

UNITED RENTALS, INC.

EXCH.	SYM.	REC. PRICE	P/E RATIO	YLD.	MKT. CAP.	RANGE (52-WK.)	'02 Y/E PR.
NYSE	URI	8.63 (2/28/03)	...	...	$0.63 bill.	30.83 - 5.88	10.76

LOWER MEDIUM GRADE. IN 2003, EARNINGS ARE EXPECTED TO WEAKEN SLIGHTLY AS REVENUE IS ANTICIPATED TO BE FLAT.

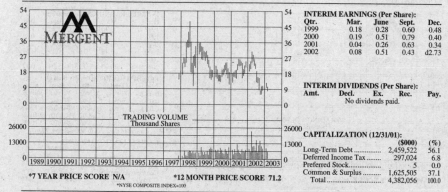

INTERIM EARNINGS (Per Share):

Qtr.	Mar.	June	Sept.	Dec.
1999	0.18	0.28	0.60	0.48
2000	0.19	0.51	0.79	0.40
2001	0.04	0.26	0.63	0.34
2002	0.08	0.51	0.43	d2.73

INTERIM DIVIDENDS (Per Share):

Amt.	Decl.	Ex.	Rec.	Pay.
		No dividends paid.		

TRADING VOLUME
Thousand Shares

*7 YEAR PRICE SCORE N/A   *12 MONTH PRICE SCORE 71.2
*NYSE COMPOSITE INDEX=100

CAPITALIZATION (12/31/01):

	($000)	(%)
Long-Term Debt	2,459,522	56.1
Deferred Income Tax	297,024	6.8
Preferred Stock	5	0.0
Common & Surplus	1,625,505	37.1
Total	4,382,056	100.0

BUSINESS:

United Rentals, Inc. rents equipment to construction and industrial companies, manufacturers, utilities, municipalities, and homeowners through more than 750 locations in 47 states, seven Canadian provinces, and Mexico. The Company also sells used rental equipment and acts as a distributor for certain new equipment and sells related merchandise and parts. URI offers over 600 types of rental equipment including light to heavy construction and industrial equipment, such as pumps, generators, forklifts, backhoes, cranes, bulldozers, aerial lifts and compressors. URI also rents general tools and equipment, such as hand tools and garden and landscaping equipment, and special event equipment, such as tents, tables and chairs. The mix of rental equipment varies at each of the Company's locations.

RECENT DEVELOPMENTS:

For the year ended 12/31/02, loss amounted to $109.5 million, before an accounting change charge of $288.3 million, compared with income of $122.6 million, before an extraordinary loss of $11.3 million, in 2001. Results were negatively affected by the continued slowdown in non-residential construction. Results for 2002 and 2001 included restructuring charges of $28.3 million and $28.9 million, respectively. Results for 2002 also included a goodwill impairment charge of $247.9 million. Total revenues slipped 2.3% to $2.82 billion from $2.89 billion the year before. Rental revenues were 76.4% of total revenues, sales of rental equipment were 6.2% and sales of equipment and merchandise and other revenues were 17.4%. Same-store rental revenues decreased 2.7% year over year.

PROSPECTS:

The Company reported that it has not yet seen signs of a recovery in non-residential construction, which accounts for the majority of its business, and predicts its earnings will weaken slightly in 2003 as revenue is expected to be flat. Assuming the economy remains sluggish, earnings per share in 2003 are anticipated to be $0.10 to $0.12 lower than in the prior year because of added interest expense for senior notes issued in the fourth quarter. While the Company is gaining market share from its smaller competitors even as its markets contract, the uncertain economy is its major obstacle to growth.

ANNUAL FINANCIAL DATA:

FISCAL YEAR	TOT. REVS. ($mill.)	NET INC. ($mill.)	TOT. ASSETS ($mill.)	OPER. PROFIT %	NET PROFIT %	RET. ON EQUITY %	RET. ON ASSETS %	CURR. RATIO	EARN. PER SH. $	CASH FL. PER SH. $	TANG. BK. VAL. $	PRICE RANGE	AVG. P/E RATIO
p12/31/02	2,821.0	③ d109.5							③ d5.25			30.83 - 5.88	...
12/31/01	2,886.6	② 122.6	4,761.5	16.0	4.2	7.5	2.6	11.9	② 1.30	5.90	...	26.40 - 12.75	15.1
12/31/00	2,918.9	176.4	5,123.9	18.8	6.0	11.4	3.4	9.5	1.89	5.95	...	24.31 - 11.69	9.5
12/31/99	2,233.6	142.7	4,497.7	18.3	6.4	10.2	3.2	9.6	1.53	5.23	...	35.69 - 14.31	16.3
12/31/98	1,220.3	① 34.8	2,634.7	11.9	2.9	4.8	1.3	12.5	① 0.48	3.38	...	48.06 - 10.56	61.1
12/31/97	10.6	33.6	169.1	2.2	317.0	21.3	19.9	20.4	...	11.16	4.49	18.06 - 14.38	...
12/31/96	354.5	37.7	...	13.8	10.6	...	...	...	1.67	4.96	...	...	...

Statistics are as originally reported. ① Incl. $47.2 mill. merger-related exps. & excl. $14.3 mill. extraord. item. ② Incl. $28.9 mill. restr. chg.; bef. extraord. chg. of $11.3 mill. ③ Incl. $247.9 mill. goodwill impair. chg. & $28.3 mill. restr. chg. and excl. $288.3 mill. acctg. chg.

OFFICERS:
B. S. Jacobs, Chmn., C.E.O.
J. Milne, C.F.O.

INVESTOR CONTACT: Investor Relations, (203) 622-3131

PRINCIPAL OFFICE: Five Greenwich Office Park, Greenwich, CT 06830

TELEPHONE NUMBER: (203) 622-3131
FAX: (203) 622-6080
WEB: www.unitedrentals.com
NO. OF EMPLOYEES: 13,606
SHAREHOLDERS: 348 (approx. record)
ANNUAL MEETING: In June
INCORPORATED: DE, Aug., 1997

INSTITUTIONAL HOLDINGS:
No. of Institutions: 151
Shares Held: 53,901,375
% Held: 70.4
INDUSTRY: Equipment rental & leasing, nec (SIC: 7359)
TRANSFER AGENT(S): American Stock Transfer & Trust Company, New York, NY

UNITED STATES STEEL CORPORATION

EXCH.	SYM.	REC. PRICE	P/E RATIO	YLD.	MKT. CAP.	RANGE (52-WK.)	'02 Y/E PR.
NYSE	X	11.62 (2/28/03)	22.8	1.7%	$1.04 bill.	22.00 - 10.66	13.12

LOWER MEDIUM GRADE. THE COMPANY IS INTERESTED IN ACQUIRING THE ASSETS OF NATIONAL STEEL CORPORATION.

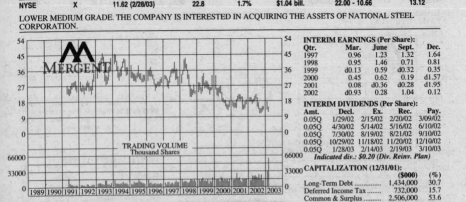

*7 YEAR PRICE SCORE 66.6   ***12 MONTH PRICE SCORE 97.7**

*NYSE COMPOSITE INDEX=100

INTERIM EARNINGS (Per Share):

Qtr.	Mar.	June	Sept.	Dec.
1997	0.96	1.23	1.32	1.64
1998	0.95	1.46	0.71	0.81
1999	d0.13	0.59	d0.32	0.35
2000	0.45	0.62	0.19	d1.57
2001	0.08	d0.36	d0.28	d1.95
2002	d0.93	0.28	1.04	0.12

INTERIM DIVIDENDS (Per Share):

Amt.	Decl.	Ex.	Rec.	Pay.
0.05Q	1/29/02	2/15/02	2/20/02	3/09/02
0.05Q	4/30/02	5/14/02	5/16/02	6/10/02
0.05Q	7/30/02	8/19/02	8/21/02	9/10/02
0.05Q	10/29/02	11/18/02	11/20/02	12/10/02
0.05Q	1/28/03	2/14/03	2/19/03	3/10/03

Indicated div.: $0.20 (Div. Reinv. Plan)

CAPITALIZATION (12/31/01):

	($000)	(%)
Long-Term Debt	1,434,000	30.7
Deferred Income Tax	732,000	15.7
Common & Surplus	2,506,000	53.6
Total	4,672,000	100.0

BUSINESS:

United States Steel Corporation (formerly USX-U.S. Steel Group) is a steel company that operates five reportable segments. Flat-rolled Products (52.9% of 2002 revenues) is involved in the production of sheet, plate and tin mill products. U. S. Steel Kosice (14.7%) is engaged in the production and sale of sheet, plate, tin, tubular, precision tube and specialty steel products, as well as coke. Tubular Products (6.4%) produce and sell both seamless and electric resistance weld tubular products. USS Real Estate (1.2%) is comprised of X's mineral interests that are not assigned to U. S. Steel Mining LLC or to the iron ore operations at Mt.

Iron, Minnesota; timber properties; and residential, commercial and industrial real estate, which is managed and developed for sale or lease. Straightline Source (0.9%) sells, processes and delivers flat rolled steel products in small to medium sized order quantities to jobs, contract manufactures, and OEM manufacturers. The Other businesses segment accounted for 23.9% of 2002 revenues. On 1/2/02, X began trading as an independent company following the spin-off from Marathon Oil Corporation (formerly USX Corporation) at the end of 2001.

RECENT DEVELOPMENTS:

For the year ended 12/31/02, net income was $62.0 million compared with a net loss of $218.0 million in 2001 due, in part, to a sharp improvement in the Company's domestic flat-rolled business. Earnings for 2002 and 2001 included nonrecurring items that resulted in a net after-tax gain of $6.0 million and a net after-tax charge of $39.0 million in 2002 and 2001, respectively. Total revenues and other income increased 10.7% to $7.05 billion.

PROSPECTS:

On 1/30/03, the Company announced that it plans to purchase the assets of National Steel Corporation in a transaction that includes substantially all of National's steelmaking and finishing assets for about $950.0 million, including the assumption of liabilities of approximately $200.0 million. The transaction is contingent on the successful negotiation of a new labor contract with the United Steelworkers of America covering the National employees, the approval of the bankruptcy court and other customary regulatory approvals.

ANNUAL FINANCIAL DATA:

FISCAL YEAR	TOT. REVS. ($mill.)	NET INC. ($mill.)	TOT. ASSETS ($mill.)	OPER. PROFIT %	NET PROFIT %	RET. ON EQUITY %	RET. ON ASSETS %	CURR. RATIO	EARN. PER SH. $	CASH FL. PER SH. $	TANG. BK. VAL. $	PRICE RANGE	AVG. P/E RATIO
p12/31/02	7,054.0	④ 62.0							④ 0.64			22.00 - 10.66	25.5
12/31/01	6,375.0	④ d218.0	8,337.0	...	...	...	...	1.6	④ d2.45	...	28.09	22.00 - 13.00	...
12/31/00	6,132.0	④ d21.0	8,711.0	1.7	...	...	...	2.0	④ d0.33	3.74	21.60	32.94 - 12.69	...
12/31/99	5,314.0	③ 51.0	7,525.0	2.8	1.0	2.5	0.7	1.6	③ 0.48	3.91	23.23	34.25 - 21.75	58.3
12/31/98	6,283.0	364.0	6,693.0	9.2	5.8	17.4	5.4	1.3	3.92	7.33	24.02	43.06 - 20.44	8.1
12/31/97	6,941.0	452.0	6,694.0	11.1	6.5	25.4	6.8	1.1	4.88	8.00	20.45	40.75 - 25.38	6.8
12/31/96	6,547.0	⑤ 275.0	6,580.0	5.5	4.2	17.6	4.2	1.1	⑤ 3.00	6.49	18.34	37.88 - 24.13	10.3
12/31/95	6,575.0	② 303.0	6,521.0	7.3	6.4	31.4	6.5	1.0	② 3.53	9.06	16.11	39.13 - 29.13	9.7
12/31/94	6,066.0	201.0	6,480.0	5.2	3.3	21.3	3.1	1.4	2.35	6.53	12.01	45.63 - 30.25	16.1
12/31/93	5,612.0	① d169.0	6,616.0	...	...	...	...	1.0	① d2.96	1.94	...	46.00 - 27.50	...

Statistics are as originally reported. ① Incl. restruct. chrg. of $42.0 mill. and excl. an acctg. chrg. of $69.0 mill. ② Bef. an extraord. loss of $7.0 mill. ③ Bef. $7.0 mill. extraord. loss on the exting. of debt. ④ Incl. nonrecurr. loss of $6.0 mill., 2002; gain of $39.0 mill., 2001; loss $98.0 mill., 2000 related to special items. ⑤ Bef. an extraord. loss of $9.0 mill.

OFFICERS:
T. J. Usher, Chmn., C.E.O.
J. P. Surma, Vice Chmn., Pres.
G. R. Haggerty, Exec. V.P., Treas., C.F.O.
INVESTOR CONTACT: Investor Relations, (412) 433-1139
PRINCIPAL OFFICE: 600 Grant Street, Pittsburgh, PA 15219-2800

TELEPHONE NUMBER: (412) 433-1121
FAX: (412) 433-4818
WEB: www.ussteel.com
NO. OF EMPLOYEES: 20,351 (avg.)
SHAREHOLDERS: 52,117
ANNUAL MEETING: In Apr.
INCORPORATED: DE, May, 1991

INSTITUTIONAL HOLDINGS:
No. of Institutions: 217
Shares Held: 76,764,528
% Held: 75.0
INDUSTRY: Blast furnaces and steel mills (SIC: 3312)
TRANSFER AGENT(S): USX Corporation Shareholder Services, Pittsburgh, PA

UNITED TECHNOLOGIES CORPORATION

EXCH.	SYM.	REC. PRICE	P/E RATIO	YLD.	MKT. CAP.	RANGE (52-WK.)	'02 Y/E PR.
NYSE	UTX	58.58 (2/28/03)	13.3	1.7%	$27.66 bill.	77.75 - 48.83	61.94

UPPER MEDIUM GRADE. THE COMPANY IS TARGETING EARNINGS PER SHARE OF $4.55 TO $4.80 IN 2003.

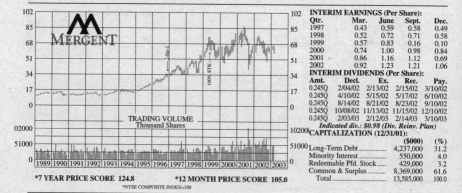

INTERIM EARNINGS (Per Share):

Qtr.	Mar.	June	Sept.	Dec.
1997	0.43	0.59	0.58	0.49
1998	0.52	0.72	0.71	0.58
1999	0.57	0.83	0.16	0.10
2000	0.74	1.00	0.98	0.84
2001	0.86	1.16	1.12	0.69
2002	0.92	1.23	1.21	1.06

INTERIM DIVIDENDS (Per Share):

Amt.	Decl.	Ex.	Rec.	Pay.
0.245Q	2/04/02	2/13/02	2/15/02	3/10/02
0.245Q	4/10/02	5/15/02	5/17/02	6/10/02
0.245Q	8/14/02	8/21/02	8/23/02	9/10/02
0.245Q	10/08/02	11/13/02	11/15/02	12/10/02
0.245Q	2/03/03	2/12/03	2/14/03	3/10/03

Indicated div.: $0.98 (Div. Reinv. Plan)

CAPITALIZATION (12/31/01):

	($000)	(%)
Long-Term Debt	4,237,000	31.2
Minority Interest	550,000	4.0
Redeemable Pfd. Stock	429,000	3.2
Common & Surplus	8,369,000	61.6
Total	13,585,000	100.0

*7 YEAR PRICE SCORE 124.8   ***12 MONTH PRICE SCORE 105.0**

*NYSE COMPOSITE INDEX=100

BUSINESS:

United Technologies Corporation provides high-technology products and support services to the aerospace, building and automotive industries. Carrier (30.5% of 2002 revenues) provides heating, ventilating and air conditioning equipment for commercial, industrial, and residential buildings. Pratt & Whitney (26.5%) consists of commercial and military aircraft engines, spare parts, and product support.

Otis (23.7%) manufactures elevators, escalators, moving walks, and shuttle systems. Flight Systems (19.3%) includes Sikorsky military and commercial helicopters, and Hamilton Sundstrand controls. The Company divested its Norden Systems subsidiary in 1994. On 5/4/99, UTX sold its automotive operations to Lear Corp. for $2.30 billion.

RECENT DEVELOPMENTS:

For the year ended 12/31/02, net income climbed 15.4% to $2.24 billion from $1.94 billion a year earlier. Results for 2002 and 2001 included pre-tax restructuring and related charges of $321.0 million and $348.0 million, respectively. Revenues totaled $28.21 billion, up 1.1% compared with

$27.90 billion in the prior year. Increased revenues at Otis and Flight Systems were partially offset by lower revenue at Carrier and Pratt & Whitney. Operating profit grew 13.1% to $3.66 billion from $3.23 billion the previous year.

PROSPECTS:

The Company is targeting full-year 2003 earnings in the range of $4.55 to $4.80 per share. Robust operating profit growth at Carrier is being fueled by UTX's efforts to reduce costs and increased volume in the transport refrigeration business and in the Latin American and North American residential heating, ventilating and air conditioning

(HVAC) market, partially offset by weakness in the commercial HVAC markets. Meanwhile, results are benefiting from strong demand for the Company's Otis elevators in Europe and Asia, along with increased demand for aftermarket services at Sikorsky and Hamilton Sundstrand's products for military aircraft.

ANNUAL FINANCIAL DATA:

FISCAL YEAR	TOT. REVS. ($mill.)	NET INC. ($mill.)	TOT. ASSETS ($mill.)	OPER. PROFIT %	NET PROFIT %	RET. ON EQUITY %	RET. ON ASSETS %	CURR. RATIO	EARN. PER SH.$	CASH FL. PER SH.$	TANG. BK. VAL.$	DIV. PER SH.$	PRICE RANGE	AVG. P/E RATIO	AVG. YIELD %
p12/31/02	28,212.0	①2,236.0							①4.42			0.98	77.75 - 48.83	14.3	1.5
12/31/01	27,897.0	①1,938.0	26,969.0	11.6	6.9	23.2	7.2	1.3	①3.83	5.63	3.32	0.90	87.50 - 40.10	16.7	1.4
12/31/00	26,583.0	1,808.0	25,364.0	11.8	6.8	23.6	7.1	1.1	3.55	5.19	1.89	0.82	79.75 - 46.50	17.8	1.3
12/31/99	24,127.0	③841.0	24,366.0	6.3	3.5	11.8	3.5	1.2	③1.65	3.33	3.11	0.76	75.97 - 51.63	38.7	1.2
12/31/98	25,715.0	1,255.0	18,375.0	8.4	4.9	25.1	6.8	1.2	2.53	4.27	7.23	0.69	56.25 - 33.50	17.8	1.5
12/31/97	24,713.0	1,072.0	16,719.0	7.9	4.3	23.4	6.4	1.3	2.11	3.72	7.84	0.62	44.47 - 32.56	18.3	1.6
12/31/96	23,512.0	906.0	16,745.0	7.6	3.9	21.0	5.4	1.3	1.73	3.31	7.61	0.55	35.22 - 22.63	16.8	1.9
12/31/95	22,802.0	750.0	15,958.0	7.0	3.3	17.3	4.7	1.3	1.47	3.24	7.68	0.51	24.44 - 15.56	13.6	2.6
12/31/94	21,197.0	②585.0	15,624.0	6.4	2.8	15.6	3.7	1.3	②1.10	2.66	6.44	0.47	18.00 - 13.75	14.4	3.0
12/31/93	21,081.0	487.0	15,618.0	5.5	2.3	13.5	3.1	1.1	0.88	2.50	7.14	0.45	16.53 - 10.94	15.6	3.3

Statistics are as originally reported. Adj. for 2-for-1 stk. split, 5/99 & 12/96. ① Incl. $321 mil pre-tax restr. chg., 2002; $348 mil, 2001. ② Bef. $59 mil ($0.03/sh) chg. for acctg. adj. ③ Bef. $690 mil ($1.36/sh) after-tax gain from sale of UT Automotive & incl. $842 mil pre-tax restr. chg.

OFFICERS:
G. David, Chmn., C.E.O.
S. F. Page, Vice-Chmn., C.F.O.
T. I. Rogan, V.P., Treas.

INVESTOR CONTACT: Paul Jackson, (860) 728-7912

PRINCIPAL OFFICE: United Technologies Building, One Financial Plaza, Hartford, CT 06103

TELEPHONE NUMBER: (860) 728-7000
FAX: (860) 728-7028
WEB: www.utc.com

NO. OF EMPLOYEES: 152,000 (avg.)

SHAREHOLDERS: 24,000 (approx.)

ANNUAL MEETING: In Apr.

INCORPORATED: DE, July, 1934

INSTITUTIONAL HOLDINGS:
No. of Institutions: 787
Shares Held: 396,035,177
% Held: 83.6

INDUSTRY: Aircraft engines and engine parts (SIC: 3724)

TRANSFER AGENT(S): First Chicago Trust Company of New York, Jersey City, NJ

UNITEDHEALTH GROUP INC.

EXCH.	SYM.	REC. PRICE	P/E RATIO	YLD.	MKT. CAP.	RANGE (52-WK.)	'02 Y/E PR.
NYSE	UNH	82.90 (2/28/03)	19.5	...	$25.59 bill.	101.00 - 67.85	83.50

INVESTMENT GRADE. THE COMPANY IS BENEFITING FROM MARKET SHARE GAINS AND MARGIN IMPROVEMENTS.

*7 YEAR PRICE SCORE 207.8   ***12 MONTH PRICE SCORE 105.7**
*NYSE COMPOSITE INDEX=100

INTERIM EARNINGS (Per Share):

Qtr.	Mar.	June	Sept.	Dec.
1998	0.32	d1.48	0.33	0.29
1999	0.36	0.38	0.41	0.46
2000	0.52	0.51	0.54	0.63
2001	0.64	0.68	0.71	0.76
2002	0.92	1.01	1.12	1.20

INTERIM DIVIDENDS (Per Share):

Amt.	Decl.	Ex.	Rec.	Pay.
0.03A	2/14/01	3/29/01	4/02/01	4/18/01
0.03A	2/14/02	3/27/02	4/01/02	4/17/02
0.03A	2/12/03	3/28/03	4/01/03	4/17/03

Indicated div.: $0.03 (Div. Reinv. Plan)

CAPITALIZATION (12/31/01):

	($000)	(%)
Long-Term Debt	900,000	18.8
Common & Surplus	3,891,000	81.2
Total	4,791,000	100.0

BUSINESS:

UnitedHealth Group Inc. offers health care coverage and related services through four lines of business. Health Care Services consists of the UnitedHealthcare and Ovations business units. UnitedHealthcare operates network-based health and well-being services including commercial, Medicare and Medicaid products for locally based employers and individuals in six broad regional markets. Ovations, which administers Medicare Supplement benefits on behalf of AARP, offers health and well-being services for Americans over 50. Uniprise provides network-based health and well-being services, business-to-business transactional infrastructure services, consumer connectivity and service, and technology support for large employers and health plans. Specialized Care Services is an expanding portfolio of health and well-being companies, each serving a specialized market need with a blend of benefits, provider networks, services and resources. Ingenix offers health care knowledge information of products and services.

RECENT DEVELOPMENTS:

For the year ended 12/31/02, net income increased 48.1% to $1.35 billion compared with $913.0 million the previous year. Total revenues rose 6.7% to $25.02 billion from $23.45 billion the year before, due to stronger growth across all business segments. Revenues from premiums climbed 5.9% to $21.91 billion and $20.68 billion, while revenues from services advanced 16.2% to $2.89 billion from $2.49 billion a year earlier. Revenues from investment and other income declined 21.7% to $220.0 million from $281.0 million the prior year. Earnings from operations jumped 39.6% to $2.19 billion versus $1.57 billion in 2001.

PROSPECTS:

The Company is benefiting from the acquisition of AmeriChoice Corporation, completed on 9/23/02. Additionally, the Company is realizing ongoing benefits from increasing operational advantages in services, systems, connectivity and health informatics that are driving market share gains and margin improvements. As a result, the Company expects full year earnings per share growth to be approximately 22.0% above $4.25 per share earned in 2001.

ANNUAL FINANCIAL DATA:

FISCAL YEAR	TOT. REVS. ($mill.)	NET INC. ($mill.)	TOT. ASSETS ($mill.)	OPER. PROFIT %	NET PROFIT %	RET. ON EQUITY %	RET. ON ASSETS %	CURR. RATIO	EARN. PER SH. $	CASH FL. PER SH. $	TANG. BK. VAL. $	DIV. PER SH. $	PRICE RANGE	AVG. P/E RATIO	AVG. YIELD %
p12/31/02	25,020.0	1,352.0							4.25			0.03	101.00 - 67.85	19.9	...
12/31/01	23,454.0	913.0	12,486.0	6.7	3.9	23.5	7.3	0.7	2.79	3.60	3.52	0.03	72.80 - 50.50	22.1	...
12/31/00	21,122.0	⑤736.0	11,053.0	5.7	3.5	20.0	6.7	0.7	⑤2.19	2.92	2.45	0.01	63.44 - 23.19	19.8	...
12/31/99	19,562.0	568.0	10,273.0	4.8	2.9	14.7	5.5	0.8	1.60	2.26	3.00	0.01	35.00 - 19.69	17.1	0.1
12/31/98	17,355.0	④d166.0	9,701.0	...	...	...	...	0.8	④d0.56	d0.08	4.13	0.01	36.97 - 14.78	...	0.1
12/31/97	11,794.0	460.0	7,623.0	6.3	3.9	10.1	6.0	0.9	1.13	1.51	5.89	0.01	30.06 - 21.22	22.7	0.1
12/31/96	10,073.8	③355.6	6,996.6	5.9	3.5	9.3	5.1	1.0	③0.88	1.24	4.55	0.01	34.50 - 15.00	28.1	0.1
12/31/95	5,670.9	②286.0	6,161.0	8.1	5.0	9.0	4.6	1.2	②0.79	1.05	4.10	0.01	32.81 - 17.06	31.8	0.1
12/31/94	3,768.9	①288.1	3,489.5	13.4	7.6	10.3	8.3	2.9	①0.82	1.01	7.21	0.01	27.69 - 18.63	28.2	0.1
12/31/93	2,527.3	194.6	1,494.0	12.1	7.7	20.3	13.0	0.8	0.62	0.78	2.46	0.01	19.69 - 10.00	23.9	0.1

Statistics are as originally reported. Adj. for 2-for-1 stock split, 12/00 & 3/94. ① Incl. one-time chrg. of $35.9 mill. & bef. extraord. gain of $1.38 bill. ② Incl. restruct. chrg. of $153.8 mill. ③ Excl. non-oper. costs assoc. with the acg. of HealthWise of $14.9 mill. & the prov. from losses on two multi-year contracts of $45.0 mill. ④ Incl. pre-tax chrgs. of $900.0 mill. ⑤ Excl. after-tax gain of $17.0 mill. rel. to disposition of UnitedHealth Capital investments.

OFFICERS: W. W. McGuire, Chmn., C.E.O. S. Hemsley, Pres., C.O.O. P. Erlandson, C.F.O., C.A.O. **INVESTOR CONTACT:** John S. Penshorn, Investor Relations, (952) 936-7214 **PRINCIPAL OFFICE:** 9900 Bren Road East, Minnetonka, MN 55343	**TELEPHONE NUMBER:** (952) 936-1300 **FAX:** (952) 936-0044 **WEB:** www.unitedheathgroup.com **NO. OF EMPLOYEES:** 30,000 (approx.) **SHAREHOLDERS:** 12,954 (record) **ANNUAL MEETING:** In May **INCORPORATED:** MN, Jan., 1977	**INSTITUTIONAL HOLDINGS:** No. of Institutions: 533 Shares Held: 330,613,210 % Held: 108.6 **INDUSTRY:** Hospital and medical service plans (SIC: 6324) **TRANSFER AGENT(S):** Wells Fargo Share- owner Services, St. Paul, MN

UNITRIN, INC.

EXCH.	SYM.	REC. PRICE	P/E RATIO	YLD.	MKT. CAP.	RANGE (52-WK.)	'02 Y/E PR.	DIV. ACH.
NYSE	UTR	24.90 (2/28/03)	...	6.7%	$1.68 bill.	42.80 - 24.30	29.22	12 yrs.

UPPER MEDIUM GRADE. THE COMPANY IS EVALUATING THE STRATEGIC ALTERNATIVES AVAILABLE FOR ITS COMMERCIAL LINES OF BUSINESSES.

*7 YEAR PRICE SCORE 105.3   *12 MONTH PRICE SCORE 86.8

*NYSE COMPOSITE INDEX=100

TRADING VOLUME
Thousand Shares

INTERIM EARNINGS (Per Share):

Qtr.	Mar.	June	Sept.	Dec.
1997	0.45	0.02	0.50	0.62
1998	1.00	0.46	4.35	0.60
1999	0.70	0.50	0.71	0.84
2000	0.60	0.37	d0.07	0.41
2001	0.24	5.25	0.30	d0.18
2002	0.13	0.06	d0.27	d0.05

INTERIM DIVIDENDS (Per Share):

Amt.	Decl.	Ex.	Rec.	Pay.
0.40Q	11/07/01	11/15/01	11/19/01	12/03/01
0.415Q	2/06/02	2/13/02	2/18/02	3/01/02
0.415Q	5/01/02	5/09/02	5/13/02	5/24/02
0.415Q	7/31/02	8/08/02	8/12/02	8/23/02
0.415Q	11/06/02	11/14/02	11/18/02	12/02/02

Indicated div.: $1.66

CAPITALIZATION (12/31/01):

	($000)	(%)
Common & Surplus	1,916,800	100.0
Total	1,916,800	100.0

BUSINESS:

Unitrin, Inc. is engaged, through its subsidiaries, in the property and casualty insurance, life and health insurance and consumer finance businesses. UTR conducts its operations through six operating segments: Multi Lines Insurance, which offers preferred and standard risk automobile, homeowners, fire, commercial liability and workers compensation; Specialty Lines Insurance, which offers automobile, motorcycle and watercraft insurance; Kemper Auto and Home, which offers personal automobile and home-

owners' insurance; Life and Health Insurance, which offers individual life, accident, health and hospitalization insurance as well as property insurance products; Consumer Finance, which offers consumer loans primarily for the purchase of used automobiles as well as thrift products in the form of investment certificates and savings accounts; and Unitrin and Kemper Direct, which offers personal automobile insurance marketed through direct mail, radio and television advertising and over the Internet.

RECENT DEVELOPMENTS:

For the year ended 12/31/02, net loss was $8.2 million compared with net income of $380.9 million the year before. Results for 2001 included an after-tax gain of $362.4 million on the disposition of UTR's interest in Litton Industries, Inc. Total revenues declined 9.3% to $2.30

billion from $2.53 billion the prior year. Revenues included a realized investment loss of $13.3 million in 2002 and a realized investment gain of $568.2 million in 2001. Revenues from premiums climbed 20.3% to $1.88 billion from $1.56 billion the year before.

PROSPECTS:

Results are being adversely affected by poor operating performance from UTR's Multi Lines Insurance segment, mainly due to adverse reserve development in its commercial lines business. Consequently, the Company is in the process of evaluating strategic alternatives available for its commercial lines. While evaluating those alternatives, UTR

will continue to reduce policies in force through extensive re-underwriting of contractors and related industries, program business, workers compensation, and product liability. Also, UTR intends to intensify aggressive pricing with higher premium rates on selected portions of the commercial lines book.

ANNUAL FINANCIAL DATA:

FISCAL YEAR	PREM. INC. ($mill.)	TOT. REVS. ($mill.)	NET INC. ($mill.)	TOT. ASSETS ($mill.)	TOT. INVST. ($mill.)	RET. ON REVS. %	RET. ON EQUITY %	RET. ON ASSETS %	EARN. PER SH. $	TANG. BK. VAL. $	AVG. YIELD %	DIV. PER SH. $	PRICE RANGE	AVG. P/E RATIO
p12/31/02	1,878.0	2,298.2	d8.2						d0.12			1.66	42.80 - 27.85	...
12/31/01	1,568.0	2,533.8	380.9	7,133.7	5,127.5	15.0	19.9	5.3	5.60	23.27	4.2	1.60	41.95 - 33.90	6.8
12/31/00	1,447.9	1,953.2	91.0	6,164.8	4,233.5	4.7	5.3	1.5	1.32	19.93	4.4	1.50	41.13 - 27.19	25.9
12/31/99	1,373.3	1,813.6	201.0	5,934.8	4,096.8	11.1	11.7	3.4	2.74	18.98	3.8	1.40	42.38 - 30.50	13.3
12/31/98	1,228.3	2,085.9	510.8	5,909.9	4,304.2	24.5	28.0	8.6	6.51	20.06	4.0	1.30	37.06 - 27.78	5.0
12/31/97	1,222.0	1,530.1	117.9	4,920.7	3,448.5	7.7	7.7	2.4	1.56	17.24	4.1	1.20	34.25 - 24.25	18.8
12/31/96	1,220.3	1,523.1	132.5	4,871.1	3,291.4	8.7	9.0	2.7	1.76	16.77	4.4	1.10	28.19 - 22.13	14.3
12/31/95	1,099.1	1,447.4	150.6	4,818.7	3,409.7	10.4	9.9	3.1	1.87	16.81	4.3	1.00	25.25 - 21.50	12.5
12/31/94	1,048.8	1,365.5	148.4	4,569.8	3,321.1	10.9	8.4	3.2	1.48	16.55	3.3	0.75	25.75 - 19.25	15.2
12/31/93	1,056.2	1,363.2	95.0	4,895.3	3,707.0	7.0	4.5	1.9	0.92	18.22	3.0	0.65	23.38 - 19.50	23.4

Statistics are as originally reported. Adj. for stk. split: 2-for-1, 3/26/99

OFFICERS:
R. C. Vie, Chmn., C.E.O.
D. G. Southwell, Pres., C.O.O.
E. J. Draut, Exec. V.P., C.F.O.
INVESTOR CONTACT: Edward J. Konar, Investor Relations, (312) 661-4930
PRINCIPAL OFFICE: One East Wacker Drive, Chicago, IL 60601

TELEPHONE NUMBER: (312) 661-4600
FAX: (312) 661-4690
WEB: www.unitrin.com
NO. OF EMPLOYEES: 8,710
SHAREHOLDERS: 7,500 (approx.)
ANNUAL MEETING: In May
INCORPORATED: DE, Feb., 1990

INSTITUTIONAL HOLDINGS:
No. of Institutions: 144
Shares Held: 16,538,033
% Held: 24.4
INDUSTRY: Fire, marine, and casualty insurance (SIC: 6331)
TRANSFER AGENT(S): First Union National Bank, Charlotte, NC

UNIVERSAL CORPORATION

EXCH.	SYM.	REC. PRICE	P/E RATIO	YLD.	MKT. CAP.	RANGE (52-WK.)	'02 Y/E PR.	DIV. ACH.
NYSE	UVV	38.11 (2/28/03)	9.5	3.8%	$1.04 bill.	43.50 - 31.15	36.96	32 yrs.

UPPER MEDIUM GRADE. THE COMPANY INDICATED THAT IT IS PLANNING TO DOWNSIZE ITS TOBACCO OPERATIONS IN ZIMBABWE.

TRADING VOLUME
Thousand Shares

*7 YEAR PRICE SCORE 123.1   *12 MONTH PRICE SCORE 109.2
*NYSE COMPOSITE INDEX=100

INTERIM EARNINGS (Per Share):

Qtr.	Sept.	Dec.	Mar.	June
1997-98	0.63	1.08	1.18	1.10
1998-99	0.78	1.23	0.88	0.91
1999-00	0.93	0.85	1.29	0.69
2000-01	0.89	1.01	1.31	0.87
2001-02	1.04	1.09	1.26	0.61
2002-03	1.09	1.04	...	...

INTERIM DIVIDENDS (Per Share):

Amt.	Decl.	Ex.	Rec.	Pay.
0.34Q	2/07/02	4/04/02	4/08/02	5/13/02
0.34Q	5/01/02	7/03/02	7/08/02	8/12/02
0.34Q	8/01/02	10/10/02	10/15/02	11/12/02
0.36Q	12/05/02	1/09/03	1/13/03	2/10/03
0.36Q	2/06/03	4/10/03	4/14/03	5/12/03

Indicated div.: $1.44 (Div. Reinv. Plan)

CAPITALIZATION (6/30/02):

	($000)	(%)
Long-Term Debt	435,592	40.8
Deferred Income Tax	16,640	1.6
Minority Interest	28,300	2.6
Common & Surplus	587,995	55.0
Total	1,068,527	100.0

BUSINESS:

Universal Corporation is an independent leaf tobacco merchant with additional operations in agri-products and the distribution of lumber and building products. UVV's tobacco business involves selecting, buying, shipping, processing, packing, storing and financing leaf tobacco in the U.S. and other tobacco growing countries for the account of, or for resale to, manufacturers of tobacco products throughout the world. The agri-products operations involve the selecting, buying, shipping, processing, storing, financing, distribution, importing, and exporting of a number of products including tea, rubber, sunflower seeds, nuts, dried fruit, and canned and frozen foods. The lumber and building products operations involve distribution to the building and construction trade in the Netherlands, Belgium and other countries in Europe. In fiscal 2002, contributions to revenues (and operating income) were tobacco, 62.4% (84.5%); lumber and building products, 20.6% (10.3%); and agri-products, 17.0% (5.2%).

RECENT DEVELOPMENTS:

For the quarter ended 12/31/02, net income declined 8.1% to $26.7 million versus $29.1 million in the same period a year earlier. Sales and other operating revenues fell 4.8% to $708.6 million. Tobacco revenues slid 7.2% to $456.0 million and operating income dropped 8.9% to $52.0 million, largely due to lower volumes shipped from Africa. Lumber/building product sales slipped to $140.4 million from $140.6 million the year before; however, operating profits rose 19.5% to $6.9 million, reflecting the continued appreciation of the euro against the U.S. dollar. Agri-products sales of $112.2 million were flat versus the prior year, while operating profits fell 18.3% to $2.6 million.

PROSPECTS:

UVV has indicated that it intends to downsize its tobacco operations in Zimbabwe, where the deteriorating economic situation is expected to contribute to a much smaller tobacco crop. UVV's equity in its net assets of subsidiaries in Zimbabwe was $47.0 million as of 6/30/02. Separately, on 1/16/03, UVV's Dutch subsidiary, N.V. Deli Universal, completed its acquisition of Willemstein's Industriele Ondernemingen B.V. (JeWe), a producer and distributor of lumber and building products to the do-it-yourself market.

ANNUAL FINANCIAL DATA:

FISCAL YEAR	TOT. REVS. ($mill.)	NET INC. ($mill.)	TOT. ASSETS ($mill.)	OPER. PROFIT %	NET PROFIT %	RET. ON EQUITY %	RET. ON ASSETS %	CURR. RATIO	EARN. PER SH.$	CASH FL.PER SH.$	TANG. BK. VAL.$	DIV. PER SH.$	PRICE RANGE	AVG. P/E RATIO	AVG. YIELD %
6/30/02	2,500.1	106.7	1,844.4	8.0	4.3	18.1	5.8	1.6	4.00	6.06	17.64	1.36	43.50 - 31.15	9.3	3.6
6/30/01	3,017.6	⑥112.7	1,782.4	7.9	3.7	20.4	6.3	1.9	⑥4.08	6.12	15.77	1.28	43.37 - 29.75	9.0	3.5
6/30/00	3,402.0	⑤113.8	1,748.1	6.9	3.3	22.9	6.5	1.2	⑤3.77	5.49	13.04	1.24	36.38 - 13.50	6.6	5.0
6/30/99	4,004.9	④127.3	1,823.1	6.4	3.2	23.6	7.0	1.3	④3.80	5.38	12.47	1.20	35.75 - 19.44	7.3	4.3
6/30/98	4,287.2	141.3	2,056.7	6.5	3.3	25.8	6.9	1.3	3.99	5.43	11.71	1.12	49.50 - 31.50	10.2	2.8
6/30/97	4,112.7	100.9	1,982.0	5.8	2.5	21.5	5.1	1.3	2.88	4.35	9.37	1.06	41.69 - 27.88	12.1	3.0
6/30/96	3,570.2	③71.4	1,889.5	5.4	2.0	17.1	3.8	1.3	③2.04	3.54	7.64	1.02	32.75 - 22.25	13.5	3.7
6/30/95	3,280.9	②25.6	1,808.0	3.8	0.8	6.6	1.4	1.3	②0.73	2.12	6.87	1.00	24.63 - 18.88	29.8	4.6
6/30/94	2,975.1	①38.6	1,667.0	3.4	1.3	10.2	2.3	1.4	①1.09	2.35	6.46	0.96	26.25 - 17.50	20.1	4.4
6/30/93	3,047.2	80.2	1,562.0	5.4	2.6	19.2	5.1	1.4	2.39	3.45	7.81	0.88	33.75 - 21.75	11.6	3.2

Statistics are as originally reported. ① Bef. acctg. change chrg. $29.4 mill. & incls. non-recurr. chrg. of $11.8 mill. ② Incl. non-recurr. chrg. of $15.6 mill. ③ Bef. extraord. gain of $900,000. ④ Incl. gain of $16.7 mill. fr. sale of invest. ⑤ Incl. after-tax restruct. chrg.: 2001, $6.0 mill.; 2000, $7.0 mill. ⑥ Incl. pre-tax restruct. costs of $8.7 mill.

OFFICERS:
H. H. Harrell, Chmn.
A. B. King, Pres., C.E.O., C.O.O.
H. H. Roper, V.P., C.F.O.
INVESTOR CONTACT: Karen M. L. Whelan,
V.P., Treas., (804) 254-8689
PRINCIPAL OFFICE: P.O. Box 25099, Richmond, VA 23260

TELEPHONE NUMBER: (804) 359-9311
FAX: (804) 254-3594
WEB: www.universalcorp.com
NO. OF EMPLOYEES: 26,000 (approx.)
SHAREHOLDERS: 2,457
ANNUAL MEETING: In Oct.
INCORPORATED: VA, Jan., 1918

INSTITUTIONAL HOLDINGS:
No. of Institutions: 148
Shares Held: 18,294,359
% Held: 71.1
INDUSTRY: Farm-product raw materials, nec
(SIC: 5159)
TRANSFER AGENT(S): Wells Fargo Shareowner Services, St. Paul, MN

UNIVERSAL HEALTH REALTY INCOME TRUST

EXCH.	SYM.	REC. PRICE	P/E RATIO	YLD.	MKT. CAP.	RANGE (52-WK.)	'02 Y/E PR.	DIV. ACH.
NYSE	UHT	26.36 (2/28/03)	14.4	7.4%	$307.9 mill.	28.50 - 23.03	26.25	15 yrs.

UPPER MEDIUM GRADE. IN 2003, A SIGNIFICANT PORTION OF THE TRUST'S REVENUES ARE LIKELY TO BE DERIVED FROM THE MEDICARE AND MEDICAID PROGRAMS.

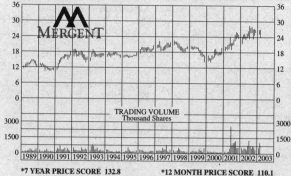

*7 YEAR PRICE SCORE 132.8   ***12 MONTH PRICE SCORE 110.1**

*NYSE COMPOSITE INDEX=100

INTERIM EARNINGS (Per Share):

Qtr.	Mar.	June	Sept.	Dec.
1998	0.40	0.39	0.39	0.42
1999	0.44	0.42	0.25	0.44
2000	0.44	0.42	0.43	0.52
2001	0.46	0.44	0.42	0.43
2002	0.53	0.44	0.43	0.43

INTERIM DIVIDENDS (Per Share):

Amt.	Decl.	Ex.	Rec.	Pay.
0.475Q	12/03/01	12/13/01	12/17/01	12/31/01
0.475Q	3/08/02	3/14/02	3/18/02	3/29/02
0.48Q	6/03/02	6/12/02	6/14/02	6/28/02
0.48Q	9/05/02	9/12/02	9/16/02	9/30/02
0.485Q	12/02/02	12/13/02	12/17/02	12/31/02

Indicated div.: $1.94 (Div. Reinv. Plan)

CAPITALIZATION (12/31/01):

	($000)	(%)
Long-Term Debt	33,432	18.2
Minority Interest	43	0.0
Common & Surplus	150,034	81.8
Total	183,509	100.0

BUSINESS:

Universal Health Realty Income Trust is an organized Maryland real estate investment trust (REIT). As of 12/31/01, the Trust had investments in 42 facilities located in 15 states consisting of investments in healthcare and human service related facilities including acute care hospitals, behavioral healthcare facilities, rehabilitation hospitals, sub-acute care facilities, surgery centers, childcare centers and medical office buildings. Six of the Trust's hospital facilities and three medical office buildings are leased to subsidiaries of Universal Health Services, Inc. As of 12/31/01, Universal Health Services owned 6.6% of the Company's outstanding shares.

RECENT DEVELOPMENTS:

For the twelve months ended 12/31/02, net income advanced 17.8% to $21.6 million compared with $18.3 million the previous year. Results for 2002 included a pre-tax loss of $217,000 on derivatives and a pre-tax gain of $1.2 million from the sale of real property. Results for 2001 included a pre-tax gain of $17,0000 from derivatives. Total revenues rose 3.1% to $28.4 million from $27.6 million a

year before. Base rental revenues grew to $24.3 million from $24.1 million, while bonus rental revenues increased 20.0% to $4.2 million from $3.5 million a year earlier. Equity in income from limited liability companies amounted to $3.7 million in 2002 and $3.6 million in the prior year.

PROSPECTS:

In 2003, a significant portion of the Trust's revenues are likely to be derived from the Medicare and Medicaid programs as well as managed care plans, which include health maintenance organizations and preferred provider organizations. In addition, the Trust anticipates investing in additional healthcare-related facilities and leasing the facilities to qualified operators, perhaps including Universal Health Services, Inc (UHS) and subsidiaries of UHS. Meanwhile, the Trust expects its hospital facilities to continue to experience increased competition and admission constraints.

ANNUAL FINANCIAL DATA:

FISCAL YEAR	TOT. INC. ($000)	NET INC. ($000)	TOT. ASSETS ($000)	NET INC. + DEPR./ ASSETS %	RET. ON EQUITY %	RET. ON ASSETS %	EARN. PER SH.$	TANG. BK. VAL.$	DIV. PER SH.$	DIV. PAYOUT %	PRICE RANGE	AVG. P/E RATIO	AVG. YIELD %
p12/31/02	28,429	④ 21,623	185,117				④ 1.84		1.92	104.3	28.50 - 21.40	13.6	7.7
12/31/01	27,574	④ 18,349	187,904	12.1	12.2	9.8	④ 1.74	12.85	1.88	107.8	26.00 - 18.75	12.9	8.4
12/31/00	27,315	①③ 16,256	183,658	11.3	16.4	8.9	①③ 1.81	11.05	1.84	101.7	19.88 - 14.25	9.4	10.8
12/31/99	23,865	①② 13,972	178,821	10.0	14.0	7.8	①② 1.56	11.09	1.81	116.0	20.50 - 14.25	11.1	10.4
12/31/98	23,234	14,337	169,406	10.8	14.1	8.5	1.76	11.32	1.75	99.7	22.50 - 17.94	11.5	8.7
12/31/97	22,764	13,967	146,755	12.1	13.6	9.5	1.56	11.47	1.71	109.3	22.38 - 18.38	13.1	8.4
12/31/96	21,923	14,158	148,566	12.0	13.6	9.5	1.58	11.62	1.70	107.3	20.63 - 17.38	12.0	8.9
12/31/95	20,417	13,584	132,770	12.8	12.9	10.2	1.52	11.74	1.68	110.5	17.88 - 15.75	11.1	10.0
12/31/94	18,826	14,312	128,907	13.6	13.4	11.1	1.60	11.90	1.67	104.1	18.00 - 15.75	10.5	9.9
12/31/93	18,263	11,888	126,657	11.9	11.1	9.4	1.45	11.96	1.66	114.5	18.88 - 14.38	11.5	9.0

Statistics are as originally reported. ① Incl. a provision of $1.6 mill. for investment losses. ② Incl. pre-tax nonrecurr. chrgs. of $5.3 mill. ③ Incl. a gain on the sale of real prop. to UHS of $1.2 mill., 2002; $1.9 mill., 2000. ④ Incl. a gain on derivatives of $17,000, 2001 & loss derivatives of $217,000, 2002.

OFFICERS:
A. B. Miller, Chmn., C.E.O.
K. E. Gorman, Pres., C.F.O., Sec.

INVESTOR CONTACT: Investor Relations, (610) 265-0688

PRINCIPAL OFFICE: Universal Corporate Center, 367 South Gulph Road, King of Prussia, PA 19406-0958

TELEPHONE NUMBER: (610) 265-0688
FAX: (610) 768-3336
WEB: www.uhrit.com

NO. OF EMPLOYEES: N/A

SHAREHOLDERS: 737 (approx.)

ANNUAL MEETING: In June

INCORPORATED: MD, July, 1986

INSTITUTIONAL HOLDINGS:
No. of Institutions: 77
Shares Held: 3,871,002
% Held: 33.1

INDUSTRY: Real estate investment trusts (SIC: 6798)

TRANSFER AGENT(S): Boston EquiServe, L.P., Boston, MA

UNIVERSAL HEALTH SERVICES, INC.

EXCH.	SYM.	REC. PRICE	P/E RATIO	YLD.	MKT. CAP.	RANGE (52-WK.)	'02 Y/E PR.
NYSE	UHS	38.84 (2/28/03)	14.2	...	$2.33 bill.	57.50 - 32.05	45.10

UPPER MEDIUM GRADE. THE COMPANY SHOULD CONTINUE TO BENEFIT FROM SOLID GROWTH IN PATIENT ADMISSIONS IN 2003.

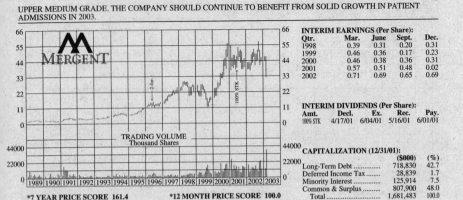

*7 YEAR PRICE SCORE 161.4 ***12 MONTH PRICE SCORE 100.0**

*NYSE COMPOSITE INDEX=100

INTERIM EARNINGS (Per Share):

Qtr.	Mar.	June	Sept.	Dec.
1998	0.39	0.31	0.20	0.31
1999	0.46	0.36	0.17	0.23
2000	0.46	0.38	0.36	0.31
2001	0.57	0.51	0.48	0.02
2002	0.71	0.69	0.65	0.69

INTERIM DIVIDENDS (Per Share):

Amt.	Decl.	Ex.	Rec.	Pay.
100% STK	4/17/01	6/04/01	5/16/01	6/01/01

CAPITALIZATION (12/31/01):

	($000)	(%)
Long-Term Debt	718,830	42.7
Deferred Income Tax	28,839	1.7
Minority Interest	125,914	7.5
Common & Surplus	807,900	48.0
Total	1,681,483	100.0

BUSINESS:

Universal Health Services, Inc. is principally engaged in the ownership and operation of acute care hospitals, behavioral health centers, ambulatory surgery centers, radiation oncology centers and women's centers. As of 12/31/02, UHS operated 72 hospitals, consisting of 34 acute care hospitals, and 38 behavioral health centers in Arkansas, California, Delaware, the District of Columbia, Florida, Georgia, Illinois, Indiana, Kentucky, Louisiana, Massachu-

setts, Michigan, Mississippi, Missouri, Nevada, New Jersey, Oklahoma, Pennsylvania, Puerto Rico, South Carolina, Tennessee, Texas, Utah, Washington and France. UHS, through its Ambulatory Treatment Centers Division, owns outright, or in partnership with physicians, and operates or manages 24 surgery and radiation oncology centers located in 12 states and Puerto Rico.

RECENT DEVELOPMENTS:

For the year ended 12/31/02, net income was $175.4 million compared with income of $100.8 million, before an extraordinary charge of $1.0 million, the previous year. Results for 2002 included a pre-tax credit of $2.2 million for recovery of facility closing costs, while 2001 results included a pre-tax charge of $40.0 million for provision of insurance settlements. Net revenues increased 14.7% to

$3.26 billion from $2.84 billion the year before. The improvement in revenues and earnings were largely due to substantial growth in admissions of patients to the Company's hospitals. Net hospital revenue from acute care services advanced 15.7% to $2.52 billion, while net hospital revenue from behavior health services grew 5.0% to $565.6 million.

PROSPECTS:

The Company should continue to benefit from growth in patient admissions in 2003. Futhermore, the Company will look selectively to acquire hospitals where it believes its skills can improve the quality and viability of the hospital. Meanwhile, the Company's return on capital, defined as net

income divided by the sum of debt plus shareholder's equity, increased to 10.8% from 9.6% in 2001. UHS expects this growth in its return on capital to continue again in 2003 as recent investments in capital expenditures and acquisitions mature.

ANNUAL FINANCIAL DATA:

FISCAL YEAR	TOT. REVS. ($mill.)	NET INC. ($mill.)	TOT. ASSETS ($mill.)	OPER. PROFIT %	NET PROFIT %	RET. ON EQUITY %	RET. ON ASSETS %	CURR. RATIO	EARN. PER SH. $	CASH FL. PER SH. $	TANG. BK. VAL. $	PRICE RANGE	AVG. P/E RATIO
p12/31/02	3,258.9	② 175.4			3.5	12.5	4.8	1.7	② 2.74		7.27	57.50 - 36.90	17.2
12/31/01	2,840.5	③ 100.8	2,114.6	7.8	3.5	12.5	4.8	1.7	③ 1.60	...	7.27	55.00 - 37.25	28.8
12/31/00	2,242.4	① 93.4	1,742.4	8.8	4.2	13.0	5.4	1.9	① 1.51	3.18	6.68	56.47 - 18.06	24.8
12/31/99	2,042.4	77.8	1,498.0	7.9	3.8	12.1	5.2	1.9	① 1.20	2.91	5.96	27.56 - 11.56	16.1
12/31/98	1,874.5	79.6	1,448.1	8.5	4.2	12.7	5.5	1.9	1.20	2.78	5.40	29.88 - 19.22	20.5
12/31/97	1,442.7	67.3	1,085.3	8.7	4.7	12.8	6.2	1.4	1.02	2.24	5.81	25.41 - 13.88	19.3
12/31/96	1,190.2	① 50.7	965.8	8.8	4.3	11.2	5.2	1.4	① 0.82	1.99	4.71	15.38 - 10.81	16.0
12/31/95	931.1	① 35.5	748.1	8.1	3.8	11.9	4.7	1.2	① 0.63	1.54	5.82	11.13 - 5.63	13.3
12/31/94	782.2	① 28.7	521.5	8.0	3.7	11.0	5.5	1.1	① 0.51	1.24	4.02	7.41 - 4.78	12.1
12/31/93	761.5	② 35.1	460.4	6.9	4.6	18.6	9.0	1.2	② 0.43	1.07	3.46	5.31 - 3.16	9.9

Statistics are as originally reported. Adj. for 100% stk. div., 6/01. ① Incl. pre-tax nonrecurr. chrgs. of $40.0 mill., 2001; $7.7 mill, 2000; $5.3 mill., 1999; $4.1 mill., 1996; $11.6 mill., 1995; $9.8 mill., 1994 ② Incl. pre-tax nonrecurr. credit of $2.2 mill., 2002; $8.8 mill., 1993. ③ Bef. extraord. chrg. of $1.0 mill.

OFFICERS:
A. B. Miller, Chmn., Pres., C.E.O.
S. G. Filton, V.P., C.F.O., Contr.
INVESTOR CONTACT: Investor Relations, (610) 768-3300
PRINCIPAL OFFICE: Universal Corporate Center, 367 South Gulph Road, King Of Prussia, PA 19406

TELEPHONE NUMBER: (610) 768-3300
FAX: (610) 768-3336
WEB: www.uhsinc.com
NO. OF EMPLOYEES: 21,200 full-time; 9,100 part-time
SHAREHOLDERS: 752
ANNUAL MEETING: In May
INCORPORATED: DE, Sept., 1978

INSTITUTIONAL HOLDINGS:
No. of Institutions: 254
Shares Held: 49,298,402
% Held: 81.4
INDUSTRY: General medical & surgical hospitals (SIC: 8062)
TRANSFER AGENT(S): Mellon Investor Services, Ridgefield Park, NJ

UNIVISION COMMUNICATIONS INC.

EXCH.	SYM.	REC. PRICE	P/E RATIO	YLD.	MKT. CAP.	RANGE (52-WK.)	'02 Y/E PR.
NYSE	UVN	24.77 (2/28/03)	72.9	..;	$5.19 bill.	47.00 - 16.40	24.50

MEDIUM GRADE. UVN RECENTLY ANNOUNCED THAT THE PROPOSED ACQUISITION OF HISPANIC BROADCAST-ING CORPORATION WAS APPROVED BY SHAREHOLDERS OF BOTH COMPANIES.

MERGENT

TRADING VOLUME
Thousand Shares

*7 YEAR PRICE SCORE N/A   ***12 MONTH PRICE SCORE 91.4**

*NYSE COMPOSITE INDEX=100

INTERIM EARNINGS (Per Share):

Qtr.	Mar.	June	Sept.	Dec.
1997	d0.01	0.12	0.11	0.14
1998	Nil	d0.02	0.02	0.05
1999	0.04	0.09	0.10	0.14
2000	0.09	0.14	0.12	0.15
2001	0.03	0.12	0.04	0.05
2002	0.03	0.09	0.08	0.14

INTERIM DIVIDENDS (Per Share):

Amt.	Decl.	Ex.	Rec.	Pay.
		No dividends paid.		

CAPITALIZATION (12/31/01):

	($000)	(%)
Long-Term Debt	985,509	52.2
Capital Lease Obligations..	84,334	4.5
Deferred Income Tax	5,657	0.3
Common & Surplus	813,280	43.1
Total	1,888,780	100.0

BUSINESS:

Univision Communications Inc. is a major Spanish-language media company. UVN's operations include: Univision Network, a Spanish-language broadcast television network reaching 97.0% of U.S. Hispanic households as of 3/20/03; TeleFutura Network, a 24-hour general-interest Spanish-language broadcast television network reaching 73.0% of U.S. Hispanic households; Univision Television Group, which owns and operates 22 Univision Network television stations and 1 non-Univision television station; TeleFutura Television Group which owns and operates 27 television stations; Galavision, a Spanish-language cable network; Univision Music Group, which includes the Univision Music label, Fonovisa Records, Rudy Perez Enterprises label and a 50.0% interest in Mexican-based Disa Records as well as Fonomusic and America Musical Publishing; and Univision Online, an Internet company.

RECENT DEVELOPMENTS:

For the year ended 12/31/02, net income was $86.5 million compared with income of $54.7 million, before an extraordinary loss of $2.3 million, the year before. Results for 2002 and 2001 included a gain on a change in Entravision ownership interest of $1.9 million and $4.6 million, and equity losses in unconsolidated subsidiaries of $15.9 million and $47.5 million, respectively. Also, results for 2001 included restructuring charges of $11.9 million. Net revenues increased 22.9% to $1.09 billion from $887.9 million a year earlier. Notably, net revenue from the television group grew 17.7% to $1.01 billion from $862.1 million the previous year.

PROSPECTS:

UVN continues to strengthen its operations through strategic developments. For instance, the Company added a second broadcast television network, restructured its cable network, acquired the leading Spanish-language record label and enhanced its Internet offerings in 2002. Also, UVN recently announced the proposed acquisition of Hispanic Broadcasting Corporation, which has been approved by shareholders of both companies and is awaiting approval by the U.S. Department of Justice and the Federal Communication Commission. Separately, UVN expects first quarter earnings of $0.04 to $0.05 per share.

ANNUAL FINANCIAL DATA:

FISCAL YEAR	TOT. REVS. ($mill.)	NET INC. ($mill.)	TOT. ASSETS ($mill.)	OPER. PROFIT %	NET PROFIT %	RET. ON EQUITY %	RET. ON ASSETS %	CURR. RATIO	EARN. PER SH. $	CASH FL. PER SH. $	TANG. BK. VAL. $	PRICE RANGE	AVG. P/E RATIO
p12/31/02	1,091.3	⑦86.5							⑦0.34			47.00 - 16.40	93.2
12/31/01	887.9	⑥54.7	3,163.5	24.4	6.2	6.7	1.7	2.2	⑥0.23	0.59	...	52.25 - 16.30	149.0
12/31/00	863.5	⑤116.9	1,448.3	30.3	13.5	16.8	8.1	0.7	⑤0.57	0.77	0.77	62.69 - 24.00	76.0
12/31/99	693.1	③83.5	974.5	29.5	12.1	16.3	8.6	1.3	③0.36	0.62	...	51.59 - 17.06	96.7
12/31/98	577.1	9.9	938.3	22.7	1.7	2.5	1.1	1.0	0.05	0.32	...	21.00 - 10.53	349.6
12/31/97	459.7	④83.2	967.8	22.7	18.1	24.0	8.6	1.0	④0.71	0.61	...	17.44 - 7.94	17.9
12/31/96	244.9	18.6	884.4	27.4	7.6	7.1	2.1	0.9	③0.16	13.39	...	10.06 - 7.38	54.5
12/31/95	173.1	②d9.4	545.9	25.3	...	...	...	0.4	d2.06	2.15	...	...	...
12/31/94	139.0	①d7.7	565.9	24.4	...	...	...	0.3	...	...	...	...	...
12/31/93	104.7	d27.2	...	8.6	...	...	...	...	...	...	...	...	...

Statistics are as originally reported. Adj. for stk splits: 100% div., 8/00; 2-for-1, 9/98. ① Excl. extraord. loss of $4.3 mill. ② Incl. nonrecurr. exp. of $1.8 mill. ③ Excl. extraord. loss of $8.2 mill., 1996; $2.6 mill., 1999. ④ Incl. nonrecurr. reversal of $1.1 mill. ⑤ Incl. nonrecurr. chrg. of $2.0 mill. ⑥ Excl. extraord. loss of $2.3 mill.; incl. non-recurr. chrgs. totaling $16.6 mill. ⑦ Incl. a gain on a chng. in Entravision ownership interest of $1.9 mill.

OFFICERS:
A. J. Perenchio, Chmn., C.E.O.
H. Cisneros, Pres., C.O.O.
G. W. Blank, Exec. V.P., C.F.O.
INVESTOR CONTACT: Diana Vesgra, (310) 556-7695
PRINCIPAL OFFICE: 1999 Avenue Of The Stars, Suite 3050, Los Angeles, CA 90067

TELEPHONE NUMBER: (310) 556-7676
FAX: (310) 556-3568
WEB: www.univision.net
NO. OF EMPLOYEES: 2,440 (approx.)
SHAREHOLDERS: 191 (Class A approx.)
ANNUAL MEETING: In May
INCORPORATED: DE, April, 1992

INSTITUTIONAL HOLDINGS:
No. of Institutions: 279
Shares Held: 157,535,546
% Held: 68.8
INDUSTRY: Television broadcasting stations (SIC: 4833)
TRANSFER AGENT(S): The Bank of New York, New York, NY

UNOCAL CORPORATION

EXCH.	SYM.	REC. PRICE	P/E RATIO	YLD.	MKT. CAP.	RANGE (52-WK.)	'02 Y/E PR.
NYSE	UCL	26.35 (2/28/03)	19.7	3.0%	$6.43 bill.	39.70 - 25.80	30.58

MEDIUM GRADE. THE COMPANY IS FORECASTING FULL-YEAR 2003 DILUTED EARNINGS OF BETWEEN $2.45 AND $2.75 PER SHARE.

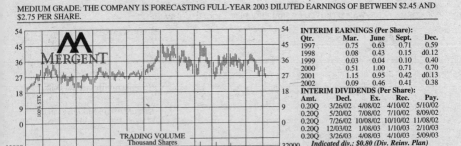

INTERIM EARNINGS (Per Share):

Qtr.	Mar.	June	Sept.	Dec.
1997	0.75	0.63	0.71	0.59
1998	0.08	0.43	0.15	d0.12
1999	0.03	0.04	0.10	0.40
2000	0.51	1.00	0.71	0.70
2001	1.15	0.95	0.42	d0.13
2002	0.09	0.46	0.41	0.38

INTERIM DIVIDENDS (Per Share):

Amt.	Decl.	Ex.	Rec.	Pay.
0.20Q	3/26/02	4/08/02	4/10/02	5/10/02
0.20Q	5/20/02	7/08/02	7/10/02	8/09/02
0.20Q	7/26/02	10/08/02	10/10/02	11/08/02
0.20Q	12/03/02	1/08/03	1/10/03	2/10/03
0.20Q	3/26/03	4/08/03	4/10/03	5/09/03

Indicated div.: $0.80 (Div. Reinv. Plan)

CAPITALIZATION (12/31/01):

	($000)	(%)
Long-Term Debt	2,897,000	38.0
Deferred Income Tax	627,000	8.2
Minority Interest	449,000	5.9
Redeemable Pfd. Stock	522,000	6.9
Common & Surplus	3,124,000	41.0
Total	7,619,001	100.0

*7 YEAR PRICE SCORE 95.9   ***12 MONTH PRICE SCORE 93.1**

NYSE COMPOSITE INDEX=100

BUSINESS:

Unocal Corporation is an independent oil and gas exploration and production company, with principal operations in North America and Asia. UCL's oil and gas exploration, development and production activities are carried out by its North America operations in the U.S. Lower 48 states, Alaska and Canada and by its International operations in about a dozen countries around the world. UCL is also a producer of geothermal energy and a provider of electrical power in Asia. Other activities include ownership in proprietary and common carrier pipelines, natural gas storage facilities and the marketing and trading of hydrocarbon commodities. As of 12/31/02, estimated proved oil and gas reserves were 1.77 billion barrels of oil equivalent.

RECENT DEVELOPMENTS:

For the year ended 12/31/02, earnings from continuing operations were $330.0 million compared with income of $599.0 million, before an accounting change charge of $1.0 million, a year earlier. Results for 2002 and 2001 excluded income of $1.0 million and $17.0 million, respectively. The decline in earnings was mainly attributable to lower North America natural gas production volumes and prices. Revenues declined 22.2% to $5.25 billion from $6.75 billion the previous year. Revenues for 2002 and 2001 included gain on the sales of assets of $42.0 million and $24.0 million, respectively. Earnings from equity investments were $154.0 million versus $144.0 million the year before.

PROSPECTS:

UCL is forecasting full-year 2003 diluted earnings of between $2.45 and $2.75 per share, excluding special items. In addition, UCL expects full-year 2003 production to be at the lower end of its previously disclosed range of 480,000 to 495,000 barrels-of-oil equivalent (BOE) per day. Fourth quarter 2002 net daily production averaged 451,000 BOE per day. The expected increase over 2002 levels reflects the start of new oil production from the West Seno field in Indonesia in the second quarter of 2003.

ANNUAL FINANCIAL DATA:

FISCAL YEAR	TOT. REVS. ($mill.)	NET INC. ($mill.)	TOT. ASSETS ($mill.)	OPER. PROFIT %	NET PROFIT %	RET. ON EQUITY %	RET. ON ASSETS %	CURR. RATIO	EARN. PER SH. $	CASH FL. PER SH. $	TANG. BK. VAL. $	DIV. PER SH. $	PRICE RANGE	AVG. P/E RATIO	AVG. YIELD %
p12/31/02	5,251.0	⑦ 330.0							⑦ 1.34			0.80	39.70 - 26.58	24.7	2.4
12/31/01	6,752.0	⑥ 599.0	10,425.0	14.0	8.9	19.2	5.7	0.9	⑥ 2.43	6.46	12.80	0.80	40.00 - 29.51	14.3	2.3
12/31/00	9,202.0	⑤ 723.0	10,010.0	14.6	7.9	26.6	7.2	1.0	⑤ 2.93	6.62	11.70	0.80	40.13 - 25.00	11.1	2.5
12/31/99	6,057.0	④ 113.0	8,967.0	8.0	1.9	5.2	1.3	1.0	④ 0.46	3.71	9.42	0.80	46.63 - 27.50	80.6	2.2
12/31/98	5,479.0	130.0	7,952.0	9.4	2.4	5.9	1.6	1.0	0.54	4.12	9.14	0.80	42.13 - 28.31	65.2	2.3
12/31/97	6,064.0	①② 669.0	7,530.0	16.3	11.0	28.5	8.9	1.3	①② 2.65	6.23	9.52	0.80	45.88 - 36.13	15.5	2.0
12/31/96	5,328.0	① 456.0	9,123.0	19.7	8.6	19.8	5.0	2.0	① 1.76	6.01	9.18	0.80	42.13 - 27.75	19.8	2.3
12/31/95	8,425.0	260.0	9,891.0	8.9	3.1	8.8	2.6	1.2	0.91	5.04	9.89	0.80	30.50 - 24.75	30.4	2.9
12/31/94	7,965.0	③ 124.0	9,337.0	7.1	1.6	4.4	1.3	1.2	③ 0.36	4.26	9.54	0.80	30.75 - 24.38	76.5	2.9
12/31/93	8,344.0	③ 343.0	9,254.0	11.0	4.1	10.9	3.7	1.3	③ 1.27	5.27	10.96	0.72	32.63 - 23.50	22.1	2.6

Statistics are as originally reported. ① Bef. loss fr. disc. ops. of $50.0 mill. 12/97; $420.0 mill., 12/96. ② Bef. extraord. chrg. $38.0 mill. ③ Bef. acctg. adj. chrg. of $277.0 mill., 12/94; $130.0 mill., 12/93. ④ Bef. inc. fr. disc. ops. $24.0 mill. ⑤ Incls. non-recurr. chrg. of $75.0 mill.; bef. inc. fr. disc. ops. of $37.0 mill. ⑥ Bef. inc. fr. disc. ops. of $17.0 mill. & acctg. chge. credit of $1.0 mill. ⑦ Bef. inc. fr. disc. ops. of $1.0 mill.

OFFICERS:
C. R. Williamson, Chmn., C.E.O.
T. H. Ling, Pres., C.O.O.
T. G. Dallas, Exec. V.P., C.F.O.

INVESTOR CONTACT: Robert E. Wright, V.P., Investor Relations, (310) 726-7665

PRINCIPAL OFFICE: 2141 Rosecrans Avenue, Suite 4000, El Segundo, CA 90245

TELEPHONE NUMBER: (310) 726-7600
FAX: (800) 344-0498
WEB: www.unocal.com

NO. OF EMPLOYEES: 6,980 (approx.)

SHAREHOLDERS: 22,959 (approx.)

ANNUAL MEETING: In May

INCORPORATED: DE, Mar., 1983

INSTITUTIONAL HOLDINGS:
No. of Institutions: 399
Shares Held: 223,387,642
% Held: 86.6

INDUSTRY: Crude petroleum and natural gas (SIC: 1311)

TRANSFER AGENT(S): Mellon Investor Services, L.L.C., Ridgefield Park, NJ

UNUMPROVIDENT CORPORATION

EXCH.	SYM.	REC. PRICE	P/E RATIO	YLD.	MKT. CAP.	RANGE (52-WK.)	'02 Y/E PR.
NYSE	UNM	13.00 (2/28/03)	8.4	4.5%	$3.15 bill.	29.70 - 12.51	17.54

UPPER MEDIUM GRADE. UNM ANNOUNCED IT IS IN DISCUSSIONS WITH THE SEC CONCERNING THE TREATMENT OF ITS BELOW-INVESTMENT-GRADE INVESTMENT LOSSES.

TRADING VOLUME Thousand Shares

*7 YEAR PRICE SCORE N/A   *12 MONTH PRICE SCORE 82.6

*NYSE COMPOSITE INDEX=100

INTERIM EARNINGS (Per Share):

Qtr.	Mar.	June	Sept.	Dec.
1998	0.66	0.70	0.74	0.47
1999	0.37	d0.80	d0.91	0.56
2000	0.56	0.59	0.57	0.62
2001	0.75	0.60	0.52	0.52
2002	0.30	0.40	0.45	0.39

INTERIM DIVIDENDS (Per Share):

Amt.	Decl.	Ex.	Rec.	Pay.
0.147Q	1/14/02	1/24/02	1/28/02	2/15/02
0.147Q	4/08/02	4/25/02	4/29/02	5/17/02
0.147Q	7/03/02	7/25/02	7/29/02	8/16/02
0.147Q	10/07/02	10/24/02	10/28/02	11/15/02
0.147Q	1/13/03	1/23/03	1/27/03	2/21/03

Indicated div.: $0.59 (Div. Reinv. Plan)

CAPITALIZATION (12/31/01):

	($000)	(%)
Long-Term Debt	2,004,200	23.7
Deferred Income Tax	509,900	6.0
Common & Surplus	5,939,900	70.3
Total	8,454,000	100.0

BUSINESS:

UnumProvident Corporation (formerly Unum Corporation), is a holding company for a group of insurance companies that collectively operate throughout North America, the United Kingdom, Japan and elsewhere around the world. The Company was created from the 6/30/99 merger between Unum Corporation and Provident Companies, Inc. UNM's principal operating subsidiaries are Unum Life Insurance Company of America, Provident Life and Accident Insurance Company, The Paul Revere Life Insurance Company, and Colonial Life & Accident Insurance Company. UNM, through its subsidiaries, is the largest provider of group and individual disability insurance in North America and the United Kingdom. UNM also provides a complementary portfolio of life insurance products, including long-term care insurance, life insurance, employer- and employee-paid group benefits, and related services.

RECENT DEVELOPMENTS:

For the year ended 12/31/02, income was $374.1 million, before an accounting change charge of $7.1 million, versus income of $582.1 million, before an extraordinary loss of $2.9 million, the year before. Results for 2002 and 2001 included after-tax net realized investment losses of $239.8 million and $25.5 million, respectively. Results for 2001 included charges of $24.0 million related to the events of 9/11/01, goodwill charges of $5.4 million and a tax benefit gain of $35.2 million. Premium income increased 5.3% to $7.45 billion from $7.08 billion the prior year.

PROSPECTS:

On 1/13/03, UNM's U.K. subsidiary, Unum Limited, announced an agreement to acquire the U.K. group income protection business together with the renewal rights to the group life business of Sun Life Financial. The acquired business covers more than 5,000 policies and is a key step in building UNM's market in the U.K. Looking ahead, UNM will focus on more selected growth opportunities, both from a product and geographic perspective, in order to achieve long-term profitability. Separately, UNM announced that it is in discussions with the SEC relating primarily to its investment disclosures and to the timing and amount of other-than-temporary losses recorded on below-investment-grade securities.

ANNUAL FINANCIAL DATA:

FISCAL YEAR	PREM. INC. ($mill.)	TOT. REVS. ($mill.)	NET INC. ($mill.)	TOT. ASSETS ($mill.)	TOT. INVST. ($mill.)	RET. ON REVS. %	RET. ON EQUITY %	RET. ON ASSETS %	EARN. PER SH.$	TANG. BK. VAL.$	AVG. YIELD %	DIV. PER SH.$	PRICE RANGE	AVG. P/E RATIO
p12/31/02	7,453.1		[6] 374.1						[6] 1.54		2.6	0.59	29.70 - 16.30	14.9
12/31/01	7,078.2	9,394.8	[5] 582.1	42,442.7	28,324.0	6.2	9.8	1.4	2.39	21.74	2.1	0.59	33.75 - 22.25	11.7
12/31/00	7,057.0	9,432.3	564.2	40,363.9	26,604.1	6.0	10.1	1.4	2.33	20.29	2.7	0.59	31.94 - 11.94	9.4
[3] 12/31/99	6,843.2	9,329.6	[4] d182.9	38,447.5	26,549.3	...	...	...	d0.77	17.79	1.3	0.59	62.50 - 26.00	...
12/31/98	3,841.7	4,641.4	363.4	15,182.9	9,837.7	7.8	13.3	2.4	2.57	19.74	1.1	0.58	60.06 - 41.75	19.8
12/31/97	3,188.7	4,076.7	[1] 370.3	13,200.3	8,934.1	9.1	15.2	2.8	2.59	17.61	1.3	0.58	54.25 - 33.63	17.0
12/31/96	3,120.4	4,042.7	238.0	15,467.5	8,724.7	5.9	10.5	1.5	1.63	15.76	1.7	0.55	36.75 - 27.38	19.7
12/31/95	3,018.2	4,122.9	281.1	14,787.8	11,692.5	6.8	12.2	1.9	1.94	15.77	2.2	0.52	28.25 - 18.81	12.2
12/31/94	2,732.4	3,623.7	[1] 154.7	13,127.2	10,433.8	4.3	8.1	1.2	1.05	13.23	2.0	0.46	29.00 - 17.56	22.3
12/31/93	2,474.1	3,397.0	[2] 312.0	12,437.3	10,095.9	9.2	14.8	2.5	[2] 1.98	13.84	1.4	0.38	30.06 - 23.88	13.6

Statistics are as originally reported. Adj. for stk. split: 2-for-1, 6/97 [1] Incl. non-recurr. chrg. 1997, $43.6 mill.; 1994, $134.5 mill. [2] Bef. acctg. change chrg. $12.1 mill. [3] Results through 1st quarter of 1999 are for UNUM Corp. only [4] Incl. pre-tax non-recurr. chrgs. $874.5 mill. [5] Bef. extraord. loss $2.9 mill.; Incl tax benef. of $35.2 mill., after-tax 9/11/01 chrgs. of $15.6 mill. & goodwill chrgs. of $5.4 mill. [6] Bef. acctg. chrg. $7.1 mill.

OFFICERS:
J. H. Chandler, Chmn., Pres., C.E.O.
T. R. Watjen, Vice-Chmn., C.O.O.
R. C. Greving, C.F.O.
INVESTOR CONTACT: Kent M. Mohnkern, V.P. Investor Relations, (207) 770-4330
PRINCIPAL OFFICE: 2211 Congress Street, Portland, ME 04122

TELEPHONE NUMBER: (207) 770-2211
FAX: (207) 770-4450
WEB: www.unum.com
NO. OF EMPLOYEES: 13,100 (approx.)
SHAREHOLDERS: 21,127
ANNUAL MEETING: In May
INCORPORATED: DE, Jan., 1985

INSTITUTIONAL HOLDINGS:
No. of Institutions: 326
Shares Held: 192,841,453
% Held: 79.9
INDUSTRY: Accident and health insurance (SIC: 6321)
TRANSFER AGENT(S): First Chicago Trust Company of New York, Jersey City, NJ

URS CORPORATION

EXCH.	SYM.	REC. PRICE	P/E RATIO	YLD.	MKT. CAP.	RANGE (52-WK.)	'02 Y/E PR.
NYSE	URS	8.89 (2/28/03)	5.1	...	$267.4 mill.	34.80 - 8.01	14.23

MEDIUM GRADE. THE COMPANY EXPECTS FISCAL 2003 EARNINGS TO BE ABOUT $1.75 PER SHARE.

*7 YEAR PRICE SCORE 134.4   *12 MONTH PRICE SCORE 55.7
*NYSE COMPOSITE INDEX=100

INTERIM EARNINGS (Per Share):

Qtr.	Jan.	Apr.	July	Oct.
1997-98	0.27	0.31	0.40	0.45
1998-99	0.35	0.42	0.53	0.68
1999-00	0.40	0.51	0.64	0.72
2000-01	0.42	0.55	0.64	0.80
2001-02	0.52	0.64	0.70	0.21
2002-03	0.18	...	...	...

INTERIM DIVIDENDS (Per Share):

Amt.	Decl.	Ex.	Rec.	Pay.
	No dividends paid.			

CAPITALIZATION (10/31/02):

	($000)	(%)
Long-Term Debt	923,863	57.8
Deferred Income Tax	40,629	2.5
Common & Surplus	633,852	39.7
Total	1,598,344	100.0

BUSINESS:

URS Corporation is an engineering services firm that provides a broad range of planning, design, program and construction management, systems integration and operations and maintenance services. URS provides these services in several markets: transportation, hazardous waste, industrial processing and petrochemical, general building, water/wastewater, military facilities and equipment platforms and security projects. URS offers services to federal, state, and local governmental agencies, as well as to private clients in the chemical, manufacturing, pharmaceutical, forest products, mining, oil and gas, and utilities industries. URS conduct business through principal offices located in more than 20 countries throughout the world.

RECENT DEVELOPMENTS:

For the quarter ended 1/31/03, net income plunged 55.2% to $6.0 million compared with $13.3 million in the equivalent 2002 quarter. Results for 2002 included a non-cash charge of $2.5 million related to the vesting of restricted stock. The decline in earnings was primarily attributed to pricing pressures due to reduced capital spending and cost cutting initiatives by large multinational corporations. Revenues increased 39.6% to $758.0 million from $543.0 million a year earlier. Gross profit advanced 29.3% to $274.2 million from $212.2 million the year before.

PROSPECTS:

As projected, difficult conditions persist for the Company's state and local government market, and its private sector business. Accordingly, URS adjusted its cost structure to match current and anticipated economic conditions. These initiatives are expected to result in cost reductions of about $30.0 million in fiscal 2003. Meanwhile, URS anticipates continued growth in the federal market. Separately, the Company has reached an agreement with its bank lenders to amend certain covenants on its senior secured credit facility for the period from the first quarter of fiscal 2003 through the first quarter of fiscal 2004. Looking ahead, URS expects earnings for fiscal year 2003 to be about $1.75 per share.

ANNUAL FINANCIAL DATA:

FISCAL YEAR	TOT. REVS. ($mill.)	NET INC. ($mill.)	TOT. ASSETS ($mill.)	OPER. PROFIT %	NET PROFIT %	RET. ON EQUITY %	RET. ON ASSETS %	CURR. RATIO	EARN. PER SH. $	CASH FL. PER SH. $	TANG. BK. VAL. $	PRICE RANGE	AVG. P/E RATIO
10/31/02	2,427.8	① 55.2	2,229.1	6.0	2.3	8.7	2.5	1.8	① 2.03	3.18	...	34.80 - 12.51	11.7
10/31/01	2,319.4	57.9	1,463.4	7.3	2.5	17.9	4.0	2.1	2.41	3.94	...	28.05 - 14.44	8.8
10/31/00	2,205.6	49.9	1,427.1	7.4	2.3	19.4	3.5	2.0	2.27	3.94	...	21.81 - 10.75	7.2
10/31/99	1,418.5	36.6	1,437.5	7.1	2.6	17.7	2.5	1.9	1.98	3.63	...	29.56 - 15.50	11.4
10/31/98	805.9	22.7	451.7	6.2	2.8	13.6	5.0	1.8	1.43	2.35	2.41	23.69 - 11.31	12.2
10/31/97	406.5	11.5	212.7	5.9	2.8	14.9	5.4	1.7	1.06	1.79	3.23	19.06 - 9.00	13.2
10/31/96	305.5	7.4	185.6	5.2	2.4	13.0	4.0	1.8	0.82	1.33	1.90	9.88 - 6.25	9.8
10/31/95	179.8	5.1	74.1	4.3	2.8	12.8	6.8	2.6	0.68	0.95	4.42	7.38 - 5.13	9.2
10/31/94	164.1	4.4	65.2	3.7	2.7	13.1	6.8	2.6	0.60	0.82	4.16	8.00 - 4.75	10.6
10/31/93	145.8	1.3	58.1	1.8	0.9	4.4	2.2	2.5	0.18	0.61	3.45	10.13 - 4.38	40.3

Statistics are as originally reported. ① Incl. a one-time, after-tax non-cash charge of $4.6 mill.

OFFICERS:
M. M. Koffel, Chmn., Pres., C.E.O.
K. P. Ainsworth, Exec. V.P., C.F.O., Sec.
D. C. Nelson, V.P., Treas.

INVESTOR CONTACT: Investor Relations,
(415) 774-2700

PRINCIPAL OFFICE: 100 California Street,
Suite 500, San Francisco, CA 94111-4529

TELEPHONE NUMBER: (415) 774-2700
FAX: (415) 398-1905
WEB: www.urscorp.com
NO. OF EMPLOYEES: 25,000 (approx.)
SHAREHOLDERS: 4,791 (approx. record)
ANNUAL MEETING: In Mar.
INCORPORATED: CA, May, 1957; reincorp.,
DE, May, 1976

INSTITUTIONAL HOLDINGS:
No. of Institutions: 103
Shares Held: 20,540,194
% Held: 68.5

INDUSTRY: Engineering services (SIC:
8711)

TRANSFER AGENT(S): Mellon Investor Services LLC, Ridgefield Park, NJ

US AIRWAYS GROUP, INC.

EXCH.	SYM.	REC. PRICE	P/E RATIO	YLD.	MKT. CAP.	RANGE (52-WK.)	'02 Y/E PR.
NYSE	U	0.16 (2/28/03)	...	...	$10.9 mill.	7.60 - 0.10	0.25

SPECULATIVE GRADE. THE COMPANY EXPECTS TO EMERGE FROM CHAPTER 11 BANKRUPTCY BY THE END OF MARCH 2003.

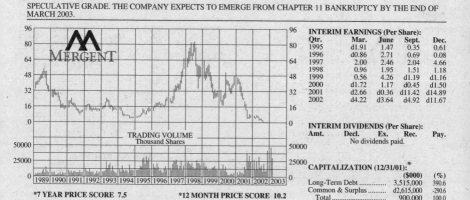

INTERIM EARNINGS (Per Share):

Qtr.	Mar.	June	Sept.	Dec.
1995	d1.91	1.47	0.35	0.61
1996	d0.86	2.71	0.69	0.08
1997	2.00	2.46	2.04	4.66
1998	0.96	1.95	1.51	1.18
1999	0.56	4.26	d1.19	d1.16
2000	d1.72	1.17	d0.45	d1.50
2001	d2.66	d0.36	d11.42	d14.89
2002	d4.22	d3.64	d4.92	d11.67

INTERIM DIVIDENDS (Per Share):

Amt.	Decl.	Ex.	Rec.	Pay.
	No dividends paid.			

TRADING VOLUME
Thousand Shares

*7 YEAR PRICE SCORE 7.5   *12 MONTH PRICE SCORE 10.2
*NYSE COMPOSITE INDEX=100

CAPITALIZATION (12/31/01):

	($000)	(%)
Long-Term Debt	3,515,000	390.6
Common & Surplus	d2,615,000	-290.6
Total	900,000	100.0

BUSINESS:

US Airways Group, Inc. (formerly USAir Group, Inc.) is the holding company for US Airways, which operated 280 aircraft, as of 12/31/02, serving the continental United States, Canada, Mexico, France, Germany, Italy, Spain, Belgium, the United Kingdom and the Caribbean. Major hubs are located in Charlotte, Philadelphia and Pittsburgh.

The Company also owns Allegheny Airlines, Piedmont Airlines, PSA Airlines, and other aviation subsidiaries. On 12/30/97, US Airways purchased Shuttle, Inc., which focuses on commuter travel, with many daily roundtrips from New York to Boston and Washington D.C. US Airways also launched a low-fare carrier, MetroJet, on 6/1/98.

RECENT DEVELOPMENTS:

For the year ended 12/31/02, net loss totaled $1.66 billion, before a $17.0 million accounting change gain, versus a loss of $2.12 billion, before a $7.0 million accounting change gain, the year before. Results included one-time after-tax net charges of $613.0 million and $951.0 million in 2002 and 2001, respectively. Total operating revenues slid 15.8% to $6.98 billion from $8.29 billion a year earlier. Passenger transportation revenues declined 19.0% to $5.80

billion, while cargo and freight revenues were down 14.6% to $140.0 million. Operating loss was $1.32 billion compared with an operating loss of $1.68 billion the previous year. US Airways' passenger load factor, or percentage of seats filled, increased to 71.0% from 68.9% in 2001. During 2002, 47.2 million passengers were carried, down 16.0% versus 56.1 million in the prior year.

PROSPECTS:

Near-term prospects appear bleak due to weak passenger demand, rising fuel prices, and the threat of war with Iraq. Meanwhile, the Company expects to emerge from Chapter 11 bankruptcy by the end of March 2003, subject to creditor approval of the Company's plan of reorginization.

Going forward, the Company's efforts to renegotiate labor contracts with employees, as well as contract terms with aircraft lessors and other vendors, are expected to generate average annual cost savings of approximately $1.90 billion over the next seven years.

ANNUAL FINANCIAL DATA:

FISCAL YEAR	TOT. REVS. ($mill.)	NET INC. ($mill.)	TOT. ASSETS ($mill.)	OPER. PROFIT %	NET PROFIT %	RET. ON EQUITY %	RET. ON ASSETS %	CURR. RATIO	EARN. PER SH.$	CASH FL. PER SH.$	PRICE RANGE	AVG. P/E RATIO
p12/31/02	6,977.0	⑥ d1,663.0		...	...	...	...		⑥ d24.45		7.60 - 0.10	...
12/31/01	8,288.0	⑤ d2,124.0	8,025.0	...	...	...	...	0.6	⑤ d31.59	d26.48	46.44 - 3.95	...
12/31/00	9,269.0	④ d166.0	9,127.0	...	...	...	...	0.9	④ d2.47	2.39	51.50 - 17.44	...
12/31/99	8,595.0	② 197.0	7,685.0	1.6	2.3	90.7	2.6	0.8	② 2.64	7.59	64.00 - 24.13	16.7
12/31/98	8,688.0	538.0	7,870.0	11.7	6.2	141.3	6.8	1.0	5.60	8.54	83.25 - 34.75	10.5
12/31/97	8,513.8	① 1,024.7	8,372.4	6.9	12.0	141.3	12.2	1.1	① 9.87	12.93	65.75 - 19.25	4.3
12/31/96	8,142.0	③ 263.0	7,531.4	5.4	3.2	...	3.5	0.8	③ 2.69	7.23	25.88 - 11.75	7.0
12/31/95	7,474.3	② 119.3	6,955.0	4.3	1.6	...	1.7	0.6	② 0.55	5.75	15.88 - 4.25	18.3
12/31/94	6,997.2	② d684.9	6,808.0	...	...	...	...	0.5	② d12.73	d6.37	15.38 - 3.88	...
12/31/93	7,083.2	① d349.4	6,877.9	...	...	...	...	0.5	① d7.68	d2.12	24.75 - 11.13	...

Statistics are as originally reported. ① Bef. $43.7 mil ($0.82/sh) chg. for acctg. adj. & incl. $112.5 mil chg. for empl. reduction. ② Incl. $181.0 mil non-recur. after-tax gain, 1999; $394.9 mil net gain, 1997; $4.1 mil non-recur. gain, 1995; & $226.1 mil chg., 1994. ③ Incl. approx. $163.1 mil in expenses & a $29.5 mil non-recur. gain. ④ Bef. $103.0 mil ($1.55/sh.) acctg. chg. ⑤ Bef. $7.0 mil ($0.11/sh) acctg. cr., incl. $810.0 mil special chg., $50.0 mil gain fr. term. of merger agree. with UAL Corp. & $320.0 mil gain fr. airline stabilization grant. ⑥ Bef. $17.0 mil ($0.25/sh) acctg. cr. & incl. $613.0 mil non-recur. after-tax chg.

OFFICERS:
S. M. Wolf, Chmn.
D. N. Siegel, Pres., C.E.O.
T. A. Mutryn, Sr. V.P., C.F.O.
INVESTOR CONTACT: Investor Relations, (703) 872-5305
PRINCIPAL OFFICE: 2345 Crystal Drive, Arlington, VA 22227

TELEPHONE NUMBER: (703) 872-7000
FAX: (703) 418-7098
WEB: www.usairways.com
NO. OF EMPLOYEES: 30,585
SHAREHOLDERS: 23,500 (approx.)
ANNUAL MEETING: In May
INCORPORATED: DE, Feb., 1983

INSTITUTIONAL HOLDINGS:
No. of Institutions: 16
Shares Held: 1,811,600
% Held: 2.7
INDUSTRY: Air transportation, scheduled (SIC: 4512)
TRANSFER AGENT(S): The Bank of New York, New York, NY

UST, INC.

EXCH.	SYM.	REC. PRICE	P/E RATIO	YLD.	MKT. CAP.	RANGE (52-WK.)	'02 Y/E PR.
NYSE	UST	28.83 (2/28/03)	...	6.9%	$5.86 bill.	41.35 - 25.30	33.43

INVESTMENT GRADE. THE COMPANY IS FORECASTING FULL-YEAR 2003 EARNINGS OF $2.99 PER DILUTED SHARE.

INTERIM EARNINGS (Per Share):

Qtr.	Mar.	June	Sept.	Dec.
1997	0.55	0.64	0.62	0.57
1998	0.60	0.64	0.63	0.57
1999	0.60	0.70	0.69	0.70
2000	0.62	0.69	0.69	0.70
2001	0.66	0.74	0.75	0.82
2002	0.61	0.80	0.77	d3.82

INTERIM DIVIDENDS (Per Share):

Amt.	Decl.	Ex.	Rec.	Pay.
0.48Q	2/21/02	3/12/02	3/14/02	3/29/02
0.48Q	5/07/02	6/12/02	6/14/02	6/28/02
0.48Q	7/29/02	9/12/02	9/16/02	9/30/02
0.48Q	10/24/02	12/12/02	12/16/02	12/31/02
0.50Q	2/20/03	3/13/03	3/17/03	3/31/03

Indicated div.: $2.00 (Div. Reinv. Plan)

*7 YEAR PRICE SCORE 119.9   *12 MONTH PRICE SCORE 102.0
*NYSE COMPOSITE INDEX=100

CAPITALIZATION (12/31/01):

	($000)	(%)
Long-Term Debt	862,575	53.0
Deferred Income Tax	183,524	11.3
Common & Surplus	581,062	35.7
Total	1,627,161	100.0

BUSINESS:

UST, Inc. is a holding company, and through its subsidiaries is a manufacturer and marketer of smokeless tobacco products with COPENHAGEN, COPENHAGEN LONG CUT, SKOAL, SKOAL LONG CUT, SKOAL BANDITS, ROOSTER, RED SEAL, BRUTON and CC as principal brands. Other consumer products made and marketed by UST subsidiaries include premium wines sold nationally under the CHA-TEAU STE. MICHELLE, COLUMBIA CREST, VILLA MT. EDEN and CONN CREEK labels, as well as sparkling wine produced under the DOMAINE STE. MICHELLE label and premium cigars including DON TOMAS and ASTRAL. Sales (operating profit) for 2001 were derived: Smokeless Tobacco, 86.9% (98.5%); Wine, 11.3% (2.6%); and Other, 1.8% (-1.1%).

RECENT DEVELOPMENTS:

For the year ended 12/31/02, UST posted a net loss of $271.5 million compared with net earnings of $491.6 million the previous year. Results for 2002 included a pre-tax litigation charge of $1.26 billion. Net sales increased 3.5% to $1.68 billion from $1.63 billion a year earlier. UST noted that the 2002 results reflected one less billing day in the smokeless tobacco segment compared with the corresponding 2001 period. On an equivalent billing day basis, consolidated net sales would have increased 5.2% versus the prior year. Moist smokeless tobacco net can sales declined 2.0% to 635.8 million cans. On an equivalent billing day basis, net can sales would have decreased 0.2%. Operating income of $862.3 million was 3.5% higher than the year before.

PROSPECTS:

UST's prospects remain solid. For full-year 2003, the Company is forecasting diluted earnings per share of $2.99, with upside potential of $3.07 if volume trends in moist smokeless tobacco and wine accelerate above expectations. UST noted that this forecast includes a significant increase in pension expense, due to a lower-than-expected return on plan assets in 2002. In addition, the Company's net interest expense is expected to climb due to the debt issuance in July 2002 and the loss of interest income on the restricted deposit in place for the Company's antitrust litigation.

ANNUAL FINANCIAL DATA:

FISCAL YEAR	TOT. REVS. ($mill.)	NET INC. ($mill.)	TOT. ASSETS ($mill.)	OPER. PROFIT %	NET PROFIT %	RET. ON EQUITY %	RET. ON ASSETS %	CURR. RATIO	EARN. PER SH.$	CASH FL. PER SH.$	TANG. BK. VAL.$	DIV. PER SH.$	PRICE RANGE	AVG. P/E RATIO	AVG. YIELD %
p12/31/02	1,682.9	⑤d271.5							⑤d1.61			1.92	41.35 - 25.30	...	5.8
12/31/01	1,670.3	491.6	2,011.7	49.9	29.4	84.6	24.4	4.0	2.97	3.23	2.86	1.84	36.00 - 23.38	10.0	6.2
12/31/00	1,547.6	441.9	1,646.4	48.6	28.6	163.3	26.8	4.1	2.70	2.94	1.32	1.76	28.88 - 13.88	7.9	8.2
12/31/99	1,512.3	③469.3	1,015.6	51.3	31.0	233.7	46.2	2.2	③2.68	2.89	0.96	1.68	34.94 - 24.06	11.0	5.7
12/31/98	1,423.2	④455.3	913.3	51.6	32.0	97.2	49.8	2.6	④2.44	2.61	2.25	1.62	36.88 - 24.56	12.6	5.3
12/31/97	1,401.7	①439.1	826.7	50.2	31.3	100.3	53.1	2.7	①2.37	2.53	2.37	1.62	36.31 - 25.50	13.0	5.2
12/31/96	1,371.7	464.0	807.4	54.3	33.8	164.5	57.5	1.5	2.48	2.63	1.53	1.48	35.88 - 28.25	12.9	4.6
12/31/95	1,325.4	429.8	784.8	53.4	32.4	146.4	54.8	1.5	2.16	2.30	1.63	1.30	36.00 - 26.50	14.5	4.2
12/31/94	1,223.0	387.4	741.2	52.4	31.7	107.1	52.3	2.4	1.87	2.00	1.84	1.12	31.50 - 23.63	14.7	4.1
12/31/93	1,110.4	②368.9	706.2	50.9	33.2	79.7	52.2	3.1	②1.71	1.83	2.30	0.96	32.75 - 24.38	16.7	3.4

Statistics are as originally reported. ① Incl. non-recurr. chrg. of $5.0 mill. ② Bef. acctg. change chrg. $19.9 mill. ($0.09/sh.) & non-recurr. credit of $22.0 mill. ③ Incl. net chrg. of $9.4 mill. ④ Incl. net chrg. of $31.7 mill. ⑤ Incl. pre-tax litigation charge of $1.26 bill.

OFFICERS:
V. A. Gierer, Jr., Chmn., Pres., C.E.O.
R. T. D'Alessandro, Sr. V.P., C.F.O.
R. H. Verheij, Exec. V.P., Gen. Couns.

INVESTOR CONTACT: Investor Relations,
(800) 730-4001

PRINCIPAL OFFICE: 100 West Putnam Avenue, Greenwich, CT 06830

TELEPHONE NUMBER: (203) 661-1100
FAX: (203) 661-1129
WEB: www.ustinc.com

NO. OF EMPLOYEES: 4,855 (avg.)

SHAREHOLDERS: 7,800 (approx.)

ANNUAL MEETING: In May

INCORPORATED: DE, Dec., 1986

INSTITUTIONAL HOLDINGS:
No. of Institutions: 292
Shares Held: 124,277,529
% Held: 73.6

INDUSTRY: Chewing and smoking tobacco
(SIC: 2131)

TRANSFER AGENT(S): EquiServe Trust
Company, N.A., Providence, RI

VALASSIS

EXCH.	SYM.	REC. PRICE	P/E RATIO	YLD.	MKT. CAP.	RANGE (52-WK.)	'02 Y/E PR.
NYSE	VCI	22.78 (2/28/03)	12.9	...	$1.22 bill.	41.28 - 21.45	29.43

LOWER MEDIUM GRADE. VCI ACQUIRED NCH MARKETING SERVICES, INC., A COUPON PROCESSING AND PROMOTION INFORMATION MANAGEMENT COMPANY, IN A TRANSACTION VALUED AT $60.0 MILLION.

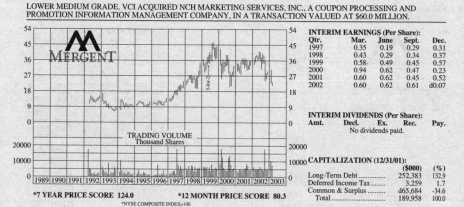

INTERIM EARNINGS (Per Share):

Qtr.	Mar.	June	Sept.	Dec.
1997	0.35	0.19	0.29	0.31
1998	0.43	0.29	0.34	0.37
1999	0.58	0.49	0.45	0.57
2000	0.94	0.62	0.47	0.23
2001	0.60	0.62	0.45	0.52
2002	0.60	0.62	0.61	d0.07

INTERIM DIVIDENDS (Per Share):

Amt.	Decl.	Ex.	Rec.	Pay.
		No dividends paid.		

CAPITALIZATION (12/31/01):

	($000)	(%)
Long-Term Debt	252,383	132.9
Deferred Income Tax	3,259	1.7
Common & Surplus	d65,684	-34.6
Total	189,958	100.0

*7 YEAR PRICE SCORE 124.0   ***12 MONTH PRICE SCORE 80.3**
*NYSE COMPOSITE INDEX=100

BUSINESS:

Valassis (formerly Valassis Communications, Inc.) provides a wide range of marketing services to consumer packaged goods manufacturers, retailers, technology companies and other customers with operations in the U.S, Europe, Mexico and Canada. VCI generates most of its revenues by printing and publishing cents-off coupons and other consumer purchase incentives primarily for packaged goods manufacturers. VCI also prints and publishes refund offers, premiums, sweepstakes and contests distributed to households throughout the U.S. The Company operates printing and manufacturing facilities in Michigan, North Carolina, Kansas and Mexico.

RECENT DEVELOPMENTS:

For the year ended 12/31/02, the Company reported net earnings of $95.3 million compared with earnings of $119.1 million, before an extraordinary loss of $1.3 million, the year before. Results for 2002 and 2001 included goodwill impairment charges and an investment write-down of $55.3 million and $6.1 million, respectively. Total revenue increased to $853.0 million from $849.5 million the year before. Interest expense decreased 24.6% to $13.3 million from $17.7 million in the prior year. Selling, general and administrative expenses grew 6.2% to $94.7 million. Earnings before taxes were $149.2 million versus $187.7 million a year earlier.

PROSPECTS:

On 2/13/03, the Company announced that it acquired Deerfield, Illinois-based NCH Marketing Services, Inc., a premier coupon processing and promotion information management company in the U.S. and worldwide, in a transaction valued at $60.0 million. The acquisition is expected to have a positive impact on earnings per share of about $0.07, with NCH generating an anticipated $60.0 million in revenue, in 2003. Looking ahead, VCI expects earnings per share of $0.48 to $0.54 in the first quarter, $0.55 to $0.61 in the second quarter, $0.50 to $0.56 in the third quarter and $0.54 to $0.60 in the fourth quarter of 2003. Additionally, free cash flow is anticipated to range from $105.0 million to $115.0 million in 2003.

ANNUAL FINANCIAL DATA:

FISCAL YEAR	TOT. REVS. ($000)	NET INC. ($000)	TOT. ASSETS ($000)	OPER. PROFIT %	NET PROFIT %	RET. ON ASSETS %	CURR. RATIO	EARN. PER SH. $	CASH FL. PER SH. $	PRICE RANGE	AVG. P/E RATIO
p12/31/02	853,019	④ 95,254	386,079					④ 1.77		41.28 - 24.00	18.4
12/31/01	849,529	②③ 119,144	363,025	24.2	14.0	32.8	1.1	②③ 2.17	2.44	37.35 - 28.00	15.1
12/31/00	863,121	③ 125,699	325,717	26.1	14.6	38.6	1.0	③ 2.27	2.47	42.63 - 20.50	13.9
12/31/99	794,566	② 121,134	247,205	27.0	15.2	49.0	0.8	② 2.09	2.31	46.50 - 29.04	18.1
12/31/98	741,383	② 84,286	232,014	23.1	11.4	36.3	0.9	② 1.42	1.69	34.50 - 19.42	19.0
12/31/97	675,496	69,930	240,885	22.7	10.4	29.0	1.0	1.13	1.38	23.92 - 12.00	15.9
12/31/96	659,108	42,902	273,734	16.8	6.5	15.7	1.1	0.67	...	14.08 - 9.75	17.9
12/31/95	613,752	① 9,574	258,932	10.3	1.6	3.7	1.0	① 0.15	0.44	12.42 - 9.08	73.1
12/31/94	279,034	② 1,923	234,330	8.5	0.7	0.8	0.8	② 0.03	0.18	13.17 - 7.00	372.1
6/30/94	542,609	5,173	239,709	6.7	1.0	2.2	0.9	0.08	0.45	13.17 - 7.00	125.9

Statistics are as originally reported. Adj. for 3-for-2 stk. split, 5/99. ① Incl. gain of $16.9 mill. from the sale of a business. ② Bef. extraord. loss of $1.3 mill. 2001; $6.9 mill. 1999; $13.6 mill. 1998; $4.2 mill. 1994. ③ Incl. a loss on investments & reserves against impaired assets of $10.1 mill. 2001; $25.9 mill. 2000. ④ Incl. goodwill impairment chrgs. & invest. write-down of $55.3 mill.

OFFICERS:
A. F. Schultz, Chmn., Pres., C.E.O.
R. L. Recchia, Exec. V.P., C.F.O.

INVESTOR CONTACT: Lynn Liddle, V.P.-Inv. & Public Rel., (734) 591-7374

PRINCIPAL OFFICE: 19975 Victor Parkway, Livonia, MI 48152

TELEPHONE NUMBER: (734) 591-3000
FAX: (734) 591-4994
WEB: www.valassis.com

NO. OF EMPLOYEES: 1,265 (approx.)

SHAREHOLDERS: 255 (approx.)

ANNUAL MEETING: In May

INCORPORATED: DE, Oct., 1986

INSTITUTIONAL HOLDINGS:
No. of Institutions: 170
Shares Held: 50,585,601
% Held: 96.2

INDUSTRY: Advertising, nec (SIC: 7319)

TRANSFER AGENT(S): American Stock Transfers & Trust Company, New York, NY

VALERO ENERGY CORPORATION

EXCH.	SYM.	REC. PRICE	P/E RATIO	YLD.	MKT. CAP.	RANGE (52-WK.)	'02 Y/E PR.
NYSE	VLO	39.01 (2/28/03)	48.2	1.0%	$4.06 bill.	49.97 - 23.15	36.94

MEDIUM GRADE. THE COMPANY ANNOUNCED AGREEMENTS TO SELL STORAGE TANKS, A PIPELINE SYSTEM AND COMMON UNITS TO VALERO L.P.

INTERIM EARNINGS (Per Share):

Qtr.	Mar.	June	Sept.	Dec.
1998	d0.11	0.70	0.08	d1.53
1999	d0.05	d0.39	0.40	0.29
2000	0.54	1.51	2.01	1.47
2001	2.13	4.23	1.58	0.82
2002	d0.37	0.10	0.27	0.81

INTERIM DIVIDENDS (Per Share):

Amt.	Decl.	Ex.	Rec.	Pay.
0.10Q	1/17/02	2/11/02	2/13/02	3/13/02
0.10Q	5/09/02	5/23/02	5/28/02	6/12/02
0.10Q	7/18/02	8/12/02	8/14/02	9/11/02
0.10Q	10/18/02	11/08/02	11/13/02	12/11/02
0.10Q	1/24/03	2/10/03	2/12/03	3/12/03

Indicated div.: $0.40

CAPITALIZATION (12/31/01):

	($000)	(%)
Long-Term Debt	2,517,398	28.3
Capital Lease Obligations..	287,849	3.2
Deferred Income Tax	1,388,123	15.6
Minority Interest	115,608	1.3
Redeemable Pfd. Stock	372,500	4.2
Common & Surplus	4,202,563	47.3
Total	8,884,041	100.0

*7 YEAR PRICE SCORE 124.5   ***12 MONTH PRICE SCORE 107.1**

*NYSE COMPOSITE INDEX=100

BUSINESS:

Valero Energy Corporation is an independent petroleum refining and marketing company. As of 3/7/03, VLO owned and operated 12 refineries in the U.S. and Canada with a combined throughput capacity of approximately 2.0 million barrels per day. Operations are involved in the production of premium petroleum products such as reformulated gasoline, low-sulfur diesel and oxygenates, and gasoline meeting specifications of the California Air Resources Board, or CARB gasoline. VLO also produces distillates, jet fuel, asphalt and petrochemicals. In addition, the Company is engaged in the retailing of petroleum products. As of 3/7/03, VLO operated about 4,200 retail outlets in the U.S. and Canada under various names including Diamond Shamrock™, Ultramar™, Valero™, Beacon™ and Total™. On 5/15/00, VLO acquired the Benicia Refinery and certain Exxon-branded supplier relationships for about $1.05 billion. On 12/31/01, VLO completed its acquisition of Ultramar Diamond Shamrock Corporation.

RECENT DEVELOPMENTS:

For the year ended 12/31/02, net income fell 83.8% to $91.5 million compared with $563.6 million a year earlier. Earnings were pressured by a 33.7% drop in refining throughput margin per barrel to $4.06, due in part to weak discounts for sour crude oil, VLO's primary feedstock. Operating revenues leapt 80.0% to $26.98 billion, reflecting the 12/31/01 acquisition of Ultramar Diamond Shamrock. Operating income slid 53.0% to $470.9 million.

PROSPECTS:

VLO's near-term prospects appear solid, reflecting recent significant improvement in refined product margins across all of the geographic regions in which the Company operates. Separately, on 3/7/03, VLO announced that it has entered into agreements with Valero L.P. to sell 58 crude oil and intermediate feedstock storage tanks and related assets for $200.0 million in cash. Additionally, VLO has entered into an agreement with Valero L.P. to sell its South Texas pipeline system and related terminals for $150.0 million. VLO also announced that it plans to sell a sufficient number of common units to Valero L.P. to reduce its aggregate ownership interest in the partnership from 73.6% to 49.5% or less. VLO noted that this transaction will deconsolidate Valero L.P. from its financial statements.

ANNUAL FINANCIAL DATA:

FISCAL YEAR	TOT. REVS. ($mill.)	NET INC. ($mill.)	TOT. ASSETS ($mill.)	OPER. PROFIT %	NET PROFIT %	RET. ON EQUITY %	RET. ON ASSETS %	CURR. RATIO	EARN. PER SH.$	CASH FL. PER SH.$	TANG. BK. VAL.$	DIV. PER SH.$	PRICE RANGE	AVG. P/E RATIO	AVG. YIELD %
p12/31/02	⑤ 26,976.2	91.5							0.83			0.40	49.97 - 23.15	44.0	1.1
12/31/01	14,988.3	563.6	⑤ 14,377.1	6.7	3.8	13.4	3.9	0.9	8.83	12.79	15.60	0.34	52.60 - 31.50	4.8	0.8
④ 12/31/00	14,671.1	339.1	4,307.7	4.2	2.3	22.2	7.9	1.2	5.60	8.46	25.10	0.32	38.63 - 18.50	5.1	1.1
12/31/99	7,961.2	14.3	2,979.0	0.9	0.2	1.3	0.5	1.2	0.25	2.70	19.35	0.32	25.31 - 16.69	84.0	1.5
12/31/98	5,539.3	③ d47.3	2,725.7	...	...	...	...	1.3	③ d0.84	1.41	19.40	0.32	36.50 - 17.63	...	1.2
12/31/97	5,756.2	① 111.8	2,493.0	3.7	1.9	9.6	4.5	1.3	① 2.03	3.62	20.64	0.42	43.00 - 26.94	17.2	1.2
12/31/96	4,990.7	72.7	3,149.6	4.0	1.5	6.7	2.3	1.0	1.40	4.55	24.49	0.52	30.00 - 20.25	17.9	2.1
12/31/95	3,019.8	59.8	2,879.7	6.3	2.0	5.8	2.1	1.3	1.10	4.20	23.56	0.52	25.88 - 16.00	19.0	2.5
12/31/94	1,837.4	26.9	2,858.8	6.9	1.5	2.7	0.9	1.2	0.40	2.82	23.21	0.52	24.13 - 16.50	50.8	2.6
12/31/93	1,222.2	② 36.4	1,796.4	6.2	3.0	4.3	2.1	1.5	② 0.82	2.66	19.48	0.46	26.13 - 19.63	27.9	2.3

Statistics are as originally reported. ① Bef. disc. ops. loss of $15.7 mill. ② Incls. non-recurr. chrg. of $12.9 mill. ③ Incls. pre-tax chrg. of $170.9 mill. ④ Incls. results from the Benicia refinery & retail assets that were acq. from ExxonMobil on 5/15/00. ⑤ Refl. 12/31/01 acq. of Ultramar Diamond Shamrock Corporation.

OFFICERS:
W. E. Greehey, Chmn., C.E.O.
G. C. King, Pres.
D. Gibbons, Exec. V.P., C.F.O.
INVESTOR CONTACT: Lee Bailey, V.P., Inv. Rel., (210) 370-2139
PRINCIPAL OFFICE: One Valero Place, San Antonio, TX 78212-0500

TELEPHONE NUMBER: (210) 370-2000
FAX: (210) 246-2646
WEB: www.valero.com
NO. OF EMPLOYEES: 22,452 (avg.)
SHAREHOLDERS: 7,265 (record)
ANNUAL MEETING: In May
INCORPORATED: DE, Nov., 1955

INSTITUTIONAL HOLDINGS:
No. of Institutions: 288
Shares Held: 88,136,646
% Held: 82.7

INDUSTRY: Petroleum refining (SIC: 2911)

TRANSFER AGENT(S): Computershare Investor Services, Chicago, IL

VALHI, INC.

EXCH.	SYM.	REC. PRICE	P/E RATIO	YLD.	MKT. CAP.	RANGE (52-WK.)	'02 Y/E PR.
NYSE	VHI	10.61 (2/28/03)	1061.0	2.3%	$1.22 bill.	19.30 - 7.35	8.30

LOWER MEDIUM GRADE. THE COMPANY ACQUIRED THE REMAINING INTEREST IN TREMONT CORPORATION THAT IT DID NOT ALREADY OWN.

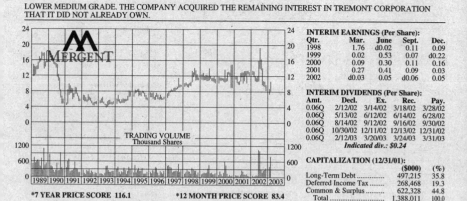

*7 YEAR PRICE SCORE 116.1   ***12 MONTH PRICE SCORE 83.4**

*NYSE COMPOSITE INDEX=100

INTERIM EARNINGS (Per Share):

Qtr.	Mar.	June	Sept.	Dec.
1998	1.76	d0.02	0.11	0.09
1999	0.02	0.53	0.07	d0.22
2000	0.09	0.30	0.11	0.16
2001	0.27	0.41	0.09	0.03
2002	d0.03	0.05	d0.06	0.05

INTERIM DIVIDENDS (Per Share):

Amt.	Decl.	Ex.	Rec.	Pay.
0.06Q	2/12/02	3/14/02	3/18/02	3/28/02
0.06Q	5/13/02	6/12/02	6/14/02	6/28/02
0.06Q	8/14/02	9/12/02	9/16/02	9/30/02
0.06Q	10/30/02	12/11/02	12/13/02	12/31/02
0.06Q	2/12/03	3/20/03	3/24/03	3/31/03

Indicated div.: $0.24

CAPITALIZATION (12/31/01):

	($000)	(%)
Long-Term Debt	497,215	35.8
Deferred Income Tax	268,468	19.3
Common & Surplus	622,328	44.8
Total	1,388,011	100.0

BUSINESS:

Valhi, Inc. is a holding company that has operations in the chemicals, component products, titanium metals and waste management industries. VHI's diverse product offerings include titanium dioxide pigments, components for office furniture and other products, and various titanium products. As of 12/31/02, VHI owned 63.0% of NL Industries Inc., a worldwide producer of titanium dioxide; 90.0% of Waste Control Specialists; 69.0% of CompX International Inc., a components products company; and 100.0% of Tremont Corporation, a holding company that owns 21.0% of NL Industries Inc. and 39.0% of Titanium Metals Corp. As of 12/31/02, Contran Corp. owned about 93.0% of VHI.

RECENT DEVELOPMENTS:

For the year ended 12/31/02, net income dropped 98.7% to $1.2 million compared with $93.2 million in 2001. Results for 2002 and 2001 included net legal settlement gains of $5.2 million and $31.9 million, and securities transaction gains of $6.4 million and $47.0 million, respectively. Results for 2002 also included a foreign currency translation gain of $6.3 million, and a gain on the disposal of fixed assets of $1.6 million. Results for 2001 included an insurance gain of $16.2 million and a gain on the sale/leaseback of land of $2.2 million. Net sales grew 1.9% to $1.08 billion from $1.06 billion a year earlier. Operating income decreased 42.4% to $81.9 million compared with $142.2 million the year before, due in part to lower average selling prices for titanium dioxide pigments.

PROSPECTS:

On 2/7/03, the Company completed the acquisition of the outstanding shares of Tremont Corporation that it did not currently own in a stock-for-stock transaction. Under the terms of the agreement, shareholders of Tremont received 3.4 shares of VHI common stock for each share held, plus cash for any fractional shares. Separately, CompX plans to consolidate two of its facilities into one facility by the end of the second quarter of 2003. This initiative is a direct result of weak market conditions in the office furniture market.

ANNUAL FINANCIAL DATA:

FISCAL YEAR	TOT. REVS. ($mill.)	NET INC. ($mill.)	TOT. ASSETS ($mill.)	OPER. PROFIT %	NET PROFIT %	RET. ON EQUITY %	RET. ON ASSETS %	CURR. RATIO	EARN. PER SH.$	CASH FL. PER SH.$	TANG. BK. VAL.$	DIV. PER SH.$	PRICE RANGE		AVG. P/E RATIO	AVG. YIELD %
p12/31/02	1,079.7	⑨ 1.2							⑨ 0.01			0.24	19.30 -	8.25	N.M.	1.7
12/31/01	1,213.5	⑧ 93.2	2,153.8	14.9	7.7	15.0	4.3	1.6	⑧ 0.80	1.44	2.37	0.24	13.45 -	9.80	14.5	2.1
12/31/00	1,319.0	⑦ 77.1	2,256.8	16.9	5.8	12.3	3.4	1.7	⑦ 0.66	1.27	2.33	0.21	15.00 -	9.00	18.2	1.8
12/31/99	1,213.7	⑥ 47.4	2,235.2	9.3	3.9	8.0	2.1	1.8	⑥ 0.41	0.96	2.02	0.20	14.00 -	10.19	29.5	1.7
12/31/98	1,538.3	⑤ 225.8	2,242.2	32.4	14.7	39.0	10.1	1.9	⑤ 1.94	2.45	2.78	0.20	14.13 -	9.06	6.0	1.7
12/31/97	1,217.9	④ 27.1	2,178.1	5.5	2.2	7.0	1.2	2.3	④ 0.24	0.77	1.11	0.20	11.50 -	6.38	37.2	2.2
12/31/96	1,232.2	② 4.2	2,145.0	0.9	0.3	1.4	0.2	1.5	② 0.04	0.65	0.40	0.20	7.75 -	5.88	169.9	2.9
③ 12/31/95	1,994.3	68.5	2,572.2	5.6	3.4	25.0	2.7	1.4	0.60	1.42	0.19	0.12	8.63 -	5.75	12.0	1.7
12/31/94	842.4	② 19.7	2,480.7	6.4	2.3	9.9	0.8	1.4	② 0.17	0.43		0.08	8.13 -	4.75	37.8	1.2
12/31/93	794.0	① d64.1	903.9	6.2	...	...	...	1.1	① d0.56	d0.34	1.77	0.05	6.50 -	3.75	...	1.0

Statistics are as originally reported. ① Bef. $15.4 mill. extraord. chg. & $429,000 acct. cr. ② Bef. $37.8 mill. gain fr. disc. ops., 1996; loss of $8.1 mill., 1994. ③ Incl. consol. results of NL Industries. ④ Bef. $33.6 mill. gain fr. disc. ops. & $4.3 mill. extraord. chg. ⑤ Bef. $6.2 mill. extraord. chg. & incl. $398.1 mill. net non-recurr. gains. ⑥ Bef. $54,000 extraord. chg. and $2.0 mill. gain fr. disc. ops. ⑦ Incl. $69.5 mill. pre-tax legal settlement gain. ⑧ Incl. $31.9 mill. settlement gain, $16.2 mill. ins. gain & $2.2 mill. gain fr. sale of land. ⑨ Incl. $5.2 mill. settlement gain, $6.4 mill. net sec. trans., $6.3 mill. foreign curr. trans. gain & $1.6 mill. gain on disp. of assets.

OFFICERS:
H. C. Simmons, Chmn., C.E.O.
G. R. Simmons, Vice-Chmn.
S. L. Watson, Pres.

INVESTOR CONTACT: Investor Relations, (972) 233-1700

PRINCIPAL OFFICE: 5430 LBJ Freeway, Suite 1700, Dallas, TX 75240-2697

TELEPHONE NUMBER: (972) 233-1700
FAX: (972) 448-1445

NO. OF EMPLOYEES: 7,015 (approx.)

SHAREHOLDERS: 2,050 (approx. record)

ANNUAL MEETING: In May

INCORPORATED: DE, Mar., 1987

INSTITUTIONAL HOLDINGS:
No. of Institutions: 39
Shares Held: 3,479,236
% Held: 3.0

INDUSTRY: Chemicals & allied products, nec (SIC: 5169)

TRANSFER AGENT(S): Computershare Investor Services, LLC, Chicago, IL

VALLEY NATIONAL BANCORP

EXCH.	SYM.	REC. PRICE	P/E RATIO	YLD.	MKT. CAP.	RANGE (52-WK.)	'02 Y/E PR.	DIV. ACH.
NYSE	VLY	25.65 (2/28/03)	15.5	3.5%	$2.32 bill.	29.04 - 24.24	26.37	11 yrs.

UPPER MEDIUM GRADE. THE COMPANY CONTINUES TO BENEFIT FROM DEMAND FOR RESIDENTIAL MORT-
GAGES, HOME EQUITY LOANS AND COMMERCIAL MORTGAGE LOANS.

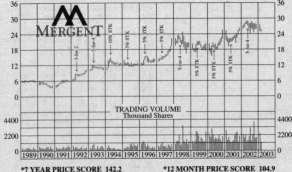

*7 YEAR PRICE SCORE 142.2   ***12 MONTH PRICE SCORE 104.9**
*NYSE COMPOSITE INDEX=100

INTERIM EARNINGS (Per Share):

Qtr.	Mar.	June	Sept.	Dec.
1999	0.31	0.30	0.33	0.32
2000	0.33	0.34	0.34	0.34
2001	0.29	0.35	0.37	0.38
2002	0.40	0.42	0.42	0.41

INTERIM DIVIDENDS (Per Share):

Amt.	Decl.	Ex.	Rec.	Pay.
5-for-4	4/10/02	5/20/02	5/03/02	5/17/02
0.225Q	5/23/02	6/05/02	6/07/02	7/01/02
0.225Q	8/20/02	9/04/02	9/06/02	10/01/02
0.225Q	11/19/02	12/04/02	12/06/02	1/02/03
0.225Q	2/27/03	3/06/03	3/10/03	4/01/03

Indicated div.: $0.90 (Div. Reinv. Plan)

CAPITALIZATION (12/31/01):

	($000)	(%)
Total Deposits	6,306,974	79.2
Long-Term Debt	975,728	12.3
Common & Surplus	678,375	8.5
Total	7,961,077	100.0

BUSINESS:

Valley National Bancorp, with $9.10 billion in assets as of 12/31/02, is a bank holding company. The Company's principal subsidiary is Valley National Bank (VNB). VNB is a national banking association, which provides a full range of commercial and retail banking services through 128 branch offices located in 82 communities serving 10 counties throughout northern New Jersey and Manhattan. These services include the following: the acceptance of demand, savings and time deposits; extension of consumer, real estate, Small Business Administration and other commercial credits; title insurance; investment services; and full personal and corporate trust, as well as pension and fiduciary services. On 1/19/01, the Company acquired Merchants New York Bancorp, Inc. for $375.0 million.

RECENT DEVELOPMENTS:

For the year ended 12/31/02, net income increased 14.4% to $154.6 million from $135.2 million the year before. Results for 2002 and 2001 included net gains on sale of loans of $6.7 million and $10.6 million, net gains on securities transactions of $7.1 million and $3.6 million, gains from bank-owned life insurance of $6.7 million and $2.1 million, and charges for distribution on capital securities of $15.7 million and $2.3 million, respectively. Net interest income grew 7.4% to $359.7 million. Provision for loan losses decreased 13.1% to $13.6 million. Total non-interest income rose 18.6% to $81.2 million, while total non-interest expense increased 10.5% to $208.0 million.

PROSPECTS:

The Company continues to benefit from demand for residential mortgages, home equity loans and commercial mortgage loans in its northern New Jersey and New York City service territories. Separately, on 1/2/03, Valley National Bank, a subsidiary of VLY, announced that it has completed the acquisition of Glen Rauch Securities, Inc., a Wall Street brokerage firm specializing in municipal securities. As of 12/31/02, assets in Glen Rauch's customer accounts totaled more than $1.00 billion and annual revenues exceeded $5.0 million. Meanwhile, during the fourth quarter of 2002, VLY opened its 128th branch in Hoboken, New Jersey.

ANNUAL FINANCIAL DATA:

FISCAL YEAR	NET INT. INC. ($mill.)	NON-INT. INC. ($mill.)	NET INC. ($mill.)	TOT. LOANS ($mill.)	TOT. ASSETS ($mill.)	TOT. DEP. ($mill.)	RET. ON EQUITY %	RET. ON ASSETS %	EQUITY/ ASSETS %	EARN. PER SH. $	TANG. BK. VAL. $	DIV. PER SH. $	PRICE RANGE	AVG. P/E RATIO
p12/31/02	359.7	81.2	④ 154.6							④ 1.65		0.87	29.04 - 24.24	16.1
12/31/01	334.8	68.5	④ 135.2	5,331.8	8,583.8	6,307.0	19.9	1.6	7.9	④ 1.38	7.10	0.82	26.36 - 19.09	16.4
12/31/00	258.1	50.9	③ 106.8	4,661.4	6,425.8	5,123.7	19.6	1.7	8.5	③ 1.33	8.65	0.77	25.62 - 15.38	15.4
12/31/99	258.4	47.3	② 106.3	4,554.8	6,360.4	5,051.3	19.2	1.7	8.7	② 1.26	9.27	0.72	21.41 - 16.93	15.3
12/31/98	229.6	43.1	② 97.3	3,977.9	5,541.2	4,674.7	17.5	1.8	10.0	② 1.21	9.12	0.65	24.88 - 16.41	16.3
12/31/97	212.3	42.3	85.0	3,622.3	5,090.7	4,403.0	17.9	1.7	9.3	1.11	10.18	0.57	22.32 - 13.36	12.3
12/31/96	178.8	26.3	67.5	3,177.2	4,686.7	4,176.2	17.0	1.4	8.5	0.97	9.04	0.51	15.66 - 11.91	10.8
12/31/95	173.4	21.0	62.6	2,794.1	4,585.8	4,083.9	15.6	1.4	8.7	0.88	8.91	0.49	13.97 - 11.53	11.0
12/31/94	149.1	22.5	59.0	2,184.7	3,743.9	3,334.0	19.7	1.6	8.0	0.98	8.16	0.44	15.09 - 10.15	9.8
12/31/93	135.5	25.7	① 54.6	1,803.2	3,413.5	3,079.8	20.7	1.6	7.7	① 0.96	7.71	0.36	12.16 - 9.90	8.6

Statistics are as originally reported. Adj. for stk. splits: 5-for-4, 5/02, 5/98 & 4/93; 5%, 5/01, 5/00, 5/99, 5/97, 5/96 & 5/95; & 10%, 5/94. ① Excl. an acctg. change chrg. $402,000. ② Incl. merger-related chrg., 1999, $3.0 mill.; 1998, $4.5 mill. ③ Incl. net gain on sale of loans of $2.0 mill. ④ Incl. a net charge of $2.1 mill., 2002; net gain of $3.7 mill. 2001.

OFFICERS:
G. H. Lipkin, Chmn., Pres., C.E.O.
S. B. Witty, Vice-Chmn.
A. D. Eskow, Exec. V.P., C.F.O.

INVESTOR CONTACT: Dianne M. Grenz, Investor Relations, (973) 305-8800

PRINCIPAL OFFICE: 1455 Valley Road, Wayne, NJ 07470

TELEPHONE NUMBER: (973) 305-8800
FAX: (973) 305-1605
WEB: www.valleynationalbank.com

NO. OF EMPLOYEES: 2,129

SHAREHOLDERS: 9,359

ANNUAL MEETING: In April

INCORPORATED: NJ, 1982

INSTITUTIONAL HOLDINGS:
No. of Institutions: 101
Shares Held: 12,530,894
% Held: 13.8

INDUSTRY: National commercial banks (SIC: 6021)

TRANSFER AGENT(S): American Stock Transfer & Trust Company, New York, NY

VALSPAR CORPORATION (THE)

EXCH.	SYM.	REC. PRICE	P/E RATIO	YLD.	MKT. CAP.	RANGE (52-WK.)	'02 Y/E PR.	DIV. ACH.
NYSE	VAL	40.94 (2/28/03)	17.1	1.5%	$2.05 bill.	50.15 - 34.80	44.18	24 yrs.

MEDIUM GRADE. THE COMPANY EXPECTS DILUTED EARNINGS PER SHARE FOR THE SECOND QUARTER OF 2003
IN THE RANGE OF $0.70 TO $0.75 PER SHARE.

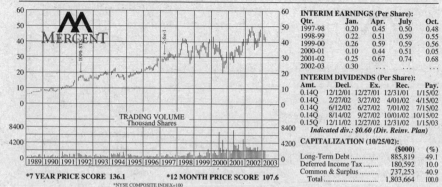

TRADING VOLUME
Thousand Shares

7 YEAR PRICE SCORE 136.1   *12 MONTH PRICE SCORE 107.6*
NYSE COMPOSITE INDEX=100

INTERIM EARNINGS (Per Share):

Qtr.	Jan.	Apr.	July	Oct.
1997-98	0.20	0.45	0.50	0.48
1998-99	0.22	0.51	0.59	0.55
1999-00	0.26	0.59	0.59	0.56
2000-01	0.10	0.44	0.51	0.05
2001-02	0.25	0.67	0.74	0.68
2002-03	0.30	...	...	...

INTERIM DIVIDENDS (Per Share):

Amt.	Decl.	Ex.	Rec.	Pay.
0.14Q	12/12/01	12/27/01	12/31/01	1/15/02
0.14Q	2/27/02	3/27/02	4/01/02	4/15/02
0.14Q	6/12/02	6/27/02	7/01/02	7/15/02
0.14Q	8/14/02	9/27/02	10/01/02	10/15/02
0.15Q	12/11/02	12/27/02	12/31/02	1/15/03

Indicated div.: $0.60 (Div. Reinv. Plan)

CAPITALIZATION (10/25/02):

	($000)	(%)
Long-Term Debt	885,819	49.1
Deferred Income Tax	180,592	10.0
Common & Surplus	737,253	40.9
Total	1,803,664	100.0

BUSINESS:

The Valspar Corporation is a global paint and coatings manufacturer. The Company manufactures and distributes a broad portfolio of coatings products. The Industrial product line includes decorative and protective coatings for wood, metal, plastic and glass. The Architectural, Automotive and Specialty product line includes interior and exterior decorative paints, primers, varnishes and specialty decorative products, such as enamels, aerosols and faux finishes for the do-it-yourself and professional markets, as well as automotive refinish and high performance floor coatings. The Packaging Coatings product line includes coatings and inks for rigid packaging containers. The Other category includes specialty polymers, composites and colorants, which are used internally and sold to other coatings manufacturers. In December 2000, VAL acquired Lilly Industries, Inc.

RECENT DEVELOPMENTS:

For the quarter ended 1/24/03, net income increased 23.9% to $15.6 million compared with $12.6 million in all equivalent 2002 quarter. The growth in earnings reflected higher sales, coupled with benefits from cost-improvement initiatives. Net sales rose 8.8% to $469.0 million from $431.0 million a year earlier. This improvement was attributed to strong sales growth with market share gains in all of VAL's product lines. Operating income advanced 10.8% to $37.2 million versus $33.5 million the year before.

PROSPECTS:

The Company is off to a solid start for 2003. However, economic uncertainties continue to cloud VAL's short-term outlook. Going forward, the Company will continue to implement its growth and cost initiatives, which should augment the Company's financial performance in this challenging business environment. The Company expects diluted earnings per share for the second quarter of 2003 in the range of $0.70 to $0.75 compared with $0.67 per share in the comparable period a year ago, assuming a continuation of current business conditions.

ANNUAL FINANCIAL DATA:

FISCAL YEAR	TOT. REVS. ($mill.)	NET INC. ($mill.)	TOT. ASSETS ($mill.)	OPER. PROFIT %	NET PROFIT %	RET. ON EQUITY %	RET. ON ASSETS %	CURR. RATIO	EARN. PER SH.$	CASH FL. PER SH.$	TANG. BK. VAL.$	DIV. PER SH.$	PRICE RANGE	AVG. P/E RATIO	AVG. YIELD %
10/25/02	2,126.9	120.1	2,419.6	11.7	5.6	16.3	5.0	1.4	2.34	3.33	...	0.56	50.15 — 34.80	18.2	1.3
10/26/01	1,921.0	③ 51.5	2,226.1	8.4	2.7	7.9	2.3	1.4	③ 1.10	2.67	...	0.54	42.00 — 26.48	31.1	1.6
10/27/00	1,483.3	④ 86.5	1,125.0	11.1	5.8	19.8	7.7	1.6	④ 2.00	3.05	5.39	0.52	43.31 — 19.75	15.8	1.6
10/29/99	1,387.7	③ 82.1	1,110.7	10.4	5.9	20.9	7.4	1.4	③ 1.87	2.78	4.07	0.46	41.88 — 29.25	19.0	1.3
10/30/98	1,155.1	72.1	801.7	10.5	6.2	21.2	9.0	1.6	1.63	2.32	5.70	0.42	42.13 — 25.75	20.8	1.2
10/31/97	1,017.3	65.9	615.5	11.0	6.5	22.3	10.7	1.4	1.49	2.07	5.68	0.36	33.06 — 26.81	20.1	1.2
10/25/96	859.8	55.9	486.4	11.0	6.5	22.0	11.5	1.5	1.26	1.76	5.79	0.33	29.31 — 20.94	19.9	1.3
10/27/95	790.2	② 47.5	398.2	10.5	6.0	22.4	11.9	1.6	② 1.08	1.54	4.82	0.30	22.31 — 16.69	18.1	1.5
10/28/94	786.8	① 45.5	363.4	10.0	5.8	26.1	12.5	1.6	① 1.04	1.48	4.03	0.26	22.94 — 15.25	18.4	1.4
10/29/93	693.7	40.2	336.8	10.0	5.8	20.4	11.9	1.7	0.93	1.40	4.57	0.22	20.75 — 15.19	19.4	1.2

Statistics are as originally reported. Adj. for stk. splits: 2-for-1, 3/97. ① Incl. pretax chrg. of $2.5 mill. from the writedown of a plant. ② Reflects the acquisition of Sunbelt Coatings on a pooling-of-interests basis. ③ Incl. restruct. chrg. of $8.3 mill., 1999; $21.9 mill., 2001. ④ Incl. restr. credit of $1.2 mill.

OFFICERS:
R. M. Rompala, Chmn., C.E.O.
J. Ballach, Pres., C.O.O.
P. C. Reyelts, Sr. V.P., C.F.O.
R. Engh, Sec.

INVESTOR CONTACT: Rolf Engh, Sec., (612) 332-7371

PRINCIPAL OFFICE: 1101 Third Street South, Minneapolis, MN 55415

TELEPHONE NUMBER: (612) 332-7371
FAX: (612) 375-7723
WEB: www.valspar.com

NO. OF EMPLOYEES: 7,058 (avg.)

SHAREHOLDERS: 1,642

ANNUAL MEETING: In Feb.

INCORPORATED: DE, Dec., 1934

INSTITUTIONAL HOLDINGS:
No. of Institutions: 191
Shares Held: 30,830,642
% Held: 61.5

INDUSTRY: Paints and allied products (SIC: 2851)

TRANSFER AGENT(S): Mellon Investor Services LLC, Ridgefield Park, NJ

VARCO INTERNATIONAL, INC.

EXCH.	SYM.	REC. PRICE	P/E RATIO	YLD.	MKT. CAP.	RANGE (52-WK.)	'02 Y/E PR.
NYSE	VRC	18.96 (2/28/03)	23.1	...	$1.82 bill.	22.00 - 12.85	17.40

MEDIUM GRADE. LOWER WORLDWIDE RIG ACTIVITY LEVELS TEMPER THE COMPANY'S NEAR-TERM OUTLOOK.

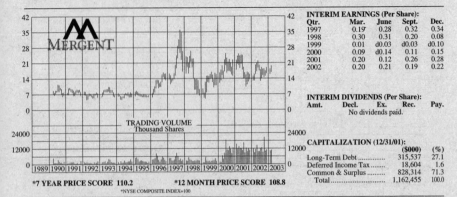

INTERIM EARNINGS (Per Share):

Qtr.	Mar.	June	Sept.	Dec.
1997	0.19	0.28	0.32	0.34
1998	0.30	0.31	0.20	0.08
1999	0.01	d0.03	d0.03	d0.10
2000	0.09	d0.14	0.11	0.15
2001	0.20	0.12	0.26	0.28
2002	0.20	0.21	0.19	0.22

INTERIM DIVIDENDS (Per Share):

Amt.	Decl.	Ex.	Rec.	Pay.
	No dividends paid.			

CAPITALIZATION (12/31/01):

	($000)	(%)
Long-Term Debt	315,537	27.1
Deferred Income Tax	18,604	1.6
Common & Surplus	828,314	71.3
Total	1,162,455	100.0

*7 YEAR PRICE SCORE 110.2   *12 MONTH PRICE SCORE 108.8

*NYSE COMPOSITE INDEX=100

BUSINESS:

Varco International, Inc. (formerly Tuboscope Inc.) is a provider of engineered drilling and well-servicing equipment, products and services to the oil and gas industry. VRC manufactures and supplies drilling systems and rig instrumentation; oilfield tubular inspections and internal tubular coating techniques; drill cuttings separation, management and disposal systems and services; and coiled tubing and pressure control equipment for land and offshore drilling and well stimulation operations. VRC also provides in-service pipeline inspections, manufactures high pressure fiberglass tubulars, and sells and rents advanced in-line inspection equipment to makers of oil country tubular goods. Drilling equipment sales accounted for 36.4% of 2002 revenues; tubular services, 26.7%; drilling services, 20.9%; and coiled tubing & wireline products, 16.0%. On 5/30/00, the Company acquired Varco International, Inc. and adopted its present name.

RECENT DEVELOPMENTS:

For the year ended 12/31/02, net income was $79.8 million compared with $83.0 million a year earlier. Results for 2002 and 2001 included merger, transaction and litigation costs of $6.5 million and $16.5 million, respectively. Results for 2001 also included goodwill amortization of $10.5 million. Total revenue increased 5.3% to $1.34 billion, aided in part by the September 2002 acquisition of the oilfield services business of ICO Inc.

PROSPECTS:

Going forward, lower worldwide rig activity levels may continue to reduce demand for certain of VRC's goods and services. A decline in the count of active drilling rigs worldwide is tempering the Company's near-term outlook. For instance, VRC's drilling equipment segment, which posted an 11.7% drop in fourth quarter 2002 revenue to $120.5 million, is being hurt by drilling contractors that are curtailing capital spending and purchases of spare parts and consumables due to lower drilling activity and dayrates. Also feeling the effects of lower demand for well service equipment is the Company's coiled tubing and wireline products segment, which reported a fourth quarter 2002 revenue decline of 22.8% to $48.9 million versus $63.3 million the year before.

ANNUAL FINANCIAL DATA:

FISCAL YEAR	TOT. REVS. ($000)	NET INC. ($000)	TOT. ASSETS ($000)	OPER. PROFIT %	NET PROFIT %	RET. ON EQUITY %	RET. ON ASSETS %	CURR. RATIO	EARN. PER SH. $	CASH FL. PER SH. $	TANG. BK. VAL. $	PRICE RANGE	AVG. P/E RATIO
p12/31/02	1,335,064	⑥ 79,807	1,429,110	12.5	6.5	10.0	5.8	2.8	⑥ 0.82	1.56	4.92	22.00 - 12.85	21.3
⑦ 12/31/01	1,267,809	⑥ 82,968	1,076,982	7.0	2.4	2.9	2.0	2.4	⑥ 0.86	0.81	4.93	25.18 - 10.25	20.6
12/31/00	866,615	⑤ 21,055	676,039	2.9	...	...	...	2.4	⑤ 0.22	0.60	2.28	25.38 - 12.00	84.9
12/31/99	385,474	④ d7,156	712,172	15.3	7.4	12.4	5.9	1.8	④ d0.16	2.28	2.32	16.88 - 5.00	...
12/31/98	567,701	41,945	686,167	19.2	10.1	17.7	7.7	2.0	0.89	1.54	1.68	26.50 - 6.31	18.4
12/31/97	525,231	③ 53,104	505,165	...	...	...	...	1.5	③ 1.14	1.68	2.39	36.00 - 11.50	20.8
12/31/96	341,431	① d43,226	306,679	14.5	4.6	7.3	2.9	1.8	① d1.17	d0.71	1.54	16.75 - 5.63	...
12/31/95	190,015	8,819	317,027	14.1	4.0	6.7	2.4	2.1	0.44	1.23	2.39	8.50 - 5.63	16.0
12/31/94	192,175	① 7,602	310,108	1.3	...	...	...	1.8	① 0.41	1.14	1.75	8.00 - 4.50	15.2
12/31/93	183,340	① ② d8,362			...	...	...	1.1	① ② d0.49	0.26	1.11	10.25 - 5.75	...

Statistics are as originally reported. ① Excl. extraord. chrg., 1996, $6.4 mill.; 1994, $764,000; 1993, $4.5 mill. ② Incl. restruct. chrg., $13.3 mill. ③ Incl. write-off of long lived assets of $63.1 mill., Drexel transaction costs of $11.3 mill., transaction costs & write-offs of $2.2 mill. ④ Incl. transaction write-off costs of $7.8 mill. ⑤ Incl. merger and transaction costs of $22.4 mill. ⑥ Incl. merger, transaction & litigation costs of $6.5 mill., 2002; $16.5 mill., 2001. ⑦ Reflects the acq. of Varco International, Inc.

OFFICERS:
G. I. Boyadjieff, Chmn.
J. F. Lauletta, Pres., C.E.O.
J. C. Winkler, Exec. V.P., C.O.O.
INVESTOR CONTACT: Clay Williams, (281) 953-2200
PRINCIPAL OFFICE: 2000 W. Sam Houston Pkwy., Suite 1700, Houston, TX 77042

TELEPHONE NUMBER: (281) 953-2200
FAX: (281) 799-1460
WEB: www.varco.com
NO. OF EMPLOYEES: 8,651 (avg.)
SHAREHOLDERS: 1,332 (approx.)
ANNUAL MEETING: In May
INCORPORATED: DE, Mar., 1988

INSTITUTIONAL HOLDINGS:
No. of Institutions: 192
Shares Held: 74,555,996
% Held: 77.0
INDUSTRY: Oil and gas field services, nec (SIC: 1389)
TRANSFER AGENT(S): Mellon Investor Services, Dallas, TX

VARIAN MEDICAL SYSTEMS, INC.

EXCH.	SYM.	REC. PRICE	P/E RATIO	YLD.	MKT. CAP.	RANGE (52-WK.)	'02 Y/E PR.
NYSE	VAR	50.55 (2/28/03)	35.1	...	$3.43 bill.	52.95 - 31.60	49.60

UPPER MEDIUM GRADE. THE COMPANY ANTICIPATES SALES GROWTH IN THE MID-TEENS AND DILUTED EARNINGS PER SHARE GROWTH OF APPROXIMATELY 26.0% FOR FISCAL 2003.

TRADING VOLUME
Thousand Shares

*7 YEAR PRICE SCORE 170.0   *12 MONTH PRICE SCORE 123.6
*NYSE COMPOSITE INDEX=100

INTERIM EARNINGS (Per Share):

Qtr	Dec.	Mar.	June	Sept.
1998-99	d0.04	d0.17	0.11	0.21
1999-00	0.09	0.16	0.22	0.36
2000-01	0.14	0.23	0.28	0.39
2001-02	0.19	0.34	0.32	0.48
2002-03	0.30	...	...	...

INTERIM DIVIDENDS (Per Share):

Amt.	Decl.	Ex.	Rec.	Pay.
100% STK	11/19/01	1/16/02	12/10/01	1/15/02

CAPITALIZATION (9/27/02):

	($000)	(%)
Long-Term Debt	58,500	11.0
Common & Surplus	472,803	89.0
Total	531,303	100.0

BUSINESS:

Varian Medical Systems, Inc. (formerly Varian Associates, Inc.) is a manufacturer of integrated cancer therapy systems. More than 4,500 Varian CLINAC® medical linear accelerators and XIMATRON® simulators systems are in service around the world, treating an estimated 200,000 cancer patients per day. VAR is also a major supplier of x-ray tubes for diagnostic imaging applications. VAR is involved in several high-growth product development opportunities, including its advanced brachytherapy system for cancer treatment and the world's first real-time, digital X-ray fluoroscopic imager. In addition, VAR is pursuing technologies and products based on molecular medicine. VAR has manufacturing sites in North America and Europe and 40 sales and support offices around the world. In April 1999, VAR completed the spin-off of the instruments and semiconductor equipment businesses.

RECENT DEVELOPMENTS:

For the three months ended 12/27/02, net earnings advanced 59.1% to $21.0 million compared with $13.2 million in the corresponding quarter of the previous year. Sales increased 18.0% to $206.7 million from $175.1 million in the year-earlier period. Oncology systems sales climbed 13.7% to $165.9 million from $145.9 million, while X-ray products sales jumped 37.7% to $34.0 million from $24.7 million in the prior-year quarter. Sales from the Ginzton Technology Center leapt 51.1% to $6.8 million from $4.5 million the year before. Operating income soared 55.3% to $32.0 million from $20.6 million in 2001. Net orders improved 26.1% to $251.1 million from $199.2 million, while order backlog grew 19.4% to $742.8 million from $621.9 million the year before.

PROSPECTS:

The Company is experiencing a stronger-than-expected first-half recovery in its X-ray Products business, while the Oncology Systems business remains on track and its backlog continues to be strong. As a result, the Company anticipates percentage sales growth in the mid-teens and diluted earnings per share growth of approximately 26.0% for fiscal 2003. Separately, the Company announced that it received U.S. FDA approval for its new PaxScan™ 4030 Medical Digital Imaging System, a portable digital radiography system.

ANNUAL FINANCIAL DATA:

FISCAL YEAR	TOT. REVS. ($Mill.)	NET INC. ($Mill.)	TOT. ASSETS ($Mill.)	OPER. PROFIT %	NET PROFIT %	RET. ON EQUITY %	RET. ON ASSETS %	CURR. RATIO	EARN. PER SH. $	CASH FL. PER SH. $	TANG. BK. VAL.$	DIV. PER SH. $	PRICE RANGE	AVG. P/E RATIO	AVG. YIELD %
p9/27/02	873.1	⑥ 93.6						⑥ 1.33							
9/28/01	773.6	⑥ 68.0	759.2	14.2	8.8	17.2	9.0	2.2	⑥ 1.00	1.34	5.86	...	38.63 - 27.00	33.0	...
9/29/00	689.7	⑤ 53.0	602.6	12.7	7.7	19.6	8.8	1.8	⑤ 0.82	1.21	4.26	...	35.50 - 13.75	30.0	...
④ 10/01/99	590.4	③ 8.2	539.2	4.1	1.4	4.4	1.5	1.4	③ 0.14	0.75	3.03	0.05	21.50 - 8.13	109.6	0.3
10/02/98	1,422.1	73.8	1,218.3	8.1	5.2	13.2	6.1	1.7	1.22	1.91	9.37	0.20	29.19 - 15.78	18.5	0.9
9/26/97	1,425.8	② 115.6	1,104.3	9.1	8.1	22.0	10.5	1.8	② 1.83	2.55	8.71	0.17	33.50 - 22.94	15.4	0.6
9/27/96	1,599.4	122.1	1,019.0	11.9	7.6	26.1	12.0	1.7	1.91	2.62	7.63	0.15	31.44 - 20.25	13.6	0.6
9/29/95	1,575.7	① 105.8	1,003.8	10.6	6.7	26.8	10.5	1.5	① 1.51	2.29	6.36	0.14	28.69 - 17.25	15.3	0.6
9/30/94	1,552.5	79.4	962.4	8.4	5.1	17.7	8.2	1.5	1.11	1.85	6.61	0.12	19.63 - 14.13	15.2	0.7
10/01/93	1,311.0	45.8	893.0	6.0	3.5	10.9	5.1	1.6	0.63	1.38	6.08	0.10	15.00 - 9.50	19.4	0.8

Statistics are as originally reported. Adj. for stk. split: 2-for-1, 3/94, 1/02. ① Bef. disc. opers. gain $33.5 mill. ($0.95/sh.) ② Incl. net gain on sale of assets $29.2 mill. ($0.96/sh.) ③ Bef. disc. oper. loss of $30.8 mill., but incl. non-recurr. chrgs. $31.0 mill. ④ Reflects spin-off of instruments and semiconductor equipment businesses. ⑤ Incl. non-recurr. chrgs. $2.2 mill. ⑥ Bef. acctg. credit of $100,000, but incl. reorg. inc. of $500,000 & $5.0 mill. write-off of equity investment. ⑦ Incl. reorg. inc. of $200,000.

OFFICERS:
R. M. Levy, Pres., C.E.O.
E. W. Finney, V.P., Fin., C.F.O.
J. B. Phair, V.P., Gen. Couns., Sec.
INVESTOR CONTACT: Elisha Finney, Investor Relations, (650) 424-6803
PRINCIPAL OFFICE: 3100 Hansen Way, Palo Alto, CA 94304-1030

TELEPHONE NUMBER: (650) 493-4000
FAX: (650) 493-0307
WEB: www.varian.com
NO. OF EMPLOYEES: 2,756
SHAREHOLDERS: 3,965 (approx.)
ANNUAL MEETING: In Feb.
INCORPORATED: CA, Apr., 1948; reincorp., DE, Apr., 1999

INSTITUTIONAL HOLDINGS:
No. of Institutions: 262
Shares Held: 58,856,654
% Held: 86.6
INDUSTRY: Special industry machinery, nec (SIC: 3559)
TRANSFER AGENT(S): First Chicago Trust Company of New York, Jersey City, NJ.

VECTREN CORPORATION

EXCH.	SYM.	REC. PRICE	P/E RATIO	YLD.	MKT. CAP.	RANGE (52-WK.)	'02 Y/E PR.	DIV. ACH.
NYSE	VVC	20.60 (2/28/03)	12.1	5.3%	$1.39 bill.	26.10 - 17.95	23.00	27 yrs.

MEDIUM GRADE. THE COMPANY EXPECTS EARNINGS FOR 2003 IN THE RANGE OF $1.80 TO $1.90 PER SHARE.

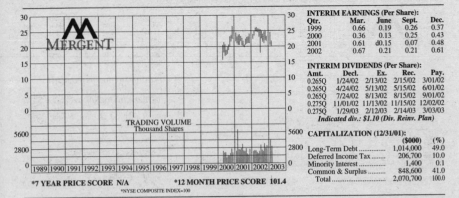

INTERIM EARNINGS (Per Share):

Qtr.	Mar.	June	Sept.	Dec.
1999	0.66	0.19	0.26	0.37
2000	0.36	0.13	0.25	0.43
2001	0.61	d0.15	0.07	0.48
2002	0.67	0.21	0.21	0.61

INTERIM DIVIDENDS (Per Share):

Amt.	Decl.	Ex.	Rec.	Pay.
0.265Q	1/24/02	2/13/02	2/15/02	3/01/02
0.265Q	4/24/02	5/13/02	5/15/02	6/01/02
0.265Q	7/24/02	8/13/02	8/15/02	9/01/02
0.275Q	11/01/02	11/13/02	11/15/02	12/02/02
0.275Q	1/29/03	2/12/03	2/14/03	3/03/03

Indicated div.: $1.10 (Div. Reinv. Plan)

CAPITALIZATION (12/31/01):

	($000)	(%)
Long-Term Debt	1,014,000	49.0
Deferred Income Tax	206,700	10.0
Minority Interest	1,400	0.1
Common & Surplus	848,600	41.0
Total	2,070,700	100.0

*7 YEAR PRICE SCORE N/A   *12 MONTH PRICE SCORE 101.4

*NYSE COMPOSITE INDEX=100

BUSINESS:

Vectren Corporation was organized to reflect the merger on 3/31/00 of Indiana Energy, Inc. and SIGCORP, Inc., both of which were Dividend Achievers. VVC is an energy and applied technology holding company. The Company's energy delivery subsidiaries provide gas and/or electricity to nearly 1.0 million customers in adjoining service territories that cover nearly two-thirds of Indiana and west central Ohio. VVC's non-regulated subsidiaries and affiliates currently offer energy-related products and services. These include gas marketing and related services, coal mining and sales, broadband communications services and utility infrastructure services, which includes underground construction and repair, facilities locating and meter reading services. VVC has three reportable segments: gas utility and electric utility, that together contributed 83.3% of 2002 net income, and non-regulated operations, which contributed 16.7% of net income.

RECENT DEVELOPMENTS:

For the year ended 12/31/02, net income soared 123.8% to $114.6 million from $51.2 million the previous year. Results for 2001 included merger, integration, restructuring and other non-recurring after-tax charges totaling $26.4 million. Net income contributed by VVC's regulated utility operations jumped 145.2% to $94.4 million from $38.5 million the year before, due to residential and commercial gas customer growth and beneficial weather conditions for both the gas and electric operations. Net income from non-regulated operations climbed 56.2% to $18.9 million from $12.1 million the year before. Comparisons were made with restated results for the prior year.

PROSPECTS:

During 2002, the Company made considerable progress in integrating its utility operations, which should allow improved customer service and help keep costs low. In addition, VVC achieved positive regulatory outcomes in several areas, especially the approval to recover capital and operating costs related to compliance with environmental regulations at electric generating plants. Looking ahead, VVC expects earnings for 2003 in the range of $1.80 to $1.90 per share, excluding the potential impact of any permanent financing completed in the coming year.

ANNUAL FINANCIAL DATA:

FISCAL YEAR	TOT. REVS. (Smill.)	NET INC. (Smill.)	TOT. ASSETS (Smill.)	OPER. PROFIT %	NET PROFIT %	NET INC./ NET PROP. %	NET INC./ TOT. CAP. %	RET. ON EQUITY %	EARN. PER SH. $	TANG. BK. VAL. $	DIV. PER SH. $	DIV. PAYOUT %	PRICE RANGE	AVG. P/E RATIO	AVG. YIELD %
p12/31/02		114.6							1.70		1.07	62.9	26.10 - 17.95	13.0	4.9
12/31/01	2,170.0	② 67.4	2,856.8	6.4	3.1	3.8	3.3	7.9	② 1.01	9.68	1.03	102.0	24.44 - 19.76	21.9	4.7
12/31/00	1,648.7	① 72.0	2,909.2	7.9	4.4	4.3	4.5	9.8	① 1.17	8.69	0.98	83.8	26.50 - 15.75	18.1	4.6
12/31/99	1,068.4	90.7	1,980.5	15.0	8.5	6.5	6.4	12.8	1.48	11.58	...	...	...	...	...
12/31/98	997.7	86.6	...	14.9	8.7	...	...	...	1.40	...	...	...	...	...	...

Statistics are as originally reported. ① Incl. nonrecurr. merger & integration chrg., $41.1 mill. ② Bef. extraord. loss of $7.7 mill. and acctg. change gain of $3.9 mill.; incl. pre-tax non-recurr. chrgs. of $21.9 mill.

OFFICERS:
N. C. Ellerbrook, Chmn., C.E.O.
A. E. Goebel, Pres., C.O.O.
J. A. Benkert Jr., Exec. V.P., C.F.O.
INVESTOR CONTACT: Steven M. Schein, V.P., Investor Relations, (812) 491-4209
PRINCIPAL OFFICE: 20 N.W. Fourth Street, Evansville, IN 47708

TELEPHONE NUMBER: (812) 491-4000
FAX: (812) 491-4149
WEB: www.vectren.com
NO. OF EMPLOYEES: 1,986 (avg.)
SHAREHOLDERS: 14,151
ANNUAL MEETING: In March
INCORPORATED: IN, June, 1999

INSTITUTIONAL HOLDINGS:
No. of Institutions: 184
Shares Held: 27,452,186
% Held: 40.5
INDUSTRY: Gas and other services combined (SIC: 4932)
TRANSFER AGENT(S): National City Bank, Cleveland, OH

VERIZON COMMUNICATIONS INC.

EXCH.	SYM.	REC. PRICE	P/E RATIO	YLD.	MKT. CAP.	RANGE (52-WK.)	'02 Y/E PR.
NYSE	VZ	34.58 (2/28/03)	21.0	4.5%	$93.94 bill.	48.70 - 26.01	38.75

MEDIUM GRADE. THE COMPANY ANTICIPATES FULL-YEAR 2003 EARNINGS OF BETWEEN $2.70 AND $2.80 PER SHARE.

*7 YEAR PRICE SCORE 87.7   *12 MONTH PRICE SCORE 110.3

*NYSE COMPOSITE INDEX=100

INTERIM EARNINGS (Per Share):

Qtr.	Mar.	June	Sept.	Dec.
1998	1.13	0.65	d0.01	0.65
1999	0.72	0.74	0.74	0.45
2000	0.56	1.79	0.97	0.62
2001	0.65	d0.38	0.69	d0.75
2002	Nil	d0.78	1.60	0.83

INTERIM DIVIDENDS (Per Share):

Amt.	Decl.	Ex.	Rec.	Pay.
0.385Q	6/06/02	7/08/02	7/10/02	8/01/02
0.385Q	9/05/02	10/08/02	10/10/02	11/01/02
0.385Q	12/05/02	1/08/03	1/10/03	2/03/03
0.385Q	3/10/03	4/08/03	4/10/03	5/01/03

Indicated div.: $1.54 (Div. Reinv. Plan)

CAPITALIZATION (12/31/01):

	($000)	(%)
Long-Term Debt	45,657,000	39.1
Deferred Income Tax	16,543,000	14.2
Minority Interest	22,149,000	18.9
Common & Surplus	32,539,000	27.8
Total	116,888,000	100.0

BUSINESS:

Verizon Communications Inc. (formerly Bell Atlantic Corp.), formed by the merger of Bell Atlantic Corporation and GTE Corp. on 6/30/00, is a provider of communications services. VZ is among the largest providers of wireline and wireless communications in the United States, with 135.8 million access line equivalents, 32.5 million wireless customers and 10.4 million long-distance customers as of 12/31/02. VZ also provides print and on-line directory information. VZ's global presence extends to 33 countries in the Americas, Europe, Asia and the Pacific. As of 12/31/02, VZ owned 55.0% of Verizon Wireless, which was formed in April 2000 through the combination of Bell Atlantic's and Vodafone AirTouch's U.S. wireless assets. In 2002, revenues were derived as follows: domestic telecom, 60.6%; domestic wireless, 28.6%; international, 4.4%; and information services, 6.4%.

RECENT DEVELOPMENTS:

For the year ended 12/31/02, income was $4.58 billion compared with $590.0 million a year earlier. Results for 2002 and 2001 included non-recurring charges of $3.79 billion and $7.62 billion, respectively. Results for 2002 and 2001 excluded extraordinary losses of $9.0 million and $19.0 million, and accounting change charges of $496.0 million and $182.0 million, respectively. Operating revenues rose to $67.63 billion from $67.19 billion in 2001.

PROSPECTS:

For full-year 2003, VZ anticipates revenue growth of nil to 2.0%, and earnings of between $2.70 and $2.80 per share. The Company expects that operational growth will contribute from $0.06 to $0.18 in earnings per share, offset $0.41 to $0.43 by reduced pension income of $0.30 to $0.32, reduced income from 2002 access line sales of $0.09, and an accounting change of $0.02 to expense stock options. Capital expenditures, including capitalized non-network software, are targeted in the $12.50 billion to $13.50 billion range, versus $13.10 billion in equivalent expenditures in 2002. Year-end 2003 net debt is targeted to drop to approximately $49.00 billion to $51.00 billion.

ANNUAL FINANCIAL DATA:

FISCAL YEAR	TOT. REVS. ($mill.)	NET INC. ($mill.)	TOT. ASSETS ($mill.)	OPER. PROFIT %	NET PROFIT %	RET. ON EQUITY %	RET. ON ASSETS %	CURR. RATIO	EARN. PER SH.$	CASH FL.PER SH.$	TANG. BK. VAL.$	DIV. PER SH.$	PRICE RANGE	AVG. P/E RATIO	AVG. YIELD %
p12/31/02	67,625.0	⑧ 4,584.0							⑧ 1.67			1.54	51.09 — 26.01	23.1	4.0
12/31/01	67,190.0	⑦ 590.0	170,795.0	17.2	0.9	1.8	0.3	0.6	⑦ 0.22	5.22	...	1.54	57.40 — 43.80	229.9	3.0
12/31/00	64,707.0	⑥ 10,810.0	164,735.0	25.9	16.7	31.3	6.6	0.6	⑥ 3.95	8.43	...	1.54	66.00 — 39.06	13.3	2.9
12/31/99	33,174.0	⑤ 4,208.0	62,614.0	25.6	12.7	26.5	6.7	0.8	⑤ 2.66	6.49	10.23	1.54	69.50 — 50.63	22.6	2.6
12/31/98	31,565.9	③ 2,990.8	55,143.9	21.0	9.5	20.7	5.3	0.9	③ 1.87	5.52	9.31	1.54	61.19 — 40.44	27.2	3.0
12/31/97	③ 30,193.9	2,454.9	53,964.1	17.7	8.1	17.7	4.5	0.7	1.57	5.23	8.82	1.49	45.88 — 28.38	23.7	4.0
12/31/96	13,081.4	② 1,739.4	24,856.2	22.4	13.3	20.9	6.1	0.5	② 1.98	4.93	9.52	1.43	37.44 — 27.56	16.4	4.4
12/31/95	13,429.5	③④ 1,861.8	24,156.3	23.0	13.9	24.1	6.7	0.5	③④ 2.13	5.12	8.81	1.40	34.44 — 24.19	13.8	4.8
12/31/94	13,791.4	⑤ 1,401.9	24,271.8	20.3	10.2	20.8	5.1	0.5	⑤ 1.61	4.64	7.73	1.37	29.81 — 24.19	16.8	5.1
12/31/93	12,990.2	⑤ 1,481.6	29,544.2	21.5	11.4	17.7	5.0	0.6	⑤ 1.70	4.61	9.62	1.33	34.56 — 24.81	17.5	4.5

Statistics are as originally reported. Results for 12/31/99 & earlier are for Bell Atlantic Corporation prior to acq. of GTE Corp. on 6/30/00. Adj. for 2-for-1 stk. split, 5/98 ① Refl. 8/97 acq. of NYNEX Corp. ② Bef. acctg. chge. chrg. of $19.8 mill. ③ Bef. extraord. chrg. 12/31/99: $6.0 mill.; 12/31/98: $25.5. mill.; 12/31/95: $3.5 mill.; 12/31/93: $58.4 mill. ④ Incl. nonrecur. cr. of $160.0 mill. ⑤ Bef. extraord. gain & acctg. chge. chrgs. of $2.16 mill. ⑥ Incl. net sales of assets of $3.79 bill. & mark-to-mark adjust. gain of $664.0 mill.; bef. extraord. gain of $1.03 bill. & acctg. chge. chrg. of $40.0 mill. ⑦ Incl. net chrg. of $7.60 bill.; bef. extraord. loss of $19.0 mill. & acctg. chge. chrg. of $182.0 mill. ⑧ Incl. net chrg. of $3.79 bill.; bef. extraord. loss of $9.0 mill. & acctg. chge. chrg. of $496.0 mill.

OFFICERS:
L. T. Babbio, Jr., Vice-Chmn., Pres.
I. G. Seidenberg, C.E.O.
D. A. Toben, Exec. V.P., C.F.O.

INVESTOR CONTACT: Shareholder Relations, (212) 395-1525

PRINCIPAL OFFICE: 1095 Avenue of the Americas, New York, NY 10036

TELEPHONE NUMBER: (212) 395-2121
FAX: (212) 921-2917
WEB: www.verizon.com
NO. OF EMPLOYEES: 229,500
SHAREHOLDERS: 1,121,000
ANNUAL MEETING: In Apr.
INCORPORATED: DE, Oct., 1983

INSTITUTIONAL HOLDINGS:
No. of Institutions: 1,093
Shares Held: 1,512,929,442
% Held: 55.3

INDUSTRY: Telephone communications, exc. radio (SIC: 4813)

TRANSFER AGENT(S): Fleet National Bank, c/o EquiServe, Boston, MA

VF CORPORATION

EXCH.	SYM.	REC. PRICE	P/E RATIO	YLD.	MKT. CAP.	RANGE (52-WK.)	'02 Y/E PR.	DIV. ACH.
NYSE	VFC	33.85 (2/28/03)	10.4	3.0%	$3.72 bill.	45.64 - 31.50	36.05	30 yrs.

UPPER MEDIUM GRADE. COST-REDUCTION EFFORTS ARE EXPECTED TO RESULT IN EARNINGS PER SHARE GROWTH OF BETWEEN 5.0% AND 10.0% IN 2003.

*7 YEAR PRICE SCORE 111.1   *12 MONTH PRICE SCORE 99.3

*NYSE COMPOSITE INDEX=100

INTERIM EARNINGS (Per Share):

Qtr.	Mar.	June	Sept.	Dec.
1997	0.54	0.61	0.86	0.74
1998	0.62	0.69	0.96	0.84
1999	0.69	0.64	0.85	0.81
2000	0.66	0.64	0.88	0.88
2001	0.67	0.60	0.90	d1.03
2002	0.69	0.79	1.15	0.63

INTERIM DIVIDENDS (Per Share):

Amt.	Decl.	Ex.	Rec.	Pay.
0.24Q	2/12/02	3/06/02	3/08/02	3/18/02
0.24Q	4/23/02	6/06/02	6/10/02	6/20/02
0.24Q	7/17/02	9/06/02	9/10/02	9/20/02
0.25Q	10/17/02	12/06/02	12/10/02	12/20/02
0.25Q	2/11/03	3/06/03	3/10/03	3/20/03

Indicated div.: $1.00 (Div. Reinv. Plan)

CAPITALIZATION (12/29/01):

	($000)	(%)
Long-Term Debt	904,035	30.0
Common & Surplus	2,112,796	70.0
Total	3,016,831	100.0

BUSINESS:

VF Corporation designs, manufactures and markets branded jeanswear, intimate apparel, playwear, workwear and daypacks. The Company's principal brands include: LEE®, RUSTLER® WRANGLER® RIDERS®, VANITY FAIR®, VASSARETTE®, BESTFORM®, LILY OF FRANCE®, LEE SPORT® HEALTHTEX®, JANSPORT®, EASTPAK®, RED KAP® AND THE NORTH FACE®. On 5/20/00, VFC acquired the Eastpak branded business and the CHIC jeans brand. On 8/16/00, VFC completed the acquisition of The North Face, Inc.

RECENT DEVELOPMENTS:

For the year ended 1/4/03, income from continuing operations advanced 67.7% to $364.4 million compared with income from continuing operations of $217.3 million in 2001. Results for 2002 and 2001 excluded a gain of $8.3 million and a loss of $79.4 million, respectively, from discontinued operations. Results for 2002 also excluded an accounting change charge of $527.3 million. Net sales declined 2.6% to $5.08 billion versus $5.22 billion in the previous year. Operating income increased 36.9% to $621.9 million compared with $454.4 million the year before, reflecting an improved sales mix and new product initiatives. Most of VFC's businesses reported improved profitability due to the benefits of its strategic repositioning program.

PROSPECTS:

Looking ahead, the Company does not expect much improvement in market conditions in 2003. However, the Company's focus on product innovation should result in increased sales for most of its businesses in 2003. In addition, the Company's cost-reduction efforts should contribute to earnings per share growth of between 5.0% and 10.0% in 2003. Sales for VFC's outdoor, international jeanswear and intimate apparel businesses are expected to report mid-single digit percentage gains, while imagewear sales are anticipated to be flat year over year. Sales for domestic jeanswear are anticipated to decrease about 3.0% due to competitive challenges in the mass channel of distribution.

ANNUAL FINANCIAL DATA:

FISCAL YEAR	TOT. REVS. ($mill.)	NET INC. ($mill.)	TOT. ASSETS ($mill.)	OPER. PROFIT %	NET PROFIT %	RET. ON EQUITY %	RET. ON ASSETS %	CURR. RATIO	EARN. PER SH.$	CASH FL. PER SH.$	TANG. BK. VAL.$	DIV. PER SH.$	PRICE RANGE	AVG. P/E RATIO	AVG. YIELD %
p1/04/03	5,083.5	③ 364.4							③ 3.24			0.97	45.64 - 31.50	11.9	2.5
12/29/01	5,518.8	② 137.8	4,103.0	6.3	2.5	6.5	3.4	2.5	② 1.19	2.67	9.97	0.93	42.70 - 28.15	29.8	2.6
12/30/00	5,747.9	① 267.1	4,358.2	8.9	4.6	12.2	6.1	2.1	① 2.27	3.76	12.56	0.89	36.90 - 20.94	12.7	3.1
1/01/00	5,551.6	366.2	4,026.5	11.8	6.6	16.9	9.1	1.7	2.99	4.37	10.08	0.85	55.00 - 27.44	13.8	2.1
1/02/99	5,478.8	388.3	3,836.7	12.5	7.1	18.8	10.1	1.8	3.10	4.40	9.33	0.81	54.69 - 33.44	14.2	1.8
1/03/98	5,222.2	350.9	3,322.8	11.6	6.7	18.8	10.6	2.1	2.70	3.91	8.68	0.77	48.25 - 32.25	14.9	1.9
1/04/97	5,137.2	299.5	3,449.5	10.8	5.8	15.2	8.7	2.2	2.27	3.61	8.68	0.73	34.94 - 23.81	12.9	2.5
12/31/95	5,062.3	157.3	3,447.1	6.9	3.1	8.9	4.6	1.9	1.19	2.55	6.97	0.69	28.56 - 23.38	21.8	2.7
12/31/94	4,971.7	274.5	3,335.6	10.8	5.5	15.8	8.2	1.7	2.05	3.35	6.41	0.65	26.88 - 22.13	12.0	2.7
1/01/94	4,320.4	246.4	2,877.3	10.0	5.7	15.9	8.6	2.3	1.86	2.91	7.54	0.61	28.25 - 19.75	12.9	2.5

Statistics are as originally reported. Adj. for stk. split: 2-for-1, 11/97. ① Incl. restr. costs of $119.9 mill.; bef. acctg. chge. chrg. of $6.8 mill. ② Incl. restr. costs of $236.8 mill. & a $0.06 per sh. gain fr. reversal of chrgs. ③ Excl. $8.3 mill. gain fr. disc. ops. & $527.3 mill. acctg. change chrg.

OFFICERS:
M. J. McDonald, Chmn., Pres., C.E.O.
R. K. Shearer, V.P., C.F.O.
C. Cummings, V.P., Gen. Couns., Sec.

INVESTOR CONTACT: Cindy Knoebel, Dir., Inv. Rel., (336) 547-6189

PRINCIPAL OFFICE: 105 Corporate Center Boulevard, Greensboro, NC 27408

TELEPHONE NUMBER: (336) 424-6000
FAX: (336) 547-7634
WEB: www.vfc.com

NO. OF EMPLOYEES: 71,000 (approx.)

SHAREHOLDERS: 6,279

ANNUAL MEETING: In Apr.

INCORPORATED: PA, Dec., 1889

INSTITUTIONAL HOLDINGS:
No. of Institutions: 283
Shares Held: 93,975,756
% Held: 86.5

INDUSTRY: Men's and boys' clothing, nec (SIC: 2329)

TRANSFER AGENT(S): First Chicago Trust Company of New York, Jersey City, NJ

VIACOM INC.

EXCH.	SYM.	REC. PRICE	P/E RATIO	YLD.	MKT. CAP.	RANGE (52-WK.)	'02 Y/E PR.
NYSE	VIAB	37.13 (2/28/03)	29.7	...	$65.22 bill.	51.89 - 29.75	40.76

MEDIUM GRADE. ON 2/4/03, VIACOM OUTDOOR INC., A DIVISION OF VIA, ANNOUNCED THAT IT HAS ACQUIRED OUTDOOR MEDIA DISPLAYS POSTERS, A BILLBOARD OPERATOR IN PUERTO RICO.

TRADING VOLUME
Thousand Shares

1989 1990 1991 1992 1993 1994 1995 1996 1997 1998 1999 2000 2001 2002 2003

*7 YEAR PRICE SCORE 121.1   ***12 MONTH PRICE SCORE 97.1**
*NYSE COMPOSITE INDEX=100

INTERIM EARNINGS (Per Share):

Qtr.	Mar.	June	Sept.	Dec.
1999	0.08	0.08	0.16	0.19
2000	0.11	d0.41	0.02	0.02
2001	Nil	0.01	d0.11	d0.02
2002	0.21	0.31	0.36	0.37

INTERIM DIVIDENDS (Per Share):

Amt.	Decl.	Ex.	Rec.	Pay.
		No dividends paid.		

CAPITALIZATION (12/31/01):

	($000)	(%)
Long-Term Debt	10,823,700	14.3
Deferred Income Tax	1,131,200	1.5
Minority Interest	1,211,800	1.6
Common & Surplus	62,716,800	82.6
Total	75,883,500	100.0

BUSINESS:

Viacom Inc. is a diversified entertainment company. VIA's operations include Infinity Broadcasting, CBS, Nickelodeon, VH1, The New TNN, TV Land, CMT: Country Music Television, Blockbuster (81.0% owned as 7/25/02), MTV Networks, BET, Paramount Pictures, Showtime Networks, and Simon & Schuster. VIA also owns Spelling Entertainment Group and the UPN television network, as well as half-interests in Comedy Central and United Cine-

mas International. National Amusements, Inc., a closely-held corporation that operates about 1,300 screens in the U.S., the U.K. and South America, is the parent company of VIA and owned 68.0% of its class A stock as of 3/31/02. On 5/4/00, VIA acquired CBS Corp. The Company acquired BET Holdings II, Inc. on 1/23/01 and Infinity Broadcasting Corporation on 2/21/01.

RECENT DEVELOPMENTS:

For the year ended 12/31/02, income was $2.21 billion, before an accounting change charge of $1.48 billion, compared with a net loss of $223.5 million the previous year. Earnings included nonrecurring items that resulted in net pre-tax charges of $523.0 million in 2001. Revenues climbed 6.0% to $24.61 million from $23.22 billion the

year before. Television revenues rose 3.3% to $7.49 billion from $7.25 billion, while video revenues grew 7.9% to $5.57 billion from $5.16 billion in 2001. Revenues from cable networks advanced 10.0% to $4.73 billion and entertainment revenues inched up 1.4% to $3.65 billion.

PROSPECTS:

On 2/4/03, Viacom Outdoor Inc., a division of VIA, announced that it has acquired Outdoor Media Displays Posters, a billboard operator in Puerto Rico. The terms of the acquisition were not disclosed. Meanwhile, the Company expects to deliver mid-single digit revenue growth

resulting in mid-teen growth in operating income and earnings per share for full-year 2003. Going forward, the Company will continue its strategic program of opportunistic acquisitions. VIAB will also focus on combining new efficiencies with investments in programming.

ANNUAL FINANCIAL DATA:

FISCAL YEAR	TOT. REVS. ($mill.)	NET INC. ($mill.)	TOT. ASSETS ($mill.)	OPER. PROFIT %	NET PROFIT %	RET. ON EQUITY %	RET. ON ASSETS %	CURR. RATIO	EARN. PER SH. $	CASH FL. PER SH. $	PRICE RANGE	AVG. P/E RATIO
p12/31/02	24,605.7	⑦ 2,206.6							⑥ 1.26		51.89 — 29.79	32.4
12/31/01	23,222.8	d219.6	90,809.9	6.3	...	...	...	1.0	⑤ d0.13	1.66	59.50 — 24.30	...
⑧ 12/31/00	20,043.7	①④ d363.8	82,646.1	6.6	...	...	...	1.0	①④ d0.30	1.53	75.88 — 44.31	...
12/31/99	12,858.8	③ 371.7	24,486.4	9.7	2.9	3.3	1.5	1.2	③ 0.51	1.72	60.44 — 35.38	93.9
12/31/98	12,096.1	②③ d43.5	23,613.1	6.2	...	...	...	0.9	②③ d0.10	1.02	37.13 — 20.25	...
12/31/97	13,206.1	①② 374.5	28,288.7	5.7	2.8	2.8	1.3	1.1	①② 0.45	1.82	21.13 — 12.63	37.9
12/31/96	12,084.2	② 170.7	28,834.0	10.5	1.4	1.4	0.6	1.3	①② 0.15	1.26	23.81 — 14.88	128.9
12/31/95	11,688.7	② 214.9	29,026.0	12.8	1.8	1.8	0.7	1.3	② 0.21	1.30	27.13 — 20.13	115.2
12/31/94	7,363.2	③④ 130.5	28,273.7	8.3	1.8	1.1	0.5	1.3	③④ 0.13	1.18	22.50 — 10.88	133.4
12/31/93	2,004.9	③④ 169.5	6,416.9	19.2	8.5	6.2	2.6	2.8	③④ 0.65	1.28	30.63 — 17.63	37.1

Statistics are as originally reported. Adj. for stk. 2-for-1 split, 3/99 ① Incl. non-recurr. chrg. 2000, $505.0 mill.; 1997, $323.0 mill.; 1996, $88.9 mill. ② Bef. disc. oper. loss 1998, $4.2 mill.; gain 1997, $419.1 mill.; 1996, $1.08 bill.; loss 1995, $7.6 mill.; 1994, $20.5 mill. ③ Bef. extraord. chrg. 1999, $37.7 mill.; 1998, $74.7 mill.; 1994, $20.4 mill.; 1993, $8.9 mill. ④ Bef. acctg. change chrg. $452.3 mill., 2000; credit $10.4 mill., 1993. ⑤ Bef. extraord. loss of $3.9 mill.; incl. pre-tax, restr. chrg. of $119.4 mill. ⑥ Ref. acq. of CBS Corp. on 5/4/00. ⑦ Bef. acctg. chng. chrg. of $1.48 bill.

OFFICERS:
S. M. Redstone, Chmn., C.E.O.
M. Karmazin, Pres., C.O.O.
R. J. Bressler, Sr. Exec. V.P., C.F.O.
INVESTOR CONTACT: Martin Shea, Sr. V.P., Inv. Rel., (212) 258-6515
PRINCIPAL OFFICE: 1515 Broadway, New York, NY 10036

TELEPHONE NUMBER: (212) 258-6000
FAX: (212) 258-6558
WEB: www.viacom.com
NO. OF EMPLOYEES: 122,770 (approx.)
SHAREHOLDERS: 6,327 (approx. class A common); 75,038 (approx. class B common)
ANNUAL MEETING: In May
INCORPORATED: DE, Nov., 1986

INSTITUTIONAL HOLDINGS:
No. of Institutions: 763
Shares Held: 1,161,374,220
% Held: 65.9
INDUSTRY: Motion picture & video production (SIC: 7812)
TRANSFER AGENT(S): First Chicago Trust Co. of New York, Jersey City, NJ

VIAD CORP.

EXCH.	SYM.	REC. PRICE	P/E RATIO	YLD.	MKT. CAP.	RANGE (52-WK.)	'02 Y/E PR.
NYSE	VVI	20.90 (2/28/03)	16.2	1.7%	$1.86 bill.	31.00 - 16.75	22.35

MEDIUM GRADE. THE COMPANY ANTICIPATES EARNINGS IN THE RANGE OF $1.50 TO $1.55 PER DILUTED SHARE FOR 2003.

*7 YEAR PRICE SCORE 103.7 ***12 MONTH PRICE SCORE 98.6**

*NYSE COMPOSITE INDEX=100

INTERIM EARNINGS (Per Share):

Qtr.	Mar.	June	Sept.	Dec.
1999	0.20	0.33	0.42	0.49
2000	0.28	0.46	0.48	0.36
2001	0.28	0.20	d0.19	0.29
2002	0.37	0.36	0.41	0.15

INTERIM DIVIDENDS (Per Share):

Amt.	Decl.	Ex.	Rec.	Pay.
0.09Q	2/21/02	3/13/02	3/15/02	4/01/02
0.09Q	5/14/02	6/05/02	6/07/02	7/01/02
0.09Q	8/15/02	9/04/02	9/06/02	10/01/02
0.09Q	11/21/02	12/04/02	12/06/02	1/02/03
0.09Q	2/20/03	3/12/03	3/14/03	4/01/03

Indicated div.: $0.36

CAPITALIZATION (12/31/01):

	($000)	(%)
Long-Term Debt	354,147	32.6
Minority Interest	5,284	0.5
Redeemable Pfd. Stock	6,679	0.6
Common & Surplus	719,673	66.3
Total	1,085,783	100.0

BUSINESS:

Viad Corp. (formerly The Dial Corporation) was formed after the spin-off of Dial's consumer products group in August 1996. The Company is a diversified business that provides services to businesses for use by their customers. Accordingly, VVI markets its services through more than 100,000 retail and financial locations (payment services), to numerous tradeshow organizers and exhibitors (convention and event services), and others. The Company's Convention and Event Services businesses are provided by VVI's GES Exposition Services and Exhibitgroup/Giltspur com-

panies. The Company's Payment Services (PS) business is conducted by the Travelers Express group of companies. VVI's Travel and Recreation Services are provided by the Brewster Transport Company Limited and Glacier Park, Inc. Net sales (and operating income) for 2002 were derived from the following: PS, 49.8% (78.8%); Convention and Event Services, 46.7% (15.5%); and Travel and Recreation Services, 3.5% (5.7%). PS' net sales and income included beneficial taxable equivalent adjustments.

RECENT DEVELOPMENTS:

For the year ended 12/31/02, VVI reported income of $113.9 million, before an accounting change charge of $37.7 million, compared with net income of $51.1 million a year earlier. Results for 2002 and 2001 included after-tax restructuring and other one-time charges of $13.1 million and $61.2 million, respectively. Total revenues decreased

0.7% to $1.65 billion from $1.66 billion a year earlier. Convention and Event Services revenues fell 11.1% to $786.2 million, while Travel and Recreation revenues declined 5.2% to $58.3 million. Taxable-equivalent Payment Services revenues climbed 10.2% to $838.7 million. Operating income advanced 13.8% to $205.8 million.

PROSPECTS:

For 2003, the Company anticipates earnings in the range of $1.50 to $1.55 per diluted share. Payment Services segment revenue is expected to grow at a high-single to low-double digit rate in the coming year, while Convention and Event

Services segment revenue is expected to decline at a mid-single to low-double digit rate year over year, primarily due to lower demand for exhibit construction.

ANNUAL FINANCIAL DATA:

FISCAL YEAR	TOT. REVS. ($mill.)	NET INC. ($mill.)	TOT. ASSETS ($mill.)	OPER. PROFIT %	NET PROFIT %	RET. ON EQUITY %	RET. ON ASSETS %	CURR. RATIO	EARN. PER SH.$	CASH FL. PER SH.$	TANG. BK. VAL.$	DIV. PER SH.$	PRICE RANGE		AVG. P/E RATIO	AVG. YIELD %
p12/31/02	1,647.0	⑨113.8							⑨1.30			0.36	31.00 -	16.75	18.4	1.5
12/31/01	1,659.4	⑧51.1	8,364.1	· 3.8	3.1	7.1	0.6	0.3	⑧0.58	1.35	1.08	0.36	27.30 -	18.00	39.0	1.6
12/31/00	1,726.8	⑦144.5	6,300.2	11.3	8.4	18.9	2.3	0.3	⑦1.58	2.34	1.25	0.36	29.81 -	19.75	15.7	1.5
12/31/99	1,581.2	⑥128.6	5,210.9	11.9	8.1	18.1	2.5	0.2	⑥1.32	1.99	0.84	0.34	33.88 -	24.00	21.9	1.2
12/31/98	2,542.1	⑤150.6	4,802.8	9.4	5.9	23.3	3.1	0.4	⑤1.52	2.40	...	0.32	30.56 -	18.56	16.2	1.3
12/31/97	2,417.5	④97.8	3,730.3	9.2	4.0	18.5	2.6	0.4	④1.03	1.88	...	0.32	20.38 -	14.63	17.0	1.8
12/31/96	2,263.2	③69.1	3,453.3	9.0	3.0	16.0	2.0	0.4	③0.74	2.02	...	0.56	33.25 -	13.38	31.5	2.4
12/31/95	3,575.1	②1.1	4,225.2	3.2	...	0.2	...	0.6	②d0.20	1.57	...	...	30.38 -	20.88	...	...
12/31/94	3,546.8	140.3	3,780.9	9.3	4.0	25.3	3.7	0.6	1.61	1.31	...	...	24.00 -	19.25	13.4	...
12/31/93	3,000.3	①110.3	3,281.1	9.2	3.7	23.5	3.4	0.6	①1.28	2.46	...	...	22.25 -	17.94	15.7	...

Statistics are as originally reported. Adj. for stk. split: 2-for-1, 7/94. ① Bef. disc. oper. gain $32.1 mill. ② Incl. nonrecur. chrg. $130.0 mill. ③ Bef. discont. oper. gain $40.7 mill.; incl. nonrecur. chrg. $2.5 mill. ④ Bef. extraord. chrg. $8.5 mill. ⑤ Bef. disc. oper. gain $32.9 mill. and a $6.9 mill. after-tax litig. settlement charge. ⑥ Bef. discont. oper. gain $219.0 mill.; incl. nonrecur. gain $6.1 mill. ⑦ Incl. nonrecur. gain $877,000. ⑧ Incl. after-tax restr. other chrg. $61.2 mill. ⑨ Inc. after-tax restr. and other chrg. $13.1 mill.

OFFICERS:
R. H. Bohannon, Chmn., Pres., C.E.O.
E. M. Ingersoll, C.F.O.
S. E. Sayre, V.P., Sec., Gen. Couns.
INVESTOR CONTACT: Patricia D. Phillips, (602) 207-1040
PRINCIPAL OFFICE: 1850 N. Central Ave., Phoenix, AZ 85077

TELEPHONE NUMBER: (602) 207-4000
FAX: (602) 207-5834
WEB: www.viad.com
NO. OF EMPLOYEES: 5,800 (approx.)
SHAREHOLDERS: 26,250
ANNUAL MEETING: In May
INCORPORATED: DE, Dec., 1991

INSTITUTIONAL HOLDINGS:
No. of Institutions: 204
Shares Held: 66,181,624
% Held: 75.1
INDUSTRY: Business services, nec (SIC: 7389)
TRANSFER AGENT(S): Wells Fargo Shareowner Services, South St. Paul, MN

VISHAY INTERTECHNOLOGY, INC.

EXCH.	SYM.	REC. PRICE	P/E RATIO	YLD.	MKT. CAP.	RANGE (52-WK.)	'02 Y/E PR.
NYSE	VSH	10.10 (2/28/03)	...	...	$1.61 bill.	26.15 - 6.70	11.18

MEDIUM GRADE. REVENUES AND EARNINGS FOR 2003 ARE EXPECTED TO BENEFIT FROM THE ACQUISITION OF BCCOMPONENTS HOLDINGS B.V.

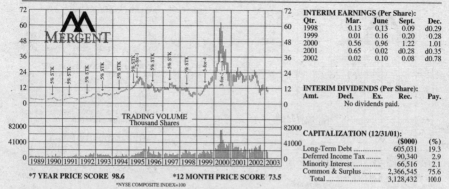

*7 YEAR PRICE SCORE 98.6   ***12 MONTH PRICE SCORE 73.5**
NYSE COMPOSITE INDEX=100

INTERIM EARNINGS (Per Share):

Qtr.	Mar.	June	Sept.	Dec.
1998	0.13	0.13	0.09	d0.29
1999	0.01	0.16	0.20	0.28
2000	0.56	0.96	1.22	1.01
2001	0.65	0.02	d0.28	d0.35
2002	0.02	0.10	0.08	d0.78

INTERIM DIVIDENDS (Per Share):

Amt.	Decl.	Ex.	Rec.	Pay.
		No dividends paid.		

CAPITALIZATION (12/31/01):

	($000)	(%)
Long-Term Debt	605,031	19.3
Deferred Income Tax	90,340	2.9
Minority Interest	66,516	2.1
Common & Surplus	2,366,545	75.6
Total	3,128,432	100.0

BUSINESS:

Vishay Intertechnology, Inc. designs and manufactures electronic components that cover a range of products and technologies. VSH's Passive Components segment consists principally of fixed resistors, solid tantalum surface mount capacitors, solid tantalum leaded capacitors, wet/foil tantalum capacitors, multi-layer ceramic chip capacitors, film capacitors and inductors. VSH's Active Components segment consists principally of diodes, transistors, power metal oxide semiconductor field effect transistor, power conversion, motor control integrated circuits, optoelectronic components and infrared data components transceivers. At 2/5/03, VSH owned 80.4% of Siliconix Inc. On 11/2/01, VSH acquired General Semiconductor, Inc. for about $555.0 million.

RECENT DEVELOPMENTS:

For the year ended 12/31/02, VSH reported a net loss of $92.6 million versus net income of $513,000 in 2001. Results for 2002 and 2001 included after-tax restructuring charges of $12.0 million and $40.0 million, and inventory write-downs of $22.5 million and $57.4 million, respectively. Results for 2002 and 2001 also included after-tax other non-recurring charges of $10.4 million and $5.4 million, respectively. In addition, results included an after-tax loss on long-term purchase commitments of $91.2 million in 2002 and purchased research and development expense of $16.0 million in 2001. Net sales advanced 10.1% to $1.82 billion from $1.66 billion a year earlier. Gross profit decreased 3.5% to $368.3 million, or 20.2% of net sales, from $381.5 million, or 23.0% of net sales, the year before.

PROSPECTS:

On 12/13/02, the Company acquired BCcomponents Holdings B.V., a manufacturer of passive components with operations in Europe, India and the Far East. BCcomponents' products include linear and non-linear resistors, ceramic, film, and aluminum electrolytic capacitors, and switches and trimming potentiometers. VSH expects to begin integrating the acquired operations with its existing passive component business in Europe and elsewhere around the world. In addition, VSH anticipates cost-savings from the integration of approximately $70.0 million.

ANNUAL FINANCIAL DATA:

FISCAL YEAR	TOT. REVS. ($mill.)	NET INC. ($mill.)	TOT. ASSETS ($mill.)	OPER. PROFIT %	NET PROFIT %	RET. ON EQUITY %	RET. ON ASSETS %	CURR. RATIO	EARN. PER SH.$	CASH FL.PER SH.$	TANG. BK. VAL.$	PRICE RANGE	AVG. P/E RATIO
p12/31/02	1,822.8	⑨d92.6							⑨d0.58			26.15 — 6.70	...
12/31/01	1,655.3	⑧0.5	3,951.5	0.9	...	...	...	3.3	⑧Nil	1.19	7.57	27.98 — 13.75	N.M.
12/31/00	2,465.1	⑦517.9	2,783.7	28.3	21.0	28.2	18.6	3.5	⑦3.77	4.79	11.15	62.67 — 13.88	10.2
12/31/99	1,760.1	⑥83.2	2,323.8	11.0	4.7	8.2	3.6	2.7	⑥0.65	1.74	4.83	21.33 — 5.93	21.1
12/31/98	1,572.7	⑤8.2	2,462.7	6.0	0.5	0.8	0.3	3.0	⑤0.06	1.07	4.49	12.51 — 4.90	135.8
12/31/97	1,125.2	④53.3	1,719.6	9.7	4.7	5.6	3.1	3.4	④0.42	1.07	5.31	16.19 — 9.37	30.3
12/31/96	1,098.0	③52.6	1,556.0	7.8	4.8	5.6	3.4	3.3	③0.42	1.02	6.70	15.78 — 8.41	29.1
12/31/95	1,224.4	②92.7	1,543.3	12.4	7.6	10.2	6.0	2.8	②0.78	1.38	6.52	20.45 — 10.59	19.8
12/31/94	987.8	58.9	1,334.0	9.9	6.0	10.4	4.4	2.4	0.55	1.09	3.46	11.49 — 6.87	16.6
12/31/93	856.3	①42.6	948.1	8.7	5.0	11.3	4.5	2.1	①0.42	0.90	2.54	7.89 — 5.32	15.7

Statistics are as originally reported. Adj. for all stk. dividends and splits through 6/00 ① Bef. acctg. change charge $1.4 mill. ② Incl. charge $4.2 mill. ③ Incl. charge $38.0 mill. for restruc. ④ Inc. pre-tax chrg. $12.6 mill. for restr. and a pre-tax charge $1.9 mill. for an unusual expense. ⑤ Incl. non-cash special charges of $55.3 million. ⑥ Incl. non-recurr. chrg. $14.6 mill. & loss on disp. of sub. $10.1 mill. ⑦ Incl. a pre-tax gain of $8.9 mill. on term. of int. swap. & incl. gain of $8.4 mill. on sale of Lite-On Power. ⑧ Incl. pre-tax restr. chrg. of $61.9 mill. ⑨ Incl. aft.-tax restr. chrg. $12.0 mill., inventory write-down $22.5 mill., loss on long-tm. purch. commit. of $91.2 mill. & oth. one-time chrg. $10.4 mill.

OFFICERS:
F. Zandman, Chmn., C.E.O.
A. D. Eden, Vice-Chmn., Exec. V.P.
M. Zandman, Vice-Chmn.

INVESTOR CONTACT: Richard N. Grubb,
Exec. V.P., C.F.O., (610) 644-1300

PRINCIPAL OFFICE: 63 Lincoln Highway,
Malvern, PA 19355-2120

TELEPHONE NUMBER: (610) 644-1300
FAX: (610) 296-0657
WEB: www.vishay.com
NO. OF EMPLOYEES: 25,000 (approx.)
SHAREHOLDERS: 1,900 (approx.)
ANNUAL MEETING: In May
INCORPORATED: DE, July, 1962

INSTITUTIONAL HOLDINGS:
No. of Institutions: 260
Shares Held: 103,402,558
% Held: 64.7

INDUSTRY: Electronic resistors (SIC: 3676)

TRANSFER AGENT(S): American Stock
Transfer & Trust, New York, NY

VISTEON CORPORATION

EXCH.	SYM.	REC. PRICE	P/E RATIO	YLD.	MKT. CAP.	RANGE (52-WK.)	'02 Y/E PR.
NYSE	VC	6.35 (2/28/03)	...	3.8%	$0.83 bill.	16.78 - 6.31	6.96

LOWER MEDIUM GRADE. THE COMPANY EXPECTS TO BENEFIT FROM NEW BUSINESS CONTRACTS AND RECENT RESTRUCTURING ACTIONS.

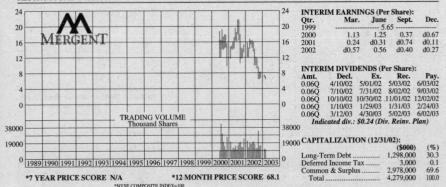

*7 YEAR PRICE SCORE N/A   *12 MONTH PRICE SCORE 68.1
*NYSE COMPOSITE INDEX=100

INTERIM EARNINGS (Per Share):

Qtr.	Mar.	June	Sept.	Dec.
1999	----	5.65	----	
2000	1.13	1.25	0.37	d0.67
2001	0.24	d0.31	d0.74	d0.11
2002	d0.57	0.56	d0.40	d0.27

INTERIM DIVIDENDS (Per Share):

Amt.	Decl.	Ex.	Rec.	Pay.
0.06Q	4/10/02	5/01/02	5/03/02	6/03/02
0.06Q	7/10/02	7/31/02	8/02/02	9/03/02
0.06Q	10/10/02	10/30/02	11/01/02	12/02/02
0.06Q	1/10/03	1/29/03	1/31/03	2/24/03
0.06Q	3/12/03	4/30/03	5/02/03	6/02/03

Indicated div.: $0.24 (Div. Reinv. Plan)

CAPITALIZATION (12/31/02):

	($000)	(%)
Long-Term Debt	1,298,000	30.3
Deferred Income Tax	3,000	0.1
Common & Surplus	2,978,000	69.6
Total	4,279,000	100.0

BUSINESS:

Visteon Corporation is a major supplier of automotive systems, modules and components to global vehicle manufacturers and the automotive aftermarket. The Automotive Operations segment (96.7% of 2002 sales) provides climate control, interior, exterior, powertrain, chassis and electronic products for vehicles. The Glass Operations segment (3.3%) produces glass products for Ford Motor Company and aftermarket customers and float glass for commercial architecture. As of 3/5/03, VC operated a delivery system of more than 180 technical, manufacturing, sales and service facilities located in 25 countries. On 6/28/00, VC was spun off from Ford.

RECENT DEVELOPMENTS:

For the year ended 12/31/02, VC reported a loss of $87.0 million, before an accounting change charge of $265.0 million, compared with a net loss of $118.0 million in the previous year. Results for 2002 and 2001 included after-tax restructuring and related charges of $142.0 million and $121.0 million, respectively. Total sales increased 3.1% to $18.40 billion from $17.84 billion a year earlier. Sales to Ford and affiliates inched up 0.8% to $14.78 billion, while sales to other customers advanced 13.5% to $3.62 billion. Cost of sales climbed 2.8% to $17.59 billion from $17.11 billion the year before. Operating loss narrowed to $81.0 million from $117.0 million in 2001.

PROSPECTS:

During 2002, the Company won more than $1.00 billion in net new non-Ford business from more than a dozen global automakers throughout the world. In addition, VC won more than $500.0 million in new business with Ford, which was primarily offset by returned and lost business. Meanwhile, VC has taken restructuring actions and achieved greater customer diversification, which should lead to improved operating results going forward. Separately, on 3/5/03, VC announced it will exit its seating business in Chesterfield, Michigan, which currently provides seating systems to Ford. Looking ahead, the Company will deliver its new thermoformed fuel tanks for future General Motors vehicles. The tank, designed to minimize evaporative emissions, integrates the fuel delivery system, fuel filters, fuel/vapor lines and on-board recovery system into the tank.

ANNUAL FINANCIAL DATA:

FISCAL YEAR	TOT. REVS. ($mill.)	NET INC. ($mill.)	TOT. ASSETS ($mill.)	OPER. PROFIT %	NET PROFIT %	RET. ON EQUITY %	RET. ON ASSETS %	CURR. RATIO	EARN. PER SH. $	CASH FL. PER SH. $	TANG. BK. VAL. $	DIV. PER SH. $	PRICE RANGE	AVG. P/E RATIO	AVG. YIELD
12/31/02	18,395.0	③ d87.0	11,170.0	...	...	...	...	1.4	③ d0.68	4.26	22.73	0.24	16.78 - 6.38	...	2.1
12/31/01	17,843.0	② d118.0	11,078.0	...	...	...	...	1.4	② d0.91	d0.90	25.12	0.24	21.72 - 10.45	...	1.5
12/31/00	19,467.0	① 270.0	11,325.0	2.3	1.4	7.7	2.4	1.3	① 2.08	7.28	26.76	0.12	19.25 - 9.75	7.0	0.8
12/31/99	19,366.0	735.0	12,449.0	6.1	3.8	49.0	5.9	0.9	5.65	10.66	10.86	...			
12/31/98	17,762.0	703.0	9,373.0	6.4	4.0	42.5	7.5	1.0	5.41	...	...	...			
12/31/97	17,220.0	511.0	...	4.9	3.0	...	...	...	3.93	...	...	...			

Statistics are as originally reported. ① Incl. non-cash impairment chrg. $220.0 mill. ② Incl. after-tax restr. chrg. $121.0 mill. ③ Bef. acctg. change chrg. $265.0 mill.; incl. after-tax restr. chrg. $142.0 mill.

OFFICERS:
P. J. Pestillo, Chmn., C.E.O.
M. F. Johnston, Pres., C.O.O.
D. R. Coulson, Exec. V.P., C.F.O.
INVESTOR CONTACT: Derek Fiebig, (313) 755-3699
PRINCIPAL OFFICE: 17000 Rotunda, Dearborn, MI 48120

TELEPHONE NUMBER: (800) 847-8366
FAX: (313) 755-2776
WEB: www.visteon.com
NO. OF EMPLOYEES: 77,000 (approx.)
SHAREHOLDERS: 126,418
ANNUAL MEETING: In May
INCORPORATED: DE, Jan., 2000

INSTITUTIONAL HOLDINGS:
No. of Institutions: 262
Shares Held: 73,123,359
% Held: 56.2
INDUSTRY: Motor vehicle parts and accessories (SIC: 3714)
TRANSFER AGENT(S): EquiServe Trust Company, N.A., Jersey City, NJ

VOLT INFORMATION SCIENCES, INC.

EXCH.	SYM.	REC. PRICE	P/E RATIO	YLD.	MKT. CAP.	RANGE (52-WK.)	'02 Y/E PR.
NYSE	VOL	11.40 (2/28/03)	...	...	$173.5 mill.	24.50 - 11.40	17.10

LOWER MEDIUM GRADE. ON 2/28/03, VMC CONSULTING CORPORATION, A WHOLLY-OWNED SUBSIDIARY OF VOL, ANNOUNCED A MERGER WITH SISTER DIVISION VOLT INTEGRATED SOLUTIONS GROUP.

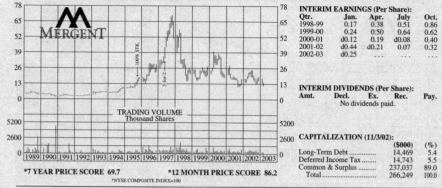

INTERIM EARNINGS (Per Share):

Qtr.	Jan.	Apr.	July	Oct.
1998-99	0.17	0.38	0.51	0.86
1999-00	0.24	0.50	0.64	0.62
2000-01	d0.12	0.19	d0.08	0.40
2001-02	d0.44	d0.21	0.07	0.32
2002-03	d0.25	...	...	...

INTERIM DIVIDENDS (Per Share):

Amt.	Decl.	Ex.	Rec.	Pay.
		No dividends paid.		

*7 YEAR PRICE SCORE 69.7 ***12 MONTH PRICE SCORE 86.2**

*NYSE COMPOSITE INDEX=100

CAPITALIZATION (11/3/02):

	($000)	(%)
Long-Term Debt	14,469	5.4
Deferred Income Tax	14,743	5.5
Common & Surplus	237,037	89.0
Total	266,249	100.0

BUSINESS:

Volt Information Sciences, Inc. is a national provider of staffing, telecommunications and information Services. Through a network of over 300 Volt Services Group branch offices as of 3/13/02, the Staffing Services segment (81.9% of sales in 2002) fulfills information technology and other technical, commercial, and industrial placement requirements of its customers, on both a temporary and permanent basis. The Telecommunications Services segment (7.3%) provides a variety of telecommunications construction, installation and engineering services. The Telecommunications Directory segment (5.6%) provides telephone directory production and directory publishing, and the Computer Systems segment (5.2%) provides advanced computer information and operator services systems.

RECENT DEVELOPMENTS:

For the first quarter ended 2/2/03, the Company reported a net loss of $3.8 million compared with a loss of $6.7 million, before a gain from discontinued operations of $4.3 million and an accounting change charge of $31.9 million, in the corresponding prior-year quarter. Net sales increased 5.8% to $358.2 million from $338.8 million a year earlier.

Net Staffing Services segment sales rose 8.8% to $302.2 million, while Telephone Directory segment sales jumped 17.4% to $12.5 million. Telecommunications Services segment sales fell 21.8% to $25.9 million, while Computer Systems segment sales declined 5.3% to $20.4 million.

PROSPECTS:

On 2/28/03, VMC Consulting Corporation, a wholly-owned subsidiary of VOL, announced a merger with sister division Volt Integrated Solutions group, the global information technology division of the Company. The combination forms a consolidated entity focused on delivering outsourced services and consulting to customers across multiple industries. VOL expects the merger will strengthen VMC Consulting's market position as a provider of cost-effective, flexible applications for managing and expediting project-based business and government services.

ANNUAL FINANCIAL DATA:

FISCAL YEAR	TOT. REVS. ($mill.)	NET INC. ($mill.)	TOT. ASSETS ($mill.)	OPER. PROFIT %	NET PROFIT %	RET. ON EQUITY %	RET. ON ASSETS %	CURR. RATIO	EARN. PER SH.$	CASH FL. PER SH.$	TANG. BK. VAL.$	PRICE RANGE	AVG. P/E RATIO
11/03/02	1,487.8	⑧d3.9	509.6	...	...	...	...	1.7	⑧d0.26	1.20	14.98	24.50 - 12.65	...
11/04/01	1,932.3	⑦6.7	637.2	0.6	0.3	2.5	1.0	1.4	⑦0.44	2.05	15.09	28.10 - 10.50	43.9
11/03/00	2,201.2	30.7	744.8	2.7	1.4	11.7	4.1	1.4	2.00	3.65	14.37	39.88 - 18.19	14.5
10/29/99	2,141.1	⑥29.0	618.3	2.3	1.4	12.6	4.7	1.5	⑥1.91	3.50	11.94	27.44 - 15.56	11.3
10/30/98	1,708.6	⑤20.9	469.3	2.3	1.2	10.4	4.5	1.9	⑤1.37	2.73	12.10	58.25 - 15.31	26.8
10/31/97	1,401.5	④40.0	418.7	3.5	2.9	22.5	9.5	2.0	④2.63	3.98	10.99	70.25 - 26.17	18.3
11/01/96	1,048.9	④23.3	337.1	3.4	2.2	17.9	6.9	1.9	④1.53	2.67	7.90	30.33 - 12.67	14.1
11/03/95	907.3	③16.4	264.0	3.6	1.8	15.3	6.2	1.5	③1.13	2.01	7.02	18.17 - 9.00	12.0
10/28/94	720.9	②12.0	226.9	1.9	1.6	12.8	5.3	1.7	②0.84	1.23	5.90	10.00 - 5.17	9.0
10/29/93	558.1	①d3.7	235.9	...	...	...	...	1.6	①d0.25	0.37	4.98	6.58 - 3.67	...

Statistics are as originally reported. Adj. for stk. splits: 3-for-2, 5/97; 2-for-1, 10/95. ① Bef. acctg. credit of $959,000 ② Bef. extraord. chrg of $271,000 & Incls. net loss on securities of $7,000 and gain on sale of joint venture of $9.8 mill. ③ Bef. extraord. chrg. of $62,000. ④ Bef. extraord. chrg. of $87,000 & incl. gain on sale of interest in subsidiary of $3.7 mill. ⑤ Bef. loss from discont. opers. of $119,000 & incl. gain on sale of joint venture of $12.8 mill. ⑥ Incls. gains on sale of joint ventures $500,000, 1998; $2.0 mill., 1999. ⑦ Bef. loss from disc. opers. of $814,000; Incl. gains on the sale of securities and a real estate partnership interest of $5.9 mill. ⑧ Bef. disc. oper. gain $4.3 mill., extr. loss $1.3 mill. & acctg. change chrg. $31.9 mill.

OFFICERS:
W. Shaw, Chmn., Pres., C.E.O.
J. J. Groberg, Sr. V.P., C.F.O.
J. Shaw, Exec. V.P., Sec.

INVESTOR CONTACT: James J. Groberg, Sr. V.P., C.F.O., (212) 704-2400

PRINCIPAL OFFICE: 560 Lexington Avenue, New York, NY 10022

TELEPHONE NUMBER: (212) 704-2400
FAX: (212) 704-2417
WEB: www.volt.com

NO. OF EMPLOYEES: 4,500 (approx.)
SHAREHOLDERS: 419 (approx.)
ANNUAL MEETING: In April
INCORPORATED: NY, March, 1957

INSTITUTIONAL HOLDINGS:
No. of Institutions: 59
Shares Held: 4,968,647
% Held: 32.7

INDUSTRY: Help supply services (SIC: 7363)

TRANSFER AGENT(S): Registrar and Transfer Company, Cranford, NJ

VORNADO REALTY TRUST

EXCH.	SYM.	REC. PRICE	P/E RATIO	YLD.	MKT. CAP.	RANGE (52-WK.)	'02 Y/E PR.
NYSE	VNO	35.00 (2/28/03)	18.9	7.8%	$3.47 bill.	47.20 - 33.20	37.20

UPPER MEDIUM GRADE. ON 1/1/03, THE COMPANY ANNOUNCED THAT IT ACQUIRED BUILDING MAINTENANCE SERVICES COMPANY FOR ABOUT $13.0 MILLION.

TRADING VOLUME
Thousand Shares

*7 YEAR PRICE SCORE 120.9   ***12 MONTH PRICE SCORE 96.6**

*NYSE COMPOSITE INDEX=100

INTERIM EARNINGS (Per Share):

Qtr.	Mar.	June	Sept.	Dec.
1999	0.49	0.49	0.51	0.45
2000	0.54	0.53	0.65	0.47
2001	0.52	0.64	0.74	0.57
2002	0.40	0.57	0.52	0.36

INTERIM DIVIDENDS (Per Share):

Amt.	Decl.	Ex.	Rec.	Pay.
0.66Q	7/26/02	8/01/02	8/05/02	8/13/02
0.68Q	10/31/02	11/07/02	11/12/02	11/20/02
0.68Q	1/24/03	1/30/03	2/03/03	2/11/03
0.68Q	3/07/03	5/01/03	5/05/03	5/13/03

Indicated div.: $2.72

CAPITALIZATION (12/31/01):

	($000)	(%)
Long-Term Debt	2,477,173	49.1
Preferred Stock	468,977	9.3
Common & Surplus	2,101,395	41.6
Total	5,047,545	100.0

BUSINESS:

Vornado Realty Trust is a fully integrated real estate investment trust. VNO operates in five business segments: Office, Retail, Merchandise Mart, Temperature Controlled Logistics and other investments. As of 12/31/02, the office segment was comprised of all or portions of 74 office properties in New York City, and in the Washington D.C. and Northern Virginia area totaling approximately 27.7 million square feet. Also, VNO owns a 100.0% limited partnership interest in Charles E. Smith Commercial Realty

L.P. The retail properties segment consists of 62 shopping centers totaling approximately 12.5 million square feet in six states and Puerto Rico as of 12/31/02. The Merchandise Mart Properties contain approximately 8.6 million square feet, including the 3.4 million square foot Merchandise Mart in Chicago as of 12/31/01. The Temperature Controlled Logistics segment consists of a 60.0% interest in partnerships that own 88 warehouse facilities nationwide.

RECENT DEVELOPMENTS:

For the year ended 12/31/02, income was $263.0 million, before an accounting change charge of $30.1 million, compared with income of $252.4 million, before an accounting change charge of $4.1 million and gain of $15.5 million from the sale of real estate, in 2002. Results for 2002 and 2001 included net non-recurring charges of $16.9 million

and a net non-recurring loss of $2.8 million, respectively. Revenues soared 45.6% to $1.44 billion from $985.8 million the year before, due to the acquisition of the remaining 66.0% interest of Charles E. Smith Commercial Realty L.P. on 1/1/02. Operating income advanced 41.5% to $554.8 million versus $385.1 million in 2001.

PROSPECTS:

On 1/1/03, the Company announced that it acquired Building Maintenance Services Company, which provides cleaning and related services primarily to VNO's Manhattan properties, for about $13.0 million. Separately, on 12/31/02, VNO and Crescent Real Estate Equities formed a

joint venture to acquire the Carthage, Missouri and Kansas City, Kansas quarries from AmeriCold Logistics for $20.0 million. VNO's future success will be affected by its ability to integrate the assets and businesses it acquires and to effectively manage those assets and businesses.

ANNUAL FINANCIAL DATA:

FISCAL YEAR	TOT. INC. ($mill.)	NET INC. ($mill.)	TOT. ASSETS ($mill.)	NET INC. +DEPR./ ASSETS %	RET. ON EQUITY %	RET. ON ASSETS %	EARN. PER SH. $	TANG. BK. VAL.$	DIV. PER SH. $	DIV. PAYOUT %	PRICE RANGE	AVG. P/E RATIO	AVG. YIELD %
p12/31/02	1,435.1	⑥ 263.0					⑥ 2.18		2.66	122.0	47.20 - 33.20	18.4	6.6
12/31/01	985.8	⑤ 376.5	6,777.3	5.8	10.4	3.9	⑤ 2.47	21.22	2.32	93.9	42.03 - 34.47	15.5	6.1
12/31/00	826.5	④ 235.1	6,370.3	5.3	11.3	3.7	④ 2.20	18.40	1.97	89.5	40.75 - 29.88	16.1	5.6
12/31/99	697.0	202.5	5,479.2	5.2	9.9	3.7	1.94	18.26	1.81	93.1	40.00 - 29.69	18.0	5.2
12/31/98	509.9	① 152.9	4,425.8	4.8	8.6	3.5	① 1.59	17.63	1.64	103.1	49.81 - 26.00	23.8	4.3
12/31/97	209.1	61.0	2,524.1	4.2	4.6	2.4	0.79	14.33	1.36	172.1	47.38 - 25.38	46.0	3.7
12/31/96	116.9	② 61.4	565.2	13.3	22.2	10.9	② 2.09	10.41	1.22	49.0	26.44 - 17.81	8.9	5.5
12/31/95	108.7	② 53.0	491.5	13.0	27.3	10.8	② 2.25	8.01	1.12	49.8	19.50 - 16.31	8.0	6.3
12/31/94	94.0	② 41.2	393.5	13.0	35.3	10.5	② 0.95	5.39	1.00	105.3	18.88 - 15.13	17.9	5.9
12/31/93	67.2	②③ 31.8	385.8	10.7	27.4	8.2	②③ 1.60	6.97	2.27	142.2	21.00 - 12.42	10.4	13.6

Statistics are as originally reported. Adj. for 2-for-1 stk. spl., 10/97 ① Incl. a net gain from ins. settle. & condemn. of $9.6 mill. ② Incl. gain on marketable secs., 1996, $913,000; 1995, $294,000; 1994, $643,000; 1993, $263,000. ③ Bef. disc. ops., $600,000 & extraord. chrg. $3.2 mill. ④ Bef. extraord. chrg., $1.1 mill.; incl. net gain of $11.0 mill. from the sale of real estate. ⑤ Bef. extraord. gain of $1.2 mill. & acctg. chng. chrg. of $4.1 mill.; incl. net gain of $7.4 mill. on sales of assets. ⑥ Bef. acctg. chng. chrg. of $30.1 mill. & incl. net non-recurr chrgs. of $16.9 mill.

OFFICERS:
S. Roth, Chmn., C.E.O.
M. D. Fascitelli, Pres.

INVESTOR CONTACT: Investor Relations,
(212) 894-7000

PRINCIPAL OFFICE: 888 Seventh Avenue,
New York, NY 10019

TELEPHONE NUMBER: (212) 894-7000
FAX: (212) 587-0600
WEB: www.vno.com

NO. OF EMPLOYEES: 1,422 (approx.)

SHAREHOLDERS: 1,750

ANNUAL MEETING: In May

INCORPORATED: MD, May, 1993

INSTITUTIONAL HOLDINGS:
No. of Institutions: 218
Shares Held: 64,160,004
% Held: 59.2
INDUSTRY: Real estate investment trusts
(SIC: 6798)
TRANSFER AGENT(S): First Union National
Bank, Charlotte, NC

VULCAN MATERIALS COMPANY

EXCH.	SYM.	REC. PRICE	P/E RATIO	YLD.	MKT. CAP.	RANGE (52-WK.)	'02 Y/E PR.	DIV. ACH.
NYSE	VMC	31.70 (2/28/03)	17.0	3.1%	$3.21 bill.	49.95 - 31.03	37.50	10 yrs.

UPPER MEDIUM GRADE. EARNINGS FOR THE CONTRUCTION MATERIALS SEGMENT SHOULD RANGE BETWEEN $350.0 MILLION AND $380.0 MILLION IN 2003.

*7 YEAR PRICE SCORE 114.5   ***12 MONTH PRICE SCORE 93.7**
*NYSE COMPOSITE INDEX=100

INTERIM EARNINGS (Per Share):
Qtr.	Mar.	June	Sept.	Dec.
1998	0.36	0.69	0.88	0.58
1999	0.26	0.61	0.84	0.64
2000	0.23	0.75	0.84	0.34
2001	0.06	0.78	0.90	0.44
2002	0.11	0.64	0.75	0.36

INTERIM DIVIDENDS (Per Share):
Amt.	Decl.	Ex.	Rec.	Pay.
0.235Q	2/08/02	2/20/02	2/22/02	3/08/02
0.235Q	5/10/02	5/22/02	5/24/02	6/10/02
0.235Q	7/12/02	8/23/02	8/27/02	9/10/02
0.235Q	10/11/02	11/22/02	11/26/02	12/10/02
0.245Q	2/14/03	2/26/03	2/28/03	3/10/03

Indicated div.: $0.98 (Div. Reinv. Plan)

CAPITALIZATION (12/31/01):
	($000)	(%)
Long-Term Debt	906,299	31.0
Deferred Income Tax	318,545	10.9
Minority Interest	95,144	3.3
Common & Surplus	1,604,274	54.9
Total	2,924,262	100.0

BUSINESS:

Vulcan Materials Company is engaged in the production, distribution and sale of construction materials and industrial and specialty chemicals. The Company is a producer of construction aggregates and other construction materials. The Company is also a chemicals manufacturer, supplying chloralkali and other industrial chemicals. Construction materials accounted for 77.8% of 2002 sales, while chemicals, such as chlorinated hydrocarbons, caustic soda and anhydrous ammonia, accounted for 22.2%. As of 12/31/01, VMC operated 202 permanent reserve-supplied aggregates production facilities in 18 states and Mexico.

RECENT DEVELOPMENTS:

For the year ended 12/31/02, the Company reported income of $190.4 million, before an accounting change charge of $20.5 million, compared with net income of $222.7 million the year before. Net sales fell 7.6% to $2.55 billion from $2.76 billion a year earlier. Construction materials net sales slid 6.3% to $1.98 billion, reflecting lower aggregates volume, partially offset by pricing improvements for aggregates. Chemicals net sales declined 12.0% to $564.5 million. This decrease was primarily due to lower caustic soda pricing and weak demand for chlorinated organic products.

PROSPECTS:

The Company's outlook for 2003 is predicated by a modest recovery in market conditions, beginning in the second half of the year. In Construction Materials, VMC anticipates aggregates demand to decrease 1.0% to 2.0% and pricing to increase modestly. Earnings for the Construction Materials segment are expected to range between $350.0 million and $380.0 million for the year. With respect to Chemicals, VMC anticipates a loss ranging from $20.0 million to $40.0 million in 2003 versus a loss of $74.0 million in 2002. Overall, earnings per share are expected to range from $1.85 to $2.15 in 2003. This estimate includes increased costs of about $0.13 per share related to pension and healthcare.

ANNUAL FINANCIAL DATA:

FISCAL YEAR	TOT. REVS. ($mill.)	NET INC. ($mill.)	TOT. ASSETS ($mill.)	OPER. PROFIT %	NET PROFIT %	RET. ON EQUITY %	RET. ON ASSETS %	CURR. RATIO	EARN. PER SH.$	CASH FL. PER SH.$	TANG. BK. VAL.$	DIV. PER SH.$	PRICE RANGE	AVG. P/E RATIO	AVG. YIELD
p12/31/02	2,545.1	④ 190.4	3,433.1			11.2	5.5		④ 1.86			0.94	49.95 - 32.35	22.1	2.3
12/31/01	2,755.3	222.7	3,398.2	12.3	7.4	13.9	6.6	2.1	2.17	4.89	10.02	0.90	55.30 - 37.50	21.4	1.9
12/31/00	2,491.7	③ 219.9	3,228.6	13.7	8.8	14.9	6.8	1.2	③ 2.16	4.43	9.00	0.84	48.88 - 36.50	19.8	2.0
12/31/99	2,355.8	239.7	2,839.5	15.2	10.2	18.1	8.4	1.6	2.35	4.37	8.63	0.78	51.25 - 34.31	18.2	1.8
12/31/98	1,776.4	255.9	1,658.6	19.3	14.4	22.2	15.4	2.7	2.50	3.85	11.47	0.69	44.66 - 31.33	15.2	1.8
12/31/97	1,678.6	209.1	1,449.2	16.9	12.5	21.1	14.4	2.3	2.03	3.21	9.81	0.63	34.64 - 18.41	13.0	2.4
12/31/96	1,568.9	② 188.6	1,320.6	17.5	12.0	21.3	14.3	2.0	② 1.79	2.85	8.42	0.56	22.16 - 17.71	11.2	2.8
12/31/95	1,461.0	② 166.2	1,215.8	17.1	11.4	20.9	13.7	2.0	② 1.54	2.57	7.59	0.49	20.12 - 16.04	11.7	2.7
12/31/94	1,253.4	① 98.0	1,181.0	11.0	7.8	13.4	8.3	1.6	① 0.89	1.86	6.79	0.44	18.83 - 14.67	18.8	2.6
12/31/93	1,133.5	88.2	1,078.6	11.5	7.8	12.6	8.2	2.1	0.80	1.72	6.45	0.42	18.71 - 13.42	20.1	2.6

Statistics are as originally reported. Adj. for 3-for-1 stk. split, 2/99. ① Incl. a pre-tax gain of $4.2 mill. on the sale of Co.'s industrial sand oper. ② Incl. gain from sales of assets: $5.2 mill., 1996; $16.5 mill., 1995. ③ Incl. a chrg. of $23.0 mill. from an arbitration settlement. ④ Bef. acctg. chrg. of $20.5 mill.

OFFICERS:
D. M. James, Chmn., C.E.O.
M. E. Tomkins, Sr. V.P., C.F.O., Treas.
W. F. Denson III, Sr. V.P., Sec., Gen. Coun.

INVESTOR CONTACT: Mark Warren, Investor Relations, (205) 298-3220

PRINCIPAL OFFICE: 1200 Urban Center Drive, Birmingham, AL 35242

TELEPHONE NUMBER: (205) 298-3000
FAX: (205) 298-2963
WEB: www.vulcanmaterials.com

NO. OF EMPLOYEES: 9,510 (approx.)

SHAREHOLDERS: 3,265 (approx.)

ANNUAL MEETING: In May

INCORPORATED: NJ, Sept., 1956

INSTITUTIONAL HOLDINGS:
No. of Institutions: 243
Shares Held: 65,823,590
% Held: 64.8

INDUSTRY: Crushed and broken limestone (SIC: 1422)

TRANSFER AGENT(S): First Chicago Trust Company of New York, Jersey City, NJ

WABTEC CORPORATION

EXCH.	SYM.	REC. PRICE	P/E RATIO	YLD.	MKT. CAP.	RANGE (52-WK.)	'02 Y/E PR.
NYSE	WAB	11.00 (2/28/03)	26.8	0.4%	$474.7 mill.	15.99 - 10.43	14.04

LOWER MEDIUM GRADE. THE COMPANY EXPECTS FULL-YEAR 2003 EARNINGS OF BETWEEN $0.50 AND $0.60 PER DILUTED SHARE.

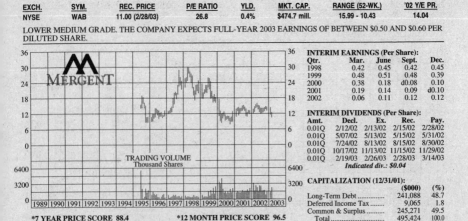

*7 YEAR PRICE SCORE 88.4   ***12 MONTH PRICE SCORE 96.5**
*NYSE COMPOSITE INDEX=100

INTERIM EARNINGS (Per Share):

Qtr.	Mar.	June	Sept.	Dec.
1998	0.42	0.45	0.42	0.45
1999	0.48	0.51	0.48	0.39
2000	0.38	0.18	d0.08	0.15
2001	0.19	0.14	0.09	d0.10
2002	0.06	0.11	0.12	0.12

INTERIM DIVIDENDS (Per Share):

Amt.	Decl.	Ex.	Rec.	Pay.
0.01Q	2/12/02	2/13/02	2/15/02	2/28/02
0.01Q	5/07/02	5/13/02	5/15/02	5/31/02
0.01Q	7/24/02	8/13/02	8/15/02	8/30/02
0.01Q	10/17/02	11/13/02	11/15/02	11/29/02
0.01Q	2/19/03	2/26/03	2/28/03	3/14/03

Indicated div.: $0.04

CAPITALIZATION (12/31/01):

	($000)	(%)
Long-Term Debt	241,088	48.7
Deferred Income Tax	9,065	1.8
Common & Surplus	245,271	49.5
Total	495,424	100.0

BUSINESS:

Wabtec Corporation (formerly Westinghouse Air Brake Company) is a manufacturer of equipment for locomotives, railway freight cars and passenger transit vehicles. Major products include electronic controls and monitors, air brakes, cooling equipment, switcher and commuter locomotives, couplers, door controls, draft gears and brake shoes. The Company's principal business segments include the freight group (63.7% of 2002 revenues) and the transit group (36.3%). WAB's products are sold to both original equipment manufacturers and the aftermarket. WAB also provides repair services and overhaul work for operators of rail vehicles such as railroads, transit authorities, utilities and leasing companies. On 11/19/99, the Company acquired MotivePower Industries.

RECENT DEVELOPMENTS:

For the twelve months ended 12/31/02, income from continuing operations was $17.5 million compared with $14.0 million a year earlier. Results for 2002 and 2001 included amortization expenses of $5.3 million and $13.0 million, respectively. Results for 2001 also included restructuring costs of $3.7 million and asset writedowns of $9.3 million.

Net sales declined 11.2% to $696.2 million from $783.7 million the previous year. Freight group sales decreased 9.5% to $443.4 million, while transit group sales dropped 13.9% to $252.8 million. Gross profit decreased 14.5% to $179.5 million, or 25.8% of net sales, versus $209.9 million, or 26.8% of net sales, the year before.

PROSPECTS:

For full-year 2003, WAB anticipates sales of about $700.0 million, with freight group sales higher and transit group sales lower compared with 2002. In addition, the Company expects full-year 2003 earnings of between $0.50 and $0.60 per diluted share. The Company has indicated that it currently plans to use its free cash primarily for debt reduction.

Separately, on 3/12/03, Wabtec Rail Ltd., the United Kingdom-based division of WAB, announced that it was awarded a $7.0 million contract to supply an additional 50 specialty freight cars plus spares to Network Rail, which owns and operates Britain's railway infrastructure. The cars and spares will be delivered during 2003.

ANNUAL FINANCIAL DATA:

FISCAL YEAR	TOT. REVS. ($mill.)	NET INC. ($mill.)	TOT. ASSETS ($mill.)	OPER. PROFIT %	NET PROFIT %	RET. ON EQUITY %	RET. ON ASSETS %	CURR. RATIO	EARN. PER SH.$	CASH FL. PER SH.$	TANG. BK. VAL.$	DIV. PER SH.$	PRICE RANGE	AVG. P/E RATIO	AVG. YIELD %
p12/31/02	696.2	⑥ 17.5							⑥ 0.40			0.04	15.99 — 11.80	34.7	0.3
12/31/01	783.7	④ 14.0	730.0	6.9	1.8	5.7	1.9	1.6	⑤ 0.32	1.30	0.05	0.04	15.24 — 10.75	40.6	0.3
12/31/00	1,028.0	④ 25.4	984.0	8.7	2.5	12.9	2.6	2.3	④ 0.59	1.55	...	0.04	17.56 — 7.81	21.5	0.3
12/31/99	1,121.1	③ 37.9	996.7	10.3	3.4	20.9	3.8	2.3	③ 0.86	1.82	...	0.04	25.94 — 16.19	24.5	0.2
12/31/98	670.9	45.0	596.2	15.6	6.7	...	7.5	1.6	1.75	2.73	...	0.04	29.81 — 17.13	13.4	0.2
12/31/97	564.4	37.3	410.9	15.9	6.6	...	9.1	1.4	1.42	2.36	...	0.04	28.94 — 12.13	14.5	0.2
12/31/96	453.5	32.7	363.2	17.6	7.2	...	9.0	1.5	1.15	1.93	...	0.04	14.13 — 8.88	10.0	0.3
12/31/95	425.0	① 35.1	263.4	21.0	8.3	...	13.3	1.5	① 1.32	2.02	...	0.01	19.00 — 8.63	10.5	0.1
12/31/94	347.5	36.8	187.7	21.2	10.6	78.7	19.6	2.1	0.92	1.32	0.56	...	... — ...	...	...
12/31/93	285.3	② 26.1	175.6	17.4	9.1	237.1	14.9	1.6	② 0.65	...	...	...	... — ...	...	...

Statistics are as originally reported. ① Bef. extraord. chrg. of $1.4 mill. ② Bef. acctg. chge. chrg. $2.0 mill. ③ Incl. merger & restruct. chrg. $43.6 mill.; excl. net extraord. loss of $1.3 mill. ④ Incl. merger & restruct. chrg. $27.1 mill. ⑤ Incl. pre-tax restruct. chrg. of $3.7 mill. & asset writedowns of $9.3 mill.; bef. inc. fr. disc. ops. of $47.8 mill. ($1.11/sh.) ⑥ Bef. loss fr. disc. ops. of $126,000, acctg. chge. chrg. of $61.7 mill. & extraord. loss of $1.2 mill.

OFFICERS:
W. E. Kassling, Chmn.
G. T. Davies, Pres., C.E.O.
A. Garcia-Tunon, Sr. V.P., C.F.O., Sec.

INVESTOR CONTACT: Tim Wesley, Inv. Rel., (412) 825-1543

PRINCIPAL OFFICE: 1001 Air Brake Avenue, Wilmerding, PA 15148

TELEPHONE NUMBER: (412) 825-1000
FAX: (412) 825-1019
WEB: www.wabtec.com

NO. OF EMPLOYEES: 4,436 (avg.)

SHAREHOLDERS: 1,115 (record)

ANNUAL MEETING: In May

INCORPORATED: DE, 1989

INSTITUTIONAL HOLDINGS:
No. of Institutions: 98
Shares Held: 29,537,787
% Held: 68.0

INDUSTRY: Railroad equipment (SIC: 3743)

TRANSFER AGENT(S): Mellon Investor Services, Pittsburgh, PA

WACHOVIA CORPORATION

EXCH.	SYM.	REC. PRICE	P/E RATIO	YLD.	MKT. CAP.	RANGE (52-WK.)	'02 Y/E PR.
NYSE	WB	35.48 (2/28/03)	13.6	2.9%	$48.32 bill.	39.88 - 28.57	36.44

INVESTMENT GRADE. THE COMPANY AND PRUDENTIAL FINANCIAL, INC. PLAN TO FORM A PREMIER RETAIL FINANCIAL ADVISORY FIRM.

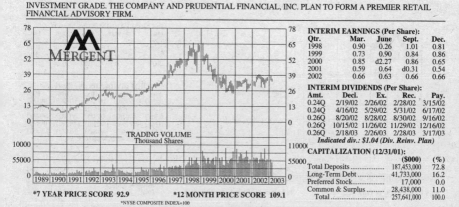

*7 YEAR PRICE SCORE 92.9 ***12 MONTH PRICE SCORE 109.1**
*NYSE COMPOSITE INDEX=100

INTERIM EARNINGS (Per Share):

Qtr.	Mar.	June	Sept.	Dec.
1998	0.90	0.26	1.01	0.81
1999	0.73	0.90	0.84	0.86
2000	0.85	d2.27	0.86	0.65
2001	0.59	0.64	d0.31	0.54
2002	0.66	0.63	0.66	0.66

INTERIM DIVIDENDS (Per Share):

Amt.	Decl.	Ex.	Rec.	Pay.
0.24Q	2/19/02	2/26/02	2/28/02	3/15/02
0.24Q	4/16/02	5/29/02	5/31/02	6/17/02
0.26Q	8/20/02	8/28/02	8/30/02	9/16/02
0.26Q	10/15/02	11/26/02	11/29/02	12/16/02
0.26Q	2/18/03	2/26/03	2/28/03	3/17/03

Indicated div.: $1.04 (Div. Reinv. Plan)

CAPITALIZATION (12/31/01):

	($000)	(%)
Total Deposits	187,453,000	72.8
Long-Term Debt	41,733,000	16.2
Preferred Stock	17,000	0.0
Common & Surplus	28,438,000	11.0
Total	257,641,000	100.0

BUSINESS:

Wachovia Corporation (formerly First Union Corporation), with assets of $341.84 billion as of 12/31/02, is a provider of financial services to 20.0 million retail, brokerage and corporate customers throughout the East Coast and the U.S. On 9/4/01, First Union acquired Wachovia Corporation and assumed its present name. The Company operates full-service banking offices in 11 East Coast states and Washington, D.C., and offers full-service brokerage with offices in 49 states and global services through more than 30 international offices. The Company operated 3,280 financial centers and 4,560 automatic teller machines, as of 12/31/02.

RECENT DEVELOPMENTS:

For the year ended 12/31/02, net income more than doubled to $3.58 billion compared with $1.62 billion the year before. Results for 2002 and 2001 included pre-tax merger-related and restructuring charges of $387.0 million and $106.0 million, respectively. Net interest income increased 26.3% to $9.82 billion from $7.78 billion in the previous year. Provision for loan losses dropped 24.0% to $1.48 million from $1.95 billion the year before. Total fee and other income increased 27.1% to $8.01 billion from $6.30 billion a year earlier. Total non-interest expense rose 18.8% to $11.68 billion compared with $9.83 billion in the prior year.

PROSPECTS:

On 2/19/03, the Company and Prudential Financial, Inc. announced that they plan to form a premier retail financial advisory firm. The new company will be the third largest brokerage firm in the U.S., based on combined client assets of $537.00 billion and 2002 estimated combined net revenue of $4.20 billion. The firm will own more than 3,500 brokerage locations, including 791 dedicated retail offices in 48 states and the District of Columbia. Under the transaction, which is expected to close in the third quarter of 2003, WB will have a 62.0% ownership interest in the new firm. The transaction is expected to be accretive to earnings per share in the first full year following the closing, excluding one-time charges.

ANNUAL FINANCIAL DATA:

FISCAL YEAR	NET INT. INC. ($mill.)	NON-INT. INC. ($mill.)	NET INC. ($mill.)	TOT. LOANS ($mill.)	TOT. ASSETS ($mill.)	TOT. DEP. ($mill.)	RET. ON EQUITY %	RET. ON ASSETS %	EQUITY/ ASSETS %	EARN. PER SH.$	TANG. BK. VAL.$	DIV. PER SH.$	PRICE RANGE	AVG. P/E RATIO
p12/31/02	9,823.0	8,005.0	③3,579.0		341,839.0					③2.60		1.00	39.88 - 28.57	13.2
12/31/01	7,775.0	6,296.0	③1,619.0	173,495.0	330,452.0	187,453.0	5.7	0.5	8.6	③1.45	11.50	0.96	36.60 - 25.22	21.3
12/31/00	7,437.0	6,712.0	③④138.0	130,242.0	254,170.0	142,668.0	0.9	0.1	6.0	③④0.12	11.92	1.92	38.88 - 23.50	259.7
12/31/99	7,452.0	6,933.0	③3,223.0	141,091.0	253,024.0	141,047.0	19.3	1.3	6.6	③3.33	11.22	1.88	65.75 - 32.00	14.7
12/31/98	7,277.0	6,555.0	③2,891.0	139,409.0	237,363.0	142,467.0	16.8	1.2	7.2	②2.95	12.36	1.58	65.94 - 40.94	18.1
12/31/97	5,743.0	3,396.0	②1,896.0	100,259.0	157,274.0	102,889.0	15.8	1.2	7.7	②2.99	14.71	1.32	53.00 - 36.31	14.9
12/31/96	4,996.0	2,357.0	②1,499.0	98,064.0	140,127.0	94,815.0	15.0	1.1	7.1	②2.68	12.46	1.10	38.88 - 25.56	12.0
12/31/95	4,634.6	1,896.5	①1,430.2	92,108.3	131,879.9	92,555.2	15.8	1.1	6.9	②2.52	11.30	0.98	29.75 - 20.69	10.0
12/31/94	3,033.7	1,159.0	925.4	54,702.1	77,313.5	58,958.3	17.1	1.2	7.0	2.49	11.68	0.86	24.00 - 19.50	8.7
12/31/93	2,765.9	1,198.3	817.5	47,210.2	70,787.0	53,742.4	15.7	1.2	7.4	2.37	12.07	0.75	26.56 - 18.63	9.6

Statistics are as originally reported. Adj. for 2-for-1 stk. split, 7/97. Financials for 12/00 and prior years reflect the operations of First Union Corporation only. ① Incl. merger with First Fidelity and after-tax merger-related charges of $72.8 mill. ② Incl. pre-tax SAIF chrg. of $133.0 mill. & merger-related chrgs. of $281.0 mill. ③ Incl. pre-tax merger-related & restr. chrgs. of $387.0 mill., 2002; $106.0 mill., 2001; $2.19 bill., 2000; $404.0 mill., 1999; $1.21 bill., 1998; $269.0 mill., 1997. ④ Bef. acctg. chrg. of $46.0 mill.

OFFICERS:
G. K. Thompson, Chmn., Pres., C.E.O.
R. P. Kelly, C.F.O.

INVESTOR CONTACT: Alice Lehman, Managing Dir. of Corp. Rel., (704) 374-2137

PRINCIPAL OFFICE: One Wachovia Center, Charlotte, NC 28288-0013

TELEPHONE NUMBER: (704) 374-6565
FAX: (704) 374-4609
WEB: www.wachovia.com

NO. OF EMPLOYEES: 80,778

SHAREHOLDERS: 191,231

ANNUAL MEETING: In April

INCORPORATED: NC, Dec., 1967

INSTITUTIONAL HOLDINGS:
No. of Institutions: 719
Shares Held: 778,563,493
% Held: 57.2

INDUSTRY: National commercial banks (SIC: 6021)

TRANSFER AGENT(S): First Union National Bank, Charlotte, NC

WADDELL & REED FINANCIAL, INC.

EXCH.	SYM.	REC. PRICE	P/E RATIO	YLD.	MKT. CAP.	RANGE (52-WK.)	'02 Y/E PR.
NYSE	WDR	16.71 (2/28/03)	15.6	3.2%	$1.34 bill.	33.10 - 15.30	19.67

MEDIUM GRADE. THE COMPANY ACQUIRED MACKENZIE INVESTMENT MANAGEMENT, INC.

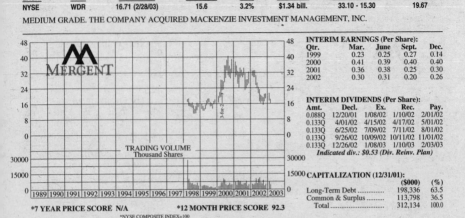

INTERIM EARNINGS (Per Share):

Qtr.	Mar.	June	Sept.	Dec.
1999	0.23	0.25	0.27	0.14
2000	0.41	0.39	0.40	0.40
2001	0.36	0.38	0.25	0.30
2002	0.30	0.31	0.20	0.26

INTERIM DIVIDENDS (Per Share):

Amt.	Decl.	Ex.	Rec.	Pay.
0.088Q	12/20/01	1/08/02	1/10/02	2/01/02
0.133Q	4/01/02	4/15/02	4/17/02	5/01/02
0.133Q	6/25/02	7/09/02	7/11/02	8/01/02
0.133Q	9/26/02	10/09/02	10/11/02	11/01/02
0.133Q	12/26/02	1/08/03	1/10/03	2/03/03

Indicated div.: $0.53 (Div. Reinv. Plan)

TRADING VOLUME
Thousand Shares

*7 YEAR PRICE SCORE N/A   ***12 MONTH PRICE SCORE 92.3**
*NYSE COMPOSITE INDEX=100

CAPITALIZATION (12/31/01):

	($000)	(%)
Long-Term Debt	198,336	63.5
Common & Surplus	113,798	36.5
Total	312,134	100.0

BUSINESS:

Waddell & Reed Financial, Inc., with assets under management of $28.12 billion as of 12/31/02, is the holding company of Waddell & Reed, Inc., Waddell & Reed Investment Management Company, and Waddell & Reed Services Company. Waddell & Reed, Inc. is a registered broker-dealer and registered investment advisor that acts as the national distributor and underwriter for shares of WPR's mutual funds and the distributor of insurance products issued primarily by Nationwide Life Insurance Company. Waddell & Reed Investment Management Company is a registered investment advisor that provides investment management and advisory services to WDR's mutual funds, institutions and other private clients. Waddell & Reed Services Company provides transfer agency and accounting services to the funds and their shareholders. On 3/31/00, WDR acquired The Legend Group. Net sales for 2002 were derived as follows: investment management fees, 42.8%; underwriting and distribution fees, 42.1%; and shareholder service fees, 15.1%.

RECENT DEVELOPMENTS:

For the year ended 12/31/02, net income decreased 18.4% to $87.4 million from $107.2 million the year before. Earnings for 2002 included one-time after-tax special charges of $1.3 million and $5.1 million, respectively. Earnings for 2002 also included a write-down of investment securities of $7.1 million. Total operating revenues declined 8.9% to $434.9 million. Investment management fees fell 13.2% to $186.0 million, while underwriting and distribution fees dropped 10.0% to $183.1 million. Comparisons were made with restated 2001 figures.

PROSPECTS:

On 12/17/02, the Company announced that it completed the acquisition of Mackenzie Investment Management, Inc., the U.S. investment management subsidiary of Mackenzie Financial Corp. and adviser of the Ivy Funds sold in the U.S. As a result of the transaction, which was valued at approximately $59.6 million, WDR should benefit from substantial subadvisory assets and future subadvisory opportunities in Canada, as well as broad U.S. retail distribution that will enhance its U.S. nonproprietary sales efforts.

ANNUAL FINANCIAL DATA:

FISCAL YEAR	TOT. REVS. ($000)	NET INC. ($000)	TOT. ASSETS ($000)	OPER. PROFIT %	NET PROFIT %	RET. ON EQUITY %	RET. ON ASSETS %	CURR. RATIO	EARN. PER SH.$	CASH FL. PER SH.$	TANG. BK. VAL.$	DIV. PER SH.$	PRICE RANGE	AVG. P/E RATIO	AVG. YIELD %
p12/31/02	434,861	③ 87,425	433,105	35.5	22.2	94.2	24.7	1.7	③ 1.07			0.49	33.10 - 15.30	22.6	2.0
12/31/01	482,562	② 107,167	433,105	35.5	22.2	94.2	24.7	1.7	② 1.28	1.44	...	0.35	37.50 - 23.00	23.6	1.2
12/31/00	520,702	139,005	422,186	43.8	26.7	98.2	32.9	1.8	1.60	1.71	...	0.35	40.50 - 16.54	17.8	1.2
12/31/99	356,657	① 81,767	335,073	37.0	22.9	64.7	24.4	0.9	① 0.89	0.95	0.15	0.35	18.67 - 12.38	17.4	2.3
12/31/98	287,289	83,735	327,179	49.5	29.1	40.4	25.6	1.6	0.85	0.89	1.18	0.27	18.67 - 10.96	17.5	1.8
12/31/97	241,772	70,292	446,964	47.6	29.1	...	15.7	0.8	0.73	0.78	...	...	...	...	...
12/31/96	220,976	66,700	429,278	47.7	30.2	28.7	15.5	1.8	...	...	2.06	...	...	...	...
12/31/95	183,504	53,501	...	46.2	29.2	...	...	...	...	...	...	...	...	...	...

Statistics are as originally reported. Adj. for 3-for-2 stk. split, 4/00. ① Incl. loss on sale of real estate of $4.6 mill. & write-off of deferred acq. costs of $19.0 mill. ② Incl. a pre-tax special chrg. of $8.2 mill. for stk. loans. ③ Incl. write-down of invest. securities of $7.1 mill. & on-time aft.-tax spec. chrg. of $1.3 mill.

OFFICERS: K. A. Tucker, Chmn., C.E.O. H. J. Herrmann, Pres. **INVESTOR CONTACT:** D. Tyler Towery, (913) 236-1880 **PRINCIPAL OFFICE:** 6300 Lamar Avenue, Overland Park, KS 66202	**TELEPHONE NUMBER:** (913) 236-2000 **FAX:** (913) 236-2017 **WEB:** www.waddell.com **NO. OF EMPLOYEES:** 1,430 **SHAREHOLDERS:** 4,746 **ANNUAL MEETING:** In April **INCORPORATED:** DE, Dec., 1981	**INSTITUTIONAL HOLDINGS:** No. of Institutions: 169 Shares Held: 63,944,916 % Held: 79.6 **INDUSTRY:** Security brokers and dealers (SIC: 6211) **TRANSFER AGENT(S):** EquiServe Trust Company, N.A., Jersey City, NJ

WALGREEN CO.

EXCH.	SYM.	REC. PRICE	P/E RATIO	YLD.	MKT. CAP.	RANGE (52-WK.)	'02 Y/E PR.	DIV. ACH.
NYSE	WAG	28.14 (2/28/03)	27.3	0.5%	$28.69 bill.	40.29 - 26.90	29.19	27 yrs.

HIGH GRADE. THE COMPANY'S EARNINGS ARE BENEFITING FROM STRONG SALES OF GENERIC PRESCRIPTION DRUGS.

MERGENT

TRADING VOLUME
Thousand Shares

| 1989 | 1990 | 1991 | 1992 | 1993 | 1994 | 1995 | 1996 | 1997 | 1998 | 1999 | 2000 | 2001 | 2002 | 2003 |

*7 YEAR PRICE SCORE 142.5   ***12 MONTH PRICE SCORE 94.9**
*NYSE COMPOSITE INDEX=100

INTERIM EARNINGS (Per Share):

Qtr.	Nov.	Feb.	May	Aug.
1998-99	0.11	0.20	0.16	0.16
1999-00	0.13	0.23	0.19	0.21
2000-01	0.15	0.29	0.21	0.21
2001-02	0.18	0.32	0.25	0.24
2002-03	0.22	...	...	...

INTERIM DIVIDENDS (Per Share):

Amt.	Decl.	Ex.	Rec.	Pay.
0.036Q	1/09/02	2/14/02	2/18/02	3/12/02
0.036Q	4/09/02	5/17/02	5/21/02	6/12/02
0.036Q	7/10/02	8/16/02	8/20/02	9/12/02
0.037Q	10/09/02	11/14/02	11/18/02	12/12/02
0.037Q	1/08/03	2/13/03	2/18/03	3/12/03

Indicated div.: $0.15 (Div. Reinv. Plan)

CAPITALIZATION (8/31/02):

	($000)	(%)
Deferred Income Tax	176,500	2.8
Common & Surplus	6,230,200	97.2
Total	6,406,700	100.0

BUSINESS:

Walgreen Co. operated 3,950 drugstores located in 43 states and Puerto Rico as of 12/31/02. The drugstores sell prescription and nonprescription drugs in addition to other products including general merchandise, cosmetics, toiletries, household items, food and beverages. Customer prescription purchases can be made at the drugstores as well as through the mail, telephone and the Internet. The Company's retail drugstore operations are supported by twelve distribution centers and a mail service facility located in Beaverton, Oregon. Prescription drugs comprised 60% of fiscal 2002 total sales; general merchandise, 29%; and nonprescription drugs, 11%.

RECENT DEVELOPMENTS:

For the three months ended 11/30/02, net earnings climbed 24.6% to $231.6 million from $185.9 million in the corresponding prior-year period. Results included after-tax gains of $10.4 million and $3.4 million in 2002 and 2001, respectively, related to litigation settlements. Net sales totaled $7.48 billion, up 14.1% compared with $6.56 billion the previous year. Comparable-store sales increased 8.6% year over year. Prescription sales, which accounted for approximately 63.0% of sales in the first quarter of fiscal 2003, climbed 19.7%. Prescription sales in comparable stores rose 14.7%. Earnings before income taxes advanced 24.5% to $372.0 million from $298.7 million the year before.

PROSPECTS:

Increased sales of generic prescription drugs and improved margins from front-end merchandise are more than offsetting higher selling, general and administrative costs and sluggish sales of promotional and seasonal items. Meanwhile, results are benefiting from WAG's aggressive store expansion program. During the first quarter, the Company opened 92 new stores. WAG anticipates spending approximately $1.00 billion in fiscal 2003 to open approximately 450 new stores, or a net increase of about 360 stores after closings and relocations, and two distribution centers.

ANNUAL FINANCIAL DATA:

FISCAL YEAR	TOT. REVS. ($mill.)	NET INC. ($mill.)	TOT. ASSETS ($mill.)	OPER. PROFIT %	NET PROFIT %	RET. ON EQUITY %	RET. ON ASSETS %	CURR. RATIO	EARN. PER SH. $	CASH FL. PER SH. $	TANG. BK. VAL. $	DIV. PER SH. $	PRICE RANGE	AVG. P/E RATIO	AVG. YIELD %
8/31/02	28,681.1	② 1,019.2	9,878.8	5.7	3.6	16.4	10.3	1.7	② 0.99	1.29	6.08	0.15	40.70 - 27.70	34.5	0.4
8/31/01	24,623.0	③ 885.6	8,833.8	5.7	3.6	17.0	10.0	1.5	③ 0.86	1.12	5.11	0.14	45.29 - 28.70	43.0	0.4
8/31/00	21,206.9	③ 776.9	7,103.7	5.8	3.7	18.3	10.9	1.5	③ 0.76	0.99	4.19	0.14	45.75 - 22.06	44.6	0.4
8/31/99	17,838.8	624.1	5,906.7	5.7	3.5	17.9	10.6	1.7	0.62	0.82	3.47	0.13	33.94 - 22.69	45.7	0.5
8/31/98	15,307.0	② 537.0	4,902.0	5.5	3.5	18.8	11.0	1.7	② 0.54	0.72	2.86	0.13	30.22 - 14.78	42.0	0.6
8/31/97	13,363.0	436.0	4,207.0	5.3	3.3	18.4	10.4	1.6	0.44	0.60	2.40	0.12	16.81 - 9.63	30.0	0.9
8/31/96	11,778.4	371.7	3,633.6	5.1	3.2	18.2	10.2	1.7	0.38	0.52	2.08	0.11	10.91 - 7.28	24.2	1.2
8/31/95	10,395.1	320.8	3,252.6	5.0	3.1	17.9	9.9	1.7	0.33	0.46	1.82	0.10	7.84 - 5.41	20.4	1.5
8/31/94	9,235.0	281.9	2,908.7	4.9	3.1	17.9	9.7	1.6	0.29	0.40	1.60	0.09	5.67 - 4.22	17.3	1.8
8/31/93	8,294.8	① 245.3	2,535.2	4.9	3.0	17.8	9.7	1.7	① 0.25	0.35	1.40	0.08	5.58 - 4.42	20.2	1.6

Statistics are as originally reported. Adj. for 2-for-1 stk. split, 2/99, 8/97, & 7/95. ① Bef. $23.6 mil chg. for acctg. adj. & incl. $4.2 mil nonrecur. chg. ② Bef. $26.4 mil ($0.03/sh) chg. for acctg. adj. & incl. $23.0 mil ($0.03/sh) after-tax gain. ③ Incl. $6.2 mil ($0.01/sh) pre-tax gain from partial payment of a prescription-drug antitrust settlement, 2002; $22.1 mil ($0.01/sh), 2001; $33.5 mil ($0.02/sh), 2000.

OFFICERS:
D. W. Bernauer, Chmn., C.E.O.
J. A. Rein, Pres., C.O.O.
R. L. Polark, Sr. V.P., C.F.O.
M. A. Wagner, Treas.

INVESTOR CONTACT: John M. Palizza, Asst. Treas., (847) 940-2935

PRINCIPAL OFFICE: 200 Wilmot Road, Deerfield, IL 60015

TELEPHONE NUMBER: (847) 940-2500
FAX: (847) 914-2654
WEB: www.walgreens.com

NO. OF EMPLOYEES: 93,000 full-time (approx.); 48,000 part-time (approx.)

SHAREHOLDERS: 96,976

ANNUAL MEETING: In Jan.

INCORPORATED: IL, Feb., 1909

INSTITUTIONAL HOLDINGS:
No. of Institutions: 743
Shares Held: 610,451,040
% Held: 59.6

INDUSTRY: Drug stores and proprietary stores (SIC: 5912)

TRANSFER AGENT(S): Computershare Investor Services, Chicago, IL

WALLACE COMPUTER SERVICES, INC.

EXCH.	SYM.	REC. PRICE	P/E RATIO	YLD.	MKT. CAP.	RANGE (52-WK.)	'02 Y/E PR.
NYSE	WCS	25.49 (2/28/03)	20.7	2.6%	$1.06 bill.	26.89 - 15.80	21.51

MEDIUM GRADE. ON 1/17/03, THE COMPANY ENTERED INTO A DEFINITIVE AGREEMENT TO BE ACQUIRED BY MOORE CORPORATION LIMITED FOR APPROXIMATELY $1.30 BILLION.

TRADING VOLUME
Thousand Shares

*7 YEAR PRICE SCORE 92.5   ***12 MONTH PRICE SCORE 131.3**
*NYSE COMPOSITE INDEX=100

INTERIM EARNINGS (Per Share):

Qtr.	Oct.	Jan.	Apr.	July
1997-98	0.49	0.48	0.41	0.33
1998-99	0.40	0.45	0.49	0.46
1999-00	0.44	0.25	d0.41	0.26
2000-01	0.41	0.41	0.34	0.14
2001-02	0.29	d0.18	0.27	0.32
2002-03	0.29	0.35	...	...

INTERIM DIVIDENDS (Per Share):

Amt.	Decl.	Ex.	Rec.	Pay.
0.165Q	12/05/01	2/27/02	3/01/02	3/20/02
0.165Q	3/12/02	5/29/02	6/01/02	6/20/02
0.165Q	6/05/02	8/29/02	9/03/02	9/20/02
0.165Q	9/12/02	11/29/02	12/03/02	12/20/02
0.165Q	12/06/02	2/27/03	3/03/03	3/20/03

Indicated div.: $0.66

CAPITALIZATION (7/31/02):

	($000)	(%)
Long-Term Debt	209,303	29.6
Deferred Income Tax	49,525	7.0
Common & Surplus	449,129	63.4
Total	707,957	100.0

BUSINESS:

Wallace Computer Services, Inc. is engaged primarily in the computer services and supply industry. The Company operates in two business segments, Forms and Labels, and Integrated Graphics. The principal products and services supplied by the Forms and Labels segment (50.5% of fiscal 2002 revenue) include the design, manufacture and sales of both paper based and electronic business forms, the manufacture of both electronic data processing labels and prime labels, and the manufacture and distribution of a standard line of office products. The Integrated Graphics segment (49.5%) includes the design and manufacture of high-color, high quality marketing and promotional materials, and the manufacture of direct response printing materials.

RECENT DEVELOPMENTS:

For the three months ended 1/31/03, net income totaled $14.8 million compared with a net loss of $7.3 million in the corresponding prior-year period. Results for 2002 included pre-tax restructuring charges of $30.3 million. Net sales slipped 4.1% to $380.0 million from $396.4 million in the previous year. Forms and Labels segment sales inched up 0.4% to $200.2 million from $199.4 million the year before, while sales for the Integrated Graphics segment declined 8.8% to $179.8 million from $197.0 million a year earlier. Operating income was $28.5 million versus an operating loss of $6.1 million in the prior year.

PROSPECTS:

On 1/17/03, the Company announced that it has entered into a definitive agreement to be acquired by Moore Corporation Limited for approximately $1.30 billion. Under the terms of the agreement, WCS shareholders will receive about $14.40 in cash and 1.05 shares of Moore common stock for each share of WCS. The transaction, which is expected to be completed in the second quarter of 2003, is subject to WCS shareholder and regulatory approvals. Upon completion, the Company's shareholders will own approximately 28.0% of the combined company, which will have annual revenues of about $3.60 billion and more than 18,500 employees worldwide.

ANNUAL FINANCIAL DATA:

FISCAL YEAR	TOT. REVS. ($mil.)	NET INC. ($mil.)	TOT. ASSETS ($mil.)	OPER. PROFIT %	NET PROFIT %	RET. ON EQUITY %	RET. ON ASSETS %	CURR. RATIO	EARN. PER SH.$	CASH FL. PER SH.$	TANG. BK. VAL.$	DIV. PER SH.$	PRICE RANGE	AVG. P/E RATIO	AVG. YIELD %
7/31/02	1,545.6	④ 29.4	930.0	4.3	1.9	6.6	3.2	2.4	④ 0.71	2.34	7.46	0.66	22.62 - 15.80	27.1	3.4
7/31/01	1,692.8	③ 53.2	1,166.7	7.0	3.1	9.2	4.6	2.2	③ 1.30	3.22	7.22	0.66	20.00 - 14.00	13.1	3.9
7/31/00	1,565.2	③ 22.6	1,249.3	5.0	1.4	4.1	1.8	2.3	③ 0.55	2.42	6.21	0.66	18.94 - 8.56	25.0	4.8
7/31/99	1,530.5	② 76.1	1,297.7	10.2	5.0	13.0	5.9	2.3	② 1.80	3.58	6.57	0.65	27.25 - 14.94	11.7	3.1
7/31/98	1,356.1	74.2	1,257.5	10.7	5.5	13.6	5.9	2.2	1.71	3.26	5.94	0.63	40.00 - 15.44	16.2	2.3
7/31/97	906.3	81.3	720.4	14.9	9.0	16.5	11.3	2.1	1.88	3.01	10.06	0.57	40.38 - 25.63	17.6	1.7
7/31/96	862.3	② 73.0	695.9	13.6	8.5	14.3	10.5	3.1	② 1.60	2.59	10.25	0.46	35.63 - 25.25	19.0	1.5
7/31/95	712.8	55.3	592.7	11.9	7.8	12.1	9.3	3.9	1.23	2.06	9.47	0.39	30.00 - 13.75	17.8	1.8
7/31/94	588.2	① 47.3	538.6	12.2	8.0	11.5	8.8	3.8	① 1.07	1.81	8.81	0.33	18.13 - 12.94	14.6	2.1
7/31/93	545.3	41.2	480.7	11.2	7.5	11.2	8.6	3.9	0.92	1.60	7.98	0.30	16.94 - 11.44	15.4	2.1

Statistics are as originally reported. Adj. for 2-for-1 stk. split, 7/96. ① Bef. $663,000 ($0.03/sh) gain from acctg. adj. ② Incl. $1.6 mil ($0.02/sh) non-recur. chg. rel to inv. adj., 1999; & $6.2 mil ($0.14/sh) non-recur. chg. rel. to takeover exp., 1996. ③ Incl. $5.9 mil ($0.14/sh) after-tax restr. & other one-time chgs., 2001; $34.7 mil ($0.84/sh), 2000. ④ Bef. $144.1 mil ($3.46/sh) acctg. chg. & incl. $43.3 mil pre-tax restr. chg.

OFFICERS:
M. D. Jones, Chmn., C.E.O.
M. O. Duffield, Pres., C.O.O.
V. L. Avril, Sr. V.P., C.F.O.
R. J. Kelderhouse, V.P., Treas., Asst. Sec.
INVESTOR CONTACT: Susan H. Fisher, Investor Relations, (630) 588-6405
PRINCIPAL OFFICE: 2275 Cabot Drive, Lisle, IL 60532

TELEPHONE NUMBER: (630) 588-5000
FAX: (630) 588-5500
WEB: www.wallace.com
NO. OF EMPLOYEES: 7,038 (avg.)
SHAREHOLDERS: 2,314 (approx.)
ANNUAL MEETING: In Nov.
INCORPORATED: DE, June, 1963

INSTITUTIONAL HOLDINGS:
No. of Institutions: 159
Shares Held: 33,994,958
% Held: 81.2

INDUSTRY: Manifold business forms (SIC: 2761)

TRANSFER AGENT(S): Boston EquiServe, L.P., Boston, MA

WAL-MART STORES, INC.

EXCH.	SYM.	REC. PRICE	P/E RATIO	YLD.	MKT. CAP.	RANGE (52-WK.)	'02 Y/E PR.	DIV. ACH.
NYSE	WMT	48.06 (2/28/03)	26.6	0.7%	...	63.94 - 43.72	50.51	21 yrs.

HIGH GRADE. THE COMPANY EXPECTS EARNINGS OF BETWEEN $0.40 AND $0.42 PER SHARE IN THE FIRST QUARTER OF THE CURRENT FISCAL YEAR.

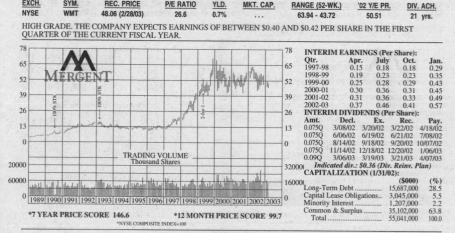

*7 YEAR PRICE SCORE 146.6   ***12 MONTH PRICE SCORE 99.7**

*NYSE COMPOSITE INDEX=100

INTERIM EARNINGS (Per Share):

Qtr.	Apr.	July	Oct.	Jan.
1997-98	0.15	0.18	0.18	0.29
1998-99	0.19	0.23	0.23	0.35
1999-00	0.25	0.28	0.29	0.43
2000-01	0.30	0.36	0.31	0.45
2001-02	0.31	0.36	0.33	0.49
2002-03	0.37	0.46	0.41	0.57

INTERIM DIVIDENDS (Per Share):

Amt.	Decl.	Ex.	Rec.	Pay.
0.075Q	3/08/02	3/20/02	3/22/02	4/18/02
0.075Q	6/06/02	6/19/02	6/21/02	7/08/02
0.075Q	8/14/02	9/18/02	9/20/02	10/07/02
0.075Q	11/14/02	12/18/02	12/20/02	1/06/03
0.09Q	3/06/03	3/19/03	3/21/03	4/07/03

Indicated div.: $0.36 (Div. Reinv. Plan)

CAPITALIZATION (1/31/02):

	($000)	(%)
Long-Term Debt	15,687,000	28.5
Capital Lease Obligations	3,045,000	5.5
Minority Interest	1,207,000	2.2
Common & Surplus	35,102,000	63.8
Total	55,041,000	100.0

BUSINESS:

Wal-Mart Stores, Inc. operated 1,568 discount department stores, 1,258 Supercenters, 525 Sam's Clubs and 49 Neighborhood Markets in the United States as of 1/31/03. WMT also operated 597 Wal-Mart stores in Mexico, 258 in the United Kingdom, 213 in Canada, 94 in Germany, 52 in Puerto Rico, 22 in Brazil, 15 in Korea, and eleven in Argentina. WMT also operated 26 stores in China under joint venture agreements. WMT's stores offer a wide assortment of merchandise to satisfy most of the clothing, home, recreational and convenience needs of the family. Supercenters combine food, general merchandise, and services including pharmacy, dry cleaning, portrait studios, photo finishing, hair salons, and optical shops. WMT also operates McLane Company, Inc., a specialty distributor serving over 50,000 convenience stores, mass merchandisers, quick-service restaurants and movie theaters. In addition, WMT owns a 34.0% interest in Seiyu, Ltd., which operates over 400 stores throughout Japan.

RECENT DEVELOPMENTS:

For the year ended 1/31/03, net income climbed 20.5% to $8.04 billion from $6.67 billion a year earlier. Net sales increased 12.3% to $244.52 billion from $217.80 billion the year before. Net sales in the Wal-Mart Stores segment, including supercenters, rose 12.9% to $157.12 billion, while net sales in the Sam's Club segment grew 7.8% to $31.70 billion. International segment net sales advanced 15.0% to $40.79 billion, while McLane's net sales were up 8.1% to $14.91 billion. Comparable-store sales increased 5.1% year over year.

PROSPECTS:

Results are benefiting from strong sales in the United Kingdom, Canada and Mexico. Meanwhile, earnings are being positively affected by increased sales of apparel, including brand-name jeans, such as WRANGLER and LEVI, and clothing sold under the FADED GLORY and MARY-KATE AND ASHLEY private labels. The Company anticipates same-store sales growth in the range of 2.0% to 4.0% and earnings of between $0.40 and $0.42 per share in the first quarter of the current fiscal year. Looking ahead, WMT is targeting earnings per share in the range of $2.00 to $2.05 for fiscal 2004, which ends in January 2004. This target includes the costs of expensing stock options and other one-time items.

ANNUAL FINANCIAL DATA:

FISCAL YEAR	TOT. REVS. ($mill.)	NET INC. ($mill.)	TOT. ASSETS ($mill.)	OPER. PROFIT %	NET PROFIT %	RET. ON EQUITY %	RET. ON ASSETS %	CURR. RATIO	EARN. PER SH. $	CASH FL. PER SH. $	TANG. BK. VAL. $	DIV. PER SH. $	PRICE RANGE	AVG. P/E RATIO	AVG. YIELD %
p1/31/03	246,525.0	8,039.0							1.81			0.30	63.94 - 43.72	29.7	0.6
1/31/02	219,812.0	6,671.0	83,451.0	5.5	3.0	19.0	8.0	1.0	1.49	2.22	5.95	0.27	58.75 - 41.50	33.6	0.5
1/31/01	193,295.0	6,295.0	78,130.0	5.9	3.3	20.1	8.1	0.9	1.40	2.04	4.99	0.23	69.00 - 41.44	39.4	0.4
1/31/00	166,809.0	① 5,575.0	70,349.0	6.1	3.3	21.6	7.9	0.9	① 1.25	1.78	3.69	0.19	70.25 - 38.69	43.6	0.3
1/31/99	139,208.0	4,430.0	49,996.0	5.8	3.2	21.0	8.9	1.3	0.99	1.41	4.18	0.15	41.38 - 18.78	30.4	0.5
1/31/98	119,299.0	3,526.0	45,384.0	5.5	3.0	19.1	7.8	1.3	0.78	1.14	4.13	0.13	20.97 - 11.00	20.5	0.8
1/31/97	106,146.0	3,056.0	39,604.0	5.4	2.9	17.8	7.7	1.6	0.67	...	3.75	0.10	14.31 - 9.55	17.8	0.9
1/31/96	94,749.0	2,740.0	37,541.0	5.5	2.9	18.6	7.3	1.5	0.60	...	3.22	0.10	13.81 - 10.25	20.2	0.8
1/31/95	83,412.0	2,681.0	32,819.0	6.0	3.2	21.1	8.2	1.5	0.59	...	2.77	0.08	14.63 - 10.50	21.5	0.6
1/31/94	67,985.0	2,333.0	26,441.0	6.2	3.4	21.7	8.8	1.6	0.51	...	2.34	0.06	17.06 - 11.50	28.0	0.4

Statistics are as originally reported. Adj. for 100% stk. div., 4/99. ① Bef. $198.0 mil ($0.04/sh) acctg. chg.

OFFICERS:
S. R. Walton, Chmn.
H. L. Scott, Jr., Pres., C.E.O.
T. M. Schoewe, Exec. V.P., C.F.O.

PRINCIPAL OFFICE: 702 S.W. Eighth Street, Bentonville, AR 72716

TELEPHONE NUMBER: (479) 273-4000
FAX: (479) 273-1986
WEB: www.wal-mart.com
NO. OF EMPLOYEES: 1,383,000 (avg.)
SHAREHOLDERS: 324,000
ANNUAL MEETING: In June
INCORPORATED: DE, Oct., 1969

INSTITUTIONAL HOLDINGS:
No. of Institutions: 1,126
Shares Held: 1,862,503,498
% Held: 42.2
INDUSTRY: Variety stores (SIC: 5331)
TRANSFER AGENT(S): EquiServe First Chicago Trust Company, Jeresy City, NJ

WASHINGTON MUTUAL, INC.

EXCH.	SYM.	REC. PRICE	P/E RATIO	YLD.	MKT. CAP.	RANGE (52-WK.)	'02 Y/E PR.	DIV. ACH.
NYSE	WM	34.53 (2/28/03)	8.7	3.4%	$32.60 bill.	39.98 - 27.80	34.53	13 yrs.

INVESTMENT GRADE. THE COMPANY PLANS TO OPEN APPROXIMATELY 250 NEW FINANCIAL STORES IN 2003, INCLUDING UP TO 70 IN THE GREATER CHICAGO AREA.

*7 YEAR PRICE SCORE 139.7   *12 MONTH PRICE SCORE 108.0

*NYSE COMPOSITE INDEX=100

INTERIM EARNINGS (Per Share):

Qtr.	Mar.	June	Sept.	Dec.
1999	0.51	0.52	0.56	0.53
2000	0.56	0.61	0.57	0.63
2001	0.76	0.91	0.85	0.62
2002	0.93	1.01	1.01	1.03

INTERIM DIVIDENDS (Per Share):

Amt.	Decl.	Ex.	Rec.	Pay.
0.25Q	1/15/02	1/29/02	1/31/02	2/15/02
0.26Q	4/16/02	4/26/02	4/30/02	5/15/02
0.27Q	7/16/02	7/29/02	7/31/02	8/15/02
0.28Q	10/15/02	10/29/02	10/31/02	11/15/02
0.29Q	1/15/03	1/29/03	1/31/03	2/14/03

Indicated div.: $1.16 (Div. Reinv. Plan)

CAPITALIZATION (12/31/01):

	($000)	(%)
Total Deposits	107,182,000	55.0
Long-Term Debt	73,758,000	37.8
Common & Surplus	14,063,000	7.2
Total	195,003,000	100.0

BUSINESS:

Washington Mutual, Inc. is a holding company for both banking and nonbanking subsidiaries. The Company's primary banking subsidiaries are Washington Mutual Bank, FA (formerly Washington Mutual Savings Bank), Washington Mutual Bank and Washington Mutual Bank fsb. These organizations provide consumer banking, full-service securities brokerage, mutual fund management, and travel and insurance underwriting services. As of 12/31/02, WM

and its subsidiaries had assets of $268.30 billion and operated more than 2,500 offices nationwide. In February 2001, WM acquired the residential mortgage banking business of PNC Financial Services Group and Bank United Corp. On 1/7/02, WM acquired Dime Bancorp. On 10/1/02, WM acquired the parent company of HomeSide Lending, Inc., the U.S. mortgage unit of the National Australia Bank Ltd., for about $1.30 billion.

RECENT DEVELOPMENTS:

For the year ended 12/31/02, net income increased 25.1% to $3.90 billion from $3.11 billion the year before. Earnings for 2002 and 2001 included net nonrecurring gains of $3.83 billion and $1.22 billion, respectively, from various items. Earnings for 2001 also included amortization of goodwill of $139.0 million. Net interest income grew 21.3% to $8.34

billion, reflecting an increase in average earnings assets, primarily from the acquisition of Dime Bancorp on 1/7/02. Provision for loan and lease losses increased 3.5% to $595.0 million. Total non-interest income rose 47.5% to $4.79 billion, while total non-interest expense grew 38.2% to $6.38 billion.

PROSPECTS:

The Company continues to perform well as multiple integrations of recent acquisitions have been successfully completed. Additionally, low interest rates continue to drive record refinancing. During the fourth quarter of 2002, the

Company opened 68 new financial center stores, including 20 in the Denver, Colorado area. The Company plans to open approximately 250 new financial stores in 2003, including up to 70 in the greater Chicago area.

ANNUAL FINANCIAL DATA:

FISCAL YEAR	NET INT. INC. ($mill.)	NON-INT. INC. ($mill.)	NET INC. ($mill.)	TOT. LOANS ($mill.)	TOT. ASSETS ($mill.)	TOT. DEP. ($mill.)	RET. ON EQUITY %	RET. ON ASSETS %	EQUITY/ ASSETS %	EARN. PER SH. $	TANG. BK. VAL. $	DIV. PER SH. $	PRICE RANGE	AVG. P/E RATIO
p12/31/02	8,341.0	4,790.0	③ 3,896.0		268,298.0		19.4	1.5		⑨ 4.05		1.06	39.98 - 27.80	8.4
12/31/01	6,876.0	2,627.0	①⑥ 2,732.0	132,991.0	242,506.0	107,182.0	19.4	1.1	5.8	①⑥ 3.15	6.29	0.90	42.99 - 26.52	11.0
12/31/00	4,311.0	1,984.0	⑥ 1,899.0	119,626.0	194,716.0	79,574.0	18.7	1.0	5.2	⑥ 2.36	9.96	0.76	37.29 - 14.42	11.0
12/31/99	4,451.8	1,509.0	⑤ 1,817.1	113,745.7	186,513.6	81,129.8	20.1	1.0	4.9	⑤ 2.11	8.41	0.65	30.50 - 16.46	11.1
⑧ 12/31/98	4,291.7	1,577.0	④ 1,486.9	107,612.2	165,493.3	85,492.1	15.9	0.9	5.6	④ 1.71	8.85	0.55	34.45 - 17.83	15.3
⑦ 12/31/97	2,656.5	750.9	③ 481.8	67,124.9	96,981.1	50,986.0	9.1	0.5	5.5	③ 0.83	7.97	0.47	32.28 - 18.78	30.9
12/31/96	1,191.0	259.3	③ 114.3	30,694.2	44,551.9	24,080.1	4.8	0.3	5.4	③ 0.38	7.98	0.40	20.39 - 11.61	42.3
12/31/95	992.6	208.3	289.9	24,428.1	42,026.6	24,463.0	11.4	0.7	6.0	1.10	8.84	0.34	13.11 - 7.39	9.3
12/31/94	571.2	107.8	172.3	12,534.6	18,457.7	9,777.9	13.2	0.9	7.1	1.13	7.99	0.31	11.11 - 7.00	8.0
12/31/93	529.4	143.9	①② 175.3	11,006.3	15,827.2	9,351.4	14.7	1.1	7.6	①② 1.22	7.19	0.22	12.61 - 7.96	8.4

Statistics are as originally reported. Adj. for stk. 3-for-2 splits: 5/01 & 6/98. ① Bef. extraord. gain of $382.0 mill., 2001; chrg. d$9.0 mill., 1993. ② Bef. acctg. credit $13.4 mill. ③ Incl. various pre-tax net exps. of $403.7 mill., 1997; $256.7 mill., 1996 ④ Incl. net pre-tax non-recurr. gains of $316.0 mill. & a write-down of $52.9 mill. ⑤ Incl. trans.-rel. exp. of $95.7 mill. ⑥ Incl. a pre-tax gain on the sale of mtge. loans of $967.0 mill., 2001; $261.6 mill., 2000. ⑦ Reflects the acq. of Great Western Financial Corp. on 7/1/97. ⑧ Reflects acq. of H. F. Ahmanson & Co. on 10/1/98. ⑨ Incl. net nonrecurr. gains of $3.83 bill. rel. to various items.

OFFICERS:	TELEPHONE NUMBER: (206) 461-2000	INSTITUTIONAL HOLDINGS:
K. K. Killinger, Chmn., Pres., C.E.O.	FAX: (206) 554-2778	No. of Institutions: 742
T. Casey, C.F.O.	WEB: www.wamu.com	Shares Held: 708,673,752
		% Held: 74.9
	NO. OF EMPLOYEES: 52,459	
INVESTOR CONTACT: JoAnn DeGrande, First Vice Pres, (206) 461-3186	SHAREHOLDERS: 42,399	INDUSTRY: Savings institutions, except federal (SIC: 6036)
	ANNUAL MEETING: In April	
PRINCIPAL OFFICE: 1201 Third Avenue, Seattle, WA 98101	INCORPORATED: WA, Nov., 1994	TRANSFER AGENT(S): ChaseMellon Shareholder Services, L.L.C., Ridgefield Park, NJ

WASHINGTON POST COMPANY (THE)

EXCH.	SYM.	REC. PRICE	P/E RATIO	YLD.	MKT. CAP.	RANGE (52-WK.)	'02 Y/E PR.
NYSE	WPO	713.50 (2/28/03)	31.6	0.8%	$6.77 bill.	764.00 - 516.00	738.00

INVESTMENT GRADE. KAPLAN, A WHOLLY-OWNED SUBSIDIARY OF THE COMPANY, PLANS TO ENHANCE ITS FINANCIAL SERVICE BUSINESSES WITH THE ACQUISITION OF THE FINANCIAL TRAINING COMPANY.

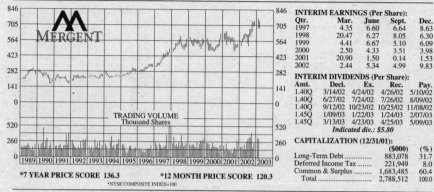

TRADING VOLUME Thousand Shares

*7 YEAR PRICE SCORE 136.3   ***12 MONTH PRICE SCORE 120.3**

*NYSE COMPOSITE INDEX=100

INTERIM EARNINGS (Per Share):

Qtr.	Mar.	June	Sept.	Dec.
1997	4.35	6.60	6.64	8.63
1998	20.47	6.27	8.05	6.30
1999	4.41	6.67	5.10	6.09
2000	2.50	4.33	3.51	3.98
2001	20.90	1.50	0.14	1.53
2002	2.44	5.34	4.99	9.83

INTERIM DIVIDENDS (Per Share):

Amt.	Decl.	Ex.	Rec.	Pay.
1.40Q	3/14/02	4/24/02	4/26/02	5/10/02
1.40Q	6/27/02	7/24/02	7/26/02	8/09/02
1.40Q	9/12/02	10/23/02	10/25/02	11/08/02
1.45Q	1/09/03	1/22/03	1/24/03	2/07/03
1.45Q	3/13/03	4/23/03	4/25/03	5/09/03

Indicated div.: $5.80

CAPITALIZATION (12/31/01):

	($000)	(%)
Long-Term Debt	883,078	31.7
Deferred Income Tax	221,949	8.0
Common & Surplus	1,683,485	60.4
Total	2,788,512	100.0

BUSINESS:

The Washington Post Company operates principally in the areas of newspaper publishing, television broadcasting, magazine publishing, cable television and education services. Newspaper operations include THE WASHINGTON POST, the HERALD, which is published in Everett, Washington, and Gazette Newspapers, Inc. As of 12/31/02, Broadcast operations were conducted primarily through six VHF stations. Magazine operations consist of the publication of a weekly news magazine, NEWSWEEK, which has one domestic and three international editions. Cable television operations provides services to about 718,000 subscribers in 19 states. Education services includes Kaplan, Inc., which provides a wide range of educational services. As of 12/31/02, WPO owned a 49.4% interest in BrassRing LLC, an Internet-based career assistance and hiring management company. On 1/1/03, WPO sold its 50.0% interest in the INTERNATIONAL HERALD TRIBUNE to The New York Times Company.

RECENT DEVELOPMENTS:

For the year ended 12/29/02, income slipped 5.8% to $216.4 million, before an accounting change charge of $12.1 million, versus $229.6 million in 2001. Results for 2002 included a net after-tax non-operating gain of $16.7 million, an after-tax goodwill impairment loss of $12.1 million, an after-tax net charge from early retirement programs of $11.3 million, and an after-tax net non-operating loss from the write-down of certain investments of $2.3 million. Results for 2001 included non-recurring gains totaling of $103.3 million. Operating revenues grew 7.2% to $2.58 billion. Operating income leapt 117.7% to $377.6 million.

PROSPECTS:

On 3/10/03, Kaplan, Inc., a wholly-owned subsidiary of WPO, agreed to acquire The Financial Training Company, a provider of test preparation services for accounting and financial service professionals with operations in the U.K. and Asia. The acquisition is valued at about $89.1 million, based on current exchange rates. The acquisition, which is subject to shareholder approval, should enhance Kaplan's financial services businesses.

ANNUAL FINANCIAL DATA:

FISCAL YEAR	TOT. REVS. ($mill.)	NET INC. ($mill.)	TOT. ASSETS ($mill.)	OPER. PROFIT %	NET PROFIT %	RET. ON EQUITY %	RET. ON ASSETS %	CURR. RATIO	EARN. PER SH. $	CASH FL. PER SH. $	TANG. BK. VAL. $	DIV. PER SH. $	PRICE RANGE	AVG. P/E RATIO	AVG. YIELD %
p12/31/02	2,584.2	⑦ 216.4							⑦ 22.72			5.60	742.00 - 516.00	27.7	0.9
12/31/01	2,416.7	⑥ 229.6	3,559.1	9.1	9.5	13.6	6.5	0.9	⑥ 24.06	46.93	50.32	5.60	651.50 - 470.00	23.3	1.0
12/31/00	2,412.2	⑤ 136.5	3,200.7	14.1	5.7	9.2	4.3	1.0	⑤ 14.32	33.41	50.03	5.40	628.75 - 467.25	38.3	1.0
1/02/00	2,215.6	225.8	2,986.9	17.5	10.2	16.5	7.6	0.6	22.30	38.45	51.03	5.20	594.50 - 490.13	24.3	1.0
1/03/99	2,110.4	④ 417.3	2,729.7	18.0	19.8	26.3	15.3	1.0	④ 41.10	54.84	69.84	5.00	605.50 - 462.00	13.0	0.9
12/28/97	1,956.3	③ 281.6	2,077.3	19.5	14.4	23.8	13.6	0.5	③ 26.23	33.00	42.64	4.80	491.06 - 325.13	15.6	1.2
12/29/96	1,853.4	220.8	1,870.4	18.2	11.9	16.7	11.8	1.4	20.05	28.70	85.25	4.60	351.75 - 276.75	15.7	1.5
12/31/95	1,719.4	② 190.1	1,732.9	15.8	11.1	16.1	11.0	1.3	② 17.15	25.92	62.96	4.40	315.00 - 237.50	16.1	1.6
1/01/95	1,614.0	② 169.7	1,696.9	17.0	10.5	15.1	10.0	1.4	② 14.65	24.08	54.16	4.20	284.00 - 221.75	17.3	1.7
1/02/94	1,498.2	① 153.8	1,622.5	16.0	10.3	14.1	9.5	2.4	① 13.10	21.15	66.44	4.20	256.50 - 212.00	17.9	1.8

Statistics are as originally reported. ① Incl. $13.4 mill. ($1.14/sh.) one-time gain & bef. $11.6 mill. ($0.98/sh.) gain fr. acct. change. ② Incl. $2.8 mill. ($0.24/sh.) net after-tax gain, 12/31/95; $8.1 mill. ($0.70/sh.), 1/1/95. ③ Incl. $44.5 mill. non-recur. gain. ④ Incl. $194.4 mill. gain fr. disp. of int. in Cowles Media, sale of 14 cable systems & disp. of Junglee. ⑤ Incl. $16.5 mill. one-time after-tax chg. & $19.8 mill. non-oper. chg. ⑥ Incl. $196.5 mill. after-tax gains. fr. sale of assets, intang. impairments & write-downs. ⑦ Incl. $16.7 mill. net non-oper. gain, $12.1 mill. goodwill impair. loss, $11.3 mill. chg. fr. early retire. prog., and $2.3 mill. net non-oper. loss fr. write-down of invest.

WASHINGTON REAL ESTATE INVESTMENT TRUST

EXCH.	**SYM.**	**REC. PRICE**	**P/E RATIO**	**YLD.**	**MKT. CAP.**	**RANGE (52-WK.)**	**'02 Y/E PR.**	**DIV. ACH.**
NYSE	WRE	25.11 (2/28/03)	18.9	5.6%	$0.97 bill.	30.15 - 20.42	25.50	41 yrs.

MEDIUM GRADE. RESULTS CONTINUE TO BE NEGATIVELY AFFECTED BY INCREASED VACANCY AND THE SEPTEMBER 2001 SALE OF 10400 CONNECTICUT AVENUE.

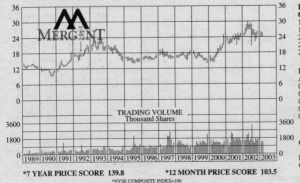

TRADING VOLUME
Thousand Shares

*7 YEAR PRICE SCORE 139.8   ***12 MONTH PRICE SCORE 103.5**
*NYSE COMPOSITE INDEX=100

INTERIM EARNINGS (Per Share):

Qtr.	Mar.	June	Sept.	Dec.
1998	0.40	0.23	0.23	0.28
1999	0.46	0.25	0.25	0.29
2000	0.31	0.28	0.36	0.32
2001	0.30	0.33	0.43	0.32
2002	0.42	0.30	0.30	0.31

INTERIM DIVIDENDS (Per Share):

Amt.	Decl.	Ex.	Rec.	Pay.
0.333Q	2/21/02	3/12/02	3/14/02	3/28/02
0.352Q	5/13/02	6/11/02	6/13/02	6/27/02
0.352Q	8/08/02	9/12/02	9/16/02	9/30/02
0.352Q	11/20/02	12/13/02	12/17/02	12/31/02
0.352Q	2/20/03	3/13/03	3/17/03	3/31/03

Indicated div.: $1.41 (Div. Reinv. Plan)

CAPITALIZATION (12/31/01):

	($000)	(%)
Long-Term Debt	359,726	52.6
Common & Surplus	323,607	47.4
Total.............................	683,333	100.0

BUSINESS:

Washington Real Estate Investment Trust is a self-administered qualified equity real estate investment trust. The trust's business consists of the ownership and operation of income-producing real estate properties principally in the Greater Washington, D.C.-Baltimore, MD area. Upon the purchase of a property, WRE begins a program of improving the real estate to increase the value and to improve its operations, with the goals of generating higher rental income and reducing expenses. As of 2/20/03, the trust owned a diversified portfolio consisting of 11 retail centers, 24 office buildings, nine multifamily buildings and 16 industrial properties. WRE's principal objective is to invest in high-quality real estate in prime locations and to monitor closely the management of these properties, which includes active leasing and ongoing capital improvement programs.

RECENT DEVELOPMENTS:

For the year ended 12/31/02, income was $48.1 million, excluding income of $3.8 million from discontinued operations, compared with income of $47.4 million, before income of $632,000 from discontinued operations, the previous year. Results for 2001 excluded a gain of $4.3 million on the sale of a real estate investment. Total income rose 3.1% to $153.6 million from $149.0 million the year before. Real estate rental revenue grew 3.8% to $152.9 million from $147.3 million, while other income fell 59.7% to $680,000 from $1.7 million a year earlier.

PROSPECTS:

Results continue to be negatively affected by increased vacancy and the September 2001 sale of 10400 Connecticut Avenue. In addition, WRE's office and industrial properties continue to be hampered by the weak economy, despite the acquisition of The Atrium Building in Rockville, Maryland for approximately $14.2 million. Nevertheless, WRE's apartment and retail portfolios should continue to perform well. Separately, WRE announced that it acquired Fullerton Industrial Center, a three building industrial property in Springfield, Virginia for $10.6 million.

ANNUAL FINANCIAL DATA:

FISCAL YEAR	TOT. INC. ($000)	NET INC. ($000)	TOT. ASSETS ($000)	NET INC. + DEPR./ ASSETS %	RET. ON EQUITY %	RET. ON ASSETS %	EARN. PER SH. $	TANG. BK. VAL.$	DIV. PER SH. $	DIV. PAYOUT %	PRICE RANGE	AVG. P/E RATIO	AVG. YIELD %
p12/31/02	153,609	② 48,080					① 1.22		1.39	113.9	30.15 - 22.24	21.5	5.3
12/31/01	148,424	① 52,353	707,935	11.2	16.2	7.4	① 1.38	8.33	1.31	94.9	25.52 - 20.80	16.8	5.7
12/31/00	134,732	① 45,139	632,047	10.7	17.5	7.1	① 1.26	7.24	1.23	97.6	25.00 - 14.31	15.6	6.3
12/31/99	118,975	① 44,301	608,480	10.5	17.2	7.3	① 1.24	7.20	1.11	93.3	18.75 - 13.81	13.1	7.1
12/31/98	103,597	① 41,064	558,707	10.1	16.2	7.3	① 1.15	7.11	1.11	96.5	18.75 - 15.06	14.7	6.6
12/31/97	79,429	30,136	468,571	8.8	12.0	6.4	0.90	7.07	1.07	118.9	19.63 - 15.50	19.5	6.1
12/31/96	65,541	27,964	338,488	11.2	14.3	8.8	0.88	6.15	1.03	117.0	17.50 - 15.25	18.6	6.3
12/31/95	52,597	26,103	241,784	12.9	13.1	10.8	0.88	6.29	0.99	112.5	16.63 - 13.88	17.3	6.5
12/31/94	45,511	23,122	178,806	15.1	15.0	12.9	0.82	5.48	0.92	112.2	21.25 - 14.75	21.9	5.1
12/31/93	39,375	23,247	162,011	16.6	14.8	14.3	0.82	5.57	0.89	108.5	24.75 - 18.63	26.4	4.1

Statistics are as originally reported. ① Incl. gain on sale of investment $4.3 mill., 2001; $3.6 mill., 2000; $7.9 mill., 1999; $6.8 mill., 1998. ② Bef. inc. of $3.8 mill. from disc. ops.

OFFICERS:
E. B. Cronin Jr., Chmn., Pres., C.E.O.
L. M. Franklin, Sr. V.P., Corp. Sec.

INVESTOR CONTACT: Investor Relations, (301) 984-9400

PRINCIPAL OFFICE: 6110 Executive Boulevard, Rockville, MD 20852-3927

TELEPHONE NUMBER: (301) 984-9400
FAX: (301) 984-9610
WEB: www.writ.com

NO. OF EMPLOYEES: 263 (avg.)

SHAREHOLDERS: 37,000 (approx.)

ANNUAL MEETING: In May

INCORPORATED: DC, Nov., 1960; reincorp., MD, June, 1996

INSTITUTIONAL HOLDINGS:
No. of Institutions: 121
Shares Held: 11,744,328
% Held: 30.0

INDUSTRY: Real estate investment trusts (SIC: 6798)

TRANSFER AGENT(S): EquiServe Trust Company N.A., Jersey City, NJ

WASTE MANAGEMENT, INC.

EXCH.	SYM.	REC. PRICE	P/E RATIO	YLD.	MKT. CAP.	RANGE (52-WK.)	'02 Y/E PR.
NYSE	WMI	19.90 (2/28/03)	14.9	0.1%	$11.83 bill.	28.89 - 19.39	22.92

LOWER MEDIUM GRADE. THE COMPANY EXPECTS ITS FULL-YEAR 2003 REVENUES TO BE ENHANCED BY ITS RECYCLE AMERICA ALLIANCE.

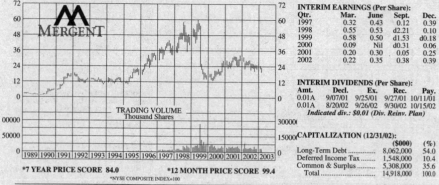

INTERIM EARNINGS (Per Share):

Qtr.	Mar.	June	Sept.	Dec.
1997	0.32	0.43	0.12	0.39
1998	0.55	0.53	d2.21	0.10
1999	0.58	0.50	d1.53	d0.18
2000	0.09	Nil	d0.31	0.06
2001	0.20	0.30	0.05	0.25
2002	0.22	0.35	0.38	0.39

INTERIM DIVIDENDS (Per Share):

Amt.	Decl.	Ex.	Rec.	Pay.
0.01A	9/07/01	9/25/01	9/27/01	10/11/01
0.01A	8/20/02	9/26/02	9/30/02	10/15/02

Indicated div.: $0.01 (Div. Reinv. Plan)

CAPITALIZATION (12/31/02):

	($000)	(%)
Long-Term Debt	8,062,000	54.0
Deferred Income Tax	1,548,000	10.4
Common & Surplus	5,308,000	35.6
Total	14,918,000	100.0

*7 YEAR PRICE SCORE 84.0   ***12 MONTH PRICE SCORE 99.4**
*NYSE COMPOSITE INDEX=100

BUSINESS:

Waste Management, Inc. (formerly USA Waste Services, Inc.) provides comprehensive waste management services to customers throughout North America. WMI provides solid waste collection, transfer, recycling and resource recovery services, and disposal services, including the landfill disposal of hazardous wastes. In addition, WMI is a developer, operator and owner of waste-to-energy facilities in the U.S. WMI's customers include commercial, industrial, municipal and residential customers, other waste management companies, governmental entities and independent power markets. On 7/16/98, WMI completed the acquisition of Waste Management Holdings, Inc. (formerly Waste Management, Inc.).

RECENT DEVELOPMENTS:

For the year ended 12/31/02, net income grew 63.6% to $823.0 million compared with $503.0 million in 2001. Results for 2002 and 2001 excluded extraordinary charges of $3.0 million and $2.0 million, respectively. Results for also excluded an accounting change credit of $2.0 million in each year. Results included gains of $34.0 million in 2002 and losses of $380.0 million in 2001 from asset impairments and unusual items. Results for 2002 included restructuring charges of $38.0 million. Operating revenues declined 1.6% to $11.1 million. Operating income grew 28.1% to $1.64 billion mostly due to WMI's various improvement initiatives.

PROSPECTS:

In January 2003, WMI formed a new recycling organization, Recycle America Alliance, which will operate with a number of other key domestic recycling processors and marketers. Recycle American Alliance will be majority-owned and a consolidated subsidiary of WMI. The Company expects full-year 2003 revenues to be around $11.60 billion, derived from acquisitions, including those related to the Recycle America Alliance. Internal revenue growth is anticipated to be 0.4% in 2003, reflecting negative volumes estimated at around 0.6% and positive price growth projected at 1.0%, excluding the adverse effect of a negative 0.3% shift in commodity prices.

ANNUAL FINANCIAL DATA:

FISCAL YEAR	TOT. REVS. ($mill.)	NET INC. ($mill.)	TOT. ASSETS ($mill.)	OPER. PROFIT %	NET PROFIT %	RET. ON EQUITY %	RET. ON ASSETS %	CURR. RATIO	EARN. PER SH.$	CASH FL. PER SH.$	TANG. BK. VAL.$	DIV. PER SH.$	PRICE RANGE	AVG. P/E RATIO
12/31/02	11,142.0	⑥823.0	19,631.0	14.8	7.4	15.5	4.2	0.9	⑥1.33	3.31	0.21	0.01	31.25 - 20.20	19.3
12/31/01	11,322.0	⑤503.0	19,490.0	11.3	4.4	9.3	2.6	0.8	⑤0.80	2.97	0.43	0.01	32.50 - 22.51	34.4
12/31/00	12,492.0	①d97.0	18,565.0	8.3	...	...	...	0.8	①d0.16	2.14	...	0.01	28.31 - 13.00	...
12/31/99	13,126.9	④d395.1	22,681.4	4.1	...	...	...	0.8	④d0.64	1.99	...	0.01	60.00 - 14.00	...
12/31/98	12,703.5	③d766.8	22,715.2	...	...	...	...	0.9	③d1.31	1.25	...	0.01	58.19 - 34.44	...
12/31/97	2,613.8	②273.3	6,622.8	20.9	10.5	10.4	4.1	1.2	②1.26	2.47	4.51	...	44.13 - 28.63	28.9
12/31/96	1,313.4	①32.9	2,830.5	8.4	2.5	2.9	1.2	1.1	①0.24	1.33	4.57	...	34.25 - 17.25	107.2
12/31/95	457.1	①30.3	908.0	12.0	6.6	7.5	3.3	1.1	①0.55	1.32	5.14	...	22.50 - 10.00	29.5
12/31/94	434.2	①d76.3	748.3	8.4	...	...	...	1.4	①d1.55	d0.41	1.43	...	15.13 - 10.38	...
12/31/93	78.1	9.6	165.7	25.2	12.3	20.5	5.8	1.0	0.80	1.48	1.79	...	15.00 - 9.75	15.5

Statistics are as originally reported. ① Incl. non-recurr. chrg. $749.0 mill.; 2000; $184.5 mill., 1996; $29.8 mill., 1995; $92.0 mill., 1994. ② Bef. extraord. loss $6.3 mill., but incl. non-recurr. chrg. $134.1 mill. ③ Bef. extraord. loss $3.9 mill., but incl. non-recurr. chrg. $2.67 bill. ④ Bef. extraord. loss $2.5 mill., but incl. non-recurr. chrg. $783.5 mill. ⑤ Bef. extraord. loss of $2.0 mill. & acctg. change benefit of $2.0 mill., but incl. nonrecurr. chrg. of $380.0 mill. ⑥ Bef. extraord. loss of $3.0 mill. & acctg. chg. chrg. of $2.0 mill., but incl. restruct. chrg. of $38.0 mill. and nonrecur. gain of $34.0 mill.

OFFICERS:
A. M. Myers, Chmn., C.E.O., Pres.
W. L. Trubeck, Exec. V.P., C.F.O.
D. Steiner, Sr. V.P., Couns., Sec.
INVESTOR CONTACT: Investor Relations, (713) 512-6548
PRINCIPAL OFFICE: 1001 Fannin Street, Suite 4000, Houston, TX 77002

TELEPHONE NUMBER: (713) 512-6200
FAX: (713) 512-6299
WEB: www.wm.com
NO. OF EMPLOYEES: 57,000 (approx.)
SHAREHOLDERS: 30,003 (record)
ANNUAL MEETING: In May
INCORPORATED: OK, Sept., 1987; reincorp., DE, June, 1995

INSTITUTIONAL HOLDINGS:
No. of Institutions: 422
Shares Held: 517,770,571
% Held: 85.1

INDUSTRY: Refuse systems (SIC: 4953)

TRANSFER AGENT(S): Mellon Investor Services, Chicago, IL

WATERS CORPORATION

EXCH.	SYM.	REC. PRICE	P/E RATIO	YLD.	MKT. CAP.	RANGE (52-WK.)	'02 Y/E PR.
NYSE	WAT	23.17 (2/28/03)	20.5	...	$3.03 bill.	34.35 - 17.86	21.78

UPPER MEDIUM GRADE. THE COMPANY IS ON TRACK TO INTRODUCE A NEW PRODUCT IN THE SECOND QUARTER OF 2003.

*7 YEAR PRICE SCORE 98.8   ***12 MONTH PRICE SCORE 98.1**
*NYSE COMPOSITE INDEX=100

TRADING VOLUME
Thousand Shares

INTERIM EARNINGS (Per Share):

Qtr.	Mar.	June	Sept.	Dec.
1997	0.10	0.12	d0.32	0.05
1998	Nil	0.15	0.17	0.25
1999	0.18	0.22	0.22	0.32
2000	0.23	0.28	0.28	0.37
2001	0.28	0.29	0.28	0.39
2002	0.26	0.28	0.29	0.30

INTERIM DIVIDENDS (Per Share):

Amt.	Decl.	Ex.	Rec.	Pay.
		No dividends paid.		

CAPITALIZATION (12/31/01):

	($000)	(%)
Common & Surplus	581,745	100.0
Total	581,745	100.0

BUSINESS:

Waters Corporation provides instruments to pharmaceutical, biotechnological and industrial chemical laboratories. WAT's customers include researchers in industry, academia and government. Waters' largest product segment, high performance liquid chromatography (HPLC), is used to identify and quantify the molecular make-up of biological and chemical samples. Through its acquisition of Micromass Limited on 9/23/97, the Company assumed a market position in mass spectrometry, a line of instruments that is complimentary to HPLC and key to proteomics and other drug discovery applications. The Company acquired TA Instruments, Inc., a provider of instruments for thermal analysis, on 5/1/96, and YMC, Inc., a manufacturer of chromatography chemicals, on 7/31/97.

RECENT DEVELOPMENTS:

For the year ended 12/31/02, net income jumped 32.9% to $152.2 million, before an accounting change charge of $4.5 million, compared with $114.5 million in 2001. Results for 2002 and 2001 included goodwill and purchased technology amortization of $3.6 million and $7.1 million, and litigation provisions of $7.9 million and $75.0 million, respectively. Results for 2002 also included an impairment of long-lived assets expense of $2.4 million and restructuring and other unusual charges of $7.4 million. Net sales rose 3.6% to $890.0 million from $859.2 million a year earlier. Gross profit grew 3.9% to $516.5 million versus $497.3 million in the previous year. Operating income increased 31.4% to $196.4 million compared with $149.5 million the year before.

PROSPECTS:

The Company has made progress on several key initiatives for continued improvements in 2003. These initiatives include new product development in mass spectrometry, as WAT is on track for the introduction in the second quarter of 2003 of a new high performance triple quadrupole system. In addition, the Company plans to pursue strategic acquisitions. Separately, on 1/16/03, the Company completed the purchase of the rheology business and net assets of Rheometric Scientific, Inc. for $17.0 million in cash and the assumption of $6.0 million in liabilities.

ANNUAL FINANCIAL DATA:

FISCAL YEAR	TOT. REVS. ($mill.)	NET INC. ($mill.)	TOT. ASSETS ($mill.)	OPER. PROFIT %	NET PROFIT %	RET. ON EQUITY %	RET. ON ASSETS %	CURR. RATIO	EARN. PER SH. $	CASH FL. PER SH. $	TANG. BK. VAL. $	PRICE RANGE	AVG. P/E RATIO
p12/31/02	890.0	⑧ 152.2	...	...	...	...	...	...	⑧ 1.12	...	...	39.25 - 17.86	25.5
12/31/01	859.2	⑦ 114.5	886.9	17.4	13.3	19.7	12.9	1.9	⑦ 0.83	1.08	3.19	85.38 - 22.33	64.9
12/31/00	795.1	⑥ 156.1	692.3	26.5	19.6	34.6	22.5	1.6	⑥ 1.14	1.36	2.21	90.94 - 21.97	49.5
12/31/99	704.4	122.3	584.4	25.1	17.4	41.9	20.9	1.3	0.92	1.14	0.98	33.84 - 18.13	28.2
12/31/98	618.8	⑤ 74.4	577.7	19.4	12.0	49.6	12.9	1.4	⑤ 0.57	0.79	...	21.88 - 9.13	27.3
12/31/97	465.5	④ d8.3	552.1	4.6	...	...	...	1.3	④ d0.08	0.10	...	12.11 - 5.78	...
12/31/96	391.1	③ 19.9	365.5	11.7	5.1	34.4	5.4	1.7	③ 0.15	0.29	...	8.41 - 4.19	42.0
12/31/95	333.0	③ 14.1	299.8	13.9	4.2	24.3	4.7	1.8	③ 0.14	0.30	...	4.56 - 3.31	29.1
② 12/31/94	131.1	d80.2	327.6	...	...	...	...	2.2	...	...	...	...	...
① 8/19/94	176.1	2.3	...	2.3	1.3	...	...	...	...	...	...	...	...

Statistics are as originally reported. Adj. for 2-for-1 split, 6/99 & 8/00. ① Results for 8/19/94 and earlier are for predecessor, Millipore Corp. ② Partial year, from 8/19/94 (date of inception). ③ Bef. $22.3 mill. ($0.71/sh.) extraord. loss, 1996; and $12.1 mill. ($0.49/sh.) extraord. loss, 1995. ④ Incl. $55.0 mill. non-recur. chg. fr. in-process R&D and $16.5 mill. non-recur. chg. fr. revaluation of Micromass inventory. ⑤ Incl. $16.5 mill. non-recur. chg. rel. to acq. of Micromass Limited. ⑥ Excl. $10.8 mill. cum. eff. of acctg. chg. ⑦ Incl. $7.1 mill. impair. chg. ⑧ Incl. $7.9 mill. litigation prov., $2.4 mill. impair. of assets & $7.4 mill. restr. chgs.

OFFICERS:
D. A. Berthiaume, Chmn., C.E.O.
J. R. Nelson, Pres., C.O.O.
J. A. Ornell, V.P., C.F.O.

INVESTOR CONTACT: Eugene Cassis, Dir., Investor Relations, (508) 482-2349

PRINCIPAL OFFICE: 34 Maple Street, Milford, MA 01757

TELEPHONE NUMBER: (508) 478-2000
FAX: (508) 872-1990
WEB: www.waters.com
NO. OF EMPLOYEES: 3,483 (avg.)
SHAREHOLDERS: 276 (approx.)
ANNUAL MEETING: In May
INCORPORATED: DE, Aug., 1994

INSTITUTIONAL HOLDINGS:
No. of Institutions: 297
Shares Held: 120,148,847
% Held: 93.0

INDUSTRY: Analytical instruments (SIC: 3826)

TRANSFER AGENT(S): BankBoston, N.A., c/o Boston EquiServe, Boston, MA

WATSCO, INC.

EXCH.	SYM.	REC. PRICE	P/E RATIO	YLD.	MKT. CAP.	RANGE (52-WK.)	'02 Y/E PR.
NYSE	WSO	13.97 (2/28/03)	13.1	1.1%	$373.6 mill.	19.48 - 12.65	16.38

MEDIUM GRADE. THE COMPANY IS USING A PORTION OF ITS CASH FLOW FROM OPERATIONS TO REDUCE DEBT.

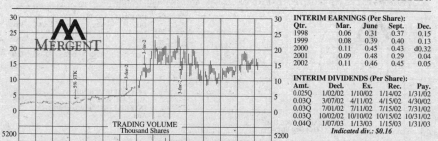

*7 YEAR PRICE SCORE 111.6   ***12 MONTH PRICE SCORE 102.9**

*NYSE COMPOSITE INDEX=100

INTERIM EARNINGS (Per Share):

Qtr.	Mar.	June	Sept.	Dec.
1998	0.06	0.31	0.37	0.15
1999	0.08	0.39	0.40	0.13
2000	0.11	0.45	0.43	d0.32
2001	0.09	0.48	0.29	0.04
2002	0.11	0.46	0.45	0.05

INTERIM DIVIDENDS (Per Share):

Amt.	Decl.	Ex.	Rec.	Pay.
0.025Q	1/02/02	1/10/02	1/14/02	1/31/02
0.03Q	3/07/02	4/11/02	4/15/02	4/30/02
0.03Q	7/01/02	7/11/02	7/15/02	7/31/02
0.03Q	10/02/02	10/10/02	10/15/02	10/31/02
0.04Q	1/07/03	1/13/03	1/15/03	1/31/03

Indicated div.: $0.16

CAPITALIZATION (12/31/01):

	($000)	(%)
Long-Term Debt	101,900	23.5
Deferred Income Tax	8,959	2.1
Common & Surplus	322,420	74.4
Total	433,279	100.0

BUSINESS:

Watsco, Inc. is primarily an independent distributor of air conditioning, heating and refrigeration equipment and related products (HVAC). The Company has two business segments, the HVAC distribution segment (97.2% of 2002 revenues) and a national temporary staffing and permanent placement services segment (2.8%). As of 2/19/03, the Company operated 283 facilities serving customers in 31

states. In addition, WSO owns Dunhill Staffing Systems, Inc., a national temporary staffing and permanent employment services business. The Company also sells products to the refrigeration market. Such products include condensing units, compressors, evaporators, valves, walk-in coolers and ice machines for industrial and commercial applications.

RECENT DEVELOPMENTS:

For the year ended 12/31/02, net income grew 16.8% to $28.5 million compared with $24.4 million the year before. Results for 2001 included pre-tax restructuring charges of $5.8 million and goodwill amortization expense of $3.6 million. Revenues declined 4.6% to $1.18 billion from $1.24 billion a year earlier, including same-store sales

decrease of 2.5% in residential and light-commercial HVAC products, as sales increases in the Company's southeastern markets were offset by declines in other markets and by lower sales of commercial products. In addition, sales were adversely affected by a 19.0% decline in same-store sales to the manufactured housing market.

PROSPECTS:

The Company's air conditioning, heating and refrigeration equipment distribution (HVAC) business is benefiting from initiatives to improve asset quality, selling margins and operating efficiency. These initiatives have allowed WSO to temper the impact of lower sales of commercial HVAC products and lower sales of residential and light-commercial HVAC products. Meanwhile, WSO's national tempo-

rary staffing and permanent placement services business is experiencing softness due to slower demand. Separately, the Company's cash flow from operations improved 27.0% to $67.0 million at 12/31/02. WSO is using these funds to reduce debt, repurchase shares of common stock and pay dividends.

ANNUAL FINANCIAL DATA:

FISCAL YEAR	TOT. REVS. ($mill.)	NET INC. ($mill.)	TOT. ASSETS ($mill.)	OPER. PROFIT %	NET PROFIT %	RET. ON EQUITY %	RET. ON ASSETS %	CURR. RATIO	EARN. PER SH.$	CASH FL. PER SH.$	TANG. BK. VAL.$	DIV. PER SH.$	PRICE RANGE		AVG. P/E RATIO	AVG. YIELD %
p12/31/02	1,181.1	28.5						1.07				0.12	19.48 -	12.65	15.0	0.7
12/31/01	1,238.6	②24.4	520.8	3.9	2.0	7.6	4.7	4.1	②0.90	1.34	7.39	0.10	14.65 -	10.25	13.8	0.8
12/31/00	1,306.6	19.1	563.5	3.5	1.5	6.3	3.4	3.4	0.69	1.13	6.62	0.10	16.38 -	8.31	17.9	0.8
12/31/99	1,246.3	29.5	588.9	4.8	2.4	9.8	5.0	3.4	0.99	1.37	6.10	0.10	19.88 -	9.75	15.0	0.7
12/31/98	1,008.8	①25.7	532.0	5.1	2.5	9.4	4.8	4.6	①0.90	1.19	6.00	0.10	24.46 -	11.75	20.1	0.5
12/31/97	635.2	①18.3	426.0	5.2	2.9	8.1	4.3	5.3	①0.68	0.86	5.67	0.09	22.92 -	14.96	27.8	0.5
12/31/96	425.4	13.0	203.6	5.7	3.1	10.8	6.4	5.5	0.62	0.83	4.58	0.09	19.42 -	7.50	21.7	0.7
12/31/95	331.0	7.3	144.9	5.4	2.2	13.5	5.0	1.6	0.48	0.73	2.60	0.08	7.95 -	4.67	13.1	1.3
12/31/94	283.7	5.8	119.7	5.3	2.0	12.3	4.8	1.7	0.40	0.59	2.43	0.08	5.04 -	3.85	11.2	1.7
12/31/93	230.7	5.0	109.7	4.9	2.2	12.1	4.6	1.8	0.38	0.53	2.07	0.07	5.04 -	3.37	11.1	1.7

Statistics are as originally reported. Adj. for 3-for-2 stk. spl., 8/98, 6/96 & 5/95 ① Bef. discontin. oper. chrg., 1998, $513,000; gain, 1997, $49,000. ② Incl. nonrecurr. chrg. of $5.8 mill.

OFFICERS:
A. H. Nahmad, Chmn., Pres., C.E.O.
B. S. Logan, V.P., C.F.O., Sec.

INVESTOR CONTACT: Barry S. Logan, (305) 714-4102

PRINCIPAL OFFICE: 2665 South Bayshore Drive, Suite 901, Coconut Grove, FL 33133

TELEPHONE NUMBER: (305) 714-4100
FAX: (305) 858-4492
WEB: www.watsco.com
NO. OF EMPLOYEES: 2,700 (approx.)
SHAREHOLDERS: 496 (common record); 226 (Class B record)
ANNUAL MEETING: In June
INCORPORATED: FL, July, 1956

INSTITUTIONAL HOLDINGS:
No. of Institutions: 94
Shares Held: 15,571,107
% Held: 60.8
INDUSTRY: Warm air heating & air-conditioning (SIC: 5075)
TRANSFER AGENT(S): First Union National Bank, Charlotte, NC

WATSON PHARMACEUTICALS, INC.

EXCH.	SYM.	REC. PRICE	P/E RATIO	YLD.	MKT. CAP.	RANGE (52-WK.)	'02 Y/E PR.
NYSE	WPI	30.93 (2/28/03)	18.9	…	$3.31 bill.	33.25 - 17.95	28.27

MEDIUM GRADE. THE COMPANY IS BENEFITING FROM ITS USE OF INTERNAL DEVELOPMENT, ALLIANCES AND ACQUISITIONS TO CREATE BROAD PORTFOLIOS OF GENERIC AND BRANDED PRODUCTS.

TRADING VOLUME
Thousand Shares

*7 YEAR PRICE SCORE 75.8   *12 MONTH PRICE SCORE 123.0*
*NYSE COMPOSITE INDEX=100

INTERIM EARNINGS (Per Share):

Qtr.	Mar.	June	Sept.	Dec.
1999	0.23	0.47	0.38	0.75
2000	1.48	0.96	d0.56	d0.02
2001	0.58	0.61	d0.55	0.43
2002	0.30	0.56	0.38	0.40

INTERIM DIVIDENDS (Per Share):

Amt.	Decl.	Ex.	Rec.	Pay.
		No dividends paid.		

CAPITALIZATION (12/31/02):

	($000)	(%)
Long-Term Debt	331,877	14.5
Deferred Income Tax	151,890	6.7
Common & Surplus	1,798,284	78.8
Total	2,282,051	100.0

BUSINESS:

Watson Pharmaceuticals, Inc. is engaged in the development, production, marketing and distribution of branded and off-patent pharmaceutical products. WPI's products include therapeutic and preventive agents generally sold by prescription or over-the-counter for the treatment of human diseases and disorders. WPI's branded pharmaceutical business operates primarily in three specialty areas: Dermatology, Women's Health and General Products. WPI is also engaged in the development, manufacture and sale of off-patent pharmaceutical products.

RECENT DEVELOPMENTS:

For the year ended 12/31/02, net income advanced 51.1% to $175.8 million compared with $116.4 million the previous year. Results for 2002 and 2001 included a net non-recurring loss of $523,000 and gain of $72.0 million, respectively. Also, results for 2001 included a pre-tax charge of $147.6 million on assets held for disposition. Net revenues grew 5.4% to $1.22 billion from $1.16 billion the year before. Revenues from branded products increased 17.8% to $649.5 million from $551.6 million, while revenues from generic products declined 10.0% to $537.5 million from $597.4 million the year before. Gross profit rose 3.9% to $677.6 million from $652.1 million a year earlier. Operating income more than doubled to $269.4 million from $101.3 million the prior year.

PROSPECTS:

On 2/6/03, WPI completed the acquisition of the U.S. rights to the FLORICET® and FLORINAL® product lines for $178.0 million from Novartis AG and its subsidiaries. The FLORICET® and FLORINAL® product lines are prescription treatments for tension headaches. Separately, the Company announced that the U.S. FDA approved OXYTROL®, a transdermal therapy to treat overactive bladder with symptoms of urge urinary incontinence, urgency and frequency. Meanwhile, the Company is benefiting from its strategy to grow through internal development, alliances and acquisitions and create broad portfolios of generic and branded products.

ANNUAL FINANCIAL DATA:

FISCAL YEAR	TOT. REVS. ($mill.)	NET INC. ($mill.)	TOT. ASSETS ($mill.)	OPER. PROFIT %	NET PROFIT %	RET. ON EQUITY %	RET. ON ASSETS %	CURR. RATIO	EARN. PER SH. $	CASH FL. PER SH. $	TANG. BK. VAL. $	PRICE RANGE	AVG. P/E RATIO
12/31/02	1,223.2	④ 175.8	2,663.5	22.0	14.4	9.8	6.6	2.5	④ 1.64	2.44	4.33	33.25 - 17.95	15.6
12/31/01	1,160.7	③ 116.4	2,528.3	8.7	10.0	7.0	4.6	3.6	③ 1.07	2.01	3.79	66.39 - 26.50	43.4
12/31/00	811.5	② 170.7	2,579.9	1.0	21.0	11.0	6.6	3.0	② 1.65	2.34	0.98	71.50 - 33.69	31.9
12/31/99	689.2	① 178.9	1,438.8	34.4	26.0	17.0	12.4	3.4	① 1.83	2.28	5.00	62.94 - 26.50	24.4
12/31/98	556.1	120.8	1,070.0	34.7	21.7	16.1	11.3	3.1	1.32	1.66	3.08	63.00 - 30.50	35.4
12/31/97	338.3	90.2	755.0	36.2	26.7	16.0	11.9	2.5	1.01	1.17	3.14	34.13 - 16.00	24.8
12/31/96	194.1	73.3	419.6	42.6	37.8	19.2	17.5	13.1	0.98	1.07	5.20	24.75 - 13.00	19.4
12/31/95	152.9	47.9	322.1	34.2	31.3	16.6	14.9	6.9	0.65	0.73	3.97	25.25 - 10.00	27.3
12/31/94	87.1	18.7	130.3	33.2	21.5	16.8	14.3	7.2	0.53	0.63	3.25	14.75 - 6.38	20.1
12/31/93	67.5	12.2	104.8	29.1	18.1	13.4	11.7	7.8	0.37	0.43	2.70	19.25 - 6.13	34.3

Statistics are as originally reported. Adj. for 100% stk. split, 10/97 ① Incl. a pre-tax merger-rel. chrg. of $20.5 mill. ② Bef. extra. loss of $1.2 mill. & acctg. chrg. of $12.0 mill.; incl. a pre-tax non-recurr. gain of $358.6 mill. & one-time chrgs. of $147.4 mill. ③ Incl. pre-tax asset impair. chrg. of $147.6 mill., pre-tax chrg. of $53.8 mill. for assets held for disp., & pre-tax gains of $125.8 mill. ④ Incl. net non-recurr. loss of $523,000

OFFICERS:
A. Chao Ph.D., Chmn., C.E.O.
J. C. Papa, Pres., C.O.O.
M. E. Boxer, Sr. V.P., C.F.O.

INVESTOR CONTACT: Patty Eisenhaur, Dir.
Inv. Rel., (270-1400

PRINCIPAL OFFICE: 311 Bonnie Circle,
Corona, CA 92880-2882

TELEPHONE NUMBER: (909) 493-5300
FAX: (909) 270-1096
WEB: www.watsonpharm.com

NO. OF EMPLOYEES: 3,729 (avg.)

SHAREHOLDERS: 3,770 (approx.)

ANNUAL MEETING: In May

INCORPORATED: CA, 1983; reincorp., NV, 1985

INSTITUTIONAL HOLDINGS:
No. of Institutions: 292
Shares Held: 82,353,408
% Held: 77.1

INDUSTRY: Pharmaceutical preparations
(SIC: 2834)

TRANSFER AGENT(S): American Stock
Transfer & Trust Company, New York, NY

WEATHERFORD INTERNATIONAL LTD.

EXCH.	SYM.	REC. PRICE	P/E RATIO	YLD.	MKT. CAP.	RANGE (52-WK.)	'02 Y/E PR.
NYSE	WFT	40.04 (2/28/03)	...	...	$5.20 bill.	54.25 - 33.10	39.93

MEDIUM GRADE. THE COMPANY'S COMPLETION SYSTEMS DIVISION HAS SIGNED A TWO YEAR CONTRACT VALUED AT OVER $34.0 MILLION WITH PETROBRAS.

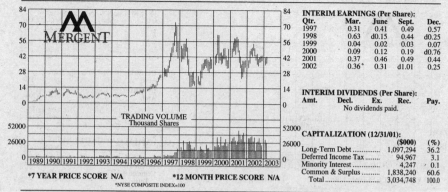

*7 YEAR PRICE SCORE N/A   *12 MONTH PRICE SCORE N/A

*NYSE COMPOSITE INDEX=100

INTERIM EARNINGS (Per Share):

Qtr.	Mar.	June	Sept.	Dec.
1997	0.31	0.41	0.49	0.57
1998	0.63	d0.15	0.44	d0.25
1999	0.04	0.02	0.03	0.07
2000	0.09	0.12	0.19	d0.76
2001	0.37	0.46	0.49	0.44
2002	0.36*	0.31	d1.01	0.25

INTERIM DIVIDENDS (Per Share):

Amt.	Decl.	Ex.	Rec.	Pay.
		No dividends paid.		

CAPITALIZATION (12/31/01):

	($000)	(%)
Long-Term Debt	1,097,294	36.2
Deferred Income Tax	94,967	3.1
Minority Interest	4,247	0.1
Common & Surplus	1,838,240	60.6
Total	3,034,748	100.0

BUSINESS:

Weatherford International Ltd. (formerly Weatherford International, Inc.) is a provider of equipment and services used for the drilling, completion and production of oil and natural gas wells. The drilling and intervention services division provides drilling systems, well installation services, cementing products and underbalanced drilling. The completion systems division provides a full range of completion products and services. The artificial lift systems division provides production optimization services and automation and monitoring of well head production. On 5/27/98, the Company acquired Weatherford Enterra, Inc. On 4/14/00, WFT spun off its Grant Prideco drilling products business to shareholders. As of 12/31/01, WFT owned 48.0% of Universal Compression Holdings, Inc., which was formed on 2/9/01 and includes essentially all of its former Compression Services Division.

RECENT DEVELOPMENTS:

For the year ended 12/31/02, WFT posted a net loss of $6.0 million compared with net income of $214.7 million a year earlier. Results for 2002 included a non-recurring charge of $232.5 million, partially offset by an income tax benefit of $76.3 million. WFT's earnings reflect a 28.1% drop in operating profits from its drilling and intervention services segment, primarily due to lower drilling activity. Net revenues of $2.33 billion were flat versus the previous year. Geographically, Eastern Hemisphere revenue fell 29.1% to $1.03 billion, U.S. revenue slid 18.4% to $774.3 million, revenues from Canada slipped 3.8% to $320.9 million, and Latin America revenue declined 17.7% to $204.6 million.

PROSPECTS:

Recent drilling activity declines in the U.S. and certain international markets, including Venezuela, Kazakhstan and the U.K. sector of the North Sea, temper the Company's near-term outlook. WFT noted that activity levels for the fourth quarter ended 12/31/02 fell about 15.0% in the U.S., 40.0% in Venezuela and more than 10.0% in the U.K. Separately, on 2/18/03, WFT announced that its completion systems division has signed a two year contract valued at over $34.0 million with Petrobras for the supply of expandable sand screens in Brazil.

ANNUAL FINANCIAL DATA:

FISCAL YEAR	TOT. REVS. ($mill.)	NET INC. ($mill.)	TOT. ASSETS ($mill.)	OPER. PROFIT %	NET PROFIT %	RET. ON EQUITY %	RET. ON ASSETS %	CURR. RATIO	EARN. PER SH. $	CASH FL. PER SH. $	TANG. BK. VAL. $	PRICE RANGE	AVG. P/E RATIO
p12/31/02	2,328.9	⑨ d6.0	4,296.4	17.6	9.2	11.7	5.0	1.6	⑨ d0.05	3.17	3.50	54.25 - 32.55	...
12/31/01	2,328.7	214.7	4,296.4	17.6	9.2	11.7	5.0	1.6	1.76	3.17	3.50	60.35 - 22.71	23.6
12/31/00	1,814.3	⑧ d38.9	3,461.6	6.6	...	...	...	2.7	d0.36	1.46	2.61	62.00 - 31.75	...
12/31/99	1,240.2	⑦ 16.2	3,513.8	5.4	1.3	0.9	0.5	1.3	⑦ 0.16	1.78	7.78	42.13 - 16.75	183.9
12/31/98	2,010.7	⑥ 64.8	2,831.7	7.4	3.2	4.3	2.3	1.9	⑥ 0.66	2.41	7.01	58.44 - 15.00	55.6
12/31/97	892.3	⑤ 83.7	1,366.1	15.9	9.4	15.9	6.1	2.0	⑤ 1.77	2.48	2.63	73.00 - 23.88	27.4
12/31/96	478.0	④ 24.5	852.8	9.7	5.1	5.4	2.9	2.4	④ 0.60	1.01	7.66	25.75 - 11.13	30.7
12/31/95	271.7	③ 2.6	453.1	6.6	1.0	1.1	0.6	3.9	③ 0.09	0.51	5.19	12.63 - 5.94	103.0
12/31/94	248.5	② 4.6	350.7	7.8	1.9	4.2	1.3	2.3	② 0.19	0.75	3.76	8.13 - 5.63	37.1
12/31/93	246.0	① 7.9	277.2	7.5	3.2	7.4	2.9	1.4	① 0.33	0.84	4.27	9.25 - 4.75	21.2

Statistics are as originally reported. ① Bef. loss of $2.1 mill. fr. disc. ops. ② Bef. extraord. chrg. of $4.0 mill. ③ Bef. inc. of $8.8 mill. fr. disc. ops. ④ Bef. net gain of $74.4 mill. fr. disc. ops. & extraord. chrg. of $731,000. ⑤ Incl. gain of $3.4 mill. on sale of mkt. sec.; bef. extraord. chgr. of $9.0 mill. ⑥ Incl. merger & oth. chrgs. of $144.1 mill. ⑦ Bef. loss of $37.1 mill. fr. disc. ops. ⑧ Incl. $67.2 mill. chrg. rel. to disp. of bus. & inc. tax chrg. of $65.9 mill. rel. to disp. of bus.; bef. loss of $3.5 mill. fr. disc. ops. ⑨ Incl. non-recurr. chrg. of $232.5 mill. & inc. tax. benefit of $76.3 mill.

OFFICERS:
B. J. Duroc-Danner, Chmn., Pres., C.E.O.
L. W. Rodriguez, Sr. V.P., C.F.O.
B. M. Martin, Sr. V.P., Sec., Gen. Couns.
INVESTOR CONTACT: Don Galletly, (713) 693-4148
PRINCIPAL OFFICE: 515 Post Oak Blvd., Suite 600, Houston, TX 77027-3415

TELEPHONE NUMBER: (713) 693-4000
FAX: (713) 297-8488
WEB: www.weatherford.com
NO. OF EMPLOYEES: 14,500 (approx.)
SHAREHOLDERS: 3,457 (record)
ANNUAL MEETING: In June
INCORPORATED: MA, 1972; reincorp., DE, Sept., 1980; Bermuda, June, 2002

WEBSTER FINANCIAL CORPORATION

EXCH.	SYM.	REC. PRICE	P/E RATIO	YLD.	MKT. CAP.	RANGE (52-WK.)	'02 Y/E PR.	DIV. ACH.
NYSE	WBS	35.60 (2/28/03)	11.3	2.1%	$1.75 bill.	40.10 - 30.28	34.80	10 yrs.

MEDIUM GRADE. THE COMPANY PLANS TO INCREASE ITS REVENUES FROM FEE-BASED SERVICES THROUGH ACQUISITIONS.

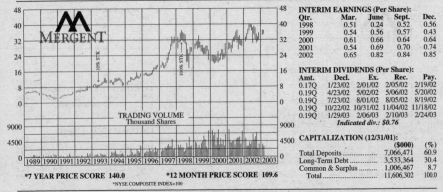

*7 YEAR PRICE SCORE 140.0   ***12 MONTH PRICE SCORE 109.6**
*NYSE COMPOSITE INDEX=100

INTERIM EARNINGS (Per Share):

Qtr.	Mar.	June	Sept.	Dec.
1998	0.51	0.24	0.52	0.56
1999	0.54	0.56	0.57	0.43
2000	0.61	0.66	0.64	0.64
2001	0.54	0.69	0.70	0.74
2002	0.65	0.82	0.84	0.85

INTERIM DIVIDENDS (Per Share):

Amt.	Decl.	Ex.	Rec.	Pay.
0.17Q	1/23/02	2/01/02	2/05/02	2/19/02
0.19Q	4/23/02	5/02/02	5/06/02	5/20/02
0.19Q	7/23/02	8/01/02	8/05/02	8/19/02
0.19Q	10/22/02	10/31/02	11/04/02	11/18/02
0.19Q	1/29/03	2/06/03	2/10/03	2/24/03

Indicated div.: $0.76

CAPITALIZATION (12/31/01):

	($000)	(%)
Total Deposits	7,066,471	60.9
Long-Term Debt	3,533,364	30.4
Common & Surplus	1,006,467	8.7
Total	11,606,302	100.0

BUSINESS:

Webster Financial Corporation, through its subsidiaries, Webster Bank and Webster Insurance, Inc., delivers business and consumer banking, mortgage, insurance, trust and investment services with $13.47 billion in assets as of 12/31/02. As of 1/22/03, the Company provided its services through more than 109 banking offices, 219 ATMs and the Internet. The Company is the majority owner of Chicago-based Duff & Phelps, LLC, a financial advisory service. Webster Bank owns the asset-based lending firm, Whitehall Business Credit Corporation, Center Capital Corporation, an equipment financing company headquartered in Farmington, Connecticut and Webster Trust Company, N.A.

RECENT DEVELOPMENTS:

For the year ended 12/31/02, net income increased 14.7% to $152.7 million compared with $133.2 million in 2001. Results for 2002 and 2001 included charges of $7.3 million and $4.5 million, respectively, for nonrecurring items. Total interest income declined 8.6% to $692.0 million from $757.2 million the year before. Total interest expense decreased 26.5% to $286.3 million versus $389.8 million a year earlier. Net interest income advanced 10.4% to $405.7 million from $367.5 million in 2001. The improvement in results were primarily attributed an increase in net interest income and growth in revenues from fee-based services. Provision for loan losses more than doubled to $29.0 million from $14.4 million the year before. Total noninterest income rose 16.7% to $185.6 million, while total noninterest expenses increased 7.6% to $328.3 million.

PROSPECTS:

On 1/24/03, the Company's subsidiary, Webster Bank, announced that it acquired Budget Installment Corp., an insurance premium financing company based in Rockville Centre, New York. Separately, on 1/6/03, Webster Bank announced that it acquired The Mathog & Moniello Companies, an East Haven Connecticut-based commercial property and casualty company that specializes in providing risk management products and services to self-insured businesses and groups. This acquisition is projected to contribute more than $11.0 million in annual insurance-related revenue for 2003. These acquisitions will broaden WBS' product offerings for commercial customers.

ANNUAL FINANCIAL DATA:

FISCAL YEAR	NET INT. INC. ($mill.)	NON-INT. INC. ($mill.)	NET INC. ($mill.)	TOT. LOANS ($mill.)	TOT. ASSETS ($mill.)	TOT. DEP. ($mill.)	RET. ON EQUITY %	RET. ON ASSETS %	EQUITY/ ASSETS %	EARN. PER SH. $	TANG. BK. VAL. $	DIV. PER SH. $	PRICE RANGE	AVG. P/E RATIO
p12/31/02	692.0	58.4	① 152.7							③ 3.16		0.74	40.10 - 30.38	2.1
12/31/01	367.5	162.1	④ 136.8	6,967.2	11,857.4	7,066.5	13.6	1.2	8.5	④ 2.68	13.97	0.67	37.10 - 25.50	11.7
12/31/00	326.5	128.8	118.3	7,053.9	11,249.5	6,941.5	13.3	1.1	7.9	2.55	11.53	0.62	30.19 - 19.69	9.8
12/31/99	303.5	92.6	③ 95.4	6,204.4	9,931.7	6,191.1	15.0	1.0	6.4	③ 2.10	10.98	0.47	34.13 - 21.56	13.3
12/31/98	245.4	74.2	③ 70.5	5,128.1	9,033.9	5,651.3	12.7	0.8	6.1	③ 1.83	12.77	0.43	37.00 - 17.50	14.9
12/31/97	191.9	36.0	② 33.8	3,907.4	7,019.6	4,365.8	8.8	0.5	5.4	② 1.22	12.20	0.39	33.75 - 17.31	20.9
12/31/96	115.8	25.5	① 25.6	2,569.3	3,917.6	3,095.9	12.4	0.7	5.3	① 1.49	10.22	0.34	19.13 - 13.38	10.9
12/31/95	87.3	22.0	① 18.3	1,941.4	3,219.7	2,400.2	8.7	0.6	6.5	① 1.22	12.70	0.32	15.50 - 9.00	10.0
12/31/94	92.4	13.6	18.7	1,869.2	3,053.9	2,431.9	11.9	0.6	5.1	1.48	14.30	0.26	12.75 - 8.63	7.2
12/31/93	63.9	8.5	12.7	1,245.6	2,167.8	1,675.3	12.1	0.6	4.9	1.37	14.67	0.25	12.63 - 7.61	7.4

Statistics are as originally reported. ① Incl. non-recurr. chrgs. $7.3 mill., 2002; $5.2 mill., 1996; $6.4 mill., 1995 ② Incl. merger and acquis. chrg. of $27.1 mill. ③ Incl. acquis.-related chrgs. of $9.5 mill., 1999; $17.4 mill., 1998. ④ Bef. extraord. chrg. of $1.2 mill. on early debt retirement and an acctg. change chrg. of $2.4 mill.

OFFICERS:
J. C. Smith, Chmn., C.E.O.
W. T. Bromage, Pres.
W. J. Healy, Exec. V.P., C.F.O.
INVESTOR CONTACT: James M. Sitro, Sr.
V.P., Inv. Rel., (203) 578-2399
PRINCIPAL OFFICE: Webster Plaza, Waterbury, CT 06720

TELEPHONE NUMBER: (203) 753-2921
FAX: (203) 755-5539
WEB: www.websterbank.com
NO. OF EMPLOYEES: 1,965 full-time; 306 part-time
SHAREHOLDERS: 12,202 (approx.)
ANNUAL MEETING: In Apr.
INCORPORATED: DE, Sept., 1986

INSTITUTIONAL HOLDINGS:
No. of Institutions: 182
Shares Held: 28,296,439
% Held: 61.5
INDUSTRY: Federal savings institutions (SIC: 6035)
TRANSFER AGENT(S): American Stock Transfer & Trust Co, New York, NY

WEINGARTEN REALTY INVESTORS

EXCH.	SYM.	REC. PRICE	P/E RATIO	YLD.	MKT. CAP.	RANGE (52-WK.)	'02 Y/E PR.	DIV. ACH.
NYSE	WRI	25.90 (Adj.; 2/28/03)	18.2	6.0%	$2.02 bill.	26.13 - 19.53	24.57	14 yrs.

UPPER MEDIUM GRADE. THE COMPANY SHOULD CONTINUE TO BENEFIT FROM RECENT ACQUISITIONS.

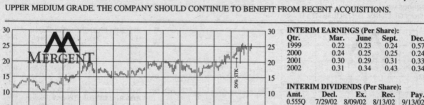

*7 YEAR PRICE SCORE 132.3   ***12 MONTH PRICE SCORE 112.7**

*NYSE COMPOSITE INDEX=100

INTERIM EARNINGS (Per Share):

Qtr.	Mar.	June	Sept.	Dec.
1999	0.22	0.23	0.24	0.57
2000	0.24	0.25	0.25	0.24
2001	0.30	0.29	0.31	0.33
2002	0.31	0.34	0.43	0.34

INTERIM DIVIDENDS (Per Share):

Amt.	Decl.	Ex.	Rec.	Pay.
0.555Q	7/29/02	8/09/02	8/13/02	9/13/02
0.555Q	10/28/02	11/06/02	11/08/02	12/16/02
0.585Q	2/24/03	3/05/03	3/07/03	3/17/03
3-for-2	2/24/03	4/16/03	4/01/03	4/15/03

Indicated div.: $1.56 (Adj.; Div. Reinv. Plan)

CAPITALIZATION (12/31/02):

	($000)	(%)
Long-Term Debt	1,296,907	57.3
Capital Lease Obligations	33,462	1.5
Preferred Stock	263	0.0
Common & Surplus	933,150	41.2
Total	2,263,782	100.0

BUSINESS:

Weingarten Realty Investors is a self-administered and self-managed real estate investment trust that acquires, develops and manages real estate, primarily anchored neighborhood and community shopping centers and, to a lesser extent, industrial properties. As of 2/24/03, the Company owned or operated under long-term leases interests in 303 developed income-producing real estate projects. WRI owned 245 shopping centers located in the Houston metropolitan area and in other parts of Texas and in California, Louisiana, Arizona, Nevada, Arkansas, New Mexico, Oklahoma, Tennessee, Kansas, Colorado, Missouri, Illinois, Florida, North Carolina, Georgia, Mississippi and Maine. WRI also owned 57 industrial projects located in Tennessee, Nevada Georgia, Florida and Houston, Austin and Dallas, Texas. Also, WRI owned one office building.

RECENT DEVELOPMENTS:

For the year ended 12/31/02, income was $110.6 million, before income of $21.3 million from discontinued operations, compared with income of $105.9 million, before income of $2.7 million from discontinued operations, the prior year. Results for 2002 and 2001 included gains of $188,000 and $8.3 million, respectively, from the sale of properties. Total revenues advanced 18.3% to $365.4 million from $309.0 million a year earlier. Rental revenues increased 18.2% to $359.0 million from $303.8 million the year before.

PROSPECTS:

On 3/10/03, the Company announced that it has completed the acquisition of a supermarket-anchored shopping center in San Marcos, California and an industrial property in Atlanta, Georgia. Including these properties, 2003 acquisition aggregate an investment of $42.8 million. Separately, on 12/20/02, the Company acquired three supermarket-anchored shopping centers for a total investment of $46.2 million. On 12/19/02, WRI and AEW Capital Management, L.P. formed a strategic joint venture to acquire up to $238.0 million of real estate using limited leveraging. The joint venture will primarily target high-quality supermarket-anchored shopping centers in the southern half of the U.S.

ANNUAL FINANCIAL DATA:

FISCAL YEAR	TOT. INC. ($mill.)	NET INC. ($mill.)	TOT. ASSETS ($mill.)	NET INC. +DEPR./ ASSETS %	RET. ON EQUITY %	RET. ON ASSETS %	EARN. PER SH. $	TANG. BK. VAL. $	DIV. PER SH. $	DIV. PAYOUT %	PRICE RANGE	AVG. P/E RATIO	AVG. YIELD %
12/31/02	365.4	③ 110.6	2,423.9	7.8	11.9	4.6	③ 1.75	11.95	1.48	126.5	26.13 - 19.53	19.6	5.1
12/31/01	314.9	② 108.5	2,095.7	8.4	11.8	5.2	② 1.23	11.92	1.40	114.5	22.51 - 17.24	16.2	7.1
12/31/00	273.4	② 79.0	1,646.0	8.4	12.5	4.8	② 0.97	10.39	1.33	137.0	20.00 - 15.36	18.2	7.5
12/31/99	230.3	①② 96.3	1,309.4	11.1	14.9	7.4	①② 1.27	10.75	1.26	99.3	20.28 - 16.45	14.4	6.9
12/31/98	198.1	① 61.8	1,107.0	9.4	11.6	5.6	① 0.92	8.88	1.19	128.8	20.83 - 15.97	19.9	6.5
12/31/97	174.5	55.0	946.8	9.8	14.1	5.8	0.91	6.50	1.14	124.8	20.28 - 17.22	20.6	6.1
12/31/96	151.1	53.9	831.1	10.6	13.5	6.5	0.90	6.71	1.10	122.2	18.11 - 15.22	18.5	6.6
12/31/95	134.2	44.8	734.8	10.2	10.9	6.1	0.75	6.89	1.07	142.0	17.11 - 14.83	21.3	6.7
12/31/94	120.8	43.8	682.0	10.4	10.3	6.4	0.74	7.14	1.01	136.6	18.00 - 14.56	21.9	6.2
12/31/93	103.3	36.2	602.0	9.9	8.5	6.0	0.67	7.31	0.96	144.0	20.11 - 16.17	27.2	5.3

Statistics are as originally reported. Adj. for 3-for-2 stk. split, 4/03; 50.0%, 4/02. ① Bef. extraord. chrg., 1999, $190,000; 1998, $1.4 mill. ② Incl. gain on sales of prop. of $8.3 mill, 2001; $382,000, 2000; $20.6 mill., 1999. ③ Bef. inc. of $21.3 mill. from disc. ops. & incl. gain of $188,000 from sale of prop.

OFFICERS:
S. Alexander, Chmn.
M. Debrovner, Vice-Chmn.
A. M. Alexander, Pres., C.E.O.
INVESTOR CONTACT: Tracy Pursell, Investor Relations, (713) 866-6050
PRINCIPAL OFFICE: 2600 Citadel Plaza Drive, P.O. Box 924133, Houston, TX 77292-4133

TELEPHONE NUMBER: (713) 866-6000
FAX: (713) 866-6049
WEB: www.weingarten.com
NO. OF EMPLOYEES: 292
SHAREHOLDERS: 3,366 (record)
ANNUAL MEETING: In Apr.
INCORPORATED: TX, 1948

INSTITUTIONAL HOLDINGS:
No. of Institutions: 178
Shares Held: 27,918,356 (Adj.)
% Held: 35.8

INDUSTRY: Real estate investment trusts (SIC: 6798)

TRANSFER AGENT(S): Mellon Investor Services, Houston, TX

WEIS MARKETS, INC.

EXCH.	SYM.	REC. PRICE	P/E RATIO	YLD.	MKT. CAP.	RANGE (52-WK.)	'02 Y/E PR.
NYSE	WMK	29.05 (2/28/03)	13.3	3.7%	$0.79 bill.	39.50 - 27.76	31.05

UPPER MEDIUM GRADE. RESULTS ARE BENEFITING FROM PRODUCTIVITY INCREASES AND THE IMPLEMENTATION OF COST-CONTROL INITIATIVES.

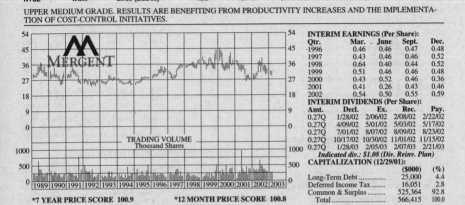

*7 YEAR PRICE SCORE 100.9   *12 MONTH PRICE SCORE 100.8
*NYSE COMPOSITE INDEX=100

INTERIM EARNINGS (Per Share):

Qtr.	Mar.	June	Sept.	Dec.
1996	0.46	0.46	0.47	0.48
1997	0.43	0.46	0.46	0.52
1998	0.64	0.40	0.44	0.52
1999	0.51	0.46	0.46	0.48
2000	0.43	0.52	0.46	0.36
2001	0.41	0.26	0.43	0.46
2002	0.54	0.50	0.55	0.59

INTERIM DIVIDENDS (Per Share):

Amt.	Decl.	Ex.	Rec.	Pay.
0.27Q	1/28/02	2/06/02	2/08/02	2/22/02
0.27Q	4/09/02	5/01/02	5/03/02	5/17/02
0.27Q	7/01/02	8/07/02	8/09/02	8/23/02
0.27Q	10/17/02	10/30/02	11/01/02	11/15/02
0.27Q	1/28/03	2/05/03	2/07/03	2/21/03

Indicated div.: $1.08 (Div. Reinv. Plan)

CAPITALIZATION (12/29/01):

	($000)	(%)
Long-Term Debt	25,000	4.4
Deferred Income Tax	16,051	2.8
Common & Surplus	525,364	92.8
Total	566,415	100.0

BUSINESS:

Weis Markets, Inc. operated 160 supermarkets in Pennsylvania, Maryland, New Jersey, New York, Virginia and West Virginia as of 10/15/02. WMK's stores operate under the names Weis Markets, Mr. Z's Food Mart, King's Supermarket, Save-A-Lot, Scot's Lo Cost and Cressler's Marketplace. The Company supplies its retail stores from distribution centers in Sunbury, Northumberland, and Milton, PA. Many of WMK's private label products are supplied by the Company's ice cream manufacturing plant, fresh meat processing plant, and milk processing plant. The Company also owns SuperPetz, an operator of 33 pet supply stores in 11 states. On 4/8/00, the Company completed the sale of Weis Food Service, its regional food service division.

RECENT DEVELOPMENTS:

For the 52 weeks ended 12/28/02, net income totaled $59.1 million, up 18.2% compared with $50.1 million in the corresponding prior-year period. Earnings for 2002 included a $3.6 million pre-tax gain stemming from the sale of closed store properties. Net sales rose 1.4% to $2.00 billion from $1.97 billion a year earlier. Identical-store sales increased 1.4% year over year. Gross profit was $527.9 million, or 26.4% of net sales, versus $514.7 million, or 26.1% of net sales, the previous year. Income from operations climbed 26.2% to $79.4 million from $62.9 million the year before.

PROSPECTS:

Earnings are being positively affected by improved gross margins, which are being fueled by supply chain productivity increases and the implementation of cost-control initiatives. Meanwhile, sales growth is being hampered by unfavorable economic conditions, lower selling prices for meat and diary products, and increased competition. Separately, the Company anticipates capital expenditures of about $72.4 million in 2003. On 2/13/03, WMK announced that it has signed a lease to build a new superstore in Honeygo, Maryland. Construction is expected to begin in early summer 2003.

ANNUAL FINANCIAL DATA:

FISCAL YEAR	TOT. REVS. ($mill.)	NET INC. ($mill.)	TOT. ASSETS ($mill.)	OPER. PROFIT %	NET PROFIT %	RET. ON EQUITY %	RET. ON ASSETS %	CURR. RATIO	EARN. PER SH. $	CASH FL. PER SH. $	TANG. BK. VAL. $	DIV. PER SH. $	PRICE RANGE	AVG. P/E RATIO	AVG. YIELD %
p12/28/02	1,999.4	① 59.1			2.5	9.5	7.1	1.7	① 2.17			1.08	39.50 - 26.90	15.3	3.3
12/29/01	1,988.2	50.1	704.2	3.2	2.5	9.5	7.1	1.7	1.55	3.13	19.31	1.08	38.25 - 25.80	20.7	3.4
12/30/00	2,061.0	① 73.8	1,085.9	3.9	3.6	7.8	6.8	5.1	① 1.77	2.99	22.74	1.06	45.25 - 32.00	21.8	2.7
12/25/99	2,004.9	① 79.7	1,058.2	4.6	4.0	8.7	7.5	5.0	① 1.91	3.02	22.03	1.02	44.31 - 32.88	20.2	2.6
12/26/98	1,867.5	① 83.7	1,029.2	4.1	4.5	9.4	8.1	5.1	① 2.00	3.11	21.33	0.98	38.88 - 33.25	18.0	2.7
12/27/97	1,818.8	78.2	971.8	4.7	4.3	9.2	8.0	5.5	1.87	2.91	20.28	0.94	36.25 - 26.88	16.9	3.0
12/28/96	1,753.2	78.9	966.3	5.2	4.5	9.6	8.2	4.6	1.87	2.77	19.47	0.88	34.88 - 27.75	16.7	2.8
12/30/95	1,646.4	79.4	923.2	5.2	4.8	10.0	8.6	5.3	1.84	2.61	18.61	0.80	29.00 - 24.00	14.4	3.0
12/31/94	1,556.7	76.3	892.1	5.1	4.9	10.0	8.5	5.5	1.75	2.45	17.53	0.74	28.00 - 23.88	14.8	2.9
12/25/93	1,441.1	73.0	844.5	5.5	5.1	9.9	8.6	6.5	1.66	2.33	16.85	0.70	29.88 - 24.00	16.2	2.6

Statistics are as originally reported. ① Incl. $3.6 mil pre-tax gain fr. sale of asets, 2002; $4.9 mil pre-tax litigation chg., 2000; $3.4 mil pre-tax gain fr. sale of asset, 1999; $8.3 mil ($0.20/sh) after-tax gain from sale of stk., 1998.

OFFICERS:
R. F. Weis, Chmn., Treas.
N. S. Rich, Pres.
R. P. Hermanns, V.P., C.O.O.
W. R. Mills, V.P., Sec.

PRINCIPAL OFFICE: 1000 South Second Street, Sunbury, PA 17801-0471

TELEPHONE NUMBER: (570) 286-4571
FAX: (570) 286-3286
WEB: www.weismarkets.com

NO. OF EMPLOYEES: 19,000 (approx.)

SHAREHOLDERS: 5,983 (approx.)

ANNUAL MEETING: In Apr.

INCORPORATED: PA, Dec., 1924

INSTITUTIONAL HOLDINGS:
No. of Institutions: 71
Shares Held: 5,129,305
% Held: 18.9

INDUSTRY: Grocery stores (SIC: 5411)

TRANSFER AGENT(S): American Stock Transfer & Trust Company, New York, NY

WELLPOINT HEALTH NETWORKS, INC.

EXCH.	SYM.	REC. PRICE	P/E RATIO	YLD.	MKT. CAP.	RANGE (52-WK.)	'02 Y/E PR.
NYSE	WLP	68.01 (2/28/03)	14.7	...	$8.69 bill.	89.20 - 57.58	71.16

UPPER MEDIUM GRADE. ON 1/24/03, THE COMPANY AND CAREFIRST, INC. ANNOUNCED THEY HAVE APPROVED AN AMENDED AND RESTATED AGREEMENT AND PLAN OF MERGER BETWEEN THE TWO COMPANIES.

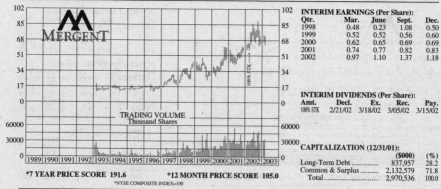

INTERIM EARNINGS (Per Share):

Qtr.	Mar.	June	Sept.	Dec.
1998	0.48	0.23	1.08	0.50
1999	0.52	0.52	0.56	0.60
2000	0.62	0.65	0.69	0.69
2001	0.74	0.77	0.82	0.83
2002	0.97	1.10	1.37	1.18

INTERIM DIVIDENDS (Per Share):

Amt.	Decl.	Ex.	Rec.	Pay.
100% STK	2/21/02	3/18/02	3/05/02	3/15/02

CAPITALIZATION (12/31/01):

	($000)	(%)
Long-Term Debt	837,957	28.2
Common & Surplus	2,132,579	71.8
Total	2,970,536	100.0

*7 YEAR PRICE SCORE 191.6 ***12 MONTH PRICE SCORE 105.0**

*NYSE COMPOSITE INDEX=100

BUSINESS:

WellPoint Health Networks, Inc. offers a broad range of network-based health products, including preferred provider organizations (PPOs), health maintenance organizations (HMOs) and point-of-service (POS) and other hybrid plans and indemnity plans to the large and small employer, individual, Medicaid and senior markets. As of 2/10/03, WLP served more than 13.0 million medical members and more than 48.0 million specialty members nationally through Blue Cross of California, Blue Cross and Blue Shield of Georgia, Blue Cross and Blue Shield of Missouri, HealthLink and UNICARE Life and Health Insurance Company throughout other parts of the country. In addition, WLP offers a variety of specialty and other products and services, including pharmacy, dental, vision, mental health, utilization management, long term care insurance, life and disability insurance, flexible spending accounts, COBRA administration, and Medicare supplements.

RECENT DEVELOPMENTS:

For the year ended 12/31/02, income was $697.9 million, before a net extraordinary gain of $5.1 million, compared with net income of $414.7 million the previous year. Revenues jumped 39.5% to $17.34 billion from $12.43 billion the prior year. Premium revenues advanced 40.0% to $16.21 billion from $11.58 billion, while management services and other revenue increased 34.2% to $818.4 million from $609.7 million the year before. Investment income improved 30.0% to $314.0 million from $241.8 million in 2001. Operating income soared 55.4% to $1.28 billion versus $823.2 million a year earlier. Total medical membership climbed 25.6% to 13.2 million.

PROSPECTS:

On 1/24/03, the Company and CareFirst, Inc. announced they have approved an amended and restated agreement and plan of merger between the two companies. The consideration payable has been increased by $70.0 million to $1.37 billion. The transaction remains subject to a number of additional closing conditions. Separately, on 12/6/02, the Company announced that it signed a definitive agreement to acquire Golden West Dental & Vision, a privately-held, stand-alone dental and vision company that serves approximately 293,000 members.

ANNUAL FINANCIAL DATA:

FISCAL YEAR	TOT. REVS. ($mill.)	NET INC. ($mill.)	TOT. ASSETS ($mill.)	OPER. PROFIT %	NET PROFIT %	RET. ON EQUITY %	RET. ON ASSETS %	CURR. RATIO	EARN. PER SH.$	CASH FL. PER SH.$	TANG. BK. VAL.$	PRICE RANGE	AVG. P/E RATIO
p12/31/02	17,338.5	⑥ 697.9							⑥ 4.64			89.20 - 57.58	15.8
⑤ 12/31/01	12,428.6	414.7	7,472.1	6.6	3.3	19.4	5.6	1.4	3.15	3.93	8.14	61.45 - 40.83	16.2
12/31/00	9,229.0	342.3	5,504.7	6.9	3.7	20.8	6.2	1.5	2.65	3.17	8.45	60.75 - 28.47	16.9
12/31/99	7,485.4	① ② 297.2	4,593.2	7.3	4.0	22.6	6.5	1.5	① ② 2.19	2.65	7.14	48.50 - 24.13	16.6
12/31/98	6,478.4	④ 319.5	4,225.8	6.9	4.9	24.3	7.6	1.6	④ 2.28	2.63	6.59	43.94 - 21.03	14.3
12/31/97	5,826.4	③ 227.4	4,533.4	7.8	3.9	18.6	5.0	1.5	③ 1.64	2.02	3.76	30.56 - 16.25	14.3
12/31/96	4,169.8	202.0	3,405.5	9.5	4.8	23.2	5.9	1.6	1.52	1.78	2.39	19.56 - 11.69	10.3
12/31/95	3,107.1	③ 180.0	2,679.3	10.2	5.8	10.8	6.7	2.9	③ 0.91	1.02	7.77	18.50 - 13.50	17.7
12/31/94	2,791.7	213.2	2,385.6	12.9	7.6	15.0	8.9	0.7	1.07	1.17	6.41	18.50 - 12.13	14.3
12/31/93	2,449.2	② 186.6	1,926.6	12.9	7.6	15.1	9.7	0.5	② 0.94	0.99	6.20	19.88 - 11.50	16.7

Statistics are as originally reported. Adj. for 2-for-1 stk. spl., 3/02. ① Bef. extraord. gain of $1.9 mill. ② Bef. acctg. chrg. of $20.6 mill.; 1999; $21.3 mill., 1993. ③ Incl. nonrecurr. chrg. of $14.5 mill.; 1997; $57.1 mill., 1995. ④ Bef. a loss of $88.3 mill. fr. disposal of workers' compensation. ⑤ Refl. the acq. of Cerulean Companies, Inc. on 3/15/01. ⑥ Bef. extra. gain of $5.1 mill.

OFFICERS:
L. D. Schaeffer, Chmn., C.E.O.
D. C. Colby, Exec. V.P., C.F.O.
T. C. Geiser, Exec. V.P., Sec., Gen. Couns.
INVESTOR CONTACT: John Cygul, V. P., Investor Relations, (805) 557-6789
PRINCIPAL OFFICE: 1 Wellpoint Way, Thousand Oaks, CA 91362

TELEPHONE NUMBER: (818) 234-4000
FAX: (818) 557-6820
WEB: www.wellpoint.com
NO. OF EMPLOYEES: 13,900 (approx.)
SHAREHOLDERS: 621 (approx.)
ANNUAL MEETING: In May
INCORPORATED: DE, Aug., 1992

INSTITUTIONAL HOLDINGS:
No. of Institutions: 481
Shares Held: 172,711,892
% Held: 116.1
INDUSTRY: Hospital and medical service plans (SIC: 6324)
TRANSFER AGENT(S): Mellon Investor Services, Ridgefield Park, NJ

WELLS FARGO & COMPANY

EXCH.	SYM.	REC. PRICE	P/E RATIO	YLD.	MKT. CAP.	RANGE (52-WK.)	'02 Y/E PR.	DIV. ACH.
NYSE	WFC	47.37 (1/31/03)	14.3	2.5%	$80.32 bill.	54.84 - 41.50	46.87	15 yrs.

INVESTMENT GRADE. THE COMPANY CONTINUES TO PERFORM WELL DESPITE THE SOFT ECONOMY AND VOLATILE MARKETS.

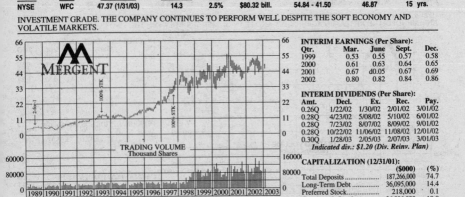

INTERIM EARNINGS (Per Share):

Qtr.	Mar.	June	Sept.	Dec.
1999	0.53	0.55	0.57	0.58
2000	0.61	0.63	0.64	0.65
2001	0.67	d0.05	0.67	0.69
2002	0.80	0.82	0.84	0.86

INTERIM DIVIDENDS (Per Share):

Amt.	Decl.	Ex.	Rec.	Pay.
0.26Q	1/22/02	1/30/02	2/01/02	3/01/02
0.28Q	4/23/02	5/08/02	5/10/02	6/01/02
0.28Q	7/23/02	8/07/02	8/09/02	9/01/02
0.28Q	10/22/02	11/06/02	11/08/02	12/01/02
0.30Q	1/28/03	2/05/03	2/07/03	3/01/03

Indicated div.: $1.20 (Div. Reinv. Plan)

CAPITALIZATION (12/31/01):

	($000)	(%)
Total Deposits	187,266,000	74.7
Long-Term Debt	36,095,000	14.4
Preferred Stock	218,000	0.1
Common & Surplus	26,996,000	10.8
Total	250,575,000	100.0

*7 YEAR PRICE SCORE 130.5   ***12 MONTH PRICE SCORE 105.9**

*NYSE COMPOSITE INDEX=100

BUSINESS:

Wells Fargo & Company (formerly Norwest Corporation), with $349.26 billion in assets as of 12/31/02, is a diversified financial services company providing banking, insurance, investments, mortgage and consumer finance through more than 5,600 financial services stores and the Internet across North America and elsewhere internationally. In early November 1998, the former Wells Fargo & Company merged with WFC Holdings, a subsidiary of Norwest Corp., with WFC Holdings as the surviving corporation. In connection with the merger, Norwest changed its name to Wells Fargo & Company. On 10/25/00, WFC acquired First Security, creating the largest banking franchise in the western region of the U.S.

RECENT DEVELOPMENTS:

For the year ended 12/31/02, WFC reported income of $5.71 billion, before an accounting charge of $276.0 million, versus net income of $3.42 billion the year before. Results for 2002 and 2001 included losses from equity investments of $327.0 million and $1.54 billion, respectively. Results also included net gains of $241.0 million in 2002 and $337.0 million in 2001 related to various items.

In addition, net earnings for 2001 included goodwill amortization of $610.0 million. Net interest income rose 19.2% to $14.86 billion due to growth in loans and mortgages held for sale. Provision for loan losses declined 2.6% to $1.73 billion. Total non-interest income grew 25.4% to $9.64 billion, while total non-interest expense rose 7.9% to $13.91 billion.

PROSPECTS:

The Company continues to perform well despite the soft economy and volatile markets. Growth in consumer loans continues to be driven by strong demand for home equity loans and lines, as well as by a solid increase in credit card balances and consumer finance receivables. Separately, WFC continues to increase its overall product breadth and diversity through strategic acquisitions, including the acquisition of a majority of the businesses of Montgomery Asset Management LLC. The acquisition includes the institutional and retail investment management business. The business lines being acquired have $4.90 billion in assets under management as of 8/31/02.

ANNUAL FINANCIAL DATA:

FISCAL YEAR	NET INT. INC. ($mill.)	NON-INT. INC. ($mill.)	NET INC. ($mill.)	TOT. LOANS ($mill.)	TOT. ASSETS ($mill.)	TOT. DEP. ($mill.)	RET. ON EQUITY %	RET. ON ASSETS %	EQUITY/ ASSETS %	EARN. PER SH.$	TANG. BK. VAL.$	DIV. PER SH.$	PRICE RANGE	AVG. P/E RATIO
p12/31/02	14,855.0	9,641.0	③⑤ 5,710.0				18.8	1.6		③⑤ 3.32		1.10	54.84 - 41.50	14.5
12/31/01	12,460.0	7,690.0	③④ 3,423.0	172,499.0	307,569.0	187,266.0	12.6	1.1	8.8	③④ 1.97	9.71	1.00	54.81 - 38.25	23.6
12/31/00	10,865.0	8,843.0	③ 4,026.0	161,124.0	272,426.0	169,559.0	15.2	1.5	9.7	③ 2.33	9.11	0.90	56.38 - 31.38	18.8
12/31/99	9,355.0	7,420.0	③ 3,747.0	119,464.0	218,102.0	132,708.0	16.9	1.7	10.1	③ 2.23	7.87	0.79	49.94 - 32.19	18.4
12/31/98	8,990.0	6,427.0	② 1,950.0	107,994.0	202,475.0	136,788.0	9.4	1.0	10.3	② 1.17	6.71	0.70	43.88 - 27.50	30.5
12/31/97	4,033.4	2,962.3	1,351.0	44,634.1	88,540.2	55,457.1	19.2	1.5	7.9	1.75	8.90	0.61	39.50 - 21.38	17.4
12/31/96	3,701.3	2,564.6	① 1,153.9	80,175.4	80,175.4	50,130.2	19.0	1.4	7.6	① 1.54	7.88	0.53	23.44 - 15.25	12.6
12/31/95	3,269.3	1,865.0	956.0	37,830.7	72,134.4	42,028.8	18.0	1.3	7.4	1.38	7.05	0.45	17.38 - 11.31	10.4
12/31/94	2,803.6	1,638.3	800.4	33,703.6	59,315.9	36,424.0	20.8	1.3	6.5	1.23	5.34	0.38	14.13 - 10.50	10.1
12/31/93	2,376.1	1,542.5	653.6	27,952.8	50,782.3	32,573.2	18.3	1.3	7.0	1.07	5.52	0.32	14.50 - 10.31	11.6

Statistics are as originally reported. Adj. for 2-for-1 stk. split, 10/97 & 6/93. Reflects 11/98 merger with Norwest Corp. & subsequent name change to Wells Fargo & Co. Yrs. prior to 12/31/98 represent the results of Norwest Corp. only. ① Incl. one-time SAIF pre-tax chg. of $19.0 mill. ② Incl. a one-time net loss of $1.85 bill. rel. to various items. ③ Incl. pre-tax net gain on dispos. of premises: gain $52.0 mill., 2002; $21.0 mill., 2001; $58.0 mill., 2000; $16.0 mill., 1999. ④ Incl. net venture capital losses of $1.63 billion. ⑤ Bef. acctg. chrge. of $276.0 mill.

OFFICERS:
R. M. Kovacevich, Chmn., Pres., C.E.O.
L. S. Biller, Vice-Chmn., C.O.O.

INVESTOR CONTACT: Robert S. Strickland, Sr. V.P., (415) 396-0523

PRINCIPAL OFFICE: 420 Montgomery Street, San Francisco, CA 94163

TELEPHONE NUMBER: (800) 411-4932
FAX: (651) 450-4033
WEB: www.wellsfargo.com
NO. OF EMPLOYEES: 119,714
SHAREHOLDERS: 98,598
ANNUAL MEETING: In April
INCORPORATED: DE, Jan., 1929

INSTITUTIONAL HOLDINGS:
No. of Institutions: 984
Shares Held: 1,103,297,124
% Held: 65.2
INDUSTRY: National commercial banks (SIC: 6021)
TRANSFER AGENT(S): Wells Fargo Shareowners Services, St. Paul, MN

WENDY'S INTERNATIONAL, INC.

EXCH.	SYM.	REC. PRICE	P/E RATIO	YLD.	MKT. CAP.	RANGE (52-WK.)	'02 Y/E PR.
NYSE	WEN	25.33 (2/28/03)	13.4	0.9%	$2.66 bill.	41.60 - 24.05	27.07

INVESTMENT GRADE. IN 2003, THE COMPANY ANTICIPATES REVENUE GROWTH OF 11.0% TO 14.0% AND EARNINGS PER SHARE INA RANGE OF $2.02 TO $2.08.

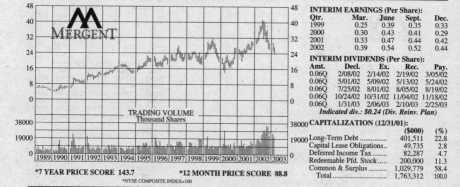

*7 YEAR PRICE SCORE 143.7   ***12 MONTH PRICE SCORE 88.8**
*NYSE COMPOSITE INDEX=100

INTERIM EARNINGS (Per Share):

Qtr.	Mar.	June	Sept.	Dec.
1999	0.25	0.39	0.35	0.33
2000	0.30	0.43	0.41	0.29
2001	0.33	0.47	0.44	0.42
2002	0.39	0.54	0.52	0.44

INTERIM DIVIDENDS (Per Share):

Amt.	Decl.	Ex.	Rec.	Pay.
0.06Q	2/08/02	2/14/02	2/19/02	3/05/02
0.06Q	5/01/02	5/09/02	5/13/02	5/24/02
0.06Q	7/25/02	8/01/02	8/05/02	8/19/02
0.06Q	10/24/02	10/31/02	11/04/02	11/18/02
0.06Q	1/31/03	2/06/03	2/10/03	2/25/03

Indicated div.: $0.24 (Div. Reinv. Plan)

CAPITALIZATION (12/31/01):

	($000)	(%)
Long-Term Debt	401,511	22.8
Capital Lease Obligations..	49,735	2.8
Deferred Income Tax	82,287	4.7
Redeemable Pfd. Stock	200,000	11.3
Common & Surplus	1,029,779	58.4
Total	1,763,312	100.0

BUSINESS:

Wendy's International, Inc., operates the third-largest quick service hamburger restaurant chain with $9.40 billion in systemwide sales during 2002. As of 1/31/03, the Company owned and franchised a total of 6,250 Wendy's Old Fashioned Hamburgers® restaurants, 2,348 Tim Hortons restaurants and 210 Baja Fresh Mexican Grill restaurants. Wendy's menu includes hamburgers, chicken sandwiches, hot stuffed baked potatoes, pita sandwiches and desserts.

The Super Value Menu offers several products each priced at $0.99. Tim Horton's restaurants sell coffee and baked goods primarily in Canada as well as in the United States. In 2001, Wendy's and Tim Hortons contributed 76.1% and 23.9%, respectively, to the Company's revenues, and 69.3% and 30.7%, respectively, to income. On 6/19/02, WEN acquired the fast-casual Baja Fresh Mexican Grill restaurant chain for $275.0 million.

RECENT DEVELOPMENTS:

For the year ended 12/29/02, net income grew 13.0% to $218.8 million from $193.6 million the year before. Systemwide sales rose 12.7% to $9.40 billion. Total revenues advanced 14.2% to $2.73 billion from $2.39 billion a year earlier. Retail sales climbed 13.6% to $2.19 billion, while

franchise revenues rose 16.5% to $542.8 million. Same-store sales grew 4.7% over the prior year at Wendy's U.S. Company restaurants. Year-over-year same-store sales at Tim Hortons restaurants in Canada rose 7.2%, while same-store sales at Tim Hortons in the U.S. increased 9.9%.

PROSPECTS:

Looking ahead, the Company anticipates revenue growth of 11.0% to 14.0% and earnings per share in a range of $2.02 to $2.08 in 2003. WEN's long-term goal for earnings per share growth continues to range from 12.0% to 15.0% per year. Additionally, the Company expects 2003 capital expenditures between $325.0 million and $365.0 million.

Moreover, the Company plans to invest $50.0 million to $60.0 million on new business opportunities and to expand its Tim Hortons joint venture facility in Canada. Meanwhile, WEN plans on opening about 560 to 605 new restaurants, primarily Wendy's, Tim Hortons and Baja Fresh restaurants, in 2003.

ANNUAL FINANCIAL DATA:

FISCAL YEAR	TOT. REVS. ($mill.)	NET INC. ($mill.)	TOT. ASSETS ($mill.)	OPER. PROFIT %	NET PROFIT %	RET. ON EQUITY %	RET. ON ASSETS %	CURR. RATIO	EARN. PER SH.$	CASH FL. PER SH.$	TANG. BK. VAL.$	DIV. PER SH.$	PRICE RANGE	AVG. P/E RATIO	AVG. YIELD %
p12/31/02	2,730.3	218.8							1.89			0.24	41.60 - 26.15	17.9	1.0
12/31/01	2,391.2	193.6	2,076.0	13.8	8.1	18.8	9.3	0.9	1.65	2.62	9.40	0.24	30.50 - 20.00	15.3	1.0
12/31/00	2,236.9	169.6	1,957.7	13.9	7.6	15.1	8.7	1.1	1.44	2.31	9.48	0.24	27.13 - 14.00	14.3	1.2
1/02/00	2,072.2	166.6	1,883.6	13.8	8.0	15.4	8.8	1.2	1.32	2.06	8.60	0.24	31.69 - 19.69	19.5	0.9
1/03/99	1,948.2	①123.4	1,837.9	12.6	6.3	11.5	6.7	1.3	①0.95	1.63	8.20	0.24	25.19 - 18.13	22.8	1.1
12/28/97	2,037.3	130.5	1,941.7	11.3	6.4	11.0	6.7	1.8	0.97	1.67	9.77	0.24	27.94 - 19.63	24.5	1.0
12/29/96	1,897.1	155.9	1,781.4	13.8	8.2	14.8	8.8	1.6	1.20	1.91	8.89	0.24	23.00 - 16.75	16.6	1.2
12/31/95	1,746.3	①110.1	1,509.2	13.0	6.3	13.4	7.3	1.1	①0.90	1.59	7.46	0.24	22.75 - 14.38	20.6	1.3
1/01/95	1,397.9	97.2	1,214.8	11.4	7.0	13.8	8.0	0.8	0.93	1.64	6.60	0.24	18.50 - 13.25	17.1	1.5
1/02/94	1,320.1	79.3	996.5	9.6	6.0	13.2	8.0	1.2	0.77	1.44	5.72	0.24	17.38 - 12.38	19.3	1.6

Statistics are as originally reported. ① Incl. non-recurr. chrg. $33.9 mill., 12/31/98; $49.7 mill., 12/31/95.

OFFICERS:
J. T. Schuessler, Chmn., Pres., C.E.O.
K. B. Anderson, Exec. V.P., C.F.O.
J. F. Brownley, Sr. V.P., Treas.
INVESTOR CONTACT: John D. Barker, (614) 764-3044
PRINCIPAL OFFICE: P.O. Box 256, 4288 West Dublin-Granville Rd., Dublin, OH 43017-0256

TELEPHONE NUMBER: (614) 764-3100
FAX: (614) 764-3330
WEB: www.wendys.com
NO. OF EMPLOYEES: 44,000 (avg.)
SHAREHOLDERS: 80,000 (approx.)
ANNUAL MEETING: In Mar.
·INCORPORATED: OH, Dec., 1969

INSTITUTIONAL HOLDINGS:
No. of Institutions: 316
Shares Held: 96,469,532
% Held: 83.6

INDUSTRY: Eating places (SIC: 5812)

TRANSFER AGENT(S): American Stock Transfer & Trust Company, New York, NY

WEST PHARMACEUTICAL SERVICES, INC.

EXCH.	SYM.	REC. PRICE	P/E RATIO	YLD.	MKT. CAP.	RANGE (52-WK.)	'02 Y/E PR.	DIV. ACH.
NYSE	WST	19.17 (2/28/03)	21.5	4.2%	$275.0 mill.	32.50 - 16.25	24.40	10 yrs.

MEDIUM GRADE. THE COMPANY EXPECTS TO INCUR PRE-TAX COSTS OF $4.0 MILLION TO $6.0 MILLION IN 2003 AS A RESULT OF THE ACCIDENT AT ITS KINSTON, NORTH CAROLINA FACILITY.

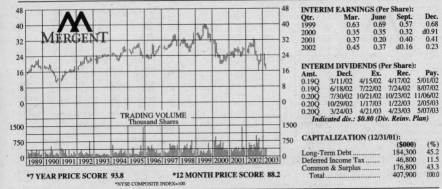

INTERIM EARNINGS (Per Share):

Qtr.	Mar.	June	Sept.	Dec.
1999	0.63	0.69	0.57	0.68
2000	0.35	0.35	0.32	d0.91
2001	0.37	0.20	0.40	0.41
2002	0.45	0.37	d0.16	0.23

INTERIM DIVIDENDS (Per Share):

Amt.	Decl.	Ex.	Rec.	Pay.
0.19Q	3/11/02	4/15/02	4/17/02	5/01/02
0.19Q	6/18/02	7/22/02	7/24/02	8/07/02
0.20Q	7/30/02	10/21/02	10/23/02	11/06/02
0.20Q	10/29/02	1/17/03	1/22/03	2/05/03
0.20Q	3/24/03	4/21/03	4/23/03	5/07/03

Indicated div.: $0.80 (Div. Reinv. Plan)

CAPITALIZATION (12/31/01):

	($000)	(%)
Long-Term Debt	184,300	45.2
Deferred Income Tax	46,800	11.5
Common & Surplus	176,800	43.3
Total	407,900	100.0

*7 YEAR PRICE SCORE 93.8   ***12 MONTH PRICE SCORE 88.2**

*NYSE COMPOSITE INDEX=100

BUSINESS:

West Pharmaceutical Services, Inc. (formerly The West Company, Inc.) is involved in drug formulation research and development, clinical research and laboratory services, and the design, development, and manufacture of components and systems for dispensing and delivering pharmaceutical, healthcare, and consumer products. Operations are divided into two business segments. The Pharmaceutical Systems segment (98.4% ot 2002 sales) designs, manufactures and sells stoppers, closures, medical device components and assemblies made from elastomers, metal, and plastics and provides contract laboratory services for testing injectable drug packaging. The Drug Delivery Systems segment (1.6%) identifies and develops drug delivery systems for biopharmaceutical and other drugs to improve therapeutic performance and/or method of administration. This segment also provides clinical research for Phase I, II and III studies and clinical and marketing research services mostly for consumer products organizations.

RECENT DEVELOPMENTS:

For the year ended 12/31/02, income from continuing operations was $12.8 million compared with income of $19.7 million the previous year. Results for 2002 and 2001 included pre-tax restructuring charges of $9.9 million and $2.9 million, respectively. Net sales climbed 7.0% to $419.7 million from $392.3 million in 2001. Pharmaceutical systems net sales increased 9.7% to $412.8 million, while net sales from drug delivery systems fell 56.6% to $6.9 million. Operating income dropped 33.1% to $26.7 million.

PROSPECTS:

The Company is aggressively implementing its manufacturing recovery plan to restore production to pre-accident levels following the explosion and related fire at its Kinston, North Carolina facility on 1/29/03. Production will be increased by increasing the number of shifts and by utilizing all available manufacturing capacity, including tooling, machinery and personnel temporarily relocated from the damaged Kinston operation. As a result of the accident, the Company expects to incur pre-tax costs of $4.0 million to $6.0 million net of insurance recoveries in 2003. Also, the Company expects sales of up to $5.0 million will be delayed until second half of the year.

ANNUAL FINANCIAL DATA:

FISCAL YEAR	TOT. REVS. ($mill.)	NET INC. ($mill.)	TOT. ASSETS ($mill.)	OPER. PROFIT %	NET PROFIT %	RET. ON EQUITY %	RET. ON ASSETS %	CURR. RATIO	EARN. PER SH. $	CASH FL. PER SH. $	TANG. BK. VAL. $	DIV. PER SH. $	PRICE RANGE	AVG. P/E RATIO	AVG. YIELD %
p12/31/02	419.7	⑤ 12.8							⑤ 0.89			0.77	32.50 — 16.25	27.4	3.2
12/31/01	396.9	④ 19.6	511.3	10.4	4.9	11.1	3.8	2.1	④ 1.37	3.60	10.05	0.73	28.35 — 22.75	18.6	2.9
12/31/00	430.1	③ 1.6	557.4	3.5	0.4	0.8	0.3	2.2	③ 0.11	2.68	10.65	0.69	31.88 — 19.63	233.9	2.7
12/31/99	469.1	③ 38.7	551.8	14.3	8.2	16.7	7.0	1.8	③ 2.57	4.94	11.23	0.65	40.44 — 30.88	13.9	1.8
12/31/98	449.7	② 6.7	505.6	7.8	1.5	2.9	1.3	1.5	② 0.40	2.36	11.24	0.61	35.69 — 25.75	76.8	2.0
12/31/97	452.5	44.4	477.9	13.9	9.8	16.0	9.3	2.9	2.68	4.60	13.65	0.57	35.06 — 27.00	11.6	1.8
12/31/96	458.8	② 16.4	477.4	7.1	3.6	6.5	3.4	2.4	② 1.00	2.87	11.79	0.53	30.00 — 22.13	26.1	2.0
12/31/95	412.9	28.7	480.1	12.1	7.0	11.3	6.0	2.4	1.73	3.52	10.50	0.49	30.63 — 22.63	15.4	1.8
12/31/94	365.1	27.3	397.4	12.4	7.5	12.0	6.9	1.6	1.70	3.14	11.75	0.45	29.13 — 21.25	14.8	1.8
12/31/93	348.7	① 22.5	309.2	11.6	6.5	12.0	7.3	2.0	① 1.42	2.81	11.02	0.41	25.25 — 19.88	15.9	1.8

Statistics are as originally reported. ① Excl. acctg. adj. chrg. of $1.0 mill. ($0.06/sh.). ② Incl. nonrecurr. chrgs. of $32.2 mill., 1998; $21.5 mill., 1996. ③ Incl. one-time chrgs. of $700,000, 1999; $20.8 mill., 2000. ④ Incl. restruct. chrg. of $2.9 mill. & excl. loss of $24.8 mill. from disc. oper. ⑤ Incl. restr. chrg. of $9.9 mill.; excl. inc. of $5.6 mill. from disc. ops.

OFFICERS:
W. G. Little, Chmn.
D. E. Morel Jr., Pres., C.E.O.

INVESTOR CONTACT: Stephen M.Heumann, V.P., Treas., & Assist. Sec., (610) 594-3346

PRINCIPAL OFFICE: 101 Gordon Drive, P.O. Box 645, Lionville, PA 19341-0645

TELEPHONE NUMBER: (610) 594-2900
FAX: (610) 594-3000
WEB: www.westpharma.com
NO. OF EMPLOYEES: 3,960
SHAREHOLDERS: 1,792 (of record)
ANNUAL MEETING: In Apr.
INCORPORATED: PA, 1923

INSTITUTIONAL HOLDINGS:
No. of Institutions: 69
Shares Held: 10,055,569
% Held: 69.5
INDUSTRY: Fabricated rubber products, nec (SIC: 3069)
TRANSFER AGENT(S): American Stock Transfer & Trust Company, New York, NY

WESTAR ENERGY, INC.

EXCH.	SYM.	REC. PRICE	P/E RATIO	YLD.	MKT. CAP.	RANGE (52-WK.)	'02 Y/E PR.
NYSE	WR	12.45 (2/28/03)	...	6.1%	$0.89 bill.	18.00 - 8.50	9.90

LOWER MEDIUM GRADE. WR SUBMITTED A PLAN TO THE KANSAS CORPORATION COMMISSION OUTLINING ITS PLANS TO REDUCE DEBT AND REFOCUS ON ITS ELECTRIC UTILITY OPERATIONS.

*7 YEAR PRICE SCORE 54.8   *12 MONTH PRICE SCORE 93.9
*NYSE COMPOSITE INDEX=100

INTERIM EARNINGS (Per Share):

Qtr.	Mar.	June	Sept.	Dec.
1997	0.61	0.36	7.77	d1.23
1998	0.45	0.50	1.10	d1.21
1999	0.31	0.27	0.70	d1.31
2000	0.58	0.34	0.77	d0.39
2001	d0.28	d0.51	0.37	d0.48
2002	d1.92	0.09	0.60	...

INTERIM DIVIDENDS (Per Share):

Amt.	Decl.	Ex.	Rec.	Pay.
0.30Q	2/19/02	3/06/02	3/08/02	4/01/02
0.30Q	4/17/02	6/05/02	6/07/02	7/01/02
0.30Q	6/26/02	9/05/02	9/09/02	10/01/02
0.30Q	11/01/02	12/05/02	12/09/02	1/02/03
0.19Q	2/24/03	3/05/03	3/07/03	4/01/03

Indicated div.: $0.76 (Div. Reinv. Plan)

CAPITALIZATION (12/31/01):

	($000)	(%)
Long-Term Debt	2,978,382	57.2
Minority Interest	166,850	3.2
Redeemable Pfd. Stock	220,000	4.2
Preferred Stock	23,936	0.5
Common & Surplus	1,820,125	34.9
Total	5,209,293	100.0

BUSINESS:

Westar Energy, Inc. (formerly Western Resources, Inc.) is a publicly-traded consumer services company. WR is engaged in the business of providing electric generation, transmission and distribution services to approximately 647,000 customers in Kansas as of 2/6/03. The Company also provides monitored services to approximately 1.2 million customers in North America, the United Kingdom and Europe through Protection One and Protection One Europe. As of 2/6/03, the Company owned a 27.4% interest in ONEOK, Inc., a natural gas transmission and distribution company with about 1.4 million customers in Oklahoma and Kansas. Regulated electric service is provided by KPL, a division of WR, and Kansas Gas and Electric Company, a wholly-owned subsidiary.

RECENT DEVELOPMENTS:

For the quarter ended 9/30/02, income was $43.8 million, before a loss from discontinued operations of $208,000, versus income of $36.1 million, before a loss from discontinued operations of $168,000, in the prior-year quarter. Results for 2002 and 2001 included gains on extinguishment of debt of $1.9 million and $14.2 million, respectively. Results for 2001 also included a gain on dispositions of monitored services operations of $4.9 million. Total sales grew 3.0% to $529.1 million versus $513.5 million in 2001. Energy sales grew 5.9% to $442.1 million.

PROSPECTS:

WR filed a comprehensive plan with the Kansas Corporation Commission (KCC) outlining how the Company plans to reduce debt and become exclusively an electric utility. The plan calls for WR to sell its non-utility and non-core assets, reduce its common dividend and refocus solely on its electric utility operations. In accordance with the plan, WR raised $300.0 million for debt reduction through a sale of ONEOK stock to ONEOK. Also, WR is in the process of selling Protection One Europe, and in cooperation with Protection One, Inc., is exploring strategic options for divesting its investment in Protection One North America. Additionally, WR plans to sell all of its remaining shares of ONEOK stock in late 2003 and 2004. WR may issue new equity following the sale of its non-utility assets if necessary to reach debt reduction targets. The target date for completing the plan is year-end 2004.

ANNUAL FINANCIAL DATA:

FISCAL YEAR	TOT. REVS. ($mill.)	NET INC. ($mill.)	TOT. ASSETS ($mill.)	OPER. PROFIT %	NET PROFIT %	NET INC./ NET PROP. %	NET INC./ TOT. CAP. %	RET. ON EQUITY %	ACCUM. DEPR./ GROSS PROP. %	EARN. PER SH. $	TANG. BK. VAL. $	DIV. PER SH. $	DIV. PAYOUT %	PRICE RANGE		AVG. P/E RATIO	AVG. YIELD %
p12/31/02												1.20		18.00	- 8.50		9.1
12/31/01	2,186.3	④ d62.7	7,513.1	3.1	...	...	...	...	38.0	④ d0.90	13.15	1.20	...	25.88	- 15.62	...	5.8
12/31/00	2,368.5	③ 91.1	7,767.2	9.5	3.8	2.3	1.6	4.7	37.0	③ 1.30	13.28	1.67	128.5	25.88	- 14.69	15.6	8.2
12/31/99	2,036.2	② 0.7	8,008.2	13.5	...	...	...	...	36.0	② ② 0.01	11.47	2.14	N.M.	33.88	- 16.81	N.M.	8.4
12/31/98	2,034.1	① ② 46.2	7,951.4	11.3	2.3	1.2	0.8	2.4	35.1	① ② 0.65	11.38	2.13	327.6	44.19	- 32.56	59.0	5.6
12/31/97	2,151.8	① 494.1	6,977.0	6.6	23.0	13.0	10.6	23.7	33.6	① 7.51	17.73	2.09	27.8	43.44	- 29.75	4.9	5.7
12/31/96	2,046.8	① 169.0	6,647.8	15.8	8.3	3.9	3.6	10.2	32.3	① 2.41	25.14	2.05	85.1	34.88	- 28.00	13.0	6.5
12/31/95	1,572.1	181.7	5,490.7	18.7	11.6	4.2	4.1	11.5	30.9	2.71	24.71	2.01	74.2	34.00	- 28.63	11.6	6.5
12/31/94	1,617.9	187.4	5,189.6	17.8	11.6	4.4	4.7	12.5	29.6	2.82	23.93	1.97	69.9	34.88	- 26.13	10.8	6.5
12/31/93	1,909.4	177.4	5,412.0	16.1	9.3	3.9	4.3	12.3	28.9	2.76	23.08	1.93	69.9	37.25	- 30.38	12.3	5.7

Statistics are as originally reported. ① Incl. net non-recurr. chrgs. $88.1 mill., 12/99; $98.9 mill., 12/98; $776.1 mill., 12/97; $18.2 mill., 12/96. ② Bef. extraord. gain $11.7 mill., 12/99; $1.6 mill., 12/98. ③ Bef. extraord. gain $49.2 mill. extraord. gain & $3.8 mill. acctg. chg. ④ Bef. extraord. gain $23.2 mill. & acctg. chrg. $18.7 mill.; Incl. merger costs of $8.7 mill. & dispos. of monitored services opers. of $13.1 mill.

OFFICERS:
J. S. Haines, Jr., Pres., C.E.O.
P. R. Geist, Sr. V.P., C.F.O., Treas.

INVESTOR CONTACT: Carl A. Ricketts, V.P.
Investor Relations, (785) 575-8424

PRINCIPAL OFFICE: 818 Kansas Avenue, Topeka, KS 66612

TELEPHONE NUMBER: (785) 575-6300
WEB: www.wr.com
NO. OF EMPLOYEES: 5,600 (approx.)
SHAREHOLDERS: 35,839
ANNUAL MEETING: In June
INCORPORATED: KS, March, 1924

INSTITUTIONAL HOLDINGS:
No. of Institutions: 149
Shares Held: 38,846,317
% Held: 54.3
INDUSTRY: Electric and other services combined (SIC: 4931)
TRANSFER AGENT(S): Western Resources, Inc., Topeka, KS

WESTERN GAS RESOURCES, INC.

EXCH.	SYM.	REC. PRICE	P/E RATIO	YLD.	MKT. CAP.	RANGE (52-WK.)	'02 Y/E PR.
NYSE	WGR	33.00 (2/28/03)	26.8	0.6%	$1.08 bill.	40.12 - 25.00	36.85

LOWER MEDIUM GRADE. THE COMPANY ANTICIPATES CAPITAL EXPENDITURES OF APPROXIMATELY $182.3 MILLION FOR 2003, AN INCREASE OF 29.7% FROM 2002.

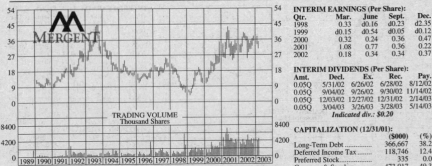

INTERIM EARNINGS (Per Share):

Qtr.	Mar.	June	Sept.	Dec.
1998	0.33	d0.16	d0.23	d2.35
1999	d0.15	d0.54	d0.05	d0.12
2000	0.32	0.24	0.36	0.47
2001	1.08	0.77	0.36	0.22
2002	0.18	0.34	0.34	0.37

INTERIM DIVIDENDS (Per Share):

Amt.	Decl.	Ex.	Rec.	Pay.
0.05Q	5/31/02	6/26/02	6/28/02	8/12/02
0.05Q	9/04/02	9/26/02	9/30/02	11/14/02
0.05Q	12/03/02	12/27/02	12/31/02	2/14/03
0.05Q	3/04/03	3/26/03	3/28/03	5/14/03

Indicated div.: $0.20

CAPITALIZATION (12/31/01):

	($000)	(%)
Long-Term Debt	366,667	38.2
Deferred Income Tax	118,746	12.4
Preferred Stock	335	0.0
Common & Surplus	473,017	49.3
Total	958,765	100.0

*7 YEAR PRICE SCORE 168.4   *12 MONTH PRICE SCORE 106.3

*NYSE COMPOSITE INDEX=100

BUSINESS:

Western Gas Resources, Inc. explores for, develops and produces, gathers, processes and treats, transports and markets natural gas and natural gas liquids. In its upstream operations, WGR explores for, develops and produces natural gas reserves primarily in the Rocky Mountain region. In its midstream operations WGR designs, constructs, owns and operates natural gas gathering, processing and treating facilities and owns and operates regulated transportation facilities and offers marketing services in order to provide its customers with a broad range of services from the wellhead to the sales delivery point. The Company's midstream operations are conducted in major gas-producing basins in the Rocky Mountain, Mid-Continent, Gulf Coast and Southwestern regions of the United States. As of 12/31/02, total proved reserves were 588.00 billion cubic feet of gas equivalent.

RECENT DEVELOPMENTS:

For the year ended 12/31/02, net income was $50.6 million versus $95.6 million a year earlier. Results included a loss of $948,000 for 2002 and a gain of $10.7 million for 2001 from assets sales. Total revenues fell 25.8% to $2.49 billion. Exploration and production operating profit rose 14.4% to $73.7 million, primarily due to volume growth from the Powder River Basin coal bed methane development and the benefit of firm transportation capacity. Gathering and processing operations operating profit slid 31.6% to $92.9 million, mainly due to lower product prices. Gas transportation and marketing operating income fell 4.8% and 25.0% to $15.7 million and $37.5 million, respectively.

PROSPECTS:

On 2/4/03, WGR announced that it has completed the purchase of 18 gathering systems in the Green River, Powder River and Wind River Basins of Wyoming from El Paso Field Services for approximately $37.0 million. Separately, WGR anticipates capital expenditures of about $182.3 million for 2003, primarily for growth and expansion projects in its Rocky Mountain upstream and midstream operations. The budget, which represents a 29.7% increase from the prior year, includes the aforementioned acquisition of El Paso gathering assets in Wyoming.

ANNUAL FINANCIAL DATA:

FISCAL YEAR	TOT. REVS. ($mill.)	NET INC. ($mill.)	TOT. ASSETS ($mill.)	OPER. PROFIT %	NET PROFIT %	NET INC./ NET PROP. %	NET INC./ TOT. CAP. %	RET. ON EQUITY %	ACCUM. DEPR./ GROSS PROP. %	EARN. PER SH.$	TANG. BK. VAL.$	DIV. PER SH.$	DIV. PAYOUT %	PRICE RANGE	AVG. P/E RATIO	AVG. YIELD %
p12/31/02	2,489.7	⑧ 50.6	...	...	...	...	...	...	...	⑧ 1.23	...	0.20	16.3	40.12 - 25.00	26.5	0.6
12/31/01	3,355.0	⑦ 95.6	1,267.9	5.0	2.9	11.3	10.0	20.2	30.0	② 2.48	14.48	0.20	8.1	43.50 - 23.90	13.6	0.6
12/31/00	3,282.0	⑥ 57.8	1,431.4	3.5	1.8	7.7	7.1	14.8	29.1	⑥ 1.39	12.10	0.20	14.4	34.69 - 10.63	16.3	0.9
12/31/99	1,910.7	⑤ d16.0	1,049.5	2.0	...	...	...	...	27.3	⑤ d0.86	10.86	0.20	...	20.00 - 3.88	...	1.7
12/31/98	2,133.6	④ d67.2	1,219.4	...	...	...	...	...	26.5	④ d2.42	11.97	0.20	...	22.13 - 5.31	...	1.5
12/31/97	2,385.3	③ 1.5	1,348.3	1.2	0.1	0.2	0.2	0.3	23.5	③ d0.28	14.55	0.20	...	25.56 - 14.88	...	1.0
12/31/96	2,091.0	② 27.9	1,361.6	3.6	1.3	3.2	3.0	5.8	22.6	② 0.66	14.95	0.20	30.3	19.88 - 11.13	23.5	1.3
12/31/95	1,257.0	① d6.1	1,176.0	2.3	...	...	...	...	19.1	① d0.84	14.42	0.20	...	24.25 - 15.00	...	1.0
12/31/94	1,063.5	7.4	1,167.4	4.1	0.7	0.8	0.8	1.7	16.9	d0.19	16.97	0.20	...	35.38 - 17.88	...	0.8
12/31/93	932.3	38.1	1,114.7	7.4	4.1	4.5	4.1	12.2	12.7	1.25	12.19	0.20	16.0	45.13 - 24.00	27.6	0.6

Statistics are as originally reported. ① Incl. net restruct. chrg. of $1.3 mill. & net chrg. of $12.4 mill. for impair. of assets. ② Incl. net gain of $1.2 mill. fr. sale of gas processing facility. ③ Incl. net gain of about $1.2 mill. fr. sale of gas processing facility & net chg. of $22.0 mill. for impair. of assets. ④ Incl. net impair. chrg. of $69.0 mill. & net gain of $10.5 mill. fr. asset sales. ⑤ Bef. extraord. loss of $1.1 mill.; incl. loss fr. asset sales of $29.8 mill. & impair. chrgs. of $1.2 mill. ⑥ Bef. extraord. loss of $1.7 mill.; incl. after-tax gain of $5.7 mill. fr. asset sales. ⑦ Incl. gain of $10.7 mill. fr. asset sales. ⑧ Incl. loss of $948,000 fr. asset sales.

OFFICERS:
B. G. Wise, Chmn.
W. L. Stonehocker, Vice-Chmn.
P. A. Dea, Pres., C.E.O.
INVESTOR CONTACT: Ron Wirth, Dir. of Investor Relations, (800) 933-5603, ext. 200
PRINCIPAL OFFICE: 12200 N. Pecos Street, Denver, CO 80234-3439

TELEPHONE NUMBER: (303) 452-5603
FAX: (303) 252-6150
WEB: www.westerngas.com
NO. OF EMPLOYEES: 639 (approx.)
SHAREHOLDERS: 226
ANNUAL MEETING: In May
INCORPORATED: DE, Oct., 1989

INSTITUTIONAL HOLDINGS:
No. of Institutions: 137
Shares Held: 24,582,922
% Held: 74.4
INDUSTRY: Natural gas transmission (SIC: 4922)
TRANSFER AGENT(S): Equiserve, L.P., Boston, MA

WESTWOOD ONE, INC.

EXCH.	SYM.	REC. PRICE	P/E RATIO	YLD.	MKT. CAP.	RANGE (52-WK.)	'02 Y/E PR.
NYSE	WON	33.32 (2/28/03)	33.0	...	$3.58 bill.	40.50 - 24.41	37.36

MEDIUM GRADE. THE COMPANY SHOULD CONTINUE TO BENEFIT FROM HIGHER REVENUES, COMBINED WITH TIGHT COST CONTROLS AND REDUCTIONS IN AFFILIATE AND PERSONNEL COSTS.

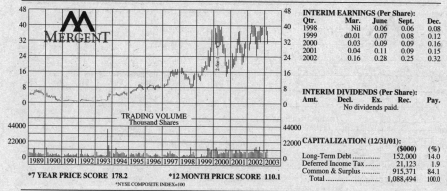

INTERIM EARNINGS (Per Share):

Qtr.	Mar.	June	Sept.	Dec.
1998	Nil	0.06	0.06	0.08
1999	d0.01	0.07	0.08	0.12
2000	0.03	0.09	0.09	0.16
2001	0.04	0.11	0.09	0.15
2002	0.16	0.28	0.25	0.32

INTERIM DIVIDENDS (Per Share):

Amt.	Decl.	Ex.	Rec.	Pay.
		No dividends paid.		

CAPITALIZATION (12/31/01):

	($000)	(%)
Long-Term Debt	152,000	14.0
Deferred Income Tax	21,123	1.9
Common & Surplus	915,371	84.1
Total	1,088,494	100.0

*7 YEAR PRICE SCORE 178.2   ***12 MONTH PRICE SCORE 110.1**

*NYSE COMPOSITE INDEX=100

BUSINESS:

Westwood One, Inc. offers radios and television stations over 150 news, sports, music, talk and entertainment programs, features, live events and 24 hour/seven days a week formats. Through its subsidiaries, Metro Networks/Shadow Broadcast Services, the Company provides local content to the radio and TV industries including news, sports, weather, traffic, video news services and other information.

SmartRoute Systems manages update information centers for state and local departments of transportation, and markets traffic and travel content to wireless, Internet, in-vehicle navigation systems and voice portal customers. The Company serves more than 7,500 radio stations. The Company is managed by Infinity Broadcasting Corporation, wholly-owned subsidiary of Viacom, Inc.

RECENT DEVELOPMENTS:

For the year ended 12/31/02, net income more than doubled to $109.1 million from $43.2 million the previous year. Gross revenues advanced 7.2% to $640.9 million from $597.7 million the year before. Revenues, less agency commissions, increased 6.7% to $550.8 million from $515.9 million the prior year, primarily due to higher advertising

rates and improved inventory management at WON's network and traffic divisions, radio broadcast of the Winter Olympics from Salt Lake City in the first quarter and new programming launches. Operating income surged 81.8% to $178.9 million from $98.4 million a year earlier.

PROSPECTS:

Going forward, the Company should continue to benefit from higher revenues, combined with tight cost controls and reductions in affiliate and personnel costs. Additionally, WON should continue to benefit from the creation of new programming and a focus on the development of new business. The Company anticipates mid-single digit reve-

nue growth and double-digit growth in operating cash flow and free cash flow per share. Moreover, WON expects full year operating cash flow to range from $210.0 million to $215.0 million. Separately, WON and NBC announced the formation of NBC News Radio, which is to begin airing on 3/31/03.

ANNUAL FINANCIAL DATA:

FISCAL YEAR	TOT. REVS. ($mill.)	NET INC. ($mill.)	TOT. ASSETS ($mill.)	OPER. PROFIT %	NET PROFIT %	RET. ON EQUITY %	RET. ON ASSETS %	CURR. RATIO	EARN. PER SH.$	CASH FL. PER SH.$	PRICE RANGE	AVG. P/E RATIO
p12/31/02	**550.8**	**109.1**							**1.00**		40.50 - 24.41	32.5
12/31/01	515.9	43.2	1,208.0	19.1	8.4	4.7	3.6	1.3	0.38	0.99	37.30 - 18.00	72.7
12/31/00	553.7	42.3	1,285.6	18.7	7.6	4.5	3.3	1.1	0.36	0.90	40.38 - 13.75	75.2
12/31/99	358.3	23.9	1,334.9	17.0	6.7	2.3	1.8	1.3	0.30	0.69	38.00 - 11.41	82.3
12/31/98	259.3	② 13.0	345.3	12.9	5.0	16.9	3.8	1.1	② 0.20	0.47	18.25 - 7.75	66.6
12/31/97	240.8	25.5	335.9	14.9	10.6	20.4	7.6	1.2	0.37	0.56	17.50 - 8.19	34.7
12/31/96	171.8	17.5	273.0	15.9	10.2	20.2	6.4	0.9	0.26	0.44	9.50 - 6.75	31.2
12/31/95	145.7	9.7	245.6	13.3	6.6	10.3	3.9	1.2	0.14	0.34	9.75 - 4.81	52.0
⑤ 12/31/94	136.3	①③ d2.7	260.1	4.4	...	...	...	1.2	①③ d0.04	0.26	5.81 - 3.56	...
11/30/93	99.6	④ d8.7	152.1	...	...	...	...	1.0	④ d1.07	0.29	4.75 - 0.80	...

Statistics are as originally reported. Adj. for 2-for-1 stk. spl., 3/00 ① Incl. restruct. costs, $2.4 mill. ② Incl. non-recurr. chrg., $551,000 ③ Bef. extraord. loss $590,000. ④ Bef. discontin. ops. chrg., $15.2 mill. ⑤ Fiscal year-end changed from 11/30 to 12/31

OFFICERS:
N. J. Pattiz, Chmn.
J. Hollander, Pres., C.E.O.
F. Suleman, C.F.O., Sec.

INVESTOR CONTACT: Jacques Tortoroli, (212) 314-9215

PRINCIPAL OFFICE: 40 West 57th Street, 5th Floor, New York, NY 10019

TELEPHONE NUMBER: (212) 641-2000
FAX: (212) 840-4052
WEB: www.westwoodone.com
NO. OF EMPLOYEES: 2,740 full-time (approx.); 920 part-time
SHAREHOLDERS: 320 (approx.); 5,000
ANNUAL MEETING: In May
INCORPORATED: CA, 1974; reincorp., DE, July, 1985

INSTITUTIONAL HOLDINGS:
No. of Institutions: 223
Shares Held: 77,412,583
% Held: 73.0

INDUSTRY: Communication services, nec (SIC: 4899)

TRANSFER AGENT(S): City National Bank, Beverly Hills, CA

WEYERHAEUSER COMPANY

EXCH.	SYM.	REC. PRICE	P/E RATIO	YLD.	MKT. CAP.	RANGE (52-WK.)	'02 Y/E PR.
NYSE	WY	49.85 (2/28/03)	41.9	3.2%	$11.03 bill.	67.95 - 37.35	49.21

MEDIUM GRADE. THE COMPANY CONTINUES TO BENEFIT FROM SALES OF SINGLE-FAMILY HOMES.

7 YEAR PRICE SCORE 110.4   **12 MONTH PRICE SCORE 100.9**

NYSE COMPOSITE INDEX=100

INTERIM EARNINGS (Per Share):

Qtr.	Mar.	June	Sept.	Dec.
1997	0.10	0.56	0.53	0.49
1998	0.43	0.34	0.56	0.15
1999	0.21	0.81	1.18	0.79
2000	1.04	0.89	0.90	0.89
2001	0.49	0.78	0.41	d0.07
2002	0.24	0.32	0.06	0.57

INTERIM DIVIDENDS (Per Share):

Amt.	Decl.	Ex.	Rec.	Pay.
0.40Q	1/08/02	1/30/02	2/01/02	3/04/02
0.40Q	4/16/02	5/01/02	5/03/02	6/03/02
0.40Q	7/09/02	7/31/02	8/02/02	9/03/02
0.40Q	10/09/02	10/30/02	11/01/02	12/02/02
0.40Q	1/07/03	1/29/03	1/31/03	3/03/03

Indicated div.: $1.60 (Div. Reinv. Plan)

CAPITALIZATION (12/29/02):

	($000)	(%)
Long-Term Debt	12,784,000	54.5
Deferred Income Tax	4,056,000	17.3
Common & Surplus	6,623,000	28.2
Total	23,463,000	100.0

BUSINESS:

Weyerhaeuser Company is a grower and harvester of timber and a manufacturer, distributor and seller of forest products, real estate development and construction, and other real estate related activities. As of 1/22/03, WY had offices or operations in 18 countries. WY owns 5.9 million acres and leases 500,000 acres of commercial forest land in North America, most of it highly productive and well located to serve both domestic and international markets. WY also has renewable, long-term licenses on 32.6 million acres of forestland located in five provinces throughout Canada. The sales breakdown in 2002 was: Wood Products, 41.3%; Containerboard, Packaging and Recycling, 22.9%; Pulp and Paper, 20.1%; Real Estate and related assets, 9.6%; and Timberlands, 6.1%.

RECENT DEVELOPMENTS:

For the year ended 12/29/02, net income declined 31.9% to $241.0 million compared with $354.0 million in 2001. Results for 2002 and 2001 included net unusual charges of $55.0 million and $57.0 million, respectively. Results for 2002 also included countervailing and anti-dumping duties and related costs of $64.0 million. Total net sales and revenues increased 27.3% to $18.5 million. Wood Products sales increased 16.8% to $7.59 billion. Containerboard, Packaging and Recycling sales rose 36.0% to $4.21 billion. Pulp and Paper sales grew 44.5% to $3.70 billion. Real Estate and related asset sales leapt 19.8% to $1.75 billion due to strong residential construction. Timberlands sales increased 42.7% to $1.12 billion.

PROSPECTS:

The Wood Products segment continues to face oversupplied markets. Consequently, first quarter results are expected to be level with fourth quarter results. Also, WY is working with U.S. and Canadian governments concerning uncertainty created by the Canadian softwood lumber issue. First quarter results for the Containerboard, Packaging and Recycling, and Timberlands segments are expected to be lower than the fourth quarter due to higher anticipated levels of maintenance and market-related downtime, and slightly weaker prices. Pulp and Paper and Real Estate and related assets results are expected to be similar to fourth quarter levels.

ANNUAL FINANCIAL DATA:

FISCAL YEAR	TOT. REVS. ($mill.)	NET INC. ($mill.)	TOT. ASSETS ($mill.)	OPER. PROFIT %	NET PROFIT %	RET. ON EQUITY %	RET. ON ASSETS %	CURR. RATIO	EARN. PER SH. $	CASH FL. PER SH. $	TANG. BK. VAL. $	DIV. PER SH. $	PRICE RANGE	AVG. P/E RATIO	AVG. YIELD %
p12/31/02	18,521.0	⑥ 241.0	28,269.0						⑥ 1.09			1.60	67.95 - 37.35	48.3	3.0
12/30/01	14,545.0	⑥ 354.0	18,293.0	5.2	2.0	4.4	1.6	1.6	⑥ 1.61	5.32	25.86	1.60	63.50 - 42.77	33.0	3.0
12/31/00	15,980.0	⑤ 840.0	18,195.0	9.3	5.3	12.3	4.6	1.2	⑤ 3.72	7.53	25.92	1.60	74.50 - 36.06	14.9	2.9
12/26/99	12,262.0	①③ 616.0	18,339.0	9.2	5.0	8.6	3.4	1.5	①③ 2.98	6.11	27.17	1.60	73.94 - 49.56	20.7	2.6
12/27/98	10,766.0	① 365.0	12,834.0	6.1	3.4	8.1	2.8	1.4	① 1.47	4.93	22.74	1.60	62.00 - 36.75	33.6	3.2
12/28/97	11,210.0	① 342.0	13,075.0	6.9	3.1	7.4	2.6	1.7	① 1.71	4.88	23.30	1.60	63.94 - 42.63	31.2	3.0
12/29/96	11,114.0	463.0	13,596.0	9.6	4.2	10.1	3.4	1.5	2.34	5.45	23.21	1.60	49.88 - 39.50	19.1	3.6
12/31/95	11,788.0	② 799.0	13,253.0	13.6	6.8	17.8	6.0	1.4	② 3.93	6.98	22.57	1.50	50.38 - 36.88	11.1	3.4
12/25/94	10,398.0	589.0	13,007.0	11.7	5.7	13.7	4.5	1.2	2.86	5.46	20.86	1.20	51.25 - 35.75	15.2	2.8
12/26/93	9,544.8	④ 527.3	12,638.5	10.3	5.5	13.3	4.2	1.8	④ 2.58	4.95	19.34	1.20	46.50 - 36.25	16.0	2.9

Statistics are as originally reported. ① Incl. a net nonrecurr. restruct. chrg. $9.0 mill., 1997; & $45.0 mill., 1998; $65.0 mill., 1999. ② Incl. spec. chrgs. of $184.0 mill. ($0.90/sh.). ③ Bef. acctg. adj. chrg. of $89.0 mill. ④ Bef. a $52.0 mill. ($0.25/sh.) gain from exting. of debt. ⑤ Incl. chrg. of $56.0 mill. for the closure of facilities & chrg. for settlement of hardboard siding claims of $130.0 mill. ⑥ Incl. nonrecurr. chrgs. of $55.0 mill., 2002; $77.0 mill., 2001; and countervailing and anti-dumping chrgs. of $64.0 mill., 2002.

OFFICERS:
S. R. Rogel, Chmn., Pres., C.E.O.
R. E. Hanson, Exec. V.P., C.O.O.

INVESTOR CONTACT: Kathryn F. McAuley, Investor Relations, (253) 924-2058

PRINCIPAL OFFICE: 33663 Weyerhaeuser Way South, Federal Way, WA 98063-9777

TELEPHONE NUMBER: (253) 924-2345
FAX: (253) 924-3332
WEB: www.weyerhaeuser.com
NO. OF EMPLOYEES: 44,843
SHAREHOLDERS: 16,127
ANNUAL MEETING: In Apr.
INCORPORATED: WA, Jan., 1900

INSTITUTIONAL HOLDINGS:
No. of Institutions: 407
Shares Held: 158,904,552
% Held: 72.6
INDUSTRY: Lumber, plywood, and millwork (SIC: 5031)
TRANSFER AGENT(S): Mellon Investor Services, Ridgefield Park, NJ

WGL HOLDINGS, INC.

EXCH.	SYM.	REC. PRICE	P/E RATIO	YLD.	MKT. CAP.	RANGE (52-WK.)	'02 Y/E PR.	DIV. ACH.
NYSE	WGL	25.14 (2/28/03)	20.3	5.1%	$1.22 bill.	27.95 - 19.25	23.92	26 yrs.

UPPER MEDIUM GRADE. GOING FORWARD, THE COMPANY EXPECTS EARNINGS PER SHARE TO BE IN THE RANGE OF $1.50 TO $1.60 FOR THE SECOND QUARTER OF 2003.

TRADING VOLUME
Thousand Shares

1989 1990 1991 1992 1993 1994 1995 1996 1997 1998 1999 2000 2001 2002 2003

*7 YEAR PRICE SCORE 103.6   ***12 MONTH PRICE SCORE 109.8**
*NYSE COMPOSITE INDEX=100

INTERIM EARNINGS (Per Share):

Qtr.	Dec.	Mar.	June	Sept.
1998-99	0.55	1.39	d0.15	d0.31
1999-00	0.85	1.39	d0.12	d0.33
2000-01	1.08	1.44	0.15	d0.48
2001-02	0.62	0.94	d0.29	d0.47
2002-03	1.06	...	...	...

INTERIM DIVIDENDS (Per Share):

Amt.	Decl.	Ex.	Rec.	Pay.
0.318Q	2/25/02	4/08/02	4/10/02	5/01/02
0.318Q	6/26/02	7/08/02	7/10/02	8/01/02
0.318Q	9/25/02	10/08/02	10/10/02	11/01/02
0.318Q	12/20/02	1/08/03	1/10/03	2/01/03
0.32Q	3/05/03	4/08/03	4/10/03	5/01/03

Indicated div.: $1.28 (Div. Reinv. Plan)

CAPITALIZATION (9/30/02):

	($000)	(%)
Long-Term Debt	667,951	39.9
Deferred Income Tax	212,631	12.7
Preferred Stock.........	28,173	1.7
Common & Surplus	766,403	45.8
Total	1,675,158	100.0

BUSINESS:

WGL Holdings, Inc. (formerly Washington Gas Light Company), through its subsidiaries, engages in the sale and distribution of natural gas and other energy-related products and services. Washington Gas Light Company is a regulated natural gas utility serving over 960,000 customers in Washington D.C., Virginia and Maryland as of 1/29/03. Hampshire Gas Company is a regulated natural gas storage business, serving Washington Gas Light Company. Washington Gas Energy Services, Inc. sells natural gas and electricity to the Washington D.C. area as well as Baltimore, Maryland and Richmond, Virginia. Washington Gas Energy Systems, Inc. designs cost-saving energy systems for the commercial and government markets. American Combustion Industries, Inc. is a contractor for the installation and service of heating, ventilating and air-conditioning (HVAC) systems. Other nonregulated activities include consumer financing and land development. WGL owned a 50.0% interest in Primary Investors, LLC. at 12/31/02.

RECENT DEVELOPMENTS:

For the three months ended 12/31/02, net income advanced 70.7% to $51.6 million compared with $30.2 million in the corresponding quarter of the previous year. The improvement in earnings growth was primarily attributed to significantly colder weather which increased gas throughput over the same quarter of 2001. Utility operations revenue soared 40.6% to $375.0 million from $266.7 million in the year-earlier period. Utility operations net revenue jumped 30.6% to $172.7 million, while utility operating income grew 47.5% to $60.4 million.

PROSPECTS:

Going forward, the Company expects earnings per share to be in the range of $1.50 to $1.60 for the second quarter of fiscal 2003. The outlook includes the effect of actual weather in the first quarter of fiscal 2003 and an expectation of normal weather thereafter. The updated guidance also anticipates an absence of non-recurring items and reflects the resolution of the pending Virginia and District of Columbia rates cases. Moreover, the Company expects earnings per share for fiscal year 2003 to range from $2.00 to $2.10 per share, with the unregulated businesses contributing $0.08 to $0.10 per share to the estimate.

ANNUAL FINANCIAL DATA:

FISCAL YEAR	TOT. REVS. ($mill.)	NET INC. ($mill.)	TOT. ASSETS ($mill.)	OPER. PROFIT %	NET PROFIT %	NET INC./ NET PROP. %	NET INC./ TOT. CAP. %	RET. ON EQUITY %	ACCUM. DEPR./ GROSS PROP. %	EARN. PER SH.$	TANG. BK. VAL.$	DIV. PER SH.$	DIV. PAYOUT %	PRICE RANGE	AVG. P/E RATIO	AVG. YIELD %
9/30/02	1,570.0	⑤ 40.4	2,113.7	5.5	2.6	2.5	2.4	5.1	35.3	⑤ 0.80	15.78	1.27	158.4	29.31 - 19.25	30.3	5.2
9/30/01	1,933.0	⑤ 83.8	2,081.1	7.2	4.3	5.5	5.2	10.3	- 35.1	⑤ 1.75	16.24	1.25	71.7	30.50 - 25.26	15.9	4.5
9/30/00	1,248.0	④ 84.6	1,939.8	10.3	6.8	5.8	5.8	11.4	34.4	④ 1.79	15.31	1.24	69.0	31.50 - 21.75	14.9	4.6
9/30/99	1,112.2	③ 68.8	1,766.7	9.7	6.2	4.9	5.0	9.7	33.6	③ 1.47	14.72	1.22	82.6	29.44 - 21.31	17.3	4.8
9/30/98	1,040.6	② 68.6	1,682.4	9.8	6.6	5.2	5.7	10.8	33.8	② 1.54	13.83	1.20	77.6	30.75 - 23.06	17.5	4.4
9/30/97	1,055.8	82.0	1,552.0	10.9	7.8	6.7	6.9	13.3	34.1	1.85	13.48	1.18	63.8	31.13 - 20.88	14.1	4.5
9/30/96	969.8	① 81.6	1,464.6	11.7	8.4	- 7.2	7.6	13.9	34.3	① 1.85	12.79	1.16	61.3	25.00 - 19.13	11.9	5.1
9/30/95	828.7	62.9	1,360.1	11.1	7.6	6.0	6.3	11.6	34.3	1.45	11.95	1.12	77.1	22.38 - 16.13	13.3	5.8
9/30/94	914.9	60.5	1,333.0	10.1	6.6	6.1	6.2	11.8	34.4	1.42	11.51	1.10	78.1	21.25 - 16.00	13.2	5.9
9/30/93	894.3	55.1	1,194.7	9.6	6.2	6.0	6.1	11.3	34.5	1.31	11.04	1.08	82.8	22.88 - 18.13	15.6	5.3

Statistics are as originally reported. Adjusted for 2-for-1 stock split 5/95. ① Incl. a nonrecurr. after-tax chg. of $3.8 mill. assoc. with the Company's reorganization. ② Incl. a net gain of $1.6 mill. from the sale of investments in venture capital funds. ③ Incl. a nonrecurr. gain of $3.0 mill. from the sale of non-utility assets and a nonrecurr. chrg. of $2.9 mill. fr. the sale of utility property. ④ Incl. a nonrecurr. gain of $711,000 mill. fr. the sale of assets. ⑤ Incl. impairment provision of $9.4 mill., 9/02; $3.9 mill. 9/01.

OFFICERS:
J. H. DeGraffenreidt Jr., Chmn., C.E.O.
T. D. McCallister, Pres., C.O.O.
F. M. Kline, V.P., C.F.O.
INVESTOR CONTACT: Melissa Adams, Dir.
Inv. Rel., (703) 750-2000
PRINCIPAL OFFICE: 1100 H Street, N.W.,
Washington, DC 20080

TELEPHONE NUMBER: (703) 750-2000
FAX: (202) 624-6196
WEB: www.washgas.com
NO. OF EMPLOYEES: 2,205 (avg.)
SHAREHOLDERS: 17,960 (record)
ANNUAL MEETING: In Feb.
INCORPORATED: DC, Mar., 1957

INSTITUTIONAL HOLDINGS:
No. of Institutions: 147
Shares Held: 21,504,150
% Held: 44.3
INDUSTRY: Natural gas distribution (SIC: 4924)
TRANSFER AGENT(S): The Riggs National Bank, Washington, D.C.

WHIRLPOOL CORPORATION

EXCH.	SYM.	REC. PRICE	P/E RATIO	YLD.	MKT. CAP.	RANGE (52-WK.)	'02 Y/E PR.
NYSE	WHR	49.26 (2/28/03)	13.0	2.8%	$3.35 bill.	79.80 - 39.23	52.22

UPPER MEDIUM GRADE. EARNINGS PER SHARE ARE EXPECTED TO RANGE FROM $6.20 TO $6.40 IN 2003.

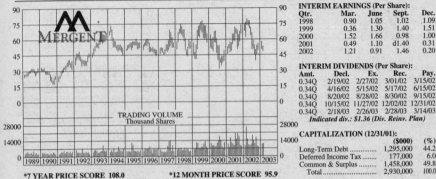

INTERIM EARNINGS (Per Share):

Qtr.	Mar.	June	Sept.	Dec.
1998	0.90	1.05	1.02	1.09
1999	0.36	1.30	1.40	1.51
2000	1.52	1.66	0.98	1.00
2001	0.49	1.10	d1.40	0.31
2002	1.21	0.91	1.46	0.20

INTERIM DIVIDENDS (Per Share):

Amt.	Decl.	Ex.	Rec.	Pay.
0.34Q	2/19/02	2/27/02	3/01/02	3/15/02
0.34Q	4/16/02	5/15/02	5/17/02	6/15/02
0.34Q	8/20/02	8/28/02	8/30/02	9/15/02
0.34Q	10/15/02	11/27/02	12/02/02	12/31/02
0.34Q	2/18/03	2/26/03	2/28/03	3/14/03

Indicated div.: $1.36 (Div. Reinv. Plan)

CAPITALIZATION (12/31/01):

	($000)	(%)
Long-Term Debt	1,295,000	44.2
Deferred Income Tax	177,000	6.0
Common & Surplus	1,458,000	49.8
Total	2,930,000	100.0

*7 YEAR PRICE SCORE 108.0   ***12 MONTH PRICE SCORE 95.9**

*NYSE COMPOSITE INDEX=100

TRADING VOLUME
Thousand Shares

BUSINESS:

Whirlpool Corporation and its consolidated subsidiaries manufacture and market a full line of major home appliances and other related products. The principal products include home laundry appliances, home refrigeration, home cooking appliances, home dishwashers, room air-conditioning equipment and small household appliances. As of 9/30/02, WHR owned nearly 50 manufacturing and technology research centers worldwide and marketed products in more than 170 countries. WHR markets WHIRLPOOL, KITCHENAID, BRASTEMP, BAUKNECHT, CONSUL and other major brand names. WHR is also the principal supplier to Sears, Roebuck and Co. of many products marketed under the KENMORE brand name. Net sales for 2001 were derived as follows: North America, 62.7%; Europe, 19.6%; Latin America, 14.2%; and Asia, 3.5%.

RECENT DEVELOPMENTS:

For the year ended 12/31/02, WHR reported income from continuing operations of $262.0 million, before an accounting charge of $613.0 million, compared with income of $34.0 million, before an accounting credit of $8.0 million, the year before. Results for 2002 and 2001 included pre-tax restructuring costs of $101.0 million and $150.0 million, and product recall costs of $9.0 million and $295.0 million, and excluded losses from discontinued operations of $43.0 million and $21.0 million, respectively. Net sales rose 6.5% to $11.02 billion. Results for 2002 reflected the Company's brand and innovation strategies and the success of its new product introductions worldwide.

PROSPECTS:

Whirlpool North America continues to perform well, reflecting the success of new products introduced in 2002 by the Whirlpool and KitchenAid brands. Additionally, Whirlpool Europe sales continue to improve due to new product innovations, productivity gains and benefits from restructuring. Meanwhile, Whirlpool Asia continues to benefit from strong growth in China and continued growth in its market position in India. Separately, when fully implemented, the Company's restructuring is anticipated to reduce annual costs by more than $200.0 million. Looking ahead, earnings per share are expected to range from $6.20 to $6.40 in 2003.

ANNUAL FINANCIAL DATA:

FISCAL YEAR	TOT. REVS. ($mill.)	NET INC. ($mill.)	TOT. ASSETS ($mill.)	OPER. PROFIT %	NET PROFIT %	RET. ON EQUITY %	RET. ON ASSETS %	CURR. RATIO	EARN. PER SH.$	CASH FL.PER SH.$	TANG. BK. VAL.$	DIV. PER SH.$	PRICE RANGE	AVG. P/E RATIO	AVG. YIELD %
p12/31/02	11,016.0	③④ 262.0	6,631.0						③④ 3.78			1.36	79.80 - 39.23	15.7	2.3
12/31/01	10,343.0	③④ 34.0	6,967.0	3.0	0.3	2.3	0.5	1.1	③④ 0.50	6.32	11.10	1.36	74.20 - 45.88	120.1	2.3
12/31/00	10,325.0	367.0	6,902.0	7.8	3.6	21.8	5.3	1.0	5.20	10.86	13.91	1.36	68.31 - 31.50	9.6	2.7
12/31/99	10,511.0	347.0	6,826.0	8.3	3.3	18.6	5.1	1.1	4.56	10.16	14.40	1.36	78.25 - 40.94	13.1	2.3
12/31/98	10,323.0	① 310.0	7,935.0	6.7	3.0	15.5	3.9	1.2	① 4.06	9.87	14.00	1.36	75.25 - 43.69	14.6	2.3
12/31/97	8,617.0	d46.0	8,270.0	0.1	...	...	...	1.2	④ d0.62	4.15	11.36	1.36	69.50 - 45.25	...	2.4
12/31/96	8,696.0	② 156.0	8,015.0	3.4	1.8	8.1	1.9	0.9	② 2.08	6.79	14.19	1.36	61.00 - 44.25	25.3	2.6
12/31/95	8,347.0	209.0	7,800.0	4.7	2.5	11.1	2.7	0.9	2.80	6.95	12.77	1.36	60.88 - 49.25	19.7	2.5
12/31/94	8,104.0	② 158.0	6,655.0	4.9	1.9	9.2	2.4	1.0	② 2.10	5.92	13.45	1.22	73.50 - 44.63	28.1	2.1
12/31/93	7,533.0	③ 231.0	6,047.0	6.4	3.1	14.0	3.8	1.0	③ 3.19	7.25	12.63	1.19	68.00 - 43.25	17.4	2.1

Statistics are as originally reported. ① Bef. $15.0 mill. inc. fr. discont. opers. ② Incl. $19.0 mill. after-tax chg., 1996; $190.0 mill. pre-tax chg., 1994 ③ Bef. acctg. chrg. of $613.0 mill., 2002; cred. $8.0 mill., 2001; chrg. $180.0 mill., 1993. ④ Bef. a loss fr. discont. opers. of $43.0 mill., 2002; $21.0 mill., 2001; gain $11.0 mill., 1997; incl. a net chrg. of $110.0 mill., 2002; $445.0 mill., 2001; $252.0 mill., 1997.

OFFICERS:
D. R. Whitwam, Chmn., C.E.O.
J. M. Fettig, Pres., C.O.O.

INVESTOR CONTACT: Thomas C. Filstrup, Dir., Investor Relations, (616) 923-3189

PRINCIPAL OFFICE: 2000 M-63, Benton Harbor, MI 49022-2692

TELEPHONE NUMBER: (269) 923-5000
FAX: (269) 923-3978
WEB: www.whirlpoolcorp.com
NO. OF EMPLOYEES: 59,408 (avg.)
SHAREHOLDERS: 8,720 (approx.)
ANNUAL MEETING: In April
INCORPORATED: DE, Aug., 1955

INSTITUTIONAL HOLDINGS:
No. of Institutions: 285
Shares Held: 64,381,417
% Held: 94.4
INDUSTRY: Household appliances, nec (SIC: 3639)
TRANSFER AGENT(S): EquiServe Trust Company, N.A., Jersey City, NJ

WILEY (JOHN) & SONS INC.

EXCH.	SYM.	REC. PRICE	P/E RATIO	YLD.	MKT. CAP.	RANGE (52-WK.)	'02 Y/E PR.
NYSE	JWA	22.70 (2/28/03)	19.1	0.9%	$1.40 bill.	27.63 - 19.26	24.01

UPPER MEDIUM GRADE. REVENUE GROWTH CONTINUES TO BE DRIVEN BY THE COMBINED EFFECTS OF ACQUISITIONS AND ORGANIC GROWTH IN THE COMPANY'S PROFESSIONAL/TRADE SEGMENT.

*7 YEAR PRICE SCORE 146.1   ***12 MONTH PRICE SCORE 106.5**

*NYSE COMPOSITE INDEX=100

INTERIM EARNINGS (Per Share):

Qtr.	July	Oct.	Jan.	Apr.
1998-99	0.16	0.15	0.20	0.10
1999-00	0.20	0.22	0.26	0.13
2000-01	0.26	0.27	0.27	0.13
2001-02	0.31	0.28	0.34	d0.02
2002-03	0.32	0.55	...	...

INTERIM DIVIDENDS (Per Share):

Amt.	Decl.	Ex.	Rec.	Pay.
0.045Q	3/13/02	3/27/02	4/01/02	4/16/02
0.05Q	6/21/02	7/02/02	7/05/02	7/19/02
0.05Q	9/19/02	9/30/02	10/02/02	10/17/02
0.05Q	12/11/02	12/19/02	12/23/02	1/16/03
0.05Q	3/12/03	3/31/03	4/02/03	4/16/03

Indicated div.: $0.20

CAPITALIZATION (4/30/02):

	($000)	(%)
Long-Term Debt	235,000	44.7
Deferred Income Tax	14,275	2.7
Common & Surplus	276,650	52.6
Total	525,925	100.0

BUSINESS:

John Wiley & Sons, Inc. develops, publishes and markets textbooks, reference works, consumer books, periodicals, including journals and other subscription-based products and electronic media products, to colleges and universities, libraries, bookstores, professional groups, industrial organizations, government agencies and individuals in the United States and abroad. In addition, JWA imports, adapts, markets and distributes books from other publishers. JWA also develops and markets computer software and electronic databases for educational use and professional research and training. On 9/21/01, JWA acquired the publisher Hungry Minds, Inc. for about $185.0 million.

RECENT DEVELOPMENTS:

For the quarter ended 10/31/02, net income surged 93.9% to $34.7 million from $17.9 million in the corresponding prior-year period. Earnings for 2002 included a one-time tax benefit of $12.0 million. Revenues advanced 26.6% to $223.0 million from $176.2 million in the previous year. Revenues for the professional/trade segment rose 55.6% to $89.7 million, primarily due to the acquisition of Hungry Minds, Inc. Scientific, technical, and medical segment revenues grew 1.5% to $42.4 million, principally due to new and renewed Wiley InterScience licenses and journal subscriptions. Higher education revenues improved 4.7% to $36.6 million from $34.9 million a year earlier.

PROSPECTS:

Revenue growth continues to be driven by the combined effects of acquisitions, particularly Hungry Minds, Inc., which was acquired in September 2001, and organic growth in JWA's professional/trade segment, as well as improvement in Asian markets, excluding Japan. Separately, the Company announced a strategic alliance with MindLeaders to extend the For Dummies brand into an online product for the corporate market. JWA also entered into a publishing alliance with Morningstar, Inc., an investment research firm, to publish the 2003 editions of Stocks 500 and Funds 500, as well as new branded titles. Looking ahead, JWA expects revenue growth in the mid-teens and earnings per share growth in the high-teens, excluding relocation charges and a one-time tax benefit, in 2003.

ANNUAL FINANCIAL DATA:

FISCAL YEAR	TOT. REVS. ($000)	NET INC. ($000)	TOT. ASSETS ($000)	OPER. PROFIT %	NET PROFIT %	RET. ON EQUITY %	RET. ON ASSETS %	CURR. RATIO	EARN. PER SH.$	CASH FL. PER SH.$	TANG. BK. VAL.$	DIV. PER SH.$	PRICE RANGE	AVG. P/E RATIO	AVG. YIELD %
4/30/02	734,396	⑤ 57,316	896,145	12.0	7.8	20.7	6.4	0.9	④ 0.91	1.85	...	0.17	24.10 - 17.90	23.1	0.8
4/30/01	613,790	58,918	588,002	15.5	9.6	26.8	10.0	0.8	0.93	1.78	...	0.15	26.00 - 13.75	21.4	0.7
4/30/00	594,815	52,388	569,337	15.0	8.8	30.3	9.2	0.7	0.81	1.63	...	0.14	24.91 - 14.94	24.6	0.7
4/30/99	508,435	39,709	528,552	12.5	7.8	24.5	7.5	1.3	0.60	1.21	...	0.12	24.16 - 12.25	30.3	0.7
4/30/98	467,081	③ 36,588	506,914	13.3	7.8	22.8	7.2	1.3	③ 0.56	1.18	...	0.11	14.25 - 7.03	19.2	1.0
4/30/97	431,974	20,340	457,944	8.1	4.7	15.8	4.4	1.2	0.31	0.83	...	0.09	8.88 - 6.66	25.0	1.2
4/30/96	362,704	② 24,680	284,501	9.1	6.8	20.9	8.7	1.2	② 0.37	0.78	1.02	0.08	8.75 - 5.47	19.1	1.2
4/30/95	331,091	① 18,311	247,481	8.1	5.5	18.5	7.4	1.1	① 0.28	0.63	0.71	0.07	5.75 - 4.38	18.1	1.4
4/30/94	294,289	12,117	243,940	6.4	4.1	14.7	5.0	1.3	0.19	...	0.61	0.07	4.63 - 2.63	19.1	1.9
4/30/93	272,894	7,718	220,593	4.8	2.8	10.8	3.5	1.3	0.13	...	0.46	0.07	3.14 - 1.94	20.3	2.7

Statistics are as originally reported. Adj. for 2-for-1 stk. split: 5/99, 10/98, 10/95 & 6/94. ① Incl. a $2.6 mill. after-tax gain from a favorable resolution of amended tax return claims. ② Incl. $4.4 mill. in amortization & financing exps. related to the acq. of VCH Publishing Group in June 1996. ③ Incl. $21.3 mill. gain on sale of publishing assets. ④ Incl. after-tax relocation expenses of $7.7 mill.

OFFICERS:
B. Wiley, Chmn.
W. J. Pesce, Pres., C.E.O.
E. E. Cousens, Exec. V.P., C.F.O., C.O.O.

INVESTOR CONTACT: Ellis E. Cousens, (201) 748-6534

PRINCIPAL OFFICE: 111 River Street, Hoboken, NJ 07030

TELEPHONE NUMBER: (201) 748-6000
FAX: (201) 748-6088
WEB: www.wiley.com
NO. OF EMPLOYEES: 3,100 (approx.)
SHAREHOLDERS: 1,220 (approx., Class A); 164 (approx., Class B)
ANNUAL MEETING: In Sept.
INCORPORATED: NY, Jan., 1904

INSTITUTIONAL HOLDINGS:
No. of Institutions: 128
Shares Held: 31,664,684
% Held: 51.4

INDUSTRY: Book publishing (SIC: 2731)

TRANSFER AGENT(S): Registrar and Transfer Company, Cranford, NJ

WILLIAMS COMPANIES, INC. (THE)

EXCH.	SYM.	REC. PRICE	P/E RATIO	YLD.	MKT. CAP.	RANGE (52-WK.)	'02 Y/E PR.
NYSE	WMB	3.81 (2/28/03)	...	1.0%	$1.96 bill.	24.50 - 0.78	2.70

SPECULATIVE GRADE. THE COMPANY COMPLETED THE SALE OF ITS MEMPHIS, TENNESSEE, REFINING OPERATIONS FOR APPROXIMATELY $455.0 MILLION CASH.

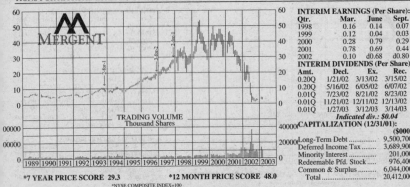

INTERIM EARNINGS (Per Share):

Qtr.	Mar.	June	Sept.	Dec.
1998	0.16	0.14	0.07	d0.02
1999	0.12	0.04	0.03	0.12
2000	0.28	0.79	0.29	0.57
2001	0.78	0.69	0.44	d0.20
2002	0.10	d0.68	d0.80	d0.22

INTERIM DIVIDENDS (Per Share):

Amt.	Decl.	Ex.	Rec.	Pay.
0.20Q	1/21/02	3/13/02	3/15/02	3/25/02
0.20Q	5/16/02	6/05/02	6/07/02	6/24/02
0.01Q	7/23/02	8/21/02	8/23/02	9/09/02
0.01Q	11/21/02	12/11/02	12/13/02	12/30/02
0.01Q	1/27/03	3/12/03	3/14/03	3/31/03

Indicated div.: $0.04

CAPITALIZATION (12/31/01):

	($000)	(%)
Long-Term Debt	9,500,700	46.5
Deferred Income Tax	3,689,900	18.1
Minority Interest	201,000	1.0
Redeemable Pfd. Stock	976,400	4.8
Common & Surplus	6,044,000	29.6
Total	20,412,000	100.0

TRADING VOLUME Thousand Shares

*7 YEAR PRICE SCORE 29.3 ***12 MONTH PRICE SCORE 48.0**

*NYSE COMPOSITE INDEX=100

BUSINESS:

The Williams Companies, Inc. is engaged in natural gas transmission and energy services. WMB is organized into three industry groups: Energy Marketing and Trading; Gas Pipeline and Energy Services, which includes Exploration and Production, International, Midstream Gas and Liquids, Petroleum Services; and Williams Energy Partners. On 4/23/01, WMB completed the spin-off of Williams Communications (WCG) to its shareholders, retaining about 4.9% of the outstanding class A common stock of WCG. On 8/2/01, WMB acquired Barrett Resources Corporation.

RECENT DEVELOPMENTS:

For the year ended 12/31/02, WMB posted a loss from continuing operations of $483.3 million versus income from continuing operations of $802.7 million a year earlier. Results for 2002 and 2001 included nonrecurring charges of $633.6 million and $303.8 million, respectively. Results included an Energy Marketing and Trading segment loss of $624.8 million versus segment profit of $1.30 billion in 2001. WMB attributed this loss primarily to the segment's limited ability to manage market risks for operations that were exposed to negative market conditions.

PROSPECTS:

On 3/4/03, WMB announced that it has completed the sale of its Memphis, Tennessee, refining operations to Premcor Inc. for approximately $455.0 million in cash. Additionally, in February 2003, WMB completed the sale of its retail travel center operations to Pilot Travel Centers LLC for approximately $189.0 million. The sale comprised 60 travel centers, including their working inventories, in 15 states. Also in February 2003, WMB announced that it had signed a definitive agreement to sell its equity interest in Williams Bio-Energy L.L.C. for about $75.0 million. Lastly, WMB stated that it is currently engaged in negotiations for the sale of its Alaska operations. All of the aforementioned transactions are components of the Company's ongoing plan to reduce debt and increase liquidity. Looking ahead, WMB expects its core gas pipeline, exploration and production, and midstream gas and liquids businesses to generate full-year 2003 segment profit of between $1.30 billion and $1.80 billion.

ANNUAL FINANCIAL DATA:

FISCAL YEAR	TOT. REVS. ($mill.)	NET INC. ($mill.)	TOT. ASSETS ($mill.)	OPER. PROFIT %	NET PROFIT %	NET INC./ NET PROP. %	NET INC./ TOT. CAP. %	RET. ON EQUITY %	ACCUM. DEPR./ GROSS PROP. %	EARN. PER SH.$	TANG. BK. VAL.$	DIV. PER SH.$	DIV. PAYOUT %	PRICE RANGE		AVG. P/E RATIO	AVG. YIELD %
p12/31/02		⑧ d483.3								⑧ d1.11		0.42	...	26.35	0.78	...	3.1
12/31/01	11,034.7	⑦ 835.4	38,906.2	22.2	7.6	4.7	4.1	13.8	23.9	⑦ 1.67	9.43	0.68	40.7	46.44	20.80	20.1	2.0
12/31/00	10,398.0	⑥ 873.2	40,197.0	17.0	8.4	4.4	4.2	14.8	20.0	⑥ 1.95	13.26	0.60	30.8	49.75	29.50	20.3	1.5
12/31/99	8,593.1	⑤ 161.8	25,288.5	9.9	1.9	1.1	0.9	2.7	21.3	⑤ 0.36	11.59	0.60	166.6	53.75	28.00	113.5	1.5
12/31/98	7,658.3	④ 146.6	18,647.3	9.5	1.9	1.2	1.1	3.4	22.3	④ 0.32	8.34	0.60	187.4	36.94	20.00	88.9	2.1
12/31/97	4,409.6	③ 350.5	13,879.0	21.0	7.9	3.5	3.5	9.8	18.1	③ 1.04	9.50	0.54	51.9	28.38	18.06	22.3	2.3
12/31/96	3,531.2	② 362.3	12,418.8	25.5	10.3	3.9	3.8	10.6	16.3	② 2.17	20.70	0.47	21.7	19.50	14.17	7.8	2.8
12/31/95	2,855.7	② 299.4	10,561.2	23.5	10.5	3.7	3.9	9.4	15.4	② 1.86	29.04	0.36	19.4	14.83	8.17	6.2	3.1
12/31/94	1,751.1	② 164.9	5,226.1	19.5	9.4	5.3	4.7	11.0	27.5	③ 1.52	14.85	0.28	18.4	11.13	7.38	6.1	3.0
12/31/93	2,438.2	② 270.2	5,020.4	16.9	11.1	10.3	6.8	15.7	34.0	② 2.20	15.75	0.26	11.8	10.63	5.98	3.8	3.1

Statistics are as originally reported. Adj. for 2-for-1 stk. split, 12/97; 3-for-2, 12/96. ① Incl. non-recurr. cr. of $44.5 mill.; bef. extraord. chrg. of $79.1 mill. ② Incl. non-recurr. pre-tax cr. 12/31/96, $15.7 mill.; aft-tax cr. 12/31/95, $14.0 mill.; pre-tax cr. 12/31/93, $97.5 mill. ③ Bef. gain of $94.0 mill. fr. disc. ops. & extraord. cr. of $12.2 mill. ④ Incl. chrg. of $80.0 mill.; bef. disc. oper. loss of $14.3 mill.; bef. extraord. gain of $4.8 mill. ⑤ Bef. extraord. gain of $65.2 mill.; bef. acctg. chge. chrg. of $5.6 mill. ⑥ Bef. loss fr. disc. ops. of $348.9 mill. ⑦ Incl. impair. chrg. of $170.0 mill.; bef. loss fr. disc. ops. of $1.31 bill. ⑧ Incl. non-recurr. chrgs. of $633.6 mill.

OFFICERS:
S. J. Malcolm, Chmn., Pres., C.E.O.
G. R. Belitz, Interim C.F.O., Contr.
J. J. Bender, Sr. V.P., Gen. Couns.
INVESTOR CONTACT: Richard George or Courtney Baugher, (800) 600-3782
PRINCIPAL OFFICE: One Williams Center, Tulsa, OK 74172

TELEPHONE NUMBER: (918) 573-2000
FAX: (918) 588-2334
WEB: www.williams.com
NO. OF EMPLOYEES: 12,433 (approx.)
SHAREHOLDERS: 15,017 (approx.)
ANNUAL MEETING: In May
INCORPORATED: NE, Feb., 1949; reincorp., DE, Feb., 1987

INSTITUTIONAL HOLDINGS:
No. of Institutions: 344
Shares Held: 237,742,220
% Held: 46.0
INDUSTRY: Natural gas transmission (SIC: 4922)
TRANSFER AGENT(S): EquiServe Trust Company, N.A., Jersey City, NJ

WILLIAMS-SONOMA, INC.

EXCH.	SYM.	REC. PRICE	P/E RATIO	YLD.	MKT. CAP.	RANGE (52-WK.)	'02 Y/E PR.
NYSE	WSM	23.28 (2/28/03)	22.2	...	$2.67 bill.	33.50 - 19.37	27.15

UPPER MEDIUM GRADE. THE COMPANY IS TARGETING NET REVENUES OF $2.64 BILLION TO $2.73 BILLION AND EARNINGS OF $1.20 TO $1.24 PER SHARE IN THE UPCOMING FISCAL YEAR.

*7 YEAR PRICE SCORE 176.9   ***12 MONTH PRICE SCORE 103.5**

*NYSE COMPOSITE INDEX=100

INTERIM EARNINGS (Per Share):

Qtr.	Apr.	July	Oct.	Jan.
1998-99	0.02	0.04	0.05	0.38
1999-00	0.03	0.06	0.08	0.41
2000-01	0.04	0.05	0.02	0.40
2001-02	0.01	0.01	0.04	0.60
2002-03	0.13	0.12	0.13	0.67

INTERIM DIVIDENDS (Per Share):

Amt.	Decl.	Ex.	Rec.	Pay.
2-for-1	4/17/02	5/10/02	4/29/02	5/09/02

CAPITALIZATION (2/3/02):

	($000)	(%)
Long-Term Debt	151,719	21.9
Deferred Income Tax	8,792	1.3
Common & Surplus	532,541	76.8
Total..............................	693,052	100.0

BUSINESS:

Williams-Sonoma, Inc. is a specialty retailer of products for the home. As of 2/2/03, the Company operated 478 retail stores including 236 Williams-Sonoma, 159 Pottery Barn, 56 Pottery Barn Kids, 13 Hold Everything and 14 outlet stores. Williams-Sonoma stores offer a selection of culinary and serving equipment, including cookware, cookbooks, cutlery, informal dinnerware, glassware and table linens, along with a variety of foods including gourmet coffees and pasta sauces. Pottery Barn stores feature an assortment of items in casual home furnishings, flatware and table accessories from around the world, while Hold Everything stores provide products for household storage needs. The Company also sells merchandise through seven mail-order catalogs and four e-commerce web sites.

RECENT DEVELOPMENTS:

For the 52 weeks ended 2/2/03, net earnings jumped 65.7% to $124.4 million from $75.1 million in the corresponding 53-week period the previous year. Net revenues climbed 13.1% to $2.36 billion from $2.09 billion the year before. Comparable-store sales were up 2.7% year over year. Gross profit was $951.6 million, or 40.3% of net revenues, versus $794.0 million, or 38.1% of net revenues, a year earlier. Earnings from operations totaled $202.3 million, up 58.1% compared with $128.0 million the prior year.

PROSPECTS:

The Company is targeting fiscal 2003 net revenues of between $2.64 billion and $2.73 billion, comparable-store sales growth of 1.0% to 3.0%, and earnings in the range of $1.20 to $1.24 per share. Leased retail square footage is expected to increase 9.0% to 11.0% in fiscal 2003. During the year, the Company plans to open 55 new stores and close 21 existing locations, including ten stores that will be temporarily closed for remodeling. Separately, in late April 2003, WSM plans to launch PBteen, a new catalog focused exclusively on the teenage market. PBteen will feature furniture, rugs, lighting, bedding and accessories for bedrooms and study and lounge areas.

ANNUAL FINANCIAL DATA:

FISCAL YEAR	TOT. REVS. ($mill.)	NET INC. ($mill.)	TOT. ASSETS ($mill.)	OPER. PROFIT %	NET PROFIT %	RET. ON EQUITY %	RET. ON ASSETS %	CURR. RATIO	EARN. PER SH. $	CASH FL. PER SH. $	TANG. BK. VAL. $	PRICE RANGE	AVG. P/E RATIO
p2/02/03	2,360.8	124.4							1.04			33.50 - 19.37	25.4
2/03/02	2,086.7	75.1	994.9	6.1	3.6	14.1	7.5	1.4	0.65	1.27	4.65	22.00 - 10.00	24.6
1/28/01	1,829.5	56.8	891.9	5.4	3.1	13.3	6.4	1.3	0.50	0.94	3.83	23.00 - 7.75	31.1
1/30/00	1,384.0	① 68.1	738.9	8.2	4.9	17.8	9.2	1.9	① 0.58	0.89	3.40	30.16 - 12.63	36.9
1/31/99	1,104.0	54.9	576.2	8.3	5.0	18.2	9.5	2.1	0.48	0.71	2.71	20.38 - 8.72	30.3
2/01/98	933.3	41.3	477.2	7.9	4.4	21.4	8.7	2.0	0.38	0.58	1.87	12.50 - 6.13	24.8
2/02/97	811.8	22.7	404.4	5.4	2.8	15.6	5.6	1.7	0.22	0.41	1.43	9.09 - 3.13	28.1
1/28/96	644.7	2.5	319.1	1.4	0.4	2.1	0.8	1.3	0.03	0.16	1.20	7.59 - 3.91	229.6
1/29/95	528.5	19.6	217.9	6.6	3.7	16.6	9.0	1.6	0.19	0.29	1.17	8.81 - 3.94	34.0
1/30/94	410.1	11.2	167.6	5.0	2.7	11.8	6.7	1.7	0.11	0.21	0.95	4.69 - 1.11	26.4

Statistics are as originally reported. Adj. for stk. splits: 2-for-1, 5/02 & 5/98; 3-for-2, 9/94 & 2/94. ① Incl. $4.0 mil pre-tax gain fr. sale of assets.

OFFICERS:
W. H. Lester, Chmn.
E. A. Mueller, C.E.O.
S. L. McCollam, Sr. V.P., C.F.O.

INVESTOR CONTACT: Christy M. Chanslor, Investor Relations, (415) 616-8332

PRINCIPAL OFFICE: 3250 Van Ness Avenue, San Francisco, CA 94109

TELEPHONE NUMBER: (415) 421-7900
FAX: (415) 434-0881
WEB: www.williams-sonoma.com

NO. OF EMPLOYEES: 6,000 full-time (approx.); 21,000 part-time (approx.)

SHAREHOLDERS: 519 (approx. record).

ANNUAL MEETING: In May

INCORPORATED: CA, Apr., 1973

INSTITUTIONAL HOLDINGS:
No. of Institutions: 268
Shares Held: 90,753,963
% Held: 78.0

INDUSTRY: Misc. homefurnishings stores
(SIC: 5719)

TRANSFER AGENT(S): Mellon Investor Services, San Francisco, CA

WILMINGTON TRUST CORPORATION

EXCH.	SYM.	REC. PRICE	P/E RATIO	YLD.	MKT. CAP.	RANGE (52-WK.)	'02 Y/E PR.	DIV. ACH.
NYSE	WL	28.40 (2/28/03)	14.1	3.6%	$1.86 bill.	34.63 - 25.05	31.68	21 yrs.

INVESTMENT GRADE. IN 2003, CREDIT QUALITY AND THE NET INTEREST MARGIN ARE EXPECTED TO REMAIN RELATIVELY STABLE.

*7 YEAR PRICE SCORE 122.1   *12 MONTH PRICE SCORE 105.7

*NYSE COMPOSITE INDEX=100

INTERIM EARNINGS (Per Share):

Qtr.	Mar.	June	Sept.	Dec.
1998	0.40	0.41	0.43	0.44
1999	0.44	0.45	0.46	0.27
2000	0.47	0.47	0.48	0.44
2001	0.46	0.47	0.48	0.48
2002	0.49	0.52	0.52	0.49

INTERIM DIVIDENDS (Per Share):

Amt.	Decl.	Ex.	Rec.	Pay.
0.51Q	4/18/02	4/29/02	5/01/02	5/15/02
100% STK	4/18/02	6/18/02	6/03/02	6/17/02
0.255Q	7/18/02	7/30/02	8/01/02	8/15/02
0.255Q	10/17/02	10/30/02	11/01/02	11/15/02
0.255Q	1/16/03	1/30/03	2/03/03	2/17/03

Indicated div.: $1.02 (Div. Reinv. Plan)

CAPITALIZATION (12/31/01):

	($000)	(%)
Total Deposits	5,590,785	86.9
Long-Term Debt	160,500	2.5
Common & Surplus	682,530	10.6
Total	6,433,815	100.0

BUSINESS:

Wilmington Trust Corporation, with assets of $8.13 billion as of 12/31/02, is a financial services holding company with offices in California, Delaware, Florida, Georgia, Maryland, Nevada, New Jersey, New York, Pennsylvania, Tennessee, the Cayman and Channel Islands, Dublin, London, and Milan. The Company provides wealth management and specialized corporate services to clients throughout the United States and in more than 50 other countries, and commercial banking services throughout the Delaware Valley region. In addition, the Company is authorized to do business in Luxembourg and the Netherlands.

RECENT DEVELOPMENTS:

For the year ended 12/31/02, the Company reported net income of $133.2 million compared with income of $124.0 million, before an accounting credit of $1.1 million, the year before. Earnings for 2002 and 2001 included amortization of other intangibles and goodwill of $1.3 million and $8.2 million, respectively. Net interest income improved 6.8% to $276.5 million from $258.8 million a year earlier, Provision for loan losses grew 10.9% to $22.0 million from $19.9 million in 2001. Total other income improved 15.0% to $262.2 million from $228.0 million in the previous year. Total other expense increased 11.9% to $309.9 million from $276.9 million a year earlier. As of 12/31/02, combined assets under management were $28.95 billion, down 20.0% from $36.17 billion the year before.

PROSPECTS:

In 2003, wealth advisory revenue is expected to continue to grow at double-digit rates, primarily as a result of the acquisition of Balentine & Company in January 2002. Balentine is expected to add $1.00 billion in new assets. The corporate client business is anticipated to report double-digit increases, reflecting WL's acquisition of SPV Management, which serves European markets, in April 2002. Meanwhile, credit quality and the net interest margin are expected to remain relatively stable in 2003. Additionally, commercial loan balances are projected to grow in the low double-digit range, while modest, single-digit growth is anticipated in the retail portfolio.

ANNUAL FINANCIAL DATA:

FISCAL YEAR	NET INT. INC. ($mill.)	NON-INT. INC. ($mill.)	NET INC. ($mill.)	TOT. LOANS ($mill.)	TOT. ASSETS ($mill.)	TOT. DEP. ($mill.)	RET. ON EQUITY %	RET. ON ASSETS %	EQUITY/ ASSETS %	EARN. PER SH. $	TANG. BK. VAL. $	DIV. PER SH. $	PRICE RANGE	AVG. P/E RATIO
p12/31/02	276.5	262.2	133.2							2.01	7.25	1.01	34.63 - 25.05	14.8
12/31/01	258.8	228.0	① 124.0	5,488.8	7,518.5	5,590.8	18.2	1.6	9.1	① 1.89	6.48	0.94	33.50 - 25.10	15.5
12/31/00	255.1	216.2	120.9	5,189.0	7,321.6	5,286.0	20.4	1.7	8.1	1.85	6.48	0.89	31.69 - 20.28	14.0
12/31/99	245.9	191.5	107.3	4,821.6	7,201.9	5,369.5	21.5	1.5	6.9	1.61	5.17	0.82	31.75 - 22.38	16.9
12/31/98	237.7	183.9	114.3	4,324.4	6,300.6	4,536.8	20.9	1.8	8.7	1.67	6.07	0.77	34.25 - 23.19	17.2
12/31/97	230.0	157.5	106.0	4,004.8	6,122.4	4,169.0	21.1	1.7	8.2	1.54	7.51	0.70	33.00 - 19.63	17.1
12/31/96	214.2	138.2	97.3	3,783.9	5,564.4	3,913.7	20.9	1.7	8.4	1.42	6.86	0.65	20.88 - 15.13	12.7
12/31/95	197.4	127.6	90.0	3,527.6	5,372.2	3,587.6	19.6	1.7	8.6	1.28	6.55	0.58	16.25 - 11.38	10.8
12/31/94	184.3	113.1	85.2	3,283.0	4,742.4	3,308.8	20.4	1.8	8.8	1.19	5.90	0.53	14.25 - 11.00	10.7
12/31/93	174.8	113.7	82.8	3,039.8	4,637.8	3,391.4	20.9	1.8	8.5	1.12	5.44	0.49	15.50 - 12.38	12.4

Statistics are as originally reported. Adj. for stk. split: 2-for-1, 6/02 & 5/92. ① Bef. an after-tax acctg. credit of $1.1 mill.

OFFICERS:
T. T. Cecala, Chmn., C.E.O.
R. V. Harra, Jr., Pres., C.O.O., Treas.
D. R. Gibson, Sr. V.P., C.F.O.
INVESTOR CONTACT: Ellen J. Roberts, Media & Investor Relations, (302) 651-8069
PRINCIPAL OFFICE: Rodney Square North, 1100 North Market St., Wilmington, DE 19890-0001

TELEPHONE NUMBER: (302) 651-1000
FAX: (302) 651-8010
WEB: www.wilmingtontrust.com
NO. OF EMPLOYEES: 2,316 (avg.)
SHAREHOLDERS: 8,841
ANNUAL MEETING: In April
INCORPORATED: DE, Mar., 1901

INSTITUTIONAL HOLDINGS:
No. of Institutions: 213
Shares Held: 26,820,966
% Held: 40.9
INDUSTRY: State commercial banks (SIC: 6022)
TRANSFER AGENT(S): Wells Fargo Shareowner Services, St. Paul, MN

WINN-DIXIE STORES, INC.

EXCH.	SYM.	REC. PRICE	P/E RATIO	YLD.	MKT. CAP.	RANGE (52-WK.)	'02 Y/E PR.
NYSE	WIN	12.20 (2/28/03)	7.4	1.6%	$1.72 bill.	20.40 - 11.30	15.28

MEDIUM GRADE. RESULTS ARE BENEFITING FROM LOWER PRODUCT COSTS AND THE COMPANY'S MARKETING INITIATIVES.

*7 YEAR PRICE SCORE 57.0   ***12 MONTH PRICE SCORE 96.1**

*NYSE COMPOSITE INDEX=100

INTERIM EARNINGS (Per Share):

Qtr.	Sept.	Dec.	Mar.	June
1997-98	0.32	0.38	0.41	0.22
1998-99	0.10	0.35	0.40	0.38
1999-00	0.15	d0.13	0.07	d1.70
2000-01	0.07	0.09	0.08	0.09
2001-02	0.22	0.37	0.38	0.37
2002-03	0.25	0.65	...	...

INTERIM DIVIDENDS (Per Share):

Amt.	Decl.	Ex.	Rec.	Pay.
0.05Q	1/22/02	1/30/02	2/01/02	2/15/02
0.05Q	4/19/02	4/29/02	5/01/02	5/15/02
0.05Q	7/22/02	7/30/02	8/01/02	8/15/02
0.05Q	10/21/02	10/30/02	11/01/02	11/15/02
0.05Q	1/21/03	1/30/03	2/03/03	2/14/03

Indicated div.: $0.20 (Div. Reinv. Plan)

CAPITALIZATION (6/26/02):

	($000)	(%)
Long-Term Debt	540,612	39.2
Capital Lease Obligations..	24,787	1.8
Common & Surplus	812,384	59.0
Total	1,377,783	100.0

BUSINESS:

Winn-Dixie Stores, Inc. operated a chain of 1,075 stores in 12 states and the Bahamas as of 1/8/03 that offer a broad line of groceries, meats, seafood, fresh produce, deli/bakery, pharmaceuticals and general merchandise items. Stores operate under the names WINN-DIXIE, WINN-DIXIE MARKETPLACE, THRIFTWAY, CITY MEAT MARKETS, SACK & SAVE and SAVE RITE. In addition, the Company also operated 34 fuel centers, 31 liquor stores, along with 15 distribution centers and 16 manufacturing plants. At 6/26/02, the Davis family owned approximately 41.0% of the Company's common stock.

RECENT DEVELOPMENTS:

For the 16 weeks ended 1/8/03, net earnings totaled $91.4 million, up 75.7% compared with earnings from continuing operations of $52.0 million in the corresponding period the year before. Results for the recent period included a pre-tax gain of $52.7 million from the termination of a bank agreement. Net sales rose 0.5% to $3.79 billion from $3.77 billion a year earlier. Identical-store sales increased 1.3%, while comparable-store sales, which include replacement stores, grew 1.3% year over year. Gross profit was $1.09 billion, or 28.9% of net sales, versus $1.05 billion, or 27.9% of net sales, the year before. Operating income slipped 7.6% to $97.2 million from $105.1 million in the prior year.

PROSPECTS:

Earnings are being positively affected by gross margin improvement stemming from lower product costs, due to improvements in procurement. Meanwhile, sales are benefiting from WIN's marketing initiatives, including expansion of its customer-reward program into new areas. WIN introduced the program into stores located in North and South Carolina, Virginia, Kentucky and Tennessee during the second quarter of fiscal 2003. Separately, the Company anticipates capital expenditures of $235.0 million for retail and support facilities, including operating leases, in the current fiscal year.

ANNUAL FINANCIAL DATA:

FISCAL YEAR	TOT. REVS. ($mill.)	NET INC. ($mill.)	TOT. ASSETS ($mill.)	OPER. PROFIT %	NET PROFIT %	RET. ON EQUITY %	RET. ON ASSETS %	CURR. RATIO	EARN. PER SH. $	CASH FL. PER SH. $	TANG. BK. VAL. $	DIV. PER SH. $	PRICE RANGE	AVG. P/E RATIO	AVG. YIELD %
6/26/02	12,334.4	② 189.5	2,937.6	3.0	1.5	23.3	6.5	1.5	② 1.35	2.60	5.15	0.20	20.40 - 11.71	11.9	1.2
6/27/01	12,903.4	① 45.3	3,041.7	1.0	0.4	5.9	1.5	1.4	① 0.32	1.63	4.83	0.85	33.12 - 10.22	67.7	3.9
6/28/00	13,697.5	① d228.9	2,747.1	...	...	...	...	1.0	① d1.57	0.19	6.03	1.02	24.75 - 13.44	...	5.3
6/30/99	14,136.5	182.3	3,149.1	1.5	1.3	12.9	5.8	1.2	1.23	3.19	9.50	1.02	46.63 - 22.31	28.0	3.0
6/24/98	13,617.5	① 198.6	3,068.7	1.7	1.5	14.5	6.5	1.2	① 1.33	3.55	9.22	1.02	62.81 - 28.63	34.4	2.2
6/25/97	13,218.7	204.4	2,921.4	1.7	1.5	15.3	7.0	1.1	1.36	3.30	8.98	0.98	44.00 - 29.88	27.2	2.7
6/26/96	12,955.5	255.6	2,648.6	2.2	2.0	19.0	9.7	1.3	1.69	3.32	8.85	0.93	39.00 - 31.00	20.7	2.6
6/28/95	11,787.8	232.2	2,482.8	2.2	2.0	18.7	9.4	1.4	1.56	2.90	8.21	0.81	37.63 - 25.56	20.3	2.6
6/29/94	11,082.2	216.1	2,146.6	2.4	2.0	20.4	10.1	1.6	1.45	2.50	7.13	0.74	29.31 - 21.31	17.4	3.0
6/30/93	10,831.5	236.4	2,062.6	2.3	2.2	24.0	11.5	1.6	1.56	2.52	6.57	0.69	39.88 - 26.38	21.3	2.1

Statistics are as originally reported. Adj. for 2-for-1 stk. split, 11/95. ① Incl. $94.0 mil ($0.67/sh) after-tax non-recur. chg., 2001; $304.1 mil ($2.09/sh), 2000; & $11 mil ($0.07/sh), 1998. ② Bef. $100.3 mil ($0.71/sh) loss fr. disc. opers. & $2.3 mil ($0.02/sh) extraord. chg.

OFFICERS:
A. D. Davis, Chmn.
A. R. Rowland, Pres., C.E.O.
F. Lazaran, Exec. V.P., C.O.O.

INVESTOR CONTACT: Rick McCook, Sr.
V.P. & C.F.O., (904) 783-5221

PRINCIPAL OFFICE: 5050 Edgewood Court, Jacksonville, FL 32254-3699

TELEPHONE NUMBER: (904) 783-5000
FAX: (904) 783-5548
WEB: www.winn-dixie.com
NO. OF EMPLOYEES: 41,000 full-time; 71,400 part-time
SHAREHOLDERS: 46,491 (record)
ANNUAL MEETING: In Oct.
INCORPORATED: FL, Dec., 1928

INSTITUTIONAL HOLDINGS:
No. of Institutions: 214
Shares Held: 47,211,825
% Held: 33.5

INDUSTRY: Grocery stores (SIC: 5411)

TRANSFER AGENT(S): First Chicago Trust Company of New York, Jersey City, NJ

WINNEBAGO INDUSTRIES, INC.

EXCH.	SYM.	REC. PRICE	P/E RATIO	YLD.	MKT. CAP.	RANGE (52-WK.)	'02 Y/E PR.
NYSE	WGO	29.35 (2/28/03)	8.9	0.7%	$0.55 bill.	51.48 - 28.85	39.23

UPPER MEDIUM GRADE. LONG-TERM PROSPECTS FOR THE COMPANY REMAIN SOLID DUE TO INCREASED POPULARITY OF RECREATIONAL VEHICLES.

*7 YEAR PRICE SCORE 234.9   ***12 MONTH PRICE SCORE 91.1**
*NYSE COMPOSITE INDEX=100

INTERIM EARNINGS (Per Share):

Qtr.	Nov.	Feb.	May	Aug.
1997-98	0.21	0.18	0.31	0.32
1998-99	0.43	0.45	0.65	0.44
1999-00	0.55	0.54	0.74	0.37
2000-01	0.45	0.30	0.61	0.74
2001-02	0.51	0.45	0.93	0.86
2002-03	0.85	0.64	...	...

INTERIM DIVIDENDS (Per Share):

Amt.	Decl.	Ex.	Rec.	Pay.
0.10S	3/14/01	6/06/01	6/08/01	7/09/01
0.10S	10/17/01	12/05/01	12/07/01	1/07/02
0.10S	3/20/02	6/05/02	6/07/02	7/08/02
0.10S	10/10/02	12/04/02	12/06/02	1/06/03
0.10S	3/20/03	6/04/03	6/06/03	7/07/03

Indicated div.: $0.20

CAPITALIZATION (8/31/02):

	($000)	(%)
Common & Surplus	179,815	100.0
Total	179,815	100.0

BUSINESS:

Winnebago Industries, Inc. is a major manufacturer of motor homes, self-contained recreation vehicles used primarily in leisure travel and outdoor recreation activities. Motor home sales by the Company represented more than 89.0% of its revenues in each of the past five fiscal years. These vehicles are sold through dealer organizations primarily under the WINNEBAGO®, ITASCA®, RIALTA® and ULTIMATE® brand names. The Company builds motor homes with computer-aided design and manufacturing systems on automotive-styled assembly lines. Other products manufactured by WGO consist of a variety of component products such as extruded aluminum and commercial vehicles for other manufacturers. Finance revenues consist of revenues from floor plan unit financing for a limited number of WGO's dealers.

RECENT DEVELOPMENTS:

For the quarter ended 3/1/03, net income grew 30.3% to $12.3 million compared with $9.4 million in the equivalent 2002 quarter. Earnings reflected an improved product mix, reduced inventory levels and lower stock-based incentive compensation expense. This was partially offset by the start-up costs of the new production facility in Charles City, Iowa. Net revenues advanced 2.0% to $186.7 million. Factory shipments of WGO's Class A motor homes increased 3.6% to 1,523, while Class C motor homes decreased 24.7% to 978.

PROSPECTS:

Near-term results are likely to be dampened by weak consumer confidence and geopolitical turmoil. As a result, the Company has temporarily scheduled four-day work weeks for its factories. The Company believes that long-term prospects remain positive due to increased popularity of recreational vehicles, growth in WGO's prime target audience of people over age 50, and broadening age range of people who are buying its motor homes. Separately, the Company has a new production facility in Charles City, Iowa, which should contribute to future results.

ANNUAL FINANCIAL DATA:

FISCAL YEAR	TOT. REVS. ($mill.)	NET INC. ($mill.)	TOT. ASSETS ($mill.)	OPER. PROFIT %	NET PROFIT %	RET. ON EQUITY %	RET. ON ASSETS %	CURR. RATIO	EARN. PER SH.$	CASH FL. PER SH.$	TANG. BK. VAL.$	DIV. PER SH.$	PRICE RANGE	AVG. P/E RATIO	AVG. YIELD %
8/31/02	828.4	54.7	337.1	9.8	6.6	30.4	16.2	2.6	2.68	3.07	9.63	0.20	51.48 - 31.85	15.5	0.5
8/25/01	681.8	①43.8	342.0	8.1	6.4	21.1	12.8	3.5	①2.08	2.43	9.99	0.20	41.32 - 15.60	13.7	0.7
8/26/00	743.3	48.4	308.7	9.5	6.5	27.7	15.7	3.0	2.20	2.50	8.22	0.20	21.75 - 10.75	7.4	1.2
8/28/99	667.7	44.3	285.9	9.6	6.6	29.6	15.5	2.5	1.96	2.22	6.70	0.20	28.75 - 12.88	10.6	1.0
8/29/98	525.1	24.4	230.6	6.3	4.6	20.9	10.6	2.5	1.00	1.23	5.11	0.20	16.38 - 8.25	12.3	1.6
8/30/97	438.1	④6.6	213.5	1.2	1.5	5.3	3.1	3.4	④0.26	0.51	4.79	0.20	9.63 - 6.25	30.5	2.5
8/31/96	484.8	③14.4	220.6	4.3	3.0	13.7	6.5	2.0	③0.57	0.95	4.15	0.20	10.38 - 6.75	15.0	2.3
8/26/95	460.1	27.9	211.6	3.9	6.1	27.8	13.2	2.4	1.11	1.45	3.96	0.40	10.75 - 7.38	8.2	4.4
8/27/94	452.1	②17.4	184.0	3.7	3.9	21.9	9.5	2.1	②0.69	1.00	3.16	...	13.88 - 7.63	15.6	...
8/28/93	384.1	9.3	157.1	2.2	2.4	11.4	5.9	1.9	0.37	0.69	3.26	...	10.50 - 5.63	21.8	...

Statistics are as originally reported. ① Bef. acctg. chrg. of $1.0 mill. ② Bef. a chrg. of $20.4 mill. for acctg. changes. ③ Bef. income from discont. oper. of $593,000 and loss on disposal of electronic component assembly segment of $2.6 mill. ④ Bef. gain from sale of discont. oper. of $16.5 mill. ($0.65/sh.).

OFFICERS:	TELEPHONE NUMBER: (641) 585-3535	INSTITUTIONAL HOLDINGS:
B. D. Hertzke, Chmn., Pres., C.E.O. E. F. Barker, V.P., C.F.O. R. M. Beebe, V.P., Sec., Gen. Couns.	FAX: (641) 585-6966 WEB: www.winnebagoind.com NO. OF EMPLOYEES: 3,685 (approx.)	No. of Institutions: 151 Shares Held: 11,779,261 % Held: 62.8
INVESTOR CONTACT: Sheila Davis, (641) 585-6803	SHAREHOLDERS: 4,922 ANNUAL MEETING: In Jan.	INDUSTRY: Motor homes (SIC: 3716)
PRINCIPAL OFFICE: P. O. Box 152, Forest City, IA 50436	INCORPORATED: IA, Feb., 1958	TRANSFER AGENT(S): Wells Fargo Shareowner Services, St. Paul, MN

WISCONSIN ENERGY CORPORATION

EXCH.	SYM.	REC. PRICE	P/E RATIO	YLD.	MKT. CAP.	RANGE (52-WK.)	'02 Y/E PR.
NYSE	WEC	22.85 (2/28/03)	16.0	3.5%	$2,637.36 bill.	26.60 - 20.17	25.20

MEDIUM GRADE. THE COMPANY COMPLETED THE SALE OF ITS WISVEST-CONNECTICUT LLC SUBSIDIARY TO PSEG FOSSIL, LLC FOR APPROXIMATELY $280.0 MILLION.

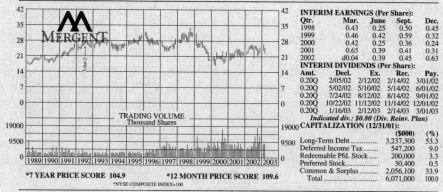

*7 YEAR PRICE SCORE 104.9   ***12 MONTH PRICE SCORE 109.6**
*NYSE COMPOSITE INDEX=100

INTERIM EARNINGS (Per Share):

Qtr.	Mar.	June	Sept.	Dec.
1998	0.43	0.25	0.50	0.45
1999	0.46	0.42	0.59	0.32
2000	0.42	0.25	0.36	0.24
2001	0.65	0.39	0.41	0.31
2002	d0.04	0.39	0.45	0.63

INTERIM DIVIDENDS (Per Share):

Amt.	Decl.	Ex.	Rec.	Pay.
0.20Q	2/05/02	2/12/02	2/14/02	3/01/02
0.20Q	5/02/02	5/10/02	5/14/02	6/01/02
0.20Q	7/24/02	8/12/02	8/14/02	9/01/02
0.20Q	10/22/02	11/12/02	11/14/02	12/01/02
0.20Q	1/16/03	2/12/03	2/14/03	3/01/03

Indicated div.: $0.80 (Div. Reinv. Plan)

CAPITALIZATION (12/31/01):

	($000)	(%)
Long-Term Debt	3,237,300	53.3
Deferred Income Tax	547,200	9.0
Redeemable Pfd. Stock	200,000	3.3
Preferred Stock	30,400	0.5
Common & Surplus	2,056,100	33.9
Total	6,071,000	100.0

BUSINESS:

Wisconsin Energy Corporation is a Milwaukee-based holding company with subsidiaries in utility and non-utility businesses. As of 2/10/02, the Company served more than 1.0 million electric and 970,000 natural gas customers in Wisconsin and Michigan's Upper Peninsula through its subsidiaries, Wisconsin Electric, Wisconsin Gas and Edison Sault Electric. WEC's non-utility subsidiaries include energy services and development, pump manufacturing, waste-to-energy and real estate businesses. On 4/26/00, the Company acquired WICOR, a Milwaukee-based diversified holding company, for $1.20 billion in cash.

RECENT DEVELOPMENTS:

For the year ended 12/31/02, net income was $167.0 million compared with income of $209.0 million, before an accounting change charge of $10.0 million, the previous year. Results for 2002 included pre-tax asset valuation charges of $141.0 million. Operating revenues declined 4.9% to $3.74 billion from $3.93 billion the prior year. Electric utility revenues increased 2.4% to $1.90 billion supported by favorable weather and the full-year impact of an increase in electric prices implemented during 2001. However, natural gas utility revenues fell 16.5% to $918.0 million, reflecting a decrease in natural gas, partially offset by higher volumes. Revenues in the manufacturing segment improved 17.1% to $685.0 million. Operating income decreased 24.3% to $458.0 million from $605.0 million in 2001.

PROSPECTS:

Going forward, the Company should benefit from the integration of recent acquisitions, growing its core businesses and its penetration into new markets. The Company estimates diluted earnings for 2003 in the range of $2.20 to $2.40 per share. Separately, on 12/6/02, the Company announced it had completed the sale of its Wisvest-Connecticut LLC subsidiary to PSEG Fossil, LLC of New Jersey for approximately $280.0 million, including reimbursement for capital expenditures, inventory and tax benefits.

ANNUAL FINANCIAL DATA:

FISCAL YEAR	TOT. REVS. ($mill.)	NET INC. ($mill.)	TOT. ASSETS ($mill.)	OPER. PROFIT %	NET PROFIT %	NET INC./ NET PROP. %	NET INC./ TOT. CAP. %	RET. ON EQUITY %	ACCUM. DEPR./ GROSS PROP. %	EARN. PER SH.$	TANG. BK. VAL.$	DIV. PER SH.$	DIV. PAYOUT %	PRICE RANGE	AVG. P/E RATIO	AVG. YIELD %
p12/31/02	3,736.0	⑥ 167.0								⑥ 1.44		0.80	55.6	26.48 - 20.17	16.2	3.4
12/31/01	3,928.5	⑤ 208.5	8,328.7	15.4	5.3	5.0	3.4	10.0	49.2	⑤ 1.77	10.60	0.80	45.2	24.62 - 19.13	12.4	3.7
12/31/00	3,354.7	④ 154.2	8,406.1	13.3	4.6	3.7	2.8	7.5	50.0	④ 1.27	10.03	1.37	107.9	23.56 - 16.81	15.9	6.8
12/31/99	2,272.6	③ 562.0	6,233.1	20.1	24.7	14.6	11.2	27.6	47.7	③ 1.79	16.89	1.56	87.1	31.56 - 19.06	14.1	6.2
12/31/98	1,980.0	496.5	5,361.8	14.0	25.1	14.1	11.7	25.7	46.7	1.65	16.46	1.55	94.2	34.00 - 27.00	18.5	5.1
12/31/97	1,789.6	② 372.7	5,037.7	11.1	20.8	11.2	9.4	19.7	45.6	② 0.54	16.51	1.53	284.2	29.06 - 23.00	48.2	5.9
12/31/96	1,773.8	513.8	4,810.8	17.2	29.0	16.1	13.2	26.0	44.0	1.97	17.42	1.51	76.5	32.00 - 26.00	14.7	5.2
12/31/95	1,770.5	537.6	4,568.3	18.6	30.4	17.7	14.3	28.3	43.4	2.13	16.89	1.46	68.3	30.88 - 25.75	13.3	5.1
12/31/94	1,742.2	① 466.7	4,408.3	15.1	26.8	15.2	13.2	26.3	41.4	① 1.67	16.01	1.40	83.6	27.50 - 23.13	15.2	5.5
12/31/93	1,643.7	451.9	4,223.1	16.0	27.5	15.4	13.1	26.8	40.6	1.81	15.67	1.34	74.1	29.38 - 24.75	15.0	5.0

Statistics are as originally reported. ① Incl. non-recurr. chrg. $190.1 mill. related to restructuring. ② Incl. non-recurr. after-tax chrg. $10.8 mill. related to the settlement of litigation. ③ Incl. non-recurr. chrg. of $36.9 mill. ④ Incl. a gain of $54.6 mill. on invest. & pre-tax non-recurr. chrg. of $83.3 mill. ⑤ Bef. acctg. chng. credit of $10.5 mill.; incl. gain of $27.5 mill. from asset sales. ⑥ Incl. pre-tax asset val. chrgs. of $141.0 mill.

OFFICERS:
R. A. Abdoo, Chmn., Pres., C.E.O.
P. Donovan, Exec. V.P., C.F.O.
L. Salustro, Sr. V.P., Gen. Couns.
INVESTOR CONTACT: Colleen Henderson, Investor Relations, (414) 221-2592
PRINCIPAL OFFICE: 231 West Michigan Street, P.O. Box 2949, Milwaukee, WI 53201

TELEPHONE NUMBER: (414) 221-2345
FAX: (414) 221-2172
WEB: www.wisenergy.com
NO. OF EMPLOYEES: 9,459 (avg.)
SHAREHOLDERS: 68,253
ANNUAL MEETING: In May
INCORPORATED: WI, June, 1981

INSTITUTIONAL HOLDINGS:
No. of Institutions: 271
Shares Held: 58,382,682
% Held: 50.5

INDUSTRY: Electric and other services combined (SIC: 4931)

TRANSFER AGENT(S): EquiServe, Canton, MA

WORTHINGTON INDUSTRIES, INC.

EXCH.	SYM.	REC. PRICE	P/E RATIO	YLD.	MKT. CAP.	RANGE (52-WK.)	'02 Y/E PR.
NYSE	WOR	13.78 (2/28/03)	13.8	4.6%	$1.18 bill.	20.40 - 13.20	15.24

UPPER MEDIUM GRADE. NEAR-TERM RESULTS MAY BE HAMPERED BY TIGHTENING MARGINS IN PROCESSED STEEL PRODUCTS AND CONTINUED CONTRACTION IN THE COMMERCIAL CONSTRUCTION MARKET.

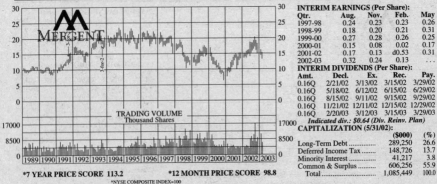

INTERIM EARNINGS (Per Share):

Qtr.	Aug.	Nov.	Feb.	May
1997-98	0.24	0.23	0.23	0.26
1998-99	0.18	0.20	0.21	0.31
1999-00	0.27	0.28	0.26	0.25
2000-01	0.15	0.08	0.02	0.17
2001-02	0.17	0.13	d0.53	0.31
2002-03	0.32	0.24	0.13	...

INTERIM DIVIDENDS (Per Share):

Amt.	Decl.	Ex.	Rec.	Pay.
0.16Q	2/21/02	3/13/02	3/15/02	3/29/02
0.16Q	5/18/02	6/12/02	6/15/02	6/29/02
0.16Q	8/15/02	9/11/02	9/15/02	9/29/02
0.16Q	11/21/02	12/11/02	12/15/02	12/29/02
0.16Q	2/20/03	3/12/03	3/15/03	3/29/03

Indicated div.: $0.64 (Div. Reinv. Plan)

CAPITALIZATION (5/31/02):

	($000)	(%)
Long-Term Debt	289,250	26.6
Deferred Income Tax	148,726	13.7
Minority Interest	41,217	3.8
Common & Surplus	606,256	55.9
Total	1,085,449	100.0

*7 YEAR PRICE SCORE 113.2   ***12 MONTH PRICE SCORE 98.8**

*NYSE COMPOSITE INDEX=100

BUSINESS:

Worthington Industries, Inc. is a diversified metal processing company that focuses on steel processing and metals-related businesses. The Company manufactures metal products such as automotive past model service stampings, pressure cylinders, and metal framing and, through joint ventures, metal ceiling grid systems and laser welded blanks. As of 3/19/03, WOR operated 62 facilities in 10 countries. The Company is involved in three business segments: Processed Steel Products (65.4% of 2002 sales),

Metal Framing (17.7%) and Pressure Cylinders (16.9%). The Processed Steel Products segment includes The Worthington Steel Company business unit and The Gerstenslager Company business unit. The Metal Framing segment is made up of Dietrich Industries, Inc. and the Pressure Cylinders segment consists of Worthington Cylinder Corporation. In addition, the Company held an equity position in seven joint ventures as of 5/31/02. On 7/31/02, the Company acquired Unimast Incorporated.

RECENT DEVELOPMENTS:

For the quarter ended 2/28/03, net income amounted to $11.3 million compared with a net loss of $45.9 million in the equivalent 2002 quarter. Results for 2002 included an after-tax nonrecurring charge of $54.5 million. Total net sales grew 32.2% to $536.6 million. Net sales for the

Processed Steel Products segment rose 22.5% to $321.9 million. Metal Framing segment net sales climbed 97.0% to $135.0 million due to the Unimast acquisition and higher selling prices. Net sales for the Pressure Cylinders segment grew 7.1% to $75.7 million.

PROSPECTS:

Going forward, the Company may continue to experience tightening margins in Processed Steel Products and continued contraction in the commercial construction market served by WOR's Metal Framing business segment. Elevated inventory levels may also be an issue in the near-term as pricing continues to fall from recent highs. Short-term

economic and business conditions are expected to deteriorate further; however, WOR is well positioned for an economic recovery and has yet to fully realize the benefits of the 7/31/02 acquisition of Unimast Incorporated and its consolidation plan.

ANNUAL FINANCIAL DATA:

FISCAL YEAR	TOT. REVS. ($mill.)	NET INC. ($mill.)	TOT. ASSETS ($mill.)	OPER. PROFIT %	NET PROFIT %	RET. ON EQUITY %	RET. ON ASSETS %	CURR. RATIO	EARN. PER SH.$	CASH FL. PER SH.$	TANG. BK. VAL.$	DIV. PER SH.$	PRICE RANGE	AVG. P/E RATIO	AVG. YIELD %
5/31/02	1,745.0	④ 6.5	1,457.3	2.0	0.4	1.1	0.4	1.4	④ 0.08	0.88	6.21	0.64	15.24 - 7.63	142.7	5.6
5/31/01	1,826.1	④ 35.6	1,475.9	3.6	1.9	5.5	2.4	1.5	④ 0.42	1.24	6.67	0.63	17.00 - 6.38	27.8	5.4
5/31/00	1,962.6	94.2	1,673.9	8.6	4.8	14.0	5.6	1.4	1.06	1.86	6.92	0.59	17.69 - 11.06	13.6	4.1
5/31/99	1,763.1	①②83.6	1,687.0	8.3	4.7	12.1	5.0	1.5	①②0.90	1.74	6.74	0.55	19.56 - 10.38	16.6	3.7
5/31/98	1,624.4	①③82.3	1,842.3	8.3	5.1	10.5	4.5	1.6	①③0.85	1.48	7.08	0.51	22.00 - 15.13	21.8	2.7
5/31/97	1,911.7	91.3	1,561.2	8.1	4.9	13.0	6.0	2.4	0.97	1.50	6.38	0.47	22.50 - 17.50	20.6	2.4
5/31/96	1,477.8	93.3	1,220.1	8.5	6.2	14.3	7.5	3.1	1.01	1.66	6.32	0.43	23.25 - 16.63	19.7	2.2
5/31/95	1,483.6	116.7	917.0	10.4	7.9	19.8	12.7	2.5	1.29	1.66	6.50	0.39	23.50 - 17.50	15.9	1.9
5/31/94	1,285.1	84.9	798.6	9.3	6.6	16.8	10.6	2.3	0.94	1.30	5.56	0.34	21.67 - 15.00	19.5	1.9
5/31/93	1,115.7	66.2	686.1	9.7	5.9	15.3	9.6	2.5	0.74	1.06	4.81	0.39	17.58 - 12.42	20.3	2.6

Statistics are as originally reported. Adj. for stk. splits: 3-for-2, 10/25/93. ① Bef. disc. oper. loss 5/31/99: $20.9 mill.; gain 5/31/98: $17.3 mill. ② Bef. acctg. change chrg. $7.8 mill. ③ Bef. extraord. credit $18.8 mill. ④ Incl. nonrecurr. loss of $21.2 mill., 2002. Restruct. chrg. of $64.6 mill., 2002; $6.5 mill., 2001.

OFFICERS:
J. P. McConnell, Chmn., C.E.O.
J. S. Christie, Pres., C.O.O.
J. T. Baldwin, V.P., C.F.O.
INVESTOR CONTACT: Investor Relations, (614) 438-3210
PRINCIPAL OFFICE: 1205 Dearborn Drive, Columbus, OH 43085

TELEPHONE NUMBER: (614) 438-3210
FAX: (614) 438-3256
WEB: www.worthingtonindustries.com
NO. OF EMPLOYEES: 8,000 (approx.)
SHAREHOLDERS: 10,717
ANNUAL MEETING: In Sept.
INCORPORATED: DE, Dec., 1996; reincorp., OH, Sept., 1998

INSTITUTIONAL HOLDINGS:
No. of Institutions: 223
Shares Held: 39,623,216
% Held: 46.2
INDUSTRY: Cold finishing of steel shapes (SIC: 3316)
TRANSFER AGENT(S): Fleet National Bank, Boston, MA

WPS RESOURCES CORPORATION

EXCH.	SYM.	REC. PRICE	P/E RATIO	YLD.	MKT. CAP.	RANGE (52-WK.)	'02 Y/E PR.	DIV. ACH.
NYSE	WPS	37.83 (2/28/03)	11.0	5.7%	$1.19 bill.	42.68 - 30.47	38.82	44 yrs.

UPPER MEDIUM GRADE. IN THE LONG TERM, THE COMPANY EXPECTS EARNINGS TO GROW FROM 6.0% TO 8.0% ON AN AVERAGE ANNUALIZED BASIS.

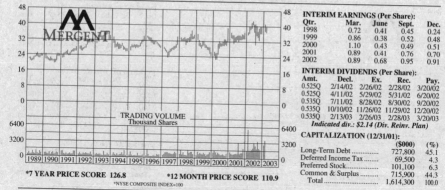

*7 YEAR PRICE SCORE 126.8 ***12 MONTH PRICE SCORE 110.9**
*NYSE COMPOSITE INDEX=100

INTERIM EARNINGS (Per Share):

Qtr.	Mar.	June	Sept.	Dec.
1998	0.72	0.41	0.45	0.24
1999	0.86	0.38	0.52	0.48
2000	1.10	0.43	0.49	0.51
2001	0.89	0.41	0.76	0.70
2002	0.89	0.68	0.95	0.91

INTERIM DIVIDENDS (Per Share):

Amt.	Decl.	Ex.	Rec.	Pay.
0.525Q	2/14/02	2/26/02	2/28/02	3/20/02
0.525Q	4/11/02	5/29/02	5/31/02	6/20/02
0.535Q	7/11/02	8/28/02	8/30/02	9/20/02
0.535Q	10/10/02	11/26/02	11/29/02	12/20/02
0.535Q	2/13/03	2/26/03	2/28/03	3/20/03

Indicated div.: $2.14 (Div. Reinv. Plan)

CAPITALIZATION (12/31/01):

	($000)	(%)
Long-Term Debt	727,800	45.1
Deferred Income Tax	69,500	4.3
Preferred Stock	101,100	6.3
Common & Surplus	715,900	44.3
Total	1,614,300	100.0

BUSINESS:

WPS Resources Corporation (formerly Wisconsin Public Service Corp.) operates as a holding company with both regulated utility and non-regulated business units. The Company's principal wholly-owned subsidiaries are: Wisconsin Public Service Corporation (WPSC), a regulated electric and gas utility in Wisconsin and Michigan; Upper Peninsula Power Company, a regulated electric utility in Michigan; and WPS Energy Service, Inc. and WPS Power Development, Inc., both non-regulated subsidiaries. As of 12/31/01, WPSC served 400,862 electric retail and 290,353 gas retail customers.

RECENT DEVELOPMENTS:

For the year ended 12/31/02, net income jumped 39.4% to $112.5 million compared with $80.7 million the previous year. Results for 2002 and 2001 included after-tax gains of $22.8 million and $1.3 million, respectively, on the sale of part of the synthetic fuel operations of WPS Power Development, which occurred in the fourth quarter of 2001. Earnings benefited from warmer-than-normal weather during the heating season in 2001. Total revenues slipped 1.0% to $2.67 billion. Nonregulated revenue declined 4.5% to $1.62 billion, while utility revenue climbed 7.7% to $1.05 billion. Operating income advanced 40.8% to $151.1 million from $107.3 million in 2001.

PROSPECTS:

In the long term, the Company expects earnings to grow from 6.0% to 8.0% on an average annualized basis. For 2003, the Company estimates earnings per share to be in the range of $2.75 to $2.95. Looking ahead, the Company should continue to benefit from the acquisition of gas utility operations in the spring of 2001 and a rate increase approved by regulators. Separately, on 12/17/02, Wisconsin Public Service Corporation, a subsidiary of WPS, announced that it closed a prior $120.0 million agreement to buy the 180-megawatt De Pere Energy Center from Calpine Corporation.

ANNUAL FINANCIAL DATA:

FISCAL YEAR	TOT. REVS. ($mill.)	NET INC. ($mill.)	TOT. ASSETS ($mill.)	OPER. PROFIT %	NET PROFIT %	NET INC./ NET PROP. %	NET INC./ TOT. CAP. %	RET. ON EQUITY %	ACCUM. DEPR./ GROSS PROP. %	EARN. PER SH. $	TANG. BK. VAL. $	DIV. PER SH. $	DIV. PAYOUT %	PRICE RANGE	AVG. P/E RATIO	AVG. YIELD %
p12/31/02	2,674.9	① 112.5	3,207.9							① 3.42		2.12	62.0	42.68 - 30.47	10.7	5.8
12/31/01	2,675.5	① 77.6	2,870.0	4.0	2.9	5.3	4.8	10.8	51.3	① 2.74	22.73	2.08	75.9	36.80 - 31.00	12.4	6.1
12/31/00	1,951.6	67.0	2,816.1	5.8	3.4	5.6	4.8	11.3	53.6	2.53	20.21	2.04	80.6	39.00 - 22.63	12.2	6.6
12/31/99	1,098.5	59.6	1,816.5	10.9	5.4	5.2	4.5	10.1	53.2	2.24	19.97	2.00	89.3	35.75 - 24.44	13.4	6.6
12/31/98	1,063.7	46.6	1,510.4	9.4	4.6	4.6	4.3	8.2	54.9	1.76	19.48	1.96	111.4	37.50 - 29.94	19.2	5.8
12/31/97	878.3	53.7	1,299.6	11.4	6.1	6.1	5.6	10.2	54.3	2.25	20.00	1.92	85.3	34.25 - 23.38	12.8	6.7
12/31/96	858.3	55.2	1,637.2	11.5	5.4	5.3	3.8	9.2	52.2	2.00	19.56	1.88	94.0	34.38 - 28.25	15.7	6.0
12/31/95	719.8	55.2	1,573.3	15.1	7.7	6.4	4.4	10.7	51.4	2.32	19.39	1.84	79.3	34.25 - 26.25	13.5	6.0
12/31/94	673.8	52.4	1,527.2	15.7	7.8	6.1	4.2	10.5	50.1	2.21	18.69	1.80	81.4	33.63 - 26.25	13.1	1.5
12/31/93	680.6	61.8	1,198.8	12.0	9.1	7.3	6.6	12.7	49.2	2.47	18.18	1.76	71.3	36.50 - 30.13	13.5	...

Statistics are as originally reported. ① Incl. after-tax gains of $22.8 mill., 2002; $1.3 mill., 2001, from the sale of part of the synthetic fuel operation of WPS Power Development

OFFICERS:
L. L. Weyers, Chmn., Pres., C.E.O.
J. P. O'Leary, Sr. V.P., C.F.O.
B. A. Johnson, Treas.

INVESTOR CONTACT: Donna M. Sheedy, Inv. Rel. Supervisor, (920) 433-1857

PRINCIPAL OFFICE: 700 North Adams Street, P.O. Box 19001, Green Bay, WI 54307-9001

TELEPHONE NUMBER: (920) 433-4901
FAX: (920) 433-1526
WEB: www.wpsr.com

NO. OF EMPLOYEES: 2,856 (avg.)

SHAREHOLDERS: 23,478

ANNUAL MEETING: In May

INCORPORATED: WI, July, 1883

INSTITUTIONAL HOLDINGS:
No. of Institutions: 158
Shares Held: 11,679,822
% Held: 36.6

INDUSTRY: Electric and other services combined (SIC: 4931)

TRANSFER AGENT(S): American Stock Transfer & Trust, Brooklyn, NY

WRIGLEY (WM.) JR. COMPANY

EXCH.	SYM.	REC. PRICE	P/E RATIO	YLD.	MKT. CAP.	RANGE (52-WK.)	'02 Y/E PR.	DIV. ACH.
NYSE	WWY	53.63 (2/28/03)	30.0	1.6%	$12.06 bill.	58.90 - 44.21	54.88	22 yrs.

HIGH GRADE. NEW PRODUCT INITIATIVES SHOULD CONTINUE TO DRIVE THE COMPANY'S RESULTS UPWARD IN 2003.

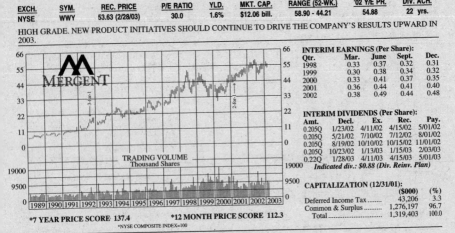

*7 YEAR PRICE SCORE 137.4 ***12 MONTH PRICE SCORE 112.3**
*NYSE COMPOSITE INDEX=100

INTERIM EARNINGS (Per Share):

Qtr.	Mar.	June	Sept.	Dec.
1998	0.33	0.37	0.32	0.31
1999	0.30	0.38	0.34	0.32
2000	0.33	0.41	0.37	0.35
2001	0.36	0.44	0.41	0.40
2002	0.38	0.49	0.44	0.48

INTERIM DIVIDENDS (Per Share):

Amt.	Decl.	Ex.	Rec.	Pay.
0.205Q	1/23/02	4/11/02	4/15/02	5/01/02
0.205Q	5/21/02	7/10/02	7/12/02	8/01/02
0.205Q	8/19/02	10/10/02	10/15/02	11/01/02
0.205Q	10/23/02	1/13/03	1/15/03	2/03/03
0.22Q	1/28/03	4/11/03	4/15/03	5/01/03

Indicated div.: $0.88 (Div. Reinv. Plan)

CAPITALIZATION (12/31/01):

	($000)	(%)
Deferred Income Tax	43,206	3.3
Common & Surplus	1,276,197	96.7
Total	1,319,403	100.0

BUSINESS:

Wm. Wrigley Jr. Company is the world's largest chewing gum producer. Main brands are WRIGLEY'S SPEARMINT, DOUBLEMINT, JUICY FRUIT, WINTERFRESH, BIG RED, EXTRA, FREEDENT and ECLIPSE. Additional brands include ORBIT, HUBBA BUBBA®, AIRWAVES, ICEWHITE, EXCEL, ARROWMINT, COOL CRUNCH, P.K. and COOL AIR. Through its Amurol Confections Company subsidiary, the Company also manufactures and markets various non-gum items,

such as a line of suckers, dextrose candy, liquid gel candy and hard roll candies. As of 12/31/02, Wrigley brands were produced in 14 factories, including three plants in North America four in Europe, one in Africa and five in the Asia/Pacific region. WWY's largest non-U.S. markets by shipments were Australia, Canada, China, France, Germany, Philippines, Poland, Russia, Taiwan and the United Kingdom.

RECENT DEVELOPMENTS:

For the year ended 12/31/02, net earnings advanced 10.6% to $401.5 million compared with $363.0 million in the previous year. Results for 2002 included a charge of about $10.0 million related to the exploration of a business combination with Hershey Foods Corporation. Net sales climbed 14.4% to $2.75 billion from $2.40 billion a year

earlier. The increase reflected favorable currency gains and strong growth in the Americas and overseas with worldwide shipment volume up 8.0% for 2002. Gross profit as percentage of net sales decreased to 58.1% from 58.5% the year before, reflecting somewhat higher product costs. Operating income increased 14.0% to $585.1 million.

PROSPECTS:

The Company continues to benefit from the strength of its established product brands, and anticipates that strong volume growth and a positive sales mix from a significant number of new product initiatives will drive results in 2003. Meanwhile, WWY has made substantial additional

investments in brand support, technology infrastructure and strategic initiatives to ensure long-term performance. Separately, the Company recently signed Grupo Bimbo to exclusively distribute WWY's products in Mexico, taking advantage of Bimbo's established distribution network.

ANNUAL FINANCIAL DATA:

FISCAL YEAR	TOT. REVS. ($mill.)	NET INC. ($mill.)	TOT. ASSETS ($mill.)	OPER. PROFIT %	NET PROFIT %	RET. ON EQUITY %	RET. ON ASSETS %	CURR. RATIO	EARN. PER SH.$	CASH FL. PER SH.$	TANG. BK. VAL.$	DIV. PER SH.$	PRICE RANGE		AVG. P/E RATIO	AVG. YIELD %
p12/31/02	2,746.3	③ 401.5		21.3	14.6				③ 1.78			0.81	58.90 - 44.21		29.0	1.6
12/31/01	2,429.6	363.0	1,765.6	21.1	14.9	28.4	20.6	2.7	1.61	1.91	5.67	0.74	53.30 - 42.94		29.9	1.5
12/31/00	2,145.7	328.9	1,574.7	21.6	15.3	29.0	20.9	2.9	1.45	1.70	5.02	0.70	48.31 - 29.94		27.0	1.8
12/31/99	2,079.2	308.2	1,547.7	21.4	14.8	27.1	19.9	3.2	1.33	1.59	4.97	0.67	50.31 - 33.25		31.4	1.6
12/31/98	2,023.4	② 304.5	1,520.9	21.3	15.0	26.3	20.0	3.9	② 1.32	1.55	4.98	0.65	52.16 - 35.47		33.3	1.5
12/31/97	1,954.2	① 271.6	1,343.1	20.4	13.9	27.6	20.2	3.5	① 1.17	1.39	4.25	0.58	41.03 - 27.28		29.2	1.7
12/31/96	1,850.6	① 230.3	1,233.5	20.5	12.4	25.7	18.7	3.3	① 1.00	1.20	3.87	0.51	31.44 - 24.19		27.9	1.8
12/31/95	1,769.7	223.7	1,099.2	19.9	12.6	28.1	20.4	3.1	0.97	1.15	3.43	0.48	27.00 - 21.44		25.1	2.0
12/31/94	1,661.3	① 230.5	978.8	21.4	13.9	33.5	23.6	3.0	① 0.99	1.17	2.96	0.45	26.94 - 19.06		23.2	2.0
12/31/93	1,440.4	174.9	815.3	19.5	12.1	30.4	21.5	3.2	0.75	0.90	2.47	0.38	23.06 - 14.75		25.2	2.0

Statistics are as originally reported. Adj. for 2-for-1 stk. split, 2/01. ① Incls. non-recurring net chrg. 12/31/97: $3.3 mill.; chrg. 12/31/96: $13.0 mill.; credit 12/31/94: $24.8 mill. ② Incls. one-time gain of $10.4 mill. ③ Incl. business combination exploration chrg. of $10.0 mill.

OFFICERS:
W. Wrigley Jr., Pres., C.E.O.
R. V. Waters III, Sr. V.P., C.F.O.
A. J. Schneider, V.P., Treas.

INVESTOR CONTACT: Shareholder Relations, (800) 874-0474

PRINCIPAL OFFICE: 410 North Michigan Avenue, Chicago, IL 60611

TELEPHONE NUMBER: (312) 644-2121
FAX: (312) 645-4083
WEB: www.wrigley.com
NO. OF EMPLOYEES: 10,800 (approx.)
SHAREHOLDERS: 38,100 (common); 3,215 (class B common)
ANNUAL MEETING: In March
INCORPORATED: DE, Oct., 1927

INSTITUTIONAL HOLDINGS:
No. of Institutions: 398
Shares Held: 85,367,446
% Held: 37.9

INDUSTRY: Chewing gum (SIC: 2067)

TRANSFER AGENT(S): EquiServe Trust Company, N.A., Jersey City, NJ

WYETH

EXCH.	SYM.	REC. PRICE	P/E RATIO	YLD.	MKT. CAP.	RANGE (52-WK.)	'02 Y/E PR.
NYSE	WYE	35.25 (2/28/03)	10.6	2.6%	$46.55 bill.	66.51 - 28.25	37.40

UPPER MEDIUM GRADE. IN 2003, THE COMPANY EXPECTS NET REVENUE GROWTH TO BE IN THE RANGE OF 6.0% TO 9.0%.

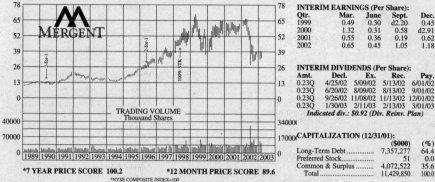

INTERIM EARNINGS (Per Share):

Qtr.	Mar.	June	Sept.	Dec.
1999	0.49	0.30	d2.20	0.45
2000	1.32	0.31	0.58	d2.91
2001	0.55	0.36	0.19	0.62
2002	0.65	0.45	1.05	1.18

INTERIM DIVIDENDS (Per Share):

Amt.	Decl.	Ex.	Rec.	Pay.
0.23Q	4/25/02	5/09/02	5/13/02	6/01/02
0.23Q	6/20/02	8/09/02	8/13/02	9/01/02
0.23Q	9/26/02	11/08/02	11/13/02	12/01/02
0.23Q	1/30/03	2/11/03	2/13/03	3/01/03

Indicated div.: $0.92 (Div. Reinv. Plan)

CAPITALIZATION (12/31/01):

	($000)	(%)
Long-Term Debt	7,357,277	64.4
Preferred Stock	51	0.0
Common & Surplus	4,072,522	35.6
Total	11,429,850	100.0

TRADING VOLUME
Thousand Shares

*7 YEAR PRICE SCORE 100.2   ***12 MONTH PRICE SCORE 89.6**

*NYSE COMPOSITE INDEX=100

BUSINESS:

Wyeth (formerly American Home Products Corporation) is one of the world's largest research-based pharmaceutical and health care product companies. WYE is engaged in the discovery, development, manufacturing and marketing of prescription drugs and over-the-counter medications. In addition, WYE is engaged in vaccines, biotechnology, and animal health care. Prescription drug subsidiaries include

Wyeth-Ayerst Laboratories, Whitehall-Robbins Healthcare, Fort, Dodge Animal Health and Scientific Protein Laboratories, Inc. In addition, WYE is the largest shareholder of Immunex Corporation, a biopharmaceutical company. WYE produces medications such as PREMARIN®, EFFEXOR®XR and ENBREL®. Pharmaceuticals accounted for 84.9% of 2002 sales.

RECENT DEVELOPMENTS:

For the year ended 12/31/02, net income leapt 94.6% to $4.45 billion compared with $2.29 billion the previous year. Results for 2002 included after-tax gains of $2.63 billion related to Immunex/Amgen common stock transactions, after-tax litigation charges of $910.0 million, and an after-tax special charge of $233.5 million. The 2001 results

included an after-tax litigation charge of $615.0 million. Net revenues rose 4.3% to $14.58 billion from $13.98 billion the year before. Worldwide pharmaceuticals net revenue climbed 6.0% to $12.39 billion, while consumer health care net revenue declined 3.0% to $2.20 billion.

PROSPECTS:

In 2003, the Company expects net revenue growth to be in the range of 6.0% to 9.0%. Furthermore, WYE estimates selling, general and administrative expenses and research and development expenses combined are projected to grow by less than the net revenue growth due primarily to

increased marketing for certain product lines such as EFFEXOR and ALAVERT and increased pension expense offset, in part, by continued cost management efforts, resulting from the restructuring program.

ANNUAL FINANCIAL DATA:

FISCAL YEAR	TOT. REVS. ($mill.)	NET INC. ($mill.)	TOT. ASSETS ($mill.)	OPER. PROFIT %	NET PROFIT %	RET. ON EQUITY %	RET. ON ASSETS %	CURR. RATIO	EARN. PER SH. $	CASH FL. PER SH. $	TANG. BK. VAL. $	DIV. PER SH. $	PRICE RANGE	AVG. P/E RATIO	AVG. YIELD %
p12/31/02	14,584.0	⑨ 4,447.2	...	...	...	...	...	...	⑨ 3.33	...	...	0.92	66.51 - 28.25	14.2	1.9
12/31/01	14,128.5	⑧ 2,285.3	22,967.9	19.4	16.2	56.1	9.9	1.3	⑧ 1.72	2.17	0.17	0.92	63.80 - 52.00	33.7	1.6
12/31/00	13,262.8	⑦ d901.0	21,092.5	...	...	...	...	1.0	⑦ d0.69	d0.28	...	0.92	65.25 - 39.38	...	1.8
12/31/99	13,550.2	⑥ d1,227.1	23,906.3	...	...	...	...	1.4	⑥ d0.94	d0.42	...	0.91	70.25 - 36.50	...	1.7
12/31/98	13,462.7	⑤ 2,474.3	20,857.8	21.7	18.4	25.7	11.9	1.9	⑤ 1.85	2.35	1.23	0.87	58.75 - 37.75	26.1	1.8
12/31/97	14,196.0	④ 2,043.1	21,391.5	22.9	14.4	23.4	9.6	1.7	④ 1.56	2.09	0.31	0.83	42.44 - 28.50	22.7	2.3
12/31/96	14,088.3	③ 1,883.4	20,869.2	21.1	13.4	26.7	9.0	1.7	③ 1.48	2.00	...	0.78	33.25 - 23.53	19.2	2.8
12/31/95	13,376.1	①② 1,680.4	21,477.9	17.4	12.6	29.7	7.8	1.8	①② 1.36	1.90	...	0.76	24.97 - 15.44	14.9	3.7
12/31/94	8,966.2	① 1,528.3	21,864.3	22.4	17.0	34.4	7.0	1.7	① 1.24	1.49	...	0.73	16.81 - 13.84	12.3	4.5
12/31/93	8,304.9	1,469.3	7,939.8	24.0	17.7	35.6	18.5	3.0	1.18	1.38	2.75	0.71	17.25 - 13.88	13.2	4.6

Statistics are as originally reported. Adj. for 2-for-1 stock split, 5/98 & 5/96. ① Incl. one-time chg. of $308.3 mil., 1995; & $97.0 mil., 1994. ② Incl. Amer. Cyanamid Co., a non-recurr. gain of $623.9 mil. & a spl. restr. chg. of $117.2 mil. ③ Incl. net gain on sale of bus. of $706.3 mil. & spl. chgs. of $697.9 mil. ④ Incl. a spec. net chg. of $180.0 mill. ⑤ Incl. a net gain of $330.8 mill. & a net restr. chg. of $343.6 mill. ⑥ Incl. a net spec. chg. of $53.0 mill. & a net chg. of $3.29 bill. of litigation brought by users of Pondimin & Redux, & oth. net chgs. ⑦ Incl. pre-tax credits of $1.71 bill. fr. the termin. merger agree. w/ Warner-Lambert & $2.06 bill fr. resale of Immunex stk., $7.50 bill. in litig. chrgs. & other chrgs. totaling $748.0 million. ⑧ Incl. a pre-tax litig. chrg. of $950.0 mill. ⑨ Incl. net non-recurr. after-tax gain. of $1.48 bill.

OFFICERS:
J. R. Stafford, Chmn.
R. Essner, Pres., C.E.O.
B. J. Poussot, Exec. V.P., C.F.O.

INVESTOR CONTACT: Justin R. Victoria, Investor Relations, (973) 660-5706

PRINCIPAL OFFICE: Five Giralda Farms, Madison, NJ 07940-0874

TELEPHONE NUMBER: (973) 660-5000
FAX: (973) 660-5012
WEB: www.wyeth.com
NO. OF EMPLOYEES: 52,289 (avg.)
SHAREHOLDERS: 64,653 (record)
ANNUAL MEETING: In Apr.
INCORPORATED: DE, Feb., 1926

INSTITUTIONAL HOLDINGS:
No. of Institutions: 972
Shares Held: 1,017,268,412
% Held: 76.7
INDUSTRY: Pharmaceutical preparations (SIC: 2834)

TRANSFER AGENT(S): Mellon Investor Services, Ridgefield Park, NJ

XCEL ENERGY, INC.

EXCH.	SYM.	REC. PRICE	P/E RATIO	YLD.	MKT. CAP.	RANGE (52-WK.)	'02 Y/E PR.
NYSE	XEL	11.09 (2/28/03)	...	6.8%	$3.83 bill.	26.71 - 5.12	11.00

LOWER MEDIUM GRADE. THE COMPANY IS IN THE PROCESS OF NEGOTIATING WITH CREDITORS TO REACH AN AGREEMENT ON A FINANCIAL RESTRUCTURING OF NRG ENERGY.

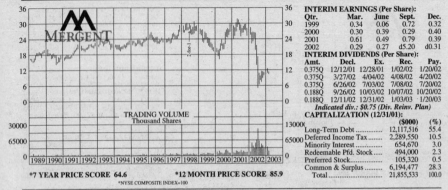

*7 YEAR PRICE SCORE 64.6   *12 MONTH PRICE SCORE 85.9
*NYSE COMPOSITE INDEX=100

INTERIM EARNINGS (Per Share):

Qtr.	Mar.	June	Sept.	Dec.
1999	0.34	0.06	0.72	0.32
2000	0.30	0.39	0.29	0.40
2001	0.61	0.49	0.79	0.39
2002	0.29	0.27	d5.20	d0.31

INTERIM DIVIDENDS (Per Share):

Amt.	Decl.	Ex.	Rec.	Pay.
0.375Q	12/12/01	12/28/01	1/02/02	1/20/02
0.375Q	3/27/02	4/04/02	4/08/02	4/20/02
0.375Q	6/26/02	7/03/02	7/08/02	7/20/02
0.188Q	9/26/02	10/03/02	10/07/02	10/20/02
0.188Q	12/11/02	12/31/02	1/03/03	1/20/03

Indicated div.: $0.75 (Div. Reinv. Plan)

CAPITALIZATION (12/31/01):

	($000)	(%)
Long-Term Debt	12,117,516	55.4
Deferred Income Tax	2,289,550	10.5
Minority Interest	654,670	3.0
Redeemable Pfd. Stock	494,000	2.3
Preferred Stock	105,320	0.5
Common & Surplus	6,194,477	28.3
Total	21,855,533	100.0

BUSINESS:

Xcel Energy, Inc. (formerly Northern States Power Company), is a public utility holding company formed on 8/18/00 upon the merger of New Century Energies and Northern States Power Company. As of 3/7/03, XEL provided energy-related products and services to 3.2 million electricity customers and 1.7 million natural gas customers. XEL, with operations in 12 Western and Midwestern states, has six public utility subsidiaries: Southwestern Public Service Company, Public Service Company of Colorado, Cheyenne Light, Fuel and Power Company, Northern States Power Company Minnesota, Northern States Power Company Wisconsin, and Black Mountain Gas Company. XEL also operates numerous non-utility subsidiaries. On 6/3/02, XEL acquired NRG Energy, Inc.

RECENT DEVELOPMENTS:

For the year ended 12/31/02, net loss was $2.01 billion versus net income of $795.0 million the previous year. Results for 2002 included pre-tax charges of $3.00 billion for asset impairments and disposal losses. Also, results for 2002 included a tax benefit of $676.0 million for XEL's investment in NRG. Total operating revenue dropped 11.2% to $10.34 billion from $11.65 billion in 2001. Revenue from electric and gas utility and trading margins slid 19.9% to $6.84 billion from $8.54 billion in 2001. NGR revenue and equity income rose 2.3% to $3.10 billion.

PROSPECTS:

On 1/17/03, XEL completed the sale of Viking Gas Transmission, including Viking's one-third interest in Guardian Pipeline, to Northern Border Partners, L.P. This action, together with a new $100.0 million, nine-month term loan facility, increases XEL's liquidity to about $300.0 million. Separately, XEL noted that it is negotiating with NRG's creditors to reach an agreement on a financial restructuring of NRG. However, there is no assurance that NRG's creditors will accept any restructuring plan, or whether NRG's lenders and bondholders will forebear from exercising any or all remedies available to them, including acceleration of NRG's indebtedness, commencement of involuntary proceeding in bankruptcy and, in the case of certain lenders, realization on the collateral for their indebtedness.

ANNUAL FINANCIAL DATA:

FISCAL YEAR	TOT. REVS. ($mill.)	NET INC. ($mill.)	TOT. ASSETS ($mill.)	OPER. PROFIT %	NET PROFIT %	NET INC./ NET PROP. %	NET INC./ TOT. CAP. %	RET. ON EQUITY %	ACCUM. DEPR./ GROSS PROP. %	EARN. PER SH.$	TANG. BK. VAL.$	DIV. PER SH.$	DIV. PAYOUT %	PRICE RANGE	AVG. P/E RATIO	AVG. YIELD %
p12/31/02	10,341.0	⑥ d2,006.0								⑥ d5.26	1.31	...	28.49 – 5.12	...	7.8
12/31/01	15,028.2	⑤ 784.7	28,735.1	12.9	5.2	3.7	3.6	12.5	31.2	⑤ 2.27	17.91	1.50	66.1	31.85 – 24.19	12.3	5.4
12/31/00	11,591.8	④ 545.8	21,768.8	13.6	4.7	3.6	3.5	9.6	36.4	④ 1.60	16.32	1.47	91.8	30.00 – 16.13	14.4	6.4
③ 12/31/99	2,869.0	② 224.3	9,767.7	12.0	7.8	5.0	3.1	8.4	54.5	② 1.43	15.97	1.44	100.7	27.94 – 19.31	16.5	6.1
12/31/98	2,819.2	282.4	7,396.3	12.9	10.0	6.4	5.2	10.9	53.4	1.84	15.62	1.42	77.2	30.81 – 25.69	15.4	5.0
12/31/97	2,733.7	① 237.3	7,144.1	13.2	8.7	5.4	4.4	9.2	51.9	① 1.61	15.27	1.40	86.6	29.44 – 22.25	16.1	5.4
12/31/96	2,654.2	274.5	6,636.9	13.8	10.3	6.3	5.8	11.6	50.4	1.91	14.71	1.36	71.5	26.69 – 22.25	12.8	5.6
12/31/95	2,568.6	275.8	6,228.6	13.5	10.7	6.4	5.9	12.2	48.7	1.96	14.24	1.33	68.1	24.75 – 21.25	11.7	5.8
12/31/94	2,486.5	243.5	5,953.6	12.4	9.8	5.7	5.5	11.4	47.3	1.73	13.57	1.30	75.4	23.50 – 19.38	12.4	6.1
12/31/93	2,404.0	211.7	5,587.7	12.6	8.8	5.0	5.1	10.2	45.8	1.51	13.13	1.27	84.4	23.94 – 20.06	14.6	5.8

Statistics are as originally reported. Adj. for stk. splits: 2-for-1, 6/1/98 ① Incl. non-recurr. chrg. $29.0 mill. fr. termination of merger. ② Incl. spec. chrgs. of $31.1 mill. ③ Results for 12/31/99 and prior are for Northern States Power Company. ④ Incl. spec. chrgs. rel. to merger of $241.0 mill., excl. extraord. item of $19.0 mill. ⑤ Incl. spec. chrgs. of $62.2 mill.; excl. extraord. gain $10.3 mill. ⑥ Incl. $3.00 billion for asset impair. & a tax benefit of $676.0 mill.

OFFICERS:
J. J. Howard, Chmn.
W. H. Brunetti, Pres., C.E.O.
R. C. Kelley, V.P., C.F.O.

INVESTOR CONTACT: Richard J. Kolkmann, Dir. Inv. Rel., (612) 215-4559

PRINCIPAL OFFICE: 8000 Nicollet Mall, Minneapolis, MN 55402

TELEPHONE NUMBER: (612) 330-5500
FAX: (612) 330-5688
WEB: www.xcelenergy.com

NO. OF EMPLOYEES: 16,595 (avg.)

SHAREHOLDERS: 134,410

ANNUAL MEETING: In April

INCORPORATED: MN, June, 1909

INSTITUTIONAL HOLDINGS:
No. of Institutions: 337
Shares Held: 181,528,639
% Held: 45.5

INDUSTRY: Electric and other services combined (SIC: 4931)

TRANSFER AGENT(S): Wells Fargo Shareowner Services, South St. Paul, MN

XEROX CORPORATION

EXCH.	SYM.	REC. PRICE	P/E RATIO	YLD.	MKT. CAP.	RANGE (52-WK.)	'02 Y/E PR.
NYSE	XRX	9.00 (2/28/03)	30.0	...	$6.50 bill.	11.15 - 4.20	8.05

SPECULATIVE GRADE. THE COMPANY ANTICIPATES EARNINGS OF BETWEEN $0.50 AND $0.55 PER SHARE FOR 2003.

MERGENT

TRADING VOLUME
Thousand Shares

*7 YEAR PRICE SCORE 30.0   *12 MONTH PRICE SCORE 121.0
*NYSE COMPOSITE INDEX=100

INTERIM EARNINGS (Per Share):

Qtr.	Mar.	June	Sept.	Dec.
1998	0.42	d1.10	0.53	0.85
1999	0.48	0.62	0.47	0.41
2000	d0.38	0.19	d0.26	d0.19
2001	0.23	d0.43	d0.29	d0.01
2002	0.12	0.12	0.05	0.01

INTERIM DIVIDENDS (Per Share):

Amt.	Decl.	Ex.	Rec.	Pay.
Last dist. 0.05Q, 4/01/01				

CAPITALIZATION (12/31/01):

	($000)	(%)
Long-Term Debt	10,128,000	80.7
Preferred Stock	605,000	4.8
Common & Surplus	1,820,000	14.5
Total	12,553,000	100.0

BUSINESS:

Xerox Corporation is engaged in the developing, manufacturing, marketing and servicing of document processing products and systems. XRX distributes its products in the Western Hemisphere through divisions and wholly-owned subsidiaries, and in Europe, Africa, the Middle East, India and parts of Asia through Xerox Limited. In the Pacific Rim, Australia and New Zealand, Xerox products are distributed by Fuji Xerox Co. Ltd., an unconsolidated joint venture owned 75.0% by Fuji Photo Film Co., Ltd. and 25.0% by Xerox Limited, as of 12/31/02.

RECENT DEVELOPMENTS:

For the year ended 12/31/02, XRX reported income of $154.0 million, before a $63.0 million accounting change charge, compared with a loss of $92.0 million, before a $2.0 million accounting change charge, in the prior year. Results included pre-tax charges of $670.0 million and $715.0 million in 2002 and 2001, respectively, related to restructuring and asset impairments. Results for 2001 also included a $777.0 million pre-tax gain, stemming primarily from the sale of half of XRX's interest in Fuji Xerox. Total revenues slipped 6.8% to $15.85 billion from $17.01 billion in the previous year, due in part to the exit from the small office/home office equipment business in 2001 and declines in developing markets operations. Sales declined 9.3% to $6.75 billion, while service, outsourcing and rental revenues slid 4.0% to $8.10 billion. Comparisons were made with restated prior-year results.

PROSPECTS:

The Company is targeting full-year 2003 earnings of between $0.50 and $0.55 per share. Earnings are being positively affected by gross margin improvement stemming from the lower cost design of the Company's new products and increased manufacturing and service productivity, partially offset by planned lower new product pricing and competitive pricing pressures. Looking ahead, results should continue to benefit from the implementation of aggressive cost-reduction initiatives and higher equipment sales driven by new product introductions.

ANNUAL FINANCIAL DATA:

FISCAL YEAR	TOT. REVS. ($mill.)	NET INC. ($mill.)	TOT. ASSETS ($mill.)	OPER. PROFIT %	NET PROFIT %	RET. ON EQUITY %	RET. ON ASSETS %	CURR. RATIO	EARN. PER SH. $	CASH FL. PER SH. $	TANG. BK. VAL. $	DIV. PER SH. $	PRICE RANGE	AVG. P/E RATIO	AVG. YIELD %
p12/31/02	15,849.0	⑥ 154.0			...	...	...		⑥ 0.10			...	11.45 - 4.20	78.3	...
12/31/01	17,008.0	⑤ d109.0	27,689.0	0.4	...	...	...	1.2	⑤ d0.17	1.74	0.52	0.10	11.35 - 4.69	...	1.2
12/31/00	18,701.0	④ d257.0	29,475.0	...	...	...	...	2.1	④ d0.44	1.04	2.88	0.80	29.31 - 3.75	...	4.8
12/31/99	19,228.0	1,424.0	28,814.0	12.1	7.4	25.5	4.9	1.5	1.96	3.20	4.79	0.78	63.94 - 19.00	21.2	1.9
12/31/98	19,449.0	③ 585.0	30,024.0	5.2	3.0	10.6	1.9	1.5	③ 0.80	2.08	4.76	0.70	60.81 - 33.00	58.7	1.5
12/31/97	18,166.0	1,452.0	27,732.0	12.3	8.0	25.5	5.2	1.4	2.02	3.03	5.54	0.63	44.00 - 25.75	17.3	1.8
12/31/96	17,378.0	1,206.0	26,818.0	11.6	6.9	23.7	4.5	1.4	1.75	2.88	5.74	0.56	29.13 - 19.00	14.0	2.3
12/31/95	16,611.0	② 1,174.0	25,969.0	11.9	7.1	25.3	4.5	1.4	② 1.70	2.69	5.02	0.50	24.10 - 16.08	11.8	2.5
12/31/94	17,837.0	794.0	38,585.0	10.0	4.5	15.9	2.1	3.2	1.12	2.30	6.12	0.50	18.79 - 14.63	14.8	3.0
12/31/93	17,410.0	① d189.0	38,750.0	11.5	...	...	...	3.7	① d0.41	0.77	5.90	0.50	15.00 - 11.65	...	3.8

Statistics are as originally reported. Adj. for stk. splits: 2-for-1, 2/99; 3-for-1, 6/96. ① Bef. $63 mil cr. fr. discont. opers. & incl. $813 mil special chg. ② Bef. $1.65 bil gain fr. discont. opers. & incl. $98 mil Brazilian tax benefit. ③ Bef. $190 mil chg. fr. discont. opers. & incl. $1.11 bil after-tax restr. chg. ④ Incl. $540 mil pre-tax restr. chg.; $170 mil pre-tax chg. rel. to XRX's Mexican opers.; $119 mil pre-tax inventory chgs.; $27 mil pre-tax chg. for Tektronix in-process R&D; $200 mil pre-tax gain fr. sale of China opers.; & $21 mil gain fr. affil. sale of stk. ⑤ Bef. $40 mil extraord. gain and $2 mil acctg. chg.; incl. $715 mil pre-tax restr. and asset impair.; & $773 mil pre-tax gain fr sale of 50% int. in Fuji Xerox; & $4 mil gain fr. affil. sale of stk. ⑥ Bef. $63 mil acctg. chg. & incl. $670 mil pre-tax restr. and asset impair chg.

OFFICERS:
A. M. Mulcahy, Chmn., C.E.O.
L. A. Zimmerman, Sr. V.P., C.F.O.

INVESTOR CONTACT: Leslie F. Varon, Dir., Investor Relations, (203) 968-4406

PRINCIPAL OFFICE: 800 Long Ridge Road, P.O. Box 1600, Stamford, CT 06904-1600

TELEPHONE NUMBER: (203) 968-3000
FAX: (203) 968-4566
WEB: www.xerox.com
NO. OF EMPLOYEES: 69,900 (approx.)
SHAREHOLDERS: 59,830
ANNUAL MEETING: In Aug.
INCORPORATED: NY, Apr., 1906

INSTITUTIONAL HOLDINGS:
No. of Institutions: 332
Shares Held: 661,162,222
% Held: 89.9
INDUSTRY: Photographic equipment and supplies (SIC: 3861)
TRANSFER AGENT(S): BankBoston N.A., Boston, MA

YORK INTERNATIONAL CORPORATION

EXCH.	SYM.	REC. PRICE	P/E RATIO	YLD.	MKT. CAP.	RANGE (52-WK.)	'02 Y/E PR.
NYSE	YRK	21.40 (2/28/03)	10.5	2.8%	$0.84 bill.	39.08 - 20.70	25.57

MEDIUM GRADE. THE COMPANY IS FACING CHALLENGING SHORT-TERM ECONOMIC CONDITIONS IN ADDITION TO SIGNIFICANT EXTERNAL COST INCREASES.

*7 YEAR PRICE SCORE 84.3   *12 MONTH PRICE SCORE 84.9

*NYSE COMPOSITE INDEX=100

INTERIM EARNINGS (Per Share):

Qtr.	Mar.	June	Sept.	Dec.
1997	0.34	0.97	0.55	d0.81
1998	0.36	1.03	1.16	0.81
1999	0.44	1.01	0.09	0.36
2000	0.60	1.20	0.40	0.59
2001	d0.23	0.84	0.42	0.14
2002	d0.38	1.21	0.65	0.55

INTERIM DIVIDENDS (Per Share):

Amt.	Decl.	Ex.	Rec.	Pay.
0.15Q	3/08/02	3/18/02	3/20/02	3/29/02
0.15Q	5/23/02	6/17/02	6/19/02	6/28/02
0.15Q	9/04/02	9/16/02	9/18/02	9/27/02
0.15Q	12/05/02	12/16/02	12/18/02	12/30/02
0.15Q	3/06/03	3/17/03	3/19/03	3/28/03

Indicated div.: $0.60 (Div. Reinv. Plan)

CAPITALIZATION (12/31/01):

	($000)	(%)
Long-Term Debt	724,378	49.5
Common & Surplus	739,434	50.5
Total	1,463,812	100.0

BUSINESS:

York International Corporation is a full-line, global manufacturer of heating, ventilating, air conditioning and refrigeration (HVAC&R) products. The Company is one of the largest independent suppliers of HVAC&R equipment in the U.S. As of 2/18/03, the Company's products were sold in more than 125 countries. Engineered Systems products (46.1% of 2002 sales) consist of large institutional heating, air conditioning, process cooling, industrial and thermal storage equipment. Refrigeration products (23.0%) include refrigeration and gas-compression equipment serving the food, beverage, marine, chemical and petrochemical processing industries. Unitary products (18.2%) include central air conditioning systems, heat pumps, gas and oil furnaces, and indoor air-quality accessories. Bristol compressors (12.7%) are used in air conditioning and heat pump systems.

RECENT DEVELOPMENTS:

For the year ended 12/31/02, income leapt 76.5% to $81.2 million compared with net income of $46.0 million in 2001. Results included restructuring credits of $111,000 in 2002 and charges of $70.5 million in 2001. Results for 2002 included a loss on divestitures of $10.3 million. Net sales slid 2.0% to $3.84 billion due to weak commercial equipment markets. Revenues for the Engineered Systems group decreased 3.2% to $1.87 billion. Revenues for the York Refrigeration group slid 0.6% to $931.2 million, while revenues for the Unitary Products group fell 2.5% to $736.8 million. Revenues for Bristol Compressors advanced 1.1% to $515.4 million.

PROSPECTS:

Given the current economic and political environments, the Company expects weak markets to continue to adversely affect results in 2003. This is expected to result in continued weak equipment markets with pricing and margin levels remaining consistent with 2002. YRK expects its service businesses to continue to grow and to realize further benefits from cost reduction actions implemented in 2002. Meanwhile, externally driven cost increases in pension expense, insurance and medical costs and sharply rising steel prices will substantially offset the realized benefits during the year. Consequently, YRK expects full-year 2003 earnings per share of about $2.50.

ANNUAL FINANCIAL DATA:

FISCAL YEAR	TOT. REVS. ($mill.)	NET INC. ($mill.)	TOT. ASSETS ($mill.)	OPER. PROFIT %	NET PROFIT %	RET. ON EQUITY %	RET. ON ASSETS %	CURR. RATIO	EARN. PER SH.$	CASH FL. PER SH.$	TANG. BK. VAL.$	DIV. PER SH.$	PRICE RANGE	AVG. P/E RATIO	AVG. YIELD %
p12/31/02	3,843.4	⑤ 81.2							⑤ 2.04			0.60	39.08 - 21.35	14.8	2.0
12/31/01	3,930.7	④ 46.0	2,572.5	2.6	1.2	6.2	1.8	1.6	④ 1.17	3.39	2.24	0.60	40.00 - 26.65	28.5	1.8
12/31/00	3,897.4	② 106.6	2,774.2	4.3	2.7	14.2	3.8	1.6	② 2.78	5.18	1.44	0.60	30.88 - 18.13	8.8	2.4
12/31/99	3,866.6	①② 76.8	2,874.5	4.2	2.0	10.5	2.7	1.5	①② 1.93	4.14	...	0.60	47.50 - 21.00	17.7	1.8
12/31/98	3,289.2	136.5	2,106.5	7.0	4.1	18.7	6.5	1.7	3.36	5.20	9.84	0.48	52.75 - 27.50	11.9	1.2
12/31/97	3,193.7	③ 47.4	1,996.3	3.6	1.5	7.3	2.4	1.8	③ 1.10	2.70	7.44	0.48	55.38 - 37.63	42.3	1.0
12/31/96	3,218.5	147.9	2,074.8	7.4	4.6	19.0	7.1	1.7	3.37	4.89	9.86	0.36	57.00 - 43.88	15.0	0.7
12/31/95	2,929.9	② d96.1	1,927.0	...	...	...	...	1.5	② d2.36	d0.85	6.37	0.24	48.50 - 34.13	...	0.6
12/31/94	2,421.9	89.8	1,588.0	7.1	3.7	17.0	5.7	1.4	2.40	3.73	3.52	0.16	42.50 - 33.88	15.9	0.4
12/31/93	2,031.9	① 75.5	1,335.2	7.3	3.7	16.5	5.7	1.3	① 2.01	3.18	2.16	0.08	41.50 - 31.50	18.2	0.3

Statistics are as originally reported. ① Bef. after-tax acctg. chg., $442,000, 1999; $70.3 mill. ($1.87/sh), 1993. ② Incl. $26.9 mil pre-tax gain fr sale of Northfield Freezing & other one-time pre-tax chgs. of $49.7 mil, 2000; $54.5 mil pre-tax acq-rel. chg. & $9.6 mil pre-tax gain on sale of Viron Corp., 1999; impair. chrg. $244.5 mill., 1995. ③ Incl. $75.1 mil chg. for facil. closings & downsizing of German opers. ④ Incl. nonrecurr. chrg. of $70.5 mill. ⑤ Bef. acctg. change chrg. of $179.4 mill., but incl. restruct. gain of $111,000 and loss on divest. of $10.3 mill.

OFFICERS:
G. C. McDonough, Chmn.
M. R. Young, Pres., C.E.O.
C. D. Myers, V.P., C.F.O.
INVESTOR CONTACT: David Myers, V.P.,
C.F.O., (717) 771-6183
PRINCIPAL OFFICE: 631 South Richland
Avenue, York, PA 17403

TELEPHONE NUMBER: (717) 771-7890
FAX: (717) 771-7381
WEB: www.york.com
NO. OF EMPLOYEES: 23,600 (approx.)
SHAREHOLDERS: 4,792
ANNUAL MEETING: In May
INCORPORATED: DE, 1874

INSTITUTIONAL HOLDINGS:
No. of Institutions: 173
Shares Held: 34,636,830
% Held: 87.8
INDUSTRY: Refrigeration and heating equipment (SIC: 3585)
TRANSFER AGENT(S): Mellon Investor Services, Ridgefield Park, NJ

YUM! BRANDS, INC.

EXCH.	SYM.	REC. PRICE	P/E RATIO	YLD.	MKT. CAP.	RANGE (52-WK.)	'02 Y/E PR.
NYSE	YUM	23.81 (2/28/03)	12.7	...	$6.95 bill.	33.17 - 20.35	24.22

MEDIUM GRADE. IN 2003, THE COMPANY EXPECTS EARNINGS PER SHARE OF AT LEAST $2.00 AND REVENUE GROWTH OF 7.0% TO 8.0%.

*7 YEAR PRICE SCORE N/A   *12 MONTH PRICE SCORE 93.9

*NYSE COMPOSITE INDEX=100

INTERIM EARNINGS (Per Share):

Qtr.	Mar.	June	Sept.	Dec.
1998	0.18	0.39	0.41	0.48
1999	0.33	0.55	0.62	0.47
2000	0.40	0.36	0.20	0.43
2001	0.30	0.38	0.41	0.54
2002	0.40	0.45	0.47	0.56

INTERIM DIVIDENDS (Per Share):

Amt.	Decl.	Ex.	Rec.	Pay.
100% STK	5/07/02	6/18/02	6/06/02	6/17/02

CAPITALIZATION (12/29/01):

	($000)	(%)
Long-Term Debt	1,552,000	93.7
Common & Surplus	104,000	6.3
Total	1,656,000	100.0

BUSINESS:

Yum! Brands, Inc. (formerly Tricon Global Restaurants, Inc.) operates and franchises KFC, Pizza Hut and Taco Bell as well as Long John Silver's and A&W All-American Food restaurants, which were acquired in May 2002. Each of YUM's operating restaurant divisions is engaged in the operation, development, franchising and licensing of a system of both traditional and non-traditional quick-service-

restaurant units. Non-traditional units include express units and kiosks, which have a more limited menu and operate in non-traditional locations like airports, gas and convenience stores and colleges. The Company owned, franchised and licensed nearly 33,000 restaurants worldwide at 2/27/03. On 10/6/97, YUM was spun off from PepsiCo Inc.

RECENT DEVELOPMENTS:

For the year ended 12/28/02, net income advanced 18.5% to $583.0 million from $492.0 million the year before. Results for 2002 and 2001 included one-time net gains of $27.0 million and $3.0 million, and net charges from facility actions of $32.0 million and $1.0 million, respectively.

Total revenues increased 11.6% to $7.76 billion from $6.95 billion in 2001. Company sales grew 12.3% to $6.89 billion, while franchise and license fees climbed 6.3% to $866.0 million. Blended same-store sales at YUM's U.S. restaurants increased 4.0% versus the previous year.

PROSPECTS:

During 2002, the Company opened a record 1,051 systemwide international traditional restaurants. In 2003, YUM expects net growth in international restaurants of 5.0% to 6.0%. Looking ahead, in 2003, the Company expects earnings per share of at least $0.38 and revenue growth of 9.0% to 10.0% in the first quarter, and earnings per share of at least $2.00 and revenue growth of 7.0% to 8.0% for the full year. These increases reflect the positive

impact of the acquisitions of Long John Silver's and A&W All-American Food restaurants, which were acquired in May 2002. Additionally, international system sales are anticipated to increase 7.0% prior to foreign currency conversion, primarily due to growth from the KFC and Pizza Hut brands. Meanwhile, cash flow from ongoing operations is expected to total more than $1.00 billion.

ANNUAL FINANCIAL DATA:

FISCAL YEAR	TOT. REVS. ($mill.)	NET INC. ($mill.)	TOT. ASSETS ($mill.)	OPER. PROFIT %	NET PROFIT %	RET. ON EQUITY %	RET. ON ASSETS %	CURR. RATIO	EARN. PER SH. $	CASH FL. PER SH. $	PRICE RANGE	AVG. P/E RATIO
12/28/02	7,757.0	④ 583.0							④ 1.88		33.17 - 20.35	14.2
12/29/01	6,953.0	④ 492.0	4,388.0	12.8	7.1	473.1	11.2	0.3	④ 1.62	2.78	26.66 - 15.78	13.1
12/30/00	7,093.0	③ 413.0	4,149.0	12.1	5.8	...	10.0	0.6	③ 1.39	2.57	19.28 - 11.78	11.2
12/25/99	7,822.0	② 627.0	3,961.0	15.9	8.0	...	15.8	0.4	② 1.96	3.17	36.94 - 17.50	13.9
12/26/98	8,468.0	445.0	4,531.0	12.1	5.3	...	9.8	0.4	1.42	2.76	25.44 - 12.53	13.4
12/27/97	9,681.0	① d111.0	5,098.0	2.5	...	...	...	0.4	① d0.36	...	20.00 - 13.94	...
12/28/96	10,232.0	① d53.0	6,520.0	3.6	...	...	...	0.7	...	...	...	...
12/30/95	10,250.0	d132.0	6,908.0	2.5	...	...	...	0.3	...	...	...	...
12/31/94	9,565.0	119.0	...	6.1	1.2	...	...	...	...	...	...	...

Statistics are as originally reported. Adj. for 100% stk. div., 6/17/02. ① Incl. non-recurr. chrg. 1997, $174.0 mill.; 1996, $246.0 mill. ② Incl. after-tax net gain of $226.0 mill. & after-tax non-recurr. chrgs. totaling $29.0 mill. ③ Incl. after-tax net gain of $68.0 mill. & after-tax unusual chrgs. of $106.0 mill. ④ Inc. pre-tax net chrg. for facility actions of $32.0 mill., 2002; $1.0 mill., 2001 and pre-tax gain from unusual items of $27.0 mill., 2002; $3.0 mill., 2001.

OFFICERS:
D. C. Novak, Chmn., Pres., C.E.O.
D. J. Deno, C.F.O.
A. B. Lewis, C.O.O.
INVESTOR CONTACT: Tim Jerzyk, V.P., Investor Relations, (502) 874-2543
PRINCIPAL OFFICE: 1441 Gardiner Lane, Louisville, KY 40213

TELEPHONE NUMBER: (502) 874-8300
WEB: www.yum.com
NO. OF EMPLOYEES: 210,000 (avg.)
SHAREHOLDERS: 116,000 (approx.)
ANNUAL MEETING: In May
INCORPORATED: NC, 1997

INSTITUTIONAL HOLDINGS:
No. of Institutions: 395
Shares Held: 237,205,373
% Held: 80.3
INDUSTRY: Eating places (SIC: 5812)
TRANSFER AGENT(S): Boston EquiServe, LP, Boston, MA

ZENITH NATIONAL INSURANCE CORP.

EXCH.	SYM.	REC. PRICE	P/E RATIO	YLD.	MKT. CAP.	RANGE (52-WK.)	'02 Y/E PR.
NYSE	ZNT	20.01 (2/28/03)	133.4	5.0%	$371.2 mill.	32.25 - 19.50	23.52

LOWER MEDIUM GRADE. GOING FORWARD, THE COMPANY SHOULD BENEFIT FROM GROWING DEMAND FOR ITS WORKERS' COMPENSATION POLICIES.

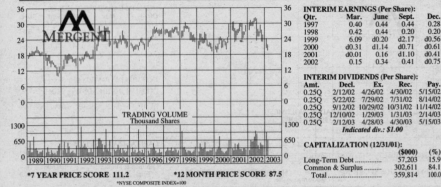

*7 YEAR PRICE SCORE 111.2 ***12 MONTH PRICE SCORE 87.5**

*NYSE COMPOSITE INDEX=100

INTERIM EARNINGS (Per Share):

Qtr.	Mar.	June	Sept.	Dec.
1997	0.40	0.44	0.44	0.28
1998	0.42	0.44	0.20	0.20
1999	6.09	d0.20	d2.17	d0.56
2000	d0.31	d1.14	d0.71	d0.61
2001	d0.01	0.16	d1.10	d0.41
2002	0.15	0.34	0.41	d0.75

INTERIM DIVIDENDS (Per Share):

Amt.	Decl.	Ex.	Rec.	Pay.
0.25Q	2/12/02	4/26/02	4/30/02	5/15/02
0.25Q	5/22/02	7/29/02	7/31/02	8/14/02
0.25Q	9/12/02	10/29/02	10/31/02	11/14/02
0.25Q	12/10/02	1/29/03	1/31/03	2/14/03
0.25Q	2/12/03	4/28/03	4/30/03	5/15/03

Indicated div.: $1.00

CAPITALIZATION (12/31/01):

	($000)	(%)
Long-Term Debt	57,203	15.9
Common & Surplus	302,611	84.1
Total	359,814	100.0

BUSINESS:

Zenith National Insurance Corp. is a holding company engaged through its wholly-owned insurance subsidiaries Zenith Insurance Company, ZNAT Insurance Company and Zenith Star Insurance Company, in the property-casualty insurance business. On 12/31/96, Zenith Insurance acquired Associated General Commerce Self-Insurers' Trust Fund, a Florida workers' compensation self-insurers'

fund. On 4/1/98, Zenith Insurance acquired RISCORP, Inc. As of 12/31/02, Fairfax Financial Holdings Limited, through its subsidiaries, owned approximately 42.0% of ZNT's common stock. Contributions to property/casualty premiums earned in 2002 were as follows: workers' compensation, 90.5% and reinsurance, 9.5%.

RECENT DEVELOPMENTS:

For the year ended 12/31/02, the Company posted income of $1.0 million, before income from discontinued operations of $9.2 million, versus a loss of $29.6 million, before income from discontinued operations of $3.7 million, the previous year. Results for 2002 included an after-tax charge of $30.1 million related to an increase in workers' compensation loss reserves. Total revenues advanced 12.1% to

$602.3 million from $537.2 million a year earlier. Revenues included a realized investment loss of $3.6 million in 2002 and a realized investment gain of $9.2 million in 2001. Net premiums earned climbed 16.8% to $557.1 million from $476.9 million the prior year. Net investment income slipped 4.6% to $48.8 million. Comparisons were made with restated prior-year figures.

PROSPECTS:

The Company is encouraged by the demand for its workers' compensation policies, the return to profitability and more favorable pricing trends that continue in both the workers' compensation and reinsurance businesses. These strengths are expected to continue into 2003. Healthcare and indemnity cost increases are necessitating continued

price increases, which are currently about 21.0% for 2003 and include 30.0% increases in California, up from 18.0% in the prior year. Meanwhile, the Company will continue to focus on profitability through maintaining underwriting discipline and pricing risk.

ANNUAL FINANCIAL DATA:

FISCAL YEAR	PREM. INC. ($mill.)	TOT. REVS. ($mill.)	NET INC. ($mill.)	TOT. ASSETS ($mill.)	TOT. INVST. ($mill.)	RET. ON REVS. %	RET. ON EQUITY %	RET. ON ASSETS %	EARN. PER SH.$	TANG. BK. VAL.$	AVG. YIELD %	DIV. PER SH.$	PRICE RANGE	AVG. P/E RATIO
p12/31/02	557.1	602.2	⑤ 1.0						⑤ 0.05		3.6	1.00	32.25 - 23.00	552.5
12/31/01	476.9	622.0	④ d23.8	1,540.1	944.7	...	...	...	④ d1.35	15.15	3.7	1.00	30.70 - 22.80	...
12/31/00	338.8	459.6	① d47.8	1,472.2	852.7	...	...	...	① d2.78	16.47	4.1	1.00	29.75 - 18.75	...
12/31/99	369.4	492.1	③ 54.1	1,573.8	901.7	11.0	15.3	3.4	③ 3.15	19.32	4.4	1.00	26.69 - 19.25	7.3
12/31/98	529.9	636.8	19.1	1,818.7	1,048.7	3.0	5.5	1.1	1.11	18.73	3.7	1.00	30.50 - 22.88	24.0
12/31/97	488.7	600.5	28.1	1,252.2	880.0	4.7	7.8	2.2	1.57	19.66	3.7	1.00	28.75 - 24.63	17.0
12/31/96	452.9	556.4	37.6	1,242.7	852.8	6.8	11.1	3.0	2.11	19.17	4.0	1.00	28.88 - 21.13	11.8
12/31/95	437.5	519.0	② 19.7	1,115.4	835.2	3.8	6.0	1.8	② 1.08	18.58	4.5	1.00	24.63 - 19.38	20.4
12/31/94	463.2	595.1	37.9	1,840.8	1,463.0	6.4	12.2	2.1	1.99	16.25	4.2	1.00	27.38 - 20.63	12.1
12/31/93	469.8	585.8	53.2	1,857.8	1,500.4	9.1	15.2	2.9	2.76	18.45	4.1	1.00	29.25 - 19.63	8.9

Statistics are as originally reported. ① Bef. extraord. gain $993,000 ② Bef. disc. oper. loss $13.1 mill. ③ Incl. $160.3 million gain from sale of CalFarm Insurance Co., chrg. $34.8 mill. associated with RISCORP-related adj. & chrg. $2.3 mill. for catastrophe losses. ④ Incl. chrg. of $27.1 mill. for catastrophe losses ⑤ Bef. inc. fr. disc. opers of $9.2 mill.; Incl. after-tax chrg. of $30.1 mill. for workers' comp. loss reserves.

OFFICERS:
S. R. Zax, Chmn., Pres.
W. J. Owen, Sr. V.P., C.F.O.
J. J. Tickner, Sr. V.P., Sec.
INVESTOR CONTACT: Juliane Sorice, Investor Relations, (818) 676-3925
PRINCIPAL OFFICE: 21255 Califa Street, Woodland Hills, CA 91367-5021

TELEPHONE NUMBER: (818) 713-1000
FAX: (818) 713-0177
WEB: www.thezenith.com
NO. OF EMPLOYEES: 1,200 (approx.)
SHAREHOLDERS: 247
ANNUAL MEETING: In May
INCORPORATED: DE, June, 1971

INSTITUTIONAL HOLDINGS:
No. of Institutions: 79
Shares Held: 8,175,168
% Held: 43.6
INDUSTRY: Fire, marine, and casualty insurance (SIC: 6331)
TRANSFER AGENT(S): Mellon Investor Services, Los Angeles, CA

ZIMMER HOLDINGS, INC.

EXCH.	SYM.	REC. PRICE	P/E RATIO	YLD.	MKT. CAP.	RANGE (52-WK.)	'02 Y/E PR.
NYSE	ZMH	44.39 (2/28/03)	33.6	...	$8.61 bill.	45.55 – 28.00	41.52

UPPER MEDIUM GRADE. FOR FULL-YEAR 2003, THE COMPANY EXPECTS EARNINGS OF AT LEAST $1.51 TO $1.53 PER SHARE.

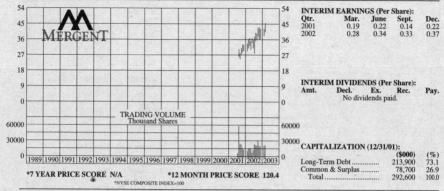

*7 YEAR PRICE SCORE N/A   ***12 MONTH PRICE SCORE 120.4**

*NYSE COMPOSITE INDEX=100

INTERIM EARNINGS (Per Share):

Qtr.	Mar.	June	Sept.	Dec.
2001	0.19	0.22	0.14	0.22
2002	0.28	0.34	0.33	0.37

INTERIM DIVIDENDS (Per Share):

Amt.	Decl.	Ex.	Rec.	Pay.
	No dividends paid.			

CAPITALIZATION (12/31/01):

	($000)	(%)
Long-Term Debt	213,900	73.1
Common & Surplus	78,700	26.9
Total	292,600	100.0

BUSINESS:

Zimmer Holdings, Inc. was formed as a result of the 7/25/01 spin-off of the orthopaedic businesses of Bristol-Meyers Squibb. The Company designs, develops, manufactures and markets orthopaedic reconstructive implants and trauma products. Orthopaedic reconstructive implants (77.4% of net sales in 2002) restore joint function lost due to disease or trauma in joints such as knees, hips, shoulders and elbows. Trauma products (9.7%) are devices used primarily to reattach or stabilize damaged bone and tissue to support the body's natural healing process. In addition, the Company manufactures and markets orthopaedic surgical products (12.9%) which include surgical supplies and instruments designed to aid in orthopaedic and general surgical procedures.

RECENT DEVELOPMENTS:

For the year ended 12/31/02, net earnings advanced 72.1% to $257.8 million compared with $149.8 million in the previous year. Earnings for 2001 were negatively affected by costs associated with ZMH's separation from Bristol-Meyers Squibb. Net sales increased 16.4% to $1.37 billion from $1.18 billion a year earlier. Sales of reconstructive implants climbed 19.8% to $1.06 billion. Sales of trauma products rose 4.3% to $133.8 million, while sales of orthopaedic surgical products grew 8.0% to $176.9 million. Gross profit jumped 19.9% to $1.03 billion from $857.0 million the year before. Operating income increased 61.5% to $400.9 million from $248.3 million in the prior year.

PROSPECTS:

On 3/14/03, the Company announced that it expects its financial performance for the first quarter of 2003 to significantly exceed previously issued guidance. The Company projects revenue for the quarter will be $15.0 million to $20.0 million higher than its earlier guidance of $367.0 million. The new projection indicates year-over-year sales growth of 20.0% or more for the first quarter. Earnings for the quarter are expected to be in the range of $0.37 to $0.38 per share, implying earnings per share growth of more than 30.0% versus the first quarter of 2002. For full-year 2003, ZMH expects earnings of at least $1.51 to $1.53 per share, with revenue growth of approximately 15.0% to 17.0%.

ANNUAL FINANCIAL DATA:

FISCAL YEAR	TOT. REVS. ($mill.)	NET INC. ($mill.)	TOT. ASSETS ($mill.)	OPER. PROFIT %	NET PROFIT %	RET. ON EQUITY %	RET. ON ASSETS %	CURR. RATIO	EARN. PER SH.$	CASH FL. PER SH.$	TANG. BK. VAL.$	PRICE RANGE	AVG. P/E RATIO
p12/31/02	1,372.4	257.8							1.31			43.00 – 28.00	27.1
⬜ 12/31/01	1,178.6	149.8	745.0	21.1	12.7	190.3	20.1	1.4	0.77	0.89	0.41	33.30 – 24.70	37.7
12/31/00	1,041.0	176.0	597.0	25.7	16.9	67.4	29.5	1.2	...	...	0.08	...	...
12/31/99	939.0	150.0	606.0	24.6	16.0	38.4	24.8	2.0	...	...	...	...	...
12/31/98	861.0	145.0	...	24.5	16.8	...	...	...	...	...	...	...	...

Statistics are as originally reported. ⬜ Results for 12/31/01 and prior are pro forma as a result of the Company's spin-off from Bristol-Meyers Squibb.

OFFICERS:
J. R. Elliott, Chmn., Pres., C.E.O.
S. R. Leno, Sr. V.P., C.F.O.
D. C. Dvorak, Sr. V.P., Gen. Couns.

INVESTOR CONTACT: Sam Leno, Sr. V.P., C.F.O., (574) 372-4790

PRINCIPAL OFFICE: 345 East Main Street, Warsaw, IN 46580

TELEPHONE NUMBER: (574) 267-6131
FAX: (574) 372-4988

NO. OF EMPLOYEES: 3,600 (approx.)

SHAREHOLDERS: 620,581

ANNUAL MEETING: In May

INCORPORATED: DE, Jan., 2001

INSTITUTIONAL HOLDINGS:
No. of Institutions: 549
Shares Held: 140,062,490
% Held: 71.8

INDUSTRY: Surgical appliances and supplies (SIC: 3842)

TRANSFER AGENT(S): Mellon Investor Services, South Hackensack, NJ

CONDENSED
STATISTICAL
TABULATION

The tab section consists statistical highlights for all U.S. companies listed on the New York Stock Exchange.

Statistics for companies whose fiscal year ends prior to June 30 are listed under the prior calendar year. Statistics for companies whose fiscal year ends June 30 or after are listed under the current calendar year. Dividends and price ranges are on a calendar year basis.

Because of editorial constraints a column for fourth quarter results was not included. At fiscal year-end, full fiscal year per share earnings are listed and quarterly figures are eliminated. Quarterly per share earnings are inserted as the company reports in the current fiscal year.

NOTE: Figures listed under "Earnings Per Share" for investment companies are net asset value per share.

For abbreviations, see the blue section of the Handbook.

SYMBOL	COMPANY	NATURE OF BUSINESS	FISCAL YEAR-END	TOTAL REV. $MILL	NET INCOME $MILL	TOTAL ASSETS $MILL	NET STK EQUITY $MILL	NO. OF INST.	INST. HOLDINGS (SHARES)
HMC			3/31/02	—	—	—	—	115	16739561
BDF	1838 Bond-Debenture Trading F	Investment company	3/31/02	5.8		74.0	74.0	12	293886
TW	21st Century Insurance Group	Property & casualty insurance	12/31/02		pd12.3	—	—	51	64071638
MMM	3M Co	Conglomerate	12/31/02					925	383371188
KDE	4 Kids Entertainment Inc. (Un	Services	12/31/01	41.5	12.2	143.7	118.5	80	9329451
SE	7-Eleven Inc.	Grocery chain	12/31/01		p2097.8			63	8715539
NDN	99 Cents Only Stores	Discount & variety stores	12/31/02	p713.9	p772.9			146	37781474
AIR	AAR Corp		5/31/02	638.7	d58.9	710.2	310.2	93	29588485
RNT	Aaron Rents, Inc. (United Sta	Furniture & fixtures	12/31/02	p640.7	p640.7	—	—	100	13984378
RNT A	Aaron Rents, Inc. (United Sta	Furniture & fixtures	12/31/02	p640.7	p640.7	—	—	19	876668
ABB	ABB Ltd (Switzerland)		12/31/01					9	1106978
SUA	Abbey National Plc	Financial services	12/31/01					4	46000
SUD	Abbey National Plc	Financial services	12/31/01					3	15400
SXA	Abbey National Plc	Financial services	12/31/02					4	106200
ABT	Abbott Laboratories	Medical & dental equipment	12/31/02	17684.7	2793.7	24259.1	10664.6	1067	1007067333
ANF	Abercrombie & Fitch Co.	Specialty stores	2/1/03	p1595.8	p1473.3	—	—	280	84003758
FCO	Aberdeen Global Income Fund,	Investment company	10/31/02	6.8	4.8	129.1	97.0	12	1294588
ABM	ABM Industries, Inc.	Maint. & security services	10/31/02	2192.0	46.7	704.9	386.7	123	31007909
ABN	ABN AMRO Holding N.V.		12/31/01					75	46722857
AKR	Acadia Realty Trust	Real estate investment trust	12/31/02	p69.3	p69.3	—	—	42	14369941
ACN	Accenture Ltd. (Bermuda)	Services	8/31/02	13105.0	244.9	5478.9	438.6	164	186965456
ACE	ACE, Ltd. (Cayman Islands)	Property & casualty insurance	12/31/01					315	232990861
AOF	ACM Govt. Opportunity Fd, Inc	Investment company	7/31/02	9.6	7.7	141.8	100.6	9	81959
ACG	ACM Income Fund, Inc.	Investment company	12/31/02	232.0	200.1	3135.3	1785.2	48	2274134
ADF	ACM Managed Dollar Income Fd	—	9/30/02	22.3	18.7	201.5	124.8	12	67455
AMF	ACM Managed Income Fund, Inc.	Investment company	8/31/01	15.5	13.1	190.5	99.5	12	620941
AMU	ACM Municipal Secs Income Fd	Investment company	10/31/01	14.5	12.5	230.1	222.2	6	33270
ATN	Action Performance Cos., Inc	Recreation	9/30/02	406.9	45.8	337.9	443.6	101	9680140
ATU	Actuant Corp.	Engineering & construction	8/31/02	462.9	25.3	294.6	402.0	119	26282864
AYI	Acuity Brands, Inc.		8/31/02	1972.8	52.0	1358.0	1024.8	54	3402777
ADX	Adams Express Co.	Investment company	12/31/02	20.8	16.7	1094.3	—	41	6785171
ADO	Adecco S.A. (Switzerland)	Services	12/31/01					12	1529004
PVD	Admin de Fondos de Pensiones	Finance	12/31/01					101	19844874
ASF	Administaff, Inc.	Services	12/31/02	p4587.7	p4587.7	—	—	142	25984144
AAP	Advance Auto Parts Inc (Unite		12/28/02	p3288.0	p3288.0	—	—	74	11845927
MKT	Advanced Marketing Services,	Publishing	3/31/02	756.1	23.1	402.9	132.3	137	23250858
AVO	Advanced Medical Optics Inc		12/31/02	p538.1	p538.1	—	—	269	186665398
AMD	Advanced Micro Devices Inc	Electronic components	12/31/02	p2697.0	p2077.4	—	—	29	8623622
ASX	Advanced Semiconductor Eng.	Electronic components	12/31/01					20	2961552
ATE	Advantest Corp. (Japan)	Meas. & control instruments	3/31/02	1130.1	42.0	330.1	36.3	117	16393132
AD	ADVO, Inc.		9/28/02					180	31084647
AEG	AEGON N.V. (Netherlands)	Insurance	12/31/01					76	14264088
ARO	Aeropostale Inc		8/4/01	304.8	10.9	121.1	26.3	310	366496665
AES	AES Corp. (United States)	Electric power	12/31/02	p8632.0	p8632.0	—	—	320	145338395
AET	Aetna Inc. (New)	Insurance	12/31/02	19878.7	393.2	40047.5	6980.0	5	86475
AEF	Aetna Inc. (New)	Insurance	12/31/02	19878.7	393.2	40047.5	6980.0	349	119159782
ACS	Affiliated Computer Services	Computer services	6/30/02	3062.9	229.6	3403.6	2095.4	189	27577934
AMG	Affiliated Managers Group In	Financial services	12/31/02	p482.5	p438.9	—	—	517	304217724
AFL	AFLAC Inc.	Insurance	12/31/02	p10.3	p10.3	—	—	24	2488933
ASV	AG Services of America, Inc.	Services	2/28/02	387.4	5.5	273.8	71.5	165	73054318
AG	AGCO Corp.		12/31/02	2922.7	d60.3	2349.0	717.6	265	604653645
AGR A	Agere Systems Inc.	Comp. components & periphs.	9/30/02	2177.0	d1811.0	2864.0	732.0	285	473827386
AGR B	Agere Systems Inc.	Comp. components & periphs.	9/30/02	2177.0	d1811.0	2864.0	732.0	442	295410365
A	Agilent Technologies, Inc.	Electrical equipment	10/31/02	6010.0	d1022.0	8203.0	4627.0	191	29805748
ATG	AGL Resources Inc.	Natural gas distributor	12/31/02	p868.9	p868.9	—	—	11	150031
ADC	Agree Realty Corp.	Real estate investment trust	12/31/02	p25.8	p25.8	0.6	—		
RRE	Aim Select Real Estate Income	Investment company	5/21/02					456	192242110
APD	Air Products & Chemicals, In	Specialty chemicals	9/30/02	5401.2	525.4	8495.0	3460.4	140	41520400
ABF	Airborne, Inc. (United State	Freight transportation	12/31/02	3343.7	14.8	1879.1	839.2	179	45456861
ARG	Airgas Inc.	Specialty chemicals	3/31/02	1636.0	48.6	1717.1	503.1		
ANS	AirNet Systems, Inc.		12/31/02	p148.9	p148.8	—	—	23	6328513
AAI	Airtran Holdings, Inc.		12/31/02	p733.4	p733.4	—	—	78	27311098
AKS	AK Steel Holding Corp	Steel producer	12/31/01	3994.1	d92.4	5225.8	1033.3	165	79922635
ABJ	Alabama Power Co.	Electric power	12/31/01	3586.4	401.9	10418.3	3628.4	1	200
ALQ	Alabama Power Co.	Electric power	12/31/01	3586.4	401.9	10418.3	3628.4	1	3100
ALG	Alamo Group, Inc.	Machinery & equipment	12/31/02	259.4	259.4	—	—	31	2846244
APS	Alamosa Holdings Inc.	Telecommunications	12/31/02	p555.7	p555.7	—	—	41	15945401
ALK	Alaska Air Group, Inc.		12/31/02	p816.0	p309.7	—	—	117	20828319
AIN	Albany International Corp (N	Paper	12/31/02	980.2	74.7	1193.0	569.7	137	22304243
ALB	Albemarle Corp.	Chemicals	9/30/02					165	19405208
ACV A	Alberto-Culver Co.	Cosmetics & toiletries	9/30/02	2651.0	137.7	1729.5	862.5	90	18469828
ACV	Alberto-Culver Co.	Cosmetics & toiletries	9/30/02	2651.0	137.7	1729.5	862.5	217	24842513
ABS	Albertson's, Inc.	Grocery chain	1/31/03	37931.0	501.0	15967.0	5915.0	396	277908307
ALA	Alcatel (France)	Telecommunications	12/31/01					118	122549850
AA	Alcoa, Inc.	Metal products	12/31/01					633	674620618
ACL	Alcon, Inc. (Switzerland)		12/31/01					123	66401337
ALX	Alexander's Inc.	Real estate	12/31/02	76.2	13.3	664.9	68.7	36	1486237
ARE	Alexandria Real Estate Equiti	Real estate investment trust	12/31/01		p40.0	—	—	123	15803555
Y	Alleghany Corp. (New)	Property & casualty insurance	12/31/02	925.0	430.6	1875.0	1390.6	108	4501243
AYE	Allegheny Energy, Inc.	Electric power	12/31/01	10378.9	448.9	11167.6	2784.0	259	56090213
ATI	Allegheny Technologies, Inc (	Conglomerate	12/31/02	p1907.8	p1907.8	—	—	179	41530124
ALN	Allen Telecom Inc.	Telecommunications	12/31/02	p417.0	p98.2	—	—	125	29228814
AGN	Allergan, Inc	Medical & dental equipment	12/31/02	1425.3	64.0	1806.6	808.3	347	127415890
ALE	ALLETE Inc.	Electric power	12/31/02	1506.9	119.0	3147.2	1232.4	190	32039477
AMO	Alliance All-Market Advantage	Investment company	9/30/02	0.5	d0.9	53.2	49.5	6	48093
AKP	Alliance California Municipal	Investment company	1/23/02			0.4	0.1		
AC	Alliance Capital Management	Financial services	12/31/02		p162.0	—	—	186	12870658
ADS	Alliance Data Systems Corp.	Computer services	12/31/01	871.5	26.7	1453.4	542.7	85	18949630
AGI	Alliance Gaming Corp.	Gaming	6/30/02	594.1	63.8	459.9	46.0	154	34989243
AIQ	Alliance Imaging, Inc.	Medical & dental equipment	12/31/02	p412.0	p410.9	—	—	123	12275984
AFB	Alliance National Municipal I	Investment company	1/23/02			0.6	0.1		
AYN	Alliance New York Municipal I	Investment company	1/23/02			0.4	0.1		
AWF	Alliance World Dlr Govt Fd II	Investment company	3/31/02	114.2	99.4	952.1	823.8	33	1883149
AWG	Alliance World Dollar Govt Fd	Investment company	10/31/02	11.1	9.4	110.1	88.7	15	254371
LNT	Alliant Energy Corp.	Electric power	12/31/02	p2608.8	p2639.4	—	—	191	23495503
ATK	Alliant Techsystems Inc.	Defense systems & equip.	3/31/02	1801.6	86.1	2211.3	556.8	246	33881409

| EARNINGS PER SHARE | | | | | | P/E RATIO | DIVIDENDS PER SHARE | | | AV. YLD. % | DIV. DECLARED | | PRICE RANGE |
| QUARTERLY | | | ANNUAL | | | | | | | | | | 2002 |
1st	2nd	3rd	2002	2001	2000		2002	2001	2000		AMOUNT	PAYABLE	
—	—	—	—	—	—	—	0.11	0.09	0.09	0.5	0.05742U	3/26/03	23.85 - 17.01
20.34	20.61	—	—	—	—	—	1.40	1.45	1.45	7.1	0.34Q	5/6/03	20.80 - 18.61
—	—	—	—	—	—	—	0.24	0.32	0.48	1.6	0.02Q	3/28/03	21.80 - 9.15
—	—	—	pd4.99	3.58	4.64	26.4 - 20.0	2.48	2.40	2.32	2.1	0.66Q	3/12/03	131.55 - 100.00
0.11	0.09	0.14	—	0.92	2.96	—	—	—	—	—	2-for-1	9/13/99	29.86 - 15.06
—	—	—	—	0.83	0.97	25.4 - 13.9	—	—	—	—	—	—	12.20 - 6.65
—	—	—	p0.48	0.69	0.56	39.8 - 24.4	—	—	—	—	4-for-3	4/3/02	33.00 - 20.26
d0.15	d0.02	—	p0.83	2.08	0.69	—	0.08	0.28	0.34	0.9	0.025Q	9/4/02	14.00 - 2.92
—	—	—	p1.29	0.61	1.37	22.1 - 11.2	0.04	0.04	0.04	0.2	0.02S	1/2/03	28.49 - 14.45
—	—	—	p1.29	0.61	1.37	21.3 - 8.1	0.04	0.04	0.04	0.2	0.02S	1/2/03	27.50 - 10.50
—	—	—	—	—	—	—	—	—	—	—	—	—	11.22 - 1.10
—	—	—	—	—	—	—	1.75	1.75	1.75	7.1	0.4375Q	4/15/03	25.59 - 23.70
—	—	—	—	—	—	—	1.81	1.81	1.81	7.2	0.45313Q	3/17/03	25.95 - 24.10
—	—	—	—	—	—	—	1.89	0.49	—	7.6	—	2/18/03	25.90 - 24.12
—	—	—	1.78	0.99	1.78	32.6 - 16.7	0.91	0.82	0.74	2.1	0.245Q	5/15/03	58.00 - 29.80
—	—	—	p1.94	1.65	1.55	17.4 - 7.7	—	—	—	—	2-for-1	6/15/99	33.85 - 14.97
—	—	—	10.46	9.99	10.20	—	0.73	0.84	0.86	7.6	0.06M	4/11/03	10.65 - 8.60
—	—	—	0.92	0.65	0.93	21.5 - 14.0	0.36	0.33	0.31	2.2	0.095Q	5/5/03	19.75 - 12.92
—	—	—	—	—	—	—	0.86	0.83	0.80	5.6	0.4815U	6/4/03	20.44 - 10.20
—	—	—	p0.77	0.37	d0.75	11.2 - 8.0	0.51	0.48	0.48	6.9	0.145Q	4/15/03	8.65 - 6.16
—	—	—	0.56	—	—	54.5 - 20.2	—	—	—	—	—	—	30.50 - 11.30
—	—	—	—	—	—	—	0.64	0.56	0.48	1.9	0.17Q	4/14/03	44.98 - 22.01
—	—	—	7.95	7.99	7.90	—	0.72	0.72	0.74	8.3	0.06M	3/21/03	9.65 - 7.80
—	—	—	7.91	7.87	8.45	—	0.96	0.82	0.80	12.2	0.0725M	3/21/03	8.50 - 7.28
p0.22	—	—	0.84	0.98	1.08	9.4 - 6.0	0.83	1.02	1.19	12.8	0.0675M	3/21/03	7.93 - 5.00
p4.06	—	—	4.06	4.71	5.31	—	0.51	0.55	0.83	12.1	0.0425M	3/21/03	4.85 - 3.60
—	23.28	—	—	12.10	11.71	—	0.87	0.87	0.87	7.3	0.0725M	3/21/03	12.62 - 11.15
0.44	—	—	2.46	1.39	d3.52	21.1 - 6.4	0.03	—	—	0.1	0.03Q	4/14/03	51.99 - 15.80
0.15	—	—	2.39	2.93	3.50	19.7 - 12.1	—	—	—	—	—	—	47.00 - 29.00
0.25	—	—	1.26	0.99	—	15.4 - 8.7	0.60	—	—	3.9	0.15Q	2/3/03	19.40 - 11.00
—	—	—	12.12	16.05	23.72	—	0.76	1.65	1.85	6.2	0.02Q	3/1/03	14.55 - 9.86
—	—	—	—	—	—	—	0.15	0.60	0.10	1.4	0.09393U	5/29/03	16.95 - 5.75
—	—	—	pd0.15	0.36	0.58	—	1.04	1.00	0.58	4.3	0.3672U	10/25/02	26.90 - 20.85
—	—	—	p1.80	0.59	0.58	34.5 - 22.1	—	—	—	—	2-for-1	10/16/00	28.40 - 1.99
—	—	—	—	—	—	—	—	—	—	—	—	—	62.19 - 39.85
0.12	0.23	0.45	1.16	1.06	—	—	0.04	0.01	0.04	0.2	0.04A	3/14/03	27.00 - 11.70
—	—	—	p0.58	—	—	21.3 -	—	—	—	—	—	—	12.35 - 0.00
—	—	—	pd2.00	d0.18	2.95	—	—	—	—	—	2-for-1	8/21/00	20.60 - 3.10
—	—	—	—	—	—	—	—	—	—	—	17%	9/17/01	5.68 - 2.19
0.55	—	—	2.07	2.47	2.35	22.5 - 12.5	0.06	0.04	—	0.4	0.01787U	3/26/03	23.00 - 7.30
0.01	d0.06	0.39	0.28	0.24	—	—	—	—	—	—	10.00Q	3/5/96	46.58 - 25.78
—	—	—	pd6.51	0.87	1.42	—	0.74	0.70	0.56	4.0	4%	5/13/03	27.46 - 9.05
—	—	—	2.57	d2.03	d0.90	20.2 - 11.6	—	—	—	—	2-for-1	6/1/00	29.50 - 5.25
0.50	0.53	—	2.57	d2.03	d0.90	10.3 - 9.6	0.04	0.04	—	0.1	0.04A	11/29/02	17.92 - 0.92
—	—	—	1.76	1.03	1.43	32.4 - 18.6	2.13	0.96	—	8.3	0.53125Q	2/28/03	51.91 - 29.90
—	—	—	p2.48	2.20	2.49	30.0 - 15.6	—	—	—	—	100%	2/22/02	26.40 - 24.75
—	—	—	—	—	—	—	—	—	—	—	—	—	57.05 - 32.70
—	—	—	—	—	—	—	—	—	—	—	—	—	74.50 - 38.75
0.39	0.45	0.25	p1.55	1.28	1.26	21.6 - 14.9	0.23	0.19	0.17	0.8	0.07Q	12/1/03	33.45 - 23.10
—	—	—	d0.81	0.34	0.06	—	—	—	—	—	2-for-1	7/29/94	14.50 - 6.24
d0.09	—	—	d1.11	d3.46	d0.07	—	—	0.01	0.04	—	0.01Q	3/1/01	26.39 - 14.60
d0.09	—	—	d1.11	d3.46	d0.07	—	—	—	—	—	—	—	6.10 - 0.50
d0.24	—	—	d2.20	d0.89	1.66	—	—	—	—	—	—	—	4.33 - 0.51
—	—	—	—	—	—	—	—	—	—	—	—	—	38.00 - 10.50
—	—	—	p1.82	1.62	1.29	13.7 - 9.5	1.08	1.08	1.08	5.1	0.27Q	3/21/03	25.00 - 17.25
—	—	—	p1.97	1.83	1.61	10.2 - 7.3	1.84	1.84	1.84	10.7	0.48Q	4/15/03	20.00 - 14.40
—	—	—	—	14.33	—	—	0.50	—	—	4.0	0.102M	6/27/03	15.05 - 10.30
0.58	—	—	2.36	2.33	0.57	22.7 - 16.9	0.82	0.78	0.74	1.8	0.21Q	5/12/03	53.52 - 40.00
—	—	—	0.31	d0.40	0.30	75.3 - 33.2	0.16	0.16	—	1.0	0.04Q	3/4/03	23.34 - 10.20
0.20	0.27	0.23	—	0.69	0.42	—	—	—	—	—	2-for-1	4/15/96	20.74 - 11.75
—	—	—	p0.15	0.49	0.68	73.7 - 26.7	—	—	—	—	2-for-1	11/21/95	11.05 - 4.00
—	—	—	p0.15	d0.03	0.69	49.7 - 15.6	—	—	—	—	0.0625Q	5/30/01	7.45 - 2.34
—	—	0.15	—	d0.87	1.20	—	—	—	—	—	—	—	14.85 - 6.45
d0.24	0.22	0.15	—	—	—	—	1.75	1.75	1.75	7.0	0.4375Q	3/31/03	25.90 - 24.00
—	—	—	—	—	—	—	1.69	1.69	1.69	6.5	—	3/31/03	27.95 - 24.31
—	—	—	p0.65	1.11	1.11	26.4 - 17.3	0.24	0.24	0.24	1.7	0.06Q	2/5/03	11.95 - 0.23
—	—	—	pd4.33	d1.65	—	—	—	—	—	—	0.05Q	11/5/92	33.90 - 13.66
—	—	—	pd4.47	d1.49	d0.51	—	0.20	—	—	0.8	0.055Q	4/3/03	30.65 - 16.90
—	—	—	p1.68	1.06	1.24	18.2 - 10.1	0.53	0.52	0.43	1.9	0.14Q	4/1/03	33.00 - 21.90
—	—	—	1.73	1.47	2.18	19.1 - 12.7	0.36	0.33	0.30	0.8	0.105Q	2/20/03	51.95 - 37.15
0.60	—	—	2.32	1.91	1.83	22.4 - 16.0	0.36	0.33	0.30	0.8	0.105Q	2/20/03	57.91 - 41.55
0.20	0.62	0.49	—	1.23	1.83	—	0.76	0.76	0.75	2.8	0.19Q	5/10/03	35.49 - 18.95
—	—	—	—	—	—	—	0.12	0.36	0.33	1.4	0.1206U	5/13/02	19.15 - 2.03
—	—	—	p0.92	1.05	1.81	43.2 - 19.2	0.60	0.60	0.50	2.1	0.15Q	2/25/03	39.75 - 17.62
—	—	—	—	—	—	—	—	—	—	—	—	—	43.35 - 26.75
—	—	—	2.66	4.77	1.04	29.2 - 21.0	—	—	—	—	—	—	77.76 - 55.75
—	—	—	p1.76	1.64	1.52	28.1 - 21.5	1.96	1.81	1.72	4.5	0.53Q	4/11/03	49.50 - 37.80
3.48	1.11	2.98	—	59.02	4.42	—	—	—	—	—	2%	4/25/03	194.00 - 170.50
0.81	d0.26	—	3.73	—	—	—	1.29	1.72	1.72	5.6	0.43Q	9/30/02	43.86 - 2.95
—	—	—	p0.82	d0.31	1.60	23.3 - 6.4	0.66	0.80	0.80	5.4	0.06Q	3/11/03	19.10 - 5.21
—	—	—	p0.14	d0.06	0.38	73.1 - 23.3	—	—	—	—	—	—	10.23 - 3.26
—	—	—	0.49	1.69	1.61	153.3 - 100.1	0.36	0.36	0.32	0.6	0.09Q	3/20/03	75.10 - 49.05
—	—	—	1.46	1.68	2.11	21.3 - 12.7	1.10	1.07	1.07	4.4	0.2825Q	3/1/03	31.10 - 18.50
—	—	—	13.65	19.68	42.58	—	1.95	7.12	7.44	11.5	0.341Q	1/3/03	21.95 - 12.05
—	—	—	—	15.00	—	—	0.68	—	—	0.8	0.076M	3/21/03	15.06 - 13.21
—	—	—	p2.11	2.10	2.93	24.1 - 11.0	2.30	2.84	3.18	6.2	0.52Q	2/20/03	50.81 - 23.20
—	—	—	0.35	d0.17	d0.60	74.9 - 39.2	—	—	—	—	—	—	26.20 - 13.73
0.13	0.24	—	1.34	0.42	d0.37	13.6 - 8.0	—	—	—	—	2-for-1	4/8/02	18.20 - 10.72
—	—	—	p0.72	0.29	d0.06	21.4 - 6.8	—	—	—	—	—	—	15.40 - 4.86
—	—	—	—	15.00	—	—	0.72	—	—	5.1	0.0795M	3/21/03	15.05 - 12.90
—	9.22	—	—	15.00	—	—	0.69	—	—	4.9	0.0765M	3/21/03	15.11 - 13.08
—	—	—	10.58	10.58	10.37	—	1.07	1.26	1.14	11.6	0.0825M	3/21/03	10.60 - 8.00
—	—	—	9.98	9.43	10.45	—	1.08	1.32	1.32	10.5	0.08M	3/21/03	11.50 - 8.95
—	—	—	p0.84	2.30	4.82	36.9 - 17.0	2.00	2.00	2.00	8.8	0.25Q	2/15/03	31.01 - 14.28
0.74	0.73	0.91	—	2.45	2.13	—	—	—	—	—	3-for-2	6/10/02	76.94 - 47.07

SYMBOL	COMPANY	NATURE OF BUSINESS	FISCAL YEAR-END	TOTAL REV. $MILL	NET INCOME $MILL	TOTAL ASSETS $MILL	NET STK EQUITY $MILL	NO. OF INST.	INST. HOLDINGS (SHARES)
AZ	Allianz Aktiengesellschaft Ho	Insurance brokerage	12/31/01	—	—	—	—	31	4704775
ALD	Allied Capital Corp. (New)	Investment company	12/31/02	—	p228.3	—	—	191	43460876
AED	Allied Domecq PLC (UK)	Investment company	8/31/02	—	—	—	—	19	908133
AIB	Allied Irish Banks Plc	—	12/31/01	—	—	—	—	93	23180760
AW	Allied Waste Industries, Inc	Pollution control	12/31/02	p5517.3	p5517.3	—	—	213	158251768
AFC	Allmerica Financial Corp.	Insurance	12/31/02	—	pd306.1	—	—	138	33143354
ALM	Allmerica Securities Trust	Investment company	12/31/02	5.6	4.9	98.5	90.8	15	581818
ALL	Allstate Corp. (The)	Insurance	12/31/02	—	—	—	—	617	490221730
AT	ALLTEL Corp. (United States)	Telecommunications	12/31/02	p7983.4	p7983.4	—	—	555	199336090
AYZ	ALLTEL Corp. (United States)	Telecommunications	12/31/02	p7983.4	p7983.4	—	—	—	—
ALO	Alpharma, Inc.	Drugs	12/31/02	p1238.0	p530.3	—	—	156	37911340
ALS	Alstom S.A. (France)	—	3/31/02	—	—	—	—	22	8960101
AAA	Altana AG (Germany)	Chemicals	12/31/01	—	—	—	—	15	399052
AWC	Alumina Ltd	Mining & processing	12/31/01	3676.2	401.7	10012.3	4853.4	6	344498
AMB	AMB Property Corp.	Real estate investment trust	12/31/02	p615.8	p124.2	—	—	178	65730572
ABK	Ambac Financial Group, Inc.	Finance	12/31/02	p740.5	p740.5	—	—	382	106419805
AKB	Ambac Financial Group, Inc.	Finance	12/31/02	p740.5	p740.5	—	—	4	33512
AFK	Ambac Financial Group, Inc.	Finance	12/31/02	p740.5	p740.5	—	—	—	—
AIZ	Amcast Industrial Corp.	Metal products	8/31/02	576.2	d21.1	450.2	91.3	15	1064521
ACO	AMCOL International Corp.	Mining & processing	12/31/02	p298.9	p64.5	—	—	47	11539538
DOX	Amdocs Ltd.	Telecommunications	9/30/02	1613.6	d5.1	2540.1	1416.3	177	113801124
BSP	Amer Strategic Incm Ptf II	Investment company	5/31/02	20.4	18.0	295.1	212.0	15	3885321
AHC	Amerada Hess Corp.	Oil	12/31/01	13613.0	914.0	15369.0	4907.0	307	73666202
AEE	Ameren Corp.	Electric power	12/31/02	p3841.0	p3841.0	—	—	304	74042959
AMX	America Movil, S.A. de C.V. (	Telecommunications	12/31/01	—	—	—	—	184	234804925
AWA	America West Holding Corp.	—	12/31/02	p2047.1	p2088.5	—	—	35	13225215
AXL	American Axle & Manufacturing	—	12/31/02	p3480.2	p394.0	—	—	154	25110626
AEP	American Electric Power Co.	Electric power	12/31/02	—	—	—	—	408	197817654
AXP	American Express Co. (United	Financial services	12/31/02	—	—	—	—	938	1082044779
AM	American Greetings Corp.	Printing & engraving	2/28/02	2355.7	d122.3	2615.0	902.4	212	86066002
MRF	American Income Fund Inc	Investment company	10/31/02	7.5	6.6	116.0	82.3	11	894415
AIG	American International Group	Insurance	12/31/02	p5518.9	p2128.4	—	—	1252	1749604490
PLB	American Italian Pasta, Co.	Food processing	9/30/02	380.8	41.3	640.6	297.1	169	21098804
ANL	American Land Lease, Inc.	Real estate investment trust	12/31/02	p23.4	p23.4	—	—	24	714392
AMZ	American Medical Security Gro	Insurance	12/31/02	p789.5	p789.5	—	—	75	9748048
CXT	American Mun Term Tr Inc III	Investment company	12/31/02	4.0	3.4	57.8	57.0	7	304240
XAA	American Municipal Incm Port	Investment company	1/31/02	7.0	6.0	129.4	127.9	5	29298
ACP	American Real Estate Partners	Real estate	12/31/01	297.3	67.5	1451.6	—	19	40438600
ARL	American Realty Investors, I	Real estate	12/31/01	208.9	15.1	758.8	85.9	12	24346
ACR	American Retirement Corp.	Hospitals & nursing homes	12/31/01	256.2	d34.6	850.2	107.5	13	4220694
ASI	American Safety Insurance Gro	Insurance	12/31/01	102.3	4.2	297.3	60.0	1	109700
SLA	American Select Portfolio Inc	Investment company	11/30/02	14.1	12.0	172.6	143.7	14	1460649
ASD	American Standard Cos Inc DE	Machinery & equipment	12/31/02	7795.4	371.0	5143.8	229.8	268	83613227
AWR	American States Water Co. (U	Water company	12/31/02	p209.2	p209.2	—	—	101	5448267
ASP	American Strategic Income Ptf	Investment company	11/30/01	5.1	4.4	75.6	53.4	11	853696
CSP	American Strtgic Incm Ptf III	Investment company	5/31/02	26.1	23.1	367.9	267.9	13	2245037
AMT	American Tower Corp.	Communications electronics	12/31/01	1134.2	d4501.1	6829.7	2869.2	156	142489939
ACF	AmeriCredit Corp.	Industrial	6/30/02	1190.2	347.5	4224.9	1432.3	192	165831725
APU	AmeriGas Partners, L.P. (Uni	Oil producer	9/30/02	1307.9	55.4	1472.6	—	48	977719
AGP	Amerigroup Corp	—	12/31/02	p1160.7	p1160.7	—	—	130	20325738
ABC	AmerisourceBergen Corp. (Uni	Drugs	9/30/02	45234.8	344.9	11213.0	3316.3	381	110734291
AFG	Amern Financial Grp Inc Hldg	Property & casualty insurance	12/31/02	p3830.2	p3830.2	—	—	146	29283572
AMN	Ameron International Corp.	—	11/30/02	539.5	28.1	462.9	211.8	60	2552817
AHM	Amersham Plc (United Kingdom	Drugs	12/31/01	—	—	—	—	29	3531833
AMH	AmerUs Group Co. (United Sta	Life Insurance	12/31/02	1428.4	62.9	20293.7	1262.9	161	20526703
AME	Ametek, Inc. (New)	Machinery & equipment	12/31/02	1040.5	83.7	1030.0	420.2	182	26457369
AML	Amli Residential Properties	Real estate investment trust	12/31/02	—	p40.4	—	—	97	9237918
AHS	AMN Healthcare Services, Inc.	—	12/31/02	p775.7	p774.8	—	—	110	23611853
AP	Ampco-Pittsburgh Corp.	Metal products	12/31/02	212.4	5.2	235.1	150.0	26	5351227
APH	Amphenol Corp. (New)	Electronic components	12/31/02	p1062.0	p1062.0	—	—	120	20743353
AMR	AMR Corp. (DE)	—	12/31/02	—	—	—	—	229	122962829
AAR	AMR Corp. (DE)	—	12/31/02	—	—	—	—	6	6952
AXR	AMREP Corp.	Home-building	4/30/02	83.4	3.7	149.7	93.5	7	792001
ASO	AmSouth Bancorporation (Unit	Banking - South	12/31/02	—	p609.1	—	—	344	137168652
AVZ	AMVESCAP Plc (United Kingdom	Investment company	12/31/01	—	—	—	—	48	7185422
APC	Anadarko Petroleum Corp	Oil	12/31/02	p3860.0	p3860.0	—	—	603	218284833
ADI	Analog Devices, Inc.	Electronic components	11/2/02	1707.5	105.3	4980.2	2900.0	426	305529371
AGL	Angelica Corp.	—	1/26/02	350.1	1.6	290.9	141.5	85	6704916
BUD	Anheuser-Busch Cos., Inc.	—	12/31/02	—	—	—	—	770	596441541
AXE	Anixter International Inc. (	Electrical equipment	1/3/03	p2520.1	p2490.7	—	—	137	24407699
ANN	Ann Taylor Stores Corp.	Specialty stores	2/1/03	p1381.0	p1381.0	—	—	198	42729692
NLY	Annaly Mortgage Management In	Real estate investment trust	12/31/02	—	p219.5	—	—	146	34685455
ANR	Annuity & Life Re (Holdings)	Life Insurance	12/31/01	362.7	d38.7	2330.2	404.9	24	10950097
ANT	Anteon International Corp. (U	Computer services	12/31/02	p825.8	p114.5	—	—	101	16453516
ATH	Anthem, Inc.	Insurance	12/31/01	—	—	—	—	388	135550059
ATV	Anthem, Inc.	Insurance	12/31/01	—	—	—	—	—	—
AHR	Anthracite Capital, Inc.	Real estate investment trust	12/31/02	—	p6.3	—	—	88	19398597
AOL	AOL Time Warner Inc.	Computer services	12/31/02	—	—	—	—	973	1457553211
AOC	AON Corp.	Insurance	12/31/02	—	—	—	—	299	236200979
APA	Apache Corp.	Oil	12/31/02	p8822.0	p8822.0	—	—	532	126812886
AIV	Apartment Investment & Mgmt	Real estate investment trust	12/31/02	1506.2	175.2	10316.6	3163.4	195	77574518
APX	Apex Municipal Fund, Inc.	Investment company	6/30/02	12.9	11.3	184.7	181.1	12	80169
AOT	Apogent Technologies, Inc.	Medical & dental equipment	9/30/02	1074.6	135.2	2036.1	975.1	191	101204354
AJB	Appalachian Power Co.	Electric power	12/31/01	6999.4	161.8	5107.9	1144.5	2	9425
AJC	Appalachian Power Co.	Electric power	12/31/01	6999.4	161.8	5107.9	1144.5	1	34000
APN	Applica Inc	'Wholesaler, distributor'	12/31/02	p727.4	p727.4	—	—	84	13838777
AIT	Applied Indl Technologies In	Services	6/30/02	1446.6	14.8	534.6	298.1	91	12580858
AHG	Apria Healthcare Group Inc.	Hospitals & nursing homes	12/31/02	p1252.2	p1199.8	—	—	184	50840331
ATS	APT Satellite Holdings Ltd.	Telecommunications	12/31/01	—	—	—	—	5	1930376
ATR	AptarGroup Inc.	Containers	12/31/01	926.7	66.6	1047.7	594.5	167	31652668
ILA	Aquila Inc (New) (DE)	Electric power	12/31/01	80753.6	40656.2	11948.3	2551.6	166	60129575
ILD	Aquila Inc (New) (DE)	Electric power	12/31/01	80753.6	40656.2	11948.3	2551.6	—	—
ARA	Aracruz Celulose S.A.	Paper	12/31/01	—	—	—	—	87	28839051
RMK	Aramark Corp. (New)	—	9/27/02	8769.8	269.9	4259.3	858.2	114	62054137
ARB	Arbitron Inc.	Computers	12/31/02	p249.8	p249.8	—	—	155	29308164
ARJ	Arch Chemicals Inc	Chemicals	12/31/02	p939.4	p929.9	—	—	108	17501386

EARNINGS PER SHARE — QUARTERLY 1st	2nd	3rd	ANNUAL 2002	2001	2000	P/E RATIO	DIVIDENDS PER SHARE 2002	2001	2000	AV. YLD. %	DIV. DECLARED AMOUNT	PAYABLE	PRICE RANGE 2002
—	—	—	—	—	—	—	0.11	0.09	—	0.7	0.11118U	6/20/02	25.35 - 7.35
—	—	—	—	—	—	—	2.20	2.01	1.82	9.6	0.57Q	3/28/03	29.00 - 16.90
—	—	—	—	—	—	—	—	—	—	—	0.52627U	2/14/03	26.50 - 23.00
—	—	—	—	—	—	—	0.84	0.73	0.66	3.5	0.68251U	4/25/03	29.35 - 18.20
—	—	—	p0.71	0.01	0.36	20.5 - 7.8	—	—	—	—	—	—	14.55 - 5.54
—	—	—	pd5.79	d0.06	3.70	—	—	0.25	0.25	—	0.25A	11/20/01	50.80 - 7.04
—	—	—	10.57	10.56	10.87	—	0.58	0.76	0.85	6.0	0.1325Q	3/31/03	10.55 - 9.10
—	—	—	p1.60	1.60	2.95	—	0.82	0.74	0.66	2.2	0.23Q	4/1/03	41.95 - 31.03
—	—	—	p3.24	3.34	6.20	26.2 - 19.4	1.36	1.32	1.28	2.8	0.35Q	4/3/03	63.25 - 35.33
—	—	—	p3.24	3.34	6.20	19.5 - 10.9	2.06	—	—	4.4	0.9688Q	2/18/03	54.89 - 39.50
—	—	—	pd1.98	d0.87	1.60	16.9 - 12.2	0.18	0.18	0.18	4.4	0.045Q	1/24/03	28.00 - 6.50
—	—	—	—	—	—	—	0.55	0.41	0.40	6.4	0.5519U	7/8/02	14.29 - 3.05
—	—	—	—	0.36	0.68	—	0.39	0.74	0.73	2.6	0.316U	4/18/03	55.10 - 35.97
—	—	—	—	—	—	—	—	—	—	—	—	—	19.55 - 10.60
—	—	—	p1.37	1.47	1.35	22.7 - 18.0	1.23	1.58	1.48	4.4	0.415Q	4/15/03	31.10 - 24.70
—	—	—	p3.97	3.97	3.41	17.9 - 12.6	0.38	0.34	0.31	0.6	0.10	3/5/03	71.25 - 49.86
—	—	—	p3.97	3.97	3.41	6.6 - 6.1	1.77	1.77	1.77	7.0	0.4425Q	3/31/03	26.30 - 24.26
d0.83	—	—	p3.97	3.97	3.41	6.9 - 6.0	1.75	0.36	—	6.8	0.4375Q	3/31/03	27.40 - 23.80
—	—	—	d2.45	4.38	0.38	—	—	0.14	0.56	—	0.14Q	3/26/01	6.49 - 1.60
—	—	—	p0.43	0.43	0.11	17.4 - 10.6	0.08	0.05	14.22	1.3	0.03Q	3/4/03	7.50 - 4.55
—	—	—	d0.02	0.29	0.03	—	—	—	—	—	—	—	39.25 - 5.85
—	13.25	—	13.29	13.06	—	—	1.14	1.09	1.04	9.0	0.095M	3/26/03	13.57 - 11.65
1.58	1.66	d1.54	10.25	11.38	—	—	1.20	1.05	0.60	1.8	0.30Q	3/31/03	84.70 - 49.40
—	—	—	p2.60	3.45	3.33	17.4 - 13.4	2.54	2.54	2.54	6.0	0.635Q	3/31/03	45.19 - 34.72
—	—	—	—	—	—	—	0.09	0.04	—	0.5	0.02102U	4/3/03	20.48 - 11.54
—	—	—	pd4.68	d4.39	0.22	—	—	—	—	—	—	—	6.45 - 0.90
—	—	—	p3.38	2.36	2.60	10.8 - 5.8	—	—	—	—	—	—	36.67 - 19.55
—	—	—	pd1.57	3.11	0.94	—	2.40	2.40	2.40	7.5	0.60Q	3/10/03	48.80 - 15.10
0.60	d0.24	0.62	p2.01	0.98	2.07	22.3 - 13.2	0.32	0.32	0.32	0.9	0.08Q	2/10/03	44.91 - 26.55
—	—	—	d1.92	d1.46	—	—	—	0.40	0.82	—	0.10Q	12/7/01	23.80 - 11.98
—	—	—	8.70	9.19	8.90	—	0.69	0.67	0.72	8.1	0.0575M	3/26/03	8.88 - 8.12
0.49	—	—	p2.10	2.07	2.41	38.1 - 22.7	0.18	0.16	0.14	0.3	0.047Q	6/20/03	80.00 - 47.61
—	—	—	2.21	1.53	1.50	23.8 - 14.3	—	—	—	—	—	—	52.56 - 31.50
—	—	—	p0.86	0.89	0.16	17.9 - 15.1	1.00	1.00	1.00	7.0	0.25Q	2/27/03	15.39 - 13.00
—	—	—	pd2.72	0.29	0.18	—	—	—	—	—	—	—	24.09 - 11.00
—	—	—	10.76	11.01	10.97	—	0.75	0.60	0.59	6.8	0.0475M	3/26/03	11.37 - 10.68
—	15.00	—	29.34	14.50	—	—	0.90	0.81	0.79	6.5	0.078M	3/26/03	14.79 - 13.12
0.33	0.24	0.30	1.19	1.29	—	—	—	—	—	—	—	—	13.95 - 4.51
0.05	d1.85	d1.34	1.07	0.03	—	—	—	—	—	—	—	—	11.50 - 6.40
d2.16	d1.12	d0.93	d2.01	d0.34	—	—	—	—	—	—	—	—	3.14 - 1.00
—	—	—	0.84	d0.25	—	—	0.36	—	—	4.5	0.12Q	1/6/03	9.75 - 6.35
—	—	—	13.48	13.38	12.85	—	1.20	1.09	1.01	9.2	0.0875M	3/26/03	14.10 - 11.91
—	—	—	5.04	4.04	4.36	15.7 - 11.5	—	—	—	—	—	—	79.00 - 58.20
—	—	—	p1.34	1.33	1.27	21.6 - 15.1	0.87	0.87	0.86	3.5	0.221Q	3/1/03	29.01 - 20.25
—	12.59	—	12.63	12.51	—	—	1.00	1.07	0.95	8.2	0.0725M	3/26/03	13.40 - 11.21
—	12.55	—	12.55	12.37	—	—	1.05	1.03	1.04	8.7	0.0875M	3/26/03	12.75 - 11.29
d0.36	d0.43	d1.81	d2.35	d1.13	—	—	—	—	—	—	—	—	10.40 - 0.60
0.81	d0.29	—	3.87	2.60	1.48	12.1 - 1.5	—	—	—	—	100%	9/30/98	46.93 - 5.90
0.82	—	—	1.12	1.18	0.36	22.1 - 15.3	2.20	2.20	2.20	10.5	0.55Q	2/18/03	24.73 - 17.11
—	—	—	p2.19	2.08	1.55	16.2 - 9.2	—	—	—	—	—	—	35.49 - 20.25
0.84	—	—	3.16	2.10	1.90	26.2 - 15.9	0.10	0.03	—	0.2	0.025Q	3/3/03	82.85 - 50.20
—	—	—	p1.22	p0.07	0.80	24.8 - 14.7	0.50	1.00	1.00	2.1	0.125Q	1/25/03	30.30 - 17.90
—	—	—	6.97	6.89	6.41	11.2 - 6.2	1.28	1.28	1.28	2.1	0.32Q	2/18/03	78.00 - 43.55
—	—	—	1.56	2.12	2.43	25.6 - 16.5	0.55	0.47	0.45	1.2	—	6/2/03	54.95 - 34.21
—	—	—	2.49	1.98	2.11	16.3 - 10.5	0.40	0.40	0.50	1.2	0.40A	12/3/02	39.98 - 25.69
—	—	—	p1.80	2.12	3.59	15.0 - 10.5	0.24	0.24	0.24	0.7	0.06Q	3/31/03	40.71 - 26.15
—	—	—	p1.12	0.04	d0.23	33.4 - 11.6	1.92	1.89	1.86	8.4	0.48Q	2/25/03	26.98 - 18.84
—	—	—	0.53	d0.10	1.68	24.2 - 18.5	—	—	—	—	—	—	37.40 - 13.00
—	—	—	p1.85	1.95	2.52	28.0 - 14.8	0.40	0.40	0.40	3.5	0.10Q	1/31/03	12.81 - 9.81
—	—	—	—	—	—	—	—	—	—	—	2-for-1	4/25/00	51.75 - 27.47
—	—	—	pd22.57	d11.43	4.81	—	—	—	—	—	0.00U	3/15/00	29.20 - 3.01
—	—	—	pd22.57	d11.43	4.81	—	1.97	1.97	1.97	12.8	—	1/31/03	24.00 - 6.85
0.12	0.19	—	0.56	0.38	—	—	—	—	—	—	3-for-2	12/1/86	8.85 - 6.50
—	—	—	p1.68	1.45	0.86	13.7 - 10.6	0.88	0.84	0.80	4.3	0.23Q	4/1/03	23.06 - 17.75
—	—	—	—	—	—	—	0.35	0.30	0.29	1.8	0.2127U	5/12/03	31.80 - 7.62
—	—	—	p3.21	d0.73	4.16	18.2 - 11.5	0.33	0.22	0.20	0.7	0.10Q	3/26/03	58.55 - 36.77
p0.16	—	—	0.28	0.93	1.59	174.4 - 63.9	—	—	—	—	2-for-1	3/15/00	48.84 - 17.88
0.26	0.37	0.40	0.19	0.76	—	—	0.32	0.32	0.64	1.8	0.10Q	4/1/03	24.31 - 10.80
—	—	—	p2.20	1.89	1.69	25.0 - 19.8	0.75	0.69	0.63	1.5	0.195Q	3/10/03	55.00 - 43.65
—	—	—	p0.15	0.89	2.03	210.0 - 125.3	—	—	—	—	2-for-1	10/25/95	31.50 - 18.80
—	—	—	p1.72	0.67	1.17	19.3 - 11.2	—	—	—	—	50%	5/20/02	33.19 - 19.25
—	—	—	p2.67	2.21	1.15	8.1 - 5.2	2.59	1.40	1.25	14.6	0.60Q	4/30/03	21.50 - 13.90
—	—	—	d1.51	1.46	—	—	0.20	0.20	0.16	1.4	0.05Q	11/28/02	26.09 - 1.80
—	—	—	p0.86	d0.02	d0.22	34.1 - 22.0	—	—	—	—	—	—	29.35 - 18.90
—	—	—	p4.51	3.30	—	16.7 - 10.3	—	—	—	—	—	—	75.50 - 46.40
—	—	—	p4.51	3.30	—	34.2 - 0.0	3.11	—	—	4.0	0.75Q	2/18/03	154.14 - 0.01
—	—	—	p1.18	1.40	1.28	11.2 - 8.0	1.40	1.23	1.16	12.4	0.35Q	4/30/03	13.25 - 9.40
—	—	—	pd22.15	d1.11	0.45	—	—	—	—	—	—	—	32.92 - 8.70
—	—	—	p1.64	0.73	1.82	24.2 - 8.1	0.82	0.90	0.87	3.1	0.15Q	2/25/03	39.63 - 13.30
—	—	—	p3.60	4.73	4.96	16.0 - 11.7	0.38	0.24	0.24	0.8	0.10Q	5/22/03	57.75 - 42.25
—	—	—	0.94	0.23	0.52	54.7 - 36.1	3.28	3.12	2.80	0.7	0.82Q	2/18/03	51.46 - 33.90
—	—	—	9.24	9.45	—	—	0.56	0.59	0.62	6.8	0.047M	3/28/03	8.78 - 7.60
0.27	—	—	1.24	1.02	0.81	21.4 - 13.5	—	—	—	—	0.00U	12/1/00	26.50 - 16.70
—	—	—	—	—	—	—	1.80	1.80	1.80	7.3	0.45Q	3/31/03	25.25 - 23.75
—	—	—	—	—	—	—	1.82	1.82	1.82	7.5	0.45625Q	3/31/03	25.40 - 23.51
0.20	0.20	—	pd3.10	d1.23	d0.92	—	—	—	—	—	0.00001Q	4/1/03	12.45 - 4.10
—	—	—	p2.08	1.32	1.06	13.7 - 9.0	0.48	0.48	0.48	2.2	0.12Q	2/14/03	21.25 - 14.70
—	—	—	—	—	—	—	—	—	—	—	—	—	28.50 - 18.80
—	—	—	—	—	—	—	0.05	0.15	0.41	2.2	0.0512U	7/8/02	3.60 - 1.15
—	—	—	1.82	1.61	1.78	21.3 - 13.6	0.24	0.22	0.20	0.8	0.06Q	2/27/03	38.74 - 24.84
0.32	d5.69	d1.01	—	2.42	2.21	—	0.77	1.20	1.20	5.4	0.175Q	9/12/02	26.95 - 1.56
0.32	d5.69	d1.01	—	2.42	2.21	—	1.48	—	—	8.6	—	3/3/03	24.90 - 9.70
—	—	—	—	—	—	—	0.73	0.64	0.56	4.0	0.7299U	5/20/02	22.88 - 13.92
0.31	—	—	1.34	0.97	0.88	21.1 - 13.7	—	—	—	—	—	—	28.30 - 18.39
—	—	—	p1.42	1.24	1.54	26.8 - 20.1	—	—	—	—	—	—	37.99 - 28.60
—	—	—	p0.13	0.08	0.02	197.5 - 120.8	0.80	0.80	0.80	3.9	0.20Q	3/12/03	25.68 - 15.70

SYMBOL	COMPANY	NATURE OF BUSINESS	FISCAL YEAR-END	TOTAL REV. $MILL	NET INCOME $MILL	TOTAL ASSETS $MILL	NET STK EQUITY $MILL	NO. OF INST.	INST. HOLDINGS (SHARES)
ACI	Arch Coal, Inc.	Coal	12/31/01	1488.7	7.2	2203.6	570.7	147	41860876
ADM	Archer Daniels Midland Co.	Food -grain & agriculture	6/30/02	23453.6	511.1	15416.3	6754.8	359	407965818
ASN	Archstone-Smith Trust	Real estate investment trust	12/31/01	1082.3	271.5	8855.1	3843.8	235	144204378
ARI	Arden Realty, Inc.	Real estate investment trust	12/31/02	p414.6	p416.0	—	—	141	44320685
AGY	Argosy Gaming Co.	Gaming	12/31/02	p936.8	p879.4	—	—	142	25896915
AH	Armor Holdings, Inc.	Defense systems & equip.	12/31/02	p305.1	p94.4	—	—	118	25253522
ARW	Arrow Electronics, Inc	Consumer electronics	12/31/02	p7390.2	p7400.4	—	—	202	93198881
ARM	ArvinMeritor, Inc.	—	9/30/02	6882.0	149.0	4651.0	741.0	192	40774150
ASA	ASA Ltd.	Investment company	11/30/02	—	—	—	—	39	2036020
ABG	Asbury Automotive Group, Inc.	—	12/31/02	p4486.0	p4486.0	—	—	51	3742827
ASH	Ashland, Inc.	—	9/30/02	7792.0	129.0	6725.0	2173.0	231	48103905
APB	Asia Pacific Fund, Inc.	Investment company	3/31/02	2.9	d0.5	161.8	161.0	20	647683
SAT	Asia Satellite Telecommunicat	Telecommunications	12/31/01	—	—	—	—	14	1194280
GRR	Asia Tigers Fund, Inc. (The)	Investment company	10/31/02	2.6	0.1	101.1	100.4	28	5809840
AEC	Associated Estates Rlty Corp	Real estate investment trust	12/31/02	p162.4	p162.4	—	—	48	3566439
AF	Astoria Financial Corp. (Uni	Banking - Northeast	12/31/01	1539.5	225.2	22667.7	1542.6	227	60067142
AZN	AstraZeneca Plc (UK)	Chemicals	12/31/01	—	—	—	—	136	84227973
T	AT&T Corp	Telecommunications	12/31/01	—	—	—	—	584	502163295
AWE	AT&T Wireless Services, Inc	Telecommunications	12/31/01	—	—	—	—	625	1404673197
ATL	Atalanta/Sosnoff Capital Corp	Financial services	12/31/01	—	—	—	—	9	516625
CGO	Atlas Air Worldwide Holdings,	—	12/31/01	763.8	d61.3	2084.8	489.9	64	13034473
ATO	Atmos Energy Corp.	Natural gas	9/30/02	950.8	59.7	1980.2	573.2	125	16642550
ATW	Atwood Oceanics, Inc. (United	Oil service & equipment	9/30/02	149.2	28.3	444.5	276.1	110	11726704
AUO	AU Optronics Corp. (Taiwan)	Electronic components	12/31/01	37588.6	d6710.2	103469.0	43947.3	28	7073379
AOR	Aurora Foods Inc	Food processing	12/31/02	p771.9	p604.5	—	—	58	9034737
ANZ	Australia and New Zealand Ban	—	9/30/02	6988.0	2322.0	183105.0	11465.0	28	36968200
ALV	Autoliv Inc. (United States)	—	12/31/02	p4443.4	p4443.4	—	—	128	28526133
ADP	Automatic Data Processing In	Computer services	6/30/02	7004.3	1100.8	18276.5	5114.2	799	462839215
AN	AutoNation, Inc.	Pollution control	12/31/01	19478.5	381.6	8584.8	3910.2	179	192114222
AZO	AutoZone, Inc.	—	8/31/02	5325.5	428.1	3477.8	689.1	361	98037279
AVB	AvalonBay Communities, Inc.	Real estate investment trust	12/31/02	p639.0	p639.0	—	—	211	53207807
AV	Avaya Inc	—	9/30/02	4956.0	d666.0	3897.0	—	276	193148678
AVE	Aventis (France)	Chemicals	12/31/01	—	—	—	—	142	29745341
AVY	Avery Dennison Corp.	Office equipment & supplies	12/28/02	p4206.9	p4184.3	—	—	402	85977648
AVL	Aviall, Inc.	—	12/31/02	p803.3	p64.4	—	—	82	13129965
AVA	Avista Corp.	Electric power	12/31/02	p980.4	p980.4	—	—	117	24277711
AVT	Avnet, Inc. (United States)	Electronic components	6/28/02	8920.2	d84.4	4682.0	1804.5	223	104327021
AVP	Avon Products, Inc.	Cosmetics & toiletries	12/31/01	6228.3	534.6	3327.5	d127.7	441	207339337
AVX	AVX Corp.	Electronic components	3/31/02	1250.0	d7.2	1691.6	1476.0	129	32196104
AXA	AXA (France)	Insurance	12/31/01	—	—	—	—	126	33244658
AZR	Aztar Corp.	Gaming	1/2/03	834.3	58.9	1210.7	515.4	136	31618634
AZZ	AZZ incorporated	Services	2/28/02	152.9	7.8	147.0	54.8	16	2624788
BZ	Bairnco Corp.	Plastics & plastic products	12/31/02	p154.4	p45.0	—	—	12	2554361
BHI	Baker Hughes Inc.	Oil service & equipment	12/31/02	5020.4	223.7	6400.8	3397.2	391	320208022
BEZ	Baldor Electric Co.	Electrical equipment	12/28/02	p549.5	p138.7	—	—	111	17698513
BLL	Ball Corp. (United States)	Containers	12/31/02	p3858.9	p3856.2	—	—	248	46975648
BFT	Bally Total Fitness Hldg Corp	Recreation	12/31/02	p968.1	p968.1	—	—	105	27663371
BBV	Banco Bilbao Vizcaya Argenta	—	12/31/02	—	—	—	—	69	65298928
BBD	Banco Bradesco S.A. (Brazil)	—	12/31/02	—	—	—	—	12	7928940
BPC	Banco Comercial Portugues	—	12/31/01	—	—	—	—	4	501971
BCH	Banco de Chile	—	12/31/01	—	—	—	—	10	1036985
ITU	Banco Itau S.A.	—	12/31/01	—	—	—	—	7	1866946
BLX	Banco Latinoamericano	—	12/31/01	—	—	—	—	16	4828176
STD	Banco Santander Cent Hispano	—	12/31/01	—	—	—	—	66	42120873
SAN	Banco Santander Chile (New)	—	12/31/01	—	—	—	—	38	10292325
CIB	BanColombia, S.A.	—	12/31/01	—	—	—	—	1	40000
BXS	BancorpSouth Inc.	Banking - South	12/31/02	—	pd79.3	—	—	100	12959516
BDG	Bandag, Inc. (United States)	Tires and/or rubber goods	12/31/02	p912.0	p843.2	—	—	107	5334621
BDG A	Bandag, Inc. (United States)	Tires and/or rubber goods	12/31/02	p912.0	p843.2	—	—	28	4367921
BAC	Bank of America Corp.	Banking - South	12/31/02	45732.0	9249.0	660458.0	50319.0	984	1074236243
IKJ	Bank of America Corp.	Banking - South	12/31/02	45732.0	9249.0	660458.0	50319.0	—	—
BOH	Bank of Hawaii Corp (DE) (Un	Banking - West	12/31/02	715.8	121.2	9516.4	1015.8	164	41865046
IRE	Bank of Ireland (Ireland)	—	3/31/02	—	—	—	—	46	3006458
BK	Bank of New York Co., Inc.	Banking - Northeast	12/31/02	5756.0	902.0	77564.0	6684.0	624	510378592
ONE	Bank One Corp. (United State	—	12/31/02	22171.0	3295.0	277383.0	22440.0	692	774214057
BBX	BankAtlantic Bancorp, Inc. (	Savings & loan	12/31/02	—	p50.3	—	—	115	31364248
BNK	Bankorth Group Inc (New)	Bank	12/31/02	1509.6	298.6	23418.9	2063.5	281	84731521
BN	Banta Corp.	Printing & engraving	12/31/02	p1366.5	p303.5	—	—	165	20509475
BCS	Barclays PLC	—	12/31/01	—	—	—	—	81	24991049
BCR	Bard (C.R.), Inc.	Medical & dental equipment	12/31/02	p1273.8	p1252.8	—	—	281	47580984
BKS	Barnes & Noble, Inc. (United	Specialty stores	2/2/02	4870.4	64.0	2623.2	888.1	186	41854582
B	Barnes Group Inc.	—	12/31/02	784.0	27.2	652.5	208.2	81	8591557
BRL	Barr Laboratories, Inc.	Drugs	6/30/02	1189.0	212.4	888.6	666.5	260	28010797
RGB	Barry (R.G.) Corp.	Shoe manufacturing	12/31/02	p122.6	p122.6	—	—	15	4510555
BF	BASF AG (Germany)	Chemicals	12/31/01	—	—	—	—	53	17348138
BOL	Bausch & Lomb, Inc.	Photo & optical	12/28/02	p1816.7	p1816.7	—	—	222	55837726
BAX	Baxter International Inc.	Medical & dental equipment	12/31/02	p8110.0	p3792.0	—	—	668	487089671
BVC	Bay View Capital Corp. (DE)	Savings & loan	12/31/02	409.9	d101.2	4014.1	336.2	93	41829586
BAY	Bayer AG (Germany)	—	12/31/01	—	—	—	—	55	9596087
BBT	BB&T Corp. (Lumberton, NC) (	Financial services	12/31/02	—	—	—	—	380	142463740
BB	BBVA Banco BHIF (Chile)	—	12/31/01	—	—	—	—	2	45604
BFR	BBVA Banco Frances S.A. (Arg	—	12/31/01	—	—	—	—	8	1708848
BSC	Bear Stearns Cos., Inc. (The	Securities brokerage	11/30/02	6890.8	878.3	184854.4	6382.1	329	74550885
BE	Bearingpoint Inc	—	6/30/02	2367.6	53.1	895.1	601.9	152	122719476
BZH	Beazer Homes USA, Inc. (Unit	Home-building	9/30/02	2641.2	122.6	1892.8	799.5	154	11597331
BEC	Beckman Coulter, Inc.	Medical & dental equipment	12/31/02	p2059.4	p2035.6	—	—	234	51390261
BDX	Becton, Dickinson & Co.	Medical & dental equipment	9/30/02	4033.1	480.0	5040.5	2488.0	407	228901731
BED	Bedford Ppty Investors Inc.	Real estate investment trust	12/31/02	99.9	36.7	635.9	281.0	92	8271370
BWC	Belden Inc.	Electrical equipment	12/31/02	p813.3	p126.9	—	—	117	23325796
BLS	Bellsouth Corp.	Telecommunications	12/31/02	22440.0	2708.0	49479.0	17686.0	838	1038835143
BLC	Belo Corp.	Publishing	12/31/02	1427.8	131.1	3614.6	1413.2	225	69597171
BMS	Bemis Co., Inc.	—	12/31/02	p2369.0	p2369.0	—	—	253	35083143
BHE	Benchmark Electronics, Inc.	Communications electronics	12/31/02	p1630.0	p1630.0	—	—	180	26479310
BNG	Benetton Group SPA	—	12/31/01	—	—	—	—	12	466901
BER	Berkley (W. R.) Corp. (Unite	Property & casualty insurance	12/31/01	1941.8	d91.5	5633.5	931.6	168	45270780
BRK A	Berkshire Hathaway Inc.	Property & casualty insurance	12/31/01	37668.0	795.0	162752.0	57950.0	418	49973741

EARNINGS PER SHARE — QUARTERLY 1st	2nd	3rd	ANNUAL 2002	2001	2000	P/E RATIO 2002	DIVIDENDS PER SHARE 2002	2001	2000	AV. YLD %	DIV. DECLARED AMOUNT	PAYABLE	PRICE RANGE 2002
d0.14	0.04	0.03	—	0.15	d0.33	—	0.23	0.23	0.23	1.2	0.0575Q	3/14/03	25.25 - 14.30
0.17	0.20	—	0.78	0.58	0.45	19.0 - 12.8	0.22	0.19	0.18	1.8	0.06Q	3/4/03	14.85 - 10.00
—	—	—	1.34	1.81	1.78	21.8 - 15.9	1.70	0.41	—	6.7	0.4275Q	2/28/03	29.19 - 21.31
—	—	—	p1.09	1.53	1.52	27.1 - 19.0	2.00	1.94	1.84	8.0	0.505Q	4/23/03	29.56 - 20.73
—	—	—	p2.43	2.25	1.56	17.1 - 6.8	—	—	—	—	—	—	41.50 - 16.49
—	—	—	pd0.57	0.41	0.73	—	—	—	—	—	—	—	29.55 - 12.00
—	—	—	pd6.12	pd0.75	3.62	—	—	—	—	—	2-for-1	10/15/97	32.97 - 8.60
0.47	—	—	2.22	0.53	4.12	14.6 - 6.5	0.40	0.64	0.44	1.7	0.10Q	3/17/03	32.50 - 14.39
—	—	—	—	—	—	—	0.80	0.80	0.60	2.6	0.15Q	2/21/03	42.85 - 19.45
0.04	—	—	1.83	5.77	4.10	25.7 - 12.9	1.10	1.10	1.10	3.1	0.275Q	3/15/03	46.98 - 23.60
—	9.78	—	11.67	10.05	—	—	—	—	0.14	—	0.14A	1/14/00	11.25 - 7.77
—	—	—	—	—	—	—	0.26	0.26	0.26	1.7	0.0769U	11/29/02	19.00 - 10.95
—	—	—	7.65	6.89	9.55	—	—	0.29	0.07	—	0.29A	1/12/01	8.80 - 6.00
—	—	—	pd0.21	d0.02	d0.03	—	1.00	1.00	1.25	12.5	0.17Q	2/1/03	10.80 - 5.18
0.69	0.73	0.72	2.38	2.16	—	—	0.77	0.61	0.51	2.7	0.20Q	3/3/03	35.17 - 21.60
—	—	—	—	—	—	—	0.70	0.70	0.70	1.7	0.47U	4/7/03	52.04 - 28.00
—	—	—	p1.26	d6.65	4.40	76.4 - 19.9	—	—	—	—	0.1875Q	5/1/03	96.25 - 25.11
—	—	—	pd0.82	0.05	0.21	—	—	—	—	—	—	—	14.60 - 3.15
—	—	—	pd0.25	0.03	1.27	—	—	0.45	—	—	0.20A	12/31/01	23.70 - 0.01
d0.17	d0.89	—	—	d1.61	2.31	—	—	—	—	—	50%	2/8/99	17.35 - 1.01
0.60	—	—	1.45	1.47	1.14	16.9 - 12.1	1.18	1.17	1.14	5.6	0.30Q	3/10/03	24.55 - 17.56
0.07	—	—	2.02	1.96	1.66	24.9 - 12.1	—	—	—	—	2-for-1	11/19/97	50.32 - 24.39
—	—	—	2.34	1.20	—	—	—	—	—	—	—	—	13.20 - 4.45
—	—	—	pd6.59	d0.26	d0.99	—	—	—	—	—	—	—	6.35 - 0.25
—	—	—	1.47	1.16	1.03	39.5 - 30.1	2.39	1.85	1.82	4.7	1.2988U	12/23/02	57.90 - 44.10
—	—	—	p1.84	0.49	1.67	14.1 - 9.1	0.44	0.44	0.44	2.1	0.13Q	6/5/03	25.90 - 16.75
0.34	0.43	—	1.75	1.44	1.31	34.0 - 17.8	0.46	0.41	0.35	1.0	0.12Q	4/1/03	59.53 - 31.15
—	—	—	1.19	0.73	0.91	15.7 - 7.6	—	—	—	—	0.00U	6/30/00	18.73 - 9.05
1.04	p0.79	—	4.00	1.54	2.00	22.3 - 14.8	—	—	—	—	100%	4/20/94	89.34 - 59.20
—	—	—	p2.23	3.12	2.53	23.6 - 16.3	2.74	2.48	2.20	6.2	0.70Q	4/15/03	52.65 - 36.38
d0.33	—	—	d2.44	d1.33	—	—	—	—	—	—	—	5/30/03	12.73 - 1.12
—	—	—	p2.59	2.47	2.84	26.9 - 20.1	0.41	0.32	0.32	0.7	—	5/30/03	74.21 - 48.00
—	—	—	p0.19	0.18	0.58	77.9 - 31.6	1.35	1.23	1.11	2.2	0.36Q	3/19/03	69.70 - 52.06
—	—	—	—	—	—	—	—	—	—	—	0.01Q	1/2/96	14.80 - 6.01
—	—	—	p0.60	1.20	1.47	27.7 - 14.6	0.48	0.48	0.48	3.8	0.12Q	3/14/03	16.60 - 8.75
—	d0.49	—	—	d0.71	0.13	—	0.07	0.30	0.38	0.4	0.075Q	1/2/02	29.24 - 5.55
—	—	—	2.22	1.79	2.02	25.7 - 19.6	0.80	0.76	0.74	1.6	0.21Q	3/3/03	57.10 - 43.49
0.01	0.01	—	—	d0.04	3.22	—	0.15	0.15	0.14	0.9	0.0375Q	2/28/03	25.40 - 7.31
—	—	—	—	—	—	—	0.43	0.81	0.98	2.7	0.43U	6/7/02	23.19 - 9.05
—	—	—	1.51	1.48	1.23	17.2 - 7.3	—	—	—	—	—	—	25.90 - 11.00
0.49	0.49	0.37	1.50	1.63	—	—	—	0.16	0.16	—	0.16A	4/27/01	21.45 - 10.95
—	—	—	p0.19	d0.04	1.07	32.1 - 24.7	0.20	0.20	0.20	3.7	0.05Q	3/28/03	6.10 - 4.69
—	—	—	0.66	1.30	0.31	60.5 - 34.2	0.46	0.46	0.46	1.5	0.115Q	2/21/03	39.95 - 22.60
—	—	—	p0.69	0.65	1.34	36.6 - 25.1	0.52	0.52	0.49	2.4	0.13Q	3/31/03	25.24 - 17.30
—	—	—	2.71	d1.85	1.07	20.1 - 12.0	0.36	0.30	0.30	0.8	0.09Q	3/17/03	54.49 - 32.60
—	—	—	p0.11	2.70	2.84	219.1 - 51.8	—	—	—	—	—	—	24.10 - 5.70
—	—	—	—	—	—	—	0.30	0.25	0.29	3.0	0.0805U	1/21/03	12.90 - 6.92
—	—	—	—	—	—	—	1.05	0.44	1.06	4.8	0.3699U	2/24/03	33.69 - 9.67
—	—	—	—	—	—	—	0.46	—	0.55	3.1	0.3985U	3/24/03	20.65 - 8.90
—	—	—	—	—	—	—	0.30	—	—	1.7	0.016U	5/12/03	20.75 - 14.25
—	—	—	—	—	—	—	0.26	—	—	0.9	0.47Q	12/6/01	43.97 - 14.25
—	—	—	—	—	—	—	—	1.88	1.25	—	0.05523U	5/9/03	29.70 - 2.00
—	—	—	—	—	—	—	0.22	0.21	0.17	3.1	0.1218U	4/2/02	9.54 - 4.70
—	—	—	—	—	—	—	1.22	1.01	0.68	6.6	0.0295U	1/13/03	20.15 - 16.50
—	—	—	—	—	—	—	0.12	0.05	—	5.5	—	—	2.88 - 1.35
—	—	—	p1.39	1.19	0.88	16.0 - 11.4	0.60	0.56	0.52	3.1	0.16Q	4/1/03	22.21 - 15.90
—	—	—	p2.52	2.12	2.90	16.7 - 10.3	1.26	1.22	1.18	3.7	0.32Q	4/17/03	42.01 - 26.00
—	—	—	p2.52	2.12	2.90	14.7 - 9.1	1.26	1.22	1.18	4.2	0.32Q	4/17/03	36.98 - 23.00
—	—	—	5.91	4.18	4.52	13.0 - 9.1	2.44	2.28	2.06	3.7	0.20Q	3/28/03	77.09 - 53.95
—	—	—	5.91	4.18	4.52	4.4 - 4.2	0.73	0.72	0.71	2.7	0.40625Q	4/15/03	25.87 - 24.80
—	—	—	1.70	1.46	1.42	18.3 - 13.4	1.28	1.04	0.90	2.9	0.19Q	3/14/03	31.05 - 22.79
—	—	—	1.24	1.81	1.92	37.5 - 16.8	0.76	0.72	0.66	2.3	0.5492U	1/17/03	52.99 - 33.75
—	—	—	2.80	2.28	pd0.45	15.3 - 11.3	0.84	0.84	1.47	2.3	0.19Q	2/6/03	46.50 - 20.85
—	—	—	p0.81	0.63	0.38	16.1 - 8.6	0.12	0.11	0.10	1.2	0.21Q	4/1/03	42.88 - 31.60
—	—	—	1.99	1.71	1.32	13.8 - 10.4	0.16	0.50	0.50	2.4	0.031Q	4/18/03	13.01 - 7.00
—	—	—	p1.71	2.01	2.35	22.9 - 17.0	0.64	0.61	0.60	1.9	0.16Q	2/10/03	27.45 - 20.68
—	—	—	—	—	—	—	1.03	0.89	0.80	3.5	0.16Q	5/1/03	39.10 - 29.05
—	—	—	p2.94	2.75	2.09	21.7 - 15.0	0.86	0.84	0.82	1.6	0.7781U	4/28/03	38.00 - 21.37
d0.25	0.02	0.05	—	0.94	d0.81	—	—	—	—	—	0.22Q	1/31/03	63.94 - 44.10
—	—	—	1.42	1.01	1.90	18.8 - 12.2	0.80	0.80	0.79	3.6	2-for-1	9/22/97	35.00 - 16.77
—	—	—	—	—	—	—	—	—	—	—	0.20Q	3/11/03	26.75 - 17.30
0.61	0.63	—	3.12	1.11	0.79	17.1 - 10.6	—	—	—	—	3-for-2	3/17/03	53.34 - 32.93
—	—	—	pd1.23	0.10	d0.09	—	—	—	—	—	5-for-4	1/17/96	6.45 - 3.06
—	—	—	—	—	—	—	0.92	1.31	0.73	2.3	1.2169U	5/19/03	46.85 - 31.84
—	—	—	p1.34	0.78	1.49	33.4 - 20.3	0.78	1.04	1.04	2.2	0.13Q	4/1/03	44.80 - 27.16
—	—	—	p1.26	1.09	1.24	47.5 - 19.1	0.58	0.58	0.15	1.4	0.582A	1/6/03	59.90 - 24.07
0.11	d0.07	4.39	p1.99	d10.00	—	—	—	—	0.30	—	0.10Q	8/25/00	7.65 - 5.25
—	—	—	—	—	—	—	0.64	0.91	0.86	2.4	0.7642U	5/12/03	36.00 - 16.77
—	—	—	p2.70	2.12	1.55	14.6 - 11.5	1.10	0.98	0.86	3.1	0.29Q	5/1/03	39.47 - 31.03
—	—	—	—	—	—	—	0.48	0.43	0.39	3.6	0.4905U	4/17/03	27.00 - 0.01
—	—	—	—	—	—	—	—	1.05	0.60	—	1.05U	5/9/01	7.33 - 1.20
—	—	—	6.47	4.27	5.35	10.4 - 7.8	0.62	0.60	0.55	1.1	0.17Q	1/31/03	67.55 - 50.50
0.09	0.09	—	0.34	d1.19	d0.58	26.5 - 14.8	—	—	—	—	—	—	9.02 - 5.03
2.75	—	—	10.74	8.26	5.05	8.9 - 4.8	0.35	0.34	0.33	0.9	0.09Q	3/13/03	95.05 - 51.40
0.43	—	—	p2.08	2.21	2.03	25.5 - 12.1	0.39	0.38	0.37	1.2	0.10Q	3/31/03	53.00 - 25.20
0.47	0.49	0.48	1.79	1.63	1.49	21.6 - 13.8	1.94	1.83	1.71	8.1	0.50Q	4/15/03	38.60 - 24.70
—	—	—	—	2.16	3.69	—	0.20	0.20	0.20	1.1	0.05Q	4/3/03	27.50 - 20.67
—	—	—	pd0.64	1.26	2.14	—	0.78	0.76	0.76	2.6	0.21Q	5/1/03	25.75 - 10.90
—	—	—	1.44	1.36	2.23	28.4 - 12.7	0.30	0.30	0.28	1.4	0.075Q	6/6/03	40.90 - 18.32
—	—	—	1.15	d0.02	1.29	21.3 - 15.4	1.04	1.00	0.96	2.1	0.28Q	3/3/03	24.52 - 17.75
—	—	—	p3.08	2.64	2.44	18.9 - 12.8	—	—	—	—	2-for-1	8/14/97	58.24 - 39.40
—	—	—	p1.51	d2.77	1.06	22.1 - 9.4	—	—	—	—	—	—	33.39 - 14.25
—	—	—	—	—	—	—	0.55	0.58	1.35	2.4	0.5495U	5/31/02	28.67 - 16.55
0.66	0.52	0.78	—	d2.09	0.93	—	0.39	0.35	0.35	1.1	0.10Q	4/1/03	40.80 - 29.90
598.00	681.00	744.00	—	521.00	2185.00	—	—	—	—	—	—	—	1000000 - 1000000

T7

SYMBOL	COMPANY	NATURE OF BUSINESS	FISCAL YEAR-END	TOTAL REV. $MILL	NET INCOME $MILL	TOTAL ASSETS $MILL	NET STK EQUITY $MILL	NO. OF INST.	INST. HOLDINGS (SHARES)
BRK B	Berkshire Hathaway Inc.	Property & casualty insurance	12/31/01	37668.0	795.0	162752.0	57950.0	557	77973876
BRY	Berry Petroleum, Co.	Oil	12/31/02	p132.6	p132.6	—	—	63	8957170
BBY	Best Buy Co., Inc. (United S	Specialty stores	3/2/02	19597.0	570.0	7375.0	2521.0	460	226024524
BEV	Beverly Enterprises, Inc.	Hospitals & nursing homes	12/31/02	p2424.7	p2347.5	—	—	105	70284719
BRG	BG Group Plc (United Kingdom)	Industrial	12/31/01	—	—	—	—	34	5069020
BHP	BHP Billiton Ltd. (Australia)	Mining & processing	6/30/02	17285.0	1648.0	29862.0	13153.0	94	29921805
BLI	Big Lots, Inc. (United States	Specialty stores	2/1/03	p3868.6	p3868.6	—	—	222	113420871
BSG	Bisys Group, Inc. (The) (Uni	Services	6/30/02	865.7	115.9	1246.2	682.6	236	109928394
BJS	BJ Services Co. (United Stat	Oil service & equipment	9/30/02	1865.8	166.5	2442.4	1418.6	333	166394361
BJ	BJ's Wholesale Club, Inc. (	Discount & variety stores	2/1/03	p5859.7	p5859.7	—	—	232	63658773
BKF	BKF Capital Group Inc	Investment company	12/31/01	91.5	1.5	146.9	103.5	44	3507094
BDK	Black & Decker Corp.	Hardware & tools	12/31/02	4394.0	229.7	4130.5	599.6	313	74500263
BKH	Black Hills Corp.	Electric power	12/31/02	p423.9	p422.2	—	—	148	11216479
BAT	BlackRock Advantage Term Trus	Investment company	12/31/01	10.8	9.5	146.3	110.7	13	1458689
BFC	BlackRock CA Insd Mun 2008 Tr	Investment company	12/31/01	15.3	13.4	280.2	279.0	6	156416
BCK	Blackrock California Insured	Investment company	10/21/02	—	—	0.2	0.2	—	—
BFZ	BlackRock California Municip	Investment company	10/31/02	18.6	16.7	353.0	212.2	3	29882
BJZ	Blackrock California Municipa	Investment company	10/18/01	—	d0.0	0.1	0.1	—	—
BHK	Blackrock Core Bond Trust	Investment company	11/19/01	—	d0.0	0.1	0.1	—	—
BRF	BlackRock FL Insd Mun 2008 Tr	Investment company	12/31/01	12.4	10.8	224.6	223.5	11	220297
BAF	Blackrock Florida Insured Mu	Investment company	10/21/02	—	—	0.1	0.1	—	—
BBF	BlackRock Florida Municipal	Investment company	10/31/02	8.0	7.1	157.5	96.8	6	185079
BHY	BlackRock High Yield Trust	Investment company	10/31/02	8.6	7.6	58.6	39.0	6	38164
BNA	BlackRock Income Opportunity	Investment company	10/31/02	43.3	39.6	669.4	407.5	25	11081550
BKT	BlackRock Income Trust Inc.	Investment company	10/31/02	67.4	62.2	732.7	511.4	30	1185596
BMT	BlackRock Insured Mun Term Tr	Investment company	12/31/01	26.1	23.1	460.9	451.1	23	912207
BRM	BlackRock Insured Muni 2008	Investment company	12/31/01	40.9	36.2	747.8	728.1	21	1801348
BYM	Blackrock Insured Municipal	Investment company	10/21/02	—	—	0.2	0.2	—	—
BKN	BlackRock Investment Qual Mun	Investment company	10/31/02	22.7	19.9	401.9	253.7	16	271130
BQT	BlackRock Invt Quality Term	Investment company	12/31/01	24.0	20.3	361.6	345.7	20	2518013
BMN	BlackRock Mun Target Term Tr	Investment company	12/31/01	42.5	37.8	802.4	779.3	28	1741030
BPK	Blackrock Municipal 2018 Term	Investment company	10/18/01	—	d0.0	0.1	0.1	—	—
BFK	BlackRock Municipal Income Tr	Investment company	10/31/02	57.2	52.3	978.4	579.7	21	620021
BNJ	Blackrock New Jersey Municipa	Investment company	10/31/02	9.1	8.1	170.5	106.0	3	37588
BSE	Blackrock New York Insured M	Investment company	10/21/02	—	—	0.1	0.1	—	—
BNY	Blackrock New York Municipal	Investment company	10/31/02	15.3	13.7	292.1	181.2	5	130800
BLH	Blackrock New York Municipal BlackRock NY InsMun 2008	Investment company	10/18/01	—	d0.0	0.1	0.1	—	—
BLN	Term	Investment company	12/31/02	16.0	14.0	293.4	292.2	11	100941
BHD	Blackrock Strategic Bond Trus	Investment company	2/20/02	—	d0.0	0.1	0.1	—	—
BSD	Blackrock Strategic Municipal	Investment company	12/31/01	10.0	9.0	166.5	165.8	7	35915
BLK	BlackRock, Inc.	—	12/31/01	533.1	107.4	684.5	486.1	90	13524969
HRB	Block (H. & R.), Inc.	Services	4/30/02	3317.7	434.4	4230.8	1369.4	450	147428439
BBI	Blockbuster, Inc.	—	12/31/02	p5565.9	p5565.9	—	—	127	31944768
BLT	Blount International Inc (New	Engineering & construction	12/31/02	p479.5	p161.2	—	—	17	27481396
BLU	Blue Chip Value Fund, Inc.	Investment company	12/31/02	2.3	0.9	132.0	128.7	15	235949
BSI	Blue Square - Israel Ltd.	Grocery chain	12/31/01	5577.5	144.3	3214.6	1397.0	2	23399
BXG	Bluegreen Corp. (United Stat	Real estate	3/31/02	287.8	11.7	435.2	149.7	17	3128348
BTH	Blyth, Inc. (United States)	—	1/31/02	1198.5	68.0	794.3	468.1	148	28295685
BMM	BMC Industries, Inc.	Photo & optical	12/31/02	p248.1	p195.8	—	—	20	12070273
BMC	BMC Software, Inc.	Computer services	3/31/02	1288.9	d184.1	2676.2	1506.6	303	190042137
BOX	BOC Group Plc (UK)	Conglomerate	9/30/02	—	—	—	—	23	3521166
RST	Boca Resorts, Inc.	Motel/hotel lodging	6/30/02	273.0	6.3	916.7	516.3	52	12844070
BA	Boeing Co.	—	12/31/02	54069.0	2319.0	52342.0	7696.0	693	531798509
BCC	Boise Cascade Corp.	Paper	12/31/02	p7412.3	p7422.7	—	—	211	52623806
BEP	Boise Cascade Corp.	Paper	12/31/02	p7412.3	p7422.7	—	—	—	—
BBA	Bombay Co., Inc. (The)	Furniture & fixtures	2/2/02	437.5	3.7	206.9	158.7	57	16726791
BGP	Borders Group, Inc.	Specialty stores	1/27/02	3387.9	87.4	2179.3	949.9	193	73975831
BWA	Borg Warner Inc	—	12/31/02	p2731.1	p208.4	—	—	214	22771936
SAM	Boston Beer Co., Inc	—	12/28/02	p215.4	p100.0	—	—	74	5264632
BXP	Boston Properties, Inc.	Real estate investment trust	12/31/02	p1234.8	p295.0	—	—	236	80729608
BSX	Boston Scientific Corp. (Uni	Medical & dental equipment	12/31/02	p2919.0	p1873.0	—	—	404	263633439
BIF	Boulder Growth & Income Fund	Investment company	11/30/02	0.8	0.1	37.9	37.3	—	—
BTF	Boulder Total Return Fund Inc	Investment company	11/30/02	8.6	4.6	219.6	219.1	14	283124
BOW	Bowater Inc. (United States)	Paper	12/31/02	p2581.1	p2581.1	—	—	186	57132144
BNE	Bowne & Co., Inc.	Printing & engraving	12/31/02	p1003.3	p1003.3	—	—	106	23316970
BYD	Boyd Gaming Corp.	+	12/31/02	p1228.9	p1228.9	—	—	121	21536692
FOB	Boyds Collection Ltd (The)	—	12/31/02	p131.3	p131.3	—	—	38	11273139
BOY	Boykin Lodging Co	Real estate investment trust	12/31/02	p263.1	p263.1	—	—	71	6773402
BP	BP p.l.c. (United Kingdom)	Oil	12/31/01	—	—	—	—	888	5186615867
BPT	BP Prudhoe Bay Royalty Trust	Oil producer	12/31/01	60.0	59.3	19.1	18.6	40	1002938
BRC	Brady Corp.	—	7/31/02	517.0	28.3	420.5	324.2	88	16001679
BDN	Brandywine Realty Trust	Real estate investment trust	12/31/02	p296.7	p296.7	—	—	130	27015103
BRP	Brasil Telecom Participacoes	Telecommunications	12/31/01	—	—	—	—	28	2768682
BTM	Brasil Telecom S.A. (Brazil)	Telecommunications	12/31/01	—	—	—	—	1	32700
BAK	Braskem S A	Specialty chemicals	12/31/01	—	—	—	—	—	—
BZF	Brazil Fund, Inc.	Investment company	6/30/02	13.3	8.8	255.9	253.8	20	6047706
BZL	Brazilian Equity Fund, Inc.	Investment company	3/31/02	1.4	0.7	32.4	32.0	4	1861395
BRE	BRE Properties, Inc. (United	Real estate investment trust	12/31/02	271.8	84.0	2108.7	851.2	147	28149471
BGG	Briggs & Stratton Corp.	Machinery & equipment	6/30/02	1529.4	53.1	1349.0	449.6	170	17869825
CBA	Brilliance China Automotive	—	12/31/01	—	—	—	—	7	225279
EAT	Brinker International, Inc.	Restaurants	6/26/02	2887.1	152.7	1783.3	977.1	287	88274891
BMY	Bristol-Myers Squibb Co.	Drugs	12/31/01	19423.0	2527.0	27057.0	10736.0	1090	1255926989
BAB	British Airways Plc	—	3/31/02	—	—	—	—	39	5904892
BSY	British Sky Broadcasting Gr	Broadcasting	6/30/02	—	—	—	—	23	2295247
BRW	Broadwing, Inc.	Telecommunications	12/31/01	2350.5	d286.2	6312.0	1678.4	179	145209507
BRO	Brown & Brown, Inc.	Insurance	12/31/02	p455.7	p404.2	—	—	184	39959680
TBI	Brown (Tom), Inc.	Oil	12/31/02	235.6	9.9	851.0	563.6	134	29240647
BWS	Brown Shoe Co., Inc. (United	Shoe manufacturing	2/1/03	p1841.4	p1841.4	—	—	112	12463387
BF A	Brown-Forman Corp.	Distilling	4/30/02	2208.0	228.0	2016.0	1311.0	44	17107298
BF B	Brown-Forman Corp.	Distilling	4/30/02	2208.0	228.0	2016.0	1311.0	196	33394853
BRT	BRT Realty Trust	Real estate investment trust	9/30/02	18.0	12.6	134.9	114.3	10	1879254
BC	Brunswick Corp.	Recreation	12/31/02	3711.9	103.5	3407.1	1101.8	226	80201308
BW	Brush Engineered Materials In	Metal products	12/31/02	p372.8	p372.8	—	—	73	11879956
BTY	BT Group Plc (United Kingdom	Telecommunications	3/31/02	—	—	—	—	71	18625490
BPL	Buckeye Partners, L.P.	Oil	12/31/02	p247.3	p247.3	—	—	97	2731471
BKI	Buckeye Technologies Inc.	Paper	6/30/02	635.2	d14.5	1135.4	253.7	88	24083654

T8

1st	2nd	3rd	2002	2001	2000	P/E RATIO	Div 2002	Div 2001	Div 2000	AV. YLD. %	AMOUNT	PAYABLE	PRICE RANGE 2002
598.00	681.00	744.00	—	521.00	2185.00	—	—	—	—	—	—	—	2620.00 - 1925.00
—	—	—	p1.37	0.99	1.67	13.4 - 9.7	0.40	0.40	0.40	2.5	0.10Q	3/28/03	18.31 - 13.25
0.22	0.19	0.26	—	1.77	1.24	—	—	—	—	—	50%	5/10/02	53.75 - 16.99
—	—	—	pd1.39	d2.90	d0.53	—	—	—	—	—	—	—	9.50 - 1.60
—	—	—	—	—	—	—	0.23	0.21	0.71	1.1	0.12322U	5/9/03	24.05 - 18.20
—	—	—	0.27	0.54	0.43	47.4 - 32.6	0.27	0.26	0.26	2.5	0.14U	12/4/02	12.95 - 8.90
—	—	—	p0.66	d0.25	0.87	30.2 - 14.8	—	0.01	—	—	0.01U	9/10/01	19.90 - 9.75
0.14	0.24	—	0.94	0.70	0.61	38.5 - 13.9	—	—	—	—	100%	2/22/02	36.20 - 13.02
0.21	—	—	1.04	2.09	0.70	38.0 - 22.1	—	—	—	—	100%	5/31/01	39.49 - 23.00
—	—	—	p1.84	1.11	1.77	26.2 - 7.8	—	—	—	—	100%	3/2/99	48.19 - 14.42
—	—	—	—	—	—	—	—	—	—	—	—	—	32.83 - 17.11
—	—	—	2.84	1.33	3.34	17.8 - 12.3	0.48	0.48	0.48	1.1	0.12Q	3/28/03	50.50 - 35.00
—	—	—	p2.26	3.42	2.37	16.3 - 8.1	1.16	1.12	1.08	4.2	0.30Q	3/1/03	36.90 - 18.35
—	11.97	—	—	11.64	10.83	—	0.63	0.60	0.60	5.5	—	3/31/03	12.05 - 10.95
—	34.18	—	—	16.77	16.72	—	0.89	0.77	0.77	5.5	—	4/1/03	16.88 - 15.55
—	—	—	12.46	—	—	—	—	—	—	—	0.075M	4/1/03	15.01 - 14.51
—	—	—	14.16	—	—	—	0.88	0.22	—	6.5	0.07375M	4/1/03	14.35 - 12.80
—	—	—	—	12.46	—	—	0.74	—	—	5.4	0.06125M	4/1/03	14.55 - 12.90
—	14.19	—	—	10.61	—	—	1.10	—	—	8.0	0.10M	3/31/03	15.05 - 12.50
—	16.21	—	—	16.01	15.84	—	0.79	0.75	0.82	5.1	0.0625M	4/1/03	15.98 - 15.10
—	—	—	12.46	—	—	—	—	—	—	—	0.075M	4/1/03	15.08 - 14.49
—	—	—	14.57	—	—	—	0.88	0.22	—	6.3	—	4/1/03	15.00 - 13.00
—	—	—	6.13	7.20	10.60	—	1.26	1.53	1.64	12.7	—	3/31/03	11.90 - 7.89
—	—	—	11.83	11.47	11.03	—	0.75	0.75	0.84	7.2	0.07M	3/31/03	10.99 - 9.83
—	—	—	8.13	—	7.23	—	0.58	0.56	0.56	7.4	—	3/31/03	8.38 - 7.27
—	11.10	—	—	10.85	10.85	—	0.69	0.60	0.60	6.5	—	4/1/03	11.05 - 10.23
—	34.02	—	—	16.80	16.62	—	0.87	0.80	0.80	5.4	0.06625M	4/1/03	16.74 - 15.57
—	—	—	12.46	—	—	—	—	—	—	—	—	4/1/03	15.15 - 14.05
—	—	—	15.19	15.19	14.30	—	0.82	0.78	0.83	5.9	0.0725M	4/1/03	14.57 - 13.06
—	9.50	—	—	9.39	—	—	0.40	0.41	0.45	4.2	—	3/31/03	9.75 - 9.12
—	—	—	—	10.57	10.67	—	0.73	0.58	0.55	6.9	—	4/1/03	11.05 - 10.37
—	—	—	12.46	—	—	—	0.78	—	—	5.7	0.065M	4/1/03	14.31 - 12.90
—	—	—	13.33	—	—	—	0.93	0.23	—	6.8	—	4/1/03	14.47 - 12.80
—	—	—	14.29	—	—	—	0.87	0.22	—	6.2	0.0725M	4/1/03	14.90 - 13.39
—	—	—	12.46	—	—	—	—	—	—	—	0.075M	4/1/03	15.05 - 13.87
—	—	—	14.47	—	—	—	0.88	0.22	—	6.3	—	4/1/03	14.86 - 12.93
—	—	—	12.46	—	—	—	0.74	—	—	5.3	0.06125M	4/1/03	27.90 - 0.01
—	33.10	—	—	16.22	16.17	—	0.77	0.75	0.81	4.9	0.0625M	4/1/03	16.35 - 15.12
—	14.41	—	—	10.61	—	—	1.08	—	—	8.3	0.12M	3/31/03	15.05 - 11.00
—	14.83	—	—	14.33	14.75	—	0.88	0.86	0.92	6.3	—	4/1/03	14.96 - 13.02
0.48	0.53	0.51	—	1.65	1.35	—	—	—	—	—	—	—	47.60 - 33.55
d0.05	d0.21	0.73	—	2.31	1.50	—	0.66	0.61	0.56	1.6	0.18Q	4/1/03	53.50 - 29.00
—	—	—	pd8.96	d1.37	d0.43	—	0.08	0.08	0.08	0.4	0.02Q	3/10/03	30.25 - 11.80
—	—	—	pd0.19	1.04	0.04	—	—	—	—	—	—	—	5.11 - 2.70
—	—	—	4.85	6.94	8.17	—	0.61	0.81	1.57	10.4	0.0072Q	1/15/03	7.56 - 4.20
—	—	—	—	3.76	3.43	—	0.53	0.23	0.19	4.3	0.285U	12/24/02	17.60 - 7.44
0.19	0.21	p0.23	—	0.46	0.11	—	—	—	—	—	5%	3/28/96	5.75 - 2.01
0.37	0.40	0.66	—	1.44	1.69	—	0.22	0.20	0.20	0.8	0.11S	11/15/02	32.80 - 20.85
—	—	—	pd2.30	d0.83	0.54	—	0.01	0.06	0.06	0.5	0.0025Q	7/3/02	2.68 - 0.40
0.02	0.04	0.05	—	p0.75	0.17	—	—	—	—	—	2-for-1	5/15/98	23.00 - 10.85
—	—	—	—	—	—	—	1.13	1.07	1.08	3.9	0.50731U	2/10/03	32.25 - 25.58
d0.23	d0.01	—	0.16	0.34	0.33	89.1 - 60.0	—	—	—	—	—	—	14.25 - 9.60
—	—	—	2.87	3.41	2.44	17.8 - 9.9	0.68	0.68	0.56	1.7	0.17Q	3/7/03	51.07 - 28.53
—	—	—	pd0.03	d0.96	2.73	—	0.60	0.60	0.60	2.1	0.15Q	4/15/03	38.81 - 19.61
—	—	—	pd0.03	0.96	2.73	—	3.86	—	—	7.9	0.9375Q	3/17/03	97.68 - 0.01
d0.10	d0.10	—	—	0.11	0.26	—	—	—	—	—	3-for-2	12/31/93	5.25 - 2.14
0.05	0.04	d0.02	—	1.06	0.92	—	—	—	—	—	2-for-1	3/27/97	24.49 - 14.68
—	—	—	pd4.44	2.51	3.54	—	0.60	0.60	0.60	1.1	0.18Q	2/17/03	68.95 - 38.38
—	—	—	p0.52	0.47	0.62	34.6 - 22.7	—	—	—	—	—	—	18.00 - 11.82
—	—	—	p4.66	2.26	2.01	8.9 - 7.1	2.38	2.22	1.96	6.4	0.61Q	4/30/03	41.55 - 32.95
—	—	—	p0.90	d0.13	0.91	49.2 - 22.8	—	—	—	—	100%	11/30/98	44.30 - 20.48
—	6.59	—	7.15	8.65	—	—	0.25	0.67	0.74	4.1	0.065A	3/31/03	7.72 - 4.40
—	15.04	—	17.36	14.81	—	—	0.03	0.14	0.16	0.2	0.03A	12/31/02	18.55 - 12.09
—	—	—	pd2.50	1.37	3.02	—	0.80	0.80	0.80	1.8	0.20Q	4/1/03	55.80 - 31.00
—	—	—	—	—	—	1621.0	—	—	—	—	—	—	
—	—	—	p0.01	d0.23	0.20	- 866.0	0.22	0.22	0.22	1.8	0.055Q	2/19/03	16.21 - 8.66
—	—	—	p0.73	0.40	1.01	25.8 - 8.4	—	—	—	—	—	—	18.81 - 6.10
—	—	—	p0.53	0.63	0.71	16.6 - 9.8	—	—	—	—	—	—	8.80 - 5.20
—	—	—	pd0.09	d1.70	0.49	—	0.18	1.46	1.77	2.0	0.18Q	5/1/03	10.93 - 7.00
—	—	—	—	2.77	2.98	—	1.41	0.98	—	3.1	0.375U	3/24/03	53.98 - 36.25
0.35	p0.12	—	1.20	1.18	2.05	33.9 - 22.3	1.51	2.77	2.98	11.7	—	1/23/03	15.10 - 10.70
—	—	—	p1.40	0.60	1.12	18.8 - 13.2	0.77	0.73	0.69	2.3	0.20Q	4/30/03	26.30 - 18.47
—	—	—	—	—	—	—	1.76	1.67	1.61	7.9	0.44Q	1/15/03	40.70 - 26.70
—	—	—	—	—	—	—	1.20	0.80	1.09	3.6	—	2/5/03	45.30 - 20.85
—	—	—	—	—	—	—	0.92	—	—	6.9	—	2/5/03	18.78 - 8.10
—	—	—	—	—	—	—	0.36	1.13	1.86	9.4	—	5/28/02	5.05 - 2.50
—	13.46	—	15.43	19.63	24.01	—	0.72	0.92	0.30	5.5	0.27A	1/13/03	17.75 - 8.40
—	2.84	—	—	5.73	6.31	—	—	0.18	—	—	0.03A	1/10/03	5.50 - 2.55
—	—	—	1.56	1.70	1.60	22.0 - 16.9	1.95	1.86	1.70	6.4	0.4875Q	3/28/03	34.25 - 26.40
d0.32	p0.53	—	2.36	2.21	5.97	20.5 - 13.0	1.27	1.24	1.21	3.2	0.32Q	4/1/03	48.39 - 30.75
—	—	—	—	—	—	—	0.12	0.11	0.07	—	0.0512U	11/12/02	37.20 - 0.01
0.45	0.38	—	—	1.52	1.42	—	—	—	—	—	50%	1/16/01	36.00 - 24.07
0.30	0.23	—	—	1.29	2.05	—	1.12	1.10	0.98	3.1	0.28Q	5/1/03	51.95 - 19.49
—	—	—	—	—	—	—	—	2.56	2.73	—	1.8214U	8/7/01	36.76 - 14.50
—	—	—	—	—	—	—	—	—	—	—	3-for-2	12/23/02	48.64 - 28.13
d0.17	d0.10	0.01	—	d1.36	d1.82	—	—	—	—	—	0.10Q	8/3/99	10.62 - 1.09
—	—	—	p1.22	0.85	0.58	30.3 - 19.7	0.20	0.21	0.14	0.7	0.0575Q	2/19/03	37.00 - 24.00
—	—	—	0.25	1.68	1.76	119.2 - 82.8	—	—	—	—	1-for-20	9/8/88	29.80 - 20.70
—	—	—	p2.52	0.05	2.04	11.2 - 5.5	0.40	0.40	0.40	1.9	0.10Q	4/1/03	28.10 - 13.80
0.53	1.18	1.02	—	3.33	3.40	—	1.40	1.32	1.24	2.0	0.375Q	4/1/03	80.50 - 58.00
0.53	1.18	1.02	—	3.33	3.40	—	1.40	1.32	1.24	2.0	0.375Q	4/1/03	80.54 - 58.69
0.38	—	—	1.68	1.49	1.05	8.3 - 6.9	1.04	0.44	—	8.1	0.30Q	4/2/03	14.00 - 11.65
—	—	—	1.14	0.96	2.28	26.3 - 16.1	0.50	0.50	0.50	2.1	0.50A	12/13/02	30.01 - 18.30
—	—	—	pd2.15	0.62	0.86	—	—	0.36	0.24	—	0.12Q	7/6/01	14.25 - 4.50
—	—	—	—	—	—	—	0.31	—	—	0.9	0.36623U	2/18/03	42.05 - 24.00
—	—	—	p2.65	2.55	2.38	15.2 - 10.0	2.50	2.45	2.40	7.5	0.625Q	2/28/03	40.20 - 26.50
d0.01	0.01	—	d0.42	1.23	1.65	—	—	—	—	—	100%	2/17/98	13.05 - 5.10

T9

SYMBOL	COMPANY	NATURE OF BUSINESS	FISCAL YEAR-END	TOTAL REV. $MILL	NET INCOME $MILL	TOTAL ASSETS $MILL	NET STK EQUITY $MILL	NO. OF INST.	INST. HOLDINGS (SHARES)
BKE	Buckle, Inc. (The)	—	2/1/03	p401.1	p401.1	—	—	41	5606723
BUH	Buhrmann NV	Office equipment & supplies	12/31/01	—	—	—	—	8	1000678
BG	Bunge Ltd. (Bermuda)	—	12/31/01	11484.0	124.0	5443.0	1376.0	131	38336806
BNL	Bunzl Plc (United Kingdom)	Paper	12/31/01	—	—	—	—	8	130907
BCF	Burlington Coat Fact Whse	—	6/1/02	2604.6	66.9	1273.8	722.5	106	15229021
BNI	Burlington Northern Santa Fe	Railroads	12/31/02	8979.0	760.0	25767.0	7932.0	420	292929168
BSH	Bush Industries, Inc.	Furniture & fixtures	12/28/02	p340.2	p337.8	—	—	35	7355250
BBR	Butler Manufacturing Co.	—	12/31/02	828.2	d1.8	455.8	149.2	61	3191963
CHP	C&D Technologies Inc.	Electrical equipment	1/31/03	p335.7	p335.7	—	—	130	25533122
CWP	Cable & Wireless Plc (UK)	Telecommunications	3/31/02	—	—	—	—	63	11784591
CDT	Cable Design Technologies Cor	Electronic components	7/31/02	553.8	3.6	585.8	356.9	114	39489179
CVC	Cablevision Systems Corp-New	—	12/31/02	p4003.4	p4003.4	—	—	225	196589255
CBT	Cabot Corp.	Specialty chemicals	9/30/02	1557.0	105.0	2067.0	977.0	188	39638283
COG	Cabot Oil & Gas Corp.	Oil	12/31/01	353.8	16.1	1054.9	350.7	135	28900507
CAI	CACI International, Inc.	Computer services	6/30/02	681.9	31.9	480.7	367.2	200	24021886
CSG	Cadbury Schweppes PLC	Soft drinks	12/30/01	—	—	—	—	101	21038463
CDN	Cadence Design Systems, Inc.	Comp. components & periphs.	12/31/02	p1293.1	p1195.8	—	—	243	236829942
CHI	Calamos Conv Opportunities &	Investment company	6/14/02	—	—	1.0	—	70	27211484
CCC	Calgon Carbon Corp.	Chemicals	12/31/02	p258.1	p80.1	—	—	70	27211484
CFP	California Federal Preferred	Real estate investment trust	12/31/01	64.8	64.7	1012.7	1011.9	7	1226900
CWT	California Water Service Gro	Water company	12/31/01	p263.2	p263.2	—	—	68	2869334
ELY	Callaway Golf Co. (DE)	Recreation	12/31/02	792.1	69.4	679.8	543.4	181	61912636
CPE	Callon Petroleum Co. (DE)	Oil	12/31/01	61.8	1.8	372.1	147.2	30	4837706
CPN	Calpine Corp. (United States	Electric power	12/31/01	p7482.8	p7488.6	—	—	341	226028502
CBM	Cambrex Corp	Specialty chemicals	12/31/02	p530.7	p207.0	—	—	137	23397847
CPT	Camden Property Trust	Real estate investment trust	12/31/01	p411.0	p443.1	—	—	143	29333130
CPB	Campbell Soup Co.	Food processing	7/28/02	6133.0	525.0	5721.0	d114.0	310	143329953
CAJ	Canon, Inc. (Japan)	Office equipment & supplies	12/31/01	—	—	—	—	116	17354882
CMN	Cantel Medical Corp (United	Medical & dental equipment	7/31/02	120.0	7.2	107.8	57.9	45	3386348
COF	Capital One Financial Corp.	Financial services	12/31/02	9647.6	899.6	37382.4	4623.2	419	194442385
CSU	Capital Senior Living Corp. (	Hospitals & nursing homes	12/31/01	p61.5	p61.5	—	—	6	3310868
CT	Capital Trust, Inc. (MD)	Real estate	12/31/01	78.7	9.4	678.8	102.6	16	9416281
CMO	Capstead Mortgage Corp.	Real estate investment trust	12/31/02	—	p96.1	—	—	48	5568871
CRR	Carbo Ceramics Inc.	Mining & processing	12/31/02	p0.1	p0.0	—	—	83	9208008
CAH	Cardinal Health, Inc. (Unite	Drugs	6/30/02	51135.7	1126.3	16438.0	6393.0	763	397865484
CMX	Caremark Rx, Inc.	Hospitals & nursing homes	12/31/01	p6805.3	p7287.8	—	—	321	217719548
CSL	Carlisle Cos., Inc.	Conglomerate	12/31/01	p1971.3	p1927.5	—	—	161	18421995
KMX	Carmax Inc.	—	2/28/02	3201.7	90.8	720.2	485.5	186	87938291
CCL	Carnival Corp.	Recreation	11/30/02	—	—	—	—	446	336840260
CG	Carolina Group	—	12/31/01	4529.6	672.7	2769.4	1274.5	99	31103062
CRS	Carpenter Tech. Corp.	Steel producer	6/30/02	977.1	d6.0	1479.5	508.3	108	12247195
CRE	CarrAmerica Realty Corp. (Un	Real estate investment trust	12/31/01	527.7	86.1	2815.7	997.8	161	46928912
CSV	Carriage Services, Inc.	Services	12/31/01	p154.2	p154.2	—	—	25	6532179
CAE	Cascade Corp.	Machinery & equipment	1/31/02	252.7	5.3	247.3	113.3	71	5568904
CGC	Cascade Natural Gas Corp	Natural gas distributor	9/30/02	321.0	10.8	367.7	114.2	35	5106704
PWN	Cash America Intl., Inc.	Finance	12/31/01	p387.8	p388.6	—	—	97	18174307
POS	Catalina Marketing Corp.	—	3/31/02	446.7	61.9	403.8	254.9	176	47101814
CDX	Catellus Development Corp.	Real estate	12/31/02	—	p100.7	—	—	15	65462999
CAT	Caterpillar Inc	Machinery & equipment	12/31/02	—	—	—	—	541	268940543
CTR	Cato Corp.	—	2/2/02	705.7	43.1	332.0	234.7	95	15867403
CAV	Cavalier Homes, Inc.	Mobile homes	12/31/02	—	pd34.7	—	—	15	3385364
CBL	CBL & Associates Properties	Real estate investment trust	12/31/02	p599.1	p596.4	—	—	158	23951107
CDI	CDI Corp.	Services	12/31/02	p1169.5	p1169.5	—	—	104	9246835
CEC	CEC Entertainment, Inc.	Restaurants	12/29/02	p602.2	p602.2	—	—	113	27050590
FUN	Cedar Fair, L.P.	—	12/31/02	p502.9	p485.7	—	—	113	10001113
CZ	Celanese AG (Germany)	Chemicals	12/31/01	—	—	—	—	35	13319092
CRA	Celera Genomics Group	—	6/30/01	89.4	d186.2	1220.1	1110.7	159	43844280
CLL	Celltech Group Plc (UK)	—	12/31/01	—	—	—	—	26	2055242
CX	Cemex, S.A. de C.V. (Mexico)	Cement & gypsum	12/31/01	—	—	—	—	149	100819412
CD	Cendant Corp.	Services	12/31/02	14088.0	1081.0	35897.0	9315.0	525	809256088
JCD	Cendant Corp.	Services	12/31/02	14088.0	1081.0	35897.0	9315.0	8	751653
CNP	Centerpoint Energy, Inc (Unit	Electric power	12/31/02	7922.5	386.3	19634.3	1422.0	225	136484284
CNT	CenterPoint Properties Trust	Real estate	12/31/02	—	p75.4	—	—	125	19998137
CEP	Centerpulse, Ltd. Switzerlan	Medical & dental equipment	12/31/01	—	—	—	—	11	1257120
CXP	Centex Construction Products	Cement & gypsum	3/31/02	471.1	39.7	743.4	427.8	69	5790405
CTX	Centex Corp.	Home-building	3/31/02	7748.4	382.2	8985.5	2116.8	314	56883426
CEE	Central European Equity Fund	Investment company	10/31/02	1.4	d0.6	127.6	126.5	17	1343181
CPC	Central Parking Corp. (Unite	Services	9/30/02	1107.3	43.1	998.9	415.8	105	19584474
CV	Central Vermont Pub Svc Corp	Electric power	12/31/02	p303.4	p303.4	—	—	71	5090498
CTL	CenturyTel, Inc. (United Sta	Telecommunications	12/31/02	p1972.0	p1917.0	—	—	339	122336496
CEN	Ceridian Corp. (New)	Services	12/31/02	p1192.7	p1192.7	—	—	181	138846878
CEY	Certegy, Inc. (United States	Telecommunications	12/31/02	1008.0	90.0	702.1	198.4	207	58350572
CHG	CH Energy Group, Inc.	Electric power	12/31/02	695.5	36.5	1210.1	520.4	125	6995515
CHB	Champion Enterprises, Inc	Mobile homes	12/28/02	p1372.3	p1372.3	—	—	87	49881262
MPH	Championship Auto Racing Team	—	12/31/01	70.3	d0.9	132.9	117.9	41	6529490
CRL	Charles River Laboratories In	—	12/31/02	p554.6	p536.4	—	—	215	43450403
CTI	Chart Industries, Inc.	Machinery & equipment	12/31/02	328.0	d5.1	409.0	49.3	53	4370878
CF	Charter One Financial, Inc.	Banking - Midwest	12/31/02	2834.0	577.7	41896.1	3083.8	375	149930321
CWF	Chartwell Dividend & Income F	Investment company	11/30/02	14.4	10.5	172.1	120.1	9	403959
CPJ	Chateau Communities, Inc.	Real estate investment trust	12/31/02	p269.7	p269.7	—	—	107	13842709
CKP	Checkpoint Systems Inc	Electronic components	12/31/01	p639.5	p639.5	—	—	122	24758790
CPG	Chelsea Property Group, Inc.	Real estate investment trust	12/31/02	p283.2	p283.2	—	—	155	32535549
CHE	Chemed Corp.	Specialty chemicals	12/31/01	477.1	d6.7	396.5	208.3	93	7469578
CSK	Chesapeake Corp.	Paper	12/31/02	p822.2	p822.2	—	—	100	9406812
CHK	Chesapeake Energy Corp. (Uni	Oil producer	12/31/02	p737.8	p737.8	—	—	220	118725803
CPK	Chesapeake Utilities Corp.	Natural gas distributor	12/31/02	p142.2	p140.3	—	—	28	918972
CVX	ChevronTexaco Corp.	Oil	12/31/02	99049.0	1132.0	77359.0	31604.0	1085	698805016
CBI	Chicago Bridge & Iron Co., N.	Engineering & construction	12/31/01	—	—	—	—	66	21713426
CME	Chicago Mercantile Exchange	Finance	12/31/02	—	p94.1	—	—	71	4129004
CHS	Chico's FAS, Inc. (United Sta	Specialty stores	2/1/03	p531.1	p531.1	—	—	241	74880927
CH	Chile Fund, Inc.	Investment company	12/31/01	6.8	2.8	138.8	134.3	22	3666339
CEA	China Eastern Airlines Corp.	—	12/31/01	—	—	—	—	3	50200
CHN	China Fund, Inc.	Investment company	10/31/02	4.2	1.1	152.1	150.3	21	5112522
CHL	China Mobile (Hong Kong) Ltd.	Telecommunications	12/31/01	—	—	—	—	98	28225144
SNP	China Petroleum & Chemical Co	Oil	12/31/01	—	—	—	—	23	3982712
ZNH	China Southern Airlines Co Lt	—	12/31/01	—	—	—	—	5	346489

EPS 1st Qtr	EPS 2nd Qtr	EPS 3rd Qtr	Annual 2002	Annual 2001	Annual 2000	P/E RATIO	Div 2002	Div 2001	Div 2000	AV. YLD. %	DIV. AMOUNT	DIV. PAYABLE	PRICE RANGE 2002
—	—	—	p1.47	1.52	1.63	17.3 - 10.7	—	—	—	—	50%	6/8/98	25.46 - 15.72
—	—	—	—	—	—	—	0.11	0.39	0.40	1.3	0.1098U	5/30/02	14.00 - 2.43
—	—	—	—	1.72	0.34	—	0.39	0.10	—	1.8	0.10Q	5/30/03	26.32 - 16.98
—	—	—	—	—	—	—	0.78	0.67	0.64	2.3	0.5955U	7/11/03	39.80 - 29.25
d0.36	0.93	—	—	1.51	1.62	—	0.02	0.02	0.02	0.1	0.02A	11/30/02	23.50 - 14.90
—	—	—	2.00	1.89	2.36	15.9 - 11.6	0.48	0.49	0.48	1.7	0.12Q	4/1/03	31.75 - 23.18
—	—	—	pd0.10	0.02	1.60	—	0.20	0.20	0.20	2.3	0.05Q	11/29/02	13.90 - 3.85
—	—	—	d0.29	1.28	3.86	—	0.72	0.69	0.65	3.0	0.18Q	4/4/03	29.10 - 18.59
—	—	—	p0.74	1.35	2.05	33.3 - 16.9	0.07	0.06	0.06	0.4	0.01375Q	4/2/03	24.65 - 12.50
d0.16	—	—	0.08	0.52	1.25	190.9 - 55.0	0.72	0.72	0.67	8.2	3-for-2	8/21/00	15.45 - 1.91
—	—	—	p0.28	7.55	1.29	172.3 - 16.7	—	—	—	—		3/13/03	15.27 - 4.40
—	—	—	—	—	—	—	—	—	—	—	0.00U	3/29/01	48.25 - 4.67
0.48	—	—	1.48	1.62	1.46	25.1 - 13.1	0.52	0.50	0.44	1.8	0.13Q	3/14/03	37.22 - 19.45
—	—	—	0.50	1.53	1.06	53.1 - 35.5	0.16	0.16	0.16	0.7	0.04Q	2/21/03	26.55 - 17.75
0.32	0.36	—	1.24	0.90	0.76	34.8 - 22.1	—	—	—	—	100%	12/6/01	43.10 - 27.43
—	—	—	p0.27	0.27	0.55	90.3 - 32.0	0.66	0.61	0.59	2.4	0.5152U	6/2/03	31.91 - 24.10
—	—	—	—	14.32	—	—	—	—	—	—	2-for-1	11/14/97	24.39 - 8.65
—	—	—	pd0.68	0.20	0.25	—	0.54	—	—	3.7	0.125M	3/28/03	16.35 - 13.00
—	—	—	—	—	—	—	0.12	0.20	0.20	1.7	0.03Q	3/7/03	9.89 - 4.00
—	—	—	—	—	—	—	2.28	2.28	2.28	8.9	0.54487Q	3/27/03	26.65 - 24.60
—	—	—	p1.25	0.97	1.31	21.5 - 16.4	1.12	1.11	1.10	4.7	0.28125Q	2/21/03	26.89 - 20.45
—	—	—	1.03	0.82	1.14	20.1 - 9.1	0.28	0.28	0.28	1.9	0.07Q	4/3/03	20.68 - 9.42
d0.21	0.15	d0.12	—	0.04	0.80	—	—	—	—	—			9.40 - 3.20
—	—	—	p0.19	1.85	1.11	90.9 - 8.2	—	—	—	—	2-for-1	11/14/00	17.28 - 1.55
—	—	—	p1.37	1.00	1.90	32.6 - 17.5	0.12	0.12	0.12	0.3	0.03Q	2/21/03	44.61 - 24.00
—	—	—	p1.73	1.42	1.63	24.1 - 16.7	2.52	2.39	2.21	7.1	0.635Q	4/17/03	41.66 - 28.95
0.47	p0.56	—	1.28	1.55	1.65	23.4 - 15.4	0.63	0.83	0.90	2.5	0.1575Q	1/31/03	30.00 - 19.65
—	—	—	—	—	—	—	0.18	0.16	0.13	0.5	0.12392U	4/8/03	41.00 - 30.00
0.13	0.24	—	0.74	0.57	0.42	26.9 - 12.8	—	—	—	—	50%	5/14/02	19.90 - 9.50
—	—	—	3.93	2.91	2.24	16.9 - 6.1	0.11	0.11	0.11	0.2		2/20/03	66.50 - 24.05
—	—	—	p0.24	0.15	0.06	17.7 - 8.5	—	—	—	—			4.25 - 2.03
0.08	0.06	0.08	—	0.37	0.33	—	—	—	—	—	1-for-3	4/2/03	5.75 - 3.51
—	—	—	p4.85	5.68	d6.60	5.3 - 2.8	5.90	3.06	—	29.9			25.71 - 13.80
—	—	—	p1.28	1.74	1.00	32.8 - 23.1	0.36	0.35	0.30	1.0	0.09Q	2/14/03	42.00 - 29.60
0.65	0.82	—	2.45	1.88	1.59	30.1 - 19.0	0.10	0.09	0.07	0.2	0.025Q	4/15/03	73.70 - 46.60
—	—	—	p3.01	0.73	0.43	7.3 - 4.1	—	—	—	—			21.95 - 12.24
0.35	—	0.14	p0.94	0.82	3.14	50.2 - 34.4	0.85	0.82	0.76	2.1	0.215Q	3/1/03	47.23 - 32.36
—	—	—	—	0.82	0.43	—	—	—	—	—			20.47 - 12.90
—	—	—	—	—	—	—	0.42	0.42	0.42	1.5	0.105Q	3/14/03	34.64 - 22.07
d0.51	d0.34	—	d0.35	1.50	2.31	—	1.33	—	—	5.3	0.445Q	3/17/03	34.05 - 16.80
—	—	—	1.04	0.71	1.65	32.0 - 21.1	1.07	1.32	1.32	5.3	0.0825Q	3/6/03	30.55 - 10.25
—	—	—	p1.16	0.51	d5.80	4.8 - 2.5	2.00	1.85	1.85	7.2	0.50Q	2/28/03	33.30 - 21.94
0.35	0.36	0.36	—	0.44	0.97	—	—	—	—	—			5.54 - 2.90
0.60	—	—	0.97	1.56	1.39	24.9 - 16.0	0.10	—	0.30	0.7	0.10Q	4/11/03	16.74 - 11.70
—	—	—	p0.78	0.51	d0.07	13.2 - 8.3	0.96	0.96	0.96	4.8	0.24Q	2/14/03	24.17 - 15.50
0.19	0.19	0.31	—	1.08	1.00	—	0.05	0.05	0.05	0.6	0.0125Q	2/19/03	10.33 - 6.50
—	—	—	p1.13	0.94	1.02	18.9 - 14.5	—	—	—	—	200%	8/17/00	39.70 - 17.15
—	—	—	—	—	—	—	—	—	—	—			21.35 - 16.35
—	—	—	p2.30	2.32	3.02	26.1 - 14.7	1.40	1.38	1.33	3.0	0.35Q	2/20/03	59.99 - 33.75
0.71	0.47	0.21	—	1.66	1.53	—	0.57	0.52	0.38	2.7	0.15Q	3/31/03	27.75 - 14.17
—	—	—	pd1.16	0.80	1.88	—	0.01Q	—	0.09	—	0.01Q	8/15/00	4.44 - 1.60
—	—	—	p2.49	2.63	2.38	16.4 - 12.4	2.20	2.11	2.02	6.1	0.655Q	4/18/03	40.94 - 30.90
—	—	—	pd0.48	0.82	1.73	—	—	—	—	—	100%	8/30/89	32.55 - 18.58
—	—	—	p2.46	2.24	1.98	20.3 - 9.7	—	—	—	—	50%	7/23/99	49.95 - 23.90
—	—	—	p1.39	1.13	1.02	17.8 - 14.1	1.65	1.58	1.50	7.4	0.44Q	5/15/03	24.80 - 19.59
—	—	—	—	—	—	—	—	0.40	0.10	—	0.44Q	4/2/03	25.52 - 15.74
pd0.25	pd1.82	—	—	d3.07	d1.73	—	—	—	—	—	100%	2/18/00	27.00 - 6.00
—	—	—	—	—	—	—	—	—	—	—			26.50 - 9.00
—	—	—	—	—	—	—	1.02	0.90	0.73	3.9		6/12/02	33.00 - 19.25
—	—	—	1.04	0.36	0.78	19.4 - 8.6	—	—	—	—	3-for-2	10/21/96	20.15 - 8.90
—	—	—	1.04	0.36	0.78	47.4 - 28.5	3.86	1.19	—	9.8	0.96875Q	2/18/03	49.31 - 29.69
—	—	—	1.29	—	2.09	21.0 - 3.3	0.16	—	—	1.0	0.10Q	3/31/03	27.10 - 4.24
—	—	—	p2.77	0.84	2.07	21.5 - 17.5	2.31	2.10	2.01	4.3	0.6075Q	4/25/03	59.49 - 48.40
0.90	0.87	0.83	—	2.15	3.22	—	0.43	0.34	0.29	2.9		10/15/02	17.90 - 11.05
1.38	1.83	2.50	—	6.11	4.65	—	0.20	0.20	0.20	0.5	0.05Q	4/22/03	45.25 - 30.17
—	—	—	15.93	13.83	16.14	—	0.16	0.16	0.16	0.3	0.04Q	4/9/03	63.09 - 38.31
0.15	—	—	1.19	0.73	0.99	22.7 - 15.1	—	0.23	—	—	0.23A	11/29/01	15.38 - 11.55
—	—	—	p1.53	0.08	1.42	12.8 - 10.3	0.06	0.06	0.06	0.3	0.015Q	1/14/03	27.00 - 18.01
—	—	—	p5.61	2.41	1.63	6.3 - 3.8	0.88	0.88	0.88	5.0	0.22Q	5/15/03	19.66 - 15.69
—	—	—	p0.77	0.33	0.54	29.9 - 14.8	0.21	0.20	0.19	0.7	0.055Q	3/21/03	35.50 - 21.13
—	—	—	1.32	1.26	—	33.7 - 12.7	—	—	—	—			23.05 - 11.40
—	—	—	—	—	—	—	—	—	—	—			44.49 - 16.70
—	—	—	2.53	3.11	3.05	20.7 - 15.8	2.16	2.16	2.16	4.7	0.54Q	5/2/03	52.39 - 39.90
d0.04	d0.21	d0.56	pd5.22	0.59	3.12	—	—	—	—	—	2-for-1	5/31/96	12.85 - 2.03
—	—	—	—	d0.06	0.97	—	—	—	—	—			17.00 - 3.30
d0.14	0.01	d0.03	p1.06	0.92	0.56	39.0 - 25.9	—	—	—	—	0.05Q	6/15/99	41.35 - 27.41
—	—	—	—	pd0.21	0.09	—	—	—	—	—			2.80 - 0.60
—	—	—	2.45	2.10	1.81	14.2 - 9.8	0.83	0.72	0.61	2.8	0.22Q	2/20/03	34.77 - 23.89
—	—	—	7.47	9.76	10.33	—	1.10	1.24	1.24	11.6	0.0833M	3/31/03	12.48 - 6.42
—	—	—	p0.53	0.90	1.32	59.9 - 39.6	1.65	2.18	2.54	6.3	0.55Q	4/15/03	31.75 - 21.00
—	—	—	pd0.10	0.21	0.07	—	—	—	—	—	0.005U	4/8/97	19.15 - 8.55
0.47	0.46	0.32	p1.05	1.37	1.26	34.2 - 22.8	1.86	1.56	1.50	6.2	0.535Q	4/14/03	35.91 - 23.93
—	—	—	—	d0.69	2.07	—	0.45	0.44	0.40	1.3	0.12Q	3/10/03	39.78 - 29.20
—	—	—	—	p0.69	0.70	—	0.88	0.88	0.88	4.1	0.22Q	5/15/03	30.80 - 12.62
—	—	—	p0.17	1.51	3.01	50.3 - 26.5	0.03	—	—	0.5	0.03Q	4/15/03	8.55 - 4.50
—	—	—	p0.68	1.24	1.40	32.3 - 24.3	1.10	1.09	1.06	5.7	0.275Q	4/7/03	21.99 - 16.50
—	—	—	1.07	3.70	7.97	85.6 - 61.1	2.80	2.65	2.60	3.6	0.70Q	3/10/03	91.60 - 65.41
—	—	—	—	—	—	—	0.12	0.12	0.12	0.9	0.04Q	3/31/03	16.50 - 11.57
—	—	—	p3.13	2.37	d0.21	14.4 - 12.4	—	—	—	—	0.14Q	3/25/03	45.06 - 38.90
—	—	—	p0.78	0.51	0.35	30.4 - 15.9	—	—	—	—	2-for-1	7/29/02	23.73 - 12.42
—	—	—	—	9.93	11.43	—	0.21	1.42	0.04	2.7	0.02A	1/10/03	9.35 - 6.10
—	—	—	—	—	—	—	0.24	0.24	—	1.6	0.242U	8/2/02	18.50 - 11.00
—	—	—	14.92	13.19	12.37	—	0.13	—	0.11	1.0	0.00069A	1/15/03	15.46 - 11.25
—	—	—	—	—	—	—	—	—	—	—	0.2051U	6/2/03	18.11 - 11.18
—	—	—	—	—	—	—	1.21	0.97	—	7.5		9/10/02	18.84 - 13.37
—	—	—	—	—	—	—	0.12	—	—	0.7	0.1208U	8/2/02	22.25 - 10.25

SYMBOL	COMPANY	NATURE OF BUSINESS	FISCAL YEAR-END	TOTAL REV. $MILL	NET INCOME $MILL	TOTAL ASSETS $MILL	NET STK EQUITY $MILL	NO. OF INST.	INST. HOLDINGS (SHARES)
CHU	China Unicom Ltd. (China, Peo	Telecommunications	12/31/01	29392.9	4456.8	127904.9	61681.2	25	3663845
CQB	Chiquita Brands International	Food processing	12/31/02	p1443.0	p231.7	—	—	129	31028344
CHZ	Chittenden Corp (VT)	Banking - Northeast	12/31/02	324.1	63.6	4920.5	418.8	120	17423456
CHH	Choice Hotels Intl Inc (New)	Motel/hotel lodging	12/31/01	341.4	14.3	321.2	d64.5	86	13539215
CPS	ChoicePoint, Inc.	Insurance brokerage	12/31/02	p791.6	p720.3	—	—	256	71189703
CBK	Christopher & Banks Corp.		3/2/02	275.9	32.9	128.6	112.0	124	23067575
CRC	Chromcraft Revington Inc.	Furniture & fixtures	12/31/02	p214.2	p187.5	—	—	18	3281738
CB	Chubb Corp.	Property & casualty insurance	12/31/02	p8085.3	p8085.3	—	—	466	146622436
CHD	Church & Dwight Co., Inc.	Soaps & cleansers	12/31/01	1080.9	47.0	949.1	282.3	164	24956907
CSB	Ciba Specialty Chemicals Hld	Chemicals	12/31/02	—	—	—	—	10	791890
CBR	CIBER, Inc. (United States)	Computer services	12/31/02	p608.3	p608.3	—	—	114	37143636
CI	CIGNA Corp.	Insurance	12/31/02	19348.0	d397.0	88950.0	3867.0	374	119794283
HIS	CIGNA High Income Shares	Investment company	12/31/01	35.6	29.1	242.3	161.7	23	646739
IIS	Cigna Investment Securities (	Investment company	12/31/01	5.6	4.8	116.4	87.5	14	422000
XEC	Cimarex Energy Co	Oil	12/31/02	p152.1	p152.1	—	—	236	47294998
JRL	Cincinnati Gas & Electric Co	Electric power	12/31/01	4693.8	326.7	5359.7	1757.6	1	400
CIN	Cinergy Corp (United States)	Electric power	12/31/02	—	—	—	—	317	110457908
CIR	Circor International Inc	Oil service & equipment	12/31/02	p331.4	p331.4	—	—	65	9431772
CC	Circuit City Group	Specialty stores	2/28/02	9589.8	190.8	4133.2	2560.3	282	154196453
CIT	CIT Group Inc. (DE)	Financial services	12/31/01	951.5	141.3	41932.4	4870.7	184	206206140
C	Citigroup Inc	Financial services	12/31/02	—	—	—	—	1300	d651075922
TLI	Citigroup Investments Loan F	Investment company	9/30/02	11.7	8.9	214.9	214.6	—	—
CZN	Citizens Communications Co	Telecommunications	12/31/02	p2669.3	p2809.4	—	—	253	217972341
CZB	Citizens Communications Co	Telecommunications	12/31/02	p2669.3	p2809.4	—	—	4	611003
CIA	Citizens, Inc. (Austin, TX)	Life Insurance	12/31/01	67.3	4.0	282.1	82.7	30	2593061
CYN	City National Corp.(CA)	Banking - West	12/31/02	—	p183.1	—	—	215	31759577
CKR	CKE Restaurants, Inc. (Unite	Restaurants	1/31/02	1438.1	d84.0	931.6	261.7	70	18094735
CLE	Claire's Stores, Inc. (Unit		2/2/02	918.7	41.1	611.6	404.2	189	35075647
CLC	Clarcor Inc.		11/30/02	715.6	46.6	546.1	315.5	148	18897222
CBC	Clark / Bardes Inc.	Life Insurance	12/31/02	p278.6	p278.6	—	—	54	8830844
CMH	Clayton Homes Inc. (United S	Mobile homes	6/30/02	1198.8	124.1	1828.4	1262.0	180	93572312
CCU	Clear Channel Communications	Broadcasting	12/31/02	8421.1	724.8	27672.2	14210.1	556	480213707
CNL	Cleco Corp. (New)	Electric power	12/31/02	721.2	71.9	2344.6	580.0	156	26257417
CLF	Cleveland-Cliffs, Inc.	Mining & processing	12/31/02	617.1	d66.4	730.1	79.3	93	8925268
CLX	Clorox Co.	Soaps & cleansers	6/30/02	4061.0	322.0	3630.0	1354.0	433	127758648
CMS	CMS Energy Corp	Electric power	12/31/01	9597.0	d331.0	17128.0	1960.0	233	95482323
CNA	CNA Financial Corp.	Property & casualty insurance	12/31/02	—	pd57.0	—	—	117	219925844
SUR	CNA Surety Corp.	Property & casualty insurance	12/31/02	p316.3	p311.4	—	—	77	40965409
CNF	CNF, Inc.	Trucking lines	12/31/02	p4762.0	p4762.0	—	—	184	43141656
CNH	CNH Global N.V. (Netherlands		12/31/01	9715.0	d332.0	17212.0	1909.0	46	68921377
CEO	Cnooc Ltd. (Hong Kong)	Oil	12/31/01	—	—	—	—	43	7517443
COH	Coach, Inc.		6/29/02	719.4	85.8	440.6	260.4	283	81161229
COA	Coachmen Industries, Inc.	Mobile homes	12/31/02	p665.2	p665.2	—	—	74	12649599
CBZ	Cobalt Corp.	Services	12/31/01	1451.2	d22.3	726.8	208.2	60	7217426
KO	Coca-Cola Co.	Soft drinks	12/31/02	—	—	—	—	1025	1550305004
CCE	Coca-Cola Enterprises, Inc.	Soft drinks	12/31/01	—	—	—	—	274	178031568
KOF	Coca-Cola FEMSA, S.A. de C.V.	Soft drinks	12/31/01	—	—	—	—	94	16939814
CCH	Coca-Cola Hellenic Bottling	Soft drinks	12/31/01	—	—	—	—		
CDE	Coeur d'Alene Mines Corp. (I	Mining & processing	12/31/02	71.9	d51.3	210.4	26.8	44	9596324
RLF	Cohen & Steers Advantage Inc	Investment company	12/31/01	23.3	20.5	481.1	476.6	18	905338
RPF	Cohen & Steers Premium Incom		8/12/02	—	—	0.2	0.1	—	—
RQI	Cohen & Steers Quality Income		2/15/02	—	—	0.1	—	—	—
RFI	Cohen & Steers Total Return	Investment company	12/31/01	9.6	8.3	124.6	124.1	15	384829
KCP	Cole (Kenneth) Productions,		12/31/02	p433.0	p433.0	—	—	85	9921774
CNJ	Cole National Corp (New) (Uni	Specialty stores	2/2/02	1101.3	5.2	604.2	155.6	56	10778110
CM	Coles Myer Ltd. (AU)	Discount & variety stores	7/28/02	26737.4	353.8	8289.4	3307.6	8	575444
CL	Colgate-Palmolive Co.	Soaps & cleansers	12/31/02	p9294.3	p9294.3	—	—	762	439086094
CKC	Collins & Aikman Corp. (New)	Textiles	12/31/02	p3885.8	p3895.3	—	—	55	15407048
CNB	Colonial Bancgroup Inc.	Banking - South	12/31/02	—	p140.0	—	—	171	45724768
CXE	Colonial High Income Mun Tr	Investment company	11/30/02	20.8	17.7	327.7	322.8	9	104024
CIF	Colonial Interm High Incm Fd	Investment company	10/31/02	10.6	7.9	84.3	58.1	17	341143
CMK	Colonial InterMkt Inc Tr I	Investment company	11/30/02	7.8	6.9	97.5	94.7	9	93612
CXH	Colonial Invt Grade Mun Tr	Investment company	11/30/02	10.6	9.0	188.5	187.1	10	220145
CMU	Colonial Munic. Inc. Tr.	Investment company	11/30/02	16.1	13.8	254.1	251.0	11	57802
CLP	Colonial Properties Trust AL	Real estate investment trust	12/31/02	p329.9	p329.9	—	—	127	11177114
CCZ	Comcast Holdings Corp		12/31/01	9674.2	225.6	38131.8	14473.0	3	135966542
CMA	Comerica, Inc.	Banking - Midwest	12/31/02	p3604.0	p594.0	—	—	52	13587191
FIX	Comfort Systems USA, Inc.	Services	12/31/01	1546.3	13.1	876.6	413.8	240	43266702
CBH	Commerce Bancorp, Inc. (NJ)	Banking - Northeast	12/31/02	—	p144.8	—	—	83	7397233
CGI	Commerce Group, Inc. (MA) (U	Property & casualty insurance	12/31/02	p1257.1	p1199.2	—	—	140	31301731
CFB	Commercial Federal Corp.	Savings & loan	12/31/02	—	p108.5	—	—	107	16057318
CMC	Commercial Metals Co.	Metal products	8/31/02	2446.8	40.5	1230.1	501.3	99	12426988
NNN	Commercial Net Lease Realty,	Real estate investment trust	12/31/02	p93.8	p95.8	—	—	141	47046192
CTV	Commscope, Inc.	Communications electronics	12/31/02	p598.5	p552.6	—	—	88	4645419
CBU	Community Bank System, Inc.	Banking - Northeast	12/31/02	—	p38.5	—	—	129	55014921
CYH	Community Health Systems, Inc	Hospitals & nursing homes	12/31/02	1693.6	48.6	2460.7	1115.7	3	563741
GGY	Compagnie Generale de Geophy.	Oil service & equipment	12/31/01	—	—	—	—	45	14850042
CBD	Companhia Brasileira de Distr	Grocery chain	12/31/01	—	—	—	—	5	209989
ABV C	Companhia de Bebidas de Amer		12/31/01	—	—	—	—	31	18290711
ABV	Companhia de Bebidas das Amer		12/31/01	—	—	—	—	9	1273633
SBS	Companhia de Saneamento Basico	Water company	12/31/01	—	—	—	—	15	4539554
CIG	Companhia Energetica de Minas	Electric power	12/31/01	—	—	—	—	15	4539554
ELP	Companhia Paranaense De Energ	Electric power	12/31/01	—	—	—	—	19	17970100
SID	Companhia Siderurgica Naciona	Steel producer	12/31/01	—	—	—	—	26	4031987
RIO	Companhia Vale Do Rio Doce	Mining & processing	12/31/02	—	—	—	—	92	54317890
VNT	Compania Anonima Nacional	Telecommunications	12/31/01	—	—	—	—	59	35013807
CU	COMPANIA CERVECERIAS UNIDAS		12/31/01	—	—	—	—	17	2378588
BVN	Compania de Minas Buenaventu	Mining & processing	12/31/01	—	—	—	—	62	20030089
CTC	Compania de Telecomunicacione	Telecommunications	12/31/01	—	—	—	—	58	40549951
CA	Computer Associates Internat	Computer services	3/31/02	2964.0	d1102.0	12226.0	4617.0	357	378053927
CSC	Computer Sciences Corp.	Computer services	3/29/02	11426.0	344.1	8610.5	3623.6	390	144054557
CTG	Computer Task Group, Inc.	Computer services	12/31/02	p263.3	p226.2	—	—	51	10564764
CIX	CompX International, Inc.	Hardware & tools	12/31/01	p196.1	p32.9	—	—	71	14198583
CRK	Comstock Resources, Inc.	Oil	12/31/02	p150.2	p150.2	—	—	71	4966164
CAG	ConAgra Foods, Inc.	Food -grain & agriculture	5/26/02	27629.6	785.0	15496.2	4308.2	484	347400956
CE	Concord EFS, Inc.	Services	12/31/01	1707.0	216.4	2729.4	1858.6	492	417353877

EARNINGS PER SHARE QUARTERLY 1st	2nd	3rd	ANNUAL 2002	2001	2000	P/E RATIO	DIVIDENDS PER SHARE 2002	2001	2000	AV. YLD. %	DIV. DECLARED AMOUNT	PAYABLE	PRICE RANGE 2002
—	—	—	—	0.36	0.29								11.60 - 5.32
—	—	—	p0.33	d1.78	d1.68	57.1 - 31.8							18.85 - 10.49
—	—	—	1.96	1.80	1.72	17.4 - 11.8	0.79	0.77	0.75	2.8	0.20Q	2/14/03	34.18 - 23.18
0.20	0.38	0.54	—	0.32	0.80								27.00 - 16.30
—	—	—	p1.01	0.58	0.52	47.7 - 29.5					33%	6/6/02	48.15 - 29.75
0.37	0.26	0.43	—	1.26	1.50						50%	12/12/01	44.80 - 18.80
—	—	—	pd3.09	1.09	1.57						2-for-1	6/10/98	16.50 - 10.30
—	—	—	p1.29	0.63	4.01	61.0 - 40.2	1.39	1.35	1.31	2.1	0.35Q	1/7/03	78.64 - 51.91
0.36	p0.45	0.42	—	1.15	0.84		0.30	0.29	0.28	1.0	0.075Q	3/3/03	36.50 - 25.54
—	—	—	—	—	—		0.94	0.59	0.57	2.6		7/8/02	40.60 - 30.83
—	—	—	p0.22	0.03	d1.15	53.2 - 20.3					2-for-1	3/31/98	11.70 - 4.46
—	—	—	d2.83	6.59	6.08		1.31	1.27	1.23	1.8	0.33Q	4/10/03	111.00 - 34.70
—	2.71	—	—	—	—		0.39	0.60	0.73	13.0	0.023M	4/10/03	3.99 - 2.02
—	18.09	—	—	18.26	18.11		1.12	1.20	1.19	6.7	0.24Q	3/10/03	33.30 - 0.01
—	—	—	p1.31	0.1735	2530.00	13.7 - 10.1							18.00 - 13.23
—	—	—	—	—	—		2.07	2.07	2.07	8.0	0.5175Q	3/31/03	26.60 - 25.01
—	—	—	p2.13	2.75	2.50	17.5 - 11.9	1.80	1.80	1.80	5.8	0.46Q	2/15/03	37.19 - 25.40
—	—	—	p1.00	1.04	0.78	22.4 - 11.8	0.15	0.15	0.11	0.9	0.0375Q	3/17/03	22.38 - 11.75
0.08	0.04	—	—	0.92	0.73		0.07	0.07	0.07	0.4	0.0175Q	4/15/03	31.40 - 6.95
—	—	—	0.67	d31.66	0.86	35.9 - 20.6	0.12	—	—	0.6	0.12Q	2/28/03	24.05 - 13.80
—	—	—	p2.94	2.75	2.62	17.8 - 8.3	0.70	0.60	0.49	1.8	0.20Q	2/28/03	52.20 - 24.48
—	—	—	13.24	14.15	15.14		0.79	1.11	1.43	6.4	0.062M	3/28/03	12.23 - 11.10
—	—	—	pd2.43	d0.28	d0.15						0.75%	12/31/98	11.52 - 2.51
—	—	—	pd2.43	d0.28	d0.15		1.69	0.69	—	10.0	0.4219Q	2/18/03	24.40 - 9.50
0.06	0.04	0.01	—	0.14	0.07						15%	6/1/02	13.25 - 5.30
—	—	—	p3.56	2.96	2.72	15.8 - 11.3	0.78	0.74	0.70	1.6	0.205Q	2/18/03	56.42 - 40.10
0.23	0.18	0.17	—	d1.66	d3.84		—	—	0.04		0.04S	5/4/00	12.85 - 3.01
0.17	0.31	0.25	—	0.84	1.30		0.16	0.16	0.16	0.8	0.04Q	3/21/03	26.97 - 14.70
—	—	—	1.85	1.68	1.64	18.4 - 13.5	0.48	0.47	0.46	1.6	0.1225Q	1/31/03	34.00 - 25.03
—	—	—	p0.99	1.18	1.05	31.1 - 13.2							30.78 - 13.05
0.22	0.22	—	0.89	0.77	1.03	22.0 - 10.4	0.06	0.05	0.06	0.4	0.064A	1/30/03	19.60 - 9.23
—	—	—	1.18	d1.93	0.57	46.5 - 16.9					2-for-1	7/28/98	54.90 - 20.00
—	—	—	1.47	1.51	1.46	16.9 - 6.6	0.90	0.87	0.84	5.2	0.225Q	2/15/03	24.90 - 9.74
—	—	—	d6.58	d3.19	1.73		—	0.40	1.50		0.10Q	12/3/01	32.25 - 15.70
0.71	0.39	—	1.37	1.36	1.64	35.0 - 23.3	0.86	0.84	0.82	2.2	0.22Q	5/15/03	47.95 - 31.92
2.92	d0.56	0.16	—	2.76	0.32		1.09	1.46	1.46	7.2	0.18Q	11/22/02	24.80 - 5.45
—	—	—	p0.83	d8.16	6.61	37.3 - 25.8					3-for-1	6/1/98	30.99 - 21.45
—	—	—	p0.67	0.86	1.25	24.8 - 11.1	0.45	0.54	0.32	3.7	0.15Q	10/7/02	16.60 - 7.41
—	—	—	p1.74	d9.06	2.65	22.0 - 15.7	0.40	0.40	0.40	1.2	0.10Q	3/14/03	38.28 - 27.36
—	—	—	—	d1.20	d1.79		0.10	0.10	0.55	2.2	0.05U	6/2/03	6.45 - 2.75
—	—	—	—	—	—		0.67	0.26	—	2.7	0.28204U	10/4/02	30.66 - 19.00
0.24	0.68	—	—	0.94	0.76						2-for-1	7/3/02	35.70 - 17.19
—	—	—	p0.62	d0.25	0.14	31.5 - 18.2	0.22	0.20	0.20	1.4	0.06Q	3/13/03	19.50 - 11.30
0.32	0.54	0.33	—	d0.58	d0.97		—	—	0.05		0.05A	12/27/00	23.50 - 5.33
—	—	—	p1.23	1.60	0.88	47.1 - 34.9	0.80	0.72	0.68	1.6	0.22Q	4/1/03	57.91 - 42.90
—	—	—	p1.07	d0.75	0.54	22.9 - 14.9	0.16	0.16	0.16	0.8	0.04Q	4/1/03	24.50 - 15.94
—	—	—	—	—	—		0.41	0.20	0.14	1.7	0.4122U	5/20/02	29.89 - 17.49
—	—	—	—	—	—								16.40 - 13.40
d0.23	d0.16	d0.14	—	d1.22	d1.87						0.15A	4/19/96	2.50 - 0.78
—	—	—	—	14.03	15.00		1.38	0.63	—	9.4	0.115M	6/30/03	16.70 - 12.65
—	—	—	—	—	—		0.35	—	—	2.5	0.115M	6/30/03	15.09 - 13.00
—	—	—	—	14.33	—		0.94	—	—	6.8	0.11M	6/30/03	16.00 - 11.80
—	15.71	—	—	13.41	12.35		0.99	0.96	0.99	7.2	0.085M	6/30/03	15.07 - 12.41
—	—	—	p1.27	0.80	1.75	24.0 - 12.5					3-for-2	3/27/00	30.50 - 15.89
0.18	0.16	—	—	0.32	0.14		—	—	—		0.01U	12/20/99	19.65 - 7.75
—	—	—	—	0.12	0.26	204.4 - 0.0	1.13	1.48	1.20	4.0		11/19/02	56.00 - 0.01
—	—	—	p2.19	1.89	1.70	26.9 - 20.1	0.72	0.67	0.63	1.4	0.24Q	5/15/03	58.86 - 44.05
—	—	—	pd1.15	d1.27	d0.07								18.65 - 2.00
—	—	—	p1.16	1.06	1.06	14.0 - 9.5	0.52	0.48	0.44	3.8	0.14Q	2/7/03	16.19 - 11.01
—	—	—	6.52	6.93	6.92		0.50	0.44	0.36	7.7	0.042M	3/14/03	6.94 - 6.00
—	—	—	2.79	3.51	4.83		0.36	0.55	0.71	11.2	0.027M	3/14/03	4.02 - 2.48
—	—	—	8.60	8.91	9.14		0.71	0.83	0.89	8.6	0.054M	4/1/03	8.90 - 7.55
—	—	—	11.04	11.06	10.55		0.67	0.60	0.60	6.4	0.0575M	4/1/03	11.08 - 9.80
—	—	—	5.82	6.12	6.05		0.42	0.39	0.43	7.3	0.037M	3/14/03	6.11 - 5.43
d0.09	d0.22	0.08	p2.58	2.02	1.83	15.2 - 11.2	2.64	2.52	2.40	7.7	0.665Q	2/7/03	39.20 - 28.99
—	—	—	—	0.23	2.16		1.43	1.43	1.43	4.1	0.3576Q	4/15/03	54.00 - 15.00
d0.11	0.13	0.04	p3.40	3.88	4.63	19.4 - 10.4	1.88	1.72	1.56	3.7	0.50Q	4/1/03	66.09 - 35.20
—	—	—	—	0.35	d0.45								5.00 - 2.50
—	—	—	p2.04	1.51	1.25	24.8 - 17.7	0.60	0.55	0.49	1.4	0.165Q	4/18/03	50.49 - 36.10
—	—	—	p1.42	2.75	3.87	29.7 - 20.7	1.23	1.19	1.15	3.4	0.31Q	3/14/03	42.11 - 29.45
—	—	—	p2.37	1.93	d0.92	12.7 - 8.0	0.34	0.30	0.28	1.4	0.09Q	4/10/03	30.03 - 19.01
0.08	—	—	—	1.43	0.93	17.4 - 10.8	0.29	0.26	0.26	1.4	0.08Q	4/18/03	24.87 - 15.50
—	—	—	p1.09	0.91	1.27	15.0 - 11.6	1.27	1.26	1.25	8.8	0.32Q	2/14/03	16.40 - 12.60
—	—	—	pd1.10	0.52	1.60								23.65 - 6.12
0.27	0.24	0.25	p2.93	1.62	2.85	11.7 - 8.8	1.10	1.08	1.02	3.7	0.29Q	4/10/03	34.21 - 25.91
—	—	—	—	0.54	0.14								30.55 - 18.50
—	—	—	—	—	—								9.25 - 2.50
—	—	—	—	—	—		0.19	0.54	0.10	1.0	0.1859U	7/8/02	25.50 - 10.90
—	—	—	—	—	—		0.29	0.29	0.12	1.9	0.2347U	3/10/03	22.00 - 8.01
—	—	—	—	—	—		0.32	0.32	0.12	1.9	0.2582U	3/10/03	22.00 - 10.70
—	—	—	—	—	—		0.29	—	—	3.5	0.2902U	6/25/02	11.94 - 4.49
—	—	—	—	—	—		0.92	0.34	0.60	8.7		12/24/02	16.39 - 4.80
—	—	—	—	—	—		0.11	0.34	0.20	2.2	0.1133U	6/13/03	8.47 - 1.77
—	—	—	—	—	—		0.63	16.63	0.81	4.4	0.40419U	6/19/02	21.10 - 7.70
—	—	—	—	—	—		0.60	—	—	2.3	0.59641U	12/17/02	30.40 - 21.65
—	—	—	—	—	—		2.09	3.28	0.62	14.3	0.6286U	1/23/03	19.35 - 9.80
—	—	—	—	—	—		0.32	0.72	0.40	2.2	0.77947U	3/21/03	17.70 - 12.10
—	—	—	—	—	—		0.30	0.21	0.15	1.2	0.009U	2/17/03	32.00 - 19.71
—	—	—	—	—	—		0.01	—	—	0.1		5/17/02	15.95 - 7.78
d0.11	d0.09	d0.08	—	d1.91	d1.02		0.08	0.08	0.08	0.3	0.04S	4/13/98	38.74 - 7.47
0.46	0.54	0.61	—	2.01	1.37		—	—	—		0.00166U	4/13/98	53.47 - 24.30
—	—	—	pd2.11	d0.13	d0.35		—	—	0.05		0.05A	5/26/00	6.08 - 2.36
—	—	—	p0.04	0.47	1.37	366.3 - 167.0	0.50	0.50	0.50	4.7	0.125Q	3/31/03	14.65 - 6.68
—	—	—	p0.34	1.06	1.21	28.6 - 16.2							9.74 - 5.50
0.42	0.45	—	—	1.47	1.33		0.95	0.91	0.84	3.9	0.2475Q	3/1/03	27.65 - 20.90
0.10	0.12	0.18	—	0.42	0.42		—	—	—		100%	9/28/01	35.06 - 12.60

SYMBOL	COMPANY	NATURE OF BUSINESS	FISCAL YEAR-END	TOTAL REV. $MILL	NET INCOME $MILL	TOTAL ASSETS $MILL	NET STK EQUITY $MILL	NO. OF INST.	INST. HOLDINGS (SHARES)
COE	Cone Mills Corp. (NC)	Textiles	12/29/02	p445.6	p61.3	—	—	18	3677671
COP	Conocophillips (United State	Natural gas distributor	12/31/02	26868.0	1643.0	35217.0	14340.0	726	559415129
CNX	Consol Energy Inc	Coal	12/31/02	p2183.6	p2183.6	—	—	110	15123803
ED	Consolidated Edison, Inc.	Electric power	12/31/02	p8482.0	p8482.0	—	—	365	144784417
EPB	Consolidated Edison, Inc.	Electric power	12/31/02	p8482.0	p8482.0	—	—		
CGX	Consolidated Graphics, Inc.	Printing & engraving	3/31/02	643.9	16.7	676.7	306.6	95	7982210
STZ	Constellation Brands Inc	Distilling	2/28/02	2820.5	138.0	3069.4	955.7	264	61759974
STZ B	Constellation Brands Inc	Distilling	2/28/02	2820.5	138.0	3069.4	955.7	6	43978
CEG	Constellation Energy Group I	Electric power	12/31/02	4703.0	525.6	14128.9	3862.3	281	111575708
CAL	Continental Airlines Inc (Un	—	12/31/02	8402.0	d441.0	10740.0	767.0	125	52800098
MCM	Controladora Comercial Mexico	Department stores	12/31/01	—	—	—	—	2	16901
CVG	Convergys Corp.	Computer services	12/31/02	2286.2	145.9	1619.5	1126.3	303	103024464
CAM	Cooper Cameron Corp.	Machinery & equipment	12/31/02	p1538.1	p1538.1	—	—	208	52089185
COO	Cooper Companies, Inc.	Medical & dental equipment	10/31/02	315.3	48.9	571.1	311.4	176	34925970
CBE	Cooper Industries, Ltd.	Machinery & equipment	12/31/02	p3960.5	p3894.0	—	—	268	69494157
CTB	Cooper Tire & Rubber Co.	Tires and/or rubber goods	12/31/02	3330.0	111.8	2711.0	941.7	214	51062827
RKY	Coors (Adolph) Co. (United St	—	12/29/02	p3776.3	p1266.8	—	—	243	22191234
CDA	Cordiant Communications Grou	—	12/31/01	—	—	—	—	6	3554349
CLB	Core Laboratories N.V.	Meas. & control instruments	12/31/01	—	—	—	—	75	26484952
CPO	Corn Products International	Food -grain & agriculture	12/31/02	p1870.9	p1870.9	—	—	168	26042311
CRN	Cornell Companies Inc	Services	12/31/02	p275.1	p274.2	—	—	42	10663162
TCR	Cornerstone Realty Income Tr	—	12/31/02	p162.7	p162.7	—	—	73	7547270
GLW	Corning, Inc.	Conglomerate	12/31/02	3164.0	d1780.0	11548.0	4691.0	483	686268080
CDG	Corporacion Durango S.A. de	Paper	12/31/01	—	—	—	—	1	39750
COY	Corporate High Yield Fd., Inc	Investment company	5/31/02	33.1	29.0	272.5	195.1	14	497095
KYT	Corporate High Yield Fund II	Investment company	8/31/02	10.7	9.3	80.8	59.2	11	90443
HYV	Corporate High Yield Fund V,	Investment company	11/27/01	—	—	0.4	0.1	—	—
OFC	Corporate Office Pptys Trust	Real estate investment trust	12/31/02	p148.0	p148.0	—	—	87	14787801
CPV	Correctional Properties Trust	Real estate investment trust	12/31/02	p30.2	p30.2	—	—	44	2637057
CXW	Corrections Corporation of A	Real estate investment trust	12/31/02	p962.8	p882.6	—	—	81	11963627
CGA	Corus Group Plc (UK)	Metal products	12/29/01	—	—	—	—	34	23438900
CFC	Countrywide Financial Corp	Financial services	12/31/01	—	—	—	—	369	121865286
CUZ	Cousins Properties Inc.	Real estate investment trust	12/31/02	p199.8	p197.7	—	—	125	19068378
CVD	Covance Inc.	Services	12/31/02	p924.7	p891.5	—	—	220	49527358
CVH	Coventry Health Care Inc.	Insurance	12/31/02	p3576.9	p3576.9	—	—	205	43352242
COX	Cox Communications Inc (New)	—	12/31/01	4067.0	37.9	25061.4	9675.8	319	209997310
PRI	Cox Communications Inc (New)	—	12/31/01	4067.0	37.9	25061.4	9675.8	6	4859665
CXR	Cox Radio Inc.	Telecommunications	12/31/02	p420.6	p420.6	—	—	142	40842878
CPF	CPB Inc	—	12/31/02	p29.3	p8.2	—	—	57	5729015
CPY	CPI Corp.	Photo & optical	2/2/02	318.9	6.2	172.7	65.4	59	5875218
CR	Crane & Co.	Machinery & equipment	12/31/02	1516.3	16.6	1413.7	649.1	187	36405249
CRD A	Crawford & Co.	Finance	12/31/02	p735.4	p156.2	—	—	21	15604413
CRD B	Crawford & Co.	Finance	12/31/02	p735.4	p156.2	—	—	46	18970935
BAP	CrediCorp Ltd. (Bermuda)	—	12/31/01	—	—	—	—	19	3072706
CIK	Credit Suisse Asset Mgmt Incm	Investment company	12/31/01	29.7	27.2	238.2	236.7	18	365276
CSR	Credit Suisse Group (Switzerl	Financial services	12/31/01	—	—	—	—	33	6814586
DHY	Credit Suisse High Yield Bond	Investment company	10/31/02	38.5	32.3	320.1	180.9	23	3179549
CEI	Crescent Real Estate Equitie	Real estate investment trust	12/31/01	696.1	6.1	4142.1	1405.9	168	59086858
CMM	CRIIMI MAE, Inc.	Real estate investment trust	12/31/01	134.4	d17.9	1315.0	261.0	23	3446043
CGW	Cristalerias de Chile S.A.	Plastics & plastic products	12/31/01	—	—	—	—	5	666610
CK	Crompton Corp	Specialty chemicals	12/31/02	p2546.9	p2208.3	—	—	165	92577718
CRT	Cross Timbers Royalty Trust	Oil	12/31/01	14.4	14.2	29.7	28.9	23	613533
CWN	Crown American Realty Trust	Real estate investment trust	12/31/02	p189.4	p189.4	—	—	74	10047694
CCI	Crown Castle International C	Telecommunications	12/31/02	p901.5	p901.5	—	—	126	142555603
CRY	CryoLife, Inc.	Medical & dental equipment	12/31/02	77.8	d27.8	106.4	79.8	66	6596395
CAO	CSK Auto Corp.	—	2/3/02	1438.6	d14.1	1068.6	154.3	99	35379647
CSS	CSS Industries, Inc.	Paper	3/31/02	424.3	21.5	298.5	234.8	47	3682357
CSX	CSX Corp.	Railroads	12/31/02	p8152.0	p1127.0	—	—	364	151592355
CTS	CTS Corp.	Electronic components	12/31/02	457.8	d17.9	490.0	265.0	107	25250507
CFR	Cullen/Frost Bankers, Inc.	Banking - Southwest	12/31/02	—	pd312.4	—	—	178	34965736
CFI	Culp Inc.	Textiles	4/28/02	381.9	d3.4	287.7	119.1	51	8890735
CUM	Cummins, Inc.	—	12/31/02	p5853.0	p5853.0	—	—	195	32587017
CW	Curtiss-Wright Corp.	Defense systems & equip.	12/31/01	343.2	62.9	500.4	350.0	115	4891461
CVS	CVS Corp. (DE)	Specialty stores	12/28/02	24181.5	716.6	9645.3	5197.0	550	352771237
CY	Cypress Semiconductor Corp.	Electronic components	12/31/02	p774.7	p774.7	—	—	194	80804641
CYT	Cytec Industries, Inc.	Chemicals	12/31/02	1346.2	79.3	1751.5	622.9	180	31575505
DCX	DaimlerChrysler AG (Germany)	—	12/31/01	—	—	—	—	148	22327647
DRF	Dan River, Inc. (GA)	Textiles	12/31/02	p612.9	p592.2	—	—	15	5442661
DCN	Dana Corp.	—	12/31/02	9694.0	58.0	9553.0	1482.0	251	f01745707
DHR	Danaher Corp.	—	12/31/02	p4577.2	p4180.2	—	—	386	127181287
DRI	Darden Restaurants, Inc. (Uni	Restaurants	5/26/02	4368.7	237.8	2529.7	1128.9	339	124877057
DAB	Dave & Busters, Inc.	Restaurants	2/3/02	358.0	7.6	309.1	170.1	52	4808805
DVA	Davita Inc.	Hospitals & nursing homes	12/31/02	1854.6	186.7	1775.7	70.3	155	59192821
DF	Dean Foods Co. (New) (United	Food processing	12/31/02	p8991.5	p8887.6	—	—	292	79034171
DE	Deere & Co.	—	10/31/02	13947.0	319.2	23768.0	3163.2	424	209807915
DLM	Del Monte Foods Co.	Food processing	6/30/02	1322.4	39.8	1070.0	31.7	359	116499892
DDF	Delaware Investments Dividend	Investment company	11/30/02	10.8	8.2	185.4	130.6	13	133714
DGF	Delaware Investments Global D	Investment company	11/30/02	4.4	3.0	38.5	59.5	6	29024
DPH	Delphi Corp. (United States)	—	12/31/02	27427.0	343.0	19316.0	1279.0	380	432818874
DFG	Delphi Financial Group, Inc.	Insurance	12/31/02	p761.4	p860.4	—	—	134	13667399
DLP	Delta & Pine Land Co.	—	8/31/02	257.8	30.3	383.1	202.2	136	30701013
DAL	Delta Air Lines, Inc. (DE) (U	—	12/31/02	—	—	—	—	238	89913915
DNT	Delta Air Lines, Inc. (DE) (U	—	12/31/02	—	—	—	—	4	31320
DLW	Delta Woodside Inds Inc New	Textiles	6/29/02	174.7	d12.0	165.9	75.2	12	1656919
DEL	Deltic Timber Corp. (United S	—	12/31/02	p104.5	p104.5	—	—	71	7185780
DLX	Deluxe Corp.	Printing & engraving	12/31/02	p1284.0	p721.8	—	—	261	48266111
DNR	Denbury Resources, Inc. (DE)	Oil	12/31/02	p285.2	p285.2	—	—	114	20790484
DFS	Department 56, Inc.	'Wholesaler, distributor'	12/28/02	p208.6	p201.7	—	—	84	9581290
DES	Desc, S.A. de C.V. (Mexico)	Chemicals	12/31/01	—	—	—	—	2	83810
DTA	Detroit Edison Co.	Electric power	12/31/01	4044.0	236.0	11253.0	2458.0	1	8000
DTB	Detroit Edison Co.	Electric power	12/31/01	4044.0	236.0	11253.0	2458.0	2	52000
DTH	Detroit Edison Co.	Electric power	12/31/01	4044.0	236.0	11253.0	2458.0	1	177335
DB	Deutsche Bank AG	—	12/31/01	—	—	—	—	75	10909226
DT	Deutsche Telekom AG (Germany	Communications electronics	12/31/01	—	—	—	—	111	74067688
DDR	Developers Diversified Realt	Real estate investment trust	12/31/02	357.2	100.9	2776.9	945.6	154	42415770
DV	DEVRY Inc. (DE)	—	6/30/02	648.1	67.1	467.6	353.5	178	50339214

T14

\<1st\>	2nd	3rd	2002	2001	2000	P/E RATIO	Div 2002	Div 2001	Div 2000	AV. YLD. %	AMOUNT	PAYABLE	PRICE RANGE 2002
			p0.28	1.07	d1.14	15.9 - 5.9	—	—	—	—	—		4.45 - 1.64
d0.27	0.95	d0.11	—	5.57	7.26	—	1.48	1.40	1.36	2.7	0.40Q	3/3/03	64.10 - 44.03
—	—	—	p0.15	0.01	2.33	188.8 - 65.3	0.84	1.12	1.12	4.4	0.14Q	2/28/03	28.32 - 9.80
—	—	—	p3.02	3.21	2.74	15.0 - 10.8	2.22	2.20	2.18	5.7	0.56Q	3/15/03	45.40 - 32.65
0.37	0.40	0.42	p3.02	3.21	2.74	8.9 - 8.3	0.88	—	—	3.4	—	4/1/03	26.75 - 25.00
0.40	0.53	0.69	—	1.25	1.68	—	—	—	—	—	2-for-1	1/10/97	23.97 - 14.35
0.40	0.53	0.69	—	1.57	1.30	—	—	—	—	—	2-for-1	5/13/02	32.00 - 21.05
0.40	0.53	0.69	—	1.57	1.30	—	—	—	—	—	2-for-1	5/13/02	41.33 - 11.98
—	—	—	3.20	0.52	2.30	10.1 - 6.0	0.84	0.78	1.68	3.3	0.26Q	4/1/03	32.38 - 19.30
—	—	—	d7.02	d1.72	5.54	—	—	—	—	—	2-for-1	7/16/96	35.25 - 3.59
—	—	—	—	—	—	—	0.23	0.21	0.18	1.7	—	5/1/02	18.15 - 9.70
—	—	—	0.88	0.80	1.23	43.2 - 14.2	—	—	—	—	—		37.98 - 12.50
—	—	—	p1.75	1.22	0.50	—	—	—	—	—	2-for-1	6/12/97	59.60 - 35.94
p0.44	—	—	1.57	1.22	1.01	20.0 - 12.2	0.05	0.04	0.04	0.2	0.03S	1/6/03	31.47 - 19.18
—	—	—	p2.28	2.75	3.80	19.6 - 11.9	0.35	—	—	1.0	0.35Q	4/1/03	44.60 - 27.14
—	—	—	1.51	0.25	1.31	17.3 - 8.1	0.42	0.42	0.42	2.2	0.105Q	3/28/03	26.10 - 12.25
—	—	—	p4.42	3.31	2.93	15.9 - 11.4	0.82	0.80	0.72	1.4	0.205Q	3/17/03	70.15 - 50.50
—	—	—	—	—	—	—	—	0.15	0.14	0.14	0.1474U	7/10/01	8.44 - 2.05
—	—	—	—	—	—	—	—	—	—	—	2-for-1	12/19/97	15.85 - 7.90
—	—	—	p1.77	1.60	1.35	19.6 - 13.5	0.40	0.40	0.40	1.4	0.10Q	1/24/03	34.77 - 23.85
—	—	—	p0.48	0.68	0.84	38.2 - 10.4	—	—	—	—	—		18.34 - 5.90
—	—	—	—	—	—	—	1.12	1.12	1.10	12.3	0.20Q	4/21/03	11.65 - 6.51
—	—	—	pd0.40	—	0.77	—	—	0.12	0.24	—	0.06Q	6/29/01	11.15 - 1.10
—	—	—	d1.85	d5.89	0.46	—	—	—	—	—	—		5.35 - 1.01
—	6.80	—	—	7.85	9.22	—	0.96	1.22	1.31	12.6	—	3/31/03	9.55 - 5.71
—	—	—	6.16	7.90	9.71	—	0.86	1.12	1.21	12.7	—	3/31/03	8.49 - 5.16
—	—	—	—	14.32	—	—	1.48	—	—	11.5	—	3/31/03	15.16 - 10.65
—	—	—	p0.33	0.64	0.60	44.5 - 35.2	0.85	0.81	0.77	6.5	0.22Q	4/15/03	14.69 - 11.60
—	—	—	p1.40	1.25	1.18	16.4 - 11.4	1.60	1.47	1.46	8.2	0.40Q	3/4/03	23.00 - 16.00
—	—	—	p2.75	0.20	d56.70	7.0 - 4.3	—	—	—	—	—		19.25 - 11.69
—	—	—	—	—	—	—	—	—	0.15	—	0.1452U	10/23/00	13.45 - 3.37
—	—	—	p6.49	3.89	3.14	8.5 - 5.8	0.46	0.40	0.40	1.0	0.12Q	2/28/03	55.00 - 37.60
—	—	—	p1.00	1.41	1.26	27.3 - 20.1	1.48	1.39	1.24	6.2	0.37Q	2/24/03	27.32 - 20.05
—	—	—	p0.93	0.79	0.27	26.9 - 13.0	—	—	—	—	—		25.00 - 12.11
—	—	—	p2.38	1.23	0.93	16.0 - 8.2	—	—	—	—	2-for-1	8/3/94	38.00 - 19.51
0.22	d0.86	d0.12	—	0.06	3.16	—	—	—	—	—	2-for-1	5/21/99	42.09 - 18.95
0.22	d0.86	d0.12	—	0.06	3.16	—	6.86	6.86	6.59	16.4	0.4425Q	2/18/03	60.00 - 23.75
—	—	—	p0.46	0.22	3.26	69.0 - 40.4	—	—	—	—	3-for-1	5/19/00	31.73 - 18.60
—	—	—	p0.62	1.72	1.07	50.4 - 22.3	0.38	0.33	0.29	1.7	0.16Q	4/25/03	31.24 - 13.82
0.01	d0.07	d0.54	—	0.77	1.87	—	0.56	0.56	0.56	3.6	0.14Q	2/24/03	19.49 - 11.65
—	—	—	0.28	1.47	2.03	103.5 - 63.3	0.40	0.40	0.40	1.7	0.10Q	3/12/03	28.99 - 17.72
—	—	—	p0.50	0.61	0.52	24.1 - 7.9	0.40	0.56	0.55	5.0	0.06Q	2/21/03	12.05 - 3.95
—	—	—	p0.50	0.61	0.52	30.0 - 10.0	0.40	0.56	0.55	4.0	0.06Q	2/21/03	15.00 - 5.00
—	—	—	—	—	—	—	0.40	0.10	0.10	4.7	0.30A	4/30/03	10.25 - 6.80
—	—	—	—	4.74	5.70	—	0.70	0.72	0.76	14.6	0.0375M	3/17/03	6.02 - 3.54
—	—	—	—	—	—	—	1.36	1.20	0.90	4.6	1.356U	8/19/02	45.10 - 13.25
—	—	—	3.53	4.49	6.16	—	0.80	0.86	0.97	17.6	0.0475M	3/20/03	6.00 - 3.10
0.17	0.06	0.19	—	0.07	2.05	—	1.50	2.03	2.20	9.0	0.375Q	2/14/03	20.15 - 13.18
0.22	0.16	d1.80	—	d2.35	d27.40	—	—	—	—	—	—		10.47 - 3.40
—	—	—	—	—	—	—	0.43	0.49	0.53	2.5	0.0674U	1/17/03	20.05 - 14.80
—	—	—	pd2.45	d1.10	0.78	—	0.20	0.20	0.20	2.2	0.05Q	2/28/03	13.00 - 5.44
0.30	0.29	0.42	—	2.37	1.92	—	1.40	2.40	1.89	8.1	—	3/14/03	20.23 - 14.50
—	—	—	pd0.20	d0.32	d0.28	—	0.85	0.84	0.83	9.9	0.2125Q	3/14/03	10.40 - 6.65
—	—	—	pd1.16	d2.08	d1.48	—	—	—	—	—	—		11.55 - 1.00
0.10	0.19	0.24	d1.43	0.47	0.41	—	—	—	—	—	3-for-2	12/27/00	32.00 - 1.40
—	—	—	—	d0.50	0.18	—	—	—	—	—	—		17.50 - 8.05
d0.52	1.37	3.19	—	2.40	0.69	—	—	—	—	—	0.10Q	3/20/03	38.70 - 24.51
—	—	—	p2.19	2.19	1.38	18.9 - 11.5	0.40	0.80	1.20	1.2	0.10Q	3/14/03	41.40 - 25.09
—	—	—	d0.54	1.61	2.94	—	0.12	0.12	0.12	1.0	0.03Q	4/25/03	19.56 - 3.65
—	—	—	p2.24	1.46	2.03	18.2 - 12.6	0.88	0.84	0.76	2.5	0.22Q	3/14/03	40.75 - 28.30
0.08	d0.57	—	—	d0.31	d0.74	—	—	0.04	0.14	—	0.035Q	1/9/01	17.89 - 3.79
—	—	—	p1.89	d2.66	0.20	26.6 - 10.4	1.20	1.20	1.20	3.4	0.30Q	3/3/03	50.29 - 19.60
0.90	1.03	1.08	—	6.14	4.03	—	0.60	0.54	0.52	1.0	0.15Q	4/25/03	80.20 - 45.10
—	—	—	1.75	1.00	1.83	20.4 - 13.2	0.23	0.23	0.23	0.8	0.0575Q	5/2/03	35.70 - 23.03
—	—	—	1.96	1.59	4.15	17.3 - 9.8	—	—	—	—	100%	10/31/95	25.48 - 3.60
—	—	—	—	—	—	—	—	—	—	—	3-for-1	7/23/96	34.00 - 19.20
—	—	—	pd0.60	0.33	0.96	—	0.88	2.08	2.22	2.2	1.50U	4/10/03	50.88 - 29.78
—	—	—	0.39	d2.01	2.18	59.5 - 23.8	0.04	0.94	1.24	0.2	0.01Q	3/14/03	23.22 - 9.28
—	—	—	p1.88	2.01	2.23	40.1 - 28.0	0.09	0.08	0.07	0.1	0.025Q	4/30/03	75.46 - 52.60
0.40	0.21	—	—	1.30	1.06	—	0.08	0.05	0.05	0.3	0.04S	5/1/03	29.77 - 18.00
0.22	0.07	d0.13	—	0.58	0.94	—	—	—	—	—	50%	9/15/97	13.38 - 6.25
—	—	—	2.28	1.51	0.20	11.5 - 8.3	—	—	—	—	5-for-3	10/20/97	26.21 - 19.00
—	—	—	p1.81	1.85	1.84	22.4 - 15.0	—	—	—	—	2-for-1	4/24/02	40.55 - 27.07
0.28	—	—	1.33	d0.27	2.06	38.8 - 28.2	0.88	0.88	0.88	2.0	0.22Q	5/1/03	51.60 - 37.50
0.01	—	—	0.75	0.76	2.50	16.3 - 9.3	—	—	—	—	—		12.20 - 6.95
—	—	—	10.14	—	—	—	1.42	1.50	1.50	12.1	0.10M	3/28/03	14.45 - 8.90
—	—	—	9.94	11.17	11.77	—	1.44	1.50	1.50	12.3	0.09375M	3/28/03	13.78 - 9.60
—	—	—	0.61	d0.66	1.88	28.5 - 10.8	0.28	0.28	0.28	2.3	0.07Q	1/15/03	17.40 - 6.60
—	—	—	p2.85	d0.04	d0.16	15.8 - 11.5	0.29	0.28	—	0.7	0.08Q	3/6/03	45.12 - 32.80
d0.20	—	—	0.76	0.81	1.98	30.3 - 22.2	0.20	0.17	0.12	1.0	0.06Q	3/14/03	23.00 - 16.90
—	—	—	pd10.44	d9.99	7.05	—	0.10	0.10	0.10	0.4	0.025Q	3/1/03	38.69 - 6.10
—	—	—	pd10.44	d9.99	7.05	—	2.03	2.03	2.03	13.1	—	4/1/03	24.70 - 6.40
0.24	0.05	—	—	d2.06	0.96	—	—	—	—	—	—		6.15 - 1.40
—	—	—	pd1.33	d0.05	0.04	—	0.25	0.25	0.25	0.9	0.0625Q	3/15/03	35.40 - 21.65
—	—	—	p3.36	2.69	2.34	14.9 - 9.8	1.48	1.48	1.48	3.6	0.37Q	3/3/03	50.13 - 33.02
—	—	—	p0.86	1.12	3.07	13.9 - 7.2	—	—	—	—	—		11.97 - 6.20
—	—	—	pd4.70	1.24	1.47	—	—	—	—	—	—		19.97 - 8.60
—	—	—	—	—	—	—	0.61	0.29	0.52	6.3	—	2/7/03	12.81 - 6.50
—	—	—	—	—	—	—	1.91	1.91	1.91	7.7	—	3/31/03	25.50 - 24.09
—	—	—	—	—	—	—	1.89	1.89	1.89	7.6	0.47125Q	3/31/03	25.35 - 24.27
—	—	—	—	—	—	—	1.84	1.84	1.84	7.4	—	3/31/03	25.60 - 24.00
—	—	—	—	—	—	—	1.30	—	—	2.4	1.30U	5/23/02	74.00 - 35.26
—	—	—	—	—	—	—	0.27	0.39	0.41	2.1	—	6/5/02	18.19 - 8.06
—	—	—	1.14	1.17	1.31	20.7 - 15.1	1.51	1.47	1.43	7.4	0.41Q	4/7/03	23.65 - 17.25
0.16	0.33	—	0.95	0.82	0.68	36.6 - 12.7	—	—	—	—	100%	6/19/98	34.76 - 12.10

SYMBOL	COMPANY	NATURE OF BUSINESS	FISCAL YEAR-END	TOTAL REV. $MILL	NET INCOME $MILL	TOTAL ASSETS $MILL	NET STK EQUITY $MILL	NO. OF INST.	INST. HOLDINGS (SHARES)
DEO	Diageo Plc	Food processing	6/30/02	—	—	—	—	171	48593652
DP	Diagnostic Products Corp.	Medical & dental equipment	12/31/02	p324.1	p324.1	—	—	137	16707436
DL	Dial Corp. (New)	Soaps & cleansers	12/31/02	1282.2	115.2	1149.7	149.0	246	69311353
DO	Diamond Offshore Drilling In	Oil service & equipment	12/31/02	752.6	62.5	3258.8	1807.5	170	127259077
DKS	Dick's Sporting Goods, Inc	Specialty stores	2/2/02	1074.6	23.5	322.8	63.1	37	6040264
DBD	Diebold, Inc.	Office equipment & supplies	12/31/02	1940.2	132.3	1625.1	940.8	306	52435960
DDS	Dillard's Inc.	Department stores	2/2/02	8388.3	65.8	7074.6	2668.4	210	68853160
DMN	DiMon, Inc.	Tobacco	6/30/02	1259.7	27.5	1277.1	434.7	97	25928379
DIS	Disney (Walt) Co. (The)	—	9/30/02	25329.0	1236.0	50045.0	23445.0	907	1263835621
DCQ	Disney (Walt) Co. (The)	—	9/30/02	25329.0	1236.0	50045.0	23445.0	—	—
DYS	Distribucion y Servicio (D&S)	Grocery chain	12/31/01	—	—	—	—	28	6000906
DJO	dj Orthopedics, Inc. (United	—	12/31/01	p182.6	p182.6	—	—	30	13611984
DNP	DNP Select Income Fund Inc (U	Investment company	12/31/01	210.9	178.4	3115.5	2459.7	99	4621922
DOL	Dole Food Co., Inc.	Food processing	12/31/02	p4392.1	p4392.1	—	—	205	30459578
DG	Dollar General Corp. (TN)	Discount & variety stores	2/1/02	5322.9	207.5	2552.4	1041.7	294	210267382
DTG	Dollar Thrifty Automotive Gro	—	12/31/02	p1133.2	p1133.2	—	—	101	21693607
DOM	Dominion Res Black Warrior Tr	Natural gas	12/31/01	26.0	25.2	57.8	57.7	18	337987
D	Dominion Resources Inc (New)	Electric power	12/31/01	—	—	—	—	494	186036394
DCP	Dominion Resources Inc (New)	Electric power	12/31/02	—	—	—	—	10	2085777
DCI	Donaldson Co. Inc.	Pollution control	7/31/02	1126.0	86.9	850.1	382.6	195	26468847
RHD	Donnelley (R.H.) Corp.	—	12/31/01	216.7	50.3	296.0	d111.3	146	26887546
DNY	Donnelley (R.R.) & Son	Printing & engraving	12/31/02	4754.9	142.2	3151.8	914.6	295	87448831
DRL	Doral Financial Corp.	Financial services	12/31/02	—	p221.0	—	—	161	42408324
DOV	Dover Corp. (United States)	Machinery & equipment	12/31/02	4183.7	211.1	4437.4	2394.6	377	167708471
DDE	Dover Downs Gaming & Enterta	Gaming	12/31/01	186.7	21.1	131.3	102.7	55	7320363
DVD	Dover Motorsports, Inc.	—	12/31/01	86.6	6.9	417.6	244.5	58	9076207
DOW	Dow Chemical Co.	Chemicals	12/31/02	27609.0	d405.0	39562.0	7626.0	636	617306419
DJ	Dow Jones & Co., Inc	Publishing	12/31/02	1559.2	201.5	1207.7	30.6	225	56461567
DSL	Downey Financial Corp. (DE)	Banking - West	12/31/02	699.7	112.3	11978.2	823.1	119	14013051
DPL	DPL, Inc.	Electric power	12/31/02	1186.4	87.3	4176.2	852.8	206	43564308
DQE	DQE	Electric power	12/31/02	p1019.4	p1019.4	—	—	158	32222963
RDY	Dr. Reddy's Laboratories Ltd	Drugs	3/31/02	—	—	—	—	60	8424450
DSM	Dreyfus Strategic Mun Bd Fd	Investment company	11/30/02	39.2	33.8	606.1	411.4	31	922006
LEO	Dreyfus Strategic Municipals	—	9/30/02	55.5	47.8	847.1	839.8	34	2179523
DRQ	Dril-Quip, Inc.	Oil service & equipment	12/31/02	p215.8	p215.8	—	—	75	9361112
DRS	DRS Technologies, Inc. (Unit	Electronic components	3/31/02	517.2	20.3	601.1	257.2	147	19093932
DST	DST Systems Inc. (DE)	Computer services	12/31/02	p2383.8	p2276.2	—	—	207	58757750
DTE	DTE Energy Co.	Electric power	12/31/02	p6749.0	p6749.0	—	—	317	95748051
DTF	DTF Tax-Free Income, Inc. (Un	Investment company	10/31/02	11.0	9.1	209.7	144.4	—	—
DD	Du Pont (E.I.) de Nemours &	Conglomerate	12/31/02	24522.0	1841.0	34621.0	9063.0	849	616343017
DRD	Duane Reade, Inc.	Drugs	12/31/02	p1274.5	p1258.5	—	—	133	28193677
DMH	Ducati Motor Holding, S.p.A.	—	12/31/01	—	—	—	—	7	52270
DCO	Ducommun Inc.	Electronic components	12/31/02	212.4	9.9	197.6	120.4	59	7126300
DUC	Duff & Phelps Util & Corp Bd	Investment company	12/31/02	33.3	26.1	485.5	345.1	28	261702
DUK	Duke Energy Corp.	Electric power	12/31/02	—	p1034.0	—	—	672	569810863
DUT	Duke Energy Corp.	Electric power	12/31/02	—	p1034.0	—	—	4	41350
DKE	Duke Energy Corp.	Electric power	12/31/02	—	p1034.0	—	—	35	4954400
DUR	Duke Energy Corp.	Electric power	12/31/02	—	p1034.0	—	—	—	—
DRE	Duke Realty Corp.	Real estate investment trust	12/31/02	p780.1	p780.1	—	—	273	70898900
DNB	Dun & Bradstreet Corp (DE) (	—	12/31/02	p1276.0	p1276.0	—	—	270	63955594
DQZ	Duquesne Light Co. (United S	Electric power	12/31/01	1053.6	53.4	2560.2	754.5	3	47755
DQC	Duquesne Light Co. (United S	Electric power	12/31/01	1053.6	53.4	2560.2	754.5	—	—
DVI	DVI, Inc.	Financial services	6/30/02	139.7	d4.1	1672.0	229.6	53	9829232
DY	Dycom Industries, Inc.	Electrical equipment	7/27/02	624.0	d36.1	514.6	431.3	137	36476540
DYN	Dynegy Inc (New)	Natural gas distributor	12/31/02	p4950.0	p5323.0	—	—	217	81968234
DX	Dynex Capital, Inc.	Real estate investment trust	12/31/02	222.8	3.3	2500.8	173.1	12	490036
ET	E*Trade Group, Inc. (United	Securities brokerage	12/31/02	—	pd567.2	—	—	196	206236392
EON	E.ON AG (Germany)	Electrical equipment	12/31/01	—	—	—	—	59	11235580
NGT	Eastern Amern Nat Gas Tr	Natural gas	12/31/01	13.3	11.3	45.1	43.2	13	87860
EGP	EastGroup Properties, Inc.	Real estate investment trust	12/31/02	p105.8	p105.8	—	—	89	6873244
EMN	Eastman Chemical Co.	Plastics & plastic products	12/31/02	5320.0	79.0	6273.0	1271.0	267	65317078
EK	Eastman Kodak Co.	Photo & optical	12/31/02	12835.0	793.0	13369.0	2777.0	446	246308018
ETN	Eaton Corp.	—	12/31/02	p7209.0	p7175.0	—	—	324	63092942
EV	Eaton Vance Corp	Financial services	10/31/02	523.0	121.1	616.6	372.3	183	34841430
EVN	Eaton Vance Municipal Income	Investment company	11/30/02	24.7	20.7	348.0	347.4	7	97229
EVF	Eaton Vance Senior Income Tru	Investment company	6/30/02	34.4	24.7	518.6	302.8	19	1117436
ECL	Ecolab, Inc.	Soaps & cleansers	12/31/02	p3403.6	p3403.6	—	—	330	75389111
EIX	Edison International	Electric power	12/31/02	—	—	—	—	290	224387851
EDO	EDO Corp. (United States)	Defense systems & equip.	12/31/02	328.9	14.0	481.6	168.3	107	16133158
EDP	EDP-Electricidade de Portugal	Electric power	12/31/01	—	—	—	—	17	4012732
AGE	Edwards (A.G.), Inc.	Securities brokerage	2/28/02	2363.8	71.5	4187.2	1647.8	220	40586436
EW	Edwards Lifesciences Corp	Medical & dental equipment	12/31/02	704.0	55.7	1008.2	539.4	213	46383479
EKC	Ek Chor China Motorcycle Co.	—	12/31/01	—	—	—	—	1	500
EP	El Paso Corp.	Natural gas	12/31/01	57475.0	67.0	48171.0	9356.0	463	471015379
EE	El Paso Electric Company	Electric power	12/31/02	p455.3	p455.3	—	—	123	42655217
EPN	El Paso Energy Partners, L.P.	Natural gas	12/31/02	p467.9	p467.9	—	—	85	4756887
ELN	Elan Corp. Plc	Drugs	12/31/01	—	—	—	—	194	85762887
ETT	ElderTrust	Real estate investment trust	12/31/02	p25.3	p25.1	—	—	12	991278
EDS	Electronic Data Sys Corp. (N	Services	12/31/02	—	—	—	—	533	402275177
ELK	Elkcorp	Engineering & construction	6/30/02	506.5	15.1	381.4	176.1	85	13739923
AKO A	Embotelladora Andina S.A.	Soft drinks	12/31/01	—	—	—	—	18	7365032
AKO B	Embotelladora Andina S.A.	Soft drinks	12/31/01	—	—	—	—	10	11639456
ERJ	Embraer-Empresa Brasileira de	—	12/31/01	—	—	—	—	6	1291133
EMT	Embratel Participacoes SA	Telecommunications	12/31/01	—	—	—	—	17	2497225
EMC	EMC Corp. (MA)	Comp. components & periphs.	12/31/02	7090.6	d507.7	9889.6	7600.8	817	1288982815
EME	EMCOR Group, Inc.	Electronic components	12/31/02	3968.1	62.9	1758.5	489.9	165	15289210
EMD	Emerging Markets Income Fd	Investment company	8/31/02	8.3	6.8	73.5	48.0	5	77076
ETF	Emerging Markets Telecommuni	Investment company	11/30/02	0.1	d1.6	70.1	66.9	19	2743590
EFL	Emerging Mkts Fltg Rate Fund	Investment company	2/28/02	6.2	5.4	67.9	51.8	6	87292
EDF	Emerging Mkts Income Fund II	Investment company	5/31/02	44.4	36.4	387.4	277.2	10	4443023
EMR	Emerson Electric Co.	Electrical equipment	9/30/02	13824.0	1060.0	14545.0	5741.0	802	346465772
EDE	Empire District Electric Co.	Electric power	12/31/02	p305.9	p304.9	—	—	67	6594708
EOC	Empresa Nacional de Electric	Electric power	12/31/01	—	—	—	—	35	6490860
ELX	Emulex Corporation (United S	Comp. components & periphs.	6/30/02	254.7	d96.2	1207.4	823.0	184	72330155
EEP	Enbridge Energy Partners, L.	Transportation	12/31/02	p1185.5	p1185.5	—	—	82	4638502
EAC	Encore Acquisition Co.	Oil	12/31/01	135.9	17.1	402.0	269.3	54	17400441

T16

| EARNINGS PER SHARE | | | | | | P/E RATIO | DIVIDENDS PER SHARE | | | AV. YLD. % | DIV. DECLARED | | PRICE RANGE |
| QUARTERLY | | | ANNUAL | | | | | | | | | | 2002 |
1st	2nd	3rd	2002	2001	2000		2002	2001	2000		AMOUNT	PAYABLE	
—	—	—	p1.60	1.32	1.01	33.1 - 19.0	1.44	1.29	1.25	3.0	0.6314U	4/11/03	55.40 - 40.75
—	—	—	1.22	0.76	d0.12	18.4 - 11.3	0.24	0.24	0.24	0.6	0.06Q	2/14/03	52.99 - 30.45
—	—	—	0.47	1.31	0.53	74.4 - 36.8	0.16	0.16	0.32	0.9	0.04Q	4/17/03	22.45 - 13.80
—	—	0.14	—	1.31	0.86	—	0.50	0.50	0.50	1.9	0.125Q	3/3/03	34.99 - 17.30
—	—	—	—	—	—	—	—	—	—	—	—	—	23.15 - 12.15
—	—	—	1.83	0.93	1.92	23.8 - 16.6	0.66	0.64	0.62	1.8	0.17Q	3/7/03	43.55 - 30.30
0.68	0.15	d0.07	—	0.78	1.06	—	0.16	0.16	0.16	0.7	0.04Q	5/5/03	31.20 - 12.94
0.11	0.14	—	0.61	0.56	0.40	13.6 - 8.8	0.22	0.20	0.20	3.3	0.075Q	3/21/03	8.29 - 5.35
0.13	—	—	0.60	0.11	0.57	42.0 - 22.5	—	0.21	0.21	—	0.21A	1/9/03	25.17 - 13.48
0.13	—	—	0.60	0.11	0.57	44.2 - 40.7	1.78	—	—	7.0	0.4375Q	2/3/03	26.50 - 24.40
—	—	—	—	—	—	—	0.17	0.11	0.24	1.5	0.07912U	1/24/03	15.40 - 7.50
—	—	—	pd0.85	4.94	d0.25	—	—	—	—	—	—	—	13.67 - 2.70
—	8.46	—	9.18	10.51	—	—	0.81	0.79	0.79	8.3	0.065M	6/10/03	11.62 - 7.85
—	—	—	p0.64	d0.66	1.21	53.1 - 37.7	0.60	0.40	0.40	2.1	0.15Q	3/18/03	33.99 - 24.14
0.14	0.13	0.20	—	0.62	0.21	—	0.10	0.13	0.12	0.6	0.035Q	4/17/03	19.95 - 11.70
—	—	—	p1.88	0.57	3.18	14.1 - 7.6	—	—	—	—	—	—	26.60 - 14.35
0.57	—	—	—	3.21	2.58	—	2.37	3.21	2.58	11.4	—	3/11/03	24.55 - 17.20
—	—	—	p4.82	2.15	1.76	13.9 - 7.3	2.58	2.58	2.58	5.0	0.645Q	3/20/03	67.06 - 35.40
—	—	—	p4.82	2.15	1.76	13.0 - 7.9	4.75	5.19	—	9.4	1.1875Q	2/18/03	62.70 - 38.00
0.50	0.45	—	1.90	1.66	1.51	23.7 - 15.7	0.33	0.30	0.29	0.9	0.09Q	3/14/03	44.99 - 29.91
0.44	0.70	0.83	—	1.62	3.85	—	—	—	—	—	0.175Q	12/10/98	32.17 - 22.02
—	—	—	1.24	0.21	2.17	25.9 - 14.9	0.98	0.94	0.90	3.9	0.25Q	3/1/03	32.10 - 18.50
—	—	—	2.84	1.88	1.23	10.7 - 7.1	0.42	0.32	0.25	1.7	0.14Q	3/7/03	30.26 - 20.18
—	—	—	1.04	0.82	2.61	41.9 - 22.6	0.54	0.52	0.48	1.6	0.135Q	3/14/03	43.55 - 23.54
d0.12	0.19	0.10	—	0.18	0.42	—	0.13	—	—	1.1	0.05Q	3/10/03	14.90 - 7.41
—	—	—	d0.44	d0.46	2.22	—	0.10	0.18	0.18	1.5	0.01Q	3/10/03	9.75 - 3.29
—	—	—	2.40	1.14	d1.35	25.1 - 12.3	1.34	1.25	1.16	4.4	0.335Q	4/30/03	37.00 - 23.66
—	—	—	3.99	4.25	3.51	14.1 - 7.6	1.00	1.00	1.00	2.2	0.25Q	2/28/03	60.20 - 29.50
—	—	—	0.72	1.70	2.14	37.8 - 18.9	0.36	0.36	0.36	0.8	0.09Q	2/21/03	56.42 - 30.44
—	—	—	pd3.28	d2.75	2.15	—	0.94	0.94	0.94	4.6	0.235Q	3/14/03	27.25 - 13.60
—	—	—	—	—	—	—	1.51	1.68	1.60	9.1	0.25Q	4/1/03	22.25 - 10.90
—	—	—	8.56	8.75	8.60	12.6 - 10.9	0.05	0.10	—	0.2	0.04618U	9/30/02	24.55 - 13.31
—	—	—	0.81	0.82	0.71	55.3 - 31.2	0.56	0.56	0.56	6.9	0.051M	3/28/03	9.00 - 7.25
—	—	—	p0.50	0.70	0.63	—	0.69	0.58	0.55	7.3	0.06M	3/28/03	10.20 - 8.80
0.31	0.44	0.41	—	1.41	1.01	—	—	—	—	—	—	—	27.64 - 15.62
—	—	—	—	—	—	—	—	—	—	—	—	—	48.66 - 28.20
—	—	—	p1.72	1.81	1.67	29.7 - 14.0	—	—	—	—	100%	10/19/00	51.15 - 24.14
—	—	—	p3.83	2.14	3.27	12.5 - 8.6	2.06	2.06	2.06	5.1	0.515Q	4/15/03	47.70 - 33.05
—	—	—	16.97	16.70	15.42	—	0.87	0.75	0.83	5.6	0.08M	3/31/03	16.39 - 14.50
—	—	—	1.84	4.15	2.19	27.1 - 19.0	1.40	1.40	1.40	3.3	0.35Q	3/14/03	49.80 - 35.02
—	—	—	p0.63	1.20	1.23	57.5 - 20.5	—	—	—	—	—	—	36.25 - 12.90
—	—	—	—	—	—	—	—	—	—	—	—	—	19.85 - 13.65
—	—	—	0.99	1.50	1.30	27.0 - 11.0	—	—	—	—	3-for-2	6/10/98	26.75 - 10.85
—	—	—	13.03	13.23	12.64	—	1.02	1.02	1.13	8.1	0.085M	3/31/03	13.85 - 11.41
—	—	—	p1.22	2.56	2.38	32.8 - 13.5	1.10	1.10	1.10	3.9	0.275Q	3/17/03	40.00 - 16.42
—	—	—	p1.22	2.56	2.38	21.9 - 20.0	1.65	1.65	1.65	6.5	0.4125Q	3/31/03	26.75 - 24.36
—	—	—	p1.22	2.56	2.38	22.0 - 12.3	2.06	1.38	—	9.8	—	2/18/03	26.90 - 15.00
—	—	—	p1.22	2.56	2.38	21.1 - 11.7	1.99	—	—	9.9	0.50Q	2/18/03	25.80 - 14.33
—	—	—	p1.19	1.75	1.66	24.3 - 18.0	1.81	1.76	1.64	7.2	0.455Q	2/28/03	28.95 - 21.40
—	—	—	p1.87	1.88	0.90	23.2 - 15.1	—	—	—	—	—	—	43.40 - 28.26
—	—	—	—	—	—	—	1.84	1.84	1.84	7.5	0.46094Q	2/3/03	25.80 - 23.44
—	—	—	—	—	—	—	0.84	—	—	3.1	0.41875Q	1/31/03	28.23 - 25.05
0.33	0.35	—	d0.28	1.22	1.54	—	—	—	—	—	—	—	21.00 - 3.47
0.09	pd0.02	—	d0.80	1.44	1.54	—	—	—	—	—	3-for-2	2/16/00	17.78 - 8.00
d0.21	d0.13	d0.52	pd8.56	1.90	1.48	—	0.15	0.30	0.25	0.9	0.075Q	6/17/02	32.19 - 0.49
—	—	—	pd0.52	d0.81	—	—	—	—	—	—	—	—	5.40 - 2.02
0.28	0.33	0.34	—	1.91	1.66	—	—	—	—	—	2-for-1	5/21/99	2.81
—	—	—	—	—	—	—	1.17	0.87	0.84	2.4	1.50501U	5/9/03	58.64 - 39.65
—	—	—	—	—	—	—	1.26	2.15	1.47	7.1	0.3671Q	3/17/03	19.29 - 16.24
—	—	—	p0.84	1.51	1.68	31.5 - 26.3	1.88	1.80	1.58	7.7	0.475Q	3/31/03	26.50 - 22.09
—	—	—	1.02	d2.33	3.94	48.6 - 33.9	1.76	1.76	1.76	4.2	0.44Q	4/1/03	49.55 - 34.53
—	—	—	2.72	0.26	4.59	14.1 - 9.4	1.80	2.21	1.76	5.6	0.90S	12/13/02	38.30 - 25.58
—	—	—	p4.39	2.39	5.00	20.2 - 13.5	1.76	1.76	1.76	2.4	0.44Q	2/21/03	88.68 - 59.10
0.37	—	—	1.70	1.60	1.58	24.1 - 13.2	0.30	0.25	0.26	0.9	0.08Q	2/10/03	41.00 - 22.46
—	—	—	13.02	12.93	11.95	—	1.05	0.79	0.78	7.5	0.0925M	3/17/03	15.09 - 12.95
—	8.11	—	8.42	8.86	9.81	—	0.55	0.77	0.91	7.7	0.04M	3/19/03	8.30 - 6.10
—	—	—	p1.60	1.45	1.58	31.5 - 22.8	0.54	0.52	0.48	1.2	0.145Q	4/15/03	50.40 - 36.53
—	—	—	p3.31	7.36	d5.84	5.9 - 2.4	—	—	1.11	—	0.28Q	10/31/00	19.60 - 7.80
—	—	—	0.81	1.09	0.05	40.7 - 19.1	0.12	0.12	0.12	0.5	0.03Q	3/28/03	33.00 - 15.50
0.48	0.33	0.40	—	—	—	—	0.88	1.00	0.23	4.8	—	6/14/02	22.19 - 14.56
—	—	—	0.91	d0.17	d4.81	32.5 - 20.2	0.64	0.64	0.63	1.7	0.16Q	4/1/03	46.70 - 26.50
—	—	—	—	—	—	—	—	—	—	—	—	—	29.60 - 18.40
0.43	0.02	d0.06	—	—	—	—	—	—	0.50	—	0.50A	6/27/02	2.95 - 0.88
—	—	—	—	0.13	2.44	—	0.86	0.84	0.82	3.4	0.04Q	4/7/03	46.89 - 4.39
—	—	—	p0.57	1.27	1.09	28.4 - 16.2	—	—	—	—	—	—	16.20 - 9.25
—	—	—	p0.80	0.38	d0.03	48.3 - 25.6	2.60	2.31	2.15	8.8	0.675Q	2/14/03	38.68 - 20.50
—	—	—	—	—	—	—	—	—	—	—	100%	6/4/99	45.18 - 1.03
—	—	—	p0.06	0.07	d3.00	141.5 - 101.0	—	—	—	—	0.30Q	5/16/00	8.49 - 6.06
—	—	—	p2.28	2.86	2.40	30.1 - 4.4	0.60	0.60	0.60	1.5	0.15Q	3/10/03	68.55 - 10.09
0.46	0.14	—	0.77	0.45	1.49	24.2 - 19.0	0.20	0.20	0.20	1.2	0.05Q	2/27/03	18.60 - 14.60
—	—	—	—	—	—	—	0.52	0.59	0.74	7.2	0.0303U	2/7/03	10.00 - 4.50
—	—	—	—	—	—	—	0.58	0.95	0.81	7.3	0.0333U	2/7/03	11.27 - 4.60
—	—	—	—	—	—	—	0.74	1.09	0.10	4.1	0.21085U	1/23/03	24.00 - 12.60
—	—	—	—	—	—	—	—	0.24	0.23	—	0.0781U	7/16/01	4.88 - 0.40
d0.03	—	0.01	—	d0.23	0.79	—	—	—	—	—	0.00U	2/7/01	32.03 - 3.67
—	—	—	4.07	3.40	2.95	15.8 - 10.8	—	—	—	—	—	—	64.35 - 43.87
—	—	—	11.80	12.91	14.01	—	1.65	1.65	1.65	12.3	0.4125Q	3/28/03	15.98 - 10.88
—	—	—	14.60	8.42	10.35	—	—	—	0.25	—	0.25A	8/25/00	7.80 - 5.40
—	9.68	—	—	12.07	11.84	—	1.13	1.55	1.59	10.9	0.092M	5/30/03	12.60 - 8.21
—	10.52	—	—	11.63	11.53	—	1.65	1.65	1.65	13.6	0.4125Q	3/28/03	14.09 - 10.25
0.52	—	—	2.52	2.40	3.30	26.2 - 16.6	1.55	1.54	1.45	2.9	0.3925Q	3/10/03	66.09 - 41.74
—	—	—	p1.19	0.59	1.35	18.5 - 12.7	1.28	1.28	1.28	6.9	0.32Q	3/15/03	21.99 - 15.06
—	—	—	—	—	—	—	0.03	0.04	—	0.4	—	5/9/02	10.73 - 6.05
0.37	0.19	—	d1.18	d0.31	0.43	—	—	—	—	—	2-for-1	12/15/04	48.17 - 7.85
—	—	—	p1.76	0.98	1.78	26.6 - 20.3	3.60	3.50	3.50	8.7	0.925Q	2/14/03	46.75 - 35.68
0.24	0.31	0.33	—	0.59	d5.81	—	—	—	—	—	—	2/14/03	20.40 - 12.40

T17

SYMBOL	COMPANY	NATURE OF BUSINESS	FISCAL YEAR-END	TOTAL REV. $MILL	NET INCOME $MILL	TOTAL ASSETS $MILL	NET STK EQUITY $MILL	NO. OF INST.	INST. HOLDINGS (SHARES)
ELE	Endesa S.A. (Spain)	Electric power	12/31/01	—	—	—	—	85	36329821
EN	ENEL S.p.A. (Italy)	Electric power	12/31/01	—	—	—	—	8	5013148
EGN	Energen Corp.	Natural gas distributor	9/30/01	785.0	67.9	1223.9	480.8	176	20322492
ENR	Energizer Holdings, Inc. (Un	Consumer electronics	9/30/02	1739.7	186.4	1588.1	704.8	235	61729087
EAS	Energy East Corp.	Electric power	12/31/02	p4008.9	p3910.4	—	—	221	67392715
EPL	Energy Partners Ltd.	Natural gas	12/31/02	p134.0	p134.0	—	—	43	3884873
ENI	Enersis S.A. (Chile)	Electric power	12/31/01	—	—	—	—	22	3400372
ENC	Enesco Group, Inc.	Specialty stores	12/31/02	p253.8	p253.8	—	—	51	8159598
EC	Engelhard Corp.	Mining & processing	12/31/02	p3753.6	p3696.7	—	—	262	116232527
E	ENI S.p.A. (Italy)	Oil	12/31/01	—	—	—	—	111	19228680
EBF	Ennis Business Forms	Office equipment & supplies	2/28/02	236.9	15.0	139.0	96.0	61	8093806
ENO	Enodis Plc (United Kingdom)	—	9/28/02	—	—	—	—	1	39050
ESV	ENSCO International Inc. (Un	Oil	12/31/02	698.1	59.3	3061.5	1967.0	299	120952423
ETS	Enterasys Networks, Inc.	Comp. components & periphs.	12/29/01	415.3	d615.1	716.7	329.7	129	113542154
ETM	Entercom Communications Corp	Broadcasting	12/31/01	391.3	55.8	1568.5	890.5	192	38663481
EHA	Entergy Arkansas, Inc.	Electric power	12/31/01	1776.8	178.2	4451.6	1344.2	—	—
EHB	Entergy Arkansas, Inc.	Electric power	12/31/01	1776.8	178.2	4451.6	1344.2	—	—
ETR	Entergy Corp.	Electric power	12/31/02	p8305.0	p8305.0	—	—	356	172660644
EHL	Entergy Louisiana, Inc. (Unit	Electric power	12/31/01	1901.9	132.6	4149.7	1328.0	—	—
EMQ	Entergy Mississippi, Inc.	Electric power	12/31/01	1093.7	39.6	1683.0	510.8	—	—
EMO	Entergy Mississippi, Inc.	Electric power	12/31/01	1093.7	39.6	1683.0	510.8	—	—
EPD	Enterprise Prods Partners LP	Natural gas	12/31/02	p3623.8	p3623.8	—	—	57	4130617
EPR	Entertainment Properties Trus	Real estate investment trust	12/31/02	—	p31.2	—	—	84	8935381
EVC	Entravision Communications C	Broadcasting	12/31/01	238.5	d10.9	1573.5	1015.0	107	46044412
ENZ	Enzo Biochem, Inc.	—	7/31/02	54.0	6.9	109.3	104.7	85	7317194
EOG	EOG Resources, Inc.	Natural gas	12/31/02	1095.0	87.2	3814.0	1672.4	297	117286495
EPC	Epcos AG (Germany)	Electronic components	9/30/02	—	—	—	—	5	40230
ENT	Equant N V (Netherlands)	Services	12/31/01	—	—	—	—	8	272829
EFX	Equifax, Inc.	Services	12/31/02	p1109.3	p972.4	—	—	316	102823762
EQT	Equitable Resources, Inc.	Natural gas	12/31/02	1069.1	150.6	2436.9	778.6	222	42528312
ENN	Equity Inns Inc.	Real estate investment trust	12/31/01	226.1	10.2	778.1	358.2	90	18957287
EOP	Equity Office Properties Tr	Real estate investment trust	12/31/02	p3506.1	p3506.1	—	—	419	331780677
EQY	Equity One, Inc.	Real estate investment trust	12/31/02	p103.0	p103.0	—	—	47	4206103
EQR	Equity Residential	Real estate investment trust	12/31/02	p1994.1	p1994.1	—	—	355	230568588
EQS	Equus II, Inc.	Investment company	12/31/01	2.7	1.2	150.8	77.0	8	607273
ESE	ESCO Technologies, Inc.	Defense systems & equip.	9/30/02	367.5	21.8	407.7	306.3	125	10882282
ESF	Espirito Santo Finl Group SA	—	12/31/01	—	—	—	—	8	4396030
ESS	Essex Property Trust, Inc.	Real estate investment trust	12/31/02	p200.1	p208.4	—	—	126	16987493
ESL	Esterline Technologies Corp.	Meas. & control instruments	10/25/02	434.8	31.3	571.0	354.4	122	18521569
ETH	Ethan Allen Interiors, Inc.	Furniture & fixtures	6/30/02	892.3	82.3	688.8	511.2	186	32794776
EY	Ethyl Corp.	Chemicals	12/31/01	724.5	d105.0	719.6	145.3	29	3167067
EF	Europe Fund Inc.	Investment company	12/31/01	2.5	0.6	122.5	121.1	21	1584095
EWF	European Warrant Fund, Inc.	Investment company	3/31/02	0.6	d0.9	67.3	62.0	14	4060241
RE	Everest Re Group Ltd (Bermuda	Property & casualty insurance	12/31/01	1801.5	99.0	7796.2	1720.5	232	44066154
EVG	Evergreen Resources, Inc.	Oil	12/31/02	p112.1	p112.1	—	—	166	18678484
EXC	Exelon Corp. (United States)	Electric power	12/31/02	—	—	—	—	427	220719312
XJT	ExpressJet Holdings Inc. (Un	—	12/31/01	1089.1	84.8	434.1	15.3	95	24724418
ESA	Extended Stay America, Inc.	Motel/hotel lodging	12/31/02	547.9	57.1	2458.7	1073.2	123	68167333
XOM	Exxon Mobil Corp.	Oil	12/31/02	—	—	—	—	1302	d657445556
FDS	FactSet Research Systems Inc.	Computer services	8/31/02	205.9	40.8	217.4	177.0	154	27575181
FIC	Fair, Isaac & Co., Inc. (Uni	Services	9/30/02	392.4	17.9	1212.5	973.5	226	46410698
FA	Fairchild Corp. (The)	—	6/30/02	635.8	d10.2	970.6	228.0	19	7578825
FCS	Fairchild Semiconductor Inter	Electronic components	12/29/02	p1411.9	p1443.2	—	—	204	97317099
FCP	Falcon Products, Inc.	Furniture & fixtures	11/2/02	277.5	0.7	273.6	61.0	20	4533014
FDO	Family Dollar Stores	Discount & variety stores	8/31/02	4162.7	216.9	1754.6	1154.9	301	149170924
FNM	Fannie Mae	Finance	12/31/02	—	p4.6	—	—	1006	904205137
FFG	FBL Financial Group, Inc.	Life Insurance	12/31/01	474.6	40.4	5629.2	565.8	56	6673855
FB	FBR Asset Investment Corp	Real estate investment trust	12/31/02	p186.0	p188.5	—	—	121	14190022
FJC	Fedders Corp.	Appliances & utensils	8/31/02	373.7	8.0	366.1	77.8	51	7693274
AGM A	Federal Agricultural Mortgag	Finance	12/31/02	—	p21.3	—	—	7	67720
AGM	Federal Agricultural Mortgag	Finance	12/31/02	—	p21.3	—	—	79	9044743
FRT	Federal Realty Invt Tr (MD)	Real estate investment trust	12/31/01	300.5	68.8	1838.0	592.4	143	26087960
FSS	Federal Signal Corp.	—	12/31/02	1057.2	46.2	1168.4	398.1	158	28864790
FD	Federated Department Stores,	Department stores	2/1/03	—	—	—	—	352	176277876
FII	Federated Investors Inc (PA)	Financial services	12/31/02	—	p203.8	—	—	188	47787975
FPT	Federated Premier Intermedia	Investment company	12/16/02	—	—	d0.1	0.1	—	—
FMN	Federated Premier Municipal	Investment company	12/16/02	—	—	d0.1	0.1	—	—
FDX	FedEx Corp	Freight transportation	5/31/02	20607.0	725.0	13812.0	6545.0	491	230594989
FCH	FelCor Lodging Trust, Inc.	Real estate investment trust	12/31/02	p1318.0	p1318.0	—	—	134	28325532
FGP	Ferrellgas Partners, L.P.	Natural gas	7/31/02	1034.8	60.0	885.1	—	41	1217915
FOE	Ferro Corp.	Specialty chemicals	12/31/01	1501.1	39.2	1732.6	300.4	142	34073739
FIA	Fiat S.p.A Torino (Italy)	—	12/31/01	—	—	—	—	18	48209854
FMK	FiberMark Inc.	Paper	12/31/01	394.3	d18.1	516.9	80.5	30	4378601
FNF	Fidelity National Financial	Insurance brokerage	12/31/02	p5082.6	p5082.6	—	—	277	69565299
FLH	Fila Holding S.p.A. (Italy)	—	12/31/01	—	—	—	—	4	4094595
FIF	Financial Federal Corp.	—	7/31/02	138.8	37.1	1447.8	248.6	101	16900300
FAF	First American Corp (The)	Insurance	12/31/02	p4704.2	p4704.2	—	—	183	41865031
FBP	First Bancorp (PR)	Banking - South	12/31/02	569.2	87.0	8197.5	602.9	100	12777161
FCF	First Commonwealth Fin (PA)	Banking - Mid-Atlantic	12/31/02	—	p43.5	—	—	69	9935159
FDC	First Data Corp. (United Sta	Financial services	12/31/02	7636.2	1237.9	26591.2	4156.3	735	718190974
FF	First Financial Fund, Inc.	Investment company	3/31/02	8.0	4.5	373.8	365.2	21	2680403
FR	First Industrial Realty Trust	Real estate investment trust	12/31/02	p371.6	p371.6	—	—	163	19202858
ISL	First Israel Fund, Inc.	Finance	9/30/02	0.3	d0.7	40.8	40.5	13	1029668
FPF	First Philippine Fund, Inc.	Investment company	6/30/02	0.6	d0.5	32.9	32.6	10	1265822
FRC	First Republic Bank (CA)	Savings & loan	12/31/02	p244.8	p142.4	—	—	88	10086155
FTN	First Tennessee National Corp	Banking - South	12/31/01	2458.5	329.6	20616.8	1477.8	291	66866420
FUR	First Union Real Est Eq & Mt	Real estate investment trust	12/31/01	31.4	16.4	185.7	122.2	26	18052208
FVB	First Virginia Banks, Inc.	Banking - Mid-Atlantic	12/31/02	p627.4	p384.1	—	—	201	19713690
FE	FirstEnergy Corp.	Electric power	12/31/02	—	—	—	—	332	211272558
FED	Firstfed Financial Corp. (DE)	Savings & loan	12/31/01	342.9	50.3	4726.3	325.7	117	12955592
FSH	Fisher Scientific Intl, Inc.	Property & casualty insurance	12/31/02	p3238.0	p3238.0	—	—	169	44564680
FLA	Fla. East Coast Industries	Railroads	12/31/02	p301.5	p89.6	—	—	74	11577641
FLA B	Fla. East Coast Industries	Railroads	12/31/02	p301.5	p89.6	—	—	46	4699905
FBC	Flagstar Bancorp, Inc. (Unite	Banking - Midwest	12/31/02	p450.1	p96.9	—	—	109	12703760
FBF	FleetBoston Financial Corp.	Banking - Northeast	12/31/02	15138.0	1524.0	190453.0	16833.0	688	727549524
FLE	Fleetwood Enterprises Inc	Mobile homes	4/28/02	2280.4	d81.3	984.9	174.7	115	44815784

| EARNINGS PER SHARE | | | | | | P/E RATIO | DIVIDENDS PER SHARE | | | AV. YLD. % | DIV. DECLARED | | PRICE RANGE |
| QUARTERLY | | | ANNUAL | | | | | | | | | | 2002 |
1st	2nd	3rd	2002	2001	2000		2002	2001	2000		AMOUNT	PAYABLE	
—	—	—	—	—	—	—	0.24	0.57	0.51	1.9		1/22/03	15.87 - 8.65
—	—	—	—	—	—	—	1.30	0.99	0.82	4.9		7/8/02	30.54 - 22.00
1.24	0.01	0.01	—	2.18	1.75	—	0.71	0.69	0.67	2.7	0.18Q	3/3/03	29.99 - 21.65
0.95	—	—	2.01	d0.42	1.87	15.9 - 9.2	—	—	—	—			31.92 - 18.50
—	—	—	p1.44	1.61	2.06	16.1 - 10.9	0.96	0.92	0.88	4.9	0.25Q	2/15/03	23.13 - 15.75
—	—	—	pd0.44	0.44	d2.27	—	—	—	—	—			11.80 - 5.90
—	—	—	—	—	—	—	—	0.15	—	—		5/4/01	13.75 - 3.70
—	—	—	pd0.60	0.08	1.11	—	—	—	0.56	—	0.28Q	4/1/00	9.21 - 5.45
—	—	—	p1.31	1.71	1.31	25.2 - 16.2	0.40	0.40	0.40	1.5	0.10Q	3/31/03	33.00 - 21.18
—	—	—	—	—	—	—	2.69	1.32	1.23	3.7	2.68521U	7/5/02	83.05 - 60.46
0.20	0.23	0.22	—	0.92	0.81	—	0.62	0.62	0.62	5.2	0.155Q	5/1/03	14.49 - 9.39
—	—	—	—	—	—	—	1.18	0.66	—	24.5	1.175U	4/22/02	7.00 - 2.60
d0.01	d0.25	d0.16	0.42	1.50	0.61	84.5 - 49.7	0.10	0.10	0.10	0.4	0.025Q	3/19/03	35.50 - 20.87
—	—	—	—	d3.24	d3.40	—	—	—	—	—	0.00U	8/6/01	11.20 - 0.78
—	—	—	1.12	0.39	1.04	53.1 - 32.0	—	—	—	—			59.45 - 35.80
—	—	—	—	—	—	—	0.85	—	—	3.3	0.41875Q	4/1/03	27.65 - 24.65
—	—	—	—	—	—	—	—	—	—	—	0.3292Q	2/3/03	25.55 - 24.70
—	—	—	p2.64	3.13	2.97	17.7 - 12.2	1.34	1.27	1.22	3.4	0.35Q	3/1/03	46.85 - 32.12
—	—	—	—	—	—	—	0.97	—	—	3.8	0.475Q	4/1/03	26.90 - 24.40
—	—	—	—	—	—	—	—	—	—	—	0.4125Q	2/3/03	25.60 - 24.70
—	—	—	—	—	—	—	—	—	—	—	0.4984Q	3/3/03	25.80 - 25.40
—	—	—	p0.48	1.40	1.33	53.8 - 31.3	1.33	1.16	1.02	6.5	0.345Q	2/12/03	25.80 - 15.00
—	—	—	p1.64	1.60	1.63	15.1 - 11.3	1.87	1.79	1.74	8.7	0.50Q	4/15/03	24.76 - 18.57
—	—	—	d0.18	d0.66	d1.34	—	—	—	—	—			17.25 - 8.55
0.13	—	—	0.24	0.23	0.23	103.8 - 46.2	—	—	—	—	5%	2/28/02	24.91 - 11.09
—	—	—	0.65	3.30	3.24	67.9 - 46.2	0.16	0.15	0.13	0.4	0.04Q	4/30/03	44.15 - 30.02
—	—	—	—	—	0.68	—	—	—	—	—	0.679U	3/14/01	53.65 - 5.60
—	—	—	—	—	—	—	—	—	—	—	0.00U	7/5/01	13.19 - 2.27
—	—	—	p1.38	0.84	1.68	22.7 - 13.7	0.08	0.23	0.37	0.3	0.02Q	3/14/03	31.30 - 18.95
—	—	—	2.36	2.30	1.60	15.9 - 12.1	0.67	0.63	0.59	2.0	0.17Q	3/1/03	37.55 - 28.67
d0.06	0.05	0.05	—	0.10	0.27	—	0.38	1.00	1.12	5.7	0.13Q	4/30/03	8.45 - 4.79
—	—	—	p1.70	1.55	1.52	18.4 - 13.4	2.00	1.90	1.74	7.4	0.50Q	4/14/03	31.36 - 22.78
—	—	—	p1.20	0.90	0.95	12.3 - 9.0	1.08	1.06	1.10	8.5	0.27Q	3/31/03	14.75 - 10.80
12.62	12.26	11.94	p1.18	1.36	1.67	26.2 - 18.3	1.73	1.68	1.57	6.6	0.4325Q	4/11/03	30.96 - 21.55
0.50	—	—	1.67	2.35	1.33	24.6 - 15.4	—	—	0.55	—	10%	12/7/01	8.10 - 5.78
—	—	—	—	—	—	—	—	—	—	—			41.15 - 25.80
—	—	—	p2.82	2.59	2.38	19.9 - 15.5	0.20	0.62	0.66	1.2	0.2008U	6/25/02	17.82 - 14.40
—	—	—	1.49	1.64	1.85	16.1 - 10.4	3.01	2.71	2.32	6.0	0.78Q	4/15/03	56.08 - 43.65
0.52	0.60	—	2.06	1.98	2.20	21.1 - 13.2	—	—	—	—	2-for-1	4/20/98	24.00 - 15.55
0.05	d0.14	0.65	—	d6.30	3.65	—	0.20	0.16	0.16	0.6	0.06Q	4/25/03	43.45 - 27.15
—	10.98	—	—	12.03	17.01	—	—	—	—	—			6.49 - 2.70
—	2.34	—	—	4.25	7.66	—	0.84	1.19	2.36	9.6	0.09926A	12/31/02	10.88 - 6.75
—	—	—	—	2.10	4.02	—	—	—	1.60	—	0.02706A	1/7/03	4.49 - 1.64
—	—	—	p0.44	1.98	0.87	106.8 - 70.2	0.32	0.28	0.24	0.5	0.09Q	3/21/03	76.50 - 42.59
—	—	—	p4.44	4.39	2.77	12.8 - 8.5	1.76	1.82	0.91	3.7	0.46Q	3/10/03	47.00 - 30.90
—	—	—	1.38	0.89	d0.72	12.6 - 5.2	—	—	—	—			56.99 - 37.85
—	—	—	0.59	0.66	0.72	30.8 - 18.5	—	—	—	—	2-for-1	7/19/96	17.40 - 7.15
—	—	—	—	—	—	—	—	—	—	—			18.20 - 10.90
0.33	—	—	p1.68	2.18	2.27	26.5 - 17.7	0.92	0.91	0.88	2.5	0.23Q	3/19/03	44.58 - 29.75
0.38	—	—	1.17	0.96	0.74	35.4 - 18.1	0.19	0.15	0.12	0.6	0.05Q	3/21/03	41.45 - 21.15
d0.29	d1.68	—	0.48	1.33	0.84	92.5 - 60.7	0.07	0.05	0.04	0.2	0.02Q	3/5/03	44.41 - 21.15
—	—	—	d0.41	d0.60	0.87	—	—	—	—	—	0.00U	4/14/00	6.24 - 2.15
pd0.03	—	—	pd0.02	0.42	2.69	—	—	—	—	—			32.03 - 6.85
0.33	—	—	0.08	d1.22	1.05	88.8 - 46.3	—	0.12	0.16	—	0.04Q	7/17/01	7.10 - 3.70
—	—	—	1.25	1.10	1.00	29.8 - 19.0	0.26	0.23	0.22	0.8	0.075Q	4/15/03	37.25 - 23.75
0.45	0.39	0.58	p4.53	5.89	4.26	18.6 - 13.0	1.32	1.20	1.12	1.8	0.39Q	2/25/03	84.10 - 58.85
—	—	—	—	1.30	1.25	—	0.40	0.40	0.36	2.1	0.10Q	3/31/03	22.30 - 15.20
d0.23	—	—	p5.72	4.17	1.84	6.5 - 4.4	5.00	3.00	2.50	16.2	1.25Q	2/3/03	36.95 - 24.90
—	—	—	0.25	d0.71	0.57	16.3 - 7.6	0.09	—	—	3.0	0.03Q	3/3/03	4.07 - 1.90
—	—	—	p1.69	1.45	0.92	30.5 - 11.4	—	—	—	—			51.60 - 19.30
—	—	—	p1.69	1.45	0.92	28.9 - 12.2	—	—	—	—	3-for-1	7/30/99	48.90 - 20.55
0.08	0.27	0.31	1.01	1.29	1.26	—	1.92	1.89	1.82	7.6	0.485Q	4/15/03	28.92 - 21.83
—	—	—	p3.21	2.59	d0.90	26.8 - 15.8	0.80	0.77	0.76	3.7	0.20Q	4/1/03	27.07 - 16.00
—	—	—	p1.74	1.44	1.27	31.8 - 7.3	—	—	—	—			44.26 - 23.59
—	—	—	14.33	—	—	20.8 - 13.5	0.22	0.18	0.14	0.7	0.057Q	2/14/03	36.18 - 23.43
—	—	—	14.33	—	—	—	—	—	—	—	0.0625Q	4/1/03	15.05 - 15.00
—	—	—	—	—	—	—	—	—	—	—	0.08375M	4/1/03	15.05 - 15.00
0.53	0.81	—	—	2.39	1.99	—	0.10	—	—	0.2	0.05Q	4/1/03	61.35 - 42.75
—	—	—	pd3.78	d1.21	0.74	—	0.50	2.20	2.20	3.1	0.15Q	1/31/03	22.00 - 10.12
d0.69	p2.31	—	1.34	1.43	d0.32	15.3 - 10.6	2.00	2.00	2.00	11.5	0.50Q	3/14/03	20.55 - 14.25
0.19	0.34	0.23	—	1.04	1.92	—	0.58	0.58	0.58	2.2	0.145Q	3/10/03	30.55 - 21.37
—	—	—	—	—	—	—	0.37	0.39	0.42	2.9	0.22197U	2/1/03	17.50 - 7.70
0.06	0.36	0.16	—	d2.74	1.84	—	—	—	—	—	3-for-2	5/13/97	9.75 - 4.65
—	—	—	p5.38	3.22	1.47	6.3 - 4.0	0.40	0.34	0.33	1.4	0.15Q	4/25/03	33.98 - 21.55
0.45	—	—	1.99	1.75	1.52	18.1 - 11.9	—	—	—	—			1.70 - 0.88
—	—	—	p2.92	2.27	1.24	7.9 - 5.5	—	—	—	—	3-for-2	7/30/97	36.00 - 23.65
0.49	0.50	0.51	—	1.76	1.47	—	0.31	0.26	0.24	1.6	0.10Q	4/15/03	23.20 - 16.14
—	—	—	p0.74	0.86	0.82	19.2 - 14.3	0.45	0.35	0.29	1.9	0.11Q	3/28/03	28.00 - 18.27
—	—	—	1.61	1.10	1.13	28.0 - 14.8	0.60	0.58	0.56	4.8	0.155Q	4/15/03	14.23 - 10.55
—	15.87	—	—	15.46	12.86	—	0.06	0.04	0.04	0.2	0.02Q	4/11/03	45.08 - 23.75
—	—	—	p2.44	2.56	2.18	15.0 - 10.6	2.96	1.66	0.10	20.5	1.348A	12/10/02	17.60 - 11.25
—	—	—	d0.17	d0.06	d0.02	—	2.72	2.63	2.48	8.7	0.685Q	4/21/03	36.50 - 25.90
—	2.67	—	3.20	3.80	5.24	—	0.17	3.15	—	1.8	0.05A	6/21/02	11.34 - 7.20
—	—	—	—	—	—	—	—	—	—	—	1.50A	1/15/97	3.49 - 2.22
0.67	0.69	0.73	p1.70	1.74	1.64	20.8 - 10.6	—	—	—	—	3-for-2	3/22/01	35.30 - 18.00
d0.06	d0.05	d0.04	—	2.51	1.77	—	1.00	0.88	0.88	2.8	0.30Q	4/1/03	41.00 - 29.76
—	—	—	—	0.39	0.98	—	—	—	0.31	9.8	0.10Q	7/31/02	2.48 - 1.60
—	—	—	p2.55	2.32	2.01	15.7 - 12.1	1.08	1.03	0.97	3.0	0.28Q	4/25/03	39.98 - 30.93
—	—	—	p2.15	2.84	2.69	18.2 - 11.6	1.50	1.50	1.50	4.7	0.375Q	3/1/03	39.12 - 24.85
0.70	0.70	0.92	—	2.85	2.20	—	—	—	—	—	2-for-1	7/30/98	30.26 - 22.93
—	—	—	pd2.94	0.31	0.51	38.4 - 26.3	—	—	—	—	5-for-1	4/1/98	33.43 - 22.85
—	—	—	—	d1.69	0.70	—	0.10	0.10	0.10	0.4	0.025Q	3/27/03	30.00 - 20.10
—	—	—	—	1.69	0.70	—	0.10	0.10	0.03	0.4	0.025Q	3/27/03	28.08 - 19.25
—	—	—	p4.18	2.78	1.04	6.2 - 3.0	0.22	0.18	0.18	1.1	0.10Q	4/15/03	25.84 - 12.67
—	—	—	1.44	0.83	3.68	26.1 - 12.3	1.40	1.32	1.20	5.1	0.35Q	4/1/03	37.56 - 17.65
d0.04	0.13	—	—	d1.53	d8.33	—	—	0.16	0.76	—	0.04Q	11/14/01	11.90 - 2.37

SYMBOL	COMPANY	NATURE OF BUSINESS	FISCAL YEAR-END	TOTAL REV. $MILL	NET INCOME $MILL	TOTAL ASSETS $MILL	NET STK EQUITY $MILL	NO. OF INST.	INST. HOLDINGS (SHARES)
FLM	Fleming Cos., Inc.	Food wholesalers	12/28/02	—	—	—	—	161	57063085
FFS	Fletcher Challenge Forests L	Forest products	6/30/02	—	—	—	—	3	21834
FFS A	Fletcher Challenge Forests L	Forest products	6/30/02	—	—	—	—		
FRK	Florida Rock Industries		9/30/02	723.7	68.9	733.3	510.6	136	14975619
FLO	Flowers Foods, Inc. (United	Food processing	12/28/02	p1652.2	p1624.5	—	—	97	16981510
FLS	Flowserve Corp.	Machinery & equipment	12/31/02	p2251.3	p2227.1	—	—	163	48350894
FLR	Fluor Corp. (New) (United St		12/31/02	p9959.0	p9862.1	—	—	236	70326899
FMC	FMC Corp.	Chemicals	12/31/02	p1852.9	p1832.2	—	—	168	27562934
FTI	FMC Technologies, Inc.		12/31/02	p2071.5	p1851.5	—	—	182	52737875
FMX	Fomento Economico Mexicano SA	Conglomerate	12/31/01	—	—	—	—	84	37388761
Z	Foot Locker, Inc.	Discount & variety stores	2/2/02	4379.0	111.0	2290.0	992.0	200	129184342
FTS	Footstar Inc.	Department stores	12/29/01	2460.5	d23.5	866.0	307.7	105	23133894
F	Ford Motor Co. (DE)		12/31/01	—	p9288.0	—	—	560	643341916
FCZ	Ford Motor Credit Co (United	Finance	12/31/01	—	p1234.0	—	—		
FCJ	Ford Motor Credit Co (United	Finance	12/31/01	—	p1234.0	—	—		
FCE A	Forest City Enterprises, Inc.	Engineering & construction	1/31/02	906.6	104.5	4417.6	662.5	77	20034122
FCE B	Forest City Enterprises, Inc.	Engineering & construction	1/31/02	906.6	104.5	4417.6	662.5	13	2202423
FRX	Forest Laboratories, Inc.	Drugs	3/31/02	1601.8	338.0	1951.9	1625.1	459	376761770
FST	Forest Oil Corp. (United Sta	Oil	12/31/02	p475.7	p475.7	—	—	155	27487293
FTD	Fort Dearborn Inc. Sec., Inc.	Investment company	9/30/02	9.3	8.3	138.2	137.9	9	133890
FO	Fortune Brands Inc		12/31/02	p5677.7	p5642.6	—	—	452	107343424
FWC	Foster Wheeler Ltd. (Bermuda)	Engineering & construction	12/28/01	3392.5	d309.1	3316.4	7.5	38	10826928
FOX	Fox Entertainment Group Inc	Broadcasting	6/30/02	9725.0	607.0	22876.0	12095.0	253	159751135
FPL	FPL Group, Inc.	Electric power	12/31/02	p8280.0	p8280.0	—	—	491	128926368
FRF	France Growth Fund Inc.	Investment company	12/31/01	1.5	d0.7	104.6	104.3	13	2801969
FTE	France Telecom S.A. (France)	Telecommunications	12/31/01	—	—	—	—	32	3012160
WFA	France Telecom S.A. (France)	Telecommunications	12/31/01	—	—	—	—	5	80218
FC	Franklin Covey Co.	Services	8/31/02	333.0	d96.5	304.7	234.6	22	4720828
FMI	Franklin Multi-Income Trust	Investment company	3/31/02	5.5	3.7	67.5	51.0	5	117750
BEN	Franklin Resources, Inc.	Financial services	9/30/02	2518.5	432.7	6422.7	4266.9	310	124615668
FT	Franklin Universal Trust	Investment company	8/31/02	25.0	17.8	201.8	141.6	16	104679
FRE	Freddie Mac	Finance	12/31/02	—	p5764.0	—	—	767	650069364
FCX	Freeport-McMoRan Copper & Go	Mining & processing	12/31/02	p1910.5	p1907.4	—	—	265	126036382
FMT	Fremont General Corp.	Property & casualty insurance	12/31/02	—	pd75.9	—	—	98	33673177
FMS	Fresenius Medical Care AG	Medical & dental equipment	12/31/01	4859.3	63.4	6516.0	2616.7	40	6178537
FDP	Fresh Del Monte Produce Inc.	Food processing	12/28/01	—	—	—	—	103	21910873
FBR	Friedman Billings Ramsey Grp	Financial services	12/31/02	p0.3	p0.3	—	—	83	15554772
FTO	Frontier Oil Corp.	Oil	12/31/02	p1813.8	p1813.8	—	—	103	19093627
FRO	Frontline Ltd.(Bermuda)	Freight transportation	12/31/01	—	—	—	—	13	3095301
FCN	FTI Consulting Inc.	Services	12/31/02	p224.1	p224.1	—	—	156	23296138
FUL	Fuller (H.B.) Co.	Specialty chemicals	11/30/02	1256.2	28.2	961.4	448.3	141	18405432
FBN	Furniture Brands Internation	Furniture & fixtures	12/31/02	p2397.7	p2397.7	—	—	187	47338922
GBL	Gabelli Asset Management, In	Banking - Northeast	12/31/02	224.4	61.1	486.4	275.3	56	4823607
GCV	Gabelli Convertible and Inco	Investment company	12/31/01	6.5	5.3	110.5	110.1	14	1475514
GAB	Gabelli Equity Trust Inc.	Investment company	12/31/01	23.4	9.8	1510.7	1465.4	46	1585204
GGT	Gabelli Global Multimedia Tr	Investment company	12/31/01	1.9	d0.3	185.6	181.5	26	1608435
GUT	Gabelli Utility Trust	Investment company	12/31/01	3.1	1.3	82.6	82.2	23	197638
GBP	Gables Residential Trust	Real estate investment trust	12/31/02	245.2	64.8	1589.2	502.8	115	18776158
AJG	Gallagher (Arthur J.) & Co.	Financial services	12/31/02	p1120.8	p1059.2	—	—	228	61486984
GLH	Gallaher Group Plc (UK)	Tobacco	12/31/01	—	—	—	—	122	12369325
GME	Gamestop Corp. (United State	Computer services	2/2/02	1121.1	7.0	606.8	d4.0	100	19977979
GCI	Gannett Co., Inc.	Broadcasting	12/29/02	6422.2	1160.1	13733.0	6911.8	665	235147536
GDI	Gardner Denver, Inc.	Machinery & equipment	12/31/02	p418.2	p418.2	—	—	78	12096453
IT	Gartner, Inc.	Services	9/30/02	907.2	48.6	824.9	d4.9	105	41855218
ITB	Gartner, Inc.	Services	9/30/02	907.2	48.6	824.9	d4.9	117	26795811
GTW	Gateway Inc	Comp. components & periphs.	12/31/02	p4171.3	p744.2	—	—	185	44267042
GMT	GATX Corp.	Equip. & vehicle leasing	12/31/02	p1281.7	p1246.8	—	—	217	16691332
GET	Gaylord Entertainment Co.	Broadcasting	12/31/01	325.2	d7.3	2167.8	658.5	125	34311277
GY	GenCorp Inc. (United States)	Defense systems & equip.	11/30/02	1135.0	30.0	1636.0	360.0	121	21464502
DNA	Genentech, Inc.		12/31/02	2719.2	63.8	6777.3	5338.9	347	169427568
GAM	General American Investors Co	Investment company	12/31/02	14.9	5.7	978.4	959.2	38	1904418
BGC	General Cable Corp (DE) (New)	Electronic components	12/31/02	p1453.9	p1453.9	—	—	67	26629865
GD	General Dynamics Corp.	Defense systems & equip.	12/31/02	—	—	—	—	600	158134483
GEA	General Electric Capital Cor		12/31/01	48545.0	6060.0	381076.0	31563.0		
GEC	General Electric Capital Cor		12/31/01	48545.0	6060.0	381076.0	31563.0	—	
GE	General Electric Co. (United	Electrical equipment	12/31/02	—	15133.0	575244.0	63706.0	1358	1100221592
GGP	General Growth Properties, I	Real estate investment trust	12/31/02	p1366.6	p1365.3	—	—	233	56209882
GMR	General Maritime Corp.	Freight transportation	12/31/02	p226.4	p226.4	—	—	37	15879311
GIS	General Mills, Inc.	Food processing	5/26/02	7949.0	461.0	16540.0	3576.0	543	228072705
GMA	General Motors Acceptance Co	Financial services	12/31/01	25475.8	1751.6	192720.9	16133.9	1	3700
GJM	General Motors Acceptance Co	Financial services	12/31/01	25475.8	1751.6	192720.9	16133.9		
GM	General Motors Corp		12/31/01	—	—	—	—	585	415076122
GMW	General Motors Corp		12/31/02	—	—	—	—	10	341660
XGM	General Motors Corp		12/31/02	—	—	—	—	6	186950
HGM	General Motors Corp		12/31/02	—	—	—	—		
RGM	General Motors Corp		12/31/02	—	—	—	—		
GXM	General Motors Corp		12/31/02	—	—	—	—		
GBM	General Motors Corp		12/31/02	—	—	—	—		
GCO	Genesco Inc. (United States)	Shoe manufacturing	2/1/03	p828.3	p828.1	—	—	117	21364729
GWR	Genesee & Wyoming Inc.	Railroads	12/31/02	p209.5	p207.0	—	—	89	9930803
GPC	Genuine Parts Co.		12/31/02	p8258.9	pd27.6	—	—	328	157850231
GGC	Georgia Gulf Corp.	Chemicals	12/31/02	1230.8	31.2	875.6	125.8	135	23204587
GPB	Georgia Power Co.	Electric power	12/31/01	4965.8	610.7	9168.5	14.6	2	12300
GPF	Georgia Power Co.	Electric power	12/31/01	4965.8	610.7	9168.5	14.6	3	12130
GP	Georgia-Pacific Corp.	Forest products	12/31/02	—	—	—	—	314	188623816
GRB	Gerber Scientific Inc.		4/30/02	502.7	d5.0	311.6	84.4	63	14867673
GGB	Gerdau S.A. (Brazil)	Steel producer	12/31/01	—	—	—	—	26	3432084
GER	Germany Fund, Inc.	Investment company	12/31/01	3.0	0.8	136.1	133.8	15	1609088
GYI	Getty Images, Inc.	Services	12/31/02	p463.0	p34.8	—	—	158	40180196
GTY	Getty Realty Corp. (New)	Real estate	12/31/02	p69.6	p69.6	—	—	66	7257374
GI	Giant Industries, Inc.	Oil	12/31/01	968.7	12.4	507.2	136.4	18	2619880
G	Gillette Co., (The)	Cosmetics & toiletries	12/31/02	8453.0	1209.0	9863.0	2260.0	731	815269100
GLT	Gtatfelter	Printing & engraving	12/31/02	652.5	7.0	960.7	353.5	118	31762040
GSK	GlaxoSmithKline Plc (UK)	Drugs	12/31/01	—	—	—	—	414	139421472
GLB	Glenborough Realty Trust, Inc	Real estate investment trust	12/31/02	200.5	45.6	1388.4	646.1	114	17085565
GRT	Glimcher Realty Trust	Real estate investment trust	12/31/02	p270.2	p272.4	—	—	104	16962964

| EARNINGS PER SHARE | | | | | | P/E RATIO | DIVIDENDS PER SHARE | | | AV. YLD. % | DIV. DECLARED | | PRICE RANGE 2002 | |
QUARTERLY 1st	2nd	3rd	ANNUAL 2002	2001	2000		2002	2001	2000		AMOUNT	PAYABLE		
—	—	—	pd1.67	0.60	d3.15	—	0.08	0.08	0.08	0.6	0.02Q	6/10/03	26.10	2.60
—	—	—	—	—	—	—	—	—	—	—	—	—	5.07	4.61
0.43	—	—	—	—	—	—	—	—	—	—	—	—	5.04	4.63
—	—	—	2.38	2.42	2.10	18.5 - 12.1	0.37	0.33	0.28	1.0	0.10Q	4/1/03	44.13	28.72
—	—	—	pd0.56	d0.61	d1.41	—	0.05	—	—	0.2	0.05Q	3/21/03	26.66	16.76
—	—	—	p1.02	0.42	0.40	34.4 - 7.4	—	—	—	—	0.14Q	12/3/99	35.09	7.58
—	—	—	p2.13	1.61	d0.05	21.1 - 9.4	0.64	0.48	—	2.0	0.16Q	4/1/03	44.95	20.06
—	—	—	p2.01	d9.85	5.62	21.0 - 11.4	—	—	—	—	0.00U	12/31/01	42.30	22.90
—	—	—	p0.96	0.60	0.92	24.8 - 14.9	—	—	—	—	—	—	23.83	14.30
—	—	—	—	—	—	—	0.70	0.45	0.50	1.7	—	5/27/03	49.79	33.25
0.26	0.22	0.29	—	0.77	0.77	—	—	—	—	—	0.03Q	5/2/03	17.95	8.20
d0.30	d0.03	—	—	d1.16	2.97	—	—	—	—	—	—	—	32.82	3.30
—	—	—	p0.54	d3.02	3.59	33.8 - 12.8	0.40	1.05	0.30	3.2	0.10Q	3/3/03	18.23	6.90
—	—	—	—	—	—	—	1.86	—	—	9.1	0.46Q	4/15/03	25.15	15.60
—	—	—	—	—	—	—	1.45	—	—	6.8	0.475Q	3/3/03	25.39	17.40
0.21	0.25	0.18	—	2.20	2.01	—	0.22	0.18	0.15	0.6	0.06Q	6/16/03	41.00	28.65
0.21	0.25	0.18	—	2.20	2.01	—	0.22	0.18	0.15	0.6	0.06Q	6/16/03	40.75	30.25
0.34	0.39	0.47	—	0.91	0.59	—	—	—	—	—	2-for-1	1/8/03	54.99	32.13
—	—	—	p0.44	2.22	2.64	73.7 - 47.0	—	—	—	—	—	—	32.44	20.69
—	—	—	15.71	—	15.05	—	0.98	1.19	1.04	6.6	0.22Q	3/26/03	15.70	14.10
—	—	—	p3.41	2.49	d0.88	17.0 - 10.8	1.02	0.97	0.93	2.2	0.27Q	3/3/03	57.86	36.85
d0.60	d2.08	d3.68	—	d7.56	0.97	—	—	—	—	—	—	—	5.39	1.06
0.25	0.32	—	—	0.72	0.28	0.20	—	—	—	39.4 - 22.4	—	—	28.40	16.13
—	—	—	p2.73	4.62	4.14	23.8 - 16.5	2.32	2.24	2.16	4.2	0.60Q	3/17/03	64.99	45.00
—	8.15	—	—	8.64	12.05	—	—	1.00	4.96	—	0.3615Q	4/12/01	7.75	5.01
—	—	—	—	—	—	—	0.84	0.72	0.80	3.4	0.8402U	7/29/02	43.25	6.84
d0.51	—	—	d5.29	d0.95	d0.61	—	—	—	—	—	—	—	14.53	10.10
—	6.12	—	—	8.71	9.80	—	—	—	—	—	—	—	6.14	0.90
0.43	—	—	1.65	1.91	2.28	27.0 - 16.9	0.65	0.67	0.73	9.0	0.035M	4/15/03	8.90	5.60
—	—	—	5.13	7.32	8.21	—	0.28	0.26	0.24	0.8	0.075Q	4/15/03	44.48	27.90
—	—	—	p7.95	5.96	3.39	8.7 - 6.6	0.74	0.80	0.80	11.3	0.046M	4/30/03	8.73	4.42
—	—	—	p0.88	0.53	0.26	23.7 - 11.3	0.88	0.80	0.68	1.4	0.26Q	3/31/03	69.50	52.60
—	—	—	p0.36	0.76	d8.23	21.6 - 8.3	—	—	—	—	0.05Q	11/1/98	20.83	9.95
—	—	—	—	1.33	4.78	—	0.10	0.10	0.28	1.9	0.03Q	4/30/03	7.79	2.98
—	—	—	—	—	—	—	0.21	0.16	0.16	1.4	0.26452U	6/2/03	21.60	6.86
—	—	—	—	—	—	—	0.20	—	—	0.9	0.10Q	6/4/03	29.70	13.50
—	—	—	p1.08	d0.29	0.36	11.9 - 4.7	—	—	—	—	—	—	12.88	5.05
—	—	—	p0.04	4.00	1.34	568.8 - 267.0	0.20	0.10	—	1.2	0.05Q	4/14/03	22.75	10.68
—	—	—	—	—	—	—	0.05	—	—	0.6	0.15Q	3/24/03	13.05	3.19
—	—	—	p1.53	0.84	0.67	28.1 - 13.7	—	—	—	—	50%	6/4/03	42.93	20.89
—	—	—	0.98	1.59	1.74	34.0 - 24.6	0.44	0.43	0.42	1.5	0.11Q	2/21/03	33.32	24.15
—	—	—	p2.11	1.13	2.15	20.3 - 8.7	—	—	—	—	—	—	22.74	18.40
0.51	0.46	0.38	—	2.03	1.94	—	—	—	—	—	—	—	44.45	24.40
—	9.12	—	—	9.92	10.02	—	0.75	0.81	1.30	7.5	0.20Q	3/25/03	11.65	8.40
—	7.59	—	—	8.97	10.89	—	0.95	1.08	1.31	11.1	0.27Q	3/25/03	11.68	5.51
—	8.16	—	—	10.52	12.21	—	0.49	0.06	1.57	6.8	0.495A	3/26/02	9.55	5.00
—	6.95	—	—	7.32	8.21	—	0.72	0.88	0.80	8.2	0.06M	6/24/03	10.25	7.21
0.95	0.25	0.28	—	2.29	2.43	—	2.41	2.34	2.20	8.9	—	3/31/03	32.90	21.25
—	—	—	p1.41	1.39	1.05	26.4 - 15.4	0.58	0.51	0.45	2.0	0.18Q	4/15/03	37.24	21.70
—	—	—	—	0.18	d0.33	—	1.56	1.37	1.33	4.5	1.2015U	5/30/03	44.52	25.20
0.08	0.10	0.16	—	—	—	—	—	—	—	—	—	—	24.30	8.92
—	—	—	4.31	3.12	3.63	18.5 - 14.6	0.93	0.89	0.85	1.3	0.24Q	4/1/03	79.90	62.76
—	—	—	p1.22	1.40	1.21	—	—	—	—	—	3-for-2	12/29/97	28.00	14.34
pd0.18	—	—	0.47	d0.77	0.30	29.1 - 10.4	—	—	—	—	—	—	13.70	4.90
pd0.18	—	—	0.47	d0.77	0.30	28.7 - 11.1	—	—	—	—	—	—	13.50	5.20
—	—	—	pd0.95	d3.14	0.73	—	—	—	—	—	2-for-1	9/7/99	10.60	2.61
—	—	—	—	p0.15	0.63	—	1.28	1.24	1.20	4.9	0.32Q	3/31/03	35.91	16.30
d0.19	0.50	0.47	—	d0.22	d4.60	—	—	—	—	—	0.20Q	12/20/99	29.26	16.16
—	—	—	0.69	3.00	1.31	23.6 - 9.2	0.12	0.12	0.12	1.1	0.03Q	2/28/03	16.25	6.38
—	—	—	0.12	0.29	d0.03	459.6 - 209.2	—	—	—	—	100%	10/24/00	55.15	25.10
—	—	—	26.48	35.14	39.91	—	0.62	4.16	8.08	2.2	0.03S	2/10/03	34.89	22.17
—	—	—	pd0.73	1.13	0.79	—	0.15	0.20	0.20	1.8	0.05Q	8/23/02	14.85	2.10
—	—	—	p5.18	4.65	4.48	21.5 - 14.1	1.18	1.10	1.02	1.3	0.32Q	5/9/03	111.18	73.25
—	—	—	—	—	—	—	0.83	—	—	3.2	—	3/28/02	26.90	24.25
—	—	—	—	—	—	—	—	—	—	—	0.38125Q	2/18/03	25.63	24.75
—	—	—	1.51	1.41	1.27	27.7 - 14.2	0.72	0.64	0.55	2.3	0.19Q	4/25/03	41.84	21.40
—	—	—	p2.95	1.61	2.18	17.7 - 12.9	2.67	2.24	2.04	5.9	0.72Q	4/30/03	52.29	38.00
—	—	—	pd0.26	1.74	1.60	—	—	—	—	—	—	—	14.20	4.78
0.47	0.73	—	—	1.35	2.28	—	1.10	1.10	1.10	2.5	0.275Q	5/1/03	51.73	37.38
—	—	—	—	—	—	—	1.82	1.37	—	7.8	0.45625Q	3/10/03	25.70	20.80
—	—	—	—	—	—	—	0.46	—	—	2.0	—	2/10/03	25.56	19.90
—	—	—	p3.37	1.77	6.68	20.2 - 9.1	2.00	2.00	2.00	4.0	0.50Q	3/10/03	68.17	30.80
—	—	—	p3.37	1.77	6.68	7.6 - 6.2	1.81	0.83	—	7.8	—	4/15/03	25.60	21.00
—	—	—	p3.37	1.77	6.68	7.5 - 6.2	1.81	0.48	—	7.9	—	4/15/03	25.35	20.80
—	—	—	p3.37	1.77	6.68	7.6 - 6.1	1.83	—	—	7.9	—	4/1/03	25.70	20.45
—	—	—	p3.37	1.77	6.68	7.6 - 6.1	1.36	—	—	5.9	—	2/18/03	25.49	20.50
—	—	—	p3.37	1.77	6.68	8.6 - 6.3	0.55	—	—	2.2	0.5625S	3/3/03	29.00	21.35
—	—	—	p3.37	1.77	6.68	9.0 - 5.8	0.64	—	—	2.6	0.65625S	3/3/03	30.20	19.51
—	—	—	p1.47	1.54	1.35	19.3 - 7.2	—	—	—	—	—	—	28.30	10.65
—	—	—	p1.48	1.48	1.38	17.8 - 10.6	—	—	—	—	3-for-2	3/14/02	26.30	15.70
—	—	—	p2.10	1.71	2.20	18.5 - 12.9	1.15	1.13	1.08	3.5	0.295Q	4/1/03	38.80	27.10
—	—	—	0.97	d0.38	2.03	28.0 - 17.7	0.32	0.30	0.32	1.4	0.08Q	4/10/03	27.20	17.20
—	—	—	—	—	—	—	1.65	1.65	1.65	6.5	0.4125Q	3/31/03	26.30	24.45
—	—	—	—	—	—	—	1.66	1.66	1.66	6.4	—	3/31/03	27.00	24.75
—	—	—	pd3.09	d2.09	1.94	—	0.50	0.50	0.50	2.4	0.125Q	2/20/03	31.60	9.81
0.10	0.14	—	—	d0.22	d1.07	—	—	0.16	0.32	—	0.22M	2/28/01	9.83	1.40
—	—	—	—	—	—	—	0.55	0.46	0.45	5.3	0.382U	2/28/03	14.05	6.68
—	—	—	—	8.02	10.89	—	0.01	0.08	2.49	0.2	0.01S	11/29/02	7.98	3.92
0.39	—	—	p0.39	d1.84	d3.41	98.7 - 33.8	—	—	—	—	—	—	38.48	13.19
—	—	—	p1.44	3.18	0.47	14.3 - 11.0	1.65	0.50	0.51	9.1	0.4125Q	4/10/03	20.55	15.87
0.01	d0.50	d0.85	—	1.39	0.79	—	—	—	—	—	0.05Q	9/30/98	12.55	1.86
—	—	—	1.14	0.86	0.77	32.7 - 24.2	0.65	0.65	0.64	2.0	0.1625Q	3/5/03	37.30	27.57
0.26	0.17	0.30	—	0.16	1.04	—	0.70	0.70	0.70	4.7	0.175Q	5/1/03	19.35	10.22
—	—	—	—	—	—	—	1.14	0.51	—	2.8	0.41868U	4/17/03	51.07	11.35
0.21	0.22	0.19	—	0.94	0.85	—	1.72	1.68	1.68	8.5	0.43Q	4/15/03	23.75	16.80
—	—	—	p0.75	1.17	0.79	27.3 - 19.4	1.92	1.92	1.92	11.0	0.4808Q	4/15/03	20.44	14.52

T21

SYMBOL	COMPANY	NATURE OF BUSINESS	FISCAL YEAR-END	TOTAL REV. $MILL	NET INCOME $MILL	TOTAL ASSETS $MILL	NET STK EQUITY $MILL	NO. OF INST.	INST. HOLDINGS (SHARES)
GHI	Global High Income Dollar Fd	Investment company	10/31/02	24.2	20.2	283.9	275.0	17	878355
GDF	Global Partners Income Fund	Investment company	8/31/02	25.2	20.4	193.1	132.9	12	125983
GPN	Global Payments, Inc.		5/31/02	462.8	39.8	431.4	296.3	143	23172507
GEG	Global Power Equipment Group	Machinery & equipment	12/31/01	p723.5	p794.9	—	—	63	23120497
GSF	GlobalSanteFe Corp. (DE) (Uni	Oil service & equipment	12/31/02	p2017.7	p2017.7	—	—	300	150600103
GFI	Gold Fields Ltd. (New)	Mining & processing	6/30/01	—	—	—	—	97	42018130
GDW	Golden West Financial	Savings & loan	12/31/02	—	p958.3	—	—	346	116163128
GS	Goldman Sachs Group, Inc.	Industrial	11/29/02	22854.0	2114.0	355574.0	19003.0	526	299519735
GR	Goodrich Corp.	Chemicals	12/31/02	3910.2	165.9	5989.6	932.9	270	89749186
GDP	Goodrich Petroleum Corp. (Hol	Oil	12/31/01	29.9	2.7	82.2	47.9	13	306044
GT	Goodyear Tire & Rubber Co.	Tires and/or rubber goods	12/31/01	14147.2	d203.6	13512.9	2864.0	238	99648885
GOT	Gottschalks, Inc.	Department stores	2/2/02	723.2	0.9	391.2	118.2	9	1505455
GPX	GP Strategies Corp.	Conglomerate	12/31/01	186.6	d0.9	163.9	95.9	18	7237726
GRA	Grace (W.R.) Co. (DE) (New)	Specialty chemicals	12/31/02	p1840.4	p1840.4	—	—	65	23933048
GGG	Graco Inc.	Machinery & equipment	12/27/02	p487.0	p487.0	—	—	145	38509034
GTI	Graftech International Ltd (	Metal products	12/31/02	p613.0	p613.0	—	—	107	52661058
GWW	Grainger (W.W.) Inc.	Hardware & tools	12/31/02	p4643.9	p4667.8	—	—	341	65371953
GVA	Granite Construction Inc.	Engineering & construction	12/31/02	p1764.7	p1764.7	—	—	126	24285691
GRP	Grant Prideco Inc		12/31/02	p639.7	p639.7	—	—	194	10513267
GPK	Graphic Packaging Internation	Conglomerate	12/31/02	p1057.8	p1057.8	—	—	44	10513267
GTN	Gray Television Inc	Broadcasting	12/31/02	p198.6	p198.6	—	—	66	34867226
GTN A	Gray Television Inc	Broadcasting	12/31/02	p198.6	p198.6	—	—	31	2066589
GFR	Great American Financial Res	Finance	12/31/02	p928.9	p928.9	—	—	35	39758193
GAP	Great Atlantic & Pacific Tea	Grocery chain	2/23/02	10973.3	d64.7	3194.3	673.0	93	12616634
GAJ	Great Atlantic & Pacific Tea	Grocery chain	2/23/02	10973.3	d64.7	3194.3	673.0	1	500
GLK	Great Lakes Chemical Corp.	Chemicals	12/31/02	1401.5	47.4	1717.7	745.7	190	46868920
GL	Great Lakes REIT, Inc.	Real estate investment trust	12/31/01	103.1	21.6	486.5	207.9	65	4235840
GNI	Great Northern Iron Ore Prop	Mining & processing	12/31/02	9.6	7.7	16.9	14.5	14	8514
GXP	Great Plains Energy, Inc.	Electric power	12/31/02	1861.9	129.2	3506.7	978.5	182	21434712
GCH	Greater China Fund, Inc (The)	Investment company	12/31/01	3.6	0.5	143.2	133.4	19	6783455
GMP	Green Mountain Power Corp	Electric power	12/31/01	283.5	11.8	330.1	101.3	45	1788594
GRX	Greenbrier Cos., Inc. (The)	Railroads	8/31/02	305.6	d6.2	527.4	103.1	19	2903804
GPT	GreenPoint Financial Corp.	Banking - Northeast	12/31/02	p1306.0	p753.2	—	—	257	61613564
GEF	Greif Bros. Corp.	Containers	10/31/02	1652.7	31.0	1758.3	569.1	65	8376475
GEF B	Greif Bros. Corp.	Containers	10/31/02	1652.7	31.0	1758.3	569.1	3	74800
GFF	Griffon Corp.	Conglomerate	9/30/02	1192.6	34.1	587.7	293.0	119	23570630
GPI	Group 1 Automotive, Inc.		12/31/01	3996.4	55.4	1054.4	392.2	116	15042586
DA	Groupe Danone (France)	Food wholesalers	12/31/01					52	5472281
GMK	Gruma, S.A. de C.V. (Mexico)	Food -grain & agriculture	12/31/01					1	41847
ASR	Grupo Aeroportuario del Sures		12/31/01					44	14007612
SAB	Grupo Casa Saba, S.A. de C.V.	Drugs	12/31/01					3	732710
EKT	Grupo Elektra S.A. de C.V.	Appliances & utensils	12/31/01					8	760719
IMY	Grupo Imsa, S.A. de C.V.	Metal products	12/31/01					11	2181907
MSK	Grupo Indl Maseca S A de C V	Food -grain & agriculture	12/31/01					5	796661
CEL	Grupo Iusacell SA de CV	Telecommunications	12/31/02					7	7787168
RC	Grupo Radio Centro S.A. de C	Broadcasting	12/31/01					7	3893100
TV	Grupo Televisa, S.A. de C.V.	Broadcasting	12/31/01					123	72759559
TMM	Grupo TMM, S.A.	Freight transportation	12/31/01					28	16616124
GTK	GTECH Holdings Corp. (United	Gaming	2/28/02	p1000.0	p1084.9	—	—	194	53938329
GSH	Guangshen Railway Co., Ltd.	Railroads	12/31/01					7	1021679
GUC	Gucci Group N.V. Netherlands	'Wholesaler, distributor'	1/31/02					80	13582246
GES	GUESS ?, Inc. (United States)		12/31/01	677.6	6.2	362.5	177.9	37	5609203
GDT	Guidant Corp.	Medical & dental equipment	12/31/02	3239.6	611.8	3716.1	2321.8	492	267241342
GSE	Gundle/SLT Environmental Inc	Pollution control	12/31/02	267.0	13.7	202.3	132.4	22	4729196
HQH	H & Q Healthcare Investors	Investment company	9/30/02	1.5	d3.6	242.5	242.0	36	1299068
HQL	H&Q Life Sciences Investors	Investment company	9/30/02	0.9	d2.5	157.9	157.6	23	639282
HAE	Haemonetics Corp.		3/30/02	320.0	27.7	364.9	236.8	101	24082251
HAL	Halliburton Co. (Holding Co.)	Oil service & equipment	12/31/02	—	—	—	—	462	322905542
HKF	Hancock Fabrics, Inc. (Unite	Specialty stores	2/2/03	p483.3	p483.3	—	—	90	12625636
HPF	Hancock John Prefered Income	Investment company	11/5/02			0.2	0.1		
HDL	Handleman Co.	'Wholesaler, distributor'	4/27/02	1337.5	37.1	605.5	289.6	94	21281482
HGR	Hanger Orthopedic Group, Inc.	Medical & dental equipment	12/31/02	p0.5	p0.5	—	—	84	15045104
HC	Hanover Compressor Co (Hldg	Machinery & equipment	12/31/02	p1028.8	p988.8	—	—	165	49654698
HAN	Hanson PLC		12/31/01					41	14135250
JH	Harland (John H.) Co.	Printing & engraving	12/31/01	743.2	39.0	467.0	202.0	136	20387069
HDI	Harley-Davidson, Inc.		12/31/01	p4091.0	p3785.4	—	—	530	230258002
HAR	Harman International Inds In	Electronic components	6/30/02	1826.2	57.5	1480.3	526.6	204	32356961
HMY	Harmony Gold Mining Co. Ltd.	Mining & processing	6/30/02					78	20643508
HET	Harrah's Entertainment, Inc	Gaming	12/31/02	p4136.4	p4046.8	—	—	301	101181903
HRS	Harris Corp.	Defense systems & equip.	6/28/02	1875.8	82.6	1858.5	1149.9	256	55066971
HSC	Harsco Corp.	Metal products	12/31/02	p1976.7	p1976.7	—	—	166	20096732
HHS	Harte-Hanks, Inc. (United Sta		12/31/02	p908.8	p908.8	—	—	180	44818454
HIG	Hartford Financial Svcs Grou	Property & casualty insurance	12/31/02	15907.0	1000.0	182043.0	10734.0	435	217836694
HSF	Hartford Income Shares Fund,	Investment company	7/31/02	8.9	8.2	86.5	85.8	—	—
HMX	Hartmarx Corp.		11/30/01	604.7	d13.9	455.4	187.0	26	10003205
HNR	Harvest Natural Resources In	Oil	12/31/02	p126.7	p126.7	—	—	67	15960348
HAS	Hasbro, Inc.		12/31/02	p2816.2	p2816.2	—	—	245	145899615
HAT	Hatteras Income Securities	Investment company	12/31/02	3.0	2.5	65.5	49.5	5	304076
HVT A	Haverty Furniture Cos., Inc.	Specialty stores	12/31/02	p704.0	p339.4	—	—		407472
HVT	Haverty Furniture Cos., Inc.	Specialty stores	12/31/02	p704.0	p339.4	—	—	89	12136129
HE	Hawaiian Electric Ind.Inc.	Electric power	12/31/01	1727.3	107.7	8517.9	929.7	190	10999258
HWK	Hawk, Corp.		12/31/02	197.3	d1.0	193.9	44.8	11	3494970
HCA	HCA, Inc.	Hospitals & nursing homes	12/31/02	—	—	—	—	492	488997665
HCC	HCC Insurance Holdings, Inc.		12/31/02	p669.4	p669.4	—	—	181	59699820
HDB	HDFC Bank Ltd (India)	Finance	3/31/02					39	8028886
HED	Head N.V. (Netherlands)		12/31/01	392.0	9.4	416.5	212.4	8	6587276
HCP	Health Care Property Invs In	Real estate investment trust	12/31/01	359.6	137.2	2748.4	1280.9	222	24890857
HCN	Health Care REIT, Inc.	Real estate investment trust	12/31/02	p163.1	p163.4	—	—	133	15383679
HMA	Health Management Assoc Inc	Hospitals & nursing homes	9/30/02	2262.6	246.4	2364.3	1346.8	337	228768165
HNT	Health Net, Inc.	Services	12/31/01					216	111747240
HR	Healthcare Realty Trust, Inc	Real estate investment trust	12/31/02	p197.9	p197.9	—	—	171	20757654
HRC	HEALTHSOUTH Corp.	Hospitals & nursing homes	12/31/02	p4310.8	p4310.8	—	—	287	272969947
HTV	Hearst-Argyle Television Inc.	Broadcasting	12/31/02	p721.3	p655.1	—	—	118	19085287
HL	Hecla Mining Co.	Mining & processing	12/31/01	85.2	d9.6	153.1	58.0	71	18420319
HEI	Heico Corp. (New) (United St		10/31/02	172.1	15.2	336.3	207.1	36	3227613
HEI A	Heico Corp. (New) (United St		10/31/02	172.1	15.2	336.3	207.1	29	5472646

| EARNINGS PER SHARE | | | | | | P/E RATIO | DIVIDENDS PER SHARE | | | AV. YLD. % | DIV. DECLARED | | PRICE RANGE |
| QUARTERLY | | | ANNUAL | | | | | | | | | | 2002 |
1st	2nd	3rd	2002	2001	2000		2002	2001	2000	%	AMOUNT	PAYABLE	
—	—	—	14.14	14.16	14.42	—	1.58	1.60	1.62	11.2	0.1381M	3/31/03	15.88 - 12.29
—	—	—	8.88	10.77	11.94	—	1.42	1.42	1.42	12.8	0.11875M	5/30/03	13.39 - 8.90
0.39	0.36	—	—	1.05	0.82	—	0.16	0.12	—	0.5	0.04Q	2/28/03	39.70 - 21.00
0.33	0.32	0.22	—	—	p3.31	—	—	—	—	—	—	—	15.02 - 3.74
—	—	—	p1.18	1.50	0.92	31.4 - 16.0	0.13	0.13	0.13	0.5	0.0375Q	4/15/03	37.05 - 18.93
—	—	—	—	—	—	—	0.27	0.16	0.03	2.5	0.1846U	3/6/03	17.15 - 4.81
—	—	—	p6.12	5.11	3.41	12.1 - 9.2	0.30	0.26	0.22	0.5	0.085Q	3/10/03	73.75 - 56.20
—	—	—	4.03	4.26	6.00	24.1 - 14.5	0.48	0.48	0.48	0.6	0.12Q	2/27/03	97.25 - 58.57
—	—	—	1.57	1.65	2.68	21.9 - 9.0	0.95	1.10	1.10	3.9	0.20Q	4/1/03	34.45 - 14.17
0.05	d0.05	d0.03	—	d0.01	0.35	—	—	—	—	—	—	—	4.94 - 2.05
d0.39	0.18	0.20	—	d1.27	0.25	—	—	—	—	—	—	—	28.85 - 6.50
d0.21	d0.17	d0.20	—	0.06	0.56	—	0.48	1.02	1.20	2.7	0.12Q	12/16/02	3.88 - 1.17
0.01	d0.01	0.25	—	d0.09	d2.04	—	—	—	—	—	1-for-4	10/6/95	5.75 - 3.23
—	—	—	p0.34	1.20	d1.34	11.7 - 2.8	—	—	—	—	—	—	3.99 - 0.95
—	—	—	p1.57	1.38	1.51	19.5 - 14.1	0.29	0.27	0.25	1.1	0.0825Q	5/7/03	30.57 - 22.13
—	—	—	pd0.33	d1.75	0.50	—	—	—	—	—	—	—	14.30 - 3.35
—	—	—	p2.24	1.84	2.05	26.5 - 17.5	0.72	0.69	0.67	1.5	0.18Q	3/1/03	59.40 - 39.20
—	—	—	p1.21	1.24	1.38	21.3 - 11.3	0.32	0.35	0.29	1.6	0.08Q	4/15/03	25.80 - 13.64
—	—	—	p0.06	0.25	d0.13	282.3 - 135.7	—	—	—	—	—	—	16.94 - 8.14
—	—	—	pd5.77	d0.11	d0.37	—	—	—	—	—	0.00U	1/3/00	9.25 - 3.45
—	—	—	pd1.53	d0.89	d0.47	—	0.08	0.08	0.08	0.8	0.02Q	3/31/03	11.75 - 7.95
—	—	—	pd1.53	d0.89	d0.47	—	0.08	0.08	0.08	0.7	0.02Q	3/31/03	13.65 - 10.15
—	—	—	p1.49	1.00	1.26	13.4 - 9.0	0.10	0.10	0.10	0.6	0.10A	12/19/02	20.00 - 13.35
0.06	d3.76	d0.77	—	d1.69	d0.65	—	—	—	0.40	—	0.10Q	11/3/00	28.44 - 5.34
0.06	d3.76	d0.77	—	d1.69	d0.65	—	2.34	2.34	2.34	12.4	0.5859Q	2/3/03	25.49 - 12.45
—	—	—	0.94	d5.76	2.42	31.2 - 22.6	0.33	0.32	0.32	1.3	0.09Q	4/30/03	29.31 - 21.24
0.26	0.31	0.57	—	1.08	1.84	—	1.48	1.60	1.91	8.6	0.135M	7/10/03	18.98 - 15.48
—	—	—	5.11	5.76	7.19	14.7 - 10.6	5.50	6.80	6.00	8.5	1.50Q	4/30/03	75.10 - 54.35
—	—	—	2.04	d0.68	2.05	13.2 - 7.7	1.66	1.66	1.66	7.8	0.415Q	3/20/03	26.98 - 15.69
—	11.49	—	—	10.59	10.84	—	0.04	0.06	0.03	0.4	0.0403A	12/30/02	11.35 - 7.55
0.57	0.32	0.52	—	1.88	d0.06	—	0.60	0.55	0.55	3.3	0.19Q	3/31/03	21.08 - 15.75
d0.01	—	—	d0.30	0.08	1.01	9.3 - 6.2	—	0.33	0.36	—	0.06Q	12/12/01	8.00 - 4.10
—	—	—	p5.58	4.50	2.34	—	1.00	1.00	1.00	2.3	0.3125Q	3/10/03	51.86 - 34.76
p0.38	—	—	2.74	7.84	6.68	13.9 - 8.4	0.56	0.54	0.52	1.8	0.14Q	4/1/03	38.21 - 23.00
p0.38	—	—	2.74	7.84	6.68	13.0 - 8.6	0.83	0.80	0.77	2.8	0.21Q	4/1/03	35.75 - 23.50
0.32	—	—	0.97	0.92	0.75	21.2 - 10.4	—	—	—	—	10%	9/4/01	20.60 - 10.11
0.64	0.78	0.84	—	2.59	1.88	—	—	—	—	—	—	—	50.80 - 18.00
—	—	—	—	—	—	—	0.39	0.32	0.65	1.6	—	7/18/02	27.88 - 21.88
—	—	—	—	—	—	—	—	—	—	—	1.6666%	5/28/99	10.00 - 0.01
—	—	—	—	—	—	—	1.51	—	—	11.1	1.5129U	6/10/02	17.50 - 9.85
—	—	—	—	—	—	—	—	—	—	—	0.1666U	5/28/98	12.51 - 6.60
—	—	—	—	—	—	—	—	—	—	—	—	—	16.00 - 9.10
—	—	—	—	—	—	—	0.31	0.23	—	2.6	0.3141U	4/29/02	16.00 - 8.50
—	—	—	—	—	—	—	0.19	1.19	0.17	3.0	—	5/14/02	8.15 - 4.70
—	—	—	—	—	—	—	—	—	—	—	—	—	4.58 - 0.37
—	—	—	—	—	—	—	—	0.60	2.17	—	—	3/16/01	6.35 - 1.65
—	—	—	—	—	—	—	—	—	—	—	10-for-1	3/1/00	49.09 - 23.87
—	—	—	—	—	—	—	—	—	—	—	—	—	11.23 - 4.60
0.49	0.66	0.57	—	—	p1.25	—	—	—	—	—	2-for-1	5/23/02	30.49 - 17.62
—	—	—	—	—	—	—	0.60	0.60	0.72	6.6	0.6042U	8/5/02	10.30 - 7.90
d0.08	d0.15	0.08	—	—	—	—	0.38	5.63	0.34	0.4	0.375U	8/7/02	99.45 - 82.53
—	—	—	2.00	1.58	1.21	25.5 - 12.4	—	—	—	—	—	—	9.35 - 3.30
—	—	—	1.17	0.12	0.31	8.5 - 2.2	—	—	—	—	—	—	10.00 - 2.61
—	—	—	18.16	27.35	46.15	—	—	—	—	—	0.08Q	6/30/03	25.95 - 12.82
—	—	—	15.14	23.09	39.37	—	2.63	3.48*	4.54	13.6	0.35Q	3/26/03	25.95 - 12.82
—	—	—	—	—	—	—	—	3.14	4.16	—	0.00Q	3/26/03	21.70 - 10.80
0.26	0.27	0.42	—	1.02	0.28	—	—	—	—	—	2-for-1	1/8/93	34.80 - 18.02
—	—	—	pd0.79	1.28	0.42	—	0.50	0.50	0.50	3.3	0.125Q	3/27/03	21.65 - 8.60
—	—	—	p1.06	0.85	0.65	19.2 - 12.0	0.28	0.14	0.10	1.7	0.10Q	4/15/03	20.40 - 12.70
—	—	—	15.61	—	—	—	—	—	—	—	0.18M	4/1/03	25.10 - 25.00
0.10	0.61	—	—	1.39	1.53	—	—	—	—	—	0.05Q	1/10/96	15.00 - 7.50
—	—	—	p0.86	d0.73	d0.98	20.9 - 6.7	—	—	—	—	—	—	17.95 - 5.80
—	—	—	pd1.46	0.95	0.88	—	—	—	—	—	2-for-1	6/13/00	25.52 - 6.20
—	—	—	—	—	—	—	1.05	1.00	1.01	3.5	—	5/23/03	39.69 - 21.15
0.29	0.42	0.53	—	1.31	1.00	—	0.30	0.30	0.30	1.1	0.075Q	2/28/03	34.81 - 18.20
—	—	—	p1.43	1.13	—	—	0.14	0.11	0.10	0.3	0.035Q	3/24/03	57.25 - 42.60
0.29	0.81	—	1.70	0.96	2.06	38.4 - 22.5	0.10	0.10	0.10	0.2	0.025Q	2/26/03	65.30 - 38.18
—	—	—	—	—	—	—	0.43	0.13	0.16	3.4	0.1539U	3/13/03	19.00 - 6.31
—	—	—	p2.99	1.81	d0.09	17.2 - 11.7	—	—	—	—	—	—	51.35 - 34.95
0.30	0.25	—	—	1.25	0.32	—	0.26	0.20	0.20	0.8	0.03Q	3/19/03	38.70 - 24.09
—	—	—	p2.21	1.79	2.42	20.1 - 11.0	1.00	0.96	0.94	2.9	0.2625Q	5/15/03	44.48 - 24.20
—	—	—	p0.96	0.82	0.79	23.6 - 16.7	0.10	0.08	0.07	0.5	0.03Q	3/14/03	22.68 - 16.05
—	—	—	3.97	2.27	4.34	17.7 - 9.4	1.04	1.00	0.96	1.9	0.27Q	4/1/03	70.24 - 37.25
—	—	—	6.66	7.95	8.17	—	0.63	0.67	0.70	9.2	0.05M	4/15/03	7.10 - 6.55
d0.02	d0.01	0.05	—	d0.46	0.29	—	—	—	—	—	0.15Q	11/15/91	3.02 - 1.18
—	—	—	p2.78	1.27	0.53	2.8 - 1.2	—	—	—	—	2-for-1	2/26/91	7.78 - 3.20
—	—	—	pd0.99	0.35	d0.82	—	0.12	0.12	0.24	0.9	0.03Q	5/15/03	17.30 - 9.87
—	—	—	14.73	14.74	14.78	—	0.95	1.02	1.07	6.9	0.065M	3/31/03	14.54 - 13.24
—	—	—	p1.10	1.06	1.31	26.1 - 8.5	0.21	0.20	0.19	1.1	0.0525Q	2/26/03	28.66 - 9.30
—	—	—	p1.10	1.06	1.31	19.5 - 8.5	0.22	0.21	0.20	1.4	0.0575Q	2/26/03	21.45 - 9.40
0.75	0.85	0.89	—	3.18	1.40	—	2.48	2.48	2.48	6.0	0.62Q	3/10/03	48.65 - 34.55
—	—	—	d0.14	d0.52	0.66	—	—	—	—	—	—	—	5.50 - 1.70
—	—	—	p1.59	1.68	0.39	32.7 - 22.8	0.08	0.08	0.08	0.2	0.02Q	3/14/03	52.05 - 36.21
—	—	—	p1.68	0.51	1.10	17.2 - 11.4	0.25	0.24	0.21	1.1	0.065Q	1/17/03	28.95 - 19.11
—	—	—	—	0.24	0.86	—	0.14	—	—	0.9	0.13682U	6/11/02	16.99 - 12.16
—	—	—	—	—	—	—	0.10	0.18	—	3.7	0.0987U	6/14/02	3.54 - 1.85
—	—	—	1.93	1.78	2.13	23.4 - 18.5	3.26	3.10	2.94	8.3	0.83Q	2/20/03	45.08 - 35.80
—	—	—	p1.48	1.52	1.91	21.5 - 16.2	2.34	2.34	2.33	8.4	0.585Q	2/20/03	31.82 - 24.02
0.24	—	—	0.97	0.76	0.68	23.7 - 16.7	0.02	—	—	0.1	0.02Q	3/3/03	22.99 - 16.24
—	—	—	p1.82	0.69	1.33	16.6 - 11.2	—	—	—	—	—	—	30.15 - 20.35
—	—	—	p1.55	1.81	1.82	20.9 - 15.3	2.39	2.31	2.23	8.5	0.61Q	3/6/03	32.35 - 23.75
—	—	—	pd0.68	0.51	0.71	—	—	—	—	—	2-for-1	3/17/97	15.90 - 2.79
—	—	—	p1.15	0.32	0.44	24.8 - 16.3	—	—	—	—	—	—	28.48 - 18.80
d0.01	0.04	d0.19	—	d0.25	d1.39	—	—	—	—	—	0.05Q	12/21/90	5.90 - 0.90
0.13	—	—	0.68	0.71	1.26	25.8 - 11.3	0.05	0.05	0.05	0.4	0.025S	1/23/03	17.55 - 7.65
0.13	—	—	0.68	0.71	1.26	21.3 - 8.6	0.05	0.05	0.05	0.5	0.025S	1/23/03	14.49 - 5.85

SYMBOL	COMPANY	NATURE OF BUSINESS	FISCAL YEAR-END	TOTAL REV. $MILL	NET INCOME $MILL	TOTAL ASSETS $MILL	NET STK EQUITY $MILL	NO. OF INST.	INST. HOLDINGS (SHARES)
HNZ	Heinz (H.J.) Co.	Food processing	5/1/02	9431.0	833.9	10278.4	1718.6	535	239712213
OTE	Hellenic Telecommunications	Telecommunications	12/31/01	—	—	—	—	46	14607861
HP	Helmerich & Payne, Inc.	Oil service & equipment	9/30/02	510.9	53.7	1227.3	895.2	223	39146690
HPC	Hercules Inc.	Chemicals	12/31/02	p1705.0	p1705.0	—	—	189	84154492
HPG	Heritage Propane Partners L P	Services	8/31/02	621.4	4.9	717.3	—	25	317835
HTG	Heritage Property Investment	—	12/31/02	p420.0	p278.0	—	—	84	20081467
HSY	Hershey Foods Corp.	—	12/31/02	p4120.3	p4120.3	—	—	418	66032372
HEW	Hewitt Associates Inc (Unite	—	9/30/02	1750.1	190.4	1219.3	532.6	60	14474201
HPQ	Hewlett-Packard Co. (DE) (Un	Computers	10/31/02	56588.0	d923.0	70710.0	36262.0	937	1912436467
HXL	Hexcel Corp. (New)	Metal products	12/31/02	p850.8	p850.8	—	—	40	11533241
HIB	Hibernia Corp.	Banking - South	12/31/02	1340.0	249.9	17392.7	1680.9	229	80735214
HIO	High Income Opportunity Fd	Investment company	9/30/02	55.9	49.8	443.7	441.6	35	3577724
HYI	High Yield Income Fund, Inc.	Investment company	8/31/02	7.6	6.3	73.3	51.8	10	265273
HYP	High Yield Plus Fund, Inc.	Investment company	3/31/02	11.7	9.6	85.6	61.3	9	119181
HIW	Highwoods Properties, Inc.	Real estate investment trust	12/31/01	540.6	131.9	3648.3	1605.6	165	27232531
HRH	Hilb, Rogal and Hamilton Co.	Life Insurance	12/31/02	p452.7	p456.7	—	—	183	28195441
HB	Hillenbrand Industries, Inc.	Conglomerate	9/30/02	1757.0	d10.0	5442.0	999.0	212	26468396
HLT	Hilton Hotels Corp.	Motel/hotel lodging	12/31/02	p3847.0	p3847.0	—	—	265	273306690
HLN	Hilton Hotels Corp.	Motel/hotel lodging	12/31/02	p3847.0	p3847.0	—	—		
HSP	Hispanic Broadcasting Corp	Broadcasting	12/31/01	240.8	31.0	1241.7	1096.8	186	67239744
HIT	Hitachi, Ltd. (Japan)	Electrical equipment	3/31/02	—	—	—	—	68	19260109
HLR	Hollinger International, Inc	Newspapers ·	12/31/01	1146.3	d337.5	1981.8	325.8	98	59319252
HD	Home Depot, Inc.	Specialty stores	2/2/03	—	p3622.0	—	—	1093	1432258534
HME	Home Properties of New York,	Real estate investment trust	12/31/01	367.5	64.6	2063.8	620.6	119	21353114
HNI	Hon Industries Inc.	Furniture & fixtures	12/28/02	p1692.6	p1692.6	—	—	138	28303430
HON	Honeywell International, Inc	Conglomerate	12/31/01	—	—	—	—	683	614215928
HMN	Horace Mann Educators Corp.	Property & casualty insurance	12/31/02	p771.8	p775.4	—	—	111	39536506
HRL	Hormel Foods Corp.	Meat packing & processing	10/26/02	3910.3	189.3	2220.2	1115.3	174	33615934
DHI	Horton (D.R.) Inc. (United St	Home-building	9/30/02	6738.8	404.7	6017.5	2269.9	243	117084364
HPT	Hospitality Properties Trust	Real estate investment trust	12/31/02	p348.7	p347.1	—	—	199	22022215
HMT	Host Marriott Corp. (REIT)	Motel/hotel lodging	12/31/02	p3767.0	p3780.0	—	—	205	211357836
HI	Household International, Inc	Finance	12/31/02	—	p1558.0	—	—	458	394088833
THX	Houston Exploration Co.	Natural gas	12/31/02	345.4	70.5	1138.8	592.8	100	9259276
HOV	Hovnanian Enterprises, Inc.	Real estate	10/31/02	2551.1	138.3	1678.1	562.5	127	13462912
HRP	HRPT Properties Trust	Real estate investment trust	12/31/02	p417.0	p417.0	—	—	157	43749414
HBC	HSBC Holdings Plc (UK)	Financial services	12/31/01	—	—	—	—	151	55047075
HUB A	Hubbell Inc.	Electrical equipment	12/31/02	p1587.8	p1562.4	—	—	37	6646605
HUB B	Hubbell Inc.	Electrical equipment	12/31/02	p1587.8	p1562.4	—	—	214	36077093
HU	Hudson United Bancorp	Banking - Mid-Atlantic	12/31/02	—	p123.2	—	—	173	21702936
HUF	Huffy Corp.	Recreation	12/31/02	372.9	4.6	282.2	71.7	45	5305380
GMH	Hughes Electronics Corp	Electronic components	12/31/02	p8934.9	p4063.9	—	—	384	729520274
HUG	Hughes Supply, Inc.	'Wholesaler, distributor'	1/25/02	3037.7	44.1	1293.3	594.5	133	19826306
HGT	Hugoton Royalty Trust (TX)	Natural gas	12/31/01	79.4	79.1	217.1	215.3	38	3882991
HUM	Humana Inc.	Hospitals & nursing homes	12/31/02	—	—	—	—	272	111108030
HBP	Huttig Building Products, In	—	12/31/02	p871.2	p6.5	—	—	32	4794998
HYC	Hypercom Corp	Computer services	12/31/01	291.7	d19.9	337.7	211.4	59	18331673
HTO	Hyperion 2005 Investmen	Investment company	12/31/02	15.4	9.6	249.4	168.5	11	3264859
HSM	Hyperion Strategic Mortgage I	Investment company	7/10/02	—	—	0.1	0.1	—	—
HTR	Hyperion Tot Return Fund Inc	Investment company	11/30/01	26.4	20.3	405.1	280.1	15	208117
IBN	ICICI Bank Ltd (India)	—	3/31/02	—	—	—	—	53	64378626
ICN	ICN Pharmaceuticals, Inc.	Drugs	12/31/01	858.1	85.2	1754.4	810.7	170	64368857
IDA	Idacorp, Inc. (United States	Electric power	12/31/02	928.8	61.7	3252.6	874.8	154	11559778
IEX	IDEX Corp.	Hardware & tools	12/31/02	p742.0	p251.7	—	—	126	27609320
IDT C	IDT Corp. (United States)	Telecommunications	7/31/02	1531.6	d156.4	1607.9	869.5	98	14156028
IDT	IDT Corp. (United States)	Telecommunications	7/31/02	1531.6	d156.4	1607.9	869.5	62	17480329
IHP	IHOP Corp. (New) (United Stat	Restaurants	12/31/02	p365.9	p365.9	—	—	99	18682183
IKN	Ikon Office Solutions, Inc.	Paper	9/30/02	4827.5	150.3	6472.6	1534.9	164	96481767
ITW	Illinois Tool Works, Inc.	Plastics & plastic products	12/31/02	9467.7	931.8	10623.1	6649.1	599	256355764
IGI	Imagistics International, In	Machinery & equipment	12/31/02	p629.9	p629.9	—	—	121	12532278
IMN	Imation Corp.	Comp. components & periphs.	12/31/02	p1066.7	p1075.3	—	—	209	29053249
IGL	IMC Global, Inc.	Fertilizer	12/31/02	p2057.4	p176.8	—	—	179	107101414
IMR	IMCO Recycling, Inc.	Metal products	12/31/02	p687.2	p46.5	—	—	72	6798483
ICI	Imperial Chemical Industries	Chemicals	12/31/01	—	—	—	—	65	21306956
ITY	Imperial Tobacco Group Plc	Tobacco	9/29/01	—	—	—	—	44	22754310
RX	IMS Health, Inc.	Services	12/31/02	1428.1	266.1	1618.5	222.3	393	270021475
IFN	India Fund, Inc. (The)	Investment company	12/31/01	9.0	2.3	371.6	366.5	31	10899473
IGF	India Growth Fund, Inc.	Investment company	6/30/02	1.5	d0.4	56.7	56.3	9	292517
IMJ	Indiana Michigan Power Co (Un	Electric power	12/31/01	4803.6	75.8	4817.0	934.3	1	900
IMK	Indiana Michigan Power Co (Un	Electric power	12/31/01	4803.6	75.8	4817.0	934.3	1	127000
IDU	Indiana Michigan Power Co (Un	Electric power	12/31/01	4803.6	75.8	4817.0	934.3		
IDG	Industrial Distr Group Inc	Industrial	12/31/02	p492.4	p492.4	—	—	5	1190450
IBA	Industrias Bachoco SA de CV	Meat packing & processing	12/31/01	—	—	—	—	3	374981
NDE	IndyMac Bancorp Inc	Real estate investment trust	12/31/02	859.3	143.4	9574.5	850.0	169	44473390
IFX	Infineon Technologies AG	Electronic components	9/30/02	—	—	—	—	32	7270273
IN	Infonet Services Corp.	Services	3/31/02	645.8	d13.3	1410.1	1097.8	51	19434500
IHI	Information Holdings, Inc.	Publishing	12/31/01	105.3	7.8	346.6	266.9	77	11295697
ING	ING Groep N.V.	—	12/31/01	—	—	—	—	127	45037262
IND	ING Groep N.V.	—	12/31/01	—	—	—	—		
INZ	ING Groep N.V.	—	12/31/01	—	—	—	—		
PPR	ING Prime Rate Trust (United	Investment company	2/28/02	139.6	101.8	1721.1	986.0	—	—
IR	Ingersoll-Rand Co. Ltd. (Berm	Machinery & equipment	12/31/02	p8951.3	p2124.8	—	—	404	123269712
IM	Ingram Micro Inc.	Comp. components & periphs.	12/28/02	p1228.3	—	—	—	138	83261875
KPA	Innkeepers USA Trust	Real estate investment trust	12/31/02	p89.3	p86.0	—	—	98	24964168
IO	Input/Output, Inc.	—	12/31/02	p118.6	p63.6	—	—	93	·40842873
IFS	Insignia Financial Group Inc	Real estate	12/31/01	741.7	5.7	918.3	399.9	45	16389427
PIF	Insured Municipal Income Fund	Investment company	3/31/02	25.3	20.8	466.5	462.6	22	2150669
IFF	Int'l. Flavors & Fragrances	Cosmetics & toiletries	12/31/02	p1809.2	p90.5	—	—	295	75890517
IDE	Integrated Defense Technologi	—	12/31/02	p304.4	p81.5	—	—	57	7595689
IES	Integrated Electrical Svcs	Electrical equipment	9/30/02	1475.4	9.9	721.6	254.4	61	21239746
IDC	Interactive Data Corp.	Securities brokerage	12/31/01	p375.0	p375.0	—	—	86	23021836
ICM	Internacional de Ceramica, SA	Floor coverings	12/31/01	—	—	—	—	5	5873
IAL	International Aluminum Corp.	—	6/30/02	193.7	1.0	184.7	110.8	17	796653
IGT	International Game Technolog	Gaming	9/28/02	1847.6	276.7	3315.8	1433.1	334	80269805
IMC	International Multifoods	Food processing	3/2/02	2849.1	9.6	1124.7	272.1	105	12863684
IP	International Paper Co.	Paper	12/31/02	24976.0	295.0	33792.0	7374.0	548	412531108
IPR	International Power Plc (Unit	Electrical equipment	12/31/01	—	—	—	—	8	705461

T24

1st	2nd	3rd	2002	2001	2000	P/E RATIO	2002	2001	2000	AV. YLD. %	AMOUNT	PAYABLE	PRICE RANGE 2002
EARNINGS PER SHARE — QUARTERLY / ANNUAL						P/E RATIO	**DIVIDENDS PER SHARE**			AV. YLD. %	**DIV. DECLARED**		PRICE RANGE
0.50	0.60	0.37	—	2.36	1.41	—	1.62	1.58	1.49	4.4	0.27Q	4/10/03	43.48 - 29.60
0.01	—	—	—	—	—	—	0.34	0.32	0.29	5.0	0.341U	8/22/02	8.51 - 5.10
—	—	—	1.07	2.84	1.64	40.4 - 21.9	0.31	0.30	0.29	0.9	0.08Q	6/2/03	43.24 - 23.45
—	—	—	pd5.65	d0.54	0.91	—	—	—	0.62	—	0.08Q	9/29/00	13.70 - 8.45
0.06	—	—	0.25	1.42	d0.37	119.6 - 90.0	2.55	2.42	2.26	9.7	0.6375Q	1/14/03	29.90 - 22.50
—	—	—	pd0.01	d4.71	d2.40	—	0.89	—	—	3.6	0.525Q	4/15/03	26.98 - 22.30
—	—	—	p2.93	1.50	2.42	27.1 - 19.3	1.26	1.17	1.08	1.9	0.3275Q	3/14/03	79.49 - 56.45
0.15	—	—	p0.27	—	—	—	—	—	—	—	—	—	33.84 - 21.20
0.24	—	—	d0.37	0.32	1.73	—	0.32	0.32	0.32	1.8	0.08Q	4/9/03	24.12 - 10.75
—	—	—	p0.35	d11.47	1.32	—	—	—	—	—	—	—	5.40 - 1.25
—	—	—	1.56	1.35	1.04	13.9 - 10.4	0.57	0.53	0.49	3.0	0.15Q	2/20/03	21.71 - 16.25
—	—	—	6.10	7.15	9.42	—	0.71	0.97	1.01	10.8	0.057M	6/27/03	7.87 - 5.26
—	—	—	4.53	5.42	6.07	—	0.56	0.60	0.62	11.2	0.0425M	3/31/03	6.14 - 3.76
—	3.04	—	—	3.92	5.02	—	0.48	0.81	0.89	11.8	0.0325M	6/10/03	5.45 - 2.70
0.36	0.34	0.16	—	1.84	1.78	—	2.34	2.31	2.25	9.7	0.585Q	2/24/03	29.45 - 18.97
0.12	—	—	p2.01	1.07	0.78	23.0 - 13.3	0.36	0.35	0.34	1.0	0.09Q	3/31/03	46.15 - 26.67
—	—	—	d0.16	2.71	2.44	—	1.02	0.84	0.80	1.8	0.25Q	3/31/03	66.48 - 46.55
—	—	—	p0.53	0.45	0.73	32.2 - 18.0	0.08	0.08	0.08	0.6	0.02Q	3/21/03	17.09 - 9.56
0.06	0.09	0.11	p0.53	0.45	0.73	47.5 - 42.5	2.00	0.47	—	8.4	0.50Q	2/18/03	25.20 - 22.50
—	—	—	—	0.28	0.38	—	—	—	—	—	2-for-1	6/15/03	32.00 - 13.80
—	—	—	—	—	—	—	0.21	0.58	0.66	0.4	—	3/27/03	77.95 - 34.30
d0.65	d0.03	d0.33	—	d3.42	1.11	—	0.41	0.55	0.55	3.6	0.05Q	4/15/03	13.75 - 8.65
1.29	—	—	p1.29	1.29	1.10	40.8 - 17.8	0.21	0.17	0.16	0.6	0.06Q	3/27/03	52.60 - 23.01
0.24	0.28	0.37	—	2.11	1.41	—	2.41	2.31	2.16	7.3	0.61Q	2/27/03	37.94 - 28.28
—	—	—	p1.55	1.26	1.77	19.9 - 14.8	0.50	0.48	0.44	1.9	0.13Q	2/28/03	30.85 - 22.88
—	—	—	pd0.27	d0.12	2.05	—	0.75	0.75	0.75	2.5	0.1875Q	3/10/03	40.95 - 18.77
—	—	—	p0.28	0.63	0.51	86.0 - 48.6	0.42	0.42	0.42	2.2	0.105Q	3/17/03	24.08 - 13.61
0.34	—	—	1.35	1.30	1.20	20.9 - 14.8	0.39	0.37	0.35	1.6	0.105Q	2/15/03	28.20 - 20.02
0.75	—	—	2.87	2.21	1.69	10.2 - 5.6	0.22	0.13	0.09	1.0	0.07Q	2/14/03	29.17 - 16.03
—	—	—	p2.15	2.12	2.24	17.1 - 12.0	2.86	2.82	2.77	9.1	0.72Q	2/20/03	36.75 - 25.80
—	—	—	pd0.19	0.09	0.64	—	—	1.04	0.86	—	0.26Q	10/12/01	12.25 - 7.50
—	—	—	p3.22	4.08	3.55	19.6 - 6.2	0.94	0.82	0.72	2.3	0.25Q	1/15/03	63.25 - 20.00
—	—	—	2.28	4.00	3.02	14.9 - 10.4	—	—	—	—	—	—	34.00 - 23.80
p1.35	—	—	4.30	2.29	1.50	9.4 - 4.4	—	—	—	—	—	—	40.56 - 18.80
—	—	—	p0.61	0.52	1.09	15.4 - 10.9	0.80	0.80	1.04	10.0	0.20Q	2/21/03	9.37 - 6.63
—	—	—	—	—	—	—	2.47	2.38	1.78	4.3	1.625U	5/6/03	64.55 - 50.29
—	—	—	p1.38	0.82	2.25	25.4 - 17.8	1.32	1.32	1.30	4.4	0.33Q	4/11/03	35.00 - 24.62
—	—	—	p1.38	0.82	2.25	27.0 - 18.6	1.32	1.32	1.30	4.2	0.33Q	4/11/03	37.30 - 25.73
—	—	—	p2.72	2.00	0.92	12.1 - 8.4	1.10	1.01	0.91	3.9	0.28Q	3/3/03	33.00 - 22.90
—	—	—	0.38	d0.82	1.03	23.6 - 14.4	—	—	—	—	0.085Q	8/2/99	8.95 - 5.48
—	—	—	—	—	—	—	—	—	—	—	3-for-1	6/30/00	17.55 - 8.00
0.52	0.78	0.84	—	1.88	1.97	—	0.34	0.34	0.34	0.9	0.10Q	5/16/03	46.96 - 25.31
0.18	0.13	0.22	—	1.98	1.42	20.5 - 11.5	0.70	2.08	1.38	6.2	—	3/14/03	13.19 - 9.44
—	—	—	p0.85	0.70	0.54	—	—	—	—	—	—	—	17.45 - 9.78
—	—	—	pd0.59	0.28	0.68	—	—	—	—	—	—	—	6.48 - 2.51
d0.02	0.01	d0.58	—	d0.54	d0.91	—	—	—	—	—	—	—	8.15 - 1.50
—	—	—	—	9.92	9.69	—	0.54	0.51	0.45	5.5	0.04167M	3/27/03	10.10 - 9.45
—	—	—	14.25	—	—	—	0.43	—	—	3.0	0.108M	3/27/03	15.35 - 13.10
—	—	—	—	9.17	9.41	—	0.90	0.87	0.86	9.7	0.075M	3/27/03	9.99 - 8.50
—	—	—	—	—	—	—	0.08	0.09	—	1.3	0.082U	3/15/02	8.31 - 4.00
0.36	0.65	d0.62	—	1.02	1.14	—	0.31	0.30	0.29	1.5	0.0775Q	4/23/03	33.88 - 6.51
—	—	—	1.63	3.35	3.72	25.1 - 12.8	1.86	1.86	1.86	6.0	0.465Q	5/30/03	40.99 - 20.87
d0.05	—	—	p1.67	1.05	2.07	23.7 - 15.4	0.56	0.56	0.56	1.7	0.14Q	1/31/03	39.66 - 25.70
d0.05	—	—	d2.08	7.12	6.22	—	—	—	—	—	0.00U	5/31/01	23.32 - 15.05
—	—	—	d2.08	7.12	6.22	—	—	—	—	—	—	—	20.35 - 13.09
—	—	—	p1.92	1.94	1.74	19.0 - 11.0	0.16	0.16	0.16	—	2-for-1	5/27/79	36.46 - 21.08
0.21	—	—	0.99	0.10	0.18	14.4 - 6.4	0.16	0.16	0.16	1.6	0.04Q	3/10/03	14.25 - 6.38
—	—	—	3.02	2.62	3.15	25.8 - 18.2	0.89	0.82	0.74	1.3	0.23Q	4/21/03	77.80 - 55.03
—	—	—	p0.86	0.65	3.29	25.4 - 14.2	—	—	—	—	—	—	21.85 - 12.25
—	—	—	p1.86	d0.05	d0.03	23.0 - 11.3	—	—	—	—	—	—	42.75 - 21.00
—	—	—	p0.10	d0.24	0.73	155.5 - 85.2	0.08	0.08	0.32	0.7	0.02Q	3/31/03	15.55 - 8.52
—	—	—	pd3.54	d0.18	0.02	—	—	—	0.24	—	0.06Q	12/29/00	11.55 - 4.95
—	—	—	—	—	—	—	0.75	1.47	1.95	4.0	0.2952U	4/29/03	24.85 - 12.48
—	—	—	—	—	—	—	6.13	0.93	0.90	20.1	—	2/28/03	35.40 - 25.65
—	12.23	—	0.93	0.46	0.39	24.3 - 13.9	0.08	0.08	0.08	0.5	0.02Q	3/31/03	22.59 - 12.90
—	—	—	—	11.93	16.18	—	0.07	—	—	0.7	0.085A	1/10/03	11.50 - 8.65
—	—	—	10.54	10.60	17.75	—	0.30	0.47	—	3.5	0.301A	1/11/02	10.01 - 7.30
—	—	—	—	—	—	—	2.00	2.00	2.00	8.3	0.50Q	3/31/03	25.65 - 22.31
—	—	—	—	—	—	—	1.90	1.90	1.90	8.5	0.475Q	3/31/03	25.46 - 19.20
—	—	—	pd5.44	d0.16	d1.09	—	—	—	—	—	0.5375Q	3/31/03	25.60 - 24.98
—	—	—	—	—	—	—	—	—	—	—	—	—	3.86 - 1.45
—	—	—	—	—	—	—	0.55	0.62	0.30	6.3	0.1771U	10/15/02	10.40 - 7.15
—	—	—	2.41	2.00	1.69	11.2 - 6.7	—	—	—	—	0.10Q	3/13/03	26.89 - 16.14
d0.08	d0.01	0.04	—	d0.03	0.06	—	—	0.43	—	—	0.4304U	4/17/01	25.89 - 5.01
0.13	0.14	—	—	0.36	0.34	—	—	—	—	—	—	—	2.78 - 1.60
—	—	—	—	—	—	—	—	—	—	—	—	—	32.08 - 11.50
—	—	—	—	—	—	—	0.92	1.06	0.81	4.5	0.5243U	6/2/03	27.75 - 12.76
—	—	—	—	—	—	—	0.72	—	—	2.9	0.44Q	3/17/03	25.70 - 24.05
—	—	—	—	—	—	—	—	—	—	—	0.47Q	3/31/03	25.30 - 25.00
7.25	6.82	—	—	7.20	8.09	—	0.46	0.69	0.85	7.5	0.033M	3/24/03	6.97 - 5.20
—	—	—	pd1.02	1.48	3.36	—	0.68	—	—	1.6	0.17Q	3/3/03	54.40 - 29.69
—	—	—	pd1.81	0.06	1.51	—	—	—	—	—	—	—	18.85 - 10.00
—	—	—	pd0.31	0.47	1.02	—	0.25	1.18	1.12	2.7	0.08Q	4/29/03	11.95 - 6.42
—	—	—	pd2.37	0.07	d0.26	—	—	—	—	—	2-for-1	1/9/96	10.00 - 3.54
d0.03	12.00	0.14	—	20.00	d0.35	—	0.82	0.72	0.77	5.9	0.07M	3/31/03	11.82 - 5.25
—	15.96	—	—	15.15	15.30	—	0.60	0.60	1.52	1.9	0.15Q	4/10/03	14.68 - 13.10
—	—	—	p1.84	1.20	1.22	20.4 - 14.2	—	—	—	—	—	—	37.45 - 26.05
0.10	—	—	pd0.21	0.15	0.13	—	—	—	—	—	—	—	33.00 - 9.51
—	—	—	0.25	0.70	0.52	26.0 - 12.4	—	—	—	—	—	—	6.50 - 3.10
—	—	—	p0.65	0.05	d1.68	31.9 - 17.1	—	0.29	—	—	0.2948U	1/16/01	20.75 - 11.11
—	—	—	—	—	—	—	—	—	—	—	—	—	13.00 - 0.01
0.16	0.13	—	0.24	1.09	0.29	99.4 - 64.6	1.20	1.20	1.20	6.1	0.30Q	4/10/03	23.85 - 15.50
1.00	—	—	3.21	2.80	2.00	25.0 - 14.9	—	—	—	—	0.03Q	3/1/99	80.10 - 47.75
0.25	0.22	0.66	—	0.50	1.12	—	—	0.20	0.80	—	0.20Q	1/16/01	28.92 - 16.95
—	—	—	0.61	d2.37	0.32	75.7 - 51.4	1.00	1.00	1.00	2.6	0.25Q	3/14/03	46.20 - 31.35
—	—	—	—	—	—	—	—	—	—	—	0.00U	10/2/00	31.76 - 13.00

SYMBOL	COMPANY	NATURE OF BUSINESS	FISCAL YEAR-END	TOTAL REV. $MILL	NET INCOME $MILL	TOTAL ASSETS $MILL	NET STK EQUITY $MILL	NO. OF INST.	INST. HOLDINGS (SHARES)
IRF	International Rectifier Corp	Electrical equipment	6/30/02	720.2	48.7	1813.2	1058.6	221	45959845
IPX	Interpool Inc	—	12/31/01	305.1	43.0	1917.8	362.5	51	8440234
IPG	Interpublic Group of Cos. In	—	12/31/02	p6203.6	p6203.6	—	—	417	340400044
IBC	Interstate Bakeries Corp.	Food processing	6/1/02	3532.4	69.8	1602.9	301.2	172	38446647
IHR	Interstate Hotels & Resorts,	Motel/hotel lodging	12/31/01	305.9	d18.9	242.9	57.1	27	4384492
ITN	InterTan Inc	Consumer electronics	6/30/02	393.8	13.6	145.1	88.4	60	15854278
IBM	Intl Business Machines Corp	Computers	12/31/02	81186.0	5334.0	96484.0	22782.0	1237	1140256320
ISH	Intl Shipholding Corp.	Freight transportation	12/31/02	p227.4	p227.4	—	—	17	2565350
IVC	Invacare Corp.	Medical & dental equipment	12/31/02	p1089.2	p1089.2	—	—	126	24302295
PPM	Investment Grade Municipal In	Investment company	9/30/02	13.9	11.5	255.9	250.5	10	37155
ITG	Invt Technology Group Inc	Securities brokerage	12/31/02	p387.6	p387.6	—	—	171	38907361
IOM	Iomega Corp. (United States)	Comp. components & periphs.	12/31/02	p614.4	p146.9	—	—	111	22375672
ION	Ionics, Inc.	Machinery & equipment	12/31/01	466.7	44.7	633.3	423.4	107	13340796
IRM	Iron Mountain Inc (PA) (New)	Services	12/31/02	p1318.5	p1316.2	—	—	146	72671377
IRS	Irsa Inversiones y Represent	Real estate	6/30/02	—	—	—	—	19	5947681
IFC	Irwin Financial Corp. (IN)	Banking - Midwest	12/31/02	p213.6	p213.6	—	—	96	11979025
IST	ISPAT International, N.V.	Steel producer	12/31/01	—	—	—	—	10	7082653
SFI	iStar Financial Inc	Real estate investment trust	12/31/02	p525.7	p525.7	—	—	188	47178756
ESI	ITT Educational Services, In	—	12/31/02	464.9	43.9	247.7	89.0	341	43860267
ITT	ITT Industries Inc.	Electronic components	12/31/02	p4985.3	p1773.4	—	—	940	1352833564
JPM	J.P. Morgan Chase & Co.	—	12/31/02	p1663.0	p1663.0	—	—	—	—
JBL	Jabil Circuit, Inc.	Machinery & equipment	8/31/02	3545.5	34.7	2547.9	1507.0	309	136020518
JBX	Jack in the Box, Inc. (Unite	Restaurants	9/29/02	1966.4	83.0	1063.5	464.1	143	30011880
JEC	Jacobs Engineering Group, In	Engineering & construction	9/30/02	4555.7	109.7	1674.0	689.6	227	41791304
JNS	Janus Capital Group Inc	Financial services	12/31/02	p1144.8	p985.5	—	—	38	12316835
JEQ	Japan Equity Fund, Inc.	Investment company	10/31/02	0.4	d0.9	49.2	49.1	16	731639
JOF	Japan Smaller Capitalization	Investment company	2/28/02	0.8	d0.9	93.3	92.8	—	—
JAH	Jarden Corp.	Metal products	12/31/02	368.2	36.3	366.8	76.8	92	11805340
JFC	Jardine Fleming China Fd	Investment company	12/31/01	1.1	d0.6	39.3	38.2	9	1479861
JFI	Jardine Fleming India Fd Inc	Investment company	11/30/01	0.9	d1.1	57.8	54.2	14	3595893
JEF	Jefferies Group, Inc. (New)	Finance	12/31/02	p754.8	p754.8	—	—	124	14240519
JP	Jefferson-Pilot Corp.	Insurance	12/31/02	—	—	—	—	350	88807117
JLG	JLG Industries, Inc. (United	Machinery & equipment	7/31/02	770.1	12.9	778.2	236.0	116	28433653
JAS A	Jo-Ann Stores, Inc. (United	Specialty stores	2/1/03	p1682.0	p1682.0	—	—	105	7770204
JAS B	Jo-Ann Stores, Inc. (United	Specialty stores	2/1/03	p1682.0	p1682.0	—	—	29	5428834
BTO	John Hancock Bk & Thrift Opp	Investment company	10/31/01	25.1	12.9	831.2	823.4	63	18177938
JHF	John Hancock Financial Servi	Insurance	12/31/02	—	—	—	—	316	142300702
JHS	John Hancock Income Sec Tr	Investment company	12/31/02	11.2	9.7	203.8	178.6	23	830640
JHI	John Hancock Investors Trust	Investment company	12/31/02	11.0	9.6	191.3	170.0	18	481633
PGD	John Hancock Patriot Global	Investment company	7/31/02	11.5	9.4	157.3	96.9	8	207509
PPF	John Hancock Patriot Preferr	Investment company	5/31/02	10.4	8.6	142.7	89.9	10	189762
PDF	John Hancock Patriot Prm Dv I	Investment company	9/30/02	14.2	11.7	193.6	193.3	19	173121
PDT	John Hancock Patriot Prm DvII	Investment company	10/31/02	18.0	14.8	251.8	250.4	15	156760
DIV	John Hancock Patriot Select	Investment company	6/30/02	14.2	11.7	206.9	136.3	4	2270
HPI	John Hancock Pfd Inc Fd	—	8/9/02	—	—	0.2	0.1	—	—
JNJ	Johnson & Johnson	Medical & dental equipment	12/31/02	—	p6651.0	—	—	1357	2146413557
JCI	Johnson Controls Inc (United	Services	9/30/02	20103.4	600.5	11165.3	3499.7	416	68088498
JNY	Jones Apparel Group, Inc.	—	12/31/02	p4340.9	p4273.3	—	—	354	125901054
JLL	Jones Lang LaSalle Inc. (Unit	Real estate	12/31/01	881.7	d15.4	835.7	314.4	102	20323708
JRC	Journal Register Co.	Newspapers	12/31/02	p407.8	p406.6	—	—	73	11060900
KTO	K2 Inc.	—	12/31/02	p582.2	p582.2	—	—	45	1062036
KPP	Kaneb Pipeline Partners, L.P.	Oil	12/31/01	207.8	69.9	548.4	—	30	2942488
KSL	Kaneb Services, LLC	—	12/31/02	p669.8	p669.8	—	—	158	41538600
KSU	Kansas City Southern	Railroads	12/31/02	p566.2	p566.2	—	—	162	30255286
KT	Katy Industries, Inc.	Machinery & equipment	12/31/01	506.0	d62.1	348.0	157.9	12	2981649
KDN	Kaydon Corp.	Engineering & construction	12/31/02	p279.4	p279.4	—	—	125	22237535
KBH	KB HOME	Home-building	11/30/02	5030.8	314.4	4025.5	1274.4	251	40613672
KCS	KCS Energy, Inc.	Oil	12/31/01	192.0	65.6	346.7	d39.5	22	8395949
KEI	Keithley Instruments, Inc.	Meas. & control instruments	9/30/02	96.9	d3.1	120.4	92.4	75	6783369
K	Kellogg Co	Food processing	12/28/02	8304.1	720.9	10219.3	895.1	391	348784497
KWD	Kellwood Co.	—	1/31/02	2281.8	37.7	1044.4	456.7	152	20922530
KEM	KEMET Corp.	Electronic components	3/31/02	508.6	d27.3	1171.7	855.0	166	52660797
KMT	Kennametal Inc.	Metal products	6/30/02	1583.7	38.5	1523.6	714.0	155	30257767
KPC	Kentucky Power Co.	Electric power	12/31/01	1659.4	21.6	1153.2	256.1	1	20000
KMG	Kerr-McGee Corp.	Oil	12/31/02	p3700.0	p3785.5	—	—	343	88545058
KMD	Kerr-McGee Corp.	Oil	12/31/02	p3700.0	p3785.5	—	—	13	1527453
KZL	Kerzner International Ltd. (	Motel/hotel lodging	12/31/01	533.0	31.7	1357.0	678.4	30	10812584
KEG	Key Energy Services, Inc.	Oil	6/30/02	802.6	41.2	1243.0	536.9	182	101873705
KEY	KeyCorp (New)	Banking - Midwest	12/31/02	—	p976.0	—	—	424	257090406
KSE	KeySpan Corp.	Natural gas distributor	12/31/02	p5970.7	p5951.0	—	—	307	90691049
KTR	Keystone Property Trust Corp	Real estate investment trust	12/31/02	p96.5	p93.3	—	—	71	11722770
KRC	Kilroy Realty Corp.	Real estate investment trust	12/31/02	p210.3	p210.3	—	—	111	23800143
KMB	Kimberly-Clark Corp.	Paper	12/31/02	13566.3	1686.0	15585.8	5650.3	823	409903714
KIM	Kimco Realty Corp.	Real estate investment trust	12/31/02	p450.8	p450.8	—	—	208	55829937
KMP	Kinder Morgan Energy Partner	Natural gas distributor	12/31/02	4237.1	608.4	8353.6	—	226	27235599
KMR	Kinder Morgan Management, LL	Oil service & equipment	12/31/02	—	45.3	1439.2	1384.9	85	31153983
KMI	Kinder Morgan, Inc. (KS)	Natural gas	12/31/02	1015.3	309.2	10102.8	2355.0	349	189706176
KG	King Pharmaceuticals, Inc.	Drugs	12/31/02	p1179.5	p1102.7	—	—	312	148722317
KEX	Kirby Corp.	Freight transportation	12/31/02	535.4	27.4	791.8	323.3	112	14872237
KRI	Knight-Ridder, Inc.	Newspapers	12/29/02	2841.6	281.7	4164.7	1461.5	286	71907495
KE	Koger Equity, Inc.	Real estate investment trust	12/31/02	p129.8	p129.8	—	—	88	11023789
KSS	Kohl's Corp. (United States	Department stores	2/1/03	p9120.3	p9120.3	—	—	519	298449561
AHO	Koninklijke Ahold NV	Grocery chain	12/31/01	—	—	—	—	79	18403114
KPN	Koninklijke KPN N.V. (Netherl	Telecommunications	12/31/01	—	—	—	—	32	2068266
PHG	Koninklijke Philips Electroni	Communications electronics	12/31/01	—	—	—	—	208	100682836
KB	Kookmin Bank (New) (South Ko	—	12/31/01	—	—	—	—	124	29029453
KOR	Koor Industries Ltd.	Conglomerate	12/31/01	7142.9	d2509.1	12882.9	2101.5	9	248030
KEP	Korea Electric Power Corp.	Electric power	12/31/01	—	—	—	—	116	98861409
KEF	Korea Equity Fund, Inc.	Investment company	10/31/02	0.5	d0.4	36.6	36.0	8	3548770
KF	Korea Fund, Inc.	Investment company	6/30/02	15.5	5.6	1010.9	1008.9	40	20783891
KFY	Korn/Ferry International	Services	4/30/02	393.9	d98.3	377.6	179.3	88	18947150
KFT	Kraft Foods, Inc.	Food processing	12/31/02	—	—	—	—	431	225706701
KRT	Kramont Realty Trust	Real estate investment trust	12/31/01	112.7	25.8	769.2	219.0	56	7360870
KKD	Krispy Kreme Doughnuts Inc (U	—	2/3/02	394.4	26.4	255.4	187.7	165	29446295
KR	Kroger Co.	Grocery chain	2/1/03	—	—	—	—	498	534860477
KTC	KT Corp (Korea)	Telecommunications	12/31/01	—	—	—	—	155	200288539

T26

EARNINGS PER SHARE — QUARTERLY			ANNUAL			P/E RATIO		DIVIDENDS PER SHARE			AV. YLD.	DIV. DECLARED		PRICE RANGE 2002	
1st	2nd	3rd	2002	2001	2000	2002		2002	2001	2000	%	AMOUNT	PAYABLE		
0.17	d1.90	—	0.75	1.35	1.27	67.3	14.2	—	—	—	—	2-for-1	12/22/95	50.50	10.65
0.39	0.21	0.12	—	1.48	1.54	—	—	0.22	0.18	0.15	1.2	0.0625Q	4/15/03	25.99	11.29
0.60	0.26	—	p0.26	d1.37	1.15	134.5	37.9	0.38	0.38	0.37	1.7	0.095Q	12/16/02	34.98	9.85
d0.25	d2.08	d1.12	—	1.36	1.13	—	—	0.28	0.28	0.28	1.3	0.07Q	2/3/03	29.22	14.40
0.09	0.40	—	—	d2.55	d1.35	—	—	—	—	—	—	—	—	4.90	2.40
—	—	—	0.53	0.82	0.82	26.3	8.8	—	—	—	—	50%	1/13/00	13.95	4.65
—	—	—	3.13	4.35	4.44	51.3	17.3	0.59	0.55	0.51	0.6	0.15Q	3/10/03	160.50	54.01
—	—	—	pd0.02	d10.59	0.03	—	—	—	0.13	0.25	—	0.0625Q	6/15/01	13.60	0.01
—	—	—	p2.05	1.11	1.95	19.5	14.1	0.05	0.05	0.05	0.1	0.0125Q	4/7/03	39.92	28.87
—	—	—	16.46	16.15	15.91	—	—	1.13	0.93	1.09	7.4	0.08M	3/31/03	15.93	14.47
—	—	—	p1.51	1.62	1.35	36.0	13.5	—	—	—	—	3-for-2	12/7/01	54.41	20.40
—	—	—	p0.68	d1.74	3.05	20.4	10.9	—	—	—	—	—	—	13.90	7.40
0.11	0.12	0.02	—	2.59	d0.12	—	—	—	—	—	—	100%	1/6/95	33.90	17.64
—	—	—	p0.68	d0.39	d0.31	50.3	29.6	—	—	—	—	50%	12/31/01	34.20	20.14
—	—	—	—	—	—	—	—	—	—	—	—	—	12/23/02	6.56	3.33
—	—	—	p1.89	1.99	1.67	10.9	7.0	0.27	0.26	0.24	1.6	0.07Q	3/28/03	20.60	13.20
—	—	—	—	—	—	—	—	—	—	0.11	—	0.1125U	6/8/00	3.10	1.26
—	—	—	p1.93	2.19	2.10	16.5	12.4	2.52	3.05	2.37	9.0	0.63Q	12/30/02	31.80	23.98
—	—	—	0.94	0.70	0.57	28.4	15.0	—	—	—	—	100%	6/5/02	26.65	14.14
—	—	—	p4.06	2.39	2.94	17.5	11.3	0.60	0.60	0.60	1.0	0.16Q	4/1/03	70.85	45.80
—	—	—	p0.80	0.80	2.86	49.6	19.1	1.36	1.34	1.23	5.0	0.34Q	4/30/03	39.68	15.26
0.04	—	—	0.17	0.59	0.78	157.6	65.5	—	—	—	—	100%	3/30/00	26.79	11.13
p0.56	—	—	2.07	2.11	2.55	16.5	6.9	—	—	—	—	—	—	34.20	14.25
0.54	—	—	1.98	1.61	0.96	21.7	13.2	—	—	—	—	100%	4/1/02	42.90	26.10
—	—	—	p0.31	1.31	2.90	94.3	28.9	0.05	0.04	0.01	0.3	0.04A	7/31/02	29.24	8.97
—	7.14	—	4.54	5.59	8.35	—	—	—	—	—	—	0.042A	12/27/96	6.99	3.88
—	—	—	—	5.86	7.59	—	—	—	0.08	0.82	—	0.08U	12/14/01	9.94	5.11
—	16.40	—	2.52	d6.71	0.39	11.0	6.7	—	—	—	—	2-for-1	6/3/02	27.70	17.00
—	8.59	—	—	8.14	9.34	—	—	—	—	—	—	0.04A	12/30/99	7.80	5.68
—	—	—	—	9.24	13.86	—	—	—	1.48	—	—	0.003A	11/30/01	8.65	6.30
—	—	—	p2.29	2.28	2.26	22.8	14.5	0.20	0.20	0.20	0.5	0.05Q	3/14/03	52.10	33.14
—	—	—	p3.04	3.34	3.29	17.4	12.0	1.18	1.07	0.96	2.6	0.33Q	6/5/03	53.00	36.35
0.01	—	—	0.30	0.80	1.37	58.7	22.6	0.02	0.04	0.04	0.2	0.005Q	4/1/03	17.61	6.78
—	—	—	p2.23	d0.78	d0.75	15.2	3.2	—	—	—	—	3-for-2	1/25/91	33.98	7.15
—	—	—	p2.23	d0.78	d0.75	12.0	3.2	—	—	—	—	—	—	26.84	7.21
—	10.38	—	—	9.76	9.53	—	—	0.86	1.22	0.77	10.9	0.11649A	12/30/02	8.92	6.79
—	—	—	p1.76	1.99	2.51	24.0	14.7	0.32	0.31	0.30	0.9	0.32A	12/11/02	42.30	25.84
—	—	—	16.31	16.06	15.89	—	—	0.92	1.02	1.07	6.2	0.2275Q	3/31/03	15.45	14.16
—	—	—	21.21	20.98	20.79	—	—	1.22	1.34	1.42	6.3	0.33Q	3/31/03	20.00	18.45
—	—	—	11.62	13.82	12.66	—	—	0.97	0.97	0.97	8.4	0.081M	3/31/03	13.07	10.00
—	11.23	—	—	12.39	12.96	—	—	0.86	0.86	0.86	7.4	0.072M	3/31/03	13.00	10.40
—	—	—	8.30	9.74	10.13	—	—	0.65	0.65	0.65	7.6	0.054M	3/31/03	9.88	7.20
—	—	—	10.01	12.06	12.24	—	—	1.02	0.78	0.78	10.0	0.065M	4/15/03	11.29	9.01
—	12.25	—	13.77	—	13.97	—	—	0.99	1.08	1.08	7.3	0.09M	3/31/03	15.10	11.86
—	—	—	—	—	—	—	—	0.36	—	—	1.5	0.18M	4/1/03	25.40	22.00
1.48	—	—	p2.18	2.16	1.84	30.2	19.0	0.79	0.88	0.62	1.5	0.205Q	3/11/03	65.89	41.40
—	—	—	6.35	5.11	5.09	14.7	10.9	1.32	1.24	1.12	1.6	0.36Q	3/31/03	93.20	69.10
—	—	—	p2.36	1.82	2.48	17.7	11.1	—	—	—	—	2-for-1	6/25/98	41.68	26.18
d0.16	0.11	0.32	—	d0.51	d2.30	—	—	—	—	—	—	—	—	24.80	14.04
—	—	—	p1.14	1.83	3.72	19.5	14.1	—	—	—	—	—	—	22.20	16.07
—	—	—	p0.67	d0.43	0.93	16.8	9.3	—	—	—	—	0.11Q	4/1/99	11.24	6.20
0.76	0.78	0.77	—	3.32	2.43	—	—	3.12	2.85	2.80	8.3	0.81Q	5/15/03	44.00	30.89
—	—	—	p4.02	2.54	—	6.0	4.0	1.60	0.36	—	8.0	0.4375Q	5/15/03	23.98	16.21
—	—	—	p0.87	0.51	0.43	20.1	13.4	—	—	0.08	—	1-for-2	7/12/00	17.50	11.70
d1.22	d1.10	d2.32	—	p7.14	d0.65	—	—	—	0.07	0.30	—	0.075Q	1/29/01	6.75	2.50
—	—	—	p0.41	0.95	1.30	71.4	42.0	0.48	0.48	0.44	2.1	0.12Q	3/31/03	29.27	17.20
p1.25	—	—	7.15	5.50	5.24	7.6	5.2	0.30	0.30	0.30	0.7	0.075Q	2/26/03	54.39	37.13
d0.03	p0.38	0.09	—	1.69	1.42	—	—	—	—	—	—	0.02Q	2/25/99	4.01	1.14
d0.03	—	—	d0.20	1.05	1.30	—	—	0.15	0.15	0.11	0.9	0.0375Q	3/31/03	25.40	8.00
—	—	—	1.75	1.18	1.45	21.1	16.6	1.01	1.01	0.99	3.1	0.2525Q	3/14/03	37.00	29.02
0.37	0.16	0.82	—	1.65	2.57	—	—	0.64	0.64	0.64	2.5	0.16Q	3/28/03	32.50	19.70
0.04	d0.13	d0.37	—	d0.32	4.00	—	—	—	—	—	—	2-for-1	6/11/00	22.40	6.13
0.31	0.07	—	1.22	1.75	1.71	35.2	22.7	0.68	0.68	0.68	1.9	0.17Q	2/25/03	43.00	27.73
—	—	—	—	—	—	—	—	2.18	2.18	2.18	8.4	0.545Q	3/31/03	26.85	24.96
—	—	—	pd5.99	4.93	8.37	—	—	1.80	1.80	1.80	3.5	0.45Q	4/1/03	63.58	38.02
—	—	—	pd5.99	4.93	8.37	—	—	1.83	1.83	1.83	4.5	—	2/1/03	47.50	33.83
—	—	—	—	1.14	d3.86	—	—	—	—	—	—	—	—	25.20	18.10
d0.02	—	—	0.38	0.61	d0.25	33.1	18.2	—	—	—	—	3333%	7/8/83	12.59	6.90
—	—	—	p2.27	0.37	2.30	13.0	9.2	1.20	1.18	1.12	4.8	0.305Q	3/14/03	29.40	20.98
—	—	—	p2.61	1.56	2.10	14.6	10.5	1.78	1.78	1.78	5.4	0.445Q	5/1/03	38.20	27.41
—	—	—	pd0.56	1.05	0.09	—	—	1.29	1.26	1.21	8.6	0.325Q	1/31/03	17.33	12.65
—	—	—	p1.45	1.45	1.75	20.4	13.7	1.96	1.89	1.77	7.9	0.495Q	4/17/03	29.64	19.86
—	—	—	3.24	3.02	3.31	26.0	14.0	1.18	1.11	1.07	2.1	0.34Q	4/2/03	66.79	45.30
—	—	—	p2.19	2.16	1.91	15.5	11.9	2.08	1.92	1.77	7.0	0.54Q	4/15/03	33.88	25.96
—	—	—	1.96	1.56	1.33	19.8	12.2	2.36	2.08	1.60	7.5	0.625Q	2/14/03	38.89	23.90
—	—	—	1.23	0.78	—	31.8	21.1	1.14	0.55	—	3.5	0.00Q	2/14/03	39.10	25.90
—	—	—	2.50	1.97	1.60	23.0	12.0	0.30	0.20	0.20	0.7	0.15Q	2/14/03	57.50	30.05
—	—	—	p1.04	0.99	0.47	40.5	14.4	—	—	—	—	4-for-3	7/19/01	42.13	15.00
—	—	—	1.13	1.63	1.39	29.6	18.1	—	—	—	—	0.10A	9/5/89	33.50	20.40
—	—	—	3.33	2.16	3.53	21.1	15.4	1.02	1.00	0.92	1.7	0.27Q	2/24/03	70.20	51.35
—	—	—	p0.77	2.75	1.01	25.1	19.2	3.14	1.40	1.40	18.4	0.35Q	5/1/03	19.34	14.80
—	—	—	p1.87	1.45	1.10	42.2	23.5	—	—	—	—	100%	4/24/00	78.83	44.00
—	—	—	—	—	—	—	—	0.52	0.44	0.37	2.6	0.1612U	10/21/02	29.51	10.01
—	—	—	—	—	—	—	—	—	—	0.31	—	2.5%	5/23/01	6.87	3.45
—	—	—	—	—	—	—	—	0.32	0.32	—	1.4	0.31709U	4/8/02	33.00	12.75
—	—	—	—	—	—	—	—	0.13	—	—	0.3	0.0693U	12/26/02	54.10	29.40
—	—	—	—	d165195.00	17319.00	—	—	—	—	0.53	—	0.1398U	7/14/00	7.40	2.08
—	—	—	—	—	—	—	—	0.36	0.19	0.23	3.7	0.1908U	12/26/02	11.80	7.95
—	—	—	—	—	—	—	—	—	—	—	—	0.02	12/29/95	4.75	3.13
—	—	—	4.28	3.23	3.52	—	—	0.12	0.18	—	0.8	0.04S	1/13/03	18.80	12.16
—	—	—	20.20	13.01	20.04	—	—	—	—	—	—	—	—	11.91	5.78
—	—	—	—	2.62	0.81	—	—	0.54	0.13	—	1.4	0.15Q	4/4/03	43.95	32.50
d0.02	d0.48	—	p1.96	1.17	1.38	22.4	16.6	1.30	1.30	0.65	9.5	0.325Q	4/18/03	16.25	11.09
0.14	0.15	0.12	—	0.97	0.97	—	—	—	—	—	—	100%	6/14/01	44.36	27.40
0.15	0.15	0.17	—	0.45	0.28	—	—	—	—	—	—	2-for-1	6/28/99	23.81	11.00
—	—	—	p1.56	1.26	1.04	15.3	7.1	0.41	0.23	0.23	1.9	—	12/27/02	24.67	19.12

SYMBOL	COMPANY	NATURE OF BUSINESS	FISCAL YEAR-END	TOTAL REV. $MILL	NET INCOME $MILL	TOTAL ASSETS $MILL	NET STK EQUITY $MILL	NO. OF INST.	INST. HOLDINGS (SHARES)
KUB	Kubota Corp. (Japan)	Machinery & equipment	3/31/02	—	—	—	—	9	563068
KVB	KV Pharmaceutical Co.	Drugs	3/31/02	204.1	31.5	195.2	158.8	27	2244340
KV A	KV Pharmaceutical Co.	Drugs	3/31/02	204.1	31.5	195.2	158.8	90	15204748
KYO	Kyocera Corp.	Electronic components	3/31/02	—	—	—	—	53	1515622
LLL	L-3 Communications Hldgs Inc	Defense systems & equip.	12/31/02	4011.2	212.3	5242.3	2202.2	411	93015844
LQI	La Quinta Corp.	Real estate investment trust	12/31/02	p536.9	p536.9	—	—	118	79533479
LZB	La-Z-Boy Inc.	Furniture & fixtures	4/27/02	2154.0	61.8	1160.8	713.5	157	27585625
LRW	Labor Ready, Inc.	Services	12/31/02	p862.7	p862.7	—	—	111	31889621
LH	Laboratory Corp. of America	Medical & dental equipment	12/31/02	p2507.7	p2507.7	—	—	287	147840889
LAB	LaBranche & Co., Inc.	Securities brokerage	12/31/02	p452.8	p373.9	—	—	133	26389217
LG	Laclede Group, Inc. (The) (H	Natural gas distributor	9/30/02	755.2	22.4	1081.9	285.8	94	4684681
LAF	Lafarge North America, Inc.	Cement & gypsum	12/31/02	p3251.6	p3251.6	—	—	138	27235036
LR	Lafarge S.A. (France)	Cement & gypsum	12/31/01	—	—	—	—	24	966933
LMS	Lamson & Sessions Co.	Plastics & plastic products	12/31/02	p314.5	p268.2	—	—	24	7278181
LFL	Lan Chile, S.A. (Chile)	—	12/31/01	—	—	—	—	5	1046485
LFG	Landamerica Finl Group Inc	Insurance brokerage	12/31/02	p2586.6	p2586.6	—	—	137	14825106
LDR	Landauer, Inc.	Services	9/30/02	58.6	16.2	60.3	34.6	72	6042763
LNY	Landry's Restaurants, Inc.	Restaurants	12/31/02	p894.8	p136.9	—	—	150	20987903
LHO	LaSalle Hotel Properties (Un	Real estate investment trust	12/31/02	178.2	2.5	605.7	315.1	80	14488560
LAQ	Latin America Equity Fund In	Investment company	12/31/01	5.5	3.4	116.3	112.0	19	2191399
LDF	Latin American Discovery Fd.	Investment company	12/31/01	5.7	3.4	131.8	129.2	13	4437814
EL	Lauder (Estee) Cos., Inc.	Cosmetics & toiletries	6/30/02	4743.7	212.5	3416.5	1461.9	254	103862671
LF	Leapfrog Enterprises Inc	—	12/31/02	p531.8	p531.8	—	—	86	11848519
LEA	Lear Corp.	—	12/31/02	—	—	—	—	248	64048365
LEE	Lee Enterprises, Inc.	Newspapers	9/30/02	525.9	81.0	1463.8	741.3	164	25401182
LM	Legg Mason, Inc. (Canada)	Securities brokerage	3/31/02	1578.6	152.9	5939.6	1084.5	228	46260289
LEG	Leggett & Platt, Inc.	Furniture & fixtures	12/31/02	4271.8	233.1	3501.1	1976.9	262	126101659
LEH	Lehman Brothers Holdings Inc	Securities brokerage	11/30/02	6155.0	975.0	260336.0	8942.0	452	171557705
LEN	Lennar Corp.	Home-building	11/30/02	7319.8	545.1	5755.6	2229.2	290	58174518
LII	Lennox International Inc	—	12/31/02	p3025.8	p3239.1	—	—	128	27550077
LUK	Leucadia National Corp.	Conglomerate	12/31/01	375.3	64.8	2577.2	1195.5	149	21739543
LXP	Lexington Corporate Properti	Real estate investment trust	12/31/02	p100.6	p100.6	—	—	84	6420836
LXK	Lexmark International, Inc.	Office equipment & supplies	12/31/02	4356.4	366.7	2808.1	1081.6	395	128848324
LBY	Libbey Inc.	Industrial	12/31/02	p437.9	p429.3	—	—	83	13787331
LBI	Liberte Investors Inc.	Real estate investment trust	6/30/02	1.5	0.5	58.9	58.4	14	1657146
USA	Liberty All-Star Equity Fund	Investment company	12/31/01	15.4	3.2	1156.5	1133.2	36	932868
ASG	Liberty All-Star Growth Fd.	Investment company	12/31/02	0.4	d1.7	165.5	163.3	13	238453
LC	Liberty Corp.	Broadcasting	12/31/02	p206.4	p206.4	—	—	85	10499313
L	Liberty Media Corp. (New)	—	12/31/01	2059.0	d6748.0	48539.0	30123.0	636	1826303637
LMC B	Liberty Media Corp. (New)	—	12/31/01	2059.0	d6748.0	48539.0	30123.0	17	2117984
LRY	Liberty Property Trust (Unit	Real estate investment trust	12/31/02	p606.0	p606.0	—	—	195	67205105
LLY	Lilly (Eli) & Co.	Drugs	12/31/02	—	—	—	—	822	851965302
LTD	Limited Brands Inc. (United	Specialty stores	2/1/03	p8444.7	p8450.2	—	—	336	406655083
TVL	LIN TV Corp (United States)	Broadcasting	12/31/02	349.6	d13.9	2334.4	860.2	97	24987849
LNC	Lincoln National Corp. (ID)	Insurance	12/31/02	4635.5	91.6	93133.3	5296.3	366	158341778
LND	Lincoln National Incm Fd Inc	Investment company	12/31/02	10.4	8.7	134.1	93.3	15	260910
LNV	Lincoln Natl Conv Secs Fd Inc	Investment company	12/31/02	4.5	3.3	73.2	73.2	13	967975
LNN	Lindsay Manufacturing Co.	—	8/31/02	145.9	10.7	112.7	90.7	85	9099659
LIN	Linens'n Things, Inc.	Textiles	12/29/01	1823.8	29.7	927.4	498.2	191	47598268
LAD	Lithia Motors, Inc. (United S	—	12/31/02	p2380.0	p2380.0	—	—	70	11830362
LIZ	Liz Claiborne, Inc.	—	12/28/02	p3717.5	p3717.5	—	—	317	100228087
LRT	LL&E Royalty Trust Co.	Real estate investment trust	12/31/01	12.4	11.9	2.1	2.1	17	170013
LYG	Lloyds TSB Group Plc (UK)	—	12/31/01	—	—	—	—	49	45019001
LNR	LNR Property Corp	Real estate	11/30/02	472.1	143.9	2834.9	1126.2	115	17744574
LMT	Lockheed Martin Corp.	Defense systems & equip.	12/31/02	26578.0	533.0	25758.0	5865.0	534	493166287
LTR	Loews Corp.	Conglomerate	12/31/02	—	—	—	—	302	122675833
LSS	Lone Star Technologies, Inc.	Industrial	12/31/02	p523.7	p7.4	—	—	104	23354404
LDG	Longs Drug Stores Corp.	Drug stores	1/30/03	p4426.3	p4401.6	—	—	137	21779436
LFB	Longview Fibre Co.	Forest products	10/31/02	769.3	5.1	1306.4	429.0	124	30094424
LOR	Loral Space & Communications	Telecommunications	12/31/01	1069.6	d216.8	4389.9	1350.9	83	35025744
LPX	Louisiana-Pacific Corp.	Forest products	12/31/02	1942.7	d21.5	2773.1	1006.0	210	75767599
LOW	Lowe's Cos., Inc.	Specialty stores	1/31/03	—	p7138.7	—	—	746	664939246
LSI	LSI Logic Corp.	Electronic components	12/31/02	—	pd30.8	—	—	326	202027263
LTC	LTC Properties, Inc.	Real estate investment trust	12/31/02	p69.2	p82.9	—	—	42	2649033
LZ	Lubrizol Corp.	Chemicals	12/31/02	p1983.9	p1991.7	—	—	200	38078070
LUB	Luby's Inc.	Restaurants	8/28/02	399.1	d9.7	342.5	163.6	71	8465846
LU	Lucent Technologies Inc.	Telecommunications	9/30/02	12321.0	—	17791.0	d4734.0	614	1295433212
LUX	Luxottica Group S.P.A. (Italy	Photo & optical	12/31/01	—	—	—	—	77	52608354
LDL	Lydall, Inc.	Textiles	12/31/02	p253.5	p253.3	—	—	71	12459568
WLS	Lyon (William) Homes	Real estate	12/31/02	613.3	49.5	617.6	181.7	32	3712869
LYO	Lyondell Chemical Co	Specialty chemicals	12/31/02	3262.0	d133.0	7448.0	1179.0	186	107527321
MFW	M & F Worldwide Corp.	—	12/31/01	223.4	1.8	912.1	295.9	27	5869287
MTB	M & T Bank Corp	Banking - Northeast	12/31/02	2354.0	485.1	33174.5	3181.8	257	52244270
MDC	M.D.C. Holdings, Inc.	Home-building	12/31/02	2318.5	167.3	1595.2	800.6	147	18280297
MHO	M/I Schottenstein Homes, Inc.	Home-building	12/31/02	p1033.0	p990.4	—	—	79	8216870
TUC	Mac-Gray Corp.	Services	12/31/02	p150.4	p150.4	—	—	7	1277336
MRD	MacDermid, Inc.	Specialty chemicals	12/31/02	p687.6	—	—	—	111	20440810
MAC	Macerich Co. (The)	Real estate investment trust	12/31/02	p377.8	p374.2	—	—	148	39750902
CLI	Mack Cali Realty Corp	Real estate investment trust	12/31/02	569.6	139.7	3796.4	1454.2	183	42796967
MAD	Madeco S.A. (Chile)	Copper	12/31/01	—	—	—	—	2	74400
MAG	MagneTek, Inc.	Electrical equipment	6/30/02	188.2	1.4	304.9	142.8	74	18248206
MHR	Magnum Hunter Resources, Inc	Oil	12/31/01	152.8	13.8	454.4	118.0	93	29987889
MWL	Mail-Well, Inc.	Paper	12/31/02	p1728.7	p1727.0	—	—	44	25707853
MAL	Malan Realty Investors, Inc.	Real estate investment trust	12/31/01	43.9	d12.3	225.3	19.9	16	920241
MF	Malaysia Fund, Inc.	Investment company	12/31/01	1.3	0.4	49.4	48.7	13	1723132
MHY	Managed High Income Portfolio	Investment company	2/28/02	40.3	36.2	306.7	304.7	24	2878889
HYF	Managed High Yield Plus Fund	Investment company	5/31/02	44.6	38.8	297.6	200.8	16	687971
MMU	Managed Municipals Portfolio,	Investment company	5/31/02	21.8	19.7	822.9	489.3	29	1870181
MBG	Mandalay Resort Group	Gaming	1/31/02	2461.8	53.0	4037.0	940.6	187	49296276
MTW	Manitowoc Co., Inc.	—	12/31/02	p1406.6	p267.0	—	—	138	18736129
HCR	Manor Care, Inc. (New)	Hospitals & nursing homes	12/31/02	p2905.4	p130.6	—	—	236	85560681
MAN	Manpower Inc. (WI)(United St	—	12/31/02	—	p1910.4	—	—	236	74369955
MHC	Manufactured Home Communities	Real estate investment trust	12/31/02	p226.7	p226.7	—	—	100	16133704
MSV	Manufacturers Services Ltd.	Comp. components & periphs.	12/31/02	p853.7	p878.8	—	—	63	30815353
MRO	Marathon Oil Corp.	Oil	12/31/02	—	—	—	—	401	248606759
MCS	Marcus Corp.	—	5/30/02	389.8	22.5	774.8	354.1	73	15945357

| EARNINGS PER SHARE | | | | | | P/E RATIO | DIVIDENDS PER SHARE | | | AV. YLD. % | DIV. DECLARED | | PRICE RANGE |
| QUARTERLY | | | ANNUAL | | | | | | | | | | |
1st	2nd	3rd	2002	2001	2000	—	2002	2001	2000	%	AMOUNT	PAYABLE	2002
0.21	d0.04	0.29	—	0.98	0.74	—	0.21	0.20	0.23	1.5	—	3/26/03	17.25 - 11.50
0.21	d0.04	0.29	—	0.98	0.74	—	—	—	—	—	3-for-2	9/7/00	33.65 - 15.00
—	—	—	—	—	—	—	—	—	—	—	3-for-2	9/7/00	32.05 - 14.90
—	—	—	—	—	—	—	0.42	0.41	0.47	0.6	—	3/27/03	80.98 - 53.95
—	—	—	2.29	1.48	1.19	29.2 - 17.7	—	—	—	—	100%	5/20/02	66.78 - 40.60
—	—	—	pd3.55	d1.40	d2.04	—	2.25	2.81	1.69	37.5	0.5625Q	3/31/03	8.04 - 3.95
0.32	0.50	0.41	—	1.01	1.13	—	0.39	0.36	0.34	1.6	0.10Q	3/10/03	30.94 - 19.25
—	—	—	p0.28	0.23	0.24	33.7 - 15.0	—	—	—	—	3-for-2	7/12/99	9.43 - 4.20
—	—	—	p1.77	2.59	0.81	29.6 - 10.5	—	—	—	—	2-for-1	5/10/02	52.38 - 18.51
—	—	—	p1.34	1.13	1.69	27.2 - 12.1	—	—	—	—	0.08Q	2/14/03	36.41 - 16.25
0.80	—	—	1.18	1.61	1.37	21.2 - 16.1	1.34	—	—	6.1	0.335Q	4/1/03	25.00 - 19.00
—	—	—	p3.64	3.21	3.51	12.4 - 7.1	0.60	0.60	0.60	1.7	0.15Q	3/3/03	45.15 - 25.90
—	—	—	pd2.99	0.36	d0.28	—	0.42	—	—	2.0	0.4193U	8/8/02	25.92 - 16.80
—	—	—	—	—	—	—	—	—	—	—	0.05U	12/10/85	6.05 - 2.30
—	—	—	—	—	—	—	0.01	0.15	0.11	0.3	—	1/27/03	7.65 - 2.60
0.43	—	—	p8.04	3.24	d6.60	4.8 - 3.1	0.24	0.20	0.20	0.8	0.07Q	3/14/03	38.30 - 25.25
—	—	—	1.83	1.64	1.47	22.9 - 16.7	1.40	1.40	1.40	3.9	0.375Q	4/11/03	41.91 - 30.65
—	—	—	p1.54	1.19	0.62	18.9 - 11.4	0.10	0.10	0.08	0.4	0.025Q	1/24/03	29.10 - 17.55
—	—	—	d0.31	0.26	0.32	—	0.24	1.17	1.53	1.8	0.07M	4/15/03	16.47 - 10.60
—	13.48	—	—	15.06	16.60	—	0.48	0.17	—	4.2	0.21A	1/10/03	14.33 - 8.60
—	10.48	—	—	11.90	12.04	—	0.16	0.04	0.11	1.8	0.1037A	1/10/03	11.55 - 6.64
0.29	0.44	—	0.78	1.17	1.20	49.7 - 32.3	0.15	0.20	0.20	0.5	0.20A	1/3/03	38.80 - 25.20
—	—	—	p0.86	0.25	d0.07	41.5 - 15.1	—	—	—	—	—	—	35.70 - 13.00
—	—	—	p0.19	0.52	4.17	283.4 - 172.1	—	—	—	—	—	—	53.84 - 32.70
0.51	—	—	1.83	1.35	1.58	21.9 - 15.8	0.68	0.68	0.64	2.0	0.17Q	4/1/03	40.09 - 28.90
0.71	0.66	p0.70	—	2.24	2.30	—	0.41	0.37	0.33	0.9	0.11Q	4/7/03	57.15 - 37.11
—	—	—	1.17	0.94	1.32	23.4 - 15.9	0.49	0.47	0.40	2.1	0.13Q	4/15/03	27.40 - 18.60
—	—	—	3.47	4.38	6.38	20.1 - 12.2	0.36	0.28	0.22	0.6	0.12Q	2/28/03	69.90 - 42.47
—	—	—	7.72	6.01	3.64	8.3 - 5.6	0.05	0.05	0.05	0.1	0.0125Q	2/17/03	63.97 - 43.20
—	—	—	pd3.23	p0.75	1.05	—	0.38	0.38	0.29	2.7	0.095Q	4/7/03	18.42 - 9.67
0.23	0.35	d0.04	—	1.17	2.07	—	0.25	0.25	0.25	0.7	0.25A	12/27/02	40.27 - 27.62
—	—	—	p1.09	0.93	1.10	15.5 - 12.2	1.32	1.27	1.22	8.8	0.335Q	2/14/03	16.87 - 13.25
—	—	—	2.79	2.05	2.13	24.9 - 15.0	—	—	—	—	100%	6/10/99	69.50 - 41.94
d0.02	d0.01	—	p1.82	2.53	3.01	22.0 - 13.1	0.30	0.30	0.30	0.9	0.10Q	3/4/03	40.10 - 23.89
—	8.49	—	0.02	0.12	0.11	247.5 - 165.0	0.01	0.13	0.09	0.1	0.006U	6/28/02	4.95 - 3.30
—	—	—	—	10.65	13.61	—	0.94	1.31	1.40	10.4	0.17Q	3/17/03	12.39 - 5.61
—	6.36	—	8.31	—	—	—	0.72	1.06	1.32	10.9	0.13Q	3/17/03	8.78 - 4.38
—	—	—	pd0.73	0.84	1.27	—	0.88	0.88	0.88	2.4	0.24Q	4/2/03	45.00 - 28.50
0.12	d1.20	d0.03	—	d2.16	—	—	—	—	—	—	—	—	15.03 - 6.16
0.12	d1.20	d0.03	—	d2.16	—	—	—	—	—	—	—	—	15.90 - 6.38
—	—	—	p2.02	2.15	2.20	17.5 - 12.9	2.37	2.30	2.13	7.7	0.60Q	4/15/03	35.40 - 26.05
—	—	—	p2.55	2.58	2.79	31.8 - 17.2	1.24	1.12	1.04	2.0	0.335Q	3/10/03	81.09 - 43.75
—	—	—	p0.96	1.19	0.96	23.3 - 13.1	0.30	0.30	0.30	1.7	0.10Q	3/18/03	22.34 - 12.53
—	—	—	d0.33	d2.23	d1.33	—	—	—	—	—	—	—	28.35 - 17.00
—	—	—	0.49	3.05	3.19	109.5 - 51.2	1.28	1.22	1.16	3.3	0.335Q	5/1/03	53.65 - 25.11
—	—	—	12.99	12.58	12.77	—	1.34	1.00	0.99	10.5	0.14Q	1/13/03	13.90 - 11.45
—	—	—	12.56	16.76	17.19	—	0.86	0.86	0.80	6.6	0.25Q	1/13/03	15.31 - 10.85
0.24	—	—	0.90	0.67	1.06	28.7 - 20.2	0.14	0.14	0.14	0.6	0.035Q	2/28/03	25.87 - 18.20
0.12	0.13	0.41	—	0.72	1.60	—	—	—	—	—	2-for-1	5/7/98	37.35 - 15.05
—	—	—	p1.84	1.60	1.76	17.0 - 7.9	—	—	—	—	—	—	31.20 - 14.55
0.04	0.01	0.02	p2.16	1.83	1.72	15.4 - 10.9	0.23	0.23	0.23	0.8	0.05625Q	6/16/03	33.25 - 23.55
—	—	—	—	0.63	0.59	—	0.11	0.62	0.59	4.8	—	3/14/03	3.25 - 1.35
—	—	—	4.15	3.87	3.32	9.3 - 6.4	0.05	0.05	0.05	0.2	0.0125Q	5/19/03	48.85 - 27.42
—	—	—	1.18	0.18	d1.05	60.6 - 38.9	0.44	0.44	0.44	0.7	0.0125Q	2/26/03	38.44 - 26.50
—	—	—	p4.65	d2.75	9.44	13.4 - 8.1	0.60	0.57	0.50	1.2	0.15Q	3/17/03	62.30 - 37.50
—	—	—	pd1.36	0.68	1.59	—	—	—	—	—	—	—	30.25 - 9.75
—	—	—	p0.18	1.25	1.19	179.2 - 106.9	0.56	0.56	0.56	2.2	0.14Q	4/10/03	32.25 - 19.25
pd2.61	—	—	0.10	0.48	0.73	123.0 - 53.8	0.03	0.48	0.48	0.3	0.02Q	4/10/03	12.30 - 5.38
—	—	—	—	d0.86	d5.20	—	—	—	—	—	—	—	3.27 - 2.02
—	—	—	d0.21	d1.64	d0.13	—	—	0.24	0.56	—	0.05Q	8/31/01	12.55 - 5.35
—	—	—	p1.85	1.30	1.05	27.0 - 17.6	0.08	0.08	0.07	0.2	0.025Q	1/31/03	49.99 - 32.50
—	—	—	pd0.08	2.84	0.70	—	—	—	—	—	2-for-1	2/16/00	18.60 - 3.97
—	—	—	p0.91	d0.75	0.63	9.6 - 5.8	0.40	—	0.87	5.7	0.10Q	3/31/03	8.70 - 5.31
d0.14	—	—	p2.29	1.83	2.22	15.9 - 11.4	1.04	1.04	1.04	3.3	0.26Q	3/10/03	36.36 - 26.20
d0.11	—	—	d0.43	d1.42	0.41	—	—	—	0.70	—	0.10Q	9/25/00	7.33 - 2.85
—	—	—	d3.51	d4.18	0.51	—	—	0.04	0.08	—	0.00Q	5/31/02	7.50 - 0.55
—	—	—	—	—	—	—	0.12	0.11	0.06	0.7	0.1206U	7/12/02	20.90 - 11.60
—	—	—	p0.71	0.47	d0.23	22.7 - 13.5	—	—	—	—	2-for-1	6/21/95	16.10 - 9.60
—	—	—	4.73	4.44	3.69	6.3 - 3.0	—	—	—	—	—	—	29.87 - 14.33
—	—	—	p0.99	d1.24	3.99	—	—	—	—	—	0.225Q	3/17/03	17.59 - 10.33
0.07	d0.01	0.07	—	0.06	0.96	—	0.90	0.90	0.90	6.4	—	—	6.05 - 2.10
—	—	—	5.07	3.82	3.44	17.8 - 13.4	1.05	1.00	0.63	1.3	0.30Q	3/31/03	90.05 - 67.70
—	—	—	6.03	5.72	4.65	8.8 - 4.9	0.31	0.25	0.20	0.7	0.08Q	2/21/03	53.10 - 29.75
—	—	—	p4.30	3.38	2.76	9.1 - 5.3	0.10	0.10	0.10	0.3	0.025Q	4/24/03	39.29 - 23.00
—	—	—	p0.23	0.20	0.30	17.6 - 11.1	—	—	—	—	—	—	4.05 - 2.55
—	—	—	p0.29	d0.91	1.07	83.8 - 57.1	0.08	0.08	0.08	0.4	0.02Q	4/1/03	24.30 - 16.55
—	—	—	p1.62	1.76	1.14	19.5 - 15.6	2.22	2.14	2.06	7.8	0.57Q	3/7/03	31.67 - 25.25
—	—	—	2.43	2.32	3.10	14.7 - 11.0	2.49	2.45	2.35	8.0	0.63Q	1/17/03	35.73 - 26.64
0.67	d1.71	0.04	0.06	0.39	0.05	212.2 - 44.2	—	—	—	—	0.1895U	5/20/99	2.80 - 0.25
0.18	0.03	0.04	—	0.37	0.51	—	—	—	—	—	—	—	12.73 - 2.65
—	—	—	pd1.33	d0.27	0.51	—	—	—	—	—	0.00U	3/21/02	8.40 - 4.19
—	—	—	—	—	—	—	—	—	—	—	2-for-1	6/10/98	6.94 - 0.95
d0.25	d0.97	d0.53	—	d4.80	0.34	—	0.25	1.35	1.70	4.9	0.25Q	1/22/02	6.70 - 3.51
6.82	6.11	—	—	5.00	4.73	—	0.09	—	0.11	2.1	0.1034A	1/10/03	5.35 - 3.60
—	4.33	—	—	6.84	8.84	—	0.69	0.90	0.97	10.8	0.056M	5/30/03	7.53 - 5.27
12.08	11.69	—	—	4.98	6.99	—	0.78	1.08	1.38	14.9	0.05M	3/31/03	6.84 - 3.57
0.71	0.41	0.47	—	11.69	11.74	—	0.63	0.60	0.60	5.8	0.058M	5/30/03	11.25 - 10.23
—	—	—	—	0.71	1.50	—	—	—	—	—	3-for-2	7/23/93	37.00 - 21.12
—	—	—	p1.56	1.99	2.40	28.5 - 14.2	0.28	0.30	0.30	0.8	0.28A	12/9/02	44.39 - 22.10
—	—	—	p1.33	0.66	0.38	20.3 - 12.2	—	—	—	—	—	—	27.01 - 16.20
—	—	—	p1.46	1.62	2.22	29.7 - 17.1	0.20	0.20	0.20	0.6	0.10S	12/16/02	43.30 - 24.99
—	—	—	p1.64	1.49	1.51	21.7 - 16.8	1.87	1.75	1.63	5.9	0.495Q	4/11/03	35.66 - 27.50
—	—	—	pd0.55	d2.86	d0.88	—	—	—	—	—	—	—	6.64 - 2.50
—	—	—	p1.72	4.26	1.39	17.6 - 11.0	0.92	—	—	3.7	0.23Q	3/10/03	30.30 - 18.85
0.42	0.09	—	—	0.76	0.43	—	0.22	0.22	0.22	1.5	0.055Q	2/17/03	17.98 - 11.90

SYMBOL	COMPANY	NATURE OF BUSINESS	FISCAL YEAR-END	TOTAL REV. $MILL	NET INCOME $MILL	TOTAL ASSETS $MILL	NET STK EQUITY $MILL	NO. OF INST.	INST. HOLDINGS (SHARES)
HZO	MarineMax, Inc.	Specialty stores	9/30/02	540.7	17.1	301.1	145.2	38	6771641
TUG	Maritrans, Inc.	Freight transportation	12/31/01	123.4	10.2	200.4	88.1	22	3708251
MKL	Markel Corp (Holding Co) (Un	Insurance brokerage	12/31/02	p1770.2	p1770.2	—	—	136	7405774
MAR	Marriott International, Inc.	Motel/hotel lodging	1/3/03	8441.0	439.0	8296.0	3573.0	291	151108688
MMC	Marsh & McLennan Cos., Inc.	Insurance brokerage	12/31/02	—	—	—	—	657	405327874
MI	Marshall & Ilsley Corp. (Uni	Banking - Midwest	12/31/02	2650.0	480.3	32874.6	3036.7	277	97078735
MSO	Martha Stewart Living Omnimed	—	12/31/02	p295.0	p295.0	—	—	66	9421246
MLM	Martin Marietta Materials, In	—	12/31/02	p1692.4	p1680.9	—	—	181	44878831
MVL	Marvel Enterprises, Inc.	—	12/31/02	p299.0	p299.0	—	—	77	15637025
MAS	Masco Corp.	Furniture & fixtures	12/31/02	p9419.4	p9419.4	—	—	412	408167766
MYS	Masisa S.A. (Chile)	—	12/31/01	—	—	—	—	8	959412
MEE	Massey Energy Co.	Engineering & construction	12/31/02	p1629.7	p1653.0	—	—	167	67906938
MCI	Massmutual Corporate Inv. Inc	Investment company	12/31/02	18.2	13.5	195.1	171.0	20	378041
MPV	MassMutual Participation Invs	Investment company	12/31/02	10.3	8.3	108.3	83.6	11	786012
MTZ	MasTec Inc. (FL)	Water company	12/31/01	1222.6	d92.4	851.4	406.8	81	18131052
MSC	Material Sciences Corp.	Steel producer	2/28/02	250.5	d4.5	299.5	128.6	68	11217794
MC	Matsushita Electric Indl	Consumer electronics	3/31/02	—	—	—	—	78	112453413
MAT	Mattel Inc.	—	12/31/02	p4885.3	p2361.0	—	—	427	366633329
MVK	Maverick Tube Corp.	Steel producer	12/31/02	p439.0	p439.0	—	—	142	34102100
MMS	Maximus Inc.	Services	9/30/02	518.7	40.3	352.1	302.1	119	21124306
MXO	Maxtor Corp.	Comp. components & periphs.	12/28/02	p3779.5	p395.2	—	—	155	213218789
MAY	May Department Stores Co	Department stores	2/1/03	—	pd278.0	—	—	402	238757188
MYG	Maytag Co.	Appliances & utensils	12/31/02	4666.0	191.4	3104.2	42.1	273	50710253
MPY	Maytag Co.	Appliances & utensils	12/31/02	4666.0	191.4	3104.2	42.1	5	57425
MBI	MBIA, Inc.	Insurance brokerage	12/31/02	—	pd7.7	—	—	446	135212004
MBD	MBIA, Inc.	Insurance brokerage	12/31/02	—	pd7.7	—	—	1	5050
MBE	MBIA, Inc.	Insurance brokerage	12/31/02	—	pd7.7	—	—	3	20200
KRB	MBNA Corp.	Banking - Mid-Atlantic	12/31/02	—	—	—	—	647	929711724
MNI	McClatchy Co. (The)	Newspapers	12/29/02	p1081.9	p1081.9	—	—	131	16369538
MKC V	McCormick & Co., Inc.	Food processing	11/30/02	2320.0	179.8	1930.8	592.3	9	158174
MKC	McCormick & Co., Inc.	Food processing	11/30/02	2320.0	179.8	1930.8	592.3	262	91760297
MDR	McDermott International, Inc	Machinery & equipment	12/31/01	1969.8	d20.9	2103.8	770.1	144	39239067
MCD	McDonald's Corp	Restaurants	12/31/02	15405.7	992.1	23970.5	10280.9	755	829779481
MHP	McGraw-Hill Cos., Inc.	Publishing	12/31/02	4787.7	576.8	5032.2	2165.8	499	173842127
MCK	McKesson Corp. (New)	'Wholesaler, distributor'	3/31/02	50006.0	418.6	13324.0	3940.1	379	228487148
MMR	McMoRan Exploration Co. (Uni	Oil	12/31/02	p43.8	p43.8	—	—	42	5718953
MDU	MDU Resources Group, Inc.	Natural gas distributor	12/31/02	p2031.5	p2014.9	—	—	179	24399491
MIG	Meadowbrook Insurance Group	Insurance brokerage	12/31/01	p197.8	p197.4	—	—	29	14619330
MWV	MeadWestvaco Corp. (United S	Paper	12/31/02	7242.0	d3.0	12921.0	4831.0	294	155365398
MDA	Media Arts Group Inc.	Printing & engraving	12/31/01	80.9	d12.8	85.5	64.8	15	3330850
MEG	Media General, Inc.	Telecommunications	12/29/02	p836.8	p909.7	—	—	157	15788472
MRN	Medical Staffing Network Hol	Services	12/29/02	p483.5	p109.1	—	—	63	10718126
MRX	Medicis Pharmaceutical Corp.	Drugs	6/30/02	212.8	50.0	876.3	429.1	206	30907310
MDT	Medtronic, Inc. (United Stat	Medical & dental equipment	4/26/02	6410.8	984.0	10904.5	6431.1	970	898354327
MEL	Mellon Financial Corp.	Banking - Mid-Atlantic	12/31/02	p1056.0	—	—	—	522	331831457
WFR	MEMC Electronic Materials, I	Comp. components & periphs.	12/31/02	p687.2	pd5.1	—	—	66	13686805
MW	Men's Wearhouse, Inc (The)	—	2/1/03	p1295.0	p1295.0	—	—	136	30604053
MRK	Merck & Co., Inc	Drugs	12/31/02	—	—	—	—	1297	1501248661
MCY	Mercury General Corp.	Property & casualty insurance	12/31/02	p113.1	p113.1	—	—	131	24043466
MDP	Meredith Corp.	Publishing	6/30/02	987.8	91.4	1460.3	507.7	216	38090234
TMR	Meridian Resource Corp. (The)	Natural gas	12/31/01	178.1	23.0	507.7	188.2	50	9643881
MHX	Meristar Hospitality Corp (U	Real estate investment trust	12/31/01	1084.9	d37.9	3009.9	1022.6	119	39810598
MTH	Meritage Corp (United States	Real estate	12/31/02	p1112.0	p1112.0	—	—	88	8419068
MER	Merrill Lynch & Co Inc	Securities brokerage	12/27/02	—	p25.0	—	—	629	653589876
JEM	Merrill Lynch & Co Inc	Securities brokerage	12/27/02	—	p25.0	—	—	1	10000
IEM	Merrill Lynch & Co Inc	Securities brokerage	12/27/02	—	p25.0	—	—	—	—
MIJ	Merrill Lynch & Co Inc	Securities brokerage	12/27/02	—	p25.0	—	—	—	—
MTR	Mesa Royalty Trust	Oil	12/31/01	10.5	10.6	12.0	10.9	10	1111120
MSB	Mesabi Trust	—	1/31/02	4.0	3.6	2.2	1.1	16	1174523
MCC	Mestek Inc	—	12/31/01	394.1	d2.2	259.5	169.8	30	1597599
MPR	Met-Pro Corp.	—	1/31/03	p69.6	p69.6	—	—	26	2281155
MET	Metlife Inc	Insurance brokerage	12/31/02	—	—	—	—	357	286019429
MIU	Metlife Inc	Insurance brokerage	12/31/02	—	—	—	—	12	5032784
MXT	Metris Cos., Inc.	—	12/31/02	—	pd33.9	—	—	129	54438182
MGM	Metro-Goldwyn-Mayer Inc	Motion pictures/theaters	12/31/02	1654.1	d142.2	4269.0	2514.5	99	50614580
MGS	MetroGas S.A. (Argentina)	Natural gas	12/31/01	—	—	—	—	1	50200
MX	Metso Oy (Finland)	—	12/31/01	—	—	—	—	8	982234
MTD	Mettler-Toledo International	Meas. & control instruments	12/31/02	p1213.7	p1216.8	—	—	136	38516975
MXE	Mexico Equity & Income Fd In	Investment company	7/31/02	1.0	d0.1	21.8	21.6	4	4916
MXF	Mexico Fund Inc.	Investment company	10/31/02	14.6	5.5	310.4	308.8	28	19003338
MFA	MFA Mortgage Investments Inc	Real estate investment trust	12/31/02	128.0	56.1	3603.9	371.2	73	23867215
MCR	MFS Charter Income Trust	Investment company	11/30/02	36.1	31.5	628.9	546.3	39	3451935
MGF	MFS Government Mkts Income Tr	Investment company	11/30/02	25.3	21.5	517.5	433.6	37	11218797
MIN	MFS Intermediate Income Trust	Investment company	10/31/02	56.1	47.7	1006.5	958.7	53	7326485
MMT	MFS Multimarket Income Trust	Investment company	10/31/02	39.8	34.7	551.3	528.9	39	5746592
MFM	MFS Municipal Income Trust	Investment company	10/31/02	30.2	25.4	444.8	442.0	21	446285
MFV	MFS Special Value Trust	Investment	10/31/02	5.7	4.9	55.1	49.6	10	108817
MTG	MGIC Investment Corp.	Finance	12/31/02	p1565.8	p629.2	—	—	353	107702702
MGG	MGM Mirage	Motel/hotel lodging	12/31/02	p4031.3	p4031.3	—	—	202	74500742
MIK	Michaels Stores, Inc.	Specialty stores	2/2/02	2530.7	94.3	1414.6	824.6	255	59234963
MFI	MicroFinancial, Inc.	Finance	12/31/01	154.1	16.3	361.7	110.6	26	4561539
MU	Micron Technology, Inc.	Electronic components	8/29/02	2589.0	d907.0	7555.4	6306.4	360	438257998
MME	Mid Atlantic Med. Svcs. Inc.	Services	12/31/02	p2328.0	p2328.0	—	—	218	31306669
MAA	Mid-America Apartment Cmmnty	Real estate investment trust	12/31/02	—	pd1.3	—	—	97	5688614
MRR	Mid-Atlantic Realty Trust	Real estate investment trust	12/31/01	62.5	14.4	389.6	104.6	72	7763710
MDS	Midas, Inc.	—	12/31/01	p328.0	p325.1	—	—	77	9035618
MWY	Midway Games Inc. (United Sta	—	12/31/02	p191.9	p191.9	—	—	104	24161389
MEH	Midwest Express Holdings Inc	—	12/31/02	p427.0	p427.0	—	—	77	9579097
MHU	MIIX Group, Inc. (The)	Insurance	12/31/02	233.3	d152.4	1895.9	131.5	13	3915486
MZ	Milacron, Inc.	Machine tools	12/31/02	p693.2	p479.9	—	—	96	23867432
MCH	Millennium Chemicals Inc.	Chemicals	12/31/01	p1554.0	p1311.0	—	—	115	53544038
MLR	Miller Industries Inc. (TN) (	—	12/31/01	304.0	d21.6	253.0	84.8	16	2308897
MIL	Millipore Corp	Medical & dental equipment	12/31/02	p704.3	p707.2	—	—	227	48530275
MLS	Mills Corp	Real estate	12/31/02	—	p62.5	—	—	133	16571380
MTX	Minerals Technologies, Inc.	Metal products	12/31/02	p752.7	p752.7	—	—	141	20691812
MIR	Mirant Corp	Electric power	12/31/01	31502.0	563.0	22754.0	5498.0	278	169594651

T30

| EARNINGS PER SHARE | | | | | | P/E RATIO | DIVIDENDS PER SHARE | | | AV. YLD. | DIV. DECLARED | | PRICE RANGE |
| QUARTERLY | | | ANNUAL | | | | | | | | | | |
1st	2nd	3rd	2002	2001	2000		2002	2001	2000	%	AMOUNT	PAYABLE	2002
d0.03	—	—	1.10	1.01	1.41	14.0 - 6.5	—	—	—	—	—	—	15.40 - 7.15
0.32	0.32	0.20	—	0.96	0.45	—	0.42	0.40	0.40	3.2	0.11Q	3/12/03	15.70 - 10.65
—	—	—	p7.65	d14.73	d3.99	29.0 - 22.4	—	—	—	—	—	—	222.03 - 171.10
—	—	—	1.74	0.92	1.89	26.7 - 15.1	0.27	0.25	0.23	0.7	0.07Q	4/30/03	46.45 - 26.25
—	—	—	p2.45	1.70	2.05	23.4 - 14.1	1.09	1.03	0.95	2.4	0.28Q	5/15/03	57.30 - 34.61
—	—	—	2.16	1.54	1.46	14.9 - 10.7	0.55	0.57	0.52	2.0	0.16Q	3/14/03	32.12 - 23.11
—	—	—	p0.15	0.45	0.43	139.5 - 35.1	—	—	—	—	—	—	20.93 - 5.26
—	—	—	p1.77	2.19	2.39	27.9 - 15.4	0.58	0.56	0.54	1.5	0.15Q	3/31/03	49.33 - 27.30
—	—	—	pd1.18	d1.27	d3.13	—	—	—	—	—	—	—	9.50 - 3.46
—	—	—	p1.15	0.42	1.31	25.6 - 15.0	0.55	0.53	0.49	2.3	0.14Q	2/10/03	29.43 - 17.25
—	—	—	—	—	—	—	0.23	0.29	0.22	2.6	0.2333U	5/28/02	13.08 - 4.90
—	—	—	pd0.40	d0.01	1.07	—	0.16	0.16	1.00	1.2	0.04Q	4/15/03	22.41 - 4.55
—	—	—	19.40	20.07	20.74	—	1.73	2.78	2.83	8.0	0.36Q	1/14/03	25.00 - 18.30
—	—	—	8.78	9.12	9.75	—	0.90	1.51	1.37	9.1	0.20Q	1/14/03	10.70 - 9.00
0.03	0.04	0.05	—	d1.93	1.35	—	—	—	—	—	3-for-2	6/19/00	9.13 - 2.03
0.15	0.10	0.02	—	d0.32	d0.05	—	—	—	—	—	3-for-2	7/28/94	15.80 - 9.40
—	—	—	—	—	—	—	0.07	0.08	0.52	0.6	0.04527U	3/26/03	14.64 - 9.32
—	—	—	p0.52	0.71	0.40	43.0 - 28.9	0.05	0.05	0.36	0.3	0.05A	12/12/02	22.36 - 15.05
—	—	—	p0.09	1.15	0.48	212.8 - 91.2	—	—	—	—	2-for-1	8/21/97	19.15 - 8.21
0.47	—	—	1.73	1.78	1.42	24.5 - 10.5	—	—	—	—	—	—	42.35 - 18.17
—	—	—	p1.09	d3.12	0.27	7.2 - 1.6	—	—	—	—	—	—	7.90 - 1.77
—	—	—	p1.76	2.21	2.62	22.1 - 11.4	0.95	0.94	0.93	3.2	0.24Q	3/15/03	38.86 - 20.10
—	—	—	2.44	2.13	2.44	19.6 - 7.7	0.72	0.72	0.72	2.2	0.18Q	3/14/03	47.94 - 18.84
—	—	—	2.44	2.13	2.44	11.1 - 10.1	1.97	0.45	—	7.6	—	2/3/03	27.00 - 24.75
—	—	—	p3.92	3.82	3.55	15.3 - 8.9	0.66	0.59	0.55	1.4	—	—	60.11 - 34.93
—	—	—	p3.92	3.82	3.55	6.8 - 6.3	1.74	1.74	1.74	6.8	0.4344Q	2/3/03	26.78 - 24.70
—	—	—	p3.92	3.82	3.55	7.3 - 6.7	2.00	2.07	—	7.3	0.50Q	3/17/03	28.43 - 26.20
—	—	—	p1.34	1.28	1.02	19.6 - 9.7	0.26	0.23	0.21	1.3	0.08Q	4/1/03	26.30 - 12.95
—	—	—	p2.84	1.27	1.97	23.1 - 16.2	0.40	0.40	0.40	0.7	0.11Q	4/1/03	65.55 - 45.95
—	—	—	1.26	1.04	0.99	21.4 - 15.9	0.42	0.40	0.38	1.8	0.11Q	1/22/03	27.00 - 20.00
—	—	—	1.26	1.04	0.99	21.6 - 16.4	0.42	0.40	0.38	1.8	0.11Q	1/22/03	27.25 - 20.70
d0.03	d3.81	d5.88	—	d0.34	d0.37	—	—	—	0.15	—	0.05Q	7/1/00	17.29 - 2.35
—	—	—	0.77	1.25	1.46	39.8 - 19.7	0.23	0.23	0.21	1.0	0.235A	12/2/02	30.68 - 15.17
0.39	0.43	0.46	2.96	1.92	2.41	23.5 - 17.1	1.02	0.98	0.94	1.7	0.27Q	3/12/03	69.70 - 50.71
—	—	—	p0.92	d9.33	d8.88	6.9 - 2.8	0.24	0.24	0.24	0.7	0.06Q	4/1/03	42.09 - 24.99
—	—	—	—	—	—	—	—	—	—	—	—	—	6.35 - 2.54
—	—	—	p2.07	2.29	1.80	16.2 - 8.7	0.93	0.89	0.85	3.6	0.24Q	4/1/03	33.45 - 18.00
—	—	—	p0.08	d0.76	d2.05	51.7 - 19.4	—	0.12	0.12	—	0.03Q	10/5/01	4.14 - 1.55
d0.18	d0.05	0.03	d0.01	d0.21	0.87	—	0.92	—	—	3.5	0.23Q	3/3/03	36.50 - 15.57
—	—	—	p0.62	d0.97	0.67	—	—	—	—	—	—	—	4.50 - 1.57
—	—	—	p0.62	0.06	0.13	48.0 - 14.9	0.72	0.68	0.64	1.2	0.19Q	3/15/03	69.49 - 46.55
0.42	0.55	—	1.59	1.28	1.41	40.6 - 21.3	—	—	—	—	—	—	29.75 - 9.25
0.31	0.25	0.35	—	0.80	0.85	—	0.24	0.22	0.18	0.6	0.0625Q	4/25/03	64.59 - 33.85
—	—	—	p1.55	2.76	2.03	26.3 - 13.2	0.49	0.82	0.86	1.6	0.13Q	2/14/03	50.69 - 32.50
—	—	—	pd0.17	d0.48	d0.62	—	—	—	—	—	—	—	40.80 - 20.42
—	—	—	p1.04	1.04	2.00	27.6 - 9.2	—	—	—	—	50%	6/19/98	11.50 - 2.25
—	—	—	p3.14	3.14	2.90	20.5 - 12.3	1.41	1.37	1.21	2.7	0.36Q	4/1/03	28.72 - 9.61
—	—	—	—	—	—	—	—	—	—	—	—	—	64.50 - 38.50
0.32	0.38	—	p1.21	1.94	2.02	42.3 - 30.8	1.20	1.06	0.96	2.7	0.33Q	3/27/03	51.15 - 37.25
d0.03	0.06	d1.03	1.79	1.39	1.35	26.7 - 18.7	0.36	0.34	0.32	0.9	0.095Q	3/14/03	47.75 - 33.42
d0.22	0.06	d0.51	—	0.43	1.06	—	—	—	—	—	0.32U	3/5/86	4.99 - 0.50
—	—	—	—	d0.91	2.14	—	0.04	2.02	2.02	0.3	0.01Q	10/31/02	18.50 - 6.25
—	—	—	p5.31	4.32	3.13	8.9 - 4.4	—	—	—	—	100%	4/26/02	47.10 - 23.28
—	—	—	p2.69	0.57	4.11	22.1 - 10.5	0.64	0.64	0.60	1.5	0.16Q	2/28/03	59.32 - 28.21
—	—	—	p2.69	0.57	4.11	3.7 - 3.6	—	—	—	—	—	—	10.05 - 9.75
—	—	—	p2.69	0.57	4.11	4.3 - 3.7	—	—	—	—	—	—	11.50 - 10.07
—	—	—	p2.69	0.57	4.11	3.9 - 3.1	—	—	—	—	—	—	10.50 - 8.30
0.48	0.58	0.80	—	5.67	4.31	—	2.49	6.48	3.78	6.4	—	4/30/03	42.99 - 34.20
0.01	0.05	0.14	—	0.28	0.41	—	0.25	0.30	0.46	6.5	0.19Q	2/20/03	4.74 - 2.90
0.18	d0.50	0.22	—	d0.25	1.87	—	—	—	—	—	0.15Q	9/4/77	23.55 - 17.05
—	—	—	p0.95	1.01	1.26	16.9 - 13.1	0.35	0.34	0.32	2.4	0.09Q	3/10/03	16.02 - 12.45
—	—	—	p2.20	0.62	1.49	15.8 - 9.4	0.21	0.20	0.20	0.8	0.21A	12/13/02	34.85 - 20.60
—	—	—	p2.20	0.62	1.49	48.5 - 29.4	4.00	4.00	2.42	4.7	1.00Q	2/18/03	106.66 - 64.70
—	—	—	pd1.20	2.62	2.15	—	0.04	0.04	0.03	0.3	0.01Q	12/31/02	27.90 - 1.43
—	—	—	d0.57	d0.24	0.24	—	—	—	—	—	—	—	23.25 - 9.00
—	—	—	—	—	—	—	—	0.80	0.80	—	0.60U	12/3/01	7.10 - 0.75
—	—	—	—	—	—	—	0.45	0.46	0.32	4.1	0.5565U	5/9/03	14.26 - 7.81
—	—	—	p2.21	1.68	1.66	23.5 - 11.2	—	—	—	—	—	—	51.85 - 24.85
—	—	—	8.74	10.19	11.36	—	—	—	0.74	—	0.62A	12/1/00	11.14 - 6.91
—	—	—	15.46	18.98	—	—	2.79	0.17	0.18	17.5	0.453Q	1/28/03	20.14 - 11.76
—	—	—	1.35	0.25	0.89	7.2 - 5.3	1.20	0.72	0.58	14.3	0.28Q	4/30/03	9.73 - 7.10
—	—	—	9.09	9.17	9.20	—	0.58	0.68	0.78	6.9	0.044M	3/31/03	8.70 - 7.97
—	—	—	7.49	7.32	7.01	—	0.42	0.42	0.49	6.3	0.031M	3/31/03	7.12 - 6.39
—	—	—	7.57	7.54	7.06	—	0.44	0.47	0.53	6.3	0.034M	3/31/03	7.48 - 6.60
—	—	—	6.32	6.60	6.69	—	0.42	0.52	0.59	7.1	0.033M	3/31/03	6.28 - 5.44
—	—	—	7.61	7.93	7.79	—	0.53	0.53	0.53	7.0	0.044M	3/31/03	8.14 - 6.95
—	—	—	7.50	8.63	11.67	—	0.83	1.65	1.65	9.4	0.06579M	3/31/03	11.00 - 6.65
—	—	—	p6.04	5.93	5.05	12.3 - 5.6	0.10	0.10	0.10	0.2	0.025Q	3/31/03	74.40 - 33.60
—	—	—	p1.83	1.06	1.13	23.0 - 15.2	—	—	0.10	—	2-for-1	2/25/00	42.03 - 27.80
0.29	0.32	0.46	—	1.41	1.18	—	—	—	—	—	100%	11/26/01	49.33 - 28.50
0.25	0.15	d1.53	—	0.83	1.63	—	0.20	0.19	0.17	3.3	0.05Q	11/15/02	11.00 - 0.99
d0.52	—	—	d1.51	d0.88	2.56	—	—	—	—	—	100%	5/1/00	39.50 - 9.50
—	—	—	p2.34	1.41	1.00	18.5 - 9.5	—	—	—	—	100%	8/5/94	43.20 - 22.30
—	—	—	pd0.11	0.78	0.79	—	2.34	2.34	2.32	9.5	0.585Q	1/31/03	27.42 - 21.99
0.24	0.26	0.30	—	0.97	0.92	—	1.19	1.14	1.09	7.7	0.31Q	3/14/03	18.15 - 13.00
0.12	0.27	0.07	—	p0.85	—	0.10	—	0.10	0.08	—	0.08A	4/1/01	15.99 - 4.30
—	—	—	pd1.61	d0.27	d1.84	—	—	—	—	—	—	—	15.25 - 3.72
—	—	—	pd0.72	d1.08	0.37	—	—	—	—	—	50%	5/27/98	20.53 - 3.90
d3.20	d0.45	0.07	—	d11.27	d2.58	—	0.05	0.20	0.20	0.7	0.05Q	1/18/02	13.50 - 0.60
—	—	—	p1.08	1.08	2.06	—	0.04	0.37	0.48	0.4	0.01Q	3/12/03	16.60 - 3.10
—	—	—	pd4.44	d0.68	1.89	—	0.54	0.59	0.60	4.6	0.135Q	3/31/03	15.80 - 7.79
d0.03	0.03	d0.08	—	d2.31	d0.70	—	—	—	—	—	—	—	4.20 - 2.30
—	—	—	p1.67	1.32	2.53	36.5 - 16.3	0.11	0.44	0.44	0.2	0.00Q	2/27/02	60.95 - 27.25
—	—	—	p1.66	1.24	1.56	18.7 - 14.1	2.17	2.11	2.05	8.0	0.565Q	5/1/03	31.05 - 23.40
—	—	—	p2.61	2.48	2.58	21.0 - 12.3	0.10	0.10	0.10	0.2	0.025Q	3/14/03	54.90 - 32.00
d0.11	d0.55	—	—	1.62	1.15	—	—	—	—	—	—	—	16.49 - 1.06

SYMBOL	COMPANY	NATURE OF BUSINESS	FISCAL YEAR-END	TOTAL REV. $MILL	NET INCOME $MILL	TOTAL ASSETS $MILL	NET STK EQUITY $MILL	NO. OF INST.	INST. HOLDINGS (SHARES)
MTF	Mitsubishi Tokyo Financial Gr	—	3/31/02	—	—	—	—	70	107781222
NUT	ML Macadamia Orchards, L.P.	Food -grain & agriculture	12/31/01	16.9	1.0	65.3	—	7	339669
OOM	mmO2 Plc (United Kingdom)	Telecommunications	3/31/02	—	—	—	—	40	9698921
MHK	Mohawk Industries, Inc. (Uni	Floor coverings	12/31/02	4522.3	284.5	3596.7	1982.9	245	56101768
MNC	Monaco Coach Corp. (United St		12/28/02	p1222.7	p1222.7	—	—	127	23148341
MON	Monsanto Co. (New)		12/31/02	4673.0	129.0	8890.0	5180.0	376	215593613
MTS	Montgomery Str Incme Secs Inc	Investment company	12/31/01	14.9	13.5	240.8	195.5	14	249980
MRH	Montpelier Re Holdings Ltd.	Property & casualty insurance	12/31/01	0.9	d61.6	1021.8	860.7	44	19773692
MNY	MONY Group, Inc.	Life Insurance	12/31/02	p2094.5	p2050.7	—	—	134	16774037
MCO	Moody's Corp.	Services	12/31/02	p1023.3	p1023.3	—	—	392	132705755
MOG A	Moog, Inc.		9/28/02	719.0	37.6	885.5	300.0	106	10106160
MOG B	Moog, Inc.		9/28/02	719.0	37.6	885.5	300.0	4	771662
MWD	Morgan Stanley	Securities brokerage	11/30/02	32415.0	2988.0	529499.0	21885.0	710	716266444
BRX	Morgan Stanley	Securities brokerage	11/30/02	32415.0	2988.0	529499.0	21885.0	—	—
BDJ	Morgan Stanley	Securities brokerage	11/30/02	32415.0	2988.0	529499.0	21885.0	—	—
BGS	Morgan Stanley	Securities brokerage	11/30/02	32415.0	2988.0	529499.0	21885.0	—	—
RBT	Morgan Stanley	Securities brokerage	11/30/02	32415.0	2988.0	529499.0	21885.0	—	—
MWN	Morgan Stanley	Securities brokerage	11/30/02	32415.0	2988.0	529499.0	21885.0	2	1200
RNE	Morgan Stanley Eastern Europe	Investment company	12/31/01	0.7	d0.8	73.2	70.5	11	1443237
MSD	Morgan Stanley Emerg Mkt Dbt	Investment company	12/31/01	20.6	17.7	208.6	181.9	24	2376681
MSF	Morgan Stanley Emerg Mkt Fd	Investment company	12/31/01	4.1	0.4	203.4	201.1	28	7617641
IIM	Morgan Stanley Fds - Ins Mun	Investment	10/31/02	29.8	27.0	571.6	551.5	22	191892
ICB	Morgan Stanley Fds Incm Secs	Investment company	9/30/02	13.1	11.9	183.2	182.5	15	180424
ICS	Morgan Stanley Fds Ins CA Mu	Investment company	10/31/02	3.2	2.8	62.5	60.9	1	287
IMT	Morgan Stanley Fds Ins Muni	Investment	10/31/02	24.4	22.0	451.0	320.3	15	345863
IMB	Morgan Stanley Fds Ins Muni	Investment	10/31/02	5.5	4.8	103.9	73.7	3	2246
OIA	Morgan Stanley Fds Muni Incm	Investment company	5/31/02	13.1	11.6	165.3	165.0	19	389372
OIC	Morgan Stanley Fds Muni Incm	Investment company	3/31/02	6.3	5.5	88.5	88.3	10	101890
PIA	Morgan Stanley Fds Muni Prem	Investment company	5/31/02	17.2	14.6	307.2	306.8	21	J026102
IQN	Morgan Stanley Fds NY Qual	Investment company	10/31/02	4.9	4.3	93.5	69.4	3	23501
IQI	Morgan Stanley Fds Qual Muni	Investment company	10/31/02	35.9	32.4	664.1	658.6	17	178061
IQT	Morgan Stanley Fds Qual Muni	Investment	10/31/02	19.9	18.0	360.0	254.6	12	82425
IQM	Morgan Stanley Fds Qual Muni	Investment	10/31/02	17.8	16.0	347.8	245.8	14	321552
IIC	Morgan Stanley Fds-CA Ins Mu	Investment	10/31/02	13.6	12.3	259.7	248.6	4	42537
IQC	Morgan Stanley Fds-CA Qual M	Investment	10/31/02	10.6	9.5	208.5	149.2	4	40826
GVT	Morgan Stanley Fds-Govt Incm	Investment company	9/30/02	12.5	9.9	410.4	372.8	21	8848827
OIB	Morgan Stanley Fds-Muni Incm	Investment company	2/28/02	10.7	9.3	154.3	154.1	11	62656
MGB	Morgan Stanley Global Opportu	Investment company	12/31/01	5.2	4.0	41.5	30.6	5	110256
MSY	Morgan Stanley High Yield	Investment company	12/31/01	17.3	13.3	128.6	84.6	18	302882
IIF	Morgan Stanley India Investme	Investment company	12/31/01	6.0	1.5	209.7	205.0	28	4308357
MOT	Motorola, Inc.	Communications electronics	12/31/02	—	—	—	—	765	1415839624
MEU	Motorola, Inc.	Communications electronics	12/31/02	—	—	—	—	—	—
MOV	Movado Group, Inc.	Jewelry	1/31/02	299.7	17.1	290.7	172.5	52	7765809
MPS	MPS Group, Inc.	Services	12/31/02	p1155.0	p1125.9	—	—	143	86970775
APF	MS Asia-Pac Fd Inc (New)	Investment company	12/31/01	7.3	0.9	398.4	397.3	42	11031770
MSM	MSC Industrial Direct Co. Inc	Machinery & equipment	8/31/02	794.0	36.4	562.9	474.7	93	32690643
MNS	MSC-Software Corp.	Comp. components & periphs.	12/31/02	p344.2	p294.2	—	—	71	20241729
MLI	Mueller Industries, Inc.	Metal products	12/28/02	p953.0	p953.0	—	—	136	24963309
MUA	MuniAssets Fund, Inc.	Investment company	5/31/02	14.2	12.5	257.6	255.1	12	84557
MAF	Municipal Advantage Fund Inc.	Investment company	10/31/02	8.7	7.2	163.4	107.7	15	192230
MHF	Municipal High Income Fund,	Investment company	10/31/02	13.4	12.0	170.8	170.5	16	226312
MMA	Municipal Mortgage & Equity	Financial services	12/31/02	p133.6	p133.6	—	—	38	806168
MPT	Municipal Partners Fd II Inc	Investment company	6/30/02	7.1	6.0	136.6	86.1	6	14397
MNP	Municipal Partners Fund, Inc.	Investment company	12/31/02	6.9	5.7	131.2	88.4	8	72979
MEN	Munienhanced Fund, Inc.	Investment company	1/31/02	26.9	23.5	486.2	485.6	16	224241
MUC	MuniHoldings CA Insured Fund,	Investment company	6/30/01	46.8	40.6	981.2	977.9	14	437402
MFL	Muniholdings FL Insured Fd	Investment company	8/31/02	49.6	43.2	944.0	580.0	13	489068
MUH	Muniholdings Fund II, Inc.	Investment company	7/31/02	14.0	12.2	242.1	149.6	9	123077
MUE	Muniholdings Insured Fund II	Investment company	9/30/01	26.9	23.6	516.5	516.0	8	103990
MUS	Muniholdings Insured Fund, In	Investment company	4/30/02	16.0	13.7	312.9	311.3	4	33890
MHN	Muniholdings New York Ins Fd	Investment company	8/31/02	38.4	32.8	796.0	482.2	18	674394
MUJ	Muniholdings NJ Insd Fd Inc	Investment company	7/31/02	26.1	22.4	517.5	313.5	10	232482
MVT	Munivest Fund II, Inc.	Investment company	10/31/02	24.8	21.8	420.5	281.8	16	118850
MCA	MuniYield CA Insd Fd II Inc	Investment company	10/31/01	21.3	18.4	415.7	413.6	16	326139
MYC	MuniYield California Fund In	Investment company	10/31/02	25.9	22.7	464.4	322.3	13	168007
MYF	MuniYield Florida Fund	Investment company	10/31/02	16.0	13.9	299.1	202.9	11	271658
MFT	MuniYield Florida Insured Fd	Investment company	10/31/02	10.1	8.7	189.1	126.9	5	86753
MYD	MuniYield Fund, Inc.	Investment company	10/31/02	52.8	46.9	903.6	590.1	22	571726
MYI	MuniYield Insured Fund, Inc.	Investment company	10/31/02	75.5	66.5	1443.1	1381.0	24	691993
MIY	MuniYield Michigan Insured Fd	Investment company	10/31/02	23.0	20.1	429.9	285.8	11	316045
MYM	MuniYield Michigan Insured Fu	Investment company	10/31/02	11.4	9.8	271.6	179.6	10	213650
MYJ	MuniYield New Jersey Insd Inc	Investment company	11/30/02	17.1	14.9	312.4	210.7	8	142109
MJI	MuniYield New Jersey Insd Fd	Investment company	10/31/02	10.6	9.2	188.5	132.1	4	100341
MYN	MuniYield New York Insured Fd	Investment company	10/31/02	42.7	37.1	915.9	843.9	20	464372
MPA	MuniYield PA Insd Fd	Investment company	10/31/02	14.5	12.6	278.3	175.7	13	310078
MQT	MuniYield Quality Fund II	Investment company	10/31/02	24.2	21.1	450.5	296.8	19	623176
MQY	MuniYield Quality Fund, Inc.	Investment company	10/31/02	36.6	32.2	667.1	462.2	19	292606
MUR	Murphy Oil Corp.	Oil	12/31/02	p3923.3	p3923.3	—	—	239	57908528
MVC	MVC Capital	Investment company	10/31/02	3.7	d3.1	196.5	195.4	—	—
MYE	Myers Industries Inc.		12/31/02	p608.0	p608.0	—	—	97	15548825
MYK	Mykrolis Corp.		12/31/01	215.3	d67.6	289.5	243.5	128	36820031
MYL	Mylan Laboratories, Inc. (Un	Drugs	3/31/02	1104.0	260.3	1616.7	1402.2	346	119584896
NC	Nacco Industries Inc.	Conglomerate	12/31/02	p2548.1	p2540.9	—	—	64	3374775
NTE	Nam Tai Electronics, Inc.	Consumer electronics	12/31/01	—	—	—	—	39	3435729
NSH	Nashua Corp. (MA)	Office equipment & supplies	12/31/02	p283.2	p283.2	—	—	20	3622567
NTG	Natco Group Inc	Oil service & equipment	12/31/02	p289.5	p70.2	—	—	45	8200903
NAB	National Australia Bank Ltd.	—	9/30/02	16234.0	3373.0	377387.0	23251.0	60	4524389
NAU	National Australia Bank Ltd.	—	9/30/02	16234.0	3373.0	377387.0	23251.0	18	4240795
NCC	National City Corp	Banking - Midwest	12/31/02	8727.9	1593.6	118258.4	8308.0	472	323596549
NCF	National Commerce Financial C	Banking - South	12/31/02	1521.5	323.6	21472.1	2682.4	242	85703803
NFG	National Fuel Gas Co. (NJ)	Natural gas distributor	9/30/02	1464.5	117.7	3401.3	1006.9	188	36453068
NGG	National Grid Transco Plc	Electric power	3/31/02	—	—	—	—	41	3689543
NHI	National Health Investors Inc	Real estate investment trust	12/31/01	p171.8	p171.8	—	—	72	7530190
NPK	National Presto Inds., Inc.	Appliances & utensils	12/31/02	p133.7	p133.7	—	—	66	3178081
NAP	National Processing Inc.	Services	12/31/02	455.4	51.1	550.5	456.4	61	6675070
NVH	National R.V. Holdings, Inc.		12/31/01	280.0	d11.5	169.8	114.4	30	7917451

T32

EARNINGS PER SHARE — QUARTERLY 1st	2nd	3rd	ANNUAL 2002	2001	2000	P/E RATIO	DIVIDENDS PER SHARE 2002	2001	2000	AV. YLD. %	DIV. DECLARED AMOUNT	PAYABLE	PRICE RANGE 2002
—	—	—	—	—	—	—	0.04	—	—	0.6	0.0287U	3/26/03	8.42 - 5.08
d0.02	d0.03	0.01	—	0.13	d0.05	—	0.20	0.24	0.47	5.6	0.05Q	5/15/03	3.95 - 3.15
—	—	—	—	—	—	—	—	—	—	—	—	—	13.22 - 5.25
—	—	—	4.39	3.55	3.00	16.1 - 9.2	—	—	—	—	3-for-2	12/4/97	70.60 - 40.25
—	—	—	p1.51	0.85	1.47	20.3 - 9.5	—	—	—	—	50%	9/7/01	30.70 - 14.30
—	—	—	d0.49	1.13	0.68	—	0.48	0.45	—	2.0	0.12Q	5/1/03	33.99 - 13.20
—	19.04	—	—	19.00	18.83	—	1.33	1.34	1.35	7.1	0.34Q	12/31/02	19.80 - 17.90
—	—	—	d1.18	—	—	—	—	—	—	—	—	—	29.40 - 21.40
—	—	—	pd0.49	d1.25	5.49	—	0.45	0.45	0.45	1.4	0.45A	12/23/02	41.99 - 21.79
—	—	—	p1.83	1.32	0.97	28.6 - 19.6	0.18	0.18	0.60	0.4	0.045Q	3/10/03	52.40 - 35.80
0.64	—	—	2.50	2.11	1.90	17.2 - 8.5	—	—	—	—	50%	9/21/01	42.88 - 21.34
0.64	—	—	2.50	2.11	1.90	16.4 - 10.7	—	—	—	—	50%	9/21/01	41.00 - 26.75
—	—	—	2.69	3.19	4.73	22.3 - 10.7	0.92	0.92	0.80	2.1	0.23Q	1/31/03	60.02 - 28.80
—	—	—	2.69	3.19	4.73	4.1 - 3.2	—	—	—	—	—	—	10.97 - 8.70
—	—	—	2.69	3.19	4.73	7.2 - 0.0	—	—	—	—	—	—	19.40 - 0.01
—	—	—	2.69	3.19	4.73	4.2 - 3.6	—	—	—	—	—	—	11.25 - 9.65
—	—	—	2.69	3.19	4.73	3.8 - 3.0	—	—	—	—	—	—	10.30 - 8.20
—	—	—	2.69	3.19	4.73	10.0 - 9.2	—	—	—	—	—	3/17/03	27.00 - 24.75
—	20.98	—	—	18.55	15.80	—	—	—	—	—	0.0886A	1/10/03	22.50 - 15.46
—	7.96	—	—	8.25	8.22	—	0.73	1.05	0.95	9.6	0.15Q	4/15/03	8.65 - 6.63
—	11.18	—	—	10.68	11.03	—	—	2.31	—	—	0.0074A	1/10/03	11.13 - 7.29
—	—	—	15.67	15.42	14.44	—	0.83	0.78	0.85	5.9	0.075M	3/21/03	14.78 - 13.33
—	—	—	16.13	17.10	16.83	—	1.07	1.28	1.32	6.9	0.075M	3/21/03	17.22 - 13.98
—	—	—	15.56	16.00	15.24	—	0.98	1.15	0.75	6.8	0.0575M	3/21/03	15.54 - 13.49
—	—	—	15.50	15.74	15.09	—	1.08	1.35	1.06	7.6	0.075M	3/21/03	15.00 - 13.60
—	—	—	15.90	15.70	14.56	—	1.06	0.92	0.85	7.2	0.075M	3/21/03	16.25 - 13.43
—	7.82	—	—	7.88	8.03	—	0.56	0.57	0.61	7.2	0.045M	3/21/03	8.55 - 7.05
—	9.44	—	—	9.32	9.48	—	0.57	0.62	0.56	6.5	0.0475M	3/21/03	9.30 - 8.15
—	9.96	—	—	10.04	9.88	—	0.62	0.58	0.54	6.9	0.0475M	3/21/03	9.39 - 8.55
—	—	—	15.07	14.88	13.81	—	0.79	0.70	0.76	5.6	0.0675M	3/21/03	15.05 - 12.90
—	—	—	15.60	—	15.22	—	1.18	1.26	1.04	8.3	0.075M	3/21/03	14.78 - 13.52
—	—	—	15.23	15.31	14.64	—	1.03	1.07	0.94	7.2	0.08M	3/21/03	15.04 - 13.55
—	—	—	15.42	15.19	14.28	—	0.82	0.75	0.80	6.0	0.0725M	3/21/03	14.41 - 13.15
—	—	—	15.00	15.07	14.28	—	0.83	0.78	0.78	5.8	0.075M	3/21/03	15.06 - 13.83
—	—	—	14.95	14.86	13.96	—	0.79	0.70	0.76	5.8	0.07M	3/21/03	14.75 - 12.75
—	—	—	10.09	9.74	9.18	—	0.48	0.54	0.54	5.4	0.034M	3/21/03	9.40 - 8.50
—	8.43	—	—	8.44	8.46	—	0.53	0.51	0.51	6.8	0.0425M	3/21/03	8.30 - 7.25
—	6.43	—	—	7.31	9.01	—	0.76	1.13	1.05	11.8	0.155Q	4/15/03	7.65 - 5.25
—	5.98	—	—	7.26	9.31	—	0.82	1.23	1.28	11.8	0.04M	4/15/03	8.79 - 5.06
—	11.74	—	—	10.53	13.92	—	0.21	2.47	—	2.2	0.0132A	7/9/02	10.49 - 8.25
—	—	—	pd1.78	d1.78	0.58	—	0.16	0.16	0.16	1.3	0.04Q	4/15/03	17.11 - 7.30
0.03	0.44	0.73	pd1.09	d1.78	0.58	—	3.66	—	—	9.2	0.875Q	2/18/03	50.99 - 28.75
—	—	—	pd5.62	0.08	1.23	—	0.12	0.12	0.10	0.6	3-for-1	1/31/03	25.20 - 14.60
—	9.95	—	—	9.24	10.82	—	—	—	—	—	3-for-1	3/27/96	9.80 - 4.35
0.19	—	—	0.51	0.58	0.78	47.8 - 18.2	—	0.19	0.07	—	0.0077A	1/10/03	9.28 - 6.52
—	—	—	pd1.75	0.47	0.76	—	—	—	—	—	100%	5/22/98	24.36 - 9.30
—	—	—	p1.92	1.80	2.43	18.9 - 12.3	—	—	—	—	0.06Q	9/4/96	23.40 - 2.74
—	—	—	—	—	—	—	—	—	—	—	100%	5/27/98	36.35 - 23.61
—	—	—	12.55	—	—	—	0.78	0.81	0.81	6.7	0.065M	3/28/03	12.21 - 11.05
—	—	—	14.84	14.82	13.75	—	0.84	0.75	0.74	6.4	0.075M	4/1/03	13.98 - 12.43
—	—	—	8.16	8.67	8.86	—	0.57	0.58	0.58	7.2	0.0465M	5/30/03	8.49 - 7.23
—	—	—	p1.13	1.66	1.62	23.4 - 19.2	1.75	1.71	1.66	7.2	0.4425Q	2/7/03	26.40 - 21.75
—	15.04	—	14.34	13.94	13.09	—	0.78	0.75	0.75	6.0	0.068M	5/30/03	13.83 - 12.21
—	—	—	15.35	14.38	14.25	—	0.79	0.73	0.78	5.9	0.07M	5/30/03	14.14 - 12.45
—	11.61	—	—	14.46	1.31	—	0.90	0.85	0.78	6.4	0.077M	3/28/03	11.50 - 10.00
—	—	—	15.41	15.29	13.85	—	0.69	0.64	0.64	6.4	0.06M	3/28/03	14.97 - 13.20
—	—	—	13.51	12.35	12.45	—	0.95	0.85	0.76	6.8	0.08M	3/28/03	15.20 - 12.90
—	13.54	—	—	13.94	12.72	—	0.88	0.78	0.78	7.0	0.084M	3/28/03	13.42 - 11.90
—	13.95	—	—	13.78	13.29	—	0.84	0.77	0.76	6.4	0.073M	3/28/03	13.85 - 12.20
—	—	—	14.37	15.78	14.19	—	0.88	0.81	0.78	6.3	0.076M	3/28/03	14.84 - 13.12
—	—	—	14.24	14.54	14.47	—	0.88	0.78	0.74	6.4	0.076M	3/28/03	14.60 - 12.91
—	—	—	14.16	14.29	13.32	—	0.91	0.82	0.78	6.8	0.084M	3/28/03	14.09 - 12.46
—	—	—	—	15.44	14.24	—	0.81	0.81	0.81	5.9	0.073M	3/28/03	14.84 - 12.95
—	—	—	15.14	15.22	14.19	—	0.97	0.88	0.79	6.6	0.081M	3/28/03	15.60 - 14.12
—	—	—	14.97	14.81	13.78	—	0.88	0.81	0.75	6.6	0.077M	3/28/03	14.45 - 12.30
—	—	—	15.04	14.94	13.89	—	0.90	0.81	0.75	6.4	0.0765M	3/28/03	15.10 - 13.10
—	—	—	13.28	13.35	14.67	—	0.93	0.87	0.86	7.1	0.078M	3/28/03	13.68 - 12.26
—	—	—	15.15	14.16	14.16	—	0.95	0.90	0.84	6.6	0.079M	3/28/03	15.35 - 13.30
—	—	—	15.74	15.81	14.48	—	0.95	0.83	0.78	6.7	0.082M	3/28/03	14.99 - 13.12
—	—	—	14.91	14.97	13.83	—	0.89	0.81	0.76	6.6	0.0745M	3/28/03	14.35 - 12.53
—	—	—	14.84	14.78	13.99	—	0.96	0.89	0.81	6.7	0.08M	3/28/03	15.30 - 13.37
—	—	—	15.14	15.17	13.96	—	0.94	0.87	0.81	6.3	0.078M	3/28/03	15.75 - 13.92
—	—	—	14.83	—	—	—	0.83	0.79	0.77	6.2	0.0689M	3/28/03	14.24 - 12.38
—	—	—	14.37	15.19	11.75	—	0.98	0.86	0.79	6.6	0.082M	3/28/03	16.10 - 13.64
—	—	—	13.27	13.21	12.39	—	0.79	0.74	0.80	6.7	0.069M	3/28/03	15.22 - 11.14
—	—	—	15.19	15.27	13.24	—	0.92	0.86	0.81	6.6	0.081M	3/28/03	14.70 - 13.10
—	—	—	p1.06	3.63	3.38	46.9 - 30.1	0.78	0.75	0.73	1.9	0.20Q	3/1/03	49.73 - 31.90
—	—	—	11.84	15.42	18.88	—	0.04	0.34	—	0.5	—	1/3/02	8.70 - 7.98
—	—	—	p0.80	0.51	0.81	18.1 - 11.5	0.19	0.18	0.16	1.6	0.05Q	4/1/03	14.48 - 9.20
d0.32	d0.17	d0.11	—	d1.92	1.15	—	—	—	—	—	—	—	18.15 - 3.18
0.33	0.36	0.37	—	1.36	0.19	—	0.11	0.11	0.11	0.5	0.0333Q	4/15/03	24.84 - 16.73
—	—	—	p6.05	d4.24	4.63	12.6 - 6.0	0.97	0.93	0.89	1.7	0.245Q	3/14/03	76.20 - 36.39
—	—	—	—	—	—	—	1.46	0.39	1.35	6.8	0.15Q	4/21/03	27.72 - 15.26
—	—	—	p0.39	d0.43	0.95	26.2 - 13.8	—	—	0.01	—	0.01Q	5/12/00	10.20 - 5.40
—	—	—	p0.24	0.34	0.51	38.0 - 24.4	—	—	—	—	—	—	9.12 - 5.85
—	—	—	2.02	1.22	2.02	52.2 - 39.8	4.10	3.48	3.46	4.4	2.1033U	12/23/02	105.79 - 80.53
—	—	—	2.02	1.22	2.02	18.2 - 14.6	1.97	2.46	1.48	5.9	—	3/31/03	36.91 - 29.66
—	—	—	2.59	2.27	2.13	13.0 - 9.5	1.20	1.16	1.14	4.1	0.305Q	2/1/03	33.70 - 24.60
—	—	—	1.55	1.09	0.57	19.1 - 13.7	0.62	0.54	0.44	2.4	0.17Q	4/1/03	29.60 - 21.27
p0.57	—	—	1.46	0.82	1.60	17.6 - 10.7	1.02	0.98	0.95	5.0	0.26Q	4/15/03	25.70 - 15.61
—	—	—	—	—	—	—	1.20	1.09	1.08	3.5	0.00U	1/21/03	37.44 - 31.09
—	—	—	p1.31	d0.08	1.31	13.1 - 9.9	1.50	—	2.02	10.0	0.40Q	5/10/03	17.16 - 12.95
—	—	—	p1.27	0.92	2.16	27.2 - 21.1	0.92	2.00	2.10	3.0	0.92A	3/12/03	34.50 - 26.80
—	—	—	0.97	1.01	0.85	33.7 - 11.9	—	—	—	—	—	—	32.69 - 11.50
d0.34	d0.14	d1.00	—	d1.18	1.11	—	—	—	—	—	3-for-2	7/24/98	14.10 - 4.77

SYMBOL	COMPANY	NATURE OF BUSINESS	FISCAL YEAR-END	TOTAL REV. $MILL	NET INCOME $MILL	TOTAL ASSETS $MILL	NET STK EQUITY $MILL	NO. OF INST.	INST. HOLDINGS (SHARES)
NRV	National Rural Utilities Coo	—	5/31/02	1186.5	139.9	20323.3	326.4	1	18700
NRX	National Rural Utilities Coo	—	5/31/02	1186.5	139.9	20323.3	326.4	1	1160
NRY	National Rural Utilities Coo	—	5/31/02	1186.5	139.9	20323.3	326.4	1	1000
NRS	National Rural Utilities Coo	—	5/31/02	1186.5	139.9	20323.3	326.4		
NSM	National Semiconductor Corp.	Electronic components	5/26/02	1494.8	d121.9	2288.8	1781.1	275	157527821
NSI	National Service Industries	Chemicals	8/31/02	532.4	d6.9	519.1	220.6	52	5414060
NOI	National-Oilwell Inc.	Oil service & equipment	12/31/02	1521.9	73.1	1968.7	933.4	215	69573931
NBM	Nations Baj Target Mat Fd Inc	Investment company	3/31/02	3.2	2.7	52.9	53.0	4	7234
NGF	Nations Govt Incm Tr 2004 Inc	Investment company	12/31/01	6.5	6.2	121.7	121.7	9	1996757
NGI	Nations Govt Incm Trm Tr 2003	Investment company	6/30/02	6.7	6.3	145.8	145.7	8	2810995
NFS	Nationwide Financial Svcs In	Life Insurance	12/31/02	p3376.1	p3376.1	—	—	152	30753800
NHP	Nationwide Health Properties	Real estate investment trust	12/31/02	p156.5	p156.5	—	—	124	28873116
NRP	Natural Resources Partners L	Coal	4/15/02	—	—	0.0	—	11	466295
NTZ	Natuzzi S.p.A. (Italy)	Furniture & fixtures	12/31/01	—	—	—	—	38	16809293
NLS	Nautilus Group Inc.	—	12/31/01	363.9	66.6	193.9	147.4	130	19398632
NCI	Navigant Consulting, Inc.	Services	12/31/02	p258.0	p258.0	—	—	70	27928844
NAV	Navistar International Corp.	—	10/31/02	6784.0	d476.0	6943.0	251.0	186	71486411
NCS	NCI Building Systems, Inc. (	—	11/2/02	953.4	32.1	721.3	303.5	79	14287723
NCR	NCR Corp. (New)	Computer services	12/31/02	5585.0	128.0	4672.0	1325.0	265	76440894
NDC	NDCHealth Corp.	Computer services	5/31/02	353.4	15.1	658.2	257.7	142	31939069
NMG B	Neiman-Marcus Group, Inc.	Specialty stores	8/3/02	2948.3	99.6	1907.5	1055.3	55	12009097
NMG A	Neiman-Marcus Group, Inc.	Specialty stores	8/3/02	2948.3	99.6	1907.5	1055.3	145	28785459
NWK	Network Equipment Technologi	Telecommunications	3/29/02	101.5	d37.4	187.4	131.3	52	17329272
NET	Networks Associates, Inc. (U	Computer services	12/31/01	834.5	d102.4	1627.1	444.8	259	148809451
NEU	Neuberger Berman Inc (United	Financial services	12/31/01	736.4	132.7	4382.5	326.4	133	20606026
NRL	Neuberger Berman Real Estate	Investment company	11/20/02	—	—	0.4	0.1	—	—
HYB	New America High Income Fd	Investment company	12/31/02	27.7	25.2	239.3	231.2	22	684881
NEB	New England Business Svc. In	Office equipment & supplies	6/29/02	557.5	25.3	368.9	136.7	98	10243414
GF	New Germany Fund, Inc.	Investment company	12/31/02	1.6	d0.7	125.2	124.5	26	5895124
IRL	New Ireland Fund, Inc. (The)	Investment company	10/31/02	0.9	d0.4	55.8	54.9	12	901282
NJR	New Jersey Resources Corp (Un	Natural gas distributor	9/30/02	1830.8	56.8	1319.3	361.5	130	12146324
NXL	New Plan Excel Realty Trust,	Real estate investment trust	12/31/02	392.4	19.4	3515.3	1572.8	188	31757515
NSK	New Skies Satellites NV (Neth	Communications electronics	12/31/01	—	—	—	—	3	138780
NYB	New York Community Bancorp I	Banking - Northeast	12/31/02	—	p229.2	—	—	219	55122472
NYT	New York Times Co.	Newspapers	12/31/02	p3079.0	p3074.4	—	—	347	118800676
NCT	Newcastle Investment Corp (N	Real estate investment trust	6/6/02	—	—	—	—	25	4907841
NWL	Newell Rubbermaid, Inc.	Hardware & tools	12/31/01	p7453.9	p237.5	—	—	417	215436350
NFX	Newfield Exploration Co.	Oil	12/31/02	p661.8	p661.8	—	—	218	43054829
NHL	Newhall Land & Farming Co.	Real estate	12/31/02	p239.8	p239.8	—	—	57	12512315
NEM	Newmont Mining Corp. (Holdin	Mining & processing	12/31/01	1664.1	d23.3	4062.4	1480.0	382	275419279
NR	Newpark Resources, Inc.	Oil service & equipment	12/31/02	p321.2	p321.2	—	—	114	68095549
NWS	News Corp. Ltd. (The) (AU)	Newspapers	6/30/01	—	—	—	—	138	89111135
NWS A	News Corp. Ltd. (The) (AU)	Newspapers	6/30/01	—	—	—	—	68	64870404
NXY	Nexen Inc. (Canada)	Oil producer	12/31/02	—	—	—	—	43	115292584
GAS	Nicor, Inc.	Oil service & equipment	12/31/01	2544.1	143.7	2574.8	727.6	225	23457525
NJ	Nidec Corp. (Japan)	Electrical equipment	3/31/02	—	—	—	—	8	99764
NKE	NIKE, Inc. (United States)	Shoe manufacturing	5/31/02	9893.0	668.3	6443.0	3839.0	349	148279131
NTT	Nippon Teleg & Tel Corp	Telecommunications	3/31/02	—	—	—	—	91	50360641
NI	NiSource Inc. (Holding Co.)	Electric power	12/31/02	—	p372.5	—	—	340	180578216
NSE	NiSource Inc. (Holding Co.)	Electric power	12/31/02	—	p372.5	—	—	19	15060948
NIS	Nissin Co. Ltd. (Japan)	Finance	3/31/02	—	—	—	—	—	—
NL	NL Industries, Inc.	Chemicals	12/31/02	p875.2	p861.9	—	—	66	3734532
NE	Noble Corp. (Cayman Islands)	Oil service & equipment	12/31/02	p986.4	p986.4	—	—	318	112348969
NBL	Noble Energy, Inc. (United S	Oil producer	12/31/02	1443.7	17.7	2730.0	1009.4	221	51520460
NOK	Nokia Corp.	Telecommunications	12/31/01	—	—	—	—	674	754614616
NMR	Nomura Holdings Inc. (Japan)	Securities brokerage	3/31/02	—	—	—	—	31	7080170
JWN	Nordstrom, Inc.	Specialty stores	1/31/03	p5975.1	p1911.7	—	—	224	74863447
NSC	Norfolk Southern Corp.	Freight transportation	12/31/02	6270.0	460.0	19956.0	6500.0	432	267877949
NHY	Norsk Hydro ASA (Norway)	—	12/31/01	—	—	—	—	57	15362476
NTL	Nortel Inversora S.A.	Telecommunications	12/31/01	—	—	—	—	3	719719
NRT	North European Oil Royalty Tr	Real estate investment trust	10/31/02	17.5	16.9	3.5	0.1	31	740872
NFB	North Fork Bancorp, Inc (NY)	Banking - Northeast	12/31/02	—	p416.9	—	—	388	100953861
NU	Northeast Utilities	Electric power	12/31/02	p5034.9	p4947.1	—	—	166	81356611
NBP	Northern Border Partners L.P	Natural gas	12/31/02	p495.6	p495.6	—	—	94	4239976
NOC	Northrop Grumman Corp (Holdi	—	12/31/02	—	p945.0	—	—	529	175748901
NWN	Northwest Natural Gas Co. (U	Natural gas distributor	12/31/02	p641.4	p641.4	—	—	134	10775346
NOR	Northwestern Corp.	Electric power	12/31/01	4237.8	44.5	2617.4	396.4	141	19715988
NVS	Novartis AG Basel (Switzerla	Drugs	12/31/02	—	—	—	—	224	66376373
NFI	NovaStar Financial, Inc.	Financial services	12/31/02	—	p48.8	—	—	59	7047882
NVO	Novo-Nordisk A/S	Drugs	12/31/01	—	—	—	—	56	6789873
NSS	NS Group, Inc. (United State	Steel producer	12/31/02	p192.4	p193.7	—	—	48	13694404
NST	Nstar	Electric power	12/31/02	p2719.2	p2719.2	—	—	191	75236918
DCM	NTT DoCoMo Inc. (Japan)	Telecommunications	3/31/02	—	—	—	—	43	4714414
NUS	NU Skin Enterprises, Inc.	Cosmetics & toiletries	12/31/02	p964.1	p67.7	—	—	99	25508948
NUE	Nucor Corp.	Steel producer	12/31/02	p4568.3	p4568.3	—	—	309	63026099
NEV	Nuevo Energy Co.	Oil	12/31/02	p323.1	p323.1	—	—	95	15167523
NUI	NUI Corp. (Holding Co.)	Natural gas distributor	9/30/02	556.5	16.2	1041.3	288.3	101	10162960
NAZ	Nuveen Ariz Prem Incm Mun Fd	Investment company	7/31/02	5.5	4.7	94.5	62.9	4	50333
NCO	Nuveen CA Mun Mart Opp Fd Inc	Investment company	8/31/02	10.2	8.6	193.5	124.4	3	33560
NCA	Nuveen CA Mun Value Fd Inc	Investment company	8/31/02	14.7	13.0	260.7	259.3	13	154457
NCP	Nuveen CA Performance Plus	Investment company	8/31/02	16.1	13.6	306.0	198.6	8	62168
NVC	Nuveen CA Select Qlty Mun Fd	Investment company	8/31/02	29.3	25.0	553.2	358.6	13	102014
NUC	Nuveen Cal Quality Inc Mun F	Investment company	8/31/02	30.2	26.0	536.7	347.6	17	163309
NAC	Nuveen California Dividend Ad	Investment company	8/31/02	27.5	25.0	533.9	356.8	9	160388
NQC	Nuveen California Investment	Investment company	8/31/02	17.2	14.7	327.6	214.3	9	56542
NXC	Nuveen California Select Tax-	Investment company	3/31/02	5.3	4.9	91.6	90.3	4	10639
NTC	Nuveen Connecticut Premium In	Investment company	5/31/02	6.3	5.3	115.1	76.3	8	90563
NAD	Nuveen Dividend Advantage Mun	Investment company	10/31/02	49.0	44.4	888.8	586.0	20	359411
NQF	Nuveen FL Inv. Qual. Mun Fd.	Investment company	6/30/02	21.7	18.6	384.9	249.8	13	301823
NUF	Nuveen Fla Qual Inc Munic Fd	Investment company	6/30/02	19.5	16.8	341.4	216.0	12	240426
NIO	Nuveen Ins Mun Opportunity F	Investment company	10/31/02	108.0	93.1	1999.6	1283.4	48	911567
NCL	Nuveen Insd CA Prem Incm Fd 2	Investment company	8/31/02	15.0	12.7	287.9	190.9	8	59066
NCP	Nuveen Insd CA Prem Incm Mun	Investment company	8/31/02	7.9	6.7	153.9	104.1	6	19275
NFL	Nuveen Insd FL Prem Incm Mun	Investment company	6/30/02	18.0	15.3	336.4	224.0	6	265270
NNF	Nuveen Insd NY Prem Incm Mun	Investment company	10/4/02	10.4	8.8	200.4	134.6	7	74978
NPX	Nuveen Insd Prem Incm Mun Fd2	Investment company	10/31/02	43.0	36.8	803.5	527.8	24	398711

T34

| EARNINGS PER SHARE | | | | | | P/E RATIO | DIVIDENDS PER SHARE | | | AV. YLD. % | DIV. DECLARED | | PRICE RANGE |
| QUARTERLY | | | ANNUAL | | | | | | | | | | |
1st	2nd	3rd	2002	2001	2000		2002	2001	2000	%	AMOUNT	PAYABLE	2002
—	—	—	—	—	—	—	1.91	1.91	1.91	7.7		3/17/03	26.20 - 23.75
—	—	—	—	—	—	—	1.84	1.84	1.84	7.6		3/17/03	25.40 - 22.90
—	—	—	—	—	—	—	1.91	1.15	—	7.5		3/17/03	26.70 - 24.33
—	—	—	—	—	—	—	1.84	—	—	7.5	0.4625Q	2/3/03	26.05 - 23.43
0.01	0.03	pd0.20	—	d0.69	1.30	—	—	—	—		3-for-1	11/29/83	37.30 - 9.95
d0.19	—	—	d0.67	d1.48	9.80	—	0.16	—	—	1.9	0.04Q	2/3/03	11.95 - 5.01
—	—	—	0.89	1.27	0.16	32.4 - 17.1	—	—	—		2-for-1	11/18/97	28.81 - 15.19
—	10.12	—	—	10.14	10.11	—	0.50	0.44	0.44	5.1	0.11Q	3/28/03	10.84 - 8.70
—	10.38	—	—	10.36	9.92	—	0.50	0.47	0.52	4.9	0.0314M	3/28/03	10.30 - 9.98
—	—	—	10.27	10.02	9.51	—	0.40	0.45	0.50	4.0	0.0304M	2/27/03	10.23 - 10.00
—	—	—	p1.56	3.20	3.38	29.3 - 14.0	0.50	0.48	0.44	1.5	0.13Q	4/15/03	45.65 - 21.80
—	—	—	p0.59	1.30	1.35	38.6 - 24.8	1.84	1.84	1.84	9.8	0.46Q	3/7/03	22.80 - 14.64
—	—	—	—	—	—	—	—	—	—		0.4234Q	2/14/03	20.70 - 18.35
0.67	—	0.71	—	1.85	1.73	—	0.20	0.18	1.12	1.6	0.2043U	7/12/02	16.25 - 8.95
—	—	—	—	—	—	—	—	—	—		0.10Q	3/10/03	43.10 - 12.40
d1.47	—	—	p0.21	d0.14	d0.35	33.3 - 16.7	—	—	—		3-for-2	4/1/98	7.00 - 3.50
p0.20	—	—	d7.88	d0.39	2.58	—	—	0.01	—		0.01U	11/15/01	47.38 - 14.77
—	—	—	1.72	0.91	2.84	14.5 - 8.8	—	—	—		2-for-1	7/22/98	24.90 - 15.05
—	—	—	1.27	2.22	1.82	35.8 - 14.8	—	—	—				45.49 - 18.80
0.32	0.36	—	—	0.43	0.82	—	0.16	0.20	0.30	0.7	0.04Q	2/28/03	37.24 - 10.90
0.90	—	—	2.08	2.26	2.75	18.1 - 10.4	—	—	—				37.60 - 21.65
0.90	—	—	2.08	2.26	2.75	19.1 - 11.4	—	—	—		0.05Q	1/31/95	39.80 - 23.75
0.03	d0.31	d0.14	—	d1.69	d0.96	—	—	—	—				6.10 - 2.60
0.10	0.14	0.06	—	d0.74	d0.72	—	—	—	—		3-for-2	5/29/98	30.50 - 8.14
0.47	0.46	0.42	—	1.82	2.02	—	0.30	0.28	0.27	0.8	0.075Q	2/19/03	48.67 - 22.83
—	—	—	15.00	—	—	—	—	—	—		0.115M	3/31/03	15.17 - 15.00
—	—	—	2.61	2.61	2.85	—	0.30	0.36	0.42	13.6	0.0175M	3/31/03	2.87 - 1.55
0.52	0.97	—	—	1.94	1.43	—	0.80	0.80	0.80	3.4	0.20Q	2/21/03	29.31 - 18.01
—	—	—	4.53	7.50	11.66	—	—	—	1.73		1.30N	11/29/00	6.39 - 2.81
—	—	—	11.04	13.28	20.06	—	—	0.72	2.66		0.691A	12/28/01	11.32 - 7.60
0.86	—	—	4.18	3.95	1.79	8.0 - 5.8	1.20	1.17	1.15	4.1	0.31Q	4/1/03	33.60 - 24.35
—	—	—	0.06	0.77	1.13	350.0 - 258.5	1.65	1.65	1.65	9.0	0.4125Q	4/15/03	21.00 - 15.51
—	—	—	—	—	—	—	—	—	—				6.60 - 3.14
—	—	—	p2.22	1.34	0.56	14.4 - 10.2	0.76	0.54	0.44	2.8	0.25Q	2/15/03	32.02 - 22.65
—	—	—	p1.94	1.94	1.26	27.3 - 19.9	0.53	0.49	0.45	1.2	0.135Q	3/19/03	53.00 - 38.60
—	—	—	—	—	—	—	—	—	—		0.39Q	1/14/03	16.00 - 12.26
—	—	—	pd0.76	0.99	1.57	—	0.84	0.84	0.84	2.7	0.21Q	3/10/03	36.70 - 26.11
—	—	—	p1.61	2.66	2.98	24.4 - 16.9	—	—	—		2-for-1	12/30/96	39.24 - 27.16
—	—	—	p1.66	3.56	3.05	20.4 - 13.6	0.53	0.50	0.75	1.9	0.10Q	3/6/03	33.80 - 22.59
d0.04	0.16	0.06	—	d0.16	d0.06	—	0.09	—	—	0.4	0.04Q	3/19/03	32.75 - 18.52
—	—	—	p0.01	0.37	0.08	912.0 - 288.0	—	—	—		2-for-1	11/26/97	9.12 - 2.88
—	—	—	—	—	—	—	0.06	0.05	0.06	0.2		5/7/03	32.50 - 17.60
—	—	—	—	—	—	—	0.14	0.13	0.16	0.7		5/7/03	27.21 - 15.09
—	—	—	—	—	—	—	0.30	0.30	0.30	1.3	0.075Q	4/1/03	28.04 - 18.57
p0.90	0.46	0.68	—	3.17	1.00	—	1.82	1.74	1.63	5.5	0.465Q	5/1/03	49.00 - 17.25
—	—	—	—	—	—	—	0.14	—	—	0.2	0.07245U	3/26/03	78.00 - 43.75
0.81	0.57	—	—	2.46	2.16	—	0.48	0.48	0.48	0.9	0.14Q	4/1/03	64.28 - 38.53
—	—	—	—	—	—	—	0.17	0.17	0.19	0.9	0.08972U	3/26/03	23.49 - 14.01
—	—	—	p2.00	1.01	1.08	12.5 - 7.3	1.16	1.16	—	5.9	0.29Q	2/20/03	24.99 - 14.51
—	—	—	p2.00	1.01	1.08	1.2 - 0.8	—	—	—				2.46 - 1.58
—	—	—	—	—	—	—	0.04	—	—	0.3	100%	5/22/03	15.82 - 12.40
—	—	—	p0.76	2.44	3.06	24.7 - 17.1	3.30	0.80	0.65	20.7	0.20Q	3/26/03	18.80 - 13.01
—	—	—	p1.57	1.97	1.22	28.3 - 17.2	—	—	—				44.40 - 27.00
—	—	—	0.31	2.33	3.38	131.5 - 86.0	0.16	0.16	0.16	0.5	0.04Q	2/24/03	40.76 - 26.65
—	—	—	—	—	—	—	0.24	0.25	0.77	1.3		4/23/03	27.06 - 10.51
—	—	—	—	—	—	—	0.11	1.17	1.18	0.8	0.106U	7/8/02	17.40 - 8.91
—	—	—	p0.66	0.93	0.78	40.7 - 22.8	0.38	0.36	0.35	1.8	0.10Q	3/14/03	26.87 - 15.06
—	—	—	1.18	0.94	0.45	22.9 - 14.6	0.26	0.24	0.80	1.2	0.07Q	3/10/03	26.98 - 17.20
—	—	—	—	—	—	—	1.04	0.89	0.74	2.3	1.28617U	5/5/03	52.30 - 37.05
—	—	—	—	—	—	—	—	0.40	0.13		0.0139U	5/11/01	4.80 - 0.44
p0.51	—	—	1.89	2.47	1.54	13.5 - 10.1	1.89	2.46	1.56	8.5	0.51Q	2/26/03	25.50 - 19.00
—	—	—	2.58	2.05	1.39	16.6 - 12.1	0.98	0.81	0.72	2.7	0.27Q	2/18/03	42.74 - 31.22
—	—	—	p1.18	1.96	1.45	17.5 - 10.7	0.53	0.45	0.40	3.1	0.1375Q	3/31/03	20.70 - 12.66
—	—	—	p2.44	2.12	2.50	17.4 - 12.0	3.20	2.99	2.65	8.9	0.80Q	2/14/03	42.50 - 29.30
—	—	—	p5.72	4.80	8.82	23.6 - 15.6	1.60	1.20	—	1.4	0.40Q	3/15/03	135.00 - 89.00
0.65	0.49	0.25	p1.62	1.88	1.79	19.0 - 14.5	1.26	1.25	1.24	4.7	0.315Q	2/15/03	30.70 - 23.46
—	—	—	—	1.53	1.87	—	1.27	1.21	1.13	9.1	0.3175Q	11/19/02	23.64 - 4.30
—	—	—	—	—	—	—	0.46	0.42	0.82	1.2	0.59488U	4/7/03	44.10 - 33.96
—	—	—	p4.50	3.18	0.50	7.9 - 3.3	3.17	0.49	—	12.5	0.33Q	2/11/03	35.75 - 15.00
—	—	—	pd1.93	d2.68	d0.19	—	0.28	0.11	0.09	0.9	0.37647U	4/7/03	40.60 - 21.50
—	—	—	p3.03	d0.05	3.18	15.9 - 11.2	—	—	—		0.03Q	3/27/92	10.61 - 5.43
—	—	—	—	—	—	—	2.12	2.06	2.00	5.2	0.54Q	2/1/03	48.20 - 34.00
—	—	—	p0.78	0.60	0.72	19.1 - 9.1	0.03	0.01	0.01	0.1	150%	5/22/02	70.00 - 16.50
—	—	—	2.07	1.45	3.80	33.9 - 17.4	0.24	0.20	—	2.2	0.07Q	3/26/03	14.86 - 7.10
—	—	—	p1.02	d4.73	0.68	16.1 - 8.8	0.74	0.66	0.58	1.4	0.20Q	5/12/03	70.15 - 36.00
0.48	—	—	1.08	1.70	2.07	25.5 - 8.9	—	—	—				16.45 - 9.00
—	—	—	14.25	14.77	14.25	—	0.98	0.73	—	5.3	0.245Q	3/14/03	27.50 - 9.65
—	—	—	15.26	15.32	14.97	—	0.90	0.89	0.83	5.6	0.0765M	4/1/03	24.38 - 7.99
—	—	—	15.26	15.32	14.97	—	0.91	1.00	1.05	6.1	0.0755M	4/1/03	15.62 - 14.16
—	—	—	10.27	10.31	9.85	—	0.53	0.52	0.51	5.3	0.0415M	4/1/03	10.54 - 9.40
—	—	—	15.32	15.32	14.96	—	0.90	0.99	0.98	6.1	0.0775M	4/1/03	15.51 - 13.90
—	—	—	15.53	15.63	14.90	—	0.93	1.07	0.93	6.2	0.0795M	4/1/03	15.89 - 14.10
—	—	—	15.84	16.16	15.41	—	1.10	1.03	0.97	6.9	0.083M	4/1/03	16.80 - 14.94
—	—	—	15.24	15.13	13.82	—	0.88	0.82	0.82	6.1	0.08M	4/1/03	15.19 - 13.53
—	—	—	15.78	15.78	14.83	—	0.94	0.94	0.92	6.1	0.0795M	4/1/03	16.16 - 14.60
—	14.94	—	—	14.44	14.79	—	0.89	0.80	0.80	6.0	0.057M	4/1/03	16.20 - 13.26
—	14.71	—	—	14.46	14.20	—	0.87	0.82	0.82	5.3	0.0735M	4/1/03	17.65 - 15.30
—	—	—	14.94	14.84	13.59	—	0.95	0.89	0.85	6.5	0.082M	4/1/03	15.74 - 13.57
—	—	—	15.19	14.76	14.24	—	1.07	0.95	0.91	6.8	0.0825M	4/1/03	16.95 - 14.45
—	—	—	15.23	15.02	14.24	—	1.16	0.94	0.89	7.3	0.083M	4/1/03	17.10 - 14.74
—	—	—	15.83	15.72	14.51	—	1.06	0.89	0.87	7.0	0.081M	4/1/03	16.20 - 14.18
—	—	—	15.08	15.01	14.09	—	0.85	0.79	0.79	5.7	0.076M	4/1/03	16.15 - 13.85
—	—	—	16.17	16.04	15.08	—	1.01	0.84	0.87	6.5	0.076M	4/1/03	16.50 - 14.55
—	—	—	15.66	15.30	14.25	—	0.91	0.81	0.79	5.7	0.079M	4/1/03	17.75 - 14.30
—	—	—	16.17	15.26	14.24	—	0.89	0.83	0.81	5.9	0.077M	4/1/03	16.11 - 14.18
—	—	—	14.17	13.94	13.05	—	0.83	0.76	0.71	6.1	0.072M	4/1/03	14.58 - 12.56

SYMBOL	COMPANY	NATURE OF BUSINESS	FISCAL YEAR-END	TOTAL REV. $MILL	NET INCOME $MILL	TOTAL ASSETS $MILL	NET STK EQUITY $MILL	NO. OF INST.	INST. HOLDINGS (SHARES)
NQI	Nuveen Insd Quality Mun Fd	Investment company	10/31/02	49.7	42.6	964.7	601.5	32	456822
NQM	Nuveen Invt Quality Mun Fd	Investment company	10/31/02	48.0	41.3	863.2	558.6	25	440013
NMT	Nuveen Mass Prem Income Mun	Investment company	5/31/02	5.7	4.8	102.3	67.9	6	34532
NMY	Nuveen MD Prem Incm Mun Fd	Investment company	5/31/02	12.7	10.8	232.3	147.8	6	69141
NMP	Nuveen Mich Prem Incm Mun Fd	Investment	7/31/02	9.5	8.1	176.6	119.8	3	57923
NUM	Nuveen Mich Qual Inc Muni Fd	Investment company	7/31/02	15.1	12.8	274.8	179.6	6	190572
NMA	Nuveen Mun Advantage Fd Inc	Investment company	10/31/02	57.6	49.6	1023.1	662.3	28	586806
NMI	Nuveen Mun Income Fd Inc	Investment company	10/31/02	5.7	4.9	87.2	85.9	14	150154
NMO	Nuveen Mun Mkt Opp Fd Inc	Investment company	10/31/02	59.0	50.7	1048.0	664.9	29	447354
NUV	Nuveen Mun Value Fd Inc	Investment	10/31/02	111.9	99.3	1975.7	1946.4	67	5320389
NNC	Nuveen NC Prem Income Mun Fd	Investment company	5/31/02	7.6	6.4	137.0	89.3	7	98535
NXN	Nuveen New York Select Tax-Fr	Investment company	3/31/02	3.1	2.8	55.7	55.4	2	35075
NQJ	Nuveen NJ Inv. Qual. Mun. Fd.	Investment company	6/30/02	26.0	22.3	479.0	304.8	13	463501
NNJ	Nuveen NJ Prem Income Mun Fd	Investment company	6/30/02	14.9	12.7	282.3	187.4	8	120263
NQN	Nuveen NY Invt Quality Mun Fd	Investment company	9/30/02	22.6	19.2	445.2	299.5	14	159899
NNY	Nuveen NY Mun Value Fd Inc	Investment company	9/30/02	8.2	7.1	156.9	153.6	18	341789
NNP	Nuveen NY Perfomance Plus Fd	Investment company	9/30/02	19.9	17.0	388.2	255.9	7	77022
NUN	Nuveen NY Quality Inc Mun Fd	Investment company	9/30/02	30.3	25.8	593.6	394.3	14	220043
NVN	Nuveen NY Sel. Qlty.Mun. Fd	Investment company	9/30/02	29.8	25.4	581.3	386.0	18	331764
NUO	Nuveen Ohio Qual Inc Munic Fd	Investment company	7/31/02	12.8	10.9	235.4	156.4	8	169135
NQP	Nuveen PA Inv. Qual. Fd.	Investment company	6/30/02	20.7	17.6	375.8	238.9	14	264232
NPY	Nuveen PA Prem Income Mun 2	Investment company	6/30/02	19.7	16.9	375.8	238.9	16	279095
NPP	Nuveen Perfomance Plus Mun Fd	Investment company	10/31/02	76.0	65.3	1410.6	921.4	39	1442819
NIF	Nuveen Premier Ins Munc Fd	Investment company	10/31/02	25.6	21.9	475.7	301.1	15	156463
NPF	Nuveen Premier Mun Inc Fund	Investment company	10/31/02	27.0	23.1	472.6	306.0	18	546336
NPI	Nuveen Premium Incm Mun Fund	Investment company	10/31/02	81.9	70.4	1479.8	948.7	36	954568
NPM	Nuveen Premium Incm Mun 2	Investment company	10/31/02	55.9	48.3	980.7	627.7	29	1054722
NPT	Nuveen Premium Incm Mun 4	Investment company	10/31/02	51.3	43.4	927.5	582.0	32	579800
NQU	Nuveen Quality Income Mun Fd	Investment company	10/31/02	70.7	60.9	1252.9	1248.6	31	970079
JTP	Nuveen Quality Preferred Inc	Investment company	5/31/02	—	—	0.7	0.1	—	—
JPS	Nuveen Quality Preferred Inc	Investment company	9/4/02	—	—	0.7	0.1	—	—
JHP	Nuveen Quality Preferred Inc	Investment company	11/26/02	—	—	1.2	0.1	—	—
NIM	Nuveen Select Maturities Mun	Investment company	5/31/02	8.0	7.1	131.7	131.0	14	199126
NQS	Nuveen Select Quality Mun Fd	Investment company	10/31/02	44.2	37.9	790.5	508.3	22	428061
NXR	Nuveen Select Tax Free Incm 3	Investment company	3/31/02	11.3	10.5	185.9	184.8	14	100971
NXP	Nuveen Select Tax Free Income	Investment company	3/31/02	15.3	14.4	258.1	240.3	16	170661
NXQ	Nuveen Select Tax Free Ptf 2	Investment company	3/31/02	16.2	15.1	261.5	255.9	13	149354
NSL	Nuveen Senior Income Fund	Investment company	7/31/02	25.5	20.2	370.6	265.5	9	1090156
NTX	Nuveen Texas Qual Inc Muni Fd	Investment company	7/31/02	12.2	10.5	213.3	143.3	8	163945
NPV	Nuveen VA Prem Income Mum Fd	Investment company	5/31/02	10.7	9.1	193.3	128.7	10	148681
NYM	NYMAGIC, Inc.	Insurance	12/31/02	p139.5	p153.3	—	—	27	3780093
OO	Oakley, Inc.	Photo & optical	12/31/01	429.3	50.4	362.8	260.7	91	21702918
OXY	Occidental Petroleum Corp. (U	Specialty chemicals	12/31/02	p7338.0	p7328.0	—	—	385	299564205
OEI	Ocean Energy, Inc. (New) (DE	Natural gas distributor	12/31/02	1162.1	135.2	3893.4	1574.7	305	146754604
OII	Oceaneering Intl, Inc.	Oil service & equipment	12/31/02	p547.5	p97.8	—	—	127	19506381
OTL	Octel Corp.	Chemicals	12/31/01	p451.5	p451.5	—	—	64	8712566
OCN	Ocwen Financial Corp.	Banking - South	12/31/02	—	p16.2	—	—	58	22033225
ORH	Odyssey Re Holdings Corp. (U	Property & casualty insurance	12/31/02	p1691.5	p1816.6	—	—	82	18581410
ODP	Office Depot, Inc.	Specialty stores	12/28/02	11356.6	311.5	4765.8	2297.1	344	274887892
OMX	OfficeMax, Inc.	Office equipment & supplies	1/25/03	p4775.6	p4773.1	—	—	142	74653096
OLG	Offshore Logistics, Inc.	—	3/31/02	512.1	44.5	807.3	340.0	122	18635832
OGE	OGE Energy Corp.	Electric power	12/31/02	p3023.9	p868.8	—	—	181	24004165
OJB	Ohio Power Company	Electric power	12/31/01	6262.4	165.8	4916.1	1201.4	2	10000
OIS	Oil States International, Inc	—	12/31/02	p616.8	p616.8	—	—	72	12149389
ODC	Oil-Dri Corp. of America	Pollution control	7/31/02	162.3	d1.1	125.0	69.1	15	2946813
ONB	Old National Bancorp (Evansvi	Banking - Midwest	12/31/02	—	pd347.0	—	—	86	14784631
ORI	Old Republic Intl Corp	Insurance	12/31/02	p2756.4	p2588.7	—	—	281	85607060
OLN	Olin Corp.	Chemicals	12/31/01	1271.0	d9.0	1219.0	271.0	168	39154242
OMG	OM Group, Inc.	Specialty chemicals	12/31/02	p4909.4	p4912.9	—	—	117	15036550
OHI	Omega Healthcare Investors	Real estate investment trust	12/31/02	137.1	d14.6	802.6	479.7	48	2547754
ORB	Omega Healthcare Investors	Real estate investment trust	12/31/02	137.1	d14.6	802.6	479.7	1	1060
OME	Omega Protein Corp.	—	12/31/02	p117.0	p117.0	—	—	12	5347587
OMM	OMI Corp. (New)	Freight transportation	12/31/02	p198.9	p198.9	—	—	81	44225230
OCR	Omnicare Inc.	Drugs	12/31/02	p2606.4	p2529.3	—	—	214	101466158
OMC	Omnicom Group, Inc.	—	12/31/02	p7536.3	p7536.3	—	—	467	172950280
OMN	Omnova Solutions, Inc.	Chemicals	11/30/02	681.2	7.0	466.1	147.2	87	33312824
OCQ	Oneida Ltd.	Appliances & utensils	1/25/03	p480.1	p480.1	—	—	60	11259208
OKE	Oneok Inc. (New)	Natural gas	12/31/02	p975.7	p975.7	—	—	163	31846353
OMS	Oppenheimer Multi-Sect Inc Tr	Investment company	10/31/02	21.0	19.0	339.1	238.8	23	3059771
OE	Orbital Engine Corp. Ltd.	—	6/30/02	52.0	d26.8	45.0	d12.7	4	132252
ORB	Orbital Sciences Corp.	—	12/31/02	p551.6	p538.7	—	—	90	25729394
OS	Oregon Steel Mills, Inc.	Steel producer	12/31/01	1561.8	775.0	869.6	318.6	60	18306613
OEH	Orient Express Hotels Ltd. (B	Motel/hotel lodging	12/31/02	261.3	29.9	836.3	392.6	38	12286005
OFG	Oriental Financial Group Inc	—	6/30/02	172.9	38.5	2489.1	166.4	48	2842113
IX	Orix Corp. (Japan)	Financial services	3/31/02	—	—	—	—	21	894123
OCA	Orthodontic Centers of Amer	Services	12/31/02	351.0	61.1	580.5	389.5	149	38259625
OSK	Oshkosh Truck Corp.	Transportation	9/30/02	1743.6	59.6	1024.3	409.8	164	12961092
OSI	Outback Steakhouse, Inc.	Restaurants	12/31/02	p2362.1	p1372.1	—	—	221	57993923
OSG	Overseas Shipholding Grp Inc	Freight transportation	12/31/01	381.0	101.4	1964.3	813.4	93	15681566
OMI	Owens & Minor, Inc.	Medical & dental equipment	12/31/02	p3959.8	p388.9	—	—	144	31302309
OI	Owens-Illinois, Inc.	Plastics & plastic products	12/31/02	p5760.1	p5283.3	—	—	156	102571143
OHP	Oxford Health Plans, Inc.	Insurance brokerage	12/31/02	4963.4	222.0	1753.5	496.9	258	83574078
OXM	Oxford Industries, Inc.	—	5/31/02	677.3	10.6	250.5	175.2	59	4422482
IIT	P.T. Indonesian Satellite Cor	Telecommunications	12/31/01	—	—	—	—	15	3861497
TLK	P.T. Telekomunikasi Indonesia	Telecommunications	12/31/01	—	—	—	—	46	13260176
PAI	Pacific Amer. Income Shs Inc	Investment company	12/31/02	10.5	9.4	151.3	141.2	13	331710
PPX	Pacific Energy Partners L.P.	Natural gas distributor	12/31/02	p124.5	p124.5	—	—	16	269387
PKG	Packaging Corp of America	Containers	12/31/02	p1735.9	p1735.9	—	—	140	56950540
PTV	Pactiv Corp.	Plastics & plastic products	12/31/01	2812.0	165.0	4060.0	1689.0	301	129249026
PLL	Pall Corp.	Pollution control	8/3/02	1290.8	73.2	2027.2	819.7	273	109278846
PNP	Pan Pacific Retail Propertie	Real estate investment trust	12/31/01	189.0	64.2	1339.6	622.5	131	26741678
PB	Panamerican Beverages, Inc.	Soft drinks	12/31/01	—	—	—	—	90	40545635
PTC	Par Technology Corp.	Computer services	12/31/01	118.5	0.5	89.0	47.6	9	958947
PKE	Park Electrochemical Corp.	Electronic components	3/3/02	230.1	d25.5	360.6	292.5	99	14745050
PPE	Park Place Entertainment Corp	Gaming	12/31/02	p4652.0	p3671.0	—	—	230	203869656
PKD	Parker Drilling Co. (United	Oil service & equipment	12/31/02	p389.9	p316.8	—	—	103	39118294

T36

EARNINGS PER SHARE — QUARTERLY			ANNUAL			P/E RATIO	DIVIDENDS PER SHARE			AV. YLD. %	DIV. DECLARED		PRICE RANGE
1st	2nd	3rd	2002	2001	2000		2002	2001	2000		AMOUNT	PAYABLE	2002
—	—	—	15.87	15.78	14.51	—	1.05	0.87	0.89	6.8	0.0845M	4/1/03	16.57 - 14.29
—	—	—	15.63	15.71	14.67	—	0.98	0.88	0.88	6.5	0.084M	4/1/03	16.00 - 14.00
—	14.69	—	—67856459.00		14.26	—	0.85	0.82	0.83	5.4	0.0735M	4/1/03	16.87 - 14.88
—	14.33	—	—	14.04	13.83	—	0.87	0.81	0.78	5.6	0.076M	4/1/03	17.07 - 14.20
—	—	—	15.56	15.31	14.24	—	0.88	0.82	0.83	5.8	0.077M	4/1/03	15.94 - 14.25
—	—	—	15.48	15.32	14.54	—	1.01	0.96	0.92	6.5	0.078M	4/1/03	16.68 - 14.60
—	—	—	15.41	15.65	14.61	—	1.03	0.96	0.99	7.1	0.086M	4/1/03	15.65 - 13.33
—	—	—	10.61	10.92	11.01	—	0.61	0.69	0.70	6.0	0.05M	4/1/03	11.30 - 9.00
—	—	—	14.60	15.24	14.36	—	0.92	0.89	0.94	6.5	0.079M	4/1/03	15.05 - 13.25
—	—	—	9.98	10.17	9.77	—	0.55	0.52	0.53	5.9	0.0415M	4/1/03	9.77 - 8.98
—	14.54	—	—	14.18	13.94	—	0.84	0.77	0.78	5.4	0.073M	4/1/03	16.99 - 14.35
—	14.78	—	—	14.17	14.51	—	0.80	0.75	0.78	5.9	0.057M	4/1/03	14.45 - 12.88
—	—	—	15.07	15.03	14.45	—	0.98	0.92	0.92	6.5	0.078M	4/1/03	16.00 - 14.38
—	—	—	15.60	15.27	14.28	—	0.88	0.83	0.83	5.8	0.078M	4/1/03	16.15 - 14.28
—	—	—	16.92	15.67	14.50	—	0.98	0.89	0.89	6.5	0.0805M	4/1/03	16.04 - 14.34
—	—	—	10.16	9.86	9.51	—	0.48	0.51	0.51	5.2	0.039M	4/1/03	9.59 - 8.84
—	—	—	17.11	15.95	14.67	—	1.18	0.89	0.92	7.5	0.0825M	4/1/03	16.78 - 14.77
—	—	—	16.37	15.20	14.44	—	1.08	0.87	0.88	7.3	0.0765M	4/1/03	15.44 - 14.00
—	—	—	16.48	15.41	14.57	—	1.05	1.00	0.91	7.0	0.0785M	4/1/03	15.90 - 14.02
—	—	—	16.36	16.10	15.52	—	0.95	0.90	0.95	5.4	0.0835M	4/1/03	19.04 - 16.10
—	—	—	14.70	14.57	14.39	—	0.91	0.91	0.94	6.1	0.076M	4/1/03	15.86 - 13.90
—	—	—	14.70	14.44	13.48	—	0.90	0.82	0.79	6.3	0.079M	4/1/03	15.24 - 13.61
—	—	—	15.38	15.57	14.36	—	0.93	0.88	0.83	6.5	0.0795M	4/1/03	15.21 - 13.29
—	—	—	15.59	15.55	14.66	—	0.99	0.89	0.88	6.4	0.0815M	4/1/03	16.20 - 14.37
—	—	—	15.23	15.31	14.42	—	1.05	0.95	0.94	7.2	0.0825M	4/1/03	15.71 - 13.65
—	—	—	14.87	15.27	14.23	—	0.92	0.82	0.78	6.5	0.08M	4/1/03	15.05 - 13.21
—	—	—	15.27	15.53	14.75	—	1.07	0.95	0.91	7.4	0.0815M	4/1/03	15.33 - 13.77
—	—	—	13.46	14.22	13.54	—	0.85	0.82	0.81	6.6	0.071M	4/1/03	13.90 - 12.11
—	—	—	14.70	15.32	14.53	—	0.96	1.00	0.95	6.8	0.0805M	4/1/03	14.99 - 13.25
—	—	—		14.32		—	0.52	—	—	3.5	0.105M	4/1/03	15.70 - 13.50
—	—	—	14.32			—	0.21	—	—	1.4	0.105M	4/1/03	15.23 - 13.92
—	—	—	14.32			—					0.103M	4/1/03	15.05 - 15.00
—	10.32	—	—	10.57	11.21	—	0.55	0.66	0.63	5.3	0.044M	4/1/03	11.35 - 9.51
—	—	—	15.00	15.48	14.48	—	0.94	1.03	0.91	6.6	0.082M	4/1/03	15.31 - 13.50
—	14.48	—	—	14.26	14.53	—	0.85	0.80	0.82	6.3	0.0575M	4/1/03	14.14 - 12.72
—	15.17	—	—	14.67	15.05	—	1.01	0.89	0.90	7.1	0.062M	4/1/03	14.95 - 13.35
—	14.84	—	—	14.53	14.89	—	1.00	0.87	0.87	7.2	0.0605M	4/1/03	14.74 - 12.95
—	—	—	7.38	8.13	9.47	—	0.58	0.94	1.03	8.3	0.043M	4/1/03	8.11 - 5.83
—	—	—	15.14	15.16	14.26	—	0.95	0.94	0.89	6.4	0.08M	4/1/03	15.75 - 13.91
—	14.89	—	—	14.69	14.59	—	0.88	0.84	0.82	5.3	0.076M	4/1/03	18.00 - 15.05
0.08	0.32	0.18	p3.08	d1.42	d0.60	7.2 - 4.5	—	0.40	0.40	—	0.06Q	4/8/03	22.21 - 13.85
—	—	—	—	0.72	0.73	—	—	—	—	—	2-for-1	10/10/96	20.09 - 8.87
—	—	—	p2.61	3.09	4.26	11.8 - 8.8	1.00	1.00	1.00	3.7	0.26Q	4/15/03	30.75 - 22.98
—	—	—	0.74	1.55	1.22	30.9 - 21.4	0.16	0.16	—	0.8	0.04Q	4/24/03	22.85 - 15.80
—	—	—	p1.63	1.38	0.49	19.7 - 11.3	—	—	—	—			32.17 - 18.40
—	—	—	p4.15	1.35	1.41	6.4 - 3.8	0.05	—	—	0.2	0.05S	9/30/02	26.42 - 15.76
—	—	—	pd0.99	d1.89	d0.25	—	—	—	—	—	2-for-1	11/20/97	8.54 - 2.05
—	—	—	p3.20	d0.14	2.63	6.3 - 4.0	0.10	0.03	—	0.6	0.025Q	3/31/03	20.25 - 12.87
—	—	—	0.98	0.66	0.16	22.4 - 10.8	—	—	—	—	3-for-2	4/1/99	21.96 - 10.60
—	—	—	p0.59	2.72	d1.20	13.7 - 5.2	—	—	—	—	3-for-2	7/9/96	8.06 - 3.05
0.39	0.51	p0.49	p1.16	1.29	1.89	20.9 - 11.8	1.33	1.33	1.33	7.0	0.3325Q	1/30/03	24.24 - 13.70
—	—	—	—	1.84	1.84	—	1.84	1.84	1.84	7.4		3/31/03	25.73 - 23.90
—	—	—	p0.81	0.95	0.04	16.7 - 8.5	—	—	—	—			13.50 - 6.90
0.07	p0.22	—	d0.19	0.16	0.39	—	0.36	0.36	0.36	4.2	0.09Q	6/13/03	10.25 - 7.05
—	—	—	p1.84	1.42	0.93	13.7 - 11.5	0.69	0.62	0.59	3.0	0.19Q	3/17/03	25.24 - 21.24
—	—	—	p3.23	2.88	2.47	10.8 - 7.6	0.63	0.59	0.55	2.1	0.16Q	3/17/03	35.00 - 24.40
d0.26	d0.15	d0.02	—	0.22	1.80	—	0.80	0.80	0.80	4.4	0.20Q	3/10/03	22.60 - 13.85
—	—	—	pd11.69	3.28	2.95	—	0.42	0.52	0.44	1.1	0.14Q	8/30/02	73.70 - 4.00
—	—	—	d1.00	1.98	d3.32	—	—	—	1.00	—	0.25Q	11/15/00	7.66 - 3.25
—	—	—	d1.00	d1.98	d3.32	—	—	—	2.16	—		11/15/00	22.97 - 16.62
—	—	—	p0.48	0.16	d0.70	10.3 - 5.2	—	—	—	—			4.95 - 2.50
—	—	—	p0.22	1.21	0.93	23.5 - 12.8	—	—	—	—			5.18 - 2.82
—	—	—	p1.33	0.79	0.53	21.7 - 13.2	0.09	0.09	0.09	0.4	0.0225Q	3/14/03	28.83 - 17.51
—	—	—	p3.44	2.70	2.73	28.3 - 10.6	0.80	0.75	0.70	1.2	0.20Q	4/4/03	97.35 - 36.50
—	—	—	0.18	d0.17	0.11	54.4 - 20.2	—	0.10	0.20	—	0.05Q	5/31/01	9.80 - 3.63
—	—	—	p0.55	0.51	d0.09	35.9 - 19.3	0.08	0.25	0.30	0.5	0.02Q	4/30/03	19.75 - 10.60
—	—	—	p1.39	0.85	1.48	16.6 - 10.5	0.62	0.62	0.62	3.3	0.155Q	2/17/03	23.14 - 14.62
—	—	—	8.17	8.37	8.85	—	0.62	0.80	0.84	7.7	0.04M	3/28/03	9.00 - 7.22
—	—	—	p0.07	d0.76	d0.49	—	—	—	—	—	1-for-75	10/30/92	2.44 - 0.57
—	—	—	p0.30	d2.49	d6.09	28.7 - 8.2	—	—	—	—			8.60 - 2.47
d0.01	0.20	0.19	—	d0.22	d0.69	—	—	—	0.06	—	0.02Q	8/31/00	8.20 - 3.50
—	—	—	—	0.97	1.43	—	—	—	—				20.90 - 12.00
0.60	0.65	—	2.00	0.36	0.95	10.4 - 6.5	0.47	0.44	0.44	2.8	0.14Q	4/15/03	20.76 - 12.95
—	—	—	—	—	—	—	0.05	0.05	0.06	0.1		3/27/03	45.85 - 26.95
0.36	0.23	0.37	—	1.21	0.96	—	—	—	—		2-for-1	9/5/96	31.33 - 7.80
0.65	—	—	3.45	2.98	2.96	19.0 - 13.4	0.34	0.34	0.34	0.6	0.08625Q	2/13/03	65.38 - 46.11
—	—	—	p2.03	1.70	1.78	19.6 - 12.3	0.12	—	—	0.4	0.12Q	3/7/03	39.80 - 24.90
0.02	0.11	d0.86	—	2.92	2.49	—	0.60	0.60	0.60	3.0	0.15Q	3/11/03	24.80 - 14.80
—	—	—	p1.26	0.85	0.94	16.6 - 10.3	0.31	0.27	0.25	1.8	0.08Q	3/31/03	20.90 - 13.00
—	—	—	pd0.08	2.33	d2.00	—	—	—	—	—			19.19 - 9.55
—	—	—	2.45	3.21	2.24	21.2 - 11.7	—	—	—	—	2-for-1	4/1/96	51.94 - 28.64
0.60	0.56	—	—	1.40	2.05	—	0.84	0.84	0.84	3.4	0.21Q	3/4/03	30*.25 - 19.50
—	—	—	—	—	—	—	0.52	0.48	0.64	4.9	0.5214U	8/8/02	14.35 - 7.10
—	—	—	—	—	—	—	0.40	0.13	0.26	5.3	0.4045U	8/22/02	9.90 - 5.27
—	—	—	15.12	15.12	14.84	36.9 - 33.1	1.00	1.06	1.07	7.0	0.24625Q	3/14/03	15.10 - 13.35
—	—	—	p0.55	—	—	46.9 - 36.0	0.34	—	—	1.8	0.4625Q	2/14/03	20.28 - 18.20
—	—	—	p0.45	0.99	1.43	—	—	—	—				21.10 - 16.20
0.26	0.38	0.37	—	1.03	0.70	—	—	—	—				24.47 - 15.35
d0.19	0.25	—	0.59	0.95	1.18	41.5 - 24.9	0.44	0.68	0.66	2.2	0.09Q	2/17/03	24.48 - 14.68
0.49	0.50	0.52	—	1.97	1.48	—	1.90	1.82	1.94	5.8	0.50Q	2/14/03	37.00 - 28.00
—	—	—	—	—	—	—	0.24	0.24	0.24	1.7	0.06Q	3/31/03	21.10 - 7.45
0.05	0.07	0.11	—	0.07	d1.71	—	—	—	—				8.13 - 2.55
d0.03	—	d0.27	—	d1.31	2.65	—	0.24	0.24	0.22	1.1	0.06Q	2/4/03	31.78 - 13.10
—	—	—	p0.53	d0.08	0.46	24.4 - 11.4	—	—	—	—			12.93 - 6.06
—	—	—	pd0.44	0.12	d0.23	—	—	—	—	—	0.01Q	2/17/87	4.82 - 1.50

SYMBOL	COMPANY	NATURE OF BUSINESS	FISCAL YEAR-END	TOTAL REV. $MILL	NET INCOME $MILL	TOTAL ASSETS $MILL	NET STK EQUITY $MILL	NO. OF INST.	INST. HOLDINGS (SHARES)
PH	Parker-Hannifin	Electronic components	6/30/02	6149.1	130.2	5752.6	2583.5	290	91328064
PKY	Parkway Properties Inc. (Unit	Real estate	12/31/01	156.1	29.5	763.9	376.8	84	6089180
PRE	PartnerRe Ltd. (Bermuda)	Property & casualty insurance	12/31/01	1895.0	d185.3	7165.4	1748.1	132	37237359
POG	Patina Oil & Gas Corp.	Oil	12/31/02	222.4	57.7	719.1	298.6	152	23228855
PXR	Paxar Corp. (New)	Printing & engraving	12/31/01	610.6	18.8	583.8	286.1	128	28425019
PSS	Payless Shoesource Inc. (DE)	Department stores	2/1/03	p2878.0	p2878.0	—	—	174	24688609
ABI	PE Biosystem Group		6/30/01	1619.5	212.4	1677.9	1041.2	294	200638617
BTU	Peabody Energy Corp. (United	Coal	12/31/02	p2717.1	p2717.1	—	—	132	46601481
PSO	Pearson Plc (United Kingdom)	Publishing	12/31/01	—	—	—	—	55	11949664
PY	Pechiney (France)	Metal products	12/31/01	—	—	—	—	21	4403164
PDX	Pediatrix Medical Group, Inc.	Services	12/31/02	p465.5	p465.5	—	—	163	23619351
PNN A	Penn Engineering & Mfg.	Electronic components	12/31/02	p150.8	p150.8	—	—	14	1820462
PNN	Penn Engineering & Mfg.	Electronic components	12/31/02	p150.8	p150.8	—	—	44	11054284
PTA	Penn Treaty American Corp.	Life insurance	12/31/01	382.4	d48.6	940.4	192.8	24	3887801
PVA	Penn Virginia Corp.	Oil	12/31/02	p111.0	p111.0	—	—	83	6763613
PVR	Penn Virginia Resource Partn	Coal	12/31/02	p38.6	p38.6	—	—	31	1248082
PNG	Penn-America Group, Inc. (Uni	Insurance brokerage	12/31/02	p128.1	p123.7	—	—	38	8166098
JCP	Penney (J.C.) Co.,Inc. (Holdi	Department stores	1/25/03	—	—	—	—	338	246040048
PEI	Pennsylvania R.E. Invest. Tr.	Real estate investment trust	12/31/01	113.6	19.8	602.6	180.3	72	4370290
PNR	Pentair, Inc.	Machine tools	12/31/02	2580.8	129.9	2514.4	1105.7	200	33617329
PME	Penton Media, Inc. (United S	Publishing	12/31/01	371.6	d104.1	700.5	220.5	40	12741392
PGL	Peoples Energy Corp.	Natural gas distributor	9/30/02	1482.5	89.1	2723.6	806.3	211	18100442
PBY	Pep Boys-Manny, Moe & Jack (		2/2/02	2183.7	36.1	1812.7	617.8	157	36704444
POM	Pepco Holdings Inc. (United	Electric power	12/31/01	—	—	200.0	200.0	238	78246352
PBG	Pepsi Bottling Group Inc (Un	Soft drinks	12/28/02	p9216.0	p9216.0	—	—	307	165851946
PAS	PepsiAmericas, Inc. (New)	Conglomerate	12/31/02	p2329.8	p2324.3	—	—	168	59847574
PEP	Pepsico Inc.	Soft drinks	12/28/02	25112.0	3313.0	23474.0	9298.0	1101	1274666903
PDA	Perdigao S.A.	Meat packing & processing	12/31/02	—	—	—	—	2	195100
PC	Perez Companc S.A. (Argentin	Oil	12/31/01	—	—	—	—	31	9608978
PKI	PerkinElmer, Inc.	Electronic components	12/31/02	p1505.0	p1357.2	—	—	239	86883279
PBT	Permian Basin Royalty Trust	Oil	12/31/01	39.9	39.5	4.2	2.4	12	4220960
PER	Perot Systems Corp.	Computer services	12/31/02	p1332.1	p1288.2	—	—	95	46338010
PTR	PetroChina Co Ltd	Oil	12/31/01	—	—	46800.0	460874.0	38	3172367
PBR A	Petroleo Brasileiro SA	Oil	12/31/01	—	—	—	—	110	16043265
PBR	Petroleo Brasileiro SA	Oil	12/31/01	—	—	—	—	119	134608258
PEO	Petroleum & Resources Corp.	Investment company	12/31/02	11.4	9.0	500.1	451.3	26	3169970
PV	Pfeiffer Vacuum Technology AG		12/31/01	—	—	—	—	2	70480
PFB	PFF Bancorp Inc.	Banking - West	3/31/02	232.8	35.4	3042.9	284.1	80	8280577
PFE	Pfizer Inc	Drugs	12/31/01	—	—	—	—	1407	d22739773
PCG	PG&E Corp. (Holding Co.)	Electric power	12/31/01	12495.0	d57.0	33696.0	3613.0	287	226819721
PRX	Pharmaceutical Resources, Inc	Drugs	12/31/02	p381.6	p381.6	—	—	167	25164398
PHA	Pharmacia Corp	Chemicals	12/31/01	—	—	—	—	800	1047121461
PD	Phelps Dodge Corp.	Copper	12/31/02	p3722.0	p3513.7	—	—	252	78628206
PSC	Philadelphia Suburban Corp.	Water company	12/31/02	p322.0	p325.7	—	—	165	22605302
PHI	Philippine Long Dist Tel Co	Telecommunications	12/31/01	—	—	—	—	43	24680005
PVH	Phillips-Van Heusen Corp.		2/2/03	p1405.0	p1405.0	—	—	112	19344557
PNX	Phoenix Companies, Inc. (The	Insurance	12/31/02	p2452.9	p2167.3	—	—	150	44483899
PFX	Phoenix Companies, Inc. (The	Insurance	12/31/02	p2452.9	p2167.3	—	—	—	—
PLP	Phosphate Resource Partners	Mining & processing	12/31/02	p18.2	p18.2	—	—	20	32761512
PNY	Piedmont Natural Gas Co., In	Natural gas distributor	10/31/02	832.0	62.2	1445.1	589.6	143	9359459
PIR	Pier 1 Imports, Inc	Specialty stores	3/2/02	1548.6	100.2	862.7	585.7	266	74295829
CHX	Pilgrim's Pride Corp.	Meat packing & processing	9/28/02	2533.7	14.3	1227.9	394.3	48	6824952
CHX A	Pilgrim's Pride Corp.	Meat packing & processing	9/28/02	2533.7	14.3	1227.9	394.3	20	2413042
PCQ	Pimco California Municipal I	Investment company	4/30/02	16.6	14.7	398.3	396.7	5	54439
PZC	Pimco California Municipal I	Investment company	10/22/02	—	—	0.0	—	—	—
PCK	Pimco California Municipal In	Investment company	6/19/02	—	—	0.0	—	—	—
PCM	PIMCO Coml Mtg Secs Tr Inc	Investment company	12/31/01	18.8	14.1	209.1	141.7	17	412116
PCN	Pimco Corporate Income Fund	Investment company	10/31/02	44.4	40.1	745.1	430.0	—	—
PTY	Pimco Corporate Opportunity F	Investment company	12/16/02	—	—	0.1	0.1	—	—
PMX	Pimco Municipal Income Fund	Investment company	10/22/02	—	—	0.0	—	—	—
PML	Pimco Municipal Income Fund I	Investment company	6/19/02	—	—	0.0	—	—	—
PNI	Pimco New York Municipal Fund	Investment company	6/19/02	—	—	0.0	—	—	—
PYN	Pimco New York Municipal Inc	Investment company	10/22/02	—	—	0.0	—	—	—
RCS	PIMCO Strategic Global Gover	Investment company	1/31/02	33.8	29.8	814.7	382.8	—	—
PNK	Pinnacle Entertainment Inc		12/31/02	p514.0	p463.4	—	—	91	14791687
PNW	Pinnacle West Capital Corp.	Electric power	12/31/02	p2637.3	p2571.5	—	—	228	72838212
PIO	Pioneer Corp (Japan)	Consumer electronics	3/31/02	—	—	—	—	10	327318
PHH	Pioneer High Income Trust (Un	Investment company	4/22/02	—	0.7	—	—	—	—
MUO	Pioneer Interest Shares	Investment company	12/31/02	7.2	6.5	91.7	90.3	19	689141
PXD	Pioneer Natural Resources Co	Oil	12/31/02	717.4	49.1	3455.1	1374.9	245	88494920
PBI	Pitney Bowes, Inc.	Office equipment & supplies	12/31/02	4409.8	437.7	8732.3	853.3	487	188294603
PAA	Plains All American Pipeline	Oil producer	12/31/02	p8384.2	p8384.2	—	—	65	8211130
PXP	Plains Exploration & Product	Oil	12/31/02	204.1	54.7	516.8	180.1	80	11896815
PLX	Plains Resources Inc. (Unite	Oil	12/31/02	p14.9	p14.9	—	—	95	15477962
PLT	Plantronics, Inc.	Communications electronics	3/31/02	311.2	36.2	201.1	142.0	177	43040144
PTP	Platinum Underwriters Holdin	Insurance	6/30/02	—	—	0.1	0.1	—	—
PLA A	Playboy Enterprises, Inc.	Publishing	12/31/02	p277.6	p277.6	—	—	13	708409
PLA	Playboy Enterprises, Inc.	Publishing	12/31/02	p277.6	p277.6	—	—	46	12764324
PYX	Playtex Products, Inc.	Cosmetics & toiletries	12/29/01	830.0	30.9	1105.2	d44.6	109	44024243
PCL	Plum Creek Timber Co., Inc.	Forest products	12/31/02	1137.0	233.0	4289.0	2222.0	371	81796792
PMI	PMI Group, Inc. (The) (Unite	Insurance brokerage	12/31/02	p1121.4	p1143.5	—	—	240	87567553
PNC	PNC Financial Services Group	Banking - Mid-Atlantic	12/31/02	6369.0	1200.0	66377.0	6859.0	481	184063343
PNM	PNM Resources, Inc. (Holding	Electric power	12/31/02	p1169.0	p1169.0	—	—	161	33855139
PPP	Pogo Producing Co.	Oil	12/31/02	751.4	107.0	2491.6	1077.8	201	52996822
PII	Polaris Industries Inc.	Recreation	12/31/02	1521.3	103.6	608.6	277.1	196	15028758
RL	Polo Ralph Lauren Corp.		3/30/02	2363.7	172.5	1749.5	998.2	143	34614792
POL	PolyOne Corp.	Plastics & plastic products	12/31/02	p2498.2	p2440.7	—	—	147	83764876
POP	Pope & Talbot, Inc.	Forest products	12/31/02	546.3	d20.9	504.4	143.9	91	11649898
PGB	Portland General Electric Co	Electric power	12/31/01	3047.0	23.0	3474.0	1090.0	2	7725
PT	Portugal Telecom, SGPS, S.A.	Telecommunications	12/31/01	—	—	—	—	63	57172945
PKX	POSCO (South Korea)	Steel producer	12/31/01	—	—	—	—	132	60550279
PPS	Post Properties, Inc.	Real estate investment trust	12/31/02	p330.0	p330.0	—	—	127	23434787
PCH	Potlatch Corp.	Forest products	12/31/02	p1286.2	p1286.2	—	—	118	15092303
PPG	PPG Industries, Inc.	Chemicals	12/31/02	8067.0	d60.0	7863.0	2150.0	429	247217563
PPL	PPL Corp	Electric power	12/31/02	p5429.0	p4991.0	—	—	296	91395972
PX	Praxair, Inc.	Specialty chemicals	12/31/02	5176.0	548.0	7401.0	2340.0	417	146118348

EARNINGS PER SHARE — QUARTERLY 1st	2nd	3rd	ANNUAL 2002	2001	2000	P/E RATIO	DIVIDENDS PER SHARE 2002	2001	2000	AV. YLD. %	DIV. DECLARED AMOUNT	PAYABLE	PRICE RANGE 2002
0.52	0.32	—	1.12	2.99	3.31	49.0 - 30.8	0.72	0.72	0.68	1.6	0.19Q	3/7/03	54.88 - 34.52
—	—	—	1.84	1.99	2.93	20.9 - 16.0	2.56	2.45	2.12	7.5	0.65Q	3/28/03	38.37 - 29.52
—	—	—	—	d3.60	2.41	—	1.15	1.10	1.04	2.4	0.29Q	3/3/03	58.20 - 38.95
—	—	—	2.09	2.30	1.82	16.7 - 9.5	0.20	0.14	0.08	0.7	0.06Q	3/28/03	34.84 - 19.76
0.19	0.32	0.25	0.44	1.73	—	—	—	—	—	—	5-for-4	9/9/97	18.05 - 12.20
—	—	—	p4.64	2.01	5.16	13.9 - 8.9	—	—	—	—	3-for-1	3/27/03	64.70 - 41.20
—	—	—	—	0.96	0.86	—	0.17	0.17	0.17	0.7	0.0425Q	4/1/03	39.28 - 13.00
—	—	—	p1.96	0.38	2.97	15.7 - 8.9	0.40	0.20	—	1.5	0.10Q	3/5/03	30.75 - 17.50
—	—	—	—	—	—	—	0.34	0.31	0.32	3.1	0.22874U	5/19/03	13.73 - 7.85
—	—	—	—	—	—	—	0.39	0.38	0.33	1.9	0.4504U	6/3/03	28.13 - 12.17
—	—	—	p2.58	1.36	0.68	18.6 - 8.0	—	—	—	—	2-for-1	2/26/99	47.91 - 20.70
—	—	—	p0.23	0.53	1.57	83.5 - 43.3	0.30	0.24	0.26	2.1	0.06Q	3/14/03	19.20 - 9.95
—	—	—	p0.23	0.53	1.57	90.2 - 37.0	0.30	0.24	0.26	2.1	0.06Q	3/14/03	20.75 - 8.50
d0.72	0.57	d1.26	—	d3.41	2.61	—	—	—	—	—	3-for-2	5/15/95	6.85 - 1.65
—	—	—	p1.34	3.86	4.69	31.3 - 19.4	0.90	0.90	0.90	2.6	0.225Q	3/19/03	42.00 - 26.03
—	—	—	p1.57	0.24	—	16.7 - 10.7	1.84	—	—	8.5	0.50Q	2/14/03	26.25 - 16.80
—	—	—	p0.88	0.47	d0.33	13.1 - 8.0	0.15	0.14	0.14	1.7	0.04375Q	3/20/03	11.53 - 7.00
—	—	—	p1.37	0.32	d2.29	20.3 - 10.3	0.38	—	—	1.8	0.125Q	2/1/03	27.75 - 14.07
0.23	0.27	0.27	—	1.35	2.41	—	2.04	2.04	1.92	8.5	0.51Q	3/17/03	27.20 - 20.55
d0.15	d1.77	d7.49	2.61	1.17	1.68	19.1 - 11.1	0.74	0.70	0.66	1.9	0.21Q	5/9/03	49.84 - 29.02
0.87	—	—	—	d3.26	2.49	—	—	0.09	0.12	—	0.03Q	7/2/01	9.65 - 0.18
0.26	0.30	0.28	2.51	2.74	2.44	16.1 - 11.1	2.07	2.03	1.99	6.1	0.53Q	4/15/03	40.41 - 27.80
—	—	0.80	—	0.69	d1.04	—	0.27	0.27	0.27	1.9	0.0675Q	1/27/03	19.39 - 8.75
—	—	—	—	—	—	—	0.42	—	—	2.1	0.25Q	3/31/03	21.88 - 18.30
—	—	—	p1.46	1.03	0.77	23.8 - 14.8	0.04	0.04	0.04	0.1	0.01Q	3/31/03	34.80 - 21.65
—	—	—	p0.88	0.58	0.51	18.1 - 12.6	0.04	0.04	0.05	0.3	0.04A	4/1/03	15.94 - 11.12
—	—	—	1.85	1.47	1.48	28.9 - 18.9	0.59	0.57	0.55	1.3	0.15Q	3/31/03	53.50 - 35.01
—	—	—	—	—	—	—	0.67	0.39	0.06	5.1	0.0676U	9/9/02	21.04 - 5.05
—	—	—	—	—	—	—	—	0.32	0.15	—	—	5/2/01	12.90 - 3.56
—	—	—	pd0.03	d0.01	0.84	—	0.28	0.28	0.28	1.4	0.07Q	5/9/03	36.30 - 4.28
0.09	0.12	0.13	—	0.85	0.76	—	0.49	0.87	0.75	9.0	—	3/14/03	6.40 - 4.50
—	—	—	p0.68	d0.03	0.49	30.5 - 12.1	—	—	—	—	—	—	20.75 - 8.21
—	—	—	—	0.27	0.32	—	1.21	1.83	0.71	6.0	0.6056U	10/18/02	22.48 - 17.90
—	—	—	—	—	—	—	0.81	1.44	0.43	4.7	—	3/25/03	26.00 - 8.66
—	—	—	—	—	—	—	1.08	1.44	—	5.9	—	3/25/03	27.42 - 9.34
—	—	—	20.98	24.90	32.69	—	1.11	1.50	1.75	5.2	0.04Q	3/1/03	25.74 - 17.31
0.68	0.65	0.70	—	—	—	—	0.42	0.31	0.28	1.5	0.4172U	6/18/02	37.53 - 16.45
—	—	—	—	2.69	2.42	—	0.34	0.26	0.24	1.1	0.10Q	3/28/03	38.50 - 23.50
—	—	—	p1.59	1.22	0.59	26.7 - 15.8	0.52	0.44	0.36	1.5	0.15Q	2/14/03	42.46 - 25.13
—	—	—	d0.15	2.99	d9.18	—	—	—	1.20	—	0.30Q	10/15/00	23.75 - 8.00
—	—	—	p2.40	1.68	d0.03	14.1 - 6.5	—	—	—	—	—	—	33.80 - 15.60
—	—	—	p0.44	0.97	0.75	106.0 - 69.0	0.54	0.51	0.29	1.4	0.135Q	2/1/03	46.64 - 30.36
—	—	—	pd1.69	d3.47	0.37	—	—	0.75	2.00	—	0.125Q	9/7/01	42.51 - 22.90
—	—	—	p0.97	0.87	0.81	25.8 - 16.5	0.54	0.54	0.50	2.6	0.14Q	3/1/03	25.00 - 16.02
—	—	—	—	—	—	—	—	0.04	0.09	—	—	4/16/01	11.30 - 3.85
—	—	—	p1.08	0.38	1.10	15.0 - 9.6	0.15	0.15	0.15	1.1	0.0375Q	3/28/03	16.25 - 10.35
—	—	—	pd2.51	—	—	—	0.16	—	—	1.2	0.16A	7/10/02	20.25 - 6.50
—	—	—	pd2.51	—	—	—	1.49	—	—	6.6	—	4/15/03	25.85 - 19.60
—	—	—	pd0.22	d0.69	d0.18	—	—	—	0.09	—	0.09Q	2/14/00	5.20 - 1.65
p1.74	—	—	1.89	2.02	2.01	20.1 - 14.5	1.59	1.52	1.44	4.9	0.415Q	4/15/03	38.00 - 27.35
0.23	0.23	0.33	1.04	0.97	—	—	0.19	0.16	0.14	1.0	0.06Q	2/19/03	24.35 - 14.35
0.07	—	—	0.35	1.02	1.27	42.8 - 11.6	0.06	0.06	0.06	0.6	0.015Q	3/28/03	14.99 - 4.05
0.07	—	—	0.35	1.02	1.27	32.1 - 9.2	0.06	0.06	0.06	0.8	0.015Q	3/28/03	11.25 - 3.21
—	—	—	—	14.00	—	—	0.92	0.38	—	6.3	0.077M	4/1/03	15.40 - 13.95
—	—	—	—	—	—	—	—	—	—	—	0.08M	4/15/03	15.10 - 13.85
—	—	—	—	14.33	—	—	0.41	—	—	2.8	0.08125M	4/15/03	15.50 - 13.94
—	—	—	—	12.85	12.86	—	1.35	1.31	1.18	9.6	0.09375M	4/10/03	15.25 - 12.60
—	—	—	12.25	14.32	—	—	1.17	—	—	8.5	0.10625M	4/1/03	15.25 - 12.01
—	—	—	14.33	—	—	—	—	—	—	—	0.1375M	4/1/03	15.04 - 15.00
—	—	—	14.33	—	—	—	—	—	—	—	0.0831M	4/1/03	15.01 - 13.92
—	—	—	—	14.33	—	—	0.42	—	—	2.9	—	4/15/03	15.25 - 13.92
—	—	—	14.33	—	—	—	0.41	—	—	2.7	0.08125M	4/15/03	15.70 - 13.87
—	—	—	—	14.33	—	—	—	—	—	—	0.08M	4/15/03	15.03 - 13.85
—	11.04	—	—	11.20	11.14	—	0.89	1.00	1.08	7.8	0.074M	4/1/03	12.70 - 10.20
—	—	—	pd0.50	d1.11	2.90	—	—	—	—	—	25%	6/1/93	12.68 - 5.02
—	—	—	p1.76	3.85	3.56	26.5 - 12.3	1.63	1.52	1.42	4.8	0.425Q	3/26/03	46.68 - 21.70
—	—	—	—	—	—	—	0.10	0.10	0.10	0.5	—	3/26/03	25.06 - 14.83
—	—	—	—	14.32	—	—	0.96	—	—	7.3	0.1375M	4/1/03	15.25 - 11.25
—	—	—	12.22	12.33	12.36	—	0.81	0.87	0.93	7.0	0.19Q	3/31/03	12.25 - 11.03
—	—	—	0.43	1.04	1.65	64.0 - 37.4	—	—	—	—	0.05S	9/15/98	27.50 - 16.10
—	—	—	1.81	2.08	2.18	24.5 - 15.8	1.18	1.16	1.14	3.2	0.30Q	3/12/03	44.41 - 28.55
—	—	—	p1.34	1.12	2.64	20.4 - 14.6	2.11	1.95	1.82	9.0	0.5375Q	2/14/03	27.30 - 19.50
—	—	—	2.26	1.19	0.79	4.6 - —	—	—	—	—	—	—	10.30 - 0.00
—	—	—	p0.34	4.82	1.56	81.6 - 34.0	—	—	—	—	0.00U	12/18/02	27.75 - 11.55
0.21	0.24	0.20	—	0.74	1.38	—	—	—	—	—	200%	8/8/00	28.00 - 12.41
—	—	—	—	—	—	—	—	—	—	—	0.08Q	3/31/03	26.79 - 24.10
—	—	—	pd0.67	d1.20	d1.96	—	—	—	—	—	—	—	15.06 - 6.50
0.47	0.32	0.14	pd0.67	d1.20	d1.96	—	—	—	—	—	—	—	17.50 - 7.48
—	—	—	—	0.51	0.58	—	—	—	—	—	—	—	14.25 - 6.95
—	—	—	1.26	2.58	1.91	25.4 - 15.0	1.49	2.85	2.28	5.9	0.35Q	2/28/03	31.98 - 18.92
—	—	—	p3.87	3.44	2.89	11.4 - 6.4	0.09	0.08	0.08	0.3	0.025Q	4/15/03	44.00 - 24.82
—	—	—	4.20	1.26	4.09	15.0 - 7.8	1.92	1.92	1.83	4.0	0.48Q	1/24/03	62.80 - 32.70
—	—	—	p1.61	3.77	2.53	19.1 - 10.7	0.86	—	—	3.6	0.23Q	5/16/03	30.76 - 17.25
—	—	—	1.77	1.62	1.99	22.2 - 13.0	0.12	0.12	0.12	0.4	0.05Q	2/1/03	39.28 - 23.00
0.07	0.52	0.43	4.39	3.88	3.50	17.5 - 11.9	1.12	1.00	0.88	1.7	0.31Q	2/15/03	77.00 - 52.05
—	—	—	—	1.75	0.61	—	—	—	—	—	—	—	30.82 - 16.49
—	—	—	pd0.07	d0.51	0.26	—	0.25	0.25	0.06	3.0	0.0625Q	12/16/02	13.40 - 3.03
—	—	—	d1.34	d1.68	2.24	—	0.60	0.60	0.52	4.2	0.15Q	2/18/03	19.10 - 9.50
—	—	—	—	—	—	—	2.06	2.06	2.06	10.7	—	3/31/03	24.55 - 14.05
—	—	—	—	—	—	—	0.08	—	0.16	1.2	0.0756U	6/3/02	8.55 - 4.47
—	—	—	—	—	—	—	0.40	0.40	0.42	1.5	0.5007U	4/1/03	31.32 - 20.75
—	—	—	p1.33	1.98	2.22	27.0 - 16.8	3.12	3.10	2.98	10.7	0.45Q	4/14/03	35.91 - 22.40
—	—	—	pd8.23	d2.81	d1.16	—	0.60	1.17	1.74	2.0	0.15Q	6/2/03	36.45 - 23.75
—	—	—	d0.36	2.29	3.57	—	1.70	1.68	1.60	3.3	0.43Q	3/12/03	62.86 - 41.39
—	—	—	p3.54	1.15	3.37	11.3 - 7.3	1.35	1.06	1.04	4.1	0.385Q	4/1/03	39.95 - 26.00
—	—	—	3.33	2.64	2.25	18.4 - 13.4	0.76	0.68	0.62	1.4	0.215Q	3/17/03	61.11 - 44.55

SYMBOL	COMPANY	NATURE OF BUSINESS	FISCAL YEAR-END	TOTAL REV. $MILL	NET INCOME $MILL	TOTAL ASSETS $MILL	NET STK EQUITY $MILL	NO. OF INST.	INST. HOLDINGS (SHARES)
PPD	Pre-Paid Legal Services, Inc	Services	12/31/02	p350.6	p350.6	—	—	111	11684013
PCP	Precision Castparts	Metal products	3/31/02	2557.4	42.4	2564.9	951.8	206	39198236
PFO	Preferred Inc Opportunity Fd	Investment company	11/30/02	14.1	12.2	192.7	122.3	6	204652
PFD	Preferred Income Fund Inc.	Investment company	11/30/02	15.0	12.9	217.4	136.8	8	95285
PCO	Premcor Inc. (United States)	Oil service & equipment	12/31/02	6772.8	d127.1	2323.0	704.0	87	21643367
PFP	Premier Farnell Plc (UK)	Electrical equipment	2/3/02	—	—	—	—	10	632724
PP	Prentiss Properties Trust (Un	Real estate investment trust	12/31/02	p354.5	p354.5	—	—	135	32629783
PR	Price Communications Corp.	Telecommunications	12/31/01	263.5	10.9	1261.7	175.6	105	28103513
POE	Pride Intl, Inc. (DE)	Oil service & equipment	12/31/02	p1269.8	p1269.0	—	—	212	112534879
PGE	Prime Group Realty Trust	Real estate investment trust	12/31/01	219.5	d4.0	1522.4	282.1	38	8253444
PDQ	Prime Hospitality Corp.	Motel/hotel lodging	12/31/02	p402.3	p385.4	—	—	113	38146890
PRM	Primedia, Inc	Publishing	12/31/02	p1587.6	p1587.6	—	—	76	65000973
PFG	Principal Financial Group, I	Insurance	12/31/02	8822.5	619.9	89861.3	6657.2	297	161826642
PRA	ProAssurance Corp.	Property & casualty insurance	12/31/02	382.6	12.4	2238.3	413.2	87	15859770
PG	Procter & Gamble Co. (United	Soaps & cleansers	6/30/02	40238.0	4352.0	40776.0	13706.0	1105	958911684
PGN	Progress Energy, Inc.	Electric power	12/31/02	p8004.7	p8004.7	—	—	390	139521224
PGR	Progressive Corp. (OH)	Property & casualty insurance	12/31/02	—	p667.3	—	—	338	168202194
PLD	Prologis (United States)	Real estate investment trust	12/31/02	—	p248.9	—	—	225	149369247
PQE	ProQuest Co. (United States)	Comp. components & periphs.	12/28/02	p428.3	p225.5	—	—	98	26653128
PHY	Prospect Street High Income	Investment company	10/31/02	15.8	13.1	106.7	49.2	14	135896
CNN	Prospect Street Income Shares	Investment company	12/31/02	8.2	7.2	88.8	57.2	9	399548
POI	Protection One, Inc. (United	Services	12/31/02	341.0	d120.5	1748.5	1063.2	24	6888258
PL	Protective Life Corp.	Life Insurance	12/31/01	1614.2	141.1	19718.8	1400.1	224	56011759
PFV	Provident Financial Group In	Banking - Midwest	12/31/02	p233.3	pd392.6	—	—		
PVN	Providian Financial Corp.	Financial services	12/31/02	p1691.3	p1691.3	—	—	299	191104581
PRV	Province Healthcare Co. (Unit	Hospitals & nursing homes	12/31/02	p704.3	p704.3	—	—	148	53821756
PRU	Prudential Financial, Inc.	Life Insurance	12/31/02	26675.0	256.0	292746.0	21330.0	381	245143835
PFA	Prudential Financial, Inc.	Life Insurance	12/31/02	26675.0	256.0	292746.0	21330.0		
PUK	Prudential Plc (United Kingdo	Insurance brokerage	12/31/01	—	—	—	—	21	3745966
POH	Public Service Company of Okl	Electric power	12/31/02	2201.2	57.8	1917.9	485.5		
PEG	Public Service Enterprise Gr	Electric power	12/31/02	8390.0	416.0	25742.0	5387.0	338	111579304
PSA	Public Storage Inc.	Real estate investment trust	12/31/01	834.6	320.1	4625.9	3909.6	197	52912149
PSA A	Public Storage Inc.	Real estate investment trust	12/31/01	834.6	320.1	4625.9	3909.6	36	1914881
PUB	Publicis S.A. (France)		12/31/01	—	—	—	—	13	207507
PSD	Puget Energy, Inc. (Holding	Electric power	12/31/02	2392.3	117.9	5657.5	1583.8	191	34907379
PTZ	Pulitzer, Inc. (United State	Newspapers	12/29/02	p416.0	p416.0	—	—	87	8467464
PHM	Pulte Homes, Inc.	Home-building	12/31/02	p7471.8	p7480.9	—	—	246	49143303
PCF	Putnam High Income Bond Fund	Investment company	8/31/02	9.4	8.3	94.3	90.6	21	251991
PCV	Putnam High Income Opportun	Investment company	2/28/02	5.6	4.3	66.9	65.2	12	227004
PYM	Putnam High Yield Mun Trust	Investment company	3/31/02	15.6	13.6	221.9	173.4	18	221218
PGM	Putnam Invetment Grade Mun Tr	Investment company	11/30/02	23.5	20.2	367.1	221.4	13	182665
PTM	Putnam Managed High Yield Tr	Investment company	5/31/02	7.2	6.4	66.4	63.8	10	279915
PMM	Putnam Managed Mun Inc Tr	Investment company	10/31/02	37.7	32.9	548.7	370.3	22	702314
PMT	Putnam Master Income Trust	Investment company	10/31/02	32.6	29.2	365.4	339.2	27	826267
PIM	Putnam Master Interm Incm Tr	—	9/30/02	57.8	52.1	683.4	627.6	41	1739599
PMO	Putnam Mun Opportunities Tr	Investment company	4/30/02	21.8	18.8	334.2	210.1	13	124015
PMG	Putnam Municipal Bond Fund	Investment company	4/30/02	20.3	17.2	364.9	359.5	14	162517
PPT	Putnam Premier Income Trust	Investment company	7/31/02	85.3	77.4	941.3	877.6	42	1572624
PMH	Putnam Tax-Free Health Fd	Investment company	5/31/02	12.6	11.0	193.3	187.9	18	632206
PXT	PXRE Group Ltd (Bermuda)	Property & casualty insurance	12/31/02	p306.7	p306.7	—	—	34	8660417
KWR	Quaker Chemical Corp.	Specialty chemicals	12/31/02	p274.5	p274.5	—	—	66	4964546
NX	Quanex Corp. (United States)	Steel producer	10/31/02	994.4	55.5	689.1	421.4	133	13712351
PWR	Quanta Services, Inc.	Electrical equipment	12/31/02	p1750.7	p1750.7	—	—	123	23985458
DGX	Quest Diagnostics, Inc.	Services	12/31/02	4108.1	322.2	3324.2	1768.9	378	96053486
STR	Questar Corp.	Natural gas	12/31/02	p1200.7	p1200.7	—	—	234	49861331
KWK	Quicksilver Resources, Inc.	Oil producer	12/31/01	143.1	19.3	469.2	94.4	78	9190750
ZQK	Quiksilver, Inc.		10/31/02	705.5	37.6	450.6	272.9	144	22561404
LQU	Quilmes Industrial S.A.		12/31/01	—	—	—	—	16	9927370
LQ	Quinenco S.A. (Chile)	Telecommunications	12/31/01	—	—	—	—	14	8020643
Q	Qwest Communications Intl Inc	Telecommunications	12/31/02	—	p9641.0	—	—	374	1001393966
RGF	R&G Financial Corp.		12/31/02	—	pd199.3	—	—	103	12245578
ROC	R.O.C. Taiwan Fund (Taiwan)	Investment	12/31/01	—	—	—	—	24	12456872
RDN	Radian Group, Inc.	Insurance	12/31/02	p1152.1	p978.0	—	—	269	88593655
RSH	RadioShack Corp.	Specialty stores	12/31/02	4577.2	2238.3	—	—	266	129482644
RRA	RailAmerica, Inc.	Railroads	12/31/02	p428.2	p425.1	—	—	85	24701900
RAS	RAIT Investment Trust (Unite	Real estate investment trust	12/31/02	p73.7	p73.7	—	—	66	7122252
RAH	Ralcorp Holdings, Inc. (New)	Food processing	9/30/02	1280.3	53.8	832.5	436.1	142	21122437
RPT	Ramco-Gershenson Properties	Real estate investment trust	12/31/02	p91.2	p91.2	—	—	53	6095842
RRC	Range Resources Corp	Oil	12/31/01	p195.4	p197.4	—	—	70	33035583
RJF	Raymond James Financial, Inc	Financial services	9/27/02	1515.9	79.3	6040.3	839.6	168	24138179
RYN	Rayonier Inc.	Forest products	12/31/02	p1117.4	p1116.7	—	—	159	22084276
ROV	Rayovac Corp. (United States	Electronic components	9/30/02	572.7	29.2	533.2	174.8	123	33407426
RAY	Raytech Corp.	Metal products	12/30/01	146.1	d6.5	320.8	144.1	32	3614051
RTN	Raytheon Co.	Electronic components	12/31/01	—	p1739.0	—	—	529	303125891
RDO	RDO Equipment Co.		1/31/02	549.9	d2.4	216.6	87.9	10	2119746
RDA	Reader's Digest Association	Publishing	6/30/02	2368.6	91.2	2702.7	471.9	180	71604682
RIT	Real Estate Income Fund Inc (		7/16/02	—	d0.0	0.0	—		
O	Realty Income Corp.	Real estate investment trust	12/31/01	126.3	67.6	1003.7	671.8	95	6152950
OUI	Realty Income Corp.	Real estate investment trust	12/31/01	126.3	67.6	1003.7	671.8	1	800
RA	Reckson Associates Realty Cor	Real estate investment trust	12/31/02	p498.1	p500.5	—	—	144	45977487
RA B	Reckson Associates Realty Cor	Real estate investment trust	12/31/02	p498.1	p500.5	—	—	39	5006548
RWT	Redwood Trust Inc. (United St	Real estate investment trust	12/31/02	144.5	35.3	2435.6	307.8	84	8763502
RBK	Reebok International, Ltd.	Shoe manufacturing	12/31/02	3127.9	131.5	1860.8	884.6	225	46149153
ENL	Reed Elsevier N.V. (Netherla	Publishing	12/31/01	—	—	—	—	20	2210804
RUK	Reed Elsevier Plc (New) (Uni	Publishing	12/31/01	—	—	—	—	29	6971131
RGC	Regal Entertainment Group (U	Motion pictures/theaters	12/26/02	p2140.2	p2138.7	—	—	110	32939429
REG	Regency Centers Corp.	Real estate investment trust	12/31/02	388.5	100.7	3109.3	1219.1	106	53521541
RF	Regions Financial Corp.	Banking - South	12/31/02	—	p619.9	—	—	273	77968194
RHB	RehabCare Group Inc.	Hospitals & nursing homes	12/31/02	p562.6	p562.6	—	—	104	16757707
RGA	Reinsurance Group of America,	Insurance	12/31/02	2382.0	2365.6	—	—	89	27052935
RS	Reliance Steel & Aluminum Co.	Metal products	12/31/02	p1748.3	p1748.3	—	—	101	19456622
RRI	Reliant Resources, Inc.	Electric power	12/31/01	36545.7	554.4	12253.6	6103.9	214	146706396
REM	Remington Oil & Gas Corp.	Oil	12/31/01	116.1	8.3	240.4	125.3	103	16152954
RNR	RenaissanceRe Holdings Ltd.	Property & casualty insurance	12/31/01	—	—	—	—	190	57355555
RCI	Renal Care Group Inc.	Hospitals & nursing homes	12/31/02	p903.4	p903.4	—	—	182	97257529
RWY	Rent-Way, Inc. (United State	Department stores	9/30/02	626.4	d31.6	510.8	136.6	46	12137549

| EARNINGS PER SHARE | | | | | | P/E | DIVIDENDS PER SHARE | | | AV. | DIV. DECLARED | | PRICE RANGE |
| QUARTERLY | | | ANNUAL | | | RATIO | | | | YLD. | | | |
1st	2nd	3rd	2002	2001	2000		2002	2001	2000	%	AMOUNT	PAYABLE	2002
—	—	—	p1.82	1.28	2.10	17.4 - 9.2	—	—	—	—	—	—	31.75 - 16.68
0.78	0.78	0.71	—	0.81	2.45	—	0.12	0.12	0.12	0.4	0.03Q	3/31/03	38.00 - 16.85
—	—	—	10.78	11.60	10.68	—	0.96	0.88	0.88	8.2	0.073M	3/31/03	12.80 - 10.43
—	—	—	13.63	14.62	13.41	—	1.16	1.07	1.07	7.7	0.0915M	3/31/03	16.36 - 13.60
—	—	—	d2.65	4.49	2.55	—	—	—	—	—	—	—	28.25 - 13.00
—	—	—	—	—	—	—	0.27	0.26	0.27	3.8	0.12411U	10/25/02	10.10 - 4.25
0.09	0.07	6.83	p1.71	2.52	1.71	19.3 - 14.1	2.19	2.04	1.85	7.7	0.56Q	4/11/03	33.05 - 24.15
—	—	—	pd0.07	0.20	0.50	—	—	—	—	—	5%	8/25/99	19.34 - 10.52
—	—	—	—	0.67	0.01	—	—	—	—	—	—	—	19.70 - 10.80
d1.34	d0.17	d0.05	d1.04	0.37	—	—	—	1.35	1.35	—	0.3375Q	10/26/01	9.85 - 4.05
—	—	—	p0.17	0.88	1.34	82.2 - 44.2	—	—	—	—	—	—	13.98 - 7.51
—	—	—	pd2.55	d5.42	d2.48	—	—	—	—	—	—	—	4.60 - 0.76
0.08	0.04	d0.18	1.77	1.02	—	17.8 - 12.4	0.25	—	—	0.9	0.25A	12/9/02	31.50 - 22.00
1.04	1.06	—	—	0.51	1.04	—	—	—	—	—	5%	2/15/00	21.24 - 14.10
—	—	—	3.09	2.07	2.47	30.7 - 24.0	1.58	1.46	1.34	1.9	0.41Q	2/14/03	94.75 - 74.08
—	—	—	p2.53	2.64	3.03	20.8 - 13.0	2.18	2.12	1.03	5.1	0.56Q	5/1/03	52.60 - 32.84
—	—	—	p2.99	1.83	0.21	20.2 - 15.0	0.10	0.09	0.09	0.2	0.025Q	3/31/03	60.49 - 44.75
—	—	—	p1.20	0.52	0.96	21.7 - 17.5	1.42	1.38	1.34	6.0	0.36Q	2/28/03	26.00 - 20.96
—	—	—	p1.65	0.51	d0.63	26.5 - 10.8	—	—	—	—	—	—	43.80 - 17.90
—	—	—	1.77	3.12	5.30	—	0.72	0.90	0.98	18.6	0.025M	3/31/03	5.78 - 2.00
—	—	—	5.90	6.77	—	—	0.68	0.81	0.93	11.2	0.17Q	4/15/03	7.11 - 5.01
d2.29	d0.04	d0.06	—	d1.14	d0.84	—	—	—	—	—	7.00U	11/24/97	3.32 - 1.94
0.60	0.77	0.73	—	2.01	2.32	—	0.59	0.55	0.51	2.0	0.15Q	2/28/03	33.90 - 26.00
—	—	—	p2.35	0.46	1.46	10.9 - 10.1	0.51	—	—	2.1	0.52344Q	1/15/03	25.50 - 23.65
—	—	—	p0.52	0.49	2.23	16.3 - 4.8	—	0.09	0.11	—	0.03Q	9/17/01	8.49 - 2.50
—	—	—	p0.73	0.67	0.45	53.2 - 12.3	—	—	—	—	50%	4/30/02	38.85 - 8.98
—	—	—	—	—	—	—	0.40	—	—	1.3	0.40A	12/18/02	36.00 - 25.25
—	—	—	—	—	—	—	3.07	—	—	5.7	0.84375Q	2/18/03	60.75 - 46.67
—	—	—	—	—	—	—	0.76	0.71	0.69	4.4	0.53694U	6/4/03	24.27 - 10.05
—	—	—	—	—	—	—	—	—	—	—	—	3/31/03	25.85 - 24.90
0.37	0.30	0.32	1.99	3.67	3.55	23.7 - 10.1	2.16	2.16	2.16	6.4	0.54Q	3/31/03	47.25 - 20.00
—	—	—	—	1.51	1.41	—	1.80	1.69	1.48	5.4	0.45Q	3/31/03	39.29 - 27.98
0.37	0.30	0.32	—	1.51	1.41	—	2.45	2.45	2.36	9.1	0.6125Q	3/31/03	28.40 - 25.70
—	—	—	—	—	—	—	0.18	0.14	—	0.7	0.1844U	7/30/02	34.95 - 16.70
—	—	—	1.24	1.31	2.16	19.0 - 13.4	1.21	1.84	1.84	6.0	0.25Q	2/15/03	23.60 - 16.63
—	—	—	p1.62	0.58	1.60	34.4 - 24.8	0.70	0.68	0.64	1.5	0.18Q	5/1/03	55.80 - 40.12
—	—	—	p7.20	6.01	5.18	8.3 - 5.0	0.16	0.16	0.16	0.3	0.04Q	4/1/03	59.75 - 36.21
—	—	—	6.56	7.30	8.09	—	0.60	0.70	0.85	9.1	0.0465M	4/1/03	7.60 - 5.51
—	15.81	—	—	17.56	19.81	—	1.22	1.38	2.09	7.9	0.102M	4/1/03	17.20 - 13.90
—	—	—	—	7.79	8.22	—	0.53	0.54	0.58	7.2	0.0385M	4/1/03	8.04 - 6.85
—	—	—	10.41	10.96	10.88	—	0.80	0.71	0.84	7.4	0.0695M	4/1/03	12.00 - 9.85
—	7.82	—	—	8.50	9.49	—	0.87	1.09	1.22	10.2	0.06M	4/1/03	10.25 - 6.90
—	—	—	7.84	8.49	8.44	—	0.57	0.57	0.76	7.3	0.0475M	4/1/03	8.42 - 7.15
—	—	—	6.37	6.80	7.13	—	0.58	0.62	0.66	9.0	0.04M	4/1/03	7.20 - 5.67
—	—	—	0.52	0.58	0.63	12.5 - 10.9	0.54	0.59	0.64	8.9	0.038M	4/1/03	6.52 - 5.65
—	12.74	—	—	26.00	13.00	—	0.91	0.91	0.91	7.2	0.0795M	4/1/03	13.39 - 11.63
—	12.95	—	—	13.14	13.10	—	0.88	0.77	0.79	7.1	0.076M	4/1/03	13.30 - 11.48
—	—	—	6.22	6.68	7.19	—	0.54	0.59	0.64	8.9	0.045M	4/1/03	6.60 - 5.57
—	13.66	—	—	13.61	13.48	—	0.69	0.86	0.91	5.7	0.0575M	4/1/03	12.70 - 11.60
—	—	—	p3.28	d1.58	d0.95	8.2 - 5.0	0.24	0.24	0.24	1.1	0.06Q	3/31/03	27.00 - 16.51
—	—	—	p1.51	0.84	1.93	16.9 - 12.1	0.83	0.82	0.79	3.8	0.21Q	4/30/03	25.50 - 18.22
0.41	—	—	3.52	2.05	d0.73	12.6 - 8.0	0.64	0.64	0.64	1.8	0.17Q	3/31/03	44.20 - 28.04
—	—	—	pd7.77	1.10	1.42	—	—	—	—	—	50%	4/7/00	18.90 - 1.75
—	—	—	3.23	1.88	1.11	29.8 - 15.2	—	—	—	—	2-for-1	5/31/01	96.14 - 49.09
0.11	0.18	0.18	p1.74	1.94	1.94	16.9 - 10.4	0.72	0.71	0.69	3.1	0.185Q	3/17/03	29.45 - 18.01
—	—	—	—	1.00	0.95	—	—	—	—	—	—	—	26.35 - 16.79
—	—	—	1.54	1.17	1.37	18.5 - 11.0	—	—	—	—	3-for-2	4/23/99	28.51 - 16.90
—	—	—	—	—	—	—	—	0.59	—	—	0.59U	8/7/01	13.30 - 5.65
—	—	—	—	—	—	—	0.07	—	0.64	1.3	—	5/22/02	7.50 - 3.00
—	—	—	pd21.35	d2.38	d0.06	—	—	0.05	—	—	0.05A	6/29/01	15.19 - 1.07
—	—	—	p2.49	1.85	1.30	10.1 - 6.6	0.34	0.26	0.20	1.6	0.0985Q	3/27/03	25.25 - 16.40
—	—	—	—	—	—	—	—	0.37	—	—	0.37U	1/26/01	5.25 - 3.13
—	—	—	p4.41	3.88	3.22	12.6 - 6.7	0.08	0.07	0.06	0.2	0.02Q	3/19/03	55.56 - 29.40
—	—	—	p1.45	0.85	1.84	25.0 - 11.7	0.22	0.22	0.22	0.8	0.22A	12/19/02	36.21 - 16.99
—	—	—	p0.16	0.72	0.49	91.5 - 40.6	—	—	—	—	—	—	14.64 - 6.50
0.44	—	—	p2.48	2.19	1.92	9.8 - 5.8	2.39	2.12	2.04	12.4	0.62Q	12/31/02	24.19 - 14.41
—	—	—	1.77	1.33	1.19	18.0 - 11.0	—	—	—	—	—	—	31.80 - 19.43
—	—	—	p1.16	1.47	1.34	18.0 - 13.9	1.68	1.68	1.68	9.1	0.42Q	4/15/03	20.90 - 16.10
—	—	—	p0.47	0.11	0.57	12.7 - 8.6	—	—	—	—	0.01Q	9/30/99	5.96 - 4.03
0.29	—	—	1.60	1.98	2.67	23.4 - 14.2	0.36	0.36	0.30	1.2	0.09Q	4/15/03	37.50 - 22.75
—	—	—	p1.92	2.09	2.82	30.6 - 19.1	1.44	1.44	1.44	3.0	0.36Q	3/31/03	58.67 - 36.70
d0.02	—	—	0.90	0.57	1.32	21.2 - 12.4	—	—	—	—	—	—	19.10 - 11.20
0.03	0.02	d0.08	d0.13	0.01	1772.62	—	—	—	—	—	0.05A	3/17/88	9.30 - 2.70
—	—	—	p1.85	0.01	1.46	24.7 - 14.2	0.80	0.40	—	2.2	0.20Q	1/30/03	45.70 - 26.30
0.08	0.10	0.12	—	d0.18	d1.41	—	—	—	—	—	—	—	6.10 - 2.50
d0.05	0.84	—	0.89	1.26	1.61	28.2 - 15.5	0.20	0.20	0.20	1.0	0.05Q	2/10/03	25.10 - 13.76
—	—	—	—	—	—	—	0.43	—	—	3.2	0.1063M	5/30/03	15.25 - 11.50
0.48	0.48	0.47	—	1.98	1.69	—	2.30	2.24	2.18	7.2	0.19625M	4/15/03	37.10 - 26.90
0.48	0.48	0.47	—	1.98	1.69	—	2.06	2.06	2.06	7.8	—	—	27.76 - 25.35
—	—	—	p0.83	d2.14	3.04	31.6 - 24.0	1.70	1.62	1.51	7.4	0.4246Q	4/17/03	26.25 - 19.90
—	—	—	p0.83	d2.14	3.04	32.6 - 24.6	2.59	2.50	2.31	10.9	0.6471Q	4/30/03	27.07 - 20.42
0.80	0.88	0.88	—	3.11	1.82	—	2.73	2.39	1.42	10.0	0.125Q	1/21/03	31.50 - 23.00
—	—	—	2.04	1.66	1.40	14.8 - 10.4	—	—	—	—	0.075Q	10/2/96	30.25 - 21.70
—	—	—	—	—	—	—	0.55	0.50	0.43	2.2	0.17505U	9/16/02	28.44 - 21.30
—	—	—	—	—	—	—	0.63	0.57	0.57	1.8	—	9/16/02	41.25 - 30.21
—	—	—	p0.79	1.69	1.49	31.8 - 20.3	0.15	—	—	0.7	0.15Q	3/14/03	25.10 - 16.00
0.37	0.32	0.41	—	1.69	1.49	—	2.04	2.00	1.92	7.1	0.52Q	3/5/03	32.40 - 25.22
—	—	—	p2.72	2.24	2.38	14.1 - 10.0	1.15	1.11	1.06	3.5	0.30Q	4/1/03	38.40 - 27.10
—	—	—	p1.38	1.16	1.45	22.0 - 11.5	—	—	—	—	100%	6/19/00	30.30 - 15.86
—	—	—	p2.47	0.80	2.12	13.6 - 9.7	0.24	0.24	0.24	0.8	0.06Q	2/25/03	33.65 - 24.00
—	—	—	p0.95	1.28	2.28	36.1 - 20.0	0.24	0.23	0.22	0.9	0.06Q	3/31/03	34.25 - 18.99
0.33	0.61	0.20	—	2.00	1.31	—	—	—	—	—	—	—	17.45 - 0.99
0.01	0.22	0.14	—	0.35	1.99	—	—	—	—	—	—	—	13.00 - 1.00
—	—	—	p0.82	1.52	1.07	43.9 - 32.9	0.57	0.53	0.50	1.6	0.15Q	3/17/03	44.19 - 28.76
—	—	—	—	—	—	—	—	—	—	—	50%	8/24/98	36.00 - 27.00
d0.26	—	—	d1.26	d2.60	d1.20	—	—	—	—	—	3-for-2	8/18/95	13.74 - 2.41

SYMBOL	COMPANY	NATURE OF BUSINESS	FISCAL YEAR-END	TOTAL REV. $MILL	NET INCOME $MILL	TOTAL ASSETS $MILL	NET STK EQUITY $MILL	NO. OF INST.	INST. HOLDINGS (SHARES)
REP	Repsol YPF, S.A. (Spain)	Oil	12/31/02	—	—	—	—	97	94851506
RSG	Republic Services, Inc.	Pollution control	12/31/02	p2365.1	p2365.1	—	—	254	147268734
RMD	ResMed Inc.	Medical & dental equipment	6/30/02	204.1	37.5	376.2	192.9	123	12499444
RZT	ResortQuest International Inc	Motel/hotel lodging	12/31/02	p190.2	p173.0	—	—	32	9558963
REV	Revlon, Inc.	Cosmetics & toiletries	12/31/01	1321.5	d150.1	997.6	d1282.7	42	2606557
RSC	Rex Stores Corp. (United Stat	Consumer electronics	1/31/02	464.5	22.6	307.3	148.0	54	7746974
REY	Reynolds & Reynolds Co.	Office equipment & supplies	9/30/02	992.4	115.6	1137.2	455.0	202	58866177
RJR	Reynolds (R.J.) Tobacco Hldg	Tobacco	12/31/02	6211.0	418.0	14651.0	6716.0	235	72888613
RFS	RFS Hotel Investors Inc.	Real estate investment trust	12/31/02	p198.9	p196.4	—	—	113	17755044
RHA	Rhodia S.A. (France)	Chemicals	12/31/01	—	—	—	—	3	85051
RNA	RIBAPHARM, INC (United States	—	12/31/02	p270.3	p270.3	—	—	64	26667304
RHT	Right Management Consultants	Services	12/31/01	315.4	19.2	261.1	76.7	124	16996874
RTP	Rio Tinto Plc (UK)	Mining & processing	12/31/01	—	—	—	—	74	16205069
RBA	Ritchie Bros. Auctioneers Inc	—	12/31/01	—	—	—	—	23	18599989
RAD	Rite Aid Corp.	Drug stores	3/2/02	15171.1	d761.1	6479.2	9.6	167	139621426
RLI	RLI Corp.	Property & casualty insurance	12/31/02	382.2	35.9	1719.3	456.6	124	17287175
RBN	Robbins & Myers, Inc.	Electrical equipment	8/31/02	526.4	14.5	682.7	260.5	84	10242901
RHI	Robert Half International Inc	Services	12/31/02	p1905.0	p713.4	—	—	231	140677215
RKT	Rock-Tenn Co. (United States	Paper	9/30/02	1436.5	32.5	1173.7	405.1	96	11152191
ROK	Rockwell Automation, Inc. (U	—	9/30/02	3909.0	226.0	4024.0	1609.0	321	105395368
COL	Rockwell Collins, Inc.	Communications electronics	9/30/02	2492.0	236.0	2560.0	987.0	294	108737323
ROG	Rogers Corp.	—	12/29/02	p219.4	p219.4	—	—	89	11517192
ROH	Rohm & Haas Co.	Chemicals	12/31/02	p5727.0	p927.0	—	—	314	175718612
ROL	Rollins, Inc.	Services	12/31/02	665.4	27.1	317.4	90.7	87	10877517
ROP	Roper Industries, Inc.	Machinery & equipment	10/31/02	627.0	66.0	829.0	376.0	158	34361145
ROU	Rouge Industries, Inc. (DE)	Steel producer	12/31/02	1127.0	d52.3	652.4	79.5	14	8673945
RSE	Rouse Co.	Real estate	12/31/02	p1221.7	p1221.7	—	—	172	75372656
RDC	Rowan Cos., Inc.	Oil service & equipment	12/31/02	p617.3	p86.3	—	—	250	85260750
RSA	Royal & Sun Allinace Insuran	Insurance brokerage	12/31/01	—	—	—	—	16	7910407
RAM	Royal Appliance Mfg. Co.	Appliances & utensils	12/31/02	p389.7	p82.7	—	—	42	4362454
RCL	Royal Caribbean Cruises Ltd.	Recreation	12/31/02	—	—	—	—	154	70505226
RD	Royal Dutch Petroleum Co.	Oil producer	12/31/01	—	—	—	—	732	317653878
RVT	Royce Value Trust Inc.	Investment company	12/31/01	12.7	2.2	851.2	849.1	47	3569202
RES	RPC, Inc.	Oil service & equipment	12/31/02	p209.0	p209.0	—	—	41	7655468
RPM	RPM International Inc (DE)	Paints & related products	5/31/02	1986.1	101.6	2036.4	858.1	264	69597340
RTI	RTI International Metals, Inc	Metal products	12/31/01	285.9	12.3	387.8	307.0	87	16972439
RI	Ruby Tuesday, Inc.	Restaurants	6/4/02	833.2	58.3	520.3	334.4	178	54458273
RDK	Ruddick Corp.	Grocery chain	9/29/02	2644.2	52.0	1038.9	457.7	128	23642908
RUS	Russ Berrie & Co., Inc.	—	12/31/02	p321.4	p176.3	—	—	105	9694293
RML	Russell Corp.	—	1/4/03	p1164.3	p1164.3	—	—	118	20168895
R	Ryder System Inc.	Equip. & vehicle leasing	12/31/02	4776.3	112.6	4767.0	1108.2	232	54631582
RT	Ryerson Tull, Inc. (New)	Steel producer	12/31/02	2096.5	d12.4	1101.5	405.6	91	19704196
RYL	Ryland Group, Inc.	—	12/31/02	2877.2	185.6	1657.8	680.1	176	22406366
PEF	S&P 500 Protected Equity Fund	Investment company	9/30/02	3.2	0.3	294.6	293.4	3	12987732
SBR	Sabine Royalty Trust	—	12/31/01	44.4	42.8	5.9	5.7	33	773208
TSG	SABRE Holdings Corp. (United	Computer services	12/31/02	2056.5	214.1	2756.5	1641.6	233	136907533
SDA	Sadia S.A. (Brazil)	Food processing	12/31/01	—	—	—	—	1	8733
SFE	Safeguard Scientifics, Inc.	Services	12/31/02	p1685.6	p1664.2	—	—	99	27923986
SWY	Safeway Inc.	Grocery chain	12/28/02	—	—	—	—	488	357311595
SKS	Saks, Inc. (United States)	Specialty stores	2/2/02	6070.6	d15.7	4595.5	2271.4	170	83502747
SBG	Salomon Bros 2008 Worldwide	Investment company	7/31/02	34.1	31.3	613.0	312.8	16	213867
HIF	Salomon Bros High Incm Fd Inc	Investment company	12/31/01	5.9	5.3	48.2	48.1	7	35943
SBW	Salomon Bros Worldwide Income	Investment company	10/31/02	24.4	20.2	208.7	145.3	12	105137
SBF	Salomon Brothers Fund Inc.	Investment company	12/31/01	20.3	11.2	1425.4	1419.8	60	2811344
SFP	Salton Inc.	Appliances & utensils	6/29/02	922.5	30.1	825.6	245.0	85	7057228
SJT	San Juan Basin Royalty Trust	Oil	12/31/01	81.5	80.1	38.1	37.9	61	22137507
IMI	San Paolo-IMI S.p.A.	—	12/31/01	—	—	—	—	43	16254641
SNY	Sanofi-Synthelabo S.A. (Fran	Drugs	12/31/01	—	—	—	—	24	59001660
SFF	Santa Fe Energy Trust	Oil	12/31/01	19.0	18.4	17.0	17.0	16	230669
SBP	Santander Bancorp (Holding C	—	12/31/02	p364.3	pd47.8	—	—	30	2305872
SAP	Sap AG (Germany)	Computer services	12/31/01	—	—	—	—	166	51057287
SPP	Sappi Ltd. (South Africa)	Paper	9/30/01	—	—	—	—	74	37246702
SLE	Sara Lee Corp.	Food processing	6/29/02	17628.0	1010.0	13753.0	1534.0	639	494566056
SHS	Sauer-Danfoss Inc.	Machinery & equipment	12/31/02	p952.3	p219.4	—	—	52	6048282
BFS	Saul Centers, Inc.	Real estate investment trust	12/31/02	p94.0	p94.0	—	—	60	2728590
VAI	Savia, S.A. de C.V. (Mexico)	Food processing	12/31/01	—	—	—	—	4	2984136
SBC	SBC Communications, Inc.	Telecommunications	12/31/02	—	—	—	—	1030	1631547538
SBT	SBC Communications, Inc.	Telecommunications	12/31/02	—	—	—	—	9	92816
SCG	SCANA Corp (New)	Electric power	12/31/01	3451.0	539.0	7822.0	2300.0	235	42816747
SGK	Schawk, Inc.	Printing & engraving	12/31/02	p186.2	p186.2	—	—	23	2953772
SHR	Schering A.G. (Germany)	Drugs	12/31/01	—	—	—	—	39	972563
SGP	Schering-Plough Corp.	Drugs	12/31/02	10180.0	1974.0	14136.0	8142.0	847	1098761740
SLB	Schlumberger Ltd.	Oil service & equipment	12/31/02	—	—	—	—	805	436019717
SCH	Schwab (Charles) Corp.	Securities brokerage	12/31/02	p4135.0	p3848.0	—	—	460	714605968
SWM	Schweitzer-Mauduit Intl. Inc.	Paper	12/31/01	499.5	24.5	497.9	179.5	116	11840955
SFA	Scientific-Atlanta Corp	Communications electronics	6/28/02	1671.1	104.4	1914.6	1436.8	298	113874647
SCO	SCOR S.A	Insurance	12/31/01	—	—	—	—	3	17271
SCT	Scottish Annuity & Life Hldgs	Life Insurance	12/31/02	p305.9	p305.9	—	—	93	26857762
SPI	Scottish Power Plc (UK)	Electric power	3/31/02	—	—	—	—	99	35235251
SMG	Scotts Co., (The)	Services	9/30/02	1760.6	101.0	1901.4	593.9	177	19690599
SKP	SCPIE Holdings Inc. (United S	Property & casualty insurance	12/31/02	279.7	d58.0	977.6	259.4	36	2898557
SSP	Scripps (E.W.) Co. (New) (OH	Newspapers	1/1/03	p151.2	p151.2	—	—	181	33463535
LBF	Scudder Global High Income Fu	Investment company	10/31/02	8.4	6.7	76.7	59.5	11	484324
KHI	Scudder High Income Trust	Investment company	11/30/02	25.7	22.3	221.3	152.8	20	806834
KGT	Scudder Intermediate Governme	Investment company	12/31/01	14.5	12.2	296.1	248.7	18	2647565
KMM	Scudder Multi-Market Income T	Investment company	11/30/02	19.0	16.4	195.0	153.1	16	233143
KTF	Scudder Municipal Income Trus	Investment company	11/30/02	40.2	35.2	740.5	473.1	29	1428508
SAF	Scudder New Asia Fund, Inc.	Investment company	12/31/01	1.2	d0.7	84.5	84.3	24	2603021
KST	Scudder Strategic Income Trus	Investment company	11/30/02	4.4	3.7	48.1	38.6	4	30300
KSM	Scudder Strategic Municipal I	Investment company	11/30/02	12.6	10.9	198.7	197.4	10	168392
SCR B	Sea Containers Ltd. (Bermuda	Containers	12/31/02	1269.8	3.5	2652.4	477.9	3	170632
SCR A	Sea Containers Ltd. (Bermuda	Containers	12/31/01	1269.8	3.5	2652.4	477.9	46	7568513
CKH	SEACOR SMIT Inc.	Oil service & equipment	12/31/01	434.8	71.6	1298.1	743.7	116	16521325
STX	Seagate Technology (New)	Comp. components & periphs.	6/28/02	6087.0	153.0	3095.0	641.0	75	70118174
SEE	Sealed Air Corp. (New)	Plastics & plastic products	12/31/02	p3204.3	p3127.8	—	—	290	80273337
SRF	Sears Roebuck Acceptance Corp	Finance	12/29/01	1089.0	144.0	16738.0	3238.0	5	42285

| | EARNINGS PER SHARE | | | | | P/E RATIO | DIVIDENDS PER SHARE | | | AV. YLD. | DIV. DECLARED | | PRICE RANGE |
| QUARTERLY | | | ANNUAL | | | | | | | | | | |
1st	2nd	3rd	2002	2001	2000		2002	2001	2000	%	AMOUNT	PAYABLE	2002
—	—	—	—	—	—		0.15	0.36	0.30	1.2	0.1366U	2/3/03	14.63 - 10.08
—	—	—	p1.44	0.73	1.26	15.1 - 11.3	—	—	—	—			21.77 - 16.26
0.28	0.30	—	1.10	0.35	0.69	49.0 - 22.1	—	—	—	—	2-for-1	3/31/00	53.92 - 24.30
—	—	—	pd0.70	0.08	0.51	—	—	—	—	—			8.12 - 3.17
d0.88	d0.75	d0.42	d2.87	d2.54	—	—	—	—	—	—			6.75 - 1.85
0.29	0.37	0.31	—	1.67	1.21	—	—	—	—	—	50%	2/11/02	20.50 - 8.96
0.40	—	—	1.58	1.31	1.11	20.0 - 12.5	0.44	0.44	0.44	1.7	0.11Q	4/10/03	31.55 - 19.74
—	—	—	4.64	4.48	3.46	15.5 - 7.5	3.65	3.20	3.10	6.8	0.95Q	4/1/03	71.90 - 34.83
—	—	—	pd0.26	d0.47	1.20	—	1.00	1.25	1.54	7.9	0.25Q	3/31/03	15.35 - 10.00
—	—	—	—	—	—		0.09	0.29	0.31	1.0		10/4/02	11.35 - 5.75
—	—	—	p0.86	0.48	0.55	13.8 - 3.0	—	—	—	—			11.85 - 2.54
0.38	0.43	0.35	—	0.81	0.41	—	—	—	—	—	50%	10/15/02	22.38 - 9.13
—	—	—	—	—	—		2.74	1.62	0.76	3.7	1.22U	4/7/03	86.00 - 61.10
d0.01	d0.21	d0.05	—	d1.68	d5.15	—	—	—	—	—			33.00 - 24.70
—	—	—	1.75	1.38	1.35	17.3 - 12.7	0.43	0.31	0.29	1.6	0.115U	10/25/99	5.13 - 1.65
0.14	—	—	1.15	1.63	1.53	25.6 - 12.8	0.22	0.22	0.22	1.0	0.09Q	4/15/03	30.20 - 22.23
—	—	—	—	—	—	—	—	—	—	—	0.055U	1/31/03	29.48 - 14.70
—	—	—	p0.01	0.67	1.00	3090.0 - 1194.0	—	—	—	—	2-for-1	6/12/00	30.90 - 11.94
0.15	—	—	0.77	0.91	d0.46	30.9 - 14.3	0.30	0.30	0.30	1.8	0.08Q	2/15/03	23.81 - 11.00
0.22	—	—	1.20	0.68	3.35	19.0 - 12.3	0.66	0.84	1.02	3.5	0.165Q	3/10/03	22.79 - 14.71
0.27	—	—	1.28	0.72	1.35	21.9 - 14.5	0.36	0.18	—	1.5	0.09Q	3/17/03	28.00 - 18.50
—	—	—	p1.16	0.98	1.69	31.0 - 17.7	—	—	—	—	100%	5/26/00	35.95 - 20.48
—	—	—	p0.98	0.31	1.61	43.5 - 30.8	0.82	0.80	0.78	2.3	0.21Q	3/31/03	42.60 - 30.19
—	—	—	0.60	0.37	0.21	31.7 - 20.2	0.13	0.13	0.13	0.9	3-for-2	3/10/03	19.00 - 12.13
p0.25	—	—	2.08	1.77	1.58	25.4 - 13.1	0.33	0.30	0.28	0.8	0.0875Q	3/31/03	52.91 - 27.25
—	—	—	d2.35	d5.01	d5.29	—	—	0.07	0.12		0.02Q	7/20/01	1.82 - 0.55
—	—	—	p1.47	1.42	2.21	22.8 - 18.5	1.56	1.42	1.32	5.1	0.42Q	3/28/03	33.50 - 27.25
—	—	—	p0.90	0.80	0.74	30.0 - 17.8	0.25	—	—	1.2	-0.25U	6/6/02	27.03 - 16.04
—	—	—	—	—	—	—	0.83	1.84	1.81	4.5		6/6/03	30.55 - 6.70
—	—	—	p0.69	0.65	0.38	10.9 - 4.9	—	—	—	—	100%	7/17/92	7.50 - 3.40
—	—	—	—	—	—	—	0.52	0.52	0.48	2.7	0.13Q	3/28/03	24.38 - 14.00
—	—	—	—	—	—	—	1.57	1.41	1.37	3.3	0.70U	9/18/02	57.30 - 38.60
—	16.55	—	—	17.31	16.56	—	1.51	1.49	1.48	9.9	0.34Q	3/24/03	18.94 - 11.51
—	—	—	pd0.19	0.89	0.57	—	0.10	0.11	0.14	0.8	0.025Q	3/10/03	17.80 - 8.50
0.38	0.26	—	—	0.97	0.62	—	0.51	0.50	0.49	3.4	0.13Q	1/31/03	17.87 - 11.58
0.38	0.17	0.14	—	0.57	0.32	—	—	—	—				14.00 - 8.51
0.31	0.27	—	—	0.88	0.91	—	0.04	0.04	0.04	0.2	0.0225S	2/7/03	27.15 - 14.24
0.28	—	—	1.12	d0.02	1.10	16.0 - 12.0	0.36	0.36	0.36	2.3	0.09Q	4/1/03	17.97 - 13.40
—	—	—	p2.24	1.99	2.37	16.8 - 11.7	1.04	1.46	0.88	3.3	0.28Q	3/28/03	37.65 - 26.30
—	—	—	p1.06	d1.74	0.44	18.4 - 12.4	0.16	0.46	0.56	1.0	0.04Q	2/17/03	19.55 - 13.14
—	—	—	1.80	0.31	1.49	17.3 - 11.7	0.60	0.60	0.60	2.3	0.15Q	3/21/03	31.09 - 21.05
—	—	—	d0.51	d2.44	d1.03	—	0.20	0.20	0.20	2.2	0.05Q	5/1/03	12.49 - 5.60
—	—	—	6.64	4.79	2.96	8.8 - 4.7	0.08	0.08	0.08	0.2	0.02Q	4/30/03	58.40 - 31.00
—	—	—	9.31	8.87	10.16	—	0.01	0.01	—	0.1		1/10/03	9.10 - 7.61
0.45	0.39	0.51	—	2.94	2.27	—	1.88	2.86	2.27	9.1		3/31/03	26.14 - 15.00
—	—	—	1.50	d0.35	1.11	33.3 - 9.9	—	—	5.20			2/18/00	49.98 - 14.85
—	—	—	—	—	—	—	1.10	0.33	—	8.8	0.1679U	3/3/03	17.30 - 7.75
—	—	—	pd1.30	d4.27	d1.86	—	—	—	—		200%	3/17/00	4.47 - 0.86
—	—	—	pd1.75	2.44	2.13	—	—	—	—		2-for-1	2/25/98	46.90 - 18.45
0.13	d0.14	0.01	—	d0.11	0.53	—	—	—	—				15.75 - 8.55
—	9.04	—	9.06	9.55	9.75	—	0.88	1.01	0.99	8.6	0.073M	5/30/03	10.69 - 9.60
—	—	—	—	9.58	10.13	—	1.00	1.30	1.50	9.6	0.08M	5/30/03	12.30 - 8.51
—	—	—	11.29	12.24	12.96	—	1.46	1.51	1.71	11.1	0.11875M	5/30/03	15.13 - 11.25
—	12.23	—	—	14.07	—	—	0.18	0.59	2.54	1.7	0.025Q	3/28/03	12.75 - 8.01
0.26	1.64	—	—	2.00	2.87	—	—	—	—		3-for-2	7/28/99	23.60 - 7.61
0.08	0.19	0.26	—	1.72	1.27	—	0.69	1.87	1.20	6.0	0.7639U	5/31/02	13.95 - 8.95
—	—	—	—	—	—	—	0.76	0.70	0.68	4.4			32.80 - 24.90
0.46	0.38	0.43	—	2.92	2.49	—	1.77	2.92	2.49	7.9	1.29361Q	2/28/03	24.00 - 20.80
—	—	—	p0.38	1.27	1.55	57.0 - 29.7	0.41	0.40	0.20	2.5	0.11Q	4/1/03	21.66 - 11.30
—	—	—	—	—	—	—	0.10	0.09	0.09	0.4	0.1034U	5/16/02	39.04 - 9.93
—	—	—	—	—	—	—	0.26	0.25	0.19	2.1	0.28U	1/23/03	15.00 - 10.20
0.38	0.42	—	—	1.23	1.87	—	0.60	0.58	0.54	3.0	-0.155Q	4/1/03	23.84 - 16.15
—	—	—	p0.29	0.10	0.69	44.0 - 25.0	0.28	0.28	0.28	2.8	0.07Q	4/15/03	12.75 - 7.25
—	—	—	p1.31	1.31	1.18	19.8 - 15.8	1.56	1.56	1.56	6.7	0.39Q	1/31/03	25.95 - 20.75
—	—	—	—	—	—	—	—	—	—		0.1345Q	5/30/96	4.00 - 0.94
—	—	—	p2.23	2.14	2.32	18.4 - 8.8	1.07	1.02	1.00	3.5	0.27Q	2/3/03	40.99 - 19.57
—	—	—	p2.23	2.14	2.32	12.1 - 10.8	1.75	0.82	—	6.9	0.4375Q	3/3/03	26.98 - 24.02
d0.68	0.38	0.74	—	5.15	2.12	—	1.28	1.19	0.86	4.6	0.345Q	4/1/03	32.15 - 23.50
—	—	—	p0.62	0.37	0.50	18.5 - 14.6	0.13	0.13	0.13	1.3	0.0325Q	3/31/03	11.45 - 9.08
—	—	—	—	—	—	—	0.58	0.65	—	1.1	0.78513U	4/21/03	63.60 - 40.31
—	—	—	1.35	1.32	1.64	26.9 - 11.9	0.67	0.62	0.55	2.6	0.17Q	2/28/03	36.25 - 16.10
—	—	—	—	—	—	—	0.75	0.75	0.75	1.6	0.1875Q	4/4/03	62.43 - 33.40
—	—	—	p0.08	0.06	0.51	237.5 - 90.3	0.04	0.04	0.04	0.3	0.011Q	2/21/03	19.00 - 7.22
0.57	0.54	0.57	—	1.63	1.82	—	0.60	0.60	0.60	2.4	0.15Q	3/17/03	29.85 - 19.95
0.07	0.10	—	—	0.66	1.99	—	0.04	0.04	0.04	0.2	0.01Q	3/17/03	28.18 - 10.10
—	—	—	—	—	—	—	5.40	1.28	1.38	23.4	5.1706U	12/26/02	40.80 - 5.28
—	—	—	p1.23	1.00	0.50	17.7 - 11.2	0.20	0.20	0.20	1.1	0.05Q	5/12/03	21.75 - 13.80
—	—	—	—	—	—	—	1.68	1.54	2.33	7.7	0.4708U	3/14/03	24.98 - 18.84
d1.55	—	—	3.19	0.51	2.25	15.9 - 10.9	—	—	—	—			50.75 - 34.80
0.10	d1.29	d1.23	—	d6.22	1.84	—	0.40	0.40	0.40	2.4	0.10Q	3/31/03	29.60 - 3.73
—	—	—	—	p1.73	2.06	—	0.60	0.60	0.56	0.8	0.15Q	3/10/03	87.50 - 65.13
—	—	—	5.98	5.66	6.10	—	0.74	0.65	0.60	12.8	0.16Q	1/13/03	6.78 - 4.90
—	—	—	4.91	5.62	6.09	—	0.70	0.86	0.97	11.5	0.053M	3/31/03	7.63 - 4.48
—	7.32	—	7.32	7.32	7.32	—	0.46	0.49	0.54	6.6	0.03M	3/31/03	7.50 - 6.64
—	—	—	7.52	8.04	8.27	—	0.83	1.07	1.03	10.5	0.0675M	3/31/03	9.18 - 6.60
—	—	—	12.18	11.87	11.30	—	0.74	0.72	0.79	6.6	0.065M	3/31/03	11.78 - 10.50
—	—	—	9.42	10.43	12.26	—	—	2.04	0.61		0.085U	4/30/01	10.35 - 7.22
—	—	—	11.10	11.75	11.97	—	1.13	1.41	1.48	10.1	0.09M	3/31/03	12.86 - 9.55
—	—	—	11.84	11.83	11.37	—	0.79	0.75	0.81	6.8	0.07M	3/31/03	12.48 - 10.80
—	—	—	—	0.13	2.42	—	0.20	0.27	0.48	1.5	0.068Q	8/20/02	18.20 - 8.32
—	—	—	—	0.13	2.42	—	0.22	0.30	0.98	1.7	0.075Q	8/20/02	18.62 - 8.19
0.55	0.59	1.09	—	3.47	1.92	—	—	—	—		50%	6/15/00	51.70 - 37.05
—	—	—	0.36	—	—	—	—	—	—		0.03Q	2/28/03	12.00 - 9.86
—	—	—	pd4.30	1.22	1.93	—	—	—	—				48.39 - 12.70
—	—	—	—	—	—	—	1.75	2.19	1.75	7.6	0.4375Q	3/3/03	25.40 - 20.70

SYMBOL	COMPANY	NATURE OF BUSINESS	FISCAL YEAR-END	TOTAL REV. $MILL	NET INCOME $MILL	TOTAL ASSETS $MILL	NET STK EQUITY $MILL	NO. OF INST.	INST. HOLDINGS (SHARES)
SRH	Sears Roebuck Acceptance Corp	Finance	12/29/01	1089.0	144.0	16738.0	3238.0	4	65850
SRJ	Sears Roebuck Acceptance Corp	Finance	12/29/01	1089.0	144.0	16738.0	3238.0	—	—
S	Sears, Roebuck & Co.	Department stores	12/28/02	41366.0	1584.0	50409.0	6753.0	423	267035852
SEM	Select Medical Corp. (United	Hospitals & nursing homes	12/31/02	p1126.6	p1070.1	—	—	105	23527301
SQF	Seligman Quality Munic Fund	Investment company	10/31/02	5.6	4.5	102.0	68.1	7	113552
SEL	Seligman Select Mun Fd Inc	Investment	12/31/02	12.8	10.8	228.9	228.5	15	457926
SEN	SEMCO Energy Inc.	Public utility	12/31/02	481.0	17.5	876.5	110.0	49	3496631
SRE	Sempra Energy (United States	Natural gas distributor	12/31/02	p6020.0	p5874.0	—	—	279	107633935
ARK	Senior High Income Portfolio	Investment company	2/28/02	46.1	38.1	421.9	294.0	18	858775
SNH	Senior Housing Properties Tr	Real estate investment trust	12/31/02	p122.3	p122.3	—	—	99	19524366
SXT	Sensient Technologies Corp.	Food processing	12/31/02	p939.9	p939.9	—	—	183	34738285
SQA A	Sequa Corp.	—	12/31/01	1755.8	8.0	1835.8	644.5	74	3423127
SQA B	Sequa Corp.	—	12/31/01	1755.8	8.0	1835.8	644.5	9	1472353
SRA	Serono S.A. (Switzerland)	Drugs	12/31/01	—	—	—	—	55	17096609
SRV	Service Corp. International	Services	12/31/02	p2272.4	p2141.8	—	—	147	188138084
SVM	ServiceMaster Co. (The)	Services	12/31/01	3601.4	d171.8	3674.7	1221.0	245	152279068
SGG	SGL Carbon AG (Germany)	Metal products	—	—	—	—	—	5	155188
SGR	Shaw Group Inc.	—	8/31/02	3170.7	98.4	2304.2	692.3	178	30828781
SC	Shell Trans & Trading Co. PL	Oil producer	12/31/01	—	—	—	—	172	41271907
SHW	Sherwin-Williams Co.	Paints & related products	12/31/02	5184.8	310.7	3432.3	1341.9	328	110172353
SKO	Shopko Stores, Inc. (WI) (Uni	Department stores	2/2/02	3387.0	28.2	1820.0	690.0	144	29462709
SHU	Shurgard Storage Centers, In	Industrial	12/31/01	232.6	36.4	1238.8	716.3	142	16572482
SI	Siemens AG (Germany)	Electrical equipment	9/30/02	—	—	—	—	83	10287757
SIE	Sierra Health Services Inc.	Hospitals & nursing homes	12/31/02	p1278.6	p1272.8	—	—	109	18828816
SRP	Sierra Pacific Resources (Ne	Electric power	12/31/02	p2991.7	p2991.7	—	—	144	70309049
SRC	Sierra Pacific Resources (Ne	Electric power	12/31/02	p2991.7	p2991.7	—	—	—	—
SGI	Silicon Graphics Inc.	Computers	6/28/02	1341.4	d46.3	910.1	d54.6	80	65328762
SPG	Simon Property Group Inc	Real estate investment trust	12/31/02	2185.8	408.3	14904.5	3467.7	319	146856717
SSD	Simpson Manufacturing Co.Inc	Furniture & fixtures	12/31/02	465.5	51.9	396.4	349.2	107	12649591
SGF	Singapore Fund Inc.	Investment company	10/31/02	1.5	0.1	61.8	59.4	8	2581656
BYH	Sinopec Beijing Yanhua Petro	Chemicals	12/31/01	—	—	—	—	4	460229
SHI	Sinopec Shanghai Petrochemica	Oil	12/31/01	—	—	—	—	9	111338
SWW	Sitel Corp.	Services	12/31/01	725.0	d22.6	355.5	140.0	51	30746745
SXC	Six Continents Plc (United Ki	Conglomerate	9/30/02	—	—	—	—	41	46937971
PKS	Six Flags Inc	—	12/31/01	1046.0	d49.6	4246.1	1446.6	137	78972789
SIZ	Sizeler Property Investors	Real estate investment trust	12/31/01	—	p2.8	—	—	39	3955036
SKM	SK Telecom Co., Ltd.	Computer services	12/31/01	—	—	—	—	132	66571229
SKX	Skechers U S A, Inc.	Shoe manufacturing	12/31/02	p943.6	p943.6	—	—	84	11163816
SKY	Skyline Corp.	Mobile homes	5/31/02	450.7	12.3	238.8	198.2	91	5566898
SLG	SL Green Realty Corp.	Real estate investment trust	12/31/02	p246.2	p246.2	—	—	152	28584051
SL	SL Industries Inc.	Metal products	12/31/01	138.5	d6.7	107.8	33.2	12	2513807
SLM	SLM Corp. (United States)	Financial services	12/31/01	3515.1	384.0	52874.0	1672.5	389	165689731
MCC	SMALLCap Fund, Inc. (The)	Investment company	12/31/01	0.8	d1.0	134.0	127.6	14	667097
SMF	Smart & Final, Inc.	Grocery chain	12/29/02	p2016.0	p2016.0	—	—	41	9660636
SMV A	Smedvig ASA (Norway)	Oil service & equipment	12/31/01	—	—	—	—	8	269283
SMV B	Smedvig ASA (Norway)	Oil service & equipment	12/31/01	—	—	—	—	6	2974668
SNN	Smith & Nephew Plc (UK)	Medical & dental equipment	12/31/01	—	—	—	—	27	1369287
AOS	Smith (A.O.) Corp	—	12/31/02	1469.1	51.3	1224.9	511.1	126	17649488
SII	Smith International	Oil service & equipment	12/31/02	p3170.1	p3170.1	—	—	259	98186466
SFD	Smithfield Foods, Inc.	Meat packing & processing	4/28/02	7356.1	196.9	3878.0	1362.8	179	62004632
SJM	Smucker (J.M.) Co. (United St	Food processing	4/30/02	687.1	30.9	524.9	280.1	286	23846679
SNA	Snap-On, Inc.	Hardware & tools	12/28/02	2109.1	103.2	1994.1	830.4	217	47141901
SQM	Sociedad Quimica y Minera	Chemicals	12/31/01	—	—	—	—	19	1058322
SQM A	Sociedad Quimica y Minera	Chemicals	12/31/01	—	—	—	—	1	11018
SDX	Sodexho Alliance S.A. (Franc	Restaurants	8/31/02	—	—	—	—	3	65907
SOL	Sola International, Inc. (Un	Photo & optical	3/31/02	529.5	19.1	713.1	261.4	99	19278731
SLR	Solectron Corp.	Electronic components	8/31/02	12276.2	d3110.2	11014.0	4772.7	377	696036644
SOI	Solutia, Inc. (United States	Chemicals	12/31/02	p2241.0	p363.0	—	—	156	77817537
SAH	Sonic Automotive, Inc.	—	12/31/02	p5.0	p5.0	—	—	115	24491017
SON	Sonoco Products Co.	Paper	12/31/02	2812.2	135.3	2390.1	867.4	211	43012533
SNE	Sony Corp	Electrical equipment	3/31/02	—	—	—	—	196	43966580
BID	Sotheby's Holdings, Inc.	—	12/31/01	336.2	d41.7	864.1	185.9	99	41061389
SOR	Source Capital, Inc.	Investment company	12/31/02	7.9	4.0	396.7	395.2	20	147159
SJI	South Jersey Industries, Inc.	Natural gas distributor	12/31/01	837.3	26.9	987.8	220.3	81	4482322
SOA	Southern Africa Fund, Inc.	Investment company	11/30/02	1.8	0.4	54.3	53.9	7	1677915
SO	Southern Co.	Electric power	12/31/02	—	p1318.0	—	—	508	285226592
PCU	Southern Peru Copper Corp.	Mining & processing	12/31/01	657.5	48.7	1821.4	1209.5	53	3577534
SUG	Southern Union Co. (New)	Natural gas	6/30/02	1290.5	19.6	2676.5	685.4	103	19439565
LUV	Southwest Airlines Co	—	12/31/02	5521.8	241.0	8953.8	4421.6	438	606042476
SWX	Southwest Gas Corp.	Natural gas distributor	12/31/02	p1320.9	p1320.9	—	—	123	18356495
SWN	Southwestern Energy Co.	Natural gas	12/31/02	261.5	14.3	740.2	177.5	113	19825897
SOV	Sovereign Bancorp, Inc.	Savings & loan	12/31/02	—	p342.0	—	—	287	181021007
SSS	Sovran Self Storage, Inc. (U	Real estate investment trust	12/31/02	p102.1	p102.1	—	—	79	4039286
SNF	Spain Fund, Inc.	Investment company	11/30/02	1.0	d0.3	59.2	58.8	10	31725
SEH	Spartech Corp.	Plastics & plastic products	11/2/02	898.3	34.3	865.3	290.7	99	21417412
SPA	Sparton Corp.	Electronic components	6/30/02	149.7	2.9	102.4	81.6	11	1656375
SP	Specialty Laboratories, Inc.	—	12/31/01	175.2	13.1	154.0	132.7	43	7033289
TRK	Speedway Motorsports, Inc.	Recreation	12/31/02	p376.0	p376.0	—	—	68	11415683
SFN	Spherion Corp.	Services	12/27/02	p2116.0	p2116.0	—	—	113	49475096
SKE	Spinnaker Exploration Co	Natural gas	12/31/02	p188.3	p188.3	—	—	133	24017549
SPM	Spirent Plc (United Kingdom)	Electrical equipment	12/31/01	—	—	—	—	3	131110
TSA	Sports Authority, Inc. (The)	Recreation	2/2/02	1419.0	12.3	601.2	155.1	96	21299160
PCS	Sprint Corp (PCS Group)	Telecommunications	12/31/02	—	—	—	—	382	637788366
FON	Sprint Corp. (FON Group)	Telecommunications	12/31/02	—	—	—	—	455	703995688
SDE	Sprint Corp. (United States)	Telecommunications	12/31/02	26071.0	d1402.0	45793.0	12616.0	14	5660789
ST	SPS Technologies Inc.	Metal products	12/31/02	p830.3	p830.3	—	—	68	8603797
SPW	SPX Corp.	—	12/31/02	5045.8	276.0	7091.5	1692.4	283	65852735
SRX	SRA International Inc	—	6/30/02	361.2	11.3	226.3	159.4	73	8398806
JOE	St. Joe Co. (The) (United St	Forest products	12/31/02	p646.4	p795.2	—	—	139	23262303
STJ	St. Jude Medical, Inc. (Unite	Medical & dental equipment	12/31/02	p1589.9	p1589.9	—	—	344	161622965
SM	St. Mary Land & Exploration	Oil	12/31/02	p193.2	p193.2	—	—	139	20538106
SPC	St. Paul Companies, Inc. (Un	Insurance	12/31/02	p8917.7	p8845.4	—	—	388	203876488
SFG	Stancorp Financial Group Inc	Insurance	12/31/02	p380.8	p380.8	—	—	175	7007944
STW	Standard Commercial Corp.	Tobacco	3/31/02	942.3	36.2	650.6	190.7	66	9003594
SMP	Standard Motor Products	—	12/31/02	p598.4	p558.5	—	—	56	6140391
SPF	Standard Pacific Corp. (New)	—	12/31/02	p1885.2	p273.0	—	—	134	24457914

T44

EARNINGS PER SHARE QUARTERLY 1st	2nd	3rd	ANNUAL 2002	2001	2000	P/E RATIO	DIVIDENDS PER SHARE 2002	2001	2000	AV. YLD. %	DIV. DECLARED AMOUNT	PAYABLE	PRICE RANGE 2002
—	—	—	—	—	—	—	1.74	1.74	1.74	7.8	—	1/23/03	25.45 - 19.00
—	—	—	—	—	—	—	0.53	—	—	2.3	0.4375Q	4/15/03	25.49 - 20.72
—	—	—	4.94	2.24	3.88	12.1 - 4.0	0.92	0.92	0.92	2.3	0.23Q	4/1/03	59.90 - 19.71
—	—	—	p0.90	0.81	0.12	19.1 - 12.9	—	—	—	—	—	—	17.20 - 11.60
—	—	—	14.44	14.40	11.50	—	0.75	0.80	0.84	6.0	0.066M	3/27/03	13.24 - 12.00
—	—	—	—	11.56	11.65	—	0.65	0.62	0.69	6.1	0.0575M	3/27/03	11.17 - 10.10
—	—	—	0.48	d0.01	0.90	23.8 - 11.7	0.58	0.84	0.83	6.9	0.125Q	2/15/03	11.40 - 5.60
—	—	—	p2.87	2.52	2.06	9.1 - 5.4	1.00	1.00	1.14	4.8	0.25Q	4/15/03	26.25 - 15.50
—	4.64	—	—	5.40	6.63	—	0.63	0.73	0.86	12.7	—	3/31/03	6.18 - 3.82
—	—	—	p0.89	0.55	2.25	17.7 - 10.4	1.23	1.20	1.50	9.8	0.31Q	2/21/03	15.73 - 9.30
—	—	—	p1.69	1.36	1.15	15.3 - 10.6	0.54	0.53	0.53	2.5	0.14Q	3/3/03	25.84 - 17.95
d0.35	0.30	0.16	—	0.58	2.12	—	—	—	—	—	0.15Q	7/1/93	65.99 - 36.30
d0.35	0.30	0.16	—	0.58	2.12	—	—	—	—	—	0.125Q	7/1/93	66.00 - 44.50
—	—	—	—	—	—	—	0.10	0.07	—	0.6	0.0996U	7/8/02	23.19 - 10.25
—	—	—	p0.34	d2.09	d1.56	16.6 - 6.6	—	—	—	—	0.09Q	10/29/99	5.65 - 2.23
0.10	0.20	0.19	—	d0.54	0.61	—	0.41	0.40	0.38	3.4	0.321U	5/4/98	8.45 - 1.60
0.42	—	—	2.26	1.46	0.98	16.0 - 3.9	—	—	—	—	2-for-1	12/15/00	36.09 - 8.90
—	—	—	2.04	1.68	0.10	16.3 - 10.7	1.33	1.27	1.24	3.3	0.9045U	5/16/03	47.33 - 34.02
0.02	0.25	0.03	—	0.98	d1.72	—	0.60	0.58	0.54	2.2	0.155Q	3/10/03	33.24 - 21.75
0.27	0.40	0.42	—	0.68	1.47	—	—	—	—	—	0.11Q	9/15/96	22.80 - 8.76
—	—	—	—	—	—	—	2.11	2.07	2.03	6.4	0.53Q	2/25/03	37.15 - 28.49
—	—	—	—	—	—	—	0.65	—	—	1.3	0.8477U	1/31/03	70.50 - 30.45
—	—	—	p1.36	0.61	d7.37	18.0 - 5.8	—	—	—	—	3-for-2	6/8/98	24.45 - 7.89
—	—	—	pd3.01	0.34	d0.63	—	0.20	0.65	1.00	1.9	0.20Q	3/15/02	16.85 - 4.65
—	—	—	pd3.01	0.34	d0.63	—	4.49	—	—	10.5	1.125Q	2/18/03	57.82 - 27.75
d0.21	d0.08	—	—	d0.24	d2.59	—	—	—	—	—	0.00U	6/20/00	4.85 - 0.56
—	—	—	1.93	0.86	1.16	19.1 - 14.9	2.18	2.08	2.02	6.6	0.60Q	2/28/03	36.95 - 28.80
—	—	—	2.09	1.64	1.56	17.5 - 12.1	—	—	—	—	2-for-1	8/16/02	36.56 - 25.33
—	—	—	6.46	5.76	8.12	—	0.01	0.08	—	0.1	0.006A	12/26/02	6.50 - 4.50
—	—	—	—	—	—	—	—	0.24	0.36	—	0.2414U	7/18/01	7.82 - 3.90
0.04	0.05	—	—	d0.31	0.17	—	—	0.72	0.60	—	0.725U	7/18/01	16.25 - 9.10
—	—	—	—	—	—	—	—	—	—	—	2-for-1	10/21/96	3.30 - 1.10
d1.23	0.08	1.31	—	d0.85	d0.96	—	0.51	0.34	0.51	5.3	0.106U	4/15/03	11.80 - 7.27
—	—	—	—	—	—	—	—	—	—	—	2-for-1	8/7/98	18.69 - 3.00
—	—	—	p0.17	0.27	0.29	66.8 - 51.9	0.92	0.92	0.91	9.1	0.23Q	3/6/03	11.35 - 8.82
—	—	—	—	—	—	—	0.06	0.09	—	0.3	—	12/27/02	26.76 - 19.20
0.22	0.23	—	p1.20	1.24	1.20	20.3 - 5.4	—	—	—	—	—	—	24.40 - 6.52
—	—	—	—	1.46	1.32	—	0.72	0.72	0.72	2.2	0.18Q	4/1/03	37.76 - 26.30
d0.12	0.06	0.10	p2.09	1.81	1.66	17.6 - 13.0	1.77	1.55	1.45	5.5	0.465Q	4/15/03	36.70 - 27.24
2.63	0.78	d0.42	—	d1.18	0.30	—	—	—	0.10	—	0.05S	11/22/00	12.60 - 4.00
—	11.08	—	—	2.28	2.76	—	0.85	0.73	0.17	0.9	0.25Q	3/21/03	106.95 - 77.00
—	—	—	—	12.15	13.40	—	0.12	0.06	3.65	1.2	0.117A	9/16/02	11.95 - 7.00
—	—	—	p0.23	0.49	0.38	47.3 - 16.8	—	—	—	—	0.05Q	1/29/99	10.88 - 3.86
—	—	—	—	—	—	—	0.18	0.13	0.11	2.7	—	4/25/03	9.65 - 4.00
—	—	—	—	—	—	—	0.18	0.13	0.11	3.3	—	4/25/03	8.08 - 3.20
—	—	—	—	—	—	—	0.71	0.65	0.24	1.3	0.4885U	5/27/03	64.60 - 47.00
—	—	—	1.86	0.61	1.76	17.6 - 10.2	0.54	0.52	0.50	2.1	0.14Q	2/18/03	32.75 - 19.00
—	—	—	p0.93	1.51	0.72	41.6 - 24.9	—	—	—	—	100%	7/8/02	38.73 - 23.19
0.11	0.04	0.05	—	1.78	2.03	—	—	—	—	—	100%	9/14/01	26.25 - 14.59
0.39	0.58	p0.56	—	1.24	1.23	—	0.40	—	—	1.2	0.20Q	3/3/03	40.40 - 28.71
—	—	—	1.76	0.37	2.10	20.0 - 11.8	0.97	0.96	0.94	3.5	0.25Q	3/10/03	35.15 - 20.71
—	—	—	—	—	—	—	0.41	0.50	0.88	1.9	0.4074U	5/20/02	24.65 - 17.70
—	—	—	—	—	—	—	0.41	0.50	0.88	1.2	0.4074U	5/20/02	45.50 - 22.00
d0.22	0.26	d0.21	—	0.78	d2.83	—	—	—	—	—	—	3/28/03	42.10 - 18.20
d0.09	—	—	d3.98	d0.19	0.80	—	—	—	—	—	100%	3/8/00	20.47 - 7.61
—	—	—	pd1.44	d0.57	0.46	—	0.04	0.04	0.04	0.5	0.04A	12/12/02	12.42 - 1.39
—	—	—	p1.91	1.91	1.69	20.8 - 7.0	—	—	—	—	2-for-1	1/25/99	13.89 - 2.67
—	—	—	1.39	0.96	1.66	21.4 - 14.0	0.83	0.80	0.79	3.4	0.21Q	3/10/03	39.75 - 13.31
—	—	—	—	—	—	—	0.17	0.17	0.29	0.3	0.09058U	3/26/03	59.68 - 39.79
d0.38	0.29	d0.70	—	d0.69	d3.22	—	—	—	—	—	0.10Q	12/3/99	17.40 - 6.30
—	—	—	41.90	55.45	48.62	—	4.60	4.60	6.41	7.6	0.875Q	3/15/03	71.84 - 48.70
1.65	0.06	d0.27	—	2.29	2.16	—	1.88	1.47	1.46	5.8	0.385Q	4/2/03	36.65 - 28.20
—	—	—	12.42	11.19	14.72	—	0.13	1.59	0.05	1.2	0.28A	1/3/03	12.11 - 8.30
—	—	—	p1.86	1.61	1.52	16.7 - 12.5	1.35	1.34	1.34	5.0	0.3425Q	3/6/03	31.14 - 23.22
0.19	0.34	0.18	—	0.61	1.16	—	0.36	0.36	0.34	2.8	0.092Q	3/11/03	15.61 - 10.44
d0.12	0.33	—	—	0.35	0.22	54.9 - 29.0	—	—	—	—	5%	7/14/02	19.23 - 10.15
—	—	—	—	0.30	0.79	73.3 - 36.3	0.01	0.02	0.01	0.1	0.0045Q	3/27/03	22.00 - 10.90
—	—	—	p1.32	1.15	1.21	19.2 - 13.7	0.82	0.82	0.82	3.8	0.205Q	6/2/03	25.35 - 18.10
—	—	—	0.55	1.38	d1.82	27.7 - 17.3	—	—	0.12	—	0.06Q	5/5/00	15.25 - 9.51
—	—	—	p1.23	0.48	d0.18	12.9 - 9.1	0.10	0.10	0.10	0.7	0.025Q	5/15/03	15.90 - 11.20
—	—	—	p1.64	1.74	1.89	20.9 - 16.1	2.37	2.33	2.29	7.8	0.60Q	4/22/03	34.20 - 26.38
p0.21	—	—	6.81	8.39	10.30	—	0.76	1.15	4.26	9.6	0.134Q	1/3/03	10.00 - 5.90
0.45	0.27	—	1.21	1.11	1.72	22.9 - 14.6	0.38	0.38	0.34	1.7	0.10Q	4/17/03	27.75 - 17.71
0.06	d0.34	d0.15	0.36	0.20	d1.02	24.7 - 18.2	—	—	—	—	5%	2/18/03	8.95 - 6.57
—	—	—	—	0.59	0.49	—	—	—	—	—	—	—	27.50 - 6.15
—	—	—	p1.32	1.34	1.13	22.9 - 16.1	0.30	—	—	1.2	0.30A	11/14/02	30.18 - 21.25
—	—	—	pd15.20	1.73	1.16	—	—	—	—	—	100%	9/5/97	12.84 - 5.35
—	—	—	p0.97	2.34	1.61	46.3 - 19.6	—	—	—	—	—	—	44.89 - 19.00
—	—	—	—	—	—	—	0.26	0.08	—	4.5	0.0838U	11/14/02	11.10 - 0.41
0.05	0.27	d0.13	—	0.37	0.21	—	—	—	—	—	3-for-2	7/16/96	14.85 - 4.10
—	—	—	pd0.58	d1.27	d1.95	—	—	—	—	—	100%	2/4/00	25.20 - 1.75
—	—	—	p1.36	d0.16	1.45	15.1 - 4.9	0.50	0.50	0.50	—	0.125Q	3/31/03	20.47 - 6.65
0.17	—	0.53	—	d1.43	d0.50	—	1.78	0.48	—	11.6	0.4453Q	4/25/03	26.00 - 4.80
—	—	—	p0.46	1.63	3.42	99.3 - 45.2	—	—	—	—	2-for-1	8/29/97	45.70 - 20.80
—	—	—	3.33	2.33	3.13	22.7 - 10.8	—	—	—	—	100%	10/24/02	75.72 - 35.90
0.21	0.38	—	0.66	0.45	0.44	45.8 - 32.2	—	—	—	—	—	—	30.26 - 21.25
—	—	—	p2.14	0.83	1.15	15.8 - 11.4	0.08	0.08	0.08	0.3	0.08A	3/31/03	33.74 - 24.35
—	—	—	p1.51	0.96	0.76	28.6 - 20.2	—	—	—	—	100%	6/28/02	43.13 - 30.52
—	—	—	p0.97	1.42	1.97	28.2 - 19.3	0.10	0.10	0.10	0.5	0.05S	11/18/02	23.75 - 18.74
—	—	—	p1.24	d4.84	4.32	40.8 - 18.5	1.15	1.11	1.07	3.1	0.29Q	4/17/03	50.60 - 23.00
0.41	1.05	0.83	p3.73	3.44	2.95	16.4 - 12.1	0.40	0.30	0.27	0.8	0.40A	12/6/02	61.20 - 45.14
—	—	—	—	2.55	1.47	—	0.22	0.20	0.20	1.2	0.0625Q	3/14/03	23.00 - 14.50
—	—	—	p0.78	0.03	0.85	22.3 - 12.1	0.36	0.36	0.36	2.7	0.09Q	3/3/03	17.39 - 9.45
—	—	—	—	p3.63	3.39	—	0.32	0.32	0.32	1.2	0.08Q	2/25/03	35.73 - 19.85

SYMBOL	COMPANY	NATURE OF BUSINESS	FISCAL YEAR-END	TOTAL REV. $MILL	NET INCOME $MILL	TOTAL ASSETS $MILL	NET STK EQUITY $MILL	NO. OF INST.	INST. HOLDINGS (SHARES)
SR	Standard Register Co.	Office equipment & supplies	12/31/01	p1196.4	p1196.4	—	—	95	13900940
SXI	Standex International Corp.	Industrial	6/30/02	574.0	20.4	406.0	178.4	82	5818842
SWK	Stanley Works	Hardware & tools	12/31/02	p2593.5	p2593.5	—	—	231	62114945
SGU	Star Gas Partners, L.P.	Oil	9/30/02	1025.1	d11.2	943.8	—	30	674609
SGH	Star Gas Partners, L.P.	Oil	9/30/02	1025.1	d11.2	943.8	—	3	43941
SCX	Starrett (L.S.) Co.	Hardware & tools	6/29/02	184.3	d0.4	239.1	180.3	28	2396612
SRT	Startek, Inc.	—	12/31/02	p207.9	p207.9	—	—	74	4835695
HOT	Starwood Hotel&Res Wrldwide	Real estate investment trust	12/31/02	4659.0	246.0	12259.0	3997.0	295	186496814
STT	State Street Corp.	Financial services	12/31/02	5395.0	1015.0	85794.0	4787.0	554	268194060
SIB	Staten Island Bancorp, Inc.	Banking - Northeast	12/31/01	501.5	70.1	5993.4	552.2	137	26726447
STN	Station Casinos, Inc.	Gaming	12/31/01	p792.9	p779.5	—	—	138	43934092
STO	Statoil ASA (Norway)	Oil	12/31/01	—	—	—	—	29	4745677
SNS	Steak n Shake Co. (The)	Restaurants	9/25/02	460.8	23.1	395.9	167.1	93	11839085
SCS	Steelcase, Inc. (United State	Furniture & fixtures	2/22/02	3089.5	1.0	2967.5	1555.5	82	30535601
LVB	Steinway Musical Instruments	—	12/31/02	p332.3	p332.3	—	—	39	6864489
SCL	Stepan Co.	Chemicals	12/31/02	p748.5	p748.5	—	—	41	3073519
STE	Steris Corp.	Medical & dental equipment	3/31/02	866.7	46.2	841.6	487.1	228	53616352
STL	Sterling Bancorp (NY)	Banking - Northeast	12/31/02	p94.2	p15.6	—	—	67	5676011
SVC	Stewart & Stevenson Svcs Inc	Oil service & equipment	1/31/02	1329.5	45.3	649.1	391.2	117	22544593
STC	Stewart Information Services	Finance	12/31/02	p1779.7	p1779.7	—	—	103	12426215
SF	Stifel Financial Corp.	Financial services	12/31/02	p194.1	p190.6	—	—	18	2643564
SWC	Stillwater Mining Co.	Metal products	12/31/02	p275.6	p275.6	—	—	108	32885611
STM	STMicroelectronics N.V.	Electronic components	12/31/01	—	—	—	—	156	61779674
SGY	Stone Energy Corp.	Oil producer	12/31/01	398.5	d71.4	1101.8	530.0	160	20664092
SRI	Stoneridge Inc.	Electrical equipment	12/31/02	p636.5	p623.1	—	—	55	7503638
SEO	Stora Enso AB (Finland)	Paper	12/31/01	—	—	—	—	68	22533772
STK	Storage Technology Corp. (Un	Comp. components & periphs.	12/27/02	2039.6	110.0	1976.1	1157.8	216	92755147
SGL	Strategic Global Income Fd	Investment company	11/30/02	12.2	9.6	224.7	221.9	18	645213
SRR	Stride Rite Corp.	Shoe manufacturing	11/29/02	532.4	24.1	334.8	253.0	118	32069459
SYK	Stryker Corp.	Medical & dental equipment	12/31/02	3011.6	346.6	2815.5	1498.2	449	146080148
STU	Student Loan Corp. (The)	Finance	12/31/02	—	p175.5	—	—	81	19161740
RGR	Sturm, Ruger& Co., Inc.	Steel producer	12/31/02	p161.6	p36.2	—	—	99	8955007
SPH	Suburban Propane Partners LP	Natural gas distributor	9/28/02	665.1	53.5	700.1	—	60	3140584
SZE	Suez S.A. (France)	Engineering & construction	12/31/01	—	—	—	—	28	2884178
SMT	Summit Properties, Inc.	Real estate investment trust	12/31/02	p156.9	p156.9	—	—	104	16450416
SUI	Sun Communities, Inc.	Real estate	12/31/01	153.6	33.9	994.4	329.6	108	13876944
SDS	Sungard Data Systems Inc.	Computer services	12/31/02	p2593.0	p2593.0	—	—	447	244206333
SXL	Sunoco Logistics Partners L.P	Oil service & equipment	12/31/02	p1830.9	p1829.4	—	—	25	645261
SUN	Sunoco, Inc.	Natural gas	12/31/02	14384.0	d47.0	6441.0	1394.0	237	56729710
SRZ	Sunrise Assisted Living, Inc.	Hospitals & nursing homes	12/31/02	p505.9	p503.3	—	—	140	20018841
STI	Suntrust Banks, Inc.	Banking - South	12/31/02	7526.9	1331.8	117332.5	8769.5	474	147949348
SPN	Superior Energy Services, Inc	Oil service & equipment	12/31/01	449.0	51.2	665.5	269.6	169	43243061
SUP	Superior Industries Intl.	—	12/31/02	p782.6	p782.6	—	—	169	20385802
UNR	Supermercados Unimarc S.A.	Grocery chain	12/31/01	—	—	—	—	1	28525
SVU	Supervalu Inc.	Food wholesalers	2/23/02	20908.5	205.5	5824.8	1916.7	290	103325216
SFY	Swift Energy Co.	Oil	12/31/02	p150.0	p150.0	—	—	110	23306899
SWZ	Swiss Helvetia Fund Inc (The	Investment company	12/31/02	3.9	d0.8	316.1	314.4	37	5054542
SCM	SwissCom AG	Telecommunications	12/31/01	—	—	—	—	36	11395209
SWS	SWS Group, Inc.	Securities brokerage	6/28/02	332.1	d7.2	3363.7	255.3	88	9339435
SY	Sybase, Inc.	Computer services	12/31/02	p829.9	p796.4	—	—	189	81481815
SYD	Sybron Dental Specialities	Medical & dental equipment	9/30/02	456.7	35.3	569.5	131.1	122	35328865
SBL	Symbol Technologies, Inc.	Comp. components & periphs.	12/31/02	p1320.1	p1279.7	—	—	296	179348304
SYM	Syms Corp.	Discount & variety stores	3/2/02	287.7	d2.3	276.5	241.5	24	6212071
SYT	Syngenta AG (Switzerland)	—	12/31/01	—	—	—	—	62	30453557
SNV	Synovus Financial Corp. (Uni	Bank	12/31/02	—	p365.3	—	—	239	143798015
SYY	Sysco Corp.	Food wholesalers	6/29/02	23350.5	679.8	5989.8	2132.5	657	486544197
SYX	Systemax, Inc.	—	12/31/02	p1551.5	p1551.5	—	—	20	2954730
TWN	Taiwan Fund, Inc.	Investment company	8/31/02	2.5	d2.0	185.4	185.1	22	3340219
TSM	Taiwan Semiconductor Mfg Co	Electronic components	12/31/01	—	14483.2	366517.7	—	238	236110389
TLB	Talbots, Inc. (United States)	—	2/2/02	1612.5	127.0	831.1	567.9	156	21717283
SKT	Tanger Factory Outlet Centers	Real estate investment trust	12/31/02	p13.2	p13.2	—	—	74	3060620
TGT	Target Corp	Department stores	2/1/03	—	—	—	—	786	794488552
TBC	Tasty Baking Co. (United Stat	Food processing	12/29/01	164.6	6.3	116.1	55.1	48	4390589
TCO	Taubman Centers, Inc.	Real estate investment trust	12/31/02	—	p14.4	—	—	125	45641797
TCB	TCF Financial Corp.	Savings & loan	12/31/02	1150.2	232.9	12202.1	977.0	250	46806679
CVT	TCW Convertible Secs Fund Inc	Investment company	12/31/02	18.3	16.0	265.4	236.1	34	1707126
TMT	TCW/DW Term Trust 2003	Investment company	3/31/02	72.8	60.6	854.6	853.9	28	17282332
TLD	TDC A/S (Denmark)	Telecommunications	12/31/01	—	—	—	—	29	2892877
TDK	TDK Corp.	Electronic components	3/31/02	—	—	—	—	25	5774541
TKP	Technip-Coflexip (France)	Engineering & construction	12/31/01	—	—	—	—	21	3878226
TNL	Technitrol, Inc.	Electrical equipment	12/31/02	p406.4	p390.6	—	—	126	27517291
TE	TECO Energy, Inc.	Electric power	12/31/02	2675.8	298.2	8637.8	2611.7	345	106455906
TFR	Tefron Ltd. (Israel)	—	12/31/01	188.9	d10.0	227.7	57.6	1	50100
TRC	Tejon Ranch Co.	—	12/31/01	p21.7	p21.5	—	—	46	3028381
TEK	Tektronix, Inc.	Meas. & control instruments	5/25/02	843.3	30.5	1384.2	927.2	197	74726584
TSU	Tele Celular Sul Participacoe	Telecommunications	12/31/01	—	—	—	—	4	1124777
TRO	Tele Centro Oeste Celular Par	Telecommunications	12/31/01	—	—	—	—	12	643423505
TBE	Tele Leste Celular Participac	Telecommunications	12/31/01	—	—	—	—	1	19464
TCN	Tele Norte Celular Participac	Telecommunications	12/31/01	—	—	—	—	1	24900
TNE	Tele Norte Leste Participacoe	Telecommunications	12/31/01	—	—	—	—	30	15696988
TSD	Tele Sudeste Celular Particip	Telecommunications	12/31/01	—	—	—	—	1	40
TEO	Telecom Argentina Stet-France	Telecommunications	12/31/01	—	—	—	—	42	30151809
NZT	Telecom Corp. of New Zealand	Telecommunications	6/30/02	5537.0	d190.0	8246.0	1325.0	61	26134825
TI	Telecom Italia S.p.A. (New)	Telecommunications	12/31/01	—	—	—	—	66	7301835
TI A	Telecom Italia S.p.A. (New)	Telecommunications	12/31/01	—	—	—	—	5	115897
TBH	Telecomunicacoes Brasileiras	Telecommunications	12/31/01	—	—	—	—	31	26028813
TSP	Telecomunicacoes De Sao Paulo	Telecommunications	12/31/01	—	—	—	—	3	66362
TDY	Teledyne Technologies, Inc.	Engineering & construction	12/31/02	p772.7	p772.7	—	—	126	20029264
TFX	Teleflex Inc.	Medical & dental equipment	12/29/02	p2076.2	p2076.2	—	—	228	27006803
TAR	Telefonica de Argentina S.A.	Telecommunications	12/31/02	—	—	—	—	10	176103
TDP	Telefonica del Peru S.A. (Per	Telecommunications	12/31/01	—	—	—	—	6	42399
TEM	Telefonica Moviles S.A. Spai	Broadcasting	12/31/01	—	—	—	—	3	679954
TEF	Telefonica, S.A. (Spain)	Telecommunications	12/31/01	—	—	—	—	182	54864386
TMX	Telefonos de Mexico, S.A. de	Telecommunications	12/31/01	—	—	—	—	251	270371964
TKA	Telekom Austria AG (Austria)	Telecommunications	12/31/01	—	—	—	—	5	95077
TMB	Telemig Celular Participacoes	Telecommunications	12/31/01	—	—	—	—	5	193680

T46

EARNINGS PER SHARE QUARTERLY 1st	2nd	3rd	ANNUAL 2002	2001	2000	P/E RATIO	DIVIDENDS PER SHARE 2002	2001	2000	AV. YLD. %	DIV. DECLARED AMOUNT	PAYABLE	PRICE RANGE 2002
0.39	0.38	0.23	—	—	pd1.79	—	0.92	0.92	0.92	3.4	0.23Q	3/7/03	35.90 - 17.60
0.38	0.29	—	1.66	2.02	2.17	16.9 - 11.3	0.84	0.84	0.81	3.6	0.21Q	2/25/03	28.00 - 18.80
0.49	—	—	p2.14	1.81	2.22	24.3 - 12.8	0.99	0.94	0.90	2.5	0.255Q	3/28/03	52.0Q - 27.31
0.49	—	—	d0.38	d0.23	0.07	—	2.30	2.30	2.30	13.1	0.575Q	2/14/03	21.65 - 13.40
d0.39	pd0.09	—	d0.38	d0.23	0.07	—	1.32	2.30	0.50	9.2	0.25Q	2/14/03	20.35 - 8.40
—	—	—	d0.06	1.25	—	—	0.80	0.80	0.80	4.1	0.20Q	3/28/03	25.48 - 13.65
—	—	—	p1.05	0.34	1.36	26.7 - 15.3	—	—	—	—	—	—	28.00 - 16.10
—	—	—	1.20	0.73	1.96	33.3 - 15.8	0.20	0.77	0.67	0.7	0.84A	1/21/03	39.94 - 19.00
—	—	—	3.10	1.90	1.81	18.8 - 10.4	0.46	0.39	0.33	1.0	0.13Q	4/15/03	58.36 - 32.11
0.38	0.31	0.73	—	1.15	0.81	—	0.46	0.32	0.26	2.6	0.13Q	2/14/03	22.72 - 12.96
—	—	—	p0.57	0.46	1.49	33.7 - 18.9	—	—	—	—	3-for-2	7/17/00	19.20 - 10.80
—	—	—	—	—	—	—	0.30	—	—	3.9	0.3001U	6/7/02	9.32 - 6.24
0.13	—	—	0.83	0.76	0.76	19.2 - 11.7	—	—	—	—	—	—	15.90 - 9.70
d0.10	d0.05	d0.21	—	0.01	1.29	—	0.24	0.44	0.44	1.8	0.06Q	1/15/03	18.00 - 7.95
—	—	—	p1.68	1.71	1.89	14.2 - 8.9	—	—	—	—	—	—	23.83 - 15.00
—	—	—	p2.05	1.59	1.47	14.4 - 11.4	0.74	0.71	0.66	2.8	0.19Q	3/14/03	29.60 - 23.44
0.18	0.26	0.30	—	0.65	0.02	—	—	—	—	—	2-for-1	8/24/98	27.30 - 16.30
—	—	—	p1.71	1.50	1.32	17.5 - 12.4	0.64	0.51	0.41	2.5	0.19Q	3/31/03	30.00 - 21.12
0.17	0.16	0.17	—	1.57	1.23	—	0.34	0.34	0.34	2.3	0.085Q	2/14/03	19.91 - 9.54
—	—	—	p5.30	2.98	0.04	4.2 - 2.8	—	—	0.04	—	0.04Q	1/31/00	22.50 - 15.05
—	—	—	p0.34	0.25	1.20	43.1 - 30.6	0.06	0.12	0.12	0.5	0.03Q	6/6/02	14.65 - 10.40
—	—	—	p0.74	1.68	1.73	27.4 - 6.2	—	—	—	—	3-for-2	12/31/98	20.24 - 4.60
—	—	—	—	—	—	—	0.03	0.03	0.02	0.1	0.06U	4/29/03	35.53 - 11.00
0.24	0.60	0.52	—	d2.73	4.51	—	—	—	—	—	—	—	43.90 - 28.65
—	—	—	pd2.16	0.13	1.46	—	—	—	—	—	—	—	19.30 - 7.05
—	—	—	—	—	—	—	0.40	0.41	—	3.5	—	4/11/03	14.50 - 8.10
—	—	—	1.02	0.64	d0.02	25.1 - 9.5	—	—	—	—	2-for-1	6/26/98	25.65 - 9.66
—	—	—	12.15	11.99	11.92	—	1.20	1.21	1.23	9.9	0.1076M	3/31/03	13.29 - 11.03
—	—	—	0.58	0.45	0.58	16.0 - 11.2	0.20	0.20	0.20	2.5	0.05Q	3/17/03	9.30 - 6.49
—	—	—	1.70	1.34	1.10	39.7 - 25.8	0.10	0.08	0.07	0.2	0.12A	1/31/03	67.47 - 43.85
—	—	—	p8.77	6.77	5.24	11.6 - 8.4	2.80	2.80	2.40	3.2	0.77Q	3/3/03	102.00 - 73.30
0.92	—	—	p0.31	0.50	1.00	47.7 - 28.9	0.80	0.80	0.80	6.7	0.20Q	3/15/03	14.80 - 8.96
—	—	—	2.12	2.14	1.70	13.4 - 9.4	2.27	2.20	2.11	9.4	0.575Q	2/11/03	28.49 - 20.00
—	—	—	—	—	—	—	0.48	—	—	2.2	—	5/9/02	30.85 - 13.18
—	—	—	p3.33	2.09	2.41	7.8 - 4.8	1.89	1.83	1.73	9.0	0.3375Q	5/15/03	25.90 - 16.15
0.44	0.39	0.32	—	1.94	1.91	—	2.29	2.18	2.10	6.1	0.58Q	1/24/03	42.60 - 32.25
—	—	—	p1.12	0.86	0.79	31.3 - 13.1	—	—	—	—	2-for-1	6/18/01	35.10 - 14.70
—	—	—	p1.86	—	—	13.0 - 9.7	1.16	—	—	5.5	0.4875Q	2/14/03	24.25 - 18.00
—	—	—	d0.62	4.85	4.70	—	1.00	1.00	1.00	2.9	0.25Q	3/7/03	42.25 - 27.02
—	—	—	p2.23	2.08	1.10	14.7 - 8.8	—	—	—	—	—	—	32.70 - 19.60
—	—	—	4.71	4.70	4.30	14.9 - 10.9	1.72	1.60	1.48	2.8	0.45Q	3/14/03	70.20 - 51.48
0.08	0.11	0.03	—	0.73	0.30	—	—	—	—	—	—	—	11.65 - 5.95
—	—	—	p2.91	2.10	3.04	18.5 - 12.3	0.47	0.42	0.38	1.0	0.125Q	1/24/03	53.80 - 35.79
—	—	—	—	—	—	—	0.00	0.00	0.00	0.4	0.0045U	6/3/02	1.85 - 0.60
0.57	0.44	0.43	p0.45	1.53	0.62	47.2 - 14.8	0.56	0.56	0.55	2.5	0.1425Q	3/17/03	30.81 - 14.75
—	14.12	—	—	d0.89	2.53	—	—	—	—	—	10%	10/23/97	21.25 - 6.65
—	—	—	—	13.16	17.92	—	0.09	1.63	1.07	0.8	0.541S	1/14/03	12.28 - 9.03
—	—	—	—	—	—	—	1.57	1.01	0.77	5.7	0.5334U	8/23/02	31.09 - 24.38
d0.02	0.05	—	—	d0.42	1.26	—	0.40	0.35	0.28	2.2	0.10Q	4/1/03	27.26 - 9.78
—	—	—	pd0.95	2.30	0.78	—	—	—	—	—	100%	11/19/93	19.24 - 9.15
0.25	—	—	0.90	1.07	—	25.1 - 12.7	—	—	—	—	—	—	22.60 - 11.41
0.04	d0.39	0.05	p0.05	d0.24	d0.33	350.0 - 99.6	0.02	0.02	0.01	0.2	0.01S	4/28/03	17.50 - 4.98
—	—	—	—	d0.15	d0.52	—	—	—	—	—	0.05Q	8/1/94	7.81 - 5.35
—	—	—	—	—	—	—	0.08	—	—	0.7	0.1082U	4/30/03	13.20 - 9.80
0.28	0.28	—	p1.21	1.05	0.92	26.4 - 13.6	0.57	0.49	0.42	2.4	0.165Q	4/1/03	31.93 - 16.48
—	—	—	—	1.01	0.88	—	0.36	0.28	0.24	1.3	0.11Q	4/25/03	32.58 - 21.25
—	—	—	pd1.73	0.02	d1.19	—	—	—	—	—	—	—	3.75 - 1.15
—	—	—	11.31	10.75	21.42	—	—	0.20	—	—	0.20A	1/15/01	13.75 - 7.29
0.57	0.33	0.63	—	0.83	5.71	—	—	—	—	—	10%	7/23/02	19.08 - 5.31
—	—	—	—	2.00	1.80	—	0.35	0.31	0.27	1.1	0.09Q	3/24/03	41.50 - 20.59
—	—	—	p1.08	0.70	0.31	28.9 - 19.2	2.45	2.44	2.43	9.4	0.6125Q	2/14/03	31.20 - 20.75
—	—	—	p1.81	1.51	1.38	25.5 - 13.8	0.24	0.22	0.21	0.7	0.06Q	6/10/03	46.15 - 24.90
0.15	0.11	d0.05	—	0.78	1.04	—	0.48	0.48	0.48	3.5	0.05Q	3/3/03	19.35 - 8.46
—	—	—	pd0.17	d0.09	1.75	—	1.02	1.00	0.98	6.9	0.26Q	4/22/03	17.15 - 12.30
—	—	—	3.15	2.70	2.35	17.3 - 11.1	1.15	1.00	0.82	2.6	0.325Q	2/28/03	54.60 - 35.10
—	—	—	4.63	6.70	8.48	—	0.84	2.41	1.55	13.0	0.08Q	4/11/03	9.30 - 3.67
—	8.85	—	—	11.01	10.75	—	0.56	0.56	0.60	5.2	0.047M	3/21/03	11.05 - 10.52
—	—	—	—	—	—	—	0.48	0.45	0.47	3.4	0.6016U	4/28/03	18.65 - 9.63
—	—	—	—	—	—	—	0.31	0.41	0.47	0.7	—	3/27/03	59.00 - 32.95
—	—	—	—	—	—	—	0.61	—	—	2.5	0.61083U	8/5/02	37.00 - 12.26
—	—	—	pd1.17	0.07	3.02	—	0.03	0.14	0.14	0.2	0.03375Q	1/25/02	31.40 - 12.66
—	—	—	1.95	2.24	1.97	14.9 - 5.1	1.41	1.37	1.33	7.2	0.355Q	2/15/03	29.05 - 10.02
—	—	—	—	d0.81	d0.36	—	—	—	—	—	—	—	4.70 - 1.15
—	—	—	p0.02	0.02	d0.04	1756.5 - -1100.0	—	—	—	—	0.025S	12/10/99	35.13 - 22.00
0.22	0.08	—	—	0.33	1.46	—	—	—	0.06	—	2-for-1	10/31/00	26.60 - 14.64
—	—	—	—	—	—	—	0.21	0.16	0.20	1.9	0.09613U	3/19/03	16.97 - 5.70
—	—	—	—	—	—	—	0.35	0.12	0.14	7.2	0.0001U	12/27/02	7.65 - 2.09
—	—	—	—	—	—	—	0.60	—	0.47	4.4	0.5997U	9/12/02	22.50 - 4.50
—	—	—	—	—	—	—	—	0.27	0.62	—	0.2672U	5/25/01	23.76 - 3.20
—	—	—	—	—	—	—	0.35	0.29	0.37	3.3	0.318U	3/13/03	16.75 - 5.02
—	—	—	—	—	—	—	0.52	0.21	0.19	5.0	0.0336U	3/21/03	13.40 - 7.40
—	—	—	—	—	—	—	1.08	0.68	—	—	0.1799U	5/10/01	6.80 - 0.60
—	—	—	d0.10	0.36	0.45	—	0.76	0.67	1.43	4.1	—	3/21/03	20.84 - 16.41
—	—	—	—	—	—	—	3.11	1.94	2.10	—	—	7/3/03	88.98 - 70.01
—	—	—	—	—	—	—	3.81	2.42	2.60	11.9	1.74184U	7/3/03	58.50 - 5.50
—	—	—	—	—	—	—	0.82	1.18	0.95	2.9	—	3/19/03	43.22 - 13.25
—	—	—	—	—	—	—	1.43	0.06	2.05	12.7	0.0778U	3/25/03	15.55 - 7.10
—	—	—	p0.77	0.77	0.21	28.2 - 17.3	0.71	0.66	0.58	1.4	0.18Q	3/14/03	59.35 - 40.64
—	—	—	p3.15	2.86	2.83	18.8 - 12.9	—	—	—	—	—	—	13.95 - 1.80
—	—	—	—	—	—	—	—	0.17	—	—	0.1676U	7/27/01	4.00 - 1.20
—	—	—	—	—	—	—	—	—	—	—	—	—	8.00 - 5.30
—	—	—	—	—	—	—	—	—	—	—	2%	3/6/03	39.50 - 20.84
—	—	—	—	—	—	—	1.11	0.97	0.86	3.3	0.27536U	3/27/03	41.45 - 26.51
—	—	—	—	—	—	—	—	—	—	—	—	—	20.27 - 14.46
—	—	—	—	—	—	—	0.62	0.35	0.31	2.4	0.3999U	3/17/03	40.40 - 11.75

SYMBOL	COMPANY	NATURE OF BUSINESS	FISCAL YEAR-END	TOTAL REV. $MILL	NET INCOME $MILL	TOTAL ASSETS $MILL	NET STK. EQUITY $MILL	NO. OF INST.	INST. HOLDINGS (SHARES)
TDA	Telephone & Data Systems Inc	Telecommunications	12/31/01	2588.5	p213.2	8046.8	3526.4		
TCP	Telesp Celular Participacoes	Telecommunications	12/31/01					16	4963037
TLS	Telstra Corp., Ltd.	Telecommunications	6/30/02	20802.0	3650.0	37597.0	14106.0	11	22095579
TIN	Temple-Inland Inc. (United S	Paper	12/31/02	p4518.0	p4492.0	—	—	255	44657358
TCH	Templeton China World Fd Inc	Investment company	8/31/02	6.8	3.7	173.7	173.2	22	6173425
TDF	Templeton Dragon Fund, Inc.	Investment company	12/31/01	19.4	12.2	430.7	429.9	44	10537313
EMF	Templeton Emerging Markets F	Investment company	8/31/02	5.3	2.7	156.5	154.6	24	1225612
TEI	Templeton Emerging Mkts Incm	Investment company	8/31/02	60.7	54.4	529.2	522.2	31	1502344
GIM	Templeton Global Income Fund	Investment company	8/31/02	54.6	48.8	945.7	944.6	49	5824726
TRF	Templeton Russia and East Eu	Investment company	3/31/02	2.0	0.3	124.2	115.9	10	483204
THC	Tenet Healthcare Corp.	Hospitals & nursing homes	5/31/02	13913.0	1025.0	13814.0	5619.0	475	421720055
TNC	Tennant Co.	Machinery & equipment	12/31/02	p425.1	p163.2	—	—	61	6375520
TEN	Tenneco Automotive, Inc.		12/31/02	p3459.0	p3244.0	—	—	94	18469924
TVC	Tennessee Valley Authority	Electric power	9/30/02	6835.0	73.0	30889.0	1416.0	15	355941
TVE	Tennessee Valley Authority	Electric power	9/30/02	6835.0	73.0	30889.0	1416.0	8	143610
TPP	Teppco Partners L.P.	Oil	12/31/02	p3242.2	p170.2	—	—	104	6637028
TER	Teradyne Inc.	Electrical equipment	12/31/02	p1222.0	p1222.0	—	—	297	176982344
TEX	Terex Corp. (New)	Machinery & equipment	12/31/01	1812.5	16.7	2387.0	595.4	131	37834379
TRA	Terra Industries, Inc.	Fertilizer	12/31/02	p1044.0	p845.8	—	—	36	18762489
TNH	Terra Nitrogen Co., L.P.	Fertilizer	12/31/02	p326.9	p317.5	—	—	6	885871
TSO	Tesoro Petroleum Corp. (Unit	Oil	12/31/02	p7119.3	p7138.7	—	—	98	39015913
TTI	Tetra Technologies, Inc. (DE)	Industrial	12/31/02	p242.6	p242.6	—	—	106	11715263
TXI	Texas Industries, Inc.	Steel producer	5/31/02	1344.9	51.3	1773.3	762.4	113	18159645
TXN	Texas Instruments, Inc.	Electronic components	12/31/02	8383.0	d344.0	14679.0	10734.0	846	1169180587
TPL	Texas Pacific Land Trust	Real estate investment trust	12/31/02	p9.1	p9.1	—	—	20	233126
TXT	Textron Inc.		12/28/02	10658.0	364.0	15505.0	3406.0	354	95118468
TTF	Thai Fund, Inc.	Investment	12/31/01	1.2	0.2	43.8	43.4	12	376704
GPS	The Gap, Inc.	Specialty stores	2/1/03					417	539829199
TGX	Theragenics Corp.	Medical & dental equipment	12/31/02	p41.9	p41.9	—	—	92	16095783
TMO	Thermo Electron Corp.	Meas. & control instruments	12/31/02	p2086.4	p2224.7	—	—	289	131210459
TNB	Thomas & Betts Corp.	Electrical equipment	12/29/02	p1345.9	p1301.0	—	—	178	52623643
TII	Thomas Industries	Conglomerate	12/31/02	p240.6	p85.7	—	—	91	12243719
TNM	Thomas Nelson, Inc.	Publishing	3/31/02	215.6	7.8	183.5	77.6	51	6938198
TNM B	Thomas Nelson, Inc.	Publishing	3/31/02	215.6	7.8	183.5	77.6	3	43036
TMS	Thomson	Consumer electronics	12/31/01	—	—	—	—	18	445491
THO	Thor Industries, Inc.		7/31/02	1245.3	51.2	497.5	334.6	125	15077555
TMA	Thornburg Mortgage Inc	Real estate investment trust	12/31/02	—	p120.0	—	—	113	12282427
TFS	Three-Five Systems, Inc.	Electronic components	12/31/02	p88.0	p88.0	—	—	79	12867260
TDW	Tidewater Inc.	Oil service & equipment	3/31/02	729.0	136.2	1669.4	1285.8	249	45729731
TIF	Tiffany & Co.	Jewelry	1/31/03	p1706.6	p1706.6	—	—	329	141682587
TBL	Timberland Co. (The) (United	Shoe manufacturing	12/31/02	p1190.9	p1195.8	—	—	156	32730962
TKR	Timken Co. (The)	Steel producer	12/31/02	2550.1	51.5	2748.4	609.1	172	29431072
TTN	Titan Corp.	Computer services	12/31/02	p1392.2	p1128.5	—	—	193	54807390
TWI	Titan International Inc (IL)	Tires and/or rubber goods	12/31/02	462.8	d35.9	532.0	144.0	21	13882532
TJX	TJX Companies, Inc. (New)		1/25/03					420	487740798
TOD	Todd Shipyards Corp.	Defense systems & equip.	3/31/02	121.9	7.0	133.7	66.0	14	1276984
TOL	Toll Brothers Inc. (United S	Home-building	10/31/02	2329.0	219.9	2895.4	1129.5	179	38193499
TKS	Tomkins Plc (United Kingdom)		4/30/02					17	6948234
TOM	Tommy Hilfiger Corp. (UK)		3/31/02	1876.7	134.5	2594.5	1497.5	126	68431112
TOO	TOO, Inc.	Specialty stores	2/1/03		p25.1	—	—	147	30534089
TR	Tootsie Roll Industries Inc		12/31/01	423.5	65.7	618.7	508.5	135	11891389
TRU	Torch Energy Royalty Trust	Oil	12/31/01	16.9	16.2	36.7	36.5	6	62000
TMK	Torchmark Corp.	Insurance brokerage	12/31/02	p2799.8	p2799.8	—	—	294	83046571
TTC	Toro Co. (The) (United State	Machinery & equipment	10/31/02	1399.3	59.9	846.1	365.3	148	8752853
TOT	Total Fina Elf S.A.	Oil	12/31/01	—	—	—	—	204	66123201
TSS	Total System Services, Inc.	Services	12/31/02	p955.1	p955.1	—	—	82	13213642
TAA	Touch America Holdings, Inc.	Telecommunications	12/31/01	549.9	d19.8	3059.5	1176.6	76	16173667
TWR	Tower Automotive, Inc.	Metal products	12/31/02	p2754.5	p2754.5	—	—	124	42020142
TCT	Town & Country Trust (The)	Real estate investment trust	12/31/02	p130.4	p130.4	—	—	65	4000794
TM	Toyota Motor Corp.		3/31/02					75	3921932
TOY	Toys R Us Inc.	Specialty stores	2/2/02	11019.0	67.0	8076.0	3414.0	289	202343440
TP	TPG N.V. (Netherlands)	Freight transportation	12/31/01					32	3403897
TCC	Trammell Crow Co.	Real estate	12/31/02	p400.3	p400.3	—	—	68	18136822
TFD	Transamerica Finance Corp.	Finance	12/31/01	1727.9	97.0	10131.5	1344.1	6	148600
TAI	Transamerica Income Shares,	Investment company	3/31/02	11.9	10.9	150.6	146.5	13	50001
TRH	Transatlantic Holdings Inc.	Property & casualty insurance	12/31/02	p2615.5	p2615.5	—	—	94	49862942
TCI	Transcontinental Realty Inve	Real estate investment trust	12/31/01	186.2	19.8	709.2	216.8	19	330696
RIG	Transocean, Inc. (Cayman Isl	Oil	12/31/01	2820.1	271.9	17019.8	10910.3	474	248199234
TGS	Transportadora de Gas del Sur	Natural gas	12/31/01	—	—	—	—	9	4184117
TPR	TransPro, Inc.		12/31/02	p230.6	p230.6	—	—	19	4333150
TT	TransTechnology Corp.	Defense systems & equip.	3/31/02	72.3	3.2	142.1	d16.2	11	3241217
TAP A	Travelers Property Casualty	Property & casualty insurance	12/31/02	—	pd27.0	—	—	439	395860608
TPK	Travelers Property Casualty	Property & casualty insurance	12/31/02	—	pd27.0	—	—		
TAP B	Travelers Property Casualty	Property & casualty insurance	12/31/02	—	pd27.0	—	—	473	355582591
TRR	TRC Companies, Inc.	Pollution control	6/30/02	269.5	15.5	205.9	116.9	50	5121289
TG	Tredegar Corp. (United State	Plastics & plastic products	12/31/02	677.3	6.2	838.0	462.9	102	13338981
TWK	Trenwick Group Ltd.	Property & casualty insurance	12/31/01	—	—	—	—	42	17922402
TWP	Trex Co., Inc.	Plastics & plastic products	12/31/02	p167.1	p167.1	—	—	90	4807978
TY	Tri-Continental Corp.	Investment company	12/31/02	61.2	42.6	2953.8	2948.9	81	3558151
TRI	Triad Hospitals, Inc.	Hospitals & nursing homes	12/31/02	p3541.0	p3541.0	—	—	259	77502638
TRY	Triarc Companies, Inc.	Soft drinks	12/30/01	136.8	9.0	868.4	332.4	97	11679614
TRB	Tribune Co.	Newspapers	12/31/02	p5384.4	p5384.4	—	—	443	168806118
TXA	Tribune Co.	Newspapers	12/31/02	p5384.4	p5384.4	—	—	15	2385765
TDR	Tricom, S.A. (Dominican Repub	Telecommunications	12/31/01	243.8	d24.9	829.4	253.5	7	1366445
TRN	Trinity Industries, Inc.	Metal products	12/31/02	p1487.3	p1487.3	—	—	136	37423096
TPC	Triton PCS Holdings Inc	Telecommunications	12/31/01	550.0	d194.6	1683.6	d39.2	76	5175352
TGI	Triumph Group Inc.		3/31/02	612.8	49.4	773.0	453.5	107	14064005
TRZ	Trizec Properties, Inc. (Can	Finance	12/31/01	1099.2	d417.9	7254.1	1618.2	109	87620122
DJT	Trump Hotels & Casino Resort	Hotel/hotel lodging	12/31/02	p1229.0	p1229.0	—	—	16	2882750
TUP	Tupperware Corp.	Plastics & plastic products	12/28/02	p1103.5	p1117.4	—	—	194	44640551
TKF	Turkish Investment Fund Inc.	Investment company	10/31/02	0.4	d0.1	28.8	24.8	9	831400
TZA	TV Azteca S.A. de C.V.	Broadcasting	12/31/01	—	—	—	—	35	22454423
TDI	Twin Disc, Inc.		6/30/02	179.4	2.2	157.3	58.5	14	890515
TXU	TXU Corp (United States)	Electric power	12/31/02	—	pd644.0	—	—	399	208810523
TYC	Tyco International Ltd. (Ber	Services	9/30/02	—	—	—	—	743	1546424689
TYL	Tyler Technologies, Inc.	Computer services	12/31/02	133.9	6.2	169.8	118.7	61	13594524

T48

EARNINGS PER SHARE — QUARTERLY 1st	2nd	3rd	ANNUAL 2002	2001	2000	P/E RATIO	DIVIDENDS PER SHARE 2002	2001	2000	AV. YLD. %	DIV. DECLARED AMOUNT	PAYABLE	PRICE RANGE 2002
0.23	d16.24	d0.33	—	d2.87	2.39	—	1.42	—	—	6.5	0.475Q	4/1/03	25.35 - 18.17
—	—	—	—	—	—	—	—	0.10	0.05	—	0.1383U	6/27/01	10.15 - 1.63
—	—	—	0.28	0.32	0.31	72.1 - 23.2	0.60	0.48	0.47	4.4	0.3675U	5/12/03	20.55 - 6.60
—	—	—	p1.52	2.26	3.83	39.5 - 21.5	1.28	1.28	1.28	2.8	0.34Q	3/14/03	59.99 - 32.69
—	—	—	10.64	9.52	11.33	—	0.21	0.18	0.23	2.2	0.01A	1/15/03	10.85 - 7.80
—	10.32	—	—	8.82	9.91	—	—	0.98	1.17	—	0.015S	4/7/03	9.94 - 7.28
—	—	—	8.76	8.86	11.44	—	0.16	0.10	0.11	1.8	0.1499M	11/8/02	11.30 - 6.75
—	—	—	11.11	11.48	12.43	—	1.26	1.28	1.24	11.4	0.25Q	4/14/03	12.45 - 9.61
—	—	—	7.29	6.99	7.06	—	0.54	0.54	0.59	7.7	0.04M	3/31/03	7.75 - 6.35
—	18.35	—	—	21.60	13.40	—	0.19	—	0.14	0.9	0.0968A	6/18/02	27.50 - 15.20
0.68	0.64	—	—	2.04	1.39	—	—	—	0.01	—	3-for-2	6/28/02	52.50 - 13.70
—	—	—	p0.95	0.52	3.09	46.3 - 27.7	0.82	0.80	0.78	2.3	0.21Q	3/14/03	44.00 - 26.35
—	—	—	p0.74	3.43	d1.18	11.2 - 2.6	—	—	0.20	—	0.05Q	12/5/00	8.32 - 1.90
—	—	—	—	—	—	—	1.69	1.69	1.69	6.5	—	3/3/03	27.18 - 25.00
—	—	—	—	—	—	—	1.63	1.63	1.63	6.1	0.40625Q	2/3/03	28.50 - 25.00
—	—	—	p1.79	2.18	1.89	18.6 - 13.4	2.35	2.15	2.00	8.2	0.60Q	2/7/03	33.25 - 23.90
0.16	0.12	0.25	pd3.93	d1.15	2.86	—	—	—	—	—	2-for-1	8/31/99	40.20 - 7.10
—	—	—	pd0.48	d1.03	0.14	—	—	—	—	—	0.06A	6/5/91	27.50 - 9.84
—	—	—	p0.33	d0.52	1.07	22.0 - 9.8	0.40	0.44	0.22	7.6	0.25Q	2/27/03	3.97 - 1.50
—	—	—	pd1.61	2.10	1.75	—	—	—	—	—	0.10Q	8/25/86	7.25 - 3.22
—	—	—	p0.60	1.61	0.57	50.0 - 27.9	—	—	—	—	—	—	15.29 - 1.24
0.18	d0.16	—	—	2.38	1.24	—	0.30	0.30	0.30	0.9	0.075Q	2/28/03	30.00 - 16.72
—	—	—	d0.20	d0.12	1.73	—	0.09	0.09	0.09	0.3	0.02125Q	2/10/03	35.94 - 13.10
—	—	—	p2.09	2.79	1.47	20.5 - 16.5	0.40	0.40	0.40	1.0	0.40A	3/14/03	42.75 - 34.45
—	—	—	2.60	1.16	1.90	20.6 - 12.4	1.30	1.30	1.30	3.0	0.325Q	4/1/03	53.60 - 32.20
—	4.49	—	—	3.27	2.99	—	0.01	0.02	—	0.2	0.039U	1/31/03	5.85 - 3.00
—	—	—	p0.54	d0.01	1.00	43.6 - 15.5	0.09	0.09	0.09	0.6	0.0222Q	3/17/03	23.54 - 8.35
—	—	—	p0.19	0.50	0.62	55.3 - 17.6	—	—	—	—	2-for-1	4/15/98	10.50 - 3.35
—	—	—	p0.99	1.12	0.27	24.8 - 14.5	—	—	—	—	0.00U	11/15/01	24.60 - 14.33
—	—	—	p0.49	d2.39	d3.33	50.0 - 24.9	—	0.84	1.12	—	0.28Q	7/2/01	24.50 - 12.20
0.02	0.28	0.17	p2.00	1.80	1.91	15.5 - 11.2	0.34	0.33	0.30	1.3	0.085Q	4/1/03	31.02 - 22.45
0.02	0.28	0.17	—	0.54	0.40	—	—	0.12	0.16	—	0.04Q	8/20/01	13.93 - 5.00
0.02	0.28	0.17	—	0.54	0.40	—	—	0.12	0.16	—	0.04Q	8/20/01	14.00 - 6.50
—	—	—	—	—	—	—	—	—	0.11	—	0.1148U	10/24/00	32.98 - 12.12
0.72	0.53	—	1.87	1.11	1.49	22.9 - 10.0	0.04	0.04	0.04	0.1	0.01Q	4/2/03	42.78 - 18.65
—	—	—	p2.59	2.10	1.05	8.2 - 6.3	2.25	1.45	0.94	12.0	0.585Q	1/24/03	21.33 - 16.20
—	—	—	pd0.79	d0.83	0.69	—	—	—	—	—	50%	5/12/00	18.19 - 3.47
0.41	0.41	0.42	—	2.41	1.53	—	0.60	0.60	0.60	1.7	0.15Q	2/20/03	45.70 - 23.38
—	—	—	p1.28	1.15	1.26	32.0 - 15.2	0.16	0.16	0.18	0.5	0.04Q	4/10/03	41.00 - 19.40
—	—	—	p2.36	2.65	2.91	19.5 - 10.9	—	—	—	—	2-for-1	7/17/00	45.95 - 25.80
—	—	—	0.83	d0.69	0.76	33.0 - 18.0	0.52	0.67	0.72	2.5	0.13Q	3/4/03	27.41 - 14.92
—	—	—	pd0.11	d0.32	d0.32	—	—	—	—	—	0.00U	8/5/02	25.10 - 8.86
—	—	—	d1.73	d1.81	0.22	—	0.02	0.04	0.06	0.6	0.005Q	4/15/03	5.64 - 1.18
0.41	0.36	d0.02	p1.08	0.97	0.93	20.8 - 14.2	0.11	0.09	0.08	0.6	0.03Q	2/27/03	22.45 - 15.30
—	—	—	—	1.03	1.73	—	—	—	—	—	—	—	17.12 - 8.85
0.61	—	—	2.91	2.76	1.95	10.9 - 6.1	—	—	—	—	100%	3/28/02	31.80 - 17.76
—	—	—	—	—	—	—	0.73	0.70	1.03	5.4	0.5147U	—	16.00 - 10.93
—	—	—	—	1.49	1.43	—	—	—	—	—	2-for-1	7/9/99	16.65 - 6.10
—	—	—	p0.72	1.23	1.02	47.9 - 27.0	—	—	—	—	—	—	34.50 - 19.45
0.24	0.23	0.51	—	1.23	1.40	—	0.27	0.26	0.24	0.7	3%	4/16/03	46.61 - 28.25
0.24	0.21	0.28	—	1.88	1.47	—	1.01	1.89	1.47	20.5	0.308Q	3/10/03	7.10 - 2.70
—	—	—	p3.18	3.11	2.82	13.3 - 9.4	0.36	0.36	0.36	1.0	0.09Q	5/1/03	42.17 - 30.02
p0.54	—	—	4.63	3.86	3.47	14.5 - 9.7	0.24	0.24	0.24	0.4	0.12Q	4/14/03	67.19 - 45.00
—	—	—	—	—	—	—	1.48	1.20	0.95	2.1	1.8836U	6/9/03	83.24 - 60.30
d0.10	d0.32	d0.21	p0.64	0.53	0.44	46.0 - 17.2	0.07	0.06	0.05	0.3	0.0175Q	4/1/03	29.44 - 11.01
—	—	—	—	0.11	1.84	—	—	—	—	—	—	—	4.29 - 0.29
—	—	—	pd1.70	d5.87	0.34	—	—	—	—	—	2-for-1	7/15/98	15.40 - 4.11
—	—	—	p1.08	0.95	1.40	21.9 - 16.4	1.72	1.72	1.68	8.3	0.43Q	3/10/03	23.70 - 17.71
—	—	—	—	—	—	—	0.43	0.37	0.38	0.8	0.2121U	3/26/03	60.00 - 45.50
d0.02	d0.08	d0.13	—	0.33	1.88	—	—	—	—	—	3-for-2	6/29/90	23.10 - 8.51
—	—	—	p0.46	d0.15	0.98	34.5 - 18.3	0.37	0.32	0.34	1.9	0.14697U	8/20/02	22.72 - 15.30
—	—	—	—	—	—	—	—	—	—	—	—	—	15.85 - 8.40
—	—	—	—	—	—	—	1.77	1.77	1.77	7.3	0.44375Q	2/3/03	25.70 - 23.05
—	22.00	—	—	23.18	24.18	—	2.12	2.06	1.90	8.6	0.15M	4/15/03	26.70 - 22.75
—	—	—	p3.21	0.36	4.03	28.3 - 18.8	0.39	0.37	0.35	0.5	0.10Q	6/13/03	91.00 - 60.25
d0.17	d1.05	d1.46	—	2.28	3.45	—	—	—	0.54	—	0.18Q	9/29/00	21.45 - 15.50
—	—	—	0.86	0.50	—	—	0.06	0.12	0.12	0.2	0.03Q	6/13/02	39.30 - 18.10
—	—	—	—	—	—	—	—	0.59	0.60	—	—	8/29/01	5.67 - 0.61
—	—	—	p0.28	3.09	d1.43	23.2 - 10.7	—	—	0.15	—	0.05Q	7/10/00	6.50 - 3.00
0.07	0.20	0.23	—	0.12	d11.83	—	—	—	0.26	—	0.065Q	12/1/00	13.60 - 8.60
—	—	—	pd0.03	1.38	1.71	—	—	—	—	—	0.06Q	2/10/03	21.05 - 11.75
—	—	—	pd0.03	1.38	1.71	—	0.62	—	—	2.7	0.28125Q	4/15/03	27.30 - 18.66
—	—	—	pd0.03	1.38	1.71	—	—	—	—	—	3-for-2	2/28/03	19.50 - 12.09
0.26	0.26	—	1.14	0.75	0.43	29.4 - 8.4	—	—	—	—	3-for-2	3/5/02	33.50 - 9.60
—	—	—	0.16	0.21	2.86	155.6 - 74.4	0.16	0.16	0.16	0.9	0.04Q	4/15/03	24.90 - 11.90
—	—	—	—	—	—	—	0.12	0.16	0.04	2.1	0.04Q	9/30/02	10.85 - 0.43
—	18.31	—	—	—	—	—	0.26	1.39	3.55	1.6	0.05Q	3/26/03	38.99 - 16.80
—	—	—	p1.16	0.64	1.36	33.6 - 14.5	—	—	—	—	—	—	19.95 - 11.75
—	—	—	p1.89	0.10	0.13	24.7 - 14.4	—	—	—	—	5%	4/25/86	46.75 - 27.15
0.35	d0.37	d0.12	—	0.40	d0.44	—	—	—	—	—	—	—	48.73 - 21.98
—	—	—	p1.30	0.28	0.99	38.1 - 27.4	0.44	0.44	0.40	1.0	0.11Q	3/13/03	49.49 - 35.66
—	—	—	p1.30	0.28	0.99	69.6 - 45.4	3.14	3.14	3.14	4.2	0.785Q	2/18/03	90.50 - 59.90
—	—	—	—	d0.78	0.33	—	—	—	—	—	—	—	4.00 - 2.75
d0.52	d0.51	d0.54	p0.43	0.90	d1.98	—	0.36	0.72	0.72	1.7	0.06Q	4/30/03	27.33 - 14.54
0.63	0.63	p0.50	—	3.16	3.01	—	—	—	—	—	—	—	29.40 - 0.88
—	—	d1.73	—	3.11	3.11	—	—	—	—	—	—	—	49.16 - 23.53
—	p0.54	—	d2.81	d1.15	d2.12	—	0.26	—	—	2.0	0.20Q	4/15/03	17.29 - 8.60
—	—	—	—	—	—	—	—	—	—	—	—	—	3.50 - 1.13
—	—	—	p1.54	1.04	1.29	16.2 - 9.4	0.88	0.88	0.88	4.5	0.22Q	4/2/03	24.99 - 14.40
—	—	—	4.39	4.23	17.69	—	0.00	3.23	0.03	0.1	0.0043A	6/11/99	6.65 - 3.46
—	—	—	—	—	—	—	0.03	0.03	0.03	0.4	0.0258U	10/11/02	8.85 - 4.29
d0.62	d1.10	—	0.73	2.20	1.34	23.2 - 16.2	0.70	0.70	0.70	4.9	0.175Q	3/3/03	16.95 - 11.80
—	—	—	p2.21	3.12	3.43	25.8 - 4.6	2.40	2.40	2.40	7.1	0.125Q	4/1/03	57.05 - 10.10
—	—	—	—	—	—	—	0.05	0.05	0.05	0.2	0.0125Q	5/1/03	58.81 - 6.98
—	—	—	0.12	0.01	d0.17	50.1 - 25.4	—	—	—	—	—	—	6.01 - 3.05

SYMBOL	COMPANY	NATURE OF BUSINESS	FISCAL YEAR-END	TOTAL REV. $MILL	NET INCOME $MILL	TOTAL ASSETS $MILL	NET STK EQUITY $MILL	NO. OF INST.	INST. HOLDINGS (SHARES)
TSN	Tyson Foods, Inc.	Meat packing & processing	9/28/02	23367.0	383.0	10372.0	3662.0	230	134397334
USB	U.S. Bancorp (DE)	Banking - Midwest	12/31/02	15422.3	3326.4	180027.0	18101.0	726	1053052863
USI	U.S. Industries Inc (Hldg Co	—	9/28/02	1159.5	33.8	1575.3	237.7	58	51645196
USV	U.S. Restaurant Properties In	Restaurants	12/31/02	p72.1	p72.1	—	—	58	4097816
UBH	U.S.B. Holding Co., Inc.	Banking - Northeast	12/31/02	—	p27.0	—	—	36	1392095
UAL	UAL Corp	—	12/31/02	—	—	—	—	75	10006401
UBS	UBS AG (Switzerland)	—	12/31/01	—	—	—	—	110	22577675
UGI	UGI Corp. (New)	Public utility	9/30/02	2213.7	75.5	2614.4	317.3	174	14914215
UCI	UICI	Life insurance	12/31/02	p1479.0	p1479.6	—	—	107	20971959
UIL	UIL Holding Corp	Electric power	12/31/02	1131.0	43.9	1780.8	482.4	106	5704369
UGP	UltraPar Participacoes S.A. (	Specialty chemicals	12/31/01	—	—	—	—	14	3236440
UBB	Unibanco-Uniao de Bancos Bra	—	12/31/02	—	—	—	—	20	4271363
UFI	Unifi, Inc.	Textiles	6/30/02	914.7	d6.1	1003.7	498.0	119	39675811
UNF	UniFirst Corp.	—	8/31/02	578.9	26.9	494.8	309.7	59	6418254
UN	Unilever N.V.	Food processing	12/31/01	—	—	—	—	253	66706255
UL	Unilever Plc (United Kingdom)	Food processing	12/31/01	—	—	—	—	102	32904829
UNP	Union Pacific Corp. (United	Railroads	12/31/02	12491.0	1341.0	32764.0	10651.0	575	222698944
UPC	Union Planters Corp	Banking - South	12/31/02	2689.6	529.0	34144.4	3226.3	302	72022934
UB	UnionBanCal Corp.	Banking - West	12/31/02	2591.9	527.9	40169.8	3758.2	147	138229348
UNS	UniSource Energy Corp.	Electric power	12/31/02	p856.2	p856.2	—	—	123	23004418
UIS	Unisys Corp.	Computers	12/31/02	5607.4	223.0	4981.4	856.0	272	220295711
UNT	Unit Corp.	Oil service & equipment	12/31/02	p187.6	p187.6	—	—	120	26272606
UAG	United Auto Group Inc. (Unit	—	12/31/02	p7434.9	p7422.3	—	—	86	29005419
UDI	United Defense Industries Inc	—	12/31/02	p1725.3	p1723.6	—	—	111	23540186
UDR	United Dominion Realty Trust	Real estate investment trust	12/31/02	p594.3	p560.5	—	—	197	51392397
UDM	United Dominion Realty Trust	Real estate investment trust	12/31/02	p594.3	p560.5	—	—	1	500
UIC	United Industrial Corp. (Unit	Defense systems & equip.	12/31/01	238.5	15.8	252.5	120.3	56	5125160
UMC	United Microelectronics Corp.	Electronic components	12/31/01	—	—	—	—	114	117171222
UPS	United Parcel Service, Inc.	Freight transportation	12/31/02	31272.0	3254.0	26357.0	12455.0	557	384269742
UPK	United Park City Mines Co.	Real estate	12/31/01	6.0	0.2	26.1	19.2	7	29278
URI	United Rentals, Inc. (United	Equip. & vehicle leasing	12/31/02	p2821.0	p878.2	—	—	151	53901375
UZG	United States Cellular Corp	Telecommunications	12/31/02	p2184.5	p2184.5	—	—		
X	United States Steel Corp. (N	Steel producer	12/31/02	p7054.0	p7060.0	—	—	217	76764528
UTX	United Technologies Corp.	—	12/31/02	28212.0	2236.0	29090.0	8355.0	787	396035177
UU	United Utilities Plc (UK)	Water company	3/31/02	—	—	—	—	9	460901
UNH	UnitedHealth Group Inc	Hospitals & nursing homes	12/31/02	—	—	—	—	533	330613210
UTR	Unitrin, Inc.	Insurance	12/31/02	2298.2	d8.2	7705.6	1802.4	140	16702992
UCO	Universal Compression Holdin	Equip. & vehicle leasing	3/31/02	680.0	49.4	1277.2	700.3	100	15631473
UVV	Universal Corp.	Tobacco	6/30/02	2500.1	106.7	1844.4	588.0	150	17999468
UHT	Universal Health Rlty. Inc. T	Real estate investment trust	12/31/01	27.6	18.3	187.9	150.0	78	3935493
UHS	Universal Health Services In	Hospitals & nursing homes	12/31/02	p3258.9	p3258.9	—	—	254	49298402
UVN	Univision Communications Inc	Broadcasting	12/31/01	887.9	54.7	3163.5	813.3	279	157535546
UCL	Unocal Corp.	Oil producer	12/31/02	p5251.0	p5251.0	—	—	399	223387642
UNA	Unova, Inc.	Services	12/31/02	p1313.2	p1313.2	—	—	84	47714097
UNM	UNUMProvident Corp.	Life Insurance	12/31/02	p9928.0	p9928.0	—	—	326	192841453
UNN	UNUMProvident Corp.	Life Insurance	12/31/02	p9928.0	p9928.0	—	—		
UPM	UPM - Kymmene Corp. (Finland	Paper	12/31/01	—	—	—	—	40	2596748
URS	URS Corp. (United States)	Engineering & construction	10/31/02	2427.8	55.2	2229.1	633.9	103	20540194
UBP	Urstadt Biddle Properties, I	Real estate investment trust	10/31/02	44.3	14.5	353.6	220.0	19	697296
UBP A	Urstadt Biddle Properties, I	Real estate investment trust	10/31/02	44.3	14.5	353.6	220.0	62	7374311
USU	USEC, Inc.	Mining & enrichment	6/30/02	1426.2	84.2	2168.0	949.3	103	47219015
USG	USG Corp. (United States)	Cement & gypsum	12/31/02	3468.0	139.0	3617.0	535.0	83	19436632
UST	UST, Inc.	Tobacco	12/31/02	p1682.9	p1855.8	—	—	297	131751730
MTN	Vail Resorts Inc. (United Sta	Recreation	7/31/02	615.3	9.3	1447.7	507.3	51	26398878
VCI	Valassis Communications, Inc.	Printing & engraving	12/31/02	p853.0	p314.4	—	—	170	50585601
VLO	Valero Energy Corp. (New)	Natural gas	12/31/01	14988.3	563.6	14377.1	4202.6	288	88136646
VLI	Valero L.P. (United States)	Oil	12/31/02	p118.5	p118.5	—	—	27	449986
VHI	Valhi, Inc. (New)	Conglomerate	12/31/02	p1059.5	p980.2	—	—	39	3479236
VLY	Valley National Bancorp	Banking - Northeast	12/31/02	598.7	154.6	9134.7	631.7	103	11676747
VMI	Valmont Industries, Inc.	Machinery & equipment	12/28/02	p854.9	p227.7	—	—	85	8190142
VAL	Valspar Corp.	Paints & related products	10/25/02	2126.9	120.1	2419.6	737.3	191	30830642
VDM	Van der Moolen Holding N.V. (	Securities brokerage	12/31/01	—	—	—	—	14	5792488
VKA	Van Kampen Adv Mun Incm Tr	Investment company	10/31/02	27.6	23.0	518.3	510.5	21	1047793
VAP	Van Kampen Adv PA Mun Incm Tr	Investment company	10/31/02	6.3	5.2	120.1	115.4	5	64646
VBF	Van Kampen Bond Fund	Investment company	6/30/02	15.7	14.2	215.5	213.4	20	304483
VQC	Van Kampen CA Quality Mun Tr	Investment company	10/31/02	13.7	11.5	242.8	167.5	7	33547
VCV	Van Kampen CA Value Mun Incm	Investment company	10/31/02	8.6	7.1	162.9	102.6	5	77417
VFM	Van Kampen FL Quality Mun Tr	Investment company	10/31/02	8.1	6.6	162.1	160.7	7	95531
VLT	Van Kampen High Income Tr II	Investment company	12/31/02	5.6	4.9	58.8	58.5	4	102384
VIT	Van Kampen High Income Trust	Investment company	12/31/02	7.5	6.5	79.4	79.1	3	149045
VIN	Van Kampen Income Trust	Investment company	12/31/02	6.8	6.0	97.4	93.8	15	379340
VIG	Van Kampen Investment Grade	Investment company	10/31/02	3.8	3.2	74.6	48.2	4	57093
VOT	Van Kampen Mun Opport Tr II	Investment company	10/31/02	15.4	12.8	291.8	175.3	14	95254
VMT	Van Kampen Municipal Income T	Investment company	6/30/02	23.3	19.7	622.5	451.4	21	1051080
VMO	Van Kampen Municipal Opportun	Investment company	10/31/02	22.6	18.8	426.7	418.4	21	238401
VKQ	Van Kampen Municipal Trust	Investment company	10/31/02	46.4	38.6	902.5	586.2	26	1922022
VNM	Van Kampen NY Quality Mun Tr	Investment company	10/31/02	7.4	6.1	144.5	143.8	7	104151
VNV	Van Kampen NY Value Mun Inm T	Investment company	10/31/02	5.8	4.7	113.6	70.4	5	51962
VOQ	Van Kampen OH Quality Mun Tr	Investment company	10/31/02	5.9	4.9	109.1	72.9	5	65335
VPQ	Van Kampen PA Quality Mun Tr	Investment company	10/31/02	11.2	9.3	204.6	139.3	8	134445
VPV	Van Kampen PA Value Mun Incm	Investment company	10/31/02	6.3	5.1	117.7	72.1	6	41828
VKS	Van Kampen Strategic Sector	Investment company	10/31/01	14.4	12.0	255.8	254.4	9	17404
VIC	Van Kampen Tr Invt Gr CA Muns	Investment company	10/31/02	6.6	5.4	122.2	77.0	6	20290
VTF	Van Kampen Tr Invt Gr FL Muns	Investment company	10/31/02	8.1	6.6	211.4	98.9	7	100513

T50

EARNINGS PER SHARE						P/E RATIO	DIVIDENDS PER SHARE			AV. YLD.	DIV. DECLARED		PRICE RANGE
QUARTERLY			ANNUAL										2002
1st	2nd	3rd	2002	2001	2000		2002	2001	2000	%	AMOUNT	PAYABLE	
0.11	—	—	1.08	0.40	0.67	14.5 - 8.6	0.16	0.16	0.16	1.3	0.04Q	6/15/03	15.71 - 9.27
—	—	—	1.73	0.88	2.13	14.2 - 9.3	0.77	0.56	—	3.8	0.205Q	4/15/03	24.48 - 16.05
0.18	—	—	0.46	d2.43	0.43	9.2 - 3.3	—	0.05	0.20	—	0.05Q	1/22/01	4.25 - 1.50
—	—	—	p0.36	d1.38	d0.46	46.4 - 29.2	1.32	1.2	1.4	9.7	0.11M	4/15/03	16.70 - 10.51
—	—	—	p1.42	1.11	1.05	14.5 - 8.8	0.35	0.30	0.27	2.1	0.10Q	4/15/03	20.60 - 12.50
—	—	—	pd53.55	d39.90	1.89	—	—	0.68	0.94	—	0.05Q	8/1/01	17.90 - 0.64
—	—	—	—	—	—	—	1.34	—	—	3.1	2.00U	4/17/03	52.64 - 33.79
1.29	—	—	2.70	1.90	1.64	15.0 - 9.5	1.08	1.05	1.02	3.3	3-for-2	4/1/03	40.49 - 25.67
—	—	—	p1.05	1.01	0.61	20.2 - 11.7	—	—	—	—	300%	5/31/95	21.22 - 12.25
—	—	—	3.08	4.19	4.31	19.1 - 9.2	2.88	1.44	—	6.6	0.72Q	4/1/03	58.90 - 28.20
—	—	—	—	—	—	—	0.32	1.86	0.33	4.6	0.1946U	3/17/03	9.55 - 4.25
—	—	—	—	—	—	—	0.86	1.00	1.06	5.0	0.3684U	2/10/03	27.70 - 6.25
0.08	d0.04	—	d0.11	d0.83	0.65	—	—	—	—	—	0.14Q	5/8/98	11.66 - 4.66
0.33	—	—	1.39	1.20	1.01	20.7 - 13.4	0.15	0.15	0.15	0.6	0.0375Q	4/3/03	28.78 - 18.68
—	—	—	—	—	—	—	1.50	1.29	1.19	2.6	—	6/9/03	67.09 - 48.06
—	—	—	—	—	—	—	0.90	0.77	0.76	2.6	0.7006U	6/9/03	39.64 - 28.82
—	—	—	5.05	3.77	3.34	12.9 - 10.5	0.80	0.80	0.80	1.4	0.23Q	4/1/03	65.15 - 53.00
—	—	—	2.59	2.13	2.00	13.1 - 9.1	1.33	1.33	1.33	4.7	0.3334Q	2/17/03	33.80 - 23.51
—	—	—	3.38	3.04	2.72	14.7 - 10.3	1.06	1.00	1.00	2.5	0.28Q	4/4/03	49.83 - 34.70
—	—	—	p0.97	1.79	1.27	21.4 - 14.1	0.50	0.40	0.32	2.9	0.15Q	3/7/03	20.75 - 13.70
—	—	—	0.69	d0.16	0.77	20.1 - 8.6	—	—	—	—	0.25Q	8/7/90	13.84 - 5.92
—	—	—	p0.47	1.75	0.96	44.5 - 21.8	—	—	—	—	—	—	20.93 - 10.24
—	—	—	p1.51	1.31	1.16	21.2 - 7.4	—	—	—	—	—	—	32.00 - 11.12
—	—	—	p2.58	0.86	0.43	11.6 - 6.8	—	—	—	—	—	—	29.85 - 17.60
—	—	—	p0.24	0.27	0.41	70.0 - 54.9	1.10	1.08	1.07	7.4	0.285Q	4/30/03	16.81 - 13.18
—	—	—	p0.24	0.27	0.41	117.5 - 104.8	2.12	2.12	2.12	8.0	—	4/15/03	28.19 - 25.15
0.08	0.12	0.32	—	1.19	0.62	—	0.30	0.40	0.40	1.6	0.10Q	4/1/03	26.05 - 12.65
—	—	—	—	—	—	—	—	—	—	—	15%	9/9/02	10.02 - 2.93
—	—	—	2.87	2.12	2.50	23.4 - 18.9	0.76	0.74	0.81	1.3	0.21Q	3/11/03	67.10 - 54.25
d0.19	d0.18	1.13	—	0.07	0.26	—	—	—	—	—	—	—	24.30 - 17.05
—	—	—	pd5.25	1.30	1.89	—	—	—	—	—	—	—	30.83 - 5.88
—	—	—	pd2.13	2.07	2.68	—	—	—	—	—	—	2/3/03	26.05 - 24.75
—	—	—	p0.64	d2.45	d0.33	34.4 - 16.7	0.20	—	—	1.2	0.05Q	3/10/03	22.00 - 10.66
—	—	—	4.42	3.83	3.55	17.6 - 11.0	0.98	0.90	0.82	1.5	0.245Q	3/10/03	77.75 - 48.83
—	—	—	—	—	—	—	1.43	0.96	1.36	7.6	0.5048U	2/20/03	20.79 - 16.91
—	—	—	p4.25	2.79	2.19	23.8 - 16.0	0.03	0.03	0.01	0.0	0.03A	4/17/03	101.00 - 67.85
—	—	—	d0.12	5.60	1.32	—	1.66	1.60	1.50	4.7	0.415Q	2/28/03	42.80 - 27.85
0.33	0.25	0.28	—	1.63	0.34	—	—	—	—	—	—	—	29.37 - 14.60
1.09	1.04	—	4.00	4.08	3.77	10.9 - 7.8	1.36	1.28	1.24	3.6	0.36Q	5/12/03	43.50 - 31.15
0.53	0.44	0.43	—	1.74	1.81	—	1.92	1.88	1.84	7.7	0.485Q	3/31/03	28.50 - 21.40
—	—	—	p2.74	3.30	1.50	21.0 - 13.5	—	—	—	—	100%	6/1/01	57.50 - 36.90
0.03	0.09	0.08	—	0.23	0.57	—	—	—	—	—	100%	8/11/00	47.00 - 16.40
—	—	—	p1.34	2.43	2.93	29.6 - 19.8	0.80	0.80	0.80	2.4	0.20Q	2/10/03	39.70 - 26.58
—	—	—	p0.04	d5.14	d0.71	209.8 - 101.3	—	—	—	—	—	—	8.39 - 4.05
—	—	—	p1.51	2.39	2.33	19.7 - 10.8	0.59	0.59	0.59	2.6	0.1475Q	2/21/03	29.70 - 16.30
—	—	—	p1.51	2.39	2.33	16.6 - 14.1	0.86	—	—	3.7	—	3/17/03	25.04 - 21.30
—	—	—	2.03	2.41	2.27	17.1 - 6.2	0.66	0.66	1.01	2.0	2-for-1	3/25/03	34.80 - 12.51
—	—	—	1.65	1.85	1.04	7.9 - 5.8	0.74	0.72	0.70	6.5	0.19Q	4/18/03	13.00 - 9.65
—	—	—	1.65	1.85	1.04	7.4 - 5.9	0.82	0.80	0.78	7.5	0.21Q	4/18/03	12.18 - 9.74
0.01	pd0.19	—	0.20	0.97	0.10	51.0 - 26.7	0.55	0.55	0.55	7.1	0.1375Q	3/15/03	10.20 - 5.35
—	—	—	3.22	0.36	d5.62	2.8 - 1.0	—	0.03	0.60	—	0.025Q	3/21/01	9.13 - 3.30
d0.71	—	—	pd1.61	2.97	2.70	—	1.92	1.84	1.76	5.8	0.50Q	3/31/03	41.35 - 25.30
—	—	—	0.26	0.54	0.44	83.8 - 47.0	—	—	—	—	—	—	21.80 - 12.23
d0.37	0.10	0.27	p1.77	2.17	2.27	23.3 - 13.6	—	—	—	—	0.00U	9/15/99	41.28 - 24.00
—	—	—	2.72	8.83	5.60	15.5 - 11.8	0.40	0.34	0.32	1.1	0.10Q	3/12/03	49.97 - 23.15
—	—	—	p0.80	1.82	1.09	24.1 - 10.3	2.65	1.10	—	7.1	0.70Q	2/14/03	42.23 - 32.00
—	—	—	1.65	0.80	0.66	17.6 - 14.7	0.24	0.24	0.21	1.7	0.06Q	3/31/03	19.30 - 8.25
—	—	—	p1.37	1.38	1.33	18.6 - 10.3	0.87	0.82	0.77	3.3	0.225Q	4/1/03	29.04 - 24.24
—	—	—	—	1.09	1.28	—	0.28	0.26	0.26	1.4	0.075Q	4/1/03	25.50 - 14.15
p0.30	—	—	2.34	1.10	2.00	21.4 - 14.9	0.56	0.54	0.52	1.3	0.15Q	4/15/03	50.15 - 34.80
—	—	—	—	—	—	—	0.73	—	—	3.0	0.7313U	5/9/02	32.35 - 15.64
—	—	—	16.77	16.80	15.52	—	1.08	0.81	0.85	7.0	0.0925M	3/31/03	16.65 - 14.16
—	18.98	—	17.24	17.28	16.40	—	1.28	1.05	1.16	7.6	0.094M	3/31/03	18.18 - 15.59
—	—	—	18.78	19.41	18.70	—	1.28	1.37	1.38	6.9	0.29Q	3/31/03	19.64 - 17.38
—	—	—	17.29	17.57	16.58	—	1.32	1.11	1.03	7.9	0.098M	3/31/03	18.00 - 15.38
—	—	—	17.02	17.02	15.92	—	1.09	0.92	0.84	6.8	0.0925M	3/31/03	17.00 - 15.02
—	—	—	16.97	17.06	16.03	—	1.25	1.08	0.98	8.5	0.077M	3/31/03	15.90 - 13.57
—	—	—	3.79	4.77	5.40	—	0.62	0.74	0.82	12.7	0.037M	3/31/03	6.14 - 3.61
—	—	—	3.03	3.78	4.22	—	0.47	0.56	0.62	12.2	0.03M	3/31/03	4.99 - 2.76
—	—	—	6.10	6.51	6.85	—	0.47	0.58	0.60	7.8	0.033M	3/31/03	6.59 - 5.41
—	—	—	9.97	10.01	9.43	—	0.49	0.49	0.58	5.6	0.041M	3/31/03	9.34 - 8.32
—	—	—	15.01	14.91	13.77	—	0.94	0.77	0.78	6.9	0.0825M	3/31/03	14.65 - 12.76
—	—	—	9.99	9362.00	8.99	—	0.53	0.53	0.58	5.9	0.046M	3/31/03	9.64 - 8.32
—	—	—	17.48	17.59	16.29	—	1.57	1.18	0.90	9.8	0.0965M	3/31/03	17.25 - 14.75
—	—	—	16.12	16.07	14.91	—	0.93	0.82	0.92	6.5	0.078M	3/31/03	15.44 - 13.33
—	—	—	17.46	17.39	16.25	—	1.63	0.96	0.87	10.2	0.085M	3/31/03	17.00 - 14.73
—	—	—	16.40	16.12	14.98	—	0.94	0.87	0.84	6.4	0.085M	3/31/03	15.89 - 13.71
—	—	—	16.92	16.91	16.23	—	1.23	0.88	1.11	7.4	0.0875M	3/31/03	15.28 - 8.25
—	—	—	16.86	16.78	16.12	—	1.18	1.04	1.19	7.1	0.084M	3/31/03	17.72 - 15.45
—	—	—	16.12	16.04	14.89	—	1.02	0.82	0.77	6.5	0.089M	3/31/03	23.38 - 7.68
—	14.30	—	—	14.75	13.70	—	0.97	0.74	0.74	7.0	0.0825M	3/31/03	14.75 - 12.91
—	—	—	16.49	16.81	15.84	—	1.27	1.16	0.98	7.9	0.0935M	3/31/03	17.04 - 15.14
—	—	—	17.79	17.69	16.53	—	1.55	0.94	1.11	9.7	0.092M	3/31/03	17.45 - 14.52

SYMBOL	COMPANY	NATURE OF BUSINESS	FISCAL YEAR-END	TOTAL REV. $MILL	NET INCOME $MILL	TOTAL ASSETS $MILL	NET STK EQUITY $MILL	NO. OF INST.	INST. HOLDINGS (SHARES)
VTJ	Van Kampen Tr Invt Gr NJ Muns	Investment company	10/31/02	9.3	7.7	175.4	175.0	9	51888
VTN	Van Kampen Tr Invt Gr NY Muns	Investment company	10/31/02	9.1	7.5	170.9	109.1	6	97286
VTP	Van Kampen Tr Invt Gr PA Muns	Investment company	10/31/02	10.8	8.9	205.3	199.0	7	107168
VGM	Van Kampen Tr Invt Grade Muns	Investment company	10/31/02	38.3	31.8	744.2	471.6	27	2406441
VIM	Van Kampen Trust for Insd Mun	Investment company	10/31/02	13.1	10.8	258.3	164.5	12	1048310
VKV	Van Kampen Value Mun Incm Tr	Investment company	10/31/02	31.5	26.2	597.4	368.1	20	425267
VRC	Varco International Inc. (Ne	Oil service & equipment	12/31/02	p1335.1	p1330.9	—	—	192	74555996
VAR	Varian Medical Systems, Inc.	Electronic components	9/27/02	873.1	93.6	910.3	472.8	262	58856654
VGR	Vector Group Ltd	Tobacco	12/31/01	744.2	21.2	688.9	113.4	56	14560627
VVC	Vectren Corp	Natural gas distributor	12/31/01	2170.0	67.4	2856.8	848.6	192	27327035
VTR	Ventas, Inc.	Hospitals & nursing homes	12/31/01	204.6	51.6	941.9	d91.1	127	54416120
VNX	Veridian Corp. (DE) (United	Computer services	12/31/02	p834.1	p820.8	—	—	74	13767595
VTS	Veritas DGC Inc.	Oil service & equipment	7/31/02	455.7	d23.1	780.8	524.2	137	26101808
VZ	Verizon Communications Inc	Telecommunications	12/31/02	67625.0	4584.0	167468.0	32616.0	1093	1512929442
VZC	Verizon South, Inc.	Telecommunications	12/31/01	1613.1	329.3	3057.0	851.5	3	100665
VTA	Vesta Insurance Group, Inc.	Property & casualty insurance	12/31/02	p662.7	p662.7	—	—	48	17701553
VES	Vestaur Securities, Inc.	Investment company	11/30/02	7.3	6.4	91.8	91.7	10	105832
VFC	VF Corp. (United States)	—	1/4/03	p5083.5	p5083.5	—	—	286	98833327
VIA	Viacom Inc	Broadcasting	12/31/02	—	—	—	—	172	82747698
VIA B	Viacom Inc	Broadcasting	12/31/02	—	—	—	—	763	1161374220
RBV	Viacom Inc	Broadcasting	12/31/02	—	—	—	—	6	75985
VVI	Viad Corp.	Conglomerate	12/31/02	1647.0	113.8	9690.5	701.1	204	66181624
VAS	Viasys Healthcare, Inc. (Uni	Medical & dental equipment	12/29/01	358.4	16.3	405.3	299.7	121	23096723
VCO	Vina Concha y Toro S.A.	Distilling	12/31/01	—	—	—	—	15	507548
VPI	Vintage Petroleum, Inc.	Oil	12/31/02	p664.3	p642.8	—	—	143	45309317
VEA	Virginia Electric & Power Co.	Electric power	12/31/01	4944.0	446.0	13784.0	4260.0	4	38900
VPA	Virginia Electric & Power Co.	Electric power	12/31/01	4944.0	446.0	13784.0	4260.0	2	198600
VSH	Vishay Intertechnology, Inc.	Electrical equipment	12/31/02	p1822.8	p1822.8	—	—	260	103402558
VC	Visteon Corp.	—	12/31/01	18395.0	d87.0	11170.0	2978.0	262	73123359
EYE	VISX, Inc.	Industrial	12/31/01	169.6	10.9	219.9	176.3	115	38485555
VTO	Vitro, S.A. (Mexico)	Plastics & plastic products	12/31/01	—	—	—	—	9	2140284
VE	Vivendi Environnement (France	—	12/31/01	—	—	—	—	7	166576
V	Vivendi Universal (France)	Telecommunications	12/31/01	—	—	—	—	107	58124923
VOD	Vodafone Group Plc (New)	Telecommunications	3/31/02	—	—	—	—	530	344295123
VOL	Volt Information Sciences, I	Services	11/3/02	1487.8	d3.9	509.6	237.0	59	4968647
VNO	Vornado Realty Trust	Real estate investment trust	12/31/02	985.8	266.7	6777.3	2570.4	218	64160004
VCP	Votorantim Celulose e Papel S	Paper	12/31/01	—	—	—	—	32	7060379
VMC	Vulcan Materials.	Conglomerate	12/31/02	p2796.6	p2776.0	—	—	249	69576551
WHI	W Holding Co.; Inc.	—	12/31/02	p410.5	p86.0	—	—	102	20387350
WPC	W.P. Carey & Co. LLC	Real estate investment trust	12/31/01	p161.6	p161.6	—	—	54	1643878
WPL	W.P. Stewart & Co. Ltd. (Berm	Securities brokerage	12/31/02	203.3	99.1	143.3	114.0	53	11464744
WNC	Wabash National Corp.	—	12/31/02	p819.6	p819.6	—	—	82	20968070
WAB	Wabtec Corp.	Railroads	12/31/02	—	pd45.5	—	—	98	29537787
WB	Wachovia Corp. (United State	Banking - South	12/31/02	—	p3386.0	—	—	719	778563493
WHC	Wackenhut Corrections Corp.	Services	12/29/02	p568.6	p561.2	—	—	53	6436641
WDR	Waddell & Reed Financial, In	Investment company	12/31/02	p434.9	p389.7	—	—	169	63944916
WMT	Wal-Mart Stores	Discount & variety stores	1/31/03	—	—	—	—	1126	1862503498
WAG	Walgreen Co.	Drug stores	8/31/02	28681.1	1019.2	9878.8	6230.2	753	645932567
WCS	Wallace Computer Svcs, Inc.	Office equipment & supplies	7/31/02	1545.6	29.4	930.0	449.1	159	33994958
WLT	Walter Industries, Inc. (Uni	—	12/31/02	p1943.2	p1943.2	—	—	94	27686587
WM	Washington Mutual Inc.	Financial services	12/31/02	19037.0	3896.0	268298.0	20134.0	763	752143129
WPO	Washington Post Co.	Publishing	12/31/01	2416.7	229.6	3559.1	1683.5	240	27919860
WRE	Washington R.E. Inv. Trust	Real estate investment trust	12/31/02	p159.9	p163.7	—	—	121	11744328
WCN	Waste Connections, Inc.	Services	12/31/02	p498.7	p501.0	—	—	186	29279879
WMI	Waste Management, Inc. (DE)	Pollution control	12/31/02	11142.0	823.0	19631.0	5308.0	422	517770571
PIK	Water Pik Technologies, Inc.	—	12/31/02	p281.8	p276.8	—	—	59	4635920
WAT	Waters Corp.	—	12/31/02	p890.0	p868.8	—	—	297	120148847
WSO	Watsco Inc	—	12/31/02	p1181.1	p1181.1	—	—	94	15571107
WPI	Watson Pharmaceuticals, Inc.	Drugs	12/31/02	1223.2	175.8	2663.5	1798.3	292	82353408
WW	Watson Wyatt & Co. Holdings	—	6/30/02	710.5	47.1	436.8	159.2	98	13546403
WTS	Watts Industries, Inc.	Meas. & control instruments	12/31/01	548.9	26.6	520.5	249.3	104	16054604
WMO	Wausau-Mosinee Paper Corp. (U	Paper	12/31/02	p948.7	p948.7	—	—	128	33490025
WCI	WCI Communities Inc (United	—	12/31/02	p1217.5	p1215.5	—	—	48	18521444
WFT	Weatherford International, L	Oil service & equipment	12/31/02	p2328.9	p2257.3	—	—	288	98014222
WBS	Webster Financial Corp.	Savings & loan	12/31/02	—	pd7.3	—	—	176	27875222
WNI	Weider Nutrition Internationa	—	5/31/02	311.1	d7.5	158.6	76.7	13	4120507
WTW	Weight Watchers Internationa	—	12/31/02	p809.6	p809.6	—	—	172	41685686
WRI	Weingarten Realty Investors	Real estate investment trust	12/31/02	365.4	110.6	2423.9	933.4	178	18612237
WMK	Weis Markets, Inc.	Food wholesalers	12/28/02	1999.4	59.1	716.7	552.4	71	5129305
WC	Wellchoice Inc	Life Insurance	12/31/02	p5015.6	p5014.5	—	—	105	14587262
WLM	Wellman, Inc.	Textiles	12/31/02	p1014.0	p112.8	—	—	121	29208461
WLP	WellPoint Health Networks In	Services	12/31/02	—	—	—	—	481	172711892
WFC	Wells Fargo & Co. (New)	Banking - Midwest	12/31/02	—	pd276.0	—	—	993	1234072460
WEN	Wendy's International, Inc.	Restaurants	12/31/02	p2730.3	p2603.1	—	—	316	96469532
WCC	Wesco International, Inc.	Electrical equipment	12/31/02	p3325.8	p3325.8	—	—	44	11039654
WST	West Pharmaceutical Svcs Inc	Plastics & plastic products	12/31/02	p419.7	p420.3	—	—	69	10055569
WR	Westar Energy Inc (United St	Electric power	12/31/01	2186.3	d62.7	7513.1	1844.1	154	41438811
WEH	WestCoast Hospitality Corp	Motel/hotel lodging	12/31/02	p194.2	p194.2	—	—	12	4986164
WES	Westcorp, Inc.	Financial services	12/31/02	—	p79.7	—	—	58	8757095
WEA	Western Asset Premier Bond F	Investment company	12/31/02	12.8	11.0	226.2	150.6	—	—
WDC	Western Digital Corp. (Unite	Comp. components & periphs.	6/28/02	2151.2	53.2	636.7	102.9	183	125474179
WGR	Western Gas Resources, Inc.	Natural gas distributor	12/31/02	p2489.7	p2489.7	—	—	137	24582922
WRC	Westport Resources Corp. (Ne	Oil	12/31/02	p400.4	pd15.1	—	—	108	25380523
WHG	Westwood Holdings Group, Inc	—	12/31/02	p21.6	p21.6	—	—	30	1749873
WON	Westwood One, Inc.	Broadcasting	12/31/02	p550.8	p487.8	—	—	223	77412583
WY	Weyerhaeuser Co. (United Sta	Forest products	12/29/02	18521.0	241.0	28219.0	6623.0	407	158904552
WGL	WGL Holdings, Inc.	Natural gas distributor	9/30/02	1570.0	40.4	2113.7	794.6	141	21696516
WHR	Whirlpool Corp. (United Stat	Appliances & utensils	12/31/02	11016.0	262.0	6631.0	739.0	285	64381417
WTM	White Mountains Insurance Gro	Property & casualty insurance	12/31/02	—	p748.1	—	—	111	4042224
JWL	Whitehall Jewellers Inc	Jewelry	1/31/02	338.9	10.1	252.3	113.7	59	10654069
WHX	WHX Corp. (United States)	Steel producer	12/31/01	620.5	88.8	985.0	256.4	17	1237461
JW A	Wiley (John) & Sons Inc.	Publishing	4/30/02	734.4	57.3	896.1	276.6	128	31664684
JW B	Wiley (John) & Sons Inc.	Publishing	4/30/02	734.4	57.3	896.1	276.6	11	1427691
WG	Willbros Group Inc.	Oil service & equipment	12/31/02	—	—	—	—	51	14306178
WTU	Williams Coal Seam Gas Rty Tr	Oil	12/31/01	24.9	24.3	22.6	22.5	8	21701
WMB	Williams Cos., Inc (The) (Uni	Conglomerate	12/31/02	—	pd253.2	—	—	344	237742220

T52

EARNINGS PER SHARE						P/E RATIO	DIVIDENDS PER SHARE			AV. YLD. %	DIV. DECLARED		PRICE RANGE
QUARTERLY 1st	2nd	3rd	ANNUAL 2002	2001	2000		2002	2001	2000		AMOUNT	PAYABLE	2002
—	—	—	18.01	17.88	16.59	—	1.22	0.93	0.96	7.1	0.0935M	3/31/03	18.15 - 15.92
—	—	—	17.59	17.50	16.64	—	1.44	1.10	1.26	8.7	0.094M	3/31/03	17.82 - 15.38
—	—	—	17.36	17.41	16.65	—	1.32	1.12	1.20	7.9	0.089M	3/31/03	18.00 - 15.40
—	—	—	17.46	17.51	16.22	—	1.38	1.10	0.95	8.8	0.092M	3/31/03	16.87 - 14.50
—	—	—	16.87	17.00	15.88	—	1.42	1.23	1.00	8.7	0.092M	3/31/03	17.55 - 15.20
—	—	—	15.63	15.68	14.38	—	0.99	0.79	0.80	6.9	0.0845M	3/31/03	15.50 - 13.37
—	—	—	p0.82	0.86	0.22	26.8 - 15.7	—	—	—	—	—	—	22.00 - 12.85
p0.30	—	—	1.33	0.99	0.82	38.6 - 23.8	—	—	—	—	100%	1/15/02	51.32 - 31.60
d0.34	d0.10	d0.23	—	0.57	5.55	—	1.56	1.49	1.16	7.7	0.40Q	3/28/03	31.38 - 9.37
0.67	0.21	0.21	—	1.01	1.17	—	1.07	1.03	0.74	4.9	0.275Q	3/3/03	26.10 - 17.95
0.18	0.15	0.24	—	0.75	d0.90	—	0.97	0.95	0.62	8.2	0.2675Q	3/17/03	13.76 - 10.06
—	—	—	pd2.13	d1.61	d2.64	—	—	—	—	—	—	—	26.00 - 17.50
0.05	—	—	d0.71	0.71	0.26	—	—	—	—	—	—	—	18.99 - 6.70
—	—	—	1.67	0.22	3.95	30.6 - 15.6	1.54	1.54	1.54	4.0	0.385Q	5/1/03	51.09 - 26.01
—	—	—	pd0.43	d0.46	0.34	—	1.75	0.93	—	7.1	0.4375Q	1/30/03	26.25 - 23.26
—	—	—	13.22	13.79	13.44	—	0.10	0.09	0.05	1.9	0.025Q	3/25/03	8.40 - 1.95
—	—	—	pd1.38	1.19	2.27	—	0.97	1.03	1.04	7.3	0.23Q	4/15/03	14.40 - 12.10
—	—	—	p1.24	d0.13	d0.30	41.8 - 24.0	0.97	0.93	0.89	2.5	0.25Q	3/20/03	45.64 - 31.50
—	—	—	p1.24	d0.13	d0.30	41.8 - 24.0	—	—	—	—	2-for-1	3/31/99	51.89 - 29.79
—	—	—	p1.24	d0.13	d0.30	21.6 - 19.5	—	—	—	—	2-for-1	3/31/99	51.89 - 29.75
0.19	0.16	0.18	1.30	0.58	1.58	23.8 - 12.9	1.81	0.91	—	7.1	—	3/31/03	26.74 - 24.21
—	—	—	—	0.62	0.73	—	0.36	0.36	0.36	1.5	0.09Q	4/1/03	31.00 - 16.75
—	—	—	—	—	—	—	—	—	—	—	—	—	24.70 - 12.90
—	—	—	—	—	—	—	0.42	0.46	0.47	1.3	0.0759U	4/10/03	38.30 - 28.05
—	—	—	pd2.27	2.09	3.08	—	0.15	0.13	0.11	1.3	0.04Q	4/2/03	14.96 - 7.85
—	—	—	—	—	—	—	1.79	1.79	1.79	7.2	—	3/31/03	25.75 - 23.90
—	—	—	—	—	—	—	1.68	1.68	1.68	6.6	0.41875Q	3/31/03	26.00 - 24.85
—	—	—	pd0.58	—	3.77	—	—	—	—	—	3-for-2	6/9/00	26.15 - 6.70
0.12	0.11	0.08	d0.68	p0.91	2.08	—	0.24	0.24	0.12	2.1	0.06Q	6/2/03	16.78 - 6.38
—	—	—	—	0.19	0.55	—	—	—	—	—	100%	5/12/99	18.15 - 6.89
—	—	—	—	—	—	—	—	—	—	—	—	6/14/02	4.61 - 2.08
—	—	—	—	—	—	—	1.25	—	—	4.8	0.4451U	8/9/02	34.49 - 17.52
—	—	—	—	—	—	—	0.77	0.75	—	2.3	0.7743U	6/4/02	57.90 - 8.90
—	—	—	—	—	—	—	0.22	0.20	0.21	1.1	0.129U	2/18/03	26.95 - 12.10
—	—	—	d0.26	0.44	2.00	—	—	—	—	—	3-for-2	5/27/97	24.50 - 12.65
0.40	0.57	0.52	—	2.47	2.20	—	2.97	2.32	1.97	7.4	0.68Q	5/1/03	47.20 - 33.20
—	—	—	p1.66	2.17	2.16	30.1 - 19.5	0.44	0.52	0.50	2.6	0.4419U	7/1/02	21.12 - 12.50
—	—	—	p1.11	0.83	0.62	17.8 - 9.1	0.94	0.90	0.84	2.3	0.245Q	3/10/03	49.95 - 32.35
—	—	—	p1.28	1.02	d0.31	20.3 - 14.7	0.23	0.16	0.31	1.5	0.0225M	4/15/03	19.80 - 10.07
—	—	—	—	2.18	2.21	—	1.71	1.70	1.69	7.7	0.432Q	4/15/03	26.00 - 18.77
—	—	—	pd2.43	d10.17	d0.38	—	1.20	1.20	—	5.2	0.30Q	1/31/03	31.73 - 14.35
—	—	—	p0.40	0.32	0.59	40.0 - 29.5	—	0.13	0.16	—	0.01Q	10/29/01	12.15 - 3.55
—	—	—	p2.60	1.45	0.12	15.3 - 11.0	0.04	0.04	0.04	0.3	0.01Q	3/14/03	15.99 - 11.80
—	—	—	p1.01	0.91	0.80	17.3 - 10.2	1.00	0.24	—	2.9	0.26Q	3/17/03	39.88 - 28.57
—	—	—	—	—	—	—	—	—	—	—	2-for-1	6/3/96	17.50 - 10.27
0.22	—	—	p1.81 *	1.49	1.40	33.2 - 24.2	0.49	0.35	0.35	2.0	0.1326Q	5/1/03	33.10 - 15.30
—	—	—	0.99	0.86	0.76	41.1 - 28.0	0.29	0.27	0.23	0.5	0.09Q	4/7/03	63.94 - 43.72
—	—	—	—	—	—	—	0.15	0.14	0.14	0.4	0.0375Q	3/12/03	40.70 - 27.70
0.29	—	—	0.71	1.30	0.55	31.9 - 22.3	0.66	0.66	0.66	3.4	0.165Q	3/20/03	22.62 - 15.80
—	—	—	pd1.17	0.95	0.06	—	0.12	0.13	0.12	1.0	0.03Q	3/20/03	15.15 - 8.51
2.44	5.37	5.02	4.05	3.15	2.36	9.9 - 6.9	1.06	0.90	0.76	3.1	0.29Q	2/14/03	39.98 - 27.80
—	—	—	—	24.06	14.32	—	5.60	5.60	5.40	5.5	1.45Q	2/7/03	743.00 - 516.00
—	—	—	p1.32	1.38	1.26	22.8 - 15.5	1.39	1.31	1.23	5.5	0.3525Q	3/31/03	30.15 - 20.42
—	—	—	p1.90	1.11	1.17	20.8 - 12.4	—	—	—	—	—	—	39.56 - 23.49
—	—	—	1.33	0.80	d0.16	23.5 - 15.2	0.01	0.01	0.01	0.0	0.01A	10/15/02	31.25 - 20.20
—	—	—	p0.44	0.85	1.05	28.6 - 15.9	—	—	—	—	—	—	12.59 - 7.00
—	—	—	p1.09	0.83	1.14	36.0 - 16.4	—	—	—	—	100%	8/25/00	39.25 - 17.86
—	—	—	p1.07	0.90	0.69	18.2 - 11.8	0.11	0.10	0.10	0.7	0.04Q	1/31/03	19.48 - 12.65
—	—	—	1.64	1.07	1.65	20.3 - 10.9	—	—	—	—	100%	10/29/97	33.25 - 17.95
0.39	0.36	—	1.41	1.37	0.62	19.5 - 12.3	—	—	—	—	—	—	27.50 - 17.31
0.30	0.32	0.32	0.99	1.17	—	—	0.24	0.24	0.27	1.4	0.06Q	3/14/03	20.45 - 13.70
—	—	—	p0.45	0.19	0.01	31.1 - 18.1	0.34	0.34	0.34	3.1	0.085Q	2/17/03	14.00 - 8.14
—	—	—	p2.41	2.80	—	13.9 - 3.1	—	—	—	—	—	—	33.60 - 7.50
—	—	—	pd0.05	1.76	d0.36	—	—	—	—	—	—	—	46.20 - 33.10
—	—	—	p3.16	2.68	2.55	12.7 - 9.6	0.74	0.67	0.62	2.1	0.19Q	2/24/03	40.10 - 30.28
d0.42	0.09	—	d0.29	0.01	—	—	—	0.15	0.15	—	0.0375Q	12/20/01	2.25 - 1.31
—	—	—	p1.31	1.34	0.13	38.5 - 23.9	—	—	—	—	—	—	50.39 - 31.35
—	—	—	1.75	1.84	1.46	22.4 - 16.7	1.48	1.40	1.33	4.3	3-for-2	4/15/03	39.20 - 29.29
—	—	—	2.17	1.55	1.77	18.2 - 12.4	1.08	1.08	1.06	3.3	0.27Q	2/21/03	39.50 - 26.90
—	—	—	d6.07	0.26	0.87	—	—	—	—	—	—	—	28.50 - 22.15
—	—	—	p4.42	3.15	2.65	20.2 - 13.0	0.36	0.36	0.36	2.6	0.09Q	3/17/03	18.22 - 9.37
—	—	—	—	—	—	—	—	—	—	—	100%	3/15/02	89.20 - 57.58
—	—	—	p3.16	1.97	2.33	17.4 - 13.1	1.10	1.00	0.90	2.3	0.30Q	3/1/03	54.84 - 41.50
—	—	—	p1.89	1.65	1.44	22.0 - 13.8	0.24	0.24	0.24	0.7	0.06Q	2/25/03	41.60 - 26.15
—	—	—	p0.49	0.43	0.70	15.5 - 5.8	—	—	—	—	—	—	7.58 - 2.85
d1.92	0.09	0.60	p1.28	1.37	0.11	25.4 - 12.7	0.77	0.73	0.69	3.2	0.20Q	2/5/03	32.50 - 16.25
—	—	—	p0.41	0.59	0.45	19.7 - 12.0	1.20	1.20	1.67	9.1	0.19Q	4/1/03	18.00 - 8.50
—	—	—	p2.05	1.61	2.52	15.6 - 7.7	—	—	—	—	—	—	8.08 - 4.90
—	—	—	13.57	—	—	—	0.47	0.43	0.30	2.0	0.13Q	5/20/03	32.00 - 15.74
—	—	—	—	—	—	—	0.85	—	—	6.0	0.10625M	4/1/03	15.33 - 13.09
0.11	0.36	—	1.23	2.48	1.39	32.6 - 20.3	—	—	—	—	2-for-1	6/3/97	8.96 - 2.98
—	—	—	pd0.63	1.09	d1.71	—	0.20	0.20	0.20	0.8	0.05Q	5/14/03	40.12 - 25.03
—	—	—	—	—	—	—	—	—	—	—	—	—	21.40 - 13.20
—	—	—	p0.97	0.23	0.74	37.8 - 11.8	0.02	—	—	0.1	0.01Q	3/31/03	17.27 - 11.40
—	—	—	p1.00	0.38	0.36	40.5 - 24.4	—	—	—	—	2-for-1	3/22/00	40.50 - 24.41
1.06	—	—	p1.09	1.61	3.72	62.3 - 34.3	1.60	1.60	1.60	3.0	0.40Q	3/3/03	67.95 - 37.35
—	—	—	p0.80	1.75	1.79	36.6 - 24.1	1.27	1.26	1.23	5.2	0.32Q	5/1/03	29.31 - 19.25
—	—	—	3.78	0.50	5.20	21.1 - 10.4	1.36	1.36	1.36	2.3	0.34Q	3/4/03	79.80 - 39.23
—	—	—	p80.75	d86.52	52.84	4.7 - 3.5	1.00	1.00	1.20	0.3	1.00A	3/26/03	379.50 - 282.00
0.02	0.04	d0.35	—	0.69	0.65	—	—	—	—	—	3-for-2	1/4/00	22.83 - 8.00
0.21	d0.22	d3.79	—	8.46	d42.30	—	—	—	—	—	—	—	2.80 - 1.91
0.32	0.55	0.39	—	0.91	0.93	—	0.19	0.17	0.15	0.8	0.05Q	4/16/03	27.63 - 19.26
0.32	0.55	0.39	—	0.91	0.93	—	0.19	0.17	0.14	0.8	0.05Q	4/16/03	27.48 - 19.51
0.19	0.11	0.23	—	2.50	1.68	—	—	—	—	—	—	—	19.24 - 5.84
—	—	—	—	—	—	—	0.89	2.51	1.68	9.3	—	2/28/03	14.10 - 5.00
—	—	—	pd1.11	1.67	1.95	—	0.42	0.68	0.60	3.1	0.01Q	3/31/03	26.35 - 0.78

SYMBOL	COMPANY	NATURE OF BUSINESS	FISCAL YEAR-END	TOTAL REV. $MILL	NET INCOME $MILL	TOTAL ASSETS $MILL	NET STK EQUITY $MILL	NO. OF INST.	INST. HOLDINGS (SHARES)
WEG	Williams Energy Partners L.P.	—	12/31/02	p434.5	p434.5	—	—	56	1579918
WSM	Williams-Sonoma, Inc. (Unite	Appliances & utensils	2/3/02	2086.7	75.1	994.9	532.5	268	90753963
WSH	Willis Group Holdings Ltd. (B	Insurance brokerage	12/31/01	1424.0	17.0	8949.0	696.0	155	63279235
WL	Wilmington Trust Corp. (DE)	Banking - Mid-Atlantic	12/31/02	—	p133.2	—	—	202	25260221
GB	Wilson Greatbatch Technologie	Electronic components	1/3/03	p167.3	p15.5	—	—	115	19348860
WRS	Windrose Medical Properties	Finance	12/31/02	p1.9	p1.9	—	—	15	2573086
WIN	Winn-Dixie Stores, Inc.	Grocery chain	6/26/02	12334.4	189.5	2937.6	812.4	214	47211825
WGO	Winnebago Industries Inc.	Mobile homes	8/31/02	828.4	54.7	337.1	179.8	151	11779261
WXH	Winston Hotels, Inc.	Real estate investment trust	12/31/01	57.5	10.5	376.9	184.2	64	6590971
WIT	Wipro Ltd (India)	Conglomerate	3/31/02	—	—	—	—	31	2146020
WEC	Wisconsin Energy Corp.	Electric power	12/31/02	3736.2	167.0	8364.9	2169.8	271	58382682
WZR	Wiser Oil Co.	Oil	12/31/02	p79.5	p66.8	—	—	21	1761183
WMS	WMS Industries Inc.	—	6/30/02	174.7	9.9	281.2	259.5	90	18449526
WOS	Wolseley PLC (UK)	—	7/31/02	—	—	—	—	5	119886
WLV	Wolverine Tube, Inc.	Copper	12/31/02	p550.5	p58.4	—	—	59	10512920
WWW	Wolverine World Wide, Inc. (U	Shoe manufacturing	12/28/02	p827.1	p803.5	—	—	129	32195786
INT	World Fuel Services Corp. (Un	Oil service & equipment	3/31/02	1365.1	17.2	257.9	116.4	69	7091961
WWE	World Wrestling Entertainmen	—	4/30/02	425.0	37.6	487.4	389.4	53	7631824
SZ	Worldwide Restaurant Concept	Restaurants	4/30/02	267.2	4.5	133.5	55.2	19	7765846
WOR	Worthington Industries, Inc.	Steel producer	5/31/02	1745.0	6.5	1457.3	606.3	223	39623216
WPS	WPS Resources Corp.	Electric power	12/31/02	p2674.9	p2647.0	—	—	157	10979073
WWY	Wrigley (William) Jr. Co. (U	—	12/31/02	2746.3	401.5	2108.3	1522.6	410	94263620
WYE	Wyeth (United States)	Drugs	12/31/02	—	p9015.6	—	—	972	1017268412
XNR	Xanser Corp.	Oil service & equipment	12/31/01	144.7	22.4	186.2	115.5	29	8174701
XEL	Xcel Energy, Inc.	Electric power	12/31/02			—	—	337	181528639
XRX	Xerox Corp	Office equipment & supplies	12/31/02			—	—	332	661162222
XL	XL Capital Ltd.	Insurance	12/31/02			—	—	330	108298136
XTO	XTO Energy, Inc.	Oil service & equipment	12/31/02	—	p186.1	—	—	273	106172435
YCC	Yankee Candle Co., Inc. (The)		12/28/02	p444.8	p444.8	—	—	102	24004264
YZC	Yanzhou Coal Mining Co., Ltd.	Mining & processing	12/31/01			—	—	1	100
YRK	York International Corp.	—	12/31/02	3843.4	81.2	2506.1	682.8	173	34636830
YPF	YPF SA (Argentina)	Oil	12/31/01			—	—	8	54299
YUM	Yum! Brands, Inc. (United St	Restaurants	12/31/02	p7757.0	p7767.0	—	—	395	237205373
ZLC	Zale Corp. (New)	Jewelry	7/31/02	2191.7	102.6	1477.9	939.8	157	31938441
ZAP	Zapata Corp. (NV)	Food processing	12/31/01	98.8	4.4	271.7	169.9	11	603210
ZNT	Zenith National Ins. Corp.	Insurance	12/31/02	p602.2	p611.4	—	—	79	8175168
ZIF	Zenix Income Fund Inc.	Investment company	3/31/02	11.8	10.5	92.1	90.8	5	207020
ZMH	Zimmer Holdings, Inc.	Medical & dental equipment	12/31/02	1372.4	257.8	858.9	366.3	549	140062490
ZF	Zweig Fund, Inc.	Investment company	12/31/01	6.1	d0.2	490.0	489.3	32	1318712
ZTR	Zweig Total Return Fund, Inc.	Investment company	12/31/01	22.1	15.7	602.5	601.7	32	1018259

1st	2nd	3rd	2002	2001	2000	P/E RATIO	2002	2001	2000	AV. YLD. %	AMOUNT	PAYABLE	PRICE RANGE 2002
—	—	—	p3.67	1.87	—	11.9 - 6.1	2.58	1.43	—	7.8	0.725Q	2/14/03	43.80 - 22.25
0.13	0.12	0.13	—	0.65	0.49	—	—	—	—	—	2-for-1	5/9/02	33.50 - 19.37
—	—	—	—	0.01	0.07	—	—	—	—	—	0.125Q	4/15/03	37.14 - 21.50
—	.	—	p2.01	1.89	1.85	17.2 - 12.5	1.00	0.94	0.89	3.4	0.255Q	2/17/03	34.63 - 25.05
—	—	—	p0.68	0.58	0.07	55.3 - 29.6	—	—	—	—	—	—	37.60 - 20.10
—	—	—	p0.02	—	—	605.0 - 492.5	—	—	—	—	0.13Q	1/10/03	12.10 - 9.85
0.25	0.65	—	—	1.35	0.32	—	0.20	0.85	1.02	1.2	0.05Q	2/14/03	20.40 - 11.71
0.85	—	—	2.68	2.08	2.20	19.2 - 11.9	0.20	0.20	0.20	0.5	0.10S	7/7/03	51.48 - 31.85
d0.16	d0.60	0.43	—	0.21	0.52	—	0.60	1.12	1.12	7.7	0.15Q	4/16/03	9.76 - 5.78
—	—	—	—	—	—	—	0.02	0.01	—	0.1	0.01837U	8/8/02	44.00 - 22.22
—	—	—	1.44	1.77	1.27	18.4 - 14.0	0.80	0.80	1.37	3.4	0.20Q	3/1/03	26.48 - 20.17
—	—	—	pd5.59	0.67	0.37	—	—	—	—	—	0.03Q	12/11/98	6.85 - 2.15
0.02	d0.06	—	0.30	1.00	1.42	69.8 - 30.9	—	—	—	—	—	—	20.95 - 9.28
—	—	—	—	—	—	—	1.26	0.33	—	2.8	0.4398U	8/11/03	55.40 - 36.00
—	—	—	p0.45	0.91	1.88	27.0 - 10.9	—	—	—	—	—	—	12.15 - 4.90
—	—	—	p1.15	1.07	0.26	16.7 - 10.9	0.18	0.15	0.14	1.1	0.055Q	5/1/03	19.25 - 12.55
0.41	0.07	p0.43	—	1.62	1.11	—	0.30	0.35	0.20	1.5	0.075Q	4/3/03	24.40 - 15.30
0.04	d0.02	pd0.23	—	0.52	0.87	—	—	—	—	—	—	—	15.83 - 6.76
0.12	0.05	—	—	0.16	0.10	—	—	—	—	—	0.04Q	10/12/95	3.23 - 1.20
0.32	0.24	—	—	0.08	0.42	—	0.64	0.64	0.63	3.8	0.16Q	3/29/03	20.40 - 13.55
—	—	—	p3.42	2.74	2.53	12.5 - 8.9	2.12	2.08	2.04	5.8	0.535Q	3/20/03	42.68 - 30.47
—	—	—	1.78	1.61	1.45	33.1 - 24.8	0.80	0.75	0.70	1.6	0.22Q	5/1/03	58.90 - 44.21
—	—	—	p3.33	1.72	d0.69	20.0 - 8.5	0.92	0.92	0.92	1.9	0.23Q	3/1/03	66.51 - 28.25
d0.03	d0.02	d0.01	—	0.64	0.19	—	—	—	—	—	0.00Q	6/29/01	3.45 - 1.25
—	—	—	pd5.26	2.27	1.60	—	1.31	1.50	1.47	7.8	0.1875Q	1/20/03	28.49 - 5.12
—	—	—	p0.11	d0.17	d0.44	104.1 - 38.2	—	0.10	0.80	—	0.05Q	4/1/01	11.45 - 4.20
—	—	—	—	—	—	—	1.88	1.84	1.80	2.4	0.48Q	3/31/03	98.48 - 58.45
—	—	—	p1.50	1.76	0.78	13.2 - 7.3	0.03	0.03	0.02	0.2	0.01Q	4/15/03	19.79 - 11.02
—	—	—	p1.17	0.79	0.80	23.7 - 11.8	—	—	—	—	—	—	27.68 - 13.80
—	—	—	—	—	—	—	0.60	0.49	0.54	3.2	0.6044U	7/10/02	22.30 - 15.55
—	—	—	2.04	1.17	2.78	19.2 - 10.5	0.60	0.60	0.60	2.0	0.15Q	3/28/03	39.08 - 21.35
—	—	—	—	—	—	—	1.12	4.22	0.88	7.4	1.1235U	11/29/02	21.80 - 8.68
—	—	—	p1.88	1.88	1.62	17.6 - 10.8	—	—	—	—	100%	6/17/02	33.17 - 20.35
d0.20	d1.44	—	2.95	2.36	3.16	15.5 - 9.0	—	—	—	—	—	—	45.84 - 26.50
0.51	0.51	1.00	—	1.85	d10.88	—	—	—	—	—	—	—	33.80 - 19.60
—	—	—	p0.55	d1.35	d2.78	58.6 - 41.6	1.00	1.00	1.00	3.6	0.25Q	5/15/03	32.25 - 22.90
2.61	—	—	—	2.95	3.97	—	0.46	0.61	0.65	15.5	0.0375M	5/30/03	3.74 - 2.15
—	—	—	1.31	0.77	0.91	32.8 - 21.4	—	—	—	—	—	—	43.00 - 28.00
—	6.45	—	—	7.96	10.32	—	0.70	0.89	1.18	10.6	0.131Q	4/28/03	8.72 - 4.50
—	6.08	—	—	6.63	7.48	—	0.62	0.71	0.74	10.2	0.048M	3/26/03	7.35 - 4.80